W9-DAC-673

SECOND EDITION - STANDARD CATALOG OF
American Light-Duty TRUCKS

John A. Gunnell, Editor

© 1993 by Krause Publications, Inc.

Published by:

krause publications

700 E. State Street • Iola, WI 54990-0001
Telephone: 715/445-2214

Library of Congress Number 86-83144

ISBN: 0-87341-238-9

Printed in the United States of America

CONTENTS

FOREWORD

The concept behind Krause Publications "Standard Catalogs" is to compile massive amounts of information about motor vehicles and present it in a standard format which the hobbyist, collector or professional dealer can use to answer some commonly asked questions.

These questions include: What year, make and model is the vehicle? What did it sell for when new? Is it original or modified? How rare is it? What's special about it? How much is it worth today?

Some answers are provided by illustrations in the catalogs; others by information found in the charts or text.

Each catalog represents the efforts of both professional research-historians and enthusiasts who collect facts and factory literature on one make or model.

The standardized format presents the following data: (1) a contributor's personal description of the vehicle's appearance; (2) where available, a list of standard factory equipment; (3) vehicle and/or engine identification codes and advice on how to interpret these; (4) a chart giving model codes, type descriptions, original retail price, original shipping weight and available production totals; (5) engine specifications; (6) a description of chassis features in a concise, generalized manner; (7) some technical information about the drive train and running gear; (8) specific option lists or a description of accessories seen in original period photos of such vehicles; (9) a "thumbnail" history of the vehicle and/or manufacturer and, in many instances, (10) a "ballpark" estimate of current prices being paid for such (pre-1980) models in today's collector vehicle market (located in rear of the catalog).

No claims are made as to the catalogs being history textbooks or encyclopedias. They are not repair manuals or "bibles" for motor vehicle enthusiasts. They are intended as collectors' guides, much like the popular spotter's books, buyers' digests and pricing guides. However, they are much larger in size, broader in scope and more deluxe in format. In addition, they represent the combined efforts of a large research team, rather than one individual's work.

All of the catalogs published to date reflect, to some degree, a balance between generalized research carried on by professional authors, and material prepared by individuals who know many facts about a single model or make through their personal hobby interests.

Part of the catalog concept is to coordinate future assignments in such a manner that each section in the book will ultimately feel both the skilled touch of the professional writer and the in-depth enthusiasm of the hobby expert. All contributors are requested to maintain an ongoing file of new research, corrections and additional photos which can be used to refine and expand future editions.

The long-range goal of Krause Publications is to have a series of catalogs that are as near-perfect as possible. We're told that these books provide many hobbyists with hours of enjoyable reading. Some also consider them essential guides to carry along when they travel to car shows, wrecking yards and swap meets. And, of course, they can be particularly useful to the hobbyist/collector when cruising the highways or back roads in search of new vehicle acquisitions. You will know, immediately, what type of vehicle you've found, how rare it is and how much it's worth when restored.

Other catalogs currently available include *THE STANDARD CATALOG of AMERICAN CARS 1805-1942* (Second Edition); *THE STANDARD CATALOG of AMERICAN CARS 1946-1972* (Third Edition); *THE STANDARD CATALOG of AMERICAN CARS 1976-1986* (Second Edition); *THE STANDARD CATALOG of AMC 1902-1987*; *THE STANDARD CATALOG of BUICK 1903-1990*; *THE STANDARD CATALOG of CADILLAC 1903-1990*; *THE STANDARD CATALOG of CHEVROLET 1912-1990*; *THE STANDARD CATALOG of CHRYSLER 1924-1990*; *THE STANDARD CATALOG of FORD 1903-1990*; *THE STANDARD CATALOG of 4x4s 1946-1990*; and *THE STANDARD CATALOG of MILITARY VEHICLES 1940-1965*. For a complete hobby books catalog write: Krause Publications/Old Cars Weekly, 700 E. State St., Iola, WI 54990.

INTRODUCTION

You'll like the second edition of *THE STANDARD CATALOG of AMERICAN LIGHT-DUTY TRUCKS 1896-1986* because of the changes in organization and content that make it a more useful guide for truck collectors. It has many new facts and photos. It is even more accurate than the highly acclaimed first edition. There is a greater emphasis on the mainstream of truck collecting. And, of course, all of the current pricing data has been brought completely up to date.

In the five years since the first edition, the explosive growth of the light-duty truck hobby has continued. This has brought a considerable amount of new information about 1/4-ton, 1/2-ton, 3/4-ton and 1-ton commercial vehicles to the surface. Knowledge about all makes and models...particularly Chevrolet, Dodge and Ford...has increased dramatically.

Our revised Chevrolet section reflects improvements throughout, with a special concentration on the popular Advance-Design and Task-Force models of the 1940s and 1950s. A number of technical advisors from the Vintage Chevrolet Club of America helped out with this massive project. There's more advice on how to identify Chevrolet models by appearance and vehicle identification codes, plus upgraded lists of original paint colors, interior trims and factory options. Over 60 new Chevrolet truck photos appear.

While editing the Ford section from beginning to end, we worked extra hard on the F-1 and early F-100 years to improve the serial number and body coding data. The six-cylinder and V-8 models have been sorted out more carefully to show differences in original prices and weights. Colors and options information has been expanded.

As for the Dodge section, the big change you'll notice is more than 100 new photos. Dodge information in the first edition was very complete and accurate. However, we have improved the overall organization and added some missing models, particularly in the late 1930s and 1940s era. Much more detailed coverage of Dodge military vehicles is now included in our new *STANDARD CATALOG of U.S. MILITARY VEHICLES 1940-1965*, rather than in this book. Those pages have been used to give greater coverage of collectible civilian models.

Jeep lovers will notice that we have combined the Willys-Overland, Kaiser and AMC Jeeps into a single, larger and more complete Jeep section. The AMC-built Wagoneer and Cherokee station wagon models are now covered by the text as well as the photos. Over 50 new Jeep photos appear.

Additional types of trucks covered in detail include Crosley; GMC; International; Plymouth; Pontiac; Studebaker; and Willys-Overland (conventionals). While the amount of new research available on these marques is limited, we have gathered as much as possible, while focusing on improving the facts and photos. Durant and Fargo commercial vehicles, which lie outside the mainstream hobby interests, have been moved to the "Illustrated Directory of Additional Marques" in the second section of the catalog. This provides more space in the first section for covering the marques that are most collected.

The "Illustrated Directory of Additional Marques," covering truck makers from A to Z (ABC to Zimmerman), has over 100 brand new entries. In all, over 650 marques are listed and well over 600 photos of rare and unusual trucks appear.

Collectors interested in the latest market prices for light-duty trucks will find the current values in the "Price Guide," which makes up the third section of this catalog. The Price Guide model lists have been revamped, too. Values for each model in six different states of condition are presented.

Throughout the catalog, refinements have been made to the organization and content of the book. The charts were cleaned up and retabulated. Many listings are much more complete. There are fewer cross references and more direct presentations of data. Large sections on non-mainstream marques have been replaced with an added emphasis on more collected models. When you have the chance to start using this catalog to look up light-duty truck information, we think you'll be impressed with all of the improvements it includes.

John "Gunner" Gunnell

April 27, 1993

ABBREVIATIONS

AC AC........Electric Division of General Motors
AC/DC........Alternating current/direct current
AIR........Air Injection Reactor
ALAM........Association of Licensed Automobile Manufacturers
AMC........American Motors Corp.
AMP........Amperes
APPROX........Approximate
ATA........American Trucking Association
BBL........Barrel
BC........Business Car
BHP........Brake horsepower
BL........Bonus Load (pickup)
Bros........Brothers
BSW........Black sidewall
BUS........Business
CC........Commercial Car
CC........Cubic Centimeters
CAFE........Corporate Average Fuel Economy
CALIF........California
CARB........Carburetor
CB........Citizen's Band (radio)
CIBA........Cast iron block
CID........Cubic-inch diameter
CJ........Civilian Jeep
CO........Company
COBRA........Copper Brazed Engine
COE........Cab-Over-Engine
COMM........Commercial
COPO........Central Office Production Option
C.R........Compression ratio
CS........Custom (Chevrolet)
CST........Custom Sport Truck (Chevrolet)
CU. FT........Cubic Feet
CUST........Custom
CYL........Cylinder
DEL........Deluxe
DELY........Delivery
DIA........Diameter
DIV........Division
DJ........Jeep 4x2 Dispatcher
DR........(2-dr.) Door (two-door)
DRW........Dual rear wheels
EFI........Electronic fuel injection
EIGHT........Eight-cylinder engine
EPA........Enviornmental Protection Agency
ESC........Electronic spark control
EXC........Except
EXP........Express
EXT........Extended
E-Z-Eye........Tinted glass
F (3F)........Forward (three forward speeds)
FC........Forward control
F.F........Cowl Flat-face cowl
F-HEAD........Vales in head and block
FLARE........Flareside pickup (Ford)
FLEET........Fleetside pickup (Chevy)
FM........Frequency modulation (radio)
FOB........Free on board
FOUR........Four-cylinder
4x2........Two-Wheel-Drive
4x4........Four-Wheel-Drive
4-DR........Four-door
4-SPD........Four-speed (transmission)
4V........Four-barrel carburetor
FRT........Front
FS........Fender-side pickup
FT........Foot/Feet
GAL........Gallon
GATE........Tailgate
GBR........Glass-belted radial (tire)
GM........General Motors
GMAD........General Motors Assembly Division
GMC........General Motors Corp., GM Truck & Bus, GM Truck & Coach
GMR........GM Research
GT........Gran Turismo
GVW........Gross Vehicle Weight
GVWR........Gross Vehicle Weight Rating
H-D........Heavy-duty
HEI........High-Energy Ignition
HP........Horsepower
HR........Hour
HWY........Highway
I........Inline
ICC........Interstate Commerce Commission
I.D........Identification
IHC........International Harvester Co.
IN(S)........Inch(es)
INC........Incorporated
INCL........Included
I.P........Instrument Panel
JR........Junior
KM........Kilometers
L........(L-head) Side-valve engine
L........(5.0L) Engine Displacement in liters
LB(s)........Pound(s)
LBS.-FT........Pounds-feet
LCF........Low-Cab-Forward
L-D........Light-Duty
LE........Luxury Edition
LPG........Liquified Petroleum Gas
LH........Left-hand
LHD........Left-hand Drive
LTD........Limited
LUV........Light Utility Vehicle
LWB........Long Wheelbase
MAX........Maximum
MFG........Manufacturing
MM........Milimeters
MPG........Miles Per Gallon
MPH........Miles Per Hour
MX........Multi-plex
N/A........Not Available
NACC........National Automobile Chamber of Commerce
NC........No charge
NADA........National Automobile Dealers Assoc.
NHP........Net Horsepower
NO........Number
NP........New Process (Dodge/Plymouth)
NPA........National Production Authority
O.F........Open front
OHC........Overhead camshaft
OHV........Overhead valves
OPEC........Organization of Petroleum Exporting Countries
OPS........Office of Price Stability
OPT........Optional
OSRV........Outside rearview mirror
OZ........Ounce
P........Passenger
PCV........Positive Crankcase Ventilation
PDV........Parcel Delivery Van
P. FRT........Power front
PMD........Pontiac Motor Division
PR........Ply-rated (tires)
PROD........Production
PTO........Power Take-Off
RBL........Raised black letter (tires)
RDS........Roadster
REG........Regular
REMOTE........Remote Control
REQ........Requires
RH........Right-hand
RHD........Right-hand drive
RPM........Revolutions per minute
RPO........Regular Production Option
RV........Recreational Vehicle
RWL........Raised white-letter
SAE........Society of Automotive Engineers
SBR........Steel-belted radial (tires)
SC........Super Cab
SCREEN........Screenside Delivery
SDL........Sedan Delivery
SE........Special Edition
SED........Sedan
SIG........Signal
SIX........Six-cylinder
SPD........Speed
SPD. REG........Speed regulator
SPL........Special
SPT........Sport
SQ. IN........Square inch(es)
SR........Senior
SRW........Single Rear Wheel
SS........Super Sport
STA. WAG........Station Wagon
STD........Standard
STEP........Stepside pickup (Chevy)
STYLE........Styleside pickup (Ford)
SUB........Suburban
SWB........Short wheelbase
TACH........Tachometer
TAX........Taxable (horsepower)
TBI........Throttle-Body Injection
TEMP........Temperature
T-HEAD........Type of engine valve layout
THM........Turbo-Hydramatic transmission
3F/1R........3 speeds forward/1 reverse
3S........Three-seat
3x2V........Three two-barrel carburetors
TRANS........Transmission
TU-TONE........Two-Tone (Ford and Jeep)
TV........Television
2-dr........Two-door
2V........Two-barrel (carburetor)
U.S........United States
U.S.A........United States of America
UTIL........Utility
V........Venturi (carburetor)
V........Vee-block engine
VIN........Vehicle identification number
VP........Vice-president
VV........Vision & ventilating windshield
W/........With
WAG........Wagon
WB........Wheelbase
W/O........Without
WPB........War Production Authority
WS........Wide-Side Pickup (GMC)
W/S........Windshield (Chassis & W/S)
WSW........White sidewall (tires)

Many different abbreviations are used in sales literature printed by truck manufacturers over the years. We have tried to standardize the use of abbreviations. However, original sales literature is used as a reference source by many editorial contributors and some rely on the abbreviations as printed in the factory materials. Thus, there may be slight variations in the use of terms used in this catalog. (For example: 4x4 and four-wheel drive both appear). The above list shows most abbreviations used, except for those so common (months, states, etc.) that no special explanation is required.

HOW TO USE THIS CATALOG

APPEARANCE AND EQUIPMENT: Word descriptions help identify trucks down to details such as styling features, trim and interior appointments. Standard equipment lists usually begin with low-priced base models. Then, subsequent data blocks cover higher-priced lines of the same year.

VEHICLE I.D. NUMBERS: This edition features expanded data explaining the basic serial numbering system used by each postwar vehicle manufacturer. This data reveals where, when and in what order your vehicle was built. There is much more information on assembly plant, body style and original engine codes.

SPECIFICATIONS CHART: The first chart column gives series or model numbers for trucks. The second column gives body type. The third column tells factory price. The fourth column gives GVW. The fifth column gives the vehicle's original shipping weight. The sixth column provides model year production totals (if available) or makes reference to additional notes found below the specifications chart. When the same vehicle came with different engines or trim levels at different prices and weights, slashes (/) are used to separate the low price or weight from the high one. In some cases, model numbers are also presented this way. In rare cases where data is non-applicable or not available the abbreviation "N.A." appears.

BASE ENGINE DATA: According to make of vehicle, engine data will be found either below the data block for each series or immediately following the specifications chart for the last vehicle-line. Displacement, bore and stroke and horsepower ratings are listed, plus a lot more data where available. This edition has more complete engine listings for many models. In other cases, extra-cost engines are listed in the "options" section.

VEHICLE DIMENSIONS: The main data compiled here consists of wheelbase, overall length and tire size. Front and rear tread widths are given for most trucks through the early 1960s and some later models. Overall width and height appears in some cases, too.

OPTIONAL EQUIPMENT LISTS: This section includes data blocks listing all types of options and accessories. A great deal of attention has been focused on cataloging both the availability and the original factory retail prices of optional equipment. Because of size and space limitations, a degree of selectivity has been applied by concentrating on those optional features of greatest interest to collectors. Important option packages have been covered and detailed as accurately as possible in the given amount of space. When available, options prices are listed.

HISTORICAL FOOTNOTES: Trucks are already recognized as an important part of America's automotive heritage. Revealing statistics; important dates and places; personality profiles; performance milestones; and other historical facts are highlighted in this "automotive trivia" section.

SEE PRICING SECTION IN BACK OF BOOK.

1/2-TON; 3/4-TON; 1-TON CONVENTIONAL — MODEL C; K/SERIES 10; 20; 30 — SIX/ V-8: Styling changes for light-duty conventional trucks were headed by revamped grille with a larger gridwork, clear-lensed parking lights, and new front fender model identification combining model nameplates and series identification plaques. A restyled tailgate with a quick-release control was used. The C10/K10 Pickups with a 6-1/2 ft. box came on the standard 117-1/2 in. wheelbase, which was used only for these models and small chassis models. The C10/K10 Pickups with an 8 ft. box featured a 131-1/2 in. wheelbase. This wheelbase was also used for 1/2-ton chassis models and all basic C30 models. The C20/K20 trucks, except Suburbans, were on a 127 in. wheelbase. All Suburbans, both 1/2-ton and 3/4-ton, were on a 129.5 in. wheelbase. Longer wheelbases were provided for Chassis & Cab and the new Crew Cab trucks. Crew cab bodies that seated six could be had as an option on all 3/4-ton and 1-ton pickups. The Crew Cab was actually an option costing about $1,000. The box used for factory-made Crew Cab Pickups was the 8 ft. Fleetside box. Custom Deluxe was the base interior. It included a foam-padded bench seat with blue, green, red or saddle plaid upholstery; a body color steel roof panel; black rubber floor mat; padded armrests; courtesy lamps; prismatic rearview mirror; foam padded dash; bright upper and lower grille outline moldings; bright headlamps bezels; silver plastic grille insert; bright outside rearview mirror; bright door handles; bright Custom Deluxe nameplates and white-painted bumper, hubcaps and wheels. The next-step-up was Scottsdale trim ($137-$199 extra), full-depth foam padded seat; which included woodgrain door trim inserts; an ashtray cigarette lighter; door or manually-operated courtesy lamps; bright door sill plates; color-keyed rubber floor mats; a high-note horn; patterned nylon cloth upholstery with vinyl trim; and all Custom Deluxe exterior features, plus a chrome bumper; chrome hubcaps; chrome bodyside moldings on Fleetsides; bright windshield and window trim..

I.D. DATA: Serial number located. Combination VIN and rating plate located on: [El Camino] Top left side of dash; [Conventionals] left door pillar. Serial number systems: [El Camino] First symbol indicates manufacturer, 1=Chevrolet. Second symbol indicates car-line/series: C=El Camino; D=El Camino Custom. Third and fourth symbols indicate body type: 80=Sedan-Pickup. Fifth symbol indicates engine: [El Camino] H=350 cid/145 nhp two-barrel V-8; L=350 cid/160 nhp four-barrel V-8; U=402 cid/175 nhp four-barrel V-8; Y=454 cid/235 nhp four-barrel V-8. Sixth symbol indicates model year: 5=1975. Seventh symbol indicates assembly plant. Symbols 8-13 indicate the production sequence number starting at 100,001. Ending numbers not available. [All Light-Duty] The first symbol indicates manufacturer: 1=Chevrolet Motor Div. The second symbol indicates chassis type: C=96 in. or 106 in. Conventional Cab including Blazer; G=Chevy Van or Sportvan; K=106 in. wheelbase Conventional cab 4x4; P= Forward-Control.

Model	Body Type	Price	Weight	Prod. Total
1/2-Ton LUV — Model L/Series 82 — 102.4 in. w.b.				
CL10503	Mini-Pickup	2976	2380	Note 1

NOTE 1: Calendar year sales: [974] 30,328.

Model	Body Type	Price	Weight	Prod. Total
1/2-Ton Vega — Model HV/Series 14000 — 97 in. w.b. — Four				
1HV05	Panel Express	2822	2401	—
El Camino — Model C/Series 13000 — 116 in. w.b. — Six				
1AC80	Sedan-Pickup	3828	3706	Note 2
El Camino Classic — Model D/Series 13000 — 116 in. w.b.				
1AD80	Classic Sedan-Pickup	3966	3748	Note 2

NOTE 2: Total El Camino production was 33,620.

ENGINE [Optional K10/K20/El Camino — $113]: V-block. OHV. Eight-cylinder. Cast iron block. Bore & stroke: 4-1/8 in. x 4 in. Displacement: 400 cid. Compression ratio: 8.5:1. Net horsepower: 175 at 3600 rpm. Five main bearings. Hydraulic valve lifters. Carburetor: four-barrel.

ENGINE [Optional C10/C20/C30]: V-block. OHV. Eight-cylinder. Cast iron block. Bore & stroke: 4-1/8 in. x 4 in. Displacement: 454 cid. Compression ratio: 8.25:1. Net horsepower: 230 at 3800 rpm. Five main bearings. Hydraulic valve lifters. Carburetor: Rochester four-barrel Quadra-Jet.

ENGINE [El Camino]: V-block. OHV. Eight-cylinder. Cast iron block. Bore & stroke: 4-1/8 in. x 4 in. Displacement: 454 cid. Compression ratio: 8.25:1. Net horsepower: 235 at 3800 rpm. Five main bearings. Hydraulic valve lifters. Carburetor: Rochester four-barrel Quadra-Jet.

CHASSIS [P10]: Wheelbase: 102 in. Height: 75 in. Tires: G78-15B.

CHASSIS [C20]: Wheelbase: 117.5 in./131.5 in./164.5 in. Overall length: [Fleetside] 191-1/4 in./211-1/4 in./244-1/4 in.; [Step-Side] 210-1/4/244-1/4 in. Height: 69.8 in. Front tread: 65.8 in. Rear tread: 62.7 in. Tires: [Standard] 8.75 x 16.5C in. [Crew Cab] 9.50 x 16.5D

CHASSIS [K20]: Wheelbase: 131.5 in. Overall length: [Fleetside] 211-1/4 in.; [Step-Side] 210-1/4 in. Height: 73.9 in. Front tread: 65.8 in. Rear tread: 62.7 in. Tires: 8.75 x 16.5C.

CHASSIS [P20]: Wheelbase: 125 in./133 in. Overall length: 220.75 in./244.75 in. Tires: 8.75 x 16.5C.

CHASSIS [P30]: Wheelbase: 125 in./133 in./157 in. Overall length: 220.75 in./268.75 in. Tires: 8.75 x 16.5C.

OPTIONS: Radio: AM or AM/FM. Windshield embedded antenna. Gauge package (ammeter, oil pressure, temperature) available with either tachometer or clock or with exomomindor gauge only. Tachometer. Drip molding. Exterior tool and storage compartment. Air-conditioning. Stainless steel Wheelcovers. White sidewall tires (Series 10 only). Below-Eyeline mirrors. Comfortilt steering wheel. Rear step bumper. Special trim molding (Fleetside only). Chrome bumpers. Chrome front bumper with rubber impact strips. Woodgrain exterior trim (Fleetside only). Sliding rear window. Cargo area lamp. Box-mounted spare tire. Glide-out spare tire carrier.

HISTORICAL: Introduced Sept. 2, 1973. Calendar year registrations: 803,864. Calendar year registrations by weight class: [6,000 lbs. and less] 575,348; [6,000-10,000 lbs.] 228,516. Calendar year production: 838,959 units (not including Vega/El Camino/LUV). Chevrolet held 29.44 percent of the U.S. truck market. On a calendar year basis, this was Chevrolet's second best year in truck sales in history with sales of 885,362 units and production of 896,130. The model year figures were, however, even more impressive with 975,257 sales and 925,696 trucks built to 1974 specifications. This production total includes trucks built in Canada for sale here, but does not include LUVs (which are included in the sales total). An all-time production record, for the Flint, Mich. factory (339,678 trucks) was set. On a calendar year basis, 85.5 percent of Chevrolet's output was V-8 powered; 15.1 percent had six-cylinder engines and a mere 0.4 percent were diesel engined.

STANDARD CATALOG CONTRIBUTORS

MARQUE RESEARCHERS

ROBERT C. ACKERSON is a writer and historian from Schenevus, N.Y. He authored the *STANDARD CATALOG of 4x4's 1945-1993* and contributed to the *STANDARD CATALOG of AMERICAN CARS 1805-1942.* He has also written the *ENCYCLOPEDIA of the AMERICAN SUPERCAR* and the *FORD RANCHERO SOURCE BOOK.* Ackerson received special recognition from the Society of Automotive Historians for material he contributed to *THE LINCOLN MOTOR CAR; SIXTY YEARS of EXCELLENCE.* He has done numerous articles for *OLD CARS* and other periodicals. His work on this catalog includes contributions to the Chevrolet, GMC and Jeep sections.

BOB ADLER, a former research biochemist, opened his restoration business in 1978. Chevrolet Advance-Design trucks filled the need for business transportation for Adler's Antique Autos, Inc. This led to the shop's specialty of restoring these models. Bob Adler has accumulated over 70 Advance-Design trucks. He is a technical advisor on these models for both the Vintage Chevrolet Club of America and the National Chevrolet-GMC Truck Association. Adler has authored numerous articles on their restoration and preservation.

JIM BENJAMINSON has been involved with old cars since 1962 when his Aunt Clara gave him a 1932 Chevrolet pickup. Two years later he got a 1940 Plymouth. He joined the Plymouth 4 & 6 Cylinder Owners Club in 1967. Benjaminson has been membership secretary of the club since 1974 and editor of the *THE PLYMOUTH BULLETIN* for the past 12 years. In 1984, he received the M.J. Duryea award from the Antique Automobile Club of America for his article "Automobile Manufacturing in North Dakota." He founded the Powell Sport Wagon Registry in 1981. Jim Benjaminson researched the Plymouth section of this catalog.

GREG CARSON, of Penhold, Alberta, Canada, is a 1954-1955 First Series Chevrolet truck owner and enthusiast. His special interests are in the fine points of the history of these models and the four-wheel drive conversions offered for them by NAPCO Products, Division, a Minneapolis, Minn. company that built the Powr-Pak four-wheel drive system that Chevrolet dealers merchandised. Greg did a fine job re-writing the 1954-1955 First Series Chevrolet section of this catalog and improving the accuracy of the information that it includes.

DON BUNN researched the Dodge section of *THE STANDARD CATALOG of AMERICAN LIGHT-DUTY TRUCKS.* He has lived in Minnesota all of his life. When not involved in the old truck hobby, Don spends his time selling office furniture. He bought his first collector truck, a 1952 Dodge Pickup, during 1973 and restored it in 1980. Bunn's various old truck hobby activities included serving as President of the Light Commercial Vehicle Association. He was also the club's Technical Advisor for 1948-1960 Dodge Trucks. Don wrote the monthly "Light-Duty Trucking" column for *OLD CARS* for several years.

JAMES M. FLAMMANG is a freelance writer specializing in automobiles, computers and electronics. He has written extensively about automotive history and technology, the social impact of the motor car, repair and restoration and ownership of both collectible and conventional vehicles. His interest in transportation dates back to childhood and encompasses just about everything that moves; not only trucks and cars, but also trains, buses and ships. Cars and pickups of the 1930s through 1950s rank as his favorites. Jim edited the Dodge section, a project on which he did an outstanding job.

FRED K. FOX has been a car collector since 1950. He and wife Linda own 15 vehicles. Fred is feature editor of the Studebaker Drivers Club's *TURNING WHEELS* and former editor of the *AVANTI NEWSLETTER* and *THE MILESTONE CAR.* Fox has contributed to a many national hobby magazines and co-authored *STUDEBAKER-THE COMPLETE STORY* in which he wrote the truck section. He has engineering degrees from the University of California (BS) and Pennsylvania State University (MS). He is a member of the national engineering honor society Tau Beta Pi. Our Studebaker truck section was written and illustrated by Fox.

JEFF GILLIS contributed Durant information to this catalog. Jeff purchased his first true antique car in 1970. It was a 1930 Durant Coach. Over the next six years, he restored the Durant without the aid of a club. This inspired him to form The Durant Family Registry in 1976 to assist owners of Durant-built cars and trucks. The DFR has grown to a sustained membership of 400 hobbyists from all corners of the world. The club magazine *DURANT'S STANDARD* received the *OLD CARS* "Golden Quill" award. Gillis has contributed articles to national hobby magazines. He participates in hobby events with his Durant and 1954 Chevrolet.

JOHN A. GUNNELL was born in Staten Island, N.Y. and attended Brooklyn Technical High School to study industrial design. He later studied English, history and fine art and earned a Bachelor of Arts degree in art. Writing about antique cars as a creative outlet, Gunnell began working as editor of several club publications. In 1978, he took an editorial position with *OLD CARS* and relocated to Iola, Wis. Since 1975 he has written articles and books and edited six standard catalogs. John owns 1936 and 1953 Pontiacs and someday wants a 1958 Chevy Apache pickup.

STEVE HANSON (and partner Tim Huehn) operate H & H Trucks, a Rice Lake, Wis. restoration company that specializes in the sales and restoration of 1960-1972 Chevrolet trucks, as well as locating parts for such vehicles. Steve Hanson has owned dozens of these light-duty Chevrolet trucks and is well-versed in their history and technology. A large collection of original literature for these vehicles has enabled Steve to research their original features and authenticity. He has written articles about 1960-1972 Chevrolet trucks for OLD CARS and other hobby publications.

ROBERT HENSEL, of Brillion, Wis., is internationally known as an expert on vintage Chevrolet cars trucks, including a 1926 Chevrolet fire truck that he brings to many antique auto meets. Hensel's company, Chevy Acres, specializes in publications, parts and restoration services for older Chevrolets of all types. A longtime member of the Vintage Chevrolet Club of America (VCCA), Hensel serves as the group's National Coordinator of Technical Advisor Services. He is also the club's technical advisor for 1919-1920; 1923-1924; 1926-1928; 1934-1936; 1938; and 1960-1974 commercial vehicles.

TOM MELEO, of Lindsay, Calif., serves as a vice-president for the Vintage Chevrolet Club of America (VCCA). He is also the VCCA Technical Advisor for 1921-1922 Series D, Series G and Series H Chevrolet trucks. In this volunteer role, Mr. Meleo provides technical services and advice to VCCA members nationwide who are restoring Chevrolet trucks made in those years. Tom reviewed the 1921-1922 Chevrolet section of *THE STANDARD CATALOG of LIGHT-DUTY AMERICAN TRUCKS 1896-1986.*

JOEL R. MILLER operates Miller's Dodge Garage in Portland, Ore. Miller specializes in the care and feeding of vintage Dodges, particularly commercial vehicles. A frequent user of the first edition of The *STANDARD CATALOG of LIGHT-DUTY AMERICAN TRUCKS 1896-1986*, Miller completed additional research to correct and amplify information for the Dodge truck and Fargo truck sections of the second edition. Much of his knowledge and research is focused on the highly collectible C-1/T300 series manufactured from October 1953 through April 1955.

FRANK SENKBEIL serves as director of the Vintage Chevrolet Club of America's Chattahoochee Region, based in Jonesboro, Ga. In the area of Chevrolet trucks, his specialty is the 1954 commercial models and Senkbeil is the VCCA Commercial Technical Advisor for that model year. His research for the *STANDARD CATALOG of LIGHT-DUTY AMERICAN TRUCKS 1896-1986* revealed some interesting information, such as the fact that Hydra-Matic transmission was used in 13,000 Chevrolet trucks built during 1954.

BILL SIURU trained as an automotive engineer and spent 24 years with the U.S. Air Force. He was involved in the development of new aircraft, missiles and spacecraft, but never forgot the car. For the past 15 years, he has been a car collector and restorer. His main interest is the Volvo P1800. He writes for numerous enthusiast publications. Since retiring, Bill has divided his time between writing about cars and aircraft and doing research in aerodynamics at the University of Colorado in Colorado Springs. Siuru wrote *FORD RANCHERO 1957-1979 PHOTOFACTS* and researched the Crosley section of this catalog.

FOREST "CHIP" SWEET serves as 1931-1933 Commercial Vehicle Technical Advisor for the Vintage Chevrolet Club of America. A native of Lake Jackson, Texas, Sweet is well-versed in the historical background and the mechanical make-up of the Chevrolet trucks built during the lean years of the Great Depression. He has collected a great deal of factory literature and specialized information these models. His goal is to disseminate accurate information to those involved in the vehicle collecting hobby. "No one wants collectors to waste time and money as a result of improper information," he says.

CHARLES WEBB is a freelance writer and member of the Wisconsin Chapter of the Society of Automotive Historians. He is author of *THE INVESTOR'S ILLUSTRATED GUIDE to AMERICAN CONVERTIBLE and SPECIAL INTEREST AUTOMOBILES 1946-1976* and a contributor to the *STANDARD CATALOG of AMERICAN CARS 1946-1975.* Webb collects vintage truck and car television commercials and sales promotion films. He also wrote the "Cars As The Stars" video review column for OLD CARS. He did the Ford, 1980-1986 Dodge and postwar Plymouth sections of this catalog.

DONALD F. WOOD is a professor of transportation in the School of Business at San Francisco State University. He co-authored of several college textbooks and served as a consultant to numerous government and private agencies. Don writes about old trucks as a hobby. He has done over 50 articles and several books on the development of trucks and trucking. One of his works is *CHEVY EL CAMINO 1959-1982 PHOTOFACTS.* Professor Wood's contributions to this catalog included preliminary work on the "Directory of Additional Truck Manufacturers" and hundreds of truck photos from his massive collection.

LESLIE WALL is a light-duty truck collector with a specialized interest in the 1958 Chevrolet Cameo Carrier. Produced in four model years, beginning in 1955, the Cameo Carrier was a limited-production model combining the features of a sporty passenger car with the functionality of a pickup. During model year 1958, the Cameo was produced for only a few months, then replaced with a new Fleetside model featuring double-wall steel box construction with Cameo-like styling. Leslie is a native of Independence, La. who has gathered numerous factory references to document the 1958 Cameo's history.

R. PERRY ZAVITZ is an expert on post World War II vehicles and has written numerous articles and book sections covering Canadian models. Perry's special interests include collecting auto sales literature, factory photos and historical items related to passenger cars, station wagons and crew cab trucks built from 1945 on. He has served as secretary and director of The Society of Automotive Historians and was the first director of the society's Canadian chapter. He is a television production staff executive. Perry contributed numerous photos of different brands of trucks for this volume.

ARTISTS

BOB HOVORKA has done some outstanding automotive artwork that is familiar to car buffs across the country. His "The Old Filling Station" feature appeared regularly in *OLD CARS* and he has done the "Blueprints" features for *SPECIAL INTEREST AUTOS.* Hovorka's long list of accomplishments includes other renderings that have appeared in *CAR COLLECTOR*, as well as on limited-edition posters. Bob's Ford poster, used as a cover on Old Cars Weekly during 1984, won an Imperial Palace Moto Award. The Ford F-100 appearing on the cover of the second edition is based on a Bob Hovorka line drawing.

BARON LESPERANCE is responsible for the "colorized" rendition of Bob Hovorka's Ford F-100 artwork appearing on the cover of the second edition of *THE STANDARD CATALOG of AMERICAN LIGHT-DUTY TRUCKS.* A loyal reader of *OLD CARS*, Mr. Lesperance participated in the coloring contest used to promote the first edition, when it was published in 1987. His entry was so outstanding, that we decided to employ it as part of the new cover art.

BOB LICHTY is in charge of marketing, advertising, public relations and publications for Blackhawk Automobile Collection. Lichty began his career at B.F. Goodrich. He has worked for collector publications, Kruse auction and Carlisle Productions. He also operated a collector car dealership in California. Lichty has written numerous articles and compiled the first-ever directory to hobby events.

SPECIAL THANKS

In addition to the Marque Researchers listed above, Krause Publications would like to give special thanks to the following people who went above and beyond the call of duty to help make this catalog possible:

Stan Binnie, Parts of the Past, Waukesha, Wis. (Truck Literature); Terry V. Boyce, Detroit, Mich. (1960-1970s Chevrolet data); George H. Dammann, Crestline Publishing, Sarasota, Fla. (1973-1986 Chevrolet Photos); ; Seth Doulton, Golden State Pickup Parts, Santa Barbara, Calif. (proofreading Chevrolet section); Jack Down, Lansing, Mich. (research on minor makes); Ralph Dunwoodie, Sun Valley, Nev. (research on minor makes); F. Denny Freeston, Atlanta, Ga. (proofreading Willys-Overland); LaVon Gray, Bristol, Ind. (IHC "Red Baby" sales literature); Jerry Heasley, Pampa, Texas (Ford production data and photos); Elliott Kahn, Clearwater Beach, Fla. (directory information); Rochelle R. LaDoucher, public relations, GMC Truck & Bus (GMC photos and data); Edward S. Lechtzin, public relations, Chevrolet Motor Division (Chevrolet truck photos); Jack L. Martin, Society of Automotive Historians, Indianapolis, Ind. (photos of Indy 500 Official Trucks); John Perala, Richmond, Calif. (research on minor makes); Duane A. Perrin, Manassas, Va., (proofreading Willys-Overland); Robert D. Regehr, Route 6 Classics (IHC information); John M. Sawruk, historian, Pontiac Motor Division (photos of prototype Pontiac trucks); The Spokesman, Inc., Tulsa, Okla. (general photos); James A. Wren, Automotive Research, Detroit, Mich. (Extensive photos-all marques).

As with any work of this scope, scores of other researchers, hobbyists, collectors, dealers, historians, writers and experts provided much information without which this catalog would never have become a reality. We'd like to thank everyone who took the time to send letters, notes, memos, clippings and advice. It was impossible to personally answer all of the mail that arrived at the Iola office, but it has all been carefully read and considered in the creation of this second edition.

PHOTO CREDITS

Whenever possible in this catalog, we have strived to picture light-duty trucks with photographs that show them in original form. Non-original features are usually noted. Some photos show the full name (or first initial and last name) of hobbyists and collectors who are owners of light-duty trucks and sent photos of their own vehicles. Photos contributed by other sources are identified with alphabetical codes corresponding to those in the list below. Double codes, separated by a slash mark, indicate the photo came from a collector who obtained it from another source. The double codes identify both sources. Photos without codes are from the *OLD CARS* photo archives.

(A&A) Applegate & Applegate
(ABA) Anheuser-Busch Archives
(ABE) American Body & Equipment Co.
(ACE) U.S. Army Corps of Engineers
(ACD) Auburn-Cord-Duesenberg Museum
(ACTHR) American Commercial Truck History & Research
(AHS) American Humane Society
(AMC) American Motors Corporation
(ASL) Akron-Summit County Library
(ASC) Antique Studebaker Club
(ATA) American Trucking Association
(ATC) Antique Truck Club of America
(ATHS) American Truck Historical Society
(BAC) Bill & Ann Clark
(BC/BCA) Blackhawk Classic Auto Collection
(BLHU) Baker Library, Harvard University
(BMM) Bill & Mary Mason
(BOR) U.S. Bureau of Reclaimation
(BS) Bob Strand
(BWA) Burkhart Wilson Associates
(BWW) B.W. Wine
(CAC) Crosley Automobile Club
(CC) Coca-Cola Company
(CCC) Crown Coach Corporation
(CDC) C.D. Clayton
(CE) Christine Eisenberg
(CHC) Chrysler Historical Collection
(CHP) California Highway Patrol
(CL) Carl Lirenzo
(CMD) Chevrolet Motor Division
(CMW) Christie, Manson & Woods Auctioneers
(CP) Crestline Publishing Company
(CPC) Calendar Promotions Company
(CPD) Chrysler-Plymouth Division
(CS) Curly Schreckenberg
(CSC) Cities Service Company
(CTA) California Trucking Association
(CW) Charles Webb
(CWC) Charles Wacker Body Company
(DB) Don Bunn
(DE) Doctor Eldoonie
(DFR) Durant Family Registry
(DFW) Donald F. Wood (SFU)
(DH) Don Hermany
(DHL) D.H. Landis
(DJE) David J. Entler
(DJS) Donald J. Summar
(DK) Dave Kostansek
(DNP) Dodge News Photo
(DPL) Detroit Public Library (NAHC)
(DS) Dennis Schrimpf
(DSM) Dunkirk (N.Y.) Swap Meet
(DSO) Daniel S. Olsen
(EK) Elliott Kahn
(ELC) Eli Lilly Company Archives
(FA) Firestone Archives
(FKF) Fred K. Fox
(FLP) Free Library of Philadelphia
(FLW) Franklin L. Walls
(FMC) Ford Motor Company
(FMCC) Ford Motor Company of Canada

(GC) Gillig Corporation
(GCC) Gast Classic Collection
(GEM) George E. Monroe
(GFC) General Foods Corporation
(GHB) George Heiser Body Company
(GHD) George H. Dammann
(GM) Giant Manufacturing Company
(GMC) General Motors Truck & Coach Division
(G-O) Grumman-Olsen
(GYTR) Goodyear Tire & Rubber Co.
(HAC) Harrah's Automobile Collection
(HACJ) Henry Austin Clark, Jr.
(HC) Hesse Corporation
(HCC) Horseless Carriage Club of America
(HCHS) Hobart County Historical Society
(HE) Hope Emerich
(HEPO) Hydro-Electric Power of Ontario
(HFM) Henry Ford Museum & Greenfield Village
(HSM) Hoosier Swap Meet & Auto Show
(HTM) Hays Truck Museum
(IBC) Interstate Brands Company
(IBT) Illinois Bell Telephone Co.
(ICS) Iola Car Show
(IHC) International Harvester Company
(IMSC) Indianapolis Motor Speedway Corp.
(IOA) Institute of Outdoor Advertising
(IPC) Imperial Palace Auto Collection
(JAG) John A. Gunnell Collection
(JAW) James A. Wren Automotive Research
(JB) Jim Benjaminson
(JB2) Jerry Beno (1928 Chevrolet)
(JB3) Jerry Bougher (1927 Pontiac)
(JBY) John B. Yetter
(JC) John Cox
(JCL) James C. Leake (Tulsa Auction)
(JE) Joe Egle
(JG) Jeff Gillis
(JH) Jerry Heasley
(JHV) J.H. Valentine
(JL) Jon Lang
(JLB) James L. Bell
(JLC) Jefferson/Little Carlisle Auto Show
(JLM) Jack L. Martin
(JMS) John M. Sawruk
(JRH) J. Roddy Huft
(JS) John Scott
(KCMS) Kansas City Museum of Science
(KJC) Kaiser-Jeep Corporation
(KM/HW) Kissel Museum/Hardford, Wis.
(LC) Linda Clark
(LIAM) Long Island Automotive Museum
(LLD) Lewis L. Danduraud
(LOC) Library of Congress
(LS) Lorin Sorenson
(MBC/MPB) McCabe-Powers Body Company
(MC) Micheal Carbonella
(MCC) Mother's Cakes & Cookies, Co.
(MES) Missletoe Express Service
(MG) Mort Glashofer
(MM) Mike Margerum
(MPC) McCabe Powers Body Company
(MQ) Michael Querio

(MS) Mitch Stenzler
(MTFCA) Model T Ford Club of America
(MVMA) Motor Vehicle Manufacturer's Association
(NA) National Arcives
(NAHC) National Automotive History Collection (DPL)
(NDC) Nacy & Dean Cowan
(NIC) Navistar International Company (IHC)
(NSPC) National Steel Products Company
(OCW) Old Cars Weekly
(OHS) Oregon Historical Society
(PM) Paul McLaughlin
(PMD) Pontiac Motor Division
(POC) Plymouth 4 & 6 Cylinder Owners Club
(POCI) Pontiac Oakland Club International
(PS) Pierce-Arrow Society
(PTC) Pacific Telephone Company
(RAW) Raymond A. Wawrzyniak
(RB) Russell Brown
(RCA) Robert C. Ackerson
(RCK) Robert C. Krause
(RJ) Rolland Jerry
(RJT) Robert J. Theimer
(RLC) R.L. Carr
(RPZ) R. Perry Zavitz
(RSB) Rank & Sons Buick (Wally Rank)
(RT) Robert Trueax
(RVH) Richard Vander Haak
(RVM) Rearview Mirror Museum
(RWC) Ramsey Winch Company
(SAB) Saskatchewan Archives Board
(SBT) Southern Bell Telephone & Telegraph Company
(SCC) SCC Promotion Club (Tom Lutzi, V.P.)
(SI) Smithsonian Institute
(SM) Steve Mostowa
(SSP) Standard Steel Products Co.
(SWT) S. Ward Tiernan
(TDB) Tommy D. Bascom
(TL) Tom Lutzi
(TSC) The Stockland Company
(UPS) United Parcel Service
(USFS) United States Forest Service
(USPS) United States Park Service
(VCCA) Vintage Chevrolet Club of America
(VHTM) Van Horn's Truck Museum
(VVC) Vita's Vintage Collection
(VWC) Volvo-White Company, Inc.
(WAD) Walter A. Drew
(WEPS) Western Electric Photographic Services
(WJP) Willard J. Prentice
(WLB) William L. Bailey
(WOM) Walter O. McIlvain
(WPL) Wisconsin Power & Light Company
(WRHS) Western Reserve Historical Society
(WRL) Western Reserve Library
(WS) Wayne Sorenson

CHEVROLET

1918-1986

1958 Chevrolet Apache 10 Fleetside Pickup

By Robert C. Ackerson

Chevrolet's first trucks, a 1/2-ton and a 1-ton, were made in 1918. From a start of 879 production units, the total number of Chevrolet trucks on the road grew to 8,179 by the end of 1919. By 1921, the company began installing outside-sourced bodies on its truck chassis at the Chevrolet factories. An all-steel, enclosed cab model and a Panel truck were introduced in 1925.

Truck number 500,000 was made in 1929, when six-cylinder engines were adopted. By the end of the year, all-time sales hit 641,482 units. In 1930, hydraulic shocks, electric fuel gauges, vacuum wipers and outside mirrors became standard. Late that season, Martin-Parry Corp., one of the world's largest truck body makers, was acquired. This led to the offering of complete 1/2-ton Pickups, Panels and Canopy Express trucks as factory models.

Passenger car-like styling graced the trucks of 1937. Three-quarter and 1-ton models joined the line. Race driver Harry Hartz traveled the country's perimeter in a Chevrolet truck. His gas bill was under one cent per mile and he had no breakdowns. By 1939, Chevrolet offered 45 models on eight wheelbases. Cumulative output was up to two million units. World War II halted production briefly, but it resumed in 1944.

Strong fleet sales, expanded color choices and a new synchromesh transmission helped the sales of trucks in the 1930s. Chevrolet's market share was 32.7 percent in 1930 and 50 percent in 1933 when the one-millionth unit was assembled. The Suburban appeared in 1935 as an all-steel station wagon on the 1/2-ton truck chassis. The next year, one-piece all-steel cab roofs and hydraulic brakes were used on the trucks.

A war wary public gobbled up nearly 260,000 Chevrolet trucks in 1947. They had 30 advanced features including an alligator-jaw hood and a "breathing" cab. A new body and steering column gear shifting bowed in 1947. The new design would last eight years with only modest changes like vent windows (1951), push-button door latches (1952), cross-bar grilles (1954) and Hydra-Matic shifting (1954).

In mid-1955, the truck-line was revolutionized with wrap-around windshields, a 12-volt electric system, optional V-8 engines, and a limited-edition "dream truck" called the Cameo. Its load box had slab-side fiberglass outer skins for an all-new fenderless look. Chevrolet's six millionth truck was built. During 1958, Chevrolet introduced dual headlamps and began a long-term association with Union Body Co. to produce Step-Van door-to-door delivery trucks.

The El Camino, a cross between a car and truck, was a 1959 highlight. Positraction axles were introduced that year, too. Fleetside pickups took the Cameo's place in line. In 1960, Chevrolet introduced a light-duty truck first with torsion bar front suspension. A total body redesign was done

and the 3100/3600/3800 series designations were switched to the C10/C20/C30 identifiers still in use today.

Full-sized El Caminos disappeared by 1961, the same year an all-new line of Forward-Control trucks was introduced. These used the Corvair platform and its air-cooled "pancake" six-cylinder engine/transaxle setup. Panels, passenger vans and pickups were available in this Corvair 95 series. One pickup had a drop-down box wall that doubled as a cargo loading ramp.

Chevrolet's eight millionth truck sale came in 1962. Two years later, the El Camino, now based on the mid-sized Chevelle, reappeared. Full-sized trucks featured self-adjusting brakes and 6,000-mile chassis lubrication intervals. In mid-1964, a compact Chevy Van was phased-in as the Corvair truck's replacement. The nine millionth Chevrolet truck was retailed, too.

A growing recreational vehicle market brought changes in 1965. They included more powerful 325 cid V-8 engines. Long Box models with 8-1/2 or 9 ft. cargo beds grew popular with buyers wishing to install camper-backs in pickup trucks. A Camper Special option package was also introduced. It had beefed-up powertrain and chassis components. Safety equipment was emphasized after 1966, becoming standard on all light-duty trucks. Chevrolet truck number 10 million left the factory during the year.

A three-door Suburban bowed in 1967, when pickups got a redesign and new CS and CST trim packages. A 108 in. wheelbase Chevy Van was offered, along with new, more rounded van bodies having a larger windshield. Safety side-markers were added to trucks in 1968, when the El Camino became a 116 in. wheelbase model with flying buttress roofline. The following season, Chevrolet went one up on Ford with a full-sized 4x4 utility truck named Blazer. Bucket seats and a center console became available as CST-level options in pickups. In 1970, Step-Vans adopted an "Easy Access" front end design.

Front disc brakes were standardized in 1971, when vans grew larger and gained coil spring front suspensions and sliding side doors. They also had new extended hoods for easier servicing. A new PO-30 Class A motorhome chassis was available, as well as a Panel Delivery version of Chevrolet's subcompact Vega station wagon. Mini-pickups sourced from Isuzu, of Japan, bowed under the Chevy LUV name in 1972, the initials standing for "Light Utility Vehicle."

Half-ton and 3/4-ton light-duty trucks adopted optional full-time 4x4 systems in 1973, a year that saw the sale of Chevrolet's 15 millionth truck. Gas tanks were moved from in the cab and all-leaf spring rear suspensions were used. Trim levels were now called Custom, Custom Deluxe, Cheyenne and Cheyenne Super (the last with woodgrained exterior body panels). Sales zoomed to 923,189 units.

Light truck sales tapered off in 1973, due to the Arab Oil Embargo. Nevertheless, the all-new 454 cid engine was released. Hi-Cube Vans were a 1974 innovation. Silverado and Scottsdale trim packages bowed in 1975. By 1977, Chevrolet had gained domination of the 4x4 market as light-duty truck sales zoomed above the one-million-per-year level. A 5.7 liter diesel V-8 was 1978's big news. A 4x4 version of the LUV pickup was added in 1979, when Chevrolet announced a figure of 21,850,083 total sales of trucks since 1918.

In mid-1980, Chevrolet abandoned the heavy-duty truck field to concentrate on light- and medium-duty sales. 1982 brought the compact S10 pickup (replacing the LUV) and a new 6.2 liter diesel V-8. Maxi-Cab and 4x4 versions of the S10 models were a headline happening for 1983. The 5.7 liter diesel was made available in El Caminos, while the full-sized 4x2 Blazer was discontinued. Production of the downsized Astro Van started in the summer of 1984, for 1985 model year release.

1919 Chevrolet Platform Stake (DFW/FLP)

1920 Chevrolet Model T Curtain Top Express (BH)

1923 Chevrolet Superior Light Delivery (BH)

1931 Chevrolet-Hercules Commercial Station Wagon (DFW/BC)

1937 Chevrolet 1/2 Ton Pickup With Utility Box (WPL)

1937 Chevrolet Coupe-Delivery (DFW/MVMA)

1949 Chevrolet 1-Ton Series 3800 Pickup (OCW)

1952 Chevrolet 1/2-Ton Series 3100 Pickup (OCW)

1954 Chevrolet 1/2-Ton Series 3100 Pickup (OCW)

1966 Chevrolet 1/2-Ton C10 Fleetside Pickup (DFW)

1974 Chevrolet 1/2-Ton K5 Blazer Utility Wagon (JAG)

1976 Chevrolet 1/2-Ton G10 Chevy Van Panel (CP)

1978 Chevrolet 1/2-Ton LUV Mini-Pickup (DFW/TSC)

1979 Chevrolet 1/2-Ton C10 Fleetside Pickup (CP)

CHEVROLET MODEL NAMES

Various terms are used in Chevrolet factory documents and sales literature to describe light-duty commercial vehicles. Sometimes different terms are used to describe the same trucks. The following chart sorts out some of the confusion:

Model Name	Type of Truck	Other Names or Nicknames
[1918-1932]		
Light Delivery	Passenger w/heavy springs	Commercial Car
Light Truck	3/4-ton truck	Commercial Car; 3/4-ton truck
Medium-Heavy	1-ton truck	Commercial Car; 1-ton Worm-Drive truck

NOTE 1: All three types formed Chevrolet's Commercial Car series.
NOTE 2: Some literature groups Sedan Delivery with passenger cars.

Model Name	Type of Truck	Other Names or Nicknames
[1933-1934]		
Light-Delivery	Passenger car-based delivery	1/2-ton Sedan Delivery Commercial Car; Light-Delivery

NOTE 3: Some factory model listings indicate 1/2-ton Sedan Delivery for 1933 models and 1/2-ton for 1934 models. There were Pickups and Panels available in the same series, so it seems most correct to call this a 1/2-ton or 1/2-ton Light-Delivery series.

Model Name	Type of Truck	Other Names or Nicknames
[1935-1946]		
Commercial Car	Sedan Delivery; Coupe-Delivery	1/2-ton Commercial; SDL Coupe-Express
Light-Delivery	1/2-ton to 1-ton truck	Light-Duty for 1/2-ton; Medium-Duty for 3/4- to 1-ton
Dubl-Duti	Forward-Control Chassis	Commercial Dubl-Duti; Forward-Control (Chassis); 3/4-ton Heavy-Duty; Parcel Delivery; Driver-Forward; Walk-in Panel

NOTE 4: Chevrolet military vehicle model names not included.
NOTE 5: Technically, Forward-Control described the chassis and Dubl-Duti described the truck body category.
NOTE 6: Trucks heavier than 1-ton were described as Heavy-Duty, Utility, Heavy-Duty COE and Utility COE models.

Model Name	Type of Truck	Other Names or Nicknames
[1946-1957]		
Sedan Delivery	Passenger car-based delivery	Commercial Car
El Camino	Coupe-Pickup (1959-'60 only)	1/2-ton Pickup; Pickup-Car
Commercial	1/2-ton to 1-ton conventional	
Dubl-Duti	Forward-Control chassis	Commercial (Dubl-Duti); Step-Van; Parcel Delivery; Walk-in; Stand-up Delivery

NOTE 7: Commercial car was the old-fashioned term for this type vehicle rarely used after 1945.

Model Name	Type of Truck	Other Names or Nicknames
[1958-1963]		
Sedan Delivery	Station Wagon-based delivery	Commercial Car
El Camino	Passenger car-based delivery	Commercial Car; 1/2-ton Pickup; Pickup-Car
Commercial	1/2-ton to 1-ton conventional	Light-duty (1/2-ton); Medium-duty (3/4-ton to 1-ton); Conventional
Dubl-Duti	Forward-Control chassis	Commercial (Dubl-Duti); Step-Van; Parcel Delivery; Walk-in; Stand-up Delivery

Model Name	Type of Truck	Other Names or Nicknames
[1964-1969]		
El Camino	Passenger car-based Pickup	Sedan-Pickup two-door; Coupe-Pickup
Chevy Van	Compact driver-forward van	Van; Panel Van; Bus (windows)
Commercial	1/2-ton to 1-ton conventional	Light-Duty (1/2-ton); Medium-Duty (3/4-ton to 1-ton); Conventional
Step-Van	Forward-Control chassis	Dubl-Duti; Walk-in; Parcel Delivery; Stand-up Delivery
Blazer	4x4 Open Utility Pickup	Sports Utility; 4x4 Utility

Model Name	Type of Truck	Other Names or Nicknames
[1970-up]		
El Camino	Passenger car-based Pickup	Sedan-Pickup two-door
Chevy Van	Commercial Panel Van	Van; Panel Van; Compact Van
Sportvan	Passenger Window Van	Bus; Window Van; Beauville; Bonaventure
Hi-Cube Van	Van Chassis With Cargo Box	Cutaway Van
Conventional	1/2-ton to 1-ton conventional	Commercial; Light-duty (1/2-ton); Medium-duty (3/4-ton to 1-ton)
Big-Dooley	1-ton Crew Cab Fleetside Long	"Country Cadillac" Box Pickup w/dual rear wheels
Step-Van	Parcel Delivery Truck	Forward-Control
Step-Van King	High, wide, Aluminum Step-Van	Forward-Control Van (10 ft. to 14.5 ft.)
Vega	Subcompact wagon-based Panel	Panel Express; Panel
LUV	Imported Mini-Pickup	Mini-Pickup; Fleetside Mini
S10	Mini-Truck	Mini-Pickup; Maxi-Cab Mini-Pickup; Mini Fleetside; Sport Pickup
S10 Blazer	Mini-Sport Utility Wagon	Sport Utility; Sport Utility Wagon

Other descriptive terms: 1100= Sedan Delivery; 1500 or 1508=Sedan Delivery; 3100=1/2-ton; 3124=Cameo Carrier (1955-1958); 3200=Long Wheelbase 1/2-ton; 3600=3/4-ton; 3800=1-ton; 3700=3/4-ton Dubl-Duti; 3900=1-ton Dubl-Duti; C10=1/2 ton; K10=1/2-ton 4x4; C14=1/2-ton Long Wheelbase; K14=1/2-ton Long Wheelbase 4x4; C20=3/4-ton; K20=3/4-ton 4x4; C30=1-ton; K30=1-ton 4x4; C25=Heavy-Duty 3/4-ton; Carryall=Suburban; Canopy=Canopy Delivery; Panel=Panel Delivery; Step-Side=Pickup with "pontoon" rear fenders; Fleetside=Pickup with slab-side rear quarters.

Common Chevrolet trim and equipment names: Custom Cab; Apache; Long Horn; Custom/10; Custom Deluxe; Custom Sport Truck (CST); Camper-Special; Cheyenne; Cheyenne Super; Scottsdale; Silverado; Chevy Sport; Beauville; Bonaventure; El Camino Custom; El Camino SS or SS-396 (Super Sport and Super Sport with 396 cid V-8); El Camino Conquista; El Camino Royal Knight; Big Dooley; S10 Tahoe; S10 Durango; S10 High-Sierra; LUV Mikado.

1918 CHEVROLET

1918 Chevrolet 1-Ton Model T Panel (DFW/OHS)

LIGHT DELIVERY — MODEL 490 — FOUR-CYLINDER: Chevrolet began production of a Light Delivery in January, 1918. It was a version of the 490 passenger car chassis beefed-up with heavier springs. It used the cowl and 15-degree backwards-slanting windshield of open Chevrolet automobiles. Standard equipment included a speedometer, ammeter, tire pump, electric horn and demountable rims. Chevrolet manufactured only the chassis, fenders and cowl and included accessories like headlamps. Dealers or customers then had bodies built and installed by aftermarket firms. Martin-Parry Co., of Indianapolis, Ind., was one major supplier of commercial bodies for the Chevrolet chassis. The Light Delivery had a 1,000 lbs. or 1/2-ton "load for trucks" (payload) rating. Styling was simple and straightforward. Appearance features included semi-circular fenders and wood spoke wheels.

1918 Chevrolet Model T 1-Ton Eight-Post Curtain Top Express (BH)

MEDIUM/HEAVY TRUCK — MODEL T — FOUR-CYLINDER: Also new for 1918 was the Model T, Chevrolet's 1-ton medium-heavy worm drive truck. It was characterized by a honeycomb radiator with rounded Chevrolet bow tie badge, sloping seven louver hood and cowl-mounted headlights. These lights had hand-grips on the back of them to aid driver entry into the cab. Three models were available: The chassis for $1,325; the Flare Board Express for $1,460 and Eight Post Curtain Top Express for $1,545. The curtain top was supported on each side by four posts whose cross section was 1-1/2- x 2 in. It was removable by releasing the posts at the sill crossmembers. Mounted on the sides of the Model T were flareboards having a width of eight-inches on the slope and overhanging the vertical sides of the body by approximately six-inches. The flares were braced from the sill crossmembers to the undersides of the boards. Two compartments were provided under the three-man seat. One held the gas tank and one was for carrying purposes. Standard equipment included electric lights and starter (highest two-unit system); complete lamp equipment (including headlamp dimmers); electric horn; odometer; side curtains for driver's seat; windshield and complete tool equipment. The transmission was a selective type with three speeds forward and one reverse. Chevrolet's FA engine was used in this model in 1918.

I.D. DATA: [Series T]: Serial number stamped on crossmember at left front of engine. [Series 490]: Serial number located on dash nameplate. Engine numbers stamped on flywheel.

Model	Body Type	Price	Weight	Prod. Total
Light Delivery — Model 490 — 1/2-Ton — 102 in. w.b.				
490	Chassis	595	2170	Note 1

Medium-Heavy Truck — Model T — 1-Ton — 125 in. w.b.				
T	Worm Drive Chassis	1325	2840	Note 2
T	Flare Board Express	1460	3300	Note 2
T	Curtain Top Express	1545	3420	Note 2

NOTE 1: Light delivery production included with 490 passenger car total.
NOTE 2: Model T production through Sept. 23, 1919 was 359 units.

ENGINE: [490] OHV. Inline. Four-cylinder. Cast-iron block. Cast en bloc cylinders. Bore & stroke: 3-11/16 x 4 in. Displacement: 170.9 cid. Compression ratio: 4.25:1. Brake horsepower: 26 at 1800 rpm. NACC horsepower: 21.70. Three main bearings. Solid valve lifters. Carburetor: Zenith model V one-barrel.

ENGINE: [Model T] OHV. Inline. Four-cylinder. Cast iron block Cast en bloc cylinders. Bore & stroke: 3-11/16 x 5-1/4 in. Displacement: 224 cid. Compression ratio: 4.25:1. Brake horsepower: 37 at 2000 rpm. NACC horsepower: 21.75. Three main bearings. Solid valve lifters. Carburetor: Zenith improved double-jet.

CHASSIS: [Series 490] Wheelbase: 102 in. Tires: 30 x 3-1/2.

CHASSIS: [Series T] Wheelbase: 125 in. Length of body from inside of tailboard to inside of headboard was 114-1/2 in. Width inside boards was 45-3/4 in. Height of top from frame to highest point of top was 63-1/4 in. Overall length of top: 156-1/4 in. Tread: 56 in. Tires: [Front] 31 x 4 in. pneumatic, clincher type, non-skid with wrapped tread. [Rear] 32 x 4 in., solid.

1918 Chevrolet 1-Ton Model T Flare Board Express (BH)

TECHNICAL: [Series 490] Selective sliding gear transmission. Speeds: 3F/1R. Center-control floor shift. Cone clutch with adjustable compensating springs. Three-quarter floating rear axle with wheel bearing carried on wheel hub and in axle housing (not shaft). Hyatt roller bearings. Brakes: [Emergency] internal-expanding type; [Service] external-contracting type. 10 in. brake drums. Foot control. Wood artillery type wheels with demountable rims and large hub flanges.

TECHNICAL: Selective sliding gear transmission. Speeds: 3F/1R. Center floor-mounted gearshift. Cone clutch with adjustable compensating springs. Semi-floating rear axle. Brakes: Two sets internal-expanding type acting on rear wheel brake drums. Artillery type wheels of standard dimensions with 12 hickory spokes and front equipped with Timken tapered roller bearings of extra-large size.

OPTIONS: Front bumper. Rear bumper. Single sidemount. Heater. Spotlight. Cowl lamps. Rearview mirror.

HISTORICAL: Introduced in late 1917. Calendar year sales: Chevrolet reported 879 truck sales. Calendar year production: [Model T] 61 at Flint, Mich.; 270 at Tarrytown, N.Y.; 28 in Canada. Innovations: First Chevrolet commercial vehicles. Chevrolet's four-cylinder engine had first been used in 1914 on its Baby Grand and Royal Mail passenger cars. It had a four-inch stroke. The 5-1/4 in. stroke FA engine was introduced in 1918 for passenger cars and Model T trucks. The smaller 490 engine was used in Light Delivery models

1918 Chevrolet 1/2-Ton Model 490 Light Delivery Wagon (BH)

1919 CHEVROLET

LIGHT DELIVERY — MODEL 490 — FOUR-CYLINDER: Chevrolet's 1919 truck line was largely unchanged. Several improvements were made to all 490 models, including the Light Delivery Wagon. The spare tire carrier was of the 3/4-circle type with a lever. Standard equipment included windshield, speedometer, ammeter, tire pump, electric horn and demountable rims.

1919 Chevrolet 1-Ton Model T Eight-Post Curtain Top Express (BH)

MEDIUM/HEAVY TRUCK — MODEL T — FOUR-CYLINDER: The Model T 1-ton worm drive truck was also much the same as in 1918. Chevy claimed its design combined graceful good looks with maximum utility. The cab was clean and simple with features including a gearshift lever and emergency brake lever positioned right at hand for the operator. Dash equipment consisted of a conveniently arranged speedometer, carburetor choke, ammeter, oil pressure gauge, lighting and ignition switches. Chevrolet's FB engine was used this season. It had the same basic specifications as the 1918 FA truck powerplant. Its cylinders were cast in the block and integral with the upper half of the crankcase. The cylinder head was detachable. Other mechanical features included a gear-driven oil pump, Remy ignition system, water pump, worm-and-gear type steering, I-beam front axle, semi-floating rear axle, semi-elliptic front and rear springs, and 13 gallon gas tank. Standard equipment included electric lights and starter (highest two-unit system); complete lamp equipment (including headlamp dimmers); electric horn; odometer; side curtains for driver's seat; windshield and complete tool equipment. The transmission was a selective type with three speeds forward and one reverse.

I.D. DATA: [Series T]: Serial number stamped on frame crossmember at left front of engine. Also on nameplate on dash. [Series 490]: Serial number located on dash nameplate. Serial numbers: [Series T] 1-1082 to 1-2284; 2-1270 to 2-2201; 3-1000 to 3-1300; 6-1047 to 6-1644 and 9-029 to 9-355. Explanation of assembly plant code: The numerical prefix identifies manufacturing plant as follows, 1=Flint, Mich.; 2=Tarrytown, N.Y.; 3=St. Louis, Mo.; 6=Oakland Calif. and 9=Oshawa Ontario, Canada. Engine numbers: located on flywheel.

Model	Body Type	Price	Weight	Prod. Total
Light Delivery — Model 490 — 1/2-Ton — 102 in. w.b.				
490	Chassis	735	2170	Note 1
Medium-Heavy Truck — Model T — 1-Ton — 125 in. w.b.				
T	Worm Drive Chassis	1325	2840	
T	Flare Board Express	1460	3300	
T	Curtain Top Express	1545	3420	

NOTE 1: Light delivery production included with 490 passenger car total.

ENGINE: [490] OHV. Inline. Four-cylinder. Cast iron block. Cast en bloc cylinders. Bore & stroke: 3-11/16 x 4 in. Displacement: 170.9 cid. Compression ratio: 4.25:1. Brake horsepower: 26 at 1800 rpm. NACC horsepower: 21.70. Three main bearings. Solid valve lifters. Carburetor: Zenith model V one-barrel.

ENGINE: [Model T] OHV. Inline. Four-cylinder. Cast iron block. Cylinder cast en bloc. Bore & stroke: 3-11/16 x 5-1/4 in. Displacement: 224 cid. Compression ratio: 4.25:1. Brake horsepower: 37 2000 rpm. NACC H.P.: 21.75. Three main bearings. Solid valve lifters. Carburetor: Zenith improved double-jet.

CHASSIS: [Series 490] Wheelbase: 102 in. Frame thickness: 4 in. Front frame width: 30-1/2 in. Rear frame width: 35-1/8 in. Length behind seat: 109 in. Loaded frame height: 25 in. Springs: Semi-elliptic, [front] 2-1/4 x 37-1/2 in.; [rear] 2-1/2 x 53 in. Tires: 30 x 3-1/2.

CHASSIS: [Model T] Wheelbase: 125 in. Length of body from inside of tailboard to inside of headboard was 114-1/2 in. Width inside boards was 45-3/4 in. Height of top from frame to highest point: 63-1/4 in. Overall length: 156-1/4 in. Tread: 56 in. Tires: [Front] 31 x 4 in., pneumatic, non-skid with wrapped tread; [Rear] 32 x 4 in.

TECHNICAL: [Both models] Selective sliding gear transmission. Speeds: 3F/1R. Floor-mounted gearshift. Cone type clutches, same as 1918. [Model 490] three-quarter floating rear axle; [Model T] semi-floating rear axle. External contracting mechanical rear wheel brakes. Wooden spoke wheels of same types as 1918. Model T driveshaft was of high-carbon seamless steel tubing 1-3/8 in. in diameter. Center of driveshaft supported on double row of self-aligning ball bearings close to middle U-Joint. Bearing housing filled with lubricant and fitted with compression grease cup for refilling. Worm gear drive: The steel worm was cut, hardened and finish-ground by special machine. The bronze gear was of special alloy, accurately cut, with teeth burnished to reduce friction. The gear ran in oil and acted as a pump which picked up and circulated oil over the worm and through the bearings. A governor was fitted on the Model T and set for 25 mph maximum speed, with a lock to prevent operator tampering.

OPTIONS: Front bumper. Rear bumper. Heater. Cowl lamps. Rearview mirror.

HISTORICAL: Introduced: Late 1918. Calendar year sales: 8,179 trucks. Calendar year production: [Model T] 1,203 at Flint, Mich.; 932 at Tarrytown, N.Y.; 301 at St. Louis, Mo.; 597 at Oakland, Calif.; 326 in Oshawa, Canada. Innovations: The popularity of Chevrolet trucks was starting to rise. Sales of Samson (another GM branch) trucks and tractors were assigned to the Chevrolet dealer organization. Martin-Parry Co. continued as the major supplier of bodies for Chevrolet chassis. William C. Durant was in control of Chevrolet this year. The company was a branch of General Motors.

1920 CHEVROLET

1920 Chevrolet 1-Ton Model T Eight-Post Curtain Top Express (BH)

LIGHT DELIVERY — MODEL 490 — FOUR-CYLINDER: "The Chevrolet Light Delivery Wagon is designed to meet the requirements of those who have need of a commercial car with slightly less capacity and of considerably lighter weight then is afforded by a 1-ton truck," said Chevrolet's 1920 *COMMERCIAL CARS* sales catalog. "It is sturdily constructed and amply powered for all transportation needs. It is light enough to be speedy, easy riding and economical with fuel and tires." Appearance improvements for the 490 included use of a reverse-curve fender line and full-crown fenders. Headlamps were mounted to the fenders, eliminating the tie-bar previously used. A couple of technical changes were made. Chevrolet still refrained from truck body building. However, the company put out a contract to source delivery wagon bodies from outside and install them at the factory level. In addition to the Chassis & Cowl truck, two models were cataloged with express bodies. Both had a four-post curtain top. The first included driver's seat and side curtains for use in cold or stormy weather. Two extra seats were provided in the second model (one at the extreme rear and one at the center of the express box) to make it useful for Station Wagon or other passenger transportation requirements. Standard equipment included: Electric lights; self-starter; complete lamps (including adjustable headlamps); top and curtains; adjustable windshield; speedometer; electric horn; extra rim; tire carrier and complete tools including tire pump and jack.

1920 Chevrolet 1/2-Ton Model 490 Light Delivery (BH)

1920 Chevrolet Model 490 Light Delivery (BH)

MEDIUM/HEAVY TRUCK — MODEL T — FOUR-CYLINDER: Chevrolet's 1-ton Model T truck (the worm drive system was now de-emphasized in sales literature) was also back in 1920. The *COMMERCIAL CAR* sales catalog stressed the abilities of its FB powerplant

sturdy construction that insured maximum service and minimum wear. Included with the basic chassis model were radiator, hood, cowl, front fenders and runningboards. The single driver's seat was mounted atop a tall platform housing the gas tank and a storage compartment. Also available was a Flare Board Express body measuring 114-1/2 in. long from the inside of the tailboard to inside of headboard, with 44 in. width inside the boards. A third model added an eight-post curtain top. The standard equipment list included electric lights and starter (highest two-unit system); complete lamp equipment (including headlamp dimmer); electric horn; odometer; side curtain for driver's seat; windshield and complete tool equipment.

I.D. DATA: Serial number stamped on frame crossmember at left front of engine. Also on nameplate on dash. Serial numbers: [490] 2-1000 to 2A-24086 and 9-115 and up. [Model T]: 1-2285 to 4199; 2-2202 to 3616; 3-1301 to 1953; 6-1645 to 2362 and 9-356 to 9-847. The numerical prefix (such as 2-) identifies manufacturing plant as follows: 1=Flint, Mich.; 2=Tarrytown, N.Y.; 3=St. Louis, Mo.; 6=Oakland Calif. and 9=Oshawa Ontario, Canada. Engine numbers located on flywheel.

1920 Chevrolet 1/2-Ton Model 490 Light Delivery Farm Wagon (BH)

Model	Body Type	Price	Weight	Prod. Total
Light Delivery — Series 490 — 1/2-Ton — 102 in. w.b.				
490	Light Delivery Chassis	685	2170	Note 1
490	Delivery Wagon 1-seat	735	—	Note 1
490	Delivery Wagon 3-seat	770	—	Note 1
Medium-Heavy Truck — Model T — 1-Ton — 125 in. w.b.				
T	Chassis & Cowl	1325	3300	Note 2
T	Flare Board Express	1460	—	Note 2
T	Covered Flare	1545	—	Note 2

NOTE 1: Light-delivery production included with 490 passenger car total.
NOTE 2: Series production was 5,288 units at all factories.

1920 Chevrolet 1/2-Ton Light Delivery Four-Post Top & Curtains (BH)

ENGINE: [490] Inline. Cast en bloc. OHV. Four-cylinder. Cast-iron block. Bore & stroke: 3-11/16 x 4 in. Displacement: 170.9 cid. Compression ratio: 4.25:1. Brake horsepower: 26 at 1800 rpm. NACC horsepower: 21.70. Three main bearings. Solid valve lifters. Carburetor: Zenith model V.
ENGINE: [T] Inline. OHV. Cast en bloc. Four-cylinder. Cast iron block. Bore & stroke: 3-11/16 x 5-1/4 in. Displacement: 224 cid. C.R.: 4.25:1. Brake horsepower: 37 at 2000 rpm. NACC horsepower: 21.75. Three main bearings. Solid valve lifters. Carburetor: Zenith improved double-jet.

1920 Chevrolet 1-Ton Model T Chassis & Windshield (BH)

CHASSIS: [Series 490] Wheelbase: 102 in. Tires: 30 x 3-1/2 in. Steering: Spur-and-gear type (adjustable for wear) with 15 in. steering wheel.

CHASSIS: [Model T] Wheelbase: 125 in. Tires: [Front] pneumatic 33 x 4 in. demountable type, non-skid with wrapped tread. [Rear] pneumatic 35 x 5 in. cord type. Steering: Worm-and-gear type with 16 in. steering wheel. Steering arm of drop-forged steel, heat treated.

1920 Chevrolet 1-Ton Model T Flare Board Express (BH)

TECHNICAL: [490] Selective sliding gear transmission. Speeds: 3F/1R. Floor-mounted center gearshift. Cone clutch with adjustable compensating springs. Three-quarter floating rear axle. Wheel bearing carried on wheel hub in axle housing (not shaft). Hyatt roller bearings. Brakes: [Emergency] internal expanding type; [Service] external contracting type with 10 in. brake drums and foot control. Wheels: Wood artillery type, demountable rim, large hub flanges.

TECHNICAL: [T] Selective type transmission. Speeds: 3F/1R. Center floor shift control. Leather-faced cone clutch with adjustable compensating springs. Governor provided and set and locked at 25 mph maximum speed. Semi-floating rear axle made of heat treated steel. Worm gear drive has cut and hardened, finish-ground steel worm requiring no adjustment at any time. Brakes: Same as 1918-1919. Wheels: Artillery spoke, standard dimensions, 12 hickory spokes, front brakes equipped with Timken tapered roller bearings of extra large size.

1920 Chevrolet 1-Ton Model T Eight-Post Curtain Top Express (BH)

OPTIONS: Front bumper. Rear bumper. Heater. Cowl lamps. Driver's seat ($50). Pair of auxiliary seats ($85). Rearview mirror.

HISTORICAL: Introduced: January, 1920. Calendar year production: [Model T] 1,914 at Flint, Mich.; 1,414 at Tarrytown, N.Y.; 652 at St. Louis, Mo.; 717 at Oakland, Calif.; 591 in Oshawa, Canada. Innovations: New fender treatment for 490 Series commercial cars. Factory-installed aftermarket bodies. Headlamp tie-bar eliminated on 490 models. W.C. Durant was forced out of General Motors by angry stock holders. Pierre S. Durant became president of the corporation. Karl W. Zimmerschied took over as president of Chevrolet.

1920 Chevrolet 1-Ton Model T Eight-Post Curtain Top Express (BH)

Standard Catalog of Light-Duty Trucks

1921 CHEVROLET

1921 Chevrolet 1/2-Ton Model 490 Light Delivery Wagon (BH)

LIGHT DELIVERY — MODEL 490 — FOUR-CYLINDER: The 490 was basically unchanged. Chevrolet's copywriters described it as a profitable investment for all light handling and delivery purposes. Standard equipment listed in the *COMMERCIAL CARS* catalog included electric lights; self-starter; complete lamps (including adjustable headlamps); top and curtains; adjustable windshield; speedometer; electric horn; extra rim; tire carrier; and complete tools including tire pump and jack. The catalog also promoted several of the more popular bodies including a Station Wagon, Delivery Wagon, Express Wagon and Farm Wagon. All Chevrolet truck bodies were still aftermarket items sourced from outside supplier firms. However, some (as shown in the sales catalog) were mass-produced especially for delivery to and installation at Chevrolet factories. Others were purchased by dealers or buyers for aftermarket attachment to the Chevrolet chassis.

LIGHT TRUCK — MODEL G — FOUR-CYLINDER: An all-new commercial vehicle was the Model G Light Truck. It was essentially the front end of the 490 mated with the longer and heavier frame and rear axle of a truck. Chevy described it as, "the product of years of experience" and said it was "built to supply the demand for a 3/4-ton truck whose strength and performance equal(s) cars of greater capacity." This model used the larger engine. Base model offerings included the Chassis, Chassis & Cab, Open Express and Curtain Top Express. Larger in size than the 490, the Model G had slanting hood louvers, reverse curve fenders and torpedo type front-fender-mounted headlamps. Body length was 97-7/8 in. from tailboard to headboard, with a width of 46 in. between flareboards. Drive was from the left-hand side with center control. Spark and throttle were located under the steering wheel and there was a foot accelerator. Standard equipment included, electric lights and starter, highest two-unit system; complete lamp equipment; side curtains; adjustable windshield; speedometer; demountable rims; electric horn and complete tool equipment including pump and jack.

MEDIUM-HEAVY TRUCK — MODEL T — FOUR-CYLINDER: Cowl mounted headlamps remained a distinctive styling characteristic of the Model T 1-ton in 1921. It had overall larger dimensions and a narrower cowl with "scooped-out" sides. Aftermarket bodies depicted in the sales catalog included a passenger bus, fire engine, wholesale hauler, Farm Wagon and panel delivery. Standard equipment was the same as in 1920.

I.D. DATA: Serial number located on nameplate on dash. Serial numbers: [490] 1-A20821 to 57835; 2-A24086 to 54564; or 2-3020 and up. [Model G] 1-13 to 1-384; 2-77 to 2-303; 3-58 to 3-122; 6-59 to 6-182; 9-115 to 9-194. [Model T] 1-4200 to 4454; 2-3617 to 2-3631; 3-1954 to 3-2081; 6-2363 to 6-2446 and 9-356 up. The numerical prefixes (i.e. 1-) indicated the factory, as follows: 1=Flint, Mich.; 2=Tarrytown, N.Y; 3=St. Louis, Mo.; 6=Oakland, Calif.; 9=Oshawa, Canada. Engine numbers located on flywheel and left side of front motor support.

Model	Body Type	Price	Weight	Prod. Total
Light Delivery — Model 490 — 1/2-Ton — 102 in. w.b.				
490	Chassis & Cow	625	—	—
490	Open Express	820	1860	Note 1
490	Covered Express 3-seat	855	—	Note 1
Light Truck — Model G — 3/4-Ton —				
G	Chassis	920	2450	Note 2
G	Chassis & Cow	995	—	Note 2
G	Open Express	1030	—	Note 2
G	Canopy Express	1095	—	Note 2
Medium-Heavy Truck — Model T — 1-Ton				
T	Chassis	1325	3300	Note 3
T	Open Express	1460	—	Note 3
T	Canopy Express	1545	—	Note 3
T	Canopy Express 3 seat	1595	—	Note 3

NOTE 1: 490 production lumped-in with passenger cars.
NOTE 2: G production was 855 units.
NOTE 3: T production was 478 units.
NOTE 4: Prices for the Model Gs decreased during the year to: [Chassis] $745; [Chassis & Cowl] $820; [Open Express] $855; and [Canopy Express] $920.
ENGINE: [490] Inline. Cylinder cast in block. Overhead valves. Four-cylinder. Cast-iron block. Bore & stroke: 3-11/16 x 4 in. Displacement: 170.9 cid. Compression ratio: 4.25:1. Brake horsepower: 26 at 2800 rpm. SAE horsepower: 21.70. Three main bearings. Solid valve lifters. Carburetor: Zenith model one-barrel.
ENGINE: [T] Inline. Cylinders cast in block. Overhead valves. Four-cylinder. Cast iron block. Bore & Stroke: 3-11/16 x 5-1/4 in. Displacement: 224 cid. C.R.: 4.25:1. Brake horsepower: 37 at 2000 rpm. SAE H.P.: 21.75. Three main bearings. Solid valve lifters. Carburetor: Zenith improved double-jet.

CHASSIS: [490] Wheelbase: 102 in. Front axle: Drop-forged I-beam. Springs: Cantilever type front and rear. Spur-and-gear steering, adjustable for wear. 15 in. steering wheel. Tires: 30 x 3-1/2 non-skid front and rear.
CHASSIS: [G] Wheelbase: 120 in. Front axle: drop-forged I-beam. Ample sized steering knuckles and steering arms (drop-forged and heat treated). Springs: [Front] Cantilever type, 21-7/8 in. long x 1-3/4 in. wide; [Rear] One-half elliptic type, 43-1/4 in. long x 2-1/2 in. wide. Five-in. deep frame. Front frame width: 28 in. Rear frame width: 37 in. Length in back of driver's seat: 76 in. Frame height: 23-1/2 in. loaded. Tires: all-pneumatic; demountable type with wrapped tread, [Front] 31 x 4 in.; [Rear] 34 x 4-1/2 in. All-weather tread. Gas tank: 10 gallons.
CHASSIS: [T] Wheelbase: 125 in. Front axle: Drop-forged I-beam. Springs: Semi-elliptic front and rear, [Front] 38 x 2-1/4 in.; [Rear] 54 x 2-1/2 in. Worm-and-gear steering. Steering arm of drop-forged, heat-treated steel, 16 in. wheel. Tires: [Front] pneumatic, 33 x 4 in., demountable type, non-skid with wrapped tread; [Rear] 35 x 5 in. pneumatic, cord type. Gas tank capacity: 13 gallons.
TECHNICAL: [(490)] Selective sliding gear transmission. Speeds: 3F/1R. Floor-mounted gearshift. Cone type clutch with adjustable compensating springs. Three-quarter floating rear axle with Hyatt roller bearings. Brakes: [Emergency] internal expanding type; [Service] external contracting type with 10 in. brake drums and foot control. Wood artillery wheels with demountable rims and large hub flanges.
TECHNICAL: [G] Selective sliding gear transmission. Speeds: 3F/1R. Cone clutch with adjustable compensating springs. Semi-floating rear axle made of heat-treated nickel steel. Brakes: [Emergency] internal expanding type; [Service] external contracting type with 12 in. brake drums and foot control. Artillery type wheels of standard dimension with 12 hickory spokes (front wheels have Timken tapered roller bearings).
TECHNICAL: [T] Selective sliding gear transmission. Speeds: 3F/1R. Governor, lockable, with 25 mph maximum speed. Leather-faced cone clutch with adjustable compensating springs. Semi-floating rear axle made of heat-treated steel. Worm drive. Artillery wheels of standard dimension with 12 hickory spokes (front wheels have Timken tapered roller bearings).
OPTIONS: Front bumper. Rear bumper. Single sidemount. Heater. Cowl lamps.
HISTORICAL: Introduced: January, 1921. Calendar year production: [Model G] 371 at Flint, Mich.; 226 at Tarrytown, N.Y.; 64 at St. Louis, Mo.; 123 at Oakland, Calif.; and 71 in Oshawa, Canada. (Model T) 255 at Flint, Mich.; 14 at Tarrytown, N.Y.; 127 at St. Louis, Mo.; and 83 at Oakland, Calif. Innovations: New 3/4-ton Model G. Colors for new Model G varied according to body style. It was painted black when sold without cowl and Chevrolet green when sold with cowl. Standard aftermarket bodies were again listed in the Chevrolet catalog.

1922 CHEVROLET

$650
F.O.B. Flint Mich.
For specifications see page 18

1922 Chevrolet 3/4-Ton Model G Light Truck Chassis & Cowl (BH)

LIGHT DELIVERY — MODEL 490 — FOUR-CYLINDER: The 490 was basically unchanged. A number of technical changes were made. Valve adjustment was moved to the rocker arms. Larger 9/16 in. king bolts replaced the previous 1/2 in. types. An emergency brake lever was introduced to replace the old ratchet on the right-hand foot pedal. The service brakes were now operated by the right-hand pedal and the left-hand pedal was for the clutch. A spiral type of ring gear and pinion replaced the old straight-cut type. Also, a new type of differential bearing was used. Standard equipment included: Electric lights and starter (highest type two-unit system); complete lamp equipment, including adjustable headlamps; four-post top; side curtains; adjustable windshield; speedometer; electric horn; extra rim; tire carrier and complete tool equipment including pump and jack. There were no major exterior design changes. Mifflinburg Body Co. of Pennsylvania supplied some models for the factory catalogs, including: Station Wagon, Delivery Wagon, Express Wagon, and Farm Wagon.
LIGHT DELIVERY — NEW SUPERIOR — FOUR-CYLINDER: Copies of a late 1922 Chevrolet sales catalog entitled *CHEVROLET FOR ECONOMICAL TRANSPORTATION COMMERCIAL CARS* do not include the 490 Light Delivery Wagon. They shows the "New Superior" Light Delivery truck instead, plus the Model G and Model T. This indicates that the Superior was available, in calendar 1922, perhaps as a midyear model. However, most references treat the New Superior Series as a 1923 line. Refer to 1923 for details.
LIGHT TRUCK — MODEL G — FOUR-CYLINDER: For 1922, the Model G adopted a centrally mounted emergency brake lever and conventional clutch and brake pedals. Chevrolet literature noted that the "chassis and body are balanced so as to make the utmost power available for the load itself and to reduce gasoline consumption to a minimum." The Model G again measured 97-7/8 in. from tailboard to headboard, with 46 in. of width inside the boards. Standard equipment included: Electric lights and starter, highest type two-unit system; complete lamp equipment; side curtains; adjustable windshield; speedometer; demountable rims; electric horn; complete tool equipment including pump and jack. This model now used the smaller engine. Base model offerings include the Chassis, Chassis & Cab, Open Express and Curtain Top Express. Larger in size than the 490, the Model G had slanting hood louvers, reverse curve fenders and torpedo type front-fender-mounted headlamps. Body length was 97-7/8 in. from tailboard to headboard, with a width of 46 in. between flareboards. Drive was from the left-hand side with center control. Spark and throttle were located under the steering wheel and there was a foot accelerator.
MEDIUM-HEAVY TRUCK — MODEL T — FOUR-CYLINDER: Cowl mounted headlamps remained a distinctive styling characteristic of the Model T 1-ton in 1921. It had overall larger dimensions and a narrower cowl with "scooped-out" sides. Aftermarket bodies depicted in the sales catalog included a passenger bus, fire engine, wholesale hauler, Farm Wagon and Panel Delivery. New for the 1922 Model T was the provision of poured rod bearings in the FB engine. Also, the three exhaust port cylinder head, also used on FB

autos, was adopted. As had been the case since 1920, pneumatic tires were used front and rear. A cab was not provided by the factory. Standard chassis features included a platform mounted seat and a windshield. Bodies sourced from outside suppliers often had tops designed to extend out to the windshield. The frame was four-inch channel iron, 30-1/2 in. wide in the front and 35-1/8 in. wide at the rear. The front axle was the drop-forged I-beam type. The rear axle was semi-floating with worm drive. The equipment consisted of a starter, generator, horn, headlamps (with dimmers), speedometer, ammeter, side curtains for driver's seat, complete tool equipment and a governor locked at 25 mph.

1922 Chevrolet 1/2-Ton Model 490 Light Delivery Panel Body (OCW)

I.D. DATA: Serial numbers stamped on frame crossmember at left front of engine. Serial number on the 490 is found on the dash-mounted nameplate. Serial numbers: [490] 1-A59934 to 928881; 2-A55239 to 88858; 3-A53242 to 87572; 6-A54959 to 76001. [Model T] 1-4455 to 4792; 2-3632 to 4359; 3-2082 to 2107 and 6-2447 to 2631. [Model G] 1-385 to 683; 2-304 to 623; 3-123 to 229; 6-183 to 6-386 and 9-195 to 202. The numerical prefixes (i.e. 1-) indicated the factory, as follows: 1=Flint, Mich.; 2=Tarrytown, N.Y; 3=St. Louis, Mo.; 6=Oakland, Calif.; 9=Oshawa, Canada. Engine number is stamped on the flywheel.

Model	Body Type	Price	Weight	Prod. Total
Light Delivery — Model 490 — 1/2-Ton — 102 in. w.b.				
490	Wagon	510	1860	Note 1
490	Panel Delivery (*)	—	2010	Note 1
490	Station Wagon (*)	—	—	Note 1

(*) Mifflinburg body.

Model	Body Type	Price	Weight	Prod. Total
Light Truck — Model G — 3/4-Ton — 120 in. w.b.				
G	Chassis & Cowl	745	2450	Note 2
G	Chassis & Cab	820	—	Note 2
G	Express	855	2600	Note 2
G	Canopy Express	920	—	Note 2
Medium-Heavy Truck — Model T — 1-Ton — 125 in. w.b.				
T	Chassis	1125	3300	Note 3
T	Open Express	1246	3450	Note 3
T	Canopy Express	1325	—	Note 3
T	Canopy/Curtain Express	1545	—	Note 3

NOTE 1: Included with 490 passenger cars.
NOTE 2: Series production was 273 units.
NOTE 3: Series production was 1,093 units.
ENGINE: [490/G] Inline. Cylinders cast in block. Overhead valves. Four-cylinder. Cast iron block. Bore & stroke: 3-11/16 x 4 in. Displacement: 170.9 cid. Compression ratio: 4.3:1. Brake horsepower: 26 at 2000 rpm. Three main bearings. Mechanical valve lifters. Carburetor: Zenith one-barrel model.
ENGINE: [T] Inline. Cylinders cast in block. Overhead valves. Four-cylinder. Cast iron block. Bore & stroke: 3-11/16 x 5-1/4 in. Displacement: 224 cid. Compression: 4.25:1. Brake horsepower: 37 at 2000 rpm. SAE horsepower: 21.75. Three main bearings. Solid valve lifters. Carburetor: Zenith improved double-jet.

1922 Chevrolet 1/2-Ton Model 490 Vestibuled Express (L. Kuntz)

CHASSIS: [490] Wheelbase: 102 in. Tires: 30 x 3-1/2.
CHASSIS: [G] Wheelbase: 120 in. Tires: All-pneumatic, demountable type, with wrapped tread; [Front] 31 x 4 in.; [Rear] 34 x 4-1/2 in.
CHASSIS: [T] Wheelbase: 125 in. Tires: [Front] pneumatic 33 x 4 in. demountable type, non-skid, wrapped tread; [Rear] 35 x 5 in. all-weather tread.

TECHNICAL: [All] Selective sliding transmission. Speeds: 3F/1R. Floor-mounted gearshift. Cone type clutch. Rear axle: [490] Three-quarter floating; [G/T] Semi-floating. Artillery type wood spoke wheels.

OPTIONS: Front bumper. Rear bumper. Single sidemount. Heater. Cowl lamps. Motor Meter. Rearview mirror.

1922 Chevrolet 1-Ton Model T Medium-Heavy Chassis & Cowl (BH)

HISTORICAL: Introduced January, 1922. Calendar year production: [Model G] Flint, Mich.=298; Tarrytown, N.Y.=319; St, Louis, Mo.=106; Oakland, Calif.=203; and Canada=7. [Model T] Flint, Mich.=337; Tarrytown, N.Y.=727; St., Louis, Mo.=25; and Oakland, Calif.=184. Innovations: New clutch/brake pedal system. Lever-action parking brake. W.S. Knudsen became the new general manager of Chevrolet. The Janesville, Wis., factory where Samsons were built, became a Chevrolet assembly plant.

1923 CHEVROLET

1923 Chevrolet 1/2-Ton Light Delivery Hercules Panel (DFW/BC)

LIGHT DELIVERY — SUPERIOR SERIES A/SERIES B — FOUR-CYLINDER: The Superior A and B trucks were Light Delivery models with a 1/2-ton load capacity. They could be identified by their raised hoodlines, higher radiators with a flatter top surface, crown paneled fenders; and a narrower cowl section. Bodies were still sourced from outside firms, although some styles were included in Chevrolet truck catalogs as factory-installed models. Prices are listed for chassis and factory-installed body models only. The Utility Delivery had a large open flareboard express box and closed cab. Standard features included a speedometer; ammeter; generator; starter; battery; drum type integral headlamps; dimmers; taillight; complete wiring system; oil pressure gauge; choke control; license brackets; motor hood; special combination dash and instrument board; front and rear fenders; runningboards with shields; demountable rims with extra front and rear rims; tire carrier; jack; and complete tool equipment. The Series B replaced the Series A as a running production change at each factory. It had several distinctions, including a curved front axle and cable-operated brakes.

UTILITY EXPRESS — SUPERIOR SERIES D — FOUR-CYLINDER: The Superior Ds had the same general design charateristics as 1/2-ton models, but they were 1-ton Utility Express trucks. The same four-cylinder engine used in the 1/2-ton trucks was employed, but the wheelbase was 17 in. longer and larger tires were mounted.

I.D. DATA: Serial numbers located on a plate found on the left side of the front seat frame. Serial numbers were: [Series A/Series B] 1A-92882 to 1B-72773; 2A-88766 to 2B-82891; 3A-86295 to 3B-983700; 6A-72320 to 6B-41755; and 21A-1000 to 21B-22373. [Series D] 1-D-1000 to 1-D-1654; 2-D-1000 to 2-D-2236; 3-D-1000 to 3-D-2155; and 21-D-1000 to 21-D-1515. The number(s) in the prefix indicated the factory and the letter indicated the series. Factory codes were: 1=Flint, Mich.; 2=Tarrytown, N.Y.; 3=St. Louis, Mo.; 6=Oakland, Calif.; 21=Janesville, Wis. Example: 1A-92882 indicates a Flint, Mich. (1) built Superior model (A Series) with sequential production number 92882. Motor numbers were located on the flywheel.

$425
f.o.b. Flint Mich.
For Specifications
See page 13

NEW SUPERIOR COMMERCIAL CHASSIS

1923 Chevrolet 1/2-Ton Superior A/B Chassis & Cowl (BH)

Model	Body Type	Price	Weight	Prod. Total
Light Delivery — Series A/Series B — 1/2-Ton — 103 in. w.b.				
A/B	Chassis	395	1830	—
A/B	Canopy Express	510	1965	—
A/B	Panel	—	—	—
A/B	Station Wagon	—	—	—
Utility Express — Series D — 1-Ton — 120 in. w.b.				
D	Chassis	375	1860	—
D	Utility Express	—	2780	—
D	Cattle Body	—	—	—
D	Delivery	—	—	—

ENGINE: [All] Inline. Overhead valves. Four-cylinder. Cast-iron block. Bore & stroke: 3-11/16 x 4 in. Displacement: 170.9 cid. Compression ratio: 4.3:1. Brake horsepower: 35 at 1900 rpm. SAE horsepower: 21.7. Three main bearings. Mechanical valve lifters. Carburetor: Zenith one-barrel.
CHASSIS: [Series A/Series B] Wheelbase: 103 in. Length: 142 in. Height: 74.25 in. Front tread: 58 in. Rear tread: 58 in. Tires: 30 x 3.5 in.
CHASSIS: [Series D] Wheelbase: 120 in. Tires: 31 x 4 in.
TECHNICAL: Manual, sliding gear transmission. Speeds: 3F/1R. Column-mounted gearshift. Cone type clutch. Semi-floating rear axle. Overall ratio: [Series A/Series B] 3.6:1; [Series D] 3.77:1. External contracting rear wheel brakes. Wood spoke wheels.
OPTIONS: Front bumper. Rear bumper. Single sidemount. Heater. Cowl lamps. Motor Meter. Rearview mirror. Cattle body with chute type side ramps.
HISTORICAL: Introduced: Aug. 1, 1922. Innovations: [Series A/Series B] First year with crown paneled fenders; [Series D] New 120 in. wheelbase. Alfred P. Sloan, Jr. took over as president of General Motors.

1924 CHEVROLET

LIGHT DELIVERY — SUPERIOR SERIES B/SERIES F — FOUR-CYLINDER: This year, the 1/2-ton Superior four started as a continuation of the 1923 series and evolved into the Series F. Both were actually commercial cars, riding a beefed-up version of the Chevrolet passenger car chassis. Curved front axles and cable-operated brakes characterized the B models again. The F models had a straight front axle and rod-operated brakes.

1924 Chevrolet 1/2-Ton Superior F Light Delivery Panel Body (WPL)

UTILITY TRUCK — SUPERIOR SERIES D/SERIES H — FOUR-CYLINDER: Available again was the Superior Utility Express line of 1-tons. These were now simply called Utility Trucks. The D models continued into the early part of the model year, before being superseded by the H models. Body-making was still an all-aftermarket operation, with some of the more popular styles available on factory-installed basis. As a running change, the H may have been replaced by a J model late in the series.
I.D. DATA: Serial numbers located on either side of dash under cowl and seat frame. Numbers were: [Series B/Series F] 1B-72774 to 1F-36881; 2B-82892 to 2F-511400; 3B-98371 to 3F-56585; 6B-41756 to 6F-29298; 9B-1166 to 9F-27125; 12B-1064 to 12F-35270; and 21B=-22374 to 21F-33581. [Series D/Series H] 1D-1655 to 1H-1307; 2D-2237 to 2H-2383; 3D-2156 to 3H-4177; 6D-1818 to 6H-1813; 9D-1000 to 9H-1372; 12D-1000 to 12H-1732

and 21D-1516 to 21H-2106. The number(s) in the prefix indicated the factory and the letter indicated the series. Factory codes were: 1=Flint, Mich.; 2=Tarrytown, N.Y.; 3=St. Louis, Mo.; 6=Oakland, Calif.; 9=Norwood, Ohio; 12=Buffalo, N.Y. 21=Janesville, Wis. Example: 1B-72774 indicates a Flint, Mich. (1) built Superior model (B Series) with sequential production number 72774. Motor numbers were located on the flywheel.

Model	Body Type	Price	Weight	Prod. Total
Light Delivery — Superior Series B/Series F — 1/2-Ton — 103 in. w.b.				
B/F	Chassis	395	1790	—
Utility Truck — Superior Series D/Series H — 1-Ton — 120 in. w.b.				
D/H	Chassis	550	1850	—

ENGINE: [All] Inline. Overhead valves. Four-cylinder. Cast-iron block. Bore & stroke: 3-11/16 x 4 in. Displacement: 170.9 cid. Compression ratio: 4.3:1. SAE horsepower: 21.70. Brake horsepower: 35 at 1900 rpm. Three main bearings. Solid valve lifters. Carburetor: Zenith one-barrel model.
CHASSIS: [Series B/F] Wheelbase: 103 in. Length: 142 in. Front tread: 58 in. Rear tread: 58 in. Tires: 30 x 3.5 in.
CHASSIS: [Series D/H] Wheelbase: 120 in. Front tread: 56 in. Rear tread: 56 in. Tires: [Front] 30 x 3.5 in.; [Rear] 30 x 5 in.

1924 Chevrolet 1/2-Ton Superior A/B Fire Truck (DFW/WS)

TECHNICAL: Manual transmission. Speeds: 3F/1R. Floor-mounted gearshift. Cone type clutch. Semi-floating rear axle. Overall ratio: 3.82:1. External contracting mechanical rear brakes. Wooden spoke wheels.
OPTIONS: Front bumper. Rear bumper. Single sidemount. Heater. Rearview mirror. Spare tires. Bodies: [1/2-ton] Panel truck. [1-ton] Open Cab Grain truck; Open Cab Stock truck; Flareboard Express; Fully-enclosed Cab Grain truck; Fully-enclosed Cab stock truck; Panel truck; Coal truck; Three-compartment Tanker truck.
HISTORICAL: Introduced: Aug. 1, 1923. Under W.S. Knudsen's direction, Chevrolet sales began to pickup at an unpredictable pace.

1925 CHEVROLET

1925 Chevrolet 1-Ton Superior H Utility Truck Flat Bed Body (OCW)

LIGHT DELIVERY — SUPERIOR SERIES F/SERIES K — FOUR-CYLINDER: The Series F Superior models were sold as 1925 trucks from Aug. 1, 1924 to Jan. 1, 1925. At that point, a new line of 1/2-ton Light Delivery trucks was introduced as the Superior Series K. The K Series offered a new Fisher bodies with vertical ventilating (VV) windshields and 1925 models could be distinguished from 1926 Superior Ks by their fender-mounted headlamps. The VV windshield, along with a slightly-angled windshield position, contributed to a more modern appearance. The K also had a one-piece rear axle with semi-elliptic springs. Other major technical changes were announced.
UTILITY TRUCK — SUPERIOR SERIES H/SERIES M — FOUR-CYLINDER: For 1-ton truck buyers, the Series H Utility Truck was still being sold when the 1925 model year started on Aug. 1, 1924. The Series M was a running change introduced Jan. 1, 1925 as part of a second 1925 series. One way to spot an M is to look in a new location for the engine number.

I.D. DATA: Serial number located: [Series F] Nameplate on dash; [Series K] Nameplate on seat frame; [Series H/Series M] Nameplate on dash. Serial numbers: [Model F] 1F-36882 to 1K-1 up; 2F-51141 up; 3F-56586 up; 6F-29297 to 6K-1 up; 9F-27126 to 9K-1 up; 12F-33582 to 12K-1 up; and 21F-33582 to 21K-1 up. [Series K] 1K-1000 to 1K33910; 2K-1000 to 2K-45726; 3K-1000 to 3K-48220; 6K-1000 to 6K-27866; 9K-1000 to 9K-27519; 12K-1000 to 12K-36081; 21K-1000 to 21K-32541. [Model H] were 1H-1308 to 1M-1812; 2H-2384 to 2M-4188; 3H-4178 to 3M-2496; 6H-1814 to 6M-1371; 9H-1373 to 9M-1719; 12H-1733 to 12M-2185 and 21H-2107 to 21M-1721. [Model M] 1M-1000 to 1M-1812; 2M-1000 to 2M-4188; 3M-1000 to 3M-2496; 6M-1000 to 6M-1371; 9M-1000 to 9M-1719; 12M-1000 to 12M-2185; 21M-1000 to 21M-2185. The number(s) in the prefix indicated the factory and the letter indicated the series. Factory codes were: 1=Flint, Mich.; 2=Tarrytown, N.Y.; 3=St. Louis, Mo.; 6=Oakland, Calif.; 9=Norwood, Ohio; 12=Buffalo, N.Y. 21=Janesville, Wis. Engine number location: [Series F] on flywheel and left engine support; [Series K] right side of block on boss just forward of oil filler tube; [Series H] on flywheel; [Series M] right side of block on boss just forward of oil filler tube.

Model	Body Type	Price	Weight	Prod. Total
[Early 1925: See I.D. Data]				
Light Delivery — Superior Series F — 1/2-Ton — 103 in. w.b.				
F	Chassis	395	1790	—
Utility Truck — Superior Series H — 1-Ton — 120 in. w.b.				
H	Chassis	550	1850	—
[Late 1925: See I.D. Data]				
Light Delivery — Superior Series K — 1/2-Ton — 103 in. w.b.				
K	Chassis	410	1380	—
Utility Truck — Superior Series M — 1-Ton — 120 in. w.b.				
M	Chassis	550	1850	—

ENGINE: [All] Inline. Overhead valves. Four-cylinder. Cast-iron block. Bore & stroke: 3-11/16 x 4 in. Displacement: 170.9 cid. Compression ratio: 4.3:1. Brake horsepower: 35 at 1900 rpm. SAE horsepower: 21.70. Three main bearings. Mechanical valve lifters. Carburetor: Zenith or Carter RXO one-barrel. Lubrication: Force feed and splash. Radiator: Cellular. Cooling: Water pump and fan. Ignition: Storage battery. Starting System: two-unit. Lighting System: Electric, six-volts. Gasoline System: Vacuum.

CHASSIS: [Series F/Series K] Wheelbase: 103 in. Length: 142 in. Front tread: 58 in. Rear tread: 58 in. Tires: 30 x 3.5 in.
CHASSIS: [Series H/Series M] Wheelbase: 120 in. Front tread: 56 in. Rear tread: 56 in. Tires: [front] 30 x 3.5 in.; [rear] 30 x 5 in.
TECHNICAL: [All] Manual sliding gear transmission. Speeds: 3F/1R. Floor-mounted gearshift. Single-plate dry-disc clutch introduced on Series K; cone type clutch on other models. Semi-floating rear axle. External contracting mechanical rear only brakes. Wooden spoke wheels.
OPTIONS: Front bumper. Rear bumper. Single sidemount. Heater. Rearview mirror. Spare tire(s), two required for 1-ton due to different sizes front and rear. Bodies: Martin-Parry Co. Panel truck. Springfield Body Mfg. Panel truck. Mifflinburg Body Co. Station Wagon.
HISTORICAL: Introduced: Jan. 1, 1925. Innovations: Redesigned engine. Disc clutch. All-steel closed truck cabs introduced in late 1925 for 1926 model year. A Chevrolet based U.S. Army Scout Car was supplied to the government this year. On June 3, 1925 the 100,000th Chevrolet built in Janesville, Wis. was assembled. It was a Series M 1-ton Utility Express chassis. Series M trucks were the last Chevrolets to use quarter-elliptic front springs.

1926 CHEVROLET

1926 Chevrolet 1-Ton Superior Model R Truck Stake (V. Kovlak)

LIGHT DELIVERY — SUPERIOR SERIES K/SERIES V — FOUR-CYLINDER: Chevrolet's 1/2-ton Superior Series K was carried over as the early 1926 Light Delivery model from Aug. 1, 1925 to Jan. 1, 1926. A change from the 1925 Series K was that the headlights, formerly fastened to the fenders, were now mounted on a tie-rod between the fenders. On Jan. 1, 1926, a new Series V was introduced as the K's replacement. This series introduced the use of a belt-driven electric generator instead of a gear-driven type. The oil pump was driven by the camshaft, instead of a gear on the front end of the engine. One-

half inch wider brakes with a 2-1/2 in. surface was another improvement. The Series V included a chassis on which aftermarket light-duty truck bodies could be installed. Most commonly seen in old photographs are depot hack type station wagons and vestibule type panels. The term vestibule referred to a fully-enclosed cab. Express wagons and other truck body styles were also built on this chassis. Two new models were a Roadster Pickup with cargo bed instead of rumbleseat and a Commercial Roadster with enclosed cargo box in the rear.

UTILITY TRUCK — SUPERIOR SERIES R/SERIES X — FOUR-CYLINDER: The Utility Truck was rated for 1-ton loads. The R Series trucks had a new, four-inch longer wheelbase. They used the Series K passenger car engine, transmission, clutch, hood, fenders, lights and radiator. However, the truck radiator was made of pressed steel, instead of the cast aluminum used for the car radiators. From serial numbers, it would appear that a substantial number of Series R trucks were built in 1926. This line was then replaced by the new Series X, which was technically similar. The Series X used the hood, fenders, lights and running gear of the late 1926 passenger cars. However, an innovation was the availability of a production-type truck bodies, which were factory-built with all-steel enclosed cabs. This new series actually spanned two model years, with many X models sold in model-year 1927.

I.D. DATA: Serial number located: [Series K/Series V] Nameplate on seat frame; [Series R/Series X] Nameplate on dash. Serial numbers: [1926 Series K] 1K-33911 to 1V-1 up; 2K-45727 to 2V-1 up; 3K-48221 to 3V-1 up; 6K-27867 to 6V-1 up; 9K-27520 to 9V-1 up; 12K-36082 to 12V-1 up; 21K-32545 to 21V-1 up. [Series V] 1V-1000 to 1V-48370; 2V-1000 to 2V-49190; 3V-1000 to 3V-83241; 6V-1000 to 6V-27138; 9V-1000 to 9V-52906; 12V-1000 to 12V-38609; 21V-1000 to 21V-54157. [Series R] 1R-1000 to 1X-10609; 2R-1000 to 2X-1000; 3R-1000 to 3X-10000; 6R-1000 to 6X-1000; 9R-1000 to 9X-1000; 12R-1000 to 12X-1000; 21R-1000 to 21X-10000. [Series X] 1X-1000 to 1X-4050; 2X-1000 to 2X-9072; 3X-1000 to 3X-11503; 6X-1000 to 6X-2940; 9X-1000 to 9X-5724; 12X-1000 to 12X-4001; 21X-1000 to 21X-6582. The number(s) in the prefix indicated the factory and the letter indicated the series. Factory codes were: 1=Flint, Mich.; 2=Tarrytown, N.Y.; 3=St. Louis, Mo.; 6=Oakland, Calif.; 9=Norwood, Ohio; 12=Buffalo, N.Y. 21=Janesville, Wis. Engine numbers location: Engine number location: [All] right side of block on boss just forward of oil filler tube.

1926 Chevrolet 1-Ton Superior X Utility Truck Chassis & Cowl (OCW)

Model	Body Type	Price	Weight	Prod. Total
[Early 1926: See I.D. Data]				
Light Delivery — Superior K Series K — 1/2-Ton — 103 in. w.b.				
K	Chassis	425	1520	—
Utility Truck — Superior V Series R — 1-Ton — 124 in. w.b.				
R	Chassis	550	1955	—
[Late 1926: See I.D. Data]				
Light Delivery — Superior V Series V — 1/2-Ton — 103 in. w.b.				
V	Chassis	410	1520	—
Utility Truck — Superior V Series X — 1-Ton — 124 in. w.b.				
X	Chassis	—	—	—
X	Springfield Suburban	—	—	—
X	Screenside Express	—	—	—

ENGINE: [All] Inline. Overhead valves. Four-cylinder. Cast-iron block. Bore & stroke: 3-11/16 x 4 in. Displacement: 170.9 cid. Compression ratio: 4.3:1. Brake horsepower: 35 at 1900 rpm. SAE horsepower: 21.7. Three main bearings. Mechanical valve lifters. Carburetor: Carter one-barrel model.
CHASSIS: [Series K/Series V] Wheelbase: 103 in. Length: 142 in. Front tread: 58 in. Rear tread: 58 in. Tires: 29 x 4.40 in.
CHASSIS: [Series R] Wheelbase: 124 in. Front tread: 56 in. Rear tread: 56 in. Tires: [front] 30 x 3.5 in.; [rear] 30 x 5 in.
CHASSIS: [Series X] Wheelbase: 124 in. Tires: [Front] 30 x 5 in.; [Rear] 30 x 3.5 in.

1926 Chevrolet 1-Ton Superior X Utility Canopy Express Body (OCW)

TECHNICAL: Manual, sliding gear transmission. Speeds: 3F/1R. Floor-mounted gearshift. Single-plate, dry-disc type clutch. Semi-floating rear axle. Overall ratio: 3.8:1 [V-series]. Mechanical, external contracting rear brakes. Wooden spoke wheels.

OPTIONS: Front bumper. Rear bumper. Single sidemount. Heater. Side curtains. Spare tires. Rearview mirror. Optional bodies for Series X, as seen in old photos, include: (1) Springfield Panel with vestibule cab; (2) Suburban (Woodie), by Springfield Body Co.; (3) Gravity Dump body for coal delivery, by Proctor-Keefe Co.; (4) Mifflinburg combination Jitney/Express; (5) Rack Body by Springfield Body Co.; (6) Hercules Body Co. Vestibuled Panel.

HISTORICAL: Introduced: [Superior K/Superior R] Aug. 1, 1925; [Superior V/Superior X] Jan. 1, 1926. Calendar year registrations: [All series] 113,682. Innovations: New all-steel factory bodies on the 1-ton Series X chassis. Bus-like depot wagons built for 1-ton chassis. All-new series designations. Late in year, a new Peddler's Wagon was introduced and proved very popular. A rail coach was built for a Louisiana railroad using a Chevrolet Series X truck chassis. A panel version of the X was used by a Michigan college professor to search for rare fish in the Northwestern U.S. (Chevy donated the truck to him). An Australian-bodied Series X bus made a 15 mile trip, between Barwon Heads and Geelong in Australia, three times each day. It carried up to 14 passengers.

1927 Chevrolet 1/2-Ton Capitol AA Express (DFW/SAB)

1927 CHEVROLET

LIGHT DELIVERY — SUPERIOR V SERIES V — FOUR-CYLINDER: Chevrolet's 1/2-ton Superior Series V was carried over as the early 1927 Light Delivery model from Aug. 1, 1926 to Jan. 1, 1927. A change from the 1926 Series K was a new crossmember supporting the transmission. The headlamps remained mounted on a tie-rod between the fenders, but the rod was heavier and channeled. Gas and spark controls were relocated above the steering wheel.

LIGHT DELIVERY — CAPITOL AA SERIES AA — FOUR-CYLINDER: Chevrolet's newest light-duty trucks were identified by their new radiator shell with a dipped center, bullet-shaped headlights with a black enamel finish with bright trim rings, and fuller one-piece crown fenders. Other new features included a coincidental lock; air cleaner and oil filter. The 1/2-ton Series AA was marketed as a commercial car chassis for use with aftermarket bodies.

Model	Body Type	Price	Weight	Prod. Total
[Early 1927: See I.D. Data]				
Light Delivery — Superior V Series V — 1/2-Ton — 103 in. w.b.				
V	Chassis	410	1520	—
Utility Truck — Superior V Series X — 1-Ton — 124 in. w.b.				
X	Chassis	—	—	—
X	Springfield Suburban	—	—	—
X	Screenside Express	—	—	—
[Late 1927: See I.D. Data]				
Light Delivery — Capitol AA Series AA — 1/2-Ton — 103 in. w.b.				
AA	Chassis	495	2130	—
Utility Truck — Capitol AA Series LM — 1-Ton — 124 in. w.b.				
LM	Factory Panel Delivery	755	2850	—
LM	Factory Stake Bed	680	3045	—
LM	Chassis	550	1955	—

ENGINE: [All] Inline. Overhead valves. Four-cylinder. Cast-iron block. Bore & stroke: 3-11/16 x 4 in. Displacement: 170.9 cid. Compression ratio: 4.3:1. Brake horsepower: 35 at 1900 rpm. SAE horsepower: 21.8. Three main bearings. Mechanical valve lifters. Carburetor: Carter one-barrel model.

1927 Chevrolet 1/2-ton Capitol AA Light Delivery Panel (DFW/LOC)

UTILITY TRUCK — SUPERIOR V SERIES X- FOUR-CYLINDER: After Aug. 1, the Superior V Series X 1-ton Utility Truck was sold as an early 1927 model. Specifications were the same as the late 1926 Superior V.

UTILITY TRUCK — CAPITOL AA SERIES LM — FOUR-CYLINDER: This was marketed as a 1927 1-ton series between Jan. 1, 1927 and Aug. 1, 1927. The same trucks were also sold as early 1928 models, until the real 1928s arrived. General Motors' bodies, for Chevrolet factory-installation, were used on the LM chassis. Of course, the bigger model could also be purchased as a chassis, if the customer wished to add their own truck body.

I.D. DATA: Serial number located on right or left side of dash under the cowl and seat frame. Serial numbers: [1927 Series V] 1V-48371 to 1AA-1; 2V-49191 to 2AA-1; 3V-83242 to 3AA-1; 6V-27139 to 6AA-1; 9V-52907 to 9AA-1; 12V-38607 to 12AA-1; 21V-54158 to 21AA-1. [Series AA] 1AA-1000 to 1AA-81763; 2AA-1000 to 2AA-79094; 3AA-1000 to 3AA-128735; 6AA-1000 to 6AA-44695; 9AA-1000 to 9AA-44695; 12AA-1000 to 12AA-68390; 21AA-1000 to 21AA-71646. [1927 Series X] 1X-4060 to 1LM-1000; 2X-9073 to 2LM-1000; 3X-11501 to 3LM-1000; 6X-2941 to 6LM-1000; 9X-4002 to 9LM-1000; 12X-4002 to 12LM-1000; 21X-6583 to 21LM-1000. [Series LM] 1LM-1000 to 1LM-9002; 2LM-1000 to 2LM-18539; 3LM-1000 to 3LM-19889; 6LM-1000 to 6LM-5251; 9LM-1000 to 9LM-9842; 12LM-1001 to 12LM-8644; 21LM-1000 to 21LM-10911. The number(s) in the prefix indicated the factory and the letter(s) indicated the series. Factory codes were: 1=Flint, Mich.; 2=Tarrytown, N.Y.; 3=St. Louis, Mo.; 6=Oakland, Calif.; 9=Norwood, Ohio; 12=Buffalo, N.Y. 21=Janesville, Wis. Engine numbers located on block ahead of fuel filter.

1927 Chevrolet 1/2-Ton Capitol AA Light Delivery Screenside (OCW)

CHASSIS: [Series V/Series AA] Wheelbase: 103 in. Usable load space length: [Panel] 64 in.; Width: [Panel] 42 in. Tires: 29 x 4.40 in.

CHASSIS: [Series X/Series LM] Wheelbase: 124 in. Width: [Panel] 44 in. (*).

* Hercules' standard panel width. Hercules also produced a flare side panel that had a 51 in. width and appropriate wheel cutouts. This larger panel was 94.5 in. long, compared to the standard panel's 93 in. length. The factory type LM panel body was 42 in. wide by 45 in. high and had a usable load length of 102 in.

TECHNICAL: Manual transmission. Speeds: 3F/1R. Floor-mounted gearshift. Single-plate, dry-disc type clutch. Semi-floating rear axle. Overall ratio: 3.82:1. External contracting, two-wheel rear brakes. Wooden spoke wheels.

1927 Chevrolet 1-Ton Capitol AA Utility Truck Dump Body (OCW)

OPTIONS: Front bumper. Rear bumper. Single sidemount. Spare tire(s). Side curtains. Motometer. Dual taillamps. Heater. Disc wheels (on commercials). Cowl lamps. Outside rearview mirror. Optional bodies from old photos: (1) Martin-Parry Dump; (2) Hercules dump; (3) Kentucky Wagon Works' Jitney Bus/School Bus; (4) Hercules Vestibule Panel (Standard or Flare side); (5) Hercules Cattle Body.

1927 Chevrolet 1-Ton Capitol AA Utility Express (L. Kemp/CPC)

HISTORICAL: Introduced: [1927 Superior V] Aug. 1, 1926; [Capitol AA] Jan. 1, 1927; [Capitol LM] January, 1927. Calendar year registrations: [All series] 104,832. Innovations: New Capitol AA Light Delivery series. New 1-ton Capitol LM series. New bullet headlights. Dipped style radiator shell adopted. Rectangular brake and clutch pedals. New coincidental lock. A South African built series LM Series truck carried supplies and communications equipment on a Cape Town-to-Stockholm (via Cairo and London) Chevy promotional tour in 1927.

1928 CHEVROLET

1928 Chevrolet 1-Ton Capitol LP Light Delivery Suburban (ATC)

LIGHT DELIVERY — CAPITOL AA SERIES AA — FOUR-CYLINDER: As usual, a carry-over line of Capitol Series trucks was marketed as 1928 models from August to January. Capitol models could again be identified by a radiator shell with a dipped center, shiny

black enamel bullet-shaped headlights and one-piece crown fenders. Other features included a coincidental lock; air cleaner and oil filter. The 1/2-ton chassis was marketed as a commercial car for use with aftermarket bodies.

LIGHT DELIVERY — NATIONAL AB SERIES AB — FOUR-CYLINDER: The new series introduced Jan. 1, 1928 was designated National AB. These trucks were very similar to the models of the previous year, but had some distinctions. Four-wheel brakes were installed on light-duty models. The wheelbase was now 107 in., up from 103 in. in 1927. Telltale engine features included thermostatic control and a crankcase breather. With a higher compression ratio, larger valves, increased valve lift and a two-piece exhaust manifold the Chevrolet engine developed 35 hp at a higher 2200 rpm.

UTILITY TRUCK — CAPITOL AA SERIES LM — FOUR-CYLINDER: The 1-ton Utility LM Series was introduced as a 1927 model. Beginning Aug. 1, 1927, it was marketed as a 1928 truck. Styling, motor and 120 in. wheelbase were unchanged. LMs sold between the above date and Jan. 1, 1928 were simply titled as 1928 models.

UTILITY TRUCK — CAPITOL AB SERIES LO/SERIES LP — FOUR-CYLINDER: On Jan. 1, 1928 a new 1-ton line began. These LO Series trucks had the same engine as previous models, but a 124 in. wheelbase. The LP Series was a running change as the range of serial numbers for late 1928 models starts with LO-1000 at each factory and ends with numbers having LP prefixes.

1928 Chevrolet 1-Ton Capitol LP Utility Truck Panel Body (DFW/MS)

I.D. DATA: Serial number located on right or left side of dash under the cowl and seat frame; also placed on front door heel board, on either the left or right side. Serial numbers: [1928 Series AA] 1AA-81764 to 1AB-1; 2AA-79088 to 2AB-1; 3AA-128736 to 3AB-1; 6AA-44706 to 6AB-1; 9AA-66289 to 9AB-1; 12AA-68391 to 12AB-1; 21AA-71647 to 21AB-1. [1928 Series LM]: 1LM-9003 to 1LO-1000; 2LM-18540 to 2LO-1000; 3LM-19800 to 3LO-1000; 6LM-5252 to 6LO-1000; 9LM-9843 to 9LO-1000; 12LM-8645 to 12LO-1000; 21LM-10912 to 21LO-1000.[1928 Series AB] 1AB-1000 up; 2AB-1000 up; 3AB-1000 up; 6AB-1000 up; 9AA-1000 up; 12AB-1000 up; 21AB-1000 up. [1928 Series LO/Series LP]: 1LO-1000 to 1LP-7248; 2LO-1000 to 2LP-12986; 3LO-1000 to 3LP-18133; 6LO-1000 to 6LP-4355; 9LO-1000 to 9LP-7007; 12LO-1000 to 12LP-6535; 21LO-1000 to 21LO-8841. The number(s) in the prefix indicated the factory and the letter(s) indicated the series. Factory codes were: 1=Flint, Mich.; 2=Tarrytown, N.Y; 3=St. Louis, Mo.; 6=Oakland, Calif.; 9=Norwood, Ohio; 12=Buffalo, N.Y. 21=Janesville, Wis. Engine numbers located on engine block ahead of oil filter, near fuel pump.

Model	Body Type	Price	Weight	Prod. Total
[Early 1928: See I.D. Data]				
Light Delivery — Capitol AA — 1/2-Ton — 103 in. w.b.				
AA	Chassis	495	2130	—
Utility Truck — Capitol LM/LO/LP — 1-Ton — 124 in. w.b.				
LO	Factory Panel Delivery	755	2850	—
LO	Factory Stake Bed	680	3045	—
LO	Chassis	520	1955	—
[Late 1928: See I.D. Data]				
Light Delivery — National AB — 1/2-Ton — 107 in. w.b.				
AB	Chassis	495	2130	—
AB	Pickup	—	—	—
AB	Canopy	—	—	—
AB	Screenside	—	—	—
AB	Panel	—	—	—
AB	Sedan Delivery	690	2450	1004
AB	Roadster Pickup	545	2130	—
AB	Commercial Roadster	575	2190	—
AB	Henney Hearse	1500	2800	—
AB	Henney Ambulance	1600	2800	—
Utility Truck — National LP — 1-Ton — 124 in. w.b.				
LP	Chassis	520	—	—

1928 Chevrolet 1-Ton Capitol LP Utility Truck Depot Body (FLW)

ENGINE: [All] Inline. Overhead valves. Four-cylinder. Cast-iron block. Bore & stroke: 3-11/16 x 4 in. Displacement: 170.9 cid. Compression ratio: 4.5:1. Brake horsepower: 35 at 2200 rpm. SAE horsepower: 21.7. Three main bearings. Mechanical valve lifters. Carburetor: Carter one-barrel model.

CHASSIS: [Series AA] Wheelbase: 103 in. Usable load space length: [Panel] 64 in.; Width: [Panel] 42 in. Tires: 29 x 4.40 in.

CHASSIS: [Series AB] Wheelbase: 107 in. Length: 156 in. Load Space: 72 in. Front tread: 56 in. Rear tread: 56 in. Tires: 30 x 4.50 in.

CHASSIS: [Series LO] Wheelbase: 124 in.

CHASSIS: [Series LP] Wheelbase: 124 in.

1928 Chevrolet 1/2-Ton Capitol AB Light Delivery Express (OCW)

TECHNICAL: Manual transmission. Speeds: 3F/1R. Floor-mounted gearshift. Single-plate, dry-disc type clutch. Semi-floating rear axle. Overall ratio: 3.82:1. Mechanical brakes. Wooden spoke or steel disc wheels.

OPTIONS: Front bumper. Rear bumper. Heater. Wood spoke wheels. Exterior rearview mirror. Slip-in pickup box for AB roadster. Commercial cargo box for AB roadster (called Panel Carrier).

1928 Chevrolet 1/2-Ton Capitol AB Light Delivery Express Body (JB)

HISTORICAL: Introduced: January, 1928. Calendar year registrations: [All Series] 133,682. Innovations: Four-wheel brakes. New four-speed transmission standard on Series LP. Refinements to engine. Last year for 170.9 cid. four-cylinder. All-new Sedan Delivery. Chevrolet was becoming a serious threat to Ford's sales leadership in both the car and truck markets.

1929 CHEVROLET

1929 Chevrolet 1/2-Ton International AC Light Delivery Pickup (OCW)

LIGHT DELIVERY — INTERNATIONAL AC SERIES AC — SIX-CYLINDER: The 1929 Chevrolet Light Delivery models again represented a 1/2-ton Commercial Car series. They had more rectangular radiators, fewer louvers only at the rear side of the hood, bullet-shaped headlights and full-crowned fenders. Of great importance was the introduction of the "Cast-Iron Wonder," Chevy's long-lived and extremely successful overhead valve six-cylinder engine. Also new were a headlight foot control switch and electrolock feature. Features of specific 1929 models included a standard side-mounted spare on the driver's side of the Sedan Delivery. A new Deluxe Panel Delivery (built by the Geneva Body Co.) was called the Ambassador. It had wood framing with steel outer paneling, imitation Spanish black leather upholstery, and multi-tone finish. The body was medium-light blue on upper portions and dark blue on the lower portion. The hood, fenders and disc wheels were black. An orange beltline panel set off the attractive color scheme. There was only one 1929 series, since the depressed U.S. economy began changing the manner in which cars and trucks were marketed.

1929 Chevrolet 1/2-Ton International AC Roadster Delivery (OCW)

CONVENTIONAL — INTERNATIONAL AC SERIES LQ — SIX-CYLINDER: Models in both lines used passenger car sheet metal and the same black radiator shell as cars. LQ was the year's bigger truck line. It was a 1-1/2-ton series, which doesn't exactly fit into the scope of this study. However, it was essentially very similar to the late 1928 Series LO/LP Utility trucks and had the same 124 in. wheelbase, so it could probably be ordered with a 1-ton chassis option. There was also just one series of 1929 1-ton models.

I.D. DATA: Location of serial number: nameplate on dash. Starting number: [AC Series] 1AC-1001 to 1AC-111583; 2AC-1001 to 2AC-104076; 3AC-1001 to 3AC-199422; %AC-1001 to 5AC-62550; 6AC-1001 to 6AC-67343; 8AC-1001 to 8AC-48890; 9AC-1001 to 9AC-93867; 12AC-1001 to 12AC-99298; 21AC-1001 to 21AC-106392. [LQ Series] 1LQ-1001 to 1LQ-14282; 2LQ-1001 to 2LQ-20188; 3LQ-1001 to 3LQ-42724; 5LQ-1001 to 5LQ-15512; 6LQ-1001 to 6LQ-11162; 8LQ-1001 to 8LQ-13324; 12LQ-1001 to 12LQ-16356; 21LQ-1001 to 21LQ-18045. The number(s) in the prefix indicated the factory and the letter(s) indicated the series. Factory codes were: 1=Flint, Mich.; 2=Tarrytown, N.Y.; 3=St. Louis, Mo.; 5=Kansas City, Mo.; 6=Oakland, Calif.; 8=Atlanta, Ga.; 9=Norwood, Ohio; 12=Buffalo, N.Y. 21=Janesville, Wis. Engine number location: right side of cylinder block behind fuel pumps.

Model	Body Type	Price	Weight	Prod. Total
Light Delivery — International AC Series AC — 107 in. w.b.				
AC	Chassis	400	1815	—
AC	Sedan Delivery	595	2450	—
AC	Pickup	—	—	—
AC	Canopy or Screen	—	—	—
AC	Panel	—	—	9640
Utility Truck — International AC Series LQ — 124 in. w.b.				
AC/LQ	Chassis	—	—	—

ENGINE: Inline. Overhead valves. Six-cylinder. Cast-iron block. Bore & stroke: 3-5/16 x 3-3/4 in. Displacement: 194 cid. Compression ratio: 5.02:1. Brake horsepower: 46 at 2600 rpm. SAE horsepower: 26.3. Three main bearings. Solid valve lifters. Carburetor: Carter one-barrel model 150S.

CHASSIS: [Series AC] Wheelbase: 107 in. Length: 156 in. Front tread: 56 in. Rear tread: 56 in. Tires: 20 x 4.50 in.

CHASSIS: [Series LQ] Wheelbase: 124 in.

1929 Chevrolet 1/2-Ton International AC Roadster Delivery (MC)

TECHNICAL: Manual transmission. Speeds: 3F/1R. Floor-mounted gearshift. Single-plate, dry-disc type clutch. Semi-floating rear axle. Overall ratio: 3.82:1. Mechanical, four-wheel brakes. Disc wheels.
OPTIONS: Front bumper. Rear bumper. Single sidemount. Heater. Cigarette lighter. Wire wheels. Exterior mirror. Slip-in pickup box for roadster. Cargo carrier for roadster.
HISTORICAL: Introduced: Nov. 24, 1928. Calendar year registrations: [All series] 160,959. Innovations: New six-cylinder engine. One-piece full crown fenders. New bullet type lamps. Electro lock. Banjo type rear axle. Chrome plated radiator shell. New multi-color finish with contrasting double belt panel. Longer 107 in. wheelbase and 17 in. rubber-covered steering wheel. New line of panel bodies by Geneva Body Co., of Geneva, N.Y. The new six-cylinder engine was a strong selling point, which carried Chevrolet's car and truck sales to record levels. During 1929, the company produced its 500,000th commercial vehicle and reported accumulated retail sales of 641,482 trucks since 1918. The majority of these were light-duty models of 1-ton or less capacity. In 1930, a military gun wagon was constructed as a U.S. Army munitions experiment. Forest "Chip" Sweet, 1931-1933 Commercial Technical Advisor for the Vintage Chevrolet Club of America, believes it was probably on a 1929 Series AC 1/2-ton chassis. It had an armored gun turret and 50 caliber machine gun.

1930 CHEVROLET

LIGHT DELIVERY — UNIVERSAL SERIES AD — SIX-CYLINDER: Chevrolet trucks for light-duty use, like the Chevrolet passenger cars, were fitted with a new instrument panel. An electric gasoline gauge was included in its array of circular gauges on the dash. The rear brakes were fully enclosed and a stronger rear axle was used. The Chevrolet commercial engine developed 46 hp. Chevrolet factory-assembled the Commercial Chassis, Chassis & Cab (including Roadster Delivery)) and the Sedan Delivery. Until Chevrolet's November, 1930 purchase of Martin Parry Body Co., all other commercial bodies were sourced from manufacturers, such as Hercules, the maker of Panel Delivery bodies. The Sedan Delivery used cowl and body panels similar to a coach in the passenger car line, which meant it had a new sloping windshield. The Roadster Delivery (an open cab pickup) used the same cowl as the roadster and the phaeton in Chevrolet's passenger car line, plus roadster doors. A different cowl was used in the other 1/2-ton Light Delivery models. It was called the cowl and dash. Chevrolet supplied the cowl and dash beginning in 1929 and continuing through 1933. Door and windshield frames bolted to it. In most models, the windshield was a fold-out type that pivoted at the top on a piano hinge. The Open Cab windshield pivoted approximately three-quarters of its height.

1930 Chevrolet 1/2-Ton Universal AD Light Delivery (DFW/ABA)

UTILITY TRUCK — UNIVERSAL AD SERIES LR — SIX-CYLINDER: The Utility truck may have come in 1-ton chassis options for 1930. Wheelbases up to 124 in. were available. Bodies were still supplied by independent body makers. Cabs for two-unit bodies were supplied by Chevrolet.
I.D. DATA: Location of serial number: on plate nailed to side of passenger seat bottom cushion support. Starting number: [AD] 1AD-1001 up; 2AD-1001 up, etc.; [LR] 1LR-1001 up; 2LR-1001 up, etc. The number(s) in the prefix indicated the factory and the letter(s) indicated the series. Factory codes were: 1=Flint, Mich.; 2=Tarrytown, N.Y.; 3=St. Louis, Mo.; 5=Kansas City, Mo.; 6=Oakland, Calif.; 8=Atlanta, Ga.; 9=Norwood, Ohio; 12=Buffalo, N.Y. 21=Janesville, Wis. There was also a model identification plate screwed to the firewall

above the starter motor on the passenger side. Engine number location: on right side of motor block behind fuel pump. Engine number was located between the distributor and fuel pump.

Model	Body Type	Price	Weight	Prod. Total
Light Delivery — 1/2-Ton — Universal AD — 107 in. w.b.				
[Factory assembled]				
AD	Chassis	365	1835	—
AD	Sedan Delivery	595	2490	6522
[Aftermarket bodies]				
AD	Roadster Delivery	440	2045	—
AD	Panel Delivery	—	—	—
AD	Deluxe Delivery	—	—	—
AD	Deluxe Panel Body	—	—	—
AD	Pickup	—	—	—
AD	Canopy Delivery	—	—	—
AD	Screenside Delivery	—	—	—
Utility Truck — 1 to 1-1/2-Ton — Universal LR — 124 in. w.b.				

NOTE 1: Aftermarket bodies or pickup box not manufactured or serviced by Chevrolet. Other suppliers such as Martin-Parry Co., etc., supplied bodies through the Chevrolet factory and dealer network. The chassis included rear fenders and spare tire rim supplied by Chevrolet.

1930 Chevrolet 1-Ton Universal LR Utility Vending (R. Barbour/CPC)

ENGINE: [All] Inline. Overhead valves. Six-cylinder. Cast-iron block. Bore & stroke: 3-5/16 x 3-3/4 in. Displacement: 194 cid. Compression ratio: 5.0:1. Brake horsepower: 46 at 2600 rpm. SAE horsepower: 26.3. Three main bearings. Mechanical valve lifters. Carburetor: Carter one-barrel model RJH08-150S, casting no. 863409.

CHASSIS: [Series AD] Wheelbase: 107 in. Tires: 4.75 x 19 in.

CHASSIS: [Series LR] Wheelbase: 124 in.

1930 Chevrolet 1/2-Ton Universal AD Light Delivery Canopy (MC)

TECHNICAL: [Typical] Manual transmission. Speeds: 3F/1R. Floor-mounted gearshift. Single-plate type clutch. Shaft drive. Semi-floating rear axle. Overall ratio: 4.1:1. Internal, expanding four-wheel mechanical brakes. The brakes changed to fully-enclosed design. Wire or disc wheels.

OPTIONS: Front bumper. Wire wheels. Hinged radiator cap. Thermostat. Tire cover. Fender well tire lock. Dash lamp. Single sidemount. Side curtains. Special paint. Cargo box-tarpaulin. Heater. Spare tire(s). Cigarette lighter. Lettering stencils. External sun shade. Spotlight. Rearview mirror. [Sedan Delivery] Rear bumper. Right-hand taillamp. Cowl lamps.

1930 Chevrolet 1-Ton Universal LR Utility Tank (K. Moore)

HISTORICAL: Introduced: Dec. 4, 1929. Calendar year registrations: [All series] 118,253. Innovations: More powerful six-cylinder engine. New Deluxe Sedan Delivery. New Roadster Delivery (open cab pickup) becomes a separate model, rather than roadster with slip-in cargo box. The U.S. Department of Agriculture maintained a large fleet of Chevrolet sedan deliveries for use in Midwestern states during a corn blight.

1931 CHEVROLET

1931 Chevrolet 1/2-Ton Model AE Canopied Express (OCW)

1/2-TON LIGHT DELIVERY — INDEPENDENCE SERIES AE — SIX-CYLINDER: A new Independence Series of Chevrolet trucks featured a 1/2-ton Light Delivery line and a 1-1/2-ton Conventional Truck line. The 1/2-ton models featured longer set of side hood louvers than the 1930 models. Early versions of the optional front bumpers were of a two-piece design, but this was changed during the model run to a single-piece design. Bumpers were not available for the rear of commercial models, with the exception of the Sedan Delivery. Some collectors believe that special bumper or "fender guards" brackets were available for other 1/2-ton models, but Chip Sweet, who is 1931-1933 Commercial Technical Adviser for the Vintage Chevrolet Club of America, has been unable to confirm this. The size of the 1931 radiator was unchanged from 1930. However, the lower portion of the radiator shell was open and not covered with a guard, which can make the radiator look larger in photographs. A black steel radiator shell and headlamp buckets were standard. A Deluxe Sedan Delivery was available. It had a bright radiator shell, bright headlight buckets, wire wheels and a sidemount on the driver's side. It was shown in advertising literature with whitewall tires. Also available was a Panel with insulated side panels, a coupe-like driver's compartment and disc wheels. It had a load space 72 in. long by 45 in. wide and 48 in. high. Another 1/2-ton was the Canopy Express. It had similar body dimensions but open bodysides with curtain or screen options. Its standard equipment included waterproof curtains for the sides and rear (screens were optional), a sedan-type roof, coupe-type cab and disc wheels. There was also an Open Cab Pickup with a cargo box 66 in. long, 45 in. wide and 13 in. deep. Its body sides were designed to meet the floor at right angles. Equipment included a roadster-type cab and disc wheels. Chevrolet changed from the worm-and-gear steering used through 1930 to worm-and-sector steering. A new three-spoke steering wheel also replaced last year's four-spoke design.

I.D. DATA: Serial number located on dash-mounted nameplate. Starting number: AE-1001 and up. Engine number on right side of motor block behind fuel pump.

Model	Body Type	Price	Weight	Prod. Total
AE	Chassis	355	1880	—
AE	Sedan Delivery	575	2585	4340
AE	Chassis & Cab	460	2215	—
AE	Chassis & Open Cab	—	2100	—
AE	Closed Cab Pickup	488	2425	—
AE	Canopy	550	—	—
AE	Screenside	569	—	—
AE	Panel	555	2710	—
AE	Open Cab Pickup	440	2310	—

1931 Chevrolet 1/2-Ton Model AE Canopy (OCW)

ENGINE: Inline. OHV. Six-cylinder. Cast-iron block. Bore & stroke: 3-5/16 x 3-3/4 in. Displacement: 194 cid. Compression ratio: 5.0:1. Brake horsepower: 50 at 2600 rpm. SAE-horsepower: 26.3. Three main bearings. Mechanical valve lifters. Carburetor: Carter one-barrel model RJHO8-150S. Casting number RJHO8.

1931 Chevrolet 1/2-Ton Model AE Quality Mower Truck (B. Beard)

CHASSIS: [Series AE] Wheelbase: 109 in. Tires: 4.75 x 19 in.
TECHNICAL: Manual transmission. Speeds: 3F/1R. Floor-mounted gearshift. Single disc type clutch. Semi-floating rear axle. Overall ratio: 4.1:1. Four-wheel, internal-expanding mechanical brakes. Steel disc or wire wheels.
OPTIONS: [All] Hinged radiator cap. Thermostat. Tire cover. Fender well tire lock. Dash lamp. Front bumper. Single sidemount. White sidewall tires. Sidemount cover(s). Wire wheels. Deluxe hood ornament. Outside rearview mirror. Heater. Cigarette lighter. Screensides for canopy. Special paint colors. Stencils for company name application. Spotlight. Wheel trim rings. Deluxe equipment. [Sedan Delivery only] Rear bumper. Right-hand taillamp. Lovejoy shock absorbers.
HISTORICAL: Introduced: November, 1930. Calendar year registrations: [All series] 99,600. Innovations: New vibrator horn below left headlight. Revised hood louver design. Two-inch longer wheelbase wheelbase. New crankshaft vibration dampener. Late in 1930, Chevrolet purchased the Martin-Parry Co. of Indianapolis, Ind., which allowed the company to finally offer factory truck bodies. A new deluxe 1/2-ton chassis was introduced using passenger car front end sheet metal. It became the basis of many station wagons, hearses, ambulances and other special bodies where a non-truck appearance was preferable. This was the first year that a variety of finish colors were available. Before 1929, trucks were painted black. From 1929 to this year, Blue Bell blue was the standard color. Chevrolet had about 32.7 percent sales penetration in the light-truck market this year. The acquisition of Martin-Parry Co. would send this figure skyrocketing upwards. The model referred to as a Roadster Pickup or Open Cab Pickup is called a Roadster Delivery in Chevrolet factory literature.

1932 CHEVROLET

1/2-TON LIGHT DELIVERY — CONFEDERATE SERIES BB — SIX-CYLINDER: The 1932 Chevrolet Sedan Deliveries had the 1932 Chevrolet passenger car front end appearance, including a new hood with louver doors. Deluxe 1/2-tons used the 1931 passenger series fenders, splash aprons, runningboards, black steel radiator shell, chrome headlamps and horn. They had the 1931 style hood, too. Light Deliveries were now equipped with a Silent Synchromesh transmission. Trucks did not get the same engine improvements as cars and had a less powerful 53 hp six. They also retained the 1929-1931 style solid rear engine mounting. A spring mount was used at the front of the engine, in place of the rubber mount used on passenger cars. Standard trucks had flat-side bodies and black-finished radiators and headlamp buckets. Equipment varied by model. The standard 1/2-ton Panel included an insulated interior; flush floor straps; locks on all doors; and hinged seats. The Special 1/2-ton Panel featured an insulated body; chrome-plated headlamps; chrome-plated radiator tie-bar; and five wire wheels. The Deluxe 1/2-ton Panel included fully lined interior

23

with dome light; hinged seats; chrome moldings; embossed panels; French-style roof; plate glass windows; five wire wheels; front fenderwell; automatic windshield wiper; and rear vision mirror. The Sedan Delivery included a chrome-plated front end and adjustable hood ports. Rear bumper brackets were listed for the Panel, Canopy and Deluxe Panel.

1932 Chevrolet Model BB Sedan Delivery (DFW/ABA)

I.D. DATA: Serial number located on dash-mounted nameplate. Starting number: BB-1001 and up. Engine number on right side of motor block behind fuel pump.

Model	Body Type	Price	Weight	Prod. Total
Confederate Series — 1/2-Ton				
BB	Chassis	355/345	1935	—
BB	Chassis & Cab	460/440	2270	—
BB	Special Chassis	365	1970	—
BB	Chassis & Open Cab	—	2155	—
BB	Open Cab & Box	440/430	Note 2	—
BB	Closed Cab Pickup	470/440	2465	—
BB	Canopy	560	2735	—
BB	Open Cab Canopy	500/470	—	—
BB	Special Canopy	580	—	—
BB	Screenside	579/510	2735	—
BB	Panel	560/565	2755	—
BB	Special Panel	580	—	—
BB	Deluxe Panel	595/585	2730	—
BB	Sedan Delivery	575	2630	3628
BB	Deluxe Delivery	—	—	—

NOTE 1: Slash indicates midyear price changes due to the Depression.
NOTE 2: Factory literature shows 2,045/2,370/2,350 lbs. weights for Open Cab.

1932 Chevrolet Model BB Sedan Delivery (OCW)

ENGINE: Inline. OHV. Six-cylinder. Cast-iron block. Bore & stroke: 3-5/16 x 3-3/4 in. Displacement: 194 cid. Compression ratio: 5.2:1. Brake horsepower: 53 at 2800 rpm. Net horsepower: 26.3. Three main bearings. Mechanical valve lifters. Carburetor: Carter one-barrel downdraft type W-1, model 222S or 222SA.

CHASSIS: [Series BB] Wheelbase: 109 in. Tires: 5.25 x 18 in.

1932 Chevrolet 1/2-Ton Model BB Panel (DFW)

TECHNICAL: Manual, synchromesh (without freewheeling on Light Delivery models). Speeds: 3F/1R. Floor-mounted gearshift. Improved single-plate dry-disc clutch (pressure plate operated by three throwout levers; clutch plate resilient-mounted and driven through eight springs). Dash operated manifold heat control valve. Torque tube drive (longer torque tube than passenger cars in 1932 Light Delivery models). Semi-floating rear axle. Axle shafts of finest alloy and increased in size; axle bearings larger and stronger. Overall drive ratio: 4.1:1. Four-wheel internal-expanding mechanical brakes with 12 in. drums and linings increased from 1.5 to 1.75 in. wide. Wire wheels. New counter-balanced crankshaft. New harmonic balancer. Built-in air cleaner with flame arrestor, accelerating pump and carburetor heat control.

1932 Chevrolet 1/2-Ton Model BB C Walk-in Delivery (DFW/SI)

OPTIONS: Tire mirror. Electric clock. Gearshift ball. Tire chains. Tire locks. Hub protectors. Snap spokes. Hot water heater. Spotlight. Radiator cap. Dash lamp. Front bumper. Single sidemount. Cowl lamps. Dual wipers. Fenderwell tire lock. Metal tire cover. Standard tire cover. Deluxe models were offered with a chrome-plated radiator shell; chrome-plated headlamps; chrome-plated headlamp tie-bar; and four hydraulic shock absorbers. A rear bumper was now available on three different 1/2-ton models: Panel, Canopy and Deluxe Panel. A wide assortment of Chevrolet built bodies was available in attractive colors.

HISTORICAL: Introduced: December, 1931. Calendar year registrations: [All series] 60,784. Innovations: Higher horsepower engine. First year for different styling appearance on cars and trucks. New 18 in. wire wheels standard for all models. Greater emphasis on marketing deluxe equipment for trucks. Chevrolet began placing great emphasis on improvements of its fleet sales program during this model-year. William S. Knudsen was general manager of Chevrolet from 1922-1932.

1933 CHEVROLET

1933 Chevrolet 1/2-Ton Model CB Sedan Delivery (OCW)

1/2-TON SEDAN DELIVERY — EAGLE/MASTER EAGLE SERIES CB — SIX-CYLINDER: In 1933, the Chevrolet Sedan Delivery continued to be related more to passenger vehicles than other commercial vehicles. It was actually what was called a "Commercial Car." However, it wasn't until 1934 that Chevrolet officially recognized the difference by giving the Sedan Delivery different coding than Light Delivery models. This year, the Sedan Delivery (which is often coded SDL in factory literature) was still part of the Series CB 1/2-ton line. There was also a Deluxe Sedan Delivery with coach lamps on the body rear quarters, a sidemount cover, bright metal trim parts and, in some cases, the ventilator door style hood. A single sidemounted spare tire was now standard equipment on 1/2-tons, since the gas tank was relocated to the location where the spare tire had been carried. Dual sidemounts were optionally available on most models. Safety plate glass was used in the 1933 windshield.

1933 Chevrolet 1/2-Ton Model CB Canopy (R. Streval)

1/2-TON LIGHT DELIVERY — EAGLE/MASTER EAGLE SERIES CB — SIX-CYLINDER:
This was the last year Chevrolet used names such as Eagle and Master, as well as letters, to identify its truck models. On some models, Chevrolet continued its inconsistent policy of fitting some light-duty trucks with a grille virtually identical to that introduced one year earlier on passenger cars. The hood louver design, however, was still of the 1931 style. Providing 56 hp at 2750 rpm was the commercial version of the Chevrolet "Stovebolt Six." A four-speed transmission was now optional in light-duty models. Standard equipment varied by model. The Pickup truck came with a 66 x 45 x 13 in. cargo box, all-steel box construction, double security chains and left-hand sidemount spare. The standard Sedan Delivery had a load space 57 x 50 x 44.5 in. and 36 in. wide curbside opening rear door. Its sheet metal was truck-like, but bright metal headlamp shells, radiator shell and cowl molding were standard, as well as a left-hand sidemount (a single sidemounted spare tire was now standard equipment on 1/2-tons, since the gas tank was relocated to the location where the spare tire had been carried). A safety plate glass windshield was adopted for 1933. The 1/2-ton Special Panel came with a recessed-panel body; chrome headlamps and radiator shell; bright metal headlight tie-bar; chrome bumpers; and a bright outside rearview mirror. Its load space was 72 x 45 x 48 in. Insulation and a dome lamp were found inside. The Canopy was similar-sized, with 18 in. deep steel sides, chrome trim parts and a slanted windshield. (*) Measurements given above are length x width x height.

I.D. DATA: Serial number located on dash-mounted nameplate. The serial number consists of a group of numerals and letters which indicate the assembly plant, the model year, the series, the month of assembly, and the number of units (plus 1,000) assembled at that plant. The first symbol indicates assembly plant: 1=Flint, Mich.; 2=Tarrytown, N.Y.; 3=St. Louis, Mo.; 5=Kansas City, Kan.; 6=Oakland, Calif.; 8=Atlanta, Ga.; 9=Norwood, Ohio; 14=Baltimore, Md.; 20=Los Angeles, Calif.; 21=Janesville, Wis. The second and third symbols indicate series symbols. The fourth symbol indicates month of assembly: A=Jan.; B=Feb., etc. Remaining numbers are the sequential unit production numbe. Each series is separately numbered in sequence beginning with 1001 at each plant. Starting number: CB-1001 and up. Engine number on right side of motor block behind fuel pump.

Model	Body Type	Price	Weight	Prod. Total
CB	Chassis	330	1995	—
CB	Chassis & Cab	420	2345	—
CB	Special Chassis	345	2025	—
CB	Sedan Delivery	545	2750	3628
CB	Special Sedan Delivery	560	—	Note 1
CB	Standard Panel	530	2750	—
CB	Closed Cab Pickup	440	2565	—
CB	Special Panel	545	2775	—
CB	Open Cab Canopy	—	—	—
CB	Closed Cab Canopy	—	—	—

NOTE 1: Special Sedan Delivery price estimated; production for Special Delivery model included with Sedan Delivery.
ENGINE: Inline. OHV. Six-cylinder. Cast-iron block. Bore & stroke: 3-5/16 x 4 in. Displacement: 206.8 cid. Compression ratio: 5.2:1. Brake horsepower: 56 at 2750 rpm. SAE horsepower: 26.3. Three main bearings. Mechanical valve lifters. Carburetor: Carter one-barrel model W1 model 260S.
CHASSIS: [Series CB] Wheelbase: 109 in. Tires: 5.25 x 18 in.
TECHNICAL: Manual, synchromesh (without freewheeling on Light Delivery models). Speeds: 3F/1R. Floor-mounted gearshift. Improved single-plate dry-disc clutch (pressure plate operated by three throwout levers; clutch plate resilient-mounted and driven through eight springs). Heat control valve is thermostatically controlled. Torque tube drive (longer torque tube than passenger cars in 1933 Light Delivery models). Semi-floating rear axle. Axle shafts of finest alloy and increased in size; axle bearings larger and stronger. Overall drive ratio: 4.1:1. Four-wheel internal-expanding mechanical brakes with 12 in. drums and linings increased from 1.5 to 1.75 in. wide. Wire wheels. Counter-balanced crankshaft. Harmonic balancer. Dual spark control and octane selector. Built-in air cleaner with flame arrestor, accelerating pump and carburetor heat control. New center camshaft bearing. Safety plate glass was used in the windshield.
OPTIONS: [All] Front bumper. Outside rearview mirror. Special paint. Bumper guards. Right-hand taillight. Heater. Dual windshield wipers. Seat covers. White sidewall tires. Lettering stencils. Spotlight. Dual sidemounts (most models). Pedestal mirrors for sidemounts. Leatherette sidemount cover. [Deluxe Equipment] Chrome radiator shell. Chrome headlamp buckets. Chrome headlamp tie-bar. Four hydraulic shock absorbers. [Sedan Delivery] Rear bumper. Coachlights. [Deluxe Panel] Spare tire. Highly-polished Duco finish. [Special Chassis Equipment] Chrome radiator shell. Chrome headlamp buckets. Chrome headlamp tie-bar. Four hydraulic shock absorbers.
HISTORICAL: Introduced: December, 1932. Calendar year registrations: [All series] 99,880. Innovations: New larger, more powerful Blue Flame six-cylinder engine. Completely new appearance with 1932 car-type radiator grille, fenders and headlights and 1931 car type hoods (except vent-door hoods optional on Deluxe Sedan Delivery) but had the hold-down mechanism the same as the 1932 cars. That being a locking handle in the middle of the hood bottom that controlled a lever type of locking mechanism. Brackets were attached to the radiator shell and cowl. Factory built body availability and the strong sales to fleet operators and government agencies increased Chevrolet's penetration of the light-truck market to nearly 50 percent in 1933. The company produced its one-millionth commercial vehicle during the model-year. Chevrolet was now selling as many trucks in the 1/2-ton and 1-1/2-ton weight classes as all other makers put together. M.E. Coyle took over as general manager of Chevrolet when William S. Knudsen was promoted to a GM Executive Vice-Presidency.

1934 CHEVROLET

1934 Chevrolet 1/2-Ton Model DB Closed Cab Pickup (DFW/SI)

SEDAN DELIVERY — MODEL DA — SIX-CYLINDER: During the early part of the 1934 model year, the Sedan Delivery (Chevrolet Job Number 34570) was offered. This was no longer considered a part of the 1/2-ton Light Delivery Series. It was moved to the Series DA passenger car line. The passenger style hood with three horizontal louvers that descended in length was used. Standard models had painted trim; Deluxe models had chrome trim. The early 1934 Sedan Delivery had a 112 in. wheelbase, which was the same as 1934 Series DB 1/2-ton trucks, but it was a DA Master Series model. The DA Master Series passenger car line also had a 112 in. wheelbase. Interestingly, this was the last Sedan Delivery that factory literature specified as a 1/2-ton. Later Sedan Deliveries were never (or rarely) referred to, by Chevrolet, in terms of tonnage class.

1934 Chevrolet 1/2-Ton Model EA/EC Canopy Top Pickup (DFW/SI)

SEDAN DELIVERY — MODEL EA/EC — SIX-CYLINDER: Thanks to Chip Sweet, Commercial Technical Adviser for the Vintage Chevrolet Club of America, we have discovered that some truck collectors have 1935 Chevrolet Sedan Deliveries that are titled/registered as 1934 models. This indicates that the new EC line was brought out in the middle or late part of the 1934 model year. Chevrolet coded these as 1935 models. The Model EC standard Sedan Delivery (with straight axle suspension) was coded with Fisher Body Style Number 35-1271A (35=1935; 12=1200 Series; 71=Sedan Delivery; A=straight axle). There was also a Model EA deluxe-chassis Sedan Delivery (also with straight axle) coded with Fisher Body Style Number 35-1271 (35=1935; 12=1200 Series; 71=Sedan Delivery). The deluxe description identified that Deluxe trim or equipment features were used. Although these were manufactured as 1935 vehicles, states with title/registration laws based on the calendar-year date of the actual registration, would have registered the trucks as 1934 models. Also, Chip Sweet reports that some Chevrolet factory literature describes the Model EA chassis as a "1934 DC" chassis (which it was identical to) and the Model EC chassis as a "1935 EC" chassis (which was new). These trucks are considered 1935 models in this book and details about them are in the next section.

1934 Chevrolet 1/2-Ton Model DB Pickup With Utility Body (DFW)

1/2-TON LIGHT DELIVERY — SERIES DB — SIX-CYLINDER: Dramatic new styling was a highlight of the latest Chevrolet trucks. Accentuating the smoother body contours and more fully-crowned fenders were two-tone color combinations available on most body styles. The elimination of the front tie-bar support for the headlights gave the Chevrolets a fresh contemporary look. Standard models had a hood with four vertical louvers that slanted slightly backwards. Deluxe models used the same front end trim parts, but they

were painted on lower-priced trucks and plated on the fancier ones. Dimensions for specific models, following the previous format, were: Pickup: 72 x 45 x 54 in.; Panel: 72 x 52 x 51 in.; Canopy: 72 x 52 x 54 in.

I.D. DATA: Serial number located on dash-mounted nameplate. The serial number consists of a group of numerals and letters which indicate the assembly plant, the model year, the series, the month of assembly, and the number of units (plus 1,000) assembled at that plant. The first symbol indicates assembly plant: 1=Flint, Mich.; 2=Tarrytown, N.Y.; 3=St. Louis, Mo.; 5=Kansas City, Kan.; 6=Oakland, Calif.; 8=Atlanta, Ga.; 9=Norwood, Ohio; 14=Baltimore, Md.; 20=Los Angeles, Calif. The second and third symbols indicate the model/series symbols. The fourth symbol indicates month of assembly: A=Jan.; B=Feb., etc. Remaining numbers are the sequential unit production number. Each series is separately numbered in sequence beginning with 1001 at each plant. Starting number: [DA Series] DA-1001 up; [EA/EC Series] EA-1001; EC-1001; [DB Series] DB-1001 and up. Engine number on right side of motor block behind fuel pump.

Model	Body Type	Price	Weight	Prod. Total
Sedan Delivery — Series DA — 112 in. w.b.				
DA	Sedan Delivery	600	—	—
Light Delivery — Series DB — 112 in. w.b.				
DB	Chassis	355	2120	—
DB	Chassis & Closed Cab	445	2465	—
DB	Closed Cab Pickup	465	2695	—
DB	Canopy Top Pickup	495	2850	—
DB	Special Chassis	375	2150	—
DB	Special Chassis & Cab	465	2485	—
DB	Special Pickup	485	2720	—
DB	Panel	575	2935	—
DB	Special Panel	615q1	2960	—

NOTE 1: See 1935 section for EA/EC Sedan Delivery data.

ENGINE: Inline. OHV. Six-cylinder. Cast-iron block. Bore & stroke: 3-5/16 x 4 in. Displacement: 206.8 cid. Compression ratio: 5.2:1. Brake horsepower: 60 at 2750 rpm. SAE horsepower: 26.3. Three main bearings. Mechanical valve lifters. Carburetor: Carter one-barrel model W1 model 285S.

CHASSIS: [Series DA] Wheelbase: 112 in. Tires: 5.50 x 17 in.

CHASSIS: [Series DB] Wheelbase: 112 in. Tires: 5.50 x 17 in.

CHASSIS: [Series EA/EC] See 1935 section.

TECHNICAL: Manual, synchromesh transmission. Speeds: 3F/1R. Floor-mounted gearshift. Semi-floating rear axle. Overall ratio: 4.11:1. Mechanical four-wheel brakes. Wire spoke wheels.

OPTIONS: Front bumper. Single sidemount. Dual sidemount. Sidemount (cover)s. Heater. Seat covers. [Sedan Delivery/Panel] Rear bumper.

HISTORICAL: Introduced: December, 1933. Calendar year registrations: [All Series] 157,507. Innovations: All-new styling. Sedan Delivery adopts shorter wheelbase. Engine moved further forward in chassis. For the first time since 1918, Chevrolet trucks (except Sedan Delivery) had their own exclusive front sheet metal, which was non-interchangeable with passenger car components.

1935 CHEVROLET

1935 Chevrolet 1-Ton-Rated Parcel Delivery Van (JAW)

SEDAN DELIVERY — MODEL EC/EA — SIX-CYLINDER: The Sedan Delivery was again part of the passenger car line. Frontal styling of the Model EC was virtually identical to that of standard 1935 passenger cars, which had a hood with three horizontal louvers that grew smaller from top-to-bottom. The Model EA front was styled similar to Master Series cars, which had only two horizontal hood louvers (the top one slightly longer). The EC Sedan Delivery was smaller, with a 107 in. wheelbase. It had a straight, I-beam front axle. The Model EA Sedan Delivery had a 113 in. wheelbase. It also had the straight front axle. Trucks in both lines were brought out in the middle or late part of the 1934 model year and are sometimes registered as 1934 models, but Chevrolet manufactured and coded them as 1935 vehicles. The Model EC standard Sedan Delivery was coded with Fisher Body Style Number 35-1271A (35=1935; 12=1200 Series; 71=Sedan Delivery; A=straight axle). The Model EC Deluxe Sedan Delivery was coded with Fisher Body Style Number 35-1271 (35=1935; 12=1200 Series; 71=Sedan Delivery). Although these were manufactured as 1935 vehicles, states with title/registration laws based on the calendar date of the actual registration, would have registered the trucks as 1934 models. A passenger side sidemounted spare tire was standard equipment.

1935 Chevrolet 1/2-Ton Model EB Suburban (OCW)

1/2-TON LIGHT DELIVERY — MODEL EB — SIX-CYLINDER: Changes for 1935 were very minor, except for the introduction of a new model that would have great significance upon the light-duty truck field. This was the Suburban Carryall, an all-steel eight-passenger station wagon, which was part of the upper-level Master series. An unusual thing about this truck was that it would eventually be sold with several entry-door configurations including two-, three- and four-doors. The original had two, plus a tailgate type rear load entrance. There were also some braking improvements in 1935. The 1/2-ton trucks had four curved vertical louvers on the rearmost surface of the hoodsides. Wire wheels, chrome hubcaps and a right-hand sidemount were standard. Chrome headlights, a chrome grille screen, radiator shell band, headlamp supports, spare tire hold-down and shock absorbers were part of the year's special equipment package. Rear bumpers were optional.

I.D. DATA: Serial Number located: on nameplate and dash. The serial number consists of a group of numerals and letters which indicate the assembly plant, the model year, the series, the month of assembly, and the number of units (plus 1,000) assembled at that plant. The first symbol indicates assembly plant: 1=Flint, Mich.; 2=Tarrytown, N.Y.; 3=St. Louis, Mo.; 5=Kansas City, Kan.; 6=Oakland, Calif.; 8=Atlanta, Ga.; 9=Norwood, Ohio; 14=Baltimore, Md.; 20=Los Angeles, Calif.; 21=Janesville, Wis. The second and third symbols indicate the model/series symbols. The fourth symbol indicates month of assembly: A=Jan.; B=Feb., etc. Remaining numbers are the sequential unit production number. Each series is separately numbered in sequence beginning with 1001 at each plant. Starting numbers: [EC Sedan Delivery] EC-1001 and up; [EA Sedan Delivery] EA-1001 up; [EB] EB-1001 and up. Engine number on right side of motor block behind fuel pump. Engine numbers: 4708995 and up.

Model	Body Type	Price	Weight	Prod. Total
Sedan Delivery — Series EC — 107 in. w.b.				
EC	Sedan Delivery	515	2675	538
Sedan Delivery — Series EA — 113 in. w.b.				
EA	Sedan Delivery	625	2920	4688
1/2-Ton Light Delivery — Series EB — 112 in. w.b.				
EB	Chassis	355	2135	—
EB	Special Chassis	375	2235	—
EB	Panel Delivery	500	2920	—
EB	Special Panel	580	3035	—
EB	Chassis & Cab	445	2480	—
EB	Pickup	465	2700	—
EB	Special Pickup	485	2810	—
EB	Canopy	495	2795	—
EC	Sedan Delivery	515	2675	6192

1935 Chevrolet Model EA Sedan Delivery (OCW)

ENGINE: Inline. OHV. Six-cylinder. Cast-iron block. Bore & stroke: 3-5/16 x 4 in. Displacement: 206.8 cid. Compression ratio: 5.45:1. Brake horsepower: 60 at 3000 rpm. SAE horsepower: 26.33. Three main bearings. Mechanical valve lifters. Carburetor: Carter one-barrel model W1 model 284S.

CHASSIS: [Series EC] Wheelbase: 107 in. Tires: 5.25 x 17 in.

CHASSIS: [Series EA] Wheelbase: 113 in. Tires: 5.50 x 17 in.

CHASSIS: [Series EB] Wheelbase: 112 in. Tires: 5.50 x 17 in.

TECHNICAL: Manual, synchromesh transmission. Speeds: 3F/1R. Floor-mounted gearshift. Semi-floating rear axle. Overall ratio: 4.11:1. Mechanical four-wheel brakes. Wire spoke wheels.

OPTIONS: Deluxe equipment. Rear bumper. Single sidemount. Metal sidemount covers. Fabric sidemount covers. Fender skirts. Bumper guards. Radio. Heater. Clock. Cigarette lighter. Radio antenna. Seat covers. Foglights. Spotlight. Special paint. Wheel trim rings. Canopy top for pickup. License plate frames. Two-tone paint. Lettering stencils. Screensides for Canopy Express. Pickup box tarpaulin. Outside rearview mirror. Pedestal mirrors for sidemounts.

1936 CHEVROLET

1936 Chevrolet 1/2-Ton Model FB Pickup (DFW)

STANDARD SERIES COMMERCIAL CAR — MODEL FC — SIX-CYLINDER: This year a Coupe Delivery joined the Sedan Delivery in the small Commercial Car Series. Both were based on the standard I-beam front axle Chevrolet Model FC passenger cars, which grew two inches in wheelbase. Front end appearance was similar to FC cars with an oval-shaped grille with vertical moldings, grille shell-mounted headlamps and hood with two horizontal louvers, the shorter on the bottom. The Sedan Delivery had panel bodysides and a curbside opening rear door.

1936 Chevrolet Model FC Coupe-Delivery (DFW/DPL)

MASTER SERIES COMMERCIAL CAR — MODEL FD — SIX-CYLINDER: Also available was a line of Commercial Cars on the longer 113 in. wheelbase Master Series chassis. These had larger tires.
1/2-TON LIGHT DELIVERY — MODEL FB — SIX-CYLINDER: The Light Delivery line included the 1/2-ton conventional trucks. All 1936 Chevrolet trucks had horizontal hood louvers in place of the vertical openings found on the 1935 models. Above the louvers, in the center, was a large Chevrolet bow tie emblem. The radiator grille resembled that of 1935 passenger cars, as did the new valanced (deep-skirted) front fenders.

1936 Chevrolet 1/2-Ton Model FB Pickup (OCW)

I.D. DATA: Serial Number located on nameplate on dash. The serial number consists of a group of numerals and letters which indicate the assembly plant, the model year, the series, the month of assembly, and the number of units (plus 1,000) assembled at that plant. The first symbol indicates assembly plant: 1=Flint, Mich.; 2=Tarrytown, N.Y.; 3=St. Louis, Mo.; 5=Kansas City, Kan.; 6=Oakland, Calif.; 8=Atlanta, Ga.; 9=Norwood, Ohio; 14=Baltimore, Md.; 20=Los Angeles, Calif.; 21=Janesville, Wis. The second and third symbols indicate the model/series symbols. The fourth symbol indicates month of assembly: A=Jan.; B=Feb., etc. Remaining numbers are the sequential unit production numbe. Each series is separately numbered in sequence beginning with 1001 at each plant. Starting numbers: [FC Sedan Delivery] FC-1001 and up; [FD Sedan Delivery] FD-1001 up; [FB] EB-1001 and up. Engine on right side of motor block behind fuel pump. Engine numbers: K-5500179 and up.

Model	Body Type	Price	Weight	Prod. Total
Commercial Cars — Series FC — 109 in. w.b. — Six				
FC	Sedan Delivery	535	2705	9404
FC	Coupe Pickup	535	2760	3183
Commercial Cars — Series FD — 113 in. w.b. — Six				
FD	Sedan Delivery	—	—	Note 1
FD	Coupe Pickup	—	—	Note 1
1/2-Ton Light Delivery — Series FB — 112 in. w.b. — Six				
FB	Chassis	360	2095	—
FB	Chassis & Cab	450	2450	—
FB	Pickup	475	2075	—
FB	Panel	565	2895	—
FB	Special Panel	577	3000	—
FB	Suburban Carryall	685	3255	—

NOTE 1: Commercial car production believed to be FC/FD combined total.
ENGINE: Inline. OHV. Six-cylinder. Cast-iron block. Bore & stroke: 3-5/16 x 4 in. Displacement: 206.8 cid. Compression ratio: 6.0:1. Brake horsepower: 79 at 3200 rpm. SAE horsepower: 26.3. Three main bearings. Mechanical valve lifters. Carburetor: Carter one-barrel Model 319S.

1936 Chevrolet 1/2-Ton Model FB Pickup (OCW)

CHASSIS: [Series FC] Wheelbase 109 in. Tires: 17 x 5.25 in.
CHASSIS: [Series FD] Wheelbase 113 in. Tires: 5.50 x 17 in.
CHASSIS: [Series FB] Wheelbase 112 in. Tires: 5.50 x 17 in.
TECHNICAL: Manual, synchromesh transmission. Speeds: 3F/1R. Floor-mounted gearshift. Diaphragm type clutch. Semi-floating rear axle. Overall ratio: [FC] 4.11:1; [Others] Not available. Four-wheel hydraulic brakes. Short-spoke wheels.
OPTIONS: Deluxe equipment package. Rear bumper. Single sidemount. Pedestal mirrors for sidemounts. Sidemount cover(s). Fender skirts. Bumper guards. Radio. Heater. Clock. Cigarette lighter. Radio antenna. Seat covers. Fog lamps. Spotlight. Screensides for canopy express. White sidewall tires. Wheel trim rings. Outside rearview mirror. Special paint. Stencils for lettering. Pickup box tarpaulin. Pressed steel wheels. Deluxe radiator ornament. License plate frames. Dual windshield wipers. Side curtains. Right-hand taillight.
HISTORICAL: Introduced: Nov. 2, 1935. Calendar year registrations: [All Series] 204,344. Innovations: Introduction of hydraulic brakes. New Carter carburetor. Coupe-pickup model bows. All new truck cabs with one-piece, all-steel construction brought out at midyear. Dupont paint company sales representatives drove a fleet of standard Chevrolet Sedan Deliveries.

1937 CHEVROLET

COMMERCIAL CAR — MODEL GB — SIX-CYLINDER: This year the Sedan Delivery and Coupe Delivery were based on the Model GB line of Master Series passenger car without Knee-Action front suspension. The year's new "waterfall" style passenger car grille was seen on all small trucks. However, the Commercial Cars also used the car-type front sheet metal with spear-shaped embossments on the hoodsides and a streamline groove running from the fenders onto the doors, where it faded into the sheet metal. There were three small slashes at the front upper corner ahead of the hood feature line and multiple chrome slashes along the hoodside embossments. The Sedan Delivery had a 68 x 54 x 41 in. load space. The Coupe Delivery was again a standard Business Coupe with a right-hand sidemount, a cargo box inside the luggage compartment and step pads on the rear bumper. A trunk lid was supplied and could be swapped for the cargo box by loosening four bolts and substituting one accessory for the other. A change was the spare tire carried under the floor of the Sedan Delivery.

1937 Chevrolet Model GB Sedan Delivery (JAW)

1/2-TON LIGHT DELIVERY — MODEL GC — SIX-CYLINDER: The Light Delivery trucks had a similar grille design, but the rest of their styling was different. There were again twin horizontal hood louvers, but both of the same length. A large Chevrolet bow tie emblem was above the center of the top louver. Double-bead belt moldings with a scallop at the side of the cowl were seen. Chevrolet offered many important new features for 1937 beginning with an all-steel cab and steel stream styling. The result was a modern looking truck with rounded, fuller fenders and smoother lines. The 1/2-ton pickup box was 77 x 45 in. with 16 in. high sidewalls. Dimensions for the GC 1/2-ton Panel were 86 x 54 x 51 in. Headlights on all models were torpedo-shaped and mounted on the side of the hood.

3/4-TON LIGHT TRUCK — MODELS GD — SIX-CYLINDER: Important to Chevrolet's marketing strategy was the return 3/4-ton models midway through the year. These had the same general design as the smaller trucks, but missing was the bow tie badge above the hood louvers. The 3/4-tons were had a longer wheelbase than the 1/2-tons, and longer bodies and boxes. A larger, more powerful engine was standard.

1-TON LIGHT-MEDIUM TRUCK — MODEL GE — SIX-CYLINDER: A new 1-ton series with a 122-1/4 in. wheelbase was also added in 1937. Styling was again basically of similar design in larger proportions. The wheelbase was the same as the 3/4-tons, but longer bodies were fitted.

I.D. DATA: Serial Number located on nameplate on dash. The serial number consists of a group of numerals and letters which indicate the assembly plant, the model year, the series, the month of assembly, and the number of units (plus 1,000) assembled at that plant. The first symbol indicates assembly plant: 1=Flint, Mich.; 2=Tarrytown, N.Y.; 3=St. Louis, Mo.; 5=Kansas City, Kan.; 6=Oakland, Calif.; 8=Atlanta, Ga.; 9=Norwood, Ohio; 14=Baltimore, Md.; 20=Los Angeles, Calif.; 21=Janesville, Wis. The second and third symbols indicate the model/series symbols. The fourth symbol indicates month of assembly: A=Jan.; B=Feb., etc. Remaining numbers are the sequential unit production number. Each series is separately in sequence beginning with 1001 at each plant. Starting numbers: [GB Commercial Cars] GB-1001 and up; [GC Light Delivery] GC-1001 up; [GD Light Truck] GD-1001 and up; [GE Light-Medium Truck] GE-1001 and up. Engine number on right side of motor block behind fuel pump. Engine numbers: [GB/GC] K-1 and up; [Others] T-1 and up.

Model	Body Type	Price	Weight	Prod. Total
Commercial Cars — Series GB — 112.25 in. w.b.				
GB	Sedan Delivery	595	2810	9404
GB	Coupe Delivery	—	—	—
1/2-Ton Light Delivery — Series GC — 112 in. w.b.				
GC	Chassis	390	2190	—
GC	Chassis & Cab	485	2575	—
GC	Pickup	515	2805	—
GC	Panel	605	3030	—
GC	Canopy	600	3050	—
GC	Suburban	725	3330	—
3/4-Ton Light Truck — Series GD — 112.25 in. w.b.				
GD	Chassis	460	2410	—
GD	Chassis & Cab	555	2780	—
GD	Pickup	595	3020	—
GD	Stake	630	3290	—
1-Ton Light-Medium Truck — Series GE — 122.25 in. w.b.				
GE	Chassis	495	2585	—
GE	Chassis & Cab	590	2955	—
GE	Pickup	630	3195	—
GE	Stake	665	3465	—

1937 Chevrolet 1/2-Ton Model GC Pickup (WPL)

ENGINE: [GB/GC] Inline. OHV. Six-cylinder. Cast-iron block. Bore & stroke: 3-5/16 x 4 in. Displacement: 206.8 cid. Compression ratio: 6.0:1. Brake horsepower: 79 at 3200 rpm. SAE horsepower: 26.3. Three main bearings. Mechanical valve lifters. Carburetor: Carter one-barrel model 319S. (Code K)

ENGINE: [GD/GE] Inline. OHV. Six-cylinder. Cast-iron block. Bore & stroke: 3.5 x 3.75 in. Displacement: 216.5 cid. Compression ratio: 6.25:1. Brake horsepower: 85 at 3200 rpm. SAE horsepower: 29.4. Four main bearings. Mechanical valve lifters. Carburetor: Carter one-barrel type W1 Model 838938. (Code T)

CHASSIS: [Model GB] Wheelbase: 112-1/4 in. Tires: 6.00 x 16 in. (7.50 x 15 in. available).

CHASSIS: [Model GC] Wheelbase: 112 in.

CHASSIS: [Model GD] Wheelbase: 122.25 in.

CHASSIS: [Model GE] Wheelbase: 122.25 in.

TECHNICAL: Manual, synchromesh transmission. Speeds: [GB/GC/GD] 3F/1R; [GE] 4F/1R. Floor-mounted gearshift. Diaphragm type clutch. [1/2-ton Models] Semi-floating rear axle; [All others] full-floating rear axle. Overall ratio: [GC] 4.11:1; [Others] 3.82:1. Hydraulic, four-wheel brakes. Pressed steel wheels.

OPTIONS: Deluxe equipment package. Rear bumper. Single sidemount. Pedestal mirrors for sidemounts. Sidemount cover(s). Fender skirts. Bumper guards. Radio. Heater. Clock. Cigarette lighter. Radio antenna. Seat covers. Fog lamps. Spotlight. Screensides for canopy express. White sidewall tires. Wheel trim rings. Outside rearview mirror. Special paint. Stencils for lettering. Pickup box tarpaulin. Deluxe radiator ornament. License plate frames. Dual windshield wipers. Side curtains. Right-hand taillight.

HISTORICAL: Introduced: November, 1936. Calendar year registrations: [All Series] 183,674. Innovations: New 3/4-ton and 1-ton series. New Diamond Crown styling. Safety glass introduced. Trucks again share appearance features with current Chevrolet cars. Larger and more powerful Blue Flame six used. Chevrolet produced some unusual 1/2-ton Dubl-Duti (walk-in delivery) trucks on the 1/2-ton chassis. One used a body by Metro Body Co., which later become a part of International-Harvester Corp. Race driver Harry Hartz drove a 1/2-ton pickup on a "Round the Nation Economy Run" sponsored by Chevrolet under American Automobile Association (AAA) Sanction. Hartz was at the wheel of the truck as it rolled off the assembly line in Flint, Mich. The 72 day excursion covered 10,244.8 miles around the rim of America and did it without mechanical failure, for less than a penny-a-mile.

1938 CHEVROLET

1938 Chevrolet Model HB Coupe-Delivery (DFW/BLHU)

COMMERCIAL CAR — MODEL HB — SIX-CYLINDER: The 1938 Chevrolet grille was made up of horizontal bars on either side of a vertical center divider. More massive horizontal bars were used to divide the thinner ones into six segments on each side. The top bar of the grille was lower and straighter than the 1937 style; on the same level as the horizontal feature line of the hood. The Coupe-Pickup and Sedan Delivery had long, horizontal louver vents similar to those of cars. These had sort of an "ice cube tray" look. The Coupe-Delivery had a cargo box measuring 66 x 38 x 12 in.

1/2-TON LIGHT DELIVERY — MODEL HC — SIX-CYLINDER: Conventional trucks had a different hoodside treatment with four, somewhat shorter horizontal louvers. They were angled at the front. A Chevrolet bow tie emblem was seen above them. Unlike the year's passenger cars, trucks had a flat, one-piece windshield. A double-bead belt molding with scalloped front was used. The 1/2-ton Pickup's load area was 77 x 45 x 16 in. Measurements for the 1/2-ton Model HC Panel body were 86 x 56 x 51 in. The Panel's rear door opening was 47 in. wide by 43 in. high.

1938 Chevrolet 3/4-Ton Model HD Panel (OCW)

Standard Catalog of Light-Duty Trucks

3/4-TON LIGHT TRUCK — MODEL HD — SIX-CYLINDER: The 3/4-ton conventional trucks also had a hood with horizontal louvers angled at the front and a flat, one-piece windshield. A double-bead belt molding with scalloped front was used. The wheelbase was 10-1/4 inches longer than that of the 1/2-ton. The Pickup had a longer, sturdier Express type cargo box. A Stake Truck was in this series.

1-TON MEDIUM-LIGHT TRUCK — MODEL HC — SIX-CYLINDER: The 1-ton conventional trucks also had a hood with horizontal louvers angled at the front and a flat, one-piece windshield. A double-bead belt molding with scalloped front was used. The wheelbase was 10-1/4 inches longer than that of the 1/2-ton and the same as that of the 3/4-ton. The Pickup had a longer, sturdier Express type cargo box. A Stake Truck was in this series. A four-speed transmission, heftier springs and larger tires were standard.

I.D. DATA: Serial Number located for all models on nameplate positioned on firewall. The serial number consists of a group of numerals and letters which indicate the assembly plant, the model year, the series, the month of assembly, and the number of units (plus 1,000) assembled at that plant. The first symbol indicates assembly plant: 1=Flint, Mich.; 2=Tarrytown, N.Y.; 3=St. Louis, Mo.; 5=Kansas City, Kan.; 6=Oakland, Calif.; 8=Atlanta, Ga.; 9=Norwood, Ohio; 14=Baltimore, Md.; 21=Los Angeles, Calif.; 21=Janesville, Wis. The second and third symbols indicate the model/series symbols. The fourth symbol indicates month of assembly: A=Jan.; B=Feb.; etc. Remaining numbers are the sequential unit production number. Each series is separately numbered in sequence beginning with 1001 at each plant. Starting: [HB] HB-1001 and up; [HC] HC-1001 and up; [HD] HD-1001 and up; [HE] HE-1001 and up. Engine numbers located: Serial numbers for all models placed on right side of cylinder block behind fuel pump, and/or stamped on a milled pad on right side of engine at rear of distributor. Starting: [HB] 1187822 and up; [HC] K-1187822 and up; [HD] AT-1187822 and up; [HE] AT-1187822 and up.

1938 Chevrolet 1/2-Ton Model HC Pickup (DFW/C. Chasteen)

Model	Body Type	Price	Weight	Prod. Total
Commercial Car — Model HB — 112.25 in. w.b				
HB	Coupe-Delivery	689	2945	—
HB	Sedan Delivery	694	2835	5742
1/2-Ton Light-Delivery — Model HC — 112 in. w.b.				
HC	Chassis	465	2200	—
HC	Chassis & Cab	562	2580	—
HC	Pickup	592	2805	—
HC	Panel	684	3015	—
HC	Canopy	678	3030	—
HC	Suburban	834	3295	—
3/4-Ton Light Truck — Model HD — 122.25 in. w.b.				
HD	Chassis	543	2420	—
HD	Chassis & Cab	639	2785	—
HD	Pickup	680	3035	—
HD	Stake	716	3300	—
HD	Panel	792	3280	—
1-Ton Light-Medium Truck — Model HE — 122.25 in. w.b.				
HE	Chassis	585	2575	—
HE	Chassis & Cab	681	2950	—
HE	Pickup	722	3200	—
HE	Stake	757	3440	—
HE	Panel	833	3445	—

1938 Chevrolet 1-Ton Model HE Platform Body (OCW)

ENGINE: [HB/HC] Inline. OHV. Six-cylinder. Cast-iron block. Bore & stroke: 3-5/16 x 4 in. Displacement: 206.8 cid. Compression ratio: 6.0:1. Brake horsepower: 79 at 3200 rpm. SAE horsepower: 26.3. Three main bearings. Mechanical valve lifters. Carburetor: Carter one-barrel model 319S. (Code K)

ENGINE: [HD/HE] Inline. OHV. Six-cylinder. Cast-iron block. Bore & stroke: 31/2 x 3-3/4 in. Displacement: 216.5 cid. Compression ratio: 6.25:1. Brake horsepower: 90 at 3200 rpm. SAE horsepower: 29.4. Four main bearings. Mechanical valve lifters. Carburetor: Carter one-barrel W-1 model 838938.

CHASSIS: [Model HB] Wheelbase: 112-1/4 in. Tires: 6.00 x 16 four-ply.

CHASSIS: [Model HC] Wheelbase: 112 in. Overall length: 188 in. Height: 71 in. Tires: 6.00 x 16 four-ply.

CHASSIS: [Model HD] Wheelbase: 122 in. Tires: 6.00 x 15 six-ply.

CHASSIS: [Model HE] Wheelbase: 122 in. Tires: 6.00 x 20 eight-ply, single rear.

TECHNICAL: Manual transmission. Speeds: [HB/HC/HD] 3F/1R; [HE] 4F/1R. Floor-mounted gearshift. Diaphragm type clutch. [HB/HC] Semi-floating rear axle; [HD/HE] Full-floating rear axle. Overall ratio: Various. Four-wheel hydraulic brakes. Steel short spoke wheels.

OPTIONS: Deluxe equipment. Rear bumper. Outside rearview mirror. Spotlight. Foglights. Cargo bed tarpaulin. Bumper guards. Radio. Heater. Clock. Cigarette lighter. Radio antenna. Seat covers. External sun shade. Dual windshield wipers. Right-hand taillight. White sidewall tires. Wheel trim rings. License plate frames. Sidemounted spare tires (special order). Two-tone paint. Special paint colors. [Canopy Delivery] Side curtains. Screensides.

HISTORICAL: Introduced: Oct. 23, 1937. Calendar year registrations: [All Series] 119,479. Innovations: Heavier valve springs. Larger water pump. New ball bearing water pump introduced at midyear. New diaphragm spring type clutch. New voltage regulator and generator. M.E. Coyle was general manager of Chevrolet.

1939 CHEVROLET

1939 Chevrolet 1/2-Ton Model JC Pickup (J. Prodoehl)

COMMERCIAL CARS — MODEL JB — SIX-CYLINDER: The JB models had the passenger car's more rounded horizontal bar grille and "ice cube tray" hoodside vents. Both models, the Coupe-Delivery and Sedan Delivery, also had larger, more streamlined headlamp buckets. A new body with a straighter back was used for the Sedan Delivery, which had a 66 x 54 x 41 in. load space.

1939 Chevrolet Model JB Sedan Delivery (MVMA)

1/2-TON LIGHT DELIVERY — MODEL JC — SIX-CYLINDER: Chevrolet used a new front end design with heavier horizontal members and straighter vertical edges. A Chevrolet script was found on the top grille bar. Chevrolet also adopted a two-piece, V-shaped windshield that replaced the old one-piece flat windshield. The hood now had a single louver and a single side trim strip was used. The same image characterized all light-duty trucks. Popular models included the Pickup with steel cargo box and wooden load floor (the box being the same size as 1938); the Panel with a one-inch wider load space; and the Suburban. This was again a two-door station wagon type vehicle having a front seat on which the right third of the backrest folded forward for passenger ingress/egress. Also somewhat changed was the Canopy Express, which gained a partition behind the driver's seat. This reduced the load space to a length of 80 in., from last season's 86 in.

1939 Chevrolet 3/4-Ton Model JD Chassis Cab Utility Body (Joe Egle)

3/4-TON LIGHT TRUCK — MODEL JD — SIX-CYLINDER: The 3/4-ton trucks had the same general front end and cab styling updates as the 1/2-ton Light Delivery line with a wheelbase nearly 10 in. longer. The Pickup had a larger, Express type cargo box and longer runningboards. The Panel had larger dimensions. There was a Stake truck in this series, but no Suburban.

3/4-TON HEAVY-DUTY TRUCK — MODEL JE — SIX-CYLINDER: The JE models were a heavy-duty version of the JD models.

1-TON MEDIUM-LIGHT TRUCK — MODEL VA — SIX-CYLINDER: The VA Chevrolet trucks had a 133 in. wheelbase. This line is listed as a 1-1/2-ton series in some Chevrolet literature. Apparently, a 1-ton chassis option was available. The VAs came in two chassis configurations and a Panel. In Kentucky, Pennsylvania and North Carolina, they came with light eight-leaf rear springs and were designated VA-S models on license applications, though not on the chassis plate.

I.D. DATA: Serial Number located on plate on right front side of under hood; [JB/JD/JE] On plate on front of firewall. The serial number consists of a group of numerals and letters which indicate the assembly plant, the model year, the series, the month of assembly, and the number of units (plus 1,000) assembled at that plant. The first symbol indicates assembly plant: 1=Flint, Mich.; 2=Tarrytown, N.Y.; 3=St. Louis, Mo.; 5=Kansas City, Kan.; 6=Oakland, Calif.; 8=Atlanta, Ga.; 9=Norwood, Ohio; 14=Baltimore, Md.; 20=Los Angeles, Calif.; 21=Janesville, Wis. The second and third symbols indicate the model/series symbols. The fourth symbol indicates month of assembly: A=Jan.; B=Feb., etc. Remaining numbers are the sequential unit production number. Each series is separately numbered in sequence beginning with 1001 at each plant. Serial numbers: [JB] JB-1001 to 33221; [JC] JC-1001 to 12094; [JD] JD-1001 to 12094; [VA] VA-1001 to 12094. Engine number located on right side of engine block behind fuel pump. Engine numbers: [JB-Coupe-Delivery] 1915447 to 2697267; [JB-Sedan Delivery] B-10503 to 105461; [JC-Chassis/Chassis & Cab/Pickup] K-1915447 to 2697267; [JC-all others] B-10503 to 105461; [JD-Chassis/Chassis & Cab/Pickup] AT-1915447 to 2697267; [JD-all others] B-10503 to 105461; [VA] — T-1915447 to 2697267. The B prefix indicates motor built in Chevrolet's new plant in Buffalo, N.Y.

1939 Chevrolet 1/2-Ton Model JC Pickup (OCW)

Model	Body Type	Price	Weight	Prod. Total
Commercial Car — Model JB — 112.25 in. w.b.				
JB	Coupe Delivery	669	2925	
JB	Sedan Delivery	673	2825	8090
1/2-Ton Light Delivery — Model JC — 113.5 in. w.b.				
JC	Chassis	450	2185	—
JC	Chassis & Cab	542	2580	—
JC	Pickup	572	2785	—
JC	Panel	658	3030	—
JC	Canopy	714	3025	—
JC	Suburban	808	3210	—
3/4-Ton Light Truck — Model JD — 123.75 in. w.b.				
JD	Chassis	528	2355	
JD	Chassis & Cab	619	2745	
JD	Pickup	660	3035	
JD	Stake	690	3305	
JD	Panel	767	3275	

3/4-Ton Light Truck — Model JE — 123.75 in. w.b.

JE	Chassis	528	2355	—
JE	Chassis & Cab	619	2745	—
JE	Panel	767	3275	—

1- to 1-1/2-Ton Medium Light Truck — Model VA/VA-S — 133 in. w.b.

VA	Chassis	552	2920	—
VA	Chassis & Cab	644	3295	—
VA	Panel	821	3975	—

1939 Chevrolet 1-Ton Model VA Stake Truck (A. Lovick/CPC)

ENGINE: Inline. OHV. Six-cylinder. Cast-iron block. Bore & stroke: 3-1/2 x 3-3/4 in. Displacement: 216.5 cid. Compression ratio: 6.25:1. Brake horsepower: 90 at 3200 rpm. SAE horsepower: 29.4. Four main bearings. Mechanical valve lifters. Carburetor: Carter one-barrel model 838938.

CHASSIS: [Model JB] Wheelbase: 112-1/4 in. Tires: 6.00 x 16 four-ply.

CHASSIS: [Model JC] Wheelbase: 113-1/2 in. Tires: 6.00 x 16 four-ply.

CHASSIS: [Model JD] Wheelbase: 123-3/4 in. Tires: 6.00 x 15 six-ply.

CHASSIS: [Model JE] Wheelbase: 123-3/4 in. Tires: 6.50 x 15 six-ply.

CHASSIS: [Model VA] Wheelbase: 133 in. Tires: 6.00 x 20 eight-ply, single rear.

TECHNICAL: Manual, synchromesh transmission. Speeds: [1-ton] 4F/1R; [Others] 3F/1R. Floor-mounted gearshift. Diaphragm type clutch. Shaft-drive. [1/2-ton models] Semi-floating rear axle; [All others] full-floating rear axle. Four-wheel hydraulic brakes. Steel disc wheels.

OPTIONS: [All Trucks and Commercial Cars] White sidewall tires. Wheel trim rings. License plate frames. Outside rearview mirror. Spotlight. Foglights. Radio and antenna. Bumper guards. Radio. Heater. Clock. Cigarette lighter. Seat covers. External sun shade. Dual windshield wipers. Two-tone paint. Special paint colors. [All Trucks] Deluxe equipment. Rear bumper. Cargo bed tarpaulin. Right-hand taillight. [All Trucks, Special order option] Sidemounted spare tire. [Canopy Delivery] Side curtains. Screenside equipment.

1939 Chevrolet 1/2-Ton Model JC Canopy (OCW)

HISTORICAL: Introduced: October, 1938. Calendar year registrations: [All Series] 169,457. Innovations: New carburetor. New Sedan Delivery partition added to Canopy model. A vacuum gearshift option was available at $10 extra. Chevrolet built and sold its two millionth truck in the 1939 model year, which (including larger capacities) featured 45 models on eight wheelbases. A new 1-1/2-ton COE truck was introduced this season.

1940 CHEVROLET

COMMERCIAL CARS — MODEL KB/KH — SIX-CYLINDER: This year's Sedan Delivery looked particularly handsome with its 1940 passenger car styling. It had a 65 x 55 x 41 in. cargo area and 34 x 34 in. rear door opening. It could be had with Knee-Action suspension for the first time. Its counterpart, the Coupe-Delivery, was available with Master Deluxe trim on special order. A special left-hand taillight was required to show up when the removable box was carried. In its place, the conventional trunk lid could be substituted. The KB model commercial cars had Special Deluxe trim. The KH models had fancier Master Deluxe trim.

1940 Chevrolet 1/2-Ton Model KC Pickup (DFW/R. McFarland)

1/2-TON LIGHT DELIVERY — MODEL KC — SIX-CYLINDER: Sealed beam headlights became a feature of 1940 Chevrolet trucks. Parking lights were now positioned on the fender. The top grille bar was wider than in 1939. A new dash panel, similar to that used on Chevrolet automobiles, was introduced for the trucks. The Pickup had a slightly longer, 78 in. load floor. Standard equipment on the Panel Delivery included an insulated roof and side panels, adjustable seat, wood floor with steel skid rails, and latex-impregnated horse-hair seat padding. Either a tailgate or double rear load doors could be had on the Suburban. The Canopy came with a tailgate that latched automatically when slammed shut. Side curtains were standard on this model, but screenside equipment was optional.

1940 Chevrolet 1-Ton Model WA Open Express (DFW/ASL)

1/2-TON DUBL-DUTI — MODEL KP — SIX-CYLINDER: This new Cab-Over-Engine (COE) line offered a Forward-Control chassis for a walk-in delivery truck. Bodies were supplied by various independent contractors, some factory-recommended. The term "Dubl-Duti" was used to describe the chassis. The finished trucks were called Walk-in Delivery Vans and later Step-Vans . They are similar to the truck your UPS man drives.

3/4-TON LIGHT TRUCK — MODEL KD — SIX-CYLINDER: The 3/4-ton trucks had the same general front end and cab styling updates as the 1/2-ton Light Delivery line with a wheelbase nearly 10 in. longer. The Pickup had a larger, Express type cargo box and longer runningboards. The Panel had larger dimensions. There was a Stake truck in this series, but no Suburban. Technical improvements included a 4.55:1 rear axle.

3/4-TON HEAVY-DUTY TRUCK — MODEL KE — SIX-CYLINDER: The JE models were a heavy-duty version of the JD models. Technical improvements included a 4.55:1 rear axle. These are called Special Commercial models.

1-TON MEDIUM-LIGHT TRUCK — MODEL KF — SIX-CYLINDER: Chevrolet factory literature lists a new KF 1-ton model for 1940. Some aftermarket sources list this as a 3/4-ton. With tire and chassis options, it probably came with different payload ratings. The only model was a large panel.

1-TON MEDIUM-LIGHT TRUCK — MODEL WA — SIX-CYLINDER: This line is listed as a 1-1/2-ton series in some Chevrolet literature, but a 1-ton chassis option was available. The WAs came in two chassis configurations and Panel, Canopy, Open Express, Platform, and Stake bodied models. In Kentucky, Pennsylvania and North Carolina, they came with light eight-leaf rear springs and were designated WA-S models on license applications, though not on the chassis plates. They came with single rear wheels.

1940 Chevrolet 1/2-Ton Model KC Pickup (E.F. Higgins)

I.D. DATA: Serial Number located on plate on right side of cowl underhood; on plate on dash; on right or left side of seat frame, and on left-hinge pillar post. The serial number consists of a group of numerals and letters which indicate the assembly plant, the model year, the series, the month of assembly, and the number of units (plus 1,000) assembled at that plant. The first symbol indicates assembly plant: 1=Flint, Mich.; 2=Tarrytown, N.Y.; 3=St. Louis, Mo.; 5=Kansas City, Kan.; 6=Oakland, Calif.; 8=Atlanta, Ga.; 9=Norwood, Ohio; 14=Baltimore, Md.; 20=Los Angeles, Calif.; 21=Janesville, Wis. The second and third symbols indicate the model/series symbols. The fourth symbol indicates month of assembly: A=Jan.; B=Feb., etc. Remaining numbers are the sequential unit production number. Each series is separately numbered in sequence beginning with 1001 at each plant. Last indicates month of manufacture. Serial numbers: [KB]: KB-1001 to 20946; [KH] KH-1001 to 37644; [KC]: KC-1001 to 17658; [KP] KP-1001 to 17658; [KD] KD-1001 to 17658; [KF] KF-1001 to 17658; [WA] WA-1001 to 18041*. (*) was designation for Kentucky, Pennsylvania, North Carolina. Plate with letter S added. Engine number location same as 1939. Starting engine number: [KB, KH] 2697268 to 3665902; [KC] K-2697268 to 3665902; [KD] AT-2697268 to 3665902; [ATB] 105462 to 221935; [WA] T-2697268 to 3665902; [TB] 105462 to 221935.

Model	Body Type	Price	Weight	Prod. Total
Commercial Cars (Special Deluxe) — Model KB — 113 in. w.b.				
KB	Sedan Delivery	694	2915	2590
KB	Coupe-Delivery	699	3025	538
Commercial Cars (Master Deluxe) — Model KH — 113 in. w.b.				
KH	Sedan Delivery	719	2970	—
KH	Coupe-Delivery	725	3090	—
1/2-Ton Light Delivery — Model KC — 113.5 in. w.b.				
KC	Chassis	450	2195	—
KC	Chassis & Cab	541	2595	—
KC	Pickup	572	2840	—
KC	Panel	658	3050	—
KC	Canopy	694	3050	—
KC	Suburban	808	3300	—
1/2-Ton Dubl-Duti — Model KP — 113.5 in. w.b.				
KP	Walk-in	1028	3650	—
3/4-Ton Light Truck — Model KD — 123.75 in. w.b.				
KD	Chassis	528	2355	—
KD	Chassis & Cab	619	2755	—
KD	Pickup	660	3110	—
KD	Platform	670	3150	—
KD	Stake	691	3330	—
KD	Panel	766	3325	—
1-Ton Commercial — Model KF — 133 in. w.b.				
KF	Panel	813	3700	—
1- to 1-1/2-Ton Light-Medium Truck — Model WA — 133 in. w.b.				
WA	Chassis	558	2940	—
WA	Chassis & Cab	649	3335	—
WA	Platform	704	3850	—
WA	Stake	730	4115	—
WA	Open Express	735	3835	—
WA	Panel	826	3985	—
WA	Canopy	867	3970	—

1940 Chevrolet 1/2-Ton Model KC Pickup (DFW)

ENGINE: Inline. OHV. Six-cylinder. Cast-iron block. Bore & stroke: 3-1/2 x 3-3/4 in. Displacement: 216.5 cid. Compression ratio: 6.25:1. Brake horsepower: 85 at 3400 rpm. SAE horsepower: 29.4. Four main bearings. Mechanical valve lifters. Carburetor: Carter one-barrel model 838938.

CHASSIS: [KB] Wheelbase: 113 in. Tires: 6.00 x 16 four-ply.

CHASSIS: [KH] Wheelbase: 113 in. Tires: 6.00 x 16 four-ply.

CHASSIS: [KC] Wheelbase: 113-1/2 in. Overall length: 193 in. Tires: 6.00 x 16 four-ply.

CHASSIS: [KP] Wheelbase: 113-1/2 in. Tires: 6.00 x 16 six-ply.

CHASSIS: [KD] Wheelbase: 123.75 in. Tires: 6.00 x 15 six-ply.

CHASSIS: [KF] Wheelbase: 133 in. Overall length: 208 in. Tires: 7.00 x 17 six-ply.

CHASSIS: [WA] Wheelbase: 133 in. Tires: [front] 6.00 x 20 in., [rear, single] 6.00 x 32 eight-ply.

1940 Chevrolet Model KH Sedan Delivery (OCW)

TECHNICAL: Manual, synchromesh transmission. Speeds: [1-ton] 4F/1R; [Others] 3F/1R. Floor-shift controls. Diaphragm type clutch. Shaft-drive. [1/2-ton] Semi-floating rear axle; [Others] Full-floating rear axle. Four-wheel hydraulic brakes. Pressed steel disc wheels.

OPTIONS: Deluxe equipment. Rear bumper. Chrome trim rings. White sidewall tires. Outside rearview mirror(s). Bumper guards. Radio. Heater. Clock. Cigarette lighter. Radio antenna. Seat covers. External sun shade. Spotlight. Two-tone paint. Special paint. Bumper step-pads. License plate frames. Fog lights. [Commercial Cars] Oversize tires on Master Deluxe Coupe-Delivery. Knee-Action. Vacuum gear shift. Column-mounted gear control. [Suburban] Panel doors in lieu of tailgate. [Canopy Express] Screenside equipment.

HISTORICAL: Introduced: October, 1939. Calendar year registrations: [All series] 185,636. Innovations: New Dubl-Duti package delivery truck added to 1/2-ton KP line. Knee-Action available on Sedan Delivery. Coupe-Pickup and Sedan Delivery have all-new styled body. The Foster Parents Plan for War Children purchased a number of Series KF 1-ton Panels fitted with dual rear wheels and special interiors for ambulance service and other wartime use in France and other parts of Europe.

1941 CHEVROLET

SEDAN DELIVERY — MODEL AG — SIX-CYLINDER: A new front end treatment was found on the 1941 Coupe-Delivery and Sedan Delivery, both of which used current passenger car sheet metal and trim. Both were now on a three-inch longer wheelbase. The Sedan Delivery had a usable load space measuring 66 in. long, 56 in. wide, and 41 in. high. Its rear door opening was 34 x 34 in. The same rear door panel was used on all 1941-1948 Sedan Deliveries. Standard features included Knee-Action front suspension, hydraulic shock absorbers front and rear, and vacuum-assisted gearshift. Interestingly, the Sedan Delivery used the same windshield as the four-door Sport Sedan, rather than the Station Wagon.

1941 Chevrolet Model AG Master Deluxe Coupe-Delivery (BMM)

1/2-TON LIGHT DELIVERY — MODEL AK — SIX-CYLINDER: The 1941 models were easily identified by their new front end with fender-mounted headlight pods which were crowned by swept-back parking lights. The grille had two distinct sections. The upper unit was similar to the 1940 version with two thick horizontal bars capped by a top bar with a thin divider and a bottom bar with Chevrolet lettering. The remaining grille elements consisted of broad vertical bars sweeping outward from a center post carrying a Chevrolet logo. No hood ornament was fitted. Side hood trim consisted of a single horizontal chrome stripe extending backward from the upper grille region and three shorter horizontal stripes dividing the side hood louvers into three sections. A 115 in. wheelbase made the new trucks larger. However, the base GVW rating for 1/2-ton models dropped from 4,600 lbs. in 1940 to 4,400 lbs. in 1941.

1/2-TON DUBL-DUTI — MODEL AJ — SIX-CYLINDER: The Dubl-Duti package delivery truck chassis was moved to the new 115 in. wheelbase. This Forward-Control truck chassis had a base 5,000 lb. GVW. Standard bodies were sourced from factory-approved manufacturers, or the buyer could add his own body.

3/4-TON LIGHT TRUCK — MODEL AL — SIX-CYLINDER: The 3/4-ton truck shared the year's new styling. The Pickup had a larger load box and longer runningboards. Platform Stake and Panel body models were also offered, along with a bare chassis and the Chassis & Cab. The standard GVW rating for trucks in this series was 5,200 lbs.

3/4-TON HEAVY-DUTY — MODEL AM — SIX-CYLINDER: The 3/4-ton heavy-duty truck also shared the year's new styling. The Pickup had a larger load box and longer runningboards. Platform Stake and Panel body models were also offered, along with a bare chassis and the Chassis & Cab. The standard GVW rating for trucks in this series was 5,600 lbs.

1-TON MEDIUM-LIGHT — MODEL AN — SIX-CYLINDER: The 1-ton series consisted of only a very large panel body truck called the Special Panel. The standard GVW rating for trucks in this series was 5,800 lbs.

1941 Chevrolet 1/2-Ton Model AK Pickup (OCW)

I.D. DATA: Serial Number located, [Sedan Delivery] On right side of floor pan ahead of seat; [Cab models/Panels/Suburbans] On plate on right side of cowl under hood; [Chassis models] On plate temporarily attached near steering column, with final location per body maker. The first symbol indicated the assembly plant: 1=Flint, Mich.; 2=Tarrytown, N.Y.; 3=St. Louis, Mo.; 5=Kansas City, Kan.; 6=Oakland, Calif.; 8=Atlanta, Ga.; 9=Norwood, Ohio; 14=Baltimore, Md.; 20=Los Angeles, Calif.; and 21=Janesville, Wis. The second and third symbols indicate model/series as follows: AG=2100; AK=3100; AL=3600; AM=3600 (This model was called a 3/4-ton Special in sales department terminology); AN=3800 (This model was called a 3/4-ton Long Wheelbase Panel in sales department terminology). The fourth symbol indicates month of assembly; A=Jan.; B=Feb., C=March; D=April; E=May; F=June; G=July [end of 1941 model production; system changes in 1942]. The following symbols indicated the sequential production number. Each series was separately numbered in sequence, starting with 1001 at each assembly plant. Starting number: [AG] AG-1001 & up; [AJ] AJ-1001 & up; [AK] AK-1001 & up; [AL] AL-1001 & up; [AN] AN-1001 & up; [YR] YR-1001 & up; [AC] AC-1001 & up*; [AE] AE-1001 & up*; [AAN] AAN-1001 & up*; [AN] AN-1001 & up*. Engine number location: Same location as 1940. Starting engine number: [AG] AA-1001 & up; [AJ] AM-1001 & up; [AK] AD-1001 & up; [AL/AN] AAF-1001 & up; [YR] AF-1001 & up. * For trucks built at Tonawanda.

1941 Chevrolet 1/2-Ton Model AK Pickup (R. Troutman)

Model	Body Type	Price	Weight	Prod. Total
Commercial Car — Series AG — 116 in. w.b.				
AG	Sedan Delivery	748	3045	9918
AG	Coupe-Delivery	754	3195	1135
1/2-Ton Dubl-Duti — Model AJ — 115 in. w.b.				
AJ	Chassis	1058	3665	—
1/2-Ton Light Delivery — Model AK — 115 in. w.b.				
AK	Chassis	478	2235	—
AK	Chassis & Cab	569	2630	—
AK	Pickup	600	2870	—
AK	Panel	686	3090	—
AK	Canopy	722	3090	—
AK	Suburban	837	3320	—
3/4-Ton Light Truck — Model AL — 125.25 in. w.b.				
AL	Chassis	556	2400	—
AL	Chassis & Cab	648	2795	—
AL	Pickup	689	3120	—
AL	Platform	699	3205	—
AL	Stake	719	3355	—
AL	Panel	795	3355	—

NOTE 1: Model designation AM used on 3/4-tons with heavy-duty chassis equipment.

1-Ton Medium-Light Truck — Model AN — 134.5 in. w.b.

AN	Special Panel	848	3770	—

ENGINE: Inline. OHV. Six-cylinder. Cast-iron block. Bore & stroke: 3-1/2 x 3-3/4 in. Displacement: 216.5 cid. Compression ratio: 6.5:1. Brake horsepower: 90 at 3300 rpm. SAE-horsepower: 29.4. Torque: 174 lbs.-ft. at 1200-2000 rpm. Four main bearings. Mechanical valve lifters. Carburetor: Carter model W1-483S.
CHASSIS: [Model AG] Wheelbase: 116 in. Overall length: 195-3/4 in. Height: 65-7/8 in. Front tread: 57-5/8 in. Rear tread: 60.0 in. Tires: 6.00 x 16 four-ply.
CHASSIS: [Model AK] Wheelbase: 115 in. Overall length: 195-198 in. Tires: 6.00 x 16 four-ply.
CHASSIS: [Model AJ] Wheelbase: 115 in. Overall length: 195 in. Tires: 6.00 x 16 four-ply.
CHASSIS: [Model AL] Wheelbase: 125-1/4 in. Tires: 6.00 x 15 six-ply.
CHASSIS: [Model AM] Wheelbase: 134-1/2 in. Tires: 7.00 x 17 six-ply.
CHASSIS: [Model AN] Wheelbase: 134-1/2 in. Tires: 7.00 x 17 six-ply.
TECHNICAL: Manual, synchromesh transmission. Speeds: [1-ton] 4F/1R; [Others] 3F/1R. Floor-shift controls. Clutch: Single-plate dry-disc.; diaphragm type; 9-1/8 in. clutch. Shaft drive. Rear axle: [AG/AK] Semi-floating rear axle; [All others] full-floating rear axle. Hydraulic, four-wheel brakes. Wheels: [AG/AJ] One-piece drop-center; [Others] Multi-piece split rims.
OPTIONS: [General, all] Chrome trim rings. White sidewall tires. Outside rearview mirror(s). Bumper guards. Radio. Heater. Clock. Cigarette lighter. Radio antenna. Seat covers. External sun shade. Spotlight. Two-tone paint. Special paint. Oversize tires (standard on Suburban). License plate frames. Fog lights. [Light Deliveries/Trucks] Deluxe cab equipment. Rear bumper. [Canopy Express] Screenside equipment. [Coupe-Pickup] Bumper step-pads. [Coupe-Pickup/Sedan Delivery]. Master Deluxe trim. Vacuum gearshift. Column-mounted gear control.

1941 Chevrolet Model AG Sedan Delivery (DFW/HTM)

1942 CHEVROLET
(EARLY SERIES)

1942 Chevrolet 3/4-Ton Model BL Pickup (OCW)

COMMERCIAL CAR — MODEL BG/SERIES 1500 — SIX-CYLINDER: The Commercial Car series included the Sedan Delivery and the Stylemaster Business Coupe when equipped with an optional, slide-in-the-trunk load box. They had the new "American Eagle" grille used on 1942 passenger cars. It was a heavier-looking design with lower and wider horizontal chrome bars. There was also a lower, longer and more massive body appearance; longer and deeper front fenders and a longer, larger hood. A splash shield was added between the bumper and grille. Parking lights were built into the grille, instead of mounted on the fenders. A stronger, deeper-crowned bumper was fitted. Technical changes included heavier front coil springs; improved front wheel bearings; larger flywheel bolts; an improved accelerator; and a redesigned headlamp switch. Both models remained on a 116 in. wheelbase. The Sedan Delivery had a usable load space measuring 66 in. long, 56 in. wide, and 41 in. high. Its rear door opening was 34 x 34 in. The same rear door panel was used on all 1941-1948 Sedan Deliveries. The windshield was the same specified for the four-door Sport Sedan. Standard features included Knee-Action front suspension, hydraulic shock absorbers front and rear. Even though Chevrolet did not promote a truck tonnage rating for the Sedan Delivery, this year the company made a heavy-duty truck clutch optional. This was indicated with a BY engine prefix. In addition, a deep oil pan better-suited for climbing 45 percent grades, became a Central Office Production Option (COPO).
1/2-TON LIGHT DELIVERY — MODEL BK/SERIES 3100 — SIX-CYLINDER: The 1942 had the 1941 style front end. The grille had two distinct sections. The upper grille had two horizontal bars curving around the nose. The bottom grille elements consisted of broad vertical bars sweeping outward from a center post carrying a Chevrolet logo. The headlamps were fender-mounted with parking lights on top of them. No hood ornament was fitted. Side hood trim consisted of a single horizontal chrome stripe extending backward from the upper grille region and three shorter horizontal stripes dividing the side hood louvers into three sections. A 115 in. was used again. The base GVW rating for 1/2-ton models climbed back up to 4,600 lbs.
1/2-TON DUBL-DUTI — MODEL BJ/SERIES 3100 — SIX-CYLINDER: The Forward-Control Dubl-Duti package delivery truck chassis remained on the 115 in. wheelbase. It had a base 5,000 lbs. GVW. Standard bodies were sourced from factory-approved manufacturers, or the buyer could add his own.
3/4-TON LIGHT TRUCK — MODEL BL/SERIES 3600 — SIX-CYLINDER: The 3/4-ton truck shared the year's new styling. The Pickup had a larger load box and longer running-boards. Platform Stake and Panel body models were also offered, along with a bare chassis and the Chassis & Cab. The standard GVW rating for trucks in this series was 5,200 lbs.
3/4-TON HEAVY-DUTY — MODEL BM/SERIES 3600 — SIX-CYLINDER: Series BM coding was used for 3/4-tons with heavy-duty equipment.
1-TON MEDIUM-LIGHT — MODEL BN/SERIES 3800 — SIX-CYLINDER: The 1-ton series consisted of only a very large panel body truck called the Special Panel. The standard GVW rating for trucks in this series was 5,800 lbs.

1942 Chevrolet "BK" Pickup (OCW)

I.D. DATA: Serial Number located, [Sedan Delivery] On right side of floor pan ahead of seat; [Cab models/Panels/Suburbans] On plate on right side of cowl under hood; [Chassis models] On plate temporarily attached near steering column, with final location per body maker. The first symbol indicated the assembly plant: 1=Flint, Mich.; 2=Tarrytown, N.Y.; 3=St. Louis, Mo.; 5=Kansas City, Kan.; 6=Oakland, Calif.; 8=Atlanta, Ga.; 9=Norwood,

Ohio; 14=Baltimore, Md.; 20=Los Angeles, Calif.; and 21=Janesville, Wis. The second and third symbols indicate model/series as follows: BG=1500; BK=3100; BL=3600; BM=3600 (This model was called a 3/4-ton Special in sales department terminology); BN=3800 (This model was called a 3/4-ton Long Wheelbase Panel in sales department terminology). The fourth and fifth symbols indicate month of assembly. Due to unusual circumstances during World War II, Chevrolet had to modify its date code system to identify "1942 models" built in 1941-1943 (civilian and military) and 1944-1945 (civilian). The 1942 trucks assembled late in 1941 had the month codes: 08=August; 09=September; 10=October; 11=November; 12=December. Codes for units built early in 1942 were 01=Jan.; 02=Feb., 03=March; 04=April; 05=May; 06=June; 07=July. For trucks made in late 1942, the month codes were determined by adding 12 months to the codes used on late 1941 models and were: 20=August; 21=September; 22=October; 23=November; 24=December. For trucks made in early 1943, the month codes were determined by adding 12 months to the codes used on early 1942 models and were: 13=Jan.; 14=Feb., 15=March; 16=April; 17=May; 18=June; 19=July. For trucks made in late 1943, the month codes were determined by adding 12 months to the codes used on late 1942 models and were: 32=August; 33=September; 34=October; 35=November; 36=December. (Chevrolet engineering bulletins do not specifically indicate any light-duty truck production during 1943, but we assume the same coding was used on big trucks built for the military.) This modified system was used through 1945. The symbols following the date code were the sequential production number. Each series was separately numbered in sequence, starting with 1001 at each assembly plant. Starting number: Serial numbers starting: [BG] 2AA-1001 and up; [BJ] 2AM-1001 and up; [BK] 2AD-1001 and up; [BL] 2AAF-1001 and up; [BN] 2AAF-1001 and up. Engine number location: On right side of engine block behind fuel pump. Starting engine number: [BG] BA-1001 and up; [BJ] BM-1001 and up; [BK] BD-1001 and up; [BL] ABF-1001 and up; [BN] ABF-1001 and up. Note: Some engines with 1941 engine numbers were used in 1942 trucks. These have a 2 stamped ahead of the regular engine prefix.

Model	Body Type	Price	Weight	Prod. Total
Commercial Car — Model BG — 116 in. w.b.				
BG	Sedan Delivery	853	3080	2996
BG	Coupe-Delivery	865	3230	206
1/2-Ton Light Delivery — Model BK — 115 in. w.b.				
BK	Chassis	536	2235	—
BK	Chassis & Cab	629	2630	—
BK	Pickup	660	2870	—
BK	Panel	748	3090	—
BK	Canopy	785	3085	—
BK	Suburban	905	3320	—
1/2-Ton Dubl-Duti — Model BJ — 115 in. w.b.				
BJ	Chassis	1127	3665	—
3/4-Ton Light Truck — Model BL — 125.25 in. w.b.				
BL	Chassis	617	2400	—
BL	Chassis & Cab	710	2795	—
BL	Pickup	752	3120	—
BL	Platform	763	3205	—
BL	Stake	783	3355	—
BL	Panel	860	3355	—

NOTE 1: BM designation was used for 3/4-ton trucks with heavy-duty equipment.

1-Ton Light-Medium Truck — Model BN — 134.5 in. w.b.

BN	Panel	915	3770	—

ENGINE: Inline. OHV. Six-cylinder. Cast-iron block. Bore & stroke: 3-1/2 x 3-3/4 in. Displacement: 216.5 cid. Compression ratio: 6.50:1. Brake horsepower: 90 at 3300 rpm. SAE horsepower: 29.4. Four main bearings. Hydraulic valve lifters. Carburetor: Carter type W-1, downdraft, one-barrel Model 839534.

CHASSIS: [Model BG] Wheelbase: 116 in. Tires: 6.00 x 16 four-ply.

CHASSIS: [Model BJ] Wheelbase: 115 in. Tires: 6.00 x 16 six-ply.

CHASSIS: [Model BK] Wheelbase: 115 in. Tires: 6.00 x 16 four-ply.

CHASSIS: [Model BL] Wheelbase: 125.25 in. Tires: 6.00 x 15 six-ply.

CHASSIS: [Model BM] Wheelbase: 125.25 in. Tires: 6.00 x 15 six-ply.

CHASSIS: [Model BN] Wheelbase: 134.5 in. Tires: 7.00 x 16 six-ply.

TECHNICAL: Manual, synchromesh transmission. Speeds: [1-ton] 4F/1R; [Others] 3F/1R. Floor-shift controls. Clutch: Single-plate dry-disc.; diaphragm type; 9-1/8 in. clutch. Shaft drive. Rear axle: [BG/BK] Semi-floating rear axle; [All others] full-floating rear axle. Hydraulic, four-wheel brakes. Wheels: [BG/BJ] One-piece drop center; [Others] Multi-piece split rims. Pressed steel disc wheels.

OPTIONS: [General, all] Chrome trim rings. White sidewall tires. Outside rearview mirror(s). Bumper guards. Radio. Heater. Clock. Cigarette lighter. Radio antenna. Seat covers. External sun shade. Spotlight. Two-tone paint. Special paint. Oversize tires (standard on Suburban). License plate frames. Fog lights. [Light Deliveries/Trucks] Deluxe cab equipment. Rear bumper. [Canopy Express] Screenside equipment. [Suburban] Double rear doors in place of tailgate. [Coupe-Pickup] Bumper step-pads. [Coupe-Pickup/Sedan Delivery] Master Deluxe trim. Vacuum gearshift. Column-mounted gear control.

HISTORICAL: Introduced: October, 1941. Calendar year production [Trucks up to 1-ton] 119,077 (This does not include Sedan Deliveries). Innovations: New styling and trim for passenger car based commercial vehicles. Regular panel door option for Suburban reinstated. Black-out trim used on late-production models. Civilian truck production ended in January, 1942, with America's entry into World War II. Chevrolet was later given permission to produce trucks for high-priority civilian use. This allowed more BK/BL/BN trucks to be built on a limited basis between Jan. 1, 1944 and Aug. 31, 1945. Factory literature indicates that Chevrolet's engineering department called these "1942" models. However, it's likely that they were sold/titled as new models in the calendar year they were purchased, either 1944 or 1945. All Chevrolet plants participated in the war effort, except the Saginaw service and manufacturing facility, which was used to supply replacement parts for trucks on the road at that time. Chevrolet changed the date coding system used in the truck serial numbers so that military trucks built in 1942-1943 and civilian trucks built in 1944-1945 can be dated to the month of manufacture. This was the last year that the Coupe-Delivery model was offered.

1944-1945 CHEVROLET (1942-LATE)

1/2-TON LIGHT DELIVERY — MODEL BK/SERIES 3100 — SIX-CYLINDER: Production of a limited line of Chevrolet trucks for the civilian market started up again Jan. 1, 1944. It represented a continuation of the 1942 series. Chevrolet engineering department bulletins refer to these as 1942 models. However, the trucks were titled in the calendar years that they were built and sold (1944-1945). Date codes in the serial number can be used to determine which year and month a truck was built. In the under 1-ton category, this was a continuation of the 1941 conventional truck Models BK, BL and BN. Larger conventionals, buses, and Cab-Over-Engine trucks were also put back into production. Styling and features were unchanged from 1941, except that all (or nearly all) of the 1944-1945 and early 1946 trucks came with painted grilles, bumpers, hubcaps and hood trim. Most were painted Turret gray. White, cream, yellow, and orange finishes were also available.

3/4-TON LIGHT TRUCK — MODEL BL/SERIES 3600 — SIX-CYLINDER: The 3/4-ton truck returned to production. The Pickup had a larger load box and longer runningboards. Platform Stake and Panel body models were also offered, along with a bare chassis and the Chassis & Cab. The standard GVW rating for trucks in this series was 5,200 lbs.

3/4-TON HEAVY-DUTY — MODEL BM/SERIES 3600 — SIX-CYLINDER: Series BM coding was used for 3/4-tons with heavy-duty equipment.

1-TON MEDIUM-LIGHT — MODEL BN/SERIES 3800 — SIX-CYLINDER: The 1-ton series consisted of only a very large panel body truck called the Special Panel. The standard GVW rating for trucks in this series was 5,800 lbs.

I.D. DATA: Serial Number located: [Cab models/Panels/Suburbans] On plate on right side of cowl under hood; [Chassis models] On plate temporarily attached near steering column, with final location per body maker. The first symbol indicated the assembly plant: 1=Flint, Mich.; 2=Tarrytown, N.Y.; 3=St. Louis, Mo.; 5=Kansas City, Kan.; 6=Oakland, Calif.; 8=Atlanta, Ga.; 9=Norwood, Ohio; 14=Baltimore, Md.; 20=Los Angeles, Calif.; and 21=Janesville, Wis. The second and third symbols indicate model/series as follows: BK=3100; BL=3600; BN=3800 (This model was called a 3/4-ton Long Wheelbase Panel in sales department terminology). The fourth and fifth symbols indicate month of assembly. Due to unusual circumstances during World War II, Chevrolet had to modify its date code system to identify "1942 models" built in 1944-1945 (civilian). For trucks made in early 1944, the month codes were determined by adding 12 months to the codes used on early 1943 models and were: 25=Jan.; 26=Feb.; 27=March; 28=April; 29=May; 30=June; 31=July. For trucks made in late 1944, the month codes were determined by adding 12 months to the codes used on late 1943 models and were: 44=August; 45=September; 46=October; 47=November; 48=December. For trucks made in early 1945, the month codes were determined by adding 12 months to the codes used on early 1944 models and were: 37=Jan.; 38=Feb.; 39=March; 40=April; 41=May; 42=June; 43=July. (A new series went into production in August, 1945 and the month codes changed to the regular Chevrolet system.) The numbers following the date codes indicated the sequential production number. Each series was separately numbered in sequence, starting with 1001 at each assembly plant. Starting number: Serial numbers starting: [BK] BK-2127 up; [Others] not available. Engine number location: On right side of engine block behind fuel pump. Starting engine numbers BG-580921 up.

Model	Body Type	Price	Weight	Prod. Total
1/2-Ton Light Delivery — Series 3100/Model BK — 115 in. w.b.				
BK	Pickup	757	2870	—
3/4-Ton Light Truck — Series 3600/Model BL — 125.25 in. w.b.				
BL	Chassis	617	2400	—
BL	Chassis & Cab	710	2795	—
BL	Pickup	752	3120	—
BL	Platform	763	3205	—
BL	Stake	783	3355	—
BL	Panel	860	3355	—

NOTE 1: BM designation was used for 3/4-ton trucks with heavy-duty equipment.

1-Ton — Light-Medium Truck — Series 3800/Model BN — 134.5 in. w.b.

BN	Special Panel	—	—	—

NOTE 1: List prices authorized by Office of Price Administration (OPA).
NOTE 2: Higher prices allowed for synthetic tires after April 18, 1944.
NOTE 3: Most sources list only 3100 Pickup.
NOTE 4: Chevrolet references indicate 3600/3800 trucks also built.

ENGINE: Inline. OHV. Six-cylinder. Cast-iron block. Bore & stroke: 3-1/2 x 33/4 in. Displacement: 216.5 cid. Compression ratio: 6.50:1. Brake horsepower: 90 at 3300 rpm. SAE horsepower: 29.4. Four main bearings. Hydraulic valve lifters. Carburetor: Carter type W-1, downdraft, one-barrel Model 839534.

CHASSIS: [Model BK] Wheelbase: 115 in. Tires: 6.00 x 16 four-ply.

CHASSIS: [Model BL/BM] Wheelbase: 125.25 in. Tires: 6.00 x 15 six-ply.

CHASSIS: [Model BN] Wheelbase: 134.5 in. Tires: 7.00 x 16 six-ply.

TECHNICAL: Manual, synchromesh transmission. Speeds: [1-ton] 4F/1R; [Others] 3F/1R. Floor-shift controls. Clutch: Single-plate dry-disc.; diaphragm type; 9-1/8 in. clutch. Shaft drive. Rear axle: [BK] Semi-floating. [All others] full-floating rear axle. Overall drive ratio: 3.73:1. Hydraulic, four-wheel brakes. Wheels: [BK] Single-piece drop center rims; [Others] Multi-piece split rims.

OPTIONS: Outside rearview mirror(s). Bumper guards. Heater. Seat covers. Special paint. Fog lights. Rear bumper.

HISTORICAL: After a massive national mobilization, production of nearly all military vehicles for World War II was completed in 1943. Chevrolet then got permission to put the 1942 models back into limited production to turn out trucks for essential users on the homefront. Chevrolet factory records show that BK (1/2-ton); BL (3/4-ton) and BN (1-ton) trucks were built between Jan. 1, 1944 and Aug. 31, 1945. The Coupe-Delivery and Sedan Delivery were discontinued. The Sedan Delivery would be reintroduced as a May, 1946 addition to the new line of Chevrolet passenger cars that debuted on Oct. 30, 1945. Chevrolet factory literature indicates that the Dubl-Duti models did not go back into production until after May 31, 1947.

1946 CHEVROLET
(INTERIM SERIES)

1946 Chevrolet 1/2-Ton Model CK Pickup (OCW)

1/2-TON COMMERCIAL — MODEL CK/SERIES 3100 — SIX-CYLINDER: Between Sept. 1, 1945 and May 1, 1946, Chevrolet built a line of trucks that were called "Interim" models. Factory service bulletins said, "These are not to be considered postwar models, but they do represent a continuation of the regular 1942 lines, which are being produced under War Production Board (WPB) authorization from Sept. 1, 1942 to the release of the postwar models." These trucks had no significant changes from the 1942 BK/BL/BM light-duty trucks. In fact, they continued to come with painted grilles, bumpers, hubcaps and hood trim. Paint color choices were unchanged. Turret gray was the color most often seen. Factory nomenclature was slightly modified to favor use of the term Commercial over Light Delivery, although the latter was still seen in technical service bulletins.

3/4-TON COMMERCIAL — MODEL CL/SERIES 3600 — SIX-CYLINDER: The CL was a 3/4-ton model in the interim series and had a 125-1/4 in. wheelbase. Longer load boxes and bodies were used with the longer wheelbase. The standard GVW rating was 5,200 lbs.

3/4-TON COMMERCIAL — MODEL CM/SERIES 3600 — SIX-CYLINDER: The CM was the 3/4-ton model with HDE (heavy-duty equipment) in the interim series. It had the 125-1/4 in. wheelbase. The same longer load box and bodies were used, but the standard GVW rating was 5,800 lbs. Regular tires were size 7.00-17 six-ply; optional tires were size 7.50-17 eight-ply. Larger wheels than used on the regular 3/4-ton were standard.

1-TON — MODEL CN/SERIES 3800 — SIX-CYLINDER: This series was comprised of one model, which Chevrolet literature describes as follows, "3/4-ton Special Panel truck of 5,800 lbs. GVW." A longer wheelbase and frame, huge panel body, and larger wheel rims and tires characterized these 1-ton interim trucks. 6.00-20 six-ply tires were standard on 20 x 5 in. five-slot heavy-duty wheels. There were numerous larger tire and wheel options, too.

I.D. DATA: Serial Number located: [Cab models/Panels/Suburbans] On plate on right side of cowl under hood; [Chassis models] On plate temporarily attached near steering column, with final location per body maker. The first symbol indicated the assembly plant: 1=Flint, Mich.; 2=Tarrytown, N.Y.; 3=St. Louis, Mo.; 5=Kansas City, Kan.; 6=Oakland, Calif.; 8=Atlanta, Ga.; 9=Norwood, Ohio; 14=Baltimore, Md.; 20=Los Angeles, Calif.; and 21=Janesville, Wis. The second and third symbols indicate model/series as follows: CK=3100; CL=3600; CM=3600; CN=3800 (This model was called a 3/4-ton Long Wheelbase Panel in sales department terminology). The fourth and fifth symbols indicate month of assembly: 09=September; 10=October; 11=November; 12=December; 1=January (1946); 2=February (1946); 3=March (1946); 4=April (1946). The numbers following the date codes indicated the sequential production number. Each series was separately numbered in sequence, starting with 1001 at each assembly plant. Starting number: [CK] 1001 up; [CL] CL-1001 up; [CN] CN-1001 up. Engine number on right side of engine block behind fuel pump.

Model	Body Type	Price	Weight	Prod. Total
1/2-Ton Commercial — Model CK/Series 3100 — 115 in. w.b.				
CK	Chassis	637	2235	—
CK	Chassis & Cab	727	2630	—
CK	Pickup	757	2870	—
CK	Panel	842	3090	—
CK	Suburban (door)	987	3320	—
CK	Suburban (gate)	987	3330	—
CK	Canopy	877	3085	—
3/4-Ton Light Truck — Model CL (CM)/Series 3600 — 125.25 in. w.b.				
CL/CM	Pickup	—	—	—

NOTE 1: The CM was the CL with heavy-duty equipment.

1-Ton Light Truck — Model CN/Series 3800 — 134.5 in. w.b.				
CN	Panel	—	—	—

ENGINE: Inline. OHV. Six-cylinder. Cast-iron block. Bore & stroke: 3-1/2 x 3-3/4 in. Displacement: 216.5 cid. Compression ratio: 6.5:1. Brake horsepower: 90 at 3300 rpm. SAE-horsepower: 29.4. Four main bearings. Mechanical valve lifters. Carburetor: Downdraft one-barrel model W1-574S.

CHASSIS: [Model CK] Wheelbase: 115 in. Overall length: 198 in. (Suburban). Tires: 6.00 x 16.

CHASSIS: [Model CL] Wheelbase: 125.25 in.

CHASSIS: [Model CN] Wheelbase: 133.5 in.

TECHNICAL: Manual transmission. Speeds: 3F/1R. Floor-mounted gearshift. [Model CK] Semi-floating rear axle; [All others] full-floating rear axle. Single disc clutch, 9-1/8 in. Four-wheel hydraulic brakes. Wheels: [CK] One-piece drop center rims; [Others] Multi-piece split rims.

OPTIONS: Rear bumper. Bumper guards. Radio. Heater. Clock. Cigarette lighter. Radio antenna. Seat covers.

HISTORICAL: Production began Sept. 1 1945; ended May 1, 1946. Calendar year production: [All, except Sedan Delivery] 270,140 (not limited to CK/CL/CM/CN models). Market share: 28.567 percent. Innovations: M.E. Coyle was elevated to a new position as executive vice-president of General Motors Corporation. Cadillac general manager Nicholas Dreystadt was appointed to Coyle's former position as president of Chevrolet.

1946 CHEVROLET
(LATE SERIES)

1946 Chevrolet 1/2-Ton Model DP Pickup (P. George)

SEDAN DELIVERY — MODEL DJ/SERIES 1500 — SIX-CYLINDER: Production of 1946 Chevrolet passenger cars started very soon after World War II ended. A Chevrolet Technical Service Bulletin of Oct. 30, 1945 announced the new Stylemaster 1500 (serial prefix DJ) and Fleetmaster 2000 (serial prefix DK) models. However, it was not until May, 1946 that the Sedan Delivery was brought back as a running addition in the Stylemaster DJ line. The Coupe-Delivery did not return, although this model is listed in some early postwar used car guides. Perhaps Chevrolet considered bringing it back, then decided not to. Essentially, the Stylemaster models were updated 1942 Master Deluxe models. The grille was modified, the parking lamps were relocated and chrome-plated trim returned. The Sedan Delivery continued to share the windshield of the four-door Sport Sedan. Its rear panel door was the same part used on 1942 Sedan Deliveries.

1946 Chevrolet 1/2-Ton Model DP Panel (OCW)

1/2-TON LIGHT-DUTY COMMERCIAL — MODEL DP/SERIES 3100 — SIX-CYLINDER: A new series of light-duty trucks started production May 1, 1946. These were officially considered the first postwar models. However, they still had the prewar appearance. Chevrolet promoted many refinements, saying, "To help refill the war-depleted highways of America as soon as possible, Chevrolet presents, with no engineering delay, new lines of time-tested trucks for 1946. Based on the 1941 model vehicles, our last truly prewar trucks and the best-designed trucks Chevrolet has ever manufactured heretofore, the new trucks are improved by the experience gained in five years of developing military trucks, five years of intense research in materials, five years of study of the operation of Chevrolet trucks on the largest proving ground in the world...the highways of America...in the particularly tough job of war transportation." There was said to be a general refinement of design to make all trucks more efficient, stronger and more durable. These trucks had the 1941 style polished chrome grille with curved horizontal front hood louvers and vertical bars in the lower radiator grille. The bottom of the front hood louver had stripes accented with Swift's red. It also had Chevrolet lettering painted in red enamel. At the top of the center bar in the radiator grille was a chrome badge with red and blue enamel finish. A polished chrome regular (curved-type) front bumper was standard. A similar chrome rear bumper was standard on all 3100s as well. Other bright-finished parts included outside door handles; windshield division molding; cab assist handles; headlamp rims; and taillamp rims. Front and rear hubcaps with chrome plating were standard. The 3100 hubcaps had small blue Chevrolet letters surrounded by blue speedlines and red-painted "hood ornament" decorations. Standard features for all 3100s marked a return to 1941 equipment levels and included Synco-perlite beige-finished metal panels in driver's compartment; hair and cotton seat cushion pads; rubber floor mats; rubber anti-squeak and sealing parts; improved windshield and window glass sealing; all-rubber windshield wiper hoses; more secure rear door weatherstrips; more durable side door locks, check links and window sash channels; more comfortable, reshaped and reconstructed cab seat and back cushions with more attractive and durable plastic (vinyl resin) upholstery; and double-laced seat cushion springs with filled-in tops. Paint colors included Brewster green; Apple green; white; Omaha orange; Hollywood tan (Oakland only); Bordeaux maroon (Tarrytown and Baltimore only); Swift's

red; Medium cream; Armour yellow; Export blue; and Boatswain blue. An Airdale brown and Circassian brown combination was available for the Suburban. Black was the regular color for all fenders, which could be painted body color when requested. The 1/2-ton Dubl-Duti truck was discontinued. All 1/2-ton 3100s had a 4,600 lbs. GVW rating.

1946 Chevrolet 1/2-Ton Model DP Pickup (A. Kaylor)

3/4-TON LIGHT-DUTY COMMERCIAL — MODEL DR/SERIES 3600 — SIX-CYLINDER: The 3/4-ton trucks had a longer wheelbase. The Pickup load box was longer and had more stake pockets. Long runningboards were used. No Suburban was offered in this line. There were Platform and Stake models. Hubcaps were larger and had only red Chevrolet lettering. The regular curved-type chrome bumper was standard on all models. The regular chrome rear bumper was standard on all except the Platform and Stake models. Base tires on 3600s were 15 in. six-ply rated on 15 x 5.50 semi-drop-center rims. There were numerous tire options. The 3/4-ton heavy-duty model was discontinued. Standard GVWs for these trucks were 5,200-5,800 lbs.

1946 Chevrolet 1/2-Ton Model DP Suburban (OCW)

1-TON COMMERCIAL — MODEL DS/SERIES 3800 — SIX-CYLINDER: The Special Panel (Model 3805) was discontinued. The 1-ton line now had a full range of models including an Express (large Pickup), Panel, Canopy, Platform and Stake. The Platform and Stake were also available with dual rear wheels. General styling and features were the same as on 3100/3600 models. The Express had a longer wheelbase than the 3600 Pickup, longer runningboards, and a longer load box with extra stake pockets. A chrome-plated hood louver and radiator grille were standard on Pickup, Panel and Canopy models. A heavy-duty, channel section front bumper was standard for chassis models and Platform and Stake trucks. A regular chrome rear bumper was standard on Panels and Canopy models only. The standard tires were 7.00 x 17 six-ply rated for trucks with single rear wheels or 7.00 x 18 eight-ply rated for trucks with dual rear wheels. They were mounted on new wider five-inch rims of advanced design. There were many tire and wheel options. Hubcaps were shared with 3600s and had only red Chevrolet lettering. No hubcaps were fitted on the 18 x 5 in. wheels used for the Chassis & Cab, Platform and Stake models. The standard GVWs for these trucks were 6,000-6,700 lbs. (depending on tire options) with single rear wheels; or 8,800 lbs. with a new dual rear wheels option. A four-speed manual transmission was standard.

1946 Chevrolet 1/2-Ton Model DP Pickup (OCW)

I.D. DATA: Serial Number located, [Sedan Delivery] On right hinge pillar about nine inches above the rocker panel; [Cab models/Panels/Suburbans] On plate on right side of cowl under hood; [Chassis models] On plate temporarily attached near steering column, with final location per body maker. The first symbol indicated the assembly plant: 1=Flint, Mich.; 2=Tarrytown, N.Y.; 3=St. Louis, Mo.; 5=Kansas City, Kan.; 6=Oakland, Calif.; 8=Atlanta, Ga.; 9=Norwood, Ohio; 14=Baltimore, Md.; 20=Los Angeles, Calif.; and 21=Janesville, Wis. The second and third symbols indicate model prefix/series as follows: DJ=Series 1500; DP=3100; DR=3600; DS=3800. The fourth symbol indicates month of assembly; A=Jan.; B=Feb., etc. The following symbols indicated the sequential production number. Each series was separately numbered in sequence, starting with 1001 at each assembly plant: [DJ] DJ-1001 and up; [DP] DP-1001 and up; [DR] DR-1001 and up; [DS] DS-1001 and up. Engine number location: Engine number on right side of engine block behind fuel pump.

1946 Chevrolet 1/2-Ton Model DP Panel (OCW)

Model	Body Type	Price	Weight	Prod. Total
Sedan Delivery — Model DJ/Series 1500 — 116 in. w.b.				
1508	Sedan Delivery	1173	3135	—
1/2-Ton Commercial — Model DP/Series 3100 — 115 in. w.b.				
3102	Chassis	796	2300	—
3103	Chassis & Cab	922	2680	—
3104	Pickup	963	2925	—
3105	Panel	1077	3145	—
3107	Canopy	1126	3135	—
3106	Suburban (door)	1283	3370	—
3116	Suburban (gate)	1281	3385	—
3112	Chassis & W/S	817	2350	—
3/4-Ton Commercial — Model DR/Series 3600 — 125.25 in. w.b.				
3602	Chassis	891	2495	—
3603	Chassis & Cab	1016	2890	—
3604	Pickup	1069	3215	—
3605	Panel	1212	3450	—
3608	Platform	1101	3300	—
3609	Stake	1127	3450	—
3612	Chassis & W/S	911	—	—
1-Ton Commercial — Model DS/Series 3800 — 134.5 in. w.b.				
[Single Rear Wheels]				
3802	Chassis	892	2835	—
3803	Chassis & Cab	—	—	—
3812	Chassis & W/S	914	2885	—
3804	Express	1139	4095	—
3805	Panel	1264	4080	—
3807	Canopy	1318	4095	—
3808	Platform	—	—	—
3809	Stake	—	—	—
[Dual Rear Wheels]				
3803	Chassis & Cab	1106	3560	—
3808	Platform	1200	4065	—
3809	Stake	1235	4315	—

1946 Chevrolet 1/2-Ton Model DP Pickup (OCW)

ENGINE: Inline. OHV. Six-cylinder. Cast-iron block. Bore & stroke: 3-1/2 x 3-3/4 in. Displacement: 216.5 cid. Compression ratio: 6.5:1. Brake horsepower: 90 at 3300 rpm. SAE horsepower: 29.4. Four main bearings. Mechanical valve lifters. Carburetor: Carter downdraft one-barrel model W1-574S.

CHASSIS: [Model DJ] Wheelbase: 116 in. Tires: 6.00 x 16 four-ply.

CHASSIS: [Model DP] Wheelbase: 115 in. Tires: 6.00 x 16 six-ply.

CHASSIS: [Model DR] Wheelbase: 125.25 in. Tires: 15 in. six-ply.

NOTE: What is a 15 in. six-ply tire? This obsolete size is comparable to size 7.50 x 15 according to Chevrolet truck expert Bob Adler, who adds, "The 15 in. tires are 'beefier' than the 16 in. tires and the 15 in. wheels weigh considerably more than the 16 in. wheels."

CHASSIS: [Model DS] Wheelbase: 134.50 in. Tires: [Single rear wheels] 7.00 x 17 six-ply; [Dual rear wheels] 7.00 x 18 eight-ply.

1946 Chevrolet 1/2-Ton Model DP Pickup (EK)

TECHNICAL: Manual transmission. Speeds: [1500/3100/3600] 3F/1R; [3800] 4F/1R. Floor-mounted gearshift. Single-disc dry-plate clutch. [1500/3100] Semi-floating rear axle. [3600/3800] Full-floating rear axle. Hydraulic brakes. Wheels: [1500/3100] One-piece drop center 16 in. wheels; [3600/3800] Multi-piece split rims.

1946 Chevrolet 1/2-Ton Model DP Pickup (OCW)

OPTIONS: [RPO] Rearview mirror(s) and bracket(s). Oil-bath air cleaner. Screenside equipment for Canopy. Spare tire and wheel carrier. Hydraulic, double-acting shock absorbers. 1-ton eight-leaf rear springs for 3600. Economy rear axle. Low-ratio rear axle. Long runningboards. Long rear fenders. Heavy-duty clutch. Frame extensions. Oil filter. Governor. Prop shaft guard. Chrome-plated bumper guards (except on rear of 3600 Platform/Stake). Radiator master grille guard. Tail and stop lamp equipment. Rear fender irons. Heavy-duty cooling system. Sun shades. Auxiliary seat for Canopy and Panel. Double-acting rear springs. Heavy-duty radiator for 3600/3800. Radiator overflow return tank. Heavy-duty three-speed transmission. Heavy-duty four-speed transmission. Advertising sign panels. Right-hand windshield wiper. Tru-Stop brake equipment. Deluxe platform body skirt. Rear bumper. Genuine leather cab seat and back upholstery. Various tire options, as follows:

Light Duty Truck Tire Options

Size	Ply Rating	Capacity (lb.)	PSI	Section (in.)
15 in.	Six	1500	40	7.74
15 in.	Eight	1700	48	7.74
6.00 x 16	Four	990	32	6.25
6.00 x 16	Six	1065	36	6.21
6.50 x 16	Six	1290	40	6.65
7.00 x 17	Six	1550	45	7.30
7.50 x 17	Eight	1725	55	7.36
7.00 x 18	Eight	1800	55	7.24

OPTIONS: [Dealer Accessories] Radio and antenna package. Floor mats. Under dash heater/defroster. Seat covers. Spotlight. Directional signals.

1946 Chevrolet 1-Ton Model DS Cantrell Woody Bus (D. Gaser)

HISTORICAL: Manufactured May 1, 1946 to May 31, 1947. Calendar year registrations: [All Chevrolet trucks] 171,618 (This does not include the Sedan Deliver total). Calendar year production: [All Chevrolet trucks, except Sedan Delivery] 335,343. Note: The registration/production totals are not limited to 1-ton and under models; production of Sedan Deliveries was included with passenger car production. Innovations: Full 1-ton series reintroduced for first time since 1941. Suburban with panel doors and Suburban with tailgate now merchandised as separate models. Dual rear wheel models in 1-ton line. Chevrolet promoted these as postwar models, although they were based on the prewar appearance. They had some technical refinements and returned to offering the bright metal trim and leather interiors last featured for 1942 models. These trucks were titled as both 1946 and 1947 models, depending upon which calendar year they were sold in. Certainly, after the fall of 1946, dealers and salesmen sold them with 1947 titles to compete with new models from other manufacturers like Dodge and Ford.

1947 CHEVROLET

1947 Chevrolet Model EJ Sedan Delivery (OCW)

SEDAN DELIVERY — MODEL EJ — SIX-CYLINDER: The 1947 Sedan Delivery entered production on May 1, 1947, along with the all-new Advance-Design trucks. There were few differences from 1946. It had a new grille with a softer, more horizontal appearance and blades contoured into three distinct sections. Chevrolet lettering appeared on the uppermost grille bar. There was a more horizontal hood emblem with Chevrolet bow tie. No bodyside moldings appeared. Short, spear-shaped hoodside nameplates said Stylemaster. The windshield was the same part used for four-door Sport Sedans. The curbside-opening rear panel door had the same part numbers as in 1941-1946. The 1947 interior was trimmed in blue-gray imitation leather, code 137. Chevrolet did not emphasize a tonnage class for the Sedan Delivery. A three-speed manual transmission was standard. A heavy-duty three-speed was optional. The Sedan Delivery had a 4,100 lbs. GVW rating.

1947 Chevrolet 3/4-Ton Model ER Pickup (K. Kutz)

1/2-TON LIGHT-DUTY COMMERCIAL — MODEL EP/SERIES 3100 — SIX-CYLINDER: On May 1, 1947, the all-new Advance-Design truck series entered production. It featured new "Unisteel" cab styling, stronger frames and revised interiors. Rear corner windows for cab models were included in a deluxe equipment option package. Trucks with this option had a different rear roof panel section. The new look was neat and uncluttered. The grille had five broad horizontal bars topped by a broad hood ornament containing a blue bow tie and vermilion Chevrolet lettering. Rectangular parking lights were placed in chrome housings at the ends of the uppermost pair of grille bars. A painted grille was standard equipment. The outer grille bar assembly was done in body color (Forester green was standard). The inner bar assemblies were finished in a grayish-green called Channel green. The outer bars each had one cream medium stripe. A chrome radiator grille package was optional. It included chrome outer grille bars, which were not striped. The inner grille bars remained Channel green. A polished chrome Chevrolet Thriftmaster nameplate was installed near the rear edge of the "alligator" hood. Underscore lines and the word Thriftmaster were painted vermilion, while the background of the nameplate was set off with black finish. Chrome-plated curved-type front bumpers were standard on all 3100s. Similar rear bumpers were standard on most models. Chrome hubcaps with vermilion Chevrolet lettering were standard. A two-piece, flat windshield was used. It had a black rubber seal and polished stainless steel divider bar. Polished stainless steel windshield reveal moldings were standard on Suburbans and optional on other models. Front and rear fenders retained their individual forms. Their rounded shape, in conjunction with the rounded corners of the body, gave the Chevrolet trucks a more up-to-date appearance. The filler tube for the under-frame-mounted gas tank came out the right-hand side of the body, ahead of the front wheels. Cab models and single-unit body models had one belt molding stripe, which was cream medium with standard finishes. Forester green was the standard truck color, but was not used on Suburbans. The Suburbans were finished with a Fathom green upper body and Channel green lower body. The following no-cost color options (pinstripe colors in parentheses) were offered on all models except the Suburban: Swift's red (Argent silver); Armour yellow (black); white (Emerald green); Jet black (Argent silver); Omaha orange (black); Cape maroon (gold); Mariner blue (cream medium); Windsor blue (cream medium); Seacrest green (cream medium); Sun beige (Totem scarlet); and cream medium (black). The interior was highlighted by wider seats, improved vision through the larger windshield, side and rear windows and a redesigned instrument panel. The instrument panel featured electric type fuel and battery charge indicators and pressure-type heat indicator and oil pressure gauge. The speedometer was driven by a flexible shaft. Interior panels were finished in slate gray enamel. Models with runningboards had black rubber runningboard mats. The 3100 (EP model prefix) trucks had a base 4,600 lbs. GVW rating.

3/4-TON LIGHT-DUTY COMMERCIAL — MODEL ER/SERIES 3600 — SIX-CYLINDER: The 3/4-ton trucks had the same new Advance-Design styling, features and finish as other conventional trucks. They rode a longer wheelbase. The Pickup load box was longer and had six stake pockets. Long runningboards were used. No Suburban was offered in this line. There were Platform and Stake models. Hubcaps looked like the ones on 3100s with vermilion Chevrolet lettering. Features and finish were similar to those for 3100 models. Curved-type chrome front bumpers were standard on all models. Base tires on 3600s were 15 in. six-ply rated on 15 x 5.50 semi-drop-center rims. Standard GVW rating for these trucks was 5,200-5,800 lbs. depending upon tire options.

1-TON MEDIUM-DUTY COMMERCIAL — MODEL ES/SERIES 3800 — SIX-CYLINDER: The 1-ton had the same new Advance-Design styling, features and finish as other conventional trucks. The basic model lineup was unchanged. It included single and dual rear wheel options for all except the Express, Canopy and Panel. The Express had a longer wheelbase than the 3600 Pickup, longer runningboards, and a longer load box with eight stake pockets. A curved-type chrome front bumper was standard on all models. Regular equipment tires were 7.00 x 17 six-ply rated for trucks with single rear wheels or 7.00 x 18 eight-ply rated for trucks with dual rear wheel options. The hubcap design was shared with 3100s and 3600s, though the 3800's hubcaps were larger. They had vermilion Chevrolet lettering. No hubcaps were used on the 18 x 5 in. wheels of the Chassis & Cab, Platform and Stake models, which had eight bolts and eight circular openings. The standard GVWs for trucks with single rear wheels were 5,700 lbs.; 6,100 lbs.; and 6,700 lbs. depending on tire options. A base GVW of 8,800 lbs. was listed for trucks with optional dual rear wheels. A four-speed manual transmission was standard.

I.D. DATA: Serial Number located: [Sedan Delivery] On right hinge pillar about nine inches above rocker panel; [Cab models/Panels/Suburbans] On plate attached to rear face of left-hand door hinge pillar; on right side of cowl under hood; [Chassis models] On plate temporarily attached near steering column, with final location per body maker. The first symbol indicated the assembly plant: 1=Flint, Mich.; 2=Tarrytown, N.Y.; 3=St. Louis, Mo.; 5=Kansas City, Kan.; 6=Oakland, Calif.; 8=Atlanta, Ga.; 9=Norwood, Ohio; 14=Baltimore, Md.; 20=Los Angeles, Calif.; and 21=Janesville, Wis. The second and third symbols indicate model prefix/series as follows: EJ=Series 1500; EP=3100; ER=3600; ES=3800. The fourth symbol indicates month of assembly; A=Jan.; B=Feb., etc. The following symbols indicated the sequential production number. Each series was separately numbered in sequence, starting with 1001 at each assembly plant: Serial numbers: [Series 1500] EJ-1001 to EJ-33745; [Series 3100] EP-1001 and up; [Series 3600] ER-1001 and up; [Series 3800] ES-1001 and up. Engine numbers: Stamped on boss on right side of cylinder block, to the rear of the distributor.

Model	Body Type	Price	Weight	Prod. Total
Sedan Delivery — Model EJ/Series 1500 — 116 in. w.b.				
1508	Sedan Delivery	1233	—	20,303
1/2-Ton Commercial — Model EP/Series 3100 — 116 in. w.b.				
3102	Chassis	843	2420	—
3103	Chassis & Cab	1030	2915	—
3104	Pickup	1087	3345	—
3105	Panel	1238	3555	—
3107	Canopy	1289	3545	—
3116	Suburban	1474	3745	—
3/4-Ton Commercial — Model ER/Series 3600 — 125.25 in. w.b.				
3602	Chassis	941	2660	—
3603	Chassis & Cab	1128	3180	—
3604	Pickup	1201	3440	—
3608	Platform	1211	3560	—
3609	Stake	1258	3720	—
1-Ton Commercial — Model ES/Series 3800 — 137 in. w.b.				
380	Chassis	988	2910	—
3803	Chassis & Cab	1176	3440	—
3804	Pickup	1279	3845	—
3805	Panel	1445	4220	—
3807	Canopy	1523	4210	—
3808	Platform	1295	3965	—
3809	Stake	1362	4195	—

1947 Chevrolet 3/4-Ton Model ER Pickup (OCW)

ENGINE: Inline. OHV. Thriftmaster Six. Six-cylinder. Cast-iron block. Bore & stroke: 3-1/2 x 3-3/4 in. Displacement: 216.5 cid. Compression ratio: 6.5:1. Gross horsepower: 90 at 3300 rpm. Gross Torque: 174 lbs.-ft. at 1200-2000 rpm. SAE horsepower: 29.4. Four main bearings. Mechanical valve lifters. Carburetor: Carter downdraft one-barrel model W1-574S.

CHASSIS: [Model 1500] Wheelbase: 116 in. Overall length: 196.75 in. Front tread: 57.6 in. Rear tread: 60 in. Tires: 6.00 x 16 in.

CHASSIS: [Model 3100] Wheelbase: 116 in. Overall length: 196.6 in. Tires: 6.00 x 16 in.

CHASSIS: [Model 3600] Wheelbase: 125.25 in. Overall length: 206 in. Tires: 6.00 x 15 in.

NOTE: What is a 15 in. six-ply tire? This obsolete size is comparable to size 7.50 x 15 according to Chevrolet truck expert Bob Adler, who adds, "The 15 in. tires are 'beefier' than the 16 in. tires and the 15 in. wheels weigh considerably more than the 16 in. wheels."

CHASSIS: [Model 3800] Wheelbase: 137 in. Overall length: 223.88 in. Tires: 7.00 x 17 in.

TECHNICAL: Manual transmission. Speeds: [1500/3100/3600] 3F/1R; [3800] [4F/1R] Floor-mounted gearshift. Single-disc, diaphragm spring clutch. [1500/3100] Semi-floating hypoid rear axle; [3600/3800] full-floating rear axle. Hydraulic, four-wheel brakes. Wheels: [1500/3100] One-piece drop center 16 in. wheels; [3600/3800] Multi-piece split rims. Standard rear axles: [1500] 4.11:1; 3.73:1; [3100] 4.11:1; [3600] 4.57:1; [3800] 5.14:1.

OPTIONS: [RPO] Rearview mirror(s) and bracket(s). Oil-bath air cleaner. Hydraulic, double-acting shock absorbers. 1-ton eight-leaf rear springs for 3600. Economy rear axle. Low-ratio rear axle. Wide runningboards. Heavy-duty clutch. Oil filter. Governor. Prop shaft guard. Chrome grille equipment. Tail and stop lamp equipment. Heavy-duty cooling system. Auxiliary seat for Canopy and Panel. Double-acting rear springs. Heavy-duty radiator for 3600/3800. Radiator overflow return tank. Heavy-duty three-speed transmission. Heavy-duty four-speed transmission. Tru-Stop brake equipment. Inside fuel tank. Heater/defroster (Fresh-Air ventilator type). Cab rear corner windows. Deluxe cab equipment. Various tire options, as follows:

Light Duty Truck Tire Options

Size	Ply Rating	Capacity (lb.)	PSI	Section (in.)
15 in.	Six	1500	40	7.74
15 in.	Eight	1700	48	7.74
6.00 x 16	Four	990	32	6.25
6.00 x 16	Six	1065	36	6.21
6.50 x 16	Six	1290	40	6.65
7.00 x 17	Six	1550	45	7.30
7.50 x 17	Eight	1725	55	7.36
7.00 x 18	Eight	1800	55	7.24

DEALER ACCESSORIES: [All Commercial] Rod type radio antenna. Locking gas tank filler cap. Auto compass. Tire air transfer connector. Spare tire outside valve. Radiator cover. Maroon seat for all cab models. Back rest cushion. Windshield defroster rubber blade fan and bracket. Windshield electric heater. Tissue dispenser. Gasoline filter. License plate frame. Curved type bumper guard. Curved type radiator grille guard. Heater and defroster with fresh air inlet (not available on Chassis & Flat-face Cowl). Deluxe heater with combined heater and blower defroster unit. Matched horns. Antifreeze hydrometer. Double Guide sealed beam fog lamps. Guide spotlamp and bracket. Unity spotlamp and bracket. Magnetic trouble lamp. Tail and stop lamps for universal use ("lollipop" lights). Underhood lamp. Package compartment light and switch. Front and rear directional signals. Cigarette lighter. Tire traction mat. Prismatic rearview mirror. Rearview mirror. Bracket for rearview mirror. Hood ornament. Ventilated seat pad. Rear axle filler plug. Transmission drain plug. Oil pan drain plug. Utility pocket. Delco receiving-radio set, plus antenna, not available with Chassis & Flat-face Cowl. Four-inch red reflex reflector. Windshield scraper. Radiator insect screen. Electric shaver. Windshield frost shield. Right-hand sunshade. Radiator overflow tank. Thermostats (151-, 161- or 180-degrees). Heater shut off valve. Windshield washer. [All except Model 3116] Left-hand or right-hand maroon door armrest. [Model 3116 only] Brown right-hand door armrest.

HISTORICAL: Production of all above models began May 1, 1947. Commercial model series production continued until March 31, 1948. It appears that the Sedan Delivery was built through August, 1947. Calendar year production was 335,343, but this included 1946 late series models produced from Jan. 1, 1947 to May 1, 1947. It also does not include Advance-Design models built after Jan. 1, 1948. The EJ/EK/ER/ES models were titled as both 1947 and 1948 models, depending upon the calendar year in which they were sold. Dealers and salesmen were unlikely to promote them as 1947 models in 1948. Calendar year registrations: [All Series] 235,803. Calendar year sales: [All Series] 259,533. Innovations: The all-new, completely restyled line featured "the cab that breathes," with 30 Advance-Design features and an alligator-jaw hood opening to make servicing easier. The capacity of Chevrolet's commercial body plant at Indianapolis, Ind. was expanded to double production capacity this year. A new assembly plant in Flint, Mich. was also opened. Late in the year, a large new plant in Los Angeles began operations. A new manufacturing plant at Cleveland was also opened.

1948 CHEVROLET

1948 Chevrolet 1-Ton Model FS Platform Stake (K. Robbins)

SEDAN DELIVERY — MODEL FJ — SIX-CYLINDER: A T-shaped vertical center bar was used to update the 148 Sedan Delivery grille. A new hood mascot and emblem appeared. This model continued to be a commercial version of the passenger car sharing few engineering features with conventional Commercial models. It had a chrome grille, chrome front and rear bumpers, a bright metal windshield division bar and black rubber gravel shields. No bodyside moldings appeared. Short, spear-shaped hoodside nameplates with a dark-finished center said Stylemaster. At the rear was a curbside-opening panel door, the same one used since 1941. The Sedan Delivery shared the windshield of the four-door Sport Sedan. The interior was trimmed in blue-black imitation leather, code 137. Chevrolet did not emphasize a tonnage class for the Sedan Delivery. A three-speed manual transmission was standard. A heavy-duty three-speed was optional. The Sedan Delivery had a 4,100 lbs. GVW rating.

1948 Chevrolet Stylemaster Model FJ Sedan Delivery (OCW)

1/2-TON LIGHT-DUTY COMMERCIAL — MODEL FP/SERIES 3100 — SIX-CYLINDER: The 1948 conventional trucks in the Light-Duty Commercial line again featured the Advance-Design "Unisteel" cab styling. There were no significant changes from 1947 specifications. The grille had five broad horizontal bars topped by a broad hood ornament containing a blue bow tie and vermilion Chevrolet lettering. Rectangular parking lights were placed in chrome housings at the ends of the uppermost pair of grille bars. A painted grille was standard equipment. The outer grille bar assembly was done in body color (Forester green was standard again). The inner bar assemblies were finished in a grayish-green called Channel green. The outer bars each had one cream medium stripe. A chrome radiator grille option was optional. The chrome front grille option included chrome outer grille bars, which were not striped. The inner grille bars remained Channel green. Rear corner windows for cab models were again included in a deluxe equipment option package. On trucks with the rear corner windows, a different rear roof panel section was used. A polished chrome Chevrolet Thriftmaster nameplate was installed near the rear edge of the "alligator" hood. Underscore lines and the word Thriftmaster were painted vermilion, while the background of the nameplate was set off with black finish. Chrome-plated curved-type front bumpers were standard on all 3100s. Similar rear bumpers were standard on most models. Chrome hubcaps with vermilion Chevrolet lettering were standard. A two-piece, flat windshield was used. It had a black rubber seal and polished stainless steel divider bar. Polished stainless steel windshield reveal moldings were standard on Suburbans and optional on other models. The filler tube for the under-frame-mounted gas tank came out the right-hand side of the body, ahead of the front wheels. Cab models and single-unit body models had one belt molding stripe, which was used with standard finishes. Forester green was the standard truck color, but was not used on Suburbans. The Suburbans were finished with a Fathom green upper body and Channel green lower body. The following no-cost color options (pinstripe colors in parentheses) were offered on all models except the Suburban: Swift's red (Argent silver); Armour yellow (black); white (Emerald green); Jet black (Argent silver); Omaha orange (black); Cape maroon (gold); Mariner blue (cream medium); Windsor blue (cream medium); Seacrest green (cream medium); Sun beige (Totem scarlet); and cream medium (black). The interior was highlighted by wider seats, improved vision through the larger windshield, side and rear windows and a redesigned instrument panel. The instrument panel featured electric type fuel and battery charge indi-

cators and pressure-type heat indicator and oil pressure gauge. The speedometer was driven by a flexible shaft. Interior panels were finished in slate gray enamel. Models with runningboards had black rubber runningboard mats. The 3100 (EP model prefix) trucks had a base 4,600 lbs. GVW rating.

3/4-TON LIGHT-DUTY COMMERCIAL — MODEL FR/SERIES 3600 — SIX-CYLINDER: The 3/4-ton trucks had the same Advance-Design styling, features and finish as other conventional trucks. They had a longer wheelbase. The Pickup load box was longer and had six stake pockets. Long runningboards were used. No Suburban was offered in this line. There were Platform and Stake models. Hubcaps looked like the ones on 3100s with vermilion Chevrolet lettering. Features and finish were similar to those for 3100 models. Curved-type chrome front bumpers were standard on all models. Base tires on 3600s were 15 in. six-ply rated on 15 x 5.50 semi-drop-center rims. The 15 in. rims had no stripe; the 16 in. rims had three cream medium stripes and 17 in. rims had two cream medium stripes. Standard GVW rating for these trucks was 5,200-5,800 lbs. depending upon tire options.

3/4-TON DUBL-DUTI — MODEL FT/SERIES 3700 — SIX-CYLINDER: Two Dubl-Duti Forward-Control chassis returned to the Chevrolet truck line. Model 3742 was the 3/4-ton version on a 125.25 in. wheelbase. Standard walk-in delivery truck bodies could be supplied by several factory-approved sources or the buyer could add his/her own truck body.

1-TON MEDIUM-DUTY COMMERCIAL — MODEL FS/SERIES 3800 — SIX-CYLINDER: The 1-ton had the same Advance-Design styling, features and finish as other conventional trucks. The basic model lineup was unchanged. It included single and dual rear wheel options for all except the Express, Canopy and Panel. The Express had a longer wheelbase than the 3600 Pickup, longer runningboards, and a longer load box with eight stake pockets. A curved-type chrome front bumper was standard on all models. Regular equipment tires were 7.00 x 17 six-ply rated for trucks with single rear wheels or 7.00 x 18 eight-ply rated for trucks with dual rear wheel options. The hubcap design was shared with 3100s and 3600s, though the 3800's hubcaps were larger. They had vermilion Chevrolet lettering. No hubcaps were used on the 18 x 5 in. wheels of the Chassis & Cab, Platform and Stake models, which had eight bolts and eight circular openings. The standard GVWs for trucks with single rear wheels were 5,700 lbs.; 6,100 lbs.; and 6,700 lbs. depending on tire options. A base GVW of 8,800 lbs. was listed for trucks with optional dual rear wheels. A four-speed manual transmission was standard.

1-TON DUBL-DUTI — MODEL FU/SERIES 3900 — SIX-CYLINDER: Two Dubl-Duti Forward-Control chassis returned to the Chevrolet truck line. Model 3942 was the 1-ton version on a 137 in. wheelbase. Standard walk-in delivery truck bodies could be supplied by several factory-approved sources or the buyer could add his/her own truck body.

I.D. DATA: Serial Number located: [All] On plate attached to rear face of left-hand door hinge pillar; on right side of cowl under hood; [Chassis models] On plate temporarily attached near steering column, with final location per body maker. The first symbol indicated the assembly plant: 1=Flint, Mich.; 2=Tarrytown, N.Y.; 3=St. Louis, Mo.; 5=Kansas City, Kan.; 6=Oakland, Calif.; 8=Atlanta, Ga.; 9=Norwood, Ohio; 14=Baltimore, Md.; 20=Los Angeles, Calif.; and 21=Janesville, Wis. The second and third symbols indicate model prefix/series as follows: FJ=Series 1500; FP=3100; FR=3600; FS=3800; FT=3700; FU=3900. The fourth symbol indicates month of assembly; A=Jan.; B=Feb.; etc. The following symbols indicated the sequential production number. Each series was separately numbered in sequence, starting with 1001 at each assembly plant: Serial numbers: [Series 1500] FJ-1001 and up; [Series 3100] FP-1001 and up; [Series 3600] FR-1001 and up; [Series 3700] FT-1001 and up; [Series 3800] FS-1001 and up; [Series 3900] FU-1001 and up. Engine numbers located: Stamped on boss on right side of cylinder block, to the rear of the distributor.

1948 Chevrolet 1/2-Ton Model FP Pickup (OCW)

Model	Body Type	Price	Weight	Prod. Total
Sedan Delivery — Model FJ/Series 1500 — 116 in. w.b.				
FJ	Sedan Delivery	1361	3075	19,490
1/2-Ton Commercial — Model FP/Series 3100 — 116 in. w.b.				
3102	Chassis	890	2430	—
3103	Chassis & Cab	1113	2960	—
3104	Pickup	1180	3215	—
3105	Panel	1377	3425	—
3107	Canopy	1429	3415	—
3116	Suburban (gate)	1627	3515	—
3/4-Ton Commercial — Model FR/Series 3600 — 125.25 in. w.b.				
3602	Chassis	1004	2660	—
3603	Chassis & Cab	1227	3180	—
3604	Pickup	1315	3460	—
3608	Platform	1320	3655	—
3609	Stake	1378	3740	—
3/4-Ton Dubl-Duti — Model FT/Series 3700 — 125.25 in. w.b.				
3742	Chassis	1097	2465	—

1-Ton Commercial — Model FS/Series 3800 — 137 in. w.b.

3802	Chassis	1087	3035	—
3803	Chassis & Cab	1310	3545	—
3804	Pickup	1425	3965	—
3805	Panel	1596	4220	—
3807	Canopy	1674	4210	—
3808	Platform	1440	4050	—
3809	Stake	1513	4300	—

1-Ton Dubl-Duti — Model FU/Series 3900 — 137 in. w.b.

3942	Deluxe Chassis	1125	2630	—

ENGINE: Inline. OHV. Thriftmaster Six. Six-cylinder. Cast-iron block. Bore & stroke: 3-1/2 x 3-3/4 in. Displacement: 216.5 cid. Compression ratio: 6.5:1. Gross horsepower: 90 at 3300 rpm. Gross Torque: 174 lbs.-ft. at 1200-2000 rpm. SAE horsepower: 29.4. Four main bearings. Mechanical valve lifters. Carburetor: Carter downdraft one-barrel model W1-574S.
CHASSIS: [Model 1500] Wheelbase: 116 in. Overall length: 196.75 in. Front tread: 57.6 in. Rear tread: 60 in. Tires: 6.00 x 16 in.
CHASSIS: [Model 3100] Wheelbase: 116 in. Overall length: 196.6 in. Tires: 6.00 x 16 in.
CHASSIS: [Model 3600] Wheelbase: 125.25 in. Overall length: 206 in. Tires: 6.00 x 15 in.
CHASSIS: [Model 3800] Wheelbase: 137 in. Overall length: 223.88 in. Tires: 7.00 x 17 in.
TECHNICAL: Manual transmission: [1500/3100/3600] 3F/1R column-mounted; [3800] [4F/1R] Floor-mounted gearshift. Single-disc, diaphragm spring clutch. [1500/3100] Semi-floating hypoid rear axle; [3600/3800] full-floating rear axles. Hydraulic, four-wheel brakes. Wheels: [1500/3100] One-piece drop center 16 in. wheels; [3600/3800] Multi-piece split rims. Standard rear axles: [1500] 4.11:1; 3.73:1; [3100] 4.11:1; [3600] 4.57:1; [3800] 5.14:1.
OPTIONS: [RPO] Rearview mirror(s) and bracket(s). Oil-bath air cleaner. Hydraulic, double-acting shock absorbers. 1-ton eight-leaf rear springs for 3600. Economy rear axle. Low-ratio rear axle. Curved type bumper guard. Wide runningboards. Heavy-duty clutch. Oil filter. Governor. Prop shaft guard. Chrome grille equipment. Tail and stop lamp equipment. Heavy-duty cooling system. Auxiliary seat for Canopy and Panel. Double-acting rear springs. Heavy-duty radiator for 3600/3800. Radiator overflow return tank. Heavy-duty three-speed transmission. Heavy-duty four-speed transmission. Tru-Stop brake equipment. Inside fuel tank. Heater/defroster (Fresh-Air ventilator type). Cab rear corner windows. Deluxe cab equipment. Various tire options, as follows:

Light Duty Truck Tire Options

Size	Ply Rating	Capacity (lb.)	PSI	Section (in.)
15 in.	Six	1500	40	7.74
15 in.	Eight	1700	48	7.74
6.00 x 16	Four	990	32	6.25
6.00 x 16	Six	1065	36	6.21
6.50 x 16	Six	1290	40	6.65
7.00 x 17	Six	1550	45	7.30
7.50 x 17	Eight	1725	55	7.36
7.00 x 18	Eight	1800	55	7.24

NOTE: What is a 15 in. six-ply tire? This obsolete size is comparable to size 7.50 x 15 according to Chevrolet truck expert Bob Adler, who adds, "The 15 in. tires are 'beefier' than the 16 in. tires and the 15 in. wheels weigh considerably more than the 16 in. wheels."
DEALER ACCESSORIES: [All Commercial] Rod type radio antenna. Locking gas tank filler cap. Auto compass. Tire air transfer connector. Spare tire outside valve. Radiator cover. Maroon seat for all cab models. Back rest cushion. Windshield defroster rubber blade fan and bracket. Windshield electric heater. Tissue dispenser. Gasoline filter. License plate frame. Curved type bumper guard. Curved type radiator grille guard. Heater and defroster with fresh air inlet (not available on Chassis & Flat-face Cowl). Deluxe heater with combined heater and blower defroster unit. Matched horns. Antifreeze hydrometer. Double Guide sealed beam fog lamps. Guide spotlamp and bracket. Unity spotlamp and bracket. Magnetic trouble lamp. Tail and stop lamps for universal use ("lollipop" lights). Underhood lamp. Package compartment light and switch. Front and rear directional signals. Cigarette lighter. Tire traction mat. Prismatic rearview mirror. Rearview mirror. Bracket for rearview mirror. Hood ornament. Ventilated seat pad. Rear axle filler plug. Transmission drain plug. Oil pan drain plug. Utility pocket. Delco receiving-radio set, plus antenna, not available with Chassis & Flat-face Cowl. Four-inch red reflex reflector. Windshield scraper. Radiator insect screen. Electric shaver. Windshield frost shield. Right-hand sunshade. Radiator overflow tank. Thermostats (151-, 161- or 180-degrees). Heater shut off valve. Windshield washer. [All except Model 3116] Left-hand or right-hand maroon door armrest. [Model 3116 only] Brown right-hand door armrest.
HISTORICAL: Introduced: [Sedan Delivery] Oct. 1, 1947; [Commercials] April 1, 1948. Calendar year registrations: [All Series] 302,219. Calendar year sales: [All Series] 323,648. Calendar year production: [All Series] 389,690. Market share: 28.46 percent. Note: None of these totals or percentages include the Sedan Delivery. Innovations: Controls for three-speed transmission moved to steering column. New foot-type parking brake on 1/2-ton models. Four-speed synchromesh transmission (with helical cut gears) introduced. Upon the death of Nicholas Dreystadt, W.F. Armstrong was temporarily named general manager of Chevrolet Motor Div. Later, T.H. Keating was promoted from the general sales manager's post to take over from Keating.

1949 CHEVROLET

SEDAN DELIVERY — MODEL GJ/SERIES 1500 — SIX-CYLINDER: For 1949, a major change was made in the Sedan Delivery. It had a new 115 in. wheelbase and shared a new lower, wider body with Chevrolet's first, true postwar passenger cars. The Sedan Delivery was a Styleline Special. Many historians say it is based on the Station Wagon, but that is an over-simplification of fact. The windshield glass was the same used on some passenger cars, but not wagons. Interestingly, tinted glass was not offered for the Sedan Delivery, though the tinted passenger car windshield should fit it. Doors were unique to the Sedan Delivery from 1949-1952. Front door window glass was the same used on 1949-1952 four-door sedans, not wagons. Lower rear quarter panel stampings were unique to the Sedan Delivery. However, the rear compartment floor panel was same one used for 1949-1952 Station Wagons. Rear bumper bars, ends and guards were also the same as wagon parts. The Sedan Delivery had a 92.5 cu. ft. load space that was 73 in. long and looked much more streamlined than the 1948 body. It had a curbside-opening rear panel door, the same door being used on all 1949-1954 models. The chrome grille had a bowed upper bar with Chevrolet lettering and a wide horizontal center bar. Round parking lamps were situated above where the curved and horizontal bars met. Seven short vertical bars divided the lower grille opening. Maryland black was the standard color for the Sedan Delivery. The interior was trimmed with brown imitation leather, code 163. Standard equipment included front and rear chrome bumpers; dual tail and stop lamp equipment; a license plate lamp; dual windshield wipers; bright metal beltline moldings; bright headlamp rims; bright rocker sill moldings; chrome hubcaps; black rubber gravel shields; and five extra-low-pressure tires.

1949 Chevrolet Styleline Model GJ Sedan Delivery (CHP)

1949 1/2-TON LIGHT-DUTY COMMERCIAL — MODEL GP/SERIES 3100 — SIX-CYLINDER: The 1949 conventional trucks had some noticeable changes from the prior Advance-Design models in appearance, features and finish. The unchanged grille again had five broad horizontal bars topped by a broad hood ornament with a cloisonne blue (metallic) bow tie emblem and vermilion Chevrolet lettering on a chrome background. Rectangular parking lights were again placed in chrome housings at the ends of the uppermost pair of grille bars. A painted grille was standard equipment on all models, except Suburban Carryalls. The outer grille bar assembly was again done in body color (Forester green remained standard). The inner bar assemblies were changed to Waldorf white finish. The outer bars were not striped. A chrome radiator grille package was standard on the Suburban Carryall and optional on other models. The chrome option included non-striped chrome outer grille bars, while the inner grille bars remained Waldorf white. Rear corner windows for cab models were again included in a deluxe equipment option package. On trucks with the rear corner windows, a different rear roof panel section was used. A polished chrome Chevrolet nameplate was installed near the rear edge of the "alligator" hood. Below it was a second nameplate indicating the series: 3100 for 1/2-tons. The background of the Chevrolet nameplate was set off with black finish. Chrome-plated curved-type front bumpers were standard on all 3100s. Similar rear bumpers were standard on all models. Chrome hubcaps with vermilion Chevrolet lettering were standard. The 3100 wheels had three pinstripes in the striping colors bracketed below. A two-piece, flat windshield was used. It had a black rubber seal and polished stainless steel divider bar. Polished stainless steel windshield reveal moldings were now standard on all models. The gas tank was now located inside cab models. Its filler tube came out rear right-hand corner of the cab, just behind the rotary type, chrome door handles. The tank and filler location were unchanged on chassis and single-unit body models. Both cab models and single-unit body models had one belt molding stripe, which was cream medium with standard finishes. Forester green was the standard truck color, except for Suburbans. The Suburban's standard two-tone paint scheme was Fathom green upper/Channel green lower body. The Suburban came with Fathom green wheels; other models came with black wheels. The following no-cost color options (pinstripe colors in parentheses) were offered on all models except the Suburban: Swift red (Argent silver); Armour yellow (black); white (Emerald green); Jet black (Argent silver); Omaha orange (black); Cape maroon (gold); Mariner blue (cream medium); Windsor blue (cream medium); Seacrest green (cream medium); Sun beige (Totem scarlet); and cream medium (black). The interior was highlighted by wide seats, a large windshield, side and rear windows and an unchanged instrument panel. The instrument panel featured AC instruments: electric fuel gauge and ammeter; pressure-type heat indicator and oil pressure gauge; and dial speedometer driven by a flexible shaft from the transmission. Panel trucks offered optional polished stainless steel rear window reveals. Cab mountings were improved by removing a single rear cab-to-frame shackle and adding two shackles to the rear sides of the cab, creating a four-point cab mounting. Removing the associated gussets freed up space behind the seat to install the interior fuel tank. The 3100 (FP model prefix) trucks had a base 4,600 lb. GVW rating.

1949 Chevrolet 1-Ton Model GS Canopy (ATC)

3/4-TON LIGHT-DUTY COMMERCIAL — MODEL GR/SERIES 3600 — SIX-CYLINDER: The 3/4-ton trucks had the same Advance-Design styling, features and finish as other conventional trucks. There was a 3800 call-out below the Chevrolet nameplate on the hood. They had a longer wheelbase. The Pickup load box was longer and had six stake pockets. Long runningboards were used. No Suburban was offered in this line. There were Platform and Stake models. Hubcaps looked like the ones on 3100s with vermilion Chevrolet lettering. The standard black wheels were of different eight-bolt design and not pinstriped. Curved-type chrome front bumpers were standard on all models. Similar rear bumpers were standard on Models 3602/3603/3604/3612. Base tires on 3600s were 15 in. six-ply rated on 15 x 5.50 semi-drop-center rims. The 15 in. rims had no stripe; the 16 in. rims had three cream medium stripes and 17 in. rims had two cream medium stripes. Standard GVW rating for these trucks was 5,200-5,800 lbs. depending upon tire options.

1949 Chevrolet 1/2-Ton Model GP Suburban (OCW)

3/4-TON DUBL-DUTI — MODEL GT/SERIES 3700 — SIX-CYLINDER: Two Dubl-Duti Forward-Control chassis returned to the Chevrolet truck line. Model 3742 was the 3/4-ton version on a 125.25 in. wheelbase. Standard walk-in delivery truck bodies could be supplied by several factory-approved sources or the buyer could add his/her own truck body. The wheels were of eight-bolt design.

1949 Chevrolet 3/4-Ton Model GR Pickup (OCW)

1-TON MEDIUM-DUTY COMMERCIAL — MODEL GS/SERIES 3800 — SIX-CYLINDER: The 1-ton had the same Advance-Design styling, features and finish as other conventional trucks. The basic model lineup was unchanged. It included single and dual rear wheel options for all except the Express, Canopy and Panel. The Express had a longer wheelbase than the 3600 Pickup, longer runningboards, and a longer load box with eight stake pockets. A curved-type chrome front bumper was standard on all models. A similar rear bumper was standard on Models 3805/3807. Regular equipment tires were 7.00 x 17 six-ply rated for trucks with single rear wheels or 7.00 x 18 eight-ply rated for trucks with dual rear wheel options. The hubcap design was shared with 3100s and 3600s, though the 3800 hubcaps were larger. They had vermilion Chevrolet lettering. The standard black wheels had two pinstripes. No hubcaps were used on the 18 x 5 in. wheels of the Chassis & Cab, Platform and Stake models, which had eight bolts and eight circular openings. The standard GVWs for trucks with single rear wheels were 5,700 lbs.; 6,100 lbs.; and 6,700 lbs. depending on tire options. A base GVW of 8,800 lbs. was listed for trucks with optional dual rear wheels. A four-speed manual synchromesh transmission was standard.

1949 Chevrolet 1/2-Ton Model GJ Suburban (OCW)

1-TON DUBL-DUTI — MODEL GU/SERIES 3900 — SIX-CYLINDER: Two Dubl-Duti Forward-Control chassis returned to the Chevrolet truck line. Model 3942 was the 1-ton version on a 137 in. wheelbase. Standard walk-in delivery truck bodies could be supplied by several factory-approved sources or the buyer could add his/her own truck body.

I.D. DATA: Serial Number located: [All] On plate attached to rear face of left-hand door hinge pillar; on right side of cowl under hood; [Chassis models] On plate temporarily attached near steering column, with final location per body maker. The first symbol indicated the assembly plant: 1=Flint, Mich.; 2=Tarrytown, N.Y.; 3=St. Louis, Mo.; 5=Kansas City, Kan.; 6=Oakland, Calif.; 8=Atlanta, Ga.; 9=Norwood, Ohio; 14=Baltimore, Md.; 20=Los Angeles, Calif.; and 21=Janesville, Wis. The second and third symbols indicate model prefix/series as follows: GJ=Series 1500; GP=3100; GR=3600; GS=3800; GT=3700; GU=3900. The fourth symbol indicates month of assembly; A=Jan., B=Feb., etc. The following symbols indicated the sequential production number. Each series was separately numbered in sequence, starting with 1001 at each assembly plant: Serial numbers:

[GJ] GJ-1001 and up; [GP] GP-1001 and up; [GR] GR-1001 and up; [GT] GT-1001 and up; [GS] GS-1001 and up; [GU] GU-1001 and up. Engine numbers located: On crankcase at rear of distributor, right side of engine.

1949 Chevrolet 3/4-Ton Model GR Platform Stake (OCW)

Model	Body Type	Price	Weight	Prod. Total
Sedan Delivery — Model GJ/Series 1508 — 115 in. w.b.				
1271	Sedan Delivery	1465	3050	9310
1/2-Ton Commercial — Model GP/Series 3100 — 116 in. w.b.				
3102	Chassis	961	2430	—
3103	Chassis & Cab	1185	2920	—
3104	Pickup	1253	3185	—
3105	Panel	1450	3425	—
3107	Canopy	1502	3385	—
3116	Suburban	1700	3710	—
3/4-Ton Commercial — Model GR/Series 3600 — 125.25 in. w.b.				
3602	Chassis	1060	2750	—
3603	Chassis & Cab	1284	3170	—
3604	Pickup	1372	3520	—
3608	Platform	1378	3550	—
3609	Stake	1435	3725	—
3/4-Ton Dubl-Duti — Model GT/Series 3700 — 125.25 in. w.b.				
3742	Chassis	1076	2465	—
1-Ton Commercial — Model GS/Series 3800 — 137 in. w.b.				
3802	Chassis	1134	3005	—
3803	Chassis & Cab	1357	3430	—
3804	Pickup	1471	3945	—
3805	Panel	1669	4220	—
3807	Canopy	1746	4180	—
3808	Platform	1487	3960	—
3809	Stake	1560	4215	—
1-Ton Dubl-Duti — Model GU/Series 3900 — 137 in. w.b.				
3942	Chassis	1169	2700	—

ENGINE: Inline. OHV. Thriftmaster Six. Six-cylinder. Cast-iron block. Bore & stroke: 3-1/2 x 3-3/4 in. Displacement: 216.5 cid. Compression ratio: 6.6:1. Gross horsepower: 90 at 3300 rpm. Gross Torque: 174 lbs.-ft. at 1200-2000 rpm. SAE horsepower: 29.4. Four main bearings. Mechanical valve lifters. Carburetor: Carter downdraft one-barrel model W1-574S.

1949 Chevrolet 1-Ton Model GS Pickup (Express)

CHASSIS: [Model 1500] Wheelbase: 116 in. Overall length: 197.5 in. Front tread: 57.6 in. Rear tread: 60 in. Tires: 6.00 x 16 in. GVW: 4,100 lbs.
CHASSIS: [Model 3100] Wheelbase: 116 in. Overall length: 196.6 in. Tires: 6.00 x 16 in. six-ply. GVWs: 4,200 lbs./4,500 lbs./4,600 lbs.
CHASSIS: [Model 3600] Wheelbase: 125.25 in. Overall length: 206 in. Tires: 15 in. six-ply. GVW: 5,200 lbs./5,400 lbs./5,800 lbs.
NOTE: What is a 15 in. six-ply tire? This obsolete size is comparable to size 7.50 x 15 according to Chevrolet truck expert Bob Adler, who adds, "The 15 in. tires are 'beefier' than the 16 in. tires and the 15 in. wheels weigh considerably more than the 16 in. wheels."
CHASSIS: [Model 3700] Wheelbase: 125.25 in. Tires: 15 in. six-ply. Maximum GVW: 7,000 lbs.
CHASSIS: [Model 3800] Wheelbase: 137 in. Overall length: 223.88 in. Tires: 7.00 x 17 in. six-ply. GVWs: 6,700 lbs./8,800 lbs.
CHASSIS: [Model 3900] Wheelbase: 137 in. Tires: 7.00 x 17 in. six-ply. Maximum GVW: 10,000 lbs.

TECHNICAL: Manual, synchromesh transmission: [1500/3100/3600] 3F/1R column-mounted; [3800] [4F/1R] Floor-mounted gearshift. Single-disc, diaphragm spring clutch. [1500/3100] Semi-floating hypoid rear axle; [3600/3800] full-floating rear axle. Hydraulic, four-wheel brakes. Wheels: [1500/3100] One-piece drop center 16 in. wheels; [3600/3800] Multi-piece split rims. Standard rear axles: [1500] 4.11:1; 3.73:1; [3100] 4.11:1; [3600] 4.57:1; [3800] 5.14:1.

OPTIONS: [RPO] Rearview mirror(s) and bracket(s): short right-hand; long left-hand bracket only; long right-hand and short left-hand bracket only. Color combinations. Genuine leather seat trim for single-unit body models. Chrome radiator grille (standard on Model 3116). Deluxe equipment (all Panel and cab models). Platform equipment for all Model 3600 high-sill platform models). Stake rack and equipment (all Stake, Stake Express and High-Rack models). Double acting front shock absorbers. Double acting rear shock absorbers. 5.43:1 ratio rear axle (3600 models). Long runningboards and rear fenders (3600/3800 model cab and chassis models). Spare wheel and tire carrier (Dubl-Duti). Front bumper equipment (Dubl-Duti). Heavy-duty radiator (3600/3800 models). Dual tail and stop lamps (Suburbans/Panels/Canopies). Heavy-duty rear springs (3100). Wide runningboards (Model 3104). School bus chassis (Dubl-Duti chassis). Oil bath air cleaner, 1-lb. dirt capacity. Oil bath air cleaner, 2-lbs. dirt capacity. Heavy-duty clutch (3100). Oil filter (3100/3600/3800). Four-speed transmission (all except Dubl-Duti). Governor (all except Dubl-Duti). Fuel and vacuum pump (all except Dubl-Duti). Various tire options, as follows:

Light Duty Truck Tire Options

Size	Ply Rating	Capacity (lb.)	PSI	Section (in.)
15 in.	Six	1500	40	7.74
15 in.	Eight	1700	48	7.74
6.00 x 16	Four	990	32	6.25
6.00 x 16	Six	1065	36	6.21
6.50 x 16	Six	1290	40	6.65
6.70 x 15	Six	n.a.	n.a.	n.a.
7.00 x 17	Six	1550	45	7.30
7.00 x 17	Eight	n.a.	n.a.	n.a.
7.50 x 17	Eight	1725	55	7.36
7.00 x 18	Eight	1800	55	7.24

DEALER ACCESSORIES: Rod type radio antenna (all). Right- or left-hand door armrest, maroon (all except Suburban). Right- or left-hand door armrest, brown (Suburban only). Locking gas cap (all). Radiator cover (all). Maroon seat cover (all cab models). Fiber seat cover (all cab models). Gasoline filter (all). License plate frame (all). Curved bumper guard (all except Dubl-Duti). Radiator grille guard for curved type bumper (all). Bumper guard for curved type bumper (all except Dubl-Duti). Outside air heater/defroster (all except Chassis & Cowl). Recirculated air type heater (all except Chassis & Cowl). Matched horns (all). Static eliminator injector (all). Powder for static eliminator injector (all). Guide dual sealed-beam fog lights (all). Guide spotlight with bracket (all). Unity spotlight with bracket (all). Magnetic trouble lamp (all). Universal stop and taillamps (all). Load compartment lamp (Panel). Underhood lamp (all). Package compartment light and switch (all). Front and rear directional signals (all). Front signal lamps, single lens (all). Front signal lamps, double lens (all). Rear signal lamp with switch (all). Cigarette lighter (all). Two tire traction mats (all). Non-glare rearview mirror (all). Long-arm adjustable outside rearview mirror (all). Bracket unit for cowl-mounted rearview mirror (all). Hood ornament (all). Ventilated seat pad (all). Rear axle magnetic filler plug (all). Magnetic transmission drain plug (all). Magnetic oil pan drain plug, (all). Delco radio receiving set, plus antenna (all except Chassis & Cowl). Four-inch red Reflex reflector (all). Windshield scraper (all). Radiator insect screen (all). Electric shaver (all). Right-hand sunshade (all). Runningboard safety tread (all). Tool kit bag and tools (all). Windshield washer (all).

HISTORICAL: Introduced to dealers January, 1949. Calendar year registrations: [All Commercial] 345,519. Calendar year production: [All Commercial] 383,543; [All Commercial below 5,000 lbs. GVW] 201,537; [All Commercials with 5,001-10,000 lb.S GVWs] 97,678. Market share: [All Commercials] 33.88 percent. The Sedan Delivery is not in the Commercial line. Innovations: All-new styling for Sedan Delivery. New four-point cab mountings. Cantrell woody station wagons and Olsen Kurbside delivery trucks were built on the Chevrolet chassis this year.

1950 CHEVROLET

1950 Chevrolet 1/2-Ton Model HP Pickup (OCW)

SEDAN DELIVERY — MODEL HJ/SERIES 1500 — SIX-CYLINDER: The passenger car-based Sedan Delivery was part of Chevrolet's Styleline Special series. It had a new frontal treatment. The grille used the same upper and center molding bars and circular parking lamps as the 1949 grille. The outer vertical moldings were the same, but the five intermediate vertical moldings of 1949 were replaced with two inner moldings with three slots in them. A completely new grille reinforcement panel was used. There was a different hood ornament. The 73 in. cargo area gave a usable cargo area of 92.5 cu. ft. Many historians say it is based on the Station Wagon, but that is an over-simplification of fact. The windshield glass (non-tinted only) was the same used on some passenger cars, but not wagons. Doors were specific to the Sedan Delivery and not used on other cars. Front door window glass was the same used on 1949-1952 four-door sedans, not wagons. Lower rear quarter panel stampings were unique to the Sedan Delivery. However, the rear compartment floor panel was same one used for 1949-1952 Station Wagons. Rear bumper bars, ends and guards were also the same as wagon parts. The brown imitation leather trim introduced in 1949 was continued for 1950. It was combination number 163.

1/2-TON LIGHT-DUTY COMMERCIAL — MODEL HP/SERIES 3100 — SIX-CYLINDER: The 1948 conventional trucks had some technical changes from the prior Advance-Design models. Appearance features and finish had only minor changes. All 3100s had improved seat cushion padding and larger, 56 in. wide seats. The Suburban Carryall with panel rear doors was reintroduced. Forester green was now the standard color for all models, including Suburbans and Suburbans were now available in all 12 colors that Chevrolet offered for trucks. Among the year's refinements were direct double-acting 1-3/8 in. rear shock absorbers, improved Rochester B carburetors, and a new circuit breaker lighting system. A revamped version of the Thriftmaster six was standard in 3100/3600/3800 models. It had a new "Power Jet" downdraft carburetor, larger exhaust valves and a straight-through muffler. The unchanged grille again had five broad horizontal bars topped by a broad hood ornament with a cloisonne blue (metallic) bow tie emblem and vermilion Chevrolet lettering on a chrome background. Rectangular parking lights were again placed in chrome housings between the ends of the uppermost pair of grille bars. A painted grille was standard equipment on all models, except Suburban Carryalls. The outer grille bar assembly was again done in body color (Forester green remained standard). The inner bar assemblies retained their Waldorf white finish. The outer bars were not striped. A chrome radiator grille package was standard on the Suburban Carryall and optional on other models. The chrome option included non-striped chrome outer grille bars, while the inner grille bars remained Waldorf white. Rear corner windows for cab models were again included in a deluxe equipment option package. On trucks with the rear corner windows, a different rear roof panel section was used. A polished chrome Chevrolet nameplate was installed near the rear edge of the "alligator" hood. Below it was a second nameplate indicating the series: 3100 for 1/2-tons. The background of the Chevrolet nameplate was set off with black finish. Chrome-plated curved-type front bumpers were standard on all 3100s. Similar rear bumpers were standard on all models. Chrome hubcaps with vermilion Chevrolet lettering were standard. The 3100 wheels had three pinstripes in the striping colors bracketed below. Forester green wheels were now standard on Suburbans. On other models, black wheels were standard, but body color wheels were used with hubcaps. A two-piece, flat windshield was used. It had a black rubber seal and polished stainless steel divider bar. Polished stainless steel windshield reveal moldings were now standard on all models. The gas tank was again located inside cab models. Its filler tube came out rear right-hand corner of the cab, just behind the rotary type, chrome door handles. The filler was just ahead of the rear wheels on single-unit body models. Both cab models and single-unit body models had one belt molding stripe, which was cream medium with standard finish. The following no-cost color options (pinstripe colors in parentheses) were offered on all models: Swift red (Argent silver); Armour yellow (black); white (Emerald green); Jet black (Argent silver); Omaha orange (black); Cape maroon (gold); Mariner blue (cream medium); Windsor blue (cream medium); Seacrest green (cream medium); Sun beige (Totem scarlet); and cream medium (black). The unchanged instrument panel featured AC instruments: electric fuel gauge and ammeter; pressure-type heat indicator and oil pressure gauge; and dial speedometer driven by a flexible shaft from the transmission. Panel trucks offered optional polished stainless steel rear window reveals. The 3100 (HP model prefix) trucks had a base 4,600 lbs. GVW rating.

3/4-TON LIGHT-DUTY COMMERCIAL — MODEL HR/SERIES 3600 — SIX-CYLINDER: The 3/4-ton trucks had the same Advance-Design styling, features and finish as other conventional trucks. Eight-leaf front springs were made standard for these 3600 models. They had 3600 hood nameplates and a longer wheelbase. The Pickup load box was longer and had six stake pockets. Long runningboards were used. No Suburban was offered in this line. There were Platform and Stake models. Hubcaps looked like the ones on 3100s with vermilion Chevrolet lettering. The standard black wheels were of different eight-bolt design and not pinstriped. Curved-type chrome front bumpers were standard on all models. Similar rear bumpers were standard on Models 3602/3603/3604/3612. Base tires on 3600s were 15 in. six-ply rated on 15 x 5.50 semi-drop-center rims. The 15 in. rims had no stripe; the 16 in. rims had three cream medium stripes and 17 in. rims had two cream medium stripes. The GVW rating range for these trucks was 5,200-5,800 lbs. depending upon tire options.

1950 Chevrolet 1/2-Ton Model HP Deluxe Cab Pickup (OCW)

3/4-TON DUBL-DUTI — MODEL HT/SERIES 3700 — SIX-CYLINDER: Two Dubl-Duti Forward-Control chassis remained in the Chevrolet truck line. Both had a new 235 cid "Loadmaster" six. Due to a less efficient updraft carburetor, this engine had the same horsepower rating as the 216 cid Thriftmaster six. Model 3742 was the 3/4-ton version on a 125.25 in. wheelbase. Standard walk-in delivery truck bodies could be supplied by several factory-approved sources or the buyer could add his/her own truck body. The wheels were of eight-bolt design.

1-TON MEDIUM-DUTY COMMERCIAL — MODEL HS/SERIES 3800 — SIX-CYLINDER: The 3800 Series had the same Advance-Design styling, features and finish as other conventional trucks. The call-out under the hood nameplate said 3800. Added to the regular production option list for 1-ton trucks were larger 1-3/8 in. diameter rear shock absorbers and auxiliary leaf springs. These models were available with an optional power brake system. This Hydrovac brake booster reduced pedal effort by two-thirds. Panel and Canopy models had a one-piece floor made of 3/4-inch thick, five-ply laminated wood. The basic model lineup was unchanged. It included single and dual rear wheel options for all except the Express, Canopy and Panel. The Express had a longer wheelbase than the 3600

Pickup, longer runningboards, and a longer load box with eight stake pockets. A curved-type chrome front bumper was standard on all models. A similar rear bumper was standard on Models 3805/3807. Regular equipment tires were 7.00 x 17 six-ply rated for trucks with single rear wheels or 7.00 x 18 eight-ply rated for trucks with dual rear wheel options. The hubcap design was shared with 3100s and 3600s, though the 3800 hubcaps were larger. They had vermilion Chevrolet lettering. The standard black wheels had two pinstripes. No hubcaps were used on the 18 x 5 in. wheels of the Chassis & Cab, Platform and Stake models, which had eight bolts and eight circular openings. The standard GVWs for trucks with single rear wheels were 5,700 lbs.; 6,100 lbs.; and 6,700 lbs. depending on tire options. A GVW of 8,800 lbs. was listed for trucks with optional dual rear wheels. A four-speed manual synchromesh transmission was standard.

1-TON DUBL-DUTI — MODEL HU/SERIES 3900 — SIX-CYLINDER: Two Dubl-Duti Forward-Control chassis returned to the Chevrolet truck line. Both had a new 235 cid "Loadmaster" six. Due to a less efficient updraft carburetor, this engine had the same horsepower rating as the 216 cid Thriftmaster six. Model 3942 was the 1-ton version on a 137 in. wheelbase. Standard walk-in delivery truck bodies could be supplied by several factory-approved sources or the buyer could add his/her own truck body.

1950 Chevrolet 1/2-Ton Model HP Suburban (OCW)

I.D. DATA: Serial Number located: [All] On plate attached to rear face of left-hand door hinge pillar; on right side of cowl under hood; [Chassis models] On plate temporarily attached near steering column, with final location per body maker. The first symbol indicated the assembly plant: 1=Flint, Mich.; 2=Tarrytown, N.Y.; 3=St. Louis, Mo.; 5=Kansas City, Kan.; 6=Oakland, Calif.; 8=Atlanta, Ga.; 9=Norwood, Ohio; 14=Baltimore, Md.; 20=Los Angeles, Calif.; and 21=Janesville, Wis. The second and third symbols indicate model prefix/series as follows: HJ=Series 1500; HP=3100; HR=3600; HS=3800; HT=3700; HU=3900. The fourth symbol indicates month of assembly; A=Jan.; B=Feb., etc. The following symbols indicated the sequential production number. Each series was separately numbered in sequence, starting with 1001 at each assembly plant. Serial numbers were as follows: [Series 1500] HJ-1001 to 49801; [Series 3100] HP-1001 to 37721; [Series 3600] HR-1001 to 12078; [Series 3742] HT-1001 to 1600; [Series 3800] HS-1001 to 5611 and [Series 3942] HJ-1001 to 1408. Engine numbers located on right side of block near fuel pump; also stamped on crankcase near rear of distributor on right side of engine. Motor numbers were as follows: [Series 1500] HA-1001 to 1320152; [Series 3100] HB-1001 to 1320152; [Series 3600] HC-1001 to 1320152; [Series 3742/3800/3942] same as 3600 Series.

Model	Body Type	Price	Weight	Prod. Total
Sedan Delivery — Model HJ/Series 1500 — 115 in. w.b.				
1271	Sedan Delivery	1455	3105	—
1/2-Ton Commercial — Model HP/Series 3100 — 116 in. w.b.				
3103	Chassis & Cab	1175	2910	—
3104	Pickup	1243	3175	—
3105	Panel	1440	3375	—
3106	Suburban (doors)	1690	3670	—
3107	Canopy	1492	3335	—
3116	Suburban (gate)	1690	3075	—
3/4-Ton Commercial — Model HR/Series 3600 — 125.25 in. w.b.				
3602	Chassis	1050	2710	—
3603	Chassis & Cab	1274	3170	—
3604	Pickup	1302	3515	—
3608	Platform	1308	3560	—
3609	Stake	1425	3700	—
3/4-Ton Dubl-Duti — Model HT/Series 3700 — 125.5 in. w.b.				
3742	Chassis	1066	2475	—
1-Ton Commercial — Model HS/Series 3800 — 137 in. w.b.				
3802	Chassis	1124	2980	—
3803	Chassis & Cab	1347	3440	—
3804	Pickup	1461	3930	—
3805	Panel	1659	4190	—
3807	Canopy Express	1736	4145	—
3808	Platform	1477	4010	—
3809	Stake Bed	1550	4255	—
1-Ton Dubl-Duti — Model HU/Series 3900 — 137 in. w.b.				
3942	Chassis	1159	2640	—

Standard Catalog of Light-Duty Trucks

1950 Chevrolet Styleline Special Model HJ Sedan Delivery

ENGINE: [Standard Series 1500/3100/3600/3800] Inline. OHV. Thriftmaster. Six-cylinder. Cast-iron block. Bore & stroke: 3-1/2 x 3-3/4 in. Displacement: 216.5 cid. Compression ratio: 6.6:1. Gross horsepower: 92 at 3400 rpm. Net horsepower: 85 at 3300 rpm. Gross torque: 176 lbs.-ft. at 1000-2000 rpm. Net torque: 170 at 1000 to 2000 rpm. SAE horsepower: 29.4. Four main bearings. Mechanical valve lifters. Carburetor: Single one-barrel model Rochester Model B Power Jet downdraft.
ENGINE: [Standard Dubl-Duti] Inline. OHV. Loadmaster. Six-cylinder. Cast-iron block. Bore & stroke: 3-9/16 x 3-15/16 in. Displacement: 235.5 cid. Compression ratio: 6.7:1. Brake horsepower: 92 at 3400 rpm. SAE horsepower: 30.4. Four main bearings. Mechanical valve lifters. Carburetor: Single one-barrel model Carter Power Jet downdraft.
CHASSIS: [Model 1500] Wheelbase: 116 in. Overall length: 197.5 in. Front tread: 57.6 in. Rear tread: 60 in. Tires: 6.00 x 16 in. GVW: 4,100 lbs.
CHASSIS: [Model 3100] Wheelbase: 116 in. Overall length: 196.6 in. Tires: 6.00 x 16 in. six-ply. GVWs: 4,200 lbs./4,500 lbs./4,600 lbs.
CHASSIS: [Model 3600] Wheelbase: 125.25 in. Overall length: 206 in. Tires: 15 in. six-ply. GVW: 5,200 lbs./5,400 lbs./5,800 lbs.
NOTE: What is a 15 in. six-ply tire? This obsolete size is comparable to size 7.50 x 15 according to Chevrolet truck expert Bob Adler, who adds, "The 15 in. tires are 'beefier' than the 16 in. tires and the 15 in. wheels weigh considerably more than the 16 in. wheels."
CHASSIS: [Model 3700] Wheelbase: 125.25 in. Tires: 15 in. six-ply. Maximum GVW: 7,000 lbs.
CHASSIS: [Model 3800] Wheelbase: 137 in. Overall length: 223.88 in. Tires: 7.00 x 17 in. six-ply. GVWs: 6,700 lbs./8,800 lbs.
CHASSIS: [Model 3900] Wheelbase: 137 in. Tires: 7.00 x 17 in. six-ply. Maximum GVW: 10,000 lbs.
TECHNICAL: Manual, synchromesh transmission: [1500/3100/3600] 3F/1R column-mounted; [3800] [4F/1R] Floor-mounted gearshift. Single-disc, diaphragm spring clutch. [1500/3100] Semi-floating hypoid rear axle; [3600/3800] full-floating rear axle. Hydraulic, four-wheel brakes. Wheels: [1500/3100] One-piece drop center 16 in. wheels; [3600/3800] Multi-piece split rims. Standard rear axles: [1500] 4.11:1; 3.73:1; [3100] 4.11:1; [3600] 4.57:1; [3800] 5.14:1.

1950 Chevrolet 1/2-Ton Model HJ Panel (OCW)

OPTIONS: [RPO] Rearview mirror(s) and bracket(s): short right-hand; long left-hand bracket only; long right-hand and short left-hand bracket only. Color combinations. Genuine leather seat trim for single-unit body models. Chrome radiator grille (standard on Model 3116). Deluxe equipment (all Panel and cab models). Platform equipment for all Model 3600 high-sill platform models. Stake rack and equipment (all Stake, Stake Express and High-Rack models). Double-acting front shock absorbers. Double-acting rear shock absorbers. 5.43:1 ratio rear axle (3600 models). Long runningboards and rear fenders (3600/3800 model cab and chassis models). Spare wheel and tire carrier (Dubl-Duti). Front bumper equipment (Dubl-Duti). Heavy-duty radiator (3600/3800 models). Dual tail and stop lamps (Suburbans/Panels/Canopies). Heavy-duty rear springs (3100). Wide runningboards (Model 3104). School bus chassis (Dubl-Duti chassis). Oil bath air cleaner, 1-lb. dirt capacity. Oil bath air cleaner, 2-lbs. dirt capacity. Heavy-duty clutch (3100). Oil filter (3100/3600/3800). Four-speed transmission (all except Dubl-Duti). Governor (all except Dubl-Duti). Fuel and vacuum pump (all except Dubl-Duti). Various tire options, as follows:

Light Duty Truck Tire Options

Size	Ply Rating	Capacity (lb.)	PSI	Section (in.)
15 in.	Six	1500	40	7.74
15 in.	Eight	1700	48	7.74
6.00 x 16	Four	990	32	6.25
6.00 x 16	Six	1065	36	6.21
6.50 x 16	Six	1290	40	6.65
6.70 x 15	Six	n.a.	n.a.	n.a.
7.00 x 17	Six	1550	45	7.30
7.00 x 17	Eight	n.a.	n.a.	n.a.
7.50 x 17	Eight	1725	55	7.36
7.00 x 18	Eight	1800	55	7.24

DEALER ACCESSORIES: Rod type radio antenna (all). Right- or left-hand door armrest, maroon (all except Suburban). Right- or left-hand door armrest, brown (Suburban only). Locking gas cap (all). Radiator cover (all). Maroon seat cover (all cab models). Fiber seat cover (all cab models). Gasoline filter (all). License plate frame (all). Curved bumper guard (all except Dubl-Duti). Radiator grille guard for curved type bumper (all except Dubl-Duti). Bumper guard for curved type bumper (all except Dubl-Duti). Outside air heater/defroster (all except Chassis & Cowl). Recirculated air type heater (all except Chassis & Cowl). Matched horns (all). Static eliminator injector (all). Powder for static eliminator injector (all). Guide dual sealed-beam fog lights (all). Guide spotlight with bracket (all). Unity spotlight with bracket (all). Magnetic trouble lamp (all). Universal stop and taillamps (all). Load compartment lamp (Panel). Underhood lamp (all). Package compartment light and switch (all). Front and rear directional signals (all). Front signal lamps, single lens (all). Front signal lamps, double lens (all). Rear signal lamp with switch (all). Two tire traction mats (all). Cigarette lighter (all). Non-glare rearview mirror (all). Long-arm adjustable outside rearview mirror (all). Bracket unit for cowl-mounted rearview mirror (all). Hood ornament (all). Ventilated seat pad (all). Rear axle magnetic filler plug (all). Magnetic transmission drain plug (all). Magnetic oil pan drain plug, (all). Delco radio receiving set, plus antenna (all except Chassis & Cowl). Four-inch red Reflex reflector (all). Windshield scraper (all). Radiator insect screen (all). Electric shaver (all). Right-hand sunshade (all). Runningboard safety tread (all). Tool kit bag and tools (all). Windshield washer (all).

1950 Chevrolet 1-Ton Model HS Panel (OCW)

HISTORICAL: Dealer introduction: January, 1950. Calendar year registrations: [All Commercials] 414,496. Calendar year production: [All Commercials] 494,573; [All Commercials 5,000 lbs. and less GVW] 265,515. [All Commercials 5,001 lbs.-10,000 lbs. GVW] 102,669. The Sedan Delivery is not a Commercial model. Innovations: Improved engines. Suburban with panel doors reintroduced. Wider seats with improved padding. This was the all-time record for sales of the Sedan Delivery to date. It was also a record year for production of Commercial models. In the month of August alone, 45,779 trucks were built.

1950 Chevrolet 1/2-Ton Model HP Pickup (P. Bachman)

1951 CHEVROLET

SEDAN DELIVERY — MODEL JJ/SERIES 1500 — SIX-CYLINDER: The passenger car-based Sedan Delivery was still a member of Chevrolet's Styleline Special series. A completely new radiator grille was used in 1951. A narrow chrome upper molding had a Chevrolet script stamped into it. Below this was a ribbed horizontal deflector, a veed horizontal chrome molding, a plain deflector with nine tabs on its lower edge and another veed horizontal molding at the bottom. The veed chrome horizontal moldings were connected together, at each end, by sideways U-shaped moldings. This gave the entire lower section of the grille a loop-like appearance. Parking lamp housings with five vertical slots fit inside the U-shaped moldings on either end. There was a different hood ornament. The 73 in. cargo area with a usable load space of 92.5 cu. ft. remained unchanged. The Sedan Delivery's windshield glass (non-tinted only) was the same used on some passenger cars, but not wagons. Doors were specific to this model and not used on other cars (although sedan doors can be modified to fit). Front door window glass was the same used on 1949-1952 four-door sedans, not wagons. Lower rear quarter panel stampings were unique to the Sedan Delivery. However, the rear compartment floor panel was same one used for 1949-1952 Station Wagons. Rear bumper bars, ends and guards were also the same as wagon parts. Standard equipment included front and rear bumpers and bumper guards; front license guard; hood ornament and emblem; chrome plated headlamp rims with doors; dual windshield wipers; dual horns; outside key locks; front and rear bumper gravel deflectors; one combination tail/stop/license plate lamp; bright, full-length rear fender crown molding; bright metal windshield divider; bright windshield reveal molding; bright rear window reveal molding; Bonderized body and sheet metal; plain plastic control knob inserts; chrome-plated radio grille; three-position ignition switch; left-hand sunshade and dome light. Interior trim

was still brown imitation leather, combination number 163. Maryland black was the standard body color for Sedan Deliveries. Other choices included Aspen green; Thistle gray; Trophy blue; Burgundy red; and Waldorf white. Two-tone color combinations were no longer a regular production option, but could be special-ordered at extra cost.

1951 Chevrolet 1/2-Ton Series 3100 Pickup (OCW)

1/2-TON LIGHT-DUTY COMMERCIAL — MODEL JP/SERIES 3100 — SIX-CYLINDER: Conventional trucks looked the same overall, but had some easy-to-spot changes. The left side cowl vent was eliminated. New ventipanes (door vent windows) were used instead. Korean War material restrictions led to discontinuance of many bright metal parts. Chrome grilles were not available, even on Suburbans, due to the war. The unchanged grille again had five broad horizontal bars topped by a broad hood ornament with a cloisonne blue (metallic) bow tie emblem and vermilion Chevrolet lettering on a chrome background. Rectangular parking lights were again placed in housings between the ends of the uppermost pair of grille bars. The outer grille bar assembly was painted body color (Forester green was standard). The inner bar assemblies were painted Waldorf white. The outer bars were not striped. A curved, chrome front bumper was standard on all 3100 models. Curved chrome rear bumpers were standard for single-unit body conventional trucks, but were not factory-supplied for cab models. Chevrolet hoodside nameplates were still used. The 1958 *CHEVROLET MASTER PARTS CATALOGS* also lists a 3100 series nameplates for 1949-1951 1/2-tons. There is anecdotal evidence that 1951 models didn't have these series designators, despite the fact that they appear in some factory illustrations. (Note, however, that there is sufficient documentation of availability in factory literature to satisfy Antique Automobile Club of America judging guidelines). A foot-operated parking brake was now used on all 3100 models. Front brake linings on 1/2-tons were larger and bonded. Brakes on 3100 models were now of the Bendix duo-servo self-energizing type, instead of the old Huck type. Rear corner windows for cab models were optional. On trucks with this option, a different rear roof section was used. Hubcaps and wheels looked the same. The 3100 wheels had three pinstripes in the striping colors bracketed below. The gas tank was inside cab models. Its filler tube came out the rear right-hand corner of the cab, just behind the rotary type, chrome door handles. The filler was just ahead of the rear wheels on single-unit body models. Both cab models and single-unit body models had one belt molding stripe, which was cream medium with standard finish. The following no-cost color options (pinstripe colors in parenthesis) were offered on all models: Swift red (Argent silver); Armour yellow (black); white (Emerald green); Jet black (Argent silver); Omaha orange (black); Cape maroon (gold); Mariner blue (cream medium); Windsor blue (cream medium); Seacrest green (cream medium); Sun beige (Totem scarlet); and cream medium (black). The unchanged instrument panel featured AC instruments: electric fuel gauge and ammeter; pressure-type heat indicator and oil pressure gauge; and dial speedometer driven by a flexible shaft from the transmission.

1951 Chevrolet 1/2-Ton Series 3100 Deluxe Panel (OCW)

3/4-TON LIGHT-DUTY COMMERCIAL — MODEL JR/SERIES 3600 — SIX-CYLINDER: The 3/4-ton trucks had the same Advance-Design styling, features and finish as other conventional trucks. A Chevrolet nameplate was on the sides of the hood. The 1958 *CHEVROLET MASTER PARTS CATALOGS* also lists a 3600 nameplate for 1949-1954 Series 3600 trucks. There is anecdotal evidence that 1951 models didn't have these series designators, despite the fact that they appear in some factory illustrations. Eight-leaf front springs were standard. They had a longer wheelbase than 1/2-tons. The Pickup load box was longer than the 3100 type and had six stake pockets. Long runningboards were used. No Suburban was offered in this line. There were Platform and Stake models. Hubcaps looked like the ones on 3100s, but the standard black wheels were of different eight-bolt design and not pinstriped. Curved-type chrome front bumpers were standard on all models. A foot-operated parking brake was now used for all 3600 models. The brakes are now Bendix's duo-servo self-energizing type. The tires on 3600s were 15 in. six-ply rated on 15 x 5.50 semi-drop-center rims. The 15 in. rims had no pinstripe; the 16 in. rims had three pinstripes and 17 in. rims had two pinstripes.

3/4-TON DUBL-DUTI — MODEL JT/SERIES 3700 — SIX-CYLINDER: Two Dubl-Duti Forward-Control chassis were in the Chevrolet truck line. Both had the 235 cid Loadmaster six with an updraft carburetor. Due to the lower efficiency of the updraft carburetor, this engine had the same horsepower rating as the 216 cid Thriftmaster six. Model 3742 was the 3/4-ton version on a 125.25 in. wheelbase. Standard walk-in delivery truck bodies could be supplied by several factory-approved sources or the buyer could add his/her own truck body. The wheels were of eight-bolt design. A painted, Anvil gray channel type front bumper was standard on the 3700 Dubl-Duti truck chassis.

1-TON MEDIUM-DUTY COMMERCIAL — MODEL JS/SERIES 3800 — SIX-CYLINDER: The 3800 Series had the same Advance-Design styling, features and finish as other conventional trucks. A Chevrolet nameplate was on the sides of the hood. The 1958 *CHEVROLET MASTER PARTS CATALOGS* also lists a 3800 nameplate for 1949-1954 Series 3800 trucks. There is anecdotal evidence that 1951 models didn't have these series designators, despite the fact that they appear in some factory illustrations. A foot-operated parking brake was also new for all 3800 models. Huck type rear brakes were still used on the 1-tons. These models were available with an optional power brake system. This Hydrovac brake booster reduced pedal effort by two-thirds. Panel and Canopy models had a one-piece floor made of 3/4-inch thick, five-ply laminated wood. The basic model lineup was unchanged. It included single and dual rear wheel options for all except the Express, Canopy and Panel. The Express had a longer wheelbase than the 3600 Pickup, longer runningboards, and a longer load box with eight stake pockets. A curved-type chrome front bumper was standard on all models. A similar rear bumper was standard on Models 3805 and 3807. Regular equipment tires were 7.00 x 17 six-ply rated for trucks with single rear wheels or 7.00 x 18 eight-ply rated for trucks with dual rear wheel options. The hubcap design was shared with 3100s and 3600s, though the 3800 hubcaps were larger. The standard black wheels had two pinstripes. No hubcaps were used on the 18 x 5 in. wheels of the Chassis & Cab, Platform, and Stake models, which had eight bolts and eight circular openings. A four-speed transmission was standard.

1-TON DUBL-DUTI — MODEL JU/SERIES 3900 — SIX-CYLINDER: Two Dubl-Duti Forward-Control chassis returned to the Chevrolet truck line. Both had a new 235 cid Loadmaster six with an updraft carburetor. Due to the lower efficiency of the updraft carburetor, this engine had the same horsepower rating as the 216 cid Thriftmaster six. Model 3942 was the 1-ton version on a 137 in. wheelbase. Standard walk-in delivery truck bodies could be supplied by several factory-approved sources or the buyer could add his/her own truck body. A painted, Anvil gray channel type front bumper was standard on the 3900 Dubl-Duti truck chassis.

1951 Chevrolet Model 1508 Sedan Delivery (OCW)

I.D. DATA: Serial Number located: [Chassis models] On plate temporarily attached near steering column, with final location per body maker; [All others] On plate attached to rear face of left-hand door hinge pillar; on right side of cowl under hood. The first symbol indicated the assembly plant: 1=Flint, Mich.; 2=Tarrytown, N.Y.; 3=St. Louis, Mo.; 5=Kansas City, Kan.; 6=Oakland, Calif.; 8=Atlanta, Ga.; 9=Norwood, Ohio; 14=Baltimore, Md.; 20=Los Angeles, Calif.; and 21=Janesville, Wis. The second and third symbols indicate model prefix/series as follows: JJ=Series 1500; JP=3100; JR=3600; JS=3800; JT=3700; JU=3900. The fourth symbol indicates month of assembly; A=Jan.; B=Feb., etc. The following symbols indicated the sequential production number. Each series was separately numbered in sequence, starting with 1001 at each assembly plant. Starting numbers for 1951, by series, were: [1500] JJ-1001; [3100] JP-1001; [3600] JR-1001; [3742] JT-1001; [3800] JS-1001 and [3942] JU-1001. Engine numbers located on right side of block behind distributor. Engine numbers were numbered in sequence, at each plant. Starting at 00-1001. Engine numbers for 1951, by series, were: [1500] JA-1001; [3100] JB-1001; [3600/3742/3800/3942] JC-1001.

Model	Body Type	Price	Weight	Prod. Total
Sedan Delivery — Model JJ/Series 1500 — 115 in. w.b.				
1271	Sedan Delivery	1532	3070	20,817
1/2-Ton Commercial — Model JP/Series 3100 — 116 in. w.b.				
3102	Chassis & Cowl	1035	2435	—
3112	Chassis & W/S	1057	2420	—
3103	Chassis & Cab	1282	2880	—
3104	Pickup	1353	3120	—
3105	Panel	1556	3350	—
3107	Canopy	1610	3325	—
3106	Suburban (doors)	1818	3640	—
3116	Suburban (gate)	1818	3635	—
3/4-Ton Commercial — Model JR/Series 3600 — 125.25 in. w.b.				
3602	Chassis & Cowl	1170	2650	—
3612	Chassis & W/S	1190	2635	—
3603	Chassis & Cab	1417	3095	—
3604	Pickup	1508	3470	—
3608	Platform	1514	3510	—
3609	Stake	1578	3690	—
3/4-Ton Dubl-Duti — Model JT/Series 3700 — 125.5 in. w.b.				
3742	Chassis	1190	2465	—
1-Ton Commercial — Model JS/Series 3800 — 137 in. w.b.				
3802	Chassis & Cowl	1258	2995	—
3812	Chassis & W/S	1280	—	—
3803	Chassis & Cab	1505	3390	—
3804	Pickup	1622	3930	—
3808	Platform	1638	3955	—
3809	Stake	1708	4205	—
3805	Panel	1836	4185	—
3807	Canopy	1916	4105	—
1-Ton Dubl-Duti — Model JU/Series 3942 — 137 in. w.b.				
3942	Chassis	1296	2670	—

ENGINE: [Standard Series 1500/3100/3600/3800] Inline. OHV. Thriftmaster. Six-cylinder. Cast-iron block. Bore & stroke: 3-1/2 x 3-3/4 in. Displacement: 216.5 cid. Compression ratio: 6.6:1. Gross horsepower: 92 at 3400 rpm. Net horsepower: 85 at 3300 rpm. Gross torque: 176 lbs.-ft. at 1000-2000 rpm. Net torque: 170 lbs.-ft. at 1000 to 2000 rpm. SAE horsepower: 29.4. Four main bearings. Mechanical valve lifters. Carburetor: Single one-barrel model Rochester Model 1B number 7002050.

ENGINE: [Standard Dubl-Duti] Inline. OHV. Loadmaster. Six-cylinder. Cast-iron block. Bore & stroke: 3-9/16 x 3-15/16 in. Displacement: 235.5 cid. Compression ratio: 6.7:1. Brake horsepower: 92 at 3400 rpm. SAE horsepower: 30.4. Four main bearings. Mechanical valve lifters. Carburetor: Single one-barrel updraft Carter model BB1-745S.

CHASSIS: [Model 1500] Wheelbase: 116 in. Overall length: 197-7/8 in. Height: 67-1/8 in. Front tread: 57.6 in. Rear tread: 60 in. Tires: 6.70 x 16 in. Maximum GVW: 4,100 lbs.

CHASSIS: [Model 3100] Wheelbase: 116 in. Overall length: 196.6 in. Tires: 6.00 x 16 in. six-ply. Maximum GVW: 4,800 lbs. (Note: 4,200 lbs. with 6.00 x 16 six-ply tires and 4,800 lbs. with 6.50 x 16 six-ply tires).

CHASSIS: [Model 3600] Wheelbase: 125.25 in. Overall length: 206 in. Tires: 15 in. six-ply. Maximum GVW: 5,800 lbs. (With optional 7.00 x 17 eight-ply tires).

NOTE: What is a 15 in. six-ply tire? This obsolete size is comparable to size 7.50 x 15 according to Chevrolet truck expert Bob Adler, who adds, "The 15 in. tires are 'beefier' than the 16 in. tires and the 15 in. wheels weigh considerably more than the 16 in. wheels."

CHASSIS: [Model 3700] Wheelbase: 125.25 in. Tires: 15 in. six-ply. Maximum GVW: 7,000 lbs. (With optional 7.00 x 17 eight-ply tires).

CHASSIS: [Model 3800] Wheelbase: 137 in. Overall length: 223.88 in. Tires: 7.00 x 17 in. six-ply. Maximum GVW: [Single rear wheels] 7,000 lbs. (With 7.50 x 17 eight-ply tires); [Dual rear wheels] 8,800 lbs. (With optional 7.00 x 18 eight-ply tires).

CHASSIS: [Model 3900] Wheelbase: 137 in. Tires: 7.00 x 17 in. six-ply. Maximum GVW: [Dual rear wheels] 10,000 lbs.

TECHNICAL: Manual, synchromesh transmission: [1500/3100/3600] 3F/1R column-mounted; [3800] [4F/1R] Floor-mounted gearshift. Single-disc, diaphragm spring clutch. [1500/3100] Semi-floating hypoid rear axle; [3600/3800] full-floating rear axle. Hydraulic, four-wheel brakes. Wheels: [1500/3100] One-piece drop center 16 in. wheels; [3600/3800] Multi-piece split rims. Standard rear axles: [1500] 4.11:1; [3100] 4.11:1; [3600] 4.57:1; 5.14:1 [3800] 5.14:1.

OPTIONS: [RPO] Rearview mirror(s) and bracket(s): short right-hand; long left-hand bracket only; long right-hand and short left-hand bracket only. Color combinations. Cab corner windows (without Deluxe Equipment bright trim). Platform equipment for all Model 3600 high-sill platform models). Stake rack and equipment (all Stake, Stake Express and High-Rack models). Double acting front shock absorbers. Double acting rear shock absorbers. 5.43:1 ratio rear axle (3600 models). Long runningboards and rear fenders (3600/3800 model cab and chassis models). Spare wheel and tire carrier (Dubl-Duti). Heavy-duty radiator (3600/3800 models). Dual tail and stop lamps (Suburbans/Panels/Canopies). Heavy-duty rear springs (3100). Wide runningboards (Model 3104). School bus chassis (Dubl-Duti chassis). Oil bath air cleaner, 1-lb. dirt capacity. Oil bath air cleaner, 2-lbs. dirt capacity. Heavy-duty clutch (3100). Oil filter (3100/3600/3800). Four-speed transmission (all except Dubl-Duti). Governor (all except Dubl-Duti). Fuel and vacuum pump (all except Dubl-Duti). Various tire options, as follows:

Light Duty Truck Tire Options

Size	Ply Rating	Capacity (lb.)	PSI	Section (in.)
15 in.	Six	1500	40	7.74
15 in.	Eight	1700	48	7.74
6.00 x 16	Four	990	32	6.25
6.00 x 16	Six	1065	36	6.21
6.50 x 16	Six	1290	40	6.65
6.70 x 15	Six	n.a.	n.a.	n.a.
7.00 x 17	Six	1550	45	7.30
7.00 x 17	Eight	n.a.	n.a.	7.30
7.50 x 17	Eight	1725	55	7.36
7.50 x 17	Ten	n.a.	n.a.	7.36
7.00 x 18	Eight	1800	55	7.24

DEALER ACCESSORIES: Rod type radio antenna (all). Locking gas cap (all). Radiator cover (all). Seat cover (all cab models). Fiber seat cover (all cab models). Gasoline filter (all). License plate frame (all). Curved bumper guard (all except Dubl-Duti). Radiator grille guard for curved type bumper (all). Bumper guard for curved type bumper (all except Dubl-Duti). Outside air heater/defroster (all except Chassis & Cowl). Recirculated air type heater (all except Chassis & Cowl). Matched horns (all). Static eliminator injector (all). Powder for static eliminator injector (all). Guide dual sealed-beam fog lights (all). Guide spotlight with bracket (all). Unity spotlight with bracket (all). Magnetic trouble lamp (all). Universal stop and taillamps (all). Load compartment lamp (Panel). Underhood lamp (all). Package compartment light and switch (all). Front and rear directional signals (all). Front signal lamps, single lens (all). Front signal lamps, double lens (all). Rear signal lamp with switch (all). Cigarette lighter (all). Two tire traction mats (all). Non-glare rearview mirror (all). Long-arm adjustable outside rearview mirror (all). Bracket unit for cowl-mounted rearview mirror (all). Hood ornament (all). Ventilated seat pad (all). Rear axle magnetic filler plug (all). Magnetic transmission drain plug (all). Magnetic oil pan drain plug, (all). Delco radio receiving set, plus antenna (all except Chassis & Cowl). Four-inch red reflex reflector (all). Windshield scraper (all). Radiator insect screen (all). Electric shaver (all). Right-hand sunshade (all). Runningboard safety tread (all). Tool kit bag and tools (all). Windshield washer (all).

HISTORICAL: Introduced: January, 1951. Calendar year registrations: [All Series; all models except Sedan Delivery] 350,344. Calendar year production: [All models except Sedan Delivery]: 426,115 (30.17 percent market share). Calendar year production by GVW: [Commercial up to 5,000 lbs.] 215,175; [5,0001 lbs.-10,000 lbs.] 76,659. The National Production Agency, which governed production restrictions during the Korean War gave Chevrolet a quota of 34.95 percent of the light-duty truck market.

1952 CHEVROLET

1952 Chevrolet 1/2-Ton Series 3100 Pickup (OCW)

1952 Chevrolet 1/2-Ton Series 3100 U.S. Navy Survey Panel (OCW)

SEDAN DELIVERY — MODEL KJ/SERIES 1500 — SIX-CYLINDER: The passenger car-based Sedan Delivery was a Styleline Special model identified by Job Number 1508 and Fisher Body Style Number 1271. The grille was somewhat similar to the previous year, except that the upper deflector was no longer grooved and five chrome "fins" or "teeth" were widely spaced across the upper horizontal chrome molding. Also, the parking lamp housings, still in sideways U-shaped end moldings, had the slotted section removed so that they could accommodate larger lenses. There was a different hood ornament. The 73 in. cargo area a usable load space of 92.5 cu. ft. remained unchanged. The Sedan Delivery's windshield glass (non-tinted only) was the same used on some passenger cars, but not wagons. Doors were specific to this model and not used on other cars (although sedan doors can be modified to fit). Front door window glass was the same used on 1949-1952 four-door sedans, not wagons. Lower rear quarter panel stampings were unique to the Sedan Delivery. However, the rear compartment floor panel was the same one used for 1949-1952 Station Wagons. Rear bumper bars, ends and guards were also the same as wagon parts. Standard equipment included front and rear bumpers and bumper guards; front license guard; hood ornament and emblem; chrome plated headlamp rims with doors; dual windshield wipers; dual horns; outside key locks; front and rear bumper gravel deflectors; one combination tail/stop/license plate lamp; bright, full-length rear fender crown molding; bright metal windshield divider; bright windshield reveal molding; bright rear window reveal molding; Bonderized body and sheet metal; plain plastic control knob inserts; chrome-plated radio grille; three-position ignition switch; left-hand sunshade and dome light. Onyx black was the standard body color for 1952 Sedan Deliveries. Options included Birch gray; Spring green; Admiral blue; Dusk gray; Emerald green; Sahara beige; Regal maroon; and Waldorf white. Interior trim was switched to dark grey imitation leather, combination number 216.

1/2-TON LIGHT-DUTY COMMERCIAL — MODEL KP/SERIES 3100 — SIX-CYLINDER: Conventional trucks looked the same as 1951 models except that new push-button type door handles were used. Chrome grilles were not available. The unchanged grille had five broad horizontal bars topped by a broad hood ornament with a cloisonne blue (metallic) bow tie emblem and vermilion Chevrolet lettering on a chrome background. Rectangular parking lights were again placed in housings between the ends of the uppermost pair of grille bars. The outer grille bars were body color (Forester green standard). The inner bars were Waldorf white. The outer bars were not striped. A curved chrome front bumper was standard on all 3100 models. Curved chrome rear bumpers were standard for single-unit body conventional trucks, but not for cab models. Chevrolet hoodside nameplates were still used. There were no series designators below them. A foot-operated parking brake was used. Brakes were Bendix's duo-servo self-energizing type. Rear corner windows for cab models were optional. On trucks with this option, a different rear roof section was used. The gas tank was inside cab models. Its filler tube came out the rear right-hand corner of the cab, just behind the rotary type, chrome door handles. The filler was just ahead of the rear wheels on single-unit body models. Both cab models and single-unit body models had one belt molding stripe, which was cream medium with standard finish. The following no-cost color options (pinstripe colors in parenthesis) were offered on all models: Swift red (Argent silver); Armour yellow (black); white (Emerald green); Jet black (Argent silver); Omaha orange (black); Cape maroon (gold); Mariner blue (cream medium); Windsor blue (cream medium); Seacrest green (cream medium); Sun beige (Totem scarlet); and cream medium (black). The unchanged instrument panel featured AC instruments; electric fuel gauge and ammeter; pressure-type heat indicator and oil pressure gauge; and dial speedometer driven by a flexible shaft from the transmission.

3/4-TON LIGHT-DUTY COMMERCIAL — MODEL KR/SERIES 3600 — SIX-CYLINDER: The 3/4-ton trucks had the same Advance-Design styling, features and finish as other conventional trucks. Eight-leaf front springs were standard. The 3600s had a longer wheelbase than 1/2-tons. The Pickup load box was longer than the half-ton type and had six stake pockets. Long runningboards were used. No Suburban was offered in this line. There were Platform and Stake models. Hubcaps looked like the ones on 3100s, but the standard wheels were of different eight-bolt design and not pinstriped. Curved-type chrome front bumpers were standard on all models. A similar rear bumper was optional on incomplete bodies and flat bed combinations. A foot-operated parking brake was used on all 3600 models. The brakes were Bendix's duo-servo self-energizing type. The tires on 3600s were 15 in. six-ply rated on 15 x 5.50 semi-drop-center rims. The 15 in. rims had no stripe; the 16 in. rims had three pinstripes and 17 in. rims had two pinstripes.

3/4-TON DUBL-DUTI — MODEL KT/SERIES 3700 — SIX-CYLINDER: Two Dubl-Duti Forward-Control chassis were in the Chevrolet truck line. Both had the 235 cid Loadmaster six with updraft carburetor. Model 3742 was the 3/4-ton version on a 125.25 in. wheelbase. Standard walk-in delivery truck bodies could be supplied by several factory-approved sources or the buyer could add his/her own truck body. The wheels were of eight-bolt design. A painted, Anvil gray channel type front bumper was standard on the 3700 Dubl-Duti truck chassis.

1-TON MEDIUM-DUTY COMMERCIAL — MODEL KS/SERIES 3800 — SIX-CYLINDER: The 3800 Series had the same Advance-Design styling, features and finish as other conventional trucks. A foot-operated parking brake was used on all 3800 models. Huck type rear brakes were still used. These models were available with an optional power brake system. This Hydrovac brake booster reduced pedal effort by two-thirds. Panel and Canopy models had a one-piece floor made of 3/4-inch thick, five-ply laminated wood. The basic model lineup was unchanged. It included single and dual rear wheel options for all except the Express, Canopy and Panel. The Express had a longer wheelbase than the 3600 Pickup, longer runningboards, and a longer load box with eight stake pockets. A curved-type chrome front bumper was standard on all models. A similar rear bumper was standard on Models 3805 and 3807. Regular equipment tires were 7.00 x 17 six-ply rated for trucks with single rear wheels or 7.00 x 18 eight-ply rated for trucks with dual rear wheel options. The hubcap design was shared with 3100s and 3600s, though the 3800's hubcaps were larger. The standard black wheels had two pinstripes. No hubcaps were used on the 18 x 5 in. wheels of the Chassis & Cab, Platform and Stake models, which had eight bolts and eight circular openings. A four-speed manual synchromesh transmission was standard. Trucks with this transmission had a new black rubber floor mat made especially for use with the floor-mounted four-speed gearshifter.

1-TON DUBL-DUTI — MODEL KU/SERIES 3900 — SIX-CYLINDER: Two Dubl-Duti Forward-Control chassis returned to the Chevrolet truck line. Both had a new 235 cid Loadmaster six with updraft carburetor. Due to the lower efficiency of the updraft carburetor, this engine had the same horsepower rating as the 216 cid Thriftmaster six. Model 3942 was the 1-ton version on a 137 in. wheelbase. Standard walk-in delivery truck bodies could be supplied by several factory-approved sources or the buyer could add his/her own truck body. A painted, Anvil gray channel type front bumper was standard on the 3900 Dubl-Duti truck chassis.

I.D. DATA: Serial Number located: [Chassis models] On plate temporarily attached near steering column, with final location per body maker; [All others] On plate attached to rear face of left-hand door hinge pillar; on right side of cowl under hood. The first symbol indicated the assembly plant: 1=Flint, Mich.; 2=Tarrytown, N.Y.; 3=St. Louis, Mo.; 5=Kansas City, Kan.; 6=Oakland, Calif.; 8=Atlanta, Ga.; 9=Norwood, Ohio; 14=Baltimore, Md.; 20=Los Angeles, Calif.; and 21=Janesville, Wis. The second and third symbols indicate model prefix/series as follows: KJ=Series 1500; KP=3100; KR=3600; KS=3800; KT=3700; KU=3900. The fourth symbol indicates month of assembly; A=Jan.; B=Feb., etc. The following symbols indicated the sequential production number. Each series was separately numbered in sequence, starting with 1001 at each assembly plant. Serial numbers by series were: [1500] KJ-1001 to 19286; [3100] KP-1001 to 27704; [3600] KR-1001 to 8132; [3742] KT-1001 to 1430; [3800] KS-1001 to 5409; and [3942] KU-1001 to 1300. Engine numbers located on right side of block near fuel pump; also stamped on crankcase near rear of distributor on right side of engine. Engine numbers for 1952, by series, were: [1500] KA-1001 to 860773; [3100] KB-1001 to 860773; [3600/3742/3800/3942] KC-1001 to 860773.

1952 Chevrolet Series 1500 Sedan Delivery (OCW)

Model No.	Body Type	Price	Weight	Prod. Total
Sedan Delivery — Model KJ/Series 1500 — 115 in. w.b.				
1508	Sedan Delivery	1648	3100	9175
1/2-Ton Commercial — Model KP/Series 3100 — 116 in. w.b.				
3102	Chassis & Cowl	1076	2435	—
3103	Chassis & Cab	1334	2880	—
3104	Pickup	1407	3120	—
3105	Panel	1620	3350	—
3107	Canopy	1676	3325	—
3112	Chassis & W/S	1099	—	—
3106	Suburban (doors)	1933	3640	—
3116	Suburban (gate)	1933	3635	—
3/4-Ton Commercial — Model KR/Series 3600 — 125.25 in. w.b.				
3602	Chassis & Cowl	1216	2655	—
3603	Chassis & Cab	1474	3095	—
3604	Pickup	1569	3470	—
3608	Platform	1575	3510	—
3609	Stake	1642	3690	—
3612	Chassis & W/S	1238	2470	—
3/4-Ton Dubl-Duti — Model KT/Series 3700 — 125.25 in. w.b.				
3742	Chassis	1238	2470	—
1-Ton Commercial — Model KS/Series 3800 — 137 in. w.b.				
3802	Chassis & Cowl	1312	3000	—
3803	Chassis & Cab	1570	3395	—
3804	Pickup	1692	3915	—
3805	Panel	1916	4140	—
3807	Canopy	2000	4110	—
3808	Platform	1709	3960	—
3809	Stake	1782	4240	—
3812	Chassis & W/S	1335	—	—
1-Ton Dubl-Duti — Model KU/Series 3900 — 137 in. w.b.				
3942	Chassis	1351	2670	—

ENGINE: [Standard Series 1500/3100/3600/3800] Inline. OHV. Thriftmaster. Six-cylinder. Cast-iron block. Bore & stroke: 3-1/2 x 3-3/4 in. Displacement: 216.5 cid. Compression ratio: 6.6:1. Gross horsepower: 92 at 3400 rpm. Net horsepower: 85 at 3300 rpm. Gross torque: 176 lbs.-ft. at 1000-2000 rpm. Net torque: 170 at 1000 to 2000 rpm. NCCA horsepower: 29.4. Four main bearings. Mechanical valve lifters. Carburetor: [Early] Single one-barrel downdraft GM (Rochester) Model B "Power Jet" number 7004475; [Late] Same type, but various different model numbers.

ENGINE: [Standard Dubl-Duti] Inline. OHV. Loadmaster. Six-cylinder. Cast-iron block. Bore & stroke: 3-9/16 x 3-15/16 in. Displacement: 235.5 cid. Compression ratio: 6.7:1. Brake horsepower: 92 at 3400 rpm. NACC horsepower: 30.4. Four main bearings. Mechanical valve lifters. Carburetor: Carter single one-barrel updraft model BB1-871S.

CHASSIS: [Model 1500] Wheelbase: 116 in. Overall length: 197-7/8 in. Height: 67-1/8 in. Front tread: 57.6 in. Rear tread: 60 in. Tires: 6.70 x 16 in. Maximum GVW: 4,100 lbs.

CHASSIS: [Model 3100] Wheelbase: 116 in. Overall length: 196.6 in. Tires: 6.00 x 16 in. six-ply. Maximum GVW: 4,800 lbs. (Note: 4,200 lbs. with 6.00 x 16 six-ply tires and 4,800 lbs. with 6.50 x 16 six-ply tires).

CHASSIS: [Model 3600] Wheelbase: 125.25 in. Overall length: 206 in. Tires: 15 in. six-ply. Maximum GVW: 5,800 lbs. (With optional 7.00 x 17 eight-ply tires).

NOTE: What is a 15 in. six-ply tire? This obsolete size is comparable to size 7.50 x 15 according to Chevrolet truck expert Bob Adler, who adds, "The 15 in. tires are 'beefier' than the 16 in. tires and the 15 in. wheels weigh considerably more than the 16 in. wheels."

CHASSIS: [Model 3700] Wheelbase: 125.25 in. Tires: 15 in. six-ply. Maximum GVW: 7,000 lbs. (With optional 7.00 x 17 eight-ply tires).

CHASSIS: [Model 3800] Wheelbase: 137 in. Overall length: 223.88 in. Tires: 7.00 x 17 in. six-ply. Maximum GVW: [Single rear wheels] 7,000 lbs. (With 7.50 x 17 eight-ply tires); [Dual rear wheels] 8,800 lbs. (With optional 7.00 x 18 eight-ply tires).

CHASSIS: [Model 3900] Wheelbase: 137 in. Tires: 7.00 x 17 in. six-ply. Maximum GVW: [Dual rear wheels] 10,000 lbs.

TECHNICAL: Manual, synchromesh transmission: [1500/3100/3600] 3F/1R column-mounted; [3800] [4F/1R] Floor-mounted gearshift. Single-disc, diaphragm spring clutch. [1500/3100] Semi-floating hypoid rear axle; [3600/3800] full-floating rear axle. Hydraulic, four-wheel brakes. Wheels: [1500/3100] One-piece drop center 16 in. wheels; [3600/3800] Multi-piece split rims. Standard rear axles: [1500] 4.11:1. [3100] 4.11:1 [3600] 4.57:1; 5.14:1 [3800] 5.14:1.

OPTIONS: [RPO] Double-acting shock absorbers. Long runningboards and rear fenders. Optional 5.14:1 rear axle ratio for 3600. Rearview mirrors and brackets. Rear shock absorber shield. Hydrovac power brakes. Propeller shaft brake. Oil bath air cleaner. Positive crankcase ventilation. Oil filter. Governor. Dual tail and stop light. Heavy-duty rear springs. Heavy-duty radiator. Auxiliary seat. Auxiliary rear springs. Vacuum reserve tank. Heavy-duty three-speed transmission. Heavy-duty four-speed transmission. High-output generators. Solenoid starter. Stand-and-drive controls (Dubl-Duti). Combination fuel and vacuum pump. Cab rear corner windows. Left-hand door key lock.

Light Duty Truck Tire Options

Size	Ply Rating	Capacity (lb.)	PSI	Section (in.)
15 in.	Six	1500	40	7.74
15 in.	Eight	1700	48	7.74
6.00 x 16	Four	990	32	6.25
6.00 x 16	Six	1065	36	6.21
6.50 x 16	Six	1290	40	6.65
6.70 x 15	Six	n.a.	n.a.	n.a.
7.00 x 17	Six	1550	45	7.30
7.00 x 17	Eight	n.a.	n.a.	7.30
7.50 x 17	Eight	1725	55	7.36
7.50 x 17	Ten	n.a.	n.a.	7.36
7.00 x 18	Eight	1800	55	7.24

DEALER ACCESSORIES: Rod type radio antenna (all). Locking gas cap (all). Radiator cover (all). Seat cover (all cab models). Fiber seat cover (all cab models). Gasoline filter (all). License plate frame (all). Curved bumper guard (all except Dubl-Duti). Painted radiator grille guard for curved type bumper (all). Painted bumper guard for curved type bumper (all except Dubl-Duti). Outside air heater/defroster (all except Chassis & Cowl). Recirculated air type heater (all except Chassis & Cowl). Matched horns (all). Static eliminator injector (all). Powder for static eliminator injector (all). Guide dual sealed-beam fog lights (all). Guide spotlight with bracket (all). Unity spotlight with bracket (all). Magnetic trouble lamp (all). Universal stop and taillamps (all). Load compartment lamp (Panel). Underhood lamp (all). Package compartment light and switch (all). Front and rear directional signals (all). Front signal lamps, single lens (all). Front signal lamps, double lens (all). Rear signal lamp with switch (all). Cigarette lighter (all). Two tire traction mats (all). Non-glare rearview mirror (all). Long-arm adjustable outside rearview mirror (all). Bracket unit for cowl-mounted rearview mirror (all). Hood ornament (all). Ventilated seat pad (all). Rear axle magnetic filler plug (all). Magnetic transmission drain plug (all). Magnetic oil pan drain plug, (all). Delco radio receiving set, plus antenna (all except Chassis & Cowl). Four-inch red reflex reflector (all). Windshield scraper (all). Radiator insect screen (all). Electric shaver (all). Right-hand sunshade (all). Runningboard safety tread (all). Tool kit bag and tools (all). Windshield washer (all).

1952 Chevrolet 1/2-Ton Series 3100 Panel (OCW)

HISTORICAL: Introduced: January, 1952. Calendar year registrations: [All Commercials] 272,249. Innovations included new push-button door handles for conventional trucks; a slightly revised GM Rochester Model B carburetor; and use of a new four-pound pressure type radiator cap. Due to the Korean War, the radiators were made lighter, with air cells placed further apart. This increased cooling capacity. Warning: Do not use higher pressure radiator caps, as the lighter cellular radiators are built for a maximum pressure of four-pounds and do not stand up to excessive radiator pressure.

1953 CHEVROLET

1953 Chevrolet 3/4-Ton Series 3600 Pickup (OCW)

SEDAN DELIVERY — MODEL D/SERIES 1500 — SIX-CYLINDER: The passenger car-based Sedan Delivery was totally new and redesigned. It was now called a One-Fifty (or 150) model, this being a shortened form of the old 1500 series designation. It could also be identified by the code 53-1271 on the Fisher Body tag under the hood. The grille consisted of a curvy upper chrome molding, with a dip in its center, positioned above a deflector and a chrome support to which three large "teeth" were attached. Large round parking lamp housings attached to the end of the support. Below it was a second deflector and a veed horizontal molding. End moldings with six horizontally grooved impressions stamped into them attached to the round parking lamp housings. The new body featured a one-piece windshield. Doors were still specific to this model and not used on other cars. Front door window glass was the same used on 1953 (and 1954) four-door sedans, not wagons. Lower rear quarter panel stampings were unique to the Sedan Delivery. However, the rear compartment floor panel was again same one used for Station Wagons. The rear panel door was the same part used since 1949. Rear bumper parts and guards were also the same as wagon parts. Standard equipment included front and rear bumpers and bumper guards; front license guard; hood ornament and emblem; chrome plated headlamp rims with doors; dual windshield wipers; dual horns; outside key locks; front and rear bumper gravel deflectors; one combination tail/stop/license plate lamp; chrome-plated radio grille; three-

position ignition switch; left-hand sunshade; and dome light. Onyx black remained the standard body color for 1953 Sedan Deliveries. Options included Driftwood gray; Surf green; Regatta blue; Dusk gray; Woodland green; Sahara beige; Madeira maroon; Thistle gray; and Moonstone Hysheen gray. The interior was trimmed with tan imitation leather, combination number 276.

1/2-TON LIGHT-DUTY COMMERCIAL — MODEL H/SERIES 3100 — SIX-CYLINDER: Conventional trucks looked the same as 1952 models except for trim and finish. A new hoodside nameplate appeared. It had the 3100 series designation above a broken loop of chrome shaped somewhat like a safety-pin. Chrome grilles were not available. The unchanged grille had five broad horizontal bars topped by a broad hood ornament with a cloisonne blue (metallic) bow tie emblem and vermilion Chevrolet lettering on a chrome background. Rectangular parking lights were again placed in housings between the ends of the uppermost pair of grille bars. The outer grille bars were body color (Juniper green with creme pinstripe standard). The inner bars were Waldorf white. The outer bars were not striped. All bumpers were also painted. A curved type Anvil gray front bumper was standard on all 3100 models. Curved painted rear bumpers were standard for single-unit body trucks only, not for cab models. When ordered as an option, bumper guards were painted, too. Hubcaps were also painted. Cab corner windows were optional and did not include chromed gasket lockstrips. On trucks with this option, a different rear roof section was used. A foot-operated parking brake was used. Brakes were Bendix's duo-servo self-energizing type. The gas tank was inside cab models. Its filler tube came out the rear right-hand corner of the cab, just behind the chrome door handles. The filler was just ahead of the rear wheels on single-unit body models. Both cab models and single-unit body models had one belt molding stripe, which was cream medium with standard finish. The following no-cost color options (pinstripe color in parenthesis) were offered: Commercial red (Argent silver); Jet black (Argent silver); Mariner blue (Cream medium); Cream medium (Jet black); Yukon yellow (Jet black); Ocean green (Jet black); Transport blue (Cream medium); Burgundy maroon (Gold bronze); Copper Tone copper (Onyx black or Shell white); Omaha orange (Jet black); Autumn brown (Shell white); and Pure white (Juniper green). The instrument panel featured AC instruments; electric fuel gauge and ammeter; pressure-type heat indicator and oil pressure; and dial speedometer driven by a flexible shaft from the transmission. Tinted glass was a new option. Even cab rear quarter windows could be ordered with tinted glass. Another new option was a side-mounted spare tire carrier. This assembly consisted of three 7/16 x 20 x 1 in. wheel mounting bolts, front and rear rail brackets measuring 1-3/16 x 2-1/2 x 17-1/2 in. and side and center wheel carrier cross braces. Also available was a wheel carrier locking mechanism. Due to their short runningboards, 3100s with side-mounted spares required a special left-hand welled rear fender (part number 3705885) to provide enough room for the fifth tire.

3/4-TON LIGHT-DUTY COMMERCIAL — MODEL J/SERIES 3600 — SIX-CYLINDER: The 3/4-ton trucks had the same Advance-Design styling, features and finish as other conventional trucks. Eight-leaf front springs were standard. The 3600s had a longer wheelbase than 1/2-tons. The Pickup load box was longer than the 1/2-ton type and had six stake pockets. Runningboards measuring 75-3/4 in. long were used. When a side-mounted spare tire carrier was used, dimpled rear fenders were not required. No Suburban was offered in this line. There were Platform and Stake models. Hubcaps were also painted on 3600s. The standard wheels were of different eight-bolt design. Painted curved-type chrome front bumpers were standard on all models. A similar rear bumper was optional on incomplete bodies and flat bed combinations. A foot-operated parking brake was used on all 3600 models. The brakes were Bendix's duo-servo self-energizing type. The standard tires on 3600s were 15 in. six-ply rated on 15 x 5.50 semi-drop-center rims. Three-quarter-ton trucks used new roller type front wheel bearings.

1953 Chevrolet 1/2-Ton Series 3100 Panel (P. Bachman)

3/4-TON DUBL-DUTI — MODEL K/SERIES 3700 — SIX-CYLINDER: Two Dubl-Duti Forward-Control chassis were in the Chevrolet truck line. Both had the 235 cid Loadmaster six with updraft carburetor. Model 3742 was the 3/4-ton version on a 125.25 in. wheelbase. Standard walk-in delivery truck bodies could be supplied by several factory-approved sources or the buyer could add his/her own truck body. The wheels were of eight-bolt design. A painted, Anvil gray channel type front bumper was standard on the 3700 Dubl-Duti truck chassis.

1-TON MEDIUM-DUTY COMMERCIAL — MODEL L/SERIES 3800 — SIX-CYLINDER: The 3800 Series had the same Advance-Design styling, features and finish as other conventional trucks. A foot-operated parking brake was used on all 3800 models. Huck type rear brakes were still used. These models were available with an optional power brake system. This Hydrovac brake booster reduced pedal effort by two-thirds. Panel and Canopy models had a one-piece floor made of 3/4-inch thick, five-ply laminated wood. The basic model lineup was unchanged. It included single and dual rear wheel options for all except the Express, Canopy and Panel. The Express had a longer wheelbase than the 3600 Pickup, a longer load box with eight stake pockets, and very long runningboards. When a side-mounted spare tire carrier was used, dimpled rear fenders were not required. A curved-type painted front bumper was standard on all models. A similar rear bumper was standard on Models 3805 and 3807. Regular equipment tires were 7.00 x 17 six-ply rated for trucks with single rear wheels or 7.00 x 18 eight-ply rated for trucks with dual rear wheel options. The hubcaps were painted. No hubcaps were used on the 18 x 5 in. wheels of the Chassis & Cab, Platform and Stake models, which had eight bolts and eight circular openings. A four-speed manual synchromesh transmission was standard. Trucks with this transmission had a black rubber floor mat made especially for use with the floor-mounted four-speed gearshifter.

1-TON DUBL-DUTI — MODEL M/SERIES 3900 — SIX-CYLINDER: Two Dubl-Duti Forward-Control chassis returned to the Chevrolet truck line. Both had the 235 cid Loadmaster six with updraft carburetor. Due to the lower efficiency of the updraft carburetor, this engine had the same horsepower rating as the 216 cid Thriftmaster six. Model 3942 was the 1-ton version on a 137 in. wheelbase. Standard walk-in delivery truck bodies could be supplied by several factory-approved sources or the buyer could add his/her own truck body. A painted, Anvil gray channel type front bumper was standard on the 3900 Dubl-Duti truck chassis.

I.D. DATA: Serial Number located: [Chassis models] On plate temporarily attached near steering column, with final location per body maker; [All others] On plate attached to rear face of left-hand door hinge pillar; on right side of cowl under hood. The first symbol indicated the series: D=1500; H=3100; J=3600; K=3700; L=3800; M=3900. The second symbol indicated the model year: 3=1953. The third symbol indicated the assembly plant: A=Atlanta, Ga.; B=Baltimore, Md.; F=Flint, Mich.; J=Janesville, Wis.; K=Kansas City, Mo.; L=Los Angeles, Calif.;N=Norwood, Ohio; O=Oakland, Calif.;S=St. Louis, Mo.; T=Tarrytown, N.Y. Each series was separately numbered in sequence, starting with 001001 at each assembly plant. Serial numbers for 1953, were as follows: [1500] D53-001001 to 228961; [3100] H53-001001 to 49126; [3600] J53-001001 to 49126; [3742] K53-001001 to 49126; [3800] L53-001001 to 49126 and [3942] M53-001001 to 49126. Engine numbers: On right side of block near fuel pump; also stamped on crankcase near rear of distributor on right side of engine. Each engine carried a letter code for model year, type and engine plant, plus a production unit number. All numbers were numbered at each source in sequence starting with 1001. Numbers used were: [1500] LA-1001 to LA-1183450; [3100] LB-1001 to LB-1183450; [3600] LC-1001 to LC-1183450; [3700] LC-1001 to LC-1183450; [3800] LC-1001 to LC-1183450; [3900] LC-1001 to LC-1183450.

1953 Chevrolet 1/2-Ton Series 3100 Suburban (OCW)

Model No.	Body Type	Price	Weight	Prod. Total
Sedan Delivery — Model D/Series 1500 — 115 in. w.b.				
1508	Sedan Delivery	1648	3160	15,523
1/2-Ton Commercial — Model H/Series 3100 — 116 in. w.b.				
3102	Chassis & Cowl	1076	2440	—
3112	Chassis & W/S	1099	2515	—
3103	Chassis & Cab	1334	2855	—
3104	Pickup	1407	3100	—
3105	Panel Delivery	1620	3335	—
3107	Canopy	1676	3305	—
3106	Suburban (doors)	1947	3625	—
3116	Suburban (gate)	1947	3635	—
3/4-Ton Commercial — Model J/Series 3600 — 125.25 in. w.b.				
3602	Chassis & Cowl	1216	2675	—
3612	Chassis & W/S	1238	2780	—
3603	Chassis & Cab	1474	3110	—
3604	Pickup	1569	3480	—
3608	Platform	1575	3515	—
3609	Stake	1642	3700	—
3/4-Ton Dubl-Duti — Model K/Series 3742 — 125.25 in. w.b.				
3742	Chassis	1238	2480	—
1-Ton Commercial — Model L/Series 3800 — 137 in. w.b.				
3802	Chassis & Cowl	1312	3000	—
3812	Chassis & W/S	1335	3080	—
3803	Chassis & Cab	1570	3405	—
3804	Pickup	1692	3920	—
3808	Platform	1709	3965	—
3809	Stake	1782	4210	—
3805	Panel Delivery	1916	4170	—
3807	Canopy	2000	4095	—
1-Ton Dubl-Duti — Model M/Series 3942 — 137 in. w.b.				
3942	Chassis	1351	2685	—

ENGINE: [Standard Series 1500/3100/3600/3800] Inline. OHV. Thriftmaster. Six-cylinder. Cast-iron block. Bore & stroke: 3-1/2 x 3-3/4 in. Displacement: 216.5 cid. Compression ratio: 6.6:1. Gross horsepower: 92 at 3400 rpm. Net horsepower: 85 at 3300 rpm. Gross torque: 176 lbs.-ft. at 1000-2000 rpm. Net torque: 170 at 1000 to 2000 rpm. NCCA horsepower: 29.4. Four main bearings. Mechanical valve lifters. Carburetor: [Early] Single one-barrel downdraft GM (Rochester) Model B.

ENGINE: [Standard Dubl-Duti] Inline. OHV. Loadmaster. Six-cylinder. Cast-iron block. Bore & stroke: 3-9/16 x 3-15/16 in. Displacement: 235.5 cid. Compression ratio: 6.7:1. Brake horsepower: 92 at 3400 rpm. NACC horsepower: 30.4. Four main bearings. Mechanical valve lifters. Carburetor: Carter single one-barrel updraft model BB1.

CHASSIS: [Model 1500] Wheelbase: 116 in. Overall length: 195-1/2 in. Height: 67-1/8 in. Front tread: 62 in. Rear tread: 62 in. Tires: 6.70 x 16 in. Maximum GVW: 4,100 lbs.

CHASSIS: [Series 3100] Wheelbase: 116 in. Overall length: [Pickup] 191.31 in.; [Panel/Suburban] 195.31 in. Height: [Panel] 80.68 in.; [Suburban] 79.5 in. Tires: 6.00 x 16 six-ply.

CHASSIS: [Series 3600] Wheelbase: 125.25 in. Overall length: [Pickup] 200-3/16 in.; [Platform/Stake] 206 in. Tires: 15 in., six-ply.

CHASSIS: [Series 3800] Wheelbase: 137 in. Overall length: [Pickup] 221.5 in.; [Panel] 229.57 in.; [Platform/Stake] 224 in. Height: [Panel] 86.5 in. Tires: [Front] 7.00 x 17 six-ply; [Rear] eight-ply.

CHASSIS: [Series 3742] Wheelbase: 125.25 in. Overall length: 197-1/8 in. Front tread: 62 in. Rear tread: 62-3/8 in. Tires: 7.00 x 17 in.

CHASSIS: [Series 3942] Wheelbase: 137 in. Overall length: 221-7/8 in. Front tread: 61-3/8 in. Rear tread: 61-3/4 in. Tires: 7.50 x 17 eight-ply or 7.50 x 18 eight-ply (Dual Rear Wheels).

TECHNICAL: Manual, synchromesh transmission: [1500/3100/3600] 3F/1R column-mounted; [3800] [4F/1R] Floor-mounted gearshift. Single-disc, diaphragm spring clutch. [1500/3100] Semi-floating hypoid rear axle; [3600/3800] full-floating rear axle. Hydraulic, four-wheel brakes. Wheels: [1500/3100] One-piece drop center 16 in. wheels; [3600/3800] Multi-piece split rims. Standard rear axles: [1500] 4.11:1 [3100] 4.11:1; [3600] 4.57:1; 5.14:1 [3800] 5.14:1.

1953 Chevrolet 3/4-Ton Series 3600 Pickup (OCW)

OPTIONS: [RPO] Double-acting shock absorbers. Long runningboards and rear fenders. Optional 5.14:1 rear axle ratio for 3600. Rearview mirrors and brackets. Rear shock absorber shield. Hydrovac power brakes. Propeller shaft brake. Oil bath air cleaner. Positive crankcase ventilation. Rear bumper. Heavy-duty clutch. Oil filter. Governor. Dual tail and stop light. Heavy-duty rear springs. Heavy-duty radiator. Auxiliary seat. Auxiliary rear springs. Heavy-duty three-speed transmission. Heavy-duty four-speed transmission. Heavy-duty generators. Solenoid starter. Combination fuel and vacuum pump. Side-mounted spare wheel carrier. Cab rear corner windows. Left-hand door key lock. Spare wheel lock equipment. E-Z-Eye glass.

Light Duty Truck Tire Options

Size	Ply Rating	Capacity (lb.)	PSI	Section (in.)
15 in.	Six	1500	40	7.74
15 in.	Eight	1700	48	7.74
6.00 x 16	Four	990	32	6.25
6.00 x 16	Six	1065	36	6.21
6.50 x 16	Six	1290	40	6.65
6.70 x 15	Six	n.a.	n.a.	n.a.
7.00 x 17	Six	1550	45	7.30
7.00 x 17	Eight	n.a.	n.a.	7.30
7.50 x 17	Eight	1725	55	7.36
7.50 x 17	Ten	n.a.	n.a.	7.36
7.00 x 18	Eight	1800	55	7.24

HISTORICAL: Introduced: January, 1953. Calendar year registrations: [All Commercials] 327,960. [Calendar year production] (GVW up to 5,000 lbs.) 203,242; (5,001 to 10,000 lbs.) 71,517. Innovations: Completely new body style for Sedan Delivery. New side-mounted spare tire option for regular trucks. E-Z-Eye glass option introduced.

1953 Chevrolet 1/2-Ton Series 3100 Pickup (JCL)

Standard Catalog of Light-Duty Trucks

1954 Chevrolet 1/2-Ton Series 3100 Panel (OCW)

SEDAN DELIVERY — MODEL D/SERIES 1500 — SIX-CYLINDER: For 1954, the Sedan Delivery used the new-for-1954 look with a different treatment at front and rear. Up front, a new full-width grille had an upper chrome molding, with curved ends, above a large full-width horizontal molding. Five large "teeth" were spaced across this bar. Large parking lamp housings had a flattened-oval shape. They wrapped around the body corners and had inner extensions that bolted to the full-width molding. Below the grille was a large body-color sheet metal filler panel. This model was again in the One-Fifty series with code 54-1271 on the Fisher Body tag under the hood. Features included a one-piece windshield. Doors were still specific to this model and not used on other cars. Front door window glass was the same used on 1953 (and 1954) four-door sedans. Lower rear quarter panel stampings were unique to the Sedan Delivery. However, the rear compartment floor panel was the same one used for Station Wagons. The rear panel door, used since 1949, was in its final year. Rear bumper parts and guards were also the same as Station Wagon parts. Standard equipment included front and rear bumpers and bumper guards; front license guard; hood ornament and emblem; chrome plated headlamp rims with doors; dual windshield wipers; dual horns; outside key locks; front and rear bumper gravel deflectors; one combination tail/stop/license plate lamp; chrome-plated radio grille; three-position ignition switch; left-hand sunshade; and dome light. Onyx black remained the standard body color for 1954 Sedan Deliveries. Options included most Chevrolet passenger car colors. The interior was trimmed with gray imitation leather, combination number 303. The Sedan Delivery was not yet available with automatic (Powerglide) transmission.

1954 Chevrolet 1-Ton Series 3800 Express (OCW)

1/2-TON COMMERCIAL — MODEL D/SERIES 3100 — SIX-CYLINDER: Conventional trucks had, what for them, was a major restyling. All-new was a one-piece windshield without vertical center molding. There was a new open radiator grille. The opening was filled with a massive cross-bar arrangement. The main horizontal bar extended the full-width of the body. Below it were rectangular parking lamps. The outer radiator grille bars were done in body color and the inner bars were Thistle gray (except trucks painted Commercial red had Argent silver inner bars and trucks painted Pure white had Pure white inner bars). The word Chevrolet was stamped into the grille header bar and lettered in Waldorf white. Bumpers were finished in Anvil gray. There was a new instrument panel with defroster openings that extended the full width of the windshield. The instruments, grouped in two clusters, were now recessed into the panel to minimize reflections. There was also a redesigned dispatch box (or glove compartment) and a restyled ash receiver. A revised steering wheel gave a full view of the instruments and incorporated finger-grips on the horizontal spokes. A new load box featured a two-inch lower loading height; flat side panel tops; deeper sides; and a grain-tight tailgate the same height as the sides. The 1954 taillights were round. When the optional rear bumper was ordered, the license plate was mounted in the center of the box under the tailgate. Some of the numerous technical changes included a more rugged three-speed manual transmission; a new optional Hydra-Matic transmission; a more durable clutch. Frame rigidity was increased by the use of a heavier crossmember at the rear of the engine. Chrome fender bars were available as Deluxe equipment on Panel trucks only. A

switch to gray and maroon interiors was made for Suburbans. Juniper green body finish with cream medium striping and black wheels was standard finish for all models. Twelve other colors were optional at no extra cost. They included the following choices (pinstripe color in parenthesis): Juniper green (standard, with cream medium pinstripe); Commercial red (Argent silver); Jet black (Argent silver); Mariner blue (Cream medium); Cream medium (Jet black); Yukon yellow (Jet black); Ocean green (Jet black); Transport blue (Cream medium); Copper Tone copper (Shell white); Omaha orange (Jet black); Autumn brown (Shell white); and Pure white (Juniper green). Standard wheels were black. On Deluxe monotone and two-tone trucks, the wheels were the color on the lower body. On two-tone trucks, Shell white was used exclusively as the upper body color and the beltline was usually striped with the lower body color. Exceptions included trucks with the lower body done in Pure white; Creme medium or Omaha orange, in which cases the striping was Jet black or Onyx black. As of about mid-February, 1954 Chevrolet introduced a new Deluxe Cab option for all 3000 series trucks. It included two-tone interior trim that harmonized with the exterior color; stainless steel windshield and side window reveals; chrome-plated ventipane frames; right-hand sunshade; left-hand armrest; cigar lighter; twin-tone horns; and cab rear corner windows. The two-tone interior colors were Light green and Juniper green; Light blue and Dark blue; Birch white and brown; and Pearl beige and maroon. This interior included a color-coordinated cloth seat; a color-coordinated rubber floor mat; color-coordinated windlacing; and special colored plastic armrests. The option also included wheels and runningboards painted lower body color, with triple striping on the wheels.

1954 Chevrolet 1/2-Ton Series 3100 Pickup (DFW)

3/4-TON LIGHT-DUTY COMMERCIAL — MODEL J/SERIES 3600 — SIX-CYLINDER:
The 3/4-ton trucks had the same Advance-Design styling, features and finish as other conventional trucks. New features included improved drivelines and universal joints. Eight-leaf front springs were standard. The 3600s had a longer wheelbase than the 1/2-tons. The new grain-tight load box was longer than the 1/2-ton type and had six stake pockets. Running-boards measuring 75-3/4 in. long were used. When a side-mounted spare tire carrier was used, dimpled rear fenders were not required. No Suburban was offered in this line. There were Platform and Stake models. Hubcaps were also painted on 3600s. The standard wheels were of different eight-bolt design. Painted curved-type chrome front bumpers were standard on all models. A similar rear bumper was optional on incomplete bodies and flat bed combinations. A foot-operated parking brake was used on all 3600 models. The brakes were Bendix's duo-servo self-energizing type. The standard tires on 3600s were 15 in. six-ply rated on 15 x 5.50 semi-drop-center rims. Three-quarter-ton trucks used roller type front wheel bearings.

1954 Chevrolet 3/4-Ton Series 3600 Stake Truck (OCW)

3/4-TON DUBL-DUTI — MODEL K/SERIES 3700 — SIX-CYLINDER: Two Dubl-Duti Forward-Control chassis were in the Chevrolet truck line. Both had the 235 cid Loadmaster six with updraft carburetor. Model 3742 was the 3/4-ton version on a 125.25 in. wheelbase. Standard walk-in delivery truck bodies could be supplied by several factory-approved sources or the buyer could add his/her own truck body. The wheels were of eight-bolt design. A painted, Anvil gray channel type front bumper was standard on the 3700 Dubl-Duti truck chassis.

1954 Chevrolet 1-Ton Series 3800 Canopy (OCW)

1-TON MEDIUM-DUTY COMMERCIAL — MODEL L/SERIES 3800 — SIX-CYLINDER:
The 3800 Series had the same Advance-Design styling, features and finish as other conventional trucks. New features included improved drivelines and universal joints. A foot-operated parking brake was used on all 3800 models. Huck type rear brakes were still used. These models were available with an optional power brake system. This Hydrovac brake booster reduced pedal effort by two-thirds. Panel and Canopy models had a one-piece floor made of 3/4-inch thick, five-ply laminated wood. The basic model lineup was unchanged. It included single and dual rear wheel options for all except the Express, Canopy and Panel. The Express had a longer wheelbase than the 3600 Pickup, a longer grain-tight load box with eight stake pockets, and very long runningboards. When a side-mounted spare tire carrier was used, dimpled rear fenders were not required. A curved-type painted front bumper was standard on all models. A similar rear bumper was standard on Models 3805 and 3807. Regular equipment tires were 7.00 x 17 six-ply rated for trucks with single rear wheels or 7.00 x 18 eight-ply rated for trucks with dual rear wheel options. The hubcaps were painted. No hubcaps were used on the 18 x 5 in. wheels of the Chassis & Cab, Platform and Stake models, which had eight bolts and eight circular openings. A four-speed manual synchromesh transmission was standard. Trucks with this transmission had a black rubber floor mat made especially for use with the floor-mounted four-speed gearshifter.

1954 Chevrolet 1/2-Ton Series 3100 Canopy (OCW)

1-TON DUBL-DUTI — MODEL M/SERIES 3900 — SIX-CYLINDER: Two Dubl-Duti Forward-Control chassis returned to the Chevrolet truck line. Both had the 235 cid Loadmaster six with updraft carburetor. Due to the lower efficiency of the updraft carburetor, this engine had the same horsepower rating as the 216 cid Thriftmaster six. Model 3942 was the 1-ton version on a 137 in. wheelbase. Standard walk-in delivery truck bodies could be supplied by several factory-approved sources or the buyer could add his/her own truck body. A painted, Anvil gray channel type front bumper was standard on the 3900 Dubl-Duti truck chassis.

1954 Chevrolet 1-Ton Series 3800 Panel (OCW)

I.D. DATA: Serial Number located: [Chassis models] On plate temporarily attached near steering column, with final location per body maker; [All others] On plate attached to rear face of left-hand door hinge pillar; on right side of cowl under hood. The first symbol indicated the series: D=1500; H=3100; J=3600; K=3700; L=3800; M=3900. The second symbol indicated the model year: 4=1954. The third symbol indicated the assembly plant: A=Atlanta, Ga.; B=Baltimore, Md.; F=Flint, Mich.; J=Janesville, Wis.; K=Kansas City, Mo.;

L=Los Angeles, Calif.;N=Norwood, Ohio; O=Oakland, Calif.;S=St. Louis, Mo.; T=Tarrytown, N.Y. Each series was separately numbered in sequence, starting with 001001 at each assembly plant. Serial numbers, by series, were as follows: [1500] D54-001001 to 174684; [3100] H54-001001 to 52112; [3600] J54-001001 to 52112; [3700] K54-001001 to 52112; [3800] L54-001001 to 52112 and [3900] M54-001001 to 52112. Engine numbers located: On right side of block near fuel pump; also stamped on crankcase near rear of distributor on right side of engine. Each engine carried a letter code for model year, type and engine plant, plus a production unit number. All numbers were numbered at each source in sequence starting with 1001. Engine numbers by series were: [1500] 01001Z54 to 1024930; [3100] 01001X54 to 1024930; [3600] 01001X54 to 1024930; [3700] 01001T54 to 1024930; [3800] 01001X54 to 1024930 and [3900] 01001T54 to 1024930. Engine numbers with X suffix indicated Thriftmaster 235 engine for 3100/3600/3800. Engine numbers with U suffix indicated Thriftmaster 235 with heavy-duty clutch for 3100/3600/3800. Engine numbers with M suffix indicated Thriftmaster 235 with Hydra-Matic for 3100/3600/3800. Engine numbers with T suffix indicated Loadmaster 235 for 3700/3900. Engine numbers with L suffix indicated Loadmaster 235 with Hydra-Matic for 3700/3900.

1954 Chevrolet Series One-Fifty Sedan Delivery (MVMA)

Model No.	Body Type	Price	Weight	Prod. Total
Sedan Delivery — Model D-54/Series 1500 — 115 in. w.b				
1508	Sedan Delivery	1632	3195	8255
1/2-Ton Commercial — Model H-54/Series 3100 — 116 in. w.b.				
3102	Chassis & Cowl	1087	2430	—
3103	Chassis & Cab	1346	2870	—
3104	Pickup	1419	3145	—
3105	Panel Delivery	1631	3375	—
3107	Canopy	1688	3325	—
3112	Chassis & W/S	1109	—	—
3106	Suburban (doors)	1958	3655	—
3116	Suburban (gate)	1958	3660	—
3/4-ton Commercial — Model J-54/Series 3600 — 125.25 in. w.b.				
3602	Chassis & Cowl	1227	2685	—
3603	Chassis & Cab	1486	3120	—
3604	Pickup	1582	3485	—
3608	Platform	1587	3540	—
3609	Stake	1654	3700	—
3612	Chassis & W/S	1249	—	—
3/4-Ton Dubl-Duti — Model K-54/Series 3700 — 125.25 in. w.b.				
3742	Chassis	1249	2460	—
1-Ton Commercial — Model L-54/Series 3800 — 137 in. w.b				
3802	Chassis & Cowl	1325	3015	—
3803	Chassis & Cab	1582	3435	—
3804	Pickup	1705	3880	—
3805	Panel Delivery	1929	4170	—
3807	Canopy	2012	4130	—
3808	Platform	1722	3950	—
3809	Stake	1794	4200	—
3812	Chassis & W/S	1347	—	—
1-Ton Dubl-Duti — Model M-54/Series 3900 — 137 in. w.b.				
3942	Chassis	1364	2700	—

1954 Chevrolet 1/2-Ton Series 3100 Panel Door Suburban (OCW)

ENGINE: [Sedan Delivery/Commercials] Inline. OHV. Six-cylinder. Cast iron block. Bore & stroke: 3-9/16 x 3-15/16 in. Displacement: 235.5 cid. Compression ratio: 6.7:1. Gross horsepower: 112 at 3700 rpm. Brake horsepower: 105 at 3600 rpm. SAE horsepower: 30.4. Four main bearings. Solid valve lifters. Carburetor: One-barrel model GM/Rochester B.

1954 Chevrolet 1-Ton Series 3800 Cantrell Station Wagon (G. Carson)

1954 CHASSIS: [Model 1500] Wheelbase: 116 in. Overall length: 195-1/2 in. Height: 67-1/8 in. Front tread: 62 in. Rear tread: 62 in. Tires: 6.70 x 16 in. Maximum GVW: 4,100 lbs.

CHASSIS: [Series 3100] Wheelbase: 116 in. Overall length: [Pickup] 191.31 in.; [Panel/Suburban] 195.31 in. Height: [Panel] 80.68 in.; [Suburban] 79.5 in. Tires: 6.00 x 16 six-ply.

CHASSIS: [Series 3600] Wheelbase: 125.25 in. Overall length: [Pickup] 200-3/16 in.; [Platform/Stake] 206 in. Tires: 15 in., six-ply.

CHASSIS: [Series 3800] Wheelbase: 137 in. Overall length: [Pickup] 221.5 in.; [Panel] 229.57 in.; [Platform/Stake] 224 in. Height: [Panel] 86.5 in. Tires: [front] 7.00 x 17 six-ply; [rear] eight-ply.

CHASSIS: [Series 3742] Wheelbase: 125.25 in. Overall length: 197-1/8 in. Front tread: 62 in. Rear tread: 62-3/8 in. Tires: 7.00 x 17 in.

CHASSIS: [Series 3942] Wheelbase: 137 in. Overall length: 221-7/8 in. Front tread: 61-3/8 in. Rear tread: 61-3/4 in. Tires: 7.50 x 17 eight-ply or 7.50 x 18 eight-ply (Dual Rear Wheels).

1954 Chevrolet 1-Ton Model 3802 16-Passenger School Bus

TECHNICAL: Manual, synchromesh transmission: [1500/3100/3600] 3F/1R column-mounted; [3800] [4F/1R] Floor-mounted gearshift. Single-disc, diaphragm spring clutch. [1500/3100] Semi-floating hypoid rear axle; [3600/3800] full-floating rear axle. Hydraulic, four-wheel brakes. Wheels: [1500/3100] One-piece drop center 16 in. wheels; [3600/3800] Multi-piece split rims. Standard rear axles: [1500] 4.11:1; [3100] 4.11:1; [3600] 4.57:1; 5.14:1 [3800] 5.14:1.

1954 Chevrolet 3/4-Ton Model 3742 Dubl-Duti Forward-Control (GC)

OPTIONS: Double-acting airplane type rear shock absorbers (All 3800). Double-acting rear cam-and-lever type shock absorbers (Model 3942). Long runningboards and rear fenders (Models 3602/3603/3612/3802/3803/3812). Rear axle, 5.14:1 ratio (Series 3600). Short left-hand rearview mirror bracket (All Chassis & Cab, except Model 3103). Short right-hand rearview mirror and bracket (All Chassis & Cabs, Pickups and single-unit body models). Long left-hand rearview mirror bracket (Models 3103/3104/3604/3804). Long right-hand rearview mirror and bracket (All cab models). Rear shock absorber shields (All, except Model 3942). Prop shaft brake (Models 3802/3812/3900). One-pint oil bath air cleaner (All). Two-pint oil bath air cleaner (All Series 3100/3600/3800). Positive crankcase ventilation system (All except Dubl-Duti). Heavy-duty clutch (All Series 3100/3600/3800). Platform body (model 3608). Eleven solid color combinations (All, except Dubl-Duti). Engine governor (All, except Dubl-Duti). Dual tail and stop lights (All

single-unit body models). Heavy-duty radiator (All, Series 3600/3800). Auxiliary seat (All Panels/Canopies). Unison seat (All cab models). Auxiliary rear springs (All 1-ton). Number 306 speedometer fittings (All Series 3600/3700/3800/3900). Number 307 speedometer fittings (All 3000). Automatic transmission (All). Heavy-duty three-speed transmission (All). Four-speed transmission (All Series 3100/3600/3700). Electric wipers (All Chassis & Cab/Pickup/Single-unit body models). 40-amp. generator (All). 45-amp. generator (All). 50-amp. generator (All). 55-amp. generator, normal and low cut-in (All except Dubl-Duti). Solenoid starter (Model 3802). Junior school bus chassis (Model 3802). Fuel and vacuum pump booster (All). Side-mounted wheel carrier (Models 3104/3604/3804). Channel type front bumper (Dubl-Duti). Spare wheel carrier (Dubl-Duti). Rear corner windows (All cab models). Deluxe equipment (Models 3106/3116). Chrome equipment (All, except Dubl-Duti). Left-hand door lock (All cab and single-unit body models). Tinted body glass (All cab and single-unit body models). Stake racks (All Platform models). Number 430 Deluxe equipment package (Models 3103/3104/3105/3603/3604/3608/3805). Number 431 Deluxe Equipment package (Models 3803/3804/3808). Number 438 two-tone color combinations (Models 3103/3104/3603/3604/3803/3804/3808). Number 439 two-tone color combinations (Models 3105/3805). Note: Option applications edited for 1/2- to 1-ton models only.

1954 Chevrolet Model 3742 Dubl-Duti 10-Ft. Forward-Control

Light Duty Truck Tire Options

Size	Ply Rating	Capacity (lb.)	PSI	Section (in.)
15 in.	Six	1500	40	7.74
15 in.	Eight	1700	48	7.74
6.00 x 16	Four	990	32	6.25
6.00 x 16	Six	1065	36	6.21
6.50 x 16	Six	1290	40	6.65
6.70 x 15	Six	n.a.	n.a.	n.a.
7.00 x 17	Six	1550	45	7.30
7.00 x 17	Eight	n.a.	n.a.	7.30
7.50 x 17	Eight	1725	55	7.36
7.50 x 17	Ten	n.a.	n.a.	7.36
7.00 x 18	Eight	1800	55	7.24

1954 Chevrolet 3/4-Ton Dubl-Duti 8-Ft. Forward-Control (GC)

OPTION PACKAGE: [RPO 430/RPO 431] Discontinued for several years due to a shortage of materials, the Deluxe Equipment option was again available in 1954. According to *CHEVROLET SERVICE NEWS* (November, 1953) it could be obtained in both cab and Panel models. A two-tone interior color combination of gray and maroon is used on all, except Panel models. Gray paint is applied on the instrument panel, garnish moldings, lower door panels, and cowl side kick-panels. The seats were trimmed in leather fabric with gray cushion and backrest and maroon facings. In addition to the two-tone interiors, the following equipment was in the option: right-hand sunshade; armrest on left-hand door; cigar lighter; dual horns; bright metal windshield and side door window reveal moldings (Panels also had rear window reveal moldings); rear corner windows on cab models; and front and rear fender moldings (bars) on Panels.

1954 Chevrolet 1-Ton Model 3802 Dubl-Duti Stand-Drive (GC)

1954 Chevrolet Series One-Fifty Sedan Delivery (OCW)

OPTIONS: [Dealer Accessories] Cowl mounted, rod type radio antenna (All). Brown armrest for left- or right-hand door (All cab or single-unit body models). Locking gas tank filler cap (All). 16 in. stainless steel hubcaps (3100 only). Radiator overflow condenser (All, except Dubl-Duti). Multi-color vertical stripe seat covers (All cab models). Rain deflectors (All). Gasoline filter (3100/3600/3800). Mud flaps (Platforms/Stakes). Guard for curved type bumper, painted or plated (Models 3100/3600). License plate frame (All). Outside air heater/defroster (All). Recirculating type heater/defroster (All). Second, high-note, horn (All). Tire static eliminator injector and powder for (All). Guide dual sealed-beam fog lamps (All). Unity spotlamp with bracket mount (All). Portable spotlamp (All with cigarette lighter). Glove compartment lamp (All). Universal, right-hand tail and stop lamp (All, except Dubl-Duti). Underhood lamp (All, except Dubl-Duti). Directional signals (All). Cigar/cigarette lighter (All). Rectangular floor mats, five colors (All). Door-mounted short-arm outside rearview mirror. (All) Five-inch round extendible arm outside rearview mirror. (All) Rectangular 5-1/2 x 7-1/2 in. extendible arm outside rearview mirror. (All) Non-glare outside rearview mirror with bracket mount (All). Hood ornament (All). Delco receiving set radio and antenna (All, except Chassis & Cowl). Reflex four-inch red reflector (All). AC/DC electric shaver (All with cigar lighter). Rear step unit (All Platform and Stake models). Right-hand sunshade (All-standard on Suburbans). Tool kit wit bag and tools (All). Outside mounted sun visor (All cab models). Foot-operated windshield wiper (All, except Dubl-Duti). Note: Option applications edited for 1/2- to 1-ton models only.

OPTIONS: [Authorized Aftermarket] A four-wheel drive (4x4) conversion by NAPCO Products, Co., of Minneapolis, Minn., was available for 1954 Chevrolet trucks. It was merchandised through Chevrolet dealers for approximately $1,200. NAPCO literature describes it as a "Powr-Pak" four-wheel drive system that shifted in and out of four-wheel drive without stopping or declutching. It featured a two-speed transfer case (eight forward speeds and two in reverse) and full-engine-torque power-take-off. NAPCO also promoted a Chevrolet "Mountain Goat" 4x4 pickup model. Also available from Cantrell Body Co. was a wood station wagon body for the Chevrolet 3600/3800 Commercial chassis.

1954 Chevrolet Series One-Fifty Sedan Delivery (JAW)

52

HISTORICAL: Introduced: December, 1953. Calendar year registrations: [All Commercials] 293,079. Calendar year production [All Chevrolet Commercials] 325,515. Light-duty calendar year production by GVW: [Below 5,000 lbs.] 170,824; [5,001 to 10,000 lbs.] 64,599. Work on a 74,000 sq.-ft. extension to the Chevrolet truck factory in Indianapolis got underway this year. Innovations included: Hydra-matic transmission. One-piece windshield. New front end styling for regular trucks.

1954 Chevrolet 1-Ton Series 3800 Panel (OCW)

1954 Chevrolet 1/2-Ton Series 3100 Pickup (MVMA)

1955 CHEVROLET
(FIRST SERIES)

1955 Chevrolet "First Series" 1-Ton Model 3808 Platform (OCW)

SEDAN DELIVERY — MODEL D/SERIES 1500 — SIX-CYLINDER: For 1955, General Motors planned the biggest revision of products it had ever attempted. At Chevrolet, all-new 1955 cars were introduced in the fall of 1954. However, the all-new trucks weren't quite ready at that time. Since the Sedan Delivery was based on the cars, it was completely changed in design. It had the all-new sheet metal of 1955 passenger cars with a slab-sided body and hooded headlamps. The front featured a narrpw upper horizontal molding, curved end moldings and a narrow lower molding all connected to completely surround the 1955 Chevrolet passenger car grille insert. The one-piece insert had 15 vertical members and seven horizontal members intersecting to form 135 small rectangular openings. The upper center rectangle was open at the top, while the others were bordered by a thin grille surround. The parking lamps were wedge-shaped and not part of the grille itself. They attached to openings in the fenders. A body-color filler panel and right- and left-hand fender

extensions completed the ensemble. The new Sedan Delivery was more directly based on a new two-door Handyman station wagon. The doors were the same as this model and the two-door sedan. Front door glass was the same as the two-door sedan. Both the rear compartment floor and the rear quarter panel sections were slightly unique to the Sedan Delivery. There was a new liftgate at the rear, instead of a panel door. This model was again in the One-Fifty series with code 55-1271 on the Fisher Body tag under the hood. Other new features included a wraparound windshield; ball joint suspension; a V-8 engine option; and Powerglide automatic transmission. Standard equipment included front and rear bumpers and bumper guards; front license guard; hood ornament and emblem; chrome plated headlamp rims with doors; dual windshield wipers; dual horns; outside key lock; front and rear bumper gravel deflectors; one combination tail/stop/license plate lamp; chrome-plated radio grille; three-position ignition switch; left-hand sunshade; and dome light. Onyx black remained the standard body color for 1954 Sedan Deliveries. Options India ivory; Sea Mist green; Glacier blue; Shadow gray; Neptune green; Skyline blue; and Gypsy red. The interior was trimmed with straw brown imitation leather, combination number 501.

1/2-TON COMMERCIAL — MODEL D/SERIES 3100 — SIX-CYLINDER: The all-new trucks were supposed to be introduced along with the new passenger car line, but due to the size of GM's massive plan, Korean War contracts and sales pressure from Ford, truck line development was delayed. When the totally new Sedan Delivery was introduced on Oct. 28, 1954, the Commercial models changed only very slightly from 1954 specifications. These "First Series 1955" trucks were available until March 25, 1955. Features again included a one-piece windshield and open radiator grille with cross-bars and rectangular parking lamps. All outer radiator grille bars were now done in Bombay ivory and the inner bars were Onyx black. The front hood ornament was the same as 1954, but striped with Bombay ivory instead of Vermillion red. The word Chevrolet was still stamped on the grille header bar, but the lettering color was changed to Onyx black. Bumpers were Bombay ivory on all trucks, except those painted Pure white, which had Pure white bumpers. There was a completely new winged hoodside nameplate that said 3100 on the upper end and Chevrolet below. The background was painted black. The dashboard with defroster openings that extended the full width of the windshield and instruments grouped in two clusters was continued. So were the glove compartment, restyled ashtray; steering wheel; grain-tight load box/tailgate; and round taillights. When the optional rear bumper was ordered, the license plate was again mounted in the center of the box under the tailgate. An important technical change for 3100s was an open Hotchkiss driveshaft replacing the old torque tube type. Hydra-Matic transmission was optional again. Chrome fender bars remained available as Deluxe equipment on Panel trucks only. Body colors stayed the same, except for the two-toning color. Juniper green body finish with cream medium striping and black wheels was standard finish for all models. Twelve other colors were optional at no extra cost. They included (pinstripe color in parenthesis): Commercial red (Argent silver); Jet black (Argent silver); Mariner blue (Cream medium); Cream medium (Jet black); Yukon yellow (Jet black); Ocean green (Jet black); Transport blue (Cream medium); Copper Tone copper (Shell white); Omaha orange (Jet black); Autumn brown (Shell white); and Pure white (Juniper green). Standard wheels were black. On Deluxe monotone and two-tone trucks, the wheels were the color on the lower body. On two-tone trucks, Bombay ivory was now used exclusively as the upper body color and the beltline was usually striped with the lower body color. Exceptions included trucks with the lower body done in Pure white; cream medium or Omaha orange, in which cases the striping was Jet black or Onyx black. Deluxe Cab models featured two-tone interior trim that harmonized with the exterior color; stainless steel windshield and side window reveals; chrome-plated ventipane frames; right-hand sunshade; left-hand armrest; cigar lighter; twin-tone horns; and cab rear corner windows. The two-tone interior colors were Light green and Juniper green; Light blue and Dark blue; Birch white and brown; and Pearl beige and maroon. This interior included a color-coordinated cloth seat; a color-coordinated rubber floor mat; color-coordinated windlacing; and special colored plastic armrests. The option also included wheels and runningboards painted lower body color, with triple striping on the wheels.

1955 Chevrolet "First Series" One-Fifty Sedan Delivery (DFW)

3/4-TON LIGHT-DUTY COMMERCIAL — MODEL J/SERIES 3600 — SIX-CYLINDER: The 3/4-ton trucks had the same Advance-Design styling, features and finish as other conventional trucks. New features included improved drivelines and universal joints. Eight-leaf front springs were standard. The 3600s had a longer wheelbase than 1/2-tons. The new grain-tight load box was longer than the 1/2-ton type and had six stake pockets. Running-boards measuring 75-3/4 in. long were used. When a side-mounted spare tire carrier was used, dimpled rear fenders were not required. No Suburban was offered in this line. There were Platform and Stake models. Hubcaps were also painted on 3600s. The standard wheels were of different eight-bolt design. The standard eight-bolt design. A similar curved-type chrome front bumper was standard on all models. A similar rear bumper was optional on incomplete bodies and flat bed combinations. A foot-operated parking brake was used on all 3600 models. The brakes were Bendix's duo-servo self-energizing type. The standard tires on 3600s were 15 in. six-ply rated on 15 x 5.50 semi-drop-center rims. Three-quarter-ton trucks used roller type front wheel bearings.

3/4-TON DUBL-DUTI — MODEL K/SERIES 3700 — SIX-CYLINDER: Two Dubl-Duti Forward-Control chassis were in the Chevrolet truck line. Both had the 235 cid Loadmaster six with updraft carburetor. Model 3742 was the 3/4-ton version on a 125.25 in. wheelbase. Standard walk-in delivery truck bodies could be supplied by several factory-approved sources or the buyer could add his/her own truck body. The wheels were of eight-bolt design. A painted, Anvil gray channel type front bumper was standard on the 3700 Dubl-Duti truck chassis.

1-TON MEDIUM-DUTY COMMERCIAL — MODEL L/SERIES 3800 — SIX-CYLINDER: The 3800 Series had the same Advance-Design styling, features and finish as other conventional trucks. New features included improved drivelines and universal joints. A foot-operated parking brake was used on all 3800 models. Huck type rear brakes were still used. These models were available with an optional power brake system. This Hydrovac brake

booster reduced pedal effort by two-thirds. Panel and Canopy models had a one-piece floor made of 3/4-inch thick, five-ply laminated wood. The basic model lineup was unchanged. It included single and dual rear wheel options for all except the Express, Canopy and Panel. The Express had a longer wheelbase than the 3600 Pickup, a longer grain-tight load box with eight stake pockets, and very long runningboards. When a side-mounted spare tire carrier was used, dimpled rear fenders were not required. A curved-type painted front bumper was standard on all models. A similar rear bumper was standard on Models 3805 and 3807. Regular equipment tires were 7.00 x 17 six-ply rated for trucks with single rear wheels or 7.00 x 18 eight-ply rated for trucks with dual rear wheel options. The hubcaps were painted. No hubcaps were used on the 18 x 5 in. wheels of the Chassis & Cab, Platform and Stake models, which had eight bolts and eight circular openings. A four-speed manual synchromesh transmission was standard. Trucks with this transmission had a black rubber floor mat made especially for use with the floor-mounted four-speed gearshifter.

1-TON DUBL-DUTI — MODEL M/SERIES 3900 — SIX-CYLINDER: Two Dubl-Duti Forward-Control chassis returned to the Chevrolet truck line. Both had the 235 cid Loadmaster six with updraft carburetor. Due to the lower efficiency of the updraft carburetor, this engine had the same horsepower rating as the 216 cid Thriftmaster six. Model 3942 was the 1-ton version on a 137 in. wheelbase. Standard walk-in delivery truck bodies could be supplied by several factory-approved sources or the buyer could add his/her own truck body. A painted, Anvil gray channel type front bumper was standard on the 3900 Dubl-Duti truck chassis.

I.D. DATA: Serial Number located: [Chassis models] On plate temporarily attached near steering column, with final location per body maker; [All others] On plate attached to rear face of left-hand door hinge pillar; on right side of cowl under hood. The first symbol indicated the series: D=1500; H=3100; J=3600; K=3700; L=3800; M=3900. The second symbol indicated the model year: 4=1954. The third symbol indicated the assembly plant: A=Atlanta, Ga.; B=Baltimore, Md.; F=Flint, Mich.; J=Janesville, Wis.; K=Kansas City, Mo.; L=Los Angeles, Calif.;N=Norwood, Ohio; O=Oakland, Calif.;S=St. Louis, Mo.; T=Tarrytown, N.Y. Each series was separately numbered in sequence, starting with 000001 at each assembly plant. Serial numbers for the 1955 First Series were a continuation of 1954 numbers. by series, were as follows: [1500] D55-001001 to 0017016; [3100] H55-001001 to 0017016; [3600] J55-001001 to 0017016; [3742] K55-001001 to 0017016; [3800] L53-001001 to 0017016 and [3942] M53-001001 to 0017016. Engine numbers: On right side of block near fuel pump; also stamped on crankcase near rear of distributor on right side of engine. Each engine carried a letter code for model year, type and engine plant, plus a production unit number. All numbers were numbered at each source in sequence starting with 1001. Engine numbers located: On right side of block near fuel pump; also stamped on crankcase near rear of distributor on right side of engine. Each engine carried a letter code for model year, type and engine plant, plus a production unit number. All numbers were numbered at each source in sequence starting with 1001. Engine numbers by series were: [1500] 01001Z55 up; [3100/3600/3800] 01001X55 up; [3700/3900] 01001T55 up. Engine numbers with X suffix indicated Thriftmaster 235 engine for 3100/3600/3800. Engine numbers with U suffix indicated Thriftmaster 235 with heavy-duty clutch for 3100/3600/3800. Engine numbers with M suffix indicated Thriftmaster 235 with Hydra-Matic for 3100/3600/3800. Engine numbers with T suffix indicated Loadmaster 235 for 3700/3900. Engine numbers with L suffix indicated Loadmaster 235 with Hydra-Matic for 3700/3900.

1955 Chevrolet First Series 1/2-Ton Model 3104 Pickup (G. Carson)

Model No.	Body Type	Price	Weight	Prod. Total
Sedan Delivery — Model D-54/Series 1500 — 115 in. w.b				
1508	Sedan Delivery	1699	3110	8255
1/2-Ton Commercial — Model H-54/Series 3100 — 116 in. w.b.				
3102	Chassis & Cowl	1098	2455	—
3103	Chassis & Cab	1357	2845	—
3104	Pickup	1430	3125	—
3105	Panel	1642	3340	—
3107	Canopy	1699	3300	—
3112	Chassis & W/S	1120	2550	—
3106	Suburban (doors)	1968	3630	—
3116	Suburban (gate)	1968	3630	—
3/4-ton Commercial — Model J-54/Series 3600 — 125.25 in. w.b.				
3602	Chassis & Cowl	1238	2685	—
3603	Chassis & Cab	1497	3135	—
3604	Pickup	1593	3525	—
3608	Platform	1598	3550	—
3609	Stake	1665	3725	—
3612	Chassis & W/S	1260	2780	—
3/4-Ton Dubl-Duti — Model K-54/Series 3700 — 125.25 in. w.b.				
3742	Chassis	1260	2465	—
1-Ton Commercial — Model L-54/Series 3800 — 137 in. w.b				
3802	Chassis & Cowl	1336	3005	—
3803	Chassis & Cab	1593	3435	—
3804	Pickup	1716	3865	—
3805	Panel Delivery	1940	4170	—
3807	Canopy	2023	4105	—
3808	Platform	1733	3990	—
3809	Stake	1805	4255	—
3812	Chassis & W/S	1358	3100	—
1-Ton Dubl-Duti — Model M-54/Series 3900 — 137 in. w.b.				
3942	Chassis	1375	2725	—

ENGINE: [Sedan Delivery/Commercials] Inline. OHV. Six-cylinder. Cast iron block. Bore & stroke: 3-9/16 x 3-15/16 in. Displacement: 235.5 cid. Compression ratio: 6.7:1. Gross horsepower: 112 at 3700 rpm. Brake horsepower: 105 at 3600 rpm. SAE horsepower: 30.4. Four main bearings. Solid valve lifters. Carburetor: One-barrel model GM/Rochester B.

ENGINE: [Dubl-Duti] The Loadmaster 235 used in 3700/3900 series model had a Gross Horsepower rating of 110 at 3600 rpm and a Net horsepower rating of 102 at 3600 rpm.

CHASSIS: [Model 1500] Wheelbase: 116 in. Overall length: 195-1/2 in. Height: 67-1/8 in. Front tread: 62 in. Rear tread: 62 in. Tires: 6.70 x 16 in. Maximum GVW: 4,100 lbs.

CHASSIS: [Series 3100] Wheelbase: 116 in. Overall length: [Pickup] 191.31 in.; [Panel/Suburban] 195.31 in. Height: [Panel] 80.68 in.; [Suburban] 79.5 in. Tires: 6.00 x 16 six-ply.

CHASSIS: [Series 3600] Wheelbase: 125.25 in. Overall length: [Pickup] 200-3/16 in.; [Platform/Stake] 206 in. Tires: 15 in., six-ply.

CHASSIS: [Series 3800] Wheelbase: 137 in. Overall length: [Pickup] 221.5 in.; [Panel] 229.57 in.; [Platform/Stake] 224 in. Height: [Panel] 86.5 in. Tires: [Front] 7.00 x 17 six-ply; [Rear] eight-ply.

CHASSIS: [Series 3742] Wheelbase: 125.25 in. Overall length: 197-1/8 in. Front tread: 62 in. Rear tread: 62-3/8 in. Tires: 7.00 x 17 in.

CHASSIS: [Series 3942] Wheelbase: 137 in. Overall length: 221-7/8 in. Front tread: 61-3/8 in. Rear tread: 61-3/4 in. Tires: 7.50 x 17 eight-ply or 7.50 x 18 eight-ply (Dual Rear Wheels).

TECHNICAL: Manual, synchromesh transmission: [1500/3100/3600] 3F/1R column-mounted; [3800] [4F/1R] Floor-mounted gearshift. Single-disc, diaphragm spring clutch. [1500/3100] Semi-floating hypoid rear axle; [3600/3800] full-floating rear axle. Hydraulic, four-wheel brakes. Wheels: [1500/3100] One-piece drop center 16 in. wheels; [3600/3800] Multi-piece split rims. Standard rear axles: [1500] 4.11:1; [3100] 4.11:1; [3600] 4.57:1; 5.14:1 [3800] 5.14:1.

OPTIONS: Double-acting airplane type rear shock absorbers (All 3800). Double-acting rear cam-and-lever type shock absorbers (Model 3942). Long runningboards and rear fenders (Models 3602/3603/3612/3802/3803/3812). Rear axle, 5.14:1 ratio (Series 3600). Short left-hand rearview mirror bracket (All Chassis & Cab, except Model 3103). Short right-hand rearview mirror and bracket (All Chassis & Cabs, Pickups and single-unit body models). Long left-hand rearview mirror bracket (Models 3103/3104/3604/3804). Long right-hand rearview mirror and bracket (All cab models). Rear shock absorber shields (All, except Model 3942). Prop shaft brake (Models 3802/3812/3900). One-pint oil bath air cleaner (All). Two-pint oil bath air cleaner (All Series 3100/3600/3800). Positive crankcase ventilation system (All except Dubl-Duti). Heavy-duty clutch (All Series 3100/3600/3800). Platform body (model 3608). Eleven solid color combinations (All, except Dubl-Duti). Oil filter (All, except Dubl-Duti). Engine governor (All, except Dubl-Duti). Dual tail and stop lights (All single-unit body models). Heavy-duty radiator (All, Series 3600/3800). Auxiliary seat (All Panels/Canopies). Unison seat (All cab models). Auxiliary rear springs (All 1-ton). Number 306 speedometer fittings (All Series 3600/3700/3800/3900). Number 307 speedometer fittings (All 3000). Automatic transmission (All). Heavy-duty three-speed transmission (All). Four-speed transmission (All Series 3100/3600/3700). Electric wipers (All Chassis & Cab/Pickup/Single-unit body models). 40-amp. generator (All). 45-amp. generator (All). 50-amp. generator (All). 55-amp. generator, normal and low cut-in (All except Dubl-Duti). Solenoid starter (Model 3802). Junior school bus chassis (Model 3802). Fuel and vacuum pump booster (All). Side-mounted wheel carrier (Models 3104/3604/3804). Channel type front bumper (Dubl-Duti). Spare wheel carrier (Dubl-Duti). Rear corner windows (All cab models). Deluxe equipment (Models 3106/3116). Chrome equipment (All, except Dubl-Duti). Left-hand door lock (All cab and single-unit body models). Tinted body glass (All cab and single-unit body models). Stake racks (All Platform models). Number 430 Deluxe equipment package (Models 3103/3104/3105/3603/3604/3608/3805). Number 431 Deluxe Equipment package (Models 3803/3804/3808). Number 438 two-tone color combinations (Models 3103/3104/3603/3604/3803/3804/3808). Number 439 two-tone color combinations (Models 3105/3805). Note: Option applications edited for 1/2- to 1-ton models only.

Light Duty Truck Tire Options

Size	Ply Rating	Capacity (lb.)	PSI	Section (in.)
15 in.	Six	1500	40	7.74
15 in.	Eight	1700	48	7.74
6.00 x 16	Four	990	32	6.25
6.00 x 16	Six	1065	36	6.21
6.50 x 16	Six	1290	40	6.65
6.70 x 15	Six	n.a.	n.a.	n.a.
7.00 x 17	Six	1550	45	7.30
7.00 x 17	Eight	n.a.	n.a.	7.30
7.50 x 17	Eight	1725	55	7.36
7.50 x 17	Ten	n.a.	n.a.	7.36
7.00 x 18	Eight	1800	55	7.24

OPTION PACKAGE: [RPO 430/RPO 431] Discontinued for several years due to a shortage of materials, the Deluxe Equipment option was made available in 1954 and continued in 1955. According to *CHEVROLET SERVICE NEWS* (November, 1953) it could be obtained in both cab and Panel models. A two-tone interior color combination of gray and maroon is used on all, except Panel models. Gray paint is applied on the instrument panel, garnish moldings, lower door panels, and cowl side kick-panels. The seats were trimmed in leather fabric with gray cushion and backrest and maroon facings. In addition to the two-tone interiors, the following equipment was in the option: right-hand sunshade; armrest on left-hand door; cigar lighter; dual horns; bright metal windshield and side door window reveal moldings (Panels also had rear window reveal moldings); rear corner windows on cab models; and front and rear fender moldings (bars) on Panels.

OPTIONS: [Dealer Accessories] Cowl mounted, rod type radio antenna (All). Brown armrest for left- or right-hand door (All cab or single-unit body models). Locking gas tank filler cap (All). 16 in. stainless steel hubcaps (3100 only). Radiator overflow condenser (All, except Dubl-Duti). Multi-color vertical stripe seat covers (All cab models). Rain deflectors (All). Gasoline filter (3100/3600/3800). Mud flaps (Platforms/Stakes). Guard for curved type bumper, painted or plated (Models 3100/3600). License plate frame (All). Outside air heater/defroster (All). Recirculating type heater/defroster (All). Second, high-note, horn (All). Tire static eliminator injector and powder for (All). Guide dual sealed-beam fog lamps (All). Unity spotlamp with bracket mount (All). Portable spotlamp (All with cigar lighter). Glove compartment lamp (All). Universal, right-hand tail and stop lamp (All, except Dubl-Duti).

Underhood lamp (All, except Dubl-Duti). Directional signals (All). Cigar/cigarette lighter (All). Rectangular floor mats, five colors (All). Door-mounted short-arm outside rearview mirror. (All) Five-inch round extendible arm outside rearview mirror. (All) Rectangular 5-1/2 x 7-1/2 in. extendible arm outside rearview mirror. (All) Non-glare outside rearview mirror with bracket mount (All). Delco receiving set radio and antenna (All, except Chassis & Cowl). Reflex four-inch red reflector (All). AC/DC electric shaver (All with cigar lighter). Rear step unit (All Platform and Stake models). Right-hand sunshade (All-standard on Suburbans). Tool kit with bag and tools (All). Outside mounted sun visor (All cab models). Foot-operated windshield wiper (All, except Dubl-Duti). Note: Option applications edited for 1/2- to 1-ton models only.

OPTIONS: [Authorized Aftermarket] A four-wheel drive (4x4) conversion by NAPCO Products, Co., of Minneapolis, Minn., was available for 1955 Chevrolet trucks. It was merchandised through Chevrolet dealers for approximately $1,200. NAPCO literature describes it as a "Powr-Pak" four-wheel drive system that shifted in and out of four-wheel drive without stopping or declutching. It featured a two-speed transfer case (eight forward speeds and two in reverse) and full-engine-torque power-take-off. NAPCO also promoted a Chevrolet "Mountain Goat" 4x4 pickup model. Also available from Cantrell Body Co. was a wood station wagon body for the Chevrolet 3600/3800 Commercial chassis.

HISTORICAL: Introduced: Oct. 28, 1954. Produced through March 25, 1955, when all-new 1955 Second Series appeared. Calendar year registrations and production are included with 1954 or 1955 Second Series models. The change to open driveshaft is important for enthusiasts making non-original engine swaps in these trucks.

1955 CHEVROLET (SECOND SERIES)

SEDAN DELIVERY — MODEL D/SERIES 1500 — SIX/V-8: Chevrolet's "Second Series" 1955 trucks were introduced on March 25, 1955. The Sedan Delivery was unchanged in appearance from the 1955 "First Series." The front featured a narrow upper horizontal molding, curved end moldings and a narrow lower molding all connected to completely surround the 1955 Chevrolet passenger car grille insert. The one-piece insert had 15 vertical members and seven horizontal members intersecting to form 135 small rectangular openings. The upper center rectangle was open at the top, while the others were bordered by a thin grille surround. The parking lamps were wedge-shaped and not part of the grille itself. They attached to openings in the fenders. A body-color filler panel and right- and left-hand fender extensions completed the ensemble. The new Sedan Delivery was more directly based on a new two-door Handyman station wagon. The doors were the same as this model and the two-door sedan. Front door glass was the same as the two-door sedan. Both the rear compartment floor and the rear quarter panel sections were slightly unique to the Sedan Delivery. There was a new liftgate at the rear, instead of a panel door. This model was again in the One-Fifty series with code 55-1271 on the Fisher Body tag under the hood. Other new features included a wraparound windshield; ball joint suspension; a V-8 engine option; and Powerglide automatic transmission. Standard equipment included front and rear bumpers and bumper guards; front license guard; hood ornament and emblem; chrome plated headlamp rims with doors; dual windshield wipers; dual horns; outside key locks; front and rear bumper gravel deflectors; one combination tail/stop/license plate lamp; chrome-plated radio grille; three-position ignition switch; left-hand sunshade; and dome light. Onyx black remained the standard body color for 1955 Sedan Deliveries. Options included India ivory; Sea Mist green; Glacier blue; Shadow gray; Neptune green; Skyline blue; and Gypsy red. The interior was trimmed with straw brown imitation leather, combination number 501.

1955 Chevrolet 1/2-Ton Model 3124 Cameo Carrier

1/2-TON COMMERCIAL — MODEL H/SERIES 3100 — SIX/V-8: Chevrolet's new "Task Force" styling was characterized by lower, flatter hood and fenderlines and rooflines. There was a Panoramic wraparound windshield and an eggcrate grille. The cabs and bodies were slab-sided. The standard Pickup still had short runningboards and protruding rear fenders. A larger, winged Chevrolet emblem decorated the hood. The front fendersides had spear-shaped nameplates with Chevrolet lettering and the series designation. They were mounted behind and above the wheel openings. On trucks with the engine option, V-8 emblems were placed on the fendersides, just below the nameplates. Interiors were trimmed with oakbark woven plastic and breathable rayon fabric in black or beige (all models) or brown and beige (cab models only). Floor mats were black rubber. Trucks with Custom Cab equipment had upgraded trims with foam padding; chrome dash knobs; cigar lighter; dual armrests and sunshades; and extra chrome trim. This was available with either the standard 10-11/16 x 35-1/8 in. rear window or the optional Panoramic rear window that wrapped around the rear cab corners. Technical changes included a new Thriftmaster six; optional V-8; shorter wheelbases; longer leaf springs; 12-volt electrics and tubeless tires on 1/2-ton (3100) models. For the second series trucks there were 13 solid and 13 two-tone color combinations. Solid colors (wheel stripe color in parenthesis) were: Juniper green (Bombay ivory); Commercial red (Argent silver); Sand beige (Bombay ivory); Jet black (Bombay ivory); Omaha orange (Bombay ivory); Granite gray (Bombay ivory); Empire blue (Bombay ivory); Cream medium (Bombay ivory);

Yukon yellow (Bombay ivory); Ocean green (Bombay ivory); Crystal blue (Bombay ivory); Russet brown (Bombay ivory); Pure white. Two-tone color combinations came with the following lower body colors and Bombay ivory upper body: Juniper green; Commercial red; Jet black; Empire blue; Cream medium; Yukon yellow; Ocean green; Crystal blue; Granite gray; Sand beige; and Omaha orange. Wheel stripe colors were the same as with solid colors. Other choices were Sand beige on top, Russet brown on bottom (Bombay ivory wheel stripe) or Commercial red upper over Bombay ivory lower body (Commercial red wheel stripe). Wheels were painted lower body color on all 3000 Series trucks. Deluxe equipment and two-tone options were no longer available for Suburbans. Only 15 x 5K or 16 x 5K wheels had pinstripes.

1955 Chevrolet 1/2-Ton Series 3100 Pickup (DFW)

1955 Chevrolet 1/2-Ton Model 3124 Cameo Carrier

1/2-TON COMMERCIAL (CAMEO) — Model H/Series 3100 — SIX/V-8: A new 1/2-ton model was the Suburban pickup, a limited-production, highly stylized 1/2-ton (Body Style No. 3124) based on the 3000 Series chassis with a 114 in. wheelbase. Special features included slab-sided rear fender skins made of fiberglass bolted onto a standard cargo box to bring the rear body width flush with the sides of the standard cab. Chrome moldings trimmed the gap between the cab and the box. A fiberglass tailgate panel over the steel tailgate hid the hinges, latches and restraining chains. A hidden compartment below the endgate held the spare tire in a fiberglass. It was accessible via a swing-down hinged rear bumper section. Unique taillights and a Chevrolet bow tie in the center of the tailgate were seen. Standard equipment included Deluxe Cab equipment and the Panoramic rear window. Cameos came finished in Bombay ivory with Commercial red accents around the side and rear windows. The inside of the cargo box was also done in red. The interior featured exclusive red and beige upholstery similar to that of a 1954 Bel Air. A red floor mat was used. A special red steering wheel had three spokes (the top two wider) and a flat horn button trimmed in black. Full wheelcovers from the 1955 Bel Air were used on ivory colored rims. Cameo Carriers had stripes on 16 x 5K wheels only.

1955 Chevrolet 1/2-Ton Series 3100 Panel (DFW)

1/2-TON COMMERCIAL — MODEL M/SERIES 3200 — SIX/V-8: This was a new long wheelbase (LWB) 1/2-ton truck on the same chassis as 3/4-ton models. It had a longer cargo box with longer runningboards and more space between the cab and rear fenders. It had the same 5,000 lbs. GVW rating as other 1/2-ton trucks.

1/2-TON DUBL-DUTI — MODEL F/SERIES 3400 — SIX/V-8: Three Dubl-Duti Forward-Control chassis were in the late-1955 Chevrolet truck line. A new model was the 1/2-ton Model 3442 a 104 in. wheelbase. Standard walk-in delivery truck bodies could be supplied by several factory-approved sources or the buyer could add his/her own truck body.

3/4-TON COMMERCIAL — MODEL J/SERIES 3600 — SIX/V-8: This series included the medium-duty cab models on a 123.5 in. wheelbase. The pickup had longer runningboards and a longer cargo box. There were also Platform and Stake models. The GVW rating was 6,900 lbs.

3/4-TON DUBL-DUTI — MODEL G/SERIES 3500 — SIX-CYLINDER: Model 3542 was the 3/4-ton Dubl-Duti on a 125 in. wheelbase. Standard walk-in delivery truck bodies could be supplied by several factory-approved sources or the buyer could add his/her own truck body. The wheels were of eight-bolt design. A painted, Anvil gray channel type front bumper was standard on the 3500 Dubl-Duti truck chassis.

3/4-TON — DUBL-DUTI — MODEL K/SERIES 3700 — SIX-CYLINDER: Model 3742 was the 3/4-ton Dubl-Duti on a 137 in. wheelbase. Standard walk-in delivery truck bodies could be supplied by several factory-approved sources or the buyer could add his/her own truck body. The wheels were of eight-bolt design. A painted, Anvil gray channel type front bumper was standard on the 3700 Dubl-Duti truck chassis.

1-TON MEDIUM-DUTY COMMERCIAL — MODEL L/SERIES 3800 — SIX-CYLINDER: The 3800 Series had the same Task-Force styling as other conventional trucks. These models were available with an optional power brake system. This Hydrovac brake booster reduced pedal effort by two-thirds. Panel models had a one-piece floor made of 3/4-inch thick, five-ply laminated wood. The basic model lineup was unchanged. The 1-ton Pickup had a longer wheelbase than the 3600 Pickup, a longer grain-tight load box with extra stake pockets, and very long runningboards. No hubcaps were used on the larger split-rim wheels of the Chassis & Cab, Platform and Stake models, which had eight bolts and eight circular openings. A four-speed manual synchromesh transmission was standard.

1955 Chevrolet 1/2-Ton Series 3100 Panel (DFW)

I.D. DATA: Serial Number located: [Chassis models] On plate temporarily attached near steering column, with final location per body maker; [All others] On plate attached to rear face of left-hand door hinge pillar; on right side of cowl under hood. The first symbol indicated the series: D=1500; H=3100; M=3200; F=3400; G=3500; J=3600; K=3700; L=3800. The second symbol was a 2 to indicate 1955 "Second Series." The third and fourth symbols indicated the model year: 55=1955. The fifth symbol indicated the assembly plant: A=Atlanta, Ga.; B=Baltimore, Md.; F=Flint, Mich.; J=Janesville, Wis.; K=Kansas City, Mo.; L=Los Angeles, Calif.; N=Norwood, Ohio; O=Oakland, Calif.; S=St. Louis, Mo.; T=Tarrytown, N.Y. Each series was separately numbered in sequence, starting with 000001 at each assembly plant. Serial numbers for 1955 second series trucks were as follows: [1500] D255-001001 to 256218; [3100] H255-001001 to 60351; [3200] M255-001001 to 60351; [3400] F255-001001 to 60351; [3500] G255-001001 to 60351; [3700] K255-001001 to 60351; [3600] J255-001001-60351 and [3800] L255-001001 to 60351. Engine numbers located on right side of engine on boss at rear of distributor. Engine numbers began with an F (Flint, Mich.) or T (Tonawanda, N.Y.) assembly plant code. On Sedan Deliveries, second symbol Z or Y indicated 235 cid six; G or F indicated 265 cid V-8. On Commercials, second symbol X, S, or M indicated 235 cid six; E indicated 265 V-8 (when available). Sequential production numbers for base 1955 engines were: [1500] 01001Z55 to 0905907; [3100] 01001X55 to 0905907; [3200] 01001X55 to 0905907; [3400/3500/3700] 01001T55 to 0905907; [3600/3800] 01001X55 to 0905907. Transmission codes: M=Muncie three-speed or overdrive transmission; S=Saginaw three-speed or overdrive transmission; W=Borg-Warner heavy-duty three-speed transmission.

Model No.	Body Type	Price	Weight	Prod. Total
Sedan Delivery — Model D255/Series 1500 — 115 in. w.b.				
1508	Sedan Delivery	1699	3110	8811
1/2-Ton Commercial — Model H255/Series 3100 — 114 in. w.b.				
3102	Chassis & Cowl	1156	2335	—
3103	Chassis & Cab	1423	2850	—
3104	Pickup	1519	3210	—
3105	Panel	1801	3440	—
3106	Suburban (doors)	2150	3715	—
3112	Chassis & W/S	1193	2460	—
3116	Suburban (gate)	2150	3725	—
1/2-Ton Commercial (Cameo) — Model H255/Series 3100 — 114 in. w.b.				
3124	Suburban Pickup	1981	3355	5220
1/2-Ton Commercial — Model M255/Series 3200 — 123.25 in. w.b.				
3204	Pickup LWB	1540	3305	—
1/2-Ton Dubl-Duti — Model F255/Series 3400 — 104 in. w.b.				
3442	Chassis	1279	2600	—
3/4-Ton Dubl-Duti — Model G255/Series 3500 — 125 in. w.b.				
3542	Chassis	1317	2720	—
3/4-Ton Dubl-Duti — Model K255/Series 3700 — 137 in. w.b.				
3742	Chassis	1350	2730	—

3/4-Ton Commercial — Model J255/Series 3600 — 123.25				
3602	Chassis & Cowl	1316	2730	—
3603	Chassis & Cab	1583	3205	—
3604	Pickup	1690	3625	—
3608	Platform	1711	3630	—
3609	Stake	1780	3815	—
3612	Chassis & W/S	1353	2815	—
1-Ton Commercial — Model L255/Series 3800 — 135 in. w.b.				
3802	Chassis & Cowl	1444	3050	—
3803	Chassis & Cab	1711	3535	—
3804	Pickup	1844	3985	—
3805	Panel	2135	4300	—
3808	Platform	1859	4075	—
3809	Stake	1944	4360	—
3812	Chassis & W/S	1481	3130	—

ENGINE: [1508/3100/3200/3600/3800] Inline. OHV. Six-cylinder. Cast iron block. Bore & stroke: 3-9/16 x 3-15/16 in. Displacement: 235.5 cid. Compression ratio: 7.5:1. Gross horsepower: 123 at 3800 rpm. Net horsepower: 109 at 3600 rpm. SAE horsepower: 30.4. Four main bearings. Solid valve lifters. Carburetor: Single-barrel downdraft. Model: Rochester B-7004468.

ENGINE: [1508 with Powerglide] Inline. OHV. Six-cylinder. Cast iron block. Bore & stroke: 3-9/16 x 3-15/16 in. Displacement: 235.5 cid. Compression ratio: 7.5:1. Gross horsepower: 136. SAE horsepower: 30.4. Four main bearings. Solid valve lifters. Carburetor: Single-barrel downdraft Rochester model B.

ENGINE: [3400/3500/3700 only] Inline. OHV. Six-cylinder. Cast iron block. Bore & stroke: 3-9/16 x 3-15/16 in. Displacement: 235.5 cid. Compression ratio: 7.5:1. Gross horsepower: 119 at 3600 rpm. Net horsepower: 105 at 3600 rpm. SAE horsepower: 30.4. Four main bearings. Solid valve lifters. Carburetor: Single-barrel downdraft Rochester model B.

1955 Chevrolet Series One-Fifty Sedan Delivery (D. Batten)

ENGINE: [Optional 3100/3200/3600/3800] Vee-block. OHV. Eight-cylinders. Cast iron block. Bore & stroke: 3-3/4 x 3 in. Displacement: 265 cid. Compression ratio: 7.5:1. Gross horsepower: 154 at 4000 rpm. Net horsepower: 126 at 4000 rpm. Five main bearings. Solid valve lifters. Carburetor: Two-barrel downdraft Rochester model 7008006.

ENGINE: [Optional 3100/3200/3600/3800] Vee-block. OHV. Eight-cylinders. Cast iron block. Bore & stroke: 3-3/4 x 3 in. Displacement: 265 cid. Compression ratio: 8.0:1. Gross horsepower: 162 at 4200 rpm. Five main bearings. Solid valve lifters. Carburetor: Two-barrel.

ENGINE: [Optional 3100/3200/3600/3800] Vee-block. OHV. Eight-cylinders. Cast iron block. Bore & stroke: 3-3/4 x 3 in. Displacement: 265 cid. Compression ratio: 8.0:1. Gross horsepower: 180 at 4800 rpm. Five main bearings. Solid valve lifters. Carburetor: Four-barrel Carter downdraft.

1955 Chevrolet 1/2-Ton Series 3100 Pickup (IMSC/Jack Martin)

CHASSIS: [Series 1500] Wheelbase: 115 in. Overall length: 200.8 in. Front tread: 58 in. Rear tread: 58.9 in. Tires: 7.15 x 14 four-ply. Maximum GVW: 4,100 lbs.

CHASSIS: [Series 3100] Wheelbase: 114 in. Overall length: 185.687 in. Front tread: 60.5 in. Rear tread: 61.0 in. Tires: 6.70 x 15 four-ply. Maximum GVW: 5,000 lbs. (4,500 lbs. for Panel).

CHASSIS: [Series 3200] Wheelbase: 123.25 in. Overall length: 205.56 in. Tires: 6.70 x 15 four-ply. Maximum GVW: 5,000 lbs.

CHASSIS: [Series 3442] Wheelbase: 104 in. Tires: 8 x 19.5 six-ply.

CHASSIS: [Series 3542] Wheelbase: 125 in. Tires: 8 x 19.5 six-ply.

CHASSIS: [Series 3742] Wheelbase: 137 in. Tires: 8 x 19.5 six-ply.

CHASSIS: [Series 3600] Wheelbase: 123.25 in. Overall length: 205.56 in. Tires: 7 x 17.5 six-ply. Maximum GVW: 6,900 lbs.

CHASSIS: [Series 3800] Wheelbase: 135 in. Overall length: 215.81 in. Tires: [front] 8 x 17.5 six-ply; [rear] 8 x 17.5 eight-ply. Maximum GVW: 8,800 lbs. (7,700 lbs. Panel).

TECHNICAL: Selective synchromesh transmission. Speeds: [3800] 4F/1R; [others] 3F/1R. Column-mounted gearshift (floor-shift on 3800). Single-plate dry-disc clutch. [3600/3800] Full-floating rear axle; [Others] Semi-floating rear axle. Overall ratio: [3100/3200] 3.90:1; [3400/3500/3700] 5.14:1; [3600] 4.57:1. Four-wheel hydraulic brakes. Steel disc wheels. Options: Heavy-duty three-speed manual transmission. Overdrive transmission. Four-speed manual transmission. Hydra-Matic transmission. Rear axles. Heavy-duty clutch. Heavy-duty radiator. Oil bath air cleaner.

1955 Chevrolet 1/2-Ton Model 3124 Cameo Carrier (Custom wheels)

OPTIONS: [RPO] Directionals. Heater/defroster. Double-action shocks. Rearview mirrors/brackets. Rear shock absorber shield. Hydrovac. Prop shaft brake. Oil bath air cleaners. PCV system. Painted or chrome rear bumper. Heavy-duty clutch. High body sills. Oil filter. Governor. Dual tail and stop lamps. Heavy-duty rear springs. Heavy-duty radiator. Foam rubber seat cushion. Auxiliary seat. Auxiliary rear springs. Airmatic seat. Wide base wheels. Speedometer fittings. Powerglide (Sedan Delivery). Hydra-Matic (Commercials). Overdrive. Heavy-duty three-speed transmission. Heavy-duty four-speed transmission. Electric wipers. Power steering. High-output generators. Side-mounted spare tire carrier ("dimpled" rear fender required 3100/3200/3600). Heavy-duty battery. Power steering. Channel type painted front bumper (Dubl-Duti.) Spare wheel carrier (Dubl-Duti). Custom Cab equipment (includes Panoramic rear window; deluxe seat; chrome instrument knobs; cigarette lighter; dual visors; dual armrests; two-tone upholstery and interior color scheme). Chrome equipment. "Full-view" Panoramic rear window. Left-hand door lock and lock for side-mounted spare. E-Z-Eye tinted glass. Trademaster V-8 engine.

OPTIONS: [Dealer Accessories] Radio antenna. Heater (Standard/Deluxe). Cigarette lighter. Seat covers. External sun shade. Hubcaps. Directional signals. Front bumper guards (painted or chrome). Rear fold-down steps (Platform/Stake). Dual sun visors. Extendible outside mirrors. Spotlight with mirror. Windshield washer. External sun visor. Traffic viewer. Backup lights (Sedan Delivery). Electric parking brake signal. Chrome hood ornament. Dual fog lamps. Red reflex reflectors. Portable spotlight. AC/DC shaver. Stainless steel door edge guards. Stainless steel door vent shades. Chrome door handle shields. Tool kit. Illuminated compass. Underhood light. Second (high-note) horn.

HISTORICAL: Introduced: March 25, 1955. Calendar year registrations: [All Commercial Series] 329,791. Calendar year production by GVW class: [All Commercial up to 5,000 lbs.] 219,805; [All Commercials, 5,001 lbs. to 10,000 lbs.] 64,589. Chevrolet was America's largest truck-maker with a 31.55 percent market share. Innovations: Completely restyled second series line. Panoramic windshield. New V-8 engine options. Limited-production Cameo Carrier with fiberglass bedliner introduced. 12-volt electrical systems. Tubeless tires. Historical notes: This was a milestone year for Chevrolet light-duty trucks due to sweeping styling revisions, technical changes and introduction of a V-8 engine.

1956 CHEVROLET

SEDAN DELIVERY — MODEL D56/SERIES 1500 — SIX/V-8: The Sedan Delivery was restyled along the lines of Chevrolet's passenger cars. Squared-off fenders more deeply hooded the headlamps. Above the new grille was a narrow reinforcement. The grille insert had six thin horizontal members and 11 vertical members. This gave the impression of 68 narrow, horizontal rectangular openings with the grille installed on the Sedan Delivery. A one-piece sheet metal filler panel was below the grille. Parking lamp housings were massive chrome panels of a square shape with square lamps inserted into their center. A short chrome molding, curved on the outer end, sat on top of the large housing. Chrome extensions were attached to the outside of the housing. They had three grooves stamped in them. Side moldings were of the One-Fifty Series style, stopping behind the side doors. The new Sedan Delivery remained based on the two-door Handyman station wagon. The doors were the same as this model and the two-door sedan. Front door glass was the same as the two-door sedan. Both the rear compartment floor and the rear quarter panel sections were slightly unique to the Sedan Delivery. The rear door was of liftgate design. This model was again in the One-Fifty series with code 56-1271 on the Fisher Body tag under the hood. Other features included a wraparound windshield; ball joint suspension; and optional Power-glide automatic transmission. The standard Chevrolet "Stovebolt" six had a higher 140 hp rating. The base rating for the 265 cid V-8 remained the same, but the four-barrel carburetor

version now produced 205 hp and had an increased compression ratio. Standard equipment included front and rear bumpers and bumper guards; front license guard; hood ornament and emblem; chrome plated headlamp rims with doors; dual windshield wipers; dual horns; outside key locks; front and rear bumper gravel deflectors; one combination tail/stop/license plate lamp; chrome-plated radio grille; three-position ignition switch; left-hand sunshade; and dome light. Onyx black remained the standard color. Optional paint colors were India ivory; Pinecrest green; Sherwood green; Nassau blue; Harbor blue; Calypso cream; and Matador red. The interior was trimmed with gold-striped charcoal gray imitation leather, combination number 615.

1956 Chevrolet One-Fifty Sedan Delivery (DFW)

1/2-TON COMMERCIAL — MODEL 3A56/SERIES 3100 — SIX/V-8: Changes for the regular Task Force trucks were minor. "The "handle-bar" hood emblem was smaller and redesigned so that the wings on it extended out from near the bottom, instead of the top. The emblem was finished in black to match the wheelcover trim. A large V-8 was added below the emblem to indicate V-8 models. Fenderside nameplates kept the same basic shape, but had a raised blade portion and center crease line. They were moved above the main body feature line, instead of below it. V-8 emblems (when appropriate) were placed below the fender nameplates. Hydra-Matic equipped trucks had fender nameplates reading "Chevrolet 3100 Hydra-Matic." There were again 13 solid colors. New colors were Forest green; Cardinal red; Golden yellow; Regal blue; and Crystal blue. Also available were Sand beige; Jet black; Omaha orange; Granite gray; Empire blue; Yukon yellow; Ocean green; and Pearl white. Twelve two-tones (eight for Cameos) were available on all, but Suburbans. Nine combinations featured Arabian ivory upper body finish in conjunction with colors listed above. New was a choice of Jet black over Golden yellow. Cardinal red over Sand beige was also available. Deluxe equipment and two-tones were not available for Suburbans. Black wheels were standard. Two-toned models had the upper body color on the wheels. Cab models, except Cameo Carriers, had standard gray seat trim. Gray and black upholstery was standard in Panels and Suburbans. Deluxe options included synthetic trim fabrics in blue, green, charcoal or gray.

1956 Chevrolet One-Fifty Sedan Delivery With Modern Tires (OCW)

1/2-TON COMMERCIAL (CAMEO) — MODEL 3A56/SERIES 3100 — SIX/V-8: The Cameo 1/2-ton Suburban pickup continued as a limited-production model. This high-style truck, Fisher Body style number 3124, was based on the 3000 chassis with a 114 in. wheelbase. It had the same basic styling changes as other models. Special features included slab-sided rear fender skins made of fiberglass bolted onto a standard cargo box to bring the rear body width flush with the sides of the standard cab. Chrome moldings trimmed the gap between the cab and the box. Bodyside moldings were the same as 1955, but with black accents to match the new black-accented hubcaps. A fiberglass tailgate panel over the steel tailgate hid the hinges, latches and restraining chains. A hidden compartment below the endgate held the spare tire in a fiberglass well. It was accessible via a swing-down hinged rear bumper section. Unique taillights and a Chevrolet bow tie in the center of the tailgate were seen. Standard equipment included Deluxe Cab equipment and the Panoramic rear window. This year's Cameo Pickup (or Suburban Pickup) came in eight two-tone combinations: Cardinal red/Bombay ivory; Cardinal red/Sand beige; Golden yellow/Jet black; Cardinal red/Arabian ivory; Regal blue/Arabian ivory; Granite gray/Arabian ivory; Ocean green/Arabian ivory; and Crystal blue/Arabian ivory. The secondary color was used on the rear cab pillars and around the back window. The roof, windshield pillars and rest of the body were done in what was called the upper color, which is listed before slashes above. The standard Cameo interior was again beige imitation leather with red nylon inserts. Options were light and dark charcoal gray; light and dark blue; and light and dark green. The steering wheel horn button now had a slight hood at the top and was trimmed with the interior color. Wheel rims were painted the upper body color. Black-accented full wheelcovers from the 1956 Bel Air were optional on the standard 15 in. wheels. Cameo Carriers had stripes on the optional 16 x 5K wheels only.

1/2-TON COMMERCIAL — MODEL 3B56/SERIES 3200 — SIX/V-8: This was the long wheelbase (LWB) 1/2-ton truck on the same chassis as 3/4-ton models. It became known as the "Long Bed" or "Long Box" Pickup because it had a long 90 in. load box. Longer runningboards were also used. There was more space between the cab and rear fenders. It still had the same 5,000 lbs. maximum GVW rating as other 1/2-ton trucks.

3/4-TON DUBL-DUTI — MODEL 3C56/SERIES 3400 — SIX/V-8: Three Dubl-Duti Forward-Control chassis remained in the truck line. The Model 3442 had a 114 in. wheelbase. Standard walk-in delivery truck bodies could be supplied by several factory-approved sources or the buyer could add his/her own body.

3/4-TON DUBL-DUTI — MODEL 3D56/SERIES 3500 — SIX-CYLINDER: Model 3542 was the 3/4-ton Dubl-Duti on a 125 in. wheelbase. Standard walk-in delivery truck bodies could be supplied by several factory-approved sources or the buyer could add his/her own body. The wheels were of eight-bolt design. A painted, Anvil gray channel type front bumper was standard on the 3500 Dubl-Duti truck chassis.

3/4-TON — DUBL-DUTI — MODEL F56/SERIES 3700 — SIX-CYLINDER: Model 3742 was the Dubl-Duti on a 137 in. wheelbase. Standard walk-in delivery truck bodies could be supplied by several factory-approved sources or the buyer could add his/her own body. The wheels were of eight-bolt design. A painted, Anvil gray channel type front bumper was standard on the 3700 Dubl-Duti truck chassis.

3/4-TON COMMERCIAL — MODEL 3E56/SERIES 3600 — SIX/V-8: The 3600 Series Task-Force trucks had the same styling and trim changes as other conventional trucks. This series included the medium-duty cab models on a 123.5 in. wheelbase. Compared to 3100 pickups, the 3600 pickup had longer runningboards and a longer cargo box with a horizontal support rib. There were also Platform and Platform/Stake models. The rail for the 3/4-ton Platform was 97-9/16 in. long. The maximum GVW rating was 6,900 lbs.

1-TON MEDIUM-DUTY COMMERCIAL — MODEL 3G/SERIES 3800 — The 3800 Series Task-Force trucks had the same styling and trim changes as other conventional trucks. These models were available with an optional power brake system. This Hydrovac brake booster reduced pedal effort by two-thirds. Panel models had a one-piece floor made of 3/4-inch thick, five-ply laminated wood. The basic model lineup was unchanged. Compared to the 3600 Pickup, the 3800 Pickup had a longer wheelbase, a longer grain-tight load box with extra stake pockets and very long runningboards. The 1-ton Platform and Platform/Stake trucks had a 115-9/16 in. long rail. No hubcaps were used on the larger split-rim wheels of the Chassis & Cab, Platform and Stake models, which had eight bolts and eight circular openings. A four-speed manual synchromesh transmission was standard.

I.D. DATA: Serial Number located: [Chassis models] On plate temporarily attached near steering column, with final location per body maker; [All others] On plate attached to rear face of left-hand door hinge pillar; on right side of cowl under hood. The first (Sedan Delivery) or first and second symbol(s) indicated the series: D=1500; 3A=3100; 3B=3200; 3C=3400; 3D=3500; 3E=3600; 3F=3700; 3G=3800. The next two symbols indicated the model year: 56=1956. The fifth symbol indicated the assembly plant: A=Atlanta, Ga.; B=Baltimore, Md.; F=Flint, Mich.; J=Janesville, Wis.; K=Kansas City, Mo.; L=Los Angeles, Calif.; N=Norwood, Ohio; O=Oakland, Calif.; S=St. Louis, Mo.; T=Tarrytown, N.Y.; W=Willow Run, Mich. Each series was separately numbered in sequence, starting with 000001 at each assembly plant. Serial numbers were: [Sedan Delivery] D56-001001 to 220555; [3100] 3A56-001001 to 033691; [3200] 3B56-001001-033691; [3600] 3E56-001001 to 033691; [3800] 3G56-001001 to 033691; [Dubl-Duti] 3C/D/F56-001001 to 033691. Engine numbers located on right side of engine on boss at rear of distributor. Engine numbers began with an F (Flint, Mich.) or T (Tonawanda, N.Y.) assembly plant code. Engine numbers consisted of an engine serial number, alphabetical factory code, two-digit model year code and letter indicating the type of truck and type of engine. For example, an engine with the number 0068025F56X would be a 235 Thriftmaster in a 3100/3200/3600/3800 Series truck (code X) made in 1956 (code 56) at the Flint plant (code F) which had engine serial number 0068025. Other common codes for trucks in these series were: (XG) for the Thriftmaster 235 with Hydra-Matic; (V) for the Thriftmaster 235 with heavy-duty clutch; (A) for the Trademaster 265 V-8; (B) for the Trademaster 265 with Hydra-Matic; (M) for the Trademaster 265 with heavy-duty clutch; (W) for the Thriftmaster 235 Special; and (WA) for the Thriftmaster 235 Special with Hydra-Matic. Codes for 3400/3500/3700 trucks were (D) for Trademaster 265 V-8; (DA) for Trademaster 265 V-8 with Hydra-Matic; and (DB) for Trademaster 265 V-8 with heavy-duty clutch.

Job No.	Body Type	Price	Weight	Prod. Total
Sedan Delivery — Model 3D56/Series 1500 — 115 in. w.b.				
1508	Sedan Delivery	1865	3145	—
1/2-Ton Commercial — Model 3A56/Series 3100 — 114 in. w.b.				
3102	Chassis & Cowl	1303	2374	—
3103	Chassis & Cab	1567	2872	—
3104	Pickup	1670	3217	—
3105	Panel	1966	3457	—
3106	Suburban (doors)	2300	3736	—
3112	Chassis & W/S	1341	2505	—
3116	Suburban (gate)	2300	3752	—
1/2-Ton Commercial (Cameo) — Model 3A56/Series 3100 — 114 in. w.b.				
3124	Cameo Pickup	2144	3373	1452
1/2-Ton Commercial (Long Box) — Model 3B56/Series 3200 — 123.25 in. w.b.				
3204	Pickup LWB	1692	3323	—
3/4-Ton Dubl-Duti — Model 3C56/Series 3400 — 114 in. w.b.				
3142	Chassis	1499	2716	—
3/4-Ton Dubl-Duti — Model 3D56/Series 3500 — 125 in. w.b.				
3542	Chassis	1537	2764	—
3/4-Ton Dubl-Duti — Model 3F56/Series 3700 — 137 in. w.b.				
3742	Chassis	1569	2784	—
3/4-Ton Commercial — Model 3E56/Series 3600 — 123.25 in. w.b.				
3602	Chassis & Cowl	1481	2736	—
3603	Chassis & Cab	1745	3252	—
3604	Pickup	1858	3633	—
3609	Platform & Stake	1950	3834	—
3612	Chassis & W/S	1519	2870	—
1-Ton Commercial — Model 3G56/Series 3800 — 135 in. w.b.				
3802	Chassis & Cowl	1611	2945	—
3803	Chassis & Cab	1875	3503	—
3804	Pickup	2009	3939	—
3805	Panel	2327	4243	—
3809	Platform & Stake	2122	4285	—
3812	Chassis & W/S	1649	3118	—

1956 Chevrolet 1/2-Ton Series 3100 Panel With Modern Tires (JLB)

ENGINE [All]: Inline. OHV. Six-cylinder. Cast iron block. Bore & stroke: 3-9/16 x 3-15/16 in. Displacement: 235.5 cid. Compression ratio: 8.0:1. Gross horsepower: 140 at 3800 rpm. SAE horsepower: 30.4. Four main bearings. Solid valve lifters. Carburetor: Single-barrel downdraft Rochester model B-7004468.

ENGINE [Optional 3100/3200/3600/3800]: Vee-block. OHV. Eight-cylinders. Cast iron block. Bore & stroke: 3-3/4 x 3 in. Displacement: 265 cid. Compression ratio: 7.5:1. Gross horsepower: 155 at 4000 rpm. Net horsepower: 126 at 4000 rpm. Five main bearings. Solid valve lifters. Carburetor: Two-barrel downdraft Rochester model 7008006.

ENGINE [Optional 1500]: Vee-block. OHV. Eight-cylinders. Cast iron block. Bore & stroke: 3-3/4 x 3 in. Displacement: 265 cid. Compression ratio: 8.0:1. Gross horsepower: 162 at 4200 rpm. Five main bearings. Solid valve lifters. Carburetor: Carter two-barrel.

ENGINE [Optional 1500]: Vee-block. OHV. Eight-cylinders. Cast iron block. Bore & stroke: 3-3/4 x 3 in. Displacement: 265 cid. Compression ratio: 9.25:1 Gross horsepower: 205 at 4800 rpm. Five main bearings. Solid valve lifters. Carburetor: Four-barrel Carter downdraft.

1956 Chevrolet 1/2-Ton Series 3100 Panel (C.H. Horst)

CHASSIS [Series 1500]: Wheelbase: 115 in. Overall length: 200.8 in. Front tread: 58 in. Rear tread: 58.9 in. Tires: 7.15 x 14 four-ply. Maximum GVW: 4,100 lbs.

CHASSIS [Series 3100]: Wheelbase: 114 in. Overall length: 185.7 in. Front tread: 60.5 in. Rear tread: 61.0 in. Tires: 6.70 x 15 four-ply. Maximum GVW: 5,000 lbs.

CHASSIS [Series 3200]: Wheelbase: 123.25 in. Overall length: 205.56 in. Tires: 6.70 x 15 four-ply. Maximum GVW: 5,000 lbs.

CHASSIS [Series 3442]: Wheelbase: 114 in. Tires: 8 x 19.5 six-ply. Maximum GVW: 7,000 lbs.

CHASSIS [Series 3542]: Wheelbase: 125 in. Tires: 8 x 19.5 six-ply. Maximum GVW: 8,800 lbs.

CHASSIS [Series 3742]: Wheelbase: 137 in. Tires: 8 x 19.5 six-ply. Maximum GVW: 10,000 lbs.

CHASSIS [Series 3600]: Wheelbase: 123.25 in. Overall length: 205.56 in. Tires: 7 x 17.5 six-ply. Maximum GVW: 6,900 lbs.

CHASSIS [Series 3800]: Wheelbase: 135 in. Overall length: 215.81 in. Tires: [Single rear wheels] 7.50 x 17.5; [Dual Rear Wheels] 8 x 17.5 six-ply; (front) 8 x 17.5 eight-ply. Maximum GVW: [Single Rear Wheels] 7,000 lbs.; [Dual Rear Wheels] 8,800 lbs.

TECHNICAL: Selective synchromesh transmission. Speeds: [3800] 4F/1R; [Others] 3F/1R. Column-mounted gearshift (floor-shift on 3800). Single-plate dry-disc clutch. [3600/3800] Full-floating rear axle; [Others] Semi-floating rear axle. Overall ratio: [3100/3200] 3.90:1; [3400/3500/3700] 5.14:1; [3600] 4.57:1. Four-wheel hydraulic brakes. Steel disc wheels. Options: Heavy-duty three-speed manual transmission. Overdrive transmission. Four-speed manual transmission. Hydra-Matic transmission. Rear axles. Heavy-duty clutch. Heavy-duty radiator. Oil bath air cleaner.

OPTIONS: [RPO] Directionals. Heater/defroster. Double-action shocks. Rearview mirrors/brackets. Rear shock absorber shield. Hydrovac. Prop shaft brake. Oil bath air cleaners. PCV system. Painted or chrome rear bumper. Heavy-duty clutch. Heavy-duty body sills. Oil filter. Governor. Dual tail and stop lamps. Heavy-duty rear springs. Heavy-duty radiator. Foam rubber seat cushion. Auxiliary seat. Auxiliary rear springs. Airmatic seat. Wide base wheels. Speedometer fittings. Powerglide (Sedan Delivery). Hydra-Matic. Overdrive. Heavy-duty three-speed transmission. Heavy-duty four-speed transmission. Electric wipers. Power steering. High-output generators. Side-mounted spare tire carrier (dimpled rear fender required 3100/3200/3600). Heavy-duty battery. Power steering. Channel type painted front bumper (Dubl-Duti.) Spare wheel carrier (Dubl-Duti). Custom Cab equipment (includes Panoramic rear window; deluxe seat; chrome instrument knobs; cigarette lighter; dual visors; dual armrests; two-tone upholstery and interior color scheme). Chrome equipment. Full-view Panoramic rear window. Left-hand door lock and lock for side-mounted spare tire. E-Z-Eye tinted glass. Trademaster V-8 engine.

OPTIONS: [Dealer Accessories] Radio antenna. Heater (Standard/Deluxe). Cigar lighter. Seat covers. External sun shade. Hubcaps. Directional signals. Front bumper guards (painted or chrome). Rear fold-down steps (Platform/Stake). Dual sun visors. Extendible

outside mirrors. Spotlight with mirror. Windshield washer. External sun visor. Traffic viewer. Backup lights (Sedan Delivery). Electric parking brake signal. Chrome hood ornament. Dual fog lamps. Red reflex reflectors. Portable spotlight. AC/DC shaver. Stainless steel door edge guards. Stainless steel door vent shades. Chrome door handle shields. Tool kit. Illuminated compass. Underhood light. Second (high-note) horn.

HISTORICAL: Introduced: Fall 1956. Calendar year production: [All Commercials] 353,509. Calendar year production, all Commercials, by GVW class: [Up to 5,000 lbs.] 194,015; [5,001 to 10,000 lbs.) 59,182. The four millionth postwar Chevrolet truck was assembled during 1956. Innovations included new paint colors and two-tone combinations; a higher compression ratio and horsepower rating for the Thriftmaster 235 six-cylinder engine and the optional four-barrel Trademaster 265 V-8. The company sent a fleet of its larger Taskmaster trucks to special displays around the country this year.

1957 CHEVROLET

1957 Chevrolet 1/2-Ton Series 3100 Pickup With Custom Wheels (DFW)

SEDAN DELIVERY — MODEL D/SERIES 1500 — SIX/V-8: The classic look for Chevrolet's 1957 cars included an oval front bumper grille with bomb type bumper guards, a flatter hood with windsplit bulges, screened headlamp housings and broad, flat tailfins. The 1957 passenger car grille used on the Sedan Delivery is one of the most famous designs. It had over 32 separate moldings, spacers, panels, supports, guards and lamp parts. The upper molding attached to the lip of the hood and was visually extended with curved moldings on either end. The delicate grille had a screen-like appearance and came with aluminum finish on Sedan Deliveries. A chrome horizontal bar with the Chevrolet emblem in a center housing and hooded parking lamp housings on either end was mounted in front of the grille insert. Round parking lamp assemblies fit inside the hooded housings. A body color sheet metal filler panel was used below the grille. The massive bumper face bar below the grille consisted of center and separate end sections. Large, round guards attached to either end of the bumper. Round inserts bolted to the front of these guards. One-Fifty style trim was used on the exterior of the body. The new Sedan Delivery remained based on the two-door Handyman station wagon. The doors were the same as this model and the two-door sedan. Front door glass was the same as the two-door sedan. Both the rear compartment floor and the rear quarter panel sections were slightly unique to the Sedan Delivery. The rear door was of liftgate design. Other features included a wraparound windshield; ball joint suspension; and optional Powerglide automatic transmission. The standard Chevrolet "Stovebolt" six again had 140 hp. The base rating for the 265 cid V-8 remained the same, but there were now 185, 220, 245, 250 and 270 hp V-8 options with dual four-barrel carburetors or fuel-injection on the hotter engines. Standard equipment included front and rear bumpers and bumper guards; front license guard; hood ornament and emblem; chrome plated headlamp rims with doors; dual windshield wipers; dual horns; outside key locks; front and rear bumper gravel deflectors; bright radio grille; three-position ignition switch; left-hand sunshade; and dome light. Onyx black remained the standard color. Optional paint colors were Imperial ivory; Surf green; Highland green; Lakespur blue; Harbor blue; and Matador red. The interior was trimmed with a black and gray imitation leather and black imitation leather two-tone upholstery combination, number 651.

1/2-TON COMMERCIAL — MODEL 3A/SERIES 3100 — SIX/V-8: Changes for conventional trucks were minor. A new grille with an oval loop in the center was attached to a more massive, trapezoid-shaped grille surround. Between the outer surround and the inner open loop, there were four short bars on both the top and bottom. Painted grilles were standard; a chrome grille was optional. Fenderside nameplates were now oval-shaped with the brand name and series number in a sculpted center depression. Trucks with Hydra-Matic transmission had this denoted on the trim. The nameplates were positioned above the feature line on the sides of the cowl. V-8 emblems were added when this option was ordered. The front hood badge was of the same general "handle-bar" shape, but larger. It had a Chevrolet bow tie in the center. On V-8 trucks, a chrome V was placed below the hood front ornament. The hood had two small windsplits sculpted into its top surface. The 3100 Pickup had short runningboards. Single-unit body models included the Suburban and Panel. Brewster green was the standard exterior body color. Options included Cardinal red; Indian turquoise; Sand beige; Jet black; Omaha orange; Granite gray; Royal blue; Golden yellow; Yukon yellow; Ocean green; Alpine blue; Pure white; and Sandstone beige. The 13 two-tones included Bombay ivory upper body with all colors except Brewster green or Golden yellow, plus Ocean green over Brewster green; Alpine blue over Royal blue; or Jet black over Golden yellow. (Custom two-tones were not available for Suburbans and the combinations were somewhat different for Cameo Carriers.) Standard interiors were gray synthetic fabric. Trucks with deluxe interiors had a non-glare satin-finish charcoal gray paint on the upper dash and light gray on the instrument panel. Doors were finished in light gray metal with charcoal gray metal door insert panels. A charcoal gray fiberboard top lining panel was used. The seats had light gray bolsters and rose-and-gray colored fabric on the cushions and back panels. Standard wheels were black. Custom Cab equipment was available for double-unit body models and included bright metal dashboard knobs, armrests, deluxe steering trim, bright window frames and chrome equipment. The wheels of two-tone trucks were done in the lower body color, except when the exterior colors were Bombay ivory over Jet black or Cardinal red over Bombay ivory, in which case the wheels were Bombay ivory and Cardinal red, respectively. Deluxe equipment was optionally available for 3100s, except Suburbans.

1/2-TON COMMERCIAL (CAMEO) — MODEL 3A/SERIES 3100 — SIX/V-8: The Cameo Carrier got the chrome version of the new grille, deluxe cab equipment and a Panoramic rear window as standard equipment. A new feature was a pair of horizontal rear quarter panel moldings with a contrast band between them. This trim ran horizontally from behind the cab to the area between the rear bumper and taillights. It carried a Chevy bow tie badge and Cameo script. The oval-shaped fenderside nameplates said 3124 and Chevrolet in a sculpted center depression. Trucks with Hydra-Matic transmission had this denoted on the trim. The nameplates were positioned above the feature line on the sides of the cowl. V-8 emblems were added when this option was ordered. Special Cameo features again included slab-sided rear fender skins made of fiberglass bolted onto a standard cargo box to bring the rear body width flush with the sides of the standard cab. Chrome moldings trimmed the gap between the cab and the box. A fiberglass tailgate panel over the steel tailgate hid the hinges, latches and restraining chains. A hidden compartment below the endgate held the spare tire in a fiberglass. It was accessible via a swing-down hinged rear bumper section. Unique taillights and a Chevrolet bow tie in the center of the tailgate were seen. Standard equipment included Deluxe Cab equipment and the Panoramic rear window. The 1957 Cameo's standard two-tone finish was Cardinal red over Bombay ivory. Also available were Bombay ivory over Sand beige; Bombay ivory over Cardinal red; Jet black over Golden yellow; Bombay ivory over Indian turquoise; Bombay ivory over Granite gray; Bombay ivory over Ocean green; Bombay ivory over Alpine blue; and Bombay ivory over Sandstone beige. The secondary color was used on the rear cab pillars and around the back window. The roof, windshield pillars and rest of the body were done in the upper color, which is listed first above. The standard Cameo interior had the same upholstery material as 1956-1957 models. Beige imitation leather with red nylon inserts was the standard color scheme. Options were light and dark charcoal gray; light and dark blue; and light and dark green. The steering wheel had a new recessed horn button and same-size spokes. It now had gray finish on the sides and top. Small chrome hubcaps and wheel trim rings were standard. The wheels were done in the lower body color, except when the exterior colors were Bombay ivory over Jet black or Cardinal red over Bombay ivory, in which case the wheels were Bombay ivory and Cardinal red, respectively. Black-accented full wheelcovers from the 1956 Bel Air (the 1957 had 14 in. wheels) were optional on the limited-edition truck's standard 15 in. wheels. Cameo Carriers had stripes only on the optional 16 x 5K wheels.

1/2-TON COMMERCIAL — MODEL 3B/SERIES 3200 — SIX/V-8: The 3200 Series Task-Force trucks had the same basic styling and trim changes as other conventional trucks. This was the long wheelbase (LWB) 1/2-ton truck on the same chassis as 3/4-ton models. It became known as the "Long Bed" or "Long Box" Pickup because it had a longer load box. Chevrolet parts catalogs indicated that a 90 in. box was used for 1955-1957 Models 3200/3600 and that a 98 in. box was used for 1957-1958 Models 3200/3600, indicating a midyear change. Longer runningboards were also used. There was more space between the cab and rear fenders. It still had the same 5,000 lbs. maximum GVW rating as other 1/2-ton trucks.

3/4-TON DUBL-DUTI — MODEL 3C/SERIES 3400 — SIX/V-8: Three Dubl-Duti Forward-Control chassis remained in the truck line. The Model 3442 had a 114 in. wheelbase. Standard walk-in delivery truck bodies could be supplied by several factory-approved sources or the buyer could add his/her own body.

3/4-TON DUBL-DUTI — MODEL 3D/SERIES 3500 — SIX-CYLINDER: Model 3542 was the 3/4-ton Dubl-Duti on a 125 in. wheelbase. Standard walk-in delivery truck bodies could be supplied by several factory-approved sources or the buyer could add his/her own body. The wheels were of eight-bolt design. A painted, Anvil gray channel type front bumper was standard on the 3500 Dubl-Duti truck chassis.

3/4-TON — DUBL-DUTI — MODEL F/SERIES 3700 — SIX-CYLINDER: Model 3742 was the Dubl-Duti on a 137 in. wheelbase. Standard walk-in delivery truck bodies could be supplied by several factory-approved sources or the buyer could add his/her own body. The wheels were of eight-bolt design. A painted, Anvil gray channel type front bumper was standard on the 3700 Dubl-Duti truck chassis.

3/4-TON COMMERCIAL — MODEL 3E56/SERIES 3600 — SIX/V-8: The 3600 Series Task-Force trucks had the same styling and trim changes as other conventional trucks. This series included the medium-duty cab models on a 123.5 in. wheelbase. Compared to 3100 pickups, the 3600 pickup had longer runningboards and a longer cargo box with a horizontal support rib. Chevrolet parts catalogs indicated that a 90 in. box was used for 1955-1957 Models 3600 and that a 98 in. box was used for 1957-1958 Models 3600, indicating a midyear change. There were also Platform and Platform/Stake models. The rail for the 3/4-ton Platform was 97-9/16 in. long. The maximum GVW rating was 6,900 lbs.

1-TON MEDIUM-DUTY COMMERCIAL — MODEL 3G/SERIES 3800 — SIX-CYLINDER: The 3800 Series Task-Force trucks had the same styling and trim changes as other conventional trucks. Panel models had a one-piece floor made of 3/4-inch thick, five-ply laminated wood. The basic model lineup was unchanged. Compared to the 3600 Pickup, the 3800 Pickup had a longer wheelbase, a longer grain-tight load box with extra stake pockets and very long runningboards. The 1-ton Platform and Platform/Stake trucks had a 115-9/16 in. long rail. No hubcaps were used on the larger split-rim wheels of the Chassis & Cab, Platform and Stake models, which had eight bolts and eight circular openings. A four-speed manual synchromesh transmission was standard.

1957 Chevrolet 1/2-Ton Model 3100 Panel (MLC)

I.D. DATA: Serial Number located: [Chassis models] On plate temporarily attached near steering column, with final location per body maker; [All others] On plate attached to rear face of left-hand door hinge pillar; on right side of cowl under hood. The first (Sedan Delivery) or first and second symbol(s) indicated the series: D=1500; 3A=3100; 3B=3200; 3C=3400; 3D=3500; 3E=3600; 3F=3700; 3G=3800. The next two symbols indicated the model year: 57=1957. The fifth symbol indicated the assembly plant: A=Atlanta, Ga.; B=Baltimore, Md.; F=Flint, Mich.; J=Janesville, Wis.; K=Kansas City, Mo.; L=Los Angeles, Calif.; N=Norwood, Ohio; O=Oakland, Calif.; S=St. Louis, Mo.; T=Tarrytown, N.Y.; W=Willow Run, Mich. Each series was separately numbered in sequence, starting with 000001 at each assembly plant. Serial numbers were: [Sedan Delivery] D56-001001 to 314393; [3100] 3A56-001001 to 144196; [3200] 3B56-001001-144196; [3600] 3E56-001001 to 144196; [3800] 3G56-001001 to 144196; [Dubl-Duti] 3C/D/F56-001001 to 144196. Engine numbers located on right side of engine on boss at rear of distributor. Engine numbers began with an F (Flint, Mich.) or T (Tonawanda, N.Y.) assembly plant code. [Sedan Delivery] Second or second and third symbols A or B=235 cid/140 hp; C=265 cid/162 hp; F or G=283 cid/185 hp; E, FC, FE or FG = 283 cid/220 hp; EA or GD=283 cid/245 hp; GF or EJ=283 cid/250 hp and EB or EK=283 cid 283 hp. [Commercials] Second or second and third symbols H or HE=235 cid/140 hp; L, LA or LB=265 cid/162 hp.

1957 Chevrolet One-Fifty Sedan Delivery (H. Fries)

ENGINE [All]: Inline. OHV. Six-cylinder. Cast iron block. Bore & stroke: 3.562 x 3.937 in. Displacement: 235.5 cid. Compression ratio: 8.0:1. Brake horsepower: 140 at 4200 rpm. Four main bearings. Hydraulic valve lifters. Carburetor: Rochester one-barrel model 7007181.
ENGINE [Optional All]: V-type. OHV. Eight-cylinder. Cast iron block. Bore & stroke: 3.75 x 3 in. Displacement: 265 cid. Compression ratio: 8.0:1. Brake horsepower: 162 at 4400 rpm. Five main bearings. Hydraulic valve lifters. Carburetor: Rochester two-barrel model 7009909.
ENGINE [Optional 1500]: V-type. OHV. Eight-cylinder. Cast iron block. Bore & stroke: 3.875 x 3 in. Displacement: 283 cid. Compression ratio: 8.5:1. Brake horsepower: 185 at 4600 rpm. Five main bearings. Hydraulic valve lifters. Carburetor: Rochester two-barrel model 7012133.

1957 Chevrolet 1/2-Ton Series 3100 Cameo Carrier (ICS)

Job No.	Body Type	Price	Weight	Prod. Total
Sedan Delivery — Model D57/Series 1500 — 115 in. w.b.				
1508	Sedan Delivery	2020	3254	7273
1/2-Ton Commercial — Model 3A/Series 3100 — 114 in. w.b.				
3102	Chassis & Cowl	1433	2374	—
3103	Chassis & Cab	1697	2871	—
3104	Pickup	1800	3217	—
3105	Panel	2101	3458	—
3106	Suburban (doors)	2435	3738	—
3112	Chassis & W/S	1471	2514	—
3116	Suburban (gate)	2435	3752	—
1/2-Ton Commercial (Cameo) — Model 3A/Series 3100 — 114 in. w.b.				
3124	Cameo Pickup	2273	3373	2244
1/2-Ton Commercial (Long Box) — Model 3B/Series 3200 — 123.25 in. w.b.				
3204	Pickup	1838	3322	—
3/4-Ton Dubl-Duti — Model 3C/Series 3400 — 114 in. w.b.				
3442	Chassis	1613	2722	—
3/4-Ton Dubl-Duti — Model 3D/Series 3500 — 125 in. w.b.				
3542	Chassis	1651	2764	—
3/4-Ton Dubl-Duti — Model 3F/Series 3700 — 137 in. w.b.				
3742	Chassis	1683	2784	—
3/4-Ton Commercial — Model 3E/Series 3600 — 123.25 in. w.b.				
3602	Chassis & Cowl	1616	2741	—
3603	Chassis & Cab	1880	3252	—
3604	Pickup	1993	3632	—
3609	Platform & Stake	2085	3876	—
3612	Chassis & W/S	1654	2881	—
1-Ton Commercial — Model 3G/Series 3800 — 135 in. w.b.				
3802	Chassis & Cowl	1763	2945	—
3803	Chassis & Cab	2027	3496	—
3804	Pickup	2160	3938	—
3805	Panel	2489	4243	—
3809	Platform & Stake	2274	4286	—
3812	Chassis & W/S	1801	3079	—

1957 Chevrolet 1/2-Ton Series 3100 Cameo Carrier (DFW)

ENGINE [Optional 1500]: V-type. OHV. Super Turbo-Fire. Eight-cylinder. Cast iron block. Bore & stroke: 3.875 x 3 in. Displacement: 283 cid. Compression ratio: 9.5:1. Brake horsepower: 220 at 4800 rpm. Five main bearings. Hydraulic valve lifters. Carburetor: Rochester four-barrel.
ENGINE [Optional 1500]: V-type. OHV. Super Turbo-Fire. Eight-cylinder. Cast iron block. Bore & stroke: 3.875 x 3 in. Displacement: 283 cid. Compression ratio: 9.5:1. Brake horsepower: 245 at 4800 rpm. Five main bearings. Carburetors: Two Rochester four-barrels.
ENGINE [Optional 1500]: V-type. OHV. Super Turbo-Fire. Eight-cylinder. Cast iron block. Bore & stroke: 3.875 x 3 in. Displacement: 283 cid. Compression ratio: 9.5:1. Brake horsepower: 250 at 4800 rpm. Five main bearings. Fuel injection.
ENGINE [Optional 1500]: V-type. OHV. Super Turbo-Fire. Eight-cylinder. Cast iron block. Bore & stroke: 3.875 x 3 in. Displacement: 283 cid. Compression ratio: 10.5:1. Brake horsepower: 270 at 5600 rpm. Five main bearings. Two four-barrel carburetors.

1957 Chevrolet One-Fifty Sedan Delivery (OCW)

CHASSIS [Series 1500]: Wheelbase: 115 in. Overall length: 200 in. Front tread: 58 in. Rear tread: 58.9 in. Tires: 7.50 x 14 four-ply. Maximum GVW: 4,100 lbs.
CHASSIS [Series 3100]: Wheelbase: 114 in. Overall length: [Cameo] 193.56 in.; [Others] 185.7 in. Front tread: 60.5 in. Rear tread: 61.0 in. Tires: 6.70 x 15 four-ply. Maximum GVW: 5,000 lbs.
CHASSIS [Series 3200]: Wheelbase: 123.25 in. Overall length: [Early] 205.56 in. [Late] 215.81 in. Tires: 7 x 7.5 six-ply. Maximum GVW: 5,000 lbs.
CHASSIS [Series 3442]: Wheelbase: 104 in. Tires: 8 x 19.5 six-ply. Maximum GVW: 7,000 lbs.
CHASSIS [Series 3542]: Wheelbase: 125 in. Tires: 8 x 19.5 six-ply. Maximum GVW: 8,800 lbs.
CHASSIS [Series 3742]: Wheelbase: 137 in. Tires: 8 x 19.5 six-ply. Maximum GVW: 10,000 lbs.
CHASSIS [Series 3600]: Wheelbase: 123.25 in. Overall length: [Early] 205.56 in. [Late] 215.81 in. Tires: 7 x 17.5 six-ply. Maximum GVW: 6,900 lbs.

CHASSIS [Series 3800]: Wheelbase: 135 in. Overall length: 215.81 in. Tires: [Single rear wheels] 7.50 x 17.5; [Dual Rear Wheels] (front) 8 x 17.5 six-ply; (rear) 8 x 17.5 eight-ply. Maximum GVW: [Single Rear Wheels] 7,000 lbs.; [Dual Rear Wheels] 9,600 lbs.
TECHNICAL: Selective synchromesh transmission. Speeds: [3800] 4F/1R; [Others] 3F/1R. Column-mounted gearshift (floor-shift on 3800). Single-plate dry-disc clutch. [3600/3800] Full-floating rear axle; [Others] Semi-floating rear axle. Overall ratio: [3100/3200] 3.90:1; [3400/3500/3700] 5.14:1; [3600] 4.57:1. Four-wheel hydraulic brakes. Steel disc wheels. Options: Heavy-duty three-speed manual transmission. Overdrive transmission. Four-speed manual transmission. Hydra-Matic transmission. Rear axles. Heavy-duty clutch. Heavy-duty radiator. Oil bath air cleaner.

1957 Chevrolet 1/2-Ton Series 3100 Panel (DFW)

OPTIONS: [RPO] Directionals. Heater/defroster. Double-action shocks. Rearview mirrors/brackets. Rear shock absorber shield. Hydrovac. Prop shaft brake. Oil bath air cleaners. PCV system. Painted or chrome rear bumper. Heavy-duty clutch. High body sills. Oil filter. Governor. Dual tail and stop lamps. Heavy-duty rear springs. Heavy-duty radiator. Foam rubber seat cushion. Auxiliary seat. Auxiliary rear springs. Airmatic seat. Wide base wheels. Speedometer fittings. Powerglide (Sedan Delivery). Hydra-Matic (Commercials). Overdrive. Heavy-duty three-speed transmission. Heavy-duty four-speed transmission. Electric wipers. Power steering. High-output generators. Side-mounted spare tire carrier (dimpled rear fender required 3100/3200/3600). Heavy-duty battery. Power steering. Channel type painted front bumper (Dubl-Duti.) Spare wheel carrier (Dubl-Duti.) Custom Cab equipment (includes Panoramic rear window; deluxe seat; chrome instrument knobs; cigarette lighter; dual visors; dual armrests; two-tone upholstery and interior color scheme. Chrome equipment. Full-view Panoramic rear window. Left-hand door lock and lock for side-mounted spare tire. E-Z-Eye tinted glass. Trademaster V-8 engine.
OPTIONS: [Dealer Accessories] Radio antenna. Heater (Standard/Deluxe). Cigar lighter. Seat covers. External sun shade. Hubcaps. Directional signals. Front bumper guards (painted or chrome). Rear fold-down steps (Platform/Stake). Dual sun visors. Extendible outside mirrors. Spotlight with mirror. Windshield washer. External sun visor. Traffic viewer. Backup lights (Sedan Delivery). Electric parking brake signal. Chrome hood ornament. Dual fog lamps. Red reflex reflectors. Portable spotlight. AC/DC shaver. Stainless steel door edge guards. Stainless steel door vent shades. Chrome door handle shields. Tool kit. Illuminated compass. Underhood light. Second (high-note) horn.
HISTORICAL: Introduced: October, 1956. Model year production: [All Series] 359,098. Innovations: New 283 cid V-8 available as optional equipment. Sedan Delivery redesigned like passenger cars. Regular trucks have new grille styling. Expanded solid color choices and two-tone color schemes. Factory-built 4x4 trucks were available for the first time from Chevrolet this year.

1958 CHEVROLET

1958 Chevrolet 1/2-Ton Apache 32 Fleetside Pickup (OCW)

SEDAN DELIVERY — MODEL G/SERIES 1171 (SIX) — MODEL H/SERIES 1271 (V-8): The new Sedan Delivery was part of the Del Ray passenger car series. General styling updates included dual headlamps in each hooded front fender, a screen-like grille and gull-wing rear fender treatment with concave sculptured upper side panels. There was a single mid-body molding that extended back along the lower edge of the concave rear side panel. The Sedan Delivery had revised six-cylinder and V-8 series/model coding to reflect its totally revised appearance and chassis. The grille was an elaborate assembly of about 40 separate parts. The upper chrome molding had center and outer sections. The grille "screen" had five full-width horizontal sections divided by tightly-spaced vertical members. Dual round parking lamps were housed in binocular-shaped ornaments that mounted to the

grille insert on either side. A filler panel was below the insert. The bumper had massive chrome "wings" on either end and an upside-down-U shaped license plate frame molding in the center. A reinforcement and ribbed lower bar bolted into the license plate frame molding. Exterior paint colors included Honey beige; Onyx black; Cashmere blue; Fathom blue; Forest green; Glen green; Rio red; and Snowcrest white. The interior was trimmed in a two-tone combination of Gun Metal gray imitation leather and metallic silver imitation leather, code number 801. The truck was based on the new two-door, six-passenger Yeoman Station Wagon and used that model's door, window glass and bumper parts. Rear quarter panels were exclusive to the Sedan Delivery, but the rear compartment floor was the same as the six-passenger Yeoman's. A rear liftgate was used again. An all-new Safety Girder X-type frame with coil springs at all four corners was featured. The six-cylinder (1100 Series) Sedan Delivery could be ordered with manual or Powerglide transmission. The V-8 (1200 Series) version could be ordered with manual or Turboglide transmission with all engines or with Powerglide on engines up to 250 hp. Manual overdrive transmission was offered with 185 or 230 hp V-8s. The 283 cid V-8 came with two-barrel or four-barrel carburetors and fuel-injection. The new 348 cid V-8 came with a single four-barrel carburetor of three two-barrel carburetors.

1/2-TON — MODEL 3A/SERIES 3100 — SIX/V-8: The new Task Force Commercial models had dual headlamps, a new grille, new trim, and technical changes. Styling-wise, the new grille consisted of narrow horizontal bars just below the hood and a more massive "barbell-shaped" lower molding extending out and under the headlamps. This molding had the Chevrolet name lettered across it and its rectangular outboard extensions surrounded the similarly-shaped parking lamp lenses. Base-level Apaches also had a cream-painted grille, bumper and headlamp buckets and cream-colored hubcaps. Chrome-plated parts could be substituted at extra-cost. A rather large, jet-plane-shaped ornament, above the front fender feature line, carried the Apache name and series identification. Two significant merchandising innovations took place this year. First, the promotional designation Apache was applied to all models. Secondly, by the end of the year, buyers were presented with a choice of two types of pickups: The traditional type with exposed rear fenders and standard width box (called the Step-Side) and a new type with slab-sided rear steel fenders and extra-wide box, which was called the Fleetside. Fleetside models had a missile-shaped bulge along the slab-sided bed exterior. Their boxes were 75 in. wide versus the Cameo Carrier's 48 in. Although the general appearance of both was similar, the Fleetline did not use bolt-on plastic panels and fiberglass parts to achieve its slab-sided look. It replaced the Cameo Carrier. The optional 4x4 drive system was also available for 3100 models. Color choices for the year were: Jet black; Dawn blue; Marine blue; Kodiak brown; Granite gray; Glade green; Oriental green; Polar green; Omaha orange; Cardinal red; Tartan turquoise; Pure white; Golden yellow; and Yukon yellow. Six two-tones used Bombay ivory as upper color, over Kodiak brown, Granite gray, Oriental green, Omaha orange, Cardinal red or Yukon yellow. A pair of two-tones used Jet black over Tartan turquoise or Golden yellow. Other two-tones included Cardinal red over black, Dawn blue over Marine blue; or Marine blue over Dawn blue. Suburbans were not available with deluxe trim or two-tone paint again. Wheels were black with solid colors and lower body color on two-tone trucks. Chevrolet's hard-wearing upholstery included new color combinations, with charcoal gray and metallic silver two-tone combinations in either all-vinyl Deluxe (now base-level) or cloth-and-vinyl Custom (extra-cost only) trims. Also featured was an 18 in. diameter deep-dish steering wheel and No-Glare instrument panel. Custom chrome and Custom cab equipment were separate options. Custom cab models had two armrests, two sun visors, a cigarette lighter, foam rubber seat cushions and backrests, bright control knobs, and chrome window moldings. The Panoramic rear window was an option. New options included Cool-Pack air-conditioning and seat belts. Maximum GVW was [4x2] 5,000 lbs.; [4x4] 5,600 lbs.

1958 Chevrolet 1-Ton Apache 36 Step-Side Pickup (OCW)

1/2-TON COMMERCIAL (CAMEO) — MODEL 3A/SERIES 3124 — SIX/V-8: The Cameo had the new 1958 dual headlights. The outside of the box was trimmed like the 1957 model. Nine two-tone color choices were used on Cameos: Cardinal red over Bombay ivory; Golden yellow over black; Bombay ivory over Cardinal red; Jet black over Tartan turquoise; Kodiak brown over Bombay ivory; Bombay ivory over Granite gray; Glade green over Polar green; Marine blue over Dawn blue; Dawn blue over Marine blue; and Bombay ivory over Oriental green. This year the upper (first) color covered the entire roof (instead of only the pillars) except for a strip below the rub rail. The seat cloth changed from star design to a charcoal horizontal stripe. Red seat material with silver trim was used with the "standard" Cardinal red over Bombay ivory paint RPO. In this case the steering wheel, mast and top of the dash were red and door panels were metallic silver. Other interior combinations were optional. Standard production wheels were Cardinal red; lower body color with paint RPOs. The Cameo again had the 114 in. wheelbase and 196.5 in. overall length. The box was 78.5 in. long. It had a 77 in. maximum outside width, but was only 50 in. wide on its interior. With standard 6.70 x 15 tires, the Cameo had a 4,600 lbs. GVW rating and could handle payloads up to about 450 lbs. With a simple change to six-ply tires, the numbers went to 4,300 lbs. and 750 lbs. With 1,550 lbs. rear springs and 6.50 x 16 six-ply tires, the GVW was 4,600 lbs. and the payload rating 1,050 lbs. Combining the heavy springs with 7-17.5 six-ply tires upped the numbers to 5,000 lbs. and 1,450 lbs. Standard equipment included: 1-pint oil bath air cleaner; 12-volt 53 amp.-hr. battery; chrome front bumper; painted rear bumper; chrome bumperettes; Custom cab equipment; single exhausts; front and integral rear fenders; fuel filter; headlamps, parking lights and dual stop/taillamps; left side mirror with eight-inch fixed bracket; two-tone paint; tubeless tires; Full-View rear window; dual vacuum wipers; tubeless tires; and three-speed manual transmission. Transmission options included Hydra-Matic, heavy-duty manual three-speed and four-speed manual. The Cameo was listed in the *CHEVROLET TRUCK DATA BOOK* issued Oct. 1, 1957. The Fleetside was later phased in to replace it. The Cameo did not come with four-wheel drive. Maximum GVW was 5,000 lbs.

1/2-TON COMMERCIAL — MODEL 3B/SERIES 3200 — SIX/V-8: The 3200 Series Task-Force trucks had the same basic styling and trim changes as other conventional trucks. A new Fleetside edition was introduced, as well as a Chassis & Cab. These were the long wheelbase (LWB) 1/2-ton trucks on the same chassis as 3/4-ton models. They are known

as "Long Bed" or "Long Box" Pickups because they had a longer load box. Chevrolet parts catalogs indicated that a 98 in. box was used for 1957-1958 Models 3200/3600. Longer runningboards were also needed because there was more space between the cab and rear fenders. They still had the same 5,000 lbs. maximum GVW rating as other 1/2-ton trucks.

3/4-TON DUBL-DUTI — MODEL 3C/SERIES 3400 — SIX/V-8: Three Dubl-Duti Forward-Control chassis remained in the truck line. The Model 3442 had a 104 in. wheelbase. Standard walk-in delivery truck bodies could be supplied by several factory-approved sources or the buyer could add his/her own body.

3/4-TON DUBL-DUTI — MODEL 3D/SERIES 3500 — SIX-CYLINDER: Model 3542 was the 3/4-ton Dubl-Duti on a 125 in. wheelbase. Standard walk-in delivery truck bodies could be supplied by several factory-approved sources or the buyer could add his/her own body. The wheels were of eight-bolt design. A painted, Anvil gray channel type front bumper was standard on the 3500 Dubl-Duti truck chassis.

3/4-TON — DUBL-DUTI — MODEL F/SERIES 3700 — SIX-CYLINDER: Model 3742 was the Dubl-Duti on a 137 in. wheelbase. Standard walk-in delivery truck bodies could be supplied by several factory-approved sources or the buyer could add his/her own body. The wheels were of eight-bolt design. A painted, Anvil gray channel type front bumper was standard on the 3700 Dubl-Duti truck chassis.

3/4-TON COMMERCIAL — MODEL 3E56/SERIES 3600 — SIX/V-8: The 3600 Series Task-Force trucks had the same styling and trim changes as other conventional trucks. A Fleetside Pickup was added to this series of medium-duty cab models on a 123.5 in. wheelbase. Compared to 3100 pickups, the 3600 pickup had longer runningboards and a longer cargo box with a horizontal support rib. Chevrolet parts catalogs indicated that a 98 in. box was used for 1957-1958 Model 3600s. There were also Platform and Platform/Stake models. The rail for the 3/4-ton Platform was 97-9/16 in. long. The maximum GVW rating was: [4x2] 6,900 lbs.; [4x4] 7,300 lbs.

1-TON MEDIUM-DUTY COMMERCIAL — MODEL 3G/SERIES 3800 — SIX-CYLINDER: The 3800 Series Task-Force trucks had the same styling and trim changes as other conventional trucks. There was no Fleetside Pickup in this line. Panel models had a one-piece floor made of 3/4-inch thick, five-ply laminated wood. The basic model lineup was unchanged. Compared to the 3600 Pickup, the 3800 Pickup had a longer wheelbase, a longer grain-tight load box with extra stake pockets and very long runningboards. The 1-ton Stake trucks had a 115-9/16 in. long rail. No hubcaps were used on the larger split-rim wheels of the Chassis & Cab and Stake models, which had eight bolts and eight circular openings. A four-speed manual synchromesh transmission was standard. GVW: [4x2] 7,400; [4x4] 9,600; [Dual Rear Wheel; 4x2] 10,000 lbs.

I.D. DATA: Serial Number located: [Chassis models] On plate temporarily attached near steering column, with final location per body maker; [All others] On plate attached to rear face of left-hand door hinge pillar; on right side of cowl under hood. The first (Sedan Delivery) or first and second symbol(s) indicated the series: G/H=1500; 3A=3100; 3B=3200; 3C=3400; 3D=3500; 3E=3600; 3F=3700; 3G=3800. The next two symbols indicated the model year: 58=1958. The fifth symbol indicated the assembly plant: A=Atlanta, Ga.; B=Baltimore, Md.; F=Flint, Mich.; J=Janesville, Wis.; K=Kansas City, Mo.; L=Los Angeles, Calif.; N=Norwood, Ohio; O=Oakland, Calif.; S=St. Louis, Mo.; T=Tarrytown, N.Y.; W=Willow Run, Mich. Each series was separately numbered in sequence, starting with 001001 at each assembly plant. Ending serial numbers not available. Engine numbers located on right side of engine on boss at rear of distributor. Engine numbers began with an F (Flint, Mich.) or T (Tonawanda, N.Y.) assembly plant code.

Job No.	Body Type	Price	Weight	Prod. Total
Sedan Delivery — Model D58/Series 1500 — 117.5 in. w.b.				
1171	Sedan Delivery	2123	3529	—
1/2-Ton Commercial — Model 3A/Series 3100 — 114 in. w.b.				
3102	Chassis	1517	2401	—
3103	Chassis & Cab	1770	2910	—
3104	Step-Side Pickup	1884	3273	—
3105	Panel	2185	3495	—
3106	Suburban (door)	2518	3794	—
3116	Suburban (gate)	2518	3799	—
3134	Fleetside Pickup	1900		—
1/2-Ton Commercial (Cameo) — Model 3A/Series 3100 — 114 in. w.b.				
3124	Cameo Carrier	2231	3423	1405
1/2-Ton Commercial (Long Box) — Model 3B/Series 3200 — 123.25 in. w.b.				
3203	Chassis & Cab	1808	3102	—
3204	Step-Side Pickup	1922	3342	—
3234	Fleetside Pickup	1938		—
3/4-Ton Dubl-Duti — Model 3C/Series 3400 — 104 in. w.b.				
3442	Chassis	1652	2687	—
3445	Walk-In Delivery	3047	4698	—
3/4-Ton Dubl-Duti — Model 3D/Series 3500 — 125 in. w.b.				
3542	Chassis	1690	2754	—
3545	Walk-In Delivery	3132	4975	—
3/4-Ton Dubl-Duti — Model 3F/Series 3700 — 137 in. w.b.				
3742	Chassis	1722	2762	—
3745	Walk-In Delivery	3243	5223	—
3/4-Ton Dubl-Duti — Model 3E/Series 3600 — 123.25 in. w.b.				
3602	Chassis	1689	2751	—
3603	Chassis & Cab	1953	3270	—
3604	Step-Side Pickup	2066	3674	—
3634	Fleetside Pickup	2082		—
3609	Stake Bed	2158	3894	—
1-Ton Commercial — Model 3G/Series 3800 — 135 in. w.b.				
3802	Chassis	1836	3030	—
3803	Chassis & Cab	2100	3496	—
3804	Step-Side Pickup	2233	3973	—
3805	Panel	2561	4265	—
3809	Stake Bed	2346	4321	—

NOTE 1: The 4x4 option was available on all 3100/3600/3800 Series trucks, except Cameo Carrier.

1958 Chevrolet 1/2-Ton Apache 31 Fleetside With Custom Wheels (RVM)

ENGINE [Standard, All]: Inline. OHV. Six-cylinder. Cast iron block. Bore & stroke: 3-9/16 x 3-15/16 in. Displacement: 235.5 cid. Compression ratio: 8.25:1. Brake horsepower: 145 at 4200 rpm. Torque: 215 lbs.-ft. at 2400 rpm. SAE horsepower: 125 at 4000 rpm. Four main bearings. Hydraulic valve lifters. Carburetor: Rochester one-barrel model 7012133.

ENGINE [Optional All, except Dubl-Duti]: Vee-block. OHV. Eight-cylinder. Cast iron block. Bore & stroke: 3-7/8 x 3 in. Displacement: 283 cid. Compression ratio: 8.5:1. Brake horsepower: 160 at 4200 rpm. Torque: 275 lbs.-ft. at 2400 rpm. SAE horsepower: 137 at 3800 rpm. Five main bearings. Hydraulic valve lifters. Carburetor: Rochester two-barrel model 7012133.8.

ENGINE [1200]: Vee-block. OHV. Eight-cylinder. Cast iron block. Bore & stroke: 3-7/8 x 3 in. Displacement: 283 cid. Compression ratio: 8.5:1. Brake horsepower: 185 at 4500 rpm. Five main bearings. Hydraulic valve lifters. Carburetor: Rochester two-barrel model 7012133.

ENGINE [1200]: Vee-block. OHV. Eight-cylinder. Cast iron block. Bore & stroke: 3-7/8 x 3 in. Displacement: 283 cid. Compression ratio: 9.5:1. Brake horsepower: 230 at 4800 rpm. Five main bearings. Hydraulic valve lifters. Carburetor: Rochester four-barrel.

ENGINE [1200]: Vee-block. OHV. Eight-cylinder. Cast iron block. Bore & stroke: 3-7/8 x 3 in. Displacement: 283 cid. Compression ratio: 9.5:1. Brake horsepower: 250 at 5200 rpm. Five main bearings. Hydraulic valve lifters. Carburetor: Rochester fuel-injection.

ENGINE [1200]: Vee-block. OHV. Eight-cylinder. Cast iron block. Bore & stroke: 3-7/8 x 3 in. Displacement: 283 cid. Compression ratio: 9.5:1. Brake horsepower: 230 at 4800 rpm. Five main bearings. Hydraulic valve lifters. Carburetor: Two Carter four-barrels.

1958 Chevrolet 1/2-Ton Apache 10 Fleetside Pickup (OCW)

CHASSIS [Series 1500]: Wheelbase: 117.5 in. Overall length: 209.1 in. Height: 57.4 in. Tires: 7.50 x 14 four-ply. Maximum GVW: 4,100 lbs.

CHASSIS [Series 3100]: Wheelbase: 114 in. Overall length: [Cameo] 193.56 in.; [Others] 185.7 in. Front tread: 60.5 in. Rear tread: 61.0 in. Tires: 6.70 x 15 four-ply. Maximum GVW: 5,000 lbs.

CHASSIS [Series 3200]: Wheelbase: 123.25 in. Overall length: [Early] 205.56; [Late] 215.81 in. Tires: 7 x 7.5 six-ply. Maximum GVW: 5,000 lbs.

CHASSIS [Series 3442]: Wheelbase: 104 in. Tires: 8 x 19.5 six-ply. Maximum GVW: 7,000 lbs.

CHASSIS [Series 3542]: Wheelbase: 125 in. Tires: 8 x 19.5 six-ply. Maximum GVW: 8,800 lbs.

CHASSIS [Series 3742]: Wheelbase: 137 in. Tires: 8 x 19.5 six-ply. Maximum GVW: 10,000 lbs.

CHASSIS [Series 3600]: Wheelbase: 123.25 in. Overall length: [Early] 205.56; [Late] 215.81 in. Tires: 7 x 17.5 six-ply. Maximum GVW: 6,900 lbs.

CHASSIS [Series 3800]: Wheelbase: 135 in. Overall length: 215.81 in. Tires: [Single rear wheels] 7.50 x 17.5; [Dual Rear Wheels] (front) 8 x 17.5 six-ply; (rear) 8 x 17.5 eight-ply. Maximum GVW: [Single Rear Wheels] 7,000 lbs.; [Dual Rear Wheels] 9,600 lbs..

TECHNICAL: Selective synchromesh transmission. Speeds: [3800] 4F/1R; [Others] 3F/1R. Column-mounted gearshift (floor-shift on 3800). Single-plate dry-disc clutch. [3600/3800] Full-floating rear axle; [Others] Semi-floating rear axle. Overall ratio: [3100/3200] 3.90:1; [3400/3500/3700] 5.14:1; [3600] 4.57:1. Four-wheel hydraulic brakes. Steel disc wheels. Options: Heavy-duty three-speed manual transmission. Overdrive transmission. Four-speed manual transmission. Hydra-Matic transmission. Rear axles. Heavy-duty clutch. Heavy-duty radiator. Oil bath air cleaner.

OPTIONS: [RPO] Directionals. Heater/defroster. Double-action shocks. Rearview mirrors/brackets. Rear shock absorber shield. Hydrovac. Prop shaft brake. Oil bath air cleaners. PCV system. Painted or chrome rear bumper. Heavy-duty clutch. High body sills. Oil filter. Governor. Dual tail and stop lamps. Heavy-duty rear springs. Heavy-duty radiator. Foam rubber seat cushion. Auxiliary seat. Auxiliary rear axle. Airmatic seat. Wide base wheels. Speedometer fittings. Powerglide (Sedan Delivery). Hydra-Matic (Commercials). Overdrive. Heavy-duty three-speed transmission. Heavy-duty four-speed transmission. Electric wipers. Power steering. High-output generators. Side-mounted spare tire carrier (dimpled

rear fender required 3100/3200/3600). Heavy-duty battery. Power steering. Channel type painted front bumper (Dubl-Duti.) Spare wheel carrier (Dubl-Duti). Custom Cab equipment (includes Panoramic rear window; deluxe seat; chrome instrument knobs; cigarette lighter; dual visors; dual armrests; two-tone upholstery and interior color scheme). Chrome equipment. Full-view Panoramic rear window. Left-hand door lock and lock for side-mounted spare. E-Z-Eye tinted glass. Trademaster V-8 engine.

1958 Chevrolet 1/2-Ton Cameo Carrier (OCW)

OPTIONS: [Dealer Accessories] Radio antenna. Heater (Standard/Deluxe). Cigar lighter. Seat covers. External sun shade. Hubcaps. Directional signals. Front bumper guards (painted or chrome). Rear fold-down steps (Platform/Stake). Dual sun visors. Extendible outside mirrors. Spotlight with mirror. Windshield washer. External sun visor. Traffic viewer. Backup lights (Sedan Delivery). Electric parking brake signal. Chrome hood ornament. Dual fog lamps. Red reflex reflectors. Portable spotlight. AC/DC shaver. Stainless steel door edge guards. Stainless steel door vent shades. Chrome door handle shields. Tool kit. Illuminated compass. Underhood light. Second (high-note) horn.

HISTORICAL: Introduced: October, 1957. Model year production: [All Chevrolet Commercial Series] 278,632. Innovations: First year for dual headlights. All-new Fleetside Pickup with double-wall cargo-box construction introduced to replace the Cameo Carrier during the model year. This was Chevrolet's 40th year of manufacturing trucks. Chevrolet's long association with Union Body Co., of Union City, Ind., began with the introduction of Step-Van forward-control (Walk-in delivery van) models.

1958 Chevrolet Delray Sedan Delivery (DFW)

1959 CHEVROLET

1959 Chevrolet 1/2-Ton Apache 10 Step-Side Pickup (DFW)

EL CAMINO — MODEL G/SERIES 1100 (SIX) — MODEL H/SERIES 1200 (V-8): The big news from Chevrolet in 1959 was the all-new El Camino, the company's first Coupe-Pickup since 1941. Replacing the (1955-1957) Cameo Pickup as a super-styled Pickup, it was a vehicle which Chevrolet depicted as, "More than a car.... More than a truck." The El Camino had the general styling of Chevrolet's passenger sedan models, while possessing a load capacity of 1,150 lbs. The box was over 6 ft. long and nearly 5-1/2 ft. wide. It had a load volume of nearly 34 cu. ft. and was of double wall design. Its steel floor had built-in skid strips over a ribbed and embossed sub-floor supported by four crossmembers. Standard for the El Camino was a six-cylinder engine, but two V-8s were available along with Powerglide, Turboglide and overdrive transmissions as alternatives to the standard three-speed manual gearbox. Trim was of the Bel Air level with a full-length side molding with painted inserts and front fender ornaments. The front fenderside scripts said El Camino. Features included all-vinyl trim, a Bel Air style steering wheel, and chrome window frames. The El Camino was offered in 13 solid and 10 two-tone color combinations. Colors were Tuxedo black; Frost blue; Harbor blue; Gothic Gold; Aspen green; Highland green; Roman red; Snow Crest white; Satin beige; Cameo coral; Classic cream; Grecian gray; and Crown Sapphire. The two-tone designs consisted of one color on the roof, upper pillar area and upper rear deck, with the rest of the vehicle in the second color. The spare tire was located behind the hinged passenger seat and the tailgate lowered to bed floor level for carrying extended loads. The maximum GVW was 4,900 lbs.

SEDAN DELIVERY — MODEL G/SERIES 1100 (SIX) — MODEL H/SERIES 1200 (V-8): The 1959 Sedan Delivery was based on the Station Wagon. It had Biscayne level trim with a solid bright metal molding across the front fenders that extended to the middle of the doors. It grew two inches longer and was two inches lower. However, the completely redesigned "Slimline" body was wider and roomier. Styling features included increased glass area; "Spread Wing" rear styling; new taillights; and a full-width rear door that swung up to protect the user unloading during rain or snow. Standard equipment included a single bucket seat; auxiliary passenger seat; cargo interior with tempered Masonite panels; and car-style cab trimmings. Colors were Tuxedo black; Frost blue; Harbor blue; Gothic Gold; Aspen green; Highland green; Roman red; and Snow Crest white.

1/2-TON — MODEL 3A/SERIES 3100 — SIX/V-8: The new Task Force Commercial models kept the dual headlamps, new grille, and basic technical features of 1958 models. The new grille consisted of narrow horizontal bars just below the hood and a more massive "barbell-shaped" lower molding extending out and under the headlamps. This molding had the Chevrolet name lettered across it and its rectangular outboard extensions surrounded the similarly-shaped parking lamp lenses. Base-level Apaches had a cream-painted grille, bumper and headlamp buckets and cream-colored hubcaps. The front hood emblem had an ornament with a somewhat "squashed T" shape. Fenderside nameplates changed from a jet plane to a rocket ship shape and were moved just behind the headlamps. They said Chevrolet Apache 31 on the 3100s. Four-wheel drive was optional. Colors included Frontier beige; Jet black; Baltic blue; Dawn blue; Cadet gray; Galway green; Glade green; Sherwood green; Omaha orange; Cardinal red; Tartan turquoise; Pure white; Golden yellow; and Yukon yellow. All colors were available as the main color in two-tone combination with Bombay ivory. "Color-Break" two-toning (with everything above the hood level feature line, except the rear of the cab in the contrasting color) was new for Fleetsides. Standard wheels were black and the wheels on two-toned trucks were the main body color. Buyers were again presented with a choice of two types of pickups: The traditional model with exposed rear fenders and standard width box (called the Step-Side) and a new type with slab-sided rear steel fenders and extra-wide box, which was called the Fleetside. Fleetside models had a missle-shaped bulge along the slab-sided bed exterior. Their boxes were 75 in. wide. Custom chrome and Custom cab equipment were separate options. Custom cab models had two armrests, two sun visors, a cigarette lighter, foam rubber seat cushions and backrests, bright control knobs, and chrome window moldings. The Panoramic rear window was a separate option. Maximum GVW was [4x2] 5,000 lbs.; [4x4] 5,600 lbs.

1959 Chevrolet 1/2-Ton Apache 10 Step-Side (OCW)

1/2-TON COMMERCIAL — MODEL 3B/SERIES 3200 — SIX/V-8: The 3200 Series Task-Force trucks had the same basic styling and trim changes as other conventional trucks. A new Step-Side with a 9 ft. box was introduced, as well as a Chassis & Cab. These were the long wheelbase (LWB) 1/2-ton trucks on the same chassis as 3/4-ton models. They are known as "Long Bed" or "Long Box" Pickups because they had a longer 98 in. load box. Longer runningboards were needed because there was more space between the cab and rear fenders. These trucks were not available with four-wheel drive. They had the same 5,000 lbs. maximum GVW rating as other 1/2-ton trucks.

3/4-TON DUBL-DUTI — MODEL 3C/SERIES 3400 — SIX/V-8: Three Dubl-Duti Forward-Control chassis remained in the truck line. The Model 3442 had a 104 in. wheelbase. Standard walk-in delivery truck bodies could be supplied by several factory-approved sources or the buyer could add his/her own body. A popular use for the Dubl-Duti chassis was as a platform for the Step-Van walk-in delivery trucks made by Union City Body Co., of Union City, Ind.

3/4-TON DUBL-DUTI — MODEL 3D/SERIES 3500 — SIX-CYLINDER: Model 3542 was the 3/4-ton Dubl-Duti on a 125 in. wheelbase. Standard walk-in delivery truck bodies, such as the Step-Van, could be supplied by several factory-approved sources or the buyer could add his/her own body. The wheels were of eight-bolt design. A painted, Anvil gray channel type front bumper was standard on the 3500 Dubl-Duti truck chassis.

3/4-TON — DUBL-DUTI — MODEL F/SERIES 3700 — SIX-CYLINDER: Model 3742 was the Dubl-Duti on a 137 in. wheelbase. Standard walk-in delivery truck bodies, such as the Step-Vans, could be supplied by several factory-approved sources or the buyer could add his/her own body. The wheels were of eight-bolt design. A painted, Anvil gray channel type front bumper was standard on the 3700 Dubl-Duti truck chassis.

3/4-TON COMMERCIAL — MODEL 3E/SERIES 3600 — SIX/V-8: The 3600 Series Task-Force trucks had the same styling and trim changes as other conventional trucks. Step-Side and Fleetside Pickups were in this series. Compared to 3100 pickups, the 3600 pickup had slightly longer runningboards and a longer cargo box with a horizontal support rib. A 98 in. box was used. There were also Platform and Platform/Stake models. The rail for the 3/4-ton Platform was 97-9/16 in. long. The maximum GVW rating was: [4x2] 6,900 lbs.; [4x4] 7,300 lbs.

1-TON MEDIUM-DUTY COMMERCIAL — MODEL 3G/SERIES 3800 — SIX-CYLINDER:
The 3800 Series Task-Force trucks had the same styling and trim changes as other conventional trucks. There was no Fleetside Pickup in this line. Panel models had a one-piece floor made of 3/4-inch thick, five-ply laminated wood. The basic model lineup was unchanged. Compared to the 3600 Pickup, the 3800 Pickup had a longer wheelbase, a longer grain-tight load box with extra stake pockets and very long runningboards. The 1-ton Stake trucks had a 115-9/16 in. long rail. No hubcaps were used on the larger split-rim wheels of the Chassis & Cab and Stake models, which had eight bolts and eight circular openings. A four-speed manual synchromesh transmission was standard. GVW: [4x2] 7,400; [4x4] 9,600.

I.D. DATA: Serial Number located: [Chassis models] On plate temporarily attached near steering column, with final location per body maker; [All others] On plate attached to rear face of left-hand door hinge pillar; on right side of cowl under hood. The first (El Camino/Sedan Delivery) or first and second symbol(s) indicated the series: G=1100; H=1200; 3A=3100; 3B=3200; 3C=3400; 3D=3500; 3E=3600; 3F=3700; 3G=3800. The next two symbols indicated the model year: 59=1959. The fifth symbol indicated the assembly plant: A=Atlanta, Ga.; B=Baltimore, Md.; F=Flint, Mich.; J=Janesville, Wis.; K=Kansas City, Mo.; L=Los Angeles, Calif.; N=Norwood, Ohio; O=Oakland, Calif.; P=Pontiac, Mich.; S=St. Louis, Mo.; T=Tarrytown, N.Y.; W=Willow Run, Mich. Each series was separately numbered in sequence, starting with 001001 at each assembly plant. Ending serial numbers not available. Engine numbers located on right side of engine on boss at rear of distributor. Engine numbers began with an F (Flint, Mich.) or T (Tonawanda, N.Y.) assembly plant code.

Job No.	Body Type	Price	Weight	Prod. Total
El Camino — Series 1100/Model G — 119 in. w.b. — Six				
1180	El Camino	2352	3605	—
Sedan Delivery — Series 1100/Model G — 119 in. w.b. — Six				
1170	Sedan Delivery	2363	3590	—
El Camino — Series 1200/Model H — 119 in. w.b. — V-8				
1180	El Camino	—	—	—
Sedan Delivery — Series 1200/Model G — 119 in. w.b. — V-8				
1170	Sedan Delivery	—	—	—
1/2-Ton Commercial — Model 3A/Series 3100 — 114 in. w.b.				
3102	Chassis	1580	2421	—
3103	Chassis & Cab	1834	2909	—
3104	Step-Side Pickup	1948	3260	—
3105	Panel	2249	3490	—
3106	Suburban (doors)	2583	3778	—
3116	Suburban (gate)	2616	3796	—
3134	Fleetside Pickup	1964	3304	—
1/2-Ton Commercial (Long Bed) — Model 3B/Series 3200 — 123.25 w.b.				
3203	Chassis & Cab	1872	2988	—
3204	Step-Side Pickup	1986	3386	—
3234	Fleetside Pickup	2002	3381	—
3/4-Ton Dubl-Duti — Model 3C/Series 3400 — 104 in. w.b.				
3442	Chassis	1716	2700	—
3445	Step-Van	3112	5042	—
3/4-Ton Dubl-Duti — Model 3D/Series 3500 — 125 in. w.b.				
3542	Chassis	1754	2795	—
3545	Step-Van	3197	5247	—
3/4-Ton Dubl-Duti — Model 3F/Series 3700 — 137 in. w.b.				
3742	Chassis	1786	2823	—
3745	Step-Van	3308	5416	—
3/4-Ton Comercial — Model 3E/Series 3600 — 123.25 in. w.b.				
3602	Chassis	1753	2780	—
3603	Chassis & Cab	2018	3275	—
3604	Step-Side Pickup	2132	3669	—
3634	Fleetside Pickup	2148	3664	—
3609	Stake	2223	3844	—
1-Ton Commercial — Model 3G/Series 3800 — 135 in. w.b.				
3802	Chassis	1899	3020	—
3803	Chassis & Cab	2164	3501	—
3804	Step-Side Pickup	2298	3954	—
3805	Panel	2626	4270	—
3809	Stake	2411	4294	—

1959 Chevrolet Series 1200 1/2-Ton El Camino Sedan-Pickup (OCW)

ENGINE [Standard All except 1200]: Inline. OHV. Six-cylinder. Cast iron block. Bore & stroke: 3.562 x 3.937 in. Displacement: 235.5 cid. Compression ratio: 8.25:1. Brake horsepower: 135 at 4000 rpm. Torque: 215 lbs.-ft. at 2400 rpm. Four main bearings. Hydraulic

valve lifters. Carburetor: Rochester two-barrel model 7013003. Name: Thriftmaster Six. Thriftmaster Special engine with lower horsepower and torque ratings available for Dubl-Duti.

ENGINE [Standard 1200; Optional 3100/3200/3600/3800]: V-type. OHV. Eight-cylinder. Cast iron block. Bore & stroke: 3.875 x 3 in. Displacement: 283 cid. Compression ratio: 8.5:1. Brake horsepower: 185. Five main bearings. Carburetor: Rochester two-barrel model 7013007. Name: Turbo-Fire V-8.

ENGINE [Optional 1200]: V-type. OHV. Eight-cylinder. Cast iron block. Bore & stroke: 3.875 x 3 in. Displacement: 283 cid. Compression ratio: 9.5:1. Brake horsepower: 230 at 4800 rpm. Maximum Torque: 300 lbs.-ft. at 3000. Five main bearings. Hydraulic valve lifters. Carburetor: Super Turbo-Fire V-8.

ENGINE [Optional 1200]: V-type. OHV. Eight-cylinder. Cast iron block. Bore & stroke: 3.875 x 3 in. Displacement: 283 cid. Compression ratio: 9.5:1. Brake horsepower: 250. Five main bearings. Fuel-injection.

ENGINE [Optional 1200]: V-type. OHV. Eight-cylinder. Cast iron block. Bore & stroke: 3.875 x 3 in. Displacement: 283 cid. Compression ratio: 10.5:1. Brake horsepower: 290. Five main bearings. Fuel-injection.

ENGINE [Optional 1200]: V-type. OHV. Eight-cylinder. Cast iron block. Bore & stroke: 4.125 x 3.25 in. Displacement: 348 cid. Compression ratio: 9.5:1. Brake horsepower: 250. Five main bearings. Carburetor: Four-barrel.

ENGINE [Optional 1200]: V-type. OHV. Eight-cylinder. Cast iron block. Bore & stroke: 4.125 x 3.25 in. Displacement: 348 cid. Compression ratio: 9.5:1. Brake horsepower: 280. Five main bearings. Carburetor: Three two-barrels.

ENGINE [Optional 1200]: V-type. OHV. Eight-cylinder. Cast iron block. Bore & stroke: 4.125 x 3.25 in. Displacement: 348 cid. Compression ratio: 11.0:1. Brake horsepower: 300. Five main bearings. Carburetor: Four-barrel.

ENGINE [Optional 1200]: V-type. OHV. Eight-cylinder. Cast iron block. Bore & stroke: 4.125 x 3.25 in. Displacement: 348 cid. Compression ratio: 11.0:1. Brake horsepower: 305. Five main bearings. Carburetor: Four-barrel.

ENGINE [Optional 1200]: V-type. OHV. Eight-cylinder. Cast iron block. Bore & stroke: 4.125 x 3.25 in. Displacement: 348 cid. Compression ratio: 11.0:1. Brake horsepower: 315. Five main bearings. Carburetor: Three two-barrels.

ENGINE [Optional 1200]: V-type. OHV. Eight-cylinder. Cast iron block. Bore & stroke: 4.125 x 3.25 in. Displacement: 348 cid. Compression ratio: 11.25:1. Brake horsepower: 320. Five main bearings. Carburetor: Four-barrel.

ENGINE [Optional 1200]: V-type. OHV. Eight-cylinder. Cast iron block. Bore & stroke: 4.125 x 3.25 in. Displacement: 348 cid. Compression ratio: 11.25:1. Brake horsepower: 335. Five main bearings. Carburetor: Three two-barrels.

1959 Chevrolet Series 1200 1/2-Ton El Camino Sedan-Pickup (OCW)

CHASSIS [1100/1200]: Wheelbase: 119 in. Overall length: 210.9 in. Height: 56.3 in. Tires: 8.00 x 14 four-ply. Maximum GVW: 4,900 lbs.

CHASSIS [Series 3100]: Wheelbase: 114 in. Overall length: [Cameo] 193.56 in.; [Others] 185.7 in. Front tread: 60.5 in. Rear tread: 61.0 in. Tires: 6.70 x 15 four-ply. Maximum GVW: 5,000 lbs.

CHASSIS [Series 3200]: Wheelbase: 123.25 in. Overall length: [Early] 205.56; [Late] 215.81 in. Tires: 7 x 7.5 six-ply. Maximum GVW: 5,000 lbs.

CHASSIS [Series 3442]: Wheelbase: 104 in. Tires: 8 x 19.5 six-ply. Maximum GVW: 7,000 lbs.

CHASSIS [Series 3542]: Wheelbase: 125 in. Tires: 8 x 19.5 six-ply. Maximum GVW: 8,800 lbs.

CHASSIS [Series 3742]: Wheelbase: 137 in. Tires: 8 x 19.5 six-ply. Maximum GVW: 10,000 lbs.

CHASSIS [Series 3600]: Wheelbase: 123.25 in. Overall length: [Early] 205.56; [Late] 215.81 in. Tires: 7 x 17.5 six-ply. Maximum GVW: 6,900 lbs.

CHASSIS [Series 3800]: Wheelbase: 135 in. Overall length: 215.81 in. Tires: [Single rear wheels] 7.50 x 17.5; [Dual Rear Wheels] (front) 8 x 17.5 six-ply; (rear) 8 x 17.5 eight-ply. Maximum GVW: [Single Rear Wheels] 7,000 lbs.; [Dual Rear Wheels] 9,600 lbs.

TECHNICAL: Selective synchromesh transmission. Speeds: [3800] 4F/1R; [others] 3F/1R. Column-mounted gearshift (floor-shift on 3800). Single-plate dry-disc clutch. [3600/3800] Full-floating rear axle; [Others] Semi-floating rear axle. Overall ratios: [1100/1200] Four from 3.08 to 4.11; [3100/3200] Five from 3.38 to 4.11; [3400/3500/3700] 4.7:1 [3600] 4.57:1.; [3800] 5.14:1. Four-wheel hydraulic brakes. Steel disc wheels. Options: Heavy-duty three-speed manual transmission. Overdrive transmission. Four-speed manual transmission. Hydra-Matic transmission. Rear axles. Heavy-duty clutch. Heavy-duty radiator. Oil bath air cleaner.

1959 Chevrolet Series 1200 1/2-Ton El Camino Sedan-Pickup (JCL)

OPTIONS: [RPO] Positraction. Directionals. Heater/defroster. Double-action shocks. Rearview mirrors/brackets. Rear shock absorber shield. Hydrovac. Prop shaft brake. Oil bath air cleaners. PCV system. Painted or chrome rear bumper. Heavy-duty clutch. High body sills. Oil filter. Governor. Dual tail and stop lamps. Heavy-duty rear springs. Heavy-duty radiator. Foam rubber seat cushion. Auxiliary seat. Auxiliary rear springs. Airmatic seat. Wide base wheels. Speedometer fittings. Powerglide (Sedan Delivery). Hydra-Matic (Commercials). Overdrive. Heavy-duty three-speed transmission. Heavy-duty four-speed transmission.

Electric wipers. Power steering. High-output generators. Side-mounted spare tire carrier (dimpled rear fender required 3100/3200/3600). Heavy-duty battery. Power steering. Channel type painted front bumper (Dubl-Duti.) Spare wheel carrier (Dubl-Duti). Custom Cab equipment (includes Panoramic rear window; deluxe seat; chrome instrument knobs; cigarette lighter; dual visors; dual armrests; two-tone upholstery and interior color scheme). Chrome equipment. Full-view Panoramic rear window. Left-hand door lock and lock for side-mounted spare. E-Z-Eye tinted glass. Trademaster V-8 engine.

OPTIONS: [Dealer Accessories] Radio antenna. Heater (Standard/Deluxe). Cigar lighter. Seat covers. External sun shade. Hubcaps. Directional signals. Front bumper guards (painted or chrome). Rear fold-down steps (Platform/Stake). Dual sun visors. Extendible outside mirrors. Spotlight with mirror. Windshield washer. External sun visor. Traffic viewer. Backup lights (Sedan Delivery). Electric parking brake signal. Chrome hood ornament. Dual fog lamps. Red reflex reflectors. Portable spotlight. AC/DC shaver. Stainless steel door edge guards. Stainless steel door vent shades. Chrome door handle shields. Tool kit. Illuminated compass. Underhood light. Second (high-note) horn.

1959 Chevrolet 1/2-Ton Apache 10 Fleetside (OCW)

HISTORICAL: Introduced: October, 1957. Model year production: [All Chevrolet Commercial Series] 278,632. Innovations: First year for dual headlights. All-new Fleetside Pickup with double-wall cargo-box construction introduced to replace the Cameo Carrier during the model year. This was Chevrolet's 40th year of manufacturing trucks. Chevrolet's long association with Union Body Co., of Union City, Ind., began with the introduction of Step-Van forward-control (walk-in delivery van) models.

HISTORICAL: Introduced: October, 1958. Calendar year registrations: [All Commercial Series] 306,237. Calendar year production: [All Commercial Series] 326,102. Innovations: El Camino personal Pickup introduced. Positraction rear axle option made available. Longer 119 in. wheelbase for Sedan Delivery and El Camino. Chevrolet sold its seventh millionth truck, since 1918, during the 1959 model run.

1960 CHEVROLET

1960 Chevrolet 1/2-Ton Apache 32 Fleetside Pickup (DFW)

EL CAMINO — SERIES 1100 (SIX)/SERIES 1200 (V-8) — SIX/V-8: Both the El Camino and Sedan Delivery, adopted the 1960 passenger car appearance changes. The grille was oval-shaped with two free-floating headlights at either end. A cross-bar arrangement of moldings held the bow tie emblem in a smaller oval at the center. They were backed by full-width horizontal bars. Parking lamps were underneath the redesigned bumper. The rear had angular gull-wing fins. Below them was a horizontal full width oval with two round taillamps at each end. The El Camino had an integral cargo bed and cab roof with rear overhang. Exterior trim for the El Camino was similar to the Bel Air level.

SEDAN DELIVERY — SERIES 1100 (SIX)/SERIES 1200 (V-8) — SIX/V-8: LIGHT TRUCK: The Sedan Delivery, adopted the 1960 passenger car appearance changes. The grille was oval-shaped with two free-floating headlights at either end. A cross-bar arrangement of moldings held the bow tie emblem in a smaller oval at the center. They were backed by full-width horizontal bars. Parking lamps were underneath the redesigned bumper. The rear had angular gull-wing fins. Below them was a horizontal full width oval with two round taillamps at each end. Sedan Deliveries looked a bit plain this year.

1/2-TON COMMERCIAL — MODEL C10 (4x2); K10 (4x4)/SERIES 1000 — SIX/V-8: Chevrolet offered 185 trucks on 18 different wheelbases. The Apache 10 models in the Series 1000 (1/2-ton) line came with C10/K10/C14 model prefixes. New design features included an elongated grille and headlamps where parking lamps were previously. The low-mounted grille consisted of full-width surround of rectangular oval-shape housing dual headlamps at each end, plus four horizontal blades between them. The bumpers, grille and inner faces of the grille surround were ivory-colored on base Apaches. Chevrolet lettering on the grille was black. At each end of the front hood face were "jet pod" air inlets with elongated parking lamps inside. The fendersides had chrome engine call-outs. A large, red bow tie in the middle of the hood face identified sixes. A Chevrolet crest with a V-shaped molding below it was on V-8 powered trucks. At the rear of the front fenders was a Chevrolet Apache 10 nameplate. The body was indented or "pinched-in" at the mid-belt level. The panels then flared out, creating a sculptured crease along the upper beltline level. The entire upper beltline seemed to have a flattened bulge to it. In front, the fenders had a flat, bulged look with a beam at the jet pods at the front. The center hood was somewhat lower and flatter. The cab looked wider, flatter and lower than in the past, but still had a wraparound windshield and side ventipanes. The bumper was a massive, but plain, full-width wraparound unit. Step-Side pickups had runningboards between the cab and pontoon style rear fenders. On these models, the pinched-in waist ended behind the cab doors and a separate crease line decorated the rear fender sides. A Custom Cab option was available and included a bright radiator grille, bright hubcaps, bright window frames, and bright, black-accented "Custom" scalp moldings on the rear upper quarter of the cab. A chrome front bumper was a separate option, as was a Full-View rear window. Paint colors were Jet black; Brigade blue; Marlin blue; Klondike gold; Garrison gray; Hemlock green; Neptune green; Omaha orange; Cardinal red; Grenadier red; Tartan turquoise; Pure white; Golden yellow; and Yukon yellow. Pickups were two-toned with the contrast color on all panels above the center of the pinched-in crease, except the roof and rear roof areas. Cab interiors were finished in metallic silver with a charcoal gray and silver dashboard. The seats had silver coverings with charcoal gray facings. A silver left-hand sun shade was used with the base deluxe interior. Custom cab interiors had charcoal upper door embossments; a silver and charcoal gray left-hand door armrest; silver right-hand sun visor; silver pattern cloth upholstery with charcoal gray vinyl facings and bolsters; chrome knobs; cigar lighter; and chrome Chevrolet nameplates. Two-toning on Suburban Carryalls was done with the contrast color on the lower body, under the pinched-in waist, and on the rear of the roof. This made them look like a pickup with a camper. Suburbans again came with either panel doors or an end-gate.

1/2-TON COMMERCIAL — MODELS C14/SERIES 1000 (4x2) — SIX/V-8: The C14 trucks in the Apache 10 Series 1000 line used a C14 model prefix. They had the same basic styling and trim changes as other conventional trucks. These were the long wheelbase (LWB) 1/2-ton trucks on the same chassis as 3/4-ton models. They are known as "Long Bed" or "Long Box" Pickups because they had a longer load box. Longer runningboards were needed on Step-Sides because there was more space between the cab and rear fenders. These trucks were not available with four-wheel drive.

3/4-TON DUBL-DUTI — MODEL P20/SERIES 2000 — SIX/V-8: Six Dubl-Duti Forward-Control chassis remained in the 2000 Series 3/4-ton truck line. The P23/P25/P26 models had wheelbases of 104 in./125 in./137 in., respectively. Standard walk-in delivery truck bodies could be supplied by several factory-approved sources. Popular models were the Step-Van walk-in delivery trucks made by Union City Body Co., of Union City, Ind. A channel type front bumper was used on Dubl-Duti trucks.

3/4-TON COMMERCIAL — MODEL C25/SERIES 2000 — SIX/V-8: The Apache 20 Series 2000 (3/4-ton) trucks had the same styling and trim changes as other conventional trucks. Step-Side and Fleetside Pickups were in this series. Compared to 3100 Pickups, the 3600 Pickup had slightly longer runningboards and a longer cargo box with a horizontal support rib. A 98 in. box was used. There were also Platform and Platform/Stake models. The rail for the 3/4-ton Platform was 97-9/16 in. long.

1960 Chevrolet 1/2-Ton Apache 10 Custom Fleetside (OCW)

1-TON DUBL-DUTI — MODEL P30/SERIES 3000 — SIX/V-8: Six Dubl-Duti Forward-Control chassis were in a new 3000 Series (1-ton) truck line. The P33/P35/P36 models had wheelbases of 104 in./125 in./137 in., respectively. Standard walk-in delivery truck bodies could be supplied by several factory-approved sources. Popular models were the Step-Van walk-in delivery trucks made by Union City Body Co., of Union City, Ind. A channel type front bumper was used on Dubl-Duti trucks.

1-TON MEDIUM-DUTY COMMERCIAL — MODEL C36/SERIES 3000 — SIX-CYLINDER: The Apache 30 Series 3000 (1-ton) trucks had the same styling and trim changes as other conventional trucks. There was no Fleetside Pickup in this line. Panel models had a one-piece floor made of 3/4-inch thick, five-ply laminated wood. The basic model lineup was unchanged. Compared to the 3600 Pickup, the 3800 Pickup had a longer wheelbase, a longer box with extra stake pockets and very long runningboards. The 1-ton Stake trucks had a 115-9/16 in. long rail. No hubcaps were used on the larger split-rim wheels of the Chassis & Cab and Stake models, which had eight bolts and eight circular openings. A four-speed manual synchromesh transmission was standard.

I.D. DATA: Serial Number located: [Chassis models] On plate temporarily attached near steering column, with final location per body maker; [All others] On plate attached to rear face of left-hand door hinge pillar; on right side of cowl under hood. The first symbol indicated model year, 0=1960. The second symbol indicated type: C=Conventional; K=4x4; G=El Camino/Sedan Delivery (six); H=El Camino/Sedan Delivery (V-8). The third and fourth symbols indicated the model prefix: El Camino/Sedan Delivery (Six)=11; El Camino/Sedan Delivery (V-8)=12; 1/2-ton standard wheelbase=14; 1/2-ton long wheelbase=15; 3/4-ton=25; 1-ton=36. The fifth symbol indicated body style: 2=Chassis & Cowl; 3=Chassis & Cab; 4=Pickup; 5=Panel; 6=Suburban Carryall; 9=Platform/Stake. The sixth symbol indicated the assembly plant: A=Atlanta, Ga.; B=Baltimore, Md.; F=Flint, Mich.; J=Janesville, Wis.; K=Kansas City, Mo.; L=Los Angeles, Calif.; N=Norwood, Ohio; O=Oakland, Calif.; S=St. Louis, Mo.; T=Tarrytown, N.Y.; and W=Willow Run, Mich. Remaining symbols were

the sequential production number starting with 100001 at each plant. Ending serial numbers not available. The Chevrolet engine had the source, date and type stamped on a serial number pad. Source codes were: F=Flint, Mich.; T=Tonawanda, N.Y.; C=Canada. Month codes were 1=Jan.; 2=Feb., etc. Date codes were 01=first of month, etc. El Camino/ Sedan Delivery engine prefix codes began with A/B/C/D/E/F/G/H (some plus second letter). Commercial model engine prefix codes were: [Thriftmaster 235] J/JB/JC/JD; [Thriftmaster 235 Special] K/KA; [Trademaster 283] M/MA. Engine serial numbers: [Six] Right side of block behind distributor; [V-8] Front of block below right-hand cylinder head. Engine serial numbers not available.

1960 Chevrolet 1/2-Ton Apache 10 Panel (DFW)

1960 Chevrolet 3/4-Ton Series 2500 Step-Side Pickup (IMSC)

Model No.	Body Type	Price	Weight	Prod. Total
El Camino — Series 1100 — 119 in. w.b. — Six				
1180	El Camino	2366	3545	—
Sedan Delivery — Series 1100 — 119 in. w.b. — Six				
1170	Sedan Delivery	2361	3605	—
El Camino — Series 1100 — 119 in. w.b. — V-8				
1180	El Camino	—	—	—
Sedan Delivery — Series 1100 — 119 in. w.b. — V-8				
1170	Sedan Delivery	—	—	—
1/2-Ton Commercial — Model C14;K14/Series 1000 — 115 in. w.b.				
[Apache 10]				
C1402	Chassis	1623	2505	—
C1403	Chassis & Cab	1877	3035	—
C1404	Step-Side	1991	3395	—
C1405	Panel	2308	3615	—
C1406	Suburban (doors)	2690	3960	—
C1416	Suburban (gate)	2723	3975	—
C1434	Fleetside	2007	3425	—

NOTE 1: K14 indicates Apache 10 4x4 trucks.

1/2-Ton Commercial (Long Bed) — Model C15/Series 1000 — 127 in. w.b.				
[Apache 10]				
C1503	Chassis & Cab	1914	3090	—
C1504	Step-Side	2028	3505	—
C1534	Fleetside	2044	3565	—
3/4-Ton Dubl-Duti — Model P23/Series 2000 — 104 in. w.b.				
P2342	Chassis	1687	2690	—
P2345	Step-Van	3083	5030	—
3/4-Ton Dubl-Duti — Model P25/Series 2000 — 125 in. w.b.				
P2542	Chassis	1725	2740	—
P2545	Step-Van	3168	5185	—
3/4-Ton Dubl-Duti — Model P26/Series 2000 — 137 in. w.b.				
P2642	Chassis	1758	2770	—
P2645	Step-Van	3279	5365	—
3/4-Ton Commercial — Model C25; K25/Series 2000 — 127 in. w.b.				
[Apache 20]				
C2502	Chassis	1795	2785	—
C2503	Chassis & Cab	2059	3370	—
C2504	Step-Side	2173	3790	—
C2509	Stake 8 ft.	2264	4000	—
C2534	Fleetside	2189	3845	—

NOTE 2: K25 indicates Apache 20 4x4 trucks.

1-Ton Commercial — Model C36/Series 3000 — 133 in. w.b.				
[Apache 30]				
C3602	Chassis	1952	3095	—
C3603	Chassis & Cab	2216	3665	—
C3604	Step-Side	2350	4120	—
C3605	Panel	2775	4405	—
C3609	Stake 9 ft.	2463	4485	—
1-Ton Dubl-Duti — Model P33/Series 3000 — 104 in. w.b.				
P3342	Chassis	1877	2865	—
P3345	Step-Van	3273	5205	—
1-Ton Dubl-Duti — Model P35/Series 3000 — 125 in. w.b.				
P3542	Chassis	1915	2930	—
P3545	Step-Van	3358	5375	—
1-Ton Dubl-Duti — Model P36/Series 3000 — 137 in. w.b.				
P3642	Chassis	1948	2960	—
P3645	Step-Van	3469	5550	—

ENGINE [Standard All except 1200]: Inline. OHV. Six-cylinder. Cast iron block. Bore & stroke: 3.562 x 3.937 in. Displacement: 235.5 cid. Compression ratio: 8.25:1. Brake horsepower: 135 at 4000 rpm. Torque: 215 lbs.-ft. at 2400 rpm. Four main bearings. Hydraulic valve lifters. Carburetor: Rochester two-barrel model 7013003. (Thriftmaster Special engine with lower horsepower and torque ratings available for Dubl-Duti.)

ENGINE [Optional 1000/2000/3000]: V-type. OHV. Eight-cylinder. Cast iron block. Bore & stroke: 3.875 x 3 in. Displacement: 283 cid. Compression ratio: 8.25:1. Brake horsepower: 160. Five main bearings. Carburetor: Two-barrel.

ENGINE [Standard 1200]: V-type. OHV. Eight-cylinder. Cast iron block. Bore & stroke: 3.875 x 3 in. Displacement: 283 cid. Compression ratio: 8.5:1. Brake horsepower: 170. Five main bearings. Carburetor: Two-barrel.

ENGINE [Optional 1200]: V-type. OHV. Eight-cylinder. Cast iron block. Bore & stroke: 3.875 x 3 in. Displacement: 283 cid. Compression ratio: 8.5:1. Brake horsepower: 230 at 4800 rpm. Maximum Torque: 300 lbs.-ft. at 3000. Five main bearings. Hydraulic valve lifters. Carburetor: Four-barrel.

ENGINE [Optional 1200]: V-type. OHV. Eight-cylinder. Cast iron block. Bore & stroke: 3.875 x 3 in. Displacement: 283 cid. Compression ratio: 9.5:1. Brake horsepower: 250. Five main bearings. Carburetor: Four-barrel.

ENGINE [Optional 1200]: V-type. OHV. Eight-cylinder. Cast iron block. Bore & stroke: 4.125 x 3.25 in. Displacement: 348 cid. Compression ratio: 9.5:1. Brake horsepower: 250. Five main bearings. Carburetor: Four-barrel.

ENGINE [Optional 1200]: V-type. OHV. Eight-cylinder. Cast iron block. Bore & stroke: 4.125 x 3.25 in. Displacement: 348 cid. Compression ratio: 9.5:1. Brake horsepower: 280. Five main bearings. Carburetor: Three two-barrels.

ENGINE [Optional 1200]: V-type. OHV. Eight-cylinder. Cast iron block. Bore & stroke: 4.125 x 3.25 in. Displacement: 348 cid. Compression ratio: 11.25:1. Brake horsepower: 320. Five main bearings. Carburetor: Four-barrel.

ENGINE [Optional 1200]: V-type. OHV. Eight-cylinder. Cast iron block. Bore & stroke: 4.125 x 3.25 in. Displacement: 348 cid. Compression ratio: 11.25:1. Brake horsepower: 335. Five main bearings. Carburetor: Three two-barrels.

1960 Chevrolet 1/2-Ton C10 Apache Suburban Carryall (BOR)

CHASSIS [1100/1200]: Wheelbase: 119 in. Overall length: 210.9 in. Height: 56.3 in. Tires: 8.00 x 14 four-ply. Maximum GVW: 4,900 lbs.

CHASSIS [C14]: Wheelbase: 115 in. Overall length: [Pickup] 186.75; [Suburban] 199.5 in. Tires: 6.70 x 15 four-ply. Maximum GVW: 5,200 lbs.

CHASSIS [C15]: Wheelbase: 127 in. Overall length: 206.25 in. Tires: 6.75 x 15 four-ply. Maximum GVW: 5,600 lbs.

CHASSIS [P23]: Wheelbase: 104 in. Tires: 7 x 17.5 six-ply.

CHASSIS [P25]: Wheelbase: 125 in. Tires: 7 x 17.5 six-ply.

CHASSIS [P26]: Wheelbase: 137 in. Tires: 7 x 17.5 six-ply.

CHASSIS [Series C25]: Wheelbase: 127 in. Overall length: 210.75 in. Tires: 7 x 17.5 six-ply.

CHASSIS [Series C36]: Wheelbase: 133 in. Overall length: 211.75 in. Tires: (front) 8 x 17.5 six-ply, (rear) 8 x 17.5 eight-ply.

CHASSIS [P33]: Wheelbase: 104 in. Tires: 8 x 19.5 six-ply.

CHASSIS [P35]: Wheelbase: 125 in. Tires: 8 x 19.5 six-ply.

CHASSIS [P36]: Wheelbase: 137 in. Tires: 8 x 17.5 six-ply.

1960 Chevrolet 1/2-Ton Delray Series 1100 Sedan-Pickup (OCW)

TECHNICAL: Selective synchromesh transmission. Speeds: [1-ton] 4F/1R; [Others] 3F/1R. Column-mounted gearshift (except four-speed). 10 or 11 in. diaphragm spring type clutch. [1-ton] Full-floating rear axle; [Others] Semi-floating rear axle. Base overall ratio: [1100/1200] 3.55:1; [C14/C15/K14/K15] 3.90:1; [C25/K25] 4.57:1; [C36] 5.14:1. Four-wheel hydraulic brakes.

OPTIONS: [RPO] Air cleaner. Air-conditioning. Positraction rear axle. Heavy-duty battery. Vacuum power brakes. Economy carburetor. Heavy-duty clutch. E-Z-Eye glass. High-output generators. Heater/defroster. Inside rearview mirror. Oil filter. Padded instrument panel. Delco AM radio. Foam rubber seat cushions. Heavy-duty rear springs. Power steering. Custom steering wheel. Powerglide automatic transmission (Now used in all models). Overdrive transmission (Sedan Delivery with 170 hp Trademaster 283 V-8 only). Full wheel discs. Windshield washers. Windshield wipers. Dual exhausts. Custom Cab Equipment package. Custom Comfort and Convenience package. Chrome Equipment package. Four-speed manual transmission (Standard in C30). Four-wheel drive system (C10 and C22 only).

1960 Chevrolet 1/2-Ton Delray Series 1100 Sedan-Pickup (OCW)

HISTORICAL: Introduced: Fall 1959. Calendar year production: [All Chevrolet Commercials] 394,017. Innovations: All-new styling for Pickups, Panels and Suburbans. First independent front suspension system for trucks. Light-duty models featured torsion bars in front and coil springs at rear. Chevrolet was America's number one truck-maker. This was the last year for a Sedan Delivery. It was also the last year for the full-size El Camino.

1961 CHEVROLET

1961 Chevrolet Corvair 95 Loadside Pickup (DFW)

CORVAIR 95 — MODEL R12/SERIES 1000 — SIX: Chevrolet's answer to the Volkswagen van was the all-new Corvair 95. These were driver-forward models built on the Corvair platform, with a rear-mounted air-cooled engine and transaxle. Dual headlamps, a small front grille with Chevrolet emblem and concave, sculptured contrast panel along the front and sides were among styling characteristics. The Panel model had steel sides in place of three side windows. There were two side load doors and double rear panel doors. It was merchandised as the Corvan and had Corvair 95 scripts on the front doors. A pickup was made by adding a cab panel-back and removing the upper sheet metal at the rear. It had a cargo box that was 105 in. long and 43-7/8 in. wide. It was called the Loadside model and featured fixed, double-wall box-side panel doors just behind the cab. Also available was the Rampside version, which had a unique door in the side of the box that dropped to the

ground to make a cargo loading ramp. Standard equipment on all Corvair 95s included: An air-cooled six-cylinder engine; three-speed synchromesh transmission; electric wipers; directional signals and five tubeless tires. Chrome hubcaps, chrome bumpers and a Custom interior/exterior appearance package were available.

1/2-TON COMMERCIAL — MODEL C14 (4x2); K14 (4x4)/SERIES 1000 — SIX/V-8: For Chevrolet's regular light-duties, the most notable exterior change involved a revised front end appearance. Each space in the "jet pod" front fender openings contained a Cameo white embossed spinner housing the parking lamps. This allowed air to enter the pods for underhood ventilation. Horizontal bars and the word Chevrolet on the lower molding disappeared from the radiator grille. It now had a silver annodized insert and a bar with Chevrolet lettering on it. The background of this center bar with lettering was painted low gloss black. The rest of the grille was Cameo white. Fenderside nameplates were raised to the upper beltline crease, just ahead of the rear hood seam. They said Apache 10 on a red bar for the Series 1000 trucks. Exterior colors were Jet black; Balboa blue; Brigade blue; Woodsmoke blue; Tahiti coral; Neptune green; Woodland green; Romany maroon; Omaha orange; Cardinal red; Tampico turquoise; Cameo white; Pure white; Flaxen yellow; and Yukon yellow. Cameo white could be teamed with one of the eight new colors for Color-Break two-toning. There were four separate Custom equipment options, which are listed in the options section below. Offered again were Step-Side (with pontoon rear fenders) and Fleetside (with slab-type rear fenders) Pickups with 6-1/2 ft. beds, plus the Panel, Suburban and the chassis models. The Apache 10 four-wheel drive 1/2-ton models had a K14 model prefix.

1/2-TON COMMERCIAL — MODELS C15 (4x2)/SERIES 1000 — SIX/V-8: The C15 trucks in the Apache 10 Series 1000 line used a C15 model prefix. Apache 10 nameplates decorated the fendersides. They had the same basic styling and trim changes as other conventional trucks. These were the long wheelbase (LWB) 1/2-ton trucks on the same chassis as 3/4-ton models. They are known as "Long Bed" or "Long Box" Pickups because they had a longer 8-ft. load box. Longer runningboards were needed on Step-Sides because there was more space between the cab and rear fenders. This series could now be had with four-wheel drive. The Apache 10 Long Bed four-wheel drive models had a K15 model prefix.

1961 Chevrolet Apache 10 Custom Fleeetside (OCW)

1/2-TON DUBL-DUTI — MODEL P13/SERIES 1000 — SIX/V-8: A 1/2-ton Dubl-Duti model resurfaced in 1961. The P13 had a 102 in. wheelbase. An approved Step-Van walk-in delivery truck made by Union City Body Co., of Union City, Ind. was most commonly mounted on the Dubl-Duti chassis. Buyers could order other bodies, too. A channel type front bumper was used on Dubl-Duti trucks, which continued to use the Special Thriftmaster Six with less horsepower than the Commercial Series base engine.

3/4-TON COMMERCIAL — MODEL C25/SERIES 2000 — SIX/V-8: The Apache 20 Series 2000 (3/4-ton) trucks had the same styling and trim changes as other conventional trucks. The fenderside nameplates said Apache 20. Step-Side and Fleetside Pickups were in this series. Compared to 3100 Pickups, the 3600 Pickup had slightly longer runningboards and a longer cargo box with a horizontal support rib. An 8 ft. bed was used. There were also Platform and Platform/Stake models. The rail for the 3/4-ton Platform was about 8 ft. long. The Apache 20 four-wheel drive 3/4-ton models had a K25 model prefix.

3/4-TON DUBL-DUTI — MODEL P23; P25; P26/SERIES 2000 — SIX/V-8: Three 3/4-ton Dubl-Duti Forward-Control chassis remained in the 3000 Series (1-ton) truck line. The P23/P25/P26 models had wheelbases of 104 in./125 in./137 in., respectively. Standard walk-in delivery truck bodies could be supplied by several factory-approved sources. Popular models were the Step-Van walk-in delivery trucks made by Union City Body Co., of Union City, Ind. A channel-type front bumper was used on Dubl-Duti trucks.

1-TON MEDIUM-DUTY COMMERCIAL — MODEL C36/SERIES 3000 — SIX-CYLINDER: The Apache 30 Series 3000 (1-ton) trucks had the same styling and trim changes as other conventional trucks. The fenderside nameplates said Apache 30. There was no Fleetside Pickup in this line. Panel models had a one-piece floor made of 3/4-inch thick, five-ply laminated wood. The basic model lineup was unchanged. Compared to the 3600 Pickup, the 3800 Pickup had a longer wheelbase, a longer 9 ft. box with extra stake pockets and very long runningboards. The 1-ton Stake trucks had a rail about 9-1/2 ft. long. No hubcaps were used on the larger split-rim wheels of the Chassis & Cab and Stake models, which had eight bolts and eight circular openings. A four-speed manual synchromesh transmission was standard. No four-wheel drive option was offered.

1-TON DUBL-DUTI — MODEL P33; P35; P36/SERIES 3000 — SIX/V-8: Three Dubl-Duti Forward-Control chassis were in the 3000 Series (1-ton) truck line. The P33/P35/P36 models had wheelbases of 104 in./125 in./137 in., respectively. Standard walk-in delivery truck bodies could be supplied by several factory-approved sources. Popular models were the Step-Van walk-in delivery trucks made by Union City Body Co., of Union City, Ind. A channel type front bumper was used on Dubl-Duti trucks.

I.D. DATA: Serial Number located: [Chassis models] On plate temporarily attached near steering column, with final location per body maker; [All others] On plate attached to rear face of left-hand door hinge pillar; on right side of cowl under hood. The first symbol indicated model year, 1=1961. The second symbol indicated type: C=Conventional; K=4x4; R=Corvair 95. The third and fourth symbols indicated the model prefix: Corvair 95=12; 1/2-ton standard wheelbase=14; 1/2-ton long wheelbase=15; 3/4-ton=25; 1-ton=36. The fifth symbol indicated body style: 2=Chassis & Cowl; 3=Chassis & Cab; 4=Panel; 5=Pickup; 6=Suburban Carryall; 9=Platform/Stake. The sixth symbol indicated the assembly plant: A=Atlanta, Ga.; B=Baltimore, Md.; F=Flint, Mich.; J=Janesville, Wis.; K=Kansas City, Mo.; L=Los Angeles, Calif.; N=Norwood, Ohio; O=Oakland, Calif.; S=St. Louis, Mo.; T=Tarrytown, N.Y.; and W=Willow Run, Mich. Remaining symbols were the sequential production number starting with 100001 at each plant. Ending serial numbers not available. The Chevrolet engine had the source, date and type stamped on a serial number pad. Source codes were: F=Flint, Mich.; T=Tonawanda, N.Y.; C=Canada. Month codes were 1=Jan.; 2=Feb., etc. Date codes were 01=first of month, etc. Corvair 95 prefix codes were V/W. Commercial model engine prefix codes were: [Thriftmaster 235] J/JB/JC; [Thriftmaster 235 Special] K; [Trademaster 283] M/MA. Engine serial numbers: [Six] Right side of block behind distribu-

tor; [V-8] Front of block below right-hand cylinder head. Engine serial numbers not available.

1961 Chevrolet Corvair 95 Rampside Pickup (CW)

Model	Body Type	Price	Weight	Prod. Total
1/2-Ton Corvair 95 — Model R12/Series 1000 — 95 in. w.b.				
R1205	Corvan	2289	2695	15,806
R1244	Loadside	2079	2595	2,475
R1254	Rampside	2133	2605	10,787
1/2 Ton Commercial 4x2 — Model C14/Series 1000 — 115 in. w.b.				
[Apache 10]				
C1403	Chassis & Cab	1877	3030	—
C1434	Fleetside	2007	3425	—
C1404	Step-Side	1991	3390	—
C1405	Panel	2308	3665	—
C1406	Suburban (doors)	2669	3970	—
C1416	Suburban (gate)	2702	4000	—
1/2 Ton Commercial 4x4 — Model K14/Series 1000 — 115 in. w.b.				
[Apache 10]				
K1434	Fleetside	2684	—	—
K1404	Step-Side	2668	—	—
K1405	Panel	2985	—	—
K1406	Suburban (doors)	3346	—	—
K1416	Suburban (gate)	3379	—	—
1/2 Ton Commercial 4x2 — Model C15/Series 1000 — 127 in. w.b.				
[Apache 10]				
C1503	Chassis & Cab	—	—	—
C1534	Fleetside	2007	3425	—
C1504	Step-Side	1991	3390	—
1/2 Ton Commercial 4x4 — Model K15/Series 1000 — 127 in. w.b.				
[Apache 10]				
K1503	Chassis & Cab	2554	3430	—
K1534	Fleetside	2684	3825	—
K1504	Step-Side	2668	3790	—
1/2-Ton Dubl-Duti — Model P23/Series 1000 — 102 in. w.b.				
P1345	Package Delivery	2546	3904	—
3/4-Ton Commercial 4x2 — Model C25/Series 2000 — 127 in. w.b.				
[Apache 20]				
C2539	Fleetside	2189	3855	—
C2504	Step-Side	2173	3810	—
C2503	Chassis & Cab	2059	3395	—
C2509	Stake 8 ft.	2264	4020	—
3/4-Ton Commercial 4x4 — Model K25/Series 2000 — 127 in. w.b.				
[Apache 20]				
K2539	Fleetside	2866	—	—
K2504	Step-Side	2850	—	—
3/4-Ton Dubl-Duti — Model P23; P25; P26/Series 2000 — 104-137 in. w.b.				
P2345	Package Delivery	3083	5030	—

NOTE 1: Data for 104 in. wheelbase. Dubl-Duti; 123 in./137 in. wheelbase optional.

Model	Body Type	Price	Weight	Prod. Total
1-Ton Commercial 4x2 — Model C36/Series 3000 — 133 in. w.b.				
[Apache 30]				
C3605	Panel	2775	4490	—
C3604	Step-Side	2350	4110	—
C3603	Chassis & Cab	2216	3655	—
C3609	Stake	2463	4485	—
1-Ton Dubl-Duti — Model P33; P35; P36/Series 3000 — 104-137 in. w.b.				
P3345	Package Delivery	3273	5185	—

NOTE 2: Data for 104 in. wheelbase. Dubl-Duti; 123.25 in./137 in. wheelbase optional.

ENGINE [Corvair 95]: Opposed. OHV. Turbo-Air. Six-cylinder. Aluminum block. Bore & stroke: 3.437 in. x 2.60 in. Displacement: 144.8 cid. Compression ratio: 8.0:1. Brake horsepower: 80 at 4400 rpm. Maximum Torque: 128 lbs.-ft. at 2300 rpm. Four main bearings. Hydraulic valve lifters. Carburetor: Two Rochester one-barrel model 7019101.
ENGINE [All except Corvair 95 and Dubl-Duti]: Inline. OHV. Thriftmaster. Six-cylinder. Cast iron block. Bore & stroke: 3-9/16 in. x 3-15/16 in. Displacement: 235.5 cid. Compression ratio: 8.25:1. Brake horsepower: 135 at 4000 rpm. Maximum Torque: 217 lbs.-ft. at

2000 rpm. Four main bearings. Hydraulic valve lifters. Carburetor: Rochester one-barrel model B7015011.
ENGINE [Optional, Except Corvair 95 and P models]: V-type. OHV. Trademaster. Eight-cylinder. Cast iron block. Bore & stroke: 3-7/8 in. x 3 in. Displacement: 283 cid. Compression ratio: 8.5:1. Brake horsepower: 160 at 4200 rpm. Maximum Torque: 270 lbs.-ft. at 2000 rpm. Five main bearings. Hydraulic valve lifters. Carburetor: Rochester two-barrel model 2G7015017.

1961 Chevrolet 1/2-Ton Series C10 Apache Fleetside Pickup (JLC)

CHASSIS [Corvair 95]: Wheelbase: 95 in. Overall length: 179.7 in. Height: 68.5 in. Front tread: 58 in. Rear tread: 58 in. Tires: 7.00 x 14 in. Maximum GVW: 4,600 lbs.
CHASSIS [C14/K14]: Wheelbase: 115 in. Overall length: 206 in.; Front tread: 63.1 in. Rear tread: 61 in. Tires: 6.70 x 15 in. Maximum GVW: [4x2] 4,600 lbs.; [4x4] 5,300 lbs.
CHASSIS [C15/K15]: Wheelbase: 127 in. Front tread: 63.1 in. Rear tread: 61.1 in. Tires: 6.70 x 15 in. Maximum GVW: [4x2] 4,600 lbs.; [4x4] 5,600 lbs.
CHASSIS [C25/K25]: Wheelbase: 127 in. Tires: 7 x 17.5 in. Maximum GVW: [4x2] 6,000 lbs.; [4x4] 6,800 lbs.
CHASSIS [C36]: Wheelbase: 133 in. Tires: 8 x 17.5 in. Maximum GVW: 7,800 lbs.
CHASSIS [P10]: Wheelbase: 102 in. Tires: 6.70 x 15 in.
CHASSIS [P20]: Wheelbase: 137 in. Tires: 7 x 17.5 in.
CHASSIS [P30]: Wheelbase: 104-137 in. Tires: 8 x 19.5 in.

1961 Chevrolet 3/4-Ton Apache K15 Fleetside 4x4 (RCA)

TECHNICAL: Manual. Synchromesh. Speeds: 3F/1R. Column-mounted gearshift lever. Single-plate dry-disc clutch. Rear axle: [1-ton] Full-floating; [Others] semi-floating. Standard axle ratio: [R12] 3.89:1; [C14/C15/K14/K15] 3.90:1; [C25/K25] 4.57:1; [C36] 5.14:1. Hydraulic four-wheel brakes. Pressed steel wheels.

OPTIONS: [Corvair 95] Positraction. Front and rear chrome bumpers. Custom Equipment package. Left-hand body door (Corvan). Level pickup box floor. Gasoline heater/defroster. Direct-Air heater/defroster. Chrome hubcaps. Two-tone exterior. Radio. Full-width front seat. Single right-hand auxiliary seat. Whitewall tires. Six-ply rated tires. Four-speed manual transmission. Powerglide automatic transmission. Two-speed electric wipers and washers. Rear bumper. Radio. Heater. Clock. Cigar lighter. Radio antenna. Seat covers.
OPTIONS: [Commercials] Air cleaner. Positraction. Special rear axle ratio. Heavy-duty battery. Spare wheel carrier. Painted rear bumper. Heavy-duty clutch. Directionals. Trademaster 283 V-8. Heavy-duty radiator fan. Ammeter. Oil pressure gauge. Generator. Alternator. Laminated glass. Engine governor. Heater and defroster. Towing hooks. Outside rearview mirror. Oil filter. Heavy-duty radiator. Delco AM radio and antenna. Bostrom seat. Shock absorbers. Rear springs. Tachometer. Fuel tank. Powerglide transmission. Heavy-duty three-speed transmission. Four-speed transmission. Positive crankcase ventilation system. Full-View rear window. Windshield washers. Electric windshield wipers. Alternator. Ammeter. Thriftmater Special economy engine.
OPTION PACKAGES: [Custom Appearance Equipment] Includes silver annodized radiator grille and headlamp door assembly; chrome-plated windshield reveal moldings; bright metal cab upper rear quarter panel trim plates; chrome horn ring steering wheel; chrome trimmed instrument panel knobs; and two-tone inside front door panels. [Custom Comfort and Convenience Equipment] Includes left door armrest; outside key lock; chrome cigar lighter; full foam rubber seat cushion; special seat trim (cab models and Suburban); and added sound insulation. [Custom Chrome Equipment] Chrome hubcaps. Not availabe with 4x4 or dual rear wheel options. [Side Trim Moldings] Bright bodyside moldings for Fleetside models.

1961 Chevrolet 1/2-Ton Apache K14 Suburban Carryall 4x4 (RCA)

HISTORICAL: Introduced: Fall 1960. Commercial model calendar year production: [All six-cylinder] 294,194; [All V-8] 48,391; [Total] 342,658. Commercial model calendar year registrations: [6,000 lbs. or less] 202,697; [6,001-10,000 lbs.] 44,903. Innovations: All-new Corvair truck-line. Alternators available (instead of generator) in electrical system. Optional heavy-duty front suspension introduced. Diesel options introduced for medium-duty series (and heavy-duties). Public acceptance of the styling and economy ·of the Corvair trucks was enthusiastic, but the lack of a single, smooth cargo load floor (due to rear engine location) proved to be a drawback to sales of these models. A fourth type of Corvair Van (Model R1206 Greenbriar) was merchandised as a passenger car (station wagon). It had a price of $2,651 and a 2,895 lbs. curb weight. Production of this model, at 18,489, was the highest of all Corvair 95s (total output was 47,557). Chevrolet was America's number one truck-maker in 1961, but only by the narrow margin of 3,670 units. Its 30.39 percent market share represented the production of 342,658 Commercial and Dubl-Duti models, down from 1960's 394,014 units. This was in contrast to production of 494,575 trucks in 1950. The company's great strength, at this time, was in the six-cylinder category. The Chevrolet six outsold its nearest competitor by nearly 100,000 units. J.E. Conlan was assistant general sales manager of the Chevrolet Truck Div.

1962 CHEVROLET

1962 Chevrolet Corvair 95 Rampside Pickup (OCW)

CORVAIR 95 — MODEL R12/SERIES 10 — SIX: The Corvair 95 trucks were virtually unchanged, except for serial numbers. A new option was a Positraction rear axle. These driver-forward models had a Corvair platform, a rear-mounted air-cooled engine and a transaxle. Dual headlamps, a small front grille with Chevrolet emblem and a sculptured contrast panel around the body were styling characteristics. The Corvan had steel panel sides, two side load doors and double rear panel doors. It had Corvair 95 scripts on the front doors. A Loadside pickup was made by adding a cab back panel and removing the upper sheet metal at the rear. The cargo box was 105 in. long and 43-7/8 in. wide. It featured a double-wall box. Also available was the Rampside pickup, which had a unique door in the side of the box. It dropped to the ground to make a cargo loading ramp. Standard equipment on all Corvair 95s included: An air-cooled six-cylinder engine; three-speed synchromesh transmission; electric wipers; directional signals and five tubeless tires. Chrome hubcaps, chrome bumpers and a Custom interior/exterior appearance package were available.

1/2-TON COMMERCIAL — MODEL C14 (4x2); K14 (4x4)/SERIES 10 — SIX/V-8: The Apache name disappeared on conventional trucks and the 1000 Series description gave way to the 10-20-30 model prefixes, still used today. A restyled hood panel gave the 1962 Chevrolet 10 Series 1/2-ton trucks a new appearance. It was lower and flatter than the "jet pod" style hood and had a bevel around its perimeter to mate with the previous lines. Rectangular parking lamps were set into the bevel at each front corner. Rectangular air slot openings were punched into the bevel on either side of center. The grille had two horizontal members and two vertical members crossing to form nine rectangular openings. Large, rectangular headlamp housings sat outside each end of the grille. The standard grille was done in Cameo white with black Chevrolet lettering on the lower molding of the grille surround. Standard hubcaps were also Cameo white. Chrome equipment was optional. The hoodside nameplates were moved slightly back to the sides of the cowl. The badge had vertical grooves and a black background with a red accented Chevrolet bow tie at the front and a 10 (for C10 or 10 Series) at the rear. Custom Fleetsides got a new silver annodized aluminum bodyside molding with white accents. Colors for the year were Desert beige; Jet black; Balboa blue; Brigade blue; Georgian gray; Seamist jade; Glenwood green; Woodland green; Omaha orange; Cardinal red; Crystal turquoise; Cameo white; Pure white; and

Yukon yellow. All colors, except the two whites, were used as lower body colors in the 12 two-tone color options. They were teamed with Cameo white on the upper body. Interiors were done in two shades of Fawn beige with Cameo white accenting the steering wheel and mast. Standard seats had medium Fawn embossed vinyl with light Fawn facings. Custom interiors had color-keyed nylon pattern cloth and pin-seal vinyl upholstery with red trim in Cameo white trucks; Georgian gray trim in Cardinal red trucks; and medium Fawn trim in other cases. There were four separate Custom equipment options, which are listed in the options section below. Offered again were Step-Side (with pontoon rear fenders) and Fleetside (with slab-type rear fenders) Pickups with 6-1/2 ft. boxes, plus the Panel, Suburban and the chassis models. Four-wheel drive 1/2-ton models were in the K10 Series had a K14 model prefix.

1/2-TON COMMERCIAL — MODELS C15 (4x2)/SERIES 10 — SIX/V-8: The C15 trucks in the 10 Series used a C15 model prefix. Their fenderside nameplates had a red bow tie and the number 10. They had the same basic styling and trim changes as other conventional trucks. These were the long wheelbase (LWB) 1/2-ton trucks on the same chassis as 3/4-ton models. They are known as "Long Bed" or "Long Box" Pickups because they had a longer 8 ft. load box. Longer runningboards were needed on Step-Sides because there was more space between the cab and rear fenders. The Apache 10 Long Bed four-wheel drive models had a K15 model prefix.

1/2-TON DUBL-DUTI — MODEL P13/SERIES 10 — SIX/V-8: The 1/2-ton Dubl-Duti returned again in 1962. The P13 had a 102 in. wheelbase. An approved Step-Van walk-in delivery truck made by Union City Body Co., of Union City, Ind. was most commonly mounted on the Dubl-Duti chassis. Buyers could order other bodies, too. A channel type front bumper was used on Dubl-Duti trucks. The P10/P13 model used the regular Thriftmaster Six.

3/4-TON COMMERCIAL — MODEL C25/SERIES 20 — SIX/V-8: The 20 Series (3/4-ton) trucks had the same styling and trim changes as other conventional trucks. The fenderside nameplates had a red bow tie emblem and the number 20. Step-Side and Fleetside Pickups were in this series. Compared to C10-14 Pickups, the C20 Pickup had slightly longer runningboards and a longer cargo box with a horizontal support rib. An 8 ft. long box was used. There were also Platform and Platform/Stake models. The rail for the 3/4-ton Platform was about 8 ft. long. The 20 Series four-wheel drive 3/4-ton models had a K25 model prefix.

1962 Chevrolet 1/2-Ton C10 Suburban Carryall (OCW)

3/4-TON DUBL-DUTI — MODEL P23; P25; P26/SERIES 20 — SIX/V-8: Three 3/4-ton Dubl-Duti Forward-Control chassis remained in the 20 Series (3/4-ton) truck line. The P23/P25/P26 models had wheelbases of 104 in./125 in./137 in., respectively. Standard walk-in delivery truck bodies could be supplied by several factory-approved sources. Popular models were the Step-Van walk-in delivery trucks made by Union City Body Co., of Union City, Ind. A channel type front bumper was used on Dubl-Duti trucks. The P20 and P30 Dubl-Duti trucks used a Trademaster Special six with slightly different horsepower rating.

1-TON MEDIUM-DUTY COMMERCIAL — MODEL C36/SERIES 30 — SIX-CYLINDER: The 30 Series (1-ton) trucks had the same styling and trim changes as other conventional trucks. The fenderside nameplates had a red bow tie logo and number 30. There was no Fleetside Pickup in this line. Panel models had a one-piece floor made of 3/4-inch thick, five-ply laminated wood. The basic model lineup was unchanged. Compared to the C20-C25 Pickup, the C30-C36 had a longer wheelbase, a longer box with extra stake pockets and very long runningboards. The 1-ton Stake trucks had a long rail nearly 9-1/2 ft. long. No hubcaps were used on the larger split-rim wheels of the Chassis & Cab and Stake models, which had eight bolts and eight circular openings. A four-speed manual synchromesh transmission was standard. No four-wheel drive option was offered.

1-TON DUBL-DUTI — MODEL P33; P35; P36/SERIES 30 — SIX/V-8: Three Dubl-Duti Forward-Control chassis were in the 30 Series (1-ton) truck line. The P33/P35/P36 models had wheelbases of 104 in./125 in./137 in., respectively. Standard walk-in delivery truck bodies could be supplied by several factory-approved sources. Popular models were the Step-Van walk-in delivery trucks made by Union City Body Co., of Union City, Ind. A channel type front bumper was used on Dubl-Duti trucks. The P20 and P30 Dubl-Duti trucks used a Trademaster Special six with slightly different horsepower rating.

I.D. DATA: Serial Number located: [Chassis models] On plate temporarily attached near steering column, with final location per body maker; [All others] On plate attached to rear face of left-hand door hinge pillar; on right side of cowl under hood. The first symbol indicated model year, 2=1962. The second symbol indicated type: C=Conventional; K=4x4; R=Corvair 95. The third and fourth symbols indicated the model prefix: Corvair 95=12; 1/2-ton standard wheelbase=14; 1/2-ton LWB=15; 3/4-ton=25; 1-ton=36. The fifth symbol indicated body style: 2=Chassis & Cowl; 3=Chassis & Cab; 4=Pickup; 5=Panel; 6=Suburban Carryall; 9=Platform/Stake. The sixth symbol indicated the assembly plant: A=Atlanta, Ga.; B=Baltimore, Md.; F=Flint, Mich.; G=Framingham, Mass.; J=Janesville, Wis.; K=Kansas City, Mo.; L=Los Angeles, Calif.; N=Norwood, Ohio; O=Oakland, Calif.; S=St. Louis, Mo.; T=Tarrytown, N.Y.; and W=Willow Run, Mich. Remaining symbols were the sequential production number starting with 100001 at each plant. Ending serial numbers not available. The Chevrolet engine had the source, date and type stamped on a serial number pad. Source codes were: F=Flint, Mich.; T=Tonawanda, N.Y.; C=Canada. Month codes were 1=Jan.; 2=Feb., etc. Date codes were 01=first of month, etc. Corvair 95 prefix codes were V/W. Commercial model engine prefix codes were: [Thriftmaster 235] J/ JB/JC; [Thriftmaster 235 Special] K/KA; [Trademaster 283] M/MA. Engine serial numbers: [Six] Right side of block behind distributor; [V-8] Front of block below right-hand cylinder head. Engine serial numbers not available.

Model	Body Type	Price	Weight	Prod. Total
1/2-Ton Corvair 95 — Model R12/Series 10 — 95 in. w.b.				
R1205	Corvan	2294	2820	13,491
R1244	Loadside	2084	2580	369
R1254	Rampside	2138	2660	4,102

1/2 Ton Commercial 4x2 — Model C14/Series 10 — 115 in. w.b.

C1403	Chassis & Cab	1897	3020	—
C1434	Fleetside	2027	3440	—
C1404	Step-Side	2011	3385	—
C1405	Panel	2328	3650	—
C1406	Suburban (doors)	2623	3980	—
C1416	Suburban (gate)	2656	3990	—

1/2 Ton Commercial 4x4 — Model K14/Series 10 — 115 in. w.b.

K1434	Fleetside	2678	—	—
K1404	Step-Side	2678	—	—
K1405	Panel	2979	—	—
K1406	Suburban (doors)	3274	—	—
K1416	Suburban (gate)	3307	—	—

1/2 Ton Commercial 4x2 — Model C15/Series 10 — 127 in. w.b.

C1503	Chassis & Cab	—	—	—
C1534	Fleetside	2027	3440	—
C1504	Step-Side	2011	3385	—

1/2 Ton Commercial 4x4 — Model K15/Series 10 — 127 in. w.b.

K1503	Chassis & Cab	2585	3430	—
K1534	Fleetside	2715	3825	—
K1504	Step-Side	2699	3790	—

1/2-Ton Dubl-Duti — Model P23/Series 10 — 102 in. w.b.

P1345	Package Delivery	2546	3695	—

3/4-Ton Commercial 4x2 — Model C25/Series 20 — 127 in. w.b.

C2534	Fleetside	2209	3905	—
C2504	Step-Side	2193	3845	—
C2503	Chassis & Cab	2080	3405	—
C2509	Stake 8 ft.	2284	4035	—

3/4-Ton Commercial 4x4 — Model K25/Series 20 — 127 in. w.b.

K2539	Fleetside	2886	—	—
K2504	Step-Side	2870	—	—

3/4-Ton Dubl-Duti — Model P23; P25; P26/Series 20 — 104-137 in. w.b.

P2345	Package Delivery	3083	4945	—

NOTE 1: Data for 104 in. wheelbase. Dubl-Duti; 123 in./137 in. wheelbase optional.

1-Ton Commercial (4x2) — Model C36/Series 30 — 133 in. w.b.

C3605	Panel	2797	4525	—
C3604	Step-Side	2372	4155	—
C3603	Chassis & Cab	2238	3700	—
C3609	Stake	2485	4530	—

1-Ton Dubl-Duti — Model P33; P35; P36/Series 30 — 104-137 in. w.b.

P3345	Package Delivery	3275	5140	—

NOTE 2: Data for 104 in. wheelbase. Dubl-Duti; 123.25 in./137 in. wheelbase optional.

1962 Chevrolet 1-Ton Series C30 Fleetside Pickup (DFW)

ENGINE [Corvair 95]: Opposed. OHV. Turbo-Air. Six-cylinder. Aluminum block. Bore & stroke: 3.437 in. x 2.60 in. Displacement: 144.8 cid. Compression ratio: 8.0:1. Brake horsepower: 80 at 4400 rpm. Maximum Torque: 128 lbs.-ft. at 2300 rpm. Four main bearings. Hydraulic valve lifters. Carburetor: Two Rochester one-barrel model 7019101.

ENGINE [All except Series 95 and P20/P30 Dubl-Duti]: Inline. OHV. Thriftmaster. Six-cylinder. Cast iron block. Bore & stroke: 3-9/16 in. x 3-15/16 in. Displacement: 235.5 cid. Compression ratio: 8.25:1. Brake horsepower: 135 at 4000 rpm. Maximum Torque: 217 lbs.-ft. at 2000 rpm. Four main bearings. Hydraulic valve lifters. Carburetor: Rochester one-barrel model B7015011. (The P20/P30 Dubl-Duti trucks had a Thriftmaster Special six with slightly less horsepower).

ENGINE [Optional, Except Corvair 95 and P models]: V-type. OHV. Trademaster. Eight-cylinder. Cast iron block. Bore & stroke: 3-7/8 in. x 3 in. Displacement: 283 cid. Compression ratio: 8.5:1. Brake horsepower: 160 at 4200 rpm. Maximum Torque: 270 lbs.-ft. at 2000 rpm. Five main bearings. Hydraulic valve lifters. Carburetor: Rochester two-barrel model 2G7015017.

1962 Chevrolet 1/2-Ton Series C10-C15 Fleetside Long Bed Pickup (OCW)

CHASSIS [Corvair 95]: Wheelbase: 95 in. Overall length: 179.7 in. Height: 68.5 in. Front tread: 58 in. Rear tread: 58 in. Tires: 7.00 x 14 in. Maximum GVW: 4,600 lbs.
CHASSIS [C14/K14]: Wheelbase: 115 in. Overall length: 206 in.; Front tread: 63.1 in. Rear tread: 61 in. Tires: 6.70 x 15 in. Maximum GVW: [4x2] 4,600 lbs.; [4x4] 5,300 lbs.
CHASSIS [C15/K15]: Wheelbase: 127 in. Front tread: 63.1 in. Rear tread: 61.1 in. Tires: 6.70 x 15 in. Maxiumu GVW: [4x2] 4,600 lbs.; [4x4] 5,600 lbs.
CHASSIS [C25/K25]: Wheelbase: 127 in. Tires: 7 x 17.5 in. Maximum GVW: [4x2] 6,000 lbs.; [4x4] 6,800 lbs.
CHASSIS [C36]: Wheelbase: 133 in. Tires: 8 x 17.5 in. Maximum GVW: 7,800 lbs.
CHASSIS [P10]: Wheelbase: 102 in. Tires: 6.70 x 15 in.
CHASSIS [P20]: Wheelbase: 137 in. Tires: 7 x 17.5 in.
CHASSIS [P30]: Wheelbase: 104-137 in. Tires: 8 x 19.5 in.

1962 Chevrolet 1/2-Ton Corvair 95 Rampside Pickup

TECHNICAL: Manual. Synchromesh. Speeds: 3F/1R. Column-mounted gearshift lever. Single-plate dry-disc clutch. Rear axle: [1-ton] Full-floating; [Others] semi-floating. Standard axle ratio: [R12] 3.89:1; [C14/C15/K14/K15] 3.90:1; [C25/K25] 4.57:1; [C36] 5.14:1. Hydraulic four-wheel brakes. Pressed steel wheels.
OPTIONS: [Corvair 95] Custom chrome, R1200 without wheelcovers ($25.10). Custom Equipment, R1205 with standard seat ($17.56). Custom Equipment, R1205 with full-width seat ($19.23). Custom Equipment, R1206 ($167.20). Custom Equipment, R1244/1254 ($19.23). Left side body doors, R1205/1206 ($62.70). Floor level pickup box, R1244/1254 ($37.65). Laminated front door glass ($4.20). Direct Air heater ($57.69). Gasoline operated heater ($71.10). Outside rearview mirror, left or right ($3.77). Two-tone paint ($20.90). Two-tone paint, 1200 pickups ($25.10). Auxiliary front seat, R1205 ($31.78). Full width seat, R1205 ($20.90). Third seat, R1206 ($29.30). Heavy-duty front springs ($8.40). Heavy-duty shock absorbers ($5.87). Whitewall tires, four-ply ($24.60). Blackwall tires, six-ply ($34.46). Whitewall tires, six-ply ($67.47). Full wheelcovers, R1206 with Custom ($6.73). Two-speed washers and wipers ($12.55).

1962 Chevrolet 1/2-Ton Series C10 Step-Side Pickup (DFW)

OPTIONS: [C10/C20/C30] Engine: 150 hp 261 High-Torque L-6 ($50.20). Trademaster 283 V-8 ($92). Oil bath air cleaner, six-cylinder with governor ($1.72); without governor ($5.06). Positraction axle, C1400/1500 ($50.20). No-Spin rear axle, C2500 ($104.50). Optional rear axle ratios: 3.38:1 with manual transmission ($5.06); 4.11:1 with manual transmission;

4.11:1 with Powerglide ($25.10). Heavy-duty battery ($5.87). Eleven-inch heavy-duty clutch, six-cylinder only ($4.20). Custom Appearance package, Panels ($33.45); others ($40.13). Custom Chrome Option, all with chrome front bumper ($16.75); pickups with both bumpers chromed ($41.80); Panels with chrome bumpers ($25.10). Custom Comfort Option, Panels ($9.21); other models ($42.66). Custom side moldings, Fleetsides ($16.75). Temperature control radiator fan ($16.75). 35-amp. generator ($5.87). 42-amp. Delcotron ($22.62). 52-amp. Delcotron ($29.30). All glass tinted ($11.74). Tinted windshield ($10.07). Deluxe heater ($53.11). Recirculating heater ($37.22). 17.5 inch outside rearview mirror, except Panels, left-hand ($1.72); right-hand ($3.77). Eight-inch outside rearview mirror, right-hand ($3.77). Oil filter, with standard six-cylinder ($2.96). Tu-tone paint, Panels ($20.90); others ($12.55). Heavy-duty radiator, except with Powerglide ($16.75). Radio ($37.22). Auxiliary seat, panels ($31.78). Full-Depth foam seat, except Panels ($25.10). Heavy-duty shock absorbers, rear ($6.73); front [requires rears] ($5.87). Heavy-duty springs, C2500 front ($2.53); all models, rear ($5.06). Heavy-duty three-speed manual transmission, C1400 ($58.55); C1500 ($62.70) and C2500 ($71.10). Heavy-duty four-speed manual transmission, C1400 ($62.70); C1500 ($66.90) and C2500 ($72.25). Powerglide transmission, all models ($146.30). Full-View rear window, except Panels ($33.45). Two-speed windshield wipers and washers ($12.55). Note: Prices above are dealer cost for 1962 options.

OPTION PACKAGES: [Custom Appearance Equipment] Includes silver annodized radiator grille and headlamp door assembly; chrome-plated windshield reveal moldings; bright metal cab upper rear quarter panel trim plates; chrome horn ring steering wheel; chrome trimmed instrument panel knobs; and two-tone inside front door panels. [Custom Comfort and Convenience Equipment] Includes left door armrest; outside key lock; chrome cigar lighter; full foam rubber seat cushion; special seat trim (cab models and Suburban); and added sound insulation. [Custom chrome equipment] Chrome hubcaps. Not availabe with 4x4 or dual rear wheel options. [Side trim moldings] Bright bodyside moldings for Fleetside models. (Package prices are given above.)

HISTORICAL: Introduced: Fall 1961. Calendar year registrations: [All Chevrolet Commercials] 425,406. Calendar year production: [All Chevrolet Commercials] 396,819. Of this total, 82 percent were six-cylinder models. Innovations: New styling for C Series models. First diesels in big Chevrolet trucks. Chevrolet was America's number one truck-maker in 1962. The eight millionth Chevrolet truck since 1918 was sold this season. J.E. Conlan remained in charge of Chevrolet's Truck and Fleet Sales Department. Model year production: 396,940.

1962 Chevrolet 1-Ton C30 Chassis & Crew Cab With Fleetside Box (OCW)

1963 CHEVROLET

1963 Chevrolet Corvair 95 Rampside Pickup (OCW)

CORVAIR 95 — MODEL R12/SERIES 1000 — SIX: The Corvair 95 trucks were virtually unchanged, except for serial numbers. A new option was a positraction rear axle. These driver-forward models had a Corvair platform, a rear-mounted air-cooled engine and a transaxle. Dual headlamps, a small front grille with Chevrolet emblem and a sculptured contrast panel around the body were styling characteristics. The Corvan had steel panel sides, two side load doors and double rear panel doors. It had Corvair 95 scripts on the front doors. A Loadside Pickup was made by adding a cab back panel and removing the upper sheet metal at the rear. The cargo box was 105 in. long and 43-7/8 in. wide. It featured a double-wall box. Also available was the Rampside Pickup, which had a unique door in the side of the box. It dropped to the ground to make a cargo loading ramp. Standard equip-

ment on all Corvair 95s included: An air-cooled six-cylinder engine; three-speed synchro-mesh transmission; electric wipers; directional signals and five tubeless tires. Chrome hubcaps, chrome bumpers and a Custom interior/exterior appearance package were available.

1/2-TON COMMERCIAL — MODEL C14 (4x2); K14 (4x4)/SERIES 10 — SIX/V-8: The 1962 style hood was carried over for 1963 Chevrolet 10 Series 1/2-ton trucks. A new technical improvement was a coil spring front suspension, replacing the 1960-1962 torsion bar type. A new radiator grille had an egg-crate appearance with round parking lamp housings at either end. The standard grille was made of steel painted Cameo white. The headlamp bezels and the Chevrolet lettering on the lower grille surround was accented in black. An anodized aluminum grille was part of the Custom Appearance Equipment package. Fenderside name badges were mounted on the cowl, behind the front wheel opening. They were vertical rectangles of satin-finished chrome with a red 10 on top and red Chevrolet bow tie emblem near the bottom. Exterior colors for the year were Desert beige; Jet black; Balboa blue; Brigade blue; Georgian gray; Seamist jade; Glenwood green; Woodland green; Omaha orange; Cardinal red; Crystal turquoise; Cameo white; Pure white; and Yukon yellow. All colors, except the two whites, were used as lower body colors in the 12 two-tone color options. They were teamed with Cameo white on the upper body. Interiors were done in two shades of Fawn beige with Cameo white accenting the steering wheel and mast. Standard seats had medium Fawn embossed vinyl with light Fawn facings. Custom interiors had color-keyed nylon pattern cloth and pin-seal vinyl upholstery with red trim in Cameo white trucks; Georgian gray trim in Cardinal red trucks; and medium Fawn trim in others. There were four separate Custom equipment options, which are listed in the options section below. Offered again were Step-Side (with pontoon rear fenders) and Fleetside (with slab type rear fenders) Pickups with 6-1/2 ft. boxes, plus the Panel, Suburban and the chassis models. The 10 Series four-wheel drive 1/2-ton models had a K14 model prefix.

1/2-TON COMMERCIAL — MODELS C15 (4x2)/SERIES 10 — SIX/V-8: The C15 trucks in the Chevrolet 10 Series long-wheelbase line used a C15 model prefix. Their fenderside nameplates had a red bow tie and the number 10. They had the same basic styling and trim changes as other conventional trucks. These were the long wheelbase (LWB) 1/2-ton trucks on the same chassis as 3/4-ton models. They are known as "Long Bed" or "Long Box" Pickups because they had a longer 8 ft. load box. Longer runningboards were needed on Step-Sides because there was more space between the cab and rear fenders. The Apache 10 Long Bed four-wheel drive models had a K15 model prefix.

1963 Chevrolet C-10 1/2-Ton Fleetside Custom Pickup (OCW)

1/2-TON DUBL-DUTI — MODEL P13/SERIES 10 — SIX/V-8: The 1/2-ton Dubl-Duti returned again in 1962. It had a 102 in. wheelbase. An approved Step-Van walk-in delivery truck made by Union City Body Co., of Union City, Ind. was most commonly mounted on the Dubl-Duti chassis. A channel type front bumper was used on Dubl-Duti trucks. The P10 now featured the four-cylinder High-Torque 153 cid/90 hp (Chevy II) engine as standard equipment.

3/4-TON COMMERCIAL — MODEL C25/SERIES 20 — SIX/V-8: The C25 trucks in the Chevrolet 20 Series 3/4-ton line had the same styling and trim changes as other conventional trucks. The fenderside nameplates had a red bow tie emblem and the number 20. Step-Side and Fleetside Pickups were in this series. Compared to C10-C14 Pickups, the C20-C25 Pickup had slightly longer runningboards and an 8-ft. long box was used. There were also Platform and Platform/Stake models. The rail for the 3/4-ton Platform was about 8 ft. long. The four-wheel drive 3/4-ton models in the 20 Series had a K25 model prefix.

3/4-TON DUBL-DUTI — MODEL P23; P25; P26/SERIES 20 — SIX/V-8: Three 3/4-ton Dubl-Duti Forward-Control chassis remained in the 20 Series (3/4-ton) truck line. The P23/P25/P26 models had wheelbases of 104 in./125 in./137 in., respectively. A channel type front bumper was used on Dubl-Duti trucks. New this year was use of a High-Torque 230 cid/140 hp engine as standard equipment in P20/P30 models.

1-TON MEDIUM-DUTY COMMERCIAL — MODEL C36/SERIES 30 — SIX-CYLINDER: The Chevrolet 30 Series 1-ton trucks had the same styling and trim changes as other conventional trucks. The fenderside nameplates had a red Chevrolet bow tie and number 30. There was no Fleetside Pickup in this line. Panel models had a one-piece floor made of 3/4-inch thick, five-ply laminated wood. The basic model lineup was unchanged. Compared to the C20-C25 Pickup, the C30-C36 Pickup had a longer wheelbase, a longer box with extra stake pockets and very long runningboards. The 1-ton Stake trucks had a long rail nearly 9-1/2 ft. long. No hubcaps were used on the larger split-rim wheels of the Chassis & Cab and Stake models, which had eight bolts and eight circular openings. A four-speed manual synchromesh transmission was standard. No four-wheel drive option was offered.

1-TON DUBL-DUTI — MODEL P33; P35; P36/SERIES 30 — SIX/V-8: Three Dubl-Duti Forward-Control chassis were in the 30 Series (1-ton) truck line. The P33/P35/P36 models had wheelbases of 104 in./125 in./137 in., respectively. A channel type front bumper was used on Dubl-Duti trucks. New this year was use of a High-Torque 230 cid/140 hp engine as standard equipment in P20/P30 models.

I.D. DATA: Serial Number located: [Chassis models] On plate temporarily attached near steering column, with final location per body maker; [All others] On plate attached to rear face of left-hand door hinge pillar; on right side of cowl under hood. The first symbol indicated model year, 3=1963. The second symbol indicated type: C=Conventional; K=4x4; R=Corvair 95. The third and fourth symbols indicated the model prefix: Corvair 95=12; 1/2-ton standard wheelbase=14; 1/2-ton long wheelbase=15; 3/4-ton=25; 1-ton=36. The fifth symbol indicated body style: 2=Chassis & Cowl; 3=Chassis & Cab; 4=Pickup; 5=Panel; 6=Suburban Carryall; 9=Platform/Stake. The sixth symbol indicated the assembly plant: A=Atlanta, Ga.; B=Baltimore, Md.; F=Flint, Mich.; G=Framingham, Mass.; J=Janesville, Wis.; K=Kansas City, Mo.; L=Los Angeles, Calif.; N=Norwood, Ohio; O=Oakland, Calif.; P=Pontiac, Mich.; S=St. Louis, Mo.; T=Tarrytown, N.Y.; and W=Willow Run, Mich. Remaining symbols were the sequential production number starting with 100001 at each plant. Ending serial numbers not available. The Chevrolet engine had the source, date and type stamped on a serial number pad. Source codes were: F=Flint, Mich.; T=Tonawanda, N.Y.;

C=Canada. Month codes were 1=Jan.; 2=Feb., etc. Date codes were 01=first of month, etc. Corvair 95 prefix codes were: [Turbo Air 145 cid/80 hp six] V/W. Commercial model engine prefix codes were: [Hi-Torque 153 cid/90 hp L-4] F/FA; [High-Torque 235 cid/135 hp L-6] J/JC; [Hi-Torque 261 cid/150 hp L-6] N/ND/NE/NK/NL/NM/NQ/NS/NU; [High-Torque 292 cid/165 hp L-6] PG/PK; [High-Torque 283 cid/175 hp V-8] M/MA. Engine serial numbers: [Six] Right side of block behind distributor; [V-8] Front of block below right-hand cylinder head. Engine serial numbers not available.

Model	Body Type	Price	Weight	Prod. Total
1/2-Ton Corvair 95 — Model R12/Series 10 — 95 in. w.b.				
R1205	Corvan	2212	2800	11,161
R1254	Rampside	2212	2800	2,046
1/2 Ton Commercial 4x2 — Model C14/Series 10 — 115 in. w.b.				
C1403	Chassis & Cab	1895	2820	—
C1434	Fleetside	2025	3235	—
C1404	Step-Side	2009	3190	—
C1405	Panel	2326	3440	—
C1406	Suburban (doors)	2620	3720	—
C1416	Suburban (gate)	2653	3735	—
1/2 Ton Commercial 4x4 — Model K14/Series 10 — 115 in. w.b.				
K1434	Fleetside	2676	—	—
K1404	Step-Side	2676	—	—
K1405	Panel	2977	—	—
K1406	Suburban (doors)	3272	—	—
K1416	Suburban (gate)	3305	—	—
1/2 Ton Commercial 4x2 — Model C15/Series 10 — 127 in. w.b.				
C1503	Chassis & Cab	—	—	—
C1534	Fleetside	2025	3235	—
C1504	Step-Side	2660	3190	—
1/2 Ton Commercial 4x4 — Model K15/Series 10 — 127 in. w.b.				
K1534	Fleetside	2676	—	—
K1504	Step-Side	2660	—	—
1/2-Ton Dubl-Duti — Model P23/Series 10 — 102 in. w.b.				
P1345	Package Delivery	2544	3450	—
3/4-Ton Commercial 4x2 — Model C25/Series 20 — 127 in. w.b.				
C2534	Fleetside	2207	3760	—
C2504	Step-Side	2193	3710	—
C2503	Chassis & Cab	2079	3280	—
C2509	Stake 8 ft.	2284	3895	—
3/4-Ton Commercial 4x4 — Model K25/Series 20 — 127 in. w.b.				
K2539	Fleetside	2884	—	—
K2504	Step-Side	2868	—	—
3/4-Ton Dubl-Duti — Model P23; P25; P26/Series 20 — 104-137 in. w.b.				
P2345	Package Delivery	3082	4805	—

NOTE 1: Data for 104 in. wheelbase. Dubl-Duti; 123 in./137 in. wheelbase optional.

Model	Body Type	Price	Weight	Prod. Total
1-Ton Commercial 4x2 — Model C36/Series 30 — 133 in. w.b.				
C3605	Panel	2797	4523	—
C3604	Step-Side	2371	3900	—
C3603	Chassis & Cab	2236	3430	—
C3609	Stake	2483	4230	—
1-Ton Dubl-Duti — Model P33; P35; P36/Series 30 — 104-137 in. w.b.				
P3345	Package Delivery	3274	5020	—

NOTE 2: Data for 104 in. wheelbase. Dubl-Duti; 123.25 in./137 in. wheelbase optional.

1963 Chevrolet 1/2-Ton Series C10 Fleetside Pickup (DFW)

ENGINE [Standard P10]: Inline. Overhead valve. High-Torque 153. Four-cylinder. Bore and stroke: 3-7/8 x 3-1/4 in. Displacement: 153 cid. Brake horsepower: 90 at 4000 rpm. Torque: 152 lbs.-ft at 2400 rpm.
ENGINE [Corvair 95]: Opposed. OHV. Turbo-Air. Six-cylinder. Aluminum block. Bore & stroke: 3.437 in. x 2.60 in. Displacement: 144.8 cid. Compression ratio: 8.0:1. Brake horsepower: 80 at 4400 rpm. Maximum Torque: 128 lbs.-ft. at 2300 rpm. Four main bearings. Hydraulic valve lifters. Carburetor: Two Rochester one-barrel model 7019101.
ENGINE [Standard C10/C20/P20/P30; Optional P10]: Inline. OHV. High-Torque 230. Six-cylinder. Cast iron block. Bore and stroke: 3-7/8 x 3-1/4. Displacement: 230 cid. Brake horsepower: 140 at 4400 rpm. Torque: 220 lbs.-ft. at 1600 rpm.
ENGINE [Standard K10/K20]: Inline. OHV. High-Torque 235. Six-cylinder. Cast iron block. Bore & stroke: 3-9/16 in. x 3-15/16 in. Displacement: 235.5 cid. Compression ratio: 8.25:1. Brake horsepower: 135 at 4000 rpm. Maximum Torque: 217 lbs.-ft. at 2000 rpm. Four main bearings. Hydraulic valve lifters. Carburetor: Rochester one-barrel model B7015011.
ENGINE [Optional K10/K20]: Inline. OHV. High-Torque 261. Six-cylinder. Cast iron block. Bore and stroke: 3-3/4 x 3-15/16. Displacement: 261 cid. Brake horsepower: 150 at 4000 rpm. Torque: 235 lbs.-ft. at 2000 rpm.

ENGINE [Optional C10/C20/C30]: Inline. OHV. High-Torque 292. Six-cylinder. Cast iron block. Bore and stroke: 3-7/8 x 4-1/8. Displacement: 292 cid. Brake horsepower: 165 at 3800 rpm. Torque: 280 lbs.-ft. at 1600 rpm.
ENGINE [Optional, Except Corvair 95 and P models]: V-type. OHV. High-Torque 283. Eight-cylinder. Cast iron block. Bore & stroke: 3-7/8 in. x 3 in. Displacement: 283 cid. Compression ratio: 8.5:1. Brake horsepower: 160 at 4200 rpm. Maximum Torque: 270 lbs.-ft. at 2000 rpm. Five main bearings. Hydraulic valve lifters. Carburetor: Rochester two-barrel model 2G7015017.
CHASSIS [Corvair 95]: Wheelbase: 95 in. Overall length: 179.7 in. Height: 68.5 in. Front tread: 58 in. Rear tread: 58 in. Tires: 7.00 x 14 in. Maximum GVW: 4,600 lbs.
CHASSIS [C14/K14]: Wheelbase: 115 in. Overall length: 206 in.; Front tread: 63.1 in. Rear tread: 61 in. Tires: 6.70 x 15 in. Maximum GVW: [4x2] 4,600 lbs.; [4x4] 5,300 lbs.
CHASSIS [C15/K15]: Wheelbase: 127 in. Front tread: 63.1 in. Rear tread: 61.1 in. Tires: 6.70 x 15 in. Maximum GVW: [4x2] 4,600 lbs.; [4x4] 5,600 lbs.
CHASSIS [C25/K25]: Wheelbase: 127 in. Tires: 7 x 17.5 in. Maximum GVW: [4x2] 6,000 lbs.; [4x4] 6,800 lbs.
CHASSIS [C36]: Wheelbase: 133 in. Tires: 8 x 17.5 in. Maximum GVW: 7,800 lbs.
CHASSIS [P10]: Wheelbase: 102 in. Tires: 6.70 x 15 in.
CHASSIS [P20]: Wheelbase: 137 in. Tires: 7 x 17.5 in.
CHASSIS [P30]: Wheelbase: 104-137 in. Tires: 8 x 19.5 in.

1963 Chevrolet 1/2-Ton C-10 Step-Side Pickup (OCW)

TECHNICAL: Manual. Synchromesh. Speeds: 3F/1R. Column-mounted gear shift lever. Single-plate dry-disc clutch. Rear axle: [1-ton] Full-floating; [Others] semi-floating. Standard axle ratio: [R12] 3.89:1; [C14/C15/K14/K15] 3.90:1; [C25/K25] 4.57:1; [C36] 5.14:1. Hydraulic four-wheel brakes. Pressed steel wheels.
OPTIONS: [Corvair 95] Custom chrome, R1200 without wheelcovers ($25.10). Custom Equipment, R1205 with standard seat ($17.56). Custom Equipment, R1205 with full-width seat ($19.23). Custom Equipment, R1206 ($167.20). Custom Equipment, R1244/1254 ($19.23). Left side body doors, R1205/1206 ($62.70). Floor level pickup box, R1244/1254 ($37.65). Laminated front door glass ($4.20). Direct Air heater ($57.69). Gasoline operated heater ($71.10). Outside rearview mirror, left or right ($3.77). Two-tone paint ($20.90). Two-tone paint, R1205 ($25.10). Auxiliary front seat, R1205 ($31.78). Full width seat, R1205 ($20.90). Third seat, R1206 ($29.30). Heavy-duty front springs ($8.40). Heavy-duty shock absorbers ($5.87). Whitewall tires, four-ply ($24.60). Blackwall tires, six-ply ($34.46). Whitewall tires, six-ply ($67.47). Full wheel covers, R1206 with Custom ($6.73). Two-speed washers and wipers ($12.55).
OPTIONS: [C10/C20/C30] Engine: 150 hp 261 High-Torque L-6 ($50.20). Trademaster 283 V-8 ($92). Oil bath air cleaner, six-cylinder with governor ($1.72); without governor ($5.06). Positraction axle, C1400/1500 ($50.20). No-Spin rear axle, C2500 ($104.50). Optional rear axle ratios: 3.38:1 with manual transmission ($5.06); 4.11:1 with manual transmission; 4.11:1 with Powerglide ($25.10). Heavy-duty battery ($5.87). Eleven-inch heavy-duty clutch, six-cylinder only ($4.20). Custom Appearance package, Panels ($33.45); others ($40.13). Custom Chrome option, all with chrome front bumper ($16.75); Pickups with both bumpers chromed ($41.80); Panels with chrome bumpers ($25.10). Custom Comfort option, panels ($9.21); other models ($42.66). Custom side moldings, Fleetsides ($16.75). Temperature control radiator fan ($16.75). 35-amp. generator ($5.87). 42-amp. Delcotron ($22.62). 52-amp. Delcotron ($29.30). All glass tinted ($11.74). Tinted windshield ($10.07). Deluxe heater ($53.11). Recirculating heater ($37.22). 17.5 inch outside rearview mirror, except panels, left-hand ($1.72); right-hand ($3.77). Eight-inch outside rearview mirror, right-hand ($3.77). Oil filter, with standard six-cylinder ($2.96). Tu-tone paint, Panels ($20.90); others ($12.55). Heavy-duty radiator, except with Powerglide ($16.75). Radio ($37.22). Auxiliary seat, panels ($31.78). Full-depth foam seat, except panels ($25.10). Heavy-duty shock absorbers, rear ($6.73); front [requires rears] ($5.87). Heavy-duty springs, C2500 front ($2.53); all models, rear ($5.06). Heavy-duty three-speed manual transmission, C1400 ($58.55); C1500 ($62.70) and C2500 ($71.10). Heavy-duty four-speed manual transmission, C1400 ($62.70); C1500 ($66.90) and C2500 ($72.25). Powerglide transmission, all models ($146.30). Full-View rear window, except panels ($33.45). Two-speed windshield wipers and washers ($12.55). Note: Prices above are dealer cost for 1963 options.
OPTION PACKAGES: [Custom Appearance Equipment] Includes silver annodized radiator grille and headlamp door assembly; chrome-plated windshield reveal moldings; bright metal cab upper rear quarter panel trim plates; chrome horn ring steering wheel; chrome trimmed instrument panel knobs; and two-tone inside front door panels. [Custom Comfort and Convenience Equipment] Includes left door armrest; outside key lock; chrome cigar lighter; full foam rubber seat cushion; special seat trim (cab models and Suburban); and added sound insulation. [Custom Chrome equipment] Chrome hubcaps. Not available with 4x4 or dual rear wheel options. [Side trim moldings] Bright bodyside moldings for Fleetside models. (Package prices are given above).
HISTORICAL: Introduced: Sept. 28, 1962. Calendar Year Production Total: 483,119. (This was 33.01 percent share of total industry). In round numbers, the total included 500 four-cylinder powered trucks; 2,200 diesels; 378,000 six-cylinder models and 102,400 trucks with V-8 powerplants. Calendar year registrations: 425,406. Corvair, total production for model year: 26,968 (including Greenbrier Sports Wagon). Innovations: New High-Torque 230 and 292 cid sixes. Light-duty trucks adopt ladder-type frame. Chevrolet commanded its largest share, ever, of the U.S. truck market in 1983. More than one-third of all trucks built this year had bow tie badges. It was also the first time since 1950 that truck deliveries went above 400,000 units. Leafing through a *CHEVROLET SILVER BOOK* for 1963 reveals some of the unusual vocational equipment available in the factory-approved aftermarket. This included roll-up doors for walk-in deliveries (from Overhead Door Corp., of Marion, Ohio); a Crew Cab conversion from Orville Metal Specialty Co., of Orrville, Ohio); a fan-belt-driven automatic snowplow from Monarch Road Machinery Co. (of Grand Rapids, Mich.) and pickup truck extension boom wrecker units from Canfield Tow Bar Co.) of Detroit, Mich. Winnebago Industries and Wolverine Camper Co. were among firms offering

slide-in campers for pickups. Perhaps the ultimate conversion, however, was the Go-Home mobile home (based on Corvair running gear) made by Ultra-Van Mfg. Co., of Oakland, Calif.

1964 CHEVROLET

1964 Chevrolet 1/2-Ton El Camino Pickup (LC)

EL CAMINO — MODEL A/SERIES 53-56 — SIX/V-8: Returning after a four-year hiatus was the El Camino, which Chevrolet described as a "personal pickup." Built on the mid-size Chevelle's 115 in. wheelbase, the El Camino was available with many passenger-car options. It came with two trim levels. El Caminos in the 53 (six-cylinder) and 54 (V-8) series were the base models, with trim and appointments comparable to the Chevelle 300. Custom El Caminos in the 55 (six-cylinder) and 56 (V-8) series had trim and appointments comparable to Chevelle Malibus. Customs had additional moldings around the wheel openings and the load box, chrome window/windshield frames and a windsplit molding on the center of the hood. The 1964 El Caminos came in Tuxedo black; Meadow green; Bahama green; Silver blue; Daytona blue; Azure aqua; Lagoon aqua; Almond fawn; Ember red; Saddle tan; Ermine white; Desert beige; Satin silver; and Palomar red. Color-keyed all-vinyl seats and sidewall trim were available in Almond fawn, Lagoon aqua or Ember red for base models. The standard interior also included an embossed vinyl headliner; dual sun visors; armrests; color-keyed vinyl floor mats; a cigar lighter; lockable glove compartment; bright instrument panel facing; and foam seat cushions. Customs featured color-keyed pattern cloth and leather-grain vinyl upholstery and had deep-twist floor carpeting, a bright glove compartment facing, two-tone steering wheel and electric clock. The El Camino had an outside width of 73-1/4 in. The pickup box inside width was 59-3/4 in. behind the cab and 64-3/4 in. near the tailgate. There was 46 in. between the wheelhousings. The bed of the box was 78-1/2 in. long. The tailgate measured 55-1/2 in. x 23 in. With the bed-level tailgate lowered, the overall bed length was 101.6 in. This box was larger than the one used on full-size 1959-1960 El Caminos.

1/2-TON CHEVY VAN — MODEL G/SERIES 10 — FOUR: A low-priced, front-engined Chevy Van was released early in calendar 1964. Styling characteristics included five-segment vents on the front with a bow tie underneath and an oval, horizontal-bar grille near the bottom of the front single headlights. It had the same general characteristics configuration and 90 in. wheelbase as the Corvan, but utilized a water-cooled 153 cid four-cylinder Chevy II engine. It was available in two models called the Carryall and Panel. The Carryall was marketed as a passenger vehicle with windows and auxiliary passenger seats were available. The Commercial Panel had double right-hand side cargo doors. It was considered a truck.

CORVAIR 95 — MODEL R12/SERIES 1000 — SIX: The Corvair 95 trucks were driver-forward models on a Corvair platform, with a rear-mounted air-cooled engine and a transaxle. Dual headlamps, a small front grille with Chevrolet emblem and a sculptured contrast panel around the body were styling characteristics. The 1964 models were virtually unchanged, except for serial numbers and new paint schemes. Colors included Meadow green; Bahama green; Daytona blue; Lagoon Aqua; Desert beige; and Goldwood yellow. The slow-selling Loadside pickup was gone. Back again was the Corvan with steel panel sides, two side load doors and double rear panel doors. It had Corvair 95 scripts on the front doors. Also available was the Rampside Pickup. It was made by adding a cab back panel and removing the upper sheet metal at the rear. The double-wall cargo box was 105 in. long and 43-7/8 in. wide. A unique door in the side of the box dropped to the ground to make a cargo loading ramp. Standard equipment on all 1964 Corvair 95s included: An air-cooled six-cylinder engine that grew from 145 to 164 cid and gained more horsepower; a three-speed synchromesh transmission; electric wipers; directional signals; and five tubeless tires. Chrome hubcaps, chrome bumpers and a Custom interior/exterior appearance package were available.

1/2-TON COMMERCIAL — MODEL C14 (4x2); K14 (4x4)/SERIES 10 — SIX/V-8: The 1963 style hood was carried over for 1964 Chevrolet 10 Series 1/2-ton trucks, but a lot of other cab sheet metal was changed due to the elimination of a wraparound windshield. The front roof pillars now slanted backwards, instead of slightly forward. This gave the door window frames a totally new shape. These rather drastic alterations were neatly integrated to the previous body, however, so overall styling was much the same. The grille also looked basically similar to the previous design with changes. The vertical and horizontal elements were slimmer and more tightly cross-hatched; the black-accented Chevrolet lettering was on the top (instead of bottom) bar; and the headlamp surrounds were square-shaped. The standard grille was made of steel painted Off-white, as were bumpers and hubcaps. An anodized aluminum grille was part of the Custom Appearance equipment package. Fenderside name badges were mounted in the same location on the cowl, behind the front wheel opening. They looked like red squares framed in chrome with a chrome 10 in the center and a chrome Chevrolet bow tie above. Exterior colors for the year were Tuxedo black; Dark blue; Light blue; fawn; gray; Gray green; Dark green; Light green; orange; red; turquoise; white; Off-white; and yellow. All colors (except the two whites) were used as lower body colors in the 12 two-tone color options. They were teamed with Off-white on the upper body. Interiors were done in two shades of fawn beige with Off-white accenting the steering wheel and mast. Standard seats had medium fawn embossed vinyl with light fawn facings. Custom interiors had color-keyed nylon-faced pattern cloth inserts and vinyl bolsters. The striped inserts were mostly Medium fawn beige. Contrasting bolsters were red or fawn, depending upon the color of the truck, with a white bottom bolster. An all-new dashboard was inside the 1964 trucks. It had a redesigned instrument cluster, glove compartment, ashtray and trim plates. Control knobs were angle-mounted at the bottom of the cluster, which was recessed to hood the instruments from glare. There were four separate Custom equipment options, which are listed in the options section below. Offered again were Step-Side (with pontoon rear fenders) and Fleetside (with slab type rear fenders) Pickups with 6-1/2 ft. boxes, plus the 7-1/2 ft. Panel and Suburban and three chassis models. The 10 Series Short Bed four-wheel drive 1/2-ton models had a K14 model prefix.

1/2-TON COMMERCIAL — MODELS C15 (4x2)/SERIES 10 — SIX/V-8: The C15 trucks in the Chevrolet 10 Series long-wheelbase line used a C15 model prefix. Their fenderside nameplates were square red badges with a chrome bow tie and number 10. They had the same basic styling and trim changes as other conventional trucks. These were the long wheelbase (LWB) 1/2-ton trucks on the same chassis as 3/4-ton models. They had a longer 8 ft. load box. Longer runningboards were needed on Step-Sides because there was more space between the cab and rear fenders. The 10 Series Long Bed four-wheel drive models had a K15 model prefix.

1/2-TON DUBL-DUTI — MODEL P13/SERIES 10 — SIX/V-8: The 1/2-ton Dubl-Duti returned again. It had a 102 in. wheelbase. An approved 7 ft. Step-Van walk-in delivery truck made by Union City Body Co., of Union City, Ind. was most commonly mounted on this Dubl-Duty chassis. A channel type front bumper and 153 High-Torque four were standard equipment.

3/4-TON COMMERCIAL — MODEL C25/SERIES 20 — SIX/V-8: The C25 trucks in the Chevrolet 20 Series 3/4-ton line had the same styling and trim changes as other conventional trucks. The fenderside nameplates were square red badges with a chrome bow tie emblem and chrome number 20. Step-Side and Fleetside Pickups were in this series. Compared to C10-C14 pickups, the C20-C25 pickup had slightly longer runningboards and an 8 ft. long box was used. There were also 8 ft. Platform and Platform/Stake models. The four-wheel drive 3/4-ton models in the 20 Series had a K25 model prefix.

1964 Chevrolet 1/2-Ton C10 Fleetside Pickup (OCW)

3/4-TON DUBL-DUTI — MODEL P23; P25; P26/SERIES 20 — SIX/V-8: Three 3/4-ton Dubl-Duti Forward-Control chassis remained in the 20 Series (3/4-ton) truck line. The P23/P25/P26 models had wheelbases of 104 in./125 in./137 in., respectively. The 104 in. wheelbase was recommended for 7 ft. to 8-1/2 ft. bodies; the 125 in. wheelbase was recommended for 9-1/2 to 10-1/2 ft. long bodies and the 137 in. wheelbase was recommended for 11-1/2 ft. to 12-1/2 ft. long bodies. Bodies could be sourced from factory approved firms or independent suppliers. A channel type front bumper and High-Torque 230 six were standard equipment.

1-TON MEDIUM-DUTY COMMERCIAL — MODEL C36/SERIES 30 — SIX-CYLINDER: The Chevrolet 30 Series 1-ton trucks had the same styling and trim changes as other conventional trucks. The fenderside nameplates were square red badges with a chrome Chevrolet bow tie and number 30. There was no Fleetside Pickup in this line. Panel models had a one-piece floor made of 3/4-in. thick, five-ply laminated wood. The basic model lineup was unchanged. Compared to the C20-C25 Pickup, the C30-C36 Pickup had a longer wheelbase, a longer box with extra stake pockets and very long runningboards. The 1-ton Stake trucks had a long rail some 9 ft. long. No hubcaps were used on the larger split-rim wheels of the Chassis & Cab and Stake models, which had eight bolts and eight circular openings. A four-speed manual synchromesh transmission was standard. No four-wheel drive option was offered.

1-TON DUBL-DUTI — MODEL P33; P35; P36/SERIES 30 — SIX/V-8: Three Dubl-Duti Forward-Control chassis were in the 30 Series (1-ton) truck line. The P33/P35/P36 models had wheelbases of 104 in./125 in./137 in., respectively. The 104 in. wheelbase was recommended for 7 ft. to 8-1/2 ft. bodies; the 125 in. wheelbase was recommended for 9-1/2 to 10-1/2 ft. long bodies and the 137 in. wheelbase was recommended for 11-1/2 ft. to 12-1/2 ft. long bodies. Bodies could be sourced from factory approved firms or independent suppliers. A channel type front bumper and High-Torque 230 six were standard equipment.

I.D. DATA: Serial Number located: [Chassis models] On plate temporarily attached near steering column, with final location per body maker; [All others] On plate attached to rear face of left-hand door hinge pillar; on right side of cowl under hood. The first symbol indicated model year, 4=1964. The second symbol (except El Caminos) indicated type: C=Conventional; K=4x4; R=Corvair 95; G=Chevy Van. The next two indicated the model prefix: Corvair 95=12; El Camino six=53; El Camino V-8=54; Custom El Camino six=55; Custom El Camino V-8=56; 1/2-ton standard wheelbase=14; 1/2-ton long wheelbase=15; 3/4-ton=25; 1-ton=36. The next symbol (or pair of symbols for El Caminos) indicated body style: 2=Chassis & Cowl; 3=Chassis & Cab; 4=Pickup; 5=Panel; 6=Suburban Carryall; 9=Platform/Stake; 80=Sedan-Pickup. The next symbol indicated the assembly plant: A=Atlanta, Ga.; B=Baltimore, Md.; C=Atlanta, Ga. BOP; F=Flint, Mich.; G=Framingham, Mass.; H=Fremont, Calif.; J=Janesville, Wis.; K=Kansas City, Mo.; L=Los Angeles, Calif.; N=Norwood, Ohio; O=Oakland, Calif.; P=Pontiac, Mich.; S=St. Louis, Mo.; T=Tarrytown, N.Y.; V=Southgate, Calif.; W=Willow Run, Mich.; Y=Wilmington, Del. (El Caminos were made at the A/B/H/K/L factories). Remaining symbols were the sequential production number starting with 100001 at each plant. Ending serial numbers not available. The Chevrolet engine had the source, date and type stamped on a serial number pad. Source codes were: F=Flint, Mich.; T=Tonawanda, N.Y.; C=Canada. Month codes were 1=Jan.; 2=Feb., etc. Date codes were 01=first of month, etc. Corvair 95 prefix codes were: [Turbo Air 164 cid/95 hp] V/W; [Turbo Air 164 cid/110 hp] VB/WB. Commercial model engine prefix codes were: [High-Torque 153 cid/90 hp L4] F/FA; [High-Torque 230 cid/140 hp L6] N/ND/NE/NK/NL/NM/NQ/NU; [High-Torque 292 cid/165 hp L6] PG/PK/PV/PL; High-Torque 283 cid/175 hp V-8] M/MA. Engine serial numbers located: [Six] Right side of block behind distributor; [V-8] Front of block below right-hand cylinder head. Engine serial numbers not available.

Model	Body Type	Price	Weight	Prod. Total
El Camino — Series 53/Series 55 — 115 in. w.b. — Six				
5380	Pickup	2267	2935	Note 1
5580	Custom Pickup	2342	2935	Note 1

El Camino — Series 54/Series 56 — 115 in. w.b. — V-8

5480	Pickup	2367	2935	Note 1
5680	Custom Pickup	2442	—	Note 1

NOTE 1: Total El Camino production was 36,615.

Chevy Van — Model G/Series 10 — 90 in. w.b. — Four

G1205	Panel	2067	2735	—

Corvair 95 — Model R12/Series 10 — 95 in. w.b. — Six

R1254	Rampside	2136	2665	851
R1205	Corvan	2212	2800	8147

1/2-Ton Commercial — Model C14/Series 10 — 115 in. w.b.

C1403	Chassis & Cab	1893	2810	—
C1434	Fleetside	2023	3205	—
C1404	Step-Side	2007	3175	—
C1405	Panel 7.5 ft.	2324	3405	—
C1406	Suburban (doors)	2629	3695	—
C1416	Suburban (gate)	2662	3705	—

1/2-Ton Commercial 4x4 — Model K14/Series 10 — 115 in. w.b.

K1434	Fleetside	2674	—	—
K1404	Step-Side	2658	—	—
K1405	Panel 7.5 ft.	2975	—	—
K1406	Suburban (doors)	3280	—	—
K1416	Suburban (gate)	3313	—	—

1/2-Ton Commercial (Long Bed) — Model C15/Series 10 — 127 in. w.b.

C1503	Chassis & Cab	—	—	—
C1534	Fleetside	2023	3205	—
C1504	Step-Side	2007	3175	—

1/2-Ton Comm. (Long Bed) 4x4 — Model K15/Series 10 — 127 in. w.b.

K1503	Chassis & Cab	2582	3430	—
K1534	Fleetside	2711	3825	—
K1504	Step-Side	2695	3790	—

1/2-Ton Dubl-Duti — Model P/Series 10 — 102 in. w.b.

P1345	Step-Van	2477	3475	—

3/4-Ton Commercial — Model C25/Series 20 — 127 in. w.b.

C2503	Chassis & Cab	2078	3230	—
C2534	Fleetside	2208	3710	—
C2504	Step-Side	2192	3665	—
C2509	Stake	2283	3855	—

3/4-Ton Commercial 4x4 — Model K25/Series 20 — 127 in. w.b.

K2534	Fleetside	2885	—	—
K2504	Step-Side	2869	—	—

3/4-Ton Dubl-Duti — Model P/Series 20 — 104-137 in. w.b.

P2345	Step-Van	3081	4825	—

1-Ton Commercial — Model C36/Series 30 — 133 in. w.b.

C3603	Chassis & Cab	2235	3410	—
C3604	Step-Side	2370	3880	—
C3609	Stake 9 ft.	2482	4240	—
C3605	Panel 10.5 ft.	2794	4240	—

1-Ton — Model P/Series 30 — 104-137 in. w.b.

P3345	Step-Van	3274	5030	—

1964 Chevrolet 1/2-Ton Series C10-C14 Fleetside Long Bed (OCW)

ENGINE [Standard El Camino; Optional G10]: Inline. OHV. Six-cylinder. Cast iron block. Bore & stroke: 3-9/16 in. x 3-1/4 in. Displacement: 194 cid. Compression ratio: 8.5:1. Brake horsepower: 120 at 4400 rpm. Maximum Torque: 177 lbs.-ft. at 2400 rpm. Seven main bearings. Hydraulic valve lifters. Carburetor: Rochester one-barrel model 7023105.

ENGINE [Standard P10/G10]: Inline. OHV. Four-cylinder. Cast iron block. Bore & stroke: 3-7/8 in. x 3-1/4 in. Displacement: 153.1 cid. Compression ratio: 8.5:1. Brake horsepower: 90 at 4000 rpm. Maximum Torque: 152 lbs.-ft. at 2400 rpm. Net horsepower: 75 at 4000 rpm. Five main bearings. Hydraulic valve lifters. Carburetor: Rochester one-barrel model 7020103.

ENGINE [Standard Corvair 95]: Opposed. OHV. Six-cylinder. Aluminum block. Bore & stroke: 3.437 in. x 2.938 in. Displacement: 163.6 cid. Compression ratio: 8.25:1. Brake horsepower: 95 at 3600 rpm. Four main bearings. Hydraulic valve lifters. Carburetor: Two Rochester one-barrel model 7019101.

ENGINE [Optional Corvair 95]: Opposed. OHV. Six-Cylinder. Aluminum block. Bore & Stroke: 3.437 in. x 2.938 in. Displacement: 163.6 cid. Compression ratio: 9.0:1. Brake horsepower: 110 at 3600 rpm. Four main bearings. Hydraulic valve lifters. Carburetor: Two Rochester single-barrel. (This engine available with three- or four-speed manual transmissions only.)

ENGINE [Standard C-K10/C-K15/C-K20/C30/P20/P30/Optional P10/El Camino]: Inline. OHV. Six-cylinder. Cast iron block. Bore & stroke: 3-7/8 in. x 3-1/4 in. Displacement: 230

cid. Compression ratio: 8.5:1. Brake horsepower: 140 at 4400 rpm. Maximum Torque: 220 lbs.-ft. at 1600 rpm. Net horsepower: 120 at 3600 rpm. Seven main bearings. Hydraulic valve lifters. Carburetor: Rochester model B-7023017.

ENGINE [Optional C-K10/C-K15/C-K20/C30/P20/P30]: Inline. OHV. Six-cylinder. Cast iron block. Bore & stroke: 3-7/8 in. x 4-1/4 in. Displacement: 292 cid. Compression ratio: 8.0:1. Brake horsepower: 165 at 3800 rpm. Maximum Torque: 280 lbs.-ft. at 1600 rpm. Net horsepower: 147 at 3600 rpm. Seven main bearings. Hydraulic valve lifters. Carburetor: Rochester one-barrel model B-7023013.

ENGINE [Optional C-K10/C-K15/C-K20/C30]: V-type. OHV. Eight-cylinder. Cast iron block. Bore & stroke: 3-7/8 in. x 3 in. Displacement: 283 cid. Compression ratio: 9.0:1. Brake horsepower: 175 at 4400 rpm. Maximum Torque: 275 lbs.-ft. at 2400 rpm. Net horsepower: 145 at 4200 rpm. Five main bearings. Hydraulic valve lifters. Carburetor: Rochester model 2G-7023010.

1964 Chevrolet Corvair 95 Rampside Pickup (OCW)

ENGINE [Optional El Camino]: V-type. OHV. Eight-cylinder. Cast iron block. Bore & stroke: 3.875 in. x 3.0 in. Displacement: 283 cid. Compression ratio: 9.25:1. Brake horsepower: 195 at 4800 rpm. Five main bearings. Hydraulic valve lifters. Carburetor: Rochester two-barrel model 7024101.

ENGINE [Optional El Camino]: V-type. OHV. Eight-cylinder. Cast iron block. Bore & stroke: 4 x 3.25 in. Displacement: 327 cid. Compression ratio: 10.5:1. Brake horsepower: 250 at 4400 rpm. Maximum torque: 350 lbs.-ft. at 2800 rpm. Carburetor: Four-barrel.

1964 Chevrolet 1/2-Ton C10 Step-Side Pickup (OCW)

CHASSIS [El Camino]: Wheelbase: 115 in. Overall length: 198-1/4 in. Front tread: 58 in. Rear tread: 58 in. Tires: 7.00 x 14 in.

CHASSIS [G10]: Wheelbase: 90 in. Tires: 6.50 x 13 in.

CHASSIS [95]: Wheelbase: 95 in. Overall length: 179.7 in. Height: 68.5 in. Front tread: 58 in. Rear tread: 58 in. Tires: 7.00 x 14 in.

CHASSIS [C10/K10]: Wheelbase: 115 in. Overall length: 206 (115 in. wheelbase) Height: 71 in. Front tread: 63.1 in. Rear tread: 61.1 in.

CHASSIS [C15/K15/C20/K20]: Wheelbase: 127 in. Height: 71 in. Front tread: 63.1 in. Rear tread: 61.1 in. Tires: [C15] 6.70 x 15; [K15/C-K20] 7 x 17.5 in.

CHASSIS [C30]: Wheelbase: 133 in.

CHASSIS [P10]: Wheelbase: 102 in. Tires: 6.70 x 15 in.

CHASSIS [P20/P30]: Wheelbase: 104 in.-137 in. Tires: 7 x 17.5 in.

TECHNICAL: Chevrolet three-speed manual transmission (Borg-Warner heavy-duty three-speed optional). [C30] 4F/1R; [Others] 3F/1R. Column-mounted gearshift lever. Single-plate, dry-disc clutch. Rear axle: [1/2-ton] semi-floating; [3/4-ton/1-Ton] full-floating. Base rear axles: [El Camino] 3.08:1; [Corvair 95] 3.55:1; [C-K10] 3.73:1; [C-K20] 4.11:1; [C30] 5.14:1. Four-wheel hydraulic, drum brakes. Brake linings: [Corvair 95] 11 x 2 in. [C-K10] 11 x 2.75 in.; [C-K20/C30] 12 x 2 in.; [El Camino] 9-1/2 x 2-1/2 in. Kelsey-Hayes pressed steel wheels.

1964 Chevrolet Corvair 95 Commercial Panel (OCW)

74

OPTIONS: [Corvair] (dealer prices): Custom Equipment Group, includes windshield molding; door inserts; nylon-and-vinyl seat; two-tone doors and steering wheel; right visor; left door armrest; cigar lighter and dispatch box trim plate: R1205 with standard seat ($17.56); R1205 with full-length seat ($19.23); R1254 ($1923). 110 hp engine ($20.90). Four-speed manual transmission ($71.10). Powerglide ($127.60). Direct Air heater ($57.69). Manual radio ($37.22). Passenger car type tires: 7.00 x 14-four-ply rated whitewall ($24.70); 7.00 x 14-six-ply rated blackwall ($34.16); 7.00 x 14 six-ply rated whitewall ($54.65); 7.00 x 14. Custom Chrome Trim, with wheelcovers ($16.75); without wheelcovers ($25.10). Two-tone paint: Pickups ($25.10); all others ($20.90). Wheelcovers for R1254 ($8.40); Greenbrier Custom ($6.73); standard Greenbrier ($8.40). Auxiliary seat, R1205 ($31.78). Air cleaner ($5.06). Positraction ($29.30). Body doors, R1205 ($62.70). Level pickup box floor, R1254 ($37.65). 35 amp. generator ($29.30). Laminated front glass ($4.20). Rear door glass ($10.07). Dual outside rearview mirrors ($7.54). Left- or right-hand fixed mirror ($3.77). Wire-control outside rearview mirror ($4.20). Heavy-duty shocks, except R1206 ($5.87). Heavy-duty front springs, includes heavy-duty shocks, except R1206 ($8.40). Windshield washer and two-speed wipers ($12.55).

OPTIONS: [Commercials] (wholesale prices): 292 cid six-cylinder engine ($75.25). 230 cid/120 hp six-cylinder engine in Step-Van ($50.20). 283 cid V-8 in C models and K20s ($92.00). Powerglide with heavy-duty radiator ($146.30). Step-Van, Borg-Warner three-speed manual transmission ($60 average). Four-speed manual transmission ($68 average). Heavy-duty battery ($5.87). Air cleaner with 230 cid six-cylinder engine ($5.06). Air cleaner with 292 cid six-cylinder engine ($1.72). Custom Appearance Group: C10/30 and K10 ($33.45); C10/20/30 and K10/20 ($40.13). No-Spin axle ($104.50). Positraction axle ($50.20). Vacuum power brakes ($35.12). Painted front bumper ($16.75). Painted front bumper ($4.20). Spare wheel carrier (average $11). Custom chrome package ($41.80). Custom Comfort package ($42.66). Economy equipment ($5.87). Fuel filter ($5.87). Gauge package ($5.87). 42-amp. generator ($16.75); 55-amp. generator ($23.43); 62-amp. generator ($69.43). Laminated glass, except Step-Vans ($4.20). Soft-Ray windshield, except Carryall/Step-Van ($10.07). E-Z-Eye windshield, P10 ($15.08). Soft-Ray glass in all windows, except Step-Van ($11.74). E-Z-Eye windshield, P20/20 ($16.75). Soft-Ray glass, all Suburban windows, ($15.08). Deluxe heater/defroster, except Step-Van ($53.11). Standard heater and defroster, except Step-Van ($41.80). Towing hooks ($10.07). Freewheeling hubs ($61.03). Lamp group ($20.90). Optional locks: Right-hand door ($1.29); Side spare wheel ($5.06); Both ($5.87). 17 in. mirrors: left ($1.72); right-extended type ($3.77). 6 x 11 in. mirrors ($4.20 each). 7 x 16 in. mirrors ($12.55 each). C10 Custom side moldings ($25.10). Two-tone paint: Pickup/cab ($12.55); Panel/Suburban ($20.90); 8 ft. Platform/Stake ($117.05). 9 ft. Platform/Stake ($142.15). 12 ft. Platform/Stake ($167.20). Heavy-duty radiator ($16.75). Radio ($37.22). Folding auxiliary seat for Panel ($31.78). Bostrom seat, except Step-Vans ($96.15). Tachometer ($37.65). Wipers and washers ($12.55).

1964 Chevrolet 1/2-Ton El Camino Custom Sedan-Pickup (OCW)

HISTORICAL: Introduced Sept. 29, 1963. Model year production: [All commercial] 523,791. Calendar year registrations: [All commercial] 483,853. Innovations: Compact van series introduced midyear. El Camino reintroduced on Chevelle platform. New features of full-size trucks include self-adjusting brakes and 6,000 mile chassis lube intervals. The nine millionth Chevrolet truck of all time was produced this season. Model year output of Corvair trucks was 15,199 units. This included 6,201 Greenbrier Sport Wagons, which were merchandised as a station wagon in the passenger car line and had a price of $2,666 and weight of 2,990 lbs.

1965 CHEVROLET

1965 Chevrolet 1/2-Ton Model C10 Fleetside With Custom Wheels (DFW)

Standard Catalog of Light-Duty Trucks

EL CAMINO — MODEL A/SERIES 13000 — SIX/V-8: The intermediate-sized El Camino had a new grille with a finer pattern and heavier horizontal center bar. Chevrolet's red, white and blue emblem was in the bar's mid-section. The front bumper was now slotted with the parking lamps being relocated to the long, horizontal slots. Built on the mid-size Chevelle's 115 in. wheelbase, the El Camino was available with many passenger-car options. It came with two trim levels. El Caminos in the 53 (six-cylinder) and 54 (V-8) series were the base models, with trim and appointments comparable to the Chevelle 300. Custom El Caminos in the 55 (six-cylinder) and 56 (V-8) series had trim and appointments comparable to Chevelle Malibu. V-8 badges, on models so-equipped, were moved ahead of the front wheel cutouts. Customs had additional moldings around the wheel openings and the load box, chrome window/windshield frames and a windsplit molding on the center of the hood. The 1965 El Caminos came in Tuxedo black; Ermine white; Mist blue; Danube blue; Willow green; Cypress green Artesian turquoise; Tahitian turquoise; Madeira maroon; Evening orchid; Regal red; Sierra tan; Cameo beige; Glacier gray; and Crocus yellow. Color-keyed all-vinyl seats and sidewall trim were featured. The standard interior also included an embossed vinyl headliner; dual sun visors; armrests; color-keyed vinyl floor mats; a cigar lighter; lockable glove compartment; bright instrument panel facing; and foam seat cushions. Customs featured color-keyed pattern cloth and leather-grain vinyl upholstery and had deep-twist floor carpeting, a bright glove compartment facing, two-tone steering wheel and electric clock. An AM/FM radio and simulated wire wheels were among new options. The 1964-1967 El Camino style pickup box was used again. Its inside width was 59-3/4 in. behind the cab and 64-3/4 in. near the tailgate. There was 46 in. between the wheelhousings. The bed of the box was 78-1/2 in. long. The tailgate measured 55-1/2 in. x 23 in. With the bed-level tailgate lowered, the overall bed length was 101.6 in.

1/2-TON CHEVY VAN — MODEL G/SERIES 10 — FOUR: The compact, front-engined Chevy Van was now the only one. The Corvair 95 series was gone. Styling characteristics again included five-segment vents on the front with a bow tie underneath and an oval, horizontal-bar grille near the bottom of the front single headlights. It had the same general characteristics, configuration and 90 in. wheelbase as the Corvan, but utilized a water-cooled 153 cid four-cylinder Chevy II engine as its base powerplant. The 194 cid and 230 cid sixes were both available at extra-cost this year. Two models called the Panel and Sportvan were offered. The Sportvan was marketed as a truck, although it was available with windows and auxiliary passenger seats. Also offered were Sportvan Custom editions. The Commercial Panel had double right-hand side cargo doors. This was clearly a truck.

1/2-TON COMMERCIAL — MODEL C14 (4x2); K14 (4x4)/SERIES 10 — SIX/V-8: The conventional trucks were unchanged in styling, trim or appointments, except for repositioning the identification badges higher up on the cowlsides, above the main feature line. New on the option list this year was a factory air-conditioning system. A new 327 cid V-8 was available in some trucks, too. An auxiliary hot water heater was available for the rear compartment of Suburbans. Even the grille was unchanged. It had thin vertical and horizontal elements in a tightly cross-hatched pattern. Black-accented Chevrolet lettering was on the top bar and the headlamp surrounds were square-shaped. The standard grille was made of steel painted Off-white, as were bumpers and hubcaps. An anodized aluminum grille and body side moldings were part of the Custom Appearance equipment packages. The cowl badges resembled a square and a rectangle separately framed in chrome. The square had a small Chevrolet bow tie. The rectangle had the series designation on a red background with vertical ribbing. Exterior colors for the year were black; Dark blue; Light blue; Fawn tan; gray; Dark green; Light green; maroon; turquoise; white; Off-white; Dark yellow; and Light yellow. Colors (except the two whites) were used as lower body colors in two-tone color options. They were teamed with Off-white on the upper body. Interiors were again done in two shades of fawn beige with Off-white accenting the steering wheel and mast. Standard seats had medium fawn embossed vinyl with light fawn facings. Custom interiors had color-keyed nylon-faced pattern cloth inserts and vinyl bolsters. The striped inserts were mostly Medium fawn beige. Contrasting bolsters were red or fawn, depending upon the color of the truck, with a white bottom bolster. There were four separate Custom equipment options, which are listed in the options section below. Offered again were Step-Side (with pontoon rear fenders) and Fleetside (with slab type rear fenders) Pickups with 6-1/2 ft. boxes, plus the 7-1/2 ft. Panel and Suburban. Three chassis models were available, too. The 10 Series Short Bed four-wheel drive 1/2-ton models had a K14 model prefix.

1/2-TON COMMERCIAL — MODELS C15; K15/SERIES 10 — SIX/V-8: The C15 trucks in the Chevrolet 10 Series long-wheelbase line used a C15 model prefix. Their cowlside nameplates were chrome and red badges with a bow tie and number 10. They had the same basic styling and trim changes as other conventional trucks. These were the long wheelbase (LWB) 1/2-ton trucks on the same chassis as 3/4-ton models. They are known as "Long Bed" or "Long Box" Pickups because they had a longer 8 ft. load box. Longer runningboards were needed on Step-Sides because there was more space between the cab and rear fenders. The 10 Series Long Bed four-wheel drive models had a K15 model prefix.

1/2-TON DUBL-DUTI — MODEL P13/SERIES 10 — SIX/V-8: The 1/2-ton Dubl-Duti returned again. It had a 102 in. wheelbase. An approved 7 ft. Step-Van walk-in delivery truck made by Union City Body Co., of Union City, Ind. was most commonly mounted on the Dubl-Duty chassis. A channel type front bumper and High-Torque 153 four-cylinder engine were standard equipment.

1965 Chevrolet 1/2-Ton C10 Fleetside Pickup (JAG)

3/4-TON COMMERCIAL — MODEL C25/SERIES 20 — SIX/V-8: The C25 trucks in the Chevrolet 20 Series 3/4-ton line had the same styling and trim changes as other conventional trucks. The cowlside nameplates were chrome and red badges with a bow tie emblem and chrome number 20. Step-Side and Fleetside Pickups were in this series. Compared to C10-C14 pickups, the C20-C25 pickup had slightly longer runningboards and an 8 ft. long box was used. There were also Platform and Platform/Stake models. The rail for the 3/4-ton Platform was about 8 ft. long. The four-wheel drive 3/4-ton models in the 20

Series had a K25 model prefix. In midyear, a truck camper package (with chassis beefed-up for camper use) was released. These trucks had distinctive "Camper Special" designation badges.

3/4-TON DUBL-DUTI — MODEL P23; P25; P26/SERIES 20 — SIX/V-8: Three 3/4-ton Dubl-Duti Forward-Control chassis remained in the 20 Series (3/4-ton) truck line. The P23/P25/P26 models had wheelbases of 104 in./125 in./137 in., respectively. The 104 in. wheelbase was recommended for 7 ft. to 8-1/2 ft. bodies; the 125 in. wheelbase was recommended for 9-1/2 to 10-1/2 ft. long bodies and the 137 in. wheelbase was recommended for 11-1/2 ft. to 12-1/2 ft. long bodies. Bodies could be sourced from factory approved firms or independent suppliers. A channel type front bumper and High-Torque 230 six were standard equipment.

1-TON MEDIUM-DUTY COMMERCIAL — MODEL C36; C38/SERIES 30 — SIX-CYLINDER: The Chevrolet 30 Series 1-ton trucks had the same styling and trim changes as other conventional trucks. The fenderside nameplates were chrome and red badges with a Chevrolet bow tie and number 30. There was no Fleetside Pickup in this line. The 10 ft. Panel model had a one-piece floor made of 3/4-in. thick, five-ply laminated wood. The basic model lineup was unchanged. Compared to the C20-C25 Pickup, the C30-C36 Pickup had a longer wheelbase, a longer 9 ft. box and very long runningboards. The 1-ton Stake trucks had a long rail some 9 ft. long. No hubcaps were used on the larger split-rim wheels of the Chassis & Cab and Stake models, which had eight bolts and eight circular openings. There was a new, midyear Camper Special package with "Camper Special" designation badges instead of 30 series call-outs. There was also a new C38 model 1-ton Chassis & Cab with a long 157 in. wheelbase that was perfectly suited for use a recreational vehicle (RV) chassis. A four-speed manual synchromesh transmission was standard. No four-wheel drive option was offered.

1-TON DUBL-DUTI — MODEL P33; P35; P36/SERIES 30 — SIX/V-8: Three Dubl-Duti Forward-Control chassis were in the 30 Series (1-ton) truck line. The P33/P35/P36 models had wheelbases of 104 in./125 in./137 in., respectively. The 104 in. wheelbase was recommended for 7 ft. to 8-1/2 ft. bodies; the 125 in. wheelbase was recommended for 9-1/2 to 10-1/2 ft. long bodies and the 137 in. wheelbase was recommended for 11-1/2 ft. to 12-1/2 ft. long bodies. Bodies could be sourced from factory approved firms or independent suppliers. A channel type front bumper and High-Torque 230 six were standard equipment.

I.D. DATA: Serial Number located: [Chassis models] On plate temporarily attached near steering column, with final location per body maker; [All others] On plate attached to rear face of left-hand door hinge pillar; on right side of cowl under hood. The first symbol (first three El Camino) indicated truck type: 133/134/135/136=El Camino; C=Conventional Cab; K=4x4; G=Chevy Van; P=Dubl-Duti Package Delivery; G=Chevy Van. The next two symbols on El Caminos indicated model (80=Sedan-Pickup); the next two symbols on other trucks indicated the series: 14=1/2-ton; 15=1/2-ton LWB; 25=3/4-ton; 36=1-ton; 38=-1-ton LWB. The next symbol indicated body type: 2=Chassis & Cowl; 3=Chassis & Cab; 4=Pickup; 5=Panel; 6=Suburban; 9=Stake. The next symbol (all) indicated model year: 5=1965. The next symbol (all) identified assembly plant: The next symbol indicated the assembly plant: [Commercial] A=Atlanta, Ga.; B=Baltimore, Md.; F=Flint, Mich.; J=Janesville, Wis.; N=Norwood, Ohio; P=Pontiac, Mich.; S=St. Louis, Mo.; T=Tarrytown, N.Y.; Z=Fremont, Calif. [El Camino] A=Lakewood; Atlanta, Ga.; B=Baltimore, Md.; G=Framingham, Mass.; K=Leeds; Kansas City, Mo.; Z=Fremont, Calif. Remaining symbols were the sequential production number starting with 100001 at each plant. Ending serial numbers not available. The Chevrolet engine had the source, date and type stamped on a serial number pad. Source codes were: F=Flint, Mich.; T=Tonawanda, N.Y.; C=Canada. Month codes were 1=Jan.; 2=Feb., etc. Date codes were 01=first of month, etc. Commercial model engine prefix codes were: [Hi-Torque 153 cid/90 hp L4] SA/SB/SC/SE; [High-Torque 194 cid/120 hp L6] SG/SI; [High-Torque 230 cid/140 hp Chevy Vans] SK/SL; [High-Torque 230 cid/140 hp L6 C/K/P] TA/TE/TF/TH/TI/TJ/TK/UH/UI/UU/UV; [High-Torque 283 cid/175 hp V-8] WA/WE/WC/WF.; [327 cid/185 hp V-8 (after midyear)] YD/YC/YR/YS/YH. Engine serial numbers: [Six] Right side of block behind distributor; [V-8] Front of block below right-hand cylinder head. Engine serial numbers not available.

Model	Body Type	Price	Weight	Prod. Total
El Camino — Model A/Series 13000 — 115 in. w.b. — Six				
13380	Pickup	2272	2925	Note 1
13580	Custom Pickup	2353	2935	Note 1
El Camino — Model A/Series 13000 — 115 in. w.b. — V-8				
13480	Pickup	2380	3060	Note 1
13680	Custom Pickup	2461	3060	Note 1

NOTE 1: Total El Camino production was 36,316.

Model	Body Type	Price	Weight	
Chevy Van — Model G/Series 10 — 90 in. w.b. — Four				
G1205	Panel	2105	2610	—
G1206	Sportvan	2355	2870	—
G1226	Custom Sportvan	2492	2970	—
G1236	Deluxe Sportvan	2717	3115	—
1/2-Ton Commercial — Model C14/Series 10 — 115 in. w.b.				
C1403	Chassis & Cab	1894	2830	—
C1434	Fleetside	2023	3205	—
C1404	Step-Side	2007	3190	—
C1405	Panel 7.5 ft.	2324	3420	—
C1406	Suburban (door)	3281	3680	—
C1416	Suburban (gate)	3314	3710	—
1/2-Ton Commercial 4x4 — Model K14/Series 10 — 115 in. w.b.				
K1434	Fleetside	2675	3825	—
K1404	Step-Side	2659	3805	—
K1405	Panel 7.5 ft.	2976	4080	—
K1406	Suburban (door)	3270	4385	—
K1416	Suburban (gate)	3303	4415	—
1/2-Ton Commercial (Long Bed) — Model C15/Series 10 — 127 in. w.b.				
C1503	Chassis & Cab	—	—	—
C1534	Fleetside	2060	3315	—
C1504	Step-Side	2044	3300	—
1/2-Ton Comm. (Long Bed) 4x4 — Model K15/Series 10 — 127 in. w.b.				
K1503	Chassis & Cab	2584	3445	—
K1534	Fleetside	2713	3840	—
K1504	Step-Side	2697	3805	—
1/2-Ton Dubl-Duti — Model P/Series 10 — 102 in. w.b.				
P1345	Step-Van	2477	3475	—

Model	Body Type	Price	Weight	
3/4-Ton Commercial — Model C25/Series 20 — 127 in. w.b.				
C2503	Chassis & Cab	2078	3230	—
C2534	Fleetside	2208	3710	—
C2504	Step-Side	2192	3665	—
C2509	Stake	2283	3855	—
3/4-Ton Commercial 4x4 — Model K25/Series 20 — 127 in. w.b.				
K2503	Chassis & Cab	2756	3805	—
K2534	Fleetside	2885	4270	—
K2504	Step-Side	2869	4225	—
3/4-Ton Dubl-Duti — Model P/Series 20 — 104-137 in. w.b.				
P2345	Step-Van	3081	4825	—
1-Ton Commercial — Model C36/Series 30 — 133 in. w.b.				
C3603	Chassis & Cab	2235	3410	—
C3604	Step-Side	2370	3880	—
C3609	Stake 9 ft.	2482	4240	—
C3605	Panel 10.5 ft.	2794	4240	—
1-Ton — Model P/Series 30 — 104-137 in. w.b.				
P3345	Step-Van	3274	5030	—

ENGINE [Standard El Camino; Optional G10]: Inline. OHV. Six-cylinder. Cast iron block. Bore & stroke: 3-9/16 in. x 3-1/4 in. Displacement: 194 cid. Compression ratio: 8.5:1. Brake horsepower: 120 at 4400 rpm. Maximum Torque: 177 lbs.-ft. at 2400 rpm. Seven main bearings. Hydraulic valve lifters. Carburetor: Rochester one-barrel model 7023105.

ENGINE [Standard P10/G10]: Inline. OHV. Four-cylinder. Cast iron block. Bore & stroke: 3-7/8 in. x 3-1/4 in. Displacement: 153.1 cid. Compression ratio: 8.5:1. Brake horsepower: 90 at 4000 rpm. Maximum Torque: 152 lbs.-ft. at 2400 rpm. Net horsepower: 75 at 4000 rpm. Five main bearings. Hydraulic valve lifters. Carburetor: Rochester one-barrel model 7020103.

ENGINE [Standard C-K10/C-K15/C-K20/C30/P20/P30/Optional P10/El Camino]: Inline. OHV. Six-cylinder. Cast iron block. Bore & stroke: 3-7/8 in. x 3-1/4 in. Displacement: 230 cid. Compression ratio: 8.5:1. Brake horsepower: 140 at 4400 rpm. Maximum Torque: 220 lbs.-ft. at 1600 rpm. Net horsepower: 120 at 3600 rpm. Seven main bearings. Hydraulic valve lifters. Carburetor: Rochester model B-7023017.

ENGINE [Optional C-K10/C-K15/C-K20/C30/P20/P30]: Inline. OHV. Six-cylinder. Cast iron block. Bore & stroke: 3-7/8 in. x 4-1/4 in. Displacement: 292 cid. Compression ratio: 8.0:1. Brake horsepower: 165 at 3800 rpm. Maximum Torque: 280 lbs.-ft. at 1600 rpm. Net horsepower: 147 at 3600 rpm. Seven main bearings. Hydraulic valve lifters. Carburetor: Rochester one-barrel model B-7023013.

ENGINE [Optional C-K10/C-K15/C-K20/C30]: V-type. OHV. Eight-cylinder. Cast iron block. Bore & stroke: 3-7/8 in. x 3 in. Displacement: 283 cid. Compression ratio: 9.0:1. Brake horsepower: 175 at 4400 rpm. Maximum Torque: 275 lbs.-ft. at 2400 rpm. Net horsepower: 145 at 4200 rpm. Five main bearings. Hydraulic valve lifters. Carburetor: Rochester model 2G-7023010.

1965 Chevrolet 1/2-Ton El Camino Sedan-Pickup With Modern Wheels

ENGINE [Optional El Camino]: V-type. OHV. Eight-cylinder. Cast iron block. Bore & stroke: 3.875 in. x 3.0 in. Displacement: 283 cid. Compression ratio: 9.25:1. Brake horsepower: 195 at 4800 rpm. Five main bearings. Hydraulic valve lifters. Carburetor: Rochester two-barrel model 7024101.

ENGINE [Optional El Camino]: V-type. OHV. Eight-cylinder. Cast iron block. Bore & stroke: 4 x 3.25 in. Displacement: 327 cid. Compression ratio: 9.25:1. Brake horsepower: 220. Carburetor: Four-barrel.

ENGINE [Optional El Camino]: V-type. OHV. Eight-cylinder. Cast iron block. Bore & stroke: 4 x 3.25 in. Displacement: 327 cid. Compression ratio: 10.5:1. Brake horsepower: 250 at 4400 rpm. Maximum torque: 350 lbs.-ft. at 2800 rpm. Carburetor: Four-barrel.

ENGINE [Optional El Camino]: V-type. OHV. Eight-cylinder. Cast iron block. Bore & stroke: 4 x 3.25 in. Displacement: 327 cid. Compression ratio: 10.5:1. Brake horsepower: 300 at 5000 rpm. Torque: 360 lbs.-ft. at 3200 rpm. Carburetor: Four-barrel.

ENGINE [Optional El Camino]: V-type. OHV. Eight-cylinder. Cast iron block. Bore & stroke: 4 x 3.25 in. Displacement: 327 cid. Compression ratio: 11.0:1. Brake horsepower: 350 at 5800 rpm. Torque: 360 lbs.-ft. at 3200 rpm. Carburetor: Four-barrel.

ENGINE [Optional El Camino]: V-type. OHV. Eight-cylinder. Cast iron block. Bore & stroke: 4.09 x 3.76 in. Displacement: 396 cid. Compression ratio: 11.0:1. Brake horsepower: 375. Carburetor: Four-barrel.

CHASSIS [El Camino]: Wheelbase: 115 in. Overall length: 197 in. Front tread: 58 in. Rear tread: 58 in. Tires: 7.35 x 14 in.

CHASSIS [G10]: Wheelbase: 90 in. Tires: 6.50 x 13 in.

CHASSIS [C10/K10]: Wheelbase: 115in./127 in. Overall length: 206 (115 in. wheelbase) Height: 71 in. Front tread: 63.1 in. Rear tread: 61.1 in. Tires: 7.75 x 15 in.

CHASSIS [P10]: Wheelbase: 102 in. Tires: 7.75 x 15 in.

CHASSIS [C15/K15/C20/K20]: Wheelbase: 127 in.

CHASSIS [C30]: Wheelbase: 133 in. Tires: 8 x 17.5 in.

CHASSIS [P20/P30]: Wheelbase: 104 in. Tires: 7.75 x 15 in.

1965 Chevrolet 1/2-Ton C10 Fleetside Pickup (JAG)

TECHNICAL: Chevrolet three-speed manual transmission (Borg-Warner heavy-duty three-speed optional). [C30] 4F/1R. [Others] 3F/1R. Column-mounted gearshift lever. Single-plate, dry-disc clutch. Rear axle: [1/2-ton] semi-floating; [3/4-ton/1-Ton] full-floating. Base rear axles: [El Camino] 3.08:1; [Corvair 95] 3.55:1; [C-K10] 3.73:1; [C-K20] 4.11:1; [C30] 5.14:1. Four-wheel hydraulic, drum brakes. Brake linings: [Corvair 95] 11 x 2 in. [C-K10] 11 x 2.75 in.; [C-K20/C30] 12 x 2 in.; [El Camino] 9-1/2 x 2-1/2 in. Kelsey-Hayes pressed steel wheels.

OPTIONS: 293 cid V-8 ($92). 292 cid six-cylinder $75.25. Oil bath air cleaner ($5.06). Positraction ($50.20). No-Spin rear axle ($104.50). Rear axle, 3.07:1 ratio, with stick ($10.07). Rear axle, 4.11:1 ratio, with stick ($6.73). Heavy-duty battery ($5.87). Painted rear bumper on pickups with painted front bumper ($16.75). Heavy-duty 11 in. clutch with six-cylinder only ($4.20). Custom Appearance option: Panel ($33.45); Others ($40.13). Custom Chrome option: Pickup with chrome front bumper ($16.75); Pickup with two chrome bumpers ($41.80); Panel with two chrome bumpers ($25.10). Custom Comfort option, Panel ($9.21); others ($42.66). Fleetside Custom side moldings ($25.10). Delcotron alternators: 42-amp. ($16.75); 52-amp. ($23.43). Tinted glass ($11.74). Tinted windshield ($10.07). Deluxe heater ($53.11). Thrift-Air heater ($41.80). Outside rearview mirrors: 17-1/4 in. left, except Panel ($1.72); right, except Panel ($3.77); 6-1/4 in. right ($3.77). Tu-tone paint: Panel ($20.90); Other trucks ($12.55). Heavy-duty radiator, except with Powerglide ($16.75). Radio ($37.22). Auxiliary Panel truck seat ($31.78). Foam seat ($16.75). Heavy-duty front shocks (average $6). Heavy-duty rear shocks ($6.73). Heavy-duty front springs, C25 ($2.53). Heavy-duty rear springs, all ($5.06). Heavy-duty three-speed transmission: C14 ($58.55); C15 ($62.70) and C25 ($71.10). Heavy-duty four-speed transmission: C14 ($62.70); C15 ($66.90) and C25 ($75.25). Powerglide, all ($146.30). Full-View rear window, except Panel ($33.45). Two-speed windshield washers and wipers ($12.55).

HISTORICAL: Introduced: Sept. 24, 1964. Model year production: [All Commercials] 619,685. Commercial model (not El Camino) calendar year registrations: 567,473. Commercial model calendar year factory shipments by GVW class: [6,000 lbs. and less] 427,100; [6,001-10,000 lbs.] 111,600. Retail sales: 574,120 units (up 15.6 percent). Innovations: Larger six-cylinder engine for vans. 327 cid V-8 released at midyear. New midyear truck-camper option. First year for factory air-conditioning. Chevrolet showcased the Turbo Titan III, a gas-turbine powered experimental truck, in 1965. Chevy called it the "Truck of Tomorrow." The 1965 Chevrolet commercial vehicles were advertised as "Work Power" trucks. This was an all-time record season for America's number one truck-maker and the first in which registrations broke the 500,000 level. Chevrolet claimed that, by the end of 1965, there were 4,751,127 Chevrolet trucks operating in the U.S.

1966 CHEVROLET

1966 Chevrolet 1/2-Ton El Camino Sedan-Pickup With Custom Wheels (DFW)

EL CAMINO — MODEL A/SERIES 13000 — SIX/V-8: An all-new Chevelle body was used for the El Camino, although the pickup box was unchanged. It had a slanted front end. The front fenders had a wraparound design. A new grille was lower and wider. It had multiple horizontal blades and wider-spaced vertical blades with a Chevrolet emblem in its center. There were two slots inside the bumper that were shorter and wider than in 1968. Following the Chevelle's every-other-year pattern, the parking lights were moved to a position inside the bumper slots, below the headlamps. There was a new dashboard and new hubcaps, too. Redesigned full wheelcovers had a spoked, rather than finned, look. There were

Standard Catalog of Light-Duty Trucks

engine designation badges on the front fender, El Camino nameplates on the rear fenders, and a tailgate with a bright latch and Chevrolet lettering. Even the standard model had bright windshield frames and a chrome hood windsplit molding. The El Camino Custom added bright side and rear window frames, moldings on the upper edge of the pickup box and wide rocker panel moldings with rear quarter panel extensions. There was no official Super Sport option this year, although the 396 cid V-8 was available as a separate option. Exterior colors for 1966 were Tuxedo black; Ermine white; Mist blue; Danube blue; Marina blue; Willow green; Artesian turquoise; Tropic turquoise; Aztec bronze; Madeira maroon; Regal red; Sandalwood tan; Cameo beige; Chateau slate; and Lemonwood yellow. The standard interior trims were fawn, blue or red vinyl. Custom interiors came with still richer all-vinyl black, fawn or red trims. Bucket seats were optional. The pickup box inside width was 59-3/4 in. behind the cab and 64-3/4 in. near the tailgate. There was 46 in. between the wheelhousings. The bed of the box was 78-1/2 in. long. The tailgate measured 55-1/2 in. x 23 in. With the bed-level tailgate lowered, the overall bed length was 101.6 in.

1/2-TON CHEVY VAN — MODEL G/SERIES 10 — FOUR: The compact, front-engined Chevy Van was basically unchanged for 1966. Styling characteristics again included five-segment vents on the front with a bow tie underneath and an oval, horizontal-bar grille near the bottom of the front single headlights. It had the same general characteristics and 90 in. wheelbase. The 153 cid four-cylinder Chevy II engine was dropped. The 194 cid six was base engine. The 230 cid six was available at extra cost. It was available in two models called the Panel and Sportvan. The Sportvan was marketed as a truck, although it was available with windows and auxiliary passenger seats. Also offered were Sportvan Custom and Sportvan Deluxe editions. The Commercial Panel had double right-hand side cargo doors and was clearly a truck. There was a new pop-up camper option.

1/2-TON COMMERCIAL — MODEL C14 (4x2); K14 (4x4)/SERIES 10 — SIX/V-8: Front end sheet metal was unchanged for 1966. Designation plates were moved below the feature line, behind the front wheel opening. They had a rectangular shape with two rectangular plaques on the surface. The narrower rectangle on top was satin-finished and carried a blue bow tie. The larger bottom rectangle had a chrome 10 (on 1/2-tons) and red background with horizontal grooves. Standard equipment on all light-duties, effective this season, included seat belts, dual long-arm mirrors, two-speed wiper washers and backup lamps. Exterior colors were Dark aqua metallic; black; Dark blue; Light blue; gray metallic; Dark green; Light green; orange; red; saddle metallic; silver metallic; white; Off-white; and School Bus yellow. All metal interior parts were medium fawn. Non-glare Dark fawn was on the instrument panel, which had a silver face plate. The steering column steps had medium fawn and the steering wheel had a chrome, half-circle horn ring. The glove box door was Silver gray with black Chevrolet lettering. Standard upholstery was medium fawn textured vinyl with embossed surfaces and fawn seat belts. A black rubber floor mat was used. The Custom Comfort Interior option included nylon-faced cloth upholstery in a medium and dark brown two-tone pattern with white vinyl backrest inserts. Custom trim also included a left armrest; right-hand sunshade; chrome cigar lighter; foam seats; insulation; and right door lock. A Custom Appearance package included bright windshield frames; "Custom" embossed roof pillar trim plates; a silver anodized aluminum grille; a medium fawn steering wheel with chrome horn ring; bright dashboard knobs; and two-tone door panels. A chrome front bumper was part of the Custom Chrome option. Silver anodized, chrome double bodyside moldings were available for Fleetside pickups. The center of the molding was accented with Off-white (or white on white trucks). Offered again were Step-Side (with pontoon rear fenders) and Fleetside (with slab type rear fenders) Pickups with 6-1/2 ft. boxes, plus the 7-1/2 ft. Panel and 7-1/2 ft. Suburban (panel door or tailgate models). There were also Chassis & Cowl, Chassis Cowl & Windshield, and Chassis & Cab models. The 10 Series Short Bed four-wheel drive 1/2-ton models had a K14 model prefix.

1/2-TON COMMERCIAL — MODELS C15 (4x2)/SERIES 10 — SIX/V-8: The C15 trucks in the Chevrolet 10 Series long-wheelbase line again used a C15 model prefix. They had the same trim changes as C14s. Designation plates were moved below the feature line, behind the front wheel opening. They had a rectangular shape with two rectangular plaques on the surface. The narrower rectangle on top was satin-finished and carried a blue bow tie. The larger bottom rectangle had a chrome 10 (on 1/2-tons) and red background with horizontal grooves. These were long wheelbase (LWB) 1/2-ton trucks on the same wheelbase as 3/4-ton models. They are known as "Long Bed" or "Long Box" Pickups because they had a longer 8 ft. load box. Longer runningboards were needed on Step-Sides because there was more space between the cab and rear fenders. The 10 Series Long Bed four-wheel drive models had a K15 model prefix.

1/2-TON DUBL-DUTI — MODEL P13/SERIES 10 — SIX/V-8: The 1/2-ton Dubl-Duti returned again. It had a 102 in. wheelbase. The small Step-Van walk-in delivery truck with a 7 ft. long body was approved for this chassis. It was made by Union City Body Co., of Union City, Ind. A channel type front bumper and 194 cid High-Torque six-cylinder engine were standard equipment.

1966 Chevrolet El Camino 1/2-Ton Sedan Pickup (OCW)

3/4-TON COMMERCIAL — MODEL C25/SERIES 20 — SIX/V-8: The C25 trucks in the Chevrolet 20 Series 3/4-ton line had the same styling and trim changes as other conventional trucks. The designation plates were had a bow tie emblem and chrome number 20. Step-Side and Fleetside Pickups were in this series. They featured the 8 ft. pickup box. There were also Platform and Platform/Stake models. The rail for the 3/4-ton Platform was 8 ft. long. The four-wheel drive 3/4-ton models in the 20 Series had a K25 model prefix. A truck camper package (with chassis beefed-up for camper use) was available.

3/4-TON DUBL-DUTI — MODEL P23; P25; P26/SERIES 20 — SIX/V-8: Three 3/4-ton Dubl-Duti Forward-Control chassis remained in the 20 Series (3/4-ton) truck line. The P23/P25/P26 models had wheelbases of 104 in./125 in./137 in., respectively. The 104 in. wheelbase was recommended for bodies 7 ft. to 8-1/2 ft. long; the 125 in. wheelbase was recommended for bodies 9-1/2 to 10-1/2 ft. long. The 137 in. wheelbase was recommended for bodies 11-1/2 to 12-1/2 ft. long. Bodies were available from factory-authorized suppliers or buyers could order them locally.

1-TON MEDIUM-DUTY COMMERCIAL — MODEL C36; C38/SERIES 30 — SIX-CYLINDER: The Chevrolet 30 Series 1-ton trucks had the same styling and trim changes as other conventional trucks. The fenderside nameplates had a Chevrolet bow tie and number 30. There was no Fleetside Pickup in this line. The 10 ft. Panel model had a one-piece floor made of 3/4-in. thick, five-ply laminated wood. The basic model lineup was unchanged. Compared to the C20-C25 Pickup, the C30-C36 Pickup had a longer wheelbase and 9 ft. long box. The 1-ton Stake trucks were also 9 ft. long. No hubcaps were used on the larger split-rim wheels of the Chassis & Cab and Stake models, which had eight bolts and eight circular openings. The Camper Special package continued. Camper Specials had their own designation plates with a Chevrolet bow tie and "Camper Special" in chrome script. The C38 model 1-ton Chassis & Cab with a long 157 in. wheelbase for use as an RV chassis was offered again. A four-speed manual synchromesh transmission was standard. No four-wheel drive option was offered.

1-TON DUBL-DUTI — MODEL P33; P35; P36/SERIES 30 — SIX/V-8: Three Dubl-Duti Forward-Control chassis were in the 30 Series (1-ton) truck line. The P33/P35/P36 models had wheelbases of 104 in./125 in./137 in., respectively. The 104 in. wheelbase was recommended for bodies 7 ft. to 8-1/2 ft. long; the 125 in. wheelbase was recommended for bodies 9-1/2 ft. to 10-1/2 ft. long. The 137 in. wheelbase was recommended for bodies 11-1/2 ft. to 12-1/2 ft. long. Bodies were available from factory-authorized suppliers or buyers could order them locally. A channel type front bumper and High-Torque 230 six were standard equipment.

I.D. DATA: Serial Number located: [Chassis models] On plate temporarily attached near steering column, with final location per body maker; [All others] On plate attached to rear face of left-hand door hinge pillar; on right side of cowl under hood. The first symbol (first three El Camino) indicated truck type: 133/134/135/136=El Camino; C=Conventional Cab; K=4x4; G=Chevy Van; P=Dubl-Duti Package Delivery; G=Chevy Van. The next two symbols on El Caminos indicated model (80=Sedan-Pickup); the next two symbols on other trucks indicated the series: 14=1/2-ton; 15=1/2-ton LWB; 25=3/4-ton; 36=1-ton; 38=-1-ton LWB. The next symbol indicated body type: 2=Chassis & Cowl; 3=Chassis & Cab; 4=Pickup; 5=Panel; 6=Suburban; 9=Stake. The next symbol (all) indicated model year: 6=1966. The next symbol indicated the assembly plant: [Commercial] A=Atlanta, Ga.; B=Baltimore, Md.; F=Flint, Mich.; J=Janesville, Wis.; N=Norwood, Ohio; P=Pontiac, Mich.; S=St. Louis, Mo.; T=Tarrytown, N.Y.; Z=Fremont, Calif. [El Camino] A=Lakewood; Atlanta, Ga.; B=Baltimore, Md.; G=Framingham, Mass.; K=Leeds; Kansas City, Mo.; Z=Fremont, Calif. Remaining symbols were the sequential production number starting with 100001 at each plant. Ending serial numbers not available. The Chevrolet engine had the source, date and type stamped on a serial number pad. Source codes were: F=Flint, Mich.; T=Tonawanda, N.Y.; C=Canada. Month codes were 1=Jan.; 2=Feb., etc. Date codes were 01=first of month, etc. Prefix codes for Commercial and Dubl-Duti models were [194 cid/120 hp High-Torque six] SC/SD/SO/SP/SG/SI/SE/SF; [230 cid/140 hp High-Torque six] SR/SS/ST/SU/SK/SL/TH/TI; [250 cid/150 hp High-Torque six] SV/SW/SX/TA/TE/TF/TJ/TK/VQ/VR/UR/UT/UU/UV; [283 cid/175 HP High-Torque V-8] WF/WH/WA/WE; [327 cid/185 hp High-Torque V-8] YC/YD/YR/YS/YH.

Model	Body Type	Price	Weight	Prod. Total
El Camino — Model A/Series 13000 — 115 in. w.b. — Six				
13380	Pickup	2318	2930	Note 1
13580	Custom Pickup	2396	2930	Note 1
El Camino — Model A/Series 13000 — 115 in. w.b. — V-8				
13480	Pickup	2426	3075	Note 1
13680	Custom Pickup	2504	3075	Note 1

NOTE 1: Total El Camino production was 35,119.

Model	Body Type	Price	Weight	Prod. Total
Chevy Van — Model G/Series 10 — 90 in. w.b. — Four				
G1205	Panel	2141	2755	28,180
G1206	Sportvan	2388	2965	4,209
G1226	Custom Sportvan	2521	3065	2,674
G1236	Deluxe Sportvan	2747	3125	2,341
1/2-Ton Commercial — Model C14/Series 10 — 115 in. w.b.				
C1403	Chassis & Cab	1927	2835	40
C1434	Fleetside	2066	3220	57,386
C1404	Step-Side	2050	3195	59,947
C1405	Panel 7.5 ft.	2361	3420	—
C1406	Suburban (door)	2598	3710	6,717
C1416	Suburban (gate)	2629	3735	5,334
1/2-Ton Ton Commercial 4x4 — Model K14/Series 10 — 115 in. w.b.				
K1434	Fleetside	2718	3825	678
K1404	Step-Side	2702	3810	1,123
K1405	Panel 7.5 ft.	3013	4085	170
K1406	Suburban (door)	3270	4385	530
K1416	Suburban (gate)	3303	4415	418
1/2-Ton Commercial (Long Bed) — Model C15/Series 10 — 127 in. w.b.				
C1503	Chassis & Cab	—	—	1,155
C1534	Fleetside	2104	3225	178,752
C1504	Step-Side	2087	3290	26,456
1/2-Ton Comm. (Long Bed) 4x4 — Model K15/Series 10 — 127 in. w.b.				
K1503	Chassis & Cab	—	—	30
K1534	Fleetside	2756	3845	1,976
K1504	Step-Side	2739	3810	457
1/2-Ton Dubl-Duti — Model P/Series 10 — 102 in. w.b.				
P1345	Step-Van	2658	3480	3,202
3/4-Ton Commercial — Model C25/Series 20 — 127 in. w.b.				
C2503	Chassis & Cab	2112	3265	6,520
C2534	Fleetside	2252	3700	55,855
C2504	Step-Side	2236	3700	9,905
C2509	Stake	2328	3890	1,499
3/4-Ton Commercial 4x4 — Model K25/Series 20 — 127 in. w.b.				
K2503	Chassis & Cab	—	—	—
K2534	Fleetside	2904	4270	1,796
K2504	Step-Side	2888	4225	924
3/4-Ton Dubl-Duti — Model P/Series 20 — 104-137 in. w.b.				
P2345	Step-Van	3432	4835	192
1-Ton Commercial — Model C36/Series 30 — 133 in. w.b.				
C3603	Chassis & Cab	2269	3455	11,852
C3604	Step-Side	2414	3930	3,646
C3609	Stake 9 ft.	2527	4285	3,651
C3605	Panel 10.5 ft.	2832	4265	3,560
1-Ton — Model P/Series 30 — 104-137 in. w.b.				
P3345	Step-Van	3432	5040	61

NOTE 1: Production totals from Chevrolet records are for model-year through Aug. 5, 1966 and include all trucks built in U.S. factories for domestic/export/Canadian markets.

ADDITIONAL PRODUCTION: [C10] Model C1412 Chassis, Cowl & Windshield=10; Model C1402 Chassis & Cowl=15; [P10] Model P1342 Chassis=107.

ENGINE [Standard P10/G10]: Inline. OHV. Six-cylinder. Cast iron block. Bore & stroke: 3-9/16 in. x 3-1/4 in. Displacement: 194 cid. Compression ratio: 8.5:1. Brake horsepower: 120 at 4400 rpm. Maximum Torque: 220 lbs.-ft. at 1600 rpm. Seven main bearings. Hydraulic valve lifters. Carburetor: Rochester one-barrel model 7023105.

ENGINE [Standard C10; Optional P10/G10/El Camino]: Inline. OHV. Six-cylinder. Cast iron block. Bore & stroke: 3-7/8 in. x 3-1/4 in. Displacement: 230 cid. Compression ratio: 8.5:1. Brake horsepower: 140 at 4400 rpm. Maximum Torque: 220 lbs.-ft. at 1600 rpm. Net horsepower: 120 at 3600 rpm. Seven main bearings. Hydraulic valve lifters. Carburetor: Rochester one-barrel model B-7023017.

ENGINE [Standard C10/K10/P20/C20/K20/P30/C30]: Inline. OHV. Six-cylinder. Cast iron block. Bore & stroke: 3.875 in. x 3.53 in. Displacement: 250 cid. Compression ratio: 8.5:1. Brake horsepower: 155 at 4200 rpm. Seven main bearings. Hydraulic valve lifters. Carburetor: Downdraft two-barrel.

ENGINE [C10/K10/P20/C20/K20/P30/C30]: Inline. OHV. Six-cylinder. Cast iron block. Bore & stroke: 3-7/8 in. x 4-1/2 in. Displacement: 292 cid. Compression ratio: 8.0:1. Brake horsepower: 170 at 4000 rpm. Maximum Torque: 275 lbs.-ft. at 1600 rpm. Net horsepower: 153 at 3600 rpm. Seven main bearings. Hydraulic valve lifters. Carburetor: Rochester model B-7024009.

ENGINE [Optional C10/C20/C30/K10/K20]: V-type. OHV. Eight-cylinder. Cast iron block. Bore & stroke: 3-7/8 in. x 3 in. Displacement: 283 cid. Compression ratio: 9.0:1. Brake horsepower: 175 at 4400 rpm. Maximum Torque: 275 lbs.-ft. at 2400 rpm. Five main bearings. Hydraulic valve lifters. Carburetor: Rochester two-barrel model 7024101.

ENGINE [Optional El Camino]: V-type. OHV. Eight-cylinder. Cast iron block. Bore & stroke: 3-7/8 in. x 3 in. Displacement: 283 cid. Compression ratio: 9.25:1. Brake horsepower: 195 at 4800 rpm. Maximum Torque: 285 lbs.-ft. at 2400 rpm. Five main bearings. Hydraulic valve lifters. Carburetor: Rochester two-barrel model 7024101.

ENGINE [Optional El Camino]: V-type. OHV. Eight-cylinder. Cast iron block. Bore & stroke: 3-7/8 in. x 3 in. Displacement: 283 cid. Compression ratio: 9.25:1. Brake horsepower: 220 at 4800 rpm. Maximum Torque: 285 lbs.-ft. at 2400 rpm. Five main bearings. Hydraulic valve lifters. Carburetor: Rochester four-barrel.

ENGINE [C10/C20/C30]: V-type. OHV. Eight-cylinder. Cast iron block. Bore & stroke: 4 in. x 3-1/4 in. Displacement: 327 cid. Compression ratio: 9.25:1. Brake horsepower: 220 at 4400 rpm. Maximum Torque: 320 lbs.-ft. at 2800 rpm. Five main bearings. Hydraulic valve lifters. Carburetor: Rochester four-barrel model 4G.

ENGINE [Optional El Camino]: V-type. OHV. Eight-cylinder. Cast iron block. Bore & stroke: 4 in. x 3-1/4 in. Displacement: 327 cid. Brake horsepower: 275 at 4800 rpm. Maximum Torque: 355 lbs.-ft. at 3200 rpm. Five main bearings. Hydraulic valve lifters. Carburetor: Rochester four-barrel.

ENGINE [Optional El Camino]: V-type. OHV. Eight-cylinder. Cast iron block. Bore & stroke: 4.094 in. x 3.76 in. Displacement: 396 cid. Compression ratio: 10.25:1. Brake horsepower: 325 at 4800 rpm. Maximum Torque: 410 lbs.-ft. at 3200 rpm. Five main bearings. Carburetor: Downdraft four-barrel.

ENGINE [Optional El Camino]: V-type. OHV. Eight-cylinder. Cast iron block. Bore & stroke: 4.094 in. x 3.76 in. Displacement: 396 cid. Compression ratio: 10.25:1. Brake horsepower: 360 at 5200 rpm. Maximum Torque: 420 lbs.-ft. at 3600 rpm. Five main bearings. Carburetor: four-barrel.

ENGINE [Optional El Camino]: V-type. OHV. Eight-cylinder. Cast iron block. Bore & stroke: 4.094 in. x 3.76 in. Displacement: 396 cid. Compression ratio: 11.25:1. Brake horsepower: 375. Five main bearings. Carburetor: four-barrel.

1966 Chevrolet 1/2-Ton C10 Fleetside Pickup (OCW)

CHASSIS [El Camino]: Wheelbase: 115 in. Overall length: 197 in. Front tread: 58 in. Rear tread: 58 in. Tires: 7.35 x 14 in. GVW: 4,300 lbs.

CHASSIS [G10]: Wheelbase: 90 in. Tires: 6.50 x 13 in. GVW: 3,900-5,000 lbs.

CHASSIS [C10-C14/K10-K14]: Wheelbase: 115 in. Overall length: 186-3/4 in. Height: 71 in. Front tread: 63.1 in. Rear tread: 61.1 in. Tires: Tires: [4x2] 7.75 x 15 in.; [Suburban] 8.15 x 15 in.; [4x4] 17.5 x 17 four-ply. GVW: [4x2] 4,400-5,000 lbs.; [4x4] 5,600 lbs.

CHASSIS [C10-C15/K10-K15]: Wheelbase: 127 in. Overall length: 206-1/4 in. Height: 71 in. Front tread: 63.1 in. Rear tread: 61.1 in. Tires: [4x2] 7.75 x 15 in. four-ply; [4x4] 17.5 x 17. GVW: [4x2] 4,400-5,000 lbs.; [4x4] 5,600 lbs.

CHASSIS [P10]: Wheelbase: 102 in. Tires: 7.75 x 15 in. GVW: 4,600-5,400 lbs.

CHASSIS [C20/K20]: Wheelbase: 127 in. Overall length: 206-1/4 in. Tires: [4x2] 7 x 17.5 in.; [4x4] 7 x 17.5 six-ply. GVW: [4x2] 5,500-7,500 lbs.]; [4x4] 5,700-7,600 lbs.

CHASSIS [P20]: Wheelbases: [P2300] 104 in.; [P2500] 125 in.; [P2600] 137 in. Base tires: 7 x 17.5. GVW: 7,000 lbs.

CHASSIS [C30]: Wheelbase: 133 in. Tires: 8 x 17.5 in. GVW: 6,700-14,000 lbs.

CHASSIS [P30]: Wheelbases: [P3300] 104 in.; [P3500] 125 in.; [P3600] 137 in. Base tires: 8 x 19.5. GVW: 7,500-14,000 lbs.

TECHNICAL: Chevrolet three-speed manual transmission (Borg-Warner heavy-duty three-speed optional). [C30] 4F/1R; [Others] 3F/1R. Column-mounted gearshift lever. Single-plate, dry-disc clutch. Rear axle: [1/2-ton] semi-floating; [3/4-ton/1-Ton] full-floating. Base rear axles: [El Camino] 3.08:1; [Corvair 95] 3.55:1; [C-K10] 3.73:1; [C-K20] 4.11:1; [C-K30] 5.14:1. Four-wheel hydraulic, drum brakes. Brake linings: [Corvair 95] 11 x 2 in. [C-K10] 11 x 2.75 in.; [C-K20/CK-30] 12 x 2 in.; [El Camino] 9-1/2 x 2-1/2 in. Kelsey-Hayes pressed steel wheels.

OPTIONS [Commercial/Dubl-Duti]: 293 cid V-8 ($92). 292 cid six-cylinder $75.25. Oil bath air cleaner ($5.06). Positraction ($50.20). No-Spin rear axle ($104.50). Rear axle, 3.07:1 ratio, with stick ($10.07). Rear axle, 4.11:1 ratio, with stick ($6.73). Heavy-duty battery ($5.87). Painted rear bumper on pickups with painted front bumper ($16.75). Heavy-duty 11 in. clutch with six-cylinder only ($4.20). Custom Appearance option: Panel ($33.45); Others ($40.13). Custom Chrome option: Pickup with chrome front bumper ($16.75); Pickup with two chrome bumpers ($41.80); Panel with two chrome bumpers ($25.10). Custom Comfort option, Panel ($9.21); Others ($42.66). Fleetside Custom side moldings ($25.10). Delcotron alternators: 42-amp. ($16.75); 52-amp. ($23.43). Tinted glass ($11.74). Tinted windshield ($10.07). Deluxe heater ($53.11). Thrift-Air heater ($41.80). Outside rearview mirrors: 17-1/4 in. left, except Panel ($1.72); right, except Panel ($3.77); 6-1/4 in. right ($3.77). Tu-tone paint: Panel ($20.90); Other trucks ($12.55). Heavy-duty radiator, except with Powerglide ($16.75). Radio ($37.22). Foam seat ($16.75). Heavy-duty rear shocks ($6.73). Heavy-duty front springs, C25 ($2.53). Heavy-duty rear springs, all ($5.06). Heavy-duty three-speed transmission: C14 ($58.55); C15 ($62.70) and C25 ($71.10). Heavy-duty four-speed transmission: C14 ($62.70); C15 ($66.90) and C25 ($75.25). Powerglide, all ($146.30). Full-View rear window, except Panel ($33.45). Two-speed windshield washers and wipers ($12.55).

OPTIONS [El Camino]: Oil bath air cleaner. Positraction. No-Spin rear axle. Heavy-duty battery. Delcotron alternators: 42-amp. Tinted glass. Tinted windshield. Deluxe heater. Outside rearview mirror. Tu-tone paint. Heavy-duty cooling. Radio. Foam seat. Heavy-duty front shocks. Heavy-duty rear shocks. Heavy-duty three-speed transmission. Four-speed transmission. Turbo-Hydramatic transmission (with V-8). Powerglide transmission (with six). Engine, 230 High-Torque six. Engine, 283 cid V-8 ($108). Engine, 327 cid/250-275 hp. Power steering ($86). Engine, 396 cid/325 hp. Engine, 396 cid/360 hp. Engine, 396 cid/375 hp. Full wheel discs. Custom interior. Bucket seats (Custom).

HISTORICAL: Model year [All El Camino]: 35,119. Model year production: [All Chevy Commercials] 621,354. Commercial model year production by GVW class: [G Vans] 37,403; [C10-C14] 115 in. wheelbase] 140,783; [K10-K14] 2,959; [K10-K15] 2,463; [P10] 3,309; [C20] 73,825; [K20] 3,151; [P20] 4,793; [C30] 23,223; [P30/157 in. wheelbase] 7,032. Light-Duty model year output by marketing category: [Domestic] 461,774; [U.S. built for export] 11,120; [U.S. built for Canada] 31,885; [Total] 504,779. Innovations: Safety equipment made standard in light-duty trucks. Expanded heavy-duty line made available. Chevrolet clinched its 10 millionth truck sale, of all time, this season.

1967 CHEVROLET

1967 Chevrolet 1/2-Ton El Camino Sedan-Pickup (DFW)

EL CAMINO — MODEL A/SERIES 13000 — SIX/V-8: The last of the second-generation El Caminos had a new radiator grille, front bumpers, fenders and hood, plus restyled wraparound taillights. The front fenders had more of a vertical downward curve. The grille again had horizontal and vertical elements, but the horizontal moldings were brighter and wider and stood out more. The widest molding, just below the hood lip, had a satin finished look and a Chevrolet emblem in its center. Dual headlamps were used. There was one wide horizontal slot, and the parking lamps were in other openings at either end. At the rear, the three-slot-styled tailights wrapped around the body corners. An El Camino script decorated the rear fenders. The front fender, just behind the headlamps, had an engine call-out: a shield with 250 on top for sixes; a V with flags for 283 V-8s; a V-with flags and 327 numbers for the bigger V-8; and an open center V with flags and a Turbo-Jet 396 plaque for the high-performance big-block. The Custom models had a thin chrome molding along the lower body feature line; a rear beauty panel between two moldings running across the tailgate; and hubcaps with Chevrolet bow ties. This was the first year for an official SS-396, although it was an option rather than a series. The SS-396 featured a blacked-out grille with SS emblem at its center. Chevelle 300 style all-vinyl upholstery, with all-vinyl embossed side panels, door armrests and vinyl-coated color-keyed floor mats was standard. The Custom interior added horizontal pleats embossed into the vinyl seat coverings, and door panels with horizontal ribs. Bucket seats were available in Customs, including those with the SS-396 option. Exterior body colors were Tuxedo black; Ermine white; Nantucket blue; Deepwater blue; Marina blue; Granada gold; Mountain green; Emerald turquoise; Tahoe turquoise; Royal plum; Madiera maroon; Bolero red; Sierra fawn; Capri cream; and Butternut yellow. The 1964 type pickup box was also in its last appearance. It was 59-3/4 in. wide behind the tailgate. There was 46 in. between the wheelhousings. The bed of the box was 78-1/2 in. long. The tailgate measured 55-1/2 in. x 23 in. With the bed-level tailgate lowered, the overall bed length was 101.6 in.

1/2-TON CHEVY VAN — MODEL G/SERIES 10 — FOUR: Chevy Vans had a more rounded configuration with a larger windshield. An additional 12 models with V-8 engines were offered in the Chevy Van and Sportvan series. Replacing the 194 cid six as base engine in G10s was the 230 cid six. The 250 cid six and 307 V-8 were optional. The compact-90 in. wheelbase G10 Chevy Van was basically unchanged, but there was a new G10 model line added. This new sub-series featured the same four models on a longer 108 in. wheelbase. Their bodies were 18 in. longer than the 90 in. wheelbase models. Styling characteristics again included five-segment vents on the front with a bow tie underneath and an

oval, horizontal-bar grille near the bottom of the front single headlights. Both lines offered Panel, Sportvan, Sportvan Custom and Sportvan Deluxe models.

1967 Chevrolet 1/2-Ton C10 Suburban (OCW)

3/4-TON CHEVY VAN — MODEL G/SERIES 10 — FOUR: The new 108 in. wheelbase driver-forward vans also came in a 3/4-ton C20 series. Styling characteristics were the same as long wheelbase C10s. The front had a bow tie underneath and an oval and a horizontal-bar grille near the bottom of the front single headlights. Panel, Sportvan, Sportvan Custom and Sportvan Deluxe models were included. Engines were the same used for G10s.

1/2-TON COMMERCIAL — MODEL C (4x2); K (4x4)/SERIES 10 — SIX/V-8: The 1967 conventional trucks were described by Chevrolet as possessing "the most significant cab and sheet metal styling change in Chevrolet history." The new styling reflected the importance of an attractive appearance in the light-duty truck field, as more and more were purchased for personal transportation and camper use. The major styling themes on the Pickup combined an inner slant above the beltline with a side body feature line nearly dividing the wheelwells into equal sections. A new lower cab with increased glass area featured a new rigid roof designed for extra strength. The front end was very attractive with single headlights recessed into square receptacles at either end of a grille with a single wide center bar. The front sheet metal also featured greatly improved protection against corrosion. The use of smooth surfaced, undercoated, full fender skirts protected the fenders and other sheet metal from mud, water and salt. In addition, minimal use of coach joints and liberal use of spot weld sealers provided additional corrosion resistance. Standard equipment included safety belts; two padded sun visors; two-speed electric wipers; rubber floor mat; dome light; new padded dash; left-hand outside mirror (right-hand mirror on Chassis and Stake models); backup lights (except Chassis models); turn signals; and hazard flashers. There was a new Fleetside box with double-wall side panels; flat-top wheelwells; and a one-hand, quick-release tailgate. Designation plates were mounted high on the sides of the cowl. Exterior body colors included black; Light green; Dark green; Medium blue poly; Light blue; Dark blue; Dark aqua poly; red; vermilion poly; Omaha orange; yellow; white; silver poly; and ivory. The standard two-tone paint scheme was white above the beltline with the second color below. Another version used white only on the roof panel, with the windshield pillars and window frames and lower body done in the second color. The standard interior featured color-keyed vinyl upholstery, foam cushions and steel spring seats. White bumpers and a white grille background were standard. A chrome front bumper was part of the Custom Chrome option. Custom equipment included a full-depth foam-padded seat; color-keyed woven fabric and vinyl trim; two door armrests; cigar lighter; cowl insulation; undercoating; and embossed vinyl door panels. There was also a new Custom Sport Truck (CST) option that included CST exterior plaques on the window sills; bucket seats; a center console/seat; chrome front bumper; bright pedal trim; chrome dash knobs; chrome horn button; silver anodized grille background; and headlamp and windshield bright trim. This year's Panel and Suburbans were switched to a 127 in. wheelbase and had a new, longer body with one entry door on the driver side and two on the passenger side. The Suburban again offered the option of a tailgate or rear panel doors. Offered again were Step-Side (with pontoon rear fenders) and Fleetside (with slab type rear fenders) Pickups with 6-1/2 ft. boxes, plus Chassis & Cowl, Chassis Cowl & Windshield, and Chassis & Cab models. The 10 Series Short Bed four-wheel drive 1/2-ton models had a K14 model prefix. There was no longer a separate C10-C15 and K10-K15 series for long wheelbase models. Instead, the 127 in. wheelbase 1/2-tons were simply coded differently under a new system that indicated cab-to-axle dimensions. An 07 code in the VIN indicated 115 in. wheelbase; an 09 indicated 127 in. wheelbase.

1/2-TON FORWARD-CONTROL — MODEL P/SERIES 10 — SIX/V-8: The 1/2-ton Forward-Control returned again. It had a 102 in. wheelbase. A small Step-Van walk-in delivery truck with a 7 ft. long body was approved for this chassis. It was made by Union City Body Co., of Union City, Ind. A channel type front bumper was standard equipment.

1967 Chevrolet 1/2-Ton C10 Fleetside Pickup (OCW)

3/4-TON COMMERCIAL — MODEL C; K/SERIES 20 — SIX/V-8: Carryover trucks in the Chevrolet 20 Series 3/4-ton line had the same styling and trim changes as other Conventional trucks. The big news for 1967 was the introduction of Suburbans and Panels in this line. These had the same dimensions as comparable 1/2-ton models, but heavier chassis components. The designation plates had a bow tie emblem and chrome number 20. Step-

Side and Fleetside Pickups were in this series. They featured the 8 ft. pickup box. There was also an 8 ft. Stake model. The four-wheel drive 3/4-ton models in the 20 Series had a K25 model prefix.

3/4-TON FORWARD-CONTROL — MODEL P/SERIES 20 — SIX/V-8: Three 3/4-ton Forward-Control chassis remained in the 20 Series (3/4-ton) truck line. The P23/P25/P26 models had wheelbases of 104 in./125 in./137 in., respectively. The 104 in. wheelbase was recommended for bodies 7 ft. to 8-1/2 ft. long; the 125 in. wheelbase was recommended for bodies 9-1/2 to 10-1/2 ft. long. The 137 in. wheelbase was recommended for bodies 11-1/2 ft. to 12-1/2 ft. long. Bodies were available from factory-authorized suppliers or buyers could order them locally. New this year was an optional three-cylinder diesel engine.

1-TON MEDIUM-DUTY COMMERCIAL — MODEL C/SERIES 30 — SIX-CYLINDER: The Chevrolet 30 Series 1-ton trucks had the same styling and trim changes as other conventional trucks. The fenderside nameplates had a Chevrolet bow tie and number 30. There was no Fleetside Pickup in this line and the Panel was dropped this year. There were chassis models, plus a 9 ft. Pickup and 9 ft. Stake. No hubcaps were used on the larger split-rim wheels of the Chassis & Cab and Stake models, which had eight bolts and eight circular openings. The Camper Special package continued. Camper models had their own designation plates with a Chevrolet bow tie and "Camper Special" chrome script. The C38 model 1-ton Chassis & Cab with a long 157 in. wheelbase for use as an RV chassis was also offered again. A four-speed manual synchromesh transmission was standard. No four-wheel drive option was offered.

1-TON FORWARD-CONTROL — MODEL P/SERIES 30 — SIX/V-8: Three Forward-Control chassis were in the 30 Series (1-ton) truck line. The P33/P35/P36 models had wheelbases of 104 in./125 in./137 in., respectively. The 104 in. wheelbase was recommended for bodies 7 ft. to 8-1/2 ft. long; 125 in. wheelbase was recommended for bodies 9-1/2 ft. to 10-1/2 ft. long. The 137 in. wheelbase was recommended for bodies 11-1/2 ft. to 12-1/2 ft. long. Bodies were available from factory-authorized suppliers or buyers could order them locally. A channel type front bumper and High-Torque 230 six were standard equipment. New this year was an optional three-cylinder diesel engine.

1967 Chevrolet 1/2-Ton C10 Fleetside Pickup (OCW)

I.D. DATA: Serial Number located: [Chassis models] On plate temporarily attached near steering column, with final location per body maker; [Others] On plate attached to rear face of left-hand door hinge pillar; on right side of cowl under hood. [El Camino]: The first symbol indicated manufacturer: 1=Chevrolet. The second and third symbols indicated series: 33=six/34=V-8/35=Custom six/36=Custom V-8. The fourth and fifth symbols indicated body type: 80=Sedan-Pickup. The sixth symbol indicate model year: 7=1967. The seventh symbol indicated assembly plant: A=Atlanta/Lakewood; B=Baltimore, Md.; G=Framingham, Mass.; K=Kansas City, Mo. (Leeds); Z=Fremont, Calif.; The remaining symbols were the sequential production number starting with 100001 at each plant. Ending serial numbers not available. The Chevrolet engine had the source, date and type stamped on a serial number pad. Various source codes were used. Month codes were 1=Jan.; 2=Feb., etc. Date codes were 01=first of month, etc. There were numerous prefix codes to indicate engines and transmission attachments. [Other models] The first symbol indicated indicated truck type: C=Conventional Cab; K=4x4; G=Chevy Van; P=Forward-Control Package Delivery. The second symbol indicated type of engine: S=six; E=eight; T=diesel. The third symbol indicated the GVW range: [GVW] 1=3,600 to 5,600 lbs.; 2=5,500 to 8,100 lbs.; 3=6,700 to 10,000 lbs.; 4=Over 10,000 lbs. The fourth and fifth symbols indicated the cab-to-axle dimension: 07=42-47 in.; 09=54-59 in.; 10=60-65 in.; 14=84-89 in. The sixth symbol indicated body type: 02=Chassis & Cowl; 03=Chassis & Cab; 04=Step-Side Pickup; 05=Panel or Panel Van; 06=Suburban (doors) or Sportvan; 09=Platform/Stake; 12=Chassis & Cowl; 13=Cab with air brakes; 16=Suburban (gate); 26=Custom Sportvan; 34=Fleetside; 36=Deluxe Sportvan; 35=Forward-Control. The eighth symbol indicates model year: 7=1967. The ninth symbol indicates assembly plant: A=Atlanta, Ga.; B=Baltimore, Md.; F=Flint, Mich.; J=Janesville, Wis.; K=Kansas City, Mo.; S=St. Louis, Mo.; T=Tarrytown, N.Y.; Z=Fremont, Calif. 1=Oshawa, Canada.

Model	Body Type	Price	Weight	Prod. Total
El Camino — Model A/Series 13000 — 115 in. w.b.				
13480	Pickup	2613	3193	Note 1
13680	Custom Pickup	2694	3210	Note 1

NOTE 1: Total El Camino production was 34,830.

1/2-Ton Chevy Van — Model G/Series 100 — 90 in. w.b.				
GS11005	Panel	2331	2849	17,956
GS11006	Sportvan	2571	3035	2398
GS11026	Custom Sportvan	2699	3138	777
GS11036	Deluxe Sportvan	2890	3174	535
1/2-Ton Chevy Van — Model G/Series 100 — 108 in. w.b.				
GS11005	Panel	—	—	13,644
GS11006	Sportvan	—	—	2,568
GS11026	Custom Sportvan	—	—	1,603
GS11036	Deluxe Sportvan	—	—	1,665
3/4-Ton Chevy Van — Model G/Series 200 — 108 in. w.b.				
GS21305	Panel	2618	3109	6013
GS21306	Sportvan	2848	3241	930
GS21326	Custom Sportvan	2975	3365	501
GS21336	Deluxe Sportvan	3166	3409	508

1/2-Ton Commercial — Model C/Series 10 — 115 in. w.b.				
CS10703	Chassis & Cab	2223	2914	2790
CS10734	Fleetside 6.5 ft.	2371	3333	43,940
CS10704	Step-Side 6.5 ft.	2333	3255	45,606
1/2-Ton Commercial — Model C/Series 10 — 127 in. w.b.				
CS10903	Chassis & Cab	—	—	39
CS10934	Fleetside 8 ft.	2408	3440	165,973
CS10904	Step-Side 8 ft.	2371	3345	19,969
CS10905	Panel	2742	3502	3827
CS10906	Suburban	2986	3670	5164
1/2-Ton Commercial 4x4 — Model K/Series 10 — 115 in. w.b.				
KS10703	Chassis & Cab	2903	—	32
KS10734	Fleetside 6.5 ft.	3051	—	1046
KS10704	Step-Side 6.5 ft.	3013	—	1,229
1/2-Ton Commercial 4x4 — Model K/Series 10 — 127 in. w.b.				
KS10903	Chassis & Cab	—	—	41
KS10934	Fleetside 8 ft.	3088	—	2,715
KS10904	Step-Side 8 ft.	3051	—	500
KS10905	Panel	3422	—	30
KS10906	Suburban	3666	3670	166
1/2-Ton Forward-Control — Model P/Series 10 — 102 in. w.b.				
PS10535	Step-Van	2864	3559	2374
3/4-Ton Commercial — Model C/Series 20 — 127 in. w.b.				
CS20903	Chassis & Cab	2403	3346	6320
CS20934	Fleetside 8 ft.	2550	3848	50,413
CS20904	Step-Side 8 ft.	2513	3753	785
CS20909	Stake	2606	3973	1415
CS20905	Panel	2884	3917	940
CS20906	Suburban	3170	4093	709
3/4-Ton Commercial 4x4 — Model K/Series 20 — 127 in. w.b.				
KS20903	Chassis & Cab	3083	—	498
KS20934	Fleetside 8 ft.	3230	—	2,773
KS20904	Step-Side 8 ft.	3193	—	8
KS20905	Panel	3286	—	8
KS20906	Suburban	3850	—	120
Long-Horn Pickup				
KS21034	Fleetside 8.5 ft.	—	—	—
3/4-Ton Forward-Control — Model P/Series 20 — 104/125/137 in. w.b.				
PS20835	Step-Van (125 in.)	3626	4970	203
1-Ton Commercial — Model C/Series 30 — 133 in. w.b.				
CS31003	Chassis & Cab	2561	3556	11,304
CS31034	Fleetside 8.5 ft.	2755	—	—
CS31004	Step-Side 9 ft.	2695	3995	4026
CS31009	Stake 9 ft.	2875	4390	3236
1-Ton Forward-Control — Model P/Series 30 — 104/125/127 in. w.b.				
PT30835	Step-Van (diesel)	5648	5931	10

NOTE 2: Production totals from Chevrolet records are for model-year through July 31, 1967 and include all trucks built in U.S. factories for domestic/export/Canadian markets. Additional production: [C10]: Chassis, Cowl & Windshield=15; Chassis & Cab=6; Chassis & Cab/127 in. wheelbase=1,066; Chassis only=140. [K20]: Chassis & Cab=498; Panel=8; Suburban=120. [P20] Chassis-only=151; Step-Van/104 in. wheelbase=143; Step-Van/125 in. wheelbase=1,313; Chassis-only/125 in. wheelbase=400; Step-Van/137 in. wheelbase=652; Chassis-only/137 in. wheelbase=240; Panel/137 in. wheelbase=76. [C30]: Chassis & Cowl= 366; Chassis, Cowl & Windshield=8; Chassis & Cab/157 in. wheelbase=4,488. [P30] Step-Van: Total gas=6, 777; Total diesel=117.

ENGINE [Standard El Camino G10/P10/G20]: Inline. OHV. Six-cylinder. Cast iron block. Bore & stroke: 3.87 in. x 3-1/4 in. Displacement: 230 cid. Compression ratio: 8.5:1. Brake horsepower: 140 at 4400 rpm. Torque 220 lbs.-ft. at 1600 rpm. Net horsepower: 120 at 3600 rpm. Seven main bearings. Hydraulic valve lifters. Carburetor: Rochester one-barrel model 7028006/7028010.

ENGINE [Standard C10/C20/C30/K10/K20/P30; Optional G10/P10/El Camino]: Inline. OHV. Six-cylinder. Cast iron block. Bore & stroke: 3.87 in. x 3.53 in. Displacement: 250 cid. Compression ratio: 8.5:1. Brake horsepower: 155 at 4200 rpm. Torque: 235 lbs.-ft. at 1600 rpm. Seven main bearings. Hydraulic valve lifters. Carburetor: Rochester one-barrel model 7028007/7028011.

ENGINE [Optional C10/C20/C30/P10/P20/P30]: Inline. OHV. Six-cylinder. Cast iron block. Bore & stroke: 3-7/8 in. x 4-1/2 in. Displacement: 292 cid. Compression ratio: 8.1:1. Brake horsepower: 170 at 4000 rpm. Torque: 275 lbs.-ft. at 1600 rpm. Seven main bearings. Hydraulic valve lifters. Carburetor: Rochester one-barrel model 7028012/7028013.

ENGINE [Optional: K Series/C10/C20/C30]: V-block. OHV. Eight-cylinder. Cast iron block. Bore & stroke: 3-7/8 in. x 3 in. Displacement: 283 cid. Brake horsepower: 175 at 4400 rpm. Torque 275 lbs.-ft. at 2400 rpm. Five main bearings. Hydraulic valve lifters.

ENGINE [Optional El Camino]: V-type. OHV. Eight-cylinder. Cast iron block. Bore & stroke: 3-7/8 in. x 3 in. Displacement: 283 cid. Compression ratio: 9.25:1. Brake horsepower: 195 at 4800 rpm. Maximum Torque: 285 lbs.-ft. at 2400 rpm. Five main bearings. Hydraulic valve lifters. Carburetor: Rochester two-barrel model 7024101.

ENGINE [Optional: C10/C20/C30/K10/K20]: V-block. OHV. Eight-cylinder. Cast iron block. Bore & stroke: 4 in. x 3.25 in. Displacement: 327 cid. Compression ratio: 9.25:1. Brake horsepower: 220. Five main bearings. Hydraulic valve lifters. Carburetor: Rochester four-barrel model 4G.

ENGINE [El Camino/standard SS-396]: V-block. OHV. Eight-cylinder. Cast iron block. Bore & stroke: 4.09 in. x 3.76 in. Displacement: 396 cid. Compression ratio: 10.25:1. Brake horsepower: 325 at 4800 rpm. Torque: 410 lbs.-ft. at 3200 rpm. Five main bearings. Hydraulic valve lifters. Carburetor: Rochester four-barrel model Quadra-Jet.

ENGINE [Optional: El Camino SS-396]: V-block. OHV. Eight-cylinder. Cast iron block. Bore & stroke: 4.09 in. x 3.76 in. Displacement: 396 cid. Compression ratio: 10.25:1. Brake horsepower: 350 at 5200 rpm. Torque: 415 lbs.-ft. at 3400 rpm. Five main bearings. Hydraulic valve lifters. Carburetor: Rochester four-barrel model Quadra-Jet.

ENGINE [Optional El Camino]: V-type. OHV. Eight-cylinder. Cast iron block. Bore & stroke: 4.094 in. x 3.76 in. Displacement: 396 cid. Compression ratio: 11.25:1. Brake horsepower: 375. Five main bearings. Carburetor: four-barrel.

1967 Chevrolet El Camino 1/2-Ton Sedan Pickup (OCW)

CHASSIS [El Camino]: Wheelbase: 115 in. Overall length: 197 in. Front tread: 58 in. Rear tread: 58 in. Tires: 7.35 x 14 in. GVW: 4,300 lbs.
CHASSIS [G10]: Wheelbase: 90 in. Tires: 6.95 x 14 in. GVW: 3,900-5,000 lbs.
CHASSIS [C10/K10]: Wheelbase: 115 in. Overall length: 186-3/4 in. Height: 71 in. Front tread: 63.1 in. Rear tread: 61.1 in. Tires: Tires: [4x2] 7.75 x 15 in.; [Suburban] 8.15 x 15 in.; [4x4] 17.5 x 17 four-ply. GVW: [4x2] 4,400-5,000 lbs.; [4x4] 5,600 lbs.
CHASSIS [C10/K10]: Wheelbase: 127 in. Overall length: 206-1/4 in. Height: 71 in. Front tread: 63.1 in. Rear tread: 61.1 in. Tires: [4x2] 7.75 x 15 in. four-ply; [4x4] 17.5 x 17. GVW: [4x2] 4,400-5,000 lbs.; [4x4] 5,600 lbs.
CHASSIS [P10]: Wheelbase: 102 in. Tires: 7.75 x 15 in. GVW: 4,600-5,400 lbs.
CHASSIS [C20/K20]: Wheelbase: 127 in. Overall length: 206-1/4 in. Tires: [4x2] 7 x 17.5 in.; [4x4] 7 x 17.5 six-ply. GVW: [4x2] 5,500-7,500 lbs.; [4x4] 5,700-7,600 lbs.
CHASSIS [P20]: Wheelbases: [P2300] 104 in.; [P2500] 125 in.; [P2600] 137 in. Base tires: 7 x 17.5. GVW: 7,000 lbs.
CHASSIS [C30]: Wheelbase: 133 in. Tires: 8 x 17.5 in. GVW: 6,700-14,000 lbs.
CHASSIS [P30]: Wheelbases: [P3300] 104 in.; [P3500] 125 in.; [P3600] 137 in. Base tires: 8 x 19.5. GVW: 7,500-14,000 lbs.
TECHNICAL: Chevrolet three-speed manual transmission (Borg-Warner heavy-duty three-speed optional). [C30] 4F/1R; [Others] 3F/1R. Column-mounted gearshift lever. Single-plate, dry-disc clutch. Rear axle: [1/2-ton] semi-floating; [3/4-ton/1-Ton] full-floating. Base rear axles: [El Camino] 3.08:1; [Corvair 95] 3.55:1; [C-K10] 3.73:1; [C-K20] 4.11:1; [C30] 5.14:1. Four-wheel hydraulic, drum brakes. Brake linings: [Corvair 95] 11 x 2 in.; [C;K10] 11 x 2.75 in.; [C-K20/C30] 12 x 2 in.; [El Camino] 9-1/2 x 2-1/2. Kelsey-Hayes pressed steel wheels.
OPTIONS: [El Camino] Tinted glass. Tinted windshield. Power windows. Custom Deluxe front seat belts. Strato bucket seats. Strato Ease headrest. Regular headrest. Safety harness. Front and rear floor mats. Deluxe foam front seat cushion. Door edge guards. Black or beige vinyl roof. Delete heater/defroster. Air-conditioning. Remote-control outside rearview mirror. Console. Heavy-duty suspension. Positraction. Rear axle ratios: 3.70; 3.36; 3.08; 3.31; 3.55; 2.73; 3.07; 3.73. Vacuum power brakes. Front disc brakes. Brake linings. Radiator fan. Air injector reactor. Cruise Control. 61-amp. Delcotron alternator. 42-amp. Delcotron alternator. Heavy-duty clutch. Overdrive transmission. Four-speed transmission. Close-ratio four-speed transmission. Powerglide transmission (with six). Three-speed Turbo-Hydramatic transmission (with V-8s). Dual exhausts. Deluxe steering wheel. Comfortilt steering wheel. Woodgrain steering wheel. Power steering. Mag style wheelcovers. Wheel trim covers. Simulated wire wheels. Heavy-duty battery. Tri-volume horn. Instrument panel gauges. Speed warning indicator. Tachometer. Underhood lamp. Glove box lamp. Ashtray lamp. Instrument panel courtesy lamps. Electric clock. Push-button AM radio and antenna. Push-button AM/FM radio and antenna. Heavy-duty radiator. Front bumper guards. SS-396 equipment.
OPTIONS: [Trucks] Oil bath air cleaner. Heavy-duty air cleaner. Air-conditioning. Positraction. Rear axle ratios. Heavy-duty battery. Vacuum power brakes. Chrome front bumper. Chrome hubcaps. Side-mounted spare wheel carrier. Heavy-duty cooling. Heavy-Duty cooling. Custom side molding package. Pickup box floor. Fuel filter. Gauges. Generator. Soft-Ray tinted glass. Air injector reactor. Engine governor. Safety harness. Heater and defroster. Towing hooks. Rear side marker lamps. Right-hand door lock. Exterior rearview mirror. Camper Special package with custom "Camper Special" nameplates. Fuel and vacuum pump booster. Heavy-duty radiator. AM radio and antenna. Auxiliary seat in Panel. Heavy-duty shock absorbers. Speed warning indicator. Auxiliary rear springs. Heavy-duty front springs. Heavy-duty rear springs. Front stabilizer bar. Heavy-duty starter. Power steering. Tachometer. Throttle control. Positive crankcase ventilation system. Full wheelcovers. Full-View rear window. Custom interior equipment. Custom chrome equipment. Custom Sport Truck equipment.

1967 Chevrolet 1/2-Ton K10 4x4 Step-Side Pickup (RCA)

OPTIONS AND INSTALLATION RATES: Heavy-duty seat (6 percent). Rear seat (44 percent). Panoramic Cab (12 percent). Tinted glass (13 percent). Bucket seats. Level-Ride seat. One-passenger auxiliary seat (61 percent). Rear center seat belt (6 percent). Center

and rear seat (59 percent). Deluxe shoulder harness (1 percent). Spare wheel lock (1 percent). Side trim moldings (34 percent). Single-speed wipers. Deluxe heater (88 percent). Air-conditioning (3 percent). Junior West Coast mirror (32 percent). Senior West Coast mirror (12 percent). Long or short Outside rearview mirror (4 percent). Front crossview mirror. Platform and stake rack (3 percent). Platform equipment (1 percent). Pickup box mounting (7 percent). Floorboard (44 percent). Special heavy-duty frame (23 percent). 9,000 lbs. front axle (16 percent). 3,500-4,000 lbs. front axle (26 percent). 5,000-7,000 lbs. front axle (14 percent). Heavy-duty front axle (16 percent). Front wheel locking hub (75 percent). Heavy rear springs (70 percent). Auxiliary springs (33 percent). Positraction (11 percent). No-Spin rear axle (8 percent). 3.07:1 rear axle (1 percent). 4.11:1 rear axle (3 percent). Vacuum gauge (74 percent). Heavy-duty air cleaner. Oil bath air cleaner (17 percent). Transistor ignition. 327 cid V-8 (21 percent). Overdrive (1 percent). Four-speed transmission (21 percent). Heavy-duty four-speed transmission (2 percent). Powerglide transmission (10 percent). Three-speed automatic transmission (3 percent). Wheel trim cover (7 percent). Chrome hubcaps (9 percent). Roof marker lamps (9 percent). Whitewall tires (8 percent). Speed warning indicator (2 percent). Speed warning indicator (2 percent). Tachometer (2 percent). Push-button radio (23 percent). Chrome bumper (17 percent). Rear painted bumpers (26 percent). Rear step bumper (9 percent). Custom Appearance equipment (17 percent). Custom Comfort and Convenience equipment (21 percent). Camper Special equipment (2 percent). Custom Sport Truck (CST) option package (3 percent). Tu-tone paint (25 percent).
NOTE: The percentage figures after each option are from Chevrolet records. They indicate what percentage of 1/2-ton to 2-ton trucks which qualified for the particular option were factory-equipped with the option. For example, the figure of 75 percent for front wheel locking hubs would apply to 4 x 4 models only.
HISTORICAL: Introduced Sept. 11, 1966. Commercials, model year production by series: [1/2-ton]: (G10) 42,133; (C10) 288,356; (K10) 6,055 and (P10) 2,514. [3/4-ton]: (G20) 8,032; (C20) 67,681; (K20) 4,271; (P20/gas) 3,178 and (P20/diesel) 10. [1-ton]: (C30) 23,428; (P30) 6,777 and (P30/diesel) 117. Commercials, model year production by engine type: [1/2-ton] (six) 207,720; (V-8) 131,338. [3/4Ton]: (six) 41,583; (V-8) 41,589. 1-ton: [six] 20,805; [V-8] 9,517. [Grand Total]: 452,552. (Note: Totals do not include El Camino.) Innovations: First year power steering was available for 4x4 models. New three-door Suburban styling. All trucks adopt 15 safety-related product improvements including dual cylinder brake systems; hazard lights; brake system warning lamp; energy-absorbing steering column; padded instrument panel; padded sun visors; folding front seatback latch; and thicker laminated windshield glass. Extensively restyled El Camino. First year for Chevy Vans with two wheelbase lengths. First year for V-8 power in vans. R.M. O'Connor was assistant general sales manager, truck & fleet sales, for Chevrolet Motor Div.

1968 CHEVROLET

1968 Chevrolet El Camino SS-396 Sedan-Pickup (OCW)

EL CAMINO — MODEL A/SERIES 13000 — SIX/V-8: For 1968, the El Camino was totally restyled. The cab had a more streamlined, "flying buttress" rear roofline. A new 116 in. wheelbase, the same used for Chevelle four-door sedans and station wagons, was featured. Overall length grew from 197 in. (1964-1967) to 207 in. (1968-1972). The new pickup box, which would also be used through 1972, had revised dimensions. Outside width increased to 75-1/2 in. Inside width behind the cab was down slightly to 59 in. Inside width near the tailgate remained at 64-1/2 in. The width between the wheelhousings fell to 44 in. The bottom bed length increased slightly to 79-1/4 in. However, tailgate measurements changed to 54-1/2 x 22-1/2 in., so lowering the tailgate added slightly less extra load length. The front end was patterned along the lines of the 1968 Chevelle passenger cars. Features included a front bumper that was slotted behind the license plate only. The parking lights were relocated to the ends of the bumper. Two headlamps on each side were set into squarish, bright metal housings. A fine, screen-like mesh grille ran the full width of the front. It had a horizontal Chevrolet badge in its center. All El Caminos had front side markers with the engine's cubic inch displacement on the front marker bezel. The base model had a chrome front bumper; Chevrolet grille badge; chrome-framed side marker lamps; an El Camino rear fender script; a bright tailgate latch; and a chrome Chevrolet script on the right-hand side of the tailgate. Added on El Camino Customs were bright window frames; pickup box upper edge moldings; rear body corner moldings; and wide rocker panel accent moldings. The SS-396 was a distinct model-option this year. On SS-396 versions, the grille was blacked-out and had an SS center badge. This option also included a special power dome hood; fat Wide-Oval tires on 6 in. JK rims; blacked-out lower body perimeter finish; chrome moldings on lower body feature line; special styled wheels; and SS tailgate moldings. The 396 cid/325 hp engine was standard. A 350 hp version of the big-block with a high-lift camshaft and dual exhausts was optional at extra cost. Rear sidemarkers were optional, at least late in the model year. Hide-Away headlamps were optional and body accent striping was available, at extra cost, for SS-396s only. Exterior body colors were Tuxedo black; Ermine white; Grotto blue; Fathom blue; Island teal; Ash gold; Grecian green; Tripoli turquoise; Teal blue; Cordovan maroon; Seafrost green; Matador red; Palomino ivory; Sequoia green; and Butternut yellow.
1/2-TON CHEVY VAN — MODEL G/SERIES 10 — FOUR: Chevy Vans were basically unchanged. The 90 in. and 108 in. Chevy Vans and Sportvans were offered in the G10 model line. The 18 in. longer body used with the longer wheelbase matched the dimensions of the G20s. The grille had six horizontal bars divided into four segments by three vertical bars. The center bar was widest. The remaining vertical bars were narrower. Sin-

81

gle, large round headlamps were at either end of the grille. Rectangular parking/directional lights were next to the headlamps. Under the windshield, five segmented vents continued to appear. Below the center vent segment was a Chevrolet bow tie emblem. There were large, rectangular sidemarker lamps. Standard models came with bumper, grille and hubcaps done in white. Chrome trim was optional. Both lines offered a Commercial Panel with double cargo doors available on the passenger side and at the rear. Both also offered window models in three levels of trim. The Sportvan was the base model. Sportvan Customs were in the middle. Sportvan Deluxe models were the fanciest. A 230 cid six was the base engine.

3/4-TON CHEVY VAN — MODEL G/SERIES 20 — SIX/V-8: The 108 in. wheelbase driver-forward vans also came as 3/4-ton G20 models. Styling characteristics were the same as long wheelbase G10s. Models included the Commercial Panel with double cargo doors available on the passenger side and at the rear. There were also window models in three levels of trim: base Sportvan, Sportvan Custom, and Sportvan Deluxe. The G20 line offered a 307 cid V-8.

1/2-TON COMMERCIAL — MODEL C; K/SERIES 10 — SIX/V-8: Safety side marker lamps were added to the front fenders of Pickups, Panels and Suburbans. A modestly revamped body had slightly more brightwork. Badges on the side of the cowl carried C10 designations for 1/2-ton models. The C10 (and K10 four-wheel drive) Chassis models and Pickups came on 115 or 127 in. wheelbases. The Chassis, Cowl & Windshield version was dropped. Panels and Suburbans came only on the longer wheelbase. The Suburban again had two-doors on the passenger side and one on the driver's side. Surburbans were available with a tailgate or Panel truck style double rear doors. Pickups on the shorter wheelbase had a 6-1/2 ft. cargo box. Those on the long wheelbase featured an 8 ft. box. Both sizes came in Step-Side or Fleetside models. Standard equipment included a painted front bumper; directional signals; Deluxe Air heater/defroster; backup lights; exterior left and right mirrors; full-width seat with vinyl interior trim; seat belts with retractors; and two-speed wipers and washers. Chrome front and rear bumpers were a separate option. The standard "pie plate" hubcaps had a wide color stripe and a Chevrolet bow tie in the center. Custom wheelcovers had a "gear sprocket" look with color-keyed finish and a bow tie in the center. The Custom Chrome option included chrome trim on the radiator grille; window frames; cab interior; steering wheel; etc. Custom equipment included Custom interior trim; right-hand sunshade; cigar lighter; bright hubcaps; bright dash knobs; dual horns; a deluxe steering wheel; and other features. There was also the Custom Comfort & Appearance option. It included bright windshield trim, rear window moldings and ventipane frames; Custom front fender nameplates; color-keyed vinyl-coated floor mats; foam seats with color-keyed vinyl trim; a cigarette lighter; bright dash knobs; cowl insulation; and full-depth armrests. On approximately four percent of production, the badges read CST10, indicating the buyer had selected the Custom Sport Truck package. This was a notch higher. The CST option had most items listed above, plus a chrome front bumper; CST plaques; full-width Western style vinyl seats; pedal trim; roof rim molding; carpeting; and extra insulation. CST equipment cost $161.40 extra. Bucket seats were $113 extra in CSTs and $139 in other cab models. Colors offered for the year were black; Light green; Dark green; Medium blue poly; Clematis (Light) blue; Dark blue; red; Metallic vermilion poly; orange; Dark yellow; Light yellow; white; silver poly; saddle poly; and ivory. Two-toning was done using Off-white as the second (upper) color. It could be applied to all sheet metal above the beltline or to only the top and rear of the cab, leaving the windshield pillar main body color. This was the 50th anniversary of Chevrolet trucks and a special Anniversary gold and Off-white two-tone paint option was available for $49.50 on Fleetside Pickups and $31.25 on Step-Sides. Interiors were available in a choice of white or black.

1/2-TON FORWARD-CONTROL — MODEL P/SERIES 10 — SIX/V-8: The 1/2-ton Forward-Control returned again. It had a 102 in. wheelbase. A small Step-Van walk-in delivery truck with a 7 ft. long body was approved for this chassis. It was made by Union City Body Co., of Union City, Ind. A channel type front bumper was standard equipment.

3/4-TON COMMERCIAL — MODEL C; K/SERIES 20 — SIX/V-8: Carryover trucks in the Chevrolet 20 Series 3/4-ton line had the same styling, trim changes and options as other conventional trucks. The big new for 1968 was the introduction of a new "Longhorn" Fleetside Pickup with a 133 in. wheelbase and 8-1/2 ft. box. The Chassis, Cowl and Windshield model was dropped. Suburbans and Panels continued in this line. These had the same dimensions as comparable 1/2-ton models, but heavier chassis components. The designation plates had a number 20. Step-Side and Fleetside Pickups were also in this series. They featured the 8 ft. pickup box. There was also an 8 ft. Stake model. The four-wheel drive 3/4-ton models in the 20 Series had a K25 model prefix.

3/4-TON FORWARD-CONTROL — MODEL P/SERIES 20 — SIX/V-8: Just two 3/4-ton Forward-Control chassis remained in the 20 Series (3/4-ton) truck line. The 104 in. wheelbase was dropped. Remaining were the 125 in. wheelbase recommended for bodies 9-1/2 ft. to 10-1/2 ft. long and the 137 in. wheelbase was recommended for bodies 11-1/2 ft. to 12-1/2 ft. long. Bodies were available from factory-authorized suppliers or buyers could order them locally. There was an optional three-cylinder diesel engine. Also new was a coil spring front suspension, as the Step-Van chassis was now starting to find its way into the growing RV market.

1-TON MEDIUM-DUTY COMMERCIAL — MODEL C/SERIES 30 — SIX-CYLINDER: The Chevrolet 30 Series 1-ton trucks had the same styling and trim changes and options as other conventional trucks. The fenderside nameplates had a number 30. The Chassis, Cowl and Windshield model was dropped. There were Chassis and Cowl and Chassis and Cab models, plus a new Fleetside Longhorn Pickup with an 8.5 ft. box, a Step-Side Pickup with a 9 ft. box and a Stake with 9 ft. rail. No hubcaps were used on the larger split-rim wheels of the Chassis & Cab and Stake models, which had eight bolts and eight circular openings. The Camper Special package continued. Camper models had their own designation plates with a Chevrolet bow tie and "Camper Special" chrome script. The C38 model 1-ton Chassis & Cab with a long 157 in. wheelbase for use as an RV chassis was also offered again. A four-speed manual synchromesh transmission was standard. No four-wheel drive option was offered.

1-TON FORWARD-CONTROL — MODEL P/SERIES 30 — SIX/V-8: Three Forward-Control chassis were in the 30 Series (1-ton) truck line, but the 104 in. wheelbase was dropped. Offered were wheelbases of 125 in., 133 in., and 157 in. respectively. The 125 in. wheelbase was recommended for bodies 9-1/2 ft. to 10-1/2 ft. long. The 137 in. wheelbase was recommended for bodies 11-1/2 ft. to 12-1/2 ft. long. The new 157 in. was used for a large Step-Van King model with a 14-1/2 ft. aluminum body. It was also suitable for RV construction. Bodies were available from factory-authorized suppliers or buyers could order them locally. A channel type front bumper and High-Torque 230 six were standard equipment. There was an optional three-cylinder diesel engine. A coil spring front suspension was featured, as the Step-Van chassis was now starting to find its way into the growing RV market.

I.D. DATA: Serial Number located: [Chassis models] On plate temporarily attached near steering column, with final location per body maker; [All others] On plate attached to rear face of left-hand door hinge pillar; on right side of cowl under hood. [El Camino]: The first symbol indicated manufacturer: 1=Chevrolet. The second and third symbols indicated series: 33=six/34=V-8/35=Custom six/36=Custom V-8/38=SS=396. The fourth and fifth symbols indicated body type: 80=Sedan-Pickup. The sixth symbol indicated model year: 8=1968. The seventh symbol indicated assembly plant: A=Atlanta (Lakewood); B=Baltimore, Md.; G=Framingham, Mass.; K=Kansas City, Mo. (Leeds); Z=Fremont, Calif.; The remaining symbols were the sequential production number starting with 100001 at each plant. Ending serial numbers not available. The Chevrolet engine had the source, date and type stamped on a serial number pad. Various source codes were used. Month codes were 1=Jan.; 2=Feb., etc. Date codes were 01=first of month, etc. The were numerous prefix codes to indicate engines and transmission attachments. The collectible 396s had the following codes: [325 hp] EK/ET/ED; [350 hp] EF/EU/EL; [375 hp] EG. [Other models] The first symbol indicated indicated truck type: C= Conventional Cab; K=4x4; G=Chevy Van; P=Forward-Control. The second symbol indicated type of engine: S=six; E=eight; T=diesel. The third symbol indicated the GVW range: [GVW] 1=3,600-5,600 lbs.; 2=5,500-8,100 lbs.; 3=6,700-10,000 lbs.; 4=Over 10,000 lbs. The fourth and fifth symbols indicated the cab-to-axle dimension: 07=42-47 in.; 09=54-59 in.; 10=60-65 in.; 14=84-89 in. The sixth symbol indicated body type: 02=Chassis & Cowl; 03=Chassis & Cab; 04=Step-Side Pickup; 05=Panel or Panel Van; 06=Suburban (doors) or Sportvan; 09=Platform/Stake; 12=Chassis & Cowl; 13=Cab with air brakes; 16=Suburban (gate); 26=Custom Sportvan; 34=Fleetside; 36=Deluxe Sportvan; 35=Forward-Control. The eighth symbol indicates model year: 8=1968. The ninth symbol indicates assembly plant: A=Atlanta, Ga.; B=Baltimore, Md.; F=Flint, Mich.; J=Janesville, Wis.; K=Kansas City, Mo.; S=St. Louis, Mo.; T=Tarrytown, N.Y.; Z=Fremont, Calif. 1=Oshawa, Canada.

Model	Body Type	Price	Weight	Prod. Total
El Camino — Model A/Series 13000 — 116 in. w.b. — Six				
13380	Pickup	2523	3169	Note 1
13580	Custom Pickup	2603	3181	Note 1
El Camino — Model A/Series 13000 — 116 in. w.b. — V-8				
13480	Pickup	2613	3193	Note 1
13680	Custom Pickup	2694	3210	Note 1
El Camino SS — Model A/Series 13000 — 116 in. w.b. — V-8				
13880	SS-396 Pickup	3138	—	5,190

NOTE 1: Total El Camino production was 41,791.

Model	Body Type	Price	Weight	Prod. Total
1/2-Ton Chevy Van — Model G/Series 100 — 90 in. w.b.				
GS11005	Panel	2458	3005	18,617
GS11006	Sportvan	2634	3191	2153
GS11026	Custom Sportvan	2758	3295	685
GS11036	Deluxe Sportvan	2945	3331	403
1/2-Ton Chevy Van — Model G/Series 100 — 108 in. w.b.				
GS11005	Panel	2522	3122	17,569
GS11006	Sportvan	2706	3241	2,961
GS11026	Custom Sportvan	2828	3359	2,158
GS11036	Deluxe Sportvan	3020	3399	1,681
3/4-Ton Chevy Van — Model G/Series 20 — 108 in. w.b.				
GS21305	Panel	2737	3262	5,504
GS21306	Sportvan	2904	3390	715
GS21326	Custom Sportvan	3028	3514	325
GS21336	Deluxe Sportvan	3215	3558	363
1/2-Ton Commercial — Model C/Series 10 — 115 in. w.b.				
CE10703	Chassis & Cab	2320	3048	2735
CE10734	Fleetside 6.5 ft.	2468	3467	46,483
CE10704	Step-Side 6.5 ft.	2430	3389	46,322
1/2-Ton Commercial — Model C/Series 10 — 127 in. w.b.				
CE10902	Chassis & Cowl	—	—	14
CE10903	Chassis & Cab	2358	3136	1,197
CE10934	Fleetside 8 ft.	2506	3572	204,286
CE10904	Step-Side 8 ft.	2468	3477	18,632
CE10905	Panel	2839	3641	4,801
CE10906	Suburban	3081	3809	11,004
1/2-Ton Commercial 4x4 — Model K/Series 10 — 115 in. w.b.				
KE10703	Chassis & Cab	2874	3435	43
KE10734	Fleetside 6.5 ft.	3022	3851	1,449
KE10704	Step-Side 6.5 ft.	2985	3771	1,706
1/2-Ton Commercial 4x4 — Model K/Series 10 — 127 in. w.b.				
KE10903	Chassis & Cab	2911	3512	41
KE10934	Fleetside 8 ft.	3060	4024	—
KE10904	Step-Side 8 ft.	3022	3916	552
KE10905	Panel	3393	4123	59
KS10906	Suburban	3667	4212	4,259
1/2-Ton Forward-Control — Model P/Series 10 — 102 in. w.b.				
PE10535	Chassis	—	—	125
PE10535	Step-Van	2864	3559	2,767
3/4-Ton Commercial — Model C/Series 20 — 127 in. w.b.				
CE20903	Chassis & Cab	2499	3458	6,636
CE20902	Chassis & Cowl	—	—	12
CE20934	Fleetside 8 ft.	2547	3960	60,646
CS20904	Step-Side 8 ft.	2610	3865	7,666
CE20909	Stake 8 ft.	2702	4085	1,103
CE20905	Panel	2981	4035	1,572
CE20906	Suburban	3264	4217	1,573
Long Horn Pickup — Model C/Series 20 — 133 in. w.b.				
CE21034	Pickup 8.5 ft.	2711	4084	1,902
3/4-Ton Commercial 4x4 — Model K/Series 20 — 127 in. w.b.				
KE20903	Chassis & Cab	3054	3590	498
KE20934	Fleetside 8 ft.	3201	4030	4,705
KE20904	Step-Side 8 ft.	3163	3940	1,047
KE20905	Panel	3534	4111	68
KE20906	Suburban	3611	4215	299
3/4-Ton Forward-Control — Model P/Series 20 — 125 in. w.b.				
PS20842	Chassis	1915	2749	404
PS20835	Steel Step-Van	3723	5070	2,314
PS20835	Alumnium Step-Van	—	—	44
PT20835	Diesel Step-Van	—	—	4
3/4-Ton Forward-Control — Model P/Series 20 — 133 in. w.b.				
PS21842	Chassis	1950	2765	188
PS21835	Step-Van	3723	5070	2314
PS21835	Steel Step-Van	—	—	735
PS21835	Aluminum Step-Van	—	—	32
PT21835	Diesel Step-Van	—	—	1

1-Ton Commercial — Model C/Series 30 — 133 in. w.b.

CE31003	Chassis & Cab	2657	3665	11,948
CE31034	Fleetside 8.5 ft.	2852	4158	213
CE31004	Step-Side 9 ft.	2791	4104	2,836
CE31009	Stake 9 ft.	2971	4499	3,272

1-Ton Forward-Control — Model P/Series 30 — 125 in. w.b.

PS30842	Chassis	3925	3764	759
PS30835	Step-Van	3902	5288	733
PS30835	Step-Van Aluminum	—	—	16
PT30835	Diesel Step-Van	—	—	2

1-Ton Forward-Control — Model P/Series 30 — 133 in. w.b.

PS31842	Chassis	3960	3784	1,043
PS31843	Chassis & Cowl	—	—	238
PS31835	Steel Step-Van	—	—	1,401
PS31835	Aluminum Step-Van	—	—	73

1-Ton Step-Van King — Model P/Series 30 — 157 in. w.b.

PE38835	Step-Van King	—	—	853

NOTE 2: Second letter in model code indicates engine: S=Six; E=V-8; T=3-cyl. diesel.

NOTE 3: Production totals from Chevrolet records are for model-year through Aug. 1, 1968 and include all trucks made in U.S. factories for domestic/export/Canadian markets. Where no production total is shown, records are not complete.

ENGINE [Standard El Camino G10/P10/G20]: Inline. OHV. Six-cylinder. Cast iron block. Bore & stroke: 3-7/8 in. x 3-1/4 in. Displacement: 230 cid. Compression ratio: 8.5:1. Brake horsepower: 140 at 4400 rpm. Torque: 220 lbs.-ft. at 1600 rpm. Net horsepower: 120 at 3600 rpm. Seven main bearings. Hydraulic valve lifters. Carburetor: Rochester one-barrel model 7028006/7028010.

ENGINE [Standard C10/C20/C30/K10/K20; Optional G10/G20/P10/El Camino]: Inline. OHV. Six-cylinder. Cast iron block. Bore & stroke: 3.875 in. x 3.53 in. Displacement: 250 cid. Compression ratio: 8.5:1. Brake horsepower: 155 at 4200 rpm. Torque: 235 lbs.-ft. at 1600 rpm. Seven main bearings. Hydraulic valve lifters. Carburetor: Rochester one-barrel model 7028007/7028011.

ENGINE [Optional C10/C20/C30; Standard P20/P30]: Inline. OHV. Six-cylinder. Cast iron block. Bore & stroke: 3.875 in. x 4-1/2 in. Displacement: 292 cid. Compression ratio: 8.1:1. Brake horsepower: 170 at 4000 rpm. Torque: 275 lbs.-ft. at 1600 rpm. Seven main bearings. Hydraulic valve lifters. Carburetor: Rochester one-barrel model 7028012/7028013.

ENGINE [Optional G10/G20/P10/P20/P30/C10/C20/C30/K10/K20/El Camino]: V-type. OHV. Eight-cylinder. Cast iron block. Bore & stroke: 3-7/8 in. x 3.25 in. Displacement: 307 cid. Compression ratio: 9.0:1. Brake horsepower: 200 at 4800 rpm. Five main bearings. Hydraulic valve lifters. Carburetor: Rochester two-barrel model 26 (numbers vary).

ENGINE [Optional: C10/C20/C30/K10/K20]: V-block. OHV. Eight-cylinder. Cast iron block. Bore & stroke: 4 in. x 3.25 in. Displacement: 327 cid. Compression ratio: 8.5:1. Brake horsepower: 220. Five main bearings. Hydraulic valve lifters. Carburetor: Rochester four-barrel model 4G.

ENGINE [Optional: El Camino]: V-block. OHV. Eight-cylinder. Cast iron block. Bore & stroke: 4 in. x 3.25 in. Displacement: 327 cid. Compression ratio: 8.75:1. Brake horsepower: 250. Five main bearings. Hydraulic valve lifters. Carburetor: Rochester four-barrel model 4G.

ENGINE [Optional: El Camino]: V-block. OHV. Eight-cylinder. Cast iron block. Bore & stroke: 4 in. x 3.25 in. Displacement: 327 cid. Compression ratio: 10.0:1. Brake horsepower: 275. Five main bearings. Hydraulic valve lifters. Carburetor: Rochester four-barrel model 4G.

ENGINE [Optional: El Camino]: V-block. OHV. Eight-cylinder. Cast iron block. Bore & stroke: 4 in. x 3.25 in. Displacement: 327 cid. Compression ratio: 11.0:1. Brake horsepower: 325. Five main bearings. Hydraulic valve lifters. Carburetor: Rochester four-barrel model 4G.

ENGINE [El Camino/standard SS-396]: V-block. OHV. Eight-cylinder. Cast iron block. Bore & stroke: 4.09 in. x 3.76 in. Displacement: 396 cid. Compression ratio: 10.25:1. Brake horsepower: 325 at 4800 rpm. Torque: 410 lbs.-ft. at 3200 rpm. Five main bearings. Hydraulic valve lifters. Carburetor: Rochester four-barrel model Quadra-Jet.

ENGINE [Optional: El Camino SS-396]: V-block. OHV. Eight-cylinder. Cast iron block. Bore & stroke: 4.09 in. x 3.76 in. Displacement: 396 cid. Compression ratio: 10.25:1. Brake horsepower: 350 at 5200 rpm. Torque: 415 lbs.-ft. at 3400 rpm. Five main bearings. Hydraulic valve lifters. Carburetor: Rochester four-barrel model Quadra-Jet.

ENGINE [Optional El Camino]: V-type. OHV. Eight-cylinder. Cast iron block. Bore & stroke: 4.094 in. x 3.76 in. Displacement: 396 cid. Compression ratio: 11.25:1. Brake horsepower: 375. Five main bearings. Carburetor: four-barrel

ENGINE [Optional P20/P30] Diesel. Model 3-53N. Three-cylinder. Bore and stroke: 3.875 x 4.5 in. Displacement: 159.2 cid. Brake horsepower: 94 at 2800 rpm. Torque: 205 lbs.-ft. at 1500 rpm.

1968 Chevrolet 1/2-Ton C10 Suburban Carryall (JAG)

CHASSIS [El Camino]: Wheelbase: 116 in. Overall length: 206 in. Front tread: 59 in. Rear tread: 59 in. Tires: 7.35 x 14 in. GVW: 4,300 lbs.

CHASSIS [G10]: Wheelbase: 90 in. Tires: 6.95 x 14 in. GVW: 3,900-5,000 lbs.

CHASSIS [C10/K10]: Wheelbase: 115 in. Overall length: 186.75 in. Height: 74.5 in. Front tread: 63.1 in. Rear tread: 61.1 in. Tires: [4x2] 8.15 x 15 in.; [Suburban] 8.15 x 15 in.; [4x4] 17.5 x 17 four-ply. GVW: [4x2] 4,400-5,000 lbs.; [4x4] 5,600 lbs.

CHASSIS [C10/K10]: Wheelbase: 127 in. Overall length: 206.25 in. Height: 71 in. Front tread: 63.1 in. Rear tread: 61.1 in. Tires: [4x2] 7.75 x 15 in. four-ply; [4x4] 17.5 x 17. GVW: [4x2] 4,400-5,000 lbs.; [4x4] 5,600 lbs.

CHASSIS [P10]: Wheelbase: 102 in. Tires: 7.75 x 15 in. GVW: 4,600-5,400 lbs.

CHASSIS [C20/K20]: Wheelbase: 127 in. Overall length: 206-1/4 in. Tires: [4x2] 7 x 17.5 in.; [4x4] 7 x 17.5 six-ply. GVW: [4x2] 5,500-7,500 lbs.; [4x4] 5,700-7,600 lbs.

CHASSIS [P20]: Wheelbases: [P2300] 104 in.; [P2500] 125 in.; [P2600] 137 in. Base tires: 7 x 17.5. GVW: 7,000 lbs.

CHASSIS [C30]: Wheelbase: 133 in. Tires: 8 x 17.5 in. GVW: 6,700-14,000 lbs.

CHASSIS [P30]: Wheelbases: [P3300] 104 in.; [P3500] 125 in.; [P3600] 137 in. Base tires: 8 x 19.5. GVW: 7,500-14,000 lbs.

TECHNICAL: Standard transmission: Chevrolet three-speed manual (Borg-Warner heavy-duty three-speed optional). Type transmission: [C30] 4F/1R; [Others] 3F/1R. Column-mounted gearshift lever. Single-plate, dry-disc clutch. Rear axle: [1/2-ton] semi-floating; [3/4-ton/1-Ton) full-floating. Base rear axles: [El Camino] 3.08:1; [C10/K10] 3.73:1; [C20/K20] 4.11:1; [C30] 5.14:1. Brakes: Four-wheel hydraulic drums. Brake linings: [C10/K10] 11 x 2.75 in.; [C20/K20/C30] 12 x 2 in.; [El Camino] 9-1/2 x 2-1/2 in. Kelsey-Hayes pressed steel wheels.

OPTIONS: [El Camino] Air-conditioning. Heavy-duty battery. Custom seat belts. Tinted glass. Tinted windshield. Power windows. Front bumper guards. Custom Deluxe front seat belts. Strato bucket seats. Strato Ease headrest. Regular headrest. Safety harness. Front and rear floor mats. Underhood trouble light. Deluxe foam front seat cushion. Door edge guards. Black or beige vinyl roof. Delete heater/defroster. Air-conditioning. Remote-control outside rearview mirror. Console. Heavy-duty suspension. Positraction. Rear axle ratios: 3.70; 3.36; 3.08; 3.31; 3.55; 2.73; 3.07; 3.73. Vacuum power brakes. Front disc brakes. Brake linings. Radiator fan. Air injector reactor. Cruise Control. 61-amp. Delcotron alternator. 42-amp. Delcotron alternator. Heavy-duty clutch. Overdrive transmission. Four-speed transmission. Close-ratio four-speed transmission. Powerglide transmission (with six). Three-speed Turbo-Hydramatic transmission (with V-8s). Dual exhausts. Deluxe steering wheel. Comfortilt steering wheel. Woodgrain steering wheel. Power steering. Mag style wheelcovers. Wheel trim covers. Simulated wire wheels. Heavy-duty battery. Tri-volume horn. Special instrumentation. Auxiliary lighting. Speed warning indicator. Tachometer. Glove box lamp. Ash ray lamp. Instrument panel courtesy lamps. Electric clock. Push-button AM radio and antenna. Push-button AM/FM radio and antenna. Heavy-duty radiator. Front bumper guards. SS-396 equipment. Vinyl roof. Deluxe front seat cushions. Concealed windshield wipers. [SS-396] Front Strato Bucket seats. Accent striping. Engine, 396 cid/350 hp V-8. Engine, 396 cid/375 hp V-8. Special mag style wheelcovers. Rally wheel rims.

OPTIONS: [Trucks] Oil bath air cleaner. Heavy-duty air cleaner. Air-conditioning. Armrests. Positraction. Rear axle ratios. Heavy-duty battery. Seat belts. Vacuum power brakes. Chrome front bumper. Chrome hubcaps. Side-mounted spare wheel carrier. Heavy-duty clutch. Heavy-duty cooling. Custom side molding package. Fuel filter. Gauges. Generator. Soft-Ray tinted glass. Engine governor. Door edge guards. Towing wire harness. Safety harness. Heater and defroster delete. Towing hooks. Rear side marker lights. Right-hand door lock. Exterior rearview mirror. Ship-to-shore power outlet. Camper Special package with custom "Camper Special" nameplates. Fuel and vacuum pump booster. AM radio and antenna. Heavy-duty shock absorbers. Speed warning indicator. Heavy-duty front springs. Heavy-duty rear springs. Front stabilizer bar. Heavy-duty starter. Power steering. Bodyside paint stripes. Throttle control. Full wheelcovers. One-passenger auxiliary seat. Panoramic rear window. Custom interior equipment. Custom chrome equipment. Custom Sport Truck equipment. Bucket seats. Trailering Special equipment.

OPTIONS AND INSTALLATION RATES: Heavy-duty seat (6 percent). Front center seat belt (2 percent). Rear seat (40 percent). Shoulder harness (1 percent). Panoramic cab (19 percent). Bucket seats (2 percent). Custom bench seat (1 percent). One-passenger auxiliary seat (55 percent). Rear center seat belt (10 percent). Center and rear seat (41 percent). Shoulder harness (not available). Spare wheel lock (2 percent). Upper bodyside molding (not available). Door edge guards (6 percent). Side trim molding (36 percent). Heater deletion (12 percent). Air-conditioning (3 percent). Roof-mounted-air-conditioning (not available). Front door armrest (2 percent). Jr. West Coast mirror (32 percent). Sr. West Coast mirror (3 percent). Non-glare inside mirror (16 percent). Body paint stripe (5 percent). Platform equipment (1 percent). Pickup box mounting (9 percent). Floorboard (28 percent). Front stabilizer (20 percent). Heavy front springs (18 percent). Front wheel locking hub (75 percent). Heavy rear spring (65 percent). Heavy shocks (11 percent). Heavy front axle (12 percent). Auxiliary springs (22 percent). Heavy-duty rear shocks (4 percent). Leaf springs (2 percent). Positraction (11 percent). No-Spin rear axle (7 percent). Pow-R-Lock rear axle (not available). Optional gear ratio (16 percent). Cruise Control (not available). Oil bath air cleaner (10 percent). 327 V-8 engine (26 percent). 396-four-barrel engine (3 percent). 396-two-barrel engine (1 percent). Overdrive (1 percent). Heavy-duty three-speed manual transmission (9 percent). Four-speed manual transmission (21 percent). Powerglide transmission (9 percent). Three-speed automatic transmission (16 percent). Wheel trim covers (10 percent). Chrome hubcaps (12 percent). Whitewall tires (9 percent). Roof marker lamps (2 percent). Speed warning indicator (not available). Tachometer (1 percent). Push-button radio (25 percent). Camper Special equipment (3 percent). Custom Sport Truck option (4 percent). Tu-tone paint (32 percent). Full gauge package (55 percent). Custom Appearance package (3 percent). Custom Comfort and Convenience package (26 percent).

NOTE: Partial list of options and installation rates based on Chevrolet cumulative model year records for 1/2-ton to 2-ton trucks built through Aug. 1, 1968. Figures do not include El Camino, which was considered a Chevelle for record-keeping purposes. The installation rate (percent) shows the percent option usage in those trucks qualifying for the particular option. For example, front wheel locking hubs were used on 75 percent of Chevrolet's four-wheel drive trucks; not 75 percent of total production. The notation not available indicates percentage installation rate not available.

HISTORICAL: Calendar Year production [All Chevrolet commercials]: 680,499. Chevrolet Commercials, model Year production by tonnage class and engine: [1/2-ton] (six-cylinder) 202,962; (V-8) 190,413; [Total] 393,375. [3/4-ton] (six-cylinder) 35,645; (V-8) 62,731; [Total] 98,376. [1-ton] (six-cylinder) 14,556; (V-8) 15,179; [Total] 29,735. [Grand Total] 521,486. Innovations: First year for front and rear safety sidemarker lights. New models included 3/4- and 1-ton Forward-Control Step-Vans equipped with independent front suspension, coil springs, power steering and V-8 engines. New 327 cid/200 hp and 396 cid/310 hp engines. Chevrolet celebrated its 50th year of truck manufacturing in 1968. Special Anniversary gold with Off-white paint was optional. Record sales and production marked Chevrolet's truck operations this season. Dealers delivered 843,990 trucks of all sizes. Most Chevrolet trucks were built at St. Louis, Mo. The home plant, at Flint, Mich., was the second highest source. However, the Fremont, Calif. factory was challenging for second place. This was the first year that production of V-8 powered trucks (410,178 units) out-paced production of sixes (269,291 units). T.L. Pritchett, assistant general sales manager, was head of the truck division.

1969 CHEVROLET

1969 Chevrolet 1/2-Ton Custom/10 Fleetside Pickup (CW)

EL CAMINO — MODEL A/SERIES 13000 — SIX/V-8: For 1969, the El Camino had a mild, but handsome facelift. A new fine-finned grille insert was dominated by bright horizontal moldings at its top, center and bottom. The center molding had a Chevrolet badge in the middle. The center bumper slot was larger. Following an every-other-year Chevelle tradition, the parking lamps were moved back inside the bumper slot backup, which was widened just enough to accommodate the lenses. At the rear, all El Caminos had large backup lamps set into the tailgate, on either side of the Chevrolet nameplate in the center. The rear bumper indentations filled by backup lamps on passenger cars had red reflectors on the Sedan-Pickup. Accenting base models was a Chevrolet script on the left fendertop; front sidemarker engine call-outs; rear sidemarker lamps; rear fender El Camino nameplates; bright windshield frames; bright tailgate latch; Chevrolet nameplate on tailgate; and narrow rocker panel moldings. Custom models had bright window frames; pickup box upper edge moldings; rear body corner moldings; two moldings across the tailgate at taillight top and bottom height; a bright rear window frame; bright moldings on lower body feature line; and silver anodized lower body perimeter finish. The SS-396 reverted to an option this year. On SS-396 versions, the grille was blacked-out. The grille center and middle of the tailgate had SS-396 badges. The engine call-outs on the front sidemarkers said Turbo-Jet 396. This option also included a special power dome hood; fat G70-14 Red Stripe tires on 14 x 7 in. rims; blacked-out lower body perimeter finish; chrome moldings on lower body feature line; special styled wheels; suspension upgrades; power disc brakes; wheel opening moldings; and SS tailgate moldings. The 396 cid/325 hp engine with chrome accents was standard. A 350 hp version of the big-block with a high-lift camshaft and dual exhausts was optional at extra cost. SS-396 models, the grille background and lower body perimeter were blacked-out. The flying buttress roofline was retained. The pickup box, used through 1972, had an outside width of to 75-1/2 in. Inside width behind the cab was 59 in. Inside width near the tailgate was 64-1/2 in. The width between the wheelhousings was 44 in. The bottom bed length measured 79-1/4 in. Tailgate measurements were 54-1/2 x 22-1/2 in. El Camino exterior body colors included Tuxedo black; Butternut yellow; Dover white; Dark blue; Garnet red; Glacier blue; Azure turquoise; Fathom green; Frost green; Burnished brown; Champagne; Olympic gold; burgundy; Cortez silver; LeMans blue; and (for SS-396s only) orange and Daytona yellow.

1/2-TON CHEVY VAN — MODEL G/SERIES 10 — SIX/V-8: Only the 1/2-ton G10 line offered the compact van body with 209 cu. ft. of payload space on a 90 in. wheelbase. The larger 256 cu. ft. body, mounted on a 108 in. wheelbase, could be ordered, too. It was 18 in. longer. Four G10 models were offered in the two lengths with six-cylinder or V-8 powerplants. Standard features included Stay-Tight integral body frame construction and durable, tapered leaf springs. Styling was basically unchanged. The grille had six horizontal bars divided into four segments by three vertical bars. The center bar was widest. The remaining vertical bars were narrower. Single, large round headlamps were at either end of the grille. Rectangular parking/directional lights were next to the headlamps. Under the windshield, five segmented vents continued to appear. Below the center vent segment was a Chevrolet bow tie emblem. There were large, rectangular sidemarker lamps. Standard models came with bumper, grille and hubcaps done in white. Chrome trim was optional. Both lines offered a Commercial Panel with double cargo doors available on the passenger side and at the rear. Both also offered window models in three levels of trim. The Sportvan was the base model. Sportvan Customs were in the middle. Sportvan Deluxe models were the fanciest. A 230 cid six was the base engine. A 307 cid V-8 was optional.

3/4-TON CHEVY VAN — MODEL G/SERIES 20 — SIX/V-8: The 108 in. wheelbase driver-forward vans also came as 3/4-ton G20 models. Styling characteristics were the same as long wheelbase G10s. Models included the Commercial Panel with double cargo doors available on the passenger side and at the rear. There were also window models in three levels of trim: base Sportvan, Sportvan Custom, and Sportvan Deluxe. The G20 line offered the same engines as G10s.

1/2-TON BLAZER — MODEL K/SERIES 5 — SIX/V-8: Attracting considerable attention was Chevrolet's entry into the expanding 4x4 off-road vehicle field...the Blazer. Its suspension system consisted of single-leaf tapered front springs with a combination of multi-leaf and tapered springs at the rear. The ball-type steering unit had a 24:1 ratio and its standard engine was Chevrolet's 155 hp six. The Blazer's single-unit body was joined to a heavy channel steel frame. The rear-mounted 23.5-gal. fuel tank was located inside the frame. Numerous options were offered for the Blazer including four-speed manual and automatic transmissions, V-8 engines, power steering, power brakes and a completely removable fiberglass top. Colors, exterior trim; upholstery and equipment were very similar or the same as used on the conventional K10 models.

1969 Chevrolet El Camino SS-396 Sedan Pickup (OCW)

1/2-TON COMMERCIAL — MODEL C; K/SERIES 10 — SIX/V-8: Pickups had a frontal redo. An aluminum centerpiece, in the grille, was embossed with the Chevrolet name and had integral, rectangular parking lamps at each end, next to the square headlamp housings. A large bow tie was at the front center of the hood. Inside was a new low-profile steering wheel, new seatback construction and new foot-operated parking brake. Standard equipment on all Pickups included: six-cylinder engine; self-adjusting four-wheel brakes; dual brake master cylinder; backup lights; directional signals; Panoramic rear window; sidemarker reflectors; left- and right-hand outside rearview mirrors; heater and defroster; padded dash; non-glare front instrument panel finish; padded sun visors; ashtray; seat belts with retractors; push-button seat belt buckles; low-profile control knobs; two-speed electric washer/wipers; windshield defrosters; safety glass; flexible fuel filler neck; deep-dish steering wheel with telescoping shaft; and thick laminate safety glass windshield; full-width seat with vinyl interior trim; and painted front bumper. Chrome front and rear bumpers were a separate option. The standard C10 had no side trim; plain black rubber window gaskets; and painted bumpers. The grille shell had bright metal finish. The hubcaps were also painted. The vent window pillars and frames were flat black. The standard "pie plate" hubcaps were painted. Rear moldings around the taillamps and tailgate were not available on standard C10. Upper and lower belt moldings were optional. Trucks equipped with the lower belt molding should have the center of the molding painted black. Chrome-plated "gear sprocket" wheelcovers with color-keyed finish and a bow tie in the center were optional. The Custom C10 was designated by Custom/10 nameplates on the front fenders. There was bright metal trim around the windshield, rear window, and vent window pillar and frame. Base bumpers and hubcaps were still painted, however. Upper and lower belt moldings were both optional and the center of the lower molding is painted. When equipped with lower side moldings, the Custom/10 also got taillamp and two tailgate moldings. These moldings were positioned above and below the Chevrolet lettering on the back. The Custom/10 grille came in bright metal with a plastic grid design for the insert. (The grille was the same for all models). Chrome hubcaps were optional on Custom/10 models. The top-of-the-line was the Custom Sport Truck, which said CST/10 on its front fendersides. The CST had all Custom/10 features, plus more. The lower belt molding was standard and had an exclusive woodgrain center insert. The upper belt molding was still optional. The CST also had special front sidemarker lamps with chrome trim, which was not available on other models. Taillight and tailgate moldings (with a woodgrain applique and chrome Chevrolet lettering) were standard on CSTs, too. Chrome "pie plate" hubcaps were standard; full wheelcovers were optional. A cab-mounted cargo lamp also came standard on CSTs. There were Custom Interior Convenience; Custom Appearance; and Custom Comfort & Convenience options, too. Bucket seats were extra in all cab models. Fifteen paint colors were available: Black; Light green; Yellow green; Dark green; Light blue; Dark blue; turquoise; red; orange; maroon; Dark yellow; yellow; white; silver; and saddle. Seat colors were saddle, blue, green, red, black and turquoise. The C10 (and K10 four-wheel drive) Chassis models and Pickups came on 115 or 127 in. wheelbases. The Chassis & Cowl model was dropped. Both Fleetside and Step-Side Pickups offered a 6-1/2 ft. box or 8 ft. box. Panels and Suburbans came only on the longer wheelbase. The Suburban again had two-doors on the passenger side and one on the driver's side. Surburbans were available with a tailgate or Panel truck style double rear doors. Both single-unit body models had coil springs on all four wheels. Optional seats, in the Suburban, converted the 181 cu. ft. payload space into a passenger compartment. Pickups on the shorter wheelbase had a 6-1/2 ft. cargo box. Those on the long wheelbase featured an 8 ft. box. Both sizes came in Step-Side or Fleetside models. Two-toning was done using Off-white as the second (upper) color. It was applied to all sheet metal above the beltline.

1/2-TON FORWARD-CONTROL — MODEL P/SERIES 10 — SIX/V-8: The 1/2-ton Forward-Control returned again. It had a 102 in. wheelbase. The Forward-Control chassis and Step-Van were designed for door-to-door delivery service. Body lengths ranged from seven to eight-feet for this Step-Van 7 series. Features included independent coil spring front suspension and two six-cylinder engines. Buyers could also get full-height doors; sliding side doors and double rear doors.

3/4-TON COMMERCIAL — MODEL C; K/SERIES 20 — SIX/V-8: Carryover trucks in the Chevrolet 20 Series 3/4-ton line had the same styling, trim changes and options as other conventional trucks. The Step-Side Pickup had the 8 ft. box. The "Longhorn" Fleetside Pickup had a 133 in. wheelbase and 8-1/2 ft. box. The Chassis & Cowl model and 4x4 Panel were dropped. The Chassis & Cab, two Suburbans and the 4x2 Panel continued in this line. These had the same dimensions as comparable 1/2-ton models, but heavier chassis components. The designation plates had a number 20. Step-Side and Fleetside Pickups were also in this series. They featured the 8 ft. pickup box. There was also an 8 ft. Stake model. The four-wheel drive 3/4-ton models in the 20 Series had a K20 model prefix.

3/4-TON FORWARD-CONTROL — MODEL P/SERIES 20 — SIX/V-8: Just two 3/4-ton Forward-Control chassis remained in the 20 Series (3/4-ton) truck line, but they were the basis for numerous steel, aluminum, and round and square styled bodies, and a number of engine choices. The P20 Forward-Control chassis and Step-Van were designed for door-to-door delivery service. Features included independent coil spring front suspension; three six-cylinder engines; two optional V-8s, plus a three-cylinder Detroit diesel engine. Buyers could also get full-height doors; sliding side doors; and double rear doors. Remaining in the 3/4-ton series were the 125 in. wheelbase chassis recommended for bodies 9-1/2 ft. to 10-1/2 ft. long and the 137 in. wheelbase chassis recommended for bodies 11-1/2 ft. to 12-1/2 ft. long. Bodies were available from factory-authorized suppliers or buyers could order them locally. The coil spring front suspension reflected the fact that the Forward-Control chassis was now starting to find its way into the growing RV market.

1-TON MEDIUM-DUTY COMMERCIAL — MODEL C/SERIES 30 — SIX-CYLINDER: The Chevrolet 30 Series 1-ton trucks had the same styling and trim changes and options as other conventional trucks. The fenderside nameplates had a number 30. The Stake with 9 ft. rail was dropped. There were four 133 in. wheelbase models: Chassis & Cowl, Chassis & Cab, Longhorn Pickup with 8.5 ft box and a Step-Side Pickup with 9 ft. box. The Stake was dropped. No hubcaps were used on the larger split-rim wheels of the Chassis & Cab models, which had eight bolts and eight circular openings. The Camper Special package continued. Camper models had their own designation plates with a Chevrolet bow tie and

"Camper Special" chrome script. The C38 model 1-ton Chassis & Cab with a long 157 in. wheelbase for use as an RV chassis was also offered again. A four-speed manual synchromesh transmission was standard. No four-wheel drive option was offered.

1-TON FORWARD-CONTROL — MODEL P/SERIES 30 — SIX/V-8: Three Forward-Control chassis were in the 30 Series (1-ton) truck line. The Forward-Control chassis and Step-Van were designed for door-to-door delivery service. Body lengths ranged up to 14-1/2 ft. for the 1-ton Step-Van King. Features included independent coil spring front suspension; three six-cylinder engines; two optional V-8s, plus a three-cylinder Detroit diesel engine. Buyers could also get full-height doors; sliding side doors and double rear doors. P30s were offered were wheelbases of 125 in., 133 in., and 157 in. respectively. The 125 in. wheelbase chassis was recommended for bodies 9-1/2 ft. to 10-1/2 ft. long. The 137 in. wheelbase was recommended for bodies 11-1/2 ft. to 12-1/2 ft. long. The new 157 in. wheelbase was used for the large aluminum-bodied Step-Van King model, as well as for RV construction. Bodies were available from factory-authorized suppliers or buyers could order them locally. A channel type front bumper and High-Torque 230 six were standard equipment.

1969 Chevrolet El Camino Custom Sedan-Pickup (DFW)

I.D. DATA: Serial Number located: [Chassis models] On plate temporarily attached near steering column, with final location per body maker; [All others] On plate attached to rear face of left-hand door hinge pillar; on right side of cowl under hood. [El Camino]: The first symbol indicated manufacturer: 1=Chevrolet. The second and third symbols indicated series: 33=six/34=V-8/35=Custom six/36=Custom V-8. The fourth and fifth symbols indicated body type: 80=Sedan-Pickup. The sixth symbol indicate model year: 9=1969. The seventh symbol indicated assembly plant: A=Atlanta (Lakewood); B=Baltimore, Md.; G=Framingham, Mass.; K=Kansas City, Mo. (Leeds); Z=Fremont, Calif.; The remaining symbols were the sequential production number starting with 100001 at each plant. Ending serial numbers not available. The Chevrolet engine had the source, date and type stamped on a serial number pad. Various source codes were used. Month codes were 1=Jan.; 2=Feb., etc. Date codes were 01=first of month, etc. The were numerous prefix codes to indicate engines and transmission attachments. The collectible 396s had the following codes: [325 hp] JA/JK/JV/KG/KH/KI; [350 hp] JC/JE/KB; [375 hp] JD/KF/KD. [Other models] The first symbol indicated indicated truck type: C=Conventional Cab; K=4x4; G=Chevy Van; P=Forward-Control. The second symbol indicated type of engine: S=six; E=eight; T=diesel. The third symbol indicated the GVW range: [GVW] 1=3,600-5,600 lbs.; 2=5,500-8,100 lbs.; 3=6,700-10,000 lbs.; 4=Over 10,000 lbs. The fourth and fifth symbols indicated the cab-to-axle dimension: 07=42-47 in.; 09=54-59 in.; 10=60-65 in.; 14=84-89 in. The sixth symbol indicated body type: 02=Chassis & Cowl; 03=Chassis & Cab; 04=Step-Side Pickup; 05=Panel or Panel Van; 06=Suburban (doors) or Sportvan; 09=Platform/Stake; 12=Chassis & Cowl; 13=Cab with air brakes; 14=Blazer; 14=Suburban (gate); 26=Custom Sportvan; 34=Fleetside; 36=Deluxe Sportvan; 35=Forward-Control. The eighth symbol indicates model year: 9=1969. The ninth symbol indicates assembly plant: A=Atlanta, Ga.; B=Baltimore, Md.; F=Flint, Mich.; J=Janesville, Wis.; K=Kansas City, Mo.; S=St. Louis, Mo.; T=Tarrytown, N.Y.; Z=Fremont, Calif. 1=Oshawa, Canada.

Model	Body Type	Price	Weight	Prod. Total
El Camino — Model A/Series 13000 — 116 in. w.b. — Six				
13380	Pickup	2552	3192	Note 1
13580	Custom Pickup	2632	3219	Note 1
El Camino — Model A/Series 13000 — 116 in. w.b. — V-8				
13480	Pickup	2642	3216	Note 1
13680	Custom Pickup	2723	3248	Note 1

NOTE 1: Total El Camino production was 48,385.

Model	Body Type	Price	Weight	Prod. Total
1/2-Ton Chevy Van — Model G/Series 100 — 90 in. w.b.				
GS11005	Panel	2531	3072	18,456
GS11006	Sportvan	2738	3266	1,730
GS11026	Custom Sportvan	2863	3375	526
GS11036	Deluxe Sportvan	3050	3415	270
1/2-Ton Chevy Van — Model G/Series 100 — 108 in. w.b.				
GS11005	Panel	2595	3189	20,730
GS11006	Sportvan	2810	3316	3,065
GS11026	Custom Sportvan	2935	3439	2,598
GS11036	Deluxe Sportvan	3125	3483	1,758
3/4-Ton Chevy Van — Model G/Series 20 — 108 in. w.b.				
GS21305	Panel	2789	3316	6,030
GS21306	Sportvan	2982	3453	625
GS21326	Custom Sportvan	3107	3586	382
GS21336	Deluxe Sportvan	3294	3629	306
1/2-Ton Blazer — Model K/Series 5 — 104 in. w.b.				
KE10514	Open Utility	2852	2947	4935
1/2-Ton Commercial — Model C/Series 10 — 115 in. w.b.				
CE10703	Chassis & Cab	2383	3116	2,343
CE10734	Fleetside 6.5 ft.	2532	3531	54,211
CE10704	Step-Side 6.5 ft.	2494	3450	49,147

Model	Body Type	Price	Weight	Prod. Total
1/2-Ton Commercial — Model C/Series 10 — 127 in. w.b.				
CE10903	Chassis & Cab	2421	3189	1,203
CE10934	Fleetside 8 ft.	2569	3623	268,233
CE10904	Step-Side 8 ft.	2532	3523	18,179
CE10905	Panel	2960	3724	5,492
CE10906	Suburban	3194	3815	14,056
1/2-Ton Commercial 4x4 — Model K/Series 10 — 115 in. w.b.				
KE10703	Chassis & Cab	2936	3316	58
KE10734	Fleetside 6.5 ft.	3085	3732	1,649
KE10704	Step-Side 6.5 ft.	3047	3652	1,698
1/2-Ton Commercial 4x4 — Model K/Series 10 — 127 in. w.b.				
KE10903	Chassis & Cab	2973	3522	35
KE10934	Fleetside 8 ft.	3123	3836	4937
KE10904	Step-Side 8 ft.	3085	36512	521
KE10905	Panel	3513	3935	—
KS10906	Suburban	3749	4024	—
1/2-Ton Forward-Control — Model P/Series 10 — 102 in. w.b.				
PE10535	Chassis	—	—	125
PE10535	Step-Van	2944	3702	2,819
3/4-Ton Commercial — Model C/Series 20 — 127 in. w.b.				
CE20903	Chassis & Cab	2614	3506	8,440
CE20934	Fleetside 8 ft.	2762	4013	74,894
CS20904	Step-Side 8 ft.	2724	3907	8,090
CE20909	Stake 8 ft.	2832	4138	—
CE20905	Panel	3172	4093	1,779
CE20906	Suburban	3447	4199	2,736
Long Horn Pickup — Model C/Series 20 — 133 in. w.b.				
CE21034	Pickup 8.5 ft.	2826	4066	8,797
3/4-Ton Commercial 4x4 — Model K/Series 20 — 127 in. w.b.				
KE20903	Chassis & Cab	3205	3626	556
KE20934	Fleetside 8 ft.	3353	4131	6,124
KE20904	Step-Side 8 ft.	3315	4025	1,071
KE20906	Suburban	4040	4316	545
3/4-Ton Forward-Control — Model P/Series 20 — 125 in. w.b.				
PS20842	Chassis	1980	2749	616
PS20835	Step-Van	3819	5175	1,843
PS20855	Alumnium Step-Van	—	—	68
3/4-Ton Forward-Control — Model P/Series 20 — 133 in. w.b.				
PS21842	Chassis	2015	2765	233
PS21835	Step-Van	3930	5410	950
PS21835	Aluminum Step-Van	4900	4760	79
1-Ton Commercial — Model C/Series 30 — 133 in. w.b.				
CE31002	Chassis & Cowl	—	—	236
CE31003	Chassis & Cab	2724	3689	16,828
CE31034	Fleetside 8.5 ft.	2919	4276	2457
CE31004	Step-Side 9 ft.	2858	4120	1,300
CE31009	Stake 9 ft.	3063	4617	—
1-Ton Commercial — Model C/Series 30 — 157 in. w.b.				
CE31103	Chassis & Cab	2839	4066	8,290
1-Ton Forward-Control — Model P/Series 30 — 125 in. w.b.				
PS30842	Chassis	2140	2968	3,447
PS30835	Step-Van King	3900	5394	855
PS30835	Step-Van Aluminum	—	—	46
PT30835	Step-Van Diesel	4020	3764	Note 2
PT30835	Step-Van King Diesel	5775	6170	Note 2
1-Ton Forward-Control — Model P/Series 30 — 133 in. w.b.				
PS31842	Chassis	2175	2987	1,170
PS31843	Chassis & Cowl	—	—	236
PS31835	Steel Step-Van	4010	5630	1,600
PS31835	Aluminum Step-Van	—	—	126
PT31042	Chassis (Diesel)	4050	3784	Note 2
PT31035	Step-Van King	5885	6405	Note 2:
1-Ton Step-Van King — Model P/Series 30 — 157 in. w.b.				
PE38842	Chassis	—	—	1,607
PE38835	Steel Step-Van	—	—	924
PE38835	Aluminum Step-Van	—	—	86

NOTE 2: Total production of diesel-powered Forward-Control models was 53.
NOTE 3: Second letter in model code indicates engine: S=Six; E=V-8; T=3-cyl. diesel.
NOTE 4: Production totals from Chevrolet records are for model-year through Aug. 1, 1969 and include all trucks made in U.S. factories for domestic/export/Canadian markets. Where no production total is shown, records are not complete.

ENGINE [Standard El Camino G10/P10/G20]: Inline. OHV. Six-cylinder. Cast iron block. Bore & stroke: 3.875 in. x 3-1/4 in. Displacement: 230 cid. Compression ratio: 8.5:1. Brake horsepower: 140 at 4400 rpm. Torque: 220 lbs.-ft. at 1600 rpm. Net horsepower: 120 at 3600 rpm. Seven main bearings. Hydraulic valve lifters. Carburetor: Rochester one-barrel model 7028006/7028010.

ENGINE [Standard C10/C20/C30/K10/K20/P30; Optional G10/G20/P10/El Camino]: Inline. OHV. Six-cylinder. Cast iron block. Bore & stroke: 3.875 in. x 3.53 in. Displacement: 250 cid. Compression ratio: 8.5:1. Brake horsepower: 155 at 4200 rpm. Torque: 235 lbs.-ft. at 1600 rpm. Seven main bearings. Hydraulic valve lifters. Carburetor: Rochester one-barrel model 7028007/7028011.

ENGINE [Optional C10/C20/C30; Standard P20/P30]: Inline. OHV. Six-cylinder. Cast iron block. Bore & stroke: 3-7/8 in. x 4-1/2 in. Displacement: 292 cid. Compression ratio: 8.1:1. Brake horsepower: 170 at 4000 rpm. Torque: 275 lbs.-ft. at 1600 rpm. Seven main bearings. Hydraulic valve lifters. Carburetor: Rochester one-barrel model 7028012/7028013.

ENGINE [Optional G10/G20/P10/P20/P30/C10/C20/C30/K10/K20/El Camino]: V-type. OHV. Eight-cylinder. Cast iron block. Bore & stroke: 3.875 in. x 3.25 in. Displacement: 307 cid. Compression ratio: 9.0:1. Brake horsepower: 200 at 4800 rpm. Five main bearings. Hydraulic valve lifters. Carburetor: Rochester two-barrel model 26 (numbers vary).

ENGINE [Optional C10/C20/C30/K10/K20/El Camino]: V-type. OHV. Eight-cylinder. Cast iron block. Bore & stroke: 4.0 in. x 3.48 in. Displacement: 350 cid. Compression ratio: 9.1. Brake horsepower: 255 at 4400 rpm. Five main bearings. Hydraulic valve lifters. Carburetor: Rochester model 4MV.

ENGINE [Optional C10/C20/C30/K10/K20]: V-type. OHV. Eight-cylinder. Cast iron block. Bore & stroke: 4.0 in. x 3.48 in. Displacement: 350 cid. Compression ratio: 10.25:1. Brake horsepower: 300 at 4800 rpm. Five main bearings. Hydraulic valve lifters. Carburetor: Rochester model 4MV.

ENGINE [Optional C10/C20/C30/K10/K20/El Camino]: V-type. OHV. Eight-cylinder. Cast iron block. Bore & stroke: 4.0 in. x 3.48 in. Displacement: 350 cid. Compression ratio: 11.0:1. Brake horsepower: 350 at 5000 rpm. Five main bearings. Hydraulic valve lifters. Carburetor: Rochester model 4MV.

ENGINE [Optional C10/C20/C30/K10/K20]: V-type. OHV. Eight-cylinder. Cast iron block. Bore & stroke: 4.09 in. x 3.76 in. Displacement: 396 cid. Compression ratio: 9.1. Brake horsepower: 310 at 4800 rpm. Maximum torque: 400 lbs.-ft. at 3200 rpm. Five main bearings. Hydraulic valve lifters. Carburetor: Rochester model 4MV 7028211.

ENGINE [Standard: El Camino With SS-396]: V-block. OHV. Eight-cylinder. Cast iron block. Bore & stroke: 4.09 in. x 3.76 in. Displacement: 396 cid. Compression ratio: 10.25:1. Brake horsepower: 325 at 4800 rpm. Torque: 410 lbs.-ft. at 3200 rpm. Five main bearings. Hydraulic valve lifters. Carburetor: Rochester four-barrel model Quadra-Jet.

ENGINE [Optional: El Camino With SS-396]: V-block. OHV. Eight-cylinder. Cast iron block. Bore & stroke: 4.09 in. x 3.76 in. Displacement: 396 cid. Compression ratio: 10.25:1. Brake horsepower: 350 at 5200 rpm. Torque: 415 lbs.-ft. at 3400 rpm. Five main bearings. Hydraulic valve lifters. Carburetor: Rochester four-barrel model Quadra-Jet.

ENGINE [Optional: El Camino With SS-396]: V-type. OHV. Eight-cylinder. Cast iron block. Bore & stroke: 4.094 in. x 3.76 in. Displacement: 396 cid. Compression ratio: 11.25:1. Brake horsepower: 375. Five main bearings. Carburetor: four-barrel.

ENGINE [Optional P20/P30]: Diesel. Model 3-53N. Three-cylinder. Bore and stroke: 3.875 x 4.5 in. Displacement: 159.2 cid. Brake horsepower: 94 at 2800 rpm. Torque: 205 lbs.-ft. at 1500 rpm.

1969 Chevrolet 1/2-Ton C10 Step-Side Pickup (OCW)

CHASSIS [El Camino]: Wheelbase: 116 in. Overall length: 201 in. Front tread: 59 in. Rear tread: 59 in. Tires: 7.35 x 14 in. GVW: 4,300 lbs.

CHASSIS [G10]: Wheelbase: 90 in. Tires: 6.95 x 14 in. GVW: 3,900-5,000 lbs.

CHASSIS [C10/K10]: Wheelbase: 115 in. Overall length: 186.75 in. Height: 74.5 in. Front tread: 63.1 in. Rear tread: 61.1 in. Tires: Tires: [4x2] 8.15 x 15 in.; [Suburban] 8.15 x 15 in.; [4x4] 17.5 x 17 four-ply. GVW: [4x2] 4,400-5,000 lbs.; [4x4] 5,600 lbs.

CHASSIS [C10/K10]: Wheelbase: 127 in. Overall length: 206.25 in. Height: 71 in. Front tread: 63.1 in. Rear tread: 61.1 in. Tires: [4x2] 7.75 x 15 in. four-ply; [4x4] 17.5 x 17. GVW: [4x2] 4,400-5,000 lbs.; [4x4] 5,600 lbs.

CHASSIS [P10]: Wheelbase: 102 in. Tires: 7.75 x 15 in. GVW: 4,600-5,400 lbs.

CHASSIS [C20/K20]: Wheelbase: 127 in. Overall length: 206.25 in. Tires: [4x2] 7 x 17.5 in.; [4x4] 7 x 17.5 six-ply. GVW: [4x2] 5,500-7,500 lbs.; [4x4] 5,700-7,600 lbs.

CHASSIS [P20]: Wheelbases: [P2300] 104 in.; [P2500] 125 in.; [P2600] 137 in. Base tires: 7 x 17.5. GVW: 7,000 lbs.

CHASSIS [C30]: Wheelbase: 133 in. Tires: 8 x 17.5 in. GVW: 6,700-14,000 lbs.

CHASSIS [P30]: Wheelbases: [P3300] 104 in.; [P3500] 125 in.; [P3600] 137 in. Base tires: 8 x 19.5. GVW: 7,500-14,000 lbs.

1969 Chevrolet 1/2-Ton C10 Fleetside Pickup (OCW)

TECHNICAL: Standard transmission: Chevrolet three-speed manual (Borg-Warner heavy-duty three-speed optional). Type: [C30] 4F/1R; [Others] 3F/1R. Column-mounted gearshift lever. Single-plate, dry-disc clutch. Rear axle: [1/2-ton] semi-floating; [3/4-ton/1-Ton] full-floating. Base rear axles: [El Camino] 3.08:1; [C10/K10] 3.73:1; [C20/K20] 4.11:1; [C30] 5.14:1. Brakes: Four-wheel hydraulic, drum brakes. Brake linings: [C10/K10] 11 x 2.75 in.; [C20/K20/C30] 12 x 2 in.; [El Camino] 9-1/2 x 2-1/2 in. Kelsey-Hayes pressed steel wheels.

OPTIONS: El Camino: Strato-bucket seats. Speed and Cruise Control. Comfortilt steering wheel. Deluxe steering wheel. Wheelcovers. Mag-style wheelcovers. Simulated wire wheelcovers. Rally wheels and trim. Concealed windshield wipers. Deluxe seat and shoulder belts. Appearance guard group. Console. Power door locks. Tinted glass. Tri-volume horn. Special instrumentation. Auxiliary lighting. Vinyl roof cover.

OPTIONS AND INSTALLATION RATES: [VANS]: Tinted windshield (15 percent). One-passenger auxiliary seat (27 percent). Heater deletion (2 percent). Jr. West Coast mirror (72 percent). Right-hand door (94 percent). Body paint stripe (1 percent). Non-glare inside mirror (not available). Front stabilizer (68 percent). Heavy front springs (73 percent). Heavy rear springs (85 percent). Positraction (9 percent). Optional rear axles (27 percent). Hydraulic brake booster (10 percent). Engine block heater (2 percent). Emission controls (9 percent). Oil bath air cleaner (4 percent). 250 six-cylinder engine (66 percent). Powerglide transmission (19 percent). Three-speed automatic transmission (16 percent). Whitewall tires (12 percent). Heavy-duty battery (16 percent). Dual electric horns (1 percent). Speed warning indicator (not available). Heavy-duty radiator (5 percent). Chrome bumper (7 percent). Gauge package (30 percent). Custom equipment (3 percent). Two-tone paint (14 percent). Cargo door lock (8 percent). Swing-out rear door glass (7 percent). Tinted side door glass (26 percent). Tinted rear door glass (77 percent). Center seat (28 percent). Center and rear seat (26 percent). Stationary auxiliary seat (53 percent).

OPTIONS AND INSTALLATION RATES: [C/K Trucks]: Heavy-duty seats (3 percent). Custom Sport Truck option (6 percent). Chrome bumper (18 percent). Custom Comfort & Appearance option (28 percent). Blazer removable top, white (94 percent). Blazer removable top, black (6 percent). Full-foam seat (23 percent). Painted rear bumper (16 percent). Rear step bumper (16 percent). Heavy-duty cooling (1 percent). Chrome rear bumper (2 percent). Courtesy lights (99 percent). Push-button radio (41 percent). Tachometer (1 percent). Speed warning indicator (not available). Sidemarker lamps (not available). Cargo lamps (not available). Camper wiring (2 percent). Roof marker lamps (2 percent). Whitewall tires (13 percent). Step-Van dual rear wheel conversion (71 percent). Side-mounted wheel carrier (11 percent). Chrome hubcaps (11 percent). Wheel trim cover (19 percent). Hydraulic steering (21 percent). 350 medium-duty V-8 (8 percent). 350 light-duty V-8 (32 percent). 292 six-cylinder (14 percent). SS-396 four-barrel V-8 (4 percent). Heavy-duty clutch (28 percent). Overdrive (1 percent). Four-speed manual transmission (17 percent). Type N heavy-duty four-speed manual transmission (1 percent). Powerglide transmission (5 percent). 300 Deluxe three-speed automatic transmission (10 percent). Hydraulic brake booster (14 percent). Positraction (7 percent). Pow-R-Lock rear axle (1 percent). No-Spin rear axle (not available). Positraction (7 percent).

NOTE: Option use rates based on Chevrolet records for model year through Dec. 31, 1969. Figures show percentage of option usage on truck qualified for the option. For example, Step-Van dual rear wheel option was used on 71 percent of all Step-Vans offering this equipment, not 71 percent of total Chevrolet production. Not available means installation rate not known.

1969 Chevrolet 1/2-Ton C10 Fleetside Pickup (OCW)

OPTION PACKAGE: [Custom]: An optional Custom Comfort & Appearance package included bright metal windshield moldings, rear window trim and ventipane frames; Custom (CS) nameplates on front fenders; color-keyed vinyl-coated rubber floor mats; full-depth foam seat with color-keyed fabric and vinyl trim; vinyl trim door panels with bright upper retainers; a cigar lighter; Chevrolet Custom nameplate on dispatch box door; bright metal control knob inserts; cowl insulation and full-depth armrests.

OPTION PACKAGE: [Custom Sport Truck] The top trim level was the Custom Sport Truck option. It included most equipment in the CS package, plus a chrome front bumper; full-width vinyl seats; bright pedal frames; bright roof drip moldings; extra insulation; matching carpets; and CST nameplates for the front fenders. Bucket seats with a center console were available on CST models.

HISTORICAL: Introduced: Fall 1968. Model year production [All Chevrolet Commercials]: 684,748. Model year Commercial production by tonnage and engine type: [1/2-ton] (six) 199,256; (V-8) 281,172; [Total] 480,428. [3/4-ton] (six) 30,991; (V-8) 93,178; [Total] 124,169. [1-ton] (six) 16,617; (V-8) 22,408; [Total] 39,025. [Grand Total] 643,622. Production of Custom Sport Truck (CST) option: 29,942. Production of CS option: 147,311. Innovations: All-new Blazer. New hinged hood on Step-Vans. New 350 cid V-8 option. New LP gas engine conversions available. Historical notes: Chevrolet production records show a model number and listing for a 4x2 Blazer, but indicate that none were built in this model year. In 1969, Chevrolet became a full-line truck-maker sharing GMC's heavy over-the-road product line with Chevrolet nameplates.

1970 CHEVROLET

1970 Chevrolet El Camino (DFW)

EL CAMINO — MODEL A/SERIES 13000 — SIX/V-8: The 1970 El Camino had a blunter, heftier front end replacing the 1968-1969 wrapover look. The dual headlamps were placed in square bezels outside the grille. A cross-hatch pattern grille insert was divided into four sections by wider chrome cross-bars. There was a bow tie in the center. Following the every-other-year pattern used since 1964, the rectangular parking lights were moved from inside the bumper air slot to the outer ends of the bumper. Regular El Caminos featured a new dash with a wide rectangular-shaped speedometer and gauges. The SS dash used circular units. At the rear, all El Caminos had large backup lamps set into the tailgate, on either side of the Chevrolet nameplate in the center. The rear bumper indentations filled by backup lamps on passenger cars had red reflectors on the Sedan-Pickup. Accenting base models was a Chevrolet script on the upper left grille section; El Camino nameplates and engine plaques above the feature line behind the front wheel openings; bright tailgate latch; and Chevrolet nameplate on tailgate. Custom models had lower bodyside and wheel opening moldings; silver anodized lower body perimeter finish; pickup box edge and rear body corner moldings; moldings running across the tailgate at top and bottom of taillamps; and a contrasting rear panel with Chevrolet nameplate. There was an SS-396 option (RPO Z25). In midyear, the 396 cid engine was actually enlarged to 402 cid, though the well-known SS-396 name was still used in sales promotion. About the same time (January, 1970) a new SS-454 option was released. Technically, it came in RPO Z15/LS5 and RPO Z15/LS6 versions. The first had a high-lift camshaft and 10.25:1 compression for 360 hp. The second had a special camshaft and 11.25:1 compression to produce 450 hp. A cowl-induction hood was available for SS models at $124. A popular option was the hood racing stripes, which were $43 extra. Super Sports included a black-accented grille with SS grille badges; special hood with locking pins; styled wheels; suspension upgrades; power disc brakes; wheel opening moldings; and SS tailgate emblems. The lower body perimeter was also blacked-out. The flying buttress roofline was retained for all El Caminos. The pickup box, used through 1972, had an outside width of 75-1/2 in. Inside width behind the cab was 59 in. Inside width near the tailgate was 64-1/2 in. The width between the wheelhousings was 44 in. The bottom bed length measured 79-1/4 in. Tailgate measurements were 54-1/2 x 22-1/2 in. El Camino exterior body colors included Tuxedo black; Classic white; Cortez silver; Cranberry red; Black cherry; Champagne gold; Autumn gold; Gobi beige; Desert sand; Green mist; Forest green; Misty turquoise; Astro blue; and Fathom blue. Upholstery in a choice of coated plain vinyl or coated patterned fabrics came in black; Medium metallic blue; and Medium metallic saddle.

1/2-TON CHEVY VAN — MODEL G/SERIES 10 — SIX/V-8: Chevy Vans continued to feature Chevrolet's so-called "Easy-Access" body design, which was popular with highly mobile businessmen. A three-range Turbo-Hydramatic transmission could be ordered. The styling, now in its last appearance, was unchanged from 1969. The grille had six horizontal bars divided into four segments by three vertical bars. The center bar was widest. The remaining vertical bars were narrower. Single, large round headlamps were at either end of the grille. Rectangular parking/directional lights were next to the headlamps. Under the windshield, five segmented vents continued to appear. Below the center vent segment was a Chevrolet bow tie emblem. There were large, rectangular sidemarker lamps. Standard models came with bumper, grille and hubcaps done in white. Chrome trim was optional. Only the 1/2-ton G10 line offered the compact van body with 209 cu. ft. of payload space on a 90 in. wheelbase. The larger 256 cu. ft. body, mounted on a 108 in. wheelbase, could be ordered, too. It was 18 in. longer. Four G10 models were offered in the two lengths with six-cylinder or V-8 powerplants. Standard features included Stay-Tight integral body frame construction and durable, tapered leaf springs. Both lines offered a Commercial Panel with double cargo doors available on the passenger side and at the rear. Both also offered window models in three levels of trim. The Sportvan was the base model. Sportvan Customs were in the middle. Sportvan Deluxe models were the fanciest. A 230 cid six was the base engine. A 307 cid V-8 was optional.

3/4-TON CHEVY VAN — MODEL G/SERIES 20 — SIX/V-8: The 108 in. wheelbase driver-forward vans also came as 3/4-ton G20 models. Styling characteristics were the same as long wheelbase G10s. Models included the Commercial Panel with double cargo doors available on the passenger side and at the rear. There were also window models in three levels of trim: base Sportvan, Sportvan Custom, and Sportvan Deluxe. The G20 line offered the same engines as G10s.

1/2-TON BLAZER — MODEL K/SERIES 10 — SIX/V-8: Blazers had a new grille with six groups of silver "dashes" above and below the horizontal aluminum center bar with Chevy's name across it. A 4x2 Blazer was produced this season, but less than 1,000 were made. The 4x4 version was more than 10 times as popular. The Blazer's suspension system consisted of single-leaf tapered front springs with a combination of multi-leaf and tapered springs at the rear. The ball-type steering unit had a 24:1 ratio and its standard engine was Chevrolet's 155 hp six. The single-unit body was joined to a heavy channel steel frame. The rear-mounted 23.5-gallon fuel tank was located inside the frame. Numerous options were offered for the Blazer including four-speed manual and automatic transmissions, V-8 engines, power steering, power brakes and a completely removable fiberglass top. Colors, exterior trims; upholstery and equipment were very similar or the same as used on the conventional K10 models.

1/2-TON COMMERCIAL — MODEL C; K/SERIES 10 — SIX/V-8: The C10s continued with the general 1969 styling. The outer grille was the same as 1969. It featured a horizontal aluminum center bar. This bar was embossed with the Chevrolet name and had integral rectangular parking lamps at each end, next to the square headlamp housings. The plastic grille insert was modified. It had a more rectangular gridwork with silver horizontal dashes against a black background. A large bow tie was at the front center of the hood. Inside was a low-profile steering wheel, full-width bench seat and foot-operated parking brake. Standard equipment on all pickups included: six-cylinder engine; self-adjusting four-wheel brakes; dual brake master cylinder with warning lights; backup lights; directional signals and four-way flashers; Panoramic rear window; left- and right-hand outside rearview mirrors; non-glare inside mirror; heater and defroster; padded dash; non-glare front instrument panel finish; padded sun visors; ashtray; seat belts with retractors; push-button seat belt buckles; low-profile control knobs; two-speed electric washer/wipers; windshield defrosters; safety glass; flexible fuel filler neck; deep-dish steering wheel with telescoping shaft; thick laminate safety glass windshield; front and rear side markers; and painted front bumper. Chrome front and rear bumpers were a separate option. The standard C10 had no side trim; plain black rubber window gaskets; and painted bumpers. The grille shell had bright metal finish. The hubcaps were also painted. The vent window pillars and frames were flat black. The standard "pie plate" hubcaps were painted. Rear moldings around the taillamps and tailgate were not available on standard C10. Upper and lower belt moldings were optional. Trucks equipped with the lower belt molding, should have the center of the molding painted black. Chrome-plated "gear sprocket" wheelcovers with color-keyed finish and a bow tie in the center were optional. The Custom C10 was designated by Custom/10 nameplates on the front fenders. There was bright metal trim around the windshield, rear window, and vent window pillar and frame. Base bumpers and hubcaps were still painted, however. Upper and lower belt moldings were both optional and the center of the lower molding was painted. When equipped with lower side moldings, the Custom/10 also got taillamp and two tailgate moldings. These moldings were positioned above and below the Chevrolet lettering on the back. The Custom/10 grille came in bright metal with a plastic grid design for the insert. (The grille was the same for all models). Chrome hubcaps were optional on Custom/10 models. The top-of-the-line was the Custom Sport Truck, which said CST/10 on its front fendersides. The CST had all Custom/10 features, plus more. The lower belt molding was standard and had an exclusive woodgrain center insert. The upper belt molding was still optional. The CST also had special front sidemarker lamps with chrome trim, which was not available on other models. Taillight and tailgate moldings (with a woodgrain applique and chrome Chevrolet lettering) were standard on CSTs, too. Chrome "pie plate" hubcaps were standard; full wheelcovers were optional. A cab-mounted cargo lamp also came standard on CSTs. There were Custom Interior Convenience; Custom Appearance; and Custom Comfort & Convenience options, too. Bucket seats were extra in all cab models. Exterior colors were black; Medium blue; Yellow green; Dark green; Dark olive; Dark blue; Medium blue; Dark blue green; Flame red; red; orange; Medium green; yellow; Light yellow; white; copper; Red orange; Medium gold; Dark gold; Dark bronze; Medium blue-green; and Dark blue. The standard interior interior featured a three-passenger bench seat; foam padding; dome light; rubber floor mat; two door armrests; and all-vinyl trim in saddle, blue, green, red, black or turquoise. The Custom interior added color-keyed floor mats; full-depth seat with color-keyed fabric-and-vinyl trim (same colors); vinyl trim door panels; cigar lighter; Custom plaque on glove compartment; and added cowl insulation. The C10 (and K10 four-wheel drive) Chassis & Cab and Pickups came on 115 or 127 in. wheelbases. Both Fleetside and Step-Side Pickups offered a 6-1/2 ft. box or 8 ft. box. Panels and Suburbans came only on the longer wheelbase. The Suburban again had two-doors on the passenger side and one on the driver's side. Surburbans were available with a tailgate or Panel truck style double rear doors. Both of these single-unit body models had coil springs on all four wheels. Optional seats, in the Suburban, converted the 181 cu. ft. payload space into a passenger compartment. Pickups on the shorter wheelbase had the 6-1/2 ft. cargo box. Two-toning was done using white as the second (upper) color. It was applied to all sheet metal above the beltline. On CSTs, the bodyside, between the upper and lower beltline moldings could also be done in white. For the first time a 402 cid V-8 (advertised as a 396 cid V-8) was available.

1970 Chevrolet 1/2-Ton K-5 Blazer Sport Utility (RCA)

1/2-TON FORWARD-CONTROL — MODEL P/SERIES 10 — SIX/V-8: The 1/2-ton Forward-Control returned again. It had a 102 in. wheelbase. A small Step-Van walk-in delivery truck was approved for this chassis. It was made by Union City Body Co., of Union City, Ind. A channel type front bumper was standard equipment. The Forward-Control chassis and Step-Van were designed for door-to-door delivery service. Body lengths ranged from seven-to-eight feet for this Step-Van 7 series. Features included independent coil spring front suspension; and three six-cylinder engines. Buyers could also get full-height doors; sliding side doors; and double rear doors.

3/4-TON COMMERCIAL — MODEL C; K/SERIES 20 — SIX/V-8: Carryover trucks in the Chevrolet 20 Series 3/4-ton line had the same styling, trim changes and options as other Conventional trucks. The Step-Side Pickup had the 8 ft. box. The "Longhorn" Fleetside pickup had a 133 in. wheelbase and 8-1/2 ft. box. The Chassis & Cowl model and 4x4 Panel were dropped. The Chassis & Cab, two Suburbans and the 4x2 Panel continued in this line. These had the same dimensions as comparable 1/2-ton models, but heavier chassis components. The designation plates had a number 20. Step-Side and Fleetside Pickups were also in this series. They featured the 8 ft. pickup box. The 8 ft. Stake model was dropped this year. The four-wheel drive 3/4-ton models in the 20 Series had a K20 model prefix.

3/4-TON FORWARD-CONTROL — MODEL P/SERIES 20 — SIX/V-8: Just two 3/4-ton Forward-Control chassis remained in the 20 Series (3/4-ton) truck line, but they were the basis for numerous steel, aluminum, and round and square styled bodies, plus a number of engine choices. The Forward-Control chassis and Step-Van were designed for door-to-

door delivery service. Body lengths ranged up to over 12 ft. for the P20 Step-Vans. Features included independent coil spring front suspension; three six-cylinder engines; two optional V-8s, plus a three-cylinder Detroit diesel engine. Buyers could also get full-height doors; sliding side doors and double rear doors. Remaining in the 3/4-ton series were the 125 in. wheelbase chassis recommended for bodies 9-1/2 ft. to 10-1/2 ft. long and the 137 in. wheelbase recommended for bodies 11-1/2 ft. to 12-1/2 ft. long. Bodies were available from factory-authorized suppliers or buyers could order them locally. The coil spring front suspension reflected the fact that the Forward-Control chassis was now starting to find its way into the growing RV market.

1-TON MEDIUM-DUTY COMMERCIAL — MODEL C/SERIES 30 — SIX-CYLINDER: The Chevrolet 30 Series 1-ton trucks had the same styling and trim changes and options as other Conventional trucks. The fenderside nameplates had a number 30. There were four 133 in. wheelbase models: Chassis & Cowl, Chassis & Cab, Longhorn Pickup with 8.5 ft box and a Step-Side Pickup with 9 ft. box. No hubcaps were used on the larger split-rim wheels of the Chassis & Cab models, which had eight bolts and eight circular openings. The Camper Special package continued. Camper models had their own designation plates with a Chevrolet bow tie and "Camper Special" chrome script. The C38 model 1-ton Chassis & Cab with a long 157 in. wheelbase for use as an RV chassis was also offered again. A four-speed manual synchromesh transmission was standard. No four-wheel drive option was offered.

1-TON FORWARD-CONTROL — MODEL P/SERIES 30 — SIX/V-8: Three Forward-Control chassis were in the 30 Series (1-ton) truck line. The Forward-Control chassis and Step-Van were designed for door-to-door delivery service. Body lengths ranged up to 14-1/2 ft. for the 1-ton Step-Van King. Features included independent coil spring front suspension; two optional V-8s; three six-cylinder engines; two optional V-8s, plus a three-cylinder Detroit diesel engine. Buyers could also get full-height doors; sliding side doors and double rear doors. Offered were wheelbases of 125 in., 133 in., and 157 in. respectively. The 125 in. wheelbase chassis was recommended for bodies 9-1/2 ft. to 10-1/2 ft. long. The 137 in. wheelbase was recommended for bodies 11-1/2 to ft. 12-1/2 ft. long. The 157 in. wheelbase was used for the large aluminum body Step-Van King model, as well as for RV construction. Bodies were available from factory-authorized suppliers or buyers could order them locally. A channel type front bumper and High-Torque 230 six were standard equipment.

1970 Chevrolet 3/4-Ton K20 Fleetside Pickup 4x4 (RCA)

I.D. DATA: Serial Number located: [Chassis models] On plate temporarily attached near steering column, with final location per body maker; [All others] On plate attached to rear face of left-hand door hinge pillar; on right side of cowl under hood. [El Camino]: The first symbol indicated manufacturer: 1=Chevrolet. The second and third symbols indicated series: 33=six/34=V-8/35=Custom six/36=Custom V-8. The fourth and fifth symbols indicated body type: 80=Sedan-Pickup. The sixth symbol indicate model year: 0=1970. The seventh symbol indicated assembly plant: A=Atlanta (Lakewood); B=Baltimore, Md.; F=Flint, Mich.; K=Kansas City, Mo. (Leeds); L=Los Angeles (Van Nuys), Calif.; R=Arlington, Texas. The remaining symbols were the sequential production number starting with 100001 at each plant. Ending serial numbers not available. The Chevrolet engine had the source, date and type stamped on a serial number pad. Various source codes were used. Month codes were 1=Jan.; 2=Feb., etc. Date codes were 01=first of month, etc. The were numerous prefix codes to indicate engines and transmission attachments. The collectible 396 cid V-8s had the following codes: [350 hp] CTW/CTX/CTZ; [375 hp] CTY; CKN/CKO/CKP/CKQ/CKT/CKU. The collectible 454 cid V-8s had the following prefixes: [360 hp] CRN/CGT/CRQ/CRM/CRT/CGU/CRU; [450 hp] CRR/CRS/CRY/CRV/CRW/CRX. [Other models] The first symbol indicated indicated truck type: C=Conventional Cab; K=4x4; G=Chevy Van; P=Forward-Control. The second symbol indicated type of engine: S=six; E=eight; T=diesel. The third symbol indicated the GVW range: [GVW] 1=3,600-5,600 lbs.; 2=5,500-8,100 lbs.; 3=6,700-10,000 lbs.; 4=Over 10,000 lbs. The fourth and fifth symbols indicated the cab-to-axle dimension: 05=30-35 in.; 07=42 to 47 in.; 09=54-59 in.; 10=60-65 in.; 14=84-89 in. The sixth symbol indicated body type: 02=Chassis & Cowl; 03=Chassis & Cab; 04=Step-Side Pickup; 05=Panel or Panel Van; 06=Suburban (doors) or Sportvan; 14=Blazer; 16=Suburban (gate); 26=Custom Sportvan; 34=Fleetside; 36=Deluxe Sportvan; 35=Forward-Control. The eighth symbol indicates model year: 0=1970. The ninth symbol indicates assembly plant: A=Atlanta, Ga.; B=Baltimore, Md.; F=Flint, Mich.; J=Janesville, Wis.; P=Pontiac, Mich.; S=St. Louis, Mo.; T=Tarrytown, N.Y.; Z=Fremont, Calif. 1=Oshawa, Canada.

Model	Body Type	Price	Weight	Prod. Total
El Camino — Model A/Series 13000 — 116 in. w.b. — Six				
13380	Pickup	2676	3302	Note 1
13580	Custom Pickup	2760	3324	Note 1
El Camino — Model A/Series 13000 — 116 in. w.b. — V-8				
13480	Pickup	2770	3418	Note 1
13680	Custom Pickup	2850	3442	Note 1

NOTE 1: Total El Camino production was 47,707.

1/2-Ton Chevy Van — Model G/Series 100 — 90 in. w.b.				
GS11005	Panel	2490	3059	3,933
GS11006	Sportvan	2725	3255	134
GS11026	Custom Sportvan	2850	3362	57
GS11036	Deluxe Sportvan	3035	3400	42
1/2-Ton Chevy Van — Model G/Series 100 — 108 in. w.b.				
GS11005	Panel	2675	3210	3,069
GS11006	Sportvan	2850	3350	422
GS11026	Custom Sportvan	2975	3480	303
GS11036	Deluxe Sportvan	3160	3425	158

3/4-Ton Chevy Van — Model G/Series 20 — 108 in. w.b.				
GS21305	Panel	2745	3281	1,195
GS21306	Sportvan	2970	3414	134
GS21326	Custom Sportvan	3095	3538	61
GS21336	Deluxe Sportvan	3280	3582	45

NOTE 2: Van production was low due to a strike and model changeover.

1/2-Ton Blazer 4x2 — Model C/Series 5 — 104 in. w.b.				
CS10514	Open Utility	2385	3375	Note 2
CE10514	Open Utility	2852	2947	Note 2

NOTE 3: 4x2 Blazer production: 985 includes CS (six) and CE (V-8) models.

1/2-Ton Blazer 4x4 — Model K/Series 5 — 104 in. w.b.				
KS10514	Open Utility	2955	3677	Note 3
KE10514	Open Utility	3050	3807	Note 3

NOTE 4: 4x4 Blazer production: 11,527 includes KS (six) and KE (V-8) models.

1/2-Ton Commercial — Model C/Series 10 — 115 in. w.b.				
CS10703	Chassis & Cab	2405	3090	2,084
CS10734	Fleetside 6.5 ft.	2560	3506	40,754
CS10704	Step-Side 6.5 ft.	2520	3426	40,754
1/2-Ton Commercial — Model C/Series 10 — 127 in. w.b.				
CS10903	Chassis & Cab	2445	3107	7,277
CS10934	Fleetside 8 ft.	2595	3605	234,904
CS10904	Step-Side 8 ft.	2560	3510	11,857
CS10905	Panel	3040	3730	3,965
CS10906	Suburban (doors)	3250	3862	11,332
1/2-Ton Commercial 4x4 — Model K/Series 10 — 115 in. w.b.				
KS10703	Chassis & Cab	2975	3295	64
KS10734	Fleetside 6.5 ft.	3158	3711	2,554
KS10704	Step-Side 6.5 ft.	3090	3631	1,629
1/2-Ton Commercial 4x4 — Model K/Series 10 — 127 in. w.b.				
KS10903	Chassis & Cab	—	—	26
KS10934	Fleetside 8 ft.	3165	3810	7,348
KS10904	Step-Side 8 ft.	3158	3715	464
KS10905	Panel	3641	3923	—
KS10906	Suburban	3849	4055	—
1/2-Ton Forward-Control — Model P/Series 10 — 102 in. w.b.				
PS10535	Chassis	1835	2120	211
PS10535	Step-Van	3139	3674	2,526
3/4-Ton Commercial — Model C/Series 20 — 127 in. w.b.				
CS20903	Chassis & Cab	2650	3496	7,277
CS20934	Fleetside 8 ft.	2790	3871	70,880
CS20904	Step-Side 8 ft.	2752	3776	5,856
CS20905	Panel	3269	3991	1,032
CS20906	Suburban	3441	4113	2,246
Long Horn Pickup — Model C/Series 20 — 133 in. w.b.				
CE21034	Pickup 8.5 ft.	2854	3912	5,281
3/4-Ton Commercial 4x4 — Model K/Series 20 — 127 in. w.b.				
KS20903	Chassis & Cab	3402	3606	582
KS20934	Fleetside 8 ft.	3540	4101	6,124
KS20904	Step-Side 8 ft.	3502	4006	953
KS20902	Panel	4019	4221	—
KS20906	Suburban	4190	4343	541
3/4-Ton Forward-Control — Model P/Series 20 — 125 in. w.b.				
PS20842	Chassis	2160	2819	421
PS20835	Step-Van	3905	5206	1,520
PS20855	Alumnium Step-Van	—	—	60
3/4-Ton Forward-Control — Model P/Series 20 — 133 in. w.b.				
PS21842	Chassis	2195	2841	184
PS21835	Step-Van	4015	5437	872
PS21835	Aluminum Step-Van	4985	4638	64
1-Ton Commercial — Model C/Series 30 — 133 in. w.b.				
CS31002	Chassis & Cowl	—	—	138
CS31003	Chassis & Cab	2735	3641	14,873
CS31034	Fleetside 8.5 ft.	2935	4157	1,404
CS31004	Step-Side 9 ft.	2875	4071	2,101
1-Ton Commercial — Model C/Series 30 — 157 in. w.b.				
CS31103	Chassis & Cab	2775	3788	—
1-Ton Forward-Control — Model P/Series 30 — 125 in. w.b.				
PS30842	Chassis	2320	2992	446
PS30835	Step-Van	4080	5379	1,520
(Diesel)				
PT30835	Step-Van King	5780	6101	3
PT30855	Step-Van King Aluminum	6570	5439	35
1-Ton Forward-Control — Model P/Series 30 — 133 in. w.b.				
PS31042	Chassis	2350	3015	1,758
PS31035	Step-Van	4190	5611	1,624
PS31035	Step-Van King	5895	6338	—
PS31055	Step-Van King Aluminum	6860	5537	68
1-Ton Forward-Control — Model P/Series 30 — 157 in. w.b.				
PS31442	Chassis	2350	—	2,608
PS31435	Step-Van King	6040	6677	1,207
PS31455	Step-Van King Aluminum	7170	5714	76

NOTE 5: All prices/weights above are for sixes (except El Camino/Blazer V-8s).
NOTE 6: Total production of diesel-powered Forward-Control models was 37or 38.
NOTE 7: Production totals from Chevrolet records are for model-year through Aug. 31, 1970 and include all trucks made in U.S. factories for domestic/export/Canadian markets. Models with no production indicated due to incomplete records.

88

ENGINE [Standard all models]: Inline. OHV. Six-cylinder. Cast iron block. Bore & stroke: 3.875 in. x 3.53 in. Displacement: 250 cid. Compression ratio: 8.5:1. Brake horsepower: 155 at 4200 rpm. Seven main bearings. Hydraulic valve lifters. Carburetor: Rochester one-barrel model M: 7028007/7028011.

ENGINE [Optional P20/C10/C20/C30/K10/K20]: Inline. OHV. Six-cylinder. Cast iron block. Bore & stroke: 3.875 in. x 4.12 in. Displacement: 292 cid. Compression ratio: 8.1:1. Brake horsepower: 170 at 4000 rpm. Maximum Torque: 275 lbs.-ft. at 1600 rpm. Seven main bearings. Hydraulic valve lifters. Carburetor: Rochester one-barrel model M: 7028012/7028013.

ENGINE [Optional El Camino/K10/G10/G20/P10/P20/C10/C20/C30/K20]: V-type. OHV. Eight-cylinder. Cast iron block. Bore & stroke: 3.875 in. x 3-1/4 in. Displacement: 307 cid. Compression ratio: 9.0:1. Brake horsepower: 200 at 4800 rpm. Five main bearings. Hydraulic valve lifters. Carburetor: Rochester two-barrel.

1970 Chevrolet CST/20 Fleetside Pickup (CW)

ENGINE [Optional El Camino]: V-type. OHV. Eight-cylinder. Cast iron block. Bore & stroke: 4 in. x 3.48 in. Displacement: 350 cid. Compression ratio: 9.0:1. Brake horsepower: 250 at 4600 rpm. Five main bearings. Hydraulic valve lifters. Carburetor: Rochester two-barrel.

ENGINE [Optional C10/K10/C20/K20/C30/G10/G20/G30/P20/P30]: V-type. OHV. Eight-cylinder. Cast iron block. Bore & stroke: 4 in. x 3.48 in. Compression ratio: 9.0:1. Brake horsepower: 255 at 4800 rpm. Maximum Torque: 365 lbs.-ft. at 3200 rpm. Five main bearings. Hydraulic valve lifters. Carburetor: Rochester four-barrel.

ENGINE [Optional El Camino]: V-type. OHV. Eight-cylinder. Cast iron block. Bore & stroke: 4 in. x 3.48 in. Displacement: 350 cid. Compression ratio: 10.25:1. Brake horsepower: 300. Five main bearings. Hydraulic valve lifters. Carburetor: Rochester four-barrel.

ENGINE [Optional El Camino]: V-type. OHV. Eight-cylinder. Cast iron block. Bore & stroke: 4.126 in. x 3.76 in. Displacement: 400 cid. Compression ratio: 9.0:1. Brake horsepower: 250. Five main bearings. Hydraulic valve lifters. Carburetor: Two-barrel.

ENGINE [Optional C5/K5/C10/C20/C30]: V-type. OHV. Eight-cylinder. Cast iron block. Bore & stroke: 4.126 in. x 3.76 in. Displacement: 400 cid. Compression ratio: 9.0:1. Brake horsepower: 310. Five main bearings. Hydraulic valve lifters. Carburetor: Four-barrel.

ENGINE [Optional El Camino]: V-type. OHV. Eight-cylinder. Cast iron block. Bore & stroke: 4.126 in. x 3.76 in. Displacement: 400 cid. Compression ratio: 10.25:1. Brake horsepower: 330. Five main bearings. Hydraulic valve lifters. Carburetor: Two-barrel.

ENGINE [Standard El Camino SS-396]: V-type. OHV. Eight-cylinder. Cast iron block. Bore & stroke: 4.09 in. x 3.76 in. Displacement: 396 cid. Compression ratio: 10.25:1. Brake horsepower: 350 at 5200 rpm. Maximum Torque: 445 lbs.-ft. at 3400 rpm. Five main bearings. Hydraulic valve lifters. Carburetor: Rochester four-barrel model Quadra-Jet.

ENGINE [Optional: El Camino With SS-396]: V-type. OHV. Eight-cylinder. Cast iron block. Bore & stroke: 4.094 in. x 3.76 in. Displacement: 396 cid. Compression ratio: 11.25:1. Brake horsepower: 375. Five main bearings. Carburetor: four-barrel.

ENGINE [Optional El Camino]: V-type. OHV. Eight-cylinder. Cast iron block. Bore & stroke: 4.251 in. x 4.0 in. Displacement: 454 cid. Compression ratio: 10.25:1. Brake horsepower: 360 at 4400 rpm. Maximum Torque: 500 lbs.-ft. at 3200 rpm. Five main bearings. Hydraulic valve lifters. Carburetor: Rochester four-barrel model Quadra-Jet.

ENGINE [Optional El Camino]: V-type. OHV. Eight-cylinder. Cast iron block. Bore & stroke: 4.251 in. x 4.0 in. Displacement: 454 cid. Compression ratio: 11.0:1. Brake horsepower: 450. Five main bearings. Carburetor: Rochester four-barrel model Quadra-Jet.

CHASSIS [Series K10 Blazer]: Wheelbase: 104 in. Overall length: 177.5 in. Height: 68.7 in. Front tread: 60.4 in. Rear tread: 60.4 in. Tires: E78-15B. GVW: 4,600-5,000 lbs.

CHASSIS [El Camino]: Wheelbase: 116 in. Overall length: 206.8 in. Height: 54.4 in. Front tread: 60.2 in. Rear tread: 59.2 in. Tires: F78-14. GVW: 4,100 lbs.

CHASSIS [G10]: Wheelbase: 90 in. Tires: 6.95 x 14 in. GVW: 3,900-5,000 lbs.

CHASSIS [Series G20]: Wheelbase: 108 in. Tires: 7.75 x 15. GVW: 5,200-6,200 lbs.

CHASSIS [C10/K10]: Wheelbase: 115 in. Overall length: 186.75 in. Height: 74.5 in. Front tread: 63.1 in. Rear tread: 61.1 in. Tires: [4x2] G78-14; [4x4] G78-15. GVW: [4x2] 4,400-5,400 lbs.; [4x4] 5,200-5,600 lbs.

CHASSIS [C10/K10]: Wheelbase: 127 in. Overall length: 206.25 in. Height: 71 in. Front tread: 63.1 in. Rear tread: 61.1 in. Tires: [4x2] H78-15; [4x4] G78-15. GVW: [4x2] 4,400-5,400 lbs.; [4x4] 5,200-5,600 lbs.

CHASSIS [P10]: Wheelbase: 102 in. Tires: G78-15. GVW: 4,600-5,400 lbs.

CHASSIS [C20/K20]: Wheelbase: 127 in. Overall length: 206.25 in. Tires: [4x2] 7 x 17.5 in.; [4x4] 7 x 17.5 six-ply. GVW: [4x2] 6,200-7,500 lbs.; [4x4] 6,400-7,500 lbs. (Longhorn Pickup has 133 in. wheelbase.)

CHASSIS [P20]: Wheelbases: 125 in.; 137 in. Base tires: 8.75 x 16.5. GVW: 6,500-7,500 lbs.

1970 Chevrolet Step-Side Pickup (DFW)

CHASSIS [C30]: Wheelbase: 133 in. Tires: 8.75 x 16.5 in. GVW: 6,600-14,000 lbs. (Chassis & Cab available with 157 in. wheelbase.)

CHASSIS [P30]: Wheelbases: 125 in.; 133 in.; 157 in. Base tires: 8.75 x 16.5. GVW: 7,300-14,000 lbs.

TECHNICAL: Chevrolet manual transmission standard. Type of transmission: [C30] 4F/1R; [Others] 3F/1R (Borg-Warner heavy-duty three-speed optional). Column-mounted gearshift lever standard. Clutch: Single-plate, dry-disc type. Rear axle: [1/2-ton] semi-floating; [3/4-ton/1-ton] full-floating. Base rear axle: [El Camino] 3.08:1; [C10/K10] 3.73:1; [C20] 4.10:1; [K20] 4.57:1; [C30] 5.14:1. Brakes: Four-wheel hydraulic, front disc/rear drum. Kelsey-Hayes pressed steel wheels.

OPTIONS: [C5/K5/C10/K10/C20/K20]: 292 six-cylinder engine ($95). 307 V-8 engine ($120). 307 V-8 engine ($120). 350 V-8 engine, for El Camino ($70). Four-speed manual transmission ($190). Powerglide transmission (average $195). Turbo-Hydramatic transmission ($280). Power brakes ($50). Power steering (average $115). Four-wheel drive system ($570). (3/4-Ton): 292 six-cilinder engine ($95). 307 V-8 engine ($95). 400 V-8 engine ($160). Powerglide transmission (average $190). Turbo-Hydramatic transmission (average $230). Power steering (average $130). Four-speed manual transmission (average $100). Four-wheel drive system ($705).

OPTIONS: [C30] 307 V-8 engine ($100). 292 six-cylinder engine ($95). 350 V-8 engine ($40). 400 V-8 engine ($160). LPG kit ($80). Turbo-Hydramatic transmission ($230). New Process transmission ($30). Nine-foot platform ($310). 12-foot platform ($370). 157 in. wheelbase ($40).

1970 Chevrolet Custom 10 Fleetside Pickup

OPTIONS AND INSTALLATION RATES: Rear seat (57 percent). Front center seat belt (1 percent). Tinted glass (28 percent). Bodyside belt molding (14 percent). Wide lower bodyside molding (46 percent). Door edge guards (12 percent). Air-conditioning (16 percent). Roof-mounted air-conditioning (15 percent). Painted camper mirror (1 percent). Stainless camper mirror (2 percent). Jr. West Coast mirror, stainless (10 percent). Dual Sr. West Coast mirrors (3 percent). Jr. painted West Coast mirror (21 percent). Body paint stripe (5 percent). Heavy-duty shocks (14 percent). Front stabilizer (28 percent). Heavy-duty front springs (24 percent). 4x4 front locking hubs (79 percent). Heavy rear springs (65 percent). Auxiliary springs (20 percent). Leaf spring suspension (20 percent). Positraction (10 percent). No-Spin rear axle (6 percent). Optional rear axles (11 percent). Hydraulic brake booster (23 percent). Oil bath air cleaner (5 percent). Engine block heater (3 percent). Manual throttle (3 percent). 292 cid six-cylinder engine (15 percent). 396 cid four-barrel V-8 (5 percent). Heavy-duty clutch (21 percent). Four-speed manual transmission (17 percent). Heavy-duty close-ratio four-speed manual transmission (2 percent). Powerglide transmission (38 percent). Three-speed manual transmission (4 percent). 4x4 auxiliary fuel tank (1 percent). Hydraulic power steering (33 percent). G78x15 whitewall tires (38 percent). H78x15B whitewall tires (3 percent). Wheel trim covers (25 percent). Chrome hubcaps (11 percent). Tachometer (1 percent). Push-button radio (48 percent). Tu-tone paint (30 percent). Special two-tone paint (15 percent). Custom Sport Truck option (10 percent). Special camper equipment (4 percent). Custom Comfort and Convenience option (24 percent). Chrome rear bumper (4 percent). Chrome bumper (6 percent). Painted rear bumper (11 percent). Rear step bumper (17 percent). Chrome front bumper (20 percent).

NOTE: Option use rates based on Chevrolet records for model year through Dec. 31, 1970. Figures show percentage of option usage on truck qualified for the option. For example, Step-Van dual rear wheel option was used on 71 percent of all Step-Vans offering this equipment, not 71 percent of total Chevrolet production.

 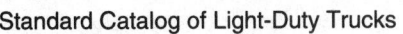

1970 Chevrolet CST/10 Fleetside Pickup (OCW)

OPTION PACKAGE: [Custom]: An optional Custom Comfort & Appearance package included bright metal windshield moldings, rear window trim and ventipane frames; Custom (CS) nameplates on front fenders; color-keyed vinyl-coated rubber floor mats; full-depth foam seat with color-keyed fabric and vinyl trim; vinyl trim door panels with bright upper retainers; a cigar lighter; Chevrolet Custom nameplate on dispatch box door; bright metal control knob inserts; cowl insulation; and full-depth armrests.

OPTION PACKAGE: [Custom Sport Truck] The top trim level was the Custom Sport Truck option. It included most equipment in the CS package, plus a chrome front bumper; full-width vinyl seats; bright pedal frames; bright roof drip moldings; extra insulation; matching carpets; and CST nameplates for the front fenders. Bucket seats with a center console were available on CST models.

1970 Chevrolet El Camino "SS" Sport Pickup (OCW)

HISTORICAL: Model year production [All Chevrolet Commercial]: 492,607. Model year production, Commercial light-duty, by tonnage and engine type: [1/2-ton] (six) 115,286; (V-8) 259,348; [Total] 374,634. [3/4-Ton]: (six) 18,644; (V-8) 88,893; [Total] 107,537. [1-Ton] (six) 10,350; (V-8) 25,552; [Total] 35,902. [Grand Total] 518,073. [RPO Production] (Custom Sport Truck) 49,717; (Custom/10) 126,848; (Camper Special) 20,900.

1971 CHEVROLET

1971 Chevrolet Cheyenne Fleetside Pickup (JLC)

1/2-TON VEGA PANEL — MODEL HV/SERIES 14000 — FOUR: New for 1971 was a Panel Express version of the sub-compact Vega. It was based on the Kammback wagon, with the rear side windows blanked-out. Chevy described it as, "the kinky way to haul around your surfboard." It came only with the standard all-vinyl interior, less passenger bucket seat, and only with black or green upholstery. The Custom interior option was not available. Standard equipment included the four-cylinder aluminum block engine, three-speed manual transmission, front disc brakes, two separate stowage compartments below the floor, many safety features and a choice of 10 colors. It had a 67.4 in. floor length, 42.6 in. between the wheelhousings and a 68.7 cu. ft. cargo volume. Payload capacity was 650 lbs.

1/2-TON EL CAMINO — MODEL AC; AD/SERIES 13000 — SIX/V-8: The El Camino models had a new look due to the use of single-unit Power Beam headlamps in square bezels. The grille had a "ice cube tray" insert and Chevrolet bow tie in its center. The front parking lamps were double-deck rectangles that angled around the body corners to double as sidemarker lights. El Camino nameplates and designation badges were mounted on the front fendersides, behind the wheel opening. The rear end appearance had hardly any changes. For the first time, the front bumper had no air slots or parking lamps in it. Standard models had bright windshield frames, backup lights on the tailgate, and a base six-cylinder engine. Customs added a V-8 as base engine; bodyside moldings; wheelhouse moldings; pickup box rim moldings; rear body corner moldings; two moldings on the tailgate; and silver anodized lower body perimeter. Super Sport equipment (RPO Z15) was available with all Custom models with V-8s other than the base 307 cid V-8. You could get an SS-350, SS-396 (actually a 402 cid engine), or SS-454. It cost $365 extra. The performance and appearance package included a black-accented grille with SS emblems; SS badges behind the front wheel cutouts; sport suspension; front power disc brakes; domed hood with lock pins; and 15 x 7 sport wheels with F60-15 raised white-letter tires. By the end of the year, the 454 cid V-8 replaced the 396 completely. A plain cloth and vinyl interior was standard. The colors were black, Dark blue, Dark Jade green and sandlewood. The Custom interior had vinyl seats with ribbed insert panels, color-keyed carpeting and imitation woodgrain trim. It came in black, Light sandalwood, Antique saddle knit vinyl, Dark saddle, Dark blue or Antique Dark jade. Exterior colors were Antique white; Nevada silver; Tuxedo black; Ascot blue; Mulsanne blue; Cottonwood green; Lime green; Antique green; Sunflower; Placer gold; sandalwood; Burnt orange; Classic copper; Cranberry red; and rosewood. The flying buttress roofline was retained for all El Caminos. The pickup box, used through 1972, had an outside width of 75-1/2 in. Inside width behind the cab was 59 in. Inside width near the tailgate was 64-1/2 in. The width between the wheelhousings was 44 in. The bottom bed length measured 79-1/4 in. Tailgate measurements were 54-1/2 x 22-1/2 in.

1/2-TON CHEVY VAN/SPORTVAN — MODEL G/SERIES 10 — SIX/V-8: The Chevrolet van models were attractively restyled. They had new 110/125 in. wheelbases, plus an extended front hood that made 26 service areas readily accessible. Van grilles consisted of seven horizontal bars with a center-mounted Chevrolet emblem. The Sportvan Deluxe became the Beauville. This fancy new model offered travel space for 12 and had a 307 cid V-8 as standard equipment. Other innovations included independent front suspension and a sliding door option. A Custom Appearance package was available, as well as Custom & Convenience interior equipment.

3/4-TON CHEVY VAN/SPORTVAN — MODEL G/SERIES 20 — SIX/V-8: The 108 in. wheelbase driver-forward vans also came as 3/4-ton G20 models. Styling characteristics were the same as G10s. Models included the Panel with double cargo doors available on the passenger side and at the rear. There were also window models in two levels of trim: base Sportvan or Beauville. The G20 line offered the same engines as G10s and a V-8 was standard in the Beauville model.

1-TON CHEVY VAN/SPORTVAN — MODEL G/SERIES 30 — SIX/V-8: For the first time ever, buyers could order a G30 (1-ton) van. Styling characteristics were the same as G10s and G20s. Models included the Panel with double cargo doors available on the passenger side and at the rear. There were also window models in two levels of trim: base Sportvan or Beauville. Officially, the G30 Sportvan and Beauville were available only on the longer 125 in. wheelbase, which was different than in the other series. However, Chevrolet production records show that nine Sportvans and eight Beauvilles were built on the 110 in. wheelbase.

1/2-TON BLAZER — MODEL C; K/SERIES 5 — SIX/V-8: Chevy's Blazer had a new, egg-crate grille. Some sources say that the 4x2 version was introduced this year, although factory records show nearly 1,000 of these were made in model year 1970. This year its production creeped up slightly to just under 1,300 units. The 4x4 version was more than 10 times as popular. The Blazer's suspension system consisted of single-leaf tapered front springs with a combination of multi-leaf and tapered springs at the rear. The ball-type steering unit had a 24:1 ratio and its standard engine was Chevrolet's 155 hp six. The single-unit body was joined to a heavy channel steel frame. The rear-mounted 23.5-gal. fuel tank was located inside the frame. Numerous options were offered for the Blazer including four-speed manual and automatic transmissions, V-8 engines, power steering, power brakes and a completely removable fiberglass top. Colors, exterior trims, upholstery and equipment were very similar or the same as used on the conventional C10/K10 models.

1/2-TON COMMERCIAL — MODEL C; K/SERIES 10 — SIX/V-8: Pickups, Panels and Suburbans featured a new egg-crate grille. It had five horizontal blades and 15 vertical members. A painted black stripe appeared around the outer edge of the grille. The Chevrolet bow tie moved from the hood to the grille center. The parking/directional lights were moved from their previous location in the grille to positions within the front bumper. Inside was a low-profile steering wheel, full-width bench seat and foot-operated parking brake. Standard equipment on all pickups included: six-cylinder engine; side terminal battery; self-adjusting four-wheel brakes (front discs); dual brake master cylinder with warning lights; backup lights; directional signals and four-way flashers; Panoramic rear window; left- and right-hand outside rearview mirrors; non-glare inside mirror; heater and defroster; padded dash; non-glare front instrument panel finish; padded sun visors; ashtray; seat belts with retractors; push-button seat belt buckles; low-profile control knobs; two-speed electric washer/wipers; windshield defrosters; safety glass; flexible fuel filler neck; deep-dish steering wheel with telescoping shaft; thick laminate safety glass windshield; right-hand coat hook; front and rear side markers; and painted front bumper. Chrome front and rear bumpers were a separate option. There were new names for different trim levels. The standard C10 became the Custom. It had no side trim; plain black rubber window gaskets; and white-painted bumpers. The grille shell had bright metal finish. The hubcaps were also painted. The vent window pillars and frames were flat black. The standard hubcaps were painted. Rear moldings around the taillamps and tailgate were not available on Customs. Upper and lower belt moldings were optional. Customs equipped with the lower belt molding, should have the center of the molding painted black. A new Custom Deluxe trim level became what the Custom/10 had been. Custom Deluxe equipment included a full-width bench seat with comfortably padded seat cushions and backrest; vinyl seat upholstery and door panels; steel roof panel painted in main exterior color; black rubber floor mat extending to firewall; padded armrests; padded sunshades; courtesy lamp; prismatic rearview mirror; foam-padded instrument panel; bright upper and lower grille outline moldings; bright headlamp bezels; bright outside rearview mirrors; bright door handles; white-painted front bumper, hubcaps and wheels; and bright Custom Deluxe nameplates. Upper and lower belt moldings were both optional. Unlike 1970, when the lower molding was black-accented, the center of the 1971 lower molding had a woodgrain insert. When equipped with lower bodyside moldings, the Custom Deluxe also got taillamp and two tailgate moldings. These moldings were positioned above and below the Chevrolet lettering on the back. Chrome hubcaps were optional on Custom Deluxe models. A new Cheyenne trim level was

comparable to the previous Custom Sport Truck option. The Cheyenne package included a bench seat with full-depth foam cushions and backrests; Custom-grained vinyl upholstery or nylon and vinyl upholstery; special door trim panels; cab headliner; deep-twist nylon carpeting extending to firewall; color-keyed garnish moldings; ashtray-mounted cigar lighter; Custom steering wheel; Cheyenne dashboard nameplates; door or manually-operated courtesy lights; extra accoustical insulation; and all Custom Deluxe exterior items, plus cab-mounted cargo lamp; bright metal cab trim and moldings; bright upper bodyside and tailgate moldings; and central taillight appliques for Fleetside and Cheyenne nameplates. When equipped with a lower bodyside molding, the Cheyenne also got woodgrained molding inserts. Bucket seats were optional for Cheyennes with the vinyl interior. A Cheyenne Super option package was introduced at midyear in 1971. This model took up where the Cheyenne left off, adding both upper and lower (woodgrained) bodyside moldings and a chrome-plated tailgate release. There were Custom Appearance; and Custom Comfort & Convenience options, too. Exterior colors were black; Dark blue; Medium blue; Medium bronze; Dark green; Medium green; yellow; Ochre; Dark olive; Medium olive; Red orange; orange; white; Dark yellow; and yellow. The standard interior interior featured a three-passenger bench seat; foam padding; dome light; rubber floor mat; two door armrests; and all-vinyl trim in green, blue, black or parchment. The Custom and Cheyenne interiors came black, blue, parchment or olive patterned cloth and vinyl. The C10 (and K10 four-wheel drive) Chassis & Cab and Pickups came on 115 or 127 in. wheelbases. Both Fleetside and Step-Side Pickups offered a 6-1/2 ft. box or 8 ft. box. Pickups on the shorter wheelbase had the 6-1/2 ft. cargo box. The Panel was discontinued. Suburbans came only on the longer wheelbase. The Suburban again had two-doors on the passenger side and one on the driver's side. Surburbans were available with tailgates or double rear doors. They had a floor space that was 9 ft. long. With second and third seats removed, cargo space totaled 190 cu. ft. Four-wheel drive was available for a price of just over $500. Both of these single-unit body models had coil springs on all four wheels. Two-toning was done using white as the second (upper) color. It was applied to all sheet metal above the beltline. On Cheyennes, the bodyside, between the upper and lower beltline moldings was usually done in white.

1971 Chevrolet 1/2-Ton C10 Fleetside Pickup (OCW)

1/2-TON FORWARD-CONTROL — MODEL P/SERIES 10 — SIX/V-8: The 1/2-ton Forward-Control returned again. It had a 102 in. wheelbase. A small Step-Van walk-in delivery truck was approved for this chassis. It was made by Union City Body Co., of Union City, Ind. A channel type front bumper was standard equipment. The Forward-Control chassis and Step-Van were designed for door-to-door delivery service. Body lengths ranged from seven-to-eight feet for this Step-Van 7 series. Features included independent coil spring front suspension; and three six-cylinder engines. Buyers could also get full-height doors; sliding side doors and double rear doors.

3/4-TON COMMERCIAL — MODEL C; K/SERIES 20 — SIX/V-8: Carryover trucks in the Chevrolet 20 Series 3/4-ton line had the same styling, trim changes and options as other Conventional trucks. Fleetside and Step-Side Pickups had an 8 ft. box. Also available was the "Longhorn" Fleetside with a 133 in. wheelbase and 8-1/2 ft. box. The Chassis & Cab and two Suburbans continued in this line. These had the same dimensions as comparable 1/2-ton models, but heavier chassis components. The designation plates had a number 20. The 8 ft. Stake model was available as an extra on the platform option for the Chassis & Cab. It cost about $400 for the platform option. The four-wheel drive 3/4-ton models in the 20 Series had a K20 model prefix. Longhorns were not built with four-wheel drive.

3/4-TON FORWARD-CONTROL — MODEL P/SERIES 20 — SIX/V-8: Just two 3/4-ton Forward-Control chassis remained in the 20 Series (3/4-ton) truck line, but they were the basis for numerous steel and aluminum body models. A number of powerplants could be had, including three six-cylinder engines; two optional V-8s, plus a three-cylinder Detroit diesel. The Forward-Control chassis and Step-Van were designed for door-to-door delivery service. Body lengths ranged up to over 12 ft. for the P20 Step-Vans. Features included independent coil spring front suspension. Buyers could also get full height doors; sliding side doors and double rear doors. Remaining in the 3/4-ton series were the 125 in. wheelbase chassis recommended for bodies 9-1/2 to 10-1/2 ft. long and the 137 in. wheelbase recommended for bodies 11-1/2 to 12-1/2 ft. long. Bodies were available from factory-authorized suppliers or buyers could order them locally. The coil spring front suspension reflected the fact that the Forward-Control chassis was now starting to find its way into the growing RV market.

1-TON MEDIUM-DUTY COMMERCIAL — MODEL C/SERIES 30 — SIX-CYLINDER: The Chevrolet 30 Series 1-ton trucks had the same styling and trim changes and options as other Conventional trucks. The fenderside nameplates had a number 30. There were four 133 in. wheelbase models: Chassis & Cowl, Chassis & Cab, Longhorn Pickup with 8.5 ft box and a Step-Side Pickup with a 9 ft. box. No hubcaps were used on the larger split-rim wheels of the Chassis & Cab models, which had eight bolts and eight circular openings. The Camper Special package continued. The C38 model 1-ton Chassis & Cab with a long 157 in. wheelbase for use as an RV chassis was also offered again. Nearly 12,000 of these were sold. A four-speed manual synchromesh transmission was standard. No four-wheel drive option was offered.

1-TON FORWARD-CONTROL — MODEL P/SERIES 30 — SIX/V-8: Three Forward-Control chassis were in the 30 Series (1-ton) truck line. The Forward-Control chassis and Step-Van were designed for door-to-door delivery service. Body lengths ranged up to 14-1/2 ft. for the 1-ton Step-Van King. Features included independent coil spring front suspension; three six-cylinder engines; two optional V-8s, plus a three-cylinder Detroit diesel engine. Buyers could also get full-height doors; sliding side doors and double rear doors. Offered for P30 buyers were wheelbases of 125 in., 133 in., and 157 in. respectively. The 125 in. wheelbase chassis was recommended for bodies 9-1/2 to 10-1/2 ft. long. The 137 in. wheelbase was recommended for Step-Van King bodies 11-1/2 to 12-1/2 ft. long. The 157 in. was also used for the large aluminum body Step-Van King models, as well as for RV construction. Bodies were available from factory-authorized suppliers or buyers could order them locally. A channel type front bumper and High-Torque 230 six were standard equipment. Chevrolet also began producing special P30 1-ton motorhome chassis on 137 in. and 157 in. wheelbases. Almost 1,600 were constructed in 1971.

I.D. DATA: Serial Number located: [Chassis models] On plate temporarily attached near steering column, with final location per body maker; [All others] On plate attached to rear face of left-hand door hinge pillar; on right side of cowl under hood. [El Camino]: The first symbol indicated manufacturer: 1=Chevrolet. The second and third symbols indicated series: 33=six/34=V-8/36=Custom V-8. The fourth and fifth symbols indicated body type: 80=Sedan-Pickup. The sixth symbol indicate model year: 1=1971. The seventh symbol indicated assembly plant: B=Baltimore, Md.; K=Kansas City, Mo. (Leeds); L=Los Angeles (Van Nuys), Calif.; R=Arlington, Texas. The remaining symbols were the sequential production number starting with 100001 at each plant. Ending serial numbers not available. The Chevrolet engine had the source, date and type stamped on a serial number pad. Various source codes were used. Month codes were 1=Jan.; 2=Feb., etc. Date codes were 01=first of month, etc. The were numerous prefix codes to indicate engines and transmission attachments. The collectible 396 (402) cid V-8s had the following codes: [300 hp] CLP/CLB/CLL/CLR/CLS. The collectible 454 cid V-8s had the following prefixes: [365 hp] CPA/CPG/CPD; [425 hp] CPP/CPR/CPZ. [Other models] The first symbol indicated indicated truck type: C=Conventional Cab; K=4x4; G=Chevy Van; P=Forward-Control. The second symbol indicated type of engine: S=six; E=eight; T=diesel. The third symbol indicated the GVW range: [GVW] 1=3,900 to 5,800 lbs.; 2=5,200 to 7,500 lbs.; 3=6,600 to 14,000 lbs. The fourth and fifth symbols indicated the cab-to-axle dimension: 05=30-35 in.; 07=42 to 47 in.; 09=54-59 in.; 10=60-65 in.; 14=84-89 in. The sixth symbol indicated body type: 02=Chassis & Cowl; 03=Chassis & Cab; 04=Step-Side Pickup; 05=Panel Van; 06=Suburban (doors)/Sportvan; 14=Blazer; 16=Suburban (gate); 32=Motorhome chassis; 34=Fleetside; 36=Beauville Van; 35=Forward-Control (steel Step-Van body); 42=Forward-Control chassis; 55=Forward-Control (aluminum Step-Van body). The eighth symbol indicates model year: 1=1971. The ninth symbol indicates assembly plant: A=Atlanta (Lakewood), Ga.; B=Baltimore, Md.; F=Flint, Mich.; J=Janesville, Wis.; K=Kansas City (Leeds), Mo.; L=Los Angeles (Van Nuys), Calif.; P=Pontiac, Mich.; R=Arlington, Texas; S=St. Louis, Mo.; T=Tarrytown, N.Y.; U=Lordstown, Ohio; Z=Fremont, Calif. 1=Oshawa, Canada. The remaining symbols were the sequential production number starting with 100001 at each plant. Ending serial numbers not available. The Chevrolet engine had the source, date and type stamped on a serial number pad. Various source codes were used. Month codes were 1=Jan.; 2=Feb., etc. Date codes were 01=first of month, etc. The were numerous prefix codes to indicate engines and transmission attachments.

Model	Body Type	Price	Weight	Prod. Total
1/2-Ton Vega — Model HV/Series 14000 — 97 in. w.b. — Four				
14105	Panel Express	2138	2152	7,800
El Camino — Model A/Series 13000 — 116 in. w.b. — Six				
13380	Sedan-Pickup	2886	3302	Note 1
El Camino — Model A/Series 13000 — 116 in. w.b. — V-8				
13480	Sedan-Pickup	2983	3418	Note 1
13680	Custom Sedan-Pickup	3069	3442	Note 1

NOTE 1: Total El Camino production was 41,606.

Model	Body Type	Price	Weight	Prod. Total
1/2-Ton Chevy Van — Model G/Series 10 — 110 in. w.b.				
GS11005	Panel	2881	3460	15,012
GS11006	Sportvan	3304	3694	1,846
1/2-Ton Chevy Van — Model G/Series 10 — 110 in. w.b. — V-8				
GE11036	Beauville	3738	3936	481
1/2-Ton Chevy Van — Model G/Series 10 — 125 in. w.b.				
GS11305	Panel	3010	3615	15,013
GS11306	Sportvan	3430	3856	2,011
1/2-Ton Chevy Van — Model G/Series 10 — 125 in. w.b. — V-8				
GS11336	Beauville	3865	4136	1,146
3/4-Ton Chevy Van — Model G/Series 20 — 110 in. w.b.				
GS21005	Panel	2976	3489	5,901
GS21006	Sportvan	3350	3761	1,774
3/4-Ton Chevy Van — Model G/Series 20 — 110 in. w.b.				
GS21036	Beauville	3817	4094	345
3/4-Ton Chevy Van — Model G/Series 20 — 125 in. w.b.				
GS21305	Panel	3105	3653	14,027
GS21306	Sportvan	3471	3929	2,796
3/4-Ton Chevy Van — Model G/Series 20 — 125 in. w.b.				
GS21336	Beauville	3943	4296	3,568
1-Ton Chevy Van — Model G/Series 30 — 110 in. w.b.				
GS31005	Panel	3087	3781	624
GS31006	Sportvan	—	—	9
GS31006	Beauville	—	—	8
1-Ton Chevy Van — Model G/Series 30 — 110 in. w.b.				
GS31305	Chevy Van	3236	3948	9,518
GS31306	Sportvan	3594	4117	1,834
1-Ton Chevy Van — Model G/Series 30 — 125 in. w.b.				
GS31336	Beauville	4060	4590	1,552
1/2-Ton Blazer 4x2 — Model C/Series 5 — 104 in. w.b.				
CS10514	Open Utility	2659	3375	1,277
1/2-Ton Blazer 4x4 — Model K/Series 5 — 104 in. w.b.				
KS10514	Open Utility	3234	3677	17,220
1/2-Ton Commercial — Model C/Series 10 — 115 in. w.b.				
CS10703	Chassis & Cab	2656	3090	1,476
CS10704	Step-Side 6.5 ft.	2816	3426	19,041
CS10734	Fleetside 6.5 ft.	2816	3506	32,865
1/2-Ton Commercial — Model C/Series 10 — 127 in. w.b.				
CS10903	Chassis & Cab	2689	3107	588
CS10904	Step-Side 8 ft.	2854	3510	7,269
CS10934	Fleetside 8 ft.	2854	3605	206,313
CS10906	Suburban (doors)	3599	3862	4,550
CS10916	Suburban (gate)	3631	3870	5,395

1/2-Ton Commercial 4x4 — Model K/Series 10 — 115 in. w.b.

KS10704	Step-Side 6.5 ft.	3414	3739	1,438
KS10734	Fleetside 6.5 ft.	3414	3824	3,068

1/2-Ton Commercial 4x4 — Model K/Series 10 — 127 in. w.b.

KS10904	Step-Side 8 ft.	3451	3832	364
KS10934	Fleetside 8 ft.	3451	3927	9,417
KS10906	Suburban (doors)	4226	4191	631
KS10916	Suburban (gate)	4256	4191	994

1/2-Ton Forward-Control — Model P/Series 10 — 102 in. w.b.

PS10542	Chassis	2119	2120	229
PS10535	Steel Step-Van	3425	3781	1.905

3/4-Ton Commercial — Model C/Series 20 — 127 in. w.b.

CS20903	Chassis & Cab	2897	3496	4,523
CS20903	Chassis & Cab With Stake	3319	—	Note 2
CS20904	Step-Side 8 ft.	3058	3896	3,406
CS20934	Fleetside 8 ft.	3058	3991	62,465
CS20906	Suburban (doors)	3760	4245	1,343
CS20916	Suburban (gate)	3791	4253	1,203

NOTE 2: Stake option included with C20 Chassis & Cab production.

3/4-Ton Long Horn — Model C/Series 20 — 133 in. w.b.

CE21034	Pickup 8.5 ft.	3236	4100	3,331

3/4-Ton Commercial 4x4 — Model K/Series 20 — 127 in. w.b.

KS20903	Chassis & Cab	3641	3659	509
KS20904	Step-Side 8 ft.	3804	4061	674
KS20934	Fleetside 8 ft.	3804	4156	10,066
KS20906	Suburban (doors)	4530	4414	256
KS20916	Suburban (gate)	4538	4414	353

3/4-Ton Forward-Control — Model P/Series 20 — 125 in. w.b.

PS20842	Chassis	2378	2819	288
PS20835	Steel Step-Van	4198	5206	819
PS20855	Aluminium Step-Van	—	—	48

3/4-Ton Forward-Control — Model P/Series 20 — 133 in. w.b.

PS21042	Chassis	2411	2841	167
PS21035	Steel Step-Van	4311	5437	654
PS21035	Aluminum Step-Van	5192	4638	37

1-Ton Commercial — Model C/Series 30 — 133 in. w.b.

CS31002	Chassis & Cowl	—	—	139
CS31003	Chassis & Cab	2735	3641	11,438
CS31003	Chassis & Cab With Stake	3530	—	Note 3
CS31004	Step-Side 9 ft.	2875	4071	1,557
CS31034	Fleetside 8.5 ft.	2935	4157	1,479

NOTE 3: Stake option included with C30 Chassis & Cab production.

1-Ton Commercial — Model C/Series 30 — 157 in. w.b.

CS31103	Chassis & Cab	2775	3788	6,071

1-Ton Forward-Control — Model P/Series 30 — 125 in. w.b.

PS30842	Chassis	2320	2992	278
PS30835	Steel Step-Van	4080	5379	561
PS30855	Aluminum Step-Van	—	—	71

1-Ton Forward-Control (King) — Model P/Series 30 — 133 in. w.b.

PS31042	King Chassis	2350	3015	853
PS31035	Steel Step-Van King	4190	5611	1,378
PS31055	Step-Van King Aluminum	6860	5537	107

1-Ton Forward-Control — Model P/Series 30 — 157 in. w.b.

PS31442	Chassis	2350	—	1,669
PS31435	Steel Step-Van King	6040	6677	1,052
PS31455	Aluminum Step-Van King	7170	5714	70

1-Ton Motorhome — Model P/Series 30 — 137 in. w.b. — V-8

PE31132	Motorhome Chassis	3353	3219	788

1-Ton Motorhome — Model P/Series 30 — 157 in. w.b. — V-8

PE31132	Motorhome Chassis	3391	3307	821

NOTE 4: Model codes, prices and weights on charts are for sixes, except where model is in a V-8 only series.
NOTE 5: Detailed Chevrolet records show above production totals with separate breakouts for country of origin and type of engine. To put these in a convenient format, the totals above show combined U.S. output, plus imports from Canada, through Aug. 31, 1971. They include both six-cylinder and V-8 trucks, although most model codes in chart are six-cylinder codes.
NOTE 6: Platform/stake options, big-block V-8s, diesel engines, and LPG conversions were options. See the options section below for partial data on options useage.

1971 Chevrolet Vega Panel Express

ENGINE [Standard Vega]: Inline. OHV. Four-cylinder. Aluminum block. Bore & stroke: 3.501 in. x 3.625 in. Displacement: 140 cid. Compression ratio: 8.0:1. Brake horsepower: 90 at 4600 rpm. Net horsepower: 72 at 4200 rpm. Maximum Torque: 136 lbs.-ft. at 2400 rpm. Five main bearings. Hydraulic valve lifters. Carburetor: one-barrel.
ENGINE [Standard: All except Vega/P20/P30]: Inline. OHV. Six-cylinder. Cast iron block. Bore & stroke: 3.9 in. x 4.5 in. Displacement: 250 cid. Compression ratio: 8.5:1. Brake horsepower: 145 at 4200 rpm. Maximum Torque: 235 lbs.-ft. at 1600 rpm. Net horsepower: 110 at 4000 rpm. Seven main bearings. Mechanical valve lifters. Carburetor: Rochester one-barrel.
ENGINE [Optional P Series]: Inline. OHV. Three-cylinder. Diesel. Cast iron block. Bore & stroke: 3.875 x 4.5 in. Displacement: 159.2 cid. Horsepower: 94 at 2800 rpm. Torque: 205 at 1500. Taxable horsepower: 18.02. Induction: Fuel-injection.
ENGINE [Standard P20/P30; optional C5/K5/C10/K10/C20/K20/C30/G10/G20/G30]: Inline. OHV. Six-cylinder. Cast iron block. Bore & stroke: 3-7/8 in. x 4-1/8 in. Displacement: 292 cid. Compression ratio: 8.0:1. Brake horsepower: 165 at 4000 rpm. Maximum Torque: 270 lbs.-ft. at 1600 rpm. Net horsepower: 125 at 3600 rpm. Seven main bearings. Hydraulic valve lifters. Carburetor: Rochester one-barrel.
ENGINE [Standard Beauville; optional El Camino/C5/K5/C10/K10/P10/P20/G10]: V-block. OHV. Eight-cylinder. Cast iron block. Bore & stroke: 3.875 in. x 3.25 in. Displacement: 307 cid. Compression ratio: 8.5:1. Brake horsepower: 200 at 4600 rpm. Maximum Torque: 300 lbs.-ft. at 2400 rpm. Net horsepower: 135 at 4000 rpm. Five main bearings. Hydraulic valve lifters. Carburetor: Rochester two-barrel.
ENGINE [Optional C20/K20/P20/C30/P30/G20/G30]: V-block. OHV. Eight-cylinder. Cast iron block. Bore & stroke: 3.875 in. x 3.25 in. Displacement: 307 cid. Compression ratio: 8.5:1. Brake horsepower: 215 at 4800 rpm. Maximum Torque: 305 lbs.-ft. at 2800 rpm. Net horsepower: 135 at 4000 rpm. Five main bearings. Hydraulic valve lifters. Carburetor: Rochester two-barrel.
ENGINE [Optional C5/K5/C10/K10/C20/K20/P20/C30/P30/G20/G30]: V-block. OHV. Eight-cylinder. Cast iron block. Bore & stroke: 4.0 in. x 3.5 in. Displacement: 350 cid. Compression ratio: 8.5:1. Brake horsepower: 250 at 4600 rpm. Maximum Torque: 350 lbs.-ft. at 3000 rpm. Net horsepower: 170 at 3600 rpm. Five main bearings. Hydraulic valve lifters. Carburetor: Rochester four-barrel.
ENGINE [El Camino]: V-block. OHV. Eight-cylinder. Cast iron block. Bore & stroke: 4.0 in. x 3.5 in. Displacement: 350 cid. Compression ratio: 8.5:1. Brake horsepower: 245 at 4400 rpm. Five main bearings. Hydraulic valve lifters. Carburetor: Rochester two-barrel.
ENGINE [El Camino]: V-block. OHV. Eight-cylinder. Cast iron block. Bore & stroke: 4.0 in. x 3.5 in. Displacement: 350 cid. Compression ratio: 8.5:1. Brake horsepower: 270 at 4800 rpm. Five main bearings. Hydraulic valve lifters. Carburetor: Rochester four-barrel.
ENGINE [Optional 400 V-8]: V-block. OHV. Eight-cylinder. Cast iron block. Bore & stroke: 4.125 in. x 3.75 in. Displacement: 402 cid. Compression ratio: 8.5:1. Brake horsepower: 300 at 4800 rpm. Net horsepower: 240 at 4400 rpm. Torque: 410 at 3200 rpm. Five main bearings. Hydraulic valve lifters. Carburetor: Rochester four-barrel.
ENGINE [Optional El Camino/SS]: V-block. OHV. Eight-cylinder. Cast iron block. Bore & stroke: 4.251 in. x 4.00 in. Displacement: 454 cid. Compression ratio: 8.5:1. Brake horsepower: 365 at 4800 rpm. Maximum Torque: 465 lbs.-ft. at 3200 rpm. Net horsepower: 285. Five main bearings. Hydraulic valve lifters. Carburetor: four-barrel.

1971 Chevrolet 3/4-Ton C20 Fleetside Pickup 4x4 (RCA)

ENGINE [SPO El Camino/SS]: V-block. OHV. Eight-cylinder. Cast iron block. Bore & stroke: 4.251 in. x 4.00 in. Displacement: 454 cid. Compression ratio: 9.0:1. Brake horsepower: 425 at 5600 rpm. Maximum Torque: 475 lbs.-ft. at 4000 rpm. Five main bearings. Hydraulic valve lifters. Carburetor: four-barrel.
CHASSIS [Vega]: Wheelbase: 97 in. Overall length: 176 in. Height: 51.8 in. Front tread: 54.8 in. Rear tread: 53.6 in. Tires: 6.00-13B. GVW: 3,300 lbs.
CHASSIS [El Camino]: Wheelbase: 116 in. Overall length: 206.8 in. Height: 54.4 in. Front tread: 60.2. Rear tread: 59.2 in. Tires: E78-14B. GVW: 4,100 lbs.
CHASSIS [G10]: Wheelbase: 110/125 in. Overall length: 178 in./202.2 in. Height 80 in. Tires: F78-14B. GVW: 4,000-5,100 lbs.
CHASSIS [G20]: Wheelbase: 110/125 in. Overall length: 178 in./202.2 in. Height: 80 in. Tires: G78-15B. GVW: 5,600-5,900 lbs.
CHASSIS [G30]: Wheelbase: 110/125 in. Overall length: 178 in./202.2 in. Height: 80 in. Tires: 8 x 16.5. GVW: 6,100-8,000 lbs.
CHASSIS [Blazer]: Wheelbase: 104 in. Overall length: 177.5 in. Height: 68.7 in. Front tread: 60.4 in. Rear tread: 60.4 in. Tires: E78-15B. GVW: 4,100 lbs.

CHASSIS [C10]: Wheelbase: 115 in./127 in. Tires: [115 in. wheelbase] G78-15B; [127 in. wheelbase] H78-15B. GVW: 4,400-5,100 lbs.

CHASSIS [K10]: Wheelbase: 115 in./127 in. Tires: [115 in. wheelbase] G78-15B; [127 in. wheelbase] H78-15B. GVW: 5,200-5,600 lbs.

CHASSIS [P10]: Wheelbase: 102 in. Height: 75 in. Tires: G78-15B. GVW: 4,600-5,400 lbs.

CHASSIS [C20]: Wheelbase: 127 in./133 in. Tires: [127 in. wheelbase] G78-15; [133 in. Longhorn] 8.75 x 16.5 six-ply. GVW: 6,200-7,500 lbs.

CHASSIS [K20]: Wheelbase: 127 in. Tires: [127 in. wheelbase] G78-15; [133 in. Longhorn] 8.75 x 16.5, six-ply. GVW: 6,400-7,500 lbs.

CHASSIS [P20]: Wheelbase: 125 in./133 in. Overall length: 220.75/244.75 in. Tires: 8.75 x 16.5. GVW: 6,500-7,500 lbs.

CHASSIS [C30]: Wheelbase: 133 in./157 in. Tires: 8.75 x 16.5. GVW: 6,600-14,000 lbs.

CHASSIS [P30]: Wheelbase: 133 in./157 in. Overall length: 220.75/265.75 in. Tires: 8.75 x 16.5. GVW: 7,300-14,000 lbs.

TECHNICAL: Saginaw manual, fully-synchronized, transmission. Speeds: 3F/1R. Column-mounted gearshift lever. Single-plate dry-disc clutch (250 cid engine); coil spring single-dry-plate (292/307/350/402/454 cid engines). Rear axle: [1/2-ton] semi-floating; [3/4-ton/1-ton] full-floating rear axle. Hydraulic, four-wheel brakes. Kelsey-Hayes pressed steel wheels.

OPTIONS: Rear bumper ($53.80). Extra wheel ($31.50). Radio ($69.95). Clock. Air-conditioning. Deluxe heater. Gauge package (Ammeter, oil, temperature). Tilt wheel. Shoulder belts. Tinted glass ($19.40). Dual outside mirrors ($21.00). Dome light switch ($4.35). Side wheel carrier ($15.10). Full foam seat ($30.15). [1/2-ton] 292 six-cylinder engine ($95). 307 V-8 engine ($120). 400 V-8 engine (average $160). 350 V-8 in El Camino ($70). Four-speed transmission ($190). Powerglide transmission ($195). Turbo-Hydramatic transmission (average $280). Power brakes (average $50). Power steering (average $115). Four-wheel drive system (average $570). [3/4-ton] 292 six-cylinder engine ($95). 307 V-8, over base six ($120). 400 V-8 over 307 ($175). Powerglide (average $210). Turbo-Hydramatic transmission (average $245). Four-speed transmission (average $120). Power steering (average $140). Four-wheel drive system ($680). [1-ton] 307 V-8 over base six ($120). 292 six-cylinder engine ($95). 350 V-8 engine, over 307 ($45). 400 V-8 engine, over 350. LPG kit ($95). Turbo-Hydramatic transmission ($245). New Process transmission ($30). Vacuum brakes ($45). Power steering (average $135). Nine-foot platform equipment ($425). 12 ft. platform equipment ($484). 157 in. wheelbase ($30).

OPTIONS: [With useage rate] Tinted glass, Van (27 percent). Cargo door lock, Van (8 percent). Body glass, Van (10 percent). Right side glass, Van (7 percent). Side door window glass, panel Van (1 percent). All tinted glass, light trucks (30 percent). Rear door glass, Van (64 percent). Sliding rear window, light truck (3 percent). Bucket seats, light truck (3 percent). Custom bench seat (used on 967 light trucks). Bodyside belt molding, light truck ($27 percent). Wide lower bodyside molding, light truck (28 percent). Upper bodyside molding, light truck (37 percent). Door edge guards, light truck (12 percent). Bodyside molding, Van (1 percent). Deluxe air-conditioning, light truck (25 percent). Roof air-conditioning, light truck (25 percent). Front air-conditioning, Van (3 percent). Rear air-conditioning, Van (1 percent). Painted camper mirror, light truck (3 percent). Stainless camper mirror, light truck (3 percent). Stainless steel West Coast Jr. mirror: Light truck (10 percent); Van (13 percent). Dual West Coast Sr. mirror, light truck (41 percent). Painted West Coast Jr. mirror: Light truck (19 percent); Van (50 percent). Body paint stripe, light truck (8 percent). Platform and Stake equipment, light truck (14 percent). Positraction: Light truck (11 percent); Van (12 percent); Step-Van (7 percent). Oil bath air cleaner: Light truck (3 percent); Van (5 percent). 350 light-duty V-8 engine: Light truck (65 percent); Van (49 percent). 292 six-cylinder engine: Light truck (14 percent); Van (68 percent). 396 V-8 engine: Step-Van (8 percent); Light truck (6 percent). LPG engine package (used on only 387 light trucks and six Vans.) Four-speed transmission: Light truck (14 percent); Van (24 percent). Heavy-duty, close-ratio, four-speed manual transmission (used on 1,122 light trucks). Powerglide transmission: Light truck (1 percent); Van (7 percent); Step-Van (6 percent). M-38 Turbo-Hydramatic transmission: Light truck (45 percent); Van (49 percent); Step-Van (22 percent). M-49 Turbo-Hydramatic transmission: Light truck (6 percent); Step-Van (17 percent). Tilt steering wheel, light truck (2 percent). Power steering: Light truck (43 percent); Van (9 percent); Step-Van (17 percent). Wheel trim cover: Light truck (53 percent); Van (37 percent). AM/FM push-button radio, light truck (1 percent). Chrome rear bumper, light truck (3 percent). Chrome front bumper, light truck (22 percent). Cheyenne Super package, light truck (2 percent). Removable hardtop, Blazer/light truck: black (78 percent); white (21 percent). Custom Appearance package, Van (9 percent). Custom Comfort and Convenience package: Light truck (21 percent); Van (10 percent). Camper Special package, light truck (18 percent). Cheyenne package, light truck (16 percent). Notes: A total of 72,609 light trucks were equipped with the Cheyenne trim package. A total of 7,190 Vans were equipped with Custom Appearance features. A total of 20,501 Pickups got the Camper Special option. A total of 9,867 trucks were Cheyenne Super models. Custom Deluxe equipment was added to 8,686 Vans and 98,895 Light trucks. Over 50 percent of the light-duty trucks were two-toned in standard colors or special colors. One two-tone paint combination ending with code 73 was used on only three trucks.

HISTORICAL: Introduction: The 1971 Chevy Vans and Sportvans were introduced in May, 1970. Production startup date for other 1971 models was Aug. 21, 1970. They hit the showrooms one month and eight days later [Sept. 29, 1970]. Calendar year Commercial model registrations, by weight class: [6,000-lbs. and less] 450,354; [6,001 to 10,000-lbs.] 145,358. Calendar year Commercial production was 739,478 units, outpacing the previous record of 683,694 set in 1969. The 1971 total included 599,207 trucks with V-8 engines; 128,660 with inline six-cylinder engines; 345 with V-6s; 9,120 Vega Panels with the four-cylinder engine and 2,146 diesels. El Caminos are not included in such production totals, as they were counted with Chevelle passenger cars. Also, 15,670 Vans were considered Nova Sportvans and their output was included with passenger car production totals. Innovations: All 1971 Chevrolet truck engines were modified to operate on unleaded gasoline. Front disc brakes were standard on all conventional light-duty models and Step-Vans. Independent front suspension was adopted for Vans. The fuel evaporative system, formerly optional in California, became standard in all 1/2-tons. A big recovery from strike-year 1970 made this a banner season. Several truck factories ran six days a week, all year, to keep up with demand. A.T. Olson was assistant general sales manager of the truck division.

1972 CHEVROLET

1972 Chevrolet El Camino (DFW)

1/2-TON LUV MINI-PICKUP — MODEL L/SERIES 82 — FOUR: An all-new LUV pickup truck was introduced in March, 1972 as a captive import sourced from Isuzu Motors of Japan. The 1972 model is readily identifiable by its 1955 Chevrolet-like egg-crate grille and total of eight round reflectors and lights on the rear end. The name LUV stood for Light Utility Vehicle. A total of 21,098 of these trucks were sold from March to December, 1972.

1/2-TON VEGA — MODEL V/SERIES 14000 — FOUR: The Vega Panel Express was available, again, in 1972. Its grille was finished in a manner that made the vertical elements slightly less prominent. A model emblem was seen on the cowl. Otherwise, there was very little change. It was again based on the Kammback wagon, with the rear side windows blanked-out. It came only with the standard all-vinyl interior, less passenger bucket seat. Standard equipment included the four-cylinder aluminum block engine, three-speed manual transmission, front disc brakes, two separate stowage compartments below the floor, many safety features and a choice of colors. It had a 67.4 in. floor length, 42.6 in. between the wheelhousings and a 68.7 cu. ft. cargo volume. Payload capacity was 650 lbs.

1/2-TON EL CAMINO — MODEL AC; AD/SERIES 13000 — SIX/V-8: Larger, one-piece corner lights were seen on the El Camino. They bent around the body corners to double as sidemarkers. The grille had a cross-hatch pattern, but four horizontal moldings with bright finish stood out the most. They split the grille into three horizontal segments. The center bow tie emblem of 1971 was replaced with Chevrolet letters at the left-hand side of the lower grille segment. El Camino nameplates and designation badges were mounted on the front fendersides, behind the wheel opening. The rear end appearance had hardly any changes. The front bumper had no air slots or parking lamps in it. Standard models had bright windshield frames, backup lights on the tailgate, and a base six-cylinder engine. Customs added a V-8 as base engine; all bright window frames; bodyside moldings; wheelhouse moldings; pickup box rim moldings; rear body corner moldings; two moldings on the tailgate; and silver anodized lower body perimeter. Super Sport equipment (RPO Z15) was available for all Custom models with V-8s other than the base 307 cid V-8. You could get an SS-350, SS-396 (actually a 402 cid engine), or SS-454. It cost less than last year...$350 extra. The SS package included a black-accented grille with SS badges; cowl badges; hood locking pins; styled wheels; special vertically pleated door panels; round instrument panel gauges; sport suspension; power front disc brakes; and 15 x 7 sport wheels with F60-15 raised white-letter tires. The 396 cid engine was gone, although the 402 cid V-8 powered trucks were promoted as SS-396 models. An unusual dealer option costing about $65 extra was a "Flame Chevy '73" decal kit. The exterior colors for the year were Antique white; Pewter silver; Ascot blue; Mulsanne blue; Spring green; Gulf green; Sequoia green; Covert tan; Placer gold; Cream yellow; Golden brown; Mohave gold; Orange flame; Midnight bronze; and Cranberry red. Interiors came in black; Antique tan; and covert vinyl and cloth-and-vinyl combinations, as well as pinta fabric combinations. The "flying buttress" roofline was retained for all El Caminos. The pickup box still had an outside width of 75-1/2 in. Inside width behind the cab was 59 in. Inside width near the tailgate was 64-1/2 in. The width between the wheelhousings was 44 in. The bottom bed length measured 79-1/4 in. Tailgate measurements were 54-1/2 x 22-1/2 in. This was the last year for this box.

1/2-TON VAN — MODEL G/SERIES 10 — SIX/V-8: Chevrolet Vans continued to come in three basic models: Chevy Van (panel), Sportvan and Beauville. The Beauville model offered travel space for 12 passengers. All G10 models could be had with 110 or 125 in. wheelbases. Panels and Sportvans used the 250 cid/145 hp inline six as base powerplant. Base engine in the 1/2-ton Beauville was the 307 cid/200 hp V-8. An extended front hood made 26 service areas readily accessible. Van grilles consisted of seven horizontal bars with a center-mounted Chevrolet emblem. Other innovations included independent front suspension and a sliding door option. A Custom Appearance package was available, as well as a Custom and Convenience interior option.

3/4-TON VAN — MODEL G/SERIES 20 — SIX/V-8: The 108 in. wheelbase driver-forward vans also came as 3/4-ton G20 models. Styling characteristics were the same as G10s. Models included the Chevy Van with double panel doors available on the passenger side and at the rear. There were also window models in two levels of trim: base Sportvan or Beauville. The G20 line offered the same engines as G10s, but a 350 cid V-8 was standard in the Beauville.

1-TON VAN — MODEL G/SERIES 30 — SIX/V-8: In the 1-ton (G30) line, only the Chevy Van panel was available with the shorter wheelbase, while the G30 Sportvan and Beauville were available only on the longer 125 in. wheelbase, which was different than in the other series. Chevrolet production records show that no 1972 Sportvans or Beauvilles were built on the 110 in. wheelbase. Only the G30 Chevy Van came with a six. In the 3/4- and 1-ton lines the 350 cid/250 hp V-8 was standard.

1/2-TON BLAZER — MODEL C; K/SERIES 5 — SIX/V-8: Light trucks, including Blazers, looked similar to the previous year's model, except that the border of the grille surround was no longer black-finished. Factory records show nearly 3,500 of the 4x2 Blazers were made in model year 1971. The 4x4 version was now nearly 15 times as popular. The Blazer's suspension system consisted of single-leaf tapered front springs with a combination of multi-leaf and tapered springs at the rear. The ball-type steering unit had a 24:1 ratio and its standard engine was Chevrolet's 155 hp six. The single-unit body was joined to a heavy channel steel frame. The rear-mounted 23.5-gallon fuel tank was located inside the frame. Numerous options were offered for the Blazer including four-speed manual and automatic transmissions, V-8 engines, power steering, power brakes and a completely removable fiberglass top. Colors, exterior trims; upholstery and equipment were very similar to or the same as used on the conventional C10/K10 models.

1/2-TON COMMERCIAL — MODEL C; K/SERIES 10 — SIX/V-8: Pickups, Panels and Suburbans looked similar to the previous year's model, except that the border of the grille surround was no longer black-finished. There were new molded door panels with integral armrests and a new Highlander interior package was available. Featured again was an egg-crate grille with five horizontal blades and 15 vertical members. A Chevrolet bow tie was on grille's center. The parking/directional lights were in the front bumper. Inside was a low-profile steering wheel, full-width bench seat and foot-operated parking brake. Standard equipment on all pickups included: six-cylinder engine; side terminal battery; self-adjusting four-wheel brakes (front discs); dual brake master cylinder with warning lights; back up lights; directional signals and four-way flashers; Panoramic rear window; left- and right-hand outside rearview mirrors; non-glare inside mirror; heater and defroster; padded dash; non-glare front instrument panel finish; padded sun visors; ashtray; seat belts with retractors; push-button seat belt buckles; low-profile control knobs; two-speed electric washer/wipers; windshield defrosters; safety glass; flexible fuel filler neck; deep-dish steering wheel with telescoping shaft; thick laminate safety glass windshield; right-hand coat hook; front and rear sidemarker lamps; and painted front bumper. Chrome front and rear bumpers were a separate option. There were different trim levels. The base Custom had no side trim; plain black rubber window gaskets; and white-painted bumpers. The grille shell had bright metal finish. The hubcaps were also painted. The vent window pillars and frames were flat black. The standard hubcaps were painted. Rear moldings around the taillamps and tailgate were not available on Customs. Upper and lower belt moldings were optional. Customs equipped with the lower belt molding, should have the center of the molding painted black. Custom Deluxe equipment included a full-width bench seat with comfortably padded seat cushions and backrest; vinyl seat upholstery and door panels; steel roof panel painted in main exterior color; black rubber floor mat extending to firewall; padded armrests; padded sunshades; courtesy lamp; prismatic rearview mirror; foam-padded instrument panel; bright upper and lower grille outline moldings; bright headlamp bezels; bright outside rearview mirrors; bright door handles; white-painted front bumper, hubcaps and wheels; and bright Custom Deluxe nameplates. Upper and lower belt moldings were both optional. The center of the 1972 lower molding had a woodgrained insert. When equipped with lower bodyside moldings, the Custom Deluxe also got taillamp and two tailgate moldings. These moldings were positioned above and below the Chevrolet lettering on the back. Chrome hubcaps were optional on Custom Deluxe models. The Cheyenne trim package included a bench seat with full-depth foam cushions and backrests; Custom-grained vinyl upholstery or nylon and vinyl upholstery; special door trim panels; cab headliner; deep-twist nylon carpeting extending to firewall; color-keyed garnish moldings; ashtray-mounted cigar lighter; Custom steering wheel; Cheyenne dashboard nameplates; door or manually-operated courtesy lights; extra acoustical insulation; and all Custom Deluxe exterior items, plus cab-mounted cargo lamp; bright metal cab trim and moldings; bright upper bodyside and tailgate moldings; and central taillight appliques for Fleetside and Cheyenne nameplates. When equipped with a lower bodyside molding, the Cheyenne also got woodgrained molding inserts. Bucket seats were optional for Cheyennes with the vinyl interior. A Cheyenne Super option package took up where the Cheyenne left off, adding both upper and lower (woodgrained) bodyside moldings and a chrome-plated tailgate release. There were Custom Appearance; and Custom Comfort & Convenience options, too. Exterior colors were Midnight black; Hawaiian blue; Mariner blue; Classic bronze; Spanish gold; Glenwood green; Meadow green; Spruce green; Willow green; Firebolt orange; Tangier orange; Crimson red; Frost white; Grapefruit yellow; and Wheatland yellow. The standard interior interior featured a three-passenger bench seat; foam padding; dome light; rubber floor mat; two door armrests; and all-vinyl trim in green, blue, black or parchment. The Custom and Cheyenne interiors came black pinta coated fabric, Antique medium tan pinta coated fabric or Antique light cover coated fabric. The C10 (and K10 four-wheel drive) Chassis & Cab and Pickups came on 115 or 127 in. wheelbases. Both Fleetside and Step-Side Pickups offered a 6-1/2 ft. box or 8 ft. box. Pickups on the shorter wheelbase had the 6-1/2 ft. cargo box. Suburbans came only on the longer wheelbase. The Suburban no longer came with the 292 cid six. It again had two-doors on the passenger side and one on the driver's side. A tailgate or double rear doors were available. They had a floor space that was 9 ft. long. With second and third seats removed, cargo space totaled 190 cu. ft. Four-wheel drive was available for a price of just over $500. Both of these single-unit body models had coil springs on all four wheels. Two-toning was done using white as the second (upper) color. It was applied to all sheet metal above the beltline or just the upper and rear cab panels. On Cheyennes, the bodyside, between the upper and lower beltline moldings was usually done in white.

1/2-TON FORWARD-CONTROL — MODEL P/SERIES 10 — SIX/V-8: The Forward-Control chassis was designed for door-to-door delivery service. Body lengths ranged from seven to eight feet for the P10 series. Step-Vans looked identical to 1971 versions. The P10 models were sold in chassis and steel Panel models on a 102 in. wheelbase. These were advertised as Step Van 7 models (due to their seven-foot long bodies). The grilles had single round headlights in the top of the housings, with rectangular parking lamps below. A channel type front bumper was standard equipment. Features included independent coil spring front suspension; and three six-cylinder engines. Buyers could also get full-height doors; sliding side doors and double rear doors.

3/4-TON COMMERCIAL — MODEL C; K/SERIES 20 — SIX/V-8: Carryover trucks in the Chevrolet 20 Series 3/4-ton line had the same styling, trim changes and options as other conventional trucks. Fleetside and Step-Side Pickups had an 8 ft. box. Also available was the "Longhorn" Fleetside with a 133 in. wheelbase and 8-1/2-ft. box. The Chassis & Cab and two Suburbans continued in this line. These had the same dimensions as comparable 1/2-ton models, but heavier chassis components. The designation plates had a number 20. The 8 ft. Stake model was available as an extra on the platform option for the Chassis & Cab. It cost about $400 for the platform option. The four-wheel drive 3/4-ton models in the 20 Series had a K20 model prefix. Longhorns were not built with four-wheel drive.

3/4-TON FORWARD-CONTROL — MODEL P/SERIES 20 — SIX/V-8: The Forward-Control chassis was designed for door-to-door delivery service. The 3/4-ton P20 models offered two wheelbases and came in Step-Van chassis form or as Step-Van King steel or aluminum panel bodies. Remaining in the series were the 125 in. wheelbase chassis recommended for bodies 9-1/2 to 10-1/2 ft. long and the 137 in. wheelbase recommended for bodies 11-1/2 to 12-1/2 ft. long. Step-Van King did not refer to the wheelbase, but to the body height and width. The Kings had their round headlamps below the rectangular parking lamps. A number of powerplants could be had, including three six-cylinder engines and two optional V-8s. The three-cylinder Detroit diesel was not listed. Features included independent coil spring front suspension. Buyers could also get full-height doors; sliding side doors and double rear doors. The coil spring front suspension reflected the fact that the Forward-Control chassis had found popularity among recreational vehicle builders.

1-TON MEDIUM-DUTY COMMERCIAL — MODEL C/SERIES 30 — SIX-CYLINDER: The Chevrolet 30 Series 1-ton trucks had the same styling and trim changes and options as other conventional trucks. The fenderside nameplates had a number 30. There were four 133 in. wheelbase models: Chassis and Cowl, Chassis and Cab, Longhorn Pickup with 8.5 ft box and a Step-Side Pickup with a 9 ft. box. No hubcaps were used on the larger split-rim wheels of the Chassis & Cab models, which had eight bolts and eight circular openings. The Camper Special package continued. The C38 model 1-ton Chassis & Cab with a long 157 in. wheelbase for use as an RV chassis was also offered again. Nearly 9,000 of these were sold. A four-speed manual synchromesh transmission was standard. No four-wheel drive option was offered.

1972 Chevrolet 1/2-Ton C10 Fleetside Pickup (OCW)

1-TON FORWARD-CONTROL — MODEL P/SERIES 30 — SIX/V-8: Two P30 models were the same sizes as P20s, but had much higher GVW ratings of 7,300-14,000 lbs. versus the 3/4-ton's 6,500-7,500 lbs. The third model featured a 157 in. wheelbase and accommodated body lengths up to 14-1/2 ft. for the 1-ton Step-Van King. More and more of these Forward-Control chassis were being used for motorhome conversions. Features included independent coil spring front suspension; three six-cylinder engines and two optional V-8s. Some Step-Vans had Liquid Petroleum Gas conversions. Buyers could also get full-height doors; sliding side doors and double rear doors. Chevrolet also produced the special P30 1-ton motorhome chassis on 137 in. and 157 in. wheelbases. Almost 5,200 were constructed in 1972.

I.D. DATA: Serial Number located: [Chassis models] On plate temporarily attached near steering column, with final location per body maker; [All others] On plate attached to rear face of left-hand door hinge pillar; on right side of cowl under hood. [LUV] The VIN consists of 10 symbols. The first three symbols are the model name. The fourth and fifth symbols are the plant code. The last five symbols are the sequential production number. [El Camino]: The first symbol indicated manufacturer: 1=Chevrolet. The second symbol indicated series: C=base; D=Custom. The third and fourth symbols indicated body style: 80=Sedan-Pickup. The fifth symbol indicated engine: D=250 cid six; F=307 cid V-8; H=350 cid V-8; J=350 cid V-8; K=350 cid V-8; L=350 cid V-8; R=400 cid V-8; S=402 cid V-8; U=402 cid V-8; V=454 cid V-8; W=454 cid V-8. The sixth symbol indicated model year: 2=1972. The seventh symbol indicated assembly plant: B=Baltimore, Md.; K=Kansas City, Mo. (Leeds); L=Los Angeles (Van Nuys), Calif.; R=Arlington, Texas. The remaining symbols were the sequential production number starting with 100001 at each plant. Ending serial numbers not available. The Chevrolet engine had the source, date and type stamped on a serial number pad. Various source codes were used. Month codes were 1=Jan.; 2=Feb., etc. Date codes were 01=first of month, etc. There were numerous prefix codes to indicate engines and transmission attachments. [C/K/G/P Series] The first symbol indicated truck type: C=Conventional Cab; K=4x4; G=Chevy Van; P=Forward-Control; Z=Motorhome. The second symbol indicated type of engine: S=six; E=eight; T=diesel. The third symbol indicated the GVW range: [GVW] 1=3,900 to 5,800 lbs.; 2=5,200 to 7,500 lbs.; 3=6,600 to 14,000 lbs. The fourth and fifth symbols indicated the cab-to-axle dimension: 05=30-35 in.; 07=42-47 in.; 09=54-59 in.; 10=60-65 in.; 14=84-89 in. The sixth symbol indicated body type: 02=Chassis & Cowl; 03=Chassis & Cab; 04=Step-Side Pickup; 05=Panel Van; 06=Suburban (doors)/Sportvan; 14=Blazer; 16=Suburban (gate); 32=Motorhome chassis; 34=Fleetside; 36=Beauville Van; 35=Forward-Control (steel Step-Van body); 42=Forward-Control chassis; 55=Forward-Control (aluminum Step-Van body). The eighth symbol indicates model year: 2=1972. The ninth symbol indicates assembly plant: A=Atlanta (Lakewood), Ga.; B=Baltimore, Md.; F=Flint, Mich.; G=Framingham, Mass.; J=Janesville, Wis.; K=Kansas City (Leeds), Mo.; L=Los Angeles (Van Nuys), Calif.; P=Pontiac, Mich.; R=Arlington, Texas; S=St. Louis, Mo.; T=Tarrytown, N.Y.; U=Lordstown, Ohio; Z=Fremont, Calif. 1=Oshawa, Canada. The remaining symbols were the sequential production number starting with 100001 at each plant. Ending serial numbers not available. The Chevrolet engine had the source, date and type stamped on a serial number pad. Various source codes were used. Month codes were 1=Jan.; 2=Feb., etc. Date codes were 01=first of month, etc. The were numerous prefix codes to indicate engines and transmission attachments.

Model	Body Type	Price	Weight	Prod. Total
1/2-Ton LUV — Model L/Series 82 — 102.4 in. w.b.				
82	Mini-Pickup	2196	2360	21,098
1/2-Ton Vega — Model V/Series 14000 — 97 in. w.b. — Four				
14105	Panel Express	2080	2152	4,114
El Camino — Model AC/Series 13000 — 116 in. w.b. — Six				
13380	Sedan-Pickup	2790	3302	Note 1
El Camino — Model AD/Series 13000 — 116 in. w.b. — V-8				
13480	Sedan-Pickup	2880	3418	Note 1
13680	Custom Sedan-Pickup	2960	3442	Note 1

NOTE 1: Total El Camino production was 57,147.

Model	Body Type	Price	Weight	Prod. Total
1/2-Ton Van — Model G/Series 10 — 110 in. w.b.				
GS11005	Panel	2775	3460	12,205
GS11006	Sportvan	3285	3694	1,346
1/2-Ton Van — Model G/Series 10 — 110 in. w.b. — V-8				
GE11036	Beauville	3685	3936	433
1/2-Ton Van — Model G/Series 10 — 125 in. w.b.				
GS11305	Panel	2910	3615	14,044
GS11306	Sportvan	3410	3856	1,593
1/2-Ton Van — Model G/Series 10 — 125 in. w.b. — V-8				
GS11336	Beauville	3805	4136	997
3/4-Ton Van — Model G/Series 20 — 110 in. w.b.				
GS21005	Panel	2890	3489	4,618
GS21006	Sportvan	3335	3761	605
3/4-Ton Van — Model G/Series 20 — 110 in. w.b.				
GS21036	Beauville	3760	4094	345
3/4-Ton Van — Model G/Series 20 — 125 in. w.b.				
GS21305	Panel	3020	3653	16,084
GS21306	Sportvan	3460	3929	3,310

3/4-Ton Van — Model G/Series 20 — 125 in. w.b.

GS21336	Beauville	3880	4296	5,581

1-Ton Van — Model G/Series 30 — 110 in. w.b.

GS31005	Panel	2996	3781	623

1-Ton Van — Model G/Series 30 — 125 in. w.b.

GS31305	Van	3130	3948	12,545
GS31306	Sportvan	3575	4117	2,036

1-Ton Van — Model G/Series 30 — 125 in. w.b.

GS31336	Beauville	3995	4590	2,020

1/2-Ton Blazer 4x2 — Model C/Series 5 — 104 in. w.b.

CS10514	Open Utility	2585	3375	3,357

1/2-Ton Blazer 4x4 — Model K/Series 5 — 104 in. w.b.

KS10514	Open Utility	3145	3677	44,266

1/2-Ton Commercial — Model C/Series 10 — 115 in. w.b.

CS10703	Chassis & Cab	2530	3090	1,640
CS10704	Step-Side 6.5 ft.	2680	3426	22,042
CS10734	Fleetside 6.5 ft.	2680	3506	39,730

1/2-Ton Commercial — Model C/Series 10 — 127 in. w.b.

CS10903	Chassis & Cab	2560	3107	717
CS10904	Step-Side 8 ft.	2715	3510	7,538
CS10934	Fleetside 8 ft.	2715	3605	273,249
CS10906	Suburban (doors)	3495	3862	6,748
CS10916	Suburban (gate)	3525	3870	10,757

1/2-Ton Commercial 4x4 — Model K/Series 10 — 115 in. w.b.

KS10704	Step-Side 6.5 ft.	3251	3766	1,736
KS10734	Fleetside 6.5 ft.	3251	3836	6,069

1/2-Ton Commercial 4x4 — Model K/Series 10 — 127 in. w.b.

KS10904	Step-Side 8 ft.	3287	3846	407
KS10934	Fleetside 8 ft.	3287	3926	18,431
KS10906	Suburban (doors)	4273	4206	993
KS10916	Suburban (gate)	4305	4206	2,145

1/2-Ton Forward-Control — Model P/Series 10 — 102 in. w.b.

PS10542	Chassis	2015	2120	196
PS10535	Steel Step-Van	3260	3781	2,063

3/4-Ton Commercial — Model C/Series 20 — 127 in. w.b.

CS20903	Chassis & Cab	2760	3496	5,974
CS20903	Chassis & Cab With Stake	3168	4163	Note 2
CS20904	Step-Side 8 ft.	2915	3896	3,973
CS20934	Fleetside 8 ft.	2915	3991	94,458
CS20906	Suburban (doors)	3650	4245	2,136
CS20916	Suburban (gate)	3680	4253	3,141

NOTE 2: Stake option included with C20 Chassis & Cab production.

3/4-Ton Long Horn — Model C/Series 20 — 133 in. w.b.

CE21034	Pickup 8.5 ft.	3088	3950	3,328

3/4-Ton Commercial 4x4 — Model K/Series 20 — 127 in. w.b.

KS20903	Chassis & Cab	3415	3651	676
KS20904	Step-Side 8 ft.	3567	4051	755
KS20934	Fleetside 8 ft.	3567	4141	19,648
KS20906	Suburban (doors)	4275	4141	503
KS20916	Suburban (gate)	43087	4585	879

3/4-Ton Forward-Control — Model P/Series 20 — 125 in. w.b.

PS20842	Chassis	2265	2819	343
PS20835	Steel Step-Van	4000	5206	1,706
PS20855	Aluminum Step-Van	—	—	92

3/4-Ton Forward-Control — Model P/Series 20 — 133 in. w.b.

PS21042	Chassis	2295	2841	189
PS21035	Steel Step-Van	4605	5437	989
PS21055	Aluminum Step-Van	4770	4638	42

1-Ton Commercial — Model C/Series 30 — 133 in. w.b.

CS31002	Chassis & Cowl	—	—	127
CS31003	Chassis & Cab	2845	3641	14,988
CS31003	Chassis & Cab With Stake	2370	4488	Note 3
CS31004	Step-Side 9 ft.	2990	4071	1,542
CS31034	Fleetside 8.5 ft.	3050	4157	2,450

NOTE 3: Stake option included with C30 Chassis & Cab production.

1-Ton Commercial — Model C/Series 30 — 157 in. w.b.

CS31103	Chassis & Cab	2885	3788	8,944

1-Ton Forward-Control — Model P/Series 30 — 125 in. w.b.

PS30842	Chassis	2435	2992	441
PS30835	Steel Step-Van	4165	5379	559
PS30855	Aluminum Step-Van	—	—	125

1-Ton Forward-Control (King) — Model P/Series 30 — 133 in. w.b.

PS31042	King Chassis	2470	3015	967
PS31035	Steel Step-Van King	4270	5611	1,710
PS31055	Step-Van King Aluminum	—	—	127

1-Ton Forward-Control — Model P/Series 30 — 157 in. w.b.

PS31442	Chassis	2350	—	1,899
PS31435	Steel Step-Van King	6040	6677	1,702
PS31455	Aluminum Step-Van King	7170	5714	231

1-Ton Motorhome — Model P/Series 30 — 137 in. w.b. — V-8

PE31132	Motorhome Chassis	3190	3219	2,267

1-Ton Motorhome — Model P/Series 30 — 157 in. w.b. — V-8

PE31132	Motorhome Chassis	3225	3307	2,942

NOTE 4: Model codes, prices and weights on charts are for sixes, except where model is in a V-8 only series.

NOTE 5: Detailed Chevrolet records show above production totals with separate breakouts for country of origin and type of engine. To put these in a convenient format, the totals above show combined U.S. output, plus imports from Canada, through Aug. 31, 1972. They include both six-cylinder and V-8 trucks, although most model codes in the chart are six-cylinder codes.

NOTE 6: Platform/stake options, big-block V-8s, diesel engines, and LPG conversions were options. See the options section below for partial data on options usage.

ENGINE [Standard LUV]: Inline. OHV. Four-cylinder. Cast iron block. Bore & stroke: 3.31 in. x 3.23 in. Displacement: 110.8 cid. Compression ratio: 8.5:1. Net horsepower: 75 at 5000 rpm. Maximum Torque: 88 lbs.-ft at 3000 rpm. Five main bearings. Hydraulic valve lifters. Carburetor: two-barrel.

ENGINE [Standard Vega]: Inline. OHV. Four-cylinder. Aluminum block. Bore & stroke: 3.501 in. x 3.625 in. Displacement: 140 cid. Compression ratio: 8.0:1. Brake horsepower: 90 at 4600-4800 rpm. Net horsepower: 72 at 4200 rpm. Maximum Torque: 115 lbs.-ft. at 2400 rpm. Five main bearings. Hydraulic valve lifters. Carburetor: one-barrel.

ENGINE [Standard El Camino; all C/K; P10]: Inline. OHV. Six-cylinder. Cast iron block. Bore & stroke: 3.9 in. x 4.5 in. Displacement: 250 cid. Compression ratio: 8.5:1. Brake horsepower: 145 at 4200 rpm. Maximum Torque: 230 lbs.-ft. at 1600 rpm. Net horsepower: 110 at 4000 rpm. Seven main bearings. Hydraulic valve lifters. Carburetor: Rochester one-barrel model 1.

ENGINE [Standard P20/P30; optional C20/C30]: Inline. OHV. Six-cylinder. Cast iron block. Bore & stroke: 3-7/8 in. x 4-1/8 in. Displacement: 292 cid. Compression ratio: 8.0:1. Brake horsepower: 165 at 4000 rpm. Maximum Torque: 270 lbs.-ft. at 1600 rpm. Net horsepower: 125 at 3600 rpm. Seven main bearings. Hydraulic valve lifters. Carburetor: Rochester one-barrel.

ENGINE [Optional El Camino; G10]: V-block. OHV. Eight-cylinder. Cast iron block. Bore & stroke: 3.875 in. x 3.25 in. Displacement: 307 cid. Compression ratio: 8.5:1. Net horsepower: 130 at 4000 rpm. Five main bearings. Hydraulic valve lifters. Carburetor: Rochester two-barrel.

ENGINE [Optional C/K]: V-block. OHV. Eight-cylinder. Cast iron block. Bore & stroke: 3.875 in. x 3.25 in. Displacement: 307 cid. Compression ratio: 8.5:1. Brake horsepower: 200 at 4600 rpm. Maximum Torque: 300 lbs.-ft. at 2400 rpm. Net horsepower: 135 at 4000 rpm. Five main bearings. Hydraulic valve lifters. Carburetor: Rochester two-barrel.

ENGINE [El Camino; standard in California]: V-block. OHV. Eight-cylinder. Cast iron block. Bore & Stroke: 4.0 in. x 3.5 in. Displacement: 350 cid. Compression ratio: 8.5:1. Net horsepower: 165 at 3400 rpm. Five main bearings. Hydraulic valve lifters. Carburetor: Rochester two-barrel.

ENGINE [Optional: El Camino; C; K; G; P20/P30]: V-block. OHV. Eight-cylinder. Cast iron block. Bore & Stroke: 4.0 x 3.5 in. Displacement: 350 cid. Compression ratio: 8.5:1. Brake horsepower: 250 at 4600 rpm. Torque: 350 lbs.-ft. at 3000 rpm. Net horsepower: 175 at 3600 rpm. Five main bearings. Hydraulic valve lifters. Carburetor: Rochester two-barrel. (Note: Standard in G20/G30 Beauville and Sportvan).

ENGINE [Optional: El Camino; C5; K5; C10; C20; K20; C30;P20/P30]: V-block. OHV. Eight-cylinder. Cast iron block. Bore & stroke: 4.125 in. x 3.75 in. Displacement: 402 cid. Compression ratio: 8.5:1. Brake horsepower: 300 at 4800 rpm. Net horsepower: 240 at 4400 rpm. Five main bearings. Hydraulic valve lifters. Carburetor: Rochester four-barrel.

ENGINE [Optional El Camino SS only; RPO LS5]: V-block. OHV. Eight-cylinder. Cast iron block. Bore & stroke: 4.251 in. x 4.00 in. Displacement: 454 cid. Compression ratio: 8.5:1. Net horsepower: 270 at 4000 rpm. Maximum Torque: 390 lbs.-ft. at 3200 rpm. Five main bearings. Hydraulic valve lifters. Carburetor: Rochester four-barrel.

CHASSIS [LUV]: Wheelbase: 102.4 in. Overall length: 173.8 in. Height: 59.3 in. Front tread: 54 in. Rear tread: 52.2 in. Tires: 6.00-14C.

CHASSIS [Vega]: Wheelbase: 97 in. Overall length: 176 in. Height: 51.8 in. Front tread: 54.8 in. Rear tread: 53.6 in. Tires: E78-14A.

CHASSIS [El Camino]: Wheelbase: 116 in. Overall length: 206.8 in. Height: 54.4 in. Front tread: 60.2 in. Rear tread: 59.2 in. Tires: E78-14B.

CHASSIS [G10]: Wheelbase: 110 in./125 in. Overall length: 178 in./202.2 in. Height 80 in. Tires: E78-14B.

CHASSIS [G20]: Wheelbase: 110 in./125 in. Overall length: 178 in./202.2 in. Height: 80 in. Tires: G78-15B.

CHASSIS [G30]: Wheelbase: 110 in./125 in. Overall length: 178 in./202.5 in. Height: 80 in. Tires: 8.75 x 16.5C.

CHASSIS [Blazer]: Wheelbase: 104 in. Overall length: 177.5 in. Height: 67.7 in. Front tread: 60.4 in. Rear tread: 60.4 in. [4x4]: Tires: E78-15B.

CHASSIS [C10]: Wheelbase: 115 in./127 in. Overall length: 200.5 in. Height: 74.5 in. Tires: [115 in. wheelbase] G78-15B; [127 in. wheelbase] H78-15B.

CHASSIS [K10]: Wheelbase: 115 in./127 in. Tires: [115 in. wheelbase] G78-15B; [127 in. wheelbase] H78-15B.

CHASSIS [P10]: Wheelbase: 102 in. Height: 75 in. Tires: G78-15B.

CHASSIS [C20]: Wheelbase: 127/133 in. Overall length: 200.5 in. Height: 74.5 in. Tires: 8.75 x 16.5C.

CHASSIS [K20]: Wheelbase: 127 in. Tires: 8.75 x 16.5.

CHASSIS [P20]: Wheelbase: 125 in./133 in. Overall length: 220.75 in./244.75 in. Tires: 8.75 x 16.5C.

CHASSIS [C30]: Wheelbase: 133 in. Tires: 8.75 x 16.5.

CHASSIS [P30]: Wheelbase: 125 in./157 in. Overall length: 220.75 in./265.75 in. Tires: 8.75 x 16C.

1972 Chevrolet 1/2-Ton C10 Fleetside Pickup (OCW)

TECHNICAL: Transmission: Three-speed synchromesh. Gears: [1-ton] 4F/1R; [Others] 3F/1R. Column-mounted gearshift lever. Single-plate, dry-disc clutch (250 cid engine); coil-spring single dry-plate (292/307/350/402 cid engines). Rear axle: [1/2-ton] semi-floating; [3/4-ton and 1-ton] full-floating. Hydraulic four-wheel brakes. Kelsey-Hayes pressed steel wheels.

OPTIONS: [1/2-ton] 292 six-cylinder engine ($90). 307 V-8 engine ($120). 400 V-8 engine (average $173). 350 V-8 engine, El Camino ($70). Four-speed transmission ($190). Power-glide transmission (average $195). Turbo-Hydramatic transmission ($242). Power brakes ($50). Power steering (average $140). Four-wheel drive ($575). [3/4-ton] 292 six-cylinder engine ($90). 307 V-8 engine, over six-cylinder ($120). 400 V-8 engine over 307 ($170). Powerglide transmission (average $210). Turbo-Hydramatic transmission (average $210). Four-speed manual transmission (average $105). Power steering (average $140). Four-wheel drive ($660). [1-ton] 307 V-8 engine over six-cylinder ($120). 292 six-cylinder engine ($97). 350 V-8 engine over 307 ($45). 400 V-8 engine ($177). Liquid Petroleum Gas kit ($97). Turbo-Hydramatic transmission ($248). Power steering ($135). 9 ft. platform ($425). 12 ft. platform ($487). 157 in. wheelbase ($40).

OPTIONS FOR 1/2- TO 1-TON CHEVROLET TRUCKS WITH FACTORY INSTALLATION RATES: [C/K Series] Bodyside belt molding (33 percent). Wide lower belt molding (54 percent). Upper bodyside molding (46 percent). Door edge guards (17 percent). Deluxe air-conditioning (33 percent). Roof-mounted air-conditioning (34 percent). Custom Comfort & Appearance group (24 percent). Camper Special package (19 percent). Removable top for Blazer: black (23 percent); white (76 percent). Gauge package (81 percent). Cheyenne Super package (7 percent). Custom Sport Truck (Cheyenne) option (22 percent). [Note: The factory records say CST, even though CST wasn't merchandised in 1972. Most likely, "CST" and "Cheyenne" meant the same thing to the factory]. Chrome front bumper (22 percent). V37 chrome bumper (7 percent). Rear step bumper (20 percent). Full foam seat (21 percent). Painted rear bumper (7 percent). Tachometer (2 percent). Push-button radio (60 percent). AM/FM radio (3 percent). VF1 rear chrome bumper (3 percent). Tool and storage box (6 percent). Camper wiring harness (4 percent). Cargo lamp (5 percent). Wheel trim cover (31 percent). Chrome hubcaps (16 percent). Tilt steering (9 percent). Blazer and C/K 4x4 skid plate (26 percent). Power steering (58 percent). Deluxe wheelcovers (8 percent). M38 Turbo-Hydramatic transmission (55 percent). M49 Turbo-Hydramatic transmission (28 percent). Four-speed manual transmission (13 percent). Liquid Petroleum Gas engine kit (used on 1,429 trucks). 396 V-8 engine (8 percent). 292 six-cylinder engine (8 percent). 350 V-8 engine (79 percent). 4x4 front locking hubs (86 percent). Positraction (15 percent). Bucket seats (4 percent). Front stabilizer (35 percent). Body paint stripe (6 percent). Platform and stake rack (13 percent).

[G Series Vans] Bodyside trim molding (1 percent). Front air-conditioning (12 percent). Rear air-conditioning (4 percent). Camper conversion (113 units). Custom Appearance package (9 percent). Custom Comfort & Appearance Option (11 percent). Gauge package (60 percent). Rear chrome bumper (14 percent). Push-button radio (42 percent). Chrome hubcaps (4 percent). Tilt steering (3 percent). M38 Turbo-Hydramatic transmission (65 percent). 350 V-8 engine (33 percent). Positraction (12 percent). Front stabilizer (57 percent). Stainless steel Jr. West Coast mirror (14 percent). Painted Jr. West Coast mirror (50 percent). Rear door glass (57 percent). Side door glass (28 percent). Swing-out rear door glass (22 percent). Stationary auxiliary seat (87 percent). Side rear door trim panel (used on 13 units). Rear door trim panel (used in 14 units). Heavy-duty rear springs (64 percent). No-Spin rear axle (8 percent). 3.73:1 rear axle (3 percent). 3.40:1 rear axle (32 percent).

[Step-Van] Body insulation (6 percent). Roof insulation (5 percent). Gauge package (96 percent). Cargo lamp (37 percent). Dual rear wheel conversion (88 percent). Roof marker clearance lamps (10 percent). Roof marker cluster bar (5 percent). M38 Turbo-Hydramatic transmission (7 percent). M49 Turbo-Hydramatic transmission (15 percent). Four-speed manual transmission (19 percent). Liquid Petroleum Gas engine kit (nine units). 396 V-8 engine (51 percent). 292 six-cylinder engine (79 percent). 350 V-8 engine (100 percent). Positraction (3 percent). 74 in. rear doors with piano hinges (4 percent); with straps (7 percent).

NOTE: All production and option use information in this section is based on Chevrolet records covering cumulative model year through July 31, 1972. Figures indicate what percentage of trucks eligible for an option were built with it. For example, the 396 cid V-8 was not available in all Step-Vans so the 77 percent figure does not apply to total Step-Van output; only to those Step-Vans available with the 396 V-8. The production total for LUV pickups is actually the number sold between March and December, 1972.

HISTORICAL: Introduced: [LUV] March 1972; [Others] Sept. 21, 1971. Calendar year registrations: [Nova Sportvan] 16,839. [Others] 774,871 including 165,829 Chevy Van/El Caminos/Blazer/Vega/LUV. Calendar year registrations by weight class: [6,000 lbs. and less] 539,242; [6,000-10,000 lbs.] 722,379. Calendar year production: 770,773 units or 31.10 percent share of total truck market. Calendar year sales: 748,478. Model year production by tons and engine: [1/2-ton] (four/six) 85,120; (V-8) 387,582; (both) 472,702. [3/4-ton] (four/six) 15,952; (V-8) 153,383; (both) 169,335. [1-ton] (four/six) 8,316; (V-8) 49,929; (both) 58,245. [Grand total] 700,282 units. Additional production breakouts: [Camper Special] 32,226; [Light truck with Custom Comfort & Convenience] 156,391; [Van with Custom Comfort & Convenience] 8,993; [Factory van-campers] 113; [Custom Sport Truck/Cheyenne] 142,636; [Cheyenne Supers] 40,636. Innovations: Front disc brakes made standard in light-duty trucks. Sliding load door made standard on vans. New cab trim and stain-resistant acrylic enamel paint finish. Stellite-faced exhaust valves in 350 and 400 cid engines. Exhaust valve rotators added to 307/350/400 cid V-8s. Four-barrel 350 cid V-8 optional in 1/2-ton vans. All-new LUV pickup introduced. Record highs of 828,961 units produced and 845,000 units sold for 1972 broke 1971's record. During 1972, Chevrolet predicted that it would have its first one-million unit truck year in 1973. A.T. Olson was assistant general sales manager, the top spot in the truck division.

1972 Chevrolet LUV Pickup (OCW)

1972 Chevrolet Blazer Convertible (OCW)

1972 Chevrolet C30 'Camper Special' Pickup

1972 Chevrolet Custom C10 Fleetside Pickup (OCW)

1972 Chevrolet El Camino Sport Pickup (OCW)

Standard Catalog of Light-Duty Trucks

1972 Chevrolet C20 Fleetside Pickup (OCW)

1972 Chevrolet Cargo Delivery Van (OCW)

1972 Chevrolet 3-Door Suburban (OCW)

1972 Chevrolet Custom C10 Fleetside Pickup (OCW)

1973 CHEVROLET

1/2-TON LUV — MODEL L/SERIES 82 — FOUR: The LUV was a badge-engineered product sourced from Isuzu Motors of Japan. It put Chevrolet in the mini-truck market until the arrival of the S-10 in mid-1981. Beginning early in 1973, the LUV model adopted rectangular-shaped headlamps in place of the circular units used since its 1972 introduction. The grille appeared to have a slightly finer gridwork. A unique (at the time) feature of this Mini-Pickup was a crank-down spare lowered by a chain-and-winch system.

1973 Chevrolet Cheyenne Fleetside Pickup (CP)

1/2-TON VEGA — MODEL V/SERIES 14000 — FOUR: The Vega Panel Express was available again. Its grille was finished in a manner that made the vertical elements slightly less prominent. There was very little change. It was again based on the Kammback wagon, with the rear side windows blanked-out. It came only with the standard all-vinyl interior, less passenger bucket seat. Standard equipment included the four-cylinder aluminum block engine, three-speed manual transmission, front disc brakes, two separate stowage compartments below the floor, many safety features and a choice of colors. It had a 67.4 in. floor length, 42.6 in. between the wheelhousings and a 68.7 cu. ft. cargo volume. Payload capacity was 650 lbs.

1/2-TON EL CAMINO — MODEL C; D/SERIES 13000 — SIX/V-8: The El Camino received its first new body since 1968. Accentuating its appearance, which was essentially that of the Chevelle, were two new trim packages: Estate and Conquista. The former was available on the standard El Camino and included a two-tone paint scheme and special moldings. The Estate version could be ordered only on the Classic model. It consisted of full bodyside and tailgate accents with a woodgrain vinyl trim. In addition, the base El Camino had its own bodyside, tailgate, drip rail and wheel opening moldings.

1/2-TON; 3/4-TON; 1-TON CHEVY VAN — MODEL G/SERIES 10; 20; 30 — SIX/V-8: Chevy Vans had no exterior changes, except that the blue Chevy badge was now painted Ochre. The G10s and G20s had rubber bushings on the inner pivots of their front suspension for a quieter ride. The G30s had a new 5,700 lbs. Salisbury axle. All series included 110 and 125 in. wheelbases. A V-8 was standard in Beauvilles.

1/2-TON BLAZER UTILITY — MODEL C; K/SERIES 5 — SIX/V-8: The 1973 Blazers had a full-time 4x4 system. Those with Cheyenne trim had a chrome circle on the rear fender. The tailgate came two ways. With the open Utility it was like the Fleetside pickup's gate. When the optional hardtop was ordered, the gate had a manually-operated roll-up window. This eliminated the lift-gate that had been used in older tops.

1973 Chevrolet Cheyenne Fleetside Pickup (DFW/TSC)

1/2-TON; 3/4-TON; 1-TON CONVENTIONAL — MODEL C; K/SERIES 10; 20; 30 — The 1973 Chevrolet light trucks were radically changed in appearance from previous models. Major styling features consisted of curved side glass, doors that opened into the roofline and the elimination of roof drip rails. Running along the beltline was a sculptured cove. Along with the very wide and flat load box, it gave the new model very clean and distinctive lines. Also contributing to the Chevrolet's good looks was a simple egg-crate grille, suggestive of the classic 1955 Chevrolet passenger car grille. A wider interior featured a powered, flow-through ventilation system. A redesigned dash, with all instruments and controls placed in a semi-circular cluster within easy reach and view of the driver, was adopted. The steering wheel was also reduced in diameter. All models had longer wheelbases. The C10/K10 Pickups with a 6-1/2 ft. box came on the standard 117-1/2 in. wheelbase, which was used only for these models and small chassis models. The C10/K10 Pickups with an 8 ft. box featured a 131-1/2 in. wheelbase. This wheelbase was also used for 1/2-ton chassis models and all basic C30 models. The C20/K20 trucks, except Suburbans, were on a 127 in. wheelbase. All Suburbans, both 1/2-ton and 3/4-ton, were on a 129.5 in. wheelbase. Longer wheelbases were provided for Chassis & Cab and the new Crew Cab trucks. Crew Cab bodies that seated six, could be had as an option on all 3/4-ton and 1-ton Pickups. The Crew Cab was actually an option costing about $1,000. The box used for factory-made Crew Cab Pickups was the 8 ft. Fleetside box. There were numerous other technical changes. C10 models used rubber control arm bushings for a quieter and smoother ride. Leaf-springs replaced the rear coil springs used in 1972 on C10/C20 models. Four-wheel drive models were fitted with longer front springs and a standard front stabilizer bar. All of the Pickups now used a Salisbury rear end. Only the C10 had this feature before. On C20 and C30 Pickups, an Eaton locking differential was optional. It locked- in upon a 100 rpm difference in the rear axles and had a governor to keep it from locking-in at above 15 mph. Gas tanks were moved from inside the cabs to under them, at the rear. Full-time four-wheel drive was introduced. It was available with only the V-8/Turbo-Hydramatic powertrain. All earlier models were continued, except the Longhorn Pickup. The C10 with 6-1/2 ft. bed was nicknamed the "Fleetwood." This truck name is rarely heard today, however. Available trim levels included Custom, Custom Deluxe, Cheyenne and Cheyenne Super, with features as follows: [Base Custom] Plain black rubber window gaskets and white-painted bumpers. The grille shell had bright metal finish. The vent window pillars and frames were flat black. The standard hubcaps were painted. Rear moldings around the taillamps and tailgate were not available on Customs. [Custom Deluxe] Includes full-width bench seat with comfortably padded seat cushions and backrest; vinyl seat upholstery and door pan-

97

els; steel roof panel painted in main exterior color; black rubber floor mat extending to firewall; padded armrests; padded sunshades; courtesy lamp; prismatic rearview mirror; foam-padded instrument panel; bright upper and lower grille outline moldings; bright headlamp bezels; bright outside rearview mirrors; bright door handles; white-painted front bumper, hubcaps and wheels; and bright Custom Deluxe nameplates. [Cheyenne] Includes bench seat with full-depth foam cushions and backrests; Custom-grained vinyl upholstery or nylon and vinyl upholstery; special door trim panels; cab headliner; deep-twist nylon carpeting extending to firewall; color-keyed garnish moldings; ashtray-mounted cigar lighter; Custom steering wheel; Cheyenne dashboard nameplates; door or manually-operated courtesy lights; extra acoustical insulation; and all Custom Deluxe exterior items, plus cab-mounted cargo lamp; bright metal cab trim and moldings; bright upper bodyside and tailgate moldings; and central taillight appliques for Fleetside and Cheyenne nameplates. [Cheyenne Super] Adds upper and lower bodyside and wheelhouse moldings and a chrome-plated tailgate release. A new offering was the "Big Doolie" type C30 pickup with dual rear wheels.

1/2-TON; 3/4-TON; 1-TON FORWARD-CONTROL — MODEL P/SERIES 10; 20; 30 — SIX/V-8: The Forward-Control chassis was designed for door-to-door delivery service. Body lengths ranged from seven-to-eight feet for the P10 series up to 14 ft. in the P30 series. Step-Vans looked identical to 1972 versions. The P10 models were sold in chassis and steel panel models on a 102 in. wheelbase. These were advertised as Step Van 7 models (due to their seven-foot long bodies). The P20 and P30 series offered larger chassis, plus Step-Van and Step-Van King models with steel or aluminum bodies. The basic body lengths were 10 ft. for the 125 in. wheelbase chassis; 12 ft. for the 133 in. wheelbase; and 14 ft. for the 157 in. chassis. The P30 chassis was also used for Chevrolet's new High-Cube vans and numerous custom motorhome conversions. The Step-Van grilles had single round headlights in the top of the housings, with rectangular parking lamps below. A channel type front bumper was standard equipment. Features included independent coil spring front suspension; and three six-cylinder engines. Buyers could also get full-height doors; sliding side doors and double rear doors.

I.D. DATA: Combination VIN and rating plate located on left door pillar. [El Camino] First symbol indicates manufacturer, 1=Chevrolet. Second symbol indicates car-line/series: C=El Camino; D=El Camino Custom. Third and fourth symbols indicate body type: 80=Sedan-Pickup. Fifth symbol indicates engine: [El Camino] H=350 cid/145 nhp two-barrel V-8; L=350 cid/160 nhp four-barrel V-8; R=400 cid/150 hp two-barrel V-8; U=402 cid/180 nhp four-barrel V-8; Y=454 cid/235 nhp four-barrel V-8. Sixth symbol indicates model year: 3=1973. Seventh symbol indicates assembly plant. Symbols 8-13 indicate the production sequence number starting at 100,001. Ending numbers not available. [All Light-Duty] The first symbol indicates manufacturer: 1=Chevrolet Motor Div. The second symbol indicates chassis type: C=96 in. or 106 in. Conventional Cab; G=Sportvan; H=92 in. Conventional Cab; J=92 in. Conventional Cab with tandem; K=4x4; L=Light-Utility; M=96 in. or 114 in. Conventional Cab with tandem; P=Forward-Control; Z=Motorhome. The third symbol indicates engine as follows: L=454 cid/245 nhp four-barrel V-8; N=110 cid/75 nhp two-barrel L4; Q=250 cid/100 nhp one-barrel L-6; S=292 cid L-6 with LPG conversion; T=292 cid/120 hp one-barrel L-6; X=307 cid/120 nhp two-barrel V-8; Y=350 cid/145 nhp two-barrel V-8; W=350 cid V-8 with LPG conversion; Y=350 cid/160 nhp four-barrel V-8; Z=454 cid/235 nhp four-barrel V-8. The fourth symbol indicates series and tonnage: 1=1/2-ton; 2=3/4-ton; 3=1-ton. The fifth symbol indicates body type: 2=Chassis & Cowl; 3=Chassis & Cab or Motorhome Chassis; 4=Cab with pickup box; 5=Panel or Panel Van; 6=Sportvan; 7=Motorhome; 8=Blazer. The sixth symbol indicates model year: 3=1973. The seventh symbol indicates the assembly plant: A=Lakewood, Ga.; B=Baltimore, Md.; F=Flint, Mich.; J=Janesville, Wis.; K=Leeds, Mo.; U=Lordstown, Ohio; V=Pontiac, Mich.; ; Z=Fremont, Calif.; 1=Oshawa, Canada; 3=GMAD, Detroit, Mich.; 8=Fujisawa, Japan. Symbols 8-13 are the production sequence number. Starting number 10001 Ending numbers not available. Engine numbers located: [Six] on pad at right-hand side of cylinder block at rear of distributor; [V-8] on pad at front, right-hand side of cylinder block.

Model	Body Type	Price	Weight	Prod. Total
1/2-Ton LUV — Model L/Series 82 — 102.4 in. w.b.				
82	Mini-Pickup	2406	2450	18,771
1/2-Ton Vega — Model HV/Series 14000 — 97 in. w.b. — Four				
1HV05	Panel Express	2106	2303	—
El Camino — Model C/Series 13000 — 116 in. w.b. — Six				
1AC80	Sedan-Pickup	2976	3725	Note 1
El Camino Custom — Model D/Series 13000 — 116 in. w.b. — V-8				
1AD80	Custom Sedan-Pickup	3038	3735	Note 1

NOTE 1: Total El Camino production was 64,987.

Model	Body Type	Price	Weight	Prod. Total
1/2-Ton Van — Model G/Series 10 — 110 in. w.b.				
CG11005	Chevy Van	2818	3486	13,408
CG11006	Sportvan	3331	3790	1,111
1/2-Ton Van — Model G/Series 10 — 110 in. w.b. — V-8				
CG11036	Beauville	3785	4078	475
1/2-Ton Van — Model G/Series 10 — 125 in. w.b.				
CG11305	Panel	2954	3651	13,956
CG11306	Sportvan	3455	3960	1,936
1/2-Ton Van — Model G/Series 10 — 125 in. w.b. — V-8				
CG11336	Beauville	3910	4308	1,045
3/4-Ton Van — Model G/Series 20 — 110 in. w.b. — V-8				
CG21005	Panel	2929	3582	5,988
CG21006	Sportvan	3381	3825	552
3/4-Ton Van — Model G/Series 20 — 110 in. w.b. — V-8				
CG21036	Beauville	3861	4150	299
3/4-Ton Van — Model G/Series 20 — 125 in. w.b. — V-8				
CG21305	Panel	3064	3708	20,515
CG21306	Sportvan	3505	3994	3,966
3/4-Ton Van — Model G/Series 20 — 125 in. w.b. — V-8				
CG21336	Beauville	3986	4379	7,750
1-Ton Van — Model G/Series 30 — 110 in. w.b. — V-8				
CG31005	Panel	3038	3886	596
1-Ton Van — Model G/Series 30 — 125 in. w.b. — V-8				
CG31305	Chevy Van	3173	3988	13,420
CG31306	Sportvan	3622	4282	2,307

Model	Body Type	Price	Weight	Prod. Total
1-Ton Van — Model G/Series 30 — 125 in. w.b. — V-8				
CG31336	Beauville	4102	4667	1,999
1/2-Ton Blazer 4x2 — Model C/Series 5 — 106.5 in. w.b.				
CC10514	Open Utility	2637	3595	3,342
1/2-Ton Blazer 4x4 — Model K/Series 5 — 106.5 in. w.b.				
CK10514	Open Utility	3200	3912	44,841
1/2-Ton Conventional — Model C/Series 10 — 117.5 in. w.b.				
CC10703	Chassis & Cab	2577	3234	1,922
CC10704	Step-Side 6.5 ft.	2763	3664	19,408
CC10734	Fleetside 6.5 ft.	2763	3560	43,987
1/2-Ton Suburban — Model C/Series 10 — 129.5 in. w.b.				
CC10906	Suburban (doors)	3560	4195	6,822
CC10916	Suburban (gate)	3590	4203	17,278
1/2-Ton Conventional — Model C/Series 10 — 131.5 in. w.b.				
CC10903	Chassis & Cab	2608	3331	877
CC10904	Step-Side 8 ft.	2799	3836	7,040
CC10934	Fleetside 8 ft.	2799	3726	309,085
1/2-Ton Conventional 4x4 — Model K/Series 10 — 117.5 in. w.b.				
CK10703	Step-Side 6.5 ft.	3510	3989	2,112
CK10703	Fleetside 6.5 ft.	3510	4108	9,605
1/2-Ton Conventional 4x4 — Model K/Series 10 — 129.5 in. w.b.				
CK10906	Suburban (doors)	4338	5200	1,128
CK10916	Suburban (gate)	—	—	3,770
1/2-Ton Conventional 4x4 — Model K/Series 10 — 131.5 in. w.b.				
CK10903	Step-Side 8 ft.	3546	4085	417
CK10903	Fleetside 8 ft.	3546	4210	29,157
1/2-Ton Forward-Control — Model P/Series 10 — 102 in. w.b.				
CP10542	Chassis	2090	2318	281
CP10542	Steel Step-Van	3458	4161	2,877
3/4-Ton Conventional — Model C/Series 20 — 131.5 in. w.b.				
CC20903	Chassis & Cab	2815	3637	8,162
CC20903	Step-Side 8 ft.	3001	4142	4,654
CC20903	Fleetside 8 ft.	3001	4032	131,624
3/4-Ton Conventional — Model C/Series 20 — 129.5 in. w.b.				
CC20906	Suburban (doors)	4009	4817	2,424
CC20916	Suburban (gate)	4040	4825	7,368

NOTE 2: Stake option included with C20 Chassis & Cab production.

Model	Body Type	Price	Weight	Prod. Total
3/4-Ton Crew Cab — Model C/Series 20 — 164.5 in. w.b.				
CE20963	Crew Cab & Chassis	—	—	712
CE20963	Crew Cab Pickup 8 ft.	4001	—	7,137

NOTE 3: Crew Cab Model 963 was an option; average price $1,000.

Model	Body Type	Price	Weight	Prod. Total
3/4-Ton Conventional 4x4 — Model K/Series 20 — 131.5 in. w.b.				
CK20903	Chassis & Cab	3562	4119	880
CK20904	Step-Side 8 ft.	3747	4514	525
CK20934	Fleetside 8 ft.	3747	4640	29,769
3/4-Ton Conventional 4x4 — Model K/Series 20 — 129.5 in. w.b.				
CK20906	Suburban (doors)	4668	5136	780
CK20916	Suburban (gate)	—	—	1,862
3/4-Ton Forward-Control — Model P/Series 20 — 125 in. w.b.				
CP20842	Chassis	2295	2902	409
CP20835	Steel Step-Van	4115	5310	2,099
CP20855	Aluminum Step-Van King	—	—	107
3/4-Ton Forward-Control — Model P/Series 20 — 133 in. w.b.				
CP21042	Chassis	2326	2942	156
CP21035	Steel Step-Van	4222	5559	1,282
CP21035	Aluminum Step-Van King	5015	4841	58
1-Ton Conventional — Model C/Series 30 — 131.5 in. w.b.				
CC30903	Chassis & Cab	3075	3811	17,422
CC30903	Step-Side 8 ft.	3087	4321	1,939
CC30903	Fleetside 8 ft.	3087	4246	7,281

NOTE 4: Stake option included with C30 Chassis & Cab production.

Model	Body Type	Price	Weight	Prod. Total
1-Ton Conventional — Model C/Series 30 — 135.5 in. w.b.				
CC31063	Crew Cab Fleetside	2915	3811	479
1-Ton Conventional — Model C/Series 30 — 159.5 in. w.b.				
CC31403	Crew Cab & Chassis	2955	3934	12,088
1-Ton Conventional — Model C/Series 30 — 164.5 in. w.b.				
CC31963	Crew Cab & Chassis	—	—	80
CC31963	Crew Cab Fleetside	—	—	2,925
1-Ton Forward-Control — Model P/Series 30 — 125 in. w.b.				
CP30842	Chassis 10 ft.	2469	2992	649
CP30842	Steel Step-Van 10 ft.	4284	5379	631
CP30842	Aluminum Step-Van King	—	—	118
CP30842	Motorhome Chassis	—	—	2,341
1-Ton Forward-Control — Model P/Series 30 — 133 in. w.b.				
CP31042	Chassis	2500	3015	—
CP31042	Steel Step-Van King 12 ft.	4392	5611	2,522
CP31042	Aluminum Step-Van King	—	—	244
CP31042	Motorhome Chassis	3285	3254	1,093

1-Ton Forward-Control — Model P/Series 30 — 157 in. w.b.

CP31442	Chassis	—	—	—
CP31442	Steel Step-Van King 14 ft.	—	6677	2,395
CP31442	Aluminum Step-Van King	—	5714	526
CP31142	Motorhome Chassis	3821	3383	4,160

NOTE 5: Model codes, prices and weights on charts are for sixes, except where model is a V-8 only truck.

NOTE 6: Detailed Chevrolet records show above production totals with separate breakouts for country of origin and type of engine. To put these in a convenient format, the totals above show combined U.S. output, plus imports from Canada. They include both six-cylinder and V-8 trucks. The model codes no longer indicate type of engine.

NOTE 7: Platform/stake options, big-block V-8s, diesel engines, and LPG conversions were options. See the options section below for partial data on options usage.

NOTE 8: Additional C30 1-ton production included 1,093 motorhomes on a 127 in. wheelbase; 7,194 motorhomes on a 158.5 in. wheelbase; and 115 motorhomes on a 178 in. wheelbase.

1973 Chevrolet El Camino SS (CP)

ENGINE [Standard: LUV]: Inline. OHV. Four-cylinder. Cast iron block. Bore & stroke: 3.31 in. x 3.23 in. Displacement: 110.8 cid. Compression ratio: 8.5:1. Net horsepower: 75 at 5000 rpm. Maximum Torque: 88 lbs.-ft. at 3000 rpm. Five main bearings. Hydraulic valve lifters. Carburetor: two-barrel.

ENGINE [Standard: Vega]: Inline. OHV. Four-cylinder. Aluminum block. Bore & stroke: 3.501 in. x 3.625 in. Displacement: 140 cid. Compression ratio: 8.0:1. Net horsepower: 72 at 4200 rpm. Maximum Torque: 115 lbs.-ft. at 2400 rpm. Five main bearings. Hydraulic valve lifters. Carburetor: one-barrel.

ENGINE [Optional: Vega]: Inline. OHV. Four-cylinder. Aluminum block. Bore & stroke: 3.501 in. x 3.625 in. Displacement: 140 cid. Compression ratio: 8.0:1. Net horsepower: 85 at 4400 rpm. Maximum Torque: 122 lbs.-ft. at 2400 rpm. Five main bearings. Hydraulic valve lifters. Carburetor: Staged two-barrel.

1973 Chevrolet Blazer (JAG)

ENGINE [Standard: all, except El Camino/LUV/Vega/K20-30/C20]: Inline. OHV. Six-cylinder. Cast iron block. Bore & stroke: 3-7/8 in. x 3-1/2 in. Displacement: 250 cid. Compression ratio: 8.25:1. Net horsepower: 100 at 3600 rpm. Maximum Torque: 175 lbs.-ft. at 2000 rpm. Seven main bearings. Hydraulic valve lifters. Carburetor: one-barrel.

ENGINE [Optional: C/K Series/P20-30]: Inline. OHV. Six-cylinder. Cast iron block. Bore & stroke: 3-7/8 in. x 4-1/8 in. Displacement: 292 cid. Compression ratio: 8.0:1. Net horsepower: 120 at 3600 rpm. Maximum Torque: 225 lbs.-ft. at 2000 rpm. Seven main bearings. Hydraulic valve lifters. Carburetor: one-barrel.

ENGINE [Optional: C10/Blazer/G10/P Series; Standard El Camino]: V-block. OHV. Eight-cylinder. Cast iron block. Bore & stroke: 3-7/8 in. x 3-1/4 in. Displacement: 307 cid. Compression ratio: 8.5:1. Net horsepower: 115 at 3600 rpm. Maximum Torque: 205 lbs.-ft. at 2000 rpm. Five main bearings. Hydraulic valve lifters. Carburetor: two-barrel.

ENGINE [Standard: C20/K20/K30; Optional: G10/G20/G30/P Series/El Camino]: V-block. OHV. Eight-cylinder. Cast iron block. Bore & stroke: 4 in. x 3.48 in. Displacement: 350 cid. Compression ratio: 8.5:1. Net horsepower: 155 at 4000 rpm. Maximum Torque: 225 lbs.-ft. at 2400 rpm. Five main bearings. Hydraulic valve lifters. Carburetor: two-barrel.

ENGINE [Optional: El Camino]: V-block. OHV. Eight-cylinder. Cast iron block. Bore & stroke: 4 in. x 3.48 in. Displacement: 350 cid. Compression ratio: 8.5:1. Net horsepower: 175 at 4000 rpm. Maximum Torque: 260 lbs.-ft. at 2800 rpm. Five main bearings. Hydraulic valve lifters. Carburetor: Rochester model Quadra-Jet, four-barrel.

ENGINE [Optional: El Camino/C20/C30/Suburban 4x2/P30]: V-block. OHV. Eight-cylinder. Cast iron block. Bore & stroke: 4.251 in. x 4.0 in. Displacement: 454 cid. Compression ratio: 8.25:1. Net horsepower: 240 at 4000 rpm. Maximum Torque: 355 lbs.-ft. at 2800 rpm. Five main bearings. Hydraulic valve lifters. Carburetor: Rochester model Quadra-Jet, four-barrel.

1973 Chevrolet 4-Door Suburban Cheyenne (CP)

CHASSIS [LUV]: Wheelbase: 102.4 in. Overall length: 173.8 in. Height: 59.3 in. Front tread: 54 in. Rear tread: 52.2 in. Tires: A78-13B.

CHASSIS [Vega]: Wheelbase: 97 in. Overall length: 176 in. Height: 51.8 in. Front tread: 54.8 in. Rear tread: 53.6 in. Tires: A78-13B.

CHASSIS [El Camino]: Wheelbase: 116 in. Overall length: 201.6 in. Height: 53.8 in. Front tread: 58.5 in. Rear tread: 57.8 in. Tires: G78-14B.

CHASSIS [All Suburbans]: Wheelbase: 129.5 in. Tires: H78-15B.

CHASSIS [G10]: Wheelbase: 110 in./125 in. Overall length: 178 in./202.2 in. Tires: E78-14A.

CHASSIS [G20]: Wheelbase: 110 in./125 in. Overall length: 178 in./202.2 in. Tires: G78-15B.

CHASSIS [G30]: Wheelbase: 110 in./125 in. Overall length: 178 in./202.2 in. Tires: 8.00 x 16.5C.

CHASSIS [Blazer]: Wheelbase: 106.5 in. Overall length: 184.5 in. Height: [4x2 without top] 67.5 in.; [4x2 with top] 69.5; [4x4 without top] 69.5; [4x4 with top] 71.5. Front tread: [4x2] 64.5 in. Rear tread: [4x2] 63.0 in. Front tread: [4x4] 65.75 in. Rear tread: [4x4] 62.75 in. Tires: E78-15B.

CHASSIS [C10]: Wheelbase: 117.5 in./131.5 in. Overall length: 191.2 in./212 in. Height: 69.8 in. Front tread: 65.8 in. Rear tread: 62.7 in. Tires: G78-15B.

CHASSIS [K10]: Wheelbase: 117.5 in./131.5 in. Overall length: 191.3 in./212 in. Height: 72 in. Front tread: 65.8 in. Rear tread: 62.7 in. Tires: G78-15B.

CHASSIS [P10]: Wheelbase: 102 in. Height: 75 in. Tires: G78-15B.

CHASSIS [C20]: Wheelbase: 117.5 in./131.5 in./164.5 in. Overall length: 191.5 in./212 in./244.43 in. Height: 69.8 in. Front tread: 65.8 in. Rear tread: 62.7 in.

CHASSIS [K20]: Wheelbase: 117.5 in./131.5 in. Overall length: 191.3 in./212 in. Height: 73.9 in. Front tread: 65.8 in. Rear tread: 62.7 in. Tires: 8.75 x 16.5C.

CHASSIS [P20]: Wheelbase: 125 in./133 in. Overall length: 220.75 in./244.75 in. Tires: 8.75 x 16.5C.

CHASSIS [C30]: Wheelbase: 131.5 in./164.5 in. Overall length: 212 in./244.43 in. Height: 71.8 in. Front tread: 65.8 in. Rear tread: 62.7 in. Tires: [Regular cab] 8.75 x 16.5C; [Crew Cab] 9.50 x 16.5E.

CHASSIS [P30]: Wheelbase: 125 in./157 in. Overall length: 220.75 in./265.75 in. Tires: 8.75 x 16.5C.

1973 Chevrolet Custom Deluxe 10 Suburban (IMSC/JLM)

TECHNICAL: Transmission: Three-speed synchromesh. Gears: [1-ton] 4F/1R; [Others] 3F/1R. Column-mounted gearshift lever. Single-plate, dry-disc clutch [250 cid engine]; coil-spring single-dry-plate (292/307/350/402 cid engines). Rear axle: [1/2-ton] semi-floating; [3/4-ton and 1-ton] full-floating. Hydraulic four-wheel brakes. Kelsey-Hayes pressed steel wheels.

OPTIONS: [Trucks] Front chrome bumper. Radio AM, AM/FM. Clock. Power steering. Custom deluxe interior. Cheyenne interior. Cheyenne super interior. Below-eyeline mirrors. Drip moldings. Sliding rear window. Cargo lamp. Gauge package. Air-conditioning. Tachometer. Comfortilt steering wheel. Chrome bumper. Exterior tool and storage compartment. Wheelcovers. Whitewall tires. Special trim molding. Woodgrain exterior trim. Rear-step bumper. Glide-out spare tire carrier. [Vega] Special ride and handling package. Rear window air deflector.

HISTORICAL: Calendar year sales: 923,189. First year for 454 cid V-8 option for standard trucks. Salisbury rear axle optional. Six-passenger model introduced. Fuel tank relocated outside cab to a position on the right frame rail. New energy-absorbing steering column.

1973 Chevrolet Vega Panel Express (CP)

1974 CHEVROLET

1974 Chevrolet 4x4 Fleetside Pickup (JAG)

Crew Cab Pickups was the 8 ft. Fleetside box. Technical developments included use of a full-time unit on all V-8 engined 4x4 drive models and the computer-matching of all brake systems to the GVW rating of each truck. The new braking system included a lining sensor on the front disc brakes. It sounded an audible signal when the pads needed replacement. In addition, all Pickups had larger front disc and rear drum brakes, as well as a new hydraulic booster power assist called Hydro-Boost. Interior refinements included foam instrument panel padding with all trim levels. All models had an energy absorbing steering column and, on all models with automatic transmission, an anti-theft ignition system was used.

1/2-TON; 3/4-TON; 1-TON FORWARD-CONTROL — MODEL P/SERIES 10; 20; 30 — SIX/V-8: The Forward-Control chassis was designed for door-to-door delivery service. Body lengths ranged from seven-to-eight feet for the P10 series up to 14 ft. in the P30 series. Step-Vans looked identical to 1973 versions. The P20 and P30 series offered larger chassis, plus Step-Van and Step-Van King models with steel or aluminum bodies. The basic body lengths were 10 ft. for the 125 in. wheelbase chassis; 12 ft. for the 133 in. wheelbase; and 14 ft. for the 157 in. chassis. The P30 chassis was also used for Chevrolet's new High-Cube vans and numerous custom motorhome conversions.

1974 Chevrolet El Camino Classic Sport Pickup (OCW)

I.D. DATA: Serial number located. Combination VIN and rating plate located on left door pillar. [El Camino] First symbol indicates manufacturer, 1=Chevrolet. Second symbol indicates car-line/series: C=El Camino; D=El Camino Custom. Third and fourth symbols indicate body type: 80=Sedan-Pickup. Fifth symbol indicates engine: [El Camino] H=350 cid/145 nhp two-barrel V-8; L=350 cid/160 nhp four-barrel V-8; R=400 cid/150 hp two-barrel V-8; U=402 cid/180 nhp four-barrel V-8; Y=454 cid/235 nhp four-barrel V-8. Sixth symbol indicates model year: 4=1974. Seventh symbol indicates assembly plant. Symbols 8-13 indicate the production sequence starting at 100,001. Ending numbers not available. [All Light-Duty] The first symbol indicates manufacturer: 1=Chevrolet Motor Div. The second symbol indicates chassis type: C=96 in. or 106 in. Conventional Cab; G=Sportvan; H=92 in. Conventional Cab; J=92 in. Conventional Cab with tandem; K=4x4; L=Light-Utility; M=96 in. or 114 in. Conventional Cab with tandem; P=Forward-Control; Z=Motorhome. The third symbol indicates engine as follows: L=454 cid/245 nhp four-barrel V-8; N=110 cid/75 nhp two-barrel L4; Q=250 cid/100 nhp one-barrel L-6; S=292 cid L-6 with LPG conversion; T=292 cid/120 hp one-barrel L-6; X=307 cid/120 nhp two-barrel V-8; Y=350 cid/145 nhp two-barrel V-8; W=350 cid V-8 with LPG conversion; Y=350 cid/160 nhp four-barrel V-8; Z=454 cid/235 nhp four-barrel V-8. The fourth symbol indicates series and tonnage: 1=1/2-ton; 2=3/4-ton; 3=1-ton. The fifth symbol indicates body type: 2=Chassis & Cowl; 3=Chassis & Cab or Motorhome Chassis; 4=Cab with pickup box; 5=Panel or Panel Van; 6=Sportvan; 7=Motorhome; 8=Blazer. The sixth symbol indicates model year: 4=1974. The seventh symbol indicates the assembly plant: A=Lakewood, Ga.; B=Baltimore, Md.; F=Flint, Mich.; J=Janesville, Wis.; K=Leeds, Mo.; U=Lordstown, Ohio; V=Pontiac, Mich.; Z=Fremont, Calif.; 1=Oshawa, Canada; 3=GMAD, Detroit, Mich.; 8=Fujisawa, Japan. Symbols 8-13 are the production sequence number. Starting number: 10001 Ending numbers not available. Engine numbers located: [Six] on pad at right-hand side of cylinder block at rear of distributor; [V-8] on pad at front, right-hand side of cylinder block.

Model	Body Type	Price	Weight	Prod. Total
1/2-Ton LUV — Model L/Series 82 — 102.4 in. w.b.				
82	Mini-Pickup	2406	2475	Note 1
NOTE 1: Calendar year sales: [1973] 39,422; [1974] 30,328.				
1/2-Ton Vega — Model HV/Series 14000 — 97 in. w.b. — Four				
1HV05	Panel Express	2404	2470	—
El Camino — Model C/Series 13000 — 116 in. w.b. — Six				
1AC80	Sedan-Pickup	3139	3950	Note 2
El Camino Classic — Model D/Series 13000 — 116 in. w.b. — V-8				
1AD80	Classic Sedan-Pickup	3277	3975	Note 2
NOTE 2: Total El Camino production was 51,223.				
1/2-Ton Sportvan — Model G/Series 10 — 110 in. w.b.				
CG11005	Chevy Van	3092	3479	Note 3
CG11006	Sportvan	3721	3806	Note 3
1/2-Ton Chevy Van — Model G/Series 10 — 110 in. w.b. — V-8				
CG11036	Beauville	4232	4109	Note 3
1/2-Ton Chevy Van — Model G/Series 10 — 125 in. w.b.— V-8				
CG11305	Panel	3228	3638	Note 3
CG11306	Sportvan	3856	3974	Note 3
1/2-Ton Chevy Van — Model G/Series 10 — 125 in. w.b. — V-8				
CG11336	Beauville	4384	4331	Note 3
3/4-Ton Chevy Van — Model G/Series 20 — 110 in. w.b. — V-8				
CG21005	Panel	3214	3576	Note 3
CG21006	Sportvan	3802	3861	Note 3
3/4-Ton Chevy Van — Model G/Series 20 — 110 in. w.b. — V-8				
CG21036	Beauville	4330	4168	Note 3
3/4-Ton Chevy Van — Model G/Series 20 — 125 in. w.b. — V-8				
CG21305	Panel	3349	3716	Note 3
CG21306	Sportvan	3937	4021	Note 3

1/2-TON LUV — MODEL L/SERIES 82 — FOUR: The LUV for 1974 adopted vertical taillights with a square backup light lens at the bottom. A Mikado trim package with striped upholstery and a sporty three-spoke steering wheel was available.

1/2-TON VEGA — MODEL V/SERIES 14000 — FOUR: The Vega Panel Express had a new front end with a divided four-louver grille and recessed headlamps. Parking lamps moved from under the bumper to between the headlamps and grille. They changed from round to tall rectangular shape. The front and rear sidemarker lamps were raised above bumper level and the rear license plate was now housed in the tailgate center, instead of below the bumper (the bumper was a thicker 5 mph crash-test type). The Vega Panel Express had the same large swing-up tailgate arrangement as the Kammback wagon. The Chevrolet brochure described it as an economy truck. It still came with just one bucket seat, rubber floor coverings and without side windows. Maximum cargo capacity was 50.2 cu. ft. All 14 Vega color combinations were available. The Panel Express used the standard interior (without dash grab handle) in choices of black, neutral, green, saddle, red and chamois colors. Technical improvements included front brake lining wear sensors, electric windshield washer and a new 16-gal. gas tank, five gallons larger than in 1973. Interestingly, Chevrolet used the same artwork in the catalog illustration both years, airbrushing in the minor changes and adding T. Tonies Bakery lettering in the panel sides.

1/2-TON EL CAMINO — MODEL C; D/SERIES 13000 — SIX/V-8: The El Camino continued to be a model of the Malibu series and carried a grille with obvious Mercedes-Benz overtones. The grille was split into six horizontal segments, three on each side of a vertical center molding. A new Classic model was added to the El Camino line. It featured a bright lower body sill molding, a full-width custom seat with a fold-down center armrest, door panel trim, deluxe vinyl-coated headliner and a black-finished rearview mirror.

1/2-TON; 3/4-TON; 1-TON VAN — MODEL G/SERIES 10; 20; 30 — SIX/V-8: Chevy Vans and Sportvans were offered with a new two-tone paint treatment. Also new were improved optional below-eyeline mirrors and new optional bright roof drip moldings. Both models also had a restyled instrument cluster and panel, as well as a new optional air-conditioning system with air outlets designed into the instrument panel. An AM/FM radio, not previously available, was new for 1974. All Vans now had a coolant recovery system, too.

1/2-TON BLAZER UTILITY — MODEL C; K/SERIES 5 — SIX/V-8: The Blazer continued with the 106.5 in. wheelbase introduced in 1973. New was a factory-padded roll bar. The limited-slip differential could be ordered with the full-time four-wheel drive system. Steel-belted radial tires were added to the option list.

1/2-TON; 3/4-TON; 1-TON CONVENTIONAL — MODEL C; K/SERIES 10; 20; 30 — SIX/V-8: After being totally restyled in 1973, the latest Chevrolet pickups and Suburbans were visually virtually unchanged. Exterior changes were highlighted by four new colors, improved below-eyeline mirrors and new optional bright roof drip moldings. The C10/K10 Pickups came with a 6-1/2 ft. box came on the standard 117-1/2 in. wheelbase, which was used only for these models and small chassis models. The C10/K10 Pickups with an 8 ft. box featured a 131-1/2 in. wheelbase. This wheelbase was also used for 1/2-ton chassis models and all basic C30 models. The C20/K20 trucks, except Suburbans, were on a 127 in. wheelbase. All Suburbans, both 1/2-ton and 3/4-ton, were on a 129.5 in. wheelbase. Longer wheelbases were provided for Chassis & Cab and the new Crew Cab trucks. Crew cab bodies that seated six, could be had as an option on all 3/4-ton and 1-ton pickups. The Crew Cab was actually an option costing about $1,000. The box used for factory-made

100

3/4-Ton Chevy Van — Model G/Series 20 — 125 in. w.b. — V-8

CG21336	Beauville	4465	4378	Note 3

1-Ton Chevy Van — Model G/Series 30 — 110 in. w.b. — V-8

CG31005	Panel	3332	3860	Note 3

1-Ton Chevy Van — Model G/Series 30 — 125 in. w.b. — V-8

CG31305	Chevy Van	3467	4007	Note 3
CG31306	Sportvan	4037	4331	Note 3

1-Ton Chevy Van — Model G/Series 30 — 125 in. w.b. — V-8

CG31336	Beauville	4585	4688	Note 3

NOTE 3: Production: [Chevy Van] 70,763; [Sportvan/Beauville] 20,779.

1/2-Ton Blazer 4x2 — Model C/Series 5 — 106.5 in. w.b.

CC10514	Open Utility	2936	3606	Note 4

1/2-Ton Blazer 4x4 — Model K/Series 5 — 106.5 in. w.b.

CK10514	Open Utility	3577	3931	Note 4

NOTE 4: Production: [4x2 and 4x4 Blazer] 56,798.

1/2-Ton Conventional — Model C/Series 10 — 117.5 in. w.b.

CC10703	Step-Side 6.5 ft.	2971	3563	Note 5
CC10703	Fleetside 6.5 ft.	2971	3664	Note 5

1/2-Ton Suburban — Model C/Series 10 — 129.5 in. w.b.

CC10906	Suburban (doors)	3832	4177	Note 6
CC10916	Suburban (gate)	3863	4185	Note 6

NOTE 6: Production: [All C10/K10/C20/K20 Suburbans] 41,882.

1/2-Ton Conventional — Model C/Series 10 — 131.5 in. w.b.

CC10903	Chassis & Cab	3104	3669	Note 5
CC10904	Step-Side 8 ft.	3007	3711	Note 5
CC10934	Fleetside 8 ft.	3007	3821	Note 5

1/2-Ton Conventional 4x4 — Model K/Series 10 — 117.5 in. w.b.

CK10703	Step-Side 6.5 ft.	3703	3973	Note 5
CK10703	Fleetside 6.5 ft.	3703	4077	Note 5

1/2-Ton Conventional 4x4 — Model K/Series 10 — 129.5 in. w.b.

CK10906	Suburban (doors)	4902	5090	Note 6
CK10916	Suburban (gate)	4933	5098	Note 6

* See Note 6 below C10 listing above.

1/2-Ton Conventional 4x4 — Model K/Series 10 — 131.5 in. w.b.

CK10903	Step-Side 8 ft.	3739	4175	Note 5
CK10903	Fleetside 8 ft.	3739	4271	Note 5

NOTE 5: Production: [All C10/K10, except Suburban] 445,699.

1/2-Ton Forward-Control — Model P/Series 10 — 102 in. w.b.

CP10542	Chassis	—	—	Note 7
CP10542	Steel Step-Van	—	—	Note 7

NOTE 7: Production [All P10/P20/P30 models] 19,759.

3/4-Ton Conventional — Model C/Series 20 — 131.5 in. w.b.

CC20903	Chassis & Cab	3104	3669	Note 8
CC20903	Step-Side 8 ft.	3271	4064	Note 8
CC20903	Fleetside 8 ft.	3271	4174	Note 8

3/4-Ton Conventional — Model C/Series 20 — 129.5 in. w.b.

CC20906	Suburban (doors)	4902	5090	Note 5
CC20916	Suburban (gate)	4040	4825	Note 5

* See Note 6 below C10 listing above.

3/4-Ton Crew Cab — Model C/Series 20 — 164.5 in. w.b.

CE20963	Crew Cab & Chassis	4214	4395	Note 8
CE20963	Crew Cab Pickup 8 ft.	4381	4904	Note 8

3/4-Ton Conventional 4x4 — Model K/Series 20 — 131.5 in. w.b.

CK20903	Chassis & Cab	3974	3981	Note 8
CK20904	Step-Side 8 ft.	4141	4372	Note 8
CK20934	Fleetside 8 ft.	4141	4486	Note 8

NOTE 8: Production [All C20/K20 except Suburbans] 178,829.

3/4-Ton Conventional 4x4 — Model K/Series 20 — 129.5 in. w.b.

CK20906	Suburban (doors)	5307	5220	Note 6
CK20916	Suburban (gate)	5276	5228	Note 6

* See Note 6 below C10 listing above.

3/4-Ton Forward-Control — Model P/Series 20 — 125 in. w.b.

CP20842	Chassis	2491	2885	Note 7
CP20835	Steel Step-Van	4471	5293	Note 7
CP20855	Aluminum Step-Van King	—	—	Note 7

3/4-Ton Forward-Control — Model P/Series 20 — 133 in. w.b.

CP21042	Chassis	2522	2915	Note 7
CP21035	Steel Step-Van	4578	5532	Note 7
CP21035	Aluminum Step-Van King	5371	4814	Note 7

* See Note 7 under P10 listing above.

1-Ton Conventional — Model C/Series 30 — 131.5 in. w.b.

CC30903	Chassis & Cab	3201	3828	Note 9
CC30903	Step-Side 8 ft.	3368	4271	Note 9
CC30903	Fleetside 8 ft.	3368	4329	Note 9

1-Ton Conventional — Model C/Series 30 — 135.5 in. w.b.

CC31063	Crew Cab Fleetside	4296	4459	Note 9

1-Ton Conventional — Model C/Series 30 — 159.5 in. w.b.

CC31403	Crew Cab & Chassis	3251	3945	Note 9

1-Ton Conventional — Model C/Series 30 — 164.5 in. w.b.

CC31963	Crew Cab & Chassis	4296	5469	Note 9

NOTE 9: Production: [All C30] 39,964.

1-Ton Forward-Control — Model P/Series 30 — 125 in. w.b.

CP30842	Chassis 10 ft.	2699	3061	Note 7
CP30842	Steel Step-Van 10 ft.	4786	5708	Note 7
CP30842	Aluminum Step-Van King	5579	4989	Note 7
CP30842	Motorhome Chassis	—	—	Note 7

1-Ton Forward-Control — Model P/Series 30 — 133 in. w.b.

CP31042	Chassis	2730	3090	Note 7
CP31042	Steel Step-Van King 12 ft.	4786	5708	Note 7
CP31042	Aluminum Step-Van King	5579	4989	Note 7
CP31042	Motorhome Chassis	—	—	Note 7

1-Ton Forward-Control — Model P/Series 30 — 157 in. w.b.

CP31442	Chassis	2766	3189	Note 7
CP31442	Steel Step-Van King 14 ft.	4786	5708	Note 7
CP31442	Aluminum Step-Van King	5579	4989	Note 7
CP31142	Motorhome Chassis	—	—	Note 7

* See Note 7 under P10 listing above.
NOTE 10: Prices/weights for V-8s, except four- or six-cylinder only trucks.
NOTE 11: Production includes trucks built in Canada for U.S. market.

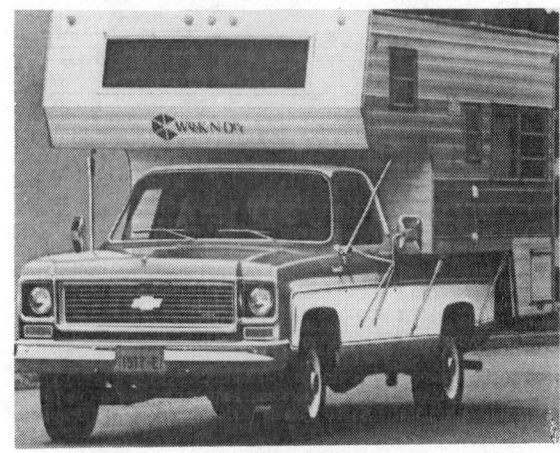

1974 Chevrolet Fleetside Pickup (CP)

ENGINE [Standard LUV]: Inline. OHV. Four-cylinder. Cast iron block. Bore & stroke: 3.31 in. x 3.23 in. Displacement: 110.8 cid. Compression ratio: 8.5:1. Net horsepower: 75 at 5000 rpm. Maximum Torque: 88 lbs.-ft at 3000 rpm. Five main bearings. Hydraulic valve lifters. Carburetor: two-barrel.

ENGINE [Standard Vega]: Inline. OHV. Four-cylinder. Aluminum block. Bore & stroke: 3.501 in. x 3.625 in. Displacement: 140 cid. Compression ratio: 8.0:1. Net horsepower: 75 at 4200 rpm. Maximum Torque: 115 lbs.-ft. at 2400 rpm. Five main bearings. Hydraulic valve lifters. Carburetor: one-barrel.

ENGINE [Standard all except El Camino/LUV/Vega]: Inline. OHV. Six-cylinder. Cast iron block. Bore & stroke: 3-7/8 in. x 3-1/2 in. Displacement: 250 cid. Compression ratio: 8.25:1. Net horsepower: 100 at 3600 rpm. Maximum Torque: 175 lbs.-ft. at 1800 rpm. Seven main bearings. Hydraulic valve lifters. Carburetor: one-barrel.

ENGINE [Optional C20/C30/K20; Standard G20/G30]: Inline. OHV. Six-cylinder. Cast iron block. Bore & stroke: 3-7/8 in. x 4.12 in. Displacement: 292 cid. Compression ratio: 8.0. Net horsepower: 120 at 3600 rpm. Maximum Torque: 215 lbs.-ft. at 2000 rpm. Seven main bearings. Hydraulic valve lifters. Carburetor: one-barrel. (An LPG conversion was available.)

1974 Chevrolet "Big Dooley" Crew Cab Pickup (CP)

ENGINE [Optional C10/G10; Standard El Camino]: Inline. OHV. Eight-cylinder. Cast iron block. Bore & stroke: 4 in. x 3.48 in. Displacement: 350 cid. Compression ratio: 8.5. Brake horsepower: 145 at 3800 rpm. Net horsepower: 145 at 3600 rpm. Maximum Torque: 250 lbs.-ft. at 2200 rpm. Five main bearings. Hydraulic valve lifters. Carburetor: two-barrel. (An LPG conversion was available.)

ENGINE [Optional C30/K10/K20/G10/G20/G30/El Camino]: Inline. OHV. Eight-cylinder. Cast iron block. Bore & stroke: 4 in. x 3.48 in. Displacement: 350 cid. Compression ratio: 8.5. Brake horsepower: 245 at 3800 rpm. Net horsepower: 160 at 3800 rpm. Maximum Torque: 255 lbs.-ft. at 2400 rpm. Five main bearings. Hydraulic valve lifters. Carburetor: four-barrel.

ENGINE [Optional: El Camino]: V-block. OHV. Eight-cylinder. Cast iron block. Bore & stroke: 4.126 in. x 3.76 in. Displacement: 400 cid. Compression ratio: 8.5:1. Net horsepower: 150. Five main bearings. Hydraulic valve lifters. Carburetor: Rochester four-barrel.

ENGINE [Optional: El Camino]: V-block. OHV. Eight-cylinder. Cast iron block. Bore & stroke: 4.125 in. x 3.75 in. Displacement: 400 cid. Compression ratio: 8.5:1. Net horsepower: 180. Five main bearings. Hydraulic valve lifters. Carburetor: Rochester four-barrel.

ENGINE [Optional C10/C20/C30/El Camino]: Inline. OHV. Eight-cylinder. Cast iron block. Bore & stroke: 1-1/4 in. x 4 in. Displacement: 454 cid. Compression ratio: 8.5. Net horsepower: 220. Five main bearings. Hydraulic valve lifters. Carburetor: Rochester four-barrel model Quadra-Jet.

ENGINE [El Camino]: Inline. OHV. Eight-cylinder. Cast iron block. Bore & stroke: 1-1/4 in. x 4 in. Displacement: 454 cid. Compression ratio: 8.5. Net horsepower: 235 at 4000 rpm. Five main bearings. Hydraulic valve lifters. Carburetor: Rochester four-barrel model Quadra-Jet.

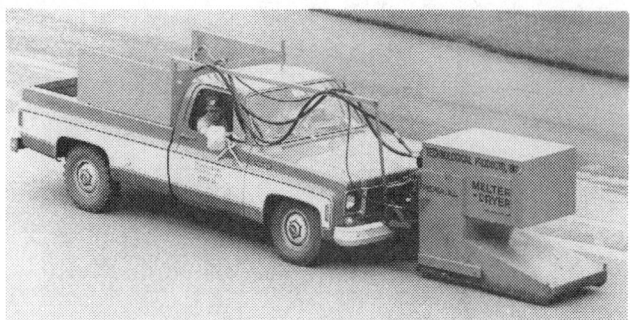

1974 Chevrolet Custom Deluxe 10 Fleetline (IMSC/JLM)

ENGINE [Optional C10/C20/C30]: Inline. OHV. Eight-cylinder. Cast iron block. Bore & stroke: 1-1/4 in. x 4 in. Displacement: 454 cid. Compression ratio: 8.5. Brake horsepower: 5. Net horsepower: 245 at 4000 rpm. Maximum Torque: 365 lbs.-ft. at 2800 rpm. Five main bearings. Hydraulic valve lifters. Carburetor: Rochester four-barrel model Quadra-Jet.

CHASSIS [El Camino]: Wheelbase: 116 in. Overall length: 201.6 in. Height: 53.8 in. Front tread: 58.5 in. Rear tread: 57.8 in. Tires: GR78-14B.

CHASSIS [LUV]: Wheelbase: 102.4 in. Overall length: 173.8 in. Height: 59.3 in. Front tread: 54 in. Rear tread: 52.2 in. Tires: A78-13B.

CHASSIS [Vega]: Wheelbase: 97 in. Overall length: 176 in. Height: 51.8 in. Front tread: 54.8 in. Rear tread: 53.6 in. Tires: A78-13B.

CHASSIS [G10]: Wheelbase: 110 in./125 in. Overall length: 178 in./202.2 in. Tires: E78-14A.

CHASSIS [G20]: Wheelbase: 110 in./125 in. Overall length: 178 in./202.2 in. Tires: G78-15B.

CHASSIS [G30]: Wheelbase: 110 in./125 in. Overall length: 178 in./202.2 in. Tires: 8.00 x 16.5C.

1974 Chevrolet Blazer (CP)

CHASSIS [Blazer]: Wheelbase: 106.5 in. Overall length: 184.5 in. Height: [4x2]: 67.5 in. [without top]; 69.5 in. [with top]. [4x4]: 69.5 in. [without top]; 71.5 in. [with top]. Front tread: 64.5 in. Rear tread: 63.0 in. [4x2]. Front tread: 65.75 in. Rear tread: 62.75 in. [4x4]. Tires: E78-15B.

CHASSIS [C10]: Wheelbase: 117.5 in./131.5 in. Overall length: 191.2 in./211.25 in. Height: 69.8 in. Front tread: 65.8 in. Rear tread: 62.7 in. Tires: G78-15B.

CHASSIS [K10]: Wheelbase: 117.5 in./131.5 in. Overall length: 191.3 in./212 in. Height: 72 in. Front tread: 65.8 in. Rear tread: 62.7 in. Tires: G78-15B.

CHASSIS [P10]: Wheelbase: 102 in. Height: 75 in. Tires: G78-15B.

1974 Chevrolet 4x4 Suburban (JAG)

CHASSIS [C20]: Wheelbase: 117.5 in./131.5 in./164.5 in. Overall length: 191.5 in./212 in./244.43 in. Height: 69.8 in. Front tread: 65.8 in. Rear tread: 62.7 in. Tires: 8.75 x 16.5C. [Crew Cab: 9.50 x 16.5D.]

CHASSIS [K20]: Wheelbase: 117.5 in./131.5 in. Overall length: 191.3 in./212 in. Height: 73.9 in. Front tread: 65.8 in. Rear tread: 62.7 in. Tires: 8.75 x 16.5C.

CHASSIS [P20]: Wheelbase: 125 in./133 in. Overall length: 220.75 in./244.75 in. Tires: 8.75 x 16.5C.

CHASSIS [C30]: Wheelbase: 131.5 in./164.5 in. Overall length: 212 in./244.43 in. Height: 71.8 in. Front tread: 65.8 in. Rear tread: 62.7 in. Tires: 8.75 x 16.5C. [Crew Cab: 9.50 x 16.5E.]

1974 Chevrolet G10 Step Van (CP)

CHASSIS [P30]: Wheelbase: 125 in./157 in. Overall length: 220.75 in./265.75 in. Tires: 8.75 x 16.5C.

TECHNICAL: Transmission: Three-speed synchromesh. Gears: [1-ton] 4F/1R; [Others] 3F/1R. Column-mounted gearshift lever. Single-plate, dry-disc clutch [250 cid engine]; coil-spring single-dry-plate (292/307/350/402 cid engines). Rear axle: [1/2-ton] semi-floating; [3/4-ton and 1-ton] full-floating. Hydraulic four-wheel brakes. Kelsey-Hayes pressed steel wheels.

1974 Chevrolet Vega Panel Express (DFW)

OPTIONS: [El Camino]: SS package ($215). Conquista package. Estate package (Classic models only). Deluxe bumpers. Power door locks. Dual sport mirrors. Turbine I wheels. Wire wheelcovers. [Vega Panel Express] Variable ratio power steering. Electro-clear rear window. Defroster. Radio AM, AM/FM. Power steering. Custom deluxe interior. Cheyenne interior. Cheyenne super interior. Below-eyeline mirrors. Drip molding. Sliding rear window. Cargo lamp. Gauge package. Air-conditioning. Tachometer. Comfortilt steering wheel. Chrome bumpers. Chromed front bumper with rubber impact strips. Exterior tool and storage compartment. Wheelcovers. White wall tires. Special trim molding. Woodgrain exterior trim. Rear step bumper. Glide-out spare tire carrier.

1974 Chevrolet El Camino SS (DFW)

OPTIONS FOR 1/2- TO 1-TON CHEVROLET TRUCKS WITH FACTORY INSTALLA-TION RATES: [El Camino] Automatic transmission (95.8 percent). Power steering (97.3 percent). AM radio (77.5 percent). AM/FM stereo radio (16.4 percent). Small V-8 (66.4 percent). Large V-8 (33.1 percent). Air-conditioning (72.4 percent). Limited-slip differential (9.9 percent). Tinted glass (90.9 percent). Steel-belted radial tires (16.8 percent). Wheelcovers (70.3 percent). Interior trim package (44.5 percent). Exterior trim package (44.5 percent). [Blazer] Automatic transmission (81.5 percent). Power steering (95 percent). AM radio (77.4 percent). AM/FM stereo radio (11.8 percent). Small V-8 (96 percent). Air-conditioning (47.4 percent). Limited-slip differential (8.6 percent). Tinted glass (63.7 percent). Steel-belted radial tires (3.8 percent). Wheelcovers (34.2 percent). Interior trim package (59.5 percent). Exterior trim package (59.5 percent). Four-wheel drive (94.6 percent). [Chevy Van]: Automatic transmission (73.5 percent). Manual disc brakes (23.3 percent). Power disc brakes (76.7 percent). Power steering (41.8 percent). AM radio (43.4 percent). AM/FM stereo radio (2.4 percent). Small V-8 (77 percent). Air-conditioning (11.6 percent). Limited-slip (3.6 percent). Tinted glass (28.3 percent). Interior trim package (21.6 percent). Exterior trim package (21.6 percent). [Sportvan]: Automatic transmission (91.5 percent). Power steering (89.1 percent). AM radio (69 percent). AM/FM stereo radio (10.3 percent). Small V-8 (94.2 percent). Air-conditioning (64 percent). Limited-slip (5.1 percent). Tinted glass (73.4 percent). Steel-belted radial tires (6.3 percent). Interior trim package (17 percent). Exterior trim package (17 percent). [Suburban]: Automatic transmission (89.3 percent). Power steering (71.5 percent). AM radio (67.7 percent). AM/FM stereo radio (12.5 percent). Small V-8 (62.7 percent). Large V-8 (33.7 percent). Air-conditioning (76 percent). Limited-slip (13 percent). Tinted glass (68.2 percent). Steel-belted radial tires (6.4 percent). Wheelcovers (24.1 percent). Interior trim package (72.5 percent). Exterior trim package (72.5 percent). [C10]: Automatic transmission (63.4 percent). Manual disc brakes (58.5 percent). Power disc brakes (41.4 percent). Power steering (63.3 percent). AM radio (71.6 percent). AM/FM stereo radio (3.6 percent). Small V-8 (74.4 percent). Large V-8 (5.9 percent). Air-conditioning (33.3 percent). Limited-slip differential (3.3 percent). Tinted glass (38.9 percent). Steel-belted radial tires (1.2 percent). Wheelcovers (29.3 percent). Interior trim package (47.3 percent). Exterior trim package (47.3 percent). Four-wheel drive (9.8 percent). [C20]: Automatic transmission (66.9 percent). Power steering (100 percent). Small V-8 (78.6 percent). Large V-8 (15.8 percent). Air-conditioning (30.7 percent). Limited-slip differential (14.3 percent). Tinted glass (40.5 percent). Interior trim package (47.3 percent). Exterior trim package (47.3 percent). Four-wheel drive (21.6 percent). [C30]: Automatic transmission (28.9 percent). Power steering (68.9 percent). AM radio (49.4 percent). AM/FM stereo radio (3.9 percent). Small V-8 (64.4 percent). Large V-8 engine (23.8 percent). Air-conditioning (20 percent). Limited-slip differential (10.1 percent). Dual rear wheels (75.6 percent). Tinted glass (29.5 percent). Wheelcovers (1.8 percent). Interior trim package (22.6 percent). Exterior trim package (22.6 percent). [P-Series]: Automatic transmission (56.2 percent). Manual disc brakes (9.2 percent). Power disc brakes (90.8 percent). Power steering (42 percent). Small V-8 (57.6 percent). Large V-8 (7 percent). Air-conditioning (2.1 percent). Limited-slip differential (1 percent). Dual rear wheels (56.1 percent). Tinted glass (11.5 percent). Wheelcovers (1.7 percent). Note: Small V-8 means 350 cid or less; large V-8 means over 350 cid.

1974 Chevrolet Beauville Sportvan (CP)

HISTORICAL: Introduced Sept. 2, 1973. Calendar year registrations: 803,864. Calendar year registrations by weight class: [6,000 lbs. and less] 575,348; [6,000-10,000 lbs.] 228,516. Calendar year production: 838,959 units (not including Vega/El Camino/LUV). Chevrolet held 29.44 percent of the U.S. truck market. On a calendar year basis, this was Chevrolet's second best year in truck sales in history with sales of 885,362 units and production of 896,130. The model year figures were, however, even more impressive with 975,257 sales and 925,696 trucks built to 1974 specifications. This production total includes trucks built in Canada for sale here, but does not include LUVs (which are included in the sales total). An all-time production record, for the Flint, Mich. factory (339,678 trucks) was set. On a calendar year basis, 85.5 percent of Chevrolet's output was V-8 powered; 15.1 percent had six-cylinder engines and a mere 0.4 percent were diesel engined.

1975 CHEVROLET

1975 Chevrolet Fleetside Pickup (CP)

1/2-TON LIGHT UTILITY (LUV) — MODEL 82 — FOUR: The LUV truck again offered the Mikado trim package including striped upholstery, a fancier steering wheel, finer seat cloth, carpets and upgraded trim throughout.
1/2-TON VEGA — MODEL V/SERIES 14000 — FOUR: The Vega Panel Express had the same appearance as 1974. A new GVW of 3,283-3,552 lbs. was listed for 1975. The Vega Panel Express had the same large swing-up tailgate arrangement as the Kammback wagon. The Chevrolet brochure described it as an economy truck. It still came with just one bucket seat, rubber floor coverings and without side windows. Maximum cargo capacity was 50.2 cu. ft. Technical features included front brake lining wear sensors, electric windshield washer and a 16-gallon gas tank.
1/2-TON EL CAMINO — MODEL C; D/SERIES 13000 — V-8: The 1975 Chevrolet El Camino continued the basic 1974 look, but had a slightly revised grille. It was vertically segmented with nine prominent members. There was now a built-in license plate holder at the center of the bumper.
1/2-TON; 3/4-TON; 1-TON VAN — MODEL G/SERIES 10; 20; 30 — SIX/V-8: Chevy Vans and Sportvans were offered again. They had no major changes. The G10 and G20 series offered Chevy Van Panels, Sportvans and V-8-only Beauvilles on 110 or 125 in. wheelbases. The G30 line offered the Chevy Van with a six or V-8 on the small wheelbase and the other styles on the 125 in. wheelbase with V-8s and a new two-tone paint treatment.
1/2-TON BLAZER UTILITY — MODEL C; K/SERIES 5 — SIX/V-8: Blazers had a revamped grille with a larger gridwork, clear-lensed parking lights, and new front fender model identification combining model nameplates and series identification plaques. A restyled tailgate with a quick-release control was used. Two types of 4x4 systems were optionally available in 1975. With a six-cylinder engine or manual gear box, a conventional 4x4 drivetrain was provided. In combination with a V-8 and Turbo-Hydramatic transmission, buyers got the full-time 4x4 system. This applied to both Pickups and Suburbans, as well as to Blazers. According to *FOUR-WHEELER* magazine's June, 1975 issue, you could not order a V-8 powered Chevrolet 4x4 with manual transmission. The magazine said, "In 1974, they did build some that way and had many problems with the New Process full-time 4x4 system. The full-time transfer case just didn't want to work with the manual transmission."

1975 Chevrolet 'Big Dooley' Crew Cab Pickup (CP)

1/2-TON; 3/4-TON; 1-TON CONVENTIONAL — MODEL C; K/SERIES 10; 20; 30 — SIX/V-8: Styling changes for light-duty conventional trucks were headed by revamped grille with a larger gridwork, clear-lensed parking lights, and new front fender identification combining model nameplates and series identification plaques. A restyled tailgate with a quick-release control was used. The C10/K10 Pickups with a 6-1/2 ft. box came on the standard 117-1/2 in. wheelbase, which was used only for these models and small chassis models. The C10/K10 Pickups with an 8 ft. box featured a 131-1/2 in. wheelbase. This wheelbase was also used for 1/2-ton chassis models and all basic C30 models. The C20/K20 trucks, except Suburbans, were on a 127 in. wheelbase. All Suburbans, both 1/2-ton and 3/4-ton, were on a 129.5 in. wheelbase. Longer wheelbases were provided for Chassis

& Cab and the new Crew Cab trucks. Crew cab bodies that seated six could be had as an option on all 3/4-ton and 1-ton pickups. The Crew Cab was actually an option costing about $1,000. The box used for factory-made Crew Cab Pickups was the 8 ft. Fleetside box. Custom Deluxe was the base interior. It included a foam-padded bench seat with blue, green, red or saddle plaid upholstery; a body color steel roof panel; black rubber floor mat; padded armrests; courtesy lamps; prismatic rearview mirror; foam padded dash; bright upper and lower grille outline moldings; bright headlamps bezels; silver plastic grille insert; bright outside rearview mirror; bright door handles; bright Custom Deluxe nameplates and white-painted bumper, hubcaps and wheels. The next-step-up was Scottsdale trim ($137-$199 extra), full-depth foam padded seat; which included woodgrain door trim inserts; an ashtray cigarette lighter; door or manually-operated courtesy lamps; bright door sill plates; color-keyed rubber floor mats; a high-note horn; patterned nylon cloth upholstery with vinyl trim; and all Custom Deluxe exterior features, plus a chrome bumper; chrome hubcaps; chrome bodyside moldings on Fleetsides; bright windshield and window trim; bright-rimmed parking, sidemarker and taillights; and Scottsdale nameplates. Cheyenne trim ($258-$315) was the next notch on the totem pole. It added full-depth foam seat cushions; a choice of custom-grained vinyl or cloth-and-vinyl seats (bucket type optional); an ashtray-mounted cigarette lighter; woodgrain door panel inserts; door or manually-operated courtesy and dome lights; extra cab insulation; and all Scottsdale exterior items, plus bright metal cab back appliques and moldings; bright upper bodyside and tailgate moldings; central appliques for Fleetsides; and Cheyenne nameplates. At the top of the line was the Silverado option ($312-$531) featuring 7 in. thick seat foam; richer basketweave nylon cloth or buffalo hide vinyl; full gauges; woodgraining on the dash panel and door panel inserts; door storage pockets; carpeting; an insulated headliner; extra body insulation; and all Cheyenne exterior items, plus lower bodyside and tailgate moldings; wheel lip moldings; Scottsdale nameplates; and a tailgate applique on Fleetsides. All Pickups could be equipped with an optional glide-out spare tire carrier. Suburbans came with the Custom DeLuxe, Scottsdale, or Silverado (but not Cheyenne) trim levels. An Estate option with woodgrain exterior paneling was offered, too. A removable rear seat was available at extra cost. Buyers still had a choice of end-gate or double panel-door rear styling. Trucks under 6,001 lbs. GVW (except LUVs) were equipped with catalytic converters. They significantly reduced hydrocarbon and carbon monoxide emissions to meet 1975 EPA standards. Chevrolet promoted them as having "newly designed engines with increased efficiency." However, one truck enthusiast publication recommended that since the converter added to cost, it might be a good idea to specify chassis equipment sufficiently heavy-duty to exceed a 6,000 lbs. GVW for C10s, K10s and Blazers. Then the converter wasn't required. Introduced on all engines, except the LUV's, was a high-energy ignition (HEI) system, which delivered a hotter and more consistent spark for better starting power. Also introduced was an outside air carburetion intake and an early fuel evaporation system which provided faster engine warm up after cold start. Chevrolet's stalwart 250 cid six-cylinder engine had a new, integrally-cast cylinder head with improved-flow intake manifold. All 1/2-ton models with this engine had a larger standard clutch. The "Big Doolie" pickup, with dual rear wheels, was one of several equipment offerings. The year's exterior colors were Skyline blue; Hawaiian blue; Catalina blue; Grecian bronze; buckskin; Yuba gold; Moss gold; Willoway green; Spring green; Glenwood green; Crimson red; Rosedale red; Saratoga silver; Sante Fe tan; and Frost white. Two-tone color options came in conventional, special and deluxe combinations, each requiring specific moldings packages.

1/2-TON; 3/4-TON; 1-TON FORWARD-CONTROL — MODEL P/SERIES 10; 20; 30 — SIX/V-8: The Forward-Control chassis was designed for door-to-door delivery service. Body lengths ranged from seven-to-eight feet for the P10 series up to 14 ft. in the P30 series. Step-Vans looked identical to 1973 versions. The P20 and P30 series offered larger chassis, plus Step-Van and Step-Van King models with steel or aluminum bodies. The basic body lengths were 10 ft. for the 125 in. wheelbase chassis; 12 ft. for the 133 in. wheelbase; and 14 ft. for the 157 in. chassis. The P30 chassis was also used for Chevrolet's new High-Cube vans and numerous custom motorhome conversions.

1975 Chevrolet Pickup (CP)

I.D. DATA: Serial number located. Combination VIN and rating plate located on: [El Camino] Top left side of dash; [Conventionals] left door pillar. Serial number systems: [El Camino] First symbol indicates manufacturer, 1=Chevrolet. Second symbol indicates car-line/series: C=El Camino; D=El Camino Custom. Third and fourth symbols indicate body type: 80=Sedan-Pickup. Fifth symbol indicates engine: [El Camino] H=350 cid/145 nhp two-barrel V-8; L=350 cid/160 nhp four-barrel V-8; U=402 cid/175 nhp four-barrel V-8; Y=454 cid/235 nhp four-barrel V-8. Sixth symbol indicates model year: 5=1975. Seventh symbol indicates assembly plant. Symbols 8-13 indicate the production sequence number starting at 100,001. Ending numbers not available. [All Light-Duty] The first symbol indicates manufacturer: 1=Chevrolet Motor Div. The second symbol indicates chassis type: C=96 in. or 106 in. Conventional Cab including Blazer; G=Chevy Van or Sportvan; K=106 in. wheelbase Conventional cab 4x4; P= Forward-Control. The third symbol indicates engine as follows: L=454 cid/245 nhp four-barrel V-8 (P-Series only); M=400 cid/175 nhp four-barrel V-8; N=110 cid/75 nhp two-barrel L4; P=250 cid/105 nhp one-barrel six; Q=250 cid/100 nhp one-barrel L-6; R=292 cid/120 hp one-barrel L-6; T=292 cid/150 nhp one-barrel L-6; U=350 cid four-barrel V-8; V=350 cid/145 nhp two-barrel V-8; Y=350 cid/160 nhp four-barrel V-8; Z=454 cid/230 nhp four-barrel V-8. The fourth symbol indicates series and tonnage: 1=1/2-ton; 2=3/4-ton; 3=1-ton. The fifth symbol indicates body type: 2=Chassis & Cowl; 3=Chassis & Cab or Motorhome Chassis; 4=Cab with pickup box; 5=Panel or Panel Van; 6=Sportvan; Suburban (doors) 7=Motorhome chassis; 8=Blazer. The sixth symbol indicates model year: 5=1975. The seventh symbol indicates the assembly plant: A=Lakewood, Ga.; B=Bal-

timore, Md.; D=Doraville, Ga.; F=Flint, Mich.; J=Janesville, Wis.; K=Leeds, Mo.; S=St. Louis, Mo.; R=Arlington, Texas; U=Lordstown, Ohio; V=Pontiac, Mich. GMAD: Z=Fremont, Calif.; 1=Oshawa, Canada; 3=GMAD, Detroit, Mich.; 4=Scarborough, Ontario, Canada; 8=Fujisawa, Japan. Symbols 8-13 are the production sequence number. Starting number: 10001 Ending numbers not available. Engine numbers located: [Six] on pad at right-hand side of cylinder block at rear of distributor; [V-8] on pad at front, right-hand side of cylinder block.

Model	Body Type	Price	Weight	Prod. Total
1/2-Ton LUV — Model L/Series 82 — 102.4 in. w.b.				
CL10503	Mini-Pickup	2976	2380	Note 1
NOTE 1: Calendar year sales: [974] 30,328.				
1/2-Ton Vega — Model HV/Series 14000 — 97 in. w.b. — Four				
1HV05	Panel Express	2822	2401	—
El Camino — Model C/Series 13000 — 116 in. w.b. — Six				
1AC80	Sedan-Pickup	3828	3706	Note 2
El Camino Classic — Model D/Series 13000 — 116 in. w.b.				
1AD80	Classic Sedan-Pickup	3966	3748	Note 2
NOTE 2: Total El Camino production was 33,620.				
1/2-Ton Van — Model G/Series 10 — 110 in./125 in. w.b.				
CG11005	Chevy Van	3443	3584	—
CG11006	Sportvan	4103	3925	—
CG11006	Beauville	4506	4088	—
NOTE 3: Add for 125 in. wheelbase.				
3/4-Ton Van — Model G/Series 20 — 110 in./125 in. w.b.				
CG21005	Panel	3653	3625	—
CG21006	Sportvan	4275	3910	—
CG21006	Beauville	4880	4583	—
NOTE 4: Add for 125 in. wheelbase.				
1-Ton Van — Model G/Series 30 — 110 in./125 in. w.b.				
CG31005	Panel	3743	3917	—
CG31006	Sportvan	4477	4369	—
CG31006	Beauville	4880	4583	—
NOTE 5: Add for 125 in. wheelbase.				
1-Ton Hi-Cube Van — Model G/Series 30 — 125 in./146 in. w.b.				
CG31303	Hi-Cube 10 ft.	4970	4998	—
CG31603	Hi-Cube 12 ft.	4477	4369	—
1/2-Ton Blazer 4x4 — Model K/Series 5 — 106.5 in. w.b.				
CK10514	Open Utility	4569	4046	—
CK10516	Hardtop Utility	4998	4313	—
NOTE 6: Deduct $1,089 for two-wheel drive Blazer.				
1/2-Ton Conventional — Model C/Series 10 — 117.5 in. w.b.				
CC10703	Chassis & Cab	3676	3318	—
CC10703	Step-Side 6.5 ft.	3609	3649	—
CC10703	Fleetside 6.5 ft.	3609	3713	—
1/2-Ton Suburban — Model C/Series 10 — 129.5 in. w.b.				
CC10906	Suburban (gate)	4707	4336	—
NOTE 7: Deduct for panel door Suburban.				
1/2-Ton Conventional — Model C/Series 10 — 131.5 in. w.b.				
CC10903	Step-Side 8 ft.	3652	3774	—
CC10903	Fleetside 8 ft.	3652	3844	—
NOTE 8: Add $1,089 for K10 (4x4) Pickups and Suburbans.				
1/2-Ton Forward-Control — Model P/Series 10 — 102 in. w.b.				
CP10542	Steel Step-Van	4532	4220	—
3/4-Ton Conventional — Model C/Series 20 — 131.5 in. w.b.				
CC20903	Chassis & Cab	3863	3737	—
CC20903	Step-Side 8 ft.	4030	4137	—
CC20903	Fleetside 8 ft.	4030	4207	—
3/4-Ton Conventional — Model C/Series 20 — 129.5 in. w.b.				
CC20916	Suburban (gate)	5045	4664	—
NOTE 9: Deduct for panel-door Suburban.				
NOTE 10: Add $1,009 for K20 (4x4) Pickups and Suburbans.				
3/4-Ton Bonus Cab — Model C/Series 20 — 164.5 in. w.b.				
CE20943	Bonus Cab Step-Side 8 ft.	4613	—	
CE20943	Bonus Cab Fleetside 8 ft.	4613	4904	
3/4-Ton Crew Cab — Model C/Series 20 — 164.5 in. w.b.				
CE20963	Crew Cab & Chassis	4835	4461	
CE20963	Crew Cab Step-Side 8 ft.	5002	4861	
CE20963	Crew Cab Fleetside 8 ft.	5002	4935	
3/4-Ton Forward-Control — Model P/Series 20 — 125 in./133 in. w.b.				
CP20842	Steel Step-Van 10 ft.	5242	5382	
NOTE 11: Add for Step-Van King; aluminum body; 12 ft. body etc.				
1-Ton Conventional — Model C/Series 30 — 131.5 in. w.b.				
CC30903	Chassis & Cab	3996	3913	
CC30903	Step-Side 8 ft.	4163	4344	
CC30903	Fleetside 8 ft.	4163	4379	

1-Ton Conventional — Model C/Series 30 — 164.5 in. w.b.

CC31963	Crew Cab & Chassis	4988	4517	—
CC31963	Crew Cab & Step-Side 8 ft.	5155	4948	—
CC31963	Crew Cab & Fleetside 8 ft.	5155	4987	—

1-Ton Step-Van — Model P/Series 30 — 125 in./133 in./157 in. w.b.

| CP30842 | Steel Step-Van 10 ft. | 5499 | 5588 | — |

NOTE 12: Add for Step-Van King; aluminum body; 12 ft./14 ft. body etc.

NOTE 13: Industry records show the following 1975 Chevrolet light-duty truck model year production breakouts: [C10/K10 Pickup] 318,234; [C20/K20 Pickup] 144,632; [C30/K30 Pickup] 44,929; [All Suburban] 30,032; [All Step-Van] 16,877; [All El Camino] 33,620; [Blazer] 50,548; [Sportvan] 21,326 and [Chevy Van] 87,290; [Grand Total] 747,488.

1975 Chevrolet El Camino (CP)

ENGINE [LUV]: Inline. OHV. Four-cylinder. Cast iron block. Bore & stroke: 3.31 in. x 3.23 in. Displacement: 110.8 cid. Compression ratio: 8.5:1. Net horsepower: 75 at 5000 rpm. Maximum Torque: 88 lbs.-ft. at 3000 rpm. Five main bearings. Hydraulic valve lifters. Carburetor: two-barrel.

ENGINE [Standard Vega]: Inline. OHV. Four-cylinder. Aluminum block. Bore & stroke: 3.501 in. x 3.625 in. Displacement: 140 cid. Compression ratio: 8.0:1. Net horsepower: 78 at 4200 rpm. Five main bearings. Hydraulic valve lifters. Carburetor: one-barrel.

ENGINE [Standard C10/K10/Blazer/El Camino/G10]: Inline. Gasoline. Six-cylinder. Cast iron block. Bore & stroke: 3-7/8 in. x 3-1/2 in. Displacement: 250 cid. Compression ratio: 8.25:1. Net horsepower: 105 at 3800 rpm. Maximum Torque: 185 lbs.-ft. at 1200 rpm. Seven main bearings. Hydraulic valve lifters. Carburetor: one-barrel.

ENGINE [Optional C10/El Camino]: V-block. Gasoline. Eight-cylinder. Cast iron block. Bore & stroke: 4 in. x 3-1/2 in. Displacement: 350 cid. Compression ratio: 8.5:1. Net horsepower: 145 at 3800 rpm. Maximum Torque: 250 lbs.-ft. at 2200 rpm. Five main bearings. Hydraulic valve lifters. Carburetor: two-barrel.

ENGINE [Standard C20/C30/K20/P10/P20/P30/G20/G30]: Inline. OHV. Six-cylinder. Cast iron block. Bore & stroke: 3-7/8 in. x 4-1/8 in. Displacement: 292 cid. Compression ratio: 8.0:1. Net horsepower: 120 at 3600 rpm. Maximum Torque: 215 lbs.-ft. at 2000 rpm. Seven main bearings. Hydraulic valve lifters. Carburetor: one-barrel.

ENGINE [Optional C10/G10; Standard El Camino]: Inline. OHV. Eight-cylinder. Cast iron block. Bore & stroke: 4 in. x 3.48 in. Displacement: 350 cid. Compression ratio: 8.5. Brake horsepower: 145 at 3800 rpm. Net horsepower: 145 at 3600 rpm. Maximum Torque: 250 lbs.-ft. at 2200 rpm. Five main bearings. Hydraulic valve lifters. Carburetor: two-barrel. (An LPG conversion was available.)

ENGINE [Optional all except Vega/LUV]: V-block. Gasoline. Eight-cylinder. Cast iron block. Bore & stroke: 4 in. x 3-1/2 in. Displacement: 350 cid. Net horsepower: 160 at 3800 rpm. Maximum Torque: 250 lbs.-ft. at 2400 rpm. Five main bearings. Hydraulic valve lifters. Carburetor: four-barrel.

1975 Chevrolet LUV Pickup (CP)

ENGINE [Optional K10/K20/El Camino — $113]: V-block. OHV. Eight-cylinder. Cast iron block. Bore & stroke: 4-1/8 in. x 4 in. Displacement: 400 cid. Compression ratio: 8.5:1. Net horsepower: 175 at 3600 rpm. Five main bearings. Hydraulic valve lifters. Carburetor: four-barrel.

ENGINE [Optional C10/C20/C30]: V-block. OHV. Eight-cylinder. Cast iron block. Bore & stroke: 4-1/8 in. x 4 in. Displacement: 454 cid. Compression ratio: 8.25:1. Net horsepower: 230 at 3800 rpm. Five main bearings. Hydraulic valve lifters. Carburetor: Rochester four-barrel Quadra-Jet.

ENGINE [El Camino]: V-block. OHV. Eight-cylinder. Cast iron block. Bore & stroke: 4-1/8 in x 4 in. Displacement: 454 cid. Compression ratio: 8.25:1. Net horsepower: 235 at 3800 rpm. Five main bearings. Hydraulic valve lifters. Carburetor: Rochester four-barrel Quadra-Jet.

ENGINE [Optional P20/P30 only]: V-block. OHV. Eight-cylinder. Cast iron block. Bore & stroke: 4-1/8 in. x 4 in. Displacement: 454 cid. Compression ratio: 8.25:1. Net horsepower: 245 at 4000 rpm. Maximum Torque: 355 lbs.-ft. at 3000 rpm. Five main bearings. Hydraulic valve lifters. Carburetor: Rochester four-barrel Quadra-Jet.

CHASSIS [LUV]: Wheelbase: 102.4 in. Overall length: 173.8 in. Height: 59.3 in. Front tread: 54 in. Rear tread: 52.2 in. Tires: 6.00 x 14C.

CHASSIS [Vega]: Wheelbase: 97 in. Overall length: 176 in. Height: 51.8 in. Front tread: 54.8 in. Rear tread: 53.6 in. Tires: A78-13B.

CHASSIS [El Camino]: Wheelbase: 116 in. Overall length: 201.60 in. Height: 53. 8 in. Front tread: 58.5 in. Rear tread: 57.8 in. Tires: GR78-15B.

CHASSIS [G10]: Wheelbase: 110 in. /125 in. Overall length: 178 in./202.2 in. Height: 78.8 x 81.2 in. Tires: E78-14A.

CHASSIS [G20]: Wheelbase: 110 in./125 in. Overall length: 178 in./202.2 in. Height: 78.8 x 81.2 in. Tires: G78-15B.

CHASSIS [G30]: Wheelbase: 125 in./146 in. Tires: 8.00 x 16.5C.

CHASSIS [Blazer]: Wheelbase: 106.5 in. Overall length: 184.5 in. Height: [4x2 without top] 66.75 in.; [4x2 with top] 68 in. ; [4x4 without top] 69 in.; [4x4 with top] 71 in. Tread: [4x2] front=64.5 in.; rear=63 in.; [4x4] front=65.75 in.; rear=62.75 in. Tires: [Six] E78-15B ; [V-8] H78-15B.

CHASSIS [C10]: Wheelbase: 117.5 in./131.5 in. Overall length: [Fleetside] 191-1/4 in./211-1/4 in.; [Step-Side] 190-1/4 in./210-1/4 in. Height: 69.8 in. Front tread: 65.8 in. Rear tread: 62.7 in. Tires: G78-15B. (Larger size tubeless and tube-type tires available for all models and series.)

CHASSIS [K10]: Wheelbase: 117.5 in./131.5 in. Overall length: [Fleetside] 191-1/4 in./211-1/4 in.; [Step-Side] 190-1/4 in./210-1/4 in. Height: 72 in. Front tread: 65.8 in. Rear tread: 62.7 in. Tires: G78-15B.

CHASSIS [P10]: Wheelbase: 102 in. Height: 75 in. Tires: G78-15B.

CHASSIS [C20]: Wheelbase: 117.5 in./131.5 in./164.5 in. Overall length: [Fleetside] 191-1/4 in./211-1/4 in./244-1/4 in.; [Step-Side] 210-1/4/244-1/4 in. Height: 69.8 in. Front tread: 65.8 in. Rear tread: 62.7 in. Tires: [Standard] 8.75 x 16.5C in. [Crew Cab] 9.50 x 16.5D

CHASSIS [K20]: Wheelbase: 131.5 in. Overall length: [Fleetside] 211-1/4 in.; [Step-Side] 210-1/4 in. Height: 73.9 in. Front tread: 65.8 in. Rear tread: 62.7 in. Tires: 8.75 x 16.5C.

CHASSIS [P20]: Wheelbase: 125 in./133 in. Overall length: 220.75 in./244.75 in. Tires: 8.75 x 16.5C.

CHASSIS [C30]: Wheelbase: 131.5 in./164.5 in. Overall length: [Fleetside] 211-1/4 in./244-1/4 in.; [Step-Side] 210-1/4 in./244-1/4 in. Height: 71.8 in. Front tread: 65.8 in. Rear tread: 62.7 in. Tires: [Standard] 8.75 x 16.5C in. [Crew Cab] 9.50 x 16.5E

CHASSIS [P30]: Wheelbase: 125 in./133 in./157 in. Overall length: 220.75 in./268.75 in. Tires: 8.75 x 16.5C.

TECHNICAL. (Selected Specifications): [C10] Three-speed manual transmission or Turbo-Hydramatic transmission with 454 cid V-8. [C20] Same as C10 except Turbo-Hydramatic with Crew Cab also. [K10/K20] Three-speed manual transmission or Turbo-Hydramatic transmission or Turbo-Hydramatic with 400 cid V-8. New Process transfer case with 4x4 trucks. Single-plate, dry-disc clutch (with base six-cylinder). Rear axle ratio (with base six-cylinder) 3.73:1 on C10s and 4.10:1 on C20s. Front disc/rear drum brakes. Standard equipment includes steel disc wheels.

1975 Chevrolet Cheyenne Blazer (CP)

OPTIONS: Radio: AM or AM/FM. Windshield embedded antenna. Gauge package (ammeter, oil pressure, temperature) available with either tachometer or clock or with exomomindor gauge only. Tachometer. Drip molding. Exterior tool and storage compartment. Air-conditioning. Stainless steel Wheelcovers. White sidewall tires (Series 10 only). Below-Eyeline mirrors. Comfortilt steering wheel. Rear step bumper. Special trim molding (Fleetside only). Chrome bumpers. Chrome front bumper with rubber impact strips. Woodgrain exterior trim (Fleetside only). Sliding rear window. Cargo area lamp. Box-mounted spare tire. Glide-out spare tire carrier.

HISTORICAL: Introduced Sept. 1, 1974. Calendar year sales: 771,518. High-energy ignition standard. Six-cylinder more efficient and powerful. Extended maintenance schedules. Catalytic converters now standard on pickups under 6,001 lbs. GVW.

Standard Catalog of Light-Duty Trucks

1976 CHEVROLET

1976 Chevrolet Crew Cab Pickup (CP)

1976 Chevrolet Blazer (CP)

1/2-TON LIGHT UTILITY VEHICLE (LUV) — MODEL L/SERIES 10500 — FOUR: Model year 1976 marked the discontinuance of the Vega Panel Express truck. The badge-engineered LUV Mini-Pickup, built by Isuzu, of Japan, returned with a Chevrolet bow tie. It had fenderless-Pickup styling, similar to the Fleetside, but in a much smaller scale. Changes for the LUV included an optional new three-speed automatic transmission. The standard all-vinyl interior had plaid pattern upholstery. A Mikado cloth trim package was available at extra cost. The EPA mileage rating for the mini-pickup was 33 highway/23 city versus the 1975 model's 29 highway/19 city rating.

1/2-TON EL CAMINO — MODEL C; D/SERIES 14000 — SIX/V-8: This season's standard El Camino had single round headlights. Classic models used dual square headlamps stacked vertically at either side. The standard grille had a tight cross-hatched pattern. Others used a mesh insert. Returning to the center of the grille was a bow tie badge. The performance edition had its SS emblem at the lower left-hand grille corner. There was also a Conquista option package.

1976 Chevrolet El Camino Classic (CP)

1/2-TON; 3/4-TON; 1-TON VAN — MODEL G/SERIES 10; 20; 30 — SIX/V-8: Chevrolet vans had the same styling as 1975. The panel-side Chevy Van, windowed Sportvan and fancy Beauville Sportvan all came on 110 in. or 125 in. wheelbases in the 1/2-ton G10 series. The 3/4-ton G20 series offered Chevy Vans and Sportvans in both sizes and a long wheelbase Beauville. In the 1-ton G30 series, all three models came on the long wheelbase and the small Chevy Van was available. All Beauvilles had a V-8 as standard equipment. New was a "Vantastic" option with wild decal graphics, side exhaust pipes, mag wheels and fat tires.

1/2-TON BLAZER — MODEL C; K/SERIES 10500 — SIX/V-8: The Blazer remained more or less a short wheelbase version of C10/K10 trucks. The front end sheet metal of the 1969-1975 models had been essentially identical to a short Chassis, Cowl & Windshield version of the regular trucks with an open cab and a short Fleetside pickup box at the rear. The box had been designed to hold a fully removable full-length roof that gave the Blazer a station wagon appearance. A major development of 1976 was a new body design. It featured a steel half-cab with an integral roll bar built into the steel front compartment roof and lock pillar structures. Available at extra cost was a removable fiberglass-reinforced plastic roof that attached to the pickup box with 16 bolts. Soft-Ride suspension was made standard. The optional Cheyenne package ($626), included a Cheyenne nameplate; front bucket seats; console; gauges; simulated woodgrain trim; chrome front and rear bumpers; bright upper and lower bodyside moldings; bright hubcaps; bright accents; and Cheyenne nameplates. The hardtop version included color-keyed carpets; door pockets; special interior trim; and woodgrain accents. body design for the 1976 model was introduced as a major change for Blazers.

1/2-TON; 3/4-TON; 1-TON — MODEL C; K/SERIES 10; 20; 30 — SIX/V-8: Conventional trucks included the Chassis & Cab, Fleetside and Step-Side Pickups, and the Suburban with its single-unit body. The four-door Suburban had its own exclusive 129.5 in. wheelbase. An end-gate was standard, but double rear panel doors were optional. Other models came on 117.5 or 131.5 in. wheelbases. Short wheelbase Pickups had a 6.5 ft. box and long wheelbase Pickups had an 8 ft. box. All these models were available in the 1/2-ton C10 series. The 3/4-ton C20 series offered the Suburban, plus long wheelbase versions of the other models. Also available were longer Bonus and Crew Cab models on a stretched 164.5 in. wheelbase. The Bonus Cab had two doors, but the cab was extended for added passenger space. The Crew Cab had four doors and a full rear seat. The 1-ton C30 series offered all models in the C30 line, except the Suburban. The C10 and C20 trucks could be had as K10/K20 four-wheel drives. In 1976, the grille texture was changed slightly and the engine call-out badges were removed from in the grille. The 400 cid (actually 402 cid) big-block V-8 was replaced with a 400 cid small-block V-8. Custom Deluxe was the base interior. It included a foam-padded bench seat with blue, green, red or saddle plaid upholstery; a body color steel roof headliner panel; black rubber floor mat; padded armrests; courtesy lamps; prismatic rearview mirror; foam padded dash; bright upper and lower grille outline moldings; bright headlamps bezels; silver plastic grille insert; bright outside rearview mirror; bright door handles; bright Custom Deluxe nameplates and white-painted bumper, hubcaps and wheels. The next-step-up was Scottsdale trim with a full-depth foam padded seat; woodgrain door trim inserts; an ashtray cigarette lighter; door or manually-operated courtesy lamps; bright door sill plates; color-keyed rubber floor mats; a high-note horn; patterned nylon cloth upholstery with vinyl trim; and all Custom Deluxe exterior features, plus a chrome bumper; chrome hubcaps; chrome bodyside moldings on Fleetsides; bright windshield and window trim; bright-rimmed parking, sidemarker and taillights; and Scottsdale nameplates. Cheyenne trim included full-depth foam seat cushions; new ribbed pattern velour or buffalo-hide vinyl upholstery (vinyl bucket seats optional); folding seatbacks; ashtray-mounted cigarette lighter; woodgrain dash insert; door or manually-operated courtesy and dome lamps; and added cab insulation. The exterior featured all Custom Deluxe and Scottsdale features, plus bright metal cab appliques and moldings; bright upper bodyside and tailgate moldings; tailgate center appliques on Fleetsides and Cheyenne nameplates. At the top of the line was the Silverado option featuring extra-thick seat padding; basket weave nylon cloth or buffalo hide vinyl trim; full gauges; woodgrain dash panel; door storage pockets; carpeting; an insulated headliner; extra body insulation; and all Custom Deluxe and Scottsdale exterior items, plus lower bodyside and tailgate moldings; wheel lip moldings; Silverado nameplates; and a tailgate applique on Fleetsides. All pickups could be equipped with an optional glide-out spare tire carrier. Step-Side Pickups with the 6-1/2-foot box were not ignored; they were available with a new trim package including special striping, chromed bumpers, Rally wheels and white-lettered tires. It was offered in four body colors: blue, orange, red or black. Exterior colors for other models were Skyline blue; Hawaiian blue; Catalina blue; Grecian bronze; buckskin; Yuba gold; Moss gold; Willoway green; Spring green; Glenwood green; Crimson red; Rosedale red; Saratoga silver; Santa Fe tan; and Frost white. Two-tone color options came in conventional, special and deluxe combinations, each requiring specific moldings packages.

1/2-TON; 3/4-TON; 1-TON FORWARD-CONTROL — MODEL P-SERIES 10; 20; 30 — SIX/V-8: Forward-Control trucks were P (parcel delivery) models available in the 10 (1/2-ton); 20 (3/4-ton) and 30 (1-ton) series The P10s had a 102 in. wheelbase and 7 ft. body. P20s came with 125 in. or 133 in. wheelbases designed for 10 ft. or 12 ft. bodies. P30s came in these sizes, plus a 157 in. wheelbase designed for 14 ft. bodies. Styling was boxy and unchanged. The grille had two horizontal rectangular openings. The bar between them said Chevrolet. Outside the grille on either end were tall rectangles housing the parking lights and headlamps. A channel type front bumper was used. An interesting thing about P models was that they were available with the most powerful engine offered in trucks, a 245 net horsepower (nhp) version of the 454 cid V-8.

I.D. DATA: Serial number location: Combination VIN and rating plate located on: [El Camino] Top left side of dash; [Conventionals] left door pillar. Serial number systems: [El Camino] First symbol indicates manufacturer, 1=Chevrolet. Second symbol indicates car-line/series: C=El Camino; D=El Camino Classic. Third and fourth symbols indicate body type: 80=Sedan-Pickup. Fifth symbol indicates engine: [El Camino] D=250 cid/105 nhp one-barrel L6; Q=305 cid/140 nhp two-barrel V-8 (except Calif.); H=350 cid/145 nhp two-barrel V-8 (except Calif.); L=350 cid/165 nhp four-barrel V-8; U=400 cid/175 nhp four-barrel V-8. Sixth symbol indicates model year: 6=1976. Seventh symbol indicates assembly plant. Symbols 8-13 indicate the production sequence number starting at 100,001. Ending numbers not available. [All Light-Duty] The first symbol indicates manufacturer: 1=Chevrolet Motor Div. The second symbol indicates chassis type: C=96 in. or 106 in. Conventional Cab including Blazer; G=Chevy Van or Sportvan; K=106 in. Conventional cab 4x4; P= Forward-Control. The third symbol indicates engine as follows: D=250 cid/105 nhp one-barrel L6; L=350 cid/160 nhp four-barrel V-8; N=110 cid/75 nhp two-barrel L4 (LUV); Q=305 cid/130 nhp two-barrel V-8 (except Calif.); S=454 cid/240 nhp four-barrel V-8 (C models only); T=292 cid/120 nhp one-barrel L-6; U=400 cid/175 nhp four-barrel V-8; V=350 cid/145 nhp two-barrel V-8; Y=454 cid/245 nhp four-barrel V-8 (P models only). The fourth symbol indicates series and tonnage: 1=1/2-ton; 2=3/4-ton; 3=1-ton. The fifth symbol indicates body type: 2=Chassis & Cowl; 3=Chassis & Cab; 4=Cab with pickup box; 5=Panel or Panel Van; 6=Sportvan; Suburban (doors) 7=Motorhome chassis; 8=Blazer. The sixth symbol indicates model year: 6=1976. The seventh symbol indicates the assembly plant: A=Lakewood, Ga.; B=Baltimore, Md.; F=Flint, Mich.; J=Janesville, Wis.; S=St. Louis, Mo.; U=Lordstown, Ohio; V=Pontiac, Mich. GMAD; Z=Fremont, Calif.; 1=Oshawa, Canada; 3=GMAD, Detroit, Mich.;

4=Scarborough, Ontario, Canada; 8=Fujisawa, Japan. Symbols 8-13 are the production sequence number. Starting number: 10001 Ending numbers not available. Engine numbers located: [Six] on pad at right-hand side of cylinder block at rear of distributor; [V-8] on pad at front, right-hand side of cylinder block.

Model	Body Type	Price	Weight	Prod. Total
1/2-Ton LUV — Model L/Series 10500 — 102.4 in. w.b.				
CL10503	Pickup	3285	2460	Note 1
NOTE 1: Calendar year sales: 45,670.				
1/2-Ton El Camino — Model C; D/Series 14000 — 116 in. w.b.				
IAC80	Sedan-Pickup	4333	3791	Note 2
IAD80	Classic Sedan-Pickup	4468	3821	Note 2
NOTE 2: Model year production: 44,890 El Camino/El Camino Classic.				
1/2-Ton Vans — Model G/Series 10 — 110 in./125 in. w.b.				
CG11005	Panel	3811	3593	Note 3
CG11006	Sportvan	4509	3917	Note 3
* Add for 125 in. wheelbase.				
1/2-Ton Van — Model G/Series 10 — 125 in. w.b.				
CG11006	Beauville	5102	4293	Note 3
3/4-Ton Vans — Model G/Series 20 — 110 in./125 in. w.b.				
CG21005	Panel Van	4022	3620	Note 3
CG21006	Sportvan	4682	3903	Note 3
* Add for 125 in. wheelbase.				
3/4-Ton Vans — Model G/Series 20 — 125 in. w.b.				
CG21306	Beauville	5220	4259	Note 3
1-Ton Vans — Model G/Series 30 — 110 in./125 in. w.b.				
CG31005	Panel Van	4143	3861	Note 3
1-Ton Vans — Model G/Series 30 — 125 in. w.b.				
CG31306	Sportvan	4915	4321	Note 3
CG31306	Beauville	5318	4508	Note 3
1-Ton High-Cube — Model G/Series 30 — 125 in. w.b.				
CG31303	Hi-Cube 10 ft.	5405	4990	Note 3
1-Ton High-Cube — Model G/Series 30 — 146 in. w.b.				
CG31603	High-Cube 12 ft.	5883	5732	Note 3
Series P10 — Step-Van — 102 in. w.b.				

NOTE 3: Model year production: [Chevy Van] 125,695; [Sportvan/Beauville] 26,860; [Hi-Cube] No separate breakout.

Model	Body Type	Price	Weight	Prod. Total
1/2-Ton Blazer 4x4 — Model K/Series 10500 — 106.5 in. w.b.				
CK10516	Utility Hardtop	5365	4017	Note 4
CK10516	Open Utility	5265	—	Note 4
NOTE 4: Model year production: 74,389.				
1/2-Ton Conventional — Model C/Series 10 — 117.5 in. w.b.				
CC10703	Chassis & Cab	3957	3449	Note 5
CC10703	Step-Side 6.5 ft.	3863	3790	Note 5
CC10703	Fleetside 6.5 ft.	3863	3848	Note 5
1/2-Ton Suburban — Model C/Series 10 — 129.5 in. w.b.				
CC10906	Suburban 9 ft. (gate)	5087	4335	Note 6
* Panel doors optional.				
1/2-Ton Conventional — Model C; K/Series 10 — 131.5 in. w.b.				
CC10903	Step-Side 6.5 ft.	3908	3877	Note 5
CC10903	Fleetside 6.5 ft.	3908	3953	Note 5
* Add for K10 (4x4) Pickup and Suburban.				

NOTE 5: Model year production: [C10/K10 Conventional] 458,424.
NOTE 6: Model year production: [C10/K10/C20/K20 Suburban] 44,977.

Model	Body Type	Price	Weight	Prod. Total
1/2-Ton Step-Van — Model P/Series 10 — 102 in. w.b.				
CP10542	Steel Step-Van 7 ft.	4855	4204	—
3/4-Ton Conventional — Model C/Series 20 — 131.5 in. w.b.				
CC20903	Chassis & Cab	4139	3730	Note 7
CC20903	Step-Side	4306	4128	Note 7
CC20903	Fleetside	4306	4204	Note 7
3/4-Ton Suburban — Model C/Series 20 — 129.5 in. w.b.				
CC10906	Suburban 9 ft. (gate)	5375	4717	Note 6
* Panel doors optional.				
CC20943	Chassis & Bonus Cab	4786	4198	Note 7
CC20943	Fleetside & Bonus Cab 8 ft.	4953	4676	Note 7
CC20963	Chassis & Crew Cab	5160	4441	Note 7
CC20963	Fleetside & Crew Cab 8 ft.	5327	4919	Note 7
* Add for K20 (4x4) Pickup and Suburban.				

NOTE 6: Model year production: [C10/K10/C20/K20 Suburban] 44,977.
NOTE 7: Model year production: [C20/K20 Conventional 172,419.

Model	Body Type	Price	Weight	Prod. Total
3/4-Ton Step-Van — Model P/Series 20 — 125 in./133 in. w.b.				
CP20842	Steel Step-Van 10 ft.	5563	5300	—
* Add for 12 ft./133 in. wheelbase P10842 model.				
1-Ton Conventional — Model C/Series 30 — 131.5 in. w.b.				
CC30903	Chassis & Cab	4279	3887	Note 8
CC30903	Step-Side 8 ft.	4446	4316	Note 8
CC30903	Fleetside 8 ft.	4446	4357	Note 8

Model	Body Type	Price	Weight	Prod. Total
1-Ton Conventional — Model C/Series 30164.5 in. w.b.				
CC30943	Chassis & Bonus Cab	5210	4420	Note 8
CC30943	Fleetside & Bonus Cab 8 ft.	5377	4894	Note 8
CC30963	Chassis & Crew Cab	5320	4497	Note 8
CC30963	Fleetside & Crew Cab 8 ft.	5487	5506	Note 8

NOTE 8: Model year production: [C30] 45,299.

Model	Body Type	Price	Weight	Prod. Total
1-Ton Step-Van — Model P/Series 30 — 125/133/157 in. w.b.				
CP30842	Steel Step-Van 10 ft.	5864	5506	—

* Add for 12 ft./133 in. wheelbase P30842 model.
** Add for 14 ft./157 in. wheelbase P31042 model.
NOTE 9: Prices/weights for base V-8s (except six-cylinder only models).

1976 Chevrolet Fleetside Pickup With Camper (CP)

ENGINE [Standard LUV]: Inline. OHV. Four-cylinder. Cast iron block. Bore & stroke: 3.31 in. x 3.23 in. Displacement: 110.8 cid. Compression ratio: 8.5:1. Net horsepower: 75 at 5000 rpm. Maximum Torque: 88 lbs.-ft. at 3000 rpm. Five main bearings. Hydraulic valve lifters. Carburetor: Rochester Quadra-Jet four-barrel.

ENGINE [Standard C10/K10/F44/El Camino/Blazer/Vans]: Inline. OHV. Six-cylinder. Cast iron block. Bore & stroke: 3-7/8 in. x 3-1/2 in. Displacement: 250 cid. Compression ratio: 8.25:1. Net horsepower: 100 at 3600 rpm. Maximum. Torque: 175 lbs.-ft. at 1800 rpm. Seven main bearings. Hydraulic valve lifters. Carburetor: one-barrel.

ENGINE [Standard C20/C30/K20/Step-Van]: Inline. OHV. Six-cylinder. Cast iron block. Bore & stroke: 3-7/8 in. x 4-1/8 in. Displacement: 292 cid. Compression ratio: 8.0:1. Net horsepower: 120 at 3600 rpm. Maximum Torque: 215 lbs.-ft. at 2000 rpm. Seven main bearings. Hydraulic valve lifters. Carburetor: one-barrel.

ENGINE [Optional El Camino]: V-block. OHV. Eight-cylinder. Cast iron block. Bore and stroke: 3.736 x 3.48 in. Displacement: 305 cid. Net horsepower: 140. Taxable horsepower: 44.66. Five main bearings. Hydraulic lifters. Carburetor: two-barrel.

ENGINE [Optional C Series]: V-block. OHV. Eight-cylinder. Cast iron block. Bore and stroke: 3.736 x 3.48 in. Displacement: 305 cid. Net horsepower: 130. Taxable horsepower: 44.66. Five main bearings. Hydraulic lifters. Carburetor: two-barrel.

ENGINE [Optional C10/El Camino]: V-block. OHV. Eight-cylinder. Cast iron block. Bore & stroke: 4 in. x 3-1/2 in. Displacement: 350 cid. Compression ratio: 8.5:1. Net horsepower: 145 at 3800 rpm. Maximum Torque: 250 lbs.-ft. at 2200 rpm. Five main bearings. Hydraulic valve lifters. Carburetor: two-barrel.

ENGINE [Optional:A except LUV/El Camino]: V-block. OHV. Eight-cylinder. Cast iron block. Bore & stroke: 4 in. x 3-1/2 in. Displacement: 350 cid. Compression ratio: 8.5:1. Net horsepower: 160 at 3800 rpm. Maximum Torque: 255 lbs.-ft. at 2800 rpm. Five main bearings. Hydraulic valve lifters. Carburetor: Rochester Quadra-Jet four-barrel.

ENGINE [Optional: El Camino]: V-block. OHV. Eight-cylinder. Cast iron block. Bore & stroke: 4 in. x 3-1/2 in. Displacement: 350 cid. Compression ratio: 8.5:1. Net horsepower: 165 at 3800 rpm. Maximum Torque: 255 lbs.-ft. at 2800 rpm. Five main bearings. Hydraulic valve lifters. Carburetor: Rochester Quadra-Jet four-barrel.

ENGINE [Optional K10/K20/Vans/Blazer-$144/El Camino-$148]: V-block. OHV. Eight-cylinder. Cast iron block. Bore & stroke: 4-1/8 in. x 4 in. Displacement: 400 cid. Compression ratio: 8.5:1. Net horsepower: 175 at 3600 rpm. Maximum Torque: 290 lbs.-ft. at 280C rpm. Five main bearings. Hydraulic valve lifters. Carburetor: Rochester four-barrel Quadra-Jet.

1976 Chevrolet Fleetside Pickup (CP)

ENGINE [Optional C10/C20/C30-$423]: V-block. OHV. Eight-cylinder. Cast iron block. Bore & stroke: 4-1/4 in. x 4 in. Displacement: 454 cid. Compression ratio: 8.25:1. Net horsepower: 240 at 3800 rpm. Maximum Torque: 370 lbs.-ft. at 2800 rpm. Five main bearings. Hydraulic valve lifters. Carburetor: Rochester Quadra-Jet four-barrel.

ENGINE [Step-Van]: V-block. OHV. Eight-cylinder. Cast iron block. Bore & stroke: 4-1/8 in. x 4 in. Displacement: 454 cid. Compression ratio: 8.25:1. Net horsepower: 245 at 3800 rpm. Five main bearings. Hydraulic valve lifters. Carburetor: Rochester four-barrel Quadra-Jet.

1976 Chevrolet "Big 10" Fleetside Pickup (CP)

CHASSIS [LUV]: Wheelbase: 102.4 in. Overall length: 173.8 in. Height: 59.3 in. Front tread: 54 in. Rear tread: 52.2 in. Tires: E78 x 14B.

CHASSIS [El Camino]: Wheelbase: 116 in. Overall length: 201.6 in. Height: 53. 8. Front tread: 58.5 in. Rear tread: 57.8 in. Tires: GR78-15B.

CHASSIS [Blazer]: Wheelbase: 106.5 in. Overall length: 184.5 in. Height: [4x2] (without top) 66.75 in.; (with top) 68.75 in. [4x4] (without top) 69 in.; (with top) 71 in. Front/rear tread: [4x2] 64.5 in./63 in.; [4x4] 65.75 in./62.75 in. Tires: [Six] E78-15B; [V-8] H78-15B.

CHASSIS [G10]: Wheelbase: 110 in./125 in. Overall length: 178 in./202.2 in. Height: 78.8 x 81.2 in. Tires: [SWB] E78 x 15B; [LWB] F78 x 15B.

CHASSIS [G20]: Wheelbase: 110 in./125 in. Overall length: 178 in./202.2 in. Height: 78.8 x 81.2 in. Tires: J78-15B.

CHASSIS [G30]: Wheelbase: 125 in./146 in. Tires: 8.00 x 16.5C.

1976 Chevrolet LUV Pickup (CP)

CHASSIS [C10/C10]: Wheelbase: 117.5/131.5 in. Overall length: Fleetside: 191.5 in./211.40 in.; Step-Side: 190.75 in./210.50 in. Height: 69.8 in. Front tread: 65.8 in. Rear tread: 62.7 in. Tires: G70-15B. Tires: [Six] L78-15B; [V-8] L78-15C [V-8].

CHASSIS [K10]: Wheelbase: 117.5 in./131.5 in. Overall length: Fleetside: 192.10 in./212 in.; Step-Side: 191.30 in./211.20 in. Height: 72 in. Front tread: 65.8 in. Rear tread: 62.7 in. Tires: L78-15B.

CHASSIS [P10]: Wheelbase: 102 in. Tires: L78-15B.

CHASSIS [C20]: Wheelbase: 131.5 in./164.5 in. Overall length: Fleetside: 211.40 in./244.40 in.; Step-Side: 210.50 in. Height: 69.8 in. Front tread: 65.8 in. Rear tread: 62.7 in. Tires: 8.75 x 16.5C. Bonus Cab tires: [Front] 8.75 x 16.5C [Rear]; 8.75 x 16.5D. Crew Cab tires: 9.50 x 16.5D.

CHASSIS [K20]: Wheelbase: 131.5 in. Overall length: Fleetside: 212 in.; Step-Side: 211.20 in. Height: 73.9 in. Front tread: 65.8 in. Rear tread: 62.7 in. Tires: 8.75 x 16.5C.

CHASSIS [P20]: Wheelbase: 125 in./133 in. Overall length: 220.75 in./244.75 in. Tires: 8.75 x 16.5C.

CHASSIS [C30]: Wheelbase: 131.5 in./164.5 in. Overall length: Fleetside: 211.40 in./244.40 in.; Step-Side: 210.50 in. Height: 69.8 in. Front tread: 65.8 in. Rear tread: 62.7 in. Tires: 8.75 x 16.5C. Bonus and Crew Cab tires: 9.50 x 16.5E.

CHASSIS [P30]: Wheelbase: 125 in./157 in. Overall length: 220.75 in./268.75 in. Tires: 8.75 x 16.5C.

1976 Chevrolet Silverado Cuburban (CP)

TECHNICAL: (Selected Specifications): [C10] Three-speed manual transmission or Turbo-Hydramatic transmission with 454 cid. [C20] Same as C10 except Turbo-Hydramatic with Crew Cab also. [K10/K20] Three-speed manual transmission or Turbo-Hydramatic with 400 cid V-8. New Process transfer case with 4x4 trucks. Single-plate, dry-disc clutch (with base six-cylinder). Rear axle ratio (with base six-cylinder) 3.73:1 on C10s and 4.10:1 on C20s. Front disc/rear drum brakes. Standard equipment includes steel disc wheels.

OPTIONS: [El Camino] SS equipment package ($226). Conquista package for El Camino Classic ($128). 350 cid V-8 ($30). 400 cid V-8 ($148). [Blazer] Cheyenne package ($626). 400 cid four-barrel V-8 engine ($144). [Pickups/Suburbans] 400 cid V-8 engine ($144). C20 eight-foot stake equipment ($595). C30 nine-foot stake equipment ($695). C10 4x4 option ($1,147). C20 4x4 option ($1,066). [Chevy Van] 350 four-barrel V-8 for G10 ($17). M40 Turbo-Hydramatic transmission ($246). Optional axle ratios ($13). Limited-slip axle ($137). Polywrap air cleaner ($11). Air-conditioning ($527). Front and rear air-conditioning ($840). Heavy-duty battery ($16). Power brakes, G10 ($55). Chrome bumpers ($33). Heavy-duty clutch ($7). Heavy-duty radiator ($24). Push-button radio ($67). AM/FM radio ($145). Painted outside rearview mirror ($19.50). Stainless outside rearview mirror ($31). Back door glass ($45). Extra heavy-duty cooling ($48). Custom Deluxe trim package ($14). Gauge package ($13). 42-amp. generator ($25). Tinted glass ($14). Body moldings ($55). Auxiliary seat ($67). Heavy-duty shocks ($16). Comfortilt steering ($58). 50-gal. fuel tank ($50). Rally wheels ($70). Custom Appearance package ($99). Step-Van: 11,000 lbs. rear axle ($152). 454 cid V-8 engine ($452). Radios: AM; AM/FM ($151.00). Tachometer. Sliding rear window. Speed and cruise control. Cargo area lamp. Below-Eyeline mirrors. Bucket seats. Two-tone paint combinations. Pickup box side rails. Rear chromed step bumper. Deluxe chromed bumper. Stainless steel wheelcovers. White-stripe or white-lettered tires, Series 10 only ($187.55). Glide-out spare tire carrier. Silverado trim package ($172.00). Scottsdale trim package.

1976 Chevrolet Beauville Sportvan (CP)

HISTORICAL: Introduced: Oct. 2, 1975. Calendar year sales: 1,048,135. Model year sales: [light-duty Pickups] 682,039; [Vans] 128,040; [Blazer] 66,368; [El Camino] 43,595; [LUV] 41,693; [Suburban] 40,122; [Medium-and heavy-duty] 43,312. [Total] 1,045,169. Innovations: All-new Blazer with station wagon type New trim packages and options. J.T. Riley was sales manager for Chevrolet Motor Div.'s truck group. All-time high output of Blazers, Vans and Suburbans in calendar year 1976. Chevrolet was America's leading truck-maker with its strong 35.02 percent market share for calendar 1976.

1977 CHEVROLET

1977 Chevrolet Cheyenne Fleetside Pickup (CP)

1/2-TON LIGHT UTILITY VEHICLE (LUV) — MODEL L/SERIES 10500 — FOUR: The badge-engineered LUV mini-pickup, built by Isuzu, of Japan, returned with a Chevrolet bow tie. It had fenderless-pickup styling like a Fleetside, but in a much smaller scale. The standard all-vinyl interior had plaid pattern upholstery. A Mikado cloth trim package was available at extra cost. For the first time, the Luv was merchandised in chassis & cab form. The main reason for this was to provide a mini-motorhome chassis. Platform and stake models were also seen. The Mighty Mike package came with a new, wide tape stripe running from doors to the rear. A "color spectrum" paint treatment was featured at the beginning of the decal, on the doors. At the rear, reversed-out lettering identified the package, which included white spoke wheels and fat white-letter tires.

1/2-TON EL CAMINO — MODEL C; D/SERIES 14000 — SIX/V-8: Standard El Caminos continued to feature single headlights and a cross-hatched grille insert. Classic models had a vertical members grille and dual stacked headlights. The grille surround molding was a much thicker piece of chrome. Classics carried a model identification script below the front fender's El Camino lettering. Their rocker panels had bright metal underscores. The sporty package included SS identification letters for the lower left-hand grille corner, plus SS decals for the cowlsides. Twin tape stripes ran from behind the decal to the rear. Styled wheels and white-letter tires were other extras. There was also a Conquista option package.

1/2-TON; 3/4-TON; 1-TON VAN — MODEL G/SERIES 10; 20; 30 — SIX/V-8: Chevrolet vans had the same styling as 1976. The panel-side Chevy Van and windowed Sportvans both came on 110 in. or 125 in. wheelbases in the 1/2-ton G10 series. The 3/4-ton G20 series offered Chevy Vans and Sportvans in both sizes and a long wheelbase Beauville Sportvan. In the 1-ton G30 series, all three models came on the long wheelbase and the small Chevy Van was available. All Beauvilles had a V-8 as standard equipment.

1/2-TON BLAZER — MODEL C; K/SERIES 10500 — SIX/V-8: The Blazer remained more or less a short wheelbase version of C10/K10 trucks. It featured a steel half-cab with an integral roll bar built into the steel front compartment roof and lock pillar structures. There was a short Fleetside pickup box at the rear. A new optional softtop came in white, black, blue or buckskin. Also available at extra cost was a removable fiberglass-reinforced plastic roof that attached to the pickup box with 16 bolts. Soft-Ride suspension was standard. For 1977 there was a restyled egg-crate grille with 15 openings (instead of 32) and dark gray metallic finish (instead of Argent silver). Custom Deluxe trim was standard. The optional Cheyenne package included a Cheyenne nameplate; front bucket seats; console; gauges; simulated woodgrain trim; chrome front and rear bumpers; bright upper and lower bodyside moldings; bright hubcaps; bright accents; and Cheyenne nameplates. Cheyenne hardtops also included color-keyed carpets; door pockets; special interior trim; and woodgrain accents.

1/2-TON; 3/4-TON; 1-TON — MODEL C; K/SERIES 10; 20; 30 — SIX/V-8: Conventional trucks included the Chassis & Cab, Fleetside and Step-Side Pickups, and the Suburban with its single-unit body. The four-door Suburban had its own exclusive 129.5 in. wheelbase. An end-gate was standard, but double rear panel doors were optional. Other models came on 117.5 or 131.5 in. wheelbases. Short wheelbase Pickups had a 6.5 ft. box and long wheelbase Pickups had an 8 ft. box. All these models were available in the 1/2-ton C10 series. The 3/4-ton C20 series offered the Suburban, plus long wheelbase versions of the other models. Also available were longer Bonus and Crew Cab models on a stretched 164.5 in. wheelbase. The Bonus Cab had four doors, but no rear seat, providing over 50 cu. ft. of lockable storage space. The Crew Cab had four doors and a full rear seat. The 1-ton C30 series offered all models in the C30 line, except the Suburban. Beginning this year, the C30 models, as well as the C10 and C20 trucks, could be had with four-wheel drive. The 4x4s were called K10s, K20s and K30s. The new K30s carried a heavier capacity 4,500 lbs. front driving axle, instead of the 3,800 lbs. axle on 3/4-ton models. Other equipment on the K30s included a modified 7,500 lbs. rear axle, power steering and a standard four-speed manual transmission. Also for 1977, all Chevrolet Conventionals had a new grille arrangement with four (rather than eight) vertical dividers and two (rather than three) horizontal bars. A secondary mesh was placed behind the major grille sections. Single unit combination tail-stop-backup lights replaced the former separate units on Step-Side models. A new Pickup option was a Sport package with special hood and bodyside striping and white-spoke or Rally wheels. The Sport tape stripes followed the body feature lines and continued in tiara fashion across the roof. "Chevy Sport" lettering appeared on the upper box sides of Fleetlines and the rear spare tire cover on Step-Sides. Appearance changes to the 1977 truck interiors consisted of new seat trim colors, fabrics and woodgrain trim. Custom Deluxe was the basic trim level. It included a foam-padded bench seat with plaid upholstery; a body color steel roof headliner panel; black rubber floor mat; padded armrests; courtesy lamps; prismatic rearview mirror; foam padded dash; bright upper and lower grille outline moldings; bright headlamp bezels; silver plastic grille insert; bright outside rearview mirror; bright door handles; bright Custom Deluxe nameplates; and white-painted bumper, hubcaps and wheels. The next-step-up was Scottsdale trim with a full-depth foam padded seat; woodgrain door trim inserts; an ashtray cigarette lighter; door or manually-operated courtesy lamps; bright door sill plates; color-keyed rubber floor mats; a high-note horn; patterned nylon cloth upholstery with vinyl trim; and all Custom Deluxe exterior features, plus a chrome bumper; chrome hubcaps; chrome bodyside moldings on Fleetsides; bright windshield and window trim; bright-rimmed parking, sidemarker and taillights; and Scottsdale nameplates. Cheyenne trim included full-depth foam seat cushions; ribbed pattern velour or buffalo-hide vinyl upholstery (vinyl bucket seats optional); folding seatbacks; ashtray-mounted cigarette lighter; chestnut woodgrain dash and door inserts; door or manually-operated courtesy and dome lamps; and added cab insulation. The exterior featured all Custom Deluxe and Scottsdale features, plus bright metal cab appliques and moldings; bright upper bodyside and tailgate moldings; tailgate center appliques on Fleetsides and Cheyenne nameplates. At the top of the line was the Silverado option featuring extra-thick seat padding; velour cloth-and-vinyl or buffalo hide vinyl trim; tilting seatbacks; full gauges; chestnut woodgrain dash panel and door inserts; door storage pockets; carpeting; an insulated headliner; extra body insulation; and all Custom Deluxe, Scottsdale and Cheyenne exterior items, plus lower bodyside and tailgate moldings; wheel lip moldings; Silverado nameplates; and a tailgate applique on Fleetsides. Joining the optional equipment list was an Operating Convenience package with power windows and power door locks. These could also be ordered separately and represented a first in the truck industry. Another new option was an Exterior Decor package. It included a spring-loaded hood emblem, two-tone paint and color-coordinated hood striping. Six new two-tone color schemes were offered in this package. They featured a secondary color on the hood, between bodyside moldings, and on the roof of cab models. Also offered were new wheelcovers for 1/2-ton models and an inside hood release. The big 454 cid V-8 was now fitted with double-honed piston walls and modified rings for improved oil consumption. Also debuting was a new method of gasketing rocker covers and redesigned distributor cap and rotor. Exterior colors for 1977 were Mariner blue; Cordova brown; Saratoga silver; Light blue; Cardinal red; Buckskin tan; Holly green; Russet metallic; Hawaiian blue; Santa Fe tan; Mahogany; Red metallic; Colonial yellow; Frost white; and Seamist green.

1977 Chevrolet Blazer (CP)

1/2-TON; 3/4-TON; 1-TON FORWARD-CONTROL — MODEL P-SERIES 10; 20; 30 — SIX/V-8: Forward-Control trucks were P (parcel delivery) models available in the 10 (1/2-ton); 20 (3/4-ton) and 30 (1-ton) series The P10s had a 102 in. wheelbase and 7 ft. body. P20s came with 125 in. or 133 in. wheelbases designed for 10 ft. or 12 ft. bodies. P30s came in these sizes, plus a 157 in. wheelbase designed for 14 ft. bodies. Styling was boxy and unchanged. The grille had two horizontal rectangular openings. The bar between them said Chevrolet. Outside the grille on either end were tall rectangles housing the parking lights and headlamps. A channel type front bumper was used. An interesting thing about P models was that they were available with the most powerful engine offered in trucks, a 240 net horsepower (nhp) version of the 454 cid V-8.

I.D. DATA: Serial number located: Combination VIN and rating plate located on: [El Camino] Top left side of dash; [Conventionals] left door pillar. Serial number systems: [El Camino] First symbol indicates manufacturer, 1=Chevrolet. Second symbol indicates car-line/series: C=El Camino; D=El Camino Classic. Third and fourth symbols indicate body type: 80=Sedan-Pickup. Fifth symbol indicates engine: [El Camino] D=250 cid/110 nhp one-barrel L6; U=305 cid/145 nhp two-barrel V-8; L=350 cid/170 nhp four-barrel V-8. Sixth symbol indicates model year: 7=1977. Seventh symbol indicates assembly plant. Symbols 8-13 indicate the production sequence number starting at 100,001. Ending numbers not available. [All Light-Duty] The first symbol indicates manufacturer: 1=Chevrolet Motor Div. The second symbol indicates chassis type: C=96 in. or 106 in. Conventional Cab including Blazer; G=Chevy Van or Sportvan; K=106 in. Conventional cab 4x4; P=Forward-Control; L=Light Utility. The third symbol indicates engine as follows: D=250 cid/110 nhp one-barrel L6; L=350 cid/165 nhp four-barrel V-8; N=110 cid/80 nhp two-barrel L4 (LUV); S=454 cid/245 nhp four-barrel V-8 (C models only); T=292 cid/120 nhp one-barrel L-6; U=305 cid/145 nhp two-barrel V-8; Y=454 cid/240 nhp four-barrel V-8 (P models only). The fourth symbol indicates series and tonnage: 1=1/2-ton; 2=3/4-ton; 3=1-ton. The fifth symbol indicates body type: 2=Chassis & Cowl; 3=Chassis & Cab; 4=Cab with pickup box or Hi-Cube van; 5=Panel or Panel Van; 6=Sportvan; Suburban (doors) 7=Motorhome chassis; 8=Utility. The sixth symbol indicates model year: 7=1977 The seventh symbol indicates the assembly plant: A=Lakewood, Ga.; B=Baltimore, Md.; F=Flint, Mich.; J=Janesville, Wis.; S=St. Louis, Mo.; U=Lordstown, Ohio; V=Pontiac, Mich. GMAD; Z=Fremont, Calif.; 1=Oshawa, Canada; 3=GMAD, Detroit, Mich.; 4=Scarborough, Ontario, Canada; 8=Fujisawa, Japan. Symbols 8-13 are the production sequence number. Starting number: 10001 Ending numbers not available. Engine numbers located: [Six] on pad at right-hand side of cylinder block at rear of distributor; [V-8] on pad at front, right-hand side of cylinder block.

Model	Body Type	Price	Weight	Prod. Total
1/2-Ton LUV — Model L/Series 10500 — 102.4 in. w.b.				
CL10503	Chassis & Cab	3084	2380	Note 1
CL10503	Pickup	3284	2380	Note 1

NOTE 1: Calendar year sales: 67,539.

Model	Body Type	Price	Weight	Prod. Total
1/2-Ton El Camino — Model C; D/Series 14000 — 116 in. w.b.				
IAC80	Sedan-Pickup	4268	3797	Note 2
IAD80	Classic Sedan-Pickup	4403	3763	Note 2

* Add $244 for SS package.

NOTE 2: Model year production: 54,321 El Camino/El Camino Classic.

Model	Body Type	Price	Weight	Prod. Total
1/2-Ton Vans — Model G/Series 10 — 110 in./125 in. w.b.				
CG11005	Panel	4112	3586	Note 3
CG11006	Sportvan	4885	3913	Note 3
* Add for 125 in. w.b.				
1/2-Ton Van — Model G/Series 10 — 125 in. w.b.				
CG11006	Beauville	5548	4314	Note 3
3/4-Ton Vans — Model G/Series 20 — 110 in./125 in. w.b.				
CG21005	Panel Van	4375	3607	Note 3
CG21006	Sportvan	5110	3890	Note 3
* Add for 125 in. w.b.				
3/4-Ton Vans — Model G/Series 20 — 125 in. w.b.				
CG21306	Beauville	5775	4267	Note 3
1-Ton Vans — Model G/Series 30 — 110 in./125 in. w.b.				
CG31005	Panel Van	4496	3840	Note 3
* Add for 125 in. w.b.				
1-Ton Vans — Model G/Series 30 — 125 in. w.b.				
CG31306	Sportvan	5368	4300	Note 3
CG31306	Beauville	5871	4508	Note 3
1-Ton High-Cube — Model G/Series 30 — 125 in. w.b.				
CG31303	Hi-Cube 10 ft.	6410	4961	Note 3
1-Ton High-Cube — Model G/Series 30 — 146 in. w.b.				
CG31603	High-Cube 12 ft.	6593	5727	Note 3

NOTE 3: Model year production: [Chevy Van] 147,377; [Sportvan/Beauville] 43,386; [Hi-Cube] No separate breakout.

Model	Body Type	Price	Weight	Prod. Total
1/2-Ton Blazer 4x4 — Model K/Series 10500 — 106.5 in. w.b.				
CK10516	Utility Hardtop	5603	4268	Note 4
CK10516	Open Utility	5503	—	Note 4

NOTE 4: Model year production: 86,838 (87.8 percent 4x4).

Model	Body Type	Price	Weight	Prod. Total
1/2-Ton Conventional — Model C/Series 10 — 117.5 in. w.b.				
CC10703	Chassis & Cab	4116	3251	Note 5
CC10703	Step-Side 6.5 ft.	4122	3585	Note 5
CC10703	Fleetside 6.5 ft.	4122	3645	Note 5
1/2-Ton Suburban — Model C/Series 10 — 129.5 in. w.b.				
CC10906	Suburban 9 ft. (gate)	5248	4315	Note 6
* Panel doors optional.				
1/2-Ton Conventional — Model C; K/Series 10 — 131.5 in. w.b.				
CC10903	Step-Side 6.5 ft.	3908	3877	Note 5
CC10903	Fleetside 6.5 ft.	3908	3953	Note 5

* Add for K10 (4x4) Pickup and Suburban.

NOTE 5: Model year production: [C10/K10 Conventional] 525,791 (21 percent 4x4).

NOTE 6: Model year production: [C10/K10/C20/K20 Suburban] 44,977 (20.9 percent 4x4).

Model	Body Type	Price	Weight	Prod. Total
1/2-Ton Step-Van — Model P/Series 10 — 102 in. w.b.				
CP10542	Steel Step-Van 7 ft.	5391	4176	—
3/4-Ton Conventional — Model C/Series 20 — 131.5 in. w.b.				
CC20903	Chassis & Cab	4399	3662	Note 7
CC20903	Step-Side	4624	4051	Note 7
CC20903	Fleetside	4624	4142	Note 7

3/4-Ton Suburban — Model C/Series 20 — 129.5 in. w.b.

CC10906	Suburban 9 ft. (gate)	5775	4671	Note 6

* Panel doors optional.

CC20943	Chassis & Bonus Cab	5046	4164	Note 7
CC20943	Fleetside & Bonus Cab 8 ft.	5271	4644	Note 7
CC20963	Chassis & Crew Cab	5420	4850	Note 7
CC20963	Fleetside & Crew Cab 8 ft.	5645	4880	Note 7

* Add for K20 (4x4) Pickup and Suburban.

NOTE 6: Model year production: [C10/K10/C20/K20 Suburban] 60,273 (20.9 percent 4x4).
NOTE 7: Model year production: [C20/K20 Conventional] 189,150 (31 percent 4x4).

3/4-Ton Step-Van — Model P/Series 20 — 125 in./133 in. w.b.

CP20842	Steel Step-Van 10 ft.	6287	5273	—

* Add for 12 ft./133 in. wheelbase P10842 model.

1-Ton Conventional — Model C/Series 30 — 131.5 in. w.b.

CC30903	Chassis & Cab	4539	3803	Note 8
CC30903	Step-Side 8 ft.	4764	4192	Note 8
CC30903	Fleetside 8 ft.	4764	4283	Note 8

1-Ton Conventional — Model C/Series 30164.5 in. w.b.

CC30943	Chassis & Bonus Cab	5470	4444	Note 8
CC30943	Fleetside & Bonus Cab 8 ft.	5695	4924	Note 8
CC30963	Chassis & Crew Cab	5580	5475	Note 8
CC30963	Fleetside & Crew Cab 8 ft.	5805	5015	Note 8

NOTE 8: Model year production: [C30] 60,779 (8 percent 4x4).

1-Ton Step-Van — Model P/Series 30 — 125/133/157 in. w.b..

CP30842	Steel Step-Van 10 ft.	6603	5493	—

* Add for 12 ft./133 in. wheelbase P30842 model.
** Add for 14 ft./157 in. wheelbase P31042 model.

NOTE 9: Prices/weights for base V-8s (except six-cylinder only models).

1977 Chevrolet Classic Pickup El Camino (CP)

ENGINE [Standard LUV]: Inline. OHV. Four-cylinder. Cast iron block. Bore & stroke: 3.31 in. x 3.23 in. Displacement: 110.8 cid. Compression ratio: 8.5:1. Net horsepower: 80 at 5000 rpm. Maximum Torque: 88 lbs.-ft. at 3000 rpm. Five main bearings. Hydraulic valve lifters. Carburetor: Rochester Quadra-Jet four-barrel.
ENGINE [Standard C10/K10/El Camino/Blazer/Vans]: Inline. OHV. Six-cylinder. Cast iron block. Bore & stroke: 3-7/8 in. x 3-1/2 in. Displacement: 250 cid. Compression ratio: 8.25:1. Net horsepower: 110 at 4800 rpm. Maximum. Torque: 175 lbs.-ft. at 1800 rpm. Seven main bearings. Hydraulic valve lifters. Carburetor: one-barrel.
ENGINE [Standard C20/C30/K20/Step-Van]: Inline. OHV. Six-cylinder. Cast iron block. Bore & stroke: 3-7/8 in. x 4-1/8 in. Displacement: 292 cid. Compression ratio: 8.0:1. Net horsepower: 120 at 3600 rpm. Maximum Torque: 215 lbs.-ft. at 2000 rpm. Seven main bearings. Hydraulic valve lifters. Carburetor: one-barrel.
ENGINE [Optional El Camino]: V-block. OHV. Eight-cylinder. Cast iron block. Bore and stroke: 3.736 x 3.48 in. Displacement: 305 cid. Net horsepower: 145. Taxable horsepower: 44.66. Five main bearings. Hydraulic lifters. Carburetor: two-barrel.
ENGINE [Optional C Series]: V-block. OHV. Eight-cylinder. Cast iron block. Bore and stroke: 3.736 x 3.48 in. Displacement: 305 cid. Net horsepower: 130. Taxable horsepower: 44.66. Five main bearings. Hydraulic lifters. Carburetor: two-barrel.
ENGINE [Optional C Series]: V-block. OHV. Eight-cylinder. Cast iron block. Bore & stroke: 4 in. x 3-1/2 in. Displacement: 350 cid. Compression ratio: 8.5:1. Net horsepower: 145 at 3800 rpm. Maximum Torque: 250 lbs.-ft. at 2200 rpm. Five main bearings. Hydraulic valve lifters. Carburetor: two-barrel.
ENGINE [Optional El Camino]: V-block. OHV. Eight-cylinder. Cast iron block. Bore & stroke: 4 in. x 3-1/2 in. Displacement: 350 cid. Compression ratio: 8.5:1. Net horsepower: 170 at 3800 rpm. Maximum Torque: 255 lbs.-ft. at 2800 rpm. Five main bearings. Hydraulic valve lifters. Carburetor: Rochester Quadra-Jet four-barrel.
ENGINE [Optional K10/K20/Vans/Blazer]: V-block. OHV. Eight-cylinder. Cast iron block. Bore & stroke: 4-1/8 in. x 4 in. Displacement: 400 cid. Compression ratio: 8.5:1. Net horsepower: 175 at 3600 rpm. Maximum Torque: 290 lbs.-ft. at 2800 rpm. Five main bearings. Hydraulic valve lifters. Carburetor: Rochester four-barrel Quadra-Jet.
ENGINE [Optional P Series]: V-block. OHV. Eight-cylinder. Cast iron block. Bore & stroke: 4-1/4 in. x 4 in. Displacement: 454 cid. Compression ratio: 8.25:1. Net horsepower: 240 at 3800 rpm. Maximum Torque: 370 lbs.-ft. at 2800 rpm. Five main bearings. Hydraulic valve lifters. Carburetor: Rochester Quadra-Jet four-barrel.
ENGINE [Step-Van]: V-block. OHV. Eight-cylinder. Cast iron block. Bore & stroke: 4-1/8 in. x 4 in. Displacement: 454 cid. Compression ratio: 8.25:1. Net horsepower: 245 at 3800 rpm. Five main bearings. Hydraulic valve lifters. Carburetor: Rochester four-barrel Quadra-Jet.
CHASSIS [LUV]: Wheelbase: 102.4 in. Overall length: 173.8 in. Height: 59.3 in. Front tread: 54 in. Rear tread: 52.2 in. Tires: E78 x 14B.
CHASSIS [El Camino]: Wheelbase: 116 in. Overall length: 210.6 in. Height: 53. 8. Front tread: 58.5 in. Rear tread: 57.8 in. Tires: GR78-15B.
CHASSIS [Blazer]: Wheelbase: 106.5 in. Overall length: 184.5 in. Height: [4x2] (without top) 66.75 in.; (with top) 68.75 in. [4x4] (without top) 69 in.; (with top) 71 in. Front/rear tread: [4x2] 64.5 in./63 in.; [4x4] 65.75 in./62.75 in. Tires: [Six] E78-15B; [V-8] H78-15B.
CHASSIS [G10]: Wheelbase: 110 in./125 in. Overall length: 178 in./202.2 in. Height: 78.8 x 81.2 in. Tires: [SWB] E78 x 15B; [LWB] F78 x 15B.
CHASSIS [G20]: Wheelbase: 110 in./125 in. Overall length: 178 in./202.2 in. Height: 78.8 x 81.2 in. Tires: J78-15B.
CHASSIS [G30]: Wheelbase: 125 in./146 in. Tires: 8.00 x 16.5C.
CHASSIS [C10/C10]: Wheelbase: 117.5/131.5 in. Overall length: Fleetside: 191.5 in./ 211.40 in.; Step-Side: 190.75 in./210.50 in. Height: 69.8 in. Front tread: 65.8 in. Rear tread: 62.7 in. Tires: G70-15B. Tires: [Six] L78-15B; [V-8] L78-15C [V-8].
CHASSIS [K10]: Wheelbase: 117.5 in./131.5 in. Overall length: Fleetside: 192.10 in./212 in.; Step-Side: 191.30 in./211.20 in. Height: 72 in. Front tread: 65.8 in. Rear tread: 62.7 in. Tires: L78-15B.
CHASSIS [P10]: Wheelbase: 102 in. Tires: L78-15B.
CHASSIS [C20]: Wheelbase: 131.5 in./164.5 in. Overall length: Fleetside: 211.40 in./ 244.40 in.; Step-Side: 210.50 in. Height: 69.8 in. Front tread: 65.8 in. Rear tread: 62.7 in. Tires: 8.75 x 16.5C. Bonus Cab tires: [Front] 8.75 x 16.5C [Rear]; 8.75 x 16.5D. Crew Cab tires: 9.50 x 16.5D.
CHASSIS [K20]: Wheelbase: 131.5 in. Overall length: Fleetside: 212 in.; Step-Side: 211.20 in. Height: 73.9 in. Front tread: 65.8 in. Rear tread: 62.7 in. Tires: 8.75 x 16.5C.
CHASSIS [P20]: Wheelbase: 125 in./133 in. Overall length: 220.75 in./244.75 in. Tires: 8.75 x 16.5C.
CHASSIS [C30]: Wheelbase: 131.5 in./164.5 in. Overall length: Fleetside: 211.40 in./ 244.40 in.; Step-Side: 210.50 in. Height: 71.8 in. Front tread: 65.8 in. Rear tread: 62.7 in. Tires: 8.75 x 16.5C. Bonus and Crew Cab tires: 9.50 x 16.5E.
CHASSIS [P30]: Wheelbase: 125 in./157 in. Overall length: 220.75 in./268.75 in. Tires: 8.75 x 16.5C.
TECHNICAL: (Selected Specifications): [C10] Three-speed manual transmission or Turbo-Hydramatic transmission with 454 cid. V-8. [C20] Same as C10 except Turbo-Hydramatic with Crew Cab also. [K10/K20] Three-speed manual transmission or Turbo-Hydramatic with 400 cid V-8. New Process transfer case with 4x4 trucks. Single-plate, dry-disc clutch (with base six-cylinder). Rear axle ratio (with base six-cylinder) 3.73:1 on C10s and 4.10:1 on C20s. Front disc/rear drum brakes. Standard equipment includes steel disc wheels.

1977 Chevrolet Beauville Sportvan (CP)

OPTIONS: [LUV] Mikado trim package. Mighty Mike package. [El Camino] 305 cid two-barrel V-8 ($120). 350 cid four-barrel V-8 ($210). Turbo-Hydramatic ($282). Power steering ($146). Power windows ($108). Front air-conditioning ($499). All tinted glass ($54). AM radio ($72). AM/FM radio ($137). Stereo tape with AM radio ($209). Stereo tape with AM/FM radio ($324). Performance axle ($14). Positraction ($54). Heavy-duty battery ($17). Heavy-duty radiator ($29). Conquista package ($138). Box tonneau ($96). Box rails ($68). SS equipment ($244). Tie down cargo box ($14). Speed and cruise control ($80). Vinyl roof ($65). Econo gauges ($47). Exterior decor package, with vinyl roof ($20); without vinyl roof ($46). Swing-out vinyl bucket seats ($129). Power seat ($137). [Chevy Vans] 305 cid two-barrel V-8 ($120). 350 cid four-barrel V-8, G10 ($210); G20 ($135). 400 cid four-barrel V-8 ($319). Turbo Hydramatic ($315). Power steering ($179). Power brakes ($62). Heavy-duty vacuum power brakes ($53). Front air-conditioning ($601). All tinted glass, Nomad ($43); other vans ($60). AM radio ($79). AM/FM radio ($155). Rear speaker ($36). Optional axle ratio ($16). Locking differential ($160). Heavy-duty battery ($31). Heavy-duty radiator ($29). Beauville trim, with Caravan ($173); without Caravan ($295). Caravan package, G10/SWB ($938); G10/LWB ($990); G20/SWB ($830); G20/LWB ($882). Custom Appearance package ($104). Custom Comfort & Convenience package, Chevy Van ($141); Sportvan/SWB ($320); Sportvan/LWB ($363). Custom vinyl bucket seats, without Caravan ($365). Custom cloth bucket seats, without Caravan ($365). 12-passenger seating option, Sportvan ($363). Front and rear air-conditioning ($964). [Blazer] 305 cid two-barrel V-8 ($120). 350 cid four-barrel V-8 ($210). 400 cid four-barrel V-8 ($369). Turbo-Hydramatic ($282). Four-speed manual transmission ($142). Power steering, with 4x2 ($169); with 4x4 ($188). Front air-conditioning ($509). All windows tinted ($43). Tinted sliding side window with hardtop ($156). AM radio ($79). AM/FM radio ($155). Rear speaker ($36). Optional axle ratio ($16). Locking differential ($160). Heavy-duty battery ($31). Auxiliary battery ($88). Heavy-duty radiator ($34). Woodgrain exterior trim, with Cheyenne ($126); without Cheyenne ($266). Cold climate package, with trailer special ($89); without ($120). Cheyenne package, with 16 in. tires ($713); without ($735). Custom vinyl seats, with Cheyenne one-seater (NC); with Cheyenne two-seater ($38); regular one-seater ($222); regular two-seater ($260). three-passenger rear seat ($179). Trailering Special package, with 4x2 ($200); with 4x4 ($219). [Suburban] 305 cid V-8, C10 ($120). 350 cid V-8, C10 ($210); C20 ($90). 400 cid V-8 ($249). 454 cid V-8, C10 ($465); C20 ($335). Turbo-Hydramatic with 454 V-8 ($330); without 454 V-8 ($315). Four-speed manual transmission ($142). Power steering, with 4x2 ($169); with 4x4 ($188). Front air-conditioning, Scottsdale/Silverado ($500); others ($599). Front/rear air-conditioning ($780). All tinted glass ($50). AM radio ($79). AM/FM radio ($155). Rear speaker ($36). Optional axle ratio ($16). Locking differential ($160). Heavy-duty battery ($31). Auxiliary battery ($88). Heavy-duty radiator ($34). Woodgrain exterior trim, Silverado ($208); Scottsdale ($210); others ($266). Scottsdale package, with 4x2 ($315); with 4x4 ($318). Silverado package, with 4x2 ($591); with 4x4 ($582). Custom vinyl seats, with Silverado ($103 or $141 depending on number of seats); with Scottsdale ($38, 88 or $216 depending on number/type of seats). Center rear seat ($265); center and rear seats, C10 ($466); K10/C20/K20 ($444). Trailering Special, 4x2 ($200); 4x4 ($219). Special Custom cloth seat, (same prices as Custom Vinyl seat options). [Pickups] 305 cid V-8 ($120). 350 cid V-8, 10 Series ($210); 20 Series ($90). 400 cid V-8, K10 ($369); K20 ($294). 454 cid V-8, C10 ($465); C20 ($380). Turbo-Hydramatic, without 454 cid V-8 ($315); with 454 cid V-8 ($330). Four-speed manual transmission ($142). Power steering, with 4x2 ($169); with 4x4 ($188). Power brakes ($62). Heavy-duty vacuum power brakes, C20 ($53). Power windows ($120). Power sliding rear window ($62) Front air-conditioning ($509). All tinted glass, Bonus Cab and Crew Cab ($34); other models ($27) AM radio ($79). AM/FM radio ($155). Optional axle ratio ($16). Locking differential ($160). Heavy-duty battery ($31). Auxiliary battery ($88). Heavy-duty radiator ($34). Speed and Cruise Control ($80). 8 ft. Pickup box floor ($63). Scottsdale package (without dual rear wheels, unless otherwise noted): For C10/C20 Step-Side with bench seat ($236); for same with bucket seats ($205). For K10/K20 Step-Side with bench seat ($239); for same with bucket seats ($208). For C10/C20 Fleetside with bench seats ($286); for same with bucket seats ($255). For Fleetside C20 Bonus Cab ($236); for C20 Crew Cab ($255). For Fleetside K10/K20 with bench seat ($289); for same with bucket seats ($258). For C10/C20 Chassis & Cab with bench seat ($236); for same with bucket seats ($205). For C20 Chassis & Bonus

Cab ($180). For C20 Chassis & Crew Cab ($210). For K10/K20 Chassis & Cab with bench seat ($239); for same with bucket seats ($208). For C20 Crew Cab with dual rear wheels ($195). Silverado package (without dual rear wheels, unless otherwise noted): For C10/C20 Step-Side with bench seat ($431); for same with bucket seats ($400). For K10/K20 Step-Side with bench seat ($422); for same with bucket seats ($391). For C10/C20 Fleetside with bench seats ($585); for same with bucket seats ($554). For Fleetside C20 Bonus Cab ($641); for C20 Crew Cab ($720). For Fleetside K10/K20 with bench seat ($575); for same with bucket seats ($545). For C10/C20 Chassis & Cab with bench seat ($431). For C20 Chassis & Bonus Cab ($487). For C20 Chassis & Crew Cab ($566). For K10/K20 Chassis & Cab with bench seat ($422); for same with bucket seats ($391). For C20 Crew Cab with dual rear wheels ($556). Operating Convenience package, including power windows ($206). Custom vinyl bucket seats ($207). Knit vinyl bench seat ($38). Special order Custom bench seat with Scottsdale Bonus Cab Pickup ($38); with Crew Cab ($76). Folding seatback ($23). Trailering Special package, includes power steering: [C10/C20] ($200); [K10/K20] ($219). Eight-foot stake body for C20 ($640).

1977 Chevrolet Scottsdale Crew Cab Pickup

HISTORICAL: Introduced: Fall 1976. Calendar year registrations: [All Series] 1,133,201. Innovations: New grilles on most models. First year for 1-ton with 4x4 chassis. New Sport Truck pickup option. Improvements in 454 cid V-8.

1978 CHEVROLET

1978 Chevrolet El Camino (CMD)

1/2-TON LIGHT UTILITY VEHICLE (LUV) — MODEL L/SERIES 10500 — FOUR: The imported LUV model moved into its Series 8 model, which provided a new grille with horizontal bars and a redesigned instrument panel. Two box lengths, 6- and 7-1/2 ft., were offered. The wheelbase on the latter extended to 117.9 in.

1/2-TON EL CAMINO — MODEL W/SERIES 14000 — SIX/V-8: The El Camino underwent its most extensive redesign since 1964. The 1978 model was on a longer 117.1 in. wheelbase, but overall length was reduced to 201.6 in. or 11.7 in. less than in 1977. A V-6 engine was now the base powerplant. Key styling features included a sweeping roofline small side quarter windows, a wraparound rear window and single rectangular headlights. Curb weight was reduced by nearly 600 lbs., but load capacity, at 800 lbs., was unchanged. The standard 3.3-liter V-6 was a derivative of the Chevrolet small-block V-8. It weighed almost 80 lbs. less than the six-cylinder engine it replaced. A second V-6, with a 3.8-liter displacement, was mandatory for California.

1/2-TON; 3/4-TON; 1-TON VAN — MODEL G/SERIES 10; 20; 30 — SIX/V-8: Chevy Vans had a facial. A new grille resembled the egg-crate version of other models. However, the headlight housings were distinct. They were sort of D-shaped and had a square headlight at top and a rectangular parking lamp on bottom. The Beauville continued to come only on the longer wheelbase with standard V-8 power. A new model was the Sporty Nomad, available only in the G20 line. It was essentially a factory custom van.

1/2-TON BLAZER — MODEL C; K/SERIES 10500 — SIX/V-8: The Blazer was a short wheelbase version of C10/K10 trucks. It featured a steel half-cab with an integral roll bar built into the steel front compartment roof and lock pillar structures. There was a short Fleetside pickup box at the rear. Softtop and hardtop models were optional. For 1978 the instrument panel trim and nameplate were changed. There was a Deluxe instrument panel option with black textured center section for Custom Deluxe models and bright brush finish for Cheyennes. Also new was an improved wiper motor; improved front seat belt system; redesigned rear compartment entry/exit system; smoother oxen textured vinyl upholstery; a new rear folding seat; and a flatter floor panel behind the rear legroom area. Power door locks and windows were added to the options list. Also new was a smaller 16 in. diameter soft vinyl steering wheel/horn button. Custom Deluxe trim was standard. The optional

1978 Chevrolet Cheyenne Blazer (CP)

Cheyenne package included front bucket seats; console; gauges; simulated chestnut woodgrain trim; chrome front and rear bumpers; bright upper and lower bodyside moldings; bright hubcaps; bright accents; and Cheyenne nameplates. Cheyenne hardtops also included color-keyed carpets; door pockets; special interior trim; and woodgrain accents. Colors were the same as those for Conventionals.

1/2-TON; 3/4-TON; 1-TON — MODEL C; K/SERIES 10; 20; 30 — SIX/V-8: All Chevrolet pickup trucks available during the 1977 model year were retained for 1978 with no additions or deletions. The C30 dual rear wheel option was called the "Big Dooley" option. Chevrolet introduced a new GM-built 5.7-liter V-8 diesel engine for use in the C10 1/2-ton two-wheel drive pickup. Among its design features were aluminum alloy pistons with three rings, a cast iron regrindable crankshaft, three-inch diameter main bearings, rotary fuel-injection plug, electric glow plugs and a seven-quart oil pump. Custom Deluxe was the basic trim level. It included a foam-padded bench seat with plaid upholstery, a body color steel roof headliner panel; black rubber floor mat; padded armrests; courtesy lamps; prismatic rearview mirror; foam padded dash; bright upper and lower grille outline moldings; bright headlamp bezels; silver plastic grille insert; bright outside rearview mirror; bright door handles; bright Custom Deluxe nameplates; and white-painted bumper, hubcaps and wheels. The next-step-up was Scottsdale trim with a full-depth foam padded seat; woodgrain door trim inserts; an ashtray cigarette lighter; door or manually-operated courtesy lamps; bright door sill plates; color-keyed rubber floor mats; a high-note horn; patterned nylon cloth upholstery with vinyl trim; and all Custom Deluxe exterior features, plus a chrome bumper; chrome hubcaps; chrome bodyside moldings on Fleetsides; bright windshield and window trim; bright-rimmed parking, sidemarker and taillights; and Scottsdale nameplates. Cheyenne trim included full-depth foam seat cushions; ribbed pattern velour or buffalo-hide vinyl upholstery (vinyl bucket seats optional); folding seatbacks; ashtray-mounted cigarette lighter; chestnut woodgrain dash and door inserts; door or manually-operated courtesy and dome lamps; and added cab insulation. The exterior featured all Custom Deluxe and Scottsdale features, plus bright metal cab appliques and moldings; bright upper bodyside and tailgate moldings; tailgate center appliques on Fleetsides and Cheyenne nameplates. At the top of the line was the Silverado option featuring extra-thick seat padding; velour cloth-and-vinyl or buffalo hide vinyl trim; tilting seatbacks; full gauges; chestnut woodgrain dash panel and door inserts; door storage pockets; carpeting; an insulated headliner; extra body insulation; and all Custom Deluxe, Scottsdale and Cheyenne exterior items, plus lower bodyside and tailgate moldings; wheel lip moldings; Silverado nameplates; and a tailgate applique on Fleetsides. Exterior colors for 1978 were again Mariner blue; Cordova brown; Saratoga silver; Light blue; Cardinal red; Buckskin tan; Holly green; Russet metallic; Hawaiian blue; Santa Fe tan; Mahogany; Red metallic; Colonial yellow; Frost white; and Seamist green.

1/2-TON; 3/4-TON; 1-TON FORWARD-CONTROL — MODEL P-SERIES 10; 20; 30 — SIX/V-8: Forward-Control trucks were P (parcel delivery) models available in the 10 (1/2-ton); 20 (3/4-ton) and 30 (1-ton) series The P10s had a 102 in. wheelbase and 7 ft. body. P20s came with 125 in. or 133 in. wheelbases designed for 10 ft. or 12 ft. bodies. P30s came in these sizes, plus a 157 in. wheelbase designed for 14 ft. bodies. Styling was boxy and unchanged.

I.D. DATA: Serial number located: Combination VIN and rating plate located on: [El Camino] Top left side of dash; [Conventionals] left door pillar. Serial number systems: [El Camino] First symbol indicates manufacturer, 1=Chevrolet. Second symbol indicates car-line/series: W=El Camino. Third and fourth symbols indicate body type: 80=Sedan-Pickup. Fifth symbol indicates engine: [El Camino] A=231 cid/105 hp two-barrel V-6; D=250 cid/105 nhp one-barrel L6; H=305 cid/140 nhp two-barrel V-8; L=350 cid/170 nhp four-barrel V-8. Sixth symbol indicates model year: 8=1978. Seventh symbol indicates assembly plant. Symbols 8-13 indicate the production sequence number starting at 100,001. Ending numbers not available. [All Light-Duty] The first symbol indicates manufacturer: 1=Chevrolet Motor Div. The second symbol indicates chassis type: C=96 in. or 106 in. Conventional Cab including Blazer; G=Chevy Van or Sportvan; K=106 in. Conventional cab 4x4; P=Forward-Control; L=Light Utility. The third symbol indicates engine as follows: D=250 cid/one-barrel L6 (horsepower rated 115 for models with GVW under 6,000 lbs.; 100 for models with GVWs over 6,000 lbs.); L=350 cid/165 nhp four-barrel V-8; N=110 nhp/80 nhp four-barrel L4 (LUV); R=400 cid/175 hp four-barrel V-8; S=454 cid nhp four-barrel V-8 for C models only (horsepower rated 205 for models with GVW under 6,000 lbs.; 240 for models with GVWs over 6,000 lbs.); T=292 cid/120 nhp one-barrel L-6; U=305 cid two-barrel V-8 (horsepower rated 145 for models with GVW under 6,000 lbs.; 140 for models with GVWs over 6,000 lbs.); Z=5.7 liter LF9 350 cid/120 hp diesel V-8. The fourth symbol indicates series and tonnage: 1=1/2-ton; 2=3/4-ton; 3=1-ton; 4=1/2-ton with heavy-duty suspension. The fifth symbol indicates body type: 2=Chassis & Cowl; 3=Chassis & Cab; 4=Cab with pickup box or van with Hi-Cube box; 5=Panel or Panel Van; 6=Sportvan; Suburban (doors) 7=Motorhome chassis; 8=Utility (Blazer). The sixth symbol indicates model year: 8=1978. The seventh symbol indicates the assembly plant: A=Lakewood, Ga.; B=Baltimore, Md.; F=Flint, Mich.; J=Janesville, Wis.; S=St. Louis, Mo.; U=Lordstown, Ohio; V=Pontiac, Mich. GMAD; Z=Fremont, Calif.; 0=Pontiac (GMC) Michigan; 1=Oshawa or London, Ontario, Canada; 3=GMAD, Detroit, Mich.; 4=Scarborough, Ontario, Canada; 8=Fujisawa, Japan. Symbols 8-13 are the production sequence number. Starting number: 10001 Ending numbers not available. Engine numbers located: [Six] on pad at right-hand side of cylinder block at rear of distributor; [V-8] on pad at front, right-hand side of cylinder block.

Model	Body Type	Price	Weight	Prod. Total
1/2-Ton LUV — Model L — 102.4/117.9 in. w.b. — Four				
CL10503	Chassis & Cab	3721	2095	—
CL10503	Pickup	3885	2315	—

1/2-Ton El Camino — Model W — 117.1 in. w.b. — V-6

1AW80	Pickup	3807	—	—
1AW80	Super Sport Pickup	3956	—	—

1/2-Ton El Camino — Model W — 117.1 in. w.b. — V-8

1AW80	Pickup	4843	3076	—
1AW80	Super Sport Pickup	5022	3076	—

1/2-Ton Van — Model G10 — 110 in. w.b. — V-8

CG11005	Panel	4609	3652	—
CG11006	Sportvan	5468	5468	—

1/2-Ton Van — Model G10 — 125 in. w.b. — V-8

CG11306	Beauville	6296	4323	—

1/2-Ton Van — Model G10 — 110 in. w.b. — Six

CG11305	Panel	4584	—	—
CG11306	Sportvan	5443	—	—

3/4-Ton Van — Model G20 — 110 in. w.b. — V-8

CG21005	Panel	4904	3661	—
CG21006	Sportvan	5726	3944	—

3/4-Ton Van — Model G20 — 125 in. w.b. — V-8

CG21306	Beauville	6439	4282	—
CG21305	Nomad	6334	3801	—

3/4-Ton Van — Model G20 — 125 in. w.b. — V-8

CG21305	Panel	3429	—	—
CG21306	Sportvan	5641	—	—

1-Ton Van — Model G30 — 110 in. w.b. — V-8

CG31005	Panel	5055	3896	—

1-Ton Van — Model G30 — 125 in. w.b. — V-8

CG31306	Sportvan	6037	4357	—
CG31306	Beauville	6590	4530	—

1-Ton Hi-Cube Van — Model G30 — 125 in. w.b. — V-8

CG31303	Van 10 ft.	6857	5047	—

1-Ton Hi-Cube Van — Model G30 — 146 in. w.b. — V-8

CG31603	Van 12 ft.	7157	5153	—

1/2-Ton Blazer — Model K10 — 106.5 in. w.b. — V-8

CK10516	Hardtop 4x4	6397	3928	—
CK10516	Softtop	4x4 6297	3780	—

* Deduct for C10 Blazer (4x2).

1/2-Ton Step-Van — Model P10 — 102 in. w.b. — Six

CP10542	Steel Step-Van	5771	4172	—

1/2-Ton Conventional 4x2 — Model C10 — 117.5 in. w.b. — V-8

CC10703	Chassis & Cab	4428	3246	—
CC10703	Step-Side	4418	3579	—
CC10703	Fleetside	4418	3639	—

1/2-Ton Suburban 4x2 — Model C10 — 129.5 in. w.b. — V-8

CC10906	Suburban (gate)	5810	4257	—

* Add for panel door Suburban.

1/2-Ton Conventional 4x2 — Model C10 — 131.5 in. w.b. — V-8

CC10903	Step-Side	4493	3694	—
CC10903	Fleetside	4493	3775	—

1/2-Ton Diesel 4x2 — Model C10 Diesel — 117.5 in. w.b. — V-8

CC10703	Step-Side	6228	3765	—
CC10703	Fleetside	6228	3824	—

1/2-Ton Diesel 4x2 — Model C10 Diesel — 131.5 in. w.b. — V-8

CC10903	Step-Side	6303	3841	—
CC10903	Fleetside	6303	3962	—

1/2-Ton Conventional 4x4 — Model K10 — 117.5 in. w.b. — V-8

CK10703	Chassis & Cab	5006	4143	—
CK10703	Step-Side	5006	4477	—
CK10703	Fleetside	5006	4537	—

1/2-Ton Suburban 4x4 — Model K10 — 129.5 in. w.b. — V-8

CK10906	Suburban (gate)	6348	5273	—

* Add for panel door Suburban.

1/2-Ton Conventional 4x4 — Model K10 — 131.5 in. w.b. — V-8

CK10903	Step-Side	5062	4639	—
CK10903	Fleetside	5062	4720	—

3/4-Ton Conventional 4x2 — Model C20 — 131.5 in. w.b. — V-8

CC20903	Chassis & Cab	4813	3665	—
CC20903	Step-Side	5038	4054	—
CC20903	Fleetside	5038	4135	—

3/4-Ton Suburban 4x4 — Model C20 — 129.5 in. w.b. — V-8

CC20906	Suburban (gate)	6795	6800	—

* Add for panel door Suburban.

3/4-Ton Conventional 4x2 — Model C20 — 164.5 in. w.b. — V-8

CC20943	Chassis & Bonus Cab	5512	4176	—
CC20943	Fleetside & Bonus Cab	5737	4646	—
CC20963	Chassis & Crew Cab	5886	4233	—
CC20963	Fleetside & Crew Cab	6111	4703	—

3/4-Ton Conventional 4x4 — Model K20 — 131.5 in. w.b. — V-8

CK20903	Chassis & Cab	5209	4485	—
CK20903	Step-Side	5434	4874	—
CK20903	Fleetside	5434	4955	—

3/4-Ton Suburban 4x4 — Model K20 — 129.5 in. w.b. — V-8

CK20906	Suburban (gate)	6381	4620	—

* Add for panel door Suburban.

3/4-Ton Step-Van — Model P20 — 125/133 in. w.b. — V-8

CP20842	Panel	6753	5283	—

* Add for 133 in. w.b. 12 ft. Step-Van Model CP20842.

CP30842	Panel (133 in. w.b.)	6978	5503	—

1-Ton Conventional 4x2 — Model C30 — 131.5 in. w.b. — V-8

CC30903	Chassis & Cab	5055	3792	—
CC30903	Step-Side	5280	4181	—
CC30903	Fleetside	5280	4262	—

1-Ton Conventional 4x2 — Model C30 — 164.5 in. w.b. — V-8

CC30943	Chassis & Cab	5937	4439	—
CC30943	Fleetside & Bonus Cab	6162	4909	—
CC30943	Chassis & Crew Cab	6047	4772	—
CC30943	Fleetwood & Crew Cab	6272	4941	—

1-Ton Conventional 4x4 — Model K30 — 131.5 in. w.b. — V-8

CK30903	Chassis & Cab	5589	4956	—
CK30903	Fleetside	5814	5426	—

1-Ton Conventional 4x4 — Model K30 — 164.5 in. w.b. — V-8

CK30943	Chassis & Bonus Cab	6250	5370	—
CK30943	Fleetside & Bonus Cab	6745	5840	—
CK30963	Chassis & Crew Cab	6630	5370	—
CK30963	Fleetwood & Crew Cab	6855	5840	—

NOTE 1: Model year production: [El Camino] 54,286; [All Chevy Van] 203,007; [All Sportvan] 44,058; [Blazer] 88,858; [C10/C20 Suburban] 57,788; [Other C10] 540,968; [Other C20] 176,735; [C30] 68,010; [P10/P20/P30] 28,127. (Includes trucks built in Canada for U.S. market).

NOTE 2: U.S. Sales of LUV: 71,145.

1978 Chevrolet El Camino "SS" (CP)

ENGINE [Standard LUV]: Inline. OHV. Four-cylinder. Cast iron block. Bore & stroke: 3.31 x 3.23 in. Displacement: 110.8 cid. Compression ratio: 8.5:1. Net horsepower: 80 at 4800 rpm. Maximum Torque: 95 lbs.-ft at 3000 rpm. Five main bearings. Hydraulic valve lifters. Carburetor: One-barrel.

ENGINE [Standard El Camino]: Vee-block. OHV. Six-cylinder. Cast iron block. Bore & stroke: 3.50 x 3.48 in. Displacement: 200 cid. Compression ratio: 8.2:1. Net horsepower: 95 at 3800 rpm. Maximum Torque: 160 lbs.-ft at 2000 rpm. Hydraulic valve lifters. Carburetor: Rochester two-barrel.

ENGINE [Optional: El Camino]: (Standard for California delivery) Available only automatic transmission. V-type. OHV. Six-cylinder. Cast iron block. Bore & stroke: 3.80 x 3.40 in. Displacement: 231 cid. Compression ratio: 8.0:1. Net horsepower: 105 at 3400 rpm. Net Torque: 185 lbs.-ft at 2000 rpm. Carburetor: Rochester two-barrel.

ENGINE [Standard: C10/Big 10/K10]: Inline. OHV. Six-cylinder. Cast iron block. Bore & stroke: 3.876 x 3.530 in. Displacement: 250 cid. Compression ratio: 8.25:1. Net horsepower: 115 at 3800 rpm. Torque: 195 lbs.-ft. at 1800 rpm. Seven main bearings. Hydraulic valve lifters. Carburetor: Mono-jet model 1ME. RPO Code: LD4.

ENGINE [Standard: C20/C30/K20/K30]: Inline. OHV. Six-cylinder. Cast iron block. Bore & stroke: 3.8764 x 4.120 in. Displacement: 292 cid. Compression ratio: 8.0:1. Net horsepower: 120 at 3600 rpm. Net torque: 215 lbs.-ft. at 2000 rpm. Seven main bearings. Hydraulic valve lifters. Carburetor: One-barrel. RPO Code: L25.

ENGINE [Optional: C10/El Camino]: Vee-block. OHV. Eight-cylinder. Cast iron block. Bore & stroke: 3.736 x 3.480 in. Displacement: 305 cid. Compression ratio: 8.5:1. Net horsepower: 145 at 3800 rpm. Net torque: 245 lbs.-ft. at 2400 rpm. Five main bearings. Hydraulic valve lifters. Carburetor: Two-barrel model 2GC. RPO Code: LG9.

ENGINE [Optional: all models]: V-type. OHV. Eight-cylinder. Cast iron block. Bore & stroke: 4.0 x 3.480 in. Displacement: 350 cid. Compression ratio: 8.5:1. Net horsepower: 165 at 3800 rpm. Net torque: 260 lbs.-ft. at 2400 rpm. Five main bearings. Hydraulic valve lifters. Carburetor: Four-barrel model M4MC/MV. RPO Code: LS9.

ENGINE [Optional: K10/K20/K30]: V-type. OHV. Eight-cylinder. Cast iron block. Bore & stroke: 4.125 x 3.750 in. Displacement: 400 cid. Compression ratio: 8.5:1. Net horsepower: 175 at 3600 rpm. Net torque: 290 lbs.-ft. at 2800 rpm. Five main bearings. Hydraulic valve lifters. Carburetor: Four-barrel model M4MC/MV. RPO Code: LF4.

ENGINE [Optional: C1500/C2500/C3500 ($235)]: V-type. OHV. Eight-cylinder. Cast iron block. Bore & stroke: 4.250 x 4.0 in. Displacement: 454 cid. Compression ratio: 8.5:1 Net horsepower: 205 at 3600 rpm. Net torque: 355 lbs.-ft. at 2800 rpm. Five main bearings. Hydraulic valve lifters. Carburetor: Four-barrel model M4MC/MV. RPO Code: LF8.

ENGINE [Optional: C10/Big 10]: V-type. OHV diesel. Eight-cylinder. Cast iron block. Bore & stroke: 4.057 x 3.385 in. Displacement: 350 cid. Compression ratio: 20.5:1. Net horsepower: 120 at 3600 rpm. Net torque: 222 lbs.-ft. at 1900 rpm. Five main bearings. Hydraulic valve lifters. RPO Code: LF9.

1978 Chevrolet Cheyenne Fleetside Pickup (CP)

CHASSIS [LUV]: Wheelbase: 102.4 in./117.9 in. Overall length: 173.8 in./190.9 in. Front tread: 54 in. Rear tread: 52.2 in. Tires: E78 x 14B in.

CHASSIS [El Camino]: Wheelbase: 117.1 in. Overall length: 201.6 in. Height: 53.8 in. Front tread: 58.5 in. Rear tread: 57.8 in. Tires: P205/75R x 14 in.

CHASSIS [G10]: Wheelbase: 110 in./125 in. Overall length: 178.2 in./202.2 in. Tires G78 x 15B in.

CHASSIS [G20]: Wheelbase: 110 in./125 in. Overall length: 178.2 in./202.2 in. Tires: J78 x 15B in.

CHASSIS [G30]: Wheelbase: 110 in./125 in. Overall length: 178.2 in./202.2 in. Tires: 8.00 x 16.5 in.

CHASSIS [K10 Blazer]: Wheelbase: 106.5 in. Overall length: 184.8 in. Height: 73.4 in. Front tread: 66.1 in. Rear tread: 63 in. Tires: H78 x 15B in.

CHASSIS [C10/C10/Big 10]: Wheelbase: 117.5 in./131.5 in. Overall length: 191.3/212 in. Height 69.8 in. Front tread: 65.8 in. Rear tread: 62.7 in. Tires: G78 x 15B in. [C10, Big 10], L78 x 15B in.

CHASSIS [K10]: Wheelbase: 117.5 in./131.5 in. Overall length: 191.3/212 in. Height: 72 in. Front tread: 65.8 in. Rear tread: 62.7 in. Tires: L78 x 15B in.

CHASSIS [P10]: Wheelbase: 102 in. Tires: L78 x 15B in.

CHASSIS [P20]: Wheelbase: 125 in./133 in. Tires: 8.75 x 16.5C in.

CHASSIS [C20]: Wheelbase: 117.5 in./131.5 in./164.5 in. Overall length: 191.3 in./212 in./244.43 in. Height: 69.8 in. Front tread: 65.8 in. Rear tread: 62.7 in. Tires: 8.75 x 16.5C in., [Bonus Cab] 8.75 x 16.5 in., [F-C, R-D], [Crew Cab] 9.50 x 16.5D in.

CHASSIS [K20]: Wheelbase: 131.5 in. Overall length: 212 in. Height: 73.9 in. Front tread: 65.8 in. Rear tread: 62.7 in. Tires: 8.75 x 16.5C in.

CHASSIS [C30]: Wheelbase: 131.5 in./164.5 in. Overall length: 212 in./244.43 in. Height: 71.8 in. Front tread: 65.8 in. Rear tread: 62.7 in. Tires: 8.75 x 16.5C in., [Bonus/Crew Cab] 9.50 x 16.5E in.

CHASSIS [K30]: Wheelbase: 131.5 in./164.5 in. Overall length: 212 in./244.43 in. Height: 74.7 in./75 in. Front tread: 65.8 in. Rear tread: 62.7 in. Tires: 9.50 x 16.5D in.

CHASSIS [P30]: Wheelbase: 125 in./157 in. Tires: 8.75 x 6.5 in.

TECHNICAL: (Selected Specifications): [C10] Three-speed manual transmission or Turbo-Hydramatic transmission with 454 cid. V-8. [C20] Same as C10 except Turbo-Hydramatic with Crew Cab also. [K10/K20] Three-speed manual transmission or Turbo-Hydramatic with 400 cid V-8. New Process transfer case with 4x4 trucks. Single-plate, dry-disc clutch (with base six-cylinder). Rear axle ratio (with base six-cylinder) 3.73:1 on C10s and 4.10:1 on C20s. Front disc/rear drum brakes. Standard equipment includes steel disc wheels.

1978 Chevrolet ChevyVan Panel (CP)

OPTIONS: [LUV]: Mikado interior. High-back bucket seats. Mighty Mike decal package. Decor package. Sliding rear window. E78 x 14B Steel-belted whitewall tires. Mud flaps. Below-Eyeline mirrors. Right-hand exterior mirror. Rear bumper. Rear-mounted spare tire. [Other Trucks] Chevy Van Custom Appearance package ($92). Chevy Van Custom Comfort package ($342). Bumper guards. Radio AM; AM/FM. Heater (deletion). Electric clock. Cigar lighter. Radio antenna. Chevy Van Caravan package ($980 to $1,050). 454 V-8 in Step-Van ($235). F44 Big 10 package. Chevy Van Sport package ($497). Scottsdale trim package, light trucks ($251). Cheyenne trim package, light trucks ($781). Silverado trim package, light trucks. Short-box Step-Side Sport package. Short-box Fleetside sport package. Rear step bumper. Cargo area lamp. Power windows. Power door locks. Glide-out spare tire carrier. Rally wheels. Styled wheels. Exterior Decor package with Silverado package only. Comfortilt steering wheel. C20 8-ft. stake($728). El Camino Conquista package ($146). Sliding rear window. Pickup box side rails. Speed and cruise controls. Bucket seats/center console. Gauges. Air-conditioning. Tachometer. Whitewall tires. Bumper guards. Auxiliary fuel tank. Chromed front and rear bumpers. Below-Eyeline mirrors. Color-keyed floor mats. Intermittent windshield wipers. Inside hoodlock release. Simulated wood grain. Exterior trim, Blazer and Suburban. Special two-tone paint. Spare tire cover (Blazer and Suburban). Rear radio speaker (Blazer and Suburban). Soft-Ray tinted glass.

Standard Catalog of Light-Duty Trucks

1978 Chevrolet Scottsdale Suburban (CP)

HISTORICAL: Introduced: Fall 1977. Calendar year registrations: 1,275,787. Calendar year sales: [All Series] 1,233,932. Innovations: El Camino downsized. New V-8 engines introduced. Big Dooley name replaces Big Dualie. New 5.7-liter V-8 diesel in half-ton pickups. Chevrolet reported an all-time record of 1.34 million truck sales in 1978. The number of trucks registered by Chevrolet dealers, per sales outlet, was 215 units, up from 187 in 1977.

1979 CHEVROLET

1979 Chevrolet LUV Pickup (CP)

1/2-TON LIGHT UTILITY VEHICLE (LUV) — MODEL L/SERIES 10500 — FOUR: Chevrolet's captive import, the LUV truck, looked the same in 1979 as it did the year before. Until you started adding some new options, that is. Four-wheel drive was now available at extra-cost. Trucks so-equipped were seen with wide striping and 4x4 decals on the sides of their cargo boxes.

1/2-TON EL CAMINO — MODEL W/SERIES 14000 — SIX/V-8: El Caminos featured a new grille with eight distinct horizontal segments formed by the bright metal molding. The moldings ran three across, with a thin one down the center. A Royal Knight dress-up package featured two dragon decals on its hood, styled wheels and other goodies. A new item was a 267 cid V-8 for all non-California trucks. The Super Sport was again merchandised as a model-option rather than an individual package.

1/2-TON; 3/4-TON; 1-TON VAN — MODEL G/SERIES 10; 20; 30 — SIX/V-8: Vans were available in various configurations. Appearance updates were mainly in terms of new decal and paint treatments. On most vans, the grille had more of a horizontal theme due to the method of finishing the grille bars with paint.

1/2-TON BLAZER — MODEL C; K/SERIES 10500 — SIX/V-8: The new Blazer had a smoother, more aerodynamic hood lip; new integral head/parking lamps; and a concealed fuel filter. Custom Deluxe interiors featured bucket seats in blue or camel houndstooth. Custom vinyl trim came in blue or camel, too. Cheyennes included Custom vinyl trim in blue, camel or carmine or Custom cloth trim in carmine or camel, plus bright trim, color-keyed carpeting, a color-keyed plastic console, full instrumentation and a new Custom steering wheel. Two-tone vinyl or cloth upholstery was optional.

1979 Chevrolet LUV 4x4 Pickup (OCW)

1/2-TON; 3/4-TON; 1-TON — MODEL C; K/SERIES 10; 20; 30 — SIX/V-8: Light-duty trucks a new front end with integral park/head lights, a bright. metal lower grille outline molding and a new paint scheme for the grille. The 1979 grille was slightly narrower top-to-bottom, but of the same basic design as last year's style. The slotted area, directly below the grille was now bright metal. An optional sport grille had only two full-width horizontal members and a center bow tie, the background being blacked-out. There was also a new concealed fuel filler. The base 250 cid six got a new staged two-barrel carburetor and dual take-down exhaust system. Custom Deluxe was the basic trim level. It included a foam-padded bench seat with plaid upholstery; a body color steel roof headliner panel; black rubber floor mat; padded armrests; courtesy lamps; prismatic rearview mirror; foam padded dash; bright upper and lower grille outline moldings; bright headlamp bezels; silver plastic grille insert; bright outside rearview mirror; bright door handles; bright Custom Deluxe nameplates; and white-painted bumper, hubcaps and wheels. The next-step-up was Scottsdale trim with a full-depth foam padded seat; woodgrain door trim inserts; an ashtray cigarette lighter; door or manually-operated courtesy lamps; bright door sill plates; color-keyed rubber floor mats; a high-note horn; patterned nylon cloth upholstery with vinyl trim; and all Custom Deluxe exterior features, plus a chrome bumper; chrome hubcaps; chrome bodyside moldings on Fleetsides; bright windshield and window trim; bright-rimmed parking, sidemarker and taillights; and Scottsdale nameplates. Cheyenne trim included full-depth foam seat cushions; ribbed pattern velour or buffalo-hide vinyl upholstery (vinyl bucket seats optional); folding seatbacks; ashtray-mounted cigarette lighter; chestnut woodgrain dash and door inserts; door or manually-operated courtesy and dome lamps; and added cab insulation. The exterior featured all Custom Deluxe and Scottsdale features, plus bright metal cab appliques and moldings; bright upper bodyside and tailgate moldings; tailgate center appliques on Fleetsides; and Cheyenne nameplates. At the top of the line was the Silverado option featuring extra-thick seat padding; basket weave nylon cloth or buffalo hide vinyl trim; full gauges; woodgrain dash panel; door storage pockets; carpeting; an insulated headliner; extra body insulation; and all Custom Deluxe and Scottsdale exterior items, plus lower bodyside and tailgate moldings; wheel lip moldings; Silverado nameplates; and a tailgate applique on Fleetsides. Exterior colors for 1979 were white; Silver metallic; Dark bright blue; Medium blue; Dark blue; Medium green metallic; Bright green metallic; Dark green; yellow; neutral; Camel metallic; Dark carmine; Bright red; Russet metallic; Dark brown metallic; Dark yellow; Charcoal; and black.

1/2-TON; 3/4-TON; 1-TON FORWARD-CONTROL — MODEL P-SERIES 10; 20; 30 — SIX/V-8: Forward-Control trucks were P (parcel delivery) models available in the 10 (1/2-ton); 20 (3/4-ton) and 30 (1-ton) series The P10s had a 102 in. wheelbase and 7 ft. body. P20s came with 125 in. or 133 in. wheelbases designed for 10 ft. or 12 ft. bodies. P30s came in these sizes, plus a 157 in. wheelbase designed for 14 ft. bodies. Styling was boxy and unchanged.

I.D. DATA: Serial number located: Combination VIN and rating plate located on: [El Camino] Top left side of dash; [Conventionals] left door pillar. Serial number systems: [El Camino] First symbol indicates manufacturer, 1=Chevrolet. Second symbol indicates car-line/series: W=El Camino. Third and fourth symbols indicate body type: 80=Sedan-Pickup. Fifth symbol indicates engine: [El Camino] A=231 cid (3.8 liter)/115 hp two-barrel V-6; J=267 cid (4.4 liter)/125 nhp two-barrel V-8; L=350 cid (5.7 liter)/170 nhp four-barrel V-8; M=200 cid (3.3 liter)/94 nhp two-barrel; V-6. Sixth symbol indicates model year: 9=1979. Seventh symbol indicates assembly plant. Symbols 8-13 indicate the production sequence number starting at 100,001. Ending numbers not available. [All Light-Duty] The first symbol indicates manufacturer. 1=Chevrolet Motor Div. The second symbol indicates chassis type: C=106 in. Conventional Cab including Blazer; G=Chevy Van or Sportvan; K=106 in. Conventional cab 4x4; P=Forward-Control; L=LUV; R=LUV (4x4). The third symbol indicates engine as follows: D=250 cid (4.1 liter)/one-barrel L6 (horsepower rated 115 for models with GVW under 6,000 lbs.; 100 for models with GVWs over 6,000 lbs.); L=350 cid (5.7 liter)/165 nhp four-barrel V-8; M=350 cid (5.7 liter)/145 nhp four-barrel V-8; N=110 cid (1.8 liter)/80 nhp two-barrel L4 (LUV); R=400 cid (6.6 liter)/175 hp four-barrel V-8; S=454 cid (7.4 liter) four-barrel V-8 for C models only (horsepower rated 205 for models with GVW under 6,000 lbs.; 245 for models with GVWs over 6,000 lbs.); T=292 cid (4.8 liter)/120 nhp one-barrel L-6; U=305 cid (5.0 liter) two-barrel V-8 (horsepower rated 145 for models with GVW under 6,000 lbs.; 140 for models with GVWs over 6,000 lbs.); Z=5.7 liter LF9 350 cid/120 hp diesel V-8. The fourth symbol indicates series and tonnage: 1=1/2-ton; 2=3/4-ton; 3=1-ton; 4=1/2-ton with heavy-duty suspension. The fifth symbol indicates body type: 2=Chassis & Cowl; 3=Chassis & Cab; 4=Cab with pickup box or van with Hi-Cube box; 5=Panel or Panel Van; 6=Sportvan; Suburban (doors) 7=Motorhome chassis; 8=Utility (Blazer). The sixth symbol indicates model year: 9=1979. The seventh symbol indicates the assembly plant: A=Lakewood, Ga.; B=Baltimore, Md.; F=Flint, Mich.; J=Janesville, Wis.; S=St. Louis, Mo.; U=Lordstown, Ohio; V=Pontiac, Mich. GMAD; Z=Fremont, Calif.; 0=Pontiac (GMC) Michigan; 1=Oshawa or London, Ontario, Canada; 3=GMAD, Detroit, Mich.; 4=Scarborough, Ontario, Canada; 8=Fujisawa, Japan. Symbols 8-13 are the production sequence number. Starting number: 10001 Ending numbers not available. Engine numbers located: [Six] on pad at right-hand side of cylinder block at rear of distributor; [V-8] on pad at front, right-hand side of cylinder block.

Model	Body Type	Price	Weight	Prod. Total
LUV — 1/2-Ton — 102.4 in. w.b. — Four				
CL10503	Chassis & Cab	4132	2095	—
CL10503	Pickup	4276	2345	—
LUV — 1/2-Ton — 117.9 in. w.b. — Four				
CL10803	Pickup	4486	2405	—

* Add $971 for 4x4 LUVs.

Model	Body Type	Price	Weight	Prod. Total
El Camino — 1/2-Ton — 117.1 in. w.b. — V-8				
1AW80	Pickup	5377	3242	—
Z15	SS Pickup	5579	3242	—
1AW80	Conquista	5532	3242	—
Chevy Van 10 — 1/2-Ton — 110 in. w.b. — V-8				
CG11005	Panel	5312	3693	—
CG11006	Sportvan	6229	3998	—
Chevy Van 10 — 1/2-Ton — 125 in. w.b. — V-8				
CG11306	Beauville	7030	4367	—
Chevy Van 20 — 3/4-Ton — 110 in. w.b. — V-8				
CG21005	Panel	5606	3689	—
CG21006	Sportvan	6397	3970	—
Chevy Van 20 — 3/4-Ton — 125 in. w.b. — V-8				
CG21306	Beauville	7198	4318	—
CG21305	Nomad	7108	3830	—
Chevy Van 30 — 1-Ton — 110 in. w.b. — V-8				
CG31005	Panel	5822	3914	—
Chevy Van 30 — 1-Ton — 125 in. w.b. — V-8				
CG31306	Sportvan	6474	4378	—
CG31306	Beauville	7410	4556	—
Hi-Cube Van — 1-Ton — 125 in. w.b. — V-8				
CG31303	Hi-Cube 10 ft.	7662	—	—
Hi-Cube Van — 1-Ton — 146 in. w.b. — V-8				
CG31603	Hi-Cube 12 ft.	7828	—	—
Blazer 4x4 — 1/2-Ton — 106.5 in. w.b. — V-8 — 4x4				
CK10516	Hardtop	7373	4371	—
CK10516	Softtop	7273	—	—

* Deduct for C10 Blazer (4x2).

Model	Body Type	Price	Weight	Prod. Total
C10 — 1/2-Ton — 117.5 in. w.b. — V-8				
CC10703	Chassis & Cab	4943	3406	—
CC10703	Step-Side Pickup	5091	3570	—
CC10703	Fleetside Pickup	5091	3629	—
C10 — 1/2-Ton — 131.5 in. w.b. — V-8				
CC10903	Step-Side Pickup	5171	3693	—
CC10903	Fleetside Pickup	5171	3767	—
C10 — 1/2-Ton — 129.5 in. w.b. — V-8				
CC10906	Suburban (gate)	6614	4285	—

* Add for K10 4x4 models (CK prefix).
* Add $1,758 and 295 lbs. for C10 diesel.

Model	Body Type	Price	Weight	Prod. Total
P10 Step-Van — 1/2-Ton — 102 in. w.b. — Six				
CP10542	Steel Step-Van	6189	4226	—
C20 — 3/4-Ton — 131.5 in. w.b. — V-8				
CC20903	Chassis & Cab	5481	3693	—
CC20903	Step-Side Pickup	5777	4077	—
CC20903	Fleetside Pickup	5777	4151	—
C20 — 3/4-Ton — 164.5 in. w.b. — V-8				
CC20943	Chassis & Bonus Cab	6233	4224	—
CC20943	Bonus Cab Pickup	6516	4682	—
CC20943	Chassis & Crew Cab	6634	—	—
CC20943	Crew Cab Pickup	6918	—	—
C20 — 3/4-Ton — 129.5 in. w.b. — V-8				
CC20906	Suburban (gate)	7075	—	—

* Add for K20 4x4 models (CK prefix).

Model	Body Type	Price	Weight	Prod. Total
P20 Step-Van — 1/2-Ton — 125/133 in. w.b. — V-8				
CP20842	Steel Step-Van	7287	5311	—
C30 — 1-Ton — 131.5 in. w.b. — V-8				
CC30903	Chassis & Cab	5941	3899	—
CC30903	Step-Side Pickup	6237	4283	—
CC30903	Fleetside Pickup	6237	4358	—
C30 — 1-Ton — 164.5 in. w.b. — V-8				
CC30943	Chassis & Bonus Cab	6740	4453	—
CC30943	Chassis & Crew Cab	7023	4911	—
CC30943	Bonus Cab Pickup	6900	—	—
CC30943	Crew Cab Pickup	7183	—	—

* Add for K30 4x4 models (CK prefix).

Model	Body Type	Price	Weight	Prod. Total
P30 Step-Van — 1-Ton — 125/133/157 in. w.b. — V-8				
CP30842	Steel Step-Van	7487	5485	—

NOTE 1: Model year production: [El Camino] 54,008; [All Chevy Van] 212,513; [All Sportvan] 40,560; [Blazer] 90,987; [C10/C20 Suburban] 54,987; [Other C10] 535,056; [Other C20] 148,782; [C30] 80,500; [P10/P20/P30] 28,536. (Includes trucks built in Canada for U.S. market).
NOTE 2: U.S. Sales of LUV: 100,192.

114

1979 Chevrolet El Camino Royal Knight (OCW)

ENGINE [Standard LUV]: Inline. OHV overhead camshaft. Four-cylinder. Cast iron block. Bore & stroke: 3.31 x 3.23 in. Displacement: 110.8 cid. Compression ratio: 8.5:1. Net horsepower: 80 at 4800 rpm. Maximum Torque: 95 lbs.-ft at 3000 rpm. Five main bearings. Hydraulic valve lifters. Carburetor: One-barrel.

ENGINE [Standard El Camino]: V-type. OHV. Six-cylinder. Cast iron block. Bore & stroke: 3.5 x 3.48 in. Displacement: 200 cid. Compression ratio: 8.2:1. Net horsepower: 95. Four main bearings. Hydraulic valve lifters. Carburetor: Rochester two-barrel model 210.

ENGINE [Optional El Camino]: V-type. OHV. Six-cylinder. Cast iron block. Bore & stroke: 3.8 x 3.4 in. Displacement: 231 cid. Compression ratio: 8.0:1. Net horsepower: 105. Four main bearings. Hydraulic valve lifters. Carburetor: Rochester two-barrel model 2GC.

ENGINE [Standard: C10/Big 10/K10]: Inline. OHV. Six-cylinder. Cast iron block. Bore & stroke: 3.876 x 3.530 in. Displacement: 250 cid. Compression ratio: 8.3:1. Net horsepower: 130 at 3800 rpm. Torque: 210 lbs.-ft. at 2400 rpm. Seven main bearings. Hydraulic valve lifters. Carburetor: Two-barrel.

NOTE: (Base engine in California) 125 horsepower at 4000 rpm. Torque: 205 lbs.-ft. at 2000 rpm.

1979 Chevrolet Blazer (CP)

ENGINE [Optional El Camino]: V-type. OHV. Eight-cylinder. Cast iron block. Bore & stroke: 3.5 x 3.48 in. Displacement: 267 cid. Five main bearings. Hydraulic valve lifters. Carburetor: two-barrel.

ENGINE [Standard: C20/C30/K20/K30]: Inline. OHV. Six-cylinder. Cast iron block. Bore & stroke: 3.876 x 4.120 in. Displacement: 292 cid. Compression ratio: 8.0:1. Net horsepower: 115 at 3400 rpm. Net torque: 215 lbs.-ft. at 3400 rpm. Seven main bearings. Hydraulic valve lifters. Carburetor: Rochester one-barrel.

ENGINE [Optional C10]: V-type. OHV. Eight-cylinder. Cast iron block. Bore & stroke: 3.736 x 3.480 in. Displacement: 305 cid. Compression ratio: 8.4:1. Net horsepower: 140 at 4000 rpm. Net torque: 235 lbs.-ft. at 2000 rpm. Five main bearings. Hydraulic valve lifters. Carburetor: Rochester two-barrel model 2GC.

NOTE: (Base engine in California) 155 horsepower at 3600 rpm. Torque: 260 lbs.-ft. at 2000 rpm. (Four-barrel California engine) 155 horsepower at 4000 rpm. Torque: 260 lbs.-ft. at 2000 rpm.

ENGINE [Optional El Camino]: V-type. OHV. Eight-cylinder. Cast iron block. Bore & stroke: 3.736 x 3.480 in. Displacement: 305 cid. Compression ratio: 8.4:1. Net horsepower: 145/135* at 3800 rpm. Five main bearings. Hydraulic valve lifters. Carburetor: Rochester two-barrel model 2GC.

* California rating.

ENGINE [Optional El Camino]: V-type. OHV. Eight-cylinder. Cast iron block. Bore & stroke: 4.0 x 3.48 in. Displacement: 350 cid. Compression ratio: 8.2:1. Net horsepower: 170/160* at 3800 rpm. Maximum torque: 270 lbs.-ft. at 2400 rpm. Hydraulic valve lifters. Carburetor: Rochester four-barrel model M4 MC/MV.

* California rating.

ENGINE [Optional: C10/Big 10]: V-type. OHV diesel. Eight-cylinder. Cast iron block. Bore & stroke: 4.057 x 3.385 in. Displacement: 350 cid. Compression ratio: 20.5:1. Net horsepower: 120 at 3600 rpm. Net torque: 222 lbs.-ft. at 1900 rpm. Five main bearings. Hydraulic valve lifters.

ENGINE [Optional: All models except LUV]: V-type. OHV. Eight-cylinder. Cast iron block. Bore & stroke: 4.0 x 3.48 in. Displacement: 350 cid. Compression ratio: 8.2:1. Net horsepower: 165 at 3600 rpm. Net torque: 270 lbs.-ft. at 2700 rpm. Five main bearings. Hydraulic valve lifters. Carburetor: Rochester four-barrel model M4 MC/MV.

ENGINE [Optional: K10/K20/K30]: V-type. OHV. Eight-cylinder. Cast iron block. Bore & stroke: 4.125 x 3.750 in. Displacement: 400 cid. Compression ratio: 8.5:1. Net horsepower: 185 at 3600 rpm. Net torque: 300 lbs.-ft. at 2400 rpm. Five main bearings. Hydraulic valve lifters. Carburetor: Rochester four-barrel model M4 MC/MV.

ENGINE [Optional: All models except Blazer/El Camino/LUV]: V-type. OHV. Eight-cylinder. Cast iron block. Bore & stroke: 4.250 x 4.0 in. Displacement: 454 cid. Compression ratio: 7.6:1. Net horsepower: 245 at 4000 rpm. Net torque: 380 lbs.-ft. at 2500 rpm. Five main bearings. Hydraulic valve lifters. Carburetor: Rochester four-barrel model M4 MC/MV.

1979 Chevrolet Blazer (CP)

CHASSIS [LUV]: Wheelbase: 102.4 in./117.9 in. Overall length: 173.8 in./190.9 in. Front tread: 54 in. Rear tread: 52.2 in. Tires: E78 x 14B in.

CHASSIS [El Camino]: Wheelbase: 117.1 in. Overall length: 201.6 in. Height: 53.8 in. Front tread: 58.5 in. Rear tread: 57.8 in. Tires: P205/75R x 14 in.

CHASSIS [G10]: Wheelbase: 110 in./125 in. Overall length: 178.2 in./202.2 in. Tires G78 x 15B in.

1979 Chevrolet 'Old Cars Weekly' Scottsdale Suburban

CHASSIS [G20]: Wheelbase: 110 in./125 in. Overall length: 178.2 in./202.2 in. Tires: J78 x 15B in.

CHASSIS [G30]: Wheelbase: 110 in./125 in. Overall length: 178.2 in./202.2 in. Tires: 8.00 x 16.5 in.

CHASSIS [K10 Blazer]: Wheelbase: 106.5 in. Overall length: 184.8 in. Height: 73.4 in. Front tread: 66.1 in. Rear tread: 63 in. Tires: H78 x 15B in.

CHASSIS [C10/Big 10]: Wheelbase: 117.5 in./131.5 in. Overall length: 191.3 in./212 in. Height 69.8 in. Front tread: 65.8 in. Rear tread: 62.7 in. Tires: [C10] G78 x 15B in. [Big 10], L78 x 15B in.

1979 Chevrolet Step-Side Pickup (CP)

CHASSIS [K10]: Wheelbase: 117.5 in./131.5 in. Overall length: 191.3 in./212 in. Height: 72 in. Front tread: 65.8 in. Rear tread: 62.7 in. Tires: L78 x 15B in.

CHASSIS [P10]: Wheelbase: 102 in. Tires: L78 x 15B in.

CHASSIS [C20]: Wheelbase: 117.5 in./131.5 in./164.5 in. Overall length: 191.3 in./212 in./244.43 in. Height: 69.8 in. Front tread: 65.8 in. Rear tread: 62.7 in. Tires: [Pickup] 8.75 x 16.5C in., [Bonus Cab] Front, 8.75 x 16.5C in.; Rear, 8.75 x 16.5D in.; [Crew Cab] 9.50 x 16.5D in.

CHASSIS [K20]: Wheelbase: 131.5 in. Overall length: 212 in. Height: 73.9 in. Front tread: 65.8 in. Rear tread: 62.7 in. Tires: 8.75 x 16.5C in.

CHASSIS [P20]: Wheelbase: 125 in./133 in. Tires: 8.75 x 16.5C in.

1979 Chevrolet Fleetside Pickup (OCW)

OPTIONS: Chrome front bumper ($33). Electric clock ($55). Chevy Van Caravan package. Custom comfort package. Chevy Sport package. F44 Big 10 package ($375). Scottsdale package. C20 Stake, 8-ft. Air-conditioning ($574). Color-keyed floor mats ($11). Tinted glass ($49). Chromed grille ($29). Exterior eye-level mirror ($55). Convenience package ($231). Comfortilt steering wheel ($78). Rally wheels ($84). Intermittent wipers ($33). Sliding side window glass, Blazer ($176). Folding rear seat, Blazer ($260). Electric tailgate window, Blazer ($65).

1979 Chevrolet Beauville Sportvan (OCW)

HISTORICAL: Introduced: Fall 1978. Calendar year registrations: 1,085,855. Calendar year sales: [Light trucks/Pickups] 644,775; [Vans] 166,850; [Suburbans] 37,215; [Blazers] 57,734; [LUV] 100,192; [El Camino] 52,803; [Sportvan] 30,135; [Total] 1,090,204. Innovations: New El Camino Black Knight model option. 4x4 introduced for LUV pickup. New 267 cid V-8.

1979 Chevrolet Silverado Suburban (CP)

1979 Chevrolet Silverado Suburban (OCW)

1980 Chevrolet Sportvan (CP)

1/2-TON LIGHT UTILITY VEHICLE (LUV) — MODEL L/SERIES 10500 — FOUR: The 1980 LUV pickup looked just like the 1979 model. New, under the hood, was an 80 hp engine. Exterior colors were the same as 1979, but the white, yellow and red paints were modified to remove lead in the formula. Standard and Mikado cloth trim came in blue, red or saddle. Sport package decals were light orange/orange/red or light blue metallic/dark blue/medium blue.

1/2-TON EL CAMINO — MODEL W/SERIES 14000 — SIX/V-8: Biggest change in the 1980 El Camino was the grille. It had 21 fine vertical members on either side of a slightly heavier vertical center molding. Base powertrain was a 229 cid. (3.8 liter) V-6 and three-speed manual transmission. The ribbed steel, six-foot cargo box provided 35.5 cu. ft. of room and a gross payload of 1,250 lbs. including passengers. Contrasting lower body perimeter finish with Super Sport shadow graphics along the door bottoms identified this model-option. Other SS features included Rally wheels, large front air dam,color sport mirrors, white-letter tires and Super Sport tailgate decals. The Royal Knight option included the double-dragon hood decal, large front air dam, Rally wheels and painted sport mirrors.

1/2-TON; 3/4-TON; 1-TON VAN — MODEL G/SERIES 10; 20; 30 — SIX/V-8: Vans and light-duty trucks had a new ice cube tray grille with 10 vertical bars and two horizontal bars forming 33 square openings. There was a Chevrolet bow tie emblem in the center. The 1-ton G30 line no longer offered the 110 in. wheelbase Chevy Van panel. Other series offered Chevy Vans and Sportvans with either wheelbase and Beauvilles on the long wheelbase only. A sporty long wheelbase 3/4-ton model was the Nomad. It had a camper-style window treatment with a door window and slider window behind the door, but panel-side styling at the rear. Model-options included Caravan and Chevy Sport packages. There was a "Van Sport" option with two-tone exterior graphics.

1980 Chevrolet Suburban (CP)

1/2-TON BLAZER — MODEL C; K/SERIES 10500 — SIX/V-8: Blazers had a new Argent-silver colored grille with 33 square openings and new gauges with international symbols. A Silverado package was now available and included rectangular headlamps, a chromed grille and larger parking lamps, plus Custom cloth or Brahman-grain vinyl interiors. Radial tires became standard equipment. The 305 cid and 400 cid V-8s were dropped, but a popular new option was styled aluminum wheels. Colors were the same as on Conventional trucks.

1/2-TON; 3/4-TON; 1-TON — MODEL C; K/SERIES 10; 20; 30 — SIX/V-8: The same new grille was used on the Conventional trucks. Silverados got the new rectangular parking lamps. The seatback angle was changed for greater comfort. There was a new thermo-static-controlled cooling fan. A single inlet dual exhaust system was new for the 292 cid six-cylinder engine. Custom Deluxe was the basic trim level. It included a foam-padded bench seat with plaid upholstery; a body color steel roof headliner panel; black rubber floor mat; padded armrests; courtesy lamps; prismatic rearview mirror; foam padded dash; bright upper and lower grille outline moldings; bright headlamp bezels; silver plastic grille insert; bright outside rearview mirror; bright door handles; bright Custom Deluxe nameplates and white-painted bumper, hubcaps and wheels. The next-step-up was Scottsdale trim with a full-depth foam padded seat; woodgrain door trim inserts; an ashtray cigarette lighter; door or manually-operated courtesy lamps; bright door sill plates; color-keyed rubber floor mats; a high-note horn; patterned nylon cloth upholstery with vinyl trim; and all Custom Deluxe exterior features, plus a chrome bumper; chrome hubcaps; chrome bodyside moldings on Fleetsides; bright windshield and window trim; bright-rimmed parking, sidemarker and tail-lights; and Scottsdale nameplates. Cheyenne trim included full-depth foam seat cushions; ribbed pattern velour or buffalo-hide vinyl upholstery (vinyl bucket seats optional); folding

seatbacks; ashtray-mounted cigarette lighter; chestnut woodgrain dash and door inserts; door or manually-operated courtesy and dome lamps; and added cab insulation. The exterior featured all Custom Deluxe and Scottsdale features, plus bright metal cab appliques and moldings; bright upper bodyside and tailgate moldings; tailgate center appliques on Fleetsides; and Cheyenne nameplates. At the top of the line was the Silverado option featuring extra-thick seat padding; basket weave nylon cloth or buffalo hide vinyl trim; full gauges; woodgrain dash panel; door storage pockets; carpeting; an insulated headliner; extra body insulation; and all Custom Deluxe and Scottsdale items, plus lower bodyside and tailgate moldings; wheel lip moldings; Silverado nameplates; and a tailgate applique on Fleetsides. The 1980 exterior colors were Frost white; Medium blue; Light blue metallic; Nordic blue metallic; Emerald green; Sante Fe tan; Carmine red; Cardinal red; Midnight black; and Burnt orange metallic. Also seen were new exterior graphics and eight new two-tones.

1/2-TON; 3/4-TON; 1-TON FORWARD-CONTROL — MODEL P-SERIES 10; 20; 30 — SIX/V-8: Forward-Control trucks were P (parcel delivery) models available in the 10 (1/2-ton); 20 (3/4-ton) and 30 (1-ton) series The P10s had a 102 in. wheelbase and 7 ft. body. P20s came with 125 in. or 133 in. wheelbases designed for 10 ft. or 12 ft. bodies. P30s came in these sizes, plus a 157 in. wheelbase designed for 14 ft. bodies. Styling was boxy and unchanged.

1980 Chevrolet Fleetside Pickup (CP)

I.D. DATA: Serial number located: Combination VIN and rating plate located on: [El Camino] Top left side of dash; [Conventionals] left door pillar. Serial number systems: [El Camino] First symbol indicates manufacturer, 1=Chevrolet. Second symbol indicates car-line/ series: W=El Camino. Third and fourth symbols indicate body type: 80=Sedan-Pickup. Fifth symbol indicates engine: [El Camino] A=229 cid (3.8 liter)/115 hp two-barrel V-6; J=267 cid (4.4 liter)/120 hp two-barrel V-8; M=305 cid (5.0 liter)/155 nhp two-barrel V-8. Sixth symbol indicates model year: A=1980. Seventh symbol indicates assembly plant. Symbols 8-13 indicate the production sequence number starting at 100,001. Ending numbers not available. [All Light-Duty] First symbol indicates manufacturer: 1=Chevrolet Motor Div. The second symbol indicates chassis type: C=106 in. Conventional Cab including Blazer; G=Chevy Van or Sportvan; P=Forward-Control; L=LUV; K=106 in. Conventional cab 4x4; R=LUV (4x4). The third symbol indicates engine as follows: D=250 cid (4.1 liter)/one-barrel L6 (horsepower rated 115 for models with GVW under 6,000 lbs.; 100 for models with GVWs over 6,000 lbs.); G=305 cid (5.0 liter)/140 hp two-barrel V-8; L=350 cid (5.7 liter)/165 nhp four-barrel V-8; M=350 cid (5.7 liter)/145 nhp two-barrel V-8; N=110 cid (1.8 liter)/80 nhp two-barrel L4 (LUV); P=350 cid (5.7 liter) 120 hp two-barrel V-8; R=400 cid (6.6 liter)/175 hp four-barrel V-8; S=454 cid (7.4 liter) four-barrel V-8 for C models only (horsepower rated 205 for models with GVW under 6,000 lbs.; 245 for models with GVWs over 6,000 lbs.); T=292 cid (4.8 liter)/120 nhp one-barrel L-6; W=454 cid (7.4 liter)/245 nhp four-barrel V-8; X=400 cid (6.6 liter)/180 nhp four-barrel V-8; Z=350 cid (5.7 liter)/120 hp diesel V-8. The fourth symbol indicates series and tonnage: 1=1/2-ton; 2=3/4-ton; 3=1-ton; 4=1/2-ton with heavy-duty suspension. The fifth symbol indicates body type: 2=Chassis & Cowl; 3=Chassis & Cab; 4=Cab with pickup box or van with Hi-Cube box; 5=Panel or Panel Van; 6=Sportvan; Suburban (doors) 7=Motorhome chassis; 8=Utility (Blazer). The sixth symbol indicates model year: A=1980. The seventh symbol indicates the assembly plant: A=Lakewood, Ga.; B=Baltimore, Md.; F=Flint, Mich.; J=Janesville, Wis.; S=St. Louis, Mo.; U=Lordstown, Ohio; V=Pontiac, Mich. GMAD; Z=Fremont, Calif.; 0=Pontiac (GMC) Michigan; 1=Oshawa or London, Ontario, Canada; 3=GMAD, Detroit, Mich.; 4=Scarborough, Ontario, Canada; 8=Fujisawa, Japan. Symbols 8-13 are the production sequence number. Starting number: 10001 Ending numbers not available. Engine numbers located: [Six] on pad at right-hand side of cylinder block at rear of distributor; [V-8] on pad at front, right-hand side of cylinder block.

Model	Body Type	Price	Weight	Prod. Total
LUV — 1/2-Ton — 102.4 in. w.b. — Four				
CL10503	Chassis & Cab	4448	2095	—
CL10503	Pickup	4612	2315	—
LUV — 1/2-Ton — 117.9 in. w.b. — Four				
CL10803	Long-Box Pickup	4787	2405	—
El Camino — 1/2-Ton — 117.1 in. w.b. — V-8				
1AW80	Pickup	5911	3238	—
RPOZ15	Super Sport Pickup	6128	3238	—
Blazer 4x4 — 1/2-Ton — 106.5 in. w.b. — V-8				
CK10516	Hardtop	8233	4429	—
CK10516	Softtop	8130	—	—
*Deduct for C10 (4x2) Blazer.				
Chevy Van 10 — 1/2-Ton — 110 in. w.b. — V-8				
CG11005	Panel	5748	3652	—
CG11006	Sportvan	6747	3971	—
Chevy Van 10 — 1/2-Ton — 125 in. w.b. — V-8				
CG11306	Beauville	7854	4203	—

Chevy Van 20 — 3/4-Ton — 110 in. w.b. — V-8				
CG21005	Panel	6183	3756	—
CG21006	Sportvan	7023	4012	—
Chevy Van 20 — 3/4-Ton — 125 in. w.b. — V-8				
CG21306	Beauville	7975	4901	—
CG21305	Nomad	7864	3915	—
Chevy Van 30 — 1-Ton — 125 in. w.b. — V-8				
CG31305	Panel	7060	4154	—
CG31306	Sportvan	7901	4450	—
CG31306	Beauville	8680	4450	—
C30 Hi-Cube Van — 1-Ton — 125 in. w.b. — V-8				
CG31303	Hi-Cube 10 ft.	7666	3524	—
C30 Hi-Cube Van — 1-Ton — 146 in. w.b. — V-8				
CG31603	Hi-Cube 12 ft.	8793	8793	—
P10 Step-Van — 1/2-Ton — 102 — Six				
CP10542	Steel Step-Van 7 ft.	6681	4226	—
CP20842	Steel Panel 10 ft.	8021	5346	—
CP20842	Steel Panel 12 ft.	8287	5522	—
C10 — 1/2-Ton — 117.5 in. w.b. — V-8				
CC10703	Chassis & Cab	5785	3243	—
CC10703	Step-Side	5505	3550	—
CC10703	Fleetside	5505	3609	—
C10 — 1/2-Ton — 129.5 in. w.b. — V-8				
CC10906	Suburban	7456	4242	—
C10 — 1/2-Ton — 131.5 in. w.b. — V-8				
CC10903	Step-Side	5590	3692	—
CC10903	Fleetside	5590	3767	—
*Add $1,120 for K10 (4x4) models.				
C20 — 3/4-Ton — 131.5 in. w.b. — V-8				
CC20903	Chassis & Cab	6216	3585	—
CC20903	Step-Side	2326	3969	—
CC20903	Fleetside	6326	4044	—
C20 — 3/4-Ton — 129.5 in. w.b. — V-8				
CC20906	Suburban	7923	4538	—
C20 — 3/4-Ton — 164.5 in. w.b. — V-8				
CC20943	Chassis & Bonus Cab	6964	4330	—
CC20943	Fleetside & Bonus Cab	7241	4789	—
CC20943	Chassis & Crew Cab	7218	—	—
CC20943	Fleetside & Crew Cab	7495	—	—
*Add for K20 (4x4) models.				
P20 — 3/4-Ton — 125 in./133 in. w.b. — V-8				
CP20842	Steel Step-Van 10 ft.	8021	5346	—
*Add for C20 12 ft. Step-Van on 133 in. wheelbase.				
C30 — 1-Ton — 131.5 in. w.b. — V-8				
CC30903	Chassis & Cab	6399	3848	—
CC30903	Step-Side	6687	4232	—
CC30903	Fleetside	6687	4307	—
C30 — 1-Ton — 164.5 in. w.b. — V-8				
CC30943	Chassis & Bonus Cab	7120	4364	—
CC30943	Fleetside & Bonus Cab	7397	—	—
CC30943	Chassis & Crew Cab	7374	—	—
CC30943	Fleetside & Crew Cab	7651	—	—
*Add for K30 (4x4) models.				
P30 Step-Van — 1-Ton — 125/133/157 in. w.b. — V-8				
CP30842	Steel Step-Van 12 ft.	8287	5522	—

* Deduct for C30 10 ft. Step-Van on 125 in. wheelbase.
** Add for C30 14 ft. Step-Van on 157 in. wheelbase.

NOTE 1: Model year production: [El Camino] 40,932; [All Chevy Van] 77,424 [All Sportvan] 14,148; [Blazer] 31,776; [C10/C20 Suburban] 30,859; [Other C10] 305,167; [Other C20] 85,553; [C30] 59,251; [P10/P20/P30] 13,232. (Includes trucks built in Canada for U.S. market).

NOTE 2: U.S. Sales of LUV: 88,447.

1980 Chevrolet ChevyVan With Sport Package (CP)

ENGINE [Standard LUV]: Inline. OHV. OHC. Four-cylinder. Cast iron block. Bore & stroke: 3.31 x 3.23 in. Displacement: 110.8 cid. Compression ratio: 8.5:1. Net horsepower: 80 at 4800 rpm. Maximum Torque: 95 lbs.-ft at 3000 rpm. Five main bearings. Hydraulic valve lifters. Carburetor: One-barrel.

ENGINE [Standard El Camino]: Vee-block. OHV. Six-cylinder. Cast iron block. Bore & stroke: 3.5 x 3.48 in. Displacement: 200 cid. Compression ratio: 8.2:1. Net horsepower: 95. Four main bearings. Hydraulic valve lifters. Carburetor: Rochester two-barrel model 210.

ENGINE: Vee-block. OHV. Six-cylinder. Cast iron block. Bore & stroke: 3.8 x 3.4 in. Displacement: 231 cid. Compression ratio: 8.0:1. Net horsepower: 105. Four main bearings. Hydraulic valve lifters. Carburetor: Rochester two-barrel model 2GC.

ENGINE [Standard: C10/Big 10/K10]: Inline. OHV. Six-cylinder. Cast iron block. Bore & stroke: 3.876 x 3.530 in. Displacement: 250 cid. Compression ratio: 8.3:1. Net horsepower: 130 at 3800 rpm. Torque: 210 lbs.-ft. at 2400 rpm. Seven main bearings. Hydraulic valve lifters. Carburetor: Two-barrel model Rochester.

ENGINE [Optional El Camino]: Vee-block. OHV. Eight-cylinder. Cast iron block. Bore & stroke: 3.5 x 3.48 in. Displacement: 267 cid. Five main bearings. Hydraulic valve lifters. Carburetor: two-barrel

1980 Chevrolet El Camino Royal Knight (CP)

ENGINE [Standard: C20/C30/K20/K30]: Inline. OHV. Six-cylinder. Cast iron block. Bore & stroke: 3.876 x 4.120 in. Displacement: 292 cid. Compression ratio: 8.0:1. Net horsepower: 115 at 3400 rpm. Torque: 215 lbs.-ft. at 3400 rpm. Seven main bearings. Hydraulic valve lifters. Carburetor: Rochester model one-barrel.

ENGINE [Optional C10]: Vee-block. OHV. Eight-cylinder. Cast iron block. Bore & stroke: 3.736 x 3.480 in. Displacement: 305 cid. Compression ratio: 8.4:1. Net horsepower: 140 at 4000 rpm. Net torque: 235 lbs.-ft. at 2000 rpm. Five main bearings. Hydraulic valve lifters. Carburetor: Rochester two-barrel model 2GC.

ENGINE [Optional El Camino]: Vee-block. OHV. Eight-cylinder. Cast iron block. Bore & stroke: 3.736 x 3.480 in. Displacement: 305 cid. Compression ratio: 8.4:1. Net horsepower: 145/135*. Five main bearings. Hydraulic valve lifters. Carburetor: Rochester two-barrel model 2GC.

* California rating.

ENGINE [Optional: C10/Big 10]: V-type. OHV Diesel. Eight-cylinder. Cast iron block. Bore & stroke: 4.057 x 3.385 in. Displacement: 350 cid. Compression ratio: 20.5:1. Net horsepower: 120 at 3600 rpm. Net torque: 222 lbs.-ft. at 1900 rpm. Five main bearings. Hydraulic valve lifters.

ENGINE [Optional: all models except LUV]: Vee-block. OHV. Eight-cylinder. Cast iron block. Bore & stroke: 4.0 x 3.48 in. Displacement: 350 cid. Compression ratio: 8.2:1. Net horsepower: 165 at 3600 rpm. Net torque: 270 lbs.-ft. at 2700 rpm. Five main bearings. Hydraulic valve lifters. Carburetor: Rochester four-barrel model M4 MC/MV.

ENGINE: V-type. OHV. Eight-cylinder. Cast iron block. Bore & stroke: 4.0 x 3.48 in. Displacement: 350 cid. Compression ratio: 8.2:1. Net horsepower: 170/160 at 3800 rpm. Maximum torque: 270 lbs.-ft. at 2400 rpm. Five main bearings. Hydraulic valve lifters. Carburetor: Rochester four-barrel model M4 MC/MV.

ENGINE [Optional: K10/K20/K30]: Vee-block. OHV. Eight-cylinder. Cast iron block. Bore & stroke: 4.125 x 3.750 in. Displacement: 400 cid. Compression ratio: 8.5:1. Net horsepower: 185 at 3600 rpm. Net torque: 300 lbs.-ft. at 2400 rpm. Five main bearings. Hydraulic valve lifters. Carburetor: Rochester four-barrel model M4 MC/MV.

ENGINE [Optional: all models except Blazer, El Camino, LUV]: Vee-block. OHV. Eight-cylinder. Cast iron block. Bore & stroke: 4.250 x 4.0 in. Displacement: 454 cid. Compression ratio: 7.6:1. Net horsepower: 245 at 4000 rpm. Net torque: 380 lbs.-ft. at 2500 rpm. Five main bearings. Hydraulic valve lifters. Carburetor: Rochester four-barrel model M4 MC/MV.

NOTE: On all engines, horsepower and torque can vary in California units.

CHASSIS [LUV]: Wheelbase: 102.4 in./117.9 in. Overall length: 173.8 in./190.9 in. Front tread: 54 in. Rear tread: 52.2 in. Tires: E78 x 14B in.

CHASSIS [El Camino]: Wheelbase: 117.1 in. Overall length: 201.6 in. Height: 53.8 in. Front tread: 58.5 in. Rear tread: 51.8 in. Tires: P205/75R x 14 in.

CHASSIS [Blazer]: Wheelbase: 106.5 in. Overall length: 184.8 in. Height: 73.4 in. Front tread: 66.1 in. Rear tread: 63 in. Tires: P215/75R x 15 in.

CHASSIS [Chevy Van 10]: Wheelbase: 110 in./125 in. Overall length: 178 in./202.2 in. Height: 78.8 in./81.2 in. Front tread: 69.5 in. Rear tread: 69.7 in. Tires: GR78 x 15B in.

CHASSIS [Chevy Van 20]: Wheelbase: 110 in./125 in. Overall length: 178.2 in./202.2 in. Height: 78.8 in./81.2 in. Front tread: 69.5 in. Rear tread: 69.7 in. Tires: JR78 x 15B in.

CHASSIS [Chevy Van 30]: Wheelbase: 125 in./146 in. Overall length: 207.6 in./231.3 in. Tires: 8.75 x 16.5E in.

CHASSIS [Series C10/K10]: Wheelbase: 117.5 in./131.5 in. Overall length: 193.3 in./212 in. Height: 72 in. Front tread: 65.8 in. Rear tread: 62.7 in. Tires: GR78 x 15B in.

CHASSIS [Step-Van 10]: Wheelbase: 102 in. Tires: L78 x 15B in.

CHASSIS [Series C20/K20]: Wheelbase: 131.5 in. Overall length: 212 in. Height: 73.9 in. Front tread: 65.8 in. Rear tread: 62.7 in. Tires: 8.75 x 16.5C in.

CHASSIS [Step-Van 20]: Wheelbase: 125 in./133 in. Tires: 8.75 x 16.5 in.

CHASSIS [C30]: Wheelbase: 131.5 in./164.5 in. Overall length: 212 in./244.43 in. Height: 71.8 in. Front tread: 65.8 in. Rear tread: 62.7 in. Tires: [Pickup] 8.75 x 16.5C in., [Bonus/Crew Cab] 16.5E in.

CHASSIS [K30]: Wheelbase: 131.5 in./164.5 in. Overall length: 212 in./244.43 in. Height: 74.7 in./75 in. Front tread: 65.8 in. Rear tread: 62.7 in. Tires: 9.50 x 16.5D in.

CHASSIS [P30]: Wheelbase: 125 in./133 in./157 in. Tires: 8.75 x 16.5 in.

TECHNICAL: Selective synchromesh transmission (Diesel with Turbo-Hydramatic only). Speeds: 3F/1R (LUV includes 4F/1R transmission). Column-mounted gearshift, except

LUV. Single dry-disc type clutch. Salisbury rear axle. Overall ratio: (C10) 3.07:1; (K10) 4.11:1; (C20) 4.10:1. Front disc/rear drum brakes. Pressed steel axle. Drivetrain options: Turbo-Hydramatic transmission ($370). Locking differential and 3.73: axle ($210). Freedom battery ($39). Engine oil cooler ($91). Heavy-duty springs and shocks ($71). Blazer towing device ($30). Dead-weight trailer hitch ($43). Uni-Royal Land Trac tires, 10.00 x 15 ($362.85). Blazer rear roll bar ($105). Big 10 package ($375).

1980 Chevrolet LUV Pickup (DFW)

OPTIONS: Chrome front bumper ($33). Radio AM, AM/FM. Electric clock ($55). Caravan package (Van). Custom comfort package. Chevy Sport package. F44 Big 10 package ($375). Scottsdale package. C20 8 ft. Stake rack body. Air-conditioning ($574). Color-keyed floor mats ($11). Tinted glass ($49). Chromed grille ($29). Exterior below-eye-level mirror ($55). Convenience package ($23). Comfortilt steering wheel ($78). Rally wheels ($84). Intermittent wipers ($33). Sliding side window glass, Blazer ($176). Folding rear seat, Blazer ($260). Electric tailgate window, Blazer ($65).

HISTORICAL: Introduced: Fall 1979. Calendar year registrations: [All Chevrolet trucks] 737,788. Calendar year sales: [Pickups] 403,487; [Vans] 86,727; [Suburbans] 19,518; [Blazer] 21,399; [LUV] 61,724; [El Camino] 33,086; [Sportvan] 13,576; [Total] 724,330. Innovations: New grilles for all series, except LUV. One-ton Chevrolet vans adopt no longer come on 110 in. chassis. Rising gasoline prices and a slackening economy made this a poor year for truck sales. At Chevrolet, calendar year registrations dropped below the one-million level for the first time since 1976. In midyear, Chevrolet discontinued its heavy, over-the-road type trucks to concentrate on the light-duty and medium-duty market products.

1981 CHEVROLET

1981 Chevrolet Step-Side Pickup (CP)

1/2-TON LIGHT UTILITY VEHICLE (LUV) — MODEL L/SERIES 10500 — FOUR: New Aerodynamic styling was seen inside and outside this year's Series 11 LUV imported compact truck. The hood was smoother and the new cab provided a larger glass area. A curved rear window was used. A major functional change added some 2-1/2 in. of legroom and about an inch of shoulder room. Wheelbase was increased to 104.3 in. with a new frame design. The grille was of egg-crate style, with a larger Chevrolet bow tie in its center. Bumper slots again numbered four, but those near the center were now the widest, while the smaller outer pair housed the parking lamps. Headlamp housings could no longer be seen in profile. The bodysides were now smoothly curved with a sculptured feature line near the bottom rather than the belt. Chevrolet medallions were positioned on the side roof panel and load tie-downs, now located on the inner side of the box. Interiors featured a restyled, color-keyed instrument panel and pad with a new instrument cluster, color-keyed steering wheel, new seat trim material, door and window regulator handles, headliner, door trim panel materials and redesigned steering column. The Mikado package was revised with new seat trim, door trim panels, steering wheel and instrument panel trim. A new color-keyed floor console was standard with automatic transmission. Realigned cab door openings made for easier exit and entry. Other improvements included weight reduction, heavier payload capacities, improved 4x2 front suspension, larger front brake area and power brake booster, improved heating/ventilation system and new electronic ignition system.

1/2-TON EL CAMINO — MODEL C; D/SERIES 14000 — SIX/V-8: The El Camino featured a new grille of horizontal design with bright upper and lower moldings. A Chevrolet name was at the lower left-hand corner of the grille, while El Camino lettering decorated the lower rear quarter, above the feature line. Attractive new wheelcovers with a turbine-fin look around a plain center disc were introduced. Inside was a redesigned instrument panel with a new pad and glossy applique, convenient door-pull straps, new seat trim and international symbols on the controls. A new 55/45 split front seat was optional, with single folding armrests. A Resume function was added to the optional automatic speed control. Standard tires were now high-pressure P205/75R models with reduced rolling resistance for better mileage. A side-lift jack replaced the former bumper type. Powertrains were carried over, but all engines were now equipped with GM's Computer Command Control (CCC) emissions system. This utilized an on-board computer for precise fuel-air ratio control. Option packages included the Conquista and Royal Knight equipment groups, while the Super Sport version was merchandised as a separate model-option, rather than individual package. New-for-1981 options also included a trip odometer.

1981 Chevrolet Fleetside Pickup (CP)

1/2-TON; 3/4-TON; 1-TON VAN — MODEL G/SERIES 10; 20; 30 — SIX/V-8: Chevy Vans were essentially unchanged in appearance. This went for Hi-Cube vans and Step-Vans, as well. A new Chevy Van model-option was the Bonaventure van. This was a mid-level passenger van with special identification nameplates, high-back bucket seats (standard in Sportvans), Custom vinyl trim, a full-length headliner, door and sidewall trim panels and deluxe instrument panel. It was available in all tonnage classes, on the 125 in. wheelbase. Offered for the first time in a Chevrolet factory van was a travel bed package consisting of a three-passenger bench seat with folding back rest and hinged extension which unfolded into a travel bed. Technical changes included improvements to the base six-cylinder engine; a new high-compression 5-liter V-8 with ESC (not available in California with ESC); and better corrosion protection measures. Anti-rust measures were the use of new, two-sided galvanized steel for rear door outer panels and the use of zinc-rich paints on brake and fuel lines.

1/2-TON BLAZER — MODEL C; K/SERIES 10500 — SIX/V-8: Blazers, for 1981, had an aerodynamically restyled front end. The smoother new hood and fenders, together with a front bumper mounted air dam, were designed to improve fuel economy. A handsome new grille (also used on pickups) continued the "ice cube tray" look with 16 taller openings running across the truck between the stacked square headlamps. A wide center horizontal molding — bright-finished with a bow tie in the middle — spanned the full width of the front end. Rectangular parking lamps/turn signals were placed in the new front bumper, directly beneath the headlamps. On the bodysides, the belt-level feature line ran the length of the Blazer and blended more smoothly into the fender edge at the front. Tu-tone paint treatments were now separated at the lower perimeter feature line. New front fender skirts with attached shields helped reduce engine compartment splash. Standard engine was still the 250 six-cylinder. A new 305 cid V-8 with electronic spark control (ESC) was optional, except in California. 4x4 models had a new aluminum transfer case and automatic locking hubs. Other technical improvements included bumpers made of lighter-weight high-strength/low-alloy steel, and a new front quad shock package. A Custom trim package included an exterior decor package or special two-tone paint. Also available were the Deluxe and Silverado options and new Deluxe Front Appearance package.

1/2-TON; 3/4-TON; 1-TON — MODEL C; K/SERIES 10; 20; 30 — SIX/V-8: Chevrolet's 1981 pickups were 87 to 300 lbs. lighter than their 1980 counterparts, while retaining the same cab size and bed size as before. They received the same new grille and sheet metal treatments described above for Blazers. The grille could be had with the square headlamps only in the top level or with a Halogen High-Beam option in which both grille levels held a square lamp unit at each end. A new one-piece instrument panel trim panel was used on the dash eliminating the vertical seam between the banks of gauges. Collectible trim options include the Chevy Sport, Cheyenne, Scottsdale and Silverado packages. Custom and Custom Deluxe trims were more commonly seen. Among light-duty powerplants was a new high-compression 5.0-liter V-8 with ESC (not used in California) that was designed to give both economy and performance improvements. Also new for the season were improved corrosion resistance; low-drag disc brakes; new 6,000-lbs. semi-floating axle (specific models); Resume Speed cruise controls; quad shock 4x4 front suspension; heavier-duty rear springs; and a water-in-fuel warning lamp for diesel-powered trucks. K20s and K10s adopted the new automatic locking hubs and shot-peened rear springs. Standard on all models were high-efficiency radiators and Delco Freedom II battery. Suburbans were restyled, along the lines of the Blazer, at the front. Like other 1981 trucks, they had reduced weights (about 200-300 lbs.). A new standard 305 cid V-8 was featured outside California. Half-tons had new drag-free disc brakes and quick-makeup master cylinder, plus lighter weight rear springs. Due to the use of new automatic-locking front hubs, Suburbans with 4x4 drive could be shifted into the 4x4 mode at speeds up to 20 mph.

1981 Chevrolet Beauville Sportvan (CP)

1/2-TON; 3/4-TON; 1-TON FORWARD-CONTROL — MODEL P-SERIES 10; 20; 30 — SIX/V-8: Forward-Control trucks were P (parcel delivery) models available in the 10 (1/2-ton); 20 (3/4-ton) and 30 (1-ton) series The P10s had a 102 in. wheelbase and 7 ft. body. P20s came with 125 in. or 133 in. wheelbases designed for 10 ft. or 12 ft. bodies. P30s came in these sizes, plus a 157 in. wheelbase designed for 14 ft. bodies. Styling was boxy and unchanged.

1981 Chevrolet Silverado Suburban (CP)

I.D. DATA: Serial number located: Combination VIN and rating plate located on: [El Camino] Top left side of dash; [Conventionals] left door pillar. Serial number systems: New system for all Light-Duty and Medium-Duty models including El Camino] The first symbol indicates country of origin: 1=U.S.A.; 2=Canada; J=Japan. The second symbol indicates manufacturer: 8=Isuzu; G=General Motors Chevrolet Motor Div. The third symbol indicates brand: C=Chevrolet Truck; 8=Chevrolet MPV; A=Chevy Van with fourth seat; Z=LUV. The fourth symbol indicates GVWR and brake system: B=3,001-4,000 lbs. (hydraulic brakes); C=4,001-5,000 lbs. (hydraulic brakes); etc. The fifth symbol indicates line and chassis type: C=106 in. Conventional Cab 4x2 including Blazer; G=Chevy Van or Sportvan; K=106 in. Conventional cab 4x4 including Blazer; P=Forward-Control 4x2; L=LUV 4x2; R=LUV 4x4; W=El Camino; Z=Special body. The sixth symbol indicates series: 1=1/2-ton; 2=3/4-ton; 3=1-ton; 8=1/2-ton El Camino; 9=Chassis & Short Sill Cowl. The seventh symbol indicates body type: 0=El Camino; 1=Hi-Cube and Cut-away Van; 2=Forward-Control; 3=Four-door Cab; 4=Two-door cab; 5=Van; 6=Suburban (doors) 7=Motorhome chassis; 8=Utility (Blazer); 9=Stake. The eighth symbol indicates engine as follows: D=250 cid (4.1 liter)/one-barrel L6 (horsepower rated 115 for models with GVW under 6,000 lbs.; 100 for models with GVWs over 6,000 lbs.; F,H=305 cid (5.0 liter) four-barrel V-8; G=305 cid (5.0 liter)/140 hp two-barrel V-8; L=350 cid (5.7 liter)/165 nhp four-barrel V-8; M=350 cid (5.7 liter)/145 nhp two-barrel V-8; N=110 cid (1.8 liter)/80 nhp two-barrel L4 (LUV); P=350 cid (5.7 liter) 120 hp two-barrel V-8; T=292 cid (4.8 liter)/120 nhp one-barrel L-6; W=454 cid (7.4 liter)/ 245 nhp four-barrel V-8; Z=350 cid (5.7 liter)/120 nhp diesel V-8. The ninth symbol indicates model year: B=1981. The 10th symbol indicates the assembly plant: A=Lakewood, Ga.; B=Baltimore, Md.; F=Flint, Mich.; J=Janesville, Wis.; S=St. Louis, Mo.; U=Lordstown, Ohio; V=Pontiac, Mich. GMAD; Z=Fremont, Calif.; 0=Pontiac (GMC) Michigan; 1=Oshawa or London, Ontario, Canada; 3=GMAD, Detroit, Mich.; 4=Scarborough, Ontario, Canada; 8=Fujisawa, Japan. Symbols 11-17 are the production sequence number. Starting number: 10001 Ending numbers not available. Engine numbers located: [Six] on pad at right-hand side of cylinder block at rear of distributor; [V-8] on pad at front, right-hand side of cylinder block.

Model	Body Type	Price	Weight	Prod. Total
LUV — 1/2-Ton — 104.3 in. w.b. — Four				
CL10503	Chassis & Cab	5913	—	—
CL10503	Pickup	6586	2315	—
LUV — 1/2-Ton — 117.9 in. w.b. — Four				
CL10803	Pickup	6795	2405	—
El Camino — 1/2-Ton — 117.1 in. w.b. — V-6				
A1AW80	Pickup	6988	3181	—
RPOZ15	Super Sport Pickup	7217	3188	—
G10 Van — 1/2-Ton — 110 in. w.b. — Six				
CG11005	Panel	6434	3577	—
CG11006	Sportvan	7465	3907	—

Standard Catalog of Light-Duty Trucks

G10 Van — 1/2-Ton — 125 in. w.b. — Six

CG11306	Bonaventure	8305	4016	—
CG11306	Beauville	8515	4016	—

G20 Van — 3/4-Ton — 110 in. w.b. — Six

CG21005	Panel	6756	3631	—
CG21006	Sportvan	7617	3928	—

G20 Van — 3/4-Ton — 125 in. w.b. — Six

CG21306	Bonaventure	8457	—	—
CG21306	Beauville	8667	—	—
CG21305	Nomad	8644	—	—

G30 Van — 1-Ton — 125 in. w.b. — V-8

CG31305	Panel	8056	4285	—
CG31306	Sportvan	8997	4602	—
CS31306	Bonaventure	9653	—	—
CG31306	Beauville	9863	—	—

G30 Hi-Cube Van — 1-Ton — 125/146 in. w.b. — V-8

CG31303	Panel & Cab 10 ft.	8921	—	—
CG31603	Panel & Cab 12 ft.	10,257	—	—

Blazer 4x4 — 1/2-Ton — 106.5 in. w.b. — Six

CK10516	Hardtop	8856	4087	—
CK10516	Softtop	8750	—	—

* Deduct for C10 (4x2) Blazer.

C10 4x2 — 1/2-Ton — 117.5 — Six

CC10703	Step-Side 6.5 ft.	6012	3328	—
CC10703	Fleetside 6.5 ft.	6012	3391	—

C10 4x2 — 1/2-Ton — 129.5 in. w.b. — V-8

CC10906	Suburban 9 ft.	8517	4276	—

C10 4x2 — 1/2-Ton — 131.5 — Six

CC10903	Step-Side 8 ft.	6099	3457	—
CC10903	Fleetside 8 ft.	6099	3518	—

* Add $1,750 for K10 (4x4) Pickups and Suburbans.

C20 — 3/4-Ton — 131.5 w.b. — Six

CC20903	Chassis & Cab	6605	3326	—
CC20903	Step-Side 8 ft.	7109	3710	—
CC20903	Fleetside 8 ft.	7109	3771	—

C20 — 3/4-Ton — 129.5 in. w.b. — V-8

CC20906	Suburban	8771	4596	—

C20 — 3/4-Ton — 164.5 in. w.b. — Six

CC20943	Chassis & Bonus Cab	7447	4246	—
CC20943	Fleetside & Bonus Cab 8 ft.	7935	—	—
CC20943	Chassis & Crew Cab	7737	—	—
CC20943	Fleetside & Crew Cab 8 ft.	8225	—	—

* Add $1,370 for K20 (4x4) Pickups and Suburbans.

P20 Step-Van — 3/4-Ton — 125/133 in. w.b. — Six

CP20842	Steel Step-Van 10 ft.	9536	5472	—

* Add for C20 12 ft. Step-Van on 133 in. wheelbase.

C30 — 1-Ton — 131.5 in. w.b. — Six

CC30903	Chassis & Cab	6720	3893	—
CC30903	Step-Side 8 ft.	7214	4251	—
CC30903	Fleetside 8 ft.	7214	4310	—

C30 — 1-Ton — 164.5 in. w.b. — Six

CC30943	Chassis & Bonus Cab	7625	4327	—
CC30943	Fleetside & Bonus Cab 8 ft.	8114	—	—
CC30943	Chassis & Crew Cab	7915	—	—
CC30943	Fleetside & Crew Cab 8 ft.	8404	—	—

* Add for K30 4x4 models; price not available.

P30 Step-Van — 1-Ton — 125/133/157 in. w.b. — V-8

CP30842	Steel Step-Van 10 ft.	9784	5671	—

* Add for P30 12 ft. Step-Van on 133 in. wheelbase.
** Add for P30 14 ft. Step-Van on 157 in. wheelbase.

NOTE 1: Model year production: [El Camino] 37,533; [All Chevy Van] 85,135 [All Sportvan] 13,844; [Blazer] 23,635; [C10/C20 Suburban] 25,983; [Other C10] 76,288; [C30] 50,250; [P10/P20/P30] 22,134. (Includes trucks built in Canada for U.S. market).
NOTE 2: U.S. Sales of LUV: 61,724.

1981 Chevrolet Blazer (CP)

ENGINE [Standard: LUV]: Inline. OHV. OHC. Four-cylinder. Cast iron block. Bore & stroke: 3.31 x 3.23 in. Displacement: 110.8 cid. Compression ratio: 8.5:1. Net horsepower: 80 at 4800 rpm. Maximum torque: 95 lbs.-ft. at 3000 rpm. Five main bearings. Hydraulic valve lifters. Carburetor: Single one-barrel.

ENGINE [Standard: El Camino (Except California)]: Vee-block. OHV. Six-cylinder. Cast iron block. Bore & stroke: 3.7 x 3.48 in. Displacement: 229 cid. Compression ratio: 8.6:1. Net horsepower: 110 at 4200 rpm. Maximum torque: 170 lbs.-ft. at 2000 rpm. Four main bearings. Hydraulic valve lifters. Order Code LC3(A).

ENGINE [Standard: El Camino (California only)]: Vee-block. OHV. Eight-cylinder. Cast iron block. Bore & stroke: 3.8 x 3.4 in. Displacement: 231 cid. Compression ratio: 8.0:1. Net horsepower: 110 at 3800 rpm. Maximum torque: 190 lbs.-ft. at 1600 rpm. Four main bearings. Hydraulic valve lifters. Order Code LD5(C).

ENGINE [Standard: C10/C20/K10/G10/G20/G30/Blazer]: Inline. OHV. Six-cylinder. Cast iron block. Bore & stroke: 3.9 x 4.5 in. Displacement: 250 cid. Compression ratio: 8.3:1. Net horsepower: 115 at 3600 rpm. Torque: 200 lbs.-ft. at 2000 rpm. Seven main bearings. Hydraulic valve lifters. Carburetor: Rochester model Staged two-barrel. Order Code LE3(A).

ENGINE [Optional El Camino (except California)]: Vee-block. OHV. Eight-cylinder. Cast iron block. Bore & stroke: 3.5 x 3.48 in. Displacement: 267 cid. Compression ratio: 8.3:1. Net horsepower: 115 at 4000 rpm. Maximum torque: 200 lbs.-ft. at 2400 rpm. Five main bearings. Hydraulic valve lifters. Carburetor: Rochester model Staged two-barrel. Order Code L39(B).

1981 Chevrolet El Camino Royal Knight (CP)

ENGINE [Standard: C20 HD (C6P)/C20 Bonus and Crew Cab/C30/C30 Bonus and Crew Cab/K20 HD (P6)]: Inline. OHV. Six-cylinder. Cast iron block. Bore & stroke: 3.876 x 4.12 in. Displacement: 292 cid. Compression ratio: 7.8:1. Net horsepower: 115 at 3400 rpm. Maximum torque: 215 lbs.-ft. at 1600 rpm. Five main bearings. Hydraulic valve lifters. Carburetor: Rochester model one-barrel. Order Code L25(B).

ENGINE [Optional C10/K10/Blazer]: Vee-block. OHV. Eight-cylinder. Cast iron block. Bore & stroke: 3.736 x 3.480 in. Displacement: 305 cid. Compression ratio: 8.5:1. Net horsepower: 130 at 4000 rpm. Maximum torque: 240 lbs.-ft. at 2000 rpm. Five main bearings. Hydraulic valve lifters. Carburetor: Rochester model Staged two-barrel. Order Code LG9(C).

ENGINE [Optional C10/C20/K10/Blazer]: Vee-block. OHV. Eight-cylinder. Cast iron block. Bore & stroke: 3.736 x 3.480 in. Displacement: 305 cid. Compression ratio: 9.2:1. Net horsepower: 160 at 4400 rpm. Maximum torque: 235 lbs.-ft. at 2000 rpm. Five main bearings. Hydraulic valve lifters. Carburetor: Rochester model Staged four-barrel with Electronic Spark Control. Order Code LE9(C). Not available for California.

ENGINE [Optional El Camino]: Vee-block. OHV. Eight-cylinder. Cast iron block. Bore & stroke: 3.7 x 3.48 in. Displacement: 305 cid. Compression ratio: 8.6:1. Net horsepower: 145 at 3800 rpm. Maximum torque: 248 lbs.-ft. at 2400 rpm. Five main bearings. Hydraulic valve lifters. Carburetor: Rochester model Staged four-barrel. Order Code LG4(B).

ENGINE [Optional: C10/C20/K10/G10/G20]: Vee-block. OHV. Eight-cylinder. Cast iron block. Bore & stroke: 3.736 x 3.480 in. Displacement: 305 cid. Compression ratio: 8.6:1. Net horsepower: 150 at 4200. Maximum torque: 240 lbs.-ft. at 2000 rpm. Five main bearings. Hydraulic valve lifters. Carburetor: Rochester model Staged four-barrel. Order Code LF3(C).

ENGINE [Standard: G30/C20/K10/K20 Suburban; Optional: C20/K20/K20 HD (CP6)/K30/C10 Suburban]: Vee-block. OHV. Eight-cylinder. Cast iron block. Bore & stroke: 4.3 x 3.5 in. Displacement: 350 cid. Compression ratio: 8.2:1. Net horsepower: 165 at 3800 rpm. Maximum torque: 275 lbs.-ft. at 1600 rpm. Five main bearings. Hydraulic valve lifters. Carburetor: Rochester model four-barrel. Order Code L59(A).

ENGINE [Optional: C10]: Vee-block. OHV Diesel. Eight-cylinder. Cast iron block. Bore & stroke: 4.06 x 3.38 in. Displacement: 350 cid. Compression ratio: 22.5:1. Net horsepower: 125 at 3600 rpm. Maximum torque: 225 lbs.-ft. at 1600 rpm. Five main bearings. Carburetor: Fuel injection. Order Code LS9(A).

ENGINE [Optional: C20/C20 HD/CP6/C30]: Vee-block. OHV. Eight-cylinder. Cast iron block. Bore & stroke: 4.250 x 4.0 in. Displacement: 454 cid. Compression ratio: 7.9:1. Net horsepower: 210 at 3800 rpm. Maximum Torque: 340 lbs.-ft at 2800 rpm. Five main bearings. Hydraulic valve lifters. Carburetor: Rochester model four-barrel. Order Code LE8(A).
NOTE: Versions of some engines used in trucks for California sale have different horse-power and torque ratings.
CHASSIS [LUV]: Wheelbase: 104.3 in./117.9 in. Overall length: 174.5 in./191.6 in. Height: [4x2] 59.3 in.; [4x4] 61.0 in. Front tread: [4x2] 53.8 in.; [4x4] 54.2 in. Rear tread: [4x2] 51.2 in.; [4x4] 52.7 in. Tires: [4x2] E78 x 14B in.; [4x4] F70 x 14B in. white-lettered.
CHASSIS [El Camino]: Wheelbase: 117.1 in. Overall length: 201.6 in. Height: 53.8 in. Front tread: 58.5 in. Rear tread: 57.8 in. Tires: P205/75R x 14 in.
CHASSIS [Chevy Van 10]: Wheelbase: 110 in./125 in. Overall length: 178.2 in./202.2 in. Height: 78.8 in./81.2 in. Front tread: 69.5 in. Rear tread: 69.7 in. Tires: FR78 x 15B in.
CHASSIS [Chevy Van 20]: Wheelbase: 110 in./125 in. Overall length: 178.2 in./202.2 in. Height: 78.8 in./81.2 in. Front tread: 69.5 in. Rear tread: 69.7 in. Tires: P225/75R x 15 in.
CHASSIS [Chevy Van 30]: Wheelbase: 125 in./146 in. Tires: 8.75 x 16.5E in.
CHASSIS [Hi-Cube Van]: Wheelbase: 125 in./146 in. Overall length: 207.3 in./231.3 in. Tires: [front] 8.75 x 16 in.; [rear] 8.00 x 16 in.
CHASSIS [Blazer 4x4]: Wheelbase: 106.5 in. Overall length: 184.8 in. Height: 73.4 in. Front tread: 66.1 in. Rear tread: 63 in. Tires: [4x2] P215/75R x 15 in.; [4x4] P215/75R x 15 in.
CHASSIS [C10 Pickups]: Wheelbase: 117.5 in./131.5 in. Overall length: 192.2 in./211.4 in. Height: [Fleetside] 69.8 in.; [Step-Side] 71.9 in. Tires: FR78 x 15B in.
CHASSIS [C10/C20 Suburban]: Wheelbase: 129.5 in. Overall length: 218.7 in. Height: 71.8 in. Tires: 8.75R x 16.5 in.
CHASSIS [C20 Pickup]: Wheelbase: 131.5 in./164.5 in. Overall length: [SWB Fleetside C10] 211.4 in.; [SWB Fleetside K10] 212.1 in. Height: [4x2] 70.8 in.; [4x4] 73.9 in. Tires: 8.75R x 16.5C in.
CHASSIS [P20 Step-Van]: Wheelbase: 125 in./133 in. Tires: 8.75 x 16.5C in.
CHASSIS [C30 Pickup]: Wheelbase: 131.5 in./164.5 in. Overall length: [SWB Fleetside] 211.4 in. Height: [SWB Fleetside 4x2] 70.9 in. Tires: 8.75 x 16.5C in.
CHASSIS [P30 Step-Van]: Wheelbase: 125 in./157 in. Tires: 8.75 x 16.5 in.
TECHNICAL: Selective, synchromesh transmission. Speeds: 3F/1R (LUV and 30 have 4F/1R speeds. Column-mounted gearshift (except LUV). Single disc-type clutch. Salisbury rear axle. Overall ratio: various. Power front disc/rear drum brakes. Pressed steel wheels.
TECHNICAL: Selective synchromesh transmission (Diesel with Turbo-Hydramatic only). Speeds: 3F/1R (LUV includes 4F/1R transmission). Column-mounted gearshift, except LUV. Single dry-disc type clutch. Salisbury rear axle. Overall ratio: (C10) 3.07:1; (K10) 4.11:1; (C20) 4.10:1. Front disc/rear drum brakes. Pressed steel wheels.

1981 Chevrolet LUV Pickup (CP)

OPTIONS: [LUV]: Air-conditioning ($603). Chrome rear step bumper ($122); Painted ($122). Chrome front bumper guards ($38). Sport stripe decals ($45). Decals and stripes ($111). California emissions ($111). Exterior Decor package, includes chrome center hub-caps and moldings for beltline, windshield and roof rails ($98). Mikado trim, with bench seat ($228); with bucket seat ($354). Stainless below-eyeline mirrors ($61). Solid paint, metallic ($75). AM radio ($98). AM/FM radio ($176). Passenger type whitewall tires, front ($19); rear, ($19); spare ($10). Automatic transmission ($420). Sliding rear window ($92). [Blazer] Silverado ($881). Custom high-back vinyl bucket seats, without Silverado and rear seat ($170); two seats without Silverado ($212); one seat with Silverado (no charge); two seats with Silverado ($42). Custom cloth high-back bucket seats, without rear seat (no charge); with rear seat ($42). Special two-tone, without Silverado ($314); with Silverado ($130). Exterior Decor package, without Silverado ($430); with Silverado ($246). 5.0 liter two-barrel V-8 ($295). 5.0 liter four-barrel V-8 ($345). 5.0 liter four-barrel V-8 with ESC ($345). Four-speed manual transmission ($170). Automatic transmission ($384). Optional axle ($26). High-altitude 3.73:1 rear axle ($26). Air-conditioning ($591). Deluxe front ($88). Locking differential ($191). Auxiliary battery ($101). Heavy-duty battery ($40). Chromed bumpers ($58). Deluxe chrome bumpers, with Silverado ($38); without Silverado ($96). Front bumper guards ($34). Quartz electric clock ($60). Power door locks ($98). Halogen high-beam headlamps ($26). Sliding side window ($184). One-way glass ($147). Below-eyeline mirror, stainless ($63); painted ($39); camper ($74). Bodyside moldings ($92). Operating Convenience package ($243). Rally wheels ($88). Aluminum forged wheels ($360). Styled wheels ($176). Power windows ($145). Tailgate ($67). Power steering ($205). Fuel tank shield ($135). AM/FM with 8-track stereo ($320). Roll bar ($108). [Chevy Van/Sportvan]: Custom vinyl high-back bucket seats ($34). Custom cloth swivel bucket seats ($420). Special two-tone paint ($185). Deluxe two-tone paint ($195). 5.0 liter four-barrel V-8 ($345). 5.7 liter four-barrel V-8 ($345). Automatic transmission ($384). Axle options ($26). Air-conditioning, front ($696); front and rear, ($1,138). Locking differential ($191). Heavy-duty battery ($40). Heavy-duty power brakes ($63). Chrome bumpers front/rear ($58). Front chrome bumper guards ($34). Electric clock ($27). Engine oil cooler ($95). Heavy-duty cooling ($42). Spare tire cover ($26). Power door locks ($147). California emissions ($80). Side rear door extender link ($29). All glass tinted ($75). Windshield tinted ($25). One-way glass ($296). Rear heater, without air conditioner ($189); with ($156). Cigar lighter ($19). Auxiliary lighting ($77). Below-eyeline mirrors, painted ($39); stainless ($63). Bodyside moldings ($102). Door edge guards ($13). Wheel opening moldings ($57). Operating Convenience package, includes power door locks and windows ($292). Passenger seats, eight-man ($219); 12-man ($467). Swivel bucket seats ($426). Travel bed with 8-passenger ($770); regular ($561). Heavy-duty shocks ($27). Automatic speed control ($132). Power steering ($217). Comfortilt steering wheel ($81). Custom steering wheel ($21). Rear door stop ($29). Front seat storage compartment ($29). Body striping ($56). Large

33-gal. fuel tank ($68). Theft deterrent system ($148). Deadweight trailer hitch ($145). Roof ventilator ($62). Special wheelcovers ($51). Forged aluminum wheels ($360). Rally wheels with trim rings ($88). Styled wheels ($176). Power windows ($145). Windshield wiper system, intermittent ($34). Deluxe front appearance ($59). Beauville trim for cargo van ($516). Trailering special ($456). Gauge package ($29). Custom vinyl high-back bucket seats in Cargo van, with auxiliary seat ($50); without auxiliary seat ($25). 5.0 liter two-barrel V-8 in cargo van ($295). Automatic transmission. [C10 Fleetside] Note: Some of this equipment was slightly less expensive on Step-Sides and slightly more expensive on Suburbans and larger pickups. Scottsdale, with bucket seats ($290); without ($310). Cheyenne, without decor and bucket seats ($452); without decor with bucket seats ($394); with decor without bucket seats ($395); with decor and bucket seats ($338). Silverado, without decor and bucket seats ($718); without decor with bucket seats ($668); with decor without bucket seats ($693) and with bucket seats and decor ($642). Regular two-tone paint, with Cheyenne or Silverado ($37); without Cheyenne or Silverado ($61). Special two-tone paint, without Scottsdale-Silverado-Cheyenne ($256); with Scottsdale ($153); with Silverado ($130); with Cheyenne ($222). 4.1 liter two-barrel six (no charge). 5.0 liter two-barrel V-8 ($295). 5.0 liter four-barrel V-8 with ESC ($345). 5.0 liter four-barrel V-8 ($345). 5.7 liter four-barrel V-8 ($315). 7.4 liter four-barrel V-8 ($425). Automatic transmission ($384). Four-speed manual transmission ($170). Deluxe two-tone paint ($288); with Scottsdale ($185); with Silverado ($138); with Cheyenne ($230). Air-conditioning ($591). Chrome bumpers ($111); with Scottsdale/Cheyenne/Silverado ($82). Chrome rear step bumper ($151); with Chevy Sport ($98). Chrome bumper with rub strip ($149); with Scottsdale/Cheyenne/Silverado ($120). Chevy Sport, with bucket seats ($722); without bucket seats ($767). AM radio ($90). AM/FM radio ($141). AM/FM stereo ($224); with 8-track ($320); with cassette tape ($325). AM/FM/CB radio with tri-band mast antenna ($420). Auxiliary rear speaker ($19). Tachometer, ($90); in combination with Silverado package ($61). Cargo lamps in combination with Scottsdale/Silverado/Cheyenne/Chevy Sport ($28); without ($49). Pickup box side rails ($77). Heavy-duty springs, front ($112); rear ($44). One-inch front stabilizer bar ($27). Trim rings ($45). Wheelcovers ($69). Sliding gear window ($88). Basic camper group C20/C30 ($48). Deluxe camper group for C20/C30 with cab-over camper bodies ($292).

OPTION PACKAGES: [Scottsdale]: includes front and rear bumpers; black bodyside moldings; cigarette lighter; headliner and dome lamp. [Silverado]: includes front and rear bumpers; wheel opening trim; deluxe molding package; visor mirror; bright bodyside moldings; deluxe front appearance headliner; carpeting; Custom steering wheel; cigarette lighter; dome lamp; voltmeter; temperature and oil pressure gauges.

HISTORICAL: Introduced: Fall 1980. Calendar year registrations: 650,460. Calendar year sales: [Pickups] 403,487; [S-10] 15,473; [Van] 86,727; [Suburban] 19,518; [Blazer] 21,399; [LUV] 61,724; [El Camino] 33,086; [Sportvan] 13,576; [Total] 654,990. Innovations: Low-alloy steel panels. New light-weight window glass. Aerodynamic Styling. Electronic spark control. Historical notes: The fuel crisis and high-interest rates continued to have a negative effect on Chevrolet's light-duty truck sales. The Chevrolet S10 Mini-Pickup was introduced in mid-1981 as a 1982 model.

1982 CHEVROLET

1982 Chevrolet 1/2-Ton LUV Pickup 4x4 (RCA)

1/2-TON LUV — MODEL L — FOUR: The Series 12 LUV pickups were similar to 1981 models. The Mikado trim option came with cloth/vinyl seat upholstery, full carpeting, a deluxe steering wheel and other goodies.

1/2-TON S10 MINI-PICKUP — MODEL S/SERIES 10 — FOUR/V-6: An important extension of the Chevy truck line was accomplished by introduction of the S10 Series. It was a new-sized compact pickup, larger than a LUV, but smaller than a C10. Styling was in the big truck mold, but with flatter bodysides. Single rectangular headlamps were featured. They had parking lamps on the outer ends that went around the body corners. The inner front edge was slanted to complement the grille design. The grille was formed with three rows of six rectangular segments, each row a little narrower than the one above. This gave an inverted trapezoid shape to the overall arrangement. A Chevrolet bow tie was in the center. Bumper-mounted turn signals and vertical taillights were other touches. Standard equipment included a 1.9-liter four-cylinder engine, four-speed manual transmission, bench seat, and dual outside rearview mirrors. Trim levels included standard, Sport and top-of-the-line Durango.

1982 Chevrolet S-10 Indy 500 Pickup (IMSC/JLM)

1/2-TON EL CAMINO — MODEL W — SIX/V-8: El Caminos adopted a new cross-hatched grille and quadruple rectangular headlights. Standard equipment included a 3.8-litre V-6 engine, three-speed automatic transmission, power brakes, cloth bench seat and carpeting. The Super Sport model-option added dual sport mirrors, front air dam, accent color on lower body and rally wheels.

1/2-TON BLAZER — MODEL C (4x2)/MODEL K (4x4) — SIX/V-8: New for 1982 Blazers was a 6.2 liter (379 cid) Chevrolet-built diesel V-8 and four-speed overdrive transmission, both costing extra. Appearance features were virtually identical to last season, except a chrome grille was standard. Standard equipment included the 4.1 liter six; three-speed manual transmission (four-speed on 4x4 models); power brakes; vinyl bucket-seats; chrome bumpers; automatic locking hubs; and, on 4x4s, power steering. Improved rust protection was promoted.

1/2-TON; 3/4-TON; 1-TON VAN/HI-CUBE VAN — MODEL G/SERIES 10; 20; 30 — SIX/V-8: Hi-Cube vans, Chevy Vans and Sportvans were pretty much devoid of any earth shaking differences from 1981.

1/2-TON; 3/4-TON; 1-TON CONVENTIONAL — MODEL C (4x2); MODEL K (4x4)/SERIES 10; 20; 30 — SIX/V-8: Since they were, more or less, longer wheelbase versions of the Blazer, Chevrolet Conventional trucks had the same type of appearance and same new options. Essentially, the 1982 models were carbon copies of 1981s, except a chrome grille was standard on all models. Standard equipment also included the trusty 250 cid six (292 cid on C30/K20/K30); column-mounted three-speed gearbox (four-speed on C30/K30); power brakes (except C10/C20); chrome bumpers; and a bench seat. Four-wheel drive models came with standard power steering and the K30s featured a two-speed transfer case. The Cheyenne trim level was eliminated. Custom Deluxe, Scottsdale and Silverado packages were still available. Improved rust protection was advertised.

3/4-TON; 1-TON FORWARD-CONTROL — MODEL P/SERIES 20; 30 — SIX/V-8: Step-Vans also had no earth shaking differences from 1981. The P20 offered two wheelbases, 125 in. for 10 ft. bodies and 133 in. for 12 ft. bodies. The P30 offered the same, plus a 157 in. wheelbase for 14 ft. bodies.

I.D. DATA: Location of serial number: The VIN is stamped on a plate attached to the left top of the instrument panel on C/K/G Series. On P Series the plate is attached to the front of the dash and the panel to the left of the steering column. The first symbol indicates country of origin: 1=U.S.; 2=Canada; J=Japan. The second symbol indicates manufacturer: G=General Motors; B=Isuzu. The third symbol indicates make: A=Chevrolet bus; B=Chevrolet (incomplete); C=Chevrolet truck; Y=LUV (incomplete); Z=LUV truck; 8=Chevy MPV. The fourth symbol indicates GVW rating (and brake system); B=3,001 lbs.-4,000 lbs. (hydraulic); C=4,001 lbs.-5,000 lbs. (hydraulic), etc. through K for hydraulic brakes. The fifth symbol indicates line and chassis type: C=Conventional cab (including Blazer and Suburban) 4x2; G=Chevy Van and Sportvan 4x2; K=Conventional cab (including Blazer and Suburban) 4x4; L=LUV 4x2; R=LUV 4x4; S=Forward-Control; W=El Camino 4x2; Z=Special body 4x2. The sixth symbol indicates series: 1=1/2-ton; 2=3/4-ton; 3=1-ton; 8=El Camino. The seventh symbol indicates body type: 0=El Camino Pickup-Delivery; 1=Hi-Cube and Cutaway Vans; 2=Forward-Control; 3=Four-door cab; 4=Two-door cab; 5=Van; 6=Suburban; 7=Motorhome chassis; 8=Blazer Utility; 9=Stake. The eighth symbol indicated engine: [El Camino] A=231 cid (3.8 liter) 110 hp two-barrel V-6); K=229 cid (3.8 liter)/110 nhp two-barrel V-6 for California; J=267 cid (4.4 liter)/115 nhp two-barrel V-8; H=305 cid (5.0 liter)/145 nhp four-barrel V-8; T=262 cid (4.3 liter)/85 nhp diesel V-8. [Trucks] A=119 cid (1.9 liter)/82 hp two-barrel Isuzu four-cylinder; B=173 cid (2.8 liter)/110 nhp two-barrel V-6; C or J=379 cid (6.2 liter)/110 nhp diesel V-8; D=250 cid (4.1 liter)/105 nhp inline six-cylinder; F or H=305 cid (5.0 liter)/140 nhp two-barrel V-8; L or M=350 cid (5.7 liter)/160 nhp two-barrel V-8; N=110.8 cid (1.8 liter) two-barrel Isuzu four-cylinder; P=350 cid (5.7 liter)/145 nhp four-barrel V-8; S=136.6 cid (2.2 liter)/58 nhp Isuzu four-cylinder diesel; T=292 cid (4.8 liter)/120 nhp one-barrel inline six-cylinder; W=454 cid (7.5 liter)/245 nhp four-barrel V-8. The ninth symbol was a check digit. The 10th symbol indicated model year: C=1982. The 11th symbol indicated the assembly plant: A=Lakewood, Ga.; B=Baltimore, Md.;C=Southgate, Calif.; D=Doraville, Ga.; E=Linden, N.J.; F=Flint, Mich.; G=Framingham, Mass.; H=Flint, Mich.; J=Janesville, Wis.; K=Leeds, Mo.; L=Van Nuys, Calif.; M=Lansing, Mich.; N=Norwood, Ohio; P=Pontiac, Mich.; R=Arlington, Texas; S=St. Louis, Mo.; T=Tarrytown, N.Y.; V=GMC, Pontiac, Mich.; W=Willow Run, Mich.; X=Fairfax, Va.; Y=Wilmington, Dela.; Z=Fremont, Calif.; O=GMAD, Pontiac, Mich.; 1=Oshawa, Canada; 2=Moraine, Ohio; 2=Ste. Therese, Quebec, Canada; 3=Chevrolet-Detroit, Mich.; 3=St. Eustache, Quebec, Canada; 4=Orion Plant, Pontiac, Mich.; 4=Scarborough, Ontario, Canada; 5=Bowling Green, Ken.; 5=London, Ontario, Canada; 6=Oklahoma City, Okla.; 7=Lordstown, Ohio; 8=Shreveport, La.; 8=Fujisawa, Japan; 9=Cadillac, Detroit, Mic. (Note: Trucks were not built at all factories). Symbols 12-17 were the production sequence number starting at 100001. Ending numbers not available. Engine number location: [Six] located on pad at right-hand side of cylinder block at rear of distributor. [V-8] located on pad at right front side of cylinder block.

Model	Body Type	Price	Weight	Prod. Total
LUV — 1/2-Ton — 104.3 in. w.b. — Four				
CL10503	Pickup	6256	2375	—
LUV — 1/2-Ton — 117.9 in. w.b. — Four				
CL10803	Pickup	6465	2470	—
S10 — 1/2-Ton — 108.3 in. w.b. — V-6				
CS10603	Pickup	6600	2476	—
S10 — 1/2-Ton — 118 in. w.b. — V-6				
CS10803	Chassis & Cab	—	2878	—
CS10803	Pickup	6750	2552	—
CS10803	Utility	—	3276	—
El Camino — 1/2-Ton — 117.1 in. w.b. — V-6				
1GW80	Sedan-Pickup	7995	3294	—
1GW80	Super Sport Sedan-Pickup	8244	3300	—
Chevy Van 10 — 110 in. w.b. — Six				
CG11005	Panel	6908	3708	—
CG11006	Sportvan	8122	4039	—
Chevy Van 10 — 125 in. w.b. — Six				
CG11306	Bonaventure	9040	—	—
CG11306	Beauville	9268	—	—
Chevy Van 20 — 110 in. w.b. — Six				
CG21005	Panel	7256	3782	—
Chevy Van 20 — 125 in. w.b. — Six				
CG21306	Sportvan	8486	4251	—
CG21306	Bonaventure	9204	—	—
CG21306	Beauville	9432	—	—
Chevy Van 30 — 125 in. w.b. — Six				
CG31305	Panel	8494	4251	—
Chevy Van 30 — 146 in. w.b. — Six				
CG31306	Sportvan	10,228	4608	—
CG31306	Bonaventure	10,946	—	—
CG31306	Beauville	11,174	—	—
G30 Hi-Cube Van — 125/146 in. w.b. — V-8				
CG31403	Hi-Cube Van 10 ft.	10,141	5515	—
CG31603	Hi-Cube Van 12 ft.	11,607	5848	—
Blazer — 1/2-Ton — 106.5 in. w.b. — Six				
CK10516	Hardtop 4x4	9874	4294	—
CK10516	Hardtop 4x2	8533	—	—
C10 Conventional — 1/2-Ton — 117.5 in. w.b. — Six				
CC10703	Step-Side 6.5 ft.	6689	3418	—
CC10703	Fleetside 6.5 ft.	6564	3461	—
C10 Suburban — 1/2-Ton — 129.5 in. w.b. — V-8				
CC10906	Suburban (gate)	9744	4295	—
C10 Conventional — 1/2-Ton — 131.5 in. w.b. — Six				
CC10903	Fleetside 8 ft.	6714	3613	—

* Add $2,185 for K10 (4x4) Pickups/Suburbans.

C20 — 3/4-Ton — 131.5 in. w.b. — Six				
CC20903	Chassis & Cab	7865	3661	—
CC20903	Step-Side 8 ft.	7857	3956	—
CC20903	Fleetside 8 ft.	7732	3999	—
C20 Suburban — 1/2-Ton — 129.5 in. w.b. — V-8				
CC20906	Suburban (gate)	9978	4677	—
C20 — 3/4-Ton — 164.5 in. w.b. — Six				
CC20943	Bonus Cab	9123	4748	—
CC20943	Crew Cab	9439	4809	—

* Add $1,974 for K20 (4x4) Fleetside/Suburban; add $1,849 for K20 (4x4) Step-Side.

P20 Step-Van — 3/4-Ton — 125/133 in. w.b. — Six				
CP20842	Step-Van 10 ft.	11,744	5777	—
C30 — 1-Ton — 131.5 in. w.b. — Six				
CC30903	Chassis & Cab	7990	3973	—
CC30903	Step-Side 8 ft.	8474	4323	—
CC30903	Fleetside 8 ft.	8349	4394	—
C30 — 1-Ton — 164.5 in. w.b. — Six				
CC30943	Chassis & Bonus Cab	8943	4400	—
CC30943	Fleetside & Bonus Cab 8 ft.	9286	4817	—
CC30943	Chassis & Crew Cab	9259	4461	—
CC30943	Fleetside & Crew Cab 8 ft.	9602	4878	—

* Add for K30 (4x4) Pickups; price not available.

P30 Step-Van — 1-Ton — 125/133/157 in. w.b. — Six				
CP30842	Steel Step-Van 10.6 ft.	11,820	5939	—

* Add for 12 ft. model on 133 in. wheelbase.

** Add for 14 ft. model on 157 in. wheelbase.

NOTE 1: Model year production: [El Camino] 23,104; [All Chevy Van] 99,019; [All Sport-Vans] 15,262; [Blazer] 24,514; [C10/C20/K10/K20 Suburbans] 28,916; [Other C10/K10, except Blazer] 243,834; [Other C20/K20] 75,714; [C30/K30] 49,230; [P10/P20/P30] 27,919. (Includes all trucks with GVWs of 10,000 lbs. or less built in U.S. and built in Canada for the U.S. market.)

NOTE 2: Percent of above totals with four-wheel drive used on chassis and Pickup trucks: [CK10] 17.5 percent; [CK20] 30.5 percent; [CK30] 16 percent.

NOTE 3: Percent of above totals with four-wheel drive used on Suburbans: [CK10/CK20 combined] 28.6 percent.

NOTE 4: U.S. sales of LUV: 22,304.

1982 Chevrolet El Camino Conquista (CP)

ENGINE [Standard: S10]: Inline. OHV. OHC. Four-cylinder. Cast iron block. Bore & stroke: 3.42 x 3.23 in. Displacement: 119 cid. Compression ratio: 8.4:1. Net horsepower: 82 at 4600 rpm. Maximum torque: 101 lbs.-ft. at 3000 rpm. Hydraulic valve lifters. Order Code LR1.
ENGINE [Standard: 4x4 LUV]: Inline. OHV. OHC. Four-cylinder. Cast iron block. Bore & stroke: 3.31 x 3.23 in. Displacement: 110.8 cid. Compression ratio: 8.5:1. Net horsepower: 80 at 4800 rpm. Maximum Torque: 95 lbs.-ft at 3000 rpm. Five main bearings. Hydraulic valve lifters. Carburetor: one-barrel. Order Code L10.
ENGINE [Standard: 4x2 LUV models; Optional: LUV 4x4]: Inline. OHV Diesel. Four-cylinder. Cast iron block. Displacement: 136.6 cid. Compression ratio: 21:1. Net horsepower: 58 at 4300 rpm. Maximum torque: 93 lbs.-ft. at 2200 rpm. Hydraulic valve lifters. Order Code LQ7.
ENGINE [Optional: S10]: Vee-block. OHV. Six-cylinder. Cast iron block. Bore & stroke: 3.50 x 2.99 in. Displacement: 173 cid. Compression ratio: 8.5:1. Net horsepower: 110 at 4800 rpm. Maximum torque: 148 lbs.-ft. at 2000 rpm. Hydraulic valve lifters. Order Code LR2.
ENGINE [Standard: El Camino (except California)]: Vee-block. OHV. Six-cylinder. Cast iron block. Bore & stroke: 3.7 x 3.48 in. Displacement: 229 cid. Compression ratio: 8.6:1. Net horsepower: 110 at 4200 rpm. Maximum torque: 170 lbs.-ft. at 2000 rpm. Four main bearings. Hydraulic valve lifters. Code LC3(A).
ENGINE [Optional El Camino, California only]: Vee-block. OHV. Six-cylinder. Cast iron block. Bore & stroke: 3.8 x 3.4 in. Displacement: 231 cid. Compression ratio: 8.0:1. Net horsepower: 110 at 3800 rpm. Maximum torque: 190 lbs.-ft. at 1600 rpm. Five main bearings. Hydraulic valve lifters. Carburetor: Rochester two-barrel. Order Code LO5(C).
ENGINE [Standard: C10/C20/K10/G10/G20/G30]: Inline. OHV. Six-cylinder. Cast iron block. Bore & stroke: 3.9 x 4.5 in. Displacement: 250 cid. Compression ratio: 8.3:1. Net horsepower: 110 at 3600 rpm. Torque: 195 lbs.-ft. at 2000 rpm. Seven main bearings. Hydraulic valve lifters. Carburetor: Rochester Staged two-barrel. Order Code LE3(A).
ENGINE [Optional: El Camino (except California)]: Vee-block. OHV. Eight-cylinder. Cast iron block. Bore & stroke: 3.5 x 3.48 in. Displacement: 267 cid. Compression ratio: 8.3:1. Net horsepower: 115 at 4000 rpm. Maximum torque: 200 lbs.-ft. at 2400 rpm. Five main bearings. Hydraulic valve lifters. Carburetor: Rochester staged two-barrel. Order Code L39(B).
ENGINE [Standard: C20 HD (C6P)/C20/C30/K20 HD (C6P)/K30 P20/P30]: Inline. OHV. Six-cylinder. Cast iron block. Bore & stroke: 3.876 x 4.12 in. Displacement: 292 cid. Compression ratio: 7.8:1. Net horsepower: 115 at 3400 rpm. Maximum torque: 215 lbs.-ft. at 1600 rpm. Seven main bearings. Hydraulic valve lifters. Carburetor: Rochester one-barrel. Order Code L25(B).
ENGINE [Optional El Camino]: Vee-block. OHV. Eight-cylinder. Cast iron block. Bore & stroke: 3.7 x 3.48 in. Displacement: 305 cid. Compression ratio: 8.6:1. Net horsepower: 150 at 3800 rpm. Maximum torque: 240 lbs.-ft. at 2400 rpm. Five main bearings. Hydraulic valve lifters. Carburetor: Rochester Staged four-barrel. Order Code LG4(B).
ENGINE [Optional C10/C20/K10]: Vee-block. OHV. Eight-cylinder. Cast iron block. Bore & stroke: 3.736 x 3.480 in. Displacement: 305 cid. Compression ratio: 9.2:1. Net horsepower: 160 at 4400 rpm. Maximum torque: 235 lbs.-ft. at 2000 rpm. Five main bearings. Hydraulic valve lifters. Carburetor: Rochester Staged four-barrel with Electronic Spark Control. Order Code LE9(C). Not available in California.
ENGINE [Optional C20/C20 HD (C6P)/C30/K20 HD (C6P)/K30/P20/P30/G10/G20]: Vee-block. OHV. Eight-cylinder. Cast iron block. Bore & stroke: 4.0 x 3.5 in. Displacement: 350 cid. Compression ratio: 8.2:1. Net horsepower: 165 at 3800 rpm. Maximum torque: 275 lbs.-ft. at 1600 rpm. Five main bearings. Hydraulic valve lifters. Carburetor: Rochester four-barrel. Order Code LS9(A). Not available in California.
ENGINE [Optional: C10/C20/C30/K10/K20/K30/C20 HD (C6P)/K20 HD (C6P)/All Suburbans]: Vee-block. OHV. Diesel. Eight-cylinder. Cast iron block. Bore & stroke: 3.98 x 3.80 in. Displacement: 379 cid. Compression ratio: 21.5:1. Net horsepower: 130 at 3600 rpm. Maximum torque: 240 lbs.-ft. at 2000 rpm. Hydraulic valve lifters. Carburetor: fuel-injection. Order Code LH6(A).
ENGINE [Optional: C20 HD (C6P)/C20/C30/K30/C20 Suburban]: Vee-block. OHV. Eight-cylinder. Cast iron block. Bore & stroke: 4.25 x 4 in. Displacement: 454 cid. Compression ratio: 7.9:1. Net horsepower: 210 at 3800 rpm. Maximum torque: 340 lbs.-ft. at 2800 rpm. Five main bearings. Hydraulic valve lifters. Carburetor: Rochester four-barrel. Order Code LE8(A).
CHASSIS [LUV]: Wheelbase: [4x2] 104.3 in./117.9 in.; [4x4] 104.3 in. Overall length: 174.5 in./191.6 in. Height: [4x2] 59.3 in.; [4x4] 61.0 in. Front tread: [4x2] 53.8 in.; [4x4] 54.2 in. Rear tread: [4x2] 51.2 in.; [4x4] 52.7 in. Tires: [4x2] E78 x 14B in.; [4x4] F70 x 14B in. white-lettered.
CHASSIS [S10]: Wheelbase: 108.3 in./117.9 in. Overall length: 178.2 in./194.1 in. Height: 59 in. Front tread: 64.7 in. Rear tread: 64.7 in. Tires: P195 in./75R x 14 in. Fiberglass-belted.
CHASSIS [El Camino]: Wheelbase: 117.1 in. Overall length: 201.6 in. Height: 53.8 in. Front tread: 58.5 in. Rear tread: 57.8 in. Tires: P205 in./75R x 14 in.
CHASSIS [C10]: Wheelbase: 117.5 in./131.5 in. Overall length: 191.3 in./212 in. Height: 69.8 in. Front tread: 65.8 in. Rear tread: 62.7 in. Tires: FR78 x 15B in.
CHASSIS [G10]: Wheelbase: 110 in./125 in. Overall length: 178.2 in./202.2 in. Height: 78.8 in./81.2 in. Front tread: 69.5 in. Rear tread: 69.7 in. Tires: FR78 x 15B in.
CHASSIS [G20]: Wheelbase: 110 in./125 in. Overall length: 178.2 in./202.2 in. Height: 78.8 in./81.2 in. Front tread: 69.5 in. Rear tread: 69.7 in. Tires: P225 in./75R x 15 in.
CHASSIS [G30]: Wheelbase: 110 in./125 in. Overall length: 178.2 in./202.2 in. Height: 78.8 in./81.2 in. Front tread: 69.5 in. Rear tread: 69.7 in. Tires: 8.75 x 16.5E in.
CHASSIS [G30 Hi-Cube]: Wheelbase: 125 in./146 in. Overall length: 207.3 in./231.3 in. Tires: [front] 8.75 x 16 in.; [rear] 8.00 x 16.5C in.
CHASSIS [K10/Blazer]: Wheelbase: 106.5 in. Overall length: 184.8 in. Height: 73.4 in. Front tread: 66.1 in. Rear tread: 63 in. Tires: [2wd] P215 /75R x 15 in.; [4wd] P215/75R x 15 in. Larger sizes available.
CHASSIS [C10/C20Suburban]: Wheelbase: 129.5 in. Overall length: 218.7 in. Height: 75.4 in. Front tread: 66.7 in. Rear tread: 63.0 in. Tires: [C10] P235/75R15; [C20] 9.50 x 16.5 in.; [K10] P215/75R15; [K20] 9.50 x 16.5 in.
CHASSIS [K10]: Wheelbase: 117.5 in./131.5 in. Overall length: 191.3/212 in. Height: 72 in. Front tread: 65.8 in. Rear tread: 62.7 in. Tires: P235/75R x 15 in.
CHASSIS [C20]: Wheelbase: 117.5 in./131.5 in./164.5 in. Overall length: 191.3 in./212 in./244.43 in. Height: 69.8 in. Front tread: 65.8 in. Rear tread: 62.7 in. Tires: 8.75R x 16.5C in.; [front] 9.50 x 16.5D in.; [rear] 9.50 x 16.5E in.; C20 HD [C6P]
CHASSIS [K20]: Wheelbase: 131.5 in. Overall length: 212 in. Height: 73.9 in. Front tread: 65.8 in. Rear tread: 62.7 in. Tires: 8.75R x 16.5C in.; 9.50 x 16.5D in. [front] E [rear] K20HD (CP6)
CHASSIS [P20]: Wheelbase: 125 in./133 in. Tires: 8.75 x 16.5C in.
CHASSIS [C30]: Wheelbase: 131.5 in./164.5 in. Overall length: 212/244.43 in. Height: 77.8 in. Front tread: 65.8 in. Rear tread: 62.7 in. Tires: 9.50 x 16.5D in.; [Bonus/Crew] 9.50 x 16.5E in.
CHASSIS [K30]: Wheelbase: 131.5 in./164.5 in. Overall length: 212 in./244.43 in. Height: 74.7/75 in. Front tread: 65.8 in. Rear tread: 62.7 in. Tires: 9.50 x 16.5D in.
CHASSIS [P30]: Wheelbase: 125 in./157 in. Tires: 8.75 x 16.5 in.
TECHNICAL: Same as 1981 except for S-10. This model has a selective synchromesh transmission with four-speeds forward/one reverse; floor-shift; single dry-disc clutch; 2.73:1 final drive ratio; front disc/rear drum brakes and pressed steel wheels.

1982 Chevrolet Silverado Blazer (CP)

OPTIONAL EQUIPMENT: [S10/El Camino/Blazer/C-Series/K-Series] 2.8 liter (173 cid) V-6 in S-10 ($215). 4.4 liter (267 cid) V-8 in El Camino ($70). 5.0 liter (305 cid) V-8 in El Camino ($70). 5.0 liter (305 cid) V-8 with electronic spark control in Blazers/Pickups without Special Economy package ($170); same in Pickups with Special Economy package ($170). 5.0 liter (305 cid) V-8 four-barrel in Blazer/Pickups ($170). 5.7 liter (350 cid) V-8 in Blazer/Pickups ($345). 5.7 liter (350 cid) V-8 in Pickups ($315). 6.2 liter (379 cid) diesel V-8 in K20 Pickups ($1,164); same in Blazer/C10/K10/C20 Pickups ($1,134). 7.4 liter (454 cid) V-8 in Pickups ($425). Four-speed manual transmission in C10 pickup ($198). Four-speed overdrive manual transmission in C10 Pickup without Special Economy package ($273); in C20/K10/K20 pickups ($75). Three-speed automatic transmission in S10/C10 pickup ($438); in C20/K20/C30/K30 Pickup ($455). Four-speed automatic transmission in C10 Blazer ($199); in K10 Blazer/C10/K10/C20/K20 Pickups ($637). Air-Conditioning: In Pickups without diesel equipment package, except K30 ($677); in Pickups with diesel equipment package, except K30 ($619); in S10 and Blazer without diesel equipment package ($677); in Blazer with diesel equipment package ($619). Deluxe front appearance package, on Blazers and Pickups ($100). Limited-slip rear axle, El Camino ($76). Locking axle/differential (except El Camino) ($217). Optional axle ratio, El Camino ($21); others ($35). Auxiliary battery in Blazer and Pickup ($118) Heavy-duty battery in El Camino ($25); in others ($45). Power brakes in Pickups and S10 ($87). Heavy-Duty Power Brakes, in C10 Pickup without diesel equipment package ($159); in C10 pickup with diesel equipment package ($72); in C20/K20 Pickups ($82). Chrome rear bumper on Pickups ($97). Painted rear step bumper, on Pickups ($106). Chromed rear step bumper on Pickups ($177). Color-keyed front bumper on S10 ($56). Color-keyed rear step bumper on S10 ($127). Deluxe chromed front and rear bumpers on Blazer ($44). Glide-out spare carrier on Pickups ($27). Slide-mount spare carrier on Pickups ($39). Electric Quartz Clock: in El Camino ($32); in Blazers/Pickups without Silverado ($70); in Blazer/Pickups with Silverado ($36). Electric digital clock on S10 ($60). Conquista package on El Camino ($183). Console in S10 ($96). Engine oil cooler, except El Camino ($112). Transmission oil cooler: On S10 without air-conditioning ($103); on S10 with air-conditioning; on others except El Camino ($55). Heavy-Duty Cooling System: On El Camino without air-conditioning ($70); on El Camino with air-conditioning ($40); on others ($48). Cargo box cover (Tonneau) on El Camino ($129). Diesel Equipment package: For Blazer ($1,125); for C10 Pickup ($1,287); for C20 Pickup ($1,723); for C30 Pickup ($1,073); for K10 and K20 Pickups ($1,041); for K30 Pickup ($783). Power door locks: For El Camino ($106); for others ($115). Dual exhaust system on Pickups ($48). Exterior Decor package: For Blazer without Silverado package ($423); for Blazer with Silverado package ($279); for Pickup without Scottsdale or Silverado ($503); for Pickup with Scottsdale package ($385); for Pickup with Silverado package ($359). Optional fuel tanks: 20 gal. tank on S10 ($39); 22 gal. tank on El Camino ($25); 31 gal. tank on Blazer ($39); Auxiliary 16 gal. on C10/K10/C20/K20 Pickups ($208). Gauges: For S10 ($51); for El Camino ($111); for others ($34). Tinted glass: For El Camino ($88); for Pickups and S10 ($40). Deep tinted glass with tinted rear window on Blazer ($119). Deep tinted glass group on Blazer ($168). Chromed grille on S10 ($53). Durango equipment group on S10 ($325). Sport equipment group on S10 ($775). Camper wiring harness on Pickups ($37). Trailer wiring harness on Blazer ($42). Five-lead trailer wiring harness on S10 ($37). Halogen headlamps: high/low beam, except El Camino ($20); high-beam on El Camino ($10); on others ($15). Headlamp warning buzzer on Blazer ($11). Headliner on Blazer ($74). Instrumentation package on El Camino ($187). Cargo area light on Pickups ($56). Dome light on Pickups ($24). Roof marker lights on Pickups ($46). Auxiliary lighting: For El Camino ($30); for S10 without Durango or Sport package ($87); for S10 with Durango or Sport package ($45). Left-hand remote-control outside rearview mirror for El Camino ($22). Left-hand remote-control sport-type and right-hand manual sport-type rearview mirror on El Camino ($55). Camper-type left- and right-hand rearview mirrors on Pickups ($86). Dual rearview mirrors (6-1/2 in. x 9 in. painted) for trucks, except El Camino ($44); same in stainless, for trucks except El Camino ($72). Senior West Coast mirrors on Pickups ($59). Custom Molding package: For Pickups without Scottsdale trim and Blazers ($144); for Pickups with Scottsdale trim ($26). Deluxe Molding package, ($157). Operating convenience group: For Blazers and Pickups ($281). Two-tone paint: On Pickups without Silverado package ($69); on Pickups with Silverado package ($42). Special two-tone paint: On Pickups without Scottsdale or Silverado packages ($291); on Pickups with Scottsdale package ($173); on Pickups and Blazers with Silverado package ($147); on Blazer without Silverado package ($291); on S10 Pickup ($275). Deluxe Two-Tone Paint: On Pickups without Scottsdale or Silverado ($328); on Pickups with Scottsdale ($210); on Pickups with Silverado ($157). Sport two-tone paint on S10 ($135). Payload capacity package of 1,500 lbs. on S10 ($173). Radio Equipment: AM in El Camino ($111); in S10 ($104); in others ($92). AM/FM in El Camino ($165); in S10 ($173); in others ($143). AM/FM Stereo in El

Camino ($196); in S10 ($256); in others ($226). AM/FM Stereo with 8-Track Tape in El Camino ($282); in others except S10 ($322). AM/FM Stereo with Cassette Tape in El Camino ($283); in others except S10 ($327). AM/FM stereo with cassette and clock in S10 ($425). AM/FM/CB with power antenna in Pickups and Blazers ($559). AM/FM stereo/CB in Blazers and Pickups ($559). Windshield antenna (not available with S10 or El Camino) ($31). Power antenna on El Camino ($55). Cargo box rails on El Camino ($81). Roll bar on Blazer ($123). Scottsdale package: For Step-Side Pickup ($208); for Fleetside Pickup without dual rear wheels ($318); for Fleetside Pickup with dual rear wheels ($217). Folding Rear Seats: For Blazer without custom trim ($308); for Blazer with custom trim ($334). Seats/trim: Custom vinyl high-back bucket seats: In Blazer without Silverado or rear seat ($193); in Blazer without Silverado, with rear seat ($241); in Blazer with Silverado without rear seat (no charge); in Blazer with Silverado and rear seat ($48); in S10 without Durango or Sport package ($166); in S10 with Durango or Sport package ($118). Custom cloth high-back bucket seats: In Blazer without rear seat (no charge); in Blazer with rear seat ($48). Special custom cloth bench seat in Pickups (no charge). Custom vinyl bench seat: In Pickup without Scottsdale or Silverado ($48); in S10 without High Sierra or Gypsy packages ($48). Fuel tank shield: For C10 Blazer; for C-Series Pickups with auxiliary fuel tank ($115); for K10 Blazer; for K-Series Pickups with auxiliary fuel tank ($154); for C-Series Pickups without auxiliary fuel tank ($45); for K-Series Pickups without auxiliary fuel tank ($84). Heavy-duty shock absorbers, front and rear (not El Camino) ($31). Quad front shock absorbers on Blazer and K10/K20 Pickups ($117). Pickup box side rails on Pickups ($88). Silverado package: For Blazer ($931); for Step-Side Pickups ($614); for Fleetside Pickups without exterior decor package or dual rear wheels ($780); for Fleetside Pickups with exterior decor package without dual rear wheels ($753); for Fleetside without special Big Dooley package ($640); for Fleetside Pickups without special Big Dooley package and dual rear wheels ($596). Special Big Dooley two-tone paint package: For Pickups without Scottsdale package ($429); for Pickups with Scottsdale package ($412); for Fleetside Pickup, add to above ($27). Automatic Speed Control: For El Camino ($155); for others with manual transmission ($169); for others with automatic transmission ($159). Heavy-Duty Front Springs: For Blazer and K10/K20 Pickups without quad shocks ($84); for Blazer and K10/K20 Pickups with quad shocks ($53); for C10/C20 Pickups ($14); combined with heavy-duty front springs on C10/C20 Pickups ($51). Extra capacity rear springs on C10 Pickup ($66). Main and auxiliary rear springs on Pickups ($91). Front stabilizer bar (not available on El Camino) ($31); Heavy-duty front stabilizer bar on C-Series Pickups ($51); Power steering on S10, except C-Series Pickups ($234); Tahoe equipment on S10 ($550); Tilt steering wheel ($95); Sport suspension on El Camino ($15). Tachometer: In S10 without Sport package ($105); in S10 with Sport package ($54). Cargo box tie downs ($23). Towing device (not S10 or El Camino) ($34). Deadweight trailer hitch on Blazer ($53). Weight distribution platform on Blazer ($145). Heavy-duty Trailering Special package: For C20/C30 Pickup without air or diesel equipment ($646); for C20/C30 Pickup with air without diesel equipment ($588); for K20 Pickup without air or diesel equipment ($412); for K20 Pickup with air without diesel equipment ($354); for K30 Pickup without diesel equipment ($354); for Blazer and Pickups with diesel equipment ($242); S10 ($187); for C10 Blazer without air-conditioning ($677); for K10 Blazer with air-conditioning ($619); for K10 Blazer without air or diesel equipment ($412); for K10 blazer with air without diesel equipment ($354). Wheelcover lock package on El Camino ($39). Bright wheelcovers on Blazer C/K10 Pickups; on S10 without Durango trim ($38). Sport wheelcovers:

For base El Camino ($62); for El Camino Super Sport ($6). Wire wheelcovers on El Camino ($153). Wheel trim rings on Pickups and Blazers ($52). Rally wheels:

For base El Camino ($56); for S10 without Durango or Sport ($83); for S10 with Durango ($31); for others ($103). Styled wheels, not available on S10 or El Camino ($201). Forged aluminum wheels, not available for El Camino ($411). Dual Rear Wheels: For C30 Fleetside without air or diesel equipment ($677); for C30 Fleetside with air or diesel equipment ($619); for K30 Pickups without air or diesel equipment ($644); for K30 Pickups with air or diesel equipment ($606). Sliding rear window on Pickups ($100). Power windows ($166). Power tailgate window on Blazer ($79). Intermittent wipers: For El Camino ($47); for others ($45).

OPTIONAL EQUIPMENT: [LUV] Air-conditioning ($677). Chrome rear step bumper ($131). Painted rear step bumper ($106). Front bumper guards ($38). Sport Stripe decals: For 104.3 in. wheelbase 4x2 ($45); for 117.9 in. wheelbase 4x2 ($50); for 104.3 in. wheelbase 4x4 ($119). Exterior decor package ($105). Mikado package: With bench seats ($244); with bucket seats ($379). Dual mirrors ($61). Metallic paint ($80). AM radio ($104). AM/FM radio ($176). Power steering ($325). Sliding rear window ($100). E78-14B whitewall tires, two for front or rear ($20). E78-14B whitewall spare tire ($10).

HISTORICAL: Introduced: Fall 1981. Calendar year registrations: 758,107. Calendar year sales: [Vans] 101,932; [Sportvan] 15,843; [S10] 177,758; [S10 Blazer] 8,161; [LUV] 22,304; [El Camino] 22,732; [Blazer] 24,103; [Suburban] 28,004; [Pickups] 393,277. Calendar year production at U.S. factories: [Blazer] 24,238; [El Camino] 22,621; [Pickups] 268,080; [Chevy Van/Sportvan] 98,764; [Suburban] 34,846; [Compact Pickups] 209,517; [Total] 658,066. Innovations: New-sized compact S10 line introduced. LUV comes with Four diesel as standard powerplant. New 6.2 liter Chevy-built diesel V-8 for larger trucks. CONSUMER GUIDE gave the 1982 Blazer 68 out of a possible 100 points in its road test covering performance, interior, utility and finish characteristics. The new S10 pickups scored 69 points on the same scale, while the standard C10 Pickup racked up 70 points. The 1982 LUV pickup earned 65 points. Chevrolet truck sales started on an upswing this season, but Ford Motor Co. was again beginning to threaten Chevrolet's ranking as the number one truck-maker. Chevrolet had held the number one position steadily from 1951 to 1968. From 1969 to 1974, Ford was on top. In 1975 and 1976, Chevrolet was back in first position again. The next five years were counted in Ford's favor. The final totals for calendar year registrations in 1982 were 758,107 for Chevy versus 733,120 for Ford.

1983 CHEVROLET

1/2-TON LUV — MODEL L — FOUR: Even though the LUV Mini-Pickup was replaced by the new S10, Chevrolet did sell 15,530 of them in the 1983 calendar year. However, these were leftover 1982 models.

1/2-TON S10 MINI-PICKUP — MODEL S/SERIES 10 — FOUR/V-6: Chevrolet entered what it called "Year II of a New Era for Chevy trucks." New four-wheel drive, extended-cab, and Blazer models were added to the S10 line. All S10 models, except Chassis & Cab and Utility Cabs, were available with four-wheel drive. The S10 Blazer, compared to the 13 year old full-size Blazer, was 15.3 in. shorter and 14.8 in. narrower. Its total floor space was only 4.8 sq. ft. less. The S10 Extended-Cab Pickup, the first such configuration ever offered by Chevrolet, added 14.5 inches to regular cab length. Added to the S10 engine line up was a new 2.0 liter 83 hp L-4. Four-wheel drive models had a new independent front suspension utilizing computer-matched torsion bars.

1983 Chevrolet 3/4-Ton K20 Scottsdale Fleetside Pickup (RCA)

1/2-TON EL CAMINO — MODEL W — SIX/V-8: This was also the first year the El Camino could be ordered with a 5.7 liter diesel V-8.

1/2-TON BLAZER — MODEL C (4x2)/MODEL K (4x4) — SIX/V-8: The full-size Blazer had a revised grille. It featured a blacked-out appearance. Parking lights were moved from the bumper to bottom of the grille. The horizontal center-bar was finished in body color. The Blazer was otherwise unchanged in appearance from 1982.

1/2-TON; 3/4-TON; 1-TON VAN/HI-CUBE VAN — MODEL G/SERIES 10; 20; 30 — SIX/V-8: For the first times G20 and G30 vans and Sportvans were available with the 6.2 liter diesel engine, as well as a four-speed overdrive automatic transmission. Other changes in the 1983 vans included a steering column angle approximating that used on pickups, floor-mounted manual transmission shift lever, and wet arms windshield washers (with nozzles located on the wiper arms). Tilt steering was available with manual transmission. There was an anti-chip coating along the lower body from front the wheelwells to the rear doors. A new rear pivot hinge, rear latch, and a floating roller mechanism improved operation of the sliding door. Also new was an inside hood release.

1983 Chevrolet S-10 'Short Box' Pickup (CMD)

1/2-TON; 3/4-TON; 1-TON CONVENTIONAL — MODEL C (4x2); MODEL K (4x4)/SERIES 10; 20; 30 — SIX/V-8: Chevrolet's Conventional-Cab C and K Pickups were unchanged, except for a revised grille treatment and parking lamp placement. The grille featured a black-out look. The parking lights were moved from the bumper to bottom of the grille. The horizontal center-bar was finished in body color. The Scottsdale trim package was upgraded slightly. Base Custom Deluxe and top-of-the-line Silverado trims were unchanged. Added corrosion protection was provided with the use of galvanized steel in the pickup box front panel and a Zincro-metal hood inner liner.

3/4-TON; 1-TON FORWARD-CONTROL — MODEL P/SERIES 20; 30 — SIX/V-8: 3/4-TON; 1-TON FORWARD-CONTROL — MODEL P/SERIES 20; 30 — SIX/V-8: Step-Vans also had no earth shaking differences from 1981. The P20 offered two wheelbases, 125 in. for 10 ft. bodies and 133 in. for 12 ft. bodies. The P30 offered the same, plus a 157 in. wheelbase for 14 ft. bodies.

1983 Chevrolet Suburban With Panel Doors (OCW)

I.D. DATA: Location of serial number: The VIN is stamped on a plate attached to the left top of the instrument panel on C/K/G Series. On P Series the plate is attached to the front of the dash and the panel to the left of the steering column. The first symbol indicates country of origin: 1=U.S.; 2=Canada; J=Japan. The second symbol indicates manufacturer: G=General Motors; 8=Isuzu. The third symbol indicates make: A=Chevrolet bus; B=Chevrolet (incomplete); C=Chevrolet truck; Y=LUV (incomplete); Z=LUV truck; 8=Chevy MPV. The fourth symbol indicates GVW rating (and brake system); B=3,001 lbs.-4,000 lbs. (hydraulic); C=4,001 lbs.-5,000 lbs. (hydraulic), etc. through K for hydraulic brakes. The

fifth symbol indicates line and chassis type: C=Conventional cab (including Blazer and Suburban) 4x2; G=Chevy Van and Sportvan 4x2; K=Conventional cab (including Blazer and Suburban) 4x4; L=LUV 4x2; R=LUV 4x4; P=Forward-Control; S=Conventional Cab 4x2; W=El Camino 4x2; Z=Special body 4x2. The sixth symbol indicates series: 1=1/2-ton; 2=3/4-ton; 3=1-ton; 8=El Camino. The seventh symbol indicates body type: 0=El Camino Pickup-Delivery; 1=Hi-Cube and Cutaway Vans; 2=Forward-Control; 3=Four-door cab; 4=Two-door cab; 5=Van; 6=Suburban; 7=Motorhome chassis; 8=Blazer Utility; 9=Stake. The eighth symbol indicated engine: [El Camino] A=231 cid (3.8 liter)/110 hp two-barrel V-6); K=229 cid (3.8 liter)/110 nhp two-barrel V-6 for California; H=305 cid (5.0 liter)/145 nhp four-barrel V-8; T=262 cid (4.3 liter)/105 nhp two-barrel V-8. [Trucks] A=119 cid (1.9 liter)/82 hp two-barrel Isuzu four-cylinder; B=173 cid (2.8 liter)/110 nhp two-barrel V-6; C or J=379 cid (6.2 liter)/110 nhp diesel V-8; D=250 cid (4.1 liter)/105 nhp two-barrel inline six-cylinder; F or H=305 cid (5.0 liter)/140 nhp two-barrel V-8; L or M=350 cid (5.7 liter)/160 nhp four-barrel V-8; P=350 cid (5.7 liter)/145 nhp two-barrel V-8; S=136.6 cid (2.2 liter)/58 nhp Isuzu four-cylinder diesel; T=292 cid (4.8 liter)/120 nhp one-barrel inline six-cylinder; W=454 cid (7.5 liter)/245 nhp four-barrel V-8. The ninth symbol was a check digit. The 10th symbol indicated model year: D=1983. The 11th symbol indicated the assembly plant: A=Lakewood, Ga.; B=Baltimore, Md.;C=Southgate, Calif.; D=Doraville, Ga.; E=Linden, N.J.; F=Flint, Mich.; G=Framingham, Mass.; H=Flint, Mich.; J=Janesville, Wis.; K=Leeds, Mo.; L=Van Nuys, Calif.; M=Lansing, Mich.; N=Norwood, Ohio; P=Pontiac, Mich.; R=Arlington, Texas; S=St. Louis, Mo.; T=Tarrytown, N.Y.; V=GMC, Pontiac, Mich.; W=Willow Run, Mich.; X=Fairfax, Va.; Y=Wilmington, Dela.; Z=Fremont, Calif.; O=GMAD, Pontiac, Mich.; 1=Oshawa, Canada; 2=Moraine, Ohio; 2=Ste. Therese, Quebec, Canada; 3=St. Eustache, Quebec, Canada; 4=Orion Plant, Pontiac, Mich.; 4=Scarborough, Ontario, Canada; 5=Bowling Green, Ken.; 5=London, Ontario, Canada; 6=Oklahoma City, Okla.; 7=Lordstown, Ohio; 8=Shreveport, La.; 8=Fujisawa, Japan; 9=Cadillac, Detroit, Mic. (Note: Trucks were not built at all factories). Symbols 12-17 were the production sequence number starting at 100001. Ending numbers not available. Engine number location: [Six] located on pad at right-hand side of cylinder block at rear of distributor. [V-8] located on pad at right front side of cylinder block.

Model	Body Type	Price	Weight	Prod. Total
El Camino — 1/2-Ton — 117.1 in. w.b. — V-6				
1GW80	Sedan Pickup	8191	3332	—
1GW80	Super Sport Pickup	8445	3337	—
1/2-Ton Mini-Truck — ModelS/Series 10 — 108.3 in. w.b. — Six				
CS10603	Pickup	6343	2537	—
1/2-Ton Mini-Truck — Model S/Series 10 — 122.0 in. w.b. — Six				
CS10803	Pickup	6496	2618	—
CS10653	Extended Pickup	6725	2647	—

* Add for S10 four-wheel drive models.

1/2-Ton Blazer 4x4 — Model S/Series 10 — 100.5 in. w.b. — V-6				
CT10516	Hardtop (gate)	9433	3106	—

* Deduct for two-wheel drive S10 Blazer.

1/2-Ton Van — Model G/Series 10 — 110 in. w.b. — Six				
CG11005	Panel	7101	3711	—
CG11006	Sportvan	8596	4039	—
1/2-Ton Van — Model G/Series 10 — 125 in. w.b. — Six				
CG11306	Bonaventure	9533	—	—
CG11306	Beauville	9789	—	—
3/4-Ton Van — Model G/Series 20 — 110 in. w.b. — Six				
CG21005	Panel	7714	3812	—
3/4-Ton Van — Model G/Series 20 — 125 in. w.b. — Six				
CG21306	Sportvan	8968	4278	—
CG21306	Bonaventure	9701	—	—
CG21306	Beauville	9957	—	—
1-Ton Van — Model G/Series 30 — 125 in. w.b. — Six				
CG31305	Panel	8718	4399	—
CG31306	Sportvan	11,371	4719	—
CG31306	Bonaventure	12,104	—	—
CG31306	Beauville	12,360	—	—
1-Ton Hi-Cube Van — Model G/Series 30 — 125 in. w.b. — V-8				
CG31305	Hi-Cube Van 10 ft.	11,151	5052	—
1-Ton Hi-Cube Van — Model G/Series 30 — 146 in. w.b. — V-8				
CG31603	Hi-Cube Van 12 ft.	12,388	5881	—
1/2-Ton Blazer 4x4 — Model K/Series 10 — 106.5 in. w.b. — V-8				
CK10516	Hardtop	10,287	4426	—
1/2-Ton Conventional — Model C/Series 10 — 117.5 in. w.b. — Six				
CC10703	Step-Side	6835	3408	—
CC10703	Fleetside	6707	3471	—
1/2-Ton Suburban — Model C/Series 10 — 129.5 in. w.b. — V-8				
CC10906	Suburban V-8	9951	4293	—
1/2-Ton Conventional — Model C/Series 10 — 131.5 in. w.b. — Six				
CC10903	Fleetside	6860	3633	—

* Add for 1/2-ton K10 four-wheel drive Pickups/Suburbans.

3/4-Ton Conventional — Model C/Series 20 — 131.5 in. w.b. — Six				
CC20903	Chassis & Cab	8032	3614	—
CC20903	Step-Side	8525	3964	—
CC20903	Fleetside	8397	4025	—
3/4-Ton Suburban — Model C/Series 20 — 129.5 in. w.b. — V-8				
CC20906	Suburban V-8	10,187	4697	—
3/4-Ton Conventional — Model C/Series 20 — 164.5 in. w.b. — V-8				
CC20943	Fleetside & Bonus Cab	9315	4745	—
CC20943	Fleetside & Crew Cab	9637	4806	—

* Add for 3/4-ton K20 four-wheel drive Pickups and Suburbans.

3/4-Ton Step-Van — Model P/Series 20 — 125/133 in. w.b. — Six				
CP20842	Steel Step-Van 10.5 ft.	12,031	5801	—

* Add for 133 in. wheelbase 12.5 ft. Step-Van.

1-Ton Conventional — Model C/Series 30 — 131.5 in. w.b. — Six				
CC30903	Chassis & Cab	8160	3965	—
CC30903	Step-Side	8654	4319	—
CC30903	Fleetside	8526	4380	—
1-Ton Conventional — Model C/Series 30 — 164.5 in. w.b. — V-8				
CC30943	Chassis & Bonus Cab	9131	4406	—
CC30943	Fleetside & Bonus Cab	9481	4817	—
CC30943	Chassis & Crew Cab	9453	4467	—
CC30943	Fleetside & Crew Cab	9803	4878	—

* Add for 1-ton K30 four-wheel drive Pickups.

1-Ton Step-Van — Model P/Series 30 — 125/133/157 in. w.b. — Six				
CP30842	Steel Step-Van 10.5 ft.	12,071	5946	—

* Add for 133 in. wheelbase 12.5 ft. Step-Van.
** Add for 157 in. wheelbase 14.5 ft. Step-Van.

NOTE 1: Model year production: [S10] 179,157; [S10 Blazer] 84,672; [El Camino] 22,429; [All Chevy Van] 126,420; [All Sportvans] 17,960; [Full-sized Blazer] 26,245; [C10/C20/K10/K20 Suburbans] 37,928; [Other C10/K10, except Blazer] 219,961; [Other C20/K20] 66,548; [C30/K30] 35,625; [P10/P20/P30] 34,369. (Includes all trucks with GVWs of 10,000 lbs. or less built in U.S. and built in Canada for the U.S. market).
NOTE 2: Percent of above totals with four-wheel drive used on chassis and Pickup trucks: [S10] 24.6 percent; [S10 Blazer] 78.8 percent; [CK10] 22.6 percent; [CK20] 38.4 percent; [CK30] 20 percent.
NOTE 3: Percent of above totals with four-wheel drive used on Suburbans: [CK10/CK20 combined] 29.6 percent.
NOTE 4: U.S. sales of LUV: 15,530.

1983 Chevrolet S-10 Blazer (CMD)

ENGINE [Standard: S10]: Inline. OHV. OHC. Four-cylinder. Cast iron block. Bore & stroke: 3.42 x 3.23 in. Displacement: 119 cid. Compression ratio: 8.4:1. Net horsepower: 82 at 4600 rpm. Maximum torque: 101 lbs.-ft. at 3000 rpm. Hydraulic valve lifters. Order Code LR1.
ENGINE [Standard: S10 Blazer/optional extended cab S10 models]: Inline. OHV. Four-cylinder. Cast iron block. Bore & stroke: 3.50 x 3.15 in. Displacement: 121 cid. Compression ratio: 9.3:1. Net horsepower: 83 at 4000 rpm. Maximum torque: 108 lbs.-ft. at 2400 rpm. Hydraulic valve lifters. Carburetor: Rochester two-barrel. Order Code LQ2.
ENGINE [Optional S10/S10 Blazer]: Inline. OHV. Diesel. Four-cylinder. Cast iron block. Bore & stroke: 3.46 x 3.62 in. Displacement: 136.6 cid. Net horsepower: 62 at 4300 rpm. Maximum torque: 96 lbs.-ft. at 2100 rpm. Hydraulic valve lifters. Order Code LQ7.
ENGINE [Optional S10/S10 Blazer]: Vee-block. OHV. Six-cylinder. Cast iron block. Bore & stroke: 3.50 x 2.99 in. Displacement: 173 cid. Compression ratio: 8.5:1. Net horsepower: 110 at 4800 rpm. Maximum torque: 145 lbs.-ft. at 2100 rpm. Hydraulic valve lifters.
ENGINE [Standard: El Camino]: Vee-block. OHV. Six-cylinder. Cast iron block. Bore & stroke: 3.7 x 3.48 in. Displacement: 229 cid. Compression ratio: 8.6:1. Net horsepower: 110 at 4200 rpm. Torque 170 lbs.-ft. at 2000 rpm. Four main bearings. Hydraulic valve lifters. Carburetor: Rochester two-barrel.
ENGINE [Standard C10/C20/K10]: Inline. OHV. Six-cylinder. Cast iron block. Bore & stroke: 3.9 x 3.5 in. Displacement: 4.1 liter (250 cid). Compression ratio: 8.3:1. Net horsepower: [C10] 120 at 4000 rpm. Torque 205 lbs.-ft. at 2000 rpm. Seven main bearings. Hydraulic valve lifters. Carburetor: Rochester two-barrel. Order Code LE3(A).

1983 Chevrolet S-10 Bonus Cab 'Long Box' Pickup (CMD)

ENGINE [Optional: C20 HD/C20/C30/K20 HD/K301]: Inline. OHV. Six-cylinder. Cast iron block. Bore & stroke: 3.9 x 4.1 in. Displacement: 4.8 liters (292 cid). Compression ratio: 7.8:1. Net horsepower: 115 at 3600 rpm. Net. torque: 215 lbs.-ft. at 1600 rpm. Five main bearings. Hydraulic valve lifters. Carburetor: Rochester one-barrel. Order Code L25(B).

ENGINE [Optional C10/C20 K10/El Camino]: Vee-block. OHV. Eight-cylinder. Cast iron block. Bore & stroke: 3.74 x 3.48 in. Displacement: 5 liters (305 cid). Compression ratio: 9.2:1. Net horsepower: [C10] 165 at 4400 rpm. Torque: 240 lbs.-ft. at 2000 rpm. Five main bearings. Hydraulic valve lifters. Carburetor: Rochester four-barrel. Order Code LE9(C).

ENGINE [Optional: El Camino]: Vee-block. OHV. Diesel. Eight-cylinder. Cast iron block. Bore & stroke: 4.0 x 3.5 in. Displacement: 350 cid. Net horsepower: 105 rpm. Five main bearings. Fuel-injected.

ENGINE [Optional: C20/C20 HD/C30/K10/K20/K20 HD/K30]: Vee-block. OHV. Eight-cylinder. Cast iron block. Bore & stroke: 4.0 x 3.5 in. Displacement: 5.7 liters (350 cid). Compression ratio: 8.2:1. Net horsepower: 165 at 3800 rpm. Torque: 275 lbs.-ft. at 1600 rpm. Five main bearings. Hydraulic valve lifters. Carburetor: Rochester four-barrel. Order Code LS9(A).

ENGINE [Optional: C10/C20/C20 HD/C30/K10/K20/K20 HD/K30]: Vee-block. OHV. Diesel. Eight-cylinder. Cast iron block. Bore & stroke: 3.98 x 3.80 in. Displacement: 6.2 liters (379 cid). Compression ratio: 21.3:1. Net horsepower: 130 at 3600 rpm. Torque: 240 lbs.-ft. at 2000 rpm. Order Code LH6(D).

ENGINE [Optional: C20 HD/C20/C30/K30]: V-block. OHV. Eight-cylinder. Cast iron block. Bore & stroke: 4.3 x 4.0 in. Displacement: 7.4 liters (454 cid). Compression ratio: 7.9:1. Net horsepower: 230 at 3800 rpm. Net. Torque: 360 lbs.-ft. at 2800 rpm. Five main bearings. Hydraulic valve lifters. Carburetor: four-barrel. Order Code LE8(A).

1983 Chevrolet El Camino (CMD)

CHASSIS [S10]: Wheelbase: 108.3 in./117.9 in. Overall length: 178.2 in./194.1 in. Height: 59 in. Front tread: 64.7 in. Rear tread: 64.7 in. Tires: P195/75R x 14 in. Fiberglass-belted.

CHASSIS [S10 Extended Cab Pickup]: Wheelbase: 122.9 in.; Height: 59.4 in. Front tread: 64.7 in. Rear tread: 64.7 in.; Tires: D195/75R x 14 in.

CHASSIS [S10 Blazer]: Wheelbase: 100.5 in. Overall length: 170.3 in. Height: 65 in. Front tread: 55.6 in. Rear tread: 55.1 in. Tires: D195/75R x 15 in.

CHASSIS [El Camino]: Wheelbase: 117.1 in. Overall length: 201.6 in. Height: 53.8 in. Front tread: 58.5 in. Rear tread: 57.8 in. Tires: P205/75R x 14 in.

CHASSIS [C10]: Wheelbase: 117.5 in./131.5 in. Overall length: 191.3 in./212 in. Height: 69.8 in. Front tread: 65.8 in. Rear tread: 62.7 in. Tires: FR78 x 15B in.

CHASSIS [G10]: Wheelbase: 110 in./125 in. Overall length: 178.2 in./202.2 in. Height: 78.8 in./81.2 in. Front tread: 69.5 in. Rear tread: 69.7 in. Tires: FR78 x 15B in.

CHASSIS [G20]: Wheelbase: 110 in./125 in. Overall length: 178.2 in./202.2 in. Height: 78.8 in./81.2 in. Front tread: 69.5 in. Rear tread: 69.7 in. Tires: P225/75R x 15 in.

CHASSIS [G30]: Wheelbase: 110 in./125 in. Overall length: 178.2 in./202.2 in. Height: 78.8 in./81.2 in. Front tread: 69.5 in. Rear tread: 69.7 in. Tires: 8.75 x 16.5E in.

CHASSIS [G30 Hi-Cube]: Wheelbase: 125 in./146 in. Overall length: 207.3/231.3 in. Tires: [front] 8.75 x 16 in.; [rear] 8.00 x 16.5C in.

CHASSIS [K10/Blazer]: Wheelbase: 106.5 in. Overall length: 184.8 in. Height: 73.4 in. Front tread: 66.1 in. Rear tread: 63 in. Tires: [2wd] P215/75R x 15 in.; [4wd] P215/75R x 15 in. Larger sizes available.

CHASSIS [C10/C20Suburban]: Wheelbase: 129.5 in. Overall length: 218.7 in. Height: 75.4 in. Front tread: 66.7 in. Rear tread: 63.0 in. Tires: [C10] P235/75R15; [C20] 9.50 x 16.5 in.; [K10] P215/75R15; [K20] 9.50 x 16.5 in.

CHASSIS [K10]: Wheelbase: 117.5 in./131.5 in. Overall length: 191.3 in./212 in. Height: 72 in. Front tread: 65.8 in. Rear tread: 62.7 in. Tires: P235/75R x 15 in.

CHASSIS [C20]: Wheelbase: 117.5 in./131.5 in./164.5 in. Overall length: 191.3 in./212 in./244.43 in. Height: 69.8 in. Front tread: 65.8 in. Rear tread: 62.7 in. Tires: 8.75R x 16.5C in.; [front] 9.50 x 16.5D in.; [rear] 9.50 x 16.5E in.; C20 HD [C6P]

CHASSIS [K20]: Wheelbase: 131.5 in. Overall length: 212 in. Height: 73.9 in. Front tread: 65.8 in. Rear tread: 62.7 in. Tires: 8.75R x 16.5C in.; 9.50 x 16.5D in. [front] E [rear] K20HD (CP6)

CHASSIS [P20]: Wheelbase: 125 IN./133 in. Tires: 8.75 x 16.5C in.

CHASSIS [C30]: Wheelbase: 131.5 in./164.5 in. Overall length: 212 in./244.43 in. Height: 77.8 in. Front tread: 65.8 in. Rear tread: 62.7 in. Tires: 9.50 x 16.5D in.; [Bonus/Crew] 9.50 x 16.5E in.

CHASSIS [K30]: Wheelbase: 131.5 in./164.5 in. Overall length: 212 in./244.43 in. Height: 74.7 in./75 in. Front tread: 65.8 in. Rear tread: 62.7 in. Tires: 9.50 x 16.5D in.

CHASSIS [P30]: Wheelbase: 125 in./157 in. Tires: 8.75 x 16.5 in.

TECHNICAL: Manual, synchromesh. 3F/1R (most models). Controls located: Column (most). Single dry-disc type clutch. Shaft drive. Salisbury rear axle. Front disc/rear drum (power on most). Pressed steel disc wheels.

1983 Chevrolet S-10 Blazer (CMD)

OPTIONS: Engine oil cooler. Heavy-duty automatic transmission. Heavy-duty battery. Heavy-duty radiator. Camper chassis equipment. Fuel tank shield. 66 amp. generator (standard on K30). Heavy-duty automatic transmission cooler. Four-speed manual transmission. Four-speed overdrive transmission. Four-speed automatic with overdrive. Three-speed automatic. Locking differential. Cruise control. Chromed front bumper. Rear bumper (chromed or painted). Radio, AM; AM/FM; AM/FM with cassette. Cigar lighter. Chromed rear step bumper. Sidemounted spare tire carrier. Glide-out spare tire carrier (Fleetside only). Cargo area lamp. Color keyed floor mats. Comfortilt steering wheel. Deluxe front appearance package. Dome lamp. Quartz electric clock. Air-conditioning. Gauge package (volt meter, temperature, oil pressure). Halogen headlamps. Intermittent windshield wipers. Tinted glass. Outside rearview mirrors: Painted or stainless steel below-eyeline type; stainless steel camper type; painted West Coast type. Sliding rear window. Durango equipment (S10). Tahoe equipment (S10). Sport equipment (S10). Body moldings; black; bright; custom package, black or bright (Fleetside only). Paint options: Conventional two-tone. (Fleetside only). Deluxe two-tone. Exterior decor. Special two-tone paint. Pickupside rails. Power door locks. Power windows. Roof marker lamps. Rally wheels. Styled wheels. Bright metal wheelcovers. Special bright metal wheelcovers. Conquista package, El Camino ($189).

HISTORICAL: Introduced: Sept. 14, 1982. Calendar year registrations: [All Chevrolet trucks] 904,672. Calendar year sales. [Vans] 141,575; [Sportvan] 18,178; [S10] 198,222; [S10 Blazer] 106,214; [El Camino] 24,010; [C/K Blazer] 31,282; [C/K Suburban] 37,222; [C/K Pickups] 412,533. Calendar year production: [C10/K10 Blazer] 35,179; [El Camino] 28,322; [C/K Pickups] 280,209; [Chevy Van/Sportvan] 142,555; [Suburban] 41,261; [S10] 321,054; [Total] 848,580. Innovations: New S10 Blazer introduced. Extend cab pickups added to S10 pickup series. Full-size 4x4s now use 15 in. wheels and tires. Chevrolet dealers recorded 176 registrations per outlet in 1983, compared to 156 the previous season. Chevrolet slipped behind Ford in calendar year registrations for all types of trucks. In van and light truck production (calendar year) in U.S. factories, Chevrolet was also behind Ford's output of 848,580 units. The big news, however, was the auto and truck industry's general recovery from the bleak period of the early 1980s. Chevrolet's overall market penetration in the light truck and van field was up 1.58 percent to a 39.72 percent share of industry.

1984 CHEVROLET

1984 Chevrolet Fleetside Pickup (CP)

1/2-TON S10 MINI-PICKUP — MODEL S/SERIES 10 — FOUR/V-6: Disappearance of the LUV Pickup made the S10 Chevy's small truck entry. While styling was unaltered, new features included a Sport suspension for regular cab 4x2 models, new quiet-set trip odometer, new ignition warning buzzer and an hydraulic, rather than cable-type, clutch. Gasoline-powered 4x2 and 4x4 models, plus the diesel 4x2 came on the short 108.3 in. wheelbase with either the 73.1 in. short box or 89 in. long box. Gas and diesel 4x2s and gas 4x4 with the extended Maxi-cab used the 122.9 in. wheelbase with short box only. The gas 4x2 chassis-cab was on the 117.9 in. stance. Standard equipment varied by trim level. Durango added such things as color-keyed floor mats, courtesy lights and Custom cloth/vinyl or special Custom cloth bench seats. The Tahoe package added carpeting, gauges, and a right-hand visor mirror. Including all Tahoe features, plus a Sport steering wheel and Sport cloth bucket-seats (with console), was the highest-priced Sport package. The standard interior was vertically pleated vinyl. Durango's interior featured rectangular pleats in three rows on each end of the seat with a plain center section. Sport upholstery used vinyl backs and bolsters with a textured woven cloth on the seat cushions and backs. Side-mounted vertically pleated jump seats were optional for Maxi-cab models. After being selected "Four wheeler of the Year" in 1983, the S10 Blazer was back with such new features as an optional off-

road package with gas-pressure shock absorbers and an hydraulic clutch. Both the 4x2 and 4x4 versions used a 2.0 liter four and four-speed gearbox as standard equipment. The only options featured on standard S10 Blazers included a cigar lighter, chrome grille and dome lamp. The Tahoe package added a right-hand visor mirror, bodyside and wheelhouse moldings, spare tire cover and wheel trim rings. On top of this, the Sport model came with a color-keyed front bumper, center console and black wheel opening moldings. Interiors included the standard type with high-back vinyl "memory" bucket seats and other niceties; the Tahoe type with Custom vinyl or special Custom cloth upholstery, side window defoggers and gauges; and the Sport type with reclining seats in charcoal or saddle Sport cloth or optional "High-Country" sheepskin front bucket seats.

1/2-TON EL CAMINO — MODEL W — SIX/V-8: The El Camino for 1984 was a very luxurious vehicle. Standard equipment included an automatic transmission, power steering, air adjustable rear shocks, notch-back seat with armrest, and color-keyed cut-pile carpeting. Both the Super Sport option and Conquista package were available again. The base El Camino had dual square headlamps on either side of a cross-hatch grille with long, narrow parking lights directly below the headlamps.

1/2-TON BLAZER — MODEL C (4x2)/MODEL K (4x4) — SIX-V-8: Chevrolet included the full-size Blazer 4x4 in its 1984 station wagon sales catalog. The big Blazer also had its own separate catalog, which noted that the Army Tank Automotive Command had recently placed an order for 23,000 diesel-powered Blazers. A bold new grille had a bi-level design with three black-finished horizontal bars and square headlamps in both sections (optional), parking lamps behind the bars on the bottom, and a yellow bow tie on the body color strip in the middle. Only 4x4 models were available. The Custom Deluxe standard interior offered foam-padded seats (front buckets) in vinyl, with color-keyed door trim panels. Also included were integrated armrests and instrument panel packs. A rear seat was optional. With the upscale Silverado package, Custom vinyl or cloth upholstery was added. Fender badges now identified these trucks as K5 models, although the series designation was actually K10500. Scottsdale versions carried an identification badge on the rear fender sides near the taillights.

1/2-TON; 3/4-TON; 1-TON VAN/HI-CUBE VAN — MODEL G/SERIES 10; 20; 30 — SIX/V-8: The Chevy Van grille also had the bi-level arrangement with quad Halogen headlamps optional. Upper and lower sections of the grille each contained three horizontal blades and seven vertical members. A body colored horizontal center piece held a yellow bow tie in the middle. (Note: If the halogen headlamp option wasn't ordered, the rectangular parking lamps were used in the lower grille section under the regular rectangular headlamps; if the option was ordered, the parking lamps were mounted behind the bars on the bottom. The G10 and G20 models offered a choice of 110 or 125 in. wheelbases. G30s came only on the larger chassis. A 146 in. wheelbase was also available for G30 RV, commercial and Hi-Cube Van applications. Power steering and heavy-duty power brakes were standard on the G20/G30 vans. RV versions of the Chevy Van 30 also came with chromed front bumpers, cigar lighters and ashtrays standard. The Hi-Cube versions included an extended-arm outside rearview mirror. In November 1983, a new 60/40 swing-out side door option was introduced. Standard interiors featured striped vinyl low-back bucket seats. Custom trim included high-back bucket seats in vinyl or Custom vinyl.

1984 Chevrolet Fleetside Pickup (CP)

1/2-TON; 3/4-TON; 1-TON CONVENTIONAL — MODEL C (4x2); MODEL K (4x4)/ SERIES 10; 20; 30 — SIX/V-8: Chevrolet's full-sized Pickup also had the bi-level grille, as used on the big Blazer. There were three horizontal bars showing prominently in each section, with seven less prominent vertical members behind them. When bright-plated, the grille had a cross-hatch look; when black-finished, it appeared more horizontal. Halogen quad headlamps were an option. New for the season were two galvanized steel interior door panels for better rust protection. Also new were semi-metallic front brake linings on 10 and 20 series trucks; new non-asbestos rear brake linings on most models and plastic fuel tank stone shields for all Pickups and Chassis & Cabs. This was the first year for optional power windows and door locks on Bonus Cab and Crew Cab models, both of which came on a 164.5 in. wheelbase with Fleetside boxes. Trucks with deluxe two-tone paint had the cab and lower perimeter finished in the secondary color. Special two-toning meant only the lower perimeter was in the secondary color and there was bright trim on the bodyside and wheel openings. The Exterior Decor package included dual-tone bodyside finish and a rear tape stripe keyed to body colors, plus a hood ornament. The secondary color was used between the decal stripes and moldings. Interior options included standard Custom Deluxe trim, plus Scottsdale and Silverado options. There were 39 models all total. C10 and K10 pickups came in short box Step-Side and long box Step-Side and Fleetside models. C20 and K20 models came in Step-Side or Fleetside form, only with the 8 ft. long box. The heavy-duty C20 added Chassis & Cab, Bonus Cab, and Crew Cab models. Heavy-duty K10s came as Fleetsides and Step-Sides with the long box. The C30 heavies offered three 4x2 and four 4x4 configurations in Chassis & Cab form for commercial and RV applications.

3/4-TON; 1-TON FORWARD-CONTROL — MODEL P/SERIES 20; 30 — SIX/V-8: Chevy issued separate 1984 sales catalogs for steel-bodied and aluminum-bodied Step-Vans. The steel models came as CP208/CP308 models on a 125 in. wheelbase; as CP210/ CP310 models on the 133 in. wheelbase and as CP314 models on the 157 in. wheelbase. Aluminum body models could be had in the same configurations, plus a model CP318 version with a 178 in. wheelbase. Load lengths were: [CP208/CP308] 129.6 in.; [CP210/ CP310] 153.6 in.; [CP314] 177.6 in. and [CP318] 178 in. wheelbase. Series 30 Hi-Cube vans came in 10 ft. models on the 125 in. wheelbase or 12 ft. models on the 146 in. wheelbase.

I.D. DATA: Location of serial number: The VIN is stamped on a plate attached to the left top of the instrument panel on C/K/G Series. On P Series the plate is attached to the front of the dash and the panel to the left of the steering column. The first symbol indicates country of origin: 1=U.S.; 2=Canada; J=Japan. The second symbol indicates manufacturer: G=General Motors; 8=Isuzu. The third symbol indicates make: A=Chevrolet bus; B=Chev-

rolet (incomplete); C=Chevrolet truck; Y=LUV (incomplete); Z=LUV truck; 8=Chevy MPV. The fourth symbol indicates GVW rating (and brake system); B=3,001 lbs.-4,000 lbs. (hydraulic); C=4,001 lbs.-5,000 lbs. (hydraulic), etc. through K for hydraulic brakes. The fifth symbol indicates line and chassis type: C=Conventional cab (including Blazer and Suburban) 4x2; G=Chevy Van and Sportvan 4x2; K=Conventional cab (including Blazer and Suburban) 4x4; L=LUV 4x2; R=LUV 4x4; P=Forward-Control; S=Conventional Cab 4x2; W=El Camino 4x2; Z=Special body 4x4. The sixth symbol indicates series: 1=1/2-ton; 2=3/4-ton; 3=1-ton; 8=El Camino. The seventh symbol indicates body type: 0=El Camino Pickup-Delivery; 1=Hi-Cube and Cutaway Vans; 2-Forward-Control; 3=Four-door cab; 4=Two-door cab; 5=Van; 6=Suburban; 7=Motorhome chassis; 8=Blazer Utility; 9=Stake. The eighth symbol indicated engine. Engine codes were generally the same as 1983. The ninth symbol was a check digit. The 10th symbol indicated model year: E=1984. The 11th symbol indicated the assembly plant: A=Lakewood, Ga.; B=Baltimore, Md.;C=Southgate, Calif.; D=Doraville, Ga.; E=Linden, N.J.; F=Flint, Mich.; G=Framingham, Mass.; H=Flint, Mich.; J=Janesville, Wis.; K=Leeds, Mo.; L=Van Nuys, Calif.; M=Lansing, Mich.; N=Norwood, Ohio; P=Pontiac, Mich.; R=Arlington, Texas; S=St. Louis, Mo.; T=Tarrytown, N.Y.; V=GMC, Pontiac, Mich.; W=Willow Run, Mich.; X=Fairfax, Va.; Y=Wilmington, Dela.; Z=Fremont, Calif.; O=GMAD, Pontiac, Mich.; 1=Oshawa, Canada; 2=Moraine, Ohio; 2=Ste. Therese, Quebec, Canada; 3=Chevrolet-Detroit, Mich.; 3=St. Eustache, Quebec, Canada; 4=Orion Plant, Pontiac, Mich.; 4=Scarborough, Ontario, Canada; 5=Bowling Green, Ken.; 5=London, Ontario, Canada; 6=Oklahoma City, Okla.; 6=Lordstown, Ohio; 8=Shreveport, La.; 8=Fujisawa, Japan; 9=Cadillac, Detroit, Mic. (Note: Trucks were not built at all factories). Symbols 12-17 were the production sequence number starting at 100001. Ending numbers not available. Engine number location: [Six] located on pad at right-hand side of cylinder block at rear of distributor. [V-8] located on pad at right front side of cylinder block.

Model	Body Type	Price	Weight	Prod. Total
S10 Pickup — 1/2-Ton — 108.3 in. w.b. — V-6				
S10	Pickup	6398	2574	—
S10 Pickup — 1/2-Ton — 122.9 in. w.b. — V-6				
S10	Pickup	6551	2649	—
S10	Maxi-Cab Pickup	6924	2705	—
S10 Blazer 4x4 — 1/2-Ton — 100.5 in. w.b. — V-6				
T10	4x4 Hardtop	9685	3146	—
*Deduct for two-wheel drive S10 Blazer.				
El Camino — 1/2-Ton — 117.1 in. w.b. — V-6				
W80	Pickup	8522	3298	—
W80	Super Sport Pickup	8781	3305	—
Chevy Van 10 — 1/2-Ton — 110 in. w.b. — Six				
G11	Panel	7541	3732	—
G11	Sportvan	9089	4085	—
Chevy Van 10 — 1/2-Ton — 125 in. w.b. — Six				
G11	Bonaventure	10,062	—	—
G11	Beauville	10,327	—	—
Chevy Van 20 — 3/4-Ton — 110 in. w.b. — Six				
G21	Panel	8176	3813	—
Chevy Van 20 — 3/4-Ton — 125 in. w.b. — Six				
G21	Sportvan	9477	4276	—
G21	Bonaventure	10,238	—	—
G21	Beauville	10,503	—	—
Chevy Van 30 — 1-Ton — 125 in. w.b. — Six				
G31	Panel	9212	4305	—
G31	Sportvan	11,964	4984	—
Chevy Van 30 — 1-Ton — 125 in. w.b. — V-8				
G31	Bonaventure	12,724	—	—
G31	Beauville	12,990	—	—
Hi-Cube Van 30 — 1-Ton — 125 in. w.b. — V-8				
G31/303	Hi-Cube 10 ft.	11,624	5860	—
Hi-Cube Van 30 — 1-Ton — 125 in. w.b. — V-8				
G31/603	Hi-Cube 12 ft	12,894	5891	—
Full-Size Blazer 4x4 — 1/2-Ton — 106.5 in. w.b. — V-8				
K10	Hardtop	10,819	4409	—
Series C10 — 1/2-Ton — 117.5 in. w.b. — Six				
C10	Step-Side	7101	3434	—
C10	Fleetside	6970	3481	—
Series C10 — 1/2-Ton — 131.5 in. w.b. — Six				
C10	Fleetside	7127	3644	—
Series C10 — 1/2-Ton — 129.5 in. w.b. — V-8				
C10	Suburban (V-8)	10,368	4310	—
*Add for four-wheel drive K10 Pickup/Suburban.				
Series C20 — 3/4-Ton — 131.5 in. w.b. — Six				
C20	Chassis & Cab	8342	3617	—
C20	Step-Side	8319	3977	—
C20	Fleetside	8188	4039	—
Series C20 — 3/4-Ton — 164.5 in. w.b. — Six				
C20	Bonus Cab	9645	4742	—
C20	Crew Cab	9975	4803	—
Series C20 — 3/4-Ton — 129.5 in. w.b. — Six				
C20	Suburban	10,579	4698	—
*Add for four-wheel drive K20 Pickup/Suburban.				
Step-Van 20 — 3/4-Ton — 125 in. w.b. — Six				
P20	Steel Step-Van 10.5 ft.	12,588	5860	—
*Add for 12.5 ft. Step-Van 20 body.				

Series C30 — 1-Ton — 131.5 in. w.b. — Six

C30903	Chassis & Cab	8474	3990	—
C30903	Step-Side	8966	4342	—
C30903	Fleetside	8834	4404	—

Series C30 — 1-Ton — 164.5 in. w.b. — Six

C30943	Chassis & Bonus Cab	9471	4412	—
C30943	Fleetside & Bonus Cab	4822	—	—
C30943	Chassis & Crew Cab	9802	4473	—
C30943	Fleetside & Crew Cab	10,146	4883	—

Step-Van 30 — 3/4-Ton — 146 in. w.b. — V-8

P30	Steel Step-Van 12.5 ft.	12,666	5998	—

* Deduct for 10.5 ft. Step-Van 30 body.
* Add for 14.5 ft. Step-Van 30 body.
* Add for four-wheel drive K30 Pickup.

NOTE 1: Model year production: [S10] 209,377; [S10 Blazer] 149,937; [El Camino] 24,244; [All Chevy Van] 172,806; [All Sportvans] 24,005; [K5 Blazer] 39,329; [C10/C20/K10/K20 Suburbans] 54,250; [Other C10/K10] 275,428; [Other C20/K20] 89,811; [C30/K30] 45,095; [P10/P20/P30] Not available (Includes all trucks with GVWs of 10,000 lbs. or less built in U.S. and built in Canada for the U.S. market).
NOTE 2: Percent of above totals with four-wheel drive used on chassis and Pickup trucks: [S10] 20.1 percent; [S10 Blazer] 72.8 percent; [CK10] 26.0 percent; [CK20] 38.5 percent; [CK30] 20.8 percent; [K5 Blazer] 100 percent.
NOTE 3: Percent of above totals with four-wheel drive used on Suburbans: [CK10/CK20 combined] 31.6 percent.

1984 Chevrolet S-10 Blazer 4x4 (CP)

ENGINE [Standard: 108.3 in. w.b. regular cab S10 models and all models with California emissions]: Inline. OHV. OHC. Four-cylinder. Cast iron block. Bore & stroke: 3.42 x 3.23 in. Displacement: 119 cid. Compression ratio: 8.4:1. Net horsepower: 82 at 4000 rpm. Maximum torque: 101 lbs.-ft. at 3000 rpm. Order Code LR1(A).

ENGINE [Standard: All S10 models except short wheelbase regular cab models not available: California]: Inline. OHV. Four-cylinder. Cast iron block. Bore & stroke: 3.50 x 3.15 in. Displacement: 121 cid. Compression ratio: 9.3:1. Net horsepower: 83 at 4600 rpm. Maximum torque: 108 lbs.-ft. at 2400 rpm. Order Code LQ2(B).

ENGINE [Optional S10 4x2 regular and Maxi-Cab models]: Inline. OHV. Diesel. Four-cylinder. Cast iron block. Bore & stroke: 3.46 x 3.62 in. Displacement: 137 cid. Compression ratio: 21:1. Net horsepower: 62 at 4300 rpm. Maximum torque: 96 lbs.-ft. at 2200 rpm. Order Code LQ7(A).

ENGINE [Optional All S10 models]: Vee-block. OHV. Six-cylinder. Cast iron block. Bore & stroke: 3.50 x 2.99 in. Displacement: 173 cid. Compression ratio: 8.5:1. Net horsepower: 110 at 4800 rpm. Maximum torque: 145 lbs.-ft. at 2100 rpm. Order Code LR2(B).

ENGINE [Standard: El Camino]: Vee-block. OHV. Six-cylinder. Cast iron block. Bore & stroke: 3.7 x 3.48 in. Displacement: 229 cid. Net horsepower: 110 at 4000 rpm. Torque: 190 lbs.-ft. at 1600 rpm. Four main bearings. Hydraulic valve lifters. Carburetor: Two-barrel.

ENGINE [Standard C10/C20/K10/G10/G20/G30]: Inline. OHV. Six-cylinder. Cast iron block. Bore & stroke: 3.9 x 3.5 in. Displacement: 250 cid. Compression ratio: 8.3:1. Net horsepower: 115 at 3600 rpm. Maximum torque: 200 lbs.-ft. at 2000 rpm. Seven main bearings. Hydraulic valve lifters. Carburetor: Rochester staged two-barrel. Order Code LE3(A).

ENGINE [Standard: C20 HD (C6P)/C20 Bonus/Crew/C30/K20 HD (C6P)/K30]: Inline. OHV. Six-cylinder. Cast iron block. Bore & stroke: 3.876 x 4.12 in. Displacement: 292 cid. Compression ratio: 7.8:1. Net horsepower: 115 at 3600 rpm. Maximum torque: 215 lbs.-ft. at 1600 rpm. Five main bearings. Hydraulic valve lifters. Carburetor: Rochester one-barrel. Order Code L25(B).

ENGINE [Optional C10/C20 K10/G10/G20; Standard: K10 Blazer/C10 Suburban]: Vee-block. OHV. Eight-cylinder. Cast iron block. Bore & stroke: 3.736 x 3.480 in. Displacement: 305 cid. Compression ratio: 9.2:1. Net horsepower: 160 at 4400 rpm. Maximum torque: 235 lbs.-ft. at 2000 rpm. Five main bearings. Hydraulic valve lifters. Carburetor: Rochester staged four-barrel (ESC). Order Code LE9(C).

ENGINE [Optional: El Camino]: Vee-block. OHV. Eight-cylinder. Cast iron block. Bore & stroke: 3.7 x 3.48 in. Displacement: 305 cid. Compression ratio: 9.2:1. Net horsepower: 160 at 4400 rpm, 235 lbs.-ft. at 2000 rpm. Five main bearings. Hydraulic valve lifters. Carburetor: Rochester model four-barrel.

ENGINE [Optional El Camino]: Vee-block. OHV. Diesel. Eight-cylinder. Cast iron block. Bore & stroke: 4.0 x 3.5 in. Displacement: 350 cid. Net horsepower: 105. Five main bearings. Hydraulic valve lifters. Fuel-injection.

ENGINE [Standard Hi-Cube Vans and Suburbans/Optional in specific other Series 10/20/30 models]: V-8. OHV. Eight-cylinder. Cast iron block. Bore & stroke: 4.0 x 3.5 in. Displacement: 350 cid. Compression ratio: 8.2:1. Net horsepower: 165 at 3800 rpm. Maximum torque: 275 lbs.-ft. at 1600 rpm. Five main bearings. Hydraulic valve lifters. Carburetor: Rochester four-barrel. Order Code LS9(A).

1984 Chevrolet S-10 Blazer 4x2 (CP)

ENGINE [Optional: All 4x2/4x4/Full Size Pickups/Suburbans/K10 Blazer/G20/G30/ C6P]: Vee-block. OHV. Diesel. Eight-cylinder. Cast iron block. Bore & stroke: 3.98 x 3.80 in. Displacement: 379 cid. Compression ratio: 21.3:1. Net horsepower: 130 at 3600 rpm. Maximum torque: 240 lbs.-ft. at 2000 rpm. Hydraulic valve lifters. Order Code LH6(D).
ENGINE [Optional: C20 HD (C6P)/C20/C30/K30]: Vee-block. OHV. Eight-cylinder. Cast iron block. Bore & stroke: 4.250 x 4 in. Displacement: 454 cid. Compression ratio: 7.9:1. Net horsepower: 230 at 3800 rpm. Maximum torque: 360 lbs.-ft. at 2800 rpm. Five main bearings. Hydraulic valve lifters. Carburetor: Rochester four-barrel. Order Code LE8(A).
CHASSIS [El Camino]: Wheelbase: 117.1 in. Overall length: 201.6 in. Height: 53.8 in. Front tread: 58.5 in. Rear tread: 57.8 in. Tires: P205/75R x 14 in.
CHASSIS [S10]: Wheelbase: 108.3 in./117.9 in./122.9 in. Overall length: 178.2 in./194.1 in. Height: 59.4 in. Front tread: 64.7 in. Rear tread: 64.7 in. Tires: P195/75R x 14 in.
CHASSIS [S10 Blazer]: Wheelbase: 100.5 Overall length: 170.3 in. Height: 65 Front tread: 55.6 in. Rear tread: 55.1 in. Tires: P195/75R x 15
CHASSIS [G10]: Wheelbase: 110 in./125 Overall length: 178.2 in./202.2 in. Height: 78.8 in./81.2 in. Front tread: 69.5 Rear tread: 69.7 in. Tires: P205/75R x 15
CHASSIS [G20]: Wheelbase: 110 in./125 Overall length: 178.2 in./202.2 in. Height: 78.8 in./81.2 in. Front tread: 69.5 Rear tread: 69.7 in. Tires: P225/75R x 15
CHASSIS [G30]: Wheelbase: 125 in. Overall length: 202.2 in. Height: 81.2 in. Front tread: 69.5 Rear tread: 69.7 in. Tires: 8.75R x 16.5D in.
CHASSIS [G30 Hi-Cube]: Wheelbase: 125 in./146 in. Overall length: 207.3 in./231.3 in. Tires: 8.75 x 16.5
CHASSIS [K10 Blazer]: Wheelbase: 106.5 Overall length: 184.8 in. Height: 73.4 in. Front tread: 66.1 in. Rear tread: 63 in. Tires: P215/75R x 15
CHASSIS [C10]: Wheelbase: 117.5 in./131.5 in. (129.5 in. Suburban). Overall length: 191.3 in./212 in. Height: 69.8 in. Front tread: 65.8 in. Rear tread: 62.7 in. Tires: P195/75R x 15; Suburban P235/75R x 15
CHASSIS [Series C20]: Wheelbase: 131.5 in./164.5 in. (129.5 in. Suburban). Overall length: 212 in./244.43 in. Height: 69.8 in. Tires: LT215/85R x 16C in.; Bonus in./Crew: LT235/85R x 16D in. (rear E).
CHASSIS [P20]: Wheelbase: 125 in./133 in. Tires: LT215/85R x 16C in.
CHASSIS [Series C30]: Wheelbase: 131.5 in./164.5 in. Overall length: 212 in./244.43 in. Height: 77.8 in. Front tread: 65.8 in. Rear tread: 62.7 in. Tires: LT235/85R x 16D in.
CHASSIS [P30]: Wheelbase: 125 in./178 in. Tires: LT215/85R x 16C in.
TECHNICAL: Selective synchromesh transmission (Automatic on Suburban and some vans). Speeds: 3F/1R (four-speed manual in 20 and 30 Series and S10s). Steering column-mounted gearshift (or four-speed on floor). Single dry-disc type clutch. Semi-floating rear axle (C30/K30/Crew and Bonus Cabs have full-floating) rear axle. Overall ratio: various. Power front disc/rear drum brakes. Pressed steel wheels.

1984 Chevrolet C10 Suburban Silverado (CP)

OPTIONS: [S10 Pickup] Color-keyed bumper. Air-conditioning. Rear step bumper, chrome or black. Chrome bumpers with rub strip. Black front bumper guards. Console. Chrome grille. Cigarette lighter. Color-keyed floor mats. Comfortilt steering wheel. Tinted glass. Deep tinted glass. Intermittent wipers. Auxiliary lighting. Cargo area lamp. Dome lamp. Halogen headlamps. Dual eyeline mirrors/painted or chrome. Right-hand visor mirror. Black bodyside/bright wheel opening moldings. Bright door edge moldings. Black or bright wheel opening moldings. Power windows. Power door locks. Special two-tone. Sport two-tone. AM radio. AM/FM radio. AM /FM stereo radio. AM/FM stereo radio with cassette and clock; same with seek-and-scan. Premium rear speakers. High-back bucket seats/with Custom vinyl; with High-Country Sheepskin; with Special Custom cloth; with adjustable seatbacks. Rear jump seats in Maxi-cab. Tinted sliding rear window. Swing-out rear quarter windows. Cast aluminum wheels. Styled wheels. Wheel trim rings. Bright wheelcovers. Resume cruise control. Sport suspension. 2.2 liter diesel engine. Insta-Trac 4x4 system. Off-road package. P235/75R x 15 steel-belted radial tires. Heavy-duty trailering package (with V-6). Heavy-duty battery. Cold climate package. Engine and oil cooler (V-6 only). Radiator and transmission oil cooler (V-6 only). 20-gal. fuel tank. Gauge package. Tachometer. 66-amp. generator. Fuel tank shield. Transfer case and differential shield. Locking rear axle differential. Heavy-duty shocks. Heavy-duty springs. Front stabilizer bar. Power steering. Two front tow hooks. Trailering wiring harness. Three-

speed automatic transmission (California only). 1.9 liter four-cylinder engine (California only; standard in California). Four-speed automatic overdrive transmission. Fully-synchronized five-speed manual transmission with overdrive. Snowplow (special order). 2.8 liter V-6 engine. Stake body (For Chassis & Cab). Durango interior trim. Tahoe interior trim. Sport interior trim. Exterior colors: Silver metallic; Frost white; Light blue metallic; Galaxy blue metallic; Doeskin tan; Indian bronze metallic/Desert Sand metallic; Apple red; Cinnamon red and Satin black (secondary). S10 Blazer: Air-conditioning. Color-keyed front bumper (requires two-tone). Black front bumper guards. Console. Chromed grille. Cigarette lighter. Color-keyed floor mats. Comfortilt steering wheel. Rear window defogger. Digital clock (requires radio). Deep-tint glass. Deep-tint with light tint rear window. Sliding rear quarter windows. Intermittent wipers. Engine compartment lamp. Dome lamp. Halogen headlamps. Luggage carrier and rear air deflector. Dual painted below-eyeline mirrors. Chrome below-eyeline mirrors. Right-hand visor mirror. Bodyside and wheel opening moldings. Door edge guards. Separate wheel opening moldings/black or bright. Operating Convenience package. Special two-tone. Sport two-tone. Striping (requires solid paint). AM radio. AM/FM radio. AM/FM stereo. AM/FM stereo with cassette and clock. Same with seek-and-scan. Premium rear speakers. Folding rear bench seat. Sliding rear tinted quarter window. Spare tire cover. 4x2 styled wheels. 4x4 cast aluminum wheels. Bright wheel trim rings. Insta-Trac 4x4 system. Cold climate package. Heavy-duty cooling with transmission oil cooler. Cruise Control. 20-gal. fuel tank. Gauges. 66-amp. generator. Heavy-duty battery. Heavy-duty front/rear shocks. Locking rear axle differential. Off-Road chassis equipment. Power steering. Tachometer. Tailgate window release. Trailering Special equipment. Transfer case shield (4x4). 1.9 liter four-cylinder engine (California only). 2.8 liter V-6. Five-speed manual transmission. Four-speed automatic overdrive transmission. Larger size tubeless tires. Dealer-installed black-finish brush guard. Tahoe interior trim (Custom vinyl, Special Custom cloth, High-Country Sheepskin). Sport cloth interior. Paint colors: Same as S10 pickups. Snow plow (special order). Full-Size Blazer: Air cleaner. Air-conditioning. Bright wheelcovers. Chrome front bumper guards. Deluxe bumpers. Cigarette lighter. Color-keyed floor mats. Comfortilt steering wheel.Deluxe front appearance. Electric Quartz clock. Deep-tint glass. Sliding side window. Halogen headlamps. Headlight warning buzzer. Full-length headliner. Intermittent wipers. Painted below-eyeline mirrors. Stainless below-eye line mirrors. Black bodyside moldings. Bright bodyside moldings. Black molding package. Bright molding package. Door edge guards.Operating Convenience package. Power door locks. Power windows. Special two-tone paint. Exterior decor package. AM radio. AM/FM radio. AM/FM stereo radio. AM/FM stereo with cassette. Windshield antenna. Folding rear seat. Electric tailgate window. Rally wheels. Styled wheels. Cold Climate package. Engine oil cooler.Transmission oil cooler. Cruise control. Deadweight trailer hitch. Front quad shocks. Front stabilizer bar. Front tow hooks. 31-gal. fuel tank. Fuel tank stone shield. Gauges package. 66-amp. generator. Heavy-duty battery. Heavy-duty springs. Heavy-duty radiator. Locking differential. Trailering Special equipment. Weight distributing hitch. Four-speed overdrive automatic. 5.0-liter V-8 engine (with Electronic Spark Control, not in California). 5.7-liter V-8 engine (California only). 6.2-liter diesel V-8. Dealer installed brush guard. Silverado interior trim. Silverado Custom cloth trim. Full-length black top. 3/4-length black top. Paint colors: Frost white, Silver metallic; Midnight black; Light blue metallic; Midnight blue; Colonial yellow; Doeskin tan; Desert Sand metallic; Indian bronze metallic and Apple red. Chevy Vans: Front air-conditioning. Front and rear air-conditioning. "Resume" Speed Control, Auxiliary lighting package. Auxiliary rear heater. Chrome bumpers. Front bumper guards. Cigar lighter & ashtray light. Comfortilt steering wheel. Custom steering wheel. Deluxe front appearance. Quartz electric clock. Floor carpeting. All windows tinted. Tinted windshield. Halogen headlights. Intermittent windshield wipers. Fixed extended arm mirrors, painted or stainless. Below-eyeline mirrors, painted or stainless. Black bodyside moldings. Wheel opening moldings. Operating Convenience Package. Power door locks. Power windows. Special two-tone paint. Power brakes. Deluxe two-tone paint. Rear door stop. AM radio. AM/FM radio. AM/FM stereo. AM/FM stereo with cassette. Roof ventilator. Front auxiliary seat. High-back front bucket seat. Sliding door extender link. Special exterior trim. Special interior trim. Right-hand sunshade. Rally wheels. Bright wheelcovers. Inside spare carrier. Spare tire cover. Side and rear windows. Auxiliary battery. Engine oil cooler. Transmission oil cooler. Dual rear wheels (Cutaway Vans). Voltmeter. Temperature gauge. Oil pressure gauge. 66-amp. generator. Heavy-duty battery. Heavy-duty power brakes. Heavy-duty cooling. Heavy-duty front springs. Heavy-duty front/rear shocks. Heavy-duty rear springs. Locking differential. Power steering (GI0). School bus equipment (G30). Deadweight trailer hitch. Weight distributing hitch. Heavy-duty Trailering Special equipment. Light-duty Trailering Special equipment. 250 cu. in.six-cylinder engine. 5.0 liter V-8 engine (with Electronic Spark Control, not available in California). 5.0 liter V-8 (California only). 5.7 liter V-8 engine. 6.2 liter Diesel V-8 engine. Four-speed automatic overdrive transmission. Four-speed manual overdrive transmission. Oversize tires. Paint colors: Galaxy blue metallic; Colonial yellow;Doeskin tan; Desert Sand metallic, Indian bronze metallic; Apple red metallic; Autumn red metallic; Frost white; Silver metallic; Light blue metallic and (Cutaway vans only) Polar white. [Step-Van]: 4.8 liter one-barrel LPG engine. (standard) 5.7 literfour-barrel V-8, engine. 6.2, liter diesel V-8 engine. Four-speed manual transmission (standard). Three-speed automatic transmission (optional, except P20 with standard six-cylinder). 125, in. wheelbase (standard). 133 in. and 157 in. wheelbases (optional). Steel panel bodies: 10.5 ft.; 12.5 ft. and 14.5 ft. Wide (74 in.) rear doors. Aluminum panel bodies (same sizes as above, plus 14 ft. 10 in.). X-950 aluminum bodies. Merchandise shelf interior. Snack food interior. Bakery pallet rack interior. Industrial laundry interior. Fiberglass skylight. Step-type bumper with recessed lights. Deluxe high-back bucket seat. Auxiliary seats with armrests. Expanded metal partition. Plywood interior lining. Right-hand sliding panel with key-locking handle. Special Custom cloth interior. All-Weather air-conditioning. Right-hand inside spare tire carrier. 66-in. wide overhead door. 60 in. wide rear door opening. Dual rear wheels. Larger size tubeless tires. P30 Step-Van 18 ft. aluminum body. High-Cube Vans: 5.7 liter V-8 engine (standard). 6.2 liter Diesel V-8 engine. Overhead rear door. Hi-back bucket seats. Three-speed automatic (with column shift) transmission (standard). Dual rear wheels on 125 in. wheelbase (Standard with extra-cost 6,200 lbs. rear axle). 7,500 lbs. rear axle also available. Loadspace skylight. Step type rear bumper. Plywood interior lining. Expanded metal partition. Right-hand sliding panel with key-locking handle; custom cloth interior trim. Inside spare tire carrier. Plywood partition with center sliding panel. C/K10/20/30: (Suburban-only): Electric tailgate window. Tailgate window defogger. Front and rear air-conditioning. Bucket seats. Deluxe front and rear bumpers. Rear right-hand heater. Three-passenger folding center seat. Three-passenger center and rear seats. 60 in. wide double panel doors. Wagon type rear tailgate. Standard transmissions for Suburbans were as follows: C10 (gas) four-speed automatic with overdrive; C20 (gas) three-speed automatic; K10 (gas) same as C10; K20 (gas) same as C20. With diesel engines the C10 came with four-speed automatic with overdrive and all other models came with four-speed manual as standard equipment). 14-gal. or 31-gal. fuel tanks. Headlamp warning buzzer. Full-length headliner. (Pickups Only): Chromed rear bumper. Chromed rear step bumper (Fleetside). Painted rear step bumper. Cargo area lamp. Dome lamp. Gauges. Conventional two-tone. Deluxe two-tone paint (Fleetside only). Sliding rear window. Side-mounted spare tire carrier (Fleetside only). Auxiliary fuel tank. Engine oil cooler. Heavy-duty automatic transmission cooler. Vacuum power brakes. Extra-capacity rear springs. G50 heavy-duty rear springs. G60 main and auxiliary rear springs. Special Camper Chassis equipment. Special commercial chassis equipment. Heavy-duty 4.8 liter six-cylinder engine (heavy-duty emissions trucks). Standard 4.1 liter six-cylinder engine. Special bright metal wheelcovers. Pickup box side rails. Painted West Coast mirrors. Glide-out spare tire carrier. (Suburbans and Pickups): Front air-conditioning. Chromed front bumper guards. Cigarette lighter. Color-keyed floor mats. Comfortilt steering wheel. Deluxe front appearance. Quartz electric clock. Deep tinted glass. Deluxe molding package, bright (Fleetside only pickups). Door edge guards. Power door locks. Power windows. Operating convenience package. Special two-tone (Fleetside only on Pickups). Exterior decor package (Fleetside only, on Pickups). AM radio. AM/FM radio. AM/FM stereo. AM/FM stereo with cassette. Windshield antenna. High-beam halogen headlamps. Intermittent windshield wipers. Painted below-eyeline mirrors. Stainless below-eyeline mirrors. Stainless camper mirrors. Black bodyside moldings (Fleetside only on Pickups). Bright bodyside moldings (Fleetside only on Pickups). Roof marker lamps. Rally wheels. Styled wheels. Bright wheelcovers. Precleaner air cleaner. Locking differential. Cold Climate package. Electronic speed control. Front quad shocks. Front stabilizer bar. Heavy-duty front stabilizer. Front tow hooks. Stone shield. Gauges. 66-amp. generator. Heavy-duty battery. Heavy-duty shocks. Heavy-duty front springs. Heavy-duty radiator. Power steering. Trailer wiring. Trailer right-hand hitches. 5.0 liter V-8 with Electronic Speed Control (not in California). 5.7 liter V-8. 6.2 liter Diesel V-8. 7.4 liter V-8 (Suburban and heavy-duty emissions pickups). Scottsdale interior trim. Silverado interior trim. Paint colors: Frost white; Silver metallic; Midnight black; Light blue metallic; Midnight blue; Colonial yellow; Doeskin tan; Desert Sand metallic; Indian bronze metallic and Apple red.

1984 Chevrolet K20 Suburban Silverado (CP)

HISTORICAL: Introduced: Fall, 1983. Calendar year sales: [All models] 1,111,839. [El Camino] 22,997. [K10 Blazer] 46,919. [S10 Blazer] 150,599. [Chevy Van] 155,421. [Sportvan] 21,902. [S10 Pickup] 199,631. [C20 Pickups] 50,823. Calendar year production: [Chevy Van/Sportvan] 120,878; [Suburban] 57,286; [Pickups] 332,404 and [Step-Van/Hi-Cube/Cutaway] 53,097. [Total] 563,665. Innovations: Newly designed grilles. S10 trucks feature hydraulic clutch in place of cable type. Improved rust protection on pickups. Improved brake linings for Blazers, Suburbans and Pickups. Step-Vans feature new exterior Velvac outside rearview mirrors, new rotary side door latches and new key-locking push-button side door handles. Chevrolet products were named as the official cars and trucks of the XIV Olympic winter games in Sarajevo. Chevrolet advertised the U.S. Army's purchase of nearly 30,000 full-sized Chevrolet 4x4 pickups and over 23,000 full-sized Blazers with 6.2 liter diesel V-8 engines. These trucks were said to be "regular production trucks like the ones you can get, except for a few specialized military adaptions like a special electrical system."

1985 CHEVROLET

1985 Chevrolet S-10 Pickup (CP)

1/2-TON S10 — MODEL S/SERIES 10 — FOUR/V-6: The easiest way to spot a 1985 Chevrolet S10 was by its larger and more stylized fender badges with the S done in red (the dash between the letter and the numbers was gone). At the rear, the taillights were framed in chrome and the large Chevrolet name (formerly running across the tailgate center) was changed to a smaller name at the right-hand side of a tailgate trim panel. A new 2.5 litre engine with EFI (electronic fuel-injection) was standard in 4x4 models. Standard, Durango, Tahoe and Sport trim treatments were available again. Trim options included Custom two-tone (second color below belt); Sport two-tone (second color on bottom below four-stripe decals or moldings) and Special two-tone (second color between beltline and lower feature line). Also standard in S10 Blazers was the 2.5 liter four-cylinder EFI engine. A new Custom vinyl interior amounted to little more than wider door panel pleats and brushed aluminum door panel trim plates. Much of the artwork used in the 1984 and 1985 sales catalogs is close to identical and even the 10 colors available (not counting Satin black) were the same. As in 1984, Satin black could only be ordered as a secondary color. Custom two-toning (with beltline decal and second color below it) was new for 1985, however.

1/2-TON EL CAMINO — MODEL W — Six/V-8: In addition to last year's standard features, the 1985 El Camino had a new 4.3 liter V-6 base engine. Standard grille was the same as last year. Also back was the El Camino SS and the Conquista. The SS had an aero-style nose cap like the Monte Carlo SS. A non-functional power blister hood, dummy side pipes and pickup bed rails were optional. Model identification decals were used on the doors, above the lower feature line. Conquista and SS Sport decors each included five distinctive two-tones.

1/2-TON ASTRO VAN — Model M/Series 10 — V-6: Chevrolet's all-new Astro was a compact van featuring a standard V-6 engine, five-speed manual transmission and rear drive axle. The mini-van body featured a sloping hood and aerodynamically rounded front end with wraparound parking lamps, single rectangular headlights and a grille with seven horizontal bars. Each bar decreased slightly in width, from top to bottom. A yellow bow tie badge was in the center. Additional standard equipment included an engine cover storage box, front arm rests, swing-out side windows, black rubber floor covering, high-back bucket seats, five-passenger seating and P195/75R15 all-season steel-belted radial tires. CS trim added color-keyed floor coverings, side window defoggers, inside fuel door release, lighted vanity mirrors and an under-the-floor spare tire carrier. The optional CL package included added features, such as bumper rub strips, a trip odometer, gauges, custom steering wheel, wheel trim rings, auxiliary lighting, cigar lighter and carpets. Cargo van versions had a standard low-back driver's seat in saddle color, black rubber floor covering, solid panel bodysides and the same arrangement of a sliding right-hand side cargo door with double panel type rear doors. Custom cloth upholstery was optional. Paint treatments included 10 solid colors; special two-tones (with decal strips at beltline and secondary color below the belt) and Sport two-tones (with secondary color on lower body perimeter). The Astro name appeared on both entry doors, just behind the front wheel openings. Taillamps were vertical units positioned on the rear body corners just below the beltline. The rear doors of all models had large windows.

1/2-TON; 3/4-TON; 1-TON VAN/HI-CUBE VAN — MODEL G/SERIES 10; 20; 30 — SIX/V-8: Chevy Vans had new grilles of the same design described below for Blazers. Model identification nameplates featured somewhat smaller and thinner lettering. Chrome trim around the taillights was no longer used. Chevrolet's new 4.3 liter Vortec V-6 was base equipment in G10/G20/G30 models, while the 6.2 liter diesel V-8 was available in G20/G30-CP6 series vans. The 5.7 liter V-8 could also be had in G30/CP6 Cutaway vans. Custom vinyl seats now used a four-pleat pattern. 60/40 style side doors were now regularly available, at no extra cost, in place of the sliding right-hand side load door. G30 Hi-Cube vans again come in 10 ft. (125 in. wheelbase) and 12 ft. (146 in. wheelbase) models, with RV and Commercial Cutaway vans available on both of these chassis as well. All manual transmissions (three-speed type standard in G10/G20) came with floor-mounted gearshifts.

1/2-TON BLAZER — MODEL K (4x4) — SIX/V-8: Full-size '85 Blazers were easier to spot. They had a much wider body color panel between upper and lower grilles and the grilles had only a single horizontal bar intersected by seven vertical bars. The headlight housing had more of a vertical look than last year's, although the rectangular lamps were stacked atop each other again. An amber-colored parking lamp was standard on the bottom, but when halogen high-beams were ordered, the parking lamps moved behind the lower grille. New features included fluidic wiper arms with built-in washers and standard color-keyed tops in a choice of four new colors, plus the old black and white. Custom Deluxe interiors were standard, with Silverado trim available at extra cost. Special two-tone and Exterior Decor packages were optional. Colonial yellow and Desert Sand metallic finishes were no longer offered. Engine and transmission selections were unchanged.

1/2-TON; 3/4-TON; 1-TON CONVENTIONAL — MODEL C (4x2); MODEL K (4x4)/ SERIES 10; 20; 30 — SIX/V-8: Full-sized pickups shared the new 1985 grille with Blazers and Suburbans. A new Custom two-tone treatment used the secondary color above the beltline on the Fleetside box, on the rear of the cab and on the doors and fendersides above the belt, but not on the hood or window frames. This gave a sportier look (something like a tapering racing stripe) to the cab and fendersides. Under the hood, as standard equipment, was the Vortec six. The trucks continued to come in a wide range of choices including 1/2-, 3/4- and 1-ton series with long or short cargo boxes; Fleetside or Step-Side styling; Crew or Bonus cabs and 4x2 or 4x4 drive. A real "Country Cadillac" was the Crew Cab "Big Dooley" with its flared rear fenders and dual rear wheels. Custom Deluxe, Scottsdale and Silverado trims were again available. Suburbans also had the new-for-1985 wide center panel grille styling. Also standard were fluidic arm window washer/wipers. Custom Deluxe trim was standard. Scottsdales had color-keyed floor mats and added cowl and headliner insulation. Door-to-door carpeting and velour or grained vinyl upholstery were featured with Silverado interiors. Special two-tone and Exterior Decor finish options were available. The latter included a hood ornament. Endgate and panel door options were still cataloged. Standard engines were all V-8s.

1985 Chevrolet Fleetside Pickup (CP)

3/4-TON; 1-TON FORWARD-CONTROL — MODEL P/SERIES 20; 30 — SIX/V-8: Chevy issued separate 1984 sales catalogs for steel-bodied and aluminum-bodied Step-Vans. The steel models came as CP208/CP308 models on a 125 in. wheelbase; as CP210/CP310 models on the 133 in. wheelbase and as CP314 models on the 157 in. wheelbase. Aluminum body models could be had in the same configurations, plus a model CP318 version with a 178 in. wheelbase. Load lengths were: [CP208/CP308] 129.6 in.; [CP210/CP310] 153.6 in.; [CP314] 177.6 in. and [CP318] 178 in. Series 30 Hi-Cube models came in 10 ft. models on the 125 in. wheelbase or 12 ft. models on the 146 in. wheelbase.

I.D. DATA: Location of serial number: The VIN is stamped on a plate attached to the left top of the instrument panel on C/K/G Series. On P Series the plate is attached to the front of the dash and the panel to the left of the steering column. The first symbol indicates country of origin: 1=U.S.; 2=Canada; J=Japan. The second symbol indicates manufacturer: G=General Motors; 8=Isuzu. The third symbol indicates make: A=Chevrolet bus; B=Chevrolet (incomplete); C=Chevrolet truck; Y=LUV (incomplete); Z=LUV truck; 8=Chevy MPV. The fourth symbol indicates GVW rating (and brake system); B=3,001 lbs.-4,000 lbs. (hydraulic); C=4,001 lbs.-5,000 lbs. (hydraulic), etc. through K for hydraulic brakes. The fifth symbol indicates line and chassis type: C=Conventional cab (including Blazer and Suburban) 4x2; G=Chevy Van and Sportvan 4x2; K=Conventional cab (including Blazer and Suburban) 4x4; L=LUV 4x2; R=LUV 4x4; P=Forward-Control; S=Conventional Cab 4x2; W=El Camino 4x2; Z=Special body 4x2. The sixth symbol indicates series: 1=1/2-ton; 2=3/4-ton; 3=1-ton; 8=El Camino. The seventh symbol indicates body type: 0=El Camino Pickup-Delivery; 1=Hi-Cube and Cutaway Vans; 2-Forward-Control; 3=Four-door cab; 4=Two-door cab; 5=Van; 6=Suburban; 7=Motorhome chassis; 8=Blazer Utility; 9=Stake. The eighth symbol indicated engine. Engine codes were generally the same as 1983. The ninth symbol was a check digit. The 10th symbol indicated model year: F=1985. The 11th symbol indicated the assembly plant: A=Lakewood, Ga.; B=Baltimore, Md.;C=Southgate, Calif.; D=Doraville, Ga.; E=Linden, N.J.; F=Flint, Mich.; G=Framingham, Mass.; H=Flint, Mich.; J=Janesville, Wis.; K=Leeds, Mo.; L=Van Nuys, Calif.; M=Lansing, Mich.; N=Norwood, Ohio; P=Pontiac, Mich.; R=Arlington, Texas; S=St. Louis, Mo.; T=Tarrytown, N.Y.; V=GMC, Pontiac, Mich.; W=Willow Run, Mich.; X=Fairfax, Va.; Y=Wilmington, Dela.; Z=Fremont, Calif.; O=GMAD, Pontiac, Mich.; 1=Oshawa, Canada; 2=Moraine, Ohio; 2=Ste. Therese, Quebec, Canada; 3=Chevrolet-Detroit, Mich.; 3=St. Eustache, Quebec, Canada; 4=Orion Plant, Pontiac, Mich.; 4=Scarborough, Ontario, Canada; 5=Bowling Green, Ken.; 5=London, Ontario, Canada; 6=Oklahoma City, Okla.; 7=Lordstown, Ohio; 8=Shreveport, La.; 8=Fujisawa, Japan; 9=Cadillac, Detroit, Mic. (Note: Trucks were not built at all factories). Symbols 12-17 were the production sequence number starting at 100001. Ending numbers not available. Engine number location: [Six] located on pad at right-hand side of cylinder block at rear of distributor. [V-8] located on pad at right front side of cylinder block.

Model	Body Type	Price	Weight	Prod. Total
El Camino — 1/2-Ton — 117.1 in. w.b. — V-6				
1GW80	Sedan Pickup	9058	3252	—
1GW80	Super Sport Pickup	9327	3263	—
S10 Pickup 4x2 — 1/2-Ton — 108.3 in. w.b. — V-6				
CS10603	Pickup	5999	2561	—
S10 Pickup 4x2 — 1/2-Ton — 122.9 in. w.b. — V-6				
CS10803	Chassis & Cab	6500	2954	—
CS10803	Pickup	6702	2623	—
CS10653	Maxi-Cab Pickup	7167	3030	—
S10 Pickup 4x4 — 1/2-Ton — 108.3 in. w.b. — V-6				
CT10603	Pickup	8258	2898	—
S10 Pickup 4x4 — 1/2-Ton — 122.9 in. w.b. — V-6				
CT10803	Pickup	8412	2623	—
CT10653	Maxi-Cab Pickup	8756	3030	—
S10 Blazer 4x2 — 1/2-Ton — 100.5 in. w.b. — V-6				
CS10516	Hardtop Utility	8881	2894	—
S10 Blazer 4x4 — 1/2-Ton — 100.5 in. w.b. — V-6				
CT10516	Hardtop Utility	10,134	3151	—
Astro Van — 1/2-Ton — 111 in. w.b. — V-6				
CM10905	Cargo Van	7821	3048	—
CM10906	Passenger Van	8195	3277	—
CM10906	CS Passenger Van	8623	3277	—
CM10906	CL Passenger Van	9359	3277	—
Chevy Van 10 — 1/2-Ton — 110 in. w.b. — V-6				
CG11006	Panal Van	9650	4802	—
Chevy Van 10 — 1/2-Ton — 125 in. w.b. — V-6				
CG11306	Sportvan	9870	4966	—
CG11306	Bonaventure	10,661	5067	—
CG11306	Beauville	10,979	5110	—
Chevy Van — 3/4-Ton — 110 in. w.b. — V-6				
CG21006	Panel Van	8581	3811	—
Chevy Van — 3/4-Ton — 125 in. w.b. — V-6				
CG21306	Sportvan	10,054	4994	—
CG21306	Bonaventure	10,845	5095	—
CG21306	Beauville	11,161	5138	—
Chevy Van 30 — 1-Ton — 125 in. w.b. — V-8				
CG31306	Panel	10,342	4402	—
CG31306	Sportvan	12,463	6915	—
CG31306	Bonaventure	13,254	7016	—
CG31306	Beauville	13,569	7059	—
Chevy Van 30 — 1-Ton — 125 in. w.b. — Diesel V-8				
CG31306	Sportvan	13,545	5971	—
CG31306	Bonaventure	14,350	6070	—
CG31306	Beauville	14,587	6113	—
Hi-Cube Vans 30 — 1-Ton — 125 in. w.b. — V-8				
CG31	Steel Hi-Cube 10 ft.	12,097	5054	—
Hi-Cube Vans 30 — 1-Ton — 146 in. w.b. — V-8				
CG31	Steel Hi-Cube 12 ft.	13,351	5891	—

* Add for 10 ft./12 ft. aluminum Hi-Cube or RV/Commercial Cutaway on 125 in./146 in. wheelbase.

Model	Body Type	Price	Weight	Prod. Total
K5 Blazer 4x4 — 1/2-Ton — 106.5 w.b. — V-8				
K10516	Hardtop Utility	11,223	4462	—

* Add $2,730 and 375 lbs. for diesel.

Model	Body Type	Price	Weight	Prod. Total
C10 — 1/2-Ton Conventional — 117.5 in. w.b. — V-6				
CC10703	Step-Side	7532	3844	—
CC10703	Fleetside	7397	3891	—
C10 — 1/2-Ton Conventional — 131.5 in. w.b. — V-6				
CC10903	Fleetside	7565	4060	—

* Add $2,322 for CK10 (4x4) Pickup with Vortec six engine.
** Add $2,913 for 6.2 liter diesel V-8 option.

C10 — 1/2-Ton Suburban — 129.5 in. w.b. — V-8

CC10906	Suburban (doors)	10,812	4755	—
CC10916	Suburban (tailgate)	10,850	4790	—

* Add $2,322 for 4x4 Suburban with larger 350 cid V-8.
** Add $2,557 for 6.2 liter diesel V-8 option.

C20 — 3/4-Ton Conventional — 131.5 in. w.b. — V-6

CC20903	Step-Side	8798	4417	—
CC20903	Fleetside	8663	4479	—

C20 — 3/4-Ton Heavy-Duty Conventional — 131.5 in. w.b. — V-6

CC20903	Chassis & Cab	9198	4057	—
CC20903	Step-Side	9756	4417	—
CC20903	Fleetside	9622	4479	—

C20 — 3/4-Ton Conventional — 164.5 in. w.b. — V-6

CC20943	Fleetside & Bonus Cab	10,584	5258	—
CC20943	Fleetside & Crew Cab	10,920	5258	—

* Add $1,525 for CK20 (4x4) pickups with 350 cid V-8.
** Add $2,276 for 6.2 liter diesel V-8 option on C20 Pickups.

C10 — 3/4-Ton Suburban — 129.5 in. w.b. — V-8

CC20906	Door Suburban with V-8	10,953	4705	—
CC20916	End-gate Suburban with V-8	10,991	4740	—

* Add $1,479 for CK20 (4x4) Suburban with larger 350 cid V-8.
** Add $2,196 for 6.2 liter diesel V-8 option on C20 Suburbans.

Step-Van — P20 — 125 in./133 in./178 in. w.b. — Six

CP20842	Steel Panel 10.5 ft.	13,119	5998	—

* Add for P20 with 12.5 ft. Step-Van body.

C30 — 1-Ton Conventional — 131.5 in. w.b. — Six

CC30903	Chassis & Cab	9332	4485	—
CC30903	Step-Side	9849	4838	—
CC30903	Fleetside	9715	4900	—

C30 — 1-Ton Conventional — 164.5 in. w.b. — V-8

CC30943	Chassis & Bonus Cab	10,349	4912	—
CC30943	Fleetside & Bonus Cab	10,715	5323	—
CC30943	Chassis & Crew Cab	9446	4520	—
CC30943	Fleetside & Crew Cab	11,053	5323	—

* Add $2,344 average for CK30 (4x4) models with six-cylinder engine.
** Add $1,800 average for 6.2 liter diesel V-8 option on C30 models.

P30 Step-Van — 1-Ton — 125 in./133 in./178 in. w.b. — Six

CP30842	Steel Panel 10.5 ft.	13,119	5998	—

* Add for P30 with 12.5 ft. Step-Van body.
** Add for P30 with 14.5 ft. Step-Van body.

1985 Chevrolet Astro Van (CP)

ENGINE: Inline. OHV. Four-cylinder. Cast iron block. Bore & stroke: 3.42 x 3.23 in. Displacement: 119 cid. Compression ratio: 8.4:1. Net horsepower: 82 at 4600 rpm. Net torque: 101 lbs.-ft. at 3000 rpm. Ordering Code LR1.
ENGINE: Inline. OHV. Diesel Four-cylinder. Cast iron block. Bore & stroke: 3.46 x 3.62 in. Displacement: 137 cid. Compression ratio: 21:1. Net horsepower: 62 at 4300 rpm. Net torque: 96 lbs.-ft. at 2200 rpm. Ordering Code LQ7.
ENGINE: Inline. OHV. Four-cylinder. Cast iron block. Bore & stroke: 4 x 3.00 in. Displacement: 151 cid. Compression ratio: 9.0:1. Net horsepower: 92 at 4400 rpm. Net torque: 132 lbs.-ft. at 2800 rpm. Electronic Fuel-injection. Ordering Code LN8.
ENGINE: Vee-block. OHV. Six-cylinder. Cast iron block. Bore & stroke: 3.50 x 2.99 in. Displacement: 173 cid. Compression ratio: 8.5:1. Net horsepower: 110 at 4800 rpm. Net torque: 145 lbs.-ft. at 2100 rpm. Electronic Fuel-injection.
ENGINE: Vee-block. OHV. Six-cylinder. Cast iron block. Bore & stroke: 4.0 x 3.48 in. Displacement: 262 cid. Compression ratio: 9.3:1. Net horsepower: 155 at 4000 rpm. Torque: 230 lbs.-ft. at 2400 rpm. Hydraulic valve lifters. Carburetor: Single four-barrel. Ordering Code LB1.
ENGINE: Vee-block. OHV. Six-cylinder. Cast iron block. Bore & stroke: 4.0 x 3.48 in. Displacement: 202 cid. Compression ratio: 9.3:1. Net horsepower: 130 at 3600 rpm. 210 lbs.-ft. at 2000 rpm. Electronic Fuel-injection. Ordering Code LB4.
ENGINE: Vee-block. OHV. Six-cylinder. Cast iron block. Bore & stroke: 3.9 x 4.1 in. Displacement: 292 cid. Compression ratio: 7.8:1. Net horsepower: 115 at 3600 rpm. Net torque: 215 lbs.-ft. at 1600 rpm. Seven main bearings. Hydraulic valve lifters. Carburetor: Rochester single one-barrel. Ordering Code L25.
ENGINE: Vee-block. OHV. Eight-cylinder. Cast iron block. Bore & stroke: 3.74 x 3.48 in. Displacement: 305 cid. Compression ratio: 9.5:1. Net horsepower: 150 at 4000 rpm. Net torque: 240 lbs.-ft. at 2000 rpm. Five main bearings. Hydraulic valve lifters. Carburetor: Single four-barrel. Ordering Code LG4.

ENGINE: Vee-block. OHV. Eight-cylinder. Cast iron block. Bore & stroke: 3.74 x 3.48 in. Displacement: 305 cid. Compression ratio: 9.2:1. Net horsepower: 160 at 4400 rpm. Net torque: 235 lbs.-ft. at 2000 rpm. Four main bearings. Hydraulic valve lifters. Carburetor: Rochester single four-barrel. Ordering Code LE9.
ENGINE: Vee-block. OHV. Eight-cylinder. Cast iron block. Bore & stroke: 4.0 x 3.5 Displacement: 350 cid. Compression ratio: 8.3:1. Net horsepower: 160 at 3800 rpm. Net torque: 250 lbs.-ft. at 2800 rpm. Five main bearings. Hydraulic valve lifters. Carburetor: Rochester four-barrel. Ordering Code LT9.
ENGINE: Vee-block. OHV. Eight-cylinder. Cast iron block. Bore & stroke: 4.0 x 3.48 in. Displacement: 350 cid. Compression ratio: 8.2:1. Net horsepower: 165 at 3800 rpm. Net torque: 275 lbs.-ft. at 1600 rpm. Carburetor: Rochester single four-barrel. Ordering Code LS9.
ENGINE: Vee-block. OHV. Diesel Eight-cylinder. Cast iron block. Bore & stroke: 3.98 x 3.82 in. Displacement: 379 cid. Compression ratio: 21.3:1. Net horsepower: 130 at 3600 rpm. Net torque: 240 lbs.-ft. at 2000 rpm. Hydraulic valve lifters. Fuel-injection. Ordering Code LH6.
ENGINE: Inline. Diesel. OHV. Eight-cylinder. Cast iron block. Bore & stroke: 3.98 x 3.80 in. Displacement: 379 cid. Compression ratio: 21.3:1. Net horsepower: 151 at 3600 rpm. Net Torque: 248 lbs.-ft. at 2000 rpm. Hydraulic valve lifters. Fuel-injection. Ordering Code LL4.
ENGINE: Vee-block. OHV. Eight-cylinder. Cast iron block. Bore & stroke: 4.3 x 4.0 in. Displacement: 454 cid. Compression ratio: 7.9:1. Net horsepower: 230 at 3800 rpm. Net torque: 360 lbs.-ft. at 2800 rpm. Five main bearings. Carburetor: Rochester single four-barrel. Ordering Code LE8.

1985 Chevrolet El Camino (CP)

CHASSIS [S10 Pickup]: Wheelbase: 108.3 in./122.9 in. Tires: P195/75R14.
CHASSIS [S10 Blazer]: Wheelbase: 100.5 in. Tires P195/75R15.
CHASSIS [El Camino]: Wheelbase: 117.1 in. Tires P205/75R14.
CHASSIS [Astro Van]: Wheelbase: 111 in. Tires P195/75R15.
CHASSIS [Chevy Van 10]: Wheelbase: 110 in. Tires: P195/75R15.
CHASSIS [Sportvan 10]: Wheelbase: 125 in. Tires: P205/75R15.
CHASSIS [Chevy Van 20]: Wheelbase: 110 in. Tires: P225/75R15.
CHASSIS [Sportvan 20]: Wheelbase: 125 in. Tires: P225/75R15.
CHASSIS [Chevy Van 30]: Wheelbase: 125 in. Tires: 8.75R-16.5C.
CHASSIS [Sportvan 30]: Wheelbase: 125 in. Tires: 8.75R-16.5D.
CHASSIS [Hi-Cube Van 10 ft.]: Wheelbase: 125 in. Tires: 8.00-16.5D.
CHASSIS [Hi-Cube Van 12 ft.]: Wheelbase: 146 in. Tires: 8.75-16.5D.
CHASSIS [K10 Blazer]: Wheelbase: 106.5 in. Tires: P215/75R15.
CHASSIS [C10 Pickup]: Wheelbase: 117.5 in./131.5 Tires: 195/75R15.
CHASSIS [C10 Suburban]: Wheelbase: 129.5 in. Tires: P233/75R15.
CHASSIS [C20 Pickup]: Wheelbase: 131.5 in. Tires: LT235/85R16C.
CHASSIS [C20 Pickup]: Wheelbase: 164.5 in. Tires: [Front] LT235/85R16D; [Rear] LT235/85R16E.
CHASSIS [C20 Suburban]: Wheelbase: 129.5. in. Tires: [Front] LT235/85R16D; [Rear] LT235/85R16E.
CHASSIS [P20 Step-Van]: Wheelbase: 125 in./133 in. Tires: LT215/85R16C.
CHASSIS [C30 Pickup]: Wheelbase: 131.5 in./164.5. in. Tires: [Front] [Rear] LT235/85R16E.
CHASSIS [P30 Step-Van]: Wheelbase: 125 in./178 in. Tires: LT215/85R16C.

1985 Chevrolet C10 Step-Side Pickup (CP)

TECHNICAL: [El Camino] Automatic transmission. Speeds: 3 F/1 R. Floor-mounted gearshift. Semi-floating rear axle. Overall ratio: 2.41, 2.56, 2.73, 3.08:1. Hydraulic power front disc/rear drum brakes. Pressed steel wheels.
TECHNICAL: [S10] Manual, synchromesh transmission. Speeds: 4 F/1 R. Floor-mounted gearshift. Semi-floating rear axle. Overall ratio: 3.08, 3.42, 3.73, 4.11:1. Hydraulic, front disc/rear drum brakes. Pressed steel wheels.
TECHNICAL: [S10 Blazer] Manual, synchromesh transmission. Speeds: 4 F/1 R. Floor-mounted gearshift. Semi-floating rear axle. Overall ratio: 2.73, 3.08, 3.42, 3.73. Hydraulic power front disc/rear drum brakes. Pressed steel, 6 in. wheels.
TECHNICAL: [Astro] Manual, synchromesh transmission. Speeds: 4 F/1 R. Floor-mounted gearshift. Semi-floating rear axle. Overall ratio: 2.56, 2.73, 3.08, 3.42, 3.73, 4.11:1. Hydraulic disc front/rear drum brakes. Pressed steel wheels.
TECHNICAL: [G10/G20] Synchromesh/manual transmission. Speeds: 3 F/1 R. Column-mounted gearshift. Semi-floating rear axle. Hydraulic front disc/rear drum brakes. Pressed steel wheels.

TECHNICAL: [G30] Automatic, overdrive transmission. Speeds: 4 F/1R. Column-mounted gearshift. Full-floating rear axle. Overall ratio: 3.73, 4.10:1. Power front disc/rear drum brakes. Pressed steel wheels.

TECHNICAL: [C10 Suburban] Automatic with overdrive transmission. Speeds: 4 F/1 R. Column-mounted gearshift. Semi-floating rear axle. Overall ratio: 3.21, 3.42, 3.73, 4.10, 3.56:1. Power hydraulic front disc/rear drum brakes. Pressed steel wheels.

TECHNICAL: [C10] Manual, synchromesh transmission. Speeds: 3 F/1 R. Column-mounted gearshift. Semi-floating rear axle. Overall ratio: 2.73, 3.08, 3.42, 3.73:1. Hydraulic front disc/rear drum brakes. Pressed steel, 6.00 in. wide wheels.

TECHNICAL: [All C20/C30] Manual, synchromesh transmission. Speeds: 4 F/1 R. Floor-mounted gearshift. Rear axle: [C30/K30] full-floating; [others] semi-floating. Overall ratio: 3.23, 3.42, 3.73, 4.10, 4.56:1 (LE 8 engine and locking differential: 3.21:1).

TECHNICAL: [C20 Suburban] Manual, synchromesh (standard on C20/K10/K20) transmission. Speeds: 4 F/1 R. Floor-mounted gearshift. Semi-floating (full-floating with 454 V-8) rear axle. Overall ratio: 3.21, 3.42, 3.73, 4.10, 4.56:1. Power hydraulic front disc/rear drum brakes. Pressed steel wheels.

OPTIONS: [S10 Models] Gauge package, S10 ($55-$113). Tinted glass, S10 ($135-$190). Exterior mirrors, S10 ($50-$83). Speed control, S10 ($195). [ASTRO] Four-speed automatic transmission ($520). Four-passenger seating CL ($552); others ($634). Seven-passenger seating, CL ($1,195); others ($1,277). Eight-passenger seating, CL ($643); others ($593). Seatback recliner and dual armrests ($230). Custom high-back buckets, 8-passenger ($150); 5-passenger ($100). Front air-conditioning, base ($740); CL/CS ($697). Front and rear air-conditioning, CL/CS ($1249). Deluxe front/rear bumpers, base and CS ($122); CL ($72). Color-keyed bumpers, base and CS ($50). Increased cargo capacity, regular 4/5 passenger seats ($314). Heavy-duty radiator ($53); with transmission cooler ($112); with transmission cooler and air-conditioning ($171). Remote fuel filler release ($25). Rubber floor covering, base ($43). Gauge package, base, CS ($58). 100 amp. alternator ($30). Tinted glass, complete ($98); standard ($71). Deluxe grille, base and CS ($25). Halogen headlamps ($22). Engine block heater ($31). Rear heater, ($256). Deluxe heater ($43). Special two-tone ($237). Sport two-tone ($162). California emissions ($99). Optional axle ratio ($36). Locking differential ($238). Heavy-duty battery ($53). Spare tire carrier, base ($21). Engine oil cooler ($120). Roof console ($79). Power door locks ($198). Carpeting in CS ($111). Rear heater ($256). Complete body glass ($121). Tinted windshield ($38). Swing-out door glass ($55). Trailer wiring harness ($39). Dome and reading lamps ($31). Auxiliary lighting, base ($142); CS ($121). Dual deluxe mirrors ($50). Black bodyside moldings, base and CS ($55). Power windows and door locks ($388). Door edge guards ($17). Right-hand visor mirror, base ($48); CL/SC ($41). Protective interior panels ($25). AM radio ($112). AM/FM stereo, base ($243); CL/CS ($283). AM/FM stereo with electronic tuning, base ($424); CL/CS ($464). Above with quadrophonic, base ($574); CL/CS ($614). Heavy-duty front/rear shocks ($34). Cruise control ($195). Front stabilizer bar ($38). Power steering ($276). Tilt steering column ($115). Custom steering wheel, base and CS ($26). Power windows ($190). Positive stop rear door, base ($35). Left-hand front seat storage compartment ($35). Left- and right-hand front seat storage compartments ($70). Body striping ($75). 27-gal. fuel tank ($66). Cargo tie-downs ($30). Dead weight trailer hitch ($64). Heavy-duty trailering package, with front and rear air-conditioning ($471); without front and rear air-conditioning ($524). Light-duty trailering package ($103). Wheel trim rings, base, CS ($56). Rally wheels, base and CS ($88); CL ($48). Cast aluminum wheels, base and CS ($299); CL ($259). Intermittent wipers ($55). Tahoe/Sierra classic equipment, S10 ($595). Sport Gypsy equipment, S10 ($972). Seat Trim, S10 ($24). High-Country bucket seats, S10 ($295). Custom two-tone paint, S10 ($200). Special two-tone paint, S10 ($311). Sport two-tone paint, S10 ($227). Air-conditioning, S10 ($705). Console, S10 ($108). [Full-size C-K Trucks] Rear step bumper, Fleetside ($189). Chromed front bumper guards ($41). Exterior mirrors ($50-$94). Bodyside molding package ($115-$173). Rally wheels for C10/K10/K5 Blazer ($115). Styled wheels for C10/K10/K5 Blazer ($174). Cast aluminum wheels for C10/K10/K5 Blazer ($299). Radio: AM/AM/FM/AM/FM, clock, AM/FM stereo and stereo cassette, AM stereo/FM stereo, seek-and-scan ($112-$594). Scottsdale/High-Sierra C-K Series ($250). Silverado/Sierra Classic C-K Series ($671). Conventional two-tone C-K Series ($72). Special two-tone C-K Series ($327). Deluxe two-tone C-K Series/Fleetside ($184-$370). Custom two-tone C-K Series/Fleetside ($531). Special Big Dooley two-tone Fleetside, dual wheels ($426-$444). Deluxe front appearance package C-K Series ($109). All-weather air-conditioning C-K Series ($678-740). Chromed rear bumper C-K Series ($103). Silverado/Sierra classic package K Blazer ($1015). Special two-tone paint K Blazer ($170-$327). Exterior decor package K Blazer ($314-$471). Deluxe front appearance K Blazer ($109). Deluxe chromed bumpers K5 Blazer ($49). Bodyside moldings K5 Blazer ($115-$173). Scottsdale/High-Sierra package for Suburban ($311-$459). Silverado/Sierra Classic ($1,111-$1,259). [El Camino] Conquista package ($195). Air-conditioning ($750). Gauge package ($115). Sport mirrors ($61). Rally wheel rims ($56). Wire wheelcovers ($199).

1985 Chevrolet El Camino "Designer Series" Pickup

HISTORICAL: Introduced Sept. 21, 1984. Calendar year production: [Pickups] 430,600; [Step-Vans] 46,978; [Vans/Sportvans] 171,329. [Total all models] 1,325,491. Innovations: New Astro Van truck line introduced. El Camino has new 4.3 liter base V-6. New 2.5 liter base engine for S10 trucks with 4x4 drive. Custom two-toning extended to S10 pickups. New 4.3 liter Vortec Six also used in Chevy Vans as standard engine. Full-sized trucks adopt new grille styling. Every new 1985 light-duty Chevy truck delivered by a Chevrolet dealer in the U.S. came with a one-year, $10,000 seat belt insurance certificate from MIC General Insurance Corp. at no additional charge. Under the policy, $10,000 would be paid to the estate of any occupant suffering fatal injuries as a result of an accident involving that vehicle while wearing a GM seat belt. The 1985 sales catalog also stated, "For three and a half decades there have been more Chevy trucks in use than any other make."

1986 Chevrolet Silverado Fleetside Pickup (CMD)

1/2-TON S10 — MODEL S/SERIES 10 — FOUR/V-6: For 1986, Chevrolet's light-duty trucks were made little changed in terms of styling and trim packages. However, a number of technical refinements were made in practically all of the product lines. Getting a new high-tech instrument cluster was the compact S10 pickup. Both the standard 2.5 liter EFI (Electronic Fuel-Injected) engine or the optional 2.8 liter V-6 were changed for improved performance, fuel economy and durability. An optional TBI (Throttle Body Injection) system for the V-6 was another technical update. It boosted the horsepower rating by nine percent. New for the S10 Blazer was a redesigned instrument cluster, TBI V-6, low-pressure Delco/Bilstein gas shocks and new paint and trim options. Chevrolet advised that the 4x2 model was rising in popularity. The 4x4 Blazer Mini-trucks came with an Insta-Trac system. It let the driver shift from 4x2 mode to 4x4 high, and back again, without stopping. The stylized fender badges had an S done in red. At the rear, the taillights were framed in chrome and the large Chevrolet name was changed to a smaller name at the right-hand side of a tailgate trim panel. Standard, Durango, Tahoe and Sport trim treatments were available again. Trim options included Custom two-tone (second color below belt); Sport two-tone (second color on bottom below four-stripe decals or moldings) and Special two-tone (second color between beltline and lower feature line). The S10 Blazer's Custom vinyl interior had wider door panel pleats and brushed aluminum door panel trim plates.

1986 Chevrolet 3/4-Ton K20 Fleetside Custom Deluxe Pickup 4x4 (RCA)

1/2-TON EL CAMINO — MODEL W — Six/V-8: The El Camino featured a new instrument panel and revised gauge cluster graphics to modernize it. It continued to offer 35.5 cu. ft. of cargo capacity and a 1,250 lbs. payload. A four-speed automatic transmission with overdrive was made available with the standard 4.3 liter V-6. Both it and the three-speed manual gearbox were offered with this engine or the optional 5.0 liter V-8. El Caminos again had a 4.3 liter V-6 base engine. Standard grille was the same as last year. Also back was the El Camino Super Sport and the Conquista. The SS had an aero nose treatment. A non-functional power blister hood, dummy side pipes and pickup bed rails were optional. Model identification decals were used on the doors, above the lower feature line. Conquista and SS Sport decors each included distinctive two-tones.

1/2-TON ASTRO VAN — Model M/Series 10 — V-6: The Astro Van was back with virtually no changes. It was a compact van featuring a standard V-6 engine, five-speed manual transmission, and rear drive axle. The Mini-Van body featured a sloping hood and aerodynamically rounded front end with wraparound parking lamps, single rectangular headlights and a grille with seven horizontal bars. Each bar decreased slightly in width, from top to bottom. A yellow bow tie badge was in the center. Additional standard equipment included an engine cover storage box; front armrests; swing-out side windows; black rubber floor covering; high-back bucket seats; five-passenger seating; and P195/75R15 all-season steel-belted radial tires. CS trim added color-keyed floor coverings; side window defoggers; inside fuel door release; lighted vanity mirrors; and an under-the-floor spare tire carrier. The optional CL package included added such features as bumper rub strips; a trip odometer; gauges; custom steering wheel; wheel trim rings; auxiliary lighting; cigar lighter; and carpets. Cargo van versions had a standard low-back driver's seat in saddle color; black rubber floor covering; solid panel bodysides; and the same arrangement of a sliding right-hand side cargo door with double panel type rear doors. Custom cloth upholstery was optional. Paint treatments included 10 solid colors; special two-tones (with decal strips at beltline and secondary color below the belt) and Sport two-tones (with secondary color on lower body perimeter). The Astro name appeared on both entry doors, just behind the front wheel openings. Taillamps were vertical units positioned on the rear body corners just below the beltline. The rear doors of all models had large windows. Standard power for the commercial versions was Chevy's 2.5 liter Tech IV powerplant with Electronic Fuel-Injection. The Vortec Six, with TBI and a five-speed manual transmission, was the standard power team for Astro passenger vans in 1986. This made them the most powerful of any small vans

1986 Chevrolet 1/2-Ton S10 Blazer 4x4 Utility Hardtop (CMD)

1/2-TON; 3/4-TON; 1-TON VAN/HI-CUBE VAN — MODEL G/SERIES 10; 20; 30 — SIX/V-8: Sportvans and Chevy Vans were again offered in G10/G20/G30 Series, with engines including the Vortec Six, a choice of two gas V-8s and Chevy's 6.2 liter diesel V-8 on G20/G30 models. One change for the season was that the conventional sliding door could be replaced, at no extra cost, by the 60/40 swing-out type incorporating a new sliding 90-degree door-check system. This change prevented fouling between the right front side door and the forward side swing-out door. G30 Hi-Cube vans again come in 10 ft. (125 in. wheelbase) and 12 ft. (146 in. wheelbase) models, with RV and Commercial Cutaway vans available on both of these chassis as well. All manual transmissions (three-speed type standard in G10/G20) came with floor-mounted gearshifts.

1/2-TON BLAZER — MODEL K (4x4) — SIX/V-8: Full-size Blazers, for 1986, had new molded front bucket seats with folding seatbacks. The cloth trim option included a reclining seatback feature and the passenger seat had the same slide-forward, easy-entry system previously used on the S10 Blazer. Three new paint colors, Canyon copper metallic, Nevada gold metallic and Steel gray metallic, were released. A new Steel gray top was designed expressly to go with the third added paint scheme. A body color panel ran between upper and lower grilles and the grilles had only a single horizontal bar intersected by seven vertical bars. The headlight housings had a vertical break with rectangular parking lamps were stacked atop each other again. An amber-colored parking lamp was standard on the bottom, but when Halogen high-beams were ordered, the parking lamps moved behind the lower grille. Features included fluidic wiper arms with built-in washers and standard color-keyed hardtops in a choice of colors or black and white. Custom Deluxe interiors were standard, with Silverado trim available at extra cost. Special two-tone and Exterior Decor packages were optional.

1986 Chevrolet 1-Ton C30 Custom Deluxe "Big Dooley" Fleetside (RCA)

1/2-TON; 3/4-TON; 1-TON CONVENTIONAL — MODEL C (4x2); MODEL K (4x4)/SERIES 10; 20; 30 — SIX/V-8: Continuing as standard equipment on full-sized Chevy pickups was the Vortec Six. Swirl-port cylinder heads helped it pump out 155 hp and 230 lbs.-ft. of torque. "It is the most powerful standard engine ever offered in a Chevrolet pickup," advised a Chevrolet press release. An electric booster fan, mounted ahead of the radiator, was a new feature used with the optional 7.4 liter V-8. The 5.0 liter and 5.7 liter gas V-8s, as well as the 6.2 liter diesel V-8, were used again. The diesel trucks came with a 50,000 mile warranty and had up to 148 hp (on trucks with over 8,500 lbs. GVW ratings.) The Suburban began its second half-century in 1986. The same three new colors available for the big Blazer were offered for the Suburban as well. New outboard armrests were made a part of the year's reclining bucket seat option. According to Chevy, the Suburban could hold nine passengers and 40.8 cu. ft. of luggage behind the third seat when outfitted for use as a station wagon. With the second seat folded and the optional rear seat removed, it became a truck with a 167 cu. ft. cargo area and payload capacity up to 3,911 lbs. The trucks continued to come in a wide range of choices including 1/2-, 3/4- and 1-ton series with long or short cargo boxes; Fleetside or Step-Side styling; Crew or Bonus cabs and 4x2 or 4x4 drive. A real "Country Cadillac" was the "Big Dooley." Custom Deluxe, Scottsdale and Silverado trims were again available. Custom Deluxe trim was standard. Scottsdales had color-keyed floor mats and added cowl and headliner insulation. Door-to-door carpeting and velour or grained vinyl upholstery were featured with Silverado interiors. Special two-tone and Exterior Decor finish options were available. The latter included a hood ornament. End-gate and panel door options were still cataloged for Suburbans, in which a V-8 was standard engine.

3/4-TON; 1-TON FORWARD-CONTROL — MODEL P/SERIES 20; 30 — SIX/V-8: Steel-bodied and aluminum-bodied Step-Vans again came in two lines. The steel models came as CP208/CP308 models on a 125 in. wheelbase. CP210/CP310 models on the 133 in. wheelbase and as CP314 models on the 157 in. wheelbase. Aluminum body models could be had in the same configurations, plus a model CP318 version with a 178 in. wheelbase. Load lengths were: [CP208] 129.6 in.; [CP210/CP310] 153.6 in.; [CP314] 177.6 in. and [CP318] 178 in. Series 30 Hi-Cube models came in 10 ft. models on the 125 in. wheelbase or 12 ft. models on the 146 in. wheelbase.

1986 Chevrolet 1/2-Ton K10 Custom Deluxe Step-Side Pickup (RCA)

I.D. DATA: Location of serial number: The VIN is stamped on a plate attached to the left top of the instrument panel on C/K/G Series. On P Series the plate is attached to the front of the dash and the panel to the left of the steering column. The first symbol indicates country of origin: 1=U.S.; 2=Canada; J=Japan. The second symbol indicates manufacturer: G=General Motors; 8=Isuzu. The third symbol indicates make: A=Chevrolet bus; B=Chevrolet (incomplete); C=Chevrolet truck; Y=LUV (incomplete); Z=LUV truck; 8=Chevy MPV. The fourth symbol indicates GVW rating (and brake system): B=3,001 lbs.-4,000 lbs. (hydraulic); C=4,001 lbs.-5,000 lbs. (hydraulic), etc. through K for hydraulic brakes. The fifth symbol indicates line and chassis type: C=Conventional cab (including Blazer and Suburban) 4x2; G=Chevy Van and Sportvan 4x2; K=Conventional cab (including Blazer and Suburban) 4x4; L=LUV 4x2; R=LUV 4x4; P=Forward-Control; S=Conventional Cab 4x2; W=El Camino 4x2; Z=Special body 4x2. The sixth symbol indicates series: 1=1/2-ton; 2=3/4-ton; 3=1-ton; 8=El Camino. The seventh symbol indicates body type: 0=El Camino Pickup-Delivery; 1=Hi-Cube and Cutaway Vans; 2=Forward-Control; 3=Four-door cab; 4=Two-door cab; 5=Van; 6=Suburban; 7=Motorhome chassis; 8=Blazer Utility; 9=Stake. The eighth symbol indicated engine. Engine codes were generally the same as 1983. The ninth symbol was a check digit. The 10th symbol indicated model year: G=1986. The 11th symbol indicated the assembly plant: A=Lakewood, Ga.; B=Baltimore, Md.; C=Southgate, Calif.; D=Doraville, Ga.; E=Linden, N.J.; F=Flint, Mich.; G=Framingham, Mass.; H=Flint, Mich.; J=Janesville, Wis.; K=Leeds, Mo.; L=Van Nuys, Calif.; M=Lansing, Mich.; N=Norwood, Ohio; P=Pontiac, Mich.; R=Arlington, Texas; S=St. Louis, Mo.; T=Tarrytown, N.Y.; V=GMC, Pontiac, Mich.; W=Willow Run, Mich.; X=Fairfax, Va.; Y=Wilmington, Dela.; Z=Fremont, Calif.; O=GMAD, Pontiac, Mich.; 1=Oshawa, Canada; 2=Moraine, Ohio; 2=Ste. Therese, Quebec, Canada; 3=Chevrolet-Detroit, Mich.; 3=St. Eustache, Quebec, Canada; 4=Orion Plant, Pontiac, Mich.; 4=Scarborough, Ontario, Canada; 5=Bowling Green, Ken.; 5=London, Ontario, Canada; 6=Oklahoma City, Okla.; 7=Lordstown, Ohio; 8=Shreveport, La.; 8=Fujisawa, Japan; 9=Cadillac, Detroit, Mich. (Note: Trucks were not built at all factories). Symbols 12-17 were the production sequence number starting at 100001. Ending numbers not available. Engine number location: [Six] located on pad at right-hand side of cylinder block at rear of distributor. [V-8] located on pad at right front side of cylinder block.

1986 Chevrolet 1/2-Ton Astro CS Passenger Mini-Van (CMD)

Model	Body Type	Price	Weight	Prod. Total
El Camino — 1/2-Ton — 117.1 in. w.b. — V-6				
W80	Sedan Pickup	9572	3234	—
W80	Super Sport Pickup	9885	3239	—
S10 Pickup — 1/2-Ton — 108.3 in. w.b. — V-6				
S14	Fleetside EL	5990	—	—
S14	Fleetside	6999	2574	—
S10 Pickup — 1/2-Ton — 122.9 in. w.b. — V-6				
S14	Fleetside	7234	2645	—
S14	Maxi-Cab	7686	2713	—
S10 Blazer 4x4 — 1/2-Ton — 100.5 in. w.b. — V-6				
T18	Utility Hardtop	10,698	3152	—
*Deduct for 4x2 Model S10 Blazer.				
Astro — 1/2-Ton — 111 in. w.b. — V-6				
M15	Cargo Van	8431	3258	—
M15	Passenger Van	9037	3434	—
M15	CS Passenger Van	9492	3509	—
M15	CL Passenger Van	10,216	3569	—
Chevy Van 10 — 1/2-Ton — 110 in. w.b. — V-6				
G15	Chevy Van	8626	3700	—
G15	Sportvan	10,232	4052	—
Chevy Van 10 — 1/2-Ton — 125 in. w.b. — V-6				
G15	Bonaventure	11,290	4153	—
G15	Beauville	11,622	4196	—
Chevy Van 20 — 3/4-Ton — 110 in. w.b. — V-6				
G25	Chevy Van	9257	3786	—

Chevy Van 20 — 3/4-Ton — 125 in. w.b. — V-6

G25	Sportvan	10,655	4244	—
G25	Bonaventure	11,482	4345	—
G25	Beauville	11,813	4388	—

Chevy Van 30 — 1-Ton — 125 in. w.b. — V-8

G35	Chevy Van (V-6)	11,128	4526	—
G35	Sportvan	13,173	5117	—
G35	Bonaventure	14,001	5218	—
G35	Beauville	14,331	5261	—
G35	Cutaway Van	10,204	3906	—

Hi-Cube Van — 1-Ton — 125 in. w.b. — V-8

G31	Hi-Cube 10 ft.	13,492	5209	—

Hi-Cube Van — 1-Ton — 146 in. w.b. — V-8

G31	Hi-Cube 12 ft.	14,803	5886	—

K10 Blazer 4x4 — 1/2-Ton — 106.5 in. w.b. — V-8

K18	Utility Hardtop	12,034	4444	—

C10 Pickup — 1/2-Ton — 117.5 in. w.b. — V-6

C14	Step-Side 6.5 ft.	7904	3385	—
C14	Fleetside 6.5 ft.	7764	3432	—

C10 Pickup — 1/2-Ton — 131.5 in. w.b. — V-6

C14	Fleetside 8 ft.	7938	3595	—

C10 Suburban — 1/2-Ton — 129.5 in. w.b. — V-8

C16	Suburban	11,476	4279	—

* Add for CK10 Pickups/Suburbans with 4x4.

C20 Pickup — 3/4-Ton — 131.5 in. w.b. — V-6

C24	Chassis & Cab	9667	3570	—
C24	Step-Side	9253	3930	—
C24	Fleetside	9113	3992	—

C20 Pickup — 3/4-Ton — 164.5 in. w.b. — L6

C24	Bonus Cab Pickup	11,103	4773	—
C24	Crew Cab Pickup	11,451	4834	—

C20 Suburban — 3/4-Ton — 129.5 in. w.b. — V-8

C24	Suburban	12,297	4771	—

* Add for CK20 Pickups/Suburbans with 4x4.

P20 Step-Van — 3/4-Ton — 125/133 in. w.b. — 6 cyl.

P22	3/4-Ton Steel Panel	14,338	5869	—

C30 Pickup — 1-Ton — 131.5 in. w.b. — L-6

C34	Chassis & Cab	9843	4011	—
C34	Step-Side	10,381	4426	—
C34	Fleetside	10,242	4426	—

C30 Pickup — 1-Ton — 164.5 in. w.b. — L-6

C34	Chassis & Bonus Cab	10,901	4451	—
C33	Fleetside & Bonus Cab	11,282	4862	—
C33	Chassis & Crew Cab	11,253	4512	—
C33	Fleetside & Crew Cab	11,633	4923	—

* Add for CK30 Pickups/Suburbans with 4x4.

P30 Step-Vans — 1-Ton — 133/178 in. w.b. — 6 cyl.

P32	1-Ton Steel Panel	14,422	6022	—

NOTE 1: All C20 and C30 Pickups have 8 ft. pickup boxes.

NOTE 2: Model year production: [S10 Maxi-Cabs] 34,865; [Other S10 cab models] 138,090; [S10 Blazer] 132,977; [Astro] 140,729; [C10/K10 cab models] 282,192; [C20/K20 regular cab models] 75,487; [C30/K30 regular cab models] 39,823; [C20/C30/K20/K30 Crew Cabs] 17,405; [K10 Blazer] 37,310; [C10/K10/C20/K20 Suburbans] 61,242; [El Camino] 16,229; [Chevy Van] 125,077; [Sportvan] 16,883. Figures include trucks built in U.S. and Canada for the U.S. market.

NOTE 3: The percentage of above trucks with four-wheel drive, by model, was: [S10 Maxi-Cabs] 26 percent; [Other S10 cab models] 24 percent; [S10 Blazer] 75 percent; [Astro] 0; [C10/K10 cab models] 31 percent; [C20/K20 regular cab models] 43 percent; [C30/K30 regular cab models] 20 percent; [C20/C30/K20/K30 Crew Cabs] 0; [K10 Blazer] 100 percent; [C10/K10/C20/K20 Suburbans] 37 percent; [El Camino] 0; [Chevy Van] 0; [Sportvan] 0.

1986 Chevrolet 1/2-Ton C10 Fleetside Pickup (OCW)

ENGINE: (Diesel). Inline. OHV. Four-cylinder. Cast iron block. Bore & stroke: 3.46 x 3.62 in. Displacement: 137 cid (2.2 liter). Brake horsepower: 62 at 4300 rpm. Taxable horsepower: 19.50. Torque: 96 lbs.-ft. at 2200 rpm. Hydraulic valve lifters. VIN Code S. Manufactured by Isuzu of Japan. Diesel optional in S10 Pickups and Blazers.

ENGINE: (Gas). Inline. OHV. Four-cylinder. Cast iron block. Bore & stroke: 4.0 x 3.0 in. Displacement: 151 cid (2.5 liter). Compression ratio: 9.0:1. Brake horsepower: 92 at 4400 rpm. Taxable horsepower: 25.6. Torque: 134 lbs.-ft. at 2800 rpm. Hydraulic valve lifters. Carburetor: Two-barrel. VIN Code E; manufactured by Pontiac. Standard in S10 Blazers and Pickups. Also standard in Astro commercial vans.

ENGINE: (Gas). Vee-block. OHV. Six-cylinder. Cast iron block. Bore & stroke: 3.5 x 2.99 in. Displacement: 173 cid (2.8 liter). Compression ratio: 8.5:1. Brake horsepower: 125 at 4800 rpm. Taxable horsepower: 29.4. Torque: 150 lbs.-ft. at 2200 rpm. Hydraulic valve lifters. Induction system: TBI. VIN Code B. Manufactured by Chevrolet. Optional in S10 Blazer and Pickups.

ENGINE: (Gas). Vee-block. OHV. Six-cylinder. Cast iron block. Bore & stroke: 4.0 x 3.48 in. Displacement: 262 cid (4.3 liter). Compression ratio: 9.3:1. Brake horsepower: 140 at 4000 rpm. Taxable horsepower: 38.4. Torque: 225 lbs.-ft. at 2000 rpm. Hydraulic valve lifters. Carburetor: Two-barrel. VIN Code Z. Manufactured by Chevrolet. Standard in El Camino.

ENGINE: (Gas). Vee-block. OHV. Six-cylinder. Cast iron block. Bore & stroke: 4.0 x 3.48 in. Displacement: 262 cid (4.3 liter). Compression ratio: 9.5:1. Brake horsepower: 155 at 4000 rpm. Taxable horsepower: 38.4. Torque: 230 lbs.-ft at 2400 rpm. Hydraulic valve lifters. Induction system: TBI. VIN Code N. Manufactured by Chevrolet. Standard in full-size pickups and Blazer and Suburbans and Vans.

ENGINE: (Gas). Inline. OHV. Six-cylinder. Cast iron block. Bore & stroke: 3.88 x 4.12 in. Displacement: 292 cid (4.8 liter). Brake horsepower: 115 at 4000 rpm. Taxable horsepower: 36.13. Torque: 210 lbs.-ft. at 2800 rpm. Hydraulic valve lifters. Carburetor: Two-barrel. VIN Code T. Manufactured by Chevrolet. Standard in Step-Vans and Crew Cab/Bonus Cab Pickups.

ENGINE: (Gas). Vee-block. OHV. Eight-cylinder. Cast iron block. Bore & stroke: 3.74 x 3.48 in. Displacement: 305 cid (5.0 liter). Compression ratio: 8.6:1. Brake horsepower: 155 at 4000 rpm. Taxable horsepower: 44.76. Torque: 245 lbs.-ft. at 1600 rpm. Hydraulic valve lifters. Carburetor: Four-barrel. VIN Code F. Manufactured by Chevrolet. Optional in full-size Pickups, Blazers, Suburban and El Camino. Also optional in light-duty vans with under 8500 lbs. GVWs and El Camino.

ENGINE: (Gas). Vee-block. OHV. Eight-cylinder. Cast iron block. Bore & stroke: 3.74 x 3.48 in. Displacement: 305 cid (5.0 liter). Brake horsepower: 160 at 4400 rpm. Taxable horsepower: 44.76. Torque: 235 lbs.-ft. at 2000 rpm. Hydraulic valve lifters. Carburetor: Four-barrel. VIN Code H. Manufactured by Chevrolet. Optional in full-sized pickups, Blazer, Suburban and El Camino. Also optional in light-duty vans with under 8,500 lbs. GVW.

ENGINE: (Gas). Vee-block. OHV. Eight-cylinder. Cast iron block. Bore & stroke: 4.0 x 3.48 in. Displacement: 350 cid (5.7 liter). Compression ratio: 8.3:1. Brake horsepower: 160 at 3800 rpm. Taxable horsepower: 51.2. Torque: 275 lbs.-ft. at 2400 rpm. Hydraulic valve lifters. Carburetor: Four-barrel. VIN Code A. This engine manufactured by various GM divisions. Optional in Pickups, full-sized Blazer and Suburbans with heavy-duty emissions.

ENGINE: (Gas). Vee-block. OHV. Eight-cylinder. Cast iron block. Bore & stroke: 4.0 x 3.48 in. Displacement: 350 cid (5.7 liter). Compression ratio: 8.2:1. Brake horsepower: 165 at 3800 rpm. Taxable horsepower: 51.2. Torque: 275 lbs.-ft. at 1600 rpm. Hydraulic valve lifters. Carburetor: Four-barrel. VIN Code L. Manufactured by Chevrolet. Optional in full-sized pickups and Blazers and Suburbans. Also optional in light-duty vans under 8,500 lbs. GVW.

ENGINE: (Gas). Vee-block. OHV. Eight-cylinder. Cast iron block. Bore & stroke: 4.0 x 3.48 in. Displacement: 350 cid (5.7 litre). Brake horsepower: 185 at 4000 rpm. Taxable horsepower: 51.2. Torque: 285 lbs.-ft. at 2400 rpm. Carburetor: Four-barrel. VIN Code M. Manufactured by Chevrolet. Optional in full-size pickups, Blazers and Suburbans.

ENGINE: (Diesel). Vee-block. OHV. Eight-cylinder. Cast iron block. Bore & stroke: 3.98 x 3.82 in. Displacement: 379 cid (6.2 liter). Brake horsepower: 130 at 3600 rpm. Taxable horsepower: 50.69. Torque: 240 lbs.-ft. at 2000 rpm. Hydraulic valve lifters. Carburetor: Four-barrel. VIN Code C. Manufactured by Chevrolet. Diesel option.

ENGINE: (Diesel). Vee-block. OHV. Eight-cylinder. Cast iron block. Bore & stroke: 3.98 x 3.82 in. Displacement: 379 cid (6.2 liter). Brake horsepower: 148 at 3600 rpm. Taxable horsepower: 50.69. Torque: 246 lbs.-ft. at 2000 rpm. Hydraulic valve lifters. Carburetor: Four-barrel. VIN Code J. Manufactured by Chevrolet. Diesel option.

ENGINE: (Gas). Vee-block. OHV. Eight-cylinder. Cast iron block. Bore & stroke: 4.25 x 4.0 in. Displacement: 454 cid (7.4 liter). Brake horsepower: 240 at 3800 rpm. Taxable horsepower: 57.8. Torque: 375 lbs.-ft. at 3200 rpm. Hydralic valve lifters. Carburetor: Four-barrel. VIN Code W. Manufactured by Chevrolet. Available for motorhome chassis.

1986 Chevrolet Fleetside Indy 500 Pace Truck (IMSC/JLM)

CHASSIS [El Camino]: Wheelbase: 117.1 in. Overall length: 201.6 in. Height: 53.8 in. Tires: P205/75R14

CHASSIS [S10 Pickup]: Wheelbase: 108.3 in. 122.9 in. Overall length: 178.2 in./194.2 in. Height: 61.3 in. Tires: P195/75R14.

CHASSIS: [S10 Blazer]: Wheelbase: 100.5 in. Overall length: 170.3 in. Height: 64.7 in. P195/75R15.

CHASSIS [Astro Van]: Wheelbase: 111 in. Overall length: 176.8 in. Height: 74.5 in. Tires: P195/75R15.

CHASSIS [G10 Vans]: Wheelbase: 110 in./125 in. Overall length: 178.2 in./202.2 in. Height: 79.4 in. Tires: [Chevy Van] P195/75R15; [Others] P205/75R15.

CHASSIS [G20 Vans]: Wheelbase: 110 in./125 in. Overall length: 178.2 in./202.2 in. Height: 79.4 in. Tires: [Chevy Van] P225/75R15; [Others] P235/75R15.

CHASSIS [G30 Vans]: Wheelbase: 125 in. Overall length: 202.2 in. Height: 79.4 in. Tires: [Chevy Van] 8.75R16.5C; [Others] 8.75R16.5D.

CHASSIS [Hi-Cube Van]: Wheelbase: 125 in./146 in. Tires: 8.75 x 16.5D.

CHASSIS [K10 Blazer]: Wheelbase: 106.5 in. Overall length: 184.8 in. Height: 73.8 in. Tires: P215/75R15.

CHASSIS [C10]: Wheelbase: 117.5 in./131.5 in. Overall length: 193.5 in./212.2 in. Height: 69.2 in. Tires: [Pickups] P195/74R15; [Suburban] P235/75R15.

CHASSIS [C20/C30]: Wheelbase: 131.5 in./164.5 in. Overall length: 212.2 in./246.4 in. Height: 72.2 in. Tires: [C20 Pickups] LT235/85R16C; [C20 Suburbans/Bonus/Crew] (Front) LT235/85R16D (Rear) LT235/85R16E. The C30 pickups also used the latter sizes.

CHASSIS [Step-Vans]: Wheelbase: 125/133/178 in. Tires: LT215/85R16C.

TECHNICAL: Same as 1985, except the El Camino now offers both the three-speed and four-speed (with overdrive) automatic transmissions with both the 4.3 liter V-6 and optional 5.0 liter V-8. The 4.3 liter engine and four-speed automatic with overdrive was standard. Also, the five-speed manual transmission (made available in May, 1985) was now standard in Astro passenger vans.

OPTIONS: [S10 Models] Gauge package, S10 ($55-$113). Tinted glass, S10 ($135-$190). Exterior mirrors, S10 ($50-$83). Speed control, S10 ($195). [ASTRO] Four-speed automatic transmission ($520). Four-passenger seating CL ($552); Others ($634). Seven-passenger seating, CL ($1,195); Others ($1,277). Eight-passenger seating, CL ($643); Others ($593). Seatback recliner and dual armrests ($230). Custom high-back buckets, 8-passenger ($150); 5-passenger ($100). Front air-conditioning, base ($740); CL/CS ($697). Front and rear air-conditioning, CL/CS ($1,249). Deluxe front/rear bumpers, base and CS ($122); CL ($72). Color-keyed bumpers, base and CS ($50). Increased cargo capacity, regular 4/5 passenger seats ($314). Heavy-duty radiator ($53); with transmission cooler ($112); with transmission cooler and air-conditioning ($171). Remote fuel filler release ($25). Rubber floor covering, base ($43). Gauge package, base and CS ($58). 100 amp. alternator ($30). Tinted glass, complete ($98); standard ($71). Deluxe grille, base and CS ($25). Halogen headlamps ($22). Engine block heater ($31). Rear heater, ($256). Deluxe heater ($43). Special two-tone ($237). Sport two-tone ($162). California emissions ($99). Optional axle ratio ($36). Locking differential ($238). Heavy-duty battery ($53). Spare tire carrier, base ($21). Engine oil cooler ($120). Power door locks ($198). Carpeting in CS ($111). Rear heater ($256). Complete body glass ($121). Tinted windshield ($38). Swing-out door glass ($55). Trailer wiring harness ($39). Dome and reading lamps ($31). Auxiliary lighting, base ($142); CS ($121). Dual deluxe mirrors ($50). Black bodyside moldings, base and CS ($55). Power windows and door locks ($388). Door edge guards ($17). Right-hand visor mirror, base ($48); CL/SC ($41). Protective interior panels ($25). AM radio ($112). AM/FM stereo, base ($243); CL/CS ($283). AM/FM stereo with electronic tuning, base ($424); CL/CS ($464). Above with quadraphonic, base ($574); CL/CS ($614). Heavy-duty front/rear shocks ($34). Cruise control ($195). Front stabilizer bar ($38). Power steering ($276). Tilt steering column ($115). Custom steering wheel, base and CS ($26). Power windows ($190). Positive stop rear door, base ($35). Left-hand front seat storage compartment ($35). Left- and right-hand front seat storage compartments ($70). Body striping ($75). 27-gal. fuel tank ($66). Cargo tie-downs ($30). Dead weight trailer hitch ($64). Heavy-duty trailering package, with front and rear air-conditioning ($471); without front and rear air-conditioning ($524). Light-duty trailering package ($103). Wheel trim rings, base and CS ($56). Rally wheels, base and CS ($88); CL ($48). Cast aluminum wheels, base and CS ($299); CL ($259). Intermittent wipers ($55). Tahoe/Sierra classic equipment, S10 ($595). Sport Gypsy equipment, S10 ($972). Seat Trim, S10 ($24). High-Country bucket seats, S10 ($295). Custom two-tone paint, S10 ($200). Special two-tone paint, S10 ($311). Sport two-tone paint, S10 ($227). Air-conditioning, S10 ($705). Console, S10 ($108). [Full-sized C-K Trucks] Rear step bumper, Fleetside ($189). Chromed front bumper guards ($41). Exterior mirrors ($50-$94). Bodyside molding package ($115-$173). Rally wheels for C10/K10/K5 Blazer ($115). Styled wheels for C10/K10/K5 Blazer ($174). Cast aluminum wheels for C10/K10/K5 Blazer ($299). Radio: AM/AM/FM/AM/FM, clock, AM/FM stereo and stereo cassette, AM stereo/FM stereo, seek-and-scan ($112-$594). Scottsdale/High-Sierra C-K Series ($250). Silverado/Sierra Classic C-K Series ($671). Conventional two-tone C-K Series ($72). Special two-tone C-K Series ($327). Deluxe two-tone C-K Series/Fleetside ($184-$370). Custom two-tone C-K Series/Fleetside ($531). Special Big Dooley two-tone Fleetside, dual wheels ($426-$444). Deluxe front appearance package C-K Series ($109). All-weather air-conditioning C-K Series ($678-740). Chromed rear bumper C-K Series ($103). Silverado/Sierra classic package K Blazer ($1015). Special two-tone paint K Blazer ($170-$327). Exterior decor package K Blazer ($314-$471). Deluxe front appearance K Blazer ($109). Deluxe chromed bumpers K5 Blazer ($49). Bodyside moldings K5 Blazer ($115-$173). Scottsdale/High-Sierra package for Suburban ($311-$459). Silverado/Sierra Classic ($1,111-$1,259). [El Camino] Conquista package ($195). Air-conditioning ($750). Gauge package ($115). Sport mirrors ($61). Rally wheel rims ($56). Wire wheelcovers ($199).

HISTORICAL: Introduced fall, 1985. Sales: [November, 1985-November, 1986]. [Chevy Van] 139,338; [Sportvan] 19,455; [Astro] 95,701; [S10] 195,620; [S10 Blazer] 170,742; [El Camino] 19,231; [Blazer] 41,866; [Suburban] 53,842; [Pickups] 438,422; [Total Chevrolet] 1,174,217. Innovations: Electronic fuel-injection used for 2.8 liter gas V-6 for nine percent horsepower boost. New high-tech instrument cluster for many models. Vortec Six has increased horsepower. Diesel V-8 gets durable steel crankshaft, modular iron crankshaft, cast-aluminum pistons and glow-plug system for fast cold-engine starts. Five-speed manual transmission standardized for Astro. New sliding 90-degree door check system made no-cost option on vans. The Chevrolet Astro Van was included in a special "Century of the Automobile" display at the 1986 Iola Old Car Show. Chevrolet kicked-off a year long celebration of its 75th year as an automaker in 1986. Of course, the 75th anniversary of Chevrolet trucks is 1993.

CROSLEY

1940-1962

1941 Crosley 1/4-Ton Model CB-41-W Covered Wagon (Donald Mizner)

By William D. Siuru, Jr.

In 1939, millionaire Powell Crosley started his automobile company. He built two-cylinder, air-cooled minicars in the days of 25-cents-a-gallon gas and $700 Chevrolets. They were not an overnight success. By 1940, light-duty trucks were added to the line.

"Here's the truck that makes sense and makes money on service and deliveries," read the sales literature. "Low cost, low operating cost, parks where no other truck can park. Gives you 35 to 50 miles on a gallon of gasoline."

Introduced in mid-1939, as a 1940 model, there was a fancy Parkway Delivery truck. The line also included a station wagon, which was considered a commercial vehicle. By the time the 1941 line bowed, in mid-1940, a Pickup, Panel and "Covered Wagon" had been added for truck buyers. These, like the cars, were powered by the twin-cylinder Waukesha engine. All rode a diminutive 80 in. wheelbase.

Critics scoffed. They said the little trucks were unsuitable for cargo carrying chores, but Crosley saw them as a modern replacement for the basket-equipped delivery bikes used by many small businesses. Powell Crosley felt that light-duty hauling had a place in the nation's commerce system.

Crosley was a good promoter. He introduced the Covered Wagon at Macy's department store in New York City. Cannonball Baker drove one of these on a cross-country

endurance run. Nevertheless, despite fame and fanfare, this model found few buyers. It was dropped in 1942, by which time it had been renamed the "Garden Wagon."

Shortly after the outbreak of World War II, Crosley took a shot at making a prototype military vehicle. He hoped to land a lucrative government contract. It was based on U.S. Army specifications for a 1/4-ton reconnaissance car; the same specifications which led to development of the Jeep. Crosley's version was called the Pup. It was intended for use by the U.S. Navy. The few that were made are now considered collectible items.

During the war, Crosley stopped car and truck production and switched to war goods manufacturing. The company developed a four-cylinder, overhead camshaft engine for the navy. It had unusual block construction of brazed copper and sheet metal and was used in refrigeration, air conditioning and aircraft applications. This COBRA engine was put in some early postwar cars and trucks. It was soon discovered to be prone to electrolysis problems that caused holes to form in the cylinders. A new CIBA (Cast Iron Block) engine was phased-in during 1946.

Trucks were not included in Crosley's 1946 model offerings, but returned in force the next season. They were completely revised, but still very small vehicles. The body was all new. Also new was the more conventional CIBA water-cooled powerplant, running gear and chassis components.

136

The postwar truck-line consisted of Pickup, Panel (a station wagon with blanked-out rear side windows) and two chassis configurations (with flat-face cowl or Chassis & Cab) that could be customized to meet the needs of the customer. A relatively popular model built off the chassis was a miniature fire engine suited for use in industrial factories.

Even though Crosley trucks weighed about one-third as much as other contemporary full-sized models from other makers, they were rated at a full 1/4-ton capacity. Where they came up short, however, was in the cargo capacity department. Being over 15 in. shorter than a Volkswagen Beetle, they were limited in the size of load they could carry.

Powell Crosley was the first to admit that his trucks were designed for inner-city use by commercial buyers whose demands were small: grocers, repairmen, and flower shops. They turned in a mere 15 ft. radius and required half as much parking space as a full-sized truck. Their economy benefits couldn't be bettered and initial prices were as low as $800.

A major restyling took place in 1949. It was seen on the two trucks, a Pickup and Panel, offered that year. A sales brochure described the panel as, "the most practical delivery truck on the streets" based on its ability to move through traffic with ease. Both models were rated for 1/4-ton payloads and sold for under $900. By way of comparison, a 1949 Chevrolet 1/2-ton Pickup listed for $1,253, a Dodge for $1,213 and a Ford for $1,302.

A new creation called the Farm-O-Road joined the line in 1950. This was an improved version of the Pup and had a 63 in. wheelbase, fold-down windshield and open two-passenger utility body. It came in pickup or dump models with hydraulic assist on the draw-bar available as a $150 option. Power-take-off attachments were provided front and rear. The Warner gear transmission featured six forward speeds. As the name implies, it could be used as a farm tractor or for road work. Only about 2,000 of these were sold.

In mid-1952, Crosley was sold to General Tire & Rubber Co. Apparently, a few leftover vehicles, including trucks, were sold and titled as 1953 models. Instead of continuing production, the new owner wrote the acquisition off as a tax loss and sold its rights on several patents to other firms.

Eventually, Crofton Diesel Engine Co. purchased rights to the powerplant. W.B. Crofton hired a man named Robert W. Jones to work out a complete redesign of the Farm-O-Road. The result was an improved version of the utility vehicle. From 1959 to 1961, some 200 of these new Crofton Bugs were produced and sold by the San Diego, Calif. company.

Powell Crosley, Jr. passed away in 1961, about the same time that the last Crofton Bugs were available. In his 74 years he had been involved in many businesses: appliances, broadcasting, baseball and automaking. Unfortunately, his light-duty truck venture seems to have taken a back seat to the others. Nevertheless, Crosley trucks are very popular with commercial vehicle collectors today, especially collectors with limited storage room.

1947 Crosley Pickup Truck (OCW)

1948 Crosley Fire Truck (OCW)

1941 Crosley Commercial Station Wagon (OCW)

1947 Crosley Pickup Truck (OCW)

Standard Catalog of Light-Duty Trucks

1948 Crosley Pickup Truck (OCW)

137

1948 Crosley Commercial Station Wagon (OCW)

1948 Crosley Panel Truck (OCW)

1950 Crosley Farm-O-Road Utility (VAN)

1951 Crosley Panel Truck (Crosley Club)

1951 Crosley Pickup Truck (OCW)

1951 Crosley Pickup Truck (OCW)

1953 Crosley Pup Utility (OCW)

1940 CROSLEY

1940 Crosley "Official Speedway" Pickup (IMSC/JM)

CROSLEY — COMMERCIAL SERIES — TWO-CYLINDER: By 1939, Powell Crosley had made millions of dollars selling appliances and radios. So, he decided to embark on building cars. The Crosley was the ultimate in economy transportation. It was powered by a two-cylinder, air-cooled Waukesha engine. The car sold for a mere $325. It was first offered in department stores, alongside Crosley radios and refrigerators. In 1940, the first Crosley aimed at the commercial vehicle market was offered. This was the Parkway Delivery, a truck designed for light, in-town delivery services by such users as grocers and florists. It was rated at 350 lbs. capacity. Besides being economical to purchase, it was cheap to operate with fuel consumption in the 45-50 mpg range. Top speed was under 50 mph.

I.D. DATA: Serial number located in engine compartment below battery shelf. Starting: [All 1940 Crosleys] 20000. Ending: 30000. Engine numbers located: On block. Starting: [All 1940 Crosleys] 12500. Ending: 21000.

Model	Body Type	Price	Weight	Prod. Total
CB-41-Y	Parkway Delivery	324	990	—

ENGINE: Waukesha, L-head. Horizontally-opposed. Air-cooled. Two-cylinder. Bore & stroke: 3 in. x 2.75 in. Displacement: 38.9 cid. Compression ratio: 5.6:1. Brake horsepower: 12 at 4000 rpm. Net horsepower: 7.2. Two main bearings. Solid valve lifters. Carburetor: Tillotson downdraft, single-barrel.

CHASSIS: Wheelbase: 80 in. Length: 120 in. Height: 56 in. Front tread: 40 in. Rear tread: 40 in. Tires: 4.25 x 12.

TECHNICAL: Three-speed manual, transmission. Speeds: 3F/1R. Floor-mounted gearshift lever. Six-inch diameter, single-disc dry-plate clutch. Semi-floating rear axle. Overall ratio: 5.57:1. Four-wheel, mechanical brakes. Pressed steel wheels.

OPTIONS: Heater ($13). Crosley five-tube radio ($30).

HISTORICAL: Introduced: October, 1939. Calendar year production, all Crosleys: 422.

1941 CROSLEY

CROSLEY — COMMERCIAL SERIES — TWO-CYLINDER: Several new models were added to Crosley's commercial series to join the Parkway Delivery. These included the Pickup Delivery and Panel Delivery. The Panel Delivery was like the Station Wagon. Its steel body had wooden side panels, but the side windows were omitted for the Panel Delivery. A chassis model consisting of hood, cowl, front fenders, square doors, windshield front seat, front floor pan and running gear was available on special order. All commercial cars were equipped with 500 lbs. capacity springs, except the Parkway Delivery, which came with 350 lbs. capacity springs. The stroke of the engine was reduced for 1941 by 0.25 in. to solve a weak crankshaft problem. Aslo, larger main bearings, improved oil cooling and a U-joint in the driveline were used. Floating brakes shoes were replaced by conventional ones.

I.D. DATA: Serial number located in engine compartment below battery shelf. Starting: [All Crosleys] 30700. Ending: 31999. Engine numbers located: On block. Starting: 21000 [All 1940 Crosleys]. Ending: 24999.

Model	Body Type	Price	Weight	Prod. Total
CB-41-V	Pickup Delivery	385	1100	—
CB-41-Y	Parkway Delivery	375	1030	—
CB-41-P	Panel Delivery	435	1125	—
CB-41-W	Chassis	—	—	—

ENGINE: Waukesha, L-head. Horizontally-opposed. Air-cooled. Two-cylinder. Bore & stroke: 3 in. x 2.5 in. Displacement: 35.3 cid. Compression ratio: 5.6:1. Brake horsepower: 12 at 4000 rpm. Net horsepower: 7.20. Two main bearings. Carburetor: Tillotson downdraft, single-barrel.

CHASSIS: Wheelbase: 80 in. Length: 120 in. Height: 56 in. Front tread: 40 in. Rear tread: 40 in. Tires: 4.25 x 12.

TECHNICAL: Three-speed manual, transmission. Speeds: 3F/1R. Floor-mounted gearshift lever. Six-inch diameter, single-disc dry-plate clutch. Semi-floating rear axle. Overall ratio: 5.57:1. Four-wheel, mechanical brakes. Pressed steel wheels.

OPTIONS: Heater ($13). Crosley five-tube radio ($30).

HISTORICAL: Introduced: October, 1940. Calendar year production: [All Crosleys] 2,289.

1941 Crosley Station Wagon

1942 CROSLEY

CROSLEY — COMMERCIAL SERIES — TWO-CYLINDER: The Crosley line was the same in 1942 as in 1941.

I.D. DATA: Serial number located inside flange of right-hand cowl panel. Starting: [All Crosleys] 32000. Ending: 35050. Engine numbers located on engine block. Starting: [All Crosleys] 25000. Ending: 27179.

Model	Body Type	Price	Weight	Prod. Total
CB-42-P	Panel Delivery	548	1080	—
CB-42-V	Pickup Delivery	493	1100	—
CB-42-Y	Parkway Delivery	493	1030	—
CB-42-W	Chassis	—	—	—

ENGINE: Waukesha, L-head. Horizontally-opposed. Air-cooled. Two-cylinder. Bore & stroke: 3 in. x 2.5 in. Displacement: 35.3 cid. Compression ratio: 5.6:1. Brake horsepower: 12 at 4000 rpm. Two main bearings. Solid valve lifters. Carburetor: Tillotson downdraft. Single-barrel.

CHASSIS: Wheelbase: 80 in. Length: 120 in. Height: 56 in. Front tread: 40 in. Rear tread: 40 in. Tires: 4.25 x 12.

TECHNICAL: Three-speed manual, synchromesh transmission. Speeds: 3F/1R. Floor-mounted gearshift lever. Six-inch single-disc, dry-plate clutch. Torque tube drive. Semi-floating rear axle. Overall ratio: 5.57:1. Four-wheel, mechanical brakes. Pressed steel wheels.

OPTIONS: Heater ($13). five-tube Crosley Radio ($30).

HISTORICAL: Introduced: August 1, 1941. Calendar year production: [All Crosleys] 1,029.

1947 CROSLEY

1947 Crosley Pickup Truck (OCW)

CROSLEY — COMMERCIAL SERIES — FOUR-CYLINDER: Unlike most other U.S. automakers, Crosley completely redesigned its postwar cars and trucks. While cars were made in model year 1946, commercial vehicles did not appear until early 1947. The slab-sided body styling was completely new. Originally, the Crosley was to have used an aluminum body. The 80 in. wheelbase was still used. Power came from Crosley's unique "Cobra Four" overhead cam engine that had a block made of sheet metal stampings copper-

brazed together. This engine was developed during World War II and used for a variety of applications, such as in aircraft and PT boat generators. The Cobra Four was much less successful in the Crosley, because electrolysis problems set in after extended periods of use. After 1949, a cast-iron block was offered and many earlier models were retrofitted with this engine. Crosley's commercial line for 1947 included a Pickup, Chassis & Cab and Chassis model.

I.D. DATA: Serial number located in engine compartment on firewall. [Jan. 1947-Oct. 10, 1947] Starting: CC47-10000. Ending: CC47-26999. [Oct. 10, 1947-December 1947] Starting: CC-27000. Ending: CC-31999. Engine numbers located on left front side of crankcase [Jan. 1947-Sept. 24, 1947] Starting: CE7-5587. Ending: CE7-21999. [Sept. 24, 1947-December 1947] Starting: 22000. Ending: 28803.

Model	Body Type	Price	Weight	Prod. Total
CC-47	Pickup	839	1180	—
CC-47	Chassis & Cab	819	1110	—

ENGINE: Inline. Water-cooled. Four-cylinder. Stamped sheet metal block with copper brazing. Bore & stroke: 2.5 in. x 2.25 in. Displacement: 44.2 cid. Compression ratio: 7.5:1. Brake horsepower: 26.5 at 5400 rpm. Net horsepower: 10. Five main bearings. Overhead cam. Carburetor: Tillotson one-barrel model DV-9B.
CHASSIS: Wheelbase: 80 in. Length: 145 in. Height: 57 in. Front tread: 40 in. Rear tread: 40 in. Tires: 4.5 x 12.
TECHNICAL: Three-speed, non-synchromesh transmission. Speeds: 3F/1R. Floor-mounted gearshift lever.
OPTIONS: Radio and Antenna. Seat covers. Bumper guards.
HISTORICAL: Introduced: Pickup Truck: January, 1947; Cab & Chassis: June 1947. Innovations: New Cobra engine with brazed sheet metal construction. Overhead cam. High-compression ratio.

1948 CROSLEY

1948 Crosley Pickup Truck (DFW)

CROSLEY — COMMERCIAL SERIES — FOUR-CYLINDER: 1948 was the best year for Crosley sales, including commercial models. Added to the line was a Panel Delivery and a flat-face cowl model. The Panel Delivery was essentially a two-door wagon without rear side windows. The Station Wagon was by far the most popular 1948 Crosley model. Economy was the key word in advertisements for Crosley trucks. Mileage claims were in the 35-50 mpg range and overall operating costs were touted as being half of a full-sized vehicle's. The 15 ft. turning circle was great for congested city traffic. The trucks were rated at a full 1/4-ton capacity. The ads also made a point of "prompt delivery," a key factor in the car-starved early postwar years.
I.D. DATA: Serial number located on firewall in engine compartment. Starting: CC-32000. Ending: CC-61256. Engine numbers located on front left side of crankcase. Starting: 28804 (other numbers from 27270-28803 were used).

1948 Crosley Pickup Truck (CAC)

Model	Body Type	Price	Weight	Prod. Total
CC	Pickup	839	1223	—
CC	Panel Delivery	899	1265	—
CC	Chassis & Cab	819	1110	—
CC	Chassis	729	—	—
CC	Flat Face Cowl	791	920	—

ENGINE: Inline. Water-cooled. Four-cylinder. Stamped sheet metal block with copper brazing. Bore & stroke: 2.5 in. x 2.25 in. Displacement: 44.2 cid. Compression ratio: 7.5:1. Brake horsepower: 26.5 at 5400 rpm. Net horsepower: 10. Five main bearings. Overhead cam. Carburetor: Tillotson, one-barrel.
CHASSIS: Wheelbase: 80 in. Length: 145 in. Height: 57 in. Front tread: 40 in. Rear tread: 40 in. Tires: 4.5 x 12 in.
TECHNICAL: Manual, non-synchromesh, transmission. Speeds: 3F/1R. Floor-mounted gearshift lever.
OPTIONS: Radio and antenna. Seat covers. Bumper guards. Cast iron engine.
HISTORICAL: Introduced: January, 1948. Calendar year registrations: 2411.

1948 Crosley Pickup Truck (BMM)

1949 CROSLEY

1949 Crosley Panel Truck (DFW/MVMA)

COMMERCIAL — SERIES CD — FOUR-CYLINDER: The Crosley was restyled for 1949. For the trucks this meant a new front end. It included a flatter hood, revised grille, wrap-around bumper, squarer front fenders, re-shaped wheel openings and headlamps that were spaced more widely apart. Crosley sales started on their downward spiral and only the Pickup and Panel were offered for commercial buyers. While the "Cobra Four" was standard until January, 1949, the "CIBA" cast-iron block, with the same internal dimensions, replaced it after Jan. 1, 1949 as standard equipment on all Crosleys.
I.D. DATA: Serial number located on firewall in engine compartment. Starting: CD-100001. Ending: CD-108628. Engine numbers located on front left side of crankcase. Starting: Engine numbers continued from 1948.

Model	Body Type	Price	Weight	Prod. Total
CD	Pickup	849	1310	—
CD	Panel Delivery	879	1343	—

ENGINE [Cobra Four]: Inline. Water-cooled. Four-cylinder. Brazed copper/sheet metal block. Bore & stroke: 2.5 in. x 2.25 in. Displacement: 44 cid. Compression ratio: 7.8:1. Brake horsepower: 26.5 at 5400 rpm. Net horsepower: 10. Five main bearings. Overhead cam. Carburetor: Tillotson, one-barrel, model DY-9C.
ENGINE [CIBA Four]: Inline. Water-cooled. Four-cylinder. Cast-iron block. Bore & stroke: 2.5 in. x 2.25 in. Displacement: 44 cid. Compression ratio: 7.8:1. Brake horsepower: 26.5 at 5400 rpm. Five main bearings. Overhead cam. Carburetor: Tillotson, one-barrel, model DY-9C.
CHASSIS: Wheelbase: 80 in. Length: 145 in. Height: 57 in. Front tread: 40 in. Rear tread: 40 in. Tires: 4.5 x 12 in.

TECHNICAL: Three-speed manual, non-synchromesh transmission. Speeds: 3F/1R. Floor-mounted gearshift lever.

OPTIONS: Crosley radio and antenna. Bumper guards. Heater and defroster. Turn signal indicators. Seat covers.

HISTORICAL: Introduced: November, 1948. Calendar year registrations: 871.

1950 Crosley Sedan Delivery (OCW)

OPTIONS: Crosley radio and antenna. Heater and defroster. Bumper guards. Seat covers. Turn signal indicators. Hydraulic draw-bar and power-take-off. Farm-O-Road ($150). Plow for Farm-O-Road ($35). Cultivator/Harrow for Farm-O-Road ($50).

HISTORICAL: Introduced: [Trucks]: October, 1949. [Farm-O-Road]: August, 1950. Calendar year registrations: [Trucks] 422. Innovations: Hydradisc brakes were a first for the industry, although disc brakes were also used on 1950 Chrysler Town & Country Newports.

1950 CROSLEY

1950 Crosley Pickup Truck (OCW)

COMMERCIAL — SERIES CD — FOUR-CYLINDER: Sales of Crosleys continued their downward trend. Changes to 1950 models over the previous year were minor. A Pickup and Panel Delivery, rated at 1/4-ton capacity, were still offered. At midyear, Crosley offered its Jeep-like Farm-O-Road, which was aimed at the small farm market. Crosley even offered farm implements as options. It came in several versions including Pickup, Dump-Truck and Buckboard for four-person capacity. The Farm-O-Road had individual rear wheel braking that allowed it to turn around, essentially, in its own length.

I.D. DATA [Pickup and Panel Delivery]: Serial number located on firewall in engine compartment. Starting: CD-200001. Ending: CD-206685. Engine numbers located on left front side of crankcase. Numbers continued from 1946.

1950 Crosley Farm-O-Road (CAC)

Model	Body Type	Price	Weight	Prod. Total
CD	Pickup	769	1310	—
CD	Panel Delivery	799	1343	—
—	Farm-O-Road	835	1100	—

ENGINE: Inline. Water-cooled. CIBA. Four-cylinder. Cast-iron block. Bore & stroke: 2.5 in. x 2.25 in. Displacement: 44 cid. Compression ratio: 7.8:1. Brake horsepower: 26.5 at 5400 rpm. Net horsepower: 10. Five main bearings. Overhead cam. Carburetor: Tillotson, one-barrel, model DY-9C.

CHASSIS [Trucks]: Wheelbase: 80 in. Length: 145 in. Height: 57 in. Front tread: 40 in. Rear tread: 40 in. Tires: 4.5 x 12.

CHASSIS [Farm-O-Road]: Wheelbase: 63 in. Length: 91.5 in. Height: 58 in. Front tread: 40 in. Rear tread: 40 in.

TECHNICAL: Non-synchromesh transmission. Speeds: 3F/1R. Four-wheel hydraulic disc brakes. Floor-mounted gearshift lever.

NOTE: Farm-O-Road has compound transmission with speeds of 6F/2R.

1951 CROSLEY

1951 Crosley Farm-O-Road (OCW)

COMMERCIAL — SERIES CD — FOUR-CYLINDER: The Crosley line was given a face-lift. It consisted of a grille with a spinner in the center and V-shaped bumpers that increased the length by over three in. The Pickup and Panel Delivery were now available as Super series models. Their main exterior feature, when so ordered, was a bodyside molding on the front fender and door.

I.D. DATA: Serial number located on firewall in engine compartment. Starting: CD-300001. Ending: CD-306958. Engine numbers located on front left side of crankcase. Numbers continued from 1950.

Model	Body Type	Price	Weight	Prod. Total
CD	Super Pickup	870	1400	—
CD	Super Panel Delivery	900	1400	—
—	Cab & Chassis	849	—	—
—	Farm-O-Road	—	1100	—

ENGINE: Inline. Water-cooled. CIBA. Four-cylinder. Cast-iron block. Bore & stroke: 2.5 in. x 2.25 in. Displacement: 44 cid. Compression ratio: 8.0:1. Brake horsepower: 26.5 at 5400 rpm. Net horsepower: 10. Five main bearings. Overhead cam. Carburetor: Tillotson, one-barrel, model DY-9C.

CHASSIS [Trucks]: Wheelbase: 80 in. Length: 148 in. Height: 57 in. Front tread: 40 in. Rear tread: 40 in. Tires: 4.5 x 12.

CHASSIS [Farm-O-Road]: Wheelbase: 63 in. Length: 91.5 in. Height: 58 in. Front tread: 40 in. Rear tread: 40 in.

TECHNICAL: Non-synchromesh transmission. Speeds: 3F/1R. Four-wheel hydraulic disc brakes. Floor-mounted gearshift lever.

NOTE: Farm-O-Road has compound transmission with speeds of 6F/2R.

OPTIONS: Crosley radio and indicator. Heater and defroster. Bumper guards. Seat covers. Plow, cultivator, harrow (Farm-O-Road).

HISTORICAL: Introduced: October, 1950. Calendar year registrations: [Trucks] 434. Historical note: Crosley returned to conventional drum brakes after experiencing problems with the Hydradisc units.

1951 Crosley Pickup Truck (EK)

CROFTON — BUG SERIES — FOUR-CYLINDER: After Crosley ceased production in 1952, other companies picked up the rights to produce the Crosley engine for industrial and marine applications. In addition, Crofton Marine Engineering Co. of San Diego, Calif., manufactured a slightly revised version of the Crosley Farm-O-Road, calling it the Bug. The main modifications came in the way of higher performance from the Crosley designed engine, a longer overall length to handle more cargo and some interior and exterior styling changes. Crofton aimed the Bug at the commercial market and off-road sportsmen. An upgraded version called the Brawny Bug included a six-speed transmission, limited-slip differential, full crash pan and either high-flotation or cleated tires as standard equipment.

1952 CROSLEY

1952 Crosley Sedan Delivery (EK)

COMMERCIAL — SERIES CD — FOUR-CYLINDER: 1952 would be the last year for the Crosley marque. After losing millions of his own dollars on this automotive venture, Powell Crosley ceased producing cars in July 1952. Crosley Motors became part of the General Tire & Rubber Co. industrial empire when it merged with the Aerojet Engineering Co. Fageol obtained the rights to the Crosley engine and, for awhile, sold an inboard boat engine based on the Crosley design. Later, rights to build the powerplant were transferred to other companies like the Homelite Corp., Fisher Pierce Co. and Crofton Diesel Engine Co. The latter firm produced a few hundred of its version of the Farm-O-Road calling it the "Bug." The slightly more than two-thousand Crosleys sold in 1952 were virtually identical to the previous year, except a Carter carburetor was now used.

I.D. DATA: Serial number located on firewall just below the hood. Starting: CD-400001 and up. Engine numbers located: Behind the distributor. Continued from previous year.

Model	Body Type	Price	Weight	Prod. Total
CD	Super Pickup	870	1310	—
CD	Super Panel Delivery	900	1343	—
CD	Farm-O-Road	—	1100	—

ENGINE: Inline. Water-cooled. Four-cylinder. Cast-iron block. Bore & stroke: 2.5 in. x 2.25 in. Displacement: 44 cid. Compression ratio: 8.0:1. Brake horsepower: 25.5 at 5200 rpm. Net horsepower: 10. Five main bearings. Carburetor: Carter, one-barrel, model WO-870S.

CHASSIS [Trucks]: Wheelbase: 80 in. Length: 148 in. Height: 57 in. Front tread: 40 in. Rear tread: 40 in. Tires: 4.5 x 12 in.

CHASSIS [Farm-O-Road]: Wheelbase: 63 in. Length: 91.5 in. Height: 58 in. Front tread: 40 in. Rear tread: 40 in.

TECHNICAL: Manual transmission. Non-synchromesh. Speeds: 3F/1R. Four-wheel hydraulic drum brakes.

OPTIONS: Crosley radio and antenna. Heater and defroster. Bumper guards. Seat covers. Plow, cultivator, harrow (Farm-O-Road).

HISTORICAL: Introduced: November, 1951. Calendar year registrations: [Trucks] [1952] 243; [1953] 32.

1960 Crofton-Bug Utility (Reggie Rapp)

I.D. DATA: Serial numbers not available. Engine numbers not available.

Model	Body Type	Price	Weight	Prod. Total
—	Bug Utility	1350	1100	—
—	Brawny Bug Utility	1800	1300	—

NOTE: All information in this section is based on the 1961 sales catalog.

ENGINE: Crosley. Inline. Water-cooled. Four-cylinder. Cast iron block. Bore & stroke: 2.5 in. x 2.25 in. Displacement: 44 cid. Compression ratio: 9.0:1. Brake horsepower: 35 at 5200 rpm. Five main bearings. Overhead Cam.

CHASSIS: Wheelbase: 63 in. Length: 105 in. Height: 59 in. Front tread: 40 in. Rear tread: 40 in. Tires: [Bug] 5.3 x 12; 9.00 x 10 high-flotation; [Brawny Bug] 7.5 x 10 cleated.

TECHNICAL: Synchromesh transmission. Speeds: 3F/1R. Floor-mounted gearshift lever. 6.5 in. single-plate clutch. Overall ratio: 5.38:1. Four-wheel, hydraulic drum brakes. Drivetrain options: Six-speed compound transmission with two-speed reverse ($100). Power-Lok differential ($40).

OPTIONS: Tow bar assembly ($28.50). Snowplow ($160). Bumper jack ($5.95). Wheel lug wrench ($1.44). Rubber front floor mat ($4.50). Tinted windshield ($10). Rear seats each ($26.65). Spare tire and wheel, 5.30 x 12 in. ($23.50). Spare tire and wheel, 6.00 x 13 in. ($39.65). Spare tire and wheel, 9.00 x 10 in. ($53.85). Dual rear wheels with wider rear fenders ($90). Folding canvas top ($100). All weather enclosure ($196). Hot water heater ($48.50). Deluxe high back seats each ($10). Optional paint color ($20). Power-take-off unit ($150). Right side windshield wiper ($9.95). Oil Filter ($12). Towing eye ($4.50). Trailer hitch ($8.50). Pintle hook ($18.50). Set of 6.00 x 9 tires ($60). Set of 6.00 x 13 tires ($55). Enginair tire pump ($10.40). Electric win. ($122.50).

HISTORICAL: Total production of Bugs and Brawny Bugs is estimated to be between 200 and 250. Listed in Crofton catalog as late as 1963.

DODGE
1914-1986

1937 Dodge Model MD-16 1-Ton 136 in. wheelbase Panel (JAG)

By Don Bunn and Charles Webb
Edited by James M. Flammang

The first Dodge Bros. car was built on Nov. 14, 1914. One day later, the first Dodge commercial chassis rolled off a production line. A Dodge dealer in Brooklyn, N.Y. fitted it with a utility body.

An article in the Nov. 29, 1916 issue of *MOTOR TRACTION* magazine described a Dodge Bros. van in London, England. That was a full year before Dodge produced such a vehicle here. It called this light-duty truck, "a smart looking vehicle rated at 12 cwt load capacity." Bare chassis were shipped to Britain. The body was built by Charles Jarrott & Hetts Ltd., Dodge representatives in London.

The American factory was continuously asked to produce such a vehicle, based on the Dodge car chassis. Demand for the cars ran at such a torrid pace, though, that the factory was not quick to attempt a commercial model. Eventually, dealer insistence and the U.S. Army forced Dodge Bros. to enter the commercial vehicle field.

The rugged Dodge car made its military mark in 1916, serving with General Pershing during the Mexican expedition against Pancho Villa. Pershing was so impressed by the Dodge's performance that he ordered his staff to use only Dodge cars. As a result, just a few years later, Dodge Bros.

began building the first of thousands of commercial vehicles for World War I use as troop carriers, ambulances and light utility trucks. The first civilian Dodge commercial vehicle, produced in 1917, was virtually a duplicate of the screenside panel built for the army.

The commercial vehicle differed from the car in its use of heavier springs, a higher-angled steering column, an underseat gas tank and screen delivery type body. A panel truck was added in 1918. Sscreenside and panel trucks, along with a chassis-only, made up the entire line of factory models until 1926.

Historians identify four series of early Dodge-related "commercial cars." In 1921, Dodge signed an agreement with Graham Bros. to source parts for Graham trucks to be marketed through Dodge dealers. The second series Dodge/Graham trucks used Dodge passenger car fronts and were made in 1923 only. Third series models (1924-1925) had longer wheelbases. On July 7, 1925, the fourth series, with totally enclosed cab and roll-up windows, appeared. It lasted through 1926.

Walter P. Chrysler purchased Dodge Bros. on June 1, 1928. He immediately changed the name of all products...including light-duty trucks...back to Dodge Bros. He substituted the four-cylinder engine from his new Plymouth and added a six-cylinder engine. Otherwise, the truck line continued, until 1933, generally unchanged.

The 1933 models were Chrysler Corp's first totally revised trucks. They were new from the wheels up. Included was Chrysler's inline six-cylinder engine (standard powerplant through 1960), attractive modernized styling and the famous "humpback" type panel truck.

In 1936, styling was changed to echo cars of that year. A ladder-type frame was adopted, converting the commercial cars into full-fledged trucks. The commercial sedan was the surviving model built on a beefed-up car chassis. Dodge's first ever, specifically-designed 3/4-ton was seen in 1937. The last year for the raised roof panel was 1938.

All-new styling ushered in 1939. This was the first year pickup box floors were made of oak with steel skid strips. A new truck plant opened. Parking lights on 1940 models moved to the top of the headlamp housings, due to a change to sealed beam headlights. In 1941, the parking lights moved to the cowl. Engine lineups were changed in 1942.

The Power-Wagon, an adaption of the 3/4-ton military 4x4 made for World War II, joined the line in 1946. No changes were apparent in 1947 models. Announcement date for Dodge's first all-new postwar models was January 1948. These B-1 models were revised from the frame up. A Route-Van was a midyear introduction.

Fluid Drive for all light-duties arrived in 1950, along with steering column gearshifting for three-speed manual transmissions. A low side cargo box became available for 1/2-ton pickups. New grilles, hoods and instrument panels characterized the 1951-1952 B-3s, which also had double-acting Oriflow shocks for improved ride quality.

The B-4 Series of 1953 brought an era to a close. Dodge made its first attempts to target light-duty truck marketing efforts towards women by upgrading interior quality and comfort and adding an automatic transmission. Only two of the early postwar years, 1950 and 1953, showed drops in market share. Years 1946 and 1947 were outstanding. Not until 1968 would sales of Dodge trucks exceed the 1947 figure.

In 1954, the Dodge C-1 series featured all-new cab styling with a one-piece curved windshield and redesigned instrument panel. It continued until April, 1955, when the C-3 line replaced it. Highlights of the C-3 were a wraparound windshield, full-width rear window and further interior upgrades. The Town Wagon, a vehicle similar to GM's Suburban, was added in 1956. So was a roof-mounted radio.

An important year in Dodge truck history was 1957. Frontal styling was changed; the Sweptside D100 pickup was introduced; V-8s grew to 315 cid; Power-Wagons with conventional cabs were added; push-button LoadFlite automatic appeared and a one-piece alligator hood was adopted. In 1958, full-width hoods and double headlights were among innovations. A new "cab-wide" Sweptline pickup was added in 1959, but the Sweptside D100 disappeared in midyear. Also new were suspended brake and clutch pedals, concealed runningboards, an hydraulically-operated clutch, a 318 cid V-8 and a restyled instrument panel. Changes were very minor in 1960.

Dodge lost market share virtually every year in the late '50s, except for 1959. Sales fell again in 1960. They hit an all-time low (in terms of market share) the next season. After 1961, the trend was reversed.

Dodge built a vast range of products between 1961 and 1971, becoming a true full-line light-duty truck maker. This period started with use of the one-year-only Dart name. Cabs were seven inches lower, four inches wider and mounted on all-new frames with changed wheelbases. Two slant-six engines replaced the old inline six as base equipment. An alternator was an industry first.

Revisions to grilles and nameplates were the only changes for 1962. In midyear, Dodge announced it would no longer make model year changes. There were no changes for 1963. A Custom Sports Special was among the news of 1964. It included racing stripes and could be ordered with V-8s up to 426 cid. At midyear, the A100 forward-control compact van line was released. It included pickup and (passenger) wagon models.

January 1965 saw a return to single headlights, the use of a new grille and the adoption of double-wall box construction. Additional emphasis was placed on penetrating the growing RV and camping market. A dash-mount lever was now used for gear selection with automatic transmissions. Among technical changes of 1966 was a close-ratio four-speed manual gearbox.

Mid-1967 saw introduction of a 108 inch wheelbase A100 van. The 273 cid V-8 was dropped in favor of the 318 cid as a van option. The 383 cid V-8 became available for all other light-duties. Dodge combined work with pleasure in the new-for-1968 high-styled Adventurer pickup. An attractive grille and vinyl top were among new options. This was the final season for the military-type Power-Wagon as a domestic offering. After all this excitement, 1969 was another no change year.

Dodge's second-generation van models were introduced in 1970. They had engines moved forward, improved front suspensions and new looks. They now came in all three light-duty weight classes in two wheelbase lengths and three sizes. A 198 cid slant six became base engine. Dodge was the industry's leading van maker. Standard pickups got a facelift. The Adventurer was heavily promoted. And all of this was carried over for 1971.

All-new 1972 models featured independent front suspension, lower and wider cabs, all-new interior and dash trims and a growing options list. Electronic ignition was added to the list, at mid-season, as a first for a light-duty truck. A landmark innovation of 1973 was the industry's first (extended) Club Cab model. A new grille graced the 1974 trucks and the Ramcharger 4x4 sport utility was launched. Vans had sliding cargo doors and the Club Cab option was available teamed with 4x4 running gear.

Innovations of the late-1970s included the release of full-time 4x4 systems and a 4x2 Ramcharger in 1975; a dual rear wheel option for 1-ton pickups in 1976; the introduction of the Dodge "Street Van" package (also in 1976); an "adult toys" marketing program for 1977 and the availability of the "Li'l Red Truck" in 1978. Some annual changes in grilles and trim were seen, too. Quad rectangular headlamps characterized the 1979 models, which also had new hoods, new front ends and an optional Mitsubishi-built diesel engine option. Dodge began importing two small pickups from this Japanese maker.

There were no major changes in the 1980 lineup. For 1981, Chrysler's new chairman, Lee Iacocca, made more news than the annual product changes. The year's revisions included single headlights and eggcrate grilles in regular Dodge trucks. A "new" accessory was a ram's head hood ornament.

In general, the 1981-1986 period was marked by enhanced aerodynamics and the down-sizing of products to make Dodge trucks more efficient. The Dodge light-duty truck lineup continued into 1980 pretty much unchanged. A novel addition appeared in 1982. Somewhat similar to the Ranchero/El Camino in concept, the front-wheel drive Rampage was also distinct. This little car/pickup had a definite

144

sports car look and feel about it. Just one glimpse and a person knew the primary purpose of this truck was to have fun.

Perhaps the most significant Dodge truck of the 1980s was the Caravan minivan. As the name suggested it was a car and a van combined into one unique vehicle. Sales literature described it as part of a "transportation revolution." That wasn't exaggerating too much. Caravan was an instant success and a trendsetter. Even two years after its introduction, and despite new competition from other makes, Caravans were selling very well. Dodge had a winner. At the same time, sports/performance options like the Rampage 2.2 package brought a missing touch of excitement to the line.

Other 1980s Dodge truck highlights included release of the Miser package in 1983, the appearance of the mini-Ram Van wagon, the introduction of a shift-on-the-go feature for 4x4 Ramchargers and an all-new front-wheel drive Caravan series. In these same years, the Ram 50 mini-pickup gained a reputation for being one of the best trucks of its type available in America.

1962 Dodge W100 Power Wagon Town Wagon (RCA)

1964 Dodge W200 Sweptline Crew Cab Power Wagon (RAC)

1965 Dodge A100 1/2-Ton Pickup (OCW)

Standard Catalog of Light-Duty Trucks

1966 Dodge WM300 1-Ton Power Wagon Utiline (RAC)

1967 Dodge W100 Sweptline Power Wagon (RAC)

1968 Dodge Sweptline Pickup (CW)

1969 Dodge W100 Sweptline Pickup power Wagon (RAC)

1970 Dodge W100 Sweptline Power Wagon (RAC)

1971 Dodge W200 Sweptline Power Wagon (RAC)

1977 Dodge W100 Utiline Power Wagon (RAC)

1978 Dodge W150 Sweptline Power Wagon (RAC)

1980 Dodge Power Wagon Utiline Pickup (CW)

1983 Dodge Rampage 2.2L Sport Pickup (OCW)

1983 Dodge Ram Maxi-Wagon (DNP)

1986 Dodge Ram Utiline Pickup (DNP)

Standard Catalog of Light-Duty Trucks

1917 DODGE

1917 Dodge Commercial Car Series 1/2-Ton Panelside (OCW)

ENGINE: Inline. L-Head. Four-cylinder. Cast iron block. Bore & stroke: 3-7/8 x 4-1/2 in. Displacement: 212.3 cid. Compression ratio: 4.0:1. Brake horsepower: 35 at 2000 rpm. Net (Taxable) horsepower: 24.03. Four main bearings. Solid valve lifters. Carburetor: Special design 7-6-24 Stewart.
CHASSIS: Wheelbase: 114 in. Tread: 56 in. Tires: 33 x 4 in.
TECHNICAL: Selective sliding gear transmission. Speeds: 3F/1R. Floor shift control. Dry plate disc clutch. Full-floating rear axle; spiral bevel gears. Shaft drive. Two-wheel mechanical brakes. Springs: (front) semi-elliptic; (rear) three-quarters elliptic. Vacuum feed fuel system. 12-volt Northeast single-unit starter-generator. Wheels: 12 hickory spokes (front and rear).
HISTORICAL: Introduced: November, 1917. Innovations: Passenger car styling on heavy-duty chassis. Historical notes: Commercial Car production began in late October, 1917. Deliveries to dealers began in November. These first Commercial Cars were considered 1918 models, since the Dodge Bros. model year ran from July 1 through June 30. Dodge Bros. also built thousands of vehicles for the U.S. Army during 1917, including touring cars, ambulances, screensides, troop carriers, and light repair trucks. During World War I, the company also erected a plant to build recoil mechanisms for the French 155mm field piece after two other manufacturers failed. Dodge engineered the pieces, built the machines and plant, and produced the product. The Dodge Bros. factory was in Hamtramck, Michigan. Dodge was the fifth largest U.S. automaker in 1917.

1917 Dodge Commercial Car Series 1/2-Ton Screenside (DFW/SI)

1/2-TON DELIVERY — SERIES ONE — FOUR-CYLINDER: The first Dodge Bros. screenside commercial car was driven off the line on Oct. 18, 1917. It had an all-steel body built by Budd Body Co. The wheelbase was identical to passenger cars, but the chassis was longer, heavier, and sturdier. *AUTOMOBILE TOPICS* magazine described the debut as follows: "Frequent and increasing demands for its passenger car chassis to be used for commercial purposes has resulted in the production by Dodge Bros., Detroit, of a light commercial car with pressed steel panel body with a black enamel finish, similar to that of the passenger models. The car has a standing roof with removable wire screen sides, a set of substantial oiled duck side curtains for both sides and the rear of the body, as well as for both sides and rear of the driver's seat, and, all told, it is precisely the kind of light delivery car that one would expect Dodge Bros. to build." Series One styling, from the front bumper to the windshield, was exactly the same as the Dodge Bros. car. So were the engine, transmission and axles. Springs were heavier, and the tire size was increased to 33 x 4 in. The steering column sat at a higher angle and the gas tank was under the driver's seat, which was upholstered in genuine leather. Driver's doors were roadster type. An extra rim was carried outside, on the left side just back of the driver's seat. Payload capacity was 1,000 lbs. Body loading space was 72 x 43 in. wide, with 54-inch inside height. Standard equipment included: Oiled duck curtains for complete enclosure; two wire screens; electric horn; license brackets; tire pump, jack and tool kit; plus complete instrument panel with 60-mph speedometer, total/trip mileage recorder, oil pressure gauge, current indicator, locking ignition and lighting switch, choke, and instrument light.

1918 DODGE

1918 Dodge 1-Ton Express Truck (DFW/FLP)

1/2-TON DELIVERY — SERIES ONE — FOUR-CYLINDER: Series One Commercial Cars continued basically unchanged except for mechanical improvements from 1917 to 1922. The Dodge Bros. did not believe in annual model introductions, or change for change's sake. Instead, they stated that improvements would be made at any time. The annual series for registration purposes ran from July 1 through the following June 30. On March 26, the first panel model was built, with chassis details and size duplicating the screenside. Dodge called the panel a Business Car (BC) and the screenside a Commercial Car (CC).
I.D. DATA: Serial-numbers on Commercial cars ran concurrently with those on Dodge passenger cars. The serial numbers were die-cut on a 2.75 x 5 in. aluminum plate attached to the right front upper toe-board. They were also stamped into the chassis on the center crossmember, under the front floorboard and near the right front door. Starting: 217,926. Ending: 303,126. Engine numbers not available.

Model	Body Type	Price	Weight	Prod. Total
1/2-Ton — 114 in. w.b.				
CC	Screenside	985	2610	2335
BC	Panel	1085	2640	1728

NOTE: Calendar year shipments to dealers. Production figures by type not available.
ENGINE: Inline. L-Head. Four-cylinder. Cast iron block. Bore & stroke: 3-7/8 x 4-1/2 in. Displacement: 212.3 cid. Compression ratio: 4.0:1. Brake horsepower: 35 at 2000 rpm. Net (Taxable) horsepower: 24.03. Four main bearings. Solid valve lifters. Carburetor: Special design 7-6-24 Stewart.
CHASSIS: Wheelbase: 114 in. Tread: 56 in. Tires: 33 x 4 in.

1917 Dodge 1/2-Ton Ambulance (OCW)

I.D. DATA: Serial-numbers on Commercial cars ran concurrently with those on Dodge passenger cars. The serial numbers were die-cut on a 2.75 x 5 in. aluminum plate attached to the right front upper toe-board. They were also stamped into the chassis on the center crossmember, under the front floorboard and near the right front door. Starting Serial-No.: 116339. Ending: 217925. Engine numbers were stamped on a pad above the carburetor, on the left side of the cylinder block. Engine numbers are not available.

Model	Body Type	Price	Weight	Prod. Total
1/2-Ton — 114 in. w.b.				
CC	Screenside	885	2610	Note 1

NOTE: Commercial Cars (CC) were built on the same line as passenger cars; no production records available by type. Total calendar year shipments to dealers: 720 units.

Standard Catalog of Light-Duty Trucks

TECHNICAL: Selective sliding gear transmission. Speeds: 3F/1R. Floor shift control. Dry-plate disc clutch. Full-floating rear axle; spiral bevel gears. Shaft drive. Two-wheel mechanical brakes. Springs: (front) semi-elliptic; (rear) three-quarters elliptic. Vacuum feed fuel system. 12-volt Northeast single-unit starter-generator. Wheels: 12 hickory spokes (front and rear).

HISTORICAL: Introduced: Continuation of model year that began in October, 1917. Calendar year shipments to dealers: 10,271 (including chassis alone). Innovations: Heavier engine crankshaft. Roadster-type door curtains, with curved rod that opened with the door, replaced the original roll curtains over driver's door in June, 1918. Historical notes: In addition to screen and panel models, Dodge Bros. continued to produce a commercial chassis only. Customers could mount their own bodies. This dependable chassis soon became a favorite with custom body builders. They used the Dodge chassis for many special-duty vehicles, including hearses, hucksters, ambulances, station buses, suburbans, carry-alls, fire engines, paddy wagons and light delivery vehicles. A total of 6,133 commercial chassis were shipped in calendar year 1917. Dodge continued to rank fifth in auto sales.

1919 DODGE

1/2-TON DELIVERY — SERIES ONE — FOUR-CYLINDER: Screenside and panel trucks were unchanged in appearance for 1919. The Dodge Bros. were convinced that their policy of no annual model changes contributed heavily to the company's success. Hubcaps were changed to a light aluminum stamping with the Dodge Bros. monogram on their faces. Cab floorboards were now covered with durable linoleum and the four floorboard sections were individually bound on each edge with heavy aluminum strips.

I.D. DATA: Serial numbers on Commercial cars ran concurrently with those on Dodge passenger cars. The serial numbers were die-cut on a 2.75 x 5 in. aluminum plate attached to the right front upper toe-board. They were also stamped into the chassis on the center crossmember, under the front floorboard and near the right front door. Starting: 303,127. Ending: 378,971. Engine numbers not available.

Model	Body Type	Price	Weight	Prod. Total
1/2-Ton — 114 in. w.b.				
CC	Screenside	1085	2610	8055
BC	Panel	1085	2640	2715

NOTE: Calendar year shipments to dealers. Production figures by type not available.
ENGINE: Inline. L-Head. Four-cylinder. Cast iron block. Bore & stroke: 3-7/8 x 4-1/2 in. Displacement: 212.3 cid. Compression ratio: 4.0:1. Brake horsepower: 35 at 2000 rpm. Net (Taxable) horsepower: 24.03. Four main bearings. Solid valve lifters. Carburetor: Special design 7-6-24 Stewart.
CHASSIS: Wheelbase: 114 in. Tread: 56 in. Tires: 33 x 4 in.
TECHNICAL: Selective sliding gear transmission. Speeds: 3F/1R. Floor shift control. Dry-plate disc clutch. Full-floating rear axle; spiral bevel gears. Shaft drive. Two-wheel mechanical brakes. Springs: (front) semi-elliptic; (rear) three-quarters elliptic. Vacuum feed fuel system. 12-volt Northeast single-unit starter-generator. Wheels: 12 hickory spokes (front and rear).
HISTORICAL: Model year began July 1, 1918. Total calendar year shipments to dealers were 15,612 (including chassis only). The first Dodge Bros. taxi was built on Sept. 9, 1919; the first limousine in October. Total vehicle production (passenger and commercial cars) climbed to 105,398. The Dodges won their long-standing lawsuit against Henry Ford and were paid $25 million for their stock, which had originally been purchased for $10,000. Dodge ended the year fourth in automobile sales.

1920 DODGE

1920 Dodge Business Car Series 1/2-Ton Panel (DFW/OHS)

1/2-TON DELIVERY — SERIES ONE — FOUR-CYLINDER: A sales brochure for 1920 claimed that "Dodge Bros. Business Cars offer a definite solution of the light transportation problem." The public must have agreed, as they purchased every unit the Dodges could push through their strained factory. Apart from the adoption of Kelsey steel-felloe wheels, product changes were minimal. Late in the model year, wheel size was reduced to 32 x 4. Standard equipment was the same as before.
I.D. DATA: Serial numbers on Commercial cars ran concurrently with those on Dodge passenger cars. The serial-numbers were die-cut on a 2.75 x 5 in. aluminum plate attached to the right front upper toe-board. They were also stamped into the chassis on the center

crossmember, under the front floorboard and near the right front door. Starting: 378,972. Ending: 569,548. Engine numbers are not available.

1920 Dodge Commercial Car Series 1/2-Ton Screenside (DB)

Model	Body Type	Price	Weight	Prod. Total
1/2-Ton — 114 in. w.b.				
CC	Screenside	1270	2610	9064
BC	Panel	1330	2640	5106

NOTE: Calendar year shipments to dealers. Production figures by type are not available.
ENGINE: Inline. L-Head. Four-cylinder. Cast iron block. Bore & stroke: 3-7/8 x 4-1/2 in. Displacement: 212.3 cid. Compression ratio: 4.0:1. Brake horsepower: 35 at 2000 rpm. Net (Taxable) horsepower: 24.03. Four main bearings. Solid valve lifters. Carburetor: Special design 7-6-24 Stewart.
CHASSIS: Wheelbase: 114 in. Tread: 56 in. Tires: 33 x 4 in.
TECHNICAL: Selective sliding gear transmission. Speeds: 3F/1R. Floor shift control. Dry plate disc clutch. Full-floating rear axle; spiral bevel gears. Shaft drive. Two-wheel mechanical brakes. Springs: (front) semi-elliptic; (rear) three-quarters elliptic. Vacuum feed fuel system. 12-volt Northeast single-unit starter-generator. Wheels: 12 hickory spokes (front and rear).
HISTORICAL: Model year began July 1, 1919. Total calendar year shipments to dealers: 16,198 (including chassis alone). Business was very good for Dodge Bros. During late 1919, the plants were hard pressed to turn out enough vehicles to meet the demand. Production continued to include chassis alone, as well as screen and panel models. John Dodge caught pneumonia and died Jan. 14, 1920 at the Ritz-Carlton Hotel, where the brothers were staying while attending the New York auto show. Horace Dodge died in December of the same year. He fell victim to influenza, while visiting Palm Beach, Florida. One of the brothers' last accomplishments was a plant expansion project that would double production capacity at the Hamtramck, Michigan factory from 300 to 600 vehicles per day. Dodge rose to America's second best selling automobile in 1920.

1921 DODGE

1921 Dodge Commercial Car Series 1/2-Ton Screenside (OCW)

1/2-TON DELIVERY — SERIES ONE — FOUR-CYLINDER: Frederick J. Haynes became the new company president on Jan. 11, 1921, following the death of Horace Dodge. Haynes continued the Dodge family's policies. A severe economic depression cut deeply into the car market. Even though the Dodge work force would be drastically reduced by March, $2 million in bonuses were paid to employees in January, 1921. One of Haynes' first official acts was to work out an agreement whereby Dodge would become the exclusive distributor of Graham Bros. trucks and buses. The Graham company agreed to use only Dodge engines, transmissions and front-end assemblies. Graham benefitted from Dodge Bros.' excellent dealer and parts organization and consumer confidence in Dodge products. Dodge Bros., in return, gained the experience, management and engineering skills of the Graham brothers. So, Dodge became an instant full-line truck manufacturer without diluting its own management and engineering staff. Meanwhile, the half-ton screenside and panel Dodge commercial cars continued with minor changes. Top and windshield

148

supports were added to the screenside in March. In May, both received redesigned fenders, runningboards and splash shields. A heater was also added.

I.D. DATA: Serial numbers were located on a small plate fastened to the upper toe-board in the truck's front compartment. They were also stamped on the right side member of the frame, under the front fender, near the front spring's rear bracket. Starting: 569,549. Ending: 663,096. Engine numbers are not available.

Model	Body Type	Price	Weight	Prod. Total
1/2-Ton — 114 in. w.b.				
CC	Screenside	1270	2610	5915
BC	Panel	1330	2640	3073

NOTE: Calendar year shipments to dealers. Production figures by type are not available.
ENGINE: Inline. L-Head. Four-cylinder. Cast iron block. Bore & stroke: 3-7/8 x 4-1/2 in. Displacement: 212.3 cid. Compression ratio: 4.0:1. Brake horsepower: 35 at 2000 rpm. Net (Taxable) horsepower: 24.03. Four main bearings. Solid valve lifters. Carburetor: Special design 7-6-24 Stewart.
CHASSIS: Wheelbase: 114 in. Tread: 56 in. Tires: 33 x 4 in.
TECHNICAL: Selective sliding gear transmission. Speeds: 3F/1R. Floor shift control. Dry plate disc clutch. Full-floating rear axle; spiral bevel gears. Shaft drive. Two-wheel mechanical brakes. Springs: (front) semi-elliptic; (rear) three-quarters elliptic. Vacuum feed fuel system. 12-volt Northeast single-unit starter-generator. Wheels: 12 hickory spokes (front and rear).

1921 Dodge Business Car Series 1/2-Ton Panel (OCW)

HISTORICAL: Model year began July 1, 1920. Total calendar year shipments of half-ton trucks: 10,731 (including chassis alone). Innovations: Heater available. A March 1920 article in *AUTOMOTIVE INDUSTRIES* announced a new Graham Bros. truck model. It was a 1-1/2-ton truck, powered by a four-cylinder Continental engine. In August, *AUTOMOBILE TRADE JOURNAL* reported a new 18-passenger bus built on the Graham Bros. 1-1/2-ton chassis. Graham Bros. produced and sold 1,086 trucks and buses using Dodge engines, transmissions and front-end sheet metal. That pattern, which gave Graham success with their assembled trucks, would last until Chrysler Corp. purchased Dodge Bros. in 1928. Light commercials, screenside and panel models would be built by Dodge Bros., while heavier trucks were made by the Graham Bros.. Upon signing the agreement with Dodge, Graham Bros. immediately moved to Detroit and built a modern new factory. Dodge produced a total of 81,000 vehicles in 1921, ranking third in sales for the U.S. auto industry.

1922 DODGE

1922 Dodge Commercial Car Series Open-Cab Pickup (DFW/JRH)

1/2-TON DELIVERY — SERIES ONE — FOUR-CYLINDER: Early in the new year, the panel model received the new top and windshield supports given to the screenside in 1921. Tire size was changed to 33 x 4.5 inches in November, 1921. Headlight lenses went from plain glass to rippled or fluted type. A major appearance change occurred on all Dodge Bros. cars in April, 1922. It consisted of a 3.5 in. higher radiator, hood and cowl. The higher hood went on the panel Business Car beginning with serial number 725468, on May 31; and on the screenside starting with number 725961, on June 5. Semi-floating rear axles replaced the full-floating type in a gradual phase-out that began on May 8. Finally, a North

East speedometer replaced the Johns-Manville unit on June 20. Standard equipment also included an ammeter, windshield, electric horn, ignition-theft lock, demountable rims and tire pump.

I.D. DATA: Serial numbers were located on a small plate fastened to the upper toe-board in the truck's front compartment. They were also stamped on the right side member of the frame, under the front fender, near the front spring's rear bracket. Starting: 663097. Ending: 826,400. Engine numbers are not available.

Model	Body Type	Price	Weight	Prod. Total
1/2-Ton — 114 in. w.b.				
CC	Screenside	1035	2610	9810
BC	Panel	1135	2640	5845

NOTE: Calendar year shipments to dealers. Production figures by type are not available.
ENGINE: Inline. L-Head. Four-cylinder. Cast iron block. Bore & stroke: 3-7/8 x 4-1/2 in. Displacement: 212.3 cid. Compression ratio: 4.0:1. Brake horsepower: 35 at 2000 rpm. Net (Taxable) horsepower: 24.03. Four main bearings. Solid valve lifters. Carburetor: Special design 7-6-24 Stewart.
CHASSIS: Wheelbase: 114 in. Tires: 33 x 4 in. (33 x 4.5 inch beginning in November, 1921). Wood-spoke wheels. GVW rating: 3,850 lbs. (including chassis and payload).
TECHNICAL: Selective sliding gear transmission. Speeds: 3F/1R. Dry disc clutch. Semi-floating rear axle, spiral bevel gear drive. Rear-wheel mechanical brakes; emergency brake on rear wheels. Worm and worm wheel steering gear. Tubular radiator. Single-unit starter-generator. 12-volt electric system. Vacuum feed fuel system.

1922 Dodge Commercial Car Cantrell Station Wagon (CHC)

HISTORICAL: Model year began July 1, 1921. Total calendar year shipments of 1/2-ton trucks: 18,595 (including chassis alone). Model year vehicle production (passenger and commercial): 152,673. This was a very good year for Dodge Bros. as the company maintained third place in sales. Dodge's business coupe was the first all-steel enclosed-type ever marketed by any automaker in the world. This was the final year for Series One commercial models. Dodge continued to supply Graham Bros. with chassis and engines. Graham produced 3,401 trucks and buses using Dodge components. Two models were a 1-ton and 1-1/2-ton, both on a 140 in. wheelbase

1923 DODGE

3/4-TON DELIVERY — SERIES TWO — FOUR-CYLINDER: More changes hit Dodge Bros.' commercial vehicles in the 1923 model year than at any time since production began. Beginning with serial number 723615, all commercial vehicles were up-rated to 3/4-ton capacity. Early in the model year, the radiator was enlarged. In October, 1922, a new caution plate was affixed to all commercial cars. Appearance changes included slanting windshields and outside handles on the driver's door. Panel models were made with one continuous side panel, eliminating the vertical half-round molding, which had been located in back of the driver's door. Steel runningboards replaced the original wooden boards, the horn button moved from the left front door to the steering wheel center, and the steering wheel's style was changed. Series Two vehicles were built only during this one model year. The 114 in. wheelbase trucks began to be phased out just before the model year ended, on June 26, 1923. The last 114 in. wheelbase units were serial number 927227 (panel) and 928100 (screenside). Standard equipment included a speedometer, ammeter, electric horn, ignition-theft lock, windshield wiper, demountable rims, rear wheel puller, and tire pump.

I.D. DATA: Serial numbers were located on a small plate fastened to the upper toe-board in the truck's front compartment. They were also stamped on the right side member of the frame, under the front fender, near the front spring's rear bracket. Starting: 826401. Ending: 928140. Engine numbers are not available.

Model	Body Type	Price	Weight	Prod. Total
3/4-Ton — 114 in. w.b.				
CC	Screenside	880	2735	10,732
BC	Panel	980	2695	6737

NOTE: Calendar year shipments to dealers. Production figures by type are not available.
ENGINE: Inline. L-head. Four-cylinder. Cast iron block. Bore & stroke: 3-7/8 x 4-1/2 in. Displacement: 212.3 cid. Compression ratio: 4.0:1. Brake horsepower: 35 at 2000 rpm Net (Taxable) horsepower: 24.03. Three main bearings. Solid valve lifters. Carburetor: Stewart.
CHASSIS: Wheelbase: 114 in. Tires: 32 x 4 pneumatic (cord). Tread: 56 in. GVW rating: 4405 lbs.
TECHNICAL: Selective sliding gear transmission. Speeds: 3F/1R. Dry disc clutch. Floor shift control. Semi-floating rear axle with spiral bevel drive. Rear-wheel mechanical (contracting) brakes; emergency brakes (expanding) on rear wheels. Worm and worm wheel steering. 12-volt electrical system. Engine lubrication: Splash with circulating pump. Water pump cooling. Vacuum feed fuel system.
HISTORICAL: Model year began July 1, 1922. Total calendar year shipments of 3/4-ton trucks, including chassis alone, were 21,681. Calendar year sales (screenside and panel) were 18,427. Innovations included slanting windshields, steel runningboards, and horn button on steering wheel. For the first time, Dodge Bros. advertisements began to use the

famous word "Dependable." Customers regularly told the factory how they could depend on Dodge cars, which led the ad writers to "Dodge Dependability." They also boasted that, since production of commercial vehicles began, Dodge had sold "the unusual total of 102,000 units." Graham Bros. built and sold 6,971 trucks and buses using Dodge engines and transmissions. Though constructed mainly of Dodge components, Graham truck chassis were built to carry heavier loads. They now had radiator and hubcaps of their own design rather than the former Dodge style. This year, too, Graham began stamping Dodge serial numbers on the chassis under the right front fender, at the spring shackle. Graham Bros. trucks also carried the Dodge number on an aluminum toe-board plate, as on Dodge vehicles. Graham built seven truck series and three bus series of one and 1-1/2-ton capacity. America's greatest World War I hero, Sergeant Alvin York, acquired a Dodge dealership in his native state of Tennessee. Dodge dropped to sixth place in car sales in 1923.

1924 DODGE

1924 Dodge 3/4-Ton Commercial Station Wagon (OCW)

3/4-TON DELIVERY — SERIES THREE — FOUR-CYLINDER: Built only during the 1924 and 1925 model years, the Series Three retained most of the basic Dodge Bros. characteristics. Appearance changes included a taller radiator and higher hood line. Hoods were louvered. Headlamps were the popular drum style. The taillamp housing included a brake light, and was combined with a license plate bracket. Front fenders and runningboards were new. Wheelbase grew to 116 in. Rear springs were now underslung semi-elliptic, rather than 3/4-elliptic. They were lengthened to 55 in. Front springs were longer too, with thinner and wider leaves. Engine, transmission and rear axle remained as before. Gearshift and parking brake hand levers were relocated farther forward, while the steering column angle was lowered. Overall vehicle weight was increased, but the center of gravity was lowered. The screenside cargo box was enlarged to 84 cu. ft. of loading space and 1,500 lbs. payload capacity. Brake and clutch pedal pads were now rectangular rather than oval. Rubber floor mats were new and the driver's seatback gained coil spring construction. Standard equipment included a speedometer, ammeter, electric horn, ignition-theft lock, windshield wiper, demountable rims, rear wheel puller, and tire pump.

I.D. DATA: Serial numbers were located on a small plate fastened to the upper toeboard in the truck's front compartment. They were also stamped on the right side member of the frame, under the front fender, near the front spring's rear bracket. During the model year, a new numbering system began, beginning with A-1001. [Early series] Starting: 930312. Ending: 982625. [New series] Starting: A-2386.

Model	Body Type	Price	Weight	Prod. Total
3/4-Ton — 116 in. w.b.				
CC	Screenside	895	2847	10,198
BC	Panel	995	2794	5151

NOTE: Calendar year shipments to dealers. Production figures by type are not available.

ENGINE: Inline. L-head. Four-cylinder. Cast iron block. Bore & stroke: 3-7/8 x 4-1/2 in. Displacement: 212.3 cid. Compression ratio: 4.0:1. Brake horsepower: 35 at 2000 rpm Net (Taxable) horsepower: 24.03. Three main bearings. Solid valve lifters. Carburetor: Stewart.

CHASSIS: Wheelbase: 116 in. Tires: 32 x 4 (cord). Tread: 56 in. GVW rating: 4,405 lbs.

TECHNICAL: Selective sliding gear transmission. Speeds: 3F/1R. Dry disc clutch. Floor shift control. Semi-floating rear axle with spiral bevel drive. Rear wheel mechanical (contracting) brakes; emergency brakes (expanding) on rear wheels. Worm and worm wheel steering. 12-volt electrical system. Engine lubrication: Splash with circulating pump. Water pump cooling. Vacuum feed fuel system.

HISTORICAL: Model year began July 1, 1923. Total calendar year shipments of 3/4-ton trucks, including chassis alone, were 20,525. Model year production of passenger and commercial cars was 207,687. Dodge Bros. invested heavily in production facilities during 1924, spending $5 million to increase capacity. This would allow daily production of 1,000 vehicles, about 200 more than the peak reached early in the year. On Dec. 12, 1923, the one-millionth Dodge Bros. vehicle (a touring car) was built. Dodge had a great year, as demand outstripped production even after the plant expansion. Their reputation for quality continued to grow, as the company regained third place among U.S. automakers. A total of 141,662 Dodge commercial vehicles had been built and sold since 1917, not including the bare chassis on which other companies mounted special bodies. Graham Bros. had its best year ever, selling 10,743 vehicles. The line consisted of 13 truck and 12 bus models, rated 1-ton or 1-1/2-ton. All Graham trucks used the standard Dodge four-cylinder engine.

1925 DODGE

1925 Dodge 96-inch Business Car Series Panel (DFW/WRL)

3/4-TON DELIVERY — SERIES THREE — FOUR-CYLINDER: Series Three commercial cars continued with little change. They were again offered in screenside and panel models, as well as the basic chassis. Improvements included automatic windshield wipers, cowl vents, one-piece windshield, silchrome exhaust valves, oil drain piston rings, and balloon tires.

I.D. DATA: Serial numbers were located on a small plate fastened to the upper toe-board in the truck's front compartment. They were also stamped on the right side member of the frame, under the front fender, near the front spring's rear bracket. Starting: A-132707. Engine numbers were in the same locations. Starting Engine no.: A-205208.

Model	Body Type	Price	Weight	Prod. Total
3/4-Ton — 116 in. w.b.				
CC	Screenside	910	2847	13,215
BC	Panel	995	2794	8754

NOTE: Calendar year shipments to dealers. Production figures by type are not available.

1925 Dodge Commercial Car Series Huckster (DFW/WAD)

ENGINE: Inline. L-head. Four-cylinder. Cast iron block. Bore & stroke: 3-7/8 x 4-1/2 in. Displacement: 212.3 cid. Compression ratio: 4.0:1. Brake horsepower: 35 at 2000 rpm Net (Taxable) horsepower: 24.03. Three main bearings. Solid valve lifters. Carburetor: Stewart.

CHASSIS: Wheelbase: 116 in. Tires: 32 x 4 (cord). Tread: 56 in. GVW rating: 4,405 lbs.

TECHNICAL: Selective sliding gear transmission. Speeds: 3F/1R. Dry disc clutch. Floor shift control. Semi-floating rear axle with spiral bevel drive. Rear-wheel mechanical (contracting) brakes; emergency brakes (expanding) on rear wheels. Worm and worm wheel steering. 12-volt electrical system. Engine lubrication: Splash with circulating pump. Water pump cooling. Vacuum feed fuel system.

HISTORICAL: Introduced: July 1, 1924. Total calendar year shipments to dealers of 3/4-ton trucks, including chassis alone, were 26,696. Dodge was the fifth best-selling car in 1925, but the year's major event had to do with the organization rather than the product. On May 1, 1925, ownership of Dodge Bros. Inc. passed to Dillon, Read and Co., a New York banking syndicate. The widows of John and Horace Dodge were paid $146 million. Stock went public, but control remained in the hands of Dillon, Read and Co. Officers, management and policies remained as before. Robert C. Graham was named director of the Commercial Car and Truck Div. Earlier in the model year, in fact, a stronger bond between Graham and Dodge had been announced. On Oct. 6, 1924, Graham Bros. became a division of Dodge Bros. Inc., while maintaining its own organization and product identity. Graham Bros. continued to operate its factory in Detroit and a plant in Evansville, Indiana. Graham had another great year, nearly doubling 1924 production with a total of 24,298 trucks and buses built and sold. The 12 truck and 12 bus models were all of either 1-ton or 1-1/2-ton capacity. Beginning in May, 1925, the Graham frame serial numbers carried a D, E or S prefix, denoting where the truck was assembled (D=Detroit, Michigan; E=Evansville, Indiana; S=Stockton, California).

1925 Dodge Commercial Car Series 3/4-Ton Panel (OCW)

TECHNICAL: Selective sliding gear transmission. Speeds: 3F/1R. Dry disc clutch. Floor shift control. Semi-floating rear axle with spiral bevel drive. Rear-wheel mechanical (contracting) brakes; emergency brakes (expanding) on rear wheels. Worm and worm wheel steering. 12-volt electrical system. Engine lubrication: Splash with circulating pump. Water pump cooling. Vacuum feed fuel system.

1926 DODGE

1926 Dodge Commercial Car Series 3/4-Ton Screenside (OCW)

3/4-TON DELIVERY — SERIES FOUR — FOUR-CYLINDER: The new model year ushered in the first Dodge commercial cars with a totally enclosed cab. Dodge Bros.' policy, from the beginning, had been to make running changes at any time, rather than to coincide with the new model year. A 140 in. wheelbase chassis with 96 in. panel body was added to the shorter wheelbase models in the lineup. Intended for businesses that handled large, bulky loads, the new panel had the same payload rating as the smaller trucks. Radiators were larger this year and the spare tire carrier was underslung.

I.D. DATA: Serial numbers were located on a small plate fastened to the upper toe-board in the truck's front compartment. They were also stamped on the right side member of the frame, under the front fender, near the front spring's rear bracket. Starting: A-372475. Ending: A-702242. No engine numbers are available.

1926 Dodge Commercial Car Series 3/4-Ton Panelside (OCW)

HISTORICAL: Introduced: July 1, 1925. Total calendar year shipments to dealers of 3/4-ton trucks (including chassis alone) were 29,830. Calendar year production of all commercial vehicles (except Graham) was 24,281. Model year production (passenger and commercial) was 249,869. Innovations included a change to S.A.E. standard gearshift pattern, disc wheels with balloon tires, oil drain piston rings and a change from 12-volt to 6-volt electrical system. Separate starters and generators were made standard. In November, 1925, Dodge Bros. bought a majority interest in the Graham Bros.' company. Dodge President Frederick J. Haynes took on the additional job of chairman of the executive committee, while E.G. Wilmer became chairman of the board. Joseph B. and Robert C. Graham were elected to the Dodge board, while Ray A. Graham became general manager of Dodge Bros. Inc. Graham continued to operate its truck division independently, selling through Dodge dealers. Early in 1926, Graham added a new factory in Stockton, Caliorniaf. Joseph was named vice president of manufacturing in January, 1926. The Graham lineup consisted of 17 trucks and four buses rated 1-ton, 1-1/2-ton and 2-ton. Graham built and sold 37,463 vehicles during 1926. Early in the model year, work began on an $8 million plant expansion. By February, daily production reached 1,500 vehicles, but it couldn't meet the goal of 2,000. Thus, production still lagged behind demand. Early in 1926, Dodge Bros. began the practice of allowing dealers to sit on its board. This was an industry first. Late in the model year, all three Grahams resigned from their posts to start a new firm, Graham-Paige. Dodge Bros. purchased all the Graham stock. Wilmer became president, Haynes chairman. This was the last year that light delivery vehicles were marketed under the Dodge Bros. name by the original Dodge company. All trucks built in 1927 and 1928 would be sold as Graham Bros. trucks, even though Dodge wholly owned the Graham company, which actually built the vehicles. Dodge was the auto industry's fourth largest producer in 1926.

1926 Dodge Commercial Car Series 3/4-Ton Screenside (DFW/JC)

1927 DODGE
(GRAHAM)

1926 Dodge Series 4 Commercial Car 3/4-Ton Express (JAW)

Model	Body Type	Price	Weight	Prod. Total
3/4-Ton — 116 in. w.b.				
CC	Screenside	885	2929	14,318
BC	Panel (72 in.)	960	2952	11,354
3/4-Ton — 140 in. w.b.				
BC	Panel (96 in.)	1225	3208	591

NOTE 1: Calendar year shipments to dealers. Production figures by type are not available.
ENGINE: Inline. L-head. Four-cylinder. Cast iron block. Bore & stroke: 3-7/8 x 4-1/2 in. Displacement: 212.3 cid. Compression ratio: 4.0:1. Brake horsepower: 35 at 2000 rpm Net (Taxable) horsepower: 24.03. Three main bearings. Solid valve lifters. Carburetor: Stewart.

3/4-TON DELIVERY — GRAHAM BROTHERS DC SERIES — FOUR-CYLINDER: For the first time, Graham Bros. took over all truck production under its own name, even though the company was now wholly owned by Dodge. Graham Bros.' truck line consisted of a new 3/4-ton series, which was basically the former Dodge 3/4-ton panel and screenside; two 1-ton series; plus 1-1/2-ton and 2-ton truck and bus models. All used Dodge Bros. engines, transmissions and front-end sheet metal. Appearance changes of the 3/4-tons, now wearing the Graham nameplate, were minimal. However, the roof line now extended over the windshield to form a sun shade. Windshields were of one-piece design and a double belt molding was added to cab doors. The major styling difference between new and former 3/4-ton trucks was the oblong quarter window that Graham Bros. added directly in back of the driver's door. This helped illuminate the load compartment. It also contributed to safety by giving better visibility. In addition, quarter windows gave all Graham Bros. models a "big truck" look. This year also brought a reworking of the venerable old Dodge four-cylinder engine. A five-bearing crankshaft contributed to smoother performance. Bore and stroke remained the

same, and developed horsepower remained at 35. All five-bearing engines had a C prefix with the engine number. On March 22, 1927, a new Morse chain drive replaced the timing gears, the oil pump was moved inside the crankcase, and both manifolds were placed on the engine's right-hand side. The water pump, generator and distributor were also relocated. The new engine was designated the 124. Graham Bros.' trucks first received this engine on April 14, 1927. Beginning on Jan. 3, 1927, a single plate Borg and Beck clutch replaced the Dodge-built dry disc type. Engines with the new clutch had a D prefix to their engine number. D models were known as Series 126, the first official series designation ever given to a line of Dodge Bros. vehicles. Standard equipment included a speedometer, ammeter, electric head and taillamps, electric horn, air cleaner, automatic tire pump, jack, tools and tool box. Upholstery was leather over curled hair and coil springs.

1927 Graham Bros. Enclosed-Cab Express (OCW)

1-TON — GRAHAM BROTHERS BD/ID SERIES — FOUR-CYLINDER: Introduced by Graham in 1926 as the famous G-Boy series, the BD continued essentially unchanged for 1927. The only difference was company ownership. Graham Bros.' truck division had been totally taken over by Dodge. However, Dodge Bros. continued to build trucks in the Graham factories and sold them under the Graham name. Appearance was much like the 3/4-ton line, except that 1-tons were built on two longer wheelbase chassis and were equipped with steel spoke wheels. Standard equipment was the same as the 3/4-ton models.
I.D. DATA: Serial numbers were located on the left side member of the frame, just in back of the front spring's front bracket. Starting: A-702243. Ending serial number not available. Engine numbers not available.

Model	Body Type	Price	Weight	Prod. Total
3/4-Ton — 116 in. w.b.				
DC	Chassis	670	4495	2742
DC	Canopy	870	4495	1012
DC	Express	845	4495	1473
DC	Panel	895	4495	8986
DC	Screen	885	4495	6757
1-Ton — 126 in. w.b.				
BD	Chassis	895	5415	Note 2
BD	Canopy	1120	5415	Note 2
BD	Express	1085	5415	Note 2
BD	Farm Box	1115	5415	Note 2
BD	Panel	1160	5415	Note 2
BD	Stake	1115	5415	Note 2
1-Ton — 137 in. w.b.				
ID	Chassis	980	5415	Note 2
ID	Canopy	1275	5415	Note 2
ID	Express	1240	5415	Note 2
ID	Panel	1320	5415	Note 2

NOTE 1: Calendar year shipments to dealers.
NOTE 2: Total calendar year shipments to dealers of 1-ton trucks: 16,992.
NOTE 3: Weights shown are GVW rating.
ENGINE: Inline. L-head. Four-cylinder. Cast iron block. Bore & stroke: 3-7/8 x 4-1/2 in. Displacement: 212.3 cid. Compression ratio: 4.0:1. Brake horsepower: 35 at 2000 rpm. Net (Taxable) horsepower: 24.03. Five main bearings. Solid valve lifters. Carburetor: Stewart.
CHASSIS [3/4-Ton]: Wheelbase: 116 in. Tires: 31 x 5.25 balloon on wood wheels.
CHASSIS [Series BD]: Wheelbase: 126 in. Tires: 30 x 5 pneumatic on steel-spoke wheels.
CHASSIS [Series ID]: Wheelbase: 137 in. Tires: Same as Series BD.

1927 Graham Bros. Model SD-770 Panel (HACJ)

TECHNICAL: Selective sliding gear transmission. Speeds: 3F/1R. Floor shift control. Dry multiple-disc clutch (later, single plate Borg & Beck). Semi-floating rear axle. Rear-wheel mechanical brakes. Hand brake (expanding) on rear wheels. Worm and wheel steering. Shaft drive. Springs: (front) semi-elliptic; (rear) semi-elliptic, underslung. Vacuum feed fuel system. Six-volt electrical system.

HISTORICAL: Introduced: July 1, 1926. Calendar year sales (Graham Bros. trucks): 42,359. Calendar year shipments to dealers were (3/4-Ton) 20,969; (1-ton) 16,992. Model year production (cars and trucks) was 146,001. Innovations included a five-bearing crankshaft. Two-unit 6-volt electrical system. Single plate clutch. Four-point engine suspension. Convertible 3/4-ton bodies used standardized parts, so owners could switch easily to another type. Dodge ranked seventh in U.S. car sales and third in trucks. Graham Bros. built a wide range of truck bodies in its own plants, in Detroit, Michigan; Evansville, Indiana; and Stockton, California. The lineup included 13 truck models in 1-1/2- and 2-ton capacity, plus three bus models. Dodge Bros. began to sell a commercial conversion for its sedan, coupe and roadster. Coupe/roadster conversions, offered in box and sliding-drawer form for the rear deck compartment, could be dealer-installed or ordered from the factory. Sedan conversions were available only from the Millspaugh and Irish Co. A removable rear seat was installed and the rear end was fitted with a single door, as in a panel or Sedan Delivery.

1927 Graham Bros. 1-Ton Panel Delivery (OCW)

1928 DODGE
(GRAHAM)

1928 Graham Bros. 3/4-Ton Panel Delivery (OCW)

1/2-TON — SERIES SD — FOUR-CYLINDER: The all new SD panel delivery was based on Dodge Bros.' Fast Four automobile, which had been introduced in July, 1927 for the 1928 model year. Much lighter in weight, with a wheelbase shortened to 108 in., the Fast Four gave sparkling performance using the Dodge Bros. four-cylinder engine. Production of the SD, or Merchant's Express, began in September, 1927, and ran until July, 1928. Its handsome, low panel body featured a smart cadet front and sun visor. The spare tire sat in the recessed left front fender. Built in the Graham Bros. factories and carrying that name, the SD was promoted for its ability to make prompt deliveries, with fast getaways and high-speed runs. Standard equipment included front and rear fenders, front bumper, spare rim, air cleaner, electric head and taillights, stoplight horn, speedometer and ammeter, windshield wipers, rearview mirrors, and a tire pump.
3/4-TON — SERIES DD — FOUR-CYLINDER: Carried over unchanged from 1927, the DD was powered by the improved Dodge Bros. four-cylinder, five-bearing engine. Outselling all other Graham Bros. trucks, the panel body was padded to reduce road rumble. Convertible bodies were featured. Any standard body could be changed easily by adding or removing various units. If the owner of a pickup truck wanted to convert it into a canopy type, a standard canopy top could be mounted on the pickup. The pickup could also be used as the basis for a panel or screen truck. Equipment was the same as the 1/2-ton model.
1-TON — SERIES BD/ID — FOUR-CYLINDER: Both the BD (126 in. wheelbase) and ID (137 in.) continued unchanged from 1927, powered by the improved Dodge four-cylinder engine. The BD was available as a chassis only, or a canopy, express, farm box, panel and stake truck. The ID came in chassis form, plus canopy, express and panel bodies were available. All bodies were standardized, like those in the DD series. Trucks were built in Graham Bros. plants and carried that nameplate. Equipment was the same as the 1/2-ton SD.
I.D. DATA: Serial numbers were located on the left side member of the frame, just in back of the front spring's front bracket. (Detroit) Starting: D-151237. Ending: D-175589. (Evans-

Standard Catalog of Light-Duty Trucks

1928 Graham Bros. 1-Ton Panel Delivery (OCW)

Model	Body Type	Price	Weight	Prod. Total
Series SD — 1/2-Ton — 108 in. w.b.				
SD	Panel	770	3780	—
Series DD — 3/4-Ton — 116 in. w.b.				
DD	Chassis	670	2170	—
DD	Pickup	845	4570	—
DD	Panel	895	4570	—
Series BD — 1-Ton — 126 in. w.b.				
BD	Chassis	895	2530	—
BD	Canopy	1130	5415	—
BD	Pickup	1095	5415	—
BD	Farm Box	1125	5415	—
BD	Panel	1170	5415	—
BD	Stake	1125	5415	—
Series ID — 1-Ton — 137 in. w.b.				
ID	Chassis	980	2860	—
ID	Canopy	1235	5415	—
ID	Pickup	1200	5415	—
ID	Panel	1280	5415	—

NOTE: All weights, except chassis alone, are GVW.

ENGINE [All Models]: Inline. L-head. Four-cylinder. Cast iron block. Bore & stroke: 3-7/8 x 4-1/2 in. Displacement: 212.3 cid. Compression ratio: 4.1:1. Brake horsepower: 35. Net horsepower: 24.03. Five main bearings. Solid valve lifters. Carburetor: Stewart.
CHASSIS [Series SD]: Wheelbase: 108 in. Tires: 29 x 5.00 balloon. Payload: 1,000 lbs.
CHASSIS [Series DD]: Wheelbase: 116 in. Tires: 31 x 5.25 in. Payload: 1,500 bs.
CHASSIS [Series BD]: Wheelbase: 126 in. Tires: 30 x 5 in. Payload: 2,000 lbs.
CHASSIS [Series ID]: Wheelbase: 137 in. Tires: 30 x 5 in. Payload: 2,000 lbs.
TECHNICAL: Selective sliding gear transmission. Speeds: 3F/1R. Floor shift control. Single-plate dry-disc clutch. Semi-floating rear axle. Two-wheel mechanical brakes. Hand brake: [SD] contracting on propellor shaft; [others] expanding on rear wheels. Steering: [SD] worm and sector; [others] cam and lever. Vacuum fuel feed. Wood-spoke wheels.
HISTORICAL: Introduced: September, 1927. Calendar year registrations (all Graham Bros. trucks and buses) were 36,542. Production figures not available. Dodge/Graham ranked third in sales among U.S. truck producers. Hotchkiss drive replaced torque tube drive. A new spiral bevel-gear rear axle was again of semi-floating type. Millspaugh and Irish Corp. developed an All-Purpose Sedan commercial conversion for the Fast Four car. A new six-cylinder Dodge car engine was used in Graham Bros. 2- and 3-ton trucks and buses. It would be ready for smaller trucks in the next model year. This was the final production year for the Dodge Bros. Co. On July 30, 1928, Walter P. Chrysler...who had wanted the company for years...purchased Dodge Bros. for a $170 million exchange of stock. Chrysler wanted a car to compete with Ford. He also wanted the excellent Dodge dealer network and the company's huge manufacturing capabilities. On the night the deal was closed, Chrysler's people moved into the Dodge Bros. factories, taking over completely. They dismissed staff members, including president Wilmer. K.T. Keller was then appointed as the new president of Dodge Div. Dodge Bros. began producing six-cylinder cars in February, 1928 and the last four-cylinder models were built on July 27, 1928.

1928-1929 DODGE

1/2-TON MERCHANT'S EXPRESS — MODEL SE — SIX-CYLINDER: After Dodge Bros. was sold to Chrysler Corp. in July, 1928, the new management had little time to plan, prepare and introduce new trucks for the 1929 model year. The 1/2-ton SD panel was discontinued in April, 1928, and immediately replaced by a Merchant's Express SE with 110 in. wheelbase (two inches longer than before). Essentially the same as its predecessor, the SE had a six-cylinder engine developed from the "Victory Six" passenger car line. It replaced the familiar Dodge Bros. four-cylinder motor. Only a panel body was offered. It had a load space 67.75 in. long by 44.5 in. wide (48.75 in. at the beltline) and 44 in. high. The radiator shell, front bumper and filler cap were nickel plated. Standard equipment included full-length runningboards, spare tire carrier with extra rim, oil filter, air cleaner, electric horn, tail/stop light, instrument light, rearview mirror, windshield wipers, and tool kit.
3/4-TON COMMERCIAL TRUCK — SERIES DA-120 — SIX-CYLINDER: This new model appeared, late in the model year, to replace the Series DD. Appearance was similar to the DD, but the new truck sat on a longer 120 in. wheelbase and was powered by a six-cylinder

engine, rather than the original Dodge four-cylinder. Model availability was expanded to include stake and platform body styles. Painted in blue lacquer, with gold moldings and cream-colored wheels, the 3/4-ton had a chrome-plated radiator shell and filler cap. Standard equipment included full-length runningboards, front bumper, electric starter and horn, tail/stop light, dash light, oil filter, radiator shutter, speedometer, oil pressure and temperature gauges, ammeter, choke, locking ignition switch, license bracket, and tool kit. A spare rim sat in a tire carrier under the frame at rear.
1-TON — SERIES DA-130/DA-140 — SIX-CYLINDER: The DA-130 (130 in. wheelbase) and DA-140 (140 in.) trucks were identical in appearance, except for longer wheelbases than the BD and ID models of 1928, which they replaced. Both were powered by the new six-cylinder engine. The 130 in. chassis held an 8 ft. body, while the longer one mounted a 9-ft body. Model availability of the smaller truck was the same as in 1928, but the DA-140 added side-door panel, platform and stake bodies. Standard equipment was identical to the DA-120, but with short runningboards and a thermostat.
I.D. DATA: Serial numbers were on the left side member of the frame, just in back of the front spring's front bracket. [ModeL SE] Starting number, Detroit: D-203830. Starting number, Evansville: E-141527. Starting number, Stockton: S-112553. [3/4-Ton/1-Ton] Starting number, Detroit: D-175590 (April, 1928). Ending number, Detroit: D-237361 (January, 1932). Starting number, Evansville: E-133097 (May, 1928). Ending number, Evansville: E-151171 (May, 1932). Starting number, Stockton: S-109835 (June, 1928). Ending number, Stockton: S-116399 (November, 1932). Engine numbers were located on the left front corner of cylinder block. [Model SE] Starting number: J-31810. [3/4-Ton and 1-Ton] Starting: M-120553.

1928 Dodge DA-130 1-Ton Panel Delivery (JAW)

Model	Body Type	Price	Weight	Prod. Total
Series SE — 1/2-Ton — 110 in. w.b.				
SE	Chassis	665	1965	—
SE	Panel	845	—	—
Series DA-120 — 3/4-Ton — 120 in. w.b.				
DA-120	Chassis	775	2510	—
DA-120	Chassis & Cab	920	—	—
DA-120	Canopy	970	—	—
DA-120	Express	955	—	—
DA-120	Panel	995	—	—
DA-120	Screen	985	—	—
DA-120	Platform	975	—	—
DA-120	Stake	1020	—	—
Series DA-130 — 1-Ton — 130 in. w.b.				
DA-130	Chassis	995	2920	—
DA-130	Chassis & Cab	1140	—	—
DA-130	Canopy	1240	—	—
DA-130	Express	1205	—	—
DA-130	Panel	1280	—	—
DA-130	Screen	1265	—	—
DA-130	Farm	1245	—	—
DA-130	Platform	1205	—	—
DA-130	Stake	1250	—	—
Series DA-140 — 1-Ton — 140 in. w.b.				
DA-140	Chassis	1065	2955	—
DA-140	Chassis & Cab	1130	—	—
DA-140	Canopy	1330	—	—
DA-140	Carryall	1385	—	—
DA-140	Express	1295	—	—
DA-140	Panel	1375	—	—
DA-140	Side Door Panel	1425	—	—
DA-140	Screen	1365	—	—
DA-140	Platform	1280	—	—
DA-140	Stake	1330	—	—

ENGINE [All Models]: Inline. L-head. Six-cylinder. Cast iron block. Bore & stroke: 3-3/8 x 3-7/8 in. Displacement: 208 cid. Compression ratio: 5.18:1. Brake horsepower: 63. Net horsepower: 27.34. Seven main bearings. Solid valve lifters. Carburetor: Stromberg or Stewart (buyer's choice).
CHASSIS [Model SE]: Wheelbase: 110 in. Tires: 29 x 5.00 balloon (6-ply). Payload: 1,000 lbs.
CHASSIS [Series DA-120]: Wheelbase: 120 in. Tires: 31 x 5.25 balloon (6-ply) on 21 x 4 rims. Payload: 1,500 lbs.
CHASSIS [Series DA-130]: Wheelbase: 130 in. Tires: 30 x 5 (8-ply) on 20 x 5 rims. Payload: 2,000 lbs.
CHASSIS [Series DA-140]: Wheelbase: 140 in. Tires: 30 x 5 (8-ply) on 20 x 5 rims. Payload: 2,000 lbs.
TECHNICAL: Selective sliding gear transmission. Speeds: [SE and DA-120] 3F/1R. [DA-130/140] 4F/1R with provision for power-take-off. Floor shift control. Single-plate dry-disc clutch. Semi-floating rear axle. Overall ratio: [SE] 4.455:1; [others] 5.1:1 (5.667:1 optional on DA-130/140). Spiral bevel gear drive. Four-wheel brakes: [SE] Steeldraulic mechanical with 2 x 12 in. drums; [others] Lockheed hydraulic. Hand brake on propeller shaft. Semi-elliptical springs: [SE] front 1.75 x 37 in., nine-leaves; rear 2 x 54 in., eight-leaves. [DA-120] front 2 x 39 in., eight-leaves; rear 2.5 x 48 in., nine-leaves. [DA-130/140] front 2 x 39 in.,

eight-leaves; rear 2.5 x 48 in., 10-leaves. Steering: [SE] worm and sector; [others] cam and lever (varying ratio). Fuel: [DA-120/130/140] vacuum feed; air cleaner and gas filter; 15-gallon gas tank under driver's seat. Maximum allowable speed: [DA-120/130/140] 35 mph. Drop forged I-beam front axle. Wheels: [SE/DA-120] wood-spoke with steel felloes on demountable rims; [others] malleable iron spoke.

OPTIONS: [DA-120]: 33 x 4-1/2 high-pressure tires, front and rear ($15). 30 x 5 eight-ply tires, front and rear ($55). Screen section hinged at top for rear end above tailgate ($15). [DA-130/140] 33 x 5 tires, front and rear ($35). 32 x 6 eight-ply tires, front and rear ($45). 32 x 6 10-ply tires, front and rear ($125). Power tire pump ($12). Heavy-duty power tire pump ($12.50). Screen section hinged at top for rear end above tailgate ($15). Extra farm sides for 8 ft. stake ($40). Extra standard stake sides for 8 ft. farm box($45).

HISTORICAL: Introduced: [Model SE] April, 1928; [Series DA-120/DA-130/DA-140] late in 1927 model year. Calendar year production for 1929 was 47,014. Calendar year registrations for 1929 were 28,759. Production figures by model year and type are not available. Four-wheel brakes (hydraulic on larger trucks) introduced. One effect of the new Chrysler Corp. influence was the abandonment of the Graham Bros. name on trucks. Beginning on Jan. 1, 1929, all trucks, buses and motorcoaches would carry the Dodge Bros. nameplate. That Dodge name was thought to have wider public acceptance and be more generally known. Besides that, the Graham Bros. were back in business building cars after a merger with the Paige-Detroit Co.

1929 DODGE

1929 Dodge Merchant's Express 1/2-Ton Panel (OCW)

1/2-TON PANEL — MERCHANT'S EXPRESS — FOUR-CYLINDER: In May 1929, the first all-new truck designed and built by Chrysler Corp. was introduced. This 1/2-ton panel used a Plymouth four-cylinder, 175.4 cid engine. At $545, this was the lowest-priced chassis ever offered by Dodge for commercial use. In less than one model year, Dodge 1/2-ton production went from a 108 in. wheelbase model with Dodge Bros. four, to the 110 in. wheelbase SE with a six-cylinder engine, to this 109 in. wheelbase version powered by a smaller four. The new Merchant's Express was an attractive little truck with forward-sweeping roof line and cadet type overhanging sun shield. Front end appearance borrowed much from Chrysler's passenger cars. The windshield was flat and vertical and the spare was carried in the left front fender. Two full-length rear doors gave access to cargo space. Interior dimensions were slightly larger than the SE it replaced: 72 in. long, 45.5 in. between wheelwells (50 in. at the beltline), and 50 in. high. This gave a load space of 102 cu. ft. Brakes were hydraulic. The 6-foot panel body was painted blue, with a gray interior. Wood-spoke wheels were cream with black hubs. The fenders were black. The radiator shell and headlight rims were chrome plated. Standard equipment included full-length running-boards, tail/stop light, panel light, automatic wipers, electric horn, electric starter, speedometer, oil pressure gauge, ammeter, choke, locking ignition switch, license bracket, and tool kit.

I.D. DATA: Serial number was located on left side member of frame, just in back of the front spring's front bracket. Starting: P-1001. Engine number was on the left front corner of the cylinder block. Starting: UT-1001.

1929 Dodge Commercial Station Wagon (CHC)

Model	Body Type	Price	Weight	Prod. Total
Merchant`s Express — 1/2-Ton — 109 in. w.b.				
—	Chassis	545	1900	—
—	Panel	795	2850	—

ENGINE: Inline. L-head. Four-cylinder. Cast iron block. Bore & stroke: 3-7/8 in. x 4 in. Displacement: 175.4 cid. Compression ratio: 4.6:1. Brake horsepower: 45 at 2800 rpm. Net horsepower: 21.03. Three main bearings. Solid valve lifters. Carburetor: Plain tube.

CHASSIS: Wheelbase: 109 in. Tires: 29 x 4.75 (six-ply) on 20 in. wheels. Payload: 1,000 lbs.

TECHNICAL: Selective sliding gear transmission. Speeds: 3F/1R. Floor shift control. Single-plate dry-disc clutch. Semi-floating rear axle. Overall ratio: 4.7:1. Spiral bevel gear drive. Hydraulic four-wheel brakes; 1-1/2 x 11 in. drums. Hand brake on propeller shaft. Springs: Front 1-3/4 x 35-1/2 in., 9 leaves; rear 1-3/4 x 53-1/2 in., 13 leaves. Drop forged I-beam front axle. Worm and sector steering. Vacuum feed fuel system. Air cleaner. 11-gallon gas tank under frame at rear. Allowable speed: 40 mph. Wood-spoke wheels with steel felloes on demountable rims.

OPTIONS: Extra seat ($20). Bumpers, front and rear ($15).

HISTORICAL: Introduced: May 1929. Calendar year production (1929): 47,014. Calendar year sales (1929): 28,759. Production figures by model type not available. Innovations: Hydraulic brakes. The new Merchant's Express, designed and engineered by Chrysler, began a trend that has lasted to the present time: Dodge trucks powered by one of the corporate engines. The 1/2-ton was powered by a Plymouth four, while 3/4- and 1-ton models carried the Dodge car's six-cylinder engine. Dodge built a full line of trucks, up to 3-ton capacity. They were basically the former Graham Bros. trucks with new nameplates. Dodge trucks ranked fourth in sales for 1929.

1930 DODGE

1930 Dodge Cantrell Commercial Station Wagon (CHC)

1/2-TON MERCHANT'S EXPRESS — SERIES U1-A-109 — FOUR-CYLINDER: The four-cylinder Merchant's Express entered its second year without appearance changes or engineering refinements. Three new body styles were added, including the first 1/2-ton pickup available from Dodge Truck Div. The perky little pickup was constructed with its cab integral to the body. It featured two small, rectangular rear cab windows. Solid-panelled wood box sides were covered outside by sheet metal. Full-length flare boards and a full-width tailgate were constructed in the same manner. The pickup's cab shared with its larger mates the traditional Graham Bros. type rear quarter windows, which enhanced its business-like good looks. Pickups were painted Dodge Blue with yellow moldings, black stripes and cream-colored wood-spoke wheels. Other models used the same scheme, except for gold stripes on the screen side truck. Pickup box inside dimensions were 60-1/2 in. long by 45-1/8 in. wide and 13-1/4 in. high. New screen and canopy models measured the same as the panel body, which continued without change. Standard equipment was the same as in 1929.

3/4 TON COMMERCIAL TRUCK — SERIES UI-8-124 — FOUR-CYLINDER: An all-new 3/4-ton truck with a 124 in. wheelbase, four inches longer than the previous version, came with hydraulic brakes and a choice of four- or six-cylinder engines. Appearance reflected the corporate styling. It was cleaner and crisper than the former Graham Bros. look. The 3/4-ton looked much like a large version of the Merchant's Express. Six body styles were available. Roomy, comfortable cabs had larger windshields and slender steel corner posts.

Upholstery was leather. The paint scheme was again Dodge Blue with yellow moldings, black stripes and cream wheels. Standard equipment included a chrome-plated radiator shell and filler cap, full-length runningboards, spare rim under frame at rear, electric horn and starter, tall/stop light, air cleaner, crankcase ventilator, speedometer, oil pressure gauge, ammeter, choke, locking ignition switch, license brackets, and tool kit.

3/4 TON COMMERCIAL TRUCK — SERIES DA1-B-124 — SIX-CYLINDER: The trucks in this series were the same as those in the UI-B-124 series, but with six-cylinder engines.

1-TON — SERIES UI-C-133 — FOUR-CYLINDER: Dodge 1-ton trucks for 1930 mixed the new with the old. At 133 in. wheelbase length, the new four-cylinder was a stretched version of the 3/4-ton with an eight-foot body rather than seven-foot. Priced lower than any 1-ton in Dodge history, it used the same Plymouth-based four-cylinder engine as the smaller trucks. The radiator shell and filler cap were chrome plated. Standard equipment included a cowl ventilator, short or long runningboards (depending on body type), spare rim under frame at rear, electric horn and starter, tail/stop light, thermostat, speedometer, oil pressure gauge, ammeter, choke, locking ignition switch, governor, and tool kit.

1-TON — SERIES DA1-C-133/DA1-C-140 — SIX-CYLINDER: Six-cylinder powered 1-ton trucks came on 133 or 140 in. wheelbases. The 140 in. models were carried over unchanged from 1929, continuing the old Graham Bros. styling with distinctive rear quarter cab windows. Standard equipment was the same as for the four-cylinder models.

I.D. DATA: Serial numbers were on the left side member of the frame, just in back of the front spring's front bracket. Serial numbers: [Four; 1/2-ton] P3488 and up; [Four; 3/4-Ton] 221142 up; [Four; 1-Ton] 218623 and up; [Six; 3/4-Ton] 221339 and up; [Six;1-Ton; 133 in. w.b.] 220380 and up; [Six; 1-Ton; 140 in. w.b.] 218711 and up. Engine numbers were located on the left front corner of the cylinder block. Engine numbers not available.

1930 Dodge 1/2-Ton Pickup (JAW)

Model	Body Type	Price	Weight	Prod. Total
1/2-Ton — 109 in. w.b.				
U1-A	Chassis	545	1900	—
U1-A	Pickup	754	—	—
U1-A	Canopy	770	—	—
U1-A	Screen	795	—	—
U1-A	Panel	795	—	—
3/4-Ton — 124 in. w.b.				
U1-B	Chassis	695	2260	—
U1-B	Chassis & Cab	845	—	—
U1-B	Platform	905	—	—
U1-B	Pickup	935	—	—
U1-B	Canopy	960	—	—
U1-B	Stake	955	—	—
U1-B	Screen	985	—	—
U1-B	Panel	985	—	—
DA1-B	Chassis	795	2360	—
DA1-B	Chassis & Cab	945	—	—
DA1-B	Platform	1005	—	—
DA1-B	Express	1035	—	—
DA1-B	Canopy	1060	—	—
DA1-B	Stake	1055	—	—
DA1-B	Screen	1085	—	—
DA1-B	Panel	1085	—	—
1-Ton — 133 in. w.b.				
U1-C	Chassis	795	2590	—
U1-C	Chassis & Cab	945	—	—
U1-C	Platform	1015	—	—
U1-C	Farm	1055	—	—
U1-C	Stake	1065	—	—
U1-C	Express	1088	—	—
U1-C	Canopy	1103	—	—
U1-C	Screen	1153	—	—
U1-C	Panel	1153	—	—
DA1-C	Chassis	895	2690	—
DA1-C	Chassis & Cab	1045	—	—
DA1-C	Platform	1115	—	—
DA1-C	Farm	1155	—	—
DA1-C	Stake	1165	—	—
DA1-C	Express	1188	—	—
DA1-C	Canopy	1203	—	—
DA1-C	Screen	1253	—	—
DA1-C	Panel	1253	—	—
1-Ton — 140 in. w.b.				
DA1-C	Chassis	1095	2955	—
DA1-C	Chassis Cab	1255	—	—
DA1-C	Platform	1335	—	—
DA1-C	Express	1385	—	—
DA1-C	Stake	1385	—	—
DA1-C	Canopy	1410	—	—
DA1-C	Screen	1440	—	—
DA1-C	Panel	1440	—	—
DA1-C	Carryall	1470	—	—
DA1-C	Side Door Panel	1475	—	—

ENGINE [U1-A-109/U1-B-124/U1-C-133]: Inline. L-head. Four-cylinder. Cast iron block. Bore & stroke: 3-5/8 in. x 4-1/4 in. Displacement: 175.4 cid. Compression ratio: 4.6:1. Brake horsepower: 45 at 2800 rpm. Net horsepower: 21.03. Three main bearings. Solid valve lifters.

ENGINE [DA1-B-124/DAI-C-133/DAi-B-140]: Inline. L-head. Six cylinder. Cast iron block. Bore & stroke: 3-3/8 in. x 3-1/8 in. Displacement: 208 cid. Compression ratio: 5.18:1. Brake horsepower: 63 at 3000 rpm. Net horsepower: 27.34. Seven main bearings. Solid valve lifters. Carburetor: [DA1-B-124] Zenith. [DA1-C-140] Stewart. Carburetor: Carter.

CHASSIS: [U1-A-109] Wheelbase: 109 in. Tires: 20 x 5 (six-ply). Payload: 1,000 lbs.

CHASSIS: [U1-B-124] Wheelbase: 124 in. Tires: 20 x 5.50 (six-ply). Body length: Seven-feet. Payload: 1,500 lbs.

CHASSIS: [U1-C-133 and DA1-C-133] Wheelbase: 133 in. Tires: 20 x 6.00 (six-ply) front and 32 x 6 (eight-ply) rear. Payload: 2,000 lbs.

CHASSIS: [DA1-C-140] Wheelbase: 140 in. Tires: 30 x 5 (eight-ply).

TECHNICAL: Selective sliding gear transmission. Speeds [1/2- and 3/4-ton] 3F/1R; [1-ton] 4F/1R with provision for power-take-off. Floor shift control. Single-plate dry-disc clutch. Semi-floating rear axle. Spiral bevel gear drive. Overall ratio: [1/2-ton] 4.7:1; [3/4-ton] 5.63:1 [6.00:1 and 5.11:1 optional]; [1-ton/UI-C-133, DA1-C-133] 5.6:1 (6.375:1 optional); [DA1-C-140] 5.1l (5.667:1 optional). Hydraulic four-wheel brakes. Hand-brake on propeller shaft. Semi-elliptic springs; [1/2-ton] front 35 in., nine-leaves; rear 53-1/2 in., 13-leaves. [3/4-ton] front 39 in., eight-leaves; rear 48 in., nine-leaves. [One-ton] front 39 in., eight-leaves; rear 48 in., 11-leaves. Steering [1/2-ton] worm and sector; [others] nut and lever (varying ratio). Vacuum feed fuel system. Air cleaner. Gas tank: [1/2-ton] 11-gallon, under frame at rear; [others] 15-gallon, under driver's seat. Allowable speed: 40 mph (except DAI-C-140: 35 mph). Wood-spoke wheels with steel felloes on demountable rims (except DA1-C-140 has malleable iron spokes.)

OPTIONS: [1/2-ton] Extra seat ($20). Bumpers, front and rear ($15). Front bumpers only ($8.50). Rear bumper only ($6.50). [3/4-ton] 33 x 4-1/2 in. tires with wood wheels ($17.50). 30 x 5 in. eight-ply tires with metal spoke wheels ($50). Front bumper ($8.50). [1-ton] 30 x 5 in. eight-ply tires on metal spoke wheels ($15). 20 x 6 in. eight-ply tires front; 32 x 6 in. eight-ply tires rear, with metal spoke wheels ($12). 20 x 6 in. six-ply front; 32 x 6 in. 10-ply rear ties on metal spoke wheels ($32.50). Extra farm box sides for eight-foot stake body ($40). Extra standard stake sides for eight-foot farm box body ($50). Front bumper ($8.50). Long runningboards and rear fenders for chassis only ($12.50). Power tire pump ($18.50).

HISTORICAL: U1-C-133 introduced September, 1929. Calendar year production was 23,316 trucks. Calendar year registrations were 15,558. Production figures not available by model year or type. Four-cylinder engine. Fuel vacuum from oil pump rather than intake manifold. A 22 percent drop in U.S. truck registrations signalled the beginning of the Great Depression. Dodge truck sales suffered even worse, dropping 45.9 percent from 1929. However, the company still ranked fourth in truck sales. The full Dodge line included four- and six-cylinder engines, but only sixes were used to power 1-1/2 to 3-ton trucks. As before, Dodge trucks were built at factories in Detroit, Michigan; Evansville, Indiana; and Stockton, California.

1931 DODGE

1931 Dodge Model UF10 with Open Passenger Body (DFW/CCC)

1/2-TON — SERIES UF-10 — FOUR-CYLINDER; 1/2-TON — SERIES F-10 — SIX-CYLINDER: Dodge entered the second year of the Great Depression fighting for sales. Two steps were taken in the 1/2-ton truck series to strengthen its position in the marketplace. First was the addition of a six-cylinder model, the F-10. Second was a substantial price cut of $110 for each model. The new series was identical in appearance to the 1930 Merchant's Express. Technical features varied only slightly and all body types were carried over. Radiator shell was black enamel with a chrome-plated cap. Standard equipment included full-length runningboards, cowl vent, automatic wipers, electric horn and starter, tail/stop light, speedometer, oil pressure gauge, ammeter, locking ignition switch, choke, thermostat, rearview mirror, license brackets, spare rim in right front fenderwell, and tool kit.

3/4-TON — SERIES UI-B-124 — FOUR-CYLINDER; 3/4-TON — SERIES DA1-B-124 — SIX-CYLINDER: These trucks were carried over from 1930 without change in either appearance or engineering specifications. Unlike the 1/2-ton and 1-ton models, their prices were not reduced. Body types and standard equipment were the same as before.

1-TON — SERIES UI-C-133 — FOUR-CYLINDER; 1-TON — SERIES DA1-C-133 — SIX-CYLINDER: No changes were made in the carryover 1-ton trucks, except that the 140 in. wheelbase model was discontinued and prices for the others were cut substantially. Standard equipment was the same as 1930.

I.D. DATA: [1/2-ton] Serial numbers were stamped on the left side member of the frame, just in back of the front spring's front bracket. They were also on a serial number plate on the engine side of the cowl. [UF-10] Starting: 8000001 (August, 1930). Ending: 8007264 (December, 1932). Starting: 9200001 (December 1930). Ending: 9200313 (October, 1932). [F-10] Starting: 8100001 (August, 1930). Ending: 8102959 (January, 1933). Starting: 9212501 (January, 1931). Ending: 9212717 (January, 1933). Engine numbers were stamped on the top left front of the engine block. [UF-10] Starting Engine Number: UT21101. [F-10] Starting Engine Number: DD2T1001. [3/4-ton] Serial numbers same as 1930. [1-ton] Serial numbers same as 133 in. wheelbase models of 1930.

1931 Dodge Model DA1-C One-Ton Screenside (OCW)

Model	Body Type	Price	Weight	Prod. Total
1/2-Ton — 109 in. w.b.				
UF-10	Chassis	435	1900	—
UF-10	Pickup	644	—	—
UF-10	Canopy	660	—	—
UF-10	Screen	685	—	—
UF-10	Panel	685	—	—
F-10	Chassis	535	2000	—
F-10	Pickup	744	—	—
F-10	Canopy	760	—	—
F-10	Screen	785	—	—
F-10	Panel	785	—	—
3/4-Ton — 124 in. w.b.				
UI-B	Chassis	695	2260	—
UI-B	Chassis & Cab	845	—	—
UI-B	Platform	905	—	—
UI-B	Pickup	935	—	—
UI-B	Canopy	960	—	—
UI-B	Stake	955	—	—
UI-B	Screen	985	—	—
UI-B	Panel	985	—	—
DA1-B	Chassis	795	2360	—
DA1-B	Chassis & Cab	945	—	—
DA1-B	Platform	1005	—	—
DA1-B	Express	1035	—	—
DA1-B	Canopy	1060	—	—
DA1-B	Stake	1055	—	—
DA1-B	Screen	1085	—	—
DA1-B	Panel	1085	—	—
1-Ton — 133 in. w.b.				
UI-C	Chassis	495	2590	—
UI-C	Chassis & Cab	645	—	—
UI-C	Platform	715	—	—
UI-C	Farm	755	—	—
UI-C	Stake	765	—	—
UI-C	Express	787.50	—	—
UI-C	Canopy	802.50	—	—
UI-C	Screen	852.50	—	—
UI-C	Panel	852.50	—	—
DA1-C	Chassis	595	2690	—
DA1-C	Chassis & Cab	745	—	—
DA1-C	Platform	815	—	—
DA1-C	Farm	855	—	—
DA1-C	Stake	865	—	—
DA1-C	Express	887.50	—	—
DA1-C	Canopy	902.50	—	—
DA1-C	Screen	952.50	—	—
DA1-C	Panel	952.50	—	—

ENGINE [UF-10]: Inline. L-head. Four-cylinder. Cast iron block. Bore & stroke: 3-5/8 in. x 4-3/4 in. Displacement: 196.1 cid. Compression ratio: 4.6:1. Brake horsepower: 48 at 2800 rpm. Net horsepower: 21.02. Max. torque: 124 lbs.-ft. at 1200 rpm. Three main bearings. Solid valve lifters. Carburetor: Carter.

ENGINE [F-10]: Inline. L-head. Six-cylinder. Cast iron block. Bore & stroke: 3-1/8 in. x 4-1/8 in. Displacement: 189.8 cid. Compression ratio: 5.2:1. Brake horsepower: 60 at 3400 rpm. Net horsepower: 23.4. Max. torque: 120 lbs.-ft. at 1200 rpm. Four main bearings. Solid valve lifters. Carburetor: Carter.

CHASSIS: [1/2-ton] Wheelbase: 109 in. Tires: 19 x 5.00 (four-ply). Payload: 1,200 lbs.

CHASSIS: [3/4-ton] Wheelbase: 124 in. Tires: 20 x 5.50 (six-ply). Payload: 1,500 lbs.

CHASSIS: [1-ton] Wheelbase: 133 in. Tires: 20 x 6 (six-ply) front and 32 x 6 (eight-ply) rear. Payload: 2,000 lbs.

TECHNICAL: [1/2-ton] Selective sliding gear transmission. Speeds: 3F/1R; [1-ton] 4F/1R with PTO provision. Floor shifters. Single-plate dry-disc clutch (9 in. on 1/2-ton). Semi-floating rear axle. Overall ratio: [1/2-ton] 4.66:1.; [3/4-ton] 5.63:1 (6.0:1 and 5.11:1 optional); [1-ton/UI-C-133 & DA1C-133] 5.6:1 (6.375:1 optional); [1-ton/DA1C-140] 5.1:1 (5.677:1 optional). Spiral bevel gear drive. Hydraulic four-wheel brakes; 11 in. drums. Hand-brake on propeller shaft. Semi-elliptical springs: [1/2-ton] front 1-3/4 x 35-1/2 in., eight-leaves; rear 1-11/16 x 53-1/2 in., 15-leaves; [3/4-ton] front 39 in., eight-leaves and rear 48 in., nine-leaves; [1-ton] front 39 in., eight-leaves; rear 48 in., 11-leaves. Steering: [1/2-ton] semi-irreversible worm and sector steering; [Others] nut-and-lever, varying ratios. I-beam front axle. Gas filter. Fuel pump. [1/2-ton] 12-gallon gas tank under frame at rear; [others] 15-gallon gas tank under seat. Allowable speed: 40 mph. Wood-spoke wheels with steel felloes on demountable rims (except 140 in. wheelbase models come with malleable iron spokes).

OPTIONS: [1/2-ton] Chrome plated spring-type front and rear bumpers. [3/4-ton] 33 x 4-1/2 in. tires with wood wheels ($17.50). 30 x 5 in. eight-ply tires with metal spoke wheels ($50). Front bumper ($8.50). [1-ton] 30 x 5 in. eight-ply tires on metal spoke wheels ($15). 20 x 6 in. six-ply tires front; 32 x 6 in. eight-ply tires rear, with metal spoke wheels ($12). 20 x 6 in. six-ply front; 32 x 6 in. 10-ply rear ties on metal spoke wheels ($32.50). Extra farm box sides for eight-foot stake body ($40). Extra standard stake sides for eight-foot farm box body ($50). Front bumper ($8.50). Long runningboards and rear fenders for chassis only ($12.50. Power tire pump ($18.50).

HISTORICAL: Introduced: September, 1930. Calendar year production was 17,509. Calendar year registrations were 13,518. Production figures by model year and type not available. Fuel pump replaced vacuum feed on 1/2-ton models. All Dodge trucks, except 1/2-tons, had full floating rear axle. Dodge began, in 1931, to divide its truck line into two categories. The Standard Line included 1/2-, 3/4-, 1- and 1-1/2-ton trucks, powered by four- and six-cylinder engines. The Heavy Duty Line consisted of 2-ton and 3-ton trucks, all with sixes. This separation allowed more effective competition in the marketplace. The 1/2-ton had been developed along passenger car lines, following the modern trend. As the depression strengthened its grip on the economy, Dodge sales fell 13.1 percent. However, total industry sales dropped 23.6 percent, so Dodge still captured fourth place in U.S. truck sales.

1932 DODGE

1932 Dodge Model UF-10 1/2-Ton Panel (DFW/CHC)

1/2-TON — MODEL E — FOUR-CYLINDER: Three Dodge Model E chassis-only trucks were offered. The 1/2-ton had a 109 inch wheelbase. The 3/4-ton and 1-ton had 124-133 inch wheelbases. The same engine used in the UF-10 series was employed in these trucks.

1/2-TON — SERIES UF-10 — FOUR-CYLINDER; 1/2-TON — SERIES F-10 — SIX-CYLINDER: Introduced for 1931, the two 1/2-ton Dodge trucks continued into their second year without appearance changes or engineering refinements. Prices were again reduced as the depression continued its hold on the economy. Standard equipment was the same as in 1931.

3/4-TON — SERIES UI-B-124 — FOUR-CYLINDER; 3/4-TON — SERIES DA1-B-124 — SIX-CYLINDER: Except for price cuts to meet the lowered demand, these trucks entered 1932 unchanged.

1-TON — SERIES UI-C-133 — FOUR-CYLINDER; 1-TON — SERIES DA1-C-133 — SIX-CYLINDER: Additional price cuts, beyond the substantial reductions of 1931, were the only changes for the Dodge 1-ton lineup.

I.D. DATA: [1/2-ton] Serial numbers were stamped on the left side member of the frame, just in back of the front spring's front bracket. They were also on a serial number plate on the engine side of the cowl. Serial numbers continued from 1931 and began with a letter designating the assembly point: D=Detroit, Michigan; E=Evansville, Indiana; S=Stockton, California. Starting numbers: [Model E] P-8184; D-236959; E-151192; S-116098; [Model UF-109] D-8003540; E-9000001; S-9200081; [Model F-10] D-8101570; E-9025001; S-9212573; [Model UG20/UG21] D-8350001; S-9243501; [Model G20/G21] D-8480001; S-9258501. Ending numbers not available.

1932 Dodge Model U1-C 1-Ton Farm Truck (OCW)

Model	Body Type	Price	Weight	Prod. Total
MODEL E — 109/124/133 in. w.b.				
E	1/2-ton Chassis	435	—	—
E	3/4-ton Chassis	499	2260	—
E	1-ton Chassis	495	2590	—
1/2-Ton — 109 in. w.b.				
UF-10	Chassis	375	1900	—
UF-10	Pickup	584	—	—
UF-10	Canopy	600	—	—
UF-10	Screen	625	—	—
UF-10	Panel	625	—	—
F-10	Chassis	475	2000	—
F-10	Pickup	684	—	—
F-10	Canopy	700	—	—
F-10	Screen	725	—	—
F-10	Panel	725	—	—
3/4-Ton — 124 in. w.b.				
UI-B	Chassis	490	2260	—
UI-B	Chassis & Cab	640	—	—
UI-B	Platform	700	—	—
UI-B	Pickup	730	—	—
UI-B	Canopy	755	—	—
UI-B	Stake	750	—	—
UI-B	Screen	780	—	—
UI-B	Panel	780	—	—
DA1-B	Chassis	595	2360	—
DA1-B	Chassis & Cab	745	—	—
DA1-B	Platform	805	—	—
DA1-B	Express	835	—	—
DA1-B	Canopy	860	—	—
DA1-B	Stake	855	—	—
DA1-B	Screen	885	—	—
DA1-B	Panel	885	—	—
1-Ton — 133 in. w.b.				
UI-C	Chassis	495	2590	—
UI-C	Chassis & Cab	645	—	—
UI-C	Platform	715	—	—
UI-C	Farm	755	—	—
UI-C	Stake	765	—	—
UI-C	Express	787.50	—	—
UI-C	Canopy	802.50	—	—
UI-C	Screen	852.50	—	—
UI-C	Panel	852.50	—	—
DA1-C	Chassis	595	2690	—
DA1-C	Chassic & Cab	745	—	—
DA1-C	Platform	815	—	—
DA1-C	Farm	855	—	—
DA1-C	Stake	865	—	—
DA1-C	Express	887.50	—	—
DA1-C	Canopy	902.50	—	—
DA1-C	Screen	952.50	—	—
DA1-C	Panel	952.50	—	—

ENGINE [E/UF-10]: Inline. L-head. Four-cylinder. Cast iron block. Bore & stroke: 3-5/8 in. x 4-3/4 in. Displacement: 196.1 cid. Compression ratio: 4.6:1. Brake horsepower: 48 at 2800 rpm. Net horsepower: 21.02. Max. torque: 124 lbs.-ft. at 1200 rpm. Three main bearings. Solid valve lifters. Carburetor: Carter.

ENGINE [F-10]: Inline. L-head. Six-cylinder. Cast iron block. Bore & stroke: 3-1/8 in. x 4-1/8 in. Displacement: 189.8 cid. Compression ratio: 5.2:1. Brake horsepower: 60 at 3400 rpm. Net horsepower: 23.4. Max. torque: 120 lbs.-ft. at 1200 rpm. Four main bearings. Solid valve lifters. Carburetor: Carter.

CHASSIS: [1/2-ton] Wheelbase: 109 in. Tires: 19 x 5.00 (four-ply). Payload: 1,200 lbs. **CHASSIS:** [3/4-ton] Wheelbase: 124 in. Tires: 20 x 5.50 (six-ply). Payload: 1,500 lbs. **CHASSIS:** [1-ton] Wheelbase: 133 in. Tires: 20 x 6 (six-ply) front and 32 x 6 (eight-ply) rear. Payload: 2,000 lbs.

TECHNICAL: [1/2-ton] Selective sliding gear transmission. Speeds: 3F/1R. Single-plate dry-disc clutch (9 in.). Semi-floating rear axle. Overall ratio: 4.66:1. Spiral bevel gear drive. Hydraulic four-wheel brakes; 11 in. drums. Handbrake on propellor shaft. Semi-elliptical springs: Front 1-3/4 x 35-1/2 in., eight-leaves; rear 1 11/16 x 53-1/2 in., 15-leaves. Semi-irreversible worm and sector steering. I-beam front axle. Gas filter. Fuel pump. 12-gallon gas tank under frame at rear. Allowable speed: 40 mph. Wood-spoke wheels with steel felloes on demountable rims. [3/4-ton/1-ton] Same as 1930 models.

1932 Dodge Model DA1-C 1-Ton Express (JAW)

HISTORICAL: Introduced: Calendar year production was 10,713. Calendar year registrations were 8,744. Production figures for model year and body type not available. This was the all-time record low year for both the truck industry and Dodge truck sales, as truckers tried to weather the storm of the depression. Industry sales were down 42.5 percent to only 180,413 trucks. Dodge fell 35.3 percent from 1931. Beginning in 1933, sales would again begin an upward climb. Dodge made no changes in its light-duty line for 1932, planning all new products for 1933. An eight-cylinder engine went into one of the Heavy-duty models and two new 1-1/2-ton models were introduced. The new G-80 eight-cylinder chassis handled a 15,000 lbs. payload or 50,000 lbs. GVW. It also had automatic chassis lubrication from Alemite, providing constant oil to the chassis when the truck was in motion.

1933 DODGE

![1933 Dodge Model HC 1/2-Ton Commercial Sedan]

1933 Dodge Model HC 1/2-Ton Commercial Sedan (DFW/WRL)

1/2-TON — COMMERCIAL SERIES HC — SIX-CYLINDER: An all-new, fully restyled, modern series of Commercial Cars was announced in January, 1933. Front end appearance was similar to that of new Dodge passenger cars with a sloping, V-shaped radiator, chrome-plated radiator shell, chromed windshield frame with rounded headers and fenders that concealed the chassis. The long hood extended almost to the base of the windshield. Narrow, yet rigid, cowl posts improved visibility. Doors were also of passenger car type, hinged at the rear. They had a large window, operated by a hand crank. The Sedan Delivery featured a full-size rear door with large, rectangular glass window. This allowed easy access to the load compartment. Inside, 1/8 in. thick rubber matting covered a heavy plywood floor. The body interior was finished in mahogany-look plywood veneer, illuminated by a dome light. The driver's seat and steering column were adjustable and the hinged right-hand seat could be pushed forward and out of the way. Body dimensions of the Commercial Sedan were 53 in. long, 44-3/4 in. wide and 44 in. high. The door opening was 35 in. wide by 37 in. high and the floor was 26 in. above the ground. The Commercial Pickup had a load space 63 in. long, 45-3/4 in. wide on the floor (50 in. at top) and 15-1/2 in. high. Loading height was also 26 inches. The spare tire sat in a welled right-hand front fender.

1/2-TON — COMMERCIAL SERIES HCL — SIX-CYLINDER: The 119 in. wheelbase HCL lineup consisted of a chassis-only, chassis with cab and panel body truck. The panel model was the first of the famous "humpback" panels, with cab roof lower than the roof of the load compartment. Loading dimensions were 81 in. long at the beltline (73 in. on floor), 57 in. wide at beltline (44-3/4 in. between wheelhousings) and 50-5/8 in. high. Floor height was 26 inches. The wheelbase was the only difference between the HC and HCL series.

1/2-TON — SERIES UF10 — FOUR-CYLINDER; 1/2-TON — SERIES F-10 — SIX-CYLINDER: Introduced for 1931, the two 1/2-ton Dodge trucks continued into their third year without appearance changes or engineering refinements. Prices were again reduced as the depression continued its hold on the economy. Standard equipment was the same as in 1931. The 1933 model would be Dodge's last four-cylinder truck for many years.

1/2-TON — SERIES F10 — SIX-CYLINDER: This line was continued into 1933 without change. The F-10 was also in its final year as a Dodge offering.

3/4-TON TO ONE-TON — SERIES H20 — SIX-CYLINDER: Another new series rated at 3/4- to 1-ton, the H20 was introduced in October, 1932. Available only with a panel body, it was a special model built from the 1-1/2-ton H30 model. The wheelbase was 131 in. The GVW rating was 6,000 lbs. It had a four-speed transmission and a 203.1 cid engine.

3/4-TON TO ONE-TON — SERIES UG20/UG21 — FOUR-CYLINDER: These trucks were actually 1932-1933 models. They came with 131 in. and 157 in. wheelbases.

I.D. DATA: [1/2-ton] Serial numbers were stamped on a number plate on the engine side of the cowl. [HC] 8007301-8017443. [HCL] 9201001 to 9201576. [UF10] (Detroit) 9200300-9300313; (Evansville) 8007133-8007264; (Los Angeles) 8102731-8102959. [F10] (Detroit) 9212689-9212724. [H20] 8483101-8492872. [UG20/UG21] (Detroit) 8351688-up; (Los Angeles) 9243544-up; [G20/G21] (Detroit) 8481871-up; (Los Angeles) 9258645-up. Engine numbers were stamped on top left side of block between cylinders one and two. Starting engine numbers were, [HC] TPD1001; [HCL] DTPP-1001; [UF10] UT-21101; [F10] DD-2-T1001; [H20] not available.

Model	Body Type	Price	Weight	Prod. Total
Commercial Series HC — 1/2-Ton — 111.25 in. w.b.				
HC	Chassis & Cab	430	1775	—
HC	Pickup	450	2465	—
KC	Comm. Sedan	555	2600	—
HC	Canopy	535	2525	—
KC	Panel	—	—	—
Commercial Series HCL — 1/2-Ton — 119 in. w.b.				
HCL	Chassis & Cowl	365	2015	—
HCL	Chassis & Cab	455	—	—
HCL	Panel	630	545	—
UF10 Series — 1/2-Ton — 109 in. w.b.				
UF10	Chassis	375	1925	—
UF10	Screen	570	—	—
UF10	Pickup	500	—	—
UF10	Canopy	570	—	—
UF10	Panel	570	—	—
F10 Series — 1/2-Ton — 109 in. w.b.				
F10	Chassis	445	1975	—
F10	Screen	655	—	—
F10	Pickup	580	—	—
F10	Canopy	655	—	—
F10	Panel	655	—	—
H20 Series — 3/4-Ton to 1-Ton — 131 in. w.b.				
H20	Chassis	502	2559	—
H20	Panel	765	—	—

UG20 Series — 3/4-Ton to 1-Ton — 131 in. w.b.

UG20	Chassis	537	2520	—
UG20	Pickup	—	—	—
UG20	Canopy	—	—	—
UG20	Panel	—	—	—
UG20	Sedan Delivery	—	—	—

G20 Series — 3/4-Ton to 1-Ton — 131 in. w.b.

G20	Chassis	597	2520	—
G20	Pickup	—	—	—
G20	Canopy	—	—	—
G20	Panel	—	—	—
G20	Sedan Delivery	—	—	—

1933 Dodge Bros. 1-Ton Armored Car (JE/NSPC)

ENGINE [HC/HCL]: Inline. L-head. Six-cylinder. Cast iron block. Bore & stroke: 3-1/8 x 4-1/8 in. Displacement: 189.8 cid. Compression ratio: 5.5:1. Brake horsepower: 70 at 3600 rpm. Net horsepower: 23.44. Torque: 130 lbs.-ft. at 1200 rpm. Four main bearings. Solid valve lifters. Carburetor: Downdraft.
ENGINE [UF10/F10]: Inline. L-head. Six-cylinder. Cast iron block. Bore & stroke: 3-1/8 in. x 4-1/8 in. Displacement: 189.8 cid. Compression ratio: 5.2:1. Brake horsepower: 60 at 3400 rpm. Net horsepower: 23.4. Max. torque: 120 lbs.-ft. at 1200 rpm. Four main bearings. Solid valve lifters. Carburetor: Carter.
ENGINE [H20]: Inline. L-head. Six-cylinder. Cast iron block. Bore & stroke: 3-1/8 x 4-3/8 in. Displacement: 201.3 cid. Compression ratio: 5.8:1. Brake horsepower: 75 at 3600 rpm. Net horsepower: 23.44. Torque: 138 lbs.-ft. at 1200 rpm. Four main bearings. Solid valve lifters.
ENGINE [UG20]: Inline. L-head. Four-cylinder. Cast iron block. Bore & stroke: 3-5/8 x 4-3/4 in. Displacement: 196.1 cid. Compression ratio: 4.6:1. Brake horsepower: 48 at 2800 rpm. Net horsepower: 21.02. Torque: 124 lbs.-ft. at 1200 rpm. Three main bearings. Solid valve lifters. Carburetor: Carter.
ENGINE [G20]: Inline. L-head. Six-cylinder. Cast iron block. Bore & stroke: 3-1/8 x 4-3/8 in. Displacement: 201.3 cid. Compression ratio: 5.8:1. Brake horsepower: 75 at 3600 rpm. Net horsepower: 23.44. Torque: 138 lbs.-ft. at 1200 rpm. Four main bearings. Solid valve lifters. Carburetor: Carter.
CHASSIS [HC]: Wheelbase: 111.25 in. Tires: 5.25 x 17 four-ply non-skid balloon.
CHASSIS [HCL]: Wheelbase: 119 in. Tires: 5.25 x 17 four-ply,
CHASSIS [UF10/F10]: Wheelbase: 109 in. Tires: 5.00 x 19 four-ply. Payload: 1,200 lbs.
CHASSIS [H20]: Wheelbase: 131 in. Tires: 7.50 x 17.
CHASSIS [UG20/UG21]: Wheelbase: 131 in.
CHASSIS [G20/G21]: Wheelbase: 131 in. and 157 in.
TECHNICAL: Selective sliding gear transmission. Speeds: 3F/1R (except H20 has 4F/1R). Floor shift control. Single-plate dry-disc clutch: [HC/HCL] nine-inch. Semi-floating rear axle (except H20 is full-floating). Overall ratio: [HC/HCL] 4.37:1; [UF10/F10] 4.66:1. Hotchkiss drive. Hydraulic four-wheel brakes: [HC/HCL] 10-inch drums with 1-1/2 in. linings; [UF10/F10] 11-inch. Semi-elliptic springs: [HC/HCL] 36 in. long seven-leaves front/53-1/2 in. eight-leaves rear; [UF10/F10] 38 in. eight-leaves front/53-1/2 15-leaves rear. Steering: Semi-irreversible worm-and-sector. Front axle: [HC/HCL] tubular; [UF10/F10] I-beam. Gas tank: [HC/HCL] 15-gallon rear-mounted. Air cleaner. Mechanical fuel pump. Foot headlight dimmer. Wheels: [HC/HCL] Demountable wire wheels with drop-center rims; [H20] Wire wheels.
OPTIONS: [HC/HCL] Chrome front bumper ($7.50). Chrome rear bumper ($7.50). Allowance for Commercial Sedan in primer ($8 net). Panel body ($6 net). Duplate safety plate glass on sedan, panel or cab ($14.50). Auxiliary seat for panel or canopy ($10). Screen sides for canopy model ($12.50). Rear screen lift for canopy ($10). Double rear screen doors ($15). Dual trumpet horns ($12.50). Dual taillights ($5). Auxiliary windshield wiper ($4.50). Metal tire cover ($5 each). Inside sun visor ($2 each). Freewheeling ($8). Freewheeling and automatic clutch ($17.50). Duplex air cleaner ($5). Vortex air cleaner ($16). Crankcase to air intake vent ($3.50). Monarch governor ($8.50). Hardy governor ($15). Duplate safety plate glass windshield ($3.50). Ornamental radiator cap ($2). Tire lock ($1.20). Side-mounted coach lamps for Commercial Sedan ($8). Chrome-plated radiator shell and headlamps ($5). Shock absorbers: Double-acting hydraulic, front/rear ($10). [Note on HC/HCL options: Unless dealer indicated otherwise on order, ornamental radiator cap and tire lock were shipped.] Bumper equipment was handled as follows: On Commercial Sedan, front and rear bumpers; pickup and canopy, front bumper only; panel, front and rear bumpers. [UF10/F10] Chrome-plated spring-type front and rear bumpers.
HISTORICAL: HC models were introduced January, 1933. H20 models were introduced October, 1932. Model year began Oct. 1, 1932. Calendar year registrations were 28,034. Calendar year production was 38,841 trucks. Passenger car styling on Commercial Car series. First "humpback" Dodge panel model HCL. Freewheeling and automatic clutch available. This was a transitional year for Dodge Truck Div. Several new series of totally redesigned trucks, ranging in size from 1/2-ton to two-tons, were brought to market over a period of several months. Designated the Standard Line, they included five series: HC/HCL (1/2-ton Commercial Car); H20 (3/4-ton to 1-ton); H30 (1-1/2-ton); and H43 (two-ton) trucks. In the light-duty lineup, the UF10 and F10 1/2-ton series and G/UG 3/4-ton to 1-ton series were carried over, from 1932, basically unchanged. Those two series retained the 1920s styling with the old Graham Bros. look. Seven different six-cylinder engine sizes were offered. Larger three-ton and four-ton models were also carried over from 1932. Dodge bounced back with the new lineup to recapture third place in the truck sales race. The truck industry, as a whole, also recovered nicely by gaining 36.3 percent in registrations. Dodge Truck Div. sales rose a whopping 321 percent! Dodge trucks were manufactured in Hamtramck, Michigan and Los Angeles, California.

1934 Dodge Model KC 1/2-Ton Pickup (R. Klawitter)

1/2-TON — COMMERCIAL SERIES KC — SIX-CYLINDER: All new in 1933, the Commercial Series continued with only two changes. A drop-forged I-beam front axle replaced the former tubular type and engine size was increased to 201.3 cid and the engine was now rated for 75 hp. New canopy and screen models were added.

1934 Dodge Model KC 1/2-Ton Commercial Sedan (OCW)

1/2-TON — COMMERCIAL SERIES KCL — SIX-CYLINDER: The longer-wheelbase (119 in.) Commercial Series continued with the same two changes as the KC. Only a panel body and basic chassis were offered.

1934 Dodge Model KC 1/2-Ton Pickup (J.F. Cadwallader)

3/4-TON — SERIES K-20 — SIX-CYLINDER; 1-TON — SERIES K-20X — SIX-CYLINDER; 1-TON — SERIES K-30 — SIX-CYLINDER: All 3/4- and 1-ton trucks were carried over for 1934, with a greatly expanded lineup. Only a panel model had been available in 1933. Pickup, canopy and screen models were added in May 1934. The panel was again the popular "humpback" style, while canopy and screen bodies were not. One-ton models differed only in optional tire equipment and rear axle ratio. All were powered by the 217.7 cid engine. An underslung tire carrier was standard on all models. Standard equipment included a cowl vent, black-enamel radiator shell, chrome filler cap, crown front fenders, short runningboards (long on Panel/Canopy/Screen), spare wheel, electric horn, stop/taillight, dash light, gas gauge, speedometer, ammeter, oil pressure gauge, heat indicator, locking ignition switch, choke, throttle, license brackets, and tool kit.
I.D. DATA: Serial numbers on a number plate on the engine side of the cowl. [Series KC] Starting: 8023001. Ending: 8048626. [KCL] Starting: 9202001. Ending: 9203885. [K-20]

Starting: 8103001. Ending: 8105509. [K-20X/K-30] Starting: 9260001. Ending: 9260137. Engine numbers were in the same location. [Series KC] Starting: T5-1001. [KCL] DT5-1001. [K-20/K-20X/K-30] Starting: T6-1000.

Model	Body Type	Price	Weight	Prod. Total
Commercial Series KC — 1/2-Ton — 111.25 in. w.b.				
KC	Chassis & Cowl	385	1775	—
KC	Chassis & Cab	480	—	—
KC	Pickup	500	2465	—
KC	Comm. Sedan	595	2600	—
KC	Canopy	610	2525	—
KC	Screen	630	2550	—
Commercial Series KCL — 1/2-Ton — 119 in. w.b.				
KCL	Chassis & Cowl	415	2015	—
KCL	Chassis & Cab	510	—	—
KCL	Panel	630	2860	—
Series K-20 — 3/4-Ton — 131 in. w.b.				
K-20	Chassis	540	2800	—
K-20	Chassis & Cab	635	3260	—
K-20	Canopy	810	3575	—
K-20	Screen	830	3650	—
K-20	Panel	820	4050	—
K-20	Pickup	715	—	—

NOTE 1: K-20X and K-30 1-ton models were priced the same as equivalent K-20 series 3/4-ton models.

1934 Dodge Model KC 1/2-Ton Pickup (J.F. Cadwallader)

ENGINE [Series KC/KCL]: Inline. L-head. Six-cylinder. Cast iron block. Bore & stroke: 3-1/8 x 4-3/8 in. Displacement: 201.3 cid. Compression ratio: 5.8:1. Brake horsepower: 75 at 3600 rpm. Net horsepower: 23.44. Torque: 138 lbs.-ft. at 1200 rpm. Four main bearings. Solid valve lifters.
ENGINE [Series K-20/K-20X, K-30]: Inline. L-head. Six-cylinder. Cast iron block. Bore & stroke: 3-1/4 x 4-3/8 in. Displacement: 217.76 cid. Compression ratio: 5.6:1. Brake horsepower: 70 at 3000 rpm. Net horsepower: 25.35. Torque: 150 lbs.-ft. at 1200 rpm. Four main bearings. Solid valve lifters.
CHASSIS [Series KC]: Wheelbase: 111-1/4 in. Tires: 5.25 x 17 four-ply (front/rear). Payload: 1,000 lbs.
CHASSIS [Series KCL]: Wheelbase: 119 in. Tires: 5.25 x 17 four-ply (front/rear). Payload: 1,200 lbs.
CHASSIS [Series K-20/K-20X/K-30]: Wheelbase: 131 in. Tires: (front) 6.00 x 20 six-ply; (rear) 32 x 6 eight-ply, except panel has 7.50 x 17 (front/rear). Max. GVW: [K-20] 5,500 lbs.; [K-20X] 6,075 lbs.; [K-30] 8,400 lbs.
TECHNICAL: [Series KC/KCL] Same as HC/HCL series of 1933, except front axle was now reverse Elliott type drop-forged I-beam and overall axle ratio was 4.11:1. [K-20/K-20X/K-30] Selective sliding gear transmission. Speeds: 4F/1R. Floor shift control. Single-plate dry-disc 10 in. clutch. Full-floating rear axle. Overall ratio: 4.875:1. Hydraulic four-wheel brakes with 12 in. front and 14 in. rear drums. Roller tooth steering. Drop-forged I-beam front axle. Semi-elliptic Silico Manganese springs: (front) 36 in. long, eight-leaves; (rear) 48 in. long, eight-leaves. 15-gallon gas tank under driver's seat. Fuel pump. Ventilated disc steel wheels (wire wheels standard on panel model).
OPTIONS: [Series KC/KCL] Chrome front bumper ($6). Chrome rear bumper ($7). Dual trumpet horns, dual taillights and auxiliary windshield wiper ($20). Auxiliary wiper alone ($4). Inside sun visor ($2 each). Metal tire cover ($6.50 each). Freewheeling ($11.50). Freewheeling and automatic clutch ($20). Duplate safety windshield ($5). Duplate safety glass throughout ($14). Auxiliary seat for Commercial Sedan ($8). Ornamental radiator cap ($2). Tire lock ($1.20). Chrome-plated radiator shell and headlamps, plus single-acting hydraulic shock absorbers, front/rear ($15). Duplex air cleaner ($2.50). Long-arm rearview mirror ($2.50). Five wood wheels with four 5.25 x 17 four-ply tires ($10). Six wood wheels with four 5.25 x 17 four-ply tires, extra fenderwell and tire lock ($20). Six wire wheels with four 5.25 x 17 four-ply tires, extra fender well and tire lock ($10). Five wire wheels with four 6.00 x 16 four-ply tires ($20). Six wire wheels with four 6.00 x 16 four-ply tires, extra fender well and tire lock ($25). Five steel spoke wheels with four 6.00 x 16 four-ply tires ($20). Six steel spoke wheels with four 6.00 x 16 four-ply tires, extra fender well and tire lock ($30). [Series K-20/K-20X/K-30] Black enamel front bumper ($5). Chrome front bumper ($7). Chrome rear bumper for panel model ($12). Auxiliary seat for panel or canopy ($3.50). Tire carrier for chassis or chassis/cab ($3.50). Chrome-plated radiator shell ($6). Chrome-plated headlights ($3). Duplate safety glass windshield ($5). Duplate safety glass throughout ($14). Auxiliary windshield wiper ($4). Long-arm rearview mirror ($2.50). Ornamental radiator cap ($2). Double-acting shock absorbers, front or rear ($10/pair). Duplex air cleaner ($2). Coach type lamps for panel ($8). Monarch governor ($8.50). 7.50 x 17 six-ply tires front/rear with wire wheels ($13.50). 6.00 x 20 six-ply front and 32 x 6 10-ply rear tires ($25). 7.00 x 20 eight-ply front and 7.00 x 20 eight-ply rear tires ($26.50). 6.50 x 20 six-ply tires front/rear (no charge). Dual rear wheels were not available.
HISTORICAL: Introduced: October, 1933. Calendar year registrations: 48,252. Calendar year production: 68,469. Production figures by model year or series not available. Dodge Div. reorganized and split the truck line completely from automobile operations. Four-cylinder engines were out of the lineup, but an eight powered the largest models. This was the final year for an inline eight in a Dodge truck. Dodge again placed third in truck sales, with

registrations up 72 percent over 1933. The truck industry continued its recovery from the depression with a 64.3 percent gain in registrations. This was the first year for the famous Dodge Airflow trucks. These were monstrous K-52 four-ton fuel tankers, powered by a 310 cid six with 3-5/8 in. bore and 5 in. stroke. Their distinctive styling is a favorite with truck lovers. Once seen, it is never forgotten. All Dodge trucks were built in Hamtramck, Michigan. It was the last time, for many years, that all trucks were Michigan-made.

1935 DODGE

1935 Dodge Model KC 1/2-Ton Commercial Sedan (OCW)

1/2-TON — COMMERCIAL SERIES KC — SIX-CYLINDER: The very attractive, good selling KC series entered another year without change. Pickup, Canopy, Screen and Sedan bodies again were offered. When introduced in 1933, the Commercial Series front end looked the same as that used on Dodge passenger cars. However, by 1935, the car lines had changed to keep up with the dictates of fashion. Truck sheet metal continued as before, though. One new body style was added: The wood-bodied Suburban Sedan (station wagon). It built by U.S. Body and Forging Co. of Tell City, Indiana. The styling of Suburban Sedans was car-like, but they were considered trucks. Sheet metal from the cowl forward was shared with other commercial models, except that the radiator shell and headlight housings were chrome plated.

1/2-TON — COMMERCIAL SERIES KCL — SIX-CYLINDER: Differing from the KC only in its longer 119 in. wheelbase, the KCL model also continued unchanged. Only the basic chassis-only and panel models were available.

1935 Dodge Model KC 1/2-Ton Pickup (M. Magnuson)

3/4-TON — SERIES KH15/KH16/KH17/KH18 — SIX-CYLINDER; 1-TON — SERIES KH20/KH21/KH22/KH23 — SIX-CYLINDER: The 3/4- and 1-ton truck lineup expanded substantially for 1935. Trucks with 131 in. wheelbases were a carryover of the K-20 and K-20X models of 1934. Those with 136, 148 and 161 in. wheelbases were 1-1/2-ton trucks scaled down to 3/4- and 1-ton capacities through the use of smaller wheels and tires, as well as lighter springs and axles. Powered by the same engine as KC/KCL trucks, these models would show up only in the 1935 model year. No appearance or mechanical changes were made, but factory list prices were cut considerably. Standard equipment was the same as in 1934.

3/4-TON — SERIES KH16V/KH17V/KH18V — SIX-CYLINDER; 1-TON — SERIES KH21V/KH22V/KH23V — SIX-CYLINDER: These 3/4- and 1-ton trucks were similar to the KH models, but had one inch longer wheelbases. They cost about $5-10 more, depending on model, and were about 300 lbs. heavier.

I.D. DATA: Serial numbers were located on a number plate on the engine side of the cowl. [Series KC/KCL]: (Detroit) 8042422-8072550; (California) 9203202-9201587. [Series KH] (Detroit) 8222759-8234001; (California) 9242917-9243500. [Series KH..V] (Detroit) 8234301-8242776; (California) 9260151-9260514. Engine numbers were on a plate on the side of the motor. [Series KC and KCL] Starting: T12-1001. [Series KH] Starting: T17-1001.

159

1935 Dodge Model KH-15 3/4-Ton Panel (OCW)

Model	Body Type	Price	Weight	Prod. Total
Commercial Series KC — 1/2-Ton — 111.25 in. w.b.				
KC	Chassis & Cowl	365	1775	—
KC	Chassis & Cab	465	2235	—
KC	Pickup	480	2465	—
KC	Canopy	590	2525	—
KC	Screen	610	2550	—
KC	Commercial Sedan	595	2600	—
KC	Suburban Sedan	715	2996	—
KC	Suburban (Note 1)	735	2996	—

NOTE 1: Suburban Sedan with movable glass windows in front doors.

Model	Body Type	Price	Weight	Prod. Total
Commercial Series KCL — 1/2-Ton — 119 in. w.b.				
KCL	Chassis & Cowl	395	2015	—
KCL	Chassis & Cab	490	2800	—
KCL	Panel	595	2860	—
KCL	Express	—	—	—
Series KH15 — 3/4-Ton — 131 in. w.b.				
KH15	Chassis	490	2550	—
KH15	Chassis & Cab	585	3080	—
KH15	Pickup	665	3480	—
KH15	Canopy	720	3575	—
KH15	Screen	740	3650	—
KH15	Panel	740	3850	—
Series KH16 — 3/4-Ton — 136 in. w.b.				
KH16	Chassis	490	2575	—
KH16	Chassis & Cab	615	3085	—
Series KH17 — 3/4-Ton — 148 in. w.b.				
KH17	Chassis	520	2625	—
KH17	Chassis & Cab	615	3085	—
Series KH18 — 3/4-Ton — 161 in. w.b.				
KH18	Chassis	520	2700	—
KH18	Chassis & Cab	615	3085	—
Series KH16V — 3/4-Ton — 137 in. w.b.				
KH16V	Chassis	495	2850	—
KH16V	Chassis & Cab	595	3225	—
KH16V	Panel	760	4150	—
KH16V	Express	675	3780	—
KH16V	Canopy	740	3688	—
KH16V	Screen	740	3688	—
Series KH17 — 3/4-Ton — 149 in. w.b.				
KH17V	Chassis	525	2925	—
KH17V	Chassis & Cab	625	3300	—
Series KH18 — 3/4-Ton — 162 in. w.b.				
KH18V	Chassis	550	3000	—
KH18V	Chassis & Cab	625	3375	—
Series KH20 — 1-Ton — 131 in. w.b.				
KH20	Chassis	490	2800	—
KH20	Chassis & Cab	585	3260	—
KH20	Pickup	665	—	—
KH20	Canopy	720	3575	—
KH20	Screen	740	3650	—
KH20	Panel	740	4050	—
Series KH21 — 1-Ton — 136 in. w.b.				
KH21	Chassis	490	—	—
KH21	Chassis & Cab	585	—	—
Series KH22 — 1-Ton — 148 in. w.b.				
KH22	Chassis	520	—	—
KH22	Chassis & Cab	615	—	—
Series KH23 — 1-Ton — 161 in. w.b.				
KH23	Chassis	520	—	—
KH23	Chassis & Cab	615	—	—
Series KH21V — 1-Ton — 137 in. w.b.				
KH21V	Chassis	495	2850	—
KH21V	Chassis & Cab	595	3225	—
KH21V	Panel	760	4150	—
KH21V	Express	675	3780	—
KH21V	Canopy	740	3688	—
KH21V	Screen	740	3688	—

Model	Body Type	Price	Weight	Prod. Total
Series KH22V — 1-Ton — 149 in. w.b.				
KH22V	Chassis	525	2925	—
KH22V	Chassis & Cab	625	3300	—
Series KH23V — 1-Ton — 162 in. w.b.				
KH23V	Chassis	550	3000	—
KH23V	Chassis & Cab	625	3375	—

1935 Dodge Delivery Truck (OCW)

ENGINE: Inline. L-head. Six-cylinder. Cast iron block. Bore & stroke: 3-1/8 x 4-3/8 in. Displacement: 201.3 cid. Compression ratio: 5.8:1. Brake horsepower: 70 at 3600 rpm. Net horsepower: 23.44. Torque: 138 lbs.-ft. at 1200 rpm. Four main bearings. Solid valve lifters. Carburetor: Carter.

1935 Dodge Model KC 1/2-Ton Pickup (D.S. Olsen)

1935 Dodge Model KC 1/2-Ton Pickup (S. Glasbrenner)

CHASSIS [Series KC]: Wheelbase: 111.25 in. Tires: 5.25 x 17 four-ply (front/rear). Payload: 1,000 lbs.
CHASSIS [Series KCL]: Wheelbase: 119 in. Tires: 5.25 x 17 four-ply (front/rear). Payload: 1,200 lbs.
CHASSIS [Series KH15/KH20]: Wheelbase: 131 in.
CHASSIS [Series KH16/KH21]: Wheelbase: 136 in.
CHASSIS [Series KH16V/KH21V]: Wheelbase: 137 in.
CHASSIS [Series KH17/KH22]: Wheelbase: 148 in.
CHASSIS [Series KH17V/KH22V]: Wheelbase: 149 in.
CHASSIS [Series KH18/KH23]: Wheelbase: 161 in.
CHASSIS [Series KH18V/KH23V]: Wheelbase: 162 in.
TECHNICAL: Selective sliding gear transmission. Speeds: [KC/KCL] 3F/1R; [KH] 4F/1R. Floor shift control. Single-plate dry-disc clutch. Rear axle: [KC/KCL] Semi-floating; [KH] full-floating. Overall ratio: [KC/KCL] 3.7:1 and 4.125:1; [KH] 4.875:1. Hydraulic four-wheel brakes. Semi-elliptic springs: [KC/KCL] (front) 36 in. long, seven-leaves; (rear) 53-1/2 in., eight-leaves; [KH] (front) 36 in. long, eight-leaves; (rear) 48 in., eight-leaves. Drop-forged I-beam front axle. Steering: [KC/KCL] Semi-irreversible worm and sector; [KH] Roller tooth. 15-gallon gas tank: [KC/KCL] at rear; [KH] under driver's seat. Fuel pump. Wheels: [KC/KCL] Demountable wire wheels with drop-center rims; [KH] Ventilated disc steel except panel model.

OPTIONS: [Series KC/KCL] Chrome front bumper ($6). Chrome rear bumper ($7). Dual trumpet horns, dual taillights and auxiliary windshield wiper ($20). Auxiliary wiper alone ($4). Inside sun visor ($2 each). Metal tire cover ($6.50 each). Freewheeling ($11.50). Freewheeling and automatic clutch ($20). Duplate safety windshield ($5). Duplate safety glass throughout ($14). Auxiliary seat for panel ($10). Side-mounted coach lamps for Commercial Sedan ($8). Ornamental radiator cap ($2). Tire lock ($1.20). Chrome-plated radiator shell and headlamps, plus single-acting hydraulic shock absorbers, front/rear ($15). Duplex air cleaner (2.50). Long-arm rearview mirror ($2.50). Five wood wheels with four 5.25 x 17 four-ply tires ($10). Six wood wheels with four 5.25 x 17 four-ply tires, extra fender well and tire lock ($20). Five wire wheels with four 5.25 x 17 four-ply tires ($20). Six wire wheels with four 5.25 x 17 four-ply tires, extra fender well and tire lock ($20). Five wire wheels with four 6.00 x 16 four-ply tires ($20). Six wire wheels with four 6.00 x 16 four-ply tires, extra fender well and tire lock ($25). Five steel spoke wheels with four 6.00 x 16 four-ply tires ($20). Six steel spoke wheels with four 6.00 x 16 four-ply tires, extra fender well and tire lock ($30). [Series KH/KVH] Black enamel front bumper ($5). Chrome front bumper ($7). Chrome rear bumper for panel model ($12). Auxiliary seat for panel or canopy ($10). Tire carrier for chassis or chassis/cab ($3.50). Chrome-plated radiator shell ($6). Chrome-plated headlights ($3). Duplate safety glass windshield ($5). Duplate safety glass throughout ($14). Auxiliary windshield wiper ($4). Long-arm rearview mirror ($2.50). Ornamental radiator cap ($2). Double-acting shock absorbers, front or rear ($10/pair). Duplex air cleaner ($2). Coach type lamps for panel ($8). Monarch governor ($8.50). 7.50 x 17 six-ply tires front/rear with wire wheels ($13.50). 6.00 x 20 six-ply front and 32 x 6 10-ply rear tires ($25). 7.00 x 20 eight-ply front and 7.00 x 20 eight-ply rear tires ($26.50). 6.50 x 20 six-ply tires front/rear (no charge). Dual rear wheels were not available.

1935 Dodge Model KH-15 3/4-Ton Panel (OCW)

HISTORICAL: Introduced: October, 1934. Calendar year registrations: 61,488. Calendar year production: 83,701. Innovations: Wood-bodied station wagon added to line. This was another strong year for the truck industry, with sales close to 1929, when the all-time record was set. Total industry sales came to 510,683 trucks, up 26.2 percent over 1934. Dodge also had a very good year, with registrations up 27.4 percent. Truck production began in Los Angeles and Canada. Of the total trucks built, 5,766 were made in California and 1,500 in Canada. Once again, Dodge marketed three truck lines: The 1/2-ton Commercial Series, the 1-1/2- to 2-ton mid-range standard series, and the 3- and 4-ton heavy-duty units. Those heavy-duty trucks still had the familiar old Graham styling of the late 1920s. In July, 1935, Dodge announced an all-new 3-ton series with modern styling. A 4-ton was no longer available. As in 1934, all Dodge trucks were powered by 6-cyl. engines. The U.S. Government ordered over 5,000 Dodge trucks for Army use, including 1/2-ton panels and 1-1/2-ton cargo trucks, some with four-wheel-drive.

1935 Dodge Model KC 1/2-Ton Pickup (OCW)

1936 DODGE

1/2-TON — COMMERCIAL SERIES LC — SIX-CYLINDER; 1/2-TON — COMMERCIAL SEDAN MODEL D2 — SIX-CYLINDER: An all-new line of trucks, including a new commercial series, was announced for 1936. The new trucks featured beautiful styling and Amola springs, plus "fore point" load distribution. That meant the engine and cab had been shifted forward, putting more payload weight on the front axle and wheels. The longer cab-to-rear-axle distance also permitted the use of longer bodies. One welcome styling change was the adoption of front-hinged doors. All Commercial Series models sat on a 116 in. wheelbase, rather than the two wheelbase choices of 1935. The unchanged six-cylinder

engine was mounted on Chrysler's famous three-point suspension system, cushioned with rubber. Springs were all made of Amola steel, a recent metallurgical development from Chrysler engineering. The series consisted of the pickup, panel, screen, canopy and Westchester Suburban station wagon, plus the Commercial Sedan, which was the only model built on a passenger-car chassis. For the first time, the balance of the series used a truck-type double-drop chassis. The Commercial Sedan used a 218 cid engine, rather than the 201 cid six found in other LC models. The spare tire sat in the right side fender well. Standard equipment included an ammeter, speedometer, fuel gauge, oil pressure gauge, heat indicator, glove compartment, choke, throttle and vacuum wiper. The 17-inch three-spoke steering wheel was height-adjustable. The Commercial Sedan, panel, screen and canopy models had only one bucket seat.

1936 Dodge Model LE-15 3/4-Ton Express (DFW/BLHU)

3/4-TON — SERIES LE-15/LE-16/LE-17 — SIX-CYLINDER; 1-TON SERIES LE-20/LE-21/LE-22 — SIX-CYLINDER: Like the smaller trucks, the LE series was totally restyled for 1936. More massive and rugged in appearance, the 3/4- and 1-ton models looked more truck-like than the LC. Three wheelbase lengths were available: 129, 136 or 162 in. Doors now hinged at the front. Fore point load distribution shifted the engine and cab forward. Only in the 136 in. size were all body types available. As before, the 3/4- and 1-ton trucks were basically 1-1/2-ton models built down by using smaller wheels and lighter springs. Standard equipment included a cowl vent, painted radiator shell, electric horn, tail/stop light, dash light, gas gauge, speedometer, ammeter, oil pressure gauge, heat indicator, choke, throttle, license bracket and tool kit. The 17-1/2 in. three-spoke steering wheel had an adjustable column.

1936 Dodge Model LE 3/4-Ton Dog Catcher Truck (DFW/AHS)

I.D. DATA: Serial numbers were again on a number plate on the engine side of the cowl. [LC] (Detroit) 8105601-8156402. (Los Angeles) 9287701-9293583. [D2] (Detroit) 4015051 up. [LE-15/LE-20] (Detroit) 8242801-8263157. [LE-16/LE-21] (Detroit) 8378051-8380000. [LE-17/LE-22] (Los Angeles) 9260551-9264974. Engine numbers were stamped on top left side of block, between cylinders one and two. [LC/D2] Starting: T23-1001. [LE] Starting: T25-1001.

1936 Dodge Model LC 1/2-Ton Panel (OCW)

Model	Body Type	Price	Weight	Prod. Total
Commercial Series D2 — 1/2-Ton — 116 in. w.b.				
D2	Commercial Sedan	665	2844	Note 1

Commercial Series LC — 1/2-Ton — 116 in. w.b.

LC	Chassis & Cowl	370	1935	Note 1
LC	Chassis & Cab	470	2450	Note 1
LC	Pickup	500	2685	Note 1
LC	Canopy	600	2735	Note 1
LC	Screen	620	2755	Note 1
LC	Panel	585	2985	Note 1
LC	Westchester Suburban	725	2985	Note 1
LC	Westchester Suburban*	750	2990	Note 1

NOTE 1: LC/D2 calendar year shipments, U.S. only: (Domestic) 51,229; (Government) 1,214. (Export) 4,783; (Total) 57,226. * With windows.

Series LE-15 — 3/4-Ton — 129 in. w.b.

LE-15	Chassis	550	—	Note 2
LE-15	Chassis & Cab	657	—	Note 2

Series LE-16 — 3/4 -Ton — 136 in. w.b.

LE-16	Chassis	550	—	Note 2
LE-16	Chassis & Cab	657	—	Note 2
LE-16	Pickup	734	—	Note 2
LE-16	Canopy	799	—	Note 2
LE-16	Screen	819	—	Note 2
LE-16	Panel	824	—	Note 2
LE-16	Platform	709	—	Note 2
LE-16	Stake	739	—	Note 2

Series LE-17 — 3/4-Ton — 162 in. w.b.

LE-17	Chassis	580	—	Note 2
LE-17	Chassis & Cab	687	—	Note 2
LE-17	Platform	759	—	Note 2
LE-17	Stake	799	—	Note 2

Series LE-20/LE-21/LE-22 (Note 3)

NOTE 2: LE series calendar year shipments, U.S. only: 2,399 (804 3/4-ton trucks and 1,595 1-ton trucks).
NOTE 3: 1-ton models were priced the same as equivalent 3/4-ton models LE-15/LE-16/LE-17, respectively.

1936 Dodge Model LC 1/2-Ton Pickup (JAW)

ENGINE [Series LC/LE]: Inline. L-head. Six-cylinder. Cast iron block. Bore & stroke: 31/8 x 4-3/8 in. Displacement: 201.3 cid. Compression ratio: 5.8:1. Brake horsepower: 70 at 3000 rpm. Net horsepower: 23.44. Torque: 138 lbs.-ft. at 1200 rpm. Four main bearings. Solid valve lifters. Carburetor: Downdraft.

ENGINE [D2 Commercial Sedan]: Inline. L-head. Six-cylinder. Cast iron block. Bore & stroke: 3-1/4 x 4-3/8 in. Displacement: 217.8 cid. Compression ratio: 6.5:1, Brake horsepower: 87 at 3600 rpm, Net horsepower: 25.35, Torque: 155 lbs.-ft. at 1200 rpm. Four main bearing. Solid valve lifters.

CHASSIS [Series LC/D2]: Wheelbase: 116 in. Tires: 6.00 x 16 four-ply (front/rear). Payload: 1000 lbs.

CHASSIS [Series LE-15/LE-20]: Wheelbase: 129 in. Tires: (front) 6.00 x 20 six-ply; (rear) 32 x 6 eight-ply on chassis, chassis & cab, platform and stake; 6.50 x 20 six-ply front/rear on panel, pickup, canopy and screen models.

CHASSIS [Series LE-16/LE-21]: Wheelbase: 136 in. Tires: Same as LE-15.

CHASSIS (Series LE-17/LE-22): Wheelbase: 162 in. Tires: Same as LE-15.

TECHNICAL: Transmission: [LC/D2] Synchro-silent shift; [LE] Selective sliding gear. Speeds: [LC/D2] 3F/1 R; [LE] 4F/1R with power-take-off on right side of case. Floor shift control. Single-plate dry-disc clutch. Rear axle: [LC/D2] Semi-floating; [LE] full-floating. Overall ratio: [LC/D2] 4.l:1 (3.7:1 optional at no extra cost); [LE] 4.875:1 (5.428:1 and 5.857:1 optional). Spiral bevel gear drive. Hydraulic four-wheel brakes: [LC/D2] 10 in. drums, 2 in. lining; [LE] 14-1/8 in. drums, 1-3/4 in. lining. Steering: [LC/D2] Semi-irreversible worm and roller gear; [LE] Worm and sector type. Reverse Elliott type I-beam front axle. Semi-elliptic springs; [LC/D2] (front) 36 in.; (rear) 48 in., eight-leaves; [LE] (front) 1-3/4 x 39 in., seven-leaves; (rear) 2-1/4 x 48 in., eight- or nine-leaves. 15-gallon gas tank. Wheels: [LC/D2] Pressed steel spoke; [LE] Ventilated disc.

1936 Dodge Model LC 1/2-Ton Pickup (OCW)

OPTIONS: [Series LC/D2] Chrome-plated front bumper ($6). Chrome-plated rear bumper ($7). Chrome radiator shell and headlamps ($7.50). Safety glass in windshield ($4). Safety glass throughout for cab, panel, canopy or screen ($7.50). Auxiliary seat for panel, canopy or screen body ($10). Inside sun visor ($2 each). Auxiliary windshield wiper ($4). Oil-bath air cleaner ($2.50). Vortex air cleaner with standard breather cap ($17.50). Vortex air cleaner with vortex cap ($19.50). Crankcase ventilator ($3.50). Governor ($10). Coach lamps for panel ($8). Oil filter ($2.75). Metal tire cover ($6.50 each). Tire lock ($1.20). Rearview mirror, long-arm ($1). Adjustable mirror ($2.50). Shock absorbers, front and rear ($10). Six steel spoke wheels with four 6.00 x 16 four-ply tires, extra fender well and tire lock ($10). Five 20 in. wheels with four 5.25 x 20 four-ply tires, 4.875:1 rear axle and shock absorbers ($25). Six 20 in. wheels with four 5.25 x 20 four-ply tires, 4.875:1 rear axle, shocks, extra fender well and tire lock ($35). [Series LE] Chrome bumper ($2 added). Chrome headlamps ($2). Chrome radiator shell ($6). Rearview mirror, long-arm ($l). Adjustable mirror ($2.50). Black front bumper ($5). Tire carrier ($3.50). Safety glass throughout ($7.50). Auxiliary windshield wiper ($4). Long runningboards with rear fenders: 126 or 136 in. ($16.50); 162 in. ($27). Governor ($5). Oil-bath air cleaner ($2.50). Shock absorbers, double-acting, front or rear ($10 pair). Auxiliary springs ($10).

1936 Dodge Model LC 1/2-Ton Pickup (OCW/DSM)

HISTORICAL: Introduced: November, 1935. Calendar year registrations: 85,295. Calendar year production: 109,392 (8,599 in Los Angeles and 2,764 in Canada). Innovations: Front-hinged doors for safety. Once again, Dodge ranked third in truck sales with a production gain of 31 percent over 1935. All U.S. trucks were made either in Hamtramck, Michigan or Los Angeles, California.Trucks up to three-ton capacity made up the standard line and a four-ton Airflow was also produced. All trucks were powered by six-cylinder engines. Truck registrations were up 38.7 percent. The year's totals included 4,783 1/2-ton trucks exported and 1,214 shipped to the government. Rapidly-growing truck sales had made necessary two plant expansions in the previous two years. In Detroit, Dodge had the capacity to build 500 units a day in 546,000 square feet of floor space. A rumor circulated that Dodge was ready to announce a diesel-powered truck, but that was not to happen until 1939.

1937 DODGE

1/2-TON — COMMERCIAL SERIES MC — SIX-CYLINDER: Commercial Series trucks were carried over from 1936 basically unchanged in appearance. Model offerings remained the same, including a Commercial Sedan and Westchester Suburban station wagon. Only the Commercial Sedan was built on a passenger car chassis; all others shared a 116 in. wheelbase truck-type chassis. The only difference between the panel and Commercial Sedan was the panel's familiar raised-roof style. A new 218 cid, 75 hp engine replaced the former 201 cid six. A chromed front bumper was standard. Chrome-plated front and rear bumpers came on the Commercial Sedan, while the Westchester Suburban carried a chrome front bumper and shock absorbers all around. The spare wheel sat in a right side fender well. Standard equipment was the same as in 1936.

1937 Dodge Model MC 1/2-Ton Panel (ATC)

1937 Dodge Model MC 1/2-Ton Pickup (front view)

3/4-TON and 1-TON — SERIES MD/ME/MF — SIX-CYLINDER: All-new appearance highlighted the 3/4- and 1-ton lineup, due to sharing sheet metal with the MC 3/4-ton series rather than the 1-1/2-tons. Dodge called this series its "in-between" trucks. They were a cross between the light Commercial Car series and the larger 1-1/2-ton models. Prior to this year, a 3/4- to 1-ton series had been built by reducing spring capacity and substituting smaller tires to carry bulky, but not heavy, loads. Only two wheelbases were now available: 120 and 136 in. The 120 in. wheelbase series carried seven-foot bodies, while the 136 in. wheelbase accomodated nine-foot bodies. All used the same new 218 cid engine as the MC. The 17 in. steering wheel had an adjustable column. Standard equipment included a cowl ventilator, glove compartment, hood ornament, electric horn, tail/stop lamp, dash light, gas gauge, ammeter, oil pressure gauge, heat indicator, speedometer, choke, throttle, license bracket, vacuum windshield wiper and tool kit, plus a chrome front bumper. The panel model had chrome bumpers front and rear. Dual wheels were not available.

1937 Dodge Model MC 1/2-Ton Panel (OCW)

I.D. DATA: Serial numbers were located on a plate on the right front door pillar. [MC] (Detroit) 8156701-8186617; (Los Angeles) 9247201-9250807. [MD/ME] (Detroit) 8072601-8082022; (Los Angeles) 9282601-9283704. [MF] (Detroit) 8407601-8421824; (California) 9293701-9294756. Engine numbers were on the top front, left side of the block between cylinders one and two. [MC] Starting: T38-1001. [MD/ME/MF] Starting: T30-1001.

1937 Dodge Model MC 1/2-Ton Westchester Suburban (OCW)

Model	Body Type	Price	Weight	Prod. Total
Series MC — 1/2-Ton — 116 in. w.b.				
MC	Chassis & Cowl	410	1975	—
MC	Chassis & Cab	510	2450	—
MC	Pickup	540	2700	—
MC	Panel	625	2975	—
MC	Canopy	640	2695	—
MC	Screen	660	2710	—
MC	Commercial Sedan	670	2845	—
MC	Westchester Suburban	755	2915	—

NOTE 1: MC Series calendar year shipments, U.S. only: (Domestic) 52,610; (Government) 80; (Export) 6,973; [Total] 59,663.

1937 Dodge Model MD-21 1-Ton Canopy (OCW)

Series MD — 3/4-Ton — 120 in. w.b.				
MD15	Chassis & Cowl	505	2425	—
MD15	Chassis & Cab	605	2900	—
MC15	Express 7 ft.	685	3200	—
MD15	Stake 7 ft.	685	3500	—
MD15	Platform 7 ft.	655	3225	—
Series MD — 3/4-Ton — 136 in. w.b.				
MD16	Chassis & Cowl	520	2450	—
MD16	Chassis & Cab	620	2925	—
MD16	Panel	800	3565	—
MD16	Canopy	765	3310	—
MD16	Screen	785	3330	—
MD16	Express 9 ft.	700	3275	—
MD16	Stake 9 ft.	705	3675	—
MD16	Platform 9 ft.	675	3500	—

1937 Dodge Model MD-21 1-Ton Panel (OCW)

Series MD20 — One-Ton — 120 in. w.b.				
MD20	Chassis & Cowl	505	2425	—
MD20	Chassis & Cab	605	2900	—
MC20	Express 7 ft.	685	3200	—
MD20	Stake 7 ft.	685	3500	—
MD20	Platform 7 ft.	655	3225	—
Series MD 21 — One-Ton — 136 in. w.b.				
MD21	Chassis & Cowl	520	2450	—
MD21	Chassis & Cab	620	2925	—
MD21	Panel	800	3565	—
MD21	Canopy	765	3310	—
MD21	Screen	785	3330	—
MD21	Express 9 ft.	700	3275	—
MD21	Stake 9 ft.	705	3675	—
MD21	Platform 9 ft.	675	3500	—

NOTE 2: MD Series calendar year shipments, U.S. only: (Domestic) 12,076; (Government) 2; (Export) 1,556; [Total] 13,634.

1937 Dodge Model MD-21 1-Ton 9 ft. Express (OCW)

Series ME15 — 3/4-Ton — 126 in. w.b.

ME15	Chassis	555	2925	—
ME15	Chassis & Cab	655	3300	—

Series ME16 — 3/4-Ton — 133 in. w.b.

ME16	Chassis	555	2950	—
ME16	Chassis & Cab	655	3325	—
ME16	Express	735	3765	—
ME16	Stake	740	4275	—

Series ME17 — 3/4-Ton — 159 in. w.b.

ME17	Chassis	585	3075	—
ME17	Chassis & Cab	685	3450	—
ME17	Stake	800	—	—

Series ME20 — 1-Ton — 126 in. w.b.

ME20	Chassis	555	2925	—
ME20	Chassis & Cab	655	3300	—

Series ME21 — 1-Ton — 133 in. w.b.

ME21	Chassis	555	2950	—
ME21	Chassis & Cab	655	3325	—
ME21	Express	735	3765	—
ME21	Stake	740	4275	—

Series ME22 — 1-Ton — 159 in. w.b.

ME22	Chassis	585	3075	—
ME22	Chassis & Cab	685	3450	—
ME22	Stake	800	—	—

Series MF28 — 3/4-Ton — 126 in. w.b.

MF28	Chassis	605	3425	—
MF28	Chassis & Cab	705	3800	—

1937 Dodge Model MC 1/2-Ton Commercial Sedan (OCW)

ENGINE: Inline. L-head. Six-cylinder. Cast iron block. Bore & stroke: 3-3/8 x 4-1/16 in. Displacement: 218.06 cid. Compression ratio: 6.5:1. Brake horsepower: 75 at 3000 rpm. Net horsepower: 27.34. Torque: 155 lbs.-ft. Four main bearings. Solid valve lifters. Carburetor: Carter.

1937 Dodge Model MC 1/2-Ton Panel (rear view)

CHASSIS [Series MC]: Wheelbase: 116 in. Tires: 6.00 x 16 four-ply (front/rear). Payload: 1,000 lbs.

1937 Dodge Model MD-15 3/4-Ton 7 ft. Express (rear)

CHASSIS [Series MD16/MD21]: Wheelbase: 136 in. Tires: (front) 7.00 x 16 six-ply; (rear) 7.50 x 16 six-ply.

1937 Dodge MD-16 3/4-Ton Panel (OCW)

CHASSIS [Series ME15/ME20]: Wheelbase: 126 in.

CHASSIS [Series ME16/ME21]: Wheelbase: 133 in.

CHASSIS [Series ME17/ME22]: Wheelbase: 159 in.

TECHNICAL: Transmission: [Series MC] Synchro-silent shift; [MD] Selective sliding gear. Speeds: [MC] 3F/1R; [MD/ME/MF] 3F/1R with power-take-off opening on right side of case. Floor shift control. Single-plate dry-disc clutch. Semi-floating rear axle. Overall ratio: [MC] 4.1:1 (3.7:1 optional); [MD/ME/MF] 4.3:1 (3.9:1 and 4.78:1 optional at no extra cost). Hotchkiss drive. Hydraulic four-wheel brakes: [MC] 10 in. drums, 2 in. lining; [MD] 11 in. front and 13 in. rear drums, 2 in. lining. Steering: [MC] Semi-irreversible worm and roller gear; [MD/ME/MF] Worm and sector. Reverse Elliott I-beam front axle. Semi-elliptic springs: [MC] (front) 36 in. long; (rear) 48 in., eight-leaves; [MD] (front) 1-3/4 x 36 in., 12-leaves; (rear) 1-3/4 x 52 in., 11-leaves. 16-gallon gas tank under left side of seat [MD]. 17 in. cooling fan [MD]. Pressed steel disc wheels.

1937 Dodge Model MC 1/2-Ton Canopy (OCW)

OPTIONS: [All Models] Chrome rear bumper ($8.50). Dual horns ($7.50). Coach lamps ($8). Stationary rearview mirror ($1.50). Adjustable mirror ($2.50). Auxiliary seat ($10). Inside sun visor ($2 each). Tire lock, except 136 in. wheelbase ($2.50). Auxiliary windshield wiper ($4). Double-acting hydraulic shock absorbers, front or rear ($4.75/pair). Four-speed transmission ($25). Oil-bath air cleaner ($3.25). Oil filter ($3.25). Leibing governor ($5). Monarch governor ($7.50). Handy governor ($10). (1/2-ton only) Bumper guards ($1.50/pair). Metal tire cover ($6.50 each). 6.00 x 16 six-ply tires, front and rear ($11.40). Five 20 in. wheels with 5.25 x 20 six-ply tires, 4.78:1 rear axle ratio and front/rear shock absorbers ($40). (3/4- and 1-ton only) Underslung tire carrier for 136 in. wheelbase ($3.50). 7.00 x 16 six-ply tires front and rear ($15 net allowance). 7.00 x 16 six-ply front and 7.50 x 16 eight-ply rear tires ($7.50). 7.50 x 16 six-ply tires front and rear ($20.50). 7.50 x 16 six-ply front and 7.50 x 16 eight-ply rear tires ($28).

Standard Catalog of Light-Duty Trucks

1937 Dodge Model MC 1/2-Ton Screenside (OCW)

HISTORICAL: Introduced December, 1936. Calendar year registrations were 64,098. Calendar year production was 121,917. Production figures by model year and type not available. Dodge truck registrations fell by 24.8 percent, while total industry sales were up slightly. So, Dodge slipped down to fourth position, even though total production actually increased. Of the total production, 7,409 trucks were made in Los Angeles and 5,383 in Canada. Sizes ranged from 1/2- to 3-tons in the standard line, plus 4-ton Airflow trucks. All were six-cylinder powered. For the first time, Dodge offered a cab-over-engine (COE) model. It was a conversion made for Dodge by the Montpelier Co. It came in 1-1/2- and 3-ton ratings. Plymouth marketed a line of 1/2-ton pickups this year. They were based on the Dodge MC series.

1937 Dodge Model MD-21 1-Ton Canopy (OCW)

1938 DODGE

1938 Dodge Model RC 1/2-Ton Pickup (DFW)

1/2-TON — COMMERCIAL SERIES RC — SIX-CYLINDER: Only appearance changes hit the 1938 half-tons. A new grille, following Dodge car styling gave the series a fresh new look. Though similar in appearance, Dodge cars and light trucks were not identical. Car headlights were now fender-mounted, while bullet-shaped truck lamps sat alongside the radiator shell. Dropped this year was the Westchester Suburban wagon on the commercial chassis. Instead, it was offered as a passenger car, using automobile front end sheet metal and chassis componentry. All other commercial body types remained the same, as did engine and mechanical components including the frame. Dodge was busy preparing an all-new line for 1939, so it could afford only a quick cosmetic facelift this year. Bodies were six-feet long. Standard equipment included an ammeter, speedometer, fuel gauge, oil pressure gauge, heat indicator, glove compartment, choke, throttle, and vacuum windshield wiper. Sedan, panel, screen and canopy models had only one bucket seat.

1938 Dodge Model RC 1/2-Ton Pickup (OCW)

3/4-TON and 1-TON — SERIES RD/RE/RF — SIX-CYLINDER: Like the smaller trucks, the larger models continued with only front end sheet metal appearance changes. Body types, engine and mechanical equipment were the same as 1937 models. The 3/4-ton models differed from the 1-ton only in tire size and spring capacities, which affected total GVW ratings. The 120 in. wheelbase RD-15 and RD-20 carried seven-foot bodies; the 136 in. wheelbase RD16 and RD21 models had nine-foot bodies. Standard equipment was the same as 1937. All models included a chrome front bumper, but the panel had chrome bumpers front and rear. Prices included a spare tire and tube, in the rear tire's size and ply.

1938 Dodge Model RC 1/2-Ton Pickup (OCW)

I.D. DATA: Serial numbers were located on a plate on the right front door pillar. [RC] (Detroit) 8186701-8204334; (Los Angeles) 9251001-9252540. [RD] (Detroit) 8082101-8087863; (Los Angeles) 9283801-9284247 [RE] (Detroit) 8276801-8284456; (California) 9263401-9263709. [RF] (Detroit) 8423601-8436063; (Los Angeles) 9295201-9295663. Engine numbers were on the top front, left side of the block between cylinders one and two. [RC] Starting: T58-1001. [RD/RE/RF] Starting: T60-1001.

1938 Dodge Model RD-21 1-Ton Canopy

Model	Body Type	Price	Weight	Prod. Total
Series RC — 1/2-Ton — 116 in. w.b.				
RC	Chassis & Cowl	475	1975	—
RC	Chassis & Cab	575	2450	—
RC	Pickup 6 ft.	600	2700	—
RC	Canopy	690	2695	—
RC	Screen	710	2710	—
RC	Panel	695	2975	—
RC	Commercial Sedan	710	2845	—

NOTE 1: RC Series calendar year shipments, U.S. only: (Domestic) 17,299; (Government) 242; (Export) 3,236; [Total] 20,777.

1938 Dodge Model RD-21 1-Ton Screen (OCW)

Series RD10 — 3/4-Ton — 120 in. w.b.

RD10	Chassis	555	2375	—
RD10	Chassis & Cab	653	2750	—
RD10	Express	694	3150	—
RD10	Platform	694	3175	—
RD10	Stake	727	3450	—

Series RD11 — 3/4-Ton — 136 in. w.b.

RD11	Chassis	605	2400	—
RD11	Chassis & Cab	703	2775	—
RD11	Express	746	3225	—
RD11	Platform	746	3450	—
RD11	Stake	781	3625	—
RD11	Canopy	828	3260	—
RD11	Screen Express	848	3320	—
RD11	Panel	855	—	—

1938 Dodge Model RD-21 1-Ton Panel (OCW)

Series RD15 — 3/4-Ton — 120 in. w.b.

RD15	Chassis & Cowl	584	2450	—
RD15	Chassis & Cab	682	2825	—
RD15	Pickup 7 ft.	725	3225	—
RD15	Platform 7 ft.	725	3250	—
RD15	Stake 7 ft.	758	3525	—

1938 Dodge Model RC 1/2-Ton Panel (OCW)

Series RD16 — 3/4-Ton — 136 in. w.b.

RD16	Chassis	635	2450	—
RD16	Chassis & Cab	733	2850	—
RD16	Pickup 9 ft.	776	3300	—
RD16	Platform 9 ft.	776	3525	—
RD16	Stake 9 ft.	809	3700	—
RD16	Canopy	858	3335	—
RD16	Screen	878	3395	—
RD16	Panel	885	3565	—

Series RD20 — 1-Ton — 120 in. w.b.

RD20	Chassis & Cowl	584	2475	—
RD20	Chassis & Cab	682	2900	—
RD20	Pickup 7 ft.	725	3200	—
RD20	Platform 7 ft.	725	3250	—
RD20	Stake 7 ft.	758	3525	—

Series RD21 — 1-Ton — 136 in. w.b.

RD21	Chassis	635	2450	—
RD21	Chassis & Cab	733	2925	—
RD21	Pickup 9 ft.	776	3275	—
RD21	Platform 9 ft.	776	3525	—
RD21	Stake 9 ft.	809	3700	—
RD21	Canopy	858	3310	—
RD21	Screen	878	3330	—
RD21	Panel	885	3565	—

NOTE 2: RD Series calendar year shipments, U.S. only: (Domestic) 4,988; (Government) 13; (Export) 760; [Total] 5,761.

Series RF28 — 3/4-Ton — 126 in. w.b.

RF28	Chassis	655	3425	—
RF28	Chassis & Cab	755	3800	—
RF28	Platform	815	4400	—
RF28	Stake	845	4750	—

1938 Dodge RD-21 1-Ton 9 ft. Express (OCW)

ENGINE: Inline. L-head. Six-cylinder. Cast iron block. Bore & stroke: 3-3/8 x 4-1/16 in. Displacement: 218.06 cid. Compression ratio: 6.5:1. Brake horsepower: 75 at 3000 rpm. Net horsepower: 27.34. Torque: 155 lbs.-ft. Four main bearings. Solid valve lifters. Carburetor: Carter.

1938 Dodge Model RD-15 3/4-Ton 7 ft. Pickup (OCW)

CHASSIS [Series RC]: Wheelbase: 116 in. Tires: 6.00 x 16 four-ply front/rear). Payload: 1,000 lbs.

1938 Dodge Model RD-15 3/4-Ton 7 ft. Stake (OCW)

CHASSIS [Series RD15/RD-20]: Wheelbase: 120 in. Tires: (front) 7.00 x 16 six-ply; (rear) 7.50 x 16 six-ply.

1938 Dodge Model RD-15 3/4-Ton Walk-in Delivery (OCW)

Standard Catalog of Light-Duty Trucks

CHASSIS [Series RD16/RD21]: Wheelbase: 136 in. Tires: (front) 7.00 x 16 six-ply; (rear) 7.50 x 16 six-ply.

CHASSIS [Series RE15/RE20]: Wheelbase: 126 in.

CHASSIS [Series RE16/RE21]: Wheelbase: 133 in.

CHASSIS [Series RE17/RE22]: Wheelbase: 159 in.

1938 Dodge Model RD-15 3/4 Ton 7 ft. Platform (OCW)

TECHNICAL: Transmission: [Series RC] Synchro-silent shift; [RD] Selective sliding gear. Speeds: [RC] 3F/1R; [RD/RE/RF] 3F/1R with power-take-off opening on right side of case. Floor shift control. Single-plate dry-disc clutch. Semi-floating rear axle. Overall ratio: [RC] 4.1:1 (3.7:1 optional); [RD/RE/RF] 4.3:1 (3.9:1 and 4.78:1 optional at no extra cost). Hotchkiss drive. Hydraulic four-wheel brakes: [RC] 10 in. drums, 2 in. lining; [RD] 11 in. front and 13 in. rear drums, 2 in. lining. Steering: [RC] Semi-irreversible worm and roller gear; [RD/RE/RF] Worm and sector. Reverse Elliott I-beam front axle. Semi-elliptic springs: [RC] (front) 36 in. long; (rear) 48 in., eight-leaves; [RD] (front) 1-3/4 x 36 in., 12-leaves; (rear) 1-3/4 x 52 in., 11-leaves. 16-gallon gas tank under left side of seat [RD]. 17 in. cooling fan [RD]. Pressed steel disc wheels.

1938 Dodge Model RC 1/2-Ton Chassis & Cab (DFW/FLP)

OPTIONS: [1/2-ton] Chrome rear bumper ($8.50). Chrome-plated headlamps ($2.75). Dual horns ($7.50). Chrome-plated radiator shell ($6). Coach lamps ($8.50). Full-width partition behind driver's seat on canopy, screen, panel models ($15). Auxiliary seat ($10). Stationary rearview mirror ($1.50). Adjustable mirror ($2.50). Inside sun visors ($2 each). Auxiliary windshield wiper ($4). Oil-bath air cleaner ($3.75). Oil filter ($3.25). Shock absorbers, front or rear ($4.75). Leibing governor ($5). Monarch governor ($5). Handy governor ($10). Four-speed transmission ($25). Six 6.00 x 16 six-ply tires ($14.68). Six steel disc wheels with five 6.00 x 14 four-ply tires, extra fender well and tire lock ($10.30). Five 20 in. wheels with 5.25 x 20 four-ply tires and 4.78:1 rear axle ratio ($10.82). Five 20 in. wheels with 5.25 x 20 six-ply tires and 4.78:1 axle ($31.42). Six 20 in. wheels with five 5.25 x 20 four-ply tires, 4.78:1 axle, extra fender well and tire lock ($26.27). Six 20 in. wheels with five 5.25 x 20 six-ply tires, 4.78:1 axle, extra fender well and tire lock ($41.72). [3/4- and 1-ton] Same as 1937, except: 7.00 x 16 six-ply front and 7.50 x 16 eight-ply rear tires ($10). 7.50 x 16 six-ply tires, front and rear ($24). 7.50 x 16 six-ply front and 7.50 x 16 eight-ply rear tires ($34).

1938 Dodge Model RD-21 1-Ton Screenside (OCW)

HISTORICAL: Calendar year registrations were 33,676. Calendar year production was 53,613. Production figures by model year and type not available. 1938 was a disastrous year for Dodge truck sales, as registrations plummeted 47.5 percent. Total industry sales were little better, down 40.9 percent. The depression was still very much alive, though this would be the last truly lean year. Of the total production, 2,563 trucks were made in Los Angeles, 5,704 in Canada, and the remainder at Hamtramck, Michigan. The truck lineup ranged from 1/2- to 3-ton ratings, including 2 and 3-ton Montpelier cab-over-engine conversions. Airflow 4-tons were custom-built. This would be the last year for the famous and popular raised-roof (humpback) panel model. Dodge finished fourth in the truck sales race.

Standard Catalog of Light-Duty Trucks

1938 Dodge Model RD-21 1-Ton 9 ft. Stake (OCW)

1939 DODGE

1939 Dodge Furniture Delivery Truck (DFW/HC)

LIGHT TRUCK — TC SERIES — 1/2-TON — SIX-CYLINDER: Dodge called it "The truck of the year." For Dodge Truck Div., 1939 was "the year of the truck." In addition to a totally redesigned truck line, Dodge opened the world's largest truck factory. This modern new facility cost over $6 million. It was built to be an exclusive truck building facility. This plant is located in Warren, Mich, and is still the home of Dodge trucks today. The 1/2-ton TC series sported all new sheet metal on the previous model's 116 in. wheelbase. Gone were the Commercial Sedan, Westchester Suburban and the raised roof panel. The new line consisted of Pickup, Panel, Canopy and Screen models, There was a family resemblance between the Dodge car and truck lines, but trucks were definitely acquiring a look of their own. The new trucks were particularly handsome and modern looking. The 1/2-ton truck engine for 1939 actually took a backward step. It was reduced from 218 cid to 201 cid. Dodge continued to refer to the 1/2-ton series as its "Commercial" series, but at long last, Dodge was beginning to recognize the popular tonnage classification of 1/2-, 3/4-, 1-1/2, 2-, 2-1/2 and 3-tons and designate its models this way. Standard equipment included: Front and rear shock absorbers. Spare tire and tube. Front bumper. Rear bumper on panel. Hood ornament. Safety glass. Electric horn. Combination stop lamp and taillamp. License brackets. Tool kit. Speedometer. Fuel gauge. Oil pressure gauge. Ammeter. Engine temperature indicator, Choke. Throttle. High-low beam headlights. Glove compartment. Cowl vent. Vacuum windshield wipers. Panel, Canopy and Screen models, one bucket seat only.

1939 Dodge 1/2-Ton Pickup (Express)

LIGHT TRUCK — SERIES TD15 — 3/4-TON — SIX-CYLINDER: For the first time since the early '30s Dodge built a true 3/4-ton series. It consisted of pickup, platform and stake with 7,5-foot bodies on a 120 in. wheelbase. Styling of the TD15 Series was the same as the TC, since they essentially shared all the same sheet metal from front bumper to back of cab. Pickup bodies were similar, only longer. Mechanicals were shared with the TC line, except TDs had a larger 218 cid engine.

1939 Dodge 1/2-Ton Canopy (OCW)

LIGHT TRUCK — SERIES TD-20/TD-21 — ONE-TON — SIX-CYLINDER: The 1-ton series completed the new light truck line-up for 1939. One-ton trucks were available in two wheelbase lengths, 120 in. TD-20 and 133 in. TD-21. The TD-20 series was basically the 3/4-ton series with beefier wheels and springs increasing payload by 500 lbs. to 2,000 lbs. total. Model offerings in the TD-20 line were the same as the 3/4-ton line, 7-1/2 foot pickup, stake and platform. The longer wheelbase TD-21 series mirrored the model offerings of the 1/2-ton series, plus added platform and stake models. Both 1-ton series used the same 218 cu. in. engine which they shared with the 3/4-ton trucks. Cabs and mechanicals used on one tons were the same as 1/2-ton and 3/4-ton models.

1939 Dodge 1/2-Ton Screenside (OCW)

LIGHT TRUCK — SERIES TE21/TE22 — ONE-TON — SIX-CYLINDER: These trucks were related to the 1-1/2-ton Dodge models and came on three different wheelbases, including a long box pickup in the TE21 line.

1939 Dodge 3/4-Ton Express (OCW)

I.D. DATA: Serial number plate is located on the right front door hinge pillar. Engine number is stamped on a pad on left side of cylinder block between cylinder numbers one and two. [TC] (Detroit) 8520301-8542929; (Los Angeles) 9252601-9254160. Engine numbers T81-1001 and up. [TD15]: (Detroit) 8204401-8207021; Los Angeles 9200321-9200465. Engine numbers T70-1001 and up. [TD-20/TD-21]: (Detroit) 8087901-8093438; (Los Angeles) 9284301-9284669. Engine numbers T72-1001 and up. [TE20/TE21/TE22] (Detroit) 8284501-8292512; (Los Angeles) 9263751-9264077. Engine numbers not available.

1939 Dodge 3/4-Ton Chassis & Cab (OCW)

Model	Body Type	Price	Weight	Prod. Total
Model TC — 1/2-Ton — 116 in. w.b.				
TC	Chassis	465	2175	—
TC	Chassis & Cab	560	2600	—
TC	Pickup	590	2925	—
TC	Panel	680	3025	—
TC	Canopy	690	3125	—
TC	Screen	710	3020	—

NOTE 1: Shipments, U.S. Only (Calendar Year) (Domestic) 30,536; (Government) 905; (Export) 3,017; [Total] 34,458.

Model	Body Type	Price	Weight	Prod. Total
Model TD15 — 3/4-Ton — 120 in. w.b.				
TD15	Chassis	535	2350	—
TD15	Chassis & Cab	630	2775	—
TD15	Pickup 7.5 ft.	670	3150	—
TD15	Stake 7.5 ft.	705	3375	—
TD15	Platform 7.5 ft.	680	3150	—

NOTE 2: Shipments, U.S. Only (Calendar Year) (Domestic) 2,878; (Government) 40; (Export) 111; [Total] 3,029.

1939 Dodge 3/4-Ton Platform (OCW)

Model	Body Type	Price	Weight	Prod. Total
Model TD20 — 1-Ton — 120 in. w.b.				
TD20	Chassis	580	2625	—
TD20	Chassis & Cab	675	3050	—
TD20	Pickup 7.5 ft.	715	3400	—
TD20	Stake 7.5 ft.	750	3650	—
TD20	Platform 7.5 ft.	725	3465	—
Model TD21 — 1-Ton — 133 in. w.b.				
TD21	Chassis	620	2650	—
TD21	Chassis & Cab	715	3075	—
TD21	Panel	855	3650	—
TD21	Canopy	840	3675	—
TD21	Screen	860	—	—
TD21	Pickup 9 ft.	765	3475	—
TD21	Stake 9 ft.	790	3825	—
TD21	Platform 9 ft.	760	3550	—

NOTE 3: Shipments, U.S. Only (Calendar Year) (Domestic) 5,414; (Government) 193; (Export) 980; [Total] 6,587.

Model	Body Type	Price	Weight	Prod. Total
Model TE20 — 1-Ton — 126.5 in. w.b.				
TE20	Chassis	590	3050	—
TE20	Chassis & Cab	685	3475	—
Model TE21 — 1-Ton — 133 in. w.b.				
TE21	Chassis	590	3075	—
TE21	Chassis & Cab	685	3500	—
TE21	Platform	745	4050	—
TE21	Express	755	3890	—
TE21	Stake	780	4400	—
Model TE22 — 1-Ton — 160 in. w.b.				
TE22	Chassis	615	3200	—
TE22	Chassis & Cab	710	3625	—
TE22	Platform	785	4325	—
TE22	Stake	825	4725	—

1939 Dodge 1-ton Panel Bread Van (OCW)

ENGINE [TC]: Inline. L-head. Six-cylinder. Cast iron block. Bore & stroke: 3-1/8 in. x 4-3/8 in. Displacement: 201.3 cid. Compression ratio: 6.7:1. Taxable horsepower: 23.44. Brake horsepower: 70 at 3000 rpm. Maximum Torque: 148 lbs.-ft. at 1200 rpm. Four main bearings. Solid valve lifters.

1939 Dodge 3/4-Ton Stake (OCW)

ENGINE [TD15/TD20/TD21/TE20/TE21]: Inline. L-head. Six-cylinder. Cast iron block. Bore & stroke: 3-1/4 in. x 4-3/8 in. Displacement: 217.76 cu. in. Compression ratio: 6.5:1. Taxable horsepower: 25.35. Brake horsepower: 77 at 3000 rpm. Maximum Torque: 158 lbs.-ft. at 1200 rpm. Four main bearings. Solid valve lifters.

1939 Dodge 3/4-Ton Montpelier Urban Panel (OCW)

CHASSIS [TC]: Wheelbase: 116 in. Wheels: Five steel disc with five 6.00 x 16, four-tires with underslung tire carrier for spare wheel and tire. Payload 1,000 lbs.

1939 Dodge 1-Ton 9 ft. Express (OCW)

CHASSIS [TD15]: Wheelbase: 120 in. Standard wheels are five steel disc with five six-ply tires front and rear. Underslung tire carrier for the spare wheel and tire. Gross weight: 5,000 lbs. Payload: 1,500 lbs.

1939 Dodge 1-Ton 9 ft. Stake (OCW)

CHASSIS [TD20/TD21]: Wheelbase: 120/133 in. Wheels and tires for both: Steel disc with semi-drop center rim. Tires: 7.00/16 six-ply front, 7.50/16 six-ply rear. Spare underslung at rear of frame. Gross weight rating 6,000 lbs. both series. Payload 2,000 lbs. both series. Rear axle ratios 4.3, 3.9 or 4.89:1.

Standard Catalog of Light-Duty Trucks

1939 Dodge 1/2-Ton Panel (0CW)

TECHNICAL [TC/TD15;TD20/TD21]: Maximum gross weight: Dodge said "has no gross rating, but will carry 1,000 lbs. payload." Mechanical fuel pump fed from 18 gallon gas tank mounted inside frame at left side. Air cleaner and gas filter. Dry, single plate clutch. Selective sliding gear transmission. Speeds: 3F/1R. Hotchkiss drive. Tubular steel propeller shaft. Reverse Elliot type front axle, I-beam section. Rear axles on 1/2- and 3/4-ton models have hypoid drive gears, 1-ton model has spiral bevel drive gears. Worm and sector gears steering. 17-inch, three-spoke steering wheel, adjustable for height. Four-wheel hydraulic brakes. Independent hand-brake operating on propeller shaft. Amola steel springs. Rear axle ratios: Standard 4.1, 3.73, 4.3 or 4.78 to 1.

1939 Dodge 1-Ton 9 ft. Platform (OCW)

OPTIONS: Oil bath air cleaner ($3.25). Rear bumper ($6). Generator for slow speed operation ($27.50). Governors: Leibing ($5), Monarch ($5), Handy ($10). Chrome headlamps ($2.75). Dual horns ($7.50). 6.00 x 16 six-ply tires front and rear ($14.50). 6.50 x 16 six-ply tires front and rear ($28.25). 5.25 x 20 four-ply tires front and rear and 20 in. wheels ($18). 5.25 x 20 six-ply tires front and rear and 20 in. wheels ($35). Coach lamps ($8.50). Oil filter ($3.25). Partition behind driver's seat: Panel, Screen and Canopy ($15). Stationary rearview mirror ($1.50). Adjustable rearview mirror ($2.50). Auxiliary seat ($10). Sun visors interior each ($2). Auxiliary taillight ($4). Four speed transmission ($17.50). Chrome windshield frame ($3). Auxiliary windshield wiper/vacuum ($4). Dual electric wipers ($8).

1939 Dodge 1-Ton 9 ft. Canopy (OCW)

HISTORICAL: Model year began Dec. 1, 1938. Dodge truck sales rebounded significantly from the low of 1938 gaining 42.8 percent in sales. Total registrations were 48,049. Total production was 89,364, of which 3,403 were built in Los Angeles and 5,704 were built in Canada. Dodge exported 19,336 trucks of all sizes and delivered 5,997 trucks to the government. Of the government sales, 905 were 1/2-ton, 40 3/4-ton and 193 1-tons. Dodge came in fourth in the U.S. truck sales race, while the car division came in fifth place in the car sales race. Dodge startled the truck industry by announcing a Dodge-built diesel engine for use in its heavy-duty 2-1/2 and 3-ton models. This engine was developed and built in-house. Dodge, like Ford and Chevrolet, offered an economy model again for 1939. It was on the 1/2-, 3/4-, and 1-ton series. Economy models were supplied with a smaller carburetor. Dodge also introduced two series of forward-control panel delivery models built on 3/4- and 1-ton chassis. Body builders were Metroplitan and Montpelier. Dodge, for 1939, continued to build trucks ranging from 1/2- to 3-tons. Montpelier continued to produce a Dodge COE conversion and Dodge continued their popular, but low volume 4-ton Airflow truck line.

1939 Dodge 1-Ton 133 in. wheelbase Panel (OCW)

1940 DODGE

1940 Dodge 1/2-Ton Panel (CHC)

Model	Body Type	Price	Weight	Prod. Total
Model VC — 1/2-Ton — 116 in. w.b.				
VC	Chassis & Flat-Face Cowl	465	2200	—
VC	Chassis & Cab	560	2600	—
VC	Pickup	590	2950	—
VC	Panel	680	3050	—
VC	Canopy	690	3150	—
VC	Screen	710	3150	—

NOTE 1: Shipments, U.S. Only (Calendar Year) (Domestic) 36,583; (Government) 10,107; (Export) 3,022; [Total] 49,712.

Model	Body Type	Price	Weight	Prod. Total
Model VD15 — 3/4-Ton — 120 in. w.b.				
VD15	Chassis & Flat Face Cowl	535	2325	—
VD15	Chassis & Cab	630	2725	—
VD15	Pickup 7.5 ft.	670	3025	—
VD15	Stake 7.5 ft.	705	3350	—
VD15	Platform 7.5 ft.	680	3125	—

NOTE 2: Shipments, U.S. Only (Calendar Year). (Domestic) 4,433; (Government) none; (Export) 81; [Total] 4,514.

Model	Body Type	Price	Weight	Prod. Total
Model VD20 — 1-Ton — 120 in. w.b.				
VD20	Chassis & Flat Face Cowl	580	2550	—
VD20	Chassis & Cab	675	2950	—
VD20	Pickup 7.5 ft.	715	3250	—
VD20	Stake 7.5 ft.	750	3575	—
VD20	Platform 7.5 ft.	725	3350	—
Model VD21 — 1-Ton — 133 in. w.b.				
VD21	Chassis & Flat Face Cowl	620	2650	—
VD21	Chassis & Cab	715	3050	—
VD21	Panel	855	3575	—
VD21	Canopy	840	3675	—
VD21	Screen	860	3675	—
VD21	Pickup 9 ft.	765	3375	—
VD21	Stake 9 ft.	790	3775	—
VD21	Platform 9 ft.	760	3500	—

NOTE 3: Shipments, U.S. Only (Calendar Year) (Domestic) 6,666; (Government) 23; (Export) 834; [Total] 7,523.

Model	Body Type	Price	Weight	Prod. Total
Model VF 20 — Heavy-Duty 1-Ton — 126.5 in. w.b.				
VF20	Chassis & Flat Face Cowl	610	3325	—
VF20	Chassis Cab	705	3700	
Model VF21 — Heavy-Duty 1-Ton — 133 in. w.b.				
VF21	Chassis & Flat Face Cowl	610	3325	—
VF21	Chassis Cab	705	3725	—
VF21	Pickup 9 ft.	775	—	—
VF21	Stake 9 ft.	800	4225	—
VF21	Platform 9 ft.	765	3875	—
Model VF22 — Heavy-Duty 1-Ton — 160 in. w.b.				
VF22	Chassis & Flat Face Cowl	635	3450	—
VF22	Chassis Cab	730	3850	—
VF22	Stake 9 ft.	845	4550	—
VF22	Platform 9 ft.	805	4150	—

ENGINE [Series VC]: Inline. L-head. Six-cylinder. Cast iron block. Bore & stroke: 3-1/8 in. x 4-3/8 in. Displacement: 201.3 cid. Compression ratio: 6.7:1. Taxable horsepower: 23.44. Brake horsepower: 79 at 3000 rpm. Maximum Torque: 154 lbs.-ft. at 1200 rpm. Four main bearings. Solid valve lifters.

ENGINE [Series VD15/VD20/VD21]: Inline. L-head. Six-cylinder. Cast iron block. Bore & stroke: 3-1/4 in. x 4-3/8 in. Displacement: 217.76 cid. Compression ratio: 6.5:1. Taxable horsepower: 25.35. Brake horsepower: 82 at 3000 rpm. Maximum Torque: 166 lbs.-ft.-at 1200 rpm. Four main bearings. Solid valve lifters.

ENGINE [Series VF20/VF21/VF22]: Inline. L-head. Six-cylinder. Cast iron block. Bore & stroke: 3-3/8 in. x 4-1/4 in. Taxable horsepower: 27.34.

CHASSIS [VC]: Wheelbase: 116 in. Wheels: Five steel disc with five 6.00 x 16, four- tires with underslung tire carrier for spare wheel and tire. Payload 1,000 lbs.

CHASSIS [VD15]: Wheelbase: 120 in. Standard wheels are five steel disc with five six-ply tires front and rear. Underslung tire carrier for the spare wheel and tire. Gross weight: 5,000 lbs. Payload: 1,500 lbs.

CHASSIS [VD20/VD21]: Wheelbase: 120/133 in. Wheels and tires for both: Steel disc with semi-drop center rim. Tires: 7.00/16 six-ply front, 7.50/ 16 six-ply rear. Spare underslung at rear of frame. GVW 6,400 lbs. both series. Payload 2,000 lbs. both series. Rear axle ratios 4.3; 3.9; or 4.89:1.

CHASSIS [VF20/VF21/VF22]: Wheelbase: 126.5 on VF20; 133 in. on VF21; 160 in. on VF22.

TECHNICAL [VC/VD15;VD20/VD21]: Maximum gross weight: Dodge said "has no gross rating, but will carry 1,000 lbs. payload." Mechanical fuel pump fed from 18 gallon gas tank mounted inside frame at left side. Air cleaner and gas filters on 1/2- and 3/4-ton models have hypoid drive gears, 1-ton model has spiral bevel drive gears. Worm and sector gears steering. 17 in., three-spoke steering wheel, adjustable for height. Four-wheel hydraulic brakes. Independent hand-brake operating on propeller shaft. Amola steel springs. Rear axle ratios: Standard 4.1, 3.73, 4.3, or 4.78 to 1.

TECHNICAL [VF21/VF22/VF23]: Single-plate, dry-disc clutch. Selective sliding gear transmission. Speeds: 4F/1R. Hotchkiss drive. Tubular steel propeller shaft. Reverse Elliot type front axle, I-beam section. Rear axle: One-ton model has spiral bevel drive gears. Worm and sector gears steering.

OPTIONS: Oil bath air cleaner ($3.25). Rear bumper ($6). Generator for slow speed operation ($27.50). Governors: Leibing ($5), Monarch ($5), Handy ($10). Chrome headlamps ($2.75). Dual horns ($7.50). 6.00 x 16 6-ply tires front and rear ($14.50). 6.50 x 16 six-ply tires front and rear ($28.25). 5.25 x 20 four-ply tires front and rear and 20 in. wheels ($18). 5.25 x 20 six-ply tires front and rear and 20 in. wheels ($35). Coach lamps ($8.50). Oil filter ($3.25). Partition behind driver's seat: Panel,Screen and Canopy ($15). Stationary rearview mirror ($1.50). Adjustable rearview mirror ($2.50). Auxiliary seat ($10). Sun visors interior each ($2). Auxiliary taillight ($4). Four-speed transmission ($17.50). Chrome windshield frame ($3). Auxiliary windshield wiper/vacuum ($4). Dual electric wipers ($8)

HISTORICAL: Model year began Oct. 1, 1939. Dodge truck sales for 1940 were up by 13.1 percent to 54,323 keeping Dodge in fourth place in the truck sales race. Total production was 117,588 of which 4,860 were produced in Los Angeles and 7,790 were produced in Canada. Government sales in 1940 were very good as the Army geared itself up for the European War. Dodge sold 10,107 half-ton models, 23 one-ton models, 8,006 1-1/2-tons

LIGHT TRUCK — VC SERIES — 1/2-TON — SIX-CYLINDER: The 1/2-ton TC series, began in 1939, continued as it was, with very minimal changes. Series designation changed to VC. Engine gross horsepower was increased to 79 from 70 and maximum engine torque increased to 154 lbs.-ft. from 148 lbs.-ft. Sealed beam headlights were new, as well as a new 35 ampere capacity generator to power them. Maximum gross allowable weight was increased from 4,000 lbs. to 4,200 lbs. Another new feature was a new wheel attaching bolt which was made in right-hand and left-hand threads to prevent loosening. Front end appearance was changed by redesigning the chrome strips on the "V" shaped grille. The chrome strips were moved upward, to give a better balanced overall look. Dodge nameplates were removed from the grille sides and replaced with the Dodge name embossed and painted on the front chrome strip. Model lineups remained as before. Standard equipment included: Shocks, front and rear. Spare tire and tube. Front bumper. Rear bumper on panel body models. Hood ornament. Safety glass. Electric horn. Combination stop and taillamp. License brackets. Tool kit. Speedometer. Fuel gauge. Oil pressure gauge. Ammeter and 35 ampere generator. Engine temperature indicator. Choke. Throttle. Sealed beam headlamps. Glove compartment. Cowl vent. Vacuum windshield wipers. The panel, screenside and canopy models came standard with just one bucket seat.

LIGHT TRUCK — SERIES VD15 — 3/4-TON — SIX-CYLINDER: This series was carried over with but few changes. The engine maximum gross horsepower was increased to 82 from 77 and maximum torque increased from 158 lbs.-ft. to 166 lbs.-ft. at 1200 rpm. Front end styling treatment was changed as per the changes in the VC series. Sealed beam headlights and 35-ampere generator were added. Maximum gross weight remained unchanged at 5,000 lbs.

LIGHT TRUCK — SERIES VD20/VD21/VF20/VF21/VF22 — ONE-TON — SIX-CYLINDER: The 1-ton series were also carried over from 1939 with minimal changes. Maximum gross weight was increased from 6,000 lbs. to 6,400 lbs. Engine gross horsepower and torque was increased. The rear axle (VD models) was changed to a new hypoid type with a new barrel type differential. This permitted the use of larger and stronger differential gears. Sealed beam headlights and a 35-ampere generator were also added. The same front end appearance changes seen on the VC models were also made. A larger engine was found in the VF Series heavy-duty 1-ton models.

I.D. DATA: [Series VC] Serial number plate on right front door hinge pillar. Engine number stamped on left side of cylinder block. Beginning serial numbers [Detroit] 8543001, ending 8562183, [Los Angeles] 9254201, ending 9256160. Engine numbers T105-1001 and up. [Series VD-15]: Beginning serial number: [Detroit] 8207101, ending 8210295. [Los Angeles] 9200471, ending 9200755. Engine numbers T94-1001 and up. [Series VD20/VD21]: Beginning serial numbers [Detroit] 8093476, ending 8098913. [Los Angeles] 9284701, ending 9285132. Engine numbers T96-1001 and up; [VF20/VF21/VF22] Beginning serial numbers: [Detroit] 8766001 and up. [Los Angeles] 9275001 and up.

and 22 two-ton models to the government. Export sales were also very good, totalling 17,599 from 1/2- to 3-ton capacity. Dodge continued to produce a full line of trucks including Diesels. Dodge also began producing their own line of cab-over-engine trucks this year. In February 1940, the last Airflow model was built. The DeKalb Wagon Company of DeKalb, Ill. produced a Brooks Stevens designed Urban Delivery for Dodge for use on its 120 inch 3/4-ton chassis. This ultra-modern designed truck was the smartest looking truck on the road featuring an egg-shape and two-tone paint schemes.

1941 DODGE

1941 Dodge 1/2-Ton Canopy (DFW/DPL)

LIGHT TRUCK — WC SERIES — 1/2-TON — SIX-CYLINDER: Minimal changes were made in the 1941 Dodge WC series. Appearance changes included moving the headlight mountings to a pocket formed in the front fenders, and new style parking lights mounted on the cowl. Also, all 1/2-, 3/4- and 1-ton models were available in a score of two-tone paint finishes at no extra cost. Standard Dodge truck paint colors remained the same since 1939. They were light blue, dark blue, orange, dark green, gray, red and black. Engine horsepower and torque was increased by addition of a new high-lift camshaft. Oil bath air cleaners were made standard equipment and a second fuel filter was mounted at the carburetor. Also, a floating-type oil pump screen was new. The hinged intake screen floated just below the surface of the oil in the crankcase. Models available in the 1/2-ton series remained the same as 1940. Standard equipment included: Shocks, front and rear. Spare tire and tube. Front bumper. Rear bumper on Panel body models. Hood ornament. Safety glass. Electric horn. Combination stop and taillamp. License brackets. Tool kit. Speedometer. Fuel gauge. Oil pressure gauge. Ammeter and 35 ampere generator. Engine temperature indicator. Choke. Throttle. Sealed beam headlamps. Glove compartment. Cowl vent. Vacuum windshield wipers. Two-tone color combinations. Oil bath air cleaner. Spare wheel and tire. The Panel, Screenside and canopy models came standard with just one bucket seat.

1941 Dodge 3/4-Ton "Brush Fire" Express (OCW)

LIGHT TRUCK — SERIES WD15 — 3/4-TON — SIX-CYLINDER: Carried over from 1940 with the same changes as WC series. Standard equipment: Same as WC series.

LIGHT TRUCK — SERIES WD20/WD21/WF20/WF21/WF22 — ONE-TON — SIX-CYLINDER: All 1-ton series were carried over intact from 1940, with the same changes as outlined above for the WC models. One-ton models were now available with dual rear wheels. On Panel, Canopy and Screen models dual rear wheels were supplied when dual wheels were specified. On platform and stake models, bodies were six inches wider when ordered with dual wheels. Standard equipment same as WC series.

I.D. DATA [Series WC]: Serial number plate on right front door hinge pillar. Engine number stamped on left side of cylinder block. (Detroit) 8562201-8584879, ending in 1947. (Los Angeles) 9212801-9215035, ending in 1947 . Starting engine number T125-1001. [Series WD15]: Engine number and serial number locations same as WC models. (Detroit) 8210351-82147541, ending in 1947; (Los Angeles) 9199101-9199515, ending in 1947. Engine numbers T114-1001. [WD20 Series] (Detroit) 81200101-81207016, ending in 1947. (Los Angeles) 9285201-9285810, ending in 1947 . Beginning engine number T116-1001. [Series WD21] serial numbers: (Detroit) 81200101-81207016, ending in 1947. (Los Angeles) 9285201 up. Beginning engine number T116-1001. [Series WF20/WF21/WF22] serial numbers: (Detroit) 8788151 up; (Los Angeles) 9276201 up. Engine number T118-42001 up.

Model	Body Type	Price	Weight	Prod. Total
Series WC — 1/2-Ton — 116 in. w.b.				
WC	Chassis & Cowl	500	2375	—
WC	Chassis & Cab	595	2775	—
WC	Pickup 6.5 ft.	630	2975	—
WC	Canopy	740	3000	—
WC	Panel	730	3175	—
WC	Screen	760	3020	—

NOTE 1: Shipments, U.S. Only (Calendar Year) (Domestic) 32,617; (Government) 54,235; (Export) 2,051; [Total] 88,903.

Model	Body Type	Price	Weight	Prod. Total
Series WD — 3/4-Ton — 120 in. w.b.				
WD-15	Chassis & Cowl	570	2525	—
WD-15	Chassis & Cab	665	2925	—
WD-15	Pickup 7.5 ft.	705	3225	—
WD-15	Platform 7.5 ft.	715	3325	—
WD-15	Stake 7.5 ft.	740	3550	—

NOTE 2: Shipments, U.S. Only (Calendar Year). (Domestic) 5,692; (Export) 149; [Total] 5,841.

Model	Body Type	Price	Weight	Prod. Total
Model WD20 — 1-Ton — 120 in. w.b.				
WD20	Chassis & Cowl	635	2825	—
WD20	Chassis & Cab	730	3250	—
WD20	Pickup 7.5 ft.	770	3600	—
WD20	Platform 7.5 ft.	780	3625	—
WD20	Stake 7.5 ft.	805	3850	—

Model	Body Type	Price	Weight	Prod. Total
Series WD21 — 1-Ton — 133 in. w.b.				
WD21	Chassis & Cowl	655	2850	—
WD21	Chassis & Cab	750	3275	—
WD21	Pickup	800	3675	—
WD21	Canopy	895	3400	—
WD21	Panel	890	3850	—
WD21	Platform	805	3750	—
WD21	Stake	825	4025	—
WD21	Screen	915	3420	—

NOTE 3: Shipments, U.S. Only (Calendar Year) (Domestic) 7,837; (Export) 756; [Total] 8,593.

Model	Body Type	Price	Weight	Prod. Total
Model WF20 — Heavy-Duty 1-Ton — 126.5 in. w.b.				
WF20	Chassis & Flat Face Cowl	645	3300	—
WF20	Chassis & Cab	740	3925	—

Model	Body Type	Price	Weight	Prod. Total
Model WF21 — Heavy-Duty 1-Ton — 135-5/16 in. w.b.				
WF21	Chassis & Flat Face Cowl	645	3325	—
WF21	Chassis & Cab	740	3950	—
WF21	Pickup 9 ft.	810	4250	—
WF21	Stake 9 ft.	800	4225	—
WF21	Platform 9 ft.	835	4850	—

Model	Body Type	Price	Weight	Prod. Total
Model WF22 — Heavy-Duty 1-Ton — 160 in. w.b.				
WF22	Chassis & Flat Face Cowl	670	3450	—
WF22	Chassis & Cab	765	4075	—
WF22	Stake 9 ft.	980	5175	—
WF22	Platform 9 ft.	835	4775	—

ENGINE [Series WC]: Inline. L-head. Six-cylinder. Cast iron block. Bore & stroke: 3-1/8 in. x 4-3/8 in. Displacement: 201.3 cid. Compression ratio: 6.7:1. Brake horsepower: 82.5 at 3000 rpm. Net horsepower: 23.44. Maximum Torque: 160 lbs.-ft. at 1200 rpm. Four main bearings. Solid valve lifters.

ENGINE [Series WD20/WD21]: Inline. L-head. Six-cylinder. Cast iron block. Bore & stroke: 3-1/4 in. x 4-3/8 in. Displacement: 217.76 cid. Compression ratio: 6.5:1. Brake horsepower: 85 at 3000 rpm. Net horsepower: 25.35. Maximum Torque: 170 lbs.-ft. at 1200 rpm. Four main bearings. Solid valve lifters.

ENGINE [Series WF20/WF21/WF22]: Inline. L-head. Six-cylinder. Cast iron block. Bore & stroke: 3-3/8 in. x 4-1/4 in. Taxable horsepower: 27.34.

CHASSIS [WC]: Wheelbase: 116 in. Wheels: Five steel disc with five 6.00 x 16, four-ply tires with underslung tire carrier for spare wheel and tire. Payload 1,000 lbs.

CHASSIS [WD15]: Wheelbase: 120 in. Standard wheels are five steel disc with five six-ply tires. Tires: TA-15 front and rear. Underslung tire carrier for the spare wheel and tire. Gross weight: 5,000 lbs. Payload: 1,500 lbs.

CHASSIS [WD20/WD21]: Wheelbase: 120/133 in. Wheels and tires for both: Steel disc with semi-drop center rim. Tires: 6.50 x 16 six-ply front, 7.00 x 16 six-ply rear. Spare underslung at rear of frame. Gross weight rating 6,400 lbs. both series. Payload 2,000 lbs. both series. Rear axle ratios 4.3, 3.9, or 4.89:1.

CHASSIS [WF20/WF21/WF22]: Wheelbase: 126.5 on WF20; 135-5/16 in. on WF21; 160 in. on WF22.

TECHNICAL: Clutch 10 inch single dry plate. Selective sliding transmission 3F/1R. Drop forged I-Beam front axle. Rear axle semi-floating with hypoid gears. Front springs 39 in. x 13/4 in.; quantity eight. Rear springs 52 in. x 1-3/4 in. quantity nine for WC, 10 for WD-15 and 11 WD20-21. Hotchkiss drive. Steering ratio 17:1. Fuel tank 18 gallons, located inside left frame rail. [WF21/WF22/WF22]: Dry, single plate clutch. Selective sliding gear transmission. Speeds: 4F/1R. Hotchkiss drive. Tubular steel propeller shaft. Reverse Elliot type front axle, I-beam section. Rear axle: One-ton model has spiral bevel drive gears. Worm and sector gears steering.

OPTIONS: Inside rearview mirror ($1). Long-arm type rearview mirror ($1.50). Long-arm adjustable types ($2.50). Auxiliary seat ($12). Adjustable auxiliary seat ($14.50). Sun visors each ($2). Auxiliary taillight ($2.50). Tow hooks (two front only) ($4). Four- speed transmission ($17.50). Chrome plated windshield frame ($3). Auxiliary vacuum wiper ($4). Dual electric ($13). Single auxiliary electric wiper ($8). Air Cleaners: Vortox ($17.50), Vortox with Vortox breather cap ($19.50). Airfoam seat cushion and back ($10). Battery 119 ampere hours ($2.50). Rear bumper ($6). DeLuxe Cab Equipment consisting of: Leather upholstery, air foam seat and back cushions, armrest on left door, single electric windshield wiper, dome light, one interior sun visor and chrome windshield frame ($25). Dome light in cab ($2.50). Generator for slow operations ($8). Glove compartment door lock ($1.50). Governor ($5). Chrome headlight and parking lights ($3.50). Heater and defroster ($25). Dual horns ($5). Coach lights ($8.50). Oil filter ($3.25). Cartridge type oil filter ($6). Partition behind drivers seat ($20). Partition behind drivers seat with full width seat ($25). Grille guard ($7.50).

HISTORICAL: Model year began Sept. 1, 1940. Total registrations were 62,925 or a 15.8 percent increase over 1940. However, total production increased to 166,602 of which 7,164 were built in Los Angeles and 12,376 were built in Canada. This was a very good year for government business, as the U.S. Army continued to prepare for war. Dodge delivered to the government 57,692 trucks. Of these, 54,235 were 1/2-ton models and 3,457 were 1-1/

2-ton models. In addition to the government business, Dodge exported 18,592 trucks. Most of these were 1-1/2-ton models. Dodge ended in fourth place in U. S. truck sales this year, while the car division came in seventh place. Dodge continued to produce a fall line of trucks from 1/2 to three-ton capacity, including a diesel model. Dodge also cataloged an Urban Panel Delivery. It was a forward control truck built on either a 3/4- or 1-ton chassis. The body was custom built by Montpelier Manufacturing Co. of Montpelier, Ohio. This was also the first year in which Dodge used their famous "Job-Rated" advertising slogan. It was an advertising theme they would continue for many years.

1942-1943 DODGE

LIGHT TRUCK — WC SERIES — 1/2-TON — SIX-CYLINDER: This series was now in its fourth year and still selling well. For 1942, it was a direct carryover of the 1940 version without major change. Even the series code was the same. A larger 217 cid engine was made standard in the WC series, boosting horsepower from 82 to 90. Clutch housings on all 1/2-ton through 2-ton models were made stronger, through the use of reinforcing ribs. Frames of the WC series trucks were strengthened by an increase in stock thickness. Bumpers on 1/2-ton and 3/4-ton models were now painted gray or black enamel, instead of the former aluminum color. A redesigned radiator core, on 1/2-ton models, provided for more efficient cooling. No appearance changes were made. No further appearance changes would be made to the W Series through the 1947 model year. Standard equipment included: Shocks, front and rear. Spare tire and tube. Front bumper. Rear bumper on panel body models. Hood ornament. Safety glass. Electric horn. Combination stop and taillamp. License brackets. Tool kit. Speedometer. Fuel gauge. Oil pressure gauge. Ammeter and 35 ampere generator. Engine temperature indicator. Choke. Throttle. Sealed beam headlamps. Glove compartment. Cowl vent. Vacuum windshield wipers. The panel, screenside and canopy models came standard with just one bucket seat.

LIGHT TRUCK — SERIES WD15 — 3/4-TON — SIX-CYLINDER: As with the WC series the WD15 series was carried forward with very little change. The WD series also received the same new engine as did the WC series. A pattern of using the 218 cid in the 1/2- and 3/4-ton trucks was now set and would last well into the 1950s. No appearance changes were made. Standard equipment: Same as WC above.

LIGHT TRUCK — SERIES WD20/WD21 — ONE-TON — SIX-CYLINDER: One-ton models were carried over without appearance changes and with but few mechanical changes. However, a new engine displacing 230.2 cid and producing 105 horsepower gave the new models added performance. Other mechanical changes were a strengthened clutch housing and a larger diameter radiator fan. The 230.2 cid engine was used in 1-ton trucks through the 1950s.

HEAVY-DUTY ONE-TON — SERIES WF20/WF21/WF22 — ONE-TON -SIX-CYLINDER: Dodge's biggest 1-ton line now used the 3-7/16 x 4-1/4 inch bore and stroke six that came from the WF30/WF31/WF32 Dodge 1-1/2-ton models. These two lines shared body dimensions and wheelbases and were essentially the same trucks in two different GVW configurations.

I.D. DATA: Serial number plate on right front door hinge pillar. Engine number stamped on left side of cylinder block. [Series WC]: Serial numbers (Detroit) 81100101-81115301, ending in 1947; (Los Angeles) 9215036-9216935, ending in 1947 9216935. Beginning engine number T112-42001. [Series WD15]: (Detroit) 8214755-8217538, ending in 1947; (Los Angeles) 9199516-9199890, ending in 1947. Beginning engine number T112-42001. [WD20] Serial numbers (Detroit) 81207017-81210967, ending in 1947; (Los Angeles) 9285811-9286180, ending in 1947. Beginning engine number T116-42001. [WD21] Serial numbers (Detroit) 81207017-81210967, ending in 1947; (Los Angeles) 9285811-9286180, ending in 1947. Beginning engine number T116-42001. [WF20/WF21/WF22] Serial numbers (Detroit) 81302818 and up; (Los Angeles) 9277517 and up.

1943 Dodge 1-Ton Panel with windows (ATC)

Model	Body Type	Price	Weight	Prod. Total
Series WC — 1/2-Ton — 116 in. w.b.				
WC	Chassis & Cowl	522	2375	—
WC	Chassis & Cab	617	2775	—
WC	Pickup 6.5 ft.	651	2975	—
WC	Canopy	762	3000	—
WC	Panel	751	3175	—

NOTE 1: Shipments, U.S. Only (Calendar Year) (Domestic) 2,466; (Government) 19,600; (Export) 566; [Total] 22,572.

Series WD15 — 3/4-Ton — 120 in. w.b.				
WD15	Chassis & Cowl	571	2525	—
WD15	Chassis & Cab	666	2925	—
WD15	Pickup 7.5 ft.	705	3225	—
WD15	Platform 7.5 ft.	716	3325	—
WD15	Stake 7.5 ft.	742	3550	—

NOTE 2: Shipments, U.S. Only (Calendar Year). (Domestic) 640; (Government) 77,046; (Export) 8; [Total] 77,694.

Series WD20 — 1-Ton — 120 in. w.b.				
WD20	Chassis & Cowl	651	2825	—
WD20	Chassis & Cab	746	3250	—
WD20	Pickup 7.5 ft.	787	3600	—
WD20	Platform 7.5 ft.	796	3625	—
WD20	Stake 7.5 ft.	821	3850	—

Series WD21 — 1-Ton — 133 in. w.b.				
WD21	Chassis & Cowl	672	2850	—
WD21	Chassis & Cab	767	3275	—
WD21	Pickup 9 ft.	817	3675	—
WD21	Canopy	912	3400	—
WD21	Panel	907	3850	—
WD21	Platform 9 ft.	821	3750	—
WD21	Stake 9 ft.	842	4025	—

NOTE 3: Shipments, U.S. Only (Calendar Year) (Domestic) 978; (Government) 3; (Export) 157; [Total] 1,138.

Model WF 20 — Heavy-Duty 1-Ton — 126.5 in. w.b.				
WF20	Chassis & Flat Face Cowl	666	3175	—
WF20	Chassis & Cab	761	3800	—

Model WF21 — Heavy-Duty 1-Ton — 135-5/16 in. w.b.				
WF21	Chassis & Flat Face Cowl	666	3200	—
WF21	Chassis & Cab	761	3825	—
WF21	Pickup 9 ft.	830	4125	—
WF21	Stake 9 ft.	855	4725	—
WF21	Platform 9 ft.	816	4375	—
WF21	Spl. Panel	987	—	—

Model WF22 — Heavy-Duty 1-Ton — 160 in. w.b.				
WF22	Chassis & Flat Face Cowl	691	3325	—
WF22	Chassis & Cab	786	3950	—
WF22	Stake 9 ft.	900	5050	—
WF22	Platform 9 ft.	855	4650	—

ENGINE [Series WC/WD]: Inline. L-head. Six-cylinder. Cast iron block. Bore & stroke: 3-1/4 in. x 4-3/8 in. Displacement: 217.76 cid Compression ratio: 6.8:1. Brake horsepower: 95 at 3600 rpm. Net horsepower: 25.35. Maximum Torque: 172 lbs.-ft. at 1200 rpm. Four main bearings. Solid valve lifters.

ENGINE [WD20/WD21]: Inline. L-head. Six-cylinder. Cast iron block. Bore & stroke: 3-1/4 in. x 4-5/8 in. Displacement: 230.2 cid. Compression ratio: 6.8:1. Brake horsepower: 105 at 3600 rpm. Net horsepower: 25.35. Maximum Torque: 184 lbs.-ft. at 1200 rpm. Four main bearings. Solid valve lifters.

ENGINE [Series WF20/WF21/WF22]: Inline. L-head. Six-cylinder. Cast iron block. Bore & stroke: 3-7/16 in. x 4-1/4 in. Taxable horsepower: 28.35.

CHASSIS [Series WC]: Wheelbase: 116 in. Tires: 6.00 x 16, four-ply (front & rear).

CHASSIS [Series WD15]: Wheelbase: 120 in. Tires: TA15 six-ply (front & rear).

CHASSIS [Series WD20/WD21]: Wheelbase: 120/133 in. Tires: (front) 6.50 x 16 six-ply; (rear) 7.00 x 16 six-ply.

CHASSIS [WF20/WF21/WF22]: Wheelbase: 126.5 on WF20; 135-5/16 in. on WF21; 160 in. on WF22.

TECHNICAL: Clutch 10-inch single dry plate. Selective sliding transmission 3F/1R. Drop forged I-Beam front axle. Rear axle semi-floating with hypoid gears. Front springs 39 in. x 1 3/4 in.; quantity eight. Rear springs 52 in. x 1-3/4 in. quantity nine for WC, 10 for WD-15 and 11 WD20-21. Hotchkiss drive. Steering ratio 17:1. Fuel tank 18 gallons, located inside left frame rail. [WF21/WF22/WF23]: Dry, single plate clutch. Selective sliding gear transmission. Speeds: 4F/1R. Hotchkiss drive. Tubular steel propeller shaft. Reverse Elliot type front axle, I-beam section. Rear axle: One-ton model has spiral bevel drive gears. Worm and sector gears steering.

OPTIONS: Inside rearview mirror ($1). Long-arm type rearview mirror ($1.50). Long-arm adjustable types ($2.50). Auxiliary seat ($12). Adjustable auxiliary seat ($14.50). Sun visors each ($2.50). Auxiliary taillight ($2.50). Tow hooks (two front only) ($4). Four- speed transmission ($17.50). Chrome-plated windshield frame ($3). Auxiliary vacuum wiper ($4). Dual electric ($13). Single auxiliary electric wiper ($8). Air Cleaners: Vortox ($17.50), Vortox with Vortox breather cap ($19.50). Airfoam seat cushion and back ($10). Battery 119 ampere hours ($2.50). Rear bumper ($6). DeLuxe Cab Equipment consisting of: Leather upholstery, air foam seat and back cushions, armrest on left door, single electric windshield wiper, dome light, one interior sun visor and chrome windshield frame ($25). Dome light in cab ($2.50). Generator for slow operations ($8). Glove compartment door lock ($1.50). Governor ($5). Chrome headlight and parking lights ($3.50). Heater and defroster ($25). Dual horns ($5). Coach lights ($8.50). Oil filter ($3.25). Cartridge type oil filter ($6). Partition behind drivers seat ($20). Partition behind drivers seat with full width seat ($25). Grille guard ($7.50).

HISTORICAL: Model year began Sept. 1, 1941. Registration figures for 1942 are not available. Civilian truck production ceased on April 30, 1942. Total production for the calendar year, however, was very good due to purchases by the military. Total production was 169,837 of which 2,420 were built in Los Angeles and 41,665 were built in Canada. Total government purchases were 109,665. They broke down as follows: 1/2-ton 19,600, 3/4-ton 77,046, 1-ton , 1-1/2-ton 12,919, 2-ton 39 and 3-ton 58. Also, 4,445 trucks were exported. Much of the Canadian production was military vehicles delivered to the Canadian government. Dodge built a full line of civilian trucks this year consisting of 112 standard chassis and body models on 18 wheelbase lengths ranging in size from 1/2- to 3-tons. This was the last year for the Dodge built Diesel engine. Civilian auto production at Chrysler ceased on Jan. 31, 1942. Dodge cars came in sixth place in the U.S. car sale race.

1946 DODGE

1946 Dodge 1/2-Ton Pickup (Mel Kay)

LIGHT TRUCK — SERIES WC — 1/2-TON — SIX-CYLINDER: To meet the pent up demand for trucks after World War II, Dodge continued its dependable proven models rather than design a new series. The WC Series continued with very minimal changes. No appearance changes were made. Seat cushions and backs were of a new design and equipped with a manually-operated air control valve by which the driver could regulate the amount of air in the seat cushion according to his weight. New spring construction in seats and backs afforded more comfort. Steering gear was improved and made heavier. Steering gear ratios were increased. Axle shafts were made larger in diameter for added strength. The WC series was given a new four pinion type differential replacing the former two pinion type. No changes were made to the engine. Models available continued unchanged from 1942. Standard equipment included: Shocks, front and rear. Spare tire and tube. Front bumper. Rear bumper on panel body models. Hood ornament. Safety glass. Electric horn. Combination stop and taillamp. License brackets. Tool kit. Speedometer. Fuel gauge. Oil pressure gauge. Ammeter and 35 ampere generator. Engine temperature indicator. Choke. Throttle. Sealed beam headlamps. Glove compartment. Cowl vent. Vacuum windshield wipers. The panel, screenside and canopy models came standard with just one bucket seat.

LIGHT TRUCK — SERIES WD15 — 3/4-TON — SIX-CYLINDER: No changes were made to the WD15 series except those noted for WC series. Engine remained the same 218 cid. L-6 as in 1942. No changes in model lineup. Standard equipment same as 1/2-ton.

LIGHT TRUCK — SERIES WD20/WD21 — ONE-TON — SIX-CYLINDER: As with the 3/4-ton series, no changes except those noted for WC series were made. Engine and model lineup remained the same.

LIGHT TRUCK — SERIES WDX — ONE-TON POWER-WAGON — SIX-CYLINDER: The famous Dodge Power-Wagon was a civilian adaptation of a four-wheel drive, 3/4-ton military vehicle which Dodge built in great numbers during World War II. Dodge engineered the Power-Wagon to be a self-propelled powerplant. It was capable of a wide range of industrial and agricultural applications. Dodge engineers set out to create the most useful and versatile vehicle ever manufactured. The Power-Wagon was capable of carrying a 3,000 pound payload in off-highway service. In addition, the Power-Wagon provided power for driving various items of auxiliary equipment. A transmission power-take-off was available with front and rear driveshafts. The Power-Wagon was equipped with a four-speed transmission and a two-speed transfer case, providing a total of eight speeds forward and two reverse. The Power-Wagon was powered by Dodge's 230 cid six as used in 1-ton trucks. Standard equipment included: Heavy duty shocks in front. One quart oil bath air cleaner. Front bumper. Channel type reinforcements inside frame side-rails. Velocity type engine governor set at 3200 rpm. Dual vacuum windshield wipers. Interior sun visor on left side. DeLuxe seat cushion and back. Rear axle gear ratio 4.89:1 with 7.50 x 16 eight-ply tires; 5.83:1 with 9.00 x 16 eight-ply tires. Power Wagon colors: Seawolf Submarine green was standard. Also available at no extra cost were red, dark blue and dark green.

HEAVY-DUTY ONE-TON — SERIES WF21/WF22 — ONE-TON -SIX-CYLINDER: Dodge's biggest 1-ton line again used the 3-7/16 x 4-1/4 inch bore and stroke six that came from the WF30/WF31/WF32 Dodge 1-1/2-ton models. These two lines shared body dimensions and wheelbases and were essentially the same trucks in two different GVW configurations. The 126.5 inch wheelbase WF20 chassis models were dropped. The WF21 and WF22 lines continued, although the Special Panel of 1942 was no longer offered.

1946 Dodge 1-Ton 9 ft. Express (Mel Kay)

I.D. DATA: Serial number plate on right front door hinge pillar. Engine number stamped on left side of cylinder block. [Series WC] Serial numbers (Detroit) 81121158-81172528; (Los Angeles) 9217001-9221269. Beginning engine number not available. [Series WD15]: Serial numbers (Detroit) 83300001-83303424; (Los Angeles) 85500001-85500431. Beginning engine number T112-7001. [WD20/WD21] Serial numbers (Detroit) 81211001-81224002; (Los Angeles) 86000001-86001388. Beginning engine number T116-69200. [WDX] (Detroit 83900001-83902665; (Los Angeles) 88750001-88750225. Engine numbers not available. [Series WF21/WF22] (Detroit) 81350578-81395479; (Los Angeles) 85500001-86502851. Engine numbers not available.

Model	Body Type	Price	Weight	Prod. Total
Series WC — 1/2-Ton — 116 in. w.b.				
WC	Chassis & Cowl	682	2375	—
WC	Chassis & Cab	813	2775	—
WC	Pickup 6.5 ft.	861	2975	—
WC	Canopy	1008	3000	—
WC	Panel	995	3175	—

NOTE 1: Shipments, U.S. Only (Calendar Year) (Domestic) 42,404; (Export) 3,108; [Total] 45,512.

Model	Body Type	Price	Weight	Prod. Total
Series WD15 — 3/4-Ton — 120 in. w.b.				
WD15	Chassis & Cowl	768	2525	—
WD15	Chassis & Cab	900	2925	—
WD15	Pickup 7.5 ft.	954	3225	—
WD15	Platform 7.5 ft.	973	3325	—
WD15	Stake 7.5 ft.	1012	3550	—

NOTE 2: Shipments, U.S. Only (Calendar Year). (Domestic) 3,834; (Export) 1; [Total] 3,835.

Model	Body Type	Price	Weight	Prod. Total
Series WD20 — 1-Ton — 120 in. w.b.				
WD20	Chassis & Cowl	849	2825	—
WD20	Chassis & Cab	981	3250	—
WD20	Pickup 7.5 ft.	1036	3600	—
WD20	Platform 7.5 ft.	1053	3625	—
WD20	Stake 7.5 ft.	1093	3850	—
Series WD21 — 1-Ton — 133 in. w.b.				
WD21	Chassis & Cowl	877	2850	—
WD21	Chassis & Cab	1008	3275	—
WD21	Pickup 9.5 ft.	1076	3675	—
WD21	Platform 9.5 ft.	1091	3750	—
WD21	Stake 9.5 ft.	1123	4025	—
WD21	Canopy	1203	3400	—
WD21	Panel	1197	3850	—

NOTE 3: Shipments, U.S. Only (Calendar Year) (Domestic) 15,784; (Export) 1,615; [Total] 17,399.

Model	Body Type	Price	Weight	Prod. Total
Power-Wagon — Series WDX — 1-Ton (4x4) — 126 in. w.b.				
WDX	Chassis & Cab	1555	4475	—
WDX	Express	1627	4900	—
Model WF21 — Heavy-Duty 1-Ton — 135-5/16 in. w.b.				
WF21	Chassis & Flat Face Cowl	888	3200	—
WF21	Chassis & Cab	1020	3600	—
WF21	Pickup 9 ft.	1115	4125	—
WF21	Stake 9 ft.	1162	4725	—
WF21	Platform 9 ft.	1103	4375	—
Model WF22 — Heavy-Duty 1-Ton — 160 in. w.b.				
WF22	Chassis & Flat Face Cowl	922	3325	—
WF22	Chassis & Cab	1054	3725	—
WF22	Stake 9 ft.	1230	5050	—
WF22	Platform 9 ft.	1161	4650	—

1946 Dodge 1/2-Ton Canopy (OCW)

ENGINE [Series WC/WD15]: Inline. L-head. Six-cylinder. Cast iron block. Bore & stroke: 3-1/4 in. x 4-3/8 in. Displacement: 217.76 cid. Compression ratio: 6.6:1. Brake horsepower: 95 at 3600 rpm. Net horsepower: 25.35. Maximum Torque: 172 lbs.-ft. at 1200 rpm. Four main bearings. Solid valve lifters. Carburetor: Stromberg model BXV-3.

ENGINE [Series WD20/WD21]: Inline. L-head. Six-cylinder. Cast iron block. Bore & stroke: 3-1/4 in. x 4-5/8 in. Displacement: 230.2 cid. Compression ratio: 6.7:1. Brake horsepower: 102 at 3600 rpm. Net horsepower: 25.35. Maximum Torque: 184 lbs.-ft. at 1200 rpm. Four main bearings. Solid valve lifters. Carburetor: Stromberg.

ENGINE [Series WDX]: Same as WD20 except brake horsepower: 94 at 3200 rpm. Torque: 185 lbs.-ft. at 1200 rpm.

ENGINE [Series WF20/WF21/WF22]: Inline. L-head. Six-cylinder. Cast iron block. Bore & stroke: 3-7/16 in. x 4-1/4 in. Taxable horsepower: 28.35.

CHASSIS [Series WC]: Wheelbase: 116 in. Tires: 6.00 x 16 four-ply (front & rear).

CHASSIS [Series WD15]: Wheelbase: 120 in. Tires: TA15 six-ply (front & rear).

CHASSIS [Series WD20/WD21]: Wheelbase: 120/133 in. Tires: (front) 6.50 x 16 six-ply; (rear) 7.00 x 16 six-ply.

CHASSIS [Series WDX]: Wheelbase: 126 in. Tires: (16 x 5.50 wheels) 7.50 x 16 eight-ply. (16 x 6.50 wheels) 9.00 x 16 eight-ply.

CHASSIS [WF20/WF21/WF22]: Wheelbase: 126.5 on WF20; 135-5/16 in. on WF21; 160 in. on WF22.

1946 Dodge 1-Ton Power Wagon (Wrecker Body)

TECHNICAL: Front and rear axles were of full floating hypoid-drive type. Ratio 5.83 to 1. Springs were semi-elliptic type. Front 11-leaves, 39 inches long by 1-3/4 inches wide. Rear 14-leaves, 52-1/4 inches long by 1-3/4 inch wide. Hotchkiss drive. Heavy-duty double-acting telescopic type shocks on front (extra cost on rear). Mud and snow all-service tread. Spare wheel and tire carrier mounted vertically on right side of pickup immediately behind cab. Single-plate 10-inch diameter clutch. Selective sliding gear type transmission with two-speed transfer case gives 8F/2R. Steering worm-and-sector type, 23.2:1 ratio with 17-inch diameter steering wheel. Electrical: Six-volt system with 35-ampere generator. Fuel tank 18 gallons. Maximum gross weight rating with 7.50 x 16 eight-ply tires was 7,600 lbs.; with 9.00 x 16 eight-ply tires 8,700 lbs.

OPTIONS [Trucks]: Air cleaner, one quart instead of standard one pint ($3.70). Rear bumper ($6.35). Deluxe cab equipment, includes hair pad seat cushion and back, armrest (left side), dome light, dual vacuum windshield wipers, one sun visor, plastic coated trim ($26.65). Generator 230 watt, six- to eight-volt/32 amp. hour. High charging at low engine speed ($8.30). Governor ($5.15). Oil filter, replaceable cartridge type ($6.35). Rearview mirror: Long-arm adjustable-left side ($1.50); Long-arm adjustable-right side ($2.60). Transmission: Four-speed ($31.45). Auxiliary vacuum windshield wiper ($4.10).

OPTIONS [Power-Wagon]: Power-take-off mounted on left side of transmission; transfers power forward to winch or to tailshaft. Power winch (7,500 lbs.) mounted directly on frame in front of radiator and provided with 250 inches of 7/16-inch steel cable. Tail shaft: Consists of two tubular driveshafts and one pillow-block shaft (pillow-block is attached to center of frame crossmember). Pulley Drive: Mounted on pillow-block at center of frame rear crossmember (9 x 6-5/8 in. pulley. Mechanical Govenor. Deluxe cab equipment. Draw Bar. Pintle Hook. Front tow hooks.

HISTORICAL: Model year started December, 1945. Sales for 1946 hit an all-time record high for Dodge, topping off at 96,490. This moved Dodge into third place in U.S. truck sales. Dodge truck production, at 144,968, was not a record-setter. Government sales slowed down to a trickle with the war over. Of the total produced, 12,919 were built in Canada and 9,251 were built in Los Angeles. The government purchased 2,076 three-ton trucks and 22,099 trucks were exported. For the industry as a whole, 1946 sales were below the level of 1941. However, Dodge sales were up 53.3 percent. Civilian truck sales, unlike car sales, did not completely cease during World War II. A number of civilian trucks were produced to meet the requirements of those industries deemed vital to the war effort. Dodge built 1,580 civilian trucks in 1942, after general sales to the public ceased. Nine were built in 1943; 7,983 in 1944 and in 1945, before restrictions were lifted, 28,405 civilian trucks were built (alongside military trucks on the same production lines). Dodge was very proud of the fact that, two hours after the last military truck rolled off the line, they had the Detroit truck plant reconverted for volume output of civilian trucks. Dodge built 400,000 military trucks during World War II. Dodge began the 1946 model year building trucks of 1/2- to 2-ton capacity and, as a midyear introduction, brought out redesigned 2-1/2 and 3-ton series. The new heavy-duty series featured a redesigned grille, which gave these trucks a more massive appearance.

1947 DODGE

1947 Dodge Series WC 1/2-Ton Pickup (J. Owens)

1/2-TON — SERIES WC — SIX-CYLINDER: The only change in the 1/2-ton line was an across-the-board price increase. All models were carried over untouched. Standard equipment included: Shocks, front and rear. Spare tire and tube. Front bumper. Rear bumper on panel body models. Hood ornament. Safety glass. Electric horn. Combination stop and taillamp. License brackets. Tool kit. Speedometer. Fuel gauge. Oil pressure gauge. Ammeter and 35 ampere generator. Engine temperature indicator. Choke. Throttle. Sealed beam headlamps. Glove compartment. Cowl vent. Vacuum windshield wipers. The panel, screenside and canopy models came standard with just one bucket seat.

1947 Dodge Series WC 1/2-Ton Pickup (D. Brusegard)

3/4-TON — SERIES WD15 — SIX-CYLINDER: There were no basic changes in styling or engineering. Standard equipment included: Shocks, front and rear. Spare tire and tube. Front bumper. Rear bumper on panel body models. Hood ornament. Safety glass. Electric horn. Combination stop and taillamp. License brackets. Tool kit. Speedometer. Fuel gauge. Oil pressure gauge. Ammeter and 35 ampere generator. Engine temperature indicator. Choke. Throttle. Sealed beam headlamps. Glove compartment. Cowl vent. Vacuum windshield wipers.

ONE-TON — POWER WAGON — SERIES WDX — SIX-CYLINDER: This civilian adaptation of Dodge's 3/4-ton military 4x4 was carried over unchanged. Standard equipment included: PTO with front/rear driveshafts. Four-speed transmission and two-speed transfer case (eight speeds forward/two reverse). Dodge 230 cid six-cylinder engine. Heavy-duty shocks in front. One-quart oil bath air cleaner. Front bumper. Channel type reinforcements inside frame side-rails. Velocity type engine governor set at 3,200 rpm. Dual vacuum windshield wipers. Interior sun visor on left side. DeLuxe seat cushion and back. Rear axle gear ratio 4.89:1 with 7.50 x 16 eight-ply tires; 5.83:1 with 9.00 x 16 eight-ply tires. Seawolf Submarine green was standard color. Red, dark blue and dark green also available at no extra cost.

ONE-TON — SERIES WD20/21 — SIX-CYLINDER: These were also a carryover from 1946. A larger engine than that used in 1/2- and 3/4-ton trucks was installed.

HEAVY-DUTY ONE-TON — SERIES WF21/WF22 — SIX-CYLINDER: The WF models were identical to the 1-1/2-ton Dodge trucks, but had lower GVW ratings. The engine used in them was the same used in 1-1/2-tons.

1947 Dodge 1/2-Ton Canopy (OCW)

I.D. DATA: Serial numbers on dash under hood. On front end of left frame member, to rear of front spring hanger or just above rear front spring hanger. Motor numbers on plate on side of motor. Serial numbers: [WC] (Detroit)81172529-84506112; (Los Angeles) 9221270-9225013; [WD15] (Detroit) 83303425—83312388; (Los Angeles) 85500432-85501169. [WD20] (Detroit) 81224003-81243970; (Los Angeles) 86001389-86002923. [WD21] (Detroit) 81224003-81243970; (Los Angeles) 86001389-86002923. [WDX] (Detroit) 83902666-83906216; (Los Angeles)88750226-88750894; [WF21/WF22] (Detroit) 81395480-8143605; (Los Angeles) 86502852-86505883. Engine numbers not available.

Model	Body Type	Price	Weight	Prod. Total
Series WC — 1/2-Ton — 116 in. w.b.				
WC	Chassis	789	2375	Note 1
WC	Chassis & Cab	944	2775	Note 1
WC	Pickup 6.5 ft.	989	2975	Note 1
WC	Canopy	1119	3000	Note 1
WC	Panel	1184	3175	Note 1

NOTE 1: Total U.S. calendar year production, WC Series: (Domestic) 37,532: (Export) 5,010; [Total] 42,542.

Model	Body Type	Price	Weight	Prod. Total
Series WD15 — 3/4-Ton — 120 in. w.b.				
WD15	Chassis & Cowl	886	2525	Note 2
WD15	Chassis & Cab	1041	2925	Note 2
WD15	Pickup 7.5 ft.	1096	3225	Note 2
WD15	Platform 7.5 ft.	1121	3325	Note 2
WD15	Stake 7.5 ft.	1166	3550	Note 2

NOTE 2: Total U.S. calendar year production, Series WD15: 9,992.

Model	Body Type	Price	Weight	Prod. Total
Series WD20 — 1-Ton — 120 in. w.b.				
WD20	Chassis & Cowl	952	2825	Note 3
WD20	Chassis & Cab	1107	3250	Note 3
WD20	Pickup 7.5 ft.	1162	3600	Note 3
WD20	Platform 7.5 ft.	1187	3625	Note 3
WD20	Stake 7.5 ft.	1232	3850	Note 3

174

Series WD21 — 1-Ton — 133 in. w.b.

WD21	Chassis	972	2850	Note 3
WD21	Chassis & Cab	1127	3275	Note 3
WD21	Pickup	1187	3675	Note 3
WD21	Platform	1222	3750	Note 3
WD21	Stake	1272	4025	Note 3
WD21	Canopy	1352	3400	Note 3

NOTE 3: Total U.S. calendar year production, Series WD20/21: (Domestic) 24,615 (Export) 3,158; [Total] 27,773,

Series WDX — 1-Ton — 126 in. w.b.

WDX	Chassis & Cab	1679	4475
WDX	Pickup	1764	4900

Model WF21 — Heavy-Duty 1-Ton — 135-5/16 in. w.b.

WF21	Chassis & Flat Face Cowl	1010	3200	—
WF21	Chassis & Cab	1165	3600	—
WF21	Pickup 9 ft.	1260	4125	—
WF21	Stake 9 ft.	1330	4500	—
WF21	Platform 9 ft.	1275	4150	—

Model WF22 — Heavy-Duty 1-Ton — 160 in. w.b.

WF22	Chassis & Flat Face Cowl	1030	3325	—
WF22	Chassis Cab	1185	3725	—
WF22	Stake 9 ft.	1390	4725	—
WF22	Platform 9 ft.	1320	4325	—

1947 Dodge Series WC 1/2-Ton Pickup

ENGINE [Series WC/WD15]: Inline. L-head. Six-cylinder. Cast iron block. Bore & stroke: 3-1/4 in. x 4-3/8 in. Displacement: 217.76 cid. Compression ratio: 6.6:1. Brake horsepower: 95 at 3600 rpm. Net horsepower: 25.35. Torque: 172 lbs.-ft. at 1200 rpm. Four main bearings. Solid valve lifters.

ENGINE [Series WD20/21]: Inline. L-head. Six-cylinder. Cast iron block. Bore & stroke: 3-1/4 in. x 4-5/8 in, Displacement: 230.2 cu. in. Compression ratio: 6.7:1. Brake horsepower: 102 at 3600 rpm. Net horsepower: 25.35. Torque: 184 lbs.-ft. at 1200 rpm. Four main bearings. Solid valve lifters.

ENGINE [Series WDX]: Same as WD20 except Brake horsepower: 94 at 3200 rpm. Torque: 185 lbs.-ft. at 1200 rpm.

ENGINE [Series WF20/WF21/WF22]: Inline. L-head. Six-cylinder. Cast iron block. Bore & stroke: 3-7/16 in. x 4-1/4 in. Taxable horsepower: 28.35.

1947 Dodge 1-Ton Screenside (OCW)

CHASSIS [Series WC]: Wheelbase: 116 in. Tires: 6.00 x 16 four-ply. Body: 6-1/2 ft.

CHASSIS [Series WD15]: Wheelbase: 120 in. Tires: TA-15 six-ply. Body: 7-1/2 ft.

CHASSIS [Series WD20]: Wheelbase: 120 in. Tires: (front) 6.50 x 16 six-ply; (rear) 7.00 x 16 six-ply. Body: 7-1/2 ft.

CHASSIS [Series WD21]: Wheelbase: 133 in. Tires: (front) 6.50 x 16 six-ply; (rear) 7.00 x 16 six-ply. Body: 9 ft.

CHASSIS [Series WDX]: Wheelbase: 126 in. Tires: 7.50 x 16 eight-ply.

CHASSIS [WF20/WF21/WF22]: Wheelbase: 126.5 on WF20; 135-5/16 in. on WF21; 160 in. on WF22.

Standard Catalog of Light-Duty Trucks

1947 Dodge Commercial Station Wagon (JAG)

TECHNICAL: Front and rear axles were of full floating hypoid-drive type. Ratio 5.83 to 1. Springs are semi-elliptic type. Front 11-leaves, 39 in. long by 1-3/4 in. wide. Rear 14-leaves, 52-1/4 in. long by 1-3/4 in. wide. Hotchkiss drive. Heavy-duty double-acting telescopic type shocks on front (extra cost on rear). Mud and snow all-service tread. Spare wheel and tire carrier mounted vertically on right side of pickup immediately behind cab. Single-plate 10 in. diameter clutch. Selective sliding gear type transmission with two-speed transfer case gives 8F/2R. Steering worm-and-sector type, 23.2:1 ratio with 17-in. diameter steering wheel. Electrical: Six-volt system with 35-ampere generator. Fuel tank 18 gallons. Maximum gross weight rating with 7.50 x 16 eight-ply tires was 7,600 lbs.; with 9.00 x 16 eight-ply tires 8,700 lbs.

1947 Dodge Commercial Station Wagon (JAG)

OPTIONS [Trucks]: Air cleaner, one quart instead of standard one pint ($3.70). Rear bumper ($6.35). Deluxe cab equipment, includes hair pad seat cushion and back, armrest (left side), dome light, dual vacuum windshield wipers, one sun visor, plastic coated trim ($26.65). Generator 230 watt, six- to eight-volt/32 amp. High charging at low engine speed ($8.30). Governor ($5.15). Oil filter, replaceable cartridge type ($6.35). Rearview mirror: Long-arm adjustable-left side ($1.50); Long-arm adjustable-right side ($2.60). Transmission: Four-speed ($31.45). Auxiliary vacuum windshield wiper ($4.10).

OPTIONS [Power-Wagon]: Power-take-off mounted on left side of transmission; transfers power forward to winch or to tailshaft. Power winch (7,500 lbs.) mounted directly on frame in front of radiator and provided with 250 in. of 7/16 in. steel cable. Tail shaft: Consists of two tubular driveshafts and one pillow-block shaft (pillow-block is attached to center of frame crossmember). Pulley Drive: Mounted on pillow-block at center of frame rear crossmember (9 x 6-5/8 in. pulley). Mechanical Govenor. Deluxe cab equipment. Draw Bar. Pintle Hook. Front tow hooks.

1947 Dodge WDX 1-Ton Power Wagon 8 ft. Express (RCA)

HISTORICAL: Introduced in December 1946. Calendar year registrations: 126,736. Calendar year production: 183,953. Dodge trucks sales were up 31.3 percent over 1946, just a trifle better than the overall industry increase. This was Dodge truck's best year ever for both sales and production. Of the total, 17,378 trucks were Canadian built and 13,320 were made in California. No trucks were shipped to the government, but 32,907 were exported. Dodge placed third in truck sales, claiming that its full line from 1/2- to 3-tons satisfied 97 percent of the truck market. The Job-Rated advertising that began in 1941 continued this year.

1947 Dodge Panel Delivery (OCW)

1948 Dodge 1/2-Ton High Side Pickup (H. Kruger)

1948-1949 DODGE

1948 Dodge 1/2-Ton High Side Pickup (H. Kruger)

1948 Dodge 1-Ton Truck Cab (RPZ)

1/2-TON — SERIES B-1-B-108 — SIX-CYLINDER: Dodge introduced a completely new truck line, the first new models since 1939. The lineup totalled 248 basic chassis models, ranging from 4,250 to 23,000 lbs. GVW. Front axles were moved back and engines forward, to place more weight on the front axle and improve weight distribution. Wheelbases for conventional models through 2-tons were reduced. The B-1-Bs had a 108 in. w.b. The new trucks were engineered so that, even with shorter wheelbase, their cab-to-axle dimensions remained the same. This permitted the same lengths as before. Ease of handling and driving was provided by the shorter wheelbase and a wide-tread front axle. Cross steering was a new feature of all conventional cab models. It allowed a 37-degree turning angle, both right and left. Turning diameters were as tight as 38 feet. Road shock through the steering wheel was also greatly reduced, as cross steering had the drag link running parallel with the axle. Standard, deluxe and custom cabs gave the driver more room, visibility, safety and comfort. Deluxe and custom cabs offered "360-degree vision" through increased glass area, including cab rear quarter windows. Windshield and windows of the new "Pilot House Cabs" were higher and wider. Comfort in any season was provided by an all-weather heating/ventilating system combining the heater, defroster, vent windows, cowl vent and fresh air intake. Braking systems were larger and improved. Front and rear axles had increased load capacity. Front springs were longer. Redesigned radiator cores gave better cooling and the frame was made heavier. One major improvement was a much larger pickup with sides 5-7/16 in. higher than before. They were wider and longer, giving a total 40 percent increase in load capacity. Pickup styling used simple, cycle-type rear fenders that were easy and inexpensive to repair or replace. Drivelines, engines, clutches, transmissions and rear axles were carried over virtually unchanged from 1947. Discontinued models included the 1/2-ton canopy express. Standard, deLuxe and custom cabs were not separate series, but optional extra-cost upgrades.

3/4-TON — SERIES B-1-C-116 — SIX-CYLINDER: The 3/4-ton trucks had the same basic styling changes as the 1/2-ton models. A 116 inch wheelbase was featured. There were three chassis versions, an express (pickup) and a platform model that could be had with a 7-1/2-foot stake bed. The same carryover engine employed for B-1-Bs was found in B-1-Cs.

3/4-TON ROUTE-VAN DELIVERY — SERIES DUL — SIX-CYLINDER: Introduced late in 1948, the all new Route-Van had many industry firsts. Foremost was the first use of Fluid Drive in a volume-production truck, making the driver's job easier as well as increasing vehicle life and cutting maintenance costs. Route-Vans had two rear axles — one to support the load and another to move it. The sole function of the driving axle was to drive the wheels. Its differential assembly was rubber-mounted on the chassis frame, moving up and down with the frame rather than the wheels. It connected to the wheels by open-type axle shafts and universal joints. Axle shaft length and angularity changed with the deflection of the springs. The two shafts telescoped to compensate for loads, with two U joints on each adjusting for angular fluctuations. An electro-hydraulic service brake holder, available on all models, made it unnecessary for the operator to reach for the hand-brake at every door-to-door stop. The driver merely flicked a switch on the steering column to apply the brakes. Extremely low floor and step heights, large door openings (76 in.), headroom and width (72 in.), plus a windshield with 1,870 sq. in. of unobstructed vision, combined to make the delivery person's job easier. The Route-Van's floor was about 10 in. closer to the pavement than any other truck floor, due to the Dodge-designed rear driving axle. The engine was offset to the right to permit better use of front-end space. Gas, oil and water intakes, and the oil level indicator, were easily reached by raising the front hood. An engine hood inside the body gave access for service and adjustments. All Route-Van bodies were Dodge-built. Dodge had one new line of Route-Vans rated for 3/4-ton. There were two models in it, the B-1-DUL-102 and the B-1-DUL-117 (the last three symbols in the model code indicated the wheelbase). These trucks were actually light-duty (signified by the L in DUL) versions of the new-for-1948 one-ton Route-Van, but with a lower GVW rating.

1948 Dodge WDX 1-Ton Power Wagon 8 ft. Pickup (OCW)

Standard Catalog of Light-Duty Trucks

1-TON — SERIES B-1-D-116/B-1-D-126 — SIX-CYLINDER: The standard 1-tons continued to come in two series. The first shared the 3/4-ton wheelbase of 116 in. The second had a distinct 125-3/4 in. wheelbase. Both used the larger 230 cid six-cylinder Dodge engine and offered the same models found in the 3/4-ton lineup.

1948 Dodge 1/2-Ton Panel Delivery (OCW)

1-TON ROUTE VAN DELIVERY — SERIES DU/EUL — SIX-CYLINDER: Dodge also had two new lines of 1-ton Route-Vans. One was the heavy-duty 1-ton (7,900 lbs. GVW), which the 3/4-ton DUL was derived from. It included two models, one called the B-1-DU-102 (102 in. wheelbase) and one called the B-1-DU-117 (117 in. wheelbase). The second line also had two models, which were actually light-duty versions of a new model EU 1-1/2-ton Route-Van. (Thus, they were coded EULs.) The B-1-EUL-102 had the smaller wheelbase and the B-1-EUL-117 had the longer wheelbase that were also used for 3/4-ton Route Vans. However, there was also a B-1-EUL-142 with a 142 inch wheelbase that was offered only on the 1-ton and 1-1/2-ton Route-Vans.

1948 Dodge Commercial Station Wagon (DB)

1-TON POWER-WAGON — SERIES B-1-PW — SIX-CYLINDER: The Power-Wagon was unchanged, except for new series coding and the addition of a chassis and cowl configuration that aftermarket companies could use to build their own complete truck body. The chassis and cab and express model offered previously also returned. The GVW rating remained at 8,700 lbs.

I.D. DATA: Serial numbers were located on a plate on left front door hinge post. Serial numbers: [1948 Model B-1-B-108] (Detroit) 82044001-82092114; (California) 9227001-9234691. [1949 Model B-1-B-108] (Detroit) 82092129-82127008; (Los Angeles) 9234692-9238500. [1948 Model B-1-C-116] (Detroit) 83314001-83323945; (Los Angeles) 85502001-85503862. [1949 Model B-1-C-116] (Detroit) 83323946-83332940; (Los Angeles) 85503863-85505264. [1948 Model B-1-D-116 or -126] (Detroit) 81245001-81268731; (Los Angeles) 86003501-86006645. [1949 Model B-1-D-116 or -126] (Detroit) 81268732-81278472; (Los Angeles) 86006646-86007552. [1948 B-1-DU/DUL-All] (Detroit) 84202001-84202693. [1949 Model B-1-/DU/DUL-All] (Detroit) 84202694-84204553. [1948-

1949 Model B-1-EUL] (Detroit) 84000001-84000167. [1948-1949 Model B-1-EUL] (Detroit) 84000168-84000911. [1948 Model B-1-PW] (Detroit) 83907001-83911548; (Los Angeles) 88759501-88759912. [1949 Model B-1-PW] (Detroit) 83911549-83915078; (Los Angeles) 88759913-88760162. [1948-1949 B-1-FL] (Detroit) 80306001 up; (Los Angeles) 86506501 up. Engine numbers were on top left side of block between cylinders two and three. The first letter and three digits of the engine number were the engineering code numbers. Engine numbers not available.

1949 Dodge WDX 1-Ton Power Wagon 8 ft. Pickup (OCW)

Model	Body Type	Price	Weight	Prod. Total
Series B-1-B-108 — 1/2-Ton — 108 in. w.b.				
B-1-B	Chassis & Cowl	987	2475	Note 1
B-1-B	Chassis & Windshield	1032	—	Note 1
B-1-B	Chassis & Cab	1197	2975	Note 1
B-1-B	Pickup 6.5 ft.	1263	3275	Note 1
B-1-B	Panel	1448	3375	Note 1

NOTE 1: Total U.S. calendar year production, 1948-1949, Series B-1-B: (Domestic) 106,794; (Export) 11,570; (Total) 118,364.

Series B-1-C-116 — 3/4-Ton — 116 in. w.b.				
B-1-C	Chassis & Cowl	1070	2650	Note 2
B-1-C	Chassis & Windshield	1115	—	Note 2
B-1-C	Chassis & Cab	1280	3150	Note 2
B-1-C	Pickup 7.5 ft.	1371	3525	Note 2
B-1-C	Platform 7.5 ft.	1377	3475	Note 2
B-1-C	Stake 7.5 ft.	1430	3700	Note 2

NOTE 2: Total U.S. production, calendar years 1948-1949, Series B-1-C: (Domestic) 29,686.

Series B-1-D-116 — 1-Ton — 116 in. w.b.				
B-1-D	Chassis & Cowl	1134	2900	Note 3
B-1-D	Chassis & Windshield	1179	—	Note 3
B-1-D	Chassis & Cab	1344	3375	Note 3
B-1-D	Pickup 7.5 ft.	1435	3725	Note 3
B-1-D	Platform 7.5 ft.	1441	3725	Note 3
B-1-D	Stake 7.5 ft.	1494	3905	Note 3

Series B-1-D-126 — 1-Ton — 126 in. w.b.				
B-1-D	Chassis & Cowl	1154	2950	Note 3
B-1-D	Chassis & Windshield	1199	—	Note 3
B-1-D	Chassis & Cab	1364	3375	Note 3
B-1-D	Pickup 9 ft.	1465	3800	Note 3
B-1-D	Platform 9 ft.	1473	3825	Note 3
B-1-D	Stake 9 ft.	1539	4055	Note 3

Series B-1-PW Power-Wagon — 1-Ton — 126 in. w.b.				
B-1-PW	Chassis & Cowl	1790	4075	Note 3
B-1-PW	Chassis & Cab	1940	4675	Note 3
B-1-PW	Pickup 8 ft.	2045	5100	Note 3

Series B-1-DUL Route-Van — 3/4-Ton				
102 in. w.b.				
B-1-DUL	Cab & Body 7 ft.	—	—	
117 in. w.b.				
B-1-DUL	Cab & Body 9.5 ft.	—	—	

Series B-1-DU/EUL Route-Van — 1-Ton				
102 in. w.b.				
B-1-DU	Cab & Body 7 ft.	2595	4510	Note 3
B-1-EUL	Cab & Body 7 ft.	—	—	Note 3
117 in. w.b.				
B-1-DU	Cab & Body 9.5 ft.	2690	4950	Note 3
B-1-EUL	Cab & Body 9.5 ft.	—	—	Note 3
142 in. w.b.				
B-1-EUL	Cab & Body 12.5 ft.	—	—	Note 3

NOTE 3: Total U.S. production, calendar years 1948-1949, all 1-ton series B-1-D, B-1-PW and B-1-DUL/DU/EUL: (Domestic) 45,272; (Export) 9,483; [Total] 54,755.

1949 Dodge 1/2-Ton Pickup (L. Anderson)

ENGINE [Series B-1-B/B-1-C]: Inline. L-head. Six-cylinder. Cast iron block. Bore & stroke: 3-1/4 x 4-3/8 in. Displacement: 217.8 cid. Compression ratio: 6.6:1. Brake horsepower: 95 at 3600 rpm. Net horsepower: 25.35. Torque: 172 lbs.-ft. at 1200 rpm. Four main bearings. Solid valve lifters. Carburetor: Carter.

ENGINE [B-1-D/Route Van/Power Wagon]: Inline. L-head. Six-cylinder. Cast iron block. Bore & stroke: 3-1/4 x 4-5/8 in. Displacement: 230.2 cid. Compression ratio: 6.7:1. Brake horsepower: 102 at 3600 rpm. Net horsepower: 25.35. Torque: 184 lbs.-ft. at 1200 rpm. Four main bearings. Solid valve lifters. Carburetor: Stromberg.

ENGINE [B-1-FL]: Inline. L-head. Six-cylinder. Cast iron block. Bore & stroke: 3-7/16 x 4-1/4 in. Brake horsepower at 3600 rpm.

CHASSIS [Series B-1-B-108]: Wheelbase: 108 in. Tires: 6.00 x 16 four-ply front and rear on 4.00 drop-center safety-rim wheels. GVW: 4,200 lbs. (4,500 lbs. with 6.50 x 16 six-ply tires; 4,800 lbs. with 6.50 x 16 six-ply tires on 4.50 wheels).

1949 Dodge 1/2-Ton Panel (MC)

CHASSIS [Series B-1-C-116]: Wheelbase: 116 in. Tires: 7.00 x 15TA six-ply on 5.50 drop-center rims. GVW: 5,500 lbs. (5,500 lbs. with 6.00 x 16 six-ply front tires on 4.50 semi-drop center rims and 7.00 x 16 six-ply rear tires on 5.50 rims; 6,000 lbs. with 7.00 x 16 six-ply front and 7.50 x 16 six-ply rear tires on 5.50 semi-drop center rims).

CHASSIS [Series B-1-D-116]: Wheelbase: 116 in. Tires: (front) 6.00 x 16 six-ply on 4.50 semi-drop-center rims; (rear) 7.00 x 16 six-ply on 5.50 rims. GVW: 5,500 lbs. (6,800 lbs. with 6.00 x 16 six-ply front tires and dual rears on 4.50 rims; 7,500 lbs. with 6.50 x 16 six-ply front and dual rear tires on 4.50 rims).

CHASSIS [Series B-1-D-126]: Wheelbase: 126 in. Tires: (front) 6.00 x 16 six-ply; (rear) 7.00 x 16 six-ply. GVW: 6,000 lbs. with 7.00 x 16 six-ply single rear tires on 5.50 rims; 6,800 lbs. with 6.00 x 16 six-ply front and dual rear tires on 4.50 rims; 7,500 lbs. with 6.50 x 16 six-ply front and dual rear tires on 4.50 rims with 2,300 lbs. rear springs.

CHASSIS [Series B-1-PW-126 Power Wagon]: Wheelbase: 126 in. Tires: 7.50 x 16 eight-ply front and rear on 5.50 wheels. GVW: 7,600 lbs. (8,700 lbs. with 9.00 x 16 eight-ply tires on 6.50 rims).

CHASSIS [Model B-1-DUL-102]: Wheelbase: 102 in. GVW: 6,200 lbs. Tires: 7.00 x 16 six-ply.

CHASSIS [Model B-1-DUL-117]: Wheelbase: 117 in. GVW: 6,900 lbs. Tires: 7.00 x 16 six-ply front and 7.50 x 16 six-ply rear.

CHASSIS [Model B-1-DU-102]: Wheelbase: 102 in. GVW: 7,500 lbs. Tires: 7.00 x 16 six-ply, front and rear. Higher GVW with 7.50 x 16 eight-ply front and rear tires.

CHASSIS [Model B-1-DU-117]: Wheelbase: 117 in. GVW: 7,900 lbs. with 8.25 x 16 eight-ply tires front and rear.

CHASSIS [Model B-1-EUL-102]: Wheelbase: 102 in. Tires: 7.50 x 16 six-ply front and 8.25 x 16 eight-ply rear. GVW: 8,000 with 8.25 x 16 eight-ply tires front and rear tires; also available 8,700 lbs. with 9.00 x 16 eight-ply front and rear; 9,600 lbs. with 9.00 x 16 ten-ply front and rear.

CHASSIS [Model B-1-EUL-142]: Wheelbase: 142 in. Tires: (front) 7.50 x 16 six-ply; (rear) 8.25 x 16 eight-ply. GVW: 8,500 lbs. with 8.25 x 16 eight-ply front and rear; 9,200 lbs. with 9.00 x 16 eight-ply front and rear; 10,100 lbs. with 9.00 x 16 ten-ply front and rear.

CHASSIS [Series B1-FL-128]: Wheelbase: 128 in. Tires: 6.00 x 20 six-ply front, 6.50 x 20 eight-ply rear. GVW: 9,500 lbs. Add $69 for dual rear wheel equipment.

CHASSIS [Series B1-FL-152]: Wheelbase: 152 in. Tires: 6.00 x 20 six-ply front, 6.50 x 20 eight-ply rear. GVW: 9,500 lbs. Add $69 for dual rear wheel equipment.

TECHNICAL: [Series B-1-B/C]. Selective sliding gear transmission. Speeds: 3F/1R; optional 4F/1R with power-take-off. Floor shift control. Single-plate dry-disc clutch, 10 in. diameter (11 in. optional). Semi-floating rear axle. Rear axle ratio: 4.1:1 (4.78:1 optional). Hotchkiss drive with hypoid drive gears. Hydraulic four-wheel brakes. Parking brake: Band and drum type, mounted at rear of transmission. Worm and roller steering. Shock absorbers front and rear.

TECHNICAL: [Series B-1-D]. Speeds: 3F/1R standard; 4F/1R optional. Rear axle ratios: 3.9 or 4.89:1. All other specs same as 1/2-ton.

TECHNICAL: [DUL Route-Van] Speeds: 3F/1R; (4F/1R optional). [EU/EUL Route-Van] 4F/1R only. Floor shift control. Single-plate dry-disc clutch: [DU] 10-inch; [EU] 11 in. Full-floating single-speed rear drive axle with hypoid gears. Frame-mounted differential. Open-type telescoping driveshafts to wheels with two cross-and-trunnion "U" joints on each side. Hotchkiss drive. Rear axle ratios: [DU] 4.89:1; [EU] 5.83:1. Semi-elliptic springs front and rear. Reverse Elliott I-beam front axle. Steel I-beam rear supporting axle. Worm and roller steering. (Note: Other axle ratios supplied with optional heavy-duty tires).

OPTIONS: [B-1-B/B-1-C/B-1-D, installed at factory] Rear bumper for pickup ($7). Deluxe cab equipment consisting of vent wings in cab door and rear quarter windows ($25). Custom cab equipment: Includes vent wings in cab door and rear quarter windows, deluxe seat cushion and back, dome light, left armrest, dual interior sun visors and dual electric windshield wipers ($46). Deluxe panel equipment: Includes vent wings in cab door windows, left armrest, dual sun visors, dual electric wipers ($30). Bumper guards, set of three ($5). Rearview mirror, long-arm adjustable, left side ($2); same for right side ($3). Dual electric horns ($12). Auxiliary seat, stationary type, panel truck only ($27). Seat cushion with special air foam padding, cab models only ($10). Paint: Pickup body and rear fenders painted to match cab, Dodge Truck red or Armour yellow only, ($5). Oil-bath air cleaner, one-quart ($1.75). Oil filter with replaceable element ($8.50). Clutch, 11-inch diameter, replacing standard ($6.50). Generator: 256 watt, 32 ampere-hour ($9.50). Engine governor ($7). Rear springs, 750 lbs. nominal capacity each (no charge). Taillamp, right side ($6). Four-speed transmission replacing standard three-speed ($30). (Note: Replaceable-element oil filter was standard on heavy-duty models with optional tires and high GVW ratings).

OPTIONS: [Route-Van, installed at factory] Rear bumper with step-plate. Radiator grille (bumper) guards, set of three. Rearview mirror (left or right). Ventilating wings in driver compartment side windows. Windshield header roof cap. Jackknife type side doors, left and right. Jackknife type rear doors. Interior lining and insulation equipment: Complete roof steel liner, 1/2 in. roof insulation, steel side liners above beltline, and dome light in driver's section. Side rub rails. Driver's seat assembly, stationary type, with standard seat cushion or air foam padding. Dual auxiliary taillamps. Tire carrier inside body above wheelhouse, right or left side. Undercoating. Paint: Body and fenders Ecuador blue, Judson green, Charlotte ivory, or black. Wheels black; all body sizes (standard paint was primer). Windshield wiper: Vacuum, right side; electric, left and right side. Oil-bath air cleaner (one-quart capacity). Oil filter (replaceable element type). Battery: 120 ampere-hour capacity. Generator: 280 watt, 35-ampere, for high charging at low engine speeds. Governor (engine velocity type). Shock absorbers, front and rear. Tool kit (wheel wrench, jack and handle in cloth bag). Four-speed transmission with 10-inch clutch, Fluid-Drive and auxiliary parking brake.

OPTIONS: [Power Wagon, installed at factory] Deluxe cab equipment: Includes vent wings in cab door windows, dome light, left armrest, dual interior sun visors and dual electric windshield wipers ($40). Rearview mirror, long-arm adjustable, left side ($2); right side ($3). Taillamp, right side ($6). Generator: 256 watt, 32 ampere-hour ($18.50). Governor, mechanical, for use with rear driveshaft assembly ($63). Oil filter, replaceable element type ($7). Radiator overflow tank ($6). Shock absorbers, telescopic type, rear ($31). Draw bar ($20). Pintle hook ($10). Power-take-off assembly ($65). Pulley drive — pulley unit only ($73). Rear driveshaft assembly only ($72). Tow hooks, front only ($5.00/pair). Winch assembly: Front winch and driveshaft assembly ($200).

NOTE: Since the majority of orders for Power Wagons specified deluxe cab equipment, it was decided to expedite production by furnishing deluxe equipment on all chassis with cab and pickup models at the established prices.

OPTIONS: [Dealer installed for all models]. Recirculating hot water heater. Defroster package. Fresh air intake heater. Radio. Fog lamps. Cigar lighter. Fire extinguisher. Flares. Grille guards. Windshield washers. Rear fender step plate (for pickups). Directional signal lamps.

HISTORICAL: Introduced in December, 1947, except for the Route-Vans, which bowed in October, 1948. Calendar year registrations: (1948) 114,431; (1949) 116,956. Calendar year production: (1948) 172,020; (1949) 151,513. Production breakdown by size: [1948 1/2-ton]: Domestic = 45,196; export = 6,898. [1949 1/2-ton]: Domestic = 61,598; export = 4,672. [1948 3/4-ton] domestic only = 11,279. [1949 3/4-ton] domestic only = 18,407. [1948 1-ton/Power Wagon/Route-Van]: Domestic = 26,288; export = 4,822. [1949 1-ton/Power Wagon/Route-Van]: Domestic = 18,984; export = 4,661.

NOTE: Power-Wagon production for 1949 was 8,198 units. Innovations included cross steering for tight turning angle. Route-Vans had Fluid-Drive, an electro-hydraulic service brake switch, separate drive and support rear axles, telescoping axle shafts, offset engine, and very low floor/step heights. B-1 Series trucks continued unchanged through the 1948-1949 period. Dodge ranked fourth in industry sales in 1948, rising to third the following year. The U.S. Government purchased 377 Power Wagons for various agencies. Dodge opened a new truck and car assembly plant in San Leandro, California. L.L. Colbert was president of Dodge Div. and L.J. Purdy was vice-president in charge of trucks.

1949 Dodge 1/2-Ton Pickup (R. Cenowa/DB)

Standard Catalog of Light-Duty Trucks

1950 DODGE

1950 Dodge Light-Duty Truck Cab (D. Sagvold)

1/2-TON — SERIES B-2-B — SIX-CYLINDER: Dodge truck styling continued in the 1948-1949 appearance. Three horizontal bars, increasing in width from top to bottom, crossed the grille opening. Round parking lamps were situated under the headlamps. The first technical improvements to the B-series came on the 1950 models. Cycle bonded brake linings, previously offered only on 1/2-tons, were made standard on all models. Brake shoes were attached without rivets. The three-speed transmission now had a steering column gearshift handle. A "Right Spot" hand-pull parking brake control sat under the dash, to the right of the steering wheel. Starting in spring 1950, Fluid-Drive was offered as an extra-cost option on all 1/2-, 3/4- and 1-ton trucks. This was a response to its popularity on the Route-Van. A new standard 1/2-ton pickup had 17 in. high sides, reduced from 22-7/16 in. The two pickup bodies were called "high side" and "low side." The latter was identical to the body on the W-series pickups offered through 1947. Model availability was the same as in the B-1 series. The 1/2-ton line offered three chassis models, a pickup with a 6-1/2-foot load bed and a panel. Standard equipment was also the same as in 1948-1949.

3/4-TON — SERIES B-2-C — SIX-CYLINDER: There were three chassis models, a pickup with a one-foot longer bed and 7-1/2 ft. platform/stake models in the 116 in. wheelbase 3/4-ton line.

1950 Dodge B-2-PW Power Wagon 8 ft. Express (RAC)

1-TON — SERIES B-2-D — SIX-CYLINDER: The regular 1-ton line offered the same models as the 3/4-ton series on two wheelbases. The 116 in. wheelbase models were the same size as the 3/4-tons, but had higher GVWs. The 126 in. wheelbase models had 1-1/2-foot longer bodies. Both lines included a 9-foot bed pickup called an express.

1-TON SPECIAL — SERIES B-2-FL — SIX-CYLINDER: As part of its "Job-Rated" marketing program, Dodge offered lighter-duty (note the L suffix on the F series code) editions of certain models that were better-suited to some user applications. The FLs came on two wheelbases, both longer than the B-2-Ds offered, and looked identical to 1-1/2 tons. However, the axles, springs, tire sizes and tire ply ratings were changed to lower the GVW into the 1-ton range. There was no express. The platform/stake models were 9 ft. and 12 ft. long, respectively.

1-TON POWER WAGON — SERIES B-2-PW — SIX-CYLINDER: Power Wagon models continued unchanged.

3/4-TON SPECIAL ROUTE-VAN — SERIES B-1-DUL/DULF — SIX-CYLINDER: Route-Van models continued unchanged, except that a new Deluxe option was offered for $145 extra. Basically, they were so unchanged, that the 1950 models retained the B-1 designa-

tion, rather than adopting the B-2 designation that other light-duty trucks switched to. The 3/4-ton Route Vans also came on 102 in. and 117 in. wheelbases with 7 ft. and 9.5 ft. bodies, respectively. They were similar to the regular 1-ton jobs, but had lower GVWs. The Route-Vans came as a chassis with front end section (Chassis w/frt.), to which aftermarket bodies could be added, or with Dodge's standard, cab-integral panel bodies installed. Approximate weight of the 7 ft. body was 1,860 lbs., while the 9.5 ft. body tipped the scales at about 2,210 lbs.

1-TON ROUTE-VAN — SERIES B-1-DU/DUF — SIX-CYLINDER: The 1-ton Route Vans also came on 102 in. and 117 in. wheelbases, but had higher GVWs than the 3/4-ton Special models.

1-TON SPECIAL ROUTE-VAN — SERIES B-1-EUL/EULF: As the Ls in the model codes indicate, these were Job-Rated versions of the 1-1/2-ton stand-up delivery truck. In addition to the 102 and 117 in. wheelbases, a longer 142 in. wheelbase was available to carry a 12-1/2 ft. body. This body weighed approximately 2,650 lbs.

I.D. DATA: Serial numbers on plate on dash under hood; also on frame in back of left front spring shackle. Serial numbers were: [B-2-B] (Detroit) 82140001-82212862; (San Leandro) 85300001-85307000. [B-2-C] (Detroit) 83340001-83361096; (San Leandro) 85506001-85508219. [B-2-D] (Detroit) 81280001-81295887; (San Leandro) 86008501-86009522. [B-2-FL] (Detroit) 80380001X and up; (San Leandro) 86513001X and up. [B-2-PW] (Detroit) 83917001-83921140; (San Leandro) 88766001-88766296. [B-2-DU/DUF] (Detroit) 84204554-84206127. [B-2-EU/EUL/EULF] (Detroit) 84000912-84001405. Engine numbers on left side of motor, below cylinder head; on front right side of motor. Starting engine numbers were: [B-2-B] T172-1001. [B-2-C] T174-1001. [B-2-D] T176-1001. [B-2-PW] [T137-1001. [B-2-DU] T164-1001. [B-2-EU] T165-1001.

Model	Body Type	Price	Weight	Prod. Total
Series B-2-B — 1/2-Ton — 108 in. w.b.				
B-2-B	Chassis & Cowl	987	2350	Note 1
B-2-B	Chassis & Windshield	1032	—	Note 1
B-2-B	Chassis & Cab	1197	2850	Note 1
B-2-B	Pickup 6.5 ft.	1263	3150	Note 1
B-2-B	Panel	1448	3250	Note 1

NOTE 1: Total U.S. calendar year production: (Domestic) 46,950; (Export) 4,300; [Total] 51,250.

Model	Body Type	Price	Weight	Prod. Total
Series B-2-C — 3/4-Ton — 116 in. w.b.				
B-2-C	Chassis & Cowl	1070	2450	Note 2
B-2-C	Chassis & Windshield	1115	—	Note 2
B-2-C	Chassis & Cab	1280	2950	Note 2
B-2-C	Pickup 7.5 ft.	1371	3325	Note 2
B-2-C	Platform 7.5 ft.	1377	3275	Note 2
B-2-C	Stake 7.5 ft.	1430	3500	Note 2

NOTE 2: Total U.S. calendar year production: (all Domestic) 14,928.

Model	Body Type	Price	Weight	Prod. Total
Series B-2-D-116 — 1-Ton — 116 in. w.b.				
B-2-D	Chassis & Cowl	1134	2775	Note 3
B-2-D	Chassis & Windshield	1179	—	Note 3
B-2-D	Chassis & Cab	1344	3275	Note 3
B-2-D	Pickup 7.5 ft.	1433	3625	Note 3
B-2-D	Platform 7.5 ft.	1441	3625	Note 3
B-2-D	Stake 7.5 ft.	1494	3805	Note 3
Series B-2-D-126 — 1-Ton — 125.75 in. w.b.				
B-2-D	Chassis & Cowl	1154	2850	Note 3
B-2-D	Chassis & Windshield	1199	—	Note 3
B-2-D	Chassis & Cab	1364	3350	Note 3
B-2-D	Pickup 9 ft.	1465	3725	Note 3
B-2-D	Platform 9 ft.	1473	3800	Note 3
B-2-D	Stake 9 ft.	1539	4030	Note 3
Series B-2-PW Power Wagon — 1-Ton (4x4) — 126 in. w.b.				
B-2-PW	Chassis & Cowl	1750	4075	Note 3
B-2-PW	Chassis & Windshield	1790	—	Note 3
B-2-PW	Chassis & Cab	1940	4575	Note 3
B-2-PW	Pickup 8 ft.	2045	5000	Note 3

NOTE 3: Total U.S. calendar year production, 1-Ton models with 116 and 126 in. wheelbase: (Domestic) 11,640; (Export) 3,221; [Total] 14,861.

Model	Body Type	Price	Weight	Prod. Total
Series B-2-FL-128 — Special 1-Ton — 128 in. w.b.				
B-2-FL	Chassis & Cowl	1234	3425	—
B-2-FL	Chassis & Windshield	1279	—	—
B-2-FL	Chassis & Cab	1444	3925	—
B-2-FL	Platform 9 ft.	1571	4350	—
B-2-FL	Stake 9 ft.	1639	4700	—
Series B-2-FL-152 — Special 1-Ton — 152 in. w.b.				
B-2-FL	Chassis & Cowl	1254	3500	—
B-2-FL	Chassis & Windshield	1279	—	—
B-2-FL	Chassis & Cab	1464	4000	—
B-2-FL	Platform 12 ft.	1617	4525	—
B-2-FL	Stake 12 ft.	1701	4925	—
Series B-1-DUL/DULF-102 — 3/4-Ton Special Route-Van — 102 in. w.b.				
B-1-DUL	Panel Body 7 ft.	2295	4510	—
B-1-DULF	Panel Body 7 ft.	2350	4510	—
Series B-1-DUL/DUFL-117 — 3/4-Ton Special Route-Van — 117 in. w.b.				
B-1-DUL	Panel Body 9.5 ft.	2380	4950	—
B-1DULF	Panel Body 9.5 ft.	2435	4950	—
Series B-1-DU/DUF/EUL/EUFL — 1-Ton Route-Van — 102 in. w.b.				
B-1-DU	Chassis & front	1795	2650	—
B-1-DU	Panel Body 7 ft.	2395	4510	—
B-1-DU	Deluxe Panel 7 ft.	2540	4510	—
B-1-DUF	Panel 7 ft.	2450	4510	—
B-1-DUF	Deluxe Panel 7 ft.	2595	4510	—
B-1-EUL	Chassis & front	—	—	—
B-1-EUL	Panel 7 ft.	—	2455	4855
B-1-EUL	Deluxe Panel 7 ft.	2600	4855	—
B-1EUFL	Panel 7 ft.	2510	4855	—
B-1EUFL	Deluxe Panel 7 ft.	2655	4855	—

Standard Catalog of Light-Duty Trucks

Series B-1-DU/DUF/EUL/EUFL — 1-Ton Route-Van — 117 in. w.b.

B-1-DU	Chassis & front	1818	2749	—
B-1-DU	Panel Body 9.5 ft.	2480	4950	—
B-1-DU	Deluxe Panel 9.5 ft.	2625	4950	—
B-1-DUF	Panel 9.5 ft.	2535	4950	—
B-1-DUF	Deluxe Panel 9.5 ft.	2690	4950	—
B-1-EUL	Chassis & front	—	—	—
B-1-EUL	Panel 9.5 ft.	2540	5280	—
B-1-EUL	Deluxe Panel 9.5 ft.	5325	5280	—
B-1EUFL	Panel 9.5 ft.	2595	5280	—
B-1EUFL	Deluxe Panel 9.5 ft.	2640	5280	—

NOTE 4: EUL/EULF are "Special" Job-Rated models.

Series B-1-EUL/EUFL — 1-Ton Special Route-Van — 142 in. w.b.

B-1-EUL	Chassis & front 12.5 ft.	—	—	—
B-1-EUL	Panel 12.5 ft.	2670	5865	—
B-1-EUL	Deluxe Panel 12.5 ft.	2815	5865	—
B-1EUFL	Panel 12.5 ft.	2725	5865	—
B-1EUFL	Deluxe Panel 12.5 ft.	2870	5865	—

ENGINE [Series B-2-B/B-2-C]: Inline. L-head. Six-cylinder. Cast iron block. Bore & stroke: 3-1/4 x 4-3/8 in. Displacement: 217.8 cid. Compression ratio: 6.6:1. Brake horsepower: 95 at 3600 rpm. Net horsepower: 25.35. Torque: 172 lbs.-ft. at 1200 rpm. Four main bearings. Solid valve lifters. Carburetor: Carter.

ENGINE [B-2-D/Route Van/Power Wagon]: Inline. L-head. Six-cylinder. Cast iron block. Bore & stroke: 3-1/4 x 4-5/8 in. Displacement: 230.2 cid. Compression ratio: 6.7:1. Brake horsepower: 102 at 3600 rpm. Net horsepower: 25.35. Torque: 184 lbs.-ft. at 1200 rpm. Four main bearings. Solid valve lifters. Carburetor: Stromberg.

ENGINE [B-2-FL]: Inline. L-head. Six-cylinder. Cast iron block. Bore & stroke: 3-7/16 x 4-1/4 in. Displacement: 236.6 cid. Brake horsepower: 109 at 3600 rpm. Compression: 7.):1. Four main bearings.

CHASSIS (Series B-2-B): Wheelbase: 108 in. Tires: 6.00 x 16 four-ply front and rear; disc wheels with 4.00 drop-center rims. Underslung tire carrier. GVW: 4,850 lbs.

CHASSIS (Series B-2-C): Wheelbase: 116 in. Tires: 7.00 x 15 six-ply front and rear; disc wheels with 5.50 drop-center rims. Underslung tire carrier. GVW: 5,500 lbs.

CHASSIS (Series B-2-D): Wheelbase: 116 and 126 in. Tires: (front 6.00 x 16 six-ply; (rear) 7.00 x 16 six-ply. Disc wheels on 4.50 semi-drop-center rims (front); 5.50 (rear and spare). Underslung tire carrier. GVW: 7,500 lbs.

CHASSIS [Series B-1-FL-128]: Wheelbase: 128 in. Tires: 6.00 x 20 six-ply front, 6.50 x 20 eight-ply rear. GVW: 9,500 lbs. Add $69 for dual rear wheel equipment.

CHASSIS [Series B-1-FL-152]: Wheelbase: 152 in. Tires: 6.00 x 20 six-ply front, 6.50 x 20 eight-ply rear. GVW: 9,500 lbs. Add $69 for dual rear wheel equipment.

CHASSIS [Series B-2-PW-126]: Wheelbase: 126 in. Tires: 7.50 x 16 eight-ply. Four-wheel-drive chassis. GVW: 8,700 lbs.

CHASSIS [Model B-1-DUL-102]: Wheelbase: 102 in. GVW: 6,900 lbs. Tires: 7.00 x 16 six-ply.

CHASSIS [Model B-1-DUL-117]: Wheelbase: 117 in. GVW: 6,900 lbs. Tires: 7.00 x 16 six-ply front and 7.50 x 16 six-ply rear.

CHASSIS [Model B-1-DU-102]: Wheelbase: 102 in. GVW: 7,900 lbs. Tires: 6.50 x 16 six-ply front/7.00 x 16 six-ply rear. Higher GVW with 7.50 x 16 eight-ply front and rear tires.

CHASSIS [Model B-1-DU-117]: Wheelbase: 117 in.; Tires: 6.50 x 16 six-ply front/7.00 x 16 six-ply rear. GVW: 7,900 lbs. (Available with 8.25 x 16 eight-ply tires front and rear).

CHASSIS [Model B-1-EUL-102]: Wheelbase: 102 in. Tires: 7.50 x 16 six-ply front and 8.25 x 16 eight-ply rear. GVW: 8,000 with 8.25 x 16 eight-ply tires front and rear tires; also available 8,700 lbs. with 9.00 x 16 eight-ply front and rear; 9,600 lbs. with 9.00 x 16 ten-ply front and rear.

CHASSIS [Model B-1-EUL-142]: Wheelbase: 142 in. Tires: (front) 7.50 x 16 six-ply; (rear) 8.25 x 16 eight-ply. GVW: 8,500 lbs. with 8.25 x 16 eight-ply front and rear; 9,200 lbs. with 9.00 x 16 eight-ply front and rear; 10,100 lbs. with 9.00 x 16 ten-ply front and rear.

TECHNICAL: [Series B-2-B/B-2-C]. Selective sliding gear transmission. Speeds: 3F/1R; optional 4F/1R with power-take-off. Floor shift control. Single-plate dry-disc clutch, 10 in. diameter (11 in. optional). Semi-floating rear axle. Rear axle ratio: 4.1:1 (4.78:1 optional). Hotchkiss drive with hypoid drive gears. Hydraulic four-wheel brakes. Parking brake: Band and drum type, mounted at rear of transmission. Worm and roller steering. Shock absorbers front and rear.

TECHNICAL: [Series B-2-D/B-2-FL]. Speeds: 3F/1R standard; 4F/1R optional. Rear axle ratios: 3.9 or 4.89:1. All other specs same as 1/2-ton.

TECHNICAL: [Route-Van] Speeds: 3F/1R; (4F/1R optional). [EU/EUL Route-Van] 4F/1R only. Floor shift control. Single-plate dry-disc clutch: [DU] 10-inch; [EU] 11 in. Full-floating single-speed rear drive axle with hypoid gears. Frame-mounted differential. Open-type telescoping driveshafts to wheels with two cross-and-trunnion "U" joints on each side. Hotchkiss drive. Rear axle ratios: [DU] 4.89:1; [EU] 5.83:1. Semi-elliptic springs front and rear. Reverse Elliott I-beam front axle. Steel I-beam rear supporting axle. Worm and roller steering. (Note: Other axle ratios supplied with optional heavy-duty tires).

OPTIONS: [B-1-B/B-1-C/B-1-D, installed at factory] Rear bumper for pickup ($7). Deluxe cab equipment consisting of vent wings in cab door and rear quarter windows ($25). Custom cab equipment: Includes vent wings in cab door and rear quarter windows, deluxe seat cushion and back, dome light, left armrest, dual interior sun visors and dual electric windshield wipers ($46). Deluxe panel equipment: Includes vent wings in cab door windows, left armrest, dual sun visors, dual electric wipers ($30). Bumper guards, set of three ($5). rearview mirror, long-arm adjustable, left side ($2); same for right side ($3). Dual electric horns ($12). Auxiliary seat, stationary type, panel truck only ($27). Seat cushion with special air foam padding, cab models only ($10). Paint: Pickup body and rear fenders painted to match cab, Dodge Truck red or Armour yellow only, ($5). Oil-bath air cleaner, one-quart ($1.75). Oil filter with replaceable element ($8.50). Clutch, 11-inch diameter, replacing standard ($6.50). Generator: 256 watt, 32 ampere-hour ($9.50). Engine governor ($7). Rear springs, 750 lbs. nominal capacity each (no charge). Taillamp, right side ($6). Four-speed transmission replacing standard three-speed ($30). (Note: Replaceable-element oil filter was standard on heavy-duty models with optional tires and high GVW ratings).

OPTIONS: [Route-Van, installed at factory] Rear bumper with step-plate. Radiator grille (bumper) guards, set of three. Rearview mirror (left or right). Ventilating wings in driver compartment side windows. Windshield header roof cap. Jackknife type side doors, left and right. Jackknife type rear doors. Interior lining and insulation equipment: Complete roof steel liner, 1/2 in. roof insulation, steel side liners above beltline, and dome light in driver's section. Side rub rails. Driver's seat assembly, stationary type, with standard seat cushion or air foam padding. Dual auxiliary taillamps. Tire carrier inside body above wheelhouse, right or left side. Undercoating. Paint: Body and fenders Ecuador blue, Judson green, Charlotte ivory, or black. Wheels black; all body sizes (standard paint was primer). Windshield wiper: Vacuum, right side; electric, left and right side. Oil-bath air cleaner (one-quart capacity). Oil filter (replaceable element type). Battery: 120 ampere-hour capacity. Generator: 280 watt, 35-ampere, for high charging at low engine speeds. Governor (engine velocity type). Shock absorbers, front and rear. Tool kit (wheel wrench, jack and handle in cloth bag). Four-speed transmission with 10-inch clutch, Fluid-Drive and auxiliary parking brake.

OPTIONS: [Power Wagon, installed at factory] Deluxe cab equipment: Includes vent wings in cab door windows, dome light, left armrest, dual interior sun visors and dual electric windshield wipers ($40). Rearview mirror, long-arm adjustable, left side ($2); right side ($3). Taillamp, right side ($6). Generator: 256 watt, 32 ampere-hour ($18.50). Governor, mechanical, for use with rear driveshaft assembly ($63). Oil filter, replaceable element type ($7). Radiator overflow tank ($6). Shock absorbers, telescopic type, rear ($31). Draw bar ($20). Pintle hook ($10). Power-take-off assembly ($65). Pulley drive — pulley unit only ($73). Rear driveshaft assembly only ($72). Tow hooks, front only ($5.00/pair). Winch assembly: Front winch and driveshaft ($200).

HISTORICAL: Introduced: October, 1949. Calendar year registrations: 99,716. Calendar year production: 122,324 (U.S. only). Model year figures not available. Innovations: Bonded brake linings on all light-duty trucks. Steering column three-speed gearshift. Sales dropped by 14.7 percent for 1950. Dodge offered 396 models rated 1/2- to 4-ton. Of the total production, 9,471 trucks were built in San Leandro, California.Dodge sold 400 1/2-ton panel trucks and 3,750 special-bodied 1-tons to the U.S. Post Office. Early in 1950, Dodge announced a new line of 4-ton trucks in five wheelbases. They were powered by a huge 337 cid L-head six. They had GVW ratings of 28,000 lbs. and combined GVW of 50,000 lbs. Chrysler Corp. suffered a 100-day labor strike from January to April, 1950. Stepped-up production after the strike ended could not make up for the loss. On Jan. 10, 1950, Dodge cut truck prices by $40 to $125.

1951 DODGE

1951 Dodge 1/2-Ton High Sides Pickup (OCW)

1/2-TON — SERIES B-3-B — SIX-CYLINDER: A new grille had a rectangular opening with heavy body-colored molding around it. Two horizontal bars crossed the grille opening. The bottom bar carried a round parking lamp near each outer end. A bright metal "Job-Rated" nameplate connected the horizontal bars at the center of the grille. The hood had an all-new appearance. The dash was redesigned, with instruments moved directly in front of driver. Cab trim details and colors were improved. The steering wheel got an attractive horn ring and turn signal switch. A higher compression ratio added more power. Oriflow shocks improved ride quality. Other new technical advances were a narrow wedge fan belt and annodized brake cylinders. The 1/2-tons had the 108 in. wheelbase and included a panel and a 6-1/2 ft. pickup with low sides standard and high sides available at extra cost. Standard equipment included front/rear hydraulic shocks; front bumper; underslung tire carrier; left outside mirror; one-pint oil bath air cleaner; dual vacuum wipers; and left interior sun visor. The Dodge ram hood ornament was changed to an option.

3/4-TON — SERIES B-3-C — SIX-CYLINDER: The styling changes on 1/2-tons were seen on 3/4-tons also. There were again three chassis models, a pickup with a one-foot longer bed and 7-1/2 ft. platform/stake models in the 116 in. wheelbase 3/4-ton line. The 3/4-ton pickup now came with the low sides as standard and high sides as an extra cost option.

1-TON — SERIES B-3-D — SIX-CYLINDER: The regular 1-ton line offered the same styling and models as the 3/4-ton series on two wheelbases. The 116 in. wheelbase models were the same size as the 3/4-tons, but had higher GVWs. The 126 in. wheelbase models had 1-1/2-foot longer bodies. Both lines included a 9-foot bed pickup called an express. Only front hydraulic shocks were standard on 1-tons; rears were optional.

1-TON POWER WAGON — SERIES B-3-PW — SIX-CYLINDER: Power Wagon models continued unchanged. It had the 126 in. wheelbase and four-wheel drive. The pickup had an 8 ft. bed. Deluxe cab features were included in the base price.

3/4-TON SPECIAL ROUTE-VAN — SERIES B-3-DUL/DULF — SIX-CYLINDER: Route-Van models continued unchanged. Dodge adopted the B-3 designation that other light-duty trucks used. The 3/4-ton Route Vans also came on 102 in. and 117 in. wheelbases with 7 ft. (1,860 lbs.) and 9.5 ft. (2,210 lbs.) bodies, respectively. They were similar to the regular 1-ton jobs, but had lower GVWs. There was a chassis with front end section (Chassis w/frt.), to which aftermarket bodies could be added, or with Dodge's standard, cab-integral panel body.

1-TON ROUTE-VAN — SERIES B-3-DU/DUF — SIX-CYLINDER: The 1-ton Route Vans also came on 102 in. and 117 in. wheelbases, but had higher GVWs than the 3/4-ton Special models.

1-TON SPECIAL ROUTE-VAN — SERIES B-3-EUL/EULF: These were Job-Rated versions of the 1-1/2-ton stand-up delivery truck. In addition to the 102 and 117 in. wheelbases, a longer 142 in. wheelbase was available to carry a 12-1/2 ft. (2,650 lbs.) body.

I.D. DATA: Serial numbers on plate on dash under hood; also on frame in back of left front spring shackle. Serial numbers were: [B-3-B] (Detroit) 82215001-82256916; (San Leandro) 85308001-85313574. [B-3-C] (Detroit) 83362001-83372821; (San Leandro) 85510001-85511859. [B-3-D] (Detroit) 81435001-81446940; (San Leandro) 86010001-86011065. [B-3-FL] (Detroit) 80392001 and up; (San Leandro) 86514001 and up. [B-3-PW] (Detroit) 83922501-83926471; (San Leandro) 88766501-88766833. [B-3-DU/DUF] (Detroit) 84206501-84207490. [B-3-EU/EUL/EULF] (Detroit) 84001701-84002151. Engine numbers on left side of motor, below cylinder head; on front right side of motor. Starting engine numbers were: [B-3-B] T306-1001. [B-3-C] T308-1001. [B-3-D] T310-1001. [B-3-PW] [T137-1001. [B-3-DU] T164-1001. [B-3-EU] T165-1001.

Model	Body Type	Price	Weight	Prod. Total
Series B-3-B — 1/2-Ton — 108 in. w.b.				
B-3-B	Chassis & Cowl	1017	2475	Note 1
B-3-B	Chassis & Windshield	1062	—	Note 1
B-3-B	Chassis & Cab	1227	2975	Note 1
B-3-B	Pickup 6.5 ft.	1293	3275	Note 1
B-3-B	Panel	1493	3375	Note 1

NOTE 1: Total U.S. calendar year production: (Domestic) 53,563; (Export) 5,429; [Total] 58,992.

Model	Body Type	Price	Weight	Prod. Total
Series B-3-C — 3/4-Ton — 116 in. w.b.				
B-3-C	Chassis & Cowl	1140	2650	Note 2
B-3-C	Chassis & Windshield	1185	—	Note 2
B-3-C	Chassis & Cab	1350	3150	Note 2
B-3-C	Pickup 7.5 ft.	1441	3525	Note 2
B-3-C	Platform 7.5 ft.	1457	3425	Note 2
B-3-C	Stake 7.5 ft.	1515	3700	Note 2

NOTE 2: Total U.S. calendar year production: (Domestic) 15,619; (Government) 11,246; [Total] 26,865.

Model	Body Type	Price	Weight	Prod. Total
Series B-3-D-116 — 1-Ton — 116 in. w.b.				
B-3-D	Chassis & Cowl	1199	2900	Note 3
B-3-D	Chassis & Windshield	1244	—	Note 3
B-3-D	Chassis & Cab	1409	3375	Note 3
B-3-D	Pickup 7.5 ft.	1500	3725	Note 3
B-3-D	Platform 7.5 ft.	1516	3725	Note 3
B-3-D	Stake 7.5 ft.	1574	3905	Note 3
Series B-3-D-126 — 1-Ton — 125.75 in. w.b.				
B-3-D	Chassis & Cowl	1219	2950	Note 3
B-3-D	Chassis & Windshield	1264	—	Note 3
B-3-D	Chassis & Cab	1429	3375	Note 3
B-3-D	Pickup 9 ft.	1530	3800	Note 3
B-3-D	Platform 9 ft.	1548	3825	Note 3
B-3-D	Stake 9 ft.	1619	4055	Note 3
Series B-3-PW Power Wagon — 1-Ton (4x4) — 126 in. w.b.				
B-3-PW	Chassis & Cowl	1875	4075	Note 3
B-3-PW	Chassis & Windshield	1915	—	Note 3
B-3-PW	Chassis & Cab	2065	4675	Note 3
B-3-PW	Pickup 8 ft.	2170	5100	Note 3

NOTE 3: Total U.S. calendar year production, 1-Ton models with 116 and 126 in. wheelbase: (Domestic) 17,489; (Export) 5,947; (Total) 23,436.

Model	Body Type	Price	Weight	Prod. Total
Series B-3-FL-128 — Special 1-Ton — 128 in. w.b.				
B-3-FL	Chassis & Cowl	1365	3400	—
B-3-FL	Chassis & Windshield	1414	—	—
B-3-FL	Chassis & Cab	1596	4025	—
B-3-FL	Platform 9 ft.	1737	4450	—
B-3-FL	Stake 9 ft.	1639	4550	—
Series B-3-FL-152 — Special 1-Ton — 152 in. w.b.				
B-3-FL	Chassis & Cowl	1387	3500	—
B-3-FL	Chassis & Windshield	1436	—	—
B-3-FL	Chassis & Cab	1619	4000	—
B-3-FL	Platform 12 ft.	1788	4525	—
B-3-FL	Stake 12 ft.	1881	4925	—
Series B-3-DUL/DULF-102 — 3/4-Ton Special Route-Van — 102 in. w.b.				
B-3-DUL	Panel Body 7 ft.	1942	2650	—
B-3-DULF	Panel Body 7 ft.	2647	2650	—
Series B-3-DUL/DUFL-117 — 3/4-Ton Special Route-Van — 117 in. w.b.				
B-3-DUL	Panel Body 9.5 ft.	2679	2740	—
B-1DULF	Panel Body 9.5 ft.	2739	2740	—
Series B-3-DU/DUF/EUL/EUFL — 1-Ton Route-Van — 102 in. w.b.				
B-3-DU	Chassis & front	1795	2650	—
B-3-DU	Panel Body 7 ft.	2846	—	—
B-3-DUF	Panel 7 ft.	2450	4510	—
B-3-EUL	Chassis & front	2248	—	—
B-3-EUL	Panel 7 ft.	2826	2995	—
B-3EUFL	Panel 7 ft.	2887	2995	—
Series B-3-DU/DUF/EUL/EUFL — 1-Ton Route-Van — 117 in. w.b.				
B-3-DU	Chassis & front	—	—	
B-3-DU	Panel Body 9.5 ft.	1963	2740	—
B-3-DUF	Panel 9.5 ft.	2535	2740	—
B-3-DUF	Deluxe Panel 9.5 ft.	2690	2740	—
B-3-EUL	Chassis & front	2187	—	—
B-3-EUL	Panel 9.5 ft.	2920	3070	—
B-3EUFL	Panel 9.5 ft.	2981	3070	—

NOTE 4: EUL/EULF are "Special" Job-Rated models.

Model	Body Type	Price	Weight	Prod. Total
Series B-3-EUL/EUFL — 1-Ton Special Route-Van — 142 in. w.b.				
B-3-EUL	Chassis & front 12.5 ft.	—	—	—
B-3-EUL	Panel 12.5 ft.	3063	3215	—
B-3EUFL	Panel 12.5 ft.	3124	3215	—

ENGINE [Series B-3-B/B-3-C]: Inline. L-head. Six-cylinder. Cast iron block. Bore & stroke: 3-1/4 x 4-3/8 in. Displacement: 217.8 cid. Compression ratio: 6.6:1. Brake horsepower: 95 at 3600 rpm. Net horsepower: 25.35. Torque: 172 lbs.-ft. at 1200 rpm. Four main bearings. Solid valve lifters. Carburetor: Carter.

ENGINE [B-3-D/Route Van/Power Wagon]: Inline. L-head. Six-cylinder. Cast iron block. Bore & stroke: 3-1/4 x 4-5/8 in. Displacement: 230.2 cid. Compression ratio: 6.7:1. Brake horsepower: 102 at 3600 rpm. Net horsepower: 25.35. Torque: 184 lbs.-ft. at 1200 rpm. Four main bearings. Solid valve lifters. Carburetor: Stromberg.

ENGINE [B-3-FL]: Inline. L-head. Six-cylinder. Cast iron block. Bore & stroke: 3-7/16 x 4-1/4 in. Displacement: 236.6 cid. Compression ratio: 7.0:1. Brake horsepower: 109 at 3600 rpm. Net horsepower: 28.35. Four main bearings.

CHASSIS (Series B-3-B): Wheelbase: 108 in. Tires: 6.00 x 16 four-ply front and rear; disc wheels with 4.00 drop-center rims. Underslung tire carrier. GVW: 4,850 lbs.

CHASSIS (Series B-3-C): Wheelbase: 116 in. Tires: 7.00 x 15 six-ply front and rear; disc wheels with 5.50 drop-center rims. Underslung tire carrier. GVW: 5,500 lbs.

CHASSIS (Series B-3-D): Wheelbase: 116 and 126 in. Tires: (front 6.00 x 16 six-ply; (rear) 7.00 x 16 six-ply. Disc wheels on 4.50 semi-drop-center rims (front); 5.50 (rear and spare). Underslung tire carrier. GVW: 7,500 lbs.

CHASSIS [Series B-3-FL-128]: Wheelbase: 128 in. Tires: 6.00 x 20 six-ply front, 6.50 x 20 eight-ply rear. GVW: 9,500 lbs. Add $69 for dual rear wheel equipment.

CHASSIS [Series B-3-FL-152]: Wheelbase: 152 in. Tires: 6.00 x 20 six-ply front, 6.50 x 20 eight-ply rear. GVW: 9,500 lbs. Add $69 for dual rear wheel equipment.

CHASSIS [Series B-3-PW-126]: Wheelbase: 126 in. Tires: 7.50 x 16 eight-ply. Four-wheel-drive chassis. GVW: 8,700 lbs.

CHASSIS [Model B-3-DUL-102]: Wheelbase: 102 in. GVW: 6,900 lbs. Tires: 7.00 x 16 six-ply.

CHASSIS [Model B-3-DUL-117]: Wheelbase: 117 in. GVW: 6,900 lbs. Tires: 7.00 x 16 six-ply front and 7.50 x 16 six-ply rear.

CHASSIS [Model B-3-DU-102]: Wheelbase: 102 in. GVW: 7,900 lbs. Tires: 6.50 x 16 six-ply front/7.00 x 16 six-ply rear. Higher GVW with 7.50 x 16 eight-ply front and rear tires.

CHASSIS [Model B-3-DU-117]: Wheelbase: 117 in.; Tires: 6.50 x 16 six-ply front/7.00 x 16 six-ply rear. GVW: 7,900 lbs. (Available with 8.25 x 16 eight-ply tires front and rear).

CHASSIS [Model B-3-EUL-102]: Wheelbase: 102 in. Tires: 7.50 x 16 six-ply front and 8.25 x 16 eight-ply rear. GVW: 8,000 with 8.25 x 16 eight-ply tires front and rear tires; also available 8,700 lbs. with 9.00 x 16 eight-ply front and rear; 9,600 lbs. with 9.00 x 16 ten-ply front and rear.

CHASSIS [Model B-3-EUL-142]: Wheelbase: 142 in. Tires: (front) 7.50 x 16 six-ply; (rear) 8.25 x 16 eight-ply. GVW: 8,500 lbs. with 8.25 x 16 eight-ply front and rear; 9,200 lbs. with 9.00 x 16 eight-ply front and rear; 10,100 lbs. with 9.00 x 16 ten-ply front and rear.

TECHNICAL: [Series B-3-B/B-3-C]. Selective sliding gear transmission. Speeds: 3F/1R; optional 4F/1R with power-take-off. Floor shift control. Single-plate dry-disc clutch, 10 in. diameter (11 in. optional). Semi-floating rear axle. Rear axle ratio: 4.1:1 (4.78:1 optional). Hotchkiss drive with hypoid drive gears. Hydraulic four-wheel brakes. Parking brake: Band and drum type, mounted at rear of transmission. Worm and roller steering. Shock absorbers front and rear.

TECHNICAL: [Series B-3-D/B-3-FL]. Speeds: 3F/1R standard; 4F/1R optional. Rear axle ratios: 3.9 or 4.89:1. All other specs same as 1/2-ton.

TECHNICAL: [Route-Van] Speeds: 3F/1R; (4F/1R optional). [EU/EUL Route-Van] 4F/1R only. Floor shift control. Single-plate dry-disc clutch: [DU] 10-inch; [EU] 11 in. Full-floating single-speed rear drive axle with hypoid gears. Frame-mounted differential. Open-type telescoping driveshafts to wheels with two cross-and-trunnion "U" joints on each side. Hotchkiss drive. Rear axle ratios: [DU] 4.89:1; [EU] 5.83:1. Semi-elliptic springs front and rear. Reverse Elliott I-beam front axle. Steel I-beam rear supporting axle. Worm and roller steering. (Note: Other axle ratios supplied with optional heavy-duty tires).

OPTIONS: [B-3-B/B-3-C/B-3-D, installed at factory] Rear bumper for pickup ($8). Deluxe cab equipment consisting of vent wings in cab door and rear quarter windows ($30). Custom cab equipment: Includes vent wings in cab door and rear quarter windows, deluxe seat cushion and back, dome light, left armrest, dual interior sun visors and dual electric windshield wipers ($56). Deluxe panel equipment: Includes vent wings in cab door windows, left armrest, dual sun visors, dual electric wipers ($30). Bumper guards ($3.50 pair). Chrome grab handles ($8). Rearview mirror, long-arm adjustable, left side ($2); same for right side ($3). Stainless steel grille panel moldings ($10). Dual electric horns ($12). Auxiliary seat, stationary type, panel truck only ($30). Seat cushion with special air foam padding, cab models only ($10). Dual electric windshield wipers ($8). Door ventilating wings ($15). Auxiliary taillamp for panel ($3); for other models ($6). Paint: Pickup body and rear fenders painted to match cab, Dodge Truck red or Armour yellow only, ($5). Oil-bath air cleaner, one-quart ($1.75). Ashtray ($2). Sealed oil filter ($5). Clutch, 11-inch diameter, replacing standard ($7.50). Battery: 120 amp. hour ($5). Fluid-Drive ($38). Electric fuel pump ($13). Engine governor ($7). Four-speed transmission replacing standard three-speed ($50). Rear shocks for 1-tons ($11). Dome light ($5).

OPTIONS: [Route-Van, installed at factory] Rear bumper with step-plate. Radiator grille (bumper) guards, set of three. Rearview mirror (left or right). Ventilating wings in driver compartment side windows. Windshield header roof cap. Jackknife type side doors, left and right. Jackknife type rear doors. Interior lining and insulation equipment: Complete roof steel liner, 1/2 in. roof insulation, steel side liners above beltline, and dome light in driver's section. Side rub rails. Driver's seat assembly, stationary type, with standard seat cushion or air foam padding. Dual auxiliary tailamps. Tire carrier inside body above wheelhouse, right or left side. Undercoating. Paint: Body and fenders Ecuador blue, Judson green, Charlotte ivory, or black. Wheels black; all body sizes (standard paint was primer). Windshield wiper: Vacuum, right side; electric, left and right side. Oil-bath air cleaner (one-quart capacity). Oil filter (replaceable element type). Battery: 120 ampere-hour capacity. Generator: 280 watt, 35-ampere, for high charging at low engine speeds. Governor (engine velocity type). Shock absorbers, front and rear. Tool kit (wheel wrench, jack and handle in cloth bag). Four-speed transmission with 10-inch clutch, Fluid-Drive and auxiliary parking brake.

OPTIONS: [Power Wagon, installed at factory] Deluxe cab equipment: Includes vent wings in cab door windows, dome light, left armrest, dual interior sun visors and dual electric windshield wipers ($40). Rearview mirror, long-arm adjustable, left side ($2); right side ($3). Taillamp, right side ($6). Generator: 256 watt, 32 ampere-hour ($18.50). Governor, mechanical, for use with rear driveshaft assembly ($63). Oil filter, replaceable element type ($7). Radiator overflow tank ($6). Shock absorbers, telescopic type, rear ($31). Draw bar ($20). Pintle hook ($10). Power-take-off assembly ($65). Pulley drive — pulley unit only ($73). Rear driveshaft assembly only ($72). Tow hooks, front only ($5.00/pair). Winch assembly: Front winch and driveshaft ($200).

HISTORICAL: Introduced: December 1950. Calendar year registrations: 106,600. Calendar year production: 169,088 (U.S. only). Model year production for 1951-1952 combined: (Series B-3-B) 118,094; (Series B-3-C) 27,194; (Series B-3-D-116) 9,085; (Series B-3-D-126) 25,704. [Total] 192,886. Truck production rose 38.2 percent. Of the total, 14,081 built in San Leandro, California; 20,876 in Canada. On Jan. 15, 1951, Dodge began building military trucks for the Koren War. A new truck engine plant was completed at Trenton, Michigan, in November. A six-week labor strike at Midland Steel Co., caused a Dodge production loss of 7,500 units, due to a shortage of frames. Six of nine American Truck Assoc. (ATA) rodeo winners drove Dodges in the 1951 competition.

1952 DODGE

1/2-TON — SERIES B-3-B — SIX-CYLINDER: The entire B-3 series was carried over without change in appearance, model availability, equipment, or mechanical details. The only exterior clue to model year was that the 1951 models used a chrome-finished medallion in the center of the grille, while the 1952 medallion was painted argent silver. Standard colors were: Armour yellow, Dodge Truck red or dark green, deep blue, or black. Gray was discontinued. Pickup bodies (including rear fenders) were black, regardless of cab color. Only for additional cost were pickup bodies and rear fenders painted cab color. Running

boards and bumpers were always black. Wheels were Dodge Truck cream (black optional). The 1/2-tons retained a 108 in. wheelbase. The pickup had the 6-1/2 ft. bed. A panel was available only in this line.

1952 Dodge 1-Ton Stake (D. Sagvold)

3/4-TON — SERIES B-3-C — SIX-CYLINDER: The 3/4-ton had the same styling and engine, an eight-inch longer wheelbase, and one-foot longer pickup and platform/stake bodies. The 7-1/2 ft. pickup was officially called an express.

1-TON — SERIES B-3-D — SIX-CYLINDER: The 1-ton offered 116 in. and 126 in. wheelbases. The B-3-D-116 pickup and platform/stake had the same 7-1/2 ft. bodies as 3/4-tons. The B-3-D-126 had 1-1/2 ft. longer truck bodies on all models. A larger six was standard in 1-tons.

1-TON — POWER-WAGON SERIES B-3-PW — SIX-CYLINDER: The Power Wagon was unchanged. It had the 126 in. wheelbase and four-wheel drive. The pickup had an 8 ft. load bed. Deluxe cab equipment was featured.

1-TON SPECIAL — SERIES B-3-FL — SIX-CYLINDER: As part of its "Job-Rated" marketing program, Dodge offered lighter-duty (L series code suffix) editions of certain models that were better-suited to some user applications. These "Special" FLs came on two wheelbases, both longer than the B-3-Ds offered. They looked identical to the 1-1/2 tons. However, the axles, springs, tire sizes and tire ply ratings were changed to lower the GVW into the 1-ton range. There was no express. The platform/stake models were 9 ft. and 12 ft. long, respectively. Dual rear wheel equipment was optional.

3/4-TON SPECIAL ROUTE-VAN — SERIES B-3-DUL/DULF — SIX-CYLINDER: Route-Van models continued unchanged. The 3/4-ton Job-Rated Route Vans came on 102 in. and 117 in. wheelbases with 7 ft. (1,860 lbs.) and 9.5 ft. (2,210 lbs.) bodies, respectively. They were similar to the regular 1-ton jobs, but had lower GVWs. There was a chassis with front end section for aftermarket bodies and Dodge's standard, cab-integral panel body.

1-TON ROUTE-VAN — SERIES B-3-DU/DUF — SIX-CYLINDER: The 1-ton Route Vans also came on 102 in. and 117 in. wheelbases, but had higher GVWs than the 3/4-ton Special models that were based on them.

1-TON SPECIAL ROUTE-VAN — SERIES B-3-EUL/EULF — These were Job-Rated versions of the 1-1/2-ton stand-up delivery truck. In addition to the 102 and 117 in. wheelbases, a longer 142 in. wheelbase was available to carry a 12-1/2 ft. (2,650 lbs.) body.

1952 Dodge 1/2-Ton High Side Pickup (OCW)

I.D. DATA: Serial numbers on plate on left door hinge. Starting and ending numbers were: [B-3-B] (Detroit) 83373001-83388000; (San Leandro) 85512001-85515000. [B-3-C] (Detroit) 81447301-81463000; (San Leandro) 86011201-86013000. [B-3-D] (Detroit) 81447301-81463000; (San Leandro) 86011201-86013000. [B-3-PW] (Detroit) 83926501-83934000; (San Leandro) 88766901-88767500. [B-3-FL] (Detroit) 80392001A-80398301A; (San Leandro) 86514001A-86514601A. [B-3-DU] (Detroit) 84207601-84208500. [B-3-EU] (Detroit) 84002201-84003000. Engine numbers: [B-3-B] T306-1001. [B-3-C] T308-1001. [B-3-D] T310-1001. [B-3-PW] T137-1001. [B-3-DU/EU] T165-1001.

Model	Body Type	Price	Weight	Prod. Total
Series B-3-B — 1/2-Ton 108 in. w.b.				
B-3-B	Chassis & Cowl	1125	2475	Note 1
B-3-B	Chassis & Cab	1365	2975	Note 1
B-3-B	Pickup 6.5 ft.	1440	3275	Note 1
B-3-B	Panel	1650	3375	Note 1

NOTE 1: Calendar year production of 1/2-ton trucks, U.S. only: (Domestic) 48,497; (Export) 3,675; [Total] 52,172.

Model	Body Type	Price	Weight	Prod. Total
Series B-3-C — 3/4-Ton — 116 in. w.b.				
B-3-C	Chassis & Cowl	1235	2650	Note 2
B-3-C	Chassis & Cab	1473	3150	Note 2
B-3-C	Pickup 7.5 ft.	1578	3525	Note 2
B-3-C	Platform 7.5 ft.	1585	3475	Note 2
B-3-C	Stake 7.5 ft.	1646	3700	Note 2

NOTE 2: Calendar year production of 3/4-ton trucks, U.S. only: (Domestic) 14,420; (Government) 26,143; [Total] 40,563.

Model	Body Type	Price	Weight	Prod. Total
Series B-3-D — 1-Ton — 116 in. w.b.				
B-3-D	Chassis & Cowl	1293	2900	Note 3
B-3-D	Chassis & Cab	1531	3375	Note 3
B-3-D	Pickup 7.5 ft.	1636	3725	Note 3
B-3-D	Platform 7.5 ft.	1642	3725	Note 3
B-3-D	Stake 7.5 ft.	1702	3905	Note 3
Series B-3-D — 1-Ton — 126 in. w.b.				
B-3-D	Chassis & Cowl	1315	2950	Note 3
B-3-D	Chassis & Cab	1555	3375	Note 3
B-3-D	Pickup 9 ft.	1669	3800	Note 3
B-3-D	Platform 9 ft.	1678	3825	Note 3
B-3-D	Stake 9 ft.	1755	4055	Note 3
Series B-3-PW — Power Wagon — 1-Ton — 126 in. w.b.				
B-3-PW	Chassis & Cab	2232	4675	Note 3
B-3-PW	Pickup 8 ft.	2353	5100	Note 3

NOTE 3: Calendar year production of 1-ton trucks (including Power Wagon and Route-Van), U.S. only: (Domestic) 14,282; (Export) 5,997; [Total] 20,279.

Model	Body Type	Price	Weight	Prod. Total
Series B-3-FL-128 — Special 1-Ton — 128 in. w.b.				
B-3-FL	Chassis & Cowl	1499	3400	—
B-3-FL	Chassis & Cab	1741	4025	—
B-3-FL	Platform 9 ft.	1886	4450	—
B-3-FL	Stake 9 ft.	1965	4550	—
Series B-3-FL-152 — Special 1-Ton — 152 in. w.b.				
B-3-FL	Chassis & Cowl	1521	3500	—
B-3-FL	Chassis & Cab	1763	4000	—
B-3-FL	Platform 12 ft.	1939	4525	—
B-3-FL	Stake 12 ft.	2036	4925	—
Series B-3-DUL-102 — 3/4-Ton Special Route-Van — 102 in. w.b.				
B-3-DUL	Chassis & front	2021	2650	—
B-3DULF	Panel Body 7 ft.	2692	4510	—
Series B-3-DUL-117 — 3/4-Ton Special Route-Van — 117 in. w.b.				
B-3-DUL	Chassis & front	2043	2740	—
B-1DULF	Panel Body 9.5 ft.	2768	4950	—
Series B-3-DU-102 — 1-Ton Route-Van — 102 in. w.b.				
B-3-DU	Chassis & front	1795	2743	—
B-3-DU	Panel Body 7 ft.	2846	4510	—
Series B-3-DU-117 — 1-Ton Route-Van — 117 in. w.b.				
B-3-DU	Chassis & front	—	2740	—
B-3-DU	Panel Body 9.5 ft.	2863	4950	—

NOTE 4: EUL/EULF are "Special" Job-Rated models.

Model	Body Type	Price	Weight	Prod. Total
Series B-3-EUL-142 — 1-Ton Special Route-Van — 142 in. w.b.				
B-3-EUL	Chassis & front 12.5 ft.	2329	3120	—
B-3-EUL	Panel 12.5 ft.	3186	5815	—

ENGINE [Series B-3-B/B-3-C]: Inline. L-head. Six-cylinder. Cast iron block. Bore & stroke: 3-1/4 x 4-3/8 in. Displacement: 217.8 cid. Compression ratio: 6.6:1. Brake horsepower: 95 at 3600 rpm. Net horsepower: 25.35. Torque: 172 lbs.-ft. at 1200 rpm. Four main bearings. Solid valve lifters. Carburetor: Carter.

ENGINE [B-3-D/Route Van/Power Wagon]: Inline. L-head. Six-cylinder. Cast iron block. Bore & stroke: 3-1/4 x 4-5/8 in. Displacement: 230.2 cid. Compression ratio: 6.7:1. Brake horsepower: 102 at 3600 rpm. Net horsepower: 25.35. Torque: 184 lbs.-ft. at 1200 rpm. Four main bearings. Solid valve lifters. Carburetor: Stromberg.

ENGINE [B-3-FL]: Inline. L-head. Six-cylinder. Cast iron block. Bore & stroke: 3-7/16 x 4-1/4 in. Displacement: 236.6 cid. Compression ratio: 7.0:1. Brake horsepower: 109 at 3600 rpm. Net horsepower: 28.35. Four main bearings.

CHASSIS (Series B-3-B): Wheelbase: 108 in. Tires: 6.00 x 16 four-ply front and rear; disc wheels with 4.00 drop-center rims. Underslung tire carrier. GVW: 4,850 lbs.

CHASSIS (Series B-3-C): Wheelbase: 116 in. Tires: 7.00 x 15 six-ply front and rear; disc wheels with 5.50 drop-center rims. Underslung tire carrier. GVW: 5,500 lbs.

CHASSIS (Series B-3-D): Wheelbase: 116 and 126 in. Tires: (front 6.00 x 16 six-ply; (rear) 7.00 x 16 six-ply. Disc wheels on 4.50 semi-drop-center rims (front); 5.50 (rear and spare). Underslung tire carrier. GVW: 7,500 lbs.

CHASSIS [Series B-3-FL-128]: Wheelbase: 128 in. Tires: 6.00 x 20 six-ply front, 6.50 x 20 eight-ply rear. GVW: 9,500 lbs. Add $69 for dual rear wheel equipment.

CHASSIS [Series B-3-FL-152]: Wheelbase: 152 in. Tires: 6.00 x 20 six-ply front, 6.50 x 20 eight-ply rear. GVW: 9,500 lbs. Add $69 for dual rear wheel equipment.

CHASSIS [Series B-3-PW-126]: Wheelbase: 126 in. Tires: 7.50 x 16 eight-ply. Four-wheel-drive chassis. GVW: 8,700 lbs.

CHASSIS [Model B-3-DUL-102]: Wheelbase: 102 in. GVW: 6,900 lbs. Tires: 7.00 x 16 six-ply.

CHASSIS [Model B-3-DUL-117]: Wheelbase: 117 in. GVW: 6,900 lbs. Tires: 7.00 x 16 six-ply front and 7.50 x 16 six-ply rear.

CHASSIS [Model B-3-DU-102]: Wheelbase: 102 in. GVW: 7,900 lbs. Tires: 6.50 x 16 six-ply front/7.00 x 16 six-ply rear. Higher GVW with 7.50 x 16 eight-ply front and rear tires.

CHASSIS [Model B-3-DU-117]: Wheelbase: 117 in.; Tires: 6.50 x 16 six-ply front/7.00 x 16 six-ply rear. GVW: 7,900 lbs. (Available with 8.25 x 16 eight-ply tires front and rear).

CHASSIS [Model B-3-EUL-102]: Wheelbase: 102 in. Tires: 7.50 x 16 six-ply front and 8.25 x 16 eight-ply rear. GVW: 8,000 with 8.25 x 16 eight-ply tires front and rear tires; also available 8,700 lbs. with 9.00 x 16 eight-ply front and rear; 9,600 lbs. with 9.00 x 16 ten-ply front and rear.

CHASSIS [Model B-3-EUL-142]: Wheelbase: 142 in. Tires: (front) 7.50 x 16 six-ply; (rear) 8.25 x 16 eight-ply. GVW: 8,500 lbs. with 8.25 x 16 eight-ply front and rear; 9,200 lbs. with 9.00 x 16 eight-ply front and rear; 10,100 lbs. with 9.00 x 16 ten-ply front and rear.

TECHNICAL: [Series B-3-B/B-3-C]. Selective sliding gear transmission. Speeds: 3F/1R; optional 4F/1R with power-take-off. Floor shift control. Single-plate dry-disc clutch, 10 in. diameter (11 in. optional). Semi-floating rear axle. Rear axle ratio: 4.1:1 (4.78:1 optional). Hotchkiss drive with hypoid drive gears. Hydraulic four-wheel brakes. Parking brake: Band and drum type, mounted at rear of transmission. Worm and roller steering. Shock absorbers front and rear.

TECHNICAL: [Series B-3-D/B-3-FL]. Speeds: 3F/1R standard; 4F/1R optional. Rear axle ratios: 3.9 or 4.89:1. All other specs same as 1/2-ton.

TECHNICAL: [Route-Van] Speeds: 3F/1R; (4F/1R optional). [EU/EUL Route-Van] 4F/1R only. Floor shift control. Single-plate dry-disc clutch; [DU] 10-inch; [EU] 11 in. Full-floating single-speed rear drive axle with hypoid gears. Frame-mounted differential. Open-type telescoping driveshafts to wheels with two cross-and-trunnion "U" joints on each side. Hotchkiss drive. Rear axle ratios: [DU] 4.89:1; [EU] 5.83:1. Semi-elliptic springs front and rear. Reverse Elliott I-beam front axle. Steel I-beam rear supporting axle. Worm and roller steering. (Note: Other axle ratios supplied with optional heavy-duty tires).

OPTIONS: Rear bumper ($8.25). Deluxe cab equipment ($30.59). Custom cab equipment ($69.36). Deluxe panel equipment ($40.73). High side pickup ($8.27). Bumper guards ($4.44). Long-arm adjustable mirror, left ($2.10); right ($3.23). Dual electric horns ($12.42). Auxiliary seat for panel ($31.36). Air foam seat cushion ($9.52). Pickup body and rear fenders painted to match cab ($6.44). Auxiliary taillamp ($6.63). Ashtray ($1.53). Oil-bath air cleaner, one-quart ($1.47). Oil filter ($9.27). Electric fuel pump ($13.96). High-charging generator ($10.38). Governor ($7.17). Fluid Drive ($43.14). Four-speed transmission ($61.01).

1952 Dodge B-3-PW Power Wagon 8 ft. Express (J.C. Lowe)

HISTORICAL: Introduced: October 15, 1951. Calendar year registrations: 102,129. Calendar year production: 127,716. See 1951 for combined model year production figures. Dodge produced a full line of trucks from 1/2- to 4-ton capacity, including a six-wheeler and 26,143 3/4-ton 4x4 trucks for the Army. Due to the Korean War, the government, through the National Production Authority, limited car and truck output to ensure availability of vital war equipment. The NPA assigned a quota of civilian trucks to each manufacturer by weight class. Dodge's NPA percentages were a bit over 13 percent of total industry output for each category. In spite of the NPA, U.S. truck production was only 14 percent less than 1951. Dodge's sales and production figures fell modestly. During 1952, Dodge created two new executive posts: Sales manager for cars and sales manager for trucks.

1953 DODGE

1953 Dodge 1/2-Ton Pickup (DB)

1/2-TON — SERIES B-4-B — SIX-CYLINDER: Extensive changes were made for this final year of the B series. A new Dodge nameplate on the front featured modern, wider-spaced letters connected by a red stripe. Chrome headlight rims replaced the black enameled ones. Parking light rims were also chrome. Striping was omitted from the grille molding. Pickup rear fenders were redesigned to a modern, streamlined look. These fenders are used on Dodge pickups up to 1985. Hubcaps, changed for the first time since 1948, were now stainless steel with a raised circular flange, inset with red Dodge letters. Dual taillamps were now standard on the panel model. Inside the cab, seat trim fabrics sported a new maroon/gray color combination. All accessories including armrests, sun visors and door handle escutcheons were color-matched. For the first time in the B series, the Dodge nameplate stood on the instrument panel. The 108 in. wheelbase 1/2-ton pickup with the short (6-1/2 ft.) bed carried a low side box. An industry first was the addition of a new 1/2-ton pickup with 90 in. (7-1/2 ft.) bed. It was for customers who needed to haul light, but bulky loads. Built on a 116 in. wheelbase chassis like the 3/4-ton pickups, this model had

the high side box. The panel was offered only on the smaller wheelbase chassis. Dodge offered an industry first with its automatic transmission. It was optional on all light-duty models. This Truck-O-Matic transmission was similar in operation to the automatic used in DeSoto and Chrysler cars. This was also the first year Dodge Truck Div. offered tinted windows. Engines were unchanged. Standard equipment included a front bumper, front and rear shocks, oil-bath air cleaner, dual vacuum windshield wipers, vent wings in cab doors, left side sun visor and a dome light (Town Panel only). Standard colors were: Armour yellow, Dodge Truck red or dark green, deep blue, or black. Gray was discontinued. Pickup bodies (including rear fenders) were black, regardless of cab color. Only for additional cost were pickup bodies and rear fenders painted cab color. Runningboards and bumpers were always black. Wheels were Dodge Truck cream (black optional).

3/4-TON — SERIES B-4-C — SIX-CYLINDER: The 3/4-ton had the same styling and engine, an 8-in. longer wheelbase, and one-foot longer pickup and platform/stake bodies. The 7-1/2 ft. pickup was officially called an Express.

1-TON — SERIES B-4-D — SIX-CYLINDER: The 1-ton offered 116 in. and 126 in. wheelbases. The B-4-D-116 pickup and platform/stake had the same 7-1/2 ft. bodies as 3/4-tons. The B-4-D-126 had 1-1/2 ft. longer truck bodies on all models. A larger six was standard in 1-tons.

1-TON — POWER-WAGON SERIES B-4-PW — SIX-CYLINDER: The Power Wagon was unchanged. It had the 126 in. wheelbase and four-wheel drive. The pickup had an 8 ft. load bed. Deluxe cab equipment was featured. A boost in power was realized by raising compression from 6.7:1 to 7.0:1 and use of a new carburetor. Horsepower and torque ratings were increased.

1-TON SPECIAL — SERIES B-4-FL — SIX-CYLINDER: As part of its "Job-Rated" marketing program, Dodge offered lighter-duty (L series code suffix) editions of certain models that were better-suited to some user applications. These "Special" FLs came on two wheelbases, both longer than the B-4-D offered. They looked identical to 1-1/2 tons. However, the axles, springs, tire sizes and tire ply ratings were changed to lower the GVW into the 1-ton range. There was no express. The platform/stake models were 9 ft. and 12 ft. long, respectively. Dual rear wheel equipment was optional. Dual-wheeled 1-ton pickups kept the previous rear fenders.

3/4-TON SPECIAL ROUTE-VAN — SERIES B-4-DUL/DULF — SIX-CYLINDER: Route-Van models continued unchanged. The 3/4-ton Job-Rated Route Vans came on 102 in. and 117 in. wheelbases with 7 ft. (1,860 lbs.) and 9.5 ft. (2,210 lbs.) bodies, respectively. They were similar to the regular 1-ton jobs, but had lower GVWs. There was a chassis with front end section for aftermarket bodies and Dodge's standard, cab-integral panel body.

1-TON ROUTE-VAN — SERIES B-4-DU/DUF — SIX-CYLINDER: The 1-ton Route Vans also came on 102 in. and 117 in. wheelbases, but had higher GVWs than the 3/4-ton Special models that were based on them.

1-TON SPECIAL ROUTE-VAN — SERIES B-4-EUL — These were Job-Rated versions of the 1-1/2-ton Stand-up Delivery Truck. In addition to the 102 and 117 in. wheelbases, a longer 142 in. wheelbase was available to carry a 12-1/2 ft. (2,650 lbs.) body.

I.D. DATA: Serial numbers on plate on left door hinge. [B-4-B] (Detroit) 82302001-82335036; (San Leandro) 85322001-85327718. [B-4-C] (Detroit) 83388001-83396360; (San Leandro) 85515001-85516395. [B-4-D] (Detroit) 81463001-81470822; (San Leandro) 86013001-86013850. [B-4-PW] (Detroit) 83934001-83937729; (San Leandro) 88767501-88767693. [B-4-FL] (Detroit) 80404001 up. (San Leandro) 86515501 up. [B-4-DU] (Detroit) 84208501-84208886. [B-4-EU] (Detroit) 84003001-84003150. Engine numbers: [B-4-B] T306-1001 up. [B-4-C] T308-1001 up. [B-4-D] T310-1001 up. [B-4-PW] T137-1001 up. [B-4-DU] T164-1001 up. [B-4-EU] T165-1001 up.

NOTE: All new and unlicensed (1952) B-3 series trucks bearing high serial numbers that were delivered to retail purchases after Oct. 15, 1952 were considered 1953 models for registration purposes. The starting serial numbers for these trucks were: [B-3-B] (Detroit) 82257601; (San Leandro) 85313701. [B-3-C] (Detroit) 83373001; (San Leandro) 85512001. [B-3-D] (Detroit) 81447301; (San Leandro) 86011201. [B-3-DU/DUF/DUFL/DUL] (Detroit) 84207601. [B-3-EU/EUL] (Detroit) 84022201. [B-3-PW] (Detroit) 83926501; (San Leandro) 88766901. [B-3-FL] (Detroit) 80398301; (San Leandro) 86514601.

Model	Body Type	Price	Weight	Prod. Total
Series B-4-B — 1/2-Ton — 108 in. w.b.				
B-4-B	Chassis & Cowl	1028	2425	Note 1
B-4-B	Chassis & Cab	1265	2975	Note 1
B-4-B	Pickup 6.5 ft.	1344	3275	Note 1
B-4-B	Panel	1541	3375	Note 1
Series B-4-B — 1/2-Ton — 116 in. w.b.				
B-4-B	Chassis & Cowl	1043	2650	Note 1
B-4-B	Chassis & Cab	1280	3150	Note 1
B-4-B	Pickup 7.5 ft.	1379	3525	Note 1

NOTE 1: Calendar year production of 1/2-ton trucks, U.S. only: (Domestic) 32,506; (Export) 3,903; [Total] 36,409.

Model	Body Type	Price	Weight	Prod. Total
Series B-4-C — 3/4-Ton — 116 in. w.b.				
B-4-C	Chassis & Cowl	1119	2650	Note 2
B-4-C	Chassis & Cab	1358	3150	Note 2
B-4-C	Pickup 7.5 ft.	1471	3525	Note 2
B-4-C	Platform	1469	3475	Note 2
B-4-C	Stake	1528	3200	Note 2

NOTE 2: Calendar year production of 3/4-ton trucks, U.S. only: (Domestic) 9,702; (Export) 15; (Government) 20,207; [Total] 29,924.

Model	Body Type	Price	Weight	Prod. Total
Series B-4-D — 1-Ton — 116 in. w.b.				
B-4-D	Chassis & Cowl	1182	2900	Note 3
B-4-D	Chassis & Cab	1417	3375	Note 3
B-4-D	Pickup 7.5 ft.	1536	3725	Note 3
B-4-D	Platform 7.5 ft.	1527	3725	Note 3
B-4-D	Stake 7.5 ft.	1586	3905	Note 3
Series B-4-D — 1-Ton — 126 in. w.b.				
B-4-D	Chassis & Cowl	1204	2950	Note 3
B-4-D	Chassis & Cab	1441	3375	Note 3
B-4-D	Pickup 9 ft.	1568	3800	Note 3
B-4-D	Platform 9 ft.	1562	3825	Note 3
B-4-D	Stake	1638	4055	Note 3

NOTE 3: Calendar year production of 1-ton models (including Power Wagon and Route-Van), U.S. only: (Domestic) 8,231; (Export) 4,921; [Total] 13,152.

Model	Body Type	Price	Weight	Prod. Total
Series B-4-PW Power-Wagon — 1-Ton — 126 in. w.b.				
Series B-4-FL-128 — Special 1-Ton — 128 in. w.b.				
B-4-FL	Chassis & Cowl	1403	3575	—
B-4-FL	Chassis & Cab	1645	—	—
B-4-FL	Platform 9 ft.	1790	—	—
B-4-FL	Stake 9 ft.	1869	—	—

Standard Catalog of Light-Duty Trucks

Series B-4-FL-152 — Special 1-Ton — 152 in. w.b.				
B-4-FL	Chassis & Cowl	1425	3675	—
B-4-FL	Chassis & Cab	1667	—	—
B-4-FL	Platform 12 ft.	1843	—	—
B-4-FL	Stake 12 ft.	1940	—	—

Series B-4-PW Power-Wagon — 1-Ton — 126 in. w.b.				
B-4-PW	Chassis & Cab	2190	3800	Note 4
B-4-PW	Pickup 8 ft.	2307	—	Note 4

NOTE 4: Model year production of Power Wagons: (Domestic) 1,215; (Export) 2,781; [Total] 3,996.

Series B-4-DUL-102 — 3/4-Ton Special Route-Van — 102 in. w.b.				
B-4-DUL	Chassis & front	2021	2665	—
B-3DULF	Panel Body 7 ft.	2692	4625	—

Series B-4-DUL-117 — 3/4-Ton Special Route-Van — 117 in. w.b.				
B-4-DUL	Chassis & front	2043	2665	—
B-1DULF	Panel Body 9.5 ft.	2788	4900	—

Series B-4-DU-102 — 1-Ton Route-Van — 102 in. w.b.				
B-4-DU	Chassis & front	—	—	—
B-4-DU	Panel Body 7 ft.	—	—	—

Series B-4-DU-117 — 1-Ton Route-Van — 117 in. w.b.				
B-4-DU	Chassis & front	—	—	—
B-4-DU	Panel Body 9.5 ft.	—	—	—

Series B-4-EUL-142 — 1-Ton Special Route-Van — 142 in. w.b.				
B-4-EUL	Chassis & front 12.5 ft.	2339	3120	—
B-4-EUL	Panel 12.5 ft.	3186	5850	—

1953 Dodge 3/4-Ton 7-1/2 ft. Pickup (R.L. Miracle)

ENGINE (Series B-4-B, B-4-C): Inline. L-head. Six-cylinder. Cast iron block. Bore & stroke: 3-1/4 x 4-3/8 in. Displacement: 217.8 cid. Compression ratio: 7.1:1. Brake horsepower: 100 at 3600 rpm. Net horsepower: 25.35. Torque: 177 lbs.-ft. at 1600 rpm. Four main bearings. Solid valve lifters.

ENGINE (Series B-4-D): Inline. L-head. Six-cylinder. Cast iron block. Bore & stroke: 3-1/4 x 4-5/8 in. Displacement: 230.2 cid. Compression ratio: 7.0:1. Brake horsepower: 103 at 3600 rpm. Net horsepower: 25.35. Torque: 190 lbs.-ft. at 1200 rpm. Four main bearings. Solid valve lifters.

ENGINE (Series B-4-PW): Inline. L-head. Six-cylinder. Cast iron block. Bore & stroke: 3-1/4 x 4-5/8 in. Displacement: 230.2 cid. Compression ratio: 7.0:1. Brake horsepower: 99 at 3600 rpm. Net horsepower: 25.35. Torque: 190 lbs.-ft. at 1200 rpm. Four main bearings. Solid valve lifters.

ENGINE [B-3-FL]: Inline. L-head. Six-cylinder. Cast iron block. Bore & stroke: 3-7/16 x 4-1/4 in. Displacement: 236.6 cid. Compression ratio: 7.0:1. Brake horsepower: 109 at 3600 rpm. Net horsepower: 28.35. Four main bearings.

CHASSIS (Series B-4-B): Wheelbase: 108 in. or 116 in. Tires: 6.00 x 16 four-ply. GVW: 4900 lbs.

CHASSIS (Series B-4-C): Wheelbase: 116 in. Tires: 7.00 x 15 six-ply. GVW: 5,800 lbs.

CHASSIS (Series B-4-D): Wheelbase: 116 in. or 126 in. Tires: (front) 6.00 x 16 six-ply; (rear) 7.00 x 16 six-ply. GVW: 8000 lbs.

CHASSIS [Series B-4-FL-128]: Wheelbase: 128 in. Tires: 6.00 x 20 six-ply front, 6.50 x 20 eight-ply rear. GVW: 9,500 lbs. Add $69 for dual rear wheel equipment.

CHASSIS [Series B-4-FL-152]: Wheelbase: 152 in. Tires: 6.00 x 20 six-ply front, 6.50 x 20 eight-ply rear. GVW: 9,500 lbs. Add $69 for dual rear wheel equipment.

CHASSIS [Series B-4-PW-126]: Wheelbase: 126 in. Tires: 7.50 x 16 eight-ply. Four-wheel-drive chassis. GVW: 8,700 lbs.

CHASSIS [Model B-4-DUL-102]: Wheelbase: 102 in. GVW: 6,900 lbs. Tires: 7.00 x 16 six-ply.

CHASSIS [Model B-4-DUL-117]: Wheelbase: 117 in. GVW: 6,900 lbs. Tires: 7.00 x 16 six-ply front and 7.00 x 16 six-ply rear.

CHASSIS [Model B-4-DU-102]: Wheelbase: 102 in. GVW: 7,900 lbs. Tires: 6.50 x 16 six-ply front/7.00 x 16 six-ply rear. Higher GVW with 7.50 x 16 eight-ply front and rear tires.

CHASSIS [Model B-4-DU-117]: Wheelbase: 117 in.; Tires: 6.50 x 16 six-ply front/7.00 x 16 six-ply rear. GVW: 7,900 lbs. (Available with 8.25 x 16 eight-ply tires front and rear).

CHASSIS [Model B-4-EUL-102]: Wheelbase: 102 in. Tires: 7.50 x 16 six-ply front and 8.25 x 16 eight-ply rear. GVW: 8,000 with 8.25 x 16 eight-ply tires front and rear tires; also available 8,700 lbs. with 8.25 x 16 eight-ply front and rear; 9,600 lbs. with 9.00 x 16 ten-ply front and rear.

CHASSIS [Model B-4-EUL-142]: Wheelbase: 142 in. Tires: (front) 7.50 x 16 six-ply; (rear) 8.25 x 16 eight-ply. GVW: 8,500 lbs. with 8.25 x 16 eight-ply front and rear; 9,200 lbs. with 9.00 x 16 eight-ply front and rear; 10,100 lbs. with 9.00 x 16 ten-ply front and rear.

TECHNICAL: [Series B-4-B/B-4-C]. Selective sliding gear transmission. Speeds: 3F/1R; optional 4F/1R with power-take-off. Floor shift control. Single-plate dry-disc clutch, 10 in. diameter (11 in. optional). Semi-floating rear axle. Rear axle ratio: 4.1:1 (4.78:1 optional). Hotchkiss drive with hypoid drive gears. Hydraulic four-wheel brakes. Parking brake: Band and drum type, mounted at rear of transmission. Worm and roller steering. Shock absorbers front and rear.

TECHNICAL: [Series B-4-D/B-4-FL]. Speeds: 3F/1R standard; 4F/1R optional. Rear axle ratios: 3.9 or 4.89:1. All other specs same as 1/2-ton.

TECHNICAL: [Route-Van] Speeds: 3F/1R; (4F/1R optional). [EU/EUL Route-Van] 4F/1R only. Floor shift control. Single-plate dry-disc clutch: [DU] 10-inch; [EU] 11 in. Full-floating single-speed rear drive axle with hypoid gears. Frame-mounted differential. Open-type telescoping driveshafts to wheels with two cross-and-trunnion "U" joints on each side. Hotchkiss drive. Rear axle ratios: [DU] 4.89:1; [EU] 5.83:1. Semi-elliptic springs front and rear. Reverse Elliott I-beam front axle. Steel I-beam rear supporting axle. Worm and roller steering. (Note: Other axle ratios supplied with optional heavy-duty tires).

OPTIONS: Rear bumper ($8.25). Deluxe cab equipment ($30.59). Custom cab equipment ($69.36). Deluxe panel equipment ($40.73). High side pickup($8.27). Bumper guards ($4.44). Long-arm adjustable mirror, left ($2.10); right ($3.23). Dual electric horns ($12.42). Auxiliary seat for panel ($31.36). Air foam seat cushion ($9.52). Pickup body and rear fenders painted to match cab ($6.44). Auxiliary taillamp ($6.63). Ashtray ($1.53). Oil-bath air cleaner, one-quart ($1.47). Oil filter ($9.27). Electric fuel pump ($13.96). High-charging generator ($10.38). Governor ($7.17). Fluid Drive ($43.14). Four-speed transmission ($61.01). Dodge-Tint glass on all Cab models, all glass areas ($12.30); on Panel model ($10.20). Truck-O-Matic transmission ($110). Rear quarter windows for Standard and Deluxe models ($12.33).

HISTORICAL: Introduced: Dec. 4, 1952. Calendar year registrations: 82,345. Calendar year production: 105,208. Model year production: [Series B-4-B-108] 40,412; [Series B-4-B-116] 9002; [Series B-4-C] 9760; [Series B-4-D-116] 967; [Series B-4-D-126] 11,178; [Total] 75,859. Innovations: Automatic transmission. Tinted glass. Long-box -1/2-ton pickup model. Prices of the new B-4 were reduced from 1952, and cut again in March 1953. In February, 1953, the government removed the National Production Authority restrictions on civilian truck manufacturing. This action didn't help Dodge, as 1953 was a disaster. Sales fell 19.4 percent, in a year when industry sales increased by 14.6 percent. Production dropped 35.2 percent. Dodge sunk from third to fifth place in the industry's ranking. The Army purchased 20,207 4x4 military 3/4-ton trucks. Light-duty exports totalled 8,839. Of the total U.S. production, 8,122 trucks were built at San Leandro, California; the remainder at the main truck plant in Warren, Michigan. Canadian production was 16,535. Dodge truck plants worked four-day weeks in February-March 1953. The 4-ton model, raised to 60,000 lbs. maximum GVW, gained a new 413 cid six-cylinder engine with dual carburetors and exhausts.

1953 Dodge 1/2-Ton Town Panel (Al Doerman)

1954 DODGE

1954 Dodge 3/4-Ton 7-1/2 ft. Pickup (IMSC/JLM)

1/2-TON — SERIES C-1-B6/C-1-B8 — SIX-CYLINDER/V-8: Dodge brought an all-new truck to market for 1954, with new frames and cab styling, plus a curved one-piece windshield. The appearance followed the Dodge look, but had many differences. The grille had a trapezoid shape. Two horizontal bars spanned the inside of the grille opening. The top bar was shorter. The bottom bar no longer extended past the opening to house the parking lamps. Each bar had a fluted chrome trim piece at its center. Three short horizontal chrome bars seemed to link the headlamps and parking lamps. Bodyside trimplates were on the fenders, not the hood. The wheel lips were not as deeply flared. The hood's center support extended down to the grille in front and had a round emblem at its center. Wheelbases and model lineups remained the same as those offered in the previous B-4 series. Both 108 in. and 116 in. wheelbase models were offered, the Town Panel on the smaller wheelbase only. The smaller pickup had a 6-1/2 ft. bed; the larger pickup had the 7-1/2 ft. express

184

body. Restyled cab interiors gave more driver comfort. Cabs were available in three trim levels: Standard, deluxe and custom. All were trimmed in attractive two-tone gray, including headliners and door trim panels. Cabs sat lower on the frame, to make entry and exit easier. Rear quarter windows were optional and larger in size. Brake and clutch pedals were now frame-mounted to reduce vibration. All dials on the new instrument panel were positioned in front of the driver, with a glove box in the center. Control buttons were conveniently placed on the driver's right. Six-cylinder engines in the C-1-B6 light-duty line carried over unchanged. V-8s, new for 1954, first came only in medium- and heavy-duty models. However, a 241 cid V-8 became available for 1/2-, 3/4- and 1-ton C-1-B8 trucks in August, 1954. The option cost $120. The venerable 218 cid six was then dropped and a higher output 230 cid six became the base engine for light-duty models. New standard paint colors were: Armour yellow, Banner green, Sonora blue, black, Dodge Truck red, Dodge Truck Ponchartrain green and Ecuador blue. Wheels were painted chrome metallic. Half-ton rear fenders and pickup boxes were black regardless of cab color. Pickup bodies painted cab color were standard on 3/4- and 1-ton models, but an extra-cost option on 1/2-tons. Low side boxes were standard on 1/2-ton pickups. High side boxes were available at extra cost. The Town Panel was extensively restyled. It was much sleeker and more modern with smooth, flowing lines. It featured dual rounded taillights, larger rear doors, smaller wheel housings, and a longer floor. Since Dodge did not make a sedan delivery, the Town Panel had to fill that role. An inside-mounted tire carrier was available for Town Panels; a side-mounted carrier for pickups. Standard equipment included a front bumper, front and rear shocks, oil-bath air cleaner, dual vacuum windshield wipers, vent wings in cab doors, left side sun visor, and a dome light (Town Panel only).

1954 Dodge 1/2-Ton Town Panel (J.K. Sheely)

1954 Dodge 1/2-Ton Town Panel (OCW)

3/4-TON — SERIES C-1-C6/C-1-C8 — SIX-CYLINDER/V-8: The new styling was seen on the standard 3/4-tons, which had the same technical distinctions as before. The 116 in. wheelbase was used. Models included the 7-1/2. ft. pickup and platform/stake. GVW was 5,800 lbs. A V-8 was made available for $120

3/4-TON SPECIAL — SERIES C-1-DL6/C-1-DL8 — SIX-CYLINDER/V-8: A Job-Rated version of the D6 1-ton brought down to 3/4-tons. It offered the 116 in. wheelbase (7-1/2 ft. body) pickup and platform/stake, plus 126 in. wheelbase (9 ft. body) versions of the same models. Chassis models were available in both lines.

1-TON — SERIES C-1-D6/C-1-D8 — SIX-CYLINDER/V-8: Same as the DL, but with beefier axles and tires for an 8,000 lbs. GVW rating. Also includes Forward Control truck chassis on both 116 and 126. in. wheelbases. Add $120 for V-8.

1-TON POWER-WAGON — SERIES C-1-PW6 — SIX-CYLINDER: Power Wagon with 126 in. wheelbase. Two chassis models and the 8 ft. pickup. All with four-wheel drive. No V-8s. No important changes.

1-TON SPECIAL — C-1-FL6 — SIX-CYLINDER: The Special 1-ton was the light-duty version of the C-1-F6 Dodge 1-1/2-ton offering one-inch longer 129 and 153 in. wheelbases for 1954. In addition to chassis versions, it included 9 ft. platform/stakes on the shorter stance and 12 ft. platform/stakes on the longer wheelbase. A 9,500 GVW was noted, as compared to the 1-1/2-ton C-1-FL's 14,000 lbs. Our sources indicate six-cylinder only in 1954.

3/4-TON SPECIAL ROUTE-VAN — SERIES C-1-DUL6 — SIX-CYLINDER: Route-Vans retained their 1948-1949 styling. The Special 3/4-ton Route-Van was the light-duty version of the C-1-DU6 ton and offered the same 102 and 117 in. wheelbases. Only sixes were offered.

1-TON ROUTE-VAN — SERIES C-1-DU6 — SIX-CYLINDER: The regular 1-ton Route-Vans also retained their 1948 styling and shared wheelbases with the DUL series. The cab-integral panel body came in a 7-1/2 ft. size and 9 ft. size, depending on whether the short or long wheelbase was ordered.

1-TON SPECIAL EXTENDED ROUTE-VAN — SERIES C-1-EUL6 — SIX-CYLINDER: This was a light version of the 1-1/2-ton with the same 12 ft. delivery body, but a lower GVW rating due to differences in running gear and tires. It had a 142 in. wheelbase.

I.D. DATA: Serial numbers were located on the left side of the cowl, under the hood. Engine numbers were stamped on a pad on the left side of the cylinder block, between cylinders two and three. Six-cylinder: [C-1-B] (Detroit) 82338001-82372344; (California) 85328001-85330985. [C-1-C] (Detroit) 83398001-83404307; (California) 85517001-85517631. [C-1-DL] (Detroit) 81472001 up; (San Leandro) 86014001 up. [C-1-D] (Detroit) 81472001-81481925; (California) 86014001-86014376. [C-1-PW] (Detroit) 83938001-83943347; (California) 88768001-88768126. [C-1-FL] (Detroit) 80407001 up; (San Leandro) 86516001 up. Eight-cylinder: [C-1-B] (Detroit) 84250001-84262923; (California) 86100001-86100446. [C-1-C] (Detroit) 84650001-84652998; (California) 86300001-86300105. [C-1-DL] (Detroit) 84800001 up; (San Leandro) 86400001 up. [C-1-D] (Detroit) 84800001-84802208; (California) 86400001-86400055.

Model	Body Type	Price	Weight	Prod. Total
Series C-1-B6-108 — 1/2-Ton — 108 in. w.b. — (6-cyl.)				
C-1-B6	Chassis & Cowl	1017	2475	Note 1
C-1-B6	Chassis & Cab	1252	2975	Note 1
C-1-B6	Pickup 6.5 ft.	1331	3275	Note 1
C-1-B6	Town Panel	1528	3375	Note 1

Add $120 and 100 lbs. for C-1-B8-108 with V-8 engine.

Model	Body Type	Price	Weight	Prod. Total
Series C-1-B6-116 — 1/2-Ton — 116 in. w.b. — (6-cyl.)				
C-1-B6	Chassis & Cowl	1032	2650	Note 1
C-1-B6	Chassis & Cab	1267	3150	Note 1
C-1-B6	Pickup 7.5 ft.	1357	3525	Note 1

Add $120 and 100 lbs. for C-1-B8-116 with V-8 engine.

NOTE 1: Calendar year production, 1/2-ton trucks; (Domestic) 26,973; (Export) 8,697; [Total] 35,670. Model year production total: (108 in. w.b.) 35,862; (116 in. w.b.) 6,570.; [Total] 42,432.

Model	Body Type	Price	Weight	Prod. Total
Series C-1-C6 — 3/4-Ton — 116 in. w.b. — (6-cyl.)				
C-1-C6	Chassis & Cowl	1114	2650	Note 2
C-1-C6	Chassis & Cab	1349	3150	Note 2
C-1-C6	Pickup 7.5 ft.	1462	3525	Note 2
C-1-C6	Platform	1459	3475	Note 2
C-1-C6	Stake 7.5 ft.	1518	3700	Note 2

Add $120 and 100 lbs. for C-1-C8 with V-8 engine.

Model	Body Type	Price	Weight	Prod. Total
Series C-1-DL6 — Special 3/4-Ton — 116 in. w.b. — (6-cyl.)				
C-1-DL6	Chassis & Cab	—	—	Note 2
C-1-DL6	Pickup 7.5 ft.	—	—	Note 2
C-1-DL6	Platform	—	—	Note 2
C-1-DL6	Stake 7.5 ft.	—	—	Note 2

Add $120 and 100 lbs. for C-1-DL8 with V-8 engine.

Model	Body Type	Price	Weight	Prod. Total
Series C-1-DL6 — Special 3/4-Ton — 126 in. w.b. — (6-cyl.)				
C-1-DL6	Chassis & Cab	—	—	Note 2
C-1-DL6	Pickup 9 ft.	—	—	Note 2
C-1-DL6	Platform	—	—	Note 2
C-1-DL6	Stake 9 ft.	—	—	Note 2

Add $120 and 100 lbs. for C-1-DL8 with V-8 engine.

Model	Body Type	Price	Weight	Prod. Total
Series C-1-C6 Forward Control — 3/4-Ton — 116 in. w.b.				
C-1-D6	Chassis	1042	2325	Note 2

Model	Body Type	Price	Weight	Prod. Total
Series C-1-DL6 Forward Control — 3/4-Ton — 116 in. w.b.				
C-1-D6	Chassis	1119	2600	Note 2

Model	Body Type	Price	Weight	Prod. Total
Series C-1-DL6 Forward Control — 3/4-Ton — 126 in. w.b.				
C-1-D6	Chassis	1143	2625	Note 2

NOTE 2: Calendar year production, 3/4-ton trucks: (Domestic) 6,639; (Export) 166; (Government) 5,586; [Total] 12,391. Model year production total: 6,808.

Model	Body Type	Price	Weight	Prod. Total
Series C-1-D6 — 1-Ton — 116 in. w.b. — (6-cyl.)				
C-1-D6	Chassis & Cowl	1182	2900	Note 3
C-1-D6	Chassis & Cab	1417	3375	Note 3
C-1-D6	Pickup 7.5 ft.	1536	3725	Note 3
C-1-D6	Platform	1527	3725	Note 3
C-1-D6	Stake 7.5 ft.	1586	3905	Note 3

Add $120 and 100 lbs. for C-1-D8 with V-8 engine.

Model	Body Type	Price	Weight	Prod. Total
Series C-1-D6 — 1-Ton — 126 in. w.b. — 6-cyl.				
C-1-D6	Chassis & Cowl	1206	2950	Note 3
C-1-D6	Chassis & Cab	1441	3375	Note 3
C-1-D6	Pickup 9 ft.	1568	3800	Note 3
C-1-D6	Platform	1562	3825	Note 3
C-1-D6	Stake 9 ft.	1638	4055	Note 3

Add $120 and 100 lbs. for C-1-D8 with V-8 engine.

Model	Body Type	Price	Weight	Prod. Total
Series C-1-D6 Forward Control — 1-Ton — 116 in. w.b.				
C-1-D6	Chassis	1129	2600	Note 3

Model	Body Type	Price	Weight	Prod. Total
Series C-1-D6 Forward Control — 1-Ton — 126 in. w.b.				
C-1-D6	Chassis	1153	2625	Note 3

Series C-1-F6L — Special 1-Ton — 129 in. w.b.

C-1-FL6	Chassis & Cowl	1398	3525	Note 3
C-1-FL6	Chassis & Cab	1633	—	Note 3
C-1-FL6	Platform	1778	—	Note 3
C-1-FL6	Stake 9 ft.	1857	—	Note 3

Dual rear wheel equipment available.

Series C-1-F6L — Special 1-Ton — 153 in. w.b.

C-1-FL6	Chassis & Cowl	1420	3650	Note 3
C-1-FL6	Chassis & Cab	1655	—	Note 3
C-1-FL6	Platform	1830	—	Note 3
C-1-FL6	Stake 9 ft.	1927	—	Note 3

Dual rear wheel equipment available.

NOTE 3: Calendar year production, 1-ton trucks: (Domestic) 7,711; (Export) 6,195; [Total] 13,906. Model year production total: (116 in. w.b.) 1,616; (126 in. w.b.) 10,597.

Series C-1-PW Power Wagon — 1-Ton — 126 in. w.b.

C-1-PW6	Chassis & Cowl	1955	4075	Note 4
C-1-PW6	Chassis & Cab	2190	4675	Note 4
C-1-PW6	Pickup 8 ft.	2307	5100	Note 4

NOTE 4: Model year production: 5,601.

Series C-1-DUL — Special Route Van — 3/4-Ton — 102/117 in. w.b.

| C-1-DUL | Panel 7 ft. | 2021 | 4300 | 61 |
| C-1-DUL | Panel 9.5 ft. | 2692 | 4600 | 458 |

Series C-1-DU — Route-Van — 1-Ton — 102/117 in. w.b.

| C-1-EU | Panel 7 ft. | 2043 | 4300 | 32 |
| C-1-EU | Panel 9.5 ft. | 2788 | 4600 | 2 |

Series C-1-EUL — Special Route-Van — 1-Ton — 142 in. w.b.

| C-1-EUL | Panel 12.5 ft. | 3186 | 4830 | 205 |

1954 Dodge 1/2-Ton Town Panel (OCW)

ENGINE [C-1-B/C-1-C]: Inline. L-head. Six-cylinder. Cast iron block. Bore & stroke: 3-1/4 x 4-3/8 in. Displacement: 217.8 cid. Compression ratio: 7.1:1. Brake horsepower: 100 at 3600 rpm. Net horsepower: 25.35. Torque: 177 lbs.-ft. at 1600 rpm. Four main bearings. Solid valve lifters.

ENGINE [Series C-1-D]: Inline. L-head. Six-cylinder. Cast iron block. Bore & stroke: 3-1/4 x 4-5/8 in. Displacement: 230.2 cid. Compression ratio: 7.25:1. Brake horsepower: 110 at 3600 rpm. Net horsepower: 25.35. Torque: 194 lbs.-ft. at 1600 rpm. Four main bearings. Solid valve lifters.

ENGINE [Power-Wagon]: Inline. L-head. Six-cylinder. Cast iron block. Bore & stroke: 3-1/4 x 4-5/8 in. Displacement: 230.2 cid. Compression ratio: 7.0:1. Brake horsepower: 99 at 3600 rpm. Net horsepower: 25.35. Torque: 190 lbs.-ft. at 1200 rpm. Four main bearings. Solid valve lifters.

ENGINE [C-1-FL]: Inline. L-head. Six-cylinder. Cast iron block. Bore & stroke: 3-7/16 x 4-1/4 in. Displacement: 236.6 cid. Compression ratio: 7.0:1. Brake horsepower: 109 at 3600 rpm. Net horsepower: 28.35. Four main bearings.

ENGINE [C-1/FC-1]: V-8. Overhead valve. Eight-cylinder. Cast iron block. Bore & stroke: 3-7/16 x 3-1/4 in. Displacement: 241.4 cid. Compression ratio: 7.5:1. Brake horsepower: 145 at 4400 rpm. Net horsepower: 37.8. Torque: 215 lbs.-ft. at 2400 rpm. Five main bearings. Hydraulic valve lifters. (T300 Engineering Code).

CHASSIS [Series C-1-B]: Wheelbase: 108 or 116 in. Tires: 6.00 x 16 four-ply. GVW: 4,900 lbs. Rear axle rating: 3,300 lbs. Front axle rating: 2,200 lbs.

CHASSIS [Series C-1-C]: Wheelbase: 116 in. Tires: 7.00 x 15 six-ply. GVW: 5,800 lbs. Rear axle rating: 3600 lbs. Front axle rating: 2,500 lbs.

CHASSIS [Series C-1-DL]: Wheelbase: 116 or 126 in.

CHASSIS [Series C-1-D]: Wheelbase: 116 or 126 in. Tires: (front) 6.00 x 16 six-ply; (rear) 7.00 x 16 six-ply. GVW: 8,000 lbs. Rear axle rating: 5,800 lbs. Front axle rating: 2,500 lbs.

CHASSIS [Series C-1-FL-129]: Wheelbase: 129 in. Tires: 6.00 x 20 six-ply front, 6.50 x 20 eight-ply rear. GVW: 9,500 lbs. Add $69 for dual rear wheel equipment.

CHASSIS [Series C-1-FL-153]: Wheelbase: 153 in. Tires: 6.00 x 20 six-ply front, 6.50 x 20 eight-ply rear. GVW: 9,500 lbs. Add $69 for dual rear wheel equipment.

CHASSIS [Series C-1-PW-126]: Wheelbase: 126 in. Tires: 7.50 x 16 eight-ply. Four-wheel-drive chassis. GVW: 8,700 lbs.

CHASSIS [Model C-1-DUL-102]: Wheelbase: 102 in. GVW: 6,900 lbs. Tires: 7.00 x 16 six-ply.

CHASSIS [Model C-1-DUL-117]: Wheelbase: 117 in. GVW: 6,900 lbs. Tires: 7.00 x 16 six-ply front and 7.50 x 16 six-ply rear.

CHASSIS [Model C-1-DU-102]: Wheelbase: 102 in. GVW: 7,900 lbs. Tires: 6.50 x 16 six-ply front/7.00 x 16 six-ply rear. Higher GVW with 7.50 x 16 eight-ply front and rear tires.

CHASSIS [Model C-1-DU-117]: Wheelbase: 117 in.; Tires: 6.50 x 16 six-ply front/7.00 x 16 six-ply rear. GVW: 7,900 lbs. (Available with 8.25 x 16 eight-ply tires rear.)

CHASSIS [Model C-1-EUL-102]: Wheelbase: 102 in. Tires: 7.50 x 16 six-ply front and 8.25 x 16 eight-ply rear. GVW: 8,000 lbs. with 8.25 x 16 eight-ply tires front and rear tires; also available 8,700 lbs. with 9.00 x 16 eight-ply front and rear, 9,600 lbs. with 9.00 x 16 ten-ply front and rear.

CHASSIS [Model C-1-EUL-142]: Wheelbase: 142 in. Tires: (front) 7.50 x 16 eight-ply; (rear) 8.25 x 16 eight-ply. GVW: 8,500 lbs. with 8.25 x 16 eight-ply front and rear; 9,200 lbs. with 9.00 x 16 eight-ply front and rear; 10,100 lbs. with 9.00 x 16 ten-ply front and rear.

TECHNICAL: (General) Selective sliding gear transmission. Speeds: 3F/1R; optional 4F/1R. Column or floor shift. Single-plate dry-disc clutch: 10 in., except 11 in. with optional

four-speed transmission. Fluid-Drive optional with three-speed transmission on 1/2- and 3/4-ton models; with four-speeds on 1-ton models. Automatic transmission optional on 1/2- and 3/4-ton models. Rear axle ratio: [1/2- and 3/4-ton] 4.1:1 and 4.78:1; [1-ton] 4.1:1 and 4.89:1. I-beam front axle. Worm and roller steering. Hydraulic four-wheel brakes.

1954 Dodge 1/2-Ton Town Panel (RPZ)

OPTIONS (Factory Installed): Rear bumper ($8.25). Bumper guards ($4.40). High side pickup box, 6-1/2 ft. ($8.25); same on 7-1/2 ft. models ($9). Deluxe cab equipment ($23.50). Custom cab equipment ($49). Deluxe panel equipment ($20). Door armrest ($3). Dodge Tint glass: All cabs ($12.30), panel ($10.20). Turn signals: Panel ($11), pickup ($16). Dome light ($4.15). Auxiliary taillight ($6.60). Rear quarter windows ($12.30). Dual electric wipers ($8.40). Dual horns ($12.40). Horn ring on steering wheel ($2.50). Long-arm mirror: Right ($3.20); left ($2.10). Inside rearview mirror ($2.75). Set of stainless wheelcovers ($13). Bright finish hubcaps ($1.50). Bright metal grille moldings ($2.75). Bright metal moldings for Town Panel ($13). Inside sun visor ($2.55). Auxiliary seat for Town Panel: Standard ($31.35), deluxe ($39.90). Deluxe seat back padding: Standard cab ($11.50), deluxe cab ($7.50). Deluxe seat cushion ($9). Heater: Standard ($40), deluxe ($60). Paint to match pickup body with cab ($6.40). One-quart air cleaner ($1.45). Oil filter ($9.25). Electric fuel pump ($13.95). Governor ($7.15). Hand throttle ($2.50). Ashtray ($1.50). Heavy-duty three-speed transmission ($20). Three-speed transmission with Fluid-Drive ($63). Four-speed transmission ($71.90). Truck-O-Matic transmission ($110).

1954 Dodge 1/2-Ton Town Panel (OCW)

HISTORICAL: Introduced: October, 1953. Calendar year sales: 60,658. Calendar year production: 94,887. Model year production, light trucks with six-cylinder engines: 67,812, including Route-Vans; (domestic only) 41,603. Joel R. Miller of Miller's Dodge Garage, Portland, Ore. has done research that shows series production of Dodge C-1/Fargo T300 models during 1954 and 1955 as follows: [1/2-Ton/six] (Warren) 34,344; (San Leandro) 2,985; (combined) 37,329. [1/2-ton/ V-8] (Warren) 12,923; (San Leandro) 446; (combined) 13,369. [3/4-ton/six] (Warren) 6,307; (San Leandro) 631; (combined) 6,938. [3/4-ton/V-8] (Warren) 2,998; (San Leandro) 105; (combined) 3,103. [1-ton/six] (Warren) 9,925; (San Leandro) 376; (combined) 10,301. [1-Ton/V-8] (Warren) 2,208; (San Leandro) 55; (combined) 2,263. [Power Wagon/six] (Warren) 5,347; (San Leandro) 126; (combined) 5,473. Innovations: Curved one-piece windshield. V-8 engine. Frame-mounted brake and clutch pedals. Despite the major product changes, 1954 was not a good year for Dodge truck. Sales were down 26.3 percent, well beyond the industry drop of 10.9 percent. Dodge's market share eroded to 7.3 percent. Of the total U.S. production, 3,690 trucks were made in California. Canadian production also dropped drastically, down to 7,201. Dodge exported 15,058 trucks and sold 5,586 to the government. The V-8 engine introduced on light-duty trucks in August, 1954 was not a hemi. The V-8 with hemispherical combustion chambers was used only in medium- and heavy-duty trucks. To publicize the light-duty V-8, Dodge ran a 1/2-ton pickup 50,198 miles in 50 days on the Chrysler Proving Grounds, setting a world endurance record. Dodge advertised the new 1/2-ton V-8 as the most powerful low-tonnage engine in the world. In November, 1954, the AAA certified the V-8's gas economy at 22.21 mpg. Dodge also began development work on an all-aluminum army truck. In December, the U.S. Post Office purchased 1,890 Dodge trucks. The largest Dodge models continued to use the monstrous 413 cid six, which debuted in 1953.

1955 DODGE

ALL — SERIES C-1 — SIX/V-8: The model year began by continuing the C-1 series without change. As Dodge told its dealers, "All new, unused and unlicensed C-1 series Dodge Job-Rated trucks delivered to a retail purchaser on and after Nov. 1, 1954 may, for registration purposes only, be considered as part of the 1955 series." Early in 1955, truck manufacturing was terminated at the San Leandro, California facility. All production came from the Warren truck plant in Detroit, Michigan. That factory was changed over and new C-3 series trucks were unveiled on April 11, 1955.

1/2-TON — SERIES C-3-B6 — SIX-CYLINDER/V-8: The C-3 Series featured a new "Pilot-House" cab. Wraparound windshields and rear windows gave almost unobstructed vision in all directions. Interior appointments were more deluxe, featuring colorful woven saron and nylon fabrics trimmed in vinyl. Seat construction was upgraded through the use of coil springs and foam rubber padding. Cabs were available with three upholstery color schemes, in four trim levels: Standard, deluxe, Custom and Custom Regal. Body paint colors were carried over, but the Custom Regal added chrome exterior accents. Half-ton models came on two wheelbases with GVW ratings of 5,100 lbs. for the 108 in. wheelbase. The Town Panel continued on the smaller wheelbase only. Sometime during the year, Dodge issued a press release photo promoting a new model called the Town Wagon. It was a passenger carrying vehicle, based on the Town Panel, but adding rear quarter windows and six- or eight-passenger seating. (Note: The same photo, with only the year in the caption changed, was also used to promote the 1956 Town Wagon). New models, never available before from Dodge, were 1/2-ton, 116 in. wheelbase stake and platform trucks. The six was unchanged, but the V-8 was enlarged to 259 cid (from 241 cid). Two new transmissions were available: A three-speed with overdrive, and a new Powerflite automatic. Truck-O-Matic and Fluid-Drive were discontinued. Standard equipment included front and rear shock absorbers, front bumper, rear bumper (Town Panel only), underslung tire carrier, one-pint oil-bath air cleaner, dual vacuum wipers, inside sun visor, plus dome light and dual taillamps (Town Panel only).

1/2-TON SPECIAL — SERIES C-3-BL6 — SIX: Extending its Job-Rated chassis classification system, Dodge now offered a light-duty (L suffix) 1/2-ton series or sub-series consisting of just one model. It was a pickup that looked the same as the 1/2-tons on the 108 in. wheelbase, but had a lower GVW of 4,250 lbs. Only a six was offered as base engine in this model. This truck was about $100-160 less costly than the C-3-B6 pickups. A limited range of optional equipment was available for this model.

3/4-TON — SERIES C-3-C6 — SIX/V-8: The regular Dodge 3/4-tons had the same new wraparound windshield styling. They continued to come on an eight-inch longer wheelbase, with the express type long bed pickup bed used.

3/4-TON SPECIAL–SERIES C-3-DL6 — SIX/V-8: This was a 3/4-ton Job-Rated version of the 1-ton truck line with both the 116 and 126 in. wheelbase lines included. Both lines included chassis models, an express and platform/stake bodies. The bodies were 7-1/2 ft. long on the 116 in. chassis and 9 ft. on the 126 in. wheelbase.

1-TON — SERIES C-3-D6 — SIX/V-8: Same models as the C-3-DL6 with heavier-duty equipment and a 1-ton rating.

1-TON SPECIAL — SERIES C-3-FL — SIX/V-8: Job-Rated 1-ton versions of Dodge's 1-1/2-ton models on 129 or 153 in. wheelbase. Chassis and platform/stakes only, the latter with 9 ft. or 12 ft. bodies. A change from 1954 was the availability of a V-8 in this series.

1-TON SPECIAL — SERIES C-3-GL/C-3-GAL — SIX/V-8: With the proliferation of models, these were other lines available in a Job-Rated 1-ton format with 129, 153 or 171 in. wheelbases.

standard equipment in Power-Wagons.

1955 Dodge 1-Ton Power Wagon 8 ft. Express (RAC)

1-TON POWER-WAGON — SERIES C-3-PW — SIX: The Power-Wagon continued without change.

3/4-TON SPECIAL ROUTE-VAN — SERIES C-3-DUL — SIX: Some Route-Vans were titled as 1955 C-3 models. The 3/4-tons were Job-Rated versions of the 1-ton. They came as 108 or 117 in. wheelbase chassis suited for aftermarket bodies or with factory cowl-integral panel delivery bodies installed.

1-TON; 1-TON SPECIAL ROUTE-VAN — SERIES C-3-DU/C-3-EUL — SIX: Some Route-Vans were titled as 1955 C-3 one-ton models. The DUs were regular 1-tons on 102 or 117 in. wheelbases. EULs were Job-Rated versions of the extended-wheelbase (142 in.) 1-1/2-ton.

3/4-TON; 3/4-TON SPECIAL FORWARD CONTROL — C-3-CN6/C-3-DNL6 — SIX: A regular 3/4-ton Forward Control truck chassis was offered to accomodate aftermarket delivery chassis. Naturally, a 3/4-ton Job-Rated edition of the 1-ton version was marketed, too. Both offered a 116 in. wheelbase, but the Job-Rated DNL came on a 126 in. chassis as well.

1-TON; 1-TON SPECIAL FORWARD CONTROL — C-3-DN6/C-3-FNL6 — SIX: The regular 1-ton Forward Control truck chassis (DN) offered the mid-size 116 and 126 in. wheelbases. Strangely, the heavier-duty Job-Rated 1-ton (the 1-1/2-ton derived FNL) came on either a smaller 108 in. wheelbase or a larger 129 in. wheelbase.

I.D. DATA: Serial numbers were on a plate on the left side of the cowl, under the hood. Serial numbers: Six-cylinder [C-3-B] 82373001-82397181. [C-3-C] 83405001-83409905. [C-3-D] 81483001-81489600. [C-3-FL] 80410001 up. [C-3-GL] 80112001 up. [C-3-PW] 83744001-83749000. [C-3-DU/DUL] 84210001 up. [C-3-EUL] 84004001 up. [C-3-CN] 80200101 up. [C-3-DN/DNL] 80002501 up. [[C-3-FNL] 80,800,001 up. Eight cylinder [C-3-B] 84265001-84284000. [C-3-C] 84654001-84658200. [C-3-D] 84803001-84806500. [C-3-FL] 83100001 up. [C-3-GL] 83202001 up. Engine numbers were stamped on a pad on the

left side of the cylinder block, between cylinders two and three. Engine numbers: [C-3-B] T334-1001; VT334-1001. [C-3-B] T336-1001; VT336-1001. [C-3-D] T338-1001; VT338-1001. [C-3-PW] T137-1001.

Model	Body Type	Price	Weight	Prod. Total
Series C-3-BL6 — 1/2-Ton — 108 in. w.b. — (6-cyl.)				
C-3-BL6	Pickup (Lowside)	1446	2175	Note 1
Series C-3-B6 — 1/2-Ton — 108 in. w.b. — (6-cyl.)				
C-3-B6	Chassis & Cowl	1195	2200	Note 1
C-3-B6	Chassis & Cab	1431	2675	Note 1
C-3-B6	Pickup (Lowside)	1530	2975	Note 1
C-3-B6	Pickup (Highside)	1499	3025	Note 1
C-3-B6	Town Panel	1760	3150	Note 1
C-3-B6	Town Wagon	—	—	Note 1
Series C-3-B6 — 1/2-Ton — 116 in. w.b. — (6-cyl.)				
C-3-B6	Chassis & Cowl	1208	2225	Note 1
C-3-B6	Chassis & Cab	1444	2700	Note 1
C-3-B6	Pickup (Lowside)	1512	3025	Note 1
C-3-B6	Pickup (Highside)	1556	3075	Note 1
C-3-B6	Platform	1563	—	Note 1
C-3-B6	Stake 7.5 ft.	1629	3250	Note 1

Add $120/100 lbs. for C-3-B8 models with V-8 engine.

NOTE 1: Calendar year production: (Domestic) 29,553; (Export) 8,214; [Total] 37,767. Model year production [Six] (108 in.) 26,067; (116 in.) 3,197. [V-8] (108 in.) 6,595; (116 in.) 8,704.

Model	Body Type	Price	Weight	Prod. Total
Series C-3-C — 3/4-Ton — 116 in. w.b. — (6-cyl.)				
C-3-C6	Chassis & Cowl	1305	2325	Note 2
C-3-C6	Chassis & Cab	1541	2800	Note 2
C-3-C6	Pickup 7.5 ft.	1653	3175	Note 2
C-3-C6	Platform	1660	3150	Note 2
C-3-C6	Stake 7.5 ft.	1726	3350	Note 2

Add $120/100 lbs. for C-3-C8 models with V-8 engine.

NOTE 2: Calendar year production: (Domestic) 6,600; (Export) 422; (Government) 7; (Total) 7,029. Model year production [Six] 5,122; [V-8] 4,083.

Model	Body Type	Price	Weight	Prod. Total
Series C-3-DL6 — 3/4-Ton — 116 in. w.b. — (6-cyl.)				
C-3-DL6	Chassis & Cowl	1236	2625	—
C-3-DL6	Chassis & Cab	1473	3100	—
C-3-DL6	Pickup 7.5 ft.	1584	3475	—
C-3-DL6	Platform	1584	3450	—
C-3-DL6	Stake 7.5 ft.	1650	3650	—
Series C-3-DL6 — 3/4-Ton — 126 in. w.b. — (6-cyl.)				
C-3-DL6	Chassis & Cowl	1262	2650	—
C-3-DL6	Chassis & Cab	1499	3125	—
C-3-DL6	Pickup 9 ft.	1624	3550	—
C-3-DL6	Platform	1624	3600	—
C-3-DL6	Stake 9 ft.	1690	3775	—

Add $120/100 lbs. for C-3-DL8 models with V-8 engine.

Model	Body Type	Price	Weight	Prod. Total
Series C-3-D — 1-Ton — 116 in. w.b. — (6-cyl.)				
C-3-D6	Chassis & Cowl	1363	2625	Note 3
C-3-D6	Chassis & Cab	1599	3100	Note 3
C-3-D6	Pickup 7.5 ft.	1711	3475	Note 3
C-3-D6	Platform	1718	3450	Note 3
C-3-D6	Stake 7.5 ft.	1784	3650	Note 3
Series C-3-D — 1-Ton — 126 in. w.b. — (6-cyl.)				
C-3-D6	Chassis & Cowl	1389	2650	Note 3
C-3-D6	Chassis & Cab	1625	3125	Note 3
C-3-D6	Pickup 9 ft.	1750	3550	Note 3
C-3-D6	Platform	1770	3600	Note 3
C-3-D6	Stake 9 ft.	1836	3775	Note 3

Add $120/100 lbs. for C-3-D8 models with V-8 engine.

NOTE 3: Calendar year production (including Power-Wagons): (Domestic) 8,257; (Export) 7,025; [Total] 15,282. Model year production [Six] (116 in.) 314; (126 in.) 236; [V-8] (116 in.) 252; (126 in.) 3,100.

Model	Body Type	Price	Weight	Prod. Total
Series C-3-FL6 — 1-Ton — 116 in. w.b. — (6-cyl.)				
C-3-FL6	Chassis & Cowl	1453	3450	—
C-3-FL6	Chassis & Cab	1690	3925	—
C-3-FL6	Platform	1815	4400	—
C-3-FL6	Stake 7.5 ft.	1880	4700	—
Series C-3-FL6 — 1-Ton — 126 in. w.b. — (6-cyl.)				
C-3-FL6	Chassis & Cowl	1486	3575	—
C-3-FL6	Chassis & Cab	1723	4050	—
C-3-FL6	Platform	1880	4650	—
C-3-FL6	Stake 9 ft.	1966	4975	—

Add $120/100 lbs. for C-3-FL8 models with V-8 engine.

Model	Body Type	Price	Weight	Prod. Total
Series C-3-PW Power-Wagon — 1-Ton 4x4 — 126 in. w.b.				
C-3-PW	Chassis & Cowl	1965	4075	Note 4
C-3-PW	Chassis & Cab	2200	4675	Note 4
C-3-PW	Pickup 8 ft.	2317	5100	Note 4

NOTE 4: Model year production: 5,058.

Model	Body Type	Price	Weight	Prod. Total
Series C-3-DUL6 — Special Route Van — 3/4-Ton — (6-cyl.)				
102 in. w.b.				
C-3-DUL	Chassis 7.5 ft.	2031	2545	—
C-3-DUL	Panel 7.5 ft.	2702	4625	—
Series C-3-DUL6 — Special Route Van — 3/4-Ton — (6-cyl.)				
117 in. w.b.				
C-3-DUL	Chassis 9 ft.	2053	2665	—
C-3-DUL	Panel 9 ft.	2798	4900	—

Series C-1-DU6 — Route-Van — 1-Ton — (6-cyl.)

102 in. w.b.

C-3-EU	Chassis 7.5 ft.	2043	2545	—
C-3-EU	Panel 7.5 ft.	—	4900	—

Series C-1-DU6 — Route-Van — 1-Ton — (6-cyl.)

117 in. w.b.

C-3-EU	Chassis 9 ft.	—	—	—
C-3-EU	Panel 9 ft.	—	—	—

Series C-1-EUL — Special Route-Van — 1-Ton — (6-cyl.)

142 in. w.b.

C-3 EUL	Chassis 12 ft.	2359	3120	—
C-3-EUL	Panel 12.5 ft.	3206	5850	—

Series C-3-DNL — Special 3/4-Ton Forward Control — (6-cyl.)

116 in. w.b.

C-3-DNL	Chassis	1262	2400	—

126 in. w.b.

C-3-DNL	Chassis	1288	2425	—

Series C-3-CN6 — 1-Ton Forward Control — (6-cyl.)

116 in. w.b.

C-3-CN	Chassis	1209	2175	—

Series C-3-FNL6 — Special 1-Ton Forward Control — (6-cyl.)

108 in. w.b.

C-3-FNL	Chassis 1446		3200	—

129 in. w.b.

C-3-FNL	Chassis	1479	3275	—

1955 Dodge 1/2-Ton Town Wagon (DB)

ENGINES [First Series C-1]: Same as 1954.

ENGINE [BL6/B6/C6/DL6/FL6/DU6/CN6/DN6/DNL6]: Inline. L-head. Six-cylinder. Cast iron block. Bore & stroke: 3.25 x 4.625 in. Displacement: 230.2 cid. Compression ratio: 7.6:1. Brake horsepower: 115 at 3600 rpm. Net horsepower: 25.35. Torque: 201 lbs.-ft. at 1600 rpm. Four main bearings. Solid valve lifters.

ENGINE: [FNL6] Inline. L-head. Cast iron block. Bore & stroke: 3.563 x 3.25 in. Net horsepower: 40.62.

ENGINE [C-3-PW Power-Wagon]: Inline. L-head. Six-cylinder. Cast iron block. Bore & stroke: 3.25 x 4.625 in. Displacement: 230.2 cid. Compression ratio: 7.6:1. Brake horsepower: 111 at 3600 rpm. Net horsepower: 25.35. Torque: 198 lbs.-ft. at 1600 rpm. Four main bearings. Solid valve lifters.

ENGINE [ALL V-8 MODELS]: V-8. Overhead valves. Eight-cylinder. Cast iron block. Bore & stroke: 3.563 x 3.25 in. Displacement: 259.2 cid. Compression ratio: 7.6:1. Brake horsepower: 169 at 4400 rpm. Net horsepower: 40.6. Torque: 243 lbs.-ft. at 2400 rpm. Five main bearings. Hydraulic valve lifters.

CHASSIS [Series C-1]: Same as 1954.

CHASSIS [Series C-3-BL6]: Wheelbase: 108 in. Tires: 6.70 x 15 four-ply (front and rear). GVW: 4,250 lbs.

CHASSIS [Series C-3-B]: Wheelbase: 108 in. and 116 in. Tires: 6.70 x 15 four-ply (front and rear). GVW: 5,100 lbs. Front axle capacity: 2,500 lbs. Rear axle capacity: 3,300 lbs.

CHASSIS [Series C-3-C]: Wheelbase: 116 in. Tires: 7.00 x 15 six-ply (front and rear). GVW: 5,800 lbs. Front axle capacity: 2,500 lbs. Rear axle capacity: 3300 lbs.

CHASSIS [Series C-3-D/C-3-DL]: Wheelbase: 116 in. and 126 in. Tires: (front) 6.00 x 16 six-ply; (rear) 7.00 x 16 six-ply. GVW: 8,800 lbs. Front axle capacity: 2,800 lbs. Rear axle capacity: 3,600 lbs.

CHASSIS [Series C-3-PW Power-Wagon]: Wheelbase: 126 in. Tires: 7.50 x 16 eight-ply (front and rear). GVW: 9,500 lbs.

CHASSIS [Route-Van/Forward Control]: Wheelbase: 102; 108; 116; 117;126;129 and 142 in. wheelbases. GVWs: [DUL/DU] 7,900 lbs.; [EUL] 10,100 lbs.; [CN] 6,000 lbs.; [DN/ DNL] 9,000 lbs.; [[FNL] 9,500 lbs. Tires: Various.

TECHNICAL: Selective sliding gear transmission. Speeds: 3F/1R; optional 4F/1R, or 3F/ 1R with overdrive. Column or floor shift. Automatic transmission optional. Single-plate dry-disc clutch: 10 in., except 11 in. with optional heavy-duty or four-speed transmission. Rear axle ratio: [3/4-ton] 3.73:1, 4.1:1 and 4.78:1; [1-ton] 4.1:1 and 4.89:1. Hydraulic four-wheel brakes.

1955 Dodge 1/2-Ton High Side Pickup (DB)

OPTIONS (Factory Installed): Rear bumper ($11.25). Bumper guards ($5.50). Deluxe cab equipment ($26). Custom equipment ($51). Custom Regal equipment ($79). Left door armrest ($3.30). Town Panel Deluxe equipment ($22.50); Custom Regal equipment ($51). Long-arm mirror: Left side ($2.50); right side ($3.95). Inside rearview mirror ($3). Bright metal molding package for Town Panel ($14.50). Dodge Tint glass, all models ($17.50). Right inside sun visor ($3). Auxiliary taillamp ($7.25). Dual electric horns ($14.50). Horn ring ($3). Cab corner marker lights ($10). Set of four bright hubcaps ($1.65); set of five ($3). Set of four 15 inch wheelcovers ($16.50). Dome light ($5.50). Heater: Standard ($41.50); Deluxe ($62). Deluxe seat for Town Panel ($11.25). Auxiliary seat for Town Panel ($45). Deluxe seat back and cushion ($11.25 each). Dual electric wipers ($11.25). Wraparound rear window ($29). Inside tire carrier, Town Panel ($6). Side tire carrier for pickup ($10.25). Hand throttle control ($3). One-quart oil-bath air cleaner: [Six] ($1.65); [V-8] ($3.95). Increased cooling capacity ($10). Ashtray ($1.65). Oil filter ($12). Electric fuel pump ($16). Three-speed transmission with overdrive ($100). Heavy-duty three-speed transmission with 10 in. clutch ($40); with 11 in. clutch ($45). Four-speed transmission ($70). PowerFlite automatic transmission ($165). Governor ($10). [C-3-BL6-108 Model Only] Rear bumper ($11.25). Increased cooling capacity ($10). Turn signals ($23.50). Heater ($41.50). Oil filter ($12). Auxiliary taillight ($7.25). (Power-Wagon Only) Deluxe cab equipment ($10). Turn signals ($30.50). Dodge Tint glass ($17.50). Long-arm mirror: Left side ($2.50); right ($3.95). Inside mirror ($3). Front and rear fenders painted cab color ($7.50). Auxiliary taillight ($8.75). Brake booster with 7-1/2 in. diaphragm ($42.50). Governor ($69.10). Draw bar ($23.05). Heater ($41.50). Oil filter ($12). Pintle hook ($12.50). Power-take-off ($75.70). Pulley drive ($85.55). Radiator overflow tank ($10). Rear drive-shaft assembly ($85.55). Rear shock absorbers ($34.90). Front springs with 1,600 lbs. capacity ($7.90). Rear main springs, 3,000 lbs. ($8.75). Front tow hooks ($8.25/pair). Winch assembly ($243.45).

HISTORICAL: Introduced: [C-1] carried over from 1954. [C-3] April, 1955. Calendar year sales: 66,208. Calendar year production: 95,430. Model year production: (Six) 40,246; (V-8) 22,734; [Total C-3 light-duty] 62,980. Model year production (U.S. only): (Six) 24,626; (V-8) 21,538; [Total] 46,164. "Pilot-House" cabs with wraparound windshield and rear window were introduced. A basic low-cost pickup model appeared. V-8 engine was enlarged. PowerFlite automatic transmission added to option list. Dodge truck sales improved by 9.1 percent over 1954, as production gained slightly. All trucks were now built at the Warren plant in Detroit, Michigan. Canadian production totaled 11,054 units. This was the end of Korean War truck production, as only seven 3/4-ton 4x4s were made in January, 1955. A total of 15,661 trucks were built for export. Dodge models met 98 percent of all hauling needs, with a total of seven six-cylinder and V-8 engines and a GVW rating range from 4,250 to 60,000 lbs. For the first time, Dodge produced a clutchless automatic transmission for light-duty trucks and built medium-duty trucks with automatic shift.

1956 DODGE

1/2-TON — SERIES C-4-B — SIX/V-8: All models, engines, features and options of the C-3 series, introduced in April 1955, continued without change for the C-4 series. Dodge even used the same factory photos to promote the new models in some cases, changing only the year in the photo caption. In January 1956, Dodge did announce one important new addition to the line. A Town Wagon was created by adding sliding glass windows and seats to the Town Panel. This versatile 1/2-ton looked like a station wagon, hauling six people on two seats with a large load space. A second version accomodated up to eight people on three seats, but had a bit less room for their luggage. With both rear seats removed, however, it could serve as a truck rated for 1,650 lbs. payloads. In Custom Regal trim, the Town Wagon was a luxurious and beautiful people/cargo hauler. PowerFlite automatic and overdrive transmissions were available. Four new paint colors were added: Chilean beige, Rackham blue, Terra Cotta and Canyon coral. Sonora blue was dropped. Standard equipment included front and rear shock absorbers, front bumper, rear bumper (Town Panel only), underslung tire carrier, one-pint oil-bath air cleaner, dual vacuum wipers, inside sun visor, plus dome light and dual taillamps (Town Panel only).

1956 Dodge 1/2-Ton Town Wagon (DFW)

3/4-TON — SERIES C-4-C6 — SIX/V-8: The regular Dodge 3/4-tons continued to come on an eight-inch longer wheelbase.

3/4-TON SPECIAL-SERIES C-4-DL6 — SIX/V-8: This was a 3/4-ton Job-Rated version of the 1-ton truck line with both the 116 and 126 in. wheelbase lines included. Both lines included chassis models, an express and platform/stake bodies. The bodies were 7-1/2 ft. long on the 116 in. chassis and 9 ft. on the 126 in. wheelbase.

1-TON — SERIES C-4-D6 — SIX/V-8: Same models as the C-4-DL6 with heavier-duty equipment and a 1-ton rating.

1-TON SPECIAL — SERIES C-4-GL/C-4-GAL — SIX/V-8: The Job-Rated 1-ton models with 129, 153 or 171 in. wheelbases returned.

1-TON POWER-WAGON — SERIES C-4-PW — SIX: The Power-Wagon continued without change.

3/4-TON; 3/4-TON SPECIAL FORWARD CONTROL — C-4-DNL6 — SIX/V-8: Route-Vans were dropped. Regular and Job-Rated 3/4-ton Forward Control truck chassis were offered to accomodate aftermarket delivery chassis. They were a 1955 carryover, except that V-8 engines could now be ordered.

1-TON; 1-TON SPECIAL FORWARD CONTROL — C-4-DN6/C-4-GNL6 — SIX/V-8: The regular 1-ton Forward Control truck chassis (DN) again offered the mid-size 116 and 126 in. wheelbases. The GNL replaced the FNL as the Job-Rated 1-ton (derived from the 1-1/2-ton) on either a 108 in. or 129 in. wheelbase.

I.D. DATA: Serial numbers were on a plate on the left side of the cowl, under the hood. Serial numbers: Six-cylinder [C-4-B] 82398001-82407868. [C-4-C] 83411001-83413368. [C-4-D] 81490001-81492874. [C-4-GL] 80117001 up. [C-4-PW] 83949001-83951794. [C-4-CN] 80200101 up. [C-4-DN/DNL] 80000301 up. Eight cylinder [C-4-B] 84284001-84287960. [C-4-C] 84660001-84661053. [C-4-D] 84807001-84808342. [C-4-GL] 83203501 up. [C-4-DN/DNL] 84004501 up. Engine numbers were stamped on a pad on the left side of the cylinder block, between cylinders two and three. Engine numbers: [C-4-B] T434-1001; VT434-1001. [C-4-B] T436-1001; VT436-1001. [C-4-D] T438-1001; VT438-1001. [C-4-PW] T137-1001. (T prefix for six-cylinder; VT for V-8)

Model	Body Type	Price	Weight	Prod. Total
Series C-4-B — 1/2-Ton — 108 in. w.b. — (6-cyl.)				
C-4-B6	Chassis & Cowl	1195	2200	Note 1
C-4-B6	Chassis & Cab	1431	2675	Note 1
C-4-B6	Pickup (Lowside)	1530	2975	Note 1
C-4-B6	Town Panel	1760	3150	Note 1
C-4-B6	Town Wagon (6P)	2057	—	Note 1
C-4-B6	Town Wagon (8P)	2103	—	Note 1
Series C-4-B — 1/2-Ton — 116 in. w.b. — (6-cyl.)				
C-4-B6	Chassis & Cowl	1208	2225	Note 1
C-4-B6	Chassis & Cab	1444	2700	Note 1
C-4-B6	Pickup (Highside)	1556	3075	Note 1
C-4-B6	Platform 7.5 ft.	1563	—	Note 1
C-4-B6	Stake 7.5 ft.	1629	—	Note 1

Add $120/100 lbs. for C-4-B8 models with V-8 engine.

NOTE 1: Calendar year production: (Domestic) 27,498; (Export) 5,346; [Total] 32,844. Model year production: [Six] (108 in.) 11,285; (116 in.) 2,782. [V-8] (108 in. 1,765; (116 in.) 2,530.

Model	Body Type	Price	Weight	Prod. Total
Series C-4-C — 3/4-Ton — (116 in.w.b.) — (6-cyl.)				
C-4-C6	Chassis & Cowl	1305	2325	Note 2
C-4-C6	Chassis & Cab	1541	2800	Note 2
C-4-C6	Pickup 7.5 ft.	1653	3175	Note 2
C-4-C6	Platform	1780	3250	Note 2
C-4-C6	Stake 7.5 ft.	1846	3450	Note 2

Add $120/100 lbs. for C-4-C8 models with V-8 engine.

Model	Body Type	Price	Weight	Prod. Total
Series C-4-DL6 — 3/4-Ton Special — 116 in. w.b. — (6-cyl.)				
C-4-DL6	Chassis & Cowl	1363	2675	Note 2
C-4-DL6	Chassis & Cab	1599	3150	Note 2
C-4-DL6	Pickup 7.5 ft.	1711	3525	Note 2
C-4-DL6	Platform	1718	3500	Note 2
C-4-DL6	Stake 7.5 ft.	1784	3700	Note 2
Series C-4-DL6 — 3/4-Ton Special — 126 in. w.b. — (6-cyl.)				
C-4-DL6	Chassis & Cowl	1389	2700	Note 2
C-4-DL6	Chassis & Cab	1625	3175	Note 2
C-4-DL6	Pickup 9 ft.	1750	3600	Note 2
C-4-DL6	Platform	1770	3650	Note 2
C-4-DL6	Stake 9 ft.	1836	3825	Note 2

Add $120/100 lbs. for C-4-DL8 models with V-8 engine.

NOTE 2: Calendar year production: (Domestic) 9,100; (Export) 452; (Government) 7; [Total] 9,552. Model year production [Six]: 1,406 (plus 1,089 special models); [V-8] 1,171.

Model	Body Type	Price	Weight	Prod. Total
Series C-4-D — 1-Ton — 116 in. w.b. — (6-cyl.)				
C-4-D6	Chassis & Cowl	1327	—	Note 3
C-4-D6	Chassis & Cab	1563	—	Note 3
C-4-D6	Pickup 7.5 ft.	1675	—	Note 3
C-4-D6	Platform	1682	—	Note 3
C-4-D6	Stake 7.5 ft.	1748	—	Note 3
Series C-4-D — 1-Ton — 126 in. w.b. — (6-cyl.)				
C-4-D6	Chassis & Cowl	1353	—	Note 3
C-4-D6	Chassis & Cab	1589	—	Note 3
C-4-D6	Pickup 9 ft.	1714	—	Note 3
C-4-D6	Platform	1734	—	Note 3
C-4-D6	Stake 9 ft.	1800	—	Note 3

Add $120/100 lbs. for C-4-D8 models with V-8 engine.

NOTE 3: Calendar year production (including Power-Wagons): (Domestic) 7,702; (Export) 6,592; [Total] 14,294. Model year production: [Six] (116 in.) 631; (126 in.) 3,434. [V-8] (116 in.) 132; (126 in.) 1,353.

Model	Body Type	Price	Weight	Prod. Total
Series C4-GL6 — 1-Ton — 129 in. w.b. — (6-cyl.)				
C4-GL6	Chassis & Cowl	1644	3775	—
C4-GL6	Chassis & Cab	1881	—	—
C4-GL6	Platform	2026	—	—
C4-GL6	Stake 9 ft.	2092	—	—
Series C4-GL6 — 1-Ton — 153 in. w.b. — (6-cyl.)				
C4-GL6	Chassis & Cowl	1677	3875	—
C4-GL6	Chassis & Cab	1914	—	—
C4-GL6	Platform	2078	—	—
C4-GL6	Stake 12 ft.	2164	—	—
Series C4-GL6 — 1-Ton — 171 in. w.b. — (6-cyl.)				
C4-GL6	Chassis & Cowl	1710	3900	—
C4-GL6	Chassis & Cab	1942	—	—
C4-GL6	Platform	2131	—	—
C4-GL6	Stake 14 ft.	2236	—	—
Series C-4-PW Power-Wagon — (1-Ton) — (126 in. w.b.)				
C-4-PW	Chassis & Cowl	2157	3800	Note 4
C-4-PW	Chassis & Cab	2393	4275	Note 4
C-4-PW	Pickup 8 ft.	2510	5100	Note 4

NOTE 4: Model year production: 2,730.

Model	Body Type	Price	Weight	Prod. Total
Series C4-DNL — Special 3/4-Ton Forward Control — (6-cyl.)				
116 in. w.b.				
C4-DNL	Chassis	1374	2400	
126 in. w.b.				
C4-DNL	Chassis	1400	2425	

Add $120/100 lbs. for C4-Add $120/100 lbs. for C4-DNL8 models with V-8 engine.

Model	Body Type	Price	Weight	Prod. Total
Series C4-GNL6 — Special 1-Ton Forward Control — (6-cyl.)				
108 in. w.b.				
C4-GNL	Chassis	1589	3175	—
129 in. w.b.				
C4-GNL	Chassis	1622	3275	—

Add $120/100 lbs. for C4-GNL8 models with V-8 engine.

ENGINE [BL6/B6/C6/DL6/GL6/DN6/DNL6]: Inline. L-head. Six-cylinder. Cast iron block. Bore & stroke: 3.25 x 4.625 in. Displacement: 230.2 cid. Compression ratio: 7.6:1. Brake horsepower: 115 at 3600 rpm. Net horsepower: 25.35. Torque: 201 lbs.-ft. at 1600 rpm. Four main bearings. Solid valve lifters.

ENGINE [GNL6]: Inline. L-head. Cast iron block. Bore & stroke: 3.563 x 3.25 in. Net horsepower: 40.62.

ENGINE [C-4-PW Power-Wagon]: Inline. L-head. Six-cylinder. Cast iron block. Bore & stroke: 3.25 x 4.625 in. Displacement: 230.2 cid. Compression ratio: 7.6:1. Brake horsepower: 111 at 3600 rpm. Net horsepower: 25.35. Torque: 198 lbs.-ft. at 1600 rpm. Four main bearings. Solid valve lifters.

ENGINE [All V-8 Models]: V-8. Overhead valves. Eight-cylinder. Cast iron block. Bore & stroke: 3.563 x 3.25 in. Displacement: 259.2 cid. Compression ratio: 7.6:1. Brake horsepower: 169 at 4400 rpm. Net horsepower: 40.6. Torque: 243 lbs.-ft. at 2400 rpm. Five main bearings. Hydraulic valve lifters.

CHASSIS [Series C-4-B]: Wheelbase: 108 in. and 116 in. Tires: 6.70 x 15 four-ply (front and rear). GVW: 5,100 lbs. Front axle capacity: 2,500 lbs. Rear axle capacity: 3,300 lbs.

CHASSIS [Series C-4-C]: Wheelbase: 116 in. Tires: 7.00 x 15 six-ply (front and rear). GVW: 5,800 lbs. Front axle capacity: 2,500 lbs. Rear axle capacity: 3,300 lbs.

CHASSIS [Series C-4-D/C-4-DL]: Wheelbase: 116 in. and 126 in. Tires: (front) 6.00 x 16 six-ply; (rear) 7.00 x 16 six-ply. GVW: 8,800 lbs. Front axle capacity: 2,800 lbs. Rear axle capacity: 3,600 lbs.

CHASSIS [Series C-4-PW Power-Wagon]: Wheelbase: 126 in. Tires: 7.50 x 16 eight-ply (front and rear). GVW: 9,500 lbs.

CHASSIS [Forward Control]: Wheelbase: 108; 116;126; and 142 in. GVWs: [CN] 6,000 lbs.; [DN/DNL] 9,000 lbs.; [[FNL] 9,500 lbs. Tires: Various.

TECHNICAL: Selective sliding gear transmission. Speeds: 3F/1R; optional 4F/1R, or 3F/1R with overdrive. Column or floor shift. Automatic transmission optional. Single-plate dry-disc clutch: 10 in., except 11 in. with optional heavy-duty or four-speed transmission. Rear axle ratio: [3/4-ton] 3.73:1, 4.1:1 and 4.78:1; [1-ton] 4.1:1 and 4.89:1. Hydraulic four-wheel brakes.

OPTIONS (Factory Installed): Rear bumper ($11.25). Bumper guards ($5.50). Deluxe cab equipment ($26). Custom equipment ($51). Custom Regal equipment ($79). Left door armrest ($3.30). Town Panel Deluxe equipment ($22.50); Custom Regal equipment ($51). Long-arm mirror: Left side ($2.50); right side ($3.95). Inside rearview mirror ($3). Bright metal molding package for Town Panel ($14.50). Dodge Tint glass, all models ($17.50). Right inside sun visor ($3). Auxiliary taillamp ($7.25). Dual electric horns ($14.50). Horn ring ($3). Cab corner marker lights ($10). Set of four bright hubcaps ($1.65); set of five ($3). Set of four 15 inch wheelcovers ($16.50). Dome light ($5.50). Heater: Standard ($41.50); Deluxe ($62). Deluxe seat for Town Panel ($11.25). Auxiliary seat for Town Panel ($45). Deluxe seat back and cushion ($11.25 each). Dual electric wipers ($11.25). Wrap-around rear window ($29). Inside tire carrier, Town Panel ($6). Side tire carrier for pickup ($10.25). Hand throttle control ($3). One-quart oil-bath air cleaner: [Six] ($1.65); [V-8] ($3.95). Increased cooling capacity ($10). Ashtray ($1.65). Oil filter ($12). Electric fuel pump ($16). Three-speed transmission with overdrive ($100). Heavy-duty three-speed transmission with 10 in. clutch ($40); with 11 in. clutch ($45). Four-speed transmission

automatic transmission ($165). Governor ($10). [C-4-BL6-108 Model Only] Rear bumper ($11.25). Increased cooling capacity ($10). Turn signals ($23.50). Heater ($41.50). Oil filter ($12). Auxiliary taillight ($7.25). (Power-Wagon Only) Deluxe cab equipment ($10). Turn signals ($30.50). Dodge Tint glass ($17.50). Long-arm mirror: Left side ($2.50); right ($3.95). Inside mirror ($3). Front and rear fenders painted cab color ($7.50). Auxiliary taillight ($8.75). Brake booster with 7-1/2 in. diaphragm ($42.50). Governor ($69.10). Draw bar ($23.05). Heater ($41.50). Oil filter ($12). Pintle hook ($12.50). Power-take-off ($75.70). Pulley drive ($85.55). Radiator overflow tank ($10). Rear driveshaft assembly ($85.55). Rear shock absorbers ($34.90). Front springs with 1,600 lbs. capacity ($7.90). Rear main springs, 3,000 lbs. ($8.75). Front tow hooks ($8.25/pair). Winch assembly ($243.45).

HISTORICAL: The C-4 was a continuation of C-3 series. Calendar year sales: 57,651. Calendar year production: 91,383. Model year production: [Six] 23,795; [V-8] 6982; [Total light-duty C-4 Series] 30,777. Model year production (U.S. only): (Six) 12,631; [V-8] 6,249; [Total] 18,880. Dodge truck sales fell 12.9 percent from their 1955 level, more than the industry drop of 6.5 percent. Total exports came to 12,390. In January, 1956, Dodge received an order for 2,000 special sit/stand 3/4-ton trucks for the U.S. Post Office. Equipped with automatic transmissions, their bodies were built by Twin Coach. Dodge also built a line of 1- and 1-1/2-ton forward control chassis-only models, powered by sixes or V-8s, with bodies supplied by other companies. This was a period of rising demand for heavy-duty trucks, due to the multi-billion dollar federal highway building program which would put a national freeway system in place. To capitalize on this trend, Dodge discontinued the 413 cid six in its 4-ton series, replacing it with a 354 cid hemi V-8. Two new V-8s were also made available to Dodge's cab-over-engine models, a 269.6 cid and a 331 cid hemi. A 2-ton 4x4 truck was added to the Power-Wagon line. It had a 265 cid six.

1957 DODGE

1957 Dodge D100 1/2-Ton Sweptside Pickup (OCW)

1/2-TON — K SERIES D100 — SIX/V-8: To stay as stylish as Dodge cars, the trucks got the "Forward Look." The front fender line extended forward and the headlights were hooded. There was a feeling of motion, even if the truck was at rest. The entire front clip was redesigned, as were the hood and front bumper. A first was an alligator type, rear-hinged hood. It had two positions: 45 degrees for engine servicing and 90 degrees for full accessibility. The panel just below the hood had Dodge lettering above a large air inlet. Six short vertical "stripes" were just below the air inlet and above a full-width chrome horizontal bar that ran above the grille. The lower grille had an air slot inside a pained recessed panel. A chrome horizontal bar extended out, in both directions, from a vertical center piece. Round parking lamps were placed in the painted bumper outside the horizontal bar. Pull-type door handles, safety door latches, locks on both doors, adjustable tilting seatbacks and chrome grille bars were all new. The hand-brake could be adjusted from inside the cab by turning a knob at the end of the handle. Two basic cabs were available: Standard and Custom. Standard cab equipment included dual electric wipers, ashtray, dome light, left armrest, sound-deadened door panels, rubber floor mats, left side mirror and sun visor, and two-tone interior trim. Custom cabs added a glove box lock, Saron and Rayon seat covering, foam rubber seat cushion, right sun visor, wraparound rear window, and two-speed wipers. Exterior trim consisted of an almost-oval series badge with arrowhead-shaped chrome embellishments. V-shaped decoration brightened the front of the hood on V-8s. New colors were: Stone gray, Mojave beige, Pacific blue, Bermuda coral, Bayview green and Omaha orange. Six old colors were dropped. Beginning this year, all pickup boxes were painted cab color; wood pickup box floors were black. Push-button three-speed PowerFlite automatic transmission was an extra-cost option on D100/D200/D300 models. The base six gained a horsepower boost by raising its compression ratio to 8.0:1. A larger new (315 cid/204 hp) V-8 was now standard. It was the largest engine in the light-duty truck field. All models had shock absorbers front and rear. The GVW rating was 5,100 lbs.

1957 Dodge D200 3/4-Ton Pickup (DFW)

NEW P1/2-TON SPECIAL — K SERIES D110 — SIX/V-8: This was a lighter-duty Job-Rated version of the regular 1/2-ton series with a 4,250 lbs. GVW rating. Both 108 and 116 in. models were offered.

1/2-TON SPECIAL — K SERIES D100 SWEPTSIDE PICKUP — SIX/V-8: A midyear addition entered the lineup in May, 1957. This famous Sweptside D110 pickup was Dodge's answer to Chevrolet's Cameo Carrier of 1955 and Ford's 1957 Ranchero. Dodge created the Sweptside by grafting rear fenders from its two-door station wagon onto the sides of its 116 in. wheelbase "long box" half-ton pickup. The station wagon's rear bumper was also used. In addition, the Sweptside got chrome rear quarter moldings to complete the lines running forward from the station wagon fenders. All Sweptside cabs were of Custom type. They had a 5,100 lbs. GVW rating.

1957 Dodge W100 1/2-Ton 4x4 Pickup (RCA)

1/2-TON — K SERIES D210 — SIX/V-8: Sharing the new K Series styling was a Job-Rated 1/2-ton version of the D200 Dodge 3/4-ton with a 5,800 lbs. GVW rating. This fell between the regular 1/2-ton's 5,100 lbs. GVW and the normal GVW of the 3/4-ton on which it was based. It shared the D200's 116 in. wheelbase.

3/4-TON — K SERIES D200 — SIX/V-8: The regular 3/4-ton line featured two chassis models, a long bed (7.5-ft) pickup and platform/stake models, as well as the year's new "Forward Look." It had a 7,500 lbs. GVW rating.

3/4-TON SPECIAL — K SERIES D310 — SIX/V-8: This was a Job-Rated version of the regular 1-ton with the 126 in. wheelbase. It had a lower 5,800 lbs. GVW than the D200.

3/4-TON SPECIAL — K SERIES D320 — SIX/V-8: This was a second Job-Rated version of the regular 1-ton with a 7,500 lbs. GVW rating, which was the same as the D200 had.

1-TON SPECIAL — K SERIES D220 — SIX/V-8: Is there no end to this madness? This was the regular 3/4-ton up-rated to a GVW in the 1-ton range. It had the 116 in. wheelbase.

1-TON — K SERIES D300 — SIX/V-8: This is the regular 1-ton. It had the new Forward-Look styling. It had the 126 in. wheelbase. It also had a 9,000 lbs. GVW rating.

1-TON — K SERIES D410 — SIX/V-8: Naturally, there was a 1-ton version of the 1-1/2 base model. This Job-Rated 1-ton on the 129, 153 or 171 in. wheelbases had an 11,000 lbs. GVW. That compared to 15,000 lbs. for the same model in the 1-1/2-ton format.

3/4-TON/1-TON — K SERIES; W100/W200 (4x4) — SIX/V-8: The Power-Wagon had proven so successful that customers were demanding additional models. So, Dodge now offered 1/2-ton (W100) and 3/4-ton (W200) conventional models with four-wheel drive. It was available with all body types, from pickups through Town Wagons. All had shock absorbers in front only. There is no indication that Job-Rated GVW options (i.e. D110) offered 4x4 equipment.

1-TON POWER-WAGON — K SERIES W300 — SIX: After 1957, the Power-Wagon would be designated WM300 (W300 would denote a conventional 1-ton 4x4). Power-Wagon front and rear fenders were painted black, regardless of cab color.

FORWARD CONTROL — K SERIES P300/P400 — SIX: P300 Forward Control models were the 1/2-ton P310 and 3/4-ton P320 and the 1-Ton P300 that they were based on. These models shared 116 or 126 in. wheelbases. Additional 3/4-ton (P410) and 1-ton (P420) models were offered as GVW options for the 1-1/2-ton P400 model.

I.D. DATA: Beginning with 1957, Dodge used a new identifying system. A letter indicated the year (K=1957), while a number ranked the individual models according to truck size: 100=1/2-ton; 200=3/4-ton; 300=1-ton and so on, up to 900. Model types were identified by a letter preceding the number: D=conventional 4x2; C=cab-over-engine; T=tandem axle; P=forward-control; W=conventional 4x4; WM=Military Type Power-Wagon 4x4. Serial number information was found on a ticket in the glove box. Starting Serial Numbers: (D100 Six) 82413001; (D100 V-8) 84289001; (D200 Six) 83414001; (D200 V-8) 84662001; (D300 Six) 81494001; (D300 V-8) 84809001; (W100 Six) 8191001; (W100 V-8) 82901001; (W200 Six) 82701001; (W200 V-8) 83250001; (W300) 83952001. Six-cylinder engine numbers were located on the left side of the block at the front, below the cylinder head. V-8 engine numbers were on top of the cylinder block, behind the water pump. Starting Engine Numbers: (D100 Six) T534-1001; (D100 V-8) VT534-1001; (D200 Six) T536-1001; (D200 V-8) VT536-1001; (D300 Six) T538-1001; (D300 V-8) VT538-1001; (W100 Six) T500-1001; (W100 V-8) VT500-1001; (W200 Six) T502-1001; (W200 V-8) VT502-1001; (W300) T137-1001. Ending serial and engine numbers are not available.

190

1957 Dodge D100 1/2-Ton Town Wagon (OCW)

1957 Dodge D100 1/2-Ton Sweptside Pickup (OCW)

Model	Body Type	Price	Weight	Prod. Total
K6-D100 Series — 1/2-Ton — 108 in. w.b. — (6-cyl.)				
D100	Chassis & Cowl	1279	2400	—
D100	Chassis & Cab	1524	2875	—
D100	Pickup 6.5 ft.	1620	3225	-
D100	Town Panel 7.5 ft.	1873	3825	—
D100	Town Wagon (6P)	2164	3925	—
D100	Town Wagon (8P)	2210	3975	—
K6-D100 Series — 1/2-Ton — 116 in. w.b. — (6-cyl.)				
D100	Chassis & Cowl	1295	2425	—
D100	Chassis & Cab	1540	2900	—
D100	Pickup 7.5 ft.	1646	3250	—
D100	Platform	1665	3250	—
D100	Stake 7.5 ft.	1731	3450	—
D100	Sweptside Pickup	1614	3425	1050

Add $105.30 and 100 lbs. for K8-D100 with 314.61 cid V-8.
Also available as 1/2-ton K6-D110 or K8-D110 (4,250 lbs. GVW).

K6-D200 Series — 3/4-Ton — 116 in. w.b. — (6-cyl.)				
D200	Chassis & Cowl	1449	2925	—
D200	Chassis & Cab	1694	3400	—
D200	Pickup	1800	3775	—
D200	Platform	1819	3750	—
D200	Stake	1885	3950	—

Add $105.30 and 100 lbs. for K8-D200 with 314.61 cid V-8.
Also available as 1/2-Ton K6-D210/K8-D210 (5,800 lbs. GVW).
Also available as 1-Ton K6-D220/K8-D220 (GVW n.a.).

K6-D300 Series — 1-Ton — 126 in. w.b.				
D300	Chassis & Cowl	1482	3025	—
D300	Chassis & Cab	1727	3500	—
D300	Pickup	1852	3925	—
D300	Platform	1881	3900	—
D300	Stake	1947	4150	—

Add $105.30 and 100 lbs. for K8-D300 with 314.61 cid V-8.
Also available as 3/4-ton K6-D310/K8-D310 (5,800 lbs. GVW).
Also available as 3/4-ton K6-D320/K8-D320 (7,500 lbs. GVW).

K6-D410 Series — 1-Ton — 129/153/171 in. w.b.				
D410	Chassis & Cowl	—	—	—
D410	Chassis & Cab	—	—	—
D410	Platform	—	—	—
D410	Stake	—	—	—

Job-Rated 1-ton versions of 1-1/2-ton (11,000 lbs. GVW).
Prices/weights for the three lines (129/153/171) not available.
The base V-8 was only $79 extra in D400s.

Series K6-W100 (4x4) — 1/2-Ton — 108 in. w.b.				
W100	Chassis & Cowl	2253	3100	—
W100	Chassis & Cab	2489	3575	—
W100	Pickup 6.5 ft.	2594	3925	—
W100	Town Panel	2865	4525	—
W100	Town Wagon (6P)	3143	4625	—
W100	Town Wagon (8P)	3189	4675	—

Add $105.30 and 100 lbs. for K8-W100 with 314.61 cid V-8.

Series K6-W100 (4x4) — 1/2-Ton — 116 in. w.b.				
W100	Chassis & Cowl	2289	3125	—
W100	Chassis & Cab	2524	3600	—
W100	Pickup 7.5 ft.	2629	3950	—
W100	Platform	2660	3950	—
W100	Stake 7.5 ft.	2715	4150	—

Add $105.30 and 100 lbs. for K8-W100 with 314.61 cid V-8.

Series K6-W200 (4x4) — 3/4-Ton — 116 in. w.b.				
W200	Chassis & Cowl	2397	3975	—
W200	Chassis & Cab	2641	4450	—
W200	Pickup 7.5 ft.	2747	4875	—
W200	Platform	2777	4850	—
W200	Stake 7.5 ft.	2832	5100	—

Add $105.30 and 100 lbs. for K8-W100 with 314.61 cid V-8.

Series K6-MW300 Power-Wagon (4x4) — 1-Ton — 126 in. w.b.				
MW300	Chassis & Cowl	2266	4650	—
MW300	Chassis & Cab	2511	5075	—
MW300	Pickup	2636	5450	—

Series 6K-P300 Forward Control — 1-TON — 116/126 in. w.b.

116 in. w.b.

P300	Chassis	1462	2400	—

126 in. w.b.

P300	Chassis	1493	2425	—

Series 6K-P410/P420 Forward Control — 3/4 to 1-ton — 108/129 in. w.b.

108 in. w.b.

P400	Chassis	1736	3175	—
P400	Chassis	1797	3275	—

Prices/weights are for 1-1/2-ton P400 base model (15,000 lbs. GVW)
Also available as 3/4-ton K6-P410 (GVW 7,500 lbs.)
Also available as 1-ton K6-P420 (GVW 9,500 lbs.)

1957 Dodge D100 1/2-Ton Sweptside Pickup (rear view)

ENGINE [All except PW/D410]: Inline. L-head. Six-cylinder. Cast iron block. Bore & stroke: 3.25 x 4.625 in. Displacement: 230.2 cid. Compression ratio: 8.0:1. Brake horsepower: 120 at 3600 rpm. Net horsepower: 25.35. Torque: 202 lbs.-ft. at 1600 rpm. Four main bearings. Solid valve lifters.

ENGINE [D410]: Inline. L-head. Six-cylinder. Cast iron block. Bore & stroke: 3.47 x 4.5. Displacement: 250.6 cid. Compression ratio: 7.1:1. Brake horsepower: 125 at 3600 rpm. Net horsepower: 28.35. Torque: 216 lbs.-ft. at 1600 rpm. Four main bearings. Solid valve lifters.

ENGINE [All except PW/P300P310/P320/P410/P420]: V-8. Overhead valve. Eight-cylinder. Cast iron block. Bore & stroke: 3.63 x 3.80 in. Displacement: 314.6 cid. Compression ratio: 8.5:1. Brake horsepower: 204 at 4400 rpm. Net horsepower: 42.16. Torque: 290 lbs.-ft. at 2400 rpm. Five main bearings. Hydraulic valve lifters.

ENGINE [Power-Wagon]: Inline. L-head. Six-cylinder. Cast iron block. Bore & stroke: 3.25 x 4.625 in. Displacement: 230.2 cid. Compression ratio: 7.9:1. Brake horsepower: 113 at 3600 rpm. Net horsepower: 25.35. Torque: 198 lbs.-ft. at 1600 rpm. Four main bearings. Solid valve lifters.

CHASSIS [D100-108]: Wheelbase: 108 in. Tires: 6.70 x 15 four-ply; tubeless passenger-car type (front and rear). GVW: 4250 lbs. Front axle capacity: 2,500 lbs. Rear axle: 3,600 lbs. Front spring capacity: 900 lbs. Rear spring: 1,200 lbs.

CHASSIS [D110-108]: Wheelbase: 108 in. GVW: 4,250 lbs. GVW.

CHASSIS [D100-116]: Wheelbase: 116 in. Tires and capacities: Same as D100-108 except 5,100 lbs. GVW.

CHASSIS [D200]: Wheelbase: 116 in. Tires: 7 x 17.5 six-ply (front and rear); tubeless truck type. GVW: 7,500 lbs. Front axle capacity: 2,800 lbs. Rear axle: 6,500 lbs. Front spring capacity: 1,000 lbs. Rear spring: 1,950 lbs.

CHASSIS [D210]: Wheelbase: 116 in. Tires: 7 x 17.5 six-ply (front and rear); tubeless truck type. GVW: 5,800 lbs.

CHASSIS [D220]: Wheelbase: 116 in. Tires: 7 x 17.5 six-ply (front and rear); tubeless truck type. GVW: n.a..

CHASSIS [D300]: Wheelbase: 126 in. GVW: 8,800 lbs.

CHASSIS [D310]: Wheelbase: 126 in. GVW: 5,800 lbs.

CHASSIS [D320]: Wheelbase: 126 in. GVW: 7,500 lbs.

CHASSIS [D410]: Wheelbase: 129/153/171 in. GVW: 11,000 lbs.

CHASSIS [W100]: Wheelbase: 108 in. and 116 in. Tires: 7 x 17.5 six-ply (front and rear). GVW: 5,100 lbs. Front axle capacity: 3,000 lbs. Rear axle: 3,600 lbs. Front spring capacity: 1,050 lbs. Rear springs: 1,250 lbs.

CHASSIS [W200]: Wheelbase: 116 in. Tires: 7 x 17.5 six-ply (front and rear). GVW: 8,000 lbs. Front axle capacity: 3,000 lbs. Rear axle: 6,500 lbs. Front spring capacity: 1,050 lbs. Rear springs: 1,750 lbs.

CHASSIS [W300 Power-Wagon]: Wheelbase: 126 in. Tires: 7.50 x 16 eight-ply (front and rear). GVW: 9,500 lbs. Front axle capacity: 3,750 lbs. Rear axle: 6,500 lbs. Front spring capacity: 1,150 lbs. Rear springs: 2,500 lbs.

CHASSIS [P300 Forward Control]: Wheelbase: 116/126 in. GVW: 9,000 lbs.

CHASSIS [P310 Forward Control]: Wheelbase: 116/126 in. GVW: 6,000 lbs.

CHASSIS [P320 Forward Control]: Wheelbase: 116/126 in. GVW: 7,800 lbs.

CHASSIS [P410 Forward Control]: Wheelbase: 108/129 in. GVW: 7,500 lbs.

CHASSIS [P420 Forward Control]: Wheelbase: 108/129 in. GVW: 9,500 lbs.

1957 Dodge W100 1/2-Ton 4x4 7-1/2 ft. Stake (RCA)

TECHNICAL: Selective sliding gear transmission. Speeds: 3F/1R (heavy-duty on 3/4- and 1-ton). Four-speed, overdrive and automatic transmissions available. Single-plate dry-disc clutch (11 in.). Column shift control (push-button automatic). One-pint oil bath air cleaner. Standard rear axle ratio: 4.1:1. Optional axle ratios: [1/2-ton] 3.73:1; [3/4- and 1-ton] 4.89:1. Hydraulic four-wheel brakes. Five disc wheels: [1/2-ton] 4.50 in.; [3/4- and 1-ton] 5.25 in. [W100/W200] Same, except two-speed transfer case with three-speed transmission. Standard axle ratio: 4.09:1 front, 4.11:1 rear, or 4.89:1 front and rear. Six-hole 5.25 in. wheels. [W300 Power-Wagon] Four-speed transmission. Front/rear axle ratio: 4.89:1 with 7.50 x 16 tires; 5.83:1 with 9.00 x 16 tires. Two-speed transfer case. Velocity-type governor. One-quart oil bath air cleaner. Five 5.50 in. wheels.

1957 Dodge D100 1/2-Ton Sweptside Pickup (DB)

OPTIONS [Factory Installed]: [Conventional] Chrome front bumper ($13.20). Painted rear bumper ($19.20). Chrome plated rear bumper ($25). Bumper guards: Painted ($5.30); chrome ($11.90). Bright hubcaps, set of our ($7.30); set of five for pickup with side tire carrier ($8.70). Chrome wheelcovers, set of four ($16.50); set of five ($20.60). Custom equipment ($46.10). Turn signals ($23.10). Dodge Tint glass ($17.20). Chrome headlight doors ($2). Cab corner marker lights ($9.90). Dual electric horns ($14.50). Horn ring ($3). Cigar lighter ($4.70). Glove box lock ($4). Inside rearview mirror ($3). Adjustable mirror: Left side ($2.40); right side ($4.30). Bright metal windshield molding ($7). Grab handles ($8.50). Two-tone paint ($15.20). Wraparound rear window ($29). Dual electric wipers ($7.20). Windshield washer ($11.60). Auxiliary taillamp ($7.30). Right side sun visor ($3). Foam padded seatback ($11.20); seat cushion ($11.20). Rear shocks for D200 or D300 ($17.80). Tire carrier on side of pickup ($10.20). Hand throttle on dash ($3). One-quart oil bath air cleaner: Six-cylinder ($1.70); V-8 ($4). Right door armrest ($3.30). One-quart oil filter ($11.90); two-quart ($15.80). Electric fuel pump ($25). Increased cooling capacity ($9.90). Vacuum brake booster ($42.50). Velocity type governor, manual transmission only ($9.90). Perforated headliner ($5.60). Heater ($46.10). Deluxe heater ($65.80). Power steering ($112). V-8 engine ($105.30). Three-ton jack ($7.90). Heavy-duty three-speed transmission ($57). Three-speed with overdrive transmission, D100 only ($100). Four-speed transmission: D100 ($65); D200 or D300 ($46.20). Three-speed automatic transmission with push-button control ($203.75). [Town Panel/Town Wagon only] Chrome plated rear bumper ($13.20). Custom Town Panel equipment ($19.80). Turn signals ($18.50). Headliner roof insulation ($7.20). Recessed rear license plate light ($8.60). Bright metal molding package ($14.50). Two-tone paint ($25). Auxiliary seat, standard panel ($34.90). Auxiliary seat, custom panel ($46.10). Tire carrier inside ($6). Side windows in panel, stationary clear glass ($50). Dodge Tint glass ($17.20). [W300 Power-Wagon] Deluxe cab equipment ($19). Dodge Tint glass ($17.20). Turn signals ($30.30). Grab handles ($8.50/pair). Inside rearview mirror ($3). Long- arm adjustable mirror: Left side ($2.40); right ($4.30). Heater ($46.10). Front and rear fenders painted to match cab color ($13.20). Auxiliary taillight ($7.30). Windshield washer ($11.60). Vacuum brake booster, 7-1/2 in. diaphragm ($42.50). Draw bar ($23.10). Oil filter, two-quart ($6). Pintle hook ($12.50). Power-take-off ($75.20). Pulley drive ($85.60). Rear driveshaft assembly ($85.60). Rear shocks ($34.90). Springs, 1,600 lbs. capacity ($164.50). Winch ($243.45). Three-ton jack ($7.90).

HISTORICAL: Introduced: October 30, 1956. Calendar year sales: 49,431. Calendar year production: 76,601. Innovations: 12-volt electrical system. Ignition key starter switch. "Forward Look" styling taken from Chrysler Corp. passenger cars. Half-ton and 3/4-ton four-wheel drive models. Sweptside pickup mating station wagon and pickup styling. Sales fell again this year. They went down by 14.2 percent; some 10 percent more than the total industry drop. Dodge ranked fifth in truck sales, with seven percent of the total manufacturing output. V-8 truck sales rose from 38 percent in 1954 to 54 percent in 1957. In March, Chrysler Corp. received over $12 million in defense contracts. One was for 2,900 4x4 trucks; another for $3.5 million worth of spare parts for World War II type military trucks. Also in March, Dodge offered for commercial sale a modification of the compact Post Office truck, for door-to-door delivery use. This forward control truck was built on a D100 or D200 chassis, shortened to 95 in. wheelbase and powered by a six-cylinder engine with push-button automatic transmission. Other forward control chassis were in the regular lineup, in four wheelbase lengths of the P300 or P400 series (3/4- or 1-ton). Dodge made significant inroads into the heavy-duty market, due to the outstanding performance of their hemi-head V-8s. Advertisements proclaimed the 1957 Dodge truck line as "Power Giants."

1957 Dodge W100 1/2-Ton 4x4 Town Wagon (RCA)

1958 DODGE

1958 Dodge D100 1/2-Ton Sweptside Pickup w/camper (OCW)

ALL — L SERIES — SIX/V-8: In 1958, it was possible to order at least 228 Dodge trucks in 1/2-, 3/4- or 1-ton weight classes (or Job-Rated options), with six-cylinder or V-8 powerplants and 4x2 (two-wheel drive) or 4x4 (four-wheel drive) running gear. This total did not include additional options, such as standard or Custom cab equipment. The following descriptions outline the basic truck lines offered for the year.

1/2-TON — L SERIES D100/D110 — SIX/V-8: The 1/2-ton Dodge 4x2 truck line had six offerings on both the 108 in. and 116 in. wheelbases. The small 230 cid six or base 315 cid V-8 was available in all models. The 1958 Power Giant models featured all new styling from the cowl forward with a full-width hood, quad headlights, new grille and heavy-duty bumper. New fender housings and two-piece splash shields created an engine compartment as wide as possible. Engine access was greatly improved. The battery was moved from under the driver's floor to under the hood. All models available in 1957 were carried forward, including the Sweptside pickup (on the 116 in. wheelbase only). A new Tradesman utility, was available on D100 and D200 chassis. It featured two large horizontal storage compartments and one vertical compartment on each side, all lockable. Tradesman bodies were a favorite with utility companies. New progressive-type rear springs and redesigned front springs with lowered deflection rates improved D100 ride quality. The D100s retained a 5,100 lbs. GVW rating. Those rear springs gave a smoother ride while the truck was empty, stiffening with a load, for support and smoothness. A new chrome trim package including chromed grille bars, sweeping side moldings, chromed hood ornament, and anodized headlight trim plates was optional. Thirteen body colors were available, plus 12 two-tone combinations. New colors were Marlin blue, Arctic blue, Valley green, Bell green, Ranch brown, Alaska white, Angus black, Klondike yellow and Sahara beige. Two-tones had

Sahara beige at the top. Standard and Custom cabs were available. Cabs featured new colors, a hooded instrument panel to reduce glare, red warning lights (replacing ammeter and oil pressure gauge), deep-dish steering wheel, a turn-signal switch integral with steering column and an available roof-mounted transistor radio. Standard equipment was the same as in 1957. The D100 models were available as Job-Rated D110s with lower GVW ratings from 4,250 lbs. In all, there were 48 basic 1/2-ton 4x2 trucks.

1/2-TON — L SERIES W100 — SIX/V-8: In 4x4 format, the 1/2-ton was called the W100. The model lineup was similar to the D100s, except that Sweptline pickups did not come with four-wheel drive. Also, there was no "W110" Job-Rated GVW option. There were 22 varieties here.

1958 Dodge D100 1/2-Ton Sweptside Pickup (JAW)

3/4-TON — L SERIES D200/D210/D220 — SIX/V-8: The D200 was the regular 3/4-ton Dodge 4x2 truck. This line included two chassis models, an express and platform/stake trucks on a 116 in. wheelbase. They had a 7,500 lbs. GVW rating. The small six or base V-8 were available, giving 30 offerings in all.

3/4-TON — L SERIES W200/W210 — SIX/V-8: This was Dodge's 3/4-ton 4x4 truck line with five offerings in the 116 in. wheelbase. For the first time, this type of truck was available as a W210 (1/2-ton) with lower Job-Rated GVW. In all, there were 20 base models.

1-TON — L SERIES D300/D310/D320 — SIX/V-8: The description "4x2 Dodge 1-ton conventional" could be used on over 30 trucks in 1958. The D300s were the "real" 1-tons with five offerings on a 126 in. wheelbase. Two Job-Rated GVW options were available: The D310 and D320. All could have either engine.

1-TON — L SERIES W300/W310 — SIX/V-8: A new 4x4 Dodge 1-ton added 20 distinct offerings to the lineup. There were five base models on a 129 in. wheelbase, all available with a six or V-8 and all with a W310 (3/4-ton) Job-Rated option.

1-TON — L SERIES D410 — SIX/V-8: If you wanted a big 1-ton Dodge 4x2 truck, the company would sell you a 1-1/2-ton-based D410 Job-Rated down to 1-ton (11,000 lbs. GVW, instead of the normal 15,000 lbs. Wheelbases of 129, 153 and 171 in. were listed for the 1-1/2-tons. The largest models had 14 ft. stake rack bodies and dual rear wheels. There were 24 offerings with a six or V-8.

1-TON — L SERIES W300M/W310M — SIX: The 4x4 Power Wagon series offered two chassis jobs and an eight-foot express on the 126 in. wheelbase. Only the small six, with a distinct horsepower rating, was installed. For the first time, there was a Job-Rated W310M (3/4-ton) option. Dodge added the M suffix to the Power Wagon model code to indicate "military" style truck and to distinguish it from the new W300 conventional 1-ton 4x4.

1-TON — L SERIES P300/P310/P320 — SIX/V-8: These 1-ton Forward Control delivery trucks came on 104 and 126 in. wheelbases with two Job-Rated 3/4-ton GVW options (P310 and P320). There were six chassis models in all, with a V-8 option increasing offerings to 12. For $467.20 extra, the factory would install a body front end section.

1-TON — L SERIES P410/P420 — SIX/V-8: Job-Rated 1-ton versions of the 1-1/2-ton Forward Control; the P410 was classed a 3/4-ton with 7,500 lbs. GVW and the P420, with its 9,500 GVW, was considered a 1-ton. These were for buyers who wanted 108, 125, 137 or 153 in. wheelbase stand-up delivery vehicles for lighter loads. With both engines available, this totaled 16 chassis variations.

I.D. DATA: Serial numbers were on a plate on the left door hinge pillar. Starting Serial Numbers: [D100 Six] L6D10-L01001; [D100 V-8] L8D10-L01001; [D200 Six] L6D20-L01001; [D200 V-8] L8D20-L01001; [D300 Six] L6D30-L01001; [D300 V-8] L8D30-L01001; [D410 Six] L6D4-HO1001; [D410 V-8] L8D4-HO1001; [P300 Six] L6P3-L01001; [P300 V-8] L8P3-L01001; [P410/P420] L6P4-HO1001; [P410/P420 V-8] L8P4-HO1001; [W100 Six] L6W10-L01001; [W100 V-8] L8W10-L01001; [W200 Six] L6W20-L01001; [W200 V-8] L8W20-L01001; [W300 Six] L6W30-L01001; [W300 V-8] L8W30-L01001; [W300M Power-Wagon] L6WM30-L01001. Engine numbers stamped on pad on left side of block. Starting Engine Numbers: [D100 Six] L6-D1-1001; [D100 V-8] L8-D1-1001; [D200 Six] L6-D2-1001; [D200 V-8] L8-D2-1001; [D300 Six] L6-D3-1001; [D300 V-8] L8-D3-1001; [W100 Six] L6-W1-1001; [W100 V-8] L8-W1-1001; [W200 Six] L6-W2-1001; [W200 V-8] L8-W2-1001; [W300 Six] L6-W3-1001; [W300 V-8] L8-W3-1001; [W300M Power-Wagon] L6-WM3-1001. Ending serial and engine numbers are not available.

1958 Dodge Compact Mini-Van (James A. Wren)

Model	Body Type	Price	Weight	Prod. Total
Series L6-D100 — 1/2-Ton — 108 in. w.b.				
D100	Chassis & Cowl	1373	2400	Note 1
D100	Chassis & Cab	1608	2875	Note 1
D100	Pickup	1714	3225	Note 1
D100	Town Panel	1985	3350	Note 1
D100	Town Wagon (6P)	2262	3575	Note 1
D100	Town Wagon (8P)	2308	3575	Note 1

(*) D110 (1/2-ton) Job-Rated GVW option available.
NOTE 1: Model year production, D100-108: (Six) 11,862; (V-8) 2,435.

Series L6-D100 — 1/2-Ton — 116 in. w.b.				
D100	Chassis & Cowl	1411	2450	Note 2
D100	Chassis & Cab	1647	2925	Note 2
D100	Pickup	1752	3300	Note 2
D100	Platform	1782	3300	Note 2
D100	Stake	1837	3475	Note 2
D100	Sweptside Pickup	2124	3425	Note 2

(*) D110 (1/2-ton) Job-Rated GVW option available.
NOTE 2: Model year production, D100-116: (Six) 4,199; (V-8) 6,067.

Series L6-D200 — 3/4-Ton — 116 in. w.b.				
D200	Chassis & Cowl	1595	2875	Note 3
D200	Chassis & Cab	1840	3350	Note 3
D200	Pickup	1945	3725	Note 3
D200	Platform	1975	3725	Note 3
D200	Stake	2031	3900	Note 3

(*) D210 (1/2-ton) and D220 (1-ton) Job-Rated GVW options available.
NOTE 3: Model year production: (Six) 1,899; (V-8) 1,508.

Series L6-D300 — 1-Ton — 126 in. w.b.				
D300	Chassis & Cowl	1631	3025	Note 4
D300	Chassis & Cab	1875	3500	Note 4
D300	Pickup	2000	3925	Note 4
D300	Platform	2041	3950	Note 4
D300	Stake	2106	4150	Note 4

(*) D310 (3/4-ton) and D320 (3/4-ton) Job-Rated GVW options available.
NOTE 4: Model year production: (Six) 2973; (V-8) 2148.

Series L6-W100 4x4 — 1/2-Ton — 108 in. w.b.				
W100	Chassis & Cowl	2253	3100	Note 5
W100	Chassis & Cab	2489	3575	Note 5
W100	Pickup	2594	3925	Note 5
W100	Town Panel	2865	4050	Note 5
W100	Town Wagon (6P)	3143	4275	Note 5
W100	Town Wagon (8P)	3189	4300	Note 5

(*) No Job-Rated GVW options available for W100.
NOTE 5: Model year production: (Six) 406; (V-8) 290.

Series L6-W100 4x4 — 1/2-Ton — 116 in. w.b.				
W100	Chassis & Cowl	2289	3125	Note 6
W100	Chassis & Cab	2524	3600	Note 6
W100	Pickup	2629	3975	Note 6
W100	Platform	2660	3975	Note 6
W100	Stake	2715	4150	Note 6

(*) No Job-Rated GVW options available for W100.
NOTE 6: Model year production: (Ssix) 196; (V-8) 564.

Series L6-W200 4x4 — 3/4-Ton — 116 in. w.b.				
W200	Chassis & Cowl	2397	3400	Note 7
W200	Chassis & Cab	2641	3875	Note 7
W200	Pickup	2747	4250	Note 7
W200	Platform	2777	4250	Note 7
W200	Stake	2832	4425	Note 7

(*) W210 (1/2-ton) Job-Rated GVW option available.
NOTE 7: Model year production: (Six) 396; (V-8) 331.

Series L6-W300 4x4 — 1-Ton — 129 in. w.b.				
W300	Chassis & Cowl	2803	3975	Note 8
W300	Chassis & Cab	3048	4450	Note 8
W300	Pickup	3173	4875	Note 8
W300	Platform	3214	4900	Note 8
W300	Stake	3278	5100	Note 8

(*) W310 (3/4-ton) Job-Rated GVW option available.
NOTE 8: Model year production: (Six) 143; (V-8) 194.

Series L6-W300M Power-Wagon — 1-Ton — 126 in. w.b.				
W300M	Chassis & Cowl	2481	4600	Note 9
W300M	Chassis & Cab	2725	5025	Note 9
W300M	Pickup	2850	5400	Note 9

(*) W310M (3/4-ton) Job-Rated GVW option available.
NOTE 9: Model year production, Power-Wagon: 2,387.

Series L6-D410 — 1-Ton — 129/152/171 in. w.b.				
D410	Chassis & Cowl	—	—	—
D410	Chassis & Cab	—	—	—
D410	Platform	—	—	—
D410	Stake	—	—	—

(*) D410 is Job-Rated (1-ton) option on 1-1/2-ton Dodge D400.

Series L6-P300 Forward Control — 1-Ton — 104/126 in. w.b.				
(104 in. w.b.)				
P300	Chassis	1517	2400	—
(126 in. w.b.)				
P300	Chassis	1555	2424	—

(*) P310 (1/2-ton) and P320 (3/4-ton) Job-Rated GVW options available.

Series L6-P410/P420 Forward Control — 3/4-/1-Ton — 108/125/137/153 in. w.b.

(108 in. w.b.)

410/420	Chassis	—	—	—

(125 in. w.b.)

410/420	Chassis	—	—	—

(137 in. w.b.)

410/420	Chassis	—	—	—

(153 in. w.b.)

410/420	Chassis	—	—	—

(*) P410 (3/4-ton) and P420 (1-ton) are Job-Rated GVW options for P400.

NOTE 10: Weights and prices shown are for 6-cyl. models. For V-8 equipped trucks (prefix L8) add 100 lbs. to weight and $105.30 to price.

1958 Dodge W100 1/2-Ton Power Wagon 4x4 (RCA)

ENGINE [D100/D200/D300/W100/W200]: Inline. L-head. Six-cylinder. Cast iron block. Bore & stroke: 3.25 in. x 4.625 in. Displacement: 230.2 cid. Compression ratio: 7.9:1. Brake Horsepower: 120 at 3600 rpm. Net (Taxable) horsepower: 25.35. Torque: 202 lbs.-ft. at 1600 rpm. Four main bearings. Solid valve lifters.
ENGINE [W300/D400/D410/D420]: Inline. L-head. Six-cylinder. Cast iron block. Bore & stroke: 3.437 in. x 4.5 in. Displacement: 250.6 cid. Compression ratio: 7.1:1. Brake horsepower: 125 at 3600 rpm. Net Horsepower: 28.35. Torque: 216 lbs.-ft. at 1600 rpm. Four main bearings. Solid valve lifters.
ENGINE [Power-Wagon]: Same as D100 except — Brake horsepower: 113 at 3600 rpm. Torque: 198 lbs.-ft. at 1600 rpm.
ENGINE [Optional, except Power-Wagon]: V-8. Overhead valves. Eight-cylinder. Cast iron block. Bore & stroke: 3.63 in. x 3.8 in. Displacement: 314.6 cid. Compression ratio: 8.1:1. Brake horsepower: 204 at 4400 rpm. Net horsepower: 42.16. Torque: 290 lbs.-ft. at 2400 rpm. Five main bearings. Hydraulic valve lifters.

1958 Dodge D100 1/2-Ton Sweptside Pickup (OCW)

CHASSIS [D110]: Wheelbase: 108 in. and 116 in. GVW: 4,250 lbs.
CHASSIS [D100]: Wheelbase: 108 in. and 116 in. Tires: 6.70 x 15 four-ply (front and rear). GVW: 5,100 lbs. Axle capacity: (front) 2,500 lbs.; (rear) 3,600 lbs.
CHASSIS [D200]: Wheelbase: 116 in. Tires: 7-17.5 six-ply (front and rear). GVW: 7,500 lbs. Axle capacity: (front) 2,800 lbs.; (rear) 6,500 lbs.
CHASSIS [D210]: Wheelbase: 116 in. GVW: 5,800 lbs.
CHASSIS [D220]: Wheelbase: 116 in. GVW: 7,500 lbs.
CHASSIS [D300]: Wheelbase: 126 in. Tires: 7-17.5 six-ply (front and rear). GVW: 9,000 lbs. Axle capacity: (front) 2,800 lbs.; (rear) 6,500 lbs.
CHASSIS [D310]: Wheelbase: 126 in. GVW: 5,800 lbs.
CHASSIS [D320]: Wheelbase: 126 in. GVW: 7,500 lbs.
CHASSIS [W100]: Wheelbase: 108 in. and 116 in. Tires: 7-17.5 six-ply (front and rear). GVW: 5,100 lbs. Axle capacity: (front) 3,000 lbs.; (rear) 3,600 lbs.
CHASSIS [W200]: Wheelbase: 116 in. Tires: 7-17.5 six-ply (front and rear). GVW: 8,000 lbs. Axle capacity: (front) 3,000 lbs.; (rear) 6,500 lbs.
CHASSIS [W210]: Wheelbase: 116 in. GVW: 6,000 lbs.
CHASSIS [W300]: Wheelbase: 129 in. Tires: 8-19.5 eight-ply (front and rear). GVW: 9,000 lbs. Axle capacity: (front) 4,500 lbs.; (rear) 8,000 lbs.
CHASSIS [W310]: Wheelbase: 129 in. GVW: 5,800 lbs.
CHASSIS [W320]: Wheelbase: 129 in. GVW: 7,500 lbs.
CHASSIS [W300M]: Wheelbase: 126 in. Tires: 7.50 x 16 eight-ply (front and rear). GVW: 9,500 lbs. Axle capacity: (front) 3,750 lbs.; (rear) 6,500 lbs.
CHASSIS [W310M]: Wheelbase: 126 in. GVW: 7,600 lbs.
CHASSIS [P300]: Wheelbase: 104 or 125 in. Tires: 7x17.5 six-ply. GVW: 9,000 lbs.
CHASSIS [P310]: Wheelbase: 104 or 125 in. GVW: 6,000 lbs.
CHASSIS [P320]: Wheelbase: 104 or 125 in. GVW: 7,800 lbs.
CHASSIS [P410]: Wheelbase: 108/125/137/153 in. Tires: 8x19.5 six-ply. GVW: 7,500 lbs.

CHASSIS [P420]: Wheelbase: 108/125/137/153 in. GVW: 9,500 lbs.

1958 Dodge W100 Power Wagon 4x4 Town Wagon (RCA)

TECHNICAL: Selective sliding gear transmission. Speeds: 3F/1R except W300 and W300M, 4F/1R. Column or floor shift. Automatic transmission and overdrive optional. Overall axle ratio: [D100] 3.73:1, 4.1:1 and 4.89:1; [D200/300] 4.1:1 and 4.89:1; [W100/200] 4.11:1 and 4.89:1; [W300] 4.88:1 and 5.87:1 (front and rear); [W300M] 4.89:1 and 5.83:1 (front and rear). Single-plate dry-disc clutch: 11 in. Hydraulic four-wheel brakes: [D100] 11 in. drums; [W100] 12-1/8 in.; [D200/D300/W200] 12-1/8 in. (front) and 13 in. (rear); [W300] 13 in.; [W300M] 14-1/8 in. Fuel tank: 17.4 gallons except W100/200/W300M, 18-gallon; W300, 25-gallon. Wheels: [D100] 15 x 4.50; [W300M] 16 x 5.50; [W300] 19.5 x 5.25; [others] 17.5 x 5.25. One-pint oil bath air cleaner.
OPTIONS: [D100/D200/D300] Chrome front bumper ($13.20). Painted rear bumper ($19.20). Chrome plated rear bumper ($25). Bumper guards: Painted ($5.30); chrome ($11.90). Bright hubcaps, set of our ($7.30); set of five for pickup with side tire carrier ($8.70). Chrome wheelcovers, set of four ($16.50); set of five ($20.60). Custom equipment ($46.10). Turn signals ($23.10). Dodge Tint glass ($17.20). Chrome headlight doors ($2). Cab corner marker lights ($9.90). Dual electric horns ($14.50). Horn ring ($3). Cigar lighter ($4.70). Glove box lock ($4). Inside rearview mirror ($3). Adjustable mirror: Left side ($2.40); right side ($4.30). Bright metal windshield molding ($7). Grab handles ($8.50). Two-tone paint ($15.20). Wraparound rear window ($29). Dual electric wipers ($7.20). Windshield washer ($11.60). Auxiliary taillamp ($7.30). Right side sun visor ($3). Foam padded seatback ($11.20); seat cushion ($11.20). Rear shocks for D200 or D300 ($17.80). Tire carrier on side of pickup ($10.20). Hand throttle on dash ($3). One-quart oil bath air cleaner: Six-cylinder ($1.70); V-8 ($4). Right door armrest ($3.30). One-quart oil filter ($11.90); two-quart ($15.80). Electric fuel pump ($25). Increased cooling capacity ($9.90). Vacuum brake booster ($42.50). Velocity type governor, manual transmission only ($9.90). Perforated headliner ($5.60). Heater ($46.10). Deluxe heater ($65.80). Power steering ($112). V-8 engine ($105.30). Three-ton jack ($7.90). Heavy-duty three-speed transmission ($57). Three-speed with overdrive transmission, D100 only ($100). Four-speed transmission: D100 ($65); D200 or D300 ($46.20). Three-speed automatic transmission with push-button control ($203.75). [Town Panel/Town Wagon only] Chrome plated rear bumper ($13.20). Custom Town Panel equipment ($19.20). Turn signals ($18.50). Headliner roof insulation ($7.20). Recessed rear license plate light ($8.60). Bright metal molding package ($14.50). Two-tone paint ($25). Auxiliary seat, standard panel ($34.90). Auxiliary seat, custom panel ($46.10). Tire carrier inside($6). Side windows in panel, stationary clear glass ($50). Dodge Tint glass ($56.60). Chrome trim package, all models except Sweptside ($32.90). Hood ornament for Sweptside ($2.40). Electric tachometer ($52.00). Full-traction differential for D100 only (46.10). [W300/Power Wagon] Deluxe cab equipment ($19). Dodge Tint glass ($17.20). Turn signals ($30.30). Grab handles ($8.50/pair). Inside rearview mirror ($3). Long-arm adjustable mirror: Left side ($2.40); right ($4.30). Heater ($46.10). Front and rear fenders painted to match cab color ($13.20). Auxiliary taillight ($7.30). Windshield washer ($11.60). Vacuum brake booster, 7-1/2 in. diaphragm ($42.50). Draw bar ($23.10). Oil filter, two-quart ($6). Pintle hook ($12.50). Power-take-off ($75.20). Pulley drive ($85.60). Rear driveshaft assembly ($85.60). Rear shocks ($34.90). Springs, 1,600 lbs. capacity ($164.50). Winch ($243.45). Three-ton jack ($7.90).

1958 Dodge W300M 1-Ton Power Wagon 8 ft. Express (RCA)

HISTORICAL: Introduced: October 31, 1957. Calendar year sales: 36,972. Calendar year production: 58,668. Model year production: (six-cylinder) 28,276; (V-8) 13,610; [Total] 41,886. Model year production (U.S. only): (six) 25,760; (V-8) 12,180; [Total] 37,940. Innovations: Quad headlights. Tradesman utility body. Hooded instrument panel. Oil/amp warning lights. For the first time, Dodge styled three distinct front end appearances: One for light and medium-duty, another for heavy-duty and a third for cab-over-engine models. Production fell 23.4 percent, the lowest total since World War II. Sales suffered a similar decrease. As a result of the general business recession, total industry sales were down 15.4 percent. Foreign trucks (mainly Volkswagen) became a factor for the first time, capturing nearly four percent of total U.S. sales. Dodge extended a new six-speed automatic transmission to medium and heavy-duty trucks. The full line included trucks from 4,250 to 46,000 lbs. GVW and 65,000 lbs. GVW. Four six-cylinder engines and three V-8s were available. A 315 cid hemi powered medium-tonnage models; a 354 cid hemi with dual carburetion and dual

exhaust went into heavy trucks. During 1958, Dodge opened 13 new truck centers, bringing the nationwide network total to 23. Chrysler Corp. previewed its new car and truck line at the Americana Hotel in Bal Harbour, Fla. in September. It was the first full line preview held outside of Detroit.

1959 DODGE

1959 Dodge D100 1/2-Ton Sweptline Pickup (OCW)

[CONVENTIONALS]
1/2-TON — M SERIES D100 — SIX/V-8: An all new, smooth-sided pickup called the Sweptline was the only major change for 1959. Sweptlines, now offered on 1/2-, 3/4- and 1-ton chassis, featured a cab-wide pickup body for greater hauling ability and cleaner, more modern styling. The traditional fender-sided pickup, now called a Utiline, was available on both D and W series chassis. Other styling changes included a new Dodge nameplate above a cleaner one-piece grille, plus new concealed runningboards. New features included a hydraulically operated clutch, suspended brake and clutch pedals and a 318 cid V-8 engine. All gauges on the new dash sat directly in front of the driver and the glove box was moved to the far right, from the center. Four body colors were added: Heron gray, Buckskin tan, Vista green and Sand Dune white. Four colors were dropped, but 13 solid colors were still available. Two-tones featured Sand Dune white at the top. Hubcaps were also Sand Dune white. All 1958 models were continued. The Sweptside D100 pickup was dropped in January, 1959. New this year was the Minivan package delivery vehicle, only 169 in. long on a 95 in. wheelbase but with 164 cu. ft. of load space. LoadFlite push-button automatic transmission was standard on the Minivan. Standard equipment included the 230 cid 6-cyl. engine, underslung tire carrier, a short-arm outside mirror, dual electric single-speed wipers, and front and rear shock absorbers (front only on 1-ton). The D100 line offered two wheelbases and a 5,100 lbs. GVW rating.

1959 Dodge D100 1/2-Ton Town Panel (OCW)

1/2-TON — M SERIES D110 — SIX/V-8: D110s were lighter-duty Job-Rated versions of the D100 with both wheelbases and a 4,250 lbs. GVW.
1/2-TON — M SERIES W100 — SIX/V-8: Four-wheel drive (4x4) models continued unchanged. Standard equipment was the same as the D Series, but with two-speed transfer case and spare tire carrier inside the pickup box. There was no Job-Rated version.
1/2-TON — M SERIES D210 — SIX/V-8: A Job-Rated version of the 3/4-ton classed as a 1/2-ton with its 5,800 lbs. GVW equipment. See D200 below.
1/2-TON — M SERIES W210 — SIX/V-8: A Job-Rated version of the 3/4-ton 4x4 classed as a 1/2-ton with its 6,000 lbs. GVW equipment. See W200 below.
3/4-TON — M SERIES D200 — SIX/V-8: This was the regular 3/4-ton conventional truck with 4x2 driveline on the 116 in. wheelbase. It had a 7,500 lbs. GVW rating.
3/4-TON — M SERIES W200 — SIX/V-8: This was the regular 3/4-ton conventional truck with 4x4 driveline on the 116 in. wheelbase, but with two-speed transfer case and spare tire carrier inside the pickup box. It had a 8,000 lbs. GVW.
3/4-TON — M SERIES D310/D320 — SIX/V-8: Both of these were Job-Rated versions of the regular 1-ton with GVWs of 5,800 lbs. and 7,500 lbs., respectively See D300 below.
3/4-TON — M SERIES W310 — SIX/V-8: A Job-Rated version of the 1-ton 4x4 classed as a 3/4-ton with its 8,500 lbs. GVW on a 129 in. wheelbase. (There is no W320, though). See W300 below.

1-TON — M SERIES D300 — SIX/V-8: This was the regular 1-ton conventional truck with 4x2 driveline on a 126 in. wheelbase. It had a 9,000 lbs. GVW rating.
1-TON — M SERIES D220 — SIX/V-8: A Job-Rated version of the 3/4-ton 4x2 with a 116 in. wheelbase and 7,500 lbs. GVW. See D200.
1-TON — M SERIES W300 — SIX/V-8: This was the regular 1-ton conventional model with 4x4 driveline on a 129 in. wheelbase. It had a 9,500 lbs. GVW rating.
1-TON — M SERIES D410 — SIX/V-8: This was a Job-Rated version of the 1-1/2-ton conventional 4x2 series with its 11,000 lbs. GVW equipment giving it a 1-ton classification. There were 129, 133 and 171 in. wheelbases.
[POWER WAGONS]
3/4 TON POWER WAGON — M SERIES W310M — SIX: This is the Job-Rated version of the military style Power Wagon with a 126 in. wheelbase and 7,600 lbs. GVW.
1-TON POWER WAGON — M SERIES W300M — SIX: This was the regular Power Wagon with the same 126 in. wheelbase, but a higher 9,500 lbs. GVW rating. Styling was continued without change. Standard equipment included an oil filter, single taillight, side-mounted tire carrier, four-speed transmission and two-speed transfer case, and front bumper. Only the 230 cid six was available; a special version with less horsepower.
[FORWARD CONTROLS]
1/2 TON — M SERIES P310 — SIX/V-8: A Job-Rated version of the 1-ton P300 with lower 6,000 lbs. GVW and the same 104 in. and 126 in. wheelspans.
3/4-TON — M SERIES P320/P410 — SIX/V-8: Both Job-Rated versions of other Forward Controls with the P320 (7,800 lbs. GVW) based on the P300 and the P410 (7,500 lbs. GVW) based on the 1-1/2-ton P400.
1-TON — M SERIES P300 — SIX/V-8: This was the regular 1-ton Forward Control. 104 in. and 126 in. wheelbases. GVW: 9,000 lbs. A front end body section cost $467 more than the stripped chassis.
1-TON — M SERIES P420/P450 — SIX/V-8: The P420 and P450 were 1-ton Job-Rated versions of the P400 1-1/2-ton Forward Control with 108, 125, 137, and 153 in. wheelbases. GVWS: [P420] 9,500 lbs.; [P450] 11,000 lbs.

1959 Dodge D100 1/2-Ton Sweptside Pickup (OCW)

I.D. DATA: Serial numbers were on a plate on the left lock pillar post. Starting Serial numbers: [D100 Six] M6D1-L01001; [D100 V-8] M8D1-L01001; [D200 Six] M6D2-1001; [D200 V-8] M8D2-L01001; [D300 Six] M6D3-L01001; [D300 V-8] M8D3-L01001; [W100 Six] M6W1-L01001; [W100 V-8] M8W1-L01001; [W200 Six] M6W2-L01001; [W200 V-8] M8W2-L01001; [W300 Six] M6W3-L01001; [W300 V-8] M8W3-L01001; [D410 Six] L6D4-HO1001; [D410 V-8] L8D4-HO1001. [W300M Power-Wagon] M6W3M-L01001. [P300/P310/P320 Six] L6D3-LO1001; [P300/P310/P320 V-8] L8P3-LO1001. [P410 Six] L6P4-HO1001; [P410 V-8] L8P4-HO1001. Engine numbers were stamped on pad on left of block. Starting Engine Numbers: [D100 Six] M6-D1-1001; [D100 V-8] M8-D1-1001; [D200 Six] M6-D2-1001; [D200 V-8] M8-D2-1001; [D300 Six] M6-D3-1001; [D300 V-8] M8-D3-1001; [W100 Six] M6-W1-1001; [W100 V-8] M8-W1-1001; [W200 Six] M6-W2-1001; [W200 V-8] M8-W2-1001; [W300 Six] M6-W3-1001; [W300 V-8] M8-W3-1001; [W300M Power-Wagon] M6-W3M-1001. Ending serial and engine numbers are not available.

1959 Dodge D100 1/2-Ton Sweptline Pickup (S. Saloy)

Model	Body Type	Price	Weight	Prod. Total
M6-D100 Series — 1/2-Ton — 108 in. w.b.				
D100	Chassis & Cowl	1440	2475	—
D100	Chassis & Cab	1675	2950	—
D100	Utiline Pickup	1781	3250	—
D100	Sweptline Pickup	1797	3325	—
D100	Town Panel	2062	3425	—
D100	Town Wagon (6P)	2336	3650	—
D100	Town Wagon (8P)	2382	3700	—

(*) D110 (1/2-ton) Job-Rated GVW option available.

M6-D100 Series — 1/2-Ton — 116 in. w.b.

D100	Chassis & Cowl	1475	2500	—
D100	Chassis & Cab	1711	2975	—
D100	Utiline Pickup	1816	3325	—
D100	Sweptline Pickup	1832	3425	—
D100	Sweptside Pickup	2189	3475	—
D100	Platform	1852	3175	—
D100	Stake	1902	3375	—

(*) D110 (1/2-ton) Job-Rated GVW option available.

M6-D200 Series — 3/4-Ton — 116 in. w.b.

D200	Chassis & Cowl	1549	2950	—
D200	Chassis & Cab	1794	3425	—
D200	Utiline Pickup	1899	3775	—
D200	Sweptline Pickup	1915	3875	—
D200	Platform	1935	3625	—
D200	Stake	1985	3825	—

(*) D210 (1/2-ton) and D220 (1-ton) Job-Rated GVW options available.

M6-300 Series — 1-Ton — 126 in. w.b.

D300	Chassis & Cowl	1693	3125	—
D300	Chassis & Cab	1937	3600	—
D300	Utiline Pickup	2062	4000	—
D300	Sweptline Pickup	2078	4025	—
D300	Platform	2108	3875	—
D300	Stake	2168	4075	—

(*) D310 (3/4-ton) and D320 (3/4-ton) Job-Rated GVW options available.

M6-W100 Series 4x4 — 1/2-Ton — 108 in. w.b.

W100	Chassis & Cowl	2248	3275	—
W100	Chassis & Cab	2483	3750	—
W100	Utiline Pickup	2589	4050	—
W100	Town Panel	2870	4225	—
W100	Town Wagon (6P)	3144	4450	—
W100	Town Wagon (8P)	3190	4500	—

(*) No Job-Rated GVW options available for W100.

M6-W100 Series 4x4 — 1/2-Ton — 116 in. w.b.

W100	Chassis & Cowl	2283	3300	—
W100	Chassis & Cab	2519	3775	—
W100	Utiline Pickup	2624	4125	—
W100	Platform	2660	3975	—
W100	Stake	2710	4175	—

(*) No Job-Rated GVW options available for W100.

M6-W200 Series 4x4 — 3/4-Ton — 116 in. w.b.

W200	Chassis & Cowl	2379	3475	—
W200	Chassis & Cab	2624	3950	—
W200	Utiline Pickup	2729	4300	—
W200	Platform	2765	4150	—
W200	Stake	2815	4350	—

(*) W210 (1/2-ton) Job-Rated GVW option available.

M6-W300 Series 4x4 — 1-Ton — 129 in. w.b.

W300	Chassis & Cowl	2932	4050	—
W300	Chassis & Cab	3177	4525	—
W300	Utiline Pickup	3302	4925	—
W300	Platform	3348	4800	—
W300	Stake	3407	5000	—

(*) W310 (3/4-ton) Job-Rated GVW option available.

M6-W300M Series Power-Wagon — 1-Ton — 126 in. w.b.

W300M	Chassis & Cowl	2811	4600	—
W300M	Chassis & Cab	3056	5025	—
W300M	Utiline Pickup	3197	5400	—

(*) W310M (3/4-ton) Job-Rated GVW option available.

Series M6-D410 — 1-Ton — 129/152/171 in. w.b. — (V-8)

D410	Chassis & Cowl	1957	3875	—
D410	Chassis & Cab	2202	4350	—
D410	Platform	2377	4550	—
D410	Stake	2437	4850	—

Add $25 and 100 lbs. for 153 in. wheelbase models.
Add $80 and 125 lbs. for 171 in. wheelbase models.

(*) D410 is Job-Rated (1-ton) option on 1-1/2-ton Dodge D400.

Series L6-P300 Forward Control — 1-Ton — 104/126 in. w.b.

(104 in. w.b.)

P300	Chassis	1528	2400	—

(126 in. w.b.)

P300	Chassis	1554	2425	—

(*) P310 (1/2-ton) and P320 (3/4-ton) Job-Rated GVW options available.

Series L6-P410/P420 Forward Control — 3/4-/1-Ton — 108/125/137/153 in. w.b.

(108 in. w.b.)

410/420	Chassis	1922	3175	—

(125 in. w.b.)

410/420	Chassis	1948	3275	—

(137 in. w.b.)

410/420	Chassis	1974	3325	—

(153 in. w.b.)

410/420	Chassis	2000	3375	—

(*) P410 (3/4-ton) and P420 (1-ton) are Job-Rated GVW options for P400.

NOTE 1: Weights and prices shown are for six-cylinder trucks. For V-8 equipped trucks (prefix M8), add $120.75 to price.

196

NOTE 2: Production figures by model and series are not available.

1959 Dodge D200 3/4-Ton Milk Truck (DFW)

ENGINE [D100/D200/D300/W100/W200]: Inline. L-head. Six-cylinder. Cast iron block. Bore & stroke: 3.25 in. x 4.625 in. Displacement: 230.2 cid. Compression ratio: 7.9:1. Brake Horsepower: 120 at 3600 rpm. Net (Taxable) horsepower: 25.35. Torque: 202 lbs.-ft. at 1600 rpm. Four main bearings. Solid valve lifters.

ENGINE [W300/D400/D410/D420]: Inline. L-head. Six-cylinder. Cast iron block. Bore & stroke: 3.437 in. x 4.5 in. Displacement: 250.6 cid. Compression ratio: 7.1:1. Brake horsepower: 125 at 3600 rpm. Net (Taxable) horsepower: 28.35. Torque: 216 lbs.-ft. at 1600 rpm. Four main bearings. Solid valve lifters.

ENGINE [Power-Wagon]: Same as D100, except brake horsepower is 113 at 3600 rpm; torque is 198 lbs.-ft. at 1600 rpm.

ENGINE [Optional: All, except W300/W300M]: 90-degree, overhead valve. Eight-cylinder. Cast iron block. Bore & stroke: 3.91 x 3.312 in. Displacement: 318.1 cid. Compression ratio: 8.25:1. Brake horsepower: 205 at 4400 rpm. Net (Taxable) horsepower: 42.16. Torque: 290 lbs.-ft. at 2400 rpm. Five main bearings. Hydraulic valve lifters.

ENGINE [Optional: W300]: Same as V-8 above, but with heavy-duty features to meet demands of more rugged use. Brake horsepower: 207 at 4400 rpm. Torque: 292 lbs.-ft. at 2400 rpm.

1959 Dodge 1-Ton Walk-in Panel Delivery Van (DFW)

CHASSIS [D100]: Wheelbase: 108 in. and 116 in. Tires: 6.70 x 15 four-ply tubeless (front/rear). GVW: 5,100 lbs. Rear axle capacity: 3,600 lbs. Front axle: 2,800 lbs.

CHASSIS [D110]: Wheelbase: 108 in. and 116 in. GVW: 4,250 lbs.

CHASSIS (D200): Wheelbase: 116 in. Tires: 6.50 x 16 six-ply tubeless (front/rear). GVW: 7500 lbs. Rear axle: 5,500 lbs. Front axle: 2,800 lbs.

CHASSIS [D210]: Wheelbase: 116 in. GVW: 5,800 lbs.

CHASSIS [D220]: Wheelbase: 116 in. GVW: 7,500 lbs.

CHASSIS (D300): Wheelbase: 126 in. Tires: 7 x 17.5 six-ply tubeless (front/rear). GVW: 9000 lbs. Rear axle: 6,500 lbs. Front axle: 2,800 lbs.

CHASSIS [D310]: Wheelbase: 126 in. GVW: 5,800 lbs.

CHASSIS [D320]: Wheelbase: 126 in. GVW: 7,500 lbs.

CHASSIS (W100): Wheelbase: 108 in. and 116 in. Tires: 7 x 17.5 six-ply tubeless (front/rear). GVW: 6,000 lbs. Axle capacity: (front) 3,000 lbs.; (rear) 4,500 lbs.

CHASSIS (W200): Wheelbase: 116 in. Tires: 7 x 17.5 six-ply tubeless (front/rear). GVW: 8000 lbs. Axle capacity: (front) 3,000 lbs.; (rear) 6,500 lbs.

CHASSIS [W210]: Wheelbase: 116 in. GVW: 6,000 lbs.

CHASSIS [W300]: Wheelbase: 129 in. Tires: 8-19.5 eight-ply (front and rear). GVW: 9,000 lbs. Axle capacity: (front) 4,500 lbs.; (rear) 7,500 lbs.

CHASSIS [W310]: Wheelbase: 129 in. GVW: 5,800 lbs.

CHASSIS [W320]: Wheelbase: 129 in. GVW: 7,500 lbs.

CHASSIS (Power-Wagon): Wheelbase: 126 in. Tires: 7.50 x 16 eight-ply tubeless (front/rear). GVW: 9500 lbs. Axle capacity: (front) 3,750 lbs.; (rear) 6,500 lbs.

CHASSIS [W310M]: Wheelbase: 126 in. GVW: 7,600 lbs.

CHASSIS [P300]: Wheelbase: 104 or 125 in. Tires: 7x17.5 six-ply. GVW: 9,000 lbs.

CHASSIS [P310]: Wheelbase: 104 or 125 in. GVW: 6,000 lbs.

CHASSIS [P320]: Wheelbase: 104 or 125 in. GVW: 7,800 lbs.

CHASSIS [P410]: Wheelbase: 108/125/137/153 in. Tires: 8x19.5 six-ply. GVW: 7,500 lbs.

CHASSIS [P420]: Wheelbase: 108/125/137/153 in. GVW: 9,500 lbs.

CHASSIS [P450]: Wheelbase: 108/125/137/153 in. GVW: 11,000 lbs.

1959 Dodge W300 Power Wagon 4x4 Utiline Pickup (RCA)

TECHNICAL: Selective sliding gear transmission. Speeds: 3F/1R except 1-ton models, 4F/1R. Column or floor shift. Automatic transmission optional. Single-plate dry-disc clutch: 11 in. Overall axle ratio: [D100] 3.54:1, 4.1:1 or 4.89:1; [D200, W100] 4.1:1 or 4.88:1. [D300, W200] 4.1:1 or 4.89:1; [W300] 4.88:1 or 5.87:1; [Power-Wagon] 4.89:1 or 5.83:1. Hydraulic four-wheel brakes. Oil bath air cleaner: [W300M] one quart; [others] one pint. Fuel tank: [D Series] 17.4 gallon mounted inside frame; [W100-300] 17.4 gallon mounted outboard on right side; [Power-Wagon] 18 gallon, at rear of frame. Governor: [Power-Wagon] velocity type. Wheels: [D100] 5-stud disc; [D200, W100] 8-stud disc; [Power-Wagon] five-stud ventilated disc; [others] six-stud disc.

OPTIONS: [All models, except Power-Wagon] Chromed front bumper ($13.20). Rear bumper ($20.40). Chrome rear bumper ($33.60). Bumper guards ($5.30). Chrome bumper guards ($11.85). Chrome hubcaps: Set of four ($5.95); set of five ($9.35). Painted hubcaps for D200: Four ($8.60); five ($10.70). Chrome wheelcovers for Town Panel and Town Wagon ($16.45); for other D100 models ($22.40). Custom cab equipment ($36.85). Armrest, left or right ($3.70). Dodge-Tint glass ($19.25). Interior lining package, Town Panel ($39.50). Glove box lock ($3.95). Inside rearview mirror ($3). Adjustable long-arm mirror: Left ($2.35); right ($5.95). 5 x 7 in. mirror: Left ($11.85); right ($15.50). Right sun visor ($2.65). Chrome trim package No. 1, pickups ($23.05). Chrome trim package No. 2, Town Wagon and Town Panel ($39.50). Wraparound rear window ($40.15). Side glass in panel ($50). Dual electric variable-speed wipers ($7.15). Windshield washer ($11.85). Turn signals ($26.35). Heater: Standard ($46.10); deluxe ($63.20). Hood ornament ($4.65). Dual electric horns ($14.50). Grab handles ($8.50). Heavy-duty instrument cluster ($59.25). Cab corner marker lights ($9.90). Bright metal moldings, Town Panel and Town Wagon ($14.50); Sweptline pickup ($19.75). Bright windshield molding ($6.95). Roof-mounted radio ($55.30). Auxiliary seat: Standard panel ($38.20); Custom panel ($46.10). Foam padding, seat back or bottom ($15.80 each). Auxiliary taillight ($7.25). Electric tachometer ($52). Hand throttle control ($4.90). Dual rear fender for D300 Utiline ($27.65). Two-tone paint: Town Panel or Town Wagon ($25); others, except Sweptside ($31.60). Inside tire carrier for panel or pickup, or outside for Utiline ($8.60). One-quart oil bath air cleaner: 6-cyl. ($3.95); V-8 ($5.60). Oil filter: One-quart ($8.60); two-quart ($12.05); all V-8 ($3.50). Electric fuel pump ($25). Vacuum brake booster ($39.50). Power steering ($111.85). Rear shocks, D300 ($25). Full-traction differential, D100 ($59.25). V-8 engine ($120.75). Governor ($10.20). 3-ton jack ($9.90). Increased cooling capacity ($9.90). Heavy-duty three-speed transmission ($5.30). LoadFlite automatic transmission ($221.10).

OPTIONS: [Power-Wagon only] Vacuum brake booster ($42.15). Deluxe cab equipment ($19.75). Forced-draft crankcase vent system ($19.75). Heater ($46.10). Fenders painted to match cab ($13.20). Draw bar ($23.05). Governor for rear driveshaft ($98.70). Two-quart oil filter ($12.05). Drive pulley ($85.55). Rear driveshaft assembly ($85.55). Winch assembly ($251.35). Heavy-duty springs: 1,600 lbs. front ($7.90); 3,000 lbs. rear ($10.70).

1959 Dodge W100 Power Wagon 4x4 Town Wagon (RCA)

HISTORICAL: Introduced: Oct. 24, 1958. Calendar year sales: 52,107. Calendar year production: 71,680. Model year production figures not available. Innovations: Cab-wide pickup body (Sweptline). Hydraulic clutch. Suspended pedals. Large-capacity Minivan. "Today it's real smart to choose Dodge trucks" was the new advertising slogan. Dodge dropped the terms "Power Giant" and "Job-Rated" in ads. Truck sales bounced back from their 1958 low, chalking up a gain of 40.7 percent. Production gained 22.2 percent, giving Dodge a 6.29 percent share of total industry production and 5.55 percent of total sales. Dodge cut prices on 21 of its basic 1959 model trucks. The full Dodge truck line covered 98 percent of the market. Prices ranged from $1,440 for a D100 chassis to $10,474 for a 4-ton tandem. Engines rated 113 to 234 horsepower were available.

1960 Dodge D100 Sweptline Pickup (S. Saloy)

1/2-TON — P SERIES D100 — SIX/V-8; 3/4-TON — P SERIES D200 — SIX/V-8; 1-TON — P SERIES D300 — SIX/V-8: Dodge marked time in 1960, preparing for an all-new line of light-duty trucks that would be unveiled for the next model year. A new bright-finished grille was the only appearance change. Cabs, engines, mechanical details and model availability were unchanged. The Minivan was dropped. Six new colors brought the total to 14: Nile green, Mustang gray, Toreador red, Indian turquoise, Pine green, and School Bus Chrome yellow. Body colors dropped were Heron gray, Alaska white, Buckskin tan, Vista green, and Poncharrain green. Two-tones combined Sand Dune white with any of the other 13 colors. Standard equipment was the same as in 1959.

1960 Dodge W200 3/4-Ton Power Wagon Utiline Pickup (RCA)

1/2-TON (4x4) — P SERIES W100 — SIX/V-8; 3/4-TON (4x4) — P SERIES W200 — SIX/V-8; 1-TON (4x4) — P SERIES W300 — SIX/V-8; 1-TON POWER-WAGON — P SERIES WM200 — SIX: W Series 4x4s received the new grille design, while the familiar Power-Wagon continued without change. So did the 1-ton Forward Control chassis.

I.D. DATA: Serial numbers were on a plate on the left door lock pillar. The first digit indicates model year (0=1960, 1=1961, etc.); the second digit reveals number of cylinders; the next letter indicates model ("D" for conventional, "W" for four-wheel drive, etc.); next is the nominal weight rating (1=1/2-ton, 2=3/4-ton, 3=1-ton); next is "L" (light duty), "M" (medium) or "H" (heavy); and the final six digits are the sequence number. Starting serial numbers: [D100 Six] 06D1-L100001; [D100 V-8] 08D1-L100001; [D200 Six] 06L2-L100001; [D200 V-8] 08D2-L100001; [D300 Six] 06D3-L100001; [D300 V-8] 08D3-L100001; [W100 Six] 06W1-L100001; [W100 V-8] 08W1-L100001; [W200 Six] 06W2-L100001; [W200 V-8] 08W2-L100001; [W300 Six] 06W3-L100001; [W300 V-8] 08W3-L100001; [WM300] 06WM3-L100001. Six-cylinder engine numbers were on the left side of the block at the front, below the cylinder head; V-8 numbers were on the left front of the block. A new engine numbering system began with the P-Series. The first two letters designate the series ("T" stands for truck, "P" for P series); the next two digits indicate engine displacement ("23" means 230.2 cid); the next two digits show the month and date of manufacture; and the final digits are the sequence number. (Note: The 318 cid V-8 uses three digits to designate its size.) Starting engine numbers: [230.2 cid six] TP-23-8-3-1001; [251 cid six] TP-25-8-3-1001; [318 cid V-8] TP-318-8-3-1001. Ending serial and engine numbers are not available.

1960 Dodge W100 1/2-Ton Power Wagon Town Wagon (RCA)

Model	Body Type	Price	Weight	Prod. Total
P6-D100 Series — 1/2-Ton — 108 in. w.b.				
D100	Chassis & Cowl	1471	2475	Note 1
D100	Chassis & Cab	1706	2950	Note 1
D100	Utiline Pickup	1812	3250	Note 1
D100	Sweptline Pickup	1826	3325	Note 1
D100	Town Panel	2119	3425	Note 1
D100	Town Wagon (6P)	2384	3650	Note 1
D100	Town Wagon (8P)	2431	3700	Note 1
P6-D100 Series — 1/2-Ton — 116 in. w.b.				
D100	Chassis & Cowl	1506	2500	Note 2
D100	Chassis & Cab	1740	2975	Note 2
D100	Utiline Pickup	1847	3325	Note 2
D100	Sweptline Pickup	1860	3425	Note 2
D100	Platform	1883	3175	Note 2
D100	Stake	1931	3375	Note 2

NOTE 1: Total model year production: (six-cylinder) 12,983; (V-8) 2,837.
NOTE 2: Total model year production: (six-cylinder) 10,712; (V-8) 6,922.

P6-D200 Series — 3/4-Ton — 116 in. w.b.				
D200	Chassis & Cowl	1602	2950	Note 3
D200	Chassis & Cab	1846	3425	Note 3
D200	Utiline Pickup	1952	3775	Note 3
D200	Sweptline Pickup	1966	3875	Note 3
D200	Platform	1988	3625	Note 3
D200	Stake	2036	3825	Note 3

NOTE 3: Total model year production: (six-cylinder) 3,031; (V-8) 1,578.

P6-D300 Series — 1-Ton — 126 in. w.b.				
D300	Chassis & Cowl	1727	3125	Note 4
D300	Chassis & Cab	1971	3600	Note 4
D300	Utiline Pickup	2096	4000	Note 4
D300	Sweptline Pickup	2110	4025	Note 4
D300	Platform	2143	3875	Note 4
D300	Stake	2202	4075	Note 4

NOTE 4: Total model year production: (six-cylinder) 3,737; (V-8) 2,468.

P6-W100 Series 4x4 — 1/2-Ton — 108 in. w.b.				
W100	Chassis & Cowl	2236	3275	Note 5
W100	Chassis & Cab	2471	3750	Note 5
W100	Utiline Pickup	2578	4050	Note 5
W100	Sweptline Pickup	2591	4125	Note 5
W100	Town Panel	2884	4225	Note 5
W100	Town Wagon (6P)	3150	4450	Note 5
W100	Town Wagon (8P)	3196	4500	Note 5
P6-W200 Series 4x4 — 1/2-Ton — 116 in. w.b.				
W100	Chassis & Cowl	2271	3300	Note 6
W100	Chassis & Cab	2506	3775	Note 6
W100	Utiline Pickup	2612	4125	Note 6
W100	Sweptline Pickup	2626	4150	Note 6
W100	Platform	2648	3975	Note 6
W100	Stake	2696	4175	Note 6

NOTE 5: Total model year production: (six-cylinder) 352; (V-8) 165.
NOTE 6: Total model year production: (six-cylinder) 189; (V-8) 262.

P6-W200 Series 4x4 — 3/4-Ton — 116 in. w.b.				
W200	Chassis & Cowl	2368	3475	Note 7
W200	Chassis & Cab	2612	3950	Note 7
W200	Utiline Pickup	2719	4300	Note 7
W200	Sweptline Pickup	2732	4400	Note 7
W200	Platform	2755	4150	Note 7
W200	Stake	2803	4350	Note 7

NOTE 7: Total model year production: (six-cylinder) 262; (V-8) 150.

W300 Series 4x4 — 1-Ton — 129 in. w.b.				
P6-W300	Chassis & Cowl	2928	4050	Note 8
W300	Chassis & Cab	3172	4525	Note 8
W300	Utiline Pickup	3299	4925	Note 8
W300	Sweptline Pickup	3346	5050	Note 8
W300	Platform	3405	4800	Note 8
W300	Stake	—	5000	Note 8

NOTE 8: Total model year production: (six-cylinder) 141; (V-8) 171.

P6-WM300 Series Power-Wagon — 1-Ton — 126 in. w.b.				
WM300	Chassis & Cowl	2848	4600	Note 9
WM300	Chassis & Cab	3096	5025	Note 9
WM300	Utiline Pickup	3239	5425	Note 9

NOTE 9: Total model year production: 1,517.
NOTE 10: Weights and prices shown are for six-cylinder models. For V-8 equipped trucks (prefix P8) add $120.75 to price.

1960 Dodge W100 Power Wagon 4x4 Sweptline Pickup (RCA)

ENGINE [D100/D200/D300/W100/W200]: Inline. L-head. Six-cylinder. Cast iron block. Bore & stroke: 3.25 x 4.625 in. Displacement: 230.2 cid. Compression ratio: 7.9:1. Brake horsepower: 120 at 3600 rpm. Net horsepower: 25.35. Torque: 202 lbs.-ft. at 1600 rpm. Four main bearings. Solid valve lifters.
ENGINE [W100M]: Inline. L-head. Six-cylinder. Cast iron block. Bore & stroke: 3.25 x 4.625 in. Displacement: 230.2 cid. Compression ratio: 7.9:1. Brake horsepower: 113 at 3600 rpm. Net horsepower: 25.35. Torque: 198 lbs.-ft. at 1600 rpm. Four main bearings. Solid valve lifters.
ENGINE [W300/WM300]: Inline. L-head. Six-cylinder. Cast iron block. Bore & stroke: 3.437 x 4.5 in. Displacement: 250.6 cid. Compression ratio: 7.1:1. Brake horsepower: 125 at 3600 rpm. Net horsepower: 28.35. Torque: 216 lbs.-ft. at 1600 rpm. Four main bearings. Solid valve lifters.
ENGINES [Optional, except W100M/W300]: 90-degree, overhead valve. Eight-cylinder. Cast iron block. Bore & stroke: 3.91 x 3.312 in. Displacement: 318.1 cid. Compression ratio: 8.25:1. Brake horsepower: 200 at 3900 rpm. Net (Taxable) horsepower: 48.92. Torque: 286 lbs.-ft. at 2400 rpm. Five main bearings. Hydraulic valve lifters.
ENGINE [Optional W300]: Same as V-8 above, but heavy-duty. Brake horsepower: 202 at 3900 rpm. Torque: 288 lbs.-ft. at 2400 rpm.
($4) for "D" models.
CHASSIS [D100]: Wheelbase 108 in. and 116 in. Tires: 6.70 x 15 four-ply tubeless (front/rear). GVW: 5,100 lbs. Rear axle capacity: 3,600 lbs. Front axle: 2,800 lbs. (Also: [D110] Wheelbase: 108 in. and 116 in. GVW: 4,250 lbs.)
CHASSIS (D200): Wheelbase: 116 in. Tires: 6.50 x 16 six-ply tubeless (front/rear). GVW: 7500 lbs. Rear axle: 5,500 lbs. Front axle: 2,800 lbs. (Also: [D210] Wheelbase: 116 in. GVW: 5,800 lbs.; [D220] Wheelbase: 116 in. GVW: 7,500 lbs.)
CHASSIS (D300): Wheelbase: 126 in. Tires: 7 x 17.5 six-ply tubeless (front/rear). GVW: 9000 lbs. Rear axle: 6,500 lbs. Front axle: 2,800 lbs. (Also: [D310] Wheelbase: 126 in. GVW: 5,800 lbs.; [D320] Wheelbase: 126 in. GVW: 7,500 lbs.)
CHASSIS (W100): Wheelbase: 108 in. and 116 in. Tires: 7 x 17.5 six-ply tubeless (front/rear). GVW: 6,000 lbs. Axle capacity: (front) 3,000 lbs.; (rear) 4,500 lbs.
CHASSIS (W200): Wheelbase: 116 in. Tires: 7 x 17.5 six-ply tubeless (front/rear). GVW: 8000 lbs. Axle capacity: (front) 3,000 lbs.; (rear) 6,500 lbs. (Also: [W210] Wheelbase: 116 in. GVW: 6,000 lbs.)
CHASSIS [W300]: Wheelbase: 129 in. Tires: 8-19.5 eight-ply (front and rear). GVW: 9,000 lbs. Axle capacity: (front) 4,500 lbs.; (rear) 7,500 lbs. (Also: [W310] Wheelbase: 129 in. GVW: 5,800 lbs.; [W320] Wheelbase: 129 in. GVW: 7,500 lbs.)
CHASSIS (Power-Wagon): Wheelbase: 126 in. Tires: 7.50 x 16 eight-ply tubeless (front/rear). GVW: 9,500 lbs. Axle capacity: (front) 3,750 lbs.; (rear) 6,500 lbs. (Also: [W310M] Wheelbase: 126 in. GVW: 7,600 lbs.). (Also: [P300] Wheelbase: 104 or 125 in. Tires: 7x17.5 six-ply. GVW: 9,000 lbs.)
CHASSIS [P310]: Wheelbase: 104 or 125 in. GVW: 6,000 lbs.; [P320] Wheelbase: 104 or 125 in. GVW: 7,800 lbs.
CHASSIS [P410]: Wheelbase: 108/125/137/153 in. Tires: 8x19.5 six-ply. GVW: 7,500 lbs.; [P420] Wheelbase: 108/125/137/153 in. GVW: 9,500 lbs.; [P450] Wheelbase: 108/125/137/153 in. GVW: 11,000 lbs.
TECHNICAL: Selective sliding gear transmission. Speeds: 3F/1R except 1-ton models, 4F/1R. Column or floor shift. Automatic transmission optional. Single-plate dry-disc clutch: 11 in. Overall axle ratio: [D100] 3.54:1, 4.1:1 or 4.89:1; [D200, W100] 4.1:1 or 4.88:1. [D300, W200] 4.1:1 or 4.89:1; [W300] 4.88:1 or 5.87:1; [Power-Wagon] 4.89:1 or 5.83:1. Hydraulic four-wheel brakes. Oil bath air cleaner: [W300M] one quart; [others] one pint. Fuel tank: [D Series] 17.4 gallon mounted inside frame; [W100-300] 17.4 gallon mounted outboard on right side; [Power-Wagon] 18 gallon, at rear of frame. Governor: [Power-Wagon] velocity type. Wheels: [D100] 5-stud disc; [D200, W100] 8-stud disc; [Power-Wagon] five-stud ventilated disc; [others] six-stud disc.
OPTIONS: [All models, except Power-Wagon] Chromed front bumper ($13.20). Rear bumper ($20.40). Chrome rear bumper ($33.60). Bumper guards ($5.30). Chrome bumper guards ($11.85). Chrome hubcaps: Set of four ($5.95); set of five ($9.35). Painted hubcaps for D200: Four ($8.60); five ($10.70). Chrome wheelcovers for Town Panel and Town Wagon ($16.45). Chrome wheelcovers for other D100 models ($22.40). Custom cab equipment ($36.85). Armrest, left or right ($3.70). Dodge-Tint glass ($19.25). Interior lining package, Town Panel ($39.50). Glove box lock ($3.95). Inside rearview mirror ($3). Adjustable long-arm mirror: Left ($2.35); right ($5.95). 5 x 7 in. mirror: Left ($11.85); right ($15.50). Right sun visor ($2.65). Chrome trim package No. 1, pickups ($23.05). Chrome trim package No. 2, Town Wagon and Town Panel ($39.50). Wraparound rear window ($40.15). Side glass in panel ($50). Dual electric variable-speed wipers ($7.15). Windshield washer ($11.85). Turn signals ($26.35). Heater: Standard ($46.10); deluxe ($63.20). Hood ornament ($4.65). Dual electric horns ($14.50). Grab handles ($8.50). Heavy-duty instrument cluster ($59.25). Cab corner marker lights ($9.90). Bright metal moldings, Town Panel and Town Wagon ($14.50). Sweptline pickup ($19.75). Bright windshield molding ($6.95). Roof-mounted radio ($55.30). Auxiliary seat: Standard ($38.20); Custom panel ($46.10). Foam padding, seat back or bottom ($15.80 each). Auxiliary taillight ($7.25). Electric tachometer ($52). Hand throttle control ($4.90). Dual rear fender for D300 Utiline ($27.65). Two-tone

198

paint: Town Panel or Town Wagon ($25); others, except Sweptside ($31.60). Inside tire carrier for panel or pickup, or outside for Utiline ($8.60). One-quart oil bath air cleaner: 6-cyl. ($3.95); V-8 ($5.60). Oil filter: One-quart ($8.60); two-quart ($12.05); all V-8 ($3.50). Electric fuel pump ($25). Vacuum brake booster ($39.50). Power steering ($111.85). Rear shocks, D300 ($25). Full-traction differential, D100 ($59.25). V-8 engine ($120.75). Governor ($10.20). 3-ton jack ($9.90). Increased cooling capacity ($9.90). Heavy-duty three-speed transmission ($5.30). LoadFlite automatic transmission ($221.10). [D Models] 20 in. steering wheel ($4).

OPTIONS: [Power-Wagon only] Vacuum brake booster ($42.15). Deluxe cab equipment ($19.75). Forced-draft crankcase vent system ($19.75). Heater ($46.10). Fenders painted to match cab ($13.20). Draw bar ($23.05). Governor for rear driveshaft ($98.70). Two-quart oil filter ($12.05). Drive pulley ($85.55). Rear driveshaft assembly ($85.55). Winch assembly ($251.35). Heavy-duty springs: 1,600 lbs. front ($7.90); 3,000 lbs. rear ($10.70).

HISTORICAL: Introduced: Oct. 9, 1959. Calendar year sales: 44,998. Calendar year production: 70,305. Model year production: (Six-cylinder) 33,408; (V-8) 14,591; (Total) 47,999. Model year production, U.S. only: (Six-cylinder) 31,522; (V-8) 13,454; (Total) 44,976. History: Dodge's advertising theme for 1960 was "You Can Depend on Dodge to Save You Money in Trucks." Despite a 20 percent increase in advertising budget, sales dropped 13.6 percent. While the light-duty line stood still, Dodge in May, 1959 introduced a new series of medium and heavy-duty cab-forward trucks, featuring "Servi-Swing" fenders that swung out at 110 degrees for easy service access. The new cab-forward C line had a short (89-3/4 in.) bumper-to-back-of-cab dimension, able to pull the maximum length trailers allowed by law. Gone were the hemi-head engines, replaced by a whole new series of 361 and 413 cid V-8s. Available for the first time were four turbocharged Cummins diesels. GVW ratings ranged all the way to 76,800 lbs. The expanding federal highway construction program continued to be a good market for trucks. The Pennsylvania State Highway Dept. ordered 250 heavy-duty D700 models. Dodge also received a contract from the Army to test Chrysler's gas turbine engine in a 14,000 lbs. GVW Dodge truck. Dodge announced in March 1960 a nationwide sales campaign based on the theme: "Take 5 to Drive the New Dodge Sweptline." This campaign, supported by national newspaper advertising, local billboards and direct mail, was intended to encourage five-minute demonstration drives.

1960 Dodge W300M 1-Ton Power Wagon 8 ft. Express (RCA)

1961 DODGE

1/2-TON — R SERIES D100 — SIX/V-8; 3/4-TON — R SERIES D200 — SIX/V-8; 1-TON — R SERIES D300 — SIX/V-8: For the first time since 1954, Dodge announced an all new light and medium duty truck line. The heavy-duty line had been redesigned and re-engineered for 1960. This year, the light-duty lineup was truly new from the ground up. New styling lowered overall heights by up to seven-inches, while widths grew by four-inches. The new Dart pickup had a low, wide silhouette with clean lines that flowed smoothly from front to rear. Dodge aimed for passenger-car styling and handling characteristics in its new truck lineup. Even the name Dart was borrowed from Dodge's popular new car line. However, it lasted only one season in the truck division. All the basic 1960 models were carried over, including the Town Panel and Town Wagon. The only innovation was a new 3/4-ton Forward Control chassis to round out that line. New drop-center frames, in 1/2- and 3/4-ton models, lowered the center of gravity and cab position. Extra rear crossmembers provided greater frame strength and rigidity. One-ton models had a new straight frame at SAE standard 34 in. width. Combined with heavier front and rear axles, it produced a 10,000 lbs. GVW rating. Tread was widened and wheelbase lengths were stretched to improve stability. New front and rear springs were longer and softer, for a passenger car ride. A new heavy-duty New Process A745 transmission was made standard for 1/2- and 3/4-ton models. New alternators replaced the old generators, at no increase in cost. They produced an electrical charge, even at idle. Cabs were available with standard or Custom equipment. Increased cab width made the seat four-inches wider, while the seven-inch reduced height made entry easier...and with no loss of ground clearance. Once again, both Utiline (fender side) and Sweptline (flush side) pickups were available. Sweptline boxes were four-inches wider, gaining 10 percent more load space. Base engine was now an overhead valve 225 cid slant six-cylinder. It was tilted 30 degrees to reduce its height. This provided space for individual branch intake manifolding and lowered the center of gravity. In standard form, the slant six was rated 140 horsepower and developed 215 lbs.-ft. of torque. D100 models intended for extra-light duty, such as stop-and-go delivery, could have a smaller 170 cid version. The familiar old L-head 230 cid six was gone. The 318 cid V-8 continued as an extra-cost option. Fourteen paint colors were again standard, including three new ones: Desert turquoise, Sunset yellow and Turf green. Wheels and bumpers were painted Sand Dune white; hubcaps were gray metallic. Two-tone combinations on the Town Panel and Town Wagon used Sand Dune white at the top. Other two-tone options used Mustang gray or Angus black as the upper color. All inside cab surfaces matched the body color. Steering wheel and column, hand brake control, gearshift lever, seat frame and riser were painted black. Town Panel and Town Wagon models continued without appearance changes. They did not receive the new styling. Only minor trim changes differentiated the 1961 models from 1960, although the wheelbase was stretched to 114 in. like other D100 models. Load capacity remained the same.

1961 Dodge W100 Power Wagon Sweptline Pickup (RCA)

1/2-TON 4x4 — R SERIES W100 — SIX/V-8; 3/4-TON 4x4 — R SERIES W200 — SIX/V-8; 1-TON 4x4 — R SERIES W300 — SIX/V-8: All W-Series models were carried over, but with the new wheelbase, frame construction and styling of the D models. A 251 cid L-head six, used for many years in medium-duty models, became the base engine for the W300.

1961 Dodge Dart D100 Sweptline Pickup (OCW)

1-TON POWER-WAGON — R SERIES W300M — SIX: Power-Wagons continued basically unchanged, except for the new 251 cid L-head six-cylinder engine, which was three-inches longer than the former 230 cid engine.

I.D. DATA: Serial numbers were on an identification plate on the left door lock pillar. Code was the same as on 1960 models. Starting Serial numbers: [D100 Six] 16D1-100001; [D100 V-8] 18D1-L100001; [D200 Six] 16D2-L100001; [D200 V-8] 18D2-L100001; [D300 Six] 16D3-L100001; [D300 V-8] 18D3-L100001; [W100 Six] 16W1-L100001; [W100 V-8] 18W1-L100001; [W200 Six] 16W2-L10000; [W200 V-8] 18W2-L100001; [W300 Six] 16W3-L100001; [W300 V-8] 18W3-L100001; [W300M] 16WM3-L100001. Six-cylinder engine numbers were on the left side of the block at the front, below the cylinder head. V-8 engine numbers were at the left front of the block. Code was the same as on 1960 models. Starting Engine numbers: [225 cid Six] TR-22-8-3-1001; [251 cid Six] TR-25-8-3-1001; [318 cid V-8] TR-318-8-3-1001.

Model	Body Type	Price	Weight	Prod. Total
R6-D100 Series — 1/2-Ton — 114 in. w.b.				
D100	Chassis & Cowl	1471	2540	Note 1
D100	Chassis & Cab	1706	3095	Note 1
D100	Dart Utiline	1812	3405	Note 1
D100	Dart Sweptline	1826	3505	Note 1
D100	Town Panel	2119	3565	Note 1
D100	Town Wagon 6P	2384	3795	Note 1
D100	Town Wagon 8P	2435	3845	Note 1
R6-D100 Series — 1/2-Ton — 122 in. w.b.				
D100	Chassis & Cowl	1506	2565	Note 2
D100	Chassis & Cab	1740	3120	Note 2
D100	Dart Utiline	1847	3470	Note 2
D100	Dart Sweptline	1860	3600	Note 2
D100	Platform	1883	3495	Note 2
D100	Stake	1931	3695	Note

NOTE 1: Total model year production: (six-cylinder) 15,499; (V-8) 2,930.
NOTE 2: Total model year production: (six-cylinder) 8,981; (V-8) 4,298.

Model	Body Type	Price	Weight	Prod. Total
R6-D200 Series — 3/4-Ton — 122 in. w.b.				
D200	Chassis & Cowl	1602	3060	Note 3
D200	Chassis & Cab	1846	3615	Note 3
D200	Utiline Pickup	1952	3965	Note 3
D200	Sweptline Pickup	1966	4095	Note 3
D200	Platform	1988	3790	Note 3
D200	Stake	2036	4190	Note 3

NOTE 3: Total model year production: (six-cylinder) 2,527; (V-8) 1,304.

Model	Body Type	Price	Weight	Prod. Total
R6-D300 Series — 1-Ton — 133 in. w.b.				
D300	Chassis & Cowl	1760	3220	Note 4
D300	Chassis & Cab	2004	3775	Note 4
D300	Utiline Pickup	2130	4175	Note 4
D300	Platform	2176	4475	Note 4
D300	Stake	2235	4675	Note 4

NOTE 4: Total model year production: (six-cylinder) 3,894; (V-8) 1,689.

R6-W100 Series 4x4 — 1/2-Ton — 114 in. w.b.

W100	Chassis & Cowl	2427	3900	Note 5
W100	Dart Utiline	2534	4210	Note 5
W100	Dart Sweptline	2547	4310	Note 5
W100	Town Panel	2840	4380	Note 5
W100	Town Wagon 6P	3106	4600	Note 5
W100	Town Wagon 8P	3152	4640	Note 5

NOTE 5: Total model year production: (six-cylinder) 516; (V-8) 281.

R6-W200 Series 4x4 — 3/4-Ton — 122 in. w.b.

W200	Chassis & Cab	2479	4070	Note 6
W200	Utiline Pickup	2586	4420	Note 6
W200	Sweptline Pickup	2599	4550	Note 6
W200	Platform	2622	4445	Note 6
W200	Stake	2670	4645	Note 6

NOTE 6: Total model year production: (six-cylinder) 273; (V-8) 258.

R6-W300 Series 4x4 — 1-Ton — 133 in. w.b.

W300	Chassis & Cowl	2934	4090	Note 7
W300	Chassis & Cab	3178	4645	Note 7
W300	Utiline Pickup	3304	5045	Note 7
W300	Platform	3351	5345	Note 7
W300	Stake	3411	5545	Note 7

NOTE 7: Total model year production: (six-cylinder) 239; (V-8) 215.

R6-WM300 Series Power-Wagon — 1-Ton — 126 in. w.b.

WM300	Chassis & Cowl	3124	4095	Note 8
WM300	Chassis & Cab	3372	4645	Note 8
WM300	Utiline Pickup	3515	4920	Note 8

NOTE 8: Total model year production: 1,367.
NOTE 9: Weights and prices shown are for six-cylinder models. For V-8 engine (prefix R8) add $130 to price.

1961 Dodge W100 Power Wagon Town Wagon (RCA)

ENGINE [D100 extra-light duty]: Inline. Overhead valves. Slant six-cylinder. Cast iron block. Bore & stroke: 3.4 x 3.125 in. Displacement: 170.2 cid. Compression ratio: 8.6:1. Brake horsepower: 101 at 4000 rpm. Net (Taxable) horsepower: 27.70. Torque: 136 lbs.-ft. at 1600 rpm. Four main bearings. Solid valve lifters.

ENGINE [D100/D200/D300/W100/W200]: Inline. Overhead valve. Slant six-cylinder. Cast iron block. Bore & stroke: 3.4 x 4.125 in. Displacement: 224.7 cid. Compression ratio: 8.2:1. Brake horsepower: 140 at 3900 rpm. Net horsepower: 27.70. Torque: 201 lbs.-ft. at 2000 rpm. Four main bearings. Solid valve lifters.

ENGINE [W300/WM300]: Inline. L-head. Six-cylinder. Cast iron block. Bore & stroke: 3.437 x 4.5 in. Displacement: 250.6 cid. Compression ratio: 7.1:1. Brake horsepower: 125 at 3600 rpm. Net horsepower: 28.35. Torque: 216 lbs.-ft. at 1600 rpm. Four main bearings. Solid valve lifters.

ENGINE [Optional V-8]: 90-degree, overhead valve. Eight-cylinder. Cast iron block. Bore & stroke: 3.91 x 3.312 in. Displacement: 318.1 cid. Compression ratio: 8.25:1. Brake horsepower: 200 at 3900 rpm. Net (Taxable) horsepower: 48.92. Torque: 286 lbs.-ft. at 2400 rpm. Five main bearings. Hydraulic valve lifters.

ENGINE [Optional W300]: Same as V-8 above, but heavy-duty. Brake horsepower: 202 at 3900 rpm. Torque: 288 lbs.-ft. at 2400 rpm.

($4) for "D" models.

CHASSIS [D100]: Wheelbase: 114 in. or 122 in. Tires: 6.70 x 15 four-ply; tubeless (front and rear). GVW: 4,300-5,100 lbs. Axle capacity: (front) 2,500 lbs; (rear) 3,600 lbs.

CHASSIS [D200]: Wheelbase: 122 in. Tires: 8 x 19.5 eight-ply tubeless (front and rear). GVW: 5,200-7,500 lbs. Axle capacity: (front) 2,800 lbs; (rear) 5,500 lbs.

CHASSIS [D300]: Wheelbase: 133 in. Tires: 7 x 17.5 six-ply tubeless (front and rear). GVW: 6,300-9,000 lbs. Axle capacity: (front) 3,800 lbs; (rear) 7,500 lbs.

CHASSIS [W100]: Wheelbase: 114 in. Tires: 7 x 17.5 tubeless (front and rear). GVW: 5,100-6,000 lbs. Axle capacity: (front) 3,000 lbs; (rear) 4,500 lbs.

CHASSIS [W200]: Wheelbase: 122 in. Tires: 8 x 19.5 eight-ply (front and rear). GVW: 6,000-8,000 lbs. Axle capacity: (front) 3,500 lbs. (rear) 5,500 lbs.

CHASSIS [W300]: Wheelbase: 133 in. Tires: 7.50 x 16 six-ply (front and rear). GVW: 8,500-10,000 lbs. Axle capacity: (front) 4,500 lbs; (rear) 7,500 lbs.

CHASSIS [WM300]: Wheelbase: 126 in. Tires: 9.00 x 16 10-ply (front and rear). GVW: 8,700-9,500 lbs. Axle capacity: (front) 3,750 lbs; (rear) 6,500 lbs.

1961 Dodge W300 Power Wagon Utiline Pickup (RCA)

TECHNICAL: Selective sliding gear transmission. Speeds: 3F/1R except 1-ton models, 4F/1R; four-wheel drive models, two-speed two-lever transfer case. Column or floor shift. Automatic transmission optional. Single-plate dry-disc clutch: [D100/200] 10 in. hydraulic; [D200, W100-300] 11 in. hydraulic; [WM300] 11 in. mechanical. Overall axle ratio: [D100] 3.58:1, 3.91:1 or 4.56:1; [D200, W100, W200] 4.1:1 or 4.88:1; [D300] 4.8:1 or 5.87:1; [W300] 4.88:1 or 5.87:1 (front and rear); [Power-Wagon] 5.83:1 (front and rear). Hydraulic four-wheel brakes: [D100] 11 in. drums; [D200, W100-200] 12-1/8 in.; [D300] 12-1/8 in. front, 13 in. rear; [W300] 14-1/8 in. front, 13 in. rear; [WM300] 14-1/8 in. (front and rear). Recirculating ball steering except [W300] worm and roller; [WM300] worm and sector. 35-amp. alternator. One-pint oil bath air cleaner. 18-gallon gas tank inside, behind seat except [WM300] behind rear axle. Wheels: [D100] 15 x 5.00; [D200, W100] 16 x 6.00; [W200, D300] 17.5 x 5.25; [W300] 19.5 x 5.25; [WM300] 16 x 6.50.

1961 Dodge WM300 Power Wagon 8 ft. Express (RCA)

OPTIONS [Factory Installed]: Painted rear bumper. Bright rear bumper. Custom cab equipment. Bright hubcaps [D100 only]. Tinted windows. Inside rear-view mirror. Right sun visor. Dual electric variable-speed wipers. Windshield washer. Full-width rear window. Dual wheel rear fenders. Two-tone paint. Cigar lighter. Left armrest. Radio. Heater. Heavy-duty instruments. Foam rubber seat cushion. Auxiliary seat. Hand throttle. Rear shock absorbers. Vacuum power brake. Power steering. One-quart oil bath air cleaner. 40-amp. alternator. Increased cooling capacity (manual transmission). Anti-spin rear axle. 170 cid slant six engine [D100 only]. 318 cid V-8 engine. Oil pressure gauge. Oil filter. Engine governor. Four-speed synchromesh transmission. LoadFlite three-speed automatic transmission. Heavy-duty springs, front or rear. Three-ton hydraulic jack. [W Series 4x4 models only] Pintle hook. Power-take-off. Winch, 8,000 lbs.. [Power-Wagon only] Combined fuel/vacuum pump. Radiator overflow tank. Tow hooks. Winch, 10,000 lbs.

HISTORICAL: Introduced: October 1960. Calendar year sales: 40,147. Calendar year production: 64,886. Model year production: (six-cylinder) 38,021; (V-8) 10,975; [Total] 48,996. Innovations: Reduced-height design. Slant six engine. Alternator charging system. Dodge ranked fifth in truck sales, as total sales fell 7.9 percent from 1960. Truck production was hindered by a December strike at the Warren, Michigan plant. In August, 1961, Dodge was awarded government contracts for 10,254 trucks: 8,503 military vehicles (trucks, ambulances and weapons carriers) and 1,751 walk-in, forward-control trucks for the U.S. Post Office. The postal trucks had a slant six and automatic transmission, plus plastic skylights in their roof panels. The full Dodge line of 140 basic models ranged from 4,250 lbs. GVW to 76,800 lbs. GVW. It included conventional, cab-forward, four-wheel drive, forward-control, school bus chassis and tandem units.

1961 Dodge W100 Power Wagon Sweptline Wrecker (RCA)

Standard Catalog of Light-Duty Trucks

1962 DODGE

1962 Dodge D100 1/2-Ton Sweptline Pickup (OCW)

1/2-TON — S SERIES D100 — SIX/V-8; 3/4-TON — S SERIES D200 — SIX/V-8; 1-TON — S SERIES D300 — SIX/V-8: Beginning with the 1961 R Series, Dodge Truck reverted to a policy the Dodge Bros. had established when they made their first car back in 1914. There would be no annual model changes just for the sake of change. Instead, improvements came as soon as they were approved, rather than waiting for the next model year. The basic 1961 body styling would continue, with only minor appearance changes, through the 1971 model year. However, many other changes would arrive during the decade. Improvements for the 1962 S series included a new one-piece steel grille for conventional cab models. It was painted Sand Dune white with standard cabs, but chrome plated for Custom cabs. Dodge nameplates were attached to the upper rear of the front fenders. A model number plate sat at the center of the grille. Solid vinyl, heavy-duty upholstery fabrics gave longer life in conventional cab, Town Panel and Town Wagon models. Both doors on Custom cab, Town Panels and Town Wagons had key locks. D100 Town Panel/Town Wagon models gained dual electric variable-speed wipers. A new LoadFlite automatic transmission, available with any engine, had 10 percent more torque capacity. Conventional cabs had a wide, easy-to-read speedometer with black numbers against a white background for greater visibility. Sealing against air, dust and water was improved. Point life was virtually doubled by a ventilated-point distributor and more efficient condenser. A new heavy-duty solenoid-shift starter was standard on all gas models (except the Power-Wagon). Both 170 and 225 cid slant six engines and the 318 cid V-8 continued without change. The only new model was a 1/2-ton Forward Control chassis, making that line complete from 1/2- to 1-1/2-tons. A six-man crew cab pickup arrived in midyear (see 1963 listing). Standard paint colors were carried over from 1961. This was the first year for Dodge's five-year, 50,000-mile warranty.

1/2-TON 4x4 — S SERIES W100 — SIX/V-8; 3/4-TON 4x4 — S SERIES W200 — SIX/V-8; 1-TON 4x4 — S SERIES W300 — SIX/V-8; 1-TON POWER-WAGON — S SERIES WM300 — SIX: A closed-crankcase ventilating system was made standard on four-wheel drive V-8 models. On the Power-Wagon, front and rear fenders were now painted body color. Otherwise, these models continued with little change.

1962 Dodge D200 3/4-Ton Sweptline Pickup (OCW)

1962 Dodge D100 Tradesman Utility Body (OCW)
Standard Catalog of Light-Duty Trucks

I.D. DATA: Serial numbers were on an identification plate on the left door lock pillar. Starting serial numbers: [D100 Six] 26D1-L100001; [D100 V-8] 28D1-L100001; [D200 Six] 26D2-L100001; [D200 V-8] 28D2-L100001; [D300 Six] 26D3-L100001; [D300 V-8] 28D3-L100001; [W100 Six] 26W1-L100001; [W100 V-8] 28W1-L100001; [W200 Six] 26W2-L100001; [W200 V-8] 28W2-L100001; [W300 Six] 26W3-L100001; [W300 V-8] 28W3-L100001; [WM300] 26WM3-L100001. Engine numbers on left side of block. Starting engine numbers: [225 cid Six] TS-22-8-3-1001; [251 cid Six] TS-25-8-3-1001; [318 cid V-8] TS-318-8-3-1001. Ending serial and engine numbers are not available.

Model	Body Type	Price	Weight	Prod. Total
S6-D100 Series — 1/2-Ton — 114 in. w.b.				
D100	Chassis & Cowl	1459	2540	Note 1
D100	Chassis & Cab	1694	3095	Note 1
D100	Utiline Pickup	1800	3405	Note 1
D100	Sweptline Pickup	1814	3505	Note 1
D100	Town Panel	1990	3565	Note 1
D100	Town Wagon 6P	2263	3795	Note 1
D100	Town Wagon 8P	2310	3845	Note 1

NOTE 1: Total model year production: (six) 16,019; (V-8) 2,824.
NOTE 2: Total model year production: (six) 8,770; (V-8) 4,752.

Model	Body Type	Price	Weight	Prod. Total
S6-D100 Series — 1/2-Ton — 122 in. w.b.				
D100	Chassis & Cowl	1494	2565	Note 2
D100	Chassis & Cab	1728	3120	Note 2
D100	Utiline Pickup	1835	3470	Note 2
D100	Sweptline Pickup	1848	3600	Note 2
D100	Platform	1871	3495	Note 2
D100	Stake	1919	3695	Note 2

Model	Body Type	Price	Weight	Prod. Total
S6-D200 Series — 3/4-Ton — 122 in. w.b.				
D200	Chassis & Cowl	1590	3060	Note 3
D200	Chassis & Cab	1838	3615	Note 3
D200	Utiline Pickup	1940	3965	Note 3
D200	Sweptline Pickup	1954	4095	Note 3
D200	Platform	1976	3990	Note 3
D200	Stake	2024	4190	Note 3

NOTE 3: Total model year production: (six) 3,789; (V-8) 2,161.

Model	Body Type	Price	Weight	Prod. Total
S6-D300 Series — 1-Ton — 133 in. w.b.				
D300	Chassis & Cowl	1748	3220	Note 4
D300	Chassis & Cab	1992	3775	Note 4
D300	Utiline Pickup	2118	4175	Note 4
D300	Platform	2164	4475	Note 4
D300	Stake	2223	4675	Note 4

NOTE 4: Total model year production: (six) 4,358; (V-8) 1,983.

Model	Body Type	Price	Weight	Prod. Total
S6-W100 Series 4x4 — 1/2-Ton — 114 in. w.b.				
W100	Chassis & Cab	2367	3900	Note 5
W100	Utiline Pickup	2474	4210	Note 5
W100	Sweptline Pickup	2487	4310	Note 5
W100	Town Panel	2780	4370	Note 5
W100	Town Wagon (6P)	3046	4600	Note 5
W100	Town Wagon (8P)	3092	4640	Note 5

NOTE 5: Total model year production: (six) 490; (V-8) 297.

Model	Body Type	Price	Weight	Prod. Total
S6-W200 Series 4x4 — 3/4-Ton — 122 in. w.b.				
W200	Chassis & Cab	2418	4070	Note 6
W200	Utiline Pickup	2525	4420	Note 6
W200	Sweptline Pickup	2538	4550	Note 6
W200	Platform	2561	4445	Note 6
W200	Stake	2609	4645	Note 6

NOTE 6: Total model year production: (six) 805; (V-8) 375.

Model	Body Type	Price	Weight	Prod. Total
S6-W300 Series 4x4 — 1-Ton — 133 in. w.b.				
W300	Chassis & Cowl	2934	4090	Note 7
W300	Chassis & Cab	3178	4645	Note 7
W300	Utiline Pickup	3304	5045	Note 7
W300	Platform	3351	5345	Note 7
W300	Stake	3411	5545	Note 7

NOTE 7: Total model year production: (six) 221; (V-8) 280.

1962 Dodge W200 Power Wagon Sweptline Pickup (OCW)

Model	Body Type	Price	Weight	Prod. Total
S6-WM300 Series Power-Wagon — 1-Ton — 126 in. w.b.				
WM300	Chassis & Cowl	3124	4095	Note 8
WM300	Chassis & Cab	3372	4645	Note 8
WM300	Utiline Pickup	3515	4920	Note 8

NOTE 8: Total model year production: 2,141 (plus 1,544 MDAP).
NOTE 9: Weights and prices shown are for six-cylinder models. For V-8 engine (prefix S8) add $120 to price.

1962 Dodge W300 1-Ton Power Wagon Utiline Pickup (OCW)

ENGINE [D100 extra-light duty]: Inline. Overhead valves. Slant six-cylinder. Cast iron block. Bore & stroke: 3.4 x 3.125 in. Displacement: 170.2 cid. Compression ratio: 8.6:1. Brake horsepower: 101 at 4000 rpm. Net (Taxable) horsepower: 27.70. Torque: 145 lbs.-ft. at 1600 rpm. Four main bearings. Solid valve lifters.

1962 Dodge D100 Power Wagon Sweptline Wrecker (OCW)

ENGINE [D100/D200/D300/W100/W200]: Inline. Overhead valves. Slant six-cylinder. Cast iron block. Bore & stroke: 3.4 x 4.125 in. Displacement: 224.7 cid. Compression ratio: 8.2:1. Brake horsepower: 140 at 3900 rpm. Net horsepower: 27.70. Torque: 215 lbs.-ft. at 1600 rpm. Four main bearings. Solid valve lifters.

1962 Dodge WM300 Military Type Power Wagon (OCW)

ENGINE [W300/WM300]: Inline. L-head. Six-cylinder. Cast iron block. Bore & stroke: 3.437 x 4.5 in. Displacement: 250.6 cid. Compression ratio: 7.1:1. Brake horsepower: 125 at 3600 rpm. Net horsepower: 28.35. Torque: 216 lbs.-ft. at 1600 rpm. Four main bearings. Solid valve lifters.
ENGINE [Optional V-8]: 90-degree, overhead valve. Eight-cylinder. Cast iron block. Bore & stroke: 3.91 in. x 3.312 in. Displacement: 318.1 cid. Compression ratio: 8.25:1. Brake horsepower: 200 at 3900 rpm. Net (Taxable) horsepower: 48.92. Torque: 286 lbs.-ft. at 2400 rpm. Five main bearings. Hydraulic valve lifters.
ENGINE [Optional W300]: Same as V-8 above, but heavy-duty. Brake horsepower: 202 at 3900 rpm. Torque: 288 lbs.-ft. at 2400 rpm.
CHASSIS [D100]: Wheelbase: 114 in. or 122 in. Tires: 6.70 x 15 four-ply; tubeless (front and rear). GVW: 4,300-5,100 lbs. Axle capacity: (front) 2,500 lbs; [rear] 3,600 lbs.
CHASSIS [D200]: Wheelbase: 122 in. Tires: 8 x 19.5 eight-ply tubeless (front and rear). GVW: 5,200-7,500 lbs. Axle capacity: (front) 2,800 lbs; (rear) 5,500 lbs.
CHASSIS [D300]: Wheelbase: 133 in. Tires: 7 x 17.5 six-ply tubeless (front and rear). GVW: 6,300-9,000 lbs. Axle capacity: (front) 3,800 lbs; (rear) 7,500 lbs.
CHASSIS [W100]: Wheelbase: 114 in. Tires: 7 x 17.5 six-ply tubeless (front and rear). GVW: 5,100-6,000 lbs. Axle capacity: (front) 3,000 lbs; (rear) 4,500 lbs.
CHASSIS [W200]: Wheelbase: 122 in. Tires: 8 x 19.5 eight-ply (front and rear). GVW: 6,000-8,000 lbs. Axle capacity: (front) 3,500 lbs. (rear) 5,500 lbs.
CHASSIS [W300]: Wheelbase: 133 in. Tires: 7.50 x 16 six-ply (front and rear). GVW: 8,500-10,000 lbs. Axle capacity: (front) 4,500 lbs; (rear) 7,500 lbs.
CHASSIS [WM300]: Wheelbase: 126 in. Tires: 9.00 x 16 10-ply (front and rear). GVW: 8,700-9,500 lbs. Axle capacity: (front) 3,750 lbs; (rear) 6,500 lbs.
TECHNICAL: Selective sliding gear transmission. Speeds: 3F/1R except 1-ton models, 4F/1R; four-wheel drive models, two-speed two-lever transfer case. Column or floor shift. Automatic transmission optional. Single-plate dry-disc clutch: [D100/200] 10 in. hydraulic; [D200, W100-300] 11 in. hydraulic; [WM300] 11 in. mechanical. Overall axle ratio: [D100] 3.58:1, 3.91:1 or 4.56:1; [D200, W100, W200] 4.1:1 or 4.88:1; [D300] 4.8:1 or 5.87:1; [W300] 4.88:1 or 5.87:1 (front and rear); [Power-Wagon] 5.83:1 (front and rear). Hydraulic four-wheel brakes: [D100] 11 in. drums; [D200, W100-200] 12-1/8 in. [D300] 12-1/8 in. front, 13 in. rear; [W300] 14-1/8 in. front, 13 in. rear; [WM300] 14-1/8 in. (front and rear). Recirculating ball steering except [W300] worm and roller; [WM300] worm and sector. 35-

amp. alternator. One-pint oil bath air cleaner. 18-gallon gas tank inside, behind seat except [WM300] behind rear axle. Wheels: [D100] 15 x 5.00; [D200, W100] 16 x 6.00; [W200, D300] 17.5 x 5.25; [W300] 19.5 x 5.25; [WM300] 16 x 6.50.

OPTIONS [Factory Installed]: Painted rear bumper. Bright rear bumper. Custom cab equipment. Bright hubcaps [D100 only]. Tinted windows. Dual electric horns. Cab corner marker lights. Inside rearview mirror. Right sun visor. Dual electric variable-speed wipers. Windshield washer. Full-width rear window. Dual wheel rear fenders. Two-tone paint. Cigar lighter. Left armrest. Radio. Heater. Heavy-duty instruments. Foam rubber seat cushion. Auxiliary seat. Hand throttle. Rear shock absorbers. Vacuum power brake. Power steering. One-quart oil bath air cleaner. 40-amp. alternator. Increased cooling capacity (manual transmission). Anti-spin rear axle. 170 cid slant six engine [D100 only]. 318 cid V-8 engine. Oil pressure gauge. Oil filter. Engine governor. Four-speed synchromesh transmission. LoadFlite three-speed automatic transmission. Heavy-duty springs, front or rear. Three-ton hydraulic jack. [W Series 4x4 models only] Pintle hook. Power-take-off. Winch, 8,000 lbs. [Power-Wagon only] Combined fuel/vacuum pump. Radiator overflow tank. Tow hooks. Winch, 10,000 lbs..

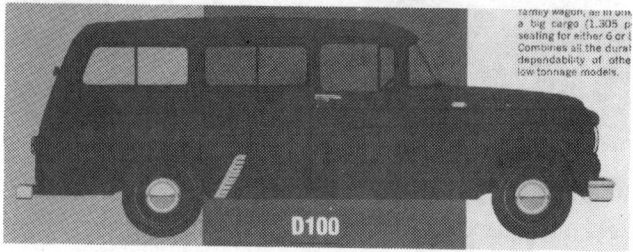

1962 Dodge D100 6/8-Passenger Town Wagon (OCW)

1962 Dodge D100 7-1/2 ft. Town Panel (OCW)

HISTORICAL: Introduced: Sept. 28, 1961. Calendar year sales: 59,118. Calendar year production: 96,102. Model year production: (Six) 53,542; (V-8) 12,672; [Total] 66,214. Dodge Truck had a very good year as production rose 48.1 percent. A heavy-duty version of the 225 cid slant six arrived in medium-duty trucks. A lightweight six-cylinder diesel from Dodge-Perkins was introduced in the spring of 1962. Dodge produced 1,000 diesel-powered trucks. Of the gasoline-powered trucks, 69.5 percent were sixes, whereas the V-8 was most popular in passenger cars. Heavy-duty truck warranty coverage on major gas engine components was extended to 100,000 miles. No appearance changes came to the medium and high-tonnage low-cab-forward [LCF] models. Dodge exhibited its gas turbine powered truck at the Chicago Automobile Show in February. The 1962 line consisted of 141 basic models from 1/2- to 5-ton capacity, all built in the Warren, Michigan truck plant.

1962 Dodge W100 Power Wagon Town Wagon (OCW)

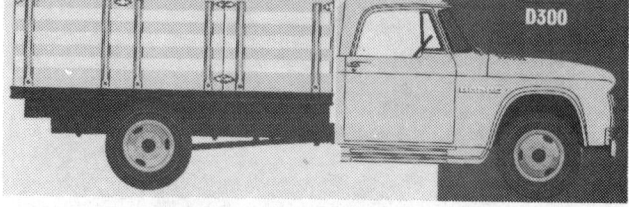

1962 Dodge D300 9 ft. Stake (OCW)

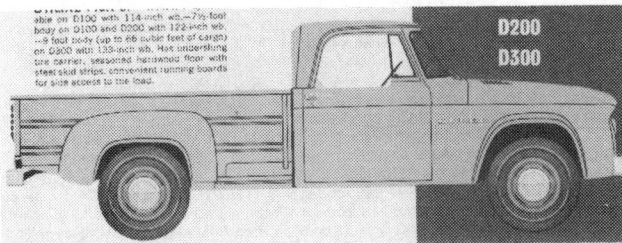

1962 Dodge D200 3/4-Ton Utiline Pickup (OCW)

1963 DODGE

1963 Dodge W200 Sweptline Crew Cab Power Wagon

1963 Dodge D100 Sweptline Pickup (D. Sagvold)

Model	Body Type	Price	Weight	Prod. Total
T6-D100 Series — 1/2-Ton — 114 in. w.b.				
T6-D100	Chassis & Cowl	1468	2540	Note 1
T6-D100	Chassis & Cab	1703	3095	Note 1
T6-D100	Utiline Pickup	1809	3405	Note 1
T6-D100	Sweptline Pickup	1823	3505	Note 1
T6-D100	Town Panel	2007	3565	Note 1
T6-D100	Town Wagon (6P)	2272	3795	Note 1
T6-D100	Town Wagon (8P)	2319	3845	Note 1

NOTE 1: Total model year production: (six) 19,375; (V-8) 4,166.

T6-D100 Series — 1/2-Ton — 122 in. w.b.				
T6-D100	Chassis & Cowl	1503	2565	Note 2
T6-D100	Chassis & Cab	1737	3120	Note 2
T6-D100	Utiline Pickup	1844	3470	Note 2
T6-D100	Sweptline Pickup	1857	3600	Note 2
T6-D100	Platform	1880	3495	Note 2
T6-D100	Stake	1928	3695	Note 2

NOTE 2: Total model year production: (six) 12,920; (V-8) 7,392.

T6-D200 Series — 3/4-Ton — 122 in. w.b.				
T6-D200	Chassis & Cowl	1599	3070	Note 3
T6-D200	Chassis & Cab	1843	3625	Note 3
T6-D200	Utiline Pickup	1949	3975	Note 3
T6-D200	Sweptline Pickup	1963	4105	Note 3
T6-D200	Platform	1985	4000	Note 3
T6-D200	Stake	2033	4200	Note 3

T6-D200 Crew Cab Series — 3/4-Ton — 146 in. w.b.				
T6-D200	Chassis	2451	3973	—
T6-D200	Utiline Pickup	2557	4285	—
T6-D200	Sweptline Pickup	2571	4385	—

NOTE 3: Total model year production: (six) 7,324; (V-8) 4,639.

T6-D300 Series — 1-Ton — 133 in. w.b.				
T6-D300	Chassis & Cowl	1757	3220	Note 4
T6-D300	Chassis & Cab	2021	3775	Note 4
T6-D300	Utiline Pickup	2147	4175	Note 4
T6-D300	Platform	2193	4475	Note 4
T6-D300	Stake	2252	4675	Note 4

NOTE 4: Total model year production: (six) 4,571; (V-8) 2,930.

T6-W100 Series 4x4 — 1/2-Ton — 114 in. w.b.				
T6-W100	Chassis & Cab	2379	3900	Note 5
T6-W100	Utiline Pickup	2486	4210	Note 5
T6-W100	Sweptline Pickup	2499	4310	Note 5
T6-W100	Town Panel	2792	4370	Note 5
T6-W100	Town Wagon (6P)	3058	4600	Note 5
T6-W100	Town Wagon (8P)	3104	4640	Note 5

NOTE 5: Total model year production: (six) 951; (V-8) 445.

T6-W200 Series 4x4 — 3/4-Ton — 122 in. w.b.				
T6-W200	Chassis & Cab	2430	4070	Note 6
T6-W200	Utiline Pickup	2537	4420	Note 6
T6-W200	Sweptline Pickup	2550	4550	Note 6
T6-W200	Platform	2573	4445	Note 6
T6-W200	Stake	2621	4645	Note 6

T6-W200 Crew Cab Series 4x4 — 3/4-Ton — 146 in. w.b.				
T6-W200	Chassis	3149	4259	—
T6-W200	Utiline Pickup	3256	4569	—
T6-W200	Sweptline Pickup	3269	4669	—

NOTE 6: Total model year production: (six) 2,385; (V-8) 764.

T6-W300 Series 4x4 — 1-Ton — 133 in. w.b.				
T6-W300	Chassis & Cowl	2943	4090	Note 7
T6-W300	Chassis & Cab	3187	4645	Note 7
T6-W300	Utiline Pickup	3313	5045	Note 7
T6-W300	Platform	3360	5345	Note 7
T6-W300	Stake	3420	5545	Note 7

NOTE 7: Total model year production: (six) 298; (V-8) 335.

T6WM300 Series Power-Wagon — 1-Ton — 126 in. w.b.				
T6WM300	Chassis & Cowl	3140	4095	Note 8
T6WM300	Chassis & Cab	3388	4520	Note 8
T6WM300	Utiline Pickup	3531	4920	Note 8

NOTE 8: Total model year production: 3,386 (plus 1,302 MDAP models).
NOTE 9: Weights and prices shown are for six-cylinder models. For V-8 engine (prefix S8) add $120 to price.

1/2-TON — T SERIES D100 — SIX-CYLINDER/V-8; 3/4-TON — T SERIES D200 — SIX-CYLINDER/V-8; 1-TON — T SERIES D300 — SIX-CYLINDER/V-8: Dodge Truck continued its policy of product improvements whenever possible throughout the year instead of automatic annual styling changes. Appearance was identical to 1962 models, including standard paint colors. Crew Cab (six-passenger) models on a 146 in. wheelbase were introduced midway in the 1962 model year. They were available as a 3/4-ton capacity D200 with 6.5 ft. Utiline or Sweptline pickup boxes, as well as in medium-tonnage models D400 through D700. Improvements included a new, more efficient oil cooler for the LoadFlite automatic transmission. Seat cushions offered more comfort and longer wear on conventional cab and cab-forward models. Full-depth foam cushioning was now standard on Custom Cab seat and optional for standard cabs. Driver's side armrests became standard on Custom Cabs, but passenger armrests cost extra. All cabs now had locks, on both doors, operated by the ignition key. All models in light-, medium- and heavy-tonnage carried over. No changes were made to Town Panel, Town Wagon or Forward Control chassis models. Standard equipment was unchanged except for the addition of a one-quart oil filter.

1/2-TON 4x4 — T SERIES W100 — SIX-CYLINDER/V-8; 3/4-TON 4x4 — T SERIES W200 — SIX-CYLINDER/V-8; 1-TON 4x4 — T SERIES W300 — SIX-CYLINDER/V-8; 1-TON POWER-WAGON — T SERIES WM300 — SIX-CYLINDER: Crew Cab models were available in the W200 series with Utiline or Sweptline pickup boxes, as well as in the heavier W500 four-wheel drive series. Other changes were the same as the D Series. Power-Wagons carried on without change. W300 models now carried a 225 cid six as standard equipment.

I.D. DATA: Serial numbers were stamped on a plate on the left door lock pillar. New serial number coding produced a 10-digit number. The first two digits indicated the model code; the third digit showed number of cylinders; and the last seven digits were the sequence number. Model codes were as follows: (D100) 11; (D200) 12; (D300) 13; (W100) 21; (W200) 22; (W300) 23; (WM300) 24; (P100/200/300 Forward Control) 30, 31 and 32. Example: 116 1,230,000 indicates model D100 with six-cylinder engine, sequence number 1,230,000. Starting serial (sequence) number: 1,230,000. Ending serial numbers are not available. Engine numbers were located as follows: (170 and 225 cid six) right side of block, on top of boss directly behind coil; (251 cid six) left front of block, at top; (318 cid V-8) left front of block, under cylinder head. The first two letters designated the series (TT/VT/AT/B/BT/C/CT). The next two digits indicated engine displacement. Third and fourth digits showed the month and date of manufacture. Then came the sequence number. Starting and ending numbers are not available.

1963 Dodge D100 Sweptline Pickup (D. Sagvold)

ENGINE (D100 extra-light duty): Inline. Overhead valves. Slant six-cylinder. Cast iron block. Bore & stroke: 3.4 x 3.125 in. Displacement: 170.2 cid. Compression ratio: 8.6:1. Brake horsepower: 101 at 4000 rpm. Net (Taxable) horsepower: 27.70. Torque: 145 lbs.-ft. at 1600 rpm. Four main bearings. Solid valve lifters.

ENGINE (D100/D200/D300/W100/W200): Inline. Overhead valves. Slant six-cylinder. Cast iron block. Bore & stroke: 3.4 x 4.125 in. Displacement: 224.7 cid. Compression ratio: 8.2:1. Brake horsepower: 140 at 3900 rpm. Net horsepower: 27.70. Torque: 215 lbs.-ft. at 1600 rpm. Four main bearings. Solid valve lifters.

ENGINE (W300): Same as W200, but heavy-duty version to meet rugged demands.

ENGINE (WM300): Inline. L-head. Six-cylinder. Cast iron block. Bore & stroke: 3.437 x 4.5 in. Displacement: 250.6 cid. Compression ratio: 7.1:1. Brake horsepower: 125 at 3600 rpm. Net horsepower: 28.35. Torque: 216 lbs.-ft. at 1600 rpm. Four main bearings. Solid valve lifters.

ENGINE (Optional: D100/D200/D300/W100/W200): 90-degree, overhead valve. Eight-cylinder. Cast iron block. Bore & stroke: 3.91 x 3.312 in. Displacement: 318.1 cid. Compression ratio: 8.25:1. Brake horsepower: 200 at 3900 rpm. Net horsepower: 48.92. Torque: 286 lbs.-ft. at 2400 rpm. Five main bearings. Hydraulic valve lifters.

ENGINE (Optional W300): Same as V-8 above, but heavy-duty. Brake horsepower: 202 at 3900 rpm. Torque: 288 lbs.-ft. at 2400 rpm. Compression ratio: 7.5:1.

CHASSIS (D100): Wheelbase: 114 in. or 122 in. Tires: 6.70 x 15 four-ply tubeless (front and rear). GVW: 4,300-5,100 lbs.

CHASSIS (D200): Wheelbase: 122 in. or 146 in. (Crew Cab). Tires: 7 x 17.5 six-ply tubeless (front and rear). GVW: 5,200-7,500 lbs.

CHASSIS (D300): Wheelbase: 133 in. Tires: 7 x 17.5 six-ply tubeless (front and rear). GVW: 6,300-9,000 lbs.

CHASSIS (W100): Wheelbase: 114 in. Tires: 7 x 17.5 six-ply tubeless (front and rear). GVW: 5,100-6,000 lbs.

CHASSIS (W200): Wheelbase: 122 in. or 146 in. (Crew Cab). Tires: 8 x 19.5 eight-ply (front/rear) except Crew Cab, 7 x 17.5 six-ply. GVW: 6,000-8,000 lbs.

CHASSIS (W300): Wheelbase: 133 in. Tires: 7.50 x 16 six-ply (front/rear). GVW: 8,500-10,000 lbs.

CHASSIS (WM300): Wheelbase: 126 in. Tires: 9.00 x 16 ten-ply (front/rear). GVW: 8,700-9,500 lbs.

TECHNICAL: Selective sliding gear transmission. Speeds: 3F/1R, except 1-ton models are 4F/1R and four-wheel drive trucks have two-speed, two-lever transfer case. Column or floor shift. Automatic transmission optional. Single-plate dry-disc clutch: (D100/D200) 10 inch hydraulic; (D200/W100/W300) 11 inch hydraulic; (WM300) 11 inch mechanical. Overall axle ratio: (D100) 3.58:1, 3.91:1 or 4.56:1; (D200/W100/W200) 4.1:1 or 4.88:1; (D300) 4.8:1 or 5.87:1; (W300) 4.88:1 or 5.87:1 (front and rear); (Power Wagon) 5.83:1 (front and rear). Hydraulic four-wheel brakes: (D100) 11 inch drums; (D200/W100/W200) 12-1/8 inch drums; (D300) 12-1/8 inch front, 13 inch rear drums; (W300) 14-1/8 inch front, 13 inch rear; (WM300) 14-1/8 inch front and rear. Recirculating ball steering, except worm-and-roller on W300 and worm-and-sector on WM300. 35-amp. alternator. One pint oil bath air cleaner. 18-gallon gas tank inside, behind seat, except behind rear axle on WM300. Wheels: (D100) 15 x 5.00; (D200/W100) 16 x 6.00; (W200/D300) 17.5 x 5.25; (W300) 19.5 x 5.25; (WM300) 16 x 6.50.

OPTIONS: (Factory-Installed) No. 1 trim package for D Series Utiline pickup, platform or stake: Bright metal moldings on hood, cowl, door and cab back. No. 2 Trim Package for D100/200 Sweptline pickup: Bright metal bumper; molding on hood, cowl, door, cab back and bodysides. Left side armrest (D/W100 panel, standard cab). Right and left armrest (D/W100 panel, standard cab). Right side armrest (Custom cab). 318 cid V-8 engine ($120). Vacuum power brakes ($45). Anti-spin rear axle ($65). LoadFlite three-speed automatic transmission ($220). Three-speed transmission on D300 ($35). Four-speed transmission on 100/200 models ($85). Undercoating.

HISTORICAL: Introduced: October, 1962. Calendar year sales: 75,025. Calendar year production: 110,987. Model year production: (six-cylinder.) 67,685; (V-8) 20,671; (Total) 88,356. Innovations: Crew Cab four-door pickup model. Dodge Truck had its best year since 1952, with a production gain of 15.5 percent and sales increase of 35 percent. Exports and government sales were substantial. Dodge produced 2,137 diesel trucks, all six-cylinder, recording an impressive sales gain. Of the total gasoline-powered trucks produced, 70,996 were six-cylinder and 37,854 were V-8 powered.

1964 DODGE

1/2-TON COMPACT — V SERIES A100 — SIX-CYLINDER; 1/2-TON — V SERIES D100 — SIX-CYLINDER/V-8; 3/4-TON — V SERIES D200 — SIX-CYLINDER/V-8; 1-TON — V SERIES D300 — SIX-CYLINDER/V-8: No changes were made, in this third year of the V-Series light-duty conventional trucks, in either appearance or specifications. Only in standard paint colors was there a change, as Sand Dune white was replaced by Dodge Truck white. All efforts went toward developing two midyear introductions, which began production in February, 1964. One was a high-tonnage tilt-cab diesel with and without sleeper. The second new entry was the compact A100 line with a light-duty, forward-control pickup, van and wagon. With a level load floor and simple, utilitarian styling, the 90 in. wheelbase A100 vans were shorter, wider and higher than a Ford Econoline or Chevrolet Greenbriar. They weighed about the same as a Greenbriar and 200 lbs. more than a Ford

Econoline. Total load space was 213 cu. ft. An A100 wagon could carry nine passengers. Both 170 and 225 cid slant sixes were available. The 225 was the largest engine in the compact truck field. Three-speed manual shift was standard, while three-speed LoadFlite automatic transmission, its shift lever conveniently located on the dash, was an option. A100 driving position was termed excellent with front bucket seats that were firm and form-fitting. Dodge also introduced the Camper Wagon, an A100 Sportsman wagon specially equipped by Travel Equipment Corp. with pop-up roof and living facilities for up to six people. Recognizing the tremendous growth in popularity of the sports/performance type truck, the Custom Sports Special. Available as an option package with either a Utiline or Sweptline box in D100 or D200 capacity, the Custom Sports carried a long list of features that set it apart from standard pickups. Those extras included black vinyl upholstered bucket seats (from a Dart GT), plush carpeting from firewall to top of gas tank behind the seat, dual armrests, a between-seat console (from Polara 500) with lighter and map light, four hood stripes, chrome front bumper and grille, chrome hubcaps, whitewall tires, twin sun visors, insulated headlining, and heat/noise insulation. In addition to the slant six or 318 cid V-8, the Custom Sports could have an optional 426 cid high-performance "wedge" V-8 engine. All Custom Sports engines had chrome air cleaners and valve covers.

1964 Dodge A100 Van/Pickup/Wagon (OCW)

1/2-TON 4x4 — V SERIES W100 — SIX-CYLINDER/V-8; 3/4-TON 4x4 — V SERIES W200 — SIX-CYLINDER/V-8; 1-TON 4x4 — V SERIES W300 — SIX-CYLINDER/V-8; 1-TON POWER-WAGON — V SERIES WM300 — SIX-CYLINDER: The Custom Sports Package described above was also available on W100 and W200 pickups. Power-Wagons entered yet another year, in their long history, without change.

I.D. DATA: Serial numbers were stamped on a plate on the left door lock pillar. Serial number coding produced a 10-digit number. The first two digits indicated the model code; the third digit showed number of cylinders; and the last seven digits were the sequence number. Model codes were as follows: (D100) 11; (D200) 12; (D300) 13; (A100 Pickup) 18; (A100 Van) 19; (A100 Wagon) 20; (W100) 21; (W200) 22; (W300) 23; (WM300) 24. Starting serial number: (A100 models) 2,000,001; (all others) 1,315,000. Ending serial numbers are not available. Engine numbers were located as follows: (170 and 225 cid six) right side of block, on top of boss directly behind coil; (251 cid six) left front of block, at top; (318 cid V-8) left front of block, under cylinder head. The first two letters designated the series. The next two digits indicated engine displacement. Third and fourth digits showed the month and date of manufacture. Then came the sequence number. Starting and ending numbers are not available.

Model	Body Type	Price	Weight	Prod. Total
V6-A100 Series — 1/2-Ton — 90 in. w.b.				
V6-A100	Pickup	1927	2770	Note 1
V6-A100	Van	2133	2790	Note 1
V6-A100	Wagon	2261	3035	7852

NOTE 1: Total model year production: 11,046.

Model	Body Type	Price	Weight	Prod. Total
V6-D100 Series — 1/2-Ton — 114 in. w.b.				
V6-D100	Chassis & Cowl	1468	2540	Note 2
V6-D100	Chassis & Cab	1703	3095	Note 2
V6-D100	Utiline Pickup	1809	3405	Note 2
V6-D100	Sweptline Pickup	1823	3505	Note 2
V6-D100	Town Panel	2007	3565	Note 2
V6-D100	Town Wagon (6P)	2272	3795	Note 2
V6-D100	Town Wagon (8P)	2319	3845	Note 2

NOTE 2: Total model year production: (six) 24,022; (V-8) 4,564.

Model	Body Type	Price	Weight	Prod. Total
V6-D100 Series — 1/2-Ton — 122 in. w.b.				
V6-D100	Chassis & Cowl	1503	2565	Note 3
V6-D100	Chassis & Cab	1737	3120	Note 3
V6-D100	Utiline Pickup	1844	3470	Note 3
V6-D100	Sweptline Pickup	1857	3600	Note 3
V6-D100	Platform	1880	3495	Note 3
V6-D100	Stake	1928	3695	Note 3

NOTE 3: Total model year production: (six) 14,469; (V-8) 11,917.

Model	Body Type	Price	Weight	Prod. Total
V6-D200 Series — 3/4-Ton — 122 in. w.b.				
V6-D200	Chassis & Cowl	1599	3070	Note 4
V6-D200	Chassis & Cab	1843	3625	Note 4
V6-D200	Utiline Pickup	1949	3975	Note 4
V6-D200	Sweptline Pickup	1963	4105	Note 4
V6-D200	Platform	1985	4000	Note 4
V6-D200	Stake	2033	4200	Note 4

Model	Body Type	Price	Weight	Prod. Total
V6-D200 Crew Cab Series — 3/4-Ton — 146 in. w.b.				
V6-D200	Chassis	2451	3973	Note 4
V6-D200	Utiline Pickup	2557	4285	Note 4
V6-D200	Sweptline Pickup	2571	4385	Note 4

NOTE 4: Total model year production: (six) 6,435; (V-8) 7,117.

Model	Body Type	Price	Weight	Prod. Total
V6-D300 Series — 1-Ton — 133 in. w.b.				
V6-D300	Chassis & Cowl	1757	3220	Note 5
V6-D300	Chassis & Cab	2021	3775	Note 5
V6-D300	Utiline Pickup	2147	4175	Note 5
V6-D300	Platform	2193	4475	Note 5
V6-D300	Stake	2252	4675	Note 5

NOTE 5: Total model year production: (six) 4,263; (V-8) 3,263.

V6-W100 Series 4x4 — 1/2-Ton — 114 in. w.b.

V6-W100	Chassis & Cab	2379	3900	Note 6
V6-W100	Utiline Pickup	2486	4210	Note 6
V6-W100	Sweptline Pickup	2499	4310	Note 6
V6-W100	Town Panel	2792	4370	Note 6
V6-W100	Town Wagon (6P)	3058	4600	Note 6
V6-W100	Town Wagon (8P)	3104	4640	Note 6

NOTE 6: Total model year production: (six) 955; (V-8) 504.

V6-W200 Series 4x4 — 3/4-Ton — 122 in. w.b.

V6-W200	Chassis & Cab	2430	4070	Note 7
V6-W200	Utiline Pickup	2537	4420	Note 7
V6-W200	Sweptline Pickup	2550	4550	Note 7
V6-W200	Platform	2573	4445	Note 7
V6-W200	Stake	2621	4645	Note 7

V6-W200 Crew Cab Series 4x4 — 3/4-Ton — 146 in. w.b.

V6-W200	Chassis	3149	4259	Note 7
V6-W200	Utiline Pickup	3256	4569	Note 7
V6-W200	Sweptline Pickup	3269	4669	Note 7

NOTE 7: Total model year production: (six) 2,058; (V-8) 989.

V6-W300 Series 4x4 — 1-Ton — 133 in. w.b.

V6-W300	Chassis & Cowl	2943	4090	Note 8
V6-W300	Chassis & Cab	3187	4645	Note 8
V6-W300	Utiline Pickup	3313	5045	Note 8
V6-W300	Platform	3360	5345	Note 8
V6-W300	Stake	3420	5545	Note 8

NOTE 8: Total model year production: (six) 289; (V-8) 333.

V6WM300 Series Power-Wagon — 1-Ton — 126 in. w.b.

V6WM300	Chassis & Cowl	3140	4095	Note 8
V6WM300	Chassis & Cab	3388	4520	Note 8
V6WM300	Utiline Pickup	3531	4920	Note 8

NOTE 9: Total model year production: 5,428 (plus 486 MDAP models).
NOTE 10: Weights and prices shown are for six-cylinder models. For V-8 engine (prefix S8) add $120 to price.

ENGINE (A100/D100 extra-light duty): Inline. Overhead valves. Slant six-cylinder. Cast iron block. Bore & stroke: 3.4 x 3.125 in. Displacement: 170.2 cid. Compression ratio: 8.5:1. Brake horsepower: 101 at 4000 rpm. Net (Taxable) horsepower: 27.70. Torque: 145 lbs.-ft. at 1600 rpm. Four main bearings. Solid valve lifters.

ENGINE (A100/D100/D200/D300/left/W200): Inline. Overhead valves. Slant six-cylinder. Cast iron block. Bore & stroke: 3.4 x 4.125 in. Displacement: 224.7 cid. Compression ratio: 8.4:1. Brake horsepower: 140 at 3900 rpm. Net horsepower: 27.70. Torque: 215 lbs.-ft. at 1600 rpm. Four main bearings. Solid valve lifters.

ENGINE (W300): Same as W200, but premium heavy-duty version to meet rugged demands.

ENGINE (WM300): Inline. L-head. Six-cylinder. Cast iron block. Bore & stroke: 3.437 x 4.5 in. Displacement: 250.6 cid. Compression ratio: 7.1:1. Brake horsepower: 125 at 3600 rpm. Net horsepower: 28.35. Torque: 216 lbs.-ft. at 1600 rpm. Four main bearings. Solid valve lifters.

ENGINE (Optional: D100/D200/D300/W100/W200): 90-degree, overhead valve. Eight-cylinder. Cast iron block. Bore & stroke: 3.91 x 3.312 in. Displacement: 318.1 cid. Compression ratio: 8.25:1. Brake horsepower: 200 at 3900 rpm. Net horsepower: 48.92. Torque: 286 lbs.-ft. at 2400 rpm. Five main bearings. Hydraulic valve lifters.

ENGINE (Optional W300): Same as V-8 above, but heavy-duty. Brake horsepower: 202 at 3900 rpm. Torque: 288 lbs.-ft. at 2400 rpm. Compression ratio: 7.5:1.

ENGINE (Custom Sports Package: D100/D200/W100/W200): 90-degree, overhead valve, single rocker. Eight-cylinder. Cast iron block. Bore & stroke: 4.25 x 3.75 in. Displacement: 426 cid. Compression ratio: 10.3:1. Brake horsepower: 365 at 4800 rpm. Net (Taxable) horsepower: 57.8. Torque: 470 lbs.-ft. at 3200 rpm. Five main bearings. Hydraulic valve lifters. Carburetor: Single four-barrel.

CHASSIS (A100): Wheelbase: 90 in. Tires: 6.50 x 13 four-ply. GVW: 3,800 lbs. Axle Capacity: (front) 2,200 lbs.; (rear) 3,000 lbs.

CHASSIS (D100): Wheelbase: 114 in. or 122 in. Tires: 6.70 x 15 four-ply. GVW: 4,300-5,100 lbs. Axle Capacity: (front) 2,500 lbs.; (rear) 3,600 lbs.

CHASSIS (D200): Wheelbase: 122 in. or 146 in. Tires: 6.50 x 16 six-ply. GVW: 5,200-7,500 lbs. Axle Capacity: (front) 2,800 lbs.; (rear) 5,500 lbs.

CHASSIS (D300): Wheelbase: 133 in. Tires: 8 x 17.5 six-ply. GVW: 6,300-9,000 lbs. Axle Capacity: (front) 3,800 lbs.; (rear) 7,500 lbs.

CHASSIS (W100): Wheelbase: 114 in. Tires: 6.50 x 16 six-ply. GVW: 5,100-6,000 lbs. Axle Capacity: (front) 3,000 lbs.; (rear) 4,500 lbs.

CHASSIS (W200): Wheelbase: 122 in. or 146 in. (Crew Cab). Tires: 7 x 17.5 six-ply. GVW: 6,000-8,000 lbs. Axle Capacity: (front) 3,000 lbs.; (rear) 5,500 lbs.

CHASSIS (W300): Wheelbase: 133 in. Tires: 8 x 19.5 eight-ply. GVW: 8,500-10,000 lbs. Axle Capacity: (front) 4,500 lbs.; (rear) 7,500 lbs.

CHASSIS (WM300): Wheelbase: 126 in. Tires: 9.00 x 16 eight-ply. GVW: 8,700-9,500 lbs. Axle Capacity: (front) 3,750 lbs.; (rear) 6,500 lbs.

TECHNICAL: Selective sliding gear transmission. Speeds: 3F/1R except 1-ton models, 4F/1R. Column or floor shift control. Transfer Case: (W models) Two-speed, two-lever. Three-speed automatic transmission optional. Single-plate dry-disc clutch: (A100) 9-1/8 in.; (D100/D200) 10 in.; (others) 11 in. Rear axle ratio: (A100) 3.55:1 or 3.91:1, (D100) 3.55:1, 3.91:1 or 4.56:1; (D200/W100/W200) 4.1:1 or 4.88:1; (D300/W300) 4.88:1 or 5.87:1; (WM300) 5.83:1. Hydraulic four-wheel brakes. Oil bath air cleaner. Fuel tank: (A100) 21 gallon; (others) 18 gallon. Alternator: (A100) 30-amp; (others) 35-amp. Shock absorbers: Front and rear except 300 models, front only. Wheels: (A100) 13 x 4.50; (D100) 15 x 5.00; (D200/W100) 16 x 6.00; (D300/W200) 17.5 x 5.25; (W300) 19.5 x 5.25; (WM300) 16 x 6.50.

1964 Dodge A100 Forward Control Pickup (LLD)

OPTIONS (Factory-Installed): Chrome front bumper (A100/D100/D200). Rear bumper (D100/D200). Bumper guards (A100). Chrome hubcaps (A100/D100/D200). Custom cab equipment (D/W models). Left armrest. Right armrest (A/D models). Radio (except WM300). Heater. Cigar lighter (except WM300). Inside mirror. Seat belts. Dual horns (except WM300). Oil pressure gauge (except WM300). Undercoating. Windshield washers. Dual electric variable-speed wipers (except WM300). Tinted glass (D/W models). Heavy-duty instruments (D/W). Cab marker lights (D/W). Auxiliary taillight (D/W/WM). Auxiliary seat (D100). Right sun visor (D/W). Full-width rear window (D/W). No. 1 Trim Package: Chrome moldings on hood, cowl, door and cab back (D100-300 Utiline, platform, stake). No. 2 Trim Package: Chrome front bumper; moldings on hood, cowl, doors, cab back and sides (D100/200 Sweptline). Full-depth foam padded seats (D models). Turn signals. Hand throttle (D/W/WM). One-quart oil bath air cleaner (except WM300). 40-amp. alternator. 3,000 or 3,600 lbs. rear axle. Two-tone paint (except WM300). Increased cooling capacity (D/W). Anti-spin rear axle (D100-300, W100/200). Engine governor (D/W). Three-ton jack (except A100). Heavy-duty front springs (D/W). Heavy-duty rear springs (D/W). Power steering (D models). Heavy-duty three-speed manual transmission (A100). LoadFlite automatic transmission (A/D models). 170 cid engine (D100). 225 cid engine (A100). 318 cid V-8 engine (D/W models). Four-speed transmission (D100/200, W100/200). Vacuum power brake (all except A100 and D100). Rear shock absorbers D/W/WM300. Front wheel locking hubs (W/WM). Pintle hook (W/WM). 8,000 lbs. winch (W models). Spare wheel (W300 dual-wheel models). Front tow hooks (WM300). 10,000 lbs. winch (WM300). Fuel/vacuum pump (WM300). Radiator overflow tank (WM300).

NOTE: High performance 426 cid V-8 in Custom Sports Package had to be ordered with: Dual exhausts, rear axle struts, power steering, heavy-duty instrument cluster, LoadFlite automatic transmission, power brakes and tachometer. (Options for Custom Sports Package) Chrome rearview mirror (left). Trim package: Bright moldings on hood, cowl, doors, cab back and bodysides. Chrome rear bumper.

HISTORICAL: Introduced: October, 1963. Calendar year sales: 101,072. Calendar year production: 135,630. Model year production: (six-cylinder) 76,075; (V-8) 28,687; (Total) 104,762. Innovations: Compact van (90 in. wheelbase). Sports-type pickup, available with 426 cid V-8 engine. Truck sales rose 31 percent over 1963...the best performance since 1953. Dodge increased its share of the U.S. market from 7.7 to 8.8 percent. Of the 141,393 gasoline-powered trucks, 64 percent had six-cylinder engines. Diesel engine production was down slightly. Dodge built 7,852 A100 wagons that were registered as passenger cars. In addition to the light-duty engines, 361 and 413 cid V-8s were available in medium- and heavy-tonnage models. Dodge opened a series of truck branch offices throughout the country, specializing in the sale of trucks over 10,000 lbs. GVW.

1965 DODGE

1965 Dodge D100 Custom Sweptline Pickup (OCW)

1/2-TON COMPACT — A SERIES A100 — SIX-CYLINDER/V-8: The A100 lineup carried over largely unchanged into its second year. Although Sportsman and Custom Sportsman wagon models were available, they were considered part of the Dodge car line. The 170 cid slant six was standard; a 225 cid slant six and 273.5 cid V-8 were optional. Dodge was the only compact van offering a V-8. Three GVW ratings were available: 3,800, 4,600 and 5,200 lbs., depending on equipment options.

205

1965 Dodge D100 Custom Sweptline Pickup (Front)

1/2-TON — A SERIES D100 — SIX-CYLINDER/V-8; 3/4-TON — A SERIES D200 — SIX-CYLINDER/V-8; 1-TON — A SERIES D300 — SIX-CYLINDER/V-8: Dodge began the model year selling an unchanged truck line. By spring 1965, in keeping with the policy of making product improvements at any time, Dodge introduced an improved line of light-duty trucks. Exterior appearance changes included a new full-width grille and headlight treatment. It gave a lower, wider look. A new full-length molding was optional on Sweptline pickups only. The series designation plate moved from the grille to the rear section of both front fenders. A wider tailgate with single-latch opening mechanism operated easily with one hand. Taillights were newly styled, slim and vertical in shape. Sweptline boxes were now perfectly vertical at the rear, better to hold an add-on camper. To improve weight distribution for big loads (such as pickup campers) the old 122 in. wheelbase models were stretched to 128 in. A new 8 ft. Utiline box replaced the 7-1/2 footer on the longer chassis. Sweptline pickup boxes had new double wall construction, plus a flat top on both wheelhousings. Custom cab options were now available in two packages, one for comfort and another for appearance. Turn signals were made standard equipment in the new models. Half- and 3/4-ton models had self-adjusting brakes. Prices did not increase when the new models arrived.

1965 Dodge D100 Custom Sweptline Pickup (Side)

1/2-TON 4x4 — A SERIES W100 — SIX-CYLINDER/V-8; 3/4-TON 4x4 — A SERIES W200 — SIX-CYLINDER/V-8; 1-TON 4x4 — A SERIES W300 — SIX-CYLINDER/V-8; 1-TON POWER-WAGON — A SERIES WM300 — SIX-CYLINDER: Four-wheel drive models continued as before, except for the changes noted in the D series. W200 models grew to 128 in. wheelbase at midyear.

1965 Dodge D100 Sweptline Pickup (Rear)

I.D. DATA: Serial numbers were stamped on a plate on the left door lock pillar. Serial number coding produced a 10-digit number. The first two digits indicated the model code; the third digit showed number of cylinders; and the last seven digits were the sequence number. Model codes were as follows: (D100) 11; (D200) 12; (D300) 13; (A100 Pickup) 18; (A100 Van) 19; (A100 Wagon) 20; (W100) 21; (W200) 22; (W300) 23; (WM300) 24. Starting serial numbers: (A100) 2,015,000; (all others) 1,430,000. Ending serial numbers are not available. Engine numbers were located as follows: (170 and 225 cid six) right side of block, on top of boss directly behind coil; (251 cid six) left front of block, at top; (318 cid V-8) left front of block, under cylinder head. The first two letters designated the series. The next two digits indicated engine displacement. Third and fourth digits showed the month and date of manufacture. Then came the sequence number. Starting and ending numbers are not available.

206

1965 Dodge A100 Sportsman Wagon (OCW)

Model	Body Type	Price	Weight	Prod. Total
A6-A100 Compact Series — 1/2-Ton — 90 in. w.b.				
A6-A100	Pickup	1756	2910	Note 1
A6-A100	Panel Van	1897	2910	Note 1
A6-A100	Van (side/rear doors)	1947	2930	Note 1
A6-A100	Sportsman Wagon	2129	—	—
A6-A100	Custom Sportsman	2434	—	—

NOTE 1: Total model year production: (six) 36,535; (V-8) 5,810.

A6-D100 Series — 1/2-Ton — 114 in. w.b.				
A6-D100	Chassis & Cowl	1482	2540	Note 2
A6-D100	Chassis & Cab	1727	3095	Note 2
A6-D100	Utiline Pickup	1833	3405	Note 2
A6-D100	Sweptline Pickup	1847	3505	Note 2
A6-D100	Town Panel	2088	3565	Note 2
A6-D100	Town Wagon (6P)	2378	3795	Note 2
A6-D100	Town Wagon (8P)	2424	3845	Note 2

NOTE 2: Total model year production: (six) 21,589; (V-8) 6,418.

A6-D100 Series — 1/2-Ton — 128 in. w.b.				
A6-D100	Chassis & Cowl	1517	2590	Note 3
A6-D100	Chassis & Cab	1761	3110	Note 3
A6-D100	Utiline Pickup	1868	3600	Note 3
A6-D100	Sweptline Pickup	1881	3660	Note 3
A6-D100	Platform	1904	3535	Note 3
A6-D100	Stake	1952	3735	Note 3

NOTE 3: Total model year production: (six) 8081; (V-8) 6789. Model year production of early 122 in. wheelbase D100: (six) 9206; (V-8) 7385.

A6-D200 Series — 3/4-Ton — 128 in. w.b.				
A6-D200	Chassis & Cowl	1613	3095	Note 4
A6-D200	Chassis & Cab	1867	3650	Note 4
A6-D200	Utiline Pickup	1973	4090	Note 4
A6-D200	Sweptline Pickup	1987	4150	Note 4
A6-D200	Platform	2009	4025	Note 4
A6-D200	Stake	2057	4225	Note 4

NOTE 4: Total model year production: (six) 3,767; (V-8) 4,366. Model year production of early 122 in. wheelbase: (six) 3,708; (V-8) 4,713.

A6-D200 Crew Cab Series — 3/4-Ton — 146 in. w.b.				
A6-D200	Chassis	2475	3973	—
A6-D200	Utiline Pickup	2581	4285	—
A6-D200	Sweptline Pickup	2595	4385	—

A6-D300 Series — 1-Ton — 133 in. w.b.				
A6-D300	Chassis & Cowl	1771	3220	Note 5
A6-D300	Chassis & Cab	2045	3775	Note 5
A6-D300	Utiline Pickup	2170	4175	Note 5
A6-D300	Platform	2217	4475	Note 5
A6-D300	Stake	2276	4675	Note 5

NOTE 5: Total model year production: (six) 4,961; (V-8) 4,155.

A6-W100 Series 4x4 — 1/2-Ton — 114 in. w.b.				
A6-W100	Chassis & Cab	2403	3900	Note 6
A6-W100	Utiline Pickup	2510	4210	Note 6
A6-W100	Sweptline Pickup	2523	4310	Note 6
A6-W100	Town Panel	2813	4370	Note 6
A6-W100	Town Wagon (6P)	3079	4600	Note 6
A6-W100	Town Wagon (8P)	3125	4640	Note 6

NOTE 6: Total model year production: (six) 843; (V-8) 631.

A6-W200 Series 4x4 — 3/4-Ton — 128 in. w.b.				
A6-W200	Chassis & Cab	2454	3945	Note 7
A6-W200	Utiline Pickup	2561	4385	Note 7
A6-W200	Sweptline Pickup	2574	4445	Note 7
A6-W200	Platform	2579	4320	Note 7
A6-W200	Stake	2645	4520	Note 7

NOTE 7: Total model year production: (six) 607; (V-8) 759. Model year production of early 122 in. wheelbase: (six) 776; (V-8) 550.

A6-W200 Crew Cab Series 4x4 — 3/4-Ton — 146 in. w.b.				
A6-W200	Chassis	3173	4259	—
A6-W200	Utiline Pickup	3280	4569	—
A6-W200	Sweptline Pickup	3293	4669	—

A6-W300 Series 4x4 — 1-Ton — 133 in. w.b.

A6-W300	Chassis & Cowl	2957	4090	Note 8
A6-W300	Chassis & Cab	3211	4645	Note 8
A6-W300	Utiline Pickup	3337	5045	Note 8
A6-W300	Platform	3384	5345	Note 8
A6-W300	Stake	3444	5545	Note 8

NOTE 8: Total model year production: (six) 223; (V-8) 573.

A6-WM300 Series Power-Wagon — 1-Ton — 126 in. w.b.

A6-WM300	Chassis & Cowl	3154	4095	Note 9
A6-WM300	Chassis & Cab	3412	4520	Note 9
A6-WM300	Utiline Pickup	3555	4920	Note 9

NOTE 9: Total model year production: 2,397 (plus 2,496 MDAP models).
NOTE 10: Weights and prices shown are for six-cylinder models. For V-8 engine (prefix AB) add $120 to price.

1965 Dodge D100 Sweptline "Indy" Pickup (IMSC/JLM)

ENGINE (A100/D100 extra-light duty): Inline. Overhead valves. Slant six-cylinder. Cast iron block. Bore & stroke: 3.4 x 3.125 in. Displacement: 170.2 cid. Compression ratio: 8.5:1. Brake horsepower: 101 at 4000 rpm. Net (Taxable) horsepower: 27.70. Torque: 145 lbs.-ft. at 1600 rpm. Four main bearings. Solid valve lifters.

1965 Dodge A100 Side/Rear Door Van (OCW)

ENGINE (A100/D100/D200/D300/W100/W200): Inline. Overhead valves. Slant six-cylinder. Cast iron block. Bore & stroke: 3.4 x 4.125 in. Displacement: 224.7 cid. Compression ratio: 8.4:1. Brake horsepower: 140 at 3900 rpm. Net horsepower: 27.70. Torque: 215 lbs.-ft. at 1600 rpm. Four main bearings. Solid valve lifters.

ENGINE (W300): Same as W200, but premium heavy-duty version to meet rugged demands.

ENGINE (WM300): Inline. L-head. Six-cylinder. Cast iron block. Bore & stroke: 3.437 x 4.5 in. Displacement: 250.6 cid. Compression ratio: 7.1:1. Brake horsepower: 125 at 3600 rpm. Net horsepower: 28.35. Torque: 216 lbs.-ft. at 1600 rpm. Four main bearings. Solid valve lifters.

ENGINE (Optional: D100/D200/D300/W100/W200): 90-degree, overhead valve. Eight-cylinder. Cast iron block. Bore & stroke: 3.91 x 3.312 in. Displacement: 318.1 cid. Compression ratio: 8.25:1. Brake horsepower: 200 at 3900 rpm. Net horsepower: 48.92. Torque: 286 lbs.-ft. at 2400 rpm. Five main bearings. Hydraulic valve lifters.

ENGINE (Optional W300): Same as V-8 above, but heavy-duty. Brake horsepower: 202 at 3900 rpm. Torque: 288 lbs.-ft. at 2400 rpm. Compression ratio: 7.5:1.

ENGINE (Custom Sports Package: D100/D200/W100/W200): 90-degree, overhead valve, single rocker. Eight-cylinder. Cast iron block. Bore & stroke: 4.25 x 3.75 in. Displacement: 426 cid. Compression ratio: 10.3:1. Brake horsepower: 365 at 4800 rpm. Net (Taxable) horsepower: 57.8. Torque: 470 lbs.-ft. at 3200 rpm. Five main bearings. Hydraulic valve lifters. Carburetor: Single four-barrel.

Standard Catalog of Light-Duty Trucks

1965 Dodge A100 Pickup (OCW)

CHASSIS (A100): Wheelbase: 90 in. Tires: 6.95 x 14-2 four-ply. GVW: 4,600 lbs. except Sportsman, 5,200 lbs. maximum.

CHASSIS (D100): Wheelbase: 114 in., 122 in. or 128 in. Tires: 6.70 x 15 four-ply except Town Panel/Wagon models, 7.10 x 15. GVW: 5,200 lbs. maximum.

CHASSIS (D200): Wheelbase: 122 in., 128 in. or 146 in. Tires: (122 in.) 6.50 x 16 six-ply; (others) 7 x 17.5 six-ply. GVW: 7,500 lbs. maximum.

CHASSIS (D300): Wheelbase: 133 in. Tires: 7 x 17.5 six-ply. GVW: 9,000 lbs. maximum.

CHASSIS (W100): Wheelbase: 114 in. Tires: 7 x 17.5 six-ply. GVW: 6,000 lbs. maximum.

CHASSIS (W200): Wheelbase: 122 in., 128 in. or 146 in. Tires: 7 x 17.5 six-ply except 128 in., 8 x 19.5 eight-ply. GVW: 8,000 lbs. maximum (Crew Cab, 6,000 lbs.)

CHASSIS (W300): Wheelbase: 133 in. Tires: 7.50 x 16 six-ply. GVW: 10,000 lbs. maximum.

CHASSIS (WM300): Wheelbase: 126 in. Tires: 9.00 x 16 ten-ply. GVW: 9,500 lbs. maximum.

TECHNICAL: Selective sliding gear transmission. Speeds: 3F/1R except 1-ton models, 4F/1R. Column or floor shift control. Transfer Case: (W models) Two-speed, two-lever. Three-speed automatic transmission optional. Single-plate dry-disc clutch: (A100) 9-1/8 in.; (D100/D200) 10 in.; (others) 11 in. Rear axle ratio: (A100) 3.55:1 or 3.91:1, (D100) 3.55:1, 3.91:1 or 4.56:1; (D200, W100, W200) 4.1:1 or 4.88:1; (D300, W300) 4.88:1 or 5.87:1; (WM300) 5.83:1. Hydraulic four-wheel brakes. Oil bath air cleaner. Fuel tank: (A100) 21 gallon; (others) 18 gallon. Alternator: (A100) 30-amp.; (others) 35-amp. Shock absorbers: Front and rear except 300 models, front only. Wheels: (A100) 13 x 4.50; (D100) 15 x 5.00; (D200/W100) 16 x 6.00; (D300/W200) 17.5 x 5.25; (W300) 19.5 x 5.25; (WM300) 16 x 6.50.

OPTIONS (Factory-Installed): Chrome front bumper (A100/D100/D200). Rear bumper (D100/D200). Bumper guards (A100). Chrome hubcaps (A100/D100/D200). Custom cab equipment (D/W models). Left armrest. Right armrest (A/D models). Radio (except WM300). Heater. Cigar lighter (except WM300). Inside mirror. Seat belts. Dual horns (except WM300). Oil pressure gauge (except WM300). Undercoating. Windshield washers. Dual electric variable-speed wipers (except WM300). Tinted glass (D/W models). Heavy-duty instruments (D/W). Cab marker lights (D/W). Auxiliary taillight (D/W/WM). Auxiliary seat (D/W). Right sun visor (D/W). Full-width rear window (D/W). No. 1 Trim Package: Chrome moldings on hood, cowl, door and cab back (D100-300 Utiline, platform, stake). No. 2 Trim Package: Chrome front bumper; moldings on hood, cowl, doors, cab back and sides (D100/200 Sweptline). Full-depth foam padded seats (D models). Turn signals. Hand throttle (D/W/WM). One-quart oil bath air cleaner (except WM300). 40-amp. alternator. 3,000- or 3,600 lbs. rear axle. Two-tone paint (except WM300). Increased cooling capacity (D/W). Anti-spin rear axle (D100/300; W100/300). Engine governor (D/W). Three-ton jack (except A100). Heavy-duty front springs (D/W). Heavy-duty rear springs (D/W). Power steering on D series ($159). Heavy-duty three-speed manual transmission (A100). Load-Flite automatic transmission in A/D models ($221). 170 cid engine (D100). 225 cid engine (A100). 318 cid V-8 engine in D/W models ($121). Four-speed transmission D100/200, W100/200). Vacuum power brake (all except A100 and D100). Rear shock absorbers D/W/WM300. Front wheel locking hubs (W/WM). Pintle hook (W/WM). Power-take-off (W/WM). 8,000 lbs. winch (W models). Spare wheel (W300 dual-wheel models). Front tow hooks (WM300). 10,000 lbs. winch (WM300). Fuel/vacuum pump (WM300). Radiator overflow tank (WM300).

NOTE: High performance 426 cid V-8 in Custom Sports Package had to be ordered with dual exhausts, rear axle struts, power steering, heavy-duty instrument cluster, LoadFlite automatic transmission, power brakes and tachometer. (Options for Custom Sports Package) Chrome rearview mirror (left). Trim package: Bright moldings on hood, cowl, doors, cab back andides. Chrome rear bumper.

HISTORICAL: Introduced: October, 1964. (128 inch wheelbase models released midway through model year). Calendar year sales: 119,365. Calendar year production: 143,452. Model year production: (six) 97,853; (V-8) 42,149; (Total) 140,002. Innovations included a V-8 engine in compact vans and double wall Sweptline pickup box construction. Dodge had a very good year, as sales rose 19 percent. Only in 1947 and 1949 had Dodge sold more trucks. Dodge ranked fourth in U.S. production. Of the total gasoline-powered trucks sold, 58.8 percent still had six-cylinder engines. Diesel sales came to 2,100. A new 860,000 sq. ft. assembly plant, to be built in St. Louis, was announced in 1965. It would turn out 200 trucks per day, with the potential for 400. A100 sales amounted to 21,333 pickups and vans. For the first time, industry sales of light trucks (6,000 lbs. or less) hit the one million mark.

1965 Dodge A100 Pickup (Louderbough)

1966 DODGE

1966 Dodge D100 Camper Special Pickup (JAG)

1/2-TON COMPACT — B SERIES A100 — SIX-CYLINDER/V-8: Compact vans, wagons and pickups entered their third year without change. Calendar year production increased by 1,015 to 22,348 units.

1/2-TON — B SERIES D100 — SIX-CYLINDER/V-8; 3/4-TON — B SERIES D200 — SIX-CYLINDER/V-8; 1-TON — B SERIES D300 — SIX-CYLINDER/V-8; 1/2-TON 4x4 — B SERIES W100 — SIX-CYLINDER/V-8; 3/4-TON 4x4 — B SERIES W200 — SIX-CYLINDER/V-8; 1-TON 4x4 — B SERIES W300 — SIX-CYLINDER/V-8: The restyling and other improvements made during the 1965 model year continued into 1966 with no further change. All models, engines and specifications carried on. Prices remained the same as in 1965. Standard equipment included a dome light, door locks, left sun visor, painted hubcaps and front bumper, glove box, seat belts, dual variable-speed wipers and dual jet washers, inside mirror, left outside mirror, front and rear shocks (front only on 1-ton) and six-cylinder engine.

1966 Dodge D100 Camper Special Pickup (OCW)

208

1966 Dodge D100 Camper Special Pickup (Front)

I.D. DATA: Serial numbers were stamped on a plate on the left door lock pillar. Serial number coding produced a 10-digit number. The first two digits indicated the model code; the third digit showed number of cylinders; and the last seven digits were the sequence number. Model codes were as follows: (D100) 11; (D200) 12; (D300) 13; (A100 Pickup) 18; (A100 Van) 19; (A100 Wagon) 20; (W100) 21; (W200) 22; (W300) 23; (WM300) 24. Starting serial numbers: (A100) 2,055,000; (all other models) 1,548,000. Ending numbers are not available. Engine numbers were located as follows: (170 and 225 cid six) right side of block, on top of boss directly behind coil; (251 cid six) left front of block, at top; (318 cid V-8) left front of block, under cylinder head. The first two letters designated the series. The next two digits indicated engine displacement. Third and fourth digits showed the month and date of manufacture. Then came the sequence number. Starting and ending numbers are not available.

1966 Dodge A100 Pickup With Camper Unit (JAG)

Model	Body Type	Price	Weight	Prod. Total
B6-A100 Series — 1/2-Ton)— 90 in. w.b.				
B6-A100	Pickup	1756	2910	Note 1
B6-A100	Panel Van	1897	2910	Note 1
B6-A100	Van (side/rear doors)	1947	2930	Note 1
B6-A100	Sportsman Wagon	2129	—	Note 1
B6-A100	Custom Sportsman	2434	—	Note 1

NOTE 1: Total model year production: (six) 35,190; (V-8) 9,536.

Model	Body Type	Price	Weight	Prod. Total
B6-D100 Series — 1/2-Ton — (114 in. w.b.)				
B6-D100	Chassis & Cowl	1482	2540	Note 2
B6-D100	Chassis & Cab	1727	3095	Note 2
B6-D100	Utiline Pickup	1833	3405	Note 2
B6-D100	Sweptline Pickup	1847	3505	Note 2
B6-D100	Town Panel	2088	3565	Note 2
B6-D100	Town Wagon (6P)	2378	3795	Note 2
B6-D100	Town Wagon (8P)	2424	3845	Note 2

NOTE 2: Total model year production: (six) 17,512; (V-8) 5,167.

Model	Body Type	Price	Weight	Prod. Total
B6-D100 Series — 1/2-Ton — 128 in. w.b.				
B6-D100	Chassis & Cowl	1517	2590	Note 3
B6-D100	Chassis & Cab	1761	3110	Note 3
B6-D100	Utiline Pickup	1868	3600	Note 3
B6-D100	Sweptline Pickup	1881	3660	Note 3
B6-D100	Platform	1904	3535	Note 3
B6-D100	Stake	1952	3735	Note 3

NOTE 3: Total model year production: (six) 17,870; (V-8) 15,991.

Model	Body Type	Price	Weight	Prod. Total
B6-D200 Series — 3/4-Ton — 128 in. w.b.				
B6-D200	Chassis & Cowl	1613	3095	Note 4
B6-D200	Chassis & Cab	1867	3650	Note 4
B6-D200	Utiline Pickup	1973	4090	Note 4
B6-D200	Sweptline Pickup	1987	4150	Note 4
B6-D200	Platform	2009	4025	Note 4
B6-D200	Stake	2057	4225	Note 4

NOTE 4: Total model year production: (six) 11,224; (V-8) 13,871.

Model	Body Type	Price	Weight	Prod. Total
B6-D200 Crew Cab Series — 3/4-Ton — 146 in. w.b.				
B6-D200	Chassis	2475	3973	—
B6-D200	Utiline Pickup	2581	4285	—
B6-D200	Sweptline Pickup	2595	4385	—

B6-D300 Series — 1-Ton — 133 in. w.b.

B6-D300	Chassis & Cowl	1771	3220	Note 5
B6-D300	Chassis & Cab	2045	3775	Note 5
B6-D300	Utiline Pickup	2170	4175	Note 5
B6-D300	Platform	2217	4475	Note 5
B6-D300	Stake	2276	4675	Note 5

NOTE 5: Total model year production: (six) 4,042; (V-8) 5,037.

B6-W100 Series 4x4 — 1/2-Ton — 114 in. w.b.

B6-W100	Chassis & Cab	2403	3900	Note 6
B6-W100	Utiline Pickup	2510	4210	Note 6
B6-W100	Sweptline Pickup	2523	4310	Note 6
B6-W100	Town Panel	2813	4370	Note 6
B6-W100	Town Wagon (6P)	3079	4600	Note 6
B6-W100	Town Wagon (8P)	3125	4640	Note 6

NOTE 6: Total model year production: (six) 1,528; (V-8) 820.

B6-W200 Series 4x4 — 3/4-Ton — 128 in. w.b.

B6-W200	Chassis & Cab	2454	3945	Note 7
B6-W200	Utiline Pickup	2561	4385	Note 7
B6-W200	Sweptline Pickup	2574	4445	Note 7
B6-W200	Platform	2579	4320	Note 7
B6-W200	Stake	2645	4520	Note 7

NOTE 7: Total model year production: (six) 1,055; (V-8) 2,258.

B6-W200 Crew Cab Series 4x4 — 3/4-Ton — 146 in. w.b.

B6-W200	Chassis	3173	4259	—
B6-W200	Utiline Pickup	3280	4569	—
B6-W200	Sweptline Pickup	3293	4669	—

B6-W300 Series 4x4 — 1-Ton — 133 in. w.b.

B6-W300	Chassis & Cowl	2957	4090	Note 8
B6-W300	Chassis & Cab	3211	4645	Note 8
B6-W300	Utiline Pickup	3337	5045	Note 8
B6-W300	Platform	3384	5345	Note 8
B6-W300	Stake	3444	5545	Note 8

NOTE 8: Total model year production: (six) 220; (V-8) 625.

B6-WM300 Series Power-Wagon — 1-Ton — 126 in. w.b.

B6-WM300	Chassis & Cowl	3154	4095	Note 9
B6-WM300	Chassis & Cab	3412	4520	Note 9
B6-WM300	Utiline Pickup	3555	4920	Note 9

NOTE 9: Total model year production: 1,245 (plus 3,371 MDAP models).
NOTE 10: Weights and prices shown are for six-cylinder models. For V-8 engine (prefix S8) add $120 to price.

1966 Dodge D100 Sweptline Custom Pickup (E.H. Terry)

CHASSIS (A100): Wheelbase: 90 in. Tires: 6.50 x 13 four-ply. GVW: 3,800-4,600 lbs. Axle Capacity: (front) 2,200 lbs.; (rear) 3,000 lbs.
CHASSIS (D100): Wheelbase: 114 in. or 128 in. Tires: 6.70 x 15 four-ply except Town Panel/Wagon, 7.10 x 15. GVW: 4,300-5,200 lbs. Axle Capacity: (front) 2,500 lbs.; (rear) 3,600 lbs.
CHASSIS (D200): Wheelbase: 128 in. or 146 in. Tires: 6.50 x 16 six-ply. GVW: 5,200-7,500 lbs. Axle Capacity: (front) 2,800 lbs.; (rear) 5,500 lbs.
CHASSIS (D300): Wheelbase: 133 in. Tires: 8 x 17.5 six-ply. GVW: 6,300-9,000 lbs. Axle Capacity: (front) 3,800 lbs.; (rear) 7,500 lbs.
CHASSIS (W100): Wheelbase: 114 in. Tires: 6.50 x 16 six-ply. GVW: 5,100-6,000 lbs. Axle Capacity: (front) 3,000 lbs.; (rear) 4,500 lbs.
CHASSIS (W200): Wheelbase: 128 in. or 146 in. Tires: 7 x 17.5 six-ply. GVW: 6,000-8,000 lbs. Axle Capacity: (front) 3,000 lbs.; (rear) 5,500 lbs.
CHASSIS (W300): Wheelbase: 133 in. Tires: 8 x 19.5 eight-ply. GVW: 8,500-10,000 lbs. Axle Capacity: (front) 4,500 lbs.; (rear) 7,500 lbs.
CHASSIS (WM300): Wheelbase: 126 in. Tires: 9.00 x 16 eight-ply. GVW: 8,700-9,500 lbs. Axle Capacity: (front) 3,750 lbs.; (rear) 6,500 lbs.

1966 Dodge D100 Camper Special Pickup (Rear)

TECHNICAL: Selective sliding gear transmission. Speeds: 3F/1R except 1-ton models, 4F/1R. Column or floor shift control. Transfer Case: (W models) Two-speed, two-lever. Single-plate dry-disc clutch: (A100) 9-1/8 in.; (D100/D200) 10 in.; (others) 11 in. Rear axle ratio: (A100) 3.23:1, 3.55:1 or 3.91:1, (D200) 3.54:1, 4.1:1 or 4.88:1; (D300) 4.1:1, 4.88:1 or 5.87:1; (W100/200) 4.1:1 or 4.88:1; (W300) 4.88:1 or 5.87:1; (WM300) 5.83:1. Hydraulic four-wheel brakes. Fuel tank: (A100) 21 gallon; (others) 18 gallon. Oil filter. Alternator: (A100) 30-amp.; (others) 35-amp. Wheels: (A100) 13 x 4.50; (D100) 15 x 5.00; (D200/W100) 16 x 6.00; (D300/W200) 17.5 x 5.25; (W300) 19.5 x 5.25; (WM300) 16 x 6.50.

1966 Dodge D200 Crew Cab Sweptline Pickup (JAG)

ENGINE (A100): Inline. Overhead valves. Slant six. Cast iron block. Bore & stroke: 3.4 x 3.125 in. Displacement: 170.2 cid. Compression ratio: 8.5:1. Brake horsepower 101 at 4000 rpm. Net (Taxable) horsepower: 27.70. Torque: 145 lbs.-ft. at 1600 rpm. Four main bearings. Solid valve lifters.

ENGINE (D100/D200/D300/W100/W200): Inline. Overhead valves. Slant six-cylinder. Cast iron block. Bore & stroke: 3.4 x 4.125 in. Displacement: 224.7 cid. Compression ratio: 8.4:1. Brake horsepower: 140 at 3900 rpm. Net horsepower: 27.70. Torque: 215 lbs.-ft. at 1600 rpm. Four main bearings. Solid valve lifters.

ENGINE (W300): Same as W200, but premium heavy-duty version to meet rugged demands.

ENGINE (WM300): Inline. L-head. Six-cylinder. Cast iron block. Bore & stroke: 3.437 x 4.5 in. Displacement: 250.6 cid. Compression ratio: 7.1:1. Brake horsepower: 125 at 3600 rpm. Net horsepower: 28.35. Torque: 216 lbs.-ft. at 1600 rpm. Four main bearings. Solid valve lifters.

ENGINE (Optional: D100/D200/D300/W100/W200): 90-degree, overhead valve. Eight-cylinder. Cast iron block. Bore & stroke: 3.91 x 3.312 in. Displacement: 318.1 cid. Compression ratio: 8.25:1. Brake horsepower: 200 at 3900 rpm. Net horsepower: 48.92. Torque: 286 lbs.-ft. at 2400 rpm. Five main bearings. Hydraulic valve lifters.

ENGINE (Optional: W300): Same V-8 as above but with premium heavy-duty features for rugged use.

ENGINE (Optional: A100): 90-degree, overhead valve. Eight-cylinder. Cast iron block. Bore & stroke: 3.63 x 3.31 in. Displacement: 273.8 cid. Compression ratio: 8.8:1. Brake horsepower: 174 at 3900 rpm. Net horsepower: 42.2. Torque: 246 lbs.-ft. at 2000 rpm. Five main bearings. Solid valve lifters.

1966 Dodge A100 Pickup (OCW)

OPTIONS: (Factory-Installed) Chrome front bumper (A100/D100/D200). Rear bumper (all except D300/WM300). Bumper guards: Painted or chrome (A100). Chrome hubcaps (A100/D100). Chrome wheelcovers (A100/D100). Spare tire carrier (D100/W100/W200). Appearance package (D100/W100/W300). Comfort package (D100/W100/W300). Tinted glass (except WM300). Left or right armrest (except WM300). Radio (except WM300). Heater/defroster. Cigar lighter (except WM300). Outside mirrors (except A100). Cab marker lights (except A100). Dual electric horns (except WM300). Heavy-duty instruments (D100/D300/W100/W300). Full-width rear window (D100/W100/W300). Custom equipment package (A100). Rear quarter cab window (A100). Right sun visor. Fenders for dual rear wheels (D/W300). Chrome trim (D100/D200/W100/W200 Sweptline).

Standard Catalog of Light-Duty Trucks

Two-tone paint (except WM300). Traffic hazard switch (except A100). Hand throttle (D100/D300/W100/W300). Foam padded seat (D100/D200/D300/W100/W200/W300). Oil pressure gauge (except WM300). Power steering on D models ($147). Vacuum power brakes (D200/W100-300/WM300). Heavy-duty front springs (except WM300). Heavy-duty rear springs (A and D models). 5,200 lbs. GVW package (A100). Rear shock absorbers (300 models). Positive crankcase ventilation system (W100-300). Cleaner air package (A100/D100). One-quart oil bath air cleaner (except W300/WM300). 46 or 59-amp. alternator. Increased cooling capacity (except WM300). 225 cid engine (A100). 273.8 cid V-8 engine (A100). 318 cid V-8 engine in D100-300/W100-300 models ($121). Heavy-duty clutch: 10 in. (A100); 11 in. (D100/200); 12 in. (W300). Governor (D/W100-300). Four-speed manual transmission (D100/W100-200). LoadFlite three-speed automatic transmision (A/D models). Three-speed heavy-duty transmission (A100). Anti-spin rear axle (except WM300). Undercoating. Three-ton jack (except A100). Locking front wheel hubs (W/WM). Pintle hook (W/WM). Radiator overflow tank (WM300). Power-take-off assembly (W/WM). Front tow hooks, pair (W/WM300). Spare wheel (W300). Fuel/vacuum pump (WM300). 8,000 lbs. winch (W100-300). 10,000 lbs. winch (WM300).

1966 Dodge A100 Side/Rear Door Van (OCW)

HISTORICAL: Introduced: October, 1965. Calendar year sales: 119,777. Calendar year production: 153,159. Model year production: (six) 96,443; (V-8) 53,305; (Total) 149,748. Truck production rose 6.8 percent, giving Dodge 8.7 percent of the industry total. Dodge ranked fourth in the truck industry, with its best production year since 1952. Sales increased only slightly over 1965. Dodge showed a good gain on both light and heavy-duty trucks. V-8 engines made up 47.5 percent of gasoline truck sales, while diesel sales fell to 1,900 units. Dodge introduced two L Series medium-duty tilt cab models, which used A100 cabs, plus a new D800 heavy-duty conventional gas model. The full line, ranging from the 90 in. wheelbase A100 up to a diesel tandem axle tilt-cab with 50,000 lbs. GVW, met nearly 97 percent of truck needs. Forward control models remained in the lineup. The only major model introduction yet to come would be the 108 in. wheelbase van, available late in 1966 as a 1967 model. To meet demand, Dodge added 40,000 square feet to its Warren, Michigan truck plant. Production also began at the new St. Louis facility.

1967 DODGE

1967 Dodge A108 King-Size Forward Control Van (JAG)

1/2-TON COMPACT — C SERIES A100 — SIX-CYLINDER/V-8; 1/2-TON COMPACT — C SERIES A108 — SIX-CYLINDER/V-8: An extended 108 in. wheelbase van and Sportsman, offering 43 cu. ft. more cargo space, were added to round out the Dodge compact truck lineup. Available gross vehicle weights for both models were now 4,000, 4,800 or 5,400 lbs. The 318 cid V-8 was made optional, replacing the 273 cid engine. Both 170 and 225 cid slant sixes were still available. Transmission options remained as before: An A903 three-speed manual, only for the 170 six; heavy-duty three-speed manual (Model A745) for the 225 cid six and 318 V-8; and three-speed automatic LoadFlite for any engine. Standard equipment for A100s included 6.95 x 14 blackwall tires; a 30-amp. alternator; directional signals; left-hand outside rearview mirror; seat belts; heater; windshield washers and variable speed wipers; 2,200 lbs. front axle and 3,000 lbs. rear axle.

1967 Dodge A100 Pickup With Camper Unit (OCW)

1/2-TON — C SERIES D100 — SIX-CYLINDER/V-8; 3/4-TON — C SERIES D200 — SIX-CYLINDER/V-8; 1-TON — C SERIES D300 — SIX-CYLINDER/V-8; 1/2-TON 4x4 — C SERIES W100 — SIX-CYLINDER/V-8; 3/4-TON 4x4 — C SERIES W200 — SIX-CYLINDER/V-8; 1-TON 4x4 — C SERIES W300 — SIX-CYLINDER/V-8: All models continued without appearance changes, but the Town Panel and Town Wagon were dropped. Both a 383 cid V-8 and the 318 cid V-8 engine were available at extra cost on all models. The 383 was the largest engine available for the Custom Sports Special pickup, replacing the 426. Dodge continued aggressive tactics in the pickup camper business, offering Camper Special packages for the entire pickup line. One interesting development was the NP435 four-speed manual transmission. Originally designed for camper use, it worked well in all pickups, offering unique spacing between second and third gears. A driver could shift down into third at highway speed and maintain speeds as high as 60 mph while pulling a load up a moderate grade. Introduced at midyear was a new, specially applied paint for cab roofs. It was stippled to create a grained effect. Viewed from a distance, it looked like a vinyl roof. Standard equipment for D100s included the 225 cid slant six; 8.15 x 15 four-ply rated tires; closed crankcase ventilation system; seat belts; 37-amp. alternator; oil bath air cleaner; left-hand outside rearview mirror; windshield washer and variable speed wipers.

1967 Dodge A108 Family Wagon (OCW)

1-TON POWER-WAGON — C SERIES WM300 — SIX-CYLINDER: Once again, Power-Wagons continued with minimal change.

I.D. DATA: Serial numbers were stamped on a plate on the left door lock pillar. Serial number coding produced a 10-digit number. The first two digits indicated the model code; the third digit showed number of cylinders; and the last seven digits were the sequence number. Model codes were as follows: (D100) 11; (D200) 12; (D300) 13; (A100 Pickup) 18; (A100 Van) 19; (A100 Wagon) 20; (W100) 21; (W200) 22; (W300) 23; (WM300) 24. Starting serial numbers: (A100/108) 2,098,000 (Michigan); 7,000,000 (Missouri). (All others) 1,668,000 (Michigan); 7,000,000 (Missouri). Ending serial numbers are not available. Engine numbers were located as follows: (170 and 225 cid six) right side of block, on top of boss directly behind coil; (251 cid six) left front of block, at top; (318 cid V-8) left front of block, under cylinder head. The first two letters designated the series. The next two digits indicated engine displacement. Third and fourth digits showed the month and date of manufacture. Then came the sequence number. Starting and ending numbers are not available.

1967 Dodge D200 Camper Special Sweptline Pickup (OCW)

Standard Catalog of Light-Duty Trucks

Model	Body Type	Price	Weight	Prod. Total
A100/A108 Compact Series — 1/2-Ton — 90 in. w.b.				
A100	Pickup	1989	2910	Note 1
A100	Panel Van (Note 2)	2076	2910	Note 1
A100	Van	2126	2930	Note 1

NOTE 1: Total model year production: (six) 22,182; (V-8) 6,352.
NOTE 2: Rear door only.

Model	Body Type	Price	Weight	Prod. Total
A100/A108 Compact Series — 1/2-Ton — 108 in. w.b.				
A108	Rear Door Panel Van	2232	3125	Note 3
A108	Van	2282	3145	Note 3

NOTE 3: Total model year production: (six) 6,599; (V-8) 7,373.

Model	Body Type	Price	Weight	Prod. Total
D100 Series — 1/2-Ton — 114 in. w.b.				
D100	Chassis & Cowl	1537	2540	Note 4
D100	Chassis & Cab	1914	3095	Note 4
D100	Utiline Pickup	2019	3405	Note 4
D100	Sweptline Pickup	2045	3505	Note 4

NOTE 4: Total model year production: (six) 9,532; (V-8) 3,342.

Model	Body Type	Price	Weight	Prod. Total
D100 Series — 1/2-Ton — 128 in. w.b.				
D100	Chassis & Cowl	1572	2590	Note 5
D100	Chassis & Cab	1948	3110	Note 5
D100	Utiline Pickup	2055	3600	Note 5
D100	Sweptline Pickup	2080	3660	Note 5
D100	Platform	2105	3535	Note 5
D100	Stake	2153	3735	Note 5

NOTE 5: Total model year production: (six) 13,419; (V-8) 15,770.

Model	Body Type	Price	Weight	Prod. Total
D200 Series — 3/4-Ton — 128 in. w.b.				
D200	Chassis & Cowl	1667	3095	Note 6
D200	Chassis & Cab	2053	3650	Note 6
D200	Utiline Pickup	2158	4090	Note 6
D200	Sweptline Pickup	2186	4150	Note 6
D200	Platform	2209	4025	Note 6
D200	Stake	2257	4225	Note 6

NOTE 6: Total model year production: (six) 6,556; (V-8) 13,469.

Model	Body Type	Price	Weight	Prod. Total
D200 Crew Cab Series — 3/4-Ton — 146 in. w.b.				
D200	Chassis	2724	3973	—
D200	Utiline Pickup	2841	4285	—
D200	Sweptline Pickup	2855	4385	—

Model	Body Type	Price	Weight	Prod. Total
D300 Series — 1-Ton — 133 in. w.b.				
D300	Chassis & Cowl	1781	3220	Note 7
D300	Chassis & Cab	2187	3775	Note 7
D300	Utiline Pickup	2324	4175	Note 7
D300	Platform	2373	4475	Note 7
D300	Stake	2432	4675	Note 7

NOTE 7: Total model year production: (six) 3,676; (V-8) 4,577.

Model	Body Type	Price	Weight	Prod. Total
W100 Series 4x4 — 1/2-Ton — 114 in. w.b.				
W100	Chassis & Cab	2559	3900	Note 8
W100	Utiline Pickup	2678	4210	Note 8
W100	Sweptline Pickup	2691	4310	Note 8

NOTE 8: Total model year production: (six) 570; (V-8) 530.

Model	Body Type	Price	Weight	Prod. Total
W200 Series 4x4 — 3/4-Ton — 128 in. w.b.				
W200	Chassis & Cab	2659	3945	Note 9
W200	Utiline Pickup	2778	4385	Note 9
W200	Sweptline Pickup	2791	4445	Note 9
W200	Platform	2815	4320	Note 9
W200	Stake	2865	4520	Note 9

NOTE 9: Total model year production: (six) 2,099; (V-8) 1,997.

Model	Body Type	Price	Weight	Prod. Total
W200 Crew Cab Series 4x4 — 3/4-Ton — 146 in. w.b.				
W200	Chassis	3416	4375	—
W200	Utiline Pickup	3534	4775	—
W200	Sweptline Pickup	3547	4785	—

Model	Body Type	Price	Weight	Prod. Total
W300 Series 4x4 — 1-Ton — 133 in. w.b.				
W300	Chassis & Cowl	3011	4090	Note 10
W300	Chassis & Cab	3395	4645	Note 10
W300	Utiline Pickup	3534	5045	Note 10
W300	Platform	3584	5345	Note 10
W300	Stake	3644	5545	Note 10

NOTE 10: Total model year production: (six) 214; (V-8) 528.

Model	Body Type	Price	Weight	Prod. Total
WM300 Series Power-Wagon — 1-Ton — 126 in. w.b.				
WM300	Chassis & Cowl	3662	4095	Note 11
WM300	Chassis & Cab	4033	4520	Note 11
WM300	Utiline Pickup	4184	4920	Note 11

NOTE 11: Total model year production: 974 (plus 2,303 MDAP models).
NOTE 12: Weights and prices shown are for six-cylinder models. For V-8 engine, add $120 to price.

Standard Catalog of Light-Duty Trucks

1967 Dodge D200 Crew Cab Sweptline Pickup (OCW)

ENGINE (A100/108): Inline. Overhead valves. Slant six. Cast iron block. Bore & stroke: 3.4 x 3.125 in. Displacement: 170.2 cid. Compression ratio: 8.5:1. Brake horsepower 101 at 4000 rpm. Net (Taxable) horsepower: 27.70. Torque: 145 lbs.-ft. at 1600 rpm. Four main bearings. Solid valve lifters.
ENGINE (D100-300/W100-300; optional A100/108): Inline. Overhead valves. Slant six-cylinder. Cast iron block. Bore & stroke: 3.4 x 4.125 in. Displacement: 224.7 cid. Compression ratio: 8.4:1. Brake horsepower: 140 at 3900 rpm. Net horsepower: 27.70. Torque: 215 lbs.-ft. at 1600 rpm. Four main bearings. Solid valve lifters.
ENGINE (WM300): Inline. L-head. Six-cylinder. Cast iron block. Bore & stroke: 3.437 x 4.5 in. Displacement: 250.6 cid. Compression ratio: 7.1:1. Brake horsepower: 125 at 3600 rpm. Net horsepower: 28.35. Torque: 216 lbs.-ft. at 1600 rpm. Four main bearings. Solid valve lifters.
ENGINE (Optional D100-300/W100-300/A100/108): 90-degree, overhead valve. Eight-cylinder. Cast iron block. Bore & stroke: 3.91 x 3.312 in. Displacement: 318.1 cid. Compression ratio: 8.5:1. Brake horsepower: 210 at 4000 rpm. Net horsepower: 48.92. Torque: 280 lbs.-ft. at 2400 rpm. Five main bearings. Hydraulic valve lifters.
ENGINE (D100-300/W100-200): 90-degree, overhead valve. Eight-cylinder. Cast iron block. Bore & stroke: 4.25 x 3.38 in. Displacement: 383 cid. Compression ratio: 9.2:1. Brake horsepower: 258 at 4400 rpm. Net horsepower: 57.8. Torque: 323 lbs.-ft. at 2400 rpm. Five main bearings. Hydraulic valve lifters.
CHASSIS (A100): Wheelbase: 90 in. Tires: 6.95 x 14-2 four-ply. (4,000 lbs. GVW); 8.15 x 15 four-ply (4,800 lbs. GVW); 8.15 x 15 eight-ply (5,400 lbs. GVW).
CHASSIS (A108): Wheelbase: 108 in. Tires: 6.95 x 14-4 eight-ply. (4,000 lbs. GVW); 8x15 x 15 four-ply (4,800 lbs. GVW); 8.15 x 15 eight-ply (5,400 lbs. GVW).
CHASSIS (D100): Wheelbase: 114 in. or 128 in. Tires: 6.70 x 15 four-ply. GVW: 5,200 lbs. max.
CHASSIS (D200): Wheelbase: 128 in. or 146 in. Tires: 7 x 17.5 six-ply. GVW: 7,500 lbs. maximum.
CHASSIS (D300): Wheelbase: 133 in. Tires: 7 x 17.5 six-ply. GVW: 9,000 lbs. max.
CHASSIS (W100): Wheelbase: 114 in. Tires: 7 x 17.5 six-ply. GVW: 6,000 lbs. max.
CHASSIS (W200): Wheelbase: 128 in. or 146 in. Tires: 8 x 19.5 eight-ply. GVW: 8,000 lbs. maximum.
CHASSIS (W300): Wheelbase: 133 in. Tires: 7.50 x 16 six-ply. GVW: 10,000 lbs. maximum.
CHASSIS (WM300): Wheelbase: 126 in. Tires: 9.00 x 16 ten-ply. GVW: 9,500 lbs. maximum.
TECHNICAL: Selective sliding gear transmission. Speeds: 3F/1R except 1-ton models, 4F/1R. Column or floor shift control. Transfer Case: (W models) Two-speed, two-lever. Single-plate dry-disc clutch: (A100) 9-1/8 in.; (D100/D200) 10 in.; (others) 11 in. Rear axle ratio: (A100) 3.23:1, 3.55:1 or 3.91:1, (D200) 3.54:1, 4.1:1 or 4.88:1; (D300) 4.1:1, 4.88:1 or 5.87:1; (W100/200) 4.1:1 or 4.88:1; (W300) 4.88:1 or 5.87:1; (WM300) 5.83:1. Hydraulic four-wheel brakes. Fuel tank: (A100) 21 gallon; (others) 18 gallon. Oil filter. Alternator: (A100) 30-amp.; (others) 35-amp. Wheels: (A100) 13 x 4.50; (D100) 15 x 5.00; (D200/W100) 16 x 6.00; (D300/W200) 17.5 x 5.25; (W300) 19.5 x 5.25; (WM300) 16 x 6.50.

1967 Dodge One-Ton Chassis and Cab (OCW)

OPTIONS: [Dealer costs shown] One-quart oil bath air cleaner ($5.30). 46 amp. alternator ($16.85). 60-amp. alternator ($23.40). Left-hand armrest in standard cab ($3.60). Right-hand front armrest in cab pickup with Comfort Package ($3.60). 59-amp. battery ($5.90). 70-amp. battery, in A100 ($9.20); in all others ($6.10). Bright finish front bumper, on A100 ($11.60); on all others ($11.10). Front bumper with bright finish and bumper guards, in A100 ($16.10). Painted rear bumper, all ($17.10). Set of four bright finish hubcaps on A100 ($4); on D100 ($11.10). Inside body tire carrier, Sweptline ($11.60). Outside tire carrier with long-arm for Utiline pickups ($11.60). Cleaner Air package, California only ($20.40).

Increased cooling capacity, all models except A100 with V-8 ($12.70). Six-cylinder engine with 10 in. clutch, all ($4.20). Dual electric horns ($6.50). Heavy-duty instrument cluster in D100 ($49.60). Three-ton hydraulic jack, all except not available for A100 ($11.10). Amber cab corner marker lights, all except A100 ($8.30). Inside rearview mirror, standard in A100 pickup; in all other cab models ($2.15). Right-hand outside rearview mirror with five inch head for D100 pickup ($4.15). Left-hand outside rearview mirror 5 x 7 in. for D100 pickup ($7.45). Left-hand and right-hand outside rearview mirrors, braced, for D100 pickup ($18.20); for cab only models ($14.90). Two-tone paint, cab models except A100 ($12.70). Power steering, D100 with V-8, except Crew Cabs ($114.50). Hand control throttle, D100 and all with manual transmission ($2.30). Four-speed manual transmission in D100 ($66.80). LoadFlite automatic transmission, all models ($173.80). Undercoating, all models ($10). Positive crankcase ventilation system, D100 with 318 cid V-8 ($6.50); all other D100s ($3.90). Sports Package, including bucket seats; custom carpeting; one inch tape stripes; bright mylar molding around windshield and rear window; Dodge Delta emblems on "B" posts; bright molding on instrument panel; textured metal door trim panels; left- and right-hand armrests; left- and right-hand sun visors; additional insulation; console with lighter and map light; black carpet over gas tank cover; bright grille; bright drip molding; custom nameplates; bright trim on instrument cluster; hood around dials and knobs; white steering wheel with bright horn ring; and bright finish front bumper. Custom Sports Package option adds short arm stationary five-inch chromed outside mirrors (left and right). Custom Sports Package was available on all conventional cab pickups.

1967 Dodge W200 Four-Wheel Drive Pickup (OCW)

HISTORICAL: Introduced: October, 1966. Calendar year sales: 101,436. Calendar year production: 141,865. Model year production: (six) 74,794; (V-8) 53,938; (Total) 128,732. Dodge placed fourth in the truck industry production race, increasing its market share slightly though total production was down 7.4 percent from 1966. This was Dodge's golden anniversary as a truck builder. In a half-century, the company had built about 4.7 million commercial vehicles. The Warren, Michigan plant produced 111,198 trucks in 1967, while 30,667 came out of St. Louis. Nearly half the trucks made carried a V-8 engine. Diesel sales rose significantly. Total industry truck shipments declined for the second straight year. Dodge exhibited an experimental truck, called Deora, at various auto shows during 1967. Based on an A100 chassis and power train, this dream truck was a fully operational prototype. Combining the creature comforts of a luxurious town sedan with the utility of a pickup truck, the Deora anticipated the tremendous future upsurge in sales of vehicles based on the pickup format.

1968 DODGE

1968 Dodge D100 Adventurer Sweptline Pickup (JAG)

1/2-TON COMPACT — A100/108 SERIES — SIX-CYLINDER/V-8: Compacts carried forward with no change in appearance, models, major mechanicals, or engine options. They shared much of the increased glamour given to the conventional light-duty models. Dodge now offered color-keyed interiors as standard equipment. Two-tone paint schemes were available. Dodge also picked up and expanded the Tradesman concept begun several years earlier. Replacing a conventional pickup, the Tradesman utility contained lockable, easy-access storage compartments on both sides. Starting in 1968, Dodge targeted its compact vans to the service trades (television, appliance, air conditioning, plumbing/heating repairmen, and so on.) Dodge offered Job-Mated interiors to allow the tradespeople to make best use of van interiors for tools and equipment. Eighteen factory-installed extra equipment packages were available, consisting of shelves, locks, drawers, hanging bars and partitions. These packages were available for both 90 in. and 108 in. wheelbase vans. They helped Dodge strengthen its leadership position in the compact van market. Dodge captured an industry first by offering power steering on compact vans and wagons with automatic transmission. Passenger vans were considered station wagons, not trucks.

1/2-TON — D100 SERIES — SIX-CYLINDER/V-8; 3/4-TON — D200 SERIES — SIX-CYLINDER/V-8; 1-TON — D300 SERIES — SIX-CYLINDER/V-8; 1/2-TON 4x4 — W100 SERIES — SIX-CYLINDER/V-8; 3/4-TON 4x4 — W200 SERIES — SIX-CYLINDER/V-8; 1-TON 4x4 — W300 SERIES — SIX-CYLINDER/V-8: Front end appearance changes set the 1968 models apart from their predecessors. A new, one-piece, full-width grille enclosed the wide-spaced headlights and new vertical parking lights. This gave the trucks a fresh new look. Gone was the plush Custom Sports Special. It was replaced by the even plusher Adventurer. A special sports-type Sweptline, the Adventurer featured vinyl bucket seats, a center console, vinyl roof, chrome moldings that swept from hood to tailgate, and color-keyed custom carpeting. Increased comfort, appearance, glamour and prestige, available through optional custom features, was the main marketing thrust this year. Dodge made a real effort to give light-duty trucks better looks and convenience. This added to their sales appeal, resale value and owner satisfaction level. Four color-keyed interiors were available, plus 13 exterior colors. Engines and models remained the same as 1967. Standard equipment included a dome light, painted front bumper and hubcaps, padded dash, backup lights, emergency flasher, heater/defroster, side reflectors, variable-speed electric wipers and dual jet washers, front and rear shocks (front only on 1-ton), and a 225-cid six-cylinder engine.

1-TON POWER-WAGON — WM300 SERIES — SIX-CYLINDER: After a lengthy career, this would be the final year for the military-style Power-Wagon. From 1969 through the late 1970s, it would be produced for export only.

I.D. DATA: Serial numbers were stamped on a plate on the left door lock pillar. Serial number coding produced a 10-digit number. The first two digits indicated the model code; the third digit showed number of cylinders; and the last seven digits were the sequence number. Model codes were as follows: (D100) 11; (D200) 12; (D300) 13; (A100 Pickup) 18; (A100 Van) 19; (A100 Wagon) 20; (W100) 21; (W200) 22; (W300) 23; (WM300) 24. Starting serial numbers: A100/108) 2,135,000 (Michigan); 7,020,000 (Missouri). (All others) 1,780,000 (Michigan); 7,020,000 (Missouri); 6,000,000 (Canada). Ending serial numbers are not available. A new engine numbering system began this year. The first two letters designated the manufacturing plant: PM (Mound Road); PT (Trenton); or DW (Windsor). The next three digits indicated displacement: 170, 225, 318, etc. The next letter designated model: R (regular gas); L (low compression); T (standard-duty); or H (heavy-duty). The next four digits designated the date of manufacture, based on a 10,000-day calendar. Last came a four-digit sequence number for each day's production, starting with 0000 for LA318 engines and 5000 for all others. Example: PT318T22040008. This engine would be made in Trenton, with 318 cid displacement, standard compression, the eighth engine built on day no. 2204. No compact vans were built in Canada.

Model	Body Type	Price	Weight	Prod. Total
A100 — Compact Series — 1/2-Ton — 90 in. w.b.				
A100	Pickup	2047	2910	Note 1
A100	Panel Van	2132	2910	Note 1
A100	Van	2183	2930	Note 1

NOTE 1: Total model year production: (six) 18,756; (V-8) 2,613.

Model	Body Type	Price	Weight	Prod. Total
A108 — King-Size Series — 1/2-Ton — 108 in. w.b.				
A108	Rear Door Panel Van	2291	3125	Note 2
A108	Van	2342	3145	Note 2

NOTE 2: Total model year production: (six) 17,548; (V-8) 16,248.

Model	Body Type	Price	Weight	Prod. Total
D100 Series — 1/2-Ton — 114 in. w.b.				
D100	Chassis & Cowl	1656	2540	Note 3
D100	Chassis & Cab	2056	3090	Note 3
D100	Utiline Pickup	2163	3470	Note 3
D100	Sweptline Pickup	2189	3520	Note 3

NOTE 3: Total model year production: (six) 10,126; (V-8) 3,930.

Model	Body Type	Price	Weight	Prod. Total
D100 Series — 1/2-Ton — 128 in. w.b.				
D100	Chassis & Cowl	1691	2590	Note 4
D100	Chassis & Cab	2090	3110	Note 4
D100	Utiline Pickup	2200	3600	Note 4
D100	Sweptline Pickup	2225	3660	Note 4
D100	Platform	2251	3535	Note 4
D100	Stake	2300	3735	Note 4

NOTE 4: Total model year production: (six) 18,505; (V-8) 27,384.

Model	Body Type	Price	Weight	Prod. Total
D200 Series — 3/4-Ton — 128 in. w.b.				
D200	Chassis & Cowl	1756	3095	Note 5
D200	Chassis & Cab	2165	3650	Note 5
D200	Utiline Pickup	2273	4090	Note 5
D200	Sweptline Pickup	2301	4150	Note 5
D200	Platform	2325	4025	Note 5
D200	Stake	2374	4225	Note 5

NOTE 5: Total model year production: (six) 7,451; (V-8) 20,422.

Model	Body Type	Price	Weight	Prod. Total
D200 Crew Cab Series — 3/4-Ton — 146 in. w.b.				
D200	Chassis	2859	3973	—
D200	Utiline Pickup	2979	4335	—
D200	Sweptline Pickup	2993	4385	—

NOTE 6: See D200 data in Note 5 above.

Model	Body Type	Price	Weight	Prod. Total
D300 Series — 1-Ton — 133 in. w.b.				
D300	Chassis & Cowl	1876	3220	Note 7
D300	Chassis & Cab	2305	3775	Note 7
D300	Utiline Pickup	2446	4355	Note 7
D300	Platform	2496	4560	Note 7
D300	Stake	2556	4760	Note 7

NOTE 7: Total model year production: (six) 3,394; (V-8) 6,979.

W100 Series 4x4 — 1/2-Ton — 114 in. w.b.

W100	Chassis & Cab	2696	3735	Note 8
W100	Utiline Pickup	2818	4095	Note 8
W100	Sweptline Pickup	2831	4145	Note 8

NOTE 8: Total model year production: (six) 721; (V-8) 752.

W200 Series 4x4 — 3/4-Ton — 128 in. w.b.

W200	Chassis & Cab	2800	3945	Note 9
W200	Utiline Pickup	2922	4385	Note 9
W200	Sweptline Pickup	2935	4445	Note 9
W200	Platform	2960	4320	Note 9
W200	Stake	3011	4520	Note 9

W200 Crew Cab Series 4x4 — 3/4-Ton — 146 in. w.b.

W200	Chassis	2582	4375	Note 9
W200	Utiline Pickup	3703	4735	Note 9
W200	Sweptline Pickup	3716	4785	Note 9

NOTE 9: Total model year production: (six) 2,759; (V-8) 3,178.

W300 Series 4x4 — 1-Ton — 133 in. w.b.

W300	Chassis & Cowl	3100	4090	Note 10
W300	Chassis & Cab	3508	4645	Note 10
W300	Utiline Pickup	3649	5140	Note 10
W300	Platform	3700	5345	Note 10
W300	Stake	3762	5545	Note 10

NOTE 10: Total model year production: (six) 175; (V-8) 693.

WM300 Series Power-Wagon — 1-Ton — 126 in. w.b.

WM300	Chassis & Cowl	3761	4095	Note 11
WM300	Chassis & Cab	4141	4520	Note 11
WM300	Utiline Pickup	4295	4920	Note 11

NOTE 11: Total model year production: 2,461 (plus 1,958 MDAP).
NOTE 12: Weights and prices shown are for six-cylinder. engines. For V-8 engine, add $120 to price.

ENGINE (A100/108): Inline. Overhead valves. Slant six. Cast iron block. Bore & stroke: 3.4 x 3.125 in. Displacement: 170.2 cid. Compression ratio: 8.5:1. Brake horsepower 101 at 4000 rpm. Net (Taxable) horsepower: 27.70. Torque: 145 lbs.-ft. at 1600 rpm. Four main bearings. Solid valve lifters.

ENGINE (D100-300/W100-300; optional A100/108): Inline. Overhead valves. Slant six-cylinder. Cast iron block. Bore & stroke: 3.4 x 4.125 in. Displacement: 224.7 cid. Compression ratio: 8.4:1. Brake horsepower: 140 at 3900 rpm. Net horsepower: 27.70. Torque: 215 lbs.-ft. at 1600 rpm. Four main bearings. Solid valve lifters.

ENGINE (WM300): Inline. L-head. Six-cylinder. Cast iron block. Bore & stroke: 3.437 x 4.5 in. Displacement: 250.6 cid. Compression ratio: 7.1:1. Brake horsepower: 125 at 3600 rpm. Net horsepower: 28.35. Torque: 216 lbs.-ft. at 1600 rpm. Four main bearings. Solid valve lifters.

ENGINE (Optional D100-300/W100-300/A100/108): 90-degree, overhead valve. Eight-cylinder. Cast iron block. Bore & stroke: 3.91 x 3.312 in. Displacement: 318.1 cid. Compression ratio: 8.5:1. Brake horsepower: 210 at 4000 rpm. Net horsepower: 48.92. Torque: 280 lbs.-ft. at 2400 rpm. Five main bearings. Hydraulic valve lifters.

ENGINE (D100-300/W100-200): 90-degree, overhead valve. Eight-cylinder. Cast iron block. Bore & stroke: 4.25 x 3.38 in. Displacement: 383 cid. Compression ratio: 9.2:1. Brake horsepower: 258 at 4400 rpm. Net horsepower: 57.8. Torque: 323 lbs.-ft. at 2400 rpm. Five main bearings. Hydraulic valve lifters.

CHASSIS (A100): Wheelbase: 90 in. Tires: 6.95 x 14 four-ply. GVW: 3,800-4,600 lbs. Axle Capacity: (front) 2,200 lbs.; (rear) 3,000 lbs.

CHASSIS (A108): Wheelbase: 108 in. Tires: 8.15 x 15-2 four-ply. GVW: 3,800-4,800 lbs. Axle Capacity: (front) 2,200 lbs.; (rear) 3,000 lbs.

CHASSIS (D100): Wheelbase: 114 in. or 128 in. Tires: 8.15 x 15 eight-ply. GVW: 4,300-5,200 lbs. Axle Capacity: (front) 2,500 lbs.; (rear) 3,600 lbs.

CHASSIS (D200): Wheelbase: 128 in. or 146 in. Tires: 8 x 19.5 eight-ply. GVW: 5,200-7,500 lbs. Axle Capacity: (front) 2,800 lbs.; (rear) 5,500 lbs.

CHASSIS (D300): Wheelbase: 133 in. Tires: 8 x 17.5 six-ply. GVW: 6,700-10,000 lbs. Axle Capacity: (front) 3,800 lbs.; (rear) 7,500 lbs.

CHASSIS (W100): Wheelbase: 114 in. Tires: 7 x 17.5 six-ply. GVW: 5,100-6.000 lbs. Axle Capacity: (front) 3,000 lbs.; (rear) 4,500 lbs.

CHASSIS (W200): Wheelbase: 128 in. or 146 in. Tires: 8 x 19.5 eight-ply. GVW: 6,000-8,000 lbs. Axle Capacity: (front) 3,000 lbs.; (rear) 5,500 lbs.

CHASSIS (W300): Wheelbase: 133 in. Tires: 7.50 x 16 six-ply. GVW: 10,000 lbs. maximum. Axle Capacity: (front) 4,500 lbs.; (rear) 7,500 lbs.

CHASSIS (WM300): Wheelbase: 126 in. Tires: 9.00 x 16 ten-ply. GVW: 8,200-9,500 lbs. Axle Capacity: (front) 3,750 lbs.; (rear) 6,500 lbs.

TECHNICAL: Selective sliding gear transmission. Speeds: 3F/1R except 1-ton models, 4F/1R. Column or floor shift control. Single-plate dry-disc clutch: (A100) 9-1/8 in.; (D100/D200) 10 in.; (others) 11 in. Rear axle ratio: (A100) 3.27:1, 3.55:1, 3.91:1 or 4.56:1; (D100) 3.23:1, 3.55:1 or 3.91:1; (D200/W100-200) 3.54:1, 4.1:1 or 4.88:1; (D300) 4.1:1, 4.88:1 or 5.87:1; (W300) 4.88:1 or 5.87:1; (WM300) 5.83:1. Hydraulic four-wheel brakes. Fuel tank: (A100) 23 gallon; (others) 18 gallon. One-quart oil filter. Air cleaner: (A100) dry; (others) oil bath. Alternator: (A100) 30-amp; (others) 37-amp. Wheels: (A100) 14 x 5.00; (D100) 15 x 5.50; (D200/W100) 16 x 6.00; (D300/W200) 17.5 x 5.25; (W300) 19.5 x 5.25; (WM300) 16 x 6.5.

OPTIONS: (Factory-Installed) Chrome front bumper (A100/D100-200). Rear bumper (except WM300). Bumper guards (A100). Wheelcovers (A100/D100). Chrome hubcaps (A100/D100-200). Spare tire carrier (D/W100-300). Adventurer package (D100-200). Appearance package (D/W100-300). Comfort package (D100-300). Tinted glass (except WM300). Radio (except WM300). Auxiliary heater (D100-300/W300). Cigar lighter (except WM300). Outside mirrors. Cab marker lights (D100-300). Dual horns (D/W100-300). Heavy-duty instruments (D/W100-300). Rear quarter cab windows (A100). Undercoating. Camper Special package (D/W200). Camper Custom package (D200). Trim molding package (D/W100-200). Two-tone paint (except WM300). Textured vinyl roof (W100). Bucket seat No. 1 or No. 2 (D100-200). Foam padded seat (D/W100-300). Third seat belt (except A100). Shoulder belt (D/W100-300). Three-ton jack (except A100). Heavy-duty front or rear springs (except WM300). Extra-heavy-duty rear springs (D100-300). Oil pressure gauge (except WM300). Power steering (D100-300). Vacuum power brake booster (D200-300, W100-300). Hand throttle (D/W100-300). Horn ring (A100). 7,500 lbs. rear axle (D300). Fenders for dual rear wheels (D/W300). Rear shock absorbers (D300). 3,500 lbs. front axle (W200). Spare wheel for dual rears (D/W300). Increased cooling capacity (D200-300/W100-300). One-quart oil bath air cleaner (except W/WM300). 46 or 60-amp. alternator (D100-300). 37-, 46- or 60-amp. alternator (A100). 10 in. clutch (A100). 11 in. clutch (D100-200). Anti-spin rear axle (except WM300). Governor (D/W100-300). 225 cid engine (A100). 318 cid V-8 engine (except WM300). 383 cid V-8 engine (D100-300/W100-200). Four-speed manual transmission, close or wide spaced ratios (D/W100-200); close only (D300). LoadFlite automatic transmission (D models). Locking front hubs (W/WM models).

Pintle hook (W/WM models). Power-take-off (W/WM models). Fuel/vacuum pump (WM300). Radiator overflow tank (WM300). Rear shocks (W/WM300). Tow hooks (W/WM300). 8,000 lbs. winch (W100-300). 10,000 lbs. winch (WM300).

HISTORICAL: Introduced: August, 1967. Calendar year sales: 138,205. Calendar year production: 173,769. Model year production: (six) 96,778; (V-8) 86,237; (Total) 183,015. Innovations: Car-like, color-keyed interiors. Tradesman compact vans with Job-Mated interiors. Power steering on compact vans. The U.S. truck industry had its best year ever, producing 1,950,713 units. Dodge shared in this record-setting feat, posting its highest production total in history. All-time record sales gained 36.2 percent over 1967. Trucks were built at three plants: Warren, Michigan (105,921 units); St. Louis (52,790); and the balance at Burt Road, Detroit. Well over half (56 percent) of Dodge trucks had V-8 engines. Dodge also built 3,488 diesel models. Dodge continued to produce a full line, from compacts to heavy-duty tilt cab diesels.

1969 DODGE

1969 Dodge D200 Adventurer Sweptline Pickup (JAG)

1/2-TON COMPACT — A100/108 SERIES — SIX-CYLINDER/V-8: Both wheelbases carried on without change. Dodge continued to promote the versatility of its Job-Mated Tradesman van. Seventeen basic Tradesman packages were available from the factory to suit every need. In the Sportsman Wagon series, a unique mobile office called the "Executive Suite" was available, as was a living room on wheels called the "Host Wagon."

1/2-TON — D100 SERIES — SIX-CYLINDER/V-8; 3/4-TON — D200 SERIES — SIX-CYLINDER/V-8; 1-TON — D300 SERIES — SIX-CYLINDER/V-8; 1/2-TON 4x4 — W100 SERIES — SIX-CYLINDER/V-8; 3/4-TON 4x4 — W200 SERIES — SIX-CYLINDER/V-8; 1-TON 4x4 — W300 SERIES — SIX-CYLINDER/V-8: Styling for 1969 did not change, as even the new grille from 1968 carried forward. Yet quite a few improvements were made. D100 and D200 models got an improved front suspension called Cushioned-Beam. The old reliable I-beam front axle was still used, but a new sway bar took out some of the lean (while cornering) and contributed to easier steering. All models, except the military style Power-Wagon, were carried over with the same engines. Transmission options also stayed the same. On D100-D300 models with three-speed LoadFlite automatic transmission, the shift lever was now conveniently column-mounted. Four-wheel drive models gained a simplified single-lever control for the transfer case. A driver could shift into and out of four-wheel drive with a flick of the wrist. Gone was the old two-lever control. Air conditioning changed from under-dash to dash-integral mounting on all models.

1969 Dodge A100 Panel Van (OCW)

I.D. DATA: Serial numbers were on a plate on the left door lock pillar. The 10-character number consisted of four elements. The first two digits gave model code; the third digit was number of cylinders (6 or 8). The fourth digit showed assembly plant (1 for Warren Truck; 2 for Warren heavy-duty; 6 for Windsor; or 7 for Missouri). The final six digits made up the sequence number. Model codes were as follows: 11 (D100); 12 (D200); 13 (D300); 18 (A100 Pickup); 19 (A100 Van); 20 (A100 Wagon); 21 (W100); 22 (W200); 23 (W300); 24 (WM300 — export only); 30 to 32 (P100-300 forward control). Starting and ending sequence numbers are not available. Engine numbers were located as follows: (six) right side of block, below no. 1 spark plug; (318 V-8) left side of block, below cylinder head; (383 V-8) right side of block, adjacent to distributor. Two engine numbering systems were used. The 170 and 225 cid six-cylinder and 318 cid V-8 engines were identified as follows: First two letters indicated manufacturing plant (GM=Mound Road; GT=Trenton; NM=Marysville; GW=Windsor). Next three digits showed displacement. Next letter gave engine type (R=regular 318 V-8; T=standard 225 cid six; H=premium 225 cid six). Next came a four-digit manufacturing date code based on a 10,000-day calendar. The final four digits were the sequence number, which began with 0001 for each day. The 383 cid V-8 and other

engines were identified as follows: First letter indicated model year; next letter indicated engine type (T=standard; H=premium); next three digits, displacement; next digit, assembly plant shift; next four digits, manufacture date; next two letters, non-standard engine indicator; followed by four-digit sequence number. Starting and ending engine numbers are not available.

Model	Body Type	Price	Weight	Prod. Total

A100 Compact Series — 1/2-Ton — 90 in. w.b.

A100	Pickup	2363	2810	Note 1
A100	Panel Van (Note 3)	2435	2795	Note 1
A100	Van	—	—	Note 1

NOTE 1: Total model year production: (six) 14,609; (V-8) 2,235.

A108 Series — 1/2-Ton —108 in. w.b.

A108	Panel Van (Note 3)	2591	3005	Note 2
A108	Van	—	—	Note 2

NOTE 2: Total model year production: (six) 14,453; (V-8) 16,354.

NOTE 3: Rear doors only.

D100 Series — 1/2-Ton — 114 in. w.b.

D100	Chassis & Cowl	—	—	Note 4
D100	Chassis & Cab	—	—	Note 4
D100	Utiline Pickup	—	—	Note 4
D100	Sweptline Pickup	2442	3432	Note 4

NOTE 4: Total model year production: (six) 10,860; (V-8) 4,587.

D100 Series — 1/2-Ton — 128 in. w.b.

D100	Chassis & Cowl	—	—	Note 5
D100	Chassis & Cab	—	—	Note 5
D100	Utiline Pickup	—	—	Note 5
D100	Sweptline Pickup	2479	3572	Note 5
D100	Platform	—	—	Note 5
D100	Stake	2527	3645	Note 5

NOTE 5: Total model year production: (six) 14,146; (V-8) 27,140.

D200 Series — 3/4-Ton — 128 in. w.b.

D200	Chassis & Cowl	—	—	Note 6
D200	Chassis & Cab	—	—	Note 6
D200	Utiline Pickup	—	—	Note 6
D200	Sweptline Pickup	2625	3807	Note 6
D200	Platform	—	—	Note 6
D200	Stake	2674	3880	Note 6

NOTE 6: Total model year production: (six) 4,282; (V-8) 17,148.

D200 Crew Cab Series — 3/4-Ton — 146 in. w.b.

D200	Chassis	—	—	Note 7
D200	Utiline Pickup	—	—	Note 7
D200	Sweptline Pickup	3341	4135	Note 7

NOTE 7: Total model year production: (six) 857; (V-8) 1,707.

D300 Series — 1-Ton — 133 in. w.b.

D300	Chassis & Cowl	—	—	Note 8
D300	Chassis & Cab	2806	3715	Note 8
D300	Utiline Pickup	2722	4050	Note 8
D300	Platform	—	—	Note 8
D300	Stake	—	—	Note 8

NOTE 8: Total model year production: (six) 2,390; (V-8) 6,136.

D300 Crew Cab Series — 1-Ton — 159 in. w.b.

D300	Chassis & Cab	2641	3810	Note 9
D300	Sweptline Pickup	3389	4505	Note 9

NOTE 9: Total model year production: (six) 245; (V-8) 1,596.

W100 Series 4x4 — 1/2-Ton — 114 in. w.b.

W100	Chassis & Cab	—	—	Note 10
W100	Utiline Pickup	—	—	Note 10
W100	Sweptline Pickup	—	—	Note 10

NOTE 10: Total model year production: (six) 766; (V-8) 1,007.

W100 Series 4x4 — 1/2-Ton — 128 in. w.b.

W100	Chassis & Cab	—	—	Note 11
W100	Utiline Pickup	—	—	Note 11
W100	Sweptline Pickup	—	—	Note 11

NOTE 11: Total model year production: (six) 218; (V-8) 878.

W200 Series 4x4 — 3/4-Ton — 128 in. w.b.

W200	Chassis & Cab	—	—	Note 12
W200	Utiline Pickup	—	—	Note 12
W200	Sweptline Pickup	—	—	Note 12
W200	Platform	—	—	Note 12
W200	Stake	—	—	Note 12

NOTE 12: Total model year production: (six) 1,091; (V-8) 3,427.

W200 Crew Cab Series 4x4 — (3/4-Ton) — (146 in. w.b.)

W200	Chassis	—	—	Note 13
W200	Utiline Pickup	—	—	Note 13
W200	Sweptline Pickup	—	—	Note 13

NOTE 13: Total model year production: (six) 698; (V-8) 438.

W300 Series 4x4 — (1-Ton) — (133 in. w.b.)

W300	Chassis & Cowl	—	—	Note 14
W300	Chassis & Cab	—	—	Note 14
W300	Utiline Pickup	—	—	Note 14
W300	Platform	—	—	Note 14
W300	Stake	—	—	Note 14

NOTE 14: Total model year production: (six) 749; (V-8) 901.

NOTE 15: Weights and prices shown are for V-8 models, except A100/108, six-cylinder.

ENGINE (A100/108): Inline. Overhead valves. Slant six. Cast iron block. Bore & stroke: 3.4 x 3.125 in. Displacement: 170.2 cid. Compression ratio: 8.5:1. Brake horsepower: 101 at 4000 rpm. Net (Taxable) horsepower: 27.70. Torque: 136 lbs.-ft. at 1600 rpm. Four main bearings. Solid valve lifters.

ENGINE (D100-300, W100-300; optional A100/108): Inline. Overhead valves. Slant six. Cast iron block. Bore & stroke: 3.4 x 4.125 in. Displacement: 224.7 cid. Compression ratio: 8.4:1. Brake horsepower: 140 at 3900 rpm. Net horsepower: 27.70. Torque: 215 lbs.-ft. at 1600 rpm. Four main bearings. Solid valve lifters.

ENGINE (Optional, all models): 90-degree, overhead valve. V-8. Cast iron block. Bore & stroke: 3.91 x 3.312 in. Displacement: 318.1 cid. Compression ratio: 8.5:1. Brake horsepower: 210 at 4000 rpm. Net horsepower: 48.92. Torque: 318 lbs.-ft. at 2800 rpm. Five main bearings. Hydraulic valve lifters.

ENGINE (Optional: D100-300, W100-200): 90-degree, overhead valve. V-8. Cast iron block. Bore & stroke: 4.25 x 3.38 in. Displacement: 383 cid. Compression ratio: 9.2:1. Brake horsepower: 258 at 4400 rpm. Net horsepower: 57.8. Torque: 375 lbs.-ft. at 2800 rpm. Five main bearings. Hydraulic valve lifters.

CHASSIS (A100): Wheelbase: 90 in. Tires: 6.95 x 14 four-ply. GVW: 3,800-4,600 lbs. Axle Capacity: (front) 2,200 lbs.; (rear) 3,000 lbs.

CHASSIS (A108): Wheelbase: 108 in. Tires: 8.15 x 15-2 four-ply. GVW: 3,800-4,800 lbs. Axle Capacity: (front) 2,200 lbs.; (rear) 3,000 lbs.

CHASSIS (D100): Wheelbase: 114 in. or 128 in. Tires: 8.15 x 15 eight-ply. GVW: 4,300-5,200 lbs. Axle Capacity: (front) 2,500 lbs.; (rear) 3,600 lbs.

CHASSIS (D200): Wheelbase: 128 in. or 146 in. Tires: 8 x 19.5 eight-ply. GVW: 5,200-7,500 lbs. Axle Capacity: (front) 2,800 lbs.; (rear) 5,500 lbs.

CHASSIS (D300): Wheelbase: 133 in. Tires: 8 x 17.5 six-ply. GVW: 6,700-10,000 lbs. Axle Capacity: (front) 3,800 lbs.; (rear) 7,500 lbs.

CHASSIS (W100): Wheelbase: 114 in. Tires: 8.15 x 15 four-ply on 5.50 wheels. GVW: 5,100-6,000 lbs. Axle Capacity: (front) 3,000 lbs.; (rear) 3,000 lbs.

CHASSIS (W200): Wheelbase: 128 in. or 146 in. Tires: 8 x 19.5 eight-ply. GVW: 6,000-8,000 lbs. Axle Capacity: (front) 3,000 lbs.; (rear) 5,500 lbs.

CHASSIS (W300): Wheelbase: 133 in. Tires: 8.76 x 16.5 ten-ply on 6.75. GVW: 10,000 lbs. maximum. Axle Capacity: (front) 4,500 lbs.; (rear) 7,500 lbs.

CHASSIS (WM300): Wheelbase: 126 in. Tires: 9.00 x 16 ten-ply. GVW: 8,200-9,500 lbs. Axle Capacity: (front) 3,750 lbs.; (rear) 6,500 lbs.

TECHNICAL: Selective sliding gear transmission. Speeds: 3F/1R except 1-ton models, 4F/1R; (A100/108) V-8 has heavy-duty three-speed transmission. Column or floor shift control. Single-plate dry-disc clutch: (A100 six) 9-1/8 in.; (A100 V-8, D100-200 six) 10 in.; (others) 11 in. Rear axle ratios: (A100) 3.27:1, 3.55:1, 3.91:1 or 4.56:1; (D100) 3.23:1, 3.55:1 or 3.91:1; (D/W200) 3.54:1, 4.1:1 or 4.88:1; ((W100) 3.54:1 or 4.1:1; (D300) 4.1:1, 4.88:1 or 5.87:1; (W300) 4.88:1 or 5.87:1. Hydraulic four-wheel brakes. Fuel tank: (A100) 23 gallon; (others) 18 gallon. One-quart oil filter. Air cleaner: (A100 and D300 V-8) dry; (others) oil bath. Alternator: (A100) 30-amp; (others) 37-amp. Wheels: (A100) 14 x 5.00; (D/W100) 15 x 5.50; (D200) 16 x 6.00; (D300, W200) 17.5 x 5.25; (W300) 16.5 x 6.75.

OPTIONS: (Factory-Installed) Air conditioner. Chrome front bumper (A100/D100-200). Rear bumper (except WM300). Bumper guards (A100). Wheelcovers (A100/D100). Chrome hubcaps (A100/D100-200). Spare tire carrier (D/W100-300). Adventurer package (D100-200). Paint stripe (with Adventurer only). Appearance package (D/W100-300). Comfort package (D/W100-300). Tinted glass (except WM300). Radio (except WM300). Auxiliary heater (D100-300/W300). Cigar lighter (except WM300). Outside mirrors. Cab marker lights (D/W100-200). Dual horns (D/W100-300). Heavy-duty instruments (D/W100-300). Rear quarter cab windows (A100). Undercoating. Camper Special package (D/W200). Camper Custom package (D200). Trim molding package (D/W100-200). Two-tone paint (except WM300). Textured vinyl roof (D100). D100 Adventurer bucket seat package. D100/D200 bucket seat package, with standard cab; or with Custom interior package in standard cab models. D100 Custom Exterior package. D100 Custom Interior package. D100 insulation package. D100 wheel lip and sill molding package. Adventurer package for 128 inch wheelbase D200 Sweptline only. D200 Adventurer bucket seat package. D200 bucket seat package with standard cab; or with Custom Interior package in standard cab. D200 Custom Special package. D200 Custom Interior package. D200 Custom Exterior package. D200 added insulation package. D200 bodyside moldings package. D200 wheel lip and sill moldings package. Black or white paint stripe package, D200 Adventurer only. D300 Custom Interior package. D300 Custom Exterior package. W100/W200 bodyside trim molding package. Foam padded seat (D/W100-300). Third seat belt (except A100). Shoulder belt (D/W100-300). Three-ton jack (except A100). Heavy-duty front or rear springs (except WM300). Extra-heavy-duty rear springs (D100-300). Oil pressure gauge (except WM300). Power steering (D100-300). Vacuum power brake booster (D200-300, W100-300). Hand throttle (D/W100-300). Horn ring (A100). 7,500 lbs. rear axle (D300). Fenders for dual rear wheels (D/W300). Rear shock absorbers (D300). 3,500 lbs. front axle (W200). Spare wheel for dual rears (D/W300). Increased cooling capacity (D200-300/W100-300). One-quart oil bath air cleaner (except W/WM300). 46 or 60-amp. alternator (except A100). 37-, 46- or 60-amp. alternator (A100). 10 in. clutch (A100). 11 in. clutch (D100-200). Anti-spin rear axle (except WM300). Governor (D/W100-300). 225 cid engine (A100). 318 cid V-8 engine (except WM300). 383 cid V-8 engine (D100-300/W100-200). Four-speed manual transmission, close or wide spaced ratios (D/W100-200); close only (D300). LoadFlite automatic transmission (D models). Locking front hubs (W/WM models). Pintle hook (W/WM models). Power-take-off (W/WM models). Fuel/vacuum pump (WM300). Radiator overflow tank (WM300). Rear shocks (W/WM300). Tow hooks (W/WM300). 8,000 lbs. winch (W100-300). 10,000 lbs. winch (WM300).

HISTORICAL: Introduced August, 1968. Calendar year sales: 177,308. Calendar year production: 165,133. Model year production: (six) 71,266; (V-8) 103,288; (Total) 174,554. Innovations: Cushioned-Beam front suspension. Total production fell from the record set in 1968. Sales dropped too, but this was still the second best year in Dodge truck history. Trucks were produced in four factories: Warren, Michigan; Burt Road, Detroit; St. Louis; and Windsor, Ontario. The Canadian plant built 7,175 trucks for sale in the U.S. market. V-8 engines accounted for 63 percent of total output. Diesel engine sales fell to just 2,512. Dodge also sold 14,739 Sportsman vans, but they were considered station wagons (passenger cars).

1970 DODGE

1/2-TON COMPACT — A100/108 SERIES — SIX-CYLINDER/V-8: No styling changes hit the compact bodies in their final year. V-8 models now had a new three-speed, fully synchronized manual transmission. A new 198 cid slant six replaced the 170 cid as standard engine. The 225 cid six and 318 V-8 remained optional. Job-Mated Tradesman van interiors were still available from the factory. Travco Corp., of Warren, Michigan, continued its Host Wagon and Executive Suite conversions. The A100/108 series was discontinued in April 1970, when an all-new B-series van (considered a 1971 model) was introduced.

1970 Dodge D100 Sweptline Pickup (DFW)

1/2-TON COMPACT — A100/108 SERIES — SIX-CYLINDER/V-8: No styling changes hit the compact bodies in their final year. V-8 models now had a new three-speed, fully synchronized manual transmission. A new 198 cid slant six replaced the 170 cid as standard engine. The 225 cid six and 318 V-8 remained optional. Job-Mated Tradesman interiors were still available from the factory. Travco Corp., of Warren, Michigan, continued its Host Wagon and Executive Suite conversions. The A100/108 series was discontinued in April, 1970, when an all-new B-series van (considered a 1971 model) was introduced.

1/2-TON — D100 SERIES — SIX-CYLINDER/V-8; 3/4-TON — D200 SERIES — SIX-CYLINDER/V-8; 1-TON — D300 SERIES — SIX-CYLINDER/V-8; 1/2-TON 4x4 — W100 SERIES — SIX-CYLINDER/V-8; 3/4-TON — W200 SERIES — SIX-CYLINDER/V-8; 1-TON 4x4 — W300 SERIES — SIX-CYLINDER/V-8: For the second year in a row light-duty trucks received a new grille. This one was anodized aluminum. It had cross-hatched bars that formed four horizontal air slots and gave the front end a wider and lower appearance. In the filler panel below the vertical center bar were two additional air slots. Parking lights within the grille were changed to horizontal style. Bright finished Junior West Coast mirrors were now available. Inside the cab, three different instrument cluster faceplates marked standard, Custom or Adventurer models. Standards had silver and black plastic; Customs had bright chrome trim; and woodgraining went on the Adventurer's faceplate. Several major engineering changes were achieved. For the first time, four-wheel drive models W100 and W200 were available with LoadFlite three-speed automatic transmission. A new three-speed, fully synchronized manual gearbox was made standard on all 1/2- and 3/4-ton conventional trucks and on six-cylinder W100-200 models. Dodge also designed the industry's first "easy-off" tailgate. It was held by retaining straps and removable, without tools, for the convenience of pickup camper owners. The tailgate could be installed by one person just as quickly as it could be removed. Camper Special models got a new hookup of the camper's electrical system to the chassis harness, plus a standard 25-gallon fuel tank. An auxiliary 23-gallon tank was optional. Tire tools were relocated to an under-hood storage area and strapped down so they wouldn't bounce around.

I.D. DATA: Serial numbers were on a plate on the left door lock pillar. The 13-character number consisted of seven elements: First two characters, model code; next digit, Body Code; next letter indicated GVW rating (A, 6000 lbs. or less; B, 6,001 to 10,001 lbs.; C, 10,001 to 14,000 lbs.); next letter indicated engine displacement; next digit showed model year; next letter was assembly plant; and final six digits were the sequence number. model code Index: A1 (A100); B1 (B100); B2 (B200); B3 (B300); D1 (D100); D2 (D200); D3 (D300); E1 (W100); E2 (W200); E3 (W300). Body Code Index: 1 (conventional cab; compact and pickup); 2 (crew cab; Tradesman van); 3 (Utiline; Low line wagon); 4 (Sweptline; Hi line wagon); 5 (Crew Utiline; Mid line wagon); 6 (crew cab Sweptline); 7 (flat face cowl); 8 (cowl with windshield). Engine Index: A (198 cid); B (225-1); C (225-2); D (251); E (LA318-1); F (360); G (LA318-3); J (383); W (230); X (Special six-cylinder.); Y (Special V-8). Assembly Plant Index: J (Canada); N (Burt Road); S (Warren No. 1); T (Warren No. 2); U (Missouri); V (Warren compact, 1971 on). Sequence numbering: 100,001 to 300,000. Engines were identified as follows: First letter indicated model year; next letter indicated engine type (T=standard; H=premium); next three digits, displacement; next digit, assembly plant shift; next four digits, manufacture date; next two letters, non-standard engine indicator; followed by four-digit sequence number. Starting and ending engine numbers are not available.

Model	Body Type	Price	Weight	Prod. Total
A100 Compact Series — 1/2-Ton — 90 in. w.b.				
A100	Pickup	2454	2834	Note 1
A100	Panel Van (Note 3)	2530	2834	Note 1
A100	Van	—	—	Note 1

NOTE 1: Total model year production: 7,273.

A108 Series — 1/2-Ton — 108 in. w.b.				
A108	Panel Van (Note 3)	2663	3044	Note 2
A108	Van	—	—	Note 2

NOTE 2: Total model year production: 11,235.
NOTE 3: Rear doors only.

D100 Series — 1/2-Ton — 114 in. w.b.				
D100	Chassis & Cowl	—	—	Note 4
D100	Chassis & Cab	—	—	Note 4
D100	Utiline Pickup	—	—	Note 4
D100	Sweptline Pickup	2667	3477	Note 4

NOTE 4: Total model year production: 15,978.

D100 Series — 1/2-Ton — 128 in. w.b.				
D100	Chassis & Cowl	—	—	Note 5
D100	Chassis & Cab	—	—	Note 5
D100	Utiline Pickup	—	—	Note 5
D100	Sweptline Pickup	2703	3617	Note 5
D100	Platform	—	—	Note 5
D100	Stake	2778	3822	Note 5

NOTE 5: Total model year production: 38,857.

D200 Series — 3/4-Ton — 128 in. w.b.				
D200	Chassis & Cowl	—	—	Note 6
D200	Chassis & Cab	—	—	Note 6
D200	Utiline Pickup	—	—	Note 6
D200	Sweptline Pickup	2915	3902	Note 6
D200	Platform	—	—	Note 6
D200	Stake	2991	4107	Note 6

NOTE 6: Total model year production: 19,911.

D200 Crew Cab Series — 3/4-Ton — 146 in. w.b.				
D200	Chassis	—	—	Note 7
D200	Utiline Pickup	—	—	Note 7
D200	Sweptline Pickup	3663	4227	Note 7

NOTE 7: Total model year production: 2,002.

D200 Crew Cab Series — 3/4-Ton — 160 in. w.b.				
D200	Chassis	—	—	Note 8
D200	Utiline Pickup	—	—	Note 8
D200	Sweptline Pickup	3825	4382	Note 8

NOTE 8: Total model year production: 678.

D300 Series — 1-Ton — 133 in. w.b.				
D300	Chassis & Cowl	—	—	Note 9
D300	Chassis & Cab	3018	3704	Note 9
D300	Utiline Pickup	2995	4087	Note 9
D300	Platform	—	—	Note 9
D300	Stake	—	—	Note 9

NOTE 9: Total model year production: 7,460.

D300 Crew Cab Series — 1-Ton — 159 in. w.b.				
D300	Chassis & Cab	3058	3799	Note 10
D300	Utiline Pickup	—	—	Note 10
D300	Sweptline Pickup	3770	4562	Note 10

NOTE 10: Total model year production: 2,300.

W100 Series 4x4 — 1/2-Ton — 114 in. w.b.				
W100	Chassis & Cab	—	—	Note 11
W100	Utiline Pickup	—	—	Note 11
W100	Sweptline Pickup	—	—	Note 11

NOTE 11: Total model year production: 1,500.

W100 Series 4x4 — 1/2-Ton — 128 in. w.b.				
W100	Chassis & Cab	—	—	Note 12
W100	Utiline Pickup	—	—	Note 12
W100	Sweptline Pickup	—	—	Note 12

NOTE 12: Total model year production: 1,897.

W200 Series 4x4 — 3/4-Ton — 128 in. w.b.				
W200	Chassis & Cab	—	—	Note 13
W200	Utiline Pickup	—	—	Note 13
W200	Sweptline Pickup	—	—	Note 13
W200	Platform	—	—	Note 13
W200	Stake	—	—	Note 13

NOTE 13: Total model year production: 5,719.

W200 Crew Cab Series 4x4 — 3/4-Ton — 146 in. w.b.				
W200	Chassis	—	—	Note 14
W200	Utiline Pickup	—	—	Note 14
W200	Sweptline Pickup	—	—	Note 14

NOTE 14: Total model year production: 914.

W300 Series 4x4 — 1-Ton — 133 in. w.b.				
W300	Chassis & Cowl	—	—	Note 15
W300	Chassis & Cab	—	—	Note 15
W300	Utiline Pickup	—	—	Note 15
W300	Platform	—	—	Note 15
W300	Stake	—	—	Note 15

NOTE 15: Total model year production: 1,053.
NOTE 16: Weights and prices shown are for V-8 models, except A100/108, six-cylinder.

ENGINE (A100/108): Inline. Overhead valve. Slant six. Cast iron block. Bore & stroke: 3.4 x 3.64 in. Displacement: 198.3 cid. Compression ratio: 8.4:1. Brake horsepower: 120 at 4000 rpm. Net (Taxable) horsepower: 27.70. Torque: 182 lbs.-ft. at 1600 rpm. Four main bearings. Solid valve lifters.
ENGINE (D100-300, W100-300; optional A100/108): Inline. Overhead valves. Slant six. Cast iron block. Bore & stroke: 3.4 x 4.125 in. Displacement: 224.7 cid. Compression ratio: 8.4:1. Brake horsepower: 140 at 3900 rpm. Net horsepower: 27.70. Torque: 215 lbs.-ft. at 1600 rpm. Four main bearings. Solid valve lifters.
ENGINE (Optional, all models): 90-degree, overhead valve. V-8. Cast iron block. Bore & stroke: 3.91 x 3.312 in. Displacement: 318.1 cid. Compression ratio: 8.5:1. Brake horsepower: 210 at 4000 rpm. Net horsepower: 48.92. Torque: 318 lbs.-ft. at 2800 rpm. Five main bearings. Hydraulic valve lifters.
ENGINE (Optional; D100-300, W100-200): 90-degree, overhead valve. V-8. Cast iron block. Bore & stroke: 4.25 x 3.38 in. Displacement: 383 cid. Compression ratio: 9.2:1. Brake horsepower: 258 at 4400 rpm. Net horsepower: 57.8. Torque: 375 lbs.-ft. at 2800 rpm. Five main bearings. Hydraulic valve lifters.
CHASSIS (A100): Wheelbase: 90 in. Tires: 6.95 x 14 four-ply. GVW: 3,800-4,600 lbs. Axle Capacity: (front) 2,200 lbs.; (rear) 3,000 lbs.
CHASSIS (A108): Wheelbase: 108 in. Tires: 8.15 x 15-2 four-ply. GVW: 3,800-4,800 lbs. Axle Capacity: (front) 2,200 lbs.; (rear) 3,000 lbs.
CHASSIS (D100): Wheelbase: 114 in. or 128 in. Tires: 8.15 x 15 eight-ply. GVW: 4,300-5,200 lbs. Axle Capacity: (front) 2,500 lbs.; (rear) 3,600 lbs.
CHASSIS (D200): Wheelbase: 128 in. or 146 in. Tires: 8 x 19.5 eight-ply. GVW: 5,200-7,500 lbs. Axle Capacity: (front) 2,800 lbs.; (rear) 5,500 lbs.
CHASSIS (D300): Wheelbase: 133 in. Tires: 8 x 17.5 six-ply. GVW: 6,700-10,000 lbs. Axle Capacity: (front) 3,800 lbs.; (rear) 7,500 lbs.
CHASSIS (W100): Wheelbase: 114 in. Tires: 8.15 x 15 four-ply on 5.50 wheels. GVW: 5,100-6,000 lbs. Axle Capacity: (front) 3,000 lbs.; (rear) 3,000 lbs.
CHASSIS (W200): Wheelbase: 128 in. or 146 in. Tires: 8 x 19.5 eight-ply. GVW: 6,000-8,000 lbs. Axle Capacity: (front) 3,000 lbs.; (rear) 5,500 lbs.

CHASSIS (W300): Wheelbase: 133 in. Tires: 8.76 x 16.5 ten-ply on 6.75. GVW: 10,000 lbs. maximum. Axle Capacity: (front) 4,500 lbs.; (rear) 7,500 lbs.

CHASSIS (WM300): Wheelbase: 126 in. Tires: 9.00 x 16 ten-ply. GVW: 8,200-9,500 lbs. Axle Capacity: (front) 3,750 lbs.; (rear) 6,500 lbs.

TECHNICAL: Selective sliding gear transmission. Speeds: 3F/1R except 1-ton models, 4F/1R; (A100/108) V-8 has heavy-duty three-speed transmission. Column or floor shift control. Single-plate dry-disc clutch: (A100 six) 9-1/8 in.; (A100 V-8, D100-200 six) 10 in.; (others) 11 in. Rear axle ratios: (A100) 3.27:1, 3.55:1, 3.91:1 or 4.56:1; (D100) 3.23:1, 3.55:1 or 3.91:1; (D/W200) 3.54:1, 4.1:1 or 4.88:1; ((W100) 3.54:1 or 4.1:1; (D300) 4.1:1, 4.88:1 or 5.87:1; (W300) 4.88:1 or 5.87:1. Hydraulic four-wheel brakes. Fuel tank: (A100) 23 gallon; (others) 18 gallon. One-quart oil filter. Air cleaner: (A100 and D300 V-8) dry; (others) oil bath. Alternator: (A100) 30-amp; (others) 37-amp. Wheels: (D/W100) 15 x 5.00; (D/W100) 15 x 5.50; (D200) 16 x 6.00; (D300, W200) 17.5 x 5.25; (W300) 16.5 x 6.75.

OPTIONS: (Factory-Installed) Air conditioner. Chrome front bumper (A100/D100-200). Rear bumper (WM300). Bumper guards (A100/D100). Wheelcovers (A100/D100). Chrome hubcaps (A100/D100-200). Spare tire carrier (D/W100-300). Adventurer package (D100-200). Paint stripe (with Adventurer only). Appearance package (D/W100-300). Comfort package (D100-300). Tinted glass (except WM300). Radio (except WM300). Auxiliary heater (D100-300/W300). Cigar lighter (except WM300). Outside mirrors. Cab marker lights (D/W100-200). Dual horns (D/W100-300). Heavy-duty instruments (D/W100-300). Rear quarter cab windows (A100). Undercoating. Camper Special package (D/W200). Camper Custom package (D200). Trim molding package (D/W100-300). Two-tone paint (except WM300). Textured vinyl roof (D100). D100 Adventurer bucket seat package. D100/D200 bucket seat package, with standard cab; or with Custom interior package in standard cab models. D100 Custom Exterior package. D100 Custom Interior package. D100 insulation package. D100 wheel lip and sill molding package. Adventurer package for 128 in. wheelbase D200 Sweptline only. D200 Adventurer bucket seat package. D200 bucket seat package with standard cab; or with Custom Interior package in standard cab. D200 Custom Special package. D200 Custom Interior package. D200 Custom Exterior package. D200 added insulation package. D200 bodyside moldings package. D200 wheel lip and sill moldings package. Black or white paint stripe package, D200 Adventurer only. D300 Custom Interior package. D300 Custom Exterior package. W100/W200 bodyside trim molding package. Foam padded seat (D/W100-300). Third seat belt (except A100). Shoulder belt (D/W100-300). Three-ton jack (except A100). Heavy-duty front or rear springs (except WM300). Extra-heavy-duty rear springs (D100-300). Oil pressure gauge (except WM300). Power steering (D100-300). Vacuum power brake booster (D200-300, W100-300). Hand throttle (D/W100-300). Horn ring (A100). 7,500 lbs. rear axle (D300). Fenders for dual rear wheels (D/W300). Rear shock absorbers (D300). 3,500 lbs. front axle (W200). Spare wheel for dual rears (D/W300). Increased cooling capacity (D200-300/W100-300). One-quart oil bath air cleaner (except W/WM300). 46 or 60-amp. alternator (except A100). 37-, 46- or 60-amp. alternator (A100). 10 in. clutch (A100). 11 in. clutch (D100-200). Anti-spin rear axle (except WM300). Governor (D/W100-300). 225 cid engine (A100). 318 cid V-8 engine (except WM300). 383 cid V-8 engine (D100-300/W100-200). Four-speed manual transmission, close or wide spaced ratios (D/W100-200); close only (D300). LoadFlite automatic transmission (D models). Locking front hubs (W/WM models). Pintle hook (W/WM models). Power-take-off (W/WM models). Fuel/vacuum pump (WM300). Radiator overflow tank (WM300). Rear shocks (W/WM300). Tow hooks (W/WM300). 8,000 lbs. winch (W100-300). 10,000 lbs. winch (WM300).

HISTORICAL: Introduced: August, 1969. Calendar year sales: 137,509. Calendar year production: (Total) 188,632; (U.S. only) 178,584. Model year production: (Total) 161,015. Innovations: Junior West Coast mirrors available. Automatic transmission on four-wheel drive models. Fully synchronized manual transmission. Easy-off pickup tailgate. This was the best year in Dodge truck history, as production gained 8.1 percent and Dodge captured more than 10 percent of the industry total. Sales rose 5.4 percent, to slightly below the 1968 record. Dodge was the only truck maker to show a gain, placing third in sales. V-8 engines went into more than two-thirds of Dodge gas trucks. Diesel production was to 3,384, giving Dodge 4.7 percent of that market. Dodge continued its leadership in the camper business by adding a 413 cid engine to the motorhome chassis. New engines of 478 and 549 cid went into the heavy-duty truck lineup.

1971 DODGE

1971 Dodge D100 Sweptline Pickup (Alvin Teeter)

1/2-TON VAN — B100 SERIES — SIX-CYLINDER/V-8; 3/4-TON VAN — B200 SERIES — SIX-CYLINDER/V-8; 1-TON VAN — B300 SERIES — SIX-CYLINDER/V-8: Introduced in April 1970, as 1971 models, the much larger "second generation" vans replaced the original A100/108 series, which dated back to 1964. The new series was developed after many interviews with the buying public. Refinements over the original vans included: Larger cargo area and increased load capacity; engine access from outside for routine maintenance; independent front suspension; longer wheelbases; and wider front and rear tracks. Exterior styling was completely new. All-new interiors had passenger car style seats and instruments. Wheelbases were 109 and 127 in., but overall lengths increased only five inches over prior models. They went to 176 and 194 in. respectively. Cargo capacities were 206 and 246 cu. ft. Passenger vans were also available. Base engine was the 198 cid slant six. Options were the 225 cid slant six and 318 V-8. Standard equipment included dual armrests, left sun visor, two-speed wipers and washers, driver's seat, brake warning light, emergency flashers, turn signals, painted bumpers, solid cargo doors, locks on all doors, glove box, heater, painted hubcaps, driver's and cargo dome light, side marker lights, backup lights, and painted outside mirrors.

1/2-TON — D100 SERIES — SIX-CYLINDER/V-8; 3/4-TON — D200 SERIES — SIX-CYLINDER/V-8; 1-TON — D300 SERIES — SIX-CYLINDER/V-8; 1/2-TON 4x4 — W100 SERIES — SIX-CYLINDER/V-8; 3/4-TON 4x4 — W200 SERIES — SIX-CYLINDER/V-8; 1-TON 4x4 — W300 SERIES — SIX-CYLINDER/V-8: This was the final year for the standard light-duty series, which had begun in 1961 and run without major changes in body styling or engineering features. Dodge merchandised its pickups in six lines. Standard models were now called Custom. Changes for 1971 included: Light argent silver paint on grille inserts; fenderside Custom 100 or Custom 200 nameplates; new Dodge decals on right corner of tailgates; and an unslotted filler panel. The standard instrument cluster faceplate was bright and black, while standard 5x7 in. mirrors were painted. Automatic choke was standard. D100 models had a new evaporative emission control system. One new pickup model was offered at the lowest end of the lineup. Built only on a 114 in. wheelbase, the D100 Sweptline Special was only available with the 198 cid slant six and 3-speed manual transmission. It had a painted grille, black wheels, five-inch round mirror, black and argent paint on instrument cluster, and black vinyl interior, with no options available. Next up the line were the Utiline (fenderside) D100 and D200 models. Standard trim included a bright grille with insert; black rubber windshield and rear window molding; Dodge decal on tailgate; and painted front bumper, hubcaps, gas cap and 5x7 in. mirror. Next came the similarly equipped Custom series with 114 or 128 in. wheelbase Sweptline or Utiline models. The Adventurer was now available in three series. The basic Adventurer package, offered on all models, sported bright windshield moldings, a bodyside molding package (Sweptline pickups only), and an Adventurer nameplate on the pickup box. Next highest, the Adventurer Sport (Sweptline models only), included bright windshield and window moldings, drip moldings, wheel lip and sill moldings; white or black paint stripes; a plain tailgate with bright plaque and Dodge identification; a Delta hood ornament; bright front bumper, hubcaps, gas cap and mirror; Dodge 100 nameplates; and an Adventurer Sport nameplate on the pickup box. Top-of-the-line, on 128 in. wheelbase Sweptlines only, was the Adventurer SE option. It included: Bright windshield and window moldings, drip molding, wheel lip and sill molding; a tailgate with bright woodgrain-filled plaque and Dodge nameplates; a Delta hood ornament; bright front bumper, hubcaps, gas cap and mirror; the Adventurer SE nameplate on the pickup box; plus lower bodyside woodgrain appliques and moldings. The engine lineup remained as before, adding the 198 cid slant six only in the D100 Sweptline Special pickup. Standard equipment included a heater/defroster; full instruments; dome and courtesy lights; side markers; backup lights; four-way flashers; armrests; rubber floor mats; two-speed wipers; and a full-width rear window.

1971 Dodge D100 Adventurer SE Sweptline Pickup (OCW)

I.D. DATA: Serial numbers were on a plate on the left door lock pillar. The 13-character number consisted of seven elements: First two characters = model code; next digit = Body Code; next letter indicates GVW rating (A=6,000 lbs. or less; B=6,001 to 10,001 lbs.; C=10,001 to 14,000 lbs.); next letter indicates engine displacement; next digit shows model year; next letter indicates assembly plant; and final six digits are the sequence number. Model codes were: A1 (A100); B1 (B100); B2 (B200); B3 (B300); D1 (D100); D2 (D200); D3 (D300); E1 (W100); E2 (W200); E3 (W300). Body Codes: 1=conventional cab; compact and pickup; 2=crew cab; Tradesman van; 3=Utiline; Low line wagon; 4= Sweptline; Highline wagon; 5=(Crew Utiline; Mid-line wagon); 6=crew cab Sweptline; 7=flat face cowl; 8=cowl with windshield. Engine codes: A=198 cid; B=225-1; C=225-2; D=251; E=LA318-1; F=360; G=LA318-3; J=383; W=230; X=Special six-cylinder; Y=Special V-8. Assembly Plant Index: J (Canada); N (Burt Road); S (Warren No. 1); T (Warren No. 2): U (Missouri); V (Warren compact, 1971 on). Sequence numbering: 300001 and up. Ending numbers are not available. Engines were identified as follows: First letter indicated model year; next letter indicated engine type (T=standard; H=premium); next three digits, displacement; next digit, assembly plant shift; next four digits, manufacture date; next two letters, non-standard engine indicator; followed by four-digit sequence number. Starting and ending engine numbers are not available.

Model	Body Type	Price	Weight	Prod. Total
B100-300 Series Van — 1/2-Ton — 109 in. w.b.				
B100-6	Van	2890	—	7673
(3/4-Ton)				
B200-6	Van	2985	—	8610
(1-Ton)				
B300-6	Van	3116	—	591

B100-300 Series Van — 1/2-Ton

(127 in. w.b.)

B100-6	Van	3027	—	6020

(3/4-Ton)

B200-6	Van (Note 1)	3451	—	23,406

(1-Ton)

B300-6	Van (Note 2)	3253	—	19,984

NOTE 1: Add $205 to price for B200 Maxivan.
NOTE 2: Add $240 to price for B300 Maxivan.

D100 Series — (1/2-Ton)

(114 in. w.b.)

D100	Chassis & Cab	2652	3095	Note 3
D100	Utiline Pickup	2811	3450	Note 3
D100	Sweptline Pickup	2811	3505	Note 3

NOTE 3: Total model year production 114 in.: 19,444.

(128 in. w.b.)

D100	Chassis & Cab	—	—	Note 4
D100	Utiline Pickup	—	—	Note 4
D100	Sweptline Pickup	—	—	Note 4

NOTE 4: Total model year production 128 in.: 33,487.

D200 Series — 3/4-Ton — 128 in. w.b.

D200	Chassis & Cab	3115	3430	Note 5
D200	Utiline Pickup	3275	3870	Note 5
D200	Sweptline Pickup	3275	3930	Note 5

NOTE 5: Total model year production: 14,094.

D200 Crew Cab Series — 3/4-Ton — 146 in. w.b.

D200	Chassis	3678	3845	Note 6
D200	Utiline Pickup	3837	4205	Note 6
D200	Sweptline Pickup	3837	4255	Note 6

(160 in. w.b.)

D200	Chassis	—	—	Note 6
D200	Utiline Pickup	—	—	Note 6
D200	Sweptline Pickup	—	—	Note 6

NOTE 6: Total model year production: (146 in.) 1,945; (160 in.) 446.

D300 Series — 1-Ton

(133 in. w.b.)

D300	Chassis & Cab	2755	3645	Note 7
D300	Utiline Pickup	2870	4140	Note 7

(159 in. w.b.)

D300	Crew Cab — Chassis	—	—	Note 7
D300	Crew Cab — Utiline	—	—	Note 7

NOTE 7: Total model year production: (133 in.) 8,904; (159 in.) 1,764.

W100 Series 4x4 — 1/2-Ton — 114 in. w.b.

W100	Chassis & Cab	3115	3555	Note 8
W100	Utiline Pickup	3275	3915	Note 8
W100	Sweptline Pickup	3275	3965	Note 8

(128 in. w.b.)

W100	Chassis & Cab	—	—	Note 8
W100	Utiline Pickup	—	—	Note 8
W100	Sweptline Pickup	—	—	Note 8

NOTE 8: Total model year production: (114 in.) 1,626; (128 in.) 2,026.

W200 Series 4x4 — 3/4-Ton

(128 in. w.b.)

W200	Chassis & Cab	3618	3785	Note 9
W200	Utiline Pickup	3777	4225	Note 9
W200	Sweptline Pickup	3777	4285	Note 9

(146 in. w.b.)

W200	Crew Cab — Chassis	4505	4260	Note 9
W200	Crew Cab — Utiline	4664	4620	Note 9
W200	Crew Cab — Sweptline	4664	4670	Note 9

NOTE 9: Total model year production: (128 in.) 4,814; (146 in.) 334.

W300 Series 4x4 — 1-Ton — 133 in. w.b.

W300	Chassis & Cab	4075	4665	Note 10
W300	Utiline Pickup	4185	5160	Note 10
W300	Platform	4395	5325	Note 10
W300	Stake	4450	5625	Note 10

NOTE 10: Total model year production: 783.
NOTE 11: Prices and weights are for six-cylinder models. For V-8 engine, add $130-150 to price.
ENGINE (Standard: B100/B200/D100): Inline. Overhead valve. Slant six. Cast iron block. Bore & stroke: 3.4 x 3.64 in. Displacement: 198.3 cid. Compression ratio: 8.4:1. Brake horsepower: 120 at 4000 rpm. Net (Taxable) horsepower: 27.70. Torque: 180 lbs.-ft. at 1600 rpm. Four main bearings. Solid valve lifters.
ENGINE (Standard: B300/D200-300/W100-300): Inline. Overhead valve. Slant six. Cast iron block. Bore & stroke: 3.4 x 4.125 in. Displacement: 224.7 cid. Compression ratio: 8.4:1. Brake horsepower: 140 at 3900 rpm. Net horsepower: 27.70. Torque: 215 lbs.-ft. at 1600 rpm. Four main bearings. Solid valve lifters.
ENGINE (Optional, all models): 90-degree, overhead valve. V-8. Cast iron block. Bore & stroke: 3.91 x 3.312 in. Displacement: 318.1 cid. Compression ratio: 8.8:1. Brake horsepower: 48.92. Torque: 318 lbs.-ft. at 2800 rpm. Five main bearings. Hydraulic valve lifters.
ENGINE (Optional: D100-300/W100-200): 90-degree, overhead valve. V-8. Cast iron block. Bore & stroke: 4.25 x 3.38 in. Displacement: 383 cid. Compression ratio: 8.7:1. Brake horsepower: 258 at 4400 rpm. Net horsepower: 57.80. Torque: 375 lbs.-ft. at 2800 rpm. Five main bearings. Hydraulic valve lifters.
CHASSIS (B100): Wheelbase: 109 in. or 127 in. Tires: E78 x 14-B four-ply. Max. GVW: 4,200-4,800 lbs. Axle Capacity: 2,700 lbs.
CHASSIS (B200): Wheelbase: 109 in. or 127 in. Tires: G78 x 15-B four-ply. Max. GVW: 5,200-5,500 lbs. Axle Capacity: (front) 3,000 lbs.; (rear) 3,300 lbs.
CHASSIS: (B300): Wheelbase: 109 in. or 127 in. Tires: 8.00 x 16.5-C six-ply or 8.00 x 16.5D eight-ply. Max. GVW: 6,100-7,700 lbs. Axle Capacity: (front) 3,300 lbs.; (rear) 3,500 lbs.
CHASSIS (D100): Wheelbase: 114 in. or 128 in. Tires: G78 x 15-B-5. Max. GVW: 4,300-5,200 lbs. Axle Capacity: (front) 2,800 lbs.; (rear) 3,600 lbs.
CHASSIS (D200): Wheelbase: 128 in., 146 in. or 160 in. Tires: 8.00 x 16.5-D-4. Max. GVW: 6,100-7,500 lbs. Axle Capacity: (front) 3,300 lbs.; (rear) 5,500 lbs.
CHASSIS (D300): Wheelbase: 133 in. or 159 in. Tires: 8.00 x 16.5-D eight-ply. Max. GVW: 6,600-10,000 lbs. Axle Capacity: (front) 3,800 lbs.; (rear) 7,500 lbs.
CHASSIS (W100): Wheelbase: 114 in. or 128 in. Tires: G78 x 15-B four-ply. Max. GVW: 5,100-5,600 lbs. Axle Capacity: (front) 3,000 lbs.; (rear) 3,600 lbs.
CHASSIS (W200): Wheelbase: 128 in. or 146 in. Tires: 8.00 x 16.5-D eight-ply. Max. GVW: 6,000-8,000 lbs. Axle Capacity: (front) 3,500 lbs.; (rear) 5,500 lbs.
CHASSIS (W300): Wheelbase: 133 in. Tires: 8.75 x 16.5-D ten-ply. Max. GVW: 8,500 lbs. Axle Capacity: (front) 4,500 lbs.; (rear) 7,500 lbs.
TECHNICAL: Selective sliding gear transmission. Speeds: 3F/1R except D/W300 1-ton models, 4F/1R; (B vans) V-8 had heavy-duty 3-speed transmission. Column (3-speed) or floor shift control. Single-plate dry-disc clutch: (B100 six) 9.25 in.; (B200 and D100-300 six) 10 in.; (all V-8) 11 in. Hydraulic four-wheel brakes. Fuel tank: (B vans) 26 gallon; (D100) 23 gallon; (others) 25 gallon. Rear Spring Capacity: (B100) 1,000/1,170 lbs.; (B200) 1,375/1,550 lbs.; (B300) 1,700/1,870 lbs.; (D100) 1,100/1,300 lbs.; (D200) 1,650/1,900 lbs.; (D300) 2,050/2,400 lbs.; (W100) 1,350/1,600 lbs.; (W200) 1,750/2,000 lbs.; (W300) 3,250/3,600 lbs. Alternator: 37 amp. Wheels: (B100) five 14 x 5.5; (B200, D100) 15 x 5.5; (B300, D200-300) 16.5 x 6.
OPTIONS (Factory-Installed): (B Series Vans) Chrome hubcaps. Chrome wheelcovers (except B300). Chrome bumpers, front and rear. Door check arms or straps. Tinted glass. Glove box door. Bright finish grille. Outside mirror. Inside mirror. Convenience package. Radio (AM or AM/FM). Heater. Insulation package. Lock package. Dual horns. Horn bar. Cigar lighter. Air conditioner. Deluxe driver's bucket seat. Passenger bucket seat. Shoulder belts. Undercoating. Window glass (side, rear, vision van, or vision van curb side). Two-tone paint. Exterior moldings: Upper side package; lower side rear package; upper side and rear and lower side package. Cargo area headliner. Oil pressure gauge. Oil-wetted air cleaner. 50 or 60-amp. alternator. Cruise control. Increased cooling capacity. One-quart oil filter. Emission control system (except B300). Padded dash. Front disc brakes (except B300). Vacuum brake booster. Power steering. Anti-spin rear axle (B300 only). 10 in. clutch (B100 with 198 cid engine). 11 in. clutch (225 cid engine). Heavy-duty shock absorbers (front and rear). Heavy-duty springs (front or rear). Three-speed automatic transmission A727. 225 cid slant six engine (B100-200). 318 cid V-8 engine. (D100-300 and W100-300) Chrome bumper (front or rear). White rear bumper. Step-type rear bumper. Spare tire carrier: Inside (Sweptlines) or outside (Utilines). Wheel covers (except 300 models). Chrome hubcaps (except 300 models). Tinted glass. Dual horns. Textured vinyl roof. Two-tone paint. Radio. Air conditioner. Cigar lighter. Heavy-duty instruments. Marker lights. Outside mirrors. Oil pressure gauge. Foam padded seat. Third seat belt. Shoulder belts (pair). Hand throttle. Undercoating. Adventurer package (except 300 models). Adventurer Sport package (except 300 models). Adventurer SE package (except 300 models). Bucket seat package (except W300). Camper package (D/W200). Dude package (except 300 models). Insulation package. Exterior trim: Upperide molding, or wheel lip and sill molding (except 300 models). NP435 4-speed transmission (except 300 models). NP445B four-speed transmission (except W300). A727 three-speed automatic transmission. Power steering. Anti-spin rear axle. One-quart oil bath air cleaner (D/W200-300). 50 or 60-amp. alternator. Heavy-duty (11 in.) clutch for 225 cid six. Auxiliary 23-gallon fuel tank. Increased cooling capacity. Three-ton jack. One-quart oil filter. Heavy-duty springs (front or rear). Heavy-duty shock absorbers (front and rear). Auxiliary springs, rear (except D300). 318 cid V-8 engine. 383 cid V-8 engine.
HISTORICAL: Introduced: August, 1970 (B Series vans in April, 1970). Calendar year sales: 159,055. Calendar year production: (U.S. only) 204,766; (including Canada) 218,337. Model year production: 175,588. Innovations: Enlarged "second generation" vans. Dodge had another record year in both sales and production — the third straight year of record-setting sales. Canadian production for the U.S. market totaled 13,571 trucks. Dodge also built 25,709 Spotsman vans, which were counted as station wagons. V-8 engines accounted for nearly 70 percent of all gasoline engine production. Diesel sales came to 2,835 units.

1972 Dodge Adventurer SE Sweptline Pickup (DNP)

1/2-TON VAN — B100 SERIES — SIX-CYLINDER/V-8; 3/4-TON VAN — B200 SERIES — SIX-CYLINDER/V-8; 1-TON VAN — B300 SERIES — SIX-CYLINDER/V-8: Dodge second generation vans changed very little in their second year. The 198 cid slant six was dropped, while the 225 cid six became standard for all vans. A 318 cid V-8 or a new 360 V-8 were options. All models, sizes and options carried forward, as did the Sportsman Wagon

lineup of passenger vans, which were counted as station wagons. Standard van equipment included painted bumpers and hubcaps, heater/defroster, locks on all doors, dome light (driver's and cargo area), four-way flashers, dual 5x7 in. mirrors, padded driver's sun visor, two-speed wipers/washers, twin armrests, and a bumper jack (axle jack for B300).

1972 Dodge Adventurer SE Sweptline Pickup (rear view)

1/2-TON — D100 SERIES — SIX-CYLINDER/V-8; 3/4-TON — D200 SERIES — SIX-CYLINDER/V-8; 1-TON — D300 SERIES — SIX-CYLINDER/V-8; 1/2-TON 4x4 — W100 SERIES — SIX-CYLINDER/V-8; 3/4-TON 4x4 — W200 SERIES — SIX-CYLINDER/V-8; 1-TON 4x4 — W300 SERIES — SIX-CYLINDER/V-8: The year 1972 heralded the beginning of a new era in Dodge truck history. The all new line of light-duty models would ultimately last even longer than the popular series that preceded it. The policy of no major yearly styling changes, ushered in with the 1961 models, would continue with the new 1972 trucks. Neither would basic chassis and mechanical components be altered on an annual basis. Light-duty trucks contributed heavily to total corporate profitability. Management was aware that the typical buyer did not expect big changes from year to year, but was more comfortable with traditional, proven appearances. Naturally, the policy of limited change, with longer runs from original tooling and development costs, added greatly to profits. Minor styling updates and engineering improvements, plus standard and optional equipment changes, would appear over the years, but the basic package would remain unchanged well into the 1980s. Dodge's new 1972 line was designed to incorporate more passenger car-like comfort and convenience, with no loss of truck function. Continued were the three basic load capacities. Two-wheel drive versions were basically as before, but four-wheel drive models received beefier chassis components, a larger clutch, wider rear brake shoes and drums, heavier front axle, and front leaf (rather than coil) springs. Standard wheelbases, across the line, grew from one to five inches for better load carrying capacity. Bigger windshields and back windows improved vision. Curved side windows added four inches to the cab shoulder room. Doors were two-inches longer and hinged to swing farther out for easier entry and exit. Cab interiors were updated for comfort, convenience and serviceability. Dashboard design put function first, with round gauges recessed to prevent glare. All gauges could be seen from the front of the dash. Both the fuse box and emergency flashers were behind the glove box door for easy service. Pedal pads and glove compartments were larger; sun visors became full-width. Enlarged seats were mounted higher. The cab noise level diminished with increased insulation and the heater and windshield wiper motors moved to the underhood area. Door latches were quieter, too. Larger vents and cowl side openings for fresh air intake improved interior airflow. Base engine remained the 225 cid slant six, while 318, 360 and 400 cid V-8s were optional. The 383 V-8 was dropped, and the 400 was not available in 4x4 models. Suspension was all new, with coil springs and independent suspension in front (four-wheel drives) and long, wide-leaf springs in the rear. Front and rear track widths increased with the wheelbases to provide better handling and load capacity. The new front end could be adjusted on standard alignment equipment. Brakes were larger, and a step-on parking brake became standard. Both Utiline and Sweptline pickup boxes were available on all models. The basic model was the Custom, with three appearance/trim packages optional: Adventurer, Adventurer Sport, and Adventurer Special Edition (SE). Two camper packages, a heavy-duty package, and a trailer-towing package also were available. Standard equipment included dual armrests; chrome front bumper and grille; heater/defroster; dome and courtesy lights; 5x7 in. chrome mirrors outside and day/night mirror inside; and two-speed wipers. New options included power-assisted disc brakes, integral power steering, cruise control and a new integral air conditioning system.

1972 Dodge Adventurer SE Camper 9000 Amerigo Cab-Over

I.D. DATA: Serial numbers were on a plate on the left door lock pillar. The seven-element serial numbers consisted of 13 alpha-numeric characters. First came a two-character model code. The next digit indicated body code. Next came a letter indicating GVW: A (6,000 lbs. or less); B (6,001 to 10,000 lbs.); C (10,001 to 14,000 lbs.); or D (14,001 to 16,000 lbs.) Next, one letter indicating engine type. The next digit showed model year 2=1972. The sixth element was a letter indicating assembly plant; J (Windsor); N (Burt Road, Detroit); S (Warren Truck No. 1); T (Warren Truck No. 2); U (St. Louis); or V (Warren compact). Finally came the six-digit sequence number. Each assembly plant began the 1972 model year with number 500001. Model code index: B1 (B100 van); B2 (B200 van); B3 (B300 van); D1 (D100); D2 ((D200); D3 (D300); G1 (Post Office); M3 (M300); P2

(P200); P3 (P300); W1 (W100); W2 (W200); W3 (W300); X3 (WM300 export). Body code index: 1=compact van (Tradesman); conventional cab; LCF cab; standard heavy-duty tilt cab. 2=compact low-line wagon (Sportsman); crew cab; long sleeper heavy-duty tilt cab. 3=compact mid-line wagon (Custom Sportsman); conventional Utiline. 4=compact hi-line wagon (Royal Sportsman); conventional Sweptline. 5=compact Maxivan (Tradesman); Utiline crew cab. 6=compact low-line Maxiwagon (Sportsman); Sweptline crew cab. 7=compact mid-line Maxiwagon (Custom Sportsman); flat face cowl. 8=compact hi-line Maxiwagon (Royal Sportsman); windshield cowl. 9=forward control or motorhome; incomplete vehicle. Gas engine index: B (225-1); C (225-2); E (LA318-1); F (360); G (LA318-3); J (400). Engine numbers were located as follows: (225 cid) right side of block below No. 1 spark plug; (318 and 360 cid V-8) left front of block, below cylinder head; (400 cid V-8) right side of block, adjacent to distributor. Engine numbers had five elements. The first two letters indicated manufacturing plant (PM=Mound Rock; PT=Trenton; NN=Marysville; GW=Windsor). The next three digits gave displacement in cid The next letter showed engine type (R=regular fuel; T=standard; H=premium). Next came a four-digit build date code, based on a 10,000-day calendar. The final four digits were the sequence number, which began with 0001 for each day's production.

1972 Dodge Adventurer SE Sweptline Pickup (DNP)

Model	Body Type	Price	Weight	Prod. Total
B100 Series Van — 1/2-Ton				
(109 in. w.b.)				
B100-6	Van	2769	3470	13,686
(127 in. w.b.)				
B100-6	Van	2898	3570	9717
B200 Series Van — 3/4-Ton				
(109 in. w.b.)				
B200-6	Van	2861	3460	12,923
(127 in. w.b.)				
B200-6	Van	2983	3570	35,919
B200-6	Maxivan	3179	3715	—
B300 Series Van — 1-Ton				
(109 in. w.b.)				
B300-6	Van	2988	3695	734
(127 in. w.b.)				
B300-6	Van	3117	3810	41,270
B300-6	Maxivan	3346	3985	—
D100 Series — 1/2-Ton				
(115 in. w.b.)				
D100	Chassis & Cab	2573	3065	Note 1
D100	Utiline Pickup	2732	3410	Note 1
D100	Sweptline Pickup	2732	3470	Note 1
(131 in. w.b.)				
D100	Chassis & Cab	2607	3105	Note 1
D100	Utiline Pickup	2765	3535	Note 1
D100	Sweptline Pickup	2765	3565	Note 1

NOTE 1: Total model year production, (115 in. wheelbase): 18,370; (131 in. wheelbase) 73,542.

D200 Series Custom — 3/4-Ton				
(131 in. w.b.)				
D200	Chassis & Cab	2809	3245	Note 2
D200	Utiline Pickup	2966	3675	Note 2
D200	Sweptline Pickup	2966	3705	Note 2

NOTE 2: Total model year production: 23,902.

D200 Crew Cab Series Custom — 3/4-Ton				
(149 in. w.b.)				
D200	Chassis & Cab	3566	3775	Note 3
D200	Utiline Pickup	3723	4120	Note 3
D200	Sweptline Pickup	3723	4160	Note 3
(165 in. w.b.)				
D200	Chassis & Cab	3651	3950	Note 3
D200	Utiline Pickup	3816	4380	Note 3
D200	Sweptline Pickup	3816	4410	Note 3

NOTE 3: Total model year production: (149 in. wheelbase) 1,881; (165 in. wheelbase) 1,057.

D300 Series Custom — 1-Ton				
(135 in. w.b.)				
D300	Chassis & Cab	2960	3795	Note 4
D300	Utiline Pickup	3077	4290	Note 4

D300	Chassis & Cab	2998	3890	2735

(165 in. w.b.)

D300	Crew Cab — Chassis & Cab	3868	4750	115

NOTE 4: Total model year production: (135 in.) 5,681.

W100 Series 4x4 — 1/2-Ton

(115 in. w.b.)

W100	Chassis & Cab	3023	3510	Note 5
W100	Utiline Pickup	3180	3855	Note 5
W100	Sweptline Pickup	3180	3893	Note 5

(131 in. w.b.)

W100	Chassis & Cab	3056	3565	Note 5
W100	Utiline Pickup	3217	3994	Note 5
W100	Sweptline Pickup	3217	4023	Note 5

NOTE 5: Total model year production: (115 in. wheelbase) 2,978; (131 in. wheelbase) 4,389.

W200 Series 4x4 Custom — 3/4-Ton

(131 in. w.b.)

W200	Chassis & Cab	3508	3810	Note 6
W200	Utiline Pickup	3666	4240	Note 6
W200	Sweptline Pickup	3666	4270	Note 6

(149 in. w.b.)

W200	Crew Cab — Chassis/Cab	4365	4145	Note 6
W200	Crew Cab— Utiline	4523	4490	Note 6
W200	Crew Cab — Sweptline	4523	4530	Note 6

NOTE 6: Total model year production: (131 in. wheelbase) 7,886; (149 in. wheelbase crew cab) 1,067.

W300 Series 4x4 Custom — 1-Ton

(135 in. w.b.)

W300	Chassis & Cab	4227	4320	Note 7
W300	Utiline Pickup	4338	4515	Note 7
W300	Platform	4640	5325	Note 7
W300	Stake	4660	5625	Note 7

NOTE 7: Total model year production: 943.
NOTE 8: Weights and prices shown are for six-cylinder. models. For V-8 engine, add $118 to $167 to price (depending on series).

1972 Dodge Adventurer Sweptline Pickup (DNP)

ENGINE (Standard: All Models): Inline. Overhead valve. Slant six. Cast iron block. Bore & stroke: 3.4 x 4.125 in. Displacement: 224.7 cid. Compression ratio: 8.4:1. Brake horsepower: 140 gross at 3900 rpm. (110 net at 4000 rpm.) Taxable horsepower: 27.70. Torque: 215 lbs.-ft. gross at 1600 rpm. (185 lbs.-ft. net at 2000 rpm.) Four main bearings. Solid valve lifters.

ENGINE (Standard V-8: All Models): 90-degree, overhead valve. V-8. Cast iron block. Bore & stroke: 3.91 x 3.312 in. Displacement: 318.1 cid. Compression ratio: 8.8:1. Brake horsepower: 210 gross (150 net) at 4000 rpm. Taxable horsepower: 48.92. Torque: 318 lbs.-ft. gross at 2800 rpm. (245 lbs.-ft. net at 1600 rpm.) Five main bearings. Hydraulic valve lifters.

ENGINE (Optional: All Models): 90-degree, overhead valve. V-8. Cast iron block. Bore & stroke: 4.00 x 3.58 in. Displacement: 359.9 cid. Compression ratio: 8.7:1. Brake horsepower: 180 (net) at 4000 rpm. Taxable horsepower: 51.2. Torque: 295 lbs.-ft. (net) at 2400 rpm. Five main bearings. Hydraulic valve lifters.

ENGINE (Optional: D100-300 only): 90-degree, overhead valve. V-8. Cast iron block. Bore & stroke: 4.34 x 3.37 in. Displacement: 400 cid. Compression ratio: 8.2:1. Brake horsepower: 200 (net) at 4400 rpm. Taxable horsepower: 60.3. Torque: 320 lbs.-ft. (net) at 2400 rpm. Five main bearings. Hydraulic valve lifters.

NOTE: Beginning in 1972, advertised brake horsepower and torque ratings were normally given as SAE net format with normal parts attached to the engine. In earlier years, gross ratings, measured with a bare engine were used.

CHASSIS (B100 Van): Wheelbase: 109 in. or 127 in. Tires: E78 x 14-B four-ply. GVW: (109) 4,600 lbs.; (127) 4,800 lbs. Axle Capacity: 2,700 lbs. (front and rear).

CHASSIS (B200 Van): Wheelbase: 109 in. or 127 in. Tires: G78 x 15-B four-ply. GVW: 5,500 lbs. max. Axle Capacity: (front) 3,000 lbs.; (rear) 3,300 lbs.

CHASSIS: (B300 Van): Wheelbase: 109 in. or 127 in. Tires: 8.00 x 16.5-C six-ply except Maxivan, 8.00 x 16.5-D eight-ply. GVW: 6,200 to 7,700 lbs. Axle Capacity: (front) 3,300 lbs.; (rear) 5,500 lbs.

CHASSIS (D100): Wheelbase: 115 in. or 131 in. Tires: G78 x 15-D four-ply. GVW: 4,600 lbs. Axle Capacity: (front) 3,000 lbs.; (rear) 3,300 lbs.

CHASSIS (D200): Wheelbase: 131 in., 149 in. or 165 in. Tires: 8.00 x 16.5-D eight-ply. GVW: 6,200-7,500 lbs. Axle Capacity: (front) 3,300/3,800 lbs.; (rear) 5,000/6,200 lbs.

CHASSIS (D300): Wheelbase: 135 in., 159 in. or 165 in. Tires: 8.00 x 16.5-D eight-ply except dual rear wheel crew cab, 8.00 x 16.5-C six-ply. GVW: 6,600-10,000 lbs. Axle Capacity: (front) 3,800 lbs.; (rear) 7,500 lbs.

CHASSIS (W100): Wheelbase: 115 in. or 131 in. Tires: G78 x 15-B four-ply. GVW: 5,100 lbs. Axle Capacity: 3,300 lbs. (front and rear).

CHASSIS (W200): Wheelbase: 131 in. or 149 in. Tires: 8.00 x 16.5-D eight-ply. GVW: 6,500 lbs. Axle Capacity: (front) 3,500 lbs.; (rear) 5,500 lbs.

CHASSIS (W300): Wheelbase: 135 in. Tires: 8.75 x 16.5-E ten-ply. GVW: 8,500 lbs. Axle Capacity: (front) 4,500 lbs.; (rear) 7,500 lbs.

TECHNICAL: Selective sliding gear transmission. Speeds: 3F/1R except (D300, W300 and 165 in. wheelbase. D200) 4F/1R. Column (3-speed) or floor shift control. Single disc dry clutch: (six-cylinder.) 10 in.; (V-8) 11 in. Hydraulic four-wheel brakes: (B100) 10 x 2-1/2 in. (front/rear); (B200) 10 x 2-1/2 (rear), 11 x 3 (front); (B300) 12 x 2-1/2 (rear), 12 x 3 (front); (D100) 10 x 2-1/2 (rear), 11 x 2-3/4 (front); (D200) 12-1/8 x 2; (D/W300) 12-1/8 x 3; (W100) 11 x 2; (W200); 12 x 2-1/2 (rear); 12-1/8 x 2 (front). Fuel tank: 25-gallon except vans, 26-gallon. Alternator: (vans) 48 amp; (others) 41 amp. Automatic transmission optional.

OPTIONS (Factory-Installed): (Vans) Chrome bumpers. Chrome grille. Chrome hubcaps. Chrome wheelcovers. Tinted glass. Dual horns. Horn bar. Radio (AM or AM/FM). Cigar lighter. Deluxe heater. Cargo area heater. Cargo area headliner. Padded dash. Convenience package. Insulation package. Lock package. Trailer-towing package. Exterior moldings: Upper side package; lower side and rear package; or upper side/rear and lower side/rear package. Oil pressure gauge. Door check arms (side and rear). Door check straps (side). Glove box door. Light switch (cargo door operated). Manual dome light switch. Chrome 5x7 in. outside mirrors. Dual Junior West Coast mirrors. Painted or chrome. Two-tone paint. Bucket seat (passenger). Deluxe bucket seat (driver's, or driver and passenger). Undercoating. Window combinations: Side glass, rear glass, vision van, or curbside vision van. Oil-wetted air cleaner. 50 or 60-amp. alternator. Anti-spin rear axle (B100-200 with 3.2:1, 3.55:1 or 3.91:1 ratio; or B300 with 4.1:1 ratio). Cruise control. Front disc brakes. Vacuum booster power brakes (standard on B200-300). 11 in. clutch (for 225 cid). Increased cooling capacity. Engine block heater. Heavy-duty shock absorbers. Heavy-duty springs (front or rear). Power steering. Three-speed automatic transmission (A727). 360-cid V-8 engine. (D100-300, W100-300) Painted rear bumper. Chrome rear bumper (D100-200). Step rear bumper. Front bumper guards. Spare tire carrier: Inside(D100-200 Sweptline); outside (Utiline); underslung (except D100). Chrome hubcaps (D100-200). Wheelcovers (except D200). Sliding rear window. Undercoating. Tinted glass. Two-tone paint. Textured vinyl roof. Dual headlamps. Cab marker lights. Chrome 5x7 in. outside mirrors (short or long-arm). Dual Junior West Coast mirrors. Radio (AM or AM/FM). Cigar lighter. Clock. Air conditioner. Heater/defroster. Deluxe foam rubber seat assembly. Shoulder belts. Adventurer package. Adventurer Sport package (131 in. w.b.). Adventurer SE package (131 in. w.b.). Bucket seat package. Convenience package. Heavy-duty package (D/W200, 131 in. w.b.). Trailer-towing package. Power steering. Electric tachometer. Hand throttle control. Oil pressure gauge. One-quart oil bath air cleaner (except D100). 50 or 60-amp. alternator. Anti-spin rear axle: D100 with 3.2:1, 3.55:1 or 3.91:1 ratio; others with 3.54:1, 4.1:1 or 4.56:1 ratio. Power front disc, rear drum brakes. Power drum brakes (D100). Power front disc, rear drum brakes. 11 in. clutch (225 cid). Increased cooling capacity. Auxiliary 25-gallon fuel tank. Engine block heater. Spare tire and wheel (except D100). Heavy-duty shock absorbers. Heavy-duty springs (front or rear). Auxiliary 500 lbs. rear springs (D100-300, W300). Front stabilizer bar (D models). NP435 four-speed manual transmission (D/W100-200). NP445B 4-speed transmission. A727 three-speed automatic transmission. 360 cid V-8 engine. 400 cid V-8 engine (D models). Tool storage box (D100-200 on 131 or 165 in. wheelbase.)

HISTORICAL: Introduced: August, 1971. Calendar year sales: 260,002. Calendar year production: 325,726 (U.S. only). Model year production: 296,397. Innovations: Curved side windows. Recessed gauges. Independent front suspension. Electronic ignition system. Dodge spent a record $50 million to completely re-engineer and restyle its line of light-duty trucks for 1972. Bolstered by a strong general economy, the U.S. truck industry produced a record 2,475,000 trucks and buses. Dodge production and sales also established new records, as the company's market share shot up to 13.2 percent (from less than 10 percent in 1971). Sales gained 63.5 percent over the previous year. For the first time, over 2 million V-8 gasoline powered trucks were sold by all manufacturers. For the model year, 71.4 percent of light-duty Dodge trucks were V-8 powered; 74.5 percent had automatic transmissions; 61.8 percent had power steering; 79.9 percent had power brakes; and 15.5 percent carried air conditioners. Dodge built 216,345 trucks in its Warren, Michigan plant and 109,381 at St. Louis. Medium and heavy-duty models were unchanged from 1971. In spring 1972, Dodge introduced its mammoth new heavy-duty conventional model, called Big Horn. Also at midyear, Dodge offered...for the first time in the industry...a fully electronic ignition system on light-duty trucks, vans and motorhomes with V-8 engines and automatic transmissions. Dodge continued its leadership role in vans and motorhomes.

1973 DODGE

1/2-TON VAN — B100 SERIES — SIX-CYLINDER/V-8; 3/4-TON VAN — B200 SERIES — SIX-CYLINDER/V-8; 1-TON VAN — B300 SERIES — SIX-CYLINDER/V-8: Second generation Dodge vans entered their third year without change in appearance or engineering features. Electronic ignition was now standard equipment on B100 and B200 vans and optional on the B300. New this year was the innovative Dodge Kary Van, with a 10 ft. body on the 127 in. wheelbase chassis. Rated up to 8,200 lbs. GVW, its 6 ft. 2 in. height gave walk-in roominess. Three rear door styles were available. All optional equipment offered on the Tradesman Van was available for the Kary Van. Its interior was readily adaptable to do-it-yourself alterations. Base engine remained the 225 cid slant six, with 318 and 360 cid V-8s optional. All models now had power brakes.

1973 Dodge Adventurer SE Sweptline Pickup (DNP)

1/2-TON — D100 SERIES — SIX-CYLINDER/V-8; 3/4-TON — D200 SERIES — SIX-CYLINDER/V-8; 1-TON — D300 SERIES — SIX-CYLINDER/V-8; 1/2-TON 4x4 — W100 SERIES — SIX-CYLINDER/V-8; 3/4-TON 4x4 — W200 SERIES — SIX-CYLINDER/V-8; 1-TON 4x4 — W300 SERIES — SIX-CYLINDER/V-8: Biggest news in 1973 pickups was the unique treatment called a Club Cab. Lengthening the cab behind the rear seat added 18 in. of interior cargo or passenger space. Two windows in the rear quarter panels gave additional visibility. Two optional jump seats, normally facing forward, fit into depressions in the side trim panel when not in use. The Club Cab was available on a D100 chassis of 133 in. wheelbase with 6-1/2 ft. Sweptline box, a 149 in. D100 chassis with 8 ft. Sweptline box, or the D200 chassis with 8 ft. Sweptline box. Club Cabs were not available on four-wheel drive models. Electronic ignition, introduced as an option on V-8 engines during 1972, was now available at extra cost for all engines. Since it eliminated breaker points and condensers, electronic ignition was essentially maintenance-free. A new extra-cost option, only on D100 and D200 Sweptline 8 ft. pickups, was a tool storage compartment under the pickup box, between the cab and rear wheel on the right side. All other 1972 models carried forward without change in styling, engines, transmissions, or engineering features. Four trim levels, as introduced for 1970, continued unchanged. They ranged from the low-end Custom up to the Adventurer, the Adventurer Sport and the top-of-the-line Adventurer Special Edition (SE).

1973 Dodge Adventurer SE Sweptline Pickup (rear view)

I.D. DATA: Serial numbers were on the left door lock pillar and consisted of 13 symbols. The first two symbols are the model code. The third symbol denotes the type of unit (conventional, crew cab, club cab, etc.). The fourth indicated GVW class. The fifth symbol denotes the engine. The sixth symbol denotes the year (3=1973). The seventh symbol denotes the assembly plant. The last six symbols are the sequential production number.

1973 Dodge Club Cab Pickup (DNP)

Model	Body Type	Price	Weight	Prod. Total
B100 Series Tradesman Van — 1/2-Ton				
(109 in. w.b.)				
B100-6	Van	2914	3470	26,980
(127 in. w.b.)				
B100-6	Van	3043	3570	17,995
B200 Series Tradesman Van — 3/4-Ton				
(109 in. w.b.)				
B200-6	Van	3049	3460	12,528
(127 in. w.b.)				
B200-6	Van	3171	3570	55,201
B200-6	Maxivan	—	3715	
B300 Series Tradesman Van — 1-Ton				
(109 in. w.b.)				
B300-6	Van	3151	3695	567
(127 in. w.b.)				
B300-6	Van	3280	3810	73,184
B300-6	Maxivan	—	3985	
CB300	Kary Van	—	—	—
D100 Series — Custom — 1/2-Ton				
(115 in. w.b.)				
D100	Chassis & Cab	2758	3065	Note 1
D100	Utiline Pickup	2914	3410	Note 1
D100	Sweptline Pickup	2914	3470	Note 1
(131 in. w.b.)				
D100	Chassis & Cab	—	3105	Note 1
D100	Utiline Pickup	—	3535	Note 1
D100	Sweptline Pickup	—	3565	Note 1

NOTE 1: Total model year production, (115 in.): 14,485; (131 in.) 61,428.

D100 Series Club Cab — Custom — 1/2-Ton

Model	Body Type	Price	Weight	Prod. Total
(133 in. w.b.)				
D100	Sweptline Pickup	—	—	4404
(149 in. w.b.)				
D100	Sweptline Pickup	—	3935	27,652

1973 Dodge Crew Cab Pickup USAC Fire-Rescue (IMSC/JLM)

D200 Series — Custom — 3/4-Ton

Model	Body Type	Price	Weight	Prod. Total
(131 in. w.b.)				
D200	Chassis & Cab	2984	3245	Note 2
D200	Utiline Pickup	3141	3675	Note 2
D200	Sweptline Pickup	3141	3705	Note 2

NOTE 2: Total model year production: 22,221.

D200 Series Club Cab — Custom — 3/4-Ton

Model	Body Type	Price	Weight	Prod. Total
(149 in. w.b.)				
D200	Sweptline Pickup	—	3935	Note 3

D200 Crew Cab — Custom — 3/4-Ton

Model	Body Type	Price	Weight	Prod. Total
(149 in. w.b.)				
D200	Chassis & Cab	3753	3775	Note 3
D200	Utiline Pickup	3910	4120	Note 3
D200	Sweptline Pickup	3910	4160	Note 3
(165 in. w.b.)				
D200	Chassis & Cab	—	3950	Note 3
D200	Utiline Pickup	—	4380	Note 3
D200	Sweptline Pickup	—	4410	Note 3

NOTE 3: Total model year production: (149 in., Club Cab and Crew Cab) 18,120; (165 in. Crew Cab) 1,325.

D300 Series — Custom — 1-Ton

Model	Body Type	Price	Weight	Prod. Total
(135 in. w.b.)				
D300	Chassis & Cab	3104	3795	Note 4
D300	Utiline Pickup	3221	4290	Note 4
(159 in. w.b.)				
D300	Chassis & Cab	—	3890	2888
(165 in. w.b.)				
D300	Crew Cab — Chassis & Cab	—	4750	151

NOTE 4: Total model year production: (135 in.) 5,856.

W100 Series 4x4 — Custom — 1/2-Ton) — 115 in. w.b.

Model	Body Type	Price	Weight	Prod. Total
W100	Chassis & Cab	3257	3510	Note 5
W100	Utiline Pickup	3414	3855	Note 5
W100	Sweptline Pickup	3414	3893	Note 5
(131 in. w.b.)				
W100	Chassis & Cab	—	3565	Note 5
W100	Utiline Pickup	—	3994	Note 5
W100	Sweptline Pickup	—	4023	Note 5

NOTE 5: Total model year production: (115 in.) 5,889; (131 in.) 10,310.

W200 Series 4x4 — Custom — 3/4-Ton

(131 in. w.b.)

W200	Chassis & Cab	3760	3810	Note 6
W200	Utiline Pickup	3914	4240	Note 6
W200	Sweptline Pickup	3914	4270	Note 6

(149 in. w.b.)

W200	Crew Cab — Chassis & Cab	4554	4145	Note 6
W200	Crew Cab — Utiline	4707	4490	Note 6
W200	Crew Cab — Sweptline	4707	4530	Note 6

NOTE 6: Total model year production: (131 in.) 13,948; (149 in.) 1,023.

W300 Series 4x4 — Custom — 1-Ton

(135 in. w.b.)

W300	Chassis & Cab	4442	4320	Note 7
W300	Utiline Pickup	4553	4515	Note 7
W300	Platform 9-1/2 ft.	4860	4977	Note 7
W300	Stake 9-1/2 ft.	4879	5275	Note 7

NOTE 7: Total model year production: 1,243.
NOTE 8: Weights and prices shown are for six-cylinder models.

1973 Dodge Club Cab Pickup (rear view)

ENGINES (STANDARD): Inline. Overhead valve. Slant six. Cast iron block. Bore & stroke: 3.4 x 4.125 in. Displacement: 224.7 cid. Compression ratio: 8.4:1. Brake horsepower: 140 gross at 3900 rpm (110 nhp at 4000 rpm). Taxable horsepower: 27.70. Torque: 215 lbs.-ft. gross at 1600 rpm (185 lbs.-ft. net at 2000 rpm). Four main bearings. Solid valve lifters.
ENGINES (STANDARD V-8): 90-degree. Overhead valve. V-8. Cast iron block. Bore & stroke: 3.91 x 3.312 in. Displacement: 318.1 cid. Compression ratio: 8.8:1. Brake horsepower: 210 gross at 4000 rpm (150 nhp at 4000 rpm). Taxable horsepower: 48.92. Torque: 318 lbs.-ft. gross at 2800 rpm (245 lbs.-ft. net at 1600 rpm). Five main bearings. Hydraulic valve lifters.
ENGINES (OPTIONAL ALL): 90-degree. Overhead valve. V-8. Cast iron block. Bore & stroke: 4.00 x 3.58 in. Displacement: 359.9 cid. Compression ratio: 8.4:1. Brake horsepower: 180 nhp at 4000 rpm. Taxable horsepower: 51.2. Torque: 295 lbs.-ft. net at 2400 rpm). Five main bearings. Hydraulic valve lifters.
ENGINES (OPTIONAL D100/D200/D300 ONLY): 90-degree. Overhead valve. V-8. Cast iron block. Bore & stroke: 4.34 x 3.37 in. Displacement: 400 cid. Compression ratio: 8.2:1. Brake horsepower: 200 nhp at 4000 rpm. Taxable horsepower: 60.3. Torque: 320 lbs.-ft. net at 2400 rpm). Five main bearings. Hydraulic valve lifters.
CHASSIS (B100): Wheelbase: 109 or 127 in. Tires: E78 x 15-B four-ply tires.
CHASSIS (B200): Wheelbase: 109 or 127 in. Tires: G78 x 15-B four-ply.
CHASSIS (B300): Wheelbase: 109 or 127 in. Tires: 8.00 x 16.5-C six-ply, except 8.00 x 16.5-D eight-ply on Maxivans.
CHASSIS (D100): Wheelbase: 115 or 131 in. Tires: G78 x 15-D four-ply.
CHASSIS (D200): Wheelbase: 131 or 149 in. Tires: 8.00 x 16.5-D eight-ply.
CHASSIS (D300): Wheelbase: 135, 159 or 165 in. Tires: 8.00 x 16.5 eight-ply, except dual rear wheels crew cab has 8.00 x 16.5-C six-ply.
CHASSIS (W100): Wheelbase: 115 or 131 in. Tires: G78 x 15-B four-ply.

1973 Dodge Club Cab With El Dorado Camper (DNP)

Standard Catalog of Light-Duty Trucks

CHASSIS (W200): Wheelbase: 131 or 149 in. Tires: 8.00 x 16.5-D eight-ply.

CHASSIS (W300): Wheelbase: 135 inches. Tires: 8.75 x 16.5-E ten-ply.

TECHNICAL: Selective sliding gear transmission. Speeds: 3F/1R (column), except D300/W300/D200 with 165 in. wheelbase have 4F/1R (floor). Single disc dry clutch. 25-gallon fuel tank, except vans (26-gallon). Alternator. Automatic transmission optional.

OPTIONS: Same as 1972, with the addition of the following: (B series Vans) Front disc brakes. Low-mount mirrors (painted or chrome). In-cab hood release lock. (D100-300, W100-300) Carpeting on Club Cabs, black only. Inside hood release. Camper 7500 and 9000 package (D/W200).

1973 Dodge Townsman KarryVan (OCW)

HISTORICAL: Introduced: August, 1972. Calendar year sales: 332,751. Calendar year production: 377,555. Model year production: 414,709 (including 51,154 passenger vans and 16,862 D200 Club Cab models). Innovations: Roomy Club Cab model and tall Kary Van. Despite a severe parts shortage and 10-day strike in the fourth quarter, Dodge set new truck sales and production records for the third straight year. Calendar year production gained almost 16 percent, while sales were up 15.2 percent. Still, Dodge's market share slipped a bit, to 12.56 percent. The Warren, Michigan factory produced 282,136 trucks; the Fenton, Missouri plant turned out 137,310 units; and 22,570 were built in Windsor, Ontario (Canada). Gasoline V-8 engines accounted for 88.6 percent of total gas engine production. Only 3,103 diesel engines were installed in 1973. Dodge continued its leadership role in manufacturing motor home chassis, completing 300 special nationwide Recreational Vehicle Service Centers. Dodge also put on the road five mobile emergency RV service vans, which operated in key camping areas to provide free servicing. Truck dealers offered a free pickup truck cap on some specially-equipped D100 Adventurer models with 131 in. wheelbase. During the year, George F. Butts, who had been with Chrysler Corp. since 1949, was appointed General Manager of Dodge Truck operations.

1973 Dodge Sportsman Passenger Van (OCW)

1973 Dodge Royal Sportsman Passenger Van (DNP)

1974 DODGE

1974 Dodge Club Cab Pickup (JAG)

1/2-TON VAN — B100 SERIES — SIX-CYLINDER/V-8; 3/4-TON VAN — B200 SERIES — SIX-CYLINDER/V-8; 1-TON VAN — B300 SERIES — SIX-CYLINDER/V-8; 1-TON KARY VAN — CB300 SERIES — SIX-CYLINDER/V-8: No major change hit the van lineup for 1974, other than the addition of a sliding side door for 127 in. wheelbase models and Maxivans. A redesigned grille gave a new frontal appearance and vans were available in nine new colors. As before, base engine was the 225 cid slant six, with 318 and 360 cid V-8 engines optional. The Kary Van continued as introduced in 1973, with the same new features as other vans. Vacuum booster brakes with 9 in. dual diaphragm were standard on B200 and B300 models, optional on the 1/2-ton.

1974 Dodge D100 Sweptline Pickup (RPZ)

1/2-TON — D100 SERIES — SIX-CYLINDER/V-8; 3/4-TON — D200 SERIES — SIX-CYLINDER/V-8; 1-TON — D300 SERIES — SIX-CYLINDER/V-8; 1/2-TON 4x4 — W100 SERIES — SIX-CYLINDER/V-8; 3/4-TON 4x4 — W200 SERIES — SIX-CYLINDER/V-8; 1-TON 4x4 — W300 SERIES — SIX-CYLINDER/V-8: Dodge had completely redesigned its light truck line two years before, so little was new for 1974. The very popular Club Cab, introduced in 1973, was now also available on W100 and W200 four-wheel drive models. A new grille changed appearance slightly, and nine new paint colors were added. An optional 440 cid V-8 engine replaced the 400 cid V-8. Electronic ignition was now standard on all models. The fuel tank on D models, formerly behind the seat, was now inside the frame rail just ahead of the left wheelwell. An optional fuel tank went behind the seat. Adventurer and Adventurer Sport trim packages now had an all-vinyl seat available as an option. Conventional seats featured full foam construction. A new coolant recovery system was optional. Base engine remained the 225 cid slant six, with three V-8 options: 318, 360 and 440 cid. Four trim options were available, as before: Custom, Adventurer, Adventurer Sport and Adventurer Special Edition (SE). In spring 1974, a new dual-wheel 1-ton pickup was announced, with Sweptline box. Rated 10,000 lbs. GVW, it came with conventional cab on 131 in. wheelbase or Club Cab on 149 in. wheelbase, with payload ratings up to 5,200 lbs.

1/2-TON RAMCHARGER 4x4 — AW100 SERIES — V-8: The long-awaited Dodge sport-utility vehicle arrived in March 1974. Called the "Rhino" during development stages, it became Ramcharger. Marketing people feared the original name would not suggest an agile, nimble, go-anywhere vehicle. Designed for commuting and personal use, the Ramcharger was sporty and luxurious. It appealed to affluent suburban drivers. Research showed that only 10-15 percent of buyers would take their vehicles off-road. High priority was placed on comfort, handling and riding quality, as well as such luxury accessories as automatic transmission and air conditioning. As many existing, proven components as possible were used to cut costs and shorten the development cycle. All front-end sheetmetal, the dashboard and many other parts came from Dodge pickups. Considerable off-road ability was provided with a full-time four-wheel drive system. Dodge used the NP203 full-time, two-speed transfer case from Chrysler's New Process Div. Dodge's product development people, expecting Ramchargers to be driven by women, directed that the styling look rugged but not too truck-like. Ramchargers rode on a 106 in. wheelbase chassis and featured the biggest V-8 (440 cid) available in any sport-utility vehicle. The slant six engine was not available. Standard equipment included twin armrests, ashtray, power brakes, front disc brakes, chrome bumpers, 318 cid base V-8 engine, chrome grille, glove box door, heater/defroster, painted hubcaps, padded dash, 5x7 in. chrome mirrors, day/night inside mirror, driver's bucket seat and color-keyed sun visor, and two-speed wipers.

1974 Dodge Crew Cab Sweptline Power Wagon (RPZ)

I.D. DATA: Serial numbers were on the left door lock pillar and consisted of 13 symbols. The first two symbols are the model code. The third symbol denotes the type of unit (conventional, Crew Cab, Club Cab, etc.). The fourth indicated GVW class. The fifth symbol denotes the engine. The sixth symbol denotes the year (4=1974). The seventh symbol denotes the assembly plant. The last six symbols are the sequential production number.

1974 Dodge Forward Control Kary Van (RPZ)

Model	Body Type	Price	Weight	Prod. Total
AW100 Ramcharger four-wheel drive — 1/2-Ton — GVW: 4,900-6,000 lbs.				
(106 in. w.b.)				
AW100	No top	4077	4085	15,810
B100 Van Series — 1/2-Ton — GVW: 4,600-4,800 lbs.				
(109 in. w.b.)				
B100-6	Van	3113	3435	39,684
(127 in. w.b.)				
B100-6	Van	3242	3550	21,364
B200 Van Series — 3/4-Ton — GVW: 5,500-6,000 lbs.				
(109 in. w.b.)				
B200-6	Van	3238	3485	13,271
(127 in. w.b.)				
B200-6	Van	3360	3610	62,257
B200-6	Maxivan	3556	—	
B300 Van Series — 1-Ton — GVW: 6,200-8,200 lbs.				
(109 in. w.b.)				
B300-6	Van	3369	3675	835
(127 in. w.b.)				
B300-6	Van	3498	3805	42,652
B300-6	Maxivan	3727	4000	—
CB300	Kary Van 10 ft.	4346	4660	5332
(145 in. w.b.)				
CB300	Kary Van 12 ft.	4618	5110	1267
D100 Series — Custom — 1/2-Ton — GVW: 5,000-5,500 lbs.				
(115 in. w.b.)				
D100	Chassis & Cab	2947	3145	Note 1
D100	Utiline Pickup	3103	3490	Note 1
D100	Sweptline Pickup	3103	3515	Note 1
(131 in. w.b.)				
D100	Chassis & Cab	2982	3160	Note 1
D100	Utiline Pickup	3137	3490	Note 1
D100	Sweptline Pickup	3137	3620	Note 1

NOTE 1: Total model year production, (115 in.): 16,852; (131 in.) 55,782.

Model	Body Type	Price	Weight	Prod. Total
D100 Series Club Cab — Custom — 1/2-Ton — GVW: 5,000-5,500 lbs.				
(133 in. w.b.)				
D100	Sweptline Pickup	3349	3730	3657
(149 in. w.b.)				
D100	Sweptline Pickup	3383	3870	17,173

D200 Series — Custom — 3/4-Ton — GVW: 6,200-9,000 lbs.

(131 in. w.b.)

D200	Chassis & Cab	3291	3325	Note 2
D200	Utiline Pickup	3448	3755	Note 2
D200	Sweptline Pickup	3448	3785	Note 2

NOTE 2: Total model year production: 19,924.

D200 Series Club Cab — Custom — 3/4-Ton — GVW: 6,200-9,000 lbs.

(149 in. w.b.)

D100	Sweptline Pickup	3694	3955	Note 3

D200 Crew Cab — Custom — 3/4-Ton — GVW: 6,200-9,000 lbs.

(149 in. w.b.)

D200	Chassis & Cab	4060	3725	Note 3
D200	Utiline Pickup	4217	4070	Note 3
D200	Sweptline Pickup	4217	4095	Note 3

(165 in. w.b.)

D200	Chassis & Cab	4290	4095	Note 3
D200	Utiline Pickup	4455	4525	Note 3
D200	Sweptline Pickup	4455	4555	Note 3

NOTE 3: Total model year production: (149 in., Club Cab and Crew Cab) 14,244; (165 in. Crew Cab) 1,400.

D300 Series — Custom — 1-Ton — GVW: 6,600-10,000 lbs.

(135 in. w.b.)

D300	Chassis & Cab	3467	3735	Note 4
D300	Utiline Pickup	3584	—	Note 4

(149 in. w.b.)

D300	Club Cab — Chassis & Cab	3960	—	461

(159 in. w.b.)

D300	Chassis & Cab	3505	3880	3990

(165 in. w.b.)

D300	Crew Cab — Chassis & Cab	4425	—	197

NOTE 4: Total model year production: (135 in.) 7,198.

W100 Series 4x4 — Custom — 1/2-Ton — GVW: 5,100-5,600 lbs.

(115 in. w.b.)

W100	Chassis & Cab	3588	3780	Note 5
W100	Utiline Pickup	3745	4125	Note 5
W100	Sweptline Pickup	3745	4150	Note 5

(131 in. w.b.)

W100	Chassis & Cab	3621	3790	Note 5
W100	Utiline Pickup	3782	4220	Note 5
W100	Sweptline Pickup	3782	4250	Note 5

NOTE 5: Total model year production: (115 in.) 7,036; (131 in.) 11,923.

W100 Series Club Cab 4x4 — Custom — 1/2-Ton — GVW: 5,100-5,600 lbs.

(133 in. w.b.)

W100	Sweptline Pickup	3991	—	1830

(149 in. w.b.)

W100	Sweptline Pickup	4028	—	3031

W200 Series 4x4 — Custom — 3/4-Ton — GVW: 6,500-8,000 lbs.

(131 in. w.b.)

W200	Chassis & Cab	4083	3845	Note 6
W200	Utiline Pickup	4237	4275	Note 6
W200	Sweptline Pickup	4237	4305	Note 6

NOTE 6: Total model year production: (131 in.) 14,549.

(149 in. w.b.)

W200	Club Cab — Sweptline	4483	4505	Note 7

W200 Crew Cab 4x4 — Custom — 3/4-Ton — GVW: 6,500-8,000 lbs.

(149 in. w.b.)

W200	Chassis & Cab	4952	4245	Note 7
W200	Utiline Pickup	5105	4590	Note 7
W200	Sweptline Pickup	5105	4615	Note 7

NOTE 7: Total model year production: (149 in. Club Cabs and Crew Cabs): 5,895.

W300 Series 4x4 — Custom — 1-Ton — GVW: 8,500-10,000 lbs.

(135 in. w.b.)

W300	Chassis & Cab	4888	4380	Note 8
W300	Utiline Pickup	4999	—	Note 8

NOTE 8: Total model year production: 1,867,
NOTE 9: Weights and prices shown are for six-cylinder. models. For V-8 engine (318 cid) add 100 lbs. to weight and $113 to $167 to price (depending on series).

1974 Dodge D100 Utiline Pickup (RPZ)

ENGINE (Standard: all models except AW100): Inline. Overhead valve. Slant six. Cast iron block. Bore & stroke: 3.4 x 4.125 in. Displacement: 224.7 cid. Compression ratio: 8.4:1. Brake horsepower: 110 (net) at 4000 rpm. Taxable horsepower: 27.70. Torque: 185 lbs.-ft. (net) at 2000 rpm. Four main bearings. Solid valve lifters.
ENGINE (Standard V-8: all models): 90-degree, overhead valve. V-8. Cast iron block. Bore & stroke: 3.91 x 3.31 in. Displacement: 318.1 cid. Compression ratio: 8.8:1. Brake horsepower: 150 (net) at 4000 rpm. Taxable horsepower: 48.92. Torque: 245 lbs.-ft. (net) at 1600 rpm. Five main bearings. Hydraulic valve lifters.
ENGINE (Optional: all models): 90-degree, overhead valve. V-8. Cast iron block. Bore & stroke: 4.00 x 3.58 in. Displacement: 359.9 cid. Compression ratio: 8.4:1. Brake horsepower: 180 (net) at 4000 rpm. Taxable horsepower: 51.2. Torque: 295 lbs.-ft. (net) at 2400 rpm. Five main bearings. Hydraulic valve lifters.

1974 Dodge Club Cab Sweptline Pickup (JAG)

ENGINE (Optional AW100 only): 90-degree, overhead valve. V-8. Cast iron block. Bore & stroke: 4.34 x 3.38 in. Displacement: 400 cid. Compression ratio: 8.2:1. Brake horsepower: 185 (net) at 4000 rpm. Taxable horsepower: 60.3. Torque: 305 lbs.-ft. (net) at 2400 rpm. Five main bearings. Hydraulic valve lifters.
ENGINE (Optional AW100/D100-300): 90-degree, overhead valve. V-8. Cast iron block. Bore & stroke: 4.32 x 3.75 in. Displacement: 440 cid. Compression ratio: 8.12:1. Brake horsepower: 230 (net) at 4000 rpm. Taxable horsepower: 59.7. Torque: 350 lbs.-ft. (net) at 3200 rpm. Five main bearings. Hydraulic valve lifters.

1974 Dodge B200 Tradesman Maxivan (RPZ)

CHASSIS (B100 Van): Wheelbase: 109 in. or 127 in. Tires: E78 x 15-B four-ply. GVW: 4,600 lbs.
CHASSIS (B200 Van): Wheelbase: 109 in. or 127 in. Tires: G78 x 15-B four-ply except (Maxivan) H78 x 15-B four-ply. GVW: 5,500 lbs.
CHASSIS: (B300 Van): Wheelbase: 109 in. or 127 in. Tires: 8.00 x 16.5-C six-ply except (Maxivan) 8.00 x 16.5-D eight-ply. GVW: 6,400 lbs.
CHASSIS (CB300 Kary Van): Wheelbase: 127 in. or 145 in. Tires: 8.75 x 16.5-E ten-ply. GVW: 7,700 lbs.
CHASSIS (D100): Wheelbase: 115 in. or 131 in. (Club Cab, 133 in. and 149 in.). Tires: G78 x 15-D four-ply. GVW: 5,000 lbs.
CHASSIS (D200): Wheelbase: 131 in., 149 in. (Crew Cab), or 165 in. Tires: 8.00 x 16.5-D eight-ply. GVW: 6,200 lbs.
CHASSIS (D300): Wheelbase: 135 in., 149 in. (Club Cab), 159 in. or 165 in. (Crew Cab). Tires: (135 in.) 8.00 x 16.5-D eight-ply; (others) 8.00 x 16.5-C eight-ply. GVW: 6,600 lbs.
CHASSIS (W100): Wheelbase: 115 in. or 131 in. (Club Cab, 133 in. or 149 in.). Tires: H78 x 15-B or G78 x 15-B. GVW: 5,400 lbs.
CHASSIS (W200): Wheelbase: 131 in. or 149 in. (Club or Crew Cab). Tires: 8.00 x 16.5-D eight-ply. GVW: 6,500 lbs.
CHASSIS (W300): Wheelbase: 135 in. Tires: 8.75 x 16.5-E ten-ply. GVW: 8,500 lbs.
CHASSIS (AW100 Ramcharger): Wheelbase: 106 in. Tires: E78 x 15-B four-ply. GVW: 4,900 lbs.

1974 Dodge Ramcharger SE Utility Wagon (CHC)

TECHNICAL: Selective sliding gear transmission. Speeds: 3F/1R except (D300, W300 and 165 in. wheelbase D200) 4F/1R. Column or floor (four-speed) shift control. Single disc dry clutch: (six-cylinder). 10 in.; (V-8) 11 in. Rear axle ratio: (AW100 Ramcharger) .3.90:1 (318 cid V-8 only); 3.55:1 or 3.23:1. Hydraulic four-wheel brakes: Front disc, rear drum. Fuel tank: (B vans) 23-gallon; (AW100) 24-gallon; (others) 22-gallon. Alternator: (Vans, AW100) 48 amp; (others) 41 amp. Automatic three-speed transmission optional.

1974 Dodge Sportsman Van (JAG)

OPTIONS: Same as 1972-73, except for the addition of the following: (B Vans) Brake vacuum booster (B100). Sliding cargo door. Banded glass in front doors and wing vents (B200-300). Glove box door and light. Heavy-duty package (B300). Chrome wheelcovers (B100-200). (D100-300, W100-300) Power brakes (D100). Heavy-duty drum brakes (D/W200-300 with 131 or 149 in. w.b.) 440 cid V-8 engine (D100-200). Chrome grip rails atop pickup box (D100-200 8 ft. Sweptline only). Two-tone paint (3 different procedures). Flip-type seat (D/W100-200 Club Cabs). (AW100 Ramcharger) Front bumper guards. Step rear bumper. Air conditioner. Cigarette lighter. Electric clock. Console. Deluxe trim. Color-keyed carpet. Tinted windshield. Tinted glass. Vented, tinted glass. Inside hood latch release. Dual horns. Chrome hubcaps. 7-1/2 x 10-1/2 in. chrome mirrors. Oil pressure gauge. Removable hardtop roof:color, white, or vinyl-textured white. Convenience package. Exterior trim molding package. SE package. Trailer-towing package. Monotone paint. Two-tone paint. Radio (AM or AM/FM). Power steering. Roll bar. Vinyl textured black roof. Passenger's bucket seat. Two deluxe front bucket seats. Passenger bucket seat and rear bench seat. Deluxe bucket seats and rear bench seat. Shoulder belts (driver's or pair). Skid plates (fuel tank or transfer case). Cruise control. Heavy-duty shock absorbers (front and rear). Electric tachometer. Hand throttle. Outside-mounted spare tire. Chrome wheelcovers. 55 or 72-amp. alternator. Anti-spin rear axle (3.55:1 or 3.90:1 ratio). Increased cooling capacity. 35-gallon fuel tank. Engine block heater. 360-cid V-8 engine. 400-cid V-8 engine. 440-cid V-8 engine. NP435 four-speed manual transmission. NP445 four-speed transmission. A727 three-speed automatic transmission.

HISTORICAL: Introduced: August, 1973. (Ramcharger, March, 1974). Calendar year sales: 292,213. Calendar year production: 362,008. Model year production: 404,619 (including 58,669 passenger vans, 5,025 Plymouth Trailbusters, and 12,609 D200 Club Cabs). Innovations: Ramcharger sport-utility model. Dodge truck sales and production saw a downturn in 1974, due to the petroleum crisis and a general slowdown in the economy. Dodge had been the industry leader in supplying chassis to the recreational vehicle industry. When the RV business collapsed because of high gas prices, Dodge lost its 85 percent share of that market. By year's end, most of the small camper manufacturers were out of business. Calendar year truck sales declined 10.1 percent; production 4.1 percent. Dodge's biggest loss was in the 10,000 to 14,000 lbs. GVW class: 1974 production fell to 6,841, from 40,086 the year before. Because of the fuel crisis, the six-cylinder engine made a comeback, increasing from 9.3 percent of total gas engine sales in 1973 to 17.5 percent in 1974. Four-wheel drive production was good, as this market remained strong. Dodge built a total of 43,324 four-wheel drive trucks, plus 10,037 Ramchargers (which counted as passenger cars). Another 57,500 Dodge Sportsman and Plymouth Voyager passenger vans were made in 1974, also counted as passenger cars. Dodge produced many trucks at its Windsor, Ontario facility (25,328 in 1974), because of a trade agreement between the two countries. Truck makers could assemble some vehicles north of the border for sale in the U.S., and could then sell U.S.-made trucks in Canada, without paying duties either way. All Dodge medium-duty trucks were made in Canada. The Warren, Michigan factory turned out 246,119 trucks; the Sherwood Avenue (Detroit) facility built 4,995 conventional trucks; 77,899 came from Fenton, Missouri; and another 17,416 knocked-down units for export were built. Dodge introduced an all new, contemporary styled medium-duty truck line. Vans and the new sport-utility vehicle were also sold by Plymouth dealers, carrying the Plymouth nameplate. They differed from Dodge models only in trim details. Dodge began work on a new truck facility in Pennyslvania, but shelved it because of uncertainty due to the oil crisis.

1975 DODGE

1/2-TON VAN — B100 SERIES — SIX-CYLINDER/V-8; 3/4-TON VAN — B200 SERIES — SIX-CYLINDER/V-8; 1-TON VAN — B300 SERIES — SIX-CYLINDER/V-8; 1-TON KARY VAN — CB300 SERIES — SIX-CYLINDER/V-8: Changes to the van line were minimal. A new optional one-piece rear door gave the back of the van an uncluttered look, made loading easier, and offered the driver a better view of the road behind. A package of more durable, heavy-duty interior trim materials was offered as an option to those owners who gave their van interiors hard service. Dodge offered a system of 50 GVW packages, covering vans as well as D and W series trucks and Ramchargers. These packages were designed to eliminate the need for dealers to specify in detail each new unit ordered from the factory. Instead, each truck ordered with a specific GVW package came equipped with the correct tires, springs, and other required components. If the buyer desired or required a part different from that in a standard package, that item could be individually coded.

1975 Dodge Ramcharger SE Utility (DNP)

1/2-TON — D100 SERIES — SIX-CYLINDER/V-8; 3/4-TON — D200 SERIES — SIX-CYLINDER/V-8; 1-TON — D300 SERIES — SIX-CYLINDER/V-8; 1/2-TON 4x4 — W100 SERIES — SIX-CYLINDER/V-8; 3/4-TON 4x4 — W200 SERIES — SIX-CYLINDER/V-8; 1-TON 4x4 — W300 SERIES — SIX-CYLINDER/V-8: For the first time in five years, Dodge did not introduce a major new light-duty truck. Between 1971 and 1974, Dodge had introduced a new van line, an all new light-duty line, the Club Cab pickup and, finally, the Ramcharger. This year's emphasis went toward refining an already broad light-duty lineup. A new instrument panel appeared on pickups. Appearance changes included new side moldings. Club Cab pickups, formerly offered in a choice of three interior trim colors, now had five. Full time four-wheel drive from Chrysler's New Process Gear Division was made standard on all W Series pickups. W100 and W200 suspensions were completely reworked to give a much more pleasant, smooth and easy ride. This was accomplished by changing spring geometry to more closely coincide with that of the Ramcharger. In addition, longer front springs were used, spring rates were softer, and new shocks were added. Vehicle height was reduced one inch. A new optional sway bar was also available for four-wheel drives, to reduce lean and increase understeer for better control through turns. The big 440 cid V-8 became optional for four-wheel drives. All 1975 Dodge trucks with a GVW rating below 6,000 lbs. carried a catalytic converter to meet new EPA emission standards.

1/2-TON RAMCHARGER 2WD — AD100 SERIES — SIX-CYLINDER/V-8; 1/2-TON RAMCHARGER 4x4 — AW100 SERIES — SIX-CYLINDER/V-8: For 1975, a two-wheel drive Ramcharger was added on the same 106 inch wheelbase, but 2-1/2 inches lower than the four-wheel drive. Ramchargers also received the pickup's new instrument panel, which could accommodate an optional clock, tachometer or combination vacuum-voltmeter gauges. To improve instrument readability, the cluster was wing-shaped with its hood redesigned to minimize glare. New interior door trim panels in high-line models included map pockets. The standard Ramcharger had a single driver's seat; a rear bench seat was optional. The SE package included carpeting, simulated woodgrain inserts, vinyl map pockets and front bucket seats, plus a lockable center console with removable canned-drink ice chest and storage area for cups, pencils, coins and maps. The slant six was made the base engine. Ramcharger roofs were optional. A dealer-installed soft top could be lowered or its rear and side panels would roll up. A removable steel roof could be ordered in white or in any of the 14 standard colors.

I.D. DATA: Serial numbers were on a vehicle identification plate attached to the driver's doorlatch post. Vehicle Identification Numbers (VIN) consisted of 13 letters and numbers, divided into seven elements. The first two characters indicated model code. Model code index: D1=D100; D2=D200; D3=D300; W1=W100; W2=W200; W3=W300; B1=B100; B2=B200; B3=B300; P1=P100; P2=P200 or P3=P300 forward-control.The next digit showed body type. Body type index: 0=forward control chassis; 1=conventional cab; 2=Crew Cab; 3=Utiline conventional cab; 4=Sweptline conventional cab; 5=Utiline Crew Cab; 6=Sweptline Crew Cab; 7=flat face cowl or Sweptline Club Cab; 8=Club Cab. The next letter designated GVW rating. GVW index: A=6,000 lbs. or less); B=6,001 to 10,000 lbs.; C=10,001 to 14,000 lbs.; D=14,000 to 16,000 lbs. etc. Next came a letter for engine type. Engine type index: B=225-1V; C=225-2V; D=440; E=318-1; F=360; G=318-3; X=Special 6; Y=Special V-8. The next digit gave model year (5=1975). The next letter indicated assembly plant: J=Windsor; S=Warren Plant No. 1; T=Warren Plant No. 2; X=Missouri. At the end came a six-digit sequence number at that assembly plant; all models began with sequence number 000,001. Engine numbers were located as follows: (225 cid six) right side of block, below No. 1 spark plug; (318 or 360 cid V-8) left front of block, below cylinder head; (440 V-8) left side of block, adjacent to front tappet rail. The first digit gave model year. The next letter indicated assembly plant (M=Mound Road). The next three digits showed displacement in cubic inches. Next came a four-digit date code, followed by a four-digit sequence number. Starting engine numbers are not available.

Model	Body Type	Price	Weight	Prod. Total
AD100/AW100 Ramcharger — 1/2-Ton — GVW: 4,600-6,100 lbs.				
(106 in. w.b.)				
AD100	4x2 without top	—	3560	1674
AW100	4x4 without top	—	4075	11,361
B100 Series Van — 1/2-Ton — GVW: 4,600-5,200 lbs.				
(109 in. w.b.)				
B100-6	Van	3202	3435	31,516
(127 in. w.b.)				
B100-6	Van	3335	3435	12,522
B200 Series Van — 3/4-Ton — GVW: 5,500-6,100 lbs.				
(109 in. w.b.)				
B200-6	Van	3331	3485	22,431
(127 in. w.b.)				
B200-6	Van	3456	3610	22,998
B200-6	Maxivan	3658	—	11,926
B300 Series Van — 1-Ton — GVW: 6,400-7,700 lbs.				
(109 in. w.b.)				
B300-6	Van	3465	3675	850

B300-6	Van	3598	3805	6638
B300-6	Maxivan	3834	4000	10,071
CB300	Kary Van 10 ft.	4776	4660	889

(145 in. w.b.)

CB300	Kary Van 12 ft.	5056	5110	2239

D100 Series — Custom — 1/2-Ton — 5,000-6,100 lbs.

(115 in. w.b.)

D100	Chassis & Cab	3051	3145	Note 1
D100	Utiline Pickup	3212	3490	Note 1
D100	Sweptline Pickup	3212	3515	Note 1

(131 in. w.b.)

D100	Chassis & Cab	3087	3160	Note 1
D100	Utiline Pickup	3247	3490	Note 1
D100	Sweptline Pickup	3247	3620	Note 1

NOTE 1: Total model year production, (115 in.): 20,921; (131 in.) 47,226.

D100 Series Club Cab — Custom — 1/2-Ton — 5,000-6,100 lbs.

(133 in. w.b.)

D100	Sweptline Pickup	3465	3730	2166

(149 in. w.b.)

D100	Sweptline Pickup	3500	3870	10,025

D200 Series — Custom — 3/4-Ton — 6,200-9,000 lbs.

(131 in. w.b.)

D200	Chassis & Cab	3385	3325	Note 2
D200	Utiline Pickup	3547	3755	Note 2
D200	Sweptline Pickup	3547	3785	Note 2

NOTE 2: Total model year production: 17,056.

D200 Series Club Cab — Custom — 3/4-Ton — 6,200-9,000 lbs.

(149 in. w.b.)

D200	Sweptline Pickup	3800	3955	7152

D200 Crew Cab — Custom — 3/4-Ton — 6,200-9,000 lbs.

(149 in. w.b.)

D200	Chassis & Cab	4176	3725	Note 3
D200	Utiline Pickup	4338	4070	Note 3
D200	Sweptline Pickup	4338	4095	Note 3

(165 in. w.b.)

D200	Chassis & Cab	4413	4095	Note 3
D200	Utiline Pickup	4583	4525	Note 3
D200	Sweptline Pickup	4583	4555	Note 3

NOTE 3: Total model year production: (149 in.) 1,935; (165 in.) 1,731.

D300 Series — Custom — 1-Ton — 6,600-11,000 lbs.

(131 in. w.b.)

D300	Sweptline Pickup	4230	—	570

(135 in. w.b.)

D300	Chassis & Cab	3556	3735	Note 4
D300	Utiline Pickup	3687	—	Note 4

(149 in. w.b.)

D300	Club Cab — Chassis & Cab	4073	—	Note 4
D300	Club Cab — Sweptline	4483	—	Note 4

(159 in. w.b.)

D300	Chassis & Cab	3605	3880	2770

(165 in. w.b.)

D300	Crew Cab — Chassis & Cab	4552	—	197

NOTE 4: Total model year production: (135 in.) 6,560; (149 in.) 687.

W100 Series 4x4 — Custom — 1/2-Ton — GVW: 5,400-6,100 lbs.

(115 in. w.b.)

W100	Chassis & Cab	3784	3780	Note 5
W100	Utiline Pickup	3945	4125	Note 5
W100	Sweptline Pickup	3945	4150	Note 5

(131 in. w.b.)

W100	Chassis & Cab	3818	3790	Note 5
W100	Utiline Pickup	3983	4220	Note 5
W100	Sweptline Pickup	3983	4250	Note 5

NOTE 5: Total model year production: (115 in.) 10,652; (131 in.) 10,974.

W100 Series Club Cab 4x4 — Custom — 1/2-Ton)— GVW: 5,400-6,100 lbs.

(133 in. w.b.)

W100	Sweptline Pickup	4198		1868

149 in. w.b.

W100	Sweptline Pickup	4236		2776

W200 Series 4x4 — Custom — 3/4-Ton

(131 in. w.b.)

W200	Chassis & Cab	4280	3845	Note 6
W200	Utiline Pickup	4438	4275	Note 6
W200	Sweptline Pickup	4438	4305	Note 6

(149 in. w.b.)

W200	Club Cab — Sweptline	4691	4505	4179

NOTE 6: Total model year production (131 in.) 13,615.

W200 Crew Cab 4x4 — Custom — 3/4-Ton — GVW: 6,500-8,000 lbs.

(149 in. w.b.)

W200	Chassis & Cab	5174	4245	Note 7
W200	Utiline Pickup	5331	4590	Note 7
W200	Sweptline Pickup	5331	4615	Note 7

NOTE 7: Total model year production: 1,683.

W300 Series 4x4 — Custom — 1-Ton — GVW: 6,600-10,000 lbs.

(135 in. w.b.)

W300	Chassis & Cab	5108	4380	Note 8
W300	Utiline Pickup	5222	—	Note 8

NOTE 8: Total model year production: 2,183.

NOTE 9: Weights and prices shown are for six-cylinder models. For V-8 engine (318 cid) add 100 lbs. to weight and $116 to $172 to price (depending on series).

ENGINE (Standard: all models): Inline. Overhead valve. Slant six. Cast iron block. Bore & stroke: 3.4 x 4.125 in. Displacement: 224.8 cid. Compression ratio: 8.4:1. Brake horsepower: 95 (net) at 3600 rpm. Taxable horsepower: 27.70. Torque: 175 lbs.-ft. (net) at 2000 rpm. Four main bearings. Solid valve lifters.

ENGINE (Standard V-8: all models): 90-degree, overhead valve. V-8. Cast iron block. Bore & stroke: 3.91 x 3.31 in. Displacement: 318.3 cid. Compression ratio: 8.6:1. Brake horsepower: 150 (net) at 4000 rpm. Taxable horsepower: 48.92. Torque: 255 lbs.-ft. (net) at 2000 rpm. Five main bearings. Hydraulic valve lifters.

ENGINE (Optional V-8: all except B100): 90-degree, overhead valve. V-8. Cast iron block. Bore & stroke: 4.00 x 3.58 in. Displacement: 360 cid. Compression ratio: 8.4:1. Brake horsepower: 175 (net) at 4000 rpm. Taxable horsepower: 51.2. Torque: 285 lbs.-ft. (net) at 2400 rpm. Five main bearings. Hydraulic valve lifters.

ENGINE (Optional V-8: D100-300, W100-300, AW100): 90-degree, overhead valve. V-8. Cast iron block. Bore & stroke: 4.32 x 3.75 in. Displacement: 440 cid. Compression ratio: 8.2:1. Brake horsepower: 235 (net) at 4000 rpm. Taxable horsepower: 58.55. Torque: 340 lbs.-ft. (net) at 2400 rpm. Five main bearings. Hydraulic valve lifters.

CHASSIS (AD100 4x2 Ramcharger): Wheelbase: 106 in. Tires: (six) H78 x 15-B four-ply; (V-8) E78 x 15-B four-ply. GVW: 4,900 lbs.

CHASSIS (AW100 4x4 Ramcharger): Wheelbase: 106 in. Tires: (six) H78 x 15-B four-ply; (V-8) E78 x 15-B four-ply. GVW: 4,900 lbs. [Six-cylinder. model rated 6,100 lbs. GVW.]

CHASSIS (B100): Wheelbase: 109 in. or 127 in. Tires: E78 x 15-B four-ply. GVW: 4,600 lbs.

CHASSIS (B200): Wheelbase: 109 in. or 127 in. Tires: G78 x 15-B four-ply except (Maxi-van) H78 x 15-B four-ply. GVW: 5,500 lbs.

CHASSIS (B300): Wheelbase: 109 in. or 127 in. Tires: 8.00 x 16.5-C six-ply except (Maxi-van) 8.00 x 16.5-D eight-ply. GVW: 6,400 lbs.

CHASSIS (CB300): Wheelbase: 127 in. or 145 in. Tires: 8.75 x 16.5-E ten-ply. GVW: 7,700 lbs.

CHASSIS (D100): Wheelbase: 115 in. or 131 in. (Club Cab, 133 or 149 in.). Tires: G78 x 15-D four-ply. GVW: 5,000 lbs.

CHASSIS (D200): Wheelbase: 131 in., 149 in. or 165 in. Tires: 8.00 x 16.5-D eight-ply. GVW: 6,200 lbs.

CHASSIS (D300): Wheelbase: 131 in., 135 in., 149 in., 159 in. or 165 in. Tires: (131 in. and 135 in.), 8.00 x 16.5-D eight-ply; (others) 8.00 x 16.5-C eight-ply. GVW: 6,600 lbs.

CHASSIS (W100): Wheelbase: 115 in. or 131 in. (Club Cab, 133 or 149 in.). Tires: (six) H78 x 15-B, (V-8) G78 x 15-B. GVW: 5,400 lbs.

CHASSIS (W200): Wheelbase: 131 in. or 149 in. Tires: 8.00 x 16.5-D eight-ply. GVW: 6,500 lbs.

CHASSIS (W300): Wheelbase: 135 in. Tires: 8.75 x 16.5-E ten-ply. GVW: 8,500 lbs.

TECHNICAL: Selective sliding gear transmission. Speeds: 3F/1R except (D300, W300 and 165 in. w.b. D200) 4F/1R. Column or floor (four-speed) shift control. Automatic 3-speed transmission optional. Single disc dry clutch: (six-cylinder) 10 in.; (V-8) 11 in. Rear axle ratio: (AW100 Ramcharger) 3.23:1, 3.55:1 or 3.90:1. Hydraulic four-wheel brakes: Front disc, rear drum. Fuel tank: (B vans) 23-gallon; (AW100) 24-gallon; (others) 22-gallon. Alternator: 48 amp.

OPTIONS: Same list as 1974, with the addition of the following: (B Vans) Door edge protectors (front only). Single rear door with fixed glass. 36-gallon fuel tank. Full-length scuff pads (side step sill). Styled road wheels (B100-200, 15 in.). (D100-300, W100-300) Carpeting (conventional cabs). Transmission oil cooler. 8-gallon auxiliary fuel tank, behind rear axle. 24-gallon auxiliary tank, in cab behind seat. Chrome styled road wheels (D100). Premium wheelcovers (D100). (Ramcharger) Transmission cooler. SE package. Protection package. Convenience package. Exterior trim molding package. Sno-fiter package. Trailer-towing package. Heavy-duty trailer-towing package. Plow lights. Deluxe wheelcovers.

HISTORICAL: Introduced: August, 1974. Calendar year sales: 286,656. Calendar year production: 344,769 (in U.S. plants); 369,484 (total). Model year production: 336,946. Early in 1975 Dodge announced that it was pulling out of the heavy-duty truck market. Sales volume could not justify the expense needed to meet new or proposed federal regulations governing heavy-duty trucks. The 10 heavy-duty models dropped amounted to only 1.2 percent of all trucks produced. Despite this loss, then, 1975 was Dodge's second best production year in history. In addition to the 344,769 units produced in the U.S., 24,715 were built at Windsor, Ontario. Additionally, 52,330 Sportsman and Voyager vans were counted as passenger cars. A total of 23,988 knocked-down units were made for export. Dodge ranked number three in truck sales. Ramcharger four-wheel drive production for 1975 was 7,382, down from 10,037 in 1974, but sales rose to 10,547. Six-cylinder engines accounted for 15.8 percent of total truck sales. The U.S. Army adopted a plan to buy regular pickup trucks for military use. For years, the military had specified specialized vehicles, at considerable extra cost, for such non-military purposes as shuttling around Army bases in the U.S. Dodge won the first order under this new program. It was for 33,759 trucks. Normally list priced at around $5,200, the Army bought these trucks for $3,825 apiece.

1976 DODGE

1976 Dodge Royal Sportsman SE Van (DNP)

1976 Dodge Champion Sportsman mini-motorhome (DNP)

1/2-TON VAN — B100 SERIES — SIX-CYLINDER/V-8; 3/4-TON VAN — B200 SERIES — SIX-CYLINDER/V-8; 1-TON VAN — B300 SERIES — SIX-CYLINDER/V-8; 1-TON KARY VAN — CB300 SERIES — SIX-CYLINDER/V-8: Van models, though unchanged in appearance, gained a major improvement in ride quality through suspension system alterations and better noise suppression with an optional heavy-duty insulation package. A new transistorized system flashed a warning light when transmission fluid was low or overheated. To benefit from the large youth market for vans, a new Street Van appeared. It featured wide tires on sport wheels, cloth-and-vinyl Boca Raton upholstery on high-back bucket seats, carpeting, and a deluxe instrument panel with woodgrained inserts. Buyers also got a Customizing Idea Kit. This kit contained suggestions for exterior paint designs and color combinations, interior design schemes, stereo installation instructions, and a list of suppliers of portholes, roof vents, fender flares, and other accessories.

1/2-TON PICKUP — D100 SERIES — SIX-CYLINDER/V-8; 3/4-TON PICKUP — D200 SERIES — SIX-CYLINDER/V-8; 1-TON PICKUP — D300 SERIES — SIX-CYLINDER/V-8; 1/2-TON 4x4 — W100 SERIES — SIX-CYLINDER/V-8; 3/4-TON 4x4 — W200 SERIES — SIX-CYLINDER/V-8; 1-TON 4x4 — W300 SERIES — SIX-CYLINDER/V-8: The basic light-duty truck line, introduced in 1972, was carried over for the fifth year with few changes. New side moldings and a grille restyling from 1975 saw another year's service. Engineering improvements included raising the fuel tank up between the frame rails, ahead of the rear axle. This moved it from its former hanging position, where it had been at risk of puncture. Pickup rear suspensions were reworked to prevent the cargo box from tilting toward the back when fully loaded. Tie rods on all four-wheel drive models were raised to give greater ground clearance for off-road driving. Sweptline pickup boxes received more corrosion protection. The seatback on bench-seat models was hinged for access to storage space behind the seat. A glide-out spare tire carrier was mounted under the pickup box. Dodge continued to build a full line of light-duty trucks, including conventional cab, Club Cab and Crew Cab models. Base engine remained the 225 cid slant six, with 318, 360, 400 and 440 cid V-8s optional. An optional overdrive four-speed manual transmission for trucks under 5,500 lbs. GVW improved fuel economy.

1/2-TON RAMCHARGER 4x2 — AD100 SERIES — SIX-CYLINDER/V-8; 1/2-TON RAMCHARGER 4x4 — AW100 SERIES — SIX-CYLINDER/V-8: Unchanged in appearance, Ramcharger continued as a topless sport-utility vehicle, with both a soft top and steel top available as options. Both two-wheel and four-wheel drive models were offered. Tie rods were raised for greater ground clearance and the spare was moved from a horizontal position to a vertical position behind the rear seat. An optional external, swing-out spare tire mount was added. Most important was the re-engineered suspension, which delivered improved handling for both highway and off-road driving.

I.D. DATA: Serial numbers were on a vehicle identification plate attached to the driver's doorlatch post. Vehicle Identification Numbers (VIN) consisted of 13 letters and numbers, divided into seven elements. The first two characters indicated model code. Model code index: D1=D100; D2=D200; D3=D300; W1=W100; W2=W200; W3=W300; B1=B100; B2=B200; B3=B300; P1=P100; P2=P200 or P3=P300 forward-control. The next digit showed body type. Body type index: 0=forward control chassis; 1=conventional cab; 2=Crew Cab; 3=Utiline conventional cab; 4=Sweptline conventional cab; 5=Utiline Crew Cab; 6=Sweptline Crew Cab; 7=flat face cowl or Sweptline Club Cab; 8=Club Cab. The next letter designated GVW rating. GVW index: A=6,000 lbs. or less); B=6,001 to 10,000 lbs.; C=10,001 to 14,000 lbs.; D=14,000 to 16,000 lbs. etc. Next came a letter for engine type. Engine type index: B=225-1V; C=225-2V; D=440; E=318-1; F=360; G=318-3; X=Special 6; Y=Special V-8. The next digit gave model year (6=1976). The next letter indicated assembly plant: J=Windsor; S=Warren Plant No. 1; T=Warren Plant No. 2; X=Missouri. At the end came a six-digit sequence number at that assembly plant; all models began with sequence number 000,001. Engine numbers were located as follows: (225 cid six) right side of block, below No. 1 spark plug; (318 or 360 cid V-8) left front of block, below cylinder head; (440 V-8) left side of block, adjacent to front tappet rail. The first digit gave model year. The next letter indicated assembly plant (M=Mound Road). The next three digits showed displacement in cubic inches. Next came a four-digit date code, followed by a four-digit sequence number. Starting engine numbers are not available.

Model	Body Type	Price	Weight	Prod. Total
AD100/AW100 Ramcharger — 1/2-Ton — 106 in. w.b.				
AD100	4x2 without top	3702	3560	1700
AW100	4x4 without top	4640	4075	12,101
B100 Series Van — 1/2-Ton — 109 in. w.b.				
B100	Van	3876	3435	28,692
(127 in. w.b.)				
B100	Van	4009	3550	11,581
B200 Series Van — 3/4-Ton — 109 in. w.b.				
B200	Van	3943	3485	28,257
(127 in. w.b.)				
B200	Van	4083	3610	27,714
B200	Maxivan	4300	—	13,567
B300 Series Van — 1-Ton — 109 in. w.b.				
B300	Van	4156	3675	262
(127 in. w.b.)				
B300	Van	4279	3805	5650
B300	Maxivan	4509	4000	9536
CB300	Kary Van 10 ft.	5594	4660	863
(145 in. w.b.)				
CB300	Kary Van 12 ft. x 80 in.	—	5110	2194
CB300	Kary Van 12 ft. x 94 in.	6683	—	Note 1

NOTE 1: 12 ft. x 94 in. Kary Van was available only with V-8.

Model	Body Type	Price	Weight	Prod. Total
D100 Series — Custom — 1/2-Ton — 115 in. w.b.				
D100	Chassis & Cab	3512	3145	Note 2
D100	Utiline Pickup	3677	3490	Note 2
D100	Sweptline Pickup	3677	3515	Note 2
(131 in. w.b.)				
D100	Chassis & Cab	3556	3160	Note 2
D100	Utiline Pickup	3721	3490	Note 2
D100	Sweptline Pickup	3721	3620	Note 2

NOTE 2: Total model year production: (115 in.) 26,153; (131 in.) 54,585.

Model	Body Type	Price	Weight	Prod. Total
D100 Series Club Cab — Custom — 1/2-Ton — 133 in. w.b.				
D100	Sweptline Pickup	3975	3730	1816
(149 in. w.b.)				
D100	Sweptline Pickup	4009	3870	8049
D200 Series — Custom — 3/4-Ton — 131 in. w.b.				
D200	Chassis & Cab	4010	3325	Note 3
D200	Utiline Pickup	4174	3755	Note 3
D200	Sweptline Pickup	4174	3785	Note 3

NOTE 3: Total model year production: 14,414.

Model	Body Type	Price	Weight	Prod. Total
D200 Series Club Cab — Custom — 3/4-Ton — 149 in. w.b.				
D200	Sweptline Pickup	4463	3955	7007
D200 Series Crew Cab — Custom — 3/4-Ton — 149 in. w.b.				
D200	Chassis & Cab	4705	3725	Note 4
D200	Utiline Pickup	4849	4070	Note 4
D200	Sweptline Pickup	4849	4095	Note 4
(165 in. w.b.)				
D200	Chassis & Cab	4932	4095	Note 4
D200	Utiline Pickup	5085	4525	Note 4
D200	Sweptline Pickup	5085	4555	Note 4

NOTE 4: Total model year production: (149 in.) 7,007 including Club Cab models above; (165 in.) 1,103.

Model	Body Type	Price	Weight	Prod. Total
D300 Series — Custom — 1-Ton — 131 in. w.b.				
D300	Sweptline Pickup	4777	—	711
(135 in. w.b.)				
D300	Chassis & Cab	4139	3775	6119
(149 in. w.b.)				
D300	Club Cab — Chassis & Cab	4667	—	Note 5
D300	Club Cab — Sweptline	5066	—	Note 5
(159 in. w.b.)				
D300	Chassis & Cab	4177	3880	1700

(165 in. w.b.)

D300	Crew Cab — Chassis & Cab	5213	—	163

NOTE 5: Total model year production: (149 in.) 888 units.

W100 Series 4x4 — Custom — 1/2-Ton — 115 in. w.b.

W100	Chassis & Cab	4419	3780	Note 6
W100	Utiline Pickup	4585	4125	Note 6
W100	Sweptline Pickup	4585	4150	Note 6

(131 in. w.b.)

W100	Chassis & Cab	4462	3790	Note 6
W100	Utiline Pickup	4628	4220	Note 6
W100	Sweptline Pickup	4628	4250	Note 6

NOTE 6: Total model year production: (115 in.) 10,580; (131 in.) 9,005.

W100 Series Club Cab 4x4 — Custom — 1/2-Ton — 133 in. w.b.

W100	Sweptline Pickup	4879	—	1440

(149 in. w.b.)

W100	Sweptline Pickup	4917	—	1921

W200 Series 4x4 — Custom — 3/4-Ton — 131 in. w.b.

W200	Chassis & Cab	5085	3845	Note 7
W200	Utiline Pickup	5251	4275	Note 7
W200	Sweptline Pickup	5251	4305	Note 7

NOTE 7: Total model year production (131 in.): 20,507.

(149 in. w.b.)

W200	Club Cab — Sweptline	5661	4605	Note 8

W200 Crew Cab 4x4 — Custom — 3/4-Ton — 149 in. w.b.

W200	Chassis & Cab	6078	4245	Note 8
W200	Utiline Pickup	6244	4590	Note 8
W200	Sweptline Pickup	6244	4615	Note 8

NOTE 8: Total model year production (all 149 in. models): 3,325.

W300 Series 4x4 — Custom — 1-Ton — 135 in. w.b.

W300	Chassis & Cab	6039	4380	1522

NOTE 9: Weights and prices shown are for six-cylinder models. For 318 cid V-8 engine, add 100 lbs. to weight and $90 to $193 (depending on series) to price; for W200 Crew Cab models, add $370 to price.

ENGINES (Standard: All models): Inline. Overhead valve. Slant six. Cast iron block. Bore & stroke: 3.4 x 4.125 in. Displacement: 224.8 cid. Compression ratio: 8.4:1. Brake horsepower: 105 (net) at 3600 rpm. Taxable horsepower: 27.70. Torque: 175 lbs.-ft. (net) at 2000 rpm. Four main bearings. Solid valve lifters.

ENGINE (Standard V-8: All models): 90-degree, overhead valve. V-8. Cast iron block. Bore & stroke: 3.91 x 3.31 in. Displacement: 318.3 cid. Compression ratio: 8.6:1. Brake horsepower: 150 (net) at 4000 rpm. Taxable horsepower: 48.92. Torque: 255 lbs.-ft. (net) at 2000 rpm. Five main bearings. Hydraulic valve lifters.

ENGINE (Optional V-8: All models): 90-degree, overhead valve. V-8. Cast iron block. Bore & stroke: 4.00 x 3.58 in. Displacement: 360 cid. Compression ratio: 8.4:1. Brake horsepower: 185 (net) at 4000 rpm. Taxable horsepower: 50.2. Torque: 290 lbs.-ft. (net) at 2400 rpm. Five main bearings. Hydraulic valve lifters.

ENGINE (Optional 400 V-8: All except B100): 90-degree, overhead valve. V-8. Cast iron block. Bore & stroke: 4.34 x 3.38 in. Displacement: 400 cid. Compression ratio: 8.2:1. Brake horsepower: 165 (net) at 4000 rpm. Taxable horsepower: 60.3. Torque: 290 lbs.-ft. (net) at 2400 rpm. Five main bearings. Hydraulic valve lifters.

ENGINE (Optional 440 V-8: D100-300, W100-300, B200-300, AW100): 90-degree, overhead valve. V-8. Cast iron block. Bore & stroke: 4.32 x 3.75 in. Displacement: 440 cid. Compression ratio: 8.2:1. Brake horsepower: 220 (net) at 4000 rpm. Taxable horsepower: 58.55. Torque: 330 lbs.-ft. (net) at 2400 rpm. Five main bearings. Hydraulic valve lifters.

CHASSIS (AD100/AW100): Wheelbase: 106 in. Tires: E78 x 15-B four-ply. GVW: 4,900 lbs.

CHASSIS (B100): Wheelbase: 109 in. or 127 in. Tires: E78 x 15-B four-ply. GVW: 4,600 lbs.

CHASSIS (B200): Wheelbase: 109 in. or 127 in. Tires: G78 x 15-B four-ply except (Maxivan) H78 x 15-B four-ply. GVW: 5,500 lbs.

CHASSIS (B300): Wheelbase: 109 in. or 127 in. Tires: 8.00 x 16.5-C six-ply except (Maxivan) 8.00 x 16.5-D eight-ply. GVW: 6,400 lbs.

CHASSIS (CB300): Wheelbase: 127 in. or 145 in. Tires: 8.75 x 16.5-E ten-ply. GVW: 7,700 lbs.

CHASSIS (D100): Wheelbase: 115 in. or 131 in. (Club Cab, 133 or 149 in.). Tires: G78 x 15-D four-ply. GVW: 5,000 lbs.

CHASSIS (D200): Wheelbase: 131 in., 149 in. or 165 in. Tires: 8.00 x 16.5-D eight-ply. GVW: 6,200 lbs.

CHASSIS (D300): Wheelbase: 131 in., 135 in., 149 in., 159 in. or 165 in. Tires: (131 in. and 135 in.), 8.00 x 16.5-D eight-ply; (others) 8.00 x 16.5-C eight-ply. GVW: 6,600 lbs.

CHASSIS (W100): Wheelbase: 115 in. or 131 in. (Club Cab, 133 or 149 in.). Tires: (six) H78 x 15-B, (V-8) G78 x 15-B. GVW: 5,400 lbs.

CHASSIS (W200): Wheelbase: 131 in. or 149 in. Tires: 8.00 x 16.5-D eight-ply. GVW: 6,500 lbs.

CHASSIS (W300): Wheelbase: 135 in. Tires: 8.75 x 16.5-E ten-ply. GVW: 8,500 lbs.

TECHNICAL: Selective sliding gear transmission. Speeds: 3F/1R except (D300, W300 and 165 in. w.b. D200) 4F/1R. Column or floor (four-speed) shift control. Automatic 3-speed transmission optional. Single disc dry clutch: (six-cylinder) 10 in.; (V-8) 11 in. Rear axle ratio: (AW100 Ramcharger) 3.23:1, 3.55:1 or 3.90:1. Hydraulic four-wheel brakes: Front disc, rear drum. Fuel tank: (B vans) 23-gallon; (AW100) 24-gallon; (others) 22-gallon. Alternator: 48 amp.

OPTIONS: Ramcharger steel hardtop ($444). Ramcharger SE package ($432). Ramcharger 400 cid V-8 ($65). Ramcharger 440 cid V-8 ($256). Custom Sportsman van package ($345). Royal Sportsman van package ($455). Royal Sportsman SE van package ($593). Eight-passenger van package ($72). Twelve-passenger van package ($184). Fifteen-passenger van package ($276). Kary Van 360 cid V-8 ($66). Kary Van 440 cid V-8 ($256). Van door edge protectors (front only). Single rear door with fixed glass. 36-gallon fuel tank. Full-length scuff pads (side step sill). Styled road wheels (B100-200, 15 in.). Premium wheelcovers (B100-200). (D100-300, W100-300) Carpeting (conventional cabs). Transmission oil cooler. 21-gallon auxiliary fuel tank, behind rear axle. 24-gallon auxiliary tank, in cab behind seat. Chrome styled road wheels (D100). Premium wheelcovers (D100). (Ramcharger) Transmission cooler. Pickup Adventurer, Adventurer Sport or Adventurers SE package. Protection package. Convenience package. Exterior trim molding package. Sno-fiter package. Trailer-towing package. Heavy-duty trailer-towing package. Plow lights. Deluxe wheelcovers. (B200-300 Vans) 400 cid V-8 engine. 440 cid V-8 engine. (Trucks under 5,500 lbs. GVW) Overdrive manual four-speed transmission.

1976 Dodge Ramcharger SE 4x4 Utility (DNP)

HISTORICAL: Introduced: August, 1975. Model year sales: 406,654. Sales breakdown: 195,864 light conventional trucks; 184,583 vans; 11,905 Ramchargers; 4,711 Trail Dusters; and 9,591 medium-duty. Calendar year production: 441,769. Model year production: 360,080. Innovations: Youth-oriented Street Van with Customizing Idea Kit. Glide-out spare tire carrier on pickups. This was a year of real recovery for Dodge trucks. A combination of an improved economy and stabilized fuel prices resulted in vastly increased sales of vans and four-wheel drive vehicles. Production rose 28 percent over 1975, while sales gained 42.9 percent. Dodge set sales records in vans, Ramchargers and medium-duty trucks. Pickup sales were up, yet below the 1973 record. Sales increased in every category except Trail Dusters, which were built by Dodge but sold by Plymouth dealers. Dodge Sportsman and Plymouth Voyager wagons were counted as passenger car sales. Dodge attributed the sales records in large measure to trucks tailored to handle specialized jobs, as well as to vehicles with special trim and option packages. Dodge offered one run of pickups with special trim and accessories for the Los Angeles market, and another package in the San Francisco area.

1977 DODGE

1977 Dodge Adventurer SE Pickup (DNP)

1/2-TON VAN — B100 SERIES — SIX-CYLINDER/V-8; 3/4-TON VAN — B200 SERIES — SIX-CYLINDER/V-8; 1-TON VAN — B300 SERIES — SIX-CYLINDER/V-8; 1-TON KARY VAN — CB300 SERIES — SIX-CYLINDER/V-8: Though unchanged in appearance for 1977, B Series vans received several interior improvements. New convenience/comfort features included high-back swivel bucket seats, improved carpeting, a quick-release mechanism for bench seats, and gray-tinted privacy glass. The single rear door became standard, but dual doors were a no-cost option. The Fuel Pacer System was now offered on vans. Five new metallic colors were available, and the Street Van option was continued. The factory offered paint schemes with six different graphic designs, plus fat tires on either five-slot chrome disc wheels or eight-spoke painted wheels. Included with each 1977 Street Van was a free membership in Mopar's Van Clan Club. Base engine remained the 225 cid slant six (except in the B300 series); options were 318, 360, 400 and 440 cid V-8s. Transmission choices included three-speed manual or automatic on all models or four-speed overdrive on the B100 only.

1/2-TON — D100 SERIES — SIX-CYLINDER/V-8 / HEAVY 1/2-TON — D150 SERIES — SIX-CYLINDER/V-8; 3/4-TON — D200 SERIES — SIX-CYLINDER/V-8; 1-TON — D300 SERIES — SIX-CYLINDER/V-8; 1/2-TON 4x4 — W100 SERIES — SIX-CYLINDER/V-8 / HEAVY 1/2-TON 4x4 — W150 SERIES — SIX-CYLINDER/V-8; 3/4-TON 4x4 — W200 SERIES — SIX-CYLINDER/V-8; 1-TON 4x4 — W300 SERIES — SIX-CYLINDER/V-8: The era of Adult toy trucks. Dodge promoted macho trucks and factory customized street trucks began with the 1977 model year. Dodge's Warlock, the first entry in this new era, was available in either a 4x2 or 4x4 version. Colors offered were bright red, medium green, sunfire metallic, and black sunfire metallic. Accent in the form of gold painted spoke wheels, gold pinstriping and chrome-plated mini runningboards made the Warlock a real standout. Warlocks were also equipped with real oak sideboards and wide tires with raised white letters. Inside were black bucket seats and gold paint accents. Warlocks sat on a 115 inch wheelbase D100 or W100 chassis with Utiline 6-1/2 ft. box. Standard engines were the 225 cid slant six and 318 cid V-8, both with two-barrel carburetors. A three-speed column shift manual transmission was standard. Optional were automatic transmission, a 360 cid V-8 (two-barrel), 400 cid V-8 (two-barrel) or a big 440 V-8 with four-barrel carburetor. A new pickup grille incorporated rectangular parking lights, with the Dodge nameplate

pressed into the top grille bar. New bodyside moldings completed the appearance changes. Three trim levels were now available on pickups: Custom, Adventurer and Adventurer SE. Gone was the Adventurer Sport. Two-tone instrument panels on all models added a more luxurious look. Interior refinements included new seat trim and style, new door trim panels, and new colors. Five metallic and five non-metallic colors were added. An optional Fuel Pacer System conserved fuel by alerting the driver, via a dash indicator light, that he was running an overly rich mixture. For improved performance, the 225 cid slant six was available with two-barrel carburetor, which produced an additional 10 horsepower. This new Super Six was developed to combine the good fuel economy of a six with the performance and feel of a V-8. The overdrive four-speed manual transmission, introduced late in the 1976 model year, continued for models up to 5,500 lbs. GVW. Fourth gear was a 27 percent overdrive. Dodge offered additional factory custom models in midyear, at a special press introduction at the Ontario Motor Speedway in Ontario, California. New models included the True Spirit, a D100 pickup with 318 V-8; a Power Wagon W100 4x4 pickup with 400 cid V-8 and four-barrel carburetor; and Street Van, a fully-tricked-out Maxivan. Dodge management was well aware of the truck boom and sought to create adult toys for a great many pickup, van and four-wheel drive enthusiasts. Dodge was intent on marketing factory custom or high-volume custom content special models to enter the "trick" truck market. Optional factory personalization of utility vehicles attracted many a recreation-oriented buyer. Optional this year was a removable tinted glass Skylite roof. Introduced at midyear 1977 were D150 and W150 heavy 1/2-ton models, with GVW ratings above 6,000 lbs.

1/2-TON RAMCHARGER 4x2 — AD100 SERIES — SIX-CYLINDER/V-8; 1/2-TON RAMCHARGER 4x4 — AW100 SERIES — SIX-CYLINDER/V-8: New two-tone paint and upper bodyside moldings gave Ramchargers a new look. They also received the same new grille as the pickups, with vertical rectangular parking lights. Dodge's exclusive high-back swivel bucket seats with movable armrests were available in the SE model. Full time four-wheel drive was standard. Transmission options on two-wheel drive models were limited to three-speed manual or automatic; but four-wheel drive Ramchargers could have a close-ratio or wide-ratio four-speed (except with 440 V-8). Engine choices ranged from the 225 cid slant six to 318, 360 and 400 cid V-8s, plus the 440 V-8 on four-wheel drive models only. Tops were again optional. The steel top's tailgate was operated by two pneumatic cylinders. Power brakes were standard.

1977 Dodge Warlock Utiline Pickup (OCW)

I.D. DATA: Serial numbers were on a vehicle identification plate attached to the driver's doorlatch post. Vehicle Identification Numbers (VIN) consisted of 13 letters and numbers, divided into seven elements. The first two characters indicated model code. Model code index: D1=D100; D2=D200; D3=D300; W1=W100; W2=W200; W3=W300; B1=B100; B2=B200; B3=B300; P1=P100; P2=P200 or P3=P300 forward-control. The next digit showed body type. Body type index: 0=forward control chassis; 1=conventional cab; 2=Crew Cab; 3=Utiline conventional cab; 4=Sweptline conventional cab; 5=Utiline Crew Cab; 6=Sweptline Crew Cab; 7=flat face cowl or Sweptline Club Cab; 8=Club Cab. The next letter designated GVW rating. GVW index: A=6,000 lbs. or less; B=6,001 to 10,000 lbs.; C=10,001 to 14,000 lbs.; D=14,000 to 16,000 lbs. etc. Next came a letter for engine type. Engine type index: B=225-1V; C=225-2V; D=440; E=318-1; F=360; G=318-3; X=Special 6; Y=Special V-8. The next digit gave model year (7=1977). The next letter indicated assembly plant: J=Windsor; S=Warren Plant No. 1; T=Warren Plant No. 2; X=Missouri. At the end came a six-digit sequence number at that assembly plant; all models began with sequence number 000,001. Engine numbers were located as follows: (225 cid six) right side of block, below No. 1 spark plug; (318 or 360 cid V-8) left front of block, below cylinder head; (440 V-8) left side of block, adjacent to front tappet rail. The first digit gave model year. The next letter indicated assembly plant (M=Mound Road). The next three digits showed displacement in cubic inches. Next came a four-digit date code, followed by a four-digit sequence number. Starting engine numbers are not available.

1977 Dodge Adventurer SE Club Cab Pickup (DNP)

Model	Body Type	Price	Weight	Prod. Total
AD100/AW100 Ramcharger Sport-Utility — 1/2-Ton — 106 in. w.b.				
AD100	4x2 without top	4377	3560	2538
AW100	4x4 without top	5392	4075	17,120
B100 Series Tradesman Van — 1/2-Ton — 109 in. w.b.				
B100	Van	4589	3435	51,602
(127 in. w.b.)				
B100	Van	4747	3550	24,723
B200 Series Tradesman Van — 3/4-Ton — 109 in. w.b.				
B200	Van	4741	3485	56,306
(127 in. w.b.)				
B200	Van	4896	3610	91,174
B200	Maxivan	5045	—	39,086
B300 Series Tradesman Van — 1-Ton — 109 in. w.b.				
B300	Van	4888	3675	517
(127 in. w.b.)				
B300	Van	5011	3805	11,465
B300	Maxivan	5241	4000	22,567
CB300	Kary Van 10 ft.	5697	4525	1648
(145 in. w.b.)				
CB300	Kary Van 12 ft.	6245	5200	5519
D100 Series — 1/2-Ton — 115 in. w.b.				
D100	Chassis & Cab	4212	3145	Note 1
D100	Utiline Pickup	4394	3490	Note 1
D100	Sweptline Pickup	4394	3515	Note 1
(131 in. w.b.)				
D100	Chassis & Cab	4261	3160	Note 1
D100	Utiline Pickup	4443	3490	Note 1
D100	Sweptline Pickup	4443	3620	Note 1
NOTE 1: Total D100 model year production: (115 in.) 32,276; (131 in.) 66,191.				
D100 Series Club Cab — 1/2-Ton — 133 in. w.b.				
D100	Sweptline Pickup	4737	3730	2459
(149 in. w.b.)				
D100	Sweptline Pickup	4773	3870	9488
D150 Series — H-D 1/2-Ton — 115 in. w.b.				
D150	Chassis & Cab	4424	—	—
D150	Utiline Pickup	4606	—	—
D150	Sweptline Pickup	4606	—	—
(131 in. w.b.)				
D150	Chassis & Cab	4473	—	—
D150	Utiline Pickup	4655	—	—
D150	Sweptline Pickup	4655	—	—
(133 in. w.b.)				
D150	Club Cab — Sweptline	4945	—	—
(149 in. w.b.)				
D150	Club Cab — Sweptline	4985	—	—
D200 Series — (3/4-Ton) — 131 in. w.b.				
D200	Chassis & Cab	4722	3325	Note 2
D200	Utiline Pickup	4983	3755	Note 2
D200	Sweptline Pickup	4983	3785	Note 2
NOTE 2: Total model year production: 18,025.				
D200 Series Club Cab — 3/4-Ton — 149 in. w.b.				
D200	Sweptline Pickup	5307	3955	Note 3
D200 Series Crew Cab — 3/4-Ton — 149 in. w.b.				
D200	Chassis & Cab	5474	3725	Note 3
D200	Utiline Pickup	5708	4070	Note 3
D200	Sweptline Pickup	5708	4095	Note 3
(165 in. w.b.)				
D200	Chassis & Cab	5701	4095	Note 3
D200	Utiline Pickup	5944	4525	Note 3
D200	Sweptline Pickup	5944	4555	Note 3

NOTE 3: Total model year production: (149 in. Club Cab and Crew Cab) 7,270; (165 in. Crew Cab) 1,257.

228

1977 Dodge Power Wagon Sweptline Pickup (JAG)

D300 Series — 1-Ton — 131 in. w.b.

D300	Sweptline Pickup	—	—	689

(135 in. w.b.)

D300	Chassis & Cab	—	3775	5921

(149 in. w.b.)

D300	Club Cab — Chassis/Cab	—	—	Note 4
D300	Club Cab — Sweptline	—	—	Note 4

(159 in. w.b.)

D300	Chassis & Cab	—	3880	2048

(165 in. w.b.)

D300	Crew — Chassis/Cab	—	—	178

NOTE 4: Total model year production: (149 in.) 1,266.

W100 Series 4x4 — 1/2-Ton — 115 in. w.b.

W100	Chassis & Cab	5256	3780	Note 5
W100	Utiline Pickup	5477	4125	Note 5
W100	Sweptline Pickup	5477	4150	Note 5

(131 in. w.b.)

W100	Chassis & Cab	5305	3790	Note 5
W100	Utiline Pickup	5525	4220	Note 5
W100	Sweptline Pickup	5525	4250	Note 5

NOTE 5: Total model year production: (115 in.) 17,523; (131 in.) 13,339.

W100 Series Club Cab 4x4 — 1/2-Ton — 133 in. w.b.

W100	Sweptline Pickup	—	—	1956

(149 in. w.b.)

W100	Sweptline Pickup	—	—	2336

W150 Series — H-D 1/2-Ton — 4x4 — 115 in. w.b.

W150	Chassis & Cab	5380	—	—
W150	Utiline Pickup	5601	—	—
W150	Sweptline Pickup	5601	—	—

(131 in. w.b.)

W150	Chassis & Cab	5429	—	—
W150	Utiline Pickup	5649	—	—
W150	Sweptline Pickup	5649	—	—

(133 in. w.b.)

W150	Club Cab — Sweptline	5848	—	—

(149 in. w.b.)

W150	Club Cab — Sweptline	—	—	—

W200 Series 4x4 — 3/4-Ton — 131 in. w.b.

W200	Chassis & Cab	5713	3845	Note 6
W200	Utiline Pickup	5970	4275	Note 6
W200	Sweptline Pickup	5970	4305	Note 6

NOTE 6: Total model year production (131 in.): 37,292.

(149 in. w.b.)

W200	Club Cab — Sweptline	6287	4605	Note 7

W200 Crew Cab 4x4 — 3/4-Ton — 149 in. w.b.

W200	Chassis & Cab	6648	4245	Note 7
W200	Utiline Pickup	6900	4590	Note 7
W200	Sweptline Pickup	6900	4615	Note 7

NOTE 7: Total model year production (all 149 in. models): 4,322.

W300 Series 4x4 — 1-Ton — 135 in. w.b.

W300	Chassis & Cab	—	4380	2365

NOTE 8: Weights and prices shown are for six-cylinder. models. For 318 cid V-8 engine, add 100 lbs. to weight and $68 to $168 to price (depending on series).

1977 Dodge Pathfinder 4x4 Custom Sportsman Van

ENGINES (Standard six: All models): Inline. Overhead valve. Slant six. Cast iron block. Bore & stroke: 3.4 x 4.125 in. Displacement: 224.8 cid. Compression ratio: 8.4:1. Brake horsepower: 100 at 3600 rpm. (110 at 3600 with two-barrel carburetor). Taxable horsepower: 27.70. Torque: 175 lbs.-ft. at 1600 rpm. (175 lbs.-ft. at 2000 with two-barrel carb). Four main bearings. Solid valve lifters.

ENGINE (Standard 318 V-8: All models): 90-degree, overhead valve. V-8. Cast iron block. Bore & stroke: 3.91 x 3.31 in. Displacement: 318.3 cid. Compression ratio: 8.6:1. Brake horsepower: 150 at 4000 rpm. Taxable horsepower: 48.92. Torque: 230 lbs.-ft. at 2400 rpm. Five main bearings. Hydraulic valve lifters.

Standard Catalog of Light-Duty Trucks

ENGINE (Optional 360 V-8: All models): 90-degree, overhead valve. V-8. Cast iron block. Bore & stroke: 4.00 x 3.58 in. Displacement: 360 cid. Compression ratio: 8.4:1. Brake horsepower: 170 at 4000 rpm. Taxable horsepower: 50.2. Torque: 280 lbs.-ft. at 2400 rpm. Five main bearings. Hydraulic valve lifters.

1977 Dodge Sportsman Passenger Van (DNP)

ENGINE (Optional 400 V-8: All except B100 and D100): 90-degree, overhead valve. V-8. Cast iron block. Bore & stroke: 4.34 x 3.38 in. Displacement: 400 cid. Compression ratio: 8.2:1. Brake horsepower: 165 at 4000 rpm. Taxable horsepower: 60.3. Torque: 290 lbs.-ft. at 2400 rpm. Five main bearings. Hydraulic valve lifters.

ENGINE (Optional 440 V-8: B200-300, D150-300, W100-300, AW100): 90-degree, overhead valve. V-8. Cast iron block. Bore & stroke: 4.32 x 3.75 in. Displacement: 439.9 cid. Compression ratio: 8.2:1. Brake horsepower: 220 at 4000 rpm. Taxable horsepower: 58.55. Torque: 320 lbs.-ft. at 2400 rpm. Five main bearings. Hydraulic valve lifters.

1977 Dodge Ramcharger SE Utility (DNP)

CHASSIS (AD100/AW100): Wheelbase: 106 in. Tires: E78 x 15-B four-ply. GVW: 4,900 lbs.

CHASSIS (B100): Wheelbase: 109 in. or 127 in. Tires: E78 x 15-B four-ply. GVW: 4,600 lbs.

CHASSIS (B200): Wheelbase: 109 in. or 127 in. Tires: G78 x 15-B four-ply except (Maxivan) H78 x 15-B four-ply. GVW: 5,500 lbs.

CHASSIS (B300): Wheelbase: 109 in. or 127 in. Tires: 8.00 x 16.5-C six-ply except (Maxivan) 8.00 x 16.5-D eight-ply. GVW: 6,400 lbs.

CHASSIS (CB300): Wheelbase: 127 in. or 145 in. Tires: 8.75 x 16.5-E ten-ply. GVW: 7,700 lbs.

CHASSIS (D100): Wheelbase: 115 in. or 131 in. (Club Cab, 133 or 149 in.). Tires: G78 x 15-D four-ply. GVW: 5,000 lbs.

CHASSIS (D200): Wheelbase: 131 in., 149 in. or 165 in. Tires: 8.00 x 16.5-D eight-ply. GVW: 6,200 lbs.

CHASSIS (D300): Wheelbase: 131 in., 135 in., 149 in., 159 in. or 165 in. Tires: (131 in. and 135 in.), 8.00 x 16.5-D eight-ply; (others) 8.00 x 16.5-C eight-ply. GVW: 6,600 lbs.

CHASSIS (W100): Wheelbase: 115 in. or 131 in. (Club Cab, 133 or 149 in.). Tires: (six) H78 x 15-B, (V-8) G78 x 15-B. GVW: 5,400 lbs.

CHASSIS (W200): Wheelbase: 131 in. or 149 in. Tires: 8.00 x 16.5-D eight-ply. GVW: 6,500 lbs.

CHASSIS (W300): Wheelbase: 135 in. Tires: 8.75 x 16.5-E ten-ply. GVW: 8,500 lbs.

1977 Dodge Tradesman Street Van (DNP)

TECHNICAL: Selective sliding gear transmission. Speeds: 3F/1R except (D300, W300 and 165 in. w.b. D200) 4F/1R. Column or floor (4-speed) shift control. Automatic 3-speed

transmission optional. Single disc dry clutch: (six-cylinder.) 10 in.; (V-8) 11 in. Rear axle ratio: (AW100 Ramcharger) 3.23:1, 3.55:1 or 3.90:1. Hydraulic four-wheel brakes: Front disc, rear drum. Fuel tank: (B vans) 23-gallon; (AW100) 24-gallon; (others) 22-gallon. Alternator: 48 amp.

1977 Dodge Sportsman Passenger Van (JAG)

OPTIONS (Factory-Installed): [B Series Vans] except for the following: Convenience package. Custom exterior package. Custom interior package. Easy-order package. Insulation package. Lock package. School bus package (B300 only). Sound control package. Street van package (B100-200). Trailer-assist package. Heavy-duty trailer-assist package (except B100). 4-speed manual overdrive transmission A833 (B100). Wide sport wheels, 15 x 7.00, chrome or painted (B100-200). AM/FM/Stereo Radio, with or without 8-track tape player. (D100-300, W100-300) Same as 1976, except for the following: Fuel Pacer. Tachometer. Vacuum gauge/voltmeter. Easy-order package. Protection package. Sound control package. Two-tone paint (procedure 4), except D/W300. Skylite sun roof. [Ramcharger] Same as 1976, except for the following: Fuel Pacer. 63 or 117-amp. alternator. Vacuum gauge/Voltmeter. Electric tachometer. Speedometer. (km/miles) and odometer (km). Easy-order package. Luxury package. Upper side molding package (for SE). Heavy-duty GVW package (5,200, 5,600, or 6,100 lbs.). Snow plow package. Deluxe vinyl interior trim. Cloth/vinyl trim. Styled road wheels. Wide sport wheels (painted spokes) Chrome disc wheels.

1977 Dodge Royal Sportsman Van (DNP)

HISTORICAL: Introduced: August, 1976 (Heavy 1/2-ton models in midyear). Calendar year production: 474,001. Model year sales: 463,218. Model year production: 623,460. Innovations: Warlock factory-custom street truck. Fuel Pacer system. Pickups and vans achieved unpredicted social acceptability in 1977. Four-wheel drive trucks boomed in popularity; both sports-utility types like Ramcharger and four-wheel drive pickups. Total industry four-wheel drive production was 762,356 units, a 24 percent jump over 1976. In fact, the four-wheel drive market grew 84 percent between 1975 and 1977. Trucks accounted for nearly one-fourth of the total motor vehicle production this year, and light-duty trucks made up over 89 percent of total truck production. Dodge set a new truck production record and sales gained 14.5 percent. Vans were Dodge's hottest seller, gaining 22.5 percent over 1976. Model year truck sales consisted of 215,409 light conventional models, 226,066 vans, 14,796 Ramchargers, and 5,926 Trail Dusters. Dodge dropped out of the medium-duty truck business this year. The factory at Windsor, Ontario was converted to build light-duty trucks. A Canadian-American Automotive Trade Treaty allowed Dodge to build light-duty trucks in Canada, for sale in the U.S., without paying duties. Output from the Canadian plant was needed to keep up with demand.

1977 Dodge Tradesman Custom Sport Van (DNP)

1978 Dodge Ramcharger 4x4 Open Utlity (DNP)

1/2-TON VAN — B100 SERIES — SIX-CYLINDER/V-8; 3/4-TON VAN — B200 SERIES — SIX-CYLINDER/V-8; 1-TON VAN — B300 SERIES — SIX-CYLINDER/V-8; 1-TON KARY VAN — CB300 SERIES — SIX-CYLINDER/V-8: Vans received their first significant exterior and interior changes since 1971, starting with a lowered beltline, which allowed deeper side windows. Side doors on 127 in. wheelbase models moved ahead 16 in., as windows were repositioned. A redesigned roof allowed installation of vents and a sun roof option. Two-tone bodies and six paint colors were new. Van rears gained a new look through new vertical taillights and body line moldings. Inside sat a new instrument panel and redesigned steering wheel. Engine covers looked less utilitarian than before. Interior trim panels and other appointments were more attractive; seats were more comfortable. The Maxivan was stretched 8 in., to 220 in. overall, providing seating space for 15 people. The Maxiwagon version could now be equipped with wraparound rear quarter windows for greatly improved visibility. The Maxi was the largest van in the industry. Radio equipment options for pickups were also available for vans. Continued for another year was the popular Street Van package, for do-it-yourself van customizers. Engine and transmission options remained the same as 1977.

1978 Dodge Power Wagon Utiline Pickup (DNP)

1/2-TON PICKUP — D100 SERIES — SIX-CYLINDER/V-8 / HEAVY 1/2-TON PICKUP — D200 SERIES — SIX-CYLINDER/V-8; 3/4-TON PICKUP — D200 SERIES — SIX-CYLINDER/V-8; 1-TON PICKUP — D300 SERIES — SIX-CYLINDER/V-8; 1/2-TON 4x4 — W150 SERIES — SIX-CYLINDER/V-8; 3/4-TON 4x4 — W200 SERIES — SIX-CYLINDER/V-8; 1-TON 4x4 — W300 SERIES — SIX-CYLINDER/V-8: Heavy 1/2-ton models D150 and W150, introduced in midyear 1977, had GVW ratings above 6,000 lbs. That was the cut-off point for the most restrictive U.S. exhaust emission regulations for light-duty trucks. Trucks rated higher had to meet only the more liberal exhaust rules, which applied to heavy models. For the first time, Dodge installed a diesel engine in light-duty trucks. An inline six of 243 cid displacement, it developed 103 hp at 3700 rpm. Diesels required two 12-volt batteries and were offered only in D/W150 and D/W200 model pickups. New this year was a D300 1-ton dual wheel Crew Cab Sweptline pickup. Appearance changes through the lineup were minimal, amounting to little more than six new colors and a new tilt-column steering wheel. A factory-installed trailer towing hitch was now optional. Other options included a sporty three-spoke steering wheel with satin chrome spokes and black rim, bucket seats in Club Cab models, Adventurer SE trim on all models and six radio options. That entertainment list included an AM radio with 40-channel CB and AM/FM/Stereo radio with CB or 8-track tape player (or alone), as well as standard AM and FM models. A new four-wheel drive transfer case shifter included a positive range detent to prevent accidental partial engagement. Sweptline pickup beds were redesigned to sit level on the chassis. All 225 cid slant six engines now had two-barrel carburetors. Dodge carried forward its line of "adult toys." They included the Street Van, Warlock, Macho Power Wagon, and 4x4 Dodge Macho Ramcharger. One more was introduced at midyear (late March 1978). This most famous toy of all was the D150 "Little Red Truck." Built on the 115 in. wheelbase Utiline 1/2-ton, the Li'l Red Truck was powered by a high-output 360 cid four-barrel V-8, through a 3.55:1 rear axle. The engine included Super-Flow cylinder heads; police type 252-degree cam (with 33-degrees of overlap), heavy-duty valve springs, Thermo-Quad four-barrel carburetor, cold air induction system, large diameter dual exhausts. A performance modified automatic transmission was included. It came from the factory with chrome-plated valve covers, air cleaner and vertical exhaust stacks. Body paint was Canyon Red, with accent stripes, genuine oak side boards and Adventurer interior trim. Interiors were black or red, with either bench or bucket seats. On the exterior gold

"Li'l Red Express Truck" decals appeared on the doors. "Li'l Red Truck" lettering also decorated the tailgate. This limited-production vehicle was designed to be a conversation-starter and traffic builder on the sales floor. Like other Utiline models, it had new rectangular stop/turn/backup lights.

1978 Dodge Ramcharger 4x4 Utility (DNP)

1/2-TON RAMCHARGER 4x2 — AD100 SERIES — SIX-CYLINDER/V-8; 1/2-TON RAMCHARGER 4x4 — AW100 SERIES — SIX-CYLINDER/V-8: Ramcharger continued with no appearance changes. As before, engine choices included the 225 cid six as well as 318, 360, 400 and 440 cid V-8s. Two four-speed manual transmissions and an automatic were available. Bucket front seats were new, as was a front bench seat for six-passenger seating. Other new options included sunscreen glass for rear quarters and tailgate, six new colors, and heavy-duty shock absorbers. The Ramcharger "Macho 4x4" continued. A Hurst shift lever and knob were standard in it.

1978 Dodge "Macho" Power Wagon Sweptline Pickup

I.D. DATA: A serial number Vehicle Identification Number (VIN) plate was on the driver's door latch post. The seven element number contained 13 alpha-numeric characters. The first two characters indicated model codes: A1=AW100; B1=B100; B2=B200; B3=B300; C3=CB300; D1=D100/150; D2=D200; R2=RD200; D3=D300; E1=AD100; W1=W150; W2=W200; W3=W300. Next came a body type code: 0=forward control, motorhome chassis, Kary Van or sport-utility; 1=Tradesman van, conventional cab/chassis; 2=Sportsman, Crew Cab/chassis; 3=Utiline conventional cab; 4=Sweptline conventional cab; 5=Maxivan, Utiline Crew Cab; 6=Sportsman Maxiwagon, Sweptline Crew Cab; 7=flat face cowl, Sweptline Club Cab; 8=cowl/windshield, Club Cab; 9=Utiline Club Cab. Next came a letter indicating GVW class: A=6,000 lbs. or less; B=6,001 to 10,000 lbs.; etc. The next letter showed engine type: A=440-3; B=225-1; C=225-2; D=440-1; E=318-1; F=360-1; G=318-3; H=400-1; K=360-3; H=243 diesel; X=special six-cylinder; V=special V-8. Next came the final digit in the year of manufacture, 8=1978. The next letter indicated assembly plant: J=Tecumseh Road; K=Pillette Road; N=Burt Road (Knocked-Down Export); S=Warren No. 1; T=Warren No. 2; X=Missouri; V=Warren No. 3 (compact). This was followed by a 6-digit sequence number. Engine numbers were in the same locations as 1975-1977.

1978 Dodge Tradesman Panel Delivery Van (DNP)

Model	Body Type	Price	Weight	Prod. Total
AD100/AW100 Ramcharger Sport — 1/2-Ton — 106 in. w.b.				
AD100	4x2 without top	4687	3560	2481
AW100	4x4 without top	5746	4075	19,123
B100 Series Tradesman Van — 1/2-Ton — 109 in. w.b.				
B100	Van	4612	3435	16,915
(127 in. w.b.)				
B100	Van	4769	3550	8586
B200 Series Tradesman Van — 3/4-Ton — 109 in. w.b.				
B200	Van	4752	3585	17,619
(127 in. w.b.)				
B200	Van	4909	3710	42,111
B200	Maxivan	5153	—	19,406
B300 Series Tradesman Van — 1-Ton — 109 in. w.b.				
B300	Van	4926	3675	193
(127 in. w.b.)				
B300	Van	5052	3805	4569
B300	Maxivan	5379	4000	9893
CB300 Series Kary Van — 1-Ton — 127 in. w.b.				
CB300	10 ft. Body	6548	4660	—
(145 in. w.b.)				
CB300	12 ft. Body	7749	5210	—
D100 Series — 1/2-Ton — 115 in. w.b.				
D100	Utiline Pickup	4171	3490	Note 1
D100	Sweptline Pickup	4171	3515	Note 1
(131 in. w.b.)				
D100	Utiline Pickup	4313	3490	Note 1
D100	Sweptline Pickup	4313	3620	Note 1

NOTE 1: Total model year production: (115 in.) 47,971; (131 in.) 64,968.

1978 Dodge Club Cab Sweptline Pickup (DNP)

Model	Body Type	Price	Weight	Prod. Total
D100 Series Club Cab — 1/2-Ton — 133 in. w.b.				
D100	Sweptline Pickup	4462	3730	3253
(149 in. w.b.)				
D100	Sweptline Pickup	4604	3870	8428
D150 Series H-D 1/2-Ton — 115 in. w.b.				
D150	Chassis & Cab	4230	3165	—
D150	Utiline Pickup	4452	3555	—
D150	Sweptline Pickup	4452	3580	—
(131 in. w.b.)				
D150	Chassis & Cab	4303	3190	—
D150	Utiline Pickup	4525	3665	—
D150	Sweptline Pickup	4525	3695	—
D150	Li'l Red Truck	—	—	2188
(133 in. w.b.)				
D150	Club Cab — Sweptline	4743	3795	—
(149 in. w.b.)				
D150	Club Cab — Sweptline	4816	3960	—
D200 Series — 3/4-Ton — 131 in. w.b.				
D200	Chassis & Cab	4571	3325	Note 2
D200	Utiline Pickup	4792	3755	Note 2
D200	Sweptline Pickup	4792	3785	Note 2

NOTE 2: Total model year production: 19,387.

D200 Series Club Cab — 3/4-Ton — 149 in. w.b.				
D200	Sweptline Pickup	5074	3955	Note 3
D200 Series Crew Cab — 3/4-Ton — 149 in. w.b.				
D200	Chassis & Cab	5354	3725	Note 3
D200	Utiline (V-8)	6945	4195	Note 3
D200	Sweptline (six)	5576	4095	Note 3
(165 in. w.b.)				
D200	Chassis & Cab	5532	4095	Note 3
D200	Sweptline	5754	4555	Note 3

NOTE 3: Total model year production: (149 in.) 7,567; (165 in.) 1,604.
NOTE 4: Models equipped with 318 cid V-8 were part of RD200 series.

D300 Series — 1-Ton — 131 in. w.b.

Model	Body Type	Price	Weight	Prod.
D300	Sweptline Pickup	5513	4300	774
(135 in. w.b.)				
D300	Chassis & Cab	4875	3735	11,408
(149 in. w.b.)				
D300	Chassis & Cab	5405	—	Note 5
D300	Sweptline Pickup	5804	—	Note 5
(159 in. w.b.)				
D300	Chassis & Cab	4949	3880	2648
(165 in. w.b.)				
D300	Crew Cab — Chassis/Cab	5955	—	Note 5
D300	Crew Cab — Sweptline	6438	—	Note 5

NOTE 5: Total model year production: (149 in.) 1,195; (165 in.) 501.

W150 Series 4x4 — (1/2-Ton) — 115 in. w.b.

Model	Body Type	Price	Weight	Prod.
W150	Chassis & Cab	5292	3780	Note 6
W150	Utiline Pickup	5514	4125	Note 6
W150	Sweptline Pickup	5514	4150	Note 6
(131 in. w.b.)				
W150	Chassis & Cab	5366	3790	Note 6
W150	Utiline Pickup	5587	4220	Note 6
W150	Sweptline Pickup	5587	4250	Note 6

NOTE 6: Total model year production: (115 in.) 24,921; (131 in.) 20,418.

1978 Dodge Adventurer Sweptline Pickup (DNP)

W150 Series Club Cab 4x4 — 1/2-Ton — 133 in. w.b.

Model	Body Type	Price	Weight	Prod.
W150	Sweptline Pickup	5805	4285	2221
(149 in. w.b.)				
W150	Sweptline Pickup	5878	4420	2283

W200 Series 4x4 — 3/4-Ton — 131 in. w.b.

Model	Body Type	Price	Weight	Prod.
W200	Chassis & Cab	5705	3945	Note 7
W200	Utiline Pickup	5927	4375	Note 7
W200	Sweptline Pickup	5927	4405	Note 7
(149 in. w.b.)				
W200	Club Cab — Sweptline	6218	4605	2822

W200 Series Crew Cab 4x4 — 3/4-Ton — 149 in. w.b.

Model	Body Type	Price	Weight	Prod.
W200	Chassis & Cab	6503	4345	Note 7
W200	Sweptline Pickup	6725	4690	Note 7

NOTE 7: Total model year production: (131 in.) 13,413; (149 in. Crew Cab) 1,709.

W300 Series 4x4 — 1-Ton — 135 in. w.b.

Model	Body Type	Price	Weight	Prod.
W300	Chassis & Cab	6872	4480	1326

NOTE 8: Weights and prices shown are for six-cylinder models, except where a V-8 was the base engine.

1978 Dodge Royal Sportsman Maxi Van (DNP)

ENGINES (Standard six: All models): Inline. Overhead valve. Slant six. Cast iron block. Bore & stroke: 3.4 in. x 4.125 in. Displacement: 224.8 cid. Compression ratio: 8.4:1. Brake horsepower: 110 at 3600 rpm. Taxable horsepower: 27.70. Torque: 175 lbs.-ft. at 1600 rpm. Four main bearings. Solid valve lifters. two-barrel carb.
ENGINES (Standard V-8: All models): 90-degree, overhead valve V-8. Cast iron block. Bore & stroke 3.91 in. x 3.31 in. Displacement: 318.3 cid. Compression ratio: 8.6:1. Brake horsepower: 145 at 4000 rpm. Taxable horsepower: 48.92. Torque: 250 lbs.-ft. at 2000 rpm. Five main bearings. Hydraulic Valve lifters.
ENGINES (Optional 360 V-8: All models): 90-degree, overhead valve V-8. Cast iron block. Bore & stroke: 4.00 in. x 3.58 in. Displacement: 360 cid. Compression ratio: 8.5:1.

Brake horsepower: 160 at 4000 rpm. Taxable horsepower: 50.2. Torque: 280 lbs.-ft. at 2000 rpm. Five main bearings. Hydraulic valve lifters.

1978 Dodge Crew Cab Sweptline "Dualie" Pickup (DNP)

ENGINES (Optional 400 V-8: All except B100/D100): 90-degree, overhead valve V-8. Cast iron block. Bore & stroke: 4.34 in. x 3.38 in. Displacement: 400 cid. Compression ratio: 8.2:1. Brake horsepower: 170 at 4000 rpm. Taxable horsepower: 60.3. Torque: 300 lbs.-ft. at 2000 rpm. Five main bearings. Hydraulic Valve lifters.
ENGINES (Optional 440 V-8: B200-300/D150-300/W150-300/AW100): 90-degree, overhead valve V-8. Cast iron block. Bore & stroke: 4.32 in. x 3.75 in. Displacement: 440 cid. Compression ratio: 8.2:1. Brake horsepower: 200 3600 rpm. Taxable horsepower: 58.55. Torque: 330 lbs.-ft. at 2800 rpm. Five main bearings. Hydraulic valve lifters.

1978 Dodge Power Wagon Sweptline Pickup (DNP)

ENGINES (Optional diesel: D150-200/W150-200): Inline. 4-cycle. Six-cylinder. Cast iron block. Bore & stroke: 3.62 in. x 3.94 in. Displacement: 243 cid. Compression ratio: 20:1. Brake horsepower: 100 at 3700 rpm. Torque: 165 lbs.-ft. at 2200 rpm. Seven main bearings. Mechanical valve lifters. Note: Diesel engine, built for Chrysler by Mitsubishi, was not available in California.

CHASSIS (B100) Wheelbase: 109 or 127 in. Tires: E78 x 15-B four-ply. GVW: 4,600 lbs.
CHASSIS (B200) Wheelbase: 109 or 127 in. Tires: G78 x 15-B four-ply. GVW: 5,500 lbs.
CHASSIS (B300) Wheelbase: 109 or 127 in. Tires: 8.00 x 16.5-C six-ply. GVW: 6,400 lbs.
CHASSIS (CB300) Wheelbase: 127 or 145 in. Tires: 8.75 x 16.5-C ten-ply. GVW: 7,700 lbs.
CHASSIS (Ramcharger) Wheelbase: 106 in. Tires: E78 x 15-B four-ply. GVW: 4,900 lbs.
CHASSIS (D100/150) Wheelbase: 115 or 131 in. (Club Cab, 133 or 149 in.) Tires: G78 x 15-B four-ply. GVW: 5,000 lbs.

1978 Dodge Royal Sportsman SE Van (DNP)

CHASSIS (D200) Wheelbase: 131, 149 (Club Cab, Crew Cab) or 165 in. (Crew Cab). Tires: 8.00 x 16.5-D eight-ply. GVW: 6,200 lbs.
CHASSIS (D300) Wheelbase: 131, 135, 149, 159 or 165 in. Tires: 8.00 x 16.5-D eight-ply. GVW: 6,600 lbs.
CHASSIS (W150) Wheelbase: 115 or 131 in. (Club Cab, 133 or 149 in.). Tires: H78 x 15-B. GVW: 5,400 lbs.
CHASSIS (W200) Wheelbase: 131 or 149 in. Tires: 8.00 x 16.5-D eight-ply. GVW: 6,500 lbs.
CHASSIS (W300) Wheelbase: 135 in. Tires: 8.75 x 16.5-E 10-ply. GVW: 8,500 lbs.

1978 Dodge Custom Sportsman Van (DNP)

TECHNICAL: Selective sliding gear column-mounted transmission. Speeds: 3F/1R, except D300/W300 and 165 in. wheelbase D200 which all come standard with floor-mounted four-speed transmission. Floor-mounted four-speed transmission optional in selected models. Three-speed automatic transmission optional. Single dry-disc clutch with manual transmissions: (six-cylinder) 10 in.; (V-8) 11 in. Various rear axle ratios. Fuel tank: (Vans) 23-gallon; (AW100) 24-gallon; (other models) 22-gallon. 48-amp. alternator.

1978 Dodge D150 "Li'l Red Truck" Utiline Pickup (JH)

OPTIONS: Same as 1977, but add the following: (Vans) Skylite sun roof. Trip computer. Unibelt restraint system. Spare tire cover. AM Radio/CB Transceiver. AM/FM/Stereo Radio with CB Transceiver. (Pickups) Four-speed overdrive transmission (floor shift) A833. Tilt steering column. AM/CB radio. AM/FM/Stereo radio. (Ramcharger) Low-back bucket seat. High-back command bucket seat. Tilt-steering column. AM/CB radio. AM/FM/Stereo/CB radio. AM/FM/Stereo radio with 8-track stereo player.

1978 Dodge D150 "Li'l Red Truck" Utiline Pickup, rear view (JH)

HISTORICAL: Introduced: August 1977. (Vans, January 1978). Calendar year sales (U.S.): 489,134. Model year sales: 480,035 (including Plymouth Trail Duster). Calendar year production: 489,074. Model year production: 383,167. Innovations: Maxivan stretched to become the largest van in the industry. Diesel engine. A strike at the van assembly plant late in 1977 delayed introduction of the 1978 vans, as old parts on hand had to be used up before production began on new models. Because the light-duty market continued to shift away from commercial applications to a personal-use market, Dodge continued to focus on those buyers with its Adult Toys collection. One specialized truck was sold only in the West: A 4x4 replica of Rod Hall's race truck, called The Force. The Force Power Wagon featured Mickey Thompson shocks, extra-leaf front springs, Hickey rollbar and grille guard, Hella driving lights, Sears Adventurer tires, Superior wheels, front and rear axle trusses, floor mats, and special paint and stripes. It sold for $1,400 more than the base price of the short-box 1/2-ton 4x4. This was another good year for the Dodge truck division, as production topped the record set in 1977. Canadian production fell 35 percent, due to factory change-over. Calendar year U.S. retail sales also set a record. For the model year, 235,160 conventional models were sold; 220,315 Tradesman vans; 17,283 Ramchargers; and 6,934 Plymouth Trail Dusters. A total of 7,717 Plymouth Voyager and 23,989 Dodge Sportsman wagons were counted in station wagon sales. The diesel engine option lasted only this one year, selling only 2,587 units. The Tradesman was the industry's most popular van, and Dodge's leading truck model. Sales of the Li'l Red Trucks came to 2,188. A pre-production version of the Li'l Red Truck was road tested by *HOT ROD* magazine and *CAR and DRIVER*. It was found to be the fastest American vehicle at speeds up to 100 mph. This pre-production test truck did the quarter-mile in 14.7 seconds at 93 mph and had a top speed of 118.8 mph. The engine used in the prototype had to be detuned for production models to meet federal regulations.

Standard Catalog of Light-Duty Trucks

1978 Dodge Tradesman Street Van (DNP)

1979 DODGE

1979 Dodge Power Wagon Sweptline Pickup (DNP)

1/2 TON VAN — B100 SERIES — SIX-CYLINDER/V-8; 3/4-TON VAN — B200 SERIES — V-8; 1-TON VAN — B300 SERIES — V-8; 1-TON KARY VAN — V-8: Vans gained a front end restyling this year, following the new side and rear appearance of 1978. This van was all-new from the windshield pillar forward. Overall length added three inches and the hood opening was made longer and wider. Larger bushings and softer spring rates in the front suspension achieved a 10 percent improvement in ride and handling. The new front styling also contributed to lowered wind resistance for better fuel mileage. A new grille with stacked rectangular quad headlamps, standard on top-of-the-line models, gave a fresh new appearance. An energy-absorbing steering column was added. Heating and air conditioning were improved. B100 models could have the 225 cid slant six or 318 cid V-8, but larger vans now came with a V-8 only. All other basic specifications were as before. New options included a tilt steering wheel, electric door locks and rear window defroster (on single rear door models). Tilt steering was available only with power steering and automatic transmission. The Street Van continued with the same appearance changes as standard models.

1979 Dodge D50 Sport Mini Pickup (DNP)

MINI PICKUP — D50 SERIES — FOUR: The only all-new vehicle for 1979 was a mini pickup designed and built for Dodge by Mitsubishi (Chrysler's Japanese partner). Sitting on a 109.4 in. wheelbase chassis, the D50 had a 6.5 ft. cargo box and carried a payload of 1,400 lbs. It came in two trim levels: Standard and Sport. Engine choices were a 2-liter (122 cid) or 2.6-liter (156 cid) four. The littlest Dodge truck gave a smooth, passenger car-like ride with its very good A-arm front suspension, solid rear axle and leaf spring layout. Styling was quite attractive, too. Interior trim on the sport model was quite pleasant, with bucket seats and carpeting on the floor. The standard model used a four-speed transmission, but the sport carried a five-speed. Automatic was optional on both.

1979 Dodge D50 Mini Pickup (DNP)

1979 Dodge Power Wagon Sweptline Pickup (DNP)

1/2-TON PICKUP — D100 SERIES — SIX-CYLINDER/V-8; HEAVY 1/2-TON PICKUP — D150 SERIES — SIX-CYLINDER/V-8; 3/4-TON PICKUP — D200 SERIES — SIX-CYLINDER/V-8; 1-TON PICKUP — D300 SERIES — V-8; 1/2-TON 4x4 — W150 SERIES — SIX-CYLINDER/V-8; 3/4-TON 4x4 — W200 SERIES — V-8; 1-TON 4x4 — W300 SERIES — V-8: Full-size pickups gained a new front end appearance. It included a new hood, cowl top panel, grille and headlight treatment. Quad rectangular headlamps became standard on top-of-the-line models, while single round headlamps remained on base models. Chassis lubrication intervals were extended to two years or 22,500 miles for trucks with less than 8,500 pound GVW ratings. Galvanized steel saw use on the inside panel of Sweptline tailgates and on cowl side outer panels of all models. An engine coolant reserve system was added. Club Cab models got rear quarter windows that opened. Other improvements included upgraded interiors for conventional and Club Cab Adventurer SE models, two new optional tape stripe packages, optional electric door locks, and air conditioning on six-cylinder models. Due to stricter federal fuel efficiency standards, the 400 and 440 cid V-8s were dropped. The D100 was now subject to federal fuel mileage standards, so its standard gear included a 225 cid six with single-barrel carburetor, radial tires, and a torque converter lockup. Dodge's popular "Adult Toys" line continued. All were based on conventional models and given the same improvements as the standard line. Paint and striping on the Macho Power Wagon and Warlock II were updated, and the Li'l Red Truck carried over for its second (and final) year. The latter looked about the same as the previous season, but had a decrease in horsepower due to a change in federal regulations governing which GVW rating classes were covered by emissions rules. Although its production nearly doubled, the Li'l Red Truck would disappear after 1979.

1979 Dodge Adventurer Club Cab Sweptline Pickup (DNP)

1/2-TON RAMCHARGER 2WD — AD100 SERIES — SIX-CYLINDER/V-8; 1/2-TON RAMCHARGER 4x4 — AW100 SERIES — V-8: Ramchargers received the same new front end treatment as the pickup models. An optional sound insulation package delivered a quieter ride. Roofs were now made of galvanized steel, and more comprehensive primer protection was applied to bodyside panels. Added to the option list were electric door locks, a tilt steering wheel and new tape stripe packages. Two-wheel drive Ramchargers could have the 225 cid six, 318 cid V-8 or 360 cid V-8. Four-wheel drive models were V-8 only. The Macho Ramcharger gained new tape striping and special tailgate designation.

1979 Dodge D150 Li'l Red Truck Utiline Pickup (OCW)

I.D. DATA: A serial number Vehicle Identification Number (VIN) plate was on the driver's door latch post. The seven element number contained 13 alpha-numeric characters. The first two characters indicated model codes: A1=AW100; B1=B100; B2=B200; B3=B300; C3=CB300; D1=D100/150; D2=D200; R2=RD200; D3=D300; E1=AD100; W1=W150; W2=W200; W3=W300. Next came a body type code: 0=forward control, motorhome chassis, Kary Van or sport-utility; 1=Tradesman van, conventional cab/chassis; 2=Sportsman, Crew Cab/chassis; 3=Utiline conventional cab; 4=Sweptline conventional cab; 5=Maxivan, Utiline Crew Cab; 6=Sportsman Maxiwagon, Sweptline Crew Cab; 7=flat face cowl, Sweptline Club Cab; 8=cowl/windshield, Club Cab; 9=Utiline Club Cab. Next came a letter indicating GVW class: A=6,000 lbs. or less; B=6,001 to 10,000 lbs.; etc. The next letter showed engine type: A=440-3; B=225-1; C=225-2; D=440-1; E=318-1; F=360-1; G=318-3; H=400-1; K=360-3; H=243 diesel; X=special six-cylinder; V=special V-8. Next came the final digit in the year of manufacture, (9=1979). The next letter indicated assembly plant: J=Tecumseh Road; K=Pillette Road; N=Burt Road (Knocked-Down Export); S=Warren No. 1; T=Warren No. 2; X=Missouri; V=Warren No. 3 (compact). This was followed by a 6-digit sequence number. Engine numbers were in the same locations as 1975-1977.

1979 Dodge Adventurer SE Sweptline Pickup (DNP)

1979 Dodge Custom Utiline Pickup (DNP)

Model	Body Type	Price	Weight	Prod. Total
D50 Series Mini Pickup — 1/4-Ton — 109.4 in. w.b.				
D50	Sweptline	4819	2410	—
D50	Sport	5608	2410	—
AD100/AW100 Ramcharger — 1/2-Ton — 106 in. w.b.				
AD100	4x2 without top	5483	3660	—
AW100	4x4 without top	6998	4175	—
B100 Series Tradesman Vans — 1/2-Ton — 109 in. w.b.				
B100	Van	4992	3435	—
(127 in. w.b.)				
B100	Van	5160	3550	—
B200 Series Tradesman Vans — 3/4-Ton — 109 in. w.b.				
B200	Van	5326	3585	—
(127 in. w.b.)				
B200	Van	5468	3710	—
B200	Maxivan	5855	—	—

Series / Model	Body	Price	Weight	
B300 Series Tradesman Vans — 1-Ton — 109 in. w.b.				
B300	Van	5523	3675	—
(127 in. w.b.)				
B300	Van	5608	3805	—
B300	Maxivan	6008	4000	—
CB300 Series Kary Van — V-8 only — 1-Ton — 127 in. w.b.				
CB300	10 ft. Body	7124	4760	
(145 in. w.b.)				
CB300	12 ft. Body	8411	5210	
D100 Series — 1/2-Ton — 115 in. w.b.				
D100	Utiline Pickup	4499	3490	—
D100	Sweptline Pickup	4499	3515	—
(131 in. w.b.)				
D100	Utiline Pickup	4651	3490	—
D100	Sweptline Pickup	4651	3620	—
D150 Series — H-D 1/2-Ton — 115 in. w.b.				
D150	Utiline Pickup	5115	3620	—
D150	Sweptline Pickup	5115	3645	—
(131 in. w.b.)				
D150	Utiline Pickup	5194	3730	—
D150	Lil Red Truck	—	—	5118
D150	Sweptline Pickup	5194	3760	—
(133 in. w.b.)				
D150	Club Cab — Sweptline	5146	3795	—
(149 in. w.b.)				
D150	Club Cab — Sweptline	5223	3950	—
D200 Series — 3/4-Ton — 131 in. w.b.				
D200	Utiline Pickup	5125	3755	—
D200	Sweptline Pickup	5125	3785	—
(149 in. w.b.)				
D200	Club Cab — Sweptline	5427	3955	—
D200 Series Crew Cab — V-8 only — 3/4-Ton — 149 in. w.b.				
D200	Sweptline Pickup	6142	4625	
(165 in. w.b.)				
D200	Sweptline Pickup	6331	4655	
D300 Series — 1-Ton — 131 in. w.b.				
D300	Sweptline Pickup	5737	4300	—
(135 in. w.b.)				
D300	Chassis & Cab	5936	3735	—
(149 in. w.b.)				
D300	Chassis & Cab	6322	—	—
D300	Sweptline Pickup	6046	—	—
(159 in. w.b.)				
D300	Chassis & Cab	6014	3880	—
(165 in. w.b.)				
D300	Crew Cab — Sweptline	6565	—	—
W150 Series 4x4 — 1/2-Ton — 115 in. w.b.				
W150	Utiline Pickup	5897	4125	—
W150	Sweptline Pickup	5897	4150	—
(131 in. w.b.)				
W150	Utiline Pickup	5902	4220	—
W150	Sweptline Pickup	5902	4250	—
W150 Series Club Cab 4x4 — V-8 only — 1/2-Ton — 133 in. w.b.				
W150	Sweptline Pickup	6416	4360	—
(149 in. w.b.)				
W150	Sweptline Pickup	6567	4495	—
W200 Series 4x4 — V-8 only — 3/4-Ton — 131 in. w.b.				
W200	Utiline Pickup	6565	4365	—
W200	Sweptline Pickup	6565	4395	—
(149 in. w.b.)				
W200	Club Cab — Sweptline	6876	4620	—
W200 Series Crew Cab 4x4 — V-8 only — 3/4-Ton — 149 in. w.b.				
W200	Sweptline Pickup	8235	4785	—
W300 Series 4x4 — 360 cid V-8 — 1-Ton — 135 in. w.b.				
W300	Chassis & Cab	8237	4525	—

NOTE 1: Weights and prices shown are for six-cylinder models, except where a 318 or 360 cid V-8 was the base engine.

Standard Catalog of Light-Duty Trucks

1979 Dodge Adventurer Club Cab Sweptline Pickup (DNP)

ENGINES (Standard six: B100/D100-200/W150/AD100): Inline. Overhead valve. Slant six. Cast iron block. Bore & stroke: 3.4 x 4.125 in. Displacement: 224.8 cid. Compression ratio: 8.4:1. Brake horsepower: 110 at 3600 rpm. Taxable horsepower: 27.70. Torque: 175 lbs.-ft. at 1600 rpm. Four main bearings. Solid valve lifters.

ENGINE (Standard V-8: B100-300/D100-200/W150-200/AD100/AW100): 90-degree, overhead valve. V-8. Cast iron block. Bore & stroke: 3.91 x 3.31 in. Displacement: 318.3 cid. Compression ratio: 8.6:1. Brake horsepower: 145 at 4000 rpm. Taxable horsepower: 48.92. Torque: 250 lbs.-ft. at 2000 rpm. Five main bearings. Hydraulic valve lifters.

ENGINE (Optional 360 V-8: B200-300/D150-200/W150-300/AD100/AW100; standard on D300): 90-degree, overhead valve. V-8. Cast iron block. Bore & stroke: 4.00 x 3.58 in. Displacement: 360 cid. Compression ratio: 8.5:1. Brake horsepower: 160 at 4000 rpm. Taxable horsepower: 50.2. Torque: 280 lbs.-ft. at 2000 rpm. Five main bearings. Hydraulic valve lifters.

1979 Dodge Ramcharger 4x4 Utility (DNP)

ENGINE (D50): Inline. Overhead cam. Four-cylinder. Cast iron block. Bore & stroke: 84.0mm x 90.0mm. Displacement: 2000 cc (122 cid). Compression ratio: 8.5:1. Brake horsepower: 93 at 5200 rpm. Torque: 108 lbs.-ft. at 3000 rpm.

ENGINE (D50 Sport): Inline. Overhead cam. Four-cylinder. Cast iron block. Bore & stroke: 91.1mm x 98.0mm. Displacement: 2555 cc (156 cid). Compression ratio: 8.2:1. Brake horsepower: 105 at 5000 rpm. Torque: 139 lbs.-ft. at 2500 rpm.

CHASSIS (D50) Wheelbase: 109.4 in.

CHASSIS (B100) Wheelbase: 109 or 127 in. Tires: E78 x 15-B four-ply. GVW: 4,600 lbs.

CHASSIS (B200) Wheelbase: 109 or 127 in. Tires: G78 x 15-B four-ply. GVW: 5,500 lbs.

CHASSIS (B300) Wheelbase: 109 or 127 in. Tires: 8.00 x 16.5-C six-ply. GVW: 6,400 lbs.

CHASSIS (CB300) Wheelbase: 127 or 145 in. Tires: 8.75 x 16.5-C ten-ply. GVW: 7,700 lbs.

CHASSIS (Ramcharger) Wheelbase: 106 in. Tires: E78 x 15-B four-ply. GVW: 4,900 lbs.

CHASSIS (D100/150) Wheelbase: 115 or 131 in. (Club Cab, 133 or 149 in.) Tires: G78 x 15-B four-ply. GVW: 5,000 lbs.

CHASSIS (D200) Wheelbase: 131, 149 (Club Cab, Crew Cab) or 165 in. (Crew Cab). Tires: 8.00 x 16.5-D eight-ply. GVW: 6,200 lbs.

CHASSIS (D300) Wheelbase: 131, 135, 149, 159 or 165 in. Tires: 8.00 x 16.5-D eight-ply. GVW: 6,600 lbs.

CHASSIS (W150) Wheelbase: 115 or 131 in. (Club Cab, 133 or 149 in.). Tires: H78 x 15-B. GVW: 5,400 lbs.

CHASSIS (W200) Wheelbase: 131 or 149 in. Tires: 8.00 x 16.5-D eight-ply. GVW: 6,500 lbs.

CHASSIS (W300) Wheelbase: 135 in. Tires: 8.75 x 16.5-E 10-ply. GVW: 8,500 lbs.

TECHNICAL: Selective sliding gear column-mounted transmission. Speeds: 3F/1R, except D300/W300 and 165 in. wheelbase D200 which all come standard with floor-mounted four-speed transmission. Floor-mounted four-speed transmission optional in selected models. Three-speed automatic transmission optional. Single dry-disc clutch with manual transmissions: (six-cylinder) 10 in.; (V-8) 11 in. Various rear axle ratios. Fuel tank: (Vans) 23-gallon; (AW100) 24-gallon; (other models) 22-gallon. 48-amp. alternator.

1979 Dodge Ramcharger SE 4x4 Utility (DNP)

1979 Dodge Royal Sportsman Maxi Van (DNP)

OPTIONS: Same as 1978, but add the following: (Vans) Quad rectangular headlamps. (Standard Pickups) Quad rectangular headlamps. Tuff type steering wheel (three-spoke). AM/FM Stereo radio with either 8-track tape player or CB transceiver. (Ramcharger) Tape stripe package. Lockable console. Quad rectangular headlamps. Skylite sun roof. Tuff type three-spoke steering wheel. AM/FM/Stereo radio with either 8-track tape player or CB transceiver. AM/CB radio/transceiver.

HISTORICAL: Introduced: August, 1978. Model year sales: 391,396 (177,937 conventional; 151,070 Tradesman vans; 15,754 Ramchargers; 6,114 Traildusters; 27,517 D50 pickups; and 13,004 Arrow pickups) Calendar year sales: 352,292. Calendar year production (U.S.): 303,075. Innovations: Mini pickup. Galvanized steel in certain panels. Gasoline shortages and higher prices caused a softening in the truck market. After a record year in 1978, total U.S. industry shipments declined 18.1 percent. Dodge's van sales were down 48 percent, pickups 30 percent, and sport-utility vehicles off 21 percent. Diminished production caused Dodge to drop to number four in the industry, behind GMC. Dodge's role as a major supplier of RV chassis proved nearly a disaster, as that business almost entirely dried up. In June, 1979, Dodge closed its RV lines. Due to more stringent corporate average fuel economy (CAFE) goals for vans and trucks in the 1980s, Dodge passenger vans were reclassified as trucks beginning on Oct. 1, 1979. Ford and GM followed suit as of January, 1980. Production of the Li'l Red Truck in this, its final year, totalled 5,118 units.

1979 Dodge Tradesman Custom Van (DNP)

1980 Dodge D50 Mini-Pickup (RPZ)

1980 Dodge D50 Sport Mini-Pickup (RPZ)

1/4-TON MINI PICKUP — D50 SERIES — FOUR-CYLINDER: This popular subcompact from Mitsubishi entered its second year with very minimal change. A lockable, sliding glass rear cab window was a new option. One paint color was added to the standard model, another to the Sport model. Color choices on the standard were Warm white, Light tan and black; but Spitfire orange, yellow, and Bright Metallic blue were available on the Sport. The Sport model also gained a macho look with black base color and wide multi-color side stripe that had colors radiating from the wheel openings.

1980 Dodge B200 Forward Control Panel Van (RPZ)

1/2-TON VAN — B100 SERIES — SIX-CYLINDER/V-8; 3/4-TON VAN — B200 SERIES — SIX-CYLINDER/V-8; 1-TON VAN — B300 SERIES — V-8: For the first time in their long history, passenger vans (Sportsman wagons) were counted as trucks, rather than cars. Changes for 1980 were slight. Four-speed overdrive manual transmission became standard on 1/2- and 3/4-ton models; TorqueFlite three-speed automatic transmission on the 1-ton B300. Large vented windows replaced dual vented windows in the sliding side cargo door, with dual vented windows on the left side. A vented window for the single rear door became optional. Other options included power front door windows, an electronic travel computer, wide-pad brake pedal (on models with automatic transmission), lighted vanity mirror in the right sun visor, reading lamp in the headliner, bright finish hitch-type towing bumper with wide center strap and halogen headlamps for better visibility. Two new entertainment packages were offered: An AM/FM/Stereo computerized radio with Search Tune and an AM/FM stereo with cassette tape player and Dolby noise reduction system. Standard van equipment included painted bumpers and grille, dual cargo doors, chrome hubcaps, driver's sun visor, power steering (on B300) and 225 cid slant six engine (318 V-8 on the B300).

1980 Dodge D150 Adventurer SE Sweptline Pickup (RPZ)

1/2-TON PICKUP — D150 SERIES — SIX-CYLINDER/V-8; 3/4-TON PICKUP — D200 SERIES — SIX-CYLINDER/V-8; 1-TON PICKUP — D300 SERIES — V-8; 1/2-TON 4x4 — W150 SERIES — SIX-CYLINDER/V-8; 3/4-TON 4x4 — W200 SERIES — V-8; 1-TON 4x4 — W300 SERIES — V-8: Full-size conventional trucks received only a minor facelift this year. Grille openings were painted black to achieve a new frontal look, but this was the only appearance change. After 23 consecutive years, the D100 model was dropped, making the D150 the lightest full-size model. D-Series improvements included a switch to four-speed manual overdrive transmission on the D150 for added fuel economy; optional power front door windows; a styled, bright-finished, hitch-type towing bumper with wide center step; halogen headlamps (on dual headlight system); and a suspended accelerator pedal. Due to pressure from higher fuel prices triggered by OPEC, W-Series 4x4 models changed to part time four-wheel drive. This improved fuel economy and front axle serviceability, while reducing weight and drive line noise. Dodge trucks used two part-time transfer cases made by Chrysler's New Process Division: NP208 on 1/2- and 3/4-ton models and NP205 on the 1-ton and 3/4-ton Crew Cab models. Standard transmission on all 4x4 models became the four-speed manual NP435, replacing the former three-speed. The popular Macho Power-Wagon, with its distinctive two-tone color scheme and large graphics, continued for 1980. Standard equipment on D/W models included chrome front bumper and grille, chrome hubcaps (D only), power brakes, 5x7 inch mirrors, bench seat, dome and courtesy lights, front/rear shocks (front only on 1-ton models), and an axle jack.

1980 Dodge Ramcharger SE "Macho" 4x4 Utility (RPZ)

1/2-TON RAMCHARGER 4x2 — AD100 SERIES — SIX-CYLINDER/V-8; 1/2-TON RAMCHARGER 4x4 — AW100 SERIES — V-8: Part time four-wheel drive was the big change for 1980 Ramchargers, which continued to be offered in standard or premium price class. Automatic transmission was standard on 4x2 models, but the NP435 manual four-speed and automatic were offered on four-wheel drive models. Fifteen paint colors (including nine new ones) were available. Other appearance items included all-new wheelcovers and hubcaps, a chrome step-type towing bumper, and aluminum road wheels. Ramchargers also offered the same new options as pickups and vans: Power front windows, two new entertainment systems and halogen headlamps. New on Ramchargers only was an optional fold-up rear bench seat. A rear compartment mat, formerly optional, was now standard. So were rear courtesy lamps and a suspended gas pedal, plus power steering on four-wheel drive models. Manual front locking hubs had to be turned by hand for four-wheel drive in the part-time system, which used the NP208 transfer case. The 318 cid V-8 now ran with a four-barrel carburetor for better performance. Ramcharger standard equipment included power brakes, chrome bumpers front and rear, chrome grille and hubcaps, map/courtesy light, rear compartment light, chrome outside mirrors, front and rear shock absorbers, and an axle jack.

1980 Dodge W150 Power Wagon Club Cab (RPZ)

Standard Catalog of Light-Duty Trucks

I.D. DATA: [D50 Imported Pickups] The 13-character VIN was stamped on a plate on the left top side of the instrument panel, visible through the windshield. The first digit showed the truck line (9=D50; 0=Plymouth Arrow). Second digit indicated GVW and number of driving wheels (J=4x2, less than 6,000 lbs.). Third digit was the price class (L=low line; P= premium). Fourth digit showed body type (4=conventional cab with Sweptline box). Fifth letter gave engine displacement (U=2-liter; W=2.6 liter). Sixth letter gave model year (A=1980). Seventh came the transmission code (1=four-speed manual, U.S.; 2=four-speed, California; 3=four-speed, Canada; 4=five-speed, U.S.; 5=five-speed, California; 6=five-speed, Canada; 7=automatic, U.S.; 8=automatic, California; 9=automatic, Canada). Trim code was denoted by the eight digit (1=low line; 3=high 1; 5=high2 2; 6=premium). The last five digits formed the sequence number, starting with 00001.

I.D. DATA: [other models] The 13-character VIN was on an identification plate on the driver's door or B post. The first two characters designated model: B1=B100; B2=B200; B3=B300; C3=CB300; D1=D150; D2=D200; R2=RD200; D3=D300; W1=W150; W2=W200; W3=W300; A1=AW100; E1=AD100. The next digit showed body type: 0=Ramcharger sport-utility, forward control, motor home chassis or incomplete chassis; 1=Dodge Van, conventional cab & chassis, CB300; 2=Sportsman, crew cab & chassis, CB300 without; 3=Utiline conventional cab; 4=Sweptline conventional cab; 5=Maxivan, Utiline Crew Cab; 6=Sportsman Maxiwagon or Sweptline Crew Cab; 7=cowl & windshield, Club Cab and chassis; 9=Utiline Club Cab. Next came a letter for GVW class: A=6,000 lbs. or less; B=6,001 to 8,500 lbs.; K=8,501 to 10,000 lbs.; etc. Next came a letter indicating engine: B=225-1-2V; C=225-2-1V; E=318-1-2V; F=360-1-2V; G=318-3-2V; K=360-3-2V; N=225-1-1V; P=318-1-4V; S=360-HP-4V; T=360-1-4V; V=special V-8; X=special six. The sixth letter indicated model year (A=1980). The next letter indicated assembly plant: C=Jefferson Ave.; K=Windsor, Pillette Rd.; N=Burt Road, Knocked-down export; S=Warren Truck No. 1; T=Warren Truck No. 2; V=Warren Truck No. 3; X=Missouri. Finally came a six digit sequence number, which began with 100001 for Warren Truck Plant No. 1, Missouri Truck and Jefferson Truck; with 300001 for the Windsor Pillette plant; with 500001 at Warren Truck No. 2, and 700001 at Warren Truck Plant No. 3. Example: B12ABAK300001 designated a Sportsman B100, rated 6,000 lbs. GVW or less, with 225 cid slant six engine and two-barrel carburetor, 1980 model, built at Windsor with serial number 300001.

Model	Body Type	Price	Weight	Prod. Total
D50 Series Mini Pickup — 1-Ton — 109.4 in. w.b.				
D50	Sweptline	4870	2573	—
D50	Sport	5683	2648	—
AD100/AW100 Ramcharger — 1/2-Ton — 106 in. w.b.				
AD100	4x2 hardtop	6793	3660	—
AW100	4x4 hardtop	8298	4150	—
B100 Series Sportsman Wagons — 1/2-Ton — 109.6 in. w.b.				
B100	Wagon	6564	3444	—
(127.6 in. w.b.)				
B100	Wagon	6736	3595	—
B200 Series Sportsman Wagons — 3/4-Ton — 109.6 in. w.b.				
B200	Wagon	6876	3460	—
(127.6 in. w.b.)				
B200	Wagon	7051	3584	—
B200	Maxiwagon	8152	4009	—
B300 Series Sportsman Wagons — 1-Ton — 127.6 in. w.b.				
B300	Wagon	8300	4121	—
B300	Maxiwagon	8659	4325	—
B100 Series Tradesman Van — 1/2-Ton — 109.6 in. w.b.				
B100	Van	5470	3232	—
(127.6 in. w.b.)				
B100	Van	5645	3351	—
B200 Series Tradesman Van — 3/4-Ton — 109.6 in. w.b.				
B200	Van	5795	3237	—
(127.6 in. w.b.)				
B200	Van	5969	3349	—
B200	Maxivan	6369	3607	—
B300 Series Tradesman Van — 1-Ton — 127.6 in. w.b.				
B300	Van	7289	3800	—
B300	Maxivan	7686	4066	—
D150 Series — 1/2-Ton — 115 in. w.b.				
D150	Utiline Pickup	5275	3288	—
D150	Sweptline Pickup	5275	3323	—
(131 in. w.b.)				
D150	Utiline Pickup	5360	3402	—
D150	Sweptline Pickup	5360	3437	—
(133 in. w.b.)				
D150	Club Cab — Sweptline	6503	3666	—
(149 in. w.b.)				
D150	Club Cab — Sweptline	6588	3796	—
D200 Series — (3/4-Ton) — 131 in. w.b.				
D200	Utiline Pickup	6052	3736	—
D200	Sweptline Pickup	6052	3771	—
(149 in. w.b.)				
D200	Club Cab — Sweptline	7010	3969	—

237

D300 Series Crew Cab — 1-Ton — 165 in. w.b.

D300	Sweptline Pickup	8461	4793	—

W150 Series 4x4 — 1/2-Ton — 115 in. w.b.

W150	Utiline Pickup	7181	3797	—
W150	Sweptline Pickup	7181	3832	—

(131 in. w.b.)

W150	Utiline Pickup	7266	3912	—
W150	Sweptline Pickup	7266	3947	—

(133 in. w.b.)

W150	Club Cab — Sweptline	7837	4090	—

(149 in. w.b.)

W150	Club Cab — Sweptline	7990	4235	—

W200 Series 4x4 — 3/4-Ton — 131 in. w.b.

W200	Utiline Pickup	7853	4120	—
W200	Sweptline Pickup	7853	4155	—

(149 in. w.b.)

W200	Club Cab — Sweptline	8503	4544	—

W200 Crew Cab 4x4 — 3/4-Ton — 149 in. w.b.

W200	Sweptline Pickup	9512	4842	—

W300 Series 4x4 — 1-Ton — 135 in. w.b.

W300	Chassis & Cab	8869	4806	—

ENGINE (standard in D150/D200/W150/B100/B200/AD100): Inline. Overhead valve. Slant six. Cast iron block. Bore x stroke: 3.4 x 4.125 in. Displacement: 224.8 cid. Compression ratio: 8.4:1. Brake horsepower: 110 at 3600 rpm. Taxable horsepower: 27.70. Torque: 175 lbs.-ft. at 1600 rpm. Four main bearings. Solid valve lifters.

ENGINE (standard V-8 in D150/D200/W150/W200/B100/B200/B300/AD100/AW100): 90-degree. Overhead valve. V-8. Cast iron block. Bore x stroke: 3.91 x 3.31 in. Displacement: 318.3 cid. Compression ratio: 8.6:1. Brake horsepower: 145 at 4000 rpm. Taxable horsepower: 48.92. Torque: 250 lbs.-ft. at 2000 rpm. Five main bearings. Hydraulic valve lifters.

ENGINE (optional V-8): 90-degree. Overhead valve. V-8. Cast iron block. Bore x stroke: 4.00 x 3.58 in. Displacement: 360 cid. Compression ratio: 8.51. Brake horsepower: 160 at 4000 rpm. Taxable horsepower: 50.2. Torque: 280 lbs.-ft. at 2000 rpm. Five main bearings. Hydraulic valve lifters.

ENGINE (D50): Inline. Overhead valve. Overhead cam. Four. Cast iron block. Bore x stroke: 84.0 mm. x 90.0 mm. Displacement: 2000 cc. (122 cid). Compression ratio: 8.5:1. Brake horsepower: 93 at 5200 rpm. Torque: 108 lbs.-ft. at 3000 rpm.

ENGINE (D50 Sport): Inline. Overhead valve. Overhead cam. Four. Cast iron block. Bore x stroke: 91.1 mm. x 98.0 mm. Displacement: 2555 cc. (156 cid). Compression ratio: 8.2:1. Brake horsepower: 105 at 5000 rpm. Torque: 139 lbs.-ft. at 2500 rpm.

1980 Dodge B200 Sportsman Maxiwagon (RPZ)

CHASSIS (D50): Wheelbase: 109.4 in. Tires: 6.00 x 14-C. GVW: 4,045-4,120 lbs.

CHASSIS (B100): Wheelbase: 109.6 or 127.6 in. Tires: P205/75R15-B. GVW: 4,700-5,100 lbs. Axle Capacity: (front) 3,300 lbs.; (rear) 3,550 lbs.

CHASSIS (B200): Wheelbase: 109.6 or 127.6 in. Tires: P22/75R15-B. GVW: 6,050 lbs. Axle Capacity: (front) 3,300 lbs.; (rear) 3,550 lbs.

CHASSIS (B300): Wheelbase: 127.6 in. Tires: 8.00 x 16.5-E. GVW: 7,000-7,200 lbs. Axle Capacity: (front) 3,600 lbs.; (rear) 5,500 lbs.

CHASSIS (D150): Wheelbase: 115 or 131 in. (Club Cab, 133 or 149 in.). Tires: P195/75R-15B. GVW: 4,800 lbs. (Club Cab 6,050). Axle Capacity: (front) 3,300 lbs.; (rear) 3,400 lbs.

CHASSIS (D200): Wheelbase: 131, 149 (Club Cab) or 165 in. (Club/Crew Cab). Tires: 8.00 x 16.5-E. GVW: 6,500 lbs. (Club Cab 7,500; Crew Cab 8,550). Axle Capacity: (front) 3,700 lbs.; (rear) 5,500 lbs.

CHASSIS (D300): Wheelbase: 149 in. or 165 in. (Crew Cab). Tires: 9.50 x 16.5-E. GVW: 9,000 lbs. (Crew, 10,000). Axle Capacity: (front) 4,000 lbs.; (rear) 6,200 lbs.

CHASSIS (W150): Wheelbase: 115 or 131 in. (Club Cab, 133 or 149 in.). GVW: 6,050 lbs. Axle Capacity: (front) 3,500 lbs.; (rear) 3,600 lbs.

CHASSIS (W200): Wheelbase: 131 or 149 in. GVW: 6,900 lbs. (Club/Crew Cab 8,550). Axle Capacity: (front) 3,500 lbs.; (rear) 5,500 lbs.

CHASSIS (W300): Wheelbase: 135 in. GVW: 10,000 lbs. Axle Capacity: (front) 4,500 lbs.; (rear) 7,500 lbs.

CHASSIS (Ramcharger): Wheelbase: 106 in. Tires: P225/75R15-B. GVW: 5,300-6,050 lbs.

TECHNICAL: Selective sliding gear transmission. Speeds: (B100-200/D150) four-speed overdrive; (B300) three-speed automatic; (D200-300/W150-300) four-speed manual. Four-wheel drive transfer case: Part time. Clutch: (B100-200/D150-300 with 115/131 in. wheelbase) 10 in.; (others) 11 in. Hydraulic brakes: Front disc, rear drum. Electronic ignition system. 48-amp. alternator. Fuel tank: (D/W) 18-gallon; (vans) 22-gallon; (Ramcharger) 24-gallon.

1980 Dodge Ramcharger SE Utility Wagon (RPZ)

OPTIONS (Factory-Installed): (B Vans) Chrome bumpers (front/rear). Bumper guards (front/rear). Chrome bumper hitch. Single rear door. Sliding side door. Door check arms. Door edge protectors. Tinted glass. Sunscreen. Banded glass. Chrome grille. Skylite sun roof. Color-keyed spare tire cover. Painted spoke white wheels (15x7.00). Chrome disc five-slot wheels. Aluminum ribbed wheels. Deluxe chrome or premium wheelcovers. Window retention. Upper, lower, upper/lower, or wheel lip molding package. Dual outside mirrors: 5x7 in. chrome, 6x9 in. painted, or 6x9 in. chrome lo-mount. Lighted vanity mirror. Dual horns. Interior reading light. Hood release lock. Rubber floor mats. Deluxe heater. Auxiliary rear heater. Cargo area headliner. Dual quad headlights. Speedometer (km/mph) and trip odometer (km). Oil pressure gauge. Cigar lighter. Digital clock. Electric rear window defroster. Air conditioning. Power brakes. Power steering. Power windows. Power door locks (front or all). Radios: AM; AM/FM; AM/FM/Stereo with search; AM/FM/Stereo with 8-track or cassette tape player; AM/FM/Stereo with CB. Rear speaker. Cruise control. Tilt steering column. Dome light switch. Unibelt restraint system (color-keyed). Deluxe windshield wipers. Front stabilizer bar. Heavy-duty shocks (rear, or front/rear). 63 or 117-amp. alternator. Maximum cooling system. Auxiliary transmission cooler. 36-gallon fuel tank. Engine block heater. (D/W models) Chrome rear bumper (D100-200/W150). Painted bumper (front or rear). Rear step bumper. Tinted glass. Quad rectangular headlights. Marker lights. In-cab hood release. Dual mirrors: 6x9 in. lo-mount; 7-1/2x10-1/2 lo-mount; or 7x10 West Coast. Upper, lower, or upper/lower molding package. Dual horns. Skylite sun roof. Inside tire carrier (D/W150-200). Underslung tire carrier (D/W200). White spoke wheels (D150). Chrome disc wheels (D150). Aluminum ribbed wheels (D150). Chrome deluxe wheelcovers (D150-200/W150). Premium wheels (D/W150). Flip-out rear quarter window (D/W150-200 Club Cab). Sliding rear window. Camper package: 7,500, 9,000 or 10,000 lbs. (D/W200-300). Big Horn package (D/W150-200). Protective package. Sound control package. Tape stripe package (except W300). Trailer-towing package. Stake 8 ft. (D200-300, W200); 9-1/2 ft. (D/W300); 12-1/2 ft. (D300). Skid plates, transfer case (W models). Front stabilizer bar. Flip-type hinged Club Cab seats (D/W150-200). Cruise control. Tilt steering. Sport steering wheel (except W200-300). Hand throttle. Unibelt restraint. Floor mats. Headliner: Oil pressure gauge. Speedometer (km/mi). Odometer (km). Cigar lighter. Clock. Air conditioning. Power brakes. Power steering. Power windows. Power door locks. Deluxe heater. Radios: AM; AM/FM/ AM/FM/Stereo; AM/FM Stereo with search, 8-track player, cassette player, or CB. Engine block heater. 63 or 117-amp. alternator. Maximum cooling system. Auxiliary transmission cooler. 21-gallon fuel tank. Heavy-duty shocks: Front or rear (D/W300); front and rear (all). (Ramcharger) Step rear bumper. Tinted glass. Privacy sun screen. Quad rectangular headlamps. Dual horns. Inside hood release. Chrome lo-mount mirrors (6x9 or 7-1/2x10-1/2). Upper, lower or upper/lowermolding package. Roll bar. Skid plates (fuel tank or transfer case). Skylite sun roof. Outside tire carrier. White spoke wheels. Chrome disc five-slot wheels. Aluminum ribbed wheels. Chrome deluxe or premium wheelcovers. SE package. Heavy-duty GVW package (5300, 5850, 6010 or 6050 lbs.). Convenience package. Insulation package. Macho four-wheel drive package. Protection package. Sound control package. Sno-Commander package. Tape stripe (Graduated Sport) package. Trailer-towing package. Rear bench seat (3-passenger). Tilt steering column. Cruise control. Front stabilizer bar (standard or heavy-duty). Cigar lighter. Clock. Lockable console. Shoulder belts. Speedometer (km/mi) and odometer (km). Oil pressure gauge. Deluxe heater. Radios (same as D/W models). Power steering. Power windows.

HISTORICAL: Introduced: August 1979. Calendar year sales: 228,500. Model year sales: 251,442 (96,468 light-duty conventional; 80,183 Tradesman vans; 22,840 Sportsman wagons; 9,411 Ramchargers; and 42,540 D50 mini-pickups). Calendar year production: 119,232. The U.S. truck industry took a severe beating in 1980, as total shipments plunged 45 percent. It was the lowest figure since 1967. Light-duty trucks did worse yet, dropping 47 percent. Dodge production took it on the chin as well, plummeting 60.6 percent to just 119,232 trucks. Sales dropped over 35 percent, due largely to high interest rates that resulted from the Federal Reserve Board's attempt to control inflation. The sole bright spot for Chrysler was its captive import mini-trucks. Sales of these subcompact Dodge and Plymouth models jumped to 63,056. In March, the plant at Fenton, Missouri was shut down. Van production from that plant was consolidated in Windsor, Ontario, Canada. Chrysler also closed its RV chassis production facility at Warren, Michigan early in 1980, bowing out of the Class A motor home business. The Jefferson Ave. pickup plant was converted, at the end of the 1980 model year, to production of the new K-cars for 1981.

1981 DODGE

1981 Dodge Ram Mini-Pickup (DNP)

RAM 50 CUSTOM PICKUP: Styling was carried over for 1981. Among standard features were: Cargo lamp. Cigarette lighter. Dome light with driver and passenger side door switches. Emergency flashers. A 15.1-gallon fuel tank. Color-keyed headliner. Inside hood release. Interior rearview mirror. Dual exterior rearview mirrors. Adjustable steering column with lock. Dual sun visors. AM radio. Tinted glass. Trip odometer. Two-speed windshield wipers with washers. Four-speed manual transmission.
RAM 50 ROYAL PICKUP: This was a new series for 1981. It came with most of the same standard features as the Custom, plus a higher level of trim inside and out.
RAM 50 SPORT PICKUP: The Sport was the flashiest Ram 50 pickup. It had high-back bucket seats, center console, oil pressure gauge, ammeter, bodyside tape stripes, spoke road wheels, and a five-speed manual transmission.
I.D. DATA (D150): There were 17 symbols in the VIN. The first three identified the manufacturer, make and type of vehicle. Next was the letter which represented the GVW range. After that came three characters which identified series and body style. After that was the character that identified the engine. It was followed by a check digit, which in turn was followed by a letter representing the model year and a character which identified the assembly plant. The last six digits were sequential production numbers.

Model	Body Type	Price	Weight	Prod. Total
9JL4	Pickup (Custom)	6145	2537	—
9JH4	Pickup (Royal)	6550	—	—
9JH4	Pickup (Sport)	7022	2648	—

ENGINE (Ram 50): 2.0L (122 cu.in.) OHC. Four-cylinder. Brake horsepower: 90 at 5000 rpm. Bore & stroke: 3.30 x 3.54 in. Compression ratio: 8.5:1. Carburetor: Two-barrel.
ENGINE (Royal, Sport): 2.6L (156 cid). Four-cylinder. Brake horsepower: 105 at 5000 rpm. Bore & stroke: 3.59 x 3.86 in. Compression ratio: 8.2:1. Carburetor: Two-barrel.
CHASSIS: Wheelbase: 109.4 in. Overall length: 184.6 in. Overall height: 60.6 in. (Custom). 59.8 in. (Royal/Sport). Overall width: 65 in. GVW: 4,045-4,120 lbs. Tires: 6.00 x 14C (Custom), 185SR14 SBR (Royal/Sport).
POWERTRAIN OPTION: Three-speed automatic transmission.
CONVENIENCE OPTIONS: Air conditioning. Chrome rear step bumper. Low-luster black rear step bumper. Front bumper guards. Electronic digital clock. Front floor mats. 18-gallon fuel tank. Front grille guard. Low-mount chrome exterior mirrors. Vinylide molding. Vinyl pickup box top edge molding. Mud guards. Power steering. Sliding rear window. Sun roof. Bodyside tape stripe. Wheel trim rings.

1981 Dodge 4x4 Ramcharger (DNP)

RAMCHARGER SPORT UTILITY VEHICLE: The 1981 Ramcharger shared front end and taillight styling with "D" series pickups. Wraparound rear quarter windows were integrated into the integral steel roof. The newly designed rear liftgate was made of light-weight fiberglass and had two pneumatic-assist cylinders. The Ramcharger was offered in two-wheel drive (AD150) and part-time four-wheel drive (AW150). Among standard features were: Dry type air cleaner. 48-amp. alternator. Ashtray. Bright front and rear bumpers. Automatic choke. Cleaner Air System. Coolant reserve system. Insulated dash liner. Color-keyed door trim panels and armrests. Electronic ignition system. Black floor mat. 35-gallon fuel tank. Tinted glass. Glove box. Aluminum grille with painted plastic insert and headlamp doors. Fresh air heater with defrosters. Single electric horn. Bright hubcaps. Front wheel locking hubs (four-wheel drive). Combination map/courtesy light on instrument panel. Dual bright finish 5 in. by 7 in. short arm exterior mirrors. 10 in. inside rearview mirror. Power front disc brakes. Power steering (four-wheel drive). Deluxe vinyl low-back bucket seats. Inside spare tire mounting. Rear roof vent. AM radio. Front stabilizer bar (four-wheel drive). Sun visors. Two-speed NP208 transfer case (four-wheel drive). Dual jet windshield washers.

Two-speed windshield wipers. Three-speed automatic transmission (two-wheel drive). Four-speed manual (four-wheel drive). Brake system warning light. Dual braking system with separate brake fluid reservoirs in the master cylinder. Ramcharger exterior colors for 1981 included: Bright silver metallic, Medium Seaspray green metallic, Impact orange, Daystar blue metallic, Cashmere, Impact red, Nightwatch blue, Ginger, Medium Crimson red, Impact blue, Coffee brown metallic, black, Light Seaspray green metallic, Graphic yellow, Pearl white.
I.D. DATA (Ramcharger): There were 17 symbols in the VIN. The first three identified the manufacturer, make and type of vehicle. Next was the letter which represented the GVW range. After that came three characters which identified series and body style. After that was the character that identified the engine. It was followed by a check digit, which in turn was followed by a letter representing the model year and a character which identified the assembly plant. The last six digits were sequential production numbers.

Model	Body Type	Price	Weight	Prod. Total
AD150	Utility	8257	—	—
AW150	Utility 4x4	9466	4174	—

ENGINES (Ramcharger): 5.2-liter (318 cid) V-8. Brake horsepower: 120 at 3600 rpm. Bore & stroke: 3.91 x 3.315 in. Compression ratio: 8.5:1. Carburetor: Two-barrel.
CHASSIS FEATURES: Wheelbase 106 in. Overall length: 184.6 in. (without bumper guards). 186.1 in. (with bumper guards). Overall width: 79.5 in. GVW. 5,300 lbs. (two-wheel drive), 5,850 lbs. (four-wheel drive). Tires: P235/75R15 BSW GBR.
POWERTRAIN OPTIONS: 5.2L (318 cid) four-barrel V-8 (four-wheel drive), 5.9L (360 cid) four-barrel V-8 (four-wheel drive). Three-speed TorqueFlite automatic transmission (four-wheel drive).
OPTION PACKAGES (Ramcharger Royal SE): Bright windshield and drip rail molding; bright taillamp housing; power steering; ram's head hood ornament; leaping ram with "150 Royal SE" plaque on front fender; bright aluminum grille with chromed plastic insert and headlamp doors; tailgate upper and lower moldings with bright applique panel; woodgrain applique on interior of door with assist strap and carpeting on lower door panel; color-keyed driver and front passenger high-back Command bucket seats with cloth and vinyl trim (included inboard fold-down armrests on seats and lockable console with removable styrofoam beverage chest); color-keyed folding rear bench seat with cloth and vinyl trim; color-keyed carpeting; color-keyed rear side and liftgate inner trim panels; woodtone instrument cluster faceplate; instrument panel plaque; black leather wrapped steering wheel with black horn pad and woodtone insert; color-keyed spare tire cover (n.a. with 10R15LT tires); cigar lighter; dual horns; bright front doorsill scuff plate; insulation under hood panel; oil pressure and engine temperature gauges; color-keyed cowl side trim panels; trip odometer.
MACHO RAMCHARGER: Royal SE trim; special two-tone exterior paint; macho tape stripe; high gloss black front and rear bumpers; five outline White lettered SBR tires; four radial-ribbed aluminum wheels on two-wheel drive (steel-spoke orange wheels with black accent on four-wheel drive); sport bar.
RAMCHARGER BIG HORN: Ram's head hood ornament; Big Horn side nameplates; Gold filigree pinstriping; Ram's hide vinyl and simulated lambs wool trim high-back bucket seats with matching rear bench seat and a center console; convenience package; electronic digital clock.
CONVENIENCE PACKAGE: Day/night 10 in. interior rearview mirror; glove box with lock and light; ash receiver light; in-cab actuated hood lock release; two-speed windshield wipers with intermittent wipe.
PROTECTION PACKAGE: Door edge protectors; bright front bumper with guards and nerf strips; bright rear bumper with nerf strips.
TRAILER TOWING PACKAGES: Light-duty; heavy-duty (four-wheel drive only).
SNO-COMMANDER PACKAGE: Four-wheel drive only, snow removal equipment.
CONVENIENCE OPTIONS: Air conditioning. Heavy-duty alternators and batteries. Painted rear step type bumper. Cigar lighter. Electronic digital clock. Lockable console. Auxiliary transmission oil to air cooler. Maximum cooling. Oil pressure, engine temperature, and trip odometer gauges; bright insert grille and bright headlamp doors; halogen headlamps; Deluxe bi-level heater; engine block heater; in cab-actuated hood lock release; dual electric horns; color-keyed rubber (accessory type) mats for driver's compartment; dual low-mount bright 6 in. x 9 in. mirrors; dual low-mount extended bright 7-1/2 in. x 10-1/2 in. mirrors; lower molding; upper molding; power door locks; power steering; power windows; Radios: AM/FM, AM/FM stereo, AM/FM stereo/cassette tape player, AM/FM stereo with 8-track tape player, AM/FM stereo with 40-channel CB, AM/FM stereo with Search-Tune; heavy-duty shocks; fuel tank skid plate; transfer case skid plate (four-wheel drive); automatic speed control; sport bar; front stabilizer bar; heavy-duty front stabilizer bar (four-wheel drive); tilt steering column; Skylite sun roof; privacy glass sunscreen; deluxe color-keyed unibelt restraint system; bright wheelcovers; premium wheelcovers (n.a. four-wheel drive); Wheels: Aluminum radial ribbed, five slot chrome disc, white painted steel spoke; two-speed windshield wipers with intermittent wipe.

1981 Dodge Ram Royal SE Maxi-Wagon (DNP)

B150 VAN: Basic styling was unchanged for 1981. Among the standard features were: Dry type air cleaner. 48-amp. alternator. Driver and front passenger armrests. Ashtray. 325-amp. battery. Power front disc brakes (except 109.6 in. and 127.6 in. wheelbase with 4,700 lbs. GVW). Painted front and rear bumpers. Double hinged right side and rear cargo doors. Electronic ignition system. Driver's compartment floor mat. 22-gallon fuel tank. Glove box. Argent finish grille. Color-keyed hardboard headliner in driver's compartment. Single electric horn. Color-keyed horn pad. Bright finish hubcaps. Ammeter, fuel gauge, odometer, oil pressure indicator light, speedometer, and temperature gauge. Duel 5 x 7 inch painted exterior mirrors. AM radio. Low-back bucket seat with vinyl trim for driver. Driver side sun visor. Spare tire carrier. Traffic hazard warning switch. Two-speed windshield wipers with washers. Brake system warning light. Energy absorbing steering column. Ignition and steering column lock. Dual braking system. The B150 Long Range Van had special trim and higher capacity.

B150 WAGON: The E150 Wagon had most of the same standard features as the van, plus (or in place of) windows all around; black full width floor mat; fresh air heater with defroster; 10 in. inside rearview mirror; two color-keyed padded sun visors; driver and front passenger low-back vinyl bucket seats and three-passenger quick-release vinyl rear bench seat including three seat belts.

B150 MINI-RAM WAGON: The new Mini-Ram van came on a 109.6 in. wheelbase and had many interior and exterior refinements such as: Bright grille. Bright front and rear bumpers. Wheelcovers. Bright 5 in. x 7 in. outside rearview mirrors. 36-gallon fuel tank. Custom SE Decor Package. Door-operated light switches. Convenience Package.

I.D. DATA: There were 17 symbols in the VIN. The first three identified the manufacturer, make and type of vehicle. Next was the letter which represented the GVW range. After that came three characters which identified series and body style. After that was the character that identified the engine. It was followed by a check digit, which in turn was followed by a letter representing the model year and a character which identified the assembly plant. The last six digits were sequential production numbers.

Model	Body Type	Price	Weight	Prod. Total
B150 Series — Van — 109.6 in. w.b.				
B150	Van	6418	3274	—
(127.6 in. w.b.)				
B150	Van	—	—	—
B150	Long Range Van	6330	—	—
(109.6 in. w.b.)				
B150	Wagon	7477	3493	—
(127.6 in. w.b.)				
B150	Wagon	—	—	—
B150	Mini-Ram Wagon	7705	—	—

ENGINE (B150): 3.7-liter (225 cid). Slant six-cylinder. Brake horsepower: 95 at 3600 rpm. Bore & stroke: 3.40 x 4.12 in. Carburetor: One-barrel.

B250 VAN: The B250 shared most of the same standard features offered on the B150. However, it was a bit more heavy-duty and could be ordered the extra long Maxi.

B250 WAGON: The 3/4-ton B250 wagon had most of the same features as the B150. It was offered in regular or extended Maxi bodies. Maxi-wagons came with an automatic transmission.

B250 MINI-RAM WAGON: This was a slightly more heavy-duty version of the B150 Mini-Ram Wagon. It came with the same standard features.

I.D. DATA: There were 17 symbols in the VIN. The first three identified the manufacturer, make and type of vehicle. Next was the letter which represented the GVW range. After that came three characters which identified series and body style. After that was the character that identified the engine. It was followed by a check digit, which in turn was followed by a letter representing the model year and a character which identified the assembly plant. The last six digits were sequential production numbers.

Model	Body Type	Price	Weight	Prod. Total
B250 Series 109.6 in. w.b.				
B250	Van	6883	3383	—
(127.6 in. w.b.)				
B250	Van	—	—	—
(109.6 in. w.b.)				
B250	Wagon	7902	3646	—
(127.6 in. w.b.)				
B150	Wagon	—	—	—
B250	Mini-Ram Wagon	8297	—	—

ENGINE (B250): Same as B150.

B350 VAN: The 1-ton B350 had most of the same standard features as the B150 plus (or in place of): Larger brakes. Higher capacity rear springs. Power steeing. Automatic transmission. Both regular, and extended "Maxi Van" bodies were offered.

B350 WAGON: This was Dodge's heftiest people hauler. It was available in regular or Maxi bodies.

I.D. DATA (D150): There were 17 symbols in the VIN. The first three identified the manufacturer, make and type of vehicle. Next was the letter which represented the GVW range. After that came three characters which identified series and body style. After that was the character that identified the engine. It was followed by a check digit, which in turn was followed by a letter representing the model year and a character which identified the assembly plant. The last six digits were sequential production numbers.

Model	Body Type	Price	Weight	Prod. Total
B350	Van	8709	3931	—
B350	Wagon	9467	4234	—

ENGINE (350): 5.2L (318 cid) V-8. Brake horsepower: 140 at 3600 rpm. Bore & stroke: 3.91 x 3.31. Compression ratio: 8.5:1. Carburetor: Two-barrel.

CB350 KARY VAN: The CB350 Kary Van was offered in three sizes and three w.b. Automatic transmission was standard.

I.D. DATA: There were 17 symbols in the VIN. The first three identified the manufacturer, make and type of vehicle. Next was the letter which represented the GVW range. After that came three characters which identified series and body style. After that was the character that identified the engine. It was followed by a check digit, which in turn was followed by a letter representing the model year and a character which identified the assembly plant. The last six digits were sequential production numbers.

Model	Body Type	Price	Weight	Prod. Total
CB350	Van 10 ft.	—	—	—
CB350	Van 12 ft.	—	—	—
CB350	Van 15 ft.	—	—	—

ENGINE (CB350): 5.2-liter (318 cid) V-8. Brake horsepower: 170 at 4000 rpm. Bore & stroke: 3.91 x 3.31 in. Compression ratio: 8.5:1. Carburetor: Four-barrel.

ENGINE: (127.6 in. w.b.) 5.9-liter (360 cid) V-8. Brake horsepower: 180 at 3600 rpm. Bore & stroke: 4.00 x 3.58. Compression ratio: 8.6:1. Carburetor: Four-barrel.

CHASSIS FEATURES: Wheelbase: 109.6 in. (B150/ B250). Wheelbase: 127.6 in, 145.6 in. (CB350). Wheelbase: 163.6 in. (CB350). Overall length: 178.9 in. (109.6 in. wheelbase), 196.9 in. (127.6 in. wheelbase), 222.9 in. (Maxivan/wagon). Overall width: 79.8 in. Overall height: 79.6 in. (109.6 in. wheelbase), 80.6 in. (Maxivan/wagon), 80.9 in. (127.6 in. wheelbase). GVW: 4,700-5,300 lbs. (B150). 6,010-6,400 lbs. (B250). 7,000-9,000 lbs. (B350). 7,500-10,000 lbs. (Kary Van). Tires: P195/75R x 15 (B150). P225/75R x 15 (B250). 8.00 x 16.5E (B350 Maxivan/wagon). 8.75 x 16.5E (Kary Van).

POWERTRAIN OPTIONS: 5.2L two-barrel V-8. 5.2L four-barrel V-8. 5.9L carburetor four-barrel V-8 (B250/B350). Three-speed automatic transmission.

VAN OPTION PACKAGES/TRAILER TOWING PACKAGES/CONVENIENCE PACKAGES: Cigar lighter; glove box lock; in-cab actuated hood lock release; two-speed windshield wipers with intermittent wipe. ROYAL EXTERIOR PACKAGE: Bright grille, front and rear bumpers, taillamp bezels, windshield molding; dual 5 in. x 7 in. exterior mirrors; dual vertically stacked quad rectangular headlamps with halogen high beam lamps. ROYAL INTERIOR PACKAGE: Color-keyed bucket seat floor risers; cigar lighter; electronic digital clock; color-keyed carpeting in driver's compartment, horn pad with woodtone applique insert, vinyl front door trim panels with woodtone applique, deluxe vinyl trimmed low-back driver's seat; garnish trim over front pillars, front door headers and around windshield; insulated dash liner; insulated headliner in drivers compartment; instrument panel nameplate; scuff pads; unibelt restraint system.

VAN/WAGON CONVENIENCE OPTIONS: Air conditioning (integral front or rear auxiliary). Heavy-duty alternators and batteries. Bright hitch type rear bumper. Bright front and rear bumpers. Front and rear bumper guards and Nerf strips. Cigar lighter. Electronic digital clock. Auxiliary transmission oil to air cooling. Maximum engine cooling. Electric rear window defroster. Dual rear doors with fixed or vented glass. Single rear door with vented glass. Sliding passenger side door. 36-gallon fuel tank. Oil pressure gauge. Trip odometer. Sunscreen privacy glass. Tinted windows. Bright grille (included dual quad rectangular headlamps, vertically stacked with halogen high beams. Passenger compartment headliner. Rear auxiliary heater. Deluxe front heater. Engine block heater. Dual electric horns. Interior reading lamp in driver's compartment. In-cab actuated hood release lock. Two color-keyed accessory type rubber mats for driver's compartment. Dual low-mount 6 in. x 9 in. bright or painted mirrors. Dual short arm bright 5 in. x 7 in. exterior mirrors. Illuminated vanity. Interior day/night rearview mirror. Lower side and rear moldings. Upper side and rear moldings and bright taillamp bezels. Upper and lower moldings. Power door locks. Power steering. Power front door windows. RADIOS: AM/FM, AM/FM stereo, AM/FM stereo with cassette tape player and Dolby Noise Reduction System, AM/FM stereo with 8-track tape player, AM/FM stereo with Search-Tune, AM/FM stereo with 40-channel CB transceiver. Rear speaker (for AM or AM/FM radios only). Heavy-duty front and rear shock absorbers. Color-keyed spare tire carrier. Automatic speed control. Front stabilizer bar. Tilt type steering column. Leather wrapped steering wheel. Skylite sun roof. Door operated dome light switch. WHEELS: Radial ribbed aluminum. Five-slot chrome disc. White painted spoke. Bright wheelcovers. Premium wheelcovers. Deluxe windshield wipers. Vinyl low-back front bucket seats (van). Driver deluxe vinyl trim low-back bucket seat (van). Driver and passenger deluxe vinyl trim low-back bucket seats (van). Cloth and vinyl trim driver and passenger high-back. Command bucket seats, non-swivel base (van). Deluxe driver and passenger high-back Command reclining bucket seats (van). Wheel lip moldings (van). Metal door check arms (van).

WAGON OPTION PACKAGES: CUSTOM SE PACKAGE: Custom nameplates; bright molding around windshield, side and rear windows (except driver and passenger door windows); bright taillamp bezels; dual vertically stacked quad rectangular headlamps with halogen high beams; instrument panel lower skirts (left and right side); cigar lighter; headliner in driver and passenger compartments; vinyl door and side trim panels with plaid insert; color-keyed carpeting; dash liner insulation; garnish trim over front doors, compartment windows and headers around rear. ROYAL PACKAGE: Includes items in Custom SE Package, plus Royal nameplates; bright lower side and rear moldings; dual vertically stacked quad rectangular headlamps with halogen high beams; bright grille; bright front and rear bumpers; dual 5 in. x 7 in. bright exterior mirrors; woodtone applique on lower face of instrument panel; horn pad with woodtone insert; spare tire cover; vinyl door and side trim panels with woodtone trim; door operated dome light switches on all doors; garnish trim over front doors, compartment windows, headers around rear compartment windows and front pillar and windshield; dual electric horns; U-belt restraint system; driver and front passenger low-back bucket seats and bench seat in deluxe vinyl trim (blue or cashmere); driver and passenger compartment soft-cloth covered headliner with insulation; accessory floor mats in driver's compartment; and electronic digital clock. ROYAL SE PACKAGE: Royal SE nameplates; bright upper side and rear moldings; bright bumper guards with nerf strips; bodyside and rear woodtone tape applique with dual gold accent stripes; vinyl door and side trim panels with woodtone trim and front door applique pull strap; color-keyed carpeted engine housing cover; oil pressure gauge and trip odometer; power steering; leather-wrapped steering wheel; 10 in. day/night interior rearview mirror; glove box lock and light; deluxe two-speed with intermittent wipe windshield wipers; in cab actuated hood release lock; ignition and headlight switch with time delay; cigar lighter light; courtesy step well lamp (front and side doors); color-keyed driver and front passenger high-back reclining command bucket seats and a three-passenger bench seat with cloth and vinyl trim in blue, cashmere or red. HEAVY-DUTY INSULATION PACKAGE: Included with integral front mounted air conditioning. For Royal and Royal SE wagons: Interior lower fiberglass insulation panels (not offered on standard single rear door or optional sliding side door); insulation under floor covering. For Custom SE wagons: Includes for Royal and Royal SE plus: Full length heading with insulation. For Custom wagons: Included items for Custom SE plus: Interior lower trip panels in passenger compartment (in blue or cashmere); color-keyed garnish trim over front door headers and around headliner and rear compartment window; dash liner insulation; sliding door track cover. Eight-passenger seating package: (B250/B350 Wagon and Maxiwagon models) included one additional quick-release three-passenger bench seat with three seat belts. Quad seating package. Eight-passenger travel seating package. Five, seven or eight-passenger convert-a-bed seating package. Twelve-passenger seating package: 127.6 in. wheelbase Maxiwagons only (requires window retention and rear doors with optional vented glass, at extra cost). Package includes three additional bench seats: Second and third seats for three passengers; fourth seat for four passengers; tire carrier relocated under fourth bench seat, plus 8,510 lbs. GVW package. CONVENIENCE PACKAGE: Cigar lighter, glove box lock. 10 in. day/night rearview mirror; cigar lighter light; automatic door switches for interior dome lights; courtesy step well lamp (front and side doors). LIGHT-DUTY TRAILER TOWING PACKAGE: (requires automatic transmission and 36-gallon fuel tank) maximum cooling; heavy-duty variable load flasher; seven wire harness; bright hitch type rear bumper; Class I ball hitch. HEAVY-DUTY TRAILER TOWING PACKAGE; B250/B350: (requires automatic transmission; V-8 engine; transmission auxiliary air cooler and 36-gallon fuel tank) includes maximum cooling; 63-amp. alternator; 430 amp. Cold Crank battery; seven-wire harness; Class IV load-equalizing tow bar hitch; heavy-duty variable load flasher; and heavy-duty front and rear shocks.

NOTE: 1981 Dodge Van exterior color included: Cashmere, Graphic yellow, Impact orange, Impact red, Ginger, Medium Crimson red, Coffee brown metallic, Impact blue, Nightwatch blue, Light Seaspray green metallic, Medium Seaspray green metallic, Daystar blue metallic, Bright silver metallic, Pearl white, black. 1981 Dodge Wagon exterior color choices were: Cashmere, Graphic yellow (n.a. on Royal or Royal SE), Impact red, Medium Crimson red, Ginger (not available on Royal or Royal SE), Coffee brown metallic, Impact blue (n.a. on Royal or Royal SE), Night-watch blue, Medium Seaspray green metallic (n.a. on Royal or Royal SE), Bright silver metallic, Daystar blue metallic, Pearl white, black.

1981 Dodge Power Ram Sweptline Pickup (DNP)

D150 SERIES — CUSTOM PICKUP: Full-sized Dodge pickups received an attractive new look for 1981. The exterior featured new aerodynamic styling. The grille had a rectangular sections theme and was bordered on each end by a slightly recessed single rectangular headlight. Amber parking lights were beneath each headlight. "Dodge" was spelled in block letters on the center face of the hood. Side marker lights were located on the lower section of the front fender, between the bumper and wheel well opening. The redesigned tailgate had caliper latches to make it easier to open and close. The instrument panel was also new. Among standard features were: All-vinyl bench seat in black, blue, cashmere, or red. Glove box. Built in dash map light. Independent front suspension. 20-gallon fuel tank. Energy absorbing steering column. Front disc brakes. Bright front bumper (painted on cab and chassis models). Cleaner air system. Coolant reserve system. Insulted dash liner. Color-keyed door interior trim panels and armrests. Black floor mat with padding. Fresh air heater with defrosters. Single electric horn. Bright hubcaps. Padded instrument panel. Dual bright finish short-arm outside rearview mirrors. 10 in. inside rearview mirror. AM radio. Color-keyed sun visors. Traffic hazard warning switch. Dual jet windshield washers. Two-speed windshield wipers. The D150 Custom pickup was offered in four wheelbases and with "smooth side" Sweptline or "rear fendered" Utiline pickup boxes. Buyers had their choice of conventional or club cabs. The Club Cab had 34 cu. ft. of in cab storage space behind the front seat.

I.D. DATA: There were 17 symbols in the VIN. The first three identified the manufacturer, make and type of vehicle. Next was the letter which represented the GVW range. After that came three characters which identified series and body style. After that was the character that identified the engine. It was followed by a check digit, which in turn was followed by a letter representing the model year and a character which identified the assembly plant. The last six digits were sequential production numbers.

Model	Body Type	Price	Weight	Prod. Total
D150	Utiline 6.5 ft.	5997	3259	—
D150	Sweptline 6.5 ft.	5997	3239	—
D150	Utiline 8 ft.	6085	3369	—
D150	Sweptline 8 ft.	6085	3339	—
D150	Club Cab 6.5 ft.	7232	3657	—
D150	Club Cab 8 ft.	7328	3786	—

ENGINE (D150): 3.7L (225 cid) Slant six-cylinder. Brake horsepower: 95 at 3600 rpm. Bore & stroke: 3.40 x 4.12 in. Compression ratio: 8.4:1. Carburetor: One-barrel (conventional cab).

ENGINE: 5.2L (318 cid) V-8. Brake horsepower: 135 at 4000 rpm. Bore & stroke: 3.91 x 3.31. Compression ratio: 8.5:1. Carburetor: Two-barrel (Club cab). Not available in California.

D250 CUSTOM PICKUP: The D250 was basically a 3/4-ton version of the 1/2-ton D150. It came with most of the same standard features, but could haul heavier loads. It was offered in three wheelbases and with conventional, club or 6-passenger Crew Cabs. The 149 in. wheelbase Crew Cab had a 6-1/2 ft. box. The 165 in. wheelbase Crew Cab had an 8 ft. box.

I.D. DATA: There were 17 symbols in the VIN. The first three identified the manufacturer, make and type of vehicle. Next was the letter which represented the GVW range. After that came three characters which identified series and body style. After that was the character that identified the engine. It was followed by a check digit, which in turn was followed by a letter representing the model year and a character which identified the assembly plant. The last six digits were sequential production numbers.

Model	Body Type	Price	Weight	Prod. Total
D250	Chassis & Cab	7079	3485	—
D250	Utiline 8 ft.	6744	3756	—
D250	Sweptline 8 ft.	6744	3726	—
D250	Club Cab 8 ft.	7753	3966	—
D250	Crew Cab 6.5 ft.	8421	4232	—
D250	Crew Cab 8 ft.	8500	4490	—

ENGINE (D150): 3.7L (225 cid) Slant six-cylinder. Brake horsepower: 95 at 3600 rpm. Bore & stroke: 3.40 x 4.12 in. Compression ratio: 8.4:1. Carburetor: One-barrel (conventional cab).

ENGINE: 5.2L (318 cid) V-8. Brake horsepower: 135 at 4000 rpm. Bore & stroke: 3.91 x 3.31. Compression ratio: 8.5:1. Carburetor: Two-barrel (Club Cab). Not available in California.

D350 CUSTOM PICKUP: The husky 1-ton D350 had most of the same standard features as the other series. In addition it had a heavier duty front axle, and rear springs. It was available in three wheelbases and with conventional, Club or Crew Cabs. The Crew Cab had dual rear wheels.

I.D. DATA: There were 17 symbols in the VIN. The first three identified the manufacturer, make and type of vehicle. Next was the letter which represented the GVW range. After that came three characters which identified series and body style. After that was the character that identified the engine. It was followed by a check digit, which in turn was followed by a letter representing the model year and a character which identified the assembly plant. The last six digits were sequential production numbers.

Model	Body Type	Price	Weight	Prod. Total
D350 Series — 131 in. w.b.				
D350	Chassis & Cab	6862	3688	—
(135 in. w.b.)				
D350	Chassis & Cab	7503	4002	—
D350	Sweptline 8 ft.	7301	4002	—
D350	Club Cab 8 ft.	7867	4371	—
(159 in. w.b.)				
D350	Chassis & Cab	7588	3876	—
D350	Crew Cab	9367	4781	—

ENGINE (D350 Custom): 5.2L (318 cid) V-8. Brake horsepower: 160 at 4000 rpm. Bore & stroke: 3.91 x 3.31. Compression ratio: 8.0:1. Carburetor: Four-barrel.

D450 CUSTOM CHASSIS & CAB: The D450 was only available with a conventional cab. It came with most of the same standard features offered on the D350, but had a higher maximum payload capacity. Dual rear wheels were standard.

I.D. DATA: There were 17 symbols in the VIN. The first three identified the manufacturer, make and type of vehicle. Next was the letter which represented the GVW range. After that came three characters which identified series and body style. After that was the character that identified the engine. It was followed by a check digit, which in turn was followed by a letter representing the model year and a character which identified the assembly plant. The last six digits were sequential production numbers.

Model	Body Type	Price	Weight	Prod. Total
D450 Series — 135 in. w.b.				
D450	Chassis & Cab	9057	3861	—
(159 in. w.b.)				
D450	Chassis & Cab	9114	3870	—

ENGINE (D450 Custom): 5.9L (360 cid) V-8. Brake horsepower: 175 at 4000 rpm. Bore & stroke: 4.0 x 3.58 in. Compression ratio: 8.0:1. Carburetor: Four-barrel.

CHASSIS FEATURES: Wheelbase 115 in. (D150), 131 in. (D150/D250/D350) 133 in. (D150 Club cab) 135 in. (D450) 149 in. (D150/D250/D350) 159 in. (D450) 165 in. (D250/D350 Crew Cab). Overall width: 79.5 in. (94.2 in. models with dual rear wheels). Overall length: 190.78 in. (D150 conventional cab with 115 in. wheelbase); 210.78 in. (131 in. wheelbase conventional cab); 208.78 in. (133 in. wheelbase Club Cab); 228.81 in. (149 in. wheelbase Club Cab); 224.78 in. (149 in. wheelbase Crew Cab); 244.78 in. (165 in. wheelbase Crew Cab). GVW: 4,800-6,010 lbs. (D150). 6,050 lbs. (W150). 6,500-8,550 lbs. (D250). 6,900-8,550 lbs. (W250). 9,000-10,000 lbs. (D350). 10,000 (W350 Chassis w/cab). 10,500 lbs. (D450). 11,000 lbs. (W450). Tires: P195/75R x 15 (D150 conventional cab). P235/75R x 15 (D150 Club Cab). 8.00 x 16.5D (D250 conventional cab/D350 Crew Cab). 8.75 x 16.5E (D250 Club Cab). 9.50 x 16.5E (D250 Crew Cab). 9.50 x 16.5E (D350). 8.00 x 16E (D450).

POWERTRAIN OPTIONS: 5.2L (318 cid) two-barrel V-8 (D150/D250/W150). 5.2L four-barrel V-8 (D150/D250/W150/W250). 5.9L (360 cid) four-barrel V-8 (D150/D250/D350/W150/W250). Four-speed manual NP 435 transmission (D150 conventional cab four-speed manual with overdrive was standard). Three-speed automatic.

OPTION PACKAGES: FOUR-WHEEL DRIVE: Pickups: W150/W250. Chassis w/cab: W250/W350/W450. Called "Power Rams" and have most of the features found on the two-wheel drive models, plus (or instead): Power steering; part-time four-wheel drive; two-speed transfer case; front wheel locking hubs; and leaf spring front suspension. STAKE BODY: An eight-foot stake body was available on D250/D350/W250. A 9.5-foot stake body was available on D350/D450/W350/W450. A 12.5-foot stake was available on D350 and D450. SNO-COMMANDER PACKAGE: Factory installed snow removal package with power angling blade with positive instrument panel mounted fingertip controls; seven way control valve, power lift, and plow lights. RETRIEVER WRECKER: Complete wrecker with five-ton capacity winch; rapid-shift winch control; tow bar with sling and towing chains; large-capacity deck-mounted tool box; sentry signal switch panel; and power-take-off assembly. D350 DYNA-TRAC PACKAGE: Dual rear wheels, 6,900 lbs. rear axle and a GVW rating of 10,000 lbs. CUSTOM SE PACKAGE: (n.a. on Club or Crew Cabs) bright windshield, backlight, drip rail, and taillamp trim; plaque on front fender with leaping ram and "Custom SE;" bench seat color-keyed with hinged seatback and cloth and vinyl trim; nameplate on instrument panel; bright seatback hinge cover; front door bright trim applique and pull strap; carpeting with underlayment; and cigar lighter. ROYAL PACKAGE: (in addition to or in place of items in Custom SE Package) upper and lower tailgate molding (Sweptlines); deluxe vinyl trimmed bench seat; two jump seats (Club cab); bright seat back hinge cover for rear seat of Crew cabs; carpeting on lower portion of door; woodgrain instrument cluster faceplate; black steering wheel horn pad with woodgrain insert; bright doorsill scuff plates (front door only); color-keyed soft headliner (n.a. Crew Cab); garnish trim over windshield, front pillar, door header, quarter trim panel upper and over backlight (n.a. Crew Cab); cowl side trim panels; dome lamp mounted center of roof (Club Cab); insulation under hood panel. ROYAL SE PACKAGE: (in addition to or in place of items in Royal Package): Ram's head hood ornament; "Dodge Ram" nameplate on Sweptline pickup tailgate; flip-out quarter window with banded glass (Club Cab pickups); dual horns; bright aluminum grille with chrome plastic insert and headlamp doors; power steering; bright tailgate applique panel (Sweptlines); deluxe cloth and vinyl trimmed bench seat; front door woodgrain trim applique, assist strap and carpeting on lower portion; black leather wrapped steering wheel; oil pressure and engine temperature gauges; trip odometer. MACHO PACKAGE: Two-tone paint scheme; bold striping; orange-painted spoke road wheels; raised outline white letter steel-belted radial tires; roll bar; black front and rear bumpers.

CONVENIENCE OPTIONS: Air conditioning. Heavy-duty alternators and batteries. Painted or bright bumpers. Rear hitch type bumper. Rear step type bumper. Cigar lighter. Electric clock. Maximum cooling. Auxiliary cooling. 30-gallon fuel tank. Oil pressure, engine temperature, and trip odometer gauges. Tinted glass. Halogen headlights. Headliner. Deluxe heater. Engine block heater. Dual electric horns. Front clearance and identification lights. In-cab hood release. Dual low mount and low mount extended mirrors. Upper, lower or upper and lower moldings. Electric door locks. Power steering. Power windows. RADIOS: AM/FM, AM/FM stereo, AM/FM stereo w/8-Track, AM/FM stereo with CB, AM/FM stereo with Search-Tune. Flip type seats (with Club Cab). Heavy-duty shocks. Skylite sun roof. Spare tire carrier. Speed control. Sport bar. Stabilizer bar. Tilt steering column. Sport steering wheel. Unibelt restraint system (color-keyed). Road type wheels. Aluminum radial ribbed wheels. Chrome disc (5-slot) wheels. Painted steel spoke (white) wheels. Wheelcovers. Sliding rear window. Rear quarter flip-out window (Club cabs). Two-speed windshield wipers with intermittent wipe. Skid plate.

NOTE: Exterior colors for full-size 1981 Dodge trucks were: Cashmere, Graphic yellow, Impact orange, Impact red, Medium Crimson red, Ginger, Coffee brown metallic, Daystar blue metallic, Impact blue, Nightwatch blue, Light Seaspray green metallic, Medium Seaspray green metallic, Bright silver metallic, Pearl white, black.

HISTORICAL: U.S. assemblies of 1981 Dodge light-duty trucks totaled 126,520 units including: [D150] 44,024; [D250] 7,589; [D350] 2,990; [W150] 5,768; [W250] 3,260; [W350] 445; [Ramcharger] 3,784; [Ram Van] 42,031; and [Ram Wagon] 16,629. Model year pro-

duction of the Ram 50 (built by Mitsubishi in Japan) came to 25,175. Model year sales totaled 172,145 units, down from 251,442 the previous model year. A decision to emphasize Dodge (and de-emphasize Plymouth), as the Chrysler Corp. truck division, was announced near the end of the year.

1982 DODGE

RAMPAGE HIGH LINE PICKUP: The new Rampage was the first front-wheel drive pickup to be offered by one of the "Big Three" automakers. It combined the comfort and conveniences of a passenger car with the utility of a pickup. It shared front end styling with the Dodge Charger. A sloping hood, deeply recessed rectangular headlights, bumper integrated rectangular slot grille, "smooth side" Sweptline box and large rectangular taillights were styling highlights. Among standard features on the Rampage High Line were: Four-speed transaxle with 3.13:1 ratio; McPherson-type Iso-strut front suspension with linkless sway bar; mini-module fan assembly; power disc brakes; tinted glass; bright sill, wheel lip and belt moldings; left-hand remote control mirror; color-keyed spot steering wheel; dual horns; front and rear bumper rub strips; AM radio; Rallye wheel dress up; day/night inside mirror; glove box lock; cigar lighter; inside hood release; black belt, windshield, and backlight moldings; key-in-ignition buzzer dome lamp; black door handle inserts; all-vinyl custom level high-back bucket seats; all-vinyl Custom door trim; and Uniconstruction.

1982 Dodge Rampage Sport Mini-Pickup (DNP)

RAMPAGE SPORT PICKUP: The Sport came with many of the same features as the High-Line plus (or instead): Two-tone paint and tape treatment; lower sill black-out finish; 14 in. color-keyed Rallye wheels; black RWL tires; cargo box flange trim molding; contoured cloth covered sport bucket seats with adjustable seatbacks; Sport door trim; shift lever console; and Rallye cluster with tach, clock, odometer.

1982 Dodge Rampage Sport Mini-Pickup (rear view)

I.D. DATA (Rampage): The VIN consisted of 17 symbols. The first three symbols revealed manufacturer, make and vehicle type. The fourth symbol indicated GVW rating. The fifth, sixth and seventh symbols indicated series and body style. The eighth symbol indicated engine. The ninth symbol was a check digit. The 10th symbol indicated model year. The 11th symbol indicated assembly plant. The last six symbols were the sequential unit production number. (**NOTE:** On imported models, the 12th symbol indicated transmission type.)

Model	Body Type	Price	Weight	Prod. Total
ZH28	High Line Pickup	6698	2246	—
ZS28	Sport Pickup	7204	2293	—

ENGINE (Rampage): 2.2L (135 cid) Four-cylinder. Brake horsepower: 84 at 4800 rpm. Bore & stroke: 3.44 x 3.62. Compression ratio: 8.5:1. Carburetor: Two-barrel.
CHASSIS FEATURES: Wheelbase: 104.2 in. Overall length: 183.6 in. Overall width: 66.8 in. Overall height: 51.8 in. GVW: 3,450 lbs. Tires: P175/75 R13 (High-Line); P195/60 R14 (Sport).
POWERTRAIN OPTIONS: TorqueFlite automatic.
CONVENIENCE OPTIONS: Air conditioning. Intermittent wipers. Heavy-duty battery. Tonneau cover. Power steering. Clock (High-Line). Heavy-duty cooling. Undercoating. Automatic speed control. Engine block heater. Rallye cluster (High-Line). 14 in. road wheels. Cloth and vinyl bucket seats (High-Line). Light package. Cargo box side rails. Dual remote control mirrors. Popular equipment package. Console (High-Line). Radios: AM/FM Stereo, AM/FM Stereo with cassette player, AM/FM Stereo with 8-track tape player.
NOTE: Rampage High-Line exterior colors for 1982 included: Graphic red, Spice tan, Manila cream, black, Burnished silver, and Charcoal gray. Sport models were offered in:

Graphic red, black, silver, and Charcoal gray; and two-tone combinations of Graphic red upper with a Spitfire orange lower and accent tape, and black upper with silver lower with a black tape.

1982 Dodge Ram 50 Custom Mini-Pickup (rear view)

RAM 50 CUSTOM PICKUP: While basic styling was unchanged, the 1982 Ram 50 did receive a new, blacked out grille and headlamp trim. Also, the Ram name on the front fenders was now placed ahead of bodyside badge. Among standard features: Argent silver painted front bumper with black rubber ends. Cargo lamp. Cigarette lighter. Dome light with driver and passenger side door switches. Emergency flashers. 18-gallon fuel tank. Tinted glass. Color-keyed headliner. Inside hood release. Bright hubcaps. Left and right sides black sport type exterior mirrors. Bright windshield molding. AM radio. Adjustable angle steering column. Dual sun visors. Trip odometer. Two-speed windshield wipers with washers. Four-speed manual transmission. This year, for the first time, the Ram 50 Custom was available with four-wheel drive drive. The 4x4 "Power Ram" version had most of the same standard features as the 4x2 version, plus all-terrain tires and power steering.
RAM 50 ROYAL PICKUP: The Royal had more deluxe interior and exterior trim than the Custom. White sidewall tires, chrome front bumper and carpeting were just a few of its luxury touches. It also came with a five-speed manual transmission.
RAM 50 SPORT PICKUP: The Sport had the most flair of any Ram 50 pickup. In addition to many of the items standard on the Custom, it also had: Center console with oil pressure gauge, ammeter and (five-speed manual) transmission shift lever. AM/FM Stereo radio. Wide spoke road wheels. Tape stripe. Bucket seats. Like the Custom, it was also available with four-wheel drive.
I.D. DATA: The VIN consisted of 17 symbols. The first three symbols revealed manufacturer, make and vehicle type. The fourth symbol indicated GVW rating. The fifth, sixth and seventh symbols indicated series and body style. The eighth symbol indicated engine. The ninth symbol was a check digit. The 10th symbol indicated model year. The 11th symbol indicated assembly plant. The last six symbols were the sequential unit production number. (Note: On imported models, the 12th symbol indicates transmission).

Model	Body Type	Price	Weight	Prod. Total
9JL4	Custom Pickup	6408	2573	—
9JL4	Cus 4x4 Pickup	8361	—	—
9JH4	Royal Pickup	6892	—	—
9JP4	Sport Pickup	7474	2648	—
9JP4	Spt 4x4 Pickup	9245	—	—

ENGINE (Ram 50): 2.0L (122 cid) OHC four-cylinder. Brake horsepower: 90 at 5000 rpm. Bore & stroke: 3.30 x 3.54. Compression ratio: 8.5:1. Carburetor: Two-barrel. (Custom). 2.6L (156 cid) four-cylinder. Brake horsepower: 105 at 5000 rpm. Bore & stroke: 3.59 x 3.86. Compression ratio: 8.2:1. Carburetor: Two-barrel. (Royal/Sport).
CHASSIS FEATURES: Wheelbase: 109.4 (two-wheel drive), 109.8 in. (four-wheel drive). Overall length: 184.6 in. Overall height: 60.6 in. (Custom), 59.8 in. (Royal/Sport). Overall width: 65 in. GVW: 4,045-4,120 lbs. Tires: 6.00 x 14C (Custom); 185SR14 SBR (Royal/Sport).
POWERTRAIN OPTIONS: Three-speed automatic transmission. Five-speed manual transmission (Custom).
CONVENIENCE OPTIONS: [Four-wheel drive]: (Custom/Sport) power steering, aluminum transfer case, Power Ram emblems. Air conditioning. Chrome rear step bumper. Low-luster black rear step bumper. Electronic digital clock. Front floor mats. Grille guard. Bright low-mount exterior mirrors. Vinyl bodyside molding. Front and rear wheel openings moldings. Mud guards. Power steering. Sliding rear window. Automatic speed control. Sport bar. Sun roof. Pickup bed liner. Bodyside tape stripe.

1982 Dodge Ramcharger 4x4 Royal SE (DNP)

RAMCHARGER SPORT UTILITY VEHICLE: Styling was carried over from 1981. As before, both two-wheel drive (AD150) and part-time four-wheel drive (AW150) were offered. With its transfer case shift selector in the "two-wheel high" mode, the four-wheel drive could drive with rear power only. When the system was in two-wheel drive, the front axle was disconnected and not in operation. Among standard Ramcharger features were: Dry type air cleaner. Ashtray. Bright front and rear bumpers. Automatic choke. Cigar lighter.

242

Insulated dash liner. Cleaner air system. Coolant reserve system. Color-keyed inner door trim panels and armrests. Electronic ignition system. Black floor mat. 35-gallon fuel tank. Tinted glass (all windows). Glove box. Aluminum grille surround molding with painted plastic insert and headlamp doors. Fresh air heater with defrosters. Insulated hood pad. In-cab hood release. Dual electric horns. Bright hubcaps. Front wheel automatic-locking type hubs (four-wheel drive). Speedometer, odometer, ammeter, fuel gauge, oil pressure and engine temperature indicator lights. Dual partial finish short arm 5 x 7 in. exterior mirrors. 10 in. day/night interior rearview mirror. Bright quarter side window and windshield moldings. Power front disc brakes. Power steering. AM radio. Rear roof vent. Deluxe vinyl low-back front bucket seats. Inside spare tire mounting. Front stabilizer bar (four-wheel drive). Sun visors. Dual jet windshield washers. Two-speed windshield wipers. Three-speed automatic transmission (two-wheel drive). Four-speed manual (four-wheel drive).

I.D. DATA (Ramcharger): The VIN consisted of 17 symbols. The first three symbols revealed manufacturer, make and vehicle type. The fourth symbol indicated GVW rating. The fifth, sixth and seventh symbols indicated series and body style. The eighth symbol indicated engine. The ninth symbol was a check digit. The 10th symbol indicated model year. The 11th symbol indicated assembly plant. The last six symbols were the sequential unit production number.

Model	Body Type	Price	Weight	Prod. Total
AD150	Sport Utility	8989	—	—
AW150	4x4 Sport Utility	10,095	4163	—

ENGINE (Ramcharger): 5.2 liter (318 cid) V-8. Brake horsepower: 120 at 3600 rpm. Bore & stroke: 3.91 x 3.31. Compression ratio: 8.5:1. Carburetor: Two-barrel. (This engine was not available in four-wheel drive Ramchargers, which used the 150 hp at 4000 rpm four-barrel version.)

CHASSIS FEATURES: Wheelbase: 106 in. Overall length: 184.6 in. (without bumper guards), 186.1 in. (with bumper guards). Overall width: 79.5 in. GVW: 5,300 lbs. (two-wheel drive); 5,850 lbs. (four-wheel drive). Tires: P235/75R15 BSW GBR.

POWERTRAIN OPTIONS: 5.2L (318 cid) four-barrel V-8 (four-wheel drive). Three-speed TorqueFlite automatic (four-wheel drive).

OPTION PACKAGES: SNO-COMMANDER PACKAGE: (four-wheel drive only) includes, power angling blade with blade markers; hydro/electric controls; powerlift; plow lights; 114-amp. alternator; 500-amp. maintenance-free battery; maximum engine cooling; Sno-Commander decal; and transmission oil temperature light with automatic transmission. SNO-PREPARATION PACKAGE: (four-wheel drive only) 114-amp. alternator; 500-amp. maintenance-free-battery; maximum engine cooling. CONVENIENCE PACKAGE: Halogen headlamps; glove box lock and light; ash receiver light; and two-speed windshield wipers with intermittent wipe. RAMCHARGER ROYAL SE: Bright drip rail molding; bright taillamp housing; ram's head hood ornament; leaping ram with "150 Royal SE" plaque on front fender; bright aluminum grille surrounded with chromed plastic insert and bright headlamp doors; liftgate upper and lower moldings with brushed finish applique panel; woodgrain interior door trim applique; assist straps; carpeting on lower door panel; driver and front passenger high-back Command bucket seats with cloth and vinyl trim (includes inboard fold-down armrests on seats, and lockable console with removable styrofoam beverage chest); folding rear bench seat with cloth and vinyl trim; color-keyed carpeting with underlayment; color-keyed cowlside trim panels; color-keyed rear side and liftgate inner trim panels; woodtone instrument cluster faceplate; nameplate on instrument panel; luxury steering wheel with woodtone insert around rim; color-keyed spare tire cover (not available with 10R15LT tires); bright front doorsill scuff plate; oil pressure and engine temperature gauges; and trip odometer. FILIGREE STRIPE PACKAGE: Included, wheel lip and hood stripes and light-reflective stripe decal with Dodge Ram on liftgate. HEAVY-DUTY TRAILER TOWING PACKAGE: (four-wheel drive only) includes, maximum cooling; 60-amp. alternator; 430-amp. maintenance-free battery; seven wire harness; class IV tow bar hitch; heavy-duty variable load turn signal flasher; heavy-duty front and rear shocks; and heavy-duty front stabilizer bar.

CONVENIENCE OPTIONS: Air conditioning. Heavy-duty alternators and batteries. Painted step type rear bumper. Front bumper and guards with rub strips and rear bumper with rub strips. Electronic digital clock. Auxiliary transmission oil to air cooler. Maximum cooling. Oil pressure and engine temperature gauges. Trip odometer. Bright grille insert and bright headlamp doors (included ram's head hood ornament). Deluxe bi-level heater. Engine block heater. Dual bright 6 x 9 in. low mount mirrors. Dual bright 7-1/2 x 10-1/2 in. low mount extended mirrors. Bright lower molding with black vinyl insert and integral wheel lip moldings. Lower and upper moldings. Bright upper moldings. Power door locks. Power windows. AM/FM Stereo Radios: With cassette tape player and electronic tuning, with 8-track tape player, with Search-Tune and electronic tuning, with 40-channel CB transceiver. Heavy-duty front and rear shocks. Fuel tank shield. Transfer case skid plate (four-wheel drive). Automatic speed control. Sport bar. Front stabilizer bar. Heavy-duty front stabilizer bar (four-wheel drive). Tilt steering column (automatic transmission required). Luxury steering wheel. Privacy glass sunscreen. Various tires. Deluxe bright wheelcovers. Aluminum radial ribbed wheels. Five-slot chrome disc wheels (not available on four-wheel drives). White-painted steel spoke wheels (not available on two-wheel drives). Two-speed windshield wipers with intermittent wipe. Deluxe split-back front bench seat in red, cashmere or blue.

NOTE: Exterior colors available on 1982 Ramchargers included: Burnished silver metallic, Medium Seaspray green metallic, Daystar blue metallic, Cashmere, Pearl white, Impact red, Ginger, Morocco red, black, Charcoal gray metallic, Dark blue metallic, Manila cream, Spice tan metallic.

1982 Dodge Van With 15 Passenger Seating (OCW)

B150 VAN: Basic styling was unchanged for 1982. Among standard features were: Brake system warning light. Dual braking system with separate brake fluid reservoirs in the master cylinder. Dry type air cleaner. 53-amp. alternator. Driver and front passenger armrests. Ashtray. 325-amp. battery. Power front disc brakes (except 109.6 in. wheelbase and 127.6 in. wheelbase with 4,700 lbs. GVW). Painted front and rear bumpers. Double hinged type cargo doors on right side and rear (no glass). Cigar lighter. Electronic ignition system. Driver's compartment floor mat. 22-gallon fuel tank. Glove box. Argent silver finish grille. Seven-inch round headlights. Hardboard headliner in driver's compartment (white). In-cab actuated hood release. Color-keyed horn pad. Dual electric horns. Bright finish hubcaps. Ammeter, fuel gauge, odometer, oil pressure indicator light, speedometer and temperature gauge. Dual bright 5 x 7 in. exterior mirrors. AM radio. Driver's low-back bucket seat with vinyl trim. Driver's side sun visor. Spare tire carrier. Traffic hazard warning switch. Two-speed non-intermittent wet arm windshield wipers with washers. The Long-Range Ram Van came with most of the same features, plus (or in place of): 36-gallon fuel tank; bright front and rear bumpers; bright wheelcovers, windshield molding, taillamp bezels; and bright grille with quad headlamps. A 109.6 in. wheelbase was standard.

B150 WAGON: Last year's attractive styling was retained for the new 1982 B150 Wagons. It came with most of the same standard features as the B150 van, plus (or in place of): Air vent doors. Right side double doors with vented glass. Single rear door with fixed glass and inside door handle and lock button. Black full width floor mat. Color-keyed driver's compartment headliner. Fresh air heater with defroster. Ten-inch day/night interior rearview mirror. Power steering. Driver and front passenger low-back vinyl bucket seats in blue or cashmere. Three-passenger matching rear bench seat. Two sun visors. Glass all around. Four-speed manual with overdrive transmission.

1982 Dodge Mini-Ram Wagon Van (DNP)

B150 MINI-RAM WAGON: The unchanged Mini-Ram Wagon came with such features as: Five-passenger seating. Bright grille. Bright front and rear bumpers. Bright wheelcovers, side window and rear window moldings. 36-gallon fuel tank. Interior lower vinyl trim panels. Convenience Package. Intermittent type windshield wipers. Full length color-keyed headliner. The 109.6 in. wheelbase was standard.

I.D. DATA (B150): The VIN consisted of 17 symbols. The first three symbols revealed manufacturer, make and vehicle type. The fourth symbol indicated GVW rating. The fifth, sixth and seventh symbols indicated series and body style. The eighth symbol indicated engine. The ninth symbol was a check digit. The 10th symbol indicated model year. The 11th symbol indicated assembly plant. The last six symbols were the sequential unit production number.

Model	Body Type	Price	Weight	Prod. Total
(109.6 in. w.b.)				
B150	Mini-Ram Van	7046	3286	—
(127.6 in. w.b.)				
B150	Sportsman Van	7477	3493	—
B150	Long Range Van	6928	—	—
(109.6 in. w.b.)				
B150	Wagon	8482	3604	—
B150	Wagon	—	—	—
(127.6 in. w.b.)				
B150	Wagon	—	—	—

ENGINE (B150): 3.7-liter (225 cid) Six-cylinder. Brake horsepower: 95 at 3600 rpm. Bore & stroke: 3.40 x 4.12. Compression ratio: 8.4:1. Carburetor: One-barrel.

B250 VAN: The B250 shared most of the same standard features offered on the B150 (plus power steering). It was a bit more heavy-duty and could be ordered with the extra long "Maxi"

B250 WAGON: The 3/4-ton B250 wagon had most of the same standard features as the B150. It was offered in regular or extra long Maxi bodies. Maxiwagons came with a three-speed TorqueFlite automatic transmission.

B250 MINI-RAM WAGON: This was a slightly heavier-duty version of the B150 Mini-Ram Wagon. It came with the same standard features, plus eight-passenger seating.

I.D. DATA (B250): The VIN consisted of 17 symbols. The first three symbols revealed manufacturer, make and vehicle type. The fourth symbol indicated GVW rating. The fifth, sixth and seventh symbols indicated series and body style. The eighth symbol indicated engine. The ninth symbol was a check digit. The 10th symbol indicated model year. The 11th symbol indicated assembly plant. The last six symbols were the sequential unit production number.

Model (109.6 in. w.b.)	Body Type	Price	Weight	Prod. Total
B250	Van	7578	3447	—
(127.6 in. w.b.)				
B250	Van	—	—	—
B250	Maxivan	—	—	—
109.6 in. w.b.				
B250	Wagon	8482	3769	—
(127.6 in. w.b.)				
B250	Wagon	—	—	—
B250	Maxiwagon	—	—	—
B250	Mini-Ram Van	—	—	9046

ENGINE (B150): 3.7-liter (225 cid) Six-cylinder. Brake horsepower: 95 at 3600 rpm. Bore & stroke: 3.40 x 4.12. Compression ratio: 8.4:1. Carburetor: One-barrel.

B350-VAN: The 1-ton B350 had most of the same standard features as the B150, plus (or in place of): Larger brakes. Power steering. Axle type jack. Three-speed automatic transmission. Both regular and extended Maxivan bodies were offered.

B350-WAGON: This was Dodge's most heavy-duty people hauler. Most standard features echoed those of the B150 wagons. It was available in regular or Maxiwagon bodies.

I.D. DATA (B350): The VIN consisted of 17 symbols. The first three symbols revealed manufacturer, make and vehicle type. The fourth symbol indicated GVW rating. The fifth, sixth and seventh symbols indicated series and body style. The eighth symbol indicated engine. The ninth symbol was a check digit. The 10th symbol indicated model year. The 11th symbol indicated assembly plant. The last six symbols were the sequential unit production number.

Model	Body Type	Price	Weight	Prod. Total
B350	Van	8929	3891	—
B350	Maxivan	—	—	—
B350	Wagon	10,159	4249	—
B350	Maxiwagon	—	—	—

ENGINE (B350): 5.2-liter (318 cid) V-8. Brake horsepower: 135 at 4000 rpm. Compression ratio: 8.5:1. Bore & stroke: 3.91 x 3.31. Carburetor: Two-barrel.

CHASSIS FEATURES: Wheelbase: 109.6 in. (B150/B250) 127.6 in. Overall length: 178.9 in. (109.6 in. wheelbase). 196.9 in. (127.6 in. wheelbase). 222.9 in. (Maxivan/wagon). Overall width: 79.8 in. Overall height: 79.6 in. (109.6 in. wheelbase) 80.6 in. (Maxivan/wagon); 80.9 in. (127.6 in. wheelbase). GVW: 4,700-5,300 lbs. (B150); 6,010-6,400 lbs. (B250); 7,500-9,000 lbs. (B350). Tires: P195/75R15 or P205/75R15 (B150); P225/65R15 or P235/75R15 (B250); P235/75R15XL (B250 Maxivan/wagon); 8.00-16.5E or 8.75-16.5E (B350).

POWERTRAIN OPTIONS: 5.2L (318 cid) two-barrel V-8 (B150/B250); 5.2L four-barrel V-8 (B150/B250); 5.9L (360 cid) four-barrel V-8 (B350). Three-speed automatic transmission (B150/B250).

VAN OPTION PACKAGES: CONVENIENCE PACKAGE: Cigar lighter light; courtesy step well lamp for front and side doors (for use with Royal interior package only); glove box lock and light; ignition and headlight switch with time delay (n.a. with tilt steering column); two-speed windshield wipers with intermittent wipe. **EXTERIOR APPEARANCE PACKAGE:** Bright grille; dual vertically stacked quad rectangular headlamps with Halogen highbeams; bright front and rear bumpers; bright taillamp bezels; bright bodyside and rear window molding for Van Window Packages; bright windshield molding. **ROYAL INTERIOR PACKAGE:** Bucket seat floor risers; electronic digital clock; color-keyed carpeting in driver's compartment; color-keyed instrument panel with woodtone applique; instrument panel lower skirts (left and right sides); color-keyed vinyl front door trim panels with woodtone applique and chrome-trimmed armrest base; deluxe vinyl-trimmed low-back driver's seat; instrument panel nameplate; insulated dash liner; insulated headliner in driver's compartment; luxury steering wheel with woodtone insert around rim; moldings over front pillars, front door headers and around windshield; scuff pads (on B150 models); scuff pads. **HEAVY-DUTY TRAILER TOWING PACKAGE:** (B250/350) requires at extra cost: 318 four-barrel V-8 or 360 four-barrel V-8; automatic transmission, transmission auxiliary oil cooler and 36-gallon fuel tank. Package then includes: 60-amp. alternator; 430-amp. battery; maximum engine cooling; seven-wire harness; heavy-duty front and rear shocks; tow bar hitch; heavy-duty variable load flasher. **LOCK PACKAGE:** Two keys: One to operate ignition and front doors; one to operate side and rear doors.

WAGON OPTION PACKAGES: ROYAL PACKAGE: (not available on Mini-Ram Wagon), includes Royal nameplates; bright lower side and rear moldings; dual vertically stacked quad rectangular headlamps with Halogen high beams and bright grille; bright front and rear bumpers; bright molding around windshield, side and rear windows (except driver and passenger door windows); bright taillamp bezels; woodtone applique on lower face of instrument panel; color-keyed vinyl spare tire cover; vinyl door and side trim panels with woodtone trim; garnish moldings over front doors, passenger compartment windows, headers around rear compartment windows and front pillar and windshield; driver and front passenger low-back bucket seats and bench seat in deluxe vinyl trim (blue, cashmere, or red); soft cloth-covered headliner with insulation; accessory floor mats in driver's compartment; electronic digital clock; instrument panel lower skirts; color-keyed carpeting; dash liner insulation; luxury steering wheel with woodtone trim. **ROYAL SE PACKAGE:** (not available Mini-Ram Wagon) includes items listed for Royal Package, plus: Royal SE nameplates; bright upper side and rear moldings; bright bumper guards with rub strips, front and rear; bodyside and rear woodtone tape applique with dual gold accent strips; vinyl door and bodyside trim panels with woodtone trim and front door applique pull straps; carpeted engine housing cover (color-keyed); oil pressure gauge and trip odometer; glove box lock and light; deluxe two-speed windshield wipers with intermittent wipe; and headlight switch with time delay; cigar lighter light; courtesy step well lamp (front and side doors); driver and front passenger color-keyed high-back reclining Command bucket seats; and a three-passenger bench seat with plaid cloth and vinyl trim (blue, cashmere, red or silver). **EXTERIOR APPEARANCE PACKAGE:** Bright grille; bright front and rear bumpers; bright taillamp bezels; bright windshield molding; dual vertically stacked quad rectangular headlamps with Halogen high beams; bright side and rear window moldings (except driver and front passenger door windows). **INSULATION PACKAGE:** Royal and Royal SE Wagons: Interior lower fiberglass insulation panels (not on standard single rear door or optional sliding side door); insulation under floor covering.

VAN AND WAGON CONVENIENCE OPTIONS: Air conditioning. Heavy-duty alternators and batteries. Bright front and rear bumpers. Bright front and rear bumper guards and rub strips. Electronic digital clock. Auxiliary transmission oil to air cooling. Maximum engine cooling. Rear window defroster. Sliding passenger side door. Dual rear door with vented glass. Single rear door with vented glass. 36-gallon fuel tank. Oil pressure and trip odometer gauges. Sunscreen privacy glass (wagon). Banded glass front door and vent window (Van). Tinted glass (all windows). Bright grille (included dual quad rectangular headlamps; vertically stacked, with halogen high beams). Deluxe front heater. Auxiliary rear heater. Engine block heater. Two color-keyed accessory type rubber floor mats in drivers compart-

ment. Dual bright low-mount 6 x 9 in. exterior mirrors. Lower molding (included side, rear and bright taillamp bezels). Upper moldings (included side, rear and bright taillamp bezels). Upper and lower moldings with bright taillamp bezels. Electronic monitor display warning indicator for engine oil level, transmission oil level, radiator coolant level, and transmission oil temperature. Power front door locks. Power front door windows. Radios: AM/FM Stereo; AM/FM Stereo electronically tuned with cassette tape player and Dolby noise reduction system; AM/FM Stereo with Search-Tune and electronic tuning; AM/FM Stereo with eight track tape player; AM/FM Stereo with 40-channel CB transceiver. Heavy-duty shocks. Automatic speed control. Front stabilizer bar. Tilt steering column. Luxury type steering wheel. Radial ribbed aluminum wheels. Five-slot chrome disc wheels. Deluxe bright wheelcovers. Deluxe two-speed windshield wipers with intermittent wipers.

NOTE: Dodge Van and Wagon exterior colors for 1982 were: Cashmere, Manila cream, Charcoal gray metallic, Impact red, Ginger, Morocco red, Spice tan metallic, Dark blue metallic, Medium Seaspray green metallic, Daystar blue metallic, Burnished silver metallic, Pearl white, black.

1982 Dodge D150 Custom Ram Sweptline Pickup (OCW)

D150 CUSTOM PICKUP: Basic styling was unchanged for 1982. Standard features included: Independent front suspension. Energy absorbing steering column. Dry type air cleaner. Ashtray. Bright front bumper. Automatic choke. Cigar lighter. Cleaner air system. Coat hooks. Coolant reserve system. Dash and plenum liner. Door inner trim panels with pull straps and armrests. Electronic ignition system. Black floor mat with padding (color-keyed carpeting on Miser models). 20-gallon fuel tank. Glove box. Aluminum grille with painted plastic insert and headlight panels. Fresh air heater with defrosters. In-cab hood release. Dual electric horns. Bright hubcaps. Padded instrument panel. Dual bright finish mirrors. Ten-inch day/night interior rearview mirror. Bright windshield molding. Power front disc brakes (except D150 with 115 in. and 131 in. wheelbases with 4,800 lbs. GVW). AM radio. All-vinyl bench seat in black, blue or cashmere (conventional cab). Sun visors. Traffic hazard warning switch. Two-speed windshield wipers. Dual jet windshield washers. As before, D150 buyers could choose from Sweptline or Utiline boxes and conventional or Club Cabs. (Club Cabs models were only available with Sweptline boxes). Flip-out side windows and flip-down rear seats were now standard in Club Cabs. A special Miser model was offered. It had most of the same standard features found in the base D150 pickup plus: Bright finish grille; bright wheelcovers; ram's head hood ornament; gold bodyside tape stripes; deluxe pleated vinyl seat; woodtoned instrument panel and color keyed carpeting.

I.D. DATA: The VIN consisted of 17 symbols. The first three symbols revealed manufacturer, make and vehicle type. The fourth symbol indicated GVW rating. The fifth, sixth and seventh symbols indicated series and body style. The eighth symbol indicated engine. The ninth symbol was a check digit. The 10th symbol indicated model year. The 11th symbol indicated assembly plant. The last six symbols were the sequential unit production number.

1982 Dodge Ram Club Cab Sweptline Pickup (DNP)

Model	Body Type	Price	Weight	Prod. Total
D150	Utiline Pickup 6.5 ft.	6847	3288	—
D150	Sweptline Pickup 6.5 ft.	6721	3268	—
D150	Utiline Pickup 8 ft.	6997	3398	—
D150	Sweptline Pickup 8 ft.	6871	3368	—
D150	Miser Pickup 6.5 ft.	5899	3239	—
D150	Miser Pickup 8 ft.	5999	—	—
D150	Club Cab Pickup 8 ft.	8381	3927	—

1982 Dodge Ram Sweptline Pickup (DNP)

ENGINE (D150 Custom): 3.7L (225 cid) slant six-cylinder. Brake horsepower: 95 at 3600 rpm. Bore & stroke: 3.40 x 4.12. Compression ratio: 8.4:1. Carburetor: One-barrel.
ENGINE (Conventional Cab): 5.2L (318 cid) V-8. Brake horsepower: 135 at 4000 rpm. Bore & stroke: 3.91 x 3.31. Compression ratio: 8.5:1. Carburetor: Two-barrel.
ENGINE (Club Cab): 5.2L (318 cid) V-8. Brake horsepower: 135 at 4000 rpm. Bore & stroke: 3.91 x 3.31. Compression ratio: 8.5:1. Carburetor: Two-barrel. (not available in California.)
D250 CUSTOM PICKUP: The 3/4-ton D250 shared most standard features with the D150. It too was offered with conventional or Club cabs.
I.D. DATA (D250): The VIN consisted of 17 symbols. The first three symbols revealed manufacturer, make and vehicle type. The fourth symbol indicated GVW rating. The fifth, sixth and seventh symbols indicated series and body style. The eighth symbol indicated engine. The ninth symbol was a check digit. The 10th symbol indicated model year. The 11th symbol indicated assembly plant. The last six symbols were the sequential unit production number.

Model	Body Type	Price	Weight	Prod. Total
D250	Chassis & Cab	7860	3521	—
D250	Utiline Pickup 8 ft.	7754	3773	—
D250	Sweptline Pickup 8 ft.	7629	3743	—
D250	Club Cab Pickup 8 ft.	8859	4124	—

ENGINE (D250 Custom): 3.7L (225 cid) slant six-cylinder. Brake horsepower: 95 at 3600 rpm. Bore & stroke: 3.40 x 4.12. Compression ratio: 8.4:1. Carburetor: One-barrel.
ENGINE (Conventional Cab): 5.2L (318 cid) V-8. Brake horsepower: 135 at 4000 rpm. Bore & stroke: 3.91 x 3.31. Compression ratio: 8.5:1. Carburetor: Two-barrel.
NOTE: Except in California. There the 3.7L six-cylinder had 90 hp and the 5.2L V-8 had a four-barrel carburetor and 160 hp.
D350 CUSTOM PICKUP: The 1-ton D350 could be had with conventional, Club, or Crew Cabs. The Crew Cab had four doors and could seat six passengers. The "smooth side" Sweptline was the only box available on D350s. Standard equipment echoed that on the D150, although Crew Cabs and Club Cabs had deluxe vinyl split-back bench seats in blue, cashmere, red, or silver.
I.D. DATA (D350): The VIN consisted of 17 symbols. The first three symbols revealed manufacturer, make and vehicle type. The fourth symbol indicated GVW rating. The fifth, sixth and seventh symbols indicated series and body style. The eighth symbol indicated engine. The ninth symbol was a check digit. The 10th symbol indicated model year. The 11th symbol indicated assembly plant. The last six symbols were the sequential unit production number.

Model	Body Type	Price	Weight	Prod. Total
(131 in. w.b.)				
D350	Chassis & Cab	8234	3563	—
D350	Sweptline 8 ft.	8661	3958	—
(135 in. w.b.)				
D350	Chassis & Cab	8664	3865	—
(149 in. w.b.)				
D350	Club Cab	9125	4181	—
D350	Crew Cab	9435	4458	—
(159 in. w.b.)				
D350	Chassis & Cab	8743	3934	—
(165 in. w.b.)				
D350	Crew Cab	9550	4592	—

ENGINE (D350 Custom): 5.2L (318 cid) V-8. Brake horsepower: 160 at 4000 rpm. Bore & stroke: 3.91 x 3.31. Compression ratio: 8.0:1. Carburetor: Four-barrel.

1982 Dodge Power Ram 50 (4x4) Mini-Pickup (DNP)

Standard Catalog of Light-Duty Trucks

CHASSIS FEATURES: Wheelbase: 115 in. (D150 conventional cab); 131 in. (D150/D250/D350 conventional cab); 149 in. (Club Cab/D350 Crew Cab); 165 in. (D350 Crew Cab). Overall width: 79.5 in. (94.2 in. with dual rear wheels). Overall length: 190.78 in. (D150 conventional cab); 210.78 in. (conventional cab); 228.81 in. (Club Cab); 224.78 in. (D350 Crew Cab); 244.78 in. (D350 Crew Cab with 165 in. wheelbase). GVW: 4,800-5,850 lbs. (D150); 6,010 lbs. (W150); 6,400-7,500 lbs. (D250); 6,900-7,500 lbs. (W250); 8,510-10,000 lbs. (D350); 8,510 lbs. (W350). Tires: P195/75R15 (D150 conventional cab); P235/75R15 (D150 Club Cab); 8.00-16.5D (D250 conventional cab); 8.75-16.5E (D250 Club Cab); 9.50-16.5E (D350).

POWERTRAIN OPTIONS: 5.2L two-barrel V-8 (D150/D250 conventional cab); 5.2L four-barrel V-8 (D150/D250); 5.9L (360 cid) four-barrel V-8 (D350/W150/W250/ W350). Three-speed automatic transmission.

1982 Dodge Power Ram 4x4 Sweptline Pickup (DNP)

OPTION PACKAGES: FOUR-WHEEL DRIVE: (Pickups W150/W250/W350/Chassis with cab W350). Called "Power Rams." Trucks had most of the features found on two-wheel drive models, plus (or in place of): Power steering, part-time four-wheel drive, two-speed transfer case, front wheel locking hubs, leaf spring front suspension. STAKE BODY: An eight-foot stake body was available on the D250 and D350; a 9-1/2 foot stake body was available on the D350 and W350; a 12-1/2 foot stake body was available on the D350. KARY VAN PACKAGE: This body was offered on D350s with 159 in. wheelbase and 10,000 lbs. GVW. RETRIEVER WRECKER: Complete wrecker with five-ton capacity winch, rapid-shift winch control, tow bar with sling and towing chains, large-capacity deck-mounted tool box, and a sentry signal switch panel with a four-bulb flashing light bar. SNO-COMMANDER PACKAGE: (W150/W250/W350 131 in. wheelbase conventional cabs and 149 in. wheelbase Club Cab four-wheel drive pickups) includes a power angling blade with positive instrument-panel-mounted fingertip controls that easily raised and lowered the plow blade and angled it to discharge snow left or right; seven-way control valve; power lift; and plow lights. (A heavy-duty version of this package was available on the W350 four-wheel drive 131 in. wheelbase conventional cab pickup). D350 DYNA-TRAC PACKAGE: Includes dual rear wheels, a 6,900 lbs. rear axle, and a GVW rating of 10,000 lbs. Trailer towing package. ROYAL PACKAGE: (not available on Club Cab, Crew Cab, or Miser) includes: Bright backlight and drip rail moldings; plaque on front fender with leaping ram and "Royal" name; bright taillamp bezels; (Sweptline) upper and lower tailgate moldings; color-keyed cloth and vinyl trim bench seat in blue, cashmere, or red; nameplate on instrument panel; front door bright trim applique and pull straps; woodtone instrument panel applique; carpeting with underlayment; insulated underhood panel; color-keyed hardboard headliner. ROYAL SE PACKAGE: (not available on Miser). Includes, in addition to or in place of Royal package features, ram's head hood ornament; "Dodge Ram" nameplate on Sweptline Pickup tailgate; bright aluminum grille with chrome plastic insert and headlamp doors; power steering; bright tailgate applique (Sweptline); premium color-keyed, cloth and vinyl trim bench seat in blue, cashmere, red, or silver; front door woodgrain trim applique; assist strap and carpeting on lower portion of doors; luxury steering wheel with woodtone insert around rim; oil pressure and engine temperature gauges; trip odometer; bright door-sill scuff plates; color-keyed soft headliner (not available Crew Cab); garnish molding over windshield, front pillar, door header, quarter trim panel upper and backlight (not on Crew Cab); cowlside trim panels; dome lamp mounted center of roof (Club Cab); and rear side and back trim panels (Club Cab). LIGHT PACKAGE: Halogen headlights, ash receiver light, glove box lock & light, exterior cargo light, map light.

CONVENIENCE OPTIONS: Air conditioning. Heavy-duty alternators and batteries. Rear step type bumper. Auxiliary transmission oil to air cooler. Maximum cooling. Thirty-gallon fuel tank. Oil pressure and engine temp gauges. Trip odometer. Tinted glass. Bright insert grille (includes ram's head hood ornament.) Deluxe bi-level heater. Engine block heater. Dual exterior low mount or low mount extended bright mirrors. Upper moldings. Lower moldings. Upper and lower moldings. Power door locks. Power steering. Power windows. Radios: AM/FM Stereo, AM/FM Stereo with electronic tuning and cassette tape player; AM/FM Stereo with 8-track tape player; AM/FM Stereo with Search-Tune and electronic tuning; AM/FM Stereo with 40-channel CB. Heavy-duty shocks. Spare tire carrier inside Automatic speed control. Front stabilizer bar. Tilt steering column. Luxury steering wheel. Transfer case skid plate. Bright wheelcovers. Wheels: Aluminum radial ribbed; chrome disc (five-slot); and painted steel spoke (White). Sliding rear window. Two-speed windshield wipers with intermittent wipe.

NOTE: D series colors for 1982 included: Cashmere, Spice tan metallic, Charcoal gray metallic, Medium Seaspray green metallic, Ginger, Daystar blue metallic, Manila cream, Dark blue metallic, Impact red, Morocco red, Burnished silver metallic, Pearl white, black.

HISTORICAL: NOTE: Dodge produced 190,346 light-duty trucks built to 1982 specifications in the U.S. This total included 17,636 Rampage pickups; 58,380 D150s; 5,132 D250s; 4,916 D350s; 7,230 W150s; 1,888 W250s; 2,447 W350s; 8,405 Ramchargers; 57,810 Ram Vans and 26,502 Ram Wagons. Calendar year sales of Mitsubishi-built Dodge Ram 50s (imported from Japan) was 34,614 units. A jump in the popularity of Dodge trucks brought Chrysler Corp. an overall 31.8 percent increase in sales of trucks during calendar year 1982. The Power Ram 50 four-wheel drive pickup was named "Four-Wheeler of the Year" by *FOUR WHEELER* and *OFF ROAD* magazine.

1983 DODGE

1983 Dodge Rampage 2.2 Sport Mini-Pickup (DNP)

RAMPAGE PICKUP: Styling of the front-wheel drive Rampage mini-pickup was unchanged for 1983. Standard features included: Iso-Strut front suspension with coil springs. Linkless-type front sway bar. Load sensing brake system. Unconstruction. Double-wall pickup box. One-piece tailgate with center release lever and covered support cables that were concealed when the tailgate was up. Power front disc brakes. Ashtray. A 335-amp. maintenance-free battery. Flexible body color front bumper integral with front end panel, backed by steel bumper bar mounted to energy absorbers. Black styled end caps on rear bumper. Front and rear bumper protective rub strip. Color-keyed carpeting. Cigarette lighter. Cleaner Air System. Quartz clock with trip odometer. Directional signals with lane-change feature. 13-gallon fuel tank. Halogen headlamps. Heater and defroster. Inside hood release. Hood silencer pad. Dual horns. Electronic ignition and voltage regulator. Dome light. Glove box lock. Left-hand remote rearview mirror (black). Day/night interior mirror. Visor vanity mirror. Black belt molding. Cargo box flange trim. Bright sill molding and wheel lip. Black window and rear window molding. Package tray. Leaf springs rear suspension. Bodyside and rear tape stripe. Four-speed manual with overdrive transmission. Lower cab back trim panel. Thirteen-inch Rallye wheels. Electric windshield washers. Deluxe windshield wipers with intermittent wipe. Payload capacity 1,145 lbs. All-vinyl low-back bucket seats in brown/beige, black or red.

1983 Dodge Rampage Mini-Pickup (rear view)

RAMPAGE 2.2 PICKUP: The 2.2 came with most of the same features as the base Rampage pickup, plus (or in place of): Cloth and vinyl high-back bucket seats with integral head restraints and reclining seatbacks in red/black. Applied hood scoop. Bodyside and rear tape stripe with 2.2 graphics. Five-speed manual transmission with overdrive. Rallye instrument cluster (included tachometer, analog clock and trip odometer). Console shift lever. AM radio. Fourteen-inch Rallye wheels.

1983 Dodge Rampage Sport 2.2 Mini-Pickup (DNP)

I.D. DATA: The VIN consisted of 17 symbols. The first three symbols revealed manufacturer, make and vehicle type. The fourth symbol indicated GVW rating. The fifth, sixth and seventh symbols indicated series and body style. The eighth symbol indicated engine. The ninth symbol was a check digit. The 10th symbol indicated model year. The 11th symbol indicated assembly plant. The last six symbols were the sequential unit production number. (NOTE: On imported models, the 12th symbol indicated transmission type.)

Model	Body Type	Price	Weight	Prod. Total
ZH28	Pickup	6683	2245	—
ZS28	Pickup 2.2	7255	2311	—

ENGINE (Rampage): 2.2L (135 cid) four-cylinder. Brake horsepower: 84 at 4800 rpm. Bore & stroke: 3.44 x 3.62. Compression ratio: 8.5:1. Carburetor: 2-bbl.

CHASSIS FEATURES: Wheelbase: 104.2 in. Overall length: 183.6 in. Overall width: 66.8 in. Overall height: 51.8 in. GVW: 3,450 lbs. Tires: P175/75R x 13 SBR black sidewall (Rampage); P195/60R x 14 SBR RWL (2.2).

POWERTRAIN OPTION: Five-speed manual with overdrive (Rampage). Three-speed TorqueFlite automatic transmission.

OPTION PACKAGES: LIGHT PACKAGE: Includes ash receiver light (standard on 2.2), glove box light, headlamps-on warning buzzer, ignition switch light with time delay, and map/courtesy light. PROTECTION PACKAGE: Includes vinyl lower bodyside corrosion protection, undercoating, floor mats. COLD WEATHER PACKAGE: Includes 430-amp. maintenance-free battery, engine block heater.

CONVENIENCE OPTIONS: Air conditioning. Front license plate bracket. Rallye cluster. Center console with storage area. High capacity engine cooling system. High-altitude emission system. Right-hand remote control mirror (painted). Power steering. RADIOS: AM; AM/FM stereo (electronically tuned); AM/FM stereo with cassette player (electronically tuned). Cargo box side rails. Automatic speed control. Tonneau cover. [Wheels]: 14 in. cast aluminum wheels; 13 in. Rallye wheels; 14 in. Rallye wheels. Cloth and vinyl low-back bucket seats with adjustable head restraints and reclining seatbacks (in brown/beige or red) [Rampage]. All-vinyl high-back bucket seats with integral head restraints and reclining seatbacks (black) [no-cost option for 2.2].

NOTE: Rampage exterior colors for 1983 were: Sable Brown (Rampage), Charcoal gray metallic (Rampage), Bright Silver Crystal Coat, Beige Crystal Coat (Rampage), Graphic Red, Pearl White, black. Two-Tone combinations were: Graphic red/Flat black, black/Burnished silver metallic, Bright Silver Crystal Coat/Flat black, Pearl white/Flat black.

1983 Dodge Ram 50 Mini-Pickup (DNP)

RAM 50 CUSTOM PICKUP: Basic styling was carried over for 1983. Sales literature claimed Ram 50s were "among the finest, most technically advanced trucks anywhere in the world." They were gaining a reputation as being one of the best compact pickups on the market. Among standard features were: Argent silver painted front bumper with black rubber ends. Cargo lamp. Cigarette lighter. Dome light with driver and passenger side door switches. Emergency flashers. 18-gallon fuel tank. Tinted glass. Color-keyed headliner. Inside hood release. Bright hubcaps. Left and right sides black sport type exterior mirrors. Bright windshield molding. AM radio. Adjustable angle steering column. Dual sun visors. Trip odometer. Two-speed windshield wipers with washers. Four-speed manual transmission. This year, as in 1982, the Ram 50 Custom was available with four-wheel drive. The 4x4 version had most of the same standard features as the 4x2 version, plus all-terrain tires and power steering.

RAM 50 ROYAL PICKUP: The Royal had more deluxe interior and exterior trim than the Custom. White sidewall tires, chrome front bumper, and carpeting were just a few of its luxury touches. It also came with a five-speed manual transmission.

RAM 50 SPORT PICKUP: The Sport had the most flair of any Ram 50 pickup. In addition to many of the items standard on the Custom, it also had: Center console with oil pressure gauge, ammeter and (five-speed manual) transmission shift lever. AM/FM stereo radio. White spoke road wheels. Tape stripe. Bucket seats. Like the Custom, it was also available with four-wheel drive.

I.D. DATA: The VIN consisted of 17 symbols. The first three symbols revealed manufacturer, make and vehicle type. The fourth symbol indicated GVW rating. The fifth, sixth and seventh symbols indicated series and body style. The eighth symbol indicated engine. The ninth symbol was a check digit. The 10th symbol indicated model year. The 11th symbol indicated assembly plant. The last six symbols were the sequential unit production number. (NOTE: On imported models, the 12th symbol indicated transmission type.)

Model	Body Type	Price	Weight	Prod. Total
9JL4	Pickup (Custom)	6266	2345	—
9JL4	Pickup (Custom 4x4)	—	—	—
9JH4	Pickup (Royal)	7135	2510	—
9JP4	Pickup (Sport)	7732	2530	—
9JP4	Pickup (Sport 4x4)	—	—	—

ENGINE (Ram 50): 2.0L (122 cid) OHC. Four-cylinder. Brake horsepower: 90 at 5000 rpm. Bore & stroke: 3.30 x 3.54 in. Compression ratio: 8.5:1. Carburetor: Two-barrel (Custom).

ENGINE (Ram 50): 2.6L (156 cid). Four-cylinder. Brake horsepower: 105 at 5000 rpm. Bore & stroke: 3.59 x 3.86 in. Compression ratio: 8.2:1. Carburetor: Two-barrel (Royal/Sport).

CHASSIS FEATURES: Wheelbase: 109.4 in. (4x2); 109.8 in. (4x4). Overall length: 184.6 in. Overall height: 60.6 in. (Custom); 59.8 in. (Royal/Sport). Overall width: 65 in. GVW: 4,045-4,120 lbs. Tires: 6.00 x 14C (Custom), 185SR x 14 SBR (Royal/Sport).

POWERTRAIN OPTIONS: Three-speed automatic transmission. Five-speed manual transmission (Custom). Four-cylinder 2.3L (140 cid) OHC turbo diesel.

CONVENIENCE OPTIONS: FOUR-WHEEL DRIVE: (Custom/Sport) power steering, aluminum transfer case, Power Ram emblems. Air conditioning. Chrome rear step bumper. Low-luster black rear step bumper. Electronic digital clock. Front floor mats. Grille guard. Bright low-mount exterior mirrors. Vinyl bodyside molding. Front and rear wheel openings moldings. Mud guards. Power steering. Sliding rear window. Automatic speed control. Sport bar. Sunroof. Pickup bed liner. Bodyside tape stripe.

1983 Dodge Power Ram 50 (4x4) Mini-Pickup (DNP)

RAMCHARGER SPORT UTILITY VEHICLE: Styling was unchanged for 1983. As before, both 4x2 (AD150) and part-time 4x4 (AW150) models were offered. With its transfer case shift selector in the two-wheel high model, the four-wheel drive could drive with rear power only. When the system was in two-wheel drive, the front axle was disconnected and not in operation. Among standard Ramcharger features were: Dry type air cleaner. Ashtray. Bright front and rear bumpers. Automatic choke. Cigar lighter. Insulated dash liner. Cleaner air system. Coolant reserve system. Color-keyed inner door trim panels and armrests. Electronic ignition system. Black floor mat. 35-gallon fuel tank. Tinted glass (all windows). Glove box. Aluminum grille with painted plastic insert and headlamp doors. Fresh air heater with defrosters. Insulated hood inner panel. In cab hood release. Dual electric horns. Bright hubcaps. Front wheel automatic-locking type hubs (four-wheel drive). Speedometer, odometer, ammeter, fuel gauge, oil pressure and engine temperature indicator lights. Dual bright finish short arm 5 in. x 7 in. exterior mirrors. 10 in. day/night interior rearview mirror. Bright quarter side window and windshield moldings. Power front disc brakes. Power steering. AM radio. Rear roof vent. Deluxe vinyl high-back front bucket seats. Inside spare tire mounting. Front stabilizer bar (four-wheel drive). Sun visors. Dual jet windshield washers. Two-speed windshield wipers. Three-speed automatic transmission.

1983 Dodge 4x4 Ramcharger Sport Utility (DNP)

I.D. DATA: The VIN consisted of 17 symbols. The first three symbols revealed manufacturer, make and vehicle type. The fourth symbol indicated GVW rating. The fifth, sixth and seventh symbols indicated series and body style. The eighth symbol indicated engine. The ninth symbol was a check digit. The 10th symbol indicated model year. The 11th symbol indicated assembly plant. The last six symbols were the sequential unit production number.

Model	Body Type	Price	Weight	Prod. Total
AD150	Utility (4x2)	9494	—	—
AW150	Utility (4x4)	11,039	4065	—

ENGINES (Ramcharger): 5.2-liter (318 cid) V-8. Brake horsepower: 120 at 3600 rpm. Bore & stroke: 3.91 x 3.31 in. Compression ratio: 8.5:1. Carburetor: Two-barrel.

CHASSIS FEATURES: Wheelbase 106 in. Overall length: 184.6 in. (without bumper guards); 186.1 in. (with bumper guards). Overall width: 79.5 in. GVW. 5,300 lbs. (4x2); 5,850 lbs. (4x4). Tires: P235/75R x 15 BSW GBR.

POWERTRAIN OPTIONS: 5.2L (318 cid) four-barrel V-8 (4x4). Four-speed manual (4x4).

OPTION PACKAGES: SNO-COMMANDER PACKAGE: (4x4 only) power angling blade with blade markers; hydro/electric controls; powerlift; plow lights; 114-amp. alternator; 500-amp. maintenance-free battery; maximum engine cooling; Sno-Commander decal; transmission oil temperature light with automatic transmission. SNO-PREPARATION PACKAGE: (4x4) 114-amp. alternator; 500-amp. maintenance-free battery; maximum engine cooling; transmission oil temperature light with automatic transmission. CONVENIENCE PACKAGE: Halogen headlamps; glove box lock and light; ash receiver light; two-speed windshield wipers with intermittent wipe. RAMCHARGER ROYAL SE: Bright drip rail molding; bright taillamp housing; ram's head hood ornament; leaping ram with "150 Royal SE" plaque on front fender; bright aluminum grille with chromed plastic insert and bright headlamp doors; liftgate upper and lower moldings with bright applique panel; woodtone interior door trim applique, assist straps, carpeting on lower door panel; driver and front passenger high-back Command bucket seats with cloth and vinyl trim (included inboard fold-down armrests on seats, and lockable console); folding rear bench seat with cloth and vinyl trim; color-keyed carpeting with underlayment; color-keyed rear side and liftgate inner trim panels; woodtone instrument cluster faceplate; nameplate on instrument panel; sport steering wheel; color-keyed spare tire cover (not available with 10R x 15LT tires); bright front doorsill scuff plate; oil pressure and engine temperature gauges; trip odometer; color-keyed cowl inner trim panels. FILIGREE TAPE STRIPE PACKAGE: Includes, wheel lip and hood

stripes, plus tape stripe decal with "Dodge Ram" on liftgate. TRAILER PREPARATION PACKAGE: (4x4 only) maximum cooling; 500-amp. maintenance-free heavy-duty battery; heavy-duty variable load flasher; heavy-duty front and rear shocks; heavy-duty front stabilizer bar.

CONVENIENCE OPTIONS: Air conditioning. Heavy-duty alternators and batteries. Painted step type rear bumper. Front bumper guards. Electronic digital clock. Auxiliary transmission oil to air cooler. Maximum cooling. Oil pressure and engine temperature gauges. Trip odometer. Bright grille insert and bright headlamp doors (included ram's head hood ornament). Engine block heater. Dual bright 6 in. x 9 in. low mount mirrors. Lower molding. Lower and upper moldings. Bright upper moldings. Power door locks. Power windows. AM/FM stereo RADIOS: With cassette tape player and electronic tuning, with electronic tuning. Heavy-duty front and rear shocks. Fuel tank shield. Transfer case skid plate (4x4). Automatic speed control. Sport bar. Front stabilizer bar. Heavy-duty front stabilizer bar (4x4). Tilt steering column (automatic transmission required). Sport steering wheel. Privacy glass sunscreen. Various tires. Bright wheelcovers. Aluminum radial ribbed wheels. Two-speed windshield wipers with intermittent wipe.

NOTE: Ramcharger exterior colors for 1983 included: Burnished silver metallic, Beige Sand, Light blue metallic, Pearl white, Graphic red, Crimson red, black, Charcoal gray metallic, Nightwatch blue, Sable brown, Spice metallic.

1983 Dodge Ram Maxi-Wagon Passenger Van (DNP)

B150 VAN: Once again, styling was unchanged for the new model year. Standard features included: Brake system warning light. Dual braking system with separate brake fluid reservoirs in the master cylinder. Dry type air cleaner. 60-amp. alternator. 370-amp. battery. Painted front and rear bumpers. Power brakes. Cigar lighter. Electronic ignition system. Floor mat. 22-gallon fuel tank. Glove box. In-cab actuated hood release. Bright hubcaps. Bumper type jack. Dual bright exterior mirrors. Double hinged type cargo doors right side and rear (no glass). Door locks. Argent grille. 7 in. round headlights. Deluxe front heater. Hardboard headliner in driver's compartment. Driver's side sun visor. Traffic warning switch. Two-speed windshield wipers with washers. Driver armrest. All-vinyl low-back driver's bucket seat in black, blue, or beige. A Long Range Ram Van was once again offered. It came with a 36-gallon fuel tank; bright front and rear bumpers; bright windshield molding, wheelcovers, taillamp bezels, and grille with quad headlights. Four-speed manual with overdrive transmission.

1983 Dodge Mini-Ram Passenger Van (DNP)

B150 WAGON: Sales literature promoted the new Dodge Wagon as a "sensible and modern people mover that's right for the times." It came with many of the same features found on the B150 Van, plus (or in place of): Driver and front passenger armrests. Hinged type right side double doors with vented glass. Single rear door with fixed glass and inside door handle and lock button. Full width black floor mat. Deluxe fresh air heater with defroster. Interior 10 in. day/night mirror. Power steering. AM radio. Driver and passenger deluxe vinyl Command bucket seats with Unibelt system and three-passenger rear bench seat in matching trim (blue or beige). Two color-keyed sun visors. Glass all around.

B150 MINI-RAM WAGON: The Mini-Ram Wagon had standard seating for five. It could reportedly carry twice as much cargo as America's largest car-type station wagon. Standard features included: Bright grille. Bright front and rear bumpers, wheelcovers, and side and rear window moldings. 36-gallon fuel tank. Interior lower vinyl trim panels. Carpeting. Dual quad stacked headlights.

I.D. DATA: The VIN consisted of 17 symbols. The first three symbols revealed manufacturer, make and vehicle type. The fourth symbol indicated GVW rating. The fifth, sixth and seventh symbols indicated series and body style. The eighth symbol indicated engine. The ninth symbol was a check digit. The 10th symbol indicated model year. The 11th symbol indicated assembly plant. The last six symbols were the sequential unit production number.

Model	Body Type	Price	Weight	Prod. Total
B150 Series — 109.6 in. w.b.				
B150	Van	7339	3299	—
(127.6 in. w.b.)				
B150	Van	—	—	—
(109.6 in. w.b.)				
B150	Wagon	9068	3585	—
(127.6 in. w.b.)				
B150	Wagon	—	—	—
B150	Long Range Ram Van	7367	—	—
B150	Mini-Ram Wagon	9154	—	—

ENGINE (B150): 3.7L (225 cid) Six-cylinder. Brake horsepower: 95 at 3600 rpm. Bore & stroke: 3.40 x 4.12 in. Compression ratio: 8.4:1. Carburetor: One-barrel.

B250 VAN: The B250 shared most of the same standard features offered on the B150, plus power steering. It was a bit heavier-duty and could be ordered with the 26 in. longer Maxi body. The B250 Maxi wagon had a payload capacity of 2,650 lbs.

B250 WAGON: The B250 Wagon had most of the same standard features as the B150. It was offered in regular or extra long Maxi bodies. Maxiwagons came with a three-speed automatic transmission.

I.D. DATA: The VIN consisted of 17 symbols. The first three symbols revealed manufacturer, make and vehicle type. The fourth symbol indicated GVW rating. The fifth, sixth and seventh symbols indicated series and body style. The eighth symbol indicated engine. The ninth symbol was a check digit. The 10th symbol indicated model year. The 11th symbol indicated assembly plant. The last six symbols were the sequential unit production number.

Model	Body Type	Price	Weight	Prod. Total
B250 Series — 109.6 in. w.b.				
B250	Van	8409	3473	—
(127.6 in. w.b.)				
B250	Van	—	—	—
B250	Maxivan	—	—	—
(109.6 in. w.b.)				
B250	Wagon	—	—	—
(127.6 in. w.b.)				
B250	Wagon	10,011	3913	—
B250	Maxiwagon	—	—	—

ENGINE (B250): Same as B150, except 5.2L. Carburetor: Two-barrel. V-8 was standard on Maxiwagon.

B350 VAN: The 1-ton B350 had most of the same standard features as the B150, plus (or in place of): Larger brakes. Power steering. Axle type jack. Three-speed automatic transmission. Both regular and extended Maxivan bodies were offered.

B350 WAGON: This continued to be Dodge's most heavy-duty people hauler. It was equipped with most of the same items found on the B150. Buyers had their choice of regular or extended (Maxi) bodies.

I.D. DATA: The VIN consisted of 17 symbols. The first three symbols revealed manufacturer, make and vehicle type. The fourth symbol indicated GVW rating. The fifth, sixth and seventh symbols indicated series and body style. The eighth symbol indicated engine. The ninth symbol was a check digit. The 10th symbol indicated model year. The 11th symbol indicated assembly plant. The last six symbols were the sequential unit production number.

Model	Body Type	Price	Weight	Prod. Total
B350	Van	9703	3981	—
B350	Maxivan	—	—	—
B350	Wagon	11,233	4309	—
B350	Maxiwagon	—	—	—

ENGINE (B350): 5.2L (318 cid) V-8, Brake horsepower: 135 at 4000 rpm. Bore & stroke: 3.91 x 3.31 in. Compression ratio: 8.5:1. Carburetor: Two-barrel. Note: Maxiwagon came with four-barrel 5.2L/160 hp V-8.

CHASSIS FEATURES: Wheelbase: 109.6 in. (B150/B250); 127.6 in. (B350). Overall length: 178.9 in. (109.6 in. wheelbase); 196.9 in. (127.6 in. wheelbase); 222.9 in. (Maxi van/wagon). Overall width: 79.8 in. Overall height: 79.6 in. (109.6 in. wheelbase); 80.6 in. (Maxi van/wagon); 80.9 in. (127.6 in. wheelbase) GVW: 4,700-6,010 lbs. (B150); 6,010-6,400 lbs. (B250); 7,500-9,000 lbs. (B350). Tires: P195/75R x 15 (109.6 in. wheelbase B150); P205/75R x 15 (127.6 in. wheelbase B150); P225/75R x 15 (B250); 8.75 x 16.5E (B350).

POWERTRAIN OPTIONS: 5.2L two-barrel V-8 (B150/B250); 5.2L four-barrel V-8 (B150/B250/B350); 5.9L (360 cid) V-8 (B350). Three-speed automatic transmission.

VAN OPTION PACKAGES: CONVENIENCE PACKAGE: Includes, cigar lighter; courtesy step well lamp for front and side doors (for use with Royal interior package only); glove box lock and light; ignition and headlight switch with time delay (not available with tilt steering column); two-speed windshield wipers with intermittent wipe. EXTERIOR APPEARANCE PACKAGE: Includes, bright grille; dual vertically stacked quad rectangular headlamps with halogen high beams; bright front and rear bumpers; bright taillamp bezels; bright rear bodyside molding for van window package; bright windshield molding. ROYAL INTERIOR PACKAGE: Includes, color-keyed bucket seat floor risers; electronic digital clock; color-keyed carpeting in driver's compartment; color-keyed instrument panel with woodtone applique; instrument panel lower skirts (right and left sides); color-keyed vinyl front door trim panels with woodtone applique and chrome trimmed armrest base; deluxe vinyl trimmed high-back Command driver and passenger seats (blue, beige or red); color-keyed garnish moldings over front pillars and front door headers and around windshield; instrument panel nameplate; insulated dash liner; insulated headliner in driver's compartment; luxury steering wheel with woodtone insert around rim; power steering on B150 models; scuff pads. TRAILER TOWING PREPARATION PACKAGE B250/B350: (requires following equipment at extra cost: 318 four-barrel V-8 or 360 four-barrel V-8, automatic transmission, transmission auxiliary oil cooler, and certain selected axle ratios) Includes 500-amp. maintenance-free heavy-duty battery; maximum engine cooling; heavy-duty shocks; heavy-duty variable load flasher; front stabilizer bar. LOCK PACKAGE: Two keys (one operates ignition and front doors; the other operates side and rear doors).

WAGON OPTION PACKAGES: ROYAL PACKAGE: Royal nameplates; bright lower bodyside and rear moldings; bright grille and dual vertically stacked quad rectangular headlamps with halogen high beams; bright front and rear bumpers; bright molding around windshield, and side and rear fixed windows (except driver and passenger door windows); bright taillamp bezels; woodtone applique on lower face of instrument panel; spare tire cover; vinyl door and side trim panels with woodtone trim; garnish trim over front doors and passenger compartment windows, the headers around rear compartment windows, front pillars and windshield; driver and front passenger high-back Command bucket seats, and three-passenger bench seat in cloth and vinyl trim (blue, beige, silver, or red); soft cloth covered headliner with insulation; accessory floor mats in driver's compartment; electronic digital clock; instrument panel lower skirts; color-keyed carpeting; dash liner insulation; luxury steering wheel with woodtone rim insert. ROYAL SE PACKAGE: Includes items in Royal Package, plus: Royal SE nameplates; bright upper side and rear moldings; bright bumper guards with rub strips; vinyl door and side trim panels with woodtone trim; front door applique pull strap; carpeted engine housing cover; oil pressure gauge and trip odometer; glove box lock and light; deluxe two-speed windshield wipers with intermittent wipe; ignition and headlight switch with time delay; cigar lighter light; courtesy step well lamp (front and side doors); driver and front passenger reclining high-back Command bucket seats and a three-passenger bench seat with deluxe cloth and vinyl trim. EXTERIOR APPEARANCE PACKAGE: Includes, bright grille; bright front and rear bumpers; bright taillamp bezels and windshield molding; dual vertically stacked quad rectangular headlamps with Halogen high beams; bright side and rear fixed window moldings (except driver and front passenger door windows). INSULATION PACKAGE [for Royal and Royal SE Wagons]: Includes, interior lower fiberglass insulation panels (not available on standard single rear door or optional sliding side door); insulation under floor covering. For Custom wagons includes Royal and Royal SE items, plus interior lower trim panels in passenger compartment (blue or beige); color-keyed garnish moldings over windshield and front door headers, and around headliner and rear compartment window; dash liner insulation; sliding side door track cover; white hardboard headliner in passenger compartment; insulation under headliner. EIGHT-PASSENGER SEATING PACKAGE: (B150 van 109.6 in. wheelbase models with 6,010 lbs. GVW Package and all B250/B350 Wagons and Maxiwagons) includes one additional quick-release three-passenger bench seat with three seat belts. EIGHT-PASSENGER TRAVEL SEATING PACKAGE. B350 12-PASSENGER SEATING PACKAGE: (requires rear doors with optional vented glass, at extra cost). Includes second (three-passenger) and third (four-passenger) extra seats; and window retention. Spare tire carrier loaded under third bench seat. B350 MAXIWAGON 15-PASSENGER SEATING PACKAGE: (requires 8,510 lbs. GVW Package and rear doors with optional vented glass, at extra cost). Includes second and third (three-passenger) and fourth (four-passenger) additional seats; window retention; and spare tire carrier relocated under fourth bench seat. B250/B350 TRAILER TOWING PREPARATION PACKAGE: (requires automatic transmission on B250 models and 318 cid four-barrel [two-barrel in California] or 360 cid V-8, transmission auxiliary oil cooler, and specified rear axle ratio). Includes maximum cooling; 500-amp. maintenance-free heavy-duty battery; heavy-duty variable load turn signal flasher; heavy-duty shocks; front stabilizer bar. CONVENIENCE PACKAGE: Includes, cigar lighter light; glove box lock and light; ignition and headlight switch with time delay (not available with tilt steering column); two-speed windshield wipers with intermittent wipers; and courtesy step well lamp for front and side doors (with Royal Package).

VAN/WAGON CONVENIENCE OPTIONS: Air conditioning. Heavy-duty alternator battery. Bright front and rear bumpers. Bright front and rear bumper guards and rub strips. Electronic digital clock. Transmission auxiliary oil cooler. Maximum engine cooling. Rear window defroster. Dual rear doors with vented and banded glass (Wagon). Single rear door with vented and banded glass. Sliding passenger side door with no glass (van), fixed glass, or with vented and banded glass. 36-gallon fuel tank. Oil pressure and trip odometer gauges. Sunscreen privacy glass (wagon). Banded front door glass and vent window (van). Bright finish grille (includes dual quad rectangular headlamps, vertically stacked, with halogen high beams). Cargo compartment white hardboard headliner (van). Power steering (B150 van). Auxiliary rear heater. Engine block heater. Scuff pads. RADIOS: AM (van); AM/FM/MX stereo, electronically tuned, with cassette tape player and Dolby Noise Reduction System; AM/FM stereo electronically tuned; AM/FM/MX stereo manually tuned. Heavy-duty shocks. Power door locks. Power windows (front doors). SEATS: (van) deluxe vinyl trim high-back Command driver's bucket; driver and passenger high-back Command buckets in cloth and vinyl trim (Royal interior trim required); driver and passenger high-back Command buckets in deluxe vinyl trim; driver and passenger low-back buckets in deluxe vinyl trim. Heavy-duty shocks. Automatic speed control. Front stabilizer bar. Tilt type steering column. Luxury type steering wheel. Sunscreen privacy glass. Tape stripes. Deluxe wheelcovers. Aluminum ribbed wheels. Intermittent type windshield wipers. Lower moldings (included side, rear and bright taillamp bezels). Upper moldings (includes side, rear and bright taillamp bezels). Upper and lower moldings (includes side, rear and bright taillamp bezels).

NOTE: Exterior colors for 1983 Dodge Vans and Wagons were: Beige Sand, Sable brown, Charcoal gray metallic, Graphic red, Crimson red, Spice metallic, Nightwatch blue, Light blue metallic, Burnished silver metallic, Pearl white, black.

1983 Dodge Ram "Miser" Sweptline Pickup (DNP)

D150 CUSTOM PICKUP: Basic styling was unchanged for 1983. Standard features included: Independent front suspension. Energy absorbing steering column. Dry type air cleaner. Ashtray. Bright front bumper. Automatic choke. Cigar lighter. Cleaner air system. Coat hooks. Coolant reserve system. Dash and plenum liner. Door inner trim panels with straps and armrests. Electronic ignition system. Black floor mat with padding (color-keyed carpeting on Miser models). 20-gallon fuel tank. Glove box. Aluminum grille with painted plastic insert and headlight doors. Fresh air heater with defrosters. In-cab hood release. Dual electric horns. Bright hubcaps. Padded instrument panel. Dual bright finish mirrors. 10 in. day/night interior rearview mirror. Bright windshield molding. Power front disc brakes (except D150 with 115 in. and 131 in. wheelbases with 4,800 lbs. GVW). Four-speed manual transmission with overdrive. All-vinyl bench seat in black, blue or cashmere. Sun visors. Traffic hazard warning switch. Two-speed windshield wipers. Dual jet windshield washers. All D150 pickups had the conventional (three-passenger) cabs. Buyers could choose from Sweptline (with smooth sides) or Utiline (with rear fenders) boxes. A special Miser model was offered. It had most of the same standard features found in the base D150 pickup, plus: Bright finish grille, bright wheelcovers, ram's head hood ornament, gold bodyside tape stripes, deluxe pleated vinyl seat, woodtoned instrument panel, and color-keyed carpeting.

1983 Dodge Royal Ram Sweptline Pickup (DNP)

I.D. DATA: The VIN consisted of 17 symbols. The first three symbols revealed manufacturer, make and vehicle type. The fourth symbol indicated GVW rating. The fifth, sixth and seventh symbols indicated series and body style. The eighth symbol indicated engine. The ninth symbol was a check digit. The 10th symbol indicated model year. The 11th symbol indicated assembly plant. The last six symbols were the sequential unit production number.

Model	Body Type	Price	Weight	Prod. Total
(6.5 ft. beds)				
D150	Utiline Pickup	6915	—	—
D150	Sweptline Pickup	6787	3244	—
D150	Miser Pickup	5989	—	—
(8 ft. beds)				
D150	Utiline Pickup	7069	3368	—
D150	Sweptline Pickup	6941	3338	—
D150	Miser Pickup	6184	—	—

ENGINE (D150 Custom): 3.7L (225 cid) Slant six-cylinder. Brake horsepower: 95 at 3600 rpm. Bore & stroke: 3.40 x 4.12 in. Compression ratio: 8.4:1. Carburetor: One-barrel

D250 CUSTOM PICKUP: The 3/4-ton D250 shared most standard features with the D150. It was available with either Sweptline or Utiline boxes and a conventional (three-passenger) cab.

I.D. DATA: The VIN consisted of 17 symbols. The first three symbols revealed manufacturer, make and vehicle type. The fourth symbol indicated GVW rating. The fifth, sixth and seventh symbols indicated series and body style. The eighth symbol indicated engine. The ninth symbol was a check digit. The 10th symbol indicated model year. The 11th symbol indicated assembly plant. The last six symbols were the sequential unit production number.

Model	Body Type	Price	Weight	Prod. Total
D250	Chassis & Cab	8387	3561	—
(8 ft. beds)				
D250	Utiline Pickup	7816	3764	—
D250	Sweptline Pickup	7688	3734	—

ENGINE (D250 Custom): 3.7L (225 cid) Slant six-cylinder. Brake horsepower: 95 at 3600 rpm. Bore & stroke: 3.40 x 4.12 in. Compression ratio: 8.4:1. Carburetor: One-barrel. Except in California, where the 3.7L six-cylinder had 84 brake horsepower.

D350 CUSTOM PICKUP: The 1-ton D350 could be had with conventional, or Crew cabs. The Crew Cab model had four doors and could seat six passengers. The smooth side Sweptline was the only box available on D350s. Standard equipment echoes that on the D150, except automatic transmission was standard. Crew Cabs had deluxe vinyl split-back bench seats in blue, beige, or red.

I.D. DATA: The VIN consisted of 17 symbols. The first three symbols revealed manufacturer, make and vehicle type. The fourth symbol indicated GVW rating. The fifth, sixth and seventh symbols indicated series and body style. The eighth symbol indicated engine. The ninth symbol was a check digit. The 10th symbol indicated model year. The 11th symbol indicated assembly plant. The last six symbols were the sequential unit production number.

Model	Body Type	Price	Weight	Prod. Total
D350 Series — 131 in. w.b.				
D350	Chassis & Cab	8553	3601	—
D350	Sweptline Pickup 8 ft.	8856	3879	—
(135 in. w.b.)				
D350	Chassis & Cab	—	—	—
(149 in. w.b.)				
D350	Crew Cab Pickup	10,010	4379	—
(159 in. w.b.)				
D350	Chassis & Cab	—	—	—
(165 in. w.b.)				
D350	Crew Cab Pickup	10,128	4513	—

ENGINE (D350 Custom): 5.2L (318 cid) V-8. Brake horsepower: 160 at 4000 rpm. Bore & stroke: 3.91 x 3.31 in. Compression ratio: 8.0:1. Carburetor: Four-barrel.

1983 Dodge Power Ram "Miser" Sweptline Pickup (DNP)

CHASSIS FEATURES: Wheelbase: 115 in. (D150 conventional cab); 131 in. (D150/D250/D350 conventional cab); 149 in. (D350 Crew Cab); 165 in. (D350 Crew Cab). Overall width: 79.5 in. (94.2 in. with dual rear wheels). Overall length: 190.78 in. (D150 conventional cab); 210.78 in. (D250/D350 conventional cab); 224.78 in. (D350 Crew Cab); 244.78 in. (D350 Crew Cab 165 in. wheelbase). GVW: 4,800-5,850 lbs. (D150); 6,010 lbs. (W150); 6,400-7,500 lbs. (D250); 6,900-7,500 lbs. (W250); 8,510-10,000 lbs. (D350); 8,510 lbs. (W350). Tires: P195/75R x 15 (D150); 8.00 x 16.5D (D250); 9.50 x 16.5E (D350).

POWERTRAIN OPTIONS: 5.2L two-barrel V-8 (D150/D250); 5.2L four-barrel V-8 (D150/D250); 5.9L (360 cid) four-barrel V-8 (D350/W150/W250/W350). Three-speed automatic transmission (D150/D250). Four-speed manual NP435 transmission (D150/D350).

OPTION PACKAGES: FOUR-WHEEL DRIVE: (Pickups: W150/W250/W350/chassis with cab W350). Called "Power Rams," these trucks had most of the features found on 4x2 models, plus (or in place of): Power steering, part-time four-wheel drive, two-speed transfer case, automatic locking hubs, and leaf spring front suspension. STAKE BODIES: An 8-foot stake body was available on the D250/D350/W350; a 9-1/2-foot stake body was available on the D350 and W350; and a 12-1/2-foot stake body was available on the D350. ONE-TON DUMP TRUCK BODIES: Offered for D350/W350 with 135 in. wheelbase and 10,000 lbs. GVW equipment. KARY VAN BODY: Offered for D350s with the 159 in. wheelbase and 10,000 lbs. GVW equipment. RETRIEVER WRECKER: Complete wrecker with five-ton capacity winch, rapid-shift winch control, tow bar with sling and towing chains, large-capacity deck-mounted tool box, a sentry signal switch panel and dual combination roof light bar. SNO-COMMANDER PACKAGE: (W150/W250/W350 MODELS [131 in. wheelbase on W350]) includes a power angling blade with positive instrument-panel-mounted fingertip controls that easily raised and lowered the plow blade and angled it to discharge snow left or right; seven-way control valve; power lift; and plow lights. (A heavy-duty version of this package was available on the W350 conventional cab pickup with 131 in. wheelbase). D350 Dyna-Trac: Includes, dual rear wheels, a 7,500 lbs. rear axle and a GVW rating of 10,000 lbs. TRAILER TOWING PACKAGE: Includes trailer towing equipment. ROYAL PACKAGE: (not available on Crew Cab), bright backlight and drip rail molding; plaque on front fender with leaping ram and "Royal" name; bright taillamp bezels (Sweptline) upper and lower tailgate moldings (Sweptline); color-keyed cloth and vinyl trim bench seat in blue, beige, or red; nameplate on instrument panel; front door bright trim applique and pull straps; woodtone instrument panel applique; carpeting with underlayment; insulation under hood panel; color-keyed hardboard headliner. ROYAL SE PACKAGE: (in addition to or in place of Royal Package features) ram's head hood ornament; "Dodge Ram" nameplate on Sweptline Pickup tailgate; bright aluminum grille with chrome plastic insert and headlamp doors; power steering; bright tailgate applique panel (Sweptline); deluxe color-keyed, cloth and vinyl trim bench seat in blue, beige, red, or silver; front door woodtone trim applique, assist strap and carpeting on lower portion; black four-spoke sport steering wheel; oil pressure and engine temperature gauges; trip odometer; bright doorsill scuff plates; color-keyed soft headliner (not available Crew Cab); garnish molding over windshield, front pillar, door header, quarter trim panel upper and over backlight (not available Crew Cab); cowl-side trim panels. LIGHT PACKAGE: Halogen headlamps, ash receiver light, glove box lock and light, exterior cargo light, map light.

CONVENIENCE OPTIONS: Air conditioning. Heavy-duty alternators and batteries. Rear step type bumper. Electric digital clock. Auxiliary transmission oil to air cooler. Maximum cooling. 30-gallon fuel tank. Oil pressure and engine temperature gauges. Trip odometer. Tinted glass. Bright insert grille (includes ram's head hood ornament). Engine block heater. Dual exterior low mount 6 in. x 9 in. bright mirrors. Upper moldings. Lower moldings. Upper and lower moldings. Power door locks. Power steering. Power windows. Radios: AM; AM/FM stereo; AM/FM stereo with electronic tuning and cassette tape player; AM/FM stereo with electronic tuning. Heavy-duty shocks. Spare tire carrier inside. Automatic speed control. Front stabilizer bar. Tilt steering column. Sport steering wheel. Transfer case skid plate. Bright wheelcovers. Wheels: Aluminum radial ribbed; chrome disc (five-slot); painted steel spokes (white). Sliding rear window. Two-speed windshield wipers with intermittent wipe.

NOTE: D series exterior colors for 1983 included: Beige Sand, Sable brown (not available on Miser), Charcoal gray metallic (not available on Miser), Graphic red, Crimson red, Spice metallic, Nightwatch blue, Light blue metallic (not available on Miser), Burnished silver metallic (not available on Miser), Pearl white. Two two-tone paint procedures and filigree pin tape stripes were optional.

HISTORICAL: Dodge produced 199,349 trucks built to 1983 specifications in the U.S. This included 8,033 Rampage pickups; 50,217 D150s; 4,979 D250s; 3,924 D350s; 10,807 W150s; 2,443 W250s; 2,795 W350s; 18,992 Ramchargers; 65,206 Ram Vans; and 31,953 Ram Wagons. Model year sales of 29,573 Ram 50 captive import trucks were also recorded. The Ram 50 was built by Mitsubishi Motors of Japan. Dodge increased its calendar year sales to 263,125 trucks, a gain of 12 percent from 1982.

1984 DODGE

1984 Dodge Rampage Mini-Pickup (DNP)

RAMPAGE PICKUP: Sales literature described Rampage as "America's only front-wheel drive sport pickup." A new grille with two rectangular slots made it look even sportier than before. That and the four rectangular halogen headlamps, new fascia with integral rub strip and new hood treatment, combined to create a more "upscale" appearance. Among standard features were: 60-amp. alternator. Instrument panel ashtray. 335-amp. maintenance-free battery. Front disc brakes. Iso-Strut front suspension with coil springs. Load sensing brake system. Unconstruction. Carpeting. Cigarette lighter. Directional signals with lane change feature. Electronic fuel control system. 13-gallon fuel tank. Tinted glass. Cloth covered headliner. Heater and defroster. Inside hood release. Hood silencer pad. Dual horns. Electronic ignition and voltage regulator. Parking brake warning light. Glove box. Black left and right remote exterior mirrors. Day/night inside rearview mirror. Black belt molding. Cargo box flange trim molding. Black windshield and rear window molding. Bright wheel lip molding. Package trays. Rack and pinion steering gear. Four-spoke type steering wheel. Leaf springs rear suspension. Black tape insert tailgate lift handle. Body side and rear tape stripe. Four-speed manual with overdrive. Lower cab back trim panel. Electric windshield washers. Deluxe windshield wipers with intermittent wipe. All vinyl-low-back bucket seats with adjustable head restraints and reclining seatbacks in Brown/Saddle, Charcoal/Silver, or Red.

1984 Dodge Rampage 2.2 Mini-Pickup (DNP)

RAMPAGE 2.2 PICKUP: The 2.2 came with most of the same features as the base Rampage pickup plus (or in place of): Cloth and vinyl high-back bucket seats with integral head restraints and reclining seatbacks in Brown/Saddle, Charcoal/Silver, or Red. Rallye instrumentation (included tach, oil pressure gauge, trip odometer, temperature gauge). Electronically tuned AM radio. 14 in. Rallye wheels. Five-speed manual with overdrive. 2.2 tape stripe graphics.

I.D. DATA: The VIN consisted of 17 symbols. The first three symbols revealed manufacturer, make and vehicle type. The fourth symbol indicated GVW rating. The fifth, sixth and seventh symbols indicated series and body style. The eighth symbol indicated engine. The ninth symbol was a check digit. The 10th symbol indicated model year. The 11th symbol indicated assembly plant. The last six symbols were the sequential unit production number.

Model	Body Type	Price	Weight	Prod. Total
ZH28	Pickup	6786	2293	—
ZS28	2.2 Pickup	7315	2357	—

NOTE: Total model year production was 11,732 trucks.

ENGINE (Rampage): 2.2L (135 cid). Four-cylinder. Brake horsepower: 84 at 4800 rpm. Bore & stroke: 3.44 x 3.62 in. Compression ratio: 8.5:1. Carburetor: Two-barrel.

CHASSIS FEATURES: Wheelbase: 104.2 in. Overall length: 183.6 in. Overall width: 66.8 in. Overall height: 51.8 in. GVW: 3,450 lbs. Tires: P175/75R x 13 SBR BSW (Rampage); P195/60R x 14 SBR RBL (2.2).

POWERTRAIN OPTION: Five-speed manual with overdrive (Rampage). Three-speed TorqueFlite automatic transmission.

OPTION PACKAGES: PROSPECTOR PACKAGE: (Rampage) Light Package, RBL tires and 14 in. wheels; console; power steering; electronically tuned AM radio with integral digital clock; cargo box side rails; Prospector decals. (2.2) Two-tone paint package; Light package; air conditioning; power steering; electronically tuned AM/FM stereo radio with integral digital clock; tonneau cover; Prospector decals. LIGHT PACKAGE: Ash receiver light; glove box light; headlamps on warning buzzer; ignition switch light with time delay; map/courtesy light. PROTECTION PACKAGE: Undercoating; floor mats. COLD WEATHER PACKAGE: 430-amp. maintenance-free battery; engine block heater.

CONVENIENCE OPTIONS: Air conditioning. Front license plate bracket. Rallye cluster (included tach, oil pressure and temperature gauges, trip odometer). Console. Engine cooling. Power steering. AM radio electronically tuned with integral digital clock. Electronically tuned AM/FM stereo radio with cassette tape player and integral digital clock. Cargo box side rails. Automatic speed control. Tonneau cover. 14 in. Rallye wheels. Cast aluminum 14 in. road wheels. Cloth and vinyl low-back bucket seats (Rampage).

NOTE: Rampage color choices for 1984 included: Charcoal gray metallic (Rampage), Garnet red Pearl Coat (Rampage), Beige Crystal Coat (Rampage), Silver Radiant Crystal Coat, Graphic red, black (Rampage), Pearl white (Rampage), brown Spice metallic. Two-Tone combinations. Graphic red/black (2.2), Brown Spice metallic/black (2.2), Beige Crystal Coat/brown Spice metallic (Rampage), Garnet red Pearl Coat/black (Rampage), silver Radiant Crystal Coat/Charcoal gray metallic.

1984 Dodge Ram Royal SE Sweptline Pickup (JG)

RAM 50 CUSTOM: Except for the standard argent (silver) painted grille, basic styling was unchanged for 1984. Other standard features included: Argent painted front bumpers with black rubber ends. Dome light with driver and passenger side door switches. Emergency flashers. 15-gallon fuel tank. Color-keyed headliner. Inside hood release. Argent hubcaps. Black left side swing-away exterior mirror. Interior rearview mirror. Adjustable angle steering column. Dual sun visors. Cargo tie-down bars (tubular low-mount on both sides of pickup box interior). Trip odometer. Door ajar, key in ignition warning buzzer. Vinyl bench seat available in beige or gray. Two-speed windshield wipers with washers. The Power Ram 50 Custom 4x4 came with most of the same standard features, plus the added pulling power of four-wheel drive. This year automatic locking front hubs were standard. Shifting from the four-wheel drive mode to the two-wheel drive mode and back again was accomplished by a flick of the shift lever.

RAM 50 ROYAL PICKUP: The Royal came with most of the same features as the Custom, plus (or in place of): Cloth and vinyl bench seat (in beige or gray). Chrome front bumper with black rubber ends. Double wall cargo box. Cargo lamp. Cigarette lighter. 18-gallon fuel tank. Chrome grille. Bright hubcaps. Black right and left swing-away exterior mirrors. Bright drip rail and windshield molding. AM radio. Tinted glass. Conventional spare tire. Two-tone tape treatment. Wheel trim rings. The Power Ram 50 Royal 4x4 came with most of the same standard features.

1984 Dodge Ram 50 Mini-Pickup (DNP)

RAM 50 SPORT PICKUP: "One of the most complete pickups for the money" is how sales literature described the Sport. It came with most of the same items found on the Royal, plus (or in place of): Center console with oil pressure gauge, ammeter, and transmission shift lever. Wide spoke road wheels. Bodyside tape stripe. Variable speed windshield wipers. Sport steering wheel. High-back velour cloth bucket seats (gray) with matching door trim panels. The Power Ram 50 Sport had four-wheel drive.

I.D. DATA: The VIN consisted of 17 symbols. The first three symbols revealed manufacturer, make and vehicle type. The fourth symbol indicated GVW rating. The fifth, sixth and seventh symbols indicated series and body style. The eighth symbol indicated engine. The ninth symbol was a check digit. The 10th symbol indicated model year. The 11th symbol indicated assembly plant. The last six symbols were the sequential unit production number.

Model	Body Type	Price	Weight	Prod. Total
4JL61	Custom Pickup	5684	2425	—
4KL61	Custom 4x4 Pickup	7870	2835	—
4JH61	Royal Pickup	6290	2447	—
4KH61	Royal 4x4 Pickup	8670	2965	—
4JP61	Sport Pickup	7018	2617	—
4KP61	Sport 4x4 Pickup	9143	2976	—

NOTE: 1984 model dealer sales in calendar 1984 totaled 42,064 trucks.

ENGINE (Custom/Royal): 2.0L (122 cid) OHC. Four-cylinder. Brake horsepower: 90 at 5000 rpm. Bore & stroke: 3.30 x 3.54 in. Compression ratio: 8.5:1. Carburetor: Two-barrel.

ENGINE (Royal 4x4/Sport): 2.6L (156 cid) OHC. Four-cylinder. Brake horsepower: 108 at 5000 rpm. Bore & stroke: 3.59 x 3.86 in. Compression ratio: 8.7:1. Carburetor: Two-barrel.

CHASSIS FEATURES: Wheelbase: 109.4 in. (4x2); 109.8 in. (4x4). Overall length: 184.6 in. Overall width: 65 in. Overall height: 60.6 in. (Custom); 59.8 in. (Royal/Sport); 63.4 in. (Power Rams). GVW: 4,045-4,520 lbs. Tires: 6.00 x 14 BSW (Custom); 185SR x 14 SBR (Royal/Sport); G78 x 15 (Power Ram).

POWERTRAIN OPTION: 2.6L OHC four-cylinder engine (Royal). 2.3L (140 cid) OHC Turbo Diesel four-cylinder (Royal/Sport). Five-speed manual with overdrive (Custom). Three-speed automatic transmission.

1984 Dodge Power Ram 50 4x4 Mini-Pickup (DNP)

CONVENIENCE OPTIONS: Air conditioning. Chrome rear step bumper (not available Custom). Electronic digital clock (not available Custom). California emissions package. High altitude emissions package. Chrome low mount exterior mirrors. Black left and right side swing-away exterior mirrors (Custom). Power steering. AM radio (Custom). Sliding rear window. Automatic speed control (not available Custom). Body side tape stripe (Custom, not available Royal). Tinted glass (not available Custom). Wheel trim rings (Custom, not available Sport). FOUR-WHEEL DRIVE: Mud guards; engine splash pan, front suspension, transfer case skid plates; front tow hook; automatic locking front hubs.

NOTE: Dodge Ram 50 exterior colors for 1984 included: [Custom] Polar white, Safari red, beige metallic, Light blue metallic. [Royal] beige metallic/cream, Safari red/white, Light blue metallic/Medium blue, silver metallic/Charcoal, Polar white/beige. [Sport] Charcoal metallic, silver metallic, Velvet black, Safari red, Polar white, Atlantic blue metallic.

1984 Dodge Ramcharger 4x2 Sport Utility (DNP)

RAMCHARGER SPORT UTILITY VEHICLE: Styling was unchanged for 1984. As before, both 4x2 (AD150) and part-time 4x4 (AW150) models were offered. With its transfer case shift selector in the "two-wheel high" mode, the four-wheel drive could drive with rear power only. When the system was in two-wheel drive, the front axle was disconnected and not in operation. Among standard Ramcharger features were: Dry type air cleaner. Ashtray. Bright front and rear bumpers. Automatic choke. Cigar lighter. Insulated dash liner. Cleaner air system. Coolant reserve system. Color-keyed inner door trim panels and armrests. Electronic ignition system. Black floor mat. 35-gallon fuel tank. Tinted glass (all windows). Glove box. Aluminum grille surround molding with painted plastic insert and headlamp doors. Fresh air heater with defrosters. Insulated hood pad. In cab hood release. Dual electric horns. Bright hubcaps. Front wheel automatic-locking type hubs (4x4). Speedometer, odometer, ammeter, fuel gauge, oil pressure and engine temperature indicator lights. Dual bright finish short arm 5 in. x 7 in. exterior mirrors. 10 in. day/night interior rearview mirror. Bright quarter side window and windshield moldings. Power front disc brakes. Power steering. AM radio. Rear roof vent. Deluxe vinyl low-back front bucket seats. Inside spare tire mounting. Front stabilizer bar (four-wheel drive). Sun visors. Dual jet windshield washers. Two-speed windshield wipers. Three-speed automatic transmission (two-wheel drive). Four-speed manual (four-wheel drive).

1984 Dodge Ramcharger Royal SE 4x4 Sport Utility (DNP)

I.D. DATA: The VIN consisted of 17 symbols. The first three symbols revealed manufacturer, make and vehicle type. The fourth symbol indicated GVW rating. The fifth, sixth and seventh symbols indicated series and body style. The eighth symbol indicated engine. The ninth symbol was a check digit. The 10th symbol indicated model year. The 11th symbol indicated assembly plant. The last six symbols were the sequential unit production number.

1984 Dodge Ramcharger 4x4 Sport Utility (DNP)

Model	Body Type	Price	Weight	Prod. Total
AD150	Utility	9844	3664	—
AW150	Utility (4x4)	10,945	4384	—

NOTE: Total model year production was 26,724 units.

ENGINE (Ramcharger): 5.2-liter (318 cid) V-8. Brake horsepower: 120 at 3600 rpm. Bore & stroke: 3.91 x 3.31 in. Compression ratio: 8.5:1. Carburetor: Two-barrel (This engine was not available in California in four-wheel drive Ramchargers.)

CHASSIS FEATURES: Wheelbase: 106 in. Overall length: 184.6 in. (without bumper guards); 186.1 in. (with bumper guards). Overall width: 79.5 in. GVW: 5,300 lbs. (4x2); 5,850 lbs. (4x4). Tires: P235/75R x 15 BSW GBR.

POWERTRAIN OPTION: 5.2L (318 cid) Carburetor: Four-barrel V-8 (four-wheel drive). Three-speed TorqueFlite automatic (four-wheel drive).

OPTION PACKAGES: SNO-COMMANDER PACKAGE: (four-wheel drive only) power angling blade with blade markers; hydro/electric controls; powerlift; plow lights; 114-amp. alternator; 500-amp. maintenance-free battery; maximum engine cooling; Sno-Commander decal; transmission oil temperature light with automatic transmission. SNO-PREPARATION PACKAGE: (four-wheel drive only) 114-amp. alternator; 500-amp. maintenance-free battery; maximum engine cooling. CONVENIENCE PACKAGE: Halogen headlamps; glove box lock and light; ash receiver light; two-speed windshield wipers with intermittent wipe. RAMCHARGER ROYAL SE: Bright drip rail molding; bright taillamp housing; ram's head hood ornament; Leaping ram with "Royal SE" plaque on front fender; bright aluminum grille with chromed plastic insert and bright headlamp doors; liftgate upper and lower moldings with applique panel; woodtone interior door trim applique, assist straps, carpeting on lower door panel; driver and front passenger high-back Command bucket seats with cloth and vinyl trim (included inboard fold-down armrests on seats, and lockable console with removable styrofoam beverage chest); folding rear bench seat with cloth and vinyl trim; color-keyed carpeting with underlayment; color-keyed cowlside trim panels; color-keyed rear side and liftgate inner trim panels; woodtone instrument cluster faceplate; nameplate on instrument panel; luxury steering wheel with woodtone insert around rim; color-keyed spare tire cover (not available with 10R x 15LT tires); bright front doorsill scuff plate; oil pressure and engine temperature gauges; trip odometer. FILIGREE STRIPE PACKAGE: Includes, wheel lip and hood stripes; light-reflective stripe decal with Dodge ram on liftgate. HEAVY-DUTY TRAILER TOWING PACKAGE: (four-wheel drive only) maximum cooling; 60-amp. alternator; 430-amp. maintenance-free battery; seven wire harness; class IV tow bar hitch; heavy-duty variable load turn signal flasher; heavy-duty front and rear shocks; heavy-duty front stabilizer bar. PROSPECTOR PACKAGES.

CONVENIENCE OPTIONS: Air conditioning. Heavy-duty alternators and batteries. Painted step type rear bumper. Front bumper and guards with rub strips and rear bumper with rub strips. Electronic digital clock. Auxiliary transmission oil to air cooler. Maximum cooling. Oil pressure and engine temperature gauges. Trip odometer. Bright grille insert and bright headlamp doors (included ram's head hood ornament). Deluxe bi-level heater. Engine block heater. Dual bright 6 in. x 9 in. low-mount mirrors. Dual bright 7-1/2 in. x 10-1/2 in. low mount extended mirrors. Bright lower molding with black vinyl insert and integral wheel lip moldings. Lower and upper moldings. Bright upper moldings. Power door locks. Power windows. AM/FM stereo RADIOS: With cassette tape player and electronic tuning; with Search-Tune and electronic tuning; with 40-channel CB transceiver. Heavy-duty front and rear shocks. Fuel tank shield. Transfer case skid plate (four-wheel drive). Automatic speed control. Sport bar. Front stabilizer bar. Heavy-duty front stabilizer bar (four-wheel drive). Tilt steering column (automatic transmission required). Sport steering wheel. Privacy glass sun screen. Various tires. Deluxe bright wheelcovers. WHEELS: Aluminum radial ribbed; 5-slot chrome disc (not available on four-wheel drive); White painted steel spoke (not available on two-wheel drive). Two-speed windshield wipers with intermittent wipe.

251

MINI-RAM VAN: The compact, front-wheel drive Mini-Ram Van shared most standard features with the Caravan. A right side, sliding cargo door without glass, and no rear seats were a couple exceptions. Its cargo compartment width between wheelhousings was 49.2 in. Maximum interior height was 48.8 in. Maximum interior width was 64.3 in. Total cargo volume was 133 cu. ft.

MINI-RAM VAN ROYAL: The Royal was a step up in trim. It came with such "extras" as: Body color front and rear bumper end caps. Front and rear bumper protective rub strips. Cloth covered front compartment headliner. Dual note horn. Luxury steering wheel. Right side sun visor. Five-speed manual with overdrive.

I.D. DATA: The VIN consisted of 17 symbols. The first three symbols revealed manufacturer, make and vehicle type. The fourth symbol indicated GVW rating. The fifth, sixth and seventh symbols indicated series and body style. The eighth symbol indicated engine. The ninth symbol was a check digit. The 10th symbol indicated model year. The 11th symbol indicated assembly plant. The last six symbols were the sequential unit production number.

Model	Body Type	Price	Weight	Prod. Total
SKE35	Mini Van	7586	2679	—
SKS35	Royal Mini Van	8345	2772	—

NOTE: Total model year production was 15,447 trucks.

ENGINE (Mini-Ram Van): 2.2L (135 cid). OHC. Transverse-mounted four-cylinder. Brake horsepower: 101 at 5600 rpm. Bore & stroke: 3.44 x 3.62 in. Compression ratio: 9.0:1. Carburetor: Two-barrel.

CHASSIS FEATURES: Wheelbase: 112 in. Overall length: 175.9 in. Overall width: 69.6 in. Overall height: 64.2 in. GVW. 3,900-4,400 lbs. Tires: P185/75R x 14.

POWERTRAIN OPTION: 2.6L (156 cid) OHC. Four-cylinder. Three-speed automatic transmission.

CONVENIENCE OPTIONS: Most of the same items offered on the Caravan, plus the following packages: Van Conversion; Basic Group; Light; and Maximum GVW.

CARAVAN: The new trendsetting front-wheel drive Caravan was part car, part station wagon, part van. It was a true multi-purpose vehicle. According to sales literature, it "might be the most exciting vehicle to hit the streets since the horseless carriage." The Caravan looked like a downsized '84 Dodge Van. It had a sloping hood with Chrysler Star ornament on it, a multi-rectangular sections grille (divided horizontally at the center), quad stacked rectangular headlights, and large wraparound taillights. The tailgate lifted up. And there was a sliding door on the right side, in addition to two front doors. Standard features included: Unit body construction. 60-amp. alternator. 335-amp. maintenance-free battery. Power front disc brakes with load sensing proportioning valve. Color-keyed front and rear bumper end caps. Bright front and rear bumpers. Carpeting. Cigarette lighter. Coolant overflow reservoir. Rear compartment sliding door with vented glass. Remote release fuel filler door. 15-gallon fuel tank. Halogen headlights. Cloth covered driver and passenger compartment headliner. Heater with upper level ventilation. Inside hood release. Single horn. Odometer. Day/night inside rearview mirror. Driver and passenger compartments dome lights. Black left outside, remote control-mirror. Black rear window and windshield molding. Clear coat paint. Loweride protective coating. Electronically tuned AM radio with integral digital clock. Low-back front bucket seats. Three passenger rear bench seat. Rack-and-pinion power steering. Vinyl-covered two-spoke steering wheel. Underslung tire carrier. Five-speed manual transmission. Two-speed windshield wipers with wet arm washers. Deluxe wheelcovers. Cloth low-back front bucket seats in beige, red, silver/charcoal. A three-passenger rear bench seat in matching trim was included.

CARAVAN SE: The SE (Special Edition) came with most of the same standard features as the base Caravan, plus (or in place of): Premium wheelcovers. Deluxe cloth low-back front bucket seats in beige, red, blue, silver/charcoal, Saddle/brown. A three-passenger bench seat in matching trim.

CARAVAN LE: The LE (Limited Edition) had most of the same standard features as the SE plus (or in place of): Dual horns. Right-hand remote control outside rearview mirror. Luxury steering wheel. Luxury cloth high-back front bucket seats in beige, red, blue silver/charcoal, saddle/brown. A three-passenger bench seat in matching trim was included.

I.D. DATA: The VIN consisted of 17 symbols. The first three symbols revealed manufacturer, make and vehicle type. The fourth symbol indicated GVW rating. The fifth, sixth and seventh symbols indicated series and body style. The eighth symbol indicated engine. The ninth symbol was a check digit. The 10th symbol indicated model year. The 11th symbol indicated assembly plant. The last six symbols were the sequential unit production number.

Model	Body Type	Price	Weight	Prod. Total
SKL36	Caravan	8280	2937	—
SKH36	Caravan SE	8517	2984	—
SKP36	Caravan LE	9105	3030	—

ENGINES (Caravan): 2.2L (135 cid). OHC. Transverse-mounted four-cylinder. Brake horsepower: 101 at 5600 rpm. Bore & stroke: 3.44 x 3.62 in. Compression ratio: 9.0:1. Carburetor: Two-barrel.

CHASSIS FEATURES: Wheelbase 112 in. Overall length: 175.9 in. Overall width: 69.6 in. Overall height: 64.2 in. GVW: 4,250-4,600 lbs. Tires: P185/75R x 14.

POWERTRAIN OPTIONS: 2.6L (156 cid) four-cylinder OHC engine. Three-speed automatic transmission.

OPTION PACKAGES: GAUGE ALERT PACKAGE: Engine temperature gauge with high temperature warning light; oil pressure gauge with low pressure warning light; low voltage warning light; trip odometer with pushbutton reset. LIGHT PACKAGE: Ash receiver light; front map/reading light (two); headlamp switch callout light; ignition switch light with time delay; instrument panel door ajar light; instrument panel low fuel warning light; instrument panel low washer fluid light; liftgate-mounted dual floodlights; underhood compartment light. DELUXE SOUND INSULATION PACKAGE: (standard on LE) door to sill seals; liftgate, passenger and cargo floor, underhood, under instrument panel, wheel housing silencers. SEVEN-PASSENGER SEATING PACKAGE: (SE and LE) included second seat (two-passenger bench with fixed back, side armrests and quick-release attachments); third seat (three-passenger bench with folding back, side armrests, adjustable feature, slid front to rear on tracks, and quick-release attachments); three storage bins (under second seat right riser cover); ash receiver in C-pillar; upgraded brakes and suspension; P195/75R x 14 SBR BSW tires.

CONVENIENCE OPTIONS: Air conditioning. 500-amp. maintenance-free battery. Electrically headed liftgate window defroster. 20-gallon fuel tank. Sunscreen glass (all windows except windshield and front doors). Roof luggage rack. Color-keyed front and rear floor accessory mats. Right-hand remote control exterior mirror. Power door locks. Power liftgate release. Power driver's bucket seat. Power front door windows (not available on base Caravan). RADIOS: AM/FM stereo with integral digital clock and cassette tape player and four speakers; AM/FM stereo with integral digital clock and four speakers. (Both radios were electronically tuned). Automatic speed control. Tilt steering column. TIRES: P195/75R x 14 SBR BSW, P205/70R x 14 SBR RBI Eagle GT, P205/70R x 14 SBR WSW. Rear cargo compartment tonneau cover (five-passenger models only). Rear quarter windows remote control vent. Wire wheelcovers. Cast aluminum road wheels. Styled steel road wheels with bright centers and trim rings. Deluxe intermittent wipe windshield wipers. Liftgate wiper/washer.

NOTE: Caravan exterior colors for 1984 included: Beige Crystal Coat, black, Mink brown Pearl Coat, Saddle brown Crystal Coat, Gunmetal blue Pearl Coat, Charcoal Crystal Coat, Garnet red Pearl Coat, Radiant silver Crystal Coat, white, Glacier blue Crystal Coat (available on SE and LE only). Two-Tone combinations included: Beige Crystal Coat/Mink brown Pearl Coat, white/Glacier blue Crystal Coat, Saddle brown Crystal Coat/black, Garnet red Pearl Coat/black, Mint brown Pearl Coat/black, white/Saddle brown Crystal Coat, Radiant silver Crystal Coat/Gunmetal blue Pearl Coat, Charcoal Crystal Coat/black, white/Charcoal Crystal Coat. Two-tones were only available on SE and LE.

1984 Dodge Long Range Ram Van (109-inch wheelbase)

B150 VAN: Styling was unchanged for 1984. Some standard features were: Independent front suspension. Computer selected front springs. Brake system warning light. Energy absorbing steering column. 60-amp. alternator. Driver armrest. Ashtray. 370-amp. battery. Power front disc brakes. Painted front and rear bumpers. Key-in-ignition, headlamps on, and fasten seat belts warning buzzer. Double hinged type right side and rear cargo doors (no glass). Cigar lighter. Door locks. Electronic ignition system. Driver's compartment floor mat. 22-gallon fuel tank. Tinted glass. Glove box. Argent finish grille. 7 in. round headlamps. Hardboard headliner in driver's compartment. Deluxe front heater. In-cab actuated hood release. Dual electric horns. Bright hubcaps. Dual 5 in. by 7 in. bright exterior mirrors. Low-back driver's bucket seat with deluxe vinyl trim in black or beige. Driver side sun visor. Spare tire carrier. Two-speed windshield wipers with washers. Four-speed manual transmission with overdrive.

B150 LONG RANGE RAM VAN: The Long Range Ram Van had bright bumpers; 36-gallon fuel tank; bright grille; quad rectangular headlights; wheelcovers. It was available in 109.6 in. and 127.6 in. wheelbases.

1984 Dodge Value Ram Wagon (127.6-inch wheelbase)

B150 WAGON: The attractive B150 Wagon came with most of the same standard features found on the B150 Van, plus (or in place of): Driver and front passenger armrests. Cleaner air system. Right side double doors with vented glass. Single rear door with fixed glass, inside door handle and lock button. Full width black floor mat. Tinted glass (all windows). Full length headliner. Deluxe fresh air heater with defroster. 10 in. interior rearview mirror. Two color-keyed sun visors.

B150 RAM VALUE WAGON: The Ram Value Wagon came with: Bright front and rear bumpers. 36-gallon fuel tank. Oil pressure and trip odometer gauges. Bright grille (included dual quad rectangular headlamps, vertically stacked, with halogen high beams). Deluxe bright wheelcovers. Color-keyed full length carpeting. Intermittent type windshield wipers.

I.D. DATA: The VIN consisted of 17 symbols. The first three symbols revealed manufacturer, make and vehicle type. The fourth symbol indicated GVW rating. The fifth, sixth and seventh symbols indicated series and body style. The eighth symbol indicated engine. The ninth symbol was a check digit. The 10th symbol indicated model year. The 11th symbol indicated assembly plant. The last six symbols were the sequential unit production number.

Model	Body Type	Price	Weight	Prod. Total
B150 Series — 109.6 in. w.b.				
B150	Van	7632	3299	—
(127.6 in. w.b.)				
B150	Van	7842	3415	—
B150	Long Range Ram Van	7812	—	—
(109.6 in. w.b.)				
B150	Wagon	9571	3585	—
(127.6 in. w.b.)				
B150	Wagon	9780	3758	—
B150	Ram Value Wagon	9659	—	—

NOTE: Total model year production was 70,929 Ram Vans and 40,313 Ram Wagons (including all wheelbases, GVW ratings and weight classes).

ENGINE (B150): 3.7 liter (225 cid). Six-cylinder. Brake horsepower: 95 at 3600 rpm. Bore & stroke: 3.40 x 4.12 in. Compression ratio: 8.4:1. Carburetor: One-barrel.

B250 VAN: The B250 Van shared most of the same standard features offered on the B150 (plus power steering). It was a bit more heavy-duty and could be ordered with the 26 in. longer Maxi body (on 127.6 in. wheelbase.)

B250 WAGON: The B250 Wagon had most of the same standard features as the B150. It was offered in regular or extra-long Maxi bodies. Maxiwagons had a three-speed automatic transmission.

I.D. DATA: The VIN consisted of 17 symbols. The first three symbols revealed manufacturer, make and vehicle type. The fourth symbol indicated GVW rating. The fifth, sixth and seventh symbols indicated series and body style. The eighth symbol indicated engine. The ninth symbol was a check digit. The 10th symbol indicated model year. The 11th symbol indicated assembly plant. The last six symbols were the sequential unit production number.

Model	Body Type	Price	Weight	Prod. Total
B250 Series — 109.6 in. w.b.				
B250	Van	8271	3359	—
(127.6 in. w.b.)				
B250	Van	8481	3475	—
B250	Maxivan	9101	3637	—
(127.6 in. w.b.)				
B250	Wagon	10,001	3799	—
B250	Maxiwagon	11,324	4182	—

NOTE: Total model year production was 70,929 Ram Vans and 40,313 Ram Wagons (including all wheelbases, GVW ratings and weight classes).

ENGINE (B250): 3.7 liter (225 cid). Six-cylinder. Brake horsepower: 95 at 3600 rpm. Bore & stroke: 3.40 x 4.12 in. Compression ratio: 8.4:1. Carburetor: One-barrel. Note: 5.2L two-barrel V-8 was standard on Maxiwagon.

B350 VAN: The 1-ton B350 had most of the same standard features as the B150, plus (or in place of): Larger brakes. Higher capacity front axle. Three-speed automatic transmission. Axle type jack. Both regular and extended Maxivan bodies were offered.

B350 WAGON: The husky B350 wagon was equipped with most of the same items found on the B150. Buyers could choose from regular or extended Maxiwagon bodies.

I.D. DATA: The VIN consisted of 17 symbols. The first three symbols revealed manufacturer, make and vehicle type. The fourth symbol indicated GVW rating. The fifth, sixth and seventh symbols indicated series and body style. The eighth symbol indicated engine. The ninth symbol was a check digit. The 10th symbol indicated model year. The 11th symbol indicated assembly plant. The last six symbols were the sequential unit production number.

Model	Body Type	Price	Weight	Prod. Total
B350	Van	9569	3867	—
B350	Maxivan	10,234	4063	—
B350	Wagon	11,292	4195	—
B350	Maxiwagon	12,119	4490	—

NOTE: Total model year production was 70,929 Ram Vans and 40,313 Ram Wagons (including all wheelbases, GVW ratings and weight classes).

ENGINE (B350): 5.2L (318 cid) V-8. Brake horsepower: 135 at 4000 rpm. Bore & stroke: 3.91 x 3.31 in. Compression ratio: 8.5:1. Carburetor: Two-barrel Maxiwagon came with 5.9L (360 cid) Carburetor: Four-barrel V-8.

CHASSIS FEATURES: Wheelbase: 109.6 in. (B150/B250); 127.6 in. (B250 Maxi/B350). Overall length: 178.9 in. (109.6 in. wheelbase); 196.9 in. (127.6 in. wheelbase); 222.9 in. (Maxi-Van/Maxi Wagon). Overall width: 79.8 in. Overall height: 79.6 in. (109.6 in. wheelbase.); 80.6 in. (Maxi-van/wagon); 80.9 in. (127.6 in. wheelbase). GVW: 4,700-6,010 lbs. (B150); 6,010-6,400 lbs. (B250); 7,500-8,510 lbs. (B350). Tires: P195/75R x 15 (4,700 lbs. GVW B150); P205/75R x 15 (B150); P225/75R x 15 (B250); P235/75R x 15XL (B250 Maxi); 8.00 x 16.5E (B350); 8.75 x 16.5E (B350 Maxi).

POWERTRAIN OPTION: 5.2L (318 cid) two-barrel V-8 (B150/B250); 5.9L (360 cid) four-barrel V-8 (B250/B350). Three-speed automatic transmission.

VAN OPTION PACKAGES: CONVENIENCE PACKAGE: Low washer fluid level warning light; glove box lock and light; ignition and headlight switch with time delay (not available with tilt steering column); two-speed windshield wipers with intermittent wipe. PROSPECTOR PACKAGES: Package No. 1: Vinyl high-back Command driver and passenger bucket seats in blue, beige or red; Convenience Package; bright grille; dual vertically stacked quad headlights with halogen high beams; bright front and rear bumpers; 36-gallon fuel tank; oil pressure gauge and trip odometer; bright wheelcovers; bright low-mount 6 in. x 9 in. mirrors; Prospector nameplates. Package No. 2: All items in Package No. 1, plus: Exterior Appearance package; electronically tuned AM radio with digital clock. Package No. 1 for Van Conversions: Includes, van conversion appearance package; convenience package; 36-gallon fuel tank; oil pressure gauge and trip odometer; bright low-mount mirrors; power door locks; scuff pads; speed control; Prospector nameplates. Package No. 2 for van conversions: Includes, all items in Package No. 1, plus: Bright bumpers, guards and nerf strips; automatic transmission; front air conditioning; dual rear cargo doors with vented glass; power windows; tilt steering column. Package No. 1 for Long Range Ram Van: Vinyl high-back Command driver and passenger bucket seats; Convenience Package; oil pressure gauge and trip odometer; bright low-mount mirrors; electronically tuned AM radio with digital clock; scuff pads; Prospector nameplates. EXTERIOR APPEARANCE PACKAGE: Bright grille; dual vertically stacked quad rectangular headlamps with halogen high beams; bright front and rear bumpers; bright taillamp bezels; bright rearside fixed window molding with Vision Van Window Package; bright windshield molding. TRAILER TOWING PREPARATION PACKAGE B250/B350: (required equipment at extra cost: 318 cid two-barrel V-8 or 360 cid four-barrel V-8, automatic transmission auxiliary cooling, and certain selected axle ratios) Includes, 500-amp. heavy-duty battery; maximum engine cooling; heavy-duty shocks; heavy-duty variable load flasher; front stabilizer bar. LOCK PACKAGE: Two keys; one operates ignition and front doors; one operates side and rear cargo doors. VAN CONVERSION APPEARANCE PACKAGE: Exterior appearance package; garnish trim over front door headers, A-pillar, around windshield; woodgrained applique instrument panel with color-keyed left and right lower skirts.

WAGON OPTION PACKAGES: ROYAL SE PACKAGE: Includes, bright front and rear bumpers; bright grille and vertically stacked quad rectangular headlamps with halogen high beams; bright moldings around windshield, and side and rear fixed windows (except driver and passenger door windows), lowerside, and rear; Leading ram plaque on front door; bright taillamp bezels; deluxe two-speed windshield wipers with intermittent wipe; carpeting on floor around engine housing cover; cigar lighter light; courtesy stepwell lamp (front and side doors); dash liner insulation; front door trim panel with assist strap; glove box lock and light; soft cloth covered headliner with insulation; ignition and headlamp switch with time of delay (not available with optional tilt steering column); instrument panel lower side skirts; dome/reading lamps (two); oil pressure gauge and trip odometer; driver and front passenger reclining high-back Command bucket seats and rear bench seat(s) in deluxe cloth and vinyl trim (in blue, beige or red); color-keyed spare tire cover; low washer fluid warning light; woodtone applique on lower face of instrument panel. EXTERIOR APPEARANCE PACKAGE: Includes, bright grille; bright front and rear bumpers; bright taillamp bezels; bright windshield moldings; dual vertically stacked quad rectangular headlamps with halogen high beams; bright side and rear fixed window moldings (except driver and front passenger door windows). EIGHT-PASSENGER SEATING PACKAGE: Includes one additional quick-release three-passenger bench seat with three seat belts. B350 MAXIWAGON 12-PASSENGER SEATING PACKAGE: (rear doors with optional vented glass required at extra cost). Includes, two additional bench seats; second (three-passenger); third (four-passenger); spare tire carrier relocated under third bench seat. B350 MAXIWAGON 15-PASSENGER SEATING PACKAGE: (8,510 lbs. GVW package, and rear doors with optional vented glass required at extra cost). Includes three additional bench seats; second and third (three-passenger); fourth (four-passenger); tire carrier relocated under fourth bench seat. B250/B350 TRAILER TOWING PREPARATION PACKAGE: (V-8 engine and transmission oil to air auxiliary cooling required). Includes maximum engine cooling; 500-amp. maintenance-free heavy-duty battery; heavy-duty variable load turn signal flasher; heavy-duty front and rear shock absorbers; front stabilizer bar.

CONVENIENCE PACKAGE: Same as Vans. PROSPECTOR PACKAGES: Package No. 1: Includes, convenience package; bright front and rear bumpers; 36-gallon fuel tank; oil pressure gauge and trip odometer; bright grille with quad headlamps and halogen high beams; bright low-mount mirrors and wheelcovers; Prospector nameplates. Package No. 2: Includes all items in Package No. 1, plus: Royal SE decor package; bright bumpers, guards and nerf strips. Package No. 3: Includes all items in Package No. 2, plus: Two-tone paint; air conditioning (front); power door locks; power windows; tilt steering column (when automatic transmission was ordered). Package No. 1 for Ram Value Wagon: Bright bumpers, guards and nerf strips; sunscreen glass; bright low-mount mirrors; Prospector nameplates.

VAN/WAGON CONVENIENCE OPTIONS: Air conditioning. Heavy-duty alternator and battery. Bright front and rear bumpers. Bright front and rear bumper guards and nerf strips. Transmission oil-to-air auxiliary cooling. Rear window defroster. Dual rear doors with vented glass (Wagon). Single rear door with fixed or vented glass (Van). Single rear door with vented glass (Wagon). Sliding passenger side door with no glass (Van), fixed glass (Van), or vented glass. 36-gallon fuel tank. Oil pressure gauge. Trip odometer. Sunscreen glass (Wagon). Banded front door glass and vent window (Van). Bright grille (included dual quad rectangular headlamps, vertically stacked, with halogen high beams). Rear auxiliary heater (Wagon). Engine block heater. Color-keyed accessory type rubber mats in driver's compartment (Wagon). Dual low-mount bright 6 in. x 9 in. exterior mirrors. Lower molding (included side and rear). Upper molding (included side, rear, and bright taillamp bezels). Heavy-duty shock absorbers. Power door locks. Power windows (front doors only). Automatic speed control. Tilt steering column. Front stabilizer bar. Luxury type steering wheel. Deluxe wheelcovers. RADIOS: Electronically tuned AM (Van); AM/FM/MX stereo; AM/FM/MX stereo with cassette tape player. Ribbed aluminum wheels. Argent painted five-slot disc wheels with bright trim ring. Intermittent type windshield wipers. SEATS: (Van) driver high-back Command buckets in deluxe vinyl trim; driver and passenger low-back buckets in deluxe vinyl trim.

NOTE: Dodge Van and Wagon exterior colors for 1984 included: Beige Sand, Charcoal metallic, Crimson red, Spice metallic, Navy blue metallic, Light blue metallic, silver metallic, Pearl white, black, Canyon red (available only with Prospector Package with two-tone paint procedure).

1984 Dodge D100 Sweptline Ram Pickup (DNP)

D100 PICKUP: The new D100 shared styling with last year's full-sized Dodge pickups. Among the many standard features were: Dry type air cleaner. Double-walled construction pickup box. Ashtray. Bright front bumper. Automatic choke. Cigar lighter. Clean air system. Coat hooks. Coolant reserve system. Insulated dash and plenum liner. Door inner trim panels with pull straps and armrests. Electronic ignition system. Exhaust emissions control system. Carpeting. 20-gallon fuel tank. Glove box. Aluminum grille with painted plastic insert and headlamp doors. Two rectangular headlamps. Heater with defrosters. In-cab hood release. Dual electric horns. Bright hubcaps. Black instrument cluster face plate with storage box and bright trim. Padded instrument panel. Dual bright finish short arm 5 in. x 7 in. exterior mirrors. 10 in. day/night interior rearview mirror. Bright windshield molding. Power front disc brakes. All-vinyl bench seat. Two sun visors. Key in ignition, headlamps on, fasten seat belts warning buzzer. Dual jet windshield wipers. Two-speed windshield wipers. Brake system warning light. Dual braking system with separate brake fluid reservoirs in the master cylinder. Recessed inside door release. The D100 was only available with the smooth sided Sweptline box in 6.5 ft. and 8 ft. lengths.

I.D. DATA: The VIN consisted of 17 symbols. The first three symbols revealed manufacturer, make and vehicle type. The fourth symbol indicated GVW rating. The fifth, sixth and seventh symbols indicated series and body style. The eighth symbol indicated engine. The ninth symbol was a check digit. The 10th symbol indicated model year. The 11th symbol indicated assembly plant. The last six symbols were the sequential unit production number.

1984 Dodge Power Ram W100 Sweptline Pickup (DNP)

Model	Body Type	Price	Weight	Prod. Total
D100	Pickup 6.5 ft.	6403	3244	—
D100	Pickup 8 ft.	6611	3338	—
W100	Pickup 6.5 ft.	8598	3888	—
W100	Pickup 8 ft.	8745	4013	—

NOTE: Separate model year production was not reported for D100 trucks.

ENGINE (D100): 3.7 liter (225 cid) Six-cylinder. Brake horsepower: 95 at 3600 rpm. Bore & stroke: 3.40 x 4.12 in. Compression ratio: 8.4:1. Carburetor: One-barrel.

D150 PICKUP: The 1/2-ton D150 could haul almost 1,000 lbs. more in payload than the D100. It was offered in 6.5 ft. and 8 ft. Utiline and Sweptline boxes. Most standard features were the same as those offered on the D100.

Model (6.5 ft. box)	Body Type	Price	Weight	Prod. Total
D150	Utiline Pickup	7237	3244	—
D150	Sweptline Pickup	7105	3264	—
(8 ft. box)				
D150	Utiline Pickup	7394	3338	—
D150	Sweptline Pickup	7262	3368	—
(6.5 ft. box)				
W150	Utiline Pickup	9487	3888	—
W150	Sweptline Pickup	9356	3909	—
(8 ft. box)				
W150	Utiline Pickup	9644	4013	—
W150	Sweptline Pickup	9514	4043	—

NOTE: Total model year production was 76,203 two-wheel drive D150s and 18,009 four-wheel drive W150s.

D250 PICKUP: The 3/4-ton D250 came with larger brakes, different four-speed manual transmission (no overdrive), higher capacity rear axle and front and rear springs, and greater maximum payload capacity than either the D100 or D150. It was available only with the eight-foot long Utiline or Sweptline boxes.

I.D. DATA: The VIN consisted of 17 symbols. The first three symbols revealed manufacturer, make and vehicle type. The fourth symbol indicated GVW rating. The fifth, sixth and seventh symbols indicated series and body style. The eighth symbol indicated engine. The ninth symbol was a check digit. The 10th symbol indicated model year. The 11th symbol indicated assembly plant. The last six symbols were the sequential unit production number.

Model	Body Type	Price	Weight	Prod. Total
D250	Chassis & Cab	8984	3459	—
D250	Utiline Pickup	8132	—	
D250	Sweptline Pickup	8009	3764	—
W250	Utiline Pickup	10,001	4154	
W250	Sweptline Pickup	9870	4184	—

NOTE: Total model year production was 13,578 two-wheel drive D250s and 6,191 four-wheel drive W250s.

ENGINE (D250): Same as D100 for pickups (except California vehicles and Chassis with cab have base 5.9L [360 cid] V-8. Brake horsepower: 185 at 4000 rpm. Bore & stroke: 4.00 x 3.58 in. Compression ratio: 8.0:1. Carburetor: Four-barrel.

1984 Dodge D350 With Retriever Wrecker Package (DNP)

D350 PICKUP: Dodge's heavy-duty pickup of 1984 was the 1-ton D350. It was offered in three wheelbase. A conventional cab was standard on the 131 in. wheelbase. The 149 in. and 165 in. wheelbase D350s came with four-door, six-passenger Crew Cabs. Most standard features were the same as those on the other series. D350 pickups were only offered with the smoothside Sweptline box.

1984 Dodge D350 With Dump Body Package (DNP)

I.D. DATA: The VIN consisted of 17 symbols. The first three symbols revealed manufacturer, make and vehicle type. The fourth symbol indicated GVW rating. The fifth, sixth and seventh symbols indicated series and body style. The eighth symbol indicated engine. The ninth symbol was a check digit. The 10th symbol indicated model year. The 11th symbol indicated assembly plant. The last six symbols were the sequential unit production number.

Model	Body Type	Price	Weight	Prod. Total
D350 Series — 131 in. w.b.				
D350	Chassis & Cab	8691	3499	—
(135 in. w.b.)				
D350	Chassis & Cab	9121	3848	—
(159 in. w.b.)				
D350	Chassis & Cab	9203	3918	—
(6.5 ft. box)				
D350	Crew Cab Pickup	10,185	4379	—
(8 ft. boxes)				
D350	Pickup 8 ft.	9003	3879	—
D350	Crew Cab Pickup	10,277	4513	—
W350 Series — 131 in. w.b.				
W350	Chassis & Cab	10,153	3849	—
(135 in. w.b.)				
W350	Chassis & Cab	11,699	4323	—
(8 ft. boxes)				
W350	Pickup	10,466	4229	—
W350	Crew Cab Pickup	12,071	4729	—

ENGINE (D350): 5.9L (360 cid) V-8. Brake horsepower: 180 at 3600 rpm. Bore & stroke: 4.00 x 3.58 in. Compression ratio: 8.0:1. Carburetor: Four-barrel

1984 Dodge D350 With 12.5 ft. Stake Body (DNP)

CHASSIS FEATURES: Wheelbase: 115 in. (D100/D150); 131 in. (All); 149 in. (D350/W350); 165 in. (D350); 135 in. and 159 in. (D350 Chassis w/cab). Overall width: 79.5 in. Overall length: [without rear bumpers] 190.78 in. (115 in. wheelbase.); 210.78 in. (131 in. wheelbase.); 224.24 in. (149 in. wheelbase.); 244.24 in. (165 in. wheelbase). GVW: 4,800 lbs. (D100); 4,800-5,850 lbs. (D150); 6,400-7,500 lbs. (D250); 8,510-10,100 lbs. (D350). Tires: P195/75R x 15 (D100/D150); 8.00 x 16.5D (D250); 9.50 x 16.5E (D350).

POWERTRAIN OPTION: 5.2L (318 cid) two-barrel V-8 (D100/D150/D250); 5.9L four-barrel V-8 (D100/D150/D250). Three-speed automatic transmission.

1984 Dodge D350 With Kary Van Package (DNP)

OPTION PACKAGES: FOUR-WHEEL DRIVE: (called Power Ram) power steering; two-speed transfer case; leaf spring front suspension; automatic locking hubs; Power Ram fender nameplates. ROYAL SE PACKAGE: Bright rear window and drip rail molding; plaque on front fender with leaping ram and Royal SE name; ram's head hood ornament; Dodge Ram nameplate on tailgate; bright taillamp housing (Sweptline); bright aluminum grille with chrome plastic insert and headlamp doors; power steering; bright tailgate applique panel (Sweptline); deluxe cloth and vinyl bench seat in red, beige, silver or blue; nameplate on instrument panel; woodtone instrument panel applique and bright trim; front door woodtone trim applique, with assist strap and carpeting on lower portions; black two-spoke 15 in. diameter steering wheel; color-keyed carpeting with underlayment; oil pressure and engine temperature gauges; trip odometer; color-keyed soft headliner (not available on Crew Cab); garnish trim over windshield, front pillar, door header, quarter trim panel upper, and over backlight (not available Crew Cab); insulation under hood panel; cowl side trim panels. PROSPECTOR RAM PICKUPS: (4x2, 4x4 D150/D250/D350/W150/W250/W350) Package No. 1: Bright low-mount mirrors, rear bumper, wheelcovers; 30-gallon fuel tank; intermittent wipers; Light Package; oil pressure and temperature gauges; trip odometer; Prospector nameplates; ram's head hood ornament; tinted glass. Package No. 2: All items in Package No. 1 plus: Royal SE Decor Package. Package No. 3: All items in Package No. 2 plus: Air conditioning; electronically tuned AM radio with integral digital clock; two-tone paint procedure. CREW CAB RAM SWEPTLINE PICKUPS: (4x2, 4x4 D350/W350) Package No.1: Bright low-mount mirrors, rear bumper, wheelcovers; cloth and vinyl bench seats; intermittent wipers; light package; oil pressure and temperature gauges; trip odometer; Prospector nameplates; ram's head hood ornament; 30-gallon fuel tank; tinted glass. Package No. 2: All items in Package No. 1 plus: Electronically tuned AM radio with integral digital clock; Royal SE Decor Package. PROSPECTOR RAM SWEPTLINE PICKUPS: (4x2

and 4x4 D100/W100) Package No. 1: Bright low-mount mirrors, rear bumper; intermittent wipers; light package; oil pressure and temperature gauges; trip odometer; Prospector nameplates; 30-gallon fuel tank; tinted glass; sliding rear window. LIGHT Package: Halogen headlamps; ash receiver light; glove box lock and light; exterior cargo light; map light on instrument panel. TRAILER TOWING PREPARATION PACKAGE: (required various extra cost items) 500-amp. maintenance-free battery; maximum engine cooling; heavy-duty variable load flasher; front stabilizer bar; heavy-duty front and rear shock absorbers.

CONVENIENCE OPTIONS: Air conditioning. 114-amp. alternator. 500-amp. battery. White painted front and/or rear bumpers. Bright rear bumper. Step type rear bumper. Transmission oil to air auxiliary cooler. 30-gallon fuel tank. Oil pressure gauge. Engine temperature gauge. Trip odometer. Tinted glass. Bright grille insert (included ram's head hood ornament). Engine block heater. Dual bright 6 in. x 9 in. exterior mirrors. Upper moldings. Lower moldings with partial wheel lip. Power steering. Power door locks. Electronically tuned AM radio. AM/FM stereo radio with cassette tape player. Heavy-duty shocks. Inside spare tire carrier. Automatic speed control. Front stabilizer bar. Tilt type steering column. Sport type steering wheel. Transfer case skid plate. Bright wheelcovers. Aluminum radial ribbed wheels. Painted five-slot disc wheels. Painted spoke wheels. Sliding rear window. Two-speed windshield wipers with intermittent wipe.

NOTE: Exterior colors for 1984 Dodge Ram pickups included: Beige Sand, black, Charcoal metallic, Light blue metallic, Graphic Red, Navy blue metallic, Pearl white, silver metallic, Spice metallic, Canyon red (available only with Prospector Package No. with two-tone paint procedure).

HISTORICAL: Thanks to introduction of the Caravan — the only true, compact minivan on the market in 1984, Dodge truck sales rose to record numbers in 1984. Production of this model was quartered at Chrysler of Canada's high-tech Windsor, Ontario factory. Also unveiled, in 1984, was the totally new N-body midsize pickup (Dakota) to be produced at the "Dodge City" truck plant in Warren, Michigan starting in 1986.

1985 DODGE

RAM 50 CUSTOM: The Ram 50 received a facelift for 1985. "Dodge" was printed in big letters on the wide top segment of the new thin rectangular slots theme grille. As before the four rectangular headlamps were slightly recessed in the grille. Among standard features were: Black front bumper with black rubber ends. Double wall cargo box. Cargo lamp. Cigarette lighter. Dome light with driver and passenger side door switches. Emergency flashers. 18-gallon fuel tank. Argent painted grille. Color-keyed headline. Inside hood release. Argent hubcaps. Day/night interior rearview mirror. Black left and right swingaway exterior mirrors. AM radio. Adjustable angle steering column. Dual sun visors. Cargo tie-down bars. Tinted glass. Conventional spare tire. Trip odometer. Door ajar, key in ignition warning buzzer. Two-speed windshield wipers with washers. The Power Ram 50 Custom had many of the same standard features, plus four-wheel drive.

RAM 50 ROYAL: The Royal came with most of the same items as the Custom, plus (or in place of): Chrome front bumper with black rubber ends. Carpeting. Black grille with bright accents. Bright hubcaps. Bright drip rail and windshield molding. Two tone treatment. The Power Ram 50 Royal had four-wheel drive.

RAM 50 SPORT: The Sport had most of the same features as the Custom, plus special interior and exterior trim. The Power Ram 50 Sport had four-wheel drive.

1985 Dodge Ram 50 Mini-Pickup (DNP)

I.D. DATA: The VIN consisted of 17 symbols. The first three symbols revealed manufacturer, make and vehicle type. The fourth symbol indicated GVW rating. The fifth, sixth and seventh symbols indicated series and body style. The eighth symbol indicated engine. The ninth symbol was a check digit. The 10th symbol indicated model year. The 11th symbol indicated assembly plant. The last six symbols were the sequential unit production number.

Model	Body Type	Price	Weight	Prod. Total
P24	Custom Pickup	5746	2310	—
K24	Custom 4x4 Pickup	8177	2720	—
P44	Royal Pickup	6456	2332	—
K44	Royal 4x4 Pickup	8743	2850	—
P44	Royal Turbo Diesel	7417	—	—
K4461	Royal 4x4 Turbo Diesel	9704	—	—
P54	Sport Pickup	7081	—	—
K54	Sport 4x4 Pickup	9368	—	—

NOTE: Total dealer sales of 1985 Ram 50 models during 1984-1985 calendar years was 66,745 trucks.

ENGINE (Ram 50): 2.0L (122 cid). OHC. Four-cylinder. Brake horsepower: 90 at 5000 rpm. Bore & stroke: 3.30 x 3.54 in. Compression ratio: 8.5:1. Carburetor: Two-barrel.

ENGINE (Custom): 2.6L (156 cid) OHC. Four-cylinder. Brake horsepower: 104 at 4800 rpm. Compression ratio: 8.7:1. Carburetor: Two-barrel (Royal/Sport).

CHASSIS FEATURES: Wheelbase: 109.4 in. (4x2); 109.8 in. (4x4). Overall length: 184.6 in. Overall width: 65 in. Overall height: 60.6 in. (Custom); 59.8 in. (Royal/Sport); 63.4 in. (4x4). GVW: 4,045-4,520 lbs. Tires: 185SR x 14 SBR BSW (4x2); GR78 x 15 SBR BSW (4x4).

POWERTRAIN OPTIONS: 2.3L (143 cid) OHC four-cylinder turbo diesel (Royal). Three-speed automatic transmission.

OPTION PACKAGES: FOUR-WHEEL DRIVE. EASY ORDER PACKAGE: (Power Ram 50 Custom) double wall pickup box; cigar lighter; AM radio; cargo light; tinted glass; day/night mirror. PREMIUM PACKAGE: (Royal) tachometer; console with gauges; full trim cab; bucket seats with deluxe cloth trim; sport steering wheel; variable intermittent wiper; AM/FM/MPX radio; power steering (4x2); tape stripes; silver painted wide spoke wheels. ROAD WHEEL PACKAGE: (available with premium package only) chrome wide spoke wheels with bright center cap; 185SR x 14 SBR RWL tires (4x2); GR78 x 15 SBR RWL tires (4x4).

CONVENIENCE OPTIONS: Air conditioning. Chrome rear step bumper (Royal). Black rear step bumper (Custom). Electronic digital clock (Royal). California emissions package. High altitude emissions package. Chrome low mount exterior mirrors. Vinylide molding (Custom). Power steering. Sliding rear window. AM/FM stereo radio (Royal). Bodyside tape stripe (Custom). Wheel trim rings (Custom).

NOTE: Ram 50 exterior colors for 1985 were: Custom: Beige metallic, Atlantic blue metallic, Safari red, Polar white, Bright silver. Royal: Beige metallic/tan, Atlantic blue metallic/white, Medium red/white, Charcoal/white, Polar white/tan. Royals with Premium Package: Medium red, Atlantic blue metallic, Charcoal metallic, beige metallic, Polar white.

1985 Dodge Ramcharger 4x4 Prospector Sport Utility

RAMCHARGER SPORT UTILITY VEHICLE: Styling was basically unchanged for 1985. However, on the AW150 four-wheel drive version, drivers were now able to shift on the go, into four-wheel drive and back into two-wheel drive at speeds up to 55 mph. There was no longer any need to stop the vehicle and get out to unlock the front hubs. Among standard features on the 4x2 (AD150) and 4x4 Ramchargers were: Dry type air cleaner. Ashtray. Bright front and rear bumpers. Key-in-Ignition, headlamps-on, and fasten-seat belts warning buzzer. Automatic choke. Cigar lighter. Cleaner air system. Coolant reserve system. Insulated dash liner. Inner door trim panels with armrests and pull straps. Electronic ignition system. Black floor mat with padding (padding not available in rear compartment). 35-gallon fuel tank. Tinted glass (all windows). Glove box. Aluminum grille with painted plastic insert and headlamp doors. Color-keyed soft cloth headliner. Fresh air heater with defrosters. Hood inner panel insulation. In-cab hood release. Dual electric horns. Bright hubcaps. Map/courtesy light on instrument panel. Rear compartment courtesy lights. Dual bright finish short arm exterior mirrors. 10 in. day/night inside rearview mirror. Bright quarter side window and windshield moldings. Power front disc brakes. Power steering. Electronically tuned AM radio with digital clock. Rear roof vent. Deluxe vinyl high-back bucket seats in red, blue or tan. Inside spare tire mounting. Front stabilizer bar (4x4). Sun visors. Dual jet windshield washers. Two-speed windshield wipers. Independent front suspension (4x2). Front leaf springs (4x4). Three speed automatic transmission (4x2). NP435 four-speed manual transmission (4x4).

I.D. DATA: The VIN consisted of 17 symbols. The first three symbols revealed manufacturer, make and vehicle type. The fourth symbol indicated GVW rating. The fifth, sixth and seventh symbols indicated series and body style. The eighth symbol indicated engine. The ninth symbol was a check digit. The 10th symbol indicated model year. The 11th symbol indicated assembly plant. The last six symbols were the sequential unit production number.

Model	Body Type	Price	Weight	Prod. Total
AD150	Utility	10,314	3664	—
AW150	Utility (4x4)	11,543	4065	—

NOTE: Total model year production was 37,055 trucks.

ENGINE (Ramcharger): 5.2L (318 cid) V-8. Brake horsepower: 120 at 3600 rpm. Bore & stroke: 3.91 x 3.31 in. Compression ratio: 8.5:1. Carburetor: Two-barrel.

CHASSIS FEATURES: Wheelbase: 106 in. Overall length: 184.6 in. (without bumper guards); 186.1 in. (with bumper guards). Overall width: 79.5 in. GVW: 5,300 lbs. (4x2); 5,850 lbs. (4x4). Tires: P235/75R x 15XL steel-belted radial.

POWERTRAIN OPTION: 5.9L (360 cid) four-barrel V-8 (not available in California). Three-speed TorqueFlite automatic transmission (4x4).

OPTION PACKAGES: RAMCHARGER ROYAL SE PACKAGE: Bright aluminum grille with chromed plastic insert, headlamp doors, and halogen headlamps; bright drip rail molding; ram hood ornament; Royal SE plaque on front fender; liftgate upper and lower moldings with bright applique panel; bright taillamp housing; color-keyed driver and front passenger high-back Command bucket seats with cloth trim (inboard fold down armrests and lockable console was included); color-keyed folding rear bench seat with cloth trim; color-keyed carpeting with underlayment throughout; bright scuff plates; woodtone door trim applique, assist strap, and carpeting on lower door panel; color-keyed rear side and lifgate inner trim panels; woodtone instrument cluster faceplate and bright trim; color-keyed spare tire cover (not available on 10R x 15LT tires); bright front doorsill scuff plate; oil pressure and engine temperature gauges; trip odometer; sport steering wheelcover; color-keyed cowl inner trim panels. PROSPECTOR PACKAGE 1: Convenience package; oil pressure and temperature gauges; trip odometer; sunscreen privacy glass; bright grille with headlamp doors, halogen headlamps, and ram's head hood ornament; bright front bumper guards; bright low-mount mirrors; deluxe wheelcovers; Prospector nameplates. PROSPECTOR PACKAGE 2: All items in Package 1, plus; AM/FM stereo radio (electronically tuned); Royal SE Decor package; power door locks. PROSPECTOR PACKAGE 3: Royal SE Decor package; two-tone paint procedure; convenience package; air conditioning; front bumper guards (4x2 only); sun screen glass; dual low-mount mirrors (4x2); power door locks (4x2); power windows; speed control; argent painted spoke road wheels with bright trim; P235/75R x 15XL SBR WLT (4x2); 10R x 15LT-B SBR WLT (4x4); Prospector nameplates. CONVENIENCE PACKAGE: Ash receiver light; glove box light and lock; two-speed windshield

wipers with intermittent wipe. FILIGREE TAPE STRIPE PACKAGE: Bodyside, wheel lip, and hood, gold pin tape stripes, plus tape stripe decal with "Dodge Ram" on liftgate. SNO-COMMANDER PACKAGE: (four-wheel drive only) power angling blade with blade markers; hydro/electric controls; power lift; plow lights; 114-amp. alternator; 500-amp. maintenance-free heavy-duty battery; maximum engine cooling; Sno-Commander decal; transmission oil temperature light with automatic transmission. SNO-PREPARATION PACKAGE: (four-wheel drive only) 114-amp. alternator; 500-amp. maintenance-free heavy-duty battery; maximum engine cooling; transmission oil temperature light with automatic transmission. TRAILER TOWING PREPARATION PACKAGE: Maximum engine cooling; 500-amp. maintenance-free heavy-duty battery; heavy-duty variable load flasher; heavy-duty front and rear shocks; front stabilizer bar on 4x2 models; heavy-duty front stabilizer bar on four-wheel drive models.

CONVENIENCE OPTIONS: Air conditioning. 114-amp. alternator. 500-amp. heavy-duty maintenance-free battery. Painted step type rear bumper. Front bumper guards. Auxiliary transmission oil to air cooler. Maximum cooling. Oil pressure and engine temperature gauges. Trip odometer. Sunscreen privacy glass (rear quarter and liftgate only). Bright grille insert and bright headlamp doors, halogen headlamps, ram's head hood ornament. Engine block heater. Dual bright low-mount mirrors. Lower side and partial wheel lip bright molding. Bright upper side and rear molding. Power door locks. Power windows. AM/FM stereo radio (electronically tuned) with integral digital clock. AM stereo/FM stereo electronically tuned radio with seek-and-scan, cassette player with automatic reverse, four speakers, and integral digital clock. Fuel tank shield. Transfer case shield (4x4). Heavy-duty shocks. Automatic speed control. Sport bar. Front stabilizer bar. Heavy-duty front stabilizer bar (4x4). Tilt steering column. Sport steering wheel. Deluxe wheelcovers. Aluminum radial ribbed wheels. Argent painted steel spoke wheels with bright trim ring. Two-speed windshield wipers with intermittent wipe. Deluxe split-back front bench seat in red, blue, or tan (this was a no-charge option).

NOTE: Ramcharger exterior colors for 1985 included: Black, Light blue metallic, Navy blue metallic, Charcoal metallic, cream, Forest green metallic, Canyon red metallic, Golden brown metallic (available with Prospector package with two-tone paint procedure only), Graphic red, silver metallic, white.

1985 Dodge Mini-Ram Van (DNP)

MINI-RAM VAN: The compact, front wheel drive Mini-Ram Van shared most standard features with the Caravan. A right side, sliding cargo door without glass, and lack of rear seats were a couple exceptions. Its cargo compartment width between wheelhousings was 49.2 in. Maximum interior height was 48.8 in. Maximum interior width was 64.3 in. And total cargo volume was 133 cu. ft.

MINI-RAM VAN ROYAL: The Royal was a step up in trim. It came with such "extras" as: Body color front and rear bumper end caps. Front and rear bumper protective rub strips. Cloth covered front compartment headliner. Chrome grille. Dual note horn. Luxury steering wheel. Right side sun visor. Five-speed manual with overdrive.

I.D. DATA: The VIN consisted of 17 symbols. The first three symbols revealed manufacturer, make and vehicle type. The fourth symbol indicated GVW rating. The fifth, sixth and seventh symbols indicated series and body style. The eighth symbol indicated engine. The ninth symbol was a check digit. The 10th symbol indicated model year. The 11th symbol indicated assembly plant. The last six symbols were the sequential unit production number.

Model	Body Type	Price	Weight	Prod. Total
K13	Van	7972	2755	—
K63	Royal Van	8760	2825	—

NOTE: Total model year production was 26,654 trucks.

ENGINE (Mini-Ram Van): 2.2L (135 cid) OHC. Transverse. Four-cylinder. Brake horsepower: 101 at 5600 rpm. Bore & stroke: 3.44 x 3.62 in. Compression ratio: 9.0:1. Carburetor: Two-barrel.

CHASSIS FEATURES: Wheelbase: 112 in. Overall length: 175.9 in. Overall width: 69.6 in. Overall height: 64.2 in. GVW: 3,900-4,400 lbs. Tires: P185/75R x 14.

POWERTRAIN OPTION: 2.6L (156 cid) OHC. Carburetor: Four-barrel. Three-speed automatic transmission.

CONVENIENCE OPTIONS: Most of the same items offered on the Caravan, (plus dual black oversized foldaway exterior mirrors; Trenton cloth low-back bucket seat(s); Tribune cloth high-back bucket seats with lockable storage drawer under passenger seat; saddle grain vinyl high-back passenger bucket seat with lockable storage drawer underneath).

OPTION PACKAGES: BASIC GROUP PACKAGE: 500-amp. battery; color-keyed driver and cargo compartment carpeting; remote control fuel filler door release; 20-gallon fuel tank; gauge with gauge alert package; maximum GVW package; full length cloth covered headliner; light package; sliding side door exterior lock; right side illuminated vanity mirror; dual black remote control exterior mirrors; power liftgate release; power steering; automatic speed control; tilt steering column; deluxe windshield wipers with intermittent wipe; rear window wiper/washer. GAUGE WITH GAUGE ALERT, LIGHT, and SPORT ROAD WHEEL (Royal only) packages same as Caravan. MAXIMUM GVW PACKAGE: Heavy-duty rear brakes; heavy-duty suspension; P195/75R x 14 SBR BSE tires. VAN CONVERSION PACKAGE: (4520 lbs. GVW package required at extra cost) black front and rear bumper nerf stripes; bright bumpers with color-keyed end caps; remote release fuel filler door; gauge with gauge alert package; chrome/argent finish grille; padded instrument panel with woodtone trim bezels; light package; bright trim around lights; exterior sliding side door lock; dual black remote control mirrors; power steering; driver and passenger seating package; two-spoke luxury steering wheel; underslung tire carrier.

NOTE: Exterior colors for 1985 Dodge Mini-Ram Vans included: Cream Crystal Coat, Black Crystal Coat, Mink Brown Pearl Coat, Gold Dust Crystal Coat, Gunmetal Blue Pearl Coat (extra cost), Crimson Red Crystal Coat, Garnet Red Pearl Coat (extra cost), Radiant Silver Crystal Coat, White Crystal Coat.

CARAVAN: Styling was unchanged for 1985. Dodge continued to promote the front wheel drive Caravan as a "transportation revolution." Standard features included: 60-amp. alternator. 335-amp. maintenance-free battery. Power brakes (front disc, rear drum) with load sensing proportioning valve. Color-keyed front and rear bumper end caps. Front and rear bright bumpers with rub strips. Carpeting. Keys-in-ignition, fasten seat belts, headlamps on warning chimes. Cigarette lighter. Coolant overflow reservoir. Front door demisters. Sliding cargo compartment door with vented glass. Electronic ignition and voltage regulator. Remote fuel filler door release. 15-gallon fuel tank. Tinted glass (all windows). Bright grille. Cloth covered driver and passenger compartment headliner. Bi-level ventilation heater. Inside hood release. Single note horn. Driver and passenger compartments dome light. Day/night inside rearview mirror. Black left-hand remote control exterior mirror. Black rear window and windshield molding. AM radio with electronic tuning and integral digital clock. Rack and pinion power steering. Two-spoke vinyl steering wheel. Compact spare tire. Five-speed manual transmission with overdrive. Deluxe wheelcovers. Two speed windshield wipers with wet arm washers. Liftgate wiper/washer. Cloth low-back front bucket seats in tan, red, silver/charcoal. A matching three-passenger bench seat was included.

CARAVAN SE: The SE came with most of the same standard features as the base Caravan, plus (or in place of): Styled road wheels with bright trim ring, hub center and nut covers. Deluxe cloth low-back front seats in tan, red, blue, silver/charcoal. A three-passenger bench seat in matching trim. Bright upper body side and liftgate moldings.

CARAVAN LE: The LE came with most of the same standard features as the SE, plus (or in addition to): Dual black remote control exterior mirrors. Bodyside and liftgate woodtone. Luxury steering wheel. Luxury cloth high-back front bucket seats with integral headrests, armrests, seatback storage pockets, and driver and passenger recliners. The seats were offered in tan, red, silver/charcoal. A three-passenger bench seat in matching trim was included.

I.D. DATA: The VIN consisted of 17 symbols. The first three symbols revealed manufacturer, make and vehicle type. The fourth symbol indicated GVW rating. The fifth, sixth and seventh symbols indicated series and body style. The eighth symbol indicated engine. The ninth symbol was a check digit. The 10th symbol indicated model year. The 11th symbol indicated assembly plant. The last six symbols were the sequential unit production number.

Model	Body Type	Price	Weight	Prod. Total
K21	Wagon	9147	2911	—
K41	Wagon (SE)	9393	2911	—
K51	Wagon (LE)	10,005	2911	—

NOTE: Total model year production was 110,844 trucks.

ENGINE (Caravan): 2.2L (135 cid). OHC. Transverse. Four-cylinder. Brake horsepower: 101 at 5600 rpm. Bore & stroke: 3.44 x 3.62 in. Compression ratio: 9.0:1. Carburetor: Two-barrel

CHASSIS FEATURES: Wheelbase: 112 in. Overall length: 175.9 in. Overall width: 69.6 in. Overall height: 64.2 in. GVW: 4,600 lbs. Tires: P185/75R x 14. SBR BSW.

POWERTRAIN OPTION: 2.6L (156 cid) OHC. Four-cylinder. Three-speed automatic transmission.

CONVENIENCE OPTIONS: Most of the same items offered on the Caravan, plus the following package: Van Conversion; Basic Group; Light; and Maximum GVW.

OPTION PACKAGES: BASIC GROUP: (Caravan) light package; deluxe intermittent windshield wipers; dual note horns; power lightgate release; 500-amp. battery; dual remote mirrors; deluxe sound insulation. POPULAR EQUIPMENT DISCOUNT PACKAGE: (SE/LE) light package; gauge with gauge alert package; deluxe windshield wipers; AM/FM stereo radio with clock; dual note horns; automatic speed control; power liftgate release; dual remote mirrors; deluxe sound insulation (standard on LE), luxury steering wheel; illuminated visor vanity mirror; overhead console (LE only). LUXURY EQUIPMENT DISCOUNT PACKAGE: (LE) popular equipment package; tilt steering column; dual power mirrors; power front door windows; power door locks; power driver's seat. TRAVEL EQUIPMENT DISCOUNT PACKAGE: (SE/LE) 2.6L four-cylinder with automatic transmission; seven passenger seating package; sunscreen glass; remote control rear vent windows; 20-gallon fuel tank; 500-amp. battery. GAUGE ALERT PACKAGE: Engine coolant temperature gauge with high temperature warning light; oil pressure gauge with low pressure warning light; low voltage warning light; trip odometer with push-button reset. LIGHT PACKAGE: Ash receiver light; front map/reading light (two); headlamp switch time delay call-out light; ignition switch light with time delay; instrument panel door-ajar light; instrument panel low fuel warning light; instrument panel low washer fluid light; underhood compartment light; liftgate mounted dual floodlights. DELUXE SOUND INSULATION PACKAGE: Door to sill seals; liftgate, passenger floor, underhood, under instrument panel, wheelhousing silencers. SEVEN PASSENGER SEATING PACKAGE: (SE/LE) included second seat (two-passenger bench with fixed back, side armrests, and quick-release attachments); third seat (three-passenger bench with folding back, side armrests, adjustable feature, and quick release attachments); three storage bins (in third seat armrests and right rear trim panel); ash receiver in C-pillar (below belt); heavy-duty suspension; heavy-duty rear brakes; P195/75R x 14 SBR BSW tires. SPORT ROAD WHEEL PACKAGE: P205/70R x 14 SBR RWL tires; cast aluminum wheels.

CONVENIENCE OPTIONS: Air conditioning. 500-amp. battery. Black front and rear bumper guards. Forward storage console. Converta-bed rear seating (Caravan and SE). Electrically head liftgate defroster. Accessory type floor mats. 20-gallon fuel tank. Sunscreen glass. Roof mounted luggage rack. Dual exterior remote control mirrors. Dual power remote control exterior mirrors. Bodyside vinyl molding. Power door locks. Power liftgate release. Power driver's seat. Power front door windows (SE, LE). RADIOS: AM/FM with electronic tuning, four speakers, integral digital clock; AM/FM stereo with electronic tuning, Seek-and-Scan, cassette player with automatic reverse, four speakers, integral digital clock; AM stereo/FM stereo 36-watt Ultimate Sound System, electronic tuning, memory scan, up-and-down scan, cassette player with automatic reverse, metal tape capability, five channel graphic equalizer, joystick balance/fader control, four speakers, ambient sound control, integral digital clock. Automatic speed control. Tilt steering column. Heavy-duty suspension (P195/75R x 14 tires included). Conventional spare tire. P195/75R x 14 SBR BSW tires. P205/70R x 14 SBR RWL or WSW tires. Rear cargo comparment tonneau cover (five-passenger models only).' Remote control rear quarter vent windows. Sport wheelcovers (SE/LE). Wire wheelcovers (SE/LE). Styled road-type wheels with bright trim ring, hub center and nut cover (Caravan). Omission of woodgrain applique when monotone paint was ordered (no-cost option only available on LE). Vinyl low-back front bucket seats (no-cost option on base Caravan). Vinyl high-back front bucket seats with integral headrest, armrest, and driver and passenger recliners (SE/LE).

NOTE: Caravan exterior colors for 1985 included: Cream Crystal Coat, Black Crystal Coat, Mink Brown Pearl Coat, Crimson Red Crystal Coat, Gunmetal Blue Pearl Coat (extra cost), Gold Dust Crystal Coat, Garnet Red Pearl Coat (extra cost), Radiant Silver Crystal Coat, White Crystal Coat, Glacier Blue Crystal Coat (SE/LE). Two-Tone Colors: Cream Crystal Coat/Gold Dust Crystal Coat, Garnet Red Pearl Coat/Black Crystal Coat, Radiant Silver Crystal Coat/Gunmetal Blue Pearl Coat, White Crystal Coat/Gold Dust Crystal Coat, Mink Brown Pearl Coat/Black Crystal Coat, Glacier Blue Crystal Coat/Black Crystal Coat. (All two-tones were only available on SE/LE models).

1985 Dodge Ram Window Van (DNP)

B150 VAN: Styling was unchanged for 1985. Standard features included: Brake warning system light. Padded instrument panel and sun visor. Ashtray. Power front disc brakes. Painted front and rear bumpers. Key in ignition, headlamps on, fasten seat belts warning buzzer. Cigar lighter. Cleaner Air System. Double hinged type right side cargo and rear doors with no glass. Electronic ignition system. Floor mat (black) for drivers side of compartment. 22-gallon fuel tank. Tinted glass. Glove box. Argent finish grille. 7 in. round headlamps. Driver's compartment headliner. Deluxe fresh air heater with defroster. In-cab activated hood release. Dual electric horns. Bright hubcaps. Dual bright 5 in. x 7 in. exterior mirrors. Nameplate on front doors. Power steering. Color-keyed steering wheel. Driver's side sun visor. Inside mounted spare tire carrier. Wiper arm mounted electric windshield washers. Two-speed windshield wipers. Four-speed manual with overdrive.
B150 LONG RANGE RAM VAN: The 1985 Long Range Ram Van came with such extras as: Bright front and rear bumpers. 35-gallon fuel tank. Bright finish grille. Wheelcovers. Quad rectangular headlamps.
B150 WAGON: The B150 Wagon kept its attractive styling for another year. It came with most of the same standard features found on the B150 Van, plus (or in place of): Driver and front passenger armrests. Right side double door with vented glass. Rear single door with fixed glass and inside door handle and lock button. Full-width black floor mat. Full length headliner. Five-passenger seating. Interior day/night rearview mirror. Electronically tuned AM radio with digital clock. Two sun visors.
B150 RAM VALUE WAGON: The Ram Value Wagon was only available on a 109.6 in. wheelbase. It came with: Bright front and rear bumpers. Oil pressure gauge. Trip odometer. Bright grille (included quad rectangular headlamps, vertically stacked, with halogen high beams). Deluxe bright wheelcovers. Full length color-keyed carpeting. Intermittent type windshield wipers.
I.D. DATA: The VIN consisted of 17 symbols. The first three symbols revealed manufacturer, make and vehicle type. The fourth symbol indicated GVW rating. The fifth, sixth and seventh symbols indicated series and body style. The eighth symbol indicated engine. The ninth symbol was a check digit. The 10th symbol indicated model year. The 11th symbol indicated assembly plant. The last six symbols were the sequential unit production number.

Model	Body Type	Price	Weight	Prod. Total
B150 Series — 109.6 in. w.b.				
B150	Van	8432	3299	—
B150	Long Range Ram Van	8522	—	—
B150	Wagon	10,118	3585	—
(127.6 in. w.b.)				
B150	Van	8664	3415	—
B150	Long Range Ram Van	—	—	—
B150	Wagon	10,333	3758	—
B150	Value Wagon	10,169	—	—

NOTE: Total model year production was 70,242 Ram Vans and 44,436 Ram Wagons including all models, wheelbases, GVW ratings and tonnage classes.

ENGINE (B150): 3.7 liter (225 cid). Six-cylinder. Brake horsepower: 95 at 3600 rpm. Bore & stroke: 3.40 x 4.12 in. Compression ratio: 8.4:1. Carburetor: One-barrel.
B250 VAN: The B250 Van shared most of the same standard features offered on the B150. It was a bit heavier-duty and could be ordered with the 26 in. longer Maxi body (on 127.6 in. wheelbase).
B250 WAGON: The B250 Wagon had most of the same standard features as the B150. It was offered in regular or extra long Maxi bodies. Maxiwagons had a three-speed automatic transmission.
I.D. DATA: The VIN consisted of 17 symbols. The first three symbols revealed manufacturer, make and vehicle type. The fourth symbol indicated GVW rating. The fifth, sixth and seventh symbols indicated series and body style. The eighth symbol indicated engine. The ninth symbol was a check digit. The 10th symbol indicated model year. The 11th symbol indicated assembly plant. The last six symbols were the sequential unit production number.

Model	Body Type	Price	Weight	Prod. Total
B250 Series — 109.6 in. w.b.				
B250	Van	8824	3359	—
B250	Wagon	—	—	—
(127.6 in. w.b.)				
B250	Van	9041	3475	—
B250	Maxivan	9624	3637	—
B250	Wagon	10,641	3799	—
B250	Maxiwagon	12,022	4182	—

NOTE: Total model year production was 70,242 Ram Vans and 44,436 Ram Wagons including all models, wheelbases, GVW ratings and tonnage classes.
ENGINE (B250): 3.7 liter (225 cid). Six-cylinder. Brake horsepower: 95 at 3600 rpm. Bore & stroke: 3.40 x 4.12 in. Compression ratio: 8.4:1. Carburetor: One-barrel. Except 5.2L two-barrel V-8 was standard on Maxiwagon.
B350 VAN: This was Dodge's top light-duty van. It had more of the same standard features as the B150, plus (or in place of): Larger brakes. Higher capacity front axle. Three-speed automatic transmission. Axle type jack. Both regular and extended Maxivan bodies were offered.
B350 WAGON: The ultimate Dodge people hauler was the B350 Maxiwagon. It could be ordered with seats for up to 15 passengers (at extra cost). The regular B150 Wagon also had a lot of carrying capacity.
I.D. DATA: The VIN consisted of 17 symbols. The first three symbols revealed manufacturer, make and vehicle type. The fourth symbol indicated GVW rating. The fifth, sixth and seventh symbols indicated series and body style. The eighth symbol indicated engine. The ninth symbol was a check digit. The 10th symbol indicated model year. The 11th symbol indicated assembly plant. The last six symbols were the sequential unit production number.

Model	Body Type	Price	Weight	Prod. Total
B350	Van	9929	3867	—
B350	Maxivan	10,613	4063	—
B350	Wagon	11,705	4195	—
B350	Maxiwagon	12,606	4490	—

NOTE: Total model year production was 70,242 Ram Vans and 44,436 Ram Wagons including all models, wheelbases, GVW ratings and tonnage classes.

ENGINE (B350): 5.2L (318 cid) V-8. Brake horsepower: 135 at 4000 rpm. Bore & stroke: 3.91 x 3.31 in. Compression ratio: 8.5:1. Carburetor: Two-barrel. (Vans and Maxivans with GVW ratings over 7,500 lbs. came with 5.9L [360 cid] four-barrel. V-8.
CHASSIS FEATURES: Wheelbase: 109.6 in. (B150/B250); 127.6 in. (All). Overall length: 178.9 in. (109.6 in. wheelbase); 196.9 in. (127.6 in. wheelbase); 222.9 in. (Maxi). Overall width: 79.8 in. Overall height: 79.6 in. (109.6 in. wheelbase); 80.9 in. (127.6 in. wheelbase); 80.6 in. (Maxi). GVW: 4,300-6,010 lbs. (B150); 6,010-6,400 lbs. (B250); 7,500-8,510 lbs. (B350). Tires: P195/75R x 15 (B150 with 4,700 lbs. GVW); P205/75R x 15 (B150); P225/75R x 15 (B250); P235/75R x 15XL (B250); 8.00 x 16.5E (B350); 8.75 x 16.5E (B350 Maxi).
POWERTRAIN OPTION: 5.2L two-barrel V-8 (B150/B250); 5.9L four-barrel V-8 (B250/B350). Three-speed automatic transmission.
VAN OPTION PACKAGES: EXTERIOR APPEARANCE PACKAGE: Includes, bright taillamp bezels; front front and rear bumpers; bright grille; dual vertically stacked rectangular headlamps with halogen high beams; rear body side fixed window with Vision Van Window Package and vented glass only, with bright moldings; bright windshield molding. CONVENIENCE PACKAGE: Cigar lighter light; low washer fluid level warning light; ignition and headlight switches lights with time delay (not available with tilt steering column); glove box lock and light; deluxe two-speed windshield wipers with intermittent wipe. LOCK PACKAGE: Two keys; one operates ignition and front doors, the other operates side and rear cargo doors. TRAILER TOWING PREPARATION PACKAGE: (B250/B350) (required equipment at extra cost: 318 two-barrel V-8 or 360 four-barrel V-8 engine, automatic transmission, auxiliary cooling and certain selected axle ratios) Includes 500-amp. battery; maximum engine cooling; heavy-duty shocks; front stabilizer bar; heavy-duty variable load flasher. B350 SCHOOL BUS PACKAGE: (with solid side panel van or Vision Van only; required equipment at extra cost includes Van Window Package for solid side panel van or Vision Van; vented glass with Van Window Package; 360 V-8; 8510 lbs. GVW Package) Package comprised of banded front door main glass and vent wings; school bus yellow paint; parking brake switch. VAN CONVERSION APPEARANCE PACKAGE: Exterior Appearance package; woodtone applique on instrument panel with color-keyed left and right lower skirts; garnish trim over front door headers, A-pillar, and around windshield. PROSPECTOR VAN CONVERSION PACKAGE: Front air conditioning; bright front and rear bumpers, guards and nerf strips; Convenience Package; power door locks; 35-gallon fuel tank; dual low-mount exterior mirrors; oil pressure gauge; Prospector nameplates; rubber scuff pads; automatic speed control; tilt steering column; automatic transmission; trip odometer; Van Conversion Appearance Package; power front door windows.
WAGON OPTION PACKAGES: ROYAL SE PACKAGE: Bright front and rear bumpers; bright grille and vertically stacked quad rectangular headlamps with halogen high beams; bright moldings around windshield and side and rear fixed windows (except driver and passenger door windows), lower body side and rear; leaping ram plaque with 150/250/350 Royal SE on front door; deluxe two-speed windshield wipers with intermittent wipe; color-keyed carpeting around engine housing cover and over fuel filler cover, cigar lighter light; courtesy step well lamp (front and side doors); dash liner insulation; front door trim panel applique with assist strap; glove box lock and light; soft cloth covered headliner with insulation; ignition and headlamp switch with time delay (not available with tilt steering column); color-keyed instrument panel lower skirts; dome/reading lamps (two); nameplates on instrument panel; oil pressure gauge and trip odometer; driver and front passenger reclining high-back Command bucket seats and rear bench seat(s) in deluxe Kincaid cloth and Saddle Grain vinyl trim; color-keyed spare tire cover; luxury steering wheel; low washer fluid warning light; woodtone applique on lower face of instrument panel. EXTERIOR APPEARANCE PACKAGE: Bright grille, front and rear bumpers, taillamp bezels, windshield molding; dual vertically stacked quad rectangular headlamps with halogen high beams; bright side and rear fixed window moldings (except driver and front passenger windows). B150 EIGHT-PASSENGER SEATING PACKAGE: Available on 109.6 in. wheelbase with 6,010 lbs. GVW package. Also available on all B250/B350 models. Includes one additional quick release three-passenger bench seat. B350 12-PASSENGER SEATING PACKAGE: (rear doors with optional vented glass required at extra cost) Includes two additional three-passenger bench seats; spare tire carrier relocated under third bench seat. B350 MAXIWAGON 15-PASSENGER SEATING PACKAGE: (8,510 lbs. GVW Package and rear doors with optional vented glass required at extra cost). Includes three additional bench seats; (second and third three-passenger]; fourth four-passenger]; tire carrier relocated under fourth seat. TRAILER TOWING PREPARATION PACKAGE, and CONVENIENCE PACKAGE same as Van. PROSPECTOR PACKAGES: (not available Ram Value Wagon) Package 1: Convenience Package; bright front and rear bumpers; 35-gallon fuel tank; oil pressure gauge and trip odometer; bright grille with quad headlamps and halogen high beams; bright low-mount mirrors and wheelcovers; Prospector nameplates. Package 2: All items in Package 1, plus: Royal SE Decor Package; bright front and rear bumpers, guards and nerf strips. Package 3: All items in Package 2, plus: Two-tone paint procedure; front air conditioning; power door locks; power windows; tilt steering column (when automatic transmission was ordered).

1985 Dodge Ram Panel Delivery Van (DNP)

VAN/WAGON CONVENIENCE OPTIONS: Front integral air conditioning. Rear auxiliary air conditioning. Heavy-duty alternator. Heavy-duty battery. Bright front and rear bumpers. Bright front and rear bumpers, guards and nerf strips. Transmission oil to air auxiliary cooling. Maximum engine cooling. Rear window defroster. Dual rear doors with vented glass. Single rear door with vented glass. Passenger side sliding door with vented glass. 35-gallon fuel tank. Oil pressure gauge. Trip odometer. Sunscreen glass. Bright grille (included quad rectangular headlamps, vertically stacked, with halogen high beams). Engine block heater. Dual bright low-mount exterior mirrors. Lower moldings (included side and rear). Upper moldings (included side, rear, and bright taillamp bezels). Power door locks. Power windows (front doors only). **RADIOS:** AM/FM stereo, electronic tuning, integral digital clock; AM stereo/FM stereo with electronic tuning, seek and scan; cassette player with automatic reverse, Dynamic Noise Reduction, four speakers, and integral digital clock; AM stereo/FM stereo 36-watt Ultimate Sound System with electronic tuning, memory scan, up and down scan, cassette player with automatic reverse, metal tape capability, Dynamic Noise Reduction, five-channel graphic equalizer, joy-stick balance/fader control, ambient sound control, four speakers, integral digital clock. Heavy-duty shocks. Automatic speed control. Front stabilizer bar. Tilt type steering column. Luxury steering wheel. Bright wheelcovers. 15 in. aluminum road wheels. 15 in. argent silver painted spoked road wheels with bright trim ring. Deluxe windshield wipers with intermittent wipe.

NOTE: 1985 Dodge Ram Van and Wagon exterior colors were: Cream, Forest green metallic, Charcoal metallic, Crimson red, Walnut brown metallic, Navy blue metallic, Light blue metallic, Medium Golden brown metallic (available only with Prospector Package with two-tone paint procedure; not available on Long Range Ram Van or Ram Value Wagon), Burnished silver metallic, white, black Crystal Coat.

1985 Dodge Ram Sweptline Pickup (DNP)

D100/W100 PICKUP: Styling was carried over from the previous year. The D100 was offered with 6.5 ft. and 8 ft. Sweptline boxes. Standard features included: Brake system warning light. Dual braking system with separate brake fluid reservoirs in the master cylinder. Dry type air cleaner. 60-amp. alternator. Ashtray. Maintenance-free battery. Bright finish front bumpers. Automatic choke. Cigar lighter. Cleaner air system. Corrosion protection (extensive use of galvanized steel). Insulated dash and plenum liner. Color-keyed door inner trim panels with pull straps and armrests. Electronic ignition system. Carpeting. 20-gallon fuel tank. Glove box. Aluminum grille with painted plastic insert and headlamp doors. Fresh air heater with defrosters. In-cab hood release. Dual electric horns. Black instrument cluster faceplate with storage box. Padded instrument panel. Interior dome light. Dual bright finish short arm exterior mirrors. 10 in. day/night inside rearview mirror. Bright windshield molding. Power front disc brakes. All vinyl, color-keyed bench seat. Sun visors. Traffic hazard warning switch. Key-in-ignition, headlamps-on, and fasten seat belts warning buzzer. Dual jet windshield wipers. Two-speed windshield wipers. Four-speed manual transmission with overdrive.
I.D. DATA: The VIN consisted of 17 symbols. The first three symbols revealed manufacturer, make and vehicle type. The fourth symbol indicated GVW rating. The fifth, sixth and seventh symbols indicated series and body style. The eighth symbol indicated engine. The ninth symbol was a check digit. The 10th symbol indicated model year. The 11th symbol indicated assembly plant. The last six symbols were the sequential unit production number.

1985 Dodge Power Ram Sweptline Pickup (DNP)

Model (6.5 ft. box)	Body Type	Price	Weight	Prod. Total
D100	Sweptline Pickup	6775	3244	—
W100	Sweptline 4x4 Pickup	8998	3888	—
(8 ft. box)				
D100	Sweptline Pickup	6991	3338	—
W100	Sweptline 4x4 Pickup	9152	4013	—

NOTE: Separate model year production for D100/W100 not recorded.

ENGINE (D100): 3.7L (225 cid). Slant six-cylinder. Brake horsepower: 95 at 3600 rpm. Bore & stroke: 3.40 x 4.12 in. Compression ratio: 8.4:1. Carburetor: One-barrel.
D150/W150 PICKUP: The D150 Pickup had an approximately 1,000 lbs. greater payload capacity than the D100. It was offered in 6.5 ft. and 8 ft. Utiline and Sweptline boxes. Most standard features were the same as that on the D100.

I.D. DATA: The VIN consisted of 17 symbols. The first three symbols revealed manufacturer, make and vehicle type. The fourth symbol indicated GVW rating. The fifth, sixth and seventh symbols indicated series and body style. The eighth symbol was a check digit. The 10th symbol indicated model year. The 11th symbol indicated assembly plant. The last six symbols were the sequential unit production number.

Model (6.5-ft box)	Body Type	Price	Weight	Prod. Total
D150	Utiline Pickup	7589	3244	—
D150	Sweptline Pickup	7456	3264	—
W150	Utiline Pickup	9785	3909	—
W150	Sweptline Pickup	9951	4043	—
(8 ft. box)				
D150	Utiline Pickup	7755	3338	—
D150	Sweptline Pickup	7622	3364	—
W150	Utiline Pickup	9918	3888	—
W150	Sweptline Pickup	10,084	4013	—

NOTE: Total model year production was 95,863 two-wheel drive D150s and 26,592 four-wheel drive W150s.

ENGINE (D150): 3.7L (225 cid). Slant six-cylinder. Brake horsepower: 95 at 3600 rpm. Bore & stroke: 3.40 x 4.12 in. Compression ratio: 8.4:1. Carburetor: One-barrel.
D250/W250 PICKUP: The 3/4-ton D250 came with larger (12.82 x 1.19 in. front, 12 x 2.5 in. rear) brakes, different four-speed manual transmission (NP435), higher capacity rear axle and front and rear springs, and 9.0 dual diaphragm vacuum booster. It was available with Utiline or Sweptline boxes.
I.D. DATA: The VIN consisted of 17 symbols. The first three symbols revealed manufacturer, make and vehicle type. The fourth symbol indicated GVW rating. The fifth, sixth and seventh symbols indicated series and body style. The eighth symbol indicated engine. The ninth symbol was a check digit. The 10th symbol indicated model year. The 11th symbol indicated assembly plant. The last six symbols were the sequential unit production number.

Model	Body Type	Price	Weight	Prod. Total
D250	Chassis & Cab	9279	3459	—
(8 ft. box)				
D250	Utiline Pickup	8522	3734	—
D250	Sweptline Pickup	8389	3764	—
W250	Utiline 4x4 Pickup	10,324	4154	—
W250	Sweptline 4x4 Pickup	10,191	4184	—

NOTE: Total model year production was 14,522 two-wheel drive D250s and 8,108 four-wheel drive W250s.

ENGINE (D250): Same as D100 for pickups. Chassis with cab had 5.9L (360 cid) V-8. Brake horsepower: 185 at 4000 rpm. Bore & stroke: 4.00 x 3.58 in. Compression ratio: 8.0:1. Carburetor: Four-barrel.
D350/W350 PICKUP: The 1-ton D350 was offered in three wheelbase. A conventional cab was standard on the 131 in. wheelbase. The 149 in. and 165 in. wheelbase D350s came with four-door, six-passenger Crew Cabs. Most standard features were the same as those on the other series. D350 pickups were only offered with the "smooth side" Sweptline box.
I.D. DATA: The VIN consisted of 17 symbols. The first three symbols revealed manufacturer, make and vehicle type. The fourth symbol indicated GVW rating. The fifth, sixth and seventh symbols indicated series and body style. The eighth symbol indicated engine. The ninth symbol was a check digit. The 10th symbol indicated model year. The 11th symbol indicated assembly plant. The last six symbols were the sequential unit production number.

Model (131 in. w.b.)	Body Type	Price	Weight	Prod. Total
D350	Chassis & Cab	8971	3499	—
D350	Sweptline Pickup	9331	3879	—
W350	Chassis & Cab 4x4	10,501	3849	—
W350	Sweptline 4x4 Pickup	10,861	4229	—
(135 in. w.b.)				
D350	Chassis & Cab	9299	3848	—
W350	Chassis & Cab 4x4	12,135	4323	—
(149 in. w.b.)				
D350	Crew Cab Pickup	10,535	4379	—
W350	Crew Cab Pickup	12,729	4729	—
(159 in. w.b.)				
D350	Chassis & Cab	9,382	3918	—
(165 in. w.b.)				
D350	Crew Cab Pickup	10,629	4513	—

NOTE: Total model year production was 14,838 two-wheel drive D350s and 7,402 four-wheel drive W350s.

ENGINE (D350): 5.9L (360 cid) V-8. Brake horsepower: 185 at 4000 rpm. Bore & stroke: 4.00 x 3.58 in. Compression ratio: 8.0:1. Carburetor: Four-barrel.
CHASSIS FEATURES: Wheelbase: 115 in. (D100/D150); 131 in. (all); 149 in. (D350); 165 in. (D350); 135 in. (D350 Chassis w/cab); 159 in. (D350 Chassis w/cab). Overall width: 79.5 in. Overall length: 190.78 in. (115 in. wheelbase); 210.78 in. (131 in. wheelbase); 224.24 in. (149 in. wheelbase Crew Cab); 244.24 in. (165 in. wheelbase Crew Cab). GVW: 4,800 lbs. (D100); 4,800-5,850 lbs. (D150); 6,010 lbs. (W100/W150); 6,400-7,500 lbs. (D250); 6,900-7,500 lbs. (W250); 8,510 lbs. (W350); 8,510-10,100 lbs. (D350). Tires: P195/75R x 15 (D100/D150); 8.00 x 16.5D (D250); 9.50 x 16.5E (D350).
POWERTRAIN OPTION: 5.2-liter (318 cid) two-barrel V-8 (not available D350); 5.9L (360 cid) four-barrel V-8. Four-speed manual NP435 transmission (D100/D150). Three-speed automatic transmission.
OPTION PACKAGES: FOUR-WHEEL DRIVE: (W100/W150/W250/W350) in addition to or in place of D series features: Two-speed transfer case, the driver could shift from two-wheel to four-wheel drive and back while the vehicle was in motion at speeds up to 55 mph. Power steering, "Power Ram" emblem on front fenders. ROYAL SE PACKAGE: Bright aluminum grille with chrome plastic insert, headlamp doors and halogen headlamps; bright drip rail and rear window molding; bright tailgate applique panel (Sweptline); bright taillamp housings (Sweptline); Dodge Ram nameplate on Sweptline pickup tailgate applique panel; plaque on front fender with "leaping ram" and Royal SE name; ram's head hood ornament; color-keyed carpeting with underlayment (rubber floor mat was a no-charge option); color-keyed cowl side trim panels; color-keyed garnish trim over windshield, front pillar, door header, quarter trim panel upper, and over backlight (not available Crew Cab); color-keyed soft headliner (not available Crew Cab); deluxe Tribune cloth bench seat (all-vinyl was a no-charge option); front door woodtone trim applique with assist strip and carpeting on lower portion; bright sill scuff plates; insulation under hood panel; oil pressure and engine temperature gauges; trip odometer; woodtone instrument panel applique and bright trim.

LIGHT PACKAGE: Ash receiver light, exterior cargo light, glove box lock and light on instrument panel. TRAILER TOWING PREPARATION PACKAGE: (not available with six, four-speed manual overdrive, or 2.94 axle ratio on D150) 500-amp. maintenance-free-battery, front stabilizer bar, heavy-duty front and rear shock absorbers, heavy-duty load flasher, maximum engine cooling. JOB RATED PACKAGE: (D250/W250 only) 114-amp. alternator, 500-amp. maintenance-free battery, argent painted rear step type bumper, maximum engine cooling, 7,500 lbs. GVW package, 30-gallon fuel tank (W250), skid plate (W250), front stabilizer bar, heavy-duty shocks (D250). PROSPECTOR PACKAGES: (D150/D250/D350/W150/W250/W350 conventional cab Sweptline pickups) Package 1: Bright front bumper guards, bright low-mount mirrors, bright wheelcovers, intermittent wipers, light package, oil pressure and temperature gauges, trip odometer, Prospector nameplates, ram's head hood ornament, 30-gallon fuel tank, tinted glass. Package 2: All the items in Package 1, plus Royal SE Decor Package. Package 3: All the items in package 2, plus: Air conditioning, AM radio (electronically tuned, with integral digital clock), power door locks, two-tone paint procedure APC. (D350/W350 Crew Cab pickups): Package 1: Bright front bumper guards, low-mount mirrors, wheelcovers; intermittent wipers; light package; oil pressure and temperature gauges; trip odometer; Prospector nameplates; ram's head hood ornament; Tempo cloth bench seats; 30-gallon fuel tank; tinted glass. Package 2: All items in Package 1, plus: Electronically tuned AM radio with integral digital clock; Royal SE Decor Package. (D100, W100 conventional cab pickups): Package 1: Same as first Package 1, except it had sliding rear window and did not have ram's head hood ornament. SNO-COMMANDER PACKAGES: (specific GVW packages, 5.2L or 5.9L V-8 engines and transmission auxiliary oil cooler with automatic transmission were required at extra cost) 500-amp. maintenance-free battery, front clearance and identification lights, hydro/electric controls, maximum engine cooling, 114-amp. alternator, plow lights, power angling blade with blade markers, power lift, Sno-Commander decal, transmission oil temperature light with automatic transmission. SNO-PREPARATION PACKAGE: (specific GVW packages, 5.2L or 5.9L V-8 engines and transmission auxiliary oil cooler with automatic transmission were required at extra cost) 114-amp. alternator, 500-amp. maintenance-free battery, maximum engine cooling, transmission oil temperature light with automatic transmission.

CONVENIENCE OPTIONS: Air conditioning with bi-level ventilation. 114-amp. alternator. 500-amp. maintenance-free battery. Front bumper guards. Rear step bumper. Auxiliary transmission oil to air cooler. 30-gallon fuel tank. Oil pressure, engine coolant temperature gauges. Trip odometer. Tinted glass. Bright insert grille, included halogen headlamps, bright headlamp doors, and ram's head hood ornament. Engine block heater. Dual lowmount exterior mirrors. Upper moldings. Lower moldings with partial wheel lip. Power door locks. Power steering. Power windows. Radios: AM, AM/FM stereo, AM stereo/FM stereo with cassette player. Heavy-duty shock absorbers. Spare tire carrier inside Automatic speed control. Front stabilizer bar. Tilt steering column. Spot type steering wheel. Transfer case skid plate. Bright wheelcovers. Aluminum radial ribbed wheels. Painted spoke wheels. Sliding rear window. Deluxe two-speed windshield wipers with intermittent wipe.

NOTE: D series exterior colors for 1985 included: Black, Light Blue Metallic, Navy Blue Metallic, Charcoal Metallic, Cream, Forest Green Metallic, Canyon Red Metallic, Golden Brown Metallic (available with Prospector Package with two-tone paint procedure only), Graphic Red, Silver Metallic, White.

HISTORICAL: Dodge trucks were built by Chrysler Corp. Truck Operations under general manager Patrick J. Keegan. The corporation scored its second consecutive record year, largely due to the sale of 243,000 Dodge and Plymouth compact minivans. Ramcharger production was moved to Mexico to provide more space at Dodge City, in Warren, Michigan, and facilitate the mid-1986 introduction of the Dakota pickup. Chrysler invested $500 million to launch this new model.

1986 DODGE

RAM 50 PICKUP: The Ram 50 received a minor facelift. The grille now had a narrower upper section with "Dodge" printed in smaller letters than in 1985. The grille "slots" were a bit larger and extended to underneath the four recessed rectangular headlights. Among standard features were: Color-keyed short armrests. Cigar lighter. Rubber mat floor covering. Inside hood release. Dome light. Day/night rearview mirror. AM radio. All vinyl bench seat. Adjustable steering column. Two-spoke plastic steering wheel. Trip odometer. Skid plates (four-wheel drive). Torsion bar front, leaf rear suspension (four-wheel drive). 45-amp. alternator. Power front disc brakes. Electronic ignition. Black front bumper. Double wall cargo box. Corrosion protection. 18-gallon fuel tank. Tinted glass (all windows). Argent grille. Argent hubcaps. Cargo box light. Black left and right swingaway outside mirrors. Two-speed windshield wipers. Five-speed manual transmission. The Power Ram 50 had most of the same features plus four-wheel drive, an aluminum transfer case with chain belt drive, and automatic locking hubs.

1986 Dodge Ram 50 Mini-Pickup (DNP)

RAM 50 SPORT: The Sport lived up to its name in looks and performance. It came with many of the same standard features as the Ram 50 plus (or in place of): Long color-keyed armrests. Electronic digital clock. Carpeting. Cloth and vinyl bench seat (high-back cloth and vinyl buckets on the four-wheel drive). Soft-feel two-spoke steering wheel. Color-keyed

scuff plate. Power steering. Chrome front bumper. Chrome/black grille. Bright drip rail and windshield moldings. Vinyl bodyside moldings. 14 in. painted wide spoke wheels (15 in. on four-wheel drive). The Power Ram 50 Sport shared most of these features plus four-wheel drive.

I.D. DATA: The VIN consisted of 17 symbols. The first three symbols revealed manufacturer, make and vehicle type. The fourth symbol indicated GVW rating. The fifth, sixth and seventh symbols indicated series and body style. The eighth symbol indicated engine. The ninth symbol was a check digit. The 10th symbol indicated model year. The 11th symbol indicated assembly plant. The last six symbols were the sequential unit production number.

Model	Body Type	Price	Weight	Prod. Total
P24	Custom Pickup	5788	2310	—
K24	Custom 4x4 Pickup	8245	2720	—
P44	Sport Pickup	6712	2332	—
P44	Sport 4x4 Pickup	9024	2850	—

NOTE: Total U.S. dealer sales of 1986 Ram 50s in the 1985-1986 calendar year was 68,800 trucks.

ENGINE (Ram 50 4x2): 2.0L (122 cid). OHC. Four-cylinder. Brake horsepower: 90 at 5000 rpm. Bore & stroke: 3.30 x 3.54 in. Compression ratio: 8.5:1. Carburetor: Two-barrel.

ENGINE (RAM 50 4x4): 2.6L (156 cid). OHC. Four-cylinder. Brake horsepower: 104 at 4800 rpm. Compression ratio: 8.7:1. Carburetor: Two-barrel.

CHASSIS FEATURES: Wheelbase: 109.4 in. (4x2); 109.8 in. (4x4). Overall length: 184.4 in. Overall width: 65 in. Overall height: 57.5 in. (4x2); 61.6 in. (4x4). Box length (inside at floor): 81.5 in. Box width (inside at floor): 60 in. GVW. 4,045-4,475 lbs. Tires: 185SR x 14 BSW (4x2); GR78 x 15 BSW (4x4).

1986 Dodge Ram 50 Sport Mini-Pickup (DNP)

POWERTRAIN OPTION: Three-speed automatic transmission.

OPTION PACKAGES: Four-wheel drive. PREMIUM PACKAGE: (Sport only) tachometer; console with oil pressure gauge and ammeter; high back premium cloth bucket seats; variable intermittent windshield wipers; AM/FM stereo radio; power steering (4x2); standard on 4x4); chrome wide spoke wheels; RWL tires. Air conditioning. Power steering. Black rear step bumper (Ram 50). Chrome rear step bumper (Sport). Chrome low-mount exterior mirrors. Vinyl bodyside molding (Ram 50). Bodyside and tailgate tape stripes (Ram 50). Wheel trim rings (Ram 50). Sliding rear window.

1986 Dodge Power Ram 50 Sport Mini-Pickup (DNP)

NOTE: Exterior Ram 50/Ram 50 Sport colors for 1986 were: Medium Blue, Charcoal, Bright Red, Bright Silver, Black, Gold, White. The last two colors had Brown/Beige interiors. The others had Gray interiors.

NOTE: Ram 50 and Power Ram 50 "Spring Specials" were offered in early 1986. They featured: Cut-pile carpeting. Cloth and vinyl bench seat. Color coordinated carpeted door panel inserts. Deluxe sport steering wheel. Chromed front bumper. Tape stripes. The Ram 50 4x2 was offered in four two-tone paint treatments with painted wide spoke wheels, or seven monotone exterior colors with chromed wheels. The Power Ram 50 had chrome wheels and a choice of seven monotone paint treatments.

1986 Dodge 4x4 Ramcharger Royal SE Sport Utility (DNP)

RAMCHARGER SPORT UTILITY VEHICLE: The 1986 Ramcharger shared the "D" series pickups attractive facelift. There was 106 cu. ft. of cargo room (with the standard rear seat removed). Both two-wheel drive (AD150) and part-time four-wheel drive (AW150) were offered. As in 1985, the four-wheel drive Ramcharger could be shifted on the run into four-wheel drive or back into two-wheel drive at speeds up to 55 mph. Among standard features were: Dry type air cleaner. 60-amp. alternator. Ashtray. 400-amp. maintenance-free battery. Power front disc brakes. Bright front and rear bumpers. Fasten seat belts, headlights on, key in ignition warning buzzers. Cigar lighter. Coolant reserve system. Corrosion protection. Insulated dash liner. Color-keyed door inner trim panels, armrests and pull straps. Electronic ignition with voltage regulation system. Black floor mats. 35-gallon fuel tank. Tinted glass (all windows). Glove box. Aluminum grille with painted plastic insert and headlamp bezels. Color-keyed soft cloth headliner. Fresh air heater with defrosters. Hood inner panel insulation. Dual note electric horns. Bright hubcaps. 10 in. day/night rearview mirror. Dual bright short arm 5 in. x 7 in. exterior mirrors. Quarter side window, rear window, and windshield bright moldings. Power steering. Deluxe vinyl high-back front bucket seats. Rear roof vent. Three-passenger rear bench seat. Inside spare tire mounting. Sun visors. Dual jet windshield washers. Two-speed windshield wipers. Three speed automatic (4x2). Four-speed manual transmission (4x4).

I.D. DATA: The VIN consisted of 17 symbols. The first three symbols revealed manufacturer, make and vehicle type. The fourth symbol indicated GVW rating. The fifth, sixth and seventh symbols indicated series and body style. The eighth symbol indicated engine. The ninth symbol was a check digit. The 10th symbol indicated model year. The 11th symbol indicated assembly plant. The last six symbols were the sequential unit production number.

1986 Dodge 4x4 Ramcharger Royal SE Sport Utility (DNP)

Model	Body Type	Price	Weight	Prod. Total
AD150	Utility	11,534	3664	—
AW150	4x4 Utility	12,763	4065	—

NOTE: Total model year production of both Ramcharger models was 20,815 trucks.

ENGINE (Ramcharger): 5.2L (318 cid) V-8. Brake horsepower: 120 at 3600 rpm. Bore & stroke: 3.91 x 3.31 in. Compression ratio: 8.5:1. Carburetor: Two-barrel.
CHASSIS FEATURES: Wheelbase: 106 in. Overall length: 184.6 in. (without bumper guards). Overall width: 79.5 in. GVW: 5,600 lbs. (4x2); 6,000-6,400 lbs. (4x4). Tires: P235/75R x 15XL SBR.
POWERTRAIN OPTION: 5.9L (360 cid). Carburetor: Four-barrel V-8 (not available in California). Three-speed automatic transmission (4x4).
OPTION PACKAGES: ROYAL SE PACKAGE: Bright drip rail molding; bright grille with bright insert and bright headlight bezels; halogen headlights; bright liftgate applique, upper and lower moldings, taillight housing; front fender leaping ram plaque "150 Royal SE"; ram's head hood ornament; bright doorsill scuff plate; center console; color-keyed carpeting throughout with underlayment; color-keyed cowl side trim panels; color-keyed rear side and liftgate inner trim panels with woodtone applique; color-keyed spare tire cover; vinyl door trim panels with woodtone trim, assist strap, armrest, and carpeting on lower door; deluxe cloth and vinyl trim high-back front bucket seats; Euro-sport steering wheel (black); folding rear bench seat in cloth with vinyl trim; nameplate on instrument panel; woodtone applique on instrument panel. HEAVY DUTY PACKAGE: Front stabilizer bar on two-wheel drive; heavy-duty front stabilizer bar on four-wheel drive; heavy-duty front and rear shocks. POWER CONVENIENCE PACKAGE: Power door locks; power windows. CONVENIENCE PACKAGE: Ash receiver light; glove box lock and light; intermittent windshield wipers. TWO-TONE PAINT PACKAGE: Lower bodyside moldings with black vinyl insert and bright partial wheel lip moldings; two-tone paint; upper side and rear exterior moldings. PROSPECTOR PACKAGES: Package 1: Convenience package; deluxe wheelcovers; grille with bright insert, headlight bezels, halogen headlights and ram's head hood ornament; power convenience package; sunscreen glass (rear quarter and liftgate windows only). Package 2: All items in package 1 except sunscreen glass, plus: Dual 6 in. by 9 in. low-mount mirrors; front bumper guards; Royal SE Decor Package. Package 3: Air conditioning; alumi-

num ribbed road wheels; AM stereo/FM stereo radio (electronically tuned) with integral clock; convenience package; dual low-mount 6 in. by 9 in. mirrors (4x2); P235/75R x 5XL RWL tires; power convenience package; Royal SE Decor Package; speed control; sunscreen glass (rear quarter and liftgate windows only); two-tone paint package.
CONVENIENCE OPTIONS: Air conditioning. Heavy-duty alternator. Antispin rear axle. Heavy-duty battery. Painted step type rear bumper. Front bumper guards. Auxiliary transmission oil to air cooling. Maximum engine cooling. Sunscreen privacy glass (rear quarter windows and liftgate only). Engine block heater. Dual bright low-mount exterior mirrors. Bright lower bodyside moldings with black vinyl insert and partial wheel lip. AM stereo/FM stereo (electronically tuned) with integral digital clock. AM stereo/FM stereo (electronically tuned) with seek-and-scan, cassette player with automatic reverse, integral digital clock. Automatic speed control. Sport bar. Tilt steering column. Argent painted steel spoke wheels with bright trim ring and hub center. Radial ribbed aluminum wheels. Two-speed windshield wipers with intermittent wipe.
NOTE: Ramcharger exterior colors for 1986 included: Light Cream, Golden Bronze Pearl Coat, Twilight Blue Pearl Coat, Graphic Red, Gold Dust, Radiant Silver, Ice Blue, White, Black, Charcoal Pearl Coat.

1986 Dodge Mini-Ram Van (DNP)

MINI-RAM VAN: The compact, front-wheel drive Mini-Ram Van shared most standard features with the Caravan. A right side, sliding cargo door without glass and no rear seats were a couple exceptions. Its cargo compartment width between wheelhousings was 49.2 in. Maximum interior height was 48.8 in. Maximum interior width was 64.3 in. And total cargo volume was 133 cu. ft.

1986 Dodge Mini-Ram Van Royal (DNP)

MINI-RAM VAN ROYAL: The Royal was a step up in trim. It came with a long list of extras: Body color front and rear bumper end caps. Front and rear bumper protective rub strips. Cloth covered front compartment headliner. Dual note horn. Luxury steering wheel. Right side sun visor. Five-speed manual with overdrive. Styled road type wheels with bright trim ring, hub cover and nut cover.
I.D. DATA: The VIN consisted of 17 symbols. The first three symbols revealed manufacturer, make and vehicle type. The fourth symbol indicated GVW rating. The fifth, sixth and seventh symbols indicated series and body style. The eighth symbol indicated engine. The ninth symbol was a check digit. The 10th symbol indicated model year. The 11th symbol indicated assembly plant. The last six symbols were the sequential unit production number.

Model	Body Type	Price	Weight	Prod. Total
K13	Minivan	8308	2754	—
K63	Royal Minivan	9128	2828	—

NOTE: See Caravan chart for combined production total.

ENGINE (Caravan): 2.2L (135 cid). OHC. Transverse-mounted four-cylinder. Brake horsepower: 101 at 5600 rpm. Compression ratio: 9.0:1. Carburetor: Two-barrel.
CHASSIS FEATURES: Wheelbase: 112 in. Overall length: 175.9 in. Overall width: 69.6 in. Overall height: 64.2 in. GVW: 3,900-4,400 lbs. Tires: P185/75R x 14.
POWERTRAIN OPTIONS: 2.6L (156 cid) OHC four-cylinder. Three-speed automatic transmission.
OPTION PACKAGES: VAN CONVERSION PACKAGE: Accessory wire harness; black front and rear rub strips; bright bumpers with color-keyed end caps; driver and passenger seating package; gauge with gauge alert package; chrome/argent finish grille; 4,500 lbs. package; light package; bright trim on front park/side marker/turn, rear backup/side marker/stop/tail/turn lights; power steering; luxury two-spoke steering wheel. BASIC GROUP PACKAGE: 500-amp. battery; remote release fuel filler door; 20-gallon fuel tank; gauge with gauge alert package; light package; sliding side door outside lock; maximum GVW package; power liftgate release; power steering; electronic speed control; tilt steering column; deluxe windshield wipers with intermittent wipe; rear window wiper/washer with fixed intermittent wipe. MAXIMUM [4,810 lbs.] GVW PACKAGE: Heavy-duty brakes; heavy-duty suspension; LT195/75R x 14 SBR BSW tires. SPORT ROAD WHEEL PACKAGE: (Mini-Ram Van Royal only, but not with 4,810 lbs. GVW package) Includes, cast aluminum 14 in.

wheels; P195/75R x 14 SBR BSW tires with 2.2L engine; P205/70R x 14 SBR BSW tires with 2.6L engine. GAUGE WITH GAUGE ALERT AND LIGHT PACKAGES: same as Caravan.

CONVENIENCE OPTIONS: Air conditioning. 500-amp. maintenance-free battery. Converta-bed rear seating (not available LE). Electric liftgate window defroster. 20-gallon fuel tank. Sunscreen glass. Roof mounted luggage rack. Dual remote control exterior mirrors (Caravan & SE). Color-keyed vinyl bodyside molding (standard woodtone applique omitted on LE models). Power door locks. Power liftgate release. Power release. Power driver's bucket seat. RADIOS: AM/FM stereo with electronic tuning and four speakers; premium AM/FM stereo with electronic tuning, seek-and-scan, Dynamic Noise Reduction, cassette tape player with automatic reverse and four speakers; AM/FM stereo 36-watt Ultimate Sound System with electronic tuning, memory scan, up and down scan, Dynamic Noise Reduction, cassette tape player with automatic reverse, metal tape capability, five band graphic equalizer, joystick balance/fader control, ambience sound control, four speakers. Electronic speed control. Tilt steering column. Heavy-suspension (P195/75R x 14 tires included). Conventional spare tire. TIRES: P195/75R x 14 SBR BSW, P205/70R x 14 SBR WSW; P205/70R x 14 SBR RWL. Rear cargo compartment tonneau cover (five- or six-passenger models only, not available with Converta-Bed). Wire wheelcovers (SE/LE). Deluxe intermittent wipe windshield wipers with wet-arm washers. Lockable storage drawer under passenger bucket seat. Dual fold-away type exterior mirrors).

NOTE: Mini-Ram Van colors for 1986 included: Light Cream, Black Golden Bronze Pearl Coat, Dark Cordovan Pearl Coat, Gunmetal Blue Pearl Coat (extra cost), Gold Dust, Garnet Red Pearl Coat (extra cost), Radiant Silver, White, Ice Blue.

CARAVAN: Styling was carried over from the previous year. Among the changes made for 1986 were: New brake proportioning valve, integrated wraparound front air dam, outside lock on sliding door, and improved manual transmission. Standard features included: 60-amp. alternator. 335-amp. maintenance-free battery. Power brakes (front disc, rear drum) with load sensing proportioning valve. Color-keyed front and rear bumper end caps. Rear passenger assist strap. Front-wheel drive. Front and rear bright bumpers with rub strips. Carpeting. Keys-in-ignition, fasten seat belts, headlamps on warning chimes. Cigarette lighter. Coolant overflow reservoir. Front door demisters. Sliding cargo compartment door with vented glass. Electronic ignition and voltage regulator. Remote fuel filler door release. 15-gallon fuel tank. Tinted glass (all windows). Bright grille. Cloth covered headliner. Bi-level ventilation heater. Inside hood release. Single note horn. Driver and passenger compartments dome light. Day/night inside rearview mirror. Black left-hand remote control exterior mirror. Black rear window and windshield molding. AM radio with electronic tuning and integral digital clock. Rack and pinion power steering. Deluxe two-spoke vinyl steering wheel. Compact spare tire. Five-speed manual transmission with overdrive. Deluxe wheelcovers. Two speed windshield wipers with wet arm washers. Liftgate wiper/washer. Cloth with vinyl trim low back front bucket seats in cordovan, almond, silver/charcoal. A matching three-passenger bench seat was included.

CARAVAN SE: The SE (Special Edition) came with most of the same standard features as the base Caravan, plus (or in place of): Bright upper bodyside and liftgate moldings. Styled road type wheels with bright trim ring, hub center and nut covers. Deluxe cloth and vinyl trim. Low-back front bucket seats in cordovan, almond, blue, silver/charcoal and three-passenger bench seat in matching trim. Dual note horn. Front folding armrests.

CARAVAN LE: The LE (Luxury Edition) came with most of the same standard features as the SE, plus (or in place of): Dual black remote control exterior rearview mirrors. Forward storage console. High-back reclining front bucket seats in luxury cloth with vinyl trim in cordovan, almond, silver/charcoal (blue was available with the optional vinyl upholstery). Three-passenger bench seat with matching trim. Deluxe sound insulation. Woodgrain center side and liftgate applique. Ash receiver light. Luxury steering wheel.

I.D. DATA: The VIN consisted of 17 symbols. The first three symbols revealed manufacturer, make and vehicle type. The fourth symbol indicated GVW rating. The fifth, sixth and seventh symbols indicated series and body style. The eighth symbol indicated engine. The ninth symbol was a check digit. The 10th symbol indicated model year. The 11th symbol indicated assembly plant. The last six symbols were the sequential unit production number.

Model	Body Type	Price	Weight	Prod. Total
K21	Caravan	9506	3005	—
K41	Caravan SE	9785	3046	—
K51	Caravan LE	10,528	3071	—

NOTE: Total model year production of all Dodge compact van (Mini-Ram and Caravan) was 111,800 trucks.

ENGINE (Caravan): 2.2L (135 cid). OHC. Transverse-mounted four-cylinder. Brake horsepower: 101 at 5600 rpm. Compression ratio: 9.0:1. Carburetor: Two-barrel.

CHASSIS FEATURES: Wheelbase: 112 in. Overall length: 175.9 in. Overall width: 69.6 in. Overall height: 64.2 in. GVW. 4,450-4,600 lbs. Tires: P185/75R x 14 SBR.

POWERTRAIN OPTIONS: 2.6L (156 cid). OHC. Four-cylinder. Three-speed automatic.

OPTION PACKAGES: BASIC GROUP: (Caravan) black front and rear bumper guards; 500-amp. maintenance-free battery; deluxe intermittent windshield wipers; deluxe sound insulation; dual-note horns; dual remote control mirrors; light package; sliding side door with outside key lock. POPULAR EQUIPMENT DISCOUNT PACKAGE: (SE/LE) accessory carpeted floor mats front and rear; AM stereo/FM stereo radio with integral clock; 500-amp. maintenance-free battery; deluxe sound insulation; deluxe intermittent windshield wipers; dual non-power remote control mirrors (SE); dual-note horns; electronic speed control; forward storage console; gauge with gauge alert package; illuminated visor vanity mirrors; light package; luxury steering wheel; overhead console (LE); power liftgate release; remote control rear quarter vent windows; sliding side door outside key lock. LUXURY EQUIPMENT DISCOUNT PACKAGE: (LE) popular equipment package; power door locks; power driver's bucket seat; power front doors windows; tilt steering column. TRAVEL EQUIPMENT DISCOUNT PACKAGE: (SE/LE) exterior right remote control mirror (SE); 500-amp. maintenance-free battery; dual-note horns (LE); 20-gallon fuel tank; 2.6L OHC four-cylinder engine with automatic transmission; remote control rear quarter vent windows; seven-passenger seating package; sliding side door outside key lock; sun screen glass. GAUGE ALERT PACKAGE: Engine coolant temperature gauge with high temperature warning light; low voltage warning light; oil pressure gauge and low pressure warning light; trip odometer with push-button reset. LIGHT PACKAGE: (500-amp. battery required on LE); ash receiver light; front map/reading lights (two); headlight switch call-out light with time delay; ignition switch light with time delay; instrument panel door-ajar; low fuel warning and low washer fluid lights; liftgate mounted dual floodlights; underhood light. SEVEN-PASSENGER SEATING: (SE/LE) included second rear seat (two-passenger bench with fixed back, side armrests and quick-release attachments); third seat (three-passenger bench with folding back, side armrests, adjustable feature and quick-release attachments); ash receiver in right C-pillar, below belt, heavy-duty rear brakes; P195/75R x 14 SBR BSW tires; dual rear storage bins with armrest covers incorporated into wheelwells. EIGHT-PASSENGER SEATING PACKAGE: (SE) included three-passenger front 40/60 bench seat in cloth vinyl trim; second seat and third seats like those in the seven-passenger seating package; heavy-duty rear brakes; heavy-duty suspension; P195/75R x 14 SBR BSW tires; dual rear storage bins with armrests covers incorporated into wheelwells. SPORT WHEEL PACKAGE: 14 in. cast aluminum wheels; P195/75R x 14 SBR BSW tires (with 2.2L engine); P205/70R x 14 SBR WLT tires with 2.6L engine.

CONVENIENCE OPTIONS: Air conditioning. 500-amp. maintenance-free battery. Converta-bed rear seating (not available LE). Electric liftgate window defroster. 20-gallon fuel tank. Sunscreen glass. Roof mounted luggage rack. Dual remote control exterior mirrors (Caravan/SE). Color-keyed vinyl bodyside molding (standard woodtone applique omitted on LE models). Power door locks. Power liftgate release. Power release. Power driver's bucket seat. RADIOS: AM/FM stereo with electronic tuning and four speakers; premium AM/FM stereo with electronic tuning, seek-and-scan, Dynamic Noise Reduction, cassette tape player with automatic reverse, four speakers; AM/FM stereo 36-watt Ultimate Sound System with electronic tuning, memory scan, up and down scan, Dynamic Noise Reduction, cassette tape player with automatic reverse, metal tape capability, five band graphic equalizer, joystick balance/fader control, ambience sound control and four speakers. Electronic speed control. Tilt steering column. Heavy-suspension (P195/75R x 14 tires included). Conventional spare tire. TIRES: P195/75R x 14 SBR BSW; P205/70R x 14 SBR WSW; P205/70R x 14 SBR RWL. Rear cargo compartment tonneau cover (five- or six-passenger models only, not available with Converta-Bed). Wire wheelcovers (SE/LE). Deluxe intermittent wipe windshield wipers with wet-arm washers.

NOTE: Caravan exterior monotone colors for 1986 included: Light Cream Black, Golden Bronze Pearl Coat, Dark Cordovan Pearl Coat, Gunmetal Blue Pearl Coat (extra cost), Gold Dust, Garnet Red Pearl Coat (extra cost), Radiant Silver, White, Ice Blue. Two-tone color combinations were: Gold Dust/Golden Bronze Pearl Coat, Garnet Red Pearl Coat/Black, Radiant Silver/Black, Light Cream/Golden Bronze Pearl Coat, Gunmetal Blue Pearl Coat/Black, Ice Blue/Gunmetal Blue Pearl Coat.

1986 Dodge Ram Wagon (JAG)

B150 VAN: Dodge Ram Vans received an attractive, though minor, facelift for 1986. The Dodge name was now centered on the face of the downward sloping hood. Directly below it was the new, large rectangular slots grille with two rectangular headlamps integrated into it. The front bumper was also revised to include an indentation for a license plate in its center. Among standard features were: 60-amp. alternator. Ashtray. 400-amp. battery. Power front disc braks. Painted front and rear bumpers. Fasten seat belts, headlights on, the key in ignition warning buzzer. Cigar lighter. Corrosion protection. Right side and rear cargo doors (with no glass). Electronic ignition and voltage regulation system. Black floor mat on driver's side. Tinted front door windows and windshield. Glove box. Argent finished grille. Deluxe fresh air heater with defroster. In-cab actuated hood release. Dual note electric horns. Bright hubcaps. Bright 5 in. by 7 in. exterior mirrors. Nameplates on front doors, hood, and rear doors. Deluxe vinyl trim low-back drivers bucket seat. Front stabilizer bar. Driver's side sun visor. Electric windshield washers. Two-speed windshield wipers. Four-speed manual transmission with overdrive.

B150 LONG RANGE RAM VAN: The 1986 Long Range Ram Van came with such "extras" as: Bright front and rear bumpers. 35-gallon fuel tank. Bright finish grille. Rectangular halogen headlights. Deluxe wheelcovers.

1986 Dodge Royal SE Ram Wagon (DNP)

B150 WAGON: The B150 Ram Wagon came with most of the same standard features found on the van, plus (or in place of); Electronically tuned AM radio with integral digital clock. Right side and single rear doors. Black full length floor mat with underlayment. All windows tinted. Rectangular halogen headlights. Full length white hardboard headliner. Deluxe heater. 10 in. day/night inside rearview mirror. Front and rear doors side step sill scuff pads. Driver and passenger side sun visors.

B150 RAM VALUE WAGON: The Ram Value Wagon was only available on a 109.6 in. wheelbase. Among its "extra" standard features were: Bright front and rear bumpers. Color-keyed full length carpeting. Insulated dash liner. Glove box with lock and light. Bright finish grille. Pecan woodtone instrument panel applique. Color-keyed instrument panel lower skirts. Cigar lighter, ignition and headlight symbol with time delay, and low washer fluid lights. Bright side and rear windows, taillight bezels, and windshield moldings. Inside mounted spare tire cover. Deluxe wheelcovers. Two-speed intermittent type windshield wipers.

I.D. DATA: The VIN consisted of 17 symbols. The first three symbols revealed manufacturer, make and vehicle type. The fourth symbol indicated GVW rating. The fifth, sixth and seventh symbols indicated series and body style. The eighth symbol indicated engine. The ninth symbol was a check digit. The 10th symbol indicated model year. The 11th symbol indicated assembly plant. The last six symbols were the sequential unit production number.

Model	Body Type	Price	Weight	Prod. Total
B150 Series — 109.6 in. w.b.				
B13	Ram Van	9040	3299	—
B13	Long Range Ram Van	9109	—	—
B11	Ram Wagon	10,987	3585	—
(127.6 in. w.b.)				
B13	Van	9266	3415	—
B13	Long Range Ram Van	—	—	—
B11	Wagon	11,215	3758	—
B11	Value Wagon	10,947	—	—

NOTE 1: Combined model year production for B150/B250/B350 Ram Vans was 66,595 trucks.
NOTE 2: Combined model year production for B150/B250/B350 Ram Wagons was 37,594 trucks.

ENGINE (B150): 3.7L (225 cid). Six-cylinder. Brake horsepower: 95 at 3600 rpm. Bore & stroke: 3.40 x 4.12 in. Compression ratio: 8.4:1. Carburetor: One-barrel.

B250 Van: The handsome 3/4-ton B250 Ram Van shared most of the same standard features offered on the 1/2-ton B150. However, it could be ordered with the 26 in. longer Maxi body on a 127.6 in. wheelbase. Maxi Ram Van cargo area capacity was an impressive 304.5 cu. ft.

B250 Wagon: The B250 Ram Wagon had most of the same standard features as the B150 version. In addition to being heavier-duty, it could be had in regular or extra-long Maxi bodies. Maxi Ram Wagons came with a payload capacity of 2,545 lbs. and automatic transmission.

I.D. DATA: The VIN consisted of 17 symbols. The first three symbols revealed manufacturer, make and vehicle type. The fourth symbol indicated GVW rating. The fifth, sixth and seventh symbols indicated series and body style. The eighth symbol indicated engine. The ninth symbol was a check digit. The 10th symbol indicated model year. The 11th symbol indicated assembly plant. The last six symbols were the sequential unit production number.

1986 Dodge Royal Ram Wagon (DNP)

Model	Body Type	Price	Weight	Prod. Total
B250 Series — 109.6 in. w.b.				
B23	Van	9489	3539	—
B21	Wagon	11,535	3799	—
(127.6 in. w.b.)				
B23	Van	9718	3475	—
B23	Maxi Van	10,329	3637	—
B21	Wagon	11,535	3799	—
B21	Maxi Wagon	13,024	4182	—

NOTE 1: Combined model year production for B150/B250/B350 Ram Vans was 66,595 trucks.
NOTE 2: Combined model year production for B150/B250/B350 Ram Wagons was 37,594 trucks.

ENGINE (B250): 3.7L (225 cid). Six-cylinder. Brake horsepower: 95 at 3600 rpm. Bore & stroke: 3.40 x 4.12 in. Compression ratio: 8.4:1. Carburetor: One-barrel. 5.2L two-barrel V-8 standard on Maxi Ram Wagon.

B350 Van: The biggest Dodge Ram Van for 1986 remained the B350. It came with most of the same standard features as the B150, plus (or in place of): Larger front and rear brakes. Three-speed automatic transmission. Axle type jack. It was offered with the regular or extended Maxivan bodies. Both were on the 127.6 in. wheelbase.

B350 Wagon: The heftiest Ram Wagon was the 1-ton B350. It could be ordered with seats for up to 12 people (regular wagon) or up to 15-passengers in the Maxi-Ram Wagon.

I.D. DATA: The VIN consisted of 17 symbols. The first three symbols revealed manufacturer, make and vehicle type. The fourth symbol indicated GVW rating. The fifth, sixth and seventh symbols indicated series and body style. The eighth symbol indicated engine. The ninth symbol was a check digit. The 10th symbol indicated model year. The 11th symbol indicated assembly plant. The last six symbols were the sequential unit production number.

Model	Body Type	Price	Weight	Prod. Total
B350 Series				
B33	Van	10,716	3867	—
B33	Maxi Van	14,593	4063	—
B31	Wagon	12,650	4195	—
B31	Maxi Wagon	13,625	4490	—

NOTE 1: Combined model year production for B150/B250/B350 Ram Vans was 66,595 trucks.
NOTE 2: Combined model year production for B150/B250/B350 Ram Wagons was 37,594 trucks.

1986 Dodge Custom Ram Van (DNP)

ENGINE (B350): 5.2L (318 cid) V-8. Brake horsepower: 135 at 4000 rpm. Bore & stroke: 3.91 x 3.31 in. Compression ratio: 8.5:1. Carburetor: Two-barrel. Maxi-Ram Wagons and Maxi-Ram Vans with GVW ratings over 7,500 lbs. came with a 5.9L (360 cid) four-barrel V-8.

CHASSIS FEATURES: Wheelbase: 109.6 in. (B150/B250); 127.6 in. (B150/B250/B350). Overall length: 178.9 in. (109.6 in. wheelbase); 196.9 in. (127.6 in. wheelbase); 222.9 in. (Maxi). Overall width: 79.8 in. Overall height: 79.6 in. (109.6 in. wheelbase); 80.9 in. (127.6 in. wheelbase); 80.6 in. (Maxi). GVW: 5,000-6,010 lbs. (B150); 6,010-6,400 lbs. (B250); 7,500-9,000 lbs. (B350). Tires: P195/75R x 15 (B150s with 5,000 lbs. GVW rating); P205/75R x 15 (B150); P225/75R x 15 or P235/75R x 15XL (B250); 8.00 x 16.5E (B350); 8.75 x 16.5E (B350 Maxi).

POWERTRAIN OPTIONS: 5.2L two-barrel V-8 (B150/B250); 5.9L four-barrel V-8 (B250/B350). Three-speed automatic transmission.

VAN OPTION PACKAGES: CONVENIENCE PACKAGE: Power door locks (all doors); deluxe two-speed windshield wipers with intermittent wipe; glove box lock and light; ignition switch light and headlight symbol light with time delay (not available with tilt steering column); low washer fluid warning light. EXTERIOR APPEARANCE PACKAGE: Bright front and rear bumpers, grille, side and rear fixed window moldings (with Vision Van Window package and vented side glass), single rear door window surround molding; taillight bezels, windshield molding; rectangular halogen headlights. LOCK PACKAGE: Two keys; one operated ignition and front doors, the other operated side and rear cargo doors. POWER CONVENIENCE PACKAGE: Power door locks; power windows (driver and front passenger doors only, front door lower trim panels included). SCHOOL BUS PACKAGE: (B350 Van with Solid Side Panel Van or Vision Van configurations only) banded glass in front doors and vent wings; parking brake switch; school bus yellow paint. VAN CONVERSION APPEARANCE PACKAGE: Accessory wiring harness, 500-amp. maintenance-free battery; Exterior Appearance Package garnish trim over front door headers; A-pillar, and around windshield; luxury steering wheel; woodtone applique instrument panel with color-keyed left and right lower skirts. PROSPECTOR VAN CONVERSION PACKAGE: Front air conditioning; automatic speed control; automatic transmission; bright bumper guards and black protective rub strips; Convenience package; dual low-mount exterior mirrors; dual rear cargo doors with vented glass; 35-gallon fuel tank; oil pressure gauge; Power Convenience package; rubber scuff pads; tilt steering column; trip odometer; Van Conversion Appearance package.

WAGON OPTION PACKAGES: EIGHT-PASSENGER SEATING PACKAGE: (For 109.6 in. wheelbase B150 with 6,010 lbs. GVW package and all B250/B350 Wagon and Maxi-Ram Wagon models), includes one additional quick-release three-passenger rear bench seat. B350 12-PASSENGER SEATING PACKAGE: (rear doors with optional vented glass required at extra cost), includes two additional rear bench seats (second three-passenger/third four-passenger) and spare tire carrier relocated under third bench seat. B350 15-PASSENGER SEATING PACKAGE: (For Maxi-Ram Wagon with 8,510 lbs. GVW package and rear doors with vented glass), includes three additional rear bench seats (second and third for three-passengers; fourth for four passengers) and spare tire carrier located under fourth bench seat. PROSPECTOR PACKAGES: (not available on Ram Value Wagon) Package 1: Automatic speed control; bright deluxe wheelcovers, front and rear bumpers, grille, 6 in. x 9 in. low-mount mirrors; 35-gallon fuel tank; Convenience Package. Package 2: All items in Package 1 plus: Bright bumper guards and black rub strips; Royal SE Decor Package. Package 3: All items in Package 2 plus: Front air conditioning; Power Convenience Package; tilt steering column (when ordered with automatic transmission); two-tone paint package. CONVENIENCE PACKAGE/POWER CONVENIENCE PACKAGE: Same as for vans. TWO-TONE PAINT PACKAGE: Bright taillight bezels; lower side and rear moldings; two-tone paint; upper side and rear moldings; the main color was used above the upper molding and below the lower molding, with the secondary color running in a wide band between the moldings. ROYAL SE PACKAGE: (not available Ram Value Wagon) bright bumpers, grille, moldings on lower bodyside and rear and around windshield and side and rear fixed windows (except driver and passenger door windows); bright taillight bezels; deluxe two-speed windshield wipers with intermittent wipe; leaping ram plaque on front door; cigar lighter light; color-keyed accessory type rubber floor mats on driver's compartment floor; color-keyed carpeting on floor, around engine housing cover and over fuel filler cover; color-keyed instrument panel lower side skirts; luxury steering wheel; spare tire carrier; courtesy stepwell light (front and side doors); dash liner insulation; dome/reading lamps; driver and front passenger reclining high-back Command bucket seats and rear bench seat(s) in color-keyed deluxe Kincaid cloth with Saddle Grain vinyl trim; front door armrests with bright trim; front door trim panel applique with pull strap; garnish trim for sliding side door track cover; glove box lock and light; ignition switch light and headlight symbol light with time delay (not available with tilt steering column); low washer fluid warning light; nameplate on instrument panel; soft cloth covered headliner with insulation; woodtone applique on lower face of instrument panel.

VAN/WAGON CONVENIENCE OPTIONS: Front air conditioning. Rear auxiliary air conditioning. 114-amp. alternator. 500-amp. battery. Bumper guards with black protective strips. Transmission oil to air auxiliary cooling. Maximum engine cooling. Rear window defroster. Single rear door with vented glass. Dual rear doors with vented glass. Engine block heater. 35-gallon fuel tank. Sunscreen privacy glass. Rear auxiliary heater. Dual bright low-mount exterior mirrors. Lower bodyside and rear moldings. Electronically tuned AM/FM stereo radio with four speakers. Electronically tuned AM/FM stereo with seek and scan, Dynamic Noise Reduction, cassette tape player with automatic reverse, and four speakers. Heavy-duty shocks. Automatic speed control. Tilt steering column. Deluxe wheelcovers. Argent painted steel spoke road type wheels with bright hub and trim rings. Deluxe windshield wipers with intermittent wipe.

NOTE: Ram Van and Wagon exterior colors for 1986 were: Light Ivory Cream, Light Blue Metallic, Forest Green Metallic, Burnished Silver Metallic, Charcoal Gray Metallic, Medium Tan Metallic, Walnut Brown Metallic, Black, Medium Blue Metallic, White, Crimson Red.

1986 Dodge Custom Ram Sweptline Pickup (DNP)

D100 PICKUP: Dodge "D" series pickups received an attractive facelift for 1986. The new grille consisted of four large slots. The headlight doors were of matching height, which made them appear to be part of the grille. The front bumper was also revised. D100 buyers had their choice of 6.5 ft. and 8 ft. Sweptline boxes. Among standard features were: Dry type air cleaners. 60-amp. alternator. Ashtray. 400-amp. maintenance-free battery. Power front disc brakes. Bright front bumper. Fasten seat belts, headlights-on, key-in-ignition warning buzzer. Cigar lighter. Coolant overflow reservoir. Corrosion protection. Insulated dash liner. Color-keyed armrest, inner trim panels, and door pull straps. Electronic ignition and voltage regulation system. Carpeting. 20-gallon fuel tank. Tinted glass. Glove box. Fresh air heater with defrosters. In cab hood release. Dual note electric horns. Wheelcovers. 10 in. day/night inside rearview mirror. Dual short-arm exterior rearview mirrors. Bright windshield molding. Color-keyed all-vinyl bench seat. Sun visors. Dual jet windshield washers. Two-speed windshield wipers. Four-speed manual transmission with overdrive.

I.D. DATA: The VIN consisted of 17 symbols. The first three symbols revealed manufacturer, make and vehicle type. The fourth symbol indicated GVW rating. The fifth, sixth and seventh symbols indicated series and body style. The eighth symbol indicated engine. The ninth symbol was a check digit. The 10th symbol indicated model year. The 11th symbol indicated assembly plant. The last six symbols were the sequential unit production number.

1986 Dodge Ram Sweptline Pickup (JAG)

Model	Body Type	Price	Weight	Prod. Total
(6.5 ft. box)				
D04	Sweptline Pickup	7291	3244	—
W04	Sweptline 4x4 Pickup	9802	3888	—
(8 ft. box)				
D04	Sweptline Pickup	7515	3545	—
W04	Sweptline 4x4 Pickup	9968	4013	—

NOTE: Model year production of D100/W100 not separately recorded.

ENGINE (D100): 3.7L (225 cid) Six-cylinder. Brake horsepower: 95 at 3600 rpm. Bore & stroke: 3.40 x 4.12 in. Compression ratio: 8.4:1. Carburetor: One-barrel.

D150 PICKUP: The D150 had most of the same features as the D100, but it could haul up to 1,000 lbs. more payload.

I.D. DATA: The VIN consisted of 17 symbols. The first three symbols revealed manufacturer, make and vehicle type. The fourth symbol indicated GVW rating. The fifth, sixth and seventh symbols indicated series and body style. The eighth symbol indicated engine. The ninth symbol was a check digit. The 10th symbol indicated model year. The 11th symbol indicated assembly plant. The last six symbols were the sequential unit production number.

Model	Body Type	Price	Weight	Prod. Total
(6.5 ft. box)				
D14	Sweptline Pickup	8010	3264	—
D14	Utiline Pickup	—	—	—
W14	Sweptline 4x4 Pickup	10,650	3909	—
W14	Utiline 4x4 Pickup	—	3888	—
(8 ft. box)				
D14	Sweptline Pickup	8184	3364	—
D14	Utiline Pickup	—	3338	—
W14	Sweptline 4x4 Pickup	10,827	4043	—
W14	Utiline 4x4 Pickup	—	4013	—

NOTE 1: Total model year production of D150s was 64,597 trucks.
NOTE 2: Total model year production of W150s was 23,314 trucks.

ENGINE (D150): 3.7L (225 cid) Six-cylinder. Brake horsepower: 95 at 3600 rpm. Bore & stroke: 3.40 x 4.12 in. Compression ratio: 8.4:1. Carburetor: One-barrel.

D250 PICKUP: The 3/4-ton D250 had most of the same features as the D100, plus (or in place of): Larger brakes. Higher capacity rear axle and front and rear springs. A different (NP435) four-speed manual transmission. And a 9.0 dual diaphragm vacuum booster.

1986 Dodge Ram Royal SE Sweptline Pickup (DNP)

I.D. DATA: The VIN consisted of 17 symbols. The first three symbols revealed manufacturer, make and vehicle type. The fourth symbol indicated GVW rating. The fifth, sixth and seventh symbols indicated series and body style. The eighth symbol indicated engine. The ninth symbol was a check digit. The 10th symbol indicated model year. The 11th symbol indicated assembly plant. The last six symbols were the sequential unit production number.

Model	Body Type	Price	Weight	Prod. Total
(131 in. w.b.)				
D24	Chassis & Cab	10,479	3459	—
W24	Chassis & Cab (4x4)	12,388	—	—
D24	Sweptline Pickup	9333	3764	—
W24	Sweptline 4x4 Pickup	11,312	4184	—
D24	Utiline Pickup	—	3734	—
W24	Utiline 4x4 Pickup	—	4154	—

NOTE 1: Total model year production of D250s was 13,382 trucks.
NOTE 2: Total model year production of W250s was 10,004 trucks.

ENGINE (D250): 3.7L (225 cid) Six-cylinder. Brake horsepower: 95 at 3600 rpm. Bore & stroke: 3.40 x 4.12 in. Compression ratio: 8.4:1. Carburetor: One-barrel.

D350 PICKUP: The 1-ton D350 pickup shared most standard features with the D250. However, it had a greater payload capacity.

I.D. DATA: The VIN consisted of 17 symbols. The first three symbols revealed manufacturer, make and vehicle type. The fourth symbol indicated GVW rating. The fifth, sixth and seventh symbols indicated series and body style. The eighth symbol indicated engine. The ninth symbol was a check digit. The 10th symbol indicated model year. The 11th symbol indicated assembly plant. The last six symbols were the sequential unit production number.

Model	Body Type	Price	Weight	Prod. Total
D350 Series — 131 in. w.b.				
D34	Chassis & Cab	10,976	3499	—
(8 ft. box)				
D34	Sweptline Pickup	11,311	4093	—
W34	Sweptline 4x4 Pickup	—	4229	—
(135 in. w.b.)				
D350	Chassis & Cab	11,256	3848	—
(159 in. w.b.)				
D350	Chassis & Cab	11,343	3918	—

NOTE 1: Total model year production of D350s was 7,543 truck.
NOTE 2: Total model year production of W350s was 744 trucks.

1986 Dodge Power Ram Royal SE Sweptline Pickup (DNP)

ENGINE (D350): 5.9L (360 cid) V-8. Brake horsepower: 185 at 4000 rpm. Bore & stroke: 4.00 x 3.58 in. Compression ratio: 8.0:1. Carburetor: Four-barrel.

CHASSIS FEATURES: Wheelbase: 115 in. (D100/D150); 131 in. (all); 135 in. (D350); 159 in. (D350). GVW: 4,950-5,000 (D100); 4,950-6,050 (D150); 6,300-6,400 (W100/W150); 6,600-8,510 (D250); 6,900-8,510 (W250); 8,700-10,500 (D350); 10,100-11,000 (W350). Tires: P195/75R x 15 (D100/D150); LT215/85R x 16C (D250); LT235/85R x 16E (D350).

POWERTRAIN OPTIONS: 5.2L (318 cid) two-barrel V-8 (D100/D150/D250); 5.9L (360 cid) four-barrel V-8. Four-speed automatic transmission.

OPTION PACKAGES: FOUR-WHEEL DRIVE: (W100/W150/W250 pickups; W250/W230 Chassis with cab): Ram Trac part time four-wheel drive system (lets driver shift from two-wheel drive to four-wheel drive while traveling at up to 55 mph); power steering; two speed transfer case; Power Ram fender emblems. HEAVY-DUTY PACKAGE: Front stabilizer bar, heavy-duty shocks. POWER CONVENIENCE PACKAGE: Power door locks, power front door windows. LIGHT PACKAGE: Ash receiver light, exterior cargo light, glove box lock and light, map light. TWO-TONE PAINT PACKAGE: (not available on chassis with cab models), Includes lower bodyside moldings with black vinyl inserts and bright partial wheel lip moldings; two-tone paint; upper side and rear exterior moldings. JOB-RATED PACKAGE: (not available with six-cylinder engine or on chassis with cab models) D250/W250 only: 114-amp. alternator, 500-amp. maintenance-free battery, front stabilizer bar, 30-gallon fuel tank, heavy-duty shocks, maximum engine cooling, 7,500 lbs. GVW, argent silver painted rear step bumper, transfer case skid plate (W250). PROSPECTOR PACKAGES: (Ram Sweptline pickups; D150/D250/D350/W150/W250) Package 1: Electronic tuning AM radio with integral digital clock; bright front bumper guards with black insert; bright deluxe wheelcovers; dual low-mount 6 in. x 9 in. mirrors; engine coolant temperature and oil pressure gauges; trip odometer, 30-gallon fuel tank, intermittent windshield wipers; light package; ram's head hood ornament. Package 2: All items in package 1 plus: Power convenience package, Royal SE Decor package. Package 3: All items in Package 2 plus: Air conditioning, two-tone paint package. SNO-COMMANDER PACKAGE LIGHT-DUTY: (W150/W150) front clearance and identification lights; hydroelectric controls; plow lights; power angling blade with blade markers; power lift with seven-way control valve; Sno-Commander decal on pickups; spare tire and wheel with 7,500 lbs. GVW package (W250 pickup only); transmission oil temperature light with automatic transmission. SNO-COMMANDER PACKAGE HEAVY DUTY: (W250/W350 models only) front clearance and identification lights; hydro-electric controls, plow lights; 96 in. long power angling blade with blade markers; power lift with seven way control valve; Sno-Commander decal on pickups; transmission oil temperature light with automatic transmission. ROYAL SE PACKAGE: (not available on D100/W100; power steering required on D150/D250 models), Includes bright drip rail and rear window molding; bright grille with bright insert and headlight bezels; bright tailgate applique panel with Dodge Ram nameplate; bright taillight housing; bright tailgate upper and lower moldings; front fender leaping ram plaque "Royal SE;" halogen headlights; ram's head hood ornament; bright doorsill scuff plate; color-keyed carpeting with underlayment; color-keyed cowl side trim panels; soft cloth headliner; upper greenhouse garnish moldings; vinyl door trim panels with woodtone trim, assists strap with bright trim, armrest, and carpeting on lower door; deluxe cloth with vinyl trim bench seats; electronically tuned AM radio with integral digital clock; Euro-sport steering wheel (black); hood inner panel insulation; nameplate on instrument panel; oil pressure and engine coolant temperature gauges; trip odometer; woodtone applique and bright trim on instrument panel.

1986 Dodge Ram Royal SE Sweptline Pickup (DNP)

CONVENIENCE OPTIONS: Air conditioning. 114-amp. alternator. Anti-spin rear axle. 500-amp. maintenance-free battery. Bright rear bumper. Step type rear bumper. Front bumper guards with black rub strip insert. Electronic digital clock integral with radio. Auxiliary transmission oil to air cooler. Maximum engine cooling. 30-gallon fuel tank. Engine block heater. Gauges for engine coolant temperature, fuel level, and oil pressure; ammeter; odometer; trip odometer, speedometer. Dual low-mount exterior mirrors. Lowerside and partial wheel lip moldings. Electronic tuning AM radio with integral digital clock. AM/FM stereo radio with integral digital clock. Automatic speed control. Power steering. Tilt steering column. Deluxe wheelcovers. Aluminum radial ribbed wheels (D150/W150 only). Argent silver painted steel spoke wheels with bright trim ring and hub center (D150/W150 only). Lockable sliding rear window. Two-speed windshield wipers with intermittent wipe.

NOTE: D series exterior colors for 1986 included: Black, Navy Blue Metallic, Cream, Medium Tan Metallic, Burnished Silver Metallic, Light Blue Metallic, Charcoal Gray Metallic, Canyon Red Metallic, Graphic Red, White.

HISTORICAL: Chrysler Corp. Truck Operations produced Dodge and Plymouth light-duty trucks in 1986. Patrick J. Keegan was general manager of truck operations. Charles Kitz was general marketing manager for trucks. Retail sales for the calendar year declined slightly from the record highs of the previous two years. A large part of the sales drop was related to the closing of the Dodge City factory to convert the assembly lines for production of the new Dakota pickup. The Dakota was introduced in the fall of 1986 as a 1987 model. Dodge and Plymouth continued to dominate the compact passenger van market. Model year production (U.S. and Canada for U.S. market) was 477,079 trucks. In addition, 68,800 Mitsubishi-built 1986 Ram 50s were made during the 1985-1986 calendar years.

FORD
1905-1986

1965 Ford Pickup

By Charles Webb

The first Ford commercial vehicle was the 1905 Delivery Car. It was essentially just a Model C automobile with a delivery top. This 10 hp vehicle cost nearly $1,000 and was discontinued at the end of the model year. From 1906 through 1911 people who wanted a Ford truck had to make it themselves. Many did. Thousands of Model C, N, and T autos were converted into commercial vehicles by their owners.

After two years of testing by John Wanamaker Stores in New York, and Bell Telephone Company branches all over the country, the Delivery Car was reintroduced in 1912. This time it was on a Model T chassis. Sales literature proclaimed it, "The car that delivers the goods. Tougher than an army mule and cheaper than a team of horses."

The 1-ton Model TT (Model T Ton) made its debut in 1917. However, aftermarket sources had been making such vehicles out of Model Ts earlier.

The first factory produced Ford Pickup arrived in the spring of 1925. It was basically a Model T Runabout with optional pickup box.

The light-duty Ford truck line was expanded in 1928, when the Model A debuted. Added to the catalog was a Delivery Car and Ford's first Panel truck. Also introduced was the Model AA 1-1/2-ton series.

A couple years later, in 1930, one of the rarest Fords ever appeared. This Town Car Delivery had an all-aluminum body and deluxe trim. Its Town Car inspired styling made it an ideal choice for exclusive shops or any business with snob appeal. Unfortunately, it was snubbed by the market and few were sold.

The big news for 1932 wasn't a new model, but the debut of a soon to be legendary powerplant; the Ford flathead V-8. However, it wasn't available on commercial vehicles until late in the model year and most 1932 Ford trucks had the four-cylinder engine.

Ford reintroduced an old idea in 1937. It was the Standard Coupe with pickup body and was offered in response to Chevrolet, who came out with a similar model the previous year. Sales were poor and it was discontinued at the end of the model year. Chevrolet kept building theirs until 1942, despite low demand.

In 1938, a series of 1-ton trucks joined the Ford light-duty truck line. A 3/4-ton series was added in late 1939. Ford made one of the best-looking 1/2-ton pickups of all time in 1940. Its front end styling was similar to, but not interchangeable with, the attractive passenger car. Even the cab was improved to give it a more car-like appearance.

In 1948, the F-1 was Ford's first truly new postwar vehicle. Handsome styling made it a standout from the start. In 1953, Ford stylists topped themselves with the beautiful F-100 series. Here was a truck anyone would be proud to park

In 1957, F-100 styling changed. The new models were attractive, but some said they lacked the classic beauty of their predecessors. Good news for the year was introduction of Ranchero. This unique vehicle was like nothing else on the road. It combined passenger car styling and interior appointments with pickup truck practicality. It would be two years before Chevrolet could catch up and offer a competitive model.

Year 1961 saw the introduction of the Econoline Van. This was one of the most significant vehicles of the postwar era. Not only did it have 39 percent more load space than a typical 1/2-ton Panel truck, but it was also easier to maneuver and could go almost twice as far on a gallon of gasoline. This was truly one of Ford's better ideas. Chevrolet came out with a Corvair-based van, in 1961, but it was the Econoline that set the standards in vans that other truck-makers (including Chevrolet) would copy.

By the 1970s, vans evolved from work vehicles into play machines for the young. Ford was first to offer a van especially for this market. In 1976, the Cruising Van came customized from the factory.

Another Ford truck, introduced in the 1960s, gained popularity in the 1970s. It was the Bronco 4x4 Sport Utility. The

first 1966 models were rather Spartan, even when fully-optioned. However, they became more luxurious as the years passed.

During the same period, Ford Pickups also evolved from being primarily work vehicles to, in some cases, replacements for the family car. It was not unusual, in the 1970s and 1980s, to see Pickups that were flashier and more pampered by their owners than passenger cars.

Ford entered the compact truck market in 1972 with the Mazda-built Courier. A decade later, it came out with a domestic-built small truck called the Ranger. The down-sized Bronco II was added to the light-duty truck line in 1984.

Ford's most radically new truck, in the 1980s, was the Aerostar. It was introduced in mid-1985 to compete with Chrysler's hot Caravan/Voyager mini-van. The Aerostar's distinctive areodynamic styling set it apart from other Ford light-duty trucks. Although it got off to a slow start, you can be sure the Aerostar will not only catch the competition, but maybe even surpass it.

1905 Ford Delivery Van (JAW)

1951 Ford 1/2-Ton F-1 Pickup (R. Forester)

1943 Ford Model GC 4x4 Military Cargo Express (OCW)

1952 Ford 1/2-Ton F-1 Pickup (JAW)

1948 Ford 1/2-Ton F-1 Pickup (OCW)

1955 Ford 1-Ton Forward-Control Parcel Delivery (S. Morgan/DB)

Standard Catalog of Light-Duty Trucks

1956 Ford 1/2-Ton F-100 Pickup (K. Leitgabel)

1956 Ford 1/2-Ton F-100 Pickup (JAW)

1957 Ford 1/2-Ton F-100 Panel (R. Warner)

1959 Ford Ranchero Custom Sedan-Pickup (DFW/GC)

Standard Catalog of Light-Duty Trucks

1964 Ford 1/2-Ton Falcon Club Wagon (JAW)

1967 Ford 1/2-Ton Econoline Panel Van (JAW)

1967 Ford 1/2-Ton Econoline Pickup (JAW)

1969 Ford 1/2-Ton Bronco Sport Utility (CW)

1971 Ford 3/4-Ton F-250 Sport Custom Styleside Pickup (JAW)

1975 Ford Ranchero 500 Sedan-Pickup (CW)

1976 Ford 1/2-Ton F-100 Ranger XLT Styleside Pickup (JAW)

1977 Ford 1/2-Ton F-150 Ranger XLT Styleside Pickup (JAW)

1984 Ford 1/2-Ton F-150 Ranger XLT Styleside Pickup (JAG)

1984 Ford Eddie Bauer Bronco II

1985 Ford F-150 Shortbed Stepside Pickup With Sport Package

1986 Ford F-Series XLT Lariat 4x2 Regular Cab Pickup

Standard Catalog of Light-Duty Trucks

1905 FORD

1905 Ford Model C Delivery Van (OCW)

FORD DELIVERY CAR: This vehicle shared most of its components with Ford's Model C passenger car. It came with a Dodge two-speed forward/one-speed reverse transmission with floor controls. There was also a cone clutch and drum brakes on the rear wheels. A nine-gallon fuel tank was provided. Chains drove the rear axle. The body was 42 in. long, 49 in. high and 40 in. wide. The Model E Delivery Car was only offered in 1905.

I.D. DATA: Serial numbers were mounted on the dash, next to the steering column.

Model	Body Type	Price	Weight	Prod. Total
T	Delivery Car	950	1350	10

ENGINE [Delivery Car]: Displacement: 120.5 cid. Two-cylinder. 10 hp. Bore & stroke: 4.25 in. x 4.5 in. Carburetor: Holley.

CHASSIS: Wheelbase: 78 in. Payload: 600-800 lbs. Tires: 2.5 in. wide.

OPTIONS: Lights.

1906-1908 FORD

MODEL N RUNABOUT: Buyers who wanted a Ford commercial vehicle from 1906 thru 1908, had to build one themselves. The Model N Runabout was a popular choice for light truck conversions. A distinctive feature of this vehicle was its plowshare front fenders. An item introduced in 1907 was the tub and fin radiator. The transmission was of the two-speed planetary type.

I.D. DATA: Serial numbers were mounted on the dash, next to the steering wheel.

Model	Body Type	Price	Weight	Prod. Total
N	Runabout	600	1050	—

ENGINE [Model N Runabout]: Displacement: 149 cid. Inline four-cylinder. 15 to 18 hp. Bore & stroke: 3-3/4 in. x 3-3/8 in. Carburetor: Holley.

CHASSIS: Wheelbase: 84 in. Tires: 30 in.

OPTIONS: Three-inch wheels. Bulb horn. Cowl lamps.

1909-1910 FORD

MODEL T CHASSIS: Once again, if you wanted a Ford truck you had to make it yourself. A Model T chassis was a good place to start. It featured front and rear transverse springs. One-piece steel engine pan. Non-tapered rear axles. I beam front axle. Brass radiator and lamps. Early 1909 Model Ts had square-tipped front fenders, built-in water pumps, two foot-pedals and two control levers. Later that year, rounded fenders with small "bills" were used. Also, the water pump was eliminated and three foot-pedals and one lever were used. The 1910 version was pretty much the same as late 1909 models, except for some changes in the rear axle.

Standard Catalog of Light-Duty Trucks

1910 Ford Model T Commercial Roadster (OCW)

I.D. DATA: Serial numbers for 1909 ranged from 1 to 11,145 (the early 1909 vehicles went up to 2,500). For 1910 the range was 11,146 to 31,532.

Model	Body Type	Price	Weight	Prod. Total
T	Chassis	—	900	—

1910 Ford Model T Wanamaker Canopy Express (OCW)

ENGINE: [Early 1909-serial number 2,500] Displacement: 176.7 cid. L-Head Four-cylinder. 22 hp at 1600 rpm. Bore & stroke: 3-3/4 in. x 4 in. Compression ratio: 4.5:1. Carburetors: Kingston 5-ball or Buffalo carburetor. [Late 1909-1910] The same basic engine, but cooled by thermo-syphon action.

CHASSIS: Wheelbase: 100 in. Length: 134.5 in. Tires: [Front] 30 x 3 in.; [Rear] 30 x 3.5 in.

OPTIONS: Windshield. Top. Gas headlights. Bumpers. Speedometer. Auto chimes. Prestolite tanks.

1911 FORD

1911 Ford Model T C-Cab Delivery Van (OCW)

MODEL T CHASSIS: If you wanted a Ford truck in 1911, you again had to make it yourself. The Model T chassis featured new wheels, fenders, radiator and front and rear axles.

I.D. DATA: Serial numbers began at approximately 31,533 and ran to about 70,749.

Model	Body Type	Price	Weight	Prod. Total
T	Chassis	—	940	248

ENGINE [Model T]: Displacement: 176.7 cid. L-Head Four-cylinder. 22 hp at 1600 rpm. Bore & stroke: 3-3/4 in. x 4 in. Compression ratio: 4.5:1. Carburetor: Kingston 5-ball; Holley 4500; or Holley H-14550.

CHASSIS: Wheelbase: 100 in. Length: 128 in. Tires: [Front] 30 x 3 in.; [Rear] 30 x 3.5 in.

1912 FORD

1912 Ford Model T C-Cab Delivery Van (DFW/PTC)

MODEL T COMMERCIAL ROADSTER: This model debuted and died in 1912. It featured a removable rumbleseat, curved rear fenders and front fenders in "lipped" or plain styles. It also had a one-piece dashboard.

MODEL T DELIVERY CAR: Also new this year was the Delivery Car. It had a wooden body and twin rear doors. Other standard items included: Speedometer; brass windshield frame; tool kit; three oil lamps; two six-inch gas lamps; horn; gas generator; and two-piece dashboard.

I.D. DATA [Model T]: Serial numbers ran from about 70,750 to approximately 157,424.

Model	Body Type	Price	Weight	Prod. Total
T	Chassis	—	940	2133
T	Commercial Roadster	590	—	13,376

(This includes the Torpedo Roadster.)

Model	Body Type	Price	Weight	Prod. Total
T	Delivery Car	700	—	1845

ENGINE [Model T]: Displacement: 176.7 cid. L-Head Four-cylinder. 22 hp at 1600 rpm. Bore & stroke: 3-3/4 in. x 4 in. Compression ratio: 4.5:1. Carburetor: Holley H-1 4550.

CHASSIS: Wheelbase: 100 in. Length: [Chassis] 128 in.; [Roadster, Delivery Car] 134.5 in. Tires: [Front] 30 x 3 in.; [Rear] 30 x 3.5 in.

1912 Ford Model T C-Cab Delivery Van (G. Teters)

1913-1916 FORD

1913 Ford Model T Depot Hack (OCW)

1913 Ford Model T Panel Delivery Van (OCW)

MODEL T DELIVERY CAR: This vehicle was withdrawn from the market early in the 1913 model year.

MODEL T CHASSIS: Ford went out of the truck business in 1913 and stayed out officially until 1917. However, that didn't stop customers from making their own trucks based on the Model T chassis, even though doing so voided their warranty. In fact, many aftermarket component suppliers produced form-a-truck kits specifically for the Model T Ford. Few changes were made to the Model T chassis during this period. Perhaps the most were made for 1915 models. These included: A different differential housing; new coils and coil box; lower louvered hood; ribbed transmission pedals; hand-operated Klaxon horn; round lensed tail and cowl lights; and lipped front fenders. In 1916, a steel hood replaced the aluminum one and the transmission cover was made of cast iron. Brass trim was replaced with less expensive materials. And metal, rather than wooden seat frames were used.

1914 Ford Model T Panel Delivery (OCW)

Standard Catalog of Light-Duty Trucks

I.D. DATA: The serial number and motor numbers were the same. The serial number was stamped on the left side of the block, directly over the water inlet. Do not confuse the serial number with the casting number of left side of block. The casting number indicates the date the cylinder block was cast (Example: 9-28-19 = Sept. 28, 1919). Numbers for 1913 models began at approximately 157,425 and ended at 248,735. For U.S.-built trucks made from Aug. 1, 1914 to April 30, 1915 the range was 539,001 to 742,313. For U.S. built trucks made from May 1, 1915 to July 31, 1915 the range was 773,488 to 855,500. For U.S. built trucks made from Aug. 1, 1915 to July 31, 1916 the range was approximately 855,501 to 1,362,714. For Canada the numbers were: [1913-1914] C-1501 to C-16500; [1914-1915] C-16501 to C-37,500; [1915-1916] C-37,501 to C-70,000.

1915 Ford Model T Canopy Top Express (DFW/HC)

1914 Ford Model T Canopy Express (DFW/PTC)

Model	Body Type	Price	Weight	Prod. Total
1913				
T	Delivery Car	625	—	513
T	Chassis	—	940	8438
1914				
T	Chassis	—	960	119
1915				
T	Chassis	410	980	13,459
1916				
T	Chassis	360	1060	11,742

1915 Ford Model T Panel Delivery Van (DFW/GFC)

1915 Ford Model T C-Cab Panel Side Delivery (OCW)

ENGINE [Model T]: Displacement: 176.7 cid. L-Head four-cylinder. 22 hp at 1600 rpm. Bore & stroke: 3-3/4 in. x 4 in. Compression ratio: 4.0:1. Carburetor: Holley S or Kingston Y (Holley G in 1914-1916).
CHASSIS: Wheelbase: 100 in. Length: 128 in. Tires: [Front] 30 x 3 in.; [Rear] 30 x 3.5 in.

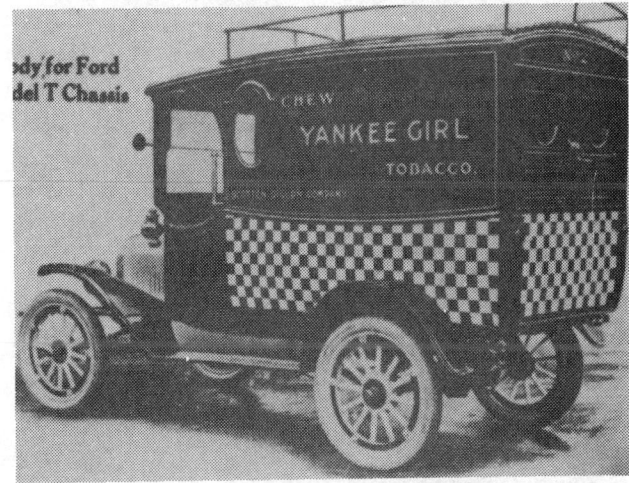

1916 Ford Model T Columbia Swell-side Panel (OCW)

1915 Ford Model T Closed Cab Express (DFW/BWW)

Standard Catalog of Light-Duty Trucks

1916 Ford Model T Open Express (DFW/RLC)

MODEL T CHASSIS: One of the most noticeable changes for 1917 was the discontinuance of the brass radiator. Other changes included: Revised windshield mounting base; nickel-plated hubcaps and steering gearbox; black radiator shell; new hood; and curved fenders. For 1919 models, the cover on the engine timing gear was changed, as were the front radius rod and rear axle.

1917 Ford Model T Panel Delivery Van (DFW/OHS)

I.D. DATA: The serial number and motor numbers were the same. The serial number was stamped on the left side of the block, directly over the water inlet. Do not confuse the serial number with the casting number of left side of block. The casting number indicates the date the cylinder block was cast (Example: 9-28-19 = Sept. 28, 1919). U.S. serial numbers: [Aug. 1, 1916-July 31, 1917] 1,362,714 to 2,113,501; [Aug. 1, 1917-July 31, 1918] 2,113,502 to 2,756,251; [Aug. 1, 1918-July 31, 1919] 2,756,252 to 3,277,851; [Aug. 1, 1919 -Dec. 31, 1919] 3,277,852 to 3,659,971. For Canada the numbers were: [1916-1917] C-70,001 to C-121,000; [1917-1918] C-121,001 to C-170,000; [1918-1919] C-170,001 to C-208,500.

Model	Body Type	Price	Weight	Prod. Total
1917				
T	Chassis	325	1060	41,165
1918				
T	Chassis	325	1060	37,648
1919				
T	Chassis	475	1060	47,125

1917 Ford Model T Roadster Pickup (OCW)

ENGINE [Model T]: Displacement: 176.7 cid. L-Head four-cylinder. 20 hp at 1600 rpm. Bore & stroke: 3-3/4 in. x 4 in. Compression ratio: 4.0:1. (1917-18). Carburetor: Kingston L2 or Holley G; [1919] Kingston L4 or Holley NH.

MODEL TT CHASSIS: Production of the new 1-ton chassis began on July 27, 1917. It was essentially a modified and beefed-up version of the Model T chassis. Standard features included: A 10-gal. gas tank; worm-drive rear axle; solid rubber tires; dual brake system; and cowl lamps. In mid-model year 1919, cowl lamps became optional. Also that year, Ford produced its 100,000th 1-ton chassis.

1918 Ford Model T Mifflinburg Model 200A Panel (OCW)

I.D. DATA: See Model T.

Model	Body Type	Price	Weight	Prod. Total
1917				
TT	Chassis	600	1450	3
1918				
TT	Chassis	600	1450	41,105
1919				
TT	Chassis	550	1477	70,816

ENGINE [Model TT]: Same as Model T.

1918 Ford Model T Fixed-Top Express (ATC/HE)

1919 Ford Model T Roadster Pickup (OCW)

CHASSIS: Wheelbase: [Model T] 100 in. [Model TT] 124 in. Length: [Model T] 128 in. Tires: [Front] 30 x 3 in.; [Rear] 30 x 3.5 in.
OPTIONS: Pneumatic tires (1919).

272

MODEL T CHASSIS: The Model T Chassis was basically the same as last year's version. However, some changes were made. Among them were a new 16 in. hard rubber steering wheel, lighter connecting rods and a stamped fan.

I.D. DATA: The serial number and motor numbers were the same. The serial number was stamped on the left side of the block, directly over the water inlet. Do not confuse the serial number with the casting number of left side of block. The casting number indicates the date the cylinder block was cast (Example: 9-28-19 = Sept. 28, 1919). U.S. serial numbers: [Jan. 1, 1920-Dec. 31, 1920] 3,659,972 to 4,698,419. For Canada the numbers were: [1919-1920] C-208,500 to C-262,500; [1920-1921] C-262501 to C-309,000.

Model	Body Type	Price	Weight	Prod. Total
T	Chassis	525	1060	35,092

ENGINE [Model T]: Displacement: 176.7 cid. L-Head four-cylinder. 20 hp at 1600 rpm. Bore & stroke: 3-3/4 in. x 4 in. Compression ratio: 4.0:1. Carburetor: Kingston L4 and Holley NH.

1921 Ford Model T Atlas 10-Passenger Bus Body (OCW)

MODEL T CHASSIS: Changes for 1921 included a slightly modified frame and different headlight lenses. Among the standard features on the Model T chassis were: Running-boards with aprons; a taillight; front fenders; two headlights; a horn; a hood; and a tool kit. In 1922, the rear axle was improved and a four-pinion differential replaced the two-pinion one.

I.D. DATA: The serial number and motor numbers were the same. The serial number was stamped on the left side of the block, directly over the water inlet. Do not confuse the serial number with the casting number of left side of block. The casting number indicates the date the cylinder block was cast (Example: 9-28-21 = Sept. 28, 1921). U.S. serial numbers: [Jan. 1, 1921-Dec. 31, 1921] 4,698,420 to 5,638,071. [Jan. 1, 1922-Dec. 31, 1922] 5,638,072 to 6,953,072. For Canada the numbers were: [1921-1922] C-309,001 to C-375,499.

Model	Body Type	Price	Weight	Prod. Total
1921				
T	Chassis	345	1060	36,792
1922				
T	Chassis	295	1060	38,541

NOTE 1: The 1922 production total includes worldwide production.

ENGINE [Model T]: Displacement: 176.7 cid. L-Head four-cylinder. 20 horsepower at 1600 rpm. Bore & stroke: 3-3/4 in. x 4 in. Compression ratio: 3.98:1. Carburetor: Kingston L4 or Holley NH.

MODEL TT CHASSIS: A feature introduced on the 1921 Model T/Model TT chassis was green visor headlight lenses. A large chunk of the upper headlight lense was tinted green, as a safety precaution to cut glare.

I.D. DATA [Model TT]: See Model T.

1920 Ford Model T Open Express (DFW/CL)

MODEL TT CHASSIS: Aside from a revised driveshaft coupling sleeve, the new Model TT chassis was pretty much left unchanged for 1920. As before, several aftermarket sources offered a wide variety of bodies for the Model TT and Model T chassis. This was the last year for the plain glass headlamp lenses.

I.D. DATA [Model TT]: See Model T truck I.D. data.

Model	Body Type	Price	Weight	Prod. Total
TT	Chassis	660	1477	135,002

NOTE: Production for Aug. 1, 1919 to July 30, 1920.

ENGINE [Model TT]: Same as Model T.

CHASSIS: Wheelbase: [Model T] 100 in. [Model TT] 124 in. Length: [Model T] 128 in. Tires: Model: T [Front] 30 x 3 in.; [Rear] 30 x 3.5 in.; Model TT: [Front] 30 x 3 in.; [Rear] 32 x 3.5 in.

OPTIONS: Starter. Demountable rims. Pneumatic rear tires. Speedometer.

1922 Ford Model T Roadster Pickup (OCW)

Model	Body Type	Price	Weight	Prod. Total
1921				
TT	Chassis	360	1477	42,860
1922				
TT	Chassis	390	1477	154,039

NOTE: Production figures for 1921 refer to domestic production from Aug. 1, 1920 to Dec. 31, 1921. The 1922 figure represents worldwide calender year production.

ENGINE [Model TT]: Same as Model T.

CHASSIS: Wheelbase: [Model T] 100 in. [Model TT] 124 in. Length: [Model T] 128 in. Tires: Model T: [Front] 30 x 3 in.; [Rear] 30 x 3.5 in.; Model TT: [Front] 30 x 3 in.; [Rear] 32 x 3.5 in.

OPTIONS: Starter. Demountable rims. 10 in. pinion rear axle.

1920 Ford Model T Closed Cab Express (OCW)

Standard Catalog of Light-Duty Trucks

1922 Ford Model T Enclosed Panel (Thomas E. Fall)

1923-1924 FORD

1923 Ford Model T Roaster Pickup (MTFCA)

MODEL T CHASSIS: Magneto headlamps and oil taillamps were a couple of standard features on the Model T chassis. In 1924, Ford began making its own truck bodies. These were dealer installed. Late in the year, the engine was improved with the use of lighter pistons. A distinguishing feature of 1924 Model Ts was their higher radiator and hood.

I.D. DATA: The serial number and motor numbers were the same. The serial number was stamped on the left side of the block, directly over the water inlet. Do not confuse the serial number with the casting number of left side of block. The casting number indicates the date the cylinder block was cast (Example: 9-28-23 = Sept. 28, 1923). U.S. serial numbers: [Jan. 1, 1923-Dec. 31, 1923] 6,953,072 to 9,008,371. [Jan. 1, 1924-Dec. 31, 1924] 9,008,372 to 10,999,901. For Canada the numbers were: [1922-1923] C-375,500 to C-458,599.

Model	Body Type	Price	Weight	Prod. Total
1923				
T	Chassis	235	1060	52,317
1924				
T	Chassis	230	1060	47,901

NOTE 1: Production figures are worldwide calendar year production.

ENGINE [Model T]: Displacement: 176.7 cid. L-Head four-cylinder. 20 hp at 1600 rpm. Bore & stroke: 3-3/4 in. x 4 in. Compression ratio: 4.0:1. Carburetor: Kingston L4 or Holley NH carburetor.

MODEL TT CHASSIS: Late 1923 Model TTs had an apron under the radiator. Among the Ford built bodies available in 1924 were: Express (Pickup) and Canopy Top trucks. Canopy models came with the sides either open, screened or curtained. Early 1924 Canopies were one-piece, but later in the year they were replaced by a two-piece design. Also available were Open Cab and Closed Cab models. The latter featured a sloping windshield and half-moon-shaped side openings which could be fitted with curtains.

1923 Ford Model T Police Paddy Wagon (JL)

I.D. DATA [Model TT]: See Model T.

Model	Body Type	Price	Weight	Prod. Total
1923				
TT	Chassis	380	1477	261,661
1924				
TT	Chassis	370	1477	204,851

NOTE 1: Figures for 1924 represent worldwide calendar year production.

ENGINE [Model TT]: Same as Model T engine.

1923 Ford Model T Closed-Cab Panel Delivery (DFW/TDB)

CHASSIS: Wheelbase: [Model T] 100 in. [Model TT] 124 in. Length: [Model T] 128 in.; Tires: Model T: [Front] 30 x 3 in.; [Rear] 30 x 3.5 in.; Model TT: [Front] 30 x 3 in.; [Rear] 32 x 4.5 in. rear.

1924 Ford Model T Panel Delivery (OCW)

OPTIONS: 30 x 5 in. eight-ply rear tires. 32 x 3.5 in. solid rubber tires. Battery. Starter. Generator. Demountable wheels. Truck rear bed.

274

1925 FORD

1926 Ford Model T Closed Cab Express (DFW/MQ)

1925 Ford Model T Express (OCW)

MODEL T RUNABOUT WITH PICKUP BODY: The first factory produced Ford Pickup truck was made April 15, 1925. Actually, the pickup box was an option for the Runabout. It had an adjustable tailgate, four stake pockets, heavy-duty rear springs and 8 in. (diameter) x 1.19 in. (wide) rear brake drums.

I.D. DATA: The serial number and motor numbers were the same. The serial number was stamped on the left side of the block, directly over the water inlet. Do not confuse the serial number with the casting number of left side of block. The casting number indicates the date the cylinder block was cast (Example: 9-28-25 = Sept. 28, 1925). U.S. serial numbers: [1925] 10,999,901-12,218,728; Canadian serial numbers: [1924-1925] 458,600 and up.

Model	Body Type	Price	Weight	Prod. Total
T	Chassis	225	1060	6523
T	Pickup	281	1471	33,795

NOTE 1: The chassis production figures represent worldwide calendar year production.

ENGINE [Model T]: Displacement: 176.7 cid. L-Head four-cylinder. 20 hp at 1600 rpm. Bore & stroke: 3-3/4 in. x 4 in. Compression ratio: 3.98:1. Carburetor: Kingston L4 or Holley NH.

MODEL TT TRUCK CHASSIS: Optional for the first time was a Ford produced Closed Cab body and a hand-operated windshield wiper. Like the Model T, the Model TT had an improved lubrication system and a 5-to-1 steering ratio. This steering ratio was optional at first. It was later made standard. The Model TT had 12 in. (diameter) x 2 in. (wide) rear brake drums.

I.D. DATA [Model TT]: See Model T.

Model	Body Type	Price	Weight	Prod. Total
TT	Chassis	365	1477	249,406

NOTE 1: The production figures refer to worldwide calendar year production.

ENGINE [Model TT]: Same as Model T.

CHASSIS: Wheelbase: [Model T] 100 in. [Model TT] 124 in. Tires: [Front] 30 x 3 in.; [Rear] 30 x 3.5 in.

OPTIONS: 30 x 5 in. rear tires. Battery headlamps. Starter. Demountable wheels. Oil lamp. Open cab. Express Canopy. Curtained Canopy. Closed Cab. Screened Ccanopy. Stake or Grain sides. Windshield wiper. Open Cab Pickup body for Runabout. Truck rear bed.

1926-1927 FORD

MODEL T RUNABOUT WITH PICKUP BODY: The new Runabout was introduced in July of 1925. It had wider runningboards; nickel-plated headlight rims; 11 in. rear brake drums; a 1-1/2 in. lower chassis; revised fenders; modified springs and front spindles; more louvers on the sides of the hood; vented cowl; and higher radiator. The slightly different pickup box was changed so a canopy top could be added. When purchased separately, the box was painted black. However, factory assembled models were painted Commercial green. In March of 1927, buyers were given three new colors to chose from: black, blue or brown.

1926 Ford Model T C-Cab Delivery Van (DFW)

I.D. DATA: The serial number and motor numbers were the same. The serial number was stamped on the left side of the block, directly over the water inlet. Do not confuse the serial number with the casting number of left side of block. The casting number indicates the date the cylinder block was cast (Example: 9-28-26 = Sept. 28, 1926). U.S. serial numbers: [1926] 12,218,729 to 14,049,029; [1927] 14,049,030 to 15,006,625. Canadian numbers no longer available.

Model	Body Type	Price	Weight	Prod. Total
1926				
T	Chassis	290	1250	—
1927				
T	Chassis	300	1250	—
1926				
T	Pickup	366	1745	75,406
1927				
T	Pickup	381	1745	28,142

ENGINE [Model T]: Displacement: 176.7 cid. L-Head four-cylinder. 22 hp at 1600 rpm. Bore & stroke: 3-3/4 in. x 4 in. Compression ratio: 3.98:1. Carburetors: Kingston L4; Holley NH; Holley Vaporizer; or Kingston Regenerator.

1926 Ford Model T Roadster Pickup (OCW)

CHASSIS [Model TT]: As before, the Model TT 1-ton truck chassis was available with several optional bodies. Balloon front and rear tires became standard in mid-1926.

I.D. DATA [Model TT]: See Model T.

Model	Body Type	Price	Weight	Prod. Total
1926				
TT	Chassis	365	1477	228,496
1927				
TT	Chassis	325	1477	83,202

ENGINE [Model TT]: Same as Model T.

1927 Ford Model T Roadster Pickup (OCW)

CHASSIS: Wheelbase: [Model T] 100 in.; [Model TT] 124 in. Tires: [Early 1926] 30 x 3.5 in.; [Late 1926] 29 x 4.40 balloon type.

OPTIONS: Pickup Windshield wiper. Front and rear bumpers. Rearview mirror. 29 x 4.40 balloon tires [early 1926]. Closed Cab body. Open Cab body. Platform Express body. Curtained Canopy body. Oversized rear tires. Starter. Oil cowl lamp. Stake body.

1928 FORD

1928 Ford Model A Roadster Pickup (HACJ)

MODEL A PICKUP: Essentially, this was a Model A chassis with a Model T Runabout Pickup body added. Only the Open Cab was offered until August, 1928. Then, a Closed Cab was made available. In midyear, the service brakes were separated from the parking brakes and the taillight was relocated. The Model A Pickup had a red phenolic steering wheel and in the center of the radiator was the new Ford script-in-oval emblem. Trucks made later in the year had higher hood louvers than early 1928 models. The interior trim was brown. The wood floors were made of beech, birch, maple, pine or oak. Like the metal skid strips, they were painted body color.

276

1928 Ford Model A Produce Truck (OCW)

DELUXE DELIVERY CAR: Basically, this was a Model A Tudor Sedan with blanked-out rear side windows, a single rear door and two folding seats. It was offered in the same colors available on regular passenger cars. The spare tire was mounted in the left front fenderwell. A battery and ignition system replaced the Model Ts magneto ignition. The Deluxe Delivery Car (a.k.a. Sedan Delivery) had to be special-ordered.

1928 Ford Model AA Platform Stake Bed (IMSC)

MODEL A PANEL: This was Ford's first Panel truck. It wasn't introduced until late in the year. It had two rear doors and two folding seats. The body was made of steel with a wood frame. The cargo area was 46.5 in. high, 57 in. long and 50 in. wide. A fifth (spare) wheel, rearview mirror and hand-operated windshield wiper were standard.

1928 Ford Model A Closed Cab Pickup (OCW)

I.D. DATA [Model A]: Serial numbers on left side of engine above water intake. Motor numbers are the same as serial numbers. Motor numbers, Oct. 20, 1927 to December 1928: 1 to 810,122.

Model	Body Type	Price	Weight	Prod. Total
A	Chassis	325	1633	—
A	Open Cab Pickup	395	2063	—
A	Closed Cab Pickup	445	2073	26,179
A	Sedan Delivery	595	—	—
A	Panel	575	—	3744

1928 Ford Model A Deluxe Delivery (DFW/LS)

ENGINE [Model A]: Displacement: 200.5 cid. L-Head four-cylinder. 40 hp at 2200 rpm. Bore & stroke: 3-7/8 in. x 4-1/4 in. Compression ratio: 4.22:1. Carburetor: Two-barrel.
CHASSIS: Wheelbase: 103.5 in. Tires: 4.75 x 19 in. balloon.
OPTIONS: Pinstripes. Special paint. Screened partition Delivery Car body. Tire cover.
NOTE: Exterior colors for 1928 Ford Commercial vehicles were black or Ross Moss green.

1928 Ford Model A Closed Cab Pickup (OCW)

1929 FORD

1929 Ford Model A U.S. Mail Delivery Van (CE)

DELUXE DELIVERY CAR: According to sales literature, the new Deluxe Delivery Car was designed for use by exclusive shops and for speedy, safe deliveries of fragile merchandise. It closely followed the lines of the Ford sedan. The body was all-steel and the front end trim was nickel-plated. There were two folding seats in the driver's compartment. They were upholstered in brown cross-cobra-grain artificial leather. The large rear door had a window in it to aid visibility. The cargo area was lined with cardboard. The Deluxe Delivery Car was

Standard Catalog of Light-Duty Trucks

available in three exterior colors. The roof covering was made of imitation black leather. There was a dome light on the windshield header.

1929 Ford Model A Deluxe Sedan Delivery (OCW)

MODEL A PICKUP: About the only difference in the 1929 Pickup was a new black steering wheel. The tailgate and enclosed cab were made of steel. The Open Cab version had an easy-to-remove top and side curtains. Its doors were similar to those used on the roadster. The one-piece windshield was made of shatter-proof glass and could be tilted in or out for ventilation. The heavy floor boards had steel batten-strips to withstand wear. The radiator shell was black. The bumper was nickel-plated.

1929 Ford Model A Closed Cab Express (M. Quesques)

MODEL A PANEL DELIVERY: You'd have to look under the hood to find much of anything new on the 1929 Panel. Like the passenger cars, it had a larger three-brush generator. The Panel Delivery was built of steel with the roof covered with bright black, heavy-coated rubber material. Double doors at the rear gave a wide opening for loading. And the small window in each door aided in visibility. There were two folding seats in the driver's compartment. A dome light was standard. The radiator shell and headlights were black.

1929 Ford Model A Closed Cab Pickup (GCC)

I.D. DATA: Serial numbers on left side of engine above water intake. Motor numbers are the same as serial numbers. Motor numbers: [Jan. 1, 1929-Dec. 31, 1929] 810,123 to 2,675,999.

Model	Body Type	Price	Weight	Prod. Total
A	Chassis	350	1650	—
130A	Sedan Delivery	550	2282	—
A	Open Cab Pickup	430	2130	—
78A	Closed Cab Pickup	460	2219	77,917
79A	Panel	590	2417	—

NOTE 1: Prices fluctuated during the model year.

1929 Ford Model A Roadster Pickup (OCW)

ENGINE [Model A]: Displacement: 200.5 cid. L-Head four-cylinder. 40 hp at 2200 rpm. Bore & stroke: 3-7/8 in. x 4-1/4 in. Compression ratio: 4.22:1. Carburetor: Two-barrel.

CHASSIS: Wheelbase: 103.5 in. Tires: 4.75 x 19 in. balloon.

1929 Ford Model A Closed Cab Pickup (Bob Strand)

OPTIONS: Rearview mirror. Removable tray (Delivery Car). Pinstripes. Special paint. Screened partition (Delivery Car).

NOTE: Exterior colors for 1929 Ford commercial vehicles were: Black, Commercial drab, L'Anse dark green, Gunmetal blue, Rock Moss green.

1929 Ford Model AA Roadster Pickup (James Leake)

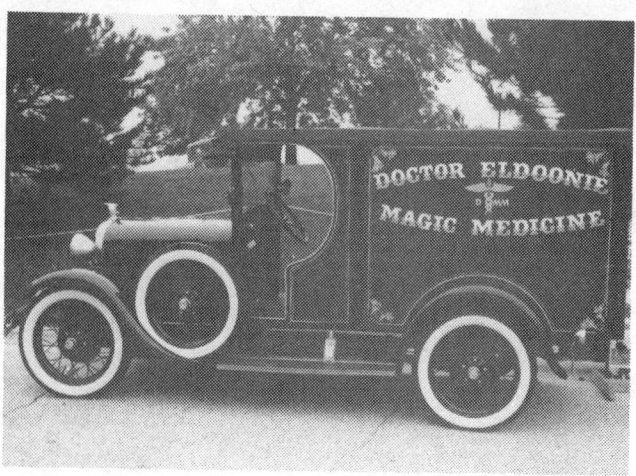

1929 Ford Model A C-Cab Panel Delivery (DE)

1929 Ford Model A Panel Delivery (George Davis)

1929 Ford Model AA Panel Delivery (OCW)

1929 Ford Model A Commercial Station Wagon (OCW)

Standard Catalog of Light-Duty Trucks

1930 FORD

1930 Ford Model A Open Cab Pickup (OCW)

MODEL A PICKUP: Early 1930 pickups were just leftover 1929 models. It wasn't until mid-year that a new truck-line was really introduced. Styling resembled the previous year's models. However, the 1930 version had Roadster type doors, wider fenders and a one-piece flat-folding windshield. The radiator shell and headlight pods were black. Early models had black cowl strips. On later models the cowl strips were painted body color. The spare tire was carried in a front fender well. The runningboards had an embossed, non-skid surface. The pickup box was carried over from 1929. Its hardwood floors were painted body color. The top was covered with rubber covered fabric. Upholstery was black cobra-cross-grain imitation leather. The headlining was also black. Both Open and Closed Cab models were available

1930 Ford Model A U.S. Mail Delivery Truck (OCW)

TOWN CAR DELIVERY: This is one of the rarest production Fords ever made. It looked like a Town Car with blanked-out rear quarter windows. It had a convertible top over the driver's section, carriage lights on the side, cowl lamps and stainless steel trim on the front end. The top was covered with black artificial leather. The wheels were painted the same color as the paint stripe. A unique feature of this vehicle was its all-aluminum body.

1930 Model A Ford Sedan Delivery (OCW)

Standard Catalog of Light-Duty Trucks

DELUXE DELIVERY CAR: The Delivery Car was, at last, more than a customized Tudor Sedan with no rear quarter windows. It now had its own distinctive body that could hold longer and wider loads. The Deluxe Delivery Car could be ordered in the same colors offered on passenger cars. The cowl molding, headlight pods and radiator shell were stainless steel. Masonite and steel paneling was used in the interior. Also inside were two seats with a tool box under them and a dome light behind.

1930 Ford Model A Canopy Express (MES/DFW)

PANEL: The new Model A Panel featured: A black-enamelled radiator shell and headlight pods; nearly foot-high steel plates inside (with wood slats above) to protect the interior from the cargo; two folding front seats; an outside sunvisor; dome light; fender well spare tire carrier; and a spacious cargo area that was 46.4 in. wide and over 59 in. long. It also had a two-bar, chrome plated bumper until August, 1930, when it was replaced by a single-bar bumper painted black. The taillight was located on the side of the body until the fall of 1930.

1930 Ford Model A Closed Cab Pickup (G. Larsen)

I.D. DATA [Model A]: Serial numbers on left side of engine above water intake. Motor numbers are the same as serial numbers. Engine numbers from Jan. 1, 1930 to Dec. 31, 1930: 2,676,000 to 4,237,500.

Model	Body Type	Price	Weight	Prod. Total
A	Chassis	345	1650	—
295A	Town Car Delivery	—	—	3
130B	Sedan Delivery	545	2282	4629
78A	Open Cab Pickup	425	2073	3429
82B	Closed Cab Pickup	435	2215	86,383
79B	Panel Delivery	590	2416	—

NOTE 1: The Sedan Delivery is also known as the Deluxe Delivery.

ENGINE [Model A]: Displacement: 200.5 cid. L-Head four-cylinder. 40 hp at 2200 rpm. Bore & stroke: 3-7/8 in. x 4-1/4 in. Compression ratio: 4.22:1. Carburetor: Two-barrel.

CHASSIS: Wheelbase: 103.5 in. Tires: 4.75 x 19 balloon.

OPTIONS: Rearview mirror. Removable tray (Delivery Car). Special paint. Screen partition (Delivery Car).

NOTE: Ford trucks in 1930 were offered in black, Blue rock green, Menelas orange, Phoenix brown, Pegex orange, Rock Moss green and Rubellite red.

1931 FORD

1931 Ford Model A Sedan Delivery (OCW)

DELUXE DELIVERY: Although the Deluxe Delivery had a distinctive body, it used passenger car stainless steel trim on the cowl molding, radiator shell and headlamps. A new rear door lock was introduced early in the model year. A formerly optional partition and shelving unit became standard. A drop floor version of this vehicle was added later in the year, but proved unpopular. It had a door-mounted taillight, headlining and no rear bumpers.

1931 Ford Model AA Panel Delivery (OCW)

TOWN CAR DELIVERY: The most prestigious Ford commercial vehicle was the aluminum-bodied Town Car Delivery. It had a canopy roof over the driver's compartment; new sloping windshield; carriage lamps; stainless steel front end trim; cowl lamps; bright metal spare tire cover bands; two dome lights; two black leather upholstered seats with a sliding door behind them; and twin fender wells. The first 50 Town Car Deliveries came with brown carpeting. Customers could choose from 40 exterior colors.

1931 Ford Model A Model 66A Deluxe Pickup (F.S. Soden)

SPECIAL DELIVERY: This was essentially a Ford station wagon with blanked-out rear windows and two doors instead of four. The body was made of maple and birch, with bass-

wood roof slats. On the inside were imitation leather seats. The hood, cowl and windshield frame were painted Manilla brown. There was a partition behind the front seats and fixed glass in the rear windows. This vehicle has also been called the Natural Wood Panel Delivery.

1931 Ford Model A Model 66A Deluxe Pickup (F.S. Soden)

DELUXE PICKUP: A distinctive feature of this model was its integral-style, wood-lined cargo box with chrome-plated brass rails on the upper part of the sides. The standard cowl lamps also gave it a refined touch. Most of these trucks were built for the Refrigeration Div. of General Electric. It was only offered with a Closed Cab body.

1931 Ford Model A Closed-Cab Pickup (CE)

MODEL A PICKUP: The type 78B Pickup debuted in mid-model year. It had nearly five more cubic-feet of cargo space than the 1930 version. The 16-gauge steel floor had a sub-floor of hardwood. New for 1931 were the fenders and one-piece splash guard shields.

DROP FLOOR PANEL: This was a new model for 1931. It was designed for customers who wanted more interior height. A section of the floor was dropped to about the center of the axle. The rear door panels were lined with Masonite until October, 1931, when they were replaced with steel panels.

1931 Ford Model A Fire Squad Truck (OCW)

PANEL: The Model A Panel featured: A black-enamelled radiator shell and headlight pods; nearly foot-high steel plates inside (with wood slats above) to protect the interior from the cargo; two folding front seats; an outside sunPvisor; dome light; fender well spare tire carrier; and a spacious cargo area that was 46.4 in. wide and over 59 in. long. It also had a single-bar bumper painted black. The taillight was located on the rear of the body.

I.D. DATA [Model A]: Serial numbers on left side of engine above water intake. Motor numbers are the same as serial numbers. Engine numbers from Jan. 1, 1931 to Dec. 31, 1931: 4,237,501 to 4,826,746.

Model	Body Type	Price	Weight	Prod. Total
A	Chassis	340	1680	—
295A	Town Car Delivery	1150	—	196
255A	Natural Wood Panel	615	2470	Note 1
66A	Deluxe Pickup	—	—	293
78B	Closed Cab Pickup	455	2215	98,166
—	Open Cab Pickup	425	2104	Note 2
225A	Drop Floor Panel	560	2568	1954
79B	Panel	535	2500	8282
130B	Deluxe Delivery	540	2465	9606

NOTE 1: Natural wood Panel: 19 made in December 1930; 841 in 1931; 40 in 1932.
NOTE 2: Open Cab Pickup bodies were used on 2,637 of the 98,166 Pickups.
NOTE 3: Production of 77 Drop Floor Panels is also included in above totals.

ENGINE [Model A]: Displacement: 200.5 cid. L-Head four-cylinder. 40 hp at 2200 rpm. Bore & stroke: 3-7/8 in. x 4-1/4 in. Compression ratio: 4.22:1. Carburetor: Two-barrel.

CHASSIS: Wheelbase: 103.5 in. Payload: [Pickup] 750 lbs. Tires: 5.00 x 19 in.

OPTIONS: Canopy top with side curtains (this top was modified when the new, larger pickup box was introduced in May of 1931). Spare tire (a spare wheel was standard). Special paint. Rearview mirror.

NOTE: 1931 Ford trucks were offered in 38 colors, including Yukon yellow, Menelous orange and Rubellite red.

1932 FORD

1932 Ford V-8 Standard Panel Delivery (J. Neal East)

SEDAN DELIVERY CAR: This was essentially what its name implied, a sedan converted into a delivery car. It featured a Deluxe Tudor Sedan body shell with blanked-out rear quarter windows and a 36 in. wide by 34 in. high rear door. The spare tire was carried in a front fender well. Early models had a hood with 20 louvers. Later 1932 model hoods had 25 louvers. This was done to improve engine cooling, a problem fairly common to models equipped with the new flathead V-8. However, a majority of 1932 Sedan Deliveries were powered by the four-cylinder engine.

I.D. DATA: Serial numbers on left side of engine above water intake. Motor numbers are the same as serial numbers. Numbers used: [Four-cylinder] B-5,000,000 and up; [V-8] 18-1 and up.

Model	Body Type	Price	Weight	Prod. Total
Series B Sedan Delivery — 1/2-Ton — 106.5 in. w.b. — Four				
68	Sedan Delivery	520	2628	401
Series B18 Sedan Delivery — 1/2-Ton — 106.5 in. w.b. — V-8				
B18	Sedan Delivery	570	2733	401

ENGINE: Displacement: 200.5 cid. L-Head four-cylinder. 50 hp at 2800 rpm. Bore & stroke: 3-7/8 in. x 4-1/4 in. Compression ratio: 4.6:1. Carburetor: Two-barrel Zenith or Holley.

ENGINE: Displacement: 221 cid. L-Head V-8. 65 hp at 3400 rpm. Bore & stroke: 3-1/16 x 3-3/4 in. Compression ratio: 5.5:1. Carburetor: One-barrel.

MODEL B PICKUP: Big news for 1932 was the introduction of Ford's V-8. However, it wasn't made available for commercial vehicles until late in the model year. So, most 1932 Ford Pickups were powered by the four-cylinder engine. Styling refinements were similar to those on the passenger car line, although the body was lengthened by almost 10 in. The spare tire was mounted in the front fender well. The grille and headlight pods were black. Buyers could choose from either Open or Closed Cab versions. A three-speed manual transmission was standard.

Standard Catalog of Light-Duty Trucks

1932 Ford United Parcel Service Delivery Van (DFW/UPS)

MODEL B STANDARD PANEL DELIVERY: The new Panel Delivery was more than a foot longer than the previous year's model. It was also nearly two inches wider, but just a fraction of an inch higher on the inside. It had all-steel construction, a 17-gal. fuel tank and a sloping windshield. Unlike the Pickup, it no longer had an outside windshield visor. The vast majority were powered by the four-cylinder engine.

DELUXE PANEL DELIVERY: This was Ford's fanciest light-duty Panel. It had the same features as the standard version, plus stainless steel cowl lights and headlights; bright-trimmed grille; high-polish exterior paint; and chrome-plated front bumper, windshield wiper and rearview mirror. Masonite paneling lined the interior.

I.D. DATA [Model B]: See Sedan Delivery I.D. Data.

See Sedan Delivery.

Model	Body Type	Price	Weight	Prod. Total
Series B — 1/2-Ton — 106.5 in. w.b. — Four				
18	Chassis	320	1688	—
76	Open Cab Pickup	410	2257	593
82	Closed Cab Pickup	435	2366	—
79	Standard Panel	520	2620	—
79	Deluxe Panel	540	2650	392
—	Station Wagon	600	2505	—
Series B18 — 1/2-Ton — 106.5 in. w.b. — V-8				
18	Chassis	370	1798	—
76	Open Cab Pickup	460	2367	593
82	Closed Cab Pickup	485	2476	—
79	Standard Panel	570	2755	—
79	Deluxe Panel	590	2815	392
—	Station Wagon	650	2635	—

ENGINE [Series B]: Displacement: 200.5 cid. L-Head four-cylinder. 50 hp at 2800 rpm. Bore & stroke: 3-7/8 in. x 4-1/4 in. Compression ratio: 4.6:1. Carburetor: Two-barrel Zenith or Holley.

ENGINE [Series B18]: Displacement: 221 cid. L-Head V-8. 65 hp at 3400 rpm. Bore & stroke: 3-1/16 x 3-3/4 in. Compression ratio: 5.5:1. Carburetor: One-barrel.

1932 Ford Model B Closed Cab Pickup (OCW)

CHASSIS: Wheelbase: 106 in. Tires: 5.25 x 18 in.

OPTIONS: Spare tire. Spare tire cover. Outside rearview mirror. Special paint.

HISTORICAL: Also introduced this year was the Model BB 1- to 1-1/2-ton truck chassis. It was offered in both the four-cylinder ($470 /2,738 lbs.) and V-8 ($520/2,858 lbs.) lines. A deluxe version was sold for $30 more. The deluxe equipment added about 77 lbs. to the weight of the Model BB.

1933 Ford Model 46 Model 850 Sedan Delivery (LS/DFW)

SEDAN DELIVERY: The Sedan Delivery had a distinctive body of its own in 1933. However, it still shared the passenger car's styling and included: A new slanted radiator with vertical bars; acorn-shaped headlight shells; a one-piece bumper with a center dip; and rear-slanting hood louvers. The instrument panel had a round 90 mph speedometer and was mounted directly in front of the steering wheel. The driver's bucket seat was fully adjustable and upholstered to match all other interior trim. The insulating board side panels and durable imitation leather headlining were finished in dark brown. The rear door glass could be lowered. A floor-shifted three-speed manual transmission was standard.

1933 Ford Model V8-46 Model 830 Closed Cab Pickup (OCW)

I.D. DATA: Serial number and motor number are the same. Serial/motor number location: [Four] Top of frame, ahead of dash. Also left side of flywheel housing. [V-8] Top of frame, left side near dash. Also top of clutch housing. Beginning engine numbers: [Four] 5,185,849; [V-8] 18-2031127. Ending numbers not available.

Model	Body Type	Price	Weight	Prod. Total
Series 46 — 1/2-Ton — 112 in. w.b. — Four				
68	Sedan Delivery	520	2628	—
Series V8-46 — 1/2-Ton — 112 in. w.b. — V-8				
68	Sedan Delivery	570	2733	—

NOTE 1: Data is for the four-cylinder model.

1933 Ford Model V8-46 Roadster Pickup (OCW)

ENGINE [Sedan Delivery]: Displacement: 200.5 cid. L-Head four-cylinder. 50 hp at 2800 rpm. Bore & stroke: 3-7/8 in. x 4-1/4 in. Compression ratio: 4.6:1. Zenith or Holley Carburetor: Two-barrel.

ENGINE [Sedan Delivery]: Displacement: 221 cid. L-Head. V-8. 75 hp at 3800 rpm. Bore & stroke: 3-1/16 x 3-3/4 in. Compression ratio: 6.3:1. Carburetor: One-barrel.

PICKUP: The 1933 Ford Pickup resembled the previous year's model, although it did have a longer wheelbase. It could be had in either Closed or Open Cab. Close-fitting side curtains were available for the Open Cab. The floor was made of steel with pressed in skid strips. There was a wood under-floor. The steel tailgate had three hinges. Sturdy corner braces supported the sides and flare boards. A floor-shifted three-speed manual transmission was standard. The front bumper was black.

1933 Ford Model V8-46 Model 850 Sedan Delivery (OCW)

STANDARD PANEL DELIVERY: The 1933 Panel Delivery had less rear overhang than the 1932 version. The quarter panels were also revised a bit and the radiator was slanted back. There was a right-hand fender well for the spare tire. The interior featured a hardwood floor interlocked with metal skid strips. There were steel panels on the lower portion of the sides and hardwood slats on the remaining area. A one-piece welded frame held the two steel rear doors. The body had a glossy satin finish.

DELUXE PANEL DELIVERY: Some items that set the Deluxe models apart from standard versions were: Cowl lamps; side panel moldings; highly-polished finish; chrome-plated rearview mirror; windshield wiper and front bumper; Masonite interior side panels; and insulated roof lined with artificial leather.

I.D. DATA: Serial number and motor number are the same. Serial/motor number location: [Four] Top of frame, ahead of dash. Also left side of flywheel housing. [V-8] Top of frame, left side near dash. Also top of clutch housing. Beginning engine numbers: [Four] 5,185,849; [V-8] 18-2031127. Ending numbers not available.

1933 Ford Model BB With Bakery Truck Body (OCW)

Model	Body Type	Price	Weight	Prod. Total
Series 46 — 1/2-Ton — 112 in. w.b. — Four				
810	Chassis & Cab	320	1688	—
820	Panel	510	2615	—
820	Deluxe Panel	530	2615	—
830	Pickup	430	2386	—
Series V8-46 — 1/2-Ton — 112 in. w.b. — V-8				
810	Chassis & Cab	370	1798	—
820	Panel	560	2750	—
820	Deluxe Panel	580	2780	—
830	Pickup	480	2496	—

ENGINE [Model 46]: Displacement: 200.5 cid. L-Head four-cylinder. 50 hp at 2800 rpm. Bore & stroke: 3-7/8 in. x 4-1/4 in. Compression ratio: 4.6:1. Zenith or Holley Carburetor: Two-barrel.

ENGINE [Model 46]: Displacement: 221 cid. L-Head. V-8. 75 horsepower at 3800 rpm. Bore & stroke: 3-1/16 in. x 3-3/4 in. Compression ratio: 6.3:1. Carburetor: One-barrel.

CHASSIS: Wheelbase: 112 in. (Sedan Delivery) Length: 176 in.; Width: 57-3/8 in.; Height: 68 in. Tires: 5.50 x 17 in.

OPTIONS: Greyhound radiator ornament. Closed face metal tire cover. Bumper guards. Dual horns. Dual windshield wipers. Spotlight. 14 in. steel-spoked wheels. Special paint.

HISTORICAL: Also available this year was the Model BB 1- to 1-1/2-ton truck chassis. It was offered in both the four-cylinder ($470 /2,770 lbs.) and V-8 ($530/2,858 lbs.) lines. A deluxe version was sold for $30 more. The deluxe equipment added about 90 lbs. to the weight of the 1933 Model BB.

1934 FORD

1934 Ford Model V8-46 Model 820 Panel Delivery (OCW)

SEDAN DELIVERY: The 1934 Sedan Delivery had a slightly changed grille with fewer vertical bars, but looked basically the same as last year. The biggest change came in the V-8 engine. It received a new fuel-induction system, a fully counter-balanced cast alloy steel crankshaft, open skirt pistons, waterline thermostats, improved fuel pump and unitized valve assemblies. The cargo area was 59 in. long and 45-3/4 in. wide. It had insulating board side panels. A single bucket seat, one sun visor and a three-speed floor-shifted manual transmission were standard.

1934 Ford Model V8-46 Model 850 Sedan Delivery (OCW)

I.D. DATA: Serial number and motor number are the same. Serial/motor number location: [Four] Top of frame, ahead of dash. Also left side of flywheel housing. [V-8] Top of frame, left side near dash. Also top of clutch housing. Beginning engine numbers: [Four] 5,189,491; [V-8] 18-457478. Ending numbers not available.

Standard Catalog of Light-Duty Trucks

Model	Body Type	Price	Weight	Prod. Total
Series 46 — 1/2-Ton — 112 in. w.b. — Four				
68	Sedan Delivery	335	1688	Note 1
Series V8-46 — 1/2-Ton — 112 in. w.b. — V-8				
68	Sedan Delivery	360	1798	Note 1

NOTE 1: Combined production: 9,021.

1934 Ford Model BB With Police Paddy Wagon Body (OCW)

ENGINE [Series 46]: Displacement: 200.4 cid. L-Head. Four. 50 horsepower at 2800 rpm. Bore & stroke: 3-7/8 in. x 4-1/4 in. Compression ratio: 6.3:1. Carburetor: One-barrel downdraft.

ENGINE [Series 18 Delivery]: Displacement: 221 cid. L-Head. V-8. 90 horsepower at 3800 rpm. Bore & stroke: 3-1/16 in. x 3-3/4- in. Compression ratio: 6.3:1. Carburetor: Two-barrel downdraft.

NOTE: A total of 281 of the 1934 Sedan Deliveries were powered by last year's four-cylinder engine.

PICKUP: The Ford script in a blue oval on the side of the hood was one of the major styling changes made for 1934 on the 112 in. wheelbase Pickup. The box was 69.75 in. long and 44 in. wide. It had a heavy steel floor panel with pressed-in skid strips and a seasoned wood under-floor. Sockets at the end of the flare boards could be used for small stake racks, advertising panels, or special tops. The Pickup was available with either Open or Closed Cab. Just 347 Open Cab Ford Pickups were built in 1934 and this style cab was then discontinued.

1934 Ford Model 46 Closed Cab Pickup (OCW)

PANEL DELIVERY: The 112 in. wheelbase Panel was basically the same vehicle as the 1933, except for some minor trim changes. It had a hardwood floor with metal skid strips. There were steel panels along the sides to the top of the wheelhousings and hardwood slats to the ceiling to protect the body from loads. Insulating board was placed over heavy wood bows in the top. The twin steel rear doors were hung in a one-piece welded steel frame that was thoroughly dust-proofed. Heavy forged hinges permitted opening the doors 180-degrees. The body had a glossy satin finish.

DELUXE PANEL DELIVERY: The 112 in. wheelbase Deluxe Panel had the same features as the standard Panel, plus a highly-polished finish, rustless steel cowl lights and chrome-plated rearview mirror windshield wiper and front bumper. The side panels were framed by moldings. The interior side panels were made of masonite. The insulated roof was lined with artificial leather and had a dome light.

I.D. DATA: Serial number and motor number are the same. Serial/motor number location: [Four] Top of frame, ahead of dash. Also left side of flywheel housing. [V-8] Top of frame, left side near dash. Also top of clutch housing. Beginning engine numbers: [Four] 5,189,491; [V-8] 18-457478. Ending numbers not available.

Model	Body Type	Price	Weight	Prod. Total
Model 46 — 1/2-Ton — 112 in. w.b. — Four				
810	Chassis & Cab	335	1688	—
820	Panel	525	2615	—
820	Deluxe Panel	540	2628	—
830	Closed Cab Pickup	445	2386	—
—	Station Wagon	635	2505	—
Model V8-46 — 1/2-Ton — 112 in. w.b. — V-8				
810	Chassis & Cab	360	1798	—
820	Panel	550	2750	—
820	Deluxe Panel	565	2780	—
830	Closed Cab Pickup	470	2496	—
—	Station Wagon	660	2635	—

ENGINE [Model 46]: Displacement: 200.4 cid. L-Head. Four. 50 horsepower at 2800 rpm. Bore & stroke: 3-7/8 in. x 4-1/4 in. Compression ratio: 6.3:1. Carburetor: One-barrel downdraft.

ENGINE [Model 18]: Displacement: 221 cid. L-Head. V-8. 85 horsepower at 3800 rpm. Bore & stroke: 3-1/16 in. x 3-3/4- in. Compression ratio: 6.3:1. Carburetor: Two-barrel downdraft.

CHASSIS: Wheelbase: 112 in. Length: [Pickup] 179-1/2 in.; [Sedan Delivery] 176 in.; [Panel] 180-3/4 in. Width: [Sedan Delivery] 57-3/8 in.; [Panel] 66-5/16 in. [Pickup] 66-1/4 in. Tires: 5.50 x 17. in.

OPTIONS: Low-compression cylinder head. Spare tire cover. Dual windshield wipers. Spare tire. Outside rearview mirror. Passenger seat (Panel). Special paint.

HISTORICAL: Also available this year was the Model BB 1- to 1-1/2-ton truck chassis. It was offered in both the four-cylinder ($460 /2,770 lbs.) and V-8 ($485/2,971 lbs.) lines. A deluxe version was sold for $25 more. The deluxe equipment added about 93 lbs. to the weight of the 1934 Model BB.

1935 FORD

1935 Ford Model V8-48 Model 780 Sedan Delivery (R.M. Bowman)

SEDAN DELIVERY: It is little wonder Fords were the best-selling trucks and cars in 1935. They were attractively restyled. The new narrower grille, with its four horizontal bars crossing the vertical ones, helped give it a more streamlined appearance. So did a longer hood. New, more rounded fenders also enhanced that image. The single rear door opened up to a cargo area that was a roomy 65 in. long, 44 in. high and 46.8 in. wide. The radiator grille and windshield frame were painted body color. A floor-shifted three-speed manual transmission was standard.

1935 Ford Model V8-50 Model 820 Panel Delivery (FMCC/DFW)

I.D. DATA [Sedan Delivery]: Serial number and engine number are identical. Serial/ engine numbers (1935-1945) located: [Four] On top of frame left side, ahead of dash; also on left side of flywheel housing; [Six] On left frame member ahead of cowl; also on top of clutch housing; [V-8] On top of frame, left side, near dash; also on top of clutch housing. Engine numbers started at 18-1,234,357.

Model	Body Type	Price	Weight	Prod. Total
Series/Model 48 — 1/2-Ton — 112 in. w.b. — V-8				
780	Sedan Delivery	585	2826	Note 1

NOTE 1: Truck production totals for 1935 available from the Henry Ford Museum & Greenfield Village are as follows: [Model 40 Station Wagon] 3; [Model 40 Sedan Delivery] 117; [Model 40 Standard Panel] 33; [Model 40 Deluxe Panel] 28; [Model 48 Sedan Delivery] 8,257; [Model 48 Standard Panel] 9,786; [Model 48 Deluxe Panel] 4,918; [Model 48 Closed Cab Pickup] 42,763; [Model 68 Station Wagon] 1,278; [Model 68 Standard Sedan Delivery] 1,796; [Model 68 Standard Panel] 3,056; [Model 68 Deluxe Panel] 1,336; and [Model 68 Standard Pickup] 18,095. Some of the model codes in these records do not match truck codes in model charts. The mixed year totals reflect the fact that Ford continued to "build out" certain trucks for several years until parts inventories were depleted.

ENGINE [Sedan Delivery]: Displacement: 221 cid. L-Head. V-8. 85 horsepower at 3800 rpm. Bore & stroke: 3-1/16 in. x 33/4- in. Compression ratio: 6.3:1. two-barrel carburetor.

PICKUP: The 1/2-ton Pickup was basically the same as the one introduced three years earlier. However, now it was all-steel and a panel was added, between the runningboards and box, to give it a more one-piece look. The graceful new fenders and sloping radiator also enhanced the truck's appearance. The front bumper had dual pinstripes. The grille added two horizontal pieces. The engine was mounted over eight in. further forward. More of the payload weight was now placed on the front wheels, so some of the rear overhang could be eliminated.

PANEL DELIVERY: Among the features of the new 1/2-ton Panel were: Steel-and-board inter-locking; hardwood plank flooring; a dome light; longer front and rear springs and revised parking brake control.

DELUXE PANEL DELIVERY: Some of the things that set the Deluxe Panel apart from the Standard were: An aluminum painted grille; color-keyed wheels; chrome-plated twin horns; a lined interior; chrome-plated windshield wiper[s] and chromed rearview mirror.

I.D. DATA [Model 50]: Serial number and engine number are identical. Serial/engine numbers (1935-1945) located: [Four] On top of frame left side, ahead of dash; also on left side of flywheel housing; [Six] On left frame member ahead of cowl; also on top of clutch housing; [V-8] On top of frame, left side, near dash; also on top of clutch housing. Engine numbers started at 18-1,234,357.

Model	Body Type	Price	Weight	Prod. Total
Series/Model 50 — 1/2-Ton — 112 in. — V-8				
810	Chassis & Cab	455	2377	Note 1
820	Panel	565	3032	Note 1
820	Deluxe Panel	580	3140	Note 1
830	Closed Cab Pickup	480	—	Note 1
840	Driveaway Chassis	360	—	Note 1

NOTE 1: Truck production totals for 1935 available from the Henry Ford Museum & Greenfield Village are as follows: [Model 40 Station Wagon] 3; [Model 40 Sedan Delivery] 117; [Model 40 Standard Panel] 33; [Model 40 Deluxe Panel] 28; [Model 48 Sedan Delivery] 8,257; [Model 48 Standard Panel] 9,786; [Model 48 Deluxe Panel] 4,918; [Model 48 Closed Cab Pickup] 42,763; [Model 68 Station Wagon] 1,278; [Model 68 Standard Sedan Delivery] 1,796; [Model 68 Standard Panel] 3,056; [Model 68 Deluxe Panel] 1,336; and [Model 68 Standard Pickup] 18,095. Some of the model codes in these records do not match truck codes in model charts. (For example, Model 50 does not appear.) The mixed year totals reflect the fact that Ford continued to "build out" certain trucks for several years until parts inventories were depleted.

1935 Ford Model V8-50 Model 830 Pickup (OCW)

ENGINE [Model 50]: Displacement: 221 cid. L-Head. V-8. 85 horsepower at 3800 rpm. Bore & stroke: 3-1/16 in. x 3-3/4 in. Compression ratio: 6.3:1. two-barrel carburetor.

CHASSIS: Wheelbase: 112 in. Length: 182-3/4 in. [Sedan Delivery] Height: 64-5/8 in. [Sedan Delivery] Tires: 6.00 x 16 in.

OPTIONS: Passenger seat (Panel/Sedan Delivery). Roll-down rear window (Panel/ Sedan Delivery). Heater. Radio. Spare tire. Bumpers. Spare tire cover. Chrome-plated outside rearview mirror. Dual windshield wipers. Cigarette lighter. Two taillights (Sedan Delivery). Bumper guards. Special paint.

1935 Ford Stretch Limousine (BLHU/DFW)

HISTORICAL: Also available this year was the Model 51 1- to 1-1/2-ton truck. It was offered as both Chassis ($500 /3,220 lbs.) and Chassis & Cab ($595/3,586 lbs.) models on a 131.5 in. wheelbase. A 157 in. wheelbase version sold for $25 more. The extra length added about 75 lbs. to the weight of the long wheelbase 1935 Model 51.

1936 FORD

1936 Ford Model 68 Model 780 Sedan Delivery (OCW)

1936 Ford Model 68 Model 830 Pickup (DFW)

SEDAN DELIVERY: The most noticeable styling changes for 1936 were the wraparound grille with vertical bars and new rear fenders. The hoodside louvers now had just one horizontal trim piece running through their center. Among the less obvious changes were: a larger capacity radiator; helical-type gears for first and second speeds; new short-spoke steel wheels; and the fact that the center of the bumpers pulled inward, rather than dipping forward. The interior featured insulating board side panels and a wood floor. A single driver's seat was standard. A small number of 1936 Sedan Deliveries had glass windows instead of the traditional steel panels. This made them look very much like two-door sedans.

PICKUP: The slightly revised radiator shell and wheels were about the only changes made to the 1936 Ford 1/2-ton Pickup. The box had a heavy steel floor panel with pressed-in skid strips. The tailgate was also all-steel.

PANEL: The new 1/2-ton Panel looked pretty much the same as the 1935 model. The wood floors had metal skid strips. The rear doors were hung in a one-piece steel frame. Boards and steel panels on the inner walls provided extra protection. Panels could be made into Station Wagons by adding rear quarter glass windows on a special order basis.

1936 Ford Model 67 Model 830 Pickup (D. Whiting)

1936 Ford Model 68 Model 830 Pickup (OCW)

DELUXE PANEL: The Deluxe Panel shared the same features as the standard models plus, an insulated interior; body color wheels; and bright-finished twin horns, windshield wipers and outside rearview mirror. There was also an aluminum-finish grille. This model was discontinued during the model year.

I.D. DATA [Sedan Delivery]: Serial number and engine number are identical. Serial/engine numbers (1935-1946) located: [Four] On top of frame left side, ahead of dash; also on left side of flywheel housing; [Six] On left frame member ahead of cowl; also on top of clutch housing; [V-8] On top of frame, left side, near dash; also on top of clutch housing. Engine numbers began at 18-2,207,111.

I.D. DATA [1/2-ton]: Serial number and engine number are identical. Serial/engine numbers (1935-1945) located: [Four] On top of frame left side, ahead of dash; also on left side of flywheel housing; [Six] On left frame member ahead of cowl; also on top of clutch housing; [V-8] On top of frame, left side, near dash; also on top of clutch housing. Engine numbers began at 18-2,207,111.

Model	Body Type	Price	Weight	Prod. Total
Series/Model 68 — 1/2-Ton — 112 in. w.b. — V-8				
780	Sedan Delivery	590	2825	Note 1

NOTE 1: Truck production totals for 1936 available from the Henry Ford Museum & Greenfield Village are as follows: [Model 48 Sedan Delivery] 19; [Model 68 Standard Sedan Delivery] 5,796; [Model 68 Deluxe Sedan Delivery] 209; [Model 78 Standard Sedan Delivery] 512; [Model 78 Deluxe Sedan Delivery] 86. Some of the model codes in these records do not match truck codes in model charts. (For example, Model 78 does not appear as a 1936 model). The mixed year totals reflect the fact that Ford continued to "build out" and sell certain trucks for several years, until parts inventories were depleted, and without regard to model year.

Model	Body Type	Price	Weight	Prod. Total
Series/Model 67 — 1/2-Ton — 112 in. w.b. — V-8/85 hp				
810	Chassis & Cab	450	2408	Note 1
820	Panel	565	3626	Note 1
820	Deluxe Panel	580	3663	Note 1
830	Pickup	480	2645	Note 1
840	Driveway Chassis	360	2027	Note 1

ENGINE [Sedan Delivery]: Displacement: 221 cid. L-Head. V-8. 85 horsepower at 3800 rpm. Bore & stroke: 3-1/16 in. x 3-3/4 in. Compression ratio: 6.3:1. Two-barrel downdraft carburetor.

NOTE 1: Truck production totals for 1936 available from the Henry Ford Museum & Greenfield Village are as follows: [Model 48 Station Wagon] 26; [Model 48 Deluxe Panel] 1; [Model 48 Standard Panel] 19; [Model 68 Station Wagon] 5,766; [Model 68 Standard Panel] 8,902; [Model 68 Deluxe Panel] 3,694; [Model 68 Standard Pickup] 49,068; [Model 68 Deluxe Pickup] 2,570; [Model 78 Station Wagon] 698; [Model 78 Standard Panel] 706; [Model 78 Deluxe Panel] 82; [Model 78 Standard Pickup] 8,975; [Model 78 Deluxe Pickup] 372. Some of the model codes in these records do not match 1936 truck codes in model charts. (For example, Models 48 and 78 do not appear). The mixed year totals reflect the fact that Ford continued to "build out" certain trucks for several years until parts inventories were depleted.

1936 Ford Model 68 Model 820 Panel Delivery (OCW)

ENGINE [Model 67]: Displacement: 221 cid. L-Head. V-8. 85 hp at 3800 rpm. Bore & stroke: 3-1/16 in. x 3-3/4 in. Compression ratio: 6.3:1. Two-barrel downdraft carburetor.

ENGINE [Model 68]: Displacement: 136 cid. L-head. V-8. 60 hp at 3600 rpm. Bore & stroke: 2-3/5 in. x 3-1/5 in. Compression ratio: 6.6:1. Two-barrel downdraft carburetor.

CHASSIS: Wheelbase: 112 in. Tires: 6.00 x 16 in.

1936 Ford Model 51 Model 820 Panel Delivery (OCW)

OPTIONS: Passenger seat for Panel and Sedan Delivery. Spare tire cover. Left-hand spare for Pickup. Canopy top for Pickup. Spotlight. Outside rearview mirror. Dual windshield wipers. Stainless steel hubcaps. Wheel trim rings. Radio. Heater. Locking gas cap. White sidewall tires. Deluxe Equipment [Sedan Delivery]: Dual windshield wipers. Two sun visors. Bright finish radiator grille, windshield frame, outside rearview mirror, horn grilles and windshield wipers. Two-tone paint.

1936 Ford Model 68 Model 830 Pickup (OCW)

HISTORICAL: Also available this year was the Model 51 1- to 1-1/2-ton truck. It was offered as both Chassis ($500/3,220 lbs.) and Chassis & Closed Cab ($590/3,559 lbs.) models on a 131.5 in. wheelbase. A 157 in. wheelbase version sold for $25 more. The extra length added about 75 lbs. to the weight of the long wheelbase 1935 Model 51.

1937 Ford Model 78 Model 770 Coupe-Express (LS/DFW)

STANDARD COUPE WITH PICKUP BODY: This was a new model that would only last a year. As its name implies, this was basically a stock 1937 Ford Business Coupe with a down-sized 1/2-ton pickup box incorporated into the trunk. The box was 33 in. wide, 64 in. long and a foot high.

1937 Ford Model 78 Model 780 Sedan Delivery (LS/DFW)

SEDAN DELIVERY: Although the body shell was basically the same as the one introduced in 1935, the front end of the Sedan Delivery was attractively restyled for 1937. The most noticeable change was the fender-integrated headlights. The V-like wraparound grille had horizontal bars and a vertical bar down its center. The sleek hoodside vents echoed the look of the grille. The windshield was now of two-piece design. The Sedan Delivery had a wide single rear door and an all-steel top. The wood floor planking was interlocked by steel skid strips. Insulation board side panels were used. A single driver's seat, front bumper guards, a lined interior, one sun visor and a three-speed manual transmission were among the standard features.

1937 Ford Model 78 Model 780 Sedan Delivery (OCW)

I.D. DATA: Serial number and engine number are identical. Serial/engine numbers (1935-1945) located: [Four] On top of frame left side, ahead of dash; also on left side of flywheel housing; [Six] On left frame member ahead of cowl; also on top of clutch housing; [V-8] On top of frame, left side, near dash; also on top of clutch housing. Serial numbers ranged from 18-3,331,857 thru 18-4,186,446.

Model	Body Type	Price	Weight	Prod. Total
Series/Model 74 — 1/2-Ton — 112 in. w.b. — V-8/60 hp				
74	Coupe-Pickup	529+	2275+	Note 1
74	Sedan Delivery	585	2765	Note 1
Model 78 — 1/2-Ton — 112 in. w.b.				
78	Coupe-Pickup	586+	2496+	Note 1
78	Sedan Delivery	649	2741	Note 1
Model 78 Deluxe — 1/2-Ton — 112 in. w.b.				
78	Coupe-Pickup	659+	2506+	Note 1
78	Sedan Delivery	712	2781	Note 1

NOTE 1: Truck production totals for 1937 available from the Henry Ford Museum & Greenfield Village are as follows: [Model 78 Standard Sedan Delivery] 7,329; [Model 78 Deluxe Sedan Delivery] 621; [Model 81A Standard five-window Coupe with Slide-in Pickup box] 14; [Model 81A Sedan Delivery] 727. Some of the model codes in these records do not match truck codes in model charts. (For example, Model 81A does not appear as a Sedan Delivery). The mixed year totals reflect the fact that Ford continued to "build out" and sell certain trucks for several years, until parts inventories were depleted, and without regard to model year.

NOTE 2: Prices/weights shown for Coupe-Pickup are for regular five-window Business Coupes. The symbol (+) indicates that the cost and weight of the slide-in Pickup box has to be added. Typically, this type of option was in the $10-$50 range..

1937 Ford Model 78 Model 780 Sedan Delivery (J. Griscon)

ENGINE: Displacement: 136 cid. L-Head. V-8. 60 hp at 3500 rpm. Bore & stroke: 2-3/5 in. x 3-1/5 in. Compression ratio: 6.6:1. Two-barrel downdraft carburetor.

ENGINE [Optional]: Displacement: 221 cid. L-Head. V-8. 85 horsepower at 3800 rpm. Bore & stroke: 3-1/16 in. x 3-3/4 in. Compression ratio: 6.3:1. Two-barrel downdraft carburetor.

1937 Ford Model 73 Model 820 Pickup (OCW)

PICKUP: Styling changes on the 1/2-ton Pickup were less dramatic than those on the Sedan Delivery. The revised grille now featured horizontal, rather than vertical bars. The windshield was two-piece. The hood louvers were shorter. The cargo box was enlarged a bit to increase load length by 4 in. It had a steel floor panel with pressed-in skid strips and a wood sub-floor. There was a new, rod-style tailgate hinge. The tailgate itself was embossed to read Ford V-8.

1937 Ford Model 77 Model 820 Panel Delivery (B. Glade)

PANEL: This model shared its looks with the Pickup. A new feature was an all-steel roof. A dome light, wood floors with interlocking steel skid plates, spare tire cover and steel dual rear doors were among the standard features. Panels could be made into Station Wagons on a special order basis.

1937 Ford Model 77 Model 805 Platform Stake Bed (LS/DFW)

PLATFORM/STAKE: The frame of the Platform/Stake was built up in order for the platform to conform to normal loading dock heights. The racks were 29.5 in. high and featured steel side panels in their forward area. The hardwood floor was interlocked by steel skid strips. A single windshield wiper and front and rear bumpers were standard.

1937 Ford Model 77 Model 800 Platform (OCW)

I.D. DATA [112 in. w.b.]: Serial number and engine number are identical. Serial/engine numbers (1935-1945) located: [Four] On top of frame left side, ahead of dash; also on left side of flywheel housing; [Six] On left frame member ahead of cowl; also on top of clutch housing; [V-8] On top of frame, left side, near dash; also on top of clutch housing. Serial numbers ranged from 18-3, 331,857 thru 18-4,186,446.

1937 Ford 1-Ton Armored Car (NSPC/JE)

Model	Body Type	Price	Weight	Prod. Total
Series/Model 73 — 1/2-Ton — 112 in. w.b. — V-8/60 hp				
800	Platform	531	2467	Note 1
805	Stake	541	2637	Note 1
810	Chassis & Cab	496	2121	Note 1
820	Panel	613	2756	Note 1
820	Deluxe Panel	623	2873	Note 1
830	Pickup	516	2397	Note 1
830	Deluxe Pickup	526	—	Note 1
840	Driveaway Chassis	406	1784	Note 1
Series/Model 77 — 1/2-Ton — 112 in. w.b. — V-8/85 hp				
800	Platform	541	2672	Note 1
805	Stake	556	2842	Note 1
810	Chassis & Cab	506	2337	Note 1
820	Panel	623	2971	Note 1
820	Deluxe Panel	633	3088	Note 1
830	Pickup	526	2594	Note 1
830	Deluxe Pickup	536	—	Note 1
840	Driveaway Chassis	416	1989	Note 1
—	Station Wagon	680	3018	Note 1
—	Station Wagon (Glass)	700	3103	Note 1

NOTE 1: Truck production totals for 1937 available from the Henry Ford Museum & Greenfield Village are as follows: [Model 48 Standard Panel] 1; [Model 78 Station Wagon] 8,498; [Model 78 Standard Panel] 5,900; [Model 78 Deluxe Panel] 351; [Model 78 Standard Panel] 5,900; [Model 78 Deluxe Panel] 351; [Model 78 Standard Pickup] 68,289; [Model 78 Deluxe Pickup] 2,248; [Model 81A Station Wagon] 932; [Model 81A Commercial chassis] 10,699. Some of the model codes in these records do not match 1936 truck codes in model charts. (For example, Models 48 and 78.) The mixed year totals reflect the fact that Ford continued to "build out" certain trucks for several years until parts inventories were depleted.

ENGINE: Displacement: 136 cid. L-Head. V-8. 60 hp at 3500 rpm. Bore & stroke: 2-3/5 in. x 3-1/5 in. Compression ratio: 6.6:1. Two-barrel downdraft carburetor.

ENGINE [Optional]: Displacement: 221 cid. L-Head. V-8. 85 hp at 3800 rpm. Bore & stroke: 3-1/16 in. x 3-3/4 in. Compression ratio: 6.12:1. Two-barrel carburetor.

1937 Ford 1-Ton Armored Car (NSPC/JE)

CHASSIS: Wheelbase: 112 in. Length: [Chassis] 186.76 in.; [Pickup] 189.63 in.; [Platform/Stake] 195.09 in.; [Panel] 178.67 in.; [Sedan Delivery] 179.5 in. Tires: [Coupe-Pickup 5.50 x 16; [Sedan Delivery] 6.00 x 16 in.

1937 Ford Model 79 Cabinet Body Utility Truck (NSPC/JE)

POWERTRAIN OPTIONS: Transmission with lower ratio gears. Four-speed manual. **CONVENIENCE OPTIONS:** Lined interior for Pickup. Radio. Heater. Stainless steel spider wheelcovers. Passenger side windshield wiper. Right-hand sun visor. Windshield defroster. Spotlight. Outside rearview mirror. Deluxe Equipment group including dual horns; twin windshield wipers; two sun visors; chrome-plated grille; outside rearview mirror; wipers; windshield frame; twin horns; and hood louver moldings. Special paint. Two-tone paint.

1937 Ford Model 78 Deluxe Sedan Delivery (G. Moyer)

HISTORICAL: Also available this year was the Series/Model 75 1-ton truck. The models, prices and weights in the Series 75 line were as follows:

Series/Model 75 — 1-Ton — 1434 in. w.b. — V-8/60 hp				
800	Platform	658	3944	—
805	Stake	683	4274	—
810	Chassis & Cab	603	3235	—
820	Panel	778	4247	—
840	Driveaway Chassis	513	2893	—

Production of the Series 75 models is not available.

1938 FORD

1938 Ford V-8 Commercial Station Wagon (OCW)

SEDAN DELIVERY: The new Sedan Delivery shared its looks with the Ford standard passenger car line. Most striking was its curved, horizontal-bar grille that wrapped around the hoodsides. The front fenders resembled the previous year's model, but were new. However, the rear fenders were the same as those used in 1937. The shell was virtually the same as the one introduced in 1935. Its styling was jazzed up a bit, early in the model year. Extra grille moldings, a bright windshield frame and stainless steel belt molding were added. The Sedan Delivery had a hardwood floor with steel skid strips. It had a load width of 52 in. and a load height of 44.75 in. A driver's seat and single windshield wiper were standard.

1938 Ford V-8 Commercial Depot Hack (OCW)

I.D. DATA [Sedan Delivery]: Serial number and engine number are identical. Serial/engine numbers (1935-1945) located: [Four] On top of frame left side, ahead of dash; also on left side of flywheel housing; [Six] On left frame member ahead of cowl; also on top of clutch housing; [V-8] On top of frame, left side, near dash; also on top of clutch housing. Serial numbers; 81A: 18-4,186,447 to 18-4,661,100. 82A: 54-358,335 & up.

Model	Body Type	Price	Weight	Prod. Total
Series/Model 82A — 1/2-Ton — 112 in. w.b. — V-8/60 hp				
780	Sedan Delivery	690	2574	Note 1
—	Coupe-Pickup	625+	2575+	Note 1
Series/Model 81A — 1/2-Ton — 112 in. w.b. — V-8/85 hp				
780	Sedan Delivery	700	2755	Note 1
—	Coupe-Pickup	685+	2606+	Note 1

NOTE 1: Truck production totals for 1938 available from the Henry Ford Museum & Greenfield Village are as follows: [Model 48 Sedan Delivery] 1; [Model 81A Standard five-window Coupe with Slide-in Pickup box] 388; [Model 81A Sedan Delivery] 3,259. Some of the model codes in these records do not match truck codes in model charts. (For example, Model 48 does not appear as a 1938 model.) The mixed year totals reflect the fact that Ford continued to "build out" and sell certain trucks for several years, until parts inventories were depleted, and without regard to model year.

NOTE 2: Prices/weights shown for Coupe-Pickup are for standard five-window Business Coupes. The symbol (+) indicates that the cost and weight of the slide-in Pickup box has to be added. Typically, this type of option was in the $10-$50 range.

1938 Ford 1/2-Ton Model 81C Model 830 Pickup (LOC/DFW)

ENGINE [Sedan Delivery]: Displacement: 136 cid. L-Head. V-8. 60 horsepower at 3500 rpm. Bore & stroke: 2-3/5 in. x 3-1/5 in. Compression ratio: 6.6:1. two-barrel carburetor.

ENGINE [Optional]: Displacement: 221 cid. L-Head. V-8. 85 hp at 3800 rpm. Bore & stroke: 3-1/16 in. x 3-3/4 in. Compression ratio: 6.12:1. Two-barrel carburetor.

1938 Ford 1/2-Ton Model 81C Model 830 Pickup (Bill Ballas photo)

ENGINE [Optional]: Displacement: 221 cid. L-Head. V-8. 85 horsepower at 3800 rpm. Bore & stroke: 3-1/16 in. x 3-3/4 in. Compression ratio: 6.12:1. Two-barrel downdraft carburetor.

1938 Ford 1/2-Ton Model 81C Model 830 Pickup (OCW)

112 IN. PICKUP: The new 1/2-ton pickup featured attractive styling. The refined, curved, almost egg-shaped grille had numerous horizontal bars with a trim piece dividing the grille vertically. The hood louvers also had a horizontal theme. The headlights were encased in new teardrop-shaped pods. Skid strips were stamped in the steel floor. A wood sub-floor gave extra support. Drop chain locking links clamped sides to the tailgate, when in the closed position. The load length was 77.75 in.

1938 Ford 3/4-Ton Model 82C Model 830 Pickup (DFW)

112 IN. PANEL: The 1/2-ton Panel received a new body to go with its new looks. Load length was now 87.78 in. at the floor. The rear door opening was 46.2 in. wide and 44 in. high. The sides of the all-steel were double-sealed at the floor, with rubber and felt to help keep out dust and moisture. The floors were made of hardwood. The spare tire carrier was located on the right-hand side of the vehicle, between the passenger side door and rear fender. A new option offered this year was fender skirts.

1938 Ford 3/4-Ton Model 810 Chassis & Cab With Utility Body (A&A)

112 IN. PLATFORM/STAKE: A couple of new features offered on the 1/2-ton Platform/Stake truck this year were a left rear fender mounted fuel filler pipe and bright-center hubcaps. The stake sides were hinged and removable for easier loading. On each forward stake section was a large metal advertising panel. The hardwood floor planking was locked together and protected by steel skid strips. Load length was 80 in. The stake sections were 29.5 in. high. A three-speed manual transmission was standard.

I.D. DATA [112 in.]: Serial number and engine number are identical. Serial/engine numbers (1935-1945) located: [Four] On top of frame left side, ahead of dash; also on left side of flywheel housing; [Six] On left frame member ahead of cowl; also on top of clutch housing; [V-8] On top of frame, left side, near dash; also on top of clutch housing. Serial numbers; 81A: 18-4,186,447 to 18-4,661,100. 82A: 54-358,335 & up.

Model	Body Type	Price	Weight	Prod. Total
Series/Model 82C — 1/2-Ton — 112 in. w.b. — V-8/60 hp				
800	Platform	600	2502	Note 1
805	Stake	615	2655	Note 1
810	Chassis & Cab	550	2199	Note 1
820	Panel (slats)	675	2780	Note 1
820	Panel (Masonite)	685	2788	Note 1
830	Pickup	580	2526	Note 1
840	Open Driveaway Chassis	455	1793	Note 1
850	Closed Driveaway Chassis	475	1820	Note 1
Series/Model 81C — 1/2-Ton — 112 in. w.b. — V-8/85 hp				
800	Platform	610	2700	Note 1
805	Stake	625	2842	Note 1
810	Chassis & Cab	560	2425	Note 1
820	Panel (slats)	685	2987	Note 1
820	Panel (Masonite)	695	2995	Note 1
830	Pickup	590	2684	Note 1
840	Open Driveaway Chassis	465	1989	Note 1
850	Closed Driveaway Chassis	485	2016	Note 1

NOTE 1: Truck production totals for 1938 available from the Henry Ford Museum & Greenfield Village are as follows: [Model 48 Station Wagon] 90; [Model 78 Station Wagon] 108; [Model 81A Station Wagon] 6,012; [Model 81A Commercial Chassis] 39,552; [Model 91A Standard Station Wagon] 818; [Model 91A Deluxe Station Wagon] 1,008; [Model 91A Commercial Chassis] 44,039. Some of the model codes in these records do not match 1938 truck codes in model charts. (For example, Models 48 and 91A.) The mixed year totals reflect the fact that Ford continued to "build out" certain trucks for several years until parts inventories were depleted.

ENGINE [112 in.]: Displacement: 136 cid. L-Head. V-8. 60 horsepower at 3500 rpm. Bore & stroke: 2-3/5 in. x 3-1/5 in. Compression ratio: 6.6:1. two-barrel carburetor.
ENGINE [Optional]: Displacement: 221 cid. L-Head. V-8. 85 hp at 3800 rpm. Bore & stroke: 3-1/16 in. x 3-3/4 in. Compression ratio: 6.12:1. Two-barrel carburetor.
122 IN. EXPRESS: This 1-ton Pickup was new for 1938. Styling resembled that of the 1/2-ton. However, it had a stronger chassis and larger body. Load length was 96 in. The hardwood floor planks were protected and inter-locked by steel skid strips. The front and side panels were reinforced and sockets were provided in the flareboards for side boards. An 18-gal. fuel tank, chrome-plated front bumper and three-speed manual transmission were among the standard features. The fuel filler pipe was located on the right-hand side of the cab, between the door and pickup box.
122 IN. PANEL: Basically, this was a larger capacity version of the 1/2-ton Panel. It featured a welded, all-steel body. The panel sides were double-sealed at the floor with felt and rubber. A welded, reinforced channel steel frame helped to maintain the alignment of the rubber-sealed rear doors. Load length was 107.25 in. at the floor. The rear opening was 46.2 in. wide by 46.5 in. high.
122 IN. PLATFORM/STAKE: The 1-ton Platform/Stake had hardwood floor planking bolted to bridge-type steel framework. The stake rack was built of hardwood with sturdy stakes. The forward section on each side was hinged to swing out for easy loading. A 28 in. wide by 34.88 in. tall metal panel on the rack could be used for advertising purposes. The cargo area was 90.4 in. long and 74 in. wide.
I.D. DATA [122 in.]: Serial number and engine number are identical. Serial/engine numbers (1935-1945) located: [Four] On top of frame left side, ahead of dash; also on left side of flywheel housing; [Six] On left frame member ahead of cowl; also on top of clutch housing; [V-8] On top of frame, left side, near dash; also on top of clutch housing. Serial numbers; 81A: 18-4,186,447 to 18-4,661,100. 82A: 54-358,335 & up.

Model	Body Type	Price	Weight	Prod. Total
Series/Model 82Y — 1-Ton — 122 in. w.b. — V-8/60 hp				
800	Platform	715	3319	Note 1
805	Stake	735	3579	Note 1
810	Chassis & Cab	660	2748	Note 1
820	Panel	840	3510	Note 1
830	Express Pickup	720	3300	Note 1
840	Open Driveaway Chassis	565	2373	Note 1
850	Closed Driveaway Chassis	585	2400	Note 1

Model	Body Type	Price	Weight	Prod. Total
Series/Model 81Y — 1-Ton — 122 in. w.b. — V-8/85 hp				
800	Platform	725	3448	Note 1
805	Stake	745	3713	Note 1
810	Chassis & Cab	670	2939	Note 1
820	Panel	850	3711	Note 1
830	Express Pickup	730	3482	Note 1
840	Open Driveaway Chassis	575	2614	Note 1
850	Closed Driveaway Chassis	595	2641	Note 1

NOTE 1: Series 82Y/81Y production figures not available.
ENGINE: Displacement: 136 cid. L-Head. V-8. 60 hp at 3500 rpm. Bore & stroke: 2-3/5 in. x 3-1/5 in. Compression ratio: 6.6:1. Two-barrel downdraft carburetor.
ENGINE [Optional]: Displacement: 221 cid. L-Head. V-8. 85 hp at 3800 rpm. Bore & stroke: 3-1/16 in. x 3-3/4 in. Compression ratio: 6.12:1. Two-barrel carburetor.
CHASSIS: 112 in. Series/Sedan Delivery: Wheelbase: 112 in. Length: [Sedan Delivery] 178.67 in.; [Pickup] 183.74 in. [Panel] 195.09 in. [Platform/Sedan] 189.6 in. Width: 72.14 in. Height: [Panel] 69.67 in.; [Sedan Delivery] 66.67 in.; [Pickup]. 71.45 in. Tires: 6.00 x 16 in.
CHASSIS: 122 In. Series: Wheelbase: 122 in. Length: [Platform/Stake] 199.89 in.; [Pickup] 217.39 in.; [Panel] 209.39 in. Width: [Pickup/Panel] 73.62 in.; [Platform/Stake] 79.24 in. Height: [Panel] 85.64 in.; [Pickup, Platform/Stake] 79.44 in. Tires: [Front] 6.00 x 17 six-ply [Rear]; 7.00 x 17.
POWERTRAIN OPTIONS: Four-speed manual.
CONVENIENCE OPTIONS: Outside mounted spare tire. Spotlight. Grille guard. Passenger side windshield wiper. Fog lights (Sedan Delivery). Radio. Wheel trim rings. Heater. Locking gas cap. License plate frame. Cigar lighter (Sedan Delivery). 6.50 x 16 six-ply tires (112 in. Series). Fender skirts (Panel). Spider wheelcovers (Sedan Delivery). Colored wheels. White sidewall tires. Over-sized tires (122 in. series). Masonite lined interior (Panel). Deluxe Equipment Package: Includes deluxe passenger car hubcaps; chrome-plated radiator grille; chrome outside rearview mirror; and bright windshield frame.

1939 FORD

1939 Ford Model 81A Sedan Delivery (LS/DFW)

SEDAN DELIVERY: The Sedan Delivery received a very minor facelift for 1939. Loop-style hoodside moldings, a different hood ornament and bright wraparound horizontal trim strips on the grille, were the most noticeable changes. Among the standard features were: Dual windshield wipers; an outside rearview mirror; hardwood floors protected by steel skid strips; friction-type door checks (to hold all doors when in open position); spare wheel mounted inside a fully lined and insulated interior; and driver's seat.
I.D. DATA [Sedan Delivery]: Serial number and engine number are identical. Serial/engine numbers (1935-1945) located: [Four] On top of frame left side, ahead of dash; also on left side of flywheel housing; [Six] On left frame member ahead of cowl; also on top of clutch housing; [V-8] On top of frame, left side, near dash; also on top of clutch housing. Serial numbers began at 54-506,501.

Model	Body Type	Price	Weight	Prod. Total
Series 922A — 1/2-Ton — 112 in. w.b. — V-8/60 hp				
780	Sedan Delivery	670	2567	—
Series 91A — 1/2-Ton — 112 in. w.b. — V-8/85 hp				
780	Sedan Delivery	685	2753	—

NOTE 1: Truck production totals for 1939 available from the Henry Ford Museum & Greenfield Village are as follows: [Series 91A Standard Station Wagon] 2,453; [Model 91A Deluxe Station Wagon] 5,147; [Model 91A Sedan Delivery] 3,434; [Model 91A Commercial Chassis] 121. Some Series 91A trucks were also sold as 1940 models as Ford continued to "build out" and sell certain trucks for several years (until parts inventories were depleted) without regard to model year.
ENGINE [Standard]: Displacement: 136 cid. L-Head. V-8. 60 hp at 3500 rpm. Bore & stroke: 2-3/5 in. x 3-1/5 in. Compression ratio: 6.6:1. Two-barrel carburetor.
ENGINE [Optional]: Displacement: 221 cid. L-Head. V-8. 85 hp at 3800 rpm. Bore & stroke: 3-1/16 in. x 3-3/4 in. Compression ratio: 6.12:1. Two-barrel carburetor.
112 IN. PICKUP: Elimination of the V-8 emblem on the grille, a sleeker hood ornament/latch handle and passenger car hubcaps were the biggest styling changes for 1939. The 112 in. Pickup had a wood sub-floor. Skid strips were stamped in the steel floor. Drop chain locking links clamped bodysides to the tailgate when in the closed position. The box had a load width of 53.6 in. and a load height of 77.7 in.
112 IN. PANEL: If you liked the 112 in. Panel of 1938, you'd like the 1939 version. They were virtually identical, although the new one had hydraulic brakes. The sides of the all-steel body were double-sealed at the floor with rubber and felt. The floors were made of hardwood. The spare tire carrier was located on the right-hand side of the vehicle, between the passenger side door and rear fender. The rear door opening was 46.2 in. wide and 44 in. high.

112 IN. PLATFORM/STAKE: The stake sides were hinged and removable for easier loading. On each forward stake section was a large metal advertising panel. The hardwood planking was locked together and protected by steel skid strips. Load length was 80 in. The hardwood stake sections were 29.5 in. high. A three-speed manual transmission was standard.

I.D. DATA [112 In.]: Serial number and engine number are identical. Serial/engine numbers (1935-1945) located: [Four] On top of frame left side, ahead of dash; also on left side of flywheel housing; [Six] On left frame member ahead of cowl; also on top of clutch housing; [V-8] On top of frame, left side, near dash; also on top of clutch housing. See Sedan Delivery number range.

1939 Ford Model 81A Business Coupe-Pickup (OCW)

Model	Body Type	Price	Weight	Prod. Total
Series 922C — 1/2-Ton — 112 in. w.b. — V-8/60 hp				
80	Platform	590	2631	—
81	Chassis & Cab	540	2175	—
82	Panel (slats)	655	2760	—
82	Panel (Masonite)	670	2784	—
83	Pickup	570	2460	—
84	Chassis & Cowl	445	1818	—
85	Chassis & W/S	465	1846	—
86	Stake	610	2773	—
Series 91C — 1/2-Ton — 112 in. w.b. — V-8/85 hp				
80	Platform	605	2817	—
81	Chassis & Cab	555	2361	—
82	Panel (slats)	670	2946	—
82	Panel (Masonite)	685	2784	—
83	Pickup	585	2646	—
84	Chassis & Cowl	460	2004	—
85	Chassis & W/S	480	2032	—
86	Stake	625	2959	—

NOTE 1: Truck production totals for 1939 available from the Henry Ford Museum & Greenfield Village are as follows: [Model 48 Station WagonI] 123; [Model 81A Commercial Chassis] 24; [Model 01A Standard Station Wagon] 980; [Model 01A Deluxe Station Wagon] 2,292; [Model 01A Sedan Delivery] 1,491; [Model 01A Panel With Slats] 2,656; [Model 01A Panel With Masonite] 235; [Model 01A Pickup] 15,742. Some of the model codes in these records do not match 1939 truck codes in model charts. (For example, Models 48 and 01A). The mixed year totals reflect the fact that Ford continued to "build out" certain trucks for several years until parts inventories were depleted.

ENGINE [Standard]: Displacement: 136 cid. L-Head. V-8. 60 hp at 3500 rpm. Bore & stroke: 2-3/5 in. x 3-1/5 in. Compression ratio: 6.6:1. Two-barrel carburetor.
ENGINE [Optional]: Displacement: 221 cid. L-Head. V-8. 85 hp at 3800 rpm. Bore & stroke: 3-1/16 in. x 3-3/4 in. Compression ratio: 6.12:1. Two-barrel carburetor.

1939 Ford 1/2-Ton Model 92D Pickup (OCW)

122 IN. 3/4-TON EXPRESS: This series was introduced in mid-model year. It shared its wheelbase, driveline, frame and suspension with the 1-ton. However it had the 1/2-ton's 12 in. brakes. Its cargo box was 96 in. long, 54 in. wide and 21.5 in. to the top of flareboards. Sockets were provided in flareboards for side boards or a top. The section corner posts were rounded. There were rolled edges on the flareboards and tailgate. The front and side panels were reinforced. The hardwood floor planks were protected and inter-locked by steel skid strips.

122 IN. 3/4-TON PANEL: Sales literature bragged that the 122 in., 3/4-ton Panel featured smart styling that brings prestige to its owner. It had a welded all-steel body. The Panel sides were double-sealed at the floor with felt and rubber. A welded, reinforced channel steel frame helped maintain the alignment of the rubber sealed doors. Its rear opening was 46.2 in. wide and 46.5 in. high.

1939 Ford 3/4-Ton Model 92D Chassis & Cab With Telephone Body (OCW)

122 IN. 3/4-TON PLATFORM/STAKE: The 3/4-ton Platform/Stake was especially designed for bulky loads. It had a sturdy steel bridge-type platform frame, hardwood floor, and smooth-surfaced rack boards with rounded corners. There was a large metal advertising panel on each forward stake section. The platform sides and end were protected by the steel frame rail. The ends of the body sills had strong steel caps riveted to the frame rail and bolted to the sills. The stake sockets were doubly reinforced, welded to the inside of the frame rail and riveted to the outside. Large steel inter-locking plates were bolted to the corners of top rack boards, tying them rigidly together to prevent fanning. The three-person, waterproof seat could be adjusted to three positions.

122 IN. 3/4-TON I.D.: Serial number and engine number are identical. Serial/engine numbers (1935-1945) located: [Four] On top of frame left side, ahead of dash; also on left side of flywheel housing; [Six] On left frame member ahead of cowl; also on top of clutch housing; [V-8] On top of frame, left side, near dash; also on top of clutch housing. See Sedan Delivery number range.

1939 Ford 1/2-Ton Model 92D Chassis & Cab With Telephone Body (OCW)

Model	Body Type	Price	Weight	Prod. Total
Series 02D — 3/4-Ton — 122 in. w.b. — V-8/60 hp				
80	Platform	650	—	Note 1
81	Chassis & Cab	595	—	Note 1
82	Panel	770	—	Note 1
83	Express-Pickup	660	3086	Note 1
84	Chassis & Cowl	500	—	Note 1
86	Stake	675	—	Note 1
Series 01D — 3/4-Ton — 122 in. w.b. — V-8/85 hp				
80	Platform	665	—	Note 1
81	Chassis & Cab	610	—	Note 1
82	Panel	785	—	Note 1
83	Express-Pickup	675	3272	Note 1
84	Chassis & Cowl	515	—	Note 1
86	Stake	690	—	Note 1

NOTE 1: Series 02D/O1D production total not available.

ENGINE [Standard]: Displacement: 136 cid. L-Head. V-8. 60 hp at 3500 rpm. Bore & stroke: 2-3/5 in. x 3-1/5 in. Compression ratio: 6.6:1. Two-barrel carburetor.
ENGINE [Optional]: Displacement: 221 cid. L-Head. V-8. 85 hp at 3800 rpm. Bore & stroke: 3-1/16 in. x 3-3/4 in. Compression ratio: 6.12:1. Two-barrel carburetor.

122 IN. 1-TON EXPRESS: This model was virtually identical to the 3/4-ton series, except for its brakes, wheels and tires. The 1-ton pickup had extra large load capacity. The cargo box featured a hardwood floor with steel skid strips. The front and side panels were reinforced. And the flareboards and tailgate had rolled edges. The spare wheel and fuel inlet were located on the right-hand side of the vehicle.

122 IN. 1-TON PANEL: The 1-ton Panel was very similar to the 3/4-ton version. Its dual rear doors were hung in a welded, one-piece channel steel frame. Panel sides were double-sealed at the floor with felt and rubber. Load length was 107.25 in. at the floor. Width was 55.25 in. and height 55 in.

122 IN. 1-TON PLATFORM/STAKE: The 1-ton Platform/Stake shared its body with the 3/4-ton version, but it could haul heavier loads. Its wheels were equipped with full, truck-type, flat-base rims. The hardwood floors were interlocked with steel skid strips. The stake pockets were doubly reinforced. The stakes themselves were made of straight-grain hardwood. The rack boards were smooth surfaced with rounded corners and edges. They had large steel inter-locking plates bolted to their corners.

122 IN. 1-TON I.D.: Serial number and engine number are identical. Serial/engine numbers (1935-1945) located: [Four] On top of frame left side, ahead of dash; also on left side of flywheel housing; [Six] On left frame member ahead of cowl; also on top of clutch housing; [V-8] On top of frame, left side, near dash; also on top of clutch housing. See Sedan Delivery number range.

Model	Body Type	Price	Weight	Prod. Total
Series 92Y — 1-Ton — 122 in. w.b. — V-8/60 hp				
80	Platform	685	3223	Note 1
81	Chassis & Cab	630	2666	Note 1
82	Panel	805	3446	Note 1
83	Express-Pickup	695	3243	Note 1
84	Chassis & Cowl	535	2335	Note 1
85	Chassis & W/S	555	2363	Note 1
86	Stake	675	—	Note 1
Series 91Y — 1-Ton — 122 in. w.b. — V-8/85 hp				
80	Platform	700	3409	Note 1
81	Chassis & Cab	645	2852	Note 1
82	Panel	820	3632	Note 1
83	Express-Pickup	710	3429	Note 1
84	Chassis & Cowl	550	2521	Note 1
85	Chassis & W/S	570	2549	Note 1
86	Stake	725	3654	Note 1

NOTE 1: Series 92Y/91Y production total not available.

ENGINE [Standard]: Displacement: 136 cid. L-Head. V-8. 60 hp at 3500 rpm. Bore & stroke: 2-3/5 in. x 3-1/5 in. Compression ratio: 6.6:1. Two-barrel carburetor.

ENGINE [Optional]: Displacement: 221 cid. L-Head. V-8. 85 hp at 3800 rpm. Bore & stroke: 3-1/16 in. x 3-3/4 in. Compression ratio: 6.12:1. Two-barrel carburetor.

1939 Ford 1/2-Ton Model 91D Pickup (OCW)

CHASSIS [112 in. Series and Sedan Delivery]: Wheelbase: 112 in. Length: [Sedan Delivery] 178.67 in.; [Pickup] 183.74 in.; [Panel] 195.09 in.; [Platform/Stake] 189.6 in. Width: 72.14 in. Height: [Panel] 69.67 in.; [Sedan Delivery] 66.67 in.; [Pickup] 71.45 in. GVW: 4,300 lbs. Tires: 6.00 x 16 in.

CHASSIS [122 in. 3/4-Ton and 1-ton]: Wheelbase: 122 in. Length: [Platform/Stake] 199.89 in.; [Pickup] 217.39 in.; [Panel] 209.39 in. Width: [Pickup/Panel] 73.62 in.; [Platform/Stake] 79.24 in. Height: [Panel] 85.64 in.; [Pickup/Platform/Stake] 79.44 in. GVW: [3/4-ton] 5,400 lbs.; [1-ton] 6,400 lbs. Tires: [3/4-Ton] 6.50 x 16 six-ply (front); 7.00 x 16 six-ply (rear); [1-ton] 6.00 x 17 six-ply (front); 7.00 x 17 six-ply (rear).

POWERTRAIN OPTIONS: 95 hp 239 cid. V-8. Four-speed manual.

CONVENIENCE OPTIONS: Plated rear bumper. Passenger seat in Panel. Outside-mounted spare tire. Spotlight. Grille guard. Passenger side windshield wiper. Fog lights for Sedan Delivery. Radio. Wheel trim rings. Heater. Locking gas cap. Cigar lighter in Sedan Delivery. Whitewall tires. Fender skirts. Right-hand sun visor.

1940 FORD

1940 Ford 1/2-Ton Model 01C Sedan Delivery (OCW)

SEDAN DELIVERY: The attractive new Sedan Delivery styling was based on the 1940 Deluxe passenger car line. Its hardbound floor was protected by steel skid strips. The interior was fully-lined and insulated. The windshield opened. There were friction-type door checks to hold all doors when in open position. The spare tire was mounted inside, under the floor. The Sedan Delivery had a single rear door and longer and wider cargo area than the previous year's model. Standard features included: Driver's seat; dual wipers; two sun visors; two ashtrays; a clock; plastic gauge panel; and three-speed manual transmission.

1940 Ford 1/2-Ton Model 01C Sedan Delivery (OCW)

I.D. DATA: Serial number and engine number are identical. Serial/engine numbers (1935-1945) located: [Four] On top of frame left side, ahead of dash; also on left side of flywheel housing; [Six] On left frame member ahead of cowl; also on top of clutch housing; [V-8] On top of frame, left side, near dash; also on top of clutch housing. Starting numbers: [60 hp] BB54-506501; [85 hp] 18-5210701.

Model	Body Type	Price	Weight	Prod. Total
Series 922A — 1/2-Ton — 112 in. w.b. — V-8/60 hp				
780	Sedan Delivery	691	2829	—
Series 91A — 1/2-Ton — 112 in. w.b. — V-8/85 hp				
780	Sedan Delivery	722	2959	—

NOTE 1: Truck production totals for 1940 available from the Henry Ford Museum & Greenfield Village are as follows: [Series 91A Station Wagon] 6; [Model 91A Sedan Delivery] 42; [Model 01A Standard Station Wagon] 3,489; [Model 01A Deluxe Station Wagon] 6,438; [Model 01A Sedan Delivery] 4,040. Ford continued to "build out" and sell certain trucks for several years (until parts inventories were depleted) without regard to model year.

ENGINE [Sedan Delivery]: Displacement: 136 cid. L-Head. V-8. 60 hp at 3500 rpm. Bore & stroke: 2-3/5 in. x 3-1/5 in. Compression ratio: 6.6:1. Carburetor: Two-barrel.

ENGINE [Optional]: Displacement: 221 cid. L-Head. V-8. 85 hp at 3800 rpm. Bore & stroke: 3-1/16 in. x 3-3/4 in. Compression ratio: 6.12:1. Carburetor: Two-barrel.

1940 Ford 1/2-Ton Model 01C Panel (OCW)

112 IN. PICKUP: Many people believe this is one of the best-looking Pickups ever made. It featured passenger car front end styling; fender-integrated headlights with egg-shaped rims; and a vertical-bars grille. The cab was strengthened and altered slightly to give it a more car-like appearance. On the inside, the seats were built with new inter-laced mattress-type coil springs. The spare tire was mounted on the right-hand side of the truck, between the cab and rear fender. Load length was 77.7 in. Load width was 60.34 in.

112 IN. PANEL: In addition to attractive styling, the 112 in. wheelbase Panel featured new tongue and groove flooring and double bodysides at the floor. An interior fully-lined with fiberboard was available at extra cost. The spare tire was located on the right-hand side, between the passenger door and the rear fender. The 112 in. Panel had a load width of 55 in., load length of 87.78 in. and load height of 78.87 in. The twin rear doors could be held open in two positions.

112 IN. PLATFORM/STAKE: The new cargo body had single-piece side rack sections that were made from hardwood boards with smooth surfaces and rounded corners. The loading height was lowered 3 in. The frame featured side rails riveted to heavy-gauge steel cross girders. The spare wheel carrier was mounted under the body at the rear. A new feature was splash shield type rear fenders. Load area was 80 in. long and 67 in. wide. The stakes were 29.5 in. high.

1940 Ford 1/2-Ton Model 01C Pickup (OCW)

I.D. DATA [112 in.]: Serial number and engine number are identical. Serial/engine numbers (1935-1945) located: [Four] On top of frame left side, ahead of dash; also on left side of flywheel housing; [Six] On left frame member ahead of cowl; also on top of clutch housing; [V-8] On top of frame, left side, near dash; also on top of clutch housing. See Sedan Delivery number range.

Model	Body Type	Price	Weight	Prod. Total
Series 02C — 1/2-Ton — 112 in. w.b. — V-8/60 hp				
80	Platform	625	2520	Note 1
81	Chassis & Cab	570	2211	Note 1
82	Panel (slats)	691	2829	Note 1
83	Pickup	595	2542	Note 1
84	Chassis & Cowl	478	1878	Note 1
85	Chassis & W/S	498	1905	Note 1
86	Stake	646	2660	Note 1
Series 01C — 1/2-Ton — 112 in. w.b. — V-8/85 hp				
80	Platform	641	2714	Note 1
81	Chassis & Cab	585	2411	Note 1
82	Panel (slats)	707	3029	Note 1
83	Pickup	610	2737	Note 1
84	Chassis & Cowl	493	2078	Note 1
85	Chassis & W/S	514	2105	Note 1
86	Stake	661	2856	Note 1

NOTE 1: Truck production totals for 1940 available from the Henry Ford Museum & Greenfield Village are as follows: [Series 01A Commercial Chassis] 121; [Series 01A Panel With Slats] 4,912; [Model 01A Panel With Masonite] 551; [Model 01A Pickup] 33,397. Some of the model codes in these records do not match 1939 truck codes in model charts. The mixed year totals reflect the fact that Ford continued to "build out" certain trucks for several years until parts inventories were depleted.

ENGINE [Standard]: Displacement: 136 cid. L-Head. V-8. 60 hp at 3500 rpm. Bore & stroke: 2-3/5 in. x 3-1/5 in. Compression ratio: 6.6:1. Two-barrel carburetor.

ENGINE [Optional]: Displacement: 221 cid. L-Head. V-8. 85 hp at 3800 rpm. Bore & stroke: 3-1/16 in. x 3-3/4 in. Compression ratio: 6.12:1. Two-barrel carburetor.

122 IN. 3/4-TON EXPRESS: A flatter-faced hood with taller vertical bar grille and fender-mounted, pod-type headlights quickly set the 3/4-ton Pickup apart from the 1/2-ton. It had a steel inter-locked wood floor and a load capacity of 59.1 cu. ft. New features included: Sealed beam headlights; higher power generator and battery; 36 x 1.75 in. longitudinal springs; and a different axle design. There were three stake sockets in each flareboard for rack or side boards. The tailgate could be lowered flush with the floor or swung all the way down.

122 IN. 3/4-TON PANEL: Like the 3/4-ton Express, the 3/4-ton Panel had a more truck-like appearance than the 1/2-ton version. However, interior features were similar. The floors were of the tongue and groove variety and the twin rear doors had two-position checks. The spare tire was located on the right-hand side, between the passenger door and the rear fender. The roof rail, top and bodysides were welded together for greater rigidity and strength. The driver's seat was upholstered in durable, waterproof-coated fabric.

1940 Ford 1/2-Ton Model 01C Pickup (OCW)

122 IN. 3/4-TON PLATFORM/STAKE: The 3/4-ton Platform/Stake was especially designed for bulky loads. It had a sturdy steel bridge-type platform frame, hardwood floor and smooth-surfaced rack boards with rounded corners. There was a large metal advertising panel on each forward stake section. The platform sides and end were protected by the steel frame rail. The ends of the body sills had strong steel caps riveted to the frame rail

and bolted to the sills. The stake sockets were doubly reinforced, welded to the inside of the frame rail and riveted to the outside. Large steel inter-locking plates were bolted to the corners of top rack boards, tying them rigidly together to prevent fanning. The three-person waterproof seat could be adjusted to three positions.

I.D. DATA [122 in. 3/4-Ton]: Serial number and engine number are identical. Serial/engine numbers (1935-1945) located: [Four] On top of frame left side, ahead of dash; also on left side of flywheel housing; [Six] On left frame member ahead of cowl; also on top of clutch housing; [V-8] On top of frame, left side, near dash; also on top of clutch housing. See Sedan Delivery number range.

Model	Body Type	Price	Weight	Prod. Total
Series 02D — 3/4-Ton — 122 in. w.b. — V-8/60 hp				
80	Platform	687	3029	Note 1
81	Chassis & Cab	631	2517	Note 1
82	Panel	804	3382	Note 1
83	Express-Pickup	697	3086	Note 1
84	Chassis & Cowl	540	2187	Note 1
85	Chassis & W/S	560	2214	Note 1
86	Stake	713	3282	Note 1
Series 01D — 3/4-Ton — 122 in. w.b. — V-8/85 hp				
80	Platform	702	3215	Note 1
81	Chassis & Cab	647	2703	Note 1
82	Panel	819	3568	Note 1
83	Express-Pickup	713	3272	Note 1
84	Chassis & Cowl	555	2373	Note 1
85	Chassis & W/S	576	2400	Note 1
86	Stake	728	3468	Note 1

NOTE 1: Series 02D/01D production total not available.

ENGINE [Standard]: Displacement: 136 cid. L-Head. V-8. 60 hp at 3500 rpm. Bore & stroke: 2-3/5 in. x 3-1/5 in. Compression ratio: 6.6:1. Two-barrel carburetor.

ENGINE [Optional]: Displacement: 221 cid. L-Head. V-8. 85 hp at 3800 rpm. Bore & stroke: 3-1/16 in. x 3-3/4 in. Compression ratio: 6.12:1. Two-barrel carburetor.

1940 Ford 1/2-Ton Model 02C Panel (OCW)

122 IN. 1-TON EXPRESS: This model was virtually identical to the 3/4-ton series, except for its brakes, wheels and tires. The 1-ton Pickup had extra large load capacity. The cargo box featured a hardwood floor with steel skid strips. The front and side panels were reinforced and the flareboards and tailgate had rolled edges. The spare wheel and fuel inlet were located on the right-hand side of the vehicle.

1940 Ford 1/2-Ton Model 01C Pickup (DFW)

122 IN. 1-TON PANEL: The 1-ton Panel was very similar to the 3/4-ton version. Its dual rear doors were hung in a welded, one-piece channel steel frame. Panel sides were double-sealed at the floor with felt and rubber. Load length was 107.25 in. at the floor. Width was 55.25 in. and height 55 in.

122 IN. 1-TON PLATFORM/STAKE: The 1-ton Platform/Stake shared its body with the 3/4-ton version, but it could haul heavier loads. Its wheels were equipped with full truck type, flat base rims. The hardwood floors were interlocked with steel skid strips. The stake pockets were doubly reinforced. The stakes themselves were made of straight-grain hardwood. The rack boards were smooth surfaced with rounded corners and edges. They had large steel inter-locking plates bolted to their corners.

I.D. DATA [122 in. 1-Tonner]: Serial number and engine number are identical. Serial/engine numbers (1935-1945) located: [Four] On top of frame left side, ahead of dash; also on left side of flywheel housing; [Six] On left frame member ahead of cowl; also on top of clutch housing; [V-8] On top of frame, left side, near dash; also on top of clutch housing. See Sedan Delivery number range.

Model	Body Type	Price	Weight	Prod. Total
Series 02Y — 1-Ton — 122 in. w.b. — V-8/60 hp				
80	Platform	723	3175	Note 1
81	Chassis & Cab	667	2732	Note 1
82	Panel	840	3482	Note 1
83	Express-Pickup	733	3257	Note 1
84	Chassis & Cowl	576	2384	Note 1
85	Chassis & W/S	596	2429	Note 1
86	Stake	748	3428	Note 1
Series 01Y — 1-Ton — 122 in. w.b. — V-8/85 hp				
80	Platform	738	3361	Note 1
81	Chassis & Cab	682	2918	Note 1
82	Panel	855	3668	Note 1
83	Express-Pickup	748	3443	Note 1
84	Chassis & Cowl	591	2570	Note 1
85	Chassis & W/S	611	2615	Note 1
86	Stake	764	3614	Note 1

NOTE 1: Series 02Y/01Y production total not available.

ENGINE [Standard]: Displacement: 136 cid. L-Head. V-8. 60 hp at 3500 rpm. Bore & stroke: 2-3/5 in. x 3-1/5 in. Compression ratio: 6.6:1. Two-barrel carburetor.

ENGINE [Optional]: Displacement: 221 cid. L-Head. V-8. 85 hp at 3800 rpm. Bore & stroke: 3-1/16 in. x 3-3/4 in. Compression ratio: 6.12:1. Two-barrel carburetor.

CHASSIS [112 In. Series and Sedan Delivery]: Wheelbase: 112 in. Length: 178.67 in. [Sedan Delivery]. 183.74 in. [Pickup]. 195.45 in. [Panel]. 189.6 in. [Platform/Stake]. Width: 72.14 in. Height: 75.85 in. [Panel]. 71.45 in. [Platform/Stake, Pickup]. GVW: 4300 lbs. Tires: 6.00 x 16 in. 122 in. 3/4-Ton and 1-ton: Wheelbase: 122 in. Length: 201.84 in. [Platform/Stake]. 203.34 in. [Pickup]. 215.57 in. [Panel]. Width: 73.62 in. [Pickup, Panel]. 79.24 in. [Platform/Stake]. Height: 82.64 in. [Panel]. 76.2 in. [Pickup, Platform/Stake]. GVW: 5,400 lbs. [3/4-ton]; 6,400 lbs. [1-ton]. Tires: 6.50 x 16 six-ply front; 7.00 x 16 six-ply rear [3/4-ton]. 6.00 x 17 six-ply front; 7.00 x 17 six-ply rear [1-ton].

POWERTRAIN OPTIONS: 95 hp 239 cid. V-8. Four-speed manual transmission.

CONVENIENCE OPTIONS: Plated rear bumper. Passenger seat for Panel. Outside mounted spare tire. Spotlight. Grille guard. Passenger side windshield wiper. Fog lights for Sedan Delivery. Radio. Wheel trim rings. Heater. Locking gas cap. Cigar lighter for Sedan Delivery. White sidewall tires. Fender skirts. Right-hand sun visor. 7.00 x 17 or 7.50 x 17 eight-ply tires on 1-ton. Two-piece sliding rear window for Pickup, Platform, Stake. A specially-formed, thick-cushioned seat of fully aerated foam rubber covered with duck. Heavy-duty 11 in. clutch.

1941 FORD

1941 Ford Model 78 Coupe-Pickup (ABE/DFW)

SEDAN DELIVERY: Rather than sharing its looks with the passenger cars, the new 1941 Sedan Delivery used slightly modified styling from the previous year. In fact, it went from being based on the 1940 Deluxe series to the Standard. It came with the Commercial Car parking lamps and vertical bar grille. The fuel filler cap was recessed. There were new, Ford script hubcaps and different optional bumper guards. The hardwood floor had steel skid plates. A door check could hold the large rear door open. The spare tire was located under the floor and could not be removed if the back door was locked. The load length was 74.6 in. A driver's seat and a three-speed manual were a couple of the standard features.

I.D. DATA [Sedan Delivery]: Serial number and engine number are identical. Serial/engine numbers (1935-1945) located: [Four] On top of frame left side, ahead of dash; also on left side of flywheel housing; [Six] On left frame member ahead of cowl; also on top of clutch housing; [V-8] On top of frame, left side, near dash; also on top of clutch housing. The VIN range for V-8 models ran from 18-5896295 through 18-6769035. Four-cylinder models went from 9A-38 through 9C-13200. And six-cylinder powered vehicles 1GC-1 through 1GC-34800.

Model	Body Type	Price	Weight	Prod. Total
Series 1NA — 1/2-Ton — 112 in. w.b. — Four				
78	Sedan Delivery	741	2705	Note 1
Series 1GA — 1/2-Ton — 112 in. w.b. — Six				
78	Sedan Delivery	746	2850	Note 1
Series 11A — 1/2-Ton — 112 in. w.b. — V-8/85 hp				
78	Sedan Delivery	761	2875	Note 1

Model	Body Type	Price	Weight	Prod. Total
Series 19A — 1/2-Ton — 112 in. w.b. — V-8/95 hp				
78	Sedan Delivery	787	2875	Note 1

NOTE 1: Combined production was 6,881 Sedan Deliveries.

ENGINE [1NA]: Displacement: 119.7 cid. L-head. Four-cylinder. 30 hp at 2800 rpm. Bore & stroke: 3.19 in. x 3.75 in. Compression ratio: 6.0:1. One-barrel updraft carburetor.

ENGINE [1GA]: Displacement: 225.8 cid. L-Head. Six-cylinder. 90 hp at 3300 rpm. Bore & stroke: 3.3 in. x 4.4 in. Compression ratio: 6.7:1. One-barrel carburetor.

ENGINE [11A]: Displacement: 221 cid. L-Head. V-8. 85 hp at 3800 rpm. Bore & stroke: 3-1/16 in. x 3-3/4 in. Compression ratio: 6.12:1. Two-barrel carburetor.

ENGINE [19A]: Displacement: 239 cid. L-Head. V-8. 95 hp at 3800 rpm. Bore & stroke: 3.19 in. x 3.75 in. Compression ratio: 6.75:1. Carburetor: Two-barrel.

112 IN. PICKUP: Styling changes were rather mild for 1941. Among them were: Different parking lamp lenses; wider hood nose moldings; and rectangular nameplates on the side of the hood. The instrument cluster graphics were revised. The V-8 logo was removed from the tailgate. And the hubcaps had the Ford script on them. The seat had mattress-type coil springs. There were 40.25 in. x 2 in. front springs and the rear springs of the Pickup were slightly longer. As before, the spare tire was placed on the right-hand side, between the cab and rear fender. Four-cylinder models came with a four-speed manual transmission. A three-speed manual was standard with the six and V-8.

112 IN. PLATFORM/STAKE: The 112 in. Platform/Stake shared the Pickups' changes. The platform frame had steel side rails riveted to heavy gauge steel cross girders. The side rack sections were made from hardwood boards with smoothed surfaces and rounded corners. The spare tire was mounted under the platform, at the rear.

1941 Ford 1/2-Ton Model 11C Pickup (Lou Harrison/DFW)

112 IN. PANEL: The 112 in. Panel lost none of its good looks in 1941. In fact, some think the minor styling changes made added to its charm. It came with tongue and groove hardwood flooring. The hardwood floor had steel skid plates. The bodysides were double sealed at the floor. Strip felt was compressed between the outer side panel and the floor plank, then sheet rubber was cemented to the top of the floor plank and the inside of the side panel. The rear doors were rubber-sealed all around. An interior light, facing the load area, was standard.

I.D. DATA [112 in.]: Serial number and engine number are identical. Serial/engine numbers (1935-1945) located: [Four] On top of frame left side, ahead of dash; also on left side of flywheel housing; [Six] On left frame member ahead of cowl; also on top of clutch housing; [V-8] On top of frame, left side, near dash; also on top of clutch housing. See Sedan Delivery number range.

1941 Ford 1/2-Ton Model 11C Sedan Delivery (OCW)

Model	Body Type	Price	Weight	Prod. Total
Series 1NC — 1/2-Ton — 112 in. w.b. — Four				
80	Platform	649	2552	Note 1
81	Chassis & Cab	588	2238	Note 1
82	Panel (slats)	710	2861	Note 1
83	Pickup	614	2575	Note 1
84	Chassis & Cowl	496	1905	Note 1
85	Chassis & W/S	517	1932	Note 1
86	Stake	670	2694	Note 1

Series 1GC — 1/2-Ton — 112 in. w.b. — Six

Model	Body Type	Price	Weight	Prod. Total
80	Platform	654	2705	Note 1
81	Chassis & Cab	593	2395	Note 1
82	Panel (slats)	715	2993	Note 1
83	Pickup	619	2732	Note 1
84	Chassis & Cowl	501	2060	Note 1
85	Chassis & W/S	522	2089	Note 1
86	Stake	675	2850	Note 1

Series 11C — 1/2-Ton — 112 in. w.b. — V-8/85 hp

Model	Body Type	Price	Weight	Prod. Total
80	Platform	670	2722	Note 1
81	Chassis & Cab	608	2408	Note 1
82	Panel (slats)	731	3031	Note 1
83	Pickup	634	2745	Note 1
84	Chassis & Cowl	517	2075	Note 1
85	Chassis & W/S	537	2102	Note 1
86	Stake	690	2864	Note 1

Series 19C — 1/2-Ton — 112 in. w.b. — V-8/95 hp

Model	Body Type	Price	Weight	Prod. Total
80	Platform	695	2722	Note 1
81	Chassis & Cab	634	2408	Note 1
82	Panel (slats)	756	3031	Note 1
83	Pickup	659	2745	Note 1
84	Chassis & Cowl	542	2075	Note 1
85	Chassis & W/S	563	2102	Note 1
86	Stake	715	2864	Note 1

NOTE 1: Combined body style production for the 1/2-Ton trucks was as follows: [Platform] 207; [Chassis & Cab] 5,129; [Panel With Slats] 11,183; [Pickup] 70,190; [Chassis & Cowl] 876; [Chassis & Windshield] 280; [Stake] 1,529.

ENGINE [1NC]: Displacement: 119.7 cid. L-head. Four-cylinder. 30 hp at 2800 rpm. Bore & stroke: 3.19 in. x 3.75 in. Compression ratio: 6.0:1. One-barrel updraft carburetor.

ENGINE [1GY]: Displacement: 225.8 cid. L-Head. Six-cylinder. 90 hp at 3300 rpm. Bore & stroke: 3.3 in. x 4.4 in. Compression ratio: 6.7:1. One-barrel carburetor.

ENGINE [11C]: Displacement: 221 cid. L-Head. V-8. 85 hp at 3800 rpm. Bore & stroke: 3-1/16 in. x 3-3/4 in. Compression ratio: 6.12:1. Two-barrel carburetor.

ENGINE [19C]: Displacement: 239 cid. L-Head. V-8. 95 hp at 3800 rpm. Bore & stroke: 3.19 in. x 3.75 in. Compression ratio: 6.75:1. Carburetor: Two-barrel.

122 IN. 3/4-TON EXPRESS: Mild styling changes were made to the 3/4-ton Pickup. Among them were: Hubcaps with the Ford name on them (this change was made during the model year, so some came with the old V-8 emblem); accent moldings placed around the hood-side louvers; and the Ford nameplate placed slightly off-center on the louvers. Wider trim was used on the hood nose with the Ford name spelled out vertically on it. The wood floor was protected and inter-locked by steel skid strips. The tailgate had truss-type rolled edge. The bodyside panels had smaller panels to increase rigidity. There were three stake pockets in each flareboard.

1941 Marmon-Harrington/Ford 3/4-Ton Model 11D Pickup 4x4 (P. McLaughlin)

122 IN. 3/4-TON PANEL: The 3/4-ton Panel had tongue and groove hardwood flooring. The bodysides were double sealed at the floor with felt and rubber. The roof rail, top and bodysides were welded together for greater rigidity and strength.

122 IN. 3/4-TON PLATFORM/STAKE: The 3/4-ton Platform/Stake had a bridge-like platform frame. The floors were made of hardwood and were inter-locked to the frame by steel skid strips. Platform sides and end were protected by the steel frame rail. The stake sockets were doubly reinforced. The stakes themselves were made of straight-grained hardwood. The rack boards were smoothly surfaced with rounded corners and edges.

1941 Ford 1/2-Ton Model 11C Pickup (OCW)

I.D. DATA [3/4-Ton]: Serial number and engine number are identical. Serial/engine numbers (1935-1945) located: [Four] On top of frame left side, ahead of dash; also on left side of flywheel housing; [Six] On left frame member ahead of cowl; also on top of clutch housing; [V-8] On top of frame, left side, near dash; also on top of clutch housing. Same as Sedan Delivery except the letter code Y replaced A and C.

Model	Body Type	Price	Weight	Prod. Total
Series 1ND — 3/4-Ton — 122 in. w.b. — Four				
80	Platform	726	3047	Note 1
81	Chassis & Cab	578	2205	Note 1
82	Panel (slats)	843	3395	Note 1
83	Express-Pickup	736	3105	Note 1
84	Chassis & Cowl	578	2205	Note 1
85	Chassis & W/S	698	2232	Note 1
86	Stake	751	3300	Note 1
Series 1GD — 3/4-Ton — 122 in. w.b. — Six				
80	Platform	716	3195	Note 1
81	Chassis & Cab	660	2683	Note 1
82	Panel (slats)	834	3472	Note 1
83	Express-Pickup	727	3252	Note 1
84	Chassis & Cowl	569	2353	Note 1
85	Chassis & W/S	589	2380	Note 1
86	Stake	742	3448	Note 1
Series 11D — 3/4-Ton — 122 in. w.b. — V-8/85 hp				
80	Platform	732	3217	Note 1
81	Chassis & Cab	676	2705	Note 1
82	Panel (slats)	849	3494	Note 1
83	Express-Pickup	742	3274	Note 1
84	Chassis & Cowl	584	2375	Note 1
85	Chassis & W/S	604	2402	Note 1
86	Stake	757	3470	Note 1
Series 19D — 3/4-Ton — 122 in. w.b. — V-8/95 hp				
80	Platform	757	3217	Note 1
81	Chassis & Cab	701	2705	Note 1
82	Panel (slats)	874	3494	Note 1
83	Express-Pickup	767	3274	Note 1
84	Chassis & Cowl	609	2375	Note 1
85	Chassis & W/S	630	2402	Note 1
86	Stake	783	3470	Note 1

NOTE 1: Combined body style production for the 3/4-Ton trucks was as follows: [Platform] 274; [Chassis & Cab] N/A; [Panel With Slats] 1,591; [Express-Pickup] 5,084; [Chassis & Cowl] N/A; [Chassis & Windshield] N/A; [Stake] 1,288.

ENGINE [1ND]: Displacement: 119.7 cid. L-head. Four-cylinder. 30 hp at 2800 rpm. Bore & stroke: 3.19 in. x 3.75 in. Compression ratio: 6.0:1. One-barrel updraft carburetor.

ENGINE [1GD]: Displacement: 225.8 cid. L-Head. Six-cylinder. 90 hp at 3300 rpm. Bore & stroke: 3.3 in. x 4.4 in. Compression ratio: 6.7:1. One-barrel carburetor.

ENGINE [11D]: Displacement: 221 cid. L-Head. V-8. 85 hp at 3800 rpm. Bore & stroke: 3-1/16 in. x 3-3/4 in. Compression ratio: 6.12:1. Two-barrel carburetor.

ENGINE [19D]: Displacement: 239 cid. L-Head. V-8. 95 hp at 3800 rpm. Bore & stroke: 3.19 in. x 3.75. Compression ratio: 6.75:1. Carburetor: Two-barrel. (At the beginning of the model year, the V-8 was rated at 85 hp.)

1941 Ford 1-Ton Model 11Y Platform Stake (OCW)

122 IN. 1-TON EXPRESS: Light-duty Pickup truck buyers who wanted extra payload capacity choose the 1-ton over the similar 3/4-ton model. The floor planking was made of hardwood and inter-locked by steel skid strips. The narrow wheelhousings helped to maximize load width. The two-position tailgate had truss-type rolled edge. The bodyside panels had smaller panels to increase rigidity. There were three stake pockets in each flareboard. The seat was adjustable to three positions. It featured interlaced mattress-type springs and was upholstered with a durable, waterproof fabric.

122 IN. 1-TON PANEL: Steel panels and hardwood boards protected the bodysides. The seasoned hardwood floor had evenly spaced steel skid strips. Side panels were double sealed at the floor with rubber and felt to exclude moisture and dust. The twin rear doors were hung in a rigid one-piece channel steel frame. They were rubber-sealed all around. An interior light was standard.

122 IN. 1-TON PLATFORM/STAKE: The 1941 Ford 1-ton Platform/Stake resembled the previous year's model, but came with an extended sub-structure and minus the sign panels. The wheels were equipped with full truck-type flat base rims. Steel skid strips were bolted to the cross girders of the platform frame. They inter-locked the hardwood floor planking. Large pressed steel gussets were used to attach the platform frame to the body sills. The ends of the body sills were protected by strong steel caps, which were riveted to the frame rail and bolted to the sills. The stakes were made of straight-grained hardwood. The rack boards were smooth surfaced with rounded corners and edges.

I.D. DATA [122 in. 1-Ton]: Serial number and engine number are identical. Serial/engine numbers (1935-1945) located: [Four] On top of frame left side, ahead of dash; also on left side of flywheel housing; [Six] On left frame member ahead of cowl; also on top of clutch housing; [V-8] On top of frame, left side, near dash; also on top of clutch housing. See 3/4-ton I.D.

Model	Body Type	Price	Weight	Prod. Total
Series 1NY — 1-Ton — 122 in. w.b. — Four				
80	Platform	762	3208	Note 1
81	Chassis & Cab	706	2813	Note 1
82	Panel (slats)	879	3511	Note 1
83	Express-Pickup	772	3272	Note 1
84	Chassis & Cowl	614	2429	Note 1
85	Chassis & W/S	634	2510	Note 1
86	Stake	787	3461	Note 1
Series 1GY — 1-Ton — 122 in. w.b. — Six				
80	Platform	753	3356	Note 1
81	Chassis & Cab	697	2961	Note 1
82	Panel (slats)	870	3639	Note 1
83	Express-Pickup	763	3420	Note 1
84	Chassis & Cowl	605	2613	Note 1
85	Chassis & W/S	625	2658	Note 1
86	Stake	778	3609	Note 1
Series 11Y — 1-Ton — 122 in. w.b. — V-8/85 hp				
80	Platform	768	3376	Note 1
81	Chassis & Cab	712	2983	Note 1
82	Panel (slats)	885	3681	Note 1
83	Express-Pickup	788	3442	Note 1
84	Chassis & Cowl	620	2635	Note 1
85	Chassis & W/S	641	2680	Note 1
86	Stake	793	3631	Note 1
Series 19Y — 1-Ton — 122 in. w.b. — V-8/95 hp				
80	Platform	793	3376	Note 1
81	Chassis & Cab	737	2983	Note 1
82	Panel (slats)	911	3681	Note 1
83	Express-Pickup	804	3442	Note 1
84	Chassis & Cowl	646	2635	Note 1
85	Chassis & W/S	666	2680	Note 1
86	Stake	819	3631	Note 1

NOTE 1: Combined body style production for the 1-Ton trucks was as follows: [Platform] 528; [Chassis & Cab] N/A; [Panel With Slats] 1,222; [Express-Pickup] 5,317; [Chassis & Cowl] N/A; [Chassis & Windshield] N/A; [Stake] 1,500.

ENGINE [1NY]: Displacement: 119.7 cid. L-head. Four-cylinder. 30 hp at 2800 rpm. Bore & stroke: 3.19 in. x 3.75 in. Compression ratio: 6.0:1. One-barrel updraft carburetor.

ENGINE [1GY]: Displacement: 225.8 cid. L-Head. Six-cylinder. 90 hp at 3300 rpm. Bore & stroke: 3.3 in. x 4.4 in. Compression ratio: 6.7:1. One-barrel carburetor.

ENGINE [11Y]: Displacement: 221 cid. L-Head. V-8. 85 hp at 3800 rpm. Bore & stroke: 3-1/16 in. x 3-3/4 in. Compression ratio: 6.12:1. Two-barrel carburetor.

ENGINE [19Y]: Displacement: 239 cid. L-Head. V-8. 95 hp at 3800 rpm. Bore & stroke: 3.19 in. x 3.75 in. Compression ratio: 6.75:1. Carburetor: Two-barrel.

CHASSIS: [112 in. Series and Sedan Delivery]: Wheelbase: 112 in. Length: [Sedan Delivery] 178.67 in.; [Pickup] 183.74 in.; [Panel] 195.45 in.; [Platform/Stake] 189.6 in. Width: 72.14 in. Height: [Panel] 75.85 in.; [Platform/Stake/Pickup] 71.45 in. GVW: 4,300 lbs. Tires: 6.00 x 16 in.

CHASSIS: [122 in. 3/4-ton/1-ton]: Wheelbase: 122 in. Length: [Platform/Stake] 201.84 in.; [Pickup] 203.34 in.; [Panel] 215.57 in. Width: [Panel, Pickup] 73.62 in.; [Platform/Stake] 79.24 in. Height: [Panel] 82.64 in.; [Pickup, Platform/Stake] 76.2 in. GVW: [3/4-ton] 5,400 lbs.; [1-ton] 6,400 lbs. Tires: [3/4-ton] 6.00 x 17 six-ply, front; 7.00 x 16 six-ply, rear; [1-ton] 6.00 x 17 six-ply, front; 7.00 x 17 six-ply, rear .

1941 Ford 1/2-Ton Model 11C Pickup (Dennis S. Olsen)

POWERTRAIN OPTIONS: 239 cid V-8. Heavy-duty four-speed manual transmission.

CONVENIENCE OPTIONS: Plated rear bumper. Passenger seat for Panel. Grille guard. Passenger side windshield wiper. Outside-mounted spare tire. Spotlight. Fog lights for Sedan Delivery. Radio. Wheel trim rings. Heater. Locking gas cap. Cigar lighter for Sedan Delivery. White sidewall tires. Fender skirts. Right-hand sun visor. 7.00 x 17 or 7.50 x 17 eight-ply tires for 1-ton. Two-piece sliding rear window [Pickup, Platform/Stake]. Heavy-duty 11 in. clutch.

1941 Ford 1/2-Ton Model 11C Pickup (OCW)

1942 FORD

1942 Ford Model 78 Sedan Delivery (OCW)

SEDAN DELIVERY: The Sedan Delivery was restyled for 1942. It had concealed running-boards and 1941 style front fenders. The grille had a narrow center section with vertical bars on either side. The parking lights were located above the painted grille frame. Super Deluxe models had a front bumper. A 120 amp.-hr. battery. The Sedan Delivery could hold up to 92.5 cu. ft. of cargo. The hardwood floor was protected by steel skid strips. The interior was fully lined and insulated. Trucks powered by a six had a 10 in. clutch. Those with V-8s had a 9 in. clutch.

I.D. DATA [Sedan Delivery]: Serial number and engine number are identical. Serial/engine numbers (1935-1945) located: [Four] On top of frame left side, ahead of dash; also on left side of flywheel housing; [Six] On left frame member ahead of cowl; also on top of clutch housing; [V-8] On top of frame, left side, near dash; also on top of clutch housing. The VINs for 90 hp V-8 models ranged from 18-67969036 thru 18-6925898; for the 100 hp V-8 models, 99A-46670 thru 99A-583000. Six-cylinder VINS were 1GC-34801 thru 1GC-227523.

Model	Body Type	Price	Weight	Prod. Total
Series 1GA — 1/2-Ton — 114 in. w.b. — Six				
78	Sedan Delivery	810	2850	Note 1
Series 21A — 1/2-Ton — 114 in. w.b. — V-8/90 hp				
78	Sedan Delivery	825	3075	Note 1
Series 29A — 1/2-Ton — 114 in. w.b. — V-8/100 hp				
78	Sedan Delivery	850	3075	Note 1

NOTE 1: Combined production was 1,316 Sedan Deliveries.

ENGINE [1GA]: Displacement: 225.8 cid. L-Head. Six-cylinder. 90 hp at 3300 rpm. Bore & stroke: 3.3 in. x 4.4 in. Compression ratio: 6.7:1. One-barrel carburetor.

ENGINE [21A]: Displacement: 221 cid. Flathead V-8. 90 hp at 3800 rpm. Bore & stroke: 3.19 in. x 3.75 in. Compression ratio: 6.2:1. Carburetor: Two-barrel.

ENGINE [29A]: Displacement: 239.4 cid. Flathead V-8. 100 hp at 3600 rpm. Bore & stroke: 3-3/16 in. x 3-3/4 in. Compression ratio: 6.75:1. Carburetor: Two-barrel.

114 IN. PICKUP: The '42 Ford 1/2-ton Pickup featured new styling that was instantly recognizable. The front end now had a slightly protruding flat faced panel. It incorporated the headlights and the waterfall painted vertical bars grille. The Ford name was printed in molding on the face of the hood, just above the grille. The parking lights were fender-mounted near the headlights. There were louvers on the side of the hood. The Ford script on the hubcaps was stylized a bit to give a winged effect. The spare tire was moved to the left-hand side of the truck. The gas tank pipe was in the tire's old position. The rectangular Shift-o-guide speedometer indicated when to shift gears for greatest pulling ability and best economy. On the left of the speedometer were the fuel and temperature gauges; on the right, the oil pressure gauge and ammeter. The floor of the welded Pickup body was metal, with strips stamped in. But there was a hardwood floor beneath. The Pickup also had a new truck type chassis.

114 IN. PANEL: The restyled 1/2-ton Panel had a lower floor, which gave it three-inches more interior height than the '41 version. It had a new straight-rail frame and truck-type front suspension. Gas tank capacity was reduced from 19-gal. to 17-gal. and the filler pipe was relocated to the left-hand side of the vehicle. Steel panels and hardwood boards were used on the interior to protect the bodysides. Steel skid strips were placed in the hardwood floors. The rear doors were rubber sealed all around.

114 IN. PLATFORM/STAKE: As before, the 1/2-ton Platform/Stake had a hardwood platform with steel skid strips bolted to a frame girder. This helped keep the planks from spreading or warping. The one-piece side rack sections featured straight grained hardwood

stakes and smooth surfaced rackboards. Steel inter-locking plates held the racks together. Some new items included: Heavy-duty shock absorbers; different runningboards; rubber-cushioned rear engine mounts; a transverse steering tie rod; and drag link.

I.D. DATA [114 in.]: Serial number and engine number are identical. Serial/engine numbers (1935-1945) located: [Four] On top of frame left side, ahead of dash; also on left side of flywheel housing; [Six] On left frame member ahead of cowl; also on top of clutch housing; [V-8] On top of frame, left side, near dash; also on top of clutch housing. Same as Sedan Delivery, plus four-cylinder VINs ranged from 9C-13201 on up.

1942 Ford 3/4-Ton Model 2ND Platform Stake (DFW)

Model	Body Type	Price	Weight	Prod. Total
Series 2NC — 1/2-Ton — 114 in. w.b. — Four				
80	Platform	655	2650	Note 1
81	Chassis & Cab	625	2377	Note 1
82	Panel (slats)	750	2929	Note 1
83	Pickup	655	2650	Note 1
84	Chassis & Cowl	535	2000	Note 1
85	Chassis & W/S	555	2023	Note 1
86	Stake	720	2748	Note 1
Series 2GC — 1/2-Ton — 114 in. w.b. — Six				
80	Platform	705	2705	Note 1
81	Chassis & Cab	630	2532	Note 1
82	Panel (slats)	755	2993	Note 1
83	Pickup	660	2805	Note 1
84	Chassis & Cowl	540	2155	Note 1
85	Chassis & W/S	560	2178	Note 1
86	Stake	725	2850	Note 1
Series 21C — 1/2-Ton — 114 in. w.b. — V-8/90 hp				
80	Platform	720	2788	Note 1
81	Chassis & Cab	645	2547	Note 1
82	Panel (slats)	770	3104	Note 1
83	Pickup	675	2820	Note 1
84	Chassis & Cowl	555	2170	Note 1
85	Chassis & W/S	575	2193	Note 1
86	Stake	740	2923	Note 1
Series 29C — 1/2-Ton — 114 in. w.b. — V-8/100 hp				
80	Platform	745	2788	Note 1
81	Chassis & Cab	670	2547	Note 1
82	Panel (slats)	795	3104	Note 1
83	Pickup	700	2820	Note 1
84	Chassis & Cowl	580	2170	Note 1
85	Chassis & W/S	600	2193	Note 1
86	Stake	765	2923	Note 1

NOTE 1: Combined body style production for the 1942 Ford 1/2-Ton trucks is not available.

ENGINE [2NC]: Displacement: 119.7 cid. L-head. Four-cylinder. 30 hp at 2800 rpm. Bore & stroke: 3.19 in. x 3.75 in. Compression ratio: 6.0:1. One-barrel updraft carburetor.

ENGINE [2GC]: Displacement: 225.8 cid. L-Head. Six-cylinder. 90 hp at 3300 rpm. Bore & stroke: 3.3 in. x 4.4 in. Compression ratio: 6.7:1. One-barrel carburetor.

ENGINE [21C]: Displacement: 221 cid. Flathead V-8. 90 hp at 3800 rpm. Bore & stroke: 3.19 in. x 3.75. Compression ratio: 6.2:1. Carburetor: Two-barrel.

ENGINE [29C]: Displacement: 239.4 cid. Flathead V-8. 100 hp at 3600 rpm. Bore & stroke: 3-3/16 in. x 3-3/4 in. Compression ratio: 6.75:1. Carburetor: Two-barrel.

ENGINE [114 in.]: Same as Sedan Delivery, plus: Displacement: 119.7 cid. L-Head Four. 30 hp at 2800 rpm. Bore & stroke: 3.19 in. x 3-3/4 in. Compression ratio: 6.0:1. Carburetor: one-barrel.

122 IN. 3/4-TON EXPRESS: The 3/4-ton now shared basic styling with the 1/2-ton series. Aside from looks, it was pretty much the same as last year, although it was about 3 in. wider. The floor planking was made of hardwood and inter-locked by steel skid strips. The tailgate could be lowered flush with the floor, or swung all the way down. There were stake pockets in the flareboards for rack or side boards.

122 IN. 3/4-TON PANEL: From the driver's seat, the 1942 3/4-ton Panel didn't seem all that much different from the 1941. The seat was a bit more comfortable, the interior was 2.5 in. wider and the truck was about 2 in. longer. A three-speed manual was standard, except on four-cylinder models. They came with a four-speed manual transmission. The hardwood floor had steel skid strips. The side panels were double sealed at the floor with felt and rubber. The rear doors were rubber sealed all around. The joints were waterproofed by sealing with a caulking compound.

122 IN. 3/4-TON PLATFORM/STAKE: The 3/4-ton Platform/Stake had double insulated stake sockets welded to the inside of the frame rail and riveted to the outside. This helped to keep the rack sided from spreading when loads pressed against them. The stakes were made of straight-grained hardwood. The rack boards were smoothly surfaced with rounded corners and edges. Large steel inter-locking plates were bolted to the corners of top rack boards.

I.D. DATA [112 in. 3/4-Ton]: Serial number and engine number are identical. Serial/engine numbers (1935-1945) located: [Four] On top of frame left side, ahead of dash; also on left side of flywheel housing; [Six] On left frame member ahead of cowl; also on top of clutch housing; [V-8] On top of frame, left side, near dash; also on top of clutch housing. Numbers same as the Sedan Delivery except the letter Y replaced letters A and C.

Series 2ND — 3/4-Ton — 122 in. w.b. — Four				
80	Platform	759	3076	Note 1
81	Chassis & Cab	709	2658	Note 1
82	Panel (slats)	879	3365	Note 1
83	Express-Pickup	764	3171	Note 1
84	Chassis & Cowl	614	2241	Note 1
85	Chassis & W/S	634	2264	Note 1
86	Stake	784	3329	Note 1
Series 2GD — 3/4-Ton — 122 in. w.b. — Six				
80	Platform	750	3214	Note 1
81	Chassis & Cab	700	2756	Note 1
82	Panel (slats)	870	3503	Note 1
83	Express-Pickup	755	3467	Note 1
84	Chassis & Cowl	605	2379	Note 1
85	Chassis & W/S	625	2402	Note 1
86	Stake	775	3467	Note 1
Series 21D — 3/4-Ton — 122 in. w.b. — V-8/90 hp				
80	Platform	765	3236	Note 1
81	Chassis & Cab	715	2778	Note 1
82	Panel (slats)	885	3525	Note 1
83	Express-Pickup	770	3331	Note 1
84	Chassis & Cowl	620	2401	Note 1
85	Chassis & W/S	640	2424	Note 1
86	Stake	790	3489	Note 1
Series 29D — 3/4-Ton — 122 in. w.b. — V-8/100 hp				
80	Platform	790	3236	Note 1
81	Chassis & Cab	740	2778	Note 1
82	Panel (slats)	910	3525	Note 1
83	Express-Pickup	795	3331	Note 1
84	Chassis & Cowl	645	2401	Note 1
85	Chassis & W/S	665	2424	Note 1
86	Stake	815	3489	Note 1

NOTE 1: Combined body style production for the 1942 Ford 3/4-Ton trucks is not available.

ENGINE [2ND]: Displacement: 119.7 cid. L-head. Four-cylinder. 30 hp at 2800 rpm. Bore & stroke: 3.19 in. x 3.75 in. Compression ratio: 6.0:1. One-barrel updraft carburetor.

ENGINE [2GD]: Displacement: 225.8 cid. L-Head. Six-cylinder. 90 hp at 3300 rpm. Bore & stroke: 3.3 in. x 4.4 in. Compression ratio: 6.7:1. One-barrel carburetor.

ENGINE [21D]: Displacement: 221 cid. Flathead V-8. 90 hp at 3800 rpm. Bore & stroke: 3.19 in. x 3.75 in. Compression ratio: 6.2:1. Carburetor: Two-barrel.

ENGINE [29D]: Displacement: 239.4 cid. Flathead V-8. 100 hp at 3600 rpm. Bore & stroke: 3-3/16 in. x 3-3/4 in. Compression ratio: 6.75:1. Carburetor: Two-barrel.

1942 Ford 1/2-ton Model 29C Pickup (WAD/DFW)

122 IN. 1-TON EXPRESS: The 1942 1-ton Pickup came with a 19-gal. fuel tank [located under the seat], a rubber-cushioned rear engine mount and a 10 in. clutch. It also had almost 2 in. more front overhang than the 1941. The truss-type rolled edge tailgate could be lowered flush with the floor or placed fully down. The bodyside panels were stamped with smaller panels to increase rigidity. There were stake pockets in each flareboard for rack or side boards.

122 IN. 1-TON PANEL: The new 1-ton Panel was slightly bigger than last year's model. Its twin rear doors were hung in a welded one-piece channel steel frame and rubber sealed all around. The drip molding was extended and welded to the roof rail. This assembly was then welded to the bodyside panel. The joints were waterproofed by sealing with a caulking compound. Steel skid strips were evenly spaced in the hardwood floors. The interior bodysides were protected by steel panels and hardwood boards.

122 IN. 1-TON PLATFORM/STAKE: The 1-ton Platform/Stake body was identical to that of the 3/4-ton Platform/Stake. However, its chassis was built to handle heavier loads. To make them easier to handle and reduce splintering, the rack boards were smooth surfaced and had rounded edges and corners. The hardwood floor planking was inter-locked with steel skid strips. Pressed steel gussets were used to attach the platform frame to the body sills.

I.D. DATA [122 in. 1-Ton]: Serial number and engine number are identical. Serial/engine numbers (1935-1945) located: [Four] On top of frame left side, ahead of dash; also on left side of flywheel housing; [Six] On left frame member ahead of cowl; also on top of clutch housing; [V-8] On top of frame, left side, near dash; also on top of clutch housing. See 3/4-ton numbers.

Model	Body Type	Price	Weight	Prod. Total
Series 2NY — 1-Ton — 122 in. w.b. — Four				
80	Platform	809	3222	Note 1
81	Chassis & Cab	754	2873	Note 1
82	Panel (slats)	924	3537	Note 1
83	Express-Pickup	809	3343	Note 1
84	Chassis & Cowl	659	2486	Note 1
85	Chassis & W/S	679	2519	Note 1
86	Stake	834	3475	Note 1
Series 2GY — 1-Ton — 122 in. w.b. — Six				
80	Platform	800	3375	Note 1
81	Chassis & Cab	745	3046	Note 1
82	Panel (slats)	915	3690	Note 1
83	Express-Pickup	800	3375	Note 1
84	Chassis & Cowl	650	2640	Note 1
85	Chassis & W/S	670	2672	Note 1
86	Stake	825	3628	Note 1
Series 21Y — 1-Ton — 122 in. w.b. — V-8/90 hp				
80	Platform	815	3397	Note 1
81	Chassis & Cab	760	3048	Note 1
82	Panel (slats)	930	3712	Note 1
83	Express-Pickup	815	3518	Note 1
84	Chassis & Cowl	665	2661	Note 1
85	Chassis & W/S	685	2694	Note 1
86	Stake	840	3650	Note 1
Series 29Y — 1-Ton — 122 in. w.b. — V-8/100 hp				
80	Platform	840	3397	Note 1
81	Chassis & Cab	785	3048	Note 1
82	Panel (slats)	955	3712	Note 1
83	Express-Pickup	840	3518	Note 1
84	Chassis & Cowl	690	2661	Note 1
85	Chassis & W/S	710	2694	Note 1
86	Stake	865	3650	Note 1

NOTE 1: Combined body style production for the 1-Ton trucks is not available.

ENGINE [2NY]: Displacement: 119.7 cid. L-head. Four-cylinder. 30 hp at 2800 rpm. Bore & stroke: 3.19 in. x 3.75 in. Compression ratio: 6.0:1. One-barrel updraft carburetor.
ENGINE [2GY]: Displacement: 225.8 cid. L-Head. Six-cylinder. 90 hp at 3300 rpm. Bore & stroke: 3.3 in. x 4.4 in. Compression ratio: 6.7:1. One-barrel carburetor.
ENGINE [21Y]: Displacement: 221 cid. Flathead V-8. 90 hp at 3800 rpm. Bore & stroke: 3.19 in. x 3.75 in. Compression ratio: 6.2:1. Carburetor: Two-barrel.
ENGINE [29Y]: Displacement: 239.4 cid. Flathead V-8. 100 hp at 3600 rpm. Bore & stroke: 3-3/16 in. x 3-3/4 in. Compression ratio: 6.75:1. Carburetor: Two-barrel.
CHASSIS [114 in. Series/Sedan Delivery]: Wheelbase: 122 in. Overall length: [Sedan Delivery] 194.3 in. Overall width: [Pickup/Panel] 72.14 in.; [Sedan Delivery] 60.2 in. Overall height: [Sedan Delivery] 68.15 in.; [Pickup/Platform/Stake] 71.45 in.; [Panel] 75.85 in. GVW: 4,300 lbs. Tires: 6.00 x 16 four-ply.
[122 in. 3/4- & 1-Ton]: Wheelbase: 122 in. Overall width: [Panel/Sedan] 79.24 in.; [Pickup/Panel] 73.62 in. GVW: [3/4-ton] 5,400 lbs.; [1-ton] 6,400 lbs. Tires: 6.00 x 16 six-ply

1942 Ford 1/2-ton Model 29C Pickup (OCW)

POWERTRAIN OPTIONS: 239 cid/100 hp V-8. Four-speed manual transmission. Heavy-duty three-speed manual transmission.
CONVENIENCE OPTIONS: Hot water heater. Rear shock absorbers. Plated rear bumper. Passenger seat for Panel. Grille guard. Passenger side windshield wiper. Outside mounted spare tire. Spotlight. Fog lights for Sedan Delivery. Radio. Locking gas cap. Cigar lighter for Sedan Delivery. White sidewall tires. Right-hand sunvisor. Heavy-duty clutch.
1945 FORD

1945 FORD

LIGHT-DUTY PICKUP: The waterfall grille found on prewar Ford Pickups was carried over on the new 1945 models. The biggest styling changes were: Application of an accent color to the lamp bezels, grille and door handles; elimination of the contrasting paint from the nameplate on the hood's face; and a larger outside rearview mirror. Some improvements were made to the chassis. Among them were a better steering gear mounting; universal joint grease fittings; and wider frame rails. Because of the rubber shortage, a spare tire was not offered. However, if a buyer was lucky enough to find one, he or she mounted it on the side of the box between the cab and rear fender.

298

1945 Ford 1/2-Ton Model 83 Pickup (OCW)

LIGHT-DUTY STAKE: This model was not offered until later in the year. It shared the same styling and improvements as the Pickup. The stakes and floors were made of hardwood. All light-duty Ford trucks were powered by the improved 100 hp flathead V-8.
I.D. DATA [Light-Duty]: Serial number and engine number are identical. Serial/engine numbers (1935-1945) located: [Four] On top of frame left side, ahead of dash; also on left side of flywheel housing; [Six] On left frame member ahead of cowl; also on top of clutch housing; [V-8] On top of frame, left side, near dash; also on top of clutch housing. VIN began at 99C-623330.

Model	Body Type	Price	Weight	Prod. Total
Series 59C — 1/2-Ton — 114 in. w.b. — V-8				
81	Chassis & Cab	888	2592	564
83	Pickup	918	2865	19,706
84	Chassis & Cowl	720	2345	230
85	Chasssis & W/S	740	—	59
86	Stake	905	3135	345

ENGINE [59C]: Displacement: 239 cid. L-Head V-8. 100 hp at 3800 rpm. Bore & stroke: 3-3/16 in. x 3-3/4 in. Compression ratio: 6.75:1. Carburetor: Two-barrel.
1-TON OPEN EXPRESS: This light-duty Pickup may have looked the same as the 1/2-ton, but it could haul a much bigger payload. Among the new standard equipment were a four-speed manual transmission and an 11 in. clutch.
1-TON STAKE: Hardwood floors and stakes from Ford's own forests were used on these trucks. As on all Ford trucks of this vintage, the cab was very Spartan. The 60 mph speedometer occupied the bulk of the rectangular instrument panel pod that included fuel, temperature and oil gauges and an ammeter.
I.D. DATA: Serial number and engine number are identical. Serial/engine numbers (1935-1945) located: [Four] On top of frame left side, ahead of dash; also on left side of flywheel housing; [Six] On left frame member ahead of cowl; also on top of clutch housing; [V-8] On top of frame, left side, near dash; also on top of clutch housing. Serial numbers: 99T-623330 up.

Model	Body Type	Price	Weight	Prod. Total
Series 59T — 1-Ton — 134 in. w.b. — V-8				
81	Chassis & Cab	960	4140	—
84	Chassis & Cowl	865	—	—
85	Chassis & W/S	885	—	—
86	Stake	1095	—	—

ENGINE [59T]: Displacement: 239 cid. L-Head V-8. 100 hp at 3800 rpm. Bore & stroke: 3-3/16 in. x 3-3/4 in. Compression ratio: 6.75:1. Carburetor: Two-barrel.
CHASSIS [Light-Duty]: Wheelbase: 114 in. Overall width: 72.14 in. GVW: 4,700 lbs. Tires: 6.50 x 16 six-ply.
CHASSIS [1-Ton]: Wheelbase: 122 in. Overall width: [Pickup] 73.62 in.; [Sedan Delivery] 79.24 in. Overall height: 76.2 in. GVW: 6,600 lbs. Tires: 7.00 x 17 six-ply, front; 7.50 x 17 eight-ply, rear.
POWERTRAIN OPTIONS: 226 cid six-cylinder engine.
CONVENIENCE OPTIONS: Passenger side sun visor. Heavy-duty battery. Heavy-duty generator. AM radio. Heater-defroster. Right-hand windshield wiper. Seat covers. Right-hand taillight.
HISTORICAL: A 1945 Light-duty 1/2-ton Pickup had the honor of being the 31,000,000th Ford built.

1946 FORD

1946 Ford Model 78 Sedan Delivery (DFW/J. Barton)

6-1/2 FT. SEDAN DELIVERY: This vehicle featured Deluxe passenger car styling. The two headlights were fender-mounted. The grille consisted of three horizontal bars with red indentations protruding from the rectangular opening. The small rectangular parking lights were on the face of the hood. The instrument panel, hubcaps, bumpers and front end ornamentation were also the same as the car type. Among the mechanical improvements for 1946 were: Self-centering brakes; improved springs and shocks; different transmission rear mount; and heavy-duty voltage regulator.

1/2-TON 6-1/2 FT. PICKUP: If you liked the 1945 Ford 1/2-ton Pickup, you'd like the 1946. For all practical purposes they were identical. About the only changes were new passenger car style hubcaps and self-centering brakes. Late in the model year, the name was changed to 6-1/2 ft. Pickup. The cab door molding grooves were painted cream. Aluminum pistons were used with the V-8.

1/2-TON 6-1/2 FT. STAKE: This was basically the same truck offered in 1945. However, it and the other Ford trucks were now available in five colors: Black, Greenfield green, light Moonstone gray, Modern blue and Vermilion. All were trimmed in Tacoma cream.

1/2-TON 7-1/2 FT. PANEL: Material shortages limited production of the 1/2-ton Panel. Unlike the Sedan Delivery, it shared styling and mechanical features with the rest of the truck line. Its hardwood floors had steel skid strips to make loading and unloading easier.

I.D. DATA: The serial number and engine number are the same. The VIN is stamped on the clutch housing and can be seen when the transmission cover is removed. [Six] The first symbol is a 1. The second and third symbols indicated the series; GA=Sedan Delivery; GC=1/2-Ton. The last six symbols are the sequential production number. [V-8] The first three or four symbols are: 99A=Sedan Delivery; 699C=1/2-Ton. The last six symbols are the sequential production number. Body type codes (two letters) are shown in first column of chart below. The serial number ranges were: [V-8] 699C-62330 thru 699C-1343165; [Six] 1GC-227524 thru 1GC-314949.

Model	Body Type	Price	Weight	Prod. Total
Series 6GC — 1/2-Ton — 114 in. w.b. — 6-Cyl.				
78A	Sedan Delivery	1186	2276	Note 1
80	Platform	—	—	Note 1
81	Chassis & Cab	924	2626	Note 1
82	Panel	1129	3238	Note 1
83	Pickup	961	2966	Note 1
84	Chassis & Cowl	792	2276	Note 1
85	Chassis & W/S	822	2306	Note 1
86	Stake	1044	3086	Note 1
Series 69C — 1/2-Ton — 114 in. w.b. — V-8				
78A	Sedan Delivery	1126	2978	Note 1
80	Platform	—	—	Note 1
81	Chassis & Cab	984	2626	Note 1
82	Panel	1189	3238	Note 1
83	Pickup	1022	2966	Note 1
84	Chassis & Cowl	852	2276	Note 1
85	Chassis & W/S	883	2306	Note 1
86	Stake	1105	3086	Note 1

NOTE 1: Combined model year production of 1/2-Ton trucks by body style was as follows: [Sedan Delivery] 3,187; [Chassis & Cab] 4,239; [7.5 ft. Panel] 5,539; [6.5 ft. Pickup] 75,088; [Chassis & Cowl] 1,258; [Chassis & Windshield] 932; [6.5 ft. Stake] 2,310.

1946 Ford 1/2-Ton Model 83 Pickup (DFW)

ENGINE [6GC]: Displacement: 226 cid. L-Head Six. 95 hp at 3300 rpm. Bore & stroke: 3.3 in. x 3.4 in. Compression ratio: 6.2:1. Carburetor: Holley one-barrel.

ENGINE [69C]: Displacement: 239.4 cid. L-Head V-8. 100 hp at 3800 rpm. Bore & stroke: 3-3/16 in. x 3-3/4 in. Compression ratio: 6.75:1. Carburetor: Two-barrel.

1-TON 8-FT. EXPRESS: The over-sized wheel and tires of the 1945 1-ton trucks were now optional. Otherwise, Ford's top light-duty Pickup was basically unchanged for 1946.

1-TON 7-1/2 FT. PLATFORM/STAKE: This was essentially a carryover from the previous year. The main difference was that buyers now had a wider choice of exterior colors. The wheels and runningboards were black. The platform was made of hardwood.

1-TON 9 FT. PANEL: The new 1-ton Panel was the largest such vehicle offered by Ford in 1946. The hardwood floors had metal skid strips. A single driver's seat was standard.

1946 Ford 1/2-Ton Model 83 Pickup (R.S. Pasquerella)

I.D. DATA: The serial number and engine number are the same. The VIN is stamped on the clutch housing and can be seen when the transmission cover is removed. [Six] The first symbol is a 1. The second and third symbols indicated the series: GY=1-ton. The last six symbols are the sequential production number. [V-8] The first three or four symbols are: 699Y=1-Ton. The last six symbols are the sequential production number. Body type codes (two letters) are shown in first column of chart below. The serial number ranges were: [V-8] 699C-62330 thru 699C-1343165; [Six] 1GC-227524 thru 1GC-314949.

Model	Body Type	Price	Weight	Prod. Total
Series 6GY — 1-Ton — 122 in. w.b. — 6-Cyl.				
80	Platform	—	—	Note 1
81	Chassis & Cab	1090	3136	Note 1
82	Panel	1348	3848	Note 1
83	Express-Pickup	1187	3606	Note 1
84	Chassis & Cowl	953	2776	Note 1
85	Chassis & W/S	983	2806	Note 1
86	Stake	1210	3751	Note 1
Series 69Y — 1-Ton — 122 in. w.b. — V-8				
80	Platform	—	—	Note 1
81	Chassis & Cab	1150	3136	Note 1
82	Panel	1408	3848	Note 1
83	Express-Pickup	1248	3606	Note 1
84	Chassis & Cowl	1013	2776	Note 1
85	Chassis & W/S	1043	2806	Note 1
86	Stake	1270	3751	Note 1

NOTE 1: Combined model year production of 1-Ton trucks by body style is not available.

ENGINE [6GY]: Displacement: 226 cid. L-Head Six. 90 hp at 3300 rpm. Bore & stroke: 3.3 in. x 3.4 in. Compression ratio: 6.2:1. Carburetor: Holley one-barrel.

ENGINE [69Y]: Displacement: 239.4 cid. L-Head V-8. 100 hp at 3800 rpm. Bore & stroke: 3-3/16 in. x 3-3/4 in. Compression ratio: 6.75:1. Carburetor: Two-barrel.

1946 Ford 3/4-Ton Model 69Y Pickup (OCW)

CHASSIS [1/2-Ton]: Wheelbase: 114 in. Overall width: 72.14 in. Overall height: 71.45 in. GVW: 4700. Tires: 6.50 x 16 [V-8]; 6.00 x 16 in. front and 6.50 x 16 in. rear [6-cyl.].

CHASSIS [1-Ton]: Wheelbase: 122 in. GVW: 6,600 lbs. Tires: 7.00 x 17 in. front, 7.50 x 17 in. rear.

1946 Ford 1/2-Ton Model 6GC Sedan Delivery (OCW)

CONVENIENCE OPTIONS: Passenger seat for Panel. Heavy-duty battery. Heavy-duty generator. AM radio. Right-hand windshield wiper. Heater-defroster. Seat covers. Right-hand taillight.

1947 FORD

1947 Ford 1/2-Ton Model 83 Pickup (A & A)

6-1/2 FT. SEDAN DELIVERY: The Sedan Delivery was the only 1947 Ford light-duty commercial vehicle to receive a facelift. It came in mid-model year and was rather mild. New round parking lamps were located below the headlights. A medallion on the face of the hood identified whether the truck was powered by a six-cylinder or V-8 engine. The grille bars were now smooth and most of the vertical identations on the trim piece above them were removed. The lines under the Ford nameplate ran horizontally, rather than vertically as before.

1947 Ford 1/2-Ton Model 7GC Pickup (OCW)

6-1/2 FT. PICKUP: The Ford 1/2-ton Pickup was unchanged for 1947. Late in the model year, an all new six-cylinder engine was made available. However, according to Ford truck expert James Wagner, it is doubtful that any trucks were built during 1947 incorporating it.

7-1/2 FT. PANEL: Although unchanged for 1947, the 7-1/2 ft. Panel was more popular than before. The main reason was increased availability of parts. This meant more could be produced for the truck-hungry postwar market.

6-1/2 FT. PLATFORM/STAKE: Hardwood floors and stakes were used on the unchanged 1947 Platform/Stake with 6-1/2 ft. bed. Black runningboards and wheels were standard.

300

1947 Ford 1/2-Ton Model 7GC Panel (L.A. Egglefield)

I.D. DATA: The serial number and engine number are the same. The VIN is stamped on the clutch housing and can be seen when the transmission cover is removed. [Six] The first symbol is a 7=1947. The second symbol and third symbols indicated the series; GA=Sedan Delivery; GC=1/2-Ton. The last six symbols are the sequential production number. [V-8] The first symbol is a 7=1947. The second and third symbols are: 99A=Sedan Delivery; 9C=1/2-Ton. The last six symbols are the sequential production number. Body type codes (two letters) are shown in first column of chart below. The serial number ranges were: [Six] 71GC-230,698 thru 71GC-410,109; [V-8] 799C-715,264 thru 799C-214,8508.

Model	Body Type	Price	Weight	Prod. Total
Series 7GC — 1/2-Ton — 114 in. w.b. — 6-Cyl.				
78	Sedan Delivery	1271	3131	Note 1
80	Platform	—	—	Note 1
81	Chassis & Cab	1067	2538	Note 1
82	Panel	1269	3150	Note 1
83	Pickup	1112	2888	Note 1
84	Chassis & Cowl	906	2188	Note 1
85	Chassis & W/S	937	2220	Note 1
86	Stake	1192	2988	Note 1
Series 79C — 1/2-Ton — 114 in. w.b. — V-8				
78	Sedan Delivery	1302	3164	Note 1
80	Platform	—	—	Note 1
81	Chassis & Cab	1098	2571	Note 1
82	Panel	1300	3183	Note 1
83	Pickup	1143	2921	Note 1
84	Chassis & Cowl	937	2221	Note 1
85	Chassis & W/S	968	2253	Note 1
86	Stake	1223	3021	Note 1

NOTE 1: Combined model year production of 1/2-Ton trucks by body style was as follows: [Sedan Delivery] 3,484; [Other models] Not available.

ENGINE [7GC]: Displacement: 226 cid. L-Head Six. 95 hp at 3300 rpm. Bore & stroke: 3.3 in. x 3.4 in. Compression ratio: 6.7:1. Carburetor: Holley one-barrel.

ENGINE [79C]: Displacement: 239.4 cid. L-Head V-8. 100 hp at 3800 rpm. Bore & stroke: 3-3/16 in. x 3-3/4 in. Compression ratio: 6.75:1. Carburetor: Two-barrel.

8 FT. EXPRESS: The 1947 Ford 8 ft. Express (Pickup) was virtually the same. It was even offered in the same five colors: black, Greenfield green, light Moonstone gray, Moden blue and vermilion. All were trimmed in Tacoma cream.

9 FT. PANEL: The hardwood floors of the 1-ton Panel had metal skid strips. A single driver's seat was standard. Styling and other features were carried over from the previous model year.

1947 Ford 3/4-Ton Model 7GY Platform/Stake (OCW)

7-1/2 FT. PLATFORM/STAKE: There was virtually no difference between the 1947 and 1946 1-ton 7-1/2 ft. Platform/Stake.

I.D. DATA: The serial number and engine number are the same. The VIN is stamped on the clutch housing and can be seen when the transmission cover is removed. [Six] The first symbol is a 7=1947. The second symbol and third symbols indicated the series; GY=1-Ton. The last six symbols are the sequential production number. [V-8] The first symbol is a 7=1947. The second and third symbols are: 9Y=1-Ton. The last six symbols are the sequential production number. Body type codes (two letters) are shown in first column of chart below. The serial number ranges were: [Six] 71GY-230,698 thru 71GY-410,109; [V-8] 799Y-715,264 thru 799Y-2148508.

Model	Body Type	Price	Weight	Prod. Total
Series 7GY — 1-Ton — 122 in. w.b. — 6-Cyl.				
80	Platform	—	—	Note 1
81	Chassis & Cab	1260	3115	Note 1
82	Panel	1514	3815	Note 1
83	Express-Pickup	1359	3615	Note 1
84	Chassis & Cowl	1099	2732	Note 1
85	Chassis & W/S	1130	2765	Note 1
86	Stake	1390	3715	Note 1
Series 79Y — 1-Ton — 122 in. w.b. — V-8				
80	Platform	—	—	Note 1
81	Chassis & Cab	1291	3148	Note 1
82	Panel	1545	3848	Note 1
83	Express-Pickup	1390	3648	Note 1
84	Chassis & Cowl	1130	2765	Note 1
85	Chassis & W/S	1161	2798	Note 1
86	Stake	1223	3021	Note 1

NOTE 1: Combined model year production of 1-Ton trucks by body style is not available.
ENGINE [7GY]: Displacement: 226 cid. L-Head Six. 90 hp at 3300 rpm. Bore & stroke: 3.3 in. x 3.4 in. Compression ratio: 6.2:1. Carburetor: Holley one-barrel.
ENGINE [79Y]: Displacement: 239.4 cid. L-Head V-8. 100 hp at 3800 rpm. Bore & stroke: 3-3/16 in. x 3-3/4 in. Compression ratio: 6.75:1. Carburetor: Two-barrel.
CHASSIS [1/2-ton]: Wheelbase: 114 in. GVW: 4,700 lbs. Tires: [Sedan Delivery] 6.00 x 16, four-ply; [Other models] 6.50 x 16, six-ply.
CHASSIS [1-Ton]: Wheelbase: 122 in. GVW: 6,600 lbs. Tires: 7.00 x 17 six-ply, front; 7.50 x 17 eight-ply, rear.

1947 Ford 1/2-Ton Series 7GC Model 78 Sedan Delivery (OCW)

CONVENIENCE OPTIONS: Passenger seat for Panel. Heavy-duty battery. Heavy-duty generator. AM radio. Right-hand windshield wiper. Heater-defroster. Seat covers.

1948 FORD

1948 Ford 1/2-Ton F-1 Pickup (OCW)

F-1 PICKUP: This was Ford's first really new postwar vehicle. The headlights were in the recessed, horizontal-bar pattern grille. The squared-off fenders and hood and a new one-piece windshield contributed to a crisp, modern look. The spare tire was relocated to underneath the box. The new, all-steel "Million Dollar" cab was wider, longer and taller than before. It was also insulated from vibration and noise via a new cab suspension system. Rubber pads and rubber insulated bolts were used at the front corners and lever- action links in torsion type rubber bushings were placed at each rear corner. Prototype trucks, seen in many factory photos, had a body-color grille/headlamp mounting panel, while early production trucks originally had Tucson tan finish there. Argent silver later replaced Tucson tan and the later trucks also had Argent silver finished grille bars with red stripes. All 1948 models had the wheels done in black. The F-1s had hubcaps first seen on late- 1947 Ford passenger cars, which were also used on 1948 passenger cars. Late in the model run, the finish on the vent window moldings was changed from chrome to black. Among the stan-·dard features were: Extra large rear cab window; ashtray; glove compartment; cowl ventilator; air-wing ventilators; three-spoke 18-in. diameter steering wheel; Synchro-Silent three-speed manual transmission; and black walls and runningboards. Colors were: vermilion; Medium-luster black; Meadow green; Birch gray; and Chrome yellow.
F-1 8 FT. PANEL: The F-1 Panel shared the same attractive styling as the rest of the 1948 truck-line. The Panel was really the only model with an all-new truck body, whiles the others had new cabs and rear fenders, but the same pickup box as before.It had a larger load area than the Panel it replaced. The floors were solid plywood with steel skid strips. To help

keep out dust, fumes and moisture, weather sealing strips joined the floor to the side panel. The driver sat on a Spiralounge seat. It floated on variable-rate spiral coil springs adjustable to the driver's weight. An hydraulic shock absorber controlled movement of the seat and back. Two-position door checks held the twin weather-sealed rear doors to either full or 90-degree opening. The runningboards were the same color as the body. A rear bumper was standard. A Deluxe Delivery version of the Panel was announced with prices of $1,443/$1,464 (six/V-8), but not scheduled into actual production. The Deluxe Delivery, as seen in factory photos, had chrome bumpers, bright vent window frames, fender moldings and below-the-belt trim, plus dual windshield wipers, a lined interior and two-tone finish. Ford did release the bright fender moldings as a dealer option.
F-1 PLATFORM/STAKE: The F-1 Platform/Stake had hardwood floors that were rabbeted and firmly inter-locked. There were long-wearing steel skid strips. The stake racks were also made of hardwood. They had steel inter-locking plates bolted on them to hold stake sections firmly. The frame, bumper and runningboards were black.
I.D. DATA: The serial number and engine number are the same. The VIN is stamped on the clutch housing and can be seen when the transmission cover is removed. [Six] The first symbol is a 8=1948. The second symbol and third symbol indicated the series; 8HC=1/2-Ton. The last six symbols are the sequential production number. [V-8] The first symbol is a 8=1948. The second and third symbols are: 8RC=1/2-Ton. The last six symbols are the sequential production number. Body type codes (two letters) are shown in first column of chart below. The VIN range for six-cylinder models: 87HC-6911 thru 87HC-166979. For V-8 models: 88RC-101 thru 88RC-139262.

1948 Ford 1/2-Ton Model F-1 Panel (DFW/LS)

Model	Body Type	Price	Weight	Prod. Total
F-1 Series 8HC — 1/2-Ton — 114 in. w.b. — six				
80	Platform	1218	2946	Note 1
81	Chassis & Cab	1141	2634	Note 1
82	Panel	1392	3216	Note 1
83	Pickup	1212	2998	Note 1
84	Chassis & Cowl	949	2205	Note 1
85	Chassis & W/S	980	2237	Note 1
86	Stake	1255	3086	Note 1
F-1 Series 8RC — 1/2-Ton — 114 in. w.b. — V-8				
80	Platform	1239	2986	Note 1
81	Chassis & Cab	1161	2680	Note 1
82	Panel	1412	3256	Note 1
83	Pickup	1239	3061	Note 1
84	Chassis & Cowl	969	2251	Note 1
85	Chassis & W/S	1000	2283	Note 1
86	Stake	1275	3126	Note 1

NOTE 1: Body style production not available.
ENGINE [8HC]: Displacement: 226.4 cid. L-Head Six. 95 hp at 3300 rpm. Bore & stroke: 3.3 in. x 3.4 in. Compression ratio: 6.2:1. Carburetor: One-barrel.
ENGINE [8RC]: Displacement: 239.4 cid. L-Head V-8. 100 hp at 3800 rpm. Bore & stroke: 3-3/16 in. x 3-3/4 in. Compression ratio: 6.2:1. Carburetor: Two-barrel.

1948 Ford 1/2-Ton F-1 Pickup (OCW)

F-2 8 FT. EXPRESS: This was Ford's first 3/4-ton since World War II. Larger tires, a 4.86:1 rear axle ratio, four-speed manual transmission, and rubber encased center bearing were a few things that set the F-2 apart from the 1/2-ton F-1. Like all 1948 Ford light-duty trucks, the F-2 got a change towards the end of the model year. The chrome-plated grille bars were replaced with painted ones. Also, the bright finish vent window division bar was phased-out for black painted ones as the 1949 model year approached.

F-2 PLATFORM/STAKE: The F-2 Platform/Stake could reportedly pull a 9.5 percent smooth concrete grade in high gear and better than a 30 percent grade in first gear. Engine speed at 35 mph was 1910 rpm. It had a load length of 90.3 in. and a load width of 74 in. The runningboards and bumper were black.

I.D. DATA: The serial number and engine number are the same. The VIN is stamped on the clutch housing and can be seen when the transmission cover is removed. [Six] The first symbol is a 8=1948. The second symbol and third symbols indicated the series; 8HD=3/4-Ton. The last six symbols are the sequential production number. [V-8] The first symbol is a 8=1948. The second and third symbols are: 8RD=3/4-Ton. The last six symbols are the sequential production number. Body type codes (two letters) are shown in first column of chart below. The VIN range for six-cylinder models: 87HC-6911 thru 87HC-166979. For V-8 models: 88RC-101 thru 88RC-139262.

Model	Body Type	Price	Weight	Prod. Total
F-2 Series 8HD — 3/4-Ton — 122 in. w.b. — Six				
80	Platform	1344	3453	Note 1
81	Chassis & Cab	1251	3053	Note 1
83	Express-Pickup	1362	3555	Note 1
84	Chassis & Cowl	1059	2624	Note 1
85	Chassis & W/S	1090	2656	Note 1
86	Stake	1391	3643	Note 1
F-2 Series 8RD — 3/4-Ton — 122 in. w.b. — V-8				
80	Platform	1365	3493	Note 1
81	Chassis & Cab	1271	3099	Note 1
83	Express-Pickup	1383	3587	Note 1
84	Chassis & Cowl	1080	2670	Note 1
85	Chassis & W/S	1111	2702	Note 1
86	Stake	1412	3683	Note 1

NOTE 1: Body style production not available.
ENGINE [8HD]: Displacement: 226.4 cid. L-Head Six. 95 hp at 3300 rpm. Bore & stroke: 3.3 in. x 3.4 in. Compression ratio: 6.2:1. Carburetor: One-barrel.
ENGINE [8RD]: Displacement: 239.4 cid. L-Head V-8. 100 hp at 3800 rpm. Bore & stroke: 3-3/16 in. x 3-3/4 in. Compression ratio: 6.2:1. Carburetor: Two-barrel.
F-3 EXPRESS: Although called a Heavy-Duty 3/4-ton, the actual payload capacity of the F-3 Pickup was nearer to 1-1/2-tons. Typical equipment on this model included: A three-spoke, 18 in. diameter steering wheel; double-acting shock absorbers on the front; cowl ventilation; 20-gal. fuel tank; spare wheel and tire; channel front bumper; and jack and tool kit. The frame, wheels and runningboard were black.
F-3 PLATFORM/STAKE: This model had hardwood floors rabbeted and firmly inter-locked with steel skid strips. The stakes were also made of hardwood.
I.D. DATA: The serial number and engine number are the same. The VIN is stamped on the clutch housing and can be seen when the transmission cover is removed. [Six] The first symbol is a 8=1948. The second symbol and third symbols indicated the series; 8HY=Heavy-duty 3/4-Ton. The last six symbols are the sequential production number. [V-8] The first symbol is a 8=1948. The second and third symbols are: 8RY=Heavy-duty 3/4-Ton. The last six symbols are the sequential production number. Body type codes (two letters) are shown in first column of chart below. The VIN range for six-cylinder models: 87HC-6911 thru 87HC-166979. For V-8 models: 88RC-101 thru 88RC-139262.

Model	Body Type	Price	Weight	Prod. Total
F-3 Series 8HY — Heavy 3/4-Ton — 122 in. w.b. — Six				
80	Platform	1412	3706	Note 1
81	Chassis & Cab	1319	3260	Note 1
83	Express-Pickup	1430	3751	Note 1
84	Chassis & Cowl	1127	2831	Note 1
85	Chassis & W/S	1158	2863	Note 1
86	Stake	1459	3896	Note 1
F-3 Series 8RY — Heavy 3/4-Ton — 122 in. w.b. — V-8				
80	Platform	1433	3736	Note 1
81	Chassis & Cab	1340	3310	Note 1
83	Express-Pickup	1451	3816	Note 1
84	Chassis & Cowl	1148	2881	Note 1
85	Chassis & W/S	1179	2913	Note 1
86	Stake	1480	3926	Note 1

NOTE 1: Body style production not available.
ENGINE [8HY]: Displacement: 226.4 cid. L-Head Six. 95 hp at 3300 rpm. Bore & stroke: 3.3 in. x 3.4 in. Compression ratio: 6.2:1. Carburetor: One-barrel.
ENGINE [8RY]: Displacement: 239.4 cid. L-Head V-8. 100 hp at 3800 rpm. Bore & stroke: 3-3/16 in. x 3-3/4 in. Compression ratio: 6.2:1. Carburetor: Two-barrel.
CHASSIS [F-1]: Wheelbase: 114 in. Overall length: [Pickup] 188.78 in.; [Panel] 202.13 in.; [Platform/Stake] 195.96 in. Overall width: [Pickup] 75.94 in.; [Panel] 75.62 in.; [Platform/Stake] 71.28 in. Overall height: [Pickup/Platform/Stake] 75.64 in.; [Panel] 79.18 in. GVW: 4,700 lbs. Tires: 6.00 x 16, four-ply.

1948 Ford 1/2-Ton F-1 Pickup (OCW)

CHASSIS [F-2/F-3]: Wheelbase: 122 in. Overall length: [Pickup] 206.96 in.; [Platform/Stake] 206.52 in. Overall width: [Pickup] 75.94 in.; [Platform/Stake] 79.24 in. Overall height: [F-2] 76.52 in.; [F-3] 77.42 in. GVW: [F-2] 5,700 lbs.; [F-3] 6,800 lbs. Tires: [F-2] 6.50 x 16, six-ply; [F-3] 7.00 x 17 six-ply.
POWERTRAIN OPTIONS: Heavy-duty three-speed transmission. Heavy-duty four-speed manual transmissions. 4.27:1 rear axle ratio.

CONVENIENCE OPTIONS: 11 in. clutch. Spiralounge bucket seat. Heavy-duty radiator. Magic Air heater-defroster. Recirculating heater-defroster. Automatic push-button tuning radio. 13 oz. nylon duck or a strong water-proofed fiber seat covers. Twin hi-way horns. Sealed beam spotlight. Sealed beam road lamps. Fire extinguisher. Reflector flare set. Grille guards. Automatic windshield washer (vacuum-operated by touch of button). See-Clear windshield washer (operated by foot plunger). Extension arm mirror. Front tow hooks. Illuminated cigar lighter. Leather door armrest. Gas tank locking cap. Radiator overflow tank. Passenger side sunvisor. Right-hand windshield wiper. Tires: [F-2] 7.00 x 16 in. and 7.5- x 16 in.; [F-3] 7.50 x 17 in.
HISTORICAL: Model year 1948 was the best year for Ford truck sales since 1929.

1948 Ford 1/2-Ton F-1 Pickup (OCW)

1949 FORD

1949 Ford 1/2-Ton Model F-1 Pickup (OCW)

F-1 6-1/2 FT. PICKUP: Body color-coordinated wheels and elimination of the red stripe on the Argent silver grille bars were the two most noticeable styling changes for 1949. The headlamp and grille mounting panel continued to be finished in Argent silver, like the late-1948 models. Vent window moldings were painted black, as were the frame, bumper, outside rearview mirror, gas cap, gas tank filler neck and runningboards. A distintion of the 1949 models was that they had runningboards that were bolted not only to the running-board supports, but also to the frame rails. Wheels were now painted body-color or black. Most 1949s also had die-cast F-series emblems on the sides of the cowl (changed to stamped stainless steel in late-1949). Interior metal was done in the body-color. The interior featured an adjustable seat with thick rubberized hair padding, individually pocketed coil springs and scientifically designed cushion contours. A sun visor, glove compartment and ashtray were standard in, what sales literature called, Ford's "Million Dollar" truck cab. Level-Action cab suspension insulated the cab from frame weave, vibration and noise. The tailgate was strengthened with a tapered, truss-type rolled edge. Anti-rattle drop chains held the tailgate flush with the floor or let it drop all the way down. The no-catch, rolled-edge flareboards strengthened the body and offered better sliding surface for objects loaded from the side. Stake pockets permitted mounting of uprights for special sides and tops. The runningboards and bumpers were painted black. A new Warner T87D heavy-duty three-speed transmission was available in all lines through F-3. Standard equipment included: Instrument panel with speedometer, water gauge, oil pressure gauge, charge indicator and choke button; light switch; left windshield wiper; treadle type accelerator pedal; spare wheel and tire; single electric horn; front and rear license plate brackets; jack; and tool kit.
F-1 8 FT. PANEL: The new F-1 Panel had solid plywood floors with steel skid strips. Weather-sealing strips joined the floor to the side panel. They helped keep out dust, fumes and moisture. The adjustable Spiralounge bucket driver's seat floated on a variable-rate, spiral coil spring which was adjustable to the driver's weight. The weather-sealed rear doors were hinged to a rugged, one-piece steel door frame. Two-position door checks held rear doors to either full or a 90-degree opening. The F-1 Panel had a total capacity of 160.3 cu. ft. The runningboards were the same color as the truck.
F-1 6-1/2 FT. PLATFORM/STAKE: The thrifty answer to loads that need headroom. So claimed sales literature for the 1949 Ford F-1 Platform/Stake truck. This was especially true of those powered by the standard 95 hp six-cylinder engine. The F-1 Platform/Stake could carry a payload up to 1,370 lbs. The floors and stake racks were made of select hardwood from Ford's own hardwood forests. The floors were rabbeted and firmly inter-locked with steel skid strips. The frame, bumper and runningboards were painted black.

I.D. DATA: The serial number and engine number are the same. The VIN is stamped on the clutch housing and can be seen when the transmission cover is removed. [Six] The first symbol is a 9=1949. The second symbol and third symbols indicated the series; 9HC=1/2-Ton. The last six symbols are the sequential production number. [V-8] The first symbol is a 9=1949. The second and third symbols are: 9RC=1/2-Ton. The last six symbols are the sequential production number. Body type codes (two letters) are shown in first column of chart below. Serial numbers: [Six] 97HC-92251 and up; [V-8] 98RC-73088 and up. Paint color codes: [M-1724] Medium-luster black; [M-1722] vermilion; [M-14283] Meadow green; [M-14286] Birch gray; [M-14301] Chrome yellow. (Note: Arabian green was renamed Meadow green in 1949.)

Model	Body Type	Price	Weight	Prod. Total
F-1 Series 9HC — 1/2-Ton — 114 in. w.b. — Six				
80	Platform	1338	2946	Note 1
81	Chassis & Cab	1224	2634	Note 1
82	Panel	1504	3216	Note 1
83	Pickup	1302	2998	Note 1
84	Chassis & Cowl	1001	2205	Note 1
85	Chassis & W/S	1038	2237	Note 1
86	Stake	1375	3086	Note 1
F-1 Series 9RC — 1/2-Ton — 114 in. w.b. — V-8				
80	Platform	1370	2986	Note 1
81	Chassis & Cab	1255	2680	Note 1
82	Panel	1536	3256	Note 1
83	Pickup	1333	3061	Note 1
84	Chassis & Cowl	1032	2251	Note 1
85	Chassis & W/S	1069	2283	Note 1
86	Stake	1406	3126	Note 1

NOTE 1: 1949-1950 production was a combined total; see 1950.

1949 Ford 1/2-Ton Model F-1 Pickup (JLC)

ENGINE [9HC]: Displacement: 226 cid. L-Head Six. 95 hp at 3300 rpm. Bore & stroke: 3.3 in. x 3.4 in. Compression ratio: 6.8:1. Carburetor: One-barrel.

ENGINE [9RC]: Displacement: 239.4 cid. L-Head V-8. 100 hp at 3800 rpm. Bore & stroke: 3-3/16 in. x 3-3/4 in. Compression ratio: 6.2:1. Carburetor: Two-barrel.

F-2 8 FT. EXPRESS: the F-2 Ford 3/4-ton Pickup had a roomy 96.05 in. long, 54 in. wide cargo box. It's payload capacity was 1,910 lbs. on 7.50 x 16, six-ply tires. The standard rear axle ratio was 4.86:1. A four-speed manual transmission was also standard. The front springs were shackled at the forward end for more stable steering. A U-type support helped relieve the radiator of road strains. The straight-through type muffer increased engine performance. The tire carrier was rear-mounted, under the frame. Rubber axle bumpers minimized shock of spring bottoming.

F-2 7-1/2 FT. PLATFORM/STAKE: Because of its slightly heavier the F-2 Platform/Stake had a payload capacity about 120 lbs. less than the F-2 Pickup. However, like the Pickup, its frame, wheels bumper and runningboards were black. The hardwood floors were interlocked with steel skid strips.

I.D. DATA: The serial number and engine number are the same. The VIN is stamped on the clutch housing and can be seen when the transmission cover is removed. [Six] The first symbol is a 9=1949. The second symbol and third symbols indicated the series; 9HD=3/4-Ton. The last six symbols are the sequential production number. [V-8] The first symbol is a 9=1949. The second and third symbols are: 9RD=3/4-Ton. The last six symbols are the sequential production number. Body type codes (two letters) are shown in first column of chart below. Serial numbers: [Six] 97HC-92251 and up; [V-8] 98RC-73088 and up. Paint color codes: [M-1724] Medium-luster black; [M-1722] vermilion; [M-14283] Meadow green; [M-14286] Birch gray; [M-14301] Chrome yellow. (Note: Arabian green was renamed Meadow green in 1949.)

Model	Body Type	Price	Weight	Prod. Total
F-2 Series HD — 3/4-Ton — 122 in. w.b. — Six				
80	Platform	1461	3453	Note 1
81	Chassis & Cab	1345	3053	Note 1
83	Express-Pickup	1466	3555	Note 1
84	Chassis & Cowl	1122	2624	Note 1
85	Chassis & W/S	1158	2656	Note 1
86	Stake	1507	3643	Note 1
F-2 Series RD — 3/4-Ton — 122 in. w.b. — V-8				
80	Platform	1492	3493	Note 1
81	Chassis & Cab	1376	3099	Note 1
83	Express-Pickup	1497	3587	Note 1
84	Chassis & Cowl	1153	2670	Note 1
85	Chassis & W/S	1189	2702	Note 1
86	Stake	1538	3683	Note 1

NOTE 1: 1949-1950 production was a combined total; see 1950.

ENGINE [9HD]: Displacement: 226 cid. L-Head Six. 95 hp at 3300 rpm. Bore & stroke: 3.3 in. x 3.4 in. Compression ratio: 6.8:1. Carburetor: One-barrel.

ENGINE [9RD]: Displacement: 239.4 cid. L-Head V-8. 100 hp at 3800 rpm. Bore & stroke: 3-3/16 in. x 3-3/4 in. Compression ratio: 6.2:1. Carburetor: Two-barrel.

1949 Ford 1-Ton Model F-3 Platform Stake (DFW/ATHS)

F-3 8 FT. EXPRESS: Standard features on the hefty F-3 Ford Heavy-Duty 3/4-ton Pickup included: Four-speed manual transmission; full-floating rear axle; double anchor type feather foot brakes; 20-gal. fuel tank; airplane type shock absorbers on the front axle; 17 in. disc wheels; 11 in. Gyro-Grip clutch; and straight-through muffler. The frame, wheels, bumper and runningboards were black.

F-3 7-1/2 FT. PLATFORM/STAKE: The F-3 Platform/Stake had a load capacity of about 2,700 lbs. That was just slightly less than the F-3 Express. Its hardwood floors were rabbeted and firmly inter-locked with long wearing steel skid strips. The stakes were also made of hardwood.

F-3 PARCEL DELIVERY: This new model was available in either 104 in. or 122 in. wheelbases. It was adaptable to many body styles. It had a large glass area which improved visiblity. The gearshift was column-mounted to maximize floor space. The low floor-to-ground height made it easier to load and unload. The front part of the engine was readily accessible by removing the grille. The bulk of the engine was hidden under a hinged cover in the cab. A heavy-duty three-speed manual transmission was standard. The frame, wheels and bumper were black. The F-3 Parcel Delivery had bright metal grille bars. The headlights, parking lamps and nameplate had a bright finish. The adjustable, tilt-forward-type driver's seat had a folding back.

I.D. DATA: The serial number and engine number are the same. The VIN is stamped on the clutch housing and can be seen when the transmission cover is removed. [Six] The first symbol is a 9=1949. The second symbol and third symbols indicated the series; 9HY=Heavy 3/4-Ton. The last six symbols are the sequential production number. [V-8] The first symbol is a 9=1949. The second and third symbols are: 9RY=Heavy 3/4-Ton. The last six symbols are the sequential production number. Body type codes (two letters) are shown in first column of chart below. Serial numbers: [Six] 97HC-92251 and up; [V-8] 98RC-73088 and up. Paint color codes: [M-1724] Medium-luster black; [M-1722] vermilion; [M-14283] Meadow green; [M-14286] Birch gray; [M-14301] Chrome yellow. (Note: Arabian green was renamed Meadow green in 1949.)

Model	Body Type	Price	Weight	Prod. Total
F-3 Series 9HY — Heavy 3/4-Ton — 122 in. w.b. — Six				
80	Platform	1540	3706	Note 1
81	Chassis & Cab	1424	3260	Note 1
83	Express-Pickup	1545	3751	Note 1
84	Chassis & Cowl	1201	2831	Note 1
85	Chassis & W/S	1238	2863	Note 1
86	Stake	1587	3896	Note 1
F-3 Series 9RY — Heavy 3/4-Ton — 122 in. w.b. — V-8				
80	Platform	1571	3736	Note 1
81	Chassis & Cab	1455	3310	Note 1
83	Express-Pickup	1576	3816	Note 1
84	Chassis & Cowl	1232	2881	Note 1
85	Chassis & W/S	1269	2913	Note 1
86	Stake	1618	3962	Note 1

NOTE 1: 1949-1950 production was a combined total; see 1950.

ENGINE [9HY]: Displacement: 226 cid. L-Head Six. 95 hp at 3300 rpm. Bore & stroke: 3.3 in. x 3.4 in. Compression ratio: 6.8:1. Carburetor: One-barrel.

ENGINE [9RY]: Displacement: 239.4 cid. L-Head V-8. 100 hp at 3800 rpm. Bore & stroke: 3-3/16 in. x 3-3/4 in. Compression ratio: 6.2:1. Carburetor: Two-barrel.

CHASSIS [F-1]: Wheelbase: 114 in. Overall length: [Pickup] 188.78 in.; [Panel] 202.13 in.; [Platform/Stake] 195.96 in. Overall width: [Pickup] 75.94 in.; [Panel] 75.62 in.; [Platform/Stake] 71.28 in. Overall height: [Pickup/Platform/Stake] 75.64 in.; [Panel] 79.18 in. GVW: 4,700 lbs. Tires: 6.00 x 16 four-ply.

CHASSIS [F-2/F-3]: Wheelbase: [Panel Delivery] 122 in. or 104 in. Overall length: [Pickup] 206.96 in.; [Platform/Stake] 206.52 in. Overall width: [Pickup] 75.94 in.; [Platform/Stake] 79.24 in. Overall height: [F-2] 76.52 in.; [F-3] 77.42 in. GVW: [F-2] 5,700 lbs.; [F-3] 6,800 lbs. Tires: [F-2] 6.50 x 16 six-ply.; [F-3] 7.00 x 17 six-ply.

POWERTRAIN OPTIONS: Heavy-duty three-speed transmission. Heavy-duty four-speed manual transmission. 4.27:1 rear axle ratio.

1949 Ford 1/2-Ton Model F-1 Pickup (Edward E. Page)

CONVENIENCE OPTIONS: 11 in. clutch. Spiralounge bucket seat. Heavy-duty radiator. Magic Air heater-defroster. Recirculating heater-defroster. Automatic push-button tuning radio. 13 oz. nylon duck or strong water-proofed fiber seat covers. Twin hi-way horns. Sealed beam spot light. Sealed beam road lamps. Fire extinguisher. Reflector flare set. Grille guards. Automatic windshield washer (vacuum operated by touch of button). "See-Clear" windshield washer (operated by foot plunger). Extension arm mirror. Front tow hooks Illuminated cigar lighter. Leather door armrest. Gas tank locking cap. Radiator overflow tank. Passenger side sunvisor. Right-hand windshield wiper. Tires: [F-2] 7.00 x 16 in. and 7.50 x 16 in.; [F-3] 7.50 x 17 in. Hubcaps. Sponge rubber seat pad. Fresh air intake heater/defroster. Heavy-duty fan. Right-hand taillight. Right-hand windshield wiper (in areas required by law).

HISTORICAL: Ford Div., the marketing arm of Ford Motor Co., was officially organized on Feb. 11, 1949. Its purpose was to sell Ford brand cars and trucks. New models were introduced in December 1948. Production for the year was 138,000 trucks.

1950 FORD

1950 Ford 1/2-Ton Model F-1 Pickup (OCW)

F-1 6-1/2 FT. PICKUP: This years trucks were almost a carbon copy of the previous year models, although minor modifications were made. The grille recess was finished in an ivory color. The 1950 runningboards ended at the edge of the cab and did not continue across to the frame, as the 1949 style did. The F-series badges on the cowlsides were now stamped out of stainless steel. Two horizontal ribs were now stamped into the firewall. Late in the year, the shift lever for the standard three-speed manual transmission was moved from the floor to the column. Among standard features were: No-Catch rolled edge flareboards on the 45 cu. ft. box; removable brake drums; two-position tailgate; semi-floating hypoid rear axle; all-steel floor with hardwood sub-floor to minimize denting; Fingertip control adjustable seat with thick rubberized hair padding; 20-gal. fuel tank; sun visor; extra large rear cab window; ashtray; glove compartment; black runningboards; three-spoke, 18 in. diameter steering wheel; and straight through type muffler.

F-1 8 FT. PANEL: The unchanged 8 ft. Panel featured the following: Solid plywood floor with steel skid strips; sealed-tight joining of floor to side panels with weather sealing strips to help exclude dust, fumes, moisture; and bucket type driver's seat floating on a variable-rate spiral coil spring adjustable to the driver's weight. An hydraulic shock absorber controled movement of seat and back. There were two-position door checks to hold the twin, weather-sealed rear doors to either full or 90-degree opening. The all-steel welded body featured heavy-gauge side and roof panels and a sturdy steel frame with reinforcing brackets. The runningboards were the same color as the truck. Panels were available with a Deluxe option. These Deluxe Deliveries, as they were called, had the body code 82A instead of 82.

F-1 6-1/2 FT. PLATFORM/STAKE: The F-1 Platform/Stake was carried over from the previous year. Its hardwood floors were rabbeted and firmly inter-locked with long-wearing steel skid strips. Floors and stake racks featured select hardwood from Ford's own forests. Steel inter-locking plates, bolted to hardwood rack boards, held stake sections firmly. The loading height was a low 32 in. from ground to floor with 6.50 x 16 in. tires. An adjustable bench seat was standard, but the Spiralounge bucket seat was available. The running-boards were black.

I.D. DATA: The serial number and engine number are the same. The VIN is stamped on the clutch housing and can be seen when the transmission cover is removed. [Six] The first symbol is a 9=1949-1950 series. The second symbol and third symbols indicated the series; 97HC=1/2-Ton. The last six symbols are the sequential production number. [V-8] The first symbol is a 9=1949-1950 series. The second and third symbols are: 98RC=1/2-Ton. The last six symbols are the sequential production number. Body type codes (two letters) are shown in first column of chart below. Serial numbers continued from 1949: [Six] 97HC-92251 and up; [V-8] 98RC-73088 and up. Paint color codes: [M-1724] Raven black; [M-1722] vermilion; [M-14283] Meadow green; [M-14286] Birch gray; [M-14341] Palisades green; [M-14285] Sheridab blue; [M-14197] Silverstone gray; [M-14344] Dover gray; [M-14343] Sunland beige; [M-4415] Prime.

1950 Ford 3/4-Ton Model F-2 Pickup (OCW)

Model	Body Type	Price	Weight	Prod. Total
F-1 Series 9HC — 1/2-Ton — 114 in. w.b. — Six				
80	Platform	1220	3010	Note 1
81	Chassis & Cab	1110	2680	Note 1
82	Panel	1370	3230	Note 1
83	Pickup	1175	3060	Note 1
84	Chassis & Cowl	895	2180	Note 1
85	Chassis & W/S	930	2210	Note 1
86	Stake	1255	3130	Note 1
F-1 Series 9RC — 1/2-Ton — 114 in. w.b. — V-8				
80	Platform	1250	3050	Note 1
81	Chassis & Cab	1140	2720	Note 1
82	Panel	1400	3270	Note 1
83	Pickup	1205	3100	Note 1
84	Chassis & Cowl	925	2220	Note 1
85	Chassis & W/S	960	2250	Note 1
86	Stake	1285	3170	Note 1

NOTE 1: Combined production of all 1949-1950 F-1 models according to body style was: [6.5 ft. Platform] 127; [Chassis & Cab] 3,935; [8 ft. Panel] 22,421; [6.5 ft. Pickup] 148,956; [Chassis & Cowl] 652; [Chassis & Windshield] 1,343; [6.5 ft. Stake] 2,259.
NOTE 2: Prices are those in effect late in the year, as reported in Nov. 1, 1950 sources. Apparently, higher prices were in effect earlier.
ENGINE [9HC]: Displacement: 226 cid. L-Head Six. 95 hp at 3300 rpm. Bore & stroke: 3.3 in. x 3.4 in. Compression ratio: 6.8:1. Carburetor: One-barrel.
ENGINE [9RC]: Displacement: 239.4 cid. L-Head V-8. 100 hp at 3800 rpm. Bore & stroke: 3-3/16 in. x 3-3/4 in. Compression ratio: 6.2:1. Carburetor: Two-barrel.
F-2 8 FT. EXPRESS: Like the F-1, the F-2 was the same as last year. It came with a four-speed manual transmission; Gyro-Grip 11 in. clutch and full-floating rear axle. The pickup box was 96.05 in. long, 54 in. wide, 21.7 in. high and had a two-position tailgate. It was just over 25 in. from the floor to the ground. This made loading and unloading easier. The cab came with the same features as the F-1 including the standard 60 mph speedometer and oil, fuel, temperature and battery gauges.
F-2 7-1/2 FT. PLATFORM/STAKE: The F-2 Platform/Stake could carry over 500 lbs. more payload than the F-1 and its standard four-speed manual transmission offered extra pulling power in first gear. It had hardwood floors and stakes. The F-2's ground to floor height was 35.14 in. The runningboards and bumper were black. The spare tire carrier was rear-mounted under the frame.
I.D. DATA: The serial number and engine number are the same. The VIN is stamped on the clutch housing and can be seen when the transmission cover is removed. [Six] The first symbol is a 9=1949-1950 series. The second symbol and third symbols indicated the series; 97HD=3/4-Ton. The last six symbols are the sequential production number. [V-8] The first symbol is a 9=1949-1950 series. The second and third symbols are: 98RD=3/4-Ton. The last six symbols are the sequential production number. Body type codes (two letters) are shown in first column of chart below. Serial numbers continued from 1949.

Model	Body Type	Price	Weight	Prod. Total
F-2 Series 9HD — 3/4-Ton — 122 in. w.b. — Six				
80	Platform	1310	3500	Note 1
81	Chassis & Cab	1210	3090	Note 1
83	Express-Pickup	1295	3570	Note 1
84	Chassis & Cowl	995	2600	Note 1
85	Chassis & W/S	1030	2630	Note 1
86	Stake	1365	3690	Note 1
F-2 Series 9RD — 3/4-Ton — 122 in. w.b. — V-8				
80	Platform	1340	3540	Note 1
81	Chassis & Cab	1240	3130	Note 1
83	Express-Pickup	1325	3610	Note 1
84	Chassis & Cowl	1025	2640	Note 1
85	Chassis & W/S	1060	2670	Note 1
86	Stake	1395	3730	Note 1

NOTE 1: Combined production of all 1949-1950 F-2 models according to body style was: [7.5 ft. Platform] 105; [Chassis & Cab] 2,207; [8 ft. Express-Pickup] 21,464; [Chassis & Cowl] 138; [Chassis & Windshield] 112; [7.5 ft. Stake] 1,545.
NOTE 2: Prices are those in effect late in the year, as reported in Nov. 1, 1950 sources. Apparently, higher prices were in effect earlier.
ENGINE [9HD]: Displacement: 226 cid. L-Head Six. 95 hp at 3300 rpm. Bore & stroke: 3.3 in. x 3.4 in. Compression ratio: 6.8:1. Carburetor: One-barrel.

ENGINE [9RD]: Displacement: 239.4 cid. L-Head V-8. 100 hp at 3800 rpm. Bore & stroke: 3-3/16 in. x 3-3/4 in. Compression ratio: 6.2:1. Carburetor: Two-barrel.

1950 Ford 1/2-Ton Model F-1 Panel With Ranger 4x4 Window Conversion (FMC)

F-3 8 FT. EXPRESS: This was, indeed, the light-duty truck for big truck loads. It could carry a payload almost twice that of the F-1. Among the standard features were: Four-speed manual transmission; 11 in. clutch; extra-large 14 x 2 in. rear brakes; full-floating rear axle with load free axle shafts; 17 in. disc wheels with advanced two-piece, wide-base rims; I-beam axle designed for fore-and-aft steering and telescopic shock absorbers. A channel rubber bumper was attached directly to the extended frame. Other features included a rubber encased center bearing; needle bearing universal joints; Loadomatic ignition with full-automatic vacuum controlled distributer; 20-gal. fuel tank; and three-spoke, 18 in. diameter steering wheel.

F-3 7-1/2 FT. PLATFORM/STAKE: The F-3 Platform/Stake was also capable of fairly heavy-duty chores. In high gear, the F-3 equipped with a 4.86:1 axle pulled its GVW up a seven percent smooth concrete grade. In first gear, a grade well over 30 percent could be handled. Engine speed, at 35 mph, was an economical 1,770 rpm with the standard 4.86 axle. Its hardwood floors were rabbeted and firmly inter-locked with long-wearing steel skid strips. The stakes were also made of select hardwoods. The frame, wheels, bumper and runningboards were black.

F-3 PARCEL DELIVERY: A column-shifted, heavy-duty three-speed manual transmission, 17-gal. fuel tank, bright grille bars and a six-cylinder engine were standard in the 1950 Parcel Delivery. The adjustable, tilt-forward type driver's seat had a folding back. The engine was hidden under a hinged cover in the cab. As in 1949, it was offered in two wheelbases, 104 or 122 in.

I.D. DATA: The serial number and engine number are the same. The VIN is stamped on the clutch housing and can be seen when the transmission cover is removed. [Six] The first symbol is a 9=1949-1950 series. The second symbol and third symbols indicated the series; 9HY=Heavy 3/4-Ton. The last six symbols are the sequential production number. [V-8] The first symbol is a 9=1949-1950 series. The second and third symbols are: 9RY=Heavy 3/4-Ton. The last six symbols are the sequential production number. Body type codes (two letters) are shown in first column of chart below. Serial numbers: continued from 1950.

Model	Body Type	Price	Weight	Prod. Total
F-3 Series 9HY — Heavy 3/4-Ton — 122 in. w.b. — Six				
80	Platform	1395	3710	Note 1
81	Chassis & Cab	1295	3300	Note 1
83	Express-Pickup	1380	3800	Note 1
84	Chassis & Cowl	1080	2810	Note 1
85	Chassis & W/S	1115	2840	Note 1
86	Stake	1450	3900	Note 1
F-3 Series 9RY — Heavy 3/4-Ton — 122 in. w.b. — V-8				
80	Platform	1425	3750	Note 1
81	Chassis & Cab	1325	3340	Note 1
83	Express-Pickup	1410	3840	Note 1
84	Chassis & Cowl	1110	2850	Note 1
85	Chassis & W/S	1145	2880	Note 1
86	Stake	1480	3940	Note 1

NOTE 1: Combined production of all 1949-1950 F-3 models according to body style was: [7.5 ft. Platform] 131; [Chassis & Cab] 3,028; [8 ft. Express-Pickup] 20,446; [Chassis & Cowl] 2,917; [Chassis & Windshield] 568; [7.5 ft. Stake] 1,992.
NOTE 2: Prices are those in effect late in the year, as reported in Nov. 1, 1950 sources. Apparently, higher prices were in effect earlier.
ENGINE [9HY]: Displacement: 226 cid. L-Head Six. 95 hp at 3300 rpm. Bore & stroke: 3.3 in. x 3.4 in. Compression ratio: 6.8:1. Carburetor: One-barrel.
ENGINE [9RY]: Displacement: 239.4 cid. L-Head V-8. 100 hp at 3800 rpm. Bore & stroke: 3-3/16 in. x 3-3/4 in. Compression ratio: 6.2:1. Carburetor: Two-barrel.
CHASSIS [F-1]: Wheelbase: 114 in. Overall length: {Pickup] 188.78 in.; [Panel] 202.13 in.; [Platform/Stake] 195.96 in. Overall width: [Pickup] 75.94 in.; [Panel]; 75.62 in.; [Platform/Stake] 71.28 in. Overall height: [Pickup/Platform/Stake] 75.64 in.; [Panel] 79.18 in. GVW: 4,700 lbs. Tires: 6.00 x 16, four-ply.
CHASSIS [F-2/F-3]: Wheelbase: 122 in. Overall length: [Pickup] 206.96 in.; [Platform/Stake] 206.52 in. Overall width: [Pickup] 75.94 in.; [Platform/Stake] 79.24 in. Overall height: [F-2] 76.52 in.; [F-3] 77.42 in. GVW: [F-2] 5,700 lbs. [F-3]; 6,800 lbs. Tires: [F-2] 6.50 x 16, six-ply; [F-3] 7.00 x 17, six-ply.
POWERTRAIN OPTIONS: Heavy-duty three-speed/heavy-duty four-speed manual transmissions. 4.27:1 rear axle ratio.
CONVENIENCE OPTIONS: 11 in. clutch. Spiralounge bucket seat. Heavy-duty radiator. Magic Air heater-defroster. Recirculating heater-defroster. Automatic push-button tuning radio. 13 oz. nylon duck or a strong waterproofed fiber seat covers. Twin hi-way horns. Sealed beam spot light. Sealed beam road lamps. Fire extinguisher. Reflector flare set. Grille guards. Automatic windshield washer (vacuum-operated by touch of button). See-Clear windshield washer (operated by foot plunger). Extension arm mirror. Front tow hooks. Illuminated cigar lighter. Leather door arm rest. Gas tank locking cap. Radiator overflow tank. Passenger side sunvisor. Right-hand windshield wiper. 7.00 x 16 and 7.50 x 16 tires [F-2]. 7.50 x 17 tires [F-3].
NOTE: Color choices for 1950 included: Black, Meadow green, Palisade green, Sheridan blue, Silvertone Gray, Vermilion.

Standard Catalog of Light-Duty Trucks

HISTORICAL: The 1950 Ford trucks were introduced Jan. 20, 1950 and marketed through Sept. 15, 1950. Available this year was the Marmon-Herrington "Ranger", a converted F-1 Panel with windows and a four-wheel drive system. Total production of Ford trucks was 345,801 units, of which over 230,000 were light-duty models. This was record for Ford commercial vehicles. A Chrysler strike that affected Dodge trucks helped Ford dealers sell more trucks. "Fifty New Ways," was the 1950 Ford truck sales slogan.

1951 FORD

1951 Ford 1/2-Ton Model F-1 Pickup (OCW)

F-1 6-1/2 FT. PICKUP: Ford restyled its light-duty trucks for 1951. They now had a wider "horizontal wing" grille supported at the ends by the parking lamps and headlight narcelles. Three "dagmar" type uprights were on the grille, one at the center and one to each side. At the upper border of the grille were three rectangular open slots. This theme was echoed on the face of the hood, just below the Ford name. Spear-shaped trim was placed on the sides of the hood. There was also a new ribbed bumper and revised front fenders. Spear-shaped hood trim had the F-series designation in a badge at the front and the Ford name on the rear. The Ford name in front moved to the nose vent trim and V-8s had a V-8 emblem above the grille. Early 1951 grilles were finished in Argent silver with chrome headlamp surrounds. The late-1951 grilles were painted cream color and had Argent silver painted headlamp surrounds due to the reduction of chrome trim to meet Korean War materials restrictions. A new pickup box featured straight corner pillars, a wood floor and level-opening grain-tight tailgate. The engine featured modified spark advance; water-proof ignition; new intake manifold; aluminum timing gear; heavier main bearings; new water pump (V-8s); and new cam wristpins. Other 1951 technical advances included a beefed-up transmission; a 3.92:1 axle; larger self-energizing brakes; and (F-2/F-3 only) a driveshaft parking brake. Among standard 1951 features were: Bright hubcaps; dual windshield wipers (except cowl); inside rearview mirror; left-hand outside rearview mirror (long-arm type on Platform/Stake; short-arm type on other models); short running boards (Panel/Stake/Platform) or long runningboards other models (straight type on Chassis & Cab; curved at rear on others); left-hand sun visor; and (on Panel) rear bumper; an improved, column mounted three-speed manual transmission; larger rear window; and the 45 cu. ft. load capacity cargo box. New this year (at extra-cost) was the Standard Five-Star Cab package. It included a 3-Way Air-Control unit with air-wing ventilators; cowl panel ventilator; tough vinyl seat with rubberized horsehair padding and coil springs; adjustable driver's side visor; dual windshield wipers; full-gauge instrumentation; dispatch box (glove compartment); ashtray; and adjustable seat. Also new (at additional extra-cost) was the Five-Star-Extra Cab package, which added dual horns; foam rubber seats; two-tone upholstery; a sound-deadening headliner with fiberglass pad; special door trim; bright window trim; door locks; armrests; cigar lighter; and automatic dome light to the standard Five-Star package contents.

1951 Ford 1/2-Ton Model F-1 Pickup (OCW)

F-1 8 FT. PANEL: The new F-1 Panel shared many of the same features as the Pickup, including a new instrument panel. A single bucket type driver' seat and twin rear doors were standard. The floor was solid plywood with steel skid strips. It could haul payloads up to 1,330 lbs.

F-1 8 FT. DELUXE PANEL: Panel buyers who wanted something with a little fancier, could order the new Deluxe model. It had a full-length glass wool headliner and the interior walls were lined with Masonite. Plus, it came with most of the other Five Star Extra cab features. This included distinctive missle-style ornaments on the sides of the hood.

F-1 6-1/2 FT. PLATFORM/STAKE: As before, the Platform/Stake had hardwood floors with steel skid strips. The removable stake racks were made of straight grained wood. There was a steel rub rail around the platform, with steel caps on the ends of the body sills. Pockets were flush with the floor, welded to the inside of the frame rail and riveted to the outside. Load space was 84.3 in. long (80 in. with stakes) and 71.28 in. wide (67 in. with stakes). The stakes were 29.54 in. high.

1951 Ford 1/2-Ton Model F-1 Pickup (OCW)

I.D. DATA [F-1]: Located on glove box door rating plate; also check clutch housing and left frame near steering gear mounting bracket. The first two symbols indicate series: F1=1/2-ton Conventional. The third symbol indicated engine: D=215 cid six; R=239 cid V-8. The fourth symbol indicated model year: 1=1951. The fifth and sixth symbols indicated the assembly plant: AT=Atlanta, Ga.; BF=Buffalo, N.Y.; CH=Chicago, Ill.; CS=Chester, Pa.; DL=Dallas, Texas; EG=Edgewater, N.J.; HM=Highland Park, Mich.; KC=Kansas City, Mo.; LB=Long Beach, Calif.; LU=Louisville, Ken.; MP=Memphis, Tenn.; NR=Norfolk, Va.; RH=Richmond, Calif.; SP=St. Paul, Minn.; and SR=Somerville, Mass. The last six symbols indicate the sequential production number starting with 100001 and each factory. Color codes were: A=black; B=Sheridan blue; D=Alpine blue; G=Sea Island green; H=Silvertone gray; M=Meadow green; N=Vermilion; P=prime; SS=special.

Model	Body Type	Price	Weight	Prod. Total
F-1 Series 1HC — 1/2-Ton — 114 in. w.b. — Six				
80	Platform	1379	2975	Note 1
81	Chassis & Cab	1265	2645	Note 1
82	Panel	1535	3195	Note 1
82B	Panel	—	—	Note 1
83	Pickup	1331	3025	Note 1
84	Chassis & Cowl	1042	2145	Note 1
85	Chassis & W/S	1078	2175	Note 1
86	Stake	1415	3095	Note 1
F-1 Series 1RC — 1/2-Ton — 114 in. w.b. — V-8				
80	Platform	1566	3235	Note 1
81	Chassis & Cab	1296	2685	Note 1
82	Panel	1566	3235	Note 1
82B	Panel	—	—	2326
83	Pickup	1363	3065	Note 1
84	Chassis & Cowl	1073	2185	Note 1
85	Chassis & W/S	1109	2215	Note 1
86	Stake	1446	3135	Note 1

NOTE 1: Combined production of 1951 models according to body style was: [6.5 ft. Platform] 85 [Chassis & Cab] 4,083; [8 ft. Panel] 14,940; [8 ft. Deluxe Panel] 2,326; [6.5 ft. Pickup] 117,414; [Chassis & Windshield] 1,007; [6.5 ft. Stake] 1,442.
ENGINE [1HC]: Displacement: 215 cid. L-Head Six. 101 hp at 3500 rpm. Bore & stroke: 3.56 in. x 3.6 in. Compression ratio: 7.0:1. Carburetor: One-barrel.
ENGINE [1RC]: Displacement: 239.4 cid. L-Head V-8. 106 hp at 3800 rpm. Bore & stroke: 3-3/16 in. x 3-3/4 in. Compression ratio: 6.8. Carburetor: Two-barrel.

1951 Ford 1/2-Ton Model F-1 Pickup (OCW)

F-2 8 FT. EXPRESS: A couple new features added during the model run on F-2 trucks were: 12 x 2 in. self-energizing front and rear brakes and a drum-type, driveshaft-mounted parking brake. Like the F-1, the F-2 Pickup had a new box with straight sided corner pillars. Dual windshield wipers were now standard.

F-2 7-1/2 FT. PLATFORM/STAKE: The powerplants of F-2 Platform/Stake were improved for the new model year, although their horsepower rating remained the same. The six-cylinder had a new water pump; level-mounted manifold; heavier-walled main bearings; aluminum timing gear; revised camshaft; and a new torsional damper. The V-8 had a new camshaft, water pump, and offset piston pins.

I.D. DATA [F-2]: Located on glove box door rating plate; also check clutch housing and left frame near steering gear mounting bracket. The first two symbols indicate series: F2=3/4 Conventional. The third symbol indicated engine: D=215 cid six; R=239 cid V-8. The fourth symbol indicated model year: 1=1951. The fifth and sixth symbols indicated the assembly plant: AT=Atlanta, Ga.; BF=Buffalo, N.Y.; CH=Chicago, Ill.; CS=Chester, Pa.; DL=Dallas, Texas; EG=Edgewater, N.J.; HM=Highland Park, Mich.; KC=Kansas City, Mo.; LB=Long Beach, Calif.; LU=Louisville, Ken.; MP=Memphis, Tenn.; NR=Norfolk, Va.; RH=Richmond, Calif.; SP=St. Paul, Minn.; and SR=Somerville, Mass. The last six symbols indicate the sequential production number starting with 100001 and each factory. Colors same as F-1.

Model	Body Type	Price	Weight	Prod. Total
F-2 Series 1HD — 3/4-Ton — 122 in. w.b. — Six				
80	Platform	1506	3450	Note 1
81	Chassis & Cab	1400	3040	Note 1
83	Express-Pickup	1490	3520	Note 1
84	Chassis & Cowl	1177	2550	Note 1
85	Chassis & W/S	1214	2580	Note 1
86	Stake	1563	3640	Note 1
F-2 Series 1RD — 3/4-Ton — 122 in. w.b. — V-8				
80	Platform	1537	3490	Note 1
81	Chassis & Cab	1432	3080	Note 1
83	Express-Pickup	1522	3560	Note 1
84	Chassis & Cowl	1209	2590	Note 1
85	Chassis & W/S	1245	2620	Note 1
86	Stake	1594	3680	Note 1

NOTE 1: Combined production of 1951 models according to body style was: [7.5 ft. Platform] 78 [Chassis & Cab] 1,494; [8 ft. Express-Pickup] 17,485; [Chassis & Cowl] 157; [Chassis & Windshield] 216; [7.5 ft. Stake] 1,039.
ENGINE [1HD]: Displacement: 215 cid. L-Head Six. 101 hp at 3500 rpm. Bore & stroke: 3.56 in. x 3.6 in. Compression ratio: 7.0:1. Carburetor: One-barrel.
ENGINE [1RD]: Displacement: 239.4 cid. L-Head V-8. 106 hp at 3800 rpm. Bore & stroke: 3-3/16 in. x 3-3/4 in. Compression ratio: 6.8. Carburetor: Two-barrel.

F-3 8 FT. EXPRESS: The F-3 remained the biggest Pickup in Ford's light-duty truck line up. It shared styling with the others and like the F-2, received new front and rear brakes and a driveshaft-mounted parking brake during the model year. Those equipped with a V-8 engine had a V-8 emblem above the grille.

F-3 7-1/2 FT. PLATFORM/STAKE: Ford's most popular light-duty stake truck in 1951 was the F-3. The increased fuel economy of available engines added to the appeal of this sturdy vehicle. As before, the wood stake sides could be snuggley locked to hold the racks firmly in place.

F-3 PARCEL DELIVERY: The 1951 Parcel Delivery had round parking lamps and a new grille that was very similar to that used on other light-duty Ford trucks.

I.D. DATA [F-3]: Located on glove box door rating plate; also check clutch housing and left frame near steering gear mounting bracket. The first two symbols indicate series: F3=Heavy-duty 3/4-ton Conventional. The third symbol indicated engine: D=215 cid six; R=239 cid V-8. The fourth symbol indicated model year: 1=1951. The fifth and sixth symbols indicated the assembly plant: AT=Atlanta, Ga.; BF=Buffalo, N.Y.; CH=Chicago, Ill.; CS=Chester, Pa.; DL=Dallas, Texas; EG=Edgewater, N.J.; HM=Highland Park, Mich.; KC=Kansas City, Mo.; LB=Long Beach, Calif.; LU=Louisville, Ken.; MP=Memphis, Tenn.; NR=Norfolk, Va.; RH=Richmond, Calif.; SP=St. Paul, Minn.; and SR=Somerville, Mass. The last six symbols indicate the sequential production number starting with 100001 and each factory. Color codes same as F-1.

Model	Body Type	Price	Weight	Prod. Total
F-3 Series 9HY — Heavy 3/4-Ton — 122 in. w.b. — Six				
80	Platform	1612	3680	Note 1
81	Chassis & Cab	1506	3270	Note 1
83	Express-Pickup	1596	3770	Note 1
84	Chassis & Cowl	1283	2780	Note 1
85	Chassis & W/S	1319	2810	Note 1
86	Stake	1669	3870	Note 1
F-3 Series 9RY — Heavy 3/4-Ton — 122 in. w.b. — V-8				
80	Platform	1643	3720	Note 1
81	Chassis & Cab	1537	3310	Note 1
83	Express-Pickup	1627	3810	Note 1
84	Chassis & Cowl	1314	2820	Note 1
85	Chassis & W/S	1350	2850	Note 1
86	Stake	1700	3910	Note 1

NOTE 1: Combined production of 1951 models according to body style was: [7.5 ft. Platform] 96 [Chassis & Cab] 2,949; [8 ft. Express-Pickup] 19,848; [Chassis & Cowl] 932; [Chassis & Windshield] 454; [7.5 ft. Stake] 1,667.
ENGINE [1HC]: Displacement: 215 cid. L-Head Six. 101 hp at 3500 rpm. Bore & stroke: 3.56 in. x 3.6 in. Compression ratio: 7.0:1. Carburetor: One-barrel.
ENGINE [1RC]: Displacement: 239.4 cid. L-Head V-8. 106 hp at 3800 rpm. Bore & stroke: 3-3/16 in. x 3-3/4 in. Compression ratio: 6.8. Carburetor: Two-barrel.
CHASSIS [F-1]: Wheelbase: 114 in. Overall length: [Pickup] 188.78 in.; [Panel] 202.13 in.; [Platform/Stake] 195.96 in. Overall width: [Pickup] 75.94 in.; [Panel]; 75.62 in.; [Platform/Stake] 71.28 in. Overall height: [Pickup/Platform/Stake] 75.64 in.; [Panel] 79.18 in. GVW: 4,700 lbs. Tires: 6.00 x 16, four-ply.
CHASSIS [F-2/F-3]: Wheelbase: 122 in. Overall length: [Pickup] 206.96 in.; [Platform/Stake] 206.52 in. Overall width: [Pickup] 75.94 in.; [Platform/Stake] 79.24 in. Overall height: [F-2] 76.52 in.; [F-3] 77.42 in. GVW: [F-2] 5,700 lbs. [F-3]; 6,800 lbs. Tires: [F-2] 6.50 x 16, six-ply; [F-3] 7.00 x 17, six-ply.
POWERTRAIN OPTIONS: Heavy-duty three-speed/heavy-duty four-speed manual transmissions. 4.27:1 and 4.09:1 rear axle ratios.
CONVENIENCE OPTIONS: Spiralounge bucket seat. Heavy-duty radiator. Magic Air heater-defroster. Radio. Seat covers. Twin horns. Sealed beam spot light. Fire extinguisher. Grille guards. Windshield washer. Gas tank locking cap. 11 in. clutch. Heavy-duty fan. Right-hand rear taillight. Rear bumper. Catridge oil filter. Electric windshield wipers. 4.27:1 axle. Six-ply tires (6x16 in. front; 6x16.5 in. rear); Five-Star cab package; Five-Star-Extra cab package; Panel truck auxiliary seat; Recirculating type heater and defroster. Fresh Air type heater/defroster. Electric windshield wipers. Rear bumper (Pickups and chassis models). Right-hand stoplamp/taillamp (standard on Panel).
OPTION PACKAGES: [Five-Star Extra Cab] Includes, dome light with door switches; deluxe door trim; chromed windshield molding; dual horns; foam rubber seat padding; vinyl and mohair seat upholstery; extra sound insulation; cigarette lighter. [Five-Star Extra Panel] Also included: uxiliary seat with two-tone upholstery, plus heavy Masonite lining above and perforated headlining on roof panel backed by thick glass wool insulating pad.
NOTE: Colors offered for 1951 were: Alpine blue, Black, Meadow green, Sea Island green, Sheridan blue, Silvertone gray and Vermilion.
HISTORICAL: Ford promoted "Step-Ahead Engineering" and a "Power Pilot" vacuum advance feature for 1951. Sales for the year amounted to 180,000 trucks.

1952 FORD

1952 Ford 1/2-Ton F-1 Pickup (OCW)

1952 Ford 1/2-Ton F-1 Panel (OCW)

COURIER CUSTOM SEDAN DELIVERY: The new Courier Sedan Delivery was based on the Ford Ranch Wagon. It shared its attractive exterior styling with the passenger car line. The grille had a three-bladed round spinner in its center. The circular, fender-mounted parking lights were located under the recessed style headlights. The Ford emblem was centered on the face of the hood. There were simulated scoops on the rear quarter panels. Tube-like round taillights protruded from the rear fenders. The interior featured a headlining, foam-padded vinyl-covered driver's seat and gray Masonite interior wall liners. Buyers had their choice of 10 colors: Raven black; Sheridan blue; Alpine blue; Woodsmoke gray; Shannon green (metallic); Meadowbrook green; Glenmist green; Carnival red; Hawaiian bronze; and Sandpiper tan. Buyers could also order vehicles in primer or special colors. Interior trim was dark brown vinyl. The Courier offered 102 cu. ft. of cargo volume with a 37 x 46.5 in. rear side-hinged door. The Courier name was on the front fenders, with a V-8 badge added on 78B models.

I.D. DATA [Courier]: VIN located on rating plate. The first symbol indicated the engine: A=215 cid six; B=239 cid V-8. The second symbol indicated the model year: 2=1952. The third symbol indicated the assembly plant: AT=Atlanta, Ga.; BF=Buffalo, N.Y.; CH=Chicago, Ill.; CS=Chester, Pa.; DA=Dearborn, Mich; DL=Dallas, Texas; EG=Edgewater, N.J.; KC=Kansas City, Mo.; LB=Long Beach, Calif.; LU=Louisville, Ken.; MP=Memphis, Tenn.; NR=Norfolk, Va.; RH=Richmond, Calif.; SP=St. Paul, Minn.; and SR=Somerville, Mass. The last six symbols were the sequential production number starting with 100001 at each plant. Color codes were: A=Raven black; B=Sheridan blue; D=Woodsmoke gray; E=Shannon green (metallic); F=Meadowbrook green; G=Glenmist green; H=Carnival red; J=Hawaiian bronze; K=Sandpiper tan; P=Primer; SS=Special color.

Model	Body Type	Price	Weight	Prod. Total
Courier — 1/2-Ton — 115 in. w.b. — Six				
78A	Sedan Delivery	1539	3109	Note 1
Courier — 1/2-Ton — 115 in. w.b. — V-8				
78B	Sedan Delivery	1571	3185	Note 1

ENGINE [78A]: Displacement: 215 cid. OHV Six-cylinder. Four main bearings. 101 hp at 3500 rpm. Torque: 185 lbs.-ft. at 1300-1700 rpm. Bore & stroke: 3.56 x 3.60 in. Compression ratio: 7.0:1. One-barrel Holley Visi-Flo carburetor. This wngine was called the "Clipper Six." It was the same used in trucks.

ENGINE [78B]: Displacement: 239.4 cid. L-head V-8. 110 hp at 3800 rpm. Bore & stroke: 3.19 in. x 3.75. Compression ratio: 7.2:1. High-lift camshaft. Carburetor: Two-barrel. This engine was called the "Strato Star" V-8. It was different than the V-8 used in trucks.

F-1 6-1/2 FT. PICKUP: Ford trucks received a minor facelift for 1952. The nose vent on the face of the hood was now painted. The word Ford was spelled out above the grille opening panel. A V-8 badge was added to models with the V-8 engine. The grille was now painted white. The hood side spears were altered. They now featured a small circular emblem toward the tip which included the F-series insignia in red. Hubcaps were changed to Argent silver finish, to reduce the use of chrome plated parts in line with Korean War materials restrictions. After midyear, the taillights also came withou bright bezels. The front fender braces, used for the last 10 years, were eliminated. Among standard equipment was: Column mounted three-speed manual transmission; dual windshield wipers; steel-floored box with level opening tailgate; and 90 amp.-hr. battery. Paint codes and colors for 1952 Ford trucks were: A=black; B=Sheridan blue; D=Woodsmoke gray; G=Glenmist green; K=Sandpiper tan; M=Vermilion; N=Meadow green; P=primer; SS=special color option.

1F-1 8 FT. PANEL: The F-1 Panel's floor was made of solid plywood with steel skid strips. A single bucket type driver's seat and twin rear doors were standard. The bezel on the taillight lenses were eliminated in midyear.

F-1 8 FT. DELUXE PANEL: In addition to the styling changes found on all Ford trucks, the Deluxe Panel came with features found in the Five Star Extra option package. One such item was chrome extentions on the side of the hood, from the F-1 insignia toward the cab.

F-1 6-1/2 FT. PLATFORM/STAKE: Aside from the mild facelift, there was little difference between this year's model and last. The wood side racks were removable. The platform was made of hardwood with a steel skid strips.

I.D. DATA [F-1]: Located on glove box door rating plate; also check clutch housing and left frame near steering gear mounting bracket. The first two symbols indicate series: F1=1/2-ton Conventional. The third symbol indicated engine: D=215 cid six; R=239 cid (Rogue) V-8. The fourth symbol indicated model year: 2=1952. The fifth and sixth symbols indicated the assembly plant: AT=Atlanta, Ga.; BF=Buffalo, N.Y.; CH=Chicago, Ill.; CS=Chester, Pa.; DA=Dearborn, Mich.; DL=Dallas, Texas; EG=Edgewater, N.J.; HM=Highland Park, Mich.; KC=Kansas City, Mo.; LB=Long Beach, Calif.; LU=Louisville, Ken.; MP=Memphis, Tenn.; NR=Norfolk, Va.; RH=Richmond, Calif.; SP=St. Paul, Minn.; and SR=Somerville, Mass. The last six symbols indicate the sequential production number starting with 100001 and each factory.

F-1 Series F1D2 — 1/2-Ton — 114 in. w.b. — Six

Model	Body Type	Price	Weight	Prod. Total
80	Platform	1367	2940	Note 1
81	Chassis & Cab	1248	2610	Note 1
82	Panel	1540	3160	Note 1
82B	Deluxe Panel	—	—	Note 1
83	Pickup	1329	2990	Note 1
84	Chassis & Cowl	1012	2110	Note 1
85	Chassis & W/S	1054	2140	Note 1
86	Stake	1405	2990	Note 1

F-1 Series F1R2 — 1/2-Ton — 114 in. w.b. — V-8

Model	Body Type	Price	Weight	Prod. Total
80	Platform	1400	3025	Note 1
81	Chassis & Cab	1281	2695	Note 1
82	Panel	1573	3245	Note 1
82B	Deluxe Panel	—	—	Note 1
83	Pickup	1362	3075	Note 1
84	Chassis & Cowl	1044	2195	Note 1
85	Chassis & W/S	1086	2215	Note 1
86	Stake	1437	3145	Note 1

NOTE 1: Combined production of 1952 models according to body style was: [6.5 ft. Platform] 19 [Chassis & Cab] 2,844; [8 ft. Panel] 6,565; [8 ft. Deluxe Panel] 1,611; [6.5 ft. Pickup] 81,537; [Chassis & Cowl] 287; [Chassis & Windshield] 252; [6.5 ft. Stake] 1,033.

ENGINE [F1D2]: Displacement: 215 cid. OHV Six-cylinder. Four main bearings. 101 hp at 3500 rpm. Torque: 185 lbs.-ft. at 1300-1700 rpm. Bore & stroke: 3.56 x 3.60 in. Compression ratio: 7.0:1. One-barrel Holley Visi-Flo carburetor. This wngine was called the "Clipper Six." It was the same used in Couriers.

ENGINE [F1R2]: Displacement: 239.4 cid. L-head V-8. 106 hp at 3500 rpm. Torque: 194 lbs.-ft. at 1900-2100 rpm. Bore & stroke: 3.19 in. x 3.75. Compression ratio: 6.8:1. Carburetor: Two-barrel. This engine was called the "Rogue" V-8. It was different than the V-8 used in Couriers.

F-2 8 FT. EXPRESS: The F-2 Pickup shared the minor styling changes found on the F-1. It, too, was basically the same as the 1951 model.

F-2 7-1/2 FT. PLATFORM/STAKE: As before, this model was a slightly heavier-duty version of its F-1 counterpart.

I.D. DATA [F-2]: Located on glove box door rating plate; also check clutch housing and left frame near steering gear mounting bracket. The first two symbols indicate series: F2=3/4 Conventional. The third symbol indicated engine: D=215 cid six; R=239 cid (Rogue) V-8. The fourth symbol indicated model year: 2=1952. The fifth and sixth symbols indicated the assembly plant: AT=Atlanta, Ga.; BF=Buffalo, N.Y.; CH=Chicago, Ill.; CS=Chester, Pa.; DA=Dearborn, Mich.; DL=Dallas, Texas; EG=Edgewater, N.J.; HM=Highland Park, Mich.; KC=Kansas City, Mo.; LB=Long Beach, Calif.; LU=Louisville, Ken.; MP=Memphis, Tenn.; NR=Norfolk, Va.; RH=Richmond, Calif.; SP=St. Paul, Minn.; and SR=Somerville, Mass. The last six symbols indicate the sequential production number starting with 100001 and each factory. Colors same as F-1.

Model	Body Type	Price	Weight	Prod. Total
F-2 Series F2D2 — 3/4-Ton — 122 in. w.b. — Six				
80	Platform	1506	3450	Note 1
81	Chassis & Cab	1400	3040	Note 1
83	Express-Pickup	1490	3520	Note 1
84	Chassis & Cowl	1177	2550	Note 1
85	Chassis & W/S	1214	2580	Note 1
86	Stake	1563	3640	Note 1
F-2 Series F2R2 — 3/4-Ton — 122 in. w.b. — V-8				
80	Platform	1537	3490	Note 1
81	Chassis & Cab	1432	3080	Note 1
83	Express-Pickup	1522	3560	Note 1
84	Chassis & Cowl	1209	2590	Note 1
85	Chassis & W/S	1245	2620	Note 1
86	Stake	1594	3680	Note 1

NOTE 1: Combined production of 1952 models according to body style was: [7.5 ft. Platform] 28 [Chassis & Cab] 1,121; [8 ft. Express-Pickup] 15,136; [Chassis & Cowl] 276; [Chassis & Windshield] 233; [7.5 ft. Stake] 785.

ENGINE [F2D2]: Displacement: 215 cid. OHV Six-cylinder. Four main bearings. 101 hp at 3500 rpm. Torque: 185 lbs.-ft. at 1300-1700 rpm. Bore & stroke: 3.56 x 3.60 in. Compression ratio: 7.0:1. One-barrel Holley Visi-Flo carburetor. This wngine was called the "Clipper Six." It was the same used in Couriers.

ENGINE [F2R2]: Displacement: 239.4 cid. L-head V-8. 106 hp at 3500 rpm. Torque: 194 lbs.-ft. at 1900-2100 rpm. Bore & stroke: 3.19 in. x 3.75. Compression ratio: 6.8:1. Carburetor: Two-barrel. This engine was called the "Rogue" V-8. It was different than the V-8 used in Couriers.

F-3 8 FT. EXPRESS: This Pickup was built for maximum light-duty hauling. It had a GVW rating over 2,000 lbs. greater than the F-1.

F-3 7-1/2 FT. PLATFORM/STAKE: Except for a minor facelift, the F-3 Platform/Stake truck was the same as last year.

I.D. DATA [F-3]: Located on glove box door rating plate; also check clutch housing and left frame near steering gear mounting bracket. The first two symbols indicate series: F3=Heavy-duty 3/4-ton Conventional. The third symbol indicated engine: D=215 cid six; R=239 cid (Rogue) V-8. The fourth symbol indicated model year: 2=1952. The fifth and sixth symbols indicated the assembly plant: AT=Atlanta, Ga.; BF=Buffalo, N.Y.; CH=Chicago, Ill.; CS=Chester, Pa.; DA=Dearborn, Mich.; DL=Dallas, Texas; EG=Edgewater, N.J.; HM=Highland Park, Mich.; KC=Kansas City, Mo.; LB=Long Beach, Calif.; LU=Louisville, Ken.; MP=Memphis, Tenn.; NR=Norfolk, Va.; RH=Richmond, Calif.; SP=St. Paul, Minn.; and SR=Somerville, Mass. The last six symbols indicate the sequential production number starting with 100001 and each factory. Colors same as F-1.

Model	Body Type	Price	Weight	Prod. Total
F-3 Series F3D2 — Heavy 3/4-Ton — 122 in. w.b. — Six				
80	Platform	1612	3680	Note 1
81	Chassis & Cab	1506	3270	Note 1
83	Express-Pickup	1596	3770	Note 1
84	Chassis & Cowl	1283	2780	Note 1
85	Chassis & W/S	1319	2810	Note 1
86	Stake	1669	3870	Note 1
F-3 Series F3R2 — Heavy 3/4-Ton — 122 in. w.b. — V-8				
80	Platform	1643	3720	Note 1
81	Chassis & Cab	1537	3310	Note 1
83	Express-Pickup	1627	3810	Note 1
84	Chassis & Cowl	1314	2820	Note 1
85	Chassis & W/S	1350	2850	Note 1
86	Stake	1700	3910	Note 1

NOTE 1: Combined production of 1952 models according to body style was: [7.5 ft. Platform] 37 [Chassis & Cab] 1,731; [8 ft. Express-Pickup] 15,771; [Chassis & Cowl] 590; [Chassis & Windshield] 204; [7.5 ft. Stake] 1,658.

ENGINE [F2D2]: Displacement: 215 cid. OHV Six-cylinder. Four main bearings. 101 hp at 3500 rpm. Torque: 185 lbs.-ft. at 1300-1700 rpm. Bore & stroke: 3.56 x 3.60 in. Compression ratio: 7.0:1. One-barrel Holley Visi-Flo carburetor. This engine was called the "Clipper Six." It was the same used in Couriers.

ENGINE [F2R2]: Displacement: 239.4 cid. L-head V-8. 106 hp at 3500 rpm. Torque: 194 lbs.-ft. at 1900-2100 rpm. Bore & stroke: 3.19 in. x 3.75. Compression ratio: 6.8:1. Carburetor: Two-barrel. This engine was called the "Rogue" V-8. It was different than the V-8 used in Couriers.

CHASSIS: [Sedan Delivery] Wheelbase: 115 in. Overall length: 197.8 in. Overall width: 73.2 in. Tread: 58 in. Tires: 6.00 x 16 in. GVW options: 4,000 lbs. with 6.70 x 15 four-ply tires. 4,200 lbs. with 7.10 x 15 four-ply tires. 4,500 lbs. with 7.10 x 15 six-ply tires.

CHASSIS [F-1]: Wheelbase: 114 in. Overall length: {Pickup} 188.78 in.; [Panel] 202.13 in.; [Platform/Stake] 195.96 in. Overall width: [Pickup] 75.94 in.; [Panel] 75.62 in.; [Platform/Stake] 71.28 in. Overall height: [Pickup/Platform/Stake] 75.64 in.; [Panel] 79.18 in. GVW: 4,700 lbs. Tires: 6.00 x 16, four-ply.

CHASSIS [F-2/F-3]: Wheelbase: 122 in. Overall length: [Pickup] 206.96 in.; [Platform/Stake] 206.52 in. Overall width: [Pickup] 75.94 in.; [Platform/Stake] 79.24 in. Overall height: [F-2] 76.52 in.; [F-3] 77.42 in. GVW: [F-2] 5,700 lbs. [F-3]; 6,800 lbs. Tires: [F-2] 6.50 x 16, six-ply; [F-3] 7.00 x 17, six-ply.

POWERTRAIN OPTIONS [COURIER]: Three-speed manual transmission. Three-speed manual transmission with overdrive. Ford-O-Matic transmission.

POWERTRAIN OPTIONS [CONVENTIONALS]: Three-speed manual transmission with overdrive, heavy-duty three-speed manual transmission or heavy-duty four-speed manual transmissions.

CONVENIENCE OPTIONS: Grille guard. Windshield washer. Heater-defroster. Heavy-duty battery. Rear bumper. Radio. Right-hand sunvisor. Turn signals. Seat covers. Fire extingisher. Right-hand visor. Deluxe Five-Star Cab package. Locking gas cap. Seat covers. Rear bumper. Radio. Grille guard. Fire extinquisher. Oil filter. Windshield washer. Heater and defroster. Four-speed manual transmission (Standard in F-2/F-3). 11 in. clutch. Heavy-duty battery. Directional signals. Heavy-duty radiator. Heavy-duty three-speed manual transmission. Panel auxlary seat.

FIVE STAR EXTRA CAB: Dome light. Glove box lock. Locks for both doors. Deluxe door trim. Chrome windshield molding. Two-tone upholstery. Foam rubber seat padding. Right-hand and left-hand sunvisors.

HISTORICAL: The new overhead valve "Clipper Six" engine was as powerful as the flathead V-8. A 14 percent economy improvement was claimed for trucks with this motor. The 1952 models were promoted as "The World's Greatest Trucks." Ford manufactured 841,000 "Bonus Built" trucks in five years. Calendar year production for 1952 was 236,753 trucks.

1953 FORD

1953 Ford 1/2-Ton Courier Sedan Delivery (OCW)

COURIER CUSTOM SEDAN DELIVERY: The Courier received a minor facelift for 1953. Rectangular parking lights were seen between the front bumper and wraparound center grille bar. A spinner was located in the middle of the bar with vertical stripes on either side of it. The trucks now had chrome plated stone shields, new hubcaps, revised instrument panel trim, and modified taillamps. A chrome Courier script decorated the front fenders and V-8s also added V-8 badges. There was also a new hood ornament and improved front suspension. The cooling system capacity of V-8 powered models was increased. The interior featured a headliner, foam-padded vinyl-covered driver's seat, Golden Anniversary horn button, and Masonite interior wall liners. A three-speed manual transmission was standard. Paint codes and colors were: A=Raven black; B=Sheridan blue; C=Glacier blue; D=Woodsmoke gray; E=Timberline green (metallic); F=Fernmist green; G=Seafoam green; H=Carnival red (metallic); J=Polynesian bronze (metallic); K=Sandpiper tan; L=Sungate ivory; M=Coral flame red; P=primer; SS=special finish.

I.D. DATA [Courier]: VIN located on rating plate. The first symbol indicated the engine: A=215 cid six; B=239 cid V-8. The second symbol indicated the model year: 3=1953. The third symbol indicated the assembly plant: A=Atlanta, Ga.; B=Buffalo, N.Y.; C=Chester, Pa.; D=Dallas, Texas; E=Edgewater, N.J.; F=Dearborn, Mich.; G=Chicago, Ill.; H=Highland Park, Mich.; K=Kansas City, Mo.; L=Long Beach, Calif.; M=Memphis, Tenn.; N=Norfolk, Va.; P=St. Paul, Minn.; R=Richmond, Va.; S=Somerville, Mass.; U=Louisville, Ken. The last six symbols were the sequential production number starting with 100001 at each plant.

Model	Body Type	Price	Weight	Prod. Total
78A	Sedan Delivery	1515	3109	Note 1

Model	Body Type	Price	Weight	Prod. Total
78B	Sedan Delivery	1547	3185	Note 1

NOTE 1: Production was 10,575 for both Courier models combined.

ENGINE [78A]: Displacement: 215 cid. OHV Six-cylinder. Four main bearings. 101 hp at 3500 rpm. Torque: 185 lbs.-ft. at 1300-1700 rpm. Bore & stroke: 3.56 x 3.60 in. Compression ratio: 7.0:1. One-barrel Holley Visi-Flo carburetor. This engine was now called the "Mileage Maker Six." It was the same used in trucks.

ENGINE [78B]: Displacement: 239.4 cid. L-head V-8. 110 hp at 3800 rpm. Bore & stroke: 3.19 in. x 3.75. Compression ratio: 7.2:1. High-lift camshaft. Carburetor: Two-barrel. This engine was called the "Strato Star" V-8. It was different than the V-8 used in trucks.

1953 Ford 1/2-Ton F-100 Pickup (OCW)

F-100 6-1/2 FT. PICKUP: The F-100 was introduced on March 13, 1953. It had a sleeker, more modern look than last year's model. The front axle was positioned four inches rearward of the previous location. A new Ford "crest" emblem was on the face of the wider hood. Chrome trimmed headlight pods were recessed and connected to the new two-bar grille. On six-cylinder trucks, the grille had a Y-shaped star in its center. V-8 powered trucks used an 8-inside-a-V type grille emblem. Deluxe models had three vertical chrome teeth on either side of the grille. Standard hoodside trim said Ford and identified the F-series number. Deluxe hoodside trim said Ford, with the F-series designation inside a chrome scallop. The cabs were roomier. The wider seats had "Counter-Shock" seat snubbers that absorbed road shocks for a softer, smoother ride. Both seat and seatback were independently adjustable. Standard cabs had metal interior door panels. A "Driverized Cab" option added foam seat padding; a thermocoustic headliner; sound deadener on the floor, doors and rear panels; two-tone seat trim; twin sun visors; dual armrests; a cigar lighter; an automatic dome light; a locking dispatch (glove) box; twin door locks; twin electric horns; distinctive bright hardware and exterior trim; and interior door trim panels. Deluxe trim trucks featured chrome grille teeth; stainless steel hood scallops; bright vent window moldings; and stainless steel drip rails. Other new features included: Overlapping windshield wipers; sound deadener on doors; push-button door handles; deeper armrest windows; a five percent bigger one-piece curved glass windshield; a four-foot wide rear window; a recessed fuel filler on driver side of cab models; rotary-latched cab doors; and a frame-mounted gas tank. The louvers on the cowl pulled in air for the Magic Aire heater. At the rear, Ford block letters were seen on the tailgate, instead of the traditional Ford script. The new bolted box had a stronger tailgate and toggle-type latches. A three-speed manual transmission was among the standard features. All 1953 Ford trucks had special "50th Anniversary" horn buttons in honor of the company's golden anniversary.

F-100 6-1/2 FT. PLATFORM/STAKE: The Platform/Stake shared the styling changes of the F-100 Pickup. The stake racks were held firmly at the top with inter-locking steel plates which were bolted to rack boards for extra strength. The stake and rack boards were made of straight grained seasoned wood. The stake pockets were flush with the floor for unobstructed open platform use. Heavy, steel rub rail and steel caps on the body ends protected the platform.

F-100 8 FT. PANEL: In addition to the other previously mentioned F-100 changes for 1953, the 8 Ft. Panel had beefed-up rear doors, steel slats above the interior bodyside panels, different runningboards and a rectangular dome light. Larger rear windows were seen, too. The Panel had a 155.8 cu. ft. cargo area. The rear door opening was 50.8 in. wide and 45.4 in. high.

F-100 8 FT. DELUXE PANEL: This was basically just a dolled-up version of the standard Panel. It came with most of the features found on the Driverized Deluxe Cab package.

Standard Catalog of Light-Duty Trucks

FORD PICKUPS
More POWER · More COMFORT · More ECONOMY

1953 Ford 1/2-Ton F-100 Pickup (IOA)

I.D. DATA: Located on glove box door rating plate; also check clutch housing and left frame near steering gear mounting bracket. The first three symbols indicate series: F10=F-100. The fourth symbol indicated engine: D=215 cid six; R=239 cid (Rogue) V-8. The fifth symbol indicated model year: 3=1953. The sixth symbol indicated the assembly plant: A=Atlanta, Ga.; B=Buffalo, N.Y.; C=Chester, Pa.; D=Dallas, Texas; E=Edgewater, N.J.; F=Dearborn, Mich.; G=Chicago, Ill.; H=Highland Park, Mich.; K=Kansas City, Mo.; L=Long Beach, Calif.; M=Memphis, Tenn.; N=Norfolk, Va.; P=St. Paul, Minn.; R=Richmond, Va.; S=Somerville, Mass.; U=Louisville, Ken. The last six symbols indicate the sequential production number starting with 100001 and each factory.

F-100 Series F10D3 — 1/2-Ton — 114 in. w.b. — Six

80	Platform	1367	2940	Note 1
81	Chassis & Cab	1259	2747	Note 1
82	Panel	1540	3392	Note 1
82B	Deluxe Panel	—	—	Note 1
83	Pickup	1330	3102	Note 1
84	Chassis & Cowl	1012	2202	Note 1
85	Chassis & W/S	1054	2140	Note 1
86	Stake	1405	3217	Note 1

F-100 Series F10R3 — 1/2-Ton — 114 in. w.b. — V-8

80	Platform	1389	2970	Note 1
81	Chassis & Cab	1279	2816	Note 1
82	Panel	1560	3461	Note 1
82B	Deluxe Panel	—	—	Note 1
83	Pickup	1350	3171	Note 1
84	Chassis & Cowl	1034	2271	Note 1
85	Chassis & W/S	1069	2190	Note 1
86	Stake	1437	3286	Note 1

NOTE 1: Combined production of 1953 models according to body style was: [6.5 ft. Platform] 64 [Chassis & Cab] 3,061; [8 ft. Panel] 9,991; [8 ft. Deluxe Panel] 2,000; [6.5 ft. Pickup] 116,437; [Chassis & Cowl] 361; [Chassis & Windshield] 48; [6.5 ft. Stake] 1,517.
ENGINE [F10D3]: Displacement: 215 cid. OHV Six-cylinder. Four main bearings. 101 hp at 3500 rpm. Torque: 185 lbs.-ft. at 1300-1700 rpm. Bore & stroke: 3.56 x 3.60 in. Compression ratio: 7.0:1. One-barrel Holley Visi-Flo carburetor. This engine was now called the "Mileage Maker Six." It was the same used in Couriers.
ENGINE [F10R3]: Displacement: 239.4 cid. L-head V-8. 106 hp at 3500 rpm. Torque: 194 lbs.-ft. at 1900-2100 rpm. Bore & stroke: 3.19 in. x 3.75. Compression ratio: 6.8:1. Carburetor: Two-barrel. This engine was called the "Rogue" V-8. It was different than the V-8 used in Couriers.
F-250 8 FT. EXPRESS: The new F-250 Pickup was not only a couple feet longer than the F-100; it could also haul heavier cargo. Some of its standard features were: Heavy-duty three-speed column shift transmission; parking brake control on dash; 10 in. clutch; 2,600 lbs. capacity front axle; Timken-Detroit hypoid rear axle; and new bolt-construction box.
F-250 7-1/2 FT. PLATFORM/STAKE: The F-250 Platform/Stake had most of the same features as its F-100 counterpart. However, it was capable of hauling heavier loads.

1953 Ford 1/2-Ton F-100 Pickup (J. Scray)

I.D. DATA: Located on glove box door rating plate; also check clutch housing and left frame near steering gear mounting bracket. The first three symbols indicate series: F25=F-250. The fourth symbol indicated engine: D=215 cid six; R=239 cid (Rogue) V-8. The fifth symbol indicated model year: 3=1953. The sixth symbol indicated the assembly plant: A=Atlanta, Ga.; B=Buffalo, N.Y.; C=Chester, Pa.; D=Dallas, Texas; E=Edgewater, N.J.; F=Dearborn, Mich.; G=Chicago, Ill.; H=Highland Park, Mich.; K=Kansas City, Mo.; L=Long Beach, Calif.; M=Memphis, Tenn.; N=Norfolk, Va.; P=St. Paul, Minn.; R=Richmond, Va.; S=Somerville, Mass.; U=Louisville, Ken. The last six symbols indicate the sequential production number starting with 100001 and each factory.

F-250 Series F25D3 — 3/4-Ton — 122 in. w.b. — Six

80	Platform	1465	3450	Note 1
81	Chassis & Cab	1359	3092	Note 1
83	Express-Pickup	1450	3482	Note 1
84	Chassis & Cowl	1111	2537	Note 1
85	Chassis & W/S	1214	2580	Note 1
86	Stake	1579	3667	Note 1

F-250 Series F25R3 — 3/4-Ton — 122 in. w.b. — V-8

80	Platform	1497	3490	Note 1
81	Chassis & Cab	1391	3161	Note 1
83	Express-Pickup	1482	3551	Note 1
84	Chassis & Cowl	1143	2606	Note 1
85	Chassis & W/S	1175	2620	Note 1
86	Stake	1590	3680	Note 1

NOTE 1: Combined production of 1952 models according to body style was: [7.5 ft. Platform] 81 [Chassis & Cab] 2,534; [8 ft. Express-Pickup] 23,363; [Chassis & Cowl] 489; [Chassis & Windshield] 137; [7.5 ft. Stake] 1,995.
ENGINE [F25D3]: Displacement: 215 cid. OHV Six-cylinder. Four main bearings. 101 hp at 3500 rpm. Torque: 185 lbs.-ft. at 1300-1700 rpm. Bore & stroke: 3.56 x 3.60 in. Compression ratio: 7.0:1. One-barrel Holley Visi-Flo carburetor. This engine was now called the "Mileage Maker Six." It was the same used in Couriers.
ENGINE [F25R3]: Displacement: 239.4 cid. L-head V-8. 106 hp at 3500 rpm. Torque: 194 lbs.-ft. at 1900-2100 rpm. Bore & stroke: 3.19 in. x 3.75. Compression ratio: 6.8:1. Carburetor: Two-barrel. This engine was called the "Rogue" V-8. It was different than the V-8 used in Couriers.
F-350 9 FT. EXPRESS: Ford's biggest 1953 light-duty Pickup was the new 9 ft. Express. Like the F-250, it came with a heavy-duty, column-shifted three-speed manual transmission. However, it had heftier front and rear axles; large 13 x 2.5 in. rear brakes; and higher-capacity front springs.
F-350 9 FT. PLATFORM/STAKE: These replaced the F-4 series of previous years. They shared most of the same standard features as the F-350 Pickup.
I.D. DATA: Located on glove box door rating plate; also check clutch housing and left frame near steering gear mounting bracket. The first three symbols indicate series: F35=F-350. The fourth symbol indicated engine: D=215 cid six; R=239 cid (Rogue) V-8. The fifth symbol indicated model year: 3=1953. The sixth symbol indicated the assembly plant: A=Atlanta, Ga.; B=Buffalo, N.Y.; C=Chester, Pa.; D=Dallas, Texas; E=Edgewater, N.J.; F=Dearborn, Mich.; G=Chicago, Ill.; H=Highland Park, Mich.; K=Kansas City, Mo.; L=Long Beach, Calif.; M=Memphis, Tenn.; N=Norfolk, Va.; P=St. Paul, Minn.; R=Richmond, Va.; S=Somerville, Mass.; U=Louisville, Ken. The last six symbols indicate the sequential production number starting with 100001 and each factory.

Model	Body Type	Price	Weight	Prod. Total
F-3 Series F3D2 — Heavy 3/4-Ton — 122 in. w.b. — Six				
80	Platform	1645	3680	Note 1
81	Chassis & Cab	1498	3406	Note 1
83	Express-Pickup	1608	3906	Note 1
84	Chassis & Cowl	1259	2851	Note 1
85	Chassis & W/S	1301	2810	Note 1
86	Stake	1695	4326	Note 1
F-3 Series F3R2 — Heavy 3/4-Ton — 122 in. w.b. — V-8				
80	Platform	1677	3720	Note 1
81	Chassis & Cab	1530	3481	Note 1
83	Express-Pickup	1640	3981	Note 1
84	Chassis & Cowl	1291	2926	Note 1
85	Chassis & W/S	1333	2850	Note 1
86	Stake	1727	4401	Note 1

NOTE 1: Combined production of 1953 models according to body style was: [7.5 ft. Platform] 86 [Chassis & Cab] 5,152; [8 ft. Express-Pickup] 7,757; [Chassis & Cowl] 375; [Chassis & Windshield] 201; [7.5 ft. Stake] 2,202.
ENGINE [F35D3]: Displacement: 215 cid. OHV Six-cylinder. Four main bearings. 101 hp at 3500 rpm. Torque: 185 lbs.-ft. at 1300-1700 rpm. Bore & stroke: 3.56 x 3.60 in. Compression ratio: 7.0:1. One-barrel Holley Visi-Flo carburetor. This engine was now called the "Mileage Maker Six." It was the same used in Couriers.
ENGINE [F35R3]: Displacement: 239.4 cid. L-head V-8. 106 hp at 3500 rpm. Torque: 194 lbs.-ft. at 1900-2100 rpm. Bore & stroke: 3.19 in. x 3.75. Compression ratio: 6.8:1. Carburetor: Two-barrel. This engine was called the "Rogue" V-8. It was different than the V-8 used in Couriers.
CHASSIS [Courier Sedan Delivery]: Wheelbase: 115 in. Overall length: 197.8 in. Overall width: 74.3 in. Tires: 7.10 x 15.
[F-100]: Wheelbase: 110 in. Overall length: [Platform/Stake] 194.3 in.; [Pickup] 189.1 in.; [Panel] 201.8 in. Overall width: [Platform/Stake] 71.3 in.; [Panel] 75.6 in.; [Pickup] 75.7 in. GVW: 4,800 lb. Tires: 6.00 x 16.
[F-250]: Wheelbase: 118 in. GVW: 6,900 lbs.. Tires: 6.50 x 16.
[F-350]: Wheelbase: 130 in. Overall length: [Pickup] 108 in. Overall width: [Pickup] 54 in. GVW: 9,500 lbs. Tires: 8 x 17.5.

1953 Ford 1-Ton F-500 Wrecker (Mike Carbonella)

POWERTRAIN OPTIONS [Courirer]: Heavy-duty three-speed manual, three-speed with overdrive or four-speed manual transmissions. Ford-O-Matic automatic.
POWERTRAIN OPTIONS [F-150/F-250/F-350]: Heavy-duty three-speed manual transmission, three-speed with overdrive transmission, four-speed manual (standard on F-350) transmission, or beefed-up Ford-O-Matic transmission.

1953 Ford 1/2-Ton F-100 Pickup (OCW)

CONVENIENCE OPTIONS: Heavy-duty battery. Rear bumper (Pickup). Right-hand sun visor. Radio. Tinted glass. Grille guard. Seat covers. Heavy-duty fan. Windshield washers. Tow hooks. Various rear axle ratios. Deluxe Five Star cab includes: Twin electric horns; two-tone seat upholstery; foam rubber seat padding; customized door and body trim; perforated therm-acoustic headlining backed by glass-wool insulation; sound deadener on floor and rear cab panels; grip type armrests on both doors; large dome light with automatic door switches; two sun visors; illuminated cigar lighter; lock on dispatch box; and distinctive chrome or bright metal hardware and exterior trim. Locking gas cap. Hand throttle. Heavy-duty generator. Flare set. Heavy-duty fan. Oil filter. Electric windshield wipers. Magic Aire heater and defroster. Deluxe radio. Directional signals. Auxiliary seat for panel. I-Rest tinted glass. After June, 1953, the Courier was also available with power steering.

1953 Ford 1/2-Ton F-100 Pickup (Ronald L. Millins)

HISTORICAL: The Ford truck crest debuted this year. It featured Ford in writing above a gear crossed by a lightning bolt. It was the company's 50th anniversary and all Fords had "Golden Jubilee" horn buttons to commemorate this milestone. Calendar year production included 177,800 light-duty trucks, of which 116,400 were F-100 models. Ford invested four years of research work and $30 million to develop the new F-series models. They were promoted as "Ford Economy Trucks."

1954 FORD

1954 Ford 1/2-Ton F-100 Pickup (A & A)

COURIER CUSTOM DELIVERY: The 1954 Courier had a new, somewhat "busier" grille design with louvered slots, round parking lights at each end of the main bar and a spinner in the center. Canted headlamp bezels and a new hood ornament were among other front end changes. The bumper was of a new ribbed design with redesigned bumper guards. There was a new hood ornament and handsome hubcaps with maroon centers. Chrome Courier signatures appeared on the front fenders, with V-8 emblems below them if appropriate. The stone shields had a more vertical appearance and less horizontal length. The taillight "tubes" were de-emphasized and decorated with new taillamp bezels and center inserts. A Fordomatic script appeared on the rear door of Couriers equipped with the optional automatic transmission. The interior featured a new "Astra-Dial" speedometer, idiot lights for the oil and generator instead of gauges and a new steering wheel and horn button. A lot of improvements were hidden. These included: Ball joint front suspension; chassis modifications; three-piece front stabilizer bar; new shock absorbers; and a heavier-duty rear axle. Suspension weight capacities were up-rated.

I.D. DATA: The VIN appeared on the rating plate. The first symbol indicated engine: A=six; V=V-8. The second symbol was the last digit of the model year. The third symbol indicated assembly plant: A=Atlanta, Ga.; B=Buffalo, N.Y.; C=Chester, Pa.; D=Dallas, Texas; E=Edgewater, N.J.; F=Dearborn, Mich.; G=Chicago, Ill.; H=Highland Park, Mich.; K=Kansas City, Kan.; L=Long Beach, Calif.; M=Memphis, Tenn.; N=Norfolk, Va.; P=Twin Cities, Minn.; R=Richmond, Va.; S=Somerville, Mass.; and U=Louisville, Ken. The fourth symbol indicated body style: S=Sedan Delivery. The next six symbols were the sequential production number starting with 100001 at each assembly plant. The body type code was 78. Paint codes and colors were: A=Raven black; B=Sheridan blue; C=Cadet blue (metallic); D=Glacier blue; E=Dovetone gray; F=Highland green (metallic); G=Killarney green metallic; H=Sea Haze green; J=Lancer maroon (metallic); L=Sandalwood tan; M=Sandstone white; N=Cameo coral; R=Torch red; P=primer; and SS=special finish.

Model	Body Type	Price	Weight	Prod. Total
Courier — 1/2-Ton — 115 in. w.b. — Six				
78A	Sedan Delivery	1515	3109	—
Courier — 1/2-Ton — 115 in. w.b. — V-8				
78V	Sedan Delivery	1586	3460	—

NOTE 1: Add 27 lbs. for overdrive and 87 lbs. for Fordomatic.
ENGINE [Cost Clipper Six]: Displacement: 223 cid. OHV. Six. Bore & stroke: 3.62 in. x 3.60 in. Horsepower: 115 hp at 3900 rpm. Torque: 193 lbs.-ft. at 1000-2200 rpm. Compression ratio: 7.2:1. Holley one-barrel carburetor.
ENGINE [Power King V-8]: Displacement: 239 cid. OHV. V-8. Bore & stroke: 3.50 in. x 3.10 in. Horsepower: 130 hp at 4200 rpm. Torque: 214 lbs.-ft. at 1800-2200 rpm. Compression ratio: 7.2:1. Carburetor: Holley two-barrel.

1954 Ford 1/2-Ton F-100 Panel (H. Brandt)

F-100 6-1/2 FT. PICKUP: Styling changes were limited primarily to the grille. It had a massive "jet-wing" grille insert with three slots at the bottom center supported by inward-slanting vertical uprights. Standard models had Ford nameplates and the F-series code on the hoodsides. There was a four-pointed star in the middle of the six-cylinder grille and an 8-inside-a-V emblem on V-8 grilles. Deluxe models had chrome spear tip outline moldings around the Ford and F-series designation on the hoodsides. The deluxe grille had the same engine identification emblems, but added chrome hash marks on either side. Deluxe models also had bright vent window and drip rail trim. The F-100 Pickups had a 45 cu. ft. payload capacity, making it one of the biggest pickup boxes in the 1/2-ton field. The box had heavy gauge steel side panels with roll-top steel flareboards. The seasoned wood floorboards were interlocked with durable steel skid strips extending the full length of the floor. Rubber cushion strips, on the sides of the tailgate, helped eliminate rattles. There were four stake pockets in corner posts to permit mounting of uprights for special tops. The cab featured a one-piece curved windshield; rearview mirror; four-foot wide rear window; weather sealing around doors and joints to keep out dust, fumes and moisture; and new two-tone upholstery of full-breathing, woven vinyl.
F-100 8 FT. PANEL: The 1954 F-100 Panel had a 155.8 cu. ft. load capacity. Standard features included: Integral rear fenders; two heavy steel rear doors that opened fully or held firmly at 90 degrees; steel side paneling; solid plywood floors with steel skid strips; fully-weatherized driver's compartment; driver's seat; two taillights; heavy-gauge steel curved channel rear bumper; center cowl ventilator; water, temperature and fuel gauges; ash receptacle; dispatch box; dual windshield wipers; right and rear door lock; left-hand outside rearview mirror; and bright hubcaps.
F-100 8 FT. DELUXE PANEL: The Deluxe Panel had most of the same features as the standard version, plus: Two-tone upholstered driver's seat with foam rubber padding; harmonizing door panel trim; full-length glass-wool insulated headliner; sound deadener on driver's compartment floor; heavy Masonite lining on panel sides; distinctive hood trim; bright metal drip molding, air wing frames and chevrons on grille; matched door locks on all doors; grip-type armrest on each front door; illuminated cigar lighter; dispatch box lock; dome light with automatic door switches; and twin, matched-tone electric horns.
F-100 6-1/2 FT. PLATFORM/STAKE: The F-100 Platform/Stake came with a frame of heavy-gauge steel side rails riveted to steel cross girders. Heavy steel brackets were riveted to girders and bolted to the sills for greater durability. All corners were reinforced with large, steel gusset plates. The stake and rack boards were straight-grained seasoned wood. The stake racks were held firmly at the top with interlocking steel plates. These were

bolted to the rack boards for added strength. The stake pockets were flush with the floor, for unobstructed open platform use. Heavy steel rub rails and steel caps on body ends protected the platform. Splash guards and a long-arm left-hand outside rearview mirror were a couple of the standard features. The spare tire carrier was located under the floor.

1954 Ford 1/2-Ton F-100 Pickup (J. Charter)

I.D. DATA: The VIN was on the rating plate. The first three symbols indicated series: F10=F-100; F25=F250; F35=F-350. The fourth symbol indicated engine: D=Six; V=V-8. The fifth symbol was the last digit of the model year. The sixth symbol identified assembly plant: A=Atlanta, Ga.; B=Buffalo, N.Y.; C=Chester, Pa.; D=Dallas, Texas; E=Edgewater, N.J.; F=Dearborn, Mich.; G=Chicago, Ill.; H=Highland Park, Mich.; K=Kansas City, Kan.; L=Long Beach, Calif.; M=Memphis, Tenn.; N=Norfolk, Va.; P=Twin Cities, Minn.; R=Richmond, Va.; S=Somerville, Mass.; and U=Louisville, Ken. The next six symbols were the sequential number. The range for six-cylinder models began at F( )D4()10001, for V-8s at F( )V4()10001. In the first two blank spaces was series code. In the third blank space was the plant code. Paint codes and colors were: A=Raven black; B=Sheridan blue; D=Glacier blue; H=Sea haze green; R=Vermilion; U=Meadow green; V=Goldenrod yellow; P=primer; SS=special finish.

Model	Body Type	Price	Weight	Prod. Total
F-100 — 1/2-Ton — 110 in. w.b. — Six				
80	Platform	1329	—	49
81	Chassis & Cab	1221	2730	5930
82A	Panel	1502	3245	8078
82B	Deluxe Panel	—	—	1015
83	Pickup	1292	3080	101,202
84	Chassis & Cowl	974	2230	275
85	Chassis & W/S	999	2255	66
86	Stake	1367	3165	972

NOTE 1: Prices and weights are for six. Add $71 for V-8.
NOTE 2: Production is for six/V-8 model of same body style combined.
ENGINE [Mileage Maker]: Displacement: 223 cid. OHV. Six. Bore & stroke: 3.62 in. x 3.60 in. Horsepower: 115 hp at 3900 rpm. Torque: 193 lbs.-ft. at 1000-2200 rpm. Compression ratio: 7.2:1. Holley one-barrel carburetor.
ENGINE [Power King V-8]: Displacement: 239 cid. OHV. V-8. Bore & stroke: 3.50 in. x 3.10 in. Horsepower: 130 hp at 4200 rpm. Torque: 214 lbs.-ft. at 1800-2200 rpm. Compression ratio: 7.2:1. Carburetor: Holley two-barrel.
F-250 8 FT. EXPRESS: A step up from the F-100 was the look-alike F-250 Pickup. It was more heavy-duty and had a larger load capacity. It came equipped with the same standard features as the F-100. The frame, runningboards and bumper were painted black.
F-250 7-1/2 FT. PLATFORM/STAKE: Among standard items on the F-250 Platform/Stake were: A curved instrument panel; charge indicator; under the floor tire carrier; right door lock; Air Wing ventilating windows in doors; left side sun visor; single electric horn; speedometer; water, oil pressure and fuel gauges; and outside rearview mirror. The frame, runningboards and bumper were painted black.
I.D. DATA [F-250]: VIN on rating plate. Same as F-100 except first five characters were: [Six] F25D4; [V-8] F25V4.

Model	Body Type	Price	Weight	Prod. Total
F-250 — 3/4-Ton — 118 in. w.b. — Six				
80	Platform	1465	3640	100
81	Chassis & Cab	1359	3063	2547
83	Express-Pickup	1450	3500	20,669
84	Chassis & Cowl	1111	2560	376
85	Chassis & W/S	1143	2595	170
86	Stake	1519	3640	1780

NOTE 1: Prices are for six-cylinder Add $71 for V-8.
NOTE 2: Production is for six/V-8 model of same body style combined.
ENGINE [F-250]: See F-100 engines.
F-350 9 FT. EXPRESS: With a maximum GVW rating of 7,100 lbs. the F-350 Pickup was certainly capable of hauling some heavy loads. Its standard features echoed those of the F-100. Fordomatic Drive was made available as an extra-cost option on the F-350 for the first time this year.
F-350 9 FT. PLATFORM/STAKE: Standard equipment on the F-350 Platform/Stake included a heavy-duty three-speed manual transmission; high-capacity front springs; parking brake control mounted on the instrument panel; and six-stud ventilated disc wheels.
I.D. DATA [F-350]: Same as F-100 except the first five characters are: [Six] F35D4; [V-8] F35V4.

Model	Body Type	Price	Weight	Prod. Total
F-350 — 1-Ton — 130 in. w.b. — Six				
80	Platform	1609	4375	217
81	Chassis & Cab	1462	3520	5642
83	Express-Pickup	1572	3990	4482
84	Chassis & Cowl	1223	3015	546
85	Chassis & W/S	1265	3050	242
86	Stake	1659	4375	2758

NOTE 1: Prices are for six-cylinder Add $71 for V-8.
NOTE 2: Production is for six/V-8 model of same body style combined.

ENGINE [F-350]: See F-100.

1954 Ford 1/2-Ton Model 78A Courier Sedan Delivery (OCW)

CHASSIS [Courier Sedan Delivery]: Wheelbase: 115 in. Overall length: 197.8 in. Overall width: 74.3 in. Tires: 7.10 x 15.
[F-100]: Wheelbase: 110 in. Overall length: [Platform/Stake] 194.3 in.; [Pickup] 189.1 in.; [Panel] 201.8 in. Overall width: [Platform/Stake] 71.3 in. ; [Panel] 75.6 in.; [Pickup] 75.7 in. GVW: 4,800 lbs. Tires: 6.00 x 16.
[F-250]: Wheelbase: 118 in. Overall length: [Pickup] 108 in. GVW: 6,900 lbs. Tires: 6.50 x 16.
[F-350]: Wheelbase: 130 in. Overall length: [Pickup] 108 in. Overall width: [Pickup] 54 in. Overall height: [Pickup] 22.2 in. GVW: 9,500 lbs. Tires: 8 x 17.5.
POWERTRAIN OPTIONS: Heavy-duty three-speed manual, three-speed with overdrive, or four-speed manual transmissions. Ford-O-matic transmission.
CONVENIENCE OPTIONS: Heavy-duty battery. Vacuum booster brakes. Rear bumper (Pickup). Side-mounted spare tire carrier (Pickup). Road lamps. Stop light. Right-hand sun visor. Radio. Tinted glass. Grille guard. Seat covers. Hand brake signal. Right-hand taillight. Heater-defroster (Magic Aire or recirculating). Heavy-duty fan. Windshield washers. Tow hooks. Various rear axle ratios. Vacuum-boosted power braking for Pickups. Side-mounted spare tire. Special Argent paint. Heavy-duty radiator. Heavy-duty or regular grille guard. Radio plus rectifier. Overhead radio speaker. See-Clear windshield washers. Spotlight with bracket. 11 in. clutch. Directional signals. Power steering. Deluxe Cab includes: Streamlined spear ornament on sides; bright metal chevrons on grille; bright metal frames around air wing vents; bright finish drip molding cap; twin electric horns; two-tone seat upholstery; foam rubber seat padding; customized door and body trim; perforated therma-coustic headlining backed by glass wool insulation; sound deadener on floor and rear cab panels; grip-type armrests on both doors; large dome light with automatic door switches; two sun visors; illuminated cigar lighter; and lock on dispatch box.

1955 FORD

1955 Ford 1/2-Ton F-100 Pickup (OCW)

COURIER CUSTOM DELIVERY: The Courier Sedan Delivery was attractively restyled for 1955. It was longer, lower and wider than the 1954 model. The hood was flatter and had an airplane type ornament. Large round, spinner-style signal lights were placed under the hooded headlights in the concave, grid pattern grille. There was a Ford crest on the hood, Courier script on the front fendersides and V-8 badge (when applicable) ahead of the front wheel opening. The sides featured some moderate sculpturing that resulted in a modest tailfin under which the circular taillights slightly protruded. The stiffer frame had a lower profile and improvements were made to the brakes, suspension and shock absorbers. The interior was upholstered in one of three copper-tone vinyl combinations. The headliner, door and cargo area trims were also coppertone. The Courier had a wraparound windshield, tubless tires, a more powerful six and new larger V-8 engine option, redesigned bumpers and restyled hubcaps.
I.D. DATA: The VIN appeared on the rating plate. The first symbol indicated engine: A=Six; U=V-8. The second symbol was the last digit of the model year. The third symbol indicated assembly plant: A=Atlanta, Ga.; B=Buffalo, N.Y.; C=Chester, Pa.; D=Dallas, Texas; E=Mahwah, N.J.; F=Dearborn, Mich.; G=Chicago, Ill.; K=Kansas City, Kan.; L=Long Beach, Calif.; M=Memphis, Tenn.; N=Norfolk, Va.; P=Twin Cities, Minn.; R=Richmond, Va.; S=Somerville, Mass.; and U=Louisville, Ken. The fourth symbol indicated body style: S=Sedan Delivery. The next six symbols were the sequential production number starting with 100001 at each assembly plant. The body type code was 78. Paint codes and colors were: A=Raven black;

B=Banner blue; C=Aquatone blue; D=Waterfall blue; E=Snowshoe white; F=Pine Tree green; G=Sea Sprite green; H=Neptune green; K=Buckskin brown; M=Regency purple; R=Torch red; T=Thunderbird blue; V=Goldenrod yellow; W=Tropical rose; P=primer; and SS=special finish.

Model	Body Type	Price	Weight	Prod. Total
Courier — 1/2-Ton — 115 in. w.b. — Six				
78A	Sedan Delivery	1725	3141	—
Courier — 1/2-Ton — 115 in. w.b. — V-8				
78U	Sedan Delivery	1824	3251	—

ENGINE [Six]: Displacement: 223 cid. OHV. Six. Bore & stroke: 3.62 in. x 3.60 in. Horsepower: 120 hp at 4000 rpm. Compression ratio: 7.5:1. Holley one-barrel carburetor.

ENGINE [V-8]: Displacement: 272 cid. OHV. V-8. 162 hp at 4400 rpm. Bore & stroke: 3.62 in. x 3.30 in. Compression ratio: 7.6:1. Carburetor: Holley two-barrel.

F-100 6-1/2 FT. PICKUP: A winged, V-styled two-bar grille quickly set the 1955 F-100 apart from the 1954. Which emblem appeared in the center of the V in the grille depended on the powerplant. An 8-inside-a-V badge meant a V-8 engine. A four-pointed star indicated the truck had a six-cylinder engine. Off-white paint was used to accent the grille, instead of the previous cream color. The hoodside medallion was changed to the Ford name in script connected to an encircled F-series designator and was the same for standard and fancy models. The fancy models were now called Custom Cab trucks, instead of Deluxes. The Custom Cab package included bright trim for the bottom edge of the main grille bar with three slots punched-in on either side of center, name plaques on the door window sills, bright vent window and drip rail moldings and additional contents described under options below. Exclusive seat shock snubbers were now built into the standard seats. They helped absorb jars and jolts to give a smoother, more comfortable ride. The seat was covered in non-sticking, easy to clean, cool woven plastic. Inside were a new key-operated ignition switch and an instrument panel changed to incorporate "idiot" lights in place of some instruments. There were larger, new Ford crest-shaped taillights (except on Panels). The F-100 came with a 45 cu. ft. pickup box with slanting flareboards, double-walled steel doors, a curved one-piece windshield and a four-foot wide rear window. Standard equipment on all F-series models included a center cowl ventilator; curved instrument panel; speedometer; water temperature gauge; fuel gauge; charge indicator; ash receptacle; dispatch box; choke button; light switch; single electric horn; one-piece curved windshield; air-wing vent windows; left sun visor; rearview mirror (inside on Express; left outside long-arm on Stake/Platform/ Chassis models); right-hand door lock; runningboards (long on Express; short on Stake/Platform/Chassis models); rear fenders (Express); spare tire carrier under frame; mechanical jack; and tools. The wheels were painted Snowshoe white on both standard and Custom Cab F-100s. Two-tone finish was available for Custom Cab models. It featured any of the regular colors as the lower hue, topped by Snowshoe white on the roof and upper cab back panel. Black finish was used on the frame; fuel tank; runningboards; outside mirror; door division bar; vent window frames; taillamp; springs; wheels and bumpers of standard models. Chassis & Cowl models came in primer, with some alterations in standard equipment.

1955 Ford 1/2-Ton F-100 Pickup (OCW)

F-100 6-1/2 FT. PLATFORM/STAKE: A new feature the Platform/Stake shared with the Pickup was 52 in. rear springs. Television commercials of the day bragged about the 1955 Ford truck's short stroke engine. This was one of the factors in Ford truck claims of triple economy. The other two were convenience of the Driverized cabs and bigger payload capacities. The F-100 Platform/Stake had straight-grained wood stakes.

F-100 8 FT. PANEL: The Panel had a 155.8 cu. ft. load capacity. It had a plywood foor with close-spaced skid strips. It was dust-sealed at the bodyside panels by a special compound. The big rear door had two-position door checks.

F-100 8 FT. CUSTOM PANEL: The nameplate under the door windows let everyone know this was the Custom Panel. It came with such customized extras as a fully-lined interior; glass-wool roof insulation; and foam-rubber seat padding. Additional standard equipment (above that listed under Pickups above) included front and rear channel type bumpers; hubcaps; long runningboards; ash receptacle; and dual windshield wipers.

I.D. DATA: The VIN was on the rating plate. The first three symbols indicated series: F10=F-100; F25=F-250; F35=F-350. The fourth symbol indicated engine: D=Six; U=V-8. The fifth symbol was the last digit of the model year. The sixth symbol identified assembly plant: A=Atlanta, Ga.; B=Buffalo, N.Y.; C=Chester, Pa.; D=Dallas, Texas; E=Mahwah, N.J.; F=Dearborn, Mich.; G=Chicago, Ill.; K=Kansas City, Kan.; L=Long Beach, Calif.; M=Memphis, Tenn.; N=Norfolk, Va.; P=Twin Cities, Minn.; R=Richmond, Va.; S=Somerville, Mass.; and U=Louisville, Ken. The next six symbols were the sequential number. The range for six-cylinder models began at F()D4()10001, for V-8s at F()U4()10001. In the first two blank spaces was series code. In the third blank space was the plant code. Paint codes and colors were: A=Raven black; B=Banner blue; C=Aquatone blue; D=Waterfall blue; E=Snowshoe white; G=Sea Sprite green; R=Vermilion; U=Meadow green; V=Goldenrod yellow; P=primer; SS=special finish.

Model	Body Type	Price	Weight	Prod. Total
F-100 — 1/2-Ton — 110 in. w.b. — Six				
80	Platform	1538	3165	69
81	Chassis & Cab	1383	2730	6477
82A	Panel	1681	3245	11,198
82B	Custom Panel	—	—	1076
83	Pickup	1460	3080	124,842
84	Chassis & Cowl	1122	2230	482
85	Chassis & W/S	1148	2355	21
86	Stake	1538	3165	997

NOTE 1: Weight and prices are for six; add $77 for V-8.
NOTE 2: Production is for six/V-8 model of same body style combined.

ENGINE [Mileage Maker]: Displacement: 223 cid. OHV. Six. Bore & stroke: 3.62 in. x 3.60 in. Horsepower: 118 hp at 3800 rpm. Torque: 195 lbs.-ft. at 1200-2400 rpm. Compression ratio: 7.5:1. Holley one-barrel carburetor.

ENGINE [Power King V-8]: Displacement: 239 cid. OHV. V-8. Bore & stroke: 3.50 in. x 3.10 in. Horsepower: 132 hp at 4200 rpm. Torque: 215 lbs.-ft. at 1800-2200 rpm. Compression ratio: 7.5:1. Carburetor: Holley two-barrel.

F-250 8 FT. EXPRESS: Except for the mild styling changes noted for the F-100, the F-250 remained pretty much the same as the previous year's model. A couple of new options were available at extra cost. These were 11-leaf rear springs and power brakes. Standard features included: Direct double-acting telescopic shocks [front and rear]; 90 amp.-hr. battery; 10 in. clutch; hydraulic brakes; 5,000 lbs. capacity rear axle; heavy-duty oil bath air cleaner; 17-gal. fuel tank; dispatch box; water temperature, oil pressure and fuel gauges; dual windshield wipers; inside rearview mirror; right-hand door lock; and spare tire carrier under the frame.

F-250 7-1/2 FT. PLATFORM/STAKE: The F-250 Platform/Stake was 74 in. wide with 32 in. high stakes. The seat was covered with dool woven plastic upholstery. A left-hand outside rearview mirror was standard. The spare tire carrier was located under the floor.

I.D. DATA [F-250]: Same as F-100 except the first five characters were: [Six] F25D5; [V-8] F25U5.

Model	Body Type	Price	Weight	Prod. Total
F-250 — 3/4-Ton — 118 in. w.b. — Six				
80	Platform	1617	3465	143
81	Chassis & Cab	1503	3075	3229
83	Express-Pickup	1602	3510	23,505
84	Chassis & Cowl	1240	2570	299
85	Chassis & W/S	1274	2605	195
86	Stake	1674	3650	1803

NOTE 1: Weight and prices are for six; add $77 for V-8.
NOTE 2: Production is for six/V-8 model of same body style combined.

ENGINE [F-250]: Same as F-100 engines.

F-350 9 FT. EXPRESS: This was the ultimate light-duty Ford Pickup for 1955. It had a big 74 cu. ft. load capacity. The box had slanting flareboards and eight deep stake pockets. The rigid tailgate had toggle-type latches.

F-350 9 FT. PLATFORM/STAKE: A distinguishing feature of the F-350 was its ventilated disc wheels. It had a one-piece curved windshield, four-foot wide rear window, cool woven plastic upholstery, double-wall steel doors and steel rub rails.

I.D. DATA [F-350]: Same as F-100 except the first five characters were: [Six] F35D5; [V-8] F35U5.

Model	Body Type	Price	Weight	Prod. Total
80	Platform	1771	4090	272
81	Chassis & Cab	1614	3520	7114
83	Express-Pickup	1732	3990	5450
84	Chassis & Cowl	1359	3015	883
85	Chassis & W/S	1404	3050	284
86	Stake	1824	4375	3504

NOTE 1: Weight and prices are for six; add $77 for V-8.
NOTE 2: Production is for six/V-8 model of same body style combined.

ENGINE [F-350]: Same as F-100 engines.

CHASSIS [Courier Sedan Delivery]: Wheelbase: 115.5 in. Overall length: 197.6 in. Overall width: 75.9 in. Tires: 7.10 x 15 in.

[F-100]: Wheelbase: 110 in. Overall length: [Pickup] 189.1 in.; [Panel] 201.8 in. Overall height: [Pickup] 75.5 in.; [Panel] 78.6 in. Overall width: [Pickup] 75.7 in.; [Panel] 75.6 in. Tread: [Front] 60.6 in.; [Rear] 60 in. GVW: 4,000-5,000 lbs. Tires: 6.00 x 16 in. four-ply.

[F-250]: Wheelbase: 118 in. Overall length: 203.2 in. GVW: 7,400 lbs. Tires: 6.50 x 16 in.

[F-350]: Wheelbase: 130 in. GVW: 9,800 lbs. Tires: 8 x 17.5 in.

POWERTRAIN OPTIONS: [F-100] Medium-duty three-speed manual. [Others] Four-speed manual, three-speed manual with overdrive transmissions or Fordomatic drive.

CONVENIENCE OPTIONS: Various rear axle ratios. Heavy-duty two-stage rear springs. Outside rearview mirror, left or right. Heavy-duty radiator. Heavy-duty radiator grille guard. Electric windshield wipers. 7.50 x 17 in. tires. 7.00 x 16 tires. Dual rear wheels for F-350 Platform/Stake. Hand brake signal. Oil filter. Radio. Magic Aire heater-defroster. Recirculating heater-defroster. Seat cover. Windshield washer. Front tow hooks. Dual air horns. Tinted glass. Argent paint finish hubcaps. Tachometer. Heavy-duty generator. Gas tank locking cap. Governors. Spare tire lock and chain. Rear bumper for Pickup. Right-hand taillight. 120 amp.-hr. battery. Vacuum booster power brakes. Side-mount spare tire. Turn signals. Engine compartment lamp. I-Rest tinted glass. Heavy-duty 11 in. clutch. Auxiliary seat for Panel. Power steering. Road lamps. Visor. Fire extinguisher. Hand-brake signal (for standard transmission). Hubcaps. Locking gas tank cap. Flare kit. Road lamps. Spotlight with bracket. Positive-action dual electric windshield wipers. [Custom Cab package] includes: Armrests; color-keyed two-tone upholstery; dual horns; light gray sun visors; seat side bolsters; kick and door panels; headliner; five-inch thick, full foam-rubber cushioning in the seat; bright Custom Cab nameplate below the windows on the doors, and bright grille trim.

HISTORICAL: Ford had a 30 percent share of the truck market in 1955. It was the second best year for Ford truck sales since the record year of 1929.

1956 FORD

1956 Ford Courier Sedan Delivery (DFW)

COURIER CUSTOM DELIVERY: "The perfect combination of distinction and utility," said an ad for the Courier. Some feel it's hard to disagree with that Ford advertising claim. As before, Courier styling was based on the passenger car line. There was a Ford crest on the front of the hood. The Courier name was written in chrome on the front fenders. Eight-cylinder trucks had V-8 emblems ahead of the front wheelwell. The side-hinged rear door could open to reveal a 6-1/2 ft. long and over 5 ft. wide cargo area. The grille resembled last year's, but had a more open grille pattern with the vertical bars more dominant. Also new were the oblong, wraparound parking lights. The taillamp bezels were redesigned. Finish seen on the center of the hubcaps was now white. On the interior there was a revamped instrument panel with driver-centered gauge cluster, plus a new deep-dished steering wheel. A driver's bucket seat was standard, but a full-width bench seat was available at extra cost. A new technical advance was a ball bearing steering sector. Buyers had their choice of 10 exterior colors.

1956 Ford 1/2-Ton F-100 Pickup (OCW)

I.D. DATA: The VIN appeared on the rating plate. The first symbol indicated engine: A=223 cid six; U=272 cid V-8; M=292 cid V-8. The second symbol was the last digit of the model year. The third symbol indicated the assembly plant: A=Atlanta, Ga.; B=Buffalo, N.Y.; C=Chester, Pa.; D=Dallas, Texas; E=Mahwah, N.J.; F=Dearborn, Mich.; G=Chicago, Ill.; K=Kansas City, Kan.; L=Long Beach, Calif.; M=Memphis, Tenn.; N=Norfolk, Va.; P=Twin Cities, Minn.; R=Richmond, Va.; S=Somerville, Mass.; and U=Louisville, Ken. The fourth symbol indicated body style: S=Sedan Delivery. The next six symbols were the sequential production number starting with 100001 at each assembly plant. The body type code was 78. Paint codes and colors were: A=Raven black; B=Nocturne blue; C=Bermuda blue; D=Diamond blue; E=Colonial white; F=Pine Ridge green; G=Meadowmist green; H=Platinum gray; J=Buckskin tan; K=Fiesta red; L=Peacock blue; M=Goldenglow yellow; N=Mandarin orange; P=primer; and SS=special finish.

Model	Body Type	Price	Weight	Prod. Total
Courier — 1/2-Ton — 115 in. w.b. — Six				
78A	Sedan Delivery	1688	3150	—
Courier — 1/2-Ton — 115 in. w.b. — V-8				
78U	Sedan Delivery	1783	3251	—

ENGINE [Six]: Displacement: 223 cid. OHV Six. 137 hp at 4200 rpm. Bore & stroke: 3.62 in. x 3.60 in. Compression ratio: 8.0:1. Holley one-barrel carburetor.

ENGINE [V-8]: Displacement: 272 cid. OHV V-8. 173 hp at 4400 rpm (176 hp with automatic). Bore & stroke: 3.62 in. x 3.30 in. Compression ratio: 8.0:1. Carburetor: Holley two-barrel.

1956 Ford 1/2-Ton F-100 Pickup (D. Hoy)

F-100 6-1/2 FT. PICKUP: The new Ford trucks for 1956 debuted Sept. 23, 1955. Sales literature boasted of new styling. A full-wrap windshield brought changes to the upper cab, doors and roof. There was a Ford crest on the front of the hood, with a Fordomatic script just below it on trucks with optional automatic transmission. The new grille was of single-unit design with large, circular headlamp surrounds on either end. It had the appearance of two horizontal members, the upper one thicker and veed down at its center. The veed section was left plain on six-cylinder trucks and trimmed with a V-8 badge on V-8 powered models. The grille had cream finish, but a chrome-plated grille (the first seen on Ford trucks since 1938) was part of the year's Custom Cab package. This option also included bright windshield moldings; black-and-white chain-stripe upholstery (with red or coppertone color-keyed facings); a dash panel insulator; and door-mounted Custom Cab nameplates. No longer included (or needed) were bright grille moldings. In addition, bright drip rail moldings; instrument panel moldings; a right-hand armrest; an automatic dome light; a second horn; and plated vent window trim were eliminated from the Custom Cab equipment content. Hoodside trim plates used on 1956 models had the F-series code inside a smaller circle, while the Ford name was on the "handle" of the can-opener-shaped molding below the circle. Another new feature was an optional large window for the rear of the cab. This so-called "big window" had bright moldings and the option group included bright windshield moldings, too. It's believed to be fairly rare today. Other new-for-1956 items were a 12-volt electrical system; optional heavy-duty three-speed manual transmission; and a new 273 cid Power King V-8. The standard Driverized cab had free-breathing woven plastic upholstery; seat shock snubbers; independent seat and seatback adjustment; High-Dial instrumentation with a shielded, indirectly-lighted instrument cluster; push-button door handles; Lifeguard door latches; double-wall safety doors; Lifeguard deep-dish steering wheel; king-size door openings; complete weather-sealing; direct line accelerator linkage; level-action cab suspension; air wing vents; full-scoop cowl ventilator; left-hand sun visor; rearview mirror; ashtray; dispatch box; and a right-hand door key lock. A new standard feature on all Ford light-duty trucks was tubeless tires. And a new 10-1/2 in. clutch was standard on F-100s with V-8 engines. Ten standard paint selections were offered. In addition, any of the standard colors used on F-series trucks could be combined with Colonial white for a two-tone effect.

F-100 8 FT. EXPRESS: This new model used the F-250's frame. It had a roomy 65.4 cu. ft. cargo area. Like all Ford light-duty trucks, it had a grille with a heavy, forward slanting upper bar and thinner lower bar. The upper bar dipped in the center and provided space for engine identification. Hooded headlights, with parking lights directly underneath, were integrated into the ends of the grille.

1956 Ford 1/2-Ton F100 Pickup With Custom Cab (OCW)

F-100 6-1/2 FT. PLATFORM/STAKE: The F-100 Platform/Stake had over 40 sq. ft. of platform area and straight-grained wood stake. It could haul payloads up to 1,615 lbs. According to sales literature, it had the highest capacity frame and axles in the 1/2-ton field.

F-100 8 FT. PANEL: This was one of the most attractive panel trucks on the road in 1956. Like other F-100s, it had a new wraparound windshield, facelifted grille, deep-dished steering wheel and Lifeguard door latches. The right-hand rearview mirror was now mounted on the upper corner of the door.

F-100 8 FT. CUSTOM PANEL: Inside or out, it was easy to identify the Custom Panel. Distinctive exterior features included a chrome-plated grille and gas filler cap and a Custom Cab nameplate under the door windows. The interior was fully-lined and had glass wool roof insulation and foam rubber seat padding.

I.D. DATA: The VIN was on the rating plate. The first three symbols indicated series: F10=F-100; F11=Low-GVW F-100. The fourth symbol indicated engine: D=Six; U=V-8. The fifth symbol was the last digit of the model year. The sixth symbol identified assembly plant: D=Dallas, Texas; E=Mahwah, N.J.; G=Chicago, Ill.; H=Detroit, Mich.; K=Kansas City, Kan.; L=Long Beach, Calif.; M=Memphis, Tenn.; N=Norfolk, Va.; P=Twin Cities, Minn.;

R=Richmond, Va.; and U=Louisville, Ken. The next six symbols were the sequential number. The range for six-cylinder models began at F( )D4( )10001, for V-8s at F( )U4( )10001. In the first two blank spaces was series code. In the third blank space was the plant code. The truck production code consisted of: (1) A number designating the day of the month the unit should be completed; (2) A letter designating the month of the year (A=Jan.; B=Feb., etc. without I); and the production item number. Paint codes and colors were: A=Raven black; B=Dark blue (metallic); D=Light blue; E=Colonial white; G=Light green; H=gray; M=yellow; P=primer; R=vermilion; S=special finish; and U=Meadow green.

Model	Body Type	Price	Weight	Prod. Total
F-100 — 1/2-Ton — 110 in. w.b. — Six				
80	Platform	1521	3030	74
81	Chassis & Cab	1393	2720	9251
82A	Panel	1759	3245	14,023
82B	Custom Panel	—	—	1190
83	Pickup 6.5 ft.	1485	3070	137,581
84	Chassis & Cowl	1147	2200	599
85	Chassis & W/S	1180	2225	12
86	Stake	1581	3155	984
F-100 — 1/2-Ton — 118 in. w.b. — Six				
81	Chassis & Cab	1519	—	Note 3
83	Pickup 8 ft.	1518	3225	25,122

NOTE 1: Weight and prices are for six; add $95 for V-8.
NOTE 2: Production is for six/V-8 model of same body style combined.
NOTE 3: Production of both size Models 81 given as combined total.

ENGINE [Six]: Displacement: 223 cid. OHV Six. Horsepower: 133 hp at 4000 rpm. Torque: 202 lbs.-ft. at 1600-2600 rpm. Bore & stroke: 3.62 in. x 3.60 in. Compression ratio: 7.8:1. One-barrel carburetor.

ENGINE [V-8]: Displacement: 272 cid. OHV V-8. Horsepower: 167 hp at 4400 rpm. Torque: 260 lbs.-ft. at 2100-2600 rpm. Bore & stroke: 3.62 in. x 3.30 in. Compression ratio: 7.8:1. Carburetor: Two-barrel.

1956 Ford 1/2-Ton F-100 Pickup (K. Leitgabel)

F-250 8 FT. EXPRESS: A sales catalog proclaimed the F-250 the first choice truck where toughness counts. Its maximum payload capacity was increased by 522 lbs. this year. Other new features were tubeless tires, standard medium-duty three-speed manual transmission, thicker brake linings and (on V-8 models) a 10-1/2 in. clutch. The F-250 Pickup had an all bolted 65.4 cu. ft. cargo area with exclusive clamp-tight tailgate and six stake pockets. The cab had the same features as the F-100.

F-250 7-1/2 FT. PLATFORM/STAKE: The F-250 Platform/Stake had a platform area of over 50 square feet and could haul a payload of up to 3,395 lbs. The straight-grained wood stakes fit into steel lined stake pockets and were easy to remove for loading. It had a heavy gauge bridge type steel frame and steel rub rail. Tubeless tires and medium-duty three-speed manual transmission were just a couple standard features.

I.D. DATA [F-250]: Same as F-100 except the first four characters were: [Six] F25D; [V-8] F25V; [Low-GVW]=F26.

Model	Body Type	Price	Weight	Prod. Total
F-250 — 3/4-Ton — 118 in. w.b. — Six				
80	Platform	1652	3460	206
81	Chassis & Cab	1523	3040	5028
83	Express-Pickup	1624	3505	28,341
84	Chassis & Cowl	1276	2545	436
85	Chassis & W/S	1309	2580	205
86	Stake	1711	3645	2173

NOTE 1: Weight and prices are for six; add $95 for V-8.
NOTE 2: Production is for six/V-8 model of same body style combined.

ENGINE [F-250]: Displacement: 223 cid. OHV Six. 133 hp at 4000 rpm. Bore & stroke: 3.62 in. x 3.60 in. Compression ratio: 7.8:1. One-barrel carburetor.

ENGINE [F-250]: Displacement: 272 cid. OHV V-8. 167 hp at 4400 rpm. Bore & stroke: 3.62 in. x 3.30 in. Compression ratio: 7.8:1. Carburetor: Two-barrel.

1956 Ford F-250 Chassis & Cab With Delivery Box (DFW/HBC)

F-350 9 FT. EXPRESS: The 1956 Ford F-350 had up to 1,200 lbs. more GVW than other 1-ton trucks. Its GVW rating increased 300 lbs. this year, thanks mainly to the use of higher capacity tubeless tires. Also new was a stronger banjo-type rear axle housing and thicker brake linings. The F-350 Pickup featured an extra large 74 cu. ft. Express body with slanting flareboards to further increase effective load capacity. There were eight deep stake pockets and a rigid tailgate with exclusive toggle-type latches. This was the only Ford 1-ton to come solely with single rear tires.

F-350 9 FT. PLATFORM/STAKE: The F-350 Platform/Stake was indeed a big payloader at light-duty cost. Its maximum payload with dual rear wheels was 5,120 lbs. It had steel stake sides and steel lined stake pockets with a swing-open center rack section for greater loading convenience. Like the F-350 Pickup, it came equipped with a heavy-duty three-speed manual transmission.

I.D. DATA [F-350]: Same as F-100 except the first four characters were: [Six] F35D; [V-8] F35V. F36 code used for low-GVW models.

Model	Body Type	Price	Weight	Prod. Total
F-350 — 1-Ton — 130 in. w.b. — Six				
80	Platform	1803	4010	387
81	Chassis & Cab	1655	3440	11,482
83	Express-Pickup	1782	3910	6226
84	Chassis & Cowl	1409	2910	1226
85	Chassis & W/S	1442	4295	5019
86	Stake	1878	4295	5019

NOTE 1: Weight and prices are for six; add $95 for V-8.
NOTE 2: Production is for six/V-8 model of same body style combined.

ENGINE [F-350]: Displacement: 223 cid. OHV Six. 133 hp at 4000 rpm. Bore & stroke: 3.62 in. x 3.60 in. Compression ratio: 7.8:1. One-barrel carburetor.

ENGINE [F-350]: Displacement: 272 cid. OHV V-8. 167 hp at 4400 rpm. Bore & stroke: 3.62 in. x 3.30 in. Compression ratio: 7.8:1. Carburetor: Two-barrel.

CHASSIS [Courier Sedan Delivery]: Wheelbase: 115.5 in. Overall length: 197.6 in. Overall width: 75.9 in. Tires: 7.10 x 15.

[F-100]: Wheelbase: 110 in. Overall length: [Pickup] 189.1 in.; Overall height: [Pickup] 75.5 in.; Overall width: [Pickup] 75.7 in. GVW: 4,000-5,000 lbs. Tires: 6.00 x 16.

[F-250]: Wheelbase: 118 in. Overall length: 203.2 in. GVW: 7,400 lbs. Tires: 6.50 x 16.

[F-350]: Wheelbase: 130 in. GVW: 9,800 lbs. Tires: 8 x 17.5.

POWERTRAIN OPTIONS: [F-100] Medium-duty three-speed manual transmission; four-speed manual or three-speed manual with overdrive transmissions. Fordomatic drive.

1956 Ford 1/2-Ton Model 78A Courier Sedan Delivery (OCW)

CONVENIENCE OPTIONS: Various rear axle ratios. Heavy-duty two-stage rear springs. Outside rearview mirror, left or right. Heavy-duty radiator. Heavy-duty radiator grille guard. Electric windshield wipers. 7.50 x 17 in. tires. 7.00 x 16 tires. Dual rear wheels on F-350 Platform/Stake. Hand brake signal. Oil filter. Radio. Magic Aire heater-defroster. Recirculating heater-defroster. Seat cover. Windshield washer. Front tow hooks. Dual air horns. Tinted glass. Argent silver paint finish hubcaps. Tachometer. Heavy-duty generator. Gas tank locking cap. Governors. Spare tire lock and chain. Rear bumper on Pickup. Right-hand taillight. Full wrap rear window. Seat belts. Power steering. Custom Cab, includes: Armrests; color-keyed two-tone upholstery; dual horns; light gray sun visors; seat side bolsters; kick and door panels; headliner; five-inch thick full foam-rubber cushioning in the seat; bright Custom Cab nameplate below the window on the doors; and bright grille trim.

HISTORICAL: Ford's share of new truck registrations dropped slightly to 29 percent of the total U.S. market.

1957 FORD

1957 Ford 1/2-Ton Ranchero Custom Sedan-Pickup (OCW)

Model	Body Type	Price	Weight	Prod. Total
Ranchero — 1/2-Ton — 116 in. w.b. — Six				
66A	Sedan-Pickup	1918	3333	6418
Custom Ranchero — 1/2-Ton — 116 in. w.b. — Six				
66B	Sedan-Pickup	2149	3276	15,277

NOTE 1: Add $93 for 272 cid V-8 in 66A; add $93 for 292 cid V-8 in 66B.
NOTE 2: Add 122 lbs. for base V-8.
ENGINE [Mileage-Maker Six]: Displacement: 223 cid. OHV Six. 144 hp at 4200 rpm. Bore & stroke: 3.62 in. x 3.60 in. Compression ratio: 8.6:1. Holley Carburetor: One-barrel.
ENGINE [Base Ranchero V-8]: Displacement: 272 cid. OHV V-8. 190 hp at 4500 rpm. Bore & stroke: 3.62 in. x 3.30 in. Compression ratio: 8.6:1. Carburetor: Holley two-barrel.
ENGINE [Base Custom Ranchero V-8]: Displacement: 292 cid. OHV. V-8. 205 hp at 4500 rpm. Bore & stroke: 3.75 x 3.30 in. Compression ratio: 9.1:1. Carburetor: Two-Barrel. Single exhausts.
ENGINE [Optional Interceptor V-8]: Displacement: 352 cid. OHV. V-8. 300 hp at 4600 rpm. Bore & stroke: 4.00 x 3.50 in. Compression ratio: 10.2:1. Carburetor: Four-Barrel. Dual exhausts.
CHASSIS: Wheelbase: 116 in. Overall length: 202 in. Overall width: 77 in. Overall height: 57.2 in. GVW: 4,600 lbs. Tires: 8.00 x 14 in.
POWERTRAIN OPTIONS: Transmissions: Fordomatic automatic or overdrive transmissions. Engines: [Ranchero] 190 hp 272 cid V-8; [Custom Ranchero] 212 hp 292 cid V-8. Axles: 3.89:1; 3.70:1; 3.56:1; and 2.92:1.
CONVENIENCE OPTIONS: Power steering. Power brakes. Power seat. Power windows. Over-size tires. Full-flow oil filter (six). Heavy-duty Super-filter air cleaner. Magic Aire heater/defroster. Console range or signal-seeking radios. Self-regulating electric clock. Fashion-Ray sunburst wheelcovers. Aquamatic windshield washer-wipers. Lifeguard padded instrument panel and cushioned sun visors. Front seat belts. I-Rest tinted safety glass. Select Aire (V-8 only) or Polar Aire air conditioners. Whitewall tires. Special fuel and vacuum pump unit. Outside rearview mirror.
COURIER SEDAN DELIVERY: The Courier was all new for 1957. Hooded headlights; a full-width horizontal-bar grille with rectangular parking lights intergrated into it; canted fins above the large, round taillights; a rear opening hood; and rear sloping windshield posts were some of the most noticeable changes. The Courier had a one-piece, lift-up tailgate with divided glass rear window. There were under-floor storage compartments behind the front seat. The interior also featured new safety-curved instrument panel with recessed controls, a restyled Lifeguard steering wheel and a safety-swivel rearview mirror. The cargo area was insulated and fully-lined. A three-speed manual transmission was standard.
I.D. DATA: The VIN appeared on the rating plate. The first symbol indicated engine: A=223 cid six; C=292 cid V-8; U=272 cid V-8 cid V-8. The second symbol was the last digit of the model year. The third symbol indicated the assembly plant: A=Atlanta, Ga.; B=Buffalo, N.Y.; C=Chester, Pa.; D=Dallas, Texas; E=Mewhah, N.J.; F=Dearborn, Mich.; G=Chicago, Ill.; K=Kansas City, Kan.; L=Long Beach, Calif.; M=Memphis, Tenn.; N=Norfolk, Va.; P=Twin Cities, Minn.; R=San Jose, Calif.; S=Somerville, Mass.; T=Metuchen, N.J.; U=Louisville, Ken.; W=Wayne, Mich.; Y=Wixom, Mich.; and Z=St. Louis, Mo. The fourth symbol indicated body style: S=Sedan-Delivery. The next six symbols were the sequential production number starting with 100001 at each assembly plant. The body type code was 66. Paint codes and colors were: A=Raven black; C=Dresden blue; E=Colonial white; F=Starmist blue; G=Cumberland green; J=Willow green; K=Silver mocha; L=Doeskin tan; N=Gunmetal gray; Q=Thunderbird bronze; T=Woodsmoke gray; V=Flame red; X=Dusk rose; Y=Inca gold; Z=Coral sand; P=primer; S=special finish.

Model	Body Type	Price	Weight	Prod. Total
Courier — 1/2-Ton — 116 in. w.b. — Six				
78A	Sedan Delivery	1989	3234	6178

NOTE 1: Add $93 for 272 cid V-8.
NOTE 2: Add 122 lbs. for base V-8.
ENGINE [Mileage-Maker Six]: Displacement: 223 cid. OHV Six. 144 hp at 4200 rpm. Bore & stroke: 3.62 in. x 3.60 in. Compression ratio: 8.6:1. Holley Carburetor: One-barrel.
ENGINE [Base Courier V-8]: Displacement: 272 cid. OHV V-8. 190 hp at 4500 rpm. Bore & stroke: 3.62 in. x 3.30 in. Compression ratio: 8.6:1. Carburetor: Holley two-barrel.
ENGINE [Ford V-8]: Displacement: 292 cid. OHV. V-8. 205 hp at 4500 rpm. Bore & stroke: 3.75 x 3.30 in. Compression ratio: 9.1:1. Carburetor: Two-Barrel. Single exhausts.
ENGINE [Interceptor V-8]: Displacement: 352 cid. OHV. V-8. 300 hp at 4600 rpm. Bore & stroke: 4.00 x 3.50 in. Compression ratio: 10.2:1. Carburetor: Four-Barrel. Dual exhausts.
CHASSIS: Wheelbase: 116 in. Overall length: 202 in. Overall width: 77 in. Overall height: 57.2 in. GVW: 4,600 lbs. Tires: 8.00 x 14 in.
POWERTRAIN OPTIONS: Transmissions: Fordomatic automatic or overdrive transmissions. Engines: [Ranchero] 190 hp 272 cid V-8; [Custom Ranchero] 212 hp 292 cid V-8. Axles: 3.89:1; 3.70:1; 3.56:1; and 2.92:1.
CONVENIENCE OPTIONS: Power steering. Power brakes. Power seat. Power windows. Over-size tires. Full-flow oil filter (six). Heavy-duty Super-filter air cleaner. Magic Aire heater/defroster. Console range or signal-seeking radios. Self-regulating electric clock. Fashion-Ray sunburst wheelcovers. Aquamatic windshield washer-wipers. Lifeguard padded instrument panel and cushioned sun visors. Front seat belts. I-Rest tinted safety glass. Select Aire (V-8 only) or Polar Aire air conditioners. Whitewall tires. Special fuel and vacuum pump unit. Outside rearview mirror.
F-100 PICKUP: "A completely new concept in Pickup design with a functional purpose," claimed Ford's sales literature. The F-100 was extensively restyled for 1957. The single bar grille (with slots in its lower half) had hooded, single headlights at either end. A V-8 insignia was at the center of the grille on V-8s, while sixes had no center badge. The flat, wrapover hood had ribs stamped in its center section. There was a Ford crest on the front of the hood and F-series identification on the sides, above the front wheel openings. The flush fenders

1957 Ford 1/2-Ton Ranchero Custom Sedan-Pickup (OCW)

RANCHERO PICKUP: The new Ranchero made its debut on Dec. 8, 1957, at the National Automobile Show in New York City. This handsome Sedan-Pickup was basically just what it looked like; a standard Ranch Wagon station wagon converted into a Pickup. Although sales literature proclaimed it a new idea in motor vehicles, it wasn't. Ford of Australia had first built Roadster-Pickups or Utes in 1934. Its success inspired the development of a car-based truck for the American market. The spare tire was stored behind the passenger seat. However, since the Ranchero's box was bolted over the same rear section used in the station wagon, some owners made a hinge and used the wagon's spare tire well. Standard features included: Bright metal windshield, back window and vent wing moldings; bright metal grille and front and rear bumpers; choice of tan-and-brown woven plastic upholstery with tan vinyl bolsters or blue vinyl upholstery with white bolsters; and three-speed manual transmission.

1957 Ford 1/2-Ton Ranchero Custom Sedan-Pickup (T. Lerdaar)

CUSTOM RANCHERO: People who wanted a little more flash, could opt for the Custom Ranchero. It had distinctive bright full-length side moldings and so-called check-mark side trim. The fancier interior of the Del Rio Ranch Wagon was available in a choice of four colors with white vinyl facings and bolsters. The choices were: Tan-and-brown or white-and-blue woven plastic or all-red or all-green vinyl. There was also a molding around the cargo box rim and rear window and a deluxe steering wheel with horn ring. Custom Rancheros came with single-tone or Style-Tone exterior colors. The latter consisted of Colonial white above the side moldings, with any of 10 other colors below the side moldings and on the cab roof. In the Custom model, the 292 cid engine was the base V-8 at the same extra cost as the 272 cid V-8 in the standard Ranchero.

I.D. DATA: The VIN appeared on the rating plate. The first symbol indicated engine: A=223 cid six; C=292 cid V-8; H=352 cid V-8. The second symbol was the last digit of the model year. The third symbol indicated the assembly plant: A=Atlanta, Ga.; B=Buffalo, N.Y.; C=Chester, Pa.; D=Dallas, Texas; E=Mewhah, N.J.; F=Dearborn, Mich.; G=Chicago, Ill.; H=Lorain, Ohio; J=Los Angeles, Calif.; K=Kansas City, Kan.; L=Long Beach, Calif.; M=Memphis, Tenn.; N=Norfolk, Va.; P=Twin Cities, Minn.; R=San Jose, Calif.; S=Somerville, Mass.; T=Metuchen, N.J.; U=Louisville, Ken.; W=Wayne, Mich.; Y=Wixom, Mich.; and Z=St. Louis, Mo. The fourth symbol indicated body style: F=Ranchero Sedan-Pickup. The next six symbols were the sequential production number starting with 100001 at each assembly plant. The body type code was 66. Paint codes and colors were: A=Raven black; C=Dresden blue; E=Colonial white; F=Starmist blue; G=Cumberland green; J=Willow green; K=Silver mocha; L=Doeskin tan; N=Gunmetal gray; Q=Thunderbird bronze; T=Woodsmoke gray; V=Flame red; X=Dusk rose; Y=Inca gold; Z=Coral sand; P=primer; S=special finish.

added to a more modern look. This was especially noticeable on Pickups with the flush Styleside box. An optional Custom Cab equipment package included a chrome grille; bright windshield trim; Custom Cab scripts (replacing nameplates); three-tone seat covers; roof insulation; foam seatback pad; and (on F-100s) chrome hubcaps. There was a new chrome front bumper option. The 1957 F-100 was also two-inches wider and 3-1/2 in. lower than the 1956. In addition it had longer and wider springs with fewer leaves for less inter-leaf friction; suspended pedals; a two-inch wider, wraparound windshield; hydraulic actuated clutch; new king pins; and a large-diameter spindle for greater durability and steering ease. Buyers had their choice of four F-100 Pickups: 6-1/2 ft. Styleside with steel floor; 6-1/2 ft. Flareside with wood floor; 8 ft. Styleside with steel floor; or 8 ft. Flareside with wood floor. Ten paint colors were standard. Trucks could also be two-toned with the top and back sides of the roof in the lower color and all other panels above the beltline done in white. Another two-tone option was white on the top and back sides of the roof only.

F-100 PLATFORM/STAKE: The new F-100 Platform/Stake shared most standard features with the F-100 Pickup. However, it had a wood platform bed with removable rack sections. The side boards and uprights were made of straight-grained wood. Body sills were protected by steel end caps.

F-100 PANEL: Like the Pickup, the 1957 F-100 Panel had new modern styling. Flush, sculptured body sides, ribs on the flat hood, elimination of the runningboards and wrap-around taillights added to the vehicle's sleek appearance. It had 158 cu. ft. of cargo capacity.

I.D. DATA: The VIN was on the rating plate. The first three symbols indicated series: F10=F-100; F11=Light-duty F-100. The fourth symbol indicated engine: J=223 cid six; K=272 cid (light-duty ECY) V-8; L=272 cid (light-duty ECY) V-8. The fifth symbol was the last digit of the model year. The sixth symbol identified assembly plant: D=Dallas, Texas; E=Mahwah, N.J.; G=Chicago, Ill.; H=Detroit, Mich.; K=Kansas City, Kan.; L=Long Beach, Calif.; M=Memphis, Tenn.; N=Norfolk, Va.; P=Twin Cities, Minn.; R=Richmond, Va.; and U=Louisville, Ken. The next six symbols were the sequential number starting at 100001. The truck production code consisted of: (1) A number designating the day of the month the unit should be completed; (2) A letter designating the month of the year (A=Jan.; B=Feb., etc. without I); and the production item number. Paint codes and colors were: A=Raven black; B=Dark blue (metallic); D=Light blue; E=Colonial white; G=Light green; H=gray; M=yellow; P=primer; R=vermilion; S=special finish; and U=Meadow green.

Model	Body Type	Price	Weight	Prod. Total
F-100 — 1/2-Ton — 110 in. w.b. -Six				
80	Platform	1658	3065	Note 1
81	Chassis & Cab	1521	2760	Note 1
82	Panel	1908	3330	Note 1
83	Styleside 6.5 ft.	1631	3110	Note 1
83	Flareside 6.5 ft.	1631	3120	Note 1
84	Chassis & Cowl	1287	2206	Note 1
85	Chassis & W/S	1323	2246	Note 1
86	Stake	1724	3200	Note 1
F-100 — 1/2-Ton — 118 in. w.b. — Six				
81	Chassis & Cab	1556	2850	Note 1
83	Styleside 8 ft.	1667	3285	Note 1
83	Flareside 8 ft.	1667	3295	Note 1

NOTE 1: Ford records show the following F-100 production breakouts: [Chassis & Cowl] 97; [Chassis & Windshield] 200; [Chassis & Cab] 6086; [Stake] 269; [Flareside Pickup] 13,122; [Styleside Flareside Pickup] 2,319; [Long Box Flareside Pickup] 64,050; [Long Box Styleside Pickup] 20,114; [Standard Panel] 6,654 and [Deluxe Panel] 711.
NOTE 2: Weight and prices are for six; add $105 for base 272 cid V-8.
NOTE 3: Production is for six/V-8 model of same body style combined.

ENGINE [Mileage-Maker Six]: Displacement: 223 cid. OHV Six. Horsepower: 139 hp at 4200 rpm. Torque: 207 lbs.-ft. at 1800-2700 rpm. Bore & stroke: 3.625 in. x 3.60 in. Compression ratio: 8.3:1. Four main bearings. Holley Carburetor: One-barrel.
ENGINE [ECW Base V-8; All F-Series]: Displacement: 272 cid. OHV. V-8. Horsepower: 171 hp at 4500 rpm. Torque: 260 lbs.-ft. at 2100-2600 rpm. Bore & stroke: 3.62 in. x 3.30 in. Compression ratio: 8.3:1. Five main bearings. Carburetor: Holley two-barrel.

F-250 EXPRESS: The large F-250 Pickup (called an Express) was all new for 1957 and not only in styling, but the king pins; parking brake location; hubcaps; dash; rear springs; and fuel filler location. Even the rear window was larger. The F-250 was available in a Flareside model (with wood floor and a runningboard between the rear fender and back of cab) or as a flush-rear-fender Styleside model. The latter model's steel floor box measured 94.4 by 73.2 in. Its tailgate was 50.2 in. wide and the taillight lenses were built into the rear section on either side of the tailgate. Only the left-hand lens had a bulb behind it unless the extra-cost turn signal option was ordered.

F-250 PLATFORM/STAKE: The F-250 Platform/Stake may have had a restyled cab, but its cargo body was virtually the same as that used for the last 19 years. Steel skid strips protected the floor. The side boards and stakes were made of strong, straight-grained wood. Body sills were protected by steel end caps. An all-steel rub rail protected the body.

I.D. DATA: Same as F-100, except first three symbols change to [3/4-ton] F25; or [Light-duty 3/4-ton] F26.

Model	Body Type	Price	Weight	Prod. Total
F-250 —3/4-Ton — 118 in. w.b. — Six				
80	Platform	1803	3475	Note 1
81	Chassis & Cab	1667	3100	Note 1
83	Styleside 8 ft.	1786	3535	Note 1
83	Flareside 8 ft.	1786	3535	Note 1
84	Chassis & Cowl	1433	2557	Note 1
85	Chassis & W/S	1469	2597	Note 1
86	Stake	1869	3650	Note 1

NOTE 1: Ford records show the following F-250 production breakouts: [Chassis & Cowl] 188; [Chassis & Windshield] 43; [Chassis & Cab] 3017; [Stake] 1,119; [Flareside Express] 4,321; and [Styleside Express] 10,936.
NOTE 2: Weight and prices are for six; add $105 for base 272 cid V-8.
NOTE 3: Production is for six/V-8 model of same body style combined.

ENGINE [Mileage-Maker Six]: Displacement: 223 cid. OHV Six. Horsepower: 139 hp at 4200 rpm. Torque: 207 lbs.-ft. at 1800-2700 rpm. Bore & stroke: 3.625 in. x 3.60 in. Compression ratio: 8.3:1. Four main bearings. Holley Carburetor: One-barrel.
ENGINE [ECW Base V-8; All F-Series]: Displacement: 272 cid. OHV. V-8. Horsepower: 171 hp at 4500 rpm. Torque: 260 lbs.-ft. at 2100-2600 rpm. Bore & stroke: 3.62 in. x 3.30 in. Compression ratio: 8.3:1. Five main bearings. Carburetor: Holley two-barrel.

F-350 EXPRESS: The F-350 was the top-of-the-line Ford Pickup. It shared the new modern styling features with the F-100 and F-250. It also had a beefed-up chassis featuring: 2,000 lbs. rear springs; heavier king pins; and a 3,800 lbs. front axle. The flush-mounted taillights on the Styleside models were flush-mounted on either side of the 50.2 in. wide tailgate. The Flareside box was also available. A four-speed manual transmission was standard.

F-350 PLATFORM/STAKE: Load space on the hefty F-350 Platform/Stake was 106 in. long, 82 in. wide and 31.2 in. to the top of the racks. The center sections of the removable racks swung open for faster side loading. It had steel channel uprights and an all-steel rub rail.

I.D. DATA [F-350]: See F-100 I.D.

Model	Body Type	Price	Weight	Prod. Total
80	Platform	1985	3965	Note 1
81	Chassis & Cab	1813	3470	Note 1
83	Styleside	1951	3875	Note 1
83	Flareside	1951	3875	Note 1
84	Chassis & Cowl	1580	2916	Note 1
85	Chassis & W/S	1615	2956	Note 1
86	Stake	2055	4325	Note 1

NOTE 1: Ford records show the following F-350 production breakouts: [Chassis & Cowl] 688; [Chassis & Windshield] 207; [Chassis & Cab] 7,339; [Stake] 2,746; [Platform] 1,370 and [Styleside Express] 1,869.
NOTE 2: Weight and prices are for six; add $105 for base 272 cid V-8.
NOTE 3: Production is for six/V-8 model of same body style combined.

ENGINE [Mileage-Maker Six]: Displacement: 223 cid. OHV Six. Horsepower: 139 hp at 4200 rpm. Torque: 207 lbs.-ft. at 1800-2700 rpm. Bore & stroke: 3.625 in. x 3.60 in. Compression ratio: 8.3:1. Four main bearings. Holley Carburetor: One-barrel.
ENGINE [ECW Base V-8; All F-Series]: Displacement: 272 cid. OHV. V-8. Horsepower: 171 hp at 4500 rpm. Torque: 260 lbs.-ft. at 2100-2600 rpm. Bore & stroke: 3.62 in. x 3.30 in. Compression ratio: 8.3:1. Five main bearings. Carburetor: Holley two-barrel.
ENGINE [ECY Optional V-8; F-350]: Displacement: 272 cid. OHV. V-8. Horsepower: 181 hp at 4400 rpm. Torque: 262 lbs.-ft. at 2200-2700 rpm. Bore & stroke: 3.62 in. x 3.30 in. Compression ratio: 8.3:1. Five main bearings. Carburetor: Holley two-barrel.

CHASSIS [Courier Sedan Delivery]: Wheelbase: 116 in. Overall length: 203.5 in. GVW: 4,600 lbs. Tires: 7.50 x 14, four-ply.

[F-100]: Wheelbase: 110 in. and 118 in. GVW: 4,000-5,000 lbs. Tires: 6.70 x 15, four-ply.

[F-250]: Wheelbase: 118 in. GVW: 4,900-7,400 lbs. Tires: 6.50 x 16, six-ply.

[F-350]: Wheelbase: 130 in. GVW: 7,600-9,800 lbs. Tires: 8 x 17.5, six-ply.

POWERTRAIN OPTIONS: 171 hp 272 cid V-8 [Courier] 190 hp 272 cid V-8. [F-100/F-250] Medium-duty three-speed transmission. [F-350] Heavy-duty three-speed transmission. Four-speed manual transmission. Three-speed with overdrive Fordomatic transmission.

1957 Ford 1/2-Ton Ranchero Custom Sedan-Pickup (DFW/DPL)

CONVENIENCE OPTIONS: Transistor-powered truck radio. [Courier] Signal-seeking radio. Magic Aire heater-defroster. Windshield washers. Power brakes. Outside rearview mirror (bright metal on Pickup, painted on others). Heavy-duty grille guard. Turn signals. Sealed beam spotlight. Seat covers. Heavy-duty rear springs. Recirculating heater-defroster. Heavy-duty radiator. Dual electric windshield wipers. Side-mounted tire carrier on Pickup. Spare tire. [Safety package]: Includes, padded instrument panel and cushioned sun visors; tinted glass; full wrap rear window; rear bumper on Pickup; front and rear chrome bumpers on Styleside Pickups, chrome front bumper other models; right-hand armrest; outside left or right telescopic mirror for cabs; outside non-telescopic mirror; tow hooks; seat belts; fire extinguishers (1-1/2 qt. or 4-lb. dry chemical); cigar lighter; dome light; splash guards; locking gas tank cap; Deluxe heater (Courier); bumper guards (Courier); Deluxe wheelcovers (Courier) and under-dash light [Courier]. [Custom Cab package] Includes two-tone seat upholstery; foam-rubber padding in seat cushion and back; Thermacoustic headlining backed by 1/2 in. of glass wool insulation; sound deadener on floor and rear cab panel; insulation on front cowl wall in cab; hardboard door and cowl side trim panels; armrest on left door; dome light with manual switch; right-hand sun visor; illuminated cigar lighter; bright metal grille; headlight assembly; windshield reveal molding; parking light rims; Custom Cab emblem on each door; and matched locks on both doors.

NOTE: The 1957 Ford truck line was introduced on Feb. 1, 1957.

1957 Ford 1/2-Ton Ranchero Standard Sedan-Pickup (OCW)

1958 FORD

1958 Ford 1/2-Ton Model 66B Ranchero Custom Sedan-Pickup (OCW)

RANCHERO PICKUP: The Ranchero received a T-Bird inspired facelift for 1958. Among new styling features were: Quad headlights, a fake air scoop on the hood and a bumper-integrated honeycomb-pattern grille. The instrument panel was also changed. However, the taillights and tailgate were carried over from 1957. Some changes were made to the chassis. These included a three-piece stabilizer bar, different shock absorbers and the upper suspension arm bushings were permanently lubricated. Standard features included: Bright metal windshield, back window, vent wing and side moldings; bright metal grille and front and rear bumpers; light and medium blue vinyl or light brown vinyl and medium brown woven plastic upholstery; and three-speed manual transmission.

CUSTOM 300 RANCHERO PICKUP: This model was a step up from the standard Ranchero. It was instantly recognized by its distinctive exterior side moldings with gold anodized aluminum inserts. The interior featured foam rubber in the seat cushions; armrests on both doors; a sun visor on the right side; a bright horn ring; and cigarette lighter. The upholstery could be had in light blue vinyl and medium blue woven plastic; light brown vinyl and medium brown woven plastic; white and red vinyl and light; and medium green vinyl. The Custom Ranchero was available in single or 11 Style-Tone color combinations. [Colonial white in combination with any of the other standard colors, plus Sun gold and Palomino tan.]

I.D. DATA [Ranchero]: VIN located on rating plate. First symbol indicates engine: A=223 cid six; C=292 cid six; H=352 cid V-8. Second symbol indicates assembly plant: A=Atlanta, Ga.; C=Chester, Pa.; D=Dallas, Texas; E=Mawhah, N.J.; F=Dearborn, Mich.; G=Chicago, Ill.; H=Lorain, Ohio; J=Los Angeles, Calif.; K=Kansas City, Kan.; L=Long Beach, Calif.; M=Memphis, Tenn.; N=Norfolk, Va.; P=Twin Cities, Minn.; R=San Jose, Calif.; S=Allen Park, Mich.; T=Metuchen, N.J.; U=Louisville, Ken.; W=Wayne, Mich.; Y=Wixom, Mich.; and Z=St. Louis, Mo.; The fourth symbol indicates body style: F=Ranchero. The last six symbols are the sequential production number.

Model	Body Type	Price	Weight	Prod. Total
Ranchero — 1/2-Ton — 116 in. w.b. — Six				
66A	Pickup	2170	3265	1471
66B	Custom Pickup	2236	3275	8479

ENGINE [Ranchero]: Displacement: 223 cid. OHV Six. 145 hp at 4200 rpm. Bore & stroke: 3.62 in. x 3.60 in. Compression ratio: 8.6:1. Holley one-barrel carburetor.
CHASSIS: Wheelbase: 116 in. Overall length: 202.9 in. Overall width: 77 in. Overall height: 57.5 in. GVW: 4,600 lbs. Tires: 7.50 x 14, four-ply.
POWERTRAIN OPTIONS: 205 hp 292 cid V-8. 300 hp 352 cid V-8. Fordomatic automatic transmission. Cruise-O-Matic with 352 cid V-8. Overdrive manual transmission.
CONVENIENCE OPTIONS: Power steering. Power brakes. Power seat. Power windows. 8.00 x 14, six-ply tires. Whitewall tires. Full-flow oil filter (six-cylinder only). Heavy-duty Super-filter air cleaner. Magic Aire system. Console Range or Signal-Seek radio. Electric clock. Fashion-Ray wheelcovers. Aquamatic windshield washer-wiper. Padded instrument panel and sun visors. Seat belts. I-Rest tinted safety glass. Select Aire (V-8 only) or Polar Aire air-conditioning. Vacuum booster windshield wipers. Outside rearview mirror.
NOTE: Colors offered on the 1958 Ranchero include: Azure blue; Silvertone blue; Seaspray green; Silvertone green; Desert beige; Bali bronze; Gunmetal gray; Torch red; Raven black; and Colonial white.

1958 Ford 1/2-Ton Courier Sedan Delivery (OCW)

COURIER SEDAN DELIVERY: The new Courier featured a restyled hood and front end. Four headlights, a Thunderbird inspired honeycomb bumper-intergrated grille with Ford printed above it; and a fake hood scoop were among the most noticeable changes. The cargo area was lined and insulated. There was storage space behind the seats. A three-speed manual transmission was standard.
I.D. DATA [Courier]: Same as Ranchero with fourth (body style) symbol S.

Model	Body Type	Price	Weight	Prod. Total
Courier — 1/2-Ton — 116 in. w.b. — Six				
78A	Sedan Delivery	2062	3303	3352

ENGINE [Courier]: Displacement: 223 cid. OHV Six. 144 hp at 4200 rpm. Bore & stroke: 3.62 in. x 3.60 in. Compression ratio: 8.6:1. Holley Carburetor: One-barrel.
F-100 PICKUP: The new thin horizontal and vertical bar grille was bordered at each side by two encased headlights. The circular parking lamps were located under the headlights. The F-100 Pickup was offered in 6-1/2 ft. and 8 ft. sizes and with two styles of boxes, the traditional Flareside with wooden floorboards and rear fenders, and the smooth side Styleside (which had an all-steel box). Among the standard features were: A Lifeguard steering wheel; safety double-grip door locks; sound deadener on doors; left-hand sun visor; Hi-Dri all-weather ventilation; ash receptacle; dispatch box; 12-volt electrical system; 10 in. clutch; 18-gal. fuel tank; front and rear double-acting telescopic shock absorbers; and three-speed manual transmission.
F-100 7-1/2 FT. PANEL: The facelifted F-100 Panel had a cargo area 91.6 in. long and 51.6 in. wide. The plywood floor was chemically treated for longer life and supported by steel cross sills. Side joints were sealed for dust-tight load protection. Among the standard features were: A white bumper; wraparound taillights (they only worked on Custom models); right and rear door locks; hubcaps; dome light; left-hand outside rearview mirror; single electric horn; under-frame spare tire carrier; and left-hand sun visor.
F-100 PLATFORM/STAKE: Except for a facelift, the new F-100 Platform/Stake was basically unchanged for 1958. However, there were several new options available on it. The Platform's loadspace was 84.3 in. long, 71.3 in. wide and had a payload rating of 1,720 lbs. The Stake's loadspace was 80 in. long, 67 in. wide and it had stakes 24.7 in. high. Sideboards and uprights were made of straight-grained wood. Body sills were protected by steel end caps.
I.D. DATA [F-100]: VIN located on rating plate. The first three symbols indicated series: F10=F100. The fourth symbol indicates engine: J=223 cid six; K=272 cid V-8. The fifth symbol indicates the model year: 8=1958. The sixth symbol indicates assembly plant: A=Atlanta, Ga.; D=Dallas, Texas; E=Mawhah, N.J.; G=Chicago, Ill.; H=Lorain, Ohio; K=Kansas City, Kan.; L=Long Beach, Calif.; N=Norfolk, Va.; P=Twin Cities, Minn.; R=San Jose, Calif.; U=Louisville, Ken. The last six symbols indicate the sequential production number.

Model	Body Type	Price	Weight	Prod. Total
F-100 — 1/2-Ton — 110 in. w.b. — Six				
80	Platform	—	3065	Note 1
81	Chassis & Cab	1758	2760	Note 1
83	Styleside	1874	3110	Note 1
83	Flareside	—	3096	Note 1
82	Panel	2167	3300	Note 1
84	Chassis	1504	2200	Note 1
86	Stake	1974	3470	Note 1
F-100 — 1/2-Ton — 118 in. w.b. — Six				
81	Chassis & Cab 118	1793	2850	Note 1
83	Styleside	1913	3285	Note 1
83	Flareside	—	3529	Note 1

NOTE 1: Ford records show the following F-100 production breakouts: [Chassis & Cowl] 84; [Chassis & Windshield] 30; [Chassis & Cab] 6,084; [cab platform and rack] 198; [Flareside Pickup] 11,818; [Styleside Pickup] 56,454; [Flareside express] 1,833; [Styleside express] 20,928; [Standard Panel] 6,560 and [Custom Panel] 592.
ENGINE [F-100]: Same as Courier, except 139 hp at 4200 rpm and 8.3:1 compression ratio.
F-250 PICKUP: The 3/4-ton F-250 was available in Styleside or Flareside versions. It came with most of the same standard features as the F-100, plus larger brakes, a higher capacity rear axle and heavier front and rear springs.
F-250 PLATFORM/STAKE: Except for the facelift, the new F-250 Platform/Stake was essentially the same as last year's model. The sideboards and uprights were made of straight-grained wood. Body sills were protected by steel end caps. The all-steel rub rail protected therfom excessive wear. Stake loadspace was 90 in. long, 74 in. wide and 28.3 in. to the top of the racks. Platform loadspace was 93.4 in. long and 79.3 in. wide.
I.D. DATA [F-250]: Same as F-100 with F25 for first three symbols.

Model	Body Type	Price	Weight	Prod. Total
F-250 — 3/4-Ton — 118 in. w.b. — Six				
80	Platform	—	3475	Note 1
81	Chassis & Cab	1912	3100	Note 1
83	Styleside	2040	3535	Note 1
83	Flareside	—	3529	Note 1
84	Chassis	1660	2545	Note 1
86	Stake	2129	3650	Note 1

NOTE 1: Ford records show the following F-250 production break-outs: [Chassis & Cowl] 176; [Chassis & Windshield] 55; [Chassis & Cab] 2,637; [Platform/Rack] 826; [Flareside express] 3,155; [Styleside express] 10,555.
F-250 ENGINE: Same as F-100.
F-350 PICKUP: This was Ford's heftiest light-duty Pickup. The Styleside version had a cargo area that was 106.44 in. long and 73.04 in. wide. Its payload capacity was 3,360 lbs. The Flareside's cargo area was 108 in. long and 54 in. wide. It had a payload capacity of 3,470 lbs. A four-speed manual transmission was standard.
F-350 PLATFORM/STAKE: The F-350 may have had a new face for 1958, but underneath it was pretty much the same as last year's model. Buyers could order dual wheels at extra cost. The F-350 Platform/Stake had steel uprights and center rack sections that swung open for faster side loading. A four-speed manual transmission was standard.
F-350 I.D.: See F-100.

Model	Body Type	Price	Weight	Prod. Total
F-350 — 1-Ton — 130 in. w.b. — Six				
80	Platform	—	3965	Note 1
81	Chassis & Cab	2072	3470	Note 1
83	Styleside	2220	3950	Note 1
83	Flareside	—	3944	Note 1
84	Chassis	1821	2910	Note 1
86	Stake	2332	4325	Note 1

NOTE 1: Ford records show the following F-350 production break-outs: [Chassis & Cowl] 598; [Chassis & Windshield] 60; [Chassis & Cab] 7,150; [Platform/Rack] 2,548; [Flareside Express] 994 and [Styleside Express] 1,974.
F-350 ENGINE: Same as F-100.
CHASSIS [Courier Sedan Delivery]: Wheelbase: 116 in. Overall length: 203.5 in. GVW: 4,600lbs. Tires: 7.50 x 14, four-ply.

[F-100]: Wheelbase: 110 in./118 in. GVW: 4,000-5,000 lbs. Tires: 6.70 x 15, four-ply.
[F-250]: Wheelbase: 118 in. GVW: 4,900-7,400 lbs. Tires: 6.50 x 16, six-ply.
[F-350]: Wheelbase: 130 in. GVW: 7,600-9,800 lbs. Tires: 8 x 17.5, six -ply.
POWERTRAIN OPTIONS: 171 hp 272 cid V-8. 190 hp 272 cid V-8 (Courier). [F-100/F-250] Medium-duty three-speed transmission; [F-350] Heavy-duty three-speed transmission. Four-speed manual transmission. Three-speed transmission with overdrive. Fordomatic.

1958 Ford 1/2-Ton Model 66A Ranchero Standard Sedan-Pickup (OCW)

CONVENIENCE OPTIONS: Transistor powered truck radio. Signal-seeking radio (Courier). Magic Aire heater-defroster. Windshield washers. Power brakes. Dual rear tires (not available on Pickup). Whitewall tires. Outside rearview mirror (bright metal on Pickup, painted on others). Heavy-duty grille guard. Turn signals. Sealed-beam spotlight. Seat covers. Heavy-duty rear springs. Recirculating heater-defroster. Heavy-duty radiator. Dual electric windshield wipers. Side-mounted tire carrier (Pickup). Spare tire. [Safety Package] Includes, padded instrument panel and cushioned sun visors; tinted glass; full wrap rear window. Rear bumper (Pickup). Front and rear chrome bumpers (Styleside Pickup). Chrome front bumper. Right-hand armrest. Outside left or right telescopic mirror for cabs. Outside non-telescopic mirror. Tow hooks. Seat belts. Fire extinguishers (1-1/2 qt. or 4 lbs. dry chemical). Cigar lighter. Dome light. Splash guards. Locking gas tank cap. Deluxe heater (Courier). Bumper guards (Courier). Deluxe wheelcovers (Courier). Under-dash light (Courier). [Custom Cab package] Includes two-tone brown and white woven nylon-saran seat upholstery in a houndstooth pattern; foam-rubber padding in seat cushion and back; thermoacoustic headlining backed by 1/2 in. of glass wool insulation; sound deadener on floor and rear cab panel; insulation on front cowl wall in cab; hardboard door and cowl side trim panels; armrest on left door; dome light with manual switch; right-hand sun visor; illuminated cigar lighter; bright metal grille, headlight assembly, windshield reveal molding, and parking light rims; Custom Cab emblem on each door; and matched locks on both doors.

NOTE: Standard Ford truck colors for 1958 were: Vermilion (red); Midnight blue; Azure blue; Gunmetal gray; Raven black; Colonial white; Meadow green; Seaspray green; Gold-enrod Yellow; or Prime. Any of the standard colors listed could be combined with Colonial white for a two-tone effect.

1959 FORD

1959 Ford 1/2-Ton F-100 Styleside Pickup (C. Webb)

CUSTOM RANCHERO: The base Ranchero was discontinued for 1959. The only model offered was the former top-of-the-line Custom. In addition to a two-inch longer wheelbase, the load area was lengthened by seven inches. The Ranchero's boxy styling mirrored that of 1959 Ford passenger cars. It had a star-pattern aluminum grille. The circular front signal lights were integrated into the bumper. Ford was spelled out on the face of the hood. A larger, compound-curved windshield was used. It provided 20 percent more visibility. The larger round taillights were placed lower than the previous year's model. Its interior was based on that offered on the Country Sedan wagon. The Ranchero's split seatbacks tilted forward for easy access to storage space behind the driver's seat or the spare tire behind passenger's seat. A three-speed manual transmission was standard.

I.D. DATA: [Ranchero] VIN located on rating plate. First symbol indicates engine: A=223 cid six; C=292 cid six; H=352 cid V-8. Second symbol indicates assembly plant: A=Atlanta, Ga.; C=Chester, Pa.; D=Dallas, Texas; E=Mahwah, N.J.; F=Dearborn, Mich.; G=Chicago, Ill.; H=Lorain, Ohio; J=Los Angeles, Calif.; K=Kansas City, Kan.; L=Long Beach, Calif.; M=Memphis, Tenn.; N=Norfolk, Va.; P=Twin Cities, Minn.; R=San Jose, Calif.; S=Allen Park, Mich.; T=Metuchen, N.J.; U=Louisville, Ken.; W=Wayne, Mich.; Y=Wixom, Mich.; and Z=St. Louis, Mo.; The fourth symbol indicates body style: F=Ranchero. The last six symbols are the sequential production number.

Model	Body Type	Price	Weight	Prod. Total
Ranchero — 1/2-Ton — 116 in. w.b. — Six				
66C	Pickup	2313	—	14,169

ENGINE [Ranchero]: Displacement: 223 cid. Six, 145 hp at 4200 rpm. Bore & stroke: 3.62 in. x 3.60 in. Compression ratio: 8.4:1. One-barrel carburetor.
CHASSIS: Wheelbase: 118 in. Overall length: 208 in. Overall width: 76.6 in. Overall height: 58 in. Tires: 7.50 x 14 four-ply.
POWERTRAIN OPTIONS: Fordomatic and Cruise-O-Matic automatics. Overdrive. Equa-lock limited slip differential. 200 hp 292 V-8. 300 hp Interceptor 352 special V-8.
NOTE: The Cruise-O-Matic was only available with the optional 300 hp 352 cid. V-8.
CONVENIENCE OPTIONS: Power steering. Power brakes. Power windows. Magic Aire or recirculating-type heater system. Console Range or Signal-Seek radio. Electric clock. bright metal wheelcovers. Aquamatic windshield washer-wiper. Padded instrument panel and sun visors. Seat belts. I-Rest tinted safety glass. Polar Aire Conditioner [V-8 only]. Dual electric windshield wipers. Outside rearview mirror. 8.00 x 14 4- or 6-ply tubeless tires. White sidewall tires.
NOTE: Colors offered on 1959 Rancheros were: Raven black. Gunsmoke gray. Colonial white. Surf blue. Wedgewood blue. Sherwood green. April green. Torch red. Tahitian bronze. Fawn tan. Inca gold. In addition, Colonial white could be combined with any color listed. And Surf blue combined with Wedgewood blue, April green with Sherwood green or Fawn tan with Tahitian bronze to create Style Tone color combinations.
COURIER SEDAN DELIVERY: The Courier was restyled for 1959. Hooded, T-bird inspired quad headlights were placed above the full width, star pattern aluminum grille. Circular parking lights were recessed in the bumper. The Courier nameplate was on the rear quarter panel. Glass side windows replaced the previous blanked out area. This, and the new two-piece tailgate made Courier look like a standard two-door Ford station wagon. However, unlike the wagons, it came with just the driver's seat. A three-speed manual transmission was standard.
I.D. DATA [Courier]: Same as Ranchero with body style symbol S.

Model	Body Type	Price	Weight	Prod. Total
Courier — 1/2-Ton — 116 in. w.b. — Six				
78A	Sedan Delivery	2424	—	5141

ENGINE [Courier]: Displacement: 223 cid. OHV Six. 145 hp at 4000 rpm. Bore & stroke: 3.62 in. x 3.60 in. Compression ratio: 8.6:1. Holley Carburetor: One-barrel.

1959 Ford 1/2-Ton F-100 Styleside Pickup With Custom Cab (OCW)

F-100 PICKUP: The F-100 received a mild, but very attractive facelift for 1959. The new hood featured the Ford name on its face in big block letters. The grille had a thick horizontal bars theme. Parking lamps were in the same location. They were now rectangular, not round. The front bumper was raised slightly (on Custom Cab models) and featured an indentation to the center for the license plate. A different Ford F-100 nameplate with the Ford truck crest was used on the front fenders. A new option was four-wheel drive. The F-100 was offered in 6-1/2 ft. and 8 ft. sizes. It came with the Styleside [flush side] welded all-metal box or Flareside box with runningboards between rear fender and back of cab and wooden floor with steel skid strips. Among the standard features were: Hi-Dri ventilation; Nylon-polyethylene-saran seat upholstery; toggle-type tailgate latches; double-acting front and rear shock absorbers; and three-speed manual transmission.

1959 Ford 1/2-Ton Model 66A Standard Ranchero Sedan-Pickup

F-100 PLATFORM/STAKE: The F-100 Platform/Stake shared the same styling changes as the Pickup. Steel skid strips protected the seasoned wood floor boards and made it easier to slide heavy cargo in or out. Sideboards and stakes were made of straight-grained wood. Bolted steel plates held sideboards firmly together at the top. Heavy-gauge steel stake pockets were set flush with the floor. Body sills were protected by steel end caps. An all-steel rub rail protected the Stake body. Load space was 80 in. long, 67 in. wide and 24.8 in. to top of racks. Platform load space was 84.3 in. long and 71.3 in. wide.

F-100 7-1/2 FT. PANEL: Standard features on the 1959 F-100 Panel included: White contour front and rear bumpers; right and rear door locks; dual vacuum booster windshield wipers; hubcaps; dome light; chrome left-hand rearview mirror; single electric horn; underframe spare tire carrier; left-hand sun visor; and tail-stop-license plate lights on left rear door. The plywood floor was supported on steel cross sills.

1959 Ford 1/2-Ton Model 66C Ranchero Custom Sedan-Pickup

I.D. DATA [F-100]: VIN located on rating plate. The first three symbols indicated series: F10=F100 or F11=F-100 four-wheel-drive. The fourth symbol indicates engine: C or D=292 cid V-8; J=223 cid six. The fifth symbol indicates the model year: 8=1958. The sixth symbol indicates assembly plant: A=Atlanta, Ga.; D=Dallas, Texas; E=Mawwah, N.J.; G=Chicago, Ill.; H=Lorain, Ohio; K=Kansas City, Kan.; L=Long Beach, Calif.; N=Norfolk, Va.; P=Twin Cities, Minn.; R=San Jose, Calif.; U=Louisville, Ken. The last six symbols indicate the sequential production number.

Model	Body Type	Price	Weight	Prod. Total
F-100 — 1/2-Ton — 110 in. w.b. — Six				
80	Platform	—	3053	Note 1
81	Chassis & Cab	1814	2748	Note 1
83	Flareside	1932	3084	Note 1
83	Styleside	1948	3098	Note 1
82	Panel	2230	3318	Note 1
84	Chassis	1558	2194	Note 1
86	Stake	2024	3458	Note 1
F-100 — 1/2-Ton — 118 in. w.b. — Six				
81	Chassis & Cab	1852	2838	Note 1
83	Flareside	1971	3262	Note 1
83	Styleside	1987	3273	Note 1

NOTE 1: Ford records show the following F-100 production break-outs: [Chassis & Cowl] 173; [Chassis & Windshield] 4; [Chassis & Cab] 8942; [Platform & Rack] 301; [Flareside Pickup] 26,616; [Styleside Pickup] 112,082; [Standard Panel] 7,963 and [Custom Panel] 982.

ENGINE [F-100]: Same as Courier except 139 hp at 4200 rpm and 8.3:1 compression ratio.

F-250 PICKUP: Like the F-100, the F-250 received an attractive facelift for 1959. Buyers had their choice of Flareside or Styleside boxes and four-wheel drive at extra cost. Most standard features were the same as those found on the F-100.

1959 Ford 3/4-Ton F-250 Styleside Pickup/Wrecker 4x4 (RCA)

F-250 PLATFORM/STAKE: The F-250 Platform/Stake had most of the same features as its F-100 counterpart. However, it could haul heavier loads. Stake load space was 90 in. long, 74 in. wide and 28.3 in. to top of racks. Platform load space was 93.4 in. long and 79.3 in. wide.

I.D. DATA [F-250]: Same as F-100, except first three symbols F25 for two-wheel drive and F26 for four-wheel drive.

Model	Body Type	Price	Weight	Prod. Total
F-250 — 3/4-Ton — 118 in. w.b. — Six				
80	Platform	—	3463	Note 1
81	Chassis & Cab	1971	3088	Note 1
83	Flareside	2090	3513	Note 1
83	Styleside	2106	3523	Note 1
84	Chassis	1704	2539	Note 1
86	Stake	2181	3638	Note 1

NOTE 1: Ford records show the following F-250 production break-outs: [Chassis & Cowl] 195; [Chassis & Windshield] 139; [Chassis & Cab] 4,016; [Platform & Rack] 1,093; [Flareside Pickup] 4,827 and [Styleside Pickup] 16,491.

ENGINE [F-250]: Same as F-100.

1959 Ford 3/4-Ton F-250 Styleside Pickup (RCA)

F-350 PICKUP: The F-350 shared styling changes and most standard features with the F-250. It was capable of hauling much heavier loads. It was available in Styleside or Flareside versions. The Flareside had wood floors protected by full-length skid strips. A four-speed manual transmission, front-only shock absorbers, and drum-and-band type parking brakes were standard.

F-350 PLATFORM/STAKE: This was the longest light-duty Ford truck of its type in 1959. It had rugged steel channel stakes for greater rigidity. Stake load space was 106 in. long, 82 in. wide and 31.2 in. to top of racks. Platform load space was 109.4 in. long and 87.3 in. wide.

I.D. DATA [F-350]: Same as F-100, except first three symbols are F35.

Model	Body Type	Price	Weight	Prod. Total
F-350 — 1-Ton — 130 in. w.b. — Six				
80	Platform	—	3953	Note 1
81	Chassis & Cab	2130	3458	Note 1
83	Flareside	2269	3932	Note 1
83	Styleside	2285	3938	Note 1
84	Chassis	1863	2904	Note 1
86	Stake	2381	4313	Note 1

NOTE 1: Ford records show the following F-350 production break-outs: [Chassis & Cowl] 749; [Chassis & Windshield] 150; [Chassis & Cab] 12,896; [Platform & Rack] 1093; [Flareside Pickup] 4827 and [Styleside Pickup] 16,491.

ENGINE [F-350]: Same as F-100.

CHASSIS [Courier Sedan Delivery]: Wheelbase: 118 in. Overall length: 208 in. Overall width: 76.6 in. GVW: 4,600 lbs. Tires: 7.50 x 14 four-ply.

[F-100]: Wheelbase: 110 in./118 in. GVW: 4,000-5,000 lbs. Tires: 6.70 x 15 four-ply.

[F-250]: Wheelbase: 118 in. GVW: 4,900-7,400 lbs. Tires: 6.50 x 16 six-ply.

[F-350]: Wheelbase: 130 in. GVW: 7,700-9,800 lbs. Tires: 8 x 17.5 six-ply.

POWERTRAIN OPTIONS: 186 hp 292 cid V-8. [Courier] 200 hp 292 cid V-8. Transmissions: [F-100/F-250] Medium-duty three-speed transmission. [F-100/Courier] Heavy-duty three-speed transmission. [F-350] Four-speed manual transmission. [F-100] Three-speed with overdrive. [Courier] Fordomatic automatic. Cruise-O-Matic automatic. [F-250/F-350] Heavy-duty Cruise-O-Matic.

CONVENIENCE OPTIONS: Transistor powered truck radio. Signal-seeking radio in Courier. Magic Aire heater-defroster. Windshield washers. Power steering. Power brakes. ICC clearance lights. 16 x 15K heavy-duty wheels on F-100. Outside rearview mirror (bright metal on Pickup, painted on others). Heavy-duty grille guard. Turn signals. Sealed beam spotlight. Seat covers. Four-wheel drive. Heavy-duty rear springs. Recirculating heater-defroster. Heavy-duty radiator. Dual electric windshield wipers. Side-mounted tire carrier for Pickup. Spare tire. [Safety Package] Includes padded instrument panel and cushioned sun visors; tinted glass; and full-wrap rear window. Rear bumper on Pickup. Front and rear chrome bumper on Styleside Pickups. Chrome front bumper. Right armrest. Outside left or right telescopic mirror for cabs. Outside non-telescopic mirror. Tow hooks. Seat belts. Fire extinguishers (1-1/2 qt. or 4 lbs. dry chemical). Cigar lighter. Dome light. Splash guards. Locking gas tank cap. Deluxe heater in Courier. Bumper guards on Courier. Deluxe wheelcovers for Courier. Underdash light in Courier. [Custom Cab package] Includes, woven nylon-saran seat upholstery in a candy-striped pattern with vinyl bolsters and seat facing; foam-rubber padding in seat cushion and back; white fleck pattern hardboard on headlining and sides of load compartment (on Panel); sound deadener on floor and rear cab panel; insulation on front cowl wall in cab; two-tone paint on doors and instrument panel; armrest on left door; white steering wheel with chrome horn ring; right sun visor; illuminated cigar lighter; bright metal grille, headlight assembly, windshield reveal molding and parking light rims; Custom Cab emblem on each door; and matched locks on both doors.

NOTE: Colors available on 1959 Ford light-duty trucks included: Academy blue, Goldenrod yellow, Vermilion, April green, Meadow green, Indian turquoise, Wedgewood blue, Colonial white, Raven black or prime. Any standard color listed could be combined with Colonial white for a two-tone effect.

HISTORICAL: Ford captured 31.09 percent of all new truck registrations in 1959.

1960 FORD

1960 Ford 1/2-Ton Falcon Ranchero Pickup (K. Buttolph)

FALCON RANCHERO: The Ranchero was now in the compact Falcon series. Sales literature proclaimed it America's lowest priced Pickup and boasted of mileage up to 30 mpg. Its styling was plain, yet attractive. The two headlights were nestled in the grille cavity. The concave aluminum grille had a pattern of horizontal and vertical lines. The slab sides had mild body sculpturing. Two large round taillights were used. Other features included: Single unitbody construction with bolt-on fenders; independent front suspension; variable-rate rear leaf springs; duo-servo hydraulic brakes; compound curved windshield; and a sloping hood. There was 31.6 cu. ft. of load space in the six-foot box, which featured an instant-lock tailgate. Standard equipment included: Bright metal windshield and drip moldings; front and rear bumpers; armrests; dome light; spare tire and wheel behind seat; sun visors; dispatch box; ashtray; double-grip door locks; Lifeguard steering wheel; foam rubber seat cushion padding; light brown Western motif vinyl seat covering with beige vinyl bolsters and seat facings; and three-speed manual transmission.

1960 Ford 1/2-Ton Falcon Ranchero Pickup (OCW)

I.D. DATA: [Ranchero] VIN located on rating plate. First symbol indicates model year: 0=1960. Second symbol indicates assembly plant: A=Atlanta, Ga.; H=Lorain, Ohio; K=Kansas City, Kan.; R=San Jose, Calif.; S=Allen Park, Mich.; T=Metuchen, N.J. The third and fourth symbols indicate model: 27=Ranchero; 29=Sedan Delivery. The fifth symbol indicates engine: S=144 cid six; D=144 cid low-compression six; U=170 cid six; E=170 cid low-compression six. The last six symbols are the sequential production number.

Model	Body Type	Price	Weight	Prod. Total
Ranchero — 1/2-Ton — 109.9 in. w.b. — Six				
66A	Pickup	1882	2435	21,027
78A	Sedan Delivery	2107	2463	—

1960 Ford 1/2-Ton Falcon Ranchero Pickup (Marley Gross)

ENGINE [Falcon Ranchero]: Displacement: 144 cid. OHV Six. 90 hp at 4200 rpm. Bore & stroke: 3.5 in. x 2.5 in. Compression ratio: 8.7:1. Holley one-barrel carburetor.

CHASSIS: Wheelbase: 109.9 in. Overall length: 189 in. Overall width: 70 in. Overall height: 54.5 in. Payload: 800 lbs. Tires: 6.50 x 13.

POWERTRAIN OPTIONS: Fordomatic transmission.

CONVENIENCE OPTIONS: Heavy-duty battery. Heavy-duty generator. [Deluxe Trim Package] Includes, bright metal exterior moldings; taillight ornaments; white steering wheel with chrome horn ring; cigar lighter; dome light door switch; Deluxe seat trim; wheelcovers; windshield washers; dual electric windshield wipers; and whitewall tires.

NOTE: Solid colors available were: Platinum; Monte Carlo red; Skymist blue; Adriatic green; Corinthian white, Meadow green; Beachwood brown; Belmont blue; Raven black; and turquoise. Two-tone combinations were: black and platinum; Skymist and Belmont blue; Adriatic and Meadow green; and Corinthian white with any other solid color.

COURIER SEDAN DELIVERY: Once again, the Courier looked like a Ford two-door Ranch wagon with just a driver's seat. It was completely restyled for 1960. The new Courier was wider, longer and lower than the 1959. It was also sleeker. The four bright-trimmed headlights were tucked into the recessed, mesh-style grille. The Ford name was printed on the face of the sloping hood. A chrome strip ran from the top of the front bumper to the length of the small horizontal tailfin. Under the fin was a semi-circular taillight. The 1960 Courier had a spacious 97.4 cu. ft. cargo area. This was the last year for the Courier Sedan Delivery.

I.D. DATA: [Courier] VIN located on rating plate. First symbol indicates model year: 0=1960. Second symbol indicates assembly plant: A=Atlanta, Ga.; C=Chester, Pa.; D=Dallas, Texas; E=Mahwah, N.J.; F=Dearborn, Mich.; G=Chicago, Ill.; H=Lorain, Ohio; J=Los Angeles, Calif.; K=Kansas City, Kan.; L=Long Beach, Calif.; M=Memphis, Tenn.; N=Norfolk, Va.; P=Twin Cities, Minn.; R=San Jose, Calif.; S=Allen Park, Mich.; T=Metuchen, N.J.; U=Louisville, Ken.; W=Wayne, Mich.; Y=Wixom, Mich.; and Z=St. Louis, Mo. The third and fourth symbols indicate model: 69=Sedan Delivery. The fifth symbol indicates engine: V=223 cid six; W=292 cid two-barrel V-8; X=352 cid two-barrel V-8; Y=352 cid four-barrel V-8; G=352 cid low-compression four-barrel V-8; T=352 cid low-compression two-barrel V-8. The last six symbols are the sequential production number.

Model	Body Type	Price	Weight	Prod. Total
Courier — 1/2-Ton — 119 in. w.b. — Six				
69	Sedan Delivery	2456	—	2,374

ENGINE [Courier]: Displacement: 223 cid. OHV Six. 145 hp at 4000 rpm. Bore & stroke: 3.62 in. x 3.60 in. Compression ratio: 8.6:1. Holley Carburetor: One-barrel.

1960 Ford 1/2-Ton F-100 Custom Cab Styleside Pickup (S. Soloy)

F-100 PICKUP: In contrast to last year's clean look, the 1960 F-100 was jazzed up considerably. The Ford truck emblem was centered on the face of the hood, between two vent slots. The new rectangular pattern grille extended down to include the parking lights. A thick bar at its top connected the larger, inward slanting headlight pods. This gave the truck a bug-eyed appearance. The hoodside ornament looked like a stylized rocket or arrow, depending on your point of view. Improvements were made to the springs, door seals, electrical and exhaust systems. The F-100 Pickup could be ordered in 110 in. or 118 in. wheelbases and with either Flareside or Styleside boxes. Among the standard features were: Lifeguard steering wheel; safety double-grip door locks; plain nylon-rayon-saran seat upholstery with gray vinyl bolster and seat facings; dome light; left-hand sun visor; ash receptacle; dispatch box; coat hook; white instrument cluster cover plate; Hi-Dri all-weather ventilation; and three-speed manual transmission. Four-wheel drive was available at extra cost, along with many other options.

1960 Ford 1/2-Ton F-100 Styleside Custom Cab Pickup (Ray Wilson)

F-100 PANEL: The 1960 F-100 Panel had a facelift and a beefed-up frame. The brakes were also improved. Among the standard features were: Bright-color plaid nylon-rayon-saran seat upholstery with vinyl bolsters and seat facings; white contour front and rear bumpers; right and rear door locks; dual vacuum booster windshield wipers; Lifeguard steering wheel; large dome light; chrome left-hand outside rearview mirror; single electric horn; under-frame type spare tire carrier; left-hand sun visor; taillight-stoplight-license plate light on left rear door; plywood floor (chemically treated for longer life and supported on steel cross sills); sealed side joints; twin rear doors hinged to one-piece channel steel door

frame; and two-position door checks. The cargo area was 91.6 in. long, 51.6 in. high and 51.6 in. wide at the floor. There was a total of 158 cu. ft. of cargo area. The sides of the body from floor to top of wheelhouses were protected by steel paneling. Smooth steel slats protected the load above these panels. This was the last conventional full-size Ford panel.

F-100 PLATFORM/STAKE: The F-100 Platform/Stake received the same facelift as the F-100 Pickup. Steel skid strips protected the floor and made it easier to slide cargo in or out. Heavy gauge steel stake pockets were set flush with the floor. Sideboards and stakes were made of straight-grained wood. Bolted steel plates held sideboards firmly together at the top yet permitted quick, easy removal of stake sections. An all-steel rub rail protected the Stakes. Load space was 80 in. long, 67 in. wide and 24.8 in. to top of racks. Platform load space was 84.3 in. long and 71.3 in. wide.

I.D. DATA [F-100]: VIN located on rating plate. The first three symbols indicated series: F10=F-100 two-wheel drive; F-11=F-100 four-wheel drive. The fourth symbol indicates engine: J=223 cid six; C=292 cid V-8. The fifth symbol indicates the model year: 0=1960. The sixth symbol indicates assembly plant: A=Atlanta, Ga.; D=Dallas, Texas; E=Mahwah, N.J.; G=Chicago, Ill.; H=Lorain, Ohio; K=Kansas City, Kan.; L=Long Beach, Calif.; N=Norfolk, Va.; P=Twin Cities, Minn.; R=San Jose, Calif.; U=Louisville, Ken. The last six symbols indicate the sequential production number.

Model	Body Type	Price	Weight	Prod. Total
F-100 — 1/2-Ton — 110 in. w.b. — Six				
80	Platform	—	3053	Note 1
81	Chassis & Cab	1839	2748	Note 1
83	Flareside	1956	3088	Note 1
83	Styleside	1972	3105	Note 1
82	Panel	2268	3248	Note 1
84	Chassis	1580	2184	Note 1
86	Stake	2049	3178	Note 1
F-100 — 1/2-Ton — 118 in. w.b. — Six				
81	Chassis & Cab	1897	2828	Note 1
83	Flareside	1994	3253	Note 1
83	Styleside	2010	3263	Note 1

* Add $566 for 4x4 option.

NOTE 1: Ford records show the following F-100 production break-outs: [Chassis & Cowl] 121; [Chassis & Windshield] 24; [Chassis & Cab] 17,159; [Platform & Rack] 245; [Flareside Pickup] 27,383; [Styleside Pickup] 113,875; [Standard Panel] 8,543; [Custom Panel] 947; [4x4 Cab] 442; [4x4 Flareside Pickup] 964 and [4x4 Styleside Pickup] 4,334.

ENGINE [F-100]: Same as Courier except 139 hp at 4200 rpm and 8.3:1 compression ratio.

1960 Ford 3/4-Ton F-250 Styleside Custom Cab Pickup 4x4 (OCW)

F-250 PICKUP: The F-250 Pickup was offered in Flareside and Styleside versions. It could also be ordered with four-wheel drive at extra cost. New standard features on that option were 1,200 lbs. front and 1,950 lbs. rear springs. Nominal payload of F-250 Pickups was 3,550 lbs.

F-250 PLATFORM/STAKE: These were also available with four-wheel drive. Nominal payload capacity on the Stake was 3,500 lbs. On the Platform it was 3,700 lbs. The F-250 Stake with 7-1/2 ft. body had two-piece side and tail racks for greater loading convenience. The sideboards and stakes were made of straight-grained wood. Steel skid strips protected the floor.

I.D. DATA [F-250]: Same as F-100, except first three symbols are: [4x2] F25; [4x4] F26.

Model	Body Type	Price	Weight	Prod. Total
F-250 — 3/4-Ton — 118 in. w.b. — Six				
80	Platform	—	—	Note 1
81	Chassis & Cab	1998	2998	Note 1
83	Flareside	2115	3423	Note 1
83	Styleside	2131	3433	Note 1
84	Chassis	1729	2444	Note 1
86	Stake	2208	3498	Note 1

* Add $609 for 4x4 option.

NOTE 1: Ford records show the following F-250 production break-outs: [Chassis & Cowl] 125; [Chassis & Windshield] 21; [Chassis & Cab] 4,811; [Platform & Rack] 1,017; [Flareside Pickup] 6,356; [Styleside Pickup] 15,518; [4x4 Cab] 411; [4x4 Platform & Rack] 98; [4x4 Flareside Pickup] 828 and [4x4 Styleside Pickup] 1,806.

Ford-built with yo cal Short Stroke

There's new ver power take-off po case to drive win or other equipmen between 2- and 4 while moving.

1960 Ford 3/4-Ton F-250 Styleside Custom Cab Pickup/Wrecker 4x4

F-250 ENGINE: Same as F-100.

F-350 PICKUP: The big light-duty Ford Pickup in 1960 was the F-350. It was offered in Flareside or Styleside versions. Among standard features were: Four-speed manual transmission; six-hole disc wheels; drum and band parking brakes; 3,800 lbs. capacity front axle; 7,200 lbs. rear axle; single-stage rear springs; and front-only shock absorbers.

F-350 PLATFORM/STAKE: Although it had most of the same standard features as the F-100 and F-250 versions, the F-350 Platform/Stake was capable of hauling heavier loads. Its payload capacity was rated at 5,075 lbs. (Stake) or 5,450 lbs. (Platform). The F-350 Stake had three-section sides, a swing-open center rack and steel stakes. A four-speed manual gearbox was standard.

I.D. DATA [F-350]: Same as F-100, except first three symbols are F35.

Model	Body Type	Price	Weight	Prod. Total
80	Platform	—	3953	Note 1
81	Chassis & Cab	2155	3458	Note 1
83	Flareside	2296	3938	Note 1
83	Styleside	2312	3938	Note 1
84	Chassis	1885	2904	Note 1
86	Stake	2407	4313	Note 1

NOTE 1: Ford records show the following F-350 production break-outs: [Chassis & Cowl] 945; [Chassis & Windshield] 175; [Chassis & Cab] 12,761; [Platform & Rack] 4,129; [Flareside Pickup] 1,213 and [Styleside Pickup] 2,140.

F-350 ENGINE: Same as F-100.

CHASSIS [Courier Sedan Delivery]: Wheelbase: 119 in. Overall length: 213.7 in. Overall width: 81.5 in. GVW: 4,600 lbs. Tires: 7.50 x 14, four-ply.

[F-100]: Wheelbase: 110 in. and 118 in. GVW: 4,000-5,000 lbs. Tires: 6.70 x 15, four-ply.

[F-250]: Wheelbase: 118 in. GVW: 4,900-7,400 lbs. Tires: 6.50 x 16, six-ply.

[F-350]: Wheelbase: 130 in. GVW: 7,700-9,800 lbs. Tires: 8 x 17.5, six-ply.

POWERTRAIN OPTIONS: 171 hp 292 cid V-8. [Courier] 185 hp 292 cid V-8. Transmissions: [F-100/F-250] Medium-duty three-speed; [F-350] Heavy-duty three-speed or four-speed manual transmission; [F-100/Courier] Three-speed with overdrive transmission; [F-100/Courier] Fordomatic transmission; [F-250/F-350] Heavy-duty Cruise-O-Matic; [Courier] Cruise-O-Matic.

CONVENIENCE OPTIONS: Transistor powered truck radio. Signal-seeking radio in Courier. Magic Aire heater-defroster. Windshield washers. Power steering. Power brakes. Four-wheel drive. Rear shocks on F-350. Outside rearview mirror (bright metal on Pickup, painted on others). Heavy-duty grille guard. Turn signals. Sealed beam spotlight. Seat covers. Auxiliary seat in Panel. ICC reflectors. ICC lights. Heavy-duty rear springs. Recirculating heater-defroster. Heavy-duty radiator. Dual electric windshield wipers. Side-mounted tire carrier for Pickup. Spare tire. [Safety package] includes: Padded instrument panel and cushioned sun visors; tinted glass; full-wrap rear window; rear bumper (Pickup); front and rear chrome bumpers (Styleside Pickup); chrome front bumper; right-hand armrest; outside left or right telescopic mirror; outside non-telescopic mirror; two hooks; seat belts; fire extinguishers (1-1/2 qt. or 4 lbs. dry chemical); cigar lighter; dome light; splash guards; locking gas tank cap; Deluxe heater in Courier; bumper guards on Courier; Deluxe wheelcovers on Courier; under-dash light for Courier. [Custom Cab] Includes: Multi-colored woven nylon-saran seat upholstery in striped pattern with vinyl bolsters and seat facings; foam-rubber padding in seat cushion and back; white splatter-pattern hardboard on headlining and sides of load compartment on panel truck; sound deadener on floor of driver's compartment; insulation on firewall; two-tone paint on doors and instrument panel; armrest on left door; white steering wheel with chrome ring; chrome-trimmed instrument cluster; bright metal grille and headlight assembly; bright metal windshield reveal molding; Custom Cab emblems on side doors; matched locks on all doors; and dual wrap-around taillights at beltline.

NOTE: 1960 Ford Diamond Lustre standard colors were: Monte Carlo red; Goldenrod yellow; Academy blue; Skymist blue; Caribbean turquoise; Adriatic green; Holly green; Corinthian white; and Raven black. Any standard color could be combined with Corinthian white for two-tone effect.

HISTORICAL: Total light-duty truck production including P-100; P-350 and P-400 Series forward-control models was 255,538. Ford was America's number two truck-maker in terms of output. Ford installed and tested a gas turbine engine in a prototype truck this year.

1961 Ford 1/2-Ton Falcon Ranchero Pickup (DFW)

1961 Ford 1/2-Ton Falcon Econoline Van (OCW)

FALCON RANCHERO PICKUP: A new convex grille with many thin vertical and horizontal pieces was the most ·noticeable change for 1961. The spring rates were lowered and the rubber upper A-arm bushings were replaced with treaded metal ones. On the inside, the dome light was moved to the ceiling. The rocker panels and all main underbody structural members were heavily zinc-coated to protect against rust and corrosion. The six-foot pickup box provided over 31.5 cu. ft. of usable load space. There was over 42 in. of flat floor width between the wheelhousings. The seat was covered with brown Western motif vinyl with beige vinyl bolsters and seat facings. Other standard features included: Chrome front and rear bumpers; bright metal windshield reveal moldings; two armrests; dome light; rearview mirror; spare tire and wheel behind seat; two sun visors; dispatch box; ashtray; Double-Grip door locks; Lifeguard steering wheel; and three-speed manual transmission.

FALCON SEDAN DELIVERY: The Falcon Sedan Delivery shared its good looks with the Ranchero. It resembled a regular Falcon wagon. However, the side windows were blanked-out from the front doors back. It had the wagon's tailgate with roll-down window. The three-passenger seat was covered in vinyl. The plywood floor was rubber-coated.

I.D. DATA: [Ranchero] VIN located on rating plate. First symbol indicates model year: 1=1961. Second symbol indicates assembly plant: A=Atlanta, Ga.; H=Lorain, Ohio; K=Kansas City, Kan.; R=San Jose, Calif.; S=Allen Park, Mich.; T=Metuchen, N.J. The third and fourth symbols indicate model: 27=Ranchero; 29=Sedan Delivery. The fifth symbol indicates engine: S=144 cid six; U=170 cid six. The last six symbols are the sequential production number.

ECONOLINE PICKUP: Ford introduced the driver-forward compact Econoline Van in 1961. The Econoline Pickup looked like an Econoline Van that had been customized and turned into a Pickup. Ford was printed in block letters on the front face of the vehicle. On either side of the name were the two headlights. They were set in large, rectangular pods which came to a point at their inner ends. The small wraparound parking lights were located just above the front bumper. Econoline was written in chrome a bit below the vent windows of both doors. The cargo area was 85.9 in. long and 63 in. wide. The sides were 22.4 in. high. The Econoline Pickup featured vinyl upholstery, a three-speed manual transmission and an insulated engine cover between the driver and passenger seats.

ECONOLINE VAN: The new Econoline Van had 39 percent more load space than a typical 1/2-ton Panel. The large interior load area was over 54 in. high and 65 in. wide. Total load space was 204.4 cu. ft. The Econoline got better gas mileage (up to 30 mpg) than standard Pickups and was easier to maneuver. Among the standard features were: Double side and rear doors; electric windshield wipers; outside rearview mirror; front and rear bumpers; dome light; single electric horn; turn signals; and I-Beam front axle.

1961 Ford 1/2-Ton Falcon Ranchero Pickup (OCW)

Model	Body Type	Price	Weight	Prod. Total
66A	Pickup	1887	2338	20,937
78A	Sedan Delivery	2109	2463	1,988

ENGINE [Falcon Ranchero/Sedan Delivery]: Displacement: 144 cid. Six-cylinder. 85 hp at 4200 rpm. Bore & stroke: 3.50 in. x 2.50 in. Compression ratio: 8.7:1. Carburetor: One-barrel.

CHASSIS: Wheelbase: 109.9 in. Overall length: 189 in. Overall width: 70 in. Overall height: 54.5 in. Payload: 800 lbs. Tires: 6.50 x 13-4 ply-rated on 13 x 4-1/2 J safety-type wheels.

POWERTRAIN OPTIONS: Fordomatic Drive automatic. 101 hp 170 cid six.

CONVENIENCE OPTIONS: Heavy-duty battery. Heater and defroster. Hydro-carbon emission control device. Radio and front-mounted antenna. Safety Package A included: Padded instrument panel and sun visors; seat belts; white sidewall tires; 6.50 x 13-6 ply-rated tires; bright metal wheelcovers; tinted windshield; windshield washers; electric windshield wipers; cigarette lighter; white steering wheel with chrome horn ring; and backup lights. [Deluxe Trim Package] includes: Bright metal molding around box and cab back; bright metal taillight trim rings; bright metal door window moldings; white steering wheel with horn ring; cigarette lighter; dome light door switch; plus black-and-white or red-and-white vinyl upholstery.

NOTE: Colors offered on 1961 Rancheros were: Raven black; Monte Carlo red; Silver gray; Chesapeake blue; Cambridge blue; Starlight blue; Laurel green; Mint green; Algiers bronze; Garden turquoise; Aquamarine; and Corinthian white. Optional two-tone combinations: Cambridge blue and Starlight blue; Laurel green and Mint green; plus Corinthian white and any solid color.

1961 Ford 1/2-Ton Falcon Econoline Station Bus (OCW)

ECONOLINE STATION BUS: "Announcing a new kind of station wagon," proclaimed sales literature. The Station Bus was essentially an Econoline Van with a view. It had windows all around. There were two front doors, a pair of rear doors and two side doors in the center, on the passenger side. Standard features included: Electric windshield wipers; rearview mirror; dome light; hubcaps; electric horn; turn signals; tire carrier; mechanical jack; contour front and rear bumpers; and three-speed manual transmission.

I.D. DATA: [Econoline] VIN located on rating plate. First symbol indicates model year: 1=1961. Second symbol indicates assembly plant: (See F-100 I.D. data.) The third and fourth symbols indicate model: 10=Econoline. The fifth symbol indicates engine: S=144 cid six. The last six symbols are the sequential production number.

Model	Body Type	Price	Weight	Prod. Total
E-100 Econoline — 1/2-Ton — 90 in. w.b. — Six				
87	Pickup	1880	2555	—
89A	Van	1981	2588	—
89B	Station Bus	2092	2778	—

NOTE 1: Ford records show the following Econoline production break-outs: [89B Standard Econoline Bus] 8,511; [89B Custom Econoline bus] 6,571; [87A Standard Pickup] 11,893; [87A Custom Pickup] 3,000; [89A Standard Van] 28,932 and [89A Custom Van] 2,228.

ENGINE [Econoline]: Displacement: 144 cid. Six-cylinder. 85 hp at 4200 rpm. Bore & stroke: 3.50 in. x 2.50 in. Compression ratio: 8.7:1. One-barrel carburetor.

CHASSIS: Wheelbase: 90 in. Overall length: 168.4 in. Overall width: 65 in. GVW: 3,300 lbs. Tires: 7.00 x 13, six-ply.

POWERTRAIN OPTIONS: None.

1961 Ford 1/2-Ton Falcon Econoline Pickup (JAG)

CONVENIENCE OPTIONS: AM radio. Fresh air heater/defroster. Windshield washers. Auxiliary gas heater. Auxiliary step. [Safety Package A] Includes: Padded instrument panels and sun visors; rear door glass (Van); flip or stationary Van seat; armrests; right-hand sun visor; interior rearview mirror; cigar lighter; horn ring; ICC four-lamp flasher; dual horns; left-hand door lock; tinted windshield; bright metal wheelcovers; front and rear chrome bumpers; cargo area dome light in Van; positive crankcase ventilation. Tires: 6.50 x 13-4 ply-rated whitewall. 7.00 x 13-6 ply-rated black- or white-sidewall. [Custom Equipment Package] Includes (On Van) right-hand air duct; armrests; cigar lighter; cargo area dome light; driver's side door lock; windows in rear doors; chrome horn ring; dual electric horns; bright metal hubcaps; passenger area dome light; foam seat padding; passenger stationary seat; twill stripe woven plastic seat upholstery; right-hand sun visor. (On Station Bus) twill-stripe woven plastic upholstery; hardboard sides and door trim; black vinyl armrests; right-hand air duct; coat hooks; passenger area dome light; driver's side door lock; cigar lighter; right-hand sun visor; full-length floor mat; fiberglass interior window molding; full-length headliner; dual electric horn; chrome horn ring; bright metal hubcaps; chrome window latches; plastic foam padding for right passenger seat; second rear passenger seat in wagon; second and third rear passenger seats; includes heavy-duty front and rear springs and 7.00 x 13 6 ply-rated tires for wagon. [Living Quarters Interior package] Includes: (Wagon) four-passenger sleeping capacity kit with cushions and window screens and heavy-duty battery.

NOTE: Color choices for the 1961 Econoline Van were: Monte Carlo red; Raven black; Academy blue; Starlight blue; Mint green; Holly green; Goldenrod yellow; Caribbean turquoise; and Corinthian white. Two-tone paint schemes included any standard color combined with Corinthian white.

F-100 PICKUP: Ford's light-duty trucks were restyled this year from the frame up. They were wider and lower than last year's models. The grille consisted of two horizontal bars with a single headlight at both ends. The rectangular parking lamps were between the bars, next to the headlights. The Ford name in block letters was centered between the upper and lower grille pieces. This entire unit was framed with a molding. Above it four rectangular slots and, centered on the face of the hood, the Ford truck badge. A rocket style emblem, on the side of the hood, carried the Ford and F-100 names. The larger windshield was of the non-wraparound variety and came with new center sweep wipers. The rear cab window was 28 percent larger. Vertical rectangular taillights were used as was a 64.5 in. wide, grain-tight tailgate. Buyers had their choice of two boxes. The Flareside box had rolled edge flareboards and runningboards between the cab and rear fender. The Styleside box was smooth-sided. Stylesides now had a one-piece cab-and-box, which helped make them appear a bit sleeker than before. Four-wheel drive was only available on Flareside pickups. Both 6.5 ft. and 8 ft. versions of these boxes were offered. Standard features included: Instant-Action tailgate with rattle-proof hinged support arms (instead of chains) on Styleside Pickup; brown basketweave vinyl seat upholstery with dark brown Morocco-grained vinyl bolsters and seat facings; a perforated and insulated headlining in Stylesides; Lifeguard steering wheel; safety double-grip door latches; dome light; left-hand sun visor; ash receptacle; dispatch box; dual electric windshield wipers; theft-retardant ignition switch; rearview mirror; all-weather venilation; concentric steering column; and three-speed manual transmission.

F-100 PLATFORM/STAKE: These shared the same styling and most other features found on F-100s. Steel skid strips protected the floor and made it easier to slide cargo in or out. Heavy gauge steel stake pockets were set flush with the floor. Side boards and stakes were made of straight-grained wood. Bolted steel plates held the removable side boards firmly together at the top. Body sills were protected by steel end caps. An all-steel rub rail protected the body.

I.D. DATA [F-100]: VIN located on rating plate. The first three symbols indicated series: F10=F-100 two-wheel drive; F-11=F-100 four-wheel drive. The fourth symbol indicates engine: J=223 cid six; C or D=292 cid V-8. The fifth symbol indicates assembly plant: D=Dallas, Texas; E=Mahwah, N.J.; G=Chicago, Ill.; H=Lorain, Ohio; K=Kansas City, Kan.; N=Norfolk, Va.; P=Twin Cities, Minn.; R=San Jose, Calif.; U=Louisville, Ken. The last six symbols indicate the sequential production number.

Model	Body Type	Price	Weight	Prod. Total
F-100 — 1/2-Ton — 114 in. w.b. — Six				
80	Platform	—	3142	—
81	Chassis & Cab	1851	2827	—
83	Flareside	1966	3167	—
83	Styleside	1981	3129	—
84	Chassis	1597	2319	—
86	Stake	2057	3267	—
F-100 — 1/2-Ton — 122 in. w.b. — Six				
81	Chassis & Cab	1882	2881	—
83	Flareside	2001	3306	—
83	Styleside	2017	3440	—

* Add $566 for 4x4 option.

NOTE 1: Ford records show the following F-100 production break-outs: [Chassis & Cowl] 46; [Chassis & Windshield] 17; [Chassis & Cab] 12,544; [Unit-body Pickup] 62,410; [Platform & Rack] 152; [Flareside Pickup] 21,474; [4x4 Chassis & Cab] 180; [Flareside Pickup] 3,361; [4x4 Flareside Pickup] 2,468 and [4x4 Styleside Pickup] 255.

ENGINE [F-100]: Displacement: 223 cid. Six-cylinder. 135 hp at 4000 rpm. Bore & stroke: 3.62 in. x 3.60 in. Compression ratio: 8.4:1. One-barrel carburetor.

F-250 PICKUP: The F-250 was a slightly more heavy-duty version of the F-100. It had larger brakes and higher capacity rear axle and rear springs. Buyers could choose from 8 ft. Flareside or Styleside versions. Four-wheel drive was only available at extra cost on the Flareside. Eight-hole disc wheels were standard.

F-250 PLATFORM/STAKE: The F-250 Platform/Stake was longer and had a higher payload capacity than the F-100. Stake load space was 90 in. long, 74 in. wide and 28.3 in. to the top of the racks. Platform load space was 93.4 in. long and 79.3 in. wide. Sideboards and stakes were made of straight-grained wood.

I.D. DATA [F-250]: Same as F-100, except first three symbols are: [4x2] F25; [4x4] F26.

Model	Body Type	Price	Weight	Prod. Total
F-250 — 3/4-Ton — 122 in. w.b. — Six				
80	Platform	—	3409	—
81	Chassis & Cab	2005	3069	—
83	Flareside	2120	3494	—
83	Styleside	2134	3499	—
84	Chassis	1741	2561	—
86	Stake	2211	3594	—

NOTE 1: Ford records show the following F-250 production break-outs: [Chassis & Cowl] 108; [Chassis & Windshield] 27; [Chassis & Cab] 3,557; [4x4 cab] 359; [Unit-body Pickup] 10,008; [4x4 Styleside Pickup] 149; [Platform & Rack] 701; [4x4 Platform & Rack] 78; [Flareside Pickup] 4,426 and [4x4 Flareside Pickup] 1,671.

ENGINE [F-250]: See F-100.

F-350 PICKUP: Although it shared F series styling changes for 1961, underneath the F-350 was pretty much the same as the previous year's model. However, its wheelbase was stretched to 132 in. Both Flareside and Styleside versions were offered. The Flareside had rolled edge flareboards and runningboards between the cab and rear fender. The Styleside had a Unit-type Pickup body with smooth sides. In addition to most of the same standard features found on the F-100, the F-350 had larger brakes, a heavy-duty clutch, front-only shock absorbers and a four-speed-manual transmission.

F-350 PLATFORM/STAKE: This continued to be the heftiest light-duty Platform/Stake Ford offered. It had steel stakes. The three-section stake sides and swing open center rack proved easier loading and unloading. Stake load space was 105.9 in. long, 82 in. wide and 31.2 in. to the top of the racks. Platform load space was 109.4 in. long and 87.3 in. wide.

I.D. DATA [F-350]: Same as F-100, except first three symbols are F35.

Model	Body Type	Price	Weight	Prod. Total
F-350 — 1-Ton — 132 in. w.b. — Six				
80	Platform	—	4017	—
81	Chassis & Cab	2171	3357	—
83	Flareside	2305	3849	—
83	Styleside	2321	3849	—
84	Chassis	1906	2849	—
86	Stake	2418	4317	—

NOTE 1: Ford records show the following F-350 production break-outs: [Chassis & Cowl] 666; [Chassis & Windshield] 72; [Chassis & Cab] 10,750; [Platform & Rack] 2,821; [Flareside Pickup] 947 and [Styleside Pickup] 1,191.

ENGINE [F-350]: See F-100.

CHASSIS: Wheelbase: [F-100] 114 in.; [F-100/F-250] 122 in.; [F-350] 132 in.; [4x4] 120 in. GVW: [F-100] 4,000-5,000 lbs.; 5,600 lbs. for 4x4. [F-250] 4,900-7,400 lbs.; [F-350] 7,600-9,600 lbs. Tires: [F-100] 6.70 x 15, four-ply; [F-250] 6.50 x 16, six-ply; [F-350] 8 x 17.5, six-ply.

POWERTRAIN OPTIONS: Transmissions: [F-100] Three-speed with overdrive; [F-100/F-250] Medium-duty three-speed; [F-350] Heavy-duty three-speed or four-speed manual transmissions; [F-100] Fordomatic transmission; [F-250/F-350] Heavy-duty Cruise-O-Matic transmission. 160 hp 292 cid V-8.

CONVENIENCE OPTIONS: Four-wheel drive for F-100/F-250 Flareside. 3,500 lbs. capacity rear axle for F-250 4x4. Radio. Left-hand armrest. Right-hand armrest. Fresh air heater.-Recirculating heater. Painted rear bumper. Chrome front and rear bumpers for Styleside. Side-mount spare wheel carrier. Heavy-duty clutch for F-100/F-250. Tinted windshield. Left and/or right outside rearview mirrors. Extra-cooling radiator. Heavy-duty front springs for F-100/ F-250. Heavy-duty two-stage rear springs for F-100/F-250. Heavy-duty rear springs for F-100/F-250. Larger tires. Whitewall tires. Woven plastic trim for standard cab. Turn signals. Windshield washer. Rear wraparound window on Styleside. Right-hand sun visor. [Custom Cab package] Includes: Twill stripe woven plastic upholstery with brown woven-in bolsters and brown Morocco-grained vinyl facings; chrome trimmed instrument cluster; white steering wheel with chrome horn ring; foam rubber in seat (five-inch deep for cushion and 1-3/4 in. deep for seatback); cigar lighter; left-hand armrest; right-hand sun visor; insulation on cowl wall in F-350 Cab (standard on F-100/F-250); bright metal grille and headlight assembly; bright metal windshield reveal molding; matched locks on both doors; two-tone interior; and coat hook.

NOTE: Standard Ford F series colors for 1961 were: Monte Carlo red; Goldenrod yellow; Raven black; Mint green; Holly green; Caribbean turquoise; Academy blue; Starlight blue; and Corinthian white. A two-tone effect was available by combining any standard color with Corinthian white (F-100 and F-250 Styleside Pickups only).

HISTORICAL: Total light truck production was 213,345 units for the model-year. This included all Rancheros, Couriers and Econolines, as well as P-100 parcel delivery trucks and P-350/P-400 chassis models.

1962 FORD

1962 Ford 1/2-Ton Falcon Ranchero Pickup (OCW)

FALCON RANCHERO PICKUP: The Ranchero featured a new squared-off grille with all vertical pieces. Parking lights were now integrated into the new front bumper. The hood was modified to give a hood scoop effect. The taillights were also revised. Other less visible changes for 1962 included: Increased brake lining; a pump-mounted in-line fuel filter; a clutch interlock that became optional later in the model year; a fully-aluminized muffler; improved carburetor and choke controls; white-lettered hubcaps; and one-inch narrower whitewall tires on vehicles so equipped. A three-speed manual transmission was standard.

1962 Ford 1/2-Ton Falcon Ranchero Pickup (OCW)

FALCON SEDAN DELIVERY: As before, this vehicle looked like a two-door Falcon wagon with blanked-out rear side windows. It even had the wagon's tailgate, with roll-down rear window. The tailgate opening was nearly four feet wide at the floor. The Sedan Delivery had a 76.2 cu. ft. load capacity with 87 in. of load space length. The driver's compartment featured a three-passenger seat covered with long-wearing vinyl in a brown or beige color scheme.

I.D. DATA: [Ranchero] VIN located on rating plate. First symbol indicates model year: 2=1962. Second symbol indicates assembly plant: A=Atlanta, Ga.; H=Lorain, Ohio; K=Kansas City, Kan.; R=San Jose, Calif.; S=Allen Park, Mich.; T=Metuchen, N.J. The third and fourth symbols indicate model: 27=Ranchero; 29=Sedan Delivery. The fifth symbol indicates engine: S=144 cid six; U=170 cid six. The last six symbols are the sequential production number.

Model	Body Type	Price	Weight	Prod. Total
Falcon — 1/2-Ton — 109.9 in. w.b. — Six				
66A	Pickup	1889	2348	20,842
78A	Sedan Delivery	2111	2463	1,568

ENGINE [Falcon Ranchero/Sedan Delivery]: Displacement: 144 cid. Six-cylinder. 85 hp at 4200 rpm. Bore & stroke: 3.50 in. x 2.50 in. Compression ratio: 8.7:1. One-barrel carburetor.

CHASSIS: Wheelbase: 109.5 in. Overall length: 189 in. Overall width: 70 in. Overall height: 54.5 in. GVW: 3,250 lbs. Tires: 6.50 x 13, four-ply.

POWERTRAIN OPTIONS: Fordomatic Drive. 101 hp 170 cid six-cylinder engine. Four-speed manual transmission.

CONVENIENCE OPTIONS: Whitewall tires. AM radio. Heater and defroster. Bright metal wheelcovers. Tinted windshield. Cigarette lighter. Backup lights. Two-speed electric windshield wipers. [Safety Package A] Includes: Padded instrument panel and sun visors. [Sedan Delivery Deluxe Package] Includes: Bright metal exterior moldings; taillamp ring ornament; white steering wheel with chrome horn ring; cigarette lighter; dome light door switch; sun visor on right side; armrests; and deluxe brown nylon-and-vinyl or red and white all-vinyl upholstery. [Ranchero Deluxe Trim Package] Includes: Bright metal molding around box and cab back; bright metal tailight trim rings; bright metal door window moldings; white steering wheel with horn ring; cigarette lighter; dome light door switch; and black-and-white or red-and-white vinyl upholstery.

1962 Ford 1/2-Ton Falcon Econoline Pickup (OCW)

ECONOLINE PICKUP: Apparently, Ford didn't want to mess with a good thing. Econoline styling was carried over to the new model year without major change. However, Econolines now had larger wheel bearings. Standard features included: Vinyl upholstery; three-speed manual transmission; and an insulated engine cover.

1962 Ford 1/2-Ton Falcon Econoline Panel Van (JAG)

ECONOLINE VAN: Standard items on the 1962 Econoline Van included: Double side and rear doors; electric windshield wipers; outside rearview mirror; front and rear bumpers; dome light; single electric horn; turn signals; I-Beam front axle; direct-acting, telescopic shock absorbers front and rear; Soft-Action rear suspension with variable-rate; and semi-elliptic leaf springs.

I.D. DATA: [Econoline] VIN located on rating plate. First symbol indicates model year: 2=1962. Second symbol indicates assembly plant: (see F-100 I.D. data. The third and fourth symbols indicate model: 10=Econoline. The fifth symbol indicates engine: S=144 cid six. The last six symbols are the sequential production number.

Model	Body Type	Price	Weight	Prod. Total
E-100 Econoline — 1/2-Ton — 90 in. w.b. — Six				
E-103	Custom Pickup	1881	2533	8140
E-104	Econovan	2070	2568	50,645

ENGINE [Econoline]: Displacement: 144 cid. Six-cylinder. 85 hp at 4200 rpm. Bore & stroke: 3.50 in. x 2.50 in. Compression ratio: 8.7:1. One-barrel carburetor.

CHASSIS: Wheelbase: 90 in. Overall length: 168.4 in. Overall width: 65 in. GVW: 3,300 lbs. Tires: 7.00 x 13.

POWERTRAIN OPTIONS: None.

CONVENIENCE OPTIONS: AM radio. Fresh air heater/defroster. Auxiliary step. Padded instrument panels and sun visors. Rear door glass in Van. Flip-up or stationary seat in Van. Armrests. Right-hand sun visor. Cigar lighter. Horn ring. ICC four lamp flasher. Dual horns. Left-hand door lock. Tinted windshield. Bright metal wheelcovers. Front and rear chrome bumpers. Cargo area domelight in Van. Positive crankcase ventilation. Tires: 6.50 x 13-4PR whitewall; 7.00 x 13-6 ply-rated blackwall or whitewall. [Custom Equipment Package] Includes: (Van) Right-hand air duct; armrests; cigar lighter; cargo area dome light; driver's side door lock; windows in rear doors; chrome horn ring; dual electric horns; bright metal hubcaps; foam seat padding; passenger stationary seat; twill stripe woven plastic seat upholstery; right-hand sun visor. (Pickup) Woven plastic upholstery; right-hand armrests; right-hand sun visor; cigar lighter; chrome horn ring; dual horns; cab rear wrap-around quarter windows; glove compartment door with cylinder lock; bright metal hubcaps; coat hook; front body interior insulation; foam padding in passenger seat cushion and back; left-hand side-mounted cargo doors; and 4,350 lbs. GVW package.

FALCON STATION BUS: The station bus was now considered part of the Falcon line. Standard equipment included: Vinyl upholstery; two-speed electric windshield wipers; foam-cushioned adjustable driver's seat; front passenger seat; front armrests; ashtray; dual horns and dome lights; left-hand air inlet; left-hand sun visor; inside rearview mirror; and retractable side step.

1962 Ford 1/2-Ton Falcon Econoline Club Wagon (OCW)

FALCON CLUB WAGON: Standard features on the Club Wagon included: Woven plastic upholstery; full-length floor mat and headlining; foam-cushioned front passenger seat; painted left-hand outside mirror; windshield washers; cigarette lighter; dual sun visors; four coat hooks; and right-hand air inlet.

FALCON DELUXE CLUB WAGON: This was the top-of-the-line model. It featured (in addition to, or in place of, items on the base Club Wagon): A padded instrument panel; all-vinyl pleated upholstery; Deluxe steering wheel; padded sun visors; bright left-hand outside mirror; bright-finished bumpers; brightside moldings; bright hubcaps; and a spare tire cover.

I.D. DATA: [Falcon-Econoline] VIN located on rating plate. First symbol indicates model year: 2=1962. Second symbol indicates assembly plant: (see F-100 I.D. data). The third and fourth symbols indicate model: 11=Station Bus; 12=Club Wagon; 13=Deluxe Club Wagon. The fifth symbol indicates engine: S=144 cid six. The last six symbols are the sequential production number.

Model	Body Type	Price	Weight	Prod. Total
Club Wagon — 1/2-Ton — 90 in. w.b. — Six				
E-11	Station Bus	2287	2712	Note 1
E-12	Club Wagon	2436	2770	Note 1
E-13	Club Wagon [Deluxe]	2673	2796	Note 1

NOTE 1: Ford Falcon production records list the Model 89B Business Club Wagon with a production total of 18,153 units. There are no separate break-outs for the three models/trim levels.

ENGINE [Falcon]: Station Bus and Club Wagon, same as Econoline. Deluxe Club Wagon: Displacement: 170 cid. Six-cylinder. 101 hp at 4400 rpm. Bore & Stroke: 3.50 in. x 2.94 in. Compression Ratio: 8.7:1, one-barrel carburetor.

CHASSIS: Wheelbase: 90 in. Overall length: 168.3 in. Overall width: 75 in. Overall height: 76.9 in. Tires: 6.50 x 13.

POWERTRAIN OPTIONS: 170 cid six-cylinder.

CONVENIENCE OPTIONS: Armrests for second/third seats. Cigarette lighter. Full wheelcovers. Gas-fired recirculating heater. Non-glare inside mirror. Outside rearview mirrors. Padded instrument panel and sun visors. AM radio. Second or second and third row three-passenger seats. Seat belts. Spare tire cover lock. Spotlight. Right-hand sun visor. Tinted windshield. Windshield washers.

E ONE-PIECE CAB-BODY DESIGN gives Ford pickups extra capacity, extra strength. Heavy duty way for heavy going all day. Car-like ride, too!

E HERE!

1962 Ford 1/2-Ton F-100 Styleside Pickup Cab (JAG)

F-100 PICKUP: The F-100 received a very minor facelift for 1962. The Ford name was now printed in smaller block letters just above the grille frame. A thin horizontal bar, divided at the center by a thin vertical bar, ran between the two larger ones. The hubcaps were also changed to solid Argent silver finish. Buyers could choose from 6.5 ft. and 8 ft. Flareside and Styleside models. Two versions of the Styleside were offered, the intergal Unit-body type, introduced in 1961, and the two-piece body type used on 1957-1960 models. Unit-body Stylelines were not available with four-wheel drive. Standard equipment included: Left-hand sun visor; dome light; oil filter; painted front bumper; electric windshield wipers; dispatch box; and rearview mirror.

2 FORD STYLESIDE PICKUPS offer a wide nge of heavy-duty options to fit your job: 5 ansmissions, Six or V-8 power, 4-wheel drive.

1962 Ford 1/2-Ton F-100 Styleside Pickup Cab (JAG)

F-100 PLATFORM/STAKE: Except for the minor styling changes noted on the Pickup, the 1962 F-100 platform/stake was basically the same as last year's model. Its sideboards and stakes were made of wood. Bolted steel plates held sideboards firmly together at top, yet permitted quick, easy removal of stake sections. Body sills were protected by steel end caps.

I.D. DATA [F-100]: VIN located on rating plate. The first three symbols indicated series: F10=F-100 two-wheel drive; F-11=F-100 four-wheel drive. The fourth symbol indicates engine: J=223 cid six; C=292 cid medium-duty V-8; D=292 cid heavy-duty V-8. The fifth symbol indicates assembly plant: D=Dallas, Texas; E=Mahwah, N.J.; G=Chicago, Ill.; H=Lorain, Ohio; K=Kansas City, Kan.; N=Norfolk, Va.; P=Twin Cities, Minn.; R=San Jose, Calif.; S=Allen Park, Mich.; U=Louisville, Ken. The last six symbols indicate the sequential production number.

Model	Body Type	Price	Weight	Prod. Total
F-100 — 1/2-Ton — 114 in. w.b. — Six				
80	Platform	—	3142	Note 1
81	Chassis & Cab	1864	2827	Note 1
83	Flareside	1979	3194	Note 1
83	Unit-body Styleside	1995	3244	Note 1
83	Styleside	2006	—	Note 1
84	Chassis	1610	2319	Note 1
86	Stake	2070	3267	Note 1
F-100 — 1/2-Ton — 122 in. w.b. — Six				
81	Chassis & Cab	1901	2939	Note 1
83	Flareside	2015	3384	Note 1
83	Unit-body Styleside	2031	3409	Note 1
83	Styleside	2042	—	Note 1

* Add $650 for 4x4.

NOTE 1: Ford records show the following F-100 production break-outs: [Chassis & Cowl] 16; [Chassis & Windshield] 11; [Chassis & Cab] 9,456; [Unit-body Pickup] 68,983; [Platform & Rack] 175; [Flareside Pickup] 29,934; and [Styleside Pickup] 24,610.

ENGINE [F-100]: Displacement: 223 cid. Six-cylinder. 135 hp at 4000 rpm. Bore & stroke: 3.62 in. x 3.60 in. Compression ratio: 8.4:1. One-barrel carburetor.

F-250 PICKUP: Three styles of F-250 pickups were offered in 1962: Flareside, Unit-body Styleside and two-piece Styleside. Four-wheel drive was available at extra cost.

F-350 PLATFORM/STAKE: The F-350 Stake had a load space 90 in. long, 74 in. wide and 28.3 in. to the top of the racks. The Platform had a load space 93.4 in. long and 79.3 in. wide. Steel skid strips protected the floor and made it easier to slide cargo in or out. The sideboards and stakes were made of straight-grained wood. An all-steel rub rail protected the body.

I.D. DATA [F-250]: Same as F-100, except first three symbols were: [4x2] F25; [4x4] F26.

Model	Body Type	Price	Weight	Prod. Total
F-250 — 3/4-Ton — 122 in. w.b. — Six				
80	Platform	3409	—	—
81	Chassis & Cab	2005	3069	—
83	Flareside	2120	3494	—
83	Unit-body Styleside	2149	3579	—
83	Styleside	2134	3499	—
84	Chassis	1741	2561	—
86	Stake	2211	3594	—

* Add $675 for 4x4.

NOTE 1: Ford records show the following F-250 production break-outs: [Chassis & Cowl] 94; [Chassis & Windshield] 130; [Chassis & Cab] 4,483; [Unit-body Styleside Pickup] 10,703; [Platform & Rack] 867; [Flareside Pickup] 7,247 and [Styleside Pickup] 6,002.

ENGINE [F-250]: See F-100.

F-350 PICKUP: The rear axle capacity of the husky F-350 pickup was more than double that of the F-100. It also had a much roomier cargo area. The F-350 was available with 9 ft. Flareside and Styleside boxes. Four-speed manual transmission was standard.

F-350 PLATFORM/STAKE: The F-350 Platform/Stake had a 9 ft. body with steel stakes. Body sills were protected by steel end caps. Heavy-gauge steel stake pockets were set flush with the floor, which had steel skid strips. The spare tire carrier was located under the frame. A four-speed manual transmission was standard.

I.D. DATA [F-350]: Same as F-100, except first three symbols were F35.

Model	Body Type	Price	Weight	Prod. Total
F-350 — 1-Ton — 132 in. w.b. — Six				
80	Platform	—	4017	—
81	Chassis & Cab	2171	3357	—
83	Flareside	2305	3849	—
83	Styleside	2321	3849	—
84	Chassis	1906	2849	—
86	Stake	2419	4317	—

NOTE 1: Ford records show the following F-350 production break-outs: [Chassis & Cowl] 794; [Chassis & Windshield] 102; [Chassis & Cab] 12,483; [Platform & Rack] 4,229; [Flareside Pickup] 1,216; and [Styleside Pickup] 1,503.

ENGINE [F-350]: See F-100.

CHASSIS: Wheelbase: [F-100] 114 in.; [F-100/F-250] 122 in.; [F-350] 132 in.; [4x4] 120 in. GVW: [F-100] 4,000-5,000 lbs.; 5,600 4x4; [F-250] 4,900-7,400 lbs.; [F-350] 7,600-9,600 lbs. Tires: [F-100] 6.70 x 15, four-ply; [F-250] 6.50 x16, six-ply; [F-350] 8 x 17.5, six-ply.

POWERTRAIN OPTIONS: Transmissions: [F-100] Three-speed with overdrive; [F-100/F-250] Medium-duty three-speed; [F-350] Heavy-duty three-speed; [F-100/F-250/4x4] Four-speed manual; [F-100] Fordomatic; [F-250/F-350] Heavy-duty Cruise-O-Matic transmissions. 160 hp 292 cid V-8.

CONVENIENCE OPTIONS: Four-wheel drive for F-100/F-250 Flaresides. 3,500 lbs. capacity rear axle for F-250 with 4x4. Radio. Left-hand armrest. Right-hand armrest. Painted rear bumper. Chrome front and rear bumpers on Stylesides. Fresh air heater. Recirculating heater. Laminated glass. Side-mount spare wheel carrier. Heavy-duty clutch for F-100/F-250. Tinted windshield. Left and/or right outside rearview mirrors. Extra-cooling radiator. Heavy-duty front springs for F-100/F-250. Heavy-duty two-stage rear springs for F-100/F-250. Heavy-duty rear springs for F-100/F-250. Larger tires. White sidewall tires. Woven plastic trim for standard cab. Turn signals. Windshield washer. Rear wrap around window for Styleside. Right-hand sun visor. [Custom Cab package] Includes: Woven plastic upholstery with vinyl bolsters and vinyl facings; chrome-trimmed instrument cluster; white steering wheel with chrome horn ring; foam rubber in seat; cigar lighter; left-hand armrest; right-hand sun visor; insulation on cowl wall in F-350 cab (standard in F-100/F-250); bright metal grille and headlight assembly; bright metal windshield reveal molding; matched locks on both doors; two-tone interior; and coat hook.

1962 Ford 1/2-Ton Falcon Econoline Pickup (OCW)

HISTORICAL: Introduced: Fall 1961. Model-year production: [Light-duty total] 267,878 including P series Parcel Vans as follows: [P-100] 227 units; [P-200] 2,269 units and [P-400] 1,149 units. This total does not include the 18,153 Falcon Business Club Wagons, which Ford lumped-in with passenger cars. Innovations: New grille with Ford name above it. Tapered seat spark plugs introduced. Ford adopted air-cooled ignition contact points for trucks. The design of multiple electrical connectors was simplified. Over 600 different truck-model variations were available this year.

1963 FORD

1963 Ford 1/2-Ton Falcon Ranchero Pickup (OCW)

FALCON RANCHERO PICKUP: The most noticeable change for 1963 was the Ranchero's new convex horizontal grid grille. The taillights were also revised. The parking lights had amber lenses. The Ford name was printed in black on the hubcaps. Other new features included: Self-adjusting brakes; an aluminized tailpipe; electric windshield wipers; hydraulic valve lifters for the six; a fully-synchronized three-speed manual transmission; and a larger front stabilizer strut. As before, the 6 ft. long, 4.5 ft. wide and 15.5 in. deep pickup box provided a total of 31.5 cu. ft. of usable load space. The integral cab and pickup box were made of heavy-gauge steel. The spare tire was still located behind the seat for easy roll-out accessibility. The upholstery had a Western motif with a steer's head pattern imprinted on beige vinyl with lighter beige vinyl bolsters and seat facings.

1963 Ford 1/2-Ton Falcon Ranchero Pickup (OCW)

FALCON SEDAN DELIVERY: According to sales literature, the 1963 Falcon Sedan Delivery was designed to haul small loads which required protection from the weather. Its seven-foot floor was constructed of steel and weather-sealed plywood with longitudinal steel strips to provide easier loading. The tailgate could be opened with a single center latch and its rear window could be manually lowered. Standard equipment included: Bright metal drip moldings; dome light; spare tire and wheel; left side sun visor; dispatch box; ashtray; Double-Grip door locks; Lifeguard steering wheel; and dual single-speed electric windshield wipers.

I.D. DATA: [Ranchero/Sedan Delivery] VIN located on rating plate. First symbol indicates model year: 3=1963. Second symbol indicates assembly plant: A=Atlanta, Ga.; H=Lorain, Ohio; J=Los Angeles, Calif.; R=San Jose, Calif.; S=Allen Park, Mich.; T=Metuchen, N.J. The third and fourth symbols indicate model: 27=Ranchero; 29=Sedan Delivery. The fifth symbol indicates engine: S=144 cid six; U=170 cid six; F=260 cid V-8. The last six symbols are the sequential production number. Body codes were: 66A=Ranchero; 66B=Deluxe Ranchero; 78A=Sedan Delivery; 78B=Deluxe Sedan Delivery.

Model	Body Type	Price	Weight	Prod. Total
Falcon — 1/2-Ton — 109.5 in. w.b. — Six				
27	Pickup	1898	2348	18,533*
29	Sedan Delivery	2111	2463	1038

NOTE 1: A total of 6,315 of the Pickups were equipped with the Deluxe option.
NOTE 2: A total of 113 Sedan Deliveries were equipped with the Deluxe option.
ENGINE [Falcon Ranchero/Sedan Delivery]: Displacement: 144 cid. Six-cylinder. 85 hp at 4200 rpm. Bore & stroke: 3.50 x 2.50 in. Compression ratio: 8.7:1. One-barrel carburetor.
CHASSIS: Wheelbase: 109.5 in. Overall length: 189 in. Overall width: 70 in. Overall height: 54.5 in. Payload Capacity: 800 lbs. Tires: 6.50 x 13-4 ply-rated on 13x4-1/2 J safety-type wheels.
POWERTRAIN OPTIONS: 101 hp 170 cid six-cylinder. 164 hp 260 cid V-8. Four-speed manual or Fordomatic transmissions.
NOTE: The V-8 was installed in mid-model year. Vehicles so-equipped had 7.00 x 13 tires, a larger rear axle and special under body reinforcements.
CONVENIENCE OPTIONS: Power steering, with V-8 only. Heavy-duty battery. Whitewall tires. 6.50 x 13 6 ply-rated tires. Heater and defroster. Air-conditioner. Push-button radio and front-mounted antenna. Seat belts. Power-operated tailgate window on Sedan Delivery. Bright metal wheelcovers. Tinted glass. Windshield washers. Two-speed electric windshield wipers. Cigarette lighter. Backup lights. [Safety Package A] Includes: Padded instrument panel and sun visors. [Deluxe Trim Package] Includes: (Sedan Delivery) Bright metal moldings on door window frames and tailgate window opening; armrests; right-hand sun visor. (Ranchero): Bright metal moldings around top of box and cab back, plus frames on door window. (Both): A black or red steering wheel with horn ring; cigarette lighter; dome light door switch; and black or red vinyl upholstery.
NOTE: Solid colors available in 1963 were: Raven black; Rangoon red; Viking blue; Oxford blue; Silver moss; Ming green; Champagne; Glacier blue; Heritage burgundy; Sandshell beige; and Corinthian white. Optional two-tone combinations were: Glacier blue and Viking blue, black and champagne, and Corinthian white with any solid color.
ECONOLINE PICKUP: Although the styling was untouched, changes were made to the Econoline for 1963. Among them were gray-toned upholstery and five-leaf springs. The standard features included: Vinyl upholstery; three-speed manual transmission; insulated engine cover; and amber parking lights lenses.
ECONOLINE VAN: Standard items on the 1963 Econoline Van included: Double side and rear doors; electric windshield wipers; outside rearview mirror; front and rear bumpers; dome light; single electric horn; turn signals; I-Beam front axle; direct-acting telescopic shock absorbers front and rear; and Soft-Action rear suspension with variable-rate, semi-elliptic leaf springs.
I.D. DATA: [Econoline] VIN located on rating plate. First symbol indicates model year: 3=1963. Second symbol indicates assembly plant: (See F-100 I.D. data.) The third and fourth symbols indicate model: 10=Econoline. The fifth symbol indicates engine: S=144 cid; U=170 cid six. The last six symbols are the sequential production number.

Model	Body Type	Price	Weight	Prod. Total
Econoline — 1/2-Ton — 90 in. w.b. — Six				
E103	Pickup	1890	2533	Note 1
E104	Van	2069	2568	Note 1

NOTE 1: Ford records show Econoline production break-outs as follows: [Standard Pickup] 10,372; [Custom Pickup] 1,022. [Standard Van] 47,119; [Custom Van] 1,501. [Stand Display Van] 3,359; [Custom Display Van] 98; [Standard Window Van] 5,376; [Custom Window Van] 332; and [Standard Cargo Van] 1,153; [Custom Cargo Van] 88.
ENGINE [Econoline]: Displacement: 144 cid. OHV. Six-cylinder. 85 hp at 4200 rpm. Bore & stroke: 3.50 in. x 2.50 in. Compression ratio: 8.7:1. One-barrel carburetor.
CHASSIS: Wheelbase: 90 in. Overall Length: 168.4 in. Overall Width: 65 in. GVW: 3,300 lbs. Tires: 6.50 x 13.
POWERTRAIN OPTIONS: 170 cis six.
CONVENIENCE OPTIONS: AM radio. Fresh air heater/defroster. Auxiliary step. Padded instrument panels and sun visors. Rear door glass on vans. Flip or stationary seat in vans. armrests. Right-hand sun visor. Cigar lighter. Horn ring. ICC four lamp flasher. Dual horns. Left-hand door lock. Tinted windshield. Bright metal wheelcovers. Front and rear chrome bumpers. Cargo area domelight for vans. Positive crankcase ventilation. Tires: 6.50 x 13 in. 4 ply-rated whitewall. 7.00 x 13 in. 6 ply-rated blackwall or whitewall. [Custom Equipment Package] Includes: (Van) Right-hand air duct; armrests; cigar lighter; cargo area dome

light; driver's side door lock; windows in rear doors; chrome horn ring; dual electric horns; bright metal hubcaps; foam seat padding; passenger stationary seat; twill stripe woven plastic seat upholstery; and right-hand sun visor. (Pickup) Woven plastic upholstery. Right-hand air duct. Armrests. Right-hand sun visor. Cigar lighter. Chrome horn ring. Dual horns. Cab rear wrap-around quarter windows. Glove compartment door with cylinder lock. Bright metal hubcaps. Coat hook. Front interior insulation. Foam padding in passenger seat cushion and back. 1-Ton payload package. Left-hand side-mounted cargo doors. 4,350 lbs. GVW package.

1963 Ford 1/2-Ton Econoline Deluxe Eight-passenger Station Bus

FALCON STATION BUS: The unchanged station bus had a 204 cu. ft. load capacity. Standard equipment included: Gray vinyl upholstery; two-speed electric windshield wipers; foam-cushioned adjustable driver's seat; front passenger seat; front armrests; ashtray; dual horns and dome lights; left-hand air inlet; left-hand sun visor; inside rearview mirror; and retractable side step.

FALCON CLUB WAGON: Standard features on the Club Wagon included: Woven plastic upholstery; full-length floor mat and headlining; foam-cushioned front passenger seat; painted left-hand outside mirror; windshield washers; cigarette lighter; dual sun visors; four coat hooks; and right-hand air inlet.

FALCON DELUXE CLUB WAGON: This was the top-of-the-line model. It featured, in addition to or in place of items on the base Club Wagon: A padded instrument panel; all-vinyl pleated upholstery; Deluxe steering wheel; padded sun visors; bright left-hand outside mirror; bright finish bumpers; bright bodyside moldings; bright hubcaps; and a spare tire cover.

I.D. DATA [Falcon]: See 1963 Econoline I.D.

Model	Body Type	Price	Weight	Prod. Total
Econoline — 1/2-Ton — 90 in. w.b.				
E11	Station Bus	2287	2712	Note 1
E12	Club Wagon	2436	2770	Note 1
E13	Deluxe Club Wagon	2673	2796	Note 1

NOTE 1: Ford records show the following production break-outs: [Standard Station Bus] 10,332; [Custom Station Bus] 4,378; and [Club Wagon] 2,923.
ENGINE [Econoline]: Displacement: 144 cid. OHV. Six-cylinder. 85 hp at 4200 rpm. Bore & stroke: 3.50 in. x 2.50 in. Compression ratio: 8.7:1. One-barrel carburetor.
ENGINE: [Deluxe Club Wagon]: Displacement: 170 cid. Six-cylinder. 101 hp at 4400 rpm. Bore & Stroke: 3.50 x 2.94 in. Compression ratio: 8.7:1. One-barrel carburetor.
CHASSIS: Wheelbase: 90 in. Overall Length: 168.3 in. Overall Width: 75 in. Overall Height: 76.9 in. Tires: 6.50 x 13.
POWERTRAIN OPTIONS: 170 cid six.
CONVENIENCE OPTIONS: Armrests for second/third seats. Cigarette lighter. Full wheel-covers. Gas-fired recirculating heater. Non-glare inside mirror. Outside rearview mirrors. Padded instrument panel and sun visors. AM radio. Second or second and third row three-passenger seats. Seat belts. Spare tire cover lock. Spotlight. Right-hand sun visor. Tinted windshield. Windshield washers.

1963 Ford 1/2-Ton F-100 Styleside Custom Cab Pickup (CW)

F-100 PICKUP: According to sales literature, the new 1963 F-100 Pickup was built for rough loading and hard use. The copy said, "It's designed to keep going no matter what, to stay out of trouble and hold down your repair bills." Like big, 20-ton trucks, the F-100 had an I-beam front axle; parallel-rail frame; variable-rate rear springs; and a straddle-mounted rear axle drive pinion. A new grille with small, stacked horizontal pieces was the main styling change for the year. The pedals' position was now closer to the floor. A three-spoke steering wheel was used. Standard transmission was a new, fully-synchronized three-speed manual unit. There were locks on both doors. The seats had new synthetic foam cushions. Plus, there was a new 20 x 12 x 2-1/2 in. storage compartment with zippered vinyl cover for extra-cost. Buyers could choose from three body styles: Flareside with wood floor and runningboard between rear fender and back of cab; integral unit-body and Styleside box with steel floor; or two-piece cab-pickup with Styleside box.

1963 Ford 1/2-Ton F-100 Standard Styleside Pickup (CW)

F-100 PLATFORM/STAKE: The new F-100 Platform/Stake shared most of the same features as the pickup. Steel skid strips protected its floor. Heavy gauge steel stake pockets were set flush with the floor. Side boards and stakes were made of straight-grained wood. Body sills were protected by steel end caps.
I.D. DATA [F-100]: VIN located on rating plate. The first three symbols indicated series: F10=F-100 (4x2); F-11=F-100 (4x4). The fourth symbol indicates engine: J=223 cid six; C=292 cid medium-duty V-8; D=292 cid heavy-duty V-8; N=302 cid V-8 (midyear). The fifth symbol indicates assembly plant: D=Dallas, Texas; E=Mawhah, N.J.; G=Chicago; H=Lorain, Ohio; K=Kansas City, Kan.; N=Norfolk, Va.; P=Twin Cities, Minn.; R=San Jose, Calif.; S=Allen Park, Mich. The last six symbols indicate the sequential production number.

1963 Ford 1/2-Ton F-100 Styleside Custom Cab Pickup (JAG)

Model	Body Type	Price	Weight	Prod. Total
F-100 — 1/2-Ton — 114 in. w.b. — Six				
80	Platform	2052	3152	Note 1
81	Chassis & Cab	1888	2837	Note 1
83	Flareside	2002	3204	Note 1
83	Styleside	2030	3254	Note 1
83	Unit-body Styleside	2019	3254	Note 1
86	Stake	2094	3277	Note 1
F-100 — 1/2-Ton — 122 in. w.b. — Six				
83	Flareside	2038	3409	Note 1
83	Styleside	2066	3389	Note 1
83	Unit-body Styleside	2055	3417	Note 1

* Add $650 for 4x4 model F-110/F-111.
NOTE 1: Ford records show the following F-100 production breakouts: [Chassis & Cowl] 20; [Chassis & Windshield] 19; [Chassis & Cab] 6,686; [4x4 cab] 179; [Unit-body Pickup] 40,535; [Platform & Rack] 190; [Flareside cab-pickup] 35,963; [Styleside cab-pickup] 76,728; [4x4 Flareside cab-pickup] 967 and [4x4 Styleside cab-pickup] 2,809.
ENGINE [F-100]: Displacement: 223 cid. Six-cylinder. 135 hp at 4000 rpm. Bore & stroke: 3.62 in. x 3.60 in. Compression ratio: 8.4:1. One-barrel carburetor.
F-250 PICKUP: The 3/4-ton F-250 pickup came with most of the same features as the F-100. It was available in 8 ft. Flareside and Unit-body or two-piece Styleside versions. Four-wheel drive was an extra-cost option.
F-250 PLATFORM/STAKE: Like all light duty Ford trucks in 1963, the F-250 Platform/Stake had 22 lbs. of sound deadening insulation. That was about eight lbs. more than Chevrolet's extra-cost cab. Stake bed was 90 x 74 in. with 28.3 in. height to top of racks. An all-steel rub rail protected the Bolted steel plates held side boards firmly together at top, yet permitted quick, easy removal of stake sections.
I.D. DATA [F-250]: Same as F-100, except first three symbols are F25 (4x2) and F26 (4x4).

Model	Body Type	Price	Weight	Prod. Total
F-250 — 3/4-Ton — 122 in. w.b. — Six				
80	Platform	2206	3459	Note 1
81	Chassis & Cab	2042	3119	Note 1
83	Flareside	2157	3569	Note 1
83	Styleside	2183	3564	Note 1
83	Unit-body Styleside	2172	3590	Note 1
86	Stake	2247	3644	Note 1

* Add $680 for 4x4 models F-260/F-261/F-262.
NOTE 1: Ford records show the following F-250 production break-outs: [Chassis & Cowl] 63; [Chassis & Windshield] 72; [Chassis & Cab] 4,273; [4x4 Chassis & Cab] 348; [Unit-body Pickup] 5,456; [Platform] 795; [4x4 Platform] 89; [Flareside Pickup] 6,673; [Styleside Pickup] 14,159; [4x4 Flareside Pickup] 865; and [4x4 Styleside Pickup] 1,835.
ENGINE [F-250]: See F-100.

Standard Catalog of Light-Duty Trucks

F-350 PICKUP: The biggest Ford pickup in 1963 was the 1-ton F-350. It was available with a 9 ft. Flareside body and had wood floors and runningboards from rear fender to back of cab. It could also be had as a smooth-side two-piece Styleside. It came with a four-speed manual transmission as standard equipment.

F-350 PLATFORM/STAKE: The 9 ft. F-350 Platform/Stake was more than adequate to handle payloads too bulky or heavy for its F-100 or F-250 counterparts. It had steel stakes and an all-steel rub rail.

I.D. DATA [F-350]: Same as F-100, except first three symbols are F35.

Model	Body Type	Price	Weight	Prod. Total
80	Platform	2410	4147	Note 1
81	Chassis & Cab	2212	3487	Note 1
83	Pickup	2345	3989	Note 1
83	Pickup	2362	3977	Note 1
86	Stake	2459	4427	Note 1

NOTE 1: Ford records show the following F-350 production break-outs: [Chassis & Cowl] 676; [Chassis & Windshield] 120; [Chassis & Cab] 15,127; [Platform] 3,808; [Flareside] 1,240; and [Styleside] 1,470.

ENGINE [F-350]: See F-100.

CHASSIS: Wheelbase: [F-100] 114 in.; [F-100/F-250] 122 in.; [F-350] 132 in.; [4x4] 120 in. GVW: [F-100]: 4,000-5,000 lbs.; [F-110] 5,600 lbs.; [F-250]: 4,900-7,400 lbs. [F-350]: 7,600-9,600 lbs. Tires: [F-100] 6.70 x 15; [F-100] 6.50 x 16, six-ply; [F-350] 8 x 17.5, six-ply.

POWERTRAIN OPTIONS: Transmissions: [F-100] Three-speed with overdrive; [F-100/F-250] Medium-duty three-speed; [F-350] Heavy-duty three-speed; [F-100/F-250/4x4] Four-speed; [F-100] Fordomatic; [F-250/F-350] Heavy-duty Cruise-O-Matic. Engine: 160 hp 292 cid V-8.

CONVENIENCE OPTIONS: Four-wheel drive for F-100/F-250 Flaresides. 3,500 lbs. capacity rear axle (F-250 4x4s). Radio. Left-hand armrest. Right-hand armrest. Heater-defroster. 42- and 60-amp. alternators. Painted rear bumper. Chrome front and rear bumpers (Styleside). Side-mount spare wheel carrier. Heavy-duty clutch (F-100/F-250). Tinted windshield. Left and/or right outside rearview mirrors. Extra-cooling radiator. Heavy-duty front springs (F-100/F-250). Heavy-duty two-stage rear springs (F-100/F-250). Heavy-duty rear springs (F-100/F-250). Larger tires. Whitewall tires. Woven plastic trim for standard cab. Turn signals. Windshield washer. Rear wraparound window (Styleside). Right-hand sun visor. [Custom Cab] Includes: Woven plastic upholstery with bolster and vinyl facings; chrome trimmed instrument cluster; white steering wheel with chrome horn ring; foam rubber in seat (five-inch in cushion); cigar lighter; left-hand armrest; right-hand sun visor; insulation on cowl wall in F-350 cab (standard in F-100/F-250); bright metal grille and headlight assembly; bright metal windshield reveal molding; matched locks on both doors; and two-tone interior and coat hook.

1963 Ford 1/2-Ton Econoline Pickup Custom Wheels (Dennis Telle)

HISTORICAL: Introduced: Fall 1961. Model Year Production: [All light-duty trucks] 315,274. This total includes: [P-100 chassis] 421; [P-350 Chassis & Windshield] 461; [P-350 stripped chassis] 1,791; [P-400 stripped chassis] 1,234 and [P-400 Chassis & Windshield] 207 trucks in the parcel delivery series. This total does not include Falcon Station Buses. Innovations: Redesigned Pickup grille. Diesel engine introduced for some larger F series trucks.

1964 FORD

1964 Ford 1/2-Ton Falcon Ranchero Pickup (OCW)

FALCON RANCHERO PICKUP: The Ranchero was restyled for 1964. Although it bore a strong resemblance to the previous model, it was different. This truck was longer, wider and heftier. It had new bumpers, a new hood, bodyside sculpturing and trim, taillights and a forward slanting grille. The interior had a new dash and shallow-dish, color-keyed steering wheel. The Ranchero standard cab's vinyl upholstery had a steer's head imprint on the seat cushion and seatback with color-matching bolsters around the sides, top and bottom. The improved chassis had larger rear springs and better front suspension lower arm bushings. The 6 x 4.5 ft. x 14.5 in. deep box provided 30 cu. ft. of usable load space. The tailgate was only 28 in. above the ground. Side loading height was just 39.5 in. Standard equipment included: Chrome front and rear bumpers; dual electric windshield wipers; dual electric horns; bright metal windshield reveal moldings, taillight trim rings and hubcaps; armrests; dome light; rearview mirror; sun visors; dispatch box; ashtray; spare tire; and spare wheel.

FALCON SEDAN DELIVERY: The Falcon Sedan Delivery shared styling and mechanical features with the Ranchero. The tailgate opening was 45.5 in. wide and 27 in. high. It had a 78 cu. ft. cargo area. Its seven-foot long floor was made of steel and weather-sealed plywood with longitudinal steel strips. All main underbody structural members were heavily galvanized for protection against rust and corrosion. Standard items included: Bright metal drip moldings; left side sun visor and most features found on the Ranchero.

I.D. DATA: [Ranchero/Sedan Delivery] VIN located on rating plate. First symbol indicates model year: 4=1964. Second symbol indicates assembly plant: A=Atlanta, Ga.; H=Lorain, Ohio; K=Kansas City, Kan.; R=San Jose, Calif.; S=Allen Park, Mich.; T=Metuchen, N.J. The third and fourth symbols indicate model: 27=Ranchero; 29=Sedan Delivery. The fifth symbol indicates engine: S=144 cid six; U=170 cid six; T=200 cid six; F=260 cid V-8. The last six symbols are the sequential production number. Body codes were: 66A=Ranchero; 66B=Deluxe Ranchero; 78A=Sedan Delivery; 78B=Deluxe Sedan Delivery.

Model	Body Type	Price	Weight	Prod. Total
Falcon — 1/2-Ton — 109.5 in. w.b. — Six				
66A	Pickup	2047	2748	9,916
78A	Sedan Delivery	2260	2858	776

ADDITIONAL PRODUCTION: In addition to the production figures given above, for the standard models, Ford records show the following production break-outs: [Model 66B Deluxe Ranchero] 7,165; [Model 66H Deluxe Ranchero with bucket seats] 235; and [Model 78B Deluxe Sedan Delivery] 98. A total of 7,400 Rancheros had the Deluxe package. Of these, 235 were equipped with bucket seats.

ENGINE [Falcon Ranchero/Sedan Delivery]: Displacement: 144 cid. OHV Six. 85 hp at 4200 rpm. Bore & stroke: 3.50 in. x 2.50 in. Compression ratio: 8.7:1. One-barrel carburetor.

CHASSIS: Wheelbase: 109.5 in. Overall length: 189.5 in. Overall width: 71.6 in. GVW: 3,340 lbs. Tires: [Six-cylinder] 6.50 x 13 6 ply-rated; [V-8] 7.00 x 13 4 ply-rated.

POWERTRAIN OPTIONS: Transmission: Four-speed manual or Fordomatic transmissions. Engines: 101 hp 170 cid six-cylinder. 116 hp 200 cid six-cylinder with automatic only. 164 hp 260 cid V-8.

CONVENIENCE OPTIONS: Power steering. Heavy-duty battery. Heater and defroster. Air-conditioner. Push-button radio and front-mounted antenna. White sidewall tires. Bright metal wheelcovers. Tinted glass. Two-speed electric windshield wipers with windshield washers. Bucket seats. Cigarette lighter. Backup lights. Bodyside moldings (Ranchero). Safety belts. Power-operated tailgate window for Sedan Delivery. [Safety Package] Includes: padded instrument panel and sun visors. [Deluxe Trim Package] Includes: (Sedan Delivery) Bright metal moldings on door window frames and tailgate window opening, armrests and right-hand sun visor. (Ranchero) Bright metal moldings around top of box and cab back, plus frames on door windows; (Both models) A black or red steering wheel with horn ring, cigarette lighter, dome light door switch and black or red pleated vinyl upholstery.

NOTE: Solid colors available on the 1964 Ranchero/Sedan Delivery were: Raven black; Rangoon red; Guardsman blue; Skylight blue; Silversmoke gray; Dynasty green; Vintage burgundy; Chantilly beige; and Wimbledon white. Optional two-tone combinations were: Guardsman blue with Skylight blue; Skylight blue with Guardsman blue; or Wimbledon white for upper body color with any of the above colors for the lower part of the body.

ECONOLINE PICKUP: You'd have to look inside to find much difference from last year's model. Among the new features were: Cab headliner; color-keyed upholstery; and a locking glove compartment. Other standard features included: A spare tire; vinyl upholstery; three-speed manual transmission; insulated engine cover; left-hand sun visor; and single horn.

ECONOLINE VAN: An 8.5 in. heavy-duty clutch and self-adjusting brakes were a couple standard items on the new Econoline Van. Other standard features were: Color-keyed vinyl upholstery; left-hand fresh air inlet; dual electric windshield wipers; left-hand sun visor; painted front and rear bumpers and hubcaps; dome lights; ashtray; matched locks for all doors; coat hook; headlining in driver's area; and armrests.

ECONOLINE PANEL VAN: This new model was basically just an Econoline van without side cargo doors.

I.D. DATA: [Econoline] VIN located on rating plate. First symbol indicates model year: 4=1964. Second symbol indicates assembly plant: (See F-100 I.D. data.) The third and fourth symbols indicate model: 10=Econoline. The fifth symbol indicates engine: S=144 cid six; U=170 cid Six. The last six symbols are the sequential production number. Model codes are in first column of chart below.

Model	Body Type	Price	Weight	Prod. Total
Econoline — 1/2-Ton — 109.5 in. w.b. — Six				
87A	Standard Pickup	1885	2530	4196
89A	Standard Van	2091	2565	44,059
89A	Standard Panel Van	2037	2565	1770

ADDITIONAL PRODUCTION: In addition to the figures given above, Ford records show the following production break-outs: [87B Custom Econoline Pickup] 988; [89E Standard Display Van] 3,621; [89F Standard Window Van] 6,289; [89G Standard Cargo Van] 1,495; [89A Custom Panel Van] 90; [89A Custom Regular Van] 2,741; [89E Custom Display Van] 138; [89F Custom Window Van] 812; and [89G Custom Cargo Van] 215.

ENGINE [Econoline]: Displacement: 144 cid. OHV six-cylinder. 85 hp at 4200 rpm. Bore & stroke: 3.50 x 2.50 in. Compression Ratio: 8.7:1. One-barrel carburetor.

CHASSIS: Wheelbase: 90 in. Overall Length: 168.4 in. Overall Width: 65 in. GVW: 3,600-4,850 lbs. Tires: 6.50 x 13.

POWERTRAIN OPTIONS: Engine: 170 cid six-cylinder. Transmission: Four-speed manual or three-speed automatic.

CONVENIENCE OPTIONS: AM radio. Fresh air heater/defroster. Padded instrument panel and sun visors. Flip-Swing or stationary passenger seat. Seat belts. Interior rearview mirror. ICC emergency lamp flasher. Tinted windshield. Windshield washer. Two-speed electric windshield wipers. Front and rear chrome bumpers. Whitewall tires. Display Van Option: Fixed windows in the right side of the cargo area. Window Van Option: Fixed windows all around. [Custom Package] Includes: Color-keyed woven plastic upholstery; right-hand fresh-air inlet and sun visor; cigar lighter; dual horns; bright metal hubcaps; chrome horn ring; cowl-wall trim panels; insulation on cowl wall; headlining on cargo area; windows in rear doors; foam padding and optional passenger seat; (Custom Pickup also has woven plastic upholstery; right-hand air duct; armrests; right-hand sun visor; cigar lighter; chrome

horn ring; dual horns; Cab rear wraparound quarter windows; glove compartment door with cylinder lock; bright metal hubcaps; coat hook; front body interior insulation; and foam padding in passenger seat cushion and back.) [1-ton Payload Package] Includes: Left-hand side-mounted cargo doors and 4,350 or 4,850 lbs. GVW Packages.

NOTE: Econoline color choices for 1964 were: Rangoon red; Bengal tan; Raven black; Pagoda green; Holly green; Caribbean turquoise; Academy blue; Skylight blue; Wimbledon white; Chrome yellow; and Pure white. A two-tone effect was available with Wimbledon white combined with any standard color except Chrome yellow or Pure white.

FALCON STATION BUS: The unchanged station bus had a 204 cu. ft. load capacity. Standard equipment included: Gray vinyl upholstery; two-speed electric windshield wipers; foam-cushioned adjustable driver's seat; front passenger seat; front armrests; ashtray; dual horns and dome lights; left-hand air inlet and sun visor; inside rearview mirror; and retractable side step.

FALCON CLUB WAGON: Standard features on the Club Wagon included: Woven plastic upholstery; full-length floor mat and headlining; foam-cushioned front passenger seat; painted left-hand outside mirror; windshield washers; cigarette lighter; dual sun visors; four coat hooks and right-hand air inlet.

1964 Ford 1/2-Ton Falcon Deluxe Club Wagon (JAG)

FALCON DELUXE CLUB WAGON: This was the top-of-the-line model. It featured (in addition to, or in place of, items on the base Club Wagon), a padded instrument panel; all-vinyl pleated upholstery; Deluxe steering wheel; padded sun visors; bright left-hand outside mirror; bright-finish bumpers; bodyside moldings and hubcaps; and a spare tire cover.

I.D. DATA [Falcon]: See 1964 Econoline I.D.

Model	Body Type	Price	Weight	Prod. Total
Club Wagon — 1/2-Ton — 90 in. w.b. — Six				
89B	Standard Station Bus	2318	2712	9249
89D	Club Wagon	2467	2770	Note 1
89D	Deluxe Club Wagon	2684	2796	Note 1

NOTE 1: Total production of both Club Wagon models was 2,687. Also listed in Ford records is the production of 4,729 Model 89C Custom Station Buses.

ENGINE [Station Bus/Club Wagon]: Displacement: 144 cid. OHV six-cylinder. 85 hp at 4200 rpm. Bore & stroke: 3.50 x 2.50 in. Compression Ratio: 8.7:1. One-barrel carburetor.

ENGINE [Deluxe Club Wagon]: Displacement: 170 cid. OHV six-cylinder. 101 hp at 4400 rpm. Bore & stroke: 3.50 in. x 2.94 in. Compression ratio: 8.7:1. One-barrel carburetor.

CHASSIS: Wheelbase: 90 in. Overall Length: 168.3 in. Overall Width: 75 in. Overall Height: 76.9 in. Tires: 6.50 x 13 in.

POWERTRAIN OPTIONS: Engine: 170 cid Six-cylinder.

CONVENIENCE OPTIONS: Armrests (for second and third seats). Cigarette lighter. Full wheelcovers. Gas-fired recirculating heater. Non-glare inside mirror. Outside rearview mirrors. Padded instrument panel and sun visor. AM radio. Second or second and third row three-passenger seats. Seat belts. Spare tire cover lock. Spotlight. Right-hand sun visor. Tinted windshield. Windshield washers.

1964 Ford 1/2-Ton F-100 Styleside Custom Cab Pickup (OCW)

F-100 PICKUP: Ford light-duty trucks received a new grille for 1964. It featured eight open rectangular stampings. Also, the Ford block letters above the grille were spaced a bit further apart. The cab roof was an inch higher. The three-spoke steering wheel was color-keyed. More padding was used in the seatback. And four more pounds of insulation were added. Buyers could choose from the wood floor Flareside or steel floor two-piece Styleside. The latter had double-walled pickup box construction and a single, center-latched tailgate that could easily be operated with one hand. The Flareside and Styleside were offered in 6.5 ft. and 8 ft. versions. The new 128 in. wheelbase Styleside was designed in particular for pickup camper applications.

F-100 PLATFORM/STAKE: These were handy for bulky, odd-shaped cargo. The platform was made of hardwood interlocked with steel skid strips. Body sills were protected by steel end caps. Side boards and stakes were made of wood. Styling and cab features were the same as those found on F-100 Pickups.

I.D. DATA [F-100]: VIN located on rating plate. The first three symbols indicated series: F10=F-100 (4x2); F-11=F-100 (4x4). The fourth symbol indicates engine: J=223 cid six; C=292 cid medium-duty V-8; D=292 cid heavy-duty V-8. The fifth symbol indicates assembly plant: A=Atlanta, Ga.; D=Dallas, Texas; E=Mawhah, N.J.; G=Chicago, Ill.; H=Lorain, Ohio; K=Kansas City, Kan.; L=Dearborn, Mich. (Truck); N=Norfolk, Va.; P=Twin Cities, Minn.; R=San Jose, Calif.; S=Allen Park, Mich.; U=Louisville, Ken. The last six symbols indicate the sequential production number.

Model	Body Type	Price	Weight	Prod. Total
F-100 — 1/2-Ton — 114 in. w.b.				
80	Platform	2000	3180	Note 1
81	Chassis & Cab	1848	2855	Note 1
83	Flareside	1964	3220	Note 1
83	Styleside	1979	3220	Note 1
86	Stake	2055	3295	Note 1
F-100 — 1/2-Ton — 128 in. w.b.				
83	Flareside	2000	3430	Note 1
83	Styleside	2016	3425	Note 1

* Add $663 for 4x4 models F-110; F-111; F-112.

NOTE 1: Ford records show the following F-100 production break-outs: [Chassis & Cowl] 13; [Chassis & Cab] 15,845; [Platform & Rack] 175; [Platform] 20; [Flareside Pickup] 28,876; [Styleside Pickup] 152,272; [4x4 cab] 330; [4x4 Flareside Pickup] 802; [4x4 Styleside Pickup] 2,922.

ENGINE [F-100]: Displacement: 223 cid. Six-cylinder. 135 hp at 4000 rpm. Bore & stroke: 3.62 in. x 3.60 in. Compression ratio: 8.4:1. One-barrel carburetor.

F-250 PICKUP: The F-250 Pickup shared most of the same features as the F-100, but was capable of hauling heavier loads. It too was offered in Flareside and two-piece Styleside versions. Both boxes were 8 ft. long.

1964 Ford 3/4-Ton F-250 Styleside Pickup 4x4 (RCA)

F-250 PLATFORM/STAKE: F-250 Platform load space was 93.4 in. long and 79.3 in. wide. F-250 Stake load space was 90 in. long, 74 in. wide and 28.3 in. to the top of the racks. Bolted steel plates held side boards firmly together at top, yet allowed fast removal of stake sections when so desired. An all-steel rub rail protected the body.

I.D. DATA [F-250]: Same F-100, except first three symbols are: [4x2] F25; [4x4] F26.

Model	Body Type	Price	Weight	Prod. Total
F-250 — 3/4-Ton — 128 in. w.b. — Six				
80	Platform	2162	3500	Note 1
81	Chassis & Cab	2011	3155	Note 1
83	Flareside	2123	3610	Note 1
83	Styleside	2140	3620	Note 1
86	Stake	2217	3690	Note 1

* Add $616 for 4x4 models F-260; F-261; F-262.

NOTE 1: Ford records show the following F-250 production break-outs: [Chassis & Cowl] 66; [Chassis & Windshield] 29; [Chassis & Cab] 5,149; [4x4 cab] 410; [Platform & Rack] 662; [Platform] 83; [4x4 Platform & Rack] 68; [4x4 Platform] 29; [Flareside Pickup] 7,621; [Styleside Pickup] 28,104; [4x4 Flareside Pickup] 1,028; and [4x4 Styleside Pickup] 2,232.

ENGINE [F-250]: See F-100.

F-350 PICKUP: The 1-ton F-350 pickup was available in two 9 ft. box versions: Flareside (with wood floor and runningboard from rear fender to back of cab) and two-piece Styleside (with steel floor and smooth outer box sides). A four-speed manual transmission was standard.

F-350 PLATFORM/STAKE: This was Ford's largest light-duty Platform/Stake. Its cargo area was nearly two-feet longer than its F-250 counterpart. And its payload capacity was greater. It had steel stakes for greater rigidity. Heavy gauge steel stake pockets were set flush with the floor, which contained steel skid strips.

I.D. DATA [F-350]: See F-100.

Model	Body Type	Price	Weight	Prod. Total
F-350 — 1-Ton — 132 in. w.b. — Six				
80	Platform	2369	4140	Note 1
81	Chassis & Cab	2176	3480	Note 1
83	Flareside	2311	3980	Note 1
83	Styleside	2322	3970	Note 1
86	Stake	2423	2423	Note 1

NOTE 1: Ford records show the following F-350 production break-outs: [Chassis & Cowl] 648; [Chassis & Windshield] 82; [Chassis & Cab] 17,686; [Platform & Rack] 3,684; [Platform] 404; [Flareside Pickup] 1,388 and [Styleside Pickup] 1,714.

ENGINE [F-350]: See F-100.

CHASSIS: Wheelbase: 114 in. (F-100); 128 in. (F-100/F-250); 132 in. (F-350). GVW: 4,200-5,000 lbs. (F-100); 4,900-5,600 lbs. (F-100 4x4); 4,800-7,500 lbs. (F-250); 4,900-7,700 lbs. (F-250 4x4); 8,000-10,000 lbs. (F-350). Tires: 6.70 x 15 (F-100); 6.50 x 16 (F-250); 8 x 17.5 (F-350).

POWERTRAIN OPTIONS: Engine: 292 V-8. Transmissions: Cruise-O-Matic; heavy-duty three-speed manual; overdrive; or four-speed manual transmissions.

CONVENIENCE OPTIONS: Four-wheel drive. Right-hand sun visor. Left- or right-hand storage compartment. Windshield washer. Two-speed electric windshield wipers. Seat belts. Radio. Safety package (padded dash and visors). Fresh air heater. Grille guard. Heavy-duty radiator. Rear shock absorbers (F-350). ICC clearance and marker lights. Bright metal bodyside molding (Styleside). Full foam cushion seat. Outside rearview mirrors. Heavy-duty rear springs. [Custom Cab Package] Includes: Striped upholstery with bolster and vinyl facings; chrome horn ring; cigar lighter; left-hand armrest; right-hand sun visor; extra insulation; bright metal grille and headlight assembly; bright metal windshield reveal molding; matched locks on both doors; and two-tone interior.

1965 FORD

1965 Ford 1/2-Ton Falcon Ranchero Pickup (Tom Kelly)

FALCON RANCHERO PICKUP: Compared to last year, styling changes were mild for 1965. The Ranchero received a new grille that featured horizontal bars divided in the center by a thin vertical bar. An ornament was added to its hood. Some improvements were made to the chassis, but most attention was placed on the powerplants. Standard equipment included: Chrome front and rear bumpers; dual electric windshield wipers; dual electric horns; tailgate steer head ornament; bright metal windshield molding, roof drip moldings, taillight trim rings and hubcaps; Palomino vinyl interior trim with armrests, door panels, cowl sides and steering wheel in matching color; dome light; dispatch box; ashtray; Double-Grip door locks; Lifeguard steering wheel; bright metal horn ring; and three-speed manual transmission.

FALCON SEDAN DELIVERY: This was the last year for this vehicle. The Sedan Delivery body type was rapidly losing popularity. It and the Panel truck were being replaced by Vans. Payloads as heavy as 6,900 lbs. could be held in the spacious 78 cu. ft. cargo area. A single center tailgate latch lowered the tailgate. The floor was constructed of steel and weather-sealed plywood with longitudinal steel skid strips that eased the sliding of heavy packages in and out. Standard features included most of the same items on the Ranchero. However, the Sedan Delivery only had one armrest and one sun visor.

I.D. DATA: [Ranchero/Sedan Delivery] VIN located on rating plate. First symbol indicates model year: 5=1965. Second symbol indicates assembly plant: A=Atlanta, Ga.; D=Dallas, Texas; E=Mawhah, N.J.; F=Dearborn, Mich.; G=Chicago, Ill.; H=Lorain, Ohio; J=Los Angeles, Calif.; K=Kansas City, Kan.; L=Michigan Truck; N=Norfolk, Va.; P=Twin Cities, Minn.; R=San Jose, Calif.; S=Allen Park, Mich.; T=Metuchen, N.J.; U=Louisville, Ken; W=Wayne, Mich.; Y=Wixom, Mich.; Z=St. Louis, Mo. The third and fourth symbols indicate model: 27=Ranchero; 29=Sedan Delivery. The fifth symbol indicates engine: A or 3=289 cid V-8; C=289 cid V-8; T or 2=200 cid six; U or 4=170 cid six. The last six symbols are the sequential production number. Body codes were: 66A=Ranchero; 66B=Deluxe Ranchero; 66G=Standard Ranchero with bucket seats; 66H=Deluxe Ranchero with bucket seats; 78A=Sedan Delivery; 78B=Deluxe Sedan Delivery.

Model	Body Type	Price	Weight	Prod. Total
Falcon — 1/2-Ton — 109.5 in. w.b.				
66A	Pickup	2095	2713	10,539
78A	Sedan Delivery	2309	2798	649

ADDITIONAL PRODUCTION: In addition to the figures given above, Ford records show the following production break-outs: [66G Standard Ranchero with bucket seats] 16; [66B Deluxe Ranchero] 7,734; [66H Deluxe Ranchero with bucket seats] 990 and [78B Deluxe Sedan Delivery] 112. A total of 16 standard and 990 (of the 7,734) Deluxe Rancheros had bucket seats.

ENGINE [Falcon Ranchero/Sedan Delivery]: Displacement: 170 cid six-cylinder. 105 hp at 4400 rpm. Bore & stroke: 3.50 in. x 2.94 in. Compression ratio: 9.1:1. Holley one-barrel carburetor.

CHASSIS: Wheelbase: 109.5 in. Overall length: 190 in. Overall width: 71.6 in. GVW: 3,340-3,640 lbs. Tires: 6.95 x 14 4 ply-rated.

POWERTRAIN OPTIONS: Engines: 120 hp 200 cid six-cylinder. 200 hp 289 cid V-8. 225 hp 289 cid V-8. Transmissions: Four-speed manual (with V-8) or three-speed dual-range Cruise-O-Matic transmissions.

1965 Ford 1/2-Ton Falcon Ranchero Pickup (DFW)

CONVENIENCE OPTIONS: Power steering. Heavy-duty battery. Fresh air heater and defroster. Air-conditioner. Seat belts. Power-operated tailgate window (Sedan Delivery). Whitewall tires. Three types of bright metal wheelcovers. Tinted glass. Two-speed electric windshield wipers with windshield washers. Outside mirror. Push-button radio. 42-amp.-hr. alternator. ICC emergency light flasher. Cigarette lighter. [Bucket Seat Packages] Bucket seats with carpeting (available with Ranchero standard interior). Bucket seats with or without console, special door trim panels, armrests and carpeting (available with Rancheros having deluxe interiors.) [Safety Package] Includes: Padded dash or dash and sun visors. [Courtesy Light Package] Includes: Ashtray; dispatch box; map; backup and door courtesy lights, plus cargo area light for Sedan Delivery. [Deluxe Trim Package] Includes: (Sedan Delivery) armrest on right side, sun visor on right side, black or red color-keyed steering wheel and black and red pleated vinyl upholstery; (Ranchero) Bright metal moldings around top of box and cab back on bodysides and on rocker panels, added sound deadener, cab front floor carpeting, deluxe instrument panel and Palomino blue, black or red pleated vinyl seat trim with color-keyed steering wheel; (Both Models) Bright metal moldings on side door window frames, dome light door switches and cigarette lighter.

1965 Ford 1/2-Ton Falcon Deluxe Ranchero Pickup (OCW)

NOTE: Solid colors available were: Raven black; Wimbledon white; Rangoon red; Vintage burgundy; Caspian blue; Silver blue; Champagne beige; Prairie bronze; Dynasty green; Ivy green; Phoenician yellow; and Twilight gray. In addition, Tropical turquoise; Honey gold; and Silversmoke gray were available with the Deluxe trim package. A special two-tone option had side moldings with Wimbledon white paint between the moldings and on the cab roof. Red was used only when the main body color was white. This option was available with any of the above colors, except Silversmoke gray.

1965 Ford 1/2-Ton Econoline Deluxe Pickup (OCW)

ECONOLINE PICKUP: Heavier bumpers and new hubcaps were the biggest styling changes for 1965. Also new were a lower seat, revised heater, different steering column bracket and license plate bracket and lamp on the rear left cargo door. Standard features included: Spare tire; vinyl upholstery; three-speed manual transmission; insulated engine cover; left-hand sun visor; and single horn.

ECONOLINE VAN: The Econoline Van had 204 cu. ft. of load space. It had a loading height of just 22.5 in. Among the standard features were: Color-keyed vinyl upholstery; left-hand fresh air inlet; dual electric windshield wipers; left-hand sun visor; painted front and rear bumpers and hubcaps; dome lights; ashtray; matched locks for all doors; coat hook; headlining in driver's area; and armrests.

ECONOLINE PANEL VAN: This new model was basically just an Econoline van with no side cargo doors.

I.D. DATA: [Econoline] VIN located on rating plate. First symbol indicates model year: 5=1965. Second symbol indicates assembly plant: (see Falcon I.D. data.) The third and fourth symbols indicate model: 10=Econoline. The fifth symbol indicates engine: S=144 cid six; U=170 cid Six. The last six symbols are the sequential production number. Model codes are in first column of chart below.

Model	Body Type	Price	Weight	Prod. Total
Eonoline — 1/2-Ton — 90 in. w.b. — Six				
E-100	Pickup	1901	2585	Note 1
E-100	Van	2108	2595	Note 1
E-100	Panel Van	2054	2595	Note 1

NOTE 1: Ford records show the following Econoline production breakouts: Pickups: [87A Standard] 4,340; [87B Custom] 3,065. Econo Vans: [89H Panel] 967; [89A Regular] 35,972; [89E Display] 2,381; [89F Window] 5,156; [89G Cargo] 1,136. Extended Van: [89S Panel] 229; [89J Regular] 7,924; [89M Display] 129; [89N Window] 1,358; and [89R Cargo] 449.

ENGINE [Econoline]: Displacement: 170 cid. Six-cylinder. 105 hp at 4400 rpm. Bore & stroke: 3.50 in. x 2.94 in. Compression Ratio: 9.1:1. One-barrel carburetor.

CHASSIS: Wheelbase: 90 in. Overall length: 168.4 in. Overall width: 65 in. GVW: 3,600-4,850 lbs. Tires: 6.95 x 14.

POWERTRAIN OPTIONS: Four-speed manual and three-speed automatic transmissions.

CONVENIENCE OPTIONS: AM radio. Fresh air heater/defroster. Super Van with an 18 in. extension to the van, with heavy-duty underbody components. Padded instrument panel and sun visors. Flip-Swing or stationary passenger seat. Seat belts. Interior rearview mirror. ICC emergency lamp flasher. Tinted windshield. Windshield washer. Two-speed elec-

tric windshield wipers. Front and rear chrome bumpers. Whitewall tires. [Display Van option] Includes: Fixed windows in the right side of the cargo area. [Window Van option] Includes: Fixed windows all around. [Custom Package] Includes: Color-keyed woven plastic upholstery; right-hand fresh-air inlet; right-hand sun visor; cigar lighter; dual horns; bright metal hubcaps; chrome horn ring; cowl-wall trim panels; insulation on cowl wall; headlining on cargo area; windows in rear doors; foam padding; and optional passenger seat, plus (in Pickups) woven plastic upholstery; right-hand air duct; armrests; right-hand sun visor; cigar lighter; chrome horn ring; dual horns; cab rear wraparound quarter windows; glove compartment door with cylinder lock; bright metal hubcaps; coat hook; front body interior insulation; and foam padding in passenger seat cushion and back. [1-ton Payload Package] Includes: left-hand side-mounted cargo doors and 4,350 or 4,850 lbs. GVW packages.

FALCON STATION BUS: Station Bus changes for 1965 echoed those on the Econoline. Among the standard features were: Vinyl upholstery; two-speed electric windshield wipers; foam-cushioned adjustable driver's seat; front passenger seat; front armrests; ashtray; dual horns and dome lights; left-hand air inlet and sun visor; inside rearview mirror and retractable side step.

FALCON CLUB WAGON: Standard features on the Club Wagon included: Woven plastic upholstery; full-length floor mat and headlining; foam-cushioned front passenger seat; painted left-hand outside mirror; windshield washers; cigarette lighter; dual sun visors; four coat hooks and right-hand air inlet.

FALCON DELUXE CLUB WAGON: This was the top-of-the-line model. It featured (in addition to, or in place of, items on the base Club Wagon): Padded instrument panel; all-vinyl pleated upholstery; Deluxe steering wheel; padded sun visors; bright left-hand outside mirror; bright finish bumpers; bright bodyside moldings; bright hubcaps; and a spare tire cover.

I.D. DATA [Falcon]: See Econoline I.D. Data.

Model	Body Type	Price	Weight	Prod. Total
Falcon Club Wagon — 1/2-Ton — 90 in. w.b. — Six				
E-11	Station Bus	2293	2778	Note 1
E-12	Club Wagon	2438	2878	Note 1
E-13	Deluxe Club Wagon	2635	2918	Note 1

NOTE 1: Ford records show the following Econo Bus production break-outs: [89B Standard] 7,116; [89K Standard Extended] 573; [89C Custom] 3,813 and [89D Club Wagon] 2,259.

ENGINE [Falcon]: Same as Econoline.

CHASSIS: Wheelbase: 90 in. Overall length: 168.3 in. Overall width: 75 in. Overall height: 76.9 in. Tires: 6.50 x 13.

POWERTRAIN OPTIONS: Engine: 240 cid six-cylinder. Transmission: Automatic transmission.

CONVENIENCE OPTIONS: Armrests (for second and third seats). Cigarette lighter. Full wheelcovers. Gas-fired recirculating heater. Non-glare inside mirror. Outside rearview mirrors. Padded instrument panel and sun visors. AM radio. Second or second and third row three-passenger seats. Seat belts. Spare tire cover lock. Spotlight. Right-hand sun visor. Tinted windshield. Windshield washers.

1965 Ford 1/2-Ton F-100 Styleside Pickup (OCW)

F-100 PICKUP: Changes for 1965 included a new grille with 18 rectangular openings. The parking lamps were relocated to above the headlights with Ford spelled out in block letters in the space between them. Series emblems were moved to the front fenders. Also new was Twin I-Beam independent front suspension, Haltenberger steering linkage and a different instrument panel. Buyers were offered 6.5 ft. and 8 ft. versions of Flareside or Styleside boxes. Four-wheel drive could be ordered at extra cost.

F-100 PLATFORM/STAKE: The F-100 Platform/Stake had most of the same features as the F-100 pickup. It could haul bulky and awkward shaped loads that might not fit properly in a Pickup. The hardwood floorboards were interlocked with steel skid strips. A steel rub rail protected the body.

1965 Ford 1/2-Ton F-100 Styleside Custom Cab Pickup (JAG)

I.D. DATA [F-100]: VIN located on rating plate. The first three symbols indicated series: F10=F-100 (4x2); F-11=F-100 (4x4). The fourth symbol indicates engine: B=300 cid six; J=240 cid six; D=292 cid heavy-duty V-8. The fifth symbol indicates assembly plant: A=Atlanta, Ga.; D=Dallas, Texas; E=Mahwah, N.J.; F=Dearborn, Mich.; G=Chicago, Ill.; H=Lorain, Ohio; J=Los Angeles, Calif.; K=Kansas City, Kan.; L=Michigan Truck; N=Norfolk, Va.;

P=Twin Cities, Minn.; R=San Jose, Calif.; S=Allen Park, Mich.; T=Metuchen, N.J.; U=Louisville, Ken.; W=Wayne, Mich.; Y=Wixom, Mich.; Z=St. Louis, Mo. The third and fourth symbols indicate model: 27=Ranchero; 29=Sedan Delivery. The last six symbols are the sequential production number.

Model	Body Type	Price	Weight	Prod. Total
F-100 — 1/2-Ton — 115 in. w.b. — Six				
80	Platform	2002	3290	Note 1
81	Chassis & Cab	1852	2850	Note 1
83	Flareside	1966	3170	Note 1
83	Styleside	1981	3225	Note 1
86	Stake	2057	3165	Note 1
F-100 — 1/2-Ton — 129 in. w.b. — Six				
83	Flareside	2002	3325	Note 1
83	Styleside	2018	3360	Note 1

* Add for 4x4 models F-110/F-111/F-112.

NOTE 1: Ford records show the following F-100 production break-outs: [Chassis & Windshield] 1; [Chassis & Cab] 7,367; [Platform & Rack] 148; [Platform] 25; [Flareside] 34,184 and [Styleside] 178,581.

1965 Ford 1/2-Ton F-100 Styleside Pickup (JAG)

ENGINE [F-100]: Displacement: 240 cid. Six-cylinder. 150 hp at 4000 rpm. Bore & stroke: 4.00 in. x 3.18 in. Compression ratio: 9.2:1. One-barrel carburetor.

F-250 PICKUP: In addition to changes made on the F-100 models, the F-250s also had a 4.56:1 rear axle ratio and a 3,000 lbs. capacity front suspension. Eight-foot Flareside and Styleside boxes were offered. Four-wheel drive could be had at extra cost.

F-250 PLATFORM/STAKE: The 3/4-ton F-250 Platform/Stake had hardwood floors with steel skid strips. Body sills were protected by steel end caps. This was the only light-duty Ford Platform/Stake available with four-wheel drive (at extra cost).

I.D. DATA [F-250]: Same as F-100, except first three symbols are: [4x2] F25; [4x4] F26.

Model	Body Type	Price	Weight	Prod. Total
F-250 — 3/4-Ton — 129 in. w.b. — Six				
80	Platform	2164	3465	Note 1
81	Chassis & Cab	2013	3110	Note 1
83	Flareside	2123	3530	Note 1
83	Styleside	2141	3570	Note 1
86	Stake	2218	3645	Note 1
F-250 Crew Cab — 3/4-Ton — 147 in. w.b. — Six				
F-250	Chassis & Cab	—	—	Note 1
F-250	Pickup	—	—	Note 1

* Add for 4x4 models F-260/F-261/F-262.

NOTE 1: Ford records show the following F-250 production break-outs: [Chassis & Windshield] 166; [Chassis & Cab] 5,995; [Platform & Rack] 874; [Platform] 150; [Flareside] 7,500 and [Styleside] 42,044.

ENGINE [F-250]: See F-100.

F-350 PICKUP: Big nine-foot Flareside and Styleside Pickup boxes were offered to buyers of Ford's heftiest light-duty truck. Unlike the F-100/F-250 models, the F-350 did not have standard Twin I-Beam front suspension.

F-350 PLATFORM/STAKE: The F-350 Platform/Stake was capable of hauling substantially heavier loads than either F-100 or F-250 versions. Steel stakes were used for greater rigidity. A four-speed manual transmission was standard.

I.D. DATA [F-350]: Same as F-100, except first three symbols are F35.

Model	Body Type	Price	Weight	Prod. Total
F-350 — 1-Ton — 132 in. w.b. — Six				
80	Platform	2370	4015	Note 1
81	Chassis & Cab	2177	3425	Note 1
83	Flareside	2313	3890	Note 1
83	Styleside	2370	3920	Note 1
86	Stake	2425	4255	Note 1
F-350 Crew Cab — 1-Ton — 152 in. w.b. — Six				
83	Chassis & Cab	—	—	Note 1
83	Pickup	—	—	Note 1

NOTE 1: Ford records show the following F-350 production break-outs: [Chassis & Cowl] 759; [Chassis & Windshield] 118; [Chassis & Cab] 17,063; [Platform & Rack] 3,996; [Platform] 424; [Flareside] 2,085 and [Styleside] 1,934.

1965 Ford 1/2-Ton F-100 Styleside Custom Cab Pickup (OCW)

ENGINE [F-350]: See F-100.
CHASSIS: Wheelbase: 115 in. (F-100); 129 in. (F-100/F-250); 132 in. (F-350); 147 in. (F-250 Crew Cab); 152 in. (F-350 Crew Cab). GVW: 4,200-5,000 lbs. (F-100); 4,600-5,600 lbs. (F-100 4x4); 4,800-7,500 lbs. (F-250); 4,900-7,700 lbs. (F-250 4x4); 6,000-10,000 lbs. (F-350). Tires: 7.15 x 15 (F-100); 6.50 x 16 (F-250); 8 x 17.5 (F-350).
POWERTRAIN OPTIONS: Engines: 352 cid V-8. 300 cid heavy-duty six-cylinder. Transmissions: Cruise-O-Matic automatic. Heavy-duty three-speed manual. Manual overdrive. Four-speed manual.
CONVENIENCE OPTIONS: Four-wheel drive. Right-hand sun visor. Left- or Right-hand storage compartment. Windshield washer. Two-speed electric windshield wiper rearview mirrors. Heavy-duty rear springs. Bucket seats. [Custom Cab] Includes: Upholstery with bolster and vinyl facings; chrome horn ring; cigar lighter; left-hand armrest; right-hand sun visor; extra insulation; bright metal grille and headlight assembly; bright metal windshield reveal molding; and matched locks on both doors. [Camper Special Package] Includes: dual Western mirrors; unique fender emblem; extra-cooling radiator; ammeter; oil pressure gauge; a 300 cid six-cylinder or 352 cid V-8; Cruise-O-Matic automatic or four-speed manual transmissions; extended tailpipe and 70 amp.-hr. battery.

1965 Ford 1/2-Ton F-100 Styleside Custom Cab Pickup (OCW)

HISTORICAL NOTES: Introduced: October 1964. Model Year Production: 391,524 including Ranchero/Sedan Delivery/Econoline Bus/F-100/F-250/F-350 and P Series. Model year output of P Series trucks included: [P-100 Parcel stripped] 205; [P-350 Parcel stripped] 2,988; and [P-400 Parcel stripped] 1,771. Ford dealers sold a record 489,510 trucks in calendar year 1965, with most gains being registered in the heavy-duty market. However, sales of conventional light-duties were up 22 percent. Philip Caldwell was Truck Operations Manager.

1966 FORD

1966 Ford 1/2-Ton Ranchero Deluxe Pickup (OCW)

RANCHERO PICKUP: The Ranchero moved from the Falcon platform to the Fairlane platform. The new taillights were vertical and the grille had horizontal bars with slightly recessed headlights integrated into it. Parking lights remained in the bumper. The rear window was slightly recessed. The standard version had no side trim. Its vinyl upholstery was available in black or parchment colors. The Ranchero's new suspension featured front coil

springs and five-leaf rear springs. There was 39.1 cu. ft. of cargo space. Standard payload capacity was 850 lbs. Standard equipment included: Fresh air heater and defroster; bright horn ring; padded dash and sun visors; seat belts; inside rearview mirror; spare tire behind seat; windshield washers; ICC emergency light flasher; cigarette lighter; Ranchero emblem on glove box door; courtesy and dome lights; armrests; left-hand outside rearview mirror; backup lights; non-glare wiper arms; chrome bumpers; bright windshield and backlight moldings; Ranchero script on front fenders; bright drip rail moldings; bright taillight bezels; bright pickup box moldings; Ranchero tailgate emblem; and bright hubcaps.

RANCHERO CUSTOM PICKUP: Buyers who wanted their Ranchero with a little more flash opted for the Custom version. It had most of the same features as the standard model, plus a Ranchero emblem on the rear roof pillars; bright door window frames; bright wheel cutout moldings; bright rocker panel moldings; bodyside contour line paint stripes; full color-keyed carpeting; Deluxe instrument panel ornamentation; Deluxe door trim panels and retainers and rear vinyl-covered trim panel. Its vinyl upholstery had a crinkle-grained pattern.

I.D. DATA: [Ranchero/Sedan Delivery] VIN located on rating plate. First symbol indicates model year: 6=1966. Second symbol indicates assembly plant: A=Atlanta, Ga.; B=Oakville, Calif.; C=Ontario, Canada; D=Dallas, Texas; E=Mahwah, N.J.; F=Dearborn, Mich.; G=Chicago, Ill.; H=Lorain, Ohio; J=Los Angeles, Calif.; K=Kansas City, Kan.; L=Michigan Truck; N=Norfolk, Va.; P=Twin Cities, Minn.; R=San Jose, Calif.; S=Allen Park, Mich.; T=Metuchen, N.J.; U=Louisville, Ken; W=Wayne, Mich.; Y=Wixom, Mich.; Z=St. Louis, Mo. The third and fourth symbols indicate model: 27=Ranchero. The fifth symbol indicates engine: A=289 cid V-8; C=289 cid V-8; T=200 cid six. The last six symbols are the sequential production number. Body codes were: 66A=Ranchero; 66B=Deluxe Ranchero; 66D=Standard Ranchero with bucket seats..

Model	Body Type	Price	Weight	Prod. Total
Ranchero — 1/2-Ton — 113 in. w.b. — Six				
66A	Pickup	2218	—	9480
66B	Deluxe Pickup	2299	—	11,038

NOTE 1: Ford also built 1,242 Model 66D Rancheros with bucket seats. A total of 1,242 of the 1966 Rancheros had bucket seats.
ENGINE [Ranchero]: Displacement: 200 cid. Six-cylinder. 120 hp at 4400 rpm. Bore & stroke: 3.68 in. x 3.13 in. Compression ratio: 9.2:1. Holley one-barrel carburetor.
CHASSIS: Wheelbase: 113 in. Overall length: 197.5 in. Overall width: 74.7 in. GVW: 3,775-4,400 lbs. Tires: 7.35 x 14.
POWERTRAIN OPTIONS: Engines: 200 hp 289 cid V-8. 225 hp 289 cid V-8. Transmissions: Four-speed manual transmission (with V-8 only). Cruise-O-Matic automatic. Axles: Limited-slip differential.
CONVENIENCE OPTIONS: Heavy-duty shock absorbers. Wheelcovers. Power steering. Heavy-duty battery. Push-button radio. SelectAire air-conditioner. Tinted glass. ICC reflectors. Two-speed electric windshield wipers. Deluxe seat belts with retractors and warning light. 7.75 x 14 4-PR tires. Whitewall tires. Higher capacity rear suspension. [Visibility Package] Includes: Two-speed electric windshield wipers; inside non-glare mirror; and outside remote-control mirror. [Courtesy Light Package] Includes: Ashtray, glove box, and map light. [Seat Package, available on Customs only] Includes: Bucket seats alone or bucket seats with console.
NOTE: Two interior vinyl colors were available on standard models: Black and parchment. Four interior vinyl colors are available on Custom models: Red; blue; black; and parchment. Exterior colors were: Raven black; Wimbledon white; Candy-apple red; Vintage burgundy; Silver Frost; Nightmist blue; Silver blue; Arcadian blue; Tahoe turquoise; Ivy green; Sauterne gold; Springtime yellow; Antique bronze; Sahara beige; and Emberglo. Bodyside contour line paint stripes for the Custom model were Raven black; Wimbledon white; or Rangoon red.

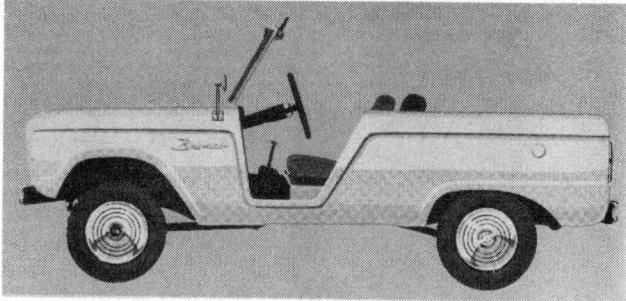

1966 Ford 1/2-Ton Model U-130 Bronco Roadster (RCA)

BRONCO ROADSTER: A TV commercial called the Bronco a stablemate of Mustang. The roadster was the base model of this new four-wheel drive vehicle and it looked it. It didn't have a roof or doors. Styling was neat, but boxy. The Ford name was printed on the center bar of the grille. Parking lights were at each end of the bar. The rectangular taillights were mounted vertically on the rear of the vehicle. Ford was printed on the far right center of the tailgate. The license plate bracket was on the opposite end. Among standard features were: A three-speed fully synchronized transmission; Mono-Beam front suspension; through-drive two-speed transfer case; 11 x 2 in. front brakes; and a folding windshield.

1966 Ford 1/2-Ton Model U-140 Bronco Sports Utility Pickup (RCA)

BRONCO SPORTS UTILITY: This looked like a Mini-Pickup. It had an all-steel, bolted-on, removable roof over the front seat. The side doors had roll-up windows. The compact rear cargo area could hold up to 32.1 cu. ft. of whatever one wanted to haul.

1966 Ford 1/2-Ton Model U-130 Bronco Wagon (RCA)

BRONCO WAGON: This was the most luxurious Bronco. It had a full length roof and large quarter windows.

I.D. DATA [U-100]: VIN located on rating plate. The first three symbols indicated series: U13=U-130; U14=U-140; U15=U-150. The fourth symbol indicates engine: A=240 cid six; F=170 cid six. The fifth symbol indicates assembly plant: H=Lorain, Ohio; L=Michigan Truck; R=San Jose, Calif.; S=Allen Park, Mich. The last six symbols are the sequential production number.

Model	Body Type	Price	Weight	Prod. Total
Bronco U-100 — 1/2-Ton — 90 in. w.b. — Six				
U-130	Roadster	2404	2750	4090
U-140	Sports Utility	2480	2955	6930
U-150	Wagon	2625	3025	12,756

ENGINE [Bronco]: Displacement: 170 cid. Six-cylinder. 105 hp at 4400 rpm. Bore & stroke: 3.50 in. x 2.94 in. Compression ratio: 9.1:1. One-barrel carburetor.
CHASSIS: Wheelbase: 90 in. Overall length: 152.1 in. Overall width: 68.8 in. GVW: 3,900-4,700 lbs. Tires: 7.35 x 15.
POWERTRAIN OPTIONS: 289 cid V-8.
CONVENIENCE OPTIONS: Bucket seats. Cigarette lighter. Cab doors. Closed crankcase emissions (required in California). Heavy-duty clutch (with six-cylinder). Tailgate mounted spare tire carrier. Rear seat. Heavy-duty battery. Front bumper guards. Heavy-duty alternator. Cooling package. GVW package. Armrests. Limited-slip front axle. Limited-slip rear axle. Chrome front and rear bumpers.
ECONOLINE PICKUP: Styling was virtually untouched for 1966. However, some changes were made. These included: Non-glare windshield wiper arms, new seat belts and a padded dash. Some standard features were: Seven-foot long cargo box; spare tire; vinyl upholstery; three-speed manual transmission; insulated engine cover; left-hand sun visor; and single horn.
ECONOLINE VAN: The Econoline Van had 204 cu. ft. of load space. It had a loading height of just 22.5 in. Among the standard features were: Color-keyed vinyl upholstery; left-hand fresh air inlet; dual electric windshield wipers; left-hand sun visor; painted front and rear bumpers and hubcaps; dome lights; ashtray; matched locks for all doors; coat hook; headlining in driver area; and armrests.
ECONOLINE PANEL VAN: This new model was basically just an Econoline Van with no side cargo doors.
I.D. DATA: [Econoline] VIN located on rating plate. First symbol indicates model year: 6=1966. Second symbol indicates assembly plant: (see Falcon I.D. data.) The third and fourth symbols indicate model: 10=Econoline. The fifth symbol indicates engine: S=144 cid six; U=170 cid Six. The last six symbols are the sequential production number. Body style codes are in first column of chart below.

Model	Body Type	Price	Weight	Prod. Total
Econoline Standard — 1/2-Ton — 90 in. w.b. — Six				
87A	Pickup	1897	2610	2578
89A	Van	2194	2670	23,861
89H	Panel Van	2139	2645	669

ADDITIONAL PRODUCTION: In addition to the above figures, Ford records show the following Econoline production break-outs: [87B Custom Pickup] 512; [89E Standard Display Van] 2,488; [89F Standard Window Van] 4,250; [89G Standard Cargo Van] 537; [89J Standard regular Super Van] 27,393; [89M Display Super Van] 381; [89N Window Super Van] 3,437; [89R Cargo Super Van] 934; [89S Panel Super Van] 558; [89A Deluxe regular Van] 563; [89E Deluxe Display Van] 119; [89F Deluxe Window Van] 252; [89G Deluxe Cargo Van] 88; [89H Deluxe Panel Van] 23; [89J Deluxe regular Super Van] 1,660; [89M Deluxe Display Super Van] 44; [89N Deluxe Window Super Van] 740; [89R Deluxe Cargo Super Van] 132 and [89S Deluxe Cargo Super Van] 41.
ENGINE [Econoline]: Displacement: 170 cid. Six-cylinder. 105 hp at 4400 rpm. Bore & stroke: 3.50 in. x 2.94 in. Compression Ratio: 9.1:1. One-barrel carburetor.
CHASSIS: Wheebase: 90 in. Overall length: 168.4 in. Overall width: 65 in. GVW: 3,600-4,930 lbs. Tires: 6.95 x 14.
POWERTRAIN OPTIONS: Transmission: Three-speed automatic.
CONVENIENCE OPTIONS: AM radio. Fresh air heater/defroster. Super Van with 18 in. extension to the Vans with heavy-duty underbody, padded instrument panel and sun visors; Flip-Swing or stationary passenger seat; seat belts; interior rearview mirror; ICC emergency lamp flasher; tinted windshield; windshield washer; two-speed electric windshield wipers; front and rear chrome bumpers and whitewall tires. [Display Van Option] Includes: fixed windows in the right side of the cargo area. [Window Van Option] Includes: fixed windows all around. [Custom Package] Includes: Color-keyed woven plastic upholstery; right-hand fresh-air inlet; right-hand sun visor; cigar lighter; dual horns; bright metal hubcaps; chrome horn ring; cowl-wall trim panels; insulation on cowl wall; headlining on cargo area; windows in rear doors; foam padding; and optional passenger seat, plus (in Pickups) woven plastic upholstery; right-hand air duct; armrests; right-hand visor; cigar lighter; chrome horn ring; dual horns; cab rear wraparound quarter windows; glove compartment door with cylinder lock; bright metal hubcaps; coat hook; front body interior insulation; and foam padding in passenger seat cushion and back. [1-ton Payload Package] Includes: Left side-mounted cargo doors, 4,350 or 4,850 lbs. GVW.
FALCON CLUB WAGON: Club Wagon changes for 1966 echoed those on the Econoline. Among the standard features were: Vinyl upholstery; two-speed electric windshield wipers; foam-cushioned adjustable driver's seat; front passenger seat; front armrests; ashtray; dual horns and dome lights; left air inlet and sun visor; inside rearview mirror; and retractable side step.

FALCON CUSTOM CLUB WAGON: Standard features on the Custom Club Wagon included: Woven plastic upholstery; full-length floor mat and headlining; foam-cushioned front passenger seat; painted left-hand outside mirror; windshield washers; cigarette lighter; dual sun visors; four coat hooks; right-hand air inlet.

FALCON DELUXE CLUB WAGON: This was the top-of-the-line model. It featured (in addition to, or in place of, items on the base Club Wagon): A padded instrument panel; all-vinyl pleated upholstery; Deluxe steering wheel; padded sun visors; bright left-hand outside rearview mirror; bright-finish bumpers; bright bodyside moldings; bright hubcaps; and spare tire cover.

I.D. DATA [Falcon]: See Econoline I.D.

Model	Body Type	Price	Weight	Prod. Total
Falcon Club Wagon — 1/2-Ton — 90 in. w.b. — Six				
E-11	Club Wagon	2462	3053	Note 1
E-12	Custom Club Wagon	2591	3163	Note 1
E-13	Deluxe Club Wagon	2779	3183	Note 1

NOTE 1: Ford records show the following Bus and Club Wagon production break-outs: [89B Standard Bus] 4,382; [89K Standard Super Bus] 2,468; [89C Club Wagon] 2,087; [89T Super Club Wagon] 1,788; [89D Deluxe Club Wagon] 1,007; and [89L Deluxe Super Club Wagon] 1,188.

ENGINE [Falcon]: Same as Econoline.

CHASSIS: Wheelbase: 90 in. Overall length: 168.3 in. Overall width: 75 in. Overall height: 76.9 in. Tires: 6.50 x 13.

POWERTRAIN OPTIONS: Transmission: Three-speed automatic transmission. Engine: 240 cid six-cylinder.

CONVENIENCE OPTIONS: Armrests (for second and third seats). Cigarette lighter. Full wheelcovers. Gas-fired recirculating heater. Non-glare inside mirror. Outside rearview mirrors. Padded instrument panel and sun visors. AM radio. Second (or second-and-third) row three-passenger seats. Seat belts. Spare tire cover lock. Spotlight. Right-hand sun visor. Tinted windshield. Windshield washers.

1966 Ford 1/2-Ton F-100 Styleside Custom Cab Pickup (OCW)

F-100 PICKUP: Except for a slightly modified series emblem and a new grille with two long rectangular slots over 18 small ones, the F-100 was about the same as last year's model. Buyers could choose from 6.5 ft. and 8 ft. box Flaresides and Stylesides. The 4x4 option could now be had on either F-100 wheelbase (at extra cost). Among standard features were: Argent silver painted hubcaps; Twin-I-Beam independent front suspension; fresh air heater/defroster; padded dash; windshield washers; and emergency flashers.

1966 Ford 1/2-Ton F-100 Styleside Pickup (OCW)

F-100 PLATFORM/STAKE: The F-100 Platform/Stake had hardwood floorboards that were interlocked with steel skid strips. Floor corners were reinforced with steel angle brackets. Standard features echoed those on the F-100 Pickup.

I.D. DATA [F-100]: VIN located on rating plate. The first three symbols indicated series: F10=F-100 (4x2); F11=F-100 (4x4). The fourth symbol indicates engine: A or 1=240 cid six; B or 2=300 cid six; Y or 8=352 cid six. The fifth symbol indicates assembly plant: A=Ontario, Canada; D=Dallas, Texas; E=Mahwah, N.J.; H=Lorain, Ohio; K=Kansas City, Kan.; L=Michigan Truck; N=Norfolk, Va.; P=Twin Cities, Minn.; R=San Jose, Calif.; S=Allen Park, Mich.; U=Louisville, Ken. The last six symbols are the sequential production number.

1966 Ford 1/2-Ton F-100 Styleside Custom Cab Camper Special

Model	Body Type	Price	Weight	Prod. Total
F-100 — 1/2-Ton — 115 in. w.b. — Six				
80	Platform	2101	3095	Note 1
81	Chassis & Cab	1951	2850	Note 1
83	Flareside	2069	3145	Note 1
83	Styleside	2085	3210	Note 1
86	Stake	2156	3220	Note 1
F-100 — 1/2-Ton — 129 in. w.b. — Six				
83	Flareside	2105	3295	Note 1
83	Styleside	2121	3310	Note 1

1966 Ford 1/2-Ton F-100 Styleside Custom Cab Pickup (RCA)

NOTE 1: Ford records show the following F-100 production break-outs; 4x2 Trucks: [Chassis & Windshield] 1; [Chassis & Cab] 4,274; [Platform & Rack] 120; [Platform] 13; [Flareside Pickup] 26,491; and [Styleside Pickup] 224,497. 4x4 Trucks: [Chassis & Cab] 145; [Flareside Pickup] 839; and [Styleside Pickup] 4,493.

ENGINE [F-100]: Displacement: 240 cid. Six-cylinder. 150 hp at 4000 rpm. Bore & stroke: 4.00 in. x 3.18 in. Compression ratio: 9.2:1. One-barrel carburetor.

1966 Ford 3/4-Ton F-250 Styleside Custom Cab Pickup (RCA)

F-250 PICKUP: Buyers of a 3/4-ton F-250 had their choice of Flareside or Styleside Pickup boxes. They could also order a six-passenger Crew Cab model. It had four doors, two bench seats and a 6.5 ft. pickup box (it could be ordered without the box). The interior was either beige, blue, green or red.

F-250 PLATFORM/STAKE: F-250 Platform/Stake styling underwent the same minor changes as its F-100 counterpart. It also had seasoned hardwood floors with interlocking steel skid strips.

I.D. DATA [F-250]: Same as F-100, except first three symbols are: [4x2] F25; [4x4] F26.

Model	Body Type	Price	Weight	Prod. Total
F-250 — 3/4-Ton — 129 in. — Six				
80	Platform	2263	3540	Note 1
81	Chassis & Cab	2113	3135	Note 1
83	Flareside	2226	3530	Note 1
83	Styleside	2244	3545	Note 1
86	Stake	2317	3720	Note 1

Model	Body Type	Price	Weight	Prod. Total
F-250 Crew Cab — 3/4-Ton — 147 in. — Six				
83	Pickup [147]	—	—	Note 1
83	Chassis & Cab [147]	—	—	Note 1

* Add for 4x4.

NOTE 1: Ford records show the following F-250 production break-outs; 4x2 Trucks: [Chassis & Windshield] 142; [Chassis & Cab] 6,187; [Platform & Rack] 1,747; [Platform] 129; [Flareside Pickup] 6,699 and [Styleside Pickup] 58,489. 4x4 Trucks: [Chassis & Cab] 644; [Platform & Rack] 125; [Platform] 29; [Flareside Pickup] 1,595 and [Styleside Pickup] 3,559.

ENGINE [F-250]: See F-100.

F-350 PICKUP: The 1-ton F-350 came with most of the same standard features as the F-100, except for Twin-I-Beam front suspension. Both Flareside (with wood floors and runningboard from rear fender to back or cab) and Styleside (smooth side) boxes were offered. Also available was a six-passenger Crew Cab with (or without) an 8 ft. pickup box.

F-350 PLATFORM/STAKE: The hardwood floorboards of the F-350 Platform/Stake could haul heavier (and bulkier) payloads than the other light-duty Ford Platform/Stakes. A four-speed manual transmission was standard.

I.D. DATA [F-350]: Same as F-100, except first three symbols are: [4x2] F35.

Model	Body Type	Price	Weight	Prod. Total
F-350 — 1-Ton — 132 in. w.b. — Six				
80	Platform	2469	4080	Note 1
81	Chassis & Cab	2276	3505	Note 1
83	Flareside	2416	3895	Note 1
83	Styleside	2425	3920	Note 1
86	Stake	2524	4320	Note 1
F-350 Crew Cab — 1-Ton — 152 in. w.b. — Six				
83	Chassis & Cab	—	—	Note 1
83	Pickup	—	—	Note 1

NOTE 1: Ford records show the following F-350 production break-outs: [Chassis & Cowl] 782; [Chassis & Windshield] 184; [Chassis & Cab] 19,716; [Platform & Rack] 4,596; [Platform] 729; [Flareside Pickup] 3,928; and [Styleside Pickup] 2,605.

ENGINE [F-350]: See F-100.

CHASSIS: Wheelbase: 115 in. (F-100); 129 in. (F-100/F-250); 132 in. (F-350); 147 in. (F-250 Crew Cab); 152 in. (F-350 Crew Cab). GVW: 4,200-5,000 lbs. (F-100); 4,600-5,600 lbs. (F-100 4x4); 4,800-7,500 lbs. (F-250); 4,900-7,700 lbs. (F-250 4x4); 6,000-10,000 lbs. (F-350). Tires: 7.75 x 15 (F-100); 6.50 x 16 (F-250); 8 x 17.5 (F-350).

POWERTRAIN OPTIONS: Engines: 300 cid six-cylinder. 352 V-8. Transmissions: Cruise-O-Matic automatic; Heavy-duty three-speed manual; Manual overdrive; and four-speed manual transmissions.

CONVENIENCE OPTIONS: Four-wheel drive. Right-hand sun visor. Left- or right-hand storage compartments. Bucket seats. Radio. Fresh air heater. Grille guard. Heavy-duty radiator. Rear shock absorbers (F-350). Power steering. ICC clearance and marker lights. Bright metal bodyside molding (Styleside). Full foam cushion seat. Outside rearview mirrors. Heavy-duty rear springs. [Custom Cab] Includes: Striped upholstery with bolster and vinyl facings; chrome horn ring; cigar lighter; left-hand armrest; right-hand sun visor; extra insulation; bright metal grille and headlight assembly; bright metal windshield reveal molding; matched locks on both doors; Custom Cab plaques; and bright hubcaps. [Camper Special Package] Includes: Dual Western mirrors; unique fender emblem; extra-cooling radiator; ammeter; oil pressure gauge; a 300 cid six-cylinder or 352 cid V-8 engine; Cruise-O-Matic or four-speed manual transmissions; extended tailpipe; 70 amp.-hr. battery; and 55-amp. alternator.

HISTORICAL: Introduced: Oct. 1, 1965. Model year production of light-duty trucks (including 171 P-100s; 2,945 P-350s and 2,239 P-400 Parcel Delivery truck chassis) was 494,909 units. Calendar year registrations included 331,498 trucks in the 6,000 lbs. or less GVW category and 98,490 trucks with GVWs between 6,001 and 10,000 lbs. Ford was America's number two truck-maker in 1966, which was an all-time best truck sales season. Calendar year sales were pegged at 536,427 units. Innovations: Ranchero redesigned. Ford Bronco introduced. Ranchero has an optional 289 cid V-8.

1967 FORD

1967 Ford 1/2-Ton Fairlane Ranchero 500XL Pickup (OCW)

FAIRLANE RANCHERO PICKUP: After a year of transition, the Ranchero was now clearly a Fairlane based vehicle. Design features included: Quad stacked headlights and a one-piece aluminum grille (its fine gridwork was accented by a wider, full-length horizontal bar in the center and three vertical bars). The rectangular taillights were divided in the center by backup lights. There were also bright metal moldings on the windshield, hood, drip rail, back of the cab and cargo box; two-speed windshield wipers; windshield washers; a pad-

ded dash and sun visors; dome light; ICC emergency flasher; horn ring; heater; cigarette lighter; left-hand remote control rearview mirror; seat belts; energy-absorbing steering wheel; color-keyed floor mat; armrests; ashtray; courtesy light door switches and three-speed manual transmission.

FAIRLANE 500 RANCHERO PICKUP: The new mid-level Ranchero had most features of the standard version, plus: Deep-pile, color-keyed wall-to-wall carpeting; instrument panel applique; electric clock; trim panel for rear of cab; bright metal wheel lip moldings and low-eride moldings; bright door window frames; bodyside paint stripes and bright wheelcovers. The full-width seat was upholstered in red, blue, parchment or ivy gold pleated vinly trim color-keyed to 13 exterior colors.

FAIRLANE 500 XL RANCHERO PICKUP: A unique medallion in the center of the grille let everyone know you were driving the new top-of-the-line Ranchero. In addition to items offered on the 500, the 500 XL had: Bucket seats; a center console; and special trim items.

I.D. DATA: [Ranchero] VIN located on rating plate. First symbol indicates model year: 7=1967. Second symbol indicates assembly plant: A=Atlanta, Ga.; B=Oakville, Calif.; C=Ontario, Canada; D=Dallas, Texas; E=Mahwah, N.J.; F=Dearborn, Mich.; G=Chicago, III.; H=Lorain, Ohio; J=Los Angeles, Calif.; K=Kansas City, Kan.; L=Michigan Truck; N=Norfolk, Va.; P=Twin Cities, Minn.; R=San Jose, Calif.; S=Allen Park, Mich.; T=Metuchen, N.J.; U=Louisville, Ken; W=Wayne, Mich.; Y=Wixom, Mich.; Z=St. Louis, Mo. The third and fourth symbols indicate model: 47=Ranchero; 48=Ranchero 500; 49=Ranchero 500 XL. The fifth symbol indicates engine: T or 2=200 cid six; C=289 cid V-8; 3=low-compression 289 cid V-8; A=premium fuel 289 cid V-8; K=high-performance 289 cid V-8; Y,H or S=390 cid V-8. The last six symbols are the sequential production number. Body codes were: 66A=Ranchero; 66B=Deluxe Ranchero; 66D=Ranchero 500XL with bucket seats.

Model	Body Type	Price	Weight	Prod. Total
Ranchero — 1/2-Ton — 113 in. w.b. — Six				
66A	Pickup	2514	3010	5858
66B	500 Pickup	2611	3020	9504
66D	500 XL Pickup	2768	3050	1881

ENGINE [Ranchero]: Displacement: 200 cid. Six-cylinder. 120 hp at 4400 rpm. Bore & stroke: 3.68 in. x 3.13 in. Compression ratio: 9.2:1. Holley one-barrel carburetor.

CHASSIS: Wheelbase: 113 in. Overall length: 199.9 in. Overall width: 74.7 in. GVW: 3,850-4,750 lbs. Tires: 7.35 x 14 4-PR.

POWERTRAIN OPTIONS: Engines: 200 hp 289 cid V-8. 225 hp 289 cid V-8 (discontinued during the model year). 270 hp 390 cid V-8. 315 hp 390 cid V-8. 320 hp 390 cid GT V-8 (mid-model year replacement for the 390 cid/315 hp V-8). Transmissions: Four-speed manual or SelectShift Cruise-O-Matic transmissions. Axle: Limited-slip rear axle.

CONVENIENCE OPTIONS: 42- or 55-amp. alternator. Heavy-duty battery. A 7-1/2 in. diameter vacuum booster for front disc brakes, including vacuum booster. Electric clock (Ranchero). Extra-cooling fan and radiator (included with Air-conditioner). Heavy-Duty Suspension Package] Includes: Heavy-duty shock absorbers and 1,165 lbs. rear springs. Linkage-type power steering. Push-button radio and antenna. Stereo-Sonic tape system (not with four-speed transmission and air-conditioner). Deluxe woodgrain steering wheel. SelectAire air-conditioner. Shoulder harness for driver and passenger. Tinted glass (windshield or all-around). Wheelcovers (Ranchero). Deluxe wheelcovers. Styled steel wheels. 7.75 x 14 4-PR and 8-PR tires. Whitewall tires.

NOTE: Interior colors: Parchment, red, or blue vinyl interiors were available on Ranchero. Parchment, red, blue, or Ivy gold vinyl interiors were available on the Ranchero 500. Parchment, red, blue, or blue vinyl interiors were available on the Ranchero 500 XL. Exterior colors: Raven black; Wimbledon white; Candyapple red; Silver Frost; Nightmist blue; Sauterne gold (500 and 500 XL); Springtime yellow; Clearwater aqua (500 and 500 XL); Dark Moss green; Vintage burgundy; Brittany blue; Frost turquoise (500 XL); Beige mist; Pebble beige; and Burnt amber. Bodyside contour line paint stripes for 500 and 500XL were white, black or red (red stripes with red interior, black stripes with black interior.)

1967 Ford 1/2-Ton Model U-130 Bronco Roadster (RCA)

BRONCO ROADSTER: The new 1967 Bronco looked about the same as last year's model. However, a few changes were made. Among them were: Variable-speed windshield wipers; padded sun visors; dual master cylinder; self-adjusting brakes; and backup lights. As before, the 4x4 Bronco roadster had no doors or roof. Its rectangular taillights were mounted vertically on the rear of the vehicle. Ford was printed on the far right-center of the tailgate. The license plate bracket was on the opposite end. Among standard features were: A three-speed fully-synchronized transmission; Mono-Beam front suspension; a through-drive two-speed transfer case; 11 x 2 in. front brakes; and a folding windshield.

1967 Ford 1/2-Ton Model U-140 Bronco Sports Utility Pickup (RCA)

BRONCO PICKUP: Last year's Sports Utility was now a Pickup. It had an all-steel, bolted-on, removable roof over the front seat. The side doors had roll-up windows. The compact rear cargo area could hold up to 32.1 cu. ft. of whatever one wanted to haul.

1967 Ford 1/2-Ton Model U-150 Bronco Wagon (RCA)

BRONCO WAGON: This was the most luxurious Bronco. It had a full-length roof and large quarter windows.

I.D. DATA [U-100]: VIN located on rating plate. The first three symbols indicated series: U13=Model U-130 Roadster; U14=Model U-140 Pickup; U15=Model U-150 Wagon. The fourth symbol indicates engine: F=170 cid six; N=289 cid V-8. The fifth symbol indicates assembly plant: H=Lorain, Ohio; L=Michigan Truck; R=San Jose, Calif.; S=Allen Park, Mich. The last six symbols are the sequential production number.

1967 Ford 1/2-Ton Model U-140 Bronco Pickup/Wrecker (RCA)

Model	Body Type	Price	Weight	Prod. Total
Bronco — 1/2-Ton — 92 in. w.b. — Six				
U-130	Roadster	2417	2775	698
U-140	Pickup	2546	2995	2602
U-150	Wagon	2633	3095	10,930

ENGINE [Bronco]: Displacement: 170 cid. Six-cylinder. 105 hp at 4400 rpm. Bore & stroke: 3.50 in. x 2.94 in. Compression ratio: 9.1:1. One-barrel. carburetor.

CHASSIS: Wheelbase: 90 in. Overall length: 152.1 in. Overall width: 68.8 in. GVW: 3,850-4,700 lbs. Tires: 7.35 x 15.

POWERTRAIN OPTIONS: Engine: 289 V-8.

CONVENIENCE OPTIONS: Bucket seats. Cigarette lighter. Cab doors. Closed crankcase emission (required by California Air Resources Board). Heavy-duty clutch (with six-cylinder). Tailgate-mounted spare tire carrier. Rear seat. Heavy-duty battery. Front bumper guards. Heavy-duty alternator. Cooling package. GVW package. Armrests. Limited-slip front axle. Limited-slip rear axle. Chrome front and rear bumpers. Auxiliary fuel tank with skid plate (11.5-gal. capacity). Wheelcovers. Tailgate moldings. Bodyside moldings. [Sport Package] Includes: (Wagon and Pickup) bright horn ring, headlight bezels, taillight bezels, tailgate handle, windshield rails, instrument panel trim, side window frames and grille (with Ford in red applique on it); chrome-plated bumpers with front bumper guards; dual armrests; trimmed headboard headliner; wheelcovers; vinyl floor mat (Wagon); and cigar lighter.

ECONOLINE PICKUP: This would be the last year for the Econoline pickup. Once again, it received only minor changes from the previous year's model. Perhaps the most important of these was the dual brake master cylinder. Among the standard features were: 7 ft. long, 5 ft. wide and nearly 2 ft. deep cargo box with reinforced stake pockets; vinyl seats; fresh air heater/defroster; two-speed windshield wipers; seat belts; spare tire; left-hand outside mirror; painted front bumper and hubcaps; ashtray; ICC emergency lamp flasher; coat hook; windshield washers; and mechanical jack.

ECONOLINE VAN: This van had right side and rear cargo doors (left-hand side doors were available). Vent type or fixed windows could be had on all right side and rear cargo doors. The Econoline Van came with most of the same standard features as the Pickup, plus dual outside rearview mirrors, painted rear bumper; and armrest for driver.

ECONOLINE PANEL VAN: This vehicle did not have side cargo doors. Fixed or vent type rear door windows were optional. Most standard features were the same as those on the Econoline Van.

I.D. DATA: [Econoline] VIN located on rating plate. First symbol indicates model year: 6=1966. Second symbol indicates assembly plant: (see Falcon I.D. data.) The third and fourth symbols indicate model: 10=Econoline. The fifth symbol indicates engine: S=144 cid six; U=170 cid Six. The last six symbols are the sequential production number. Model codes are in the first column of chart below.

Model	Body Type	Price	Weight	Prod. Total
Econoline — 1/2-Ton — 90 in. w.b. — Six				
E-100	Pickup	2111	2625	Note 1
E-100	Van	2308	2715	Note 1
E-150	Panel Van	2254	2690	Note 1

NOTE 1: Production By Body Type Number: [87A-Standard] 1,697; [87B] 318; [89A] 21,107; [89E-Standard] 3,249; [89F-Standard] 3,752; [89G-Standard] 492; [89H-Standard] 618; [89J-Standard] 23,009; [89M-Standard] 357; [89N-Standard] 3,434; [89R-Standard] 821; [89S] 431; [89A-Custom] 327; [89E-Custom] 299; [89F-Custom] 268; [89G-Custom] 23; [89H-Custom] 24; [89J-Custom] 1,027; [89M-Custom] 41; [89N-Custom] 563 and [89R-Custom] 100.

ENGINE [Econoline]: Displacement: 170 cid. Six-cylinder. 105 hp at 4400 rpm. Bore & stroke: 3.50 in. x 2.94 in. Compression Ratio: 9.1:1. One-barrel carburetor.

CHASSIS: Wheelbase: 90 in. Overall length: 168.4 in. Overall width: 65 in. GVW: 4,350-4,930 lbs. Tires: 6.95 x 14.

POWERTRAIN OPTIONS: Engine: 240 cid six-cylinder. Transmission: Three-speed automatic transmission.

CONVENIENCE OPTIONS: AM radio. Auxiliary gas or hot water heaters. Super Van with 18 in. extension to the Vans with heavy-duty underbody. Ammeter and oil pressure gauge. Western-type rearview mirrors. Flip-Swing passenger seat. Tinted glass all around (Pickup and Window Van). Tinted windshield. Front and rear chrome bumpers. Folding driver's seat. Stationary passenger seat for vans. Cargo door positioners. Whitewall tires. [Display Van Option] Includes: Fixed windows in the right side of the cargo area. [Window Van Option] Includes: Fixed windows all around. [Custom Package] Includes: Color-keyed woven plastic upholstery; right-hand armrest and (in Vans); right- and left-hand armrest; (in Pickups) lighter; dual horns; bright metal hubcaps; chrome horn ring; cowl-trim panels; insulation on cowl wall; headlining on cargo area; window in rear van doors; foam padding in passenger seat (with optional seat on Vans); rear quarter windows (Pickup); bright body moldings; heavy-duty front and rear shocks; heavy-duty front and rear springs; and safety shoulder harness. GVW Packages: 4,750 lbs. and 4,930 lbs.

NOTE: Econoline color choices for 1967 were: Rangoon red; Pebble beige; Raven black; Springtime yellow; Holly green; Lunar green; Frost turquoise; Harbor blue; Wimbledon white; Chrome yellow; and Pure white. A two-tone paint effect was available with Wimbledon white combined with any other standard color except Chrome yellow or Pure white.

FALCON CLUB WAGON: Club Wagon changes for 1967 echoed those on the Econoline. Among the standard features were: Vinyl upholstery; two-speed electric windshield wipers; foam-cushioned adjustable driver's seat; front passenger seat; front armrests; ashtray; dual horns and dome lights; left air inlet and sun visor; inside outside rearview mirror; retractable side step; backup lights; left outside rearview mirror; windshield washer; and stabilizer bar.

FALCON CUSTOM CLUB WAGON: Standard features included most of what was on the Club Wagon, plus cigar lighter; dome light in rear compartment; left outside door lock; second seat; horn ring; and emergency flashers.

FALCON DELUXE CLUB WAGON: This was the top-of-the-line model. It featured (in addition to, or in place of, items on the base Club Wagon): Cigar lighter; chrome front and rear bumpers; and chrome left outside rearview mirror.

I.D. DATA [Falcon]: See Econoline I.D.

Model	Body Type	Price	Weight	Prod. Total
Falcon Club Wagon — 1/2-Ton -90 in. w.b. — Six				
89B	Club Wagon	2532	2985	4233
89C	Custom Club Wagon	2668	3095	1538
89D	DeLuxe Club Wagon	2841	3115	741

ADDITIONAL PRODUCTION: Also produced were 2,248 Model 98K Club Wagon ELS models; 2,063 Model 89T Custom Club Wagon ELS models; and 1,261 Model 89L Deluxe Club Wagon ELS models.

ENGINE [Falcon]: Same as Econoline.

CHASSIS: Wheelbase: 90 in. Overall length: 168.3 in. Overall width: 75 in.

POWERTRAIN OPTIONS: Transmission: Three-speed automatic transmission.

CONVENIENCE OPTIONS: Armrests (for second and third seats). Cigarette lighter. Full wheelcovers. Gas-fired recirculating heater. Non-glare inside mirror. Outside rearview mirrors. Padded instrument panel and sun visor. AM radio. Second or second-and-third row three-passenger seats. Seat belts. Spare tire cover lock. Spotlight. Right-hand sun visor. Tinted windshield. Windshield washers.

F-100 PICKUP: Ford light-duty trucks were restyled for 1967. Headlights were integrated into a rectangular slots grille. Parking lights were now located directly below the headlights. Ford was placed in block letters on the face of the hood. Like Styleside bodyside panels, the hood was double-walled. Both the hood and tailgate had one-hand operation. Running-boards on Flaresides were a wide, ribbed-steel steps between the cab and rear fender. They facilitated easy loading from either side. The forward-slanting series identification emblem was moved to the side of the hood. The cabs were improved. There was nearly four more inches of shoulder room. Seats were three inches wider and deep-cushioned. A new swept-away instrument panel provided extra space. The overall effect gave the cab a more car-like look and feel. The two body styles were offered in 6.5 ft. and 8 ft. sizes. They were the wood-floored Flareside and the steel-floored Styleside. Among standard features were: Color-keyed padded dash; foot-operated parking brake; molded fiberboard glove box with push-button latch; bright aluminum door scuff plates; slide-action air vents; one-piece hardboard headlining; full-width red, blue, green or beige vinyl-trimmed seats (color-keyed to cab paint); seat belts for driver and passenger; seat belt anchorage for center passenger; padded dash and sun visors; emergency lamp flasher; backup lights; dual safety hydraulic brake system with warning light; windshield washers; dual electrical two-speed windshield wipers (with non-glare wiper arms); interior and left outside rearview mirrors; and three-speed fully-synchronized manual transmission.

F-100 PLATFORM/STAKE: The good-looking 1967 F-100 Platform/Stake could haul most lightweight bulky loads with ease. Its seasoned hardwood floorboards were interlocked with steel skid strips. Floor corners were reinforced with steel angle brackets. It came with most of the same standard features as the F-100 pickup, plus right and left outside rearview mirrors.

I.D. DATA [F-100]: VIN located on rating plate. The first three symbols indicated series: F10=F-100 (4x2); F11=F-100 (4x4). The fourth symbol indicates engine: A or 1=240 cid six; B or 2=300 cid Six; Y or 8=352 cid Six. The fifth symbol indicates assembly plant: A=Ontario, Canada; D=Dallas, Texas; E=Mawhah, N.J.; H=Lorain, Ohio; K=Kansas City, Kan.; L=Michigan Truck; N=Norfolk, Va.; P=Twin Cities, Minn.; R=San Jose, Calif.; S=Allen Park, Mich.; U=Louisville, Ken. The last six symbols are the sequential production number.

Model	Body Type	Price	Weight	Prod. Total
F-100 — 1/2-Ton — 115 in. w.b. — Six				
80	Platform and Rack	2224	3190	Note 1
81	Chassis & Cab	2072	2945	Note 1
83	Flareside	2198	3265	Note 1
83	Styleside	2237	—	Note 1
83	[86] Stake	2278	3315	Note 1
F-100 — 1/2-Ton — 131 in. w.b. — Six				
83	Flareside	2237	—	Note 1
83	Styleside	2273	—	Note 1

* Add $650 for 4x4 models F-110/F-111/F-112.

NOTE 1: Ford records show the following F-100 production break-outs: 4x2 Trucks: [Chassis & Cowl] 1; [Chassis & Windshield] 1; [Chassis & Cab] 2,905; [Platform & Rack] 80; [Platform] 17; [Flareside Pickups] 18,307; [Styleside Pickups] 204,710. 4x4 Trucks: [Chassis & Cab] 135; [Flareside Pickups] 481; and [Styleside Pickups] 3,455.

ENGINE [F-100]: Displacement: 240 cid. Six-cylinder. 150 hp at 4000 rpm. Bore & stroke: 4.0 in. x 3.18 in. Compression ratio: 9.2:1. One-barrel carburetor.

1967 Ford 3/4-Ton F-250 "Camper Special" Styleside Pickup (JAG)

F-250 PICKUP: The F-250 shared most of the same styling and other features of the F-100. However, it was a bit more heavy-duty. Its front axle had a 400 lbs. greater capacity than the F-100; its rear axle was almost 2,000 lbs. beefier. In addition, it had larger (12-7/8 x 2 in.) brakes. A new item exclusive on the F-250 for 1967 was 3.89 in. frame section modules. Both Styleside and Flareside boxes were offered. The six-passenger Crew Cab was available with or without a 6.5 ft. pickup box.

NOTE: Travel Industries, Co. designed a sleek camper specifically for the F-250 Ford 3/4-ton Pickup. It was available through many Ford dealers. The camper was made of strong, lightweight plastic. It was 33 percent larger inside and 40 percent lighter than similar size units. Prices for the 10.5 ft. camper ranged from $1,995 to $2,895.

F-250 PLATFORM/STAKE: The F-250 3/4-ton Platform/Stake had ample cargo room. Inside length was 90 in. (Stake); 93.4 in. (Platform). Rear opening was 73.7 in. (Stake); 79.3 in. (Platform). The stake height was 28.3 in. Like the F-100, it had seasoned hardwood floorboards.

I.D. DATA [F-250]: Same as F-100, except first three symbols are: [4x2] F25; [4x4] F26.

1967 Ford 3/4-Ton F-250 Styleside Pickup 4x4 (RCA)

Model	Body Type	Price	Weight	Prod. Total
F-250 — 3/4-Ton — 131 in. w.b. — Six				
80	Platform	2443	3190	Note 1
81	Chassis & Cab	2282	2945	Note 1
83	Flareside	2409	3660	Note 1
83	Styleside	2446	3675	Note 1
86	Stake	2498	3835	Note 1
F-250 Crew Cabs — 3/4-Ton — 149 in. w.b. — Six				
83	Chassis & Cab	—	—	Note 1
83	Styleside	—	—	Note 1

* Add $615 for 4x4 models F-260/F-261/F-262/F-263/F-264.

NOTE 1: Ford records show the following F-250 production break-outs: 4x2 Trucks: [Chassis & Cowl] 5; [Chassis & Windshield] 197; [Chassis & Cab] 4,316; [Platform & Rack] 438; [Platform] 76; [Flareside Pickup] 4,412; [Styleside Pickup] 58,506. 4x4 Trucks: [Chassis & Cab] 426; [Platform & Rack] 89; [Platform] 25; [Flareside Pickup] 915; and [Styleside Pickup] 3,836.

ENGINE [F-250]: See F-100.

F-350 PICKUP: Only the Flareside Pickup was offered this year in the 1-ton F-350 series. It had a new 135 in. wheelbase. There were runningboards between the cab and rear fenders; seasoned hardwood floors with steel skid strips to help when sliding cargo into place; rubber covered, forged steel chains to support the tailgate and steel side panels (with rolled edges) to provide extra strength and rigidity. It had a cargo capacity of 74 cu. ft. The F-350 now had Twin-I-Beam front suspension. A four-speed manual transmission was standard. A six-passenger crew cab, with or without a pickup box, was available.

F-350 PLATFORM/STAKE: Buyers had their choice of 9 ft. or 12 ft. Platform/Stakes this year. Both had seasoned hardwood floors with steel skid strips. The floor corners were reinforced with steel angle brackets. A four-speed manual transmission and two outside rearview mirrors were standard.

I.D. DATA [F-350]: Same as F-100, except first three symbols are: [4x2] F35.

Model	Body Type	Price	Weight	Prod. Total
F-350 — 1-Ton — 135 in./159 in. w.b. — Six				
80	Platform 9 ft.	2606	4285	Note 1
80	Platform 12 ft.	—	—	Note 1
81	Chassis & Cab	2401	2401	Note 1
83	Flareside	2550	—	Note 1
86	Stake 9 ft.	2606	4285	Note 1
86	Stake 12 ft.	—	—	Note 1
F-350 Crew Cabs — 1-Ton — 164.5 in. w.b. — Six				
F-350	Chassis & Cab	—	—	Note 1
F-350	Styleside	—	—	Note 1

NOTE 1: Ford records show the following F-350 production break-outs: [Chassis & Cowl] 320; [Chassis & Windshield] 84; [chassis and cab] 16,738; [Platform & Rack] 2,574; [Platform] 273; and [Flareside Pickup] 1,411.

ENGINE [F-350]: See F-100.

CHASSIS: Wheelbase: 115 in. (F-100). 131 in. (F-100/F250). 135 in. (F-350). 149 in. (F-250 Crew Cab). 159 in. (F-350). 164.5 in. (F-250 Crew Cab). GVW: 4,200-5,000 lbs. (F-100); 4,900-5,600 lbs. (F-100 4x4). 4,800-7,500 lbs. (F-250); 6,800-7,700 lbs. (F-250 4x4); 6,800-10,000 lbs. (F-350). Tires: 8.15 x 15 (F-100); 8.00 x 16.5 (F-250/F-350).

POWERTRAIN OPTIONS: Engines: 170 hp 300 cid six-cylinder. 208 hp 352 cid V-8. Three-speed with overdrive transmission (F-100). Four-speed manual transmission. Cruise-O-Matic.

CONVENIENCE OPTIONS: Dual rear wheels (F-350). Bucket seats. Power steering. 25-gal. under cab fuel tank with stone shield (with or without standard tank). Heavy-duty black vinyl seat trim. Deluxe fresh air heater-defroster. Radio and antenna. Dual electric horns. Shoulder safety harness. Orschein parking brake lever (F-250/F-350). Air-conditioner. Limited-slip differential. [Camper Special Package] Includes: 70 amp.-hr. battery; oil pressure gauge; ammeter; deluxe fresh air heater; dual electric horns; dual chrome 6 in. x 10 in. western type mirrors; extra-cooling radiator; extended tailpipe; camper wiring harness; rear shock absorbers (F-350); and Camper Special emblem. [Custom Cab Package] Includes, woven-plastic seat trim in red, blue, green or beige color keyed to exterior color; deep foam-cushioned full-width seat; armrests; rubber floor mat; cigar lighter; bright finish horn ring; headlining retainer molding; instrument cluster; padded dash; bright metal grille and headlight assembly; windshield reveal molding; and Custom Cab plaques. [Ranger Package] Includes: Full-width deep-cushioned seat upholstered in vinyl with a soft cloth appearance; vinyl door trim panels and nylon carpeting trimmed with bright metal moldings; color-keyed armrests; bright-finished horn ring, instrument cluster, headlining and instrument padding moldings; bright-finished front bumper, grille and headlight assembly, hubcaps, wheel lip; and rocker panel moldings.

NOTE: Standard colors for 1967 were: Rangoon red; Pebble beige; Raven black; Springtime yellow; Holly green; Lunar green; Frost turquoise; Harbor blue; Wimbledon white; Chrome yellow; and Pure white. Regular two-tone paint option included Wimbledon white applied to entire cab roof (including drip rails and entire back panel above beltline molding and extending around cab corners to door openings). Deluxe two-tone paint option was available with F-100/F250 Styleside Pickups. It included Wimbledon white applied to the sheet metal below the side molding and lower tailgate section. All other sheet metal was painted the basic color selected. This package included bright bodyside moldings, lower tailgate molding and taillight bezels and was also offered in combination with the regular two-tone paint options.

1968 FORD

1968 Ford 1/2-Ton Fairlane Ranchero GT Pickup (OCW)

RANCHERO PICKUP: Once again the Ranchero was on its own, although it still was obviously derived from the Fairlane. The quad headlights were now mounted horizontally and integrated into the horizontal recessed grille. Small wraparound corner lights were on the fenders, just above the front bumper. The taillights were vertical. Ford was printed on the tailgate. Under it, in a corner, was the Ranchero signature. Side vent windows were eliminated. There was a new, curved lower control arm in the front suspension. The color-coordinated interior was available in black, blue or parchment. The 6.5 ft. pickup box had 39.1 cu. ft. of cargo space. Sides were double-walled and the tailgate opened with one hand. A three-speed manual transmission was standard.

1968 Ford Ranchero 500 Sedan-Pickup (Ralph Utermochler)

RANCHERO 500 PICKUP: The mid-level Ranchero was the 500. Like the lower- and higher-priced versions, it had flow-through ventilation and an improved chassis. Its interior featured deep-pile carpeting, distinctive instrument panel trim, electric clock and four upholstery color choices. On the outside were high-style wheelcovers and special bodyside moldings.

RANCHERO GT PICKUP: This was the ultimate Ranchero for 1968. Sales literature called it excitingly elegant. It was easily distinguished from the others by the bold color-keyed C stripes on its sides. It had a GT emblem in the center of the radiator; GT hubcaps and 12-slot styled steel wheels; GT dash plate; deluxe interior featuring pleated vinyl bucket seats; and deep-pile carpeting.

I.D. DATA: [Ranchero] VIN located on rating plate. First symbol indicates model year: 8=1968. Second symbol indicates assembly plant: A=Atlanta, Ga.; B=Oakville, Calif.; C=Ontario, Canada; D=Dallas, Texas; E=Mahwah, N.J.; F=Dearborn, Mich.; G=Chicago, Ill.; H=Lorain, Ohio; J=Los Angeles, Calif.; K=Kansas City, Kan.; L=Michigan Truck; N=Norfolk, Va.; P=Twin Cities, Minn.; R=San Jose, Calif.; S=Allen Park, Mich.; T=Metuchen, N.J.; U=Louisville, Ken; W=Wayne, Mich.; X=St. Thomas, Canada; Y=Wixom, Mich.; Z=St. Louis, Mo. The third and fourth symbols indicate model: 47=Ranchero; 48=Ranchero 500; 49=Ranchero 500 XL. The fifth symbol indicates engine: T or 2=200 cid six; F=302 cid V-8; J=302 cid V-8; Y=390 cid V-8; X=390 cid V-8; S=390 cid GT V-8. The last six symbols are the sequential production number.

Model	Body Type	Price	Weight	Prod. Total
Ranchero -1/2-Ton — 113 in. w.b. — Six				
66A	Sedan-Pickup	2632	3135	5014
66B	500 Sedan-Pickup	2731	3140	10,029
Ranchero GT -1/2-Ton — 113 in. w.b. — V-8				
66D	GT Sedan-Pickup	2964	3150	1669

ENGINE [Ranchero]: Displacement: 200 cid. Six-cylinder. 115 hp at 3800 rpm. Bore & stroke: 3.68 in. x 3.13 in. Compression ratio: 8.8:1. Holley one-barrel carburetor.

ENGINE [Ranchero/Ranchero 500]: Displacement: 289 cid V-8. 195 hp at 4600 rpm. Bore & stroke: 4.00 in. x 2.87 in. Compression ratio: 8.7:1. Carburetor: Holley two-barrel (Ranchero GT).

CHASSIS: Wheelbase: 116 in. GVW: 3,900-4,800 lbs. Tires: 7.35 x 14.

POWERTRAIN OPTIONS: Engines: 195 hp 289 V-8 (Ranchero, 500). 210 hp 302 cid V-8. 265 hp 390 cid V-8. 280 hp 390 cid V-8. 315 hp 390 cid V-8. 335 hp 428 Cobra-Jet V-8. Transmissions: Four-speed manual transmission. SelectShift Cruise-O-Matic transmission. Axle: Limited-slip rear axle.

CONVENIENCE OPTIONS: Power steering. Tinted glass (windshield or all around). Wheelcovers. Slotted steel wheels. Courtesy lights. Electric clock (Ranchero). 55-amp. alternator. Bodyside molding (Ranchero). Power front disc brakes. Vinyl roof. Tachometer (with V-8 engines). SelectAire air-conditioner. Console (with bucket-seats in 500 or GT). AM/FM stereo radio. Heavy-duty battery. Bucket seats. [Heavy-Duty Suspension Package] Includes: Heavy-duty front and rear shocks and 1,280 lbs. rear springs.

BRONCO ROADSTER: The most noticeable change to the four-wheel drive Bronco for 1968 was the addition of side-marker lights on the front fenders and reflectors on the lower rear quarter panels. Minor revisions were made to the interior, in particular the armrest, window crank knobs and door handles. A heater and defroster were now standard. Free-running front hubs and a dry type air cleaner were also new. Among the other standard features were: Three-speed fully-synchronized transmission; Mono-Beam front suspension; through-drive two-speed transfer case; 11 x 2 in. front brakes; and folding windshield.

BRONCO PICKUP: This cute vehicle was also little changed. It had an all-steel, bolt-on removable roof over the front seat. The side doors had roll-up windows. The compact rear cargo area could hold up to 32.1 cu. ft. of whatever one wanted to haul.

BRONCO WAGON: This was the most luxurious Bronco. It had a full-length roof and large quarter windows.

I.D. DATA [U-100]: VIN located on rating plate. The first three symbols indicated series: U13=Model U-130 Roadster; U14=Model U-140 Pickup; U15=Model U-150 Wagon. The fourth symbol indicates engine: F=170 cid six; A=240 cid six; N=289 cid V-8; G=302 cid V-8. The fifth symbol indicates assembly plant: H=Lorain, Ohio; L=Michigan Truck; R=San Jose, Calif.; S=Allen Park, Mich. The last six symbols are the sequential production number.

Model	Body Type	Price	Weight	Prod. Total
Bronco — 1/2-Ton — 92 in. w.b. — Six				
U-130	Roadster	2638	2815	—
U-140	Pickup	2741	2995	—
U-150	Wagon	2851	3095	—

ENGINE [Bronco]: Displacement: 170 cid. Six-cylinder. 105 hp at 4400 rpm. Bore & stroke: 3.50 in. x 2.94 in. Compression ratio: 9.1:1. one-barrel carburetor.

CHASSIS: Wheelbase: 92 in. Overall length: 152.1 in. Overall width: 68.8 in. GVW: 3,850-4,700 lbs. Tires: 7.35 x 15.

POWERTRAIN OPTIONS: Engine: 289 V-8.

CONVENIENCE OPTIONS: Bucket seats. Cigarette lighter. Cab doors. Closed crankcase emission (required in California). Heavy-duty clutch (with six). Tailgate-mounted spare tire carrier. Rear seat. Heavy-duty battery. Front bumper guards. Heavy-duty alternator. Cooling package. GVW package. Armrests. Limited-slip front axle. Limited-slip rear axle. Chrome front and rear bumpers. Auxiliary fuel tank with skid plate (11.5-gal. capacity). Wheelcovers. Tailgate moldings. Bodyside moldings. [Sport Package] Includes: (Wagon and Pickup) frosted horn ring; headlight bezels; taillight bezels; tailgate handle; chrome windshield drip moldings; instrument panel trim and side window frames and grille (with Ford in red appliqued to it); chrome-plated bumpers with front bumper guards; dual armrests; trimmed hardboard headliner; wheelcovers; vinyl floor mat (wagon); and cigar lighter.

337

FALCON CLUB WAGON/ECONOLINE VANS: Due to a United Auto Worker (UAW) strike, the 1967 vans were carried over until early 1968. At that point, a new line of 1969 vans was marketed. (See historical notes below for production data).

F-100 PICKUP: The most noticeable change to Ford light-duty trucks in 1968 was their new grille. It was split in the center by a thick horizontal bar and had thinner, shorter horizontal bars floating above and below it. Also new were the side-marker lights, which were integrated into the series identification emblem on the sides of the hood. The interior was color-coordinated with exterior paint. It included a chair-height seat; swept-away instrument panel; padded sun visors; armrests with paddle-type door latch handles; dome light; double-grip door locks; deluxe fresh air heater with three-speed fan and illuminated controls; hardboard headlining; seat belts with push-button buckles; floor mat; and vinyl seat trim in red, blue, black or beige. F-100 buyers could choose from 6.5 ft. or 8 ft. cargo boxes in either Flareside or Styleside versions. A three-speed fully-synchronized transmission was standard.

1968-1/2 Ford 1/2-Ton 12-Passenger Club Wagon Chateau (JAG)

F-100 PLATFORM/STAKE: The F-100 Platform/Stake was ideal for hauling bulky or odd shaped items. Its seasoned hardwood floor boards were inter-locked with steel skid strips. Floor corners were reinforced with steel angle brackets. It also had side-marker lights on the front fenders and reflectors on sides and back of platform. Like the Pickup, it came with Twin-I-Beam front suspension.

I.D. DATA [F-100]: VIN located on rating plate. The first three symbols indicated series: F10=F-100 (4x2); F11=F-100 (4x4). The fourth symbol indicates engine: A=240 cid six; B=300 cid six; H=390 cid V-8; Y=390 cid V-8. The fifth symbol indicates assembly plant: C=Ontario, Canada; D=Dallas, Texas; E=Mewhah, N.J.; H=Lorain, Ohio; K=Kansas City, Kan.; L=Michigan Truck; N=Norfolk, Va.; P=Twin Cities, Minn.; R=San Jose, Calif.; S=Allen Park, Mich.; U=Louisville, Ken. The last six symbols are the sequential production number.

Model	Body Type	Price	Weight	Prod. Total
F-100 — 1/2-Ton — 115 in. w.b. — Six				
80	Platform	2343	3280	Note 1
81	Chassis & Cab	2193	3035	Note 1
83	Flareside	2318	3355	Note 1
83	Styleside	2357	3400	Note 1
86	Stake	2398	3405	Note 1
F-100 — 1/2-Ton — 131 in. w.b. — Six				
83	Flareside	2357	3490	Note 1
83	Styleside	2393	3505	Note 1

* Add $645 for 4x4.

NOTE 1: Ford records show the following F-100 production break-outs: [Chassis & Cab] 2,616; [Platform & Rack] 98; [Platform] 16; [Flareside Pickup] 16,686; and [Styleside Pickup] 285,015.

ENGINE [F-100]: Displacement: 240 cid. Six-cylinder. 150 hp at 4000 rpm. Bore & stroke: 4.0 in. x 3.18 in. Compression ratio: 9.2:1. One-barrel carburetor.

1968 Ford 3/4-Ton F-250 Styleside Pickup 4x4 (RCA)

F-250 PICKUP: The F-250 shared most features of the F-100. In addition, it came with Flex-O-Matic rear suspension, which combined longer springs with a unique device that automatically adjusted spring length for varying load conditions. Two 8 ft. cargo boxes were offered. The Styleside had sleek styling and bodyside panels extended forward to hug the contour of rear cab corners. It had double-wall side panels and tailgate, plus an all-steel floor. The Flareside came with runningboards between cab and rear fenders, seasoned hardwood floorboards with steel skid strips, rubber-covered forged steel chains to support tailgate and steel side panels with rolled edges to provide extra strength and rigidity.

F-250 PLATFORM/STAKE: The F-250 Platform/Stake could haul larger and heavier loads on its hardwood platform than the F-100. It had 10 in. more inside length and nearly four-inch higher stakes. Unlike the F-100, it was available with four-wheel drive (at extra cost).

I.D. DATA [F-250]: Same as F-100, except first three symbols are: [4x2] F25; [4x4] F26.

Model	Body Type	Price	Weight	Prod. Total
F-250 — 3/4-Ton — 131 in. w.b. — Six				
80	Platform	2576	—	Note 1
81	Chassis & Cab	2415	3275	Note 1
83	Flareside	2542	3695	Note 1
83	Styleside	2579	3710	Note 1
86	Stake	2631	3870	Note 1
F-250 Crew Cabs — 3/4-Ton — 149 in. w.b. — Six				
81	Chassis & Cab	—	—	Note 1
83	Styleside	—	—	Note 1

* Add $645 for 4x4.

NOTE 1: Ford records show the following F-250 production break-outs: [Chassis & Cowl] 7; [Chassis & Windshield] 108; [Chassis & Cab] 5,762; [Platform & Rack] 621; [Platform] 150; [Flareside Pickup] 5,298; [Styleside Pickup] 90,170.

ENGINE [F-250]: See F-100.

F-350 PICKUP: Like other 1968 light-duty Ford trucks, the 1-ton F-350 came with many safety features. Among them were: Dual hydraulic brake system with warning light; seat belts; energy absorbing instrument panel with padding; double-yoke safety door latches and safety hinges; positive door lock buttons; windshield washers; two-speed windshield wipers; padded safety sun visors; double-thick laminate safety glass windshield; inside day/night rearview mirror; backup lights; side-marker lights or reflectors; four-way emergency flashers; energy-absorbing armrests and safety-designed door handles; glare-reduced windshield wiper arms and blades; and horn button. The F-350 was only offered with the Flareside cargo box. A four-speed manual transmission was standard.

F-350 PLATFORM/STAKE: This was the largest light-duty Platform/Stake available from Ford in 1968. Dual rear wheels could be ordered for even greater payload capacity. Seasoned hardwood floors were interlocked with steel skid strips. Floor corners were reinforced with steel angle brackets. A four-speed manual transmission was standard.

I.D. DATA [F-350]: Same as F-100, except first three symbols are: [4x2] F35.

Model	Body Type	Price	Weight	Prod. Total
F-350 — 1-Ton — 135 in./159 in. w.b. — Six				
80	Platform 9 ft.	2829	4305	Note 1
80	Platform 12 ft.	2868	4580	Note 1
81	Chassis & Cab	2526	3710	Note 1
83	Flareside	2675	4170	Note 1
86	Stake 9 ft.	2883	4545	Note 1
86	Stake 12 ft.	2922	4925	Note 1
F-350 Crew Cabs — 1-Ton — 164.5 in. w.b. — Six				
81	Chassis & Cab	—	—	Note 1
83	Styleside	—	—	Note 1

NOTE 1: Ford records show the following F-350 production break-outs: [Chassis & Cowl] 388; [Chassis & Windshield] 99; [Chassis & Cab] 22,389; [Platform & Rack] 4,451; [Platform] 487; [Flareside Pickup] 1,612.

ENGINE [F-350]: See F-100.

CHASSIS: Wheelbase: 115 in. (F-100). 131 in. (F-100/F-250). 135 in. (F-350). 149 in. (F-250 Crew Cab). 159 in. (F-350). 164.5 in. (F-350 Crew Cab). GVW: 4,200-5,000 lbs. (F-100); 4,600-5,600 lbs. (F-100 4x4); 6,100-7,500 lbs. (F-250); 6,300-7,700 lbs. (F-250 4x4); 6,600-10,000 lbs. (F-350). Tires: 8.15 x 15 (F-100); 8.00 x 16.5 (F-250/F-350).

POWERTRAIN OPTIONS: Engines: 165 hp 300 cid Six. 215 hp 360 cid V-8. 255 hp 390 cid V-8. Transmissions: Three-speed overdrive (F-100). Four-speed manual. Cruise-O-Matic.

CONVENIENCE OPTIONS: Dual rear wheels (F-350). Bucket seats. Power steering. Power front disc brakes (F-250/F-350). Convenience lighting package. 25-gal. under cab fuel tank (with or without standard tank). Tinted glass. Heavy-duty black vinyl seat trim. Deluxe fresh air heater-defroster. Radio and antenna (push-button or manual). Dual electric horns. Shoulder safety harness. Heavy-duty rear springs with Flex-O-Matic suspension (F-100). Orschein parking brake lever (F-250/F-350). Air-conditioner. Limited-slip differential. [Camper Special Package] Includes: 70 amp.-hr. battery; oil pressure gauge; ammeter; dual electric horns; dual chrome 6 in. x 10 in. Western type mirrors; extra-cooling radiator; extended tailpipe; camper wiring harness; rear shock absorbers (F-350); Camper Special emblem. [Custom Cab Package] Includes: Woven-plastic seat trim on a deep foam-cushioned full width seat; color-coordinated floor mat; horn ring; headlining retainer molding; custom instrument cluster; bright metal grille and headlight assembly; windshield reveal molding; Custom Cab plaques. [Ranger Package] Includes: Full-width deep-cushioned seat upholstered in vinyl with a soft cloth appearance; door trim panels and carpeting trimmed with bright metal moldings; bright-finished horn ring; bright-finished instrument cluster; bright-finished front bumper, grille and headlight assembly; bright wheel lip and rocker panel moldings. Explorer Special Package.

NOTE: Standard colors for 1968 were: Rangoon red; Pebble Beige; Raven black; Meadowlark yellow; Holly green; Lunar green; Sky View blue; Harbor blue; Wimbledon white; Chrome yellow; and Pure white. Regular two-tone paint option: Wimbledon white applied to entire cab roof (including drip rails and back panel) above beltline molding and extending around cab corners to door openings. Deluxe two-tone paint: (F-100/F-250 Stylesides) Wimbledon white applied to the sheet metal below the side molding and lower tailgate section. All other sheet metal was painted to basic color selected. This package included bright bodyside moldings, a lower tailgate molding and taillight bezels. A combination two-tone paint option was available, too. It combined the regular and deluxe two-tone paint options.

HISTORICAL: Introduced: Fall 1967. Total light-duty truck production including Bronco/Ranchero/Econoline/Pickups/P-350/P-400 was 414,968 units. Innovations: New Flex-O-Matic rear suspension standard on F-250 and optional on F-100. Ranchero is five inches longer and has new vinyl top option. Bronco receives safety improvements and swing-away spare tire carrier. Due to a UAW strike, Econoline vans and Club Wagons were carried over from 1967. Redesigned Econoline Vans were released as 1969 models. Ford records show production break-outs for model year 1968 as follows: Econoline: [89A Standard Cargo Van] 31,983; [89C Standard Display Van] 2,207; [89E Standard Window Van] 5,933; [89B Custom Cargo Van] 1,929; [89D Custom Display Van] 111; [89F Custom Window Van] 800. Falcon: [82A Club Wagon] 5,648; [82B Custom Club Wagon] 3,292 and [82C Deluxe Club Wagon] 2,297.

1969 FORD

1969 Ford 1/2-Ton Fairlane Ranchero GT Pickup (OCW)

RANCHERO PICKUP: The most striking styling change for 1969 was the Ranchero's new hood scoop. Aside from that, and a slightly revised grille, things looked pretty much the same as last year. Rear side marker lights replaced the reflectors used in 1968. The suspension system and brake linings were also modified. On the inside, instrument dial faces were now silver and a different design was used on the three-passenger seat. It was upholstered in all-vinyl (black, blue or Nugget gold) and color-coordinated with vinyl trim panels and interior paint. Other standard features included: Deluxe seat belts with outboard retractors; vinyl-coated rubber floor mat; vinyl headlining; ventless side windows; door-operated courtesy light switches; fresh air heater/defroster with sliding controls; satin-finished horn ring; day/night inside rearview mirror; spare tire and tool storage compartments behind the split seatback; and three-speed manual transmission.

RANCHERO 500 PICKUP: In addition to (or in place of) Ranchero features, the Ranchero 500 had: Deep-pile wall-to-wall carpeting (color-coordinated with the black, red, blue, or Nugget gold-pleated upholstery); deluxe door trim panels and moldings; electric clock; spare tire cover; bright metal wheelcovers; bright metal bodyside moldings; and shiny wheel opening moldings.

RANCHERO GT PICKUP: The GT emblem was moved from the center of the grille to the lower left-hand corner next to the headlights. The upper part of the bodyside C-stripe was lowered. Special features of the GT included: A uniquely detailed grille; Sport hood scoop; deluxe wheelcovers; whitewall tires; and a distinctive GT stripe in black, white, red, or gold color-coordinated with body and interior color schemes.

I.D. DATA: [Ranchero] VIN located on rating plate. First symbol indicates model year: 9=1969. Second symbol indicates assembly plant: A=Atlanta, Ga.; B=Oakville, Calif.; C=Ontario, Canada; D=Dallas, Texas; E=Mahwah, N.J.; F=Dearborn, Mich.; G=Chicago, Ill.; H=Lorain, Ohio; J=Los Angeles, Calif.; K=Kansas City, Kan.; L=Michigan Truck; N=Norfolk, Va.; P=Twin Cities, Minn.; R=San Jose, Calif.; S=Allen Park, Mich.; T=Metuchen, N.J.; U=Louisville, Ken; W=Wayne, Mich.; X=St. Thomas, Canada; Y=Wixom, Mich.; Z=St. Louis, Mo. The third and fourth symbols indicate model: 47=Ranchero; 48=Ranchero 500; 49=Ranchero 500 GT. The fifth symbol indicates engine: L=250 cid six; F=302 cid V-8; H=351 cid V-8; M=351 cid V-8; Y=390 cid V-8; Q=428 CJ (Cobra-Jet) V-8; and R=428 CJ Ram-Air V-8. The last six symbols are the sequential production number.

1969 Ford 1/2-Ton Bronco Pickup (OCW)

Model	Body Type	Price	Weight	Prod. Total
Ranchero — 1/2-Ton — 113 in. w.b. — Six				
66A	Sedan-Pickup	2623	3185	5856
66B	500 Sedan-Pickup	2740	3190	11,214
Ranchero — 1/2-Ton — 113 in. w.b. — V-8				
66C	GT Sedan-Pickup	2954	3200	1658

NOTE 1: In addition to the production figures given, 727 Rancheros came with bucket seats.

ENGINE [Ranchero]: Displacement: 250 cid. Six-cylinder. 155 hp at 4000 rpm. Bore & stroke: 3.68 in. x 3.91 in. Compression ratio: 9.0:1. One-barrel carburetor.

Standard Catalog of Light-Duty Trucks

1969 Ford 1/2-Ton Fairlane Ranchero GT Pickup (DFW)

ENGINE [Ranchero GT]: Displacement: 302 cid V-8. 220 hp at 4600 rpm. Bore & stroke: 4.00 in. x 3.00 in. Compression ratio: 9.5:1. Carburetor: Two-barrel.
CHASSIS: Wheelbase: 116 in. GVW: 4,000-4,950 lbs. Tires: 7.35 x 14B.
POWERTRAIN OPTIONS: Engines: 220 hp 302 cid V-8. 250 hp 351 cid V-8. 290 hp 351 cid V-8. 320 hp 390 cid V-8. 335 hp 428 cid V-8. 335 hp 428 cid Cobra-Jet V-8. Transmissions: Four-speed manual transmission. SelectShift Cruise-O-Matic transmission.
NOTE: The 428 engine package included: Performance/handling suspension; extra-cooling radiator; 80-amp.-hr. battery; cast aluminum rocker covers; bright radiator cap, dipstick, oil filler cap and air-cleaner top; and 428 emblem. In addition, the 428 Ram-Air Cobra-Jet V-8 included a special induction system that forced cool outside air directly to the carburetor through a hood air scoop for peak power.

1969 Ford 1/2-Ton Fairlane Ranchero GT Pickup With 428 C-J

CONVENIENCE OPTIONS: 7.75 x 14B and D or F70 x 14B tires. Power front disc brakes. Tachometer (for V-8s). Bodyside moldings (Ranchero/500). SelectAire air-conditioner. AM/FM stereo radio. Deluxe steering wheel. Intermittent windshield wipers. Vinyl roof. Electric clock (Ranchero). Power steering. Forced ventilation system. Tinted glass (all around). Wheelcovers. Styled steel wheels. Heavy-duty suspension package. Courtesy light group. Bucket seats.
NOTE: Exterior colors offered on 1969 Rancheros were: Raven black; Wimbledon white; Candy Apple red; Royal maroon; Dresden blue; Brittany blue (metallic); Presidential blue (metallic); Aztec aqua; Gulfstream aqua (metallic); New lime; Lime gold (metallic); Meadowlark yellow; Black jade (metallic); Champagne gold (metallic); and Indian-Fire (metallic). Two-tone combinations were available with Wimbledon white roofs and all other body colors or Raven black roofs with all colors except Dresden, Brittany and Presidential blues or Black jade.

1969 Ford 1/2-Ton Bronco Wagon 4x4 (DFW/DPL)

BRONCO PICKUP: The 4x4 Bronco looked about the same as it always had. However, there were some changes. For example, the windshield no longer folded down. Also, the side-marker light pads on the lower forward section of the front fenders had a lighter color. There was a black steering wheel grommet. The cowl area was improved to reduce road noise. The insulation was improved. The doors were changed. During the model year, two-speed electric windshield wipers became standard.

1969 Ford 1/2-Ton Bronco Wagon 4x4 (JAG)

BRONCO WAGON: The wagon's body was beefed up a bit, particularly the door frames, rocker panels and roof. The roof was no longer detachable. There were fixed windows in the rear liftgate and on each side of the rear compartment.
I.D. DATA [U-100]: VIN located on rating plate. The first three symbols indicated series: U14=Model U-140 Pickup; U15=Model U-150 Wagon. The fourth symbol indicates engine: F=170 cid six; G=302 cid V-8. The fifth symbol indicates assembly plant: H=Lorain, Ohio; L=Michigan Truck; R=San Jose, Calif.; S=Allen Park, Mich. The last six symbols are the sequential production number.

1969 Ford 1/2-Ton Bronco Wagon 4x4 (DFW/DPL)

Model	Body Type	Price	Weight	Prod. Total
U-140	Pickup	2834	2990	2317
U-150	Wagon	2945	3090	18,639

ENGINE [Bronco]: Displacement: 170 cid. Six-cylinder. 105 hp at 4400 rpm. Bore & stroke: 3.50 in. x 2.94 in. Compression ratio: 9.1:1. One-barrel carburetor.
CHASSIS: Wheelbase: 90 in. Overall length: 152.1 in. Overall width: 68.8 in. GVW: 3,850-4,700 lbs. Tires: 7.35 x 15.
POWERTRAIN OPTIONS: Engine: 289 cid V-8.
CONVENIENCE OPTIONS: Bucket seats. Cigarette lighter. Closed crankcase emission (required in California). Heavy-duty clutch (with six-cylinder engine). Tailgate-mounted spare tire carrier. Rear seat. Heavy-duty battery. Front bumper guards. Heavy-duty alternator. Cooling package. GVW package. Armrests. Limited-slip front axle. Limited-slip rear axle. Chrome front and rear bumpers. Auxiliary fuel tank with skid plate (11.5-gal. capacity). Wheelcovers. Tailgate moldings. Bodyside moldings. [Sport Package] Includes: (Wagon and Pickup) Frosted horn ring, headlight bezels, taillight bezels, tailgate handle, windshield drip, instrument panel trim, side window frames and grille (with red Ford applique); chrome-plated bumpers with front bumper guards; dual armrests; trimmed hardboard headliner; wheelcovers; vinyl floor mat (wagon); cigar lighter; pleated parchment interior; and aluminum door trim appliques.
ECONOLINE E-100 CARGO VAN: Although introduced in February 1968, these were considered 1969 models. (There were no 1968 Econolines.) Styling was dramatically changed. The horizontal-bars theme grille was enlarged and had the Ford name in block letters on its upper portion. Trim rings made the two round headlights seem larger than before. Above the headlights and grille was the sloping hood. It could be opened for checking fluid levels in the radiator, battery, brake master cylinder and windshield washer reservoir. Complete access to the engine could be attained by removing the cover within the vehicle. Since the engine had been pushed forward a bit, it was now possible to swing the driver's seat into the cargo area. Vertical, rectangular taillights were used on the rear. The right-hand cargo doors had push-button handles and all doors had slam type latches. Standard features included: Vinyl color-coordinated upholstery; painted front and rear bumpers and hubcaps; left-hand fresh air inlet; dome lights in driver's compartment and cargo area; single electric horn; coat hook; mechanical jack; double-grip door locks on all doors with reversible keys; push-pull interior door locks (except rear doors); metal door checks; individual driver's seat; headlining in driver and passenger area; fresh air heater and defroster; and double cargo doors at right and rear.
ECONOLINE E-100 WINDOW VAN: As the name suggests, the window van had glass all around. On it and other E-100s the cargo area was 11.5 feet long and 53.5 in. wide. It shared most standard features with the Cargo Van.
ECONOLINE E-100 DISPLAY VAN: This model had windows at the rear and on the right-hand side. It came with the same standard features as the Cargo Van.
I.D. DATA: [Econoline] VIN located on rating plate. First symbol indicates model year: 9=1969. Second symbol indicates assembly plant. (See Ranchero/Bronco/F-100 I.D. data.) The third and fourth symbols indicate model: E10=1/2-Ton Econoline; E20=3/4-Ton Econoline; E30=1-Ton Econoline. The fifth symbol indicates engine: U=170 cid Six; G=302 V-8. The last six symbols are the sequential production number. Model codes are in the first column of the chart below.

Model	Body Type	Price	Weight	Prod. Total
Econoline — 1/2-Ton — 105.5 in. w.b. — Six				
E-140	Cargo Van	2489	3040	Note 1
E-150	Window Van	2567	3115	Note 1
E-160	Display Van	2522	3085	Note 1

NOTE 1: Available production break-outs are given at the end of the Econoline section.

ENGINE [Econoline E-100]: Displacement: 170 cid. Six-cylinder. 105 hp at 4400 rpm. Bore & stroke: 3.50 in. x 2.94 in. Compression ratio: 9.1:1. One-barrel carburetor.
ECONOLINE E-200 CARGO VAN: For heavier loads, buyers could move up to the new 3/4-ton E-200 series. Its front axle had a capacity of 2,750 lbs. It also had larger (11 x 3 in. front/11 x 2.25 in. rear) brakes. Standard features echoed those of the E-100 Cargo Van.
ECONOLINE E-200 WINDOW VAN: This vehicle shared styling with the E-100 Window Van and load capacity with other E-200 vans.
ECONOLINE E-200 DISPLAY VAN: This vehicle shared styling with the E-100 Display Vans and load capacity with other E-200 vans.
I.D. DATA [Econoline E-200]: See E-100.

Model	Body Type	Price	Weight	Prod. Total
Econoline — 3/4-Ton — 105.5 in. w.b. — Six				
E-240	Cargo Van	2592	3165	Note 1
E-250	Window Van	2670	3240	Note 1
E-260	Display Van	2625	3210	Note 1

NOTE 1: Available production break-outs are given at the end of the Econoline section.
ENGINE [Econoline E-200]: Same as E-100.
ECONOLINE E-300 CARGO VAN: For really big loads, it was hard to beat the 1-ton E-300 Cargo Van. Its front axle capacity was rated at 3,300 lbs. The rear axle was rated at 4,800 lbs. The front brakes were 12 x 3 in.; the rears 12 x 12.5 in. A 10 in. clutch was standard. Its front and rear springs were also heavy-duty.
ECONOLINE E-300 WINDOW VAN: Same features as the Cargo Van, plus windows all around.
ECONOLINE E-300 DISPLAY VAN: Had same features as the Cargo Van, plus windows on the right-hand side.
I.D. DATA [Econoline E-300]: See E-100 I.D.

Model	Body Type	Price	Weight	Prod. Total
Econoline — 1-Ton — 105.5 in. w.b. — Six				
E-340	Cargo Van	2745	3880	Note 1
E-350	Window Van	2825	3820	Note 1
E-360	Display Van	2780	3790	Note 1

NOTE 1: Ford records show the following 1969 Econoline production break-outs: [89A Standard Cargo Van] 69,806; [89C Standard Display Van] 6,337; [89E Standard Window Van] 14,383; [89B Custom Cargo Van] 4,665; [89D Custom Display Van] 1,077 and [89F Custom Window Van] 1,774.
ENGINE [Econoline E-300]: Displacement: 240 cid. Six-cylinder. 150 hp at 4000 rpm. Bore & stroke: 4.00 in. x 3.18 in. Compression ratio: 9.2:1. One-barrel carburetor.
CHASSIS: Wheelbase: 105.5 in. (123.5 in. Super Van). Tires: [E-100] E78-14B; [E-200] G78-15B; [E-300] 8.00 x 16.5.
POWERTRAIN OPTIONS: Engines: 240 cid six-cylinder engine. 302 cid V-8 engine. Transmissions: SelectShift Cruise-O-Matic transmission.
CONVENIENCE OPTIONS: Push-button radio. Stationary or flip-fold passenger seat. High output heater and defroster. Auxiliary hot water heater. Air-conditioner. Insulation package. Insulated floor mats. Inside body rub rails. Inside or Western-type rearview mirrors. Deluxe driver and/or stationary passenger seats with color-coordinated floor mats. Auxiliary step for right-side cargo doors. Dual electric horns. Courtesy light switches for front or all doors. Padded instrument panel. Shoulder harness. Stationary glass or vents in rear and/or right side cargo doors. Tinted glass. Inside rear door latch and lock. Scuff pads at front door wells. School bus package for E-200 and E-300 Window Vans with 123.5 in. wheelbase. [Custom Equipment Package] Includes (in addition to or in place of standard items): Deluxe pleated vinyl seat trim; bright metal front and rear bumpers and hubcaps; horn ring; cigarette lighter; color-coordinated floor mat on left side; glove box door with lock; and bright metal grille, taillight bezels, vent window and windshield moldings.

1969 Ford 12-Passenger Club Wagon (JAG)

CLUB WAGON: Club Wagons were basically Econolines made for hauling people. The base model held five passengers. Among standard features were: Twin-I-Beam independent front suspension; vinyl seat trim; armrests on front doors and at right side of three-passenger seats; ashtrays, front and rear; black floor mats; coat hook; two dome lights; dual sun visors; instrument panel padded on right side; bright instrument cluster trim; glove box door with lock; headlining in front compartment; dual outside rearview mirrors; backup lights; inside rearview mirror; emergency lamp flasher; retracting step for double side doors; rear reflectors; and side-marker lights at front and rear.
CUSTOM CLUB WAGON: This was a step up from the base model. Both shared many of the same features. However, the Custom also had: Pleated vinyl seat trim; interior vinyl side and door trim panels; armrests for all seats; color-coordinated front and rear floor mats; four coat hooks; full-length headlining; window trim moldings; cigarette lighter; scuff pads at front door wells; spare tire cover; horn ring; bright metal grille; instrument panel padded full width; custom ornaments; bright metal bodyside moldings; taillight bezels and hubcaps; and added insulation.
CHATEAU CLUB WAGON: At the top-of-the-line was the Chateau. It had (in addition to or in place of Custom Club Wagon features) pleated deluxe cloth seat trim with vinyl bolsters; similar trim on interior door and side panels with simulated woodgrain bands; full-length color-coordinated carpeting with dash insulator; chrome front and rear bumpers; bright metal dual outside mirrors; bright metal moldings around windshield, side and rear windows; bright metal rear body molding; and Chateau ornaments.

I.D. DATA [Club Wagon]: See E-100.

Model	Body Type	Price	Weight	Prod. Total
Club Wagon — 1/2-Ton — 105.5 in. w.b. — Six				
E-110	Standard	2897	3425	10,956
E-120	Custom	3121	3600	11,725
E-130	Chateau	3025	3630	9702
Club Wagon — 3/4-Ton — 105.5 in. w.b. — Six				
E-210	Standard	3030	3800	Note 1
E-220	Custom	3255	4040	Note 1
E-230	Chateau	3410	4270	Note 1
Club Wagon — 1/2-Ton — 123.5 in. w.b. — Six				
E-310	Standard	3370	4550	Note 1
E-320	Custom	3595	4810	Note 1
E-330	Chateau	3755	5040	Note 1

NOTE 1: Combined body style production totals for the three Club Wagon lines were: [Standard Club Wagon] 10,956; [Custom Club Wagon] 11,725; and [Chateau Club Wagon] 9,702.

ENGINE [Club Wagon]: Same as E-300.

CHASSIS: Wheelbase: 105.5 in./123.5 in. Tires: E78-14B.

POWERTRAIN OPTIONS: Engine: 302 V-8. Transmission: SelectShift Cruise-O-Matic transmission.

CONVENIENCE OPTIONS: Power steering. Ammeter and oil pressure gauge. Heavy-duty battery. Heavy-duty shocks. Whitewall tires. Chrome front and rear bumpers. Cigarette lighter. Courtesy light switches for all doors. Door positioners for all door. Air-conditioner. Insulation package. Inside body rub rails. High-output heater/defroster. Auxiliary hot water heater for passenger compartment. Tinted glass. AM radio.

1969 Ford 1/2-Ton F-100 Deluxe Styleside 8-Foot Pickup (JAG)

F-100 PICKUP: The new light-duty Ford trucks had a revised grille. It featured two thin horizontal bars crossed by three vertical ones above and below a thicker horizontal center bar. Aside from that, styling was basically carried over from the previous year. Among the standard features were: Three-speed fully-synchronized manual transmission; color-coordinated interior; dome light; Hi-Dri all-weather ventilation; deluxe fresh air heater with three-speed fan; ashtray; glove compartment; energy-absorbing armrests with paddle-type door latch handles; seat belts; hardboard headlining; black floor mat; vinyl seat trim in black, blue, red or parachment; and padded instrument panel. Both Styleside and Flareside versions were offered in either 6-.5 ft. or 8 ft. cargo box lengths.

1969 Ford 1/2-Ton F-100 Deluxe Styleside 6.5-Foot Pickup (JAG)

I.D. DATA [F-100]: VIN located on rating plate. The first three symbols indicated series: F10=F-100 (4x2); F11=F-100 (4x4). The fourth symbol indicates engine: A=240 cid six; B=300 cid six; H=390 cid V-8; Y=360 cid V-8. The fifth symbol indicates assembly plant: C=Ontario, Canada; D=Dallas, Texas; E=Mahwah, N.J.; H=Lorain, Ohio; K=Kansas City, Kan.; L=Michigan Truck; N=Norfolk, Va.; P=Twin Cities, Minn.; R=San Jose, Calif.; S=Allen Park, Mich.; U=Louisville, Ken. The last six symbols are the sequential production number.

Model	Body Type	Price	Weight	Prod. Total
F-100 — 1/2-Ton — 115 in. w.b. — Six				
81	Chassis & Cab	2230	3060	Note 1
83	Flareside 6.5 ft.	2354	3380	Note 1
83	Styleside 6.5 ft.	2393	3440	Note 1
F-100 — 1/2-Ton — 131 in. w.b. — Six				
83	Flareside 8 ft.	2393	3490	Note 1
83	Styleside 8 ft.	2430	3505	Note 1

* Add $645 for 4x4.

NOTE 1: Ford records show the following F-100 production break-outs: [4x2 Chassis & Cab] 3,058; [4x2 Flareside Pickups] 16,248; [4x2 Styleside Pickups] 315,979; [4x4 Chassis & Cab] 56; [4x4 Flareside Pickup] 465 and [4x4 Styleside Pickup] 7,940.

ENGINE [F-100]: Displacement: 240 cid. Six-cylinder. 150 hp at 4000 rpm. Bore & stroke: 4.0 in. x 3.18 in. Compression ratio: 9.2:1. One-barrel carburetor.

1969 Ford 1/2-Ton F-100 Deluxe Styleside 8-Foot Bed Pickup (JAG)

F-250 PICKUP: The F-250 Pickup had most of the same features as the F-100. Plus, it came with Flex-O-Matic rear suspension. The Styleside had double-wall side panels and tailgate; flat-top wheelhousings; stake pockets; and an all-steel floor. A single center latch mechanism opened the tailgate. Steel support straps held the tailgate in open position. The Flareside had runningboards between the cab and rear fenders. It came with seasoned hardwood floorboards and with steel skid strips to help slide cargo into place. Rubber-covered forged-steel chains supported the tailgate when open. Toggle-type latches maintained a tight seal when the tailgate was closed. Heavy gauge steel side panels with flared sides had rolled edges for extra strength and rigidity.

F-250 PLATFORM/STAKE: Floor frames of the F-250 Platform/Stake were made of steel cross sills riveted to steel siderails. Floorboards were interlocked with steel skid strips and corners were reinforced with steel brackets. Formed steel caps over the ends of the body sills acted as bumpers for loading docks. Sideboards and stakes were straight-grained hardwood.

I.D. DATA [F-250]: Same as F-100, except first three symbols were: [4x2] F25; [4x4] F26.

Model	Body Type	Price	Weight	Prod. Total
F-250 — 3/4-Ton — 131 in. w.b. — Six				
81	Chassis & Cab	2461	3290	Note 1
83	Flareside	2588	3710	Note 1
83	Styleside	2624	3725	Note 1
80	Platform	2621	3705	—
86	Stake	2677	3885	Note 1
F-250 Crew Cabs — 3/4-Ton — 147 in. w.b. — Six				
81	Chassis & Cab	—	—	Note 1
83	Styleside	—	—	Note 1

* Add $725 for 4x4.

NOTE 1: Ford records show the following F-250 production break-outs: [4x2 Chassis & Windshield] 242; [4x2 Chassis & Cab] 6,093; [4x2 Platform & Rack] 586; [4x2 Platform] 73; [4x2 Flareside Pickups] 3,827; [4x2 Styleside Pickups] 101,603; [4x4 Chassis & Cab] 641; [4x4 Platform & Rack] 102; [4x4 Platform] 30; [4x4 Flareside Pickups] 973 and [4x4 Styleside Pickups] 10,286.

ENGINE [F-250]: Same as F-100.

F-350 PICKUP: F-350 buyers had to settle for the Flareside cargo box. It had a cargo capacity of 74 cu. ft. That was almost 10 cu. ft. more than the comparable F-250 Flareside. Plus, it could haul heavier payloads. A four-speed manual transmission was standard.

F-350 PLATFORM/STAKE: The F-350 Platform/Stake had most of the same features as the F-250 version. However, rather than wood, it used reinforced steel stakes. Also, it was available with dual rear wheels (at extra cost). A four-speed manual transmission was standard.

I.D. DATA [F-350]: Same as F-100, except first three symbols were: [4x2] F35.

Model	Body Type	Price	Weight	Prod. Total
F-350 — 1-Ton — 135 in./159 in. w.b. — Six				
81	Chassis & Cab	2579	3615	Note 1
83	Flareside	2727	4075	Note 1
80	Platform 9 ft.	2881	4200	Note 1
80	Platform 12 ft.	2920	4600	Note 1
86	Stake 9 ft.	2935	4440	Note 1
86	Stake 12 ft.	2975	4945	Note 1
F-350 Crew Cab — 1-Ton — 1564.5 in. w.b. — Six				
81	Chassis & Cab	—	—	Note 1
83	Styleside	—	—	Note 1

NOTE 1: Ford records show the following F-350 production break-outs: [Chassis & Cowl] 331; [Chassis & Windshield] 206; [Chassis & Cab] 27,817; [Platform & Rack] 5,335; [Platform] 613; and Flareside Pickup [1,829].

ENGINE [F-350]: See F-100.

CHASSIS: Wheelbase: 115 in. (F-100); 131 in. (F-100/F-250); 135 in. (F-350); 149 in. (F-250 Crew Cab); 159 in. (F-350 Crew Cab); 164.5 in. (F-350 Crew Cab). GVW: 4,200-5,000 lbs.(F-100); 4,600-5,600 lbs. (F-100 4x4); 6,300-7,500 lbs. (F-250); 6,300-7,700 lbs. (F-250 4x4); 6,600-10,000 lbs. (F-350). Tires: 8.25 x 15 (F-100); 8.00 x 16.5 (F-250/F-350).

POWERTRAIN OPTIONS: Engines: 300 cid six. 360 cid V-8. 390 cid V-8. Transmissions: Three-speed with overdrive (F-100). Four-speed manual. Cruise-O-Matic automatic.

CONVENIENCE OPTIONS: Four-wheel drive. F-100 4x4s had Mono-Beam front suspension with coil springs and forged radius rods and a single-speed transfer case coupled to a four-speed transmission. The F-250 4x4 front suspension consisted of resilient front leaf springs with lubrication free shackles (They also had a standard two-speed transfer case and three-speed manual transmission). Electric power pack (under-hood 2500-watt generator). Frame mounted 25-gal. fuel tank. [Convenience Group] Includes: Cargo area light; courtesy light door switches; day/night mirror; and engine compartment light. Tool stowage box (8 ft. Styleside). Western type mirrors (fixed or swing-lock). Spare tire carrier (inside box on Styleside, ahead of left rear fender on Flareside). Bright finish grille. Rear step bumper (Styleside). Bright hubcaps. Bright or mag wheelcovers for 15 in. wheels. Extra-cooling equipment. Chrome contour front bumpers. Chrome or painted contour rear bumpers for Stylesides. Painted channel rear bumper for Flaresides. Brush-type grille guard. Free-running front hubs for 4x4s. Oil-bath engine air cleaner. Velocity-type engine governor. Vacuum brake booster. Power disc front brakes (F-250/F-350). Power steering (F-100/F-250). Flex-O-Matic rear suspension (F-100). Heavy-duty shocks. Heavy-duty front springs. Heavy-duty alternator. Heavy-duty battery. Select-Aire air-conditioner (includes standard fresh air heater in an integral unit). Push-button radio. Manual radio. Ammeter and oil pressure gauge. Bucket seats color-coordinated to exterior paint. Lockable cab storage compartment behind the seat. Remote-control outside mirror. Tinted windshield. Tinted glass all around. Cab market and identification lights.

Shoulder harnesses. Dual electric horns. Heavy-duty black vinyl seat trim. Full-width Custom Cab seat. [Custom Cab Equipment] Includes: Deep-foam seat cushion and foam padding in seatback; woven plastic seat trim; color-coordinated floor mat; custom instrument cluster; horn ring; cigarette lighter; bright metal headlining retainer and door cover plate moldings; bright metal front bumper, grille, windshield moldings; and taillamp bezels. [Ranger Package] Includes: Color-coordinated pleated vinyl upholstery with a cloth-like pattern; woodgrain inserts in instrument cluster; bright metal instrument panel molding; pleated vinyl door trim with simulated woodgrain insert and bright molding; door courtesy light switches; wall-to-wall carpeting; distinctive grille; bright metal hubcaps and trim on rocker panels, front wheel opening lips, roof drip rails and around rear window; Ranger emblem; cargo area light; bright metal tailgate release handle, rocker panel extension, rear wheel opening lip; and bright tailgate moldings. [Camper Special Package] Includes: 70 amp.-hr. battery; oil pressure gauge; ammeter; extra-cooling radiator; dual bright metal 6 x 10 in. Western type mirrors; extended tailgate; front side-marker lights; camper wiring harness; rear shock absorbers (F-350); and Camper Special emblem. [Farm & Ranch Special] Includes: (F-100/F-250 Stylesides) Heavy-duty Twin-I-Beam front suspension; heavy-duty Flex-O-Matic rear suspension; front and nine-inch high side cargo boards painted body color; rear step bumper with provision for trailer hitch; chrome Western swing-lock mirrors; heavy-duty battery; heavy-duty alternator; bright metal bodyside moldings; and Farm & Ranch Special insignia on cowl. [Contractor Special] Includes: (8 ft. Styleside) Heavy-duty Package 1 with heavy-duty front and rear springs; rear step bumper; convenience group; dual chrome western swing-lock mirrors; contractor box on both sides with key-lockable fold-down doors; and Contractor Special insignia on cowl sides. [Package 2] Includes everything on package 1, plus under-hood electric power pack.

NOTE: Standard colors for 1969 were: Raven black; Wimbledon white; Norway green; New lime; Boxwood green; Candy-apple red; Royal maroon; Cordova copper; Empire yellow; Lunar green; Reef aqua; Sky View blue; Harbor blue; Chrome yellow and Pure white. With regular two-tones the accent color was applied to the roof and upper back panel with a belt line molding from door to door, around back of the cab. Deluxe two-tones (Styleside only) had accent color applied to the area below the bodyside and lower tailgate moldings, which were included in this option. Combination two-tones (Stylesides only) featured the regular and deluxe two-tone options combined with the accent color applied as specified for these options.

1969 Ford 1/2-Ton Model U-140 Bronco Sports Utility Pickup (RCA)

HISTORICAL: Introductory dates: [Vans] Spring of 1968; [Others] Fall of 1968. Calendar year production: 639,948. Industry share: 32.60 percent. Calendar year registrations by weight class: [6,000 lbs. or under] 399,285; [6,000-10,000 lbs.] 179,082. Model year production of light-duty trucks including Ranchero, Bronco and Econoline was 647,948. (This includes 2,780 Ford P-350 Parcel Vans and 2,382 Ford P-400 Parcel Vans). Innovations: Completely redesigned and re-engineered Econoline Van introduced in Feb. 1968 as a 1969 model. The Econoline boasted more cargo space and passenger carrying room than any similar competing model. It featured Twin I-Beam front suspension; V-8 options; and two wheelbase choices. P. Caldwell was Vice-President and General Manager of the Ford Truck Division of Ford Motor Co. This was a record year for sales, with 713,699 deliveries made for the January through January period. A total of 13,915 Ford trucks of all sizes were made with diesel engines. Other engine installations included 158,521 sixes and 467,512 V-8s.

1970 FORD

1970 Ford 1/2-Ton Ranchero Squire Sedan-Pickup (OCW)

RANCHERO PICKUP: The 1970 Ranchero was sleek and stylish. It had rounded fender contours, a slightly sloping hood, hidden windshield wipers and a criss-cross pattern full-width grille with four headlights recessed in it. Standard features included: Bright left-hand remote control outside mirror; bright windshield, rear window, drip rail and top of cargo box moldings; bright taillight bezels; bright hubcaps; full-width seat upholstered in black, blue or gold vinyl with pleated seatback; color-keyed vinyl door trim panels with bright frames;

color-keyed rubber floor covering; flow-through ventilation; ventless side windows; locking steering column; fresh air heater/defroster; trim panel behind the split seatback (with spare tire and tool compartment cover); deluxe seat belts with outboard retractors and shoulder harnesses (also center passenger seat belts); armrests with integral, squeeze-type door handles; vinyl-framed day/night mirror; cigarette lighter; and emergency lamp flasher.

RANCHERO 500 PICKUP: This was the most popular Ranchero in 1970. In addition to (or in place of) standard Ranchero features, the 500 had: Pleated all-vinyl seat upholstery in black, red, blue, white or ginger; deep-pile wall-to-wall carpeting; wood-tone inlay in padded steering wheel hub; electric clock; armrests with bright base; deluxe grille with center crest; bright metal wheelcovers; bright metal side moldings with vinyl insert; bright metal wheel lip moldings; and bright metal hidden wiper lip molding.

RANCHERO GT PICKUP: The GT had (in addition to or in place of all the standard Ranchero features) a deluxe grille with center GT crest; colorful laser stripe (red, brown, green or blue color-keyed with exterior) on bodysides and tailgate; GT letters and chevrons on sides; Sport-scoop hood; deluxe wheelcovers; fiberglass-belted whitewall tires; bright metal wheel lip and hidden wiper lip moldings; pleated, all-vinyl seat upholstery in black, red, blue, white or ginger; deep-pile, wall-to-wall carpeting; wood-tone inlay panel in padded steering wheel hub; electric clock; and black lower instrument panel. The Cobra-Jet V-8 option for the Ranchero GT included: Performance handling package; 80-amp.-hr. battery; 55-amp. alternator; dual exhausts; and appearance package with bright cast aluminum rocker covers. The Cobra-Jet Ram-Air V-8 had all this, plus a ram-induction system with pop-through "shaker" hood scoop for peak performance.

RANCHERO SQUIRE PICKUP: Sales literature called this the, "New ultimate in personal Pickup luxury." The Squire had (in addition to or in place of standard Ranchero features): Color-coordinated deep-pile wall-to-wall carpeting; wood-tone panel under instruments; wood-tone inlay in padded steering wheel hub; electric clock; deluxe grille with center crest; wood-tone panels on sides and tailgate; fiberglass belted whitewall tires; Deluxe wheelcovers; bright metal hidden wiper lip molding; and Ranchero Squire script on front fenders.

I.D. DATA: [Ranchero] VIN located on rating plate. First symbol indicates model year: 0=1970. Second symbol indicates assembly plant: A=Atlanta, Ga.; B=Oakville, Calif.; D=Dallas, Texas; E=Mahwah, N.J.; F=Dearborn, Mich.; G=Chicago, Ill.; H=Lorain, Ohio; J=Los Angeles, Calif.; K=Kansas City, Kan.; N=Norfolk, Va.; P=Twin Cities, Minn.; R=San Jose, Calif.; S=Allen Park, Mich.; T=Metuchen, N.J.; U=Louisville, Ken; W=Wayne, Mich.; X=St. Thomas, Canada; Y=Wixom, Mich. The third and fourth symbols indicate model: 47=Ranchero; 48=Ranchero 500; 49=Ranchero 500 GT. The fifth symbol indicates engine: L or 3=250 cid six; F or 6=302 cid V-8; H=351 cid V-8; M=351 cid V-8; N=429 cid V-8; C=429 CJ (Cobra-Jet) V-8; and J=429 CJ Ram-Air V-8. The last six symbols are the sequential production number.

Model	Body Type	Price	Weight	Prod. Total
Ranchero — 1/2-Ton — 117 in. w.b. — Six				
661	Sedan-Pickup	2646	3285	4816
Ranchero — 1/2-Ton — 117 in. w.b. — V-8				
66B	500 Sedan-Pickup	2860	3295	8976
66C	GT Sedan-Pickup	3010	3445	3905
66D	Squire Sedan-Pickup	2965	3330	3943

ENGINE [Ranchero]: Displacement: 250 cid. OHV six-cylinder. 155 hp at 4000 rpm. Bore & stroke: 3.68 x 3.91 in. Compression ratio: 9.0:1. One-barrel carburetor.

ENGINE [Ranchero GT/500/Squire]: Displacement: 302 cid. V-8. 220 hp at 4600 rpm. Bore & stroke: 4 x 3 in. Compression ratio: 9.5:1. Carburetor: Two-barrel.

CHASSIS: Wheelbase: 117 in. Overall length: 206.2 in. Tires: E78-14 4PR.

POWERTRAIN OPTIONS: Engines: 220 hp 302 cid V-8. 250 hp 351 cid V-8. 300 hp 351 cid V-8. 360 hp 429 cid Thunder-Jet V-8. 370 hp 429 cid Cobra V-8. 370 hp 429 Cobra-Jet V-8. Transmissions: Four-speed manual transmission with Hurst shifter. SelectShift Cruise-O-Matic transmission.

CONVENIENCE OPTIONS: Rim-blow sport steering wheel (allowed one to blow the horn by squeezing the rim). AM/FM stereo radio. SelectAire air-conditioner with hi-level outlets. Hidden headlamps (Squire/GT/500). Vinyl roof in black or white. Intermittent windshield wipers. AM push-button radio. Electric clock (Ranchero). Power steering. Tinted glass. Deluxe wheelcovers. Sport-styled wheelcovers. Styled steel wheels. [Visibility Group] Includes: Ashtray, map, glove compartment and underhood lights; warning lights for seat belts and parking brake; and headlight-on reminder buzzer. Tachometer (V-8s only). High-back bucket seats in black or white knitted vinyl (Squire/GT/500). Power front disc brakes. Racing-type mirrors painted body color (left-hand mirror includes remote control). Shaker hood scoop with Ram-Air induction system (included with optional 429 Cobra-Jet V-8). Flat black paint on hood and scoop of Ranchero GT. Heavy-duty suspension package. Heavy-duty battery. Extra-cooling radiator. [Class II Trailer Towing Package] Includes: Front power disc brakes; heavy-duty suspension; cooling package; heavy-duty alternator and battery; and F78-14 4PR or E70-14 4PR or F70-14 4PR whitewall tires.

NOTE: Ranchero colors for 1970 were: Raven black; Wimbledon white; Candy-apple red; Calypso coral; Dark maroon; Dark blue; Medium blue metallic; platinum; Medium and Dark Ivy green (metallic); New lime; Champagne gold; Morning gold; Carmel bronze (metallic) and Bright yellow. Two-tone combinations were available with Wimbledon white roofs and all other colors except platinum. Raven black roofs were available with all colors except Dark blue, Medium blue and Dark ivy-green.

1970 Ford 1/2-Ton Bronco Model U-150 Sport Utility Wagon (RCA)

BRONCO PICKUP: Styling changes were minor for the four-wheel drive Bronco in 1970. The front side-marker light and rear quarter panel reflector were now flush-mounted and higher than before. Standard features included: All-vinyl seat; full-width seat; fresh air heater and defroster; lockable glove compartment; padded instrument panel; energy-absorbing

342

sun visors; vinyl-coated floor mat; floor-mounted T-bar transfer case control; Mono-Beam suspension; self-adjusting brakes; and fully-synchronized three-speed manual transmission.

BRONCO WAGON: The Bronco wagon shared the features of the Pickup, but had a full-length roof. The roof had fixed windows in the rear liftgate and on each side of the rear compartment.

I.D. DATA [U-100]: VIN located on rating plate. The first three symbols indicated series: U14=Model U-140 Pickup; U15=Model U-150 Wagon. The fourth symbol indicated engine: F=170 cid six; G=302 cid V-8. The fifth symbol indicated assembly plant: H=Lorain, Ohio; L=Michigan Truck; R=San Jose, Calif.; S=Allen Park, Mich. The last six symbols are the sequential production number.

Model	Body Type	Price	Weight	Prod. Total
Bronco — 1/2-Ton — 90 in. w.b. — Six				
U140	Pickup	3035	2990	1700
U150	Wagon	3149	3090	16,750

ENGINE [Bronco]: Displacement 170 cid. OHV six-cylinder. 105 hp at 4400 rpm. Bore & stroke: 3.50 x 2.94 in. Compression ratio: 9.1:1. One-barrel carburetor.

CHASSIS: Wheelbase: 90 in. Overall length: 152.1 in. Overall width: 68.8 in. GVW: 3,850-4,700 lbs. Tires: 7.35 x 15.

POWERTRAIN OPTIONS: Engine: 302 cid V-8.

CONVENIENCE OPTIONS: [Convenience Group] Includes: Cigarette lighter; map light (inside 10 in. day/night mirror); horn ring; one-pint oil bath air cleaner (302 V-8); right-hand chrome rearview mirror; bucket seats; shoulder harness; rear seat (Bronco Wagon with bucket seat option); chrome bumpers; skid plates for standard fuel tank and transfer case; inside tailgate-mounted spare tire carrier (included with rear seat option); exterior rear-mounted swing-away tire carrier; bright metal wheelcovers; high-flotation tires; auxiliary 11.5-gal. fuel tank (with skid plate); manual radio and antenna; bright bodyside and tailgate moldings; bright metal rocker panel moldings; Dana free-running front hubs; hand-operated throttle; and heavy-duty front axle carrier assembly (special order). [Sport Package] Includes: Bright metal Sport Bronco emblem; pleated parchment vinyl front seat; vinyl door trim panels with bright metal moldings; hardboard headlining with bright metal retainer moldings (Wagon); parchment vinyl simulated-carpet front floor mat with bright metal retainers (rear floor mat included with optional rear seat); cigarette lighter; satin-finish horn ring; bright metal drip rail moldings; bright metal windshield and window frames; bright metal grille molding and tailgate release handle; bright headlight, side light, reflector and taillight bezels; Argent silver-painted grille with bright Ford letters; chrome bumpers front and rear; chrome front bumper guards; bright metal wheelcovers (with 15 in. wheels only); and 6.50 x 16-6 ply-rated TT tires. Dealer-installed accessories: Power-take-off (front-mounted). Warn free-running front hubs (manual or automatic). Snow plows. Snow plow angling kits. Front auxiliary air springs. Front-mounted winch. Trailer hitch. Trailer towing mirror. Locking gas cap. Front tow hooks. Compass. Fire extinguisher. Tachometer. Two-way radio.

NOTE: Bronco color choices for 1970 were: Raven black; Wimbledon white; Candy-apple red; Royal maroon; Sky View blue; Harbor blue; Diamond blue; Acapulco blue; Reef aqua; Norway green; Boxwood green; Mojave tan; Chrome yellow; Pinto yellow; Carmel bronze metallic; New lime; and Yucatan gold. Bronco roofs were painted Wimbledon white.

ECONOLINE E-100 CARGO VAN: Except for a slight revision to the side-marker lamps and reflectors (the rear ones were now at the same level as the front ones), the Econoline was basically unchanged for 1970. Standard features included: Vinyl color-coordinated upholstery; painted front and rear bumpers and hubcaps; left-hand fresh air inlet; dome lights in driver's compartment and cargo area; ashtray; single electric horn; coat hook; mechanical jack; Double-grip door locks on all doors (with reversible keys); push-pull interior door locks (except rear doors); metal door checks; individual driver's seat; headlining in driver and passenger area; fresh air heater and defroster; and double cargo doors at right and rear.

ECONOLINE E-100 WINDOW VAN: As the name suggests, the window van had glass all around. Like other E-100s, its cargo area was 11.5 ft. long and 53.5 in. wide. It shared most standard features with the Cargo Van.

ECONOLINE E-100 DISPLAY VAN: This model had windows at the rear and on the right-hand side. It came with the same standard features as the Cargo Van.

I.D. DATA: [Econoline] VIN located on rating plate. First symbol indicates model year: 0=1970. Second symbol indicates assembly plant: (See Ranchero/Bronco/F-100 I.D. data.) The third and fourth symbols indicate model: E10=1/2-Ton Econoline; E20=3/4-Ton Econoline; E30=1-Ton Econoline. The fifth symbol indicates engine: U=170 cid Six; G=302 V-8. The last six symbols are the sequential production number. Model codes are in first column of chart elow.

Model	Body Type	Price	Weight	Prod. Total
Econoline — 1/2-Ton — 105.5 in. w.b. — Six				
E-140	Cargo Van	2673	3265	Note 1
E-150	Window Van	2751	3340	Note 1
E-160	Display Van	2706	3310	Note 1

NOTE 1: For production break-outs see end of Econoline listings.

ENGINE [Econoline E-100]: Displacement: 170 cid. OHV six-cylinder. 105 hp at 4400 rpm. Bore & stroke: 3.50 x 2.94 in. Compression ratio: 9.1:1. One-barrel carburetor.

ECONOLINE E-200 CARGO VAN: For heavier loads, buyers could move up to the E-200 series. Its front axle had a capacity of 2,750 lbs. The rear axle capacity was 3,300 lbs. It also had larger (11 x 3 in. front and 11 x 2.25 in. rear) brakes. Standard features echoed those of the E-100 Cargo Van.

ECONOLINE E-200 WINDOW VAN: This vehicle shared styling with the E-100 Window Van and load capacity with other E-200 vans.

ECONOLINE E-200 DISPLAY VAN: This vehicle shared styling with the E-100 Display Van and load capacity with other E-200 vans.

I.D. DATA [Econoline E-200]: See E-100.

Model	Body Type	Price	Weight	Prod. Total
Econoline — 3/4-Ton — 105.5 in. w.b. — Six				
E-240	Cargo Van	2776	3385	Note 1
E-250	Window Van	2854	3460	Note 1
E-260	Display Van	2809	3430	Note 1

NOTE 1: For production break-outs see end of Econoline listings.

ENGINE [Econoline E-200]: Same as E-100.

ECONOLINE E-300 CARGO VAN: For really big loads, it was hard to beat the E-300 Cargo Van. Its front axle capacity was rated at 3,300 lbs. Rear axle was 4,800 lbs. The front brakes were 12 x 3 in., the rears 12 x 12.5 in. A 10 in. clutch was standard. Its front and rear springs were also heavy-duty.

ECONOLINE E-300 WINDOW VAN: Had same features as the Cargo Van, plus windows all around.

ECONOLINE E-300 DISPLAY VAN: Had the same features as the Cargo Van, plus windows on the right-hand side.

I.D. DATA [Econoline E-300]: See F-100 I.D.

Model	Body Type	Price	Weight	Prod. Total
Econoline — 1-Ton — 123.5 in. w.b. — Six				
E-340	Cargo Van	2865	3790	Note 1
E-350	Window Van	3009	3920	Note 1
E-360	Display Van	2964	3890	Note 1

NOTE 1: Ford records show the following Econoline combined body style production break-outs: [89A Standard Cargo Van] 75,179; [89C Standard Display Van] 8,471; [89E Standard Window Van] 16,192; [89B Custom Cargo Van] 6,533; [89D Custom Display Van] 846 and [89F Custom Window Van] 1,884.

ENGINE [Econoline E-300]: Displacement: 240 cid. Six-cylinder. 150 hp at 4000 rpm. Bore & stroke: 4.00 x 3.18 in. Compression ratio: 9.2:1. One-barrel carburetor.

CHASSIS: Wheelbase: 105.5 in. (123.5 in. SuperVan) Tires: E78-14B (E-100); G78-15B (E-200); 8.00 x 16.5 in. (E-300).

POWERTRAIN OPTIONS: Engines: 240 six-cylinder engine. 302 V-8 engine. Transmissions: SelectShift Cruise-O-Matic transmission.

CONVENIENCE OPTIONS: Push-button radio. Stationary or flip-fold passenger seat. High-output heater and defroster. Auxiliary hot water heater. Air-conditioner. Insulation package. Insulated floor mats. Inside body rub rails. Inside or Western-type outside rear-view mirrors. Deluxe driver and/or stationary passenger seats with color-coordinated floor mats. Auxiliary step for right-side cargo doors. Dual electric horns. Courtesy light switches for front or all doors. Padded instrument panel. Shoulder harness. Stationary glass or vents in rear and/or right-side cargo doors. Tinted glass. Inside rear door latch and lock. Scuff pads at front door wells. School bus package for E-200 and E-300 Window Vans with 123.5 in. wheelbase. [Custom Equipment Package] Includes: (in addition to or in place of standard items] Deluxe pleated vinyl seat trim; bright metal front and rear bumpers and hubcaps; horn ring; cigarette lighter; color-coordinated floor mat on left side; glove box door with lock and bright metal grille, taillight bezels, vent window and windshield moldings.

NOTE: Econoline colors for 1970 were: Sky View blue; Harbor blue; Reef aqua; Cactus green; Crystal green; Tampico yellow; Pinto yellow; Chrome yellow; Baja beige; Candy-apple red; and Wimbledon white. Two-tone paint combinations were available.

CLUB WAGON: Club wagons were basically Econolines made for hauling people. The base model held five passengers. Among standard features were: Twin-I-Beam independent front suspension; vinyl seat trim; armrests on front doors and at right side of 3+ passenger seats; ashtrays front and rear; black floor mats; coat hook; two dome lights; dual sun visors; instruments panel (padded on right side); bright instrument cluster trim; glove box door with lock; headlining in front compartment; dual outside rearview mirrors; backup lights; inside rearview mirror; emergency lamp flasher; retracting step for double side doors; rear reflectors; and side-marker lights at front and rear.

CUSTOM CLUB WAGON: This was a step up from the base model. Both shared many of the same features. The Custom, however, also had: pleated vinyl seat trim; interior vinyl side and door trim panels; armrests for all seats; color-coordinated front and rear floor mats; four coat hooks; full-length headlining; window trim moldings; cigarette lighter; scuff pads at front door wells; spare tire cover; horn ring; bright metal grille; full-width padded instrument panel; Custom ornaments; bright metal bodyside moldings, taillight bezels and hubcaps; and added insulation.

CHATEAU CLUB WAGON: At the top-of-the-line was the Chateau. It had, in addition to or in place of Custom Club Wagon features: Pleated deluxe cloth seat trim with vinyl bolsters; similar trim on interior door and side panels (with simulated woodgrain bands); full-length color-coordinated carpeting with dash insulator; chrome front and rear bumpers; bright metal dual outside mirrors; bright metal molding around windshield, side and rear windows; bright metal rear body molding; and Chateau ornaments.

I.D. DATA [Club Wagon]: See E-100.

Model	Body Type	Price	Weight	Prod. Total
Club Wagon — 1/2-Ton — 105.5 in. w.b. — Six				
E-110	Club Wagon	3109	3595	Note 1
E-120	Custom Club Wagon	3334	3710	Note 1
E-130	Chateau Club Wagon	3483	4180	Note 1

NOTE 1: Body style production: [E-110] 9,951; [E-120] 11,221; [E-130] 8,118.

ENGINE [Club Wagon]: Same as E-300.

CHASSIS: Wheelbase: 105.5 in. (123.5 in. optional) Tires: E78-14B.

POWERTRAIN OPTIONS: Engine: 302 cid V-8. Transmission: SelectShift Cruise-O-Matic transmission.

CONVENIENCE OPTIONS: Power steering. Ammeter and oil pressure gauge. Heavy-duty battery. Heavy-duty shocks. Whitewall tires. Chrome front and rear bumpers. Cigarette lighter. Courtesy light switches for all doors. Door positioners for all doors. Air-conditioner. Insulation package. Inside body rub rails. High-output heater/defroster. Auxiliary hot water heater for passenger compartment. Tinted glass. AM radio.

1970 Ford 1/2-Ton F-100 Ranger XLT Styleside Pickup (JAG)

F-100 CUSTOM PICKUP: The 1970 Ford light-duty trucks had a new grille. It featured a grid-pattern divided at the center by a vertical bar. The parking lamps were slightly lower and of the wraparound variety. The rear side-marker lamps were now at the end of the bodyside spear sculpturing. Standard features included: Three-speed manual transmission; color-coordinated interior; door courtesy light switches; Hi-Dri all-weather ventilation; deluxe fresh air heater with three-speed fan; ashtray; glove compartment; aluminum scuff plates; deluxe instrument cluster bezel; seat belts; hardboard headlining; black floor mats with heel pads; vinyl seat trim with embossed patterned rib inserts in black, blue, red, parchment or green; bright grille; and chrome front bumper. Both Styleside and Flareside versions were offered in either 6.5 ft. or 8 ft. cargo box lengths.

I.D. DATA [F-100]: VIN located on rating plate. The first three symbols indicated series: F10=F-100 (4x2); F11=F-100 (4x4). The fourth symbol indicates engine: A=240 cid six; B=300 cid six; G=302 cid six; H=390 cid V-8; Y=360 cid V-8. The fifth symbol indicates assembly plant: C=Ontario, Canada; D=Dallas, Texas; E=Mahwah, N.J.; H=Lorain, Ohio;

1970 Ford 1/2-Ton F-100 Ranger XLT Styleside Pickup (JAG)

Model	Body Type	Price	Weight	Prod. Total
F-100 — 1/2-Ton — 115 in. w.b. — Six				
81	Chassis & Cab	2384	3160	Note 1
83	Flareside 6.5 ft.	2510	3475	Note 1
83	Styleside 6.5 ft.	2550	3540	Note 1
F-100 — 1/2-Ton — 131 in. w.b. — Six				
83	Flareside 8 ft.	2610	3690	Note 1
83	Styleside 8 ft.	2650	3705	Note 1

NOTE 1: Ford records show the following F-100 production figure break-outs: [Chassis & Cab] 2,688; [Flareside Pickup] 13,551.. Note: No additional break-outs are given.

1970 Ford 1/2-Ton F-100 Custom Styleside Pickup (RCA)

ENGINE [F-100]: Displacement: 240 cid. Six-cylinder. 150 hp at 4000 rpm. Bore & stroke: 4.0 in. x 3.18 in. Compression ratio: 9.2:1. One-barrel carburetor.

F-250 CUSTOM PICKUP: The F-250 Pickup had most of the same features as the F-100. It also had Flex-O-Matic rear suspension. The Styleside had double-wall side panels and tailgate, flat-top wheelhousings, stake pockets and an all-steel floor. A single center latch mechanism opened the tailgate. Steel support straps held the tailgate in open position. The Flareside had runningboards between the cab and rear fenders. It came with seasoned hardwood floorboards with steel skid strips to help slide cargo into place. Rubber-covered forged steel chains supported the the tailgate when open. Toggle-type latches maintained a tight seal when tailgate was closed. Heavy gauge steel side panels, with flared sides, had rolled edges for extra strength and rigidity.

F-250 PLATFORM/STAKE: Floor frames of the F-250 Platform/Stake were made of steel cross-sills riveted to steel side rails. Floorboards were interlocked with steel skid strips and the corners were reinforced with steel brackets. Formed steel caps over the ends of the body sills acted as bumpers for loading docks. Sideboards and stakes were straight-grained hardwood.

I.D. DATA [F-250]: Same as F-100, except first three symbols are: [4x2] F25; [4x4] F26.

Model	Body Type	Price	Weight	Prod. Total
F-250 — 3/4-Ton — 131 in. w.b. — Six				
81	Chassis & Cab	2615	3370	Note 1
83	Flareside	2740	3790	Note 1
83	Styleside	2780	3805	Note 1
80	Platform	2775	3705	Note 1
86	Stake	2830	3885	Note 1
F-250 Crew Cab — 3/4-Ton — 149 in. w.b. — Six				
81	Chassis & Cab	—	—	Note 1
83	Styleside	—	—	Note 1

NOTE 1: Ford records show the following F-250 production break-outs: [Chassis & Windshield] 131; [Chassis & Cab] 6,366; [Platform & Rack] 650; [Platform] 130; [Flareside Pickup] 4,683 and [Styleside Pickup] 121,265. Note: No additional break-outs are available.

ENGINE [F-250]: Same as F-100.

F-350 CUSTOM PICKUP: F-350 buyers had to settle for the Flareside cargo box. It had a cargo capacity of 74 cubic-feet. That was almost 10 more than the comparable F-250 Flareside. It could also haul heavier payloads. A four-speed manual transmission was standard.

F-350 PLATFORM/STAKE: The F-350 Platform/Stake had most of the features as the F-250 version. However, rather than wood, it used reinforced steel stakes. Also, it was available with dual rear wheels (at extra cost). A four-speed manual transmission was standard.

I.D. DATA [F-250]: Same as F-100, except first three symbols are: [4x2] F35.

Model	Body Type	Price	Weight	Prod. Total
F-350 — 1-Ton — 135 in./159 in. w.b. — Six				
81	Chassis & Cab	2720	3725	Note 1
83	Flareside	3505	4290	Note 1
80	Platform 9 ft.	—	4310	Note 1
80	Platform 12 ft.	—	4600	Note 1
86	Stake 9 ft.	2830	3885	Note 1
86	Stake 12 ft.	—	4945	Note 1
F-350 Crew Cab — 3/4-Ton — 164.5 in. w.b. — Six				
81	Chassis & Cab	2770	3835	Note 1
83	Styleside	—	—	Note 1

NOTE 1: Ford records show the following F-350 production break-outs: [Chassis & Cowl] 149; [Chassis & Windshield] 152; [Chassis & Cab] 27,511; [Platform & Rack] 5,341; [Platform] 609; and [Flareside] 1,570.

ENGINE [F-350]: See F-100.

CHASSIS: Wheelbase: 115 in. (F-100); 131 in. (F-100/F-250); 135 in. (F-350); 149 in. (F-250 Crew Cab); 159 in. (F-350); 164.5 in. (F-350 Crew Cab). GVW: 4,200-5,000 lbs. [F-100]; 4,600-5,600 lbs. (F-100 4x4); 6,100-7,500 lbs. (F-250); 6,300-7,700 lbs. (F-250 4x4); 6,600-10,000 lbs. (F-350). Tires: G78 x 15 (F-100); 8.00 x 16.5 (F-250/F-350).

POWERTRAIN OPTIONS: Engines: 300 cid six-cylinder engine. 302 V-8 (F-100). 360 cid V-8. 390 cid V-8. Transmissions: Four-speed manual transmission. SelectShift Cruise-O-Matic.

CONVENIENCE OPTIONS: Four-wheel drive. F-100 model 4x4s had Mono-Beam front suspension with coil springs, steering linkage shock absorber and forged radius rods. The F-100 single-speed transfer case was coupled to a four-speed transmission. The F-250 model 4x4 front suspension consisted of resilient long leaf springs with lubrication-free shackles; standard two-speed transfer case and three-speed transmission. Electric power pack (underhood 2500 watt generator). Frame mounted 25-gal. fuel tank. [Convenience Group] Includes: Cargo area light; courtesy light door switches; day/night mirror and engine compartment light. Tool storage box for eight-foot Styleside. Bright bodyside moldings (Styleside). Western-type mirrors (fixed or swing-lock). Spare tire carrier (inside box on Styleside, ahead of left rear fender on Flareside). Black-textured painted floor. Rear step bumper (Styleside). Bright hubcaps. Bright or mag wheelcovers for 15 in. wheels. Extra-cooling equipment. Chrome contour rear bumpers for Stylesides. Painted channel rear bumper for Flaresides. Brush-type grille guard. Free-running front hubs for 4x4s. Oil bath engine air cleaner. Sliding rear window (standard on F-250 Camper Special). Velocity-type engine governor. Vacuum brake booster. Power disc front brakes (F-250/F-350). Power steering (F-100/F-250). Flex-O-Matic rear suspension (F-100). Heavy-duty shocks. Heavy-duty front springs. Heavy-duty alternator. Heavy-duty battery. SelectAire air-conditioner (includes standard fresh air heater in an integral unit). Push-button radio. Manual radio. Ammeter and oil pressure gauge. Bucket seats color-coordinated to exterior paint. Lockable cab stowage compartment behind the seat. Remote-control outside mirror. Tinted windshield. Tinted glass all around. Cab marker and identification lights. Shoulder harnesses. Dual electric horns. Heavy-duty black vinyl seat trim. Full-width Custom Cab seat. [Sport Custom Cab] Includes: Deep-foam seat cushion and foam padding in seatback; pleated basketweave vinyl seat trim inserts; grained vinyl bolsters; color-coordinated floor mat; horn ring; cigarette lighter; bright rocker panel, wheel lip, windshield molding; and bright taillamp bezels (Stylesides have tailgate applique). [Ranger Package] Includes: Woodgrain inserts in instrument cluster; pleated vinyl door trim with simulated woodgrain insert and bright molding; bright seat-pivot arm covers; glove box plaque; bright metal hub-caps, roof drip rails and moldings around rear window; Ranger emblem; and bright metal tailgate release handle. [Camper Special Package] Includes: 70 amp.-hr. battery; oil pressure gauge; ammeter; extra-cooling radiator; sliding rear window (F-250); dual bright metal 6 x 10 in. Western type mirrors; camper wiring harness; rear shock absorbers (F-350); and Camper Special emblem. [Farm & Ranch Special]: (F-100/F-250 Stylesides) Includes: Front and nine-inch high side cargo boards painted body color; rear step bumper; bright Western swing-lock mirrors; and Farm & Ranch Special insignia. [Contractor Special]: (for eight-foot Styleside) Includes, rear step bumper; dual bright Western long-arm mirrors; contractor box on both sides with key-lock fold down doors; and Contractor Special insignia. [Ranger XLT Package Styleside and Chassis & Cab] Includes: (in addition to, or in place of Ranger equipment) Pleated cloth and vinyl seat upholstery; color-keyed carpeting; special insulation; convenience group; sound-absorbing perforated headlining; bright instrument panel molding on right side; heater modesty panel with wood-tone inserts; bright rocker panel and wheel lip moldings; and wood-tone tailgate panel. [Heavy-duty Special for 8 ft. Styleside] Includes: Heavy-duty front springs; battery; altenator; ammeter; oil pressure gauge; rear step bumper; dual bright Western swing-lock mirrors and Heavy-Duty Special insignia.

NOTE: Standard colors for 1970 were: Raven black; Wimbledon white; New lime; Boxwood green; Candy-apple red; Royal maroon; Mojave tan; Yucatan gold; Pinto yellow; Diamond blue; Reef aqua; Sky View blue; Harbor blue; Chrome yellow; and Pure white. On regular two-tones the accent color was applied to roof and upper back panel with a beltline molding from door-to-door around back of cab. On deluxe two-tones (Styleside only) the accent color was applied to area below the bodyside and lower tailgate moldings, which were included with this option. Combination two-tone, for Stylesides only, combined regular and deluxe two-tone options with accent color applied as specified for these two options.

HISTORICAL: Introduced: Sept. 19, 1969. Calendar year production: 626,585. Market penetration: 36.50 percent of total industry. New truck registrations by weight class, for calendar year: [6,000 lbs. and under] 399,285; [6,001-10,000 lbs.] 179,082. Model year production (light-duty including Bronco/Ranchero/Econoline): 659,722 units including 2,359 of the P-350 Parcel Delivery vans and 2,074 of Ford's P-400 Parcel Delivery vans. Calendar year retail deliveries: 682,789. Calendar year North American sales: 730,268. Engine production, by calendar year: [V-8] 478,821; [Six] 132,016; [Diesel] 15,748. Innovations: New Explorer Special option introduced featuring Shetland plaid upholstery. Automatic choke standard on light-duty trucks. F-100s get fiberglass-belted tires as a regular feature. Other new features for F-100s included a simulated vinyl cab roof and optional sliding rear cab window. Calendar year 1970 was the second best sales season in Ford truck history up to that point. The company offered over 1,300 separate models including medium- and heavy-duty trucks. J.B. Naughton became V.P. and General Manager of Ford Truck Division.

1971 FORD

1971 Ford 1/2-Ton Ranchero 500 Sedan-Pickup (OCW)

RANCHERO PICKUP: The new Ranchero looked pretty much the same as last year's model. That wasn't bad. It had a thin horizontal-bars grille, with a larger bar in the center connecting the headlights. This grille was exclusive to the standard Ranchero. All 1971 Rancheros had flared and finned brake drums, higher rate front springs and a new throttle control mechanism. Other standard features included: Full-width seat upholstered in black, blue or gold vinyl with pleated seatback; color-keyed vinyl door trim panels with bright moldings; color-keyed rubber floor covering; flow-through ventilation; ventless side windows; locking steering column; fresh air heater/defroster; trim panel behind the split seat-back (with spare tire and tool compartment cover); deluxe seat belts with outboard retractors and shoulder harnesses (also center passenger seat belts); armrests with integral, squeeze-type door handles; vinyl-framed day/night mirror; cigarette lighter; emergency lamp flasher; bright left-hand remote-control mirror; hidden windshield wipers; bright windshield, rear window, drip rail and top of cargo box moldings; bright taillight bezels and hubcaps; and fiberglass-belted tires.

RANCHERO 500 PICKUP: The major styling change was to the grille. The basic theme remained the same as in 1970, but it was now divided into two sections. Sandwiched in the center of the division was an oblong emblem. The 500 had (in addition to or in place of standard Ranchero features): Pleated all-vinyl seat upholstery in black, green, blue, vermilion or ginger; deep-pile wall-to-wall carpeting; wood-tone inlay around padded steering wheel horn bar; electric clock; armrests with bright base; deluxe grille with center crest; bright metal wheelcovers and rocker panel moldings; bright metal bodyside molding; bright wheel lips; and hidden wiper lip moldings.

RANCHERO GT PICKUP: The GT had (in addition to or in place of all the standard Ranchero features): Deluxe grille with center GT crest; ribbed Argent rocker panel molding with GT letters; Sport-scoop hood; sporty wheelcovers; fiberglass-belted whitewall tires; bright metal wheel lip and hidden wiper lip moldings; pleated, all-vinyl seat upholstery in black, green, blue, vermilion or ginger; deep-pile, wall-to-wall carpeting; wood-tone inlay panel around padded steering wheel horn bar; electric clock; and black lower instrument panel. The 429 CJ V-8 came with a 80-amp.-hr. battery, 55-amp. alternator, dual exhaust and appearance package with bright cast aluminum rocker covers. The 429 CJ Ram-Air V-8 had all the CJ equipment, plus a ram-induction system with pop-through shaker hood air scoop and special performance handling package.

RANCHERO SQUIRE PICKUP: The Squire had (in addition to or in place of all the standard Ranchero features): Color-coordinated deep-pile, wall-to wall-carpeting; wood-tone panel under instruments; wood-tone inlay around padded steering wheel horn bar; electric clock; deluxe grille with center crest; wood-tone panels on sides and tailgate; fiberglass-belted whitewall tires; deluxe wheelcovers; bright metal hidden wiper lip molding; Ranchero Squire script on front fenders; and knit-vinyl seats in black, vermilion, blue, green or ginger.

I.D. DATA: [Ranchero] VIN located on rating plate. First symbol indicates model year: 1=1971. Second symbol indicates assembly plant: A=Atlanta, Ga.; B=Oakville, Calif.; E=Mahwah, N.J.; F=Dearborn, Mich.; G=Chicago, Ill.; H=Lorain, Ohio; J=Los Angeles, Calif.; K=Kansas City, Kan.; N=Norfolk, Va.; P=Twin Cities, Minn.; R=San Jose, Calif.; S=Allen Park, Mich.; T=Metuchen, N.J.; U=Louisville, Ken; W=Wayne, Mich.; X=St. Thomas, Canada; Y=Wioxom, Mich. The third and fourth symbols indicate model: 46=Ranchero; 47=Ranchero 500; 48=Ranchero GT; 49=Ranchero Squire. The fifth symbol indicates engine: V=240 cid six; F=302 cid V-8; 6=302 cid V-8; H=351 cid V-8; M=351 cid V-8; Q=351 GT V-8; C=429 Cobra-Jet V-8; J=429 Cobra-Jet Ram-Air V-8. The last six symbols are the sequential production number.

Model	Body Type	Price	Weight	Prod. Total
Ranchero -1/2-Ton — 114 in. w.b. — Six				
66A	Sedan-Pickup	2851	3285	6041
66B	500 Sedan-Pickup	2983	3295	12,678
66E	Squire Sedan-Pickup	3192	3330	2595
Ranchero -1/2-Ton — 114 in. w.b. — V-8				
66C	GT Sedan-Pickup	3273	3445	3632

ENGINE [Ranchero]: Displacement: 250 cid. OHV. Six-cylinder. 145 hp at 4000 rpm. Bore & stroke: 3.68 x 3.91 in. Compression ratio: 9.0:1. one-barrel carburetor (Ranchero/500/Squire).

ENGINE [Optional;Standard in GT]: Displacement: 302 cid. OHV. V-8. 210 hp. Bore & stroke: 4 x 3 in. Compression ratio: 9.0:1. Carburetor: Two-barrel.

CHASSIS: Wheelbase: 117 in. Overall length: 206.2 in. GVW: Tires: E78-14 4PR.

POWERTRAIN OPTIONS: Engines: 210 hp 302 cid V-8. 240 hp 351 cid V-8. 285 hp 351 cid V-8. 360 hp 429 cid Thunder Jet V-8. 370 hp 429 cid Cobra-Jet V-8. 370 hp 429 cid CJ Ram-Air V-8. Transmissions: Four-speed manual transmission with Hurst shifter. Select Shift Cruise-O-Matic transmission.

CONVENIENCE OPTIONS: Rim-blow sport steering wheel. AM/FM stereo radio. Select Aire air-conditioner. Hidden headlamps (Squire/GT/500). Vinyl roof in black or white. Power full-width seat with four-way adjustment. Intermittent windshield wipers. AM push-button radio. Electric clock (Ranchero). Power steering. Tinted glass. Deluxe wheelcovers. Sport wheelcovers. Hubcaps and trim rings. Front bumper guards. Styled steel wheels. [Visibility Group] Includes: Ashtray, map, glove compartment and underhood lights; warning lights for seat belts and parking brake; and headlight-on warning buzzer and light. Tachometer (V-8s only). High-back bucket seats in green, ginger, black or white knit-vinyl (Squire/GT/500). Power front disc brakes. Racing-type mirrors painted body color (left-hand mirror includes remote control). Shaker hood scoop with Ram-Air induction system (included with optional 429 CJ Ram-Air V-8 and available for 351 cid four-barrel V-8). Flat back paint on hood and scoop of Ranchero GT. Heavy-duty suspension. Heavy-duty battery. extra-cooling radiator. Class II option (2,000-3,500 lbs.) [Trailer Towing Package] Includes: Front power disc brakes; heavy-duty suspension; cooling package; heavy-duty alternator and battery with 351 cid V-8s. [Ranchero Special Package] Includes: Choice of eight chromatic exterior colors and four unique matching interior trims; distinctive black, non-reflective painted hood; black vinyl roof; special accent black-painted box interior; unique bodyside stripe; twin racing mirrors (painted body color); bright hubcaps; and trim rings.

NOTE: 1971 Ranchero colors: White; Bright red; Maroon metallic; Dark blue metallic; Medium blue metallic; Grabber blue; Pastel blue; Light Pewter metallic; Dark green metallic; Medium green metallic; Grabber green metallic; Light green; Gray gold metallic; Light gold; Medium yellow gold; Grabber yellow. Black painted roofs were available with all colors, except Dark blue metallic.

1971 Ford 1/2-Ton Bronco 4x4 Utility Wagon (FMC)

BRONCO PICKUP: Styling changes were minor for the four-wheel drive Bronco in 1971. About the biggest change was a new 12.7-gal. fuel tank and a heavy-duty front driving axle. The standard features included: All-vinyl, full-width seat; fresh air heater and defroster; lockable glove compartment; padded instrument panel; energy-absorbing sun visors; vinyl-coated rubber floor mat; floor-mounted T-bar transfer case control; Mono-Beam front suspension; self-adjusting brakes and fully-synchronized three-speed manual transmission.

BRONCO WAGON: The Bronco wagon shared the features of the Pickup, but had a full-length roof. The roof had fixed windows in the rear liftgate and on each side of the rear compartment.

I.D. DATA [U-100]: VIN located on rating plate. The first three symbols indicated series: U14=Model U-140 Sport Utility Vehicle (or U-142 heavy-duty Sport Utility Vehicle); U15=Model U-150 Wagon (or U-152 heavy-duty Wagon). The fourth symbol indicates engine: F=170 cid six; G=302 cid V-8. The fifth symbol indicates assembly plant: H=Lorain, Ohio; L=Michigan Truck; R=San Jose, Calif.; S=Allen Park, Mich. The last six symbols are the sequential production number.

Model	Body Type	Price	Weight	Prod. Total
Bronco U-100 4x4 — 1.2-Ton — 90 in. w.b. — Six				
U-140	Pickup	3466	2990	1503
U-150	Wagon	3570	3090	18,281

ENGINE [Bronco]: Displacement: 170 cid. OHV. Six-cylinder. 105 hp at 4400 rpm. Bore & stroke: 3.50 x 2.94 in. Compression ratio: 9.1:1. One-barrel carburetor.

CHASSIS: Wheebase: 90 in. Overall length: 152.1 in. Overall width: 68.8 in. GVW: 3,850-4,700 lbs. Tires: 7.35 x 15.

POWERTRAIN OPTIONS: Engine: 302 cid V-8.

CONVENIENCE OPTIONS: Extra-cooling V-8 radiator. Left-hand remote-control outside mirror. Hardboard headlining (Pickup). G78-15 tires (with 4,700 lbs. GVW package). [Convenience Group] Includes: Cigarette lighter; map light; inside 10 in. day/night mirror and horn ring. One-pint oil bath air cleaner (302 V-8). Right-hand chrome rearview mirror. Bucket seats. Shoulder harness. Rear seat (Wagon with bucket seat option). Chrome bumpers. Skid plates for standard fuel tank and transfer case. Inside-tailgate-mounted spare tire carrier (included with rear seat option). Exterior rear-mounted swing-away tire carrier. Bright metal wheelcovers. High-floatation tires. Auxiliary 11.5-gal. fuel tank with skid plate. Manual radio and antenna. Bright bodyside and tailgate moldings. Bright metal rocker panel molding. Dana free-running front hubs. Hand-operated throttle. Heavy-duty front axle carrier assembly (special order). [Sport Package] Includes: Bright metal Sport Bronco emblem; pleated parchment vinyl front seat; vinyl door trim panels with bright metal moldings; hardboard headlining with bright metal retainer moldings (Wagon); parchment vinyl simulated-carpet front floor mat with bright metal retainers; rear floor mat (with optional rear seat); cigarette lighter; satin-finish horn ring; bright metal drip rail moldings; bright metal windshield and window frames; bright metal grille molding and tailgate release handle; bright headlight, side light, reflector and taillight bezels; Argent silver-painted grille with bright F-O-R-D letters; chrome bumpers, front and rear; chrome front bumper guards; bright metal wheelcovers (with 15 in. wheels only); and 6.50 x 16-6PR TT tires. Dealer-installed Accessories: Power-take-off (front-mounted). Warn free-running front hubs (manual or automatic). Snow plows. Snow plow angling kits. Front auxiliary air springs. Front-mounted winch. Trailer hitch. Trailer towing mirror. Locking gas cap. Front tow hooks. Compass. Fire extinguisher. Tachometer. Two-way radio.

NOTE: A special customized Baja Bronco, based on the wagon, was available from Bill Stroppe & Associates.

ECONOLINE E-100 CARGO VAN: Econolines receive a new grille for 1971. It now appeared to be divided into two sections. The half below the headlights used the same horizontal and vertical bars theme as before. The upper part featured a blackout section with the word Ford proportionally printed in chrome letters. There was also new interior trim and bright signal and shift levers. In addition, the fuel tank capacity dropped from 24- to 21-gals. and the front springs rates rose from 915 lbs. to 1,040 lbs. Standard features included: Vinyl color-coordinated upholstery; painted front and rear bumpers and hubcaps; left-hand fresh air inlet; dome lights in driver's compartment and cargo area; ashtray; single electric horn; coat hook; mechanical jack; double-grip door locks on all doors (with reversible keys); push-pull interior door locks (except rear doors); metal door checks; individual driver's seat; headlining in driver and passenger area; fresh air heater and defroster; and double cargo doors at right and rear.

ECONOLINE E-100 WINDOW VAN: As the name suggests, the Window Van had glass all around. On it (and other E-100s) the cargo area was 1.5 ft. long and 53.5 in. wide. It shared most standard features with the Cargo Van.

ECONOLINE E-100 DISPLAY VAN: This model had windows at the rear and on the right-hand side. It came with the same standard features as the Cargo Van.

I.D. DATA: [Econoline] VIN located on rating plate. First symbol indicates model year: 1=1971. Second symbol indicates assembly plant: (See Ranchero/Bronco/F-100 I.D. data for plant codes.) The third and fourth symbols indicate model: E10=1/2-Ton Econoline; E20=3/4-Ton Econoline; E30=1-Ton Econoline. The fifth symbol indicates engine: U=170 cid Six; G=302 V-8. The last six symbols are the sequential production number. Model codes are in first column of chart below.

Model	Body Type	Price	Weight	Prod. Total
Econoline 1/2-Ton — 105.5 in. w.b. — Six				
E-140	Cargo Van	2983	3260	Note 1
E-150	Window Van	3061	3335	Note 1
E-160	Display Van	3106	3305	Note 1

NOTE 1: See production total notes at end of Econoline section.

ENGINE [Econoline E-100]: Displacement: 170 cid. OHV. Six-cylinder. 105 hp at 4400 rpm. Bore & stroke: 3.50 x 2.94 in. Compression ratio: 9.1:1. One-barrel carburetor.

ECONOLINE E-200 CARGO VAN: For heavier loads, buyers could move up to the E-200 series. Its front axle had a capacity of 2,750 lbs. The rear axle capacity was 3,300 lbs. It also had larger (11 x 3 in. front/11 x 2-1/4 in. rear) brakes. Standard features echoed those of the E-100 Cargo Van.

ECONOLINE E-200 WINDOW VAN: This vehicle shared styling with the E-100 Window Van and load capacity with other E-200 vans.

ECONOLINE E-200 DISPLAY VAN: This vehicle shared styling with the E-100 Display Van and load capacity with other E-200 vans.

I.D. DATA [Econoline E-200]: See E-100.

Model	Body Type	Price	Weight	Prod. Total
Econoline 3/4-Ton — 105.5 in. w.b. — Six				
E-240	Cargo Van	3072	3350	Note 1
E-250	Window Van	3150	3395	Note 1
E-260	Display Van	3106	3425	Note 1

NOTE 1: See production total note at end of Econoline data.

ENGINE [Econoline E-200]: Same as E-100.

ECONOLINE E-300 CARGO VAN: For really big loads, it was hard to beat the E-300 Cargo Van. Its front axle capacity was rated at 3,300 lbs., rear axle at 4,800 lbs. The front brakes were 12 x 3 in., the rear 12 x 12-1/2 in. A 10 in. clutch was standard. Its front and rear springs were also heavy duty.

ECONOLINE E-300 WINDOW VAN: Had same features as the Cargo Van, plus windows all around.

ECONOLINE E-300 DISPLAY VAN: Had same features as the Cargo Van, plus windows on the right hand side.

I.D. DATA [Econoline E-300]: See F-100 I.D.

Model	Body Type	Price	Weight	Prod. Total
Econoline 1-Ton — 105.5 in. w.b. — Six				
E-340	Cargo Van	3094	3790	Note 1
E-350	Window Van	3172	3440	Note 1
E-360	Display Van	3108	3425	Note 1

NOTE 1: Production: [89A Cargo Van] 58,995; [89B Cargo Custom] 4,470; [89C Display Van] 5,265; [89D Custom Display Van] 410; [89E Window Van] 13,101; and [89F Custom Window Van].

ENGINE [Econoline E-300]: Displacement: 240 cid. OHV. Six-cylinder. 150 hp at 4000 rpm. Bore & stroke: 4.00 x 3.18 in. Compression ratio: 9.2:1. One-barrel carburetor.

CHASSIS: Wheelbase: 105.5 in. (123.5 in. SuperVan) Tires: E78-14B (E-100); G78-15B (E-200); 8.00 x 16.5 (E-300).

POWERTRAIN OPTIONS: Engines: 240 six-cylinder engine. 302 cid V-8. Transmission: Select Shift Cruise-O-Matic transmission.

CONVENIENCE OPTIONS: Push-button radio. Stationary or flip-fold passenger seat. High-output heater and defroster. Auxiliary hot water heater. Air-conditioner. Insulation package. Insulated floor mats. Inside or western-type rearview mirrors. Deluxe driver and/or stationary passenger seats with color-coordinated floor mats. Auxiliary step for right-side cargo doors. Dual electric horns. Courtesy light switches for front or all doors. Padded instrument panel. Shoulder harness. Stationary glass or vents in rear and/or right-side cargo doors. Tinted glass. Inside rear door latch and lock. Scuff pads at front door wells. School bus package for E-200 and E-300 Window Vans with 123.5 in. wheelbase. [Custom Equipment Package] Includes (in addition to or in place of standard items): Deluxe pleated vinyl seat trim; bright metal front and rear bumpers, hubcaps and horn ring; color-coordinated floor mat on left side; glove box door with lock and bright metal grille, taillight bezels, vent window; and windshield moldings.

NOTE: Econoline colors for 1971 were: Sky View blue; Harbor blue; Diamond blue; Reef aqua; Seafoam green; Boxwood green; Fiesta tan; Chrome yellow; Baja beige; Candy-apple red; and Wimbledon white. Two-tone paint combinations were also available.

1971 Ford 3/4-Ton E-250 Custom Club Wagon (JAG)

CLUB WAGON: Club wagons were basically Econolines made for hauling people. The base model held five passengers. Among standard features were: Twin-I-Beam independent front suspension; vinyl seat trim; armrests on front doors and at right side of three-passenger seats; ashtrays, front and rear; black floor mats; coat hook; two dome lights; dual sun visors; instrument panel padded on right side; bright instrument cluster trim; glove box door with lock; headlining in front compartment; dual outside rearview mirrors; backup lights; inside rearview mirror; emergency lamp flasher; retracting step for double side doors; rear reflectors; and side-marker lights at front and rear.

CUSTOM CLUB WAGON: This was a step up from the base model. Both shared many of the same features. However, the Custom also had: Pleated vinyl seat trim; interior vinyl side and door trim panels; armrests for all seats; color-coordinated front and rear floor mats; four coat hooks; full-length headlining; window trim moldings; cigarette lighter; scuff pads at front door wells; spare tire cover; horn ring; bright metal grille; instrument panel padded full-width; Custom ornaments; bright metal bodyside moldings; taillight bezels and hubcaps; and added insulation.

CHATEAU CLUB WAGON: At the top-of-the-line was the Chateau. It had, in addition to or in place of Custom Club Wagon features: Pleated deluxe cloth seat trim with vinyl bolsters; similar trim on interior door and side panels (with simulated woodgrain bands); full-length, color-coordinated carpeting (with dash insulator); chrome front and rear bumpers; bright metal dual outside mirrors; bright metal molding around windshield, side and rear windows; bright metal rear body molding; and Chateau ornaments.

I.D. DATA [Club Wagon]: See F-100.

Model	Body Type	Price	Weight	Prod. Total
Club Wagon 1/2-Ton — 105.5 in. w.b. — Six				
E-110	Club Wagon	3453	3595	6801
E-120	Custom Club Wagon	3678	3710	8817
E-130	Chateau Club Wagon	3827	4180	5438
Club Wagon 3/4-Ton — 105.5 in. w.b. — Six				
E-210	Club Wagon	3498	3800	—
E-220	Custom Club Wagon	3723	4040	—
E-230	Chateau Club Wagon	3878	4270	—
Club Wagon 1-Ton — 123.5 in. w.b. — Six				
E-310	Club Wagon	3850	4550	—
E-320	Custom Club Wagon	4975	4810	—
E-330	Chateau Club Wagon	5235	5040	—

ENGINE [Club Wagon]: Same as E-300.

CHASSIS: Wheelbase: 105.5 in. (123.5 in. optional) Tires: E78-14B.

POWERTRAIN OPTIONS: Engine: 302 cid V-8. Transmission: SelectShift Cruise-O-Matic transmission.

CONVENIENCE OPTIONS: Power steering. Ammeter and oil pressure gauge. Heavy-duty battery. Heavy-duty shocks. Whitewall tires. Chrome front and rear bumpers. Cigarette lighter. Courtesy light switches for all doors. Door positioners in all doors. Air-conditioner. Insulation package. Inside body rub rails. High-output heater/defroster. Auxiliary hot water heater for passenger compartment. Tinted glass. AM radio.

NOTE: Club Wagon colors for 1971 were: Wimbledon white; Sky View blue; Diamond blue; Harbor blue; Reef aqua; Seafoam green; Boxwood green; Fiesta tan; Chrome yellow; Baja beige and Candy-apple red. Custom and Chateau Club Wagons: Winter blue metallic; Scandia green metallic; Fiesta tan; Chrome yellow; Saddle tan metallic and Wimbledon white. Two-tone paint combinations were available using selected accent colors. Regular: The accent color on the roof. Deluxe: The accent color on roof and below the side and rear body moldings (included with this option) and grille area, when painted grille is used.

1971 Ford 1/2-Ton F-100 Styleside Pickup (RCA)

F-100 CUSTOM PICKUP: The grille was modified on Ford light-duty trucks for 1971. As before, it had a two-piece look. However, there was now a horizontal bar in the center of each section. Above and below it were three rectangular slots. Among the standard features were: Deluxe fresh air heater with three-speed fan; Hi-Dri ventilation; door courtesy light switches; ashtray; right-hand coat hook; Wedge-type vent window handles; Glove compartment with push-button catch; hardboard headlining; black floor mats with heel pads; aluminum scuff plates; Deluxe instrument cluster bezel; color-keyed steel door trim panels; and black, blue, red, parchment or green vinyl seat trim with chevron pattern vinyl inserts. Both 6-1/2 ft. and 8 ft. Styleside and Flareside cargo boxes were offered.

I.D. DATA [F-100]: VIN located on rating plate. The first three symbols indicated series: F10=F-100 (4x2); F11=F-100 (4x4). The fourth symbol indicates engine: A=240 cid six; B=300 cid six; G=302 cid six; H=390 cid V-8; Y=360 cid V-8. The fifth symbol indicates assembly plant: C=Ontario, Canada; E=Mahwah, N.J.; H=Lorain, Ohio; K=Kansas City, Kan.; L=Michigan Truck; N=Norfolk, Va.; P=Twin Cities, Minn.; R=San Jose, Calif.; S=Allen Park, Mich.; V=Louisville, Ken. (Truck). The last six symbols are the sequential production number.

Model	Body Type	Price	Weight	Prod. Total
F-100 — 1/2-Ton -115 in. w.b. — Six				
81	Chassis & Cab	2647	3160	Note 1
83	Flareside 6.5 ft.	2810	3475	Note 1
83	Styleside 6.5 ft.	2810	3540	Note 1
F-100 — 1/2-Ton -131.5 in. w.b. — Six				
83	Flareside 8 ft.	2928	3675	Note 1
83	Styleside 8 ft.	2928	3740	Note 1

NOTE 1: Ford records show the following F-100 production break-outs: 4x2 Models: [Chassis & Cab] 2,580; [Flareside Pickup] 10,106; [Styleside Pickup] 332,131; 4x4 Models: [Chassis & Cab] 96; [Flareside Pickup] 591 and [Styleside Pickup] 12,870.

ENGINE [F-100]: Displacement: 240 cid. OHV. Six-cylinder. 140 hp at 4000 rpm. Bore & stroke: 4.0 x 3.18 in. Compression ratio: 8.9:1. One-barrel carburetor.

F-250 PICKUP: The F-250 pickup had most of the same features as the F-100. In addition, it came with power brakes and Flex-O-Matic rear suspension. The Styleside had double-wall side panels and tailgate, flat-top wheelhousings, stake pockets and an all-steel floor. A single center latch mechanism opened the tailgate. Steel support straps held the tailgate in open position. The Flareside had runningboards between the cab and rear fenders. It had seasoned hardwood floorboards with steel skid strips to help slide cargo into place. Rubber-covered forged steel chains supported the tailgate when open. Toggle-type latches maintained tight seal when the tailgate was closed. Heavy-gauge steel side panels, with flared sides, had rolled edges for extra strength and rigidity.

F-250 PLATFORM/STAKE: Floor frames of the F-250 Platform/Stake were made of steel cross sills riveted to steel side rails. Floorboards were interlocked with steel skid strips and corners were reinforced with steel brackets. Formed steel caps over the ends of the body sills acted as bumpers for loading docks. Sideboards and stakes were straight-grained hardwood.

I.D. DATA [F-250]: Same as F-100, except first three symbols are: [4x2] F25; [4x4] F26.

Model	Body Type	Price	Weight	Prod. Total
F-250 — 3/4-Ton — 131 in. w.b. — Six				
81	Chassis & Cab	2979	3370	Note 1
83	Flareside	3145	3790	Note 1
83	Styleside	3145	3805	Note 1
80	Platform	3255	3780	Note 1
86	Stake	3288	3885	Note 1
F-250 Crew Cabs — 3/4-Ton — 149 in. w.b. — Six				
F-250	Chassis & Cab	—	—	Note 1
F-250	Styleside	—	—	Note 1

NOTE 1: Ford records show the following F-250 production break-outs: 4x2 Models: [Chassis & Windshield] 43; [Chassis & Cab] 5,467; [Platform & Rack] 398; [Platform] 40; [Flareside Pickup] 2,684; [Styleside Pickup] 117,820; 4x4 Models: [Chassis & Cab] 649; [Platform & Rack] 87; [Platform] 23; [Flareside Pickup] 635 and [Styleside Pickup] 16,164.

ENGINE [F-250]: Same as F-100.

F-350 PICKUP: F-350 buyers had to settle for the Flareside cargo box. It had a cargo capacity of 74 cu. ft. That was almost 10 more cubic-feet than comparable F-250 Flareside. Plus, it could haul heavier payloads. A four-speed manual transmission was standard.

F-350 PLATFORM/STAKE: The F-350 Platform/Stake had most of the same features as the F-250 version. However, rather than wood, it used reinforced steel stakes. Also, it was available with dual rear wheels (at extra cost). A four-speed manual transmission was standard.

I.D. DATA [F-350]: Same as F-100, except first three symbols are: [4x2] F35.

Model	Body Type	Price	Weight	Prod. Total
F-350 — 1-Ton — 135 in./159 in. w.b. — Six				
81	Chassis & Cab	3104	3615	Note 1
83	Flareside	3253	4185	Note 1
80	Platform 9 ft.	3470	4310	Note 1
80	Platform 12 ft.	3530	4600	Note 1
80	Stake 9 ft.	3508	4550	Note 1
86	Stake 12 ft.	3568	4945	Note 1
F-350 Crew Cabs — 1-Ton — 164.5 in. w.b. — Six				
83	Chassis & Cab	—	—	—
83	Styleside	—	—	Note 1

NOTE 1: Ford records show the following F-350 production totals: [Chassis & Cowl] 150; [Chassis & Windshield] 143; [Chassis & Cab] 28,432; [Platform & Rack] 5,087; [Platform] 412 and [Flareside Pickup] 1,349.

ENGINE [F-350]: See F-100.

CHASSIS: Wheelbase: 115 in. (F-100); 131 in. (F-100/F-250); 135 in. (F-350); 149 in. (F-250 crew cab); 159 in. (F-350); 164.5 in. (F-350 crew cab). GVW: 4,500-5,000 lbs. (F-100); 4,600-5,600 lbs. (F-100 4x4); 6,100-7,500 lbs. (F-250); 6,300-7,700 lbs. (F-250 4x4); 6,600-10,000 (F-350). Tires: 8.25 x 15 (F-100); 8.00 x 16.5 (F-250/F-350).

POWERTRAIN OPTIONS: Engines: 300 cid Six. 302 cid V-8 (F-100). 360 cid V-8. 390 cid V-8. Transmissions: Four-speed manual transmission. SelectShift Cruise-O-Matic transmission.

NOTE: Most 1971 light-duty Ford Trucks (86 percent) had V-8s and 43.7 percent had automatic transmission.

CONVENIENCE OPTIONS: Four-wheel drive (F-100 4x4s had Mono-Beam front suspension with coil springs; steering linkage shock absorber; forged radius rods; and a single-speed transfer case coupled to a four-speed transmission.) F-250 4x4 had a front suspension consisting of resilient long leaf springs with lubrication-free shackles. They also had a standard two-speed transfer case and three-speed transmission. Electric power pack (underhood 2500 watt generator). Frame-mounted 25-gal. fuel tank. [Convenience Group] Includes: Cargo area light; courtesy light door switches; day/night mirror and engine compartment light. Tool storage box (8 ft. Styleside). Bright bodyside moldings (Styleside). Western-type mirrors (fixed or swing-lock). Spare tire carrier (inside box on Styleside/ ahead of left rear fender on Flareside). Black-textured painted roof. Rear step bumper (Styleside). Bright hubcaps. Bright or mag wheelcovers for 15 in. wheels. Extra-cooling equipment. Chrome contour rear bumpers for Stylesides. Painted channel rear bumper for Flaresides. Brush-type grille guard. Free-running front hubs for 4x4s. Oil-bath engine air cleaner. Sliding rear window. Velocity-type engine governor. Vacuum brake booster. Power disc front brakes (F-250/F-350). Power steering (not with 4x4). Flex-O-Matic rear suspension (F-100). Heavy-duty shocks. Heavy-duty front springs. Heavy-duty alternator. Heavy-duty battery. SelectAire air-conditioner (includes standard fresh air heater in an integral unit). Push-button radio. Manual radio. Ammeter and oil pressure gauge. Bucket seats color-coordinated to exterior paint. Lockable cab stowage compartment behind the seat. Remote-control outside mirror. Tinted windshield. Tinted glass all around. Cab marker and indentification lights. Shoulder harnesses. Dual electric horns. Heavy-duty black vinyl seat trim. Full-width Custom Cab seat. [Sport Custom Cab] Includes: Deep-foam seat cushion and foam padding in seatback; pleated, basketweave vinyl seat trim inserts with grained vinyl bolsters; color-coordinated floor mats and horn ring; cigarette lighter; bright rocker panel, wheel lip, windshield molding and taillamp bezels; and black tailgate applique (on Stylesides). [Ranger Package] Includes: Color-coordinated pleated cloth-with-vinyl seat trim upholstery; wood-tone instrument panel and horn bar; vinyl door panels; heater panel with wood-tone insert; bright headlining molding; bright seat pivot covers; bright hubcaps, roof drip rails and around rear window; Ranger emblem; (Styleside Rangers included bright bodyside moldings and Argent silver tailgate panels, but rocker panel and wheel lip moldings were optional.) [Camper Special Package] Includes: 70 amp.-hr. battery; oil pressure gauge; ammeter; extra-cooling radiator; sliding rear cab window (F-250); dual bright metal 6 x 10 in. Western long-arm mirrors; camper wiring harness; rear shock absorbers (F-350); and Camper Special emblem. [Ranger XLT Package] Includes: (On Stylesides and Chassis & Cabs, in addition to or in place of Ranger equipment): Pleated cloth and vinyl seat upholstery; color-keyed carpeting; special insulation; convenience group; perforated headlining; color-keyed pleated vinyl door panels with wood-tone applique; Styleside decor including bright bodyside moldings with woodgrain accents; bright rocker panel and wheel lip moldings; and wood-tone tailgate applique. [Heavy-Duty Special Package for 8 ft. Styleside] Includes: Heavy-duty front springs and battery; alternator; ammeter; oil pressure gauge; rear step bumper; dual bright Western swing-lock mirrors and Heavy-Duty Special insignia. [Explorer Package A] Includes: Medium blue, Lime gold or Saddle tan (metallic) paint; special random-striped cloth seat trim in unique sew-style (blue, green or ginger); full-foam seat; bright front bumper guards, drip moldings and hubcaps; and Explorer glove box ornament. Package B: Includes package A contents, plus bright box rails (F-100/113 in. wheelbase only); bright spear moldings; swing-lock mirrors; and mag style wheelcovers (F-100 only). Package C: Includes package A and B contents, plus Cruise-O-Matic automatic transmission. Package D: Includes A, B and C contents, plus air-conditioning and tinted glass.

NOTE: Most 1971 light-duty Ford trucks (57.6 percent) came with an AM radio. 35.3 percent had power steering; 25.6 percent tinted glass; 42.4 percent power brakes and 9.7 percent air-conditioning.

NOTE: Standard colors for 1971 were: Raven black; Wimbledon white; Mallard green; Boxwood green; Seafoam green; Calypso coral; Candy-apple red; Regis red; Mojave tan; Prairie yellow; Diamond blue; Swiss aqua; Sky View blue; Bahama blue; Chrome yellow; and Pure white. Two-Tones: [Regular] Accent color was applied to roof and upper back panel with a belt line molding from door to door around back of cab; [Deluxe] Accent color was applied to area below the bodyside and lower tailgate moldings, which were included in this option (Stylesides only). [Combination] Regular and deluxe two-tone options were combined with accent color applied as specified for these two options (Stylesides only).

HISTORICAL: Introduced Oct. 30, 1970. Calendar year production: 628,126. Calendar year factory shipments by weight class: [Up to 6,000 lbs.] 381,900; [6,001 to 10,000 lbs.] 166,500. Calendar year registrations by weight class: [Up to 6,000 lbs.] 424,280; [6,001 to 10,000 lbs.] 188,325. Calendar year engine production: [Four] none; [Six] 104,587; [V-8] 506,518; [Diesel] 17,021; [Total all Ford trucks] 628,126. Model year production: [Light-duty] 671,053 — including 2,642 of the P-350 Parcel Delivery van chassis and 2,330 of the P-400 Parcel Delivery van chassis. Innovations: Econoline and Club Wagon models received new front end treatments. Introduced on both series were new options including power steering and a high-capacity air-conditioner. Rancheros received a new frontal treatment and throttle response mechanism improvements. J. B. Naughton was again Vice-President and General Manager of Ford's truck arm. Ford dealers delivered a record 735,370 trucks to customers in 1971. Domestic sales increased eight percent. Ford was America's number two truck-maker in 1971.

1972 FORD

1972 Ford 1/2-Ton Ranchero Squire Sedan-Pickup (OCW)

RANCHERO PICKUP: A separate body-frame, as opposed to the previous unit-type, was now used to make the Ranchero. It was bigger and bolder looking than ever in 1972. Styling was highlighted by a large, new, squared-oval, slightly protruding grille. Upper bodyside sculpturing began beneath the new recessed door handles and ran to the taillights. New link-coil rear suspension made for better roadability. Four convenient tie-down bars were located in the walls of the 6.5 ft. cargo body. With the standard model discontinued, the 500 was now the base Ranchero. Among standard features were: A high-back, full-width seat upholstered in black, blue, ginger, green or white vinyl; color-keyed vinyl door trim panels with bright trim; deep-pile wall-to-wall carpeting; hi-level, flow-through ventilation; ventless door windows; impact-absorbing steering column; padded steering wheel hub; lockable glove box; locking steering column; fresh-air heater/defroster; trim panel behind the split-back seat; vinyl headliner; seat belts with outboard retractors and shoulder harnesses (also center passenger seat belts); armrests with recessed squeeze-type door handles; vinyl-framed day/night mirror; cigarette lighter; padded, color-keyed instrument panel; emergency lamp flasher; deluxe grille with moldings; chrome bumpers; bright left-hand mirror with remote-control; hidden windshield wipers; bright metal windshield, rear window, drip rail and top of cargo box moldings; belted tires; bright metal hubcaps; and bright taillight bezels.

1972 Ford 1/2-Ton Ranchero GT Sedan-Pickup (OCW)

RANCHERO GT PICKUP: The GT had (in addition to or in place of all of the standard Ranchero 500 features): A two-tone Argent silver grille; color-keyed bodyside stripes; a hood with twin air scoop design; racing mirrors painted body colors (left side remote-control); hubcaps with trim rings; white sidewall belted tires; unique door trim panels formed of resilient plastic with long, molded armrests; a spare tire and tool compartment cover; a Ranchero GT instrument panel plaque; and a high-back bench seat with horizontal pleats in its vinyl upholstery to give a bucket seat appearance.

1972 Ford 1/2-Ton Ranchero GT Sedan-Pickup (OCW)

RANCHERO SQUIRE PICKUP: The Squire had (in addition to or in place of the standard Ranchero 500 features): Deluxe chrome wheelcovers; wood-tone panels on sides and tailgate; Ranchero Squire script on grille; Squire crest on grille; wood-tone panel around instruments; electric clock; bright armrest bases; spare tire and tool compartment cover; and Squire instrument panel plaque. Colors available on 1972 Rancheros were:

white; Bright red; maroon; Dark blue (metallic); Medium blue (metallic); Light blue; Light pewter (metallic); Dark green (metallic); Medium green (metallic); Bright green; Gold (metallic); Ginger (metallic); Medium goldenrod; Medium bright yellow; and Gray-gold (metallic.) (Ivy Glow; Gold Glow, black or white vinyl roofs were offered).

I.D. DATA [Ranchero]: VIN located on rating plate. The first symbol was the last digiti of the model year. The second symbol identified the assembly plant (same factory codes as 1971, plus X=St. Louis, Mo.) The third and fourth symbols indicated the body series: 47=Ranchero 500; 48=Ranchero GT; 49=Ranchero Squire. The fifth symbol indicated the engine: L or 3=250 cid six; F or 6=302 cid V-8; H,Q or R=351 cid V-8; S=400 cid V-8; N=429 cid V-8. The last six symbols indicate the sequential production number. Body style codes appear in first column of charts below.

Model	Body Type	Price	Weight	Prod. Total
Ranchero 500 — 1/2-Ton — 118 in. w.b. — Six				
97D	Sedan-Pickup	2850	3295	23,431
Ranchero GT — 1/2-Ton — 118 in. w.b. — Six				
97R	Sedan-Pickup	3201	3445	12,620
Ranchero Squire — 1/2-Ton — 118 in. w.b. — Six				
97K	Sedan-Pickup	3088	3330	4283

NOTE 1: Add for $95 for base 302 cid V-8 (Standard in GTs).
ENGINE [Base 500/Squire Six]: Displacement: 250 cid. Six-cylinder. 98 nhp at 3400 rpm. Bore & stroke: 3.68 in. x 3.91 in. Compression ratio: 8.0:1. One-barrel carburetor.
ENGINE [Base GT V-8]: Displacement: 302 cid. V-8. Bore & stroke: 4 in. x 3 in. 140 nhp at 4000 rpm. Compression ratio: 8.5:1. Carburetor: Two-barrel.
CHASSIS: Wheebase: 118 in. Overall length: 216 in. Tires: E78-14B (E70-14B whitewall on GT).
POWERTRAIN OPTIONS: Engines: 302 cid V-8 (two-barrel); 351 cid V-8 (two-barrel); 351 cid V-8 (four-barrel); 400 cid V-8 (two-barrel); 429 cid V-8 (four-barrel). Transmissions: Four-speed manual transmission with Hurst floor shifter. SelectShift Cruise-O-Matic transmission. A Ram-Air induction system with functional hood air scoop was available for 351 (four-barrel) and 429 cid V-8 engines in Ranchero 500 and Ranchero GT models.
CONVENIENCE OPTIONS: SelectAire air-conditioner. Power steering. [Protection Group]: Includes [500] chrome bumper guards; vinyl insert bodyside moldings; and door edge guards; plus [on 500/Squire] Flight-bench seat. Cloth upholstery for the standard seat and Sport cloth seat. [Instrumentation Group] Includes: (V-8s) tachometer; trip odometer; clock; ammeter; water temperature and oil pressure gauges. High-back bucket seats in knitted vinyl. Vinyl roof in black or white. Power front disc brakes. AM/FM stereo radio. AM radio. 15 in. wheels. Full wheelcovers. Deluxe wheelcovers. Hubcaps with trim rings. Mag-style wheels. Tinted glass. Color glow paints (Ivy or Gold Glow). Class II 2,000-3,500 lbs./Class III 3,500-6,000 lbs. trailer towing packages. Rim-blow sport steering wheel. Electric clock. Racing type mirrors painted body color. Black-painted hood. [Visibility Group] Includes: Ashtray, underhood and glove box lights; parking brake light; and seat belt warning lights. [Performance/Handling Package] (offered with 351 four-barrel and 429 cid V-8s) Includes: high-rate rear springs; heavy-duty front and rear shock absorbers; rear stabilizer bar; and heavy-duty front stabilizer bar. [Ranchero Special Package] Includes: Choice of Ivy Glow or Gold Glow paint; green vinyl roof or Ivy Glow brown vinyl roof with Gold glow; bright front bumper guards; bright wheel lip moldings; black Sport cloth interior with Ivy Glow or Ginger Sport cloth interior with Gold Glow (both with matching vinyl trim); twin color-keyed racing mirrors; bright hubcaps and bright trim rings.
BRONCO PICKUP: Styling of the 4x4 Bronco was basically the same as last year. Some changes were made to the standard equipment. It now included bucket seats and a 3.50:1 rear axle (on V-8 powered units). Also standard were: Pleated vinyl seats; floor-mounted T-bar transfer case control; suspended foot pedals; fresh air heater and defroster; lockable glove compartment; padded instrument panel; two-speed electric windshield wipers; sun visors; vinyl-coated rubber floor mat; and fully-synchronized three-speed manual transmission. Bronco color choices for 1972 were: Wimbledon white; Candy-apple red; Royal maroon; Wind blue; Bahama blue; Bay-Roc blue (metallic); Seapine green (metallic); Swiss aqua; Winter green; Chelsea green (metallic); Mallard green; Sequoia brown (metallic); Hot ginger (metallic); Prairie yellow; Calypso coral; Tampico yellow; and Chrome yellow. Bronco roofs were painted Wimbledon white when two-toning was ordered.
BRONCO WAGON: The Bronco wagon shared the features of the Pickup, but had a full-length roof. The roof had fixed windows in the rear liftgate and on each side of the rear compartment.
I.D. DATA [U-100]: VIN located on rating plate. The first three symbols indicated series: U14=Model U-140 Pickup; U15=Model U-150 Wagon. The fourth symbol indicates engine: F=170 cid six; G=302 cid V-8. The fifth symbol indicates assembly plant: H=Lorain, Ohio; L=Michigan Truck; R=San Jose, Calif.; S=Allen Park, Mich. The last six symbols are the sequential production number.

Model	Body Type	Price	Weight	Prod. Total
Bronco 4x4 — 1/2-Ton — 92 in. w.b. —Six				
U-140	Pickup	3414	2990	Note 1
U-150	Wagon	3588	3090	Note 1

NOTE 1: Ford records show total Bronco production of 21,894 units with no break-outs by body style.
NOTE 2: Add for $125 for 302 cid V-8.
ENGINE [Bronco]: Displacement: 170 cid. Six-cylinder. 105 hp at 4400 rpm. Bore & stroke: 3.50 in. x 2.94 in. Compression ratio: 9.1:1. One-barrel carburetor. (not available in California).
ENGINE [Base V-8]: Displacement: 302 cid. V-8. Bore & stroke: 4 in. x 3 in. 140 nhp at 4000 rpm. Compression ratio: 8.5:1. Carburetor: Two-barrel.
CHASSIS: Wheebase: 92 in. Overall length: 152.1 in. Overall width: 68.8 in. GVW: 4,300-4,900 lbs. Tires: E78 x 15.
POWERTRAIN OPTIONS: 302 cid V-8.
CONVENIENCE OPTIONS: Extra-cooling V-8 radiator. Left-hand remote control outside mirror. Hardboard headlining (Pickup). [Convenience Group] Includes: Cigarette lighter; map light; and inside 10 in. day/night mirror. Horn ring. Right-hand chrome rearview mirror. Bucket seats. Shoulder harness and rear seat (Wagon). Chrome bumpers. Skid plates for standard fuel tank and transfer case. Inside tailgate-mounted spare tire carrier (included with wagon). Exterior rear-mounted swing-away tire carrier. Bright metal wheelcovers. High-flotation tires. Auxiliary 7.5-gal. fuel tank with skid plate. Manual radio and antenna. Bright bodyside and tailgate moldings. Bright metal rocker panel molding. Hand-operated throttle. [Sport Package] Includes: Bright metal Sport Bronco emblem; pleated parchment vinyl front seat; vinyl door trim panels with bright metal moldings; hardboard headlining with bright metal retainer moldings (Wagon); parchment vinyl front floor mat with bright metal retainers; rear floor mat (included with optional rear seat); cigarette lighter; horn ring; bright metal drip rail moldings; bright metal windshield and window frames; bright metal grille molding and tailgate release handle; bright headlight, side light, reflector and taillight bezels; Argent silver-painted grille with bright Ford letters; chrome bumpers, front and rear; chrome front bumper guards; bright metal wheelcovers (with 15 in. wheels only) and 7.00 x 15-C TT tires.

348

DEALER-INSTALLED ACCESSORIES: Power-take-off (front-mounted). Warn free-running front hubs (manual or automatic). Snow plows. Snow plow angling kits. Front auxiliary air springs. Front-mounted winch. Trailer hitch. Trailer towing mirror. Locking gas cap. Front tow hooks. Compass. Fire extinguisher. Transmission oil cooler. Tachometer. [4,500 lb. GVW Package] Includes: 2,780 lbs. rear axle; front springs rated at 1,000 lbs.; rear springs rated at 1,475 lbs. and G78-15B tires. [4,900 lb. GVW Package] Includes: 3,300 lbs. Traction-Lok rear axle plus heavy-duty front and rear spring ratings and tires same as 4,500 lbs. package. [Ranger Package] Includes: Argent grille; bucket seats; lower bodyside stripes; fiberboard headliner; cut-pile carpeting front and rear; wheelcovers; white power dome and white spare tire carrier.
ECONOLINE E-100 CARGO VAN: The biggest news for 1972 was the availability of a sliding side cargo door for Econolines. This was especially useful for cargo handling in cramped alleys and beside loading docks. Three separate tracks, at top, bottom and center, gave bridge-like support for smooth one-handed operation. Aside from that, a smaller (20.3-gal.) fuel tank and larger (11 in.) clutch, were about the only other changes made for the new model year. Standard features included: Vinyl color-coordinated upholstery; painted front and rear bumpers and hubcaps; left-hand fresh air inlet; dome lights in driver's compartment and cargo area; ashtray; single electric horn; coat hook; mechanical jack; double-grip door locks on all doors (with reversible keys); push-pull interior door locks (except rear doors); metal door checks; individual driver's seat; headlining in driver and passenger area; fresh air heater and defroster; and double cargo doors at right and rear.

1972 Ford 1/2-Ton E-140 Econoline Cargo Van (OCW)

ECONOLINE E-100 WINDOW VAN: As the name suggests, the Window Van had glass all around. Like other E-100s, its cargo area was 11.5 feet long and 53.5 in. wide. It shared most standard features with the Cargo Van.
ECONOLINE E-100 DISPLAY VAN: This model had windows at the rear and on the right-hand side. It came with the same standard features as the Cargo Van.
I.D. DATA: [Econoline] VIN located on rating plate. First symbol indicates model year: 1=1971. Second symbol indicates assembly plant: (See Ranchero/Bronco/F-100 I.D. data for plant codes.) The third and fourth symbols indicate model: E10=1/2-Ton Econoline; E20=3/4-Ton Econoline; E30=1-Ton Econoline. The fifth symbol indicates engine: U=170 cid Six; G=302 V-8. The last six symbols are the sequential production number. Model codes are in the first column of the chart below.

Model	Body Type	Price	Weight	Prod. Total
E-100 Econoline — 1/2-Ton — 105.5 in. w.b. — Six				
E-140	Cargo Van	2757	3275	Note 1
E-150	Window Van	2829	3350	Note 1
E-160	Display Van	2787	3320	Note 1

NOTE 1: See production data at end of Econoline section.
ENGINE [Base six]: Displacement: 170 cid. Six-cylinder. 105 hp at 4400 rpm. Bore & stroke: 3.50 in. x 2.94 in. Compression ratio: 9.1:1. One-barrel carburetor.
ENGINE [Base V-8]: Displacement: 302 cid. V-8. Bore & stroke: 4 in. x 3 in. 140 nhp at 4000 rpm. Compression ratio: 8.5:1. Carburetor: Two-barrel.
ECONOLINE E-200 CARGO VAN: For heavier loads, buyers could move up to the E-200 series. Its front axle had a capacity of 2,750 lbs. The rear axle was rated for 3,300 lbs. It also had larger (11 x 3 in. front/11 x 2.25 in. rear) brakes. Standard features echoed those of the E-100 Cargo Van.
ECONOLINE E-200 WINDOW VAN: This vehicle shared styling with the E-100 Window Van and load capacity with other E-200 vans.
ECONOLINE E-200 DISPLAY VAN: This vehicle shared styling with the E-100 Display Van and load capacity with other E-200 vans.
I.D. DATA [Econoline E-200]: See E-100 I.D. Data.

Model	Body Type	Price	Weight	Prod. Total
E-200 Econoline — 3/4-Ton — 105.5 in. w.b.				
E-240	Cargo Van	2844	3345	Note 1
E-250	Window Van	2916	3420	Note 1
E-260	Display Van	2874	3390	Note 1

NOTE 1: See production data at end of Econoline section.
ENGINES [Econoline E-200]: Same as E-100 engines.
ECONOLINE E-300 CARGO VAN: For really big loads, it was hard to beat the E-300 Cargo Van. Its front axle capacity was 3,300 lbs. and rear axles were rated at 4,800 lbs. The bigger brakes were 12 x 3 in. up front/12 x 12-1/2 in. at the rear. Its front and rear springs were also heavy-duty. A larger six was standard in the 1-ton vans.
ECONOLINE E-300 WINDOW VAN: Had same features as the Cargo Van, plus windows all around.
ECONOLINE E-300 DISPLAY VAN: : Had same features as the Cargo Van, plus windows on the right-hand side.
I.D. DATA [Econoline E-300]: See E-100 I.D. Data

Model	Body Type	Price	Weight	Prod. Total
E-300 Econoline — 1-Ton — 105.5 in. w.b. — Six				
E-340	Cargo Van	3304	3450	Note 1
E-350	Window Van	3376	3525	Note 1
E-360	Display Van	3334	3495	Note 1

NOTE 1: Ford records show the following Econoline production break-outs: [89A standard Cargo Van] 60,509; [89C standard Display Van] 7,198; [89E standard Window Van] 13,382; [89B Custom Cargo Van] 5,123; [89D Custom Display Van] 94; [89F Custom Window Van] 1,828 and [33A Cut-away Van] 850.

ENGINE [Base six; E-300]: Displacement: 240 cid. Six-cylinder. 150 hp at 4000 rpm. Bore & stroke: 4.00 in. x 3.18 in. Compression ratio: 9.2:1. One-barrel carburetor.
ENGINE [Base V-8]: Displacement: 302 cid. V-8. Bore & stroke: 4 in. x 3 in. 140 nhp at 4000 rpm. Compression ratio: 8.5:1. Carburetor: Two-barrel.
CHASSIS: Wheelbase: 105.5 in. (123.5 in. SuperVan). Tires: E78-14B (E-100); G78-15B (E-200); 8.00 x 16.5 in. (E-300). GVW: 4,800 lbs. (E-100); 6,000 lbs. (E-200); 8,300 lbs. (E-300).
POWERTRAIN OPTIONS: Engines: 240 cid six. 302 cid V-8. Transmissions: SelectShift Cruise-O-Matic transmission.
CONVENIENCE OPTIONS: Push-button radio. Stationary or flip-fold passenger seat. High-output heater and defroster. Auxiliary hot water heater. Air-conditioner. Insulation package. Insulated floor mats. Inside body rub rails. Inside or Western-type rearview mirrors. Deluxe driver and/or stationary passenger seats with color-coordinated floor mats. Auxiliary step for right-side cargo doors. Dual electric horns. Courtesy light switches for front or all doors. Padded instrument panel. Shoulder harness. Stationary glass or vents in rear and/or right-side cargo doors. Tinted glass. Inside rear door latch and lock. Scuff pads at front door wells. School bus package for E-200 and E-300 Window Vans with 123.5 in. wheelbase. [Custom Equipment Package] Includes: (in addition to or in place of standard items) Deluxe pleated vinyl seat trim; bright metal front and rear bumpers and hubcaps; horn ring; cigarette lighter; color-coordinated floor mat on left-hand side; glove box door with lock; and bright metal grille, taillight bezels, vent window and windshield moldings.

1972 Ford 1/2-Ton E-110 Club Wagon (OCW)

CLUB WAGON: Club wagons were basically Econolines made for hauling people. The base model held five passengers. Among standard features were: Twin-I-Beam independent front suspension; vinyl seat trim; armrests on front doors and at right side of three-passenger seats; ashtrays, front and rear; black floor mats; coat hook; two dome lights; dual sun visors; instrument panel padded on right side; bright instrument cluster trim; glove box door with lock; headlining in front compartment; dual outside rearview mirrors; backup lights; inside rearview mirror; emergency lamp flasher; retracting step for double side doors; rear reflectors; and side-marker lights at front and rear. Paint colors standard for the 1972 Club Wagon were: Wind blue; Diamond blue; Harbor blue; Tidewater aqua; Mill Valley green; Boxwood green; Fiesta tan; Baja beige; Candy-apple red; Wimbledon white; and Chrome yellow. Custom and Chateau Club Wagons also came in: Brook blue (metallic); Scandia green (metallic); Fiesta tan; Saddle tan (metallic); Wimbledon white; and Chrome yellow. Two-tone paint combinations were available using selected accent colors: Regular two-tones had the accent color on roof. Deluxe two-tones had the accent color on roof and below the side and rear body moldings (which were included with the paint option) and on grille area, unless it was bright metal.
CUSTOM CLUB WAGON: This was a step up from the base model. Both shared many of the same features. However, the Custom also had: Pleated vinyl seat trim; interior vinyl side and door trim panels; armrests for all seats; color-coordinated front and rear floor mats; four coat hooks; a full-length headlining; window trim moldings; a cigarette lighter; scuff pads at the front door wells; a spare tire cover; a horn ring; a bright metal grille; a full-width padded instrument panel; Custom ornaments; bright metal bodyside moldings, taillight bezels and hubcaps; and added insulation.
CHATEAU CLUB WAGON: At the top-of-the-line was the Chateau. It had, in addition to or in place of Custom Club Wagon features, pleated deluxe cloth seat trim with vinyl bolsters; similar trim on interior door and bodyside panels with simulated wood-grained bands; full-length color-coordinated carpeting with a dash insulator; a bright metal rear body molding; and Chateau ornaments.
I.D. DATA [Club Wagon]: See E-100 I.D. Data.

Model	Body Type	Price	Weight	Prod. Total
E-110	Club Wagon	3309	3595	5833
E-120	Custom Club Wagon	3647	3710	6608
E-130	Chateau Club Wagon	3791	4180	4955

ENGINE [Club Wagon]: Same as E-300.
CHASSIS: Wheelbase: 105.5 in. or 123.5 in. (optional) Tires: E78-14B.
POWERTRAIN OPTIONS: Engine: 302 cid V-8. Transmission: SelectShift Cruise-O-Matic transmission.
CONVENIENCE OPTIONS: Power steering. Ammeter and oil pressure gauge. Heavy-duty battery. Heavy-duty shocks. Whitewall tires. Chrome front and rear bumpers. Cigarette lighter. Coutesy light switches for all doors. Door positioners for all door. Air-conditioner. Insulation package. Inside body rub rails. High-output heater/defroster. Auxiliary hot water heater for passenger compartment. Tinted glass. AM radio. Heavy-duty Package. Seating Packages: 8-passenger or 12-passenger.
COURIER PICKUP: This was Ford's entry into the Mini-Pickup market. According to Ford's marketing division, the typical Courier buyer was expected to be slightly younger than the average domestic Pickup buyer. About one-third would be under 35 years old, they said. The buyer was als more likely to have a high school or higher education level. The Courier was made by Mazda, in Japan, but had its own distinctive front end styling. The bright metal and plastic grille ran the full-width of the body and encased the two round headlights. The parking lights were integrated into the wraparound front bumper. The front-hinged hood was released from inside the cab and was counter-balanced to stay open. The full-width tailgate featured raised Courier letters painted a contrasting color. Among standard equipment was: 11 tie-down hooks around the box and tailgate for securing cargo or a tarpaulin; rear mud flaps; bright hubcaps; white sidewall tires; vinyl upholstery, headliner and door panels; padded armrests; padded sun visors; tool set emergency flashers; outside rearview mirror; axle type jack with crank; and four-speed manual transmission.
I.D. DATA: Serial number located on door post on driver's side and consisted of either 10 or 11 symbols. The first five symbols indicated the series and the remaining symbols were the sequential production number.

Model	Body Type	Price	Weight	Prod. Total
—	Pickup	2222	2420	26,958

NOTE 1: Production column indicates Courier sales for calendar year 1972.

ENGINE [Courier]: Displacement: 109.5 cid. Inline. 4-cyl. nhp 74 at 5000 rpm. (67 hp at 5000 rpm in California] Bore & stroke: 3.07 in. x 3.70 in. Compression ratio: 8.6:1. Carburetor: Zenith-Stromberg two-barrel.

CHASSIS: Wheelbase: 104.3 in. Overall length: 172 in. Overall width: 61.6 in. GVW Rating: 3910 lbs. Tires: 6.00 x 14.

Options: AM radio. Rear step bumper.

1972 Ford 1/2-Ton F-100 Styleside Custom Pickup (OCW)

F-100 CUSTOM PICKUP: Styling changes for 1972 were limited to a modified, rectangular slot grille. Standard features included: Deluxe fresh air heater; door courtesy light switches; ashtray; coat hook; vent window handles; glove compartment; hardboard headlining; floor mats; Deluxe instrument cluster bezel; color-keyed door trim panels; three-speed manual transmission; black, blue, parchment or green vinyl seat trim with vinyl inserts; aluminum scuff plates; windshield washers; left-hand interior mirror; day/night mirror; two-speed windshield wipers; backup lights; sun visors; armrests; seat belts; double-walled tailgate and side panels; power brakes (on F-100s over 5,500 lbs. GVW) and Twin-I-Beam front suspension. Once again, 6.5 ft. and 8 ft. Styleside and Flareside models were available. Standard colors for 1972 were: Wimbledon white; Mallard green; Seapine green (metallic); Winter green; Calypso coral; Candy-apple red; Royal maroon; Prairie yellow; Tampico yellow; Swiss aqua; Wind blue; Bahama blue; Bay Roc blue metallic; Sequoia brown (metallic); Chrome yellow; and Pure white. Two-tones came in regular with accent color applied to roof and upper back panel and a beltline molding from door-to-door around back of cab; Deluxe (for Styleside only) with accent color applied to area below the bodyside and lower tailgate moldings, which were included in this option; and Combination (also for Styleside only) with regular and Deluxe two-tone options combined and accent color applied as specified for these two options.

1972 Ford 1/2-Ton F-100 Styleside Custom Ranger XLT Pickup

I.D. DATA [F-100]: VIN located on rating plate. The first three symbols indicated series: F10=F-100 (4x2); F11=F-100 (4x4). The fourth symbol indicates engine: A or 1=240 cid six; B or 2=300 cid six; G or 3=302 cid V-8; H=390 cid V-8; Y or 8=360 cid V-8. The fifth symbol indicates assembly plant: C=Ontario, Canada; E=Mahwah, N.J.; H=Lorain, Ohio; K=Kansas City, Kan.; L=Michigan Truck; N=Norfolk, Va.; P=Twin Cities, Minn.; R=San Jose, Calif.; S=Allen Park, Mich.; V=Louisville, Ken. (Truck). The last six symbols are the sequential production number.

Model	Body Type	Price	Weight	Prod. Total
F-100 — 1/2-Ton — 115 in. w.b. — Six				
81	Chassis & Cab	2550	3160	Note 1
83	Flareside 6.5 ft.	2703	3475	Note 1
83	Styleside 6.5 ft.	2703	3540	Note 1
F-100 — 1/2-Ton — 131 in. w.b. — Six				
83	Flareside 8 ft.	2739	—	Note 1
83	Styleside 8 ft.	2739	—	Note 1

NOTE 1: Ford records show the following F-100 production break-outs: [Chassis & Cab] 2,461; [Flareside Pickup] 3,034 and [Styleside Pickup] 457,746.

ENGINE [F-100]: Displacement: 240 cid. OHV. Six-cylinder. 140 hp at 4000 rpm. Bore & stroke: 4.0 x 3.18 in. Compression ratio: 8.9:1. One-barrel carburetor.

ENGINE [Base V-8]: Displacement: 302 cid. V-8. Bore & stroke: 4 in. x 3 in. 140 nhp at 4000 rpm. Compression ratio: 8.5:1. Carburetor: Two-barrel.

1972 Ford 3/4-Ton E-250 Cut-Away Van With Cimmarron Camper

F-250 CUSTOM PICKUP: The F-250 Pickup had most of the same features as the F-100. However, it also came with power brakes and the Flex-O-Matic rear suspension, which automatically adjusted spring stiffness for varying loads. The Styleside had sleek body panels extending all the way forward to hug the rear cab corners. Its pickup box featured strong, double-wall side panel construction; a sturdy tailgate that could support a ton; wide apart flat-top wheelhousings; deep stake pockets; and an all-steel floor. The Flareside had runningboards between cab and rear fenders for easy side loading. Its seasoned hardwood floorboards had inter-locked steel skid strips. Rubber-covered forged steel chains supported the tailgate when open. Toggle type latches maintained tight seal when tailgate was closed.

I.D. DATA [F-250]: See F-100 I.D. Data.

Model	Body Type	Price	Weight	Prod. Total
F-250 — 3/4-Ton — 131 in. w.b. — Six				
81	Chassis & Cab	2870	3370	Note 1
83	Flareside	3020	3790	Note 1
83	Styleside	3020	3805	Note 1
F-250 Crew Cabs — 3/4-Ton — 149 in. w.b. — Six				
83	Chassis & Cab	3368	—	Note 1
83	Styleside	3518	—	Note 1

NOTE 1: Ford records show the following F-250 production break-outs: [Chassis & Cab] 7,674; [Flareside Pickup] 3,004; [Styleside Pickup] 187,348.

ENGINE [F-250]: Displacement: 300 cid. Six-cylinder. 165 hp at 3600 rpm. Bore & stroke: 4.0 in. x 3.98 in. Compression ratio: 8.6:1. One-barrel carburetor.

1972 Ford 3/4-Ton F-250 Ranger XLT Styleside Camper Special

F-350 CUSTOM PICKUP: The F-350 came in one pickup box style, the Flareside. Its desired payload, including driver and passenger was, 2,440 lbs. That was more than double the payload of the F-100, which shared most other features with. However, a four-speed manual transmission was standard in F-350s.

F-350 PLATFORM/STAKE: This model was offered in two sizes, 9 ft. and 12 ft. Both had floor frames formed of steel cross sills riveted to steel side rails. The floorboards were inter-locked with steel skid strips. The corners were reinforced with steel brackets. Formed steel caps over the ends of the body sills acted as bumpers against loading docks. Sideboards were straight-grained hardwood. Stakes were steel. A four-speed manual transmission was standard.

I.D. DATA [F-350]: See F-100 I.D. Data

Model	Body Type	Price	Weight	Prod. Total
F-350 — 1-Ton — 135 in. w.b. — Six				
81	Chassis & Cab	2985	3725	Note 1
83	Flareside	3120	4185	Note 1
80	Platform 9 ft.	3335	4310	Note 1
86	Stake 9 ft.	3375	4550	Note 1

F-350 Crew Cab — 1-Ton — 164.5 in. w.b. — Six

83	Chassis & Cab	—	—	Note 1
83	Styleside	—	—	Note 1

NOTE 1: Ford records show the following F-350 production break-outs: [Chassis & Cowl] 80; [Chassis & Cab] 42,084; [Platform & Rack] 6,656; [Platform] 749 and [Styleside] 11,889. Parcel van production: [P-350] 1,054; [P-400] 6,251.
ENGINE [F-350]: See F-250 engines.
CHASSIS: Wheelbase: 115 in. (F-100); 131 in. (F-100/F-250]; 135 in. (F-350]; 149 in. (F-250 Crew Cab]; 159 in. (F-350); 164.5 in. (F-350 Crew Cab). GVW: 4,500-5,500 lbs. (F-100); 6,200-8,100 lbs. (F-250); 6,600-10,000 lbs. Tires: G78 x 15 (F-100); 8.00 x 16.5D (F-250/F-350).
POWERTRAIN OPTIONS: Engines: 302 cid V-8 (F-100). 360 cid V-8. 390 cid V-8. Transmissions: Four-speed manual transmission. SelectShift Cruise-O-Matic transmission.
CONVENIENCE OPTIONS: Air-conditioner. Rear step bumper (Styleside). Spare tire carrier. [Convenience Group] Includes: Cargo light; inside 12 in. day/night mirror; glove box door lock; and engine compartment light. Remote-control mirror for driver's door. Western mirrors. Tool box with door lock (Styleside). Auxiliary fuel tank. AM/FM stereo radio. AM radio. Full wheelcovers or mag-style wheelcovers. Black-textured roof with bright belt and drip moldings. Electric Power Pak (2,500-watt underhood generator). Sliding rear window. Power steering (not with 4x4). Power brakes (F-100; Standard F-250/F-350). Ammeter and oil pressure gauge. Styleside body moldings. Bright hubcaps. Chrome contour rear bumper for Stylesides. Painted channel rear bumper for Flaresides. Tinted glass all around. Shoulder harness. Dual electric horns. Heavy-duty black vinyl seat trim. Free-running front hubs for F-100 4x4s (Standard F-250). Oil bath engine air cleaner. [Four-wheel drive package] Includes: (F-100) Mono-Beam front suspension with full-floating axle; coil springs; forged radius rods and track bar; power brakes; steering linkage shock absorber; and a single-speed transfer case with four-speed manual transmission; (F-250) Heavy-duty front suspension with long, resilient leaf springs and lube-free shackles; power brakes; free-running hubs; two-speed transfer case; and four-speed manual transmission. [Northland Special Package] Includes: Engine block heater; heavy-duty battery and alternator; 50 percent (-35 degrees F.) anti-freeze; and Traction-Lok rear axle. [Sport Custom Package] Includes: (In addition to or in place of Custom items) extra-deep foam seat cushion; pleated vinyl seat trim inserts with grained vinyl bolsters; color-keyed vinyl door panels with bright moldings; color-keyed floor mats; cigarette lighter; and bright windshield, rocker panel and wheel lip moldings. [Ranger Package] Includes: (In addition to or in place of Sport Custom features) color-keyed, pleated cloth with vinyl trim seat upholstery; wood-tone instrument panel and horn bar; heater panel with wood-tone insert; bright headlining molding; color-keyed vinyl door panels; bright seat pivot covers; bright rear window and roof drip moldings; and hubcaps (Stylesides also include bright bodyside moldings and Argent silver tailgate panel). Rocker panel and wheel lip moldings optional. [Ranger XLT Package] Includes: (In addition to or in place of Ranger items) Deluxe pleated cloth with vinyl trim seat upholstery; color-keyed pleated vinyl door panels with wood-tone applique; color-keyed wall-to-wall carpeting; and additional insulation. [Convenience Group with Styleside Decor] Includes: Bright bodyside moldings with woodgrain accents; bright rocker panel and wheel lip moldings; and wood-tone tailgate panel. [Camper Special Package] Includes: Heavy-duty battery and alternator; ammeter, oil pressure gauge; bright Western long-arm mirrors; extra-cooling package camper wiring harness; dual electric horns; rear shocks (F-350); and emblem.
PRODUCTION NOTE: Most 1972 Ford light-duty trucks (62.3 percent) had an AM radio; 1.6 percent had AM/FM radio; 45.7 percent used power steering; 12.6 percent featured air-conditioning; 88.9 percent had V-8s; 49.9 percent used automatic transmission; and 28.5 percent wore tinted glass.
HISTORICAL: Introduced: Sept. 24, 1971. Calendar year production: 795,987 (or 32.20 percent of industry.) Calendar year registrations by weight class: [Up to 6,000 lbs.] 502,219; [6,001 to 10,000 lbs.] 225,399. Dealer deliveries in the calendar year totaled 735,370 units. Model year production (light-duty only) was 886,649. Innovations: All-new Ranchero Deluxe Pickup introduced. Econolines featured new, optional sliding door and power brakes. Pickup truck grilles restyled. Ford's North American truck sales topped the previous high (786,444) by a wide margin and totaled 795,987 units for a new all-time record. D.E. Petersen was Vice-President and General Manager of Truck Operations. Ford leaped ahead of Chevrolet in calendar year production for 1972 by building 795,987 trucks to Chevy's 770,773. Chevy dropped to a 31.10 percent market share.

1973 FORD

1973 Ford 1/2-Ton Ranchero Squire Sedan-Pickup (OCW)

RANCHERO 500 PICKUP: The Ranchero received a toned down front end for 1973. The grille was smaller, flatter and contained the parking lights in its criss-cross pattern. The new straight front bumper was energy-absorbing. The front fenders were more rounded and didn't come to a point as in previous years. Also new for 1973 was an inside hood release and improved rear brakes. Among the standard features were: Four cargo tie-downs; full-width seat upholstered in black, blue, ginger, green or beige vinyl; color-keyed vinyl door trim panels with bright trim. Deep-pile wall-to-wall carpeting; hi-level, flow-through ventilation; ventless door windows; impact-absorbing steering column; padded steering wheel hub; lockable glove box; locking steering column; fresh-air heater/defroster; trim panel behind the split-back seat; vinyl headliner; seat belts with outboard retractors and shoulder harnesses (also center passenger belts); armrests with recessed door handles; vinyl-framed day/night rearview mirror; cigarette lighter; added, color-keyed instrument panel; emergency lamp flasher; deluxe grille with moldings; chrome bumpers; bright left-hand mirror with remote-control; hidden windshield wipers; bright metal windshield, rear window, drip rail and top of cargo body moldings; belted tires; bright metal hubcaps; and bright taillight bezels. Colors offered on 1973 Rancheros were: white; Bright red; Medium blue metallic; Light blue; Light pewter metallic; Dark green metallic; Light green; Medium brown metallic; tan; Medium copper metallic; and Medium-bright yellow. Color Glow paints were: Blue Glow, Ivy Glow and Gold Glow (optional). Black or white vinyl roofs were available.
RANCHERO OF PICKUP: The GT had (in addition to or in place of all of the standard Ranchero 500 features): Color-keyed bodyside stripes and racing mirrors painted body colors (left-side remote-control); black hubcaps with bright trim rings; white-lettered tires; GT grille in resilient plastic with long, molded armrests; spare tire and tool compartment cover; Ranchero GT instrument panel plaque; and high-back seats.
RANCHERO SQUIRE PICKUP: The Squire had (in addition to or in place of all the standard Ranchero features): Deluxe chrome wheelcovers; wood-tone panels on the sides and tailgate; Ranchero Squire script on front fenders; Squire crest on grille; wood-tone panel around instruments; electric clock; bright armrest bases; Squire tire and tool compartment cover; Squire instrument panel plaque; and bright trim on pedals.
I.D. DATA [Ranchero]: VIN located on rating plate. The first symbol was the last digit of the model year. The second symbol identified the assembly plant (same factory codes as 1972. The third and fourth symbols indicated the body series: 47=Ranchero 500; 48=Ranchero GT; 49=Ranchero Squire. The fifth symbol indicated the engine: L or 3=250 cid six; F or 6=302 cid V-8; H,Q or R=351 cid V-8; S=400 cid V-8; N=429 cid V-8. The last six symbols indicate the sequential production number. Body style codes appear in first column of charts below.

Model	Body Type	Price	Weight	Prod. Total
Ranchero 500 — 1/2-Ton — 118 in. w.b. — Six				
97R	Sedan-Pickup	2323	3670	4787
Ranchero 500 GT — 1/2-Ton — 118 in. w.b. — V-8				
97D	Sedan-Pickup	2904	3675	25,634
Ranchero Squire — 1/2-Ton — 118 in. w.b. — Six				
97K	Sedan Pickup	3142	3710	15,320

ENGINE [Standard 97R/97K]: Displacement: 250 cid. OHV. Six. 98 nhp at 3400 rpm. Bore & stroke: 3.68 x 3.91 in. Compression ratio: 8.0:1. Carburetor: One-barrel.
ENGINE Standard 97D]: Displacement: 302 cid. V-8. Bore & stroke: 4 x 3 in. 140 nhp at 4000 rpm. Compression ratio: 8.5:1. Carburetor: Two-barrel.
CHASSIS: Wheelbase: 118 in. Overall length: 216 in. Tires: E78-14B (E70B white-lettered on GT).
POWERTRAIN OPTIONS: Engines: 302 cid two-barrel V-8. 351 cid two-barrel V-8. 351 cid four-barrel V-8. 400 cid two-barrel V-8. 429 cid four-barrel V-8. Transmission: Four-speed manual transmission with Hurst floor shifter.
CONVENIENCE OPTIONS: SelectAire air-conditioner. Power steering. [Protection Group] Includes: (500) door edge and bumper guards; vinyl insert bodyside moldings; and front bumper rubber inserts. (500 Squire) Flight-bench seat. Cloth upholstery for standard seat in 500. Sport cloth seat. High-back vinyl bucket seats. Vinyl roof in black or white. Power front disc brakes. AM/FM stereo radio. AM radio. 15 in. wheels. Full wheelcovers. Deluxe wheelcovers. Hubcaps with trim rings. Mag-style wheels. Tinted glass. Class II (2,000-3,500 lbs.) and Class III (3,500-6,000 lbs.) trailer towing packages. Rim-blow sport steering wheel. Electric clock. Racing type mirrors painted body color. [Visibility Group] Includes: Illuminated light switch; ashtray, underhood and courtesy lights; parking brake light; and seat belt warning lights. [Peformance/Handling Package] Includes: High-rate rear springs; heavy-duty front and rear shock absorbers; rear stablizer bar; and heavy-duty front stablizer bar (offered with 351 four-barrel and 429 cid V-8s). [Heavy-duty Suspension Package] Includes: Heavy-duty shock absorbers and rear springs. [Instrument Group] Includes: (V-8) Tach; trip odometer; clock; ammeter; water temperature gauge; and oil pressure gauge.
NOTE: According to a *Popular Mechanics* poll of owners, the four things Ranchero owners liked best about their vehicles were: Handling, styling, comfort and ride. By far the biggest complaint was poor gas mileage, although many blamed this on the anti-pollution equipment. The majority were pleased with the Ranchero. In fact, 83.5 percent said they would buy another. When asked the same question, only 77.2 percent of El Camino owners said they would purchase another.
BRONCO WAGON: The Pickup was discontinued, so the four-wheel drive Wagon was the only Bronco model available in 1973. Styling was basically the same as last year. Among the standard features were: Bucket vinyl seats; a floor-mounted T-bar transfer case control; suspended foot pedals; fresh air heater and defroster; lockable glove compartment; padded instrument panel; two-speed electric windshield wipers; sun visors; vinyl-coated rubber floor mat; fully synchronized three-speed manual transmission; and full-length roof with fixed windows in the rear liftgate and on each side of the rear compartment.
I.D. DATA [U-100]: VIN located on rating plate. The first three symbols indicated series: U14=Model U-140 Pickup; U15=Model U-150 Wagon. The fourth symbol indicates engine: F=170 cid six; G=302 cid V-8. The fifth symbol indicates assembly plant: H=Lorain, Ohio; L=Michigan Truck; R=San Jose, Calif.; S=Allen Park, Mich. The last six symbols are the sequential production number.

Model	Body Type	Price	Weight	Prod. Total
Bronco 4x4 — 1/2-Ton — 92 in. w.b. — Six				
U-100	Wagon	3636	3090	21,894

ENGINE [Bronco]: Displacement: 200 cid. OHV Six. 84 nhp at 3800 rpm. Bore & stroke: 3.68 x 3.13 in. Compression ratio: 8.3:1. Carburetor: One-barrel.
CHASSIS: Wheelbase: 92 in. Overall length: 152.1 in. Overall width: 68.8 in. GVW: 4,300-4,900 lbs. Tires: E78-15.
POWERTRAIN OPTIONS: Engine: 302 cid V-8. Transmission: Cruise-O-Matic automatic.
CONVENIENCE OPTIONS: Extra-cooling V-8 radiator. Left-hand remote-control outside mirror. Power steering (with V-8). [Convenience Group] Includes: Cigarette lighter; map light; inside 10 in. day/night rearview mirror; right-hand chrome rearview mirror; shoulder harness; and rear seat. Chrome bumper. Skid plates for standard fuel tank and transfer case. Inside-tailgate-mounted spare tire carrier (included with rear seat option). Exterior rear-mounted swing-away tire carrier. Bright metal wheelcovers. High-flotation tires. Auxiliary 7.5-gal. fuel tank with skid plate. Manual radio and antenna. Bright bodyside and tailgate moldings. Bright metal rocker panel molding. Hand-operated throttle. [Sport Bronco Package] Includes: Bright metal Sport Bronco emblem; pleated parchment vinyl front seat; vinyl door trim panels with bright metal moldings; hardboard headlining with bright metal retainer moldings; parchment vinyl front floor mat with bright metal retainers; rear floor mat included with optional rear seat; cigarette lighter; horn ring; bright metal drip rail moldings; bright metal windshield and window frames; bright metal grille molding and tailgate release handle; bright headlight, side light, reflector and taillight bezels; Argent-painted grille with bright Ford letters; chrome bumpers front and rear; chrome front bumper guard; and bright metal wheelcovers (with 15 in. wheels only). Over-size 6.50 x 16 6PR TT tires.

DEALER-INSTALLED ACCESSORIES: Power-take-off (front-mounted). Warn free-running front hubs (manual or automatic). Snow plows. Snow plow angling kits. Front auxiliary air springs. Front-mounted winch. Trailer hitch. Trailer towing mirror. Locking gas cap. Front tow hooks. Compass. Fire extinguisher. Transmission oil cooler. Tachometer. [4500 lbs. GVW Package] Includes: 2,780 lbs. rear axle, front springs rated at 1,000 lbs., rear springs rated at 1,475 lbs. and G78-15B tires. [4,900 lbs. GVW Package] Includes: 3,300 lbs. Traction-Lok rear axle, heavy-duty front and rear springs rating, and tires same as 4,500 lbs. package. [Ranger Package] Includes: Argent silver grille, bucket seats, lower bodyside strips, fiberboard headliner, cut-pile carpeting front and rear, wheelcovers, white power dome and white spare tire carrier.

ECONOLINE E-100 CARGO VAN: The Econoline was little changed for the new year. However, the front axle capacity was increased 50 lbs. and the optional air-conditioning evaporator was now located under the floor. Some standard features included: Vinyl color-coordinated upholstery; painted front and rear bumpers and hubcaps; left-hand fresh air inlet; dome lights in driver's compartment and cargo area; ashtray; single electric horn; coat hook; mechanical jack; double-grip door locks on all doors with reversible keys; push-pull interior door locks (except rear doors); metal door checks; individual driver's seat; headlining in driver and passenger area; fresh air heater and defroster; and double cargo doors at right and rear.

ECONOLINE E-100 WINDOW VAN: As the name suggests, the Window Van had glass all around. Like other E-100s, its cargo area was 11-1/2 ft. long and 53.5 in. wide. It shared most standard features with the Cargo Van.

ECONOLINE E-100 DISPLAY VAN: This model had windows at the rear and on the right-hand side. It came with the same standard features as the Cargo Van.

I.D. DATA [Econoline]: VIN located on rating plate. First symbol indicates model year: 3=1973. Second symbol indicates assembly plant: (See Ranchero/Bronco/F-100 I.D. data for plant codes.) The third and fourth symbols indicate model: E10=1/2-Ton Econoline; E20=3/4-Ton Econoline; E30=1-Ton Econoline. The fifth symbol indicates engine: U=170 cid Six; G=302 V-8. The last six symbols are the sequential production number.

Model	Body Type	Price	Weight	Prod. Total
Econoline E-100 — 1/2-Ton — 105.5 in./123.5 in. w.b. — Six				
E-140	Cargo Van	2738	3240	Note 1
E-150	Window Van	2808	3285	Note 1
E-160	Display Van	2880	3240	Note 1

NOTE 1: See production data at end of Econoline section.

ENGINE [Econoline E-100]: Displacement: 170 cid. OHV. Six. 105 hp at 4400 rpm. Bore & stroke: 3.50 x 2.94 in. Compression ratio: 9.1:1. one-barrel. carburetor.

ECONOLINE E-200 CARGO VAN: For heavier loads, buyers could move up to the E-200 series. Its front axle had a capacity of 2,750 lbs. The rear axle had a 3,300 lbs. rating. It also had larger (11 x 3 in. front/11 x 2-1/4 in. rear) brakes. Standard features echoed those of the E-100 Cargo Van.

ECONOLINE E-200 WINDOW VAN: This vehicle shared styling with the E-100 Window Van and load capacity with other E-200 vans.

ECONOLINE E-200 DISPLAY VAN: This vehicle shared styling with the E-100 Display Van and load capacity with other E-200 vans.

I.D. DATA: See E-100 I.D. Data.

Model	Body Type	Price	Weight	Prod. Total
Econoline E-200 — 3/4-Ton — 105.5 in./123.5 in. w.b. — Six				
E-240	Cargo Van	2873	3290	Note 1
E-250	Window Van	2945	3365	Note 1
E-260	Display Van	2903	3335	Note 1

NOTE 1: See production data at end of Econoline section.

ENGINE [Econoline E-200]: Same as E-100.

ECONOLINE E-300 CARGO VAN: For really big loads, it was hard to beat the E-300 Cargo Van. Its front axle capacity was rated at 3,300 lbs. Its rear axle was rated at 4,800 lbs. The front brakes were 12 x 3 in., the rears 12 x 12-1/2 in. Its front and rear springs were also heavy-duty.

ECONOLINE E-300 WINDOW VAN: Had same features as the Cargo Van, plus windows all around.

ECONOLINE E-300 DISPLAY VAN: Had same features as the Cargo Van, plus windows on the right-hand side.

Model	Body Type	Price	Weight	Prod. Total
Econoline E-300 — 1-Ton — 105.5 in./123.5 in. w.b. — Six				
E-340	Cargo Van	3112	3670	Note 1
E-350	Window Van	3184	3745	Note 1
E-360	Display Van	3142	3715	Note 1

NOTE 1: Ford records show the following Econoline production break-outs: [89A Standard Cargo Van] 60,509; [89B Custom Cargo Van] 5,123; [89C Standard Display Van] 7,198; [89D Custom Display Van] 94; [89E Standard Window Van] 13,382; [89F Custom Window Van] 1,828; [33A Cutaway Camper Special] 850.

ENGINE [Econoline E-300]: Displacement: 240 cid. OHV. Six. 150 hp at 4000 rpm. Bore & stroke: 4.00 x 3.18 in. Compression ratio: 9.2:1. Carburetor: One-barrel.

CHASSIS: Wheelbase: 105.5. in. (123.5 in. SuperVan). Tires: E78-14B (E-100); G78-15B (E-200); 8.00 x 16.5 (E-300). GVW: 4,800 lbs. (E-100); 6,000 lbs. (E-200); 8,300 lbs. (E-300).

POWERTRAIN OPTIONS: Engines: 240 cid six. 300 cid six. 302 cid V-8. Transmissions: SelectShift Cruise-O-Matic automatic transmission.

CONVENIENCE OPTIONS: Push-button radio. Stationary or flip-fold passenger seat. High-output heater and defroster. Auxiliary hot water heater. Air-conditioner. Insulation package. Insulated floor mats. Inside body rub rails. Inside or Western-type rearview mirrors. Low-mount rearview mirrors. Wheelcover adapters. Wheelcovers. Deluxe driver and/or stationary passenger seats with color-coordinated floor mats. Auxiliary step for right-side cargo doors. Dual electric horns. Courtesy light switches for front or all doors. Padded instrument panel. Shoulder harness. Stationary glass or vents in rear and/or right-side cargo doors. Tinted glass. Inside rear door latch and lock. Scuff pads at front door wells. School bus package for E-200 and E-300 Window Vans with 123.5 in. wheelbase. [Custom Equipment Package] Includes: (In addition to or in place of standard items) deluxe pleated vinyl seat trim; bright metal front and rear bumpers and hubcaps; horn ring; cigarette lighter; color-coordinated floor mat on left-hand side; glove box door with lock; bright metal grille; taillight bezels; vent window trim; and windshield moldings.

CLUB WAGON: Club Wagons were basically Econolines made for hauling people. The base model held five passengers. Among standard features were: Twin-I-Beam independent front suspension; vinyl seat trim; armrests on front doors and at right side of three-passenger seats; ashtrays, front and rear; black floor mats; coat hook; two dome lights; dual sun visors; instrument panel padded on right side; bright instrument cluster trim; glove box door with lock; headlining in front compartment; dual outside rearview mirrors; backup lights; inside rearview mirror; emergency lamp flasher; retracting step for double side doors; rear reflectors; and side-marker lights at front and rear.

CUSTOM CLUB WAGON: This was a step up from the base model. Both shared many of the same features, however, the Custom also had: Pleated vinyl seat trim; interior vinyl side and door trim panels; armrests for all seats; color-coordinated front and rear floor mats; four coat hooks; full-length headlining; window trim moldings; cigarette lighter; scuff pads at front door wells; spare tire cover; horn ring; bright metal grille; full-width, padded instrument panel; Custom ornaments; bright metal bodyside moldings, taillight bezels and hubcaps; and added insulation.

CHATEAU CLUB WAGON: At the top-of-the-line was the Chateau. It had, in addition to or in place of Custom Club Wagon features, pleated deluxe cloth seat trim with vinyl bolsters; similar trim on interior door and side panels with simulated woodgrain bands; full-length color-coordinated carpeting with dash insulator; chrome front and rear bumpers; bright metal dual outside mirrors; bright metal molding around windshield, side and rear windows; bright metal rear bodyside molding; and Chateau ornaments.

I.D. DATA [Club Wagon]: See F-100 I.D. Data.

Model	Body Type	Price	Weight	Prod. Total
Club Wagon E-100 — 1/2-Ton — 105.5 in./123.5 in. w.b. — Six				
E-110	Club Wagon	3140	3555	5,833
E-120	Custom Club Wagon	3748	4090	6,608
E-130	Chateau Club Wagon	3892	4060	4,955

ENGINE [Club Wagon]: Same as E-300 engine.

CHASSIS: Wheelbase: 105.5 in. (123.5 in. optional) Tires: E78-14B.

POWERTRAIN OPTIONS: Engine: 302 cid V-8. Transmission: SelectShift Cruise-O-Matic automatic transmission.

CONVENIENCE OPTIONS: Power steering. Ammeter and oil pressure gauge. Heavy-duty battery. Heavy-duty shocks. Whitewall tires. Chrome front and rear bumpers. Cigarette lighter. Courtesy light switches for all doors. Door positioners for all door. Air-conditioner. Insulation package. Inside body rub rails. High-output heater/defroster. Auxiliary hot water heater for passenger compartment. Tinted glass. AM radio.

COURIER PICKUP: Early 1973 Couriers were identical to the 1972s. In mid-model year, the Courier name was removed from the hood and replaced with the Ford name (in block letters). The Ford nameplate was also put on the tailgate. Among the standard equipment was: 11 tie-down hooks around the box and tailgate for securing cargo or a tarpaulin; rear mud flaps; bright hubcaps; white sidewall tires; vinyl upholstery, headliner and door panels; padded armrests; padded sun visors; tool set emergency flashers; outside rearview mirror; axle type jack with crank; and four-speed manual transmission.

I.D. DATA: Serial number located on door post on driver's side and consisted of either 10 or 11 symbols. The first five symbols indicated the series and the remaining symbols were the sequential production number.

Model	Body Type	Price	Weight	Prod. Total
Courier — 1/2-Ton — 104.3 in. w.b. — Four				
—	Pickup	2508	2515	—

ENGINE [Courier]: Displacement: 109.5 cid. Inline four-cylinder nhp 74 at 5000 rpm. (67 hp at 5000 rpm in California). Bore & stroke: 3.07 x 3.70 in. Compression ratio: 8.6:1. Carburetor: Zenith or Stromberg two-barrel.

CHASSIS: Wheelbase: 104.3 in. Overall length: 172 in. Overall width: 61.6 in. GVW Rating: 3,910 lbs. Tires: 6.00 x 14.

POWERTRAIN OPTIONS: Transmission: Jatco automatic transmission.

CONVENIENCE OPTIONS: AM radio. Rear step bumper. 6 x 9 in. swing-lok mirrors. Tinted glass. Full wheelcovers. Air-conditioning. [Dress Up Package] Includes: Backlite, windshield, drip and bodyside moldings; front bumper guards.

1973 Ford 1/2-Ton F-100 Styleside Pickup With Camper Shell (DFW)

F-100 CUSTOM PICKUP: Although it bore a strong resemblance to last year's model, many changes were made for 1973. Parking lights were moved to above the headlights. In the slot between them, Ford was spelled out in block letters. The rectangular slots grille was divided at the center by a vertical bar. The former convex bodyside spear was replaced by a concave groove that ran almost the full-length of the vehicle (on Styleside models) from the parking lights back. Side-marker lights were placed in the groove. An F-series emblem was placed slightly below the groove between the door and front tire opening. The new hood had a flatter face. The cab was longer and had a behind-the-seat storage area. Ford Custom Pickups had a standard 7 in. full-foam cushioned seat. The seatback also tilted back more than last year's, for car-like comfort. Some other standard features were: Deluxe fresh air heater/defroster; seat belts; windshield washers; two-speed windshield wipers; dome light with door courtesy switch; ashtray; glove compartment with push-button latch; rubber floor mat; day/night rearview mirror; bright left-hand and right-hand exterior mirrors; hubcaps; three-speed manual transmission; color-keyed padded instrument panel; chrome front bumper; frame-mounted fuel tank; front disc brakes; long 2-1/2 in. wide rear leaf springs; Twin-I-Beam independent front suspension; new simplified box construction utilizing a single strong sheet of steel, making the inside panel, wheelhouse and part of the floor one solid piece.There was a new frame with six crossmembers (four placed at the rear half of the frame to provide extra strength under the pickup box for carrying heavy loads).

1973 Ford 1/2-Ton F-110 Custom Styleside Pickup 4x4 (RCA)

I.D. DATA: VIN located on rating plate. The first three symbols indicated series: F10=F-100 (4x2); F11=F-100 (4x4). The fourth symbol indicates engine: A or 1=240 cid six; B or 2=300 cid six; G or 3=302 cid six; H=390 cid V-8; Y or 8=360 cid V-8. The fifth symbol indicates assembly plant: C=Ontario, Canada; E=Mahwah, N.J.; H=Lorain, Ohio; K=Kansas City, Kan.; L=Michigan Truck; N=Norfolk, Va.; P=Twin Cities, Minn.; R=San Jose, Calif.; S=Allen Park, Mich.; V=Louisville, Ken. (Truck). The last six symbols are the sequential production number.

1973 Ford 1/2-Ton F-100 Ranger XLT Styleside Pickup (OCW)

Model	Body Type	Price	Weight	Prod. Total
F-100 — 1/2-Ton — 117 in. w.b. — V-8				
81	Chassis & Cab	2736	3145	Note 1
83	Styleside 6.75 ft.	2889	3495	Note 1
F-100 — 1/2-Ton — 133 in. w.b. — V-8				
83	Flareside 8 ft.	2925	3590	Note 1
83	Styleside 8 ft.	2925	3590	Note 1

NOTE 1: Ford records show the following F-100 production: [Chassis & Cab] 2,461; [Flareside] 3,034; and [Styleside] 457,746.
NOTE 2: Prices/weights for base V-8; deduct for six-cylinder.
NOTE 3: Add $575 for 4x4.
ENGINE [Base Six]: Inline. OHV. Six-cylinder. Bore and stroke: 4.0 x 3.18 in. Displacement: 240 cid. Gross bhp: 150 at 4000 rpm. Gross torque: 234 lbs.-ft. at 2200 rpm.
ENGINE [Base V-8]: V-block. OHV. Eight-cylinder. Bore and stroke: 4.0 x 3.0 in. Displacement: 302 cid. Net horsepower: 130 at 3800 rpm. Net torque: 122 lbs.-ft. at 2000 rpm.
F-250 CUSTOM PICKUP: The F-250 had most of the same standard features as the F-100, plus power brakes. The Styleside had sleek body panels extending all the way forward to hug the rear cab corners. Its pickup box featured strong, double-walled side panel construction. Each inner and outer panel was one solid piece. The tailgate was also double-walled. Flareside Pickups had runningboards between cab and fenders for easy side loading. The seasoned hardwood floorboards had interlocking steel skid strips. Rubber-covered forged-steel chains supported the tailgate when open and toggle-type latches maintained tight seal when tailgate was closed.
I.D. DATA [F-250]: Same as F-100 I.D. Data, except first three symbols are: [4x2] F-25; [4x4] F-26.

Model	Body Type	Price	Weight	Prod. Total
F-250 — 3/4-Ton — 133 in. w.b. — V-8				
F-250	Chassis & Cab	3031	3505	Note 1
F-250	Flareside	3183	3925	Note 1
F-250	Styleside	3183	3925	Note 1
F-250 Crew Cabs — 3/4-Ton — 149.5 in. w.b. — V-8				
F-250	Chassis & Cab	—	—	Note 1
F-250	Styleside	—	—	Note 1

NOTE 1: Ford records show the following F-250 production break-outs: [Chassis & Cab] 7,674; [Flareside] 3,004; [Styleside] 187,348.
NOTE 2: Prices/weights for base 360 V-8; deduct for six-cylinder.
NOTE 3: Add $575 for 4x4.
ENGINE [Base Heavy-duty Six]: Inline. OHV. Six-cylinder. Bore and stroke: 4.0 x 3.98 in. Displacement: 300 cid. Net horsepower: 101 at 3000 rpm. Net torque: 223 lbs.-ft. at 1600 rpm.

ENGINE [Base V-8]: V-block. OHV. Eight-cylinder. Bore and stroke: 4.0 x 3.5 in. Displacement: 360 cid. Net horsepower: 145 at 3800 rpm. Net torque: 264 lbs.-ft. at 2200 rpm.
F-350 CUSTOM PICKUP: The F-350 pickup was now available only with the Styleside box. It was similar in construction to F-250 Stylesides, except it was a more heavy-duty vehicle and had the spare tire location built into the outer right side. A four-speed manual transmission was standard.
F-350 PLATFORM/STAKE: This model was offered in two sizes: 9 ft. and 12 ft. Both had floor frames formed of steel cross sills riveted to steel side rails. Floorboards were interlocked with steel skid strips and corners were reinforced with steel brackets. Formed steel caps covered the ends of the body sills. Sideboards were made of hardwood and stakes were steel.
I.D. DATA: [F-350]: Same as F-100 except first three symbols are F-35.

1973 Ford 1-Ton F-350 Ranger XLT Supercab Styleside Pickup

Model	Body Type	Price	Weight	Prod. Total
F-350 — 1-Ton — 137 in. w.b. — V-8				
81	Chassis & Cab	3109	3730	Note 1
83	Styleside 8 ft.	3557	4365	Note 1
80	Platform 9 ft.	3390	4315	Note 1
86	Stake 9 ft.	3431	4365	Note 1
F-350 — 1-Ton — 140 in. w.b. — V-8				
80	Platform 12 ft.	—	—	Note 1
86	Stake 12 ft.	—	—	Note 1
F-350 Crew Cabs — 1-Ton — 161 in. w.b. — V-8				
83	Chassis & Cab	—	—	Note 1
83	Styleside	—	—	Note 1
83	Super Camper	3940	4365	Note 1

NOTE 1: Ford records show the following F-350 production break-outs: [Chassis & Cowl] 80; [Chassis & Cab] 42,084; [Platform & Rack] 6,656; [Platform] 749 and [Styleside] 11,889. Parcel Vans: [P-350] 1,054; [P-400] 6,251.
NOTE 2: Deduct for six-cylinder.
NOTE 3: Add $575 for 4x4.
ENGINE [Base Heavy-duty Six]: Inline. OHV. Six-cylinder. Bore and stroke: 4.0 x 3.98 in. Displacement: 300 cid. Net horsepower: 101 at 3000 rpm. Net torque: 223 lbs.-ft. at 1600 rpm
ENGINE [Base V-8]: V-block. OHV. Eight-cylinder. Bore and stroke: 4.0 x 3.5 in. Displacement: 360 cid. Net horsepower: 145 at 3800 rpm. Net torque: 264 lbs.-ft. at 2200 rpm.
CHASSIS: Wheelbase: 117 in. (F-100); 133 in. (F-100/F-250); 140 in. (F-350 Platform/Stake); 137 in. (F-350); 161 in. (F-350 Platform/Stake). GVW: 4,600-5,500 lbs. (F-100); 6,200-8,100 lbs. (F-250); 8,350-10,000 lbs. (F-350). Tires: G78-15B (F-100); 8.00 x 16.5D (F-250); 8.75 x 16.5E (F-350).
POWERTRAIN OPTIONS: Engines: 300 cid six (F-100); 302 cid V-8 (F-100); 360 cid V-8; 390 cid V-8; 460 cid V-8. Transmissions: Four-speed manual transmission; Cruise-O-Matic automatic.

1973 Ford 1/2-Ton F-100 Custom Styleside Pickup (JAG)

CONVENIENCE OPTIONS: Four-wheel drive. Pickup box cover: (Standard) Fiberglass construction, tinted side and rear windows, T-handle locking rear lift gate and rubber-cushioned tie-downs; (Deluxe) Sliding side windows with screens, bright side and rear window moldings, roof vent, interior dome light and color-keyed body stripe in a choice of five colors). Knitted vinyl seat trim. Heavy-duty black vinyl seat trim. Vinyl insert bodyside molding. AM/FM stereo radio. AM radio. Intermittent windshield wipers. [Super Camper Special Package] Includes: Front and rear stabilizer bars; heavy-duty frame; automatic transmission; extra-cooling; 360 cid V-8; power front disc brakes; 55 amp. alternator; 70 amp.-hr. battery; oil pressure gauge and ammeter; bright Western mirrors; dual horns; heavy-duty

shocks; and camper wiring harness. Rear step bumper. Western style mirrors. Sliding rear cab window. Concealed spare tire and wheel. Auxiliary 12-volt 70 amp.-hr. battery. Air-conditioner. Black or white texture painted roof (includes bright drip rail molding). Full wheelcovers. Mag style wheelcovers. 22.5-gal. auxiliary fuel tank (20.2 gal. F-100). Dual tape stripes. Bright tie-down hooks. Super cooling package. Slide out spare tire carrier. Tool stowage box with locking door. [Convenience Group] Includes: Cargo, engine, glove compartment and ashtray lights; glove compartment door lock; door map pockets; and 12 in. day/night mirror. [Northland Special Package] Includes: Engine block heater; 50 percent (-30 degree F. anti-freeze; 70 amp.-hr. battery; 55 amp. alternator; and limited-slip rear axle. Power steering. Power front disc brakes (4x2s). High-output heater. Trailer towing packages. Ammeter and oil pressure gauge. Bright hubcaps. Bright contour rear bumper for Stylesides. Painted channel rear bumper for Faresides. Tinted glass all around. Shoulder harness. Oil-bath engine air cleaner. Frame-anchored camper tie-down system. Heavy-duty 50-amp. camper wiring harness. [Ranger Package] Includes: (In addition to or in place of Custom features) Color-keyed pleated cloth seat upholstery with metallic vinyl bolsters; instrument panel molding with black accent; color-keyed door panels with bright moldings; additional insulation; perforated headlining (insulated) with bright molding; color-keyed vinyl coated floor mat with heel pads; cigarette lighter; bright windshield, rear window and roof drip moldings; bright rocker panel and wheel lip moldings; bright hubcaps (except with 4x4 option and dual rear wheels). Styleside Rangers also include bright tailgate moldings top and bottom; taillight bezels; and a bright recessed tailgate handle. [Ranger XLT Package] Includes: (In addition to or in place of Ranger items) Deluxe color-keyed, long-wearing cloth-with-vinyl seat upholstery; color-keyed pleated vinyl upper door panel with simulated woodgrain accent moldings; map pockets; lower panels color-keyed; wall-to-wall nylon carpeting; black steering wheel with simulated woodgrain insert; bright seat-pivot covers; additional insulation and double-wrapped muffler; convenience group; color-keyed vinyl headlining (with special insulation) and sun visors. Styleside Ranger XLTs also include bright bodyside moldings with vinyl inserts; upper tailgate applique panel and molding; and aluminum tailgate applique panel.

HISTORICAL: Introduced December, 1972. Model year production [Light-duty trucks including Parcel Vans] 886,649.

1973 Ford 1/2-Ton F-100 Custom Styleside Pickup (OCW)

1974 FORD

1974 Ford 1/2-Ton Ranchero 500 Sedan-Pickup (OCW)

RANCHERO 500 PICKUP: The Ranchero received a very mild facelift for 1974. The grille design was squared off a bit. It was divided into eight rectangular sections containing a criss-cross pattern. The parking lights were hidden in the grille. The front bumper now had a slight dip under the grille. Standard features included: Black saddle, blue, tan, or green upholstery. Color-keyed vinyl door trim panels with bright trim. Color-keyed steering wheel and column. Deep-pile carpeting. Hi-level, flow-through ventilation. Ventless door windows. Energy-absorbing steering column. Padded steering wheel hub. Lockable glove box. Locking steering column. Fresh-air heater defroster. Trim panel behind the split-back seat. Vinyl headliner. Color-keyed seat belts with outboard retractors and shoulder harnesses (also center passenger seat belts). Armrests with recessed door handles. Vinyl-framed day/night mirror. Cigarette lighter. Padded, color-keyed instrument panel. Emergency lamp flasher. Spare tire and tool compartment. Deluxe grille with moldings. Bright energy absorbing front bumper. Bright left-hand mirror with remote-control. Hidden windshield wipers. Bright metal windshield, rear window, drip rail and top of cargo body moldings. Bright metal hubcaps. Four cargo tie-downs. Colors offered on 1974 Rancheros were: white; Bright red; Medium blue metallic; Pastel blue; Bright dark blue metallic; Dark green metallic; Pastel lime; Saddle bronze metallic; Medium copper metallic; Bright green-gold metallic; Medium dark gold metallic; Medium ivy-bronze metallic; and Maize yellow. Optional Color Glow finishes were: Green Glow; Ginger Glow; Tan Glow and Gold Glow. Black, white, blue, green, brown, tan or gold vinyl roofs were available.

RANCHERO GT PICKUP: The GT had (in addition to or in place of the Ranchero 500 features): Color-keyed bodyside stripes. Sport style mirrors painted body color (both with remote-control). Black hubcaps with bright trim rings. White-lettered belted tires. GT grille crest. Spare tire and tool compartment cover. Bright trim on pedals. GT instrument panel plaque.

RANCHERO SQUIRE PICKUP: The Squire had (in addition to or in place of Ranchero 500 features): Deluxe bright wheelcovers. Simulated woodgrain panels on sides and tailgate. Ranchero Squire script on front fenders. Squire crest on grille. wood-tone panel around instruments. Electric clock. Spare tire and tool compartment cover. Bright trim on pedals. Squire instrument panel plaque.

I.D. DATA [Ranchero]: The VIN consists of 11 symbols. The first symbol is the last digit of the model year. The second symbol indicates the assembly plant. The third and fourth symbols indicate the product line and body style. The fifth symbol indicates the engine. The last six symbols are the sequential production number.

Model	Body Type	Price	Weight	Prod. Total
Ranchero 500 — 1/2-Ton — 118 in. w.b. — V-8				
97D	Sedan-Pickup	3258	3915	18,447
Ranchero GT — 1/2-Ton — 118 in. w.b. — V-8				
97R	Sedan-Pickup	3555	3980	11,328
Ranchero Squire — 1/2-Ton — 118 in. w.b. — V-8				
97K	Sedan-Pickup	3575	3940	3150

ENGINE [Ranchero]: Displacement: 302 cid. V-8. 140 nhp at 3800 rpm. Bore & stroke: 4 in. x 3 in. Compression ratio: 8.0:1. Carburetor: Two-barrel.

CHASSIS: Wheebase: 118 in. Overall length: 218.3 in. GVW: 5,480-5,950 lbs. Tires: F78-14B (F70-14B white-lettered on GT).

POWERTRAIN OPTIONS: Engines: 250 cid six-cylinder (this engine was discontinued, then reinstated later in the model year). 351 cid V-8 two-barrel. 351 cid V-8. 400 cid V-8 four-barrel. 460 cid V-8 four-barrel. Transmissions: SelectShift Cruise-O-Matic transmission (required with optional engines).

CONVENIENCE OPTIONS: [Performance Cluster] Includes: Tachometer, trip odometer, clock, ammeter, water temperature and oil pressure gauges (also includes heavy-duty battery). SelectAire air-conditioner with automatic temperature control. SelectAire air-conditioner. Power steering. [Body Protection Group/Bumpers] Includes: Front and rear bumper guards and front bumper rubber inserts. [Protection Group/Appearance] Includes: Spare tire lock, floor mats, license plate frame, and door edge guards. Vinyl insert bodyside molding. Anti-theft alarm system. Power side windows. Tilt steering wheel. Cruise control. [Convenience Group] Includes: Right and left remote-control mirrors, interval windshield wipers, vanity mirror. Restraint system. Sport flight bench seat with vinyl trim. [Brougham Decor Group] Includes: Split bench seat with super-soft vinyl or knit cloth upholstery for the standard seat in Ranchero 500 and Squire. Bucket seats. Vinyl roof. Power brakes. AM radio. 15 in. wheels. Luxury wheelcovers. Hubcaps with trim rings. Mag style wheels. Tinted glass. Electric clock. Dual sport style mirrors. [Light Group] Includes: Ashtray, underhood and glove box lights, parking brake warning light, lights-on warning buzzer and illuminated light switch. Class II (2,000-3,500 lbs.) or Class III (3,500-6,000 lbs.) trailer towing package. [Handling Suspension Package] Includes: Heavy-duty shock absorbers, rear springs and heavy-duty rear stabilizer bar.

BRONCO WAGON: Bronco styling was carried over for 1974. A few minor changes were made to this four-wheel drive vehicle. Among them, the automatic gear-selector dial had a light, a different steering gear was used and a dome light replaced the map light as standard equipment. Other standard features included: Vinyl bucket seats. Floor-mounted T-bar transfer case control. Suspended foot pedals. Fresh air heater and defroster. Lockable glove compartment. Padded instrument panel. Two-speed electric windshield wipers. Sun visors. Vinyl-coated rubber floor mat. Fully synchronized three-speed manual transmission. Full-length roof with fixed windows in the rear liftgate and on each side of the rear compartment.

I.D. DATA [Bronco]: The VIN consists of 11 symbols. The first three indicate the series. The fourth indicates the engine. The fifth shows the assembly plant. The last six are the sequential production number.

Model	Body Type	Price	Weight	Prod. Total
Bronco 4x4 — 1/2-Ton — 92 in. w.b. — V-8				
U-100	Wagon	4182	3420	18,786

NOTE 1: Prices/weights for base V-8; deduct for six.

NOTE 2: Deduct for 4x2 models.

ENGINE [Bronco]: Displacement: 200 cid. Six-cylinder. 84 nhp at 3800 rpm. Bore & stroke: 3.68 in. x 3.13 in. Compression ratio: 8.3:1. One-barrel carburetor.

CHASSIS: Wheebase: 92 in. Overall length: 152.1 in. Overall width: 68.8 in. GVW: 4,300-4,900 lbs. Tires: E78 x 15 in.

POWERTRAIN OPTIONS: Engine: 302 cid V-8. Transmission: Cruise-O-Matic transmission.

CONVENIENCE OPTIONS: Extra-cooling V-8 radiator. Left-hand remote-control outside mirror. Knitted vinyl upholstery. Power steering. [Convenience Group] Includes: Cigarette lighter, map light, 10 in. inside day/night mirror. Shoulder harness. Rear seat. Chrome bumper. Skid plates for standard fuel tank and transfer case. Inside tailgate-mounted spare tire carrier (included with rear seat option). Exterior rear-mounted swing-away tire carrier. Bright metal wheelcovers. High-flotation tires. Auxiliary 7.5-gal. fuel tank with skid plate. Manual radio and antenna. Bright bodyside and tailgate moldings. Bright metal rocker panel molding. Hand-operated throttle. [Sport Bronco Package] Includes: Bright metal Sport Bronco emblem. Pleated parchment vinyl front seat. Vinyl door trim panels with bright metal moldings. Hardboard headlining with bright metal retainer moldings. Parchment vinyl front floor mat with bright metal retainers. Rear floor mat included with optional rear seat. Cigarette lighter. Horn ring. Bright metal drip rail moldings. Bright metal windshield and window frames. Bright metal grille molding and tailgate release handle. Bright headlight, side light, reflector and taillight bezels. Argent silver-painted grille with bright Ford letters. Chrome bumpers, front and rear. Chrome front bumper guards. Bright metal wheelcovers (with 15 in. wheels only). 6.50 x 16-6 ply-rated TT tires.

DEALER-INSTALLED ACCESSORIES: Power-take-off (front-mounted). Warn free-running front hubs (manual or automatic). Snow plows. Snow plow angling kits. Front auxiliary air springs. Front-mounted winch. Trailer hitch. Trailer towing mirror. Locking gas cap. Front tow hooks. Compass. Fire extinguisher. Transmission oil cooler. Tachometer. [4,500 lbs. GVW Package] Includes: 2,780 lbs. rear axle, front springs rated at 1,000 lbs., rear springs rated at 1,475 lbs. and G78-15B tires. 4,900 lbs. GVW Package] Includes: 3,300 lbs. Traction-Lok rear axle (front and rear spring ratings and tires same as 4,500 lbs. package. [Ranger Package] Includes: Argent silver grille, bucket seats, lower bodyside stripes, fiberboard headliner, cut-pile carpeting front and rear, wheelcovers, white power dome and white spare tire carrier.

1974 Ford Econoline Custom Cargo Van (OCW)

ECONOLINE E-100 CARGO VAN: The step wells were now stamped and covered with rubber mats. Aside from that, the new Econoline was pretty much unchanged for 1974. Standard features included: Vinyl color-coordinated upholstery. Painted front and rear bumpers and hubcaps. Left-hand fresh air inlet. Dome lights in driver's compartment and cargo area. Ashtray. Single electric horn. Coat hook. Mechanical jack. Double-grip door locks on all doors with reversible keys. Push-pull interior door locks (except rear doors). Metal door checks. Individual driver's seat. Headlining in driver and passenger area. Fresh air heater and defroster. Double cargo doors at right and rear.
ECONOLINE E-100 WINDOW VAN: As the name suggests, the Window Van had glass all around. On it and other E-100s the cargo area was 11-1/2 feet long and 53.5 in. wide. It shared most standard features with the Cargo Van.
ECONOLINE E-100 DISPLAY VAN: This model had windows at the rear and on the right-hand side. It came with the same standard features as the Cargo Van.
I.D. DATA [Econoline]: The VIN consists of 11 symbols. The first three indicate the series. The fourth indicates the engine. The fifth shows the assembly plant. The last six are the sequential production number.

Model	Body Type	Price	Weight	Prod. Total
E-100 — 1/2-Ton — 105.5 in./123.5 in. w.b. — V-8				
E-140	Cargo Van	3176	3240	Note 1
E-150	Window Van	3248	3320	Note 1
E-160	Display Van	3206	3285	Note 1

NOTE 1: See production totals under E-300.
NOTE 2: Prices/weights for base V-8; deduct for six.
ENGINE [Econoline E-100]: Displacement: 170 cid. Six-cylinder. 105 hp at 4400 rpm. Bore & stroke: 3.50 in. x 2.94 in. Compression ratio: 9.1:1. One-barrel carburetor. (300 cid six-cylinder engine standard in California.)
ECONOLINE E-200 CARGO VAN: For heavier loads, buyers could move up to the E-200 series. Its front axle had a capacity of 2,750 lbs. The rear axle was rated for 3,300 lbs. It also had larger (11 x 3 in. front/11 x 2-1/4 in. rear) brakes. Standard features echoed those of the E-100 Cargo Van.
ECONOLINE E-200 WINDOW VAN: This vehicle shared styling with the E-100 Window Van and load capacity with other E-200 vans.
ECONOLINE E-200 DISPLAY VAN: This vehicle shared styling with the E-100 Display Van and load capacity with other E-200 vans.
I.D. DATA: The VIN consists of 11 symbols. The first three indicate the series. The fourth indicates the engine. The fifth shows the assembly plant. The last six are the sequential production number.

Model	Body Type	Price	Weight	Prod. Total
E-250 — 3/4-Ton — 105.5 in./123.5 in. w.b. — V-8				
E-240	Cargo Van	3241	3290	Note 1
E-250	Window Van	3313	3370	Note 1
E-260	Display Van	3271	3335	Note 1

NOTE 1: See production totals under E-300.
NOTE 2: Prices/weights for base V-8; deduct for six.
ENGINE [Econoline E-200]: Same as E-100 engine.
ECONOLINE E-300 CARGO VAN: For really big loads, it was hard to beat the E-300 Cargo Van. Its front axle capacity was rated at 3,300 lbs. and its rear axle at 4,800 lbs. The front brakes were 12 x 3 in., the rears 12 x 12-1/2 in. A 10-in. clutch was standard. The front and rear springs were also heavy-duty.
ECONOLINE E-300 WINDOW VAN: This truck had the same features as the Cargo Van, plus windows all around.
ECONOLINE E-300 DISPLAY VAN: This truck had the same features as the Cargo Van, plus windows on the right-hand side.
I.D. DATA: The VIN consists of 11 symbols. The first three indicate the series. The fourth indicates the engine. The fifth shows the assembly plant. The last six are the sequential production number.

Model	Body Type	Price	Weight	Prod. Total
E-350 — 1-Ton — 105.5 in./123.5 in. w.b. — V-8				
E-340	Cargo Van	3523	3670	Note 1
E-350	Window Van	3595	3750	Note 1
E-360	Display Van	3553	3715	Note 1

NOTE 1: Model year production: [89A Standard Congo Van] 120,205; [89B Custom Cargo Van] 11,235; [89C Standard Display Van] 11,780; [89D Custom Display Van] 248; 89E Standard Window Van] 25,056; [89F Custom Window Van] 3,211; [33A Cutaway Camper] 2,050; and [33B Base Cutaway] 8,212.
NOTE 2: Prices/weights for base V-8; deduct for six.
ENGINE [Econoline E-300]: Displacement: 240 cid. Six-cylinder. 150 hp at 4000 rpm. Bore & stroke: 4.00 in. x 3.18 in. Compression ratio: 9.2:1. One-barrel carburetor. (300 cid six-cylinder standard in California.)
CHASSIS: Wheelbase: 105.5 in. (123.5 in. SuperVan) Tires: E78-14B (E-100); G78-15B (E-200); 8.00 x 16.5 in. (E-300). GVW: 4,800 lbs. (E-100); 6,000 lbs. (E-200); 8,300 lbs. (E-300).
POWERTRAIN OPTIONS: Engines: 240 cid six. 300 cid six. 302 cid V-8. Transmission: SelectShift Cruise-O-Matic transmission.
CONVENIENCE OPTIONS: Push-button radio. Stationary or flip-fold passenger seat. High-output heater and defroster. Auxiliary hot water heater. Air-conditioner. Insulation package. Insulated floor mats. Inside body rub rails. Inside or Western-type rearview mirrors. Low-mount rearview mirrors. Wheelcover adapters. Wheelcovers. Deluxe driver and/or stationary passenger seats with color-coordinated floor mats. Auxiliary step for right-side cargo doors. Dual electric horns. Courtesy light switches for front or all doors. Padded instrument panel. Shoulder harness. Stationary glass or vents in rear and/or right-side cargo doors. Tinted glass. Inside rear door latch and lock. Scuff pads at front door wells. School bus package for E-200 and E-300 Window Vans with 123.5 in. wheelbase. [Custom Equipment Package] Includes: (In addition to or in place of standard items) Deluxe pleated vinyl seat trim, bright metal front and rear bumpers and hubcaps, horn ring, cigarette lighter, color-coordinated floor mat on left-hand side, glove box door with lock, bright metal grille, taillight bezels, vent window and windshield moldings.
CLUB WAGON: Club wagons were basically Econolines made for hauling people. The base model held five passengers. Among standard features were: Twin-I-Beam independent front suspension. Vinyl seat trim. Armrests on front doors and at right side of three-passenger seats. Ashtrays, front and rear. Black floor mats. Coat hook. Two dome lights. Dual sun visors. Instrument panel (padded on right side). Bright instrument cluster trim. Glove box door with lock. Headlining in front compartment. Dual outside rearview mirrors. Backup lights. Inside rearview mirror. Emergency lamp flasher. Retracting step for double side doors. Rear reflectors. Body side-marker lights at front and rear.
CUSTOM CLUB WAGON: This was a step up from the base model. Both shared many of the same features. However, the Custom also had: Pleated vinyl seat trim. Interior vinyl side and door trim panels. Armrests for all seats. Color-coordinated front and rear floor mats. Four coat hooks. Full-length headlining. Window trim moldings. Cigarette lighter. Scuff pads at front door wells. Spare tire cover. Horn ring. Bright metal grille. Instrument panel padded full width. Custom ornaments. Bright metal bodyside moldings, taillight bezels and hubcaps. Added insulation.
CHATEAU CLUB WAGON: At the top-of-the-line was the Chateau. It had, in addition to or in place of Custom Club Wagon features, pleated deluxe cloth seat trim with vinyl bolsters. Similar trim on interior door and die panels with simulated woodgrain bands. Full-length color coordinated carpeting with dash insulator. Chrome front and rear bumpers. Bright metal dual outside mirrors. Bright metal molding around windshield, side and rear windows. Bright metal rearmolding. Chateau ornaments.
I.D. DATA: The VIN consists of 11 symbols. The first three indicate the series. The fourth indicates the engine. The fifth shows the assembly plant. The last six are the sequential production number.

Model	Body Type	Price	Weight	Prod. Total
E-100 — 1/2-Ton — 105.5 in./123.5 in. w.b. — V-8				
E-100	Club Wagon	3869	3550	11,331
E-200	Custom Club Wagon	3943	3650	12,038
E-300	Chateau Club Wagon	4176	4060	7,459

ENGINE [Club Wagon]: Same as E-300.
CHASSIS: Wheelbase: 105.5 in. (123.5 in. optional). Tires: E78-14B.
POWERTRAIN OPTIONS: Engine: 302 cid V-8. Transmission: SelectShift Cruise-O-Matic transmission.
CONVENIENCE OPTIONS: Power steering. Ammeter and oil pressure gauge. Heavy-duty battery. Heavy-duty shocks. Whitewall tires. Chrome front and rear bumpers. Cigarette lighter. Courtesy light switches for all doors. Door positioners for doors. Air-conditioner. Insulation package. Inside body rub rails. High-output heater/defroster. Auxiliary hot water heater for passenger compartment. Tinted glass. AM radio.
COURIER PICKUP: The Courier was unchanged in 1974. Among the standard equipment was: 11 tie-down hooks around the box and tailgate for securing cargo or a tarpaulin. Rear mud flaps. Bright hubcaps. White sidewall tires. Vinyl upholstery, headliner and door panels. Padded armrests. Padded sun visors. Tool set. Emergency flashers. Outside rearview mirror. Axle type jack with crank. Four-speed manual transmission.
I.D. DATA [Courier]: The VIN consists of 11 symbols. The first indicates the manufacturer. The second indicates the assembly plant. The third indicates the series. The fourth indicates the engine. The fifth (a letter) indicates the model year. The sixth indicates the production month. The last five are the sequential production number.

Model	Body Type	Price	Weight	Prod. Total
Courier — 1/2-Ton — 104.3 w.b. — Four				
—	Pickup	2969	2510	144,491

NOTE 1: Production column shows calendar year sales total.
ENGINE [Courier]: Displacement: 109.5 cid. Inline. Four-cylinder. Horsepower: 74 nhp at 5000 rpm. [67 nhp at 5000 rpm in California). Bore & stroke: 3.07 in. x 3.70 in. Compression ratio: 8.6:1. Zenith Stromberg two-barrel carburetor.
CHASSIS: Wheelbase: 104.3 in. Overall length: 172 in. Overall width: 61.6 in. GVW Rating: 3,910 lbs. Tires: 6.00 x 14.
POWERTRAIN OPTION: Jatco automatic transmission.
CONVENIENCE OPTIONS: AM radio. Rear step bumper. 6 x 9 in. Swing-Lok mirrors. Tinted glass. Full wheelcovers. Air-conditioning. [Dress-Up Package] Includes: Backlite, windshield, drip and bodyside moldings and front bumper guards.
HISTORICAL NOTE: According to a *POPULAR MECHANICS'* reader survey, the majority of Courier buyers (68.6 percent) used it as a second car. The main reason most purchased one was for economy, although handling tied with economy as its best-liked feature.
F-100 CUSTOM PICKUP: Styling was unchanged for 1974. However, a new extended cab model was made available in June of 1974. This SuperCab was offered with either a full-width rear foam seat or two facing jump seats that folded out of the way when not in use. In all, it provided 44 cu. ft. of extra load space. The SuperCab had a stiffer frame. It was available with 6.75-ft. or 8 ft. Styleside boxes. Both sizes of Styleside and Flareside boxes were offered on the regular (three-passenger) F-100 Pickups as well. Standard F-100 features included: Deluxe fresh air heater/defroster. Energy-absorbing sun visors and instrument panel padding. Instrument cluster with green backlighting. Keyless locking doors. Color-keyed molded door panels with integral armrests and paddle-type door handles. Seat belts. Windshield washers. Two-speed windshield wipers. Dome light with door courtesy light switches. Ashtray. Large glove compartment with push-button latch. Sponge-grain headlining. Black rubber floor mat. Door scuff plates. Black, red, blue or green vinyl seat trim. 10 in. day/night rearview mirror. Left- and right-hand bright metal exterior mirrors. Taillights with integral stop, turn, backup lights and reflector. Hubcaps (except 4x4). Bright tailgate handle depression (Styleside). Three-speed manual transmission. Standard colors for 1974 were: Wimbledon white; Samoa lime; Pastel lime; Limestone green (metallic); Village green; Candy-apple red; Sandpiper yellow; Burnt orange; Raven black; Wind blue; Light Grabber blue; Midnight blue metallic; Sequoia brown metallic; and Chrome yellow. New Ivy Glow and Gold Glow colors were optional. Different two-tones could be obtained by using all standard colors, except Chrome yellow. Wimbledon white could be used as the accent color for any other color.
I.D. DATA: The VIN consists of 11 symbols. The first three indicate the series. The fourth indicates the engine. The fifth shows the assembly plant. The last six are the sequential production number.

Model	Body Type	Price	Weight	Prod. Total
F-100 — 1/2-Ton — 117 in. w.b. — V-8				
81	Chassis & Cab	3092	3125	Note 1
83	Flareside 6.75 ft.	3246	3480	Note 1
83	Styleside 6.75 ft.	3246	3480	Note 1
F-100 — 1/2-Ton — 133 in. w.b. — V-8				
83	Flareside 8 ft.	3282	3570	Note 1
83	Styleside 8 ft.	3282	3570	Note 1
F-100 Supercab — 1/2-Ton — 139 in. w.b. — V-8				
83	Styleside 6.75 ft.	4185	3820	Note 1
F-100 Supercab — 1/2-Ton — 155 in. w.b. — V-8				
83	Styleside 8 ft.	4221	3930	Note 1

NOTE 1: Ford records show the following F-100 production break-outs: [4x2] [Chassis & Cab] 2,241; [Flareside Pickup] 2,517; [Styleside] 389,407; [Supercab Pickup] 17,537. [4x4] [Chassis & Cab] 2,547; [Flareside Pickup] 176; and [Styleside Pickup] 26,788.
NOTE 2: Prices/weights for base V-8; deduct for six-cylinder.
NOTE 3: Add $600 for 4x4.
ENGINE [Base Six]: Inline. OHV. Six-cylinder. Bore and stroke: 4.0 x 3.18 in. Displacement: 240 cid. Gross bhp: 150 at 4000 rpm. Gross torque: 234 lbs.-ft. at 2200 rpm.
ENGINE [Base V-8]: V-block. OHV. Eight-cylinder. Bore and stroke: 4.0 x 3.0 in. Displacement: 302 cid. Net horsepower: 130 at 3800 rpm. Net torque: 122 lbs.-ft. at 2000 rpm.
ENGINE [Super Cab]: V-block. OHV. Eight-cylinder. Bore and stroke: 4.05 in. x 3.50 in. Displacement: 360 cid. Horsepower: 143 nhp at 3800 rpm. Net torque: 264 lbs.-ft. at 2200 rpm. Carburetor: Two-barrel.
F-250 CUSTOM PICKUP: The F-250 had most of the same features as the F-100. It too was offered with regular or Super cabs and with Flareside or Styleside boxes. Power brakes and a three-speed manual transmission were standard.
I.D. DATA: The VIN consists of 11 symbols. The first three indicate the series. The fourth indicates the engine. The fifth shows the assembly plant. The last six are the sequential production number.

Model	Body Type	Price	Weight	Prod. Total
F-250 — 3/4-Ton — 133 in. w.b. — V-8				
80	Chassis & Cab	3410	3480	Note 1
83	Flareside	3564	3900	Note 1
83	Styleside	3564	3900	Note 1
F-250 Supercab — 3/4-Ton — 140 in. w.b. — V-8				
83	Supercab	4473	4015	Note 1
F-350 Crew Cab — 3/4-Ton — 155 in.				
80	Chassis & Cab	4229	4100	Note 1
83	Styleside	4371	4455	Note 1

NOTE 1: Ford records show the following F-250 production break-outs: [4x2] [Chassis & Cab] 5,616; [Flareside Pickup] 1,787; [Styleside Pickup] 123,711; [Supercab] 10,852. [4x4] [Chassis & Cab] 1,137; [Flareside Pickup] 645; and [Styleside Pickup] 34,618.
ENGINE [Base Heavy-duty Six]: Inline. OHV. Six-cylinder. Bore and stroke: 4.0 x 3.98 in. Displacement: 300 cid. Net horsepower: 101 at 3000 rpm. Net torque: 223 lbs.-ft. at 1600 rpm.
ENGINE: [Base V-8]: V-block. OHV. Eight-cylinder. Bore and stroke: 4.0 x 3.5 in. Displacement: 360 cid. Net horsepower: 145 at 3800 rpm. Net torque: 264 lbs.-ft. at 2200 rpm.
F-350 CUSTOM PICKUP: The F-350 Pickup was only offered with the Styleside box. However, there were three choices of cabs: Regular, Supercab or Crew Cab. Standard features included: Front shocks (front and rear with Styleside), a four-speed manual transmission and heavy-duty power front disc brakes.
F-350 PLATFORM/STAKE: Two lengths of 1-ton F-350 Platform/Stakes were available: 9 ft. and 12 ft. Floor frames of the Platform/Stake were made of steel cross sills riveted to steel side rails. Floorboards were interlocked with steel brackets. Formed steel caps covered ends of the body sills. Side boards were hardwood and stakes were steel. A four-speed manual transmission was standard.
I.D. DATA: The VIN consists of 11 symbols. The first three indicate the series. The fourth indicates the engine. The fifth shows the assembly plant. The last six are the sequential production number.

Model	Body Type	Price	Weight	Prod. Total
F-350 — 1-Ton — 137 in. w.b. — V-8				
80	Platform 9 ft.	3873	4375	Note 1
81	Chassis & Cab	3510	3795	Note 1
83	Styleside	3958	4345	Note 1
86	Stake 9 ft.	3912	4615	Note 1
F-350 SuperCab — 1-Ton — 140 in. w.b. — V-8				
83	Styleside	5070	4570	Note 1
F-350 — 1-Ton — 161 in. w.b. — V-8				
80	Platform 12 ft.	4875	—	Note 1
86	Stake 12 ft.	5115	—	Note 1
F-350 Crew Cab — 1-Ton — 155 in. w.b. — V-8				
81	Chassis & Cab	4363	4290	Note 1
83	Styleside	4514	4730	Note 1

NOTE 1: Ford records show the following F-350 production break-outs: All 4x2 [Chassis & Cowl] 144; [Chassis & Cab] 48,812; [Platform & Rack] 7,546; [Platform] 786; [Supercab] 1340 and [Styleside cab] 9,929.
ENGINE [Base Heavy-duty Six]: Inline. OHV. Six-cylinder. Bore and stroke: 4.0 x 3.98 in. Displacement: 300 cid. Net horsepower: 101 at 3000 rpm. Net torque: 223 lbs.-ft. at 1600 rpm.
ENGINE [Base V-8]: V-block. OHV. Eight-cylinder. Bore and stroke: 4.0 x 3.5 in. Displacement: 360 cid. Net horsepower: 145 at 3800 rpm. Net torque: 264 lbs.-ft. at 2200 rpm.
CHASSIS: Wheelbase: 117 in. (F-100); 133 in. (F-100/F-250); 139 in. (F-100/F-250 Super Cab); 140 in. (F-350); 137 in. (F-350 Platform/Stake); 155 in. (Super Cab); 161 in. (F-350 Platform/Stake). GVW: 4,600-5,500 lbs. (F-100); 6,200-8,100 lbs. (F-250); 8,350-10,000 lbs. (F-350). Tires: G78 x 15B (F-100); 8.00 x 16.5D in. (F-250); and 8.75 x 16.5E (F-350).
POWERTRAIN OPTIONS: Engine: 300 cid six-cylinder engine (F-100). 302 cid V-8 (F-100). 360 cid V-8. 390 cid V-8. 460 cid V-8. Transmissions: Four-speed manual or Cruise-O-Matic transmissions.
CONVENIENCE OPTIONS: Four-wheel drive (F-100/F-250). [Pickup box cover] (Standard) Has fiberglass construction; tinted side and rear windows; T-handle locking rear liftgate; and rubber cushioned tie-downs. (Deluxe) has sliding side windows with screens; bright side and rear window moldings; roof vent; interior dome light; and color-keyed body strip (in a choice of five colors). Knitted vinyl seat trim. Folding bench or jump seats (Super Cab). Heavy-duty black vinyl seat trim. Vinyl insert bodyside molding. AM/FM stereo radio. AM radio. Intermittent windshield wipers. [Super Camper Special] Includes: Front and rear stablizier bars; heavy-duty frame; automatic transmission; extra-cooling system; 360 cid V-8; power front disc brakes; 55 amp. alternator; 70 amp.-hr. battery; oil pressure gauge and ammeter; bright Western mirrors; dual horns; heavy-duty shocks; and camper wiring harness. Rear step bumper. Western style mirrors. Sliding rear cab window. Concealed spare tire and wheel. Auxiliary 12-volt, 70 amp.-hr. battery. Air-conditioner. Black or white texture painted roof (includes bright drip rail molding). Full wheelcovers. Mag style covers. 22.5 gal. Auxiliary fuel tank, 20.2 gal. (F-100). Dual tape stripes. Bright tie-down hooks. Supercooling package. Slide-out spare tire carrier. Tool stowage box with locking door. [Convenience Group]: Includes cargo, engine, glove compartment and ashtray lights; glove compartment door lock; door map pockets; and 12 in. day/night mirror. [Northland Special Package] Includes: Engine block heater; 50 percent (-30 degrees F.) anti-freeze; 70 amp.-hr. battery; 55 amp. alternator; and limited-slip rear axle. Power steering. Power front disc brakes (4x2s). High-output heater. Trailer towing packages. Ammeter and oil pressure gauge. Bright hubcaps. Bright contour rear bumper for Stylesides. Painted channel rear bumper for Flaresides. Tinted glass all around. Shoulder harness. Oil-bath engine air cleaner. Frame-anchored camper tie-down system. Heavy-duty 50-amp. camper wiring harness. [Ranger Package] Includes: (In addition to or in place of Custom features) Color-keyed pleated cloth seat upholstery with metallic vinyl bolsters; instrument panel molding with black accent; color-keyed door panels with bright moldings; additional insulation; perforated headlining (insulated) with bright molding; color-keyed vinyl coated floor mat with heel pads; cigarette lighter; bright windshield, rear window and roof drip moldings; bright rocker panel and wheel lip moldings and bright hubcaps (except 4x4 option and dual rear wheel units). Styleside Pickups also included bright tailgate moldings (top and bottom), taillight bezels and bright recessed tailgate handle. [Ranger XLT Package] Includes: (In addition to or in place of Ranger items) Deluxe color-keyed, long-wearing cloth with vinyl trim seat upholstery; color-keyed pleated vinyl upper door panel with simulated woodgrain accented moldings and map pocket lower panels; color-keyed wall-to-wall nylon carpeting; black steering wheel with simulated woodgrain insert; bright seat-pivot covers; additional insulation and double-wrapped muffler; convenience group; color-keyed vinyl headlining (with special insulation); and sun visors. Styleside Pickups also included bright bodyside moldings with vinyl insert; upper tailgate applique panel and molding; and aluminum tailgate applique.

HISTORICAL: Introduced: Sept. 21, 1973. Calendar year production [All Ford trucks]: 1,028,507 or 36.10 percent of industry. Model year production: [Light-duty] 928,882; [Medium-duty] 44,452; [Heavy-duty] 80,238; [All] 1,053,572. Calendar year sales, by line: [Ranchero] 26,731; [Bronco] 18,786; [Courier] 44,491; [Econoline] 122,623; [Other light-duty] 561,108; [Medium- and heavy-duty] 84,185; and [Extra-heavy-duty] 28,784; [Total] 886,708. Calendar year registrations by weight class: [Up to 6,000 lbs.] 513,367; [6,001-10,000 lbs.] 246,989. Innovations: Ranchero face-lifted. Improved Bronco steering. Supercab pickup introduced. This was the third best truck sales year in Ford's history. The company retained its number one position in calendar year production. Its sales total of 886,708 units compared favorably to Chevrolet's 885,362, allowing Ford to regain the lead in the domestic industry. Donald E. Peterson was Vice-President and General Manager of Ford Motor Company Truck Operations.

1975 FORD

1975 Ford Econoline 500 Chateau Club Wagon (OCW)

RANCHERO 500 PICKUP: Styling was unchanged for 1975, except for a new steering wheel and different filler neck to comply with no-lead gasoline requirements. Standard features included: Vinyl upholstery and door trim. Panels with bright trim. Color-keyed steering wheel and column. Deep-pile carpeting. Hi-level, flow-through ventilation. Ventless door windows. Energy-absorbing steering column. Padded steering wheel hub. Lockable glove box. Locking steering column. Fresh-air heater defroster. Trim panel behind the split-back seat. Vinyl headliner. Color-keyed seat belts with outboard retractors and shoulder harnesses (also center passenger seat belts). Armrests with recessed door handles. Vinyl-framed day/night mirror. Cigarette lighter. Padded, color-keyed instrument panel. Emergency lamp flasher. Spare tire and tool compartment. Deluxe grille with moldings. Bright energy absorbing front bumper. Bright left-hand mirror with remote control. Hidden windshield wipers. Bright metal windshield, rear window, drip rail and top of cargo body moldings. Bright metal hubcaps. Power steering. Power brakes. Cruise-O-Matic automatic. Colors offered on 1975 Rancheros were: White; Bright red; Dark red; black; Pastel blue; Bright dark blue (metallic); Light green-gold (metallic); Light green; Saddle bronze (metallic); Dark copper (metallic); Dark yellow-green (metallic); Medium Dark gold (metallic); and Pastel yellow. Color Glow paints were: Green Glow; Ginger Glow; Tan Glow; and Silver-blue Glow. Black; white; blue; green; brown; or tan vinyl roofs were available.

RANCHERO GT PICKUP: The GT had (in addition to or in place of the Ranchero 500 features): Color-keyed bodyside stripe. Sport style mirrors painted body colors, both with remote-control. Black hubcaps with bright trim rings. Lettered belted tires. GT grille crest. Spare tire and tool compartment cover. Bright trim on pedals. GT instrument panel plaque.
RANCHERO SQUIRE PICKUP: The Squire had (in addition to or in place of Ranchero 500 features): Deluxe bright wheelcovers. Simulated woodgrain panels on sides and tailgate. Ranchero Squire script on front fenders. Squire crest on grille. Wood-tone panel around instruments. Electric clock. Spare tire and tool compartment cover. Bright trim on pedals. Squire instrument panel plaque.
I.D. DATA [Ranchero]: The VIN consists of 11 symbols. The first symbol is the last digit of the model year. The second symbol indicates the assembly plant. The third and fourth symbols indicate the product line and body style. The fifth symbol indicates the engine. The last six symbols are the sequential production number.

Model	Body Type	Price	Weight	Prod. Total
Ranchero 500 — 1/2-Ton — 118 in. w.b. — V-8				
97D	Sedan-Pickup	4049	3915	8,778
Ranchero GT — 1/2-Ton — 118 in. w.b. — V-8				
97R	Sedan-Pickup	4381	3980	6,114
Ranchero Squire — 1/2-Ton — 118 in. w.b. — V-8				
97K	Sedan-Pickup	4407	3940	1549

NOTE 1: Prices/weights for base V-8; deduct for six.
ENGINE [Base Six]: Displacement: 200 cid. Six-cylinder. 84 nhp at 3800 rpm. Bore & stroke: 3.68 in. x 3.13 in. Compression ratio: 8.3:1. Carburetor: One-barrel.
ENGINE [Base V-8; Ranchero]: Displacement: 302 cid. V-8. 140 nhp at 3800 rpm. Bore & stroke: 4 in. x 3 in. Compression ratio: 8.0:1. Carburetor: Two-barrel.
ENGINE [Base V-8; Ranchero GT]: Displacement: 351 M (modified). V-8. 148 nhp at 3800 rpm. Bore & stroke: 4 in. x 3.5 in. Compression ratio: 8.0:1. Carburetor: Two-barrel.
CHASSIS: Wheelbase: 118 in. Overall length: 218.3 in. GVW: 5,480-5,950 lbs. Tires: G78-14B (G70-14B white-lettered on GT).
POWERTRAIN OPTIONS: Engine: 351 cid V-8. 400 cid V-8. 460 cid V-8.
CONVENIENCE OPTIONS: [Performance Cluster] Includes: Tachometer; trip odometer; clock; ammeter; water temperature; and oil pressure gauges (also includes heavy-duty battery). SelectAire air-conditioner with automatic temperature control. SelectAire air-conditioner. Power steering. [Protection Group/Bumpers] Includes: Front and rear bumper guards; front bumper rubber inserts. [Protection Group/Appearance] Includes: Spare tire lock; floor mats; license plate frame; and door edge guards. Vinyl insert bodyside molding. Anti-theft alarm system. Power side windows. Tilt steering wheel. Cruise control. [Convenience Group] Includes: Right- and left-hand remote-control mirrors; interval windshield wipers; vanity mirror. Restraint system. Sport flight bench seat with vinyl trim. [Brougham Decor Group] Includes: Split bench seat with super-soft vinyl or knit cloth upholstery; Brougham door trim panels; and cut-pile carpeting. Bucket seats. Vinyl roof. Power brakes. AM radio. 15 in. wheels. Luxury wheelcovers. Hubcaps with trim rings. Mag style wheels. Tinted glass. Electric clock. Dual sport style mirrors. [Light Group] Includes: Ashtray; underhood and glove box lights; parking brake warning light; lights-on warning buzzer; and illuminated light switch. Class II (2,000-3,500 lbs.) or Class III (3,500-6,000 lbs.) trailer towing packages. [Handling Suspension Package] Includes: Heavy-duty shock absorbers; rear springs; and heavy-duty rear stabilizer bar. Fuel guard warning light. Power door locks. Heavy-duty electrical system. H78-14B/G70-14B/H70-14B tires. (White sidewall tires available).

1975 Ford 1/2-Ton Bronco Ranger Sport Utility Wagon 4x4 (RCA)

BRONCO WAGON: A heftier rear axle, revised exhaust system and fuel filler, higher riding height, and...late in the year...front disc brakes, were among major changes made on the 1975 Bronco 4x4. Other standard features included: Vinyl bucket seats. Floor-mounted T-bar transfer case control. Suspended foot pedals. Fresh air heater and defroster. Lockable glove compartment. Padded instrument panel. Two-speed electric windshield wipers. Sun visors. Vinyl-coated rubber floor mat. Fully-synchronized three-speed manual transmission. Full-length roof with fixed windows in the rear liftgate and on each side of the rear compartment.
I.D. DATA [Bronco]: The VIN consists of 11 symbols. The first three indicate the series. The fourth indicates the engine. The fifth shows the assembly plant. The last six are the sequential production number.

Model	Body Type	Price	Weight	Prod. Total
Bronco 4x4 — 1/2-Ton — 92 in. w.b. — V-8				
U-100	Wagon	4979	3490	11,273

NOTE 1: Prices/weights for base V-8; deduct for six.
ENGINE [Bronco]: Displacement: 200 cid. Six-cylinder. 84 nhp at 3800 rpm. Bore & stroke: 3.68 in. x 3.13 in. Compression ratio: 8.3:1. Carburetor: One-barrel.
ENGINE [Base V-8]: Displacement: 302 cid. V-8. 140 nhp at 3800 rpm. Bore & stroke: 4 in. x 3 in. Compression ratio: 8.0:1. Carburetor: Two-barrel.
CHASSIS: Wheebase: 92 in. Overall length: 152.1 in. Overall width: 69.1 in. Overall height: 70.1 in. GVW: 4,400-4,900 lbs. Tires: E78 x 15.
POWERTRAIN OPTIONS: Engine: 302 cid V-8. Transmission: Cruise-O-Matic transmission.
CONVENIENCE OPTIONS: Extra-cooling V-8 radiator. Left-hand remote-control outside mirror. Knitted vinyl upholstery. Power steering. [Convenience Group] Includes: Cigarette lighter; map light; inside 10 in. day/night rearview mirror; and right-hand chrome rearview mirror. Shoulder harness. Rear seat. Chrome bumper. Skid plates for standard fuel tank and transfer case. Inside tailgate-mounted spare tire carrier (included with rear seat option). Exterior rear-mounted swing-away tire carrier. Bright metal wheelcovers. High-flotation tires. Auxiliary 7.5-gal. fuel tank with skid plate. Manual radio and antenna. Bright bodyside and tailgate moldings. Bright metal rocker panel molding. Hand-operated throttle. [Sport Bronco Package] Includes: Bright metal Sport Bronco emblem; pleated parchment vinyl front seat; vinyl door trim panels with bright metal moldings; hardboard headlining with bright metal retainer moldings; parchment vinyl front floor mat with bright metal retainers; rear floor mat (included free combined with optional rear seat); cigarette lighter; horn ring; bright metal drip rail moldings; bright metal windshield and window frames; bright metal grille molding and tailgate release handle; bright headlight, side light, reflector and taillight bezels; and Argent silver painted grille with bright Ford letters. Chrome bumpers, front and rear. Chrome front bumper guards. Bright metal wheelcovers (with 15 in. wheels only). 6.50 x 16-6 ply-rated TT tires.
DEALER-INSTALLED ACCESSORIES: Power-take-off (front-mounted). Warn free-running front hubs (manual or automatic). Snow plows. Snow plow angling kits. Front auxiliary air springs. Front-mounted winch. Trailer hitch. Trailer towing mirror. Locking gas cap. Front tow hooks. Compass. Fire extinguisher. Transmission oil cooler. Tachometer. 4,600 lbs. and 4,900 lbs. GVW packages. [Ranger Package] Includes: Argent silver grille; bucket seats; lower bodyside stripes; fiberboard headliner; cut-pile carpeting front and rear; wheelcovers; white power dome; and white spare tire carrier. Reduced external sound package. [Northland Special option] Includes: Single element 600-watt engine block heater; 50 percent (-30 degrees F.) anti-freeze; 70 amp.-hr. battery; 60-amp. alternator; and limited-slip rear axle.
ECONOLINE E-100 CARGO VAN: These were the first of the third-generation Econolines. The Ford name was now printed, in smaller letters, on the face of the longer hood. The higher, rectangular theme, split-level grille was bordered by slightly recessed round headlights on either end. The entire grille and headlight section was framed by bright trim. Parking lights were located directly above the bumper, under the headlights. The side-marker lights were in the full-length concave bodyside grooves. The 1975 Econolines also featured body-on-frame construction; improved Twin-I-Beam front suspension; an 18 percent larger windshield; computer-selected front coil springs; wiper arm mounted-windshield washer jets; molded and heavily insulated engine cover console; and bolt-on front fenders. Among the standard features were: Full-foam driver's bucket seat. Color-keyed vinyl seat trim in black, blue, green or tan. Color-keyed seat belt. Color-keyed windshield trim moldings. Color-keyed engine cover with clipboard flashlight pocket and removable ashtray designed into console. Fresh air heater defroster. Fresh air vents with blend-air control. Two-speed electric windshield wipers. Energy-absorbing sun visor on driver's side. Front and cargo area dome lights. Front compartment hardboard headlining and insulated floor mat with scuff plates. Push-pull door lock buttons. Armrest. Coat hook. Electric horn. Door checks. Latch release handles on side cargo doors. Argent silver bumpers. Argent silver hubcaps. Bright windshield molding and mirrors. Econoline colors for 1975 included: Wimbledon white; Candy-apple red; Brook blue (metallic); Wind blue; Hatteras green (metallic); Baytree green; Glen green; Hot Ginger (metallic); Vineyard gold; Parrot orange; Autumn tan; and Chrome yellow. Medium Green Glow and Medium Ginger Glow were optional. Five separate and distinctive Tu-Tone paint schemes were available.
ECONOLINE E-100 WINDOW VAN: As the name suggests, the Window Van had glass all around. It shared standard features with the Cargo Van.
ECONOLINE E-100 DISPLAY VAN: This model had windows at the rear and on the right-hand side. It came with the same standard features as the Cargo Van.
I.D. DATA [Vans]: The VIN consists of 11 symbols. The first three indicate the series. The fourth indicates the engine. The fifth shows the assembly plant. The last six are the sequential production number.

Model	Body Type	Price	Weight	Prod. Total
Vans — 1/2-Ton — 124 in./138 in. — V-8				
E-140	Cargo Van	3683	3940	Note 1
E-150	Window Van	3769	3970	Note 1
E-160	Display Van	3722	3955	Note 1

NOTE 1: See production data at end of E-350 model listing.
NOTE 2: Total Ford Van sales in the 1975 model year were 113,715.
NOTE 3: Prices/weights for base V-8; deduct for six.
ENGINE [Base Six]: Displacement: 300 cid. Six. Horsepower: 101 nhp at 3000 rpm. Torque: 223 lbs.-ft. at 1600 rpm. Bore & stroke: 4.00 in. x 3.98 in. Compression ratio: 8.0:1. Carburetor: One-barrel.
ENGINE [Base V-8]: Displacement: 351 cid. V-8. Horsepower: 156 nhp at 4000 rpm. Torque: 262 lbs.-ft. at 2200 rpm. Bore & stroke: 4.00 in. x 3.50 in. Carburetor: Two-barrel.
ECONOLINE E-150 CARGO VAN: This was the first year for this series. It had a slightly higher GVW rating than the E-100. Unlike the E-100, it could be operated on either leaded or unleaded gasoline. Standard features echoed those on the E-100.
ECONOLINE E-150 DISPLAY VAN: This Van shared styling with the E-100 Display Van, but had greater load capacity.
ECONOLINE E-150 WINDOW VAN: This Van shared styling with the E-100 Window Van, but had greater load capacity.
I.D. DATA [Vans]: The VIN consists of 11 symbols. The first three indicate the series. The fourth indicates the engine. The fifth shows the assembly plant. The last six are the sequential production number.

Model	Body Type	Price	Weight	Prod. Total
Vans — 1/2-Ton — 124 in./138 in. — V-8				
E-140	Cargo Van	3903	3945	Note 1
E-160	Display Van	3942	3960	Note1
E-150	Window Van	3989	3975	Note 1

NOTE 1: See production data at end of E-350 model listing.
NOTE 2: Total Ford Van sales in the 1975 model year were 113,715.
NOTE 3: Prices/weights for base V-8; deduct for six.
ENGINE [Base six]: Displacement: 300 cid. Six. Horsepower: 101 nhp at 3000 rpm. Torque: 223 lbs.-ft. at 1600 rpm. Bore & stroke: 4.00 in. x 3.98 in. Compression ratio: 8.0:1. Carburetor: One-barrel.
ENGINE [Base V-8]: Displacement: 351 cid. V-8. Horsepower: 156 nhp at 4000 rpm. Torque: 262 lbs.-ft. at 2200 rpm. Bore & stroke: 4.00 in. x 3.50 in. Carburetor: Two-barrel.
ECONOLINE E-250 CARGO VAN: The new E-250 had a higher GVW rating and heavier-duty front and rear axles than the E-150. It also came with eight-hole, rather than five-hole, wheels. Standard features were the same as those on the E-100.
ECONOLINE E-250 DISPLAY VAN: This vehicle shared styling and features with the E-100, but had greater load capacity.
ECONOLINE E-250 WINDOW VAN: This vehicle shared styling and features with the E-100 Display Van, but had greater load capacity.
ECONOLINE E-250 CUTAWAY VAN: This Van with Camper Special Packages was designed to readily accommodate custom motorhomes.

ECONOLINE E-250 PARCEL DELIVERY: This vehicle looked more like a typical delivery truck than a van. It was basically a cutaway chassis with a large cargoadded.
I.D. DATA: [Vans]: The VIN consists of 11 symbols. The first three indicate the series. The fourth indicates the engine. The fifth shows the assembly plant. The last six are the sequential production number.

Model	Body Type	Price	Weight	Prod. Total
Vans — 3/4-Ton — 124 in./138 in. — V-8				
E-240	Cargo Van	4204	4340	Note 1
E-260	Display Van	4244	4355	Note 1
E-250	Window Van	4291	4370	Note 1
E-270	Cutaway Van	4294	3790	Note 1
E-280	Parcel Delivery	6265	5735	Note 1

NOTE 1: See production data at end of E-350 model listing.
NOTE 2: Total Ford Van sales in the 1975 model year were 113,715.
NOTE 3: Prices/weights for base V-8; deduct for six.
ENGINE [Base six]: Displacement: 300 cid. Six. Horsepower: 101 nhp at 3000 rpm. Torque: 223 lbs.-ft. at 1600 rpm. Bore & stroke: 4.00 in. x 3.98 in. Compression ratio: 8.0:1. Carburetor: One-barrel.
ENGINE [Base V-8]: Displacement: 351 cid. V-8. Horsepower: 156 nhp at 4000 rpm. Torque: 262 lbs.-ft. at 2200 rpm. Bore & stroke: 4.00 in. x 3.50 in. Carburetor: Two-barrel.
ECONOLINE E-350 CARGO VAN: This was the top-of-the-line Econoline. It had heavy-duty front and rear shocks and a greater load capacity than the other series. Standard features were the same as those on the E-100, plus automatic transmission.
ECONOLINE E-350 DISPLAY VAN: See E-250 Display Van.
ECONOLINE E-350 WINDOW VAN: See E-250 Window Van.
ECONOLINE E-350 CUTAWAY VAN: See E-250 Cutaway Van.
ECONOLINE E-350 PARCEL DELIVERY: See E-250 Parcel Delivery.
I.D. DATA [Vans]: The VIN consists of 11 symbols. The first three indicate the series. The fourth indicates the engine. The fifth shows the assembly plant. The last six are the sequential production number.

Model	Body Type	Price	Weight	Prod. Total
Vans — 1-Ton — 124 in./138 in. — V-8				
E-340	Cargo Van	4444	4520	Note 1
E-360	Display Van	4484	4535	Note 1
E-350	Window Van	4531	4550	Note 1
E-370	Cutaway Van	4400	3875	Note 1
E-380	Parcel Delivery	6265	5735	Note 1

NOTE 1: Ford records show the following production break-outs for 1975 Econolines: [89A-B Cargo Vans] 51,710; [89C-D Display Vans] 1,758; [89E-F Window Vans] 12,269; [Econoline type Cutaway/less Parcel Vans] 3,528; [Parcel Delivery Vans] 1,646. Ford also continued to produce the P series [Walk-in type] Parcel Delivery vans and built 467 of the P-350 model and 1,245 of the P-400 model during the 1975 model year.
NOTE 2: Prices/weights for base V-8; deduct for six.
NOTE 3: Total Ford Van sales in the 1975 model year were 113,715.
ENGINE [Base Six]: Displacement: 300 cid. Six. Horsepower: 101 nhp at 3000 rpm. Torque: 223 lbs.-ft. at 1600 rpm. Bore & stroke: 4.00 in. x 3.98 in. Compression ratio: 8.0:1. Carburetor: One-barrel.
ENGINE [Base V-8]: Displacement: 351 cid. V-8. Horsepower: 156 nhp at 4000 rpm. Torque: 262 lbs.-ft. at 2200 rpm. Bore & stroke: 4.00 in. x 3.50 in. Carburetor: Two-barrel.
CHASSIS: Wheelbase: 124 in. or 138 in. (158 in. available on Cutaway and Parcel Delivery) Overall width: 70.3 in. Overall length: 186.8 in. (with 124 in. wheelbase); or 206.8 in. (with 138 in. wheelbase). GVW: 5,100-10,725 lbs. Tires: F78-15B PT (E-100); H78-15D (E-150); 8.00 x 16.5D TT (E-250); 8.75 x 16.5EC on Econoline Parcel Delivery. 9.50 x 16.5D TT (E-350); 8.00 x 16.5D dual rear on Econoline parcel delivery.
POWERTRAIN OPTIONS: Transmission: Cruise-O-Matic transmission. Engines: 351 cid V-8. 460 cid V-8 (E-250/E-350).
CONVENIENCE OPTIONS: Custom Van: (in addition to or place of standard) color-keyed padded full-length instrument panel with woodgrained vinyl applique; color-keyed seat pedestal; cowl-side trim panels; vinyl front door trim panels; insulated floor mats; roof rail garnish moldings; and bright hubcaps, tailight bezels, vent and rear window frames. [Chateau Van] Includes: (In addition to or in place of Custom features) Super Soft vinyl seat trim; color-keyed cut-pile carpeting on front floor and lower section of engine cover; padded vinyl front door trim panels with woodgrained vinyl applique in center and carpeted lower panel; woodgrained vinyl horn bar insert in steering wheel; bright grille; bright bumpers; and bright bodyside and rear moldings. Wheelcovers. Right-hand sliding cargo door. Adjustable or flip-fold passenger seat. High-output heater and defroster. Auxiliary hot water heater. Bright grille and/or front and rear bumpers. Full-length, insulated carpet or mat (138 in. wheelbase only). Courtesy light switches on front, or on all doors. Two-stage door positioners for hinged cargo doors. [Northland Special Package] Includes: Engine block heater; -35 F. anti-freeze; 77 amp.-hr. battery; 60- amp. alternator; and high-output heater. Engine block heater. Locking fuel cap. Tinted glass. Full-length hardboard headlining. Dual electric horns. Insulation Package. [Protection Group] Includes: Front door edge guards and front and side sliding door stepwell pads. Interior rub rails (138 in. wheelbase only). School Bus Package for 138 in. wheelbase Window Van. Cloth insert seat trim. Shoulder harness. Spare tire and wheel. Spare tire cover. Bright hubcaps. Trailer Towing Package (for Class I, II, III and IV trailers). Front stabilizer bar. Captain's chairs. Air-conditioning. Power steering. Auxiliary fuel tank. Interval windshield wipers. Swing-Lok Western mirrors. Swing-out recreation mirrors. Swing-Lok low-mount Western mirrors. AM radio. AM/FM stereo. AM/FM stereo with tape player. Door windows for rear and/or side cargo doors. One-way glass in rear side windows and rear door. Flip-open windows for cargo doors. Job-engineered interior packages. [Low-Line Camper Package] Includes: Includes: 60-amp. alternator; 77 amp.-hr. battery; auxiliary 81 amp.-hr. battery; heavy-duty shocks (with E-250); Custom trim package; camper wiring harness; Camper Special emblem; and extra-cooling package. [High-Line Camper Special Package] Includes: Basic package plus (or in place of) 90-amp. alternator; adjustable passenger seat; external auxiliary oil cooler; fuel monitor warning light and ammeter and oil pressure gauge; front stabilizer bar; dual horns; 351 cid V-8; Chateau trim package; high-output heater; power steering; tinted windshield; and tinted glass.
E-100 CLUB WAGON: The new E-100 Club wagon shared the Econoline Vans' styling and other changes. It was offered in five- or eight-passenger versions. Among the standard features were: Full foam front bucket seats. Color-keyed patterened vinyl seat trim in black, blue, green or tan. Seat belts. Color-keyed windshield trim moldings. Fresh air heater/defroster. Fresh air vents with blend-air control. Two-speed electric windshield wipers. Wiper arm mounted washer jets. Sun visors. Rearview mirror. Dome lights. Front compartment hardboard headlining and insulated floor mat with scuff plates. Push-pull door lock buttons. Armrests. Coat hook. Electric horns. Door checks. Flip-open windows in sliding door and opposite windows. Argent silver bumpers and hubcaps. Bright windshield moldings. Outside rearview mirrors. Standard Club Wagon colors for 1975 were: Wimbledon white; Candy Apple red; Brook blue metallic; Wind blue; Hatteras green metallic; Baytree green; Glen green; Hot Ginger metallic; Vineyard gold; Parrot orange; Autumn tan and Chrome yellow. Custom and Chateau colors were: Brook blue metallic; Hatteras green metallic; Autumn tan; Chrome yellow and Wimbledon white. Medium green Glow and Medium Ginger Glow were optional on Standard, Custom and Chateau Club Wagons. Five Tu-Tone paint schemes were available.
E-150 CLUB WAGON: This was a slightly heavier-duty version of the E-100. It had a longer 138 in. wheelbase and was also offered in five- and eight-passenger versions. Standard features were same as those on the E-100.
E-250 CLUB WAGON: The E-250 Club Wagon could be had with five-, eight-, or 12-passenger capacity packages. It had most of the same features as the E-100.
I.D. DATA: [Vans]: The VIN consists of 11 symbols. The first three indicate the series. The fourth indicates the engine. The fifth shows the assembly plant. The last six are the sequential production number.

Model	Body Type	Price	Weight	Prod. Total
Vans — 1/2-Ton — 124 in./138 in. — V-8				
E-100	Club Wagon	4446	4225	Note 1
E-150	Club Wagon	4340	4340	Note 1
E-250	Club Wagon	5004	4690	Note 1

NOTE 1: Ford records show the following production break-outs for 1975 Econoline Club Wagons: [82A Standard] 3,656; [82B Custom] 4,767 and [82C Chateau] 9,008.
NOTE 2: Total Ford Van sales in the 1975 model year were 113,715.
NOTE 3: Prices/weights for base V-8; deduct for six.
ENGINE [Base Six]: Displacement: 300 cid. Six. Horsepower: 101 nhp at 3000 rpm. Torque: 223 lbs.-ft. at 1600 rpm. Bore & stroke: 4.00 in. x 3.98 in. Compression ratio: 8.0:1. Carburetor: One-barrel.
ENGINE [Base V-8]: Displacement: 351 cid. V-8. Horsepower: 156 nhp at 4000 rpm. Torque: 262 lbs.-ft. at 2200 rpm. Bore & stroke: 4.00 in. x 3.50 in. Carburetor: Two-barrel.
CHASSIS: Wheelbase: 124 in. (E-100); 138 in. (E-150/E-250). Overall width: 70.3 in. GVW: 5,600-5,900 lbs. (E-100); 6,050-6,300 lbs. (E-150); 7,100-8,550 lbs. (E-250). Tires: G78-15B (E-100); G78-15D (E-150); 8.00 x 16.5D (E-250).
POWERTRAIN OPTIONS: Engine: 351 cid V-8. 460 cid V-8. Transmissions: SelectShift Cruise-O-Matic.
CONVENIENCE OPTIONS: Auxiliary fuel tank. Speed control. Power steering. Captain's chair. AM radio. AM/FM stereo radio. AM/FM stereo with tape player. High-capacity air-conditioner. One-way glass. Wheelcovers. Swing-Lok Western mirrors. Swing-Lok low-mount Western mirrors. Bright non-telescopic mirrors. Swing-out recreation mirrors. High-output heater/defroster. Auxiliary hot water heater. Bright grille and/or bumpers. Full-length insulated floor mat. Courtesy light switches for all doors. Hinged side doors in place of sliding door. Two-stage door positioners for all hinged double doors. Locking gas cap. Intermittent two-speed windshield wipers. [Instrument Package] Includes: Fuel monitor warning light; ammeter; and oil pressure gauge. [Northland Special Package] Includes: Engine block heater; tinted glass; full-length hardboard headlining; and insulation package. [Protection Group] Includes: Front door edge guards and front and side sliding door step well pads. Shoulder harness. Spare tire cover. Bright hubcaps. Low-Line Camper Package. High-Line Camper Special Package. Light-, heavy- and extra-heavy-duty trailer towing packages. [Custom Package] Includes: (In addition to or in place of standard) color-keyed, padded, full-length instrument panel with woodgrained vinyl applique; color-keyed seat pedestal; cowl trim panels; padded vinyl door trim panels; cigarette lighter; insulated full-length floor mats; window garnish moldings; color-keyed armrests on three- and four-passenger seats; three coat hooks; aluminum scuff plates on side and rear doors; and bright hubcaps, taillight bezels and window frames. [Chateau Package] Includes: (In addition to or in place of Custom) Super Soft vinyl seat trim; color-keyed cut-pile carpeting on full-length of floor, lower section of engine cover and rear wheelwells; vinyl door trim panels with woodgrained vinyl applique in center and carpeted lower panel; color-keyed vinyl headlining (insulated); woodgrained vinyl horn bar insert; color-keyed vinyl spare tire cover; and bright grille, bumpers, lower bodyside moldings and rear moldings.
COURIER PICKUP: Styling was unchanged for 1975. Standard features included: Biscuit-pattern, full-width vinyl upholstered seat (in black or light beige). Padded instrument panel with ammeter, fuel and temperature gauges and oil pressure warning light. Cigarette lighter. Inside hood release. Tool kit. Beige vinyl headliner. Armrests. Six-leaf rear springs. Cylindrical double-acting shock absorbers. Independent front suspension. The 1975 Courier was available in six exterior colors: Red, blue, green, yellow, white and tan.
I.D. DATA: [Courier]: The VIN consists of 11 symbols. The first indicates the manufacturer. The second indicates the assembly plant. The third indicates the series. The fourth indicates the engine. The fifth (a letter) indicates the model year. The sixth indicates the production month. The last five are the sequential production number.

Model	Body Type	Price	Weight	Prod. Total
Courier — 1/2-Ton — 109.6 in. w.b. — Four				
—	Pickup	3146	2510	56,073

ENGINE [Courier]: Displacement: 110 cid. OHC. Four-cylinder.
CHASSIS: Wheelbase: 104.3 in. Overall length: 172 in. Overall height: 61.6 in. Overall width: 61.6 in. GVW Rating: 3,955 lbs. Tires: 6.00 x 14.
POWERTRAIN OPTIONS: Transmissions: Automatic tranmission with floor-mounted T-bar handle.
CONVENIENCE OPTIONS: Push-button AM radio. Pickup box cover. Deluxe pickup box cover (includes dome light, tinted side windows and woodgrain side stripe). Full wheelcovers. Bright-framed 6 x 9 in. swing-lock western mirrors. Argent silver-painted rear step bumper. Tinted glass. [Dress-up Package] Includes: Bright bodyside protective molding with black vinyl insert; bright front bumper guards with rubber inserts; bright molding around windshield and back window; and bright drip molding. Air-conditioner.
F-100 CUSTOM PICKUP: Exterior styling remained unchanged for 1975. Once again, buyers had their choice of Flareside or Styleside boxes. Regular or Super cabs were available. The latter made for 44 cu. ft. of cargo space behind the front seat. Standard F-100 features included: Deluxe fresh air heater/defroster (high-output heater with Super Cab]. Energy-absorbing sun visors and instrument panel padding. Instrument cluster with green backlighting. Keyless locking doors. Color-keyed molded door panels with integral armrests and paddle-type door handles. Seat belts. Windshield washers. Two-speed windshield wipers. Dome light with door courtesy light switches. Ashtray. Large glove compartment with push-button latch. Sponge-grain headlining. Black rubber floor mat. Door scuff plates. Black, red, blue or green vinyl seat trim. 10 in. day/night rearview mirror. Left-hand and right-hand bright metal exterior mirrors. Taillights with integral stop, turn, backup lights and reflector. Hubcaps (except 4x4s without full-time drive). Three-speed manual transmission. Standard F-Series colors for 1975 included: Wimbledon white; Vineyard gold; Viking red; Baytree green; Hatteras green (metallic); Glen green; Candy-apple red; Parrot orange; Raven black; Wind blue; Bahama blue; Midnight blue (metallic); Sequoia brown (metallic); and Chrome yellow. New Ginger Glow and Medium Green Glow colors were optional. Different two-tones could be obtained by using all the standard colors, except Chrome yellow. Wimbledon white could be used as the accent color for any color. Two-tones: [Regular} The accent color was applied to the roof and upper back panel with a beltline molding around back of cab. [Deluxe] The accent color was applied to the area below the bodyside and lower tailgate moldings, which were included in this Stylesides-only option. [Combination] In this Styleside-only combination, the regular and deluxe two-tone options were combined, with the accent color was applied as specified for these two options. [White bodyside accent Panel] For Stylesides only, with all colors (except white) on Ranger and Ranger XLT, and with regular two-tone white accent.

I.D. DATA [F-Series]: The VIN consists of 11 symbols. The first three indicate the series. The fourth indicates the engine. The fifth shows the assembly plant. The last six are the sequential production number.

Model	Body Type	Price	Weight	Prod. Total
F-100 — 1/2-Ton — 117 in. w.b. — V-8				
81	Chassis & Cab	3487	3135	Note 1
83	Flareside 6.75 ft.	3640	3505	Note 1
83	Styleside 6.75 ft.	3640	3490	Note 1
F-100 — 1/2-Ton — 133 in. w.b. — V-8				
83	Flareside 8 ft.	3676	3570	Note 1
83	Styleside 8 ft.	3676	3570	Note 1
F-100 Supercab — 1/2-Ton — 139 in. w.b. — V-8				
83	Styleside 6.75 ft.	4233	3860	Note 1
F-100 Supercab — 1/2-Ton — 155 in. w.b. — V-8				
81	Chassis & Cab	4079	3505	Note 1
83	Styleside 8 ft.	4229	3765	Note 1

NOTE 1: Ford records show the following F-100 production break-outs: [4x2 Cab Pickup] 173,965; [Supercab Pickup] 16,792. [4x4 Cab Pickup] 37,297.
NOTE 2: Prices/weights for base V-8; deduct for six-cylinder.
NOTE 3: Add $600 for 4x4.
ENGINE [Base Six]: Inline. OHV. Six-cylinder. Bore and stroke: 4.0 x 3.18 in. Displacement: 240 cid. Gross bhp: 150 at 4000 rpm. Gross torque: 234 lbs.-ft. at 2200 rpm.
ENGINE [Base V-8]: V-block. OHV. Eight-cylinder. Bore and stroke: 4.0 x 3.0 in. Displacement: 302 cid. Net horsepower: 130 at 3800 rpm. Net torque: 122 lbs.-ft. at 2000 rpm.
ENGINE [Super Cab Base V-8]: V-block. OHV. Eight-cylinder. Bore and stroke: 4.05 in. x 3.50 in. Displacement: 360 cid. Horsepower: 143 nhp at 3800 rpm. Net torque: 264 lbs.-ft. at 2200 rpm. Carburetor: Two-barrel.
F-150 CUSTOM PICKUP: This new series was basically just a slightly heavier-duty version of the F-100. It came with heftier front axle and rear springs. Regular cab models were only available on the 133 in. wheelbase and could carry a payload of 2,275 lbs. Supercab versions were offered on 133 in. and 155 in. wheelbases. Standard features were the same as those on the F-100, plus power brakes. Both Flareside and Styleside boxes were available.
I.D. DATA [F-Series]: The VIN consists of 11 symbols. The first three indicate the series. The fourth indicates the engine. The fifth shows the assembly plant. The last six are the sequential production number.

Model	Body Type	Price	Weight	Prod. Total
F-150 — 1/2-Ton — 133 in. w.b. — V-8				
81	Chassis & Cab	3849	3350	Note 1
83	Flareside	4002	3770	Note 1
83	Styleside	4002	3770	Note 1
F-150 Supercab — 1/2-Ton — 133 in. w.b. — V-8				
81	Chassis & Cab	4387	3570	Note 1
83	Styleside	4541	3925	Note 1
F-150 Supercab — 1/2-Ton — 155 in. w.b. — V-8				
83	Styleside	4644	4005	Note 1

NOTE 1: Ford records show the following F-150 production break-outs: [Cab Pickup] 80,917; [Supercab Pickup] 20,958. These records do not indicate any 4x4 production of F-150s.
NOTE 2: Prices/weights for base V-8; deduct for six.
ENGINE [Base Six]: Inline. OHV. Six-cylinder. Bore and stroke: 4.0 x 3.18 in. Displacement: 240 cid. Gross bhp: 150 at 4000 rpm. Gross torque: 234 lbs.-ft. at 2200 rpm.
ENGINE [Base V-8]: V-block. OHV. Eight-cylinder. Bore and stroke: 4.05 x 3.50 in. Displacement: 360 cid. Horsepower: 143 nhp at 3800 rpm. Net torque: 264 lbs.-ft. at 2200 rpm. Carburetor: Two-barrel.
F-250 CUSTOM PICKUP: The F-250 had most of the same features as the F-100. It, too, was offered with regular or Supercabs and with Flareside or Styleside boxes. Power brakes and a three-speed manual transmission were standard.
I.D. DATA [F-Series]: The VIN consists of 11 symbols. The first three indicate the series. The fourth indicates the engine. The fifth shows the assembly plant. The last six are the sequential production number.

Model	Body Type	Price	Weight	Prod. Total
F-250 — 3/4-Ton — 133 in. w.b. — V-8				
81	Chassis & Cab	3946	3495	Note 1
83	Flareside	4099	3915	Note 1
83	Styleside	4099	3915	Note 1
F-250 Supercab — 3/4-Ton — 155 in. w.b. — V-8				
81	Chassis & Cab	4449	3680	Note 1
83	Styleside	4603	4035	Note 1

NOTE 1: Ford records show the following F-250 production break-outs: 4x2 [Cab Pickup] 86,106; [Supercab Pickup] 29,622. 4x4 [Cab Pickup] 47,226.
NOTE 2: Prices/weights for base V-8; deduct for six.
NOTE 3: Add $600 for 4x4.
ENGINE [Base Six]: Displacement: 300 cid six-cylinder. 120 nhp at 3400 rpm. Bore & stroke: 4.00 x 3.98 in. Compression ratio: 8.0:1. One-barrel carburetor. Supercab had 360 cid V-8.
ENGINE [Base V-8]: V-block. OHV. Eight-cylinder. Bore and stroke: 4.05 in. x 3.50 in. Displacement: 360 cid. Horsepower: 143 nhp at 3800 rpm. Net torque: 264 lbs.-ft. at 2200 rpm. Carburetor: Two-barrel.
F-350 CUSTOM PICKUP: The F-350 Pickup was only offered with the Styleside box. However, there were three choices of cabs: Regular, Supercab or Crew Cab. Front-only shock absorbers (front and rear with Supercab), a four-speed manual transmission and power brakes were standard.
F-350 PLATFORM/STAKE: Two lengths of 1-ton F-350 Platform/Stakes were available: 9 ft. and 12 ft. Floor frames of the Platform/Stake were made of steel cross sills riveted to steel side rails. Floorboards were interlocked with steel brackets. Formed steel caps covered ends of the body sills. Sideboards were hardwood and stakes were steel. A four-speed manual tranmission was standard.
I.D. DATA [F-Series]: The VIN consists of 11 symbols. The first three indicate the series. The fourth indicates the engine. The fifth shows the assembly plant. The last six are the sequential production number.

Model	Body Type	Price	Weight	Prod. Total
F-350 — 1-Ton — 137 in. w.b. — V-8				
80	Stake 9 ft.	—	4620	Note 1
81	Chassis & Cab	4089	3795	Note 1
83	Styleside	4519	4535	Note 1
86	Platform 9 ft.	—	4380	Note 1
F-350 — 1-Ton — 137 in. w.b. — V-8				
80	Stake 12 ft.	—	—	Note 1
86	Platform 12 ft.	—	—	Note 1
F-350 Supercab — 1-Ton — 155 in. w.b. — V-8				
81	Chassis & Cab	4843	4100	Note 1
83	Styleside	4997	4525	Note 1
—	Camper Special	4902	4620	Note 1
F-350 Crew Cabs — 1-Ton — 161 in. w.b. — V-8				
81	Chassis & Cab	4902	4290	Note 1
83	Styleside	5063	4730	Note 1

NOTE 1: Ford records show the following F-350 production break-outs: [Cab Pickup] 41,616; [SuperCab Pickup] 2,816.
NOTE 2: Prices/weights for base V-8; deduct for six.

ENGINE [Base Six]: Displacement: 300 cid. Six-cylinder. 120 nhp at 3400 rpm. Bore & stroke: 4.00 x 3.98 in. Compression ratio: 8.0:1. One-barrel carburetor. Supercab had 360 cid V-8.

ENGINE [Base V-8]: V-block. OHV. Eight-cylinder. Bore and stroke: 4.05 in. x 3.50 in. Displacement: 360 cid. Horsepower: 143 nhp at 3800 rpm. Net torque: 264 lbs.-ft. at 2200 rpm. Carburetor: Two-barrel.

CHASSIS: Wheelbase: 117 in. (F-100); 133 in. (F-100/F-250); 139 in. (F-100/F-250 Supercab); 140 in. (F-350); 137 in. (F-350 Platform/Stake); 155 in. (SuperCab); 161 in. (F-350 Platform/Stake). GVW: 4,650-5,500 lbs. (F-100); 6,050 lbs. (F-150); 6,200-8,100 lbs. (F-250); 8,350-10,000 lbs. (F-350). Tires: G78-15B (F-100); L78-15D (F-150); 8.00 x 16.5D (F-250); 8.75 x 16.5E (F-350).

POWERTRAIN OPTIONS: Engine: V-8 engines: (F-100) 302 cid V-8 (Others). 360 cid/390 cid/460 cid V-8s (E-Series/F-Series). Transmissions: Four-speed manual Cruise-O-Matic.

CONVENIENCE OPTIONS: Four-wheel drive. [Pickup Box Cover] (Standard) Has fiberglass construction; tinted side and rear windows; roof vent; T-handle locking rear liftgate; and rubber-cushioned tie-downs; (Deluxe) Has sliding side windows with screens; bright side and rear window moldings; interior dome light; and color-keyed two-tone paint. Knitted vinyl seat trim. Heavy-duty black vinyl seat trim. Speed control. Vinyl insert bodyside molding. Folding bench or jump seats (Supercab). AM/FM stereo radio. AM radio. Intermittent windshield wipers. [Camper Special] Includes: Front and rear stabilizer bars; automatic transmission; extra-cooling package; low fuel economy warning light; power front disc brakes; 55 amp. alternator; 70 amp.-hr. battery; oil pressure gauge and ammeter; bright Western mirrors; dual horns; heavy-duty rear shocks; and camper wiring harness. Rear step bumper. Western style mirrors. Sliding rear cab window. Concealed spare tire and wheel. Auxiliary 12-volt 70 amp.-hr. battery. Air-conditioner. Flip open rear side window (Supercab). Black or white texture painted roof (included bright drip rail molding). Full wheelcovers. Mag style covers. Dual tape stripes. Bright tie-down hooks. Super-cooling package. Slide-out spare tire carrier. Tool stowage box with locking door. [Convenience Group] Includes: Cargo, engine, glove compartment, two courtesy and ashtray lights; glove compartment door lock; door map pockets; and 12 in. day/night mirror. [Northland Special Package] Includes: Engine block heater; 50 percent (-30 degree F.) antifreeze; 70 amp.-hr. battery; 55-amp. alternator; and limited-slip rear axle. Power steering. Power front disc brakes (4x2s). High-output heater. Trailer towing packages. Ammeter and oil pressure gauge. Bright hubcaps. Bright contour rear bumper for Stylesides. Painted channel rear bumper for Flaresides. Tinted glass all around. Frame-anchored camper tie-down system. Heavy-duty 50-amp camper wiring harness. [Ranger Package] Includes: (In addition to or in place of Custom features) color-keyed super soft vinyl seat upholstery in black, red (not with Supercab), blue, green or ginger; instrument panel molding with black accent; shoulder high vinyl bolster around rear area (Supercab); color-keyed door panels with bright moldings; additional insulation; perforated headlining (insulated) with bright molding; color-keyed vinyl nylon carpeting; two courtesy lights; cigarette lighter; bright windshield, rear window and roof drip moldings; bright rocker panel and wheel lip moldings; and bright hubcaps (except 4x4 option and dual rear wheel units). Styleside Pickups also include bright side moldings with vinyl inserts; tailgate moldings (top and bottom); and taillight bezels. (Note: Ranger trim not available on Crew Cab.) [Ranger XLT] Includes: (In addition to or in place of Ranger items) Deluxe color-keyed, long-wearing cloth with vinyl trim seat upholstery; color-keyed pleated vinyl upper door panel with simulated woodgrain accented moldings and map pockets; lower panels color-keyed; wall-to-wall cut-pile nylon carpeting; bright instrument panel molding with simulated woodgrain insert; bright seat-pivot covers; additional insulation; bright wheelcovers; convenience group; color-keyed vinyl headlining (with special insulation); and sun visors. On Styleside Pickups, Ranger XLT also included bright tailgate applique panel and molding and aluminum tailgate applique panel.

CUSTOM DECOR GROUP: [Regular/Supercab Pickups] Includes: Knitted vinyl seat trim in black, red, blue, green or ginger; color-keyed floor mats with insulation; bright moldings around windshield and rear window; bright drip rail moldings and bright hubcaps (except F-100 4x4s).

HISTORICAL: Ford light conventional truck sales totaled 448,081 for model year 1975.

1976 FORD

1976 Ford 1/2-Ton Ranchero GT Sedan-Pickup (JAG)

RANCHERO 500 PICKUP: Aside from modifications to the engines to improve fuel economy and some different upholstery, the 1976 Ranchero was pretty much the same as the previous year's model. Standard features included: Vinyl upholstery and door trim. Panels with bright trim. Color-keyed steering wheel and column. Deep-pile carpeting. Hi-level, flow-through ventilation. Ventless door windows. Energy-absorbing steering column. Padded steering wheel hub. Lockable glove box. Locking steering column. Fresh-air heater defroster. Trim panel behind the split-back seat. Vinyl headliner. Color-keyed seat belts with outboard retractors and shoulder harnesses. Center passenger seat belts. Armrests with recessed door handles. Vinyl-framed day/night mirror. Cigarette lighter. Padded, color-keyed instrument panel. Emergency lamp flasher. Spare tire and tool compartment. Deluxe grille with moldings. Bright energy-absorbing front bumper. Bright left-hand mirror with remote-control. Hidden windshield wipers. Bright metal windshield, rear window, drip rail and top of cargo body moldings. Bright metal hubcaps. Power steering. Power brakes. Cruise-O-Matic automatic. Colors offered on 1976 Rancheros were: White; Bright red; Dark red; black; Light blue; Bright dark-blue (metallic); silver (metallic); Light green; Saddle bronze (metallic); Dark brown (metallic); Dark yellow-green (metallic); tan; and Pastel yellow. Color-Glow paint colors Green Glow, Tan Glow and Silver-blue Glow were optional. Black; white; blue; green; brown; and tan vinyl roofs were available.

RANCHERO GT PICKUP: The GT had (in addition to or in place of the Ranchero 500 features): Color-keyed bodyside stripes. Sport style mirrors painted body colors both with remote-control. Black hubcaps with bright trim rings. Lettered belted tires. GT grille crest. Spare tire and tool compartment cover. Bright trim on pedals. GT instrument panel plaque.

RANCHERO SQUIRE PICKUP: The Squire had (in addition to or in place of Ranchero 500 features): Deluxe bright wheelcovers. Simulated woodgrain panels on sides and tailgate. Ranchero Squire script on front fenders. Squire crest on grille. Wood-tone panel around instruments. Electric clock. Spare tire and tool compartment cover. Bright trim on pedals. Squire instrument panel plaque.

I.D. DATA [Ranchero]: The VIN consists of 11 symbols. The first symbol is the last digit of the model year. The second symbol indicates the assembly plant. The third and fourth symbols indicate the product line and body style. The fifth symbol indicates the engine. The last six symbols are the sequential production number.

Model	Body Type	Price	Weight	Prod. Total
Ranchero 500 — 1/2-Ton — 118 in. w.b. — V-8				
97D	Sedan-Pickup	4315	3915	9,958
Ranchero GT — 1/2-Ton — 118 in. w.b. — V-8				
97R	Sedan-Pickup	4649	3980	4,942
Ranchero Squire — 1/2-Ton — 118 in. w.b. — V-8				
97K	Sedan-Pickup	4668	3940	1172

NOTE 1: Prices/weights for base V-8; deduct for six.

ENGINE [Base Six]: Displacement: 200 cid. Six-cylinder. 84 nhp at 3800 rpm. Bore & stroke: 3.68 in. x 3.13 in. Compression ratio: 8.3:1. Carburetor: One-barrel.

ENGINE [Base V-8; Ranchero]: Displacement: 302 cid. V-8. 140 nhp at 3800 rpm. Bore & stroke: 4 in. x 3 in. Compression ratio: 8.0:1. Carburetor: Two-barrel.

ENGINE [Base V-8; Ranchero GT]: Displacement: 351 M (modified). V-8. 148 nhp at 3800 rpm. Bore & stroke: 4 in. x 3.5 in. Compression ratio: 8.0:1. Carburetor: Two-barrel.

CHASSIS: Wheelbase: 118 in. Overall length: 218.3 in. GVW: 5,480-5,950 lbs. Tires HR78-14B steel-belted radial [G70-14B white-lettered on GT].

POWERTRAIN OPTIONS: Engines: 351 cid V-8. 400 cid V-8. 460 cid V-8.

CONVENIENCE OPTIONS: [Performance Cluster] Includes: Tachometer; trip odometer; clock; ammeter; water temperature and oil pressure gauges; and heavy-duty battery. SelectAire air-conditioner with automatic temperature control. SelectAire air-conditioner. Power steering. [Protection Group/Bumpers] Includes: Front and rear bumper guards and front bumper rubber inserts. [Protection Group/Appearance] Includes: Spare tire lock; floor mats; license plate frame; and door edge guards. Vinyl insert bodyside molding. Anti-theft alarm system. Power side windows. Tilt steering wheel. Cruise control. [Convenience Group] Includes: Right and left remote-control mirrors; interval windshield wipers; automatic parking brake release; and vanity mirror. Restraint system. [Brougham Decor Group] Includes: Split bench seat with super-soft vinyl or knit cloth upholstery for the standard seat in Ranchero 500 and Squire. Bucket seats. Vinyl roof. Power brakes. AM radio. 15-in. wheels. Luxury wheelcovers. Hubcaps with trim rings. Mag style wheels. Tinted glass. Electric clock. Dual sport style mirrors. [Light Group] Includes: Ashtray, underhood and glove box lights: parking brake warning light; lights-on warning buzzer; and illuminated light switch. Class II (2,000-3,500 lbs.) or Class III (3,500-6,000 lbs.) trailer towing packages. [Handling Suspension Package] Includes: Heavy-duty shock absorbers; rear springs; and heavy-duty rear stabilizer bar. Fuel guard warning light. Power door locks. Heavy-duty electrical system. H78-14B, G70-14B and H70-14B tires. White sidewall tires available. Power seat. [Explorer Package] Includes: Broadcloth interior (vinyl optional); sports wheelcovers; vinyl roof; white sidewall tires; white side stripe; and hood ornament.

BRONCO WAGON: Standard features on the four-wheel drive 1976 Bronco included: Mono-Beam front suspension. Solid state ignition. Front disc brakes. Variable ratio parking brake control. Vinyl bucket seat [driver's only]. Floor-mounted T-bar transfer case control. Suspended foot pedals. Double-acting shock absorbers. Fresh air heater and defroster. Lockable glove compartment. Padded instrument panel. Two-speed electric windshield wipers. Sun visors. Vinyl-coated rubber floor mat. Fully synchronized three-speed manual. Full-length roof with fixed windows in the rear liftgate and on each side of the rear compartment. Dome light. Painted channel-type steel bumpers. Bronco color choices in 1976 were: Wimbledon white; Castillo red; Candy-apple red; Midnight blue (metallic); Bahama blue; Bali blue; Hatteras green (metallic); Glen green; Dark jade (metallic); silver (metallic); Indio tan; copper (metallic); Mecca gold; Cayan red; Raven black; and Chrome yellow. Glamour color paints: Ginger Glow and Medium Green Glow were optional. Bronco roofs were painted Wimbledon white when a two-tone was desired.

I.D. DATA: [Bronco]: The VIN consists of 11 symbols. The first three indicate the series. The fourth indicates the engine. The fifth shows the assembly plant. The last six are the sequential production number.

Model	Body Type	Price	Weight	Prod. Total
Bronco 4x4 — 1/2-Ton — 92 in. w.b. — V-8				
U-100	Wagon	5078	3490	13,625

NOTE 1: Prices/weights for base V-8; deduct for six.

ENGINE [Base Six]: Displacement: 200 cid. Six-cylinder. 84 nhp at 3800 rpm. Bore & stroke: 3.68 in. x 3.13 in. Compression ratio: 8.3:1. Carburetor: One-barrel.

ENGINE [Base V-8]: Displacement: 302 cid. V-8. 140 nhp at 3800 rpm. Bore & stroke: 4 in. x 3 in. Compression ratio: 8.0:1. Carburetor: Two-barrel.

CHASSIS: Wheelbase: 92 in. Overall length: 152.1 in. Overall width: 69.1 in. Overall height: 70.1 in. GVW: 4,400-4,900 lbs. Tires: E78-15.

POWERTRAIN OPTIONS: Engine: 302 cid V-8. Transmission: Cruise-O-Matic automatic transmission.

CONVENIENCE OPTIONS: Extra-cooling V-8 radiator. Left-hand remote-control outside mirror. Passenger front bucket seat. Heavy-duty shocks. Power steering. [Convenience Group] Includes: Cigarette lighter; map light; and inside 10 in. day/night rearview mirror. Right-hand chrome rearview mirror. Shoulder harness. Rear seat. Chrome bumper with chrome front guards. Skid plates for fuel tank and transfer case. 600-watt single element engine block heater. Dual horns. Exterior rear-mounted swing-away tire carrier. Bright metal wheelcovers. High-flotation tires. Auxiliary 7.5-gal. fuel tank with skid plate. Manual radio and antenna. Bright bodyside and tailgate moldings. Bright metal rocker panel molding. Hand-operated throttle. [Sport Bronco Package] Includes: Right-hand front seat and sun visor; vinyl door trim panels with bright metal moldings; hardboard headlining with bright metal retainer moldings; steering wheel with wood-tone horn pad; vinyl front and rear floor mats with bright metal retainers; cigarette lighter; horn ring; bright metal drip rail moldings; bright metal windshield and window frames; bright metal grille molding and tailgate release handle; bright headlight, side light, reflector and taillight bezels; and Argent silver-painted grille with bright Ford letters. Chrome bumpers, front and rear. Chrome front bumper guards. Bright metal wheelcovers.

DEALER INSTALLED ACCESSORIES: Power-take-off (front-mounted). Warn free-running front hubs (manual or automatic). Snow plows. Snow plow angling kits. Front auxiliary air springs. Front-mounted winch. Trailer hitch. Trailer towing mirror. Locking gas cap. Front tow hooks. Compass. Fire extinguisher. Transmission oil cooler. Tachometer. [4,600 lbs. GVW Package] Includes: Rear springs rated at 1,240 lbs. and E78-15B tires (requires rear bench seat and right-hand front seat). [4,900 lbs. GVW Package] Includes: Rear springs rated at 1,475 lbs. and G78-15 B tires. Reduced external sound package. [Northland Special] Includes: Single element 600-watt engine block heater; 50 percent (-30 degrees F.) antifreeze; 70 amp.-hr. battery; 60-amp. alternator; and limited-slip rear axle. [Ranger Package] Includes: Color-keyed full carpeting (including tailgate and wheelhousings); color-keyed vinyl door trim panels with burl wood-tone accent; color-keyed vinyl trim with insulation on rear quarter panels; cloth-and-vinyl seat trim in tan, blue or green; color-keyed instrument panel paint; hood and lower bodyside tape stripes; white stripe with orange accent; Swing-away spare tire carrier; spare tire cover in white vinyl with orange accent; and Bronco insignia. [Special Decor Group/Available on standard and Sport Broncos] Includes: Black grille; solid exterior colors (white roof is available); color-keyed tape stripe across hood and along upper sides; bright wheelcovers; bright windshield moldings; and window frames.

ECONOLINE E-100 CARGO VAN: Econolines were basically unchanged for 1976. Power brakes and a three-speed manual transmission were standard. Other standard features were: Full-foam driver's bucket seat. Color-keyed vinyl seat trim in black, blue, green or tan. Color-keyed seat belt. Color-keyed windshield trim moldings. Color-keyed engine cover with clipboard flashlight pocket and removable ashtray designed into console. Fresh air heater defroster. Fresh air vents with blend air control. Two-speed electric windshield wipers. Energy-absorbing sun visor on driver's side. Front and cargo area dome lights. Front compartment hardboard headlining and insulated floor mat with scuff plates. Push-pull door lock buttons. Armrest. Coat hook. Electric horn. Door checks. Latch release handles on side cargo doors. Argent silver bumpers. Argent silver hubcaps. Bright windshield molding and mirrors. Econoline colors for 1976 included: Wimbledon white; Candy-apple red; Brook blue (metallic); Bali blue; Hatteras green (metallic); silver (metallic); Glen green; copper (metallic); Peppertree red; Harness tan; Indio tan; and Chrome yellow. Medium Green Glow and Medium Ginger Glow paints were optional. Five separate and distinctive Tu-Tone paint schemes were available.

ECONOLINE E-100 WINDOW VAN: As the name suggests, the Window Van had glass all around. It shared standard features with the cargo van.

ECONOLINE E-100 DISPLAY VAN: This model had windows at the rear and on the right-hand side. It came with the same standard features as Cargo Van.

I.D. DATA [Vans]: The VIN consists of 11 symbols. The first three indicate the series. The fourth indicates the engine. The fifth shows the assembly plant. The last six are the sequential production number.

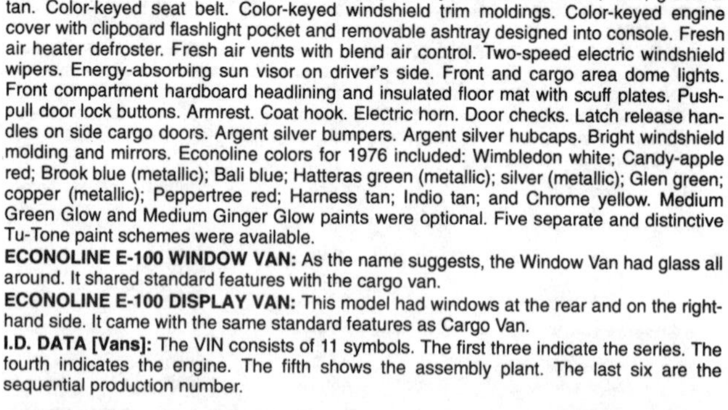

1976 Ford Club Wagon Passenger Van (JAG)

Model	Body Type	Price	Weight	Prod. Total
E-100 — 1/2-Ton — 124 in./138 in. w.b. — V-8				
E-040	Cargo Van	3882	3890	Note 1
E-050	Window Van	3968	3915	Note 1
E-060	Display Van	3921	3905	Note 1

NOTE 1: Total Ford Van sales were 179,820.
NOTE 2: Prices/weights for base V-8; deduct for six.
ENGINE [BaseSix]: Displacement: 300 cid. Six. Horsepower: 101 nhp at 3000 rpm. Torque: 223 lbs.-ft. at 1600 rpm. Bore & stroke: 4.00 in. x 3.98 in. Compression ratio: 8.0:1. Carburetor: One-barrel.
ENGINE [Base V-8]: Displacement: 351 cid. V-8. Horsepower: 156 nhp at 4000 rpm. Torque: 262 lbs.-ft. at 2200 rpm. Bore & stroke: 4.00 in. x 3.50 in. Carburetor: Two-barrel.
ECONOLINE E-150 CARGO VAN: This was the second year for this series. It had a slightly higher GVW rating than the E-100. Unlike the E-100, it could be operated on either leaded or unleaded gasoline. Standard features echoed those on the E-100.
ECONOLINE E-150 DISPLAY VAN: This Van shared styling with the E-100 Display Van but had greater load capacity.
ECONOLINE E-150 WINDOW VAN: This Van shared styling with the E-100 Window Van, but had greater load capacity.
I.D. DATA: [Vans]: The VIN consists of 11 symbols. The first three indicate the series. The fourth indicates the engine. The fifth shows the assembly plant. The last six are the sequential production number.

Model	Body Type	Price	Weight	Prod. Total
E-150 — 1/2-Ton — 124 in./138 in. w.b. — V-8				
E-140	Cargo Van	4064	3850	Note
E-160	Display Van	4103	3865	Note
E-150	Window Van	4150	3875	Note

NOTE 1: Total Ford Van sales were 179,820.
NOTE 2: Prices/weights for base V-8; deduct for six.
ENGINE [Base Six]: Displacement: 300 cid. Six. Horsepower: 101 nhp at 3000 rpm. Torque: 223 lbs.-ft. at 1600 rpm. Bore & stroke: 4.00 in. x 3.98 in. Compression ratio: 8.0:1. Carburetor: One-barrel.
ENGINE [Base V-8]: Displacement: 351 cid. V-8. Horsepower: 156 nhp at 4000 rpm. Torque: 262 lbs.-ft. at 2200 rpm. Bore & stroke: 4.00 in. x 3.50 in. Carburetor: Two-barrel.
ECONOLINE E-250 CARGO VAN: The new E-250 had a higher GVW rating and more heavy duty front and rear axles, than the E-150. It also came with eight, rather than five, hole wheels. Standard features were the same as those on the E-100.
ECONOLINE E-250 DISPLAY VAN: This vehicle shared styling and features with the E-100, but had greater load capacity.
ECONOLINE E-250 WINDOW VAN: This vehicle shared styling and features with the E-100 Window Van, but had greater load capacity.
ECONOLINE E-250 CUTAWAY VAN: This Van with Camper Special Packages was designed to readily accommodate custom motorhomes.
ECONOLINE E-250 PARCEL DELIVERY: This vehicle looked more like a typical delivery truck than a Van. It was basically a cutaway chassis with a large cargo body added.
I.D. DATA [Vans]: The VIN consists of 11 symbols. The first three indicate the series. The fourth indicates the engine. The fifth shows the assembly plant. The last six are the sequential production number.

Model	Body Type	Price	Weight	Prod. Total
E-250 — 3/4-Ton — 138 in. w.b. — V-8				
E-240	Cargo Van	4360	4380	Note
E-260	Display Van	4400	4395	Note
E-250	Window Van	4447	4410	Note
E-270	Cutaway Van	4154	3950	Note
E-280	Parcel Delivery	6129	5405	Note

NOTE 1: Total Ford Van sales were 179,820.
NOTE 2: Prices/weights for base V-8; deduct for six.
ENGINE [Base Six]: Displacement: 300 cid. Six. Horsepower: 101 nhp at 3000 rpm. Torque: 223 lbs.-ft. at 1600 rpm. Bore & stroke: 4.00 in. x 3.98 in. Compression ratio: 8.0:1. Carburetor: One-barrel.
ENGINE [Base V-8]: Displacement: 351 cid. V-8. Horsepower: 156 nhp at 4000 rpm. Torque: 262 lbs.-ft. at 2200 rpm. Bore & stroke: 4.00 in. x 3.50 in. Carburetor: Two-barrel.
ECONOLINE E-350 CARGO VAN: This was the top-of-the-line Econoline. It had heavy-duty front and rear shocks and a greater load capacity than the other series. Standard features were the same as those on the E-100.
ECONOLINE E-350 DISPLAY VAN: See E-250 Display Van.
ECONOLINE E-350 WINDOW VAN: See E-250 Window Van.
ECONOLINE E-350 CUTAWAY VAN: See E-250 Cutaway Van.
ECONOLINE F-350 PARCEL DELIVERY: See E-250 Parcel Delivery.
I.D. DATA [Vans]: The VIN consists of 11 symbols. The first three indicate the series. The fourth indicates the engine. The fifth shows the assembly plant. The last six are the sequential production number.

Model	Body Type	Price	Weight	Prod. Total
E-350 — 1-Ton — 138 in./158 in. w.b. — V-8				
E-340	Cargo Van	4543	4545	Note
E-360	Display Van	4583	4560	Note
E-350	Window Van	4630	4575	Note
E-370	Cutaway Van	4259	3995	Note
E-380	Parcel Delivery	6538	5715	Note

NOTE 1: Total Ford Van sales were 179,820.
NOTE 2: Prices/weights for base V-8; deduct for six.
ENGINE [Base Six]: Displacement: 300 cid six. Horsepower: 101 nhp at 3000 rpm. Torque: 223 lbs.-ft. at 1600 rpm. Bore & stroke: 4.00 in. x 3.98 in. Compression ratio: 8.0:1. Carburetor: One-barrel.
ENGINE [Base V-8]: Displacement: 351 cid V-8. Horsepower: 156 nhp at 4000 rpm. Torque: 262 lbs.-ft. at 2200 rpm. Bore & stroke: 4.00 in. x 3.50 in. Carburetor: Two-barrel.
CHASSIS: Wheelbase: 124 in. or 138 in. (158 in. available on Cutaway and Parcel Delivery). Overall Width: 70.3 in. Overall length: 186.8 in. (124 in. w.b.); 206.8 in. (138 in. w.b.). GVW: 5,100-10,725 lbs. Tires: F78-15B PT (E-100); H78-15D PT (E-150); 8.00 x 16.5D TT (E-250); 8.75 x 16.5E (C on Parcel Delivery Van); 9.50 x 16.5D TT (E-350); 8.00 x 16.5D (dual rear on Parcel Delivery Van).
POWERTRAIN OPTIONS: Transmissions: Cruise-O-Matic automatic. Engines: 351 cid V-8; 460 cid V-8 (E-250/E-350).
CONVENIENCE OPTIONS: [Custom Van] Includes: (In addition to or place of standard equipment) Color-keyed padded full-length instrument panel with woodgrained vinyl applique; color-keyed seat pedestal; cowl-side trim panels; vinyl front door trim panels; insulated floor mats; roof rail garnish moldings; bright hubcaps; tailight bezels; vent and rear window frames. [Chateau Van] Includes: (In addition to or in place of Custom equipment) Super Soft vinyl seat trim; color-keyed cut pile carpeting on front floor and lower section of engine cover; padded vinyl front door trim panels with woodgrained vinyl applique in center and carpeted lower panel; woodgrained vinyl horn bar insert in steering wheel; bright grille; bright bumpers; bright bodyside moldings; bright rear moldings; and wheelcovers. Right-hand sliding cargo door. Adjustable or flip-fold passenger seat. High-output heater and defroster. Auxiliary hot water heater. Bright grille and/or front and rear bumpers. Full-length, insulated carpet or mat (138 in. wheelbase models only). Courtesy light switches, front or all doors. Two-stage door positioners for hinged cargo doors. [Northland Special Package] Includes: Engine block heater (-35 F. antifreeze); 77 amp.-hr. battery; 60 amp. alternator and high-output heater. Engine block heater. Locking fuel cap. Tinted glass. Full-length hardboard headlining. Dual electric horns. Insulation package. Protection Group (front door edge guards and front and side sliding door stepwell pads). Interior rub rails (138 in. only). School Bus Package for 138 in. wheelbase Window Van. Cloth insert seat trim. Shoulder harness. Spare tire and wheel. Spare tire cover. Bright hubcaps. Trailer Towing Package (for Class I, II, III and IV trailers). Front stabilizer bar. Captain's chair. Air-conditioning. Power steering. Auxiliary fuel tank. Interval windshield wipers. Swing-Lok Western mirrors. Swing-out recreation mirrors. Swing-Lok low-mount Western mirrors. AM radio. AM/FM stereo. AM/FM stereo with tape player. Door windows for rear and/or side cargo doors. One-way glass in rear side windows and rear door. Flip-open windows for cargo doors. Job-engineered interior packages. [Low Line Camper Package] Includes: 60 amp. alternator; 77 amp.-hr. battery; auxiliary 81 amp.-hr. battery; heavy-duty shocks (with E-250); Custom trim package; camper wiring harness; Camper Special emblem; and extra-cooling package. [High Line Camper Special Package] Includes: (Basic package plus/or in place of) 90 amp. alternator; adjustable passenger seat; external auxiliary oil cooler; fuel monitor warning light and ammeter and oil pressure gauge; front stabilizer bar; dual horns; 351 cid V-8; Chateau trim package; high-output heater; power steering; and tinted windshield and glass.
NOTE: According to a *POPULAR MECHANICS* survey, most 1976 Ford van buyers (53.9 percent) used their vehicle for recreation. The four features they liked best about it were: Handling, ride, comfort and styling. Also, these owners reported having fewer mechanical problems than owners of comparable Chevy and Dodge vans. Not surprisingly, 88.2 percent said they would buy another Ford van.
E-100 CLUB WAGON: The new E-100 Club wagon shared the Econoline Van's styling and other changes. It was offered in five- or eight-passenger versions. Among the standard features were: Full foam front bucket seats. Color-keyed patterened vinyl seat trim. Seat belts. Color-keyed windshield trim moldings. Fresh air heater/defroster. Fresh air vents with blend air control. Two-speed electric windshield wipers. Wiper-arm-mounted washer jets. Sun visors. Rearview mirror. Dome lights. Front compartment hardboard headlining and insulated floor mat with scuff plates. Push-pull door lock buttons. Armrests. Coat hook. Electric horns. Door checks. Flip-open windows in sliding door and opposite windows. Argent silver bumpers and hubcaps. Bright windshield moldings. Painted outside rearview mirrors. Standard Club Wagon colors for 1976 were: Wimbledon white; silver (metallic); Candy-apple red; Brook blue (metallic); Bali blue; Hatteras green (metallic); Glen green; Copper (metallic); Peppertree red; Harness tan; Indio tan; and Chrome yellow. Custom and Chateau colors were: Silver (metallic); Brook blue (metallic); Hatteras green (metallic); Indio tan; Chrome yellow; and Wimbledon white. Medium green Glow and Ginger Glow were optional on standard, Custom and Chateau Club Wagons. Five two-tone paint schemes were available.
E-150 CLUB WAGON: This was a slightly more heavy-duty version of the E-100. It could be had 124 in. or 138 in. wheelbase and was also offered in five- and eight-passenger versions. Standard features were same as those on the E-100.
E-250 CLUB WAGON: The E-250 Club Wagon could be had with five-, eight-, or 12-passenger capacity. It had most of the same features as the E-100.
I.D. DATA [Vans]: The VIN consists of 11 symbols. The first three indicate the series. The fourth indicates the engine. The fifth shows the assembly plant. The last six are the sequential production number.

Model	Body Type	Price	Weight	Prod. Total
E-100 — 1/2-Ton — 124 in./138 in. w.b. — V-8				
E-100	Club Wagon	5018	—	—
E-150 — 1/2-Ton — 124 in./138 in. w.b. — V-8				
E-150	Club Wagon	5248	—	—
E-250 — 3/4-Ton — 138 in. w.b. — V-8				
E-250	Club Wagon	5461	—	—

NOTE 1: Total Ford Van sales were 179,820.
NOTE 2: Prices/weights for base V-8; deduct for six.
ENGINE [Base Six]: Displacement: 300 cid. Six. Horsepower: 101 nhp at 3000 rpm. Torque: 223 lbs.-ft. at 1600 rpm. Bore & stroke: 4.00 in. x 3.98 in. Compression ratio: 8.0:1. Carburetor: One-barrel.
ENGINE [Base V-8]: Displacement: 351 cid. V-8. Horsepower: 156 nhp at 4000 rpm. Torque: 262 lbs.-ft. at 2200 rpm. Bore & stroke: 4.00 in. x 3.50 in. Carburetor: Two-barrel.
CHASSIS: Wheelbase: 124 in. (E-100/E-150); 138 in. (E-150/E-250). Overall length: See Econoline. GVW: 5,600-5,900 lbs. (E-100); 6,010-6,300 lbs.; (E-150) 7,000-8,450 lbs. (E-250). Tires: G78-15B (E-100); G78-15D (E-150); 8.00 x 16.5D (E-250).
POWERTRAIN OPTIONS: Engines: 351 cid V-8; 460 cid cid V-8. Transmission: SelectShift Cruise-O-Matic automatic.
CONVENIENCE OPTIONS: Auxiliary fuel tank. Speed control. Power steering. Captain's chair. AM radio. AM/FM stereo radio. AM/FM stereo with tape player. High-capacity Air-conditioner. One way glass. Wheelcovers. Swing-Lok western mirrors. Swing-Lok low-mount western mirrors. Bright non-telescopic mirrors. Swing-out recreation mirrors. High-output heater/defroster. Auxiliary hot water heater. Bright grille and/or bumpers. Full-length insulated floor mat. Courtesy light switches for all doors. Hinged side doors in place of sliding door. Two-stage door positioners for all hinged double doors. Locking gas cap. Intermittent two-speed windshield wipers. [Instrument Package] Includes: Fuel monitor warning light, ammeter and oil pressure gauge. [Northland Special Package] Includes: Engine block heater; tinted glass; full-length hardboard headlining; and insulation package. [Protection Group] Includes: Front door edge guards and front and side sliding door step well pads; shoulder harness; spare tire cover; and bright hubcaps. Low-Line Camper Package. High-Line Camper Special Package. Trailer Towing Packages (Light-duty/heavy-duty/extra heavy-duty). [Custom Package] Includes: (In addition to or in place of standard equipment) Color-keyed padded full-length instrument panel with woodgrained vinyl applique; color-keyed seat pedestal, cowl trim panels, and padded vinyl door trim panels; cigarette lighter; insulated full-length floor mats; window garnish moldings; color-keyed armrests on three- and four-passenger seats; three coat hooks; aluminum scuff plates on side and rear doors; bright hubcaps; taillight bezels; and window frames. [Chateau Package] Includes: (In addition to or in place of Custom) Super Soft vinyl seat trim; color-keyed cut pile carpeting full-length of floor; lower section of engine cover and rear wheel wells; vinyl door trim panels with woodgrained vinyl applique in center and carpeted lower panel; color-keyed vinyl headlining (insulated); woodgrained vinyl horn bar insert; color-keyed vinyl spare tire cover; bright grille and bumpers; and lower bodyside and rear moldings. [Convenience Group] Includes: Courtesy light door switches; day/night mirror; and two-speed windshield wipers.

COURIER PICKUP: The Courier received a new grille for 1976. It resembled previous ones, except it had a horizontal-bars theme. The cab was three inches longer. Standard features included: Biscuit-pattern, full-width vinyl upholstered seat (in red, blue, tan or black). Padded instrument panel. Six- leaf rear springs. Double-acting shocks front and rear. Independent front suspension. The 1976 Courier was available in seven exterior colors.

I.D. DATA [Courier]: There were 11 symbols in the VIN. The first six were letters. They represented: Manufacturer, assembly plant, series, engine, model year and production month. The last five digits were the sequential production numbers.

Model	Body Type	Price	Weight	Prod. Total
Courier — 1/2-Ton — 104.3 in. w.b. — Four				
—	Pickup		2605	51,408

ENGINE [Courier]: Displacement: 110 cid. OHC four-cylinder.

1976 Ford 1/2-Ton Courier Mini-Pickup (JAG)

CHASSIS: Wheelbase: 104.3 in. Overall length: 171.5 in. Overall width: 63 in. Overall height: 61.5 in. GVW: 4,005 lbs. Tires: 6.00 x 14 6 ply-rated white sidewall.
POWERTRAIN OPTIONS: Transmissions: Automatic transmission with floor-mounted T-bar handle. Five-speed overdrive manual transmission.
CONVENIENCE OPTIONS: Pickup box cover. Deluxe pickup box cover (includes tinted-side windows, woodgrain vinyl side stripe and a dome light). Air-conditioner. AM or AM/FM monaural radio with push-button tuning. Tinted glass all around. Bright-framed Western mirrors. [Convenience/Decor Group] Includes: (Interior) Cut-pile carpet; day/night mirror; lights in glove box, ashtray and engine compartment; deluxe steering wheel; woodgrain vinyl instrument panel applique and manual transmission shift knob; glove box door lock; courtesy light switch; (Exterior) Bodyside molding with black vinyl insert (not available with tape stripe); chromed front bumper guards with rubber inserts; bright windshield, drip rail and back-light moldings; full wheelcovers. [Cold Weather Group] Includes: Electric rear window defroster, heavy-duty battery and high-output heater. Argent silver painted rear step bumper. Dual-accent tape stripe color-keyed to exterior paint. Concorde silver (metallic) paint.

Styleside 4x4 Pickup (JAG)

F-100 CUSTOM PICKUP: Ford light-duty trucks received a mild facelift for 1976. The two headlights were each recessed in a blacked-out square at each end of the vertically split, rectangular openings grille. A new cargo body was offered; the 6.5 ft. Flareside. It had seasoned hardwood floorboards. Early models had 40 percent flareboards. Later in the model year, 90 percent flareboards were used. In addition to these shorties, 8 ft. Flaresides and 6.75 ft. and 8 ft. Styleside cargo boxes were also available. The Stylesides could be ordered in regular or Supercab versions. The latter had a 44 cu. ft. cargo space behind the front seat (rear bench or jump seats were extra cost options). Among standard F-100 features for 1976 were: Bright grille. Chromed front bumper. Twin-I-Beam front suspension. Deluxe fresh air heater/defroster (high-output heater with Supercab). Energy-absorbing sun visors and instrument panel padding. Instrument cluster with green back lighting. Keyless locking doors. Color-keyed molded door panels with integral armrests and paddle-type door handles. 3-point restraint system. Windshield washers. Two-speed windshield wipers. Dome light with door courtesy light switches. Ashtray. Large glove compartment with push-button latch. Sponge-grain headlining. Black rubber floor mat. Door scuff plates. Black, tan, red, blue or green vinyl seat trim coordinated with exterior paint colors. 10 in. rearview mirror. Left-hand and right-hand bright metal exterior mirrors. Taillights with integral stop, turn, backup lights and reflector. Hubcaps (except 4x4s and dual rear wheel units). Three-speed manual transmission. Standard F-series colors for 1976 were: Wimbledon white; Mecca Gold; Indio tan; Castillo red; copper (metallic); Hatteras green (metallic); Glen green; Candy-apple red; Raven black; Bali blue; Bahama blue; Midnight blue (metallic); silver (metallic); and Chrome yellow. Ginger Glow and Medium Green Glow colors were optional. Different Tu-Tones could be obtained by using all the standard colors, except Chrome yellow. Wimbledon white could be used as the accent color for any color. The various Tu-Tone applications were the same as they were in 1975.

I.D. DATA [F-Series]: The VIN consists of 11 symbols. The first three indicate the series. The fourth indicates the engine. The fifth shows the assembly plant. The last six are the sequential production number.

Model	Body Type	Price	Weight	Prod. Total
F-100 — 1/2-Ton — 117 in. w.b. — V-8				
81	Chassis & Cab	3655	3145	Note 1
83	Flareside 6.5 ft.	3827	3495	Note 1
83	Styleside 6.75 ft.	3827	3495	Note 1
F-100 — 1/2-Ton — 133 in. w.b. — V-8				
83	Flareside 8 ft.	3873	3595	Note 1
83	Styleside 8 ft.	3873	3595	Note 1
F-100 Supercab — 1/2-Ton — 155 in. w.b. — V-8				
81	Chassis & Cab	4056	3765	Note 1
83	Styleside 8 ft.	4229	3765	Note 1

NOTE 1: Production: [F-100] 225,154.
NOTE 2: Prices/weights for base V-8; deduct for six-cylinder.
NOTE 3: Add $650 for 4x4.
ENGINE [Base Six]: Inline. OHV. Six-cylinder. Bore and stroke: 4.0 x 3.18 in. Displacement: 240 cid. Gross bhp: 150 at 4000 rpm. Gross torque: 234 lbs.-ft. at 2200 rpm.
ENGINE [Base V-8]: V-block. OHV. Eight-cylinder. Bore and stroke: 4.0 x 3.0 in. Displacement: 302 cid. Net horsepower: 130 at 3800 rpm. Net torque: 122 lbs.-ft. at 2000 rpm.
ENGINE [Super Cab Base V-8]: V-block. OHV. Eight-cylinder. Bore and stroke: 4.05 in. x 3.50 in. Displacement: 360 cid. Horsepower: 143 nhp at 3800 rpm. Net torque: 264 lbs.-ft. at 2200 rpm. Carburetor: Two-barrel.

1976 Ford 1/2-Ton F-100 Ranger XLT Styleside Pickup (OCW)

F-150 CUSTOM PICKUP: Sales literature called this the heavy duty 1/2-ton. Like the F-100, it had Mono-Beam front suspension with full-floating front axle, coil springs, forged-steel radius rods and track bar for ruggedness and ride. Power disc/drum brakes and a steering linkage shock absorber were also standard, along with most of the features listed for the F-100. Buyers could choose from Flareside (6.5 ft. Short Bed or 8 ft. Long Bed) and Styleside (8 ft. Long Bed) styling and regular or Supercab truck cabs.
I.D. DATA [F-Series]: The VIN consists of 11 symbols. The first three indicate the series. The fourth indicates the engine. The fifth shows the assembly plant. The last six are the sequential production number.

1976 Ford 1/2-Ton F-150 Ranger XLT Styleside Pickup 4x4 (OCW)

Model	Body Type	Price	Weight	Prod. Total
F-150 — 1/2-Ton — 133 in. w.b. — V-8				
81	Chassis & Cab	4062	3430	Note 1
83	Flareside	4235	3850	Note 1
83	Styleside	4235	3850	Note 1
F-150 Supercab — 1/2-Ton — 155 in. w.b. — V-8				
81	Chassis & Cab	4471	3655	Note 1
83	Styleside	4644	4005	Note 1

NOTE 1: Production: [F-150] 200,174.
NOTE 2: Prices/weights for base V-8; deduct for six.
ENGINE [Base Six]: Inline. OHV. Six-cylinder. Bore and stroke: 4.0 x 3.18 in. Displacement: 240 cid. Gross bhp: 150 at 4000 rpm. Gross torque: 234 lbs.-ft. at 2200 rpm.
ENGINE [Base V-8]: V-block. OHV. Eight-cylinder. Bore and stroke: 4.05 in. x 3.50 in. Displacement: 360 cid. Horsepower: 143 nhp at 3800 rpm. Net torque: 264 lbs.-ft. at 2200 rpm. Carburetor: Two-barrel.
F-250 CUSTOM PICKUP: The F-250 had most of the same features as the F-100. It too was offered with regular or Supercabs and with Flareside or Styleside boxes. Power brakes and a three-speed manual transmission were standard.

I.D. DATA [F-Series]: The VIN consists of 11 symbols. The first three indicate the series. The fourth indicates the engine. The fifth shows the assembly plant. The last six are the sequential production number.

1976 Ford 3/4-Ton F-250 Ranger XLT Styleside Pickup (OCW)

Model	Body Type	Price	Weight	Prod. Total
F-250 — 3/4-Ton — 133 in. w.b. — V-8				
81	Chassis & Cab	4141	3535	Note 1
83	Flareside	4313	3955	Note 1
83	Styleside	4313	3955	Note 1
F-250 Supercab — 3/4-Ton — 155 in. w.b. — V-8				
81	Chassis & Cab	4471	3655	Note 1
83	Styleside	4721	4110	Note 1

NOTE 1: Production: [F-250] 189,631.
NOTE 2: Prices/weights for base V-8; deduct for six.
ENGINE [F-250]: Displacement: 300 cid. Six. Horsepower: 120 nhp at 3400 rpm. Bore & stroke: 4.00 x 3.98. Compression ratio: 8.0:1. Carburetor: One-barrel. Supercab had 360 cid V-8.
ENGINE [Base V-8]: V-block. OHV. Eight-cylinder. Bore and stroke: 4.05 in. x 3.50 in. Displacement: 360 cid. Horsepower: 143 nhp at 3800 rpm. Net torque: 264 lbs.-ft. at 2200 rpm. Carburetor: Two-barrel.
F-350 CUSTOM PICKUP: The F-350 Pickup was only offered with the Styleside box. However, there were three choices of cabs: Regular, Supercab or Crew Cab. Front-only shocks (front and rear with Supercab), a four-speed manual transmission, and power brakes were standard.
F-350 PLATFORM/STAKE: Two lengths of 1-ton F-350 Platform/Stakes were available: 9 ft. and 12 ft. Floor frames of the Platform/Stake were made of steel cross sills riveted to steel siderails. Floorboards were interlocked with steel brackets. Formed steel caps covered ends of body sills. Sideboards were hardwood and stakes were steel. A four-speed manual transmission was standard.
I.D. DATA [F-Series]: The VIN consists of 11 symbols. The first three indicate the series. The fourth indicates the engine. The fifth shows the assembly plant. The last six are the sequential production number.

Model	Body Type	Price	Weight	Prod. Total
F-350 — 1-Ton — 137 in. w.b. — V-8				
80	Stake 9 ft.	4847	4665	Note 1
81	Chassis & Cab	4289	3845	Note 1
83	Styleside	4664	4415	Note 1
86	Platform 9 ft.	4806	4475	Note 1
F-350 — 1-Ton — 140 in. w.b. — V-8				
80	Stake 12 ft.	—	—	Note 1
86	Platform 12 ft.	—	—	Note 1
F-350 Supercab — 1-Ton — 155 in. w.b. — V-8				
81	Chassis & Cab	4924	4185	Note 1
83	Styleside	5097	4545	Note 1
83	Camper Special	5082	4415	Note 1
F-350 Crew Cabs — 1-Ton — 166.5 in. w.b. — V-8				
81	Chassis & Cab	5131	4345	Note 1
83	Styleside	5291	4785	Note 1

NOTE 1: Production: [F-350] 42,804.
NOTE 2: Prices/weights for base V-8; deduct for six.
ENGINE [Base Six]: Displacement: 300 cid six-cylinder. 120 nhp at 3400 rpm. Bore & stroke: 4.00 x 3.98 in. Compression ratio: 8.0:1. One-barrel carburetor.
ENGINE [Base V-8]: V-block. OHV. Eight-cylinder. Bore and stroke: 4.05 in. x 3.50 in. Displacement: 360 cid. Horsepower: 143 nhp at 3800 rpm. Net torque: 264 lbs.-ft. at 2200 rpm. Carburetor: Two-barrel.
CHASSIS: Wheelbase: 117 in. (F-100); 133 in. (F-100); 139 in. (F-100/F-250 Supercab); 137 in. (F-350); 140 in. (F-350 Platform/Stake); 155 in. (Supercab); 161 in. (F-350 Platform/Stake). GVW: 4,600-5,700 lbs. (F-100); 6,050-6,400 lbs. (F-150); 6,200-8,100 lbs. (F-250); 6,650-10,000 lbs. (F-350). Tires: G78-15B (F-100); L78-15D or 8.00 x 16.5D (F-250/F-350).
POWERTRAIN OPTIONS: Engines: 302 cid V-8 (F-100). 360 cid V-8. 390 cid V-8. 460 cid V-8. Transmissions: Four-speed manual. Cruise-O-Matic automatic.
CONVENIENCE OPTIONS: [Pickup box cover] Includes: (Standard) Fiberglass construction; tinted side and rear windows; roof vent; and T-handle locking rear lift gate; (Deluxe) Sliding side windows with screens; bright side and rear window moldings; interior dome light; and Tu-Tone paint color-keyed to the most popular truck colors. Knitted vinyl seat trim. Bright metal bodyside molding with vinyl insert. Speed control. AM/FM stereo radio. AM radio. Folding bench or jump seats (Supercab). Intermittent windshield wipers. [Super Camper Special] Includes: Front and rear stabilizer bars; heavy-duty frame; automatic transmission; extra-cooling; 360 cid V-8; power front disc brakes; 55 amp. alternator; 70 amp.-hr. battery; oil pressure gauge and ammeter; bright Western mirrors; dual horns; heavy-duty shocks; and camper wiring harness. Western style mirrors. Rear step bumper. Sliding rear cab window. Concealed spare tire and wheel. Auxiliary 12-volt 70 amp.-hr. battery. Air-conditioner. Black or white texture painted roof (includes bright drip rail molding).

Full wheelcovers. Mag style covers. Dual tape stripes. Bright tie-down hooks. Super cooling package. Slide out spare tire carrier. Tool stowage box with locking door. [Visibility Group] Includes: Cargo, engine, glove compartment and ashtray lights. [Convenience Group] Includes: Glove compartment door lock; intermittent windshield wipers; and 12 in. day/night mirror. [Northland Special Package] Includes: Engine block heater; 50 percent (-35 degrees F.) antifreeze; 70 amp.-hr. battery; 60 -amp. alternator; and limited-slip rear axle. Power steering. Power front disc brakes (4x2s). High-output heater. Trailer towing packages. Ammeter and oil pressure gauge. Bright hubcaps. Bright contour rear bumper for Stylesides. Painted channel rear bumper for Flaresides. Tinted glass all around. Frame-anchored camper tie-down system. Heavy-duty 50 amp. camper wiring harness. [Ranger Package] Includes: (In addition to or in place of Custom features) Color-keyed super soft vinyl seat upholstery; instrument panel molding with black accent; color-keyed door panels with bright moldings; shoulder high vinyl bolster around rear area (Supercab); additional insulation; perforated headling (insulated) with bright molding; color-keyed wall-to-wall carpeting; black steering wheel with woodgrain insert; cigarette lighter; bright windshield, rear window, rear quarter window (Supercab) and roof drip moldings; bright hubcaps (except trucks with 4x4 option and dual wheels). Styleside Ranger Pickups included bright bodyside moldings with vinyl inserts; tailgate moldings (top and bottom); and taillight bezels. [Ranger XLT] Includes: (In addition to or in place of Ranger items) Deluxe color-keyed, long-wearing cloth with vinyl (or Super Soft vinyl) trim seat upholstery; color-keyed pleated padded upper door panel with simulated woodgrain insert; color-keyed wall-to-wall cut-pile nylon carpeting; bright seat-pivot covers; additional insulation; convenience group; color-keyed vinyl headling (with special insulation) and sun visors; bright rocker panel moldings; and bright wheelcovers. Ranger XLT Styleside Pickups also included: Upper tailgate applique panel and molding and aluminum tailgate applique panel.
CUSTOM DECOR GROUP: [Custom Pickups, regular or Supercab] Includes: Knitted vinyl seat trim; color-keyed floor mats with insulation; bright moldings around windshield and rear window; bright drip rail moldings; bright hubcaps, except 4x4s (bright hubcaps included on F-250 4x4 with full-time drive, but not other 4x4s). [XLT Luxury Group/Texas Ranger Group in Texas] Includes unique trim features from color-keyed wheelcovers to special headliner and available only with regular cab 4x2 Styleside Pickups. Four-wheel drive (F-100/F-250).
HISTORICAL: Model year production totals were as follows: [F-100] 225,154; [F-150] 200,174; [F-250] 189,631; [F-350] 42,804; [Bronco] 13,704; [Ranchero] 15,152; Club Wagon] 38,329; [Econoline] 167,830 (Econoline includes units built in Canada for U.S. sales). In 1976, Ford Div. truck dealers narrowly missed setting a record for model year sales. Total sales were 1,003,611 vehicles, up 36 percent from the 739,185 units sold in 1975. Of these, 663,537 were conventional light trucks; 179,820 were vans; 13,625 were Broncos; 17,047 were Rancheros; 51,408 were Courier (captive imports); and 78,174 were medium-duty and heavy-duty trucks. J.A. Capolongo was Vice-President and General Manager of truck operations.

1977 FORD

1977 Ford 1/2-Ton Ranchero GT Sedan-Pickup (OCW)

RANCHERO 500 PICKUP: The Ranchero received its first styling change in years. It had rectangular, stacked headlights, a criss-cross pattern rectangular grille and fender integral wraparound parking lights. It also had new doors and revised quarter panels. Standard features included: SelectShift Cruise-O-Matic automatic. Power brakes and steering. Wiper-mounted windshield washer jets. Bright hubcaps. Bright windshield, drip rail and cargo body moldings. Carpeting. Vinyl door trim. Spare tire compartment. Vinyl covered bench seat (in blue, red, gray, jade, chamois or saddle).
RANCHERO GT PICKUP: In addition to most items on the 500, the GT had: GT strip in black, orange, silver, white or brown. Dual racing mirrors. Bright hubcaps with trim rings. Flight bench seat covered in fine grain Mateao vinyl. Sports instrument panel. Luxury steering wheel.
RANCHERO SQUIRE PICKUP: In addition to most items on the 500, the Squire had: Simulated woodgrain paneling on sides and tailgate. Deluxe wheelcovers. Colors offered on 1977 Rancheros were: Black; silver (metallic); Dark red; Dark blue (metallic); Bali blue; Dark jade (metallic); Bright saddle (metallic); champagne; Dark brown (metallic); cream; and white. Optional Color Glow Paints were Bright Blue Glow; Light Jade Glow; and Chamois Glow.
BRONCO I.D. DATA: [Ranchero]: The VIN consists of 11 symbols. The first symbol is the last digit of the model year. The second symbol indicates the assembly plant. The third and fourth symbols indicate the product line and body style. The fifth symbol indicates the engine. The last six symbols are the sequential production number.

Model	Body Type	Price	Weight	Prod. Total
Ranchero 500 — 1/2-Ton — 118 in. w.b. — V-8				
97D	Sedan-Pickup	4618	3915	9,453
Ranchero GT — 1/2-Ton — 118 in. w.b. — V-8				
97R	Sedan-Pickup	4984	3940	12,462

Ranchero Squire — 1/2-Ton — 118 in. w.b. — V-8

97K	Sedan-Pickup	4971	3980	1,126

NOTE 1: Total production: 21,850.
NOTE 2: Prices/weights for base V-8; deduct for six.
ENGINE [Base V-8; Ranchero GT]: Displacement: 351 M (modified). V-8. 148 nhp at 3800 rpm. Bore & stroke: 4 in. x 3.5 in. Compression ratio: 8.0:1. Carburetor: Two-barrel.
ENGINE [Base V-8; Ranchero]: Displacement: 302 cid. V-8, 130 nhp at 3800 rpm. Bore & stroke: 4 in. x 3 in. Compression ratio: 8.0:1. Carburetor: Two-barrel.
CHASSIS: Wheebase: 118 in. Overall length: 220.1 in. Overall height: 53.5 in. GVW: 5,452-5,904 lbs. Tires: G78-14B (G70-14B on GT).
POWERTRAIN OPTIONS: Engines: 351 cid V-8. 400 cid. V-8.
CONVENIENCE OPTIONS: Altitude-compensating carburetor. Appearance Protection Group with door edge guards, floor mat and license plate frame. Brougham Decor Group with split bench seat in cloth and vinyl trim or Mateao vinyl upholstery and individually adjustable seats. Bucket seats (include matching door trim panels and cut-pile carpet.) Bumper Protection Group with front and rear bumper guards and front bumper rub strips. Convenience Group with intermittent wipers and automatic parking brake release (on 500 and Squire includes right-hand remote control mirror and trip odometer). Engine block heater. Handling Suspension Package with 1,250 lbs. payload, heavy-duty rear springs and rear stabilizer bar. Heavy-duty alternator. Heavy-duty battery. Illuminated entry system. Light Group with under-hood, glove box and ashtray lights, headlights-on warning buzzer and door ajar light. Power door windows. Power flight bench seat covered in fine grain Mateao vinyl or optional cloth and vinyl. Racing mirror (dual, color-keyed). Leather wrapped sport steering wheel. Tinted glass all around. Class II (2,000-3,500 lbs.) trailer towing package with heavy-duty handling suspension package, extra-cooling package, 3.00:1 rear axle ratio and wiring harness (requires either 351 cid V-8 or 400 cid V-8 at extra-cost). Class III (3,500-6,000 lbs.) towing package with everything in Class II package, plus 60-amp. alternator (requires 400 cid V-8). Vinyl roof in red, black, silver, brown or white (not available with Tu-Tone finish). Wheel lip moldings. Deluxe wheelcovers. Hubcaps with trim rings. Luxury wheelcovers. Sports Instrument Panel with tachometer, trip odometer, ammeter, temperature and oil gauges and electric clock and luxury steering wheel. Fingertip speed control. AM/FM stereo with search. AM/FM monaural. AM radio. SelectAire air-conditioner (also available with automatic temperature control). Tilting steering wheel. Front cornering lamps. Mag 500 chrome wheels. Day/date digital clock. Wire wheelcovers.
BRONCO WAGON: Standard features on the four-wheel drive 1977 Bronco included: Mono-Beam front suspension. Solid state ignition. Front disc brakes. Variable ratio parking brake control. Vinyl bucket seat (driver's only). Floor-mounted T-bar transfer case control. Suspended foot pedals. Double-acting shock absorbers. Fresh air heater and defroster. Lockable glove compartment. Two-speed electric windshield wipers. 41-amp.-hr. battery. sun visors. Vinyl-coated rubber floor mat. Fully synchronized three-speed manual. Full-length roof with fixed windows in the rear liftgate and on each side of the rear compartment. Dome light. Painted channel-type steel bumpers.
I.D. DATA [Bronco]: The VIN consists of 11 symbols. The first three indicate the series. The fourth indicates the engine. The fifth shows the assembly plant. The last six are the sequential production number.

Model	Body Type	Price	Weight	Prod. Total
Bronco 4x4 — 1/2-Ton — 92 in. w.b. — V-8				
U-100	Wagon	5260	3490	13,593

ENGINE [Bronco]: Displacement: 200 cid. Six. Horsepower: 84 nhp at 3800 rpm. Bore & stroke: 3.68 in. x 3.13 in. Compression ratio: 8.3:1. Carburetor: One-barrel.
CHASSIS: Wheelbase: 92 in. Overall length: 152.1 in. Overall width: 69.1 in. Overall height: 70.1 in. GVW: 4,400-4,900 lbs. Tires: E78 x 15 in.
POWERTRAIN OPTIONS: Engine: 302 cid V-8. Transmission: Cruise-O-Matic automatic.
CONVENIENCE OPTIONS: Extra-cooling V-8 radiator. Left-hand remote-control outside mirror. Free-running hubs. Passenger front bucket seat. Heavy-duty shocks. 53- and 68-amp.-hr. batteries. Power steering. Convenience Group with cigarette lighter, map light and inside 10 in. day/night rearview mirror. Right-hand chrome rearview mirror. Shoulder harness. Rear seat. Chrome bumper with chrome front guards. Skid plates for fuel tank and transfer case 600-watt single-element engine block heater. Dual horns. Exterior rear-mounted swing-away tire carrier. Bright metal wheelcovers. High-flotation tires. Auxiliary 7.5-gal. fuel tank with skid plate. Manual radio and antenna. Bright bodyside and tailgate moldings. Bright metal rocker panel molding. Hand-operated throttle. Sport Bronco Package with right-hand front seat and sun visor; vinyl door trim panels with bright metal moldings; hardboard headlining with bright metal retainer moldings; steering wheel with wood-tone horn pad; vinyl front and rear floor mats with bright metal retainers; cigarette lighter; horn ring; passenger seat; bright metal drip rail moldings; bright metal windshield and window frames; bright metal grille molding and tailgate release handle; bright headlight, side light, reflector and taillight bezels; and Argent silver-painted grille with bright Ford letters. Chrome bumpers, front and rear. Chrome front bumper guards. Bright metal wheelcovers.
DEALER-INSTALLED ACCESSORIES: Power-take-off (front mounted). Warn free-running front hubs (manual or automatic). Snow plows. Snow plow angling kits. Front auxiliary air springs. Front mounted winch. Trailer hitch. Trailer towing mirror. Locking gas cap. Front tow hooks. Compass. Fire extinguisher. Transmission oil cooler. Tachometer. 4,600 lbs. GVW Package rear springs rated at 1,240 lbs. and E78-15B tires (requires rear bench seat and right-hand front seat.) 4,900 lbs. GVW Package with rear springs rated at 1,475 lbs., G78-15 B tires and reduced external sound package. Northland Special with single element 600-watt engine block heater, 50 percent (-30 degress F.) antifreeze, 70 amp.-hr. battery, 60-amp. alternator and limited-slip rear axle. Ranger Package with color-keyed full carpeting (including tailgate and wheelhousings); passenger seat; color-keyed vinyl door trim panels with burl wood-tone accent; color-keyed vinyl trim with insulation on rear quarter panels; cloth-and-vinyl seat trim in tan, blue or green; color-keyed padded instrument panel paint; hood and lower side tape stripes; white stripe with orange accent; Swing-away spare tire carrier; Spare tire cover (white vinyl with orange accent and Bronco insignia; and coat hooks. Special Decor Group (for standard and Sport Bronco) with black grille, solid exterior colors (white roof is available); color-keyed tape stripe across hood and along upper bodysides; bright windshield and window frames.
ECONOLINE E-100 CARGO VAN: The growing popularity of vans among the youth market was apparent on the cover of the 1977 Econoline sales catalog. It featured the photo of an Econoline with a trick paint job and fancy wheels. For the second year in a row, Ford continued to offer custom look vans straight from the factory. The rear spring rating was dropped slightly, but aside from that, the 1977 Econoline was basically the same as the 1976 version. Among the standard features were: Full-foam driver's bucket seat. Color-keyed vinyl seat trim in black, blue, jade or tan. Color-keyed seat belt. Color-keyed windshield trim moldings. Color-keyed engine cover with clipboard flashlight pocket and removable ashtray designed into console. Fresh air heater defroster. Fresh air vents with blend air control. Two-speed electric windshield wipers. Wiper-arm-mounted washer jets. Front and cargo area dome lights. Front compartment hardboard headlining and insulated floor mat with scuff plates. Push-pull door lock buttons. Armrest. Coat hook. Electric horn. Door checks. Latch release handles on side cargo doors. Argent silver bumpers. Argent silver hubcaps. Bright windshield molding. Painted mirrors.
ECONOLINE E-100 WINDOW VAN: As the name suggests, the Window Van had glass all around. It shared most standard features with the Cargo Van.
ECONOLINE E-100 DISPLAY VAN: This model had windows at the rear and on the right-hand side. It came with the same standard features as the Cargo Van. Standard Econoline colors for 1977 included: Wimbledon white; Candy-apple red; Brook blue (metallic); Light blue; Silver (metallic); Light jade; Dark brown (metallic); Indio tan; tangerine; Midnight blue (metallic); Raven black; Chrome yellow; and Dark Jade (metallic). Jade Glow and Cinnamon Glow were optional. Five Tu-Tone paint schemes were available.
I.D. DATA: [Van]: The VIN consists of 11 symbols. The first three indicate the series. The fourth indicates the engine. The fifth shows the assembly plant. The last six are the sequential production number.

Model	Body Type	Price	Weight	Prod. Total
E-100 Van — 1/2-Ton — 124 in./138 in. w.b. — V-8				
E-040	Cargo Van	4245	3875	Note
E-050	Window Van	4350	3900	Note
E-600	Display Van	4314	3890	Note

NOTE 1: Production: [Econoline] 128,818.
NOTE 2: Prices/weights for base V-8; deduct for six.
ENGINE [Base Six]: Inline. Six-cylinder. OHV. Bore & stroke: 4.00 in. x 3.98 in. Displacement: 300 cid. Net horsepower: 101 hp at 3000 rpm. Net torque: 223 lbs.-ft. at 1600 rpm. Compression ratio: 8.0:1. Carburetor: One-barrel.
ENGINE [Base V-8]: V-block. Eight-cylinder. OHV. Bore & stroke:4.0 x 3.5 in. Displacement: 351 cid. Net horsepower: 156 at 4000 rpm. Net torque: 262 lbs.-ft. at 2200 rpm.
ECONOLINE E-150 CARGO VAN: The E-150 could run on leaded or unleaded gas. It had a slightly higher GVW rating than the E-100. Unlike the E-100, it could be operated on either leaded or unleaded gasoline. Standard features echoed those on the E-100.
ECONOLINE E-150 DISPLAY VAN: This Van shared styling with the E-100 Display Van but had greater load capacity.
ECONOLINE E-150 WINDOW VAN: This Van shared styling with the E-100 Window Van but had greater load capacity.
I.D. DATA: [Van]: The VIN consists of 11 symbols. The first three indicate the series. The fourth indicates the engine. The fifth shows the assembly plant. The last six are the sequential production number.

Model	Body Type	Price	Weight	Prod. Total
E-150 Van — 1/2-Ton — 124 in./138 in. w.b. — V-8				
E-140	Cargo Van	4465	3833	Note
E-160	Display Van	4535	3850	Note
E-150	Window Van	4570	3860	Note

NOTE 1: Production: [Econoline] 128,818.
NOTE 2: Prices/weights for base V-8; deduct for six.
ENGINE [Base Six]: Inline. Six-cylinder. OHV. Bore & stroke: 4.00 in. x 3.98 in. Displacement: 300 cid. Net horsepower: 101 hp at 3000 rpm. Net torque: 223 lbs.-ft. at 1600 rpm. Compression ratio: 8.0:1. Carburetor: One-barrel.
ENGINE [Base V-8]: V-block. Eight-cylinder. OHV. Bore & stroke:4.0 x 3.5 in. Displacement: 351 cid. Net horsepower: 156 at 4000 rpm. Net torque: 262 lbs.-ft. at 2200 rpm.
ECONOLINE E-250 CARGO VAN: The new E-250 had a higher GVW rating and more heavy-duty front and rear axles, than the E-150. It also came with eight-hole, rather than five-hole, wheels. Standard features were the same as those on the E-100.
ECONOLINE E-250 DISPLAY VAN: This vehicle shared styling and features with the E-100, but had greater load capacity.
ECONOLINE E-250 WINDOW VAN: This vehicle shared styling and features with the E-100 Window Van, but had greater load capacity.
ECONOLINE E-250 CUTAWAY VAN: This Van with Camper Special Packages was designed to readily accommodate custom motor homes.
ECONOLINE E-250 PARCEL DELIVERY: The E-250 Parcel Delivery van was capable of hauling a payload up to 2,340 lbs. Its cargo area was 149.9 in. long and 74.3 in. high. The rear door opening was 84.7 in. wide.
I.D. DATA [Van]: The VIN consists of 11 symbols. The first three indicate the series. The fourth indicates the engine. The fifth shows the assembly plant. The last six are the sequential production number.

Model	Body Type	Price	Weight	Prod. Total
Van — 1/2-Ton — 138 in. w.b. — V-8				
E-240	Cargo Van	4780	4365	Note
E-260	Display Van	4850	4380	Note
E-250	Window Van	4886	4395	Note
E-270	Cutaway Van	4622	3935	Note
E-280	Parcel Delivery	6220	5390	Note

NOTE 1: Production: [Econoline] 128,818.
NOTE 2: Prices/weights for base V-8; deduct for six.
ENGINE [Base Six]: Inline. Six-cylinder. OHV. Bore & stroke: 4.00 in. x 3.98 in. Displacement: 300 cid. Net horsepower: 101 hp at 3000 rpm. Net torque: 223 lbs.-ft. at 1600 rpm. Compression ratio: 8.0:1. Carburetor: One-barrel.
ENGINE [Base V-8]: V-block. Eight-cylinder. OHV. Bore & stroke: 4.00 x 3.5 in. Displacement: 351 cid. Net horsepower: 156 at 4000 rpm. Net torque: 262 lbs.-ft. at 2200 rpm.
ECONOLINE E-350 CARGO VAN: This was the top of the line Econoline. It had heavy-duty front and rear shocks and a greater load capacity than the other series. Standard features were the same as those on the E-100.
ECONOLINE E-350 DISPLAY VAN: See E-250 Display Van.
ECONOLINE E-350 WINDOW VAN: See E-250 Window Van.
ECONOLINE E-350 CUTAWAY VAN: See E-250 Cutaway Van.
ECONOLINE E-350 PARCEL DELIVERY: This heavy-duty Van came in two wheelbases. Styling and features were the same as those offered on the E-250.
I.D. DATA: [Van]: The VIN consists of 11 symbols. The first three indicate the series. The fourth indicates the engine. The fifth shows the assembly plant. The last six are the sequential production number.

Model	Body Type	Price	Weight	Prod. Total
E-350 Van — 1-Ton — 138 in./158 in. w.b. — V-8				
E-340	Cargo Van	4962	4530	Note
E-360	Display Van	5033	4545	Note
E-350	Window Van	5068	4560	Note
E-370	Cutaway Van	4718	3980	Note
E-380	Parcel Delivery	6654	5700	Note

NOTE 1: Production: [Econoline] 128,818.
NOTE 2: Prices/weights for base V-8; deduct for six.
ENGINE [Base Six]: Inline. Six-cylinder. OHV. Bore & stroke: 4.00 in. x 3.98 in. Displacement: 300 cid. Net horsepower: 101 hp at 3000 rpm. Net torque: 223 lbs.-ft. at 1600 rpm. Compression ratio: 8.0:1. Carburetor: One-barrel.
ENGINE [Base V-8]: V-block. Eight-cylinder. OHV. Bore & stroke: 4.00 x 3.5 in. Displacement: 351 cid. Net horsepower: 156 at 4000 rpm. Net torque: 262 lbs.-ft. at 2200 rpm.

CHASSIS: Wheelbase: 124 in. 138 in. (158 in. available on Cutaway and Parcel Delivery). Overall width: 70.3 in. Overall length: 186.8 in. (124 in. w.b.); 206.8 in. (138 in. w.b.). GVW: 5,150-11,000 lbs. Tires: F78-15B. (E-100) H78-15D PT (E-150); 8.00 x 16.5D TT (E-250); 8.75 x 16.5E (C on Parcel Delivery Van) 9.50 x 16.5D TT (E-350); 8.00 x 16.5D (dual rear on Parcel Delivery Van).

POWERTRAIN OPTIONS: Transmissions: Cruise-O-Matic automatic. Engine: 351 cid V-8. 460 cid V-8 (E-250/E-350).

CONVENIENCE OPTIONS: Custom Van package with standard equipment, plus color-keyed padded full-length instrument panel with wood grained vinyl applique; color-keyed seat pedestal; cowl-side trim panels; vinyl front door trim panels; insulated floor mats; roof rail garnish moldings; bright hubcaps; taillight bezels; and vent and rear window frames. Chateau Van with (in addition to or in place of Custom equipment) Super Soft vinyl seat trim; color-keyed cut pile carpeting on front floor and lower section of engine cover; padded vinyl front door trim panels with woodgrained vinyl applique in center and carpeted lower panel; woodgrained vinyl horn bar insert in steering wheel; bright grille; bright bumpers; bright bodyside and rear moldings; wheelcovers; right-hand sliding cargo door; adjustable or flip-fold passenger seat; high-output heater and defroster; and auxiliary hot water heater. Cruising Van Interior with full carpeting and insulation and captain's chairs. Bright grille and/ or front and rear bumpers. Full-length, insulated carpet or mat (138 in. wheelbase only). Courtesy light switches, front or all doors. Two-stage door positioners for hinged cargo doors. Northland Special Package with engine block heater; -35 F. anti-freeze; 77 amp.-hr. battery; 60-amp. alternator; and high-output heater. Engine block heater. Locking fuel can. Tinted glass. Full-length hardboard headlining. Dual electric horns. Insulation Package. Protection Group with front door edge guards and front and side sliding door stepwell pads. Interior rub rails (138 in. wheelbase models only). School Bus Package for 138 in. wheelbase chassis. Window Van. Argyle cloth insert seat trim. Spare tire and wheel. Spare tire cover. Bright hubcaps. Trailer Towing Package for Class I, II, III and IV trailers. Front stabilizer bar. Captain's chair. Air-conditioning. Power steering. Auxiliary fuel tank. Interval windshield wipers. Swing-Lok Western mirrors. Swing-out recreation mirrors. Swing-Lok low-mount Western mirrors. AM radio. AM/FM monaural. AM/FM stereo. AM/FM stereo with tape player. Door windows for rear and/or side cargo doors. One-way glass in rear side windows and rear door. Flip-open windows for cargo doors. Job-engineered interior packages. Low Line Camper Package with 60 -amp. alternator; 77 amp.-hr. battery; auxiliary 81 amp.-hr. battery; and heavy-duty shocks (with E-250). Custom trim package including camper wiring harness; Camper Special emblem; and extra-cooling package. High Line Camper Special Package with basic package, plus (or in place of basic) 90-amp. alternator; adjustable passenger seat; external auxiliary oil cooler; fuel monitor warning light and ammeter and oil pressure gauge; front stabilizer bar; dual horns; and 351 cid V-8. Chateau trim package with high-output heater; power steering; tinted windshield; and tinted glass.

E-100 CLUB WAGON: Re-rated rear springs and new wheelcovers were the major changes for 1977. The E-100 was offered in five- and eight- passenger versions. Among the standard features were: Full foam front bucket seats. Color-keyed patterned vinyl seat trim in black, blue, jade or tan. Seat belts. Two-speed electric windshield wipers. Wiper-arm-mounted washer jets. 10 in. rearview mirror. Dome lights. Insulated floor mat with scuff plates. Three armrests. Dual horns. Flip-open windows in sliding door and opposite windows. Painted bumpers. 5 in. x 8 in. mirrors and hubcaps. Bright windshield molding. Standard Club Wagon colors for 1977 were: Wimbledon white; Candy-apple red; Brook blue (metallic); Light blue; silver (metallic); Light jade; Dark brown (metallic); Indio tan; tangerine; Midnight blue (metallic); Raven black; Chrome yellow; and Dark jade (metallic). Optional were: Jade and Cinnamon Glow. Five Tu-Tone paint schemes were offered.

E-150 CLUB WAGON: This was a slightly more heavy-duty version of the E-100. It could be had in 124 in. or 138 in. wheelbases and was also offered in five- and eight-passenger versions. Standard features were same as those on the E-100.

E-250 CLUB WAGON: The E-250 Club Wagon could be had with five-, eight- or 12-passenger capacity. It had most of the same features as the E-100.

I.D. DATA [Van]: The VIN consists of 11 symbols. The first three indicate the series. The fourth indicates the engine. The fifth shows the assembly plant. The last six are the sequential production number.

Model	Body Type	Price	Weight	Prod. Total
E-100 — 1/2-Ton — 124 in./138 in. w.b. — V-8				
E-100	Club Wagon	5485	4090	—
E-150 — 1/2-Ton — 124 in./138 in. w.b. — V-8				
E-150	Club Wagon	5680	4225	—
E-250 — 3/4-Ton — 138 in. w.b. in. w.b. — V-8				
E-250	Club Wagon	5921	4735	—

NOTE 1: Production: [Club Wagon] 31,980.

NOTE 2: Prices/weights for base V-8; deduct for six.

ENGINE [Base Six]: Inline. Six-cylinder. OHV. Bore & stroke: 4.00 in. x 3.98 in. Displacement: 300 cid. Net horsepower: 101 hp at 3000 rpm. Net torque: 223 lbs.-ft. at 1600 rpm. Compression ratio: 8.0:1. Carburetor: One-barrel.

ENGINE [Base V-8]: V-block. Eight-cylinder. OHV. Bore & stroke: 4.00 x 3.5 in. Displacement: 351 cid. Net horsepower: 156 at 4000 rpm. Net torque: 262 lbs.-ft. at 2200 rpm.

CHASSIS: Wheelbase: 124 in. (E-100); 138 in. (E-150/E-250). Overall length: See Econoline. GVW: 5,600-5,900 lbs. (E-100); 6,010-6,300 lbs. (E-150); 7,000-8,450 lbs. (E-250 five-passenger). Tires: G78 x 15B (E-100); H78 x 15D (E-150); 8.00 x 16D (E-250).

POWERTRAIN OPTIONS: Engine: 351 cid V-8. 460 cid V-8. Transmission: SelectShift Cruise-O-Matic automatic.

CONVENIENCE OPTIONS: Auxiliary fuel tank. Speed control. Power steering. Captain's chair. AM radio. AM/FM stereo radio. AM/FM stereo with tape player. High-capacity or front-only air-conditioner. Privacy glass. Wheelcovers. Swing-Lok Western mirrors. Swing-Lok low-mount Western mirrors. Bright non-telescopic mirrors. Swing-out recreation mirrors. High-output heater. Roof luggage carrier. Spare tire lock. Low-mount Swing-Lok bright mirrors. AM/FM monaural radio. Bright grille and/or bumpers. Full-length insulated floor mat. Free Wheeling Option with black rocker panel paint accents; painted bumpers; painted grille and mirrors; forged aluminum wheels; and raised white-lettered tires. Courtesy light switches for all doors. Hinged side doors in place of sliding door. Two-stage door positioners for all hinged double doors. Locking gas cap. Intermittent two-speed windshield wipers. Instrument Package includes fuel monitor warning light; ammeter; and oil pressure gauge. Northland Special Package with engine block heater; tinted glass; full-length hardboard headliner and insulation package. Protection Group with front door edge guards and front and side sliding door step well pads. Shoulder harness. Spare tire cover. Bright hubcaps. Low Line Camper Package. High Line Camper Special Package. Trailer Towing Packages (light-, heavy- and extra-heavy-duty). Custom Package with standard features, plus (or in place of standard) color-keyed padded full-length instrument panel with woodgrained vinyl applique; padded vinyl door trim panels; cigarette lighter; insulated full-length floor mats; window garnish moldings; color-keyed armrests on three- and four-passenger seats; three coat hooks; aluminum scuff plates on side and rear doors; bright hubcaps; taillight bezels; and window frames. Chateau Package with (in addition to or in place of Custom) Super Soft vinyl seat trim; color-keyed cut pile carpeting full-length of floor; lower section of engine cover and rear wheel wells; vinyl door trim panels with woodgrained vinyl applique in center and carpeted lower panel; color-keyed vinyl headlining (insulated); woodgrained vinyl horn bar insert; color-keyed vinyl spare tire cover; bright grille and bumpers; and bright lower bodyside and rear moldings. Convenience Group with courtesy light door switches, day/night mirror and two-speed windshield wipers.

1977 Ford 1/2-Ton Courier Mini-Pickup (OCW)

COURIER PICKUP: The restyled Courier was introduced in the spring of 1977. Between the recessed headlights was the two level, horizontal bars theme grille. New, wraparound taillights highlighted the rear end treatment. Standard items included: Vinyl headliner. Inside hood release. Full-width vinyl upholstered seat. Hinged seatback for easy access to stowage area. Independent front suspension. Six-leaf rear springs. Double-acting shocks front and rear.

I.D. DATA [Courier]: The VIN consists of 11 symbols. The first indicates the manufacturer. The second indicates the assembly plant. The third indicates the series. The fourth indicates the engine. The fifth (a letter) indicates the model year. The sixth indicates the production month. The last five are the sequential production number.

Model	Body Type	Price	Weight	Prod. Total
Courier — 1/2-Ton — 104.3 in. w.b. — Four				
—	Pickup	—	2675	13,167

ENGINE [Base Four]: Inline. Four-cylinder. OHV. Bore & stroke: 3.07 in. x 3.70 in. Displacement: 110 cid. Net horsepower: 67 nhp at 4500 rpm. Carburetor: One-barrel.

CHASSIS: Wheelbase: 106.9 in. (6 ft. box); 112.8 in. (7 ft. box). Overall length: 177.9 in. (6 ft. box); 189.4 in. (7 ft. box). Overall width: 63 in. Overall height: 61.5 in. GVW: 3,965 lbs. Tires: 6.00 x 14 in.

POWERTRAIN OPTIONS: Transmissions: Automatic transmission. Five-speed manual transmission.

CONVENIENCE OPTIONS: AM or AM/FM monaural radios. Air-conditioning. Tinted glass all around. Western rearview mirrors. Rear step bumper. Cold Weather Group with electric rear window defroster, heavy-duty battery and high-output heater. Radial tires. Cast aluminum wheels. Free Wheeling packages A and B.

F-100 CUSTOM PICKUP: Styling was unchanged for 1977. Among standard features were: Fresh air heater/defroster (high-output heater with Supercab). Energy-absorbing instrument panel padding. Instrument cluster with green back-lighting. Behind-seat storage. Molded door panels with integral armrests and paddle-type door handles. Two-speed windshield wipers. Dome light with door courtesy light switches. Ashtray. Glove compartment. Headlining. Black floor mat. Door scuff plates. Full-foam seat (7 in. of foam in seat and 5 in. in back). Black, red, tan or jade green vinyl seat trim. Twin-I-Beam front suspension. No-rust fender liners. F-100 buyers had their choice of the 6.75 ft. and 8 ft. Styleside boxes; the 6.5 ft. and 8 ft. Flareside boxes; or the 6.75 ft. and 8 ft. Styleside boxes with a Supercab style cab. The latter featured an extended cab with room for an optional folding rear seat or two jump seats behind the front bench seat. Standard F-series colors for 1977 included: Raven black; Wimbledon white; Candy-apple red; Castilo red; Silver (metallic); Midnight blue (metallic); Light blue; Bahama blue; Light jade; Dark jade (metallic); Chrome yellow; Indio tan; Medium copper; and copper (metallic). New Jade Glow and Dark Cinnamon Glow colors were optional. Wimbledon white could be used as the accent color for any exterior color except silver (metallic). Two-tone applications: [Regular] Accent on roof and upper back panel; [Deluxe/for Stylesides only] accent color inside molding; [Combination/ for Stylesides only] Combines regular and deluxe.

I.D. DATA: [F-Series]: The VIN consists of 11 symbols. The first three indicate the series. The fourth indicates the engine. The fifth shows the assembly plant. The last six are the sequential production number.

Model	Body Type	Price	Weight	Prod. Total
F-100 — 1/2-Ton — 117 in. w.b. — V-8				
81	Chassis & Cab	3846	3145	Note 1
83	Flareside 6.5 ft.	4076	3495	Note 1
83	Styleside 6.75 ft.	4076	3495	Note 1
F-100 — 1/2-Ton — 133 in. w.b. — V-8				
83	Flareside 8 ft.	3897	3595	Note 1
83	Styleside 8 ft.	3897	3595	Note 1
F-100 Supercab — 1/2-Ton — 155 in. w.b. — V-8				
81	Chassis & Cab	4372	3550	Note 1
83	Styleside 8 ft.	4602	3905	Note 1

NOTE 1: Production: [F-100] 197,822l.

NOTE 2: Prices/weights for base V-8; deduct for six-cylinder.

NOTE 3: Add $700 for 4x4.

ENGINE [Base Six]: Inline. Six-cylinder. OHV. Bore & stroke: 4.00 in. x 3.98 in. Displacement: 300 cid. Net horsepower: 101 hp at 3000 rpm. Net torque: 223 lbs.-ft. at 1600 rpm. Compression ratio: 8.0:1. Carburetor: One-barrel.

ENGINE [Base V-8]: V-block. OHV. Eight-cylinder. Bore and stroke: 4.00 x 3.00 in. Displacement: 302 cid. Net horsepower: 130 at 3800 rpm. Net torque: 222 lbs.-ft. at 2000 rpm.

ENGINE [Super Cab Base V-8]: V-block. OHV. Eight-cylinder. Bore and stroke: 4.05 in. x 3.50 in. Displacement: 360 cid. Horsepower: 145 nhp at 3800 rpm. Net torque: 264 lbs.-ft. at 2200 rpm. Carburetor: Two-barrel.

1977 Ford 1/2-Ton F-150 Ranger XLT Flareside Pickup 4x4 (RCA)

F-150 CUSTOM PICKUP: Once again, the F-150 was Ford's heavy-duty 1/2-ton. Its payload ranged from 605 lbs. to 930 lbs. greater than F-100's. However, it shared most of the standard feature with that series, with the addition of power brakes.

I.D. DATA [F-Series]: The VIN consists of 11 symbols. The first three indicate the series. The fourth indicates the engine. The fifth shows the assembly plant. The last six are the sequential production number.

Model	Body Type	Price	Weight	Prod. Total
F-150 — 1/2-Ton — 133 in. w.b. — V-8				
81	Chassis & Cab	4332	3435	Note 1
83	Flareside	4561	3855	Note 1
83	Styleside	4561	3855	Note 1
F-150 Supercab — 1/2-Ton — 155 in. w.b. — V-8				
81	Chassis & Cab	4683	3660	Note 1
83	Styleside	4913	4010	Note 1

NOTE 1: Production: [F-150] 337,068.
NOTE 2: Prices/weights for base V-8; deduct for six.
NOTE 3: Supercabs offered with either 6.75 ft. or 8 ft. Styleside boxes.

1977 Ford 1/2-Ton F-150 Ranger XLT Styleside Pickup 4x4 (RCA)

ENGINE [Base Six]: Inline. OHV. Six-cylinder. Bore and stroke: 4.0 x 3.18 in. Displacement: 240 cid. Gross bhp: 150 at 4000 rpm. Gross torque: 234 lbs.-ft. at 2200 rpm.
ENGINE [Base V-8]: V-block. OHV. Eight-cylinder. Bore and stroke: 4.05 in. x 3.50 in. Displacement: 360 cid. Horsepower: 143 nhp at 3800 rpm. Net torque: 264 lbs.-ft. at 2200 rpm. Carburetor: Two-barrel.

1977 Ford 3/4-Ton F-260 Ranger Styleside Pickup 4x4 (OCW)

F-250 CUSTOM PICKUP: The F-250 had most of the same features as the F-100. It too was offered with regular or Supercabs and with Flareside or Styleside boxes. Power brakes and a three-speed manual transmission were standard.

I.D. DATA [F-Series]: The VIN consists of 11 symbols. The first three indicate the series. The fourth indicates the engine. The fifth shows the assembly plant. The last six are the sequential production number.

1977 Ford 3/4-Ton F-250 Ranger Styleside Pickup 4x4 (JAG)

Model	Body Type	Price	Weight	Prod. Total
F-250 — 3/4-Ton — 133 in. w.b. — V-8				
81	Chassis & Cab	4438	3540	Note 1
83	Flareside	4667	3960	Note 1
83	Styleside	4667	3960	Note 1
F-250 Supercab — 3/4-Ton — 155 in. w.b. — V-8				
81	Chassis & Cab	4783	3760	Note 1
83	Styleside	5013	4115	Note 1
F-250 Crew Cabs — 3/4-Ton — 166.5 in. w.b. — V-8				
81	Chassis & Cab	5183	4180	Note 1
83	Styleside	5414	4535	Note 1

NOTE 1: Production: [F-250] 180,612
NOTE 2: Prices/weights for base V-8; deduct for six.
NOTE 3: Supercabs available with 6.75 ft. and 8 ft. styleside boxes.
ENGINE [F-250]: Displacement: 300 cid. Six. Horsepower: 120 nhp at 3400 rpm. Bore & stroke: 4.00 x 3.98. Compression ratio: 8.0:1. Carburetor: One-barrel. Supercab had 360 cid V-8.
ENGINE [Base V-8]: V-block. OHV. Eight-cylinder. Bore and stroke: 4.05 in. x 3.50 in. Displacement: 360 cid. Horsepower: 143 nhp at 3800 rpm. Net torque: 264 lbs.-ft. at 2200 rpm. Carburetor: Two-barrel.

1977 Ford 3/4-Ton F-250 Ranger Styleside Pickup 4x4 (RCA)

F-350 CUSTOM PICKUP: The F-350 Pickup was only offered with the Styleside box. However, there were three choices of cabs: Regular, Supercab or Crew Cab. Front-only shocks (front and rear with Supercab), a four-speed manual transmission and power brakes were standard.
F-350 PLATFORM/STAKE: Two lengths of 1-ton F-350 Platform/Stake were available: 9 ft. and 12 ft. Floor frames of the Platform/Stake were made of steel cross sills riveted to steel siderails. Floorboards were interlocked with steel brackets. Formed steel caps covered ends of sills. Sideboards were hardwood and stakes were steel. A four-speed manual transmission was standard.
I.D. DATA [F-Series]: The VIN consists of 11 symbols. The first three indicate the series. The fourth indicates the engine. The fifth shows the assembly plant. The last six are the sequential production number.

Model	Body Type	Price	Weight	Prod. Total
F-350 — 1-Ton — 137 in. w.b. — V-8				
80	Stake 9 ft.	5230	4670	Note 1
81	Chassis & Cab	4639	3850	Note 1
83	Styleside	5016	4415	Note 1
86	Platform 9 ft.	5187	4430	Note 1
F-350 — 1-Ton — 161 in. w.b. — V-8				
80	Stake 12 ft.	—	—	Note 1
86	Platform 12 ft.	—	—	Note 1
F-350 Supercab — 1-Ton — 155 in. w.b. — V-8				
81	Chassis & Cab	5184	4185	Note 1
83	Styleside	5414	4545	Note 1
F-350 Crew Cabs — 1-Ton — 166.5 in. w.b. — V-8				
81	Chassis & Cab	5184	4185	Note 1
83	Styleside	5615	4790	Note 1

NOTE 1: Production: [F-350] 52,493.
NOTE 2: Prices/weights for base V-8; deduct for six.
ENGINE [Base Six]: Displacement: 300 cid. Six-cylinder. 120 nhp at 3400 rpm. Bore & stroke: 4.00 x 3.98 in. Compression ratio: 8.0:1. One-barrel carburetor.
ENGINE [Base V-8]: V-block. OHV. Eight-cylinder. Bore and stroke: 4.05 in. x 3.50 in. Displacement: 360 cid. Horsepower: 143 nhp at 3800 rpm. Net torque: 264 lbs.-ft. at 2200 rpm. Carburetor: Two-barrel.

CHASSIS: Wheelbase: 117 in. (F-100); 133 in. (F-100/F-150/F-250); 139 in. (F-100/F-150/F-250 Supercab); 155 in. (Supercab); 137 in. (F-350 Platform/Stake); 140 in. (F-350); 161 in. (F-350 Platform/Stake); 150 in. (F-250 Crew Cab); 166.5 in. (F-350 Crew Cab). GVW: 4,700-5,650 lbs. (F-100); 6,050-6,200 lbs. (F-150); 6,200-8,100 lbs. (F-250); 8,300-10,000 lbs. (F-350). Tires: G78-15B (F-100); L78-15D (F-150); 8.00 x 16.5D (F-250/F-350).

POWERTRAIN OPTIONS: Engines: 302 cid V-8 (F-100 regular cab). 351 cid V-8. 400 cid V-8. 460 cid V-8 (F-150/F-250/F-350). Transmissions: Four-speed manual transmission. Cruise-O-Matic automatic transmission.

CONVENIENCE OPTIONS: Air-conditioner. Breathable knitted vinyl seat trim. Speed control. Flip-open windows on Supercabs (plain or tinted glass). Dual tape paint strips for Stylesides (available in five paint-keyed colors). Bright metal bodyside moldings with vinyl insert (Standard Ranger/Ranger XLT). Rear step bumper for Stylesides. Bright contour rear bumper. Painted channel-type bumper for Faresides. AM radio. AM/FM radio. AM/FM stereo radio (with speaker in each door). Black or white texture painted roof with bright drip and back of cab moldings. Tool stowage box with locking door (located in curbside of pickup box skirt on 8 ft. Stylesides). Fixed Western-type 6.5 ft. by 9.5 in. painted mirrors. Recreation swing-out bright mirrors. Low-profile bright mirrors. Non-telescopic painted mirrors. Box cover for 8 ft. Stylesides (Standard) Includes: Tinted side and rear windows; roof vent; and liftgate. (Deluxe) Includes: Sliding side windows with screens; dome light; Tu-Tone; and sliding front box cover window (available with white cover). Super cooling package available with 351 and bigger V-8s. Spare tire lock. Sliding rear window. Bright tie-down hooks for Stylesides (three on each side and two on tailgate). Concealed spare tire in right side of F-350 Styleside and Camper Special models. Mag style wheelcovers for 15 in. wheels. Full wheelcovers on Pickups with 15 in. and 16.5 in. wheels. Slide-out spare tire carrier. Auxiliary 12-volt 68 amp.-hr. battery with dual circuit charging system for campers. Full-width foam rear seat that folds flat when not in use (Supercab). Two jump seats with foam padded cushion and back that fold out of the way when not in use (Supercab). Convenience Package with intermittent wipers; glove box lock; and 12 in. day/night rearview mirror. Electric block heater. Electric rear window defroster. Flareside special trim package. Color-keyed rubber floor mats. Auxiliary fuel tank. Locking fuel cap. Dual electric horns. Bright hubcaps. Five amber clearance lights. Visibility Light Group including cargo glove box, ashtray, engine compartment and under instrument panel lights. Northland Special with engine block heater; 50 percent (-35 degrees F.) antifreeze mixture; 68 amp.-hr. battery; 60 -amp. alternator; and limited-slip rear axle. Protection Package with bright door edge guards, front bumper guards and front bumper rub strip. Heavy-duty black vinyl seat upholstery. Tinted glass (windshield or all around.) Trailer towing packages up to 10,000 lbs. F-250/350 Camper Special Package with 60 -amp. alternator; 68 amp.-hr. battery (77 amp.- hr, with 460 cid V-8); oil pressure gauge; ammeter; dual electric horns; bright 6.75 in. x 9-1/2 in. swing-out recreation mirrors; front and rear stabilizer bars; extra-cooling package; Camper wiring harness; heavy-duty shocks front and rear; Camper Special emblem; and heavy-duty in-tank oil cooler with Cruise-O-Matic (standard on F-350 Camper Special with 140 in. wheelbase). Pinstripe Accent Package with (6.5 ft. Flareside) black channel rear bumper; tape pinstriping; and black-out painted grille insert. Four-wheel drive (F-150/F-250). Custom Decor Group with knitted vinyl seat trim, color-keyed floor mats with insulation, bright moldings around windshield and rear window, bright drip rail moldings, bright hubcaps. Ranger package with bright moldings on windshield; rear window; rear quarter windows (Supercab) and drip rails; plus bright hubcaps (single rears); nylon carpeting; instrument panel molding with black accent; door panels with bright moldings; shoulder high vinyl bolster around rear area (Supercab); seatback cover; additional cab insulation; perforated, insulated headlining; and two courtesy lights (Supercab). Stylesides with Ranger package also include bright side moldings with vinyl inserts and bright tailgate moldings. Ranger XLT includes same equipment as 1976, plus Stylesides had new upper and lower bodyside molding combination; bright wheelcovers; wall-to-wall cut-pile carpeting; covered floor insulation; vinyl headlining with sound-absorbing backing; cloth-and-vinyl or Super Soft vinyl seat upholstery; vinyl door trim panels with insulation; convenience group features; and instrument panel with simulated woodgrain applique within bright surround moldings. Also available was a new XLT Luxury Group with plush cloth and Super Soft vinyl upholstery; padded design headliner; color-keyed wheelcovers; carpeted floor; and carpeted back panel up to rear window on behind-the-seat storage area.

HISTORICAL: Ford light conventional truck sales totaled 723,925 for 1977. Total model year production of the models featured above was 964,236. This excludes Cutaway Vans made for motorhome chassis and larger medium- and heavy-duty trucks. For the calendar year, Ford division dealers sold a record 1,214,622 commercial vehicles of all types to edge out Chevrolet in the retail sales race. Model year sales, by type, were: [Light Conventional] 723,925; [Van] 138,064; [Bronco] 13,335; [Ranchero] 21,438; [Courier] 13,167; and [Medium- and Heavy-duty] 81,459.

1978 FORD

RANCHERO 500 PICKUP: Styling was unchanged for 1978. Standard features included: SelectShift Cruise-O-Matic transmission. Power steering and brakes. Bright hubcaps. Vinyl door trim and spare tire compartment. Carpeting. Vinyl-covered bench seat in blue, russet, grey, jade, chamois or saddle. Colors offered on 1978 Rancheros were: Russet (metallic); Dove grey; Dark midnight-blue; creme; Light chamois; black; Polar white; silver (metallic); Light blue; Dark jade (metallic); Dark brown (metallic); Bright Blue Glow; Light Jade Glow; champagne (metallic). Tu-Tone option (500 only) included accent color applied on roof, hood and lower bodyside.

RANCHERO GT PICKUP: The GT was once again the most popular Ranchero. It had most of the same items as the 500 plus: Flight bench seat in Mateao vinyl or optional cloth and vinyl. Cut-pile carpeting. GT stripe. Dual sport mirrors. Bright hubcaps with trim rings.

RANCHERO SQUIRE PICKUP: In addition to most of the items on the 500, the Squire had: Simulated woodgrain paneling on sides and tailgate. Deluxe wheelcovers.

I.D. DATA [Ranchero]: The VIN consists of 11 symbols. The first symbol is the last digit of the model year. The second symbol indicates the assembly plant. The third and fourth symbols indicate the product line and body style. The fifth symbol indicates the engine. The last six symbols are the sequential production number. Most 1978 Rancheros (76 percent) came with one of the optional engines.

Model	Body Type	Price	Weight	Prod. Total
Ranchero 500 — 1/2-Ton — 118 in. w.b. — V-8				
97D	Sedan-Pickup	5179	3698	9,911
Ranchero GT — 1/2-Ton — 118 in. w.b. — V-8				
97R	Sedan-Pickup	5400	3716	12,469
Ranchero Squire — 1/2-Ton — 118 in. w.b. — V-8				
97K	Sedan-Pickup	5532	3728	907

NOTE 1: Total production: 23,287.
NOTE 2: Prices/weights for base V-8.
NOTE 3: A limited number of Shelby GT Rancheros were made for Ford Motor Co. These had a 400 cid V-8, electronic ignition, twin comfort-lounge seats, T-Bird door panels and gray dashboards with full instrumentation.

ENGINE [Base V-8]: Displacement: 351 M (modified). V-8. Net horsepower: 134 nhp at 3800 rpm. Bore & stroke: 4 in. x 3.5 in. Compression ratio: 8.4:1. Carburetor: Two-barrel.

CHASSIS: Wheebase: 118 in. Overall length: 220.1 in. Overall height: 53.5 in. GVW: 5,452-5,904 lbs. Tires: G78-14B (G70-14B on GT).

POWERTRAIN OPTIONS: Engines: 351 cid V-8. 400 cid V-8.

CONVENIENCE OPTIONS: Dual sport mirrors. Wire wheelcovers. Magnum 500 chrome wheels. SelectAire air-conditioner (available with manual or automatic temperature control). AM/FM stereo with 8-track tape. AM/FM stereo with cassette tape player. AM/FM stereo with search feature. AM/FM stereo. AM/FM monaural radio. AM radio. Day/date clock. Sports Instrumentation Group including wood-tone applique around instrument cluster pods; tachometer, temperature and oil pressure gauges; trip odometer; ammeter; electric clock; and luxury steering wheel. Tilt steering wheel. Cornering lamps. Six-way power flight bench or split bench seat. Appearance Protection Group with door edge guards, floor mat and license plate frames. Deluxe wheelcovers. Wheel trim rings. Vinyl roof in black, white, red, blue and cordovan (not available with GT or Tu-Tone paint). Wheel lip moldings. Convenience Group with intermittent windshield wipers, automatic parking brake release, right-hand remote-control mirror, trip odometer, and passenger visor vanity mirror. Fingertip speed control. Illuminated entry system. Light Group, including engine compartment, glove box and ashtray lights; plus door ajar warning light and headlights-on warning buzzer. Power door windows. Tinted glass all around. Engine block heater. Heavy-duty. Handling Suspension: Heavy-duty rear springs, and rear stablizer bar. Heavy-duty alternator. Heavy-duty battery. Medium-duty trailer towing package. Traction-lok differential (not available in California). Bumper Protection Group with front and rear bumper guards and front bumper rub strips. Bodyside protection molding with vinyl insert for 500 (not available with Tu-Tone). Lower bodyside protection (application of vinyl along the lower sides to help protect against stone pecking.) Brougham Decor Group with split bench seat in cloth and vinyl trim or Matao vinyl upholstery. Bucket seats. H78-14B, HR78-14B, G70-14B or H70-14B tires.

1978 Ford 1/2-Ton Bronco Ranger Sport Utility Wagon 4x4 (JAG)

BRONCO CUSTOM: The four-wheel drive Bronco was completely restyled for 1978. As sales literature stated, it was all-new top-to-bottom and front-to-rear. Front end design echoed that used on the full-size Pickups. The honeycomb theme grille and two recessed, rectangular headlights were surrounded by bright moldings. The amber wraparound parking lights were beneath the headlights. Ford was printed in block letters on the face of the hood. The rectangular side-marker lights were located in the bodyside sculpturing, which ran straight from the upper part of the headlight level almost the entire length of the truck. Standard features included: Deep foam bucket seats. Color-keyed instrument and door trim panel in red, black, blue, green or tan. Steering wheel and horn pad in black, sun visors in white. Bright hubcaps. Bright door-mounted mirrors on both sides. Black-painted front and rear bumpers. Power brakes. 25-gal. fuel tank. Four-speed manual transmission. Most 1978 Broncos, 78.9 percent, came with an automatic transmission. Bronco color choices for 1979 were: Raven black; Wimbledon white; Candy-apple red; Castillo red; Medium copper; silver (metallic); Midnight blue (metallic); Light blue; Bahama blue; Dark jade (metallic); Light jade; Chrome yellow; tan; cream; Dark brown (metallic); Jade Glow; Dark Cinnamon Glow; Bright emerald; and Bright yellow. A choice of black or white fiberglass rear roof section was offered to go with any exterior color. Tu-Tone choices: Special hood and roof Tu-Tone. Black or white only (to match black or white fiberglass roof) was available with all solid exterior colors. Combination: With hood/roof/body side in black or white only to match black or white roof (includes special hood/roof and Deluxe Tu-Tone with moldings). Deluxe Tu-Tone: With accent color applied within bodyside molding and upper and lower tailgate moldings (bodyside moldings included).

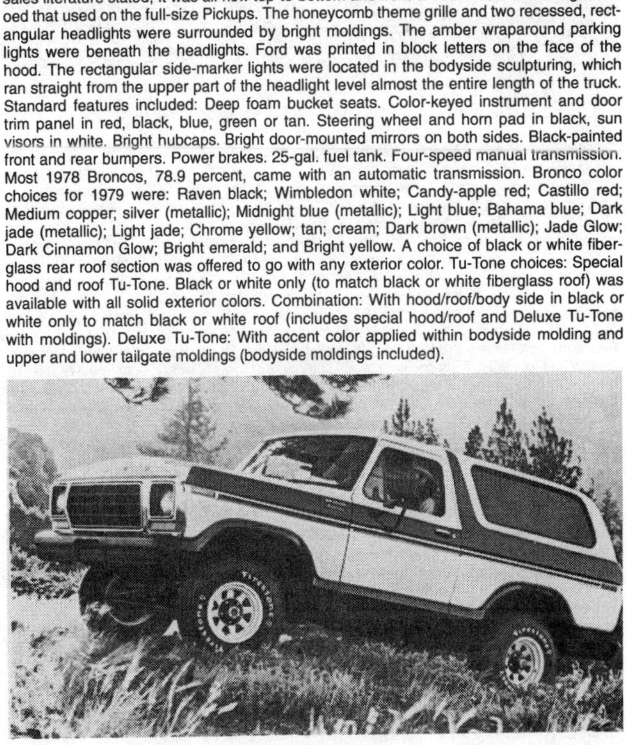

1978 Ford 1/2-Ton Bronco Custom Sport Utility Wagon 4x4 (RCA)

I.D. DATA [Bronco]: The VIN consists of 11 symbols. The first three indicate the series. The fourth indicates the engine. The fifth shows the assembly plant. The last six are the sequential production number.

Model	Body Type	Price	Weight	Prod. Total
Bronco 4x4 — 1/2-Ton — 104 in. w.b. — V-8				
U-150	Wagon	6543	4509	69,120

NOTE 1: Prices and weight for base V-8.

ENGINE [Base V-8]: V-block. OHV. Eight cylinders. Bore & stroke: 4.0 x 3.50. Displacement: 351 cid. Net horsepower: 156 at 4000 rpm. Net torque: 262 at 2200 rpm. Carburetor: Two-barrel.

CHASSIS: Wheelbase: 104 in. Overall length: 180.3 in. Overall width: 79.3 in. Overall height: 75.5 in. Tires: L78 x 15B.

POWERTRAIN OPTIONS: Transmissions: Cruise-O-Matic automatic. Engine: 400 cid V-8.

CONVENIENCE OPTIONS: Bright wheel lip moldings. Inside spare tire cover. Mag style wheelcovers. Narrow bodyside paint stripe. ComfortVent heater. Console (with front bucket seats). Convenience Group with intermittent wipers, gathered map pockets and 12 in. day/night mirror. Heavy-duty scissor-type jack. Insulation package. Lighted visor vanity mirror. Rear floor mat. Front bench seat. Folding rear bench seat (includes rear floor mat). Tinted glass all around. Visibility Group with lights in glove box, ashtray and underhood; instrument panel courtesy lights; and dome light with integral map light (not included with front bench seat). Handling Package including rear stablizer bar, quad front and heavy-duty rear shocks. Northland Special Package including 68-amp.-hr. battery, 60 -amp. alternator, dual 600-watt engine block heater and limited-slip rear axle. Rear stablizer bar. Skid plates for standard fuel tank and transfer case. Trailer towing packages (light- and heavy-duty). 32-gal. fuel tank in lieu of standard (includes skid plate). Inside locking hood release. Protection Group with bright door edge guards, front bumper guards and front bumper rub strip. Security Group with locking gas cap, inside hood release lock, spare tire lock and locking glove box. Free Wheeling Package with tri-color striping; black bumpers; dual black low-mount mirrors; sport steering wheel; black glove box applique; and five 15 x 6 styled steel wheels with raised white-letter tires (15 x 8 styled steel wheels available after Nov. 7, 1977). Ranger XLT with rectangular headlamps; bright front and rear bumpers; bright molding around front windshield; rear side windows; wheel lips and lower section of tailgate; side molding with black vinyl insert and bright taillight bezels; cut-pile carpeting; door trim panels with woodgrain accent; seat covering in vinyl or vinyl and cloth; spare tire cover; wood-tone dash with bright moldings; and Ranger XLT plaque on the glove box. Tilt steering wheel. Privacy glass. Low-mount Western mirrors. Air-conditioning. AM digital clock radio. AM/FM stereo. Quad front shock absorbers. Recreation swing-out mirrors. Sliding side windows. GT bar. Sport steering wheel. Five-slot forged aluminum 15 in. wheels. Maintenance-free battery. Speed control. Swing-away spare tire carrier. 40-channel CB radio. Front tow hooks. Front and rear contour bumpers. 10-hole forged aluminum 15 in. wheels. Painted styled steel white 15 x 6 wheels. Part-time 4x4 (with automatic). A total of 68.7 percent of 1979 Broncos had bucket seats, 63 percent tinted glass, 32.4 percent an AM radio and 53.3 percent Air-conditioning.

1978 Ford 1/2-Ton Bronco Sport Utility Wagon 4x4 (OCW)

ECONOLINE E-100 CARGO VAN: Econolines received a minor facelift for 1978. The very similar (but revised) grille had less brightwork. This gave it a semi blacked-out appearance. A different paint treatment for two-tone Vans added to the new look. The speedometer now had kilometers per hour readings beneath the miles per hour markings. Standard feaures were: Full-foam driver's bucket seat. Color-keyed vinyl seat trim in black, blue, jade green or tan. Turn indicators with lane change feature. Padded full-width instrument panels. Brake warning light. Two-speed electric windshield wipers. Wiper-arm-mounted washer jets. Dome lights. Front compartment headlining and insulated floor mat with scuff plates. Electric horn. Door checks. Argent silver-painted bumpers and hubcaps. Bright windshield molding. Painted 5 in. x 8 in. mirrors. Hinged side cargo doors (sliding door available at no extra cost). Power steering. Three-speed manual. Twin-I-Beam front suspension. Standard Econoline colors for 1978 included: Wimbledon white; Candy-apple red; Light blue; silver (metallic); Light jade; Dark brown (metallic); Indio tan Coral; Midnight blue (metallic); Raven black; Chrome yellow; Dark jade (metallic). Blue Glow, Jade Glow, and Cinnamon Glow paints were optional. Four Tu-Tone paint schemes were offered. Tu-Tone paint schemes were available.

ECONOLINE E-100 WINDOW VAN: As the name suggests, the Window Van had glass all around. It shared standard features with the cargo van.

ECONOLINE E-100 DISPLAY VAN: This model had windows at the rear and on the right-hand side. It came with the same standard features as Cargo Van.

I.D. DATA [Vans]: The VIN consists of 11 symbols. The first three indicate the series. The fourth indicates the engine. The fifth shows the assembly plant. The last six are the sequential production number.

Model	Body Type	Price	Weight	Prod. Total
E-100 Van — 1/2-Ton — 124 in./138 in. w.b. — V-8				
E-040	Cargo Van	4840	3810	Note 1
E-050	Window Van	4965	3837	Note 1
E-600	Display Van	4927	3824	Note 1

NOTE 1: Production: [Econoline] 238,833.

NOTE 2: Prices/weights for base V-8; deduct for six.

ENGINE [Base Six]: Inline. Six-cylinder. OHV. Bore & stroke: 4.00 in. x 3.98 in. Displacement: 300 cid. Net horsepower: 117 hp at 3000 rpm. Net torque: 223 lbs.-ft. at 1600 rpm. Compression ratio: 8.9:1. Carburetor: One-barrel.

ENGINE [Base V-8]: V-block. Eight-cylinder. OHV. Bore & stroke: 4.00 x 3.5 in. Displacement: 351 cid. Net horsepower: 156 at 4000 rpm. Net torque: 262 lbs.-ft. at 2200 rpm.

ECONOLINE E-150 CARGO VAN: The E-150 could run on leaded or unleaded gas. It had a slightly higher GVW rating than the E-100. Unlike the E-100, it could be operated on either leaded or unleaded gasoline. Standard features echoed those on the E-100.

ECONOLINE E-150 SUPER CARGO VAN: This van was introduced in January 1978. It had a 20 in. extended rear overhang. That allowed owners to carry longer loads. Standard features were same as on the E-100.

ECONOLINE E-150 DISPLAY VAN: The van shared styling with the E-100 Display Van but had greater load capacity.

ECONOLINE E-150 SUPER DISPLAY VAN: See E-150 Super Cargo Van.

ECONOLINE E-150 WINDOW VAN: This van shared styling with the E-100 Window Van, but had greater load capacity.

ECONOLINE E-150 SUPER WINDOW VAN: See E-150 Super Cargo Van.

I.D. DATA [Vans]: The VIN consists of 11 symbols. The first three indicate the series. The fourth indicates the engine. The fifth shows the assembly plant. The last six are the sequential production number.

Model	Body Type	Price	Weight	Prod. Total
E-150 Van — 1/2-Ton — 124 in. w.b. — V-8				
E-140	Cargo Van	5008	3741	Note 1
E-160	Display Van	5095	3755	Note 1
E-150	Window Van	5133	3768	Note 1
E-100 Super Van — 1/2-Ton — 138 in. w.b. — V-8				
E-140	Cargo Van	5232	—	Note 1
E-160	Display Van	5319	—	Note 1
E-150	Window Van	5319	—	Note 1

NOTE 1: Production: [Econoline] 238,833.

NOTE 2: Prices/weights for base V-8; deduct for six.

ENGINE [Base Six]: Inline. Six-cylinder. OHV. Bore & stroke: 4.00 in. x 3.98 in. Displacement: 300 cid. Net horsepower: 117 hp at 3000 rpm. Net torque: 223 lbs.-ft. at 1600 rpm. Compression ratio: 8.9:1. Carburetor: One-barrel.

ENGINE [Base V-8]: V-block. Eight-cylinder. OHV. Bore & stroke: 4.00 x 3.5 in. Displacement: 351 cid. Net horsepower: 156 at 4000 rpm. Net torque: 262 lbs.-ft. at 2200 rpm.

ECONOLINE E-250 CARGO VAN: The new E-250 had a higher GVW rating and more heavy duty front and rear axles, than the E-150. It also came with eight, rather than five, hole wheels. Standard features were the same as those on the E-100.

ECONOLINE E-250 SUPER CARGO VAN: See E-150 Super Cargo Van.

ECONOLINE E-250 DISPLAY VAN: This vehicle shared styling and features with the E-100, but had greater load capacity.

ECONOLINE E-250 SUPER DISPLAY VAN: See E-150 Super Cargo Van.

ECONOLINE E-250 WINDOW VAN: This vehicle shared styling and features with the E-100 Window Van, but had greater load capacity.

ECONOLINE E-250 SUPER WINDOW VAN: See E-150 Super Cargo Van.

ECONOLINE E-250 CUTAWAY VAN: This van with Camper Special Packages was designed to readily accommodate custom motor homes.

ECONOLINE E-250 PARCEL DELIVERY: The E-250 Parcel Delivery van was capable of hauling a payload up to 2,340 lbs. Its cargo area was 149.9 in. long and 74.3 in. high. The rear door opening was 84.7 in. wide.

I.D. DATA [Vans]: The VIN consists of 11 symbols. The first three indicate the series. The fourth indicates the engine. The fifth shows the assembly plant. The last six are the sequential production number.

Model	Body Type	Price	Weight	Prod. Total
E-250 Van — 3/4-Ton — 124 in. w.b. — V-8				
E-240	Cargo Van	5356	4217	Note 1
E-260	Display Van	5444	4232	Note 1
E-250	Window Van	5482	4245	Note 1
E-250 Super Van — 3/4-Ton — 138 in. w.b. — V-8				
E-240	Cargo Van	5437	—	Note 1
E-260	Display Van	5525	—	Note 1
E-250	Window Van	5563	—	Note 1
E-250 Van — 3/4-Ton — 138 in. w.b. — V-8				
E-270	Cutaway Van	5237	—	Note 1
E-280	Parcel Delivery	6553	5294	Note 1

NOTE 1: Production: [Econoline] 238,833.

NOTE 2: Prices/weights for base V-8; deduct for six.

ENGINE [Base Six]: Inline. Six-cylinder. OHV. Bore & stroke: 4.00 in. x 3.98 in. Displacement: 300 cid. Net horsepower: 117 hp at 3000 rpm. Net torque: 223 lbs.-ft. at 1600 rpm. Compression ratio: 8.9:1. Carburetor: One-barrel.

ENGINE [Base V-8]: V-block. Eight-cylinder. OHV. Bore & stroke: 4.00 x 3.5 in. Displacement: 351 cid. Net horsepower: 156 at 4000 rpm. Net torque: 262 lbs.-ft. at 2200 rpm.

ECONOLINE E-350 CARGO VAN: This was the top-of-the-line Econoline. It had heavy-duty front and rear shocks and a greater load capacity than the other series. Standard features were the same as those on the E-100.

ECONOLINE E-350 SUPER CARGO VAN: See E-150 Super Cargo Van.

ECONOLINE E-350 DISPLAY VAN: See E-250 Display Van.

ECONOLINE E-350 SUPER DISPLAY VAN: See E-150 Super Cargo Van.

ECONOLINE E-350 WINDOW VAN: See E-250 Window Van.

ECONOLINE E-350 SUPER WINDOW VAN: See E-150 Super Cargo Van.

ECONOLINE E-350 CUTAWAY VAN: See E-250 Cutaway Van.

ECONOLINE E-350 PARCEL DELIVERY: This heavy-duty Van came in two wheelbases. Styling and features were the same as those offered on the E-250.

I.D. DATA [Vans]: The VIN consists of 11 symbols. The first three indicate the series. The fourth indicates the engine. The fifth shows the assembly plant. The last six are the sequential production number.

Model	Body Type	Price	Weight	Prod. Total
E-350 Super Van — 1-Ton — 138 in. w.b. — V-8				
E-340	Cargo Van	5538	4376	Note 1
E-360	Display Van	5627	4395	Note 1
E-350	Window Van	5665	4385	Note 1
E-350 Super Van — 1-Ton — 155 in. w.b. — V-8				
E-370	Cutaway Van	5354	—	Note 1
E-380	Parcel Delivery	7318	5648	Note 1

NOTE 1: Production: [Econoline] 238,833.

NOTE 2: Prices/weights for base V-8; deduct for six.

ENGINE [Base Six]: Inline. Six-cylinder. OHV. Bore & stroke: 4.00 in. x 3.98 in. Displacement: 300 cid. Net horsepower: 117 hp at 3000 rpm. Net torque: 223 lbs.-ft. at 1600 rpm. Compression ratio: 8.9:1. Carburetor: One-barrel.
ENGINE [Base V-8]: V-block. Eight-cylinder. OHV. Bore & stroke: 4.00 x 3.5 in. Displacement: 351 cid. Net horsepower: 156 at 4000 rpm. Net torque: 262 lbs.-ft. at 2200 rpm.
CHASSIS: Wheelbase: 124 in. and 138 in. Overall length: 186 in. (E-100/E-150 124 in. wheelbase); 206.8 in. (138 in. wheelbase); 226.8 in. (Super Vans). Overall height: 79.6 in. (E-100); 81 in. (E-150 124 in. wheelbase); 81.2 in. (E-150 138 in. wheelbase); 82.6 in. (E-250); 84.5 in. (E-350). GVW: 5,750-11,000 lbs. Tires: F78-15B PT (E-100); L78-15B PT (E-150); 8.00 x 16.5D TT (E-250, 8.75 x 16.5E C Parcel Delivery Van); 9.50 x 16.5D TT (E-350); 8.00 x 16.5D Parcel Delivery Van.
POWERTRAIN OPTIONS: Transmissions: Cruise-O-Matic automatic. Four-speed manual with overdrive. Engines: 351 cid V-8. 460 cid V-8 (E-250/E-350).
CONVENIENCE OPTIONS: Custom Van with (added to or in place of standard) color-keyed padded full-length instrument panel with woodgrained vinyl applique; front side and door trim panels; insulated front floor mats; roof rail garnish moldings; bright hubcaps; tailight bezels; and vent and rear window frames. Chateau Van with (added to or in place of Custom) Super Soft Ruffino vinyl seat trim; color-keyed cut pile carpeting on front floor; padded vinyl front door trim panels with woodgrained vinyl applique in center and carpeting lower panel; woodgrained vinyl horn bar insert in steering wheel; and courtesy lights for all doors. Bright grille, bright bumpers, Bright bodyside and rear moldings. Wheelcovers. Right-hand sliding cargo door. Adjustable or flip-fold passenger seat. High-output heater and defroster. Auxiliary hot water heater. Cruising Van with captain's chairs; full-length carpeting; deluxe insulation package with woodgrain vinyl paneling and sport steering wheel. Free Wheeling with: (Interior) full-length carpeting, front door trim panels and deluxe insulation package; (Exterior) Five-slot forged aluminum wheels; raised white-letter tires; black bumpers; grille; stripe; and mirrors. Bright grille and/or front and rear bumpers. Full-length, insulated carpet or mat (138 in. wheelbase only). Courtesy light switches, front or all doors. Two-stage door positioners for hinged cargo doors. Northland Special Package includes engine block heater; -35 F antifreeze; 68 amp.-hr. battery; 60 -amp. alternator; and high-output heater. Engine block heater. Locking fuel cap. Tinted glass. Full-length hardboard headlining. Bodyside tape stripe (black, tan, white or gold). Bright grille surround molding. Black push bar. Fog lights. Ten-inch port hole windows with privacy glass. Sport rails. Tilt steering. Speed control. Dual electric horns. Insulation Package. Protection Group with front door edge guards and front and side sliding door stepwell pads and front bumper guards. Huntsman cloth seat trim. Spare tire and wheel. Spare tire cover. Bright hubcaps. Handling Package with front stablizer bar, heavy-duty shocks and heavy-duty front springs. Front stablizer bar. Captains chair. Air-conditioning. Power steering. Auxiliary fuel tank. Trailer towing packages. Swing-out recreation mirrors. Low-mount Western mirrors. AM radio. AM/FM stereo. AM/FM stereo with tape player. Door windows for rear and/or side cargo doors. One-way glass in rear side windows and rear door. Flip-open windows for cargo doors. Simulated leather wrapped steering wheel. Mag style wheelcovers. Painted styled steel wheels. Ten-hole forged aluminum wheels. Five-slot forged aluminum wheels. Step bumper. Sport steering wheel. ComfortVent heater (not available with air-conditioning).

1978 Ford Club Wagon Chateau Passenger Van (OCW)

E-100 CLUB WAGON: The new Club Wagon shared the mild styling changes found on the Econoline. E-100 was offered in five- and eight-passenger versions. Among the standard features were: Full foam front bucket seats. Color-keyed patterned vinyl seat trim. Seat belts. Color-two-speed electric windshield wipers. Wiper-arm-mounted washer jets. 10 in. rearview mirror. Dome lights. Insulated floor mat with scuff plates. Three armrests. Dual horns. Flip-open windows in sliding door and opposite windows. Painted bumpers, 5 in. x 8 in. mirrors and hubcaps. Bright windshield molding.
E-150 CLUB WAGON: This was a slightly more heavy-duty version of the E-100. It could be had in 124 in. or 138 in. wheelbase and was also offered in five- and eight-passenger versions. Standard features were same as those on the E-100.
E-150 SUPER WAGON: This was basically the same as the 138 in. wheelbase E-150, but had a 20 in. extended rear overhang.
E-250 CLUB WAGON: The E250 Club Wagon could be had with five-, eight- or 12- passenger capacity. It had most of the same features as the E-100.
E-250 SUPER WAGON: This was basically an E-250 with a 20 in. rear overhang.
I.D. DATA [Vans]: The VIN consists of 11 symbols. The first three indicate the series. The fourth indicates the engine. The fifth shows the assembly plant. The last six are the sequential production number.

Model	Body Type	Price	Weight	Prod. Total
E-100 Van — 1/2-Ton — 124 in./138 in. w.b. — V-8				
E-100	Club Wagon	5485	4090	Note 1
E-100 Van — 1/2-Ton — 124 in./138 in. w.b. — V-8				
E-150	Club Wagon	5680	4225	Note 1
E-150	Super Wagon	6194	—	Note 1
E-250 Van — 3/4-Ton — 138 in. w.b. — V-8				
E-250	Club Wagon	5921	4735	Note 1
E-250	Super Wagon	6506	—	Note 1

NOTE 1: Production: [Club Wagon] 44,484.
NOTE 2: Prices/weights for base V-8; deduct for six.

ENGINE [Base Six]: Inline. Six-cylinder. OHV. Bore & stroke: 4.00 in. x 3.98 in. Displacement: 300 cid. Net horsepower: 117 hp at 3000 rpm. Net torque: 223 lbs.-ft. at 1600 rpm. Compression ratio: 8.9:1. Carburetor: One-barrel.
ENGINE [Base V-8]: V-block. Eight-cylinder. OHV. Bore & stroke: 4.00 x 3.5 in. Displacement: 351 cid. Net horsepower: 156 at 4000 rpm. Net torque: 262 lbs.-ft. at 2200 rpm.
CHASSIS: Wheelbase: 124 in. (E-100); 138 in. (E-150/E-250). Overall length: See Econoline. GVW: 5,600-5,900 lbs. (E-100); 6,010-6,300 lbs. (E-150); 7,000-8,450 lbs. (E-250 five-passenger). Tires: G78 x 15B (E-100); H78 x 15D (E-150); 8.00 x 16D (E-250).
POWERTRAIN OPTIONS: Engines: 351 cid V-8, 460 cid V-8. Transmissions: SelectShift Cruise-O-Matic automatic.
CONVENIENCE OPTIONS: Auxiliary fuel tank. Speed control. Power steering. Captain's chair. AM radio. AM/FM stereo radio. AM/FM stereo with tape player. High-capacity or front only air-conditioner. Privacy glass. Wheelcovers. Swing-Lok Western mirrors. Swing-Lok low-mount Western mirrors. Bright non-telescopic mirrors. Swing-out recreation mirrors. High-output heater. Roof luggage carrier. Spare tire lock. Low-mount Swing-Lok bright mirrors. AM/FM monaural radio. Bright grille and/or bumpers. Full-length insulated floor mat. Free Wheeling Option with black rocker panel paint accent; painted bumpers; grille and mirrors; forged aluminum wheels; and raised white-letter tires. Courtesy light switches for all doors. Hinged side doors in place of sliding door. Two-stage door positioners for all hinged double doors. Locking gas cap. Intermittent two-speed windshield wipers. Instrument Package with fuel monitor warning light; ammeter; and oil pressure gauge. Northland Special Package. Engine block heater. Tinted glass. Full-length hardbound headlining. Insulation package. Protection Group (front door edge guards and front and side sliding door step well pads). Shoulder harness. Spare tire cover. Bright hubcaps. Low-Line Camper Package. High-Line Camper Special Package. Trailer Towing Packages. Custom Package includes (in addition to or in place of standard) color-keyed padded full-length instrument panel with woodgrained vinyl applique; color-keyed seat pedestal, cowl trim panels, padded vinyl door trim panels; cigarette lighter; insulated full-length floor mats; window garnish moldings; color-keyed armrests on three- and four-passenger seats; three coat hooks; aluminum scuff plates on side and rear doors; bright hubcaps; taillight bezels; and window frames. Chateau Package includes (in addition to or in place of Custom) Super Soft vinyl seat trim; color-keyed cut-pile carpeting full-length of floor; lower section of engine cover and rear wheel wells; vinyl door trim panels with woodgrained vinyl applique in center and carpeted lower panel; color-keyed vinyl headlining (insulated); woodgrained vinyl horn bar insert; color-keyed vinyl spare tire cover; bright grille; bumpers; lower bodyside trim; and rear moldings. Convenience Group with courtesy light door switches; day/night mirror; and two-speed windshield wipers.
COURIER PICKUP: The biggest styling change for 1978 was moving the parking lamps from the bumper to the grille. Standard features included: Vinyl headliner. Inside hood release. Full-width vinyl upholstered seat. Hinged seatback for easy access to stowage area. Independent front suspension. Six-leaf rear springs. Double-acting shocks front and rear.
I.D. DATA [Courier]: The VIN consists of 11 symbols. The first indicates the manufacturer. The second indicates the assembly plant. The third indicates the series. The fourth indicates the engine. The fifth (a letter) indicates the model year. The sixth indicates the production month. The last five are the sequential production number.

Model	Body Type	Price	Weight	Prod. Total
Courier — 1/2-Ton — 104.3 in. w.b. — Four				
—	Pickup	3895	2675	70,546

ENGINE [Base Four]: Inline. Four-cylinder. OHV. Bore & stroke: 3.07 in. x 3.70 in. Displacement: 110 cid. Net horsepower: 67 nhp at 4500 rpm. Carburetor: One-barrel.
CHASSIS: Wheelbase: 106.9 in. (6 ft. box); 112.8 in. (7 ft. box). Overall length: 177.9 in. (6 ft. box); 189.4 in. (7 ft. box). Overall width: 63 in. Overall height: 61.5 in. GVW: 3,965 lbs. Tires: 6.00 x 14 in.
POWERTRAIN OPTIONS: Transmissions: Floor-shifted automatic or five-speed manual (with overdrive).
CONVENIENCE OPTIONS: AM or AM/FM monaural radios. Air-conditioning. Tinted glass all around. Western rearview mirrors. Rear step bumper. Radial tires. Cast aluminum wheels. Cold Weather Group with electric rear window defroster, heavy-duty battery and high-output heater. Free Wheeling Packages A and B.
F-100 CUSTOM PICKUP: Ford light duty trucks had new styling for 1978. The Ford name was now spelled in block letters on the face of the hood. Wraparound amber parking lights were located below each of the headlights. The higher grille had a rectangular slots theme and was rounded slightly at the sides. Headlights and grille were encased in a thick bright trim frame (with optional chrome grille). The revised front bumper had a heftier appearance. Among standard features were: Chromed contour front bumper. Argent grille. Turn signal lever with lane change feature. Behind-seat storage area (regular cabs). Full-width, energy-absorbing instrument panel. Molded door trim panels with armrests. Large glove box with push-button latch and woodgrain vinyl applique on door. Argent silver hubcaps. Black carpet grain floor mat. Headlining. Door scuff plates. Mohave embossed vinyl seat trim. Twin-I-Beam front suspension. No rust front fender liners. Three-speed manual transmission. F-100 buyers could choose from all-steel welded construction Styleside or seasoned hardwood floor Flareside boxes in either long or short wheelbases. Supercab models were only offered with a Styleside box. Standard F-series colors for 1978 were: Raven black; Wimbledon white; Candy-apple red; Castillo red; silver (metallic); Midnight blue (metallic); Light blue; Bahama blue; Light jade; Dark jade (metallic); Chrome yellow; tan; Medium copper; and Dark brown (metallic). Dark Cinnamon Glow; Cream; Jade Glow; Maroon; Bright yellow; and tangerine were available on special order, at extra cost. Wimbledon white could be used as the accent color for any exterior colors, except silver (metallic) and cream. Regular, Deluxe and Combination Tu-Tones were available. Interior colors were: Black, blue, red, jade green or saddle.
I.D. DATA [F-Series]: The VIN consists of 11 symbols. The first three indicate the series. The fourth indicates the engine. The fifth shows the assembly plant. The last six are the sequential production number.

Model	Body Type	Price	Weight	Prod. Total
F-100 — 1/2-Ton — 117 in. w.b. — V-8				
81	Chassis & Cab	4168	3099	Note 1
83	Flareside 6.5 ft.	4399	3453	Note 1
83	Styleside 6.75 ft.	4399	3453	Note 1
F-100 — 1/2-Ton — 133 in. w.b. — V-8				
83	Flareside 8 ft.	4475	3518	Note 1
83	Styleside 8 ft.	4475	3518	Note 1
F-100 Supercab — 1/2-Ton — 155 in. w.b. — V-8				
81	Chassis & Cab	4726	3589	Note 1
83	Styleside 8 ft.	4957	3493	Note 1

NOTE 1: Production: [F-100] 158,591;
NOTE 2: Prices/weights for base V-8; deduct for six-cylinder.
NOTE 3: Add $750 for 4x4.

ENGINE [Base Six]: Inline. Six-cylinder. OHV. Bore & stroke: 4.00 in. x 3.98 in. Displacement: 300 cid. Net horsepower: 101 hp at 3000 rpm. Net torque: 223 lbs.-ft. at 1600 rpm. Compression ratio: 8.0:1. Carburetor: One-barrel.
ENGINE: [Base V-8]: V-block. OHV. Eight-cylinder. Bore and stroke: 4.0 x 3.0 in. Displacement: 302 cid. Net horsepower: 130 at 3800 rpm. Net torque: 222 lbs.-ft. at 2000 rpm.
ENGINE [Super Cab Base V-8]: V-block. OHV. Eight-cylinder. Bore and stroke: 4.00 in. x 3.50 in. Displacement: 360 cid. Horsepower: 145 nhp at 3800 rpm. Net torque: 264 lbs.-ft. at 2200 rpm. Carburetor: Two-barrel.

1978 Ford 1/2-Ton F-150 Crew Cab Styleside Pickup 4x4 (RCA)

F-150 CUSTOM PICKUP: The F-150 was a bit more heavy duty than the F-100. Its payload capacity was several hundred pounds greater. However, it came with most of the same standard features, plus power brakes. The Supercab (with area behind the front seat for an optional folding rear seat or two jump seats) was offered with the 6.75 ft. and 8 ft. Styleside box. The regular cab was only available in the 8 ft. Styleside or Flareside box.
I.D. DATA [F-Series]: The VIN consists of 11 symbols. The first three indicate the series. The fourth indicates the engine. The fifth shows the assembly plant. The last six are the sequential production number.

1978 Ford 1/2-Ton F-150 Ranger Supercab Styleside Pickup 4x4

Model	Body Type	Price	Weight	Prod. Total
F-150 — 1/2-Ton — 133 in. w.b. — V-8				
81	Chassis & Cab	4548	3190	Note 1
83	Flareside 8 ft.	4779	3579	Note 1
83	Styleside 8 ft.	4779	3579	Note 1
F-150 Supercab — 1/2-Ton — 155 in. w.b. — V-8				
81	Chassis & Cab	5030	3609	Note 1
83	Styleside	5262	3963	Note 1

NOTE 1: Production: [F-150] 422,264.
NOTE 2: Prices/weights for base V-8; deduct for six-cylinder.
ENGINE [Base Six]: Inline. Six-cylinder. OHV. Bore & stroke: 4.00 in. x 3.98 in. Displacement: 300 cid. Net horsepower: 101 hp at 3000 rpm. Net torque: 223 lbs.-ft. at 1600 rpm. Compression ratio: 8.0:1. Carburetor: One-barrel.
ENGINE [Base V-8]: V-block. OHV. Eight-cylinder. Bore and stroke: 4.0 x 3.0 in. Displacement: 302 cid. Net horsepower: 130 at 3800 rpm. Net torque: 222 lbs.-ft. at 2000 rpm.
ENGINE [Super Cab Base V-8]: V-block. OHV. Eight-cylinder. Bore and stroke: 4.00 in. x 3.50 in. Displacement: 360 cid. Horsepower: 145 nhp at 3800 rpm. Net torque: 264 lbs.-ft. at 2200 rpm. Carburetor: Two-barrel.

1978 Ford 1/2-Ton F-150 Custom Flareside Short Box Pickup 4x4

F-250 CUSTOM PICKUP: The F-250 had most of the same features as the F-100. It too was offered with regular or Supercabs and with Flareside or Styleside boxes. Power brakes and a three-speed manual transmission were standard.

I.D. DATA [F-Series]: The VIN consists of 11 symbols. The first three indicate the series. The fourth indicates the engine. The fifth shows the assembly plant. The last six are the sequential production number.

Model	Body Type	Price	Weight	Prod. Total
F-250 — 3/4-Ton — 133 in. w.b. — V-8				
81	Chassis & Cab	4856	3488	Note 1
83	Flareside	5087	3877	Note 1
83	Styleside	5087	3877	Note 1
F-250 Supercab — 3/4-Ton — 155 in. w.b. — V-8				
81	Chassis & Cab	5201	3734	Note 1
83	Styleside	5433	4088	Note 1
F-250 Crew Cabs — 3/4-Ton — 150 in. w.b. — V-8				
81	Chassis & Cab	4856	3488	Note 1
83	Styleside	5866	4455	Note 1

NOTE 1: Production: [F-250] 190,613.
NOTE 2: Prices/weights for base V-8; deduct for six.
NOTE 3: Supercabs available with 6.75 ft. and 8 ft. Styleside boxes.

1978 Ford 3/4-Ton F-250 Ranger XLT Styleside Pickup (JAG)

ENGINE [Base Six]: Displacement: 300 cid. Six. Horsepower: 120 nhp at 3400 rpm. Bore & stroke: 4.00 x 3.98. Compression ratio: 8.0:1. Carburetor: One-barrel. Supercab had 360 cid V-8.
ENGINE [Base V-8]: V-block. OHV. Eight-cylinder. Bore and stroke: 4.05 in. x 3.50 in. Displacement: 360 cid. Horsepower: 143 nhp at 3800 rpm. Net torque: 264 lbs.-ft. at 2200 rpm. Carburetor: Two-barrel.
F-350 CUSTOM PICKUP: The F-350 Pickup was only offered with the Styleside box. However, there were three choices of cabs: Regular, Super, or Crew. Front only shocks, (rear with Supercab) a four-speed manual transmission, and power front brakes were standard.
F-350 PLATFORM/STAKE: Two lengths of 1-ton F-350 Platform/Stakes were available: 9 ft. and 12 ft. Floor frames of the Platform/Stake were made of steel cross sills riveted to steel siderails. Floorboards were interlocked with steel brackets. Formed steel caps covered ends of the body sills. Side boards were hardwood and stakes were steel. A four-speed manual transmission was standard.

I.D. DATA [F-Series]: The VIN consists of 11 symbols. The first three indicate the series. The fourth indicates the engine. The fifth shows the assembly plant. The last six are the sequential production number.

Model	Body Type	Price	Weight	Prod. Total
F-350 — 1-Ton — 140 in. w.b. — V-8				
80	Stake 9 ft.	5814	4625	Note 1
81	Chassis & Cab	5187	3783	Note 1
83	Styleside	5776	4462	Note 1
86	Platform 9 ft.	5768	4385	Note 1
F-350 — 1-Ton — 137 in. w.b. — V-8				
80	Stake 12 ft.	—	—	Note 1
86	Platform 12 ft.	—	—	Note 1
F-350 Supercab — 1-Ton — 155 in. w.b. — V-8				
81	Chassis & Cab	5943	4285	Note 1
83	Styleside	6174	4674	Note 1
F-350 Crew Cabs — 1-Ton — 167 in. w.b. — V-8				
81	Chassis & Cab	5941	4307	Note 1
83	Styleside	6160	4748	Note 1

NOTE 1: Production: [F-350] 59,528.
NOTE 2: Prices/weights for base V-8; deduct for six.
ENGINE [Base Six]: Displacement: 300 cid. Six-cylinder. 120 nhp at 3400 rpm. Bore & stroke: 4.00 x 3.98. Compression ratio: 8.0:1. One-barrel carburetor.
ENGINE [Base V-8]: V-block. OHV. Eight-cylinder. Bore and stroke: 4.05 in. x 3.50 in. Displacement: 360 cid. Horsepower: 143 nhp at 3800 rpm. Net torque: 264 lbs.-ft. at 2200 rpm. Carburetor: Two-barrel.
CHASSIS: Wheelbase: 117 in. (F-100); 133 in. (F-100/F-150/F-250); 140 in. (F-350); 139 in. (F-100/F-150/F-250 Supercab); 155 in. (Supercab); 150 in. (F-250 Crew Cab); 166.5 in. (F-350 Crew Cab); 137 in. (F-350 Platform/Stake); 161 in. (F-350 Platform/Stake). Overall length: 195.1 in. (F-100 Styleside 6.75 ft.); 211.3 in. (F-100/F-150/F-250 Styleside 8 ft.); 140 in. (F-350 Styleside); 217.3 in. (F-100/F-150/F-250 6.75 ft. Supercab); 233.5 in. (8 ft. Supercab); 192.2 in. (F-100 Flareside 6.5 ft.); 208.4 in. (8 ft. Flareside); 221.8 in. (9 ft. Platform/Stake); 259.3 in. (12 ft. Platform/Stake). GVW: 4,900-5,800 lbs. (F-100); 6,050-6,400 lbs. (F-150); 6,200-7,800 lbs. (F-250); 8,300-10,000 lbs. (F-350). Tires: F78 x 15B PT (F-100); L78 x 15B PT (F-150); 8.00 x 16.5D TT (F-250); F-350).
POWERTRAIN OPTIONS: Transmissions: Four-speed manual; four-speed manual with overdrive; Cruise-O-Matic automatic. Engines: 302 cid V-8 (F-100/F-150); 351 cid V-8; 400 cid V-8; 460 cid V-8 (not available F-100).

1978 Ford 3/4-Ton F-250 Styleside Camper Special Pickup 4x4

1979 Ford 1/2-Ton Ranchero GT Sedan-Pickup (OCW)

CONVENIENCE OPTIONS: Bright box rails for 8 ft. Stylesides. Bright bodyside molding with black vinyl insert (for Custom and Ranger Stylesides and Chassis Cabs). Bright rocker panel molding (not available with Lariat, Crew Cab, Flareside, or Deluxe Tu-Tones). Bright wheel lip molding (Custom only). Narrow bodyside molding (for Custom Stylesides and Chassis Cabs). Dual narrow tape/paint stripe extending the full-length of Styleside Pickups (available in five colors with solid exterior paint or regular Tu-Tone only). Pickup box cover (has textured white fiberglass and tinted side and rear windows, adjustable roof vent and liftgate). Deluxe box cover (has sliding side windows with screens; bright side and rear window moldings; dome light; and Tu-Tone paint. Sliding front window available on white box cover. High-output heater. ComfortVent heater. Rear bench or jump seats (Supercab). Convenience Package with intermittent wipers, 12 in. day/night mirror and door map pockets. Visibility/Light Group with glove box, ashtray, under instrument panel, engine compartment and cargo box lights. Electric rear window defroster. Breathable knitted vinyl seat upholstery. Duraweave polyknit seat upholstery. Heavy-duty black vinyl seat upholstery. Rainbow tape stripe (Stylesides). GT bar (Stylesides). Forged aluminum wheels (five-slot brushed or 10-hole polished). Styled steel wheels. Step bumper. Free Wheeling Styleside with: (A) Interior in silver and black with red accents, rainbow side tape stripe, black-out grille and black front bumper (an optional black rear contour or step bumper was required); (B) Black GT bar, painted styled steel wheels in white or yellow and a spare tire lock. Free Wheeling Flareside with distinctive pinstriping (black, white or gold) and black-out grille, plus black front and rear bumpers. Four-wheel drive (now available on Supercab in addition to regular and Crew Cabs). Tilt steering wheel. CB radio. Engine block heater. Super cooling package. Trailer towing packages. Northland Special with engine block heater; -35 degrees F. antifreeze; 68 amp.-hr. battery; 60 -amp. alternator; and limited-slip rear axle. Handling Package with (F-100/F-150) front stabilizer bar, heavy-duty front and rear shocks and heavy-duty front springs (radial tires were recommended). Amber cab clearance lights (five). Locking inside hood release. Eight chromed tie-down hooks. Protection Package with bright door edge guards, front bumper guards and rub strip. Security Group with locking gas cap, glove box door, inside hood release and spare tire (regular carrier only). Recreation swing-out mirrors (6-3/4 in. x 9-1/2 in.). Low-mount Western 9 in. x 6 in. mirrors. Digital AM clock radio (displayed time and radio frequency). AM, AM/FM and AM/FM stereo radios. Air-conditioning. Illuminated vanity mirror. Speed control. Sliding rear window. Tool stowage box with locking door in curbside of pickup box skirt on 8 ft. Stylesides. Sport steering wheel with brushed spokes and simulated leather wrapped padded rim. Simulated leather wrapped steering wheel (included woodgrain vinyl horn pad with Custom and Ranger). Maintenance-free battery. Chromed or black contour rear bumpers (Styleside), black channel (Flareside). Painted styled steel 15 in. wheels. Slide-out spare tire carrier. Chrome grille and bright headlight surround (grille only with Custom). Mag-style wheelcovers for 15 in. wheels. Full wheelcovers for Pickups with 15 in. or 16.5 in. wheels. Flip open rear side windows on Supercabs (plain or tinted glass) with bright moldings and window latch. Ranger with (in addition to or in place of Custom items) rectangular headlights; bright moldings on roof drip rail and all windows; bright narrow bodyside moldings (all cabs and Stylesides); bright hubcaps (except dual rears); bright upper and lower tailgate moldings; bright taillight bezels; and chain-mail vinyl seat upholstery with color-keyed seatback cover (regular cabs); floor covering; sun visors and headliner with bright moldings; added sound insulation; and Skanda cloth upholstery optional at no extra charge. Ranger XLT Package with bright aluminum bodyside moldings on roof drip rail, windshield and rear window; trim on rear side windows (Supercab and Crew Cab); Westminster cloth seat upholstery with vinyl trim (chain-mail vinyl was a no-cost option); wall-to-wall cut-pile carpeting; covered floor insulation; vinyl headlining with sound-deadening backing; door trim panels with woodgrain vinyl insert and bright trim moldings; steering wheel horn bar with woodgrain vinyl surround; and (on Stylesides) special tailgate applique with bright back up light and wheel lip moldings. Ranger Lariat Package (Stylesides) with deluxe Tu-Tone paint treatment; "race track" moldings; special Ranger Lariat emblems; black tailgate applique (solid exterior paint colors available); Picton cloth seat upholstery trimmed with super soft vinyl; deluxe seat belts; color-keyed vinyl headliner with special sound-absorbing padding and button-quilted design; door trim panels with padded inserts above and map pockets in the lower door; wall-to-wall carpeting; and inner cowlside carpeting. Camper Special Package.

HISTORICAL NOTE: Model year production, by line, was: [F-100] 158,591; [F-150] 422,264; [F-250] 190,613; [F-350] 59,528; [Bronco] 69,120; [Ranchero] 22,519; [Econoline] 238,833; [Club Wagon] 44,484; [Total] 1,205,952. The Pickup totals include trucks produced in Canada for the U.S. market and the Econoline/Club Wagon totals exclude Cutaway vans for motorhomes.) Model year truck sales broke out as follows: [Light Conventional] 875,153; [Econoline] 228,849; [Courier] 70,553; [Bronco] 70,546; [Ranchero] 23,047; and [Medium- to Heavy-duty] 94,130; [Total] 1,362,278. Ford dealers sold a record 1,365,718 trucks for the calendar year, upping the company's previous record by 12 percent. Ford was America's number one truck maker in 1978, but Chevrolet was close behind and actually won the race in light-duty sales. The all-new, larger Bronco was the big sales success of the year.

RANCHERO 500 PICKUP: Styling was unchanged for 1979. Standard features include: SelectShift automatic transmission. Power steering and brakes. Bright hubcaps. Vinyl door trim and spare tire compartment. Carpeting. Cloth/vinyl combination trimmed bench seat. Colors offered on 1979 Rancheros were: Dark red; Dove Grey; Midnight blue (metallic); Pastel chamois; Light chamois; black; Polar white; silver (metallic); Light Medium blue; Dark jade (metallic); Dark cordovan (metallic). Optional glamour colors: Burnt Orange Glow, Light Jade Glow, Medium Blue Glow. Tu-Tone option [500 only]: accent color was applied on roof, hood and lower bodyside.

RANCHERO GT PICKUP: The GT was once again the most popular Ranchero. It had most of the same items as the 500 plus: Flight bench seat in cloth-and-vinyl with matching door trim panels and cut-pile carpet. GT stripe. Dual sport mirrors. Bright hubcaps with trim rings. Sports instrumentation group with engine turned cluster applique.

RANCHERO SQUIRE PICKUP: In addition to most of the items on the 500, the Squire had: Simulated woodgrain paneling on sides and tailgate. Deluxe wheelcovers.

I.D. DATA [Ranchero]: The VIN consists of 11 symbols. The first symbol is the last digit of the model year. The second symbol indicates the assembly plant. The third and fourth symbols indicate the product line and body style. The fifth symbol indicates the engine. The last six symbols are the sequential production number. Most 1978 Rancheros (76 percent) came with one of the optional engines.

Model	Body Type	Price	Weight	Prod. Total
Ranchero 500 — 1/2-Ton — 118 in. w.b. — V-8				
97D	Sedan-Pickup	5866	3698	12,093
Ranchero GT — 1/2-Ton — 118 in. w.b. — V-8				
97R	Sedan-Pickup	6289	3716	12,159
Ranchero Squire — 1/2-Ton — -118 in. w.b. — V-8				
97K	Sedan-Pickup	6014	3728	758

NOTE 1: Total production: 24,300.
NOTE 2: Prices/weights for base V-8.
ENGINE [Base V-8]: Displacement: 302 cid. V-8. Net horsepower: 134 nhp at 3800 rpm. Torque: 222 lbs.-ft. at 2200 rpm. Bore & stroke: 4 in. x 3 in. Compression ratio: 8.4:1. Carburetor: Two-barrel.
ENGINE [Optional V-8]: Displacement: 351 M (modified). V-8. Net horsepower: 162 nhp at 4000 rpm. Torque: 262 lbs.-ft. at 2200 rpm. Bore & stroke: 4 in. x 3.5 in. Compression ratio: 8.4:1. Carburetor: Two-barrel.
CHASSIS: Wheelbase: 118 in. Overall length: 220.1 in. Overall height: 53.5 in. GVW: 4,725-5,685 lbs. Tires: HR78-14B [raised white-letter on GT].
POWERTRAIN OPTIONS: Transmission: Automatic.
NOTE: Most 1979 Rancheros, 67.9 percent, came with the 351 cid V-8.
CONVENIENCE OPTIONS: Dual sport mirrors. Wire wheelcovers. Magnum 500 chrome wheels. SelectAire air-conditioner available with manual or automatic temperature control. AM/FM stereo with 8-track tape. AM/FM stereo with cassette tape player. AM/FM stereo with search feature. AM/FM stereo. AM/FM monaural radio. AM radio. Day/date clock. Sports Instrumentation Group with wood-tone applique around instrument cluster pods; Tachometer, temperature and oil pressure gauges, trip odometer, ammeter, electric clock and luxury steering wheel. Tilt steering wheel. Cornering lamps. Six-way power flight bench or split bench seat. Appearance Protection Group with door edge guards, floor mat and license plate frames. Deluxe wheelcovers. Wheel trim rings. Vinyl roof in black, white, red, blue and cordovan (not available with GT or Tu-Tones). Wheel lip moldings. Convenience Group with intermittent windshield wipers, automatic parking brake release, Right-hand remote-control mirror, trip odometer, and passenger visor vanity mirror. Fingertip speed control. Illuminated entry system. Light Group with engine compartment, glove box and ashtray lights; plus door ajar warning light and headlights on warning buzzer. Power door windows. Tinted glass all around. Engine block heater. Heavy-Duty Handling Suspension with heavy-duty rear springs, and rear stabilizer bar. Heavy-duty alternator. Heavy-duty battery. Medium-duty trailer towing package. Traction-lok differential (not available in California). Bumper Protection Group with front and rear bumper guards and front bumper rub strips. Bodyside protection molding with vinyl insert for 500 (not available with Tu-Tone). Lower bodyside protection (application of vinyl along the lower sides to help protect against stone pecking.) Brougham Decor Group with split bench seat in cloth and vinyl trim or Mateao vinyl upholstery. Bucket seats. Limited-Production Ranchero with leather seat; steering wheel and dash pad; T-bird or Cougar inner door panels; wide wheel opening moldings white sidewall tires; and wire wheelcovers. Just over 30 percent of 1979 Rancheros had steel styled wheels; 29.2 percent wheelcovers; 7.6 percent trailer towing equipment; 3.7 percent bucket seats; 88.9 percent air-conditioning; and 94 percent tinted glass.

1979 Ford Bronco Custom Ranger XLT Sport Utility Wagon 4x4

BRONCO CUSTOM: After last year's dramatic styling changes, the four-wheel drive Bronco was left pretty much alone for 1979. As before, the front end design echoed that used on the full-size Pickups. The honeycomb theme grille and two recessed, rectangular headlights, were surrounded by bright molding. The amber wraparound parking lights were beneath the headlights. Ford was printed in block letters on the face of the hood. The rectangular side-marker lights were located in the bodyside sculpturing, which ran straight from the upper part of the headlight level almost the entire length of the truck. Standard features included: Deep foam bucket seats. Color-keyed instrument and door trim panel in red, black, blue, jade or sand tan. Steering wheel and horn pad were black, sun visors were white. Bright hubcaps. Bright door-mounted mirrors on both sides. Bright painted front and rear bumpers. Power brakes. 25-gal. fuel tank. Four-speed manual transmission. Hardboard rear quarter panels. Bronco color choices for 1979 were: Raven black; Wimbledon white; Candy-apple red; maroon (metallic); coral; silver (metallic); Dark blue (metallic); Light Medium blue; Bright Emerald; Dark jade (metallic); Light jade; Midnight jade; Gold (metallic); Light sand; Dark brown (metallic); Medium copper (metallic); Bright yellow; Medium Blue Glow; and Walnut Glow. Standard Bronco paint scheme was solid exterior body color, with rear fiberglass roof in black, sand or white.

1979 Ford 1/2-Ton Bronco Ranger XLT Sport Utility Wagon 4x4

I.D. DATA [Bronco]: The VIN consists of 11 symbols. The first three indicate the series. The fourth indicates the engine. The fifth shows the assembly plant. The last six are the sequential production number.

Model	Body Type	Price	Weight	Prod. Total
Bronco 4x4 — 1/2-Ton — 104 in. w.b. — V-8				
U-150	Wagon	7733	4569	93,536

NOTE 1: Prices and weight for base V-8.
ENGINE [Base V-8]: V-block. OHV. Eight cylinders. Bore & stroke: 4.0 x 3.50. Displacement: 351 cid. Net horsepower: 156 at 4000 rpm. Net torque: 262 at 2200 rpm. Carburetor: Two-barrel.
CHASSIS: Wheebase: 104 in. Overall length: 180.3 in. Overall width: 79.3 in. Overall height: 75.5 in. Tires: L78 x 15B in.
POWERTRAIN OPTIONS: Transmissions: Cruise-O-Matic automatic. Engine: 400 cid V-8. Most 1979 Broncos (78.8 percent) came with automatic.
CONVENIENCE OPTIONS: Bright wheel lip moldings. Chrome bumpers. Tri-color or Chromatic tape stripe. Narrow bodyside paint stripe. ComfortVent heater. Console with front bucket seats. Convenience Group with intermittent wipers, gathered map pockets and 12 in. day/night mirror. Heavy-duty scissor-type jack. Insulation package. Lighted visor vanity mirror. Rear floor mat. Front bench seat. Folding rear bench seat (includes rear floor mat). Tinted glass all around. Visibility Group with lights in glove box, ashtray and underhood: instrument panel courtesy lights and dome light with integral map light (not included with front bench seat). Handling Package with rear stabilizer bar, quad front and heavy-duty rear shocks. Captain's chairs with fold-down armrests. Part time four-wheel drive with automatic. Trailer towing package: light (up to 2,000 lbs.), heavy-duty (over 2,000 lbs.). Thirty-two-gallon fuel tank in lieu of standard (includes skid plate). Inside locking hood release. Protection Group with bright door edge guards, front bumper guards and front bumper rub strip. Security Group with locking gas cap, inside hood release lock, spare tire lock and locking glove box. Free Wheeling Package with tri-color or chromatic tape stripe striping; black bumpers; dual black low-mount mirrors; sport steering wheel; black glove box applique; and five 15 x 6 styled steel wheels in white or chrome yellow with raised white-letter L78 x 15C tires. Ranger XLT with insulation package; rectangular headlamps; bright front and rear bumpers; bright molding around front windshield; rear side windows; wheel lips and lower section of tailgate; bodyside molding with black vinyl insert and bright taillight bezels; cut-pile carpeting; door trim panels with woodgrain accent; seat covering in vinyl or vinyl and cloth; spare tire cover; wood-tone dash with bright moldings; and Ranger XLT

plaque on the glove box. Tilt steering wheel. Privacy glass. Low-mount Western mirrors. Air-conditioning. AM digital clock radio. AM/FM stereo. Quad front shock absorbers. Recreation swing-out mirrors. Sliding side windows. GT bar. Sport steering wheel. Five-slot forged aluminum 15 in. wheels. Maintenance-free battery. Speed control. Swing-away spare tire carrier. 40-channel CB radio. Front tow hooks. Front and rear contour bumpers. 10-hole forged aluminum 15 in. wheels. Painted styled steel white 15 x 6 wheels. Five-slot forged aluminum 15 x 6 wheels. AM radio. AM/FM monaural radio. A total of 62.2 percent of 1979 Broncos had air-conditioning; 29.9 percent had cruise control; and 33.5 percent had tilt steering.

ECONOLINE E-100 CARGO VAN: The Econoline received a new criss-cross pattern grille for 1979. New, slightly recessed rectangular headlights were on each side of the grille. Rectangular parking lights were directly below the headlights. Among the standard features were: Full-foam driver's bucket seat. Vinyl seat trim in black, blue, jade or sand. Padded full-width instrument panel. Brake warning light. Two-speed electric windshield wipers. Wiper-arm-mounted washer jets. Dome lights. Front compartment headlining and insulated floor mat with scuff plates. Door checks. Argent silver-painted bumpers and hubcaps. Bright windshield molding. Painted mirrors. Hinged side cargo doors (sliding door available at no extra cost). Econoline and Club Wagon colors for 1979 were: Wimbledon white; Candy-apple red; Light-medium blue; silver (metallic); Light-medium pine; Dark brown (metallic); Light sand; coral; Dark blue (metallic); Raven black; Bright yellow; Dark jade (metallic); and maroon. Optional Glow colors available were: Medium Blue Glow; Camel Glow; and Walnut Glow. Bodyside accent tape stripe was available in Raven black; Dark blue (metallic); Dark brown (metallic); coral; Camel Glow; Walnut Glow; Light sand; Wimbledon white; and Bright yellow. Four Tu-Tone paint schemes were available.

ECONOLINE E-100 DISPLAY VAN: This model had windows at the rear and on the right hand side. It came with the same standard features as the Cargo Van.

ECONOLINE E-100 WINDOW VAN: The Window Van had glass all around. It shared features with the Cargo Van.

I.D. DATA [Vans]: The VIN consists of 11 symbols. The first three indicate the series. The fourth indicates the engine. The fifth shows the assembly plant. The last six are the sequential production number.

Model	Body Type	Price	Weight	Prod. Total
E-100 Van — 1/2-Ton — 124 in./138 in. w.b. — V-8				
E-040	Cargo Van	5441	3659	Note 1
E-050	Window Van	5578	3686	Note 1
E-600	Display Van	5532	3673	Note 1

NOTE 1: Production: [Econoline] 213,654.
NOTE 2: Prices/weights for base V-8; deduct for six.
ENGINE [Base Six]: Inline. Six-cylinder. OHV. Bore & stroke: 4.00 in. x 3.98 in. Displacement: 300 cid. Net horsepower: 117 hp at 3000 rpm. Net torque: 223 lbs.-ft. at 1600 rpm. Compression ratio: 8.9:1. Carburetor: One-barrel.
ENGINE [Base V-8]: V-block. Eight-cylinder. OHV. Bore & stroke:4.0 x 3.5 in. Displacement: 351 cid. Net horsepower: 156 at 4000 rpm. Net torque: 262 lbs.-ft. at 2200 rpm.

ECONOLINE E-150 CARGO VAN: The slightly more heavy-duty E-150 had most of the same standard features as the E-100. Four-hole wheels were a distinctive item found only on this series.
ECONOLINE E-150 SUPER CARGO VAN: This Van had the same features as the E-150 Cargo Van plus a 20 in. extended rear overhang. This allowed carrying of longer loads. The maximum cargo length (right side, without passenger's seat) was 14 feet.
ECONOLINE E-150 DISPLAY VAN: This Van shared styling with the E-100 but had greater load capacity.
ECONOLINE E-150 WINDOW VAN: This Van shared styling with the E-100 Window Van, but had greater load capacity.
ECONOLINE E-150 SUPER WINDOW VAN: See E-150 Super Cargo Van.
I.D. DATA [Vans]: The VIN consists of 11 symbols. The first three indicate the series. The fourth indicates the engine. The fifth shows the assembly plant. The last six are the sequential production number.

Model	Body Type	Price	Weight	Prod. Total
E-150 Van — 1/2-Ton — 124 in. w.b. — V-8				
E-140	Cargo Van	5722	3822	Note 1
E-160	Display Van	5814	3876	Note 1
E-150	Window Van	5860	3851	Note 1
E-100 Super Van — 1/2-Ton — 138 in. w.b. — V-8				
E-140	Cargo Van	6078	3960	Note 1
E-160	Display Van	6171	3989	Note 1
E-150	Window Van	6217	3975	Note 1

NOTE 1: Production: [Econoline] 213,654.
NOTE 2: Prices/weights for base V-8; deduct for six.
ENGINE [Base Six]: Inline. Six-cylinder. OHV. Bore & stroke: 4.00 in. x 3.98 in. Displacement: 300 cid. Net horsepower: 117 hp at 3000 rpm. Net torque: 223 lbs.-ft. at 1600 rpm. Compression ratio: 8.9:1. Carburetor: One-barrel.
ENGINE [Base V-8]: V-block. Eight-cylinder. OHV. Bore & stroke: 4.00 x 3.5 in. Displacement: 351 cid. Net horsepower: 156 at 4000 rpm. Net torque: 262 lbs.-ft. at 2200 rpm.

ECONOLINE E-250 CARGO VAN: The new E-250 had a higher GVW rating and more heavy-duty front and rear axles, than the E-150. It also came with eight-hole wheels. Standard features were the same as those on the E-100 except the three-speed manual was not available in California.
ECONOLINE E-250 SUPER CARGO VAN: See E-150 Cargo Van.
ECONOLINE E-250 DISPLAY VAN: This vehicle shared styling and features with the E-100, but had greater load capacity.
ECONOLINE E-250 SUPER DISPLAY VAN: See E-150 Super Cargo Van.
ECONOLINE E-250 WINDOW VAN: This vehicle shared styling with the E-100 Window Van, but had greater load capacity.
ECONOLINE E-250 SUPER WINDOW VAN: See E-150 Super Cargo Van.
ECONOLINE E-250 CUTAWAY VAN: This Van with Camper Special Packages, was designed to readily accommodate custom motor homes.
ECONOLINE E-250 PARCEL DELIVERY: The E-250 Parcel Delivery van was 149.9 in. long and 74.3 in. high in its cargo area. The rear door opening was 84.7 in. wide.
I.D. DATA [Vans]: The VIN consists of 11 symbols. The first three indicate the series. The fourth indicates the engine. The fifth shows the assembly plant. The last six are the sequential production number.

Model	Body Type	Price	Weight	Prod. Total
E-250 Van — 3/4-Ton — 124 in. w.b. — V-8				
E-240	Cargo Van	5994	4144	Note 1
E-260	Display Van	6087	4159	Note 1
E-250	Window Van	6133	4173	Note 1

E-250 Super Van — 3/4-Ton — 138 in. w.b. — V-8

Model	Body Type	Price	Weight	Prod. Total
E-240	Cargo Van	6535	4349	Note 1
E-260	Display Van	6628	4378	Note 1
E-250	Window Van	6674	4364	Note 1

NOTE 1: Production: [Econoline] 213,654.
NOTE 2: Prices/weights for base V-8: deduct for six.
ENGINE [Base Six]: Inline. Six-cylinder. OHV. Bore & stroke: 4.00 in. x 3.98 in. Displacement: 300 cid. Net horsepower: 117 hp at 3000 rpm. Net torque: 223 lbs.-ft. at 1600 rpm. Compression ratio: 8.9:1. Carburetor: One-barrel.
ENGINE [Base V-8]: V-block. Eight-cylinder. OHV. Bore & stroke: 4.0 x 3.5 in. Displacement: 351 cid. Net horsepower: 156 at 4000 rpm. Net torque: 262 lbs.-ft. at 2200 rpm.
ECONOLINE E-350 CARGO VAN: This was the top-of-the-line Econoline Van. It had heavy-duty front and rear shocks and a greater load capacity than the other series. Standard features were the same as the E-100.
ECONOLINE E-350 SUPER CARGO VAN: See E-150 Super Cargo Van.
ECONOLINE E-350 DISPLAY VAN: See E-250 Display Van.
ECONOLINE E-350 SUPER DISPLAY VAN: See E-150 Super Cargo Van.
ECONOLINE E-350 WINDOW VAN: See E-250 Window Van.
ECONOLINE E-350 SUPER WINDOW VAN: See E-150 Super Cargo Van.
ECONOLINE E-350 CUTAWAY VAN: See E-250 Cutaway Van.
ECONOLINE E-350 PARCEL DELIVERY: See E-250 Parcel Delivery.
I.D. DATA [Vans]: The VIN consists of 11 symbols. The first three indicate the series. The fourth indicates the engine. The fifth shows the assembly plant. The last six are the sequential production number.

Model	Body Type	Price	Weight	Prod. Total
E-350 Super Van — 1-Ton — 138 in. w.b. — V-8				
E-340	Cargo Van	6387	4323	Note 1
E-360	Display Van	6480	4338	Note 1
E-350	Window Van	6526	4352	Note 1
E-350 Super Van — 1-Ton — 138 in. w.b. — V-8				
S-340	Cargo Van	7249	4449	Note 1
S-350	Window Van	7387	4464	Note 1
S-360	Display Van	7341	4478	Note 1
E-350 Super Van — 1-Ton — 155 in. w.b. — V-8				
E-370	Cutaway Van	6188	3917	Note 1
E-380	Parcel Delivery	8187	5279	Note 1

NOTE 1: Production: [Econoline] 213,654.
NOTE 2: Prices/weights for base V-8; deduct for six.
ENGINE [Base Six]: Inline. Six-cylinder. OHV. Bore & stroke: 4.00 in. x 3.98 in. Displacement: 300 cid. Net horsepower: 117 hp at 3000 rpm. Net torque: 223 lbs.-ft. at 1600 rpm. Compression ratio: 8.9:1. Carburetor: One-barrel.
ENGINE [Base V-8]: V-block. Eight-cylinder. OHV. Bore & stroke: 4.00 x 3.5 in. Displacement: 351 cid. Net horsepower: 156 at 4000 rpm. Net torque: 262 lbs.-ft. at 2200 rpm.
CHASSIS: Wheelbase: 124 in. (E-100/E-150) 138 in. Overall length: 186.8 in. (124 in. wheelbase); 206.8 in. (138 in. wheelbase); 226.8 in. (138 in Super Van). GVW: 5,050-5,650 lbs. (E-100); 6,050-6,300 lbs. (E-150); 6,500-8,250 lbs. (E-250); 8,550-9,800 lbs. (E-350). Tires: F78 15B PT (E-100); L78 x 15B PT (E-150); 8.00 x 16.5D TT (E-250); 9.50 x 16.5D TT (E-350).
POWERTRAIN OPTIONS: Engines: 302 cid V-8. 351 cid V-8. 460 cid V-8 (E-250/E-350). 300 cid heavy-duty six-cylinder (E-350). Transmissions: Four-speed manual with overdrive. SelectShift automatic.

1979 Ford Cruising Van (OCW)

CONVENIENCE OPTIONS: Custom Van with (in addition to or in place of standard features) a wood-tone applique on instrument panel; front side cowl and door trim panels; cigarette lighter; front compartment headlining; insulated front floor mats; front roof rail garnish moldings; bright hubcaps; bright taillight bezels; and bright window frames with optional rear windows. Chateau with (in addition to or in place of Custom features) super soft vinyl or cloth-and-vinyl seat trim; cut-pile carpeting in front; courtesy light switches for all doors; chrome front and rear bumpers; bright grille surround molding; bright lower bodyside character line molding; and bright mirrors. Sports rails. Bodyside accent tape stripes. Three-color "Cruising Van" theme tape stripe. Port hole window in right and left side. Moldings with bright grille surround; deluxe accent with bright drip rail moldings; plus center bodyside and lower character line moldings; bright lower character line trim; bright drip rails; and bright window moldings. Audio with AM monaural radio. AM/FM monaural radio. AM/FM digital clock radio, AM/FM stereo with tape deck or cassette player. 40-channel CB radio. Rear speakers. Premium Sound System. Air-conditioning front or high-capacity. Heaters with high output. ComfortVent or auxiliary vent for cargo area. Roof/floor insulation package. Deluxe insulation package. Convenience group (with intermittent wipers, dome light switches in all doors and day/night mirror). Dome light courtesy switches for all doors. Western low-mount mirrors. Swing-out recreation mirrors. Sport steering wheel with simulated leather wrapping. Simulated leather wrapped steering wheel. Tilt steering. Speed control. Tinted glass all around. Privacy glass. Flip-open or fixed windows available in all cargo doors. Single sliding side cargo door in lieu of double doors. Combination three-passenger rear seat that converts into a bed. Dual or quad captain's chairs (reclining and swivel or reclining only). Passenger's seat. Flip-fold passenger seat. Cloth-and-vinyl seat trim for bucket and captain's chairs. Free Wheeling Packages with full-length carpeting, front door trim panels and the deluxe insulation package were part of the interior package. The

Free Wheeling exterior package included five-slot matte-finish aluminum wheels; raised white-letter tires; black-out grille; black-painted bumpers and mirrors; and a black lower bodyside panel bordered by a half-inch black stripe. Trailer Towing Packages with five-slot or 10-hole forged aluminum wheels. Cruising Van with tri-color tape stripes; 10-hole polished-finish forged aluminum wheels; port holes; black-out grille; black mirrors and bumpers; Chateau front door trim panels; wood-tone vinyl applique with bright surround on instrument panel; courtesy dome light switches on all doors; deluxe insulation package; full-length carpeting; Sport steering wheel; and two reclining captain's chairs. Heavy-duty shocks. Front stabilizer bar. Engine block heater. Oil pressure gauge and ammeter. Cooling Packages with (super and extra). Push bar, plus fog lights and covers. Protection Group with front and sliding door black stepwell pads, front door edge guards and front bumper guards (require chrome bumpers). Security Group with locking gas cap, inside locking hood release and spare tire lock. Inside locking hood release. Chrome or painted Argent silver step bumper. Chrome contour bumpers. Deluxe wheelcovers.

1979 Ford Econoline 100 Chateau Window Van (OCW)

E-100 CLUB WAGON: A new, quick release feature was on all three-passenger bench seats. This allowed for faster adjustment of cargo and/or seating capacity. The E-100 was offered in five- an eight-passenger versions. Among the standard features were: Front bucket and rear bench seats. Color-keyed patterned vinyl seat trim. Seat belts. Two-speed electric windshield wipers. Wiper-arm-mounted washer jets. Dome lights. Insulated floor mat with scuff plates. Three armrests. Dual horns. Flip-open windows in sliding door and opposite windows. Painted bumpers, 5 in. x 8 in. mirrors and hubcaps. Bright windshield molding. Econoline and Club Wagon colors for 1979 were: Wimbledon white; Candy-apple red; Light-medium blue; silver (metallic); Light-medium pine; Dark brown (metallic); Light sand; coral; Dark blue (metallic); Raven black; Bright yellow; Dark jade (metallic); and maroon. Optional Glow colors available were: Medium Blue Glow; Camel Glow; and Walnut Glow. Bodyside accent tape stripe was available in Raven black; Dark blue (metallic); Dark brown (metallic); coral; Camel Glow; Walnut Glow; Light sand; Wimbledon white; and Bright yellow. Four Tu-Tone paint schemes were available.
E-150 CLUB WAGON: This was a slightly more heavy-duty version of the E-100. It could be had in 124 in. or 138 in. wheelbase and was also offered in five- and eight-passenger versions. Standard features were same as those on the E-100.
E-150 SUPER WAGON: This was basically the same as the 138 in. wheelbase E-150, but it had an 20 in. extended rear overhang.
E-250 CLUB WAGON: The E-250 Club Wagon could be had with five-, eight- or 12-passenger capacity. It had most of the same features as the E-100.
E-250 SUPER WAGON: This was basically an E-250 with a 20 in. rear overhang.
E-350 SUPER WAGON: The heavy-duty E-350 provided 20 in. more inside length than regular 138 in. wheelbase Club Wagons. Heavy-duty shocks were standard.

1979 Ford Club Wagon Chateau Passenger Van (OCW)

I.D. DATA [Vans]: The VIN consists of 11 symbols. The first three indicate the series. The fourth indicates the engine. The fifth shows the assembly plant. The last six are the sequential production number.

Model	Body Type	Price	Weight	Prod. Total
E-100 Van — 1/2-Ton — 124 in./138 in. w.b. — V-8				
E-100	Club Wagon	6307	3933	Note 1
E-100 Van — 1/2-Ton — 124 in./138 in. w.b. — V-8				
E-150	Club Wagon	6410	4005	Note 1
E-150	Super Wagon	6951	4254	Note 1
E-250 Van — 3/4-Ton — 138 in. w.b. — V-8				
E-250	Club Wagon	6877	4443	Note 1
E-250	Super Wagon	7513	4570	Note 1

E-350 — 1-Ton — 138 in. w.b. — V-8

E-350	Super Wagon	8084	4815	Note 1

NOTE 1: Production: [Club Wagon] 47,712.
NOTE 2: Prices/weights for base V-8; deduct for six.
ENGINE [Base Six]: Inline. Six-cylinder. OHV. Bore & stroke: 4.00 in. x 3.98 in. Displacement: 300 cid. Net horsepower: 117 hp at 3000 rpm. Net torque: 223 lbs.-ft. at 1600 rpm. Compression ratio: 8.9:1. Carburetor: One-barrel.
ENGINE [Base V-8]: V-block. Eight-cylinder. OHV. Bore & stroke: 4.00 x 3.5 in. Displacement: 351 cid. Net horsepower: 156 at 4000 rpm. Net torque: 262 lbs.-ft. at 2200 rpm.
CHASSIS: Wheelbase: 124 in. (E-100), 138 in. (E-150/E-250/E-350). Overall length: See Econoline. GVW: 5,400-9,000 lbs. Tires: G78 x 15B (E-100), H78 x 15D (E-150), 8.00 x 16D (E-250), 9.50 x 16.5D (E-350).
POWERTRAIN OPTIONS: Engine: 302 cid V-8, 351 cid V-8, 460 cid V-8. SelectShift Cruise-O-Matic automatic. Four-speed manual with overdrive.
CONVENIENCE OPTIONS: Most of the same items available on the Econoline, plus four-passenger rear bench seat. Snack-game table.

1979 Ford 1/2-Ton Courier Sport Mini-Pickup (OCW)

COURIER PICKUP: Tough as all outdoors. That's what sales literature said of the new 1979 Courier. Styling remained the same as last year, but changes were made under the hood. A 2.0 litre engine was now standard. Other standard features included: Bright hubcaps. Color-keyed vinyl headlining, seat and door trim panels. Instrument lighting intensity control. Cigarette lighter. Brake warning light. New dome light. Door vent windows with wedge-type handles. Padded instrument panel. Hinged seatback for easy access to storage area. Inside hood release. White sidewall tires. Cargo tie-down hooks. Bright front bumper. One-hand tailgate operation. Four-speed manual transmission.
I.D. DATA [Courier]: The VIN consists of 11 symbols. The first indicates the manufacturer. The second indicates the assembly plant. The third indicates the series. The fourth indicates the engine. The fifth (a letter) indicates the model year. The sixth indicates the production month. The last five are the sequential production number.

Model	Body Type	Price	Weight	Prod. Total
Courier — 1/2-Ton — 104.3 in. w.b. — Four				
—	Chassis & Cab	4711	2430	Note 1
—	Pickup	4861	2680	Note 1

NOTE 1: Model year sales: 76,883.
ENGINE [Base Four]: Inline. Four-cylinder. OHV. Bore & stroke: 3.07 in. x 3.70 in. Displacement: 110 cid. Net horsepower: 67 nhp at 4500 rpm. Carburetor: One-barrel.
CHASSIS: Wheelbase: 106.9 in. (6 ft. box); 112.8 in. (7 ft. box). Overall length: 177.9 in. (6 ft. box); 189.4 in. (7 ft. box). Overall width: 63 in. Overall height: 61.5 in. GVW: 4,100 lbs. Tires: 6.00 x 14C white sidewall.
POWERTRAIN OPTIONS: Transmissions: Floor-shifted automatic or five-speed manual transmission (with overdrive).
CONVENIENCE OPTIONS: AM or AM/FM monaural pushbutton radios. Air-conditioning. Low-mounted Western mirrors. Tinted glass all around. Radial tires. Cast aluminum wheels. Soft Ride Package) Includes: 3,600 lbs. GVWR, 5-leaf progressive-rate rear springs, and 2,010 lbs. rated rear axle. Rear step bumper. Free Wheeling Packages with A includes black painted GT bar and push bar. B includes: Plus cast aluminum wheels, raised white-letter 70 series tires (5), and three color accent tape stripe. XLT Package includes: Interior with soft, supple vinyl seat and door trim. wood-tone upper door trim panel and transmission shift knob. Cut-pile carpeting. Day/night mirror. Ashtray, under hood and glove box lights. Glove box lock. Sport steering wheel. Temperature gauge and ammeter. Exterior with Bright grille. Bright windshield, rear window, drip rail, wheel lip and taillight surround moldings. Deluxe wheelcovers. Dual accent pinstripes. Sports Group with black sport steering wheel, bucket seats trimmed in black vinyl with black and white plaid fabric inserts, black carpet and interior trim, wood-tone applique on instrument cluster mask, temperature gauge, and ammeter. The 1979 Courier was available in seven exterior colors: Red; white; light blue; silver (metallic); dark brown; black; or yellow.
F-100 CUSTOM PICKUP: The biggest styling change for 1979 was rectangular headlights were now standard. Other standard features included: Full foam seat. Chrome contour front bumper. Vent window handle. Argent grille. Behind seat storage area (regular cabs). Full-width, energy-absorbing instrument panel. Molded door trim panels with armrests. Large glove box with push-button latch and wood-tone applique on door. Dome lamp. Argent silver hubcaps. Black carpet-grain floor mat. Headlining. Door scuff plates. Embossed vinyl seat trim. Special floor, door trim panel with headliner insulation. Three-speed manual transmission (Supercab had automatic). Buyers could choose from 6.5 ft. and 8 ft. Flaresides with regular cab or 6.75 ft. or 8 ft. Stylesides in regular or Supercabs. Standard F-series colors for 1979 were: Raven black; Wimbledon white; Candy-apple red; maroon (metallic); silver (metallic); Dark blue (metallic); Light-medium blue; Light jade; Dark jade (metallic); Bright yellow; Medium copper (metallic); Dark brown (metallic); Light sand; and coral. Optional Glow Colors: Medium Blue Glow and Walnut Glow. Tu-Tone colors: [Regular] Accent color was applied on roof and upper back panel; included a belt-line molding around back of cab; available with all type cabs and optional dual tape stripes. [Accent] Combined regular tu-tone with color-keyed dual tape stripes and had special tailgate applique. [Deluxe] Accent color was applied inside upper and lower tailgate molding; standard on Ranger Lariat; on other trim levels the tu-tone option included bright molding additions or deletions as needed to complement tu-tone scheme. [Combination] Combined regular and accent tu-tone combined.
I.D. DATA [F-Series]: The VIN consists of 11 symbols. The first three indicate the series. The fourth indicates the engine. The fifth shows the assembly plant. The last six are the sequential production number.

F-100 — 1/2-Ton — 117 in. w.b. — V-8

Model	Body Type	Price	Weight	Prod. Total
81	Chassis & Cab	4878	3094	Note 1
83	Flareside 6.5 ft.	5085	3448	Note 1
83	Styleside 6.75 ft.	5085	3448	Note 1

F-100 — 1/2-Ton — 133 in. w.b. — V-8

Model	Body Type	Price	Weight	Prod. Total
83	Flareside 8 ft.	5179	3513	Note 1
83	Styleside 8 ft.	5179	3513	Note 1

F-100 Supercab — 1/2-Ton — 155 in. w.b. — V-8

Model	Body Type	Price	Weight	Prod. Total
81	Chassis & Cab	5875	3576	Note 1
83	Styleside 8 ft.	6255	3930	Note 1

NOTE 1: Production: [F-100] 225,893.
NOTE 2: Prices/weights for base V-8; deduct for six-cylinder.
NOTE 3: Add for 4x4.
ENGINE [Base Six]: Inline. Six-cylinder. OHV. Bore & stroke: 4.00 in. x 3.98 in. Displacement: 300 cid. Net horsepower: 101 hp at 3000 rpm. Net torque: 223 lbs.-ft. at 1600 rpm. Compression ratio: 8.0:1. Carburetor: One-barrel.
ENGINE [Base V-8]: V-block. OHV. Eight-cylinder. Bore and stroke: 4.0 x 3.0 in. Displacement: 302 cid. Net horsepower: 130 at 3800 rpm. Net torque: 222 lbs.-ft. at 2000 rpm.
ENGINE [Supercab and 4x4 Base V-8]: V-block. OHV. Eight-cylinder. Bore and stroke: 4.00 in. x 3.50 in. Displacement: 351 cid. Horsepower: 156 nhp at 4000 rpm. Net torque: 262 lbs.-ft. at 2200 rpm. Carburetor: Two-barrel. (Note: By this time net horsepower ratings were calculated according to weight of the model, so exact horsepower ratings vary in different reference sources.)
F-150 CUSTOM PICKUP: Ford's heavy-duty 1/2-ton could haul several hundred pounds more payload than the F-100. It came with most of the same standard features, plus power brakes. The regular cab was available with 8 ft. all-steel Styleside or 8 ft. wood floor Flareside boxes. The Supercab, with space behind the front seat for an optional rear seat or jump seats, came with 6.75 ft. or 8 ft. Styleside boxes.
I.D. DATA [F-Series]: The VIN consists of 11 symbols. The first three indicate the series. The fourth indicates the engine. The fifth shows the assembly plant. The last six are the sequential production number.

F-150 — 1/2-Ton — 133 in. w.b. — V-8

Model	Body Type	Price	Weight	Prod. Total
81	Chassis & Cab	5018	3221	Note 1
83	Flareside 8 ft.	5489	3605	Note 1
83	Styleside 8 ft.	5489	3605	Note 1

F-150 Supercab — 1/2-Ton — 155 in. w.b. — V-8

Model	Body Type	Price	Weight	Prod. Total
81	Chassis & Cab	6075	3655	Note 1
83	Styleside	6302	4009	Note 1

NOTE 1: Production: [F-150] 400,399.
NOTE 2: Prices/weights for base V-8; deduct for six-cylinder.
ENGINE [Base Six]: Inline. Six-cylinder. OHV. Bore & stroke: 4.00 in. x 3.98 in. Displacement: 300 cid. Net horsepower: 101 hp at 3000 rpm. Net torque: 223 lbs.-ft. at 1600 rpm. Compression ratio: 8.0:1. Carburetor: One-barrel.
ENGINE [Base V-8]: V-block. OHV. Eight-cylinder. Bore and stroke: 4.0 x 3.0 in. Displacement: 302 cid. Net horsepower: 130 at 3800 rpm. Net torque: 222 lbs.-ft. at 2000 rpm.
ENGINE [Supercab and 4x4 Base V-8]: V-block. OHV. Eight-cylinder. Bore and stroke: 4.00 in. x 3.50 in. Displacement: 351 cid. Horsepower: 156 nhp at 4000 rpm. Net torque: 262 lbs.-ft. at 2200 rpm. Carburetor: Two-barrel. (Note: By this time net horsepower ratings were calculated according to weight of the model, so exact horsepower ratings vary in different reference sources.)

1979 Ford 3/4-Ton F-250 Ranger XLT Styleside Pickup (OCW)

F-250 CUSTOM PICKUP: The F-250 had most of the same features as the F-100. It too was offered with regular or Supercabs and with Flareside or Styleside boxes. Power brakes and a three-speed manual transmission were standard.
I.D. DATA [F-Series]: The VIN consists of 11 symbols. The first three indicate the series. The fourth indicates the engine. The fifth shows the assembly plant. The last six are the sequential production number.

F-250 — 3/4-Ton — 133 in. w.b. — V-8

Model	Body Type	Price	Weight	Prod. Total
81	Chassis & Cab	5525	3479	Note 1
83	Flareside	5822	3868	Note 1
83	Styleside	5822	3868	Note 1

F-250 Supercab — 3/4-Ton — 155 in. w.b. — V-8

Model	Body Type	Price	Weight	Prod. Total
81	Chassis & Cab	6074	3727	Note 1
83	Styleside	6301	4081	Note 1

F-250 Crew Cabs — 3/4-Ton — 155 in. w.b. — V-8

Model	Body Type	Price	Weight	Prod. Total
81	Chassis & Cab	6361	4025	Note 1
83	Styleside	6657	4380	Note 1

NOTE 1: Production: [F-250] 189,743.
NOTE 2: Prices/weights for base V-8; deduct for six.
NOTE 3: Add for 4x4.
NOTE 4: Supercabs available with 6.75 ft. and 8 ft. styleside boxes.
ENGINE [Base Six]: Displacement: 300 cid six. Horsepower: 120 nhp at 3400 rpm. Bore & stroke: 4.00 x 3.98. Compression ratio: 8.0:1. Carburetor: One-barrel. Supercab had 360 cid V-8.

ENGINE [Base V-8]: V-block. OHV. Eight-cylinder. Bore and stroke: 4.00 in. x 3.50 in. Displacement: 351 cid. Horsepower: 156 nhp at 4000 rpm. Net torque: 262 lbs.-ft. at 2200 rpm. Carburetor: Two-barrel. (Note: By this time net horsepower ratings were calculated according to weight of the model, so exact horsepower ratings vary in different reference sources.)

POWERTRAIN OPTIONS: Transmissions: Four-speed manual. Four-speed manual with overdrive. SelectShift automatic. Engines: 300 cid heavy-duty six (F-350); 302 cid V-8 (F-100/F-150); 351 cid V-8; 400 cid V-8; 460 cid V-8 (not available F-100).

1979 Ford F-350 1-Ton Ranger Styleside Pickup (OCW)

1979 Ford Ranger XLT Indy 500 Courtesy Pickup (IMSC/JLM)

F-350 CUSTOM PICKUP: The F-350 Pickup was only offered with the Styleside box. However, there were three choices of cabs: Regular, Super, or Crew. Front only shocks, a four-speed manual transmission and heavy-duty power front disc brakes were standard.

F-350 PLATFORM/STAKE: Two lengths of 1-ton F-350 Platform/Stakes were available: 9-ft. and 12-ft. Floor frames of the Platform/Stake were made of steel cross sills riveted to steel siderails. Floorboards were interlocked with steel brackets. Formed steel caps covered ends of the body sills. Side boards were hardwood and stakes were steel. A four-speed manual transmission was standard.

I.D. DATA [F-Series]: The VIN consists of 11 symbols. The first three indicate the series. The fourth indicates the engine. The fifth shows the assembly plant. The last six are the sequential production number.

Model	Body Type	Price	Weight	Prod. Total
F-350 — 1-Ton — 140 in. w.b. — V-8				
80	Stake 9 ft.	7181	4747	Note 1
81	Chassis & Cab	6141	3905	Note 1
83	Styleside	6739	4341	Note 1
86	Platform 9 ft.	7132	4507	Note 1
F-350 — 1-Ton — 137 in. w.b. — V-8				
80	Stake 12 ft.	—	—	Note 1
86	Platform 12 ft.	—	—	Note 1
F-350 Supercab — 1-Ton — 155 in. w.b. — V-8				
81	Chassis & Cab	6908	4121	Note 1
83	Styleside	7318	4510	Note 1
F-350 Crew Cabs — 1-Ton — 165.6 in. w.b. — V-8				
81	Chassis & Cab	6949	4325	Note 1
83	Styleside	7233	4766	Note 1

NOTE 1: Production: [F-350] 72,674.
NOTE 2: Prices/weights for base V-8; deduct for six.
NOTE 3: Add for 4x4; first time offered for F-350.

ENGINE [Base Six]: Displacement: 300 cid. Six. Horsepower: 120 nhp at 3400 rpm. Bore & stroke: 4.00 x 3.98. Compression ratio: 8.0:1. Carburetor: One-barrel. Supercab had 360 cid V-8.

ENGINE [Base V-8]: V-block. OHV. Eight-cylinder. Bore and stroke: 4.00 in. x 3.50 in. Displacement: 351 cid. Horsepower: 156 nhp at 4000 rpm. Net torque: 262 lbs.-ft. at 2200 rpm. Carburetor: Two-barrel. (Note: By this time net horsepower ratings were calculated according to weight of the model, so exact horsepower ratings vary in different reference sources.)

CHASSIS: Wheelbase: 117 in. (F-100); 133 in. (F-100/F-150/F-250); 140 in. (F-350); 139 in. (F-100/F-150/F-250 Supercab); 155 in. (Supercab); 150 in. (F-250 Crew Cab); 165.5 in. (F-350 Crew Cab); 137 in. (F-350 Platform/Stake); 161 in. (F-350 Platform/Stake). Overall length: 195.1 in. (F-100 6.75 ft. Styleside); 211.3 in. (F-100/F-150/F-250 8 ft. Styleside); 140 in. (F-100/F-150/F-250 6.75 ft. Supercab); 233.6 in. (8 ft. Supercab); 192.2 in. (F-100 6.5 ft. Flareside); 208.4 in. (8 ft. Flareside); 221.9 in. (Platform/Stake 9 ft.); 259.5 in. (Platform/Stake 12 ft.) GVW: 4,800-5,800 lbs. (F-100); 6,050-6,400 lbs. (F-150); 6,200-7,900 lbs. (F-250); 8,900-10,000 lbs. (F-350). Tires: F78 x 15B PT (F-100); L78 x 15B PT (F-150); 8.00 x 16.5D TT (F-250); 9.50 x 16.3E TT (F-350).

CONVENIENCE OPTIONS: Bright box rails for 8 ft. Stylesides. Bright bodyside molding with black vinyl insert. Bright rocker panel molding (Stylesides only). Bright wheel lip molding (Custom stylesides only). Narrow Bright bodyside molding (for Custom Stylesides). Tape/stripe dual narrow extending the full-length of Styleside Pickups, available with solid exterior paint or regular Tu-Tone only. Pickup box cover (textured white or sand, fiberglass and tinted side and rear windows, adjustable roof vent and liftgate). Deluxe box cover (sliding side windows with screens, bright side and rear window moldings, dome light.) Sliding front window available for standard or deluxe box cover. High-output heater. ComfortVent heater. Convenience Group with intermittent wipers, 12 in. day/night mirror, and map pockets. Light Group with glove box, ashtray, under instrument panel, engine compartment, and cargo box lights. Breathable knitted vinyl seat upholstery. Chain mail pattern vinyl seat upholstery. Duraweave polyknit seat upholstery. Heavy-duty black vinyl seat upholstery. Multistripe cloth inserts for Ranger regular and Supercabs. Rainbow tape stripe Stylesides. GT bar (Stylesides). Forged aluminum wheels (5-slot brushed for 10-hole polished wheels). Styled steel wheels. Rear step bumper. Free Wheeling Styleside with A: interior in silver and black with red accents, multi-color bodyside tape stripe (Chromatic tape stripe optional), blackout grille and black front bumper (an optional black rear contour or step bumper was required). B: Black GT bar, painted styled steel wheels in white or yellow, and a spare tire lock. Free Wheeling Flareside with distinctive pinstriping (black, white or orange), blackout grille plus black front and rear bumpers. Four-wheel drive (now available on F-350 series). Tilt steering wheel. CB radio. Engine block heater. Super cooling package. Trailer towing packages. High altitude emission system. Handling Package) Includes: (F-100, F-150) front stabilizer bar, heavy-duty gas-filled front and rear shocks, and heavy-duty front springs (radial tires were recommended). Roof clearance lights (five). Push bar. Locking inside hood release. Fog lamps. 8 chromed tie-down hooks. Front tow hook. Protection Package includes: Bright door edge guards, front bumper guards and front bumper rub strip. Security Group with locking gas cap, glove box door, inside hood release and spare tire. Recreation swing-out mirrors (6.75 ft. x 9.5 in.) (not available with F-100). Low-mount Western 9 in. x 6 in. mirrors, bright or black. Digitial AM clock radio. AM, AM/FM, and AM/FM stereo radios. Air-conditioning. Illuminated vanity mirror. Speed control. Sliding rear window. Tool storage box with locking door in curbside of pickup box skirt on 8-ft. Stylesides. Sport steering wheel with simulated leather wrapped padded rim. Simulated leather wrapped steering wheel. Chromed or painted argent step bumper for Styleside. Chromed or black contour rear bumpers (Styleside), black channel (Flareside). White painted styled steel 15 in. wheels. Slide-out spare tire carrier. Chrome grille insert with bright headlight doors. Chromatic tape stripe. (Stylesides). Mag-style wheelcovers for 15 in. wheels. Full wheelcovers for Pickups. Ranger with (in addition to or in place of Custom items) bright moldings, on roof drip rail, windshield, backlight and rear side windows (Supercab); bright narrowide moldings (all cabs and Stylesides); bright hubcaps (except dual rears); bright upper and lower Styleside tailgate moldings and bright tail-light bezels; bright wheel lip moldings, Chain Mail vinyl or multi-stripe cloth seat upholstery with color-keyed floor covering, sun visors and white headliner, added sound insulation. Ranger XLT Package with bright aluminum bodyside moldings on roof drip rail, windshield and rear window; trim on rear side windows (Supercab and Crew Cab); cloth seat upholstery with vinyl trim (chain-mail vinyl was a no-cost option); wall-to-wall cut-pile carpeting; covered floor insulation; vinyl headlining with sound-deadening backing; door trim panels with woodgrain vinyl insert and bright trim moldings; steering wheel horn bar with woodgrain vinyl surround; and (on Stylesides) special tailgate applique with bright back-up light and wheel lip moldings. Ranger Lariat Package (for Stylesides) with deluxe Tu-Tone paint treatment; "race track" moldings; special Ranger Lariat emblems; black tailgate applique (solid exterior paint colors available); Dura-weave polyknit cloth seat upholstery trimmed with super soft vinyl; deluxe seat belts; color-keyed vinyl headliner with special sound-absorbing padding and button-quilted design; door trim panels with padded inserts above and map pockets in the lower door; wall-to-wall carpeting; and inner cowlside carpeting. Camper Special Package.

HISTORICAL: Model year production by line: [F-100] 225,893; [F-150] 400,399; [F-250] 189,743; [F-350] 72,674; [Bronco] 93,536; [Ranchero] 24,300; [Econoline] 213,654; [Club Wagon] 47,712; [Total] 1,267,911. Model Year sales by type: [Light Conventional] 742,761; [Econoline] 184,722; [Ranchero] 18,658; [Courier] 76,883; [Bronco] 75,761; [Medium- and Heavy-duty] 99,523; [Total] 1,198,308. Ford remained the most popular nameplate in the U.S. truck field, although Chevrolet again outsold Ford in the light-duty categories. Ford sold a total of 1,053,394 light-duty trucks of all types, against Chevrolet's 1,059,569 total. Joseph A. Capolongo continued as General Manager of Ford Truck Operations.

1980 FORD

1980 Ford 1/2-Ton Bronco Custom Sport Utility Wagon 4x4 (JAG)

BRONCO CUSTOM: The 4x4 Bronco trimmed down a bit for 1980. Although the front end treatment resembled that used on 1978-79 models it was different. The grille was revised and the parking lights were now recessed directly beneath the headlights. New wraparound taillights were used. Also new was twin beam independent front suspension. And an improved four-wheel drive transfer case. In addition, the selector lever was relocated. Standard features included: Bucket seats. Vinyl sun visors. Padded instrument panel. Armrests. Dome lamp. Windshield header and A pillar moldings. Locking steering column. Anti-theft sliding door lock buttons. Inside hood release. Cowl side trim. Rubber floor mats. Black front and rear bumpers. Bright hubcaps and door-mounted mirrors. Swing-down tailgate with power window. Power brakes and steering. Four-speed manual transmission. Bronco color choices for 1980 were: Raven black; Wimbledon white; Candy-apple red; silver (metallic); Light sand; maroon; Dark chamois (metallic); Midnight blue (metallic); Medium blue; Light caramel; Dark pine (metallic); Medium grey (metallic); Dark silver-blue (metallic); Light medium pine; Chamois Glow; Walnut Glow; Sand Glow; Medium copper; and Bright yellow. Tu-Tone effects, with exterior color accented on roof, available in six different combinations. Accent tape stripe available with solid color or Victoria Tu-Tone. Deluxe Tu-Tone accent color covers center bodyside panel and lower molding is brushed aluminum on Custom. Victoria Tu-Tone accent color is on the front of roof, hood and around door window, plus the accent color also covers the lower bodyside.

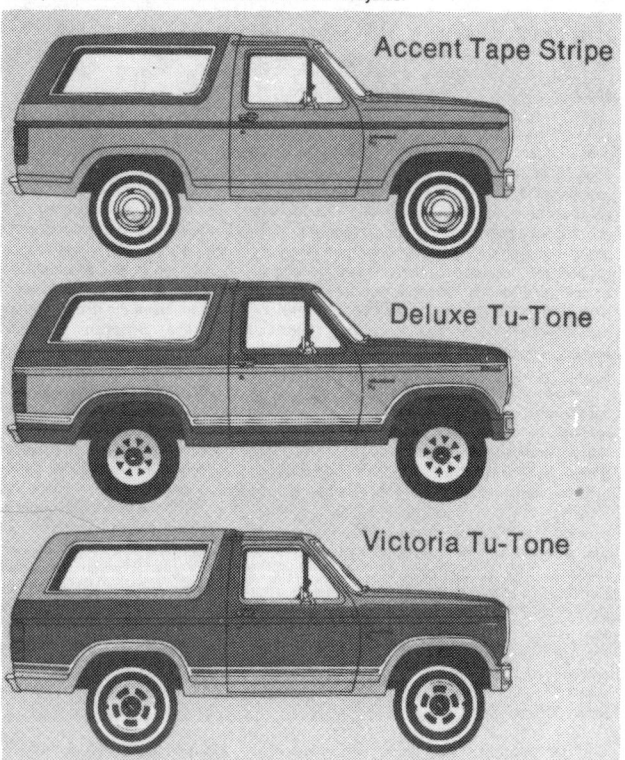

1980 Ford Bronco Exterior Trim Packages (JAG)

I.D. DATA [Bronco]: The VIN consists of 11 symbols. The first three indicate the series. The fourth indicates the engine. The fifth shows the assembly plant. The last six are the sequential production number.

Model	Body Type	Price	Weight	Prod. Total
Bronco 4x4 — 1/2-Ton — 104 in. w.b. — V-8				
U-150	Wagon	8392	4083	48,837

NOTE 1: Prices and weight for base V-8.

1980 Ford Bronco Utility With Free Wheeling Option (JAG)

ENGINE [Six]: Inline. OHV. Six. Bore & stroke: 4.00 x 3.98. Displacement: 300 cid. Net orsepower: 117 at 3000 rpm. Net torque: 223 lbs.-ft. at 1600 rpm. Compression: 8.9:1. Carburetor: One-barrel.

ENGINE [Base V-8]: V-block. OHV. Eight cylinders. Bore & stroke: 4.0 x 3.00. Displacement: 302 cid. Net horsepower: 130 at 3800 rpm. Net torque: 222 at 2000 rpm. Carburetor: Two-barrel.

CHASSIS: Wheebase: 104 in. Overall length: 180.3 in. Overall width: 79.3 in. Overall height: 75.5 in. Tires: L78 x 15B in.

1980 Ford Bronco Sport Utility Wagon (OCW)

POWERTRAIN OPTIONS: Transmission: SelectShift automatic. Engines: 302 cid V-8. 351 cid V-8. Most 1980 Broncos (42.2 percent) came with the 302 cid V-8; 41 percent had the 351 cid V-8 and 71.2 percent had automatic transmission.

CONVENIENCE OPTIONS: Bright wheel lip moldings. Chrome bumpers. Tri-color tape stripe on hood and sides. Padded black GT bar. Chrome grille. ComfortVent, high-output, or auxiliary heaters. Console. Convenience Group with intermittent wipers; map box in doors; headlamp-on warning buzzer; right-hand door courtesy light switch; and 12 in. mirror. Front bench seat. Flip/fold rear bench seat. Tinted glass all around. Privacy glass in quarter windows. Light Group with lights in glove box, ashtray and underhood; instrument panel courtesy lights; dome light with map light; right-hand door courtesy light; and headlamp-on warning buzzer (the underhood light had a 20-ft. cord). Handling Package with front stabilizer bar, quad heavy-duty hydraulic front and rear shocks. Captain's chairs. Tool storage box. Part time four-wheel drive (with optional automatic transmission). Trailer towing packages for light-duty (up to 2,000 lbs.) and heavy-duty (over 2,000 lbs.) applications. 32-gal. fuel tank in lieu of standard (includes skid plate.) Inside locking hood release. Protection Group with bright door edge guards, front bumper guards and front bumper rub strip. Security Group with locking gas cap, inside hood release lock, spare tire lock and locking glove box. Free Wheeling Packages: (A) With pinstripes along bodyside, hood, tailgate and around door windows; sport wheelcovers and bright bumpers or (B) with sports instrumentation; simulated leather wrapped steering wheel; fog lamps; bumper guards; handling package; GT bar and white styled steel wheels. Ranger XLT with brushed aluminum tailgate applique with bright letters; chrome bumpers; bright rear side window moldings; bright lower bodyside molding with black vinyl insert; Ranger XLT plaque; cloth trim or patterned vinyl interior; cut-pile carpeting; bright accents on door trims panels with lower area carpeted; rear quarter trim panels with integral armrests; storage bin and cargo lamps; front vinyl headliner on foam padding; deluxe seat belts; black vinyl spare tire cover; courtesy lighting; simulated leather wrapped steering wheel; cigar lighter; wood-tone accent around horn pad; and polished wood-tone applique on instrument panel with bright molding around instruments. Heavy-duty air cleaner. Heavy-duty shocks. Auxiliary transmission cooling package. White styled steel wheels. Chrome rear step bumper. Argent rear step bumper. Speed control. Swing-away spare tire carrier. 40-channel CB radio. Front tow hooks. Front and rear contour bumpers. 10-hole forged aluminum wheels with plastic coating. Sport wheelcovers. 5-slot forged aluminum 15 x 6 wheels. AM radio. AM/FM monaural radio. A total of 76.4 percent of 1980 Broncos had bucket seats; 61.6 percent tinted glass; 42.7 percent had styled steel wheels; 59.9 percent had air-conditioning; 23.9 percent had stereo; and 20.2 percent had AM/FM radios.

1980 Ford 1/2-Ton Econoline 100 Chateau Passenger Van (JAG)

ECONOLINE E-100 CARGO VAN: Econoline Van styling was unchanged for 1980. Among the standard features were: Full-foam driver's bucket seat. Vinyl seat trim in black, blue, red or sand. Padded full-width instrument panel. Brake warning light. Two-speed electric windshield wipers. Wiper-arm-mounted washer jets. Dome lights. Front compartment handling and insulated floor mat with scuff plates. Door checks. Argent silver-painted bumpers and hubcaps. Bright windshield molding. Painted mirrors. Hinged side cargo doors (sliding door available at no extra-cost).

ECONOLINE E-100 DISPLAY VAN: This model had windows at the rear and on the right-hand side. It came with the same standard features as the Cargo Van.

ECONOLINE E-100 WINDOW VAN: The Window Van had glass all around. It shared standard features with the Cargo Van.

I.D. DATA [Vans]: The VIN consists of 11 symbols. The first three indicate the series. The fourth indicates the engine. The fifth shows the assembly plant. The last six are the sequential production number.

Model	Body Type	Price	Weight	Prod. Total
E-100 Van — 1/2-Ton — 124 in./138 in. w.b. — V-8				
E-040	Cargo Van	5714	3680	Note 1
E-050	Window Van	5867	3813	Note 1
E-600	Display Van	5812	3802	Note 1

NOTE 1: Production: [Econoline] 92,661.
NOTE 2: Prices/weights for base V-8; deduct for six.
ENGINE [Base Six]: Inline. Six-cylinder. OHV. Bore & stroke: 4.00 in. x 3.98 in. Displacement: 300 cid. Net horsepower: 117 hp at 3000 rpm. Net torque: 223 lbs.-ft. at 1600 rpm. Compression ratio: 8.9:1. Carburetor: One-barrel.
ENGINE [Base V-8]: V-block. OHV. Eight cylinders. Bore & stroke: 4.0 x 3.00. Displacement: 302 cid. Net horsepower: 130 at 3800 rpm. Net torque: 222 at 2000 rpm. Carburetor: Two-barrel.

ECONOLINE E-150 CARGO VAN: The slightly more heavy-duty E-150 had most of the same standard features as the E-100.

ECONOLINE E-150 SUPER CARGO VAN: This Van had the same features as the E-150 Cargo Van plus a 20 in. extended rear overhang. This allowed carrying of longer loads. The maximum cargo length (right side, without passenger's seat) was 14 feet.

ECONOLINE E-150 DISPLAY VAN: This Van shared styling with the E-100 but had greater load capacity.

ECONOLINE E-150 WINDOW VAN: This Van shared styling with the E-100 Window Van, but had greater load capacity.

ECONOLINE E-150 SUPER WINDOW VAN: See E-150 Super Cargo Van.

I.D. DATA [Vans]: The VIN consists of 11 symbols. The first three indicate the series. The fourth indicates the engine. The fifth shows the assembly plant. The last six are the sequential production number.

Model	Body Type	Price	Weight	Prod. Total
E-150 Van — 1/2-Ton — 124 in. w.b. — V-8				
E-140	Cargo Van	6597	4160	Note 1
E-160	Display Van	6695	4306	Note 1
E-150	Window Van	6750	4317	Note 1
E-100 Super Van — 1/2-Ton — 138 in. w.b. — V-8				
E-140	Cargo Van	7115	4349	Note 1
E-160	Display Van	7213	4495	Note 1
E-150	Window Van	7268	4506	Note 1

NOTE 1: Production: [Econoline] 92,661.
NOTE 2: Prices/weights for base V-8; deduct for six.
ENGINE [Base Six]: Inline. Six-cylinder. OHV. Bore & stroke: 4.00 in. x 3.98 in. Displacement: 300 cid. Net horsepower: 117 hp at 3000 rpm. Net torque: 223 lbs.-ft. at 1600 rpm. Compression ratio: 8.9:1. Carburetor: One-barrel.

ECONOLINE E-250 CARGO VAN: The new E-250 had a higher GVW rating and more heavy-duty front and rear axles, than the E-150. It also came with eight-hole wheels. Standard features were the same as those on the E-100, except the three-speed manual transmission was not available in California.

ECONOLINE E-250 SUPER CARGO VAN: See E-150 Cargo Van.

ECONOLINE E-250 DISPLAY VAN: This vehicle shared styling and features with the E-100, but had greater load capacity.

ECONOLINE E-250 SUPER DISPLAY VAN: See E-150 Super Cargo Van.

ECONOLINE E-250 WINDOW VAN: This vehicle shared styling and features with the E-100 Window Van, but had greater load capacity.

ECONOLINE E-250 SUPER WINDOW VAN: See E-150 Super Cargo Van.

ECONOLINE E-250 CUTAWAY VAN: This Van with Camper Special Packages, was designed to readily accommodate custom motor homes.

ECONOLINE E-250 PARCEL DELIVERY: The E-250 Parcel Delivery van was 149.9 in. long and 74.3 in. high in its cargo area. The rear door opening was 84.7 in. wide.

I.D. DATA [Vans]: The VIN consists of 11 symbols. The first three indicate the series. The fourth indicates the engine. The fifth shows the assembly plant. The last six are the sequential production number.

Model	Body Type	Price	Weight	Prod. Total
E-250 Van — 3/4-Ton — 124 in. w.b. — V-8				
E-240	Cargo Van	6597	4160	Note 1
E-260	Display Van	6695	4306	Note 1
E-250	Window Van	6750	4317	Note 1
E-250 Super Van — 3/4-Ton — 138 in. w.b. — V-8				
E-240	Cargo Van	7115	4349	Note 1
E-260	Display Van	7213	4495	Note 1
E-250	Window Van	7268	4506	Note 1

NOTE 1: Production: [Econoline] 92,661.
NOTE 2: Prices/weights for base V-8; deduct for six.
ENGINE [Base Six]: Inline. Six-cylinder. OHV. Bore & stroke: 4.00 in. x 3.98 in. Displacement: 300 cid. Net horsepower: 117 hp at 3000 rpm. Net torque: 223 lbs.-ft. at 1600 rpm. Compression ratio: 8.9:1. Carburetor: One-barrel.
ENGINE [Base V-8]: V-block. OHV. Eight cylinders. Bore & stroke: 4.0 x 3.00. Displacement: 302 cid. Net horsepower: 130 at 3800 rpm. Net torque: 222 at 2000 rpm. Carburetor: Two-barrel.

ECONOLINE E-350 CARGO VAN: This was the top-of-the-line Econoline Van. It had heavy-duty front and rear shocks and a greater load capacity than the other series. Standard features were the same as the E-100.

ECONOLINE E-350 SUPER CARGO VAN: See E-150 Super Cargo Van.

ECONOLINE E-350 DISPLAY VAN: See E-250 Display Van.

ECONOLINE E-350 SUPER DISPLAY VAN: See E-150 Super Cargo Van.

ECONOLINE E-350 WINDOW VAN: See E-250 Window Van.

ECONOLINE E-350 SUPER WINDOW VAN: See E-150 Super Cargo Van.

ECONOLINE E-350 CUTAWAY VAN: See E-250 Cutaway Van.

ECONOLINE E-350 PARCEL DELIVERY: See E-250 Parcel Delivery.

I.D. DATA [Vans]: The VIN consists of 11 symbols. The first three indicate the series. The fourth indicates the engine. The fifth shows the assembly plant. The last six are the sequential production number.

Model	Body Type	Price	Weight	Prod. Total
E-350 Van — 1-Ton — 138 in. w.b. — V-8				
E-340	Cargo Van	6972	4352	Note 1
E-360	Display Van	7069	4498	Note 1
E-350	Window Van	7124	4509	Note 1
E-350 Super Van — 1-Ton — 155 in. w.b. — V-8				
S-340	Cargo Van	7784	4446	Note 1
S-350	Window Van	7937	4623	Note 1
S-360	Display Van	7882	4600	Note 1
E-350 Cutaway Van — 1-Ton — 155 in. w.b. — V-8				
E-370	Cutaway Van	6731	3840	Note 1
E-380	Parcel Delivery	9077	5338	Note 1

NOTE 1: Production: [Econoline] 92,661.
NOTE 2: Prices/weights for base V-8; deduct for six.
ENGINE [Base Six]: Inline. Six-cylinder. OHV. Bore & stroke: 4.00 in. x 3.98 in. Displacement: 300 cid. Net horsepower: 117 hp at 3000 rpm. Net torque: 223 lbs.-ft. at 1600 rpm. Compression ratio: 8.9:1. Carburetor: One-barrel.
ENGINE [Base V-8]: V-block. Eight-cylinder. OHV. Bore & stroke: 4.0 x 3.5. Displacement: 351 cid. Net horsepower: 156 at 4000 rpm. Net torque: 262 lbs.-ft. at 2200 rpm.
CHASSIS: Wheelbase: 124 in. (E-100/E-150) 138 in. Overall length: 186.8 in. (124 in. wheelbase); 206.8 in. (138 in. wheelbase); 226.8 in. (138 in. Super Van). GVW: 5,050-5,650 lbs. (E-100); 6,050-6,300 lbs. (E-150); 6,500-8,250 lbs. (E-250); 8,550-9,800 lbs. (E-350). Tires: F78 x 15B PT (E-100); L78 x 15B PT (E-150); 8.00 x 16.5D TT (E-250); 9.50 x 16.5D TT (E-350).

POWERTRAIN OPTIONS: Engine: 302 cid V-8. 351 cid V-8. 460 cid V-8 (E-250/E-350). 300 heavy-duty Six (E-350). Transmissions: Four-speed manual with overdrive. Select Shift automatic.

CONVENIENCE OPTIONS: Custom Van with (in addition to or in place of standard) wood-tone applique on instrument panel; front side cowl and door trim panels; cigarette lighter; front compartment headlining; insulated front floor mats; front roof rail garnish moldings; bright hubcaps; bright taillight bezels; and bright window frames with optional rear windows. Chateau Package with (in addition to or in place of Custom features) super soft vinyl or cloth and vinyl seat trim; cut-pile carpeting in front; courtesy light switches for all doors; chrome front and rear bumpers; bright grille surround molding; bright lower bodyside character line molding; and bright mirrors. Sports rails. Bodyside accent tape stripe. Three-color Cruising Van theme tape stripe. Port hole in right and left side. Bright grille surround. Deluxe accent moldings with bright drip rail moldings, plus center bodyside and lower character line molding. Bright lower character line moldings. Bright drip rail moldings. Bright window moldings. AM radio. AM/FM monaural radio. AM/FM stereo. AM/digital clock radio. AM/FM stereo with tape deck or cassette player. 40-channel CB radio. Rear speakers. Premium Sound System. Air-conditioning front or high capacity. Heaters, high output or auxiliary type for cargo area. Roof/floor insulation package. Deluxe insulation package. Convenience group (with intermittent wipers, dome light switches in all doors and day/night mirror). Dome light courtesy switches for all doors. Western low-mount mirrors (bright or black). Swing-out recreation mirrors (E-350). Sport steering wheel. Simulated leather wrapped steering wheel. Tilt steering. Speed control. Tinted glass all around. Privacy glass. Flip-open or fixed windows were available in all cargo doors. Single sliding side cargo door in lieu of hinged doors. Combination three-passenger rear seat that converts into a bed. Dual or quad captain's chairs (reclining and swivel or reclining only). Passenger seat. Flip-fold passengers seat. Cloth-and-vinyl trim for bucket and captain's chairs. Free Wheeling Packages with full-length carpeting, front door trim panels and the deluxe insulation package were part of the interior package. The Free Wheeling exterior package included five-slot matte finish aluminum wheels, black-out grille, black painted bumpers and mirrors and a black lower bodyside panel bordered by a half-inch black stripe. Trailer Towing Packages with five-slot or 10-hole forged aluminum wheels. Cruising Van with three-color tape stripes; 10-hole polished-finish forged aluminum wheels; port holes; blackout grille; black mirrors and bumpers; Chateau front door trim panels; wood-tone vinyl applique with bright surround on instrument panel; courtesy dome light switches on all doors; deluxe insulation package; full-length carpeting; Sport steering wheel; two reclining captain's chairs. Heavy-duty shocks. Front stabilizer bar. Engine block heater. Oil pressure gauge and ammeter. Cooling Packages: (super and extra). Push bar plus fog lights and covers. Protection Group with front and sliding door black stepwell pads, front door edge guards and front bumper guards (requires chrome bumpers). Security Group with locking gas cap, inside locking hood release and spare tire lock. Inside locking hood release. Chrome or painted Argent silver step bumper. Chrome contour bumpers. Deluxe wheelcovers.

Standard Catalog of Light-Duty Trucks

E-100 CLUB WAGON: Styling was carried over from the previous year. The E-100 Club Wagon was available in five- or eight-passenger versions. Among the standard features were: Front bucket and rear bench seats. Color-keyed patterned vinyl seat trim. Seat belts. Two-speed electric windshield wipers. Wiper-arm-mounted washer jets. 10 in. rearview mirror. Dome lights. Insulated floor mat with scuff plates. Three armrests. Dual horns. Flip-open windows in sliding door and opposite windows. Painted bumpers. 5 in. x 8 in. mirrors and hubcaps. Bright windshield molding. Econoline and Club Wagon colors for 1980 were: Wimbledon white; Candy-apple red; Light medium-blue; silver (metallic); Dark pine (metallic); Dark brown (metallic); Light sand; Dark silver blue (metallic); Raven black; Bright yellow; and maroon. Optional Glow colors: Sand Glow and Walnut Glow. Bodyside accent tape stripe was available in Raven black; Midnight blue (metallic); Dark brown (metallic); Sand Glow; Light sand; Wimbledon white; or Gold yellow. Four two-tone paint schemes were available.

E-150 CLUB WAGON: This was a slightly more heavy-duty version of the E-100. It could be had in 124 in. or 138 in. wheelbase and was also offered in five- and eight-passenger versions. Standard features were same as those on the E-100.

E-150 SUPER WAGON: This was basically the same as the 138 in. wheelbase E-150, but had an 20 in. extended rear overhang.

E-250 CLUB WAGON: The E-250 Club Wagon could be had with five-, eight- or 12-passenger capacity. It had most of the same features as the E-100.

E-250 SUPER WAGON: This was basically an E-250 with a 20 in. rear overhang.

E-350 SUPER WAGON: The heavy-duty E-350 provided 20 in. more inside length than regular 138 in. wheelbase Club Wagons. Heavy-duty shocks were standard.

I.D. DATA [Vans]: The VIN consists of 11 symbols. The first three indicate the series. The fourth indicates the engine. The fifth shows the assembly plant. The last six are the sequential production number.

Model	Body Type	Price	Weight	Prod. Total
E-100 Van — 1/2-Ton — 124 in./138 in. w.b. — V-8				
E-100	Club Wagon	6862	3988	Note 1
E-100 Van — 1/2-Ton — 124 in./138 in. w.b. — V-8				
E-150	Club Wagon	7078	4039	Note 1
E-150	Super Wagon	7831	4336	Note 1
E-250 Van — 3/4-Ton — 138 in. w.b. — V-8				
E-250	Club Wagon	7538	4450	Note 1
E-250	Super Wagon	8165	4625	Note 1
E-350 — 1-Ton — 138 in. w.b. — V-8				
E-350	Super Wagon	8758	4901	Note 1

NOTE 1: Production: [Club Wagon] 22,956.
NOTE 2: Prices/weights for base V-8; deduct for six.
ENGINE [Base Six]: Inline. Six-cylinder. OHV. Bore & stroke: 4.00 in. x 3.98 in. Displacement: 300 cid. Net horsepower: 117 hp at 3000 rpm. Net torque: 223 lbs.-ft. at 1600 rpm. Compression ratio: 8.9:1. Carburetor: One-barrel.
ENGINE [Base V-8; Except E-350]: V-block. OHV. Eight cylinders. Bore & stroke: 4.0 x 3.00. Displacement: 302 cid. Net horsepower: 130 at 3800 rpm. Net torque: 222 at 2000 rpm. Carburetor: Two-barrel.
ENGINE [Base V-8; E-350]: V-block. Eight-cylinder. OHV. Bore & stroke: 4.00 x 3.5 in. Displacement: 351 cid. Net horsepower: 156 at 4000 rpm. Net torque: 262 lbs.-ft. at 2200 rpm.
CHASSIS: Wheelbase: 124 in. (E-100); 138 in. (E-150/E-250/E-350). Overall length: See Econoline. GVW: 5,400-9,400 lbs. Tires: G78 x 15B (E-100); H78 x 15D (E-150); 8.00 x 16D (E-250); 9.50 x 16.5D (E-350).
POWERTRAIN OPTIONS: Engines: 302 cid V-8. 351 cid V-8. 400 cid V-8. 460 cid V-8. Transmissions: SelectShift automatic. Four-speed manual with overdrive.

1980 Ford 1/2-Ton Econoline 100 Chateau Club Wagon

CONVENIENCE OPTIONS: Most of the same items available on the Econoline, plus four-passenger rear bench seat. Snack-game table.

1980 Ford 1/2-Ton Courier Mini-Pickup (JAG)

COURIER PICKUP: If you liked the 1979 Courier, you'd like the 1980. For all practical purposes, they were the same. Buyers could still choose from a six- or seven-foot box. Among the standard features were: Color-keyed vinyl headlining, seat and door trim panels. Instrument lighting intensity control. Cigarette lighter. Brake warning light. New dome light. Door vent windows with wedge-type handles. Padded instrument panel. Hinged seatback for easy access to stowage area. Inside hood release. White sidewall tires. Cargo tie-down hooks. Bright front bumper. One-hand tailgate operation. Four-speed manual transmission.

I.D. DATA [Courier]: The VIN consists of 11 symbols. The first indicates the manufacturer. The second indicates the engine. The third indicates the series. The fourth indicates the engine. The fifth (a letter) indicates the model year. The sixth indicates the production month. The last five are the sequential production number.

Model	Body Type	Price	Weight	Prod. Total
Courier — 1/2-Ton — 104.3 in. w.b. — Four				
—	Chassis & Cab	4712	2430	Note 1
—	Pickup	4861	2680	Note 1

NOTE 1: Model year sales: 78,401.
ENGINE [Base Four]: Inline. Four-cylinder. OHV. Bore & stroke: 3.07 in. x 3.70 in. Displacement: 110 cid. Net horsepower: 77 nhp at 4500 rpm 972 nhp in California). Carburetor: Two-barrel.
CHASSIS: Wheelbase: 106.9 in. (6 ft. box); 112.8 in. (7 ft. box). Overall length: 177.9 in. (6 ft. box); 189.4 in. (7 ft. box). Overall width: 63 in. Overall height: 61.5 in. GVW: 4,100 lbs. Tires: 6.00 x 14C white sidewall.
POWERTRAIN OPTIONS: Transmissions: Floor-shifted automatic or five-speed manual transmission (with overdrive).
CONVENIENCE OPTIONS: AM or AM/FM monaural push-button radios. Air-conditioning. Low-mounted Western mirrors. Tinted glass all around. Radial tires. Cast aluminum wheels. Soft Ride Package with 3,600 lbs. GVWR, five-leaf progressive-rate rear springs and 2,010 lbs. rated rear axle. Rear step bumper. Free Wheeling Packages: (A) Includes: Black-painted GT bar and push bar; (B) Includes: Package A, plus cast aluminum wheels, five raised white-letter 70 series tires and three-color accent tape stripe. XLT Package with [Interior] soft supple vinyl seat and door trim; wood-tone upper door trim panel and transmission shift knob; cut-pile carpeting; day/night mirror; Ashtray, underhood and glove box lights; glove box lock; sport steering wheel; and temperature gauge and ammeter. [Exterior] Bright grille; bright windshield, rear window, drip rail, wheel lip and taillight surround moldings; Deluxe wheelcovers; and dual accent pinstripes. Sports Group with black sport steering wheel; bucket seats trimmed in black vinyl with black and white plaid fabric inserts; black carpet and interior trim; wood-tone applique on instrument cluster mask; temperature gauge; and ammeter.

1980 Ford 1/2-Ton F-100 Ranger XLT Styleside Pickup 4x4 (JAG)

F-100 CUSTOM PICKUP: The first new truck of the 1980s. That's what Ford advertising claimed of its new light-duty trucks. They featured a new vertical and horizontal bars theme grille. Rectangular parking lights were recessed below each rectangular headlight, which were also recessed. The Ford letters on the face of the hood were slanted back. Rectangular slots were located between the grille and new, larger front bumper. Styleside models now had wraparound taillights and the Supercab featured a distinctive twin window treatment. The interiors were also redesigned. New seats gave passengers approximately 10 percent more legroom. A new 4x4 transfer case shift pattern had the "2H" gearshift position located up out of the way. Standard features included: Bright front bumper, grille surround, windshield moldings. Left-hand and right-hand door-mounted mirrors. Argent silver hubcaps. Push-button door handles. All-vinyl seat trim. Instrument panel with cluster trim applique and full-width pad. Glove box with latch. Left-hand door courtesy light switch. Temperature gauge. Color-keyed windshield pillar, header, cowl side trim panels and door trim panels with foam-padded armrests. Scuff plates. Coat hook. Dome light. Floor insulation and carpet-texture rubber mat. Easily removable tailgate (Styleside). Radial-ply tires. Maintenance-free battery. Long windshield wiper blades with dual port washer spray nozzles. Coolant recovery system. Rubber-isolated front coil springs. Lower overall steering ratio. Locking steering column. Horizontal sliding door lock buttons. Entry shield on door latch. Door vent windows with steel push-button lock. Aerodynamic design (reportedly this reduced air drag at highway speeds as much as 13 percent). Twin-I-Beam independent front suspension. Three-speed manual transmission. The F-100 Pickup could be ordered with 6.5 ft. Flareside and 6.75 ft. or 8-ft. Styleside boxes. Only the regular cab was available. Standard F-series colors for 1980 were: Raven black; Wimbledon white; Candy-apple red; silver (metallic); Light sand; maroon; Dark chamois (metallic); Midnight blue (metallic); Medium blue; Light caramel; Dark pine (metallic); Medium gray (metallic); Dark silver-blue (metallic); and Light medium-pine. Optional glamour colors were: Chamois Glow, Walnut Glow and Sand Glow. Accent tape stripe: Bodyside tape runs from front marker lamp to taillamp. Available separately or with regular or Victoria Tu-Tone. Tu-Tones: [Regular] Accent color covered roof and upper back panel; options includes dual tape stripe to divide colors; [Deluxe] Accent color on center bodyside area and on tailgate, below upper molding; [Combination] Regular and Deluxe Tu-Tone combined; [Victoria] Accent color applied to hood, upper fender, around door window and on the lower bodyside.

I.D. DATA [F-Series]: The VIN consists of 11 symbols. The first three indicate the series. The fourth indicates the engine. The fifth shows the assembly plant. The last six are the sequential production number.

Model	Body Type	Price	Weight	Prod. Total
F-100 — 1/2-Ton — 117 in. w.b. — V-8				
83	Flareside 6.5 ft.	5549	3324	Note 1
83	Styleside 6.75 ft.	5549	3324	Note 1

378

F-100 Supercab — 1/2-Ton — 133 in. w.b. — V-8

83	Styleside 8 ft.	5633	3391	Note 1

NOTE 1: Production: [F-100] 133,590.
NOTE 2: Prices/weights for base V-8; deduct for six-cylinder.
NOTE 3: Add for 4x4.
ENGINE [Base Six]: Inline. Six-cylinder. OHV. Bore & stroke: 4.00 in. x 3.98 in. Displacement: 300 cid. Net horsepower: 117 hp at 3200 rpm. Net torque: 223 lbs.-ft. at 1600 rpm. Compression ratio: 8.0:1. Carburetor: One-barrel. Most 1980 F-100s (73 percent) came with this engine.
ENGINE [Base V-8]: V-block. OHV. Eight-cylinder. Bore and stroke: 4.0 x 3.0 in. Displacement: 302 cid. Net horsepower: 130 at 3800 rpm. Net torque: 222 lbs.-ft. at 2000 rpm.

1980 Ford Heavy 1/2-Ton F-150 Custom Flareside Pickup 4x4 (JAG)

F-150 CUSTOM PICKUP: The 150 was Ford's heavy-duty 1/2-ton. It had most of the same features as the F-100, plus power brakes. Both Flareside and Styleside boxes were available. Stylesides could be had in regular or Supercabs. The latter provided space behind the front seat for an optional rear bench seat or two jump seats. The F-150 4x4 like all F-Series with optional 4x4, had new Twin-Traction Beam Independent Suspension.
I.D. DATA [F-Series]: The VIN consists of 11 symbols. The first three indicate the series. The fourth indicates the engine. The fifth shows the assembly plant. The last six are the sequential production number.

Model	Body Type	Price	Weight	Prod. Total
F-150 — 1/2-Ton — 133 in. w.b. — V-8				
83	Flareside 6.5 ft.	5697	3388	Note 1
83	Styleside 6.75 ft.	5697	3388	Note 1
83	Styleside 8 ft.	5782	3457	Note 1
F-150 Supercab — 1/2-Ton — 155 in. w.b. — V-8				
83	Styleside	6400	3691	Note 1

NOTE 1: Production: [F-150] 173,050.
NOTE 2: Prices/weights for base V-8; deduct for six-cylinder.
NOTE 3: Add For 4x4.
ENGINE [Base Six]: Inline. Six-cylinder. OHV. Bore & stroke: 4.00 in. x 3.98 in. Displacement: 300 cid. Net horsepower: 101 hp at 3000 rpm. Net torque: 223 lbs.-ft. at 1600 rpm. Compression ratio: 8.0:1. Carburetor: One-barrel.
ENGINE [Base V-8]: V-block. OHV. Eight-cylinder. Bore and stroke: 4.0 x 3.0 in. Displacement: 302 cid. Net horsepower: 130 at 3800 rpm. Net torque: 222 lbs.-ft. at 2000 rpm.
ENGINE [Supercab and 4x4 Base V-8]: V-block. OHV. Eight-cylinder. Bore and stroke: 4.00 in. x 3.50 in. Displacement: 351 cid. Horsepower: 156 nhp at 4000 rpm. Net torque: 262 lbs.-ft. at 2200 rpm. Carburetor: Two-barrel. (Note: By this time net horsepower ratings were calculated according to weight of the model, so exact horsepower ratings vary in different reference sources.)

1980 Ford Heavy 1/2-Ton F-150 Ranger Styleside Pickup 4x4 (JAG)

F-250 CUSTOM PICKUP: The 3/4-ton F-250 was offered in regular or Supercabs. However, the only box available was the Styleside. Standard features echoed those of the F-100 with the addition of power brakes.
I.D. DATA [F-Series]: The VIN consists of 11 symbols. The first three indicate the series. The fourth indicates the engine. The fifth shows the assembly plant. The last six are the sequential production number.

Model	Body Type	Price	Weight	Prod. Total
F-250 — 3/4-Ton — 133 in. w.b. — V-8				
81	Chassis & Cab	6515	3479	Note 1
83	Styleside	6234	3636	Note 1

F-250 Supercab — 3/4-Ton — 155 in. w.b. — V-8

83	Styleside	6741	3815	Note 1

NOTE 1: Production: [F-250] 71,089.
NOTE 2: Prices/weights for base V-8; deduct for six.
NOTE 3: Add for 4x4.
NOTE 4: Supercabs available with 6.75 ft. and 8 ft. Styleside boxes.
ENGINE [Base Six]: Displacement: 300 cid. Six. Horsepower: 120 nhp at 3400 rpm. Bore & stroke: 4.00 x 3.98. Compression ratio: 8.0:1. Carburetor: One-barrel. This engine went in 22.3 percent of the 1980 Ford F-250s. Most (58.5 percent) had the base 351 cid V-8. Supercabs had 360 cid V-8s.
ENGINE [Base V-8]: V-block. OHV. Eight-cylinder. Bore and stroke: 4.00 in. x 3.50 in. Displacement: 351 cid. Horsepower: 156 nhp at 4000 rpm. Net torque: 262 lbs.-ft. at 2200 rpm. Carburetor: Two-barrel. (Note: By this time net horsepower ratings were calculated according to weight of the model, so exact horsepower ratings vary in different reference sources.)

1980 Ford 1-Ton F-350 Ranger XLT Super Cab Styleside Pickup

F-350 CUSTOM PICKUP: The 1-ton F-350 was offered in regular and Supercab versions. Both featured the smooth sides all-steel Styleside box. New for 1980 was a dual rear wheel Styleside Pickup. Except for having a four-speed manual transmission and power brakes, most F-350 features were the same as those on the F-100.
I.D. DATA [F-Series]: The VIN consists of 11 symbols. The first three indicate the series. The fourth indicates the engine. The fifth shows the assembly plant. The last six are the sequential production number.

Model	Body Type	Price	Weight	Prod. Total
F-350 — 1-Ton — 133 in./161 in. w.b. — V-8				
81	Chassis & Cab	6457	3805	Note 1
83	Styleside	6769	4080	Note 1
F-350 Supercab — 1-Ton — 133 in./161 in. w.b. — V-8				
83X	Styleside	7362	4338	Note 1

NOTE 1: Production: [F-350] 49,339.
NOTE 2: Prices/weights for base V-8; deduct for six.
NOTE 3: Add for 4x4.
NOTE 4: Supercabs available with 6.75 ft. and 8 ft. Styleside boxes.

1980 Ford 1-Ton F-350 Ranger XLT Styleside Pickup (JAG)

ENGINE [Base Six]: Displacement: 300 cid. Six. Horsepower: 120 nhp at 3400 rpm. Bore & stroke: 4.00 x 3.98. Compression ratio: 8.0:1. Carburetor: One-barrel. Only 10 percent of 1980 F-350s came with this six-cylinder engine.
ENGINE [Base V-8]: V-block. OHV. Eight-cylinder. Bore and stroke: 4.00 in. x 3.50 in. Displacement: 351 cid. Horsepower: 156 nhp at 4000 rpm. Net torque: 262 lbs.-ft. at 2200 rpm. Carburetor: Two-barrel. Supercabs had 360 cid V-8s.
(Note: By this time net horsepower ratings were calculated according to the weight of the vehicle, so horsepower ratings vary in different reference sources.)
CHASSIS: Wheelbase: 116.8 in. (F-100/F-150); 133 in. (all); 138.8 in. (F-150/F-250 Supercab); 155 in. (F-150/F-250/F-350 Supercab). Overall length: 187.8 in. (F-100/F-150 Flareside); 192.1 in. (F-100/F-150 Style); 208.3 in. (Styleside); 214.1 in. (F-150/F-250 Supercab); 230.3 in. (F-350 Supercab). GVW: 4,700-5,150 lbs. (F-100); 5,250-6,000 lbs. (F-150); 6,350-8,200 lbs. (F-250); 8,650-10,000 lbs. (F-350). Tires: P195/75R x 15SL (F-100); P215/75R x 15SL (F-150); P225/75R x 15SL (F-150 Supercab); 8.00 x 16.5D (F-250); 9.50 x 16.5E (F-350).
POWERTRAIN OPTIONS: Engines: 302 cid V-8 (F-100/F-150/F-250); 351 cid V-8 (F-150/F-250/F-350); 400 cid V-8 (F-350). Transmission: Four-speed manual. Four-speed manual with overdrive. SelectShift automatic. Most 1980 F-350s (67.7 percent) had the four-speed manual transmission. However, an automatic was the choice in 43 percent of the F-100s, 55.5 percent of F-150s and 51 percent of F-250s.

Standard Catalog of Light-Duty Trucks

1980 Ford 1-Ton F-350 Ranger XLT 4x4 Camper Special Styleside Pickup (JAG)

CONVENIENCE OPTIONS: Chrome grille. Accent tape stripe (for single rear wheel Stylesides). Lower bodyside molding with black vinyl insert (for single rear wheel Stylesides). Bright wheel lip moldings (for single rear wheel Custom Stylesides). Bright box rails for 8 ft. Styleside Pickups. GT bar with three equipment mounting tabs on top. AM radio. AM/FM monaural radio. AM/FM stereo radio (speakers mounted in door panels). AM/FM stereo with 8-track tape player. AM/FM stereo with cassette tape player. 40-channel CB radio. Air-conditioning. High-output or ComfortVent heaters. Convenience Group with intermittent wipers; 12 in. day/night mirror; map box on doors; headlamp-on warning buzzer; and courtesy light switch on right-hand door with Custom. Electronic digital clock. Fingertip speed control. Light Group with lights in glove box; in ashtray; under instrument panel; and dome lamp with map light; plus cargo box light, headlamp-on warning buzzer and courtesy light switch on right-hand door with Custom. Also new movable underhood worklight with 20 ft. retractable cord. Bright low-mount Western mirrors. Bright low-mount recreation mirrors. Power steering. Power brakes (F-100). Simulated leather-wrapped steering wheel. Tinted sliding rear window. Tilt steering wheel. Tinted glass all around. Tool storage box located under the hood (includes movable underhood worklight with 20 ft. retractable cord and inside locking hood release). Slide-out spare tire carrier. Spare tire carrier side-mounted inside Styleside box. Center console (Supercabs with captain's chairs). Reclining captain's chairs in Supercab. Forward-facing, folding rear seat in Supercab. Center-facing folding rear seats in Supercab. Heavy-duty black vinyl, knitted vinyl or all-vinyl seat trim. Cloth and vinyl inserts in Ranger. Folding seatback in Customs. Auxiliary fuel tank. Heavy-duty front and rear shocks. Oil pressure and ammeter gauges. Handling Package with front and rear stabilizer bars, heavy-duty front and rear shocks and heavy-duty front springs. Front and rear stabilizer bars. Engine block heater. Extra-cooling engine package. Super-cooling engine package. Special altitude performance package. Camper special package. Trailer towing packages. Dual horns. Fog lamps (included plastic covers and bright front bumper guards.) Inside locking hood release. Five roof clearance lights. Exterior Protection Group with bright door edge guards, front bumper guards and front bumper rub strip. Security Lock Group with locking gas cap, inside hood release, locking glove box and spare tire lock. Sports instrumentation. Eight chromed tie-down hooks on Stylesides. Argent silver step for Stylesides. Chrome step for single rear wheel Stylesides. Chrome channel type rear bumper for Flaresides. Chrome contour type rear bumper for single rear wheel Stylesides. Deluxe wheelcovers. White-painted styled steel wheels. Ten-hole polished forged aluminum wheels with clear plastic coating. Sport wheelcovers. Five-slot brushed-finished forged aluminum wheels with clear plastic coating. Free Wheeling Packages: (A) With pin-striping, black-out grille and headlamp doors and sport wheelcovers; (B) With all A group features, plus fog lamps and bumper guards; handling package; bright rear contour bumper (Stylesides) or bright channel bumper (Flaresides); 10-hole aluminum wheels in place of wheelcovers; simulated leather-wrapped steering wheel; plus sports instrumentation package with tachometer, trip odometer, ammeter and oil pressure gauge; GT bar; and styled steel wheels (Styleside 4x4). Ranger Package with (in addition to or in place of all Custom features) brushed aluminum lower bodyside molding; black insert around the back window; bright hubcaps (except with dual rear wheels); all-vinyl or cloth and vinyl seat trim; courtesy lighting with passenger side door switch as well as driver's; bright accents on door trim panels; cigarette lighter; wood-tone accent around steering wheel horn pad; polished wood-tone applique on instrument panel; color-keyed seat belts; folding seatback; and color-keyed floor mat. Ranger XLT Package with bright aluminum bodyside moldings on roof drip rail, windshield and rear window; trim on rear side windows (Supercab and Crew Cab); cloth seat upholstery with vinyl trim (chain-mail vinyl was a no-cost option); wall-to-wall cut-pile carpeting; covered floor insulation; vinyl headlining with sound-deadening backing; door trim panels with woodgrain vinyl insert and bright trim moldings; steering wheel horn bar with woodgrain vinyl surround; and (on Stylesides) special tailgate applique with bright back-up light and wheel lip moldings. Ranger Lariat Package (for Stylesides) with deluxe Tu-Tone paint treatment; "race track" moldings; special Ranger Lariat emblems; black tailgate applique (solid exterior paint colors available); unique upholstery trimmed with super soft vinyl; deluxe seat belts; color-keyed vinyl headliner with special sound-absorbing padding and button-quilted design; door trim panels with padded inserts above and map pockets in the lower door; wall-to-wall carpeting; and inner cowlside carpeting. Camper Special Package.

HISTORICAL: Model year production by line was: [F-100] 133,590; [F-150] 173,050; [F-250] 71,089; [F-350] 49,339; [Bronco] 38,563; [Econoline] 92,661; [Club Wagon] 22,956; [Total] 581,248. This total covers all trucks up to 10,000 lbs. GVRW, including those built in Canada for the U.S. market. Model year sales, by type, were: [Light Conventional] 537,476; [Econoline] 114,645; [Club Wagon] 26,498; [Courier] 78,401; [Bronco] 48,837; [Medium- and Heavy-duty] 74,662; [Total] 880,519. The Ranchero was not available for the first time since 1957. Despite a sharp drop in total sales volume, Ford remained the nation's number one truck-maker. Light-duty trucks sales were down 31 percent and reflected the concern over rising gas prices; the effect of soaring interest rates; and a generally weak economy.

1981 FORD

BRONCO CUSTOM: Styling of the four-wheel drive Bronco was unchanged for 1981. Interior colors offered were: Black; red; Medium blue; fawn; nutmeg; and spruce. Standard features included: Bucket seats; vinyl sun visors; padded instrument panel; armrests; dome lamp; windshield header and A pillar moldings; locking steering column; anti-theft sliding door lock buttons; inside hood release; cowlside trim; rubber floor mats; black front and rear bumpers; bright hubcaps and door-mounted mirrors; swing-down tailgate with power window; power brakes and steering; and four-speed manual transmission. Standard Bronco color choices for 1981 were: Raven black; Wimbledon white; silver (metallic); Medium grey (metallic); Candy-apple red; maroon; Medium blue; Midnight blue (metallic); Dark spruce (metallic); fawn; Dark cocoa (metallic); Dark chamois (metallic); Medium caramel (metallic); Light caramel; and tan. Optional colors were Bittersweet Glow; Medium Blue Glow; Medium Spruce Glow; and Fawn Glow. Tu-Tone effects included: (A) Exterior body color accented by roof available in six different colors; (B) Accent Tape Stripe available with solid exterior color; (C) Tu-Tone effect and Victoria Tu-Tone; (D) Deluxe Tu-Tone with accent color covering center bodyside panel (includes lower bodyside protection molding with black vinyl insert); and (E) Victoria Tu-Tone where accent color is on the front roof, hood and lower bodyside (includes lower bodyside protection molding with black vinyl insert).

I.D. DATA: The VIN has 17 symbols. The first three indicate the manufacturer, make, and type of vehicle. The fourth symbol indicates the GVW range. The fifth, sixth and seventh symbols indicate the series and body style. The eighth symbol indicates the type of engine. The ninth symbol is a check digit. The 10th symbol (a letter) indicates model year. The 11th symbol indicates the assembly plant. The remaining symbols are the sequential production number starting with 100001 at each plant.

Model	Body Type	Price	Weight	Prod. Total
Bronco 4x4 — 1/2-Ton — 105 in. w.b. — Six				
U-150	Wagon	9085	4038	34,850

ENGINE [Base Six]: Inline. OHV. Six-cylinder (heavy-duty). Bore & stroke: 4.0 x 3.98 in. Displacement: 300 cid (4.9 liter). Compression ratio: 8.9:1. Net horsepower: 115 at 3000 rpm. Taxable horsepower: 38.4. Net torque: 223 lbs.-ft. at 1600 rpm. Carburetor: One-barrel. (Note: Horsepower and torque may vary with specific model applications, as net horsepower ratings are relative to weight of vehicle.)

1981 Ford 1/2-Ton Bronco XLT Sport Utility Wagon 4x4 (OCW)

ENGINE [Base V-8; Mandatory in California]: V-block. OHV. Eight-cylinder. Bore & stroke: 4.0 in. x 3.0 in. Displacement: 302 cid (5.0 liter). Net horsepower: 130 at 3800 rpm. Taxable horsepower: 51.2. Net torque: 222 lbs.-ft. at 2000 rpm. Carburetor: Two-barrel. (Note: Horsepower and torque may vary with specific model applications, as net horsepower ratings are relative to weight of vehicle.)

ENGINE [Optional V-8]: V-block. OHV. Eight-cylinder. Bore & stroke: 4.0 in. x 3.5 in. Displacement: 351 cid (5.8 liter). Net horsepower: 156 at 4000 rpm. Taxable horsepower: 51.2. Net torque: 262 lbs.-ft. at 2200 rpm. Carburetor: Two-barrel. (Note: Horsepower and torque may vary with specific model applications, as net horsepower ratings are relative to weight of vehicle.)

CHASSIS: Wheebase: 104.7 in. Overall length: 177.6 in. Overall height: 73.2 in. Tires: P215/75R-15 SL.

POWERTRAIN OPTIONS: Engines: 302 cid V-8. 351 cid V-8. Transmissions: SelectShift automatic transmission. Four-speed manual transmission with overdrive. Most 1981 Broncos (66 percent) came with automatic transmission and 37 percent had the 302 cid V-8, while 38.3 percent had the 351 cid V-8.

CONVENIENCE OPTIONS: Bright wheel lip moldings. Chrome bumpers. Tri-color tape stripe. Chromatic tape. Padded black GT bar. Chrome grille. High-output or auxiliary heaters. Console. Rear window defroster. Soft wrap steering wheel. AM/FM stereo with eight-track player. Convenience Group includes intemittent wipers; map box in doors; headlamp-on warning buzzer; right-hand door courtesy light switch; 12-in. mirror and visor vanity mirror; front bench seat; flip/fold rear bench seat; power windows; tinted glass all around; and privacy glass in quarter windows. Light Group includes lights in glove box, ashtray and underhood; instrument panel courtesy lights; dome light with map light; right-hand door courtesy light; and headlamp-on warning buzzer (the underhood light had a 20 foot cord). Handling Package includes front stabilizer bar, quad heavy-duty hydraulic front shocks; and dual heavy-duty rear shocks. Captain's chair. Underhood tool box. Part-time four-wheel drive (with optional automatic transmission). Sports Instrumentation option includes tachometer; ammeter; oil pressure gauge; and trip odometer. Trailer Towing Packages in light-duty (up to 2,000 lbs.) and heavy-duty (over 2,000 lbs.) versions with 32-gal. fuel tank and skid plate. Inside locking hood release. Protection Group includes bright door edge guards; front bumper guards; and front bumper rub strip. Security Group includes locking gas cap; inside hood release lock; spare tire lock; and locking glove box. Free Wheeling Package A includes pinstripes along bodyside, hood, tailgate and around door windows; sport wheelcovers; and bright bumpers. Free Wheeling Package B includes sports instrumentation; soft-wrap steering wheel; fog lamps with covers; bumper guards; handling package; GT bar; and white styled steel wheels. Ranger XLT includes brushed aluminum tailgate applique with bright letters; chrome bumpers; bright rear side window moldings;

bright lower bodyside molding with black vinyl insert; Ranger XLT plaque; cloth trim on interior; full cut-pile carpeting; bright and wood-tone accents on door trim panels with lower area carpeted; rear quarter trim panels with integral armrests; storage bin and cargo lamp; front vinyl headliner on foam padding; deluxe seat belts; black vinyl spare tire cover; courtesy lighting; soft-wrap steering wheel; visor vanity mirror; cigar lighter; wood-tone accent around horn pad; and polished wood-tone applique on instrument panel with bright molding around instruments. Heavy-duty air cleaner. Heavy-duty shocks. Auxiliary transmission cooling package. White styled steel wheels. Chrome rear step bumper. Argent silver rear step bumper. Speed control. Swing-away spare tire carrier. 40-channel CB radio. Front tow hooks. Front and rear contour bumpers. 10-hole forged aluminum wheels with plastic coating. Sport wheelcovers. Five-slot forged aluminum 15 x 6 in. wheels. AM radio. AM/FM monaural radio. Snow plow preparation package. Special high-altitude performance package.

NOTE: A total of 78.5 percent of 1981 Broncos had bucket seats and 54.8 percent came with the Ranger XLT package.

ECONOLINE E-100 CARGO VAN: If you liked the 1980 Econoline, you'd probably like the 1981. It looked the same on the outside. However, changes were made to the standard and optional upholstery. Among the standard features were: Full-foam driver's bucket seat; ribbed vinyl seat trim in black, Medium blue, red, fawn or Nutmeg; padded full-width instrument panel; brake warning light; two-speed electric windshield wipers; wiper-arm-mounted washer jets; dome lights; front compartment headlining; column-mounted ignition switch; door checks; Argent silver-painted bumpers and hubcaps; bright windshield molding; painted mirrors; hinged side cargo doors (sliding door available at no extra cost); and halogen headlights. Econoline colors for 1981 were: Wimbledon white; Candy-apple red; Antique cream; silver (metallic); Dark pine (metallic); Raven black; Medium caramel (metallic); Dark silver blue (metallic); black; Dark cocoa; Dark chamois (metallic); and maroon. Optional Glow colors were Medium blue; fawn; and Light fawn. Three Tu-Tone combinations were available.

ECONOLINE E-100 DISPLAY VAN: This model had windows at the rear and on the right-hand side. It came with the same standard features as the Cargo Van.

ECONOLINE E-100 WINDOW VAN: The Window Van had glass all around. It shared features with the Cargo Van.

I.D. DATA: The VIN has 17 symbols. The first three indicate the manufacturer; make; and type of vehicle. The fourth symbol indicates the GVW range. The fifth, sixth and seventh symbols indicate the series and body style. The eighth symbol indicates the type of engine. The ninth symbol is a check digit. The 10th symbol (a letter) indicates model year. The 11th symbol indicates the assembly plant. The remaining symbols are the sequential production number starting with 100001 at each plant.

Model	Body Type	Price	Weight	Prod. Total
E-100 — 1/2-Ton — 124 in./138 in. w.b. — Six				
E-040	Cargo Van	6420	3650	Note 1
E-050	Window Van	6575	3677	Note 1
E-060	Display Van	6522	3664	Note 1

NOTE 1: Model year production of Econolines was 104,566.

ENGINE [Base Six]: Inline. OHV. Six-cylinder (heavy-duty). Bore & stroke: 4.0 x 3.98 in. Displacement: 300 cid (4.9 liter). Compression ratio: 8.9:1. Net horsepower: 115 at 3000 rpm. Taxable horsepower: 38.4. Net torque: 223 lbs.-ft. at 1600 rpm. Carburetor: One-barrel. (Note: Horsepower and torque may vary with specific model applications, as net horsepower ratings are relative to weight of vehicle.)

ENGINE [Base V-8; Mandatory in California]: V-block. OHV. Eight-cylinder. Bore & stroke: 4.0 in. x 3.0 in. Displacement: 302 cid (5.0 liter). Net horsepower: 130 at 3800 rpm. Taxable horsepower: 51.2. Net torque: 222 lbs.-ft. at 2000 rpm. Carburetor: Two-barrel. (Note: Horsepower and torque may vary with specific model applications, as net horsepower ratings are relative to weight of vehicle.)

ENGINE [Optional V-8]: V-block. OHV. Eight-cylinder. Bore & stroke: 4.0 in. x 3.5 in. Displacement: 351 cid (5.8 liter). Net horsepower: 156 at 4000 rpm. Taxable horsepower: 51.2. Net torque: 262 lbs.-ft. at 2200 rpm. Carburetor: Two-barrel. (Note: Horsepower and torque may vary with specific model applications, as net horsepower ratings are relative to weight of vehicle.)

ECONOLINE E-150 CARGO VAN: The slightly heavier-duty E-150 had most of the same standard features as the E-100.

ECONOLINE E-150 SUPER CARGO VAN: This Van had the same features as the E-150 Cargo Van, plus a 20 in. extended rear overhang. This allowed carrying of longer loads. The maximum cargo length (right side, without passenger seat) was 14 ft.

ECONOLINE E-150 DISPLAY VAN: This Van shared styling with the E-100, but had greater load capacity.

ECONOLINE E-150 WINDOW VAN: This Van shared styling with the E-100 Window Van, but had greater load capacity.

ECONOLINE E-150 SUPER WINDOW VAN: See E-150 Super Cargo Van.

I.D. DATA: The VIN has 17 symbols. The first three indicate the manufacturer, make, and type of vehicle. The fourth symbol indicates the GVW range. The fifth, sixth and seventh symbols indicate the series and body style. The eighth symbol indicates the type of engine. The ninth symbol is a check digit. The 10th symbol (a letter) indicates model year. The 11th symbol indicates the assembly plant. The remaining symbols are the sequential production number starting with 100001 at each plant.

Model	Body Type	Price	Weight	Prod. Total
E-150 — 1/2-Ton — 124 in./138 in. w.b. — Six				
E-140	Cargo Van	6597	4160	Note 1
E-150	Window Van	6750	4317	Note 1
E-160	Display Van	6695	4306	Note 1
E-150 Supervan — 1/2-Ton — 124 in./138 in. w.b. — Six				
S-140	Cargo Van	7115	4349	Note 1
S-150	Window Van	7268	4506	Note 1
S-160	Display Van	7213	4495	Note 1

NOTE 1: Model year production of Econolines was 104,566.

ENGINE [Base Six]: Inline. OHV. Six-cylinder (heavy-duty). Bore & stroke: 4.0 x 3.98 in. Displacement: 300 cid (4.9 liter). Compression ratio: 8.9:1. Net horsepower: 115 at 3000 rpm. Taxable horsepower: 38.4. Net torque: 223 lbs.-ft. at 1600 rpm. Carburetor: One-barrel. (Note: Horsepower and torque may vary with specific model applications, as net horsepower ratings are relative to weight of vehicle.)

ENGINE [Base V-8; Mandatory in California]: V-block. OHV. Eight-cylinder. Bore & stroke: 4.0 in. x 3.0 in. Displacement: 302 cid (5.0 liter). Net horsepower: 130 at 3800 rpm. Taxable horsepower: 51.2. Net torque: 222 lbs.-ft. at 2000 rpm. Carburetor: Two-barrel. (Note: Horsepower and torque may vary with specific model applications, as net horsepower ratings are relative to weight of vehicle.)

ENGINE [Optional V-8]: V-block. OHV. Eight-cylinder. Bore & stroke: 4.0 in. x 3.5 in. Displacement: 351 cid (5.8 liter). Net horsepower: 156 at 4000 rpm. Taxable horsepower: 51.2. Net torque: 262 lbs.-ft. at 2200 rpm. Carburetor: Two-barrel. (Note: Horsepower and torque may vary with specific model applications, as net horsepower ratings are relative to weight of vehicle.)

ENGINE [Optional V-8]: V-block. OHV. Eight-cylinder. Bore & stroke: 4.0 in. x 4.0 in. Displacement: 400 cid (6.6 liter). Net horsepower: 158 at 3800 rpm. Taxable horsepower: 52.5. Net torque: 276 lbs.-ft. at 2000 rpm. Carburetor: Two-barrel. (Note: Horsepower and torque may vary with specific model applications, as net horsepower ratings are relative to weight of vehicle.)

ECONOLINE E-250 CARGO VAN: The new E-250 had a higher GVW rating and heavier-duty front and rear axles than the E-150. It also came with eight-hole wheels. Standard features were the same as those on the E-100, but three-speed manual transmission was not available in California.

ECONOLINE E-250 SUPER CARGO VAN: See E-150 Cargo Van.

ECONOLINE E-250 DISPLAY VAN: This vehicle shared styling and features with the E-100, but had greater load capacity.

ECONOLINE E-250 SUPER DISPLAY VAN: See E-150 Super Cargo Van.

ECONOLINE E-250 WINDOW VAN: This vehicle shared styling and features with the E-100 Window Van, but had greater load capacity.

ECONOLINE E-250 SUPER WINDOW VAN: See E-150 Super Cargo Van.

ECONOLINE E-250 CUTAWAY VAN: This Van, with Camper Special packages, was designed to readily accommodate custom motorhomes.

ECONOLINE E-250 PARCEL DELIVERY: The E-250 Parcel Delivery Van was 149.9 in. long and 74.3 in. high in its cargo area. The rear door opening was 84.7 in. wide.

I.D. DATA: The VIN has 17 symbols. The first three indicate the manufacturer, make, and type of vehicle. The fourth symbol indicates the GVW range. The fifth, sixth and seventh symbols indicate the series and body style. The eighth symbol indicates the type of engine. The ninth symbol is a check digit. The 10th symbol (a letter) indicates model year. The 11th symbol indicates the assembly plant. The remaining symbols are the sequential production number starting with 100001 at each plant.

Model	Body Type	Price	Weight	Prod. Total
E-250 — 3/4-Ton — 138 in. w.b. — Six				
E-240	Cargo Van	7299	4090	Note 1
E-250	Window Van	7454	4119	Note 1
E-260	Display Van	7400	4105	Note 1
E-250 Supervan — 3/4-Ton — 138 in. w.b. — Six				
S-240	Super Cargo Van	7646	4203	Note 1
S-250	Super Window Van	7801	4232	Note 1
S-260	Super Display Van	7748	4218	Note 1

NOTE 1: Model year production of Econolines was 104,566.

ENGINE [Base Six]: Inline. OHV. Six-cylinder (heavy-duty). Bore & stroke: 4.0 x 3.98 in. Displacement: 300 cid (4.9 liter). Compression ratio: 8.9:1. Net horsepower: 115 at 3000 rpm. Taxable horsepower: 38.4. Net torque: 223 lbs.-ft. at 1600 rpm. Carburetor: One-barrel. (Note: Horsepower and torque may vary with specific model applications, as net horsepower ratings are relative to weight of vehicle.)

ENGINE [Base V-8; Mandatory in California]: V-block. OHV. Eight-cylinder. Bore & stroke: 4.0 in. x 3.0 in. Displacement: 302 cid (5.0 liter). Net horsepower: 130 at 3800 rpm. Taxable horsepower: 51.2. Net torque: 222 lbs.-ft. at 2000 rpm. Carburetor: Two-barrel. (Note: Horsepower and torque may vary with specific model applications, as net horsepower ratings are relative to weight of vehicle.)

ENGINE [Optional V-8]: V-block. OHV. Eight-cylinder. Bore & stroke: 4.0 in. x 3.5 in. Displacement: 351 cid (5.8 liter). Net horsepower: 156 at 4000 rpm. Taxable horsepower: 51.2. Net torque: 262 lbs.-ft. at 2200 rpm. Carburetor: Two-barrel. (Note: Horsepower and torque may vary with specific model applications, as net horsepower ratings are relative to weight of vehicle.)

ENGINE [Optional V-8]: V-block. OHV. Eight-cylinder. Bore & stroke: 4.0 in. x 4.0 in. Displacement: 400 cid (6.6 liter). Net horsepower: 158 at 3800 rpm. Taxable horsepower: 52.5. Net torque: 276 lbs.-ft. at 2000 rpm. Carburetor: Two-barrel. (Note: Horsepower and torque may vary with specific model applications, as net horsepower ratings are relative to weight of vehicle.)

ECONOLINE E-350 CARGO VAN: This was the top-of-the-line Econoline Van. It had heavy-duty front and rear shocks and a greater load capacity than vans in the other series. Standard features were the same as the E-100.

ECONOLINE E-350 SUPER CARGO VAN: See E-150 Super Cargo Van.

ECONOLINE E-350 DISPLAY VAN: See E-250 Display Van.

ECONOLINE E-350 SUPER DISPLAY VAN: See E-150 Super Cargo Van.

ECONOLINE E-350 WINDOW VAN: See E-250 Window Van.

ECONOLINE E-350 SUPER WINDOW VAN: See E-150 Super Cargo Van.

ECONOLINE E-350 CUTAWAY VAN: See E-250 Cutaway Van.

ECONOLINE E-350 PARCEL DELIVERY: See E-250 Parcel Delivery.

I.D. DATA: The VIN has 17 symbols. The first three indicate the manufacturer, make, and type of vehicle. The fourth symbol indicates the GVW range. The fifth, sixth and seventh symbols indicate the series and body style. The eighth symbol indicates the type of engine. The ninth symbol is a check digit. The 10th symbol (a letter) indicates model year. The 11th symbol indicates the assembly plant. The remaining symbols are the sequential production number starting with 100001 at each plant.

Model	Body Type	Price	Weight	Prod. Total
E-350 — 1-Ton — 138 in./158 in. w.b. — Six				
E-340	Cargo Van	7539	4263	Note 1
E-350	Window Van	7693	4292	Note 1
E-360	Display Van	7640	4278	Note 1
E-350 Supervan — 1-Ton — 138 in./158 in. w.b. — Six				
S-340	Super Cargo Van	8340	4428	Note 1
S-350	Super Window Van	8495	4457	Note 1
S-360	Super Display Van	8441	4443	Note 1
E-350 Stretch Van — 1-Ton — 158 in. w.b. — Six				
E-37B	Cutaway	6822	3635	Note 1
E-380	Parcel Delivery	9803	5198	Note 1

NOTE 1: Model year production of Econolines was 104,566.

ENGINE [Base Six]: Inline. OHV. Six-cylinder (heavy-duty). Bore & stroke: 4.0 x 3.98 in. Displacement: 300 cid (4.9 liter). Compression ratio: 8.9:1. Net horsepower: 115 at 3000 rpm. Taxable horsepower: 38.4. Net torque: 223 lbs.-ft. at 1600 rpm. Carburetor: One-barrel. (Note: Horsepower and torque may vary with specific model applications, as net horsepower ratings are relative to weight of vehicle.)

ENGINE [Base V-8; Mandatory in California]: V-block. OHV. Eight-cylinder. Bore & stroke: 4.0 in. x 3.0 in. Displacement: 302 cid (5.0 liter). Net horsepower: 130 at 3800 rpm. Taxable horsepower: 51.2. Net torque: 222 lbs.-ft. at 2000 rpm. Carburetor: Two-barrel. (Note: Horsepower and torque may vary with specific model applications, as net horsepower ratings are relative to weight of vehicle.)

ENGINE [Optional V-8]: V-block. OHV. Eight-cylinder. Bore & stroke: 4.0 in. x 3.5 in. Displacement: 351 cid (5.8 liter). Net horsepower: 156 at 4000 rpm. Taxable horsepower: 51.2. Net torque: 262 lbs.-ft. at 2200 rpm. Carburetor: Two-barrel. (Note: Horsepower and torque may vary with specific model applications, as net horsepower ratings are relative to weight of vehicle.)

ENGINE [Optional V-8]: V-block. OHV. Eight-cylinder. Bore & stroke: 4.0 in. x 4.0 in. Displacement: 400 cid (6.6 liter). Net horsepower: 158 at 3800 rpm. Taxable horsepower: 52.5. Net torque: 276 lbs.-ft. at 2000 rpm. Carburetor: Two-barrel. (Note: Horsepower and torque may vary with specific model applications, as net horsepower ratings are relative to weight of vehicle.)

CHASSIS: Wheelbase: 124 in. (E-100/E-150); 138 in. (E-250/E-350). Overall length: 186.8 in. (with 124 in. wheelbase); 206.8 in. (with 138 in. wheelbase); 226.8 in. (with 138 in. wheelbase Super Van). GVW: 5,200-5,600 lbs. (F-100); 5,850-6,300 lbs. (E-150); 6,500-8,250 lbs. (E-250); 8,550-9,750 lbs. (E-350). Tires: P205/75R15SL (E-100); P225/75R15SL (E-150); 8.00 x 16.5D (E-250); 9.50 x 16.5E (E-350).

POWERTRAIN OPTIONS: Engines: 302 cid V-8. 351 cid V-8. 400 cid V-8 (E350). 460 cid V-8 (E-350; special order). Transmissions: Four-speed manual with overdrive or SelectShift automatic.

CONVENIENCE OPTIONS: Custom Van includes (in addition to or in place of standard van) wood-tone applique on instrument panel; front side cowl and door trim panels; cigarette lighter; front compartment headlining; insulated front floor mats; front roof rail garnish moldings; bright hubcaps; and bright taillight bezels and bright window frames with optional rear windows. Chateau Package includes, in addition to or in place of Custom features, super-soft vinyl or cloth-and-vinyl seat trim; cut-pile carpeting in front and courtesy light switches for all doors; chrome front and rear bumpers; bright grille surround molding; bright lower bodyside character line molding; and bright mirrors. Sports rails. Bodyside accent tape stripe. Pinstripe tape in black; white or gold. Chrome grille. Deluxe Accent Molding Package includes bright drip rail; center bodyside and lower character line moldings. Bright drip rails. Bright window moldings. Console. Right-hand visor mirror. Power door locks. AM radio. AM/FM monaural radio. AM/FM stereo radio. AM/digital clock radio. AM/FM stereo radio with tape deck or cassette player. 40-channel CB. Rear speakers. Premium Sound System. Air-conditioning front or high capacity. High-Output heater. ComfortVent heater. Auxiliary heater for cargo area. Roof/floor insulation package. Deluxe insulation package. Convenience group (with intermittent wipers; dome light switches in all doors and day/night mirror). Dome light courtesy switches for all doors. Western low-mount mirrors. Swing-out recreation mirrors (E-350). Tilt steering. Speed control. Tinted glass all around. Privacy Glass. Flip-open or fixed windows available in all cargo doors. Single sliding side cargo door in lieu of double doors. Combination three-passenger rear seat that converts into a bed. Dual or quad Captain's chairs (reclining and swivel or reclining only). Passenger seat. Flip-fold passenger seat. Cloth and vinyl trim for bucket and captain's chairs. Light Group includes dual beam dome light; headlamps on buzzer; underhood light; and dome light switches on all doors. Chrome or Argent silver step bumper. 18-gal. auxiliary fuel tank (138 inch wheelbase required). Trailer towing packages. Five-slot or 10-hole forged aluminum wheels. Heavy-duty shocks. Handling Package. Power steering. Front stabilizer bar. Engine block heater. Oil pressure gauge and ammeter. Cooling Packages (super and extra). Push bar, plus fog lights and covers. Protection Group includes front and sliding door; black stepwell pads; front door edge guards; and front bumper guards (chrome bumpers required). Security Group includes locking gas cap; inside locking hood release; and spare tire lock. Inside locking hood release. Chrome or painted Argent silver step bumper. Chrome contour bumpers. Deluxe wheelcovers.

1981 Ford Club Wagon Chateau Passenger Van (OCW)

E-100 CLUB WAGON: Exterior styling features were carried over from 1980. However, different style upholstery was used. Among the standard features were: Front bucket seats and rear bench seats. Color-keyed patterned vinyl seat trim. Seat belts. Two-speed electric windshield wipers. Wiper-arm-mounted washer jets. 10 in. rearview mirror. Dome lights. Insulated floor mat with scuff plates. Three armrests. Dual horns. Flip-open windows in sliding door and opposite windows. Painted bumpers. 5x8 inch mirrors and hubcaps. Bright windshield molding. Club Wagon colors for 1981 were: Wimbledon white; Candy-apple red; Antique cream; silver (metallic); Dark pine (metallic); Raven black; Medium caramel (metallic); Dark silver blue (metallic); black; Dark cocoa; Dark chamois (metallic); and maroon. Optional Glow colors: Medium Blue Glow; Fawn Glow; and Light Fawn Glow. Three Tu-Tone combinations were available.

E-150 CLUB WAGON: This was a slightly heavier-duty version of the E-100. It could be had in 124 or 138 in. wheelbases and in five- and eight-passenger versions. Standard features were same as those on the E-100.

E-150 SUPER WAGON: This was basically the same as the 138 in. wheelbase E-150, but had a 20 in. extended rear overhang.

E-250 CLUB WAGON: This was available in 11- and 12-passenger versions only. An eight-passenger version was available with quad captain's chairs and a four-passenger bench seat.

E-350 SUPER WAGON: The heavy-duty E-350 provided 20 in. more inside length than regular 138 in. wheelbase Club Wagons. Heavy-duty shocks were standard.

I.D. DATA: The VIN has 17 symbols. The first three indicate the manufacturer, make, and type of vehicle. The fourth symbol indicates the GVW range. The fifth, sixth and seventh symbols indicate the series and body style. The eighth symbol indicates the type of engine. The ninth symbol is a check digit. The 10th symbol (a letter) indicates model year. The 11th symbol indicates the assembly plant. The remaining symbols are the sequential production number starting with 100001 at each plant.

Model	Body Type	Price	Weight	Prod. Total
E-100 Club Wagon— 1/2-Ton — 124 in./138 in. w.b. — Six				
E-100	Club Wagon	7591	3848	Note 1
E-150 Club Wagon/Super Wagon— 1/2-Ton — 124 in./138 in. w.b. — Six				
E-150	Club Wagon	7851	3869	Note 1
E-150	Super Wagon	8495	4284	Note 1
E-250 Supervan — 3/4-Ton — 138 in. w.b. — Six				
E-250	Club Wagon	10,082	4858	Note 1
E-350 Supervan — 1-Ton — 138 in. w.b. — Six				
E-350	Super Wagon	9568	4821	Note 1

NOTE 1: Total 1981 Club Wagon model year production was 23,087.

ENGINE [Base Six]: Inline. OHV. Six-cylinder (heavy-duty). Bore & stroke: 4.0 x 3.98 in. Displacement: 300 cid (4.9 liter). Compression ratio: 8.9:1. Net horsepower: 115 at 3000 rpm. Taxable horsepower: 38.4. Net torque: 223 lbs.-ft. at 1600 rpm. Carburetor: One-barrel. (Note: Horsepower and torque may vary with specific model applications, as net horsepower ratings are relative to weight of vehicle.)

ENGINE [Base V-8; Mandatory in California]: V-block. OHV. Eight-cylinder. Bore & stroke: 4.0 in. x 3.0 in. Displacement: 302 cid (5.0 liter). Net horsepower: 130 at 3800 rpm. Taxable horsepower: 51.2. Net torque: 222 lbs.-ft. at 2000 rpm. Carburetor: Two-barrel. (Note: Horsepower and torque may vary with specific model applications, as net horsepower ratings are relative to weight of vehicle.)

ENGINE [Optional V-8; All]: V-block. OHV. Eight-cylinder. Bore & stroke: 4.0 in. x 3.5 in. Displacement: 351 cid (5.8 liter). Net horsepower: 156 at 4000 rpm. Taxable horsepower: 51.2. Net torque: 262 lbs.-ft. at 2200 rpm. Carburetor: Two-barrel. (Note: Horsepower and torque may vary with specific model applications, as net horsepower ratings are relative to weight of vehicle.)

ENGINE [Optional V-8; Club Wagon 350 Only]: V-block. OHV. Eight-cylinder. Bore & stroke: 4.0 in. x 4.0 in. Displacement: 400 cid (6.6 liter). Net horsepower: 158 at 3800 rpm. Taxable horsepower: 52.5. Net torque: 276 lbs.-ft. at 2000 rpm. Carburetor: Two-barrel. (Note: Horsepower and torque may vary with specific model applications, as net horsepower ratings are relative to weight of vehicle.)

CHASSIS: Wheelbase: 124 in. (E-100); 138 in. (E-150/E-250/E-350). Overall length: See Econoline. GVW: 5,400-9,400 lbs. Tires: G78 x 15B (E-100); H78 x 15D (E-150); 8.00 x 16D (E-250); 9.50 x 16.5D (E-350).

POWERTRAIN OPTIONS: Engines: 302 cid V-8. 351 cid V-8. 400 cid V-8. 460 cid V-8. Transmissions: Select Shift automatic or four-speed manual with overdrive transmissions.

CONVENIENCE OPTIONS: Custom Van includes (in addition to or in place of standard van) wood-tone applique on instrument panel; front side cowl and door trim panels; cigarette lighter; front compartment headlining; insulated front floor mats; front roof rail garnish moldings; bright hubcaps; and bright taillight bezels and bright window frames with optional rear windows. Chateau Package includes, in addition to or in place of Custom features, super-soft vinyl or cloth-and-vinyl seat trim; cut-pile carpeting in front and courtesy light switches for all doors; chrome front and rear bumpers; bright grille surround molding; bright lower bodyside character line molding; and bright mirrors. Sports rails. Bodyside accent tape stripe. Pinstripe tape in black; white or gold. Chrome grille. Deluxe Accent Molding Package includes bright drip rail; center bodyside and lower character line moldings. Bright drip rails. Bright window moldings. Console. Right-hand visor mirror. Power door locks. AM radio. AM/FM monaural radio. AM/FM stereo radio. AM/digital clock radio. AM/FM stereo radio with tape deck or cassette player. 40-channel CB. Rear speakers. Premium Sound System. Air-conditioning front or high capacity. High-Output heater. ComfortVent heater. Auxiliary heater for cargo area. Roof/floor insulation package. Deluxe insulation package. Convenience group (with intermittent wipers; dome light switches in all doors and day/night mirror). Dome light courtesy switches for all doors. Western low-mount mirrors. Swing-out recreation mirrors (E-350). Tilt steering. Speed control. Tinted glass all around. Privacy Glass. Flip-open or fixed windows available in all cargo doors. Single sliding side cargo door in lieu of double doors. Combination three-passenger rear seat that converts into a bed. Dual or quad Captain's chairs (reclining and swivel or reclining only). Passenger seat. Flip-fold passenger seat. Cloth and vinyl trim for bucket and captain's chairs. Light Group includes dual beam dome light; headlamps on buzzer; underhood light; and dome light switches on all doors. Chrome or Argent silver step bumper. 18-gal. auxiliary fuel tank (138 inch wheelbase required). Trailer towing packages. Five-slot or 10-hole forged aluminum wheels. Heavy-duty shocks. Handling Package. Power steering. Front stabilizer bar. Engine block heater. Oil pressure gauge and ammeter. Cooling Packages (super and extra). Push bar, plus fog lights and covers. Protection Group includes front and sliding door; black stepwell pads; front door edge guards; and front bumper guards (chrome bumpers required). Security Group includes locking gas cap; inside locking hood release; and spare tire lock. Inside locking hood release. Chrome or painted Argent silver step bumper. Chrome contour bumpers. Deluxe wheelcovers. Four-passenger rear bench seat. Snack-game table.

1981 Ford 1/2-Ton Courier Mini-Pickup (OCW)

COURIER PICKUP: Once again, stylists left the Courier alone. About the only ways to tell it from last year's model was by a new lap belt for center passengers; by the visible vehicle identification number mounted on the dash; or by the bright Argent silver instrument panel appliques. Standard features included: Four-speed manual transmission; power front disc brakes; independent front suspension; one-hand tailgate operation; bright front bumper; bright hubcaps; whitewall tires; seats and door panels trimmed in pleated vinyl; seatback hinged for easy access to behind-seat storage area; inside hood release; door vent windows; dome light; and cigarette lighter.

I.D. DATA: The VIN has 17 symbols. The first three indicate the manufacturer; make and type of vehicle. The fourth, fifth and sixth symbols indicate the line, series, chassis, cab type and body style. The seventh symbol identifies the GVWR class. The eighth symbol indicates the type of engine. The ninth symbol is a check digit. The 10th symbol (a letter) indicates the model year. The 11th symbol indicates the assembly plant. The last six symbols are the sequential production numbers.

Model	Body Type	Price	Weight	Prod. Total
Courier — 1/2-Ton — 106.9 in./112.8 in. w.b. — Four				
—	Chassis & Cab	6198	2430	Note 1
—	Pickup	6404	2680	Note 1

NOTE 1: Courier dealer sales for calendar year 1981 were 63,925.

CHASSIS: Wheelbase: 106.9 in. (6 ft. box); 112.8 in. (7 ft. box). Overall length: 177.9 in. (6 ft. box); 189.4 in. (7 ft. box). Overall width: 63 in. Overall height: 61.5 in. GVW: 4,100 lbs. Tires: 6.00 x 14C White sidewall.

ENGINE [Base Four]: Inline. OHV. OHC. Bore & stroke: 3.07 x 3.70 in. Displacement: 110 cid (2.0 liter). Net horsepower: 77 at 4500 rpm (72 in California). Taxable horsepower: 15.8. Carburetor: Two-barrel.

ENGINE [Optional Four]: Inline. OHV. OHC. Bore & stroke: 3.87 x 3.12 in. Displacement: 140 cid (2.3 liter). Net horsepower: 78 at 5000 rpm. Taxable horsepower: 22.86. Carburetor: Two-barrel.

POWERTRAIN OPTIONS: Engine: 2.3 liter engine. Transmission: Automatic and five-speed manual transmissions with overdrive.

CONVENIENCE OPTIONS: AM monaural radio. AM/FM monaural radios. Air-conditioning. All tinted glass. Argent silver rear bumper. Cold Weather Group includes electric rear window defroster; heavy-duty battery and high-output heater. Low-mount Western mirrors. Soft-Ride Package includes 3,600 lbs. GVWR and five-leaf progressive-rate rear springs. Exterior Decor Group (not available with XLT/Chassis & Cab/or tri-color accent stripe) includes bright drip rail and wheel lip moldings and bright bodyside moldings with black vinyl inserts. Tri-color accent tape stripe (not available with Exterior Decor Group; replace bodyside molding with XLT). XLT Package includes exterior bright grille surround; bright moldings on windshield; bright rear window moldings; drip rail moldings; wheel lip moldings; bright taillight surrounds; bright bodyside moldings with black vinyl inserts; bright red XLT fender plaques; and deluxe wheelcovers; herringbone cloth seat trim in three color choices (tan; red and blue); contrasting accent stripe on seatback and door trim; color-keyed cut-pile carpeting; cowl trim panels; instrument panel; headlining; seats; heater shroud; ashtray; sun visors and shift boot; wood-tone upper door trim panel with contrasting accent stripe and floorshift knob; day/night mirror; ashtray light; underhood light; and glove box light. Glove box lock. Sport steering wheel with black spokes. Temperature gauge and ammeter. Free-Wheeling Package includes black-painted GT bar; push-bar; tri-color accent tape stripe and deluxe wheelcovers. Sports Group includes Sport steering wheel with bright argent spokes; temperature gauge and ammeter; individually adjustable bucket seats trimmed in black vinyl (with black-and-white plaid fabric inserts); soft black shift lever knob; bright argent instrument panel appliques; black carpeting; black interior trim; and radial tires.

F-100 CUSTOM PICKUP: The handsome aerodynamic styling was carried over for 1981. Standard features included: Bright front bumper; grille surround and windshield molding; left- and right-hand door-mounted mirrors; Argent hubcaps; push-button door handles; all-vinyl seat trim; instrument panel with cluster trim applique and full-width pad; behind-seat storage with folding seatback (on Customs built after Oct. 6, 1980); glovebox with latch; left-hand door courtesy light switch; temperature gauge; color-keyed windshield pillar; header and cowlside trim panels; door trim panels with foam-padded armrests; scuff plates; coat hook; dome light; floor insulation; carpet-texture rubber mat; easily removable tailgate (Styleside); radial-ply tires; maintenance-free battery; long windshield wiper blades with dual-port washer spray nozzles; coolant recovery system; rubber-isolated front coil springs; locking steering column; horizontal sliding door lock buttons; entry shield on door latch; door vent windows with steel push-button lock; Twin-I-Beam independent front suspension; and three-speed manual transmission. The F-100 Pickup could be ordered with 6.5 ft. Flareside or 6.75 ft. and 8 ft. Styleside boxes. Only the regular cab was available. Interior colors for 1981 were: Fawn; Medium blue; red; black; and nutmeg or spruce (except SuperCab). Exterior colors included: Raven black; Wimbledon white; silver (metallic); Medium grey (metallic); Candy-apple red; maroon; Midnight blue (metallic); Medium blue; Dark spruce (metallic); fawn; Dark chamois (metallic); Medium caramel (metallic); Light caramel; and tan. Optional glamour colors included Medium Blue Glow; Medium Spruce Glow and Fawn Glow. Tu-tones: (Regular) Accent color covered the roof and upper back panel, plus dual tape stripe included to divide colors; (Deluxe) Accent color on center bodyside area and on tailgate below upper molding; moldings were included as needed; (Combination) regular and deluxe Tu-Tones combined; (Victoria) Accent color applied to hood, upper fenders, around door window and on lower bodyside. Tape stripe treatments available included: [Accent; single rear wheel Styleside only] Bodyside tape ran from the front marker lamp to the taillamp; available separately or with regular or Victoria Tu-Tone; [Tri-color for single rear wheel Styleside only] With three stripes as name implies; [Upper Bodyside for regular and Supercab] Highlights upper portion of single rear wheel Styleside Pickup, available separately or with regular Tu-Tone.

I.D. DATA: The VIN has 17 symbols. The first three indicate the manufacturer; make; and type of vehicle. The fourth symbol indicates the GVW range. The fifth, sixth and seventh symbols indicate the series and body style. The eighth symbol indicates the type of engine. The ninth symbol is a check digit. The 10th symbol (a letter) indicates model year. The 11th symbol indicates the assembly plant. The remaining symbols are the sequential production number starting with 100001 at each plant.

Model	Body Type	Price	Weight	Prod. Total
F-100 — 1/2-Ton — 117 in. w.b. — Six				
F-10	Flareside	6026	—	Note 1
F-10	Styleside 6.8 ft	6026	3264	Note 1
F-100 — 1/2-Ton — 133 in. w.b. — Six				
F-10	Styleside 8 ft.	6112	3349	Note 1

NOTE 1: Model year production was: [F-100] 170,835.

ENGINE [Base Six]: Inline. OHV. Six-cylinder (heavy-duty). Bore & stroke: 4.0 x 3.98 in. Displacement: 300 cid (4.9 liter). Compression ratio: 8.9:1. Net horsepower: 115 at 3000 rpm. Taxable horsepower: 38.4. Net torque: 223 lbs.-ft. at 1600 rpm. Carburetor: One-barrel. (Note: Horsepower and torque may vary with specific model applications, as net horsepower ratings are relative to weight of vehicle.)

ENGINE [Base V-8]: V-block. OHV. Eight-cylinder. Bore & stroke: 3.68 in. x 3.00 in. Displacement: 255 cid (4.2 liter). Net horsepower: n.a. Taxable horsepower: 43.3. Net torque: n.a. Carburetor: Two-barrel. (Note: Horsepower and torque may vary with specific model applications, as net horsepower ratings are relative to weight of vehicle.)

ENGINE [Optional V-8; Mandatory in California]: V-block. OHV. Eight-cylinder. Bore & stroke: 4.0 in. x 3.0 in. Displacement: 302 cid (5.0 liter). Net horsepower: 130 at 3800 rpm. Taxable horsepower: 51.2. Net torque: 222 lbs.-ft. at 2000 rpm. Carburetor: Two-barrel. (Note: Horsepower and torque may vary with specific model applications, as net horsepower ratings are relative to weight of vehicle.)

1981 Ford 1/2-Ton F-150 Ranger XLT Styleside Pickup 4x4 (OCW)

F-150 CUSTOM PICKUP: The F-150 was Ford's heavy-duty 1/2-ton. It had most of the same features as the F-100, plus power brakes. Both Flareside and Styleside boxes were available. Stylesides could he had in regular or Supercabs. The latter provided space behind the front seat for an optional rear bench seat or two jump seats.

I.D. DATA: The VIN has 17 symbols. The first three indicate the manufacturer; make; and type of vehicle. The fourth symbol indicates the GVW range. The fifth, sixth and seventh symbols indicate the series and body style. The eighth symbol indicates the type of engine. The ninth symbol is a check digit. The 10th symbol (a letter) indicates model year. The 11th symbol indicates the assembly plant. The remaining symbols are the sequential production number starting with 100001 at each plant.

Model	Body Type	Price	Weight	Prod. Total
F-150 — 1/2-Ton — 117 in. w.b. — Six				
F-15	Flareside 6.5 ft.	6300	—	Note 1
F-15	Styleside 6.75 ft.	6300	3315	Note 1
F-150 — 1/2-Ton — 133 in. w.b. — Six				
F-15	Styleside 8 ft.	6387	3404	Note 1
F-150 Supercab — 1/2-Ton — 155 in. w.b. — Six				
X-15	Styleside	7197	3614	Note 1

NOTE 1: Model year production: [F-150] 210,475.

ENGINE [Base Six]: Inline. OHV. Six-cylinder (heavy-duty). Bore & stroke: 4.0 x 3.98 in. Displacement: 300 cid (4.9 liter). Compression ratio: 8.9:1. Net horsepower: 115 at 3000 rpm. Taxable horsepower: 38.4. Net torque: 223 lbs.-ft. at 1600 rpm. Carburetor: One-barrel. (Note: Horsepower and torque may vary with specific model applications, as net horsepower ratings are relative to weight of vehicle.)

ENGINE [Base V-8; Mandatory in California]: V-block. OHV. Eight-cylinder. Bore & stroke: 4.0 in. x 3.0 in. Displacement: 302 cid (5.0 liter). Net horsepower: 130 at 3800 rpm. Taxable horsepower: 51.2. Net torque: 222 lbs.-ft. at 2000 rpm. Carburetor: Two-barrel. (Note: Horsepower and torque may vary with specific model applications, as net horsepower ratings are relative to weight of vehicle.)

ENGINE [Optional V-8]: V-block. OHV. Eight-cylinder. Bore & stroke: 4.0 in. x 3.5 in. Displacement: 351 cid (5.8 liter). Net horsepower: 156 at 4000 rpm. Taxable horsepower: 51.2. Net torque: 262 lbs.-ft. at 2200 rpm. Carburetor: Two-barrel. (Note: Horsepower and torque may vary with specific model applications, as net horsepower ratings are relative to weight of vehicle.)

F-250 CUSTOM PICKUP: The 3/4-Ton F-250 was offered in regular or Supercabs. However, the only box available was the Styleside type. Standard features echoed those of the F-100, with the addition of power brakes.

I.D. DATA: The VIN has 17 symbols. The first three indicate the manufacturer; make; and type of vehicle. The fourth symbol indicates the GVW range. The fifth, sixth and seventh symbols indicate the series and body style. The eighth symbol indicates the type of engine. The ninth symbol is a check digit. The 10th symbol (a letter) indicates model year. The 11th symbol indicates the assembly plant. The remaining symbols are the sequential production number starting with 100001 at each plant.

Model	Body Type	Price	Weight	Prod. Total
F-250 — 3/4-Ton — 133 in./161 in. w.b. — Six				
—	Chassis & Cab	7182	3467	Note 1
F-25	Styleside 8 ft.	6772	3565	Note 1
F-250 — 3/4-Ton — 133 in./161 in. w.b. — Six				
X-25	SuperCab Pickup	7424	3849	Note 1

NOTE 1: Model year production: [F-250] 71,884.

ENGINE [Base Six]: Inline. OHV. Six-cylinder (heavy-duty). Bore & stroke: 4.0 x 3.98 in. Displacement: 300 cid (4.9 liter). Compression ratio: 8.9:1. Net horsepower: 115 at 3000 rpm. Taxable horsepower: 38.4. Net torque: 223 lbs.-ft. at 1600 rpm. Carburetor: One-barrel. (Note: Horsepower and torque may vary with specific model applications, as net horsepower ratings are relative to weight of vehicle.)

ENGINE [Base V-8; Mandatory in California]: V-block. OHV. Eight-cylinder. Bore & stroke: 4.0 in. x 3.0 in. Displacement: 302 cid (5.0 liter). Net horsepower: 130 at 3800 rpm. Taxable horsepower: 51.2. Net torque: 222 lbs.-ft. at 2000 rpm. Carburetor: Two-barrel. (Note: Horsepower and torque may vary with specific model applications, as net horsepower ratings are relative to weight of vehicle.)

ENGINE [Optional V-8]: V-block. OHV. Eight-cylinder. Bore & stroke: 4.0 in. x 3.5 in. Displacement: 351 cid (5.8 liter). Net horsepower: 156 at 4000 rpm. Taxable horsepower: 51.2. Net torque: 262 lbs.-ft. at 2200 rpm. Carburetor: Two-barrel. (Note: Horsepower and torque may vary with specific model applications, as net horsepower ratings are relative to weight of vehicle.)

F-350 CUSTOM PICKUP: The 1-Ton F-350 was only offered in regular cab version. It featured the smoothside all-steel Styleside box. Except for having a four-speed manual transmission and power brakes, most F-350 features were the same as those on the F-100. However; the F-350 was the only F-Series Styleside to offer dual rear wheels.

I.D. DATA: The VIN has 17 symbols. The first three indicate the manufacturer; make; and type of vehicle. The fourth symbol indicates the GVW range. The fifth, sixth and seventh symbols indicate the series and body style. The eighth symbol indicates the type of engine. The ninth symbol is a check digit. The 10th symbol (a letter) indicates model year. The 11th symbol indicates the assembly plant. The remaining symbols are the sequential production number starting with 100001 at each plant.

Model	Body Type	Price	Weight	Prod. Total
F-350 — 1-Ton — 133 in. w.b. — V-8				
F-37	Chassis & Cab	7527	3759	Note 1
F-35	Styleside	7750	4299	Note 1

NOTE 1: Model year production: [F-350] 37,120.

ENGINE [Base Six]: Inline. OHV. Six-cylinder (heavy-duty). Bore & stroke: 4.0 x 3.98 in. Displacement: 300 cid (4.9 liter). Compression ratio: 8.9:1. Net horsepower: 115 at 3000 rpm. Taxable horsepower: 38.4. Net torque: 223 lbs.-ft. at 1600 rpm. Carburetor: One-barrel. (Note: Horsepower and torque may vary with specific model applications, as net horsepower ratings are relative to weight of vehicle.)

ENGINE [Base V-8]: V-block. OHV. Eight-cylinder. Bore & stroke: 4.0 in. x 3.5 in. Displacement: 351 cid (5.8 liter). Net horsepower: 156 at 4000 rpm. Taxable horsepower: 51.2. Net torque: 262 lbs.-ft. at 2200 rpm. Carburetor: Two-barrel. (Note: Horsepower and torque may vary with specific model applications, as net horsepower ratings are relative to weight of vehicle.)

ENGINE [Optional V-8]: V-block. OHV. Eight-cylinder. Bore & stroke: 4.0 in. x 4.0 in. Displacement: 400 cid (6.6 liter). Net horsepower: 158 at 3800 rpm. Taxable horsepower: 52.5. Net torque: 276 lbs.-ft. at 2000 rpm. Carburetor: Two-barrel. (Note: Horsepower and torque may vary with specific model applications, as net horsepower ratings are relative to weight of vehicle.)

CHASSIS: Wheelbase: 116.8 in. (F-100/F-150); 133 in. (All); 138.8 in. (F-150/F-250 Supercab); 155 in. (F-150/F-250/F-350 Supercab). Overall length: 187.8 in. (F-100/F-150 Flareside); 192.1 in. (F-100/F-150 Styleside); 208.3 in. (Styleside); 214.1 in. (F-150/F-250 Supercab); 230.3 in. (F-350 Supercab). GVW: 4,700-5,150 lbs. (F-100); 5,250-6,000 lbs. (F-150); 6,350-8,200 lbs. (F-250); 8,650-10,000 lbs.(F-350). Tires: P195/75R 15SL (F-100); P215/75R 15SL (F-150); P225/75R 15SL (F-150 Supercab); 8.00 x 16.5D (F-250); and 9.50 x 16.5E (F-350).

POWERTRAIN OPTIONS: Engines: 255 cid V-8 (F-100). 302 cid V-8 (F-100/F-150/F-250). 351 cid V-8 (F-150/F-250/F-350). 400 cid V-8 (F-350). Transmissions: Four-speed manual. Four-speed manual with overdrive. SelectShift automatic transmission.

1981 Ford 1/2-Ton F-150 Ranger Styleside Pickup (OCW)

CONVENIENCE OPTIONS: Accent tape stripe. Chrome grille. Tri-color tape stripe (for regular cab Styleside). Upper bodyside protection molding. Lower bodyside molding with black vinyl insert (for Styleside). Heavy-duty air cleaner (4x4). Bright wheel lip moldings (for Custom and Ranger Styleside). Bright box rails for 8 ft. Styleside Pickups. Upper bodyside tape stripe (Styleside). Quad heavy-duty front shocks and heavy-duty rear shocks (4x4). AM radio. AM/FM monaural radio. AM/FM stereo radio. AM/FM stereo radio with 8-track tape player. AM/FM stereo radio with cassette tape player. Air-conditioning. High-output heaters. Convenience Group includes intermittent wipers; 12 in. day/night mirror; molded bin on lower doors; headlamps on warning buzzer and courtesy light switch on right-hand door (with Custom). Electronic digital clock. Fingertip speed control. Light Group includes light in glove box; ashtray and under instrument panel; dome lamp with map light; cargo box light; headlamp-on warning buzzer; courtesy light switch on right-hand door with Custom; plus movable underhood worklight with 20 ft. retractable cord. Bright low-mount swing-away Western mirrors. Remote-control low-mount Western mirrors. Bright low-mount recreation mirrors. Power steering. Soft-wrapped steering wheel. Tinted sliding rear window. Tilt steering wheel. Tinted glass all around. Tool storage box located under the hood (includes movable underhood worklight with 20 ft. retractable cord and inside locking hood release). Slide-out spare tire carrier. Spare tire carrier side-mounted inside Styleside box. Center console (Supercabs with captains chairs). Reclining captain's chairs in Supercab. Forward-facing folding rear seat in Supercab. Center-facing folding rear seats in Supercab. Heavy-duty black vinyl, knitted vinyl or all-vinyl seat trim. Cloth and vinyl inserts (Ranger/Custom). Auxiliary transmission cooler. Heavy-duty front and rear shocks. Quad heavy-duty front shocks and heavy-duty rear shocks (F-150 with 4x4). Auxiliary fuel tank. Handling Package includes front and rear stabilizer bars; heavy-duty front and rear shocks; and heavy-duty front springs. Oil pressure and ammeter gauges. Engine block heater. Extra-cooling engine package. Super-cooling engine package. Front and rear stabilizer bars. Camper Special package. Trailer towing packages. Dual note horns. Fog lamps (includes plastic covers and bright front bumper guards). Power door locks. Inside locking hood release. Five roof clearance lights. Exterior Protection Group includes bright door edge guards; front bumper guards; and front bumper rub strip. Security Lock Group includes locking gas cap; inside hood release; and glove box and spare tire lock. Sports instrumentation. Eight chrome tie-down hooks for single rear wheel Styleside. Six chrome tie-down hooks for dual rear wheel Styleside. Argent silver step bumper for Styleside. Chrome step bumper for single rear wheel Styleside. Chrome channel bumper for Flareside. Chrome contour rear bumpers for single rear wheel Styleside. Deluxe wheelcovers. White-painted styled steel wheels. Ten-hole polished forged aluminum wheels with clear plastic coating. Sport wheelcovers. Five-slot brushed forged-aluminum wheels with clear plastic coating. Free Wheeling Package A includes pinstriping or tri-color tape stripe on Styleside/Deluxe Tu-Toned trucks; or black-out grille; black-out headlamp doors and sport wheelcovers for Flareside. Free Wheeling Package B includes all features of Package A, plus fog lamps and bumper guards; handling package; bright rear contour bumper (Styleside); bright channel bumper (Flareside); white styled-steel wheels in place of wheelcovers; soft-wrapped steering wheel; and Sports Instrumentation package (with tachometer; trip odometer; ammeter; and oil pressure gauge). Ranger Package includes (in addition to or in place of Custom features) brushed aluminum upper bodyside and tailgate moldings; bright insert around the back window; bright hubcaps (except with dual rear wheels); all-vinyl or cloth and vinyl seat trim; courtesy lighting with driver/passenger side door switches; bright accents on door trim panels; cigarette lighter; ashtray light; wood-tone accent around steering wheel horn pad; polished wood-tone applique on instrument panel; color-keyed seat belts; and color-keyed floor mat. Ranger XLT Package includes (in addition to/in place of Ranger features) brushed aluminum tailgate applique (*); XLT emblems; grained vinyl upholstery with cloth seat trim inserts; color-keyed cut-pile carpeting covering floor; floor insulation padding; lower door trim panels; carpeted storage area behind seat; cloth headliner on foam padding; color-keyed moldings; and bright aluminum door scuff plates. (* Styleside tailgates had bright letters and a black tape stripe at bottom; Flaresides tailgate trim had raised Ford letters that matched the contrasting color in the surrounding dual-color tape stripe.) Ranger XLT Flaresides and dual rear wheel Ranger XLT Stylesides included dual-color narrow upper and lower bodyside tape stripes. Ranger Lariat Package included a brushed aluminum lower bodyside molding with black vinyl protective insert; tailgate applique; dual narrow tape stripe; special cushioned seat trim; new style special cloth upholstery with vinyl bolsters; Ranger Lariat scripts on the wood-tone trimmed dashboard; wood-tone appliques on door panels; map boxes on doors covered with carpeting; thick cut-pile floor carpeting; and luxury steering wheel. The 4x4 Package for F-150/F-250/F-350 included P-metric steel-belted radial tires (F-150 only); ladder-type frame; integral front axle skid plate; 4x4 indicator lamp on instrument panel; four-speed manual transmission; and free-running front hubs. Snow Preparation Package available for 4x4 trucks. Automatic locking front hubs for 4x4s.

HISTORICAL: Model year production of light-duty trucks by line was: [F-100] 170,835; [F-150] 210,475; [F-250] 71,884; [F-350] 37,120; [Bronco] 34,850; [Econoline] 104,566; [Club Wagon] 23,087; [Total] 652,817. Model year truck sales by type were: [Light Conventional] 470,756; [Econoline] 108,599; [Courier] 66,155; [Bronco] 37,396; [Club Wagon] 25,051; [Medium- to Heavy-duty] 52,345; [Total] 760,302. Ford was America's first-ranked truck manufacturer, even though sales dropped another 9.8 percent in reaction to the fuel crisis and a sick national economy. Ford made numerous changes to 1981 models to improve their fuel economy. An automatic overdrive transmission became available with the 5.0 liter V-8 powered trucks, while standard Pickups with the base 300 cid six and four-speed overdrive manual transmission received a 21 miles per gallon EPA fuel economy rating. An all-new, compact-size Ranger Pickup entered production in Louisville, Ken. in January 1981.

1982 FORD

1982 Ford 1/2-Ton Bronco XLT Lariat Sport Utility Wagon 4x4 (JAG)

BRONCO: The 4x4 Bronco received a mild facelift for 1982. The revised grille had only three vertical bars and the Ford script in an oval emblem in its center. This emblem was also placed on the lower left corner of the tailgate. Standard features included: Bucket seats; vinyl sun visors; padded instrument panel; armrests; dome lamp; windshield header and A pillar moldings; AM radio (could be deleted for credit); inside hood release; cowlside trim panels; rubber floor mats; black front and rear bumpers; bright hubcaps; bright door-mounted mirrors; swing-down tailgate with power window; power brakes and steering; four-speed manual transmission; and black grille. Bronco color choices for 1982 were: Raven black; Wimbledon white; silver (metallic); Medium grey (metallic); Candy-apple red; Midnight blue (metallic); Medium blue (metallic); Bright blue; Dark spruce (metallic); Light spruce; maroon; Dark fawn (metallic); fawn; Medium caramel (metallic); tan; Dark brown (metallic); Medium yellow; Light Spruce Glow; and Bittersweet Glow.

I.D. DATA: The VIN has 17 symbols. The first three indicate the manufacturer, make, and type of vehicle. The fourth symbol indicates the GVW range. The fifth, sixth and seventh symbols indicate the series and body style. The eighth symbol indicates the type of engine. The ninth symbol is a check digit. The 10th symbol (a letter) indicates model year. The 11th symbol indicates the assembly plant. The remaining symbols are the sequential production number starting with 100001 at each plant.

Model	Body Type	Price	Weight	Prod. Total
Bronco 4x4 — 1/2-Ton — 105 in. w.b. — Six				
U-150	Wagon	9899	4079	38,891

ENGINE [Base Six]: Inline. OHV. Six-cylinder (heavy-duty). Bore & stroke: 4.0 x 3.98 in. Displacement: 300 cid (4.9 liter). Compression ratio: 8.9:1. Net horsepower: 115 at 3000 rpm. Taxable horsepower: 38.4. Net torque: 223 lbs.-ft. at 1600 rpm. Carburetor: One-barrel. (Note: Horsepower and torque may vary with specific model applications, as net horsepower ratings are relative to weight of vehicle.)

ENGINE [Base V-8; Mandatory in California]: V-block. OHV. Eight-cylinder. Bore & stroke: 4.0 in. x 3.0 in. Displacement: 302 cid (5.0 liter). Net horsepower: 130 at 3800 rpm. Taxable horsepower: 51.2. Net torque: 222 lbs.-ft. at 2000 rpm. Carburetor: Two-barrel. (Note: Horsepower and torque may vary with specific model applications, as net horsepower ratings are relative to weight of vehicle.)

ENGINE [Optional V-8]: V-block. OHV. Eight-cylinder. Bore & stroke: 4.0 in. x 3.5 in. Displacement: 351 cid (5.8 liter). Net horsepower: 156 at 4000 rpm. Taxable horsepower: 51.2. Net torque: 262 lbs.-ft. at 2200 rpm. Carburetor: Two-barrel. (Note: Horsepower and torque may vary with specific model applications, as net horsepower ratings are relative to weight of vehicle.)

CHASSIS: Wheebase: 104.7 in. Overall length: 177.6 in. Overall height: 73.2 in. Overall width: 77.2 in. Tires: P215/75R x 15 SL.

POWERTRAIN OPTIONS: Transmissions: SelectShift automatic transmission. Four-speed manual transmission with overdrive. Engines: 302 cid V-8. 351 cid V-8.

CONVENIENCE OPTIONS: Bright wheel lip moldings. Chrome bumpers. Tri-color tape stripe. Accent tape stripe. Black GT bar. Chrome grille. Upper bodyside tape stripe. Lower bodyside molding. High-output or auxiliary heaters. Console. Rear window defroster. Soft wrap steering wheel. Convenience Group includes intermittent wipers; map box in doors; headlamp-on warning buzzer; right-hand door courtesy light switch; 12 in. mirror; visor vanity mirror; front bench seat; flip/fold rear bench seat; power windows. Tinted glass all around and privacy glass in quarter windows. Light Group includes lights in glove box; ashtray and underhood; instrument panel courtesy lights; dome light with map light; right-hand door courtesy light; and headlamp-on warning buzzer (the underhood light had a 20 ft. cord). Handling Package includes front stabilizer bar; quad heavy-duty hydraulic front shocks and dual heavy-duty rear shocks. captain's chairs. Underhood tool box. Part time 4x4 (with optional automatic transmission). Sports Instrumentation includes tachometer; ammeter; oil pressure gauge and trip odometer. Heavy-duty trailer towing package includes heavy-duty battery; ammeter; oil pressure gauge; 32-gal. fuel tank in lieu of standard (includes skid plate); inside locking hood release. Protection Group includes bright door edge guards; front bumper guards; and front bumper rub strip. Security Group includes locking gas cap; inside hood release lock; spare tire lock; and locking glove box. Super engine cooling package. Extra engine cooling package. Fog lamps. Exterior sound package. Cigarette lighter. Power door locks. XLT Lariat includes bright front and rear bumpers; black grille; bright hubcaps; windshield; quarter window and upper bodyside (with vinyl insert) protection moldings; bright wheel lip moldings; side molding accent tape stripe; brushed aluminum tailgate applique; dome lamp; left- and right-hand courtesy light switches; color-keyed carpeting; left-hand rear quarter trim panel cargo lamp; door trim panel with bright surround molding; wood-tone panel with full-length storage bins; color-keyed vinyl headliner; simulated wood-tone applique and bright moldings on instrument panel; bright scuff plates; deluxe seat belts; cloth and vinyl seat trim; soft-wrap steering wheel with wood-tone insert; molded rear quarter trim panels with armrests; speaker grilles; storage bin and light; spare tire cover; cigarette lighter; and added insulation. XLS Package includes most of the features of the XLT, plus black gloss on front and rear bumpers; black gloss grille; Argent silver styled steel wheels with black hub; black gloss windshield molding; black treatment on headlamp doors and around window; door handles; locks; mirrors and tailgate lock; XLS tape; door trim panel with bright surround; brushed aluminum applique; and steering wheel trim. Speed control. Swing-Away spare tire carrier. 40-channel CB. Front tow hooks. Cast aluminum wheels. Styled steel painted (white) wheels. Sport wheelcovers. Deluxe Argent silver styled steel wheels. AM/FM monaural; AM/FM stereo; AM/FM stereo with cassette or 8-track player. Snow plow packages. High-altitude emissions system. Heavy-duty auxiliary battery.

ECONOLINE E-100 CARGO VAN: Styling was unchanged for the new model year. Among the standard features were: Full-foam driver's bucket seat; vinyl seat trim; padded full-width instrument panel; brake warning light; two-speed electric windshield wipers; wiper-arm-mounted washer jets; dome lights; front compartment headlining; column-mounted ignition switch scuff plates; door checks; Argent silver-painted bumpers and hubcaps; bright windshield molding; painted mirrors; and hinged side cargo doors (sliding door available at no extra cost).

ECONOLINE E-100 DISPLAY VAN: This model had windows at the rear and on the right-hand side. It came with the same standard features as the Cargo Van.

ECONOLINE E-100 WINDOW VAN: The Window Van had glass all around. It shared standard features with the Cargo Van.

I.D. DATA: The VIN has 17 symbols. The first three indicate the manufacturer; make; and type of vehicle. The fourth symbol indicates the GVW range. The fifth, sixth and seventh symbols indicate the series and body style. The eighth symbol indicates the type of engine. The ninth symbol is a check digit. The 10th symbol (a letter) indicates model year. The 11th symbol indicates the assembly plant. The remaining symbols are the sequential production number starting with 100001 at each plant.

Model	Body Type	Price	Weight	Prod. Total
E-100 — 1/2-Ton — 124 in./138 in. w.b. — Six				
E-040	Cargo Van	7056	3664	Note 1
E-050	Window Van	7237	3691	Note 1
E-060	Display Van	7172	3678	Note 1

NOTE 1: Model year production of Econolines was 119,206.

ENGINE [Base Six]: Inline. OHV. Six-cylinder (heavy-duty). Bore & stroke: 4.0 x 3.98 in. Displacement: 300 cid (4.9 liter). Compression ratio: 8.9:1. Net horsepower: 115 at 3000 rpm. Taxable horsepower: 38.4. Net torque: 223 lbs.-ft. at 1600 rpm. Carburetor: One-barrel. (Note: Horsepower and torque may vary with specific model applications, as net horsepower ratings are relative to weight of vehicle.)

ENGINE [Base V-8; Mandatory in California]: V-block. OHV. Eight-cylinder. Bore & stroke: 4.0 in. x 3.0 in. Displacement: 302 cid (5.0 liter). Net horsepower: 130 at 3800 rpm. Taxable horsepower: 51.2. Net torque: 222 lbs.-ft. at 2000 rpm. Carburetor: Two-barrel. (Note: Horsepower and torque may vary with specific model applications, as net horsepower ratings are relative to weight of vehicle.)

ENGINE [Optional V-8]: V-block. OHV. Eight-cylinder. Bore & stroke: 4.0 in. x 3.5 in. Displacement: 351 cid (5.8 liter). Net horsepower: 156 at 4000 rpm. Taxable horsepower: 51.2. Net torque: 262 lbs.-ft. at 2200 rpm. Carburetor: Two-barrel. (Note: Horsepower and torque may vary with specific model applications, as net horsepower ratings are relative to weight of vehicle.)

ECONOLINE E-150 CARGO VAN: The slightly heavier-duty E-150 had most of the same standard features as the E-100.

ECONOLINE E-150 SUPER CARGO VAN: This Van had the same features as the E-150 Cargo Van, plus a 20 in. extended rear overhang. This allowed carrying of longer loads. The maximum cargo length (right side; without passenger seat) was 14 ft.

ECONOLINE E-150 DISPLAY VAN: This Van shared styling with the E-100, but had greater load capacity.

ECONOLINE E-150 WINDOW VAN: This Van shared styling with the E-100 Window Van, but had greater load capacity.

I.D. DATA: The VIN has 17 symbols. The first three indicate the manufacturer; make; and type of vehicle. The fourth symbol indicates the GVW range. The fifth, sixth and seventh symbols indicate the series and body style. The eighth symbol indicates the type of engine. The ninth symbol is a check digit. The 10th symbol (a letter) indicates model year. The 11th symbol indicates the assembly plant. The remaining symbols are the sequential production number starting with 100001 at each plant.

Model	Body Type	Price	Weight	Prod. Total
E-150 — 1/2-Ton — 124 in./138 in. w.b. — Six				
E-140	Cargo Van	7303	3617	Note 1
E-150	Window Van	7485	3644	Note 1
E-160	Display Van	7419	3631	Note 1
E-150 Supervan — 1/2-Ton — 124 in./138 in. w.b. — Six				
E-140	Cargo Van	7963	3923	Note 1
E-150	Window Van	8145	3952	Note 1
E-160	Display Van	8079	3938	Note 1

NOTE 1: Model year production of Econolines was 119,206.

ENGINE [Base Six]: Inline. OHV. Six-cylinder (heavy-duty). Bore & stroke: 4.0 x 3.98 in. Displacement: 300 cid (4.9 liter). Compression ratio: 8.9:1. Net horsepower: 115 at 3000 rpm. Taxable horsepower: 38.4. Net torque: 223 lbs.-ft. at 1600 rpm. Carburetor: One-barrel. (Note: Horsepower and torque may vary with specific model applications, as net horsepower ratings are relative to weight of vehicle.)

ENGINE [Base V-8; Mandatory in California]: V-block. OHV. Eight-cylinder. Bore & stroke: 4.0 in. x 3.0 in. Displacement: 302 cid (5.0 liter). Net horsepower: 130 at 3800 rpm. Taxable horsepower: 51.2. Net torque: 222 lbs.-ft. at 2000 rpm. Carburetor: Two-barrel. (Note: Horsepower and torque may vary with specific model applications, as net horsepower ratings are relative to weight of vehicle.)

ENGINE [Optional V-8]: V-block. OHV. Eight-cylinder. Bore & stroke: 4.0 in. x 3.5 in. Displacement: 351 cid (5.8 liter). Net horsepower: 156 at 4000 rpm. Taxable horsepower: 51.2. Net torque: 262 lbs.-ft. at 2200 rpm. Carburetor: Two-barrel. (Note: Horsepower and torque may vary with specific model applications, as net horsepower ratings are relative to weight of vehicle.)

ECONOLINE E-250 CARGO VAN: The new E-250 had a higher GVW rating and more heavy-duty front and rear axles; than the E-150. It also came with eight-hole wheels. Standard features were the same as those on the E-100 except the three-speed manual was not available in Calif.

ECONOLINE E-250 SUPER CARGO VAN: See E-150 Cargo Van.

ECONOLINE E-250 DISPLAY VAN: This vehicle shared styling and features with the E-100; but had greater load capacity.

ECONOLINE E-250 SUPER DISPLAY VAN: See E-150 Super Cargo Van.

ECONOLINE E-250 WINDOW VAN: This vehicle shared styling and features with the E-100 Window Van; but had greater load capacity.

ECONOLINE E-250 SUPER WINDOW VAN: See E-150 Super Cargo Van.

ECONOLINE E-250 CUTAWAY VAN: This Van with Camper Special Packages; was designed to readily accommodate custom motorhomes.

ECONOLINE E-250 PARCEL DELIVERY: The E-250 Parcel Delivery van was 149.9 in. long and 74.3 in. high in its cargo area. The rear door opening was 84.7 in. wide.

I.D. DATA: The VIN has 17 symbols. The first three indicate the manufacturer; make; and type of vehicle. The fourth symbol indicates the GVW range. The fifth, sixth and seventh symbols indicate the series and body style. The eighth symbol indicates the type of engine. The ninth symbol is a check digit. The 10th symbol (a letter) indicates model year. The 11th symbol indicates the assembly plant. The remaining symbols are the sequential production number starting with 100001 at each plant.

Model	Body Type	Price	Weight	Prod. Total
E-250 — 3/4-Ton — 138 in. w.b. — Six				
E-240	Cargo Van	8199	4132	Note 1
E-250	Window Van	8381	4161	Note 1
E-260	Display Van	8315	4147	Note 1
E-150 Supervan — 1/2-Ton — 138 in. w.b. — Six				
E-040	Cargo Van	8573	4245	Note 1
E-050	Window Van	8755	4274	Note 1
E-060	Display Van	8689	4260	Note 1

NOTE 1: Model year production of Econolines was 119,206.

ENGINE [Base Six]: Inline. OHV. Six-cylinder (heavy-duty). Bore & stroke: 4.0 x 3.98 in. Displacement: 300 cid (4.9 liter). Compression ratio: 8.9:1. Net horsepower: 115 at 3000 rpm. Taxable horsepower: 38.4. Net torque: 223 lbs.-ft. at 1600 rpm. Carburetor: One-barrel. (Note: Horsepower and torque may vary with specific model applications, as net horsepower ratings are relative to weight of vehicle.)

ENGINE [Base V-8; Mandatory in California]: V-block. OHV. Eight-cylinder. Bore & stroke: 4.0 in. x 3.0 in. Displacement: 302 cid (5.0 liter). Net horsepower: 130 at 3800 rpm. Taxable horsepower: 51.2. Net torque: 222 lbs.-ft. at 2000 rpm. Carburetor: Two-barrel. (Note: Horsepower and torque may vary with specific model applications, as net horsepower ratings are relative to weight of vehicle.)

ENGINE [Optional V-8]: V-block. OHV. Eight-cylinder. Bore & stroke: 4.0 in. x 3.5 in. Displacement: 351 cid (5.8 liter). Net horsepower: 156 at 4000 rpm. Taxable horsepower: 51.2. Net torque: 262 lbs.-ft. at 2200 rpm. Carburetor: Two-barrel. (Note: Horsepower and torque may vary with specific model applications, as net horsepower ratings are relative to weight of vehicle.)

ECONOLINE E-350 CARGO VAN: This was the top-of-the-line Econoline Van. It had heavy-duty front and rear shocks and a greater load capacity than the other series. Standard features were the same as the E-100.

ECONOLINE E-350 SUPER CARGO VAN: See E-150 Super Cargo Van.

ECONOLINE E-350 DISPLAY VAN: See E-250 Display Van.

ECONOLINE E-350 SUPER DISPLAY VAN: See E-150 Super Cargo Van.

ECONOLINE E-350 WINDOW VAN: See E-250 Window Van.

ECONOLINE E-350 SUPER WINDOW VAN: See E-150 Super Cargo Van.

ECONOLINE E-350 CUTAWAY VAN: See E-250 Cutaway Van.

ECONOLINE E-350 PARCEL DELIVERY: See E-250 Parcel Delivery.

I.D. DATA: The VIN has 17 symbols. The first three indicate the manufacturer; make; and type of vehicle. The fourth symbol indicates the GVW range. The fifth, sixth and seventh symbols indicate the series and body style. The eighth symbol indicates the type of engine. The ninth symbol is a check digit. The 10th symbol (a letter) indicates model year. The 11th symbol indicates the assembly plant. The remaining symbols are the sequential production number starting with 100001 at each plant.

Model	Body Type	Price	Weight	Prod. Total
E-350 — 1-Ton — 138 in. w.b. — Six				
E-340	Cargo Van	8424	4305	Note 1
E-350	Window Van	8606	4334	Note 1
E-360	Display Van	8540	4320	Note 1
E-350 Supervan — 1-Ton — 138 in. w.b. — Six				
E-340	Cargo Van	9404	4470	Note 1
E-050	Window Van	9585	4499	Note 1
E-060	Display Van	9520	4485	Note 1
E-350 Stretch Vans — 1-Ton — 158 in. w.b. — Six				
E-37B	Cutaway	—	3677	—
E-380	Parcel Delivery	—	5240	—

NOTE 1: Model year production of Econolines was 119,206.

ENGINE [Base Six]: Inline. OHV. Six-cylinder (heavy-duty). Bore & stroke: 4.0 x 3.98 in. Displacement: 300 cid (4.9 liter). Compression ratio: 8.9:1. Net horsepower: 115 at 3000 rpm. Taxable horsepower: 38.4. Net torque: 223 lbs.-ft. at 1600 rpm. Carburetor: One-barrel. (Note: Horsepower and torque may vary with specific model applications, as net horsepower ratings are relative to weight of vehicle.)

ENGINE [Base V-8; Mandatory in California]: V-block. OHV. Eight-cylinder. Bore & stroke: 4.0 in. x 3.0 in. Displacement: 302 cid (5.0 liter). Net horsepower: 130 at 3800 rpm. Taxable horsepower: 51.2. Net torque: 222 lbs.-ft. at 2000 rpm. Carburetor: Two-barrel. (Note: Horsepower and torque may vary with specific model applications, as net horsepower ratings are relative to weight of vehicle.)

ENGINE [Optional V-8]: V-block. OHV. Eight-cylinder. Bore & stroke: 4.0 in. x 3.5 in. Displacement: 351 cid (5.8 liter). Net horsepower: 156 at 4000 rpm. Taxable horsepower: 51.2. Net torque: 262 lbs.-ft. at 2200 rpm. Carburetor: Two-barrel. (Note: Horsepower and torque may vary with specific model applications, as net horsepower ratings are relative to weight of vehicle.)

CHASSIS: Wheelbase: 124 in.; (E-100/E-150) 138 in. Overall length: 186.8 in. (124 in. wheelbase); 206.8 in. (138 in. wheelbase); 226.8 in. (138 in Super Van). GVW: 5,200-5,600 lbs. (E-100); 5,800-6,300 lbs. (E-150); 6,500-7,900 lbs. (E-250); 8,550-9750 lbs. (E-350). Tires: P205/75R x 15 SL (E-100); P225/75R x 15 SL (E-150); 8.00 x 16.5D TT (E-250); 9.50 x 16.5E (E-350).

POWERTRAIN OPTIONS: Engines: 302 cid V-8. 351 cid V-8. (The 400 cid and 406 cid V-8s were no longer listed as regular production options, but probably were available on special order). Four-speed manual with overdrive or SelectShift automatic transmissions.

CONVENIENCE OPTIONS: Custom Van includes (in addition to or in place of standard) wood-tone applique on instrument panel; front side cowl and door trim panels; cigarette lighter; front compartment headlining; insulated front floor mats; front roof rail garnish moldings; bright hubcaps; bright taillight bezels; and bright window frames with optional rear windows. Chateau includes (in addition to or in place of Custom features) super soft vinyl or cloth and vinyl seat trim; cut-pile carpeting in front; courtesy light switches for all doors; chrome front and rear bumpers; bright grille surround molding; bright lower bodyside character line moldings; and bright mirrors. Sports rails. Bodyside accent tape stripe. Pinstripe tape in black, white or gold. Chrome grille. Deluxe Accent Moldings Package with bright drip rail; center bodyside and lower character line moldings. Bright drip rails. Bright window moldings. Console. Right-hand visor mirror. Power door locks. AM radio. AM/FM monaural radio. AM/FM stereo radio. AM/digital clock radio. AM/FM stereo radio with tape deck or cassette player. 40-channel tape player. 40-channel CB radio. Rear speakers. Premium Sound System. Air-conditioning front or high-capacity. Heaters, high-output or auxiliary (for cargo area) types. Roof/floor insulation package. Deluxe insulation package. Convenience group with intermittent wipers; dome light switches in all doors; and day/night mirror). Dome light courtesy switches for all doors. Western low-mount mirrors. Swing-out recreation mirrors. Tilt steering. Speed control. Tinted glass all around. Privacy glass. Flip-open or fixed windows (available in all cargo doors). Single sliding side cargo door in lieu of double doors. Combination three-passenger rear seat that converts into a bed. Dual or quad captain's chairs (reclining and swivel or reclining only). Passengers' seat. Flip-fold passengers' seat. Cloth and vinyl trim for bucket seat and captain's chairs. Light Group with dual beam dome light; headlamps-on buzzer; underhood light; and dome light switches on all doors. Chrome or argent step bumper. 18-gal. auxiliary fuel tank (138 in. wheelbase). Trailer Towing Packages. Five-slot or 10-hole forged aluminum wheels. Heavy-duty shocks. Handling Package. Power steering. Front stabilizer bar. Engine block heater. Oil pressure gauge and ammeter. Cooling Packages (super and extra). Push bar plus fog lights and covers. Protection Group with front and sliding door black stepwell pads; front door edge guards; and front bumper guards (require chrome bumpers). Security Group with Locking gas cap; inside locking hood release; and spare tire lock. Chrome or painted Argent silver step bumper. Chrome contour bumpers. Deluxe wheelcovers.

E-100 CLUB WAGON: The new E-100 Club Wagon looked the same as last year's model. That wasn't bad! Among the standard features were: front bucket seats and rear bench seats; color-keyed patterned vinyl seat trim; seat belts; two-speed electric windshield wipers; wiper-arm-mounted washer jets; 10 inch rearview mirror; dome lights; insulated floor mat with Supercabuff plates; three armrests; dual horns; flip-open windows in sliding door and opposite windows; painted bumpers; 5 x 8 in. mirrors and hubcaps and bright windshield molding.

E-150 CLUB WAGON: This was a slightly heavier-duty version of the E-100. It could be had in 124 or 138 inch wheelbases and was also offered in five- and eight-passenger versions. Standard features were same as those on the E-100.

E-150 SUPER WAGON: This was basically the same as the 138 inch wheelbase E-150; but it had a 20 inch extended rear overhang.

E-250 CLUB WAGON: This was available in 11- and 12-passenger versions. Also; an eight-passenger version was available with quad captain's chairs and a four-passenger bench seat.

E-350 SUPER WAGON: The heavy-duty E-350 provided 20 in. more inside length than regular 138 inch wheelbased Club Wagons. Heavy-duty shocks were standard.

I.D. DATA: The VIN has 17 symbols. The first three indicate the manufacturer, make, and type of vehicle. The fourth symbol indicates the GVW range. The fifth, sixth and seventh symbols indicate the series and body style. The eighth symbol indicates the type of engine. The ninth symbol is a check digit. The 10th symbol (a letter) indicates model year. The 11th symbol indicates the assembly plant. The remaining symbols are the sequential production number starting with 100001 at each plant.

Model	Body Type	Price	Weight	Prod. Total
E-100 Supervan — 1/2-Ton — 124 in./138 in. w.b. — Six				
E-100	Club Wagon	8501	3889	Note 1
E-150 Supervan — 1/2-Ton — 124 in./138 in. w.b. — Six				
E-150	Club Wagon	8794	3896	Note 1
E-150	Super Wagon	9480	4216	Note 1
E-250 Supervan — 3/4-Ton — 138 in. w.b. — Six				
E-250	Club Wagon	11,785	4751	Note 1
E-350 Supervan — 1-Ton — 138 in. w.b. — Six				
E-350	Super Wagon	10,785	4751	Note 1

NOTE 1: Total 1982 Club Wagon model year production was 30,924.

ENGINE [Base Six]: Inline. OHV. Six-cylinder (heavy-duty). Bore & stroke: 4.0 x 3.98 in. Displacement: 300 cid (4.9 liter). Compression ratio: 8.9:1. Net horsepower: 115 at 3000 rpm. Taxable horsepower: 38.4. Net torque: 223 lbs.-ft. at 1600 rpm. Carburetor: One-barrel. (Note: Horsepower and torque may vary with specific model applications, as net horsepower ratings are relative to weight of vehicle.)

ENGINE [Base V-8; Mandatory in California]: V-block. OHV. Eight-cylinder. Bore & stroke: 4.0 in. x 3.0 in. Displacement: 302 cid (5.0 liter). Net horsepower: 130 at 3800 rpm. Taxable horsepower: 51.2. Net torque: 222 lbs.-ft. at 2000 rpm. Carburetor: Two-barrel. (Note: Horsepower and torque may vary with specific model applications, as net horsepower ratings are relative to weight of vehicle.)

ENGINE [Optional V-8; All]: V-block. OHV. Eight-cylinder. Bore & stroke: 4.0 in. x 3.5 in. Displacement: 351 cid (5.8 liter). Net horsepower: 156 at 4000 rpm. Taxable horsepower: 51.2. Net torque: 262 lbs.-ft. at 2200 rpm. Carburetor: Two-barrel. (Note: Horsepower and torque may vary with specific model applications, as net horsepower ratings are relative to weight of vehicle.)

CHASSIS: Wheelbase: 124 in. (E-100); 138 in. (E-150/E-250/E-350). Overall width: 79.7 in. GVW: 5,400-9,400 lbs. Tires: P205/75R x 15 SL.

POWERTRAIN OPTIONS: Engines: 302 cid V-8. 351 cid V-8. SelectShift automatic or four-speed manual with overdrive transmissions.

CONVENIENCE OPTIONS: CONVENIENCE OPTIONS: Custom Van includes (in addition to or in place of standard) wood-tone applique on instrument panel; front side cowl and door trim panels; cigarette lighter; front compartment headlining; insulated front floor mats; front roof rail garnish moldings; bright hubcaps; bright taillight bezels; and bright window frames with optional rear windows. Chateau includes (in addition to or in place of Custom features) super soft vinyl or cloth and vinyl seat trim; cut-pile carpeting in front; courtesy light switches for all doors; chrome front and rear bumpers; bright grille surround molding; bright lower bodyside character line moldings; and bright mirrors. Sports rails. Bodyside accent tape stripe. Pinstripe tape in black, white or gold. Chrome grille. Deluxe Accent Moldings Package with bright drip rail; center bodyside and lower character line moldings. Bright drip rails. Bright window moldings. Console. Right-hand visor mirror. Power door locks. AM radio. AM/FM monaural radio. AM/FM stereo radio. AM/digital clock radio. AM/FM stereo radio with tape deck or cassette player. 40-channel tape player. 40-channel CB radio. Rear speakers. Premium Sound System. Air-conditioning front or high-capacity. Heaters, high-output or auxiliary (for cargo area) types. Roof/floor insulation package. Deluxe insulation package. Convenience group with intermittent wipers; dome light switches in all doors; and day/night mirror). Dome light courtesy switches for all doors. Western low-mount mirrors. Swing-out recreation mirrors. Tilt steering. Speed control. Tinted glass all around. Privacy glass. Flip-open or fixed windows (available in all cargo doors). Single sliding side cargo door in lieu of double doors. Combination three-passenger rear seat that converts into a bed. Dual or quad captain's chairs (reclining and swivel or reclining only). Passengers' seat. Flip-fold passengers' seat. Cloth and vinyl trim for bucket seat and captain's chairs. Light Group with dual beam dome light; headlamps-on buzzer; underhood light; and dome light switches on all doors. Chrome or argent step bumper. 18-gal. auxiliary fuel tank (138 in. wheelbase). Trailer Towing Packages. Five-slot or 10-hole forged aluminum wheels. Heavy-duty shocks. Handling Package. Power steering. Front stabilizer bar. Engine block heater. Oil pressure gauge and ammeter. Cooling Packages (super and extra). Push bar plus fog lights and covers. Protection Group with front and sliding door black stepwell pads; front door edge guards; and front bumper guards (require chrome bumpers). Security Group with Locking gas cap; inside locking hood release; and spare tire lock. Chrome or painted Argent silver step bumper. Chrome contour bumpers. Deluxe wheelcovers. Four-passenger rear bench seat. Snack-game table.

COURIER PICKUP: This was the last year for the Courier. It received a new padded steering wheel and column with stalk-mounted gear-shift controls. Other standard features included: Four-speed manual transmission; power front disc brakes; independent front suspension; one-hand tailgate operation; bright front bumper; bright hubcaps; and whitewall tires. The seats and door panels were trimmed in pleated vinyl. The seatback was hinged for easy access to behind-seat stowage area. Also included were an inside hood release; door vent windows; dome light and cigarette lighter.

I.D. DATA: The VIN has 17 symbols. The first three indicate the manufacturer; make and type of vehicle. The fourth, fifth and sixth symbols indicate the line, series, chassis, cab type and body style. The seventh symbol identifies the GVWR class. The eighth symbol indicates the type of engine. The ninth symbol is a check digiti. The 10th symbol (a letter) indivates the model year. The 11th symbol indicates the assembly plant. The last six symbols are the sequential production numbers.

Model	Body Type	Price	Weight	Prod. Total
Courier — 1/2-Ton — 106.9 in./112.8 in. w.b. — Four				
—	Chassis & Cab	6198	2430	Note 1
—	Pickup	6614	2680	Note 1

NOTE 1: Courier dealer sales for calendar year 1982 were 32,967.

CHASSIS: Wheelbase: 106.9 in. (6 ft. box); 112.8 in. (7 ft. box). Overall length: 177.9 in. (6 ft. box); 189.4 in. (7 ft. box). Overall width: 63 in. Overall height: 61.5 in. GVW: 4,100 lbs. Tires: 6.00 x 14C White sidewall.

ENGINE [Base Four]: Inline. OHV. OHC. Bore & stroke: 3.07 x 3.70 in. Displacement: 110 cid (2.0 liter). Net horsepower: 77 at 4500 rpm (72 in California). Taxable horsepower: 15.8. Carburetor: Two-barrel.

ENGINE [Optional Four]: Inline. OHV. OHC. Bore & stroke: 3.87 x 3.12 in. Displacement: 140 cid (2.3 liter). Net horsepower: 78 at 5000 rpm. Taxable horsepower: 22.86. Carburetor: Two-barrel.

CHASSIS: Wheelbase: 106.9 in. (6 ft. box); 112.8 in. (7 ft. box). Overall length: 177.9 in. (6 ft. box); 189.4 in. (7 ft. box). Overall width: 63 in. Overall height: 61.5 in. GVW: 4,100 lbs. Tires: 6.00 x 14C white sidewall.

ENGINE [Courier]: 2.0 liter OHC four-cylinder.

POWERTRAIN OPTIONS: Engine: 2.3 liter engine. Automatic and five-speed manual transmission (with overdrive).

CONVENIENCE OPTIONS: AM or AM/FM monaural radios. Air-conditioning. Tinted glass all around. Argent rear bumper. Cold Weather Group includes electric rear window defroster; heavy-duty battery and high-output heater; and low-mount Western mirrors. Soft Ride Package includes 3,600 lbs. GVWR and five-leaf progressive-rate rear springs. Exterior Decor Group (not available with XLT; chassis-cab or tri-color accent tape stripe) includes bright drip rail and wheel lip moldings; bright bodyside moldings with black vinyl inserts; tri-color accent tape stripe (not available with Exterior Decor Group and replaces side molding with XLT). XLT Package includes bright grille surround; bright moldings on windshield; rear window; drip rails; wheel lips and taillight surround; bright bodyside moldings with black vinyl inserts; bright red XLT fender plaques; and deluxe wheelcovers. Free Wheeling Package includes black-painted GT bar; push bar; tri-color accent tape stripe; and deluxe wheelcovers. Sport Group includes sport steering wheel with bright Argent silver spokes; temperature gauge and ammeter; individually adjustable bucket seats (trimmed in black vinyl with black and white plaid fabric inserts); black soft shift lever knob; bright Argent silver instrument panel appliques; black carpeting; and black interior trim. Radial tires. XLT Interior includes herringbone cloth seat trim in three color choices (tan, red and blue); contrasting accent stripe on seatback and door trim; color-keyed cut-pile carpeting; cowl trim panels; instrument panel; headlining; seats; heater shroud; ashtray; sun visors and shift boot; wood-tone upper door trim panel with contrasting accent stripe and floorshift knob; day/night mirror; ashtray; underhood and glove box lights; glove box lock; Sport steering wheel with black spokes; temperature gauge; and ammeter.

1982 Ford 1/2-Ton F-100 XLT Lariat Styleside Pickup (JAG)

F-100 PICKUP: The most noticeable styling change for 1982 was the removal of the Ford name from the face of the hood. It was replaced by the Ford oval in the center of the revised, rectangular slots theme grille. Also new were lubed-for-life ball joints and adjustable camber. Among standard features were: Chrome front bumper; bright grille surround; windshield molding and door-mount mirrors; Argent silver hubcaps; all-vinyl seat trim; full-foam seat cover springs; folding seatback access to behind seat storage area; glove box; left door courtesy light switch; temperature gauge; color-keyed windshield pillar; header and cowl side trim panels and door trim panels (with foam padded armrests); floor insulation and carpet-texture rubber mat; inside hood release; black applique instrument panel; black steering wheel; vinyl headlining (Supercab); and three-speed manual transmission. The F-100 was available with 6.5 ft. Flareside and 6.75 ft. or 8 ft. Styleside versions. Interior F-series colors in 1982 were: fawn; Dark blue; red; black; Nutmeg or spruce (except Supercab). Exterior colors included: Raven black; Wimbledon white; silver (metallic); Medium grey (metallic); Candy-apple red; Midnight blue (metallic); Medium blue (metallic); Bright blue; Dark spruce (metallic); Light spruce; Dark fawn (metallic); fawn; Medium Carmel (metallic); tan; Dark brown (metallic); maroon; and Light Spruce Glow (optional). Tu-Tones: (Regular) Accent color covered roof and upper back panel; dual-color tape strip divided colors; (Deluxe) Accent color on center bodyside area and tailgate; moldings or tapes included as needed; (Combination) Regular and deluxe Tu-Tones combined; (Victoria) Accent color applied to hood, upper fender, around door window and on the lower bodyside (tape and moldings included as needed).

I.D. DATA: The VIN has 17 symbols. The first three indicate the manufacturer; make; and type of vehicle. The fourth symbol indicates the GVW range. The fifth, sixth and seventh symbols indicate the series and body style. The eighth symbol indicates the type of engine. The ninth symbol is a check digit. The 10th symbol (a letter) indicates model year. The 11th symbol indicates the assembly plant. The remaining symbols are the sequential production number starting with 100001 at each plant.

Model	Body Type	Price	Weight	Prod. Total
F-100 — 1/2-Ton — 117 in. w.b. — Six				
F-10	Flareside 6.5 ft.	6840	—	Note 1
F-10	Styleside 6.8 ft	6713	3080	Note 1
F-100 — 1/2-Ton — 133 in. w.b. — Six				
F-10	Styleside 8 ft.	6863	3152	Note 1

NOTE 1: Model year production was: [F-100] 108,096.

ENGINE [Base Six]: Inline. OHV. Six-cylinder (heavy-duty). Bore & stroke: 4.0 x 3.98 in. Displacement: 300 cid (4.9 liter). Compression ratio: 8.9:1. Net horsepower: 115 at 3000 rpm. Taxable horsepower: 38.4. Net torque: 223 lbs.-ft. at 1600 rpm. Carburetor: One-barrel. (Note: Horsepower and torque may vary with specific model applications, as net horsepower ratings are relative to weight of vehicle.)

ENGINE [Optional V-6]: V-block. OHV. Six-cylinder. Bore & stroke: 3.81 x 3.38 in. Displacement: 232 cid (3.8 liter). Net horsepower: 109 at 3600 rpm. Net torque: 184 lbs.-ft. at 1600 rpm. Taxable horsepower: 34.83. Carburetor: Two-barrel.

ENGINE [Base V-8]: V-block. OHV. Eight-cylinder. Bore & stroke: 3.68 in. x 3.00 in. Displacement: 255 cid (4.2 liter). Net horsepower: n.a. Taxable horsepower: 43.3. Net torque: n.a. Carburetor: Two-barrel. (Note: Horsepower and torque may vary with specific model applications, as net horsepower ratings are relative to weight of vehicle.)

ENGINE [Optional V-8; Mandatory in California]: V-block. OHV. Eight-cylinder. Bore & stroke: 4.0 in. x 3.0 in. Displacement: 302 cid (5.0 liter). Net horsepower: 130 at 3800 rpm. Taxable horsepower: 51.2. Net torque: 222 lbs.-ft. at 2000 rpm. Carburetor: Two-barrel. (Note: Horsepower and torque may vary with specific model applications, as net horsepower ratings are relative to weight of vehicle.)

1982 Ford 1/2-Ton F-150 XLS Styleside Pickup 4x4 (JAG)

F-150 PICKUP: The F-150 was Ford's heavy-duty 1/2-ton. It had most of the same features as the F-100; plus power brakes. Both Flareside and Styleside boxes were available. Styleside boxes could be had with regular or Supercabs. The latter provided space behind the front seat for an optional bench seat or two jump seats.

I.D. DATA: The VIN has 17 symbols. The first three indicate the manufacturer; make; and type of vehicle. The fourth symbol indicates the GVW range. The fifth, sixth and seventh symbols indicate the series and body style. The eighth symbol indicates the type of engine. The ninth symbol is a check digit. The 10th symbol (a letter) indicates model year. The 11th

symbol indicates the assembly plant. The remaining symbols are the sequential production number starting with 100001 at each plant.

Model	Body Type	Price	Weight	Prod. Total
F-150 — 1/2-Ton — 117 in. w.b. — Six				
F-15	Flareside 6.5 ft.	7094	—	Note 1
F-15	Styleside 6.75 ft.	6969	3303	Note 1
F-150 — 1/2-Ton — 133 in. w.b. — Six				
F-15	Styleside	7119	3404	Note 1
F-150 Supercab — 1/2-Ton — 155 in. w.b. — Six				
X-15	Styleside	8010	3635	Note 1

NOTE 1: Model year production was: [F-150] 183,606.

1982 Ford 1/2-Ton Ranger XLS Styleside Pickup (JAG)

ENGINE [Base Six]: Inline. OHV. Six-cylinder (heavy-duty). Bore & stroke: 4.0 x 3.98 in. Displacement: 300 cid (4.9 liter). Compression ratio: 8.9:1. Net horsepower: 115 at 3000 rpm. Taxable horsepower: 38.4. Net torque: 223 lbs.-ft. at 1600 rpm. Carburetor: One-barrel. (Note: Horsepower and torque may vary with specific model applications, as net horsepower ratings are relative to weight of vehicle.)

ENGINE [Optional V-8; Mandatory in California]: V-block. OHV. Eight-cylinder. Bore & stroke: 4.0 in. x 3.0 in. Displacement: 302 cid (5.0 liter). Net horsepower: 130 at 3800 rpm. Taxable horsepower: 51.2. Net torque: 222 lbs.-ft. at 2000 rpm. Carburetor: Two-barrel. (Note: Horsepower and torque may vary with specific model applications, as net horsepower ratings are relative to weight of vehicle.)

ENGINE [Optional V-8]: V-block. OHV. Eight-cylinder. Bore & stroke: 4.0 in. x 3.5 in. Displacement: 351 cid (5.8 liter). Net horsepower: 150 at 3200 rpm. Taxable horsepower: 51.2. Net torque: 280 lbs.-ft. at 1800 rpm. Carburetor: Two-barrel. (Note: Horsepower and torque may vary with specific model applications, as net horsepower ratings are relative to weight of vehicle.)

1982 Ford 3/4-Ton F-250 Styleside Camper Special Pickup (RCA)

F-250 PICKUP: The regular cab F-250 was only offered with the 8 ft. Styleside box. Supercab models came with either the 6.75 ft. or 8 ft. box. Standard features were similar to those on the F-100, with the addition of power brakes. Heavy-duty F-250s also had four-speed manual transmission.

I.D. DATA: The VIN has 17 symbols. The first three indicate the manufacturer; make; and type of vehicle. The fourth symbol indicates the GVW range. The fifth, sixth and seventh symbols indicate the series and body style. The eighth symbol indicates the type of engine. The ninth symbol is a check digit. The 10th symbol (a letter) indicates model year. The 11th symbol indicates the assembly plant. The remaining symbols are the sequential production number starting with 100001 at each plant.

Model	Body Type	Price	Weight	Prod. Total
F-250 — 3/4-Ton — 133 in. w.b. — Six				
—	Chassis & Cab	7527	3481	Note 1
F-25	Styleside	7568	3579	Note 1
F-250 — 3/4-Ton — 161 in. w.b. — Six				
X-25	Supercab Pickup	8227	3906	Note 1

NOTE 1: Model year production: [F-250] 69,482.

ENGINE [Base Six]: Inline. OHV. Six-cylinder (heavy-duty). Bore & stroke: 4.0 x 3.98 in. Displacement: 300 cid (4.9 liter). Compression ratio: 8.9:1. Net horsepower: 115 at 3000 rpm. Taxable horsepower: 38.4. Net torque: 223 lbs.-ft. at 1600 rpm. Carburetor: One-barrel. (Note: Horsepower and torque may vary with specific model applications, as net horsepower ratings are relative to weight of vehicle.)

ENGINE [Optional V-8; Mandatory in California]: V-block. OHV. Eight-cylinder. Bore & stroke: 4.0 in. x 3.0 in. Displacement: 302 cid (5.0 liter). Net horsepower: 130 at 3800 rpm. Taxable horsepower: 51.2. Net torque: 222 lbs.-ft. at 2000 rpm. Carburetor: Two-barrel. (Note: Horsepower and torque may vary with specific model applications, as net horsepower ratings are relative to weight of vehicle.)

ENGINE [Optional V-8]: V-block. OHV. Eight-cylinder. Bore & stroke: 4.0 in. x 3.5 in. Displacement: 351 cid (5.8 liter). Net horsepower: 150 at 3200 rpm. Taxable horsepower: 51.2. Net torque: 280 lbs.-ft. at 1800 rpm. Carburetor: Two-barrel. (Note: Horsepower and torque may vary with specific model applications, as net horsepower ratings are relative to weight of vehicle.)

F-350 PICKUP: The F-350 was only offered with a regular cab and with a smooth side Styleside box. The F-350 Pickup could also be had with dual rear wheels. Such models had Flareside-like rear fenders, but otherwise looked like Stylesides. Except for having power brakes, power steering and a four-speed manual transmission, most F-350 standard features were the same as those on F-100s.

I.D. DATA: The VIN has 17 symbols. The first three indicate the manufacturer; make; and type of vehicle. The fourth symbol indicates the GVW range. The fifth, sixth and seventh symbols indicate the series and body style. The eighth symbol indicates the type of engine. The ninth symbol is a check digit. The 10th symbol (a letter) indicates model year. The 11th symbol indicates the assembly plant. The remaining symbols are the sequential production number starting with 100001 at each plant.

Model	Body Type	Price	Weight	Prod. Total
F-350 — 1-Ton — 133 in. w.b. — V-8				
F-37	Chassis & Cab	8648	3717	Note 1
F-35	Styleside	8901	3961	Note 1
F-350 — 1-Ton — 161 in. w.b. — V-8				
X-35	Supercab Pickup	—	—	Note 1

NOTE 1: Model year production [F-350] 28,805.

ENGINE [Base Six]: Inline. OHV. Six-cylinder (heavy-duty). Bore & stroke: 4.0 x 3.98 in. Displacement: 300 cid (4.9 liter). Compression ratio: 8.9:1. Net horsepower: 115 at 3000 rpm. Taxable horsepower: 38.4. Net torque: 223 lbs.-ft. at 1600 rpm. Carburetor: One-barrel. (Note: Horsepower and torque may vary with specific model applications, as net horsepower ratings are relative to weight of vehicle.)

ENGINE [Optional V-8]: V-block. OHV. Eight-cylinder. Bore & stroke: 4.0 in. x 3.5 in. Displacement: 351 cid (5.8 liter). Net horsepower: 150 at 3200 rpm. Taxable horsepower: 51.2. Net torque: 280 lbs.-ft. at 1800 rpm. Carburetor: Two-barrel. (Note: Horsepower and torque may vary with specific model applications, as net horsepower ratings are relative to weight of vehicle.)

1982 Ford 1/2-Ton Ranger Styleside Mini-Pickup (JAG)

CHASSIS: Wheelbase: 116.8 in. (F-100/F-150). 133 in. (All). 138.8 in. (F-150/F-250 Supercab); 155 in. (F-150/F-250 Supercab). Overall length: 189.3 in. (Flareside). 192.1 in. (F-100/F-150 Styleside); 208.3 in. (Style). 214.1 in. (F-150/F-250 Supercab); 230.3 in. (F-150/F-250 Supercab). GVW: 4,650-5,050 lbs. (F-100); 5,250-6,450 lbs. (F-150); 6,500-9,200 lbs. (F-250); 8,900-11;000 lbs. (F-350). Tires: P215/75R x 15SL (F-100/F-150); 8.00 x 16.5 (F-250); 9.50 x 16.5E (F-350).

POWERTRAIN OPTIONS: Engines: 255 cid V-8 (F-100). 302 cid V-8 (F-100/F-150/F-250). 351 cid V-8 (F-150/F-250/F-350). 400 cid V-8 (F-250 heavy-duty/F-350). Transmissions: Four-speed manual. Four-speed manual with overdrive (F-100/F-150/F-250); SelectShift automatic or automatic overdrive.

1982 Ford 1/2-Ton Ranger Styleside Mini-Pickup (JAG)

CONVENIENCE OPTIONS: Four-wheel drive (F-150/F-250/F-350). Chrome grille. Chromatic tape stripe. Tri-colored tape strip. Accent tape stripe. Lower bodyside molding with black vinyl insert. Bright box rails for 8 ft. Styleside. Wheel lip moldings. AM radio. AM/FM monaural radio. AM/FM stereo (speakers mounted in door panels). AM/FM stereo with cassette player. AM/FM stereo radio with 8-track tape player. Air-conditioning. High-output heater. Convenience Group includes interval wipers; 12 in. day/night mirror; right-hand visor vanity mirror; molded bin on lower doors; headlamps-on warning buzzer and courtesy

light switch on right-hand door. Electronic digital clock. Fingertip speed control. Vinyl headliner. Light Group includes movable underhood worklight with 20 ft. retractable cord; plus lights in glove box; ashtray and under instrument panel; dome lamp with map lights; cargo box light; headlamps-on warning buzzer and courtesy light switch on right-hand door. Power door locks. Power steering. Power windows. Tinted sliding rear window. Tilt steering wheel. Tinted glass all around. Tool storage box located under the hood (included movable underhood worklight with 20 ft. retractable cord and inside locking hood release). Slide-out spare tire carrier. Spare tire carrier side-mounted inside Styleside box. Center console (Supercab with captain's chairs). Electric remote-control swing-away mirrors. Black low-mount Western swing-away mirrors. Bright low-mount Western swing-away mirrors. Bright low-mount recreational mirrors. Bright swing-away recreational mirrors. Reclining captain's chairs. Forward-facing rear seat (folds down to form flat floor in Supercab. Center-facing folding rear seats in Supercab. Heavy-duty black vinyl upholstery. Knitted vinyl upholstery. Auxiliary fuel tank. Handling Package includes front and rear stabilizer bars; heavy-duty front and rear shocks; and heavy-duty front springs. Heavy-duty shock absorbers. Oil pressure and ammeter gauges. Front and rear stabilizer bars. Engine block heater. XL Package includes front and rear stabilizer bars. Engine block heater. Extra engine cooling package. Super engine cooling package. Camper special package. Trailer towing packages. Heavy-duty air cleaner. Dual note horns. Color-keyed floor mats in lieu of standard carpeting with XLS. Five roof clearance lights. Exterior Protection Group includes bright door edge guards; front bumper guards; and front bumper rub strip. Security Lock Group includes locking gas cap; inside hood release; and glove box; also spare tire lock (with under frame and in-box carrier). Sports instrumentation with tachometer; ammeter; oil pressure gauge; and trip odometer. Black step bumper (XLS Style). Argent silver step bumper (Styleside). Chrome step bumper (single rear wheel Styleside). Chrome channel bumper (Flareside). Chrome contour bumper (single rear wheel Styleside. Deluxe wheelcovers. White styled steel wheels. Deluxe Argent silver styled steel wheels. Spot wheelcovers. Cast aluminum wheels. XLS Package includes XLS tape stripe; Argent silver styled steel wheels with black hubs; black front and rear bumpers; black-out treatment on grille and headlamp doors; black side window surround; black door handles and locks; windshield molding; mirrors and tailgate handle (Styleside); cigarette lighter; left- and right-hand courtesy light switches; bright surround door trim panel moldings; color-keyed carpeting; brushed aluminum applique instrument panel; folding fully covered seatback; cloth and vinyl seat trim; aluminum scuff plates; brushed aluminum trim steering wheel. XL Package includes bright hubcaps; bright upper bodyside moldings; windshield; rear window; tape letters on tailgate; cigarette lighter; left- and right-hand courtesy light switches; day/night mirror; bright surround door trim panel moldings; color-keyed mat; wood-tone applique instrument panel; fully-covered folding seatback; cloth and vinyl seat trim; aluminum scuff plates; vinyl headlining; and trim panel moldings above belt line. XL Lariat includes (in addition to or in place of items on XL or XLS) vinyl upper bodyside protection; tape stripe; bright windshield, rear window and wheel lip accents; brushed aluminum tailgate applique; bright door trim panel moldings with wood-tone applique; color-keyed carpeting; wood-tone applique for instrument panel; deluxe steering wheel with wood-tone insert; and moldings and trim panels above beltline (and below on Supercabs). Explorer package.

HISTORICAL: Model year production of light-duty trucks, by model, was: [F-100] 108,096; [F-150] 183,606; [F-250] 69,482; [F-350] 28,805; [Bronco] 38,891; [Econoline] 119,206; [Club Wagon] 30,924. In addition, 108,196 of the new Ranger Pickups were counted in the 1982 model year production figures, giving Ford a total of 687,206 light-duty vehicles built in the U.S. or in Canada for the U.S. market. In addition, 32,967 Couriers were sold for the calendar year. Although Ford continued to outsell Chevrolet in six segments of the truck market, the new S-10 Pickup and S-10 Blazer pushed Chevrolet to the top sales rank for the first time in six years. Edson P. Williams became General Manager of Ford Truck Operations this year, as well as a Ford Vice-President. The down-sized Ranger Pickup made its official debut in March 1982 and was marketed as an early 1983 model.

1983 Ford Ranger XLT Pickup

1983 FORD

BRONCO CUSTOM: Styling of the four-wheel drive Bronco was carried over from the previous year. Standard features included: Bucket seats. Vinyl sun visors. Padded instrument panel. Armrests. Dome lamp. Windshield header and A pillar moldings. AM radio (could be deleted for credit). Flip/fold rear bench seat. Halogen headlights. Full instrumentation. Black grille. Black front and rear bumpers. Bright hubcaps. Black scuff plate. Twin Traction Beam independent front suspension. Power brakes and steering. Four-speed manual transmission. Black grille. Bronco color choices for 1983 were: Raven black; Wimbledon white; Candy-apple red; Dark red (metallic); Midnight blue (metallic); Bright blue; Walnut (metallic); copper; Desert tan; Light Desert tan; Light Charcoal (metallic); Dark Charcoal (metallic); blue Glow; and Light Teal Glow. Fiberglass roof colors were: Black; Midnight blue; Candy-apple red; Desert tan; and white.

1983 Ford 1/2-Ton Bronco XLS Sport Utility Wagon 4x4 (JAG)

BRONCO CUSTOM: Styling of the four-wheel drive Bronco was carried over from the previous year. Standard features included: Bucket seats. Vinyl sun visors. Padded instrument panel. Armrests. Dome lamp. Windshield header and A pillar moldings. AM radio (could be deleted for credit). Flip/fold rear bench seat. Halogen headlights. Full instrumentation. Black front and rear bumpers. Bright hubcaps. Black scuff plate. Twin Traction Beam independent front suspension. Power brakes and steering. Four-speed manual transmission. Black grille. Bronco color choices for 1983 were: Raven black; Wimbledon white; Candy-apple red; Dark red (metallic); Midnight blue (metallic); Bright blue; Walnut (metallic); copper; Desert tan; Light Desert tan; Light Charcoal (metallic); Dark Charcoal (metallic); blue Glow; and Light Teal Glow. Fiberglass roof colors were: Black; Midnight blue; Candy-apple red; Desert tan; and white.
ECONOLINE E-100 CARGO VAN: Econoline styling was unchanged for 1983. Among the standard features were: Full-foam driver's bucket seat. Vinyl seat trim. Padded full-width instrument panel. Brake warning light. Two-speed electric windshield wipers. Wiper-arm-mounted washer jets. Dome lights. Front compartment headlining. Column mounted ignition switch scuff plates. Door checks. Argent silver-painted bumpers and hubcaps. Bright windshield molding. Painted mirrors. Hinged side cargo doors (sliding door available at no extra cost).
I.D. DATA: The VIN has 17 symbols. The first three indicate the manufacturer, make, and type of vehicle. The fourth symbol indicates the GVW range. The fifth, sixth and seventh symbols indicate the series and body style. The eighth symbol indicates the type of engine. The ninth symbol is a check digit. The 10th symbol (a letter) indicates model year. The 11th symbol indicates the assembly plant. The remaining symbols are the sequential production number starting with 100001 at each plant.

Model	Body Type	Price	Weight	Prod. Total
Bronco 4x4 — 1/2-Ton — 105 in. w.b. — Six				
U-150	Wagon	10,858	4079	38,963

ENGINE [Base Six]: Inline. OHV. Six-cylinder (heavy-duty). Bore & stroke: 4.0 x 3.98 in. Displacement: 300 cid (4.9 liter). Compression ratio: 8.9:1. Net horsepower: 115 at 3000 rpm. Taxable horsepower: 38.4. Net torque: 223 lbs.-ft. at 1600 rpm. Carburetor: One-barrel. (Note: Horsepower and torque may vary with specific model applications, as net horsepower ratings are relative to weight of vehicle.)
ENGINE [Base V-8; Mandatory in California]: V-block. OHV. Eight-cylinder. Bore & stroke: 4.0 in. x 3.0 in. Displacement: 302 cid (5.0 liter). Net horsepower: 130 at 3800 rpm. Taxable horsepower: 51.2. Net torque: 222 lbs.-ft. at 2000 rpm. Carburetor: Two-barrel. (Note: Horsepower and torque may vary with specific model applications, as net horsepower ratings are relative to weight of vehicle.)
ENGINE [Optional V-8]: V-block. OHV. Eight-cylinder. Bore & stroke: 4.0 in. x 3.5 in. Displacement: 351 cid (5.8 liter). Net horsepower: 156 at 4000 rpm. Taxable horsepower: 51.2. Net torque: 262 lbs.-ft. at 2200 rpm. Carburetor: Two-barrel. (Note: Horsepower and torque may vary with specific model applications, as net horsepower ratings are relative to weight of vehicle.)
CHASSIS: Wheebase: 104.7 in. Overall length: 177.6 in. Overall height: 73.2 in. Overall width: 77.2 in. Tires: P215/75R x 15 SL.
POWERTRAIN OPTIONS: Transmissions: SelectShift automatic. Four-speed manual with overdrive. Engines: 302 cid V-8; 351 cid V-8. Axles: Limited-slip front axle.
CONVENIENCE OPTIONS: Chrome front or front and rear bumpers. Tri-color tape stripe. Accent tape stripe. Black GT bar. Chrome grille. Upper bodyside tape stripe. Lower bodyside molding. High-output heater. Center console. Electric rear window defroster. Electric remote-control swing-away rearview mirrors. Convenience Group with intemittent wipers; map box in doors; headlamp-on warning buzzer; right-hand door courtesy light switch; 12 in. mirror; visor vanity mirror. Front bench seat. Rear bench seat delete. Power windows. Tinted glass all around. Privacy glass in quarter windows. Light Group with lights in glove box, ashtray and underhood; instrument panel courtesy lights; dome light with map light; right-hand door courtesy light; headlamp-on warning buzzer (the underhood light had a 20 ft. cord). Handling Package includes front and rear stablizier bars; quad heavy-duty front and dual heavy-duty rear shocks. captains chairs. underhood tool box. Automatic locking hubs. Traction-Lok front and/or rear axle. Sports Instrumentation with tachometer and odometer. Recreational mirrors. Bright low-mount Western mirrors. Heavy-duty trailer towing package. 32-gal. fuel tank in lieu of standard (includes skid plate). Sliding rear quarter windows. Protection Group with bright door edge guards; front bumper guards; and front bumper rub strip. Security Group with locking gas cap; inside hood release lock; spare tire lock; and locking glove box. Super engine cooling package. Extra engine cooling package. Fog lamps. Exterior sound package. Cigarette lighter. Power door locks. XLT with bright front and rear bumpers; black grille; bright hubcaps; windshield; quarter window; lower bodyside protection molding with vinyl insert; brushed aluminum tailgate applique; dome lamp; left- and right-hand courtesy light switches; color-keyed carpeting; left-hand rear quarter trim panel cargo lamp; door trim panel with bright surround molding; wood-tone panel with full-length storage bins; color-keyed vinyl headliner; simulated wood-tone applique and bright moldings instrument panel; bright scuff plates; deluxe seat belts; cloth and vinyl seat; trim soft-wrap steering wheel with wood-tone insert; molded rear quarter trim panels with armrests; speaker grilles; storage bin and light; spare tire cover; cigarette lighter; and added insulation. XLS Package includes most features of the XLT, plus black gloss on front and rear bumpers; black gloss grille; Argent silver styled steel wheels with black hub; black gloss windshield molding; treatment on headlamp doors and around window; door handles; locks; mirrors and tailgate lock; XLS tape; door trim panel with bright surround; brushed aluminum applique and steering wheel trim. Speed control. Swing-away spare tire carrier. 40-channel CB. Front tow hooks. Cast aluminum wheels. Styled steel painted (white) wheels. Sport wheelcovers. Deluxe Argent silver styled steel wheels. AM/FM monaural radio. AM/FM stereo. AM/FM stereo with cassette or 8-track player. Snow plow packages. High altitude emmissions system. Heavy-duty auxiliary battery.
ECONOLINE E-100 DISPLAY VAN: This model had windows at the rear and on the right hand side. It came with the same standard features as the Cargo Van.
ECONOLINE E-100 WINDOW VAN: The Window Van had glass all around. It shared standard features with the Cargo Van.
I.D. DATA: The VIN has 17 symbols. The first three indicate the manufacturer; make; and type of vehicle. The fourth symbol indicates the GVW range. The fifth, sixth and seventh symbols indicate the series and body style. The eighth symbol indicates the type of engine. The ninth symbol is a check digit. The 10th symbol (a letter) indicates model year. The 11th symbol indicates the assembly plant. The remaining symbols are the sequential production number starting with 100001 at each plant.

Model	Body Type	Price	Weight	Prod. Total
E-100 — 1/2-Ton — 124 in./138 in. w.b. — Six				
E-040	Cargo Van	7310	3763	Note 1
E-050	Window Van	7498	3802	Note 1
E-060	Display Van	7432	3797	Note 1

NOTE 1: Model year production of Econolines was 151,180.
ENGINE [Base Six]: Inline. OHV. Six-cylinder (heavy-duty). Bore & stroke: 4.0 x 3.98 in. Displacement: 300 cid (4.9 liter). Compression ratio: 8.9:1. Net horsepower: 115 at 3000 rpm. Taxable horsepower: 38.4. Net torque: 223 lbs.-ft. at 1600 rpm. Carburetor: One-barrel. (Note: Horsepower and torque may vary with specific model applications, as net horsepower ratings are relative to weight of vehicle.)
ENGINE [Base V-8; Mandatory in California]: V-block. OHV. Eight-cylinder. Bore & stroke: 4.0 in. x 3.0 in. Displacement: 302 cid (5.0 liter). Net horsepower: 130 at 3800 rpm. Taxable horsepower: 51.2. Net torque: 222 lbs.-ft. at 2000 rpm. Carburetor: Two-barrel. (Note: Horsepower and torque may vary with specific model applications, as net horsepower ratings are relative to weight of vehicle.)
ENGINE [Optional V-8]: V-block. OHV. Eight-cylinder. Bore & stroke: 4.0 in. x 3.5 in. Displacement: 351 cid (5.8 liter). Net horsepower: 156 at 4000 rpm. Taxable horsepower: 51.2. Net torque: 262 lbs.-ft. at 2200 rpm. Carburetor: Two-barrel. (Note: Horsepower and torque may vary with specific model applications, as net horsepower ratings are relative to weight of vehicle.)
ECONOLINE E-150 CARGO VAN: The slightyly more heavy-duty E-150 had most of the same standard features as the E-100.
ECONOLINE E-150 SUPER CARGO VAN: This Van had the same features as the E-150 Cargo Van, plus a 20 in. extended rear overhang. This allowed carrying of longer loads. The maximum cargo length (right side, without passenger seat) was 14 ft.
ECONOLINE E-150 DISPLAY VAN: This Van shared styling with the E-100, but had greater load capacity.
ECONOLINE E-150 SUPER DISPLAY VAN: See E-150 Super Cargo Van.
ECONOLINE E-150 WINDOW VAN: This Van shared styling with the E-100 Window Van, but had greater load capacity.
ECONOLINE E-150 SUPER WINDOW VAN: See E-150 Super Cargo Van.
I.D. DATA: The VIN has 17 symbols. The first three indicate the manufacturer; make; and type of vehicle. The fourth symbol indicates the GVW range. The fifth, sixth and seventh symbols indicate the series and body style. The eighth symbol indicates the type of engine. The ninth symbol is a check digit. The 10th symbol (a letter) indicates model year. The 11th symbol indicates the assembly plant. The remaining symbols are the sequential production number starting with 100001 at each plant.

Model	Body Type	Price	Weight	Prod. Total
E-150 — 1/2-Ton — 124 in./138 in. w.b. — Six				
E-140	Cargo Van	7566	3736	Note 1
E-150	Window Van	7754	3775	Note 1
E-160	Display Van	7688	3770	Note 1
E-150 Supervan — 1/2-Ton — 124 in./138 in. w.b. — Six				
E-140	Cargo Van	8388	4134	Note 1
E-150	Window Van	8576	4173	Note 1
E-160	Display Van	8510	4168	Note 1

NOTE 1: Model year production of Econolines was 151,180.
ENGINE [Base Six]: Inline. OHV. Six-cylinder (heavy-duty). Bore & stroke: 4.0 x 3.98 in. Displacement: 300 cid (4.9 liter). Compression ratio: 8.9:1. Net horsepower: 115 at 3000 rpm. Taxable horsepower: 38.4. Net torque: 223 lbs.-ft. at 1600 rpm. Carburetor: One-barrel. (Note: Horsepower and torque may vary with specific model applications, as net horsepower ratings are relative to weight of vehicle.)
ENGINE [Base V-8; Mandatory in California]: V-block. OHV. Eight-cylinder. Bore & stroke: 4.0 in. x 3.0 in. Displacement: 302 cid (5.0 liter). Net horsepower: 130 at 3800 rpm. Taxable horsepower: 51.2. Net torque: 222 lbs.-ft. at 2000 rpm. Carburetor: Two-barrel. (Note: Horsepower and torque may vary with specific model applications, as net horsepower ratings are relative to weight of vehicle.)
ENGINE [Optional V-8]: V-block. OHV. Eight-cylinder. Bore & stroke: 4.0 in. x 3.5 in. Displacement: 351 cid (5.8 liter). Net horsepower: 156 at 4000 rpm. Taxable horsepower: 51.2. Net torque: 262 lbs.-ft. at 2200 rpm. Carburetor: Two-barrel. (Note: Horsepower and torque may vary with specific model applications, as net horsepower ratings are relative to weight of vehicle.)
ECONOLINE E-250 CARGO VAN: The new E-250 had a higher GVW rating and more heavy-duty front and rear axles; than the E-150. It also came with eight-hole wheels. Standard features were the same as those on the E-100 except the three-speed manual was not available in Calif.
ECONOLINE E-250 SUPER CARGO VAN: See E-150 Cargo Van.
ECONOLINE E-250 DISPLAY VAN: This vehicle shared styling and features with the E-100; but had greater load capacity.
ECONOLINE E-250 SUPER DISPLAY VAN: See E-150 Super Cargo Van.
ECONOLINE E-250 WINDOW VAN: This vehicle shared styling and features with the E-100 Window Van; but had greater load capacity.
ECONOLINE E-250 SUPER WINDOW VAN: See E-150 Super Cargo Van.
ECONOLINE E-250 CUTAWAY VAN: This Van with Camper Special Packages; was designed to readily accommodate custom motorhomes.
ECONOLINE E-250 PARCEL DELIVERY: The E-250 Parcel Delivery van was 149.9 in. long and 74.3 in. high in its cargo area. The rear door opening was 84.7 in. wide.
I.D. DATA: The VIN has 17 symbols. The first three indicate the manufacturer; make; and type of vehicle. The fourth symbol indicates the GVW range. The fifth, sixth and seventh symbols indicate the series and body style. The eighth symbol indicates the type of engine. The ninth symbol is a check digit. The 10th symbol (a letter) indicates model year. The 11th symbol indicates the assembly plant. The remaining symbols are the sequential production number starting with 100001 at each plant.

Model	Body Type	Price	Weight	Prod. Total
E-250 — 3/4-Ton — 138 in. w.b. — Six				
E-240	Cargo Van	7299	4090	Note 1
E-250	Window Van	7454	4119	Note 1
E-260	Display Van	7400	4105	Note 1
E-250 Supervan — 1/2-Ton — 138 in. w.b. — Six				
E-040	Cargo Van	7646	4203	Note 1
E-050	Window Van	7801	4232	Note 1
E-060	Display Van	7748	4218	Note 1

NOTE 1: Model year production of Econolines was 151,180.

ENGINE [Base Six]: Inline. OHV. Six-cylinder (heavy-duty). Bore & stroke: 4.0 x 3.98 in. Displacement: 300 cid (4.9 liter). Compression ratio: 8.9:1. Net horsepower: 115 at 3000 rpm. Taxable horsepower: 38.4. Net torque: 223 lbs.-ft. at 1600 rpm. Carburetor: One-barrel. (Note: Horsepower and torque may vary with specific model applications, as net horsepower ratings are relative to weight of vehicle.)

ENGINE [Base V-8; Mandatory in California]: V-block. OHV. Eight-cylinder. Bore & stroke: 4.0 in. x 3.0 in. Displacement: 302 cid (5.0 liter). Net horsepower: 130 at 3800 rpm. Taxable horsepower: 51.2. Net torque: 222 lbs.-ft. at 2000 rpm. Carburetor: Two-barrel. (Note: Horsepower and torque may vary with specific model applications, as net horsepower ratings are relative to weight of vehicle.)

ENGINE [Optional V-8]: V-block. OHV. Eight-cylinder. Bore & stroke: 4.0 in. x 3.5 in. Displacement: 351 cid (5.8 liter). Net horsepower: 156 at 4000 rpm. Taxable horsepower: 51.2. Net torque: 262 lbs.-ft. at 2200 rpm. Carburetor: Two-barrel. (Note: Horsepower and torque may vary with specific model applications, as net horsepower ratings are relative to weight of vehicle.)

ECONOLINE E-350 CARGO VAN: This was the top-of-the-line Econoline Van. It had heavy-duty front and rear shocks and a greater load capacity than the other series. Standard features were the same as the E-100.

ECONOLINE E-350 SUPER CARGO VAN: See E-150 Super Cargo Van.

ECONOLINE E-350 DISPLAY VAN: See E-250 Display Van.

ECONOLINE E-350 SUPER DISPLAY VAN: See E-150 Super Cargo Van.

ECONOLINE E-350 WINDOW VAN: See E-250 Window Van.

ECONOLINE E-350 SUPER WINDOW VAN: See E-150 Super Cargo Van.

ECONOLINE E-350 CUTAWAY VAN: See E-250 Cutaway Van.

ECONOLINE E-350 PARCEL DELIVERY: See E-250 Parcel Delivery.

I.D. DATA: The VIN has 17 symbols. The first three indicate the manufacturer; make; and type of vehicle. The fourth symbol indicates the GVW range. The fifth, sixth and seventh symbols indicate the series and body style. The eighth symbol indicates the type of engine. The ninth symbol is a check digit. The 10th symbol (a letter) indicates model year. The 11th symbol indicates the assembly plant. The remaining symbols are the sequential production number starting with 100001 at each plant.

Model	Body Type	Price	Weight	Prod. Total
E-350 — 1-Ton — 138 in. w.b. — Six				
E-340	Cargo Van	8668	4460	Note 1
E-350	Window Van	8856	4513	Note 1
E-360	Display Van	8790	4494	Note 1
E-350 Supervan — 1-Ton — 138 in. w.b. — Six				
E-340	Cargo Van	9632	4608	Note 1
E-350	Window Van	9820	4661	Note 1
E-360	Display Van	9754	4642	Note 1
E-350 Stretch Vans — 1-Ton — 158 in. w.b. — Six				
E-37B	Cutaway	8835	3815	Note 1

NOTE 1: Model year production of Econolines was 151,180.

ENGINE [Base Six]: Inline. OHV. Six-cylinder (heavy-duty). Bore & stroke: 4.0 x 3.98 in. Displacement: 300 cid (4.9 liter). Compression ratio: 8.9:1. Net horsepower: 115 at 3000 rpm. Taxable horsepower: 38.4. Net torque: 223 lbs.-ft. at 1600 rpm. Carburetor: One-barrel. (Note: Horsepower and torque may vary with specific model applications, as net horsepower ratings are relative to weight of vehicle.)

ENGINE [Base V-8; Mandatory in California]: V-block. OHV. Eight-cylinder. Bore & stroke: 4.0 in. x 3.0 in. Displacement: 302 cid (5.0 liter). Net horsepower: 130 at 3800 rpm. Taxable horsepower: 51.2. Net torque: 222 lbs.-ft. at 2000 rpm. Carburetor: Two-barrel. (Note: Horsepower and torque may vary with specific model applications, as net horsepower ratings are relative to weight of vehicle.)

ENGINE [Optional V-8]: V-block. OHV. Eight-cylinder. Bore & stroke: 4.0 in. x 3.5 in. Displacement: 351 cid (5.8 liter). Net horsepower: 156 at 4000 rpm. Taxable horsepower: 51.2. Net torque: 262 lbs.-ft. at 2200 rpm. Carburetor: Two-barrel. (Note: Horsepower and torque may vary with specific model applications, as net horsepower ratings are relative to weight of vehicle.)

CHASSIS: Wheelbase: 124 in. (E-100; E-150) 138 in. Overall length: 186.8 in. (124 in. w.b.); 206.8 in. (138 in. w.b.); 226.8 in. (138 in. Super Van). GVW: 5200 (E-100); 5850-6350 (E-150); 6750-7900 (E-250); 8750-11;000 (E-350). Tires: P205/75R x 15SL (E-100); P225/75R x 15SL (E-150); 8.00 x 16.5D (E-250); 9.50 x 16.5E (E-350).

POWERTRAIN OPTIONS: Engine: 5.0L cid V-8. 5.8L cid V-8. 6.9L Diesel V-8. 7.5L V-8 (E-350). Four-speed manual with overdrive. SelectShift automatic.

E-150 CLUB WAGON: The E-100 Club Wagon was dropped in 1983. The E-150 Club Wagon looked the same as last year's model, but that wasn't bad. Among the standard features were: Front bucket seats. A rear bench seat. Color-keyed patterned vinyl seat trim. Seat belts. Two-speed electric windshield wipers. Wiper-arm-mounted washer jets. 10 in. rearview mirror. Dome lights. Insulated floor mat with scuff plates. Three armrests. Dual horns. Flip-open windows in sliding door and opposite windows. Painted bumpers; 5 in. x 8 in. mirrors and hubcaps. Bright windshield molding. This was the last year for the E-100 Club Wagon series. It now came only with the 124 in. wheelbase. It was offered in five- and eight-passenger versions. The E-150 Super Wagon was dropped.

E-250 CLUB WAGON: This came in an eight-passenger version available with quad captain's chairs and a four-passenger bench seat.

E-250 SUPER WAGON: This was available in 11- and 12-passenger versions.

E-350 SUPER WAGON: The heavy-duty E-350 provided 20 in. more inside length than regular 138 in. wheelbase Club Wagons. Heavy-duty shocks were standard.

I.D. DATA: The VIN has 17 symbols. The first three indicate the manufacturer, make, and type of vehicle. The fourth symbol indicates the GVW range. The fifth, sixth and seventh symbols indicate the series and body style. The eighth symbol indicates the type of engine. The ninth symbol is a check digit. The 10th symbol (a letter) indicates model year. The 11th symbol indicates the assembly plant. The remaining symbols are the sequential production number starting with 100001 at each plant.

Model	Body Type	Price	Weight	Prod. Total
E-150 Supervan — 1/2-Ton — 124 in. w.b. — Six				
E-150	Club Wagon	9,122	3991	Note 1
E-250 Supervan — 3/4-Ton — 138 in. w.b. — Six				
E-250	Club Wagon	11,017	4911	Note 1
E-250	Super Wagon	11,439	4134	Note 1
E-350 Supervan — 1-Ton — 138 in. w.b. — Six				
E-350	Super Wagon	11,120	4912	Note 1

NOTE 1: Total 1983 Club Wagon model year production was 30,074.

ENGINE [Base Six]: Inline. OHV. Six-cylinder (heavy-duty). Bore & stroke: 4.0 x 3.98 in. Displacement: 300 cid (4.9 liter). Compression ratio: 8.9:1. Net horsepower: 115 at 3000 rpm. Taxable horsepower: 38.4. Net torque: 223 lbs.-ft. at 1600 rpm. Carburetor: One-barrel. (Note: Horsepower and torque may vary with specific model applications, as net horsepower ratings are relative to weight of vehicle.)

ENGINE [Base V-8; Mandatory in California]: V-block. OHV. Eight-cylinder. Bore & stroke: 4.0 in. x 3.0 in. Displacement: 302 cid (5.0 liter). Net horsepower: 130 at 3800 rpm. Taxable horsepower: 51.2. Net torque: 222 lbs.-ft. at 2000 rpm. Carburetor: Two-barrel. (Note: Horsepower and torque may vary with specific model applications, as net horsepower ratings are relative to weight of vehicle.)

ENGINE [Optional V-8; All]: V-block. OHV. Eight-cylinder. Bore & stroke: 4.0 in. x 3.5 in. Displacement: 351 cid (5.8 liter). Net horsepower: 156 at 4000 rpm. Taxable horsepower: 51.2. Net torque: 262 lbs.-ft. at 2200 rpm. Carburetor: Two-barrel. (Note: Horsepower and torque may vary with specific model applications, as net horsepower ratings are relative to weight of vehicle.)

CHASSIS: Wheelbase: 124 in. (E-100); 138 in. (E-150; E-250; E-350). Overall width: 79.7 in. Overall length: 186.8 in. (124 in. w.b.) 206.8 in. (138 in. w.b.) 226.8 in. (138 in. wheelbase Super Wagon). GVW: 6,000-9,400 lbs. Tires: P225/75R x 15SL; 8.75 x 16.5E.

POWERTRAIN OPTIONS: Engines: 5.0L V-8; 5.8L V-8; 6.9L Diesel V-8; 7.5L cid V-8. Transmissions: SelectShift automatic. Four-speed manual with overdrive.

CONVENIENCE OPTIONS: XL Package includes vinyl bucket seats; front compartment carpeting; color-keyed door trim panels; leather tone inserts on instrument panel; courtesy lights; interval wipers; bright grille; front and rear bumpers; and low-mount swingaway mirrors. Cloth-and-vinyl captain's chairs. Air-conditioning. High-capacity air-conditioner and auxiliary heater. Heavy-duty battery. Chrome rear step bumper. Chrome bumpers. Super engine cooling. Auxiliary fuel tank. Ammeter and oil pressure gauges. Privacy glass. Swing-out rear door and/or cargo door glass. Tinted glass. Handling package. Deluxe Insulation Package. Light and Convenience group. Bright low-mount swing-away mirrors. Bright swing-out recreation mirrors. Deluxe two-tone paint. Power door locks. Speed control. Tilt steering wheel. Heavy-duty front and rear springs. Trailer Towing Packages. Wheelcovers. AM/FM monaural radio. AM/FM stereo. AM/digital clock radio. AM/FM stereo with cassette player. Hinged side cargo door. Four-passenger rear bench seat. Snack-game table.

1983 Ford 1/2-Ton R-100 Ranger XLT Styleside Mini-Pickup (OCW)

RANGER PICKUP: The new Ranger was introduced in early 1982 as a 1983 model. It looked like a down-sized F-100. The grille featured a rectangular sections theme with the Ford script in an oval emblem in the left corner and a rectangular headlight on each end. This entire sectioned was framed in bright moldings. Rectangular parking lights were directly below the headlights. The rectangular side-marker lights were placed vertically on the front fenders. The Ranger nameplate was also on the front fenders. Taillights were of the wraparound variety. The double-walled box was 85 in. long and 54.3 in. wide (40.4 in. at the wheelhouses) and had a quick release tailgate. Standard features included: Halogen headlights. Four-speed manual transmission. Floor mat. Vinyl bench seat with folding backrest. Two outside rearview mirrors. Styled steel wheels.

I.D. DATA: The VIN has 17 symbols. The first three indicate the manufacturer, make, and type of vehicle. The fourth symbol indicates the GVW range. The fifth, sixth and seventh symbols indicate the series and body style. The eighth symbol indicates the type of engine. The ninth symbol is a check digit. The 10th symbol (a letter) indicates model year. The 11th symbol indicates the assembly plant. The remaining symbols are the sequential production number starting with 100001 at each plant.

Model	Body Type	Price	Weight	Prod. Total
Ranger — 1/2-Ton — 107.9 in. w.b. — Four				
R-10	Styleside	6289	2526	Note 1
Ranger — 1/2-Ton — 113.9 in. w.b. — Four				
R-10	Styleside	6446	—	Note 1

NOTE 1: Ranger model year production: [1982] 108,196; [1983] 143,100.

ENGINE [4x2]: Inline. Four-cylinder. OHV. OHC. Bore & stroke: 3.52 x 3.13 in. Displacement: 122 cid (2.0 liter). Compression ratio: 9.0:1. Net horsepower: 73 at 4000 rpm. Taxable horsepower: 19.8. Net torque: 107 lbs.-ft. at 2400 rpm. Carburetor: One-barrel.

ENGINE [4x4]: Inline. Four-cylinder. OHV. OHC. Bore & stroke: 3.78 in. x 3.13 in. Displacement: 140 cid (2.3 liter). Compression ratio: 9.0:1. Net horsepower: 79 at 4200 rpm. Taxable horsepower: 22.8. Net torque: 126 lbs.-ft. at 2200 rpm. Carburetor: One-barrel.

ENGINE [Optional]: Inline. Four-cylinder. OHV. OHC. Bore & stroke: 3.78 in. x 3.13 in. Displacement: 140 cid (2.3 liter). Compression ratio: 9.0:1. Net horsepower: 82 at 4200 rpm. Taxable horsepower: 22.8. Net torque: 126 lbs.-ft. at 2200 rpm. Carburetor: Two-barrel.

ENGINE [Diesel]: Inline. Four-cylinder. OHV. OHC. Bore & stroke: 3.5 in. x 3.5 in. Displacement: 135 cid (2.2 liter). Net horsepower: 59 at 4000 rpm. Taxable horsepower: 19.6. Net torque: 90 lbs.-ft. at 2500 rpm. Fuel-injection.

CHASSIS: Wheebase: 107.9 in.; 113.9 in. Overall length: 175.6 in. (107.9 in. wheelbase.); 187.6 in. (113.9 in. wheelbase). Overall width: 66.9 in. Overall height: 64 in. (67.1 in. 4x4). GVW: 3,740-4,220 lbs. Tires: P185/75R x 14.

POWERTRAIN OPTIONS: Engines: 2.3 liter Four. 2.3 liter two-barrel Four. 2.2 liter Diesel Four. Transmissions: Five-speed manual with overdrive. Automatic.

CONVENIENCE OPTIONS: Four-wheel drive. Twin-Traction Beam front axle. 2,700 lbs. rear axle. Power brakes. 2.3 liter Four. Two-speed part-time transfer case. Headliner. 4x4 tape stripe. AM/FM monaural radio. AM/FM stereo radio. AM/FM stereo radio with cassette tape player. Air-conditioning. Black rear step bumper. Convenience Group with dual electric horns (except with 2.2 liter diesel); interval windshield wipers; passenger's visor vanity mirror; driver's sun visor band; and cigarette lighter. Tinted glass all around. Light Group with ashtray light; cargo box light; glove box light; passenger door courtesy light switch; and headlights-on warning buzzer. Floor console (for bucket seats). Bright low-mount Western swing-away mirrors. Power steering. Power brakes. Tilt steering wheel. Sliding rear window. Eight cargo tie-down hooks. Pivoting vent windows. Fingertip speed control. Reclining bucket seats. Knitted vinyl contoured bench seat. Cloth and vinyl bench seat. Payload packages up to 1770 lbs. Heavy-duty air cleaner. Heavy-duty battery. Camper package. Extra-cooling. Auxiliary 13-gal. fuel tank. Gauge Package includes ammeter; oil pressure gauge; temperature gauge; and trip odometer. Engine block heater. Heavy-duty shocks. Tow hooks. Snow plow special package. Automatic locking hubs (4x4). Heavy-duty front suspension (4x4). Traction Lok rear axle. Limited-slip front axle (4x4). Handling Package includes heavy-duty front and rear shock absorbers and front and rear stabilizer bars (rear only with 4x4). Skid plates (4x4). California emissions system. High-altitude emissions system. Security Lock Group with glove box lock; locking gas cap; and; under-frame spare tire carrier lock. Exterior Protection Group with chrome front bumper with end caps; black front bumper guards; and black upper bodyside molding with dual red accent stripes. Chrome front bumper. Cast aluminum wheels. White sport wheels. Deluxe wheel trim. Cast aluminum spare wheel (4x4). XL Package with (in addition to or in place of standard features), bright rear window insert molding; deluxe wheel trim and chrome front bumper; wood-tone instrument cluster applique; color-keyed headliner; contoured knitted vinyl bench seat; color-keyed seat belts with tension eliminator; color-keyed steering wheel and floor mats; passenger door courtesy light switch; and aluminum scuff plates. XLS with (in addition to or in place of XL features), black-out trim components and special XLS tape stripe; bucket seats; color-keyed deluxe steering wheel; gauge package; brushed pewter-tone cluster applique on instrument panel; color-keyed cloth door trim with carpeted map pocket; and black scuff plates. XLT Package with (in addition to or in place of XLS features), chrome front bumper with black end caps; full-length lower bodyside molding; accent bodyside paint stripes; deluxe wheel trim and brushed aluminum tailgate applique; full cloth door trim with color- keyed molding and bright insert; carpeted lower portion and map pockets; cloth seat trim; carpeting; color-keyed deluxe steering wheel; and wood-tone cluster applique on instrument panel.

F-100 PICKUP: Styling was carried over from the previous year. As a means of saving horsepower and fuel, Ford light-duty trucks came with a viscous type fan clutch. It engaged the fan only as needed. The fan did not run constantly. Standard F-100 features included: Chrome front bumper. Light Argent silver grille with bright surround. Bright windshield molding. Argent silver hubcaps. Bright door-mounted mirrors. Rectangular halogen headlights. Wraparound taillights. Easily removable tailgate (Styleside). Rope tie holes in corner stake pockets (Styleside). AM radio. All-vinyl seat trim. Full-foam seat over springs. Folding seatback access to behind seat storage area. Pivoting vent windows. Glove box. Left-hand door courtesy light switch and dome lamp. Temperature gauge. Color-keyed windshield pillar, header and cowlside trim panels. Color-keyed door trim panels with foam-padded armrests. Coat hook. Floor insulation and carpet-texture rubber mat. Rearview mirror. Inside hood release. Black scuff plates. Black steering wheel. Power brakes. Three-speed manual transmission. Buyers could choose from 6.5 ft. Flareside and 6.75 ft. or 8 ft. Styleside boxes. F-series colors for 1983 included: Raven black; Candy-apple red; Dark red (metallic); Midnight blue (metallic); Bright blue; Dark teal (metallic); copper; Wimbledon white; Desert tan; Light charcoal (metallic); Light desert-tan; Dark charcoal (metallic); and walnut (metallic), plus Blue Glow and Light Teal Glow optional glamour colors. Tu-Tone treatments: (Regular) Accent color covered roof and upper back panel; dual color tape stripe divided colors; (Deluxe) Accent color on center bodyside area and tailgate; molding or tapes included as needed; (Combination) Regular and deluxe tu-tones combined; (Victoria) Accent color applied to hood, upper fender, around door window and lower bodyside; tape and moldings included as needed.

I.D. DATA: The VIN has 17 symbols. The first three indicate the manufacturer; make; and type of vehicle. The fourth symbol indicates the GVW range. The fifth, sixth and seventh symbols indicate the series and body style. The eighth symbol indicates the type of engine. The ninth symbol is a check digit. The 10th symbol (a letter) indicates model year. The 11th symbol indicates the assembly plant. The remaining symbols are the sequential production number starting with 100001 at each plant.

Model	Body Type	Price	Weight	Prod. Total
F-100 — 1/2-Ton — 117 in. w.b. — V-6				
F-10	Flareside 6.5 ft.	7068	3266	Note 1
F-10	Styleside 6.8 ft	6909	3240	Note 1
F-100 — 1/2-Ton — 133 in. w.b. — V-6				
F-10	Styleside 8 ft.	7063	3326	Note 1

NOTE 1: Model year production was: [F-100] 75,191.

ENGINE [Base V-6]: V-block. OHV. Six-cylinder. Bore & stroke: 3.81 x 3.38 in. Displacement: 232 cid (3.8 liter). Net horsepower: 109 at 3600 rpm. Net torque: 184 lbs.-ft. at 1600 rpm. Taxable horsepower: 34.83. Carburetor: Two-barrel.

ENGINE [Optional I-6]: Inline. OHV. Six-cylinder (heavy-duty). Bore & stroke: 4.0 x 3.98 in. Displacement: 300 cid (4.9 liter). Compression ratio: 8.9:1. Net horsepower: 115 at 3000 rpm. Taxable horsepower: 38.4. Net torque: 223 lbs.-ft. at 1600 rpm. Carburetor: One-barrel. (Note: Horsepower and torque may vary with specific model applications, as net horsepower ratings are relative to weight of vehicle.)

ENGINE [Optional V-8; Mandatory in California]: V-block. OHV. Eight-cylinder. Bore & stroke: 4.0 in. x 3.0 in. Displacement: 302 cid (5.0 liter). Net horsepower: 130 at 3800 rpm. Taxable horsepower: 51.2. Net torque: 222 lbs.-ft. at 2000 rpm. Carburetor: Two-barrel. (Note: Horsepower and torque may vary with specific model applications, as net horsepower ratings are relative to weight of vehicle.)

F-150 PICKUP: The heavy-duty 1/2-ton F-150 had most of the same standard features as the F-100. It was available with the 6.5 ft. Flareside and 6.75 ft. or 8 ft. Styleside boxes. Regular and Supercabs were offered (the later only with Styleside box).

I.D. DATA: The VIN has 17 symbols. The first three indicate the manufacturer; make; and type of vehicle. The fourth symbol indicates the GVW range. The fifth, sixth and seventh symbols indicate the series and body style. The eighth symbol indicates the type of engine. The ninth symbol is a check digit. The 10th symbol (a letter) indicates model year. The 11th symbol indicates the assembly plant. The remaining symbols are the sequential production number starting with 100001 at each plant.

Model	Body Type	Price	Weight	Prod. Total
F-150 — 1/2-Ton — 117 in. w.b. — Six				
F-15	Flareside 6.5 ft.	7327	3418	Note 1
F-15	Styleside 6.75 ft.	7169	3391	Note 1
F-150 — 1/2-Ton — 133 in. w.b. — Six				
F-15	Styleside	7322	3507	Note 1
F-150 Supercab- 1/2-Ton — 155 in. w.b. — Six				
X-15	Styleside	8232	3752	Note 1

NOTE 1: Model year production was: [F-150] 192,704.

ENGINE [Base Six]: Inline. OHV. Six-cylinder (heavy-duty). Bore & stroke: 4.0 x 3.98 in. Displacement: 300 cid (4.9 liter). Compression ratio: 8.9:1. Net horsepower: 115 at 3000 rpm. Taxable horsepower: 38.4. Net torque: 223 lbs.-ft. at 1600 rpm. Carburetor: One-barrel. (Note: Horsepower and torque may vary with specific model applications, as net horsepower ratings are relative to weight of vehicle.)

ENGINE [Optional V-8; Mandatory in California]: V-block. OHV. Eight-cylinder. Bore & stroke: 4.0 in. x 3.0 in. Displacement: 302 cid (5.0 liter). Net horsepower: 130 at 3800 rpm. Taxable horsepower: 51.2. Net torque: 222 lbs.-ft. at 2000 rpm. Carburetor: Two-barrel. (Note: Horsepower and torque may vary with specific model applications, as net horsepower ratings are relative to weight of vehicle.)

ENGINE [Optional V-8]: V-block. OHV. Eight-cylinder. Bore & stroke: 4.0 in. x 3.5 in. Displacement: 351 cid (5.8 liter). Net horsepower: 150 at 3200 rpm. Taxable horsepower: 51.2. Net torque: 280 lbs.-ft. at 1800 rpm. Carburetor: Two-barrel. (Note: Horsepower and torque may vary with specific model applications, as net horsepower ratings are relative to weight of vehicle.)

F-250 PICKUP: F-250 Pickups came with an 8 ft. Styleside box and either regular or Supercabs. They shared most of the same standard features as found on F-100s. However; the F-250 heavy-duty models had power steering; a four-speed manual transmission and an 11 in. clutch.

I.D. DATA: The VIN has 17 symbols. The first three indicate the manufacturer; make; and type of vehicle. The fourth symbol indicates the GVW range. The fifth, sixth and seventh symbols indicate the series and body style. The eighth symbol indicates the type of engine. The ninth symbol is a check digit. The 10th symbol (a letter) indicates model year. The 11th symbol indicates the assembly plant. The remaining symbols are the sequential production number starting with 100001 at each plant.

Model	Body Type	Price	Weight	Prod. Total
F-250 — 3/4-Ton — 133 in. w.b. — Six				
—	Chassis & Cab	7869	3472	Note 1
F-25	Styleside	7803	3695	Note 1
F-250 Supercab — 3/4-Ton — 161 in. w.b. — Six				
X-25	Styleside	9028	4127	Note 1

NOTE 1: Model year prooduction [F-250] 94,844.

ENGINE [Base Six]: Inline. OHV. Six-cylinder (heavy-duty). Bore & stroke: 4.0 x 3.98 in. Displacement: 300 cid (4.9 liter). Compression ratio: 8.9:1. Net horsepower: 115 at 3000 rpm. Taxable horsepower: 38.4. Net torque: 223 lbs.-ft. at 1600 rpm. Carburetor: One-barrel. (Note: Horsepower and torque may vary with specific model applications, as net horsepower ratings are relative to weight of vehicle.)

ENGINE [Optional V-8; Mandatory in California]: V-block. OHV. Eight-cylinder. Bore & stroke: 4.0 in. x 3.0 in. Displacement: 302 cid (5.0 liter). Net horsepower: 130 at 3800 rpm. Taxable horsepower: 51.2. Net torque: 222 lbs.-ft. at 2000 rpm. Carburetor: Two-barrel. (Note: Horsepower and torque may vary with specific model applications, as net horsepower ratings are relative to weight of vehicle.)

ENGINE [Optional V-8]: V-block. OHV. Eight-cylinder. Bore & stroke: 4.0 in. x 3.5 in. Displacement: 351 cid (5.8 liter). Net horsepower: 150 at 3200 rpm. Taxable horsepower: 51.2. Net torque: 280 lbs.-ft. at 1800 rpm. Carburetor: Two-barrel. (Note: Horsepower and torque may vary with specific model applications, as net horsepower ratings are relative to weight of vehicle.)

F-350 PICKUP: The husky F-350 was offered in regular and 6-pass. Crew cabs. All had the 8 ft. Styleside box. Standard features included most of those found on the F-100 plus power steering; an 11 in. clutch; and 4-speed manual transmission. A regular cab F-350 was available with dual rear wheels.

I.D. DATA: The VIN has 17 symbols. The first three indicate the manufacturer; make; and type of vehicle. The fourth symbol indicates the GVW range. The fifth, sixth and seventh symbols indicate the series and body style. The eighth symbol indicates the type of engine. The ninth symbol is a check digit. The 10th symbol (a letter) indicates model year. The 11th symbol indicates the assembly plant. The remaining symbols are the sequential production number starting with 100001 at each plant.

Model	Body Type	Price	Weight	Prod. Total
F-350 — 1-Ton — 133 in. w.b. — V-8				
F-37	Chassis & Cab	8953	3794	Note 1
F-35	Styleside	9212	4071	Note 1
F-350 Crew Cab — 1-Ton — 161 in. w.b. — V-8				
X-35	Styleside	10,131	4553	Note 1

NOTE 1: Model year production [F-350] 34,241.

ENGINE [Base Six]: Inline. OHV. Six-cylinder (heavy-duty). Bore & stroke: 4.0 x 3.98 in. Displacement: 300 cid (4.9 liter). Compression ratio: 8.9:1. Net horsepower: 115 at 3000 rpm. Taxable horsepower: 38.4. Net torque: 223 lbs.-ft. at 1600 rpm. Carburetor: One-barrel. (Note: Horsepower and torque may vary with specific model applications, as net horsepower ratings are relative to weight of vehicle.)

ENGINE [Optional V-8]: V-block. OHV. Eight-cylinder. Bore & stroke: 4.0 in. x 3.5 in. Displacement: 351 cid (5.8 liter). Net horsepower: 150 at 3200 rpm. Taxable horsepower: 51.2. Net torque: 280 lbs.-ft. at 1800 rpm. Carburetor: Two-barrel. (Note: Horsepower and torque may vary with specific model applications, as net horsepower ratings are relative to weight of vehicle.)

ENGINE [Optional Diesel V-8]: V-block. OHV. Eight-cylinder. Bore & stroke: 4.0 in. x 4.18 in. Displacement: 420 cid (7.5 liter). Net horsepower: 170 at 3000 rpm. Taxable horsepower: 51.2. Net torque: 315 lbs.-ft. at 1400 rpm. Fuel-injection. (Note: Horsepower and torque may vary with specific model applications, as net horsepower ratings are relative to weight of vehicle.)

CHASSIS: Wheebase: 116.8 in. (F-100/F-150); 133 in. (All Series); 138.8 in. (F-150/F-250 Supercabs); 155 in. (F-150/F-250/Supercab); 168.4 in. (F-350 Crew Cab). Overall length: 192.1 in. (F-100/F-150 Styleside); 189.3 in. (Flareside); 208.3 in. (Styleside); 214.1 in. (F-150 Supercab); 230.3 in. (F-150/F-250 Supercab); 237.6 in. (F-350 Crew Cab). GVW: 4,700 lbs. (F-100); 5,250-6,450 lbs, (F-150); 6,300-9,000 lbs. (F-250); 8,700-11;000 lbs. (F-350). Tires: P195/75R x 15SL (F-100); P215/75R x 15SL (F-150); LT215/85R x 16C (F-250); LT235/85R x 16E (F-350).

POWERTRAIN OPTIONS: Engines: 4.9 liter (300 cid) six (F-100); 5.0 liter (302 cid) V-8 (F-100/F-150/F-250); 5.8 liter (351 cid) V-8 (F-250/F-250 heavy-duty/ F-350); 7.5 liter V-8 (F-250 heavy-duty/F-350); 6.9 liter (420 cid) Diesel V-8 (F-250 heavy-duty/F-350). Transmissions: Four-speed manual (F-150/F-250); Four-speed manual with overdrive (F-100/F-150/F-250); SelectShift automatic; Automatic overdrive (F-100/F-150/F-250).

CONVENIENCE OPTIONS: Four-wheel drive. Chrome grille. Tri-colored tape stripe. Accent tape stripe (Styleside). Lower bodyside molding with black vinyl insert for single

rear wheel Stylesides with standard or XL trim. Wheel lip moldings. AM/FM monaural radio (single speaker); AM/FM stereo (speakers mounted in door panels). AM/FM stereo radio with cassette tape player. Air-conditioning. High-output heater. Cigarette lighter. Convenience Group with interval wipers; 12 in. day/night mirror; right-hand visor vanity mirror; molded bin on lower doors; headlights-on warning buzzer; and courtesy light switch on right-hand door with standard trim. Deluxe Insulation Package includes color-keyed headliner and moldings (door upper, B pillar, and rear window), plus aluminum door scuff plates with standard regular cab; also includes black fully insulated floor mat with standard trim and covered back panel. Electronic digital clock (includes date/time/elapsed time display with new stop watch feature). Fingertip speed control. Light Group with movable underhood work lights with 20 ft. retractable cord, plus lights in glove box, ashtray and under instrument panel; dual beam dome/map light; cargo box light; headlights-on warning buzzer; and courtesy light switch for right-hand door. Power door locks. Power steering. Power windows. Tinted sliding rear window. Tilt steering wheel. Tinted glass. Tool storage box located under the hood. In-box spare tire carrier side-mounted inside Styleside box. Center console (Supercab with captain's chairs). Electric remote-control swing-away mirrors. Bright lowmount swing-away Western mirrors. Bright swing-out recreational mirrors. Cloth and vinyl seat trim. Heavy-duty black vinyl or knitted vinyl seat trim. Folding rear bench seat in Supercab. Two center-facing jump seats that fold out of the way in Supercab. Auxiliary fuel tank (20-gal.). Outside of frame fuel tank for dual rear wheel Chassis & Cab model, in lieu of standard tank. Auxiliary transmission oil cooler. Handling Package includes front and rear stabilizer bars; heavy-duty front and rear shock absorbers; and heavy-duty front springs. Heavy-duty shock absorbers. Oil pressure and ammeter gauges. Engine oil cooler for 7.5 liter (460) V-8. Front and rear stabilizer bars. Engine block heater. Extra engine cooling package. Super engine cooling package. Trailer towing package. Camper package. Limited-slip axle. Traction-Lok rear axle. Heavy-duty air cleaner. Dual note horns. Five roof clearance lights. Exterior Protection Group with bright door edge guards; front bumper guards; and front bumper rub strip. Security Lock Group with locking gas cap; inside hood release; glove box lock; and spare tire lock (with under-frame and in-box carrier). Sports Instrumentation Package with tachometer; ammeter; oil pressure gauge; and trip odometer. Argent silver rear step bumper for Stylesides. Chrome step bumper for single rear wheel Stylesides. Chrome channel bumper for Flaresides. Chrome contour bumper for single rear wheel Stylesides. Cast aluminum wheels. White styled steel wheels. Sport wheelcovers. Deluxe Argent silver styled steel wheels. Deluxe wheelscovers. XL Package with (in addition to or in place of standard features) left-hand and right-hand courtesy light switches; day/night mirror; bright surround door trim panel moldings; color-keyed floor mat; woodtone applique on instrument panel; folding fully covered seatback; deluxe seat belts; clothand-vinyl seat trim; aluminum scuff plates; sun visors; headlining; moldings/trim panels above belt line; bright upper bodyside and tailgate moldings on single rear wheel Stylesides; plus bodyside surround tape strip and tailgate tape letters on Flareside and dual rear wheel Pickups; bright hubcaps (except on dual rear wheel models) and bright rear window molding. XLS Package with (in addition to or in place of items on the XL), color-keyed carpeting; brushed aluminum applique on instrument panel; brushed aluminum trim steering wheel; two-color XLS tape stripe; Argent silver styled steel wheels with black hubs; black front and rear bumpers; black-out treatment on grille and headlamp doors; black door handles; windshield molding; and low-mount Western swing-away mirrors. XLT Package with (in addition to or in place of items on the XL), door trim panel moldings with bright surround; wood-tone door panel appliques; wood-tone trimmed map box; color-keyed carpeting; deluxe steering wheel; moldings/trim panels above beltline (and below on Supercab); full-length lower bodyside molding (with protective black vinyl insert); and distinctive brushed aluminum tailgate applique.

HISTORICAL: In 1983, Ford regained its traditional first spot in sales back from Chevrolet. Total sales for the year were counted as 991,958 units, up from 791, 547 in 1982. Sales of 453,108 F-series Pickups gave that model the number one sales rank among all cars and trucks sold in the U.S. Ford's F-series models were simply America's most popular vehicle of any type.

1984 FORD

1984 Ford 1/2-Ton Bronco II Eddie Bauer Wagon 4x4 (JAG)

BRONCO II: This was the full-size Bronco's little 4x4 brother. It was meant to compete with Chevrolet's S-10 Blazer. Basic styling resembled that of the big Bronco, but there were some differences. Most noticeably, the Bronco II had a shorter grille with more vertical bars. The Ford emblem was placed in the lower left-hand area of the grille. The grille and headlights were framed by bright trim. Parking lights were beneath the headlights. Rectangular side-marker lights were placed vertically on the front fenders. A distinctive feature was the wraparound rear quarter windows. Among the standard features were: Twin-Traction Beam front axle. Power brakes and steering. Front and rear stabilizer bars. Four-speed manual transmission. Reclining front seats. Split fold-down rear bench seat. Halogen headlights. Dual outside fold-away rearview mirrors. Bright front and rear contour bumpers. Sport wheelcovers. Color-keyed carpeting. Full-length cloth headliner. Sun visors. Bronco II color choices for 1984 were: Raven black; Polar white; Light charcoal (metallic); Dark Canyon red; Light blue; Medium blue (metallic); Midnight blue (metallic); Medium desert tan; walnut (metallic); Light desert tan; Bright bittersweet; and Bright Copper Glow. Interior trim colors were: Dark blue; Canyon red; and tan.

1984 Ford 1/2-Ton Bronco II XLT Wagon 4x4 (RCA)

I.D. DATA: The VIN has 17 symbols. The first three indicate the manufacturer; make; and type of vehicle. The fourth symbol indicates the GVW range. The fifth; sixth and seventh symbols indicate the series and body style. The eighth symbol indicates the type of engine. The ninth symbol is a check digit. The 10th symbol (a letter) indicates model year. The 11th symbol indicates the assembly plant. The remaining symbols are the sequential production number starting with 100001 at each plant.

Model	Body Type	Price	Weight	Prod. Total
Bronco II 4x4 — 1/2-Ton — 94 in. w.b. — V-6				
U-14	Wagon	10,860	3237	Note 1
U-14	Eddie Bauer Wagon	13,053	3250	Note 1

NOTE 1: Model year production: [Bronco II] 144,100

1984 Ford 1/2-Ton Bronco II XLS Wagon 4x4 (RCA)

ENGINE [Bronco II]: 170 cid. V-6. Brake horsepower: 115 at 4600 rpm. Torque: 150 lbs.-ft. at 2600 rpm. Bore and stroke: 3.66 x 2.70 in. Compression ratio: 8.6:1. Carburetor: Twobarrel. [VIN Code S]

CHASSIS: Wheelbase: 94 in. Overall length: 158.4 in. Overall width: 68 in. Overall height: 68.2 in. Tires: P195/75R x 15 SL.

POWERTRAIN OPTIONS: Transmissions: Three-speed automatic or five-speed manual transmissions.

CONVENIENCE OPTIONS: Chrome grille. Tu-Tone paints. Sport tape stripe. Eddie Bauer Bronco II Package includes special Tu-Tone paint treatment; Eddie Bauer emblem; XLT level trim inside and out; cast aluminum wheels; all-terrain tires with raised white letters; ammeter; oil pressure and temperature gauges; trip odometer; dual captain's chairs; AM/FM stereo radio; tilt steering wheel; floor console; dual electric horns; interval windshield wipers; passenger visor vanity mirror; driver's sun visor band; ashtray and glove box lights; headlamps-on warning buzzer; and Eddie Bauer field bag and map holder. AM/FM monaural radio. AM/FM stereo. AM/FM stereo radio with cassette tape player. Dual or quad captain's chairs (including power lumbar support and zippered map pocket on seatback). Airconditioning. Tinted glass. Convenience Group includes interval windshield wipers; visor vanity mirror; cigarette lighter; dual electric horns; and driver's sun visor band. Light Group includes glove box; ashtray and cargo area light; passenger door and liftgate courtesy light switches; and headlights-on warning buzzer. Fingertip speed control. Tilt steering wheel. Rear window wiper/defroster. Flip-open liftgate window. Flip-up; open air roof. Flip-open removable quarter windows (gray tinted). Pivoting front vent windows. Privacy glass. Floor Console includes gauge package; trash bin; cassette tape tray; coin tray; two cup depressions; and electronic graphic warning display module. Overhead console includes digital clock and pivoting map light; bright; low-mount Western swing-away mirrors; and outside swing-away spare tire carrier. Roof rack. Rear seat delete. Carpet delete. Automatic locking hubs. Engine block heater. Super engine cooling. Heavy-duty maintenance-free battery. Heavy-duty air cleaner. Gauge Package includes ammeter; temperature and oil pressure gauges; plus resettable trip odometer. Heavy-duty shocks. Snow plow special package. Trailer towing package. Tow hooks. Limited-slip front axle. Traction-lok axle. California emissions system. High-altitude emissions system. Exterior Protection Group includes bright front and rear bumpers with black end caps; black front bumper guards; and black upper bodyside molding with two end accent strips. Transfer case skid plate. Front license plate bracket. Cast aluminum wheels. White sport styled steel wheels. Deluxe wheel trim (includes Argent silver styled steel wheel with bright trim ring; lug nuts; and black hub cover). XLT Package includes chrome grille; bodyside accent stripe; pivoting front vent windows; tinted glass; deluxe wheel trim; cloth and vinyl seat trim with full cloth door trim panels and a map pocket; carpet insert; bright headlights; color-keyed instrument panel; deluxe steering wheel; wood-tone applique on instrument cluster; color-keyed deluxe seat belts; courtesy light switches; liftgate-operated cargo area light; rear quarter trim panels (including integral padded armrests); speaker grilles; and storage compartments. XLS Package includes XLS tape striping in three colors on the lower bodysides; rocker panel molding spats; blacked-out grille surround; bumpers and bumper end caps; deluxe wheel trim; cloth door trim panels with carpet insert and map pocket; deluxe steering wheel; color-keyed instrument panel (with storage bin); and full instrumentation.

Standard Catalog of Light-Duty Trucks

1984 Ford 1/2-Ton Bronco II Standard Sports Utility Wagon 4x4 (RCA)

BRONCO: Styling of the 4x4 Bronco was carried over from the previous year. Standard features included: Bucket seats. Vinyl sun visors. Padded instrument panel. Armrests. Dome lamp. Windshield header and A pillar moldings. AM radio (could be deleted for credit). Flip/fold rear bench seat. Halogen headlights. Full instrumentation. Black front and rear bumpers. Bright hubcaps. Black scuff plate. Twin Traction Beam independent front suspension. Power brakes and steering. Four-speed transmission. Fold-down tailgate with power window.
I.D. DATA: The VIN has 17 symbols. The first three indicate the manufacturer; make; and type of vehicle. The fourth symbol indicates the GVW range. The fifth; sixth and seventh symbols indicate the series and body style. The eighth symbol indicates the type of engine. The ninth symbol is a check digit. The 10th symbol (a letter) indicates model year. The 11th symbol indicates the assembly plant. The remaining symbols are the sequential production number starting with 100001 at each plant.

Model	Body Type	Price	Weight	Prod. Total
Bronco 4x4 — 1/2-Ton — 104.7 in. w.b. — V-8				
U-150	Wagon	10,858	4079	47,423

ENGINE [Base Six]: Inline. OHV. Six-cylinder (heavy-duty). Bore & stroke: 4.0 x 3.98 in. Displacement: 300 cid (4.9 liter). Compression ratio: 8.9:1. Net horsepower: 115 at 3000 rpm. Taxable horsepower: 38.4. Net torque: 223 lbs.-ft. at 1600 rpm. Carburetor: One-barrel. (Note: Horsepower and torque may vary with specific model applications; as net horsepower ratings are relative to weight of vehicle.) [VIN Code Y]
ENGINE: [Optional V-8] V-block. OHV. Eight-cylinder. Bore & stroke: 4.0 in. x 3.0 in. Displacement: 302 cid (5.0 liter). Net horsepower: 130 at 3800 rpm. Taxable horsepower: 51.2. Net torque: 222 lbs.-ft. at 2000 rpm. Carburetor: Two-barrel. (Note: Horsepower and torque may vary with specific model applications; as net horsepower ratings are relative to weight of vehicle.) [VIN Code N]
ENGINE: [Optional V-8] V-block. OHV. Eight-cylinder. Bore & stroke: 4.0 in. x 3.5 in. Displacement: 351 cid (5.8 liter). Net horsepower: 150 at 3200 rpm. Taxable horsepower: 51.2. Net torque: 280 lbs.-ft. at 1800 rpm. Carburetor: Two-barrel. (Note: Horsepower and torque may vary with specific model applications; as net horsepower ratings are relative to weight of vehicle.) [VIN Code F]
CHASSIS: Wheebase: 104.7 in. Overall length: 177.6 in. Overall height: 73.2 in. Overall width: 77.2 in. Tires: P215/75R x 15 SL.
POWERTRAIN OPTIONS: Transmissions: SelectShift automatic. Four-speed transmission with overdrive. Engines: 302 cid V-8; 351 cid V-8; 351 cid HO V-8. Axles: Limited-slip front axle.

1984 Ford Bronco II (RCA)

CONVENIENCE OPTIONS: Chrome front or front and rear bumpers. Tri-color tape stripe. Accent tape stripe. Black GT bar. Chrome grille. Upper bodyside tape stripe. Lower bodyside molding. High-output heater. Center console. Electric rear window defroster. Electric remote control swing-away rearview mirrors. Convenience Group with intemittent wipers; map box in doors; headlamp-on warning buzzer; right-hand door courtesy light switch; 12 in. mirror; visor vanity mirror. Front bench seat. Power windows. Tinted glass all around. Privacy glass in quarter windows. Light Group with lights in glove box; ashtray and underhood; instrument panel courtesy lights; dome light with map light; right-hand door courtesy light; and headlamp-on warning buzzer (the underhood light had a 20 ft. cord). Handling Package includes front and rear stabilizer bars; quad heavy-duty front; and dual heavy-duty rear shocks. captains chairs. underhood tool box. Automatic locking hubs. Traction-Lok front and/or rear axle. Sports Instrumentation Group with tachometer and odometer. Recreational mirrors. Bright low-mount Western mirrors. Heavy-duty trailer towing package. 32-gal. fuel tank in lieu of standard (includes skid plate). Sliding rear quarter windows. Protection Group with bright door edge guards; front bumper guards; and front bumper rub strip. Security Group with locking gas cap; inside hood release lock; spare tire lock; and locking glove box. Super engine cooling package. Extra engine cooling package. Fog lamps. Exterior sound package. Cigarette lighter. Power door locks. XLT Package with bright front and rear bumpers; black grille; bright hubcaps; windshield; quarter window; lower bodyside protection molding with vinyl insert; brushed aluminum tailgate applique; dome lamp; left-hand and right-hand courtesy light switches; color-keyed carpeting; left-hand rear quarter trim panel cargo lamp; door trim panel with bright surround molding; wood-tone panel with full-length storage bins; color-keyed vinyl headliner; simulated wood-tone applique and bright moldings for instrument panel; bright scuff plates; deluxe seat belts; cloth and vinyl seat trim; soft-wrap steering wheel with wood-tone insert; molded rear quarter trim panels with armrests; speaker grilles; storage bin and light; spare tire cover; cigarette lighter; and added insulation. XLS Package includes has most of the features of the XLT, plus black gloss on front and rear bumpers; black gloss grille; Argent silver styled steel wheels with black hub; black gloss windshield molding; black gloss treatment on headlamp doors and around window; door handles; locks; mirrors and tailgate lock; XLS tape; door trim panel with bright surround; brushed aluminum applique; and steering wheel trim. Speed control. Swing away spare tire carrier. 40-channel CB. Front tow hooks. Cast aluminum wheels. Styled steel painted (white) wheels. Sport wheelcovers. Deluxe Argent silver styled steel wheels. AM/FM monaural radio. AM/FM stereo radio. AM/FM stereo radio with cassette or 8-track player. Snow plow packages. High-altitude emissions system. Heavy-duty auxiliary battery.
ECONOLINE E-150 CARGO VAN: The most noticeable styling change for 1984 was the Ford name, in script in an oval, on the center of the grille. Also, the bright outer trim that surrounded the grille was eliminated. Among the standard features were: Power brakes. Halogen headlights. AM radio. Bright hubcaps. Three-speed manual transmission. Econoline colors for 1984 were: Raven black; Polar white; Light charcoal (metallic); Dark Canyon red; Midnight Canyon red (metallic); Light blue; Midnight blue (metallic); Light desert tan; Medium desert tan; walnut (metallic); Medium copper (metallic); and Bright Copper Glow.
ECONOLINE E-150 SUPER CARGO VAN: This Van had the same features as the E-150 Cargo Van, plus a 20 in. extended rear overhang. This was especially useful for hauling longer loads.
ECONOLINE E-150 DISPLAY VAN: This Van had windows at the rear and on the right-hand side. It came with the same standard features as the Cargo Van.
ECONOLINE E-150 SUPER DISPLAY VAN: See E-150 Super Cargo Van.
ECONOLINE E-150 WINDOW VAN: This Window Van had glass all around. It shared standard features with the Cargo Van.
ECONOLINE E-150 SUPER WINDOW VAN: See E-150 Super Cargo Van.
I.D. DATA: The VIN has 17 symbols. The first three indicate the manufacturer; make; and type of vehicle. The fourth symbol indicates the GVW range. The fifth; sixth and seventh symbols indicate the series and body style. The eighth symbol indicates the type of engine. The ninth symbol is a check digit. The 10th symbol (a letter) indicates model year. The 11th symbol indicates the assembly plant. The remaining symbols are the sequential production number starting with 100001 at each plant.

Model	Body Type	Price	Weight	Prod. Total
E-150 Econoline Van — 1/2-Ton — 124 in. w.b. — Six				
E-150	Cargo Van	7759	3720	Note 1
E-150	Window Van	7946	3786	Note 1
E-150	Display Van	7880	3763	Note 1
E-150 Econoline SuperVan — 1/2-Ton — 138 in. w.b. — Six				
E-150	Super Cargo Van	8893	4039	Note 1
E-150	Super Window Van	9080	4105	Note 1
E-150	Super Display Van	9015	4082	Note 1

NOTE 1: Model year production: [All Econoline Vans] 171,952.
ENGINE [Base Six]: Inline. OHV. Six-cylinder (heavy-duty). Bore & stroke: 4.0 x 3.98 in. Displacement: 300 cid (4.9 liter). Compression ratio: 8.9:1. Net horsepower: 115 at 3000 rpm. Taxable horsepower: 38.4. Net torque: 223 lbs.-ft. at 1600 rpm. Carburetor: One-barrel. (Note: Horsepower and torque may vary with specific model applications; as net horsepower ratings are relative to weight of vehicle.) [VIN Code Y]
ENGINE: [Optional V-8] V-block. OHV. Eight-cylinder. Bore & stroke: 4.0 in. x 3.0 in. Displacement: 302 cid (5.0 liter). Net horsepower: 130 at 3800 rpm. Taxable horsepower: 51.2. Net torque: 222 lbs.-ft. at 2000 rpm. Carburetor: Two-barrel. (Note: Horsepower and torque may vary with specific model applications; as net horsepower ratings are relative to weight of vehicle.) [VIN Code F]
ENGINE: [Optional V-8] V-block. OHV. Eight-cylinder. Bore & stroke: 4.0 in. x 3.5 in. Displacement: 351 cid (5.8 liter). Net horsepower: 150 at 3200 rpm. Taxable horsepower: 51.2. Net torque: 280 lbs.-ft. at 1800 rpm. Carburetor: Two-barrel. (Note: Horsepower and torque may vary with specific model applications; as net horsepower ratings are relative to weight of vehicle.) [VIN Code G]
ECONOLINE E-250 CARGO VAN: The new E-250 had a higher GVW rating and more heavy-duty front and rear axles than the E-150. It also came with eight-hole wheels. Standard features were the same as those on the E-100, except the three-speed transmission was not available in California.
ECONOLINE E-250 SUPER CARGO VAN: See E-150 Cargo Van.
ECONOLINE E-250 DISPLAY VAN: This vehicle shared styling and features with the E-100, but had greater load capacity.
ECONOLINE E-250 SUPER DISPLAY VAN: See E-150 Super Cargo Van.
ECONOLINE E-250 WINDOW VAN: This vehicle shared styling and features with the E-100 Window Van, but had greater load capacity.
ECONOLINE E-250 SUPER WINDOW VAN: See E-150 Super Cargo Van.
ECONOLINE E-250 CUTAWAY VAN: This van with Camper Special Packages was designed to readily accommodate custom motor homes.
ECONOLINE E-250 PARCEL DELIVERY: The E-250 Parcel Delivery van was 149.9 in. long and 74.3 in. high in its cargo area. The rear door opening was 84.7 in. wide.
I.D. DATA: The VIN has 17 symbols. The first three indicate the manufacturer; make; and type of vehicle. The fourth symbol indicates the GVW range. The fifth; sixth and seventh symbols indicate the series and body style. The eighth symbol indicates the type of engine. The ninth symbol is a check digit. The 10th symbol (a letter) indicates model year. The 11th symbol indicates the assembly plant. The remaining symbols are the sequential production number starting with 100001 at each plant.

Model	Body Type	Price	Weight	Prod. Total
E-250 Econoline Van — 3/4-Ton — 138 in. w.b. — Six				
E-240	Cargo Van	8815	4146	Note 1
E-250	Window Van	9002	4212	Note 1
E-260	Display Van	8937	4189	Note 1
E-250 Econoline SuperVan — 3/4-Ton — 138 in. w.b. — Six				
S-240	Super Cargo Van	9493	4474	Note 1
S-250	Super Window Van	9680	4540	Note 1
S-260	Super Display Van	9615	4517	Note 1

NOTE 1: Model year production: [All Econoline Vans] 171,952.
ENGINE [Base Six]: Inline. OHV. Six-cylinder (heavy-duty). Bore & stroke: 4.0 x 3.98 in. Displacement: 300 cid (4.9 liter). Compression ratio: 8.9:1. Net horsepower: 115 at 3000 rpm. Taxable horsepower: 38.4. Net torque: 223 lbs.-ft. at 1600 rpm. Carburetor: One-barrel. (Note: Horsepower and torque may vary with specific model applications; as net horsepower ratings are relative to weight of vehicle.) [VIN Code Y]

ENGINE: [Optional V-8] V-block. OHV. Eight-cylinder. Bore & stroke: 4.0 in. x 3.0 in. Displacement: 302 cid (5.0 liter). Net horsepower: 130 at 3800 rpm. Taxable horsepower: 51.2. Net torque: 222 lbs.-ft. at 2000 rpm. Carburetor: Two-barrel. (Note: Horsepower and torque may vary with specific model applications; as net horsepower ratings are relative to weight of vehicle.) [VIN Code F]

ENGINE: [Optional V-8] V-block. OHV. Eight-cylinder. Bore & stroke: 4.0 in. x 3.5 in. Displacement: 351 cid (5.8 liter). Net horsepower: 150 at 3200 rpm. Taxable horsepower: 51.2. Net torque: 280 lbs.-ft. at 1800 rpm. Carburetor: Two-barrel. (Note: Horsepower and torque may vary with specific model applications; as net horsepower ratings are relative to weight of vehicle.) [VIN Code G]

ENGINE: [Optional V-8] V-block. OHV. Eight-cylinder. Bore & stroke: 4.0 in. x 3.5 in. Displacement: 351 cid (5.8 liter). Net horsepower: 210 at 4000 rpm. Taxable horsepower: 51.2. Net torque: 305 lbs.-ft. at 2800 rpm. Carburetor: Four-barrel. (Note: Horsepower and torque may vary with specific model applications; as net horsepower ratings are relative to weight of vehicle.) [VIN Code H]

ENGINE: [Optional V-8] V-block. OHV. Eight-cylinder. Diesel. Bore & stroke: 4.0 in. x 4.18 in. Displacement: 420 cid (6.9 liter). Net horsepower: 170 at 3300 rpm. Taxable horsepower: 51.2. Net torque: 315 lbs.-ft. at 1400 rpm. Fuel-injected. (Note: Horsepower and torque may vary with specific model applications; as net horsepower ratings are relative to weight of vehicle.) [VIN Code 1]

ENGINE: [Optional V-8] V-block. OHV. Eight-cylinder. Bore & stroke: 4.36 in. x 3.85 in. Displacement: 460 cid (7.5 liter). Net horsepower: 214 at 3600 rpm. Taxable horsepower: 52.5. Net torque: 362 lbs.-ft. at 1800 rpm. Carburetor: Four-barrel. (Note: Horsepower and torque may vary with specific model applications; as net horsepower ratings are relative to weight of vehicle.) [VIN Code L]

ECONOLINE E-350 CARGO VAN: This was the top-of-the-line Econoline Van. It had heavy-duty front and rear shocks and a greater load capacity than the other series. Standard features were the same as the E-100.

ECONOLINE E-350 SUPER CARGO VAN: See E-150 Super Cargo Van.

ECONOLINE E-350 DISPLAY VAN: See E-250 Display Van.

ECONOLINE E-350 SUPER DISPLAY VAN: See E-150 Super Cargo Van.

ECONOLINE E-350 WINDOW VAN: See E-250 Window Van.

ECONOLINE E-350 SUPER WINDOW VAN: See E-150 Super Cargo Van.

ECONOLINE E-350 CUTAWAY VAN: See E-250 Cutaway Van.

ECONOLINE E-350 PARCEL DELIVERY: See E-250 Parcel Delivery.

I.D. DATA: The VIN has 17 symbols. The first three indicate the manufacturer; make; and type of vehicle. The fourth symbol indicates the GVW range. The fifth; sixth and seventh symbols indicate the series and body style. The eighth symbol indicates the type of engine. The ninth symbol is a check digit. The 10th symbol (a letter) indicates model year. The 11th symbol indicates the assembly plant. The remaining symbols are the sequential production number starting with 100001 at each plant.

Model	Body Type	Price	Weight	Prod. Total
E-350 Econoline SuperVan — 1-Ton — 138 in. w.b. — Six				
E-340	Cargo Van	9043	4442	Note 1
E-350	Window Van	9231	4508	Note 1
E-360	Display Van	9165	4485	Note 1
E-350 Econoline SuperVan — 1-Ton — 138 in. w.b. — Six				
S-340	Super Cargo Van	10,511	4613	Note 1
S-350	Super Window Van	10,699	4679	Note 1
S-360	Super Display Van	10,633	4656	Note 1
E-350 Econoline Stretch Van — 1-Ton — 176 in. w.b. — Six				
E-37B	Cutaway	—	3992	Note 1
E-380	Parcel Delivery	—	5395	Note 1

NOTE 1: Model year production: [All Econoline Vans] 171,952.

ENGINE [Base Six]: Inline. OHV. Six-cylinder (heavy-duty). Bore & stroke: 4.0 x 3.98 in. Displacement: 300 cid (4.9 liter). Compression ratio: 8.9:1. Net horsepower: 115 at 3000 rpm. Taxable horsepower: 38.4. Net torque: 223 lbs.-ft. at 1600 rpm. Carburetor: One-barrel. (Note: Horsepower and torque may vary with specific model applications; as net horsepower ratings are relative to weight of vehicle.) [VIN Code Y]

ENGINE: [Optional V-8] V-block. OHV. Eight-cylinder. Bore & stroke: 4.0 in. x 3.5 in. Displacement: 351 cid (5.8 liter). Net horsepower: 210 at 4000 rpm. Taxable horsepower: 51.2. Net torque: 305 lbs.-ft. at 2800 rpm. Carburetor: Four-barrel. (Note: Horsepower and torque may vary with specific model applications; as net horsepower ratings are relative to weight of vehicle.) [VIN Code G]

ENGINE: [Optional V-8] V-block. OHV. Eight-cylinder. Diesel. Bore & stroke: 4.0 in. x 4.18 in. Displacement: 420 cid (6.9 liter). Net horsepower: 170 at 3300 rpm. Taxable horsepower: 51.2. Net torque: 315 lbs.-ft. at 1400 rpm. Fuel-injected. (Note: Horsepower and torque may vary with specific model applications; as net horsepower ratings are relative to weight of vehicle.) [VIN Code 1]

ENGINE: [Optional V-8] V-block. OHV. Eight-cylinder. Bore & stroke: 4.36 in. x 3.85 in. Displacement: 460 cid (7.5 liter). Net horsepower: 214 at 3600 rpm. Taxable horsepower: 52.5. Net torque: 362 lbs.-ft. at 1800 rpm. Carburetor: Four-barrel. (Note: Horsepower and torque may vary with specific model applications; as net horsepower ratings are relative to weight of vehicle.) [VIN Code L]

CHASSIS: Wheelbase: 124 in. (E-150); 138 in. (E-250/E-350); 176 in. (E-350). Overall length: 186.8 in. (124 in. wheelbase); 206.8 in. (138 in. wheelbase); 226.8 in. (138 in. wheelbase SuperVan). GVW: 5,250-6,350 lbs. (E-150); 6,800-7,900 lbs. (E-250); 8,750-11,000 lbs. (E-350). Tires: P225/75R x 15 SL (E-150); 8.00 x 16.5D (E-250); 9.50 x 16.5E (E-350).

POWERTRAIN OPTIONS: Engines: 5.0L V-8. 5.8L V-8. 6.5L Diesel V-8; 7.5L V-8. Transmissions: Four-speed transmission with overdrive. SelectShift automatic.

CONVENIENCE OPTIONS: XL Package includes vinyl bucket seats; front compartment carpeting; color-keyed door trim panels; leather tone inserts on instrument panel; courtesy lights; interval wipers; bright grille; front and rear bumpers; and low-mount swing-away mirrors. Cloth and vinyl captain's chairs. Air-conditioning. High-capacity air-conditioner and auxiliary heater. Heavy-duty battery. Chrome rear step bumper. Chrome bumpers. Super engine cooling. Auxiliary fuel tank. Ammeter and oil pressure gauges. Privacy glass. Swing-out rear door and/or cargo door glass. Tinted glass. Handling package. Deluxe insulation package. Light and Convenience group. Bright low-mount swing-away mirrors. Bright swing-out recreation mirrors. Deluxe two-tone paint. Power door locks. Speed control. Tilt steering wheel. Heavy-duty front and rear springs. Trailer Towing Packages. Wheelcovers. Radios: AM/FM monaural radio. AM/FM stereo radio. AM/digital clock radio; AM/FM stereo radio with cassette player. Hinged side cargo door.

1984 Ford Club Wagon Chateau Passenger Van (JAG)

E-150 CLUB WAGON: Like the Econoline, the 1984 Club Wagon received a minor facelift. Standard features included: Four-speed transmission with overdrive. 18-gal. fuel tank. Argent silver bumpers, grille and mirrors. Color-keyed vinyl seat trim. Power steering and brakes. Halogen headlights. AM radio. Sliding side doors with swing-out windows. Full-length floor mat. Bright hubcaps. Hardboard headliner (front only). Padded sun visors. Color-keyed instrument panel. Club Wagon colors for 1984 were: Raven black; Polar white; Light charcoal (metallic); Dark Canyon red; Midnight Canyon red (metallic); Light blue; Midnight blue (metallic); Light desert tan; Medium desert tan; walnut (metallic); Medium copper (metallic); and Bright Copper Glow.

E-250 CLUB WAGON: The E-250 had most of the same standard features as the E-150, with a few exceptions. They included the SelectShift automatic transmission, a 22.1-gal. fuel tank and a heavier-duty battery.

E-250 CLUB WAGON: This was basically the same as the 138 in. wheelbase E-250, but it had a 20 in. extended rear overhang.

E-350 SUPER WAGON: This heavy-duty wagon provided 20 in. more inside space than regular 138 in. wheelbase Club Wagons. It could hold up to 15 passengers with optional seating packages.

I.D. DATA: The VIN has 17 symbols. The first three indicate the manufacturer; make; and type of vehicle. The fourth symbol indicates the GVW range. The fifth; sixth and seventh symbols indicate the series and body style. The eighth symbol indicates the type of engine. The ninth symbol is a check digit. The 10th symbol (a letter) indicates model year. The 11th symbol indicates the assembly plant. The remaining symbols are the sequential production number starting with 100001 at each plant.

Model	Body Type	Price	Weight	Prod. Total
E-150 Club Wagon — 1/2-Ton — 124 in. w.b. — Six				
E-150	Club Wagon	9527	3947	Note 1
E-250 Club Wagon — 3/4-Ton — 138 in. w.b. — Six				
E-250	Club Wagon	11,388	4873	Note 1
E-250	Super Wagon	11,825	4852	Note 1
E-350 Club Wagon — 1-Ton — 138 in. w.b. — Six				
E-350	Super Wagon	11,498	4923	Note 1

NOTE 1: Model year production: [All Club Wagons] 30,903.

ENGINE [Base Six; All]: Inline. OHV. Six-cylinder (heavy-duty). Bore & stroke: 4.0 x 3.98 in. Displacement: 300 cid (4.9 liter). Compression ratio: 8.9:1. Net horsepower: 115 at 3000 rpm. Taxable horsepower: 38.4. Net torque: 223 lbs.-ft. at 1600 rpm. Carburetor: One-barrel. (Note: Horsepower and torque may vary with specific model applications; as net horsepower ratings are relative to weight of vehicle.) [VIN Code Y]

ENGINE: [Optional V-8; E-150/E-250] V-block. OHV. Eight-cylinder. Bore & stroke: 4.0 in. x 3.0 in. Displacement: 302 cid (5.0 liter). Net horsepower: 130 at 3800 rpm. Taxable horsepower: 51.2. Net torque: 222 lbs.-ft. at 2000 rpm. Carburetor: Two-barrel. (Note: Horsepower and torque may vary with specific model applications; as net horsepower ratings are relative to weight of vehicle.) [VIN Code F]

ENGINE: [Optional V-8; E-150/E-250] V-block. OHV. Eight-cylinder. Bore & stroke: 4.0 in. x 3.5 in. Displacement: 351 cid (5.8 liter). Net horsepower: 150 at 3200 rpm. Taxable horsepower: 51.2. Net torque: 280 lbs.-ft. at 1800 rpm. Carburetor: Two-barrel. (Note: Horsepower and torque may vary with specific model applications; as net horsepower ratings are relative to weight of vehicle.) [VIN Code G]

ENGINE: [Optional V-8; E-250/E-350] V-block. OHV. Eight-cylinder. Bore & stroke: 4.0 in. x 3.5 in. Displacement: 351 cid (5.8 liter). Net horsepower: 210 at 4000 rpm. Taxable horsepower: 51.2. Net torque: 305 lbs.-ft. at 2800 rpm. Carburetor: Four-barrel. (Note: Horsepower and torque may vary with specific model applications; as net horsepower ratings are relative to weight of vehicle.) [VIN Code H]

ENGINE: [Optional V-8; E-250/E-350] V-block. OHV. Eight-cylinder. Diesel. Bore & stroke: 4.0 in. x 4.18 in. Displacement: 420 cid (6.9 liter). Net horsepower: 170 at 3300 rpm. Taxable horsepower: 51.2. Net torque: 315 lbs.-ft. at 1400 rpm. Fuel-injected. (Note: Horsepower and torque may vary with specific model applications; as net horsepower ratings are relative to weight of vehicle.) [VIN Code 1]

ENGINE: [Optional V-8; E-250/E-350] V-block. OHV. Eight-cylinder. Bore & stroke: 4.36 in. x 3.85 in. Displacement: 460 cid (7.5 liter). Net horsepower: 214 at 3600 rpm. Taxable horsepower: 52.5. Net torque: 362 lbs.-ft. at 1800 rpm. Carburetor: Four-barrel. (Note: Horsepower and torque may vary with specific model applications; as net horsepower ratings are relative to weight of vehicle.) [VIN Code L]

CHASSIS: Wheelbase: 124 in. (E-150); 138 in. (E-250/E-350); 176 in. (E-350). Overall length: 186.8 in. (124 in. wheelbase); 206.8 in. (138 in. wheelbase); 226.8 in. (138 in. wheelbase SuperVan). GVW: 5,250-6,350 lbs. (E-150); 6,800-7,900 lbs. (E-250); 8,750-11,000 lbs. (E-350). Tires: P225/75R x 15 SL (E-150); 8.00 x 16.5D (E-250); 9.50 x 16.5E (E-350).

POWERTRAIN OPTIONS: Engines: 5.0L V-8. 5.8L V-8. 6.5L Diesel V-8; 7.5L V-8. Transmissions: Four-speed transmission with overdrive. SelectShift automatic.

CONVENIENCE OPTIONS: Most of the same items and packaes that were offered on the Econoline plus: 4-, 7-, 8-, 11- and 12-passenger seating packages. Club Wagon XL includes bright bumpers; taillight bezels; low-mount Western swing-away mirrors; color-keyed front; side and rear door trim panels with leather-tone inserts; color-keyed carpeting front to rear; door trim panels map pockets; full-length white hardboard headliner with insulation; instrument panel appliques and vinyl steering wheel pad with look of leather. Club Wagon XLT includes chrome grille; bright window moldings; lower bodyside moldings and lower bodyside accent paint in addition to Club Wagon XL features; front bucket seats upholstered in color-keyed cloth and vinyl (premium vinyl available at no extra cost); headliner was color-keyed vinyl (full-length in long wheelbase model and Super Wagon); color-

keyed sun visors (long wheelbase models); and spare tire cover with storage pocket; right-hand visor vanity mirror; stepwell pads for the front and sliding side doors; courtesy light switch on every door; and three-way switch for the rear dome lamp. Available on all Club Wagons was a three-passenger rear seat that could convert into a bed.

1984 Ford 1/2-Ton Ranger Long Box Mini-Pickup (JAG)

RANGER PICKUP: Ranger styling was unchanged for 1984. Like full-size Ford Pickups it had double-wall construction in hood, roof, doors, pickup box sides and tailgate. The box was all-welded with integral floor skid strips; stake pockets; and rope tie holds. The Ranger had Twin-I-Beam independent front suspension with lubed-for-life ball joints. There was 39.2 in. of headroom and 42.4 in. of legroom. Among standard features were: Black front bumper. Dual mirrors. Chrome grille and windshield moldings. Argent silver styled steel wheels with black hub covers. Tethered gas cap. Vinyl bench seat with folding covered seatback. Instrument panel storage bin and glove box. Inside hood release. Day/night rearview mirror. AM radio. Courtesy light switch for driver's door. Dome lamp. Black floor mat. Ranger interior colors for 1984 were: Dark blue; Canyon red; and tan. Exterior colors were: Raven black; Polar white; Light charcoal (metallic); Dark Canyon red; Light blue; Medium blue (metallic); Midnight blue (metallic); Medium desert tan; walnut (metallic); Light desert tan; Bright bittersweet; and Bright Copper Glow (optional). Tu-Tones included: (Regular) With accent color applied to lower bodyside and tailgate, plus two-color tape stripe; (Deluxe) Accent color was applied to mid-bodyside and tailgate, plus upper and lower two-color tape stripes; (Special) With accent color applied to mid-bodyside, inside of pickup box, rear of roof, B-pillar, back of cab and tailgate, plus upper and lower two-color tape strips. Notes: Regular and Deluxe tu-tones were not available on Ranger XLS models. When Special tu-toning was ordered on Ranger XLS models, the lower two-color tape stripe and rocker panel paint was replaced by XLS tape stripes

RANGER S PICKUP: This was a no-frills version of the base Ranger Pickup with fewer standard features.

1984 Ford 1/2-Ton Ranger XLT Mini-Pickup 4x4 (RCA)

I.D. DATA: The VIN has 17 symbols. The first three indicate the manufacturer; make; and type of vehicle. The fourth symbol indicates the GVW range. The fifth; sixth and seventh symbols indicate the series and body style. The eighth symbol indicates the type of engine. The ninth symbol is a check digit. The 10th symbol (a letter) indicates model year. The 11th symbol indicates the assembly plant. The remaining symbols are the sequential production number starting with 100001 at each plant.

Model	Body Type	Price	Weight	Prod. Total
Ranger — 1/2-Ton — 107.9 in. w.b. — Four				
R-10	Styleside	6462	2544	Note 1
R-10	Styleside	5993	—	Note 1
Ranger — 1/2-Ton — 113.9 in. w.b. — Four				
R-10	Styleside	6620	2576	Note 1
R-10	Styleside	6146	—	Note 1

NOTE 1: Model year production: [All Ranger] 277,188.
ENGINE [Base Four]: Inline. Four-cylinder. OHV. OHC. Bore & stroke: 3.52 x 3.13. Displacement: 120 cid (2.0 liter). Compression ratio: 9.0:1. Brake horsepower: 74 at 4300 rpm. Taxable horsepower: 15.87. Torque: 105 lbs.-ft. at 3500 rpm. Carburetor: One-barrel. [VIN Code C]
ENGINE [Optional Big Four]: Inline. Four-cylinder. OHV. OHC. Bore & stroke: 3.78 x 3.13. Displacement: 140 cid (2.3 liter). Compression ratio: 9.0:1. Brake horsepower: 90 at 400 rpm. Taxable horsepower: 22.8. Torque: 130 lbs.-ft. at 1800 rpm. Carburetor: One-barrel. [VIN Code B]
ENGINE [Optional V-6]: V-block. Six-cylinder. OHV. Bore & stroke: 3.66 x 2.70. Displacement: 170 cid (2.8 liter). Compression ratio: 8.7:1. Brake horsepower: 115 at 4600 rpm. Taxable horsepower: 64.8. Torque: 150 lbs.-ft. at 2600 rpm. Carburetor: Two-barrel. [VIN Code S]
ENGINE [Optional]: Inline. Four-cylinder. Diesel. OHV. OHC. Bore & stroke: 3.5 x 3.5. Displacement: 135 cid (2.2 liter). Compression ratio: 22.0:1. Brake horsepower: 59 at 4000 rpm. Taxable horsepower: 19.6. Torque: 90 lbs.-ft. at 2500 rpm. Injected. [VIN Code P]
CHASSIS: Wheelbase: 107.9 in; 113.9 in. Overall length: 175.6 in. (107.9 in. w.b.); 187.6 in. (113.9 in. w.b.). Overall width: 66.9 in. Overall height: 64 in. (67.1 in. 4x4). GVW: 3780-4500 lbs. Tires: P185/75R x 14.
POWERTRAIN OPTIONS: Engines: 2.3 liter Four. 2.2 liter Diesel Four. 2.8 liter V-6. (2.3 liter I-4 standard on 4x4s and 4x2s in California). Transmissions: Five-speed manual with overdrive. Automatic.

1984 Ford Bronco XLT Ranger (RCA)

CONVENIENCE OPTIONS: Four-wheel drive includes Twin-Traction Beam front axle; 2,700 lbs. rear axle; power brakes; 2.3 liter four; and two-speed part-time transfer case. Headliner. Tri-color sport tape stripe. 4x4 tape stripe. AM/FM monaural radio. AM/FM stereo radio. AM/FM stereo radio with cassette tape player. Air-conditioning. Black rear step bumper. Convenience Group with dual electric horns (except with 2.2 liter diesel); interval windshield wipers; passenger visor vanity mirror; driver's sun visor band; and cigarette lighter. Tinted glass all around. Light Group with ashtray; cargo box; glove box lights; passenger door courtesy light switch; and headlights-on warning buzzer. Floor console (for bucket seats). Overhead console (including pivoting map light and electronic digital clock). Bright low-mount Western swing-away mirrors. Power steering. Power brakes. Tilt steering wheel. Sliding rear window. Eight cargo tie-down hooks. Pivoting vent windows. Fingertip speed control. Reclining bucket seats. Knitted vinyl contoured bench seat. Cloth-and-vinyl bench seat. Cloth contoured bench seat. Cloth contoured bench seat. Payload packages up to 1,770 lbs. Heavy-duty air cleaner. Heavy-duty battery. Camper package. Super engine cooling. Auxiliary 13-gal. fuel tank. Gauge Package includes ammeter; oil pressure gauge; temperature gauge; and trip odometer. Engine block heater. Heavy-duty shocks. Tow hooks. Snow plow special package. Automatic locking hubs (4x4). Heavy-duty front suspension (4x4). Traction-Lok rear axle. Limited-slip front axle (4x4). Handling Package includes heavy-duty front and rear shock absorbers and front and rear stabilizer bars (rear only with 4x4). Skid plates (4x4). California emissions system. High-altitude emissions system. Security Lock Group with glove box lock; locking gas cap; and under frame spare tire carrier lock. Exterior Protection Group includes chrome front bumper with end caps; black front bumper guards; and black upper bodyside molding with dual red accent stripes. Chrome front bumper. Cast aluminum wheels. White sport wheels. Deluxe wheel trim. Cast aluminum spare wheel (4x4). XL includes (in addition to or in place of standard features) bright wheel lip moldings; bright rear window insert molding; deluxe wheel trim and chrome front bumper; wood-tone instrument cluster applique; color-keyed cloth headliner; contoured knitted vinyl bench seat; color-keyed seat belts with tension eliminator; color-keyed steering wheel and floor mats; passenger door courtesy light switch; and aluminum scuff plates. XLS Package includes (in addition to or in place of XL features) black-out trim components and special XLS three-color tape stripe; reclining cloth and vinyl bucket seats; color-keyed deluxe steering wheel; gauge package; brushed pewter-tone cluster applique on instrument panel; color-keyed cloth door trim with carpeted map pocket; black scuff plates. XLT Package includes (in addition to or in place of XLS features) chrome front bumper with black end caps; full-length black lower bodyside molding with bright accent; dual accent bodyside paint stripes; deluxe wheel trim and brushed aluminum tailgate applique; full cloth door trim with color-keyed molding and bright insert, carpeted lower portion and map pockets; cloth seat trim; full color-keyed carpeting; color-keyed deluxe steering wheel; and wood-tone cluster applique on instrument panel.

1984 Ford 1/2-Ton F-150 XLT Styleside Pickup 4x4 (JAG)

F-150 PICKUP: The F-150 was now Ford's base light-duty truck. Styling was carried over from last year. Among standard features were: Chrome front bumper. Light Argent silver grille with bright surround. New bright hubcaps. Bright door-mounted mirrors. Rectangular halogen headlights. All-vinyl seat trim. AM radio. Pivoting vent windows. Glove box. Temperature gauge. Color-keyed windshield pillar, header and cowl-side trim panels. New textured steel roof. Cloth headliner with Supercab. Color-keyed door trim panels with foam-padded armrests. Floor insulation and carpet-texture rubber mat. Day/night rearview mirror. Inside hood release. Key-in-ignition warning buzzer. Parking brake engaged warning light. Coat hook. Left-hand courtesy light. Argent silver instrument panel applique (wood-tone with diesel). Folding seatback. Black steering wheel. Three speed manual transmission. The F-150 was available with 6.5 ft. Flareside and 6.75 ft. and 8 ft. Styleside boxes. In addition to the regular cab, Styleside boxes could also be had with the Supercab. Interior colors for 1984 were: Charcoal; Dark blue; Canyon red; and tan. Exterior colors were: Raven black; Polar white; Light charcoal (metallic); Bright Canyon red; Light blue; Medium blue (metallic); Midnight blue (metallic); Medium desert tan; walnut (metallic); Light desert tan; Medium copper (metallic); and Bright Copper Glow (optional). Tu-tones were: (Regular) Accent color covers the roof and upper back panel; (Deluxe) Accent color on center body-

side area and tailgate, plus moldings or tapes included as needed; (Combination) Regular and deluxe tu-tones combined; and (Victoria) Accent color applied to hood; upper fender; around door window; and the lower bodyside; tape and moldings included as needed.

1984 Ford 1/2-Ton F-150 XLT Styleside Pickup 4x4 (RCA)

I.D. DATA: The VIN has 17 symbols. The first three indicate the manufacturer; make; and type of vehicle. The fourth symbol indicates the GVW range. The fifth; sixth and seventh symbols indicate the series and body style. The eighth symbol indicates the type of engine. The ninth symbol is a check digit. The 10th symbol (a letter) indicates model year. The 11th symbol indicates the assembly plant. The remaining symbols are the sequential production number starting with 100001 at each plant.

Model	Body Type	Price	Weight	Prod. Total
F-150 — 1/2-Ton — 116.8 in. w.b. — Six				
F-15	Flareside 6.5 ft.	7381	3400	Note 1
F-15	Styleside 6.75 ft.	7219	3390	Note 1
F-15	Styleside 8 ft.	7376	3501	Note 1
F-150 Supercab — 1/2-Ton — 116.8 in. w.b. — Six				
X-15	Styleside 6.75 ft.	8690	3765	Note 1
X-15	Styleside 8 ft.	8847	3871	Note 1

NOTE 1: Model year production: [F-150] 350,501.

ENGINE [Base Six]: Inline. OHV. Six-cylinder (heavy-duty). Bore & stroke: 4.0 x 3.98 in. Displacement: 300 cid (4.9 liter). Compression ratio: 8.9:1. Net horsepower: 115 at 3000 rpm. Taxable horsepower: 38.4. Net torque: 223 lbs.-ft. at 1600 rpm. Carburetor: One-barrel. (Note: Horsepower and torque may vary with specific model applications; as net horsepower ratings are relative to weight of vehicle.) [VIN Code Y]

ENGINE [Optional V-8]: V-block. OHV. Eight-cylinder. Bore & stroke: 4.0 in. x 3.0 in. Displacement: 302 cid (5.0 liter). Net horsepower: 130 at 3800 rpm. Taxable horsepower: 51.2. Net torque: 222 lbs.-ft. at 2000 rpm. Carburetor: Two-barrel. (Note: Horsepower and torque may vary with specific model applications; as net horsepower ratings are relative to weight of vehicle.) [VIN Code F]

1984 Ford 1/2-Ton F-150 XLT Styleside Pickup 4x4 (JAG)

ENGINE [Optional V-8]: V-block. OHV. Eight-cylinder. Bore & stroke: 4.0 in. x 3.5 in. Displacement: 351 cid (5.8 liter). Net horsepower: 150 at 3200 rpm. Taxable horsepower: 51.2. Net torque: 280 lbs.-ft. at 1800 rpm. Carburetor: Two-barrel. (Note: Horsepower and torque may vary with specific model applications; as net horsepower ratings are relative to weight of vehicle.) [VIN Code G]

1984 Ford 1/2-Ton F-150 XLT Styleside Pickup 4x4 (JAG)

F-250 PICKUP: The F-250 was only available with the 8 ft. Styleside box. However, it could be had in regular or F-250 Heavy-duty Supercab versions. The Supercab models had room behind the front seat for an optional rear seat which could fold down flat. Two center facing jump seats were standard. They too could fold out of the way to make room for cargo. Most standard F-250 features were the same as those offered on the on the F-150, plus a four-speed manual transmission and, on F-250 Heavy-Duties, an 11 in. clutch.

I.D. DATA: The VIN has 17 symbols. The first three indicate the manufacturer; make; and type of vehicle. The fourth symbol indicates the GVW range. The fifth; sixth and seventh symbols indicate the series and body style. The eighth symbol indicates the type of engine. The ninth symbol is a check digit. The 10th symbol (a letter) indicates model year. The 11th symbol indicates the assembly plant. The remaining symbols are the sequential production number starting with 100001 at each plant.

Model	Body Type	Price	Weight	Prod. Total
F-250 — 3/4-Ton — 133 in. w.b. — Six				
—	Chassis & Cab	8314	3426	Note 1
F-25	Styleside	8146	3666	Note 1
F-250 Supercab — 3/4-Ton — 155 in. w.b. — Six				
X-25	Supercab Pickup	9826	4279	Note 1

NOTE 1: Model year production: [F-250] 138,198.

ENGINE [Base Six; F-250]: Inline. OHV. Six-cylinder (heavy-duty). Bore & stroke: 4.0 x 3.98 in. Displacement: 300 cid (4.9 liter). Compression ratio: 8.9:1. Net horsepower: 115 at 3000 rpm. Taxable horsepower: 38.4. Net torque: 223 lbs.-ft. at 1600 rpm. Carburetor: One-barrel. (Note: Horsepower and torque may vary with specific model applications; as net horsepower ratings are relative to weight of vehicle.) [VIN Code Y]

ENGINE [Optional V-8; F-250]: V-block. OHV. Eight-cylinder. Bore & stroke: 4.0 in. x 3.0 in. Displacement: 302 cid (5.0 liter). Net horsepower: 130 at 3800 rpm. Taxable horsepower: 51.2. Net torque: 222 lbs.-ft. at 2000 rpm. Carburetor: Two-barrel. (Note: Horsepower and torque may vary with specific model applications; as net horsepower ratings are relative to weight of vehicle.) [VIN Code F]

ENGINE [Optional V-8; F-250]: V-block. OHV. Eight-cylinder. Bore & stroke: 4.0 in. x 3.5 in. Displacement: 351 cid (5.8 liter). Net horsepower: 150 at 3200 rpm. Taxable horsepower: 51.2. Net torque: 280 lbs.-ft. at 1800 rpm. Carburetor: Two-barrel. (Note: Horsepower and torque may vary with specific model applications; as net horsepower ratings are relative to weight of vehicle.) [VIN Code G]

ENGINE [Optional V-8; F-250 Heavy-duty]: V-block. OHV. Eight-cylinder. Bore & stroke: 4.0 in. x 3.5 in. Displacement: 351 cid (5.8 liter). Net horsepower: 210 at 4000 rpm. Taxable horsepower: 51.2. Net torque: 305 lbs.-ft. at 2800 rpm. Carburetor: Four-barrel. (Note: Horsepower and torque may vary with specific model applications; as net horsepower ratings are relative to weight of vehicle.) [VIN Code H]

ENGINE [Optional V-8; F-250 Heavy-duty]: V-block. OHV. Eight-cylinder. Diesel. Bore & stroke: 4.0 in. x 4.18 in. Displacement: 420 cid (6.9 liter). Net horsepower: 170 at 3300 rpm. Taxable horsepower: 51.2. Net torque: 315 lbs.-ft. at 1400 rpm. Fuel-injected. (Note: Horsepower and torque may vary with specific model applications; as net horsepower ratings are relative to weight of vehicle.) [VIN Code 1]

ENGINE [Optional V-8; F-250 Heavy-duty]: V-block. OHV. Eight-cylinder. Bore & stroke: 4.36 in. x 3.85 in. Displacement: 460 cid (7.5 liter). Net horsepower: 214 at 3600 rpm. Taxable horsepower: 52.5. Net torque: 362 lbs.-ft. at 1800 rpm. Carburetor: Four-barrel. (Note: Horsepower and torque may vary with specific model applications; as net horsepower ratings are relative to weight of vehicle.) [VIN Code L]

F-350 PICKUP: The F-350 was offered in regular and six-passenger Crew Cabs. Both had 8 ft. Styleside boxes. It had most of the same standard features as the F-150, plus power steering.

I.D. DATA: The VIN has 17 symbols. The first three indicate the manufacturer; make; and type of vehicle. The fourth symbol indicates the GVW range. The fifth; sixth and seventh symbols indicate the series and body style. The eighth symbol indicates the type of engine. The ninth symbol is a check digit. The 10th symbol (a letter) indicates model year. The 11th symbol indicates the assembly plant. The remaining symbols are the sequential production number starting with 100001 at each plant.

Model	Body Type	Price	Weight	Prod. Total
F-350 — 1-Ton — 133 in. w.b. — V-8				
F-37	Chassis and Cab	9403	3927	Note 1
F-35	Styleside	9666	4030	Note 1
F-350 Crew Cabs — 1-Ton — 168.4 in. w.b. — V-8				
W-35	Crew Cab Pickup	10,547	4948	Note 1

NOTE 1: Model year production: [F-350] 40,187.

ENGINE [Base V-8; F-350]: V-block. OHV. Eight-cylinder. Bore & stroke: 4.0 in. x 3.5 in. Displacement: 351 cid (5.8 liter). Net horsepower: 150 at 3200 rpm. Taxable horsepower: 51.2. Net torque: 280 lbs.-ft. at 1800 rpm. Carburetor: Two-barrel. (Note: Horsepower and torque may vary with specific model applications; as net horsepower ratings are relative to weight of vehicle.) [VIN Code G]

ENGINE [Optional V-8; F-350]: V-block. OHV. Eight-cylinder. Bore & stroke: 4.0 in. x 3.5 in. Displacement: 351 cid (5.8 liter). Net horsepower: 210 at 4000 rpm. Taxable horsepower: 51.2. Net torque: 305 lbs.-ft. at 2800 rpm. Carburetor: Four-barrel. (Note: Horsepower and torque may vary with specific model applications; as net horsepower ratings are relative to weight of vehicle.) [VIN Code H]

ENGINE [Optional V-8; F-350]: V-block. OHV. Eight-cylinder. Diesel. Bore & stroke: 4.0 in. x 4.18 in. Displacement: 420 cid (6.9 liter). Net horsepower: 170 at 3300 rpm. Taxable horsepower: 51.2. Net torque: 315 lbs.-ft. at 1400 rpm. Fuel-injected. (Note: Horsepower and torque may vary with specific model applications; as net horsepower ratings are relative to weight of vehicle.) [VIN Code 1]

ENGINE [Optional V-8; F-350]: V-block. OHV. Eight-cylinder. Bore & stroke: 4.36 in. x 3.85 in. Displacement: 460 cid (7.5 liter). Net horsepower: 214 at 3600 rpm. Taxable horsepower: 52.5. Net torque: 362 lbs.-ft. at 1800 rpm. Carburetor: Four-barrel. (Note: Horsepower and torque may vary with specific model applications; as net horsepower ratings are relative to weight of vehicle.) [VIN Code L]

CHASSIS: Wheelbase: 116.8 in. (F-150); 133 in. (Styleside); 138.8 in. (F-150 Supercab); 155 in. (F-150/F-250 Heavy-duty Supercab); 168.4 in. (F-350 Crew Cab). Overall length: 189.3 in. (Flareside); 192.1 in. (F-150 Styleside); 208.3 in. (Styleside); 214.1 in. (F-150 Supercab); 230.3 in. (F-150/F-250 Supercab); 243.6 in. (F-350 Crew Cab). GVW: 5,250-6,450 lbs. (F-150); 6,300-9,000 lbs. (F-250); 8,700-11,000 lbs. (F-350). Tires: P195/75R x 15SL (F-150); LT215/85R x 16C (F-250); LT235/85R x 16E (F-250 Heavy-duty/F-350); LT215/85R x 16D (F-350 dual rear wheels/regular cab).

POWERTRAIN OPTIONS: Engines: 5.0L V-8 (F-150/F-250); 5.8L V-8; 5.8L HO V-8 (F-150/F-250); 7.5L V-8 (F-250 Heavy-duty/F-350); 6.9L Diesel V-8 (F-250 Heavy-duty/F-350). Transmissions: Four-speed manual (F-150/F-250). Four-speed manual with overdrive (F-150/F-250). Automatic overdrive (F-150/F-250); SelectShift automatic.

CONVENIENCE OPTIONS: Four-wheel drive includes power brakes; manual locking free running hubs; power steering; two-speed transfer case; and four-speed manual transmission. Automatic locking hubs (4x4). Chrome grille. Accent tape stripe (Styleside). Lower bodyside molding with black vinyl insert (Styleside). Bright wheel lip moldings (Style). AM/FM monaural radio (single speaker). AM/FM stereo (speakers mounted in door panels). AM/FM stereo radio with cassette tape player. Radio credit option (deleted standard AM radio for credit). Air-conditioning. High-output heater (Standard with Crew Cab). Convenience Group with interval wipers; 12 in. day/night mirror; right-hand visor vanity mirror; molded bin on lower doors; headlights-on warning buzzer; and courtesy light switch on right-hand door. Deluxe Insulation Package includes color-keyed cloth headliner; floor mats with full insulation (carpet on Crew Cab); back panel cover; and moldings for headliner, B pillar, and back panel, plus aluminum door scuff plates. Electronic Digital Clock. Fingertip speed control (with resume feature). Light Group with movable underhood worklight with 20 ft. retractable cord, plus lights in glove box and under instrument panel, dual beam dome/map light, cargo box light, headlights-on warning buzzer and ashtray light and courtesy light switch on right-hand door. Power door locks/windows (not available with Crew Cab). Power steering (4x2). Tinted sliding rear window. Tilt steering wheel. Tinted glass. Tool storage box (located under the hood). Spare tire carrier side-mounted inside box (Styleside). Center console (Supercab with captain's chairs). Bright low-mount swing-away Western mirrors. Bright swing-out recreation mirrors. Reclining captain's chairs in Supercab. Folding forward-facing rear seat in Supercab. Cloth-and-vinyl seat trim. Heavy-duty charcoal vinyl or knitted vinyl seat trim. Special cloth and vinyl seat trim for XLT. Auxiliary fuel tank. Auxiliary transmission oil cooler. Handling Package includes front and rear stabilizer bars; heavy-duty front and rear shocks (quad front on F-150 regular cab 4x4); and heavy-duty front springs. Heavy-duty shocks. Heavy-Duty front suspension package includes (on 133 in. wheelbase 4x4) heavy-duty 3,800 lbs. rated front axle and springs; 3.54 axle ratio; and heavy-duty front and rear shock absorbers. (A version of this package was also offered for F-250 and F-350 4x4s.) Oil pressure and ammeter gauges. Front and rear stabilizer bars. Engine block heater. Extra engine cooling package. Super engine cooling package. Trailer towing package. Camper package. Heavy-duty air cleaner. Dual electric horns. Five roof clearance lights. Exterior Protection Group with front bumper guards and front bumper rub strip. Security Lock Group with locking gas cap; inside hood release; glove box lock; and spare tire lock. Sports Instrumentation with tachometer; ammeter; oil pressure gauge; and trip odometer. Skid plates (4x4s) include transfer and fuel tank protective plates. Argent silver step rear bumper (Styleside). Chrome step rear bumper (Styleside). Chrome channel rear bumper (Flareside). Chrome contour rear bumper (Styleside). Deluxe wheelcovers (not available with 4x4s or dual rear wheels). White styled steel wheels (F-150). Sport wheelcovers (F-150). Cast aluminum wheels (F-150). XL Package includes (in addition to or in place of items on standard model) bright wheel lip moldings and new two-color dual bodyside accent side paint stripes on single rear wheel Stylesides; or bodyside surround tape stripe and tailgate tape letters on Flareside and dual rear wheel trucks; bright insert on rear window weatherstrip; cigarette lighter; left-hand and right-hand courtesy light switches; 12 in. day/night mirror; bright-surround door trim panel moldings; color-keyed floor mat; wood-tone applique instrument panel; folding fully-covered seatbacks (with fixed trim and folding rear type in Crew Cabs); deluxe seat belts; cloth-and-vinyl seat trim; aluminum scuff plates; cloth headlining; and moldings and trim panels above beltline. XLT Package with (in addition to or in place of items on the XL), door trim panel moldings with bright surround; wood-tone door panel appliques; wood-tone trimmed map box; color-keyed carpeting; deluxe steering wheel; moldings/trim panels above beltline (and below on Supercab); full-length lower bodyside molding (with protective black vinyl insert); and distinctive brushed aluminum tailgate applique.

HISTORICAL: Model year production of light-duty trucks by line was: [Ranger] 227,188; [Bronco II] 144,100; [F-150] 350,501; [F-250] 138,198; [F-350] 40,187; [Bronco] 47,423; [Econoline] 171,952; [Club Wagon] 30,903; [Grand Total] 1,150,452. Model year sales, according to type, were: [Light Conventional] 535,043; [Ranger] 215,430; [Econoline] 173,630; [Bronco II] 98,462; [Bronco] 46,444; [Club Wagon] 32,056; [Medium- and Heavy-duty] 49,409; [Grant total] 1,150,474. Ford continued to reign as America's largest truck retailer and delivered 1,166,715 trucks of all types for the calendar year. This equated to an 18 percent sales increase. Total production of 1,170,000 trucks was the highest since 1978. December 1984 brought the start up of Aerostar Minivan production at a Ford plant in St. Louis, Mo. Edson P. Williams was Vice-President and General Manager of Ford Truck Operations. J.E. Englehart was Chief Engineer for Light Trucks.

1985 FORD

1985 Ford 1/2-Ton Bronco II XLT Sports Utility Wagon 4x4 (JAG)

BRONCO II: Styling on the compact 4x4 Bronco II was carried over from last year. Standard features included: Tinted glass. Full instrumentation. Transfer case skid plate. Power brakes and steering. Front and rear stabilizer bars. Five-speed transmission. Reclining front seats. Split fold down rear bench seat. Halogen headlights. Dual outside foldaway rearview mirrors. Bright front and rear contour bumpers. Sport wheelcovers. Color-keyed carpeting. Full-length cloth headliner. Sun visors.

I.D. DATA: The VIN has 17 symbols. The first three indicate the manufacturer; make; and type of vehicle. The fourth symbol indicates the GVW range. The fifth; sixth and seventh symbols indicate the series and body style. The eighth symbol indicates the type of engine. The ninth symbol is a check digit. The 10th symbol (a letter) indicates model year. The 11th symbol indicates the assembly plant. The remaining symbols are the sequential production number starting with 100001 at each plant.

Model	Body Type	Price	Weight	Prod. Total
Bronco II — 1/2-Ton — 94 in. w.b. — Four				
U-14	Wagon	11,507	3239	Note 1
U-14	Eddie Bauer Wagon	13,770	3250	Note 1

NOTE 1: Model year production: [Bronco II] 98,243.

ENGINE [Bronco II]: 170 cid. V-6. Brake horsepower: 115 at 4600 rpm. Torque: 150 lbs.-ft. at 2600 rpm. Bore and stroke: 3.66 x 2.70 in. Compression ratio: 8.6:1. Carburetor: Two-barrel. [VIN Code S]

ENGINE [Bronco II Diesel]: 135 cid. Four. Brake horsepower: 59 at 4000 rpm. Torque: 90 lbs.-ft. at 2500 rpm. Bore and stroke: 3.5 x 3.5 in. Compression ratio: 22.0:1. Injected. [VIN Code P]

CHASSIS FEATURES: Wheelbase: 94 in. Overall length: 158.4 in. Overall width: 68 in. Overall height: 68.2 in. Tires: P195/75R x 15SL.

POWERTRAIN OPTIONS: Engine: 2.2 liter diesel. Transmissions: Three-speed automatic. Automatic transmission with overdrive.

1985 Ford 1/2-Ton Bronco II XLT Sports Utility Wagon 4x4 (JAG)

CONVENIENCE OPTIONS: Chrome grille. Tu-Tone paints. Sport tape stripe. Eddie Bauer Bronco II with special Tu-Tone paint treatment; Eddie Bauer emblem; XLT-level trim inside and out; cast aluminum wheels; all-terrain tires with raised white letters; ammeter; oil pressure and temperature gauges; trip odometer; dual captain's chairs; AM/FM stereo radio; tilt steering wheel; floor console; dual electric horns; interval windshield wipers; passenger visor vanity mirror; dark tinted privacy glass; driver's sun visor band; ashtray and glove box lights; headlamps-on warning buzzer; Eddie Bauer field bag; and map folder. AM/FM monaural radio. AM/FM stereo. AM/FM stereo radio with cassette tape player. Dual or quad captain's chairs (include power lumbar support and zippered map pocket on seatback). Air-conditioning. Tinted glass. Convenience Group with internval windshield wipers; visor vanity mirror; cigarette lighter; dual electric horns; and driver's sun visor band. Light Group with glove box, ashtray and cargo area lights; passenger door and liftgate courtesy light switches; and headlights-on warning buzzer. Fingertip speed control. Tilt steering wheel. Rear window wiper/defroster. Flip-open liftgate window. Flip-up open-air roof. Flip-open removable quarter windows (gray-tinted). Pivoting front vent windows. Privacy glass. Floor

Console Package includes gauge package; trash bin; cassette tape tray; coin tray; two cup depressions; and electronic graphic warning display module. Overhead Console including digital clock and pivoting map light. Bright low-mount Western swing-away mirrors. Outside swing-away spare tire carrier. Roof rack. Rear seat delete. Carpet delete. Automatic locking hubs. Engine block heater. Super engine cooling. Heavy-duty maintenance-free battery. Heavy-duty air cleaner. Electronically-tuned stereo and cassette player. Premium sound system. Odometer. Heavy-duty shocks. Snow plow special package. Trailer towing package. Tow hooks. Limited-slip front axle. Traction-lok axle. California emissions system. High-altitude emissions system. Exterior Protection Group with bright front and rear bumpers with black end caps; black front bumper guards; and black upper bodyside molding with two red accent stripes. Transfer case skid plate. Front license plate bracket. Cast aluminum wheels. White sport styled steel wheels. Deluxe wheel trim (includes Argent silver styled steel wheel with bright trim ring, lug nuts and black hub cover). XLT Package includes chrome grille; bodyside accent stripe; pivoting front vent windows; tinted glass; deluxe wheel trim; cloth-and-vinyl seat trim with full cloth door trim panels and map pocket; carpet insert; bright headlights; color-keyed instrument panel; deluxe steering wheel; woodtone applique on instrument cluster; color-keyed deluxe seat belts; courtesy light switches; liftgate- operated cargo area light; rear quarter trim panels including integral padded armrests; speaker grilles; and storage compartments. XLS Package includes XLS tape striping in three colors on the lower bodysides; rocker panel molding spats; blacked-out grille surround, bumpers and bumper end caps; deluxe wheel trim; cloth door trim panels with carpet insert and map pocket; sport steering wheel; color-keyed instrument panel (with storage bin); and full instrumentation.

1985 Ford Sport Bronco (RCA)

BRONCO: Outside of some new options, the four-wheel drive Bronco was unchanged for 1985. Standard features included: Four-speed transmission. Intermittent wipers. Vinyl front bucket seats. Flip/fold rear bench seat. Power steering and brakes. Power tailgate window. AM radio. Twin-Traction Beam independent front suspension. Manual locking front hubs. Heavy-duty front shock absorbers. Padded instrument panel. Seat belts cigar lighter. Front and rear floor mats. scuff plates. Dual low-mount mirrors. Day/night rearview mirror.

I.D. DATA: The VIN has 17 symbols. The first three indicate the manufacturer; make; and type of vehicle. The fourth symbol indicates the GVW range. The fifth; sixth and seventh symbols indicate the series and body style. The eighth symbol indicates the type of engine. The ninth symbol is a check digit. The 10th symbol (a letter) indicates model year. The 11th symbol indicates the assembly plant. The remaining symbols are the sequential production number starting with 100001 at each plant.

Model	Body Type	Price	Weight	Prod. Total
Bronco — 1/2-Ton — 104.7 in. w.b. — V-8				
U-150	Wagon	11,993	4373	52,316

ENGINE [Base Six]: Inline. OHV. Six-cylinder (heavy-duty). Bore & stroke: 4.0 x 3.98 in. Displacement: 300 cid (4.9 liter). Compression ratio: 8.9:1. Net horsepower: 115 at 3000 rpm. Taxable horsepower: 38.4. Net torque: 223 lbs.-ft. at 1600 rpm. Carburetor: One-barrel. (Note: Horsepower and torque may vary with specific model applications; as net horsepower ratings are relative to weight of vehicle.) [VIN Code Y]

ENGINE [Optional V-8]: V-block. OHV. Eight-cylinder. Bore & stroke: 4.0 in. x 3.0 in. Displacement: 302 cid (5.0 liter). Net horsepower: 130 at 3800 rpm. Taxable horsepower: 51.2. Net torque: 222 lbs.-ft. at 2000 rpm. Carburetor: Two-barrel. (Note: Horsepower and torque may vary with specific model applications; as net horsepower ratings are relative to weight of vehicle.) [VIN Code N]

ENGINE [Optional H.O. V-8]: V-block. OHV. Eight-cylinder. Bore & stroke: 4.0 in. x 3.5 in. Displacement: 351 cid (5.8 liter). Net horsepower: 210 at 4000 rpm. Taxable horsepower: 51.2. Net torque: 305 lbs.-ft. at 2800 rpm. Carburetor: Four-barrel. (Note: Horsepower and torque may vary with specific model applications; as net horsepower ratings are relative to weight of vehicle.) [VIN Code H]

1985 Ford Special Eddie Bauer Bronco II

CHASSIS FEATURES: Wheelbase: 104.7 in. Overall length: 177.6 in. Overall height: 72.9 in. Overall width: 77.2 in. Tires P215/75R x 15SL.

POWERTRAIN OPTIONS: Transmissions: Three-speed automatic; Four-speed automatic with overdrive transmission. Engines: 302 cid V-8; 351 cid V-8; 351 cid HO V-8. Transmissions: Four-speed manual with overdrive. Axle: Limited-slip front axle.

CONVENIENCE OPTIONS: White styled steel wheels. Deluxe Argent silver styled steel wheels. Cloth-and-vinyl bucket and/or bench seats. High-output heater. Center console. Electric rear window defroster. Front bench seat. Rear bench seat delete. Power windows. Tinted glass all around. Privacy glass in quarter windows. Light Group with lights in glove box; ashtray and underhood: instrument panel courtesy lights; dome light with map light; right-hand door courtesy light; headlamp-on warning buzzer (the underhood light had a 20 ft. cord). Power door locks. Captain's chair. Underhood tool box. Automatic locking hubs. Traction-Lok front and/or rear axle. Sports Instrumentation with tachometer and odometer. Recreational mirrors. Trailer Towing Package includes 7-wire trailer wiring harness; 71-amp. hr. battery; super engine cooling; auxiliary transmission oil cooler; heavy-duty flasher; and handling package (automatic transmission required). Security Group with locking gas cap; inside hood release lock; spare tire lock; and locking glove box. Super engine cooling package. Extra engine cooling package. Fog lamps. Exterior sound package. Cigarette lighter. Power door locks. XLT Package includes cloth-and-vinyl bucket seats; tachometer and trip odometer; sun visors; color-keyed carpeting; color-keyed vinyl front headliner; courtesy lights; visor vanity mirror; soft-wrapped steering wheel; bodyside protection molding with vinyl insert; dome light; rear door panel armrests; and storage bin. Eddie Bauer Package includes air-conditioning; cruise control; tilt steering wheel; fuel-injected V-8; captain's chairs; full carpeting; light group; AM/FM radio; center console; privacy glass; heavy-duty battery; and special exterior trim. Cruise control. Deluxe two-tone paint. Victoria paint treatment. Heavy-duty rear shocks. Skid plate. Cast aluminum sheets. AM/FM stereo. AM/FM stereo radio with cassette player. Snow plow package. California emissions system.

ECONOLINE E-150 CARGO VAN: Exterior styling was left untouched for 1985. Power steering was now standard on E-150 Econolines. Among the other standard features were: Power brakes. Halogen headlights. AM radio. Bright hubcaps. Three-speed manual transmission.

ECONOLINE E-150 SUPER CARGO VAN: This van had the same features as the E-150 Cargo Van plus a 20 in. extended rear overhang. This was especially useful for hauling longer loads.

ECONOLINE E-150 DISPLAY VAN: This van had windows at the rear and on the right-hand bodyside. It came with the same standard features as the Cargo Van.

ECONOLINE E-150 WINDOW VAN: The Window Van had glass all around. It shared standard features with the Cargo Van.

ECONOLINE E-150 SUPER WINDOW VAN: See E-150 Super Cargo Van.

I.D. DATA: The VIN has 17 symbols. The first three indicate the manufacturer; make; and type of vehicle. The fourth symbol indicates the GVW range. The fifth; sixth and seventh symbols indicate the series and body style. The eighth symbol indicates the type of engine. The ninth symbol is a check digit. The 10th symbol (a letter) indicates model year. The 11th symbol indicates the assembly plant. The remaining symbols are the sequential production number starting with 100001 at each plant.

Model	Body Type	Price	Weight	Prod. Total
E-150 Econoline Van — 1/2-Ton — 128 in. w.b. — Six				
E-150	Cargo Van	8561	3755	Note 1
E-150	Window Van	8755	3807	Note 1
E-150	Display Van	8688	3786	Note 1
E-150 Econoline SuperVan — 1/2-Ton — 138 in. w.b. — Six				
E-150	Super Cargo Van	9688	4154	Note 1
E-150	Super Window Van	9844	4220	Note 1

NOTE 1: Model year production: [E-150/E-250/E-350] 189,155.

ENGINE [Base Six]: Inline. OHV. Six-cylinder (heavy-duty). Bore & stroke: 4.0 x 3.98 in. Displacement: 300 cid (4.9 liter). Compression ratio: 8.9:1. Net horsepower: 115 at 3000 rpm. Taxable horsepower: 38.4. Net torque: 223 lbs.-ft. at 1600 rpm. Carburetor: One-barrel. (Note: Horsepower and torque may vary with specific model applications; as net horsepower ratings are relative to weight of vehicle.) [VIN Code Y]

ENGINE [Optional V-8]: V-block. OHV. Eight-cylinder. Bore & stroke: 4.0 in. x 3.0 in. Displacement: 302 cid (5.0 liter). Net horsepower: 130 at 3800 rpm. Taxable horsepower: 51.2. Net torque: 222 lbs.-ft. at 2000 rpm. Carburetor: Two-barrel. (Note: Horsepower and torque may vary with specific model applications; as net horsepower ratings are relative to weight of vehicle.) [VIN Code N]

ENGINE [Optional V-8]: V-block. OHV. Eight-cylinder. Bore & stroke: 4.0 in. x 3.5 in. Displacement: 351 cid (5.8 liter). Net horsepower: 150 at 3200 rpm. Taxable horsepower: 51.2. Net torque: 280 lbs.-ft. at 1800 rpm. Carburetor: Two-barrel. (Note: Horsepower and torque may vary with specific model applications; as net horsepower ratings are relative to weight of vehicle.) [VIN Code G]

ENGINE [Optional H.O. V-8]: V-block. OHV. Eight-cylinder. Bore & stroke: 4.0 in. x 3.5 in. Displacement: 351 cid (5.8 liter). Net horsepower: 210 at 4000 rpm. Taxable horsepower: 51.2. Net torque: 305 lbs.-ft. at 2800 rpm. Carburetor: Four-barrel. (Note: Horsepower and torque may vary with specific model applications; as net horsepower ratings are relative to weight of vehicle.) [VIN Code H]

ECONOLINE E-250 CARGO VAN: The new E-250 had a higher GVW rating and heavier-duty front and rear axles than the E-150. It also came with eight-hole wheels. Standard features were the same as those on the E-100, except the three-speed manual transmission was not available in California.

ECONOLINE E-250 SUPER CARGO VAN: See E-150 Cargo Van.

ECONOLINE E-250 DISPLAY VAN: This vehicle shared styling and features with the E-100, but had greater load capacity.

ECONOLINE E-250 WINDOW VAN: This vehicle shared styling and features with the E-100 Window Van, but had greater load capacity.

ECONOLINE E-250 SUPER WINDOW VAN: See E-150 Super Cargo Van.

ECONOLINE E-250 CUTAWAY VAN: This van, with Camper Special Packages, was designed to readily accommodate custom motorhomes.

ECONOLINE E-250 PARCEL DELIVERY: The E-250 Parcel Delivery van was 149.9 in. long and 74.3 in. high in its cargo area. The rear door opening was 84.7 in. wbodyside.

I.D. DATA: The VIN has 17 symbols. The first three indicate the manufacturer; make; and type of vehicle. The fourth symbol indicates the GVW range. The fifth; sixth and seventh symbols indicate the series and body style. The eighth symbol indicates the type of engine. The ninth symbol is a check digit. The 10th symbol (a letter) indicates model year. The 11th symbol indicates the assembly plant. The remaining symbols are the sequential production number starting with 100001 at each plant.

Model	Body Type	Price	Weight	Prod. Total
E-250 Econoline Van — 3/4-Ton — 138 in. w.b. — Six				
E-240	Cargo Van	9817	4251	Note 1
E-250	Window Van	10,011	4294	Note 1
E-260	Display Van	9944	4317	Note 1
E-250 Econoline Super Van — 3/4-Ton — 138 in. w.b. — Six				
S-240	Super Cargo Van	10,447	4500	Note 1
S-250	Super Window Van	10,641	4566	Note 1

E-250 Econoline Cutaway Van — 3/4-Ton — 155 in. w.b. — Six

X-250	Cutaway	—	—	Note 1

NOTE 1: Model year production: [E-150/E-250/E-350] 189,155.
ENGINE [Base Six]: Inline. OHV. Six-cylinder (heavy-duty). Bore & stroke: 4.0 x 3.98 in. Displacement: 300 cid (4.9 liter). Compression ratio: 8.9:1. Net horsepower: 115 at 3000 rpm. Taxable horsepower: 38.4. Net torque: 223 lbs.-ft. at 1600 rpm. Carburetor: One-barrel. (Note: Horsepower and torque may vary with specific model applications; as net horsepower ratings are relative to weight of vehicle.) [VIN Code Y]
ENGINE [Optional V-8]: V-block. OHV. Eight-cylinder. Bore & stroke: 4.0 in. x 3.0 in. Displacement: 302 cid (5.0 liter). Net horsepower: 130 at 3800 rpm. Taxable horsepower: 51.2. Net torque: 222 lbs.-ft. at 2000 rpm. Carburetor: Two-barrel. (Note: Horsepower and torque may vary with specific model applications; as net horsepower ratings are relative to weight of vehicle.) [VIN Code N]
ENGINE [Optional V-8]: V-block. OHV. Eight-cylinder. Bore & stroke: 4.0 in. x 3.5 in. Displacement: 351 cid (5.8 liter). Net horsepower: 150 at 3200 rpm. Taxable horsepower: 51.2. Net torque: 280 lbs.-ft. at 1800 rpm. Carburetor: Two-barrel. (Note: Horsepower and torque may vary with specific model applications; as net horsepower ratings are relative to weight of vehicle.) [VIN Code G]
ENGINE [Optional H.O. V-8]: V-block. OHV. Eight-cylinder. Bore & stroke: 4.0 in. x 3.5 in. Displacement: 351 cid (5.8 liter). Net horsepower: 210 at 4000 rpm. Taxable horsepower: 51.2. Net torque: 305 lbs.-ft. at 2800 rpm. Carburetor: Four-barrel. (Note: Horsepower and torque may vary with specific model applications; as net horsepower ratings are relative to weight of vehicle.) [VIN Code H]
ECONOLINE E-350 CARGO VAN: This was the top-of-the-line Econoline Van. It had heavy-duty front and rear shocks and a greater load capacity than the other series. Standard features were the same as the E-100.
ECONOLINE E-350 SUPER CARGO VAN: See E-150 Super Cargo Van.
ECONOLINE E-350 DISPLAY VAN: See E-250 Display Van.
ECONOLINE E-350 WINDOW VAN: See E-250 Window Van.
ECONOLINE E-350 SUPER WINDOW VAN: See E-150 Super Cargo Van.
ECONOLINE E-350 CUTAWAY VAN: See E-250 Cutaway Van.
ECONOLINE E-350 PARCEL DELIVERY: See E-250 Parcel Delivery.
I.D. DATA: The VIN has 17 symbols. The first three indicate the manufacturer; make; and type of vehicle. The fourth symbol indicates the GVW range. The fifth; sixth and seventh symbols indicate the series and body style. The eighth symbol indicates the type of engine. The ninth symbol is a check digit. The 10th symbol (a letter) indicates model year. The 11th symbol indicates the assembly plant. The remaining symbols are the sequential production number starting with 100001 at each plant.

Model	Body Type	Price	Weight	Prod. Total
E-350 Econoline Van — 1-Ton — 138 in. w.b. — Six				
E-340	Cargo Van	9949	4464	—
E-350	Window Van	10;143	4530	—
E-360	Display Van	10;076	4507	—
E-350 Econoline SuperVan — 1-Ton — 138 in. w.b. — Six				
S-340	Super Cargo Van	10;948	4646	—
S-350	Super Window Van	11;142	4712	—
E-350 Econoline Cutaway Van — 1-Ton — 176 in. w.b. — Six				
E-37B	Cutaway	—	3840	—

NOTE 1: Model year production: [E-150/E-250/E-350] 189,155.
ENGINE [Base Six]: Inline. OHV. Six-cylinder (heavy-duty). Bore & stroke: 4.0 x 3.98 in. Displacement: 300 cid (4.9 liter). Compression ratio: 8.9:1. Net horsepower: 115 at 3000 rpm. Taxable horsepower: 38.4. Net torque: 223 lbs.-ft. at 1600 rpm. Carburetor: One-barrel. (Note: Horsepower and torque may vary with specific model applications; as net horsepower ratings are relative to weight of vehicle.) [VIN Code Y]
ENGINE [Optional Heavy-duty V-8]: V-block. OHV. Eight-cylinder. Bore & stroke: 4.0 in. x 3.5 in. Displacement: 351 cid (5.8 liter). Net horsepower: 210 at 4000 rpm. Taxable horsepower: 51.2. Net torque: 305 lbs.-ft. at 2800 rpm. Carburetor: Four-barrel. (Note: Horsepower and torque may vary with specific model applications; as net horsepower ratings are relative to weight of vehicle.) [VIN Code H]
ENGINE [Optional Heavy-duty Diesel V-8]: V-block. OHV. Eight-cylinder. Diesel. Bore & stroke: 4.0 in. x 4.18 in. Displacement: 420 cid (6.9 liter). Net horsepower: 170 at 3300 rpm. Taxable horsepower: 51.2. Net torque: 315 lbs.-ft. at 1400 rpm. Fuel-injected. (Note: Horsepower and torque may vary with specific model applications; as net horsepower ratings are relative to weight of vehicle.) [VIN Code 1]
ENGINE [Optional Heavy-duty V-8]: V-block. OHV. Eight-cylinder. Bore & stroke: 4.36 in. x 3.85 in. Displacement: 460 cid (7.5 liter). Net horsepower: 214 at 3600 rpm. Taxable horsepower: 52.5. Net torque: 362 lbs.-ft. at 1800 rpm. Carburetor: Four-barrel. (Note: Horsepower and torque may vary with specific model applications; as net horsepower ratings are relative to weight of vehicle.) [VIN Code L]
CHASSIS: Wheelbase: 124 in. (E-150); 138 in. (E-250/E-350). Overall length: 186.8 in. (124 in. wheelbase); 206.8 in. (138 in. wheelbase); 226.8 in. (138 in. wheelbase Super-Van). GVW: 5,250-6,300 lbs. (E-150); 6,800-7,900 lbs. (E-250); 8,900-10,900 (E-350). Tires: P235/75R x 15 (E-150); LT215/85R x 16D (E-250); LT235/85R x 16E (E-350).
POWERTRAIN OPTIONS: Engines: 5.0L V-8. 5.8L V-8 (Two-barrel/Four-barrel). 6.9L Diesel V-8. 7.5L V-8. Transmissions: Four-speed manual with overdrive. SelectShift automatic.
CONVENIENCE OPTIONS: XL Package includes vinyl bucket seats; front compartment carpeting; color-keyed door trim panels; leather tone inserts on instrument panel; courtesy lights; interval wipers; bright grille; front and rear bumpers; and low-mount swing-away mirrors. Cloth-and-vinyl captain's chairs. Air-conditioning. High capacity air-conditioner and auxiliary heater. Heavy-duty battery. Chrome rear step bumper. Chrome bumpers. Super engine cooling. Auxiliary fuel tank. Ammeter and oil pressure gauges. Privacy Glass. Swing-out rear door and/or cargo doorglass. Tinted glass. Handling package. Deluxe insulation package. Light and Convenience group. Bright low-mount swing-away mirrors. Bright swing-out recreation mirrors. Deluxe two-tone paint. Power door locks. Speed control. Tilt steering wheel. Heavy-duty front and rear springs. Trailer Towing Package. Wheelcovers. AM/FM monaural radio. AM/FM stereo radio. AM/digital clock radio. AM/FM stereo radio with cassette player. Hinged bodyside cargo door.
E-150 CLUB WAGON: Like the Econoline, the Club Wagon had styling that was unchanged for 1985. Among the standard features were: Four-speed manual overdrive transmission. 18-gal. fuel tank. Argent silver bumpers, grille and mirrors. Color-keyed vinyl seat trim. Power steering and brakes. Halogen headlights. AM radio. Sliding bodyside doors with swing-out windows. Full-length floor mat. Bright hubcaps. Hardboard headliner (front only). Padded sun visors. Color-keyed instrument panel (138 in. wheelbase models).
E-250 CLUB WAGON: The E-250 had most of the same standard features as the E-150 with a couple exceptions. SelectShift automatic was included. So was a heavier-duty battery with the diesel option.
E-350 SUPER WAGON: This heavy-duty wagon provided bodysides with 20 in. more space than regular 138 in. wheelbase Club Wagons. It could hold up to 15 passengers with optional seating packages.
I.D. DATA: The VIN has 17 symbols. The first three indicate the manufacturer; make; and type of vehicle. The fourth symbol indicates the GVW range. The fifth; sixth and seventh symbols indicate the series and body style. The eighth symbol indicates the type of engine. The ninth symbol is a check digit. The 10th symbol (a letter) indicates model year. The 11th symbol indicates the assembly plant. The remaining symbols are the sequential production number starting with 100001 at each plant.

Model	Body Type	Price	Weight	Prod. Total
E-150 Club Wagon — 1/2-Ton — 124 in. w.b. — Six				
E-150	Club Wagon	12,120	4173	Note 1
E-250 Club Wagon — 3/4-Ton — 138 in. w.b. — Six				
E-250	Club Wagon	13,619	4303	Note 1
E-350 Super Club Wagon — 1-Ton — 138 in. w.b. — Six				
E-350	Super Wagon	14,596	4950	Note 1

NOTE 1: Model year production: [Club Wagons] 34,234.
ENGINE [Base Six]: Inline. OHV. Six-cylinder (heavy-duty). Bore & stroke: 4.0 x 3.98 in. Displacement: 300 cid (4.9 liter). Compression ratio: 8.9:1. Net horsepower: 115 at 3000 rpm. Taxable horsepower: 38.4. Net torque: 223 lbs.-ft. at 1600 rpm. Carburetor: One-barrel. (Note: Horsepower and torque may vary with specific model applications; as net horsepower ratings are relative to weight of vehicle.) [VIN Code Y]
ENGINE [Optional V-8]: V-block. OHV. Eight-cylinder. Bore & stroke: 4.0 in. x 3.0 in. Displacement: 302 cid (5.0 liter). Net horsepower: 130 at 3800 rpm. Taxable horsepower: 51.2. Net torque: 222 lbs.-ft. at 2000 rpm. Carburetor: Two-barrel. (Note: Horsepower and torque may vary with specific model applications; as net horsepower ratings are relative to weight of vehicle.) [VIN Code N]
ENGINE [Optional V-8]: V-block. OHV. Eight-cylinder. Bore & stroke: 4.0 in. x 3.5 in. Displacement: 351 cid (5.8 liter). Net horsepower: 150 at 3200 rpm. Taxable horsepower: 51.2. Net torque: 280 lbs.-ft. at 1800 rpm. Carburetor: Two-barrel. (Note: Horsepower and torque may vary with specific model applications; as net horsepower ratings are relative to weight of vehicle.) [VIN Code G]
ENGINE [Optional H.O. V-8]: V-block. OHV. Eight-cylinder. Bore & stroke: 4.0 in. x 3.5 in. Displacement: 351 cid (5.8 liter). Net horsepower: 210 at 4000 rpm. Taxable horsepower: 51.2. Net torque: 305 lbs.-ft. at 2800 rpm. Carburetor: Four-barrel. (Note: Horsepower and torque may vary with specific model applications; as net horsepower ratings are relative to weight of vehicle.) [VIN Code H]
ENGINE [Optional E-350; Heavy-duty Diesel V-8]: V-block. OHV. Eight-cylinder. Diesel. Bore & stroke: 4.0 in. x 4.18 in. Displacement: 420 cid (6.9 liter). Net horsepower: 170 at 3300 rpm. Taxable horsepower: 51.2. Net torque: 315 lbs.-ft. at 1400 rpm. Fuel-injected. (Note: Horsepower and torque may vary with specific model applications; as net horsepower ratings are relative to weight of vehicle.) [VIN Code 1]
ENGINE [Optional E-350; Heavy-duty V-8]: V-block. OHV. Eight-cylinder. Bore & stroke: 4.36 in. x 3.85 in. Displacement: 460 cid (7.5 liter). Net horsepower: 214 at 3600 rpm. Taxable horsepower: 52.5. Net torque: 362 lbs.-ft. at 1800 rpm. Carburetor: Four-barrel. (Note: Horsepower and torque may vary with specific model applications; as net horsepower ratings are relative to weight of vehicle.) [VIN Code L]
CONVENIENCE OPTIONS: Club Wagons came with most of the same items and packages that were offered on the Econoline, plus: 7-, 8-, 11-, 12- and 15-passenger seating packages. A Club Wagon XL Package included bright bumpers; taillight bezels; low-mount Western swing-away mirrors; color-keyed front; bodyside and rear door trim panels with leather-tone inserts; color-keyed carpeting front to rear; door trim panels map pockets; full-length white hardboard headliner with insulation; instrument panel appliques; and vinyl steering wheel pad with look of leather. A Club Wagon XLT Package included a chrome grille; bright window moldings; lower bodyside moldings; and lower bodyside accent paint in addition to Club Wagon XL features such as front bucket seats upholstered in color-keyed cloth-and-vinyl (premium vinyl available at no extra cost); a color-keyed headliner; color-keyed sun visors; spare tire cover with storage pocket; right-hand visor vanity mirror; stepwell pads for the front and sliding bodyside doors; courtesy light switch on every door; and three-way switch for the rear dome lamp.

1985 Ford 1/2-Ton Ranger Mini-Pickup Sport 4x4 (JAG)

RANGER PICKUP: Sales literature bragged of the many features the compact Ranger shared with full-size Ford trucks. They included: A rugged ladder-type frame; double-walled body panel construction; Twin-I-Beam independent front suspension; and a high payload capacity. Steps were taken in construction of Rangers to help prevent corrosion. These included use of aluminized wax; more plastic parts; urethane anti-corrosion spraying; galvanized metal; and zinc-coated metal. Other standard features included: Black front bumper. Dual fold-away mirrors. Chrome grille and windshield moldings. Argent silver styled steel wheels with bright aluminum hub covers. Vinyl bench seat with folding; covered seatback. Soft-feel steering wheel. Instrument panel storage bin and glove box. Inside hood release. Day/night rearview mirror. AM radio dome lamp. Driver's door courtesy light switch. Right-hand passenger assist handle. Black vinyl coated rubber floor mat. Black scuff plates. Vinyl door trim. Five-speed manual with overdrive transmission. Ranger interior color choices for 1985 were: Regatta blue; Canyon red; and tan. Exterior paint colors included: Raven black; silver (metallic); Light canyon red; Midnight blue (metallic); Light regatta blue; Dark canyon red; Bright regatta blue (metallic); Wimbledon white; Light desert tan; Dark charcoal (metallic); walnut (metallic); and Dark spruce (metallic). Tu-Tone options were: [Regular] Accent color was applied to lower bodyside and tailgate with a two-color tape stripe included (not available with XLS); [Deluxe] Accent color was applied to mid-bodyside and tailgate and upper and lower two-color tape stripes were included (not available with XLS); [Special] Accent color applied to mid-bodyside; inside pickup box; rear of roof; B-pillar; back of cab; and tailgate and included upper and lower two-color tape stripes. Note: The lower two-color tape stripe and rocker panel paint was replaced by XLS tape stripe when ordered with XLS trim.

1985 Ford F-150 XL Styleside Pickup (RCA)

RANGER S PICKUP: This was a no-frills version of the base Ranger Pickup with fewer standard features.

I.D. DATA: The VIN has 17 symbols. The first three indicate the manufacturer; make; and type of vehicle. The fourth symbol indicates the GVW range. The fifth; sixth and seventh symbols indicate the series and body style. The eighth symbol indicates the type of engine. The ninth symbol is a check digit. The 10th symbol (a letter) indicates model year. The 11th symbol indicates the assembly plant. The remaining symbols are the sequential production number starting with 100001 at each plant.

Model	Body Type	Price	Weight	Prod. Total
Ranger — 1/2-Ton — 107.9 in. w.b. — Four				
R-10	Styleside	6675	2585	Note 1
R-10	Styleside S	5993	2527	Note 1
Ranger — 1/2-Ton — 113.9 in. w.b. — Four				
R-10	Styleside	6829	2614	Note 1

NOTE 1: Model year production: [Ranger] 232,771.

ENGINE [Base Four]: Inline. Overhead valve. Four-cylinder. Bore & stroke: 3.78 x 3.13. Displacement: 140 cid (2.3 liter). Compression ratio: 9.5:1. Brake horsepower: 90 at 4000 rpm. Taxable horsepower: 22.8. Torque: 130 lbs.-ft. at 1800 rpm. Electronic fuel-injection. [VIN Code A].

ENGINE [Optional Four]: Inline. Overhead valve. Four-cylinder. Bore & stroke: 3.52 x 3.13. Displacement: 122 cid (2.0 liter). Compression ratio: 9.5:1. Brake horsepower: 73 at 4400 rpm. Taxable horsepower: 19.8. Torque: 107 lbs.-ft. at 2400 rpm. Carburetor: Two-barrel. [VIN Code C]. This 2.0L four was subject to restricted availabity.

ENGINE [Optional V-6]: V-block. OHV. Six-cylinder. Bore & stroke: 3.66 x 2.83 in. Displacement: 170 cid (2.8 liter). Compression ratio: 8.7:1. Brake horsepower: 115 at 4600 rpm. Taxable horsepower: 32.1. Torque: 150 lbs.-ft. at 2600 rpm. Carburetor: Two-barrel. [VIN Code S].

CHASSIS FEATURES: Wheebase: 107.9 in.; 113.9 in. (Ranger). Overall length: 175.6 in. (107.9 in. wheelbase); 187.6 in. (113.9 in. wheelbase). Overall width: 66.9 in. Overall height: 64 in. (67.1 in. 4x4). GVW: 3,800-4,500 lbs. Tires: P185/75R x 14 SL.

POWERTRAIN OPTIONS: Engines: 2.0 liter carbureted four. 2.8 liter V-6. Transmissions: Automatic overdrive transmission.

CONVENIENCE OPTIONS: Four-wheel drive. Headliner. Sport Tape stripe (tri-color). 4x4 tape stripe. AM/FM stereo radio. AM/FM stereo radio with cassette tape player. Electronic AM/FM stereo radio with cassette tape player and two rear speakers. Premium sound system (included power amplifier and dual rear speakers.) Air-conditioning. Black rear step bumper. Chrome rear step bumper with black end caps. Convenience Group with dual electric horns; interval windshield wipers; passenger visor vanity mirror; driver's sun visor band; and cigarette lighter. Tinted glass all around. Light Group with ashtray, cargo box, glove box and engine compartment lights; headlights-on warning buzzer; and passenger door courtesy light switch. Floor console (included gauge package; graphic display module; cassette tape tray; coin holder; and storage bin. Overhead console (included pivoting map light and electonic digital clock). Bright low-mount Western swing-away mirrors. Power steering. Power brakes. Power windows with lock group. Tilt steering wheel. Speed control. Tinted sliding rear window. Cargo tie-down hooks. Pivoting vent windows. Tilt-up open-air roof (glass could be opened or completely removed). Reclining cloth-and-vinyl bucket seats. Knitted vinyl contoured bench seat. Cloth-and-vinyl bench seat. Cloth contoured bench seat. Payload packages up to 1,765 lbs. Heavy-duty air cleaner. Heavy-duty battery. Camper package. Super engine cooling (included in towing package). Auxiliary fuel tank. Gauge Package includes ammeter; oil pressure gauge; temperature gauge; and trip odometer. Engine block heater. Heavy-duty shocks. Tow hooks. Trailer towing package. Snow Plow special package (4x4). Automatic locking hubs (4x4). Traction-Lok rear axle. Limited-slip front axle (4x4). Heavy-duty front suspension (4x4). Handling Package includes heavy-duty front and rear shocks and front and rear stabilizer bars (rear only with 4x4s). Skid plates (4x4). High-altitude emissions system. Security Lock Group with glove box lock; locking gas cap; and undespare tire carrier lock. Exterior Protection Group with chrome front bumper with end caps; black front bumper guards; and black upper bodyside molding with dual red accent stripes. Chrome front bumper without end caps. Cast aluminum wheels. White sport wheels. Deluxe wheel trim. XL Package with (in addition to or in place of standard features) bright wheel lip moldings; rear window insert molding; deluxe wheel trim; chrome front bumper; wood-tone instrument cluster applique; color-keyed cloth headliner; contoured knitted vinyl bench seat; color-keyed seat belts with tension eliminator feature; color-keyed floor mat; passenger door courtesy light switch; aluminum scuff plates; and bright dome light bezel. XLS Package with (in addition to or in place of feature on the XL) black-out exterior trim and distinctive XLS three-color tape stripe; reclining cloth-and-vinyl bucket seats; leather wrapped A-frame steering wheel; gauge package; full color-keyed door trim with cloth and carpet insert and map pocket; and full carpeting. XLT Package with (in addition to or in place of features on XL) chrome front bumper with black end caps; full-length black lower bodyside moldings with bright accents; dual accent bodyside paint stripes; brushed aluminum tail gate applique; full-cloth door trim with color-keyed molding and bright insert; carpeted lower portion and map pocket; contoured bench seat with cloth seat trim; full color-keyed carpeting; leather wrapped A-frame steering wheel with center horn blow; and vent windows with tinted side windows.

1985 Ford 1/2-Ton F-150 Flareside Pickup 4x4 (JAG)

F-150 PICKUP: Basic styling was unchanged for 1985; although optional bodyside moldings now started below the front side-marker lights. Standard features included: Twin-I-Beam independent front suspension (4x4s had Twin-Traction Beam Independent front suspension). Chrome front bumper. Light Argent silver grille with bright surround molding. Bright hubcaps. Black fold-away door- mounted mirrors. Rectangular halogen headlights. Rope tie down holes (Styleside). New all-vinyl seat trim. Pivoting vent windows. Glove box. Temperature gauge. Lighted ashtray. Argent silver instrument panel appliques (wood-tone with 6.9 liter diesel). Black control knobs. Color-keyed door trim panels with foam-padded armrests. Floor insulation and rubber mat. 9-5/8 in. day/night rearview mirror. Inside hood release. Dome light. Reversible keys. AM radio. Coat hook. Left-hand courtesy light switch. Black steering wheel. Vinyl sun visors. Power brakes. Power steering. 10 in. clutch. Three-speed manual. Flareside and Styleside boxes with regular cabs or the Supercab were offered. Interior colors for 1985 were: Charcoal; Regatta blue; Canyon red; and tan. Exterior colors were: Raven black; silver (metallic); Bright canyon red; Midnight blue (metallic); Light regatta blue; Dark canyon red; Dark teal (metallic); Dark charcoal (metallic); Desert tan (metallic); Wimbledon white; Light desert tan; and Bright regatta blue (metallic). Tu-Tone options were: (Regular) Accent color covered roof and upper cab back panel; (Deluxe) Accent color covered center bodyside area and tailgate and moldings or tape were included or deleted as needed; (Combination) Regular and deluxe tu-tone combined; (Victoria) Accent color was applied to hood, upper fender, and around window and lower bodyside and tape and moldings were included or deleted as required.

I.D. DATA: The VIN has 17 symbols. The first three indicate the manufacturer; make; and type of vehicle. The fourth symbol indicates the GVW range. The fifth; sixth and seventh symbols indicate the series and body style. The eighth symbol indicates the type of engine. The ninth symbol is a check digit. The 10th symbol (a letter) indicates model year. The 11th symbol indicates the assembly plant. The remaining symbols are the sequential production number starting with 100001 at each plant.

1985 Ford 1/2-Ton F-150 XLT Styleside Pickup 4x4 (JAG)

Model	Body Type	Price	Weight	Prod. Total
F-150 — 1/2-Ton — 116.8 in. w.b. — Six				
F-15	Flareside 6.5 ft.	7962	3412	Note 1
F-15	Styleside 6.75 ft.	7799	3402	Note 1
F-15	Styleside 8 ft.	7965	3513	Note 1
F-150 SuperCab — 1/2-Ton — 138.8 in. w.b. — Six				
X-15	Styleside 6.75 ft.	9134	3756	Note 1
X-15	Styleside 8 ft.	9300	3962	Note 1

NOTE 1: Model year production: [F-150] 348,565.

ENGINE [Base Six]: Inline. OHV. Six-cylinder (heavy-duty). Bore & stroke: 4.0 x 3.98 in. Displacement: 300 cid (4.9 liter). Compression ratio: 8.9:1. Net horsepower: 115 at 3000 rpm. Taxable horsepower: 38.4. Net torque: 223 lbs.-ft. at 1600 rpm. Carburetor: One-barrel. (Note: Horsepower and torque may vary with specific model applications; as net horsepower ratings are relative to weight of vehicle.) [VIN Code Y].

ENGINE [Optional V-8]: V-block. OHV. Eight-cylinder. Bore & stroke: 4.0 in. x 3.0 in. Displacement: 302 cid (5.0 liter). Net horsepower: 150 at 3600 rpm. Taxable horsepower: 51.2. Net torque: 250 lbs.-ft. at 2600 rpm. Carburetor: Two-barrel. (Note: Horsepower and torque may vary with specific model applications; as net horsepower ratings are relative to weight of vehicle.) [VIN Code F].

ENGINE [Optional V-8]: V-block. OHV. Eight-cylinder. Bore & stroke: 4.0 in. x 3.0 in. Displacement: 302 cid (5.0 liter). Net horsepower: 190 at 3800 rpm. Taxable horsepower: 51.5. Net torque: 285 lbs.-ft. at 2400 rpm. Electronic fuel-injection. (Note: Horsepower and torque may vary with specific model applications; as net horsepower ratings are relative to weight of vehicle.) [VIN Code N].

ENGINE [Optional V-8]: V-block. OHV. Eight-cylinder. Bore & stroke: 4.0 in. x 3.5 in. Displacement: 351 cid (5.8 liter). Net horsepower: 150 at 3200 rpm. Taxable horsepower: 51.2. Net torque: 280 lbs.-ft. at 1800 rpm. Carburetor: Two-barrel. (Note: Horsepower and torque may vary with specific model applications; as net horsepower ratings are relative to weight of vehicle.) [VIN Code G]

1985 Ford 3/4-Ton F-250 XLT Styleside Pickup 4x4 (JAG)

F-250 PICKUP: The F-250 was only offered with the 8 ft. Styleside box, but it could be had in regular or F-250 Heavy-duty Supercab. The Supercab had room behind the front seat for an optional forward-facing rear seat, which could fold-down flat. Two center-facing jump seats were standard. When these were folded out of the way, there was an extra 29.8 cu. ft. of interior load space for cargo. Most standard F-250 features were the same as those offered on the F-150, plus a four-speed manual transmission and, on F-250 HDE models, an 11 in. clutch.

I.D. DATA: The VIN has 17 symbols. The first three indicate the manufacturer, make and type of vehicle. The fourth symbol indicates the GVW range. The fifth, sixth and seventh symbols indicate the series and body style. The eighth symbol indicates the type of engine. The ninth symbol is a check digit. The 10th symbol (a letter) indicates model year. The 11th symbol indicates the assembly plant. The remaining symbols are the sequential production number starting with 100001 at each plant.

Model	Body Type	Price	Weight	Prod. Total
F-250 — 3/4-Ton — 133 in. w.b. — Six				
—	Chassis and Cab	9138	3732	—
F-25	Styleside 8 ft.	8951	3785	—
F-250 Supercab — 3/4-Ton — 155 in. w.b. — Six				
X-25	Styleside 8 ft.	10,250	4305	—

ENGINE [Base Six; F-250/F-250 HDE]: Inline. OHV. Six-cylinder (heavy-duty). Bore & stroke: 4.0 x 3.98 in. Displacement: 300 cid (4.9 liter). Compression ratio: 8.9:1. Net horsepower: 115 at 3000 rpm. Taxable horsepower: 38.4. Net torque: 223 lbs.-ft. at 1600 rpm. Carburetor: One-barrel. (Note: Horsepower and torque may vary with specific model applications; as net horsepower ratings are relative to weight of vehicle.) [VIN Code Y]

ENGINE [Optional V-8; F-250/F-250 HDE]: V-block. OHV. Eight-cylinder. Bore & stroke: 4.0 in. x 3.5 in. Displacement: 351 cid (5.8 liter). Net horsepower: 150 at 3200 rpm. Taxable horsepower: 51.2. Net torque: 280 lbs.-ft. at 1800 rpm. Carburetor: Two-barrel. (Note: Horsepower and torque may vary with specific model applications; as net horsepower ratings are relative to weight of vehicle.) [VIN Code G]

ENGINE [Optional H.O. V-8]: V-block. OHV. Eight-cylinder. Bore & stroke: 4.0 in. x 3.5 in. Displacement: 351 cid (5.8 liter). Net horsepower: 210 at 4000 rpm. Taxable horsepower: 51.2. Net torque: 305 lbs.-ft. at 2800 rpm. Carburetor: Four-barrel. (Note: Horsepower and torque may vary with specific model applications; as net horsepower ratings are relative to weight of vehicle.) [VIN Code H]

ENGINE [Optional F-250/F-250 HDE; Heavy-duty Diesel V-8]: V-block. OHV. Eight-cylinder. Diesel. Bore & stroke: 4.0 in. x 4.18 in. Displacement: 420 cid (6.9 liter). Net horsepower: 170 at 3300 rpm. Taxable horsepower: 51.2. Net torque: 315 lbs.-ft. at 1400 rpm. Fuel-injected. (Note: Horsepower and torque may vary with specific model applications; as net horsepower ratings are relative to weight of vehicle.) [VIN Code 1]

ENGINE [Optional F-250 HDE Only; Heavy-duty V-8]: V-block. OHV. Eight-cylinder. Bore & stroke: 4.36 in. x 3.85 in. Displacement: 460 cid (7.5 liter). Net horsepower: 214 at 3600 rpm. Taxable horsepower: 52.5. Net torque: 362 lbs.-ft. at 1800 rpm. Carburetor: Four-barrel. (Note: Horsepower and torque may vary with specific model applications; as net horsepower ratings are relative to weight of vehicle.) [VIN Code L]

1985 Ford 3/4-Ton F-250 XLT Styleside Pickup 4x4 (RCA)

F-350 PICKUP: The F-350 was offered in 8 ft. Styleside boxes with regular or Crew Cabs. The latter featured four doors and two full-width bench seats. Both regular and Crew Cab models could be ordered with dual rear wheels. An 11 in. clutch and four-speed manual transmission were standard on all F-350s.

I.D. DATA: The VIN has 17 symbols. The first three indicate the manufacturer; make; and type of vehicle. The fourth symbol indicates the GVW range. The fifth; sixth and seventh symbols indicate the series and body style. The eighth symbol indicates the type of engine. The ninth symbol is a check digit. The 10th symbol (a letter) indicates model year. The 11th symbol indicates the assembly plant. The remaining symbols are the sequential production number starting with 100001 at each plant.

Model	Body Type	Price	Weight	Prod. Total
F-350 — 1-Ton — 133 in. w.b.				
F-37	Chassis & Cab	9138	3732	—
F-350 Supercab — 1-Ton — 155 in. w.b.				
F-35	Styleside	10,437	4004	—
F-350 Crew Cabs — 1-Ton — 133 in. w.b.				
F-37	Chassis & Cab	9234	3861	—
W-35	Styleside	10,993	4713	—

ENGINE [Base Six; F-350/F-350 HDE]: Inline. OHV. Six-cylinder (heavy-duty). Bore & stroke: 4.0 x 3.98 in. Displacement: 300 cid (4.9 liter). Compression ratio: 8.9:1. Net horsepower: 115 at 3000 rpm. Taxable horsepower: 38.4. Net torque: 223 lbs.-ft. at 1600 rpm. Carburetor: One-barrel. (Note: Horsepower and torque may vary with specific model applications; as net horsepower ratings are relative to weight of vehicle.) [VIN Code Y]

ENGINE [Optional V-8; F-350/F-350 HDE]: V-block. OHV. Eight-cylinder. Bore & stroke: 4.0 in. x 3.5 in. Displacement: 351 cid (5.8 liter). Net horsepower: 150 at 3200 rpm. Taxable horsepower: 51.2. Net torque: 280 lbs.-ft. at 1800 rpm. Carburetor: Two-barrel. (Note: Horsepower and torque may vary with specific model applications; as net horsepower ratings are relative to weight of vehicle.) [VIN Code G]

ENGINE [Optional H.O. V-8]: V-block. OHV. Eight-cylinder. Bore & stroke: 4.0 in. x 3.5 in. Displacement: 351 cid (5.8 liter). Net horsepower: 210 at 4000 rpm. Taxable horsepower: 51.2. Net torque: 305 lbs.-ft. at 2800 rpm. Carburetor: Four-barrel. (Note: Horsepower and torque may vary with specific model applications; as net horsepower ratings are relative to weight of vehicle.) [VIN Code H]

ENGINE [Optional F-350/F-350 HDE; Heavy-duty Diesel V-8]: V-block. OHV. Eight-cylinder. Diesel. Bore & stroke: 4.0 in. x 4.18 in. Displacement: 420 cid (6.9 liter). Net horsepower: 170 at 3300 rpm. Taxable horsepower: 51.2. Net torque: 315 lbs.-ft. at 1400 rpm. Fuel-injected. (Note: Horsepower and torque may vary with specific model applications; as net horsepower ratings are relative to weight of vehicle.) [VIN Code 1]

ENGINE [Optional F-350 HDE Only; Heavy-duty V-8]: V-block. OHV. Eight-cylinder. Bore & stroke: 4.36 in. x 3.85 in. Displacement: 460 cid (7.5 liter). Net horsepower: 214 at 3600 rpm. Taxable horsepower: 52.5. Net torque: 362 lbs.-ft. at 1800 rpm. Carburetor: Four-barrel. (Note: Horsepower and torque may vary with specific model applications; as net horsepower ratings are relative to weight of vehicle.) [VIN Code L]

CHASSIS: Wheelbase: 116.8 in. (F-150 Styleside/F-250); 138.8 in. (F-150 Supercab); 155 in. (F-250/F-250HD/F-350 Supercab); 168.4 in. (F-350 Crew Cab). Overall length: 189.3 in. (Flareside); 192.1 in. (F-150 Styleside); 208.3 in. (F-250 Styleside); 214.1 in. (F-150 Supercab); 230.3 in. (F-150/F-250 Supercab); 243.7 in. (F-350 Crew Cab). GVW: 5,250-6,450 lbs. (F-150); 6,300-9,000 lbs. (F-250); 8,700-11,000 lbs. (F-350). Tires: P195/75R x 15SL (F-150); LT215/85R x 16C (F-250); LT235/85R x 16E (F-250HD/F-350); LT215/85R x 16D (F-350 dual rear wheels/regular cab).

POWERTRAIN OPTIONS: Engines: 5.0L V-8 (F-150/F-250). 5.0L V-8 with Electronic Fuel Injection (F-150/F-250). 5.8L V-8. 5.8L HO V-8 (F-150/F-250). 7.5L V-8 (F-250HDE/F-350). 6.9L Diesel V-8 (F-250HDE/F-350). Four-wheel drive F-350s and those with dual rear wheels came with the 5.8L V-8, except in California. Transmissions: Four-speed manual (F-150). Four-speed manual with overdrive (F-150/F-250). Automatic overdrive (F-150/F-250). SelectShift automatic.

1985 Ford Pickup

CONVENIENCE OPTIONS: Four-wheel drive option with power brakes; manual locking free running hubs; power steering; two-speed transfer case; and four-speed manual. Automatic locking hubs (4x4). Chrome grille. Bodyside protection molding with black vinyl insert (Styleside). Bright wheel lip moldings (Styleside). Electronic AM/FM stereo radio with search and cassette tape player. AM/FM stereo (speakers mounted in door panels). AM/FM stereo radio with cassette tape player. Radio credit option (deleted standard AM radio for credit). Air-conditioning. High-output heater (Standard with Crew Cab). Convenience Group with interval wipers; 12 in. day/night mirror; right-hand visor vanity mirror; carpeted map pocket on lower doors; headlights-on warning buzzer; and courtesy light switch on right-hand door. Headliner and Deluxe Insulation Package includes color-keyed cloth headliner; black floor mats with full insulation (carpet on Crew Cab); back panel cover; and moldings for upper door, B-pillar and rear window; plus aluminum door scuff plates. Electronic digital clock. Speed control (with resume feature). Light Group with movable underhood worklight with 20 ft. retractable cord, plus lights in glove box; lights under instrument panel; dual beam dome/map light; cargo box light; headlights-on warning buzzer; and courtesy light switch on right-hand door. Power door locks/windows (not available with Crew Cab). Manual steering (F-150 regular Cab). Tinted sliding rear window. Tilt steering wheel. Tinted glass. Spare tire carrier in box, bodyside-mounted (Stylesides). Center console (Supercab with captain's chairs). Bright low-mount swing-away Western mirrors. Bright swing-out recreation mirrors. Reclining captain's chairs in Supercab. Folding forward-facing rear seat in Supercab. Cloth-and-vinyl seat trim. Knitted vinyl seat trim. Auxiliary fuel tank. Auxiliary transmission oil cooler. Handling Package includes front and rear stabilizer bars;

heavy-duty front and rear shocks (quad front on F-150 regular cab 4x4); and heavy-duty front springs. Heavy-duty shocks. Heavy-Duty Front Suspension Package includes (133 in. wheelbase F-150 4x4) heavy-duty 3,800 lbs. rated front axle and springs; 3.54:1 axle ratio; heavy-duty front shock absorbers; and heavy-duty rear shock absorbers. (A version of this package was also offered for F-250 and F-350 4x4s.) Oil pressure and ammeter gauges. Front and rear stabilizer bars. Engine block heater. Extra engine cooling package. Super engine cooling package. Trailer towing package. Camper package. Heavy-duty air cleaner. Dual electric horns. Five roof clearance lights. Exterior Protection Group with front bumper guards and front bumper rub strip. Security Lock Group with locking gas cap; inside hood release; glove box lock; and spare tire lock. Sports Instrumentation with tachometer; ammeter; oil pressure gauge; and trip odometer. Skid plates (4x4s), include transfer and fuel tank protective plates. Argent silver step type rear bumper (Styleside). Chrome step type rear bumper (Styleside). Chrome channel type rear bumper (Flarebodyside). Deluxe wheelcovers (not available with 4x4s or dual rear wheels. White styled steel wheels (F-150). Sport wheelcovers (F-150). XL Package with (in addition to or in place of items on standard model) bright wheel lip moldings and two-color full-length bodyside paint stripes on single rear wheel Stylesides or bodyside surround tape stripes and tailgate surround tape stripe on Flareside and dual rear wheel models; bright insert on rear window weather-strip; cigarette lighter; left-hand and right-hand courtesy light switch; 12 in. day/night mirror; bright dome light bezel; bright surround door trim panel moldings; color-keyed floor mat; wood-tone applique instrument panel; folding fully covered seatback (fixed front and folding rear on Crew Cab); deluxe seat belts; cloth-and-vinyl seat trim; aluminum scuff plates; cloth headlining; and moldings/trim panels above beltline. XLT Lariat Package included (in addition to or in place of items on the XL) full-length black bodyside moldings with bright insert; wheel lip moldings; distinctive brushed aluminum Styleside tailgate applique with red reflective lower portion; wall-to-wall carpeting; door trim panels with bright surrounds, cloth inserts, carpeted lower area; and map pockets; soft-wrapped steering wheel with wood-tone inserts; and trim panels above beltline.

HISTORICAL: Light-duty truck model-year production by line was: [Ranger] 232,771; [Bronco II] 98,243; [Aerostar; 1986 models] 10,301; [F-150] 348,565; [F-250] 151,619; [F-350] 57,088; [Bronco] 52,316; [Club Wagon] 34,234; [Econoline] 189,155; [Grand total] 189,155. Including Medium- and Heavy-duty models, Ford dealers retailed a total of 1,271,809 new trucks in calendar year 1985, a seven percent increase over the previous year. However, production delays that held up the launch of the all-new Aerostar Minivan caused the company the top sales rank in the industry. Ford did lead Chevrolet, however, in sales of full-size Pickups, compact Pickups, standard Sport Utility Vehicles and full-size cargo and passenger vans.

1986 FORD

1986 Ford Aerostar XL Passenger Van (FMC)

AEROSTAR: After some delays, the Aerostar was introduced in the summer of 1985 as an 1986 model. This compact van's aerodynamic styling seemed more akin to Ford's automobile line than its truck line. The Aerostar's front end steeply sloped to a blunt, four horizontal-bars grille that was sandwiched between the two rectangular headlights and wraparound parking lights. The Aerostar had a one-piece liftgate and a sliding door on the passenger side. The instrument panel was computer-designed and had a backlit speedometer and lighted speedometer needle for good legibility at night. Standard features included: Front bucket seats (wagon also had rear seats). Twin-tube low-pressure gas shock absorbers. Five-speed manual transmission with overdrive. Manual rack-and-pinion steering. Argent silver styled steel wheels with bright hubcaps. Full wrapover color-keyed door panels. Color-keyed soft vinyl steering wheel. AM radio. White fiberboard front compartment headliner. Dual aero-style fold-away mirrors. Front compartment carpeting (a rubber mat replaced the carpet if it was deleted). Aerostar color choices for 1986 were: Silver clearcoat (metallic); Bright canyon red; Dark grey clearcoat (metallic); Desert tan; Dark canyon red clearcoat (metallic); Bright copper clearcoat (metallic); Bright regatta blue clearcoat (metallic); Light chestnut clearcoat (metallic); Midnight regatta blue; Dark walnut clearcoat (metallic); Light regatta blue; and Colonial white. Two-tone paint was applied with a lower accent treatment.

I.D. DATA: The VIN has 17 symbols. The first three indicate the manufacturer, make and type of vehicle. The fourth symbol indicates the GVW range. The fifth, sixth and seventh symbols indicate the series and body style. The eighth symbol indicates the type of engine. The ninth symbol is a check digit. The 10th symbol (a letter) indicates model year. The 11th symbol indicates the assembly plant. The remaining symbols are the sequential production number starting with 100001 at each plant.

Model	Body Type	Price	Weight	Prod. Total
Aerostar Minivan — 1/2-Ton — 119 in. w.b. — V-6				
A-140	Cargo Van	8774	2755	Note 1
A-110	Wagon	9398	3123	Note 1
A-150	Window Van	9764	2893	Note 1

NOTE 1: Aerostar model year production: [Cargo Van] 33,514; [Wagon] 110,231.

ENGINE [Base Four]: Inline. Overhead valve. Four-cylinder. Bore & stroke: 3.78 x 3.13. Displacement: 140 cid (2.3 liter). Compression ratio: 9.5:1. Brake horsepower: 90 at 4000 rpm. Taxable horsepower: 22.8. Torque: 130 lbs.-ft. at 1800 rpm. Electronic fuel-injection. [VIN Code A]

ENGINE [Optional V-6]: V-block. OHV. Six-cylinder. Bore & stroke: 3.66 x 2.83 in. Displacement: 170 cid (2.8 liter). Compression ratio: 8.7:1. Brake horsepower: 115 at 4600 rpm. Taxable horsepower: 32.1. Torque: 150 lbs.-ft. at 2600 rpm. Carburetor: Two-barrel. [VIN Code S]

CHASSIS: Wheelbase: 118.9 in. Overall length: 174.9 in. Overall width: 71.7 in. Overall height: 72.6 in. Tires: P185/75R x 14SL.

POWERTRAIN OPTIONS: Transmission: Automatic with overdrive. Engine: 2.8 liter V-6.

CONVENIENCE OPTIONS: Power rack and pinion steering. Payload Packages: 1,600 lbs. and 2,000 lbs. (both include power steering). Cloth seat trim. Air-conditioning. Supercool radiator cooling. Rear window defroster and wiper/washer. AM/FM stereo radio. AM/FM stereo radio with cassette. Bright outside swing-away mirrors. Bodyside door fixed window. Polished aluminum wheels. Speed control and tilt steering wheel. Engine block heater. California emissions system. High-altitude emissions system. XL Van Package with AM/FM stereo radio; interval wipers; tinted glass; courtesy lamp switches for all doors; cargo lamps for instrument panel, glove box and vanity panel; two-tone rocker panel accent treatment; painted bodyside pinstripes; bright grille; bright aluminum full wheelcovers; deluxe high-impact color-coordinated plastic bumpers; dual reclining cloth captain's chairs with inboard armrests; and 16 oz. full-length carpeting. Bright Argent silver grille. Sliding bodyside windows. Argent silver styled steel wheels with bright hubcaps. Tinted glass. Interval wipers. Electronic digital clock. Convenience Group with courtesy light switches for all doors; cargo lamps; and instrument panel, glove box and vanity panel lights. Light Group with under-hood light; glove box light; front reading lamp; ashtray light; under instrument panel lamps; and headlamp-on alert.

1986 Ford Aerostar Mini-Van

BRONCO II: Styling on the compact 4x4 Bronco II was carried over from last year. A new feature was the tip-and-slide front passenger seat, which provided more convenient access to the rear passenger area. With four passengers seated the Bronco provided 21.1 in. of load floor length and 25.6 cu. ft. of cargo volume. With rear seatbacks down the load floor length increased to 52.5 in. and cargo volume to 64.9 cu. ft. Among the many standard features were: Tinted glass. Full instrumentation. Transfer case skid plate. Power brakes and steering. Front and rear stabilizer bars. Five-speed manual transmission. Reclining front seats. Split fold-down rear bench seat. Halogen headlights. Dual outside fold-away rear-view mirrors. Bright front and rear contour bumpers. Sport wheelcovers. Color-keyed carpeting. Full-length cloth headliner. Sun visors. A 4x2 Bronco II was reportedly offered for a short time, then discontinued. Color choices for 1986 were: Dark grey (metallic); Raven black; Medium silver (metallic); Bright canyon red; Dark canyon red; Light regatta blue; Dark shadow blue (metallic); Colonial white; Dark walnut (metallic); Light desert tan; Desert tan (metallic); and Dark spruce (metallic). The last color was for the Eddie Bauer model only. With Deluxe two-tone paint the accent color was applied to the mid-bodyside and liftgate below the chamfer, as well as above the rocker area. Also included was two-color tape stripes at the two-tone break.

I.D. DATA: The VIN has 17 symbols. The first three indicate the manufacturer; make; and type of vehicle. The fourth symbol indicates the GVW range. The fifth; sixth and seventh symbols indicate the series and body style. The eighth symbol indicates the type of engine. The ninth symbol is a check digit. The 10th symbol (a letter) indicates model year. The 11th symbol indicates the assembly plant. The remaining symbols are the sequential production number starting with 100001 at each plant.

Model	Body Type	Price	Weight	Prod. Total
Bronco II — 1/2-Ton — 94 in. w.b. — V-6				
U-14	Wagon	11,906	3072	Note 1
U-14	Eddie Bauer Wagon	12,697	3213	Note 1

NOTE 1: Model year production: [All Bronco IIs] 109,875.

ENGINE: V-block. OHV. Six-cylinder. Bore & stroke: 3.66 x 2.83. Displacement: 179 cid (2.9 liter). Compression ratio: 9.3:1. Brake horsepower: 140 at 4600 rpm. Taxable horsepower: 32.1. Torque: 170 lbs.-ft. at 2600 rpm. Electronic fuel-injection. [VIN Code T]

CHASSIS: Wheelbase: 94 in. Overall length: 158.2 in. Overall width: 68 in. Overall height: 68.4 in. Tires: P195/75R x 15 SL.

POWERTRAIN OPTIONS: Transmissions: Four-speed automatic with overdrive.

CONVENIENCE OPTIONS: Touch-Drive electric shift transfer case. Eddie Bauer Bronco II Package with Special Tu-Tone paint treatment; Eddie Bauer emblem; XLT-level trim inside and outside; cast aluminum wheels; all-terrain tires with raised white letters; ammeter; oil pressure and temperature gauges; trip odometer; dual captain's chairs; AM/FM stereo radio; tilt steering wheel; floor console; dual electric horns; interval windshield wipers; passenger visor vanity mirror; dark-tinted privacy glass; driver's sun visor band; ashtray and glove box lights; headlamps-on warning buzzer; Eddie Bauer garment bag; and Eddie Bauer tote bags. AM/FM stereo radio with cassette tape player. Dual captain's chairs. Cloth/vinyl 60/40 split bench seat. Air-conditioning. Tinted glass. Luggage rack. Cloth/vinyl reclining bucket seats. Light Group with glove box, ashtray and cargo area lights; passenger door light switches; liftgate courtesy light switches; and headlights-on warning buzzer. Fingertip speed control. Tilt steering wheel. Rear window wiper/defroster. Flip-open liftgate window. Flip-up open-air roof. Flip-open removable quarter windows (gray-tinted). Pivoting front vent windows. Privacy glass. Floor Console includes gauge package; trash bin; cassette tape tray; coin tray; two cup depressions; and electronic graphic warning display module. Overhead Console with digital clock and pivoting map light. Bright low-mount Western swing-away mirrors. Outside swing-away spare tire carrier. Rear seat delete. Carpet delete. Automatic locking hubs. Engine block heater. Super engine cooling. Heavy-duty shocks. Snow plow special package. Trailer towing package. Tow hooks. Limited-slip front axle. California emissions system. High-altitude emissions system. Plate bracket. Cast alu-

minum wheels. White sport styled steel wheels. Deluxe wheel trim (includes Argent silver styled steel wheel with bright trim ring, lug nuts and black hub cover). XLT Package includes chrome grille; bodyside accent stripe; pivoting front vent windows; tinted glass; deluxe wheel trim; cloth-and-vinyl seat trim with full cloth door trim panels and map pocket; door carpet inserts; bright headlights; courtesy light trucks; liftgate-operated cargo area light; and rear quarter trim panels.

1986 Ford 1/2-Ton Bronco Sport Utility Wagon (RCA)

BRONCO: The attractive full-size Bronco 4x4 was basically unchanged for 1986. Standard features included: Twin-Traction Beam independent front suspension. Power steering and brakes. A 32-gal. fuel tank. Front vinyl bucket seats. Color-keyed floor mat. Flip/fold back seat. Power tailgate window. Interval wipers. AM radio. Tinted glass. Pivoting front bent windows. Chrome front and rear contour bumpers. Bright swing away mirrors. Sport wheelcovers. Four-speed manual. Bronco colors for 1986 were: Raven black; Dark canyon red; Colonial white; Light regatta blue; Medium silver (metallic); Dark shadow blue (metallic); Dark grey (metallic); Light desert tan; Bright canyon red; and Desert tan (metallic). Bronco roof colors included black, Dark shadow blue, Light desert tan; and white. Tu-Tone effects featured the exterior color accented by a contrasting rear fiberglass roof. Deluxe Tu-Toning included the accent color on the center bodyside area and on the tailgate (between a tape stripe below the upper mid-bodyside depression and the lower bodyside protection moldings). Victoria Tu-Toning included the accent color on the hood, upper fender and around the door window and on lower bodyside below the lower bodyside protection molding.
I.D. DATA: The VIN has 17 symbols. The first symbol indicates the manufacturer; make; and type of vehicle. The fourth symbol indicates the GVW range. The fifth; sixth and seventh symbols indicate the series and body style. The eighth symbol indicates the type of engine. The ninth symbol is a check digit. The 10th symbol (a letter) indicates model year. The 11th symbol indicates the assembly plant. The remaining symbols are the sequential production number starting with 100001 at each plant.

1986 Ford 1/2-Ton Bronco Eddie Bauer Sport Utility Wagon (RCA)

Model	Body Type	Price	Weight	Prod. Total
Bronco — 1/2-Ton — 105 in. w.b. — Six				
U-150	Wagon	13,302	4383	57,448

ENGINE [Base Six; F-350/F-350 HDE]: Inline. OHV. Six-cylinder (heavy-duty). Bore & stroke: 4.0 x 3.98 in. Displacement: 300 cid (4.9 liter). Compression ratio: 8.9:1. Net horsepower: 115 at 3000 rpm. Taxable horsepower: 38.4. Net torque: 223 lbs.-ft. at 1600 rpm. Carburetor: One-barrel. (Note: Horsepower and torque may vary with specific model applications; as net horsepower ratings are relative to weight of vehicle.) [VIN Code Y]
ENGINE [Optional V-8]: V-block. OHV. Eight-cylinder. Bore & stroke: 4.0 in. x 3.0 in. Displacement: 302 cid (5.0 liter). Net horsepower: 190 at 3800 rpm. Taxable horsepower: 51.5. Net torque: 285 lbs.-ft. at 2400 rpm. Electronic fuel-injection. (Note: Horsepower and torque may vary with specific model applications; as net horsepower ratings are relative to weight of vehicle.) [VIN Code N]
ENGINE [Optional H.O. V-8]: V-block. OHV. Eight-cylinder. Bore & stroke: 4.0 in. x 3.5 in. Displacement: 351 cid (5.8 liter). Net horsepower: 210 at 4000 rpm. Taxable horsepower: 51.2. Net torque: 305 lbs.-ft. at 2800 rpm. Carburetor: Four-barrel. (Note: Horsepower and torque may vary with specific model applications; as net horsepower ratings are relative to weight of vehicle.) [VIN Code H]
CHASSIS: Wheebase: 104.7 in. Overall length: 177.7 in. Overall height: 74 in. Overall width: 77.2 in. Tires: P235/75R x 15 SL BSW.
POWERTRAIN OPTIONS: Engine: 5.0L EFI; 5.8L HO. Four-speed manual with overdrive Automatic. Automatic with overdrive transmission.
CONVENIENCE OPTIONS: California emissions system. High-altitude system. P235/75R x 15XL black sidewall or raised white-letter all-terrain tires. 31 x 10.5R x 15C in. raised white-letter all-terrain tires. Cloth-and-vinyl bucket seats. Cloth-and-vinyl bench seat. Cloth captain's chairs. Air-conditioner. Heavy-duty battery. Chrome rear step bumper. Floor console. Super engine cooling. Rear window defroster. Privacy glass. Handling package. Engine block heater. Automatic locking hubs. Light Group with glove box and underhood light; dual beam map/dome light; under instrument panel courtesy lights; passenger-side door courtesy light switch; headlights-on warning buzzer. Transfer case skid plate. Outside swing-away spare tire carrier. Speed control/tilt steering wheel. Heavy-duty front

suspension. Snow plow package. Trailer Towing Package includes 7-wire trailer wiring harness; 71-amp.-hr. battery; super engine cooling; auxiliary transmission oil cooler; heavy-duty flasher; and handling package. Deluxe two-tone paint. Victoria two-tone paint. Deluxe Argent silver styled steel wheels. White styled steel wheels. AM/FM stereo. AM/FM stereo radio with cassette player. Power door locks/power windows. Exterior Protection Group with front bumper guards and front bumper rub strips. Eddie Bauer Bronco with two-tone paint; dual bodyside paint stripes; privacy glass; all-terrain raised white-letter tires; deluxe Argent silver styled steel wheels; captain's chairs in special cloth trim with fold-down armrests; fully-carpeted interior; center floor console; air-conditioning; speed control/tilt steering wheel; light group; AM/FM stereo radio; heavy-duty battery; and Eddie Bauer garment and equipment bags. XLT Package with chrome front and rear bumpers; lower bodyside protection molding; rear fold-down tailgate with brushed aluminum applique; bright moldings on rear quarter windows; cloth-and-vinyl front bucket seats; 16 oz. color-keyed cut-pile carpeting; center console with a covered storage compartment (plus depressions for beverage cups); door trim panels with padded cloth insert on the upper half and carpeted lower insert with map pocket; soft-wrapped steering wheel; and AM/FM stereo radio. Econoline colors for 1986 were: Dark grey (metallic); Dark walnut (metallic); Medium silver (metallic); Dark shadow blue (metallic); Medium canyon red (metallic); Light desert tan; Light regatta blue (metallic); Desert tan (metallic); Light regatta blue; and Colonial white.

1986 Ford 1/2-Ton E-150 Econoline XL Cargo Van (FMC)

ECONOLINE E-150 CARGO VAN: The Econoline exterior styling was left untouched for 1986. Among the standard features were: Power steering. Adjustable passenger seat (could be deleted). Color-keyed continuous-loop seat belts. Inside hood release. Front door courtesy light switch (both doors). Stepwell pads for the front doors and bodyside cargo door. Day/night rearview mirror. Rear door latch and lock. Rear door positioners. Cigarette lighter. Bright hubcaps. Bright windshield moldings.
ECONOLINE E-150 SUPER CARGO VAN: This Van had the same features as the E-150 Cargo Van, plus a 20 in. extended rear overhang. This was especially useful for hauling longer loads.
ECONOLINE E-150 WINDOW VAN: This Window Van had glass all around. It shared standard features with the Cargo Van.
ECONOLINE E-150 SUPER WINDOW VAN: See E-150 Super Cargo Van.
I.D. DATA: The VIN has 17 symbols. The first three indicate the manufacturer; make; and type of vehicle. The fourth symbol indicates the GVW range. The fifth; sixth and seventh symbols indicate the series and body style. The eighth symbol indicates the type of engine. The ninth symbol is a check digit. The 10th symbol (a letter) indicates model year. The 11th symbol indicates the assembly plant. The remaining symbols are the sequential production number starting with 100001 at each plant.

Model	Body Type	Price	Weight	Prod. Total
E-150 Econoline Van — 1/2-Ton — 124 in. w.b. — Six				
E-150	Cargo Van	9439	3764	Note 1
E-150	Window Van	9710	3791	Note 1
E-150 Econoline SuperVan — 1/2-Ton — 138 in. w.b. — Six				
E-150	Super Cargo Van	10,593	4036	Note 1
E-150	Super Window Van	10,863	4096	Note 1

NOTE 1: Model year production: [All Econolines] 194,875.
ENGINE [Base Six; F-350/F-350 HDE]: Inline. OHV. Six-cylinder (heavy-duty). Bore & stroke: 4.0 x 3.98 in. Displacement: 300 cid (4.9 liter). Compression ratio: 8.9:1. Net horsepower: 115 at 3000 rpm. Taxable horsepower: 38.4. Net torque: 223 lbs.-ft. at 1600 rpm. Carburetor: One-barrel. (Note: Horsepower and torque may vary with specific model applications; as net horsepower ratings are relative to weight of vehicle.) [VIN Code Y]
ENGINE [Optional V-8]: V-block. OHV. Eight-cylinder. Bore & stroke: 4.0 in. x 3.0 in. Displacement: 302 cid (5.0 liter). Net horsepower: 190 at 3800 rpm. Taxable horsepower: 51.5. Net torque: 285 lbs.-ft. at 2400 rpm. Electronic fuel-injection. (Note: Horsepower and torque may vary with specific model applications; as net horsepower ratings are relative to weight of vehicle.) [VIN Code N]
ENGINE [Optional H.O. V-8]: V-block. OHV. Eight-cylinder. Bore & stroke: 4.0 in. x 3.5 in. Displacement: 351 cid (5.8 liter). Net horsepower: 210 at 4000 rpm. Taxable horsepower: 51.2. Net torque: 305 lbs.-ft. at 2800 rpm. Carburetor: Four-barrel. (Note: Horsepower and torque may vary with specific model applications; as net horsepower ratings are relative to weight of vehicle.) [VIN Code H]
ECONOLINE E-250 CARGO VAN: The new E-250 had a higher GVW rating and heavier-duty front and rear axles than the E-150. It also came with eight-hole wheels. Standard features were the same as those on the E-100, except the three-speed manual was not available in California.
ECONOLINE E-250 SUPER CARGO VAN: See E-150 Cargo Van.
ECONOLINE E-250 WINDOW VAN: This vehicle shared styling and features with the E-100 Window Van, but had greater load capacity.
I.D. DATA: The VIN has 17 symbols. The first three indicate the manufacturer, make and type of vehicle. The fourth symbol indicates the GVW range. The fifth, sixth and seventh symbols indicate the series and body style. The eighth symbol indicates the type of engine. The ninth symbol is a check digit. The 10th symbol (a letter) indicates model year. The 11th symbol indicates the assembly plant. The remaining symbols are the sequential production number starting with 100001 at each plant.

Model	Body Type	Price	Weight	Prod. Total
E-250 Econoline Van — 3/4-Ton — 138 in. w.b. — Six				
E-240	Cargo Van	10,561	4278	Note 1
E-250	Window Van	10,831	4307	Note 1
E-250 Econoline SuperVan — 3/4-Ton — 138 in. w.b. — Six				
S-240	Cargo Van	11,222	4586	Note 1

NOTE 1: Model year production: [All Econolines] 194,875.

ENGINE [Base Six; F-350/F-350 HDE]: Inline. OHV. Six-cylinder (heavy-duty). Bore & stroke: 4.0 x 3.98 in. Displacement: 300 cid (4.9 liter). Compression ratio: 8.9:1. Net horsepower: 115 at 3000 rpm. Taxable horsepower: 38.4. Net torque: 223 lbs.-ft. at 1600 rpm. Carburetor: One-barrel. (Note: Horsepower and torque may vary with specific model applications; as net horsepower ratings are relative to weight of vehicle.) [VIN Code Y]

ENGINE [Optional V-8]: V-block. OHV. Eight-cylinder. Bore & stroke: 4.0 in. x 3.0 in. Displacement: 302 cid (5.0 liter). Net horsepower: 190 at 3800 rpm. Taxable horsepower: 51.5. Net torque: 285 lbs.-ft. at 2400 rpm. Electronic fuel-injection. (Note: Horsepower and torque may vary with specific model applications; as net horsepower ratings are relative to weight of vehicle.) [VIN Code N]

ENGINE [Optional H.O. V-8]: V-block. OHV. Eight-cylinder. Bore & stroke: 4.0 in. x 3.5 in. Displacement: 351 cid (5.8 liter). Net horsepower: 210 at 4000 rpm. Taxable horsepower: 51.2. Net torque: 305 lbs.-ft. at 2800 rpm. Carburetor: Four-barrel. (Note: Horsepower and torque may vary with specific model applications; as net horsepower ratings are relative to weight of vehicle.) [VIN Code H]

ECONOLINE E-350 CARGO VAN: This was the top-of-the-line Econoline Van. It had heavy-duty front and rear shocks and a greater load capacity than the other models. Standard features were the same as the E-100.

ECONOLINE E-350 SUPER CARGO VAN: See E-150 Super Cargo Van.

ECONOLINE E-350 WINDOW VAN: See E-250 Window Van.

ECONOLINE E-350 SUPER WINDOW VAN: See E-150 Super Cargo Van.

ECONOLINE E-350 CUTAWAY VAN: See 1985 E-250 Cutaway Van.

ECONOLINE E-350 PARCEL DELIVERY: See 1985 E-250 Parcel Delivery.

I.D. DATA: The VIN has 17 symbols. The first three indicate the manufacturer; make; and type of vehicle. The fourth symbol indicates the GVW range. The fifth; sixth and seventh symbols indicate the series and body style. The eighth symbol indicates the type of engine. The ninth symbol is a check digit. The 10th symbol (a letter) indicates model year. The 11th symbol indicates the assembly plant. The remaining symbols are the sequential production number starting with 100001 at each plant.

Model	Body Type	Price	Weight	Prod. Total
E-350 Econoline Van — 1-Ton — 138 in. w.b. — Six				
E-340	Cargo Van	11,264	4411	Note 1
E-350	Window Van	11,534	4440	Note 1
E-350 Econoline SuperVan — 1-Ton — 138 in. w.b. — Six				
S-340	Cargo Van	12,322	4728	Note 1
S-350	Window Van	12,593	4767	Note 1
E-350 Econoline Cutaway Van — 1-Ton — 176 in. w.b. — Six				
E-37B	Cutaway	11,940	4138	Note 1
E-380	Parcel Delivery	—	—	Note 1

NOTE 1: Model year production: [All Econolines] 194,875.

ENGINE [Base Six; F-350/F-350 HDE]: Inline. OHV. Six-cylinder (heavy-duty). Bore & stroke: 4.0 x 3.98 in. Displacement: 300 cid (4.9 liter). Compression ratio: 8.9:1. Net horsepower: 115 at 3000 rpm. Taxable horsepower: 38.4. Net torque: 223 lbs.-ft. at 1600 rpm. Carburetor: One-barrel. (Note: Horsepower and torque may vary with specific model applications; as net horsepower ratings are relative to weight of vehicle.) [VIN Code Y]

ENGINE [Optional H.O. V-8]: V-block. OHV. Eight-cylinder. Bore & stroke: 4.0 in. x 3.5 in. Displacement: 351 cid (5.8 liter). Net horsepower: 210 at 4000 rpm. Taxable horsepower: 51.2. Net torque: 305 lbs.-ft. at 2800 rpm. Carburetor: Four-barrel. (Note: Horsepower and torque may vary with specific model applications; as net horsepower ratings are relative to weight of vehicle.) [VIN Code H]

ENGINE [Optional F-350/F-350 HDE; Heavy-duty Diesel V-8]: V-block. OHV. Eight-cylinder. Diesel. Bore & stroke: 4.0 in. x 4.18 in. Displacement: 420 cid (6.9 liter). Net horsepower: 170 at 3300 rpm. Taxable horsepower: 51.2. Net torque: 315 lbs.-ft. at 1400 rpm. Fuel-injected. (Note: Horsepower and torque may vary with specific model applications; as net horsepower ratings are relative to weight of vehicle.) [VIN Code 1]

ENGINE [Optional F-350 HDE Only; Heavy-duty V-8]: V-block. OHV. Eight-cylinder. Bore & stroke: 4.36 in. x 3.85 in. Displacement: 460 cid (7.5 liter). Net horsepower: 214 at 3600 rpm. Taxable horsepower: 52.5. Net torque: 362 lbs.-ft. at 1800 rpm. Carburetor: Four-barrel. (Note: Horsepower and torque may vary with specific model applications; as net horsepower ratings are relative to weight of vehicle.) [VIN Code L]

CHASSIS: Wheelbase: 124 in. (E-150); 138 in. (F-150 SuperVan/F-250/F-350); Overall length: 186.8 in. (124 in. wheelbase); 206.8 in. (138 in. wheelbase); 226.8 in. (138 in. wheelbase SuperVan). GVW: 5,250-6,300 lbs. (E-150); 6,800-7,900 lbs. (E-250); 8,900-10,900 lbs. (E-350). Tires: P205/75R x 15 XL (E-150); LT215/85R x 16D (E-250); LT235/85R x 16E (E-350)

POWERTRAIN OPTIONS: Engines: 5.0L EFI V-8. 5.8L H.O. V-8. 6.9L Diesel V-8; 7.5L V-8. Transmissions: Four-speed manual with overdrive transmission. SelectShift automatic. Automatic overdrive.

CONVENIENCE OPTIONS: XL Package includes vinyl bucket seats; front compartment carpeting; color-keyed door trim panels; leather tone inserts on instrument panel; courtesy lights; interval wipers; bright grille; front and rear bumpers; and low-mount swing-away mirrors. Cloth-and-vinyl captain's chairs. Air-conditioning. High-capacity air-conditioner and auxiliary heater. Heavy-duty battery. Chrome rear step bumper. Chrome bumpers. Super engine cooling. Auxiliary fuel tank. Ammeter and oil pressure gauges. Privacy glass. Swing-out rear door and/or cargo door glass. Tinted glass. Handling package. Deluxe insulation package. Light and Convenience group. Bright low-mount swing-away mirrors. Bright swing-out recreation mirrors. Deluxe two-tone paint. Power door locks. Speed control. Tilt steering wheel. Heavy-duty front and rear springs. Trailer Towing Packages. Wheelcovers. AM/FM monaural radio. AM/FM stereo radio. AM/digital clock radio; AM/FM stereo radio with cassette player. Hinged bodyside cargo door.

E-150 CLUB WAGON: Club Wagon styling was unchanged for 1986. Among the standard features were: Bucket front seats and rear bench seat with quick- release feature. Low-angle steering wheel with full-width horn pad on the spokes. Front door vent windows. Ashtray and pockets molded into the engine cover. Power steering and brakes. 23.4-gal. fuel tank. Four-speed manual with overdrive transmission. Gas pressurized shock absorbers. Body on frame construction. Twin-I-Beam independent front suspension. Club Wagon colors for 1986 were: Dark grey (metallic); Dark walnut (metallic); Medium silver (metallic); Dark shadow blue (metallic); Medium canyon red (metallic); Light desert tan; Light regatta blue (metallic); Desert tan (metallic); Light regatta blue; and Colonial white.

E-250 CLUB WAGON: The slightly more heavy-duty E-250 came with most of the same features as the E-150, with the exception of standard SelectShift automatic transmission.

E-350 SUPER WAGON: This heavy-duty wagon provided 20 in. more inside space than regular Club Wagons. It could hold up to 15 passengers with optional seating packages.

I.D. DATA: The VIN has 17 symbols. The first three indicate the manufacturer, make and type of vehicle. The fourth symbol indicates the GVW range. The fifth, sixth and seventh symbols indicate the series and body style. The eighth symbol indicates the type of engine. The ninth symbol is a check digit. The 10th symbol (a letter) indicates model year. The 11th symbol indicates the assembly plant. The remaining symbols are the sequential production number starting with 100001 at each plant.

Model	Body Type	Price	Weight	Prod. Total
E-150 Club Wagon — 1/2-Ton — 124 in. w.b. — Six				
E-150	Club Wagon	12,274	4326	Note 1
E-250 Club Wagon — 3/4-Ton — 138 in. w.b. — Six				
E-250	Club Wagon	13,838	4931	Note 1
E-150 Club Wagon — 1-Ton — 138 in. w.b. — Six				
E-350	Super Wagon	14,849	5238	Note 1

NOTE 1: Model year production: [All Club Wagons] 28,929.

ENGINE [Base Six; F-350/F-350 HDE]: Inline. OHV. Six-cylinder (heavy-duty). Bore & stroke: 4.0 x 3.98 in. Displacement: 300 cid (4.9 liter). Compression ratio: 8.9:1. Net horsepower: 115 at 3000 rpm. Taxable horsepower: 38.4. Net torque: 223 lbs.-ft. at 1600 rpm. Carburetor: One-barrel. (Note: Horsepower and torque may vary with specific model applications; as net horsepower ratings are relative to weight of vehicle.) [VIN Code Y]

ENGINE [Optional V-8]: V-block. OHV. Eight-cylinder. Bore & stroke: 4.0 in. x 3.0 in. Displacement: 302 cid (5.0 liter). Net horsepower: 190 at 3800 rpm. Taxable horsepower: 51.5. Net torque: 285 lbs.-ft. at 2400 rpm. Electronic fuel-injection. (Note: Horsepower and torque may vary with specific model applications; as net horsepower ratings are relative to weight of vehicle.) [VIN Code N]

ENGINE [Optional H.O. V-8]: V-block. OHV. Eight-cylinder. Bore & stroke: 4.0 in. x 3.5 in. Displacement: 351 cid (5.8 liter). Net horsepower: 210 at 4000 rpm. Taxable horsepower: 51.2. Net torque: 305 lbs.-ft. at 2800 rpm. Carburetor: Four-barrel. (Note: Horsepower and torque may vary with specific model applications; as net horsepower ratings are relative to weight of vehicle.) [VIN Code H]

ENGINE [Optional F-350/F-350 HDE; Heavy-duty Diesel V-8]: V-block. OHV. Eight-cylinder. Diesel. Bore & stroke: 4.0 in. x 4.18 in. Displacement: 420 cid (6.9 liter). Net horsepower: 170 at 3300 rpm. Taxable horsepower: 51.2. Net torque: 315 lbs.-ft. at 1400 rpm. Fuel-injected. (Note: Horsepower and torque may vary with specific model applications; as net horsepower ratings are relative to weight of vehicle.) [VIN Code 1]

ENGINE [Optional F-350 HDE Only; Heavy-duty V-8]: V-block. OHV. Eight-cylinder. Bore & stroke: 4.36 in. x 3.85 in. Displacement: 460 cid (7.5 liter). Net horsepower: 214 at 3600 rpm. Taxable horsepower: 52.5. Net torque: 362 lbs.-ft. at 1800 rpm. Carburetor: Four-barrel. (Note: Horsepower and torque may vary with specific model applications; as net horsepower ratings are relative to weight of vehicle.) [VIN Code L]

CHASSIS: Wheelbase: 124 in. (E-150); 138 in. (F-150 SuperVan/F-250/F-350); Overall length: 186.8 in. (124 in. wheelbase); 206.8 in. (138 in. wheelbase); 226.8 in. (138 in. wheelbase SuperVan). GVW: 5,250-6,300 lbs. (E-150); 6,800-7,900 lbs. (E-250); 8,900-10,900 lbs. (E-350). Tires: P205/75R x 15 XL (E-150); LT215/85R x 16D (E-250); LT235/85R x 16E (E-350)

POWERTRAIN OPTIONS: Engines: 5.0L EFI V-8. 5.8L H.O. V-8. 6.9L Diesel V-8; 7.5L V-8. Transmissions: Four-speed manual with overdrive transmission. SelectShift automatic. Automatic overdrive.

CONVENIENCE OPTIONS: Most of the same items and packages that were offered on the Econoline plus: 7-, 8-, 11-, 12- and 15-passenger seating packages. Club Wagon XL Package with AM radio; interval windshield wipers; courtesy light switches on all doors (a three-way switch on the rear dome lamp); tinted glass; inside hood release; ammeter and oil pressure gauges; a high-output heater; rear door positioners; premium vinyl seat trim; stepwell pads on the front doors and sliding bodyside door; seat belt reminder chime; bright low-mount swing-away mirrors; bright bumpers and window moldings; color-keyed front; bodyside and rear door trim panels; color-keyed carpeting; front door map pockets. (Trim Credit Options deleted the front door trim panels; the bodyside and rear trim panels; and the garnish moldings; and added a black insulated floor mat and Argent silver bumpers.) Club Wagon XLT Package with chrome grille; chrome bumpers with black rub strip; deluxe wheelcovers; lower bodyside moldings; lower bodyside accent paint; reclining front captain's chairs and rear bench seat upholstered in cloth-and-vinyl; full-length cloth headliners; electronic digital clock; headlights-on alert chime; dual beam/dome map light and underhood light; and right-hand visor mirror. A combination rear seat/bed option was available in the E150 XLT. It could be used as either a three-passenger bench seat or a larger 62 in. x 72 in. bed.

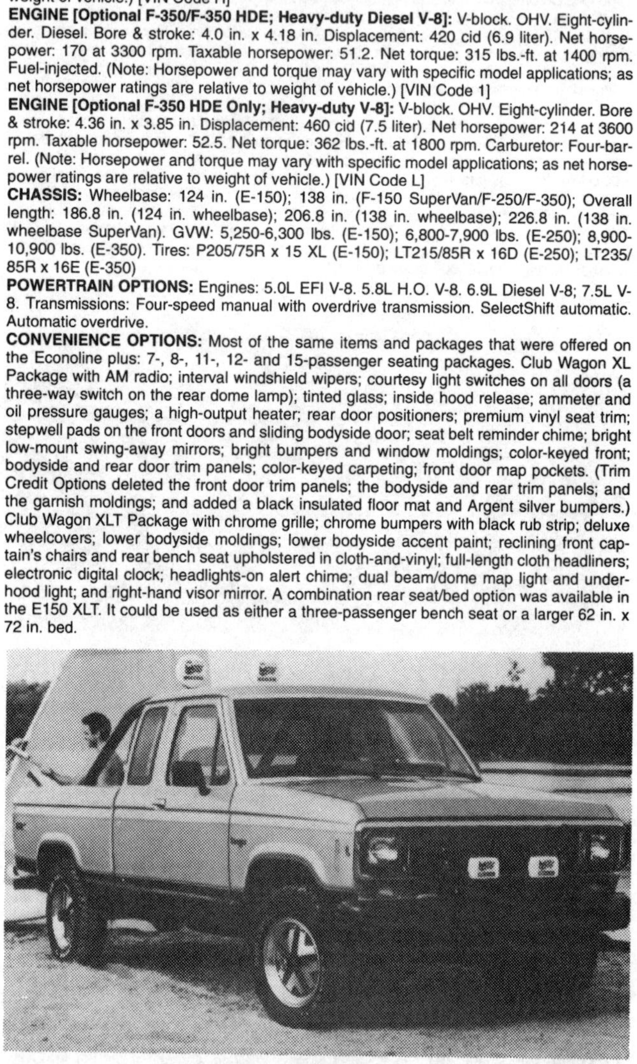

1986 Ford 1/2-Ton Ranger STX Supercab Mini-Pickup 4x4 (FMC)

RANGER PICKUP: Styling was essentially unchanged for 1986. Among standard features were: Power brakes. Ammeter, temperature and oil gauges. Trip odometer. Interval wipers. Instrument panel storage bin. Lockable glove box. Inside hood release. Day/night rearview mirror. Color-keyed seat belts with comfort regulator feature. Halogen headlights. Bright grille and windshield moldings. Black fold-away mirrrors. Five-speed manual transmission with overdrive. Ranger buyers in 1986 now had their choice of two cabs, regular or Supercab. The latter provided nearly 17 in. of additional cargo length behind the front seat. Optional rear vinyl jump seats were available at extra cost. The Supercab came only with a 6 ft. box, but the regular cab Ranger could be had with an 6 ft. or 7 ft. box. Exterior colors

for 1986 Rangers included: Dark canyon red; Medium silver (metallic); Raven black; Colonial white; Desert tan; Light regatta blue; Dark grey (metallic); Dark spruce (metallic); silver clearcoat (metallic); Dark canyon red (metallic); Dark shadow blue (metallic); Desert tan (metallic); Bright regatta blue clearcoat (metallic); Light chestnut clearcoat (metallic); Dark walnut (metallic); and Bright canyon red. Deluxe Tu-Toning featured the accent color applied to the mid-bodyside and tailgate, plus bright upper and lower bodyside molding paint breaks.

RANGER S PICKUP: The S was more basic than the base model. It had fewer frills. Low price and top economy were its main selling features. It was only offered with the regular cab.

I.D. DATA: The VIN has 17 symbols. The first three indicate the manufacturer, make and type of vehicle. The fourth symbol indicates the GVW range. The fifth, sixth and seventh symbols indicate the series and body style. The eighth symbol indicates the type of engine. The ninth symbol is a check digit. The 10th symbol (a letter) indicates model year. The 11th symbol indicates the assembly plant. The remaining symbols are the sequential production number starting with 100001 at each plant.

Model	Body Type	Price	Weight	Prod. Total
Ranger — 1/2-Ton — 107.5 in. w.b. — Four				
R-10	"S" Styleside	6388	2638	Note 1
R-10	Styleside	7229	2638	Note 1
Ranger — 1/2-Ton — 113.9 in. w.b. — Four				
R-10	Styleside	6991	2545	Note 1
Ranger Supercab — 1/2-Ton — 125 in. w.b. — Four				
R-14	Supercab Pickup	8217	2842	Note 1

NOTE 1: Model year production: [All Rangers] 279,251.

ENGINE [Four; California]: Inline. Overhead valve. Four-cylinder. Bore & stroke: 3.78 x 3.13. Displacement: 140 cid (2.3 liter). Compression ratio: 9.5:1. Brake horsepower: 90 at 4000 rpm. Taxable horsepower: 22.8. Torque: 130 lbs.-ft. at 1800 rpm. Electronic fuel-injection. [VIN Code A]

ENGINE [Four; Except California]: Inline. Overhead valve. Four-cylinder. Bore & stroke: 3.52 x 3.13. Displacement: 122 cid (2.0 liter). Brake horsepower: 73 at 4000 rpm. Taxable horsepower: 19.8. Torque: 107 lbs.-ft. at 2400 rpm. Electronic fuel-injection. [VIN Code C]

ENGINE [Four; Turbo-Diese]l: Inline. Overhead valve. Four-cylinder. Bore & stroke: 3.59 x 3.54. Displacement: 143 cid (2.3 liter). Brake horsepower: 86 at 4200 rpm. Taxable horsepower: 20.6. Torque: 134 lbs.-ft. at 2000 rpm. Fuel-injection. [VIN Code E]

ENGINE: V-block. OHV. Six-cylinder. Bore & stroke: 3.66 x 2.83. Displacement: 179 cid (2.9 liter). Compression ratio: 9.3:1. Brake horsepower: 140 at 4600 rpm. Taxable horsepower: 32.1. Torque: 170 lbs.-ft. at 2600 rpm. Electronic fuel-injection. [VIN Code T]

CHASSIS: Wheelbase: 107.9 in; 113.9 in; 125 in. in Supercab. Overall length: 175.6 in. (107.9 in. w.b.); 187.6 in. (113.9 in. w.b.); 192.7 in. in Supercab. Overall width: 66.9 in. Overall height: 64 in. (4x2); 64.1 in. (4x2 Supercab); 66.7 in. (4x4). GVW: 3820-4740. Tires: P195/75R x 14SL; P185/75R x 14SL (S); P195/75R x 15SL (4x4).

POWERTRAIN OPTIONS: Engines: 2.3 liter Turbo Diesel; 2.9L V-6 EFI. Transmissions: Automatic with overdrive transmission.

CONVENIENCE OPTIONS: Four-Wheel Drive with manual locking free-running hubs; Twin-Traction Beam independent front suspension; front stabilizer bar; two-speed manual shift transfer case; power steering. Touch-Drive electric shift (4x4). Power steering. Speed control/tilt steering wheel. Cloth contoured bench seat. Cloth 60/40 split bench seat. Sport cloth bucket seats. Overhead console/digital clock. Cloth headliner. Tachometer. AM/FM stereo radio. AM/FM stereo radio with cassette player. Electronic AM/FM stereo radio with cassette tape player. Power windows and door locks. Bright low-mount swing-away mirrors. Tinted glass. Black rear step bumper. Chrome rear step bumper. Chrome Package includes bright bumpers; low-mount swing-away mirrors; and special tailgate applique. Sliding rear window. Handling package. Heavy-duty front suspension package (4x4). Camper package. Auxiliary fuel tank. Super engine cooling. Payload packages. Limited-slip rear axle. Cast aluminum wheels (4x4). Black sidewall all-terrain tires. White sidewall all-season tires. Black sidewall all-season tires. Raised white-letter off-road tires. California emissions system. High-altitude emissions system. Cargo cover in Supercab. Dual captian's chairs in Supercab. Rear vinyl jump seat in Supercab. Pivoting quarter windows in Supercab. XL Package with (regular cab only; in addition to or in place of standard features) 2.9L V-6 engine; knitted vinyl contoured bench seat; color-keyed floor mat; cloth headliner and moldings; interval windshield wipers; power steering; bright front bumper with black rub strip; bright wheel lip moldings; bright rear window insert; deluxe wheel trim; and tinted glass. STX Package with (in addition to or in place of items on XL) gas-pressurized shocks; front stabilizer bar; P205/70R x 14SL raised white-letter tires on 4x2s; power steering; two-tone paint; black grille; black bumpers; reclining bucket seats; captain's chairs in Supercab; AM/FM stereo radio; skid plates on 4x4; and P215/75R x 15SL tires on 4x4. XLT Package for Supercab only with (in addition to or in place of items on STX) three-passenger 60/40 split bench seat with cloth upholstery; cloth door trim panels with map pockets and carpeted lower sections; tinted pivoting vent windows; 16 oz. color-keyed carpeting; color-keyed leather wrapped A-frame steering wheel; and inside cargo cover.

1986 Ford 1/2-Ton F-150 Lariat XLT Styleside Pickup (FMC)

F-150 PICKUP: Basic styling remained unchanged for 1986. Standard features included: Twin-I-Beam independent front suspension (4x4s had Twin-Traction Beam Independent front suspension). Chrome front bumper. Light Argent silver grille with bright surround molding. Bright windshield molding. Black fold-away door-mounted mirrors. Rectangular Halogen headlights. Bright hubcaps and tailgate handle. Rope tie-down holes (Styleside). All-vinyl seat trim. Pivoting vent windows. Locking glove box. Ammeter, oil pressure, fuel and temperature gauges. Lighted ashtray. Cigarette lighter. AM radio. Coat hook. Left-hand courtesy light switch. Black steering wheel. Vinyl sun visors. Power brakes. Power steering. 10 in. clutch. Three-speed manual transmission. Flareside and Styleside boxes with regular or Supercab cabs were offered. Interior colors for 1986 were: Canyon red; chestnut; Regatta blue; and Medium Gray (not available on XLT Lariat; Supercab and Crew Cab). Exterior colors included: Raven black; Dark canyon red; Colonial white; Light regatta blue; Medium silver (metallic); Dark shadow blue (metallic); Dark grey (metallic); Light desert tan; Bright canyon red; Desert tan (metallic); and Dark spruce (metallic). Tu-Tone treatments included: (Deluxe) Accent color covering center bodyside area and tailgate and includes mid-bodyside tape stripe and lower bodyside protection molding on single rear wheel regular cab and Supercab Styleside models; mid- and lower-bodyside tape on other models; (Combination) Included accent color applied to roof and Deluxe Tu-Tone treatment (as described). No tape or molding paint break was utilized on the roof; (Victoria) With accent color applied to hood; upper fenders; around windows and on lower bodyside (this included lower bodyside protection molding and tape upper paint break.)

1986 Ford Pickup

I.D. DATA: The VIN has 17 symbols. The first three indicate the manufacturer, make and type of vehicle. The fourth symbol indicates the GVW range. The fifth, sixth and seventh symbols indicate the series and body style. The eighth symbol indicates the type of engine. The ninth symbol is a check digit. The 10th symbol (a letter) indicates model year. The 11th symbol indicates the assembly plant. The remaining symbols are the sequential production number starting with 100001 at each plant.

Model	Body Type	Price	Weight	Prod. Total
F-150 — 1/2-Ton — 116.8 in. w.b. — Six				
F-15	Flareside 6.5 ft.	8625	3412	Note 1
F-15	Styleside 6.75 ft.	8373	3315	Note 1
F-15	Styleside 8 ft.	8548	3411	Note 1
F-150 Super cab — 1/2-Ton — 133 in. w.b. — Six				
X-15	Styleside 6.75 ft.	10,272	3883	Note 1
X-15	Styleside 8 ft.	10,446	3974	Note 1

NOTE 1: Model year production: [F-150] 360,698.

ENGINE [Base Six; F-350/F-350 HDE]: Inline. OHV. Six-cylinder (heavy-duty). Bore & stroke: 4.0 x 3.98 in. Displacement: 300 cid (4.9 liter). Compression ratio: 8.9:1. Net horsepower: 115 at 3000 rpm. Taxable horsepower: 38.4. Net torque: 223 lbs.-ft. at 1600 rpm. Carburetor: One-barrel. (Note: Horsepower and torque may vary with specific model applications; as net horsepower ratings are relative to weight of vehicle.) [VIN Code Y]

ENGINE [Optional V-8]: V-block. OHV. Eight-cylinder. Bore & stroke: 4.0 in. x 3.0 in. Displacement: 302 cid (5.0 liter). Net horsepower: 190 at 3800 rpm. Taxable horsepower: 51.5. Net torque: 285 lbs.-ft. at 2400 rpm. Electronic fuel-injection. (Note: Horsepower and torque may vary with specific model applications; as net horsepower ratings are relative to weight of vehicle.) [VIN Code N]

ENGINE [Optional H.O. V-8]: V-block. OHV. Eight-cylinder. Bore & stroke: 4.0 in. x 3.5 in. Displacement: 351 cid (5.8 liter). Net horsepower: 210 at 4000 rpm. Taxable horsepower: 51.2. Net torque: 305 lbs.-ft. at 2800 rpm. Carburetor: Four-barrel. (Note: Horsepower and torque may vary with specific model applications; as net horsepower ratings are relative to weight of vehicle.) [VIN Code H]

F-250 PICKUP: The F-250 was only offered with the 8 ft. Styleside box. It could be had in regular or F-250 HDE (heavy-duty engine) Supercab versions. The Supercab had room behind the front seat for a forward-facing rear seat which folded down flat. Two center facing jump seats were optional. When folded out of the way, there was an extra 29.8 cu. ft. of interior load space for cargo. Most standard F-250 features were the same as those offered on the F-150, plus a four-speed manual transmission and (on F-250 HDEs) an 11 in. clutch.

I.D. DATA: The VIN has 17 symbols. The first three indicate the manufacturer, make and type of vehicle. The fourth symbol indicates the GVW range. The fifth, sixth and seventh symbols indicate the series and body style. The eighth symbol indicates the type of engine. The ninth symbol is a check digit. The 10th symbol (a letter) indicates model year. The 11th symbol indicates the assembly plant. The remaining symbols are the sequential production number starting with 100001 at each plant.

Model	Body Type	Price	Weight	Prod. Total
F-250 — 3/4-Ton — 133 in. w.b. — Six				
F-25	Styleside 8 ft.	9646	3708	Note 1
F-250 Supercab — 3/4-Ton — 155 in. w.b. — Six				
X-25	Styleside 8 ft.	11,645	4465	Note 1

NOTE 1: Model year production: [F-250] 154,778.

ENGINE [Base Six; F-250/F-250 HDE]: Inline. OHV. Six-cylinder (heavy-duty). Bore & stroke: 4.0 x 3.98 in. Displacement: 300 cid (4.9 liter). Compression ratio: 8.9:1. Net horsepower: 115 at 3000 rpm. Taxable horsepower: 38.4. Net torque: 223 lbs.-ft. at 1600 rpm. Carburetor: One-barrel. (Note: Horsepower and torque may vary with specific model applications; as net horsepower ratings are relative to weight of vehicle.) [VIN Code Y]

ENGINE [Optional V-8]: V-block. OHV. Eight-cylinder. Bore & stroke: 4.0 in. x 3.0 in. Displacement: 302 cid (5.0 liter). Net horsepower: 190 at 3800 rpm. Taxable horsepower: 51.5. Net torque: 285 lbs.-ft. at 2400 rpm. Electronic fuel-injection. (Note: Horsepower and torque may vary with specific model applications; as net horsepower ratings are relative to weight of vehicle.) [VIN Code N]

ENGINE [Optional H.O. V-8]: V-block. OHV. Eight-cylinder. Bore & stroke: 4.0 in. x 3.5 in. Displacement: 351 cid (5.8 liter). Net horsepower: 210 at 4000 rpm. Taxable horsepower: 51.2. Net torque: 305 lbs.-ft. at 2800 rpm. Carburetor: Four-barrel. (Note: Horsepower and torque may vary with specific model applications; as net horsepower ratings are relative to weight of vehicle.) [VIN Code H]

F-350 PICKUP: The F-350 was offered in 8 ft. Styleside boxes with regular or Crew Cabs. The latter featured four doors and two full-width bench seats. The regular Cab F-350 had dual rear wheels. Crew Cab models could be ordered with dual rear wheels or single rear wheels. An 11 in. clutch and four-speed manual transmission were standard on all F-350s.

I.D. DATA: The VIN has 17 symbols. The first three indicate the manufacturer, make, and type of vehicle. The fourth symbol indicates the GVW range. The fifth, sixth and seventh symbols indicate the series and body style. The eighth symbol indicates the type of engine. The ninth symbol is a check digit. The 10th symbol (a letter) indicates model year. The 11th symbol indicates the assembly plant. The remaining symbols are the sequential production number starting with 100001 at each plant.

Model	Body Type	Price	Weight	Prod. Total
F-350 — 1-Ton — 133 in. w.b. — Six				
F-35	Chassis & Cab	10,117	3574	Note 1
F-35	Styleside	12,228	4332	Note 1
F-350 — 1-Ton — 137 in. w.b. — Six				
F-37	Chassis & Cab	10,429	3930	Note 1
F-350 Crew Cab — 1-Ton — 167 in. w.b. — Six				
W-37	Chassis & Cab	10,515	4059	Note 1
W-35	Styleside	13,171	4809	Note 1

ENGINE [Base Six; F-350/F-350 HDE]: Inline. OHV. Six-cylinder (heavy-duty). Bore & stroke: 4.0 x 3.98 in. Displacement: 300 cid (4.9 liter). Compression ratio: 8.9:1. Net horsepower: 115 at 3000 rpm. Taxable horsepower: 38.4. Net torque: 223 lbs.-ft. at 1600 rpm. Carburetor: One-barrel. (Note: Horsepower and torque may vary with specific model applications; as net horsepower ratings are relative to weight of vehicle.) [VIN Code Y]

ENGINE [Optional V-8]: V-block. OHV. Eight-cylinder. Bore & stroke: 4.0 in. x 3.0 in. Displacement: 302 cid (5.0 liter). Net horsepower: 190 at 3800 rpm. Taxable horsepower: 51.5. Net torque: 285 lbs.-ft. at 2400 rpm. Electronic fuel-injection. (Note: Horsepower and torque may vary with specific model applications; as net horsepower ratings are relative to weight of vehicle.) [VIN Code N]

ENGINE [Optional H.O. V-8]: V-block. OHV. Eight-cylinder. Bore & stroke: 4.0 in. x 3.5 in. Displacement: 351 cid (5.8 liter). Net horsepower: 210 at 4000 rpm. Taxable horsepower: 51.2. Net torque: 305 lbs.-ft. at 2800 rpm. Carburetor: Four-barrel. (Note: Horsepower and torque may vary with specific model applications; as net horsepower ratings are relative to weight of vehicle.) [VIN Code H]

CHASSIS: Wheelbase: 116.8 in. (F-150); 133 in. (Styleside); 138.8 in. (F-150 Supercab); 155 in. (F-150/F-250 HDE Supercab); 168.4 in. (F-350 Crew Cab). Overall length: 189.3 in. (Flareside); 192.1 in. (F-150 Styleside); 208.3 in. (Styleside); 214.1 in. (F-150 Supercab); 230.3 in. (F-150/F-250 Supercab); 243.7 in. (F-350 Crew Cab). GVW: 4,800-6,250 lbs. (F-150); 6,300-8,800 lbs. (F-250); 8,800-11,000 lbs. (F-350). Tires: P195/75R x 15SL (F-150); LT215/85R x 16C (F-250); LT235/85R x 16E (F-250 HDE/F-350).

POWERTRAIN OPTIONS: Engines: 5.0 liter EFI (Electronic Fuel-Injection) V-8 (F-150/F-250); 5.8 liter H.O. V-8 (All); 7.5 liter V-8 (F-250 HDE/F-350); 6.9 liter Diesel V-8 (F-250 HDE/F-350). Four-wheel drive F-350s and those with dual rear wheels came with the 5.8 liter V-8; except in California. Transmissions: Four-speed manual transmission (F-150/F-250). Four-speed manual with overdrive (F-150/F-250). Automatic overdrive (F-150/F-250). SelectShift automatic.

CONVENIENCE OPTIONS: Four-wheel drive with power brakes; manual locking free- running hubs; power steering; two-speed transfer case; and four-speed manual transmissionb. Automatic locking hubs (F-150 4x4). Chrome grille. Black vinyl bodyside molding with bright insert (Styleside). Bright wheel lip moldings (Styleside). Electronic AM/FM stereo radio with cassette player. AM/FM stereo (speakers mounted in door panels). AM/FM stereo radio with cassette tape player. Radio credit option (deleted standard AM radio for credit). Air-conditioning. High-output heater (Standard with 6.9 liter diesel). Convenience Group with interval wipers; 12 in. day/night mirror; right-hand visor vanity mirror; carpeted map pocket on lower doors; headlights-on audible warning; and courtesy light switch on right-hand door. Headliner and deluxe insulation package. Electronic digital clock. Speed control (with resume feature). Light Group with underhood work light, plus lights in glove box; under instrument panel; dual beam dome/map light; cargo box light; headlights-on audible warning; and courtesy light switch on right-hand door. Power door locks/windows (not available with Crew Cab). Manual steering (F-150 4x2). Tinted glass. Tinted sliding rear window. Tilt steering wheel. Tinted glass. Bright low-mount swing away 8 in. x 5 in. mirrors (right-hand convex glass). Bright swing out recreational mirrors (6-3/4 in. x 9-1/2 in). Reclining captain's chairs with console in Supercab. Folding center-facing jump seat in Supercab. Auxiliary fuel tank. Handling Package includes front and rear stabilizer bars; heavy-duty rear springs on 4x4 with 6.9 liter Diesel; heavy-duty front and rear shocks (quad front on F-150 regular cab 4x4); and heavy-duty front springs. Engine block heater. Super engine cooling package. Trailer towing package. Camper package. Heavy-duty battery. Tachometer with trip odometer. Roof clearance lights. Exterior Protection Group with front bumper guards and front bumper rub strip. Skid plates (4x4s). Argent silver step type rear bumper for Stylesides. Chrome step type rear bumper for Stylesides. Deluxe wheelcovers. Sport wheelcovers (F-150). XL Package with (in addition to or in place of items on standard model) bright wheel lip moldings and rear window molding insert; dual bodyside accent paint stripes on single rear wheel Stylesides; left-hand and right-hand courtesy light switches; bright dome light bezel; bright surround door trim panel moldings; color-keyed floor mat; wood-tone applique for instrument panel; folding fully-covered seatback (fixed front and folding rear on Crew Cabs); deluxe seat belts; cloth-and-vinyl seat trim; aluminum scuff plates; cloth headlining; and black steering wheel. XLT Package with (in addition to or in place of items on the XL) lower bodyside moldings with protective black vinyl insert and distinctive aluminum Styleside tailgate applique with red reflective lower section; color-keyed carpeting; door trim panels with bright molding; cloth door trim inserts; carpeted lower door panels with map pockets; and soft-wrapped steering wheel with wood-tone insert.

HISTORICAL: Model year production by line was: [Ranger] 279,251; [Bronco II] 109,875; [Aerostar Wagon] 110,231; [Aerostar Van] 33,514; [F-150] 360,698; [F-250] 154,778; [F-350] 75,920; [Bronco] 57,448; [Econoline] 194,875; [Club Wagon] 28,929; [Grand Total] 1,405,519. Calendar year sales hit a record high of 1,381,438 light-, medium- and heavy-duty models. Ford re-captured the first rank on the U.S. sales charts.

GMC

1911-1986

1936 GMC Pickup

By Robert C. Ackerson

Early GMC light-duty trucks, like their larger capacity counterparts, enjoyed a solid reputation for reliability and rugged construction. During World War I, the Model 16 1-ton truck was used extensively, by the U.S. Army, as an ambulance. After the war, it became the basis for the GMC K Series.

During the '20s, GMC turned to several manufacturers for its truck engines. In 1927, the GMC 1-ton models switched to a six-cylinder Buick-built motor. A year later, in 1928, the T-11 light-duty line evolved from a Pontiac truck that was offered just one year. Naturally, the powerplant was a Pontiac six.

The introduction of the 1-ton Model T-19, in 1928, marked a major advance in GMC truck styling. Its headlamps were relocated next to the radiator. The fenders were more deeply crowned and the radiator was chrome-plated. It was a handsome commercial vehicle and combined sales for 1928-1929 raced to 20,000 units.

The GMC-Buick connection lead, in 1931, to the manufacturing of GMC's "own" Buick engines. This development brought an extensive series of GMC trucks with engines, based on Buick designs, that had distinct bore and stroke dimensions for truck use. These powerplants were produced in various displacements. They were used in GMC

trucks with a wide variety of load capacities and remained in production even after optional V-8s were released in 1955. In fact, they survived until the V-6 engine appeared in the 1960s.

During the mid-1930s, GMC trucks gradually shed many styling items associated with the previous decade, such as exterior mounted windshield visors and highly visible hood louvers. As a result, appearance became more streamlined and attractive. By 1937, the design format that survived many years (it was essentially unchanged until the late 1940s) was well established.

The light-duty models had "veed" windshields, bullet-shaped headlamps, rounded fenders and prominent GMC identification on each side of the hood. The 1941 models, with a new 228 cid ohv six-cylinder engine, had fender-mounted headlamps and a grille consisting of a broad base and a narrower top section, both of which had wide, horizontal bars.

This appearance was continued after the war. It lasted until new models were ready for introduction in the summer of 1947. These were modern-looking vehicles with headlights mounted low in the fenders, a simple grille arrangement (with four fluted horizontal bars) and a body whose extremities were rounded and smooth. This general styling format remained virtually unchanged until 1954, but numerous technical changes were incorporated to avoid any suggestion of obsolesence. Most noteworthy, was the

availability of dual-range Hydra-Matic transmission beginning in 1953.

The following year, GMC light-duty trucks were given several major styling revisions, including a one-piece curved windshield, a much broader grille and rectangular parking lamps (positioned at the outer limits of the grille.)

These developments did not, however, change the basic character of GMC trucks. Radical change would have to wait for model year 1955. That year marked the introduction of new models with styling that possessed strong influences of the General Motors automotive divisions. Leading the list of new styling themes was a panoramic windshield. Not far behind was a grille/bumper arrangement that resembled, at least in theme, others seen earlier on Oldsmobiles.

Even Cadillac, it seemed, had a role in the styling of the latest GMC trucks, as evidenced by the visors installed over the headlights. Paralleling Chevrolet's introduction of its Cameo Carrier, GMC released a comparable model called the Suburban Pickup. Both of these models, based on the styling of Nike missile carriers that designer Chuck Jordon observed while in the military, were advanced-guard units. Both foretold the coming of the "fenderless" GMC Wide-Side models in 1958.

Eventually, the influence of automotive styling upon GMC truck design faded. Before it had run its course, a new line of 1960-1961 models appeared with futuristic front ends. By 1964, these developments had run their natural course and GMC trucks returned to front ends that were characterized by simple, horizontal forms and windshields that no longer had "dog-leg" corner posts. New to the GMC line that year were the Handi-Van models with a trim 90 in. wheelbase. They were available with either four- or six-cylinder engines.

By 1967, GMC pickups were totally restyled. The main bodyside creases were lowered. Instead of being just below the beltline, they were now on the feature line that bisected the fender cut-outs into equal semi-circles. This styling was popular. Three years later, when the first Jimmy 4x4 model was introduced, it had a similar appearance.

Introduction of the Jimmy widened GMC's role in the growing RV market and was followed, in 1971, with release of the Sprint. This was GMC's version of the Chevrolet El Camino. At the same time, GMC vans were redesigned along more contemporary lines.

When it came time to update GMC pickups in 1973, the company pulled out all stops. It extended the line to include 3+3 models with six doors and six-passenger accommodations. By 1978, GMC pickups, like those from Chevrolet, were available with diesel engines. That year, the Sprint became the Caballero.

Significant styling changes were made to GMC full-size pickups in 1981. They were intended to improve aerodynamics and, thus, have a positive effect on fuel efficiency. The following year, the company entered the mini-truck market with its S-15 model line. This move was followed by introduction of the Safari mini-van as a 1985 model.

1937 GMC 1/2-Ton Model T-14A Pickup (S. Glasbrenner)

1959 GMC 1/2-Ton Wide-Side Pickup (S. Soloy)

1937 GMC 1/2-Ton Model T-14A Pickup (OCW)

1960 GMC 1/2-Ton Suburban Carryall 4x4 (GMC)

1968 GMC 1/2-Ton Wide-Side Pickup (C. Webb)

1970 GMC 3/4-Ton Wide-Side Pickup (D. Monetti)

1972 GMC 1/2-Ton Wide-Side Pickup

1972 GMC 3/4-Ton Wide-Side "Camper Special" Pickup (GMC)

1976 GMC 1/2-Ton "Jimmy" Utility Wagon 4x4 (GMC)

1984 GMC S-15 "Indy Hauler" Club Cab Pickup (JLM/IMSC)

1912 GMC

1912 GMC Reliance Model H Stake (Steve Schmidt)

MODEL 1,000. LBS. — 1/2-TON — ELECTRIC: GMC offered an electric-powered truck with Renault-style shovel-nose hood. It was rated for a 1,000 lb. payload. This was the first year of the GMC nameplate.

MODEL 2,000 LBS. — 1-TON — ELECTRIC: GMC also offered an electric-powered 1-ton in the first year of the marque.

I.D. DATA: Not available

Model	Body Type	Price	Weight	Prod. Total
1000#	Chassis	1425	—	—
2000#	Chassis	1525	—	—

ENGINE: Electric

CHASSIS: Chain-drive.

TECHNICAL: Battery-powered.

HISTORICAL: First year for GMC nameplate. Company was formed by merger of Rapid and Reliance, two truck firms already under control of General Motors. Both electric and gasoline powered trucks were marketed, but the gasoline versions started a 2-ton capacity and went up to 5-tons. Electrics came in 1/2-, 1-, 2-, 3-, 4-, 5- and 6-ton models.

1913-1915 GMC

1914 GMC Covered Flareboard (OCW)

MODEL 1-1B — 1/2-TON — ELECTRIC: GMC again offered an electric-powered truck rated for a 1,000 lb. payload. During this three-year period, it was marketed for a lower price because batteries were optional at extra cost.

MODEL 2-2B — 1-TON — ELECTRIC: GMC also offered an electric-powered 1-ton again. It, too, was listed for three years at a lower price, which did not include batteries.

I.D. DATA: Not available

Model	Body Type	Price	Weight	Prod. Total
1-1B	Chassis	1200	—	—
2-2B	Chassis	1300	—	—

ENGINE: Electric

CHASSIS: Chain-drive.

TECHNICAL: Battery-powered.

1915 GMC Model 15 Express Truck (OCW)

HISTORICAL: During these years, the seven electric models offered in 1912 were continued, plus a 1-1/2-ton electric was offered. Gasoline trucks now started at 1-1/2-ton capacity and included one 2-ton, four 3-1/2-tons, and five 5-tons.

1916 GMC

1916 GMC 3/4-Ton Model 15 Canopy Express (OCW)

MODEL 15 — 3/4-TON — FOUR-CYLINDER: The Model 15 was the first light-duty GMC gasoline-fueled truck. Handsome express bodies were available to fit the 1,500 lb. payload chassis.

MODEL 21 — 1-TON — FOUR-CYLINDER: GMC's first 1-ton gasoline truck was introduced late in 1916.

I.D. DATA: Serial number on left-hand front spring horn. Motor number on left side of crankcase. Serial numbers: [Model 15] 15851 to 152650; [Model 21] 21101 to 21119.

Model	Body Type	Price	Weight	Prod. Total
15	Chassis	1090	2510	1800
21	Chassis	1800	3794	19

ENGINE: [Model 15] Continental. Monobloc. Four-cylinder. Bore & stroke: 3-1/2 x 5 in. NACC HP: 19.60. [Model 21] Continental. Monobloc. Four-cylinder. Bore & stroke: 3-3/4 x 5 in. NACC HP: 22.50.

CHASSIS: Shaft drive.

TECHNICAL: Three-speed transmission. Straight-bevel axle. Magneto ignition.

HISTORICAL: GMC trucks used Continental engines until 1920. Electric models were no longer offered. In 1916, William Warwick and his wife drove from Seattle to New York in a GMC truck. The trip took two months (with an appreciably longer return trip), but was successful. The Model 21 appears to have come out late in 1916. Some sources first list it as a 1917 model, although the 1916 serial number range indicates production of 19 Model 21s in 1916.

1917 GMC

MODEL 15 — 3/4-TON — FOUR-CYLINDER: The Model 15 was again available in the GMC truck line. As in 1915, a handsome express body was available to fit the 1,500 lb. payload chassis.

MODEL 16 — 3/4-TON — FOUR-CYLINDER: The Model 16 was about 400 lbs. heavier than the Model 15 and had the more powerful four-cylinder engine previously used in the Model 21 1-ton.

MODEL 21 — 1-TON — FOUR-CYLINDER: GMC's first 1-ton gasoline truck was continued from 1916.

MODEL 23 — 1-TON — FOUR-CYLINDER: GMC added a new 1-ton gasoline truck during mid-year 1917. It had a larger, more powerful four-cylinder engine.

1917 GMC 3/4-Ton Model 16 Stake (CPC/W. Wedekind)

I.D. DATA: Serial number on left-hand front spring horn. Motor number on left side of crankcase. Serial numbers: [Model 15] 152651 to 154125; [Model 16] 16100 to 162154. [Model 21] 21120 to 21593. [Model 23] 23100-2338.

Model	Body Type	Price	Weight	Prod. Total
15	Chassis	1150	2510	1475
16	Chassis	—	2940	2055
21	Chassis	1800	3794	474
23	Chassis	—	5210	339

ENGINE: [Model 15] Continental. Monobloc. Four-cylinder. Bore & stroke: 3-1/2 x 5 in. NACC HP: 19.60. [Model 16] Continental. Monobloc. Four-cylinder. Bore & stroke: 3-3/4 x 5 in. NACC HP: 22.50. [Model 21] Monobloc. Continental. Four-cylinder. Bore & stroke: 3-3/4 x 5 in. NACC HP: 22.50. [Model 23] Continental. Monobloc. Four-cylinder. Bore & stroke: 4-1/8 x 5-1/4 in. NACC HP: 27.20.

CHASSIS: Shaft drive.

TECHNICAL: Three-speed transmission. Straight-bevel axle. Magneto ignition.

HISTORICAL: GMC trucks used Continental engines until 1920. The Model 15 gained fame during World War I as an outstanding truck for use in military ambulance service. Over 5,000 such ambulances were used by the U.S. Army. After the war, it became the basis of the classic GMC K-Series truck.

1918 GMC

1918 GMC 3/4-Ton Model 16 Flatbed (CPC/P. Reynolds)

MODEL 16 — 3/4-TON — FOUR-CYLINDER: The Model 16 was offered again in 1918. There were no obvious changes in the truck's technical specifications. Even the price stayed the same. There were two distinct ranges of Model 16 serial numbers for trucks produced in different factories.

MODEL 21 — 1-TON — FOUR-CYLINDER: The 23 hp 1-ton gasoline truck was offered again. The 27 hp Model 23 1-ton was no longer produced. To get the bigger motor, you had to order at least a 2-ton truck.

I.D. DATA: Serial number on left-hand front spring horn. Motor number on left side of crankcase. Serial numbers: [Model 16/Factory 1] 162155 to 166650; [Model 16/Factory 2] 168001 to 168450. [Model 21] 21594 to 21863.

Model	Body Type	Price	Weight	Prod. Total
16	Chassis	1495	2940	4946
21	Chassis	1800	3794	270

ENGINE: [Model 16] Continental. Four-cylinder. Bore & stroke: 3-3/4 x 5 in. NACC HP: 22.50. [Model 21] Continental. Four-cylinder. Bore & stroke: 3-3/4 x 5 in. NACC HP: 22.50.

CHASSIS: Shaft drive.

TECHNICAL: Three-speed transmission. Straight-bevel axle. Magneto ignition.

1918 GMC 3/4-Ton Model 16 Military Ambulance (CMW/CE)

HISTORICAL: Increased production for military use during World War I was reflected in the output of GMC trucks during 1918. Many Model 16s were also used in military ambulance service.

1919 GMC

1919 GMC 3/4-Ton Model 16 Screenside Delivery (DFW/MPB)

MODEL 16 — 3/4-TON — FOUR-CYLINDER: The Model 16 was offered again in 1919. There were no obvious changes in the truck's technical specifications. Even the price stayed the same again. Due to wartime and postwar demand, Model 16 production was scheduled in four factories, with a distinct range of serial for each one of them.

MODEL 21 — 1-TON — FOUR-CYLINDER: The 23 hp 1-ton gasoline truck was offered again for the fourth year in a row. It was made in just one factory, but also saw a production increase due to the momentum of World War I. (Government orders still were being filled after the armistice).

I.D. DATA: Serial number on left-hand front spring horn. Motor number on left side of crankcase. Serial numbers: [Model 16/Factory 1] 166651 to 168000; [Model 16/Factory 2] 168451 to 169000. [Model 16/Factory 3] 199001 to 169201. [Model 16/Factory 4] 169601 to 1611270. [Model 21] 21864 to 211198.

Model	Body Type	Price	Weight	Prod. Total
16	Chassis	1495	2940	3772
21	Chassis	1800	3794	335

ENGINE: [Model 16] Continental. Four-cylinder. Bore & stroke: 3-3/4 x 5 in. NACC HP: 22.50. [Model 21] Continental. Four-cylinder. Bore & stroke: 3-3/4 x 5 in. NACC HP: 22.50.

CHASSIS: Shaft drive.

TECHNICAL: Three-speed transmission. Straight-bevel axle. Magneto ignition.

HISTORICAL: Many trucks ordered by the government were still uncompleted when World War I came to an end. A large number of these were diverted to use by government agencies or sold to private companies. The surplus of trucks existing after the war brought many trucks on the market at low prices and increased the general use of motor trucks in many businesses. It also inspired the government to undertake public works projects in which these commercial vehicles could be put to good use.

1920 GMC

MODEL 16 — 3/4-TON TO 1-TON — FOUR-CYLINDER: The Model 16 was now rated as a 3/4-ton to 1-ton model to cover a wider market niche with a single product. This was probably part of an effort to cut back production, due to a slackening of late postwar demand,

because of heavy inventories in the military surplus market. Production was limited to two factories. The Model 16's shipping weight did not increase, despite the wider load capacity rating.

1920 GMC 3/4-Ton Model 16 Canopy Delivery (D. Sagvold)

I.D. DATA: Serial number on left-hand front spring horn. Motor number on left side of crankcase. Serial numbers: [Model 16/Factory 1] 169202 to 169501; [Model 16/Factory 2] 1611271 to 1613513.

Model	Body Type	Price	Weight	Prod. Total
16	Chassis	1495	2940	2623

ENGINE: [Model 16] Continental. Four-cylinder. Bore & stroke: 3-3/4 x 5 in. NACC HP: 22.50. Brake HP: 37 at 1810 rpm.

CHASSIS: [Model 16] 132 in. wheelbase. Shaft drive.

TECHNICAL: Three-speed transmission. Straight-bevel axle. Magneto ignition.

HISTORICAL: During 1920, General Motor Truck Co. switched from Continental-built engines to GMC-built engines in its trucks.

1921 GMC

1921 GMC 3/4-Ton Model K-16 Panel Delivery (D. Sagvold)

MODEL K-15 — 3/4-TON — FOUR-CYLINDER: The Model K-15 was a 3/4-ton version of the new postwar K-Series GMC truck. Other Ks came in capacities up to 5-tons. They had lighter shipping weights and a new 19.6 NACC horsepower four-cylinder engine.

MODEL K-16 — 1-TON — FOUR-CYLINDER: The Model K-16 was a 1-ton version of the new postwar K-Series GMC truck. It had a slightly heavier shipping weight than the previous Model 16 and shared the new 19.6 hp engine with the K-15.

I.D. DATA: Serial number on left-hand front spring horn. Motor number on left side of crankcase. Serial numbers: [K-15] K-154201 to K-154476; [K-16] K-1614001 to K-1616026.

Model	Body Type	Price	Weight	Prod. Total
K-15	Chassis	—	2850	276
K-16	Chassis	—	3300	2026

ENGINE: [Model K-15/K-16] GMC. Four-cylinder. Bore & stroke: 3-1/2 x 5-1/2 in. NACC HP: 19.60. Brake HP: 37 at 1810 rpm.

CHASSIS: Wheelbase: [K-16] 132 in. w.b.; [Others] Data not available. Shaft drive.

TECHNICAL: Three-speed transmission. Straight-bevel axle. Magneto ignition.

HISTORICAL: New K-Series introduced.

1922 GMC

MODEL K-15 — 3/4-TON — FOUR-CYLINDER: The Model K-15 was carried over with a slightly increased shipping weight and the same 19.6 NACC horsepower four-cylinder engine.

1922 GMC 1-Ton Model K-16 Express (CPC/Ben Ostergen)

MODEL K-16 — 1-TON — FOUR-CYLINDER: The Model K-16 was a 1-ton version of the new postwar K-Series GMC truck. It had a slightly lower shipping weight than the previous K-16 and the same 19.6 hp engine.

I.D. DATA: Serial number on left-hand front spring horn. Motor number on left side of crankcase. Serial numbers: [K-15] K-154477 to K-154601; [K-16] K-1616027 to K-1619242.

Model	Body Type	Price	Weight	Prod. Total
K-15	Chassis	—	2945	325
K-16	Chassis	—	3250	3215

ENGINE: [Model K-15/K-16] GMC. Four-cylinder. Bore & stroke: 3-1/2 x 5-1/2 in. NACC HP: 19.60. Brake HP: 37 at 1810 rpm.

CHASSIS: Shaft drive.

TECHNICAL: Three-speed transmission. Straight-bevel axle. Magneto ignition.

HISTORICAL: New K-Series continued.

1923 GMC

1923 GMC 1-Ton Model 16 Canopy Express (D. Sagvold)

MODEL K-16 — 1-TON — FOUR-CYLINDER: The Model K-15 was dropped in 1923. The K-16 was carried over. With its 1-ton load capacity, it was GMC's smallest truck this year. There were no changes from 1922 specifications.

I.D. DATA: Serial number on left-hand front spring horn. Motor number on left side of crankcase. Serial numbers: [K-16] K-1619243 and up.

Model	Body Type	Price	Weight	Prod. Total
K-16	Chassis	—	3250	—

ENGINE: [K-16] GMC. Four-cylinder. Bore & stroke: 3-1/2 x 5-1/2 in. NACC HP: 19.60. Brake HP: 37 at 1810 rpm.

CHASSIS: Shaft drive.

TECHNICAL: Three-speed transmission. Straight-bevel axle. Magneto ignition.

HISTORICAL: New K-Series continued.

1924 GMC

MODEL K-16 — 1-TON — FOUR-CYLINDER: The K-16 was carried over. It was still GMC's smallest truck. There were no changes from 1923 specifications.
MODEL K-16X — 1-TON — FOUR-CYLINDER: The Model K-16X was added in 1923. The X indicated that it had a factory installed express body.
I.D. DATA: Serial number on left-hand front spring horn. Motor number on left side of crankcase. Serial numbers: [K-16] 80-7312 up; [K-16X] 80-10092 up.

Model	Body Type	Price	Weight	Prod. Total
K-16	Chassis	—	3250	—
K-16X	Chassis	—	3435	—

ENGINE: [K-16] GMC. Four-cylinder. Bore & stroke: 3-1/2 x 5-1/2 in. NACC HP: 19.60. Brake HP: 37 at 1810 rpm. [K-16X] GMC. Four-cylinder. Bore & stroke: 3-1/2 x 5-1/2 in. NACC HP: 19.60. Brake HP: 37 at 1810 rpm.
CHASSIS: Shaft drive.
TECHNICAL: Three-speed transmission. Straight-bevel axle. Magneto ignition.
HISTORICAL: New K-Series continued. New factory 1-ton express model.

1925 GMC

MODEL K-16 — 1-TON — FOUR-CYLINDER: The K-16 was carried over. It was still GMC's smallest truck. There were no changes from 1924 specifications.
MODEL K-16X — 1-TON — FOUR-CYLINDER: The Model K-16X returned in 1925. The X indicated that it had a factory installed express body.
MODEL K-17 — 1-TON — FOUR-CYLINDER: A third 1-ton model was introduced during 1925. It was an improved version of the K-16 and probably replaced it.
I.D. DATA: Serial number on left-hand front spring horn. Motor number on left side of crankcase. Serial numbers: [K-16] K-1623242 to K-1626042.; [K-16X] K-1623307 to K-1626045; [K-17] K-17101 to K-17115.

Model	Body Type	Price	Weight	Prod. Total
K-16	Chassis	—	3250	2801
K-16X	Chassis	—	3435	2739
K-17	Chassis	—		116

ENGINE: [K-16] GMC. Four-cylinder. Bore & stroke: 3-1/2 x 5-1/2 in. NACC HP: 19.60. Brake HP: 37 at 1810 rpm. [K-16X] GMC. Four-cylinder. Bore & stroke: 3-1/2 x 5-1/2 in. NACC HP: 19.60. Brake HP: 37 at 1810 rpm. [K-17] GMC. Four-cylinder. Bore & stroke: Data not available.
CHASSIS: Shaft drive.
TECHNICAL: Three-speed transmission. Straight-bevel axle. Magneto ignition.
HISTORICAL: New K-17 series.

1926 GMC

MODEL K-16 — 1-TON — FOUR-CYLINDER: The K-16 was carried over. It was still GMC's smallest truck. There were no changes from 1925 specifications.
I.D. DATA: Serial number on left-hand front spring horn. Motor number on left side of crankcase. Serial numbers: K-1626043 and up.

Model	Body Type	Price	Weight	Prod. Total
K-16	Chassis	—	3250	2801

ENGINE: [K-16] GMC. Four-cylinder. Bore & stroke: 3-1/2 x 5-1/2 in. NACC HP: 19.60. Brake HP: 37 at 1810 rpm.
CHASSIS: Shaft drive.
TECHNICAL: Three-speed transmission. Straight-bevel axle. Magneto ignition.
HISTORICAL: GMC was working on the design of a new line of light-duty models for 1927-1928 introduction.

1927 GMC

There's two ways to look at 1927 GMC light-duty truck history. Some experts say there were no 1927 GMC light-duty trucks. Others insist the GMC light-duty did exist, marketed as a Pontiac. The Pontiac Deluxe Delivery truck was introduced (as a 1927 model) in October 1926. In 1928, some details of the radiator design were changed and this truck became the GMC T-11. This change to GMC identification took place in calendar year 1927, when the second series of the trucks was released. However, these were officially considered 1928 models. See the 1928 GMC entry below and the 1927 Pontiac entry in another section of this catalog.

1928 GMC

1928 GMC 1/2-Ton Model T-11 Panel Delivery (DFW/BCA)

SERIES T-11 — 1/2-TON — SIX: In late 1927 GMC re-entered the light-duty truck field with its new T-11 series. These trucks were identical to the 1927 Pontiac models except for having a GMC radiator shield. An addition to the instrument panel was the gasoline gauge which, on the 1927 Pontiac models, was located on the fuel tank.
I.D. DATA: Serial numbers 204001 to 426022.

Model	Body Type	Price	Weight	Prod. Total
T-11	Chassis	585	1820	—
T-11	Pickup	—	—	—
T-11	Canopy	—	—	—
T-11	Screen	—	—	—
T-11	Panel	—	—	—
T-11	Sedan Delivery	—	—	—

1928 GMC Screenside Express (OCW)

1928 GMC 1/2-Ton Model T-11 Panel Delivery (OCW)

ENGINE: L-head. inline. Six-cylinder. Cast iron block. Bore & stroke: 3.25 in. x 3.75 in. Displacement: 186.5 cid. Compression ratio: 4.9:1. Brake horsepower: 36 at 2400 rpm. Mechanical valve lifters. Carburetor: Carter one-barrel.
CHASSIS [Series T-11]: Wheelbase: 110 in. Tires: 4.75 x 20 in.
TECHNICAL: Manual transmission. Speeds: 3F/1R. Floor-mounted gear shift lever. Overall ratio: 4.18:1. Four-wheel, mechanical brakes. Delco-Remy ignition.
OPTIONS: Disc wheels.
HISTORICAL: Calendar year registrations: [All models] 17,568.
Engine now used convex rather than concave interior cylinder walls. First year for fuel pump rather than vacuum feed. Also introduced was a new clutch and transmission.

1929 GMC

1929 GMC 1/2-Ton Model T-11 "Fifth Avenue" Panel Delivery (DFW/DPL)

SERIES T-11 — 1/2-TON — SIX: These trucks were identical to the 1928 models. They again had a GMC radiator shield and instrument panel gas gauge.

I.D. DATA: Serial number located on left side of frame below front fender. Starting: 410202 and up. Engine numbers located on left side of cylinder block behind oil filter.

Model	Body Type	Price	Weight	Prod. Total
T-11	Chassis	625	2135	—
T-11	Pickup	—	—	—
T-11	Canopy	—	—	—
T-11	Screen	—	—	—
T-11	Panel	—	—	—
T-11	Sedan Delivery (*)	—	—	—

NOTE 1: A deluxe "5th Ave." option was available for the Panel Delivery.

1929 GMC 1-1-1/2-Ton Canopy Delivery (OCW)

ENGINE: L-head. inline (Pontiac manufacture). Six-cylinder. Cast iron block. Bore & stroke: 3.31 in. x 3.88 in. Displacement: 200.4 cid. Compression ratio: 4.9:1. Brake horsepower: 60 at 3000 rpm. Mechanical valve lifters. Carburetor: Marvel one-barrel.

CHASSIS [Series T-11]: Wheelbase: 109.625 in. Tires: 5.00 x 19 in.

TECHNICAL: Manual, sliding gear transmission. Speeds: 3F/1R. Floor-mounted gearshift lever. Overall ratio: 4.36:1. Mechanical brakes. Four pressed steel wheels. Delco-Remy ignition.

HISTORICAL: Calendar year registrations: [All models] 14,300.

1930 GMC

SERIES T-11 — 1/2-TON — SIX: No change in exterior appearance from 1928. Mechanical alterations were extensive. The six-cylinder engine's displacement was boosted to 200.4 cid. The torque tube drive used previously was replaced by a Hotchkiss system.

SERIES T-15A — 3/4-TON — SIX: The new T-15 range was introduced. Appearances were not drastically changed. Technically, the trucks were a bit heavier-duty. The T-15A had a 109-5/8 in. wheelbase.

SERIES T-15AA — 1/2-TON — SIX: This version of the T-15 had a longer 121 in. wheelbase, but a smaller payload capacity.

SERIES T-15B — 3/4-TON — SIX: The new T-15 with a 142 in. wheelbase.

I.D. DATA: Serial number located on left side of frame below front fender. Starting: [T-11] 591519 and up. [T-15A] 101 and up; [T-15AA] T-15AA-1468 up; [T-15B] 142 up. Engine numbers located on left side of cylinder block behind oil filter.

Model	Body Type	Price	Weight	Prod. Total
Series T-11 — 1/2-Ton — 109. 6 in. w.b.				
T-11	Chassis	625	2135	—
T-11	Pickup	—	—	—
T-11	Canopy	—	—	—
T-11	Screen	—	—	—
T-11	Panel	—	—	—
T-11	Sedan Delivery	—	—	—
Series T-15A — 3/4-Ton -109.6 in. w.b.				
T-15A	Chassis	695	2500	—
T-15A	Pickup	—	—	—
T-15A	Canopy	—	—	—
T-15A	Screen	—	—	—
T-15A	Panel	—	—	—
T-15A	Sedan Delivery	—	—	—
Series T-15AA — 1/2-Ton — 121 in. w.b.				
T-15AA	Chassis	—	—	—
T-15AA	Pickup	—	—	—
T-15AA	Canopy	—	—	—
T-15AA	Screen	—	—	—
T-15AA	Panel	995	3300	—
T-15AA	Sedan Delivery	—	—	—
Series T-15B — 3/4-Ton — 142 in. w.b.				
T-15B	Chassis	—	—	—
T-15B	Pickup	—	—	—
T-15B	Canopy	1045	3645	—
T-15B	Screen	1045	3645	—
T-15B	Panel	1045	3665	—
T-15B	Sedan Delivery	—	—	—

ENGINE: [All] L-head. Inline (Pontiac manufacture). Six-cylinder. Cast iron block. Overall length: 167.73 in. Bore & stroke: 3.31 in. at 3.88 in. Displacement: 200.4 cid. Compression ratio: 4.9:1. Brake horsepower: 60 at 3000 rpm. Mechanical valve lifters. Carburetor: Marvel one-barrel.

CHASSIS [Series T-15]: Wheelbase: 109.6 in.; [T-15AA] 121 in.; [T-15B] 142 in.

TECHNICAL: [All] Manual transmission. Speeds: 3F/1R. Column-mounted gearshift lever. Single-disc, dry-plate clutch. Hypoid, semi-floating rear axle. Mechanical, four-wheel brakes. Pressed steel wheels.

OPTIONS: Front bumper. Rear bumper.

HISTORICAL: Calendar year registrations: [All models] 9,004.

1931-1932 GMC

1931 GMC Police Paddy Wagon (ATC)

SERIES T-11 — 1/2-TON — SIX: The T-11 line was carried over in 1931. It was certified to have an approximate payload capacity of 1,100 lbs., making it a "heavy" 1/2 ton. The Pontiac flathead six was again used as the powerplant both years.

T-15 — 3/4-TON-1-TON — SIX: The T-15 was also carried over for 1931. It was certified for a payload range between 1,675 lbs. and 2,875 lbs. It also used the Pontiac engine.

T-15AA — 1-TON — SIX: The T-15AA was listed for 1931, also. It used the same Pontiac L-head six.

T-17A — 1-TON — SIX: The T-17 was rated for 1,645 lb. to 3,050 lb. payloads. It, too, used the reliable Pontiac engine.

I.D. DATA: Serial number located [T-11]: on left side of frame below front fender. [T-15/T-15AA/T-17]: on right side of frame below front fender. Starting: [T-11] 591519 and up; [T-15] T-15-101 and up; [T-15AA] not available; [T-17] T-17-101 up. Engine numbers located on left side of cylinder block behind oil filter.

Model	Body Type	Price	Weight	Prod. Total
Series T-11 — 1/2-Ton — 109.56 in. w.b.				
T-11	Chassis	625	1885	—
T-11	Pickup	—	—	—
T-11	Canopy	—	—	—
T-11	Screen	—	—	—
T-11	Panel	—	—	—
T-11	Sedan Delivery	—	—	—

Series T-15A — 3/4-Ton -109.6 in. w.b.

T-15A	Chassis	645	2500	—
T-15A	Pickup	—	—	—
T-15A	Canopy	—	—	—
T-15A	Screen	—	—	—
T-15A	Panel	—	—	—
T-15A	Sedan Delivery	—	—	—

Series T-15AA — 1/2-Ton — 121 in. w.b.

T-15AA	Chassis	645	2300	—
T-15AA	Pickup	—	—	—
T-15AA	Canopy	—	—	—
T-15AA	Screen	—	—	—
T-15AA	Panel	995	3300	—
T-15AA	Sedan Delivery	—	—	—

Series T-17A — 1-Ton — 142 in. w.b.

T-17A	Chassis	665	2550	—
T-17A	Pickup	—	—	—
T-17A	Canopy	—	—	—
T-17A	Screen	—	—	—
T-17A	Panel	—	—	—
T-17A	Sedan Delivery	—	—	—

ENGINE: L-head. inline (Pontiac manufacture). Six-cylinder. Cast iron block. Bore & stroke: 3.31 in. x 3.88 in. Displacement: 200.4 cid. Compression ratio: 4.9:1. Brake horsepower: 60 at 3000 rpm. Mechanical valve lifters. Carburetor: Marvel one-barrel.

1931 GMC 1-Ton Model T-17A Stake (IMSC/Jack L. Martin)

CHASSIS: [Series T-11] Wheelbase: 109.625 in. Overall length: 167.63 in.

CHASSIS: [Series T-15] Wheelbase: 130 in.

CHASSIS: [Series T-15AA] Wheelbase: 121 in.

CHASSIS: [Series 17A] Wheelbase: 141 in. w.b.

1931 GMC Police Paddy Wagon (OCW)

TECHNICAL: Manual transmission. Speeds: 3F/1R. Column-mounted gearshift lever. Single-dry-plate clutch. Hypoid, semi-floating rear axle. Mechanical, four-wheel brakes. Pressed steel wheels.

OPTIONS: Front bumper. Rear bumper.

Standard Catalog of Light-Duty Trucks

1932 GMC 1-Ton Model T-17A Pickup (DFW/SI)

HISTORICAL: Calendar year registrations: All models: [1931] 6,919; [1932] 6,359.

1933 GMC

T-15 — 1-TON — SIX: The T-15 was carried over for 1931 as the smallest GMC model available. Every other truck this year was 1-1/2-tons or up. Even the T-15 was offered only in the early part of the year, as a "first series" model. It still had the Pontiac-built six. (When "second series" models came out, the T-15 and the Pontiac motor were dropped.)

I.D. DATA: Serial number located [T-15]: on right side of frame below front fender. Starting: Continued from 1931.

Model	Body Type	Price	Weight	Prod. Total
Series T-15 — 1-Ton -109.6 in. w.b.				
T-15	Chassis	645	2500	—
T-15	Pickup	—	—	—
T-15	Canopy	—	—	—
T-15	Screen	—	—	—
T-15	Panel	—	—	—
T-15	Sedan Delivery	—	—	—

ENGINE: L-head. inline (Pontiac manufacture). Six-cylinder. Cast iron block. Bore & stroke: 3.31 in. x 3.88 in. Displacement: 200.4 cid. Compression ratio: 4.9:1. Brake horsepower: 60 at 3000 rpm. Mechanical valve lifters. Carburetor: Marvel one-barrel.

CHASSIS: [Series T-15] Wheelbase: 130 in.

TECHNICAL: Manual transmission. Speeds: 3F/1R. Column-mounted gearshift lever. Single-dry-plate clutch. Hypoid, semi-floating rear axle. Mechanical, four-wheel brakes. Pressed steel wheels.

OPTIONS: Front bumper. Rear bumper.

HISTORICAL: New GMC six with 3-3/16 x 4-5/8 in. bore and stroke used in T-18A and T23 (1-1/2-ton) "second series" 1933 trucks.

1934 GMC

In 1934, the T-15 was replaced by the T16. This truck had a 1-1/2-ton payload rating and was the smallest GMC product available.

1935 GMC

SERIES T16L — 6-CYLINDER: GMC returned to light-duty truck manufacture with the T16L model. It was a 3/4-ton truck with a six-cylinder engine having a 3-5/16 bore and 4-5/8 in. stroke. New styling features included a sloping grille and fender mounted headlamps. Hydraulic brakes were introduced on all GMC light- and medium-duty trucks.

1935 GMC 3/4-Ton/1-Ton Model T-16 Police Paddy Wagon (OCW)

I.D. DATA: Serial number located on right frame side rail at front and on caution plate on instrument panel. Starting: T16L-4001 and up. Engine numbers located on left lower front end of cylinder block.

Model	Body Type	Price	Weight	Prod. Total
Series T16L — 3/4-Ton — 131 in. w.b.				
T16L	Chassis	595	2945	—

ENGINE: Inline. L-head. Six-cylinder. Cast iron block. Bore & stroke: 3.3125 in. x 4.125 in. Displacement: 213 cid. NACC HP: 26.3. Mechanical valve lifters. Carburetor: one-barrel.
CHASSIS: (Series T16L): Wheelbase: 131 in.
TECHNICAL: Manual transmission. Speeds: 4F/1R. Floor-mounted gearshift lever. Single-dry-disc clutch. Full-floating axle. Mechanical, four-wheel brakes. Pressed steel wheels.
OPTIONS: Front bumper. Rear bumper. Heater.
HISTORICAL: Calendar year registrations: [All models] 11,442.

1936 GMC

1936 GMC 1/2-Ton Model T-14 Panel Delivery (DFW/MVMA)

SERIES T-14 — 1/2-Ton — SIX: The latest GMC light-duty models featured skirted front and rear fenders and a rounder grille with prominent vertical bars. There was also a larger, fin-like hood ornament. The use of a "blister" type sun visor over the windshield was discontinued. Directly below the "General Motors Truck"" nameplate on the hoodsides were five bright horizontal moldings. A handsome "veed" bumper was featured up front. There was a new 1/2-ton truck called the T-14. It had the T-16L's engine.
SERIES T-16L — 3/4-TON — SIX: The T-16L was carried over, but without the "blister" type sun visor above the windshield. It had the same six-cylinder motor.
I.D. DATA: Serial number located on right-hand frame side rail at front and on caution plate on instrument panel. Serial numbers: [T-14] T-14-001 to T-14-11251; [T-16L] T-16L-9051 to T-16L -18801. Engine numbers located on left lower front of cylinder block.

Model	Body Type	Price	Weight	Prod. Total
Series T-14 — 1/2-Ton — 131 in. w.b.				
T-14	Chassis	425	2210	—
T-14	Chassis & Cab	525	—	—
T-14	Pickup	566	—	—
Series T-16L — 1/2-Ton — 131 in. w.b.				
T-16L	Chassis	525	3360	—

NOTE 1: Cab includes shatter-proof glass.
ENGINE: Inline. L-head. Six-cylinder. Cast iron block. Bore & stroke: 3.3125 in. x 4.125 in. Displacement: 213 cid. NACC HP: 26.3. Mechanical valve lifters. Carburetor: one-barrel.
CHASSIS: [Series T-14]: Wheelbase: 126 in. Tires: 6:00 x 16 four-ply in early 1936 only. [Later became an $8 option].
CHASSIS: [Series T-16L]: Wheelbase: 131 in.

TECHNICAL: Manual, synchromesh transmission. Speeds [T-14]: 3F/1R; [All others] four-speed. Floor-mounted gearshift lever. Single-dry-plate clutch. Axle: [T-14] Hypoid, semi-floating rear; [All others] full-floating.
OPTIONS: Front bumper. Rear bumper. Heater. Accessory Group #1 ($23.50). Heavy-duty shocks ($10.20). 6.50 x 16 six-ply tires ($20).
HISTORICAL: Calendar year registrations: [All models] 26,980.

1936 GMC 3/4-Ton Model T-16L Stake (CPC/Lindon's Sales & Service)

1937 GMC

1937 GMC 1/2-Ton Model T-14A Pickup (DFW/BLHU)

SERIES T-14 — 1/2-Ton — SIX: The latest GMC light-duty models featured a revamped front end design with headlights set in the fender valleys, new "Dual Tone" color designs and a grille combining three sections of horizontal bars with a broad center portion of horizontal fins. The L-head engine used for the GMC light-duty models was enlarged to displace 230 cid.
SERIES T-16L — 3/4-TON — SIX: The T-16L was carried over with the same styling changes seen on the T-14.

1937 GMC 3/4-Ton Model F-16L Walk-in Delivery (DFW/MPC)

SERIES FL-16 — 3/4-TON — SIX: A series of Model F walk-in vans was introduced.
I.D. DATA: Serial number located on right-hand frame side rail at front and on caution plate on instrument panel. Starting: T-14: T-14-11252 to 34527. T-16L: T-16L-18802 and up. F-16L: F-16L-001 and up. Engine numbers located on left lower front of cylinder block.

Model	Body Type	Price	Weight	Prod. Total
Series T-14A — 1/2-Ton				
T-14A	Chassis	425	2195	—
T-14A	Chassis & Cab	527	—	—
T-14A	Pickup Body	570	—	—

Series T-14B — 1/2-Ton				
T-14B	Chassis	395	N/A	—
T-14B	Chassis & Cab	497	—	—
T-14B	Pickup	528	—	—
Series T-16L — 3/4-Ton				
T-16L	Chassis	535	3155	—
F-16L				
Series F-16L — 3/4-Ton — Walk-in Delivery				
F-16L	Chassis	645	3230	—

1937 GMC 1/2-Ton Model T-14A Pickup (DFW/BLHU)

ENGINE: Inline. L-head. Six-cylinder. Cast iron block. Bore & stroke: 3.4375 in. x 4.125 in. Displacement: 230 cid. Brake HP: 86 at 3600 rpm. Mechanical valve lifters. Carburetor: one-barrel.

CHASSIS [Series T-14A/T-14B]: Wheelbase: 112 in. Tires: 6.00 x 16 four-ply.
CHASSIS [Series T-16L]: Wheelbase: 131.5 in.
CHASSIS [Series F-16L]: Wheelbase: 108 in.

1937 GMC 1/2-Ton Model T-14A Pickup (HAS)

1937 GMC 1/2-Ton Model T-14A Pickup (CPC/Robert Cloud)

TECHNICAL: Manual, synchromesh transmission. Speeds: [T-14] 3F/1R; [All others] 4F/1R. Floor-mounted gearshift lever. Single-dry-plate clutch. Axle: [T-14] Hypoid, semi-floating; [All others] full-floating. Hydraulic four-wheel brakes. Pressed steel wheels. Heavy-duty shocks ($10.20). 6.50 x 16 6 ply tires, T-14B ($20); 6.00 x 16 six-ply ($8). Four-speed transmission ($15.25). Shatter-proof glass ($12.50).

OPTIONS: Front bumper ($6.50). Rear bumper. Heater. Seat covers. Tire carrier, T-14B ($3.50). Tire carrier, T-14A ($10.20). Accessory Group #1 for T-14B ($29.40). Accessory Group #1 for T-14A ($26).

HISTORICAL: Calendar year registrations: [All models] 43,522.

Standard Catalog of Light-Duty Trucks

1937 GMC 1/2-Ton Model T-14A Suburban Carryall (GMC)

1938 GMC

1938 GMC 3/4-Ton Model T-15 Express (OCW)

ALL SERIES — 1/2-TON — SIX: The latest 1/2-ton GMC trucks featured hood-mounted headlights and grilles with added brightwork. No hood louvers were installed. This was the last year the light-duty models used single-piece windshields.

ALL SERIES — 3/4-TON — SIX: GMC's 1938 3/4-tonners featured the same basic styling changes as the smaller trucks. They also shared the same wheelbases.

I.D. DATA: Serial number located on right-hand frame side rail at front and on caution plate on firewall. Starting: [T-14A] T-14A-11252 to 34527; [T-14B] T-14B-34528 and up; [T-145] T-145-001 and up; [T-15] T-15-5001 and up; [T-155] T-155-001 and up. Engine numbers located right side of crankcase.

Model	Body Type	Price	Weight	Prod. Total
Series T-14A — 1/2-Ton				
T-14A	Chassis	410	2195	—
Series T-14B — 1/2-Ton				
T-14B	Chassis	445	2300	—
Series T-145 — 3/4-Ton				
T-145	Chassis	515	2470	—
Series T-15 — 3/4-Ton				
T-15	Chassis	545	2655	—
Series T-155 — 3/4-Ton				
T-155	3/4-Ton Chassis	565	2795	—

ENGINE: Inline. L-head. Six-cylinder. Cast iron block. Bore & stroke: 3.4375 in. x 4.125 in. Displacement: 230 cid. Brake H.P.: 86 at 3600 rpm. Four main bearings. Mechanical valve lifters. Carburetor: Zenith one-barrel.

CHASSIS [Series T-14]: Wheelbase: 112 in. Tires: 6.00 x 16 in.
CHASSIS [Series T-14A]: Wheelbase: 126 in.
CHASSIS [Series T-15]: Wheelbase: 131.5 in.
CHASSIS [Series T-145]: Wheelbase: 126 in.
CHASSIS [Series T-155]: Wheelbase: 131.5 in.

TECHNICAL: Manual, synchromesh transmission. Speeds: [T-14] 3F/1R; [All others] 4F/1R. Floor-mounted gearshift lever. Single-dry-plate clutch. Rear axle: Hypoid, semi-floating. Overall ratio: [T-14] 4.11:1. Hydraulic, four-wheel brakes. Pressed steel wheels. Heavy-duty shocks. Various tire sizes. Four-speed transmission.

OPTIONS: Front bumper. Rear bumper. Radio. Heater. Clock. Cigar lighter. Radio antenna. Seat covers. Tire carriers.

HISTORICAL: Calendar year registrations: [All models] 20,152.

1938 GMC 1/2-Ton Model T-14A Pickup (CPC/L.Tunker)

1939 GMC

1939 GMC 1-Ton Model ACL-300 Armored Car (NSBC/JE)

SERIES AC-100 — 1/2-TON — SIX: The restyled 1939 GMC light-duty trucks adopted V-shaped, two-piece windshields. The grille remained high and narrow, but it had a more massive appearance with thicker and sharply-angled horizontal bars attached to a center vertical bar. The design seemed to be patterned after a fish skeleton. The uppermost bar carried the GMC logo. As in earlier years, the side hood bar read "General Motors Truck," but its leading edge was more blunt than in 1938. Six 1/2-ton models were on a 113-1/2 in. wheelbase. There was also one chassis model (AC-102) with a 10-3/4 in. longer wheelbase.

AC-150 — 3/4-TON — SIX: The 3/4-ton trucks had the same changes in design. They were on the 123-3/4 in. wheelbase.

AC-250 — 1-TON — SIX: New to the line was a pair of 1-ton lines. The AC-250s were the standard tonners on a 133 in. wheelbase.

ACL-300 — 1-TON — SIX: The "L" in the model code indicated that this was a "light-duty" version of the AC-300, which also came in 1-1/2-ton formats. It also used a 133 in. w.b.

I.D. DATA: Serial number located on right-hand frame side rail at front and on caution plate on firewall. Starting: [AC-100] AC-101-001 and up; [AC-100/123.25 in. wheelbase] AC-102-001 and up; [AC-150] AC-152-001 and up; [AC-250] AC-252-001 and up; [ACL-300] ACL-302-001 up. Engine numbers located right side of crankcase.

1939 GMC 1/2-Ton Model AC-100 Panel Delivery (DFW/BLHU)

1939 GMC 3/4-Ton Model AC-250 Utility Body Truck (DFW/MVMA)

Model	Body Type	Price	Weight	Prod. Total
Series AC-100 — 1/2-Ton — 113.5 in. w.b.				
AC-100	Chassis	460	2230	—
AC-100	Chassis & Cab	557	2620	—
AC-100	Pickup	593	2855	—
AC-100	Panel	669	3495	—
Series AC-102 — 1/2-Ton — 123-3/4 in. w.b.				
AC-102	Chassis	490	2290	—
AC-102	Chassis & Cab	587	—	—
AC-102	Pickup	633	—	—
Series AC-150 — 3/4-Ton — 123-3/4 in. w.b.				
AC-150	Chassis	535	2470	—
AC-150	Chassis & Cab	632	2860	—
AC-150	Pickup	678	3135	—
AC-150	Stake	703	3480	—
AC-150	Panel	775	3800	—
Series AC-250 — 1-Ton — 133 in. w.b.				
AC-250	Chassis	555	2660	—
AC-250	Chassis & Cab	652	3050	—
AC-250	Platform	708	3565	—
AC-250	Express	728	3360	—
AC-250	Stake	734	3855	—
AC-250	Panel	825	4060	—
Series ACL-300 — 1-Ton — 133 in. w.b.				
ACL-300	Chassis	575	3050	—
ACL-300	Chassis & Cab	672	3440	—
ACL-300	Platform	728	3955	—
ACL-300	Express	753	3750	—
ACL-300	Stake	754	4245	—
ACL-300	Panel	850	4450	—

1939 GMC 1/2-Ton Model AC-100 Suburban Carryall (OCW)

ENGINE: Inline. OHV. Six-cylinder. Cast iron block. Bore & stroke: 3.5625 in. x 3.8125 in. Displacement: 228 cid. Brake H.P.: 80 at 3000 rpm. Four main bearings. Hydraulic valve lifters. Carburetor: one-barrel.
CHASSIS [Series AC-100]: Wheelbase: 113.5. Tires: 6.50 x 16 in. Wheels: 16 x 4.50 in.
CHASSIS [Series AC-102]: Wheelbase: 123.75. Tires: 6.50 x 16 in. Wheels: 16 x 4.50 in.
CHASSIS [Series AC-150]: Wheelbase: 123.75 in.
CHASSIS [Series AC-250]: Wheelbase: 133 in.
CHASSIS [Series ACL-300]: Wheelbase: 133 in.
TECHNICAL: Manual, synchromesh transmission. Speeds: 3F/1R. Floor-mounted gearshift lever. Single-plate, dry-disc clutch. Hypoid, semi-floating rear axle. Overall ratio: [AC-100]: 4.11:1. Hydraulic, four-wheel brakes. Pressed steel wheels, [AC-100] 16 x 4.50 in. Heavy-duty shocks. Larger tires. Four-speed transmission for AC-100 ($15.40).
OPTIONS: Front bumper. Rear bumper. Heater ($23.50). Clock. Cigar lighter. Seat covers. Tire carriers. Deluxe Chassis Group. Accessory Group. Chrome headlights ($3.50).
HISTORICAL: Calendar year registrations: [All models] 34,908.

1940 GMC

1940 GMC 1-Ton AC-250 Pickup (DFW)

SERIES AC-100/101 — 1/2-TON — SIX-CYLINDER: New for 1940 was a revised "Quick-Vision" instrument panel, sealed beam headlights and front fender-mounted parking lights. There were many series and sub-series and model codes can be confusing. The AC-100 line contained seven models on the 113-1/2 in. wheelbase. Basically, 1/2-tons were in the AC-100 series. Those with the short wheelbase were technically in an AC-101 sub-series and those with the longer wheelbase were AC-102s.

SERIES ACV — 1/2-TON — SIX-CYLINDER: A 1/2-ton delivery with a 113-3/4 in. wheelbase is found in some reference books. The V model suffix probably meant van. It used the same engine found in other ACs.

SERIES AC-100/102 — 1/2-TON — SIX-CYLINDER: There were now five models in the long-wheelbase (123-3/4 in.) 1/2-ton series.

SERIES AC-150/152 — 3/4-TON — SIX-CYLINDER: This series was identical to the AC-102, except the chassis was rated for 3/4-ton payloads.

SERIES AC-250/252 — 1-TON — SIX-CYLINDER: Eight 1-ton trucks were offered on a 133 in. wheelbase in this series.

SERIES ACL-300 — 1-TON — SIX-CYLINDER: This series duplicated the AC-250 in models and wheelbase, but these were "L" (light-duty) editions of the sturdier 1-1/2-ton AC-300 series with dual rear tires. The engines were the same.

SERIES AF-230/AF-241 — 1-TON — SIX-CYLINDER: This series offered GMC's smallest walk-in delivery vans on a 112 in. wheelbase. A different six-cylinder engine was employed in the AF-230 model. The AF-241 switched to the base six used in other light trucks. There was an AFP "special delivery" on a 10 in. shorter wheelbase, too.

1940 GMC AF-240 1-Ton Walk-in Bread Delivery Van (OCW)

I.D. DATA: Serial number located on right-hand frame side rail at front and on right side of firewall. VIN consisted of the model code, followed by sequential production number. Serial numbers: [AC-101] 7375-11213; [AC-102] 7375-11213; [ACV-100] 101-214; [AC-152] 2393 and up; [AF-240/250] 001-172; [AC-250] 1903 and up; [ACL-300] 10015 and up. Engine numbers located on crankcase side.

Model	Body Type	Price	Weight	Prod. Total
Series AC-100 — 1/2-Ton — 113-1/2 in. w.b.				
AC-101	Chassis	460	2285	—
AC-101	Chassis & Cab	557	2675	—
AC-101	Pickup	590	2910	—
AC-101	Panel	669	3140	—
AC-101	Canopy	705	3140	—
AC-101	Screen	723	3205	—
AC-101	Suburban	810	3275	—

Model	Body Type	Price	Weight	Prod. Total
Series AC-100 — 1/2-Ton — 123-3/4 in. w.b.				
AC-102	Chassis	475	2315	—
AC-102	Chassis & Cab	572	2705	—
AC-102	Pickup	618	2975	—
AC-102	Stake	643	3255	—
AC-102	Panel	715	3200	—
Series AC-150 — 3/4 Ton — 123-3/4 in. w.b.				
AC-152	Chassis	535	2515	—
AC-152	Chassis & Cab	632	2905	—
AC-152	Pickup	678	3175	—
AC-152	Stake	703	3455	—
AC-152	Panel	775	3400	—
Series AC-250 — 1-Ton — 133 in. w.b.				
AC-252	Chassis	555	2760	—
AC-252	Chassis & Cab	652	3150	—
AC-252	Platform	708	3740	—
AC-252	Pickup	729	3465	—
AC-252	Stake	734	3970	—
AC-252	Panel	825	3780	—
AC-252	Canopy	866	3740	—
AC-252	Screen	886	3825	—
Series ACL-300 — 1-Ton — 133 in. w.b.				
ACL-300	Chassis	575	3035	—
ACL-300	Chassis & Cab	672	3425	—
ACL-300	Platform	728	3995	—
ACL-300	Pickup	753	3740	—
ACL-300	Stake	754	4245	—
ACL-300	Panel	845	4055	—
ACL-300	Canopy	886	4015	—
ACL-300	Screen	906	4100	—
Series AF-230/AF-240 — 1-Ton — 112 in. w.b.				
AF-230	Walk-in Delivery	1365	4630	—
AF-241	Walk-in Delivery	1365	4630	—
Series AFP-241 — 1-Ton — 100 in. w.b.				
AFP-241	Special Walk-in Delivery	1495	—	

1940 GMC 1/2-Ton Model AC-101 Pickup (OCW)

ENGINE: [AF-230]: Inline. Six-cylinder. Cast iron block. Bore & stroke: 3-7/16 in. x 4-1/8 in. NACC HP: 28.40. Carburetor: one-barrel.
ENGINE: [All AC/AF-240]: Inline. OHV. Six-cylinder. Cast iron block. Bore & stroke: 3.5625 in. x 3.8125 in. Displacement: 228 cid. Brake HP: 80 at 3000 rpm. NACC HP: 30.40. Four main bearings. Hydraulic valve lifters. Carburetor: one-barrel.
CHASSIS [Series AC-100/101]: Wheelbase: 113.5 in. Tires: 6.00 x 16 in. four-ply.
CHASSIS [Series AC-100/102]: Wheelbase: 123.75 in. Tires: 6.00 x 16 in. four-ply. Wheels: 16 x 4.50 in.
CHASSIS [Series AC-150/152]: Wheelbase: 123.75 in. Tires: 7.00 x 15 in six-ply.
CHASSIS [Series AC-250/AC-252]: Wheelbase: 133 in. Tires: 7.00 x 16 six-ply. ACL-300]: Wheelbase: 133 in.
CHASSIS [ACL-300]: Wheelbase: 133 in. Tires: 6.00 x 20 in. six-ply. front/ 32 x 6 in. eight-ply dual rear.
CHASSIS [AF-230/AF-240]: Wheelbase: 112 in. Tires: 7.00 x 16 six-ply.
CHASSIS [AFP-241]: Wheelbase: 100 in. Tires: 7.00 x 16 six-ply.
TECHNICAL: Manual, transmission. Speeds: 3F/1R. Floor mounted gear shift lever. Single dry-disc clutch. Hypoid, semi-floating rear axle. Overall ratio: [AC-100]: 4.11:1. Hydraulic, four-wheel brakes. Pressed steel wheels. Four-speed transmission ($15.40). Right-side wiper ($5.50).

1940 GMC 1/2-Ton Model AC-100 Panel (DFW/LOC)

Standard Catalog of Light-Duty Trucks

HISTORICAL: Calendar year registrations: [All models] 38,841.

1941 GMC

1941 GMC 3/4-Ton Model CC-150 Pickup With Stake Sides (DFW/NA)

1941 GMC SERIES CC-100/101 — 1/2-TON — SIX-CYLINDER: The headlights were moved out onto the fenders for 1941 and now carried the parking lights. Also adopted was a new two-tier grille arrangement highlighted by horizontal bars. The many sub-series model codes can again be confusing. The CC-100 line contained nine models on a longer 115 in. wheelbase. Basically, 1/2-tons were in the CC-100 series. Those with the short wheelbase were in the CC-101 sub-series and those with the longer wheelbase were CC-102s.

SERIES ACV/CCV — 1/2-TON — SIX-CYLINDER: The 1/2-ton delivery with the V model suffix was carried over with a 113-1/2 in. wheelbase in early 1941. It was later replaced by the CCV-101 with a 1-1/2 in. longer wheelbase.

SERIES CC-100/102 — 1/2-TON — SIX-CYLINDER: There were now five models in the long-wheelbase 1/2-ton series. The wheelbase used increased to 125-1/4 in.

SERIES CC-150/152 — 3/4-TON — SIX-CYLINDER: This series was identical to the CC-102, except the chassis was rated for 3/4-ton payloads.

SERIES CC-250/CC-251 — 1-TON — SIX-CYLINDER: New this year was a short (115 in.) wheelbase 1-ton series with chassis models only.

SERIES CC-250/CC-252 — 1-TON — SIX-CYLINDER: Eight 1-ton trucks were offered on a new 134-1/2 in. wheelbase in these series.

SERIES CCX-252 — 1-TON — SIX-CYLINDER: New this year was a medium (125-1/4 in.) wheelbase 1-ton series with chassis models only.

SERIES CC-260/CC-262 — 1-TON — SIX-CYLINDER: This was a line of trucks virtually identical to CC-252s, except for larger wheels and tires.

SERIES AF-241/AFP-241 — 1-TON — SIX-CYLINDER: This series offered GMC's small-est walk-in delivery vans on a 112 in. wheelbase (or special 100 in. wheelbase for the AFP).

SERIES CCL-300 — 1-TON — SIX-CYLINDER: This series duplicated the CC-262 in models, wheelbase, engine, and (front) tire size, but these were "L" (light-duty) editions of the sturdier 1-1/2-ton CC-300 series and added larger, dual rear tires.

I.D. DATA: Serial number located on right-hand frame side rail at front and on right side of firewall. Starting: [C-101/CC-102] 001 to 10635; [ACV-101] 001 to 215; [CCV-101] 001 to 224; [CC-152] 001 to 5353; [AF-241] 001 to 221; [AFP-241] 001 to 173; [CC-251/CCX-252/CC-252] 001 to 4357; [CC-262] 001 to 1530. Engine numbers located on crankcase side. Starting: CC-100: A22800001 and up. CC-150: B22800001 and up.

1941 GMC 1/2-Ton Model CC-101 Pickup (OCW)

Model	Body Type	Price	Weight	Prod. Total
Series CC-100 — 1/2-Ton — 115 in. w.b.				
CC-101	Chassis	515	2340	—
CC-101	Chassis & Cab	615	2730	—
CC-101	Pickup	648	2965	—
CC-101	Pickup Stake	666	3030	—
CC-101	Panel	730	3195	—
CC-101	Canopy Exppress	765	3195	—
CC-101	Screen	790	3260	—
CC-101	Suburban	875	3330	—
Series CC-100 — 1/2-Ton — 125.25 in. w.b.				
CC-102	Chassis	530	2395	—
CC-102	Chassis & Cab	630	2785	—
CC-102	Pickup	675	3055	—
CC-102	Pickup Stake	695	3130	—
CC-102	Stake	700	3335	—
CC-102	Panel	775	3280	—
Series ACV-101 — 1/2-Ton — 113.25 in. w.b.				
ACV-101	Delivery	1035	3695	—
Series CCV-101 — 1/2-Ton — 115 in. w.b.				
CCV-101	Delivery	1100	3810	—
Series CC-150 — 3/4-Ton — 125.25 in. w.b.				
CC-152	Chassis	595	2455	—
CC-152	Chassis & Cab	695	2845	—
CC-152	Pickup	740	3115	—
CC-152	Pickup Stake	760	3190	—
CC-152	Stake	765	3395	—
CC-152	Panel	840	3340	—
Series AF-241 — 1-Ton — 112 in. w.b.				
AF-241	Chassis	920	—	—
AF-241	Delivery	1430	4630	—
Series AFP-241- 1-Ton — 100 in. w.b.				
AFP-241	Chassis	945	—	—
AFP-241	Delivery	1560	4955	—
Series CC-250/251 — 1-Ton — 115 in. w.b.				
CC-251	Chassis	620	2600	—
CC-251	Chassis & Cowl	635	—	—
CC-251	Chassis & Cab	720	—	—
Series CCX-250/252 — 1-Ton — 125.25 in. w.b.				
CCX-250	Chassis	620	2775	—
CCX-250	Chassis & Cab	720	—	—
CCX-250	Chassis & W/S	635	—	—
Series CC-250/252 — 1-Ton — 134.5 in. w.b.				
CC-252	Chassis	620	2685	—
CC-252	Chassis & W/S	635	—	—
CC-252	Chassis & Cab	720	3075	—
CC-252	Pickup	800	3390	—
CC-252	Pickup Stake	817	3460	—
CC-252	Stake	800	3875	—
CC-252	Panel	895	3685	—
CC-252	Canopy Express	935	3645	—
CC-252	Canopy Screen	963	3730	—
Series CC-260				
CC-262	Chassis	635	2955	—
CC-262	Chassis & Cab	735	3345	—
CC-262	Platform	790	3915	—
CC-262	Stake	815	4165	—
CC-262	Pickup	810	3660	—
CC-262	Pickup Stake	832	3750	—
CC-262	Panel	915	3975	—
CC-262	Canopy Exp.	955	3935	—
CC-262	Canopy Screen	982	4020	—
Series CCL-300				
CCL-300	Chassis	645	3075	—
CCL-300	Chassis & Cab	745	3465	—
CCL-300	Platform	800	4035	—
CCL-300	Stake	825	4285	—
CCL-300	Pickup	820	3780	—
CCL-300	Pickup Stake	842	3870	—
CCL-300	Panel	925	4095	—
CCL-300	Canopy Exp.	965	4055	—
CCL-300	Canopy Screen	992	4140	—

ENGINE: Inline. OHV. Six-cylinder. Cast iron block. Bore & stroke: 3.5625 in. x 3.8125 in. Displacement: 228 cid. Brake hp: 80 at 3000 rpm. (93 hp at 3200 rpm after June 1941.) Four main bearings. Hydraulic valve lifters. Carburetor: one-barrel.
CHASSIS [Series CC-101]: Wheelbase: 115 in. Tires: 6.00 x 16 in. four-ply.
CHASSIS [Series CC-102]: Wheelbase: 125.25 in. Wheels: 16 x 4.50 in. Tires: 6.00 x 16 four-ply.
CHASSIS [Series ACV-101]: Wheelbase: 113.5 in. Tires: 6.00 x 16 six-ply.
CHASSIS [Series CCV-101]: Wheelbase: 115 in. Tires: 6.00 x 16 six-ply.
CHASSIS [Series CC-152]: Wheelbase: 125.25 in. Tires: 7.00 x 15 in. Wheels: 15 x 5.50 in.
CHASSIS [Series AF-241]: Wheelbase: 112 in. Tires: 7.00 x 16 six-ply.
CHASSIS [Series AFP-241]: Wheelbase: 100 in. Tires: 7.00 x 16 six-ply.
CHASSIS [Series CC-251]: Wheelbase: 115 in. Tires: 7.00 x 16 six-ply.
CHASSIS [Series CCX-252/CC-252]: Wheelbase: 125.25 in. Tires: 7.00 x 16 six-ply.
CHASSIS [Series CC-262]: Wheelbase: 134.50 in. Tires: 6.00 x 20 six-ply.
CHASSIS [Series CCL-300]: Wheelbase: 134.50 in. Tires: 6.00 x 20 six-ply front; 32 x 6 eight-ply rear.
TECHNICAL: Manual transmission. Speeds: 3F/1R. Floor mounted gear shift lever. Single dry-disc clutch. Hypoid, semi-floating rear axle. Overall ratio: [CC-100] 4.11:1, [CC-150]: 4.55:1. Hydraulic brakes. Pressed steel wheels. Four-speed transmission ($15.40). Economy engine ($10).

Standard Catalog of Light-Duty Trucks

OPTIONS: Front bumper. Rear bumper. Radio. Master heater ($11.55). Clock. Cigar lighter. Radio antenna. Seat covers ($2.50). Air cleaner ($3.10). Oil filter ($4). Defroster ($6.25). Whipcord upholstery ($9.25). Heater and defroster ($17.80). Available colors: Permanent red, Pimpernal, Ferrara blue.

HISTORICAL: Calendar year registrations: [All models] 45,703.

1942 GMC

1942 GMC 1/2-Ton Model CC-101 Pickup (GMC)

SERIES CC-100/101/102 — 1/2-TON — SIX-CYLINDER: Styling was unchanged from 1941 in any significant way. The two-tier grille arrangement highlighted by horizontal bars continued. The CC-100/101 line contained nine models on a 115 in. wheelbase. Basically, 1/2-tons were in the CC-100 series. Those with the short wheelbase were in the CC-101 sub-series and those with the longer wheelbase were CC-102s.

SERIES CCV-101 — 1/2-TON — SIX-CYLINDER: The 1/2-ton delivery with the V model suffix was carried over with a 115 in. wheelbase from late 1941.

SERIES CC-100/102 — 1/2-TON — SIX-CYLINDER: There were now seven models in the long-wheelbase 1/2-ton series. The wheelbase used increased to 125-1/4 in.

SERIES CC-150/152 — 3/4-TON — SIX-CYLINDER: This series was identical to the CC-102, except the chassis was rated for 3/4-ton payloads.

SERIES CC-250/CC-251 — 1-TON — SIX-CYLINDER: Offered again this year was a short (115 in.) wheelbase 1-ton series with chassis models only.

SERIES CC-250/CC-252 — 1-TON — SIX-CYLINDER: Ten 1-ton trucks were offered on a 134-1/2 in. wheelbase in both these series.

SERIES CCX-252 — 1-TON — SIX-CYLINDER: New this year was a medium (125-1/4 in.) wheelbase 1-ton series with chassis models only.

SERIES CC-260/CC-262 — 1-TON — SIX-CYLINDER: This was a line of trucks virtually identical to CC-252s, except for larger wheels and tires.

SERIES AF-241/AFP-241 — 1-TON — SIX-CYLINDER: This series offered GMC's smallest walk-in delivery vans on a 112 in. wheelbase (or special 100 in. wheelbase for the AFP).

SERIES CCL-300 — 1-TON — SIX-CYLINDER: This series duplicated the CC-262 in models, wheelbase, engine, and (front) tire size, but these were "L" (light-duty) editions of the sturdier 1-1/2-ton CC-300 series and added larger, dual rear tires.

I.D. DATA: Serial number located on right-hand frame side rail at front and on right side of firewall. Starting: [C-101/CC-102] 10635 up; [CCV-101] 224 up; [CC-152] 5353 up; [AF-241] 221 up; [AFP-241] 173 up; [CC-251/CCX-252/CC-252] 4357 up; [CC-262] 1530 up. Engine numbers located crankcase side.

Model	Body Type	Price	Weight	Prod. Total
Series CC-100 — 1/2-Ton — 115 in. w.b.				
CC-101	Chassis	515	2340	—
CC-101	Chassis & Cab	615	2730	—
CC-101	Pickup	648	2965	—
CC-101	Pickup Stake	666	3030	—
CC-101	Panel	730	3195	—
CC-101	Canopy Express	765	3195	—
CC-101	Screen	790	3260	—
CC-101	Suburban	875	3330	—
Series CC-100 — 1/2-Ton — 125.25 in. w.b.				
CC-102	Chassis	530	2395	—
CC-102	Chassis & Cab	630	2785	—
CC-102	Pickup	675	3055	—
CC-102	Pickup Stake	695	3130	—
CC-102	Stake	700	3335	—
CC-102	Panel	775	3280	—
Series CC-150 — 3/4-Ton — 125.25 in. w.b.				
CC-152	Chassis	595	2455	—
CC-152	Chassis & Cab	695	2845	—
CC-152	Pickup	740	3115	—
CC-152	Pickup Stake	760	3190	—
CC-152	Stake	765	3395	—
CC-152	Panel	840	3340	—
Series CC-250 — 1-Ton — 115 in. w.b.				
CC-251	Chassis	620	2588	—
CC-251	Chassis & W/S	635	2630	—
CC-251	Chassis & Cab	720	2990	—

Series CCX -250 — 1-Ton — 125.25 in. w.b.				
CCX-252	Chassis	620	2775	—
CCX-252	Chassis & W/S	635	2805	—
CCX-252	Chassis & Cab	720	3165	—
Series CC-250 — 1-Ton — 134.5 in. w.b.				
CC-252	Chassis	620	2665	—
CC-252	Chassis & Cab	720	3055	—
CC-252	Platform	775	3625	—
CC-252	Pickup	795	3370	—
CC-252	Pickup Stake	817	3460	—
CC-250	Stake	800	3875	—
CC-250	Panel	895	3685	—
CC-250	Canopy Express	935	3645	—
CC-250	Canopy Screen	963	3730	—
Series CC-260 — 1-Ton — 134.5 in. w.b.				
CC-262	Chassis	635	2955	—
CC-262	Chassis & Cab	735	3345	—
CC-262	Platform	790	3915	—
CC-262	Stake	815	4165	—
CC-262	Pickup	810	3660	—
CC-262	Pickup Stake	832	3750	—
CC-262	Panel	915	3975	—
CC-262	Canopy Express	955	3935	—
CC-262	Canopy Screen	982	4020	—
Series CCL-300 — 1-Ton — 134.5 in. w.b.				
CCL-300	Chassis	645	3075	—
CCL-300	Chassis & Cab	745	3465	—
CCL-300	Platform	800	4035	—
CCL-300	Stake	825	4285	—
CCL-300	Pickup	820	3780	—
CCL-300	Pickup Stake	842	3870	—
CCL-300	Panel	925	4095	—
CCL-300	Canopy Express	965	4055	—
CCL-300	Canopy Screen	992	4140	—

ENGINE: Inline. OHV. Six-cylinder. Cast iron block. Bore & stroke: 3.5625 in. x 3.8125 in. Displacement: 228 cid. Brake hp: 93 at 3200 rpm. Four main bearings. Hydraulic valve lifters. Carburetor: one-barrel.

CHASSIS [Series CC-101]: Wheelbase: 115 in. Tires: 6.00 x 16 in. four-ply.

CHASSIS [Series CC-102]: Wheelbase: 125.25 in. Wheels: 16 x 4.50 in. Tires: 6.00 x 16 four-ply.

CHASSIS [Series CCV-101]: Wheelbase: 115 in. Tires: 6.00 x 16 six-ply.

CHASSIS [Series CC-152]: Wheelbase: 125.25 in. Tires: 7.00 x 15 in. six-ply. Wheels: 15 x 5.50 in.

CHASSIS [Series AF-241]: Wheelbase: 112 in. Tires: 7.00 x 16 six-ply.

CHASSIS [Series AFP-241]: Wheelbase: 100 in. Tires: 7.00 x 16 six-ply.

CHASSIS [Series CC-251]: Wheelbase: 115 in. Tires: 7.00 x 16 six-ply.

CHASSIS [Series CCX-252/CC-252]: Wheelbase: 125.25 in. Tires: 7.00 x 16 six-ply.

CHASSIS [Series CC-262]: Wheelbase: 134.50 in. Tires: 6.00 x 20 six-ply.

CHASSIS [Series CCL-300]: Wheelbase: 134.50 in. Tires: 6.00 x 20 six-ply front; 32 x 6 eight-ply rear.

TECHNICAL: Manual transmission. Speeds: 3F/1R. Floor mounted gear shift lever. Single dry-disc clutch. Hypoid, semi-floating rear axle. Overall ratio: [CC-100]: 4.11:1, [CC-150]: 4.55:1. Hydraulic, four-wheel brakes. Pressed steel wheels. Four-speed transmission.

OPTIONS: Front bumper. Rear bumper. Radio. Heater. Clock. Cigar lighter. Radio antenna. Seat covers. Air cleaner. Oil filter. Defroster. Whipcord upholstery.

1945-1946 GMC

1946 GMC 1/2-Ton Model CC-102 Pickup (DSO)

GMC — LIGHT-DUTY — SIX-CYLINDER: GMC resumed production with the light-duty trucks virtually identical to their prewar counterparts. The front grille was characterized by a horizontal bar scheme with the GMC logo prominently displayed on the uppermost section. The headlights extended forward from the fenders and were crowned by torpedo-shaped parking lights. The side hood section carried a long chrome spear bearing "General Motors Truck" lettering.

I.D. DATA: Serial numbers placed on front section of right side frame rail and on engine firewall. Starting: [CC-101] CC-101-16726 to CC-101-18831; [CC-102] CC-102-16726 to CC-102-18831. Engine numbers located on left side of cylinders block behind oil filler.

Model	Body Type	Price	Weight	Prod. Total
Series CC-101 — 1/2-Ton — 115 in. w.b.				
CC-101	Chassis	651	2340	—
CC-101	Chassis & Cab	761	2730	—
CC-101	Pickup	805	2965	—
CC-101	Panel	887	3195	—
Series CC-102 — 1/2-Ton — 125.25 in. w.b.				
CC-102	Chassis	666	2395	—
CC-102	Chassis & Cab	776	2785	—
CC-102	Pickup	832	3055	—

ENGINE: Inline. OHV. Six-cylinder. Cast iron block. Bore & stroke: 3.5625 in. x 3.8125 in. Displacement: 228 cid. Brake horsepower: 93. Mechanical valve lifters. Carburetor: one-barrel.

CHASSIS [Series CC-101]: Wheelbase: 115 in. Tires: 15 in. six-ply.
CHASSIS [Series CC-102]: Wheelbase: 125.25 in. Tires: 15 in. six-ply.
TECHNICAL: Manual synchromesh transmission. Speeds: 3F/1R. Floor mounted gear shift. Single plate, dry disc clutch. Semi-floating rear axle. Hydraulic, four-wheel brakes. Pressed steel wheels. Four-speed manual transmission ($15).
OPTIONS: Rear bumper. Bumper guards. Radio. Heater. Clock. Cigar lighter. Radio antenna. Seat covers. Spotlight.
HISTORICAL: Registrations 1945-1946 series: [All GMC models] 25,645.

1947 GMC
(1st Series)

GMC — LIGHT-DUTY — SIX-CYLINDER: There were three series of 1947 GMCs. The first was simply a carryover of the 1942-1946 CC Series with the 115 in./125.25 in. wheelbases. The front grille was again characterized by a horizontal bar scheme with the GMC logo prominently displayed on the uppermost section. The headlights extended forward from the fenders and were crowned by torpedo-shaped parking lights. The side hood section still carried a long chrome spear bearing "General Motors Truck" lettering.
I.D. DATA: Serial numbers placed on front section of right side frame rail and on engine firewall. Starting: [CC-101] CC-101-18832 up; [CC-102] CC-102-18832 up. Engine numbers located on left side of cylinders block behind oil filler.

Model	Body Type	Price	Weight	Prod. Total
Series CC-101 — 1/2-Ton — 115 in. w.b.				
CC-101	Chassis	721	2390	—
CC-101	Chassis & Cab	848	2780	—
CC-101	Pickup	891	3015	—
CC-101	Panel	990	3325	—
Series CC-102 — 1/2-Ton — 125.25 in. w.b.				
CC-102	Chassis	741	2440	—
CC-102	Chassis & Cab	868	2830	—
CC-102	Pickup	927	3055	—

ENGINE: Inline. OHV. Six-cylinder. Cast iron block. Bore & stroke: 3.5625 in. x 3.8125 in. Displacement: 228 cid. Brake horsepower: 93. Mechanical valve lifters. Carburetor: one-barrel.
CHASSIS [Series CC-101]: Wheelbase: 115 in. Tires: 15 in. six-ply.
CHASSIS [Series CC-102]: Wheelbase: 125.25 in. Tires: 15 in. six-ply.
TECHNICAL: Manual synchromesh transmission. Speeds: 3F/1R. Floor mounted gear shift. Single plate, dry disc clutch. Semi-floating rear axle. Hydraulic, four-wheel brakes. Pressed steel wheels. Four-speed manual transmission ($15).
OPTIONS: Rear bumper. Bumper guards. Radio. Heater. Clock. Cigar lighter. Radio antenna. Seat covers. Spotlight.
HISTORICAL: Any 1946 CC Series trucks remaining in inventory on Oct. 1, 1946 could be registered as 1947 models.

1947 GMC
(2nd Series)

SERIES EC-101 — 1/2-TON — SIX-CYLINDER: The second 1947 series was a continuation of the prewar line, with new EC Series coding. The 3/4-ton and 1-ton series also reappeared. Styling was basically unchanged from prewar and 1947 First Series models in any important way, although there were some detail variations. Prices and weights were higher and the model count was lower. Among body styles no longer offered were the pickup with stake sides and the screenside delivery. The two-tier grille arrangement highlighted by horizontal bars continued. The EC-100/101 line contained nine models on a 115 in. wheelbase. Basically, 1/2-tons were in the EC-100 series. Those with the short wheelbase were in the EC-101 sub-series and those with the longer wheelbase were EC-102s.
SERIES EC-102 — 1/2-TON — SIX-CYLINDER: There were now five models in the long-wheelbase (125-1/4 in.) 1/2-ton series.
SERIES EC-152 — 3/4-TON — SIX-CYLINDER: This series was identical to the EC-102, except the chassis was rated for 3/4-ton payloads.
SERIES EC-251 — 1-TON — SIX-CYLINDER: Reintroduced this year was a short (115 in.) wheelbase 1-ton series with chassis models only.
SERIES EC-252 — 1-TON — SIX-CYLINDER: Seven 1-ton trucks were offered on a 134-1/2 in. wheelbase in this series.
SERIES ECX-252 — 1-TON — SIX-CYLINDER: Reintroduced this year was a medium (125-1/4 in.) wheelbase 1-ton series with chassis models only.
SERIES EC-262 — 1-TON — SIX-CYLINDER: This was a line of trucks virtually identical to EC-252s, except for larger wheels and tires.
SERIES EF-241/EFP-241 — 1-TON — SIX-CYLINDER: This series offered GMC's smallest walk-in delivery vans on a 112 in. wheelbase (or special 100 in. wheelbase for the EFP).

SERIES ECL-300 — 1-TON — SIX-CYLINDER: This series duplicated the EC-262 in models, wheelbase, engine, and (front) tire size, but these were "L" (light-duty) editions of the sturdier 1-1/2-ton EC-300 series and added larger, dual rear tires.
I.D. DATA: Serial number located on right-hand frame side rail at front and on right side of firewall. Engine numbers located crankcase side.

Model	Body Type	Price	Weight	Prod. Total
Series EC-101 — 1/2-Ton — 115 in. w.b.				
EC-101	Chassis & Cab	885	2780	—
EC-101	Pickup	928	3015	—
EC-101	Panel	1029	3325	—
EC-101	Canopy Express	1076	3305	—
EC-101	Suburban	1219	3340	—
Series EC-102 — 1/2-Ton — 125.25 in. w.b.				
EC-102	Chassis	778	2440	—
EC-102	Chassis & Cab	905	2830	—
EC-102	Pickup	964	3100	—
EC-102	Stake	1012	3380	—
EC-102	Panel	1089	3405	—
Series EC-152 — 3/4-Ton — 125.25 in. w.b.				
EC-152	Chassis	881	2485	—
EC-152	Chassis & Cab	1008	2875	—
EC-152	Pickup	1067	3145	—
EC-152	Stake	1115	3425	—
EC-152	Panel	1192	3450	—
Series EC-251 — 1-Ton — 115 in. w.b.				
EC-251	Chassis	953	3060	—
EC-251	Chassis & Cab	1080	3450	—
Series ECX-252 — 1-Ton — 125.25 in. w.b.				
ECX-252	Chassis	953	3100	—
ECX-252	Chassis & Cab	1080	3490	—
Series EC-252 — 1-Ton — 134.5 in. w.b.				
EC-252	Chassis	953	3120	—
EC-252	Chassis & Cab	1080	3510	—
EC-252	Platform	1170	4088	—
EC-252	Pickup	1179	3825	—
EC-250	Stake	1203	4338	—
EC-250	Panel	1312	4220	—
EC-250	Canopy Express	1363	4160	—
Series EC-262 — 1-Ton — 134.5 in. w.b.				
EC-262	Chassis	935	3510	—
EC-262	Chassis & Cab	1062	3900	—
EC-262	Platform	1152	4478	—
EC-262	Stake	1185	4728	—
EC-262	Pickup	1161	4215	—
EC-262	Panel	1294	4610	—
EC-262	Canopy Express	1345	4550	—
Series ECL-300 — 1-Ton — 134.5 in. w.b.				
ECL-300	Chassis	974	3575	—
ECL-300	Chassis & Cab	1101	3965	—
ECL-300	Platform	1215	4714	—
ECL-300	Stake	1268	5009	—
ECL-300	Express	1288	5095	—

ENGINE: Inline. OHV. Six-cylinder. Cast iron block. Bore & stroke: 3.5625 in. x 3.8125 in. Displacement: 228 cid. Brake hp: 93 at 3200 rpm. Four main bearings. Hydraulic valve lifters. Carburetor: one-barrel.
CHASSIS [Series EC-101]: Wheelbase: 115 in. Tires: 6.00 x 16 in. four-ply.
CHASSIS [Series EC-102]: Wheelbase: 125.25 in. Wheels: 16 x 4.50 in. Tires: 6.00 x 16 four-ply.
CHASSIS [Series EC-152]: Wheelbase: 125.25 in. Tires: 7.00 x 15 in. six-ply. Wheels: 15 x 5.50 in.
CHASSIS [Series EF-241]: Wheelbase: 112 in. Tires: 7.00 x 16 six-ply.
CHASSIS [Series EFP-241]: Wheelbase: 100 in. Tires: 7.00 x 16 six-ply.
CHASSIS [Series EC-251]: Wheelbase: 115 in. Tires: 7.00 x 16 six-ply.
CHASSIS [Series ECX-252/EC-252]: Wheelbase: 125.25 in. Tires: 7.00 x 16 six-ply.
CHASSIS [Series EC-262]: Wheelbase: 134.50 in. Tires: 6.00 x 20 six-ply.
CHASSIS [Series ECL-300]: Wheelbase: 134.50 in. Tires: 6.00 x 20 six-ply front; 32 x 6 eight-ply rear.
TECHNICAL: Manual transmission. Speeds: 3F/1R. Floor mounted gear shift lever. Single dry-disc clutch. Hypoid, semi-floating rear axle. Overall ratio: [EC-100]: 4.11:1, [EC-150]: 4.55:1. Hydraulic, four-wheel brakes. Pressed steel wheels. Four-speed transmission.
OPTIONS: Front bumper. Rear bumper. Radio. Heater. Clock. Cigar lighter. Radio antenna. Seat covers. Air cleaner. Oil filter. Defroster. Whipcord upholstery.

1947 GMC
(3rd Series)

GMC — LIGHT-DUTY — SIX-CYLINDER: Mid-way through 1947 GMC introduced totally restyled light-duty trucks. They had General Motor's all-new "Advance-Design" styling for the postwar marketplace. The appearance of these models was attractive, devoid of excess trim, smooth and streamlined. Large GMC lettering was mounted at the top of a simple multi-tiered grille with broad horizontal bars. The headlights were mounted totally within the front fenders and small, circular parking lights were positioned directly below the headlights. Drivers were quick to appreciate the GMC's improved cab ventilation, improved visibility and revamped front suspension system.

1947 GMC 1-Ton Model FC-253 Panel Delivery (GMC)

I.D. DATA: Unchanged from 1946. Starting: [FC-101] FC-101-001 and up; [FC-102] FC-102-001 and up; [FC-152] FC-152-001 and up; [FC-151] FC-151-001 and up; [FC-252] FC-252-001 and up; [FC-281] FC-281-001 and up; [FC-283] FC-283-001 and up; [EF-241] EF-241-001 and up; [EF-242] EF-242-001 and up; [EFP-241] EFP-241-001 and up; [EFP-242] EFP-242-001 and up; Engine numbers located same as in 1946.

Model	Body Type	Price	Weight	Prod. Total
Series FC-101 — 1/2-Ton — 116 in. w.b.				
FC-101	Chassis	845	2580	—
FC-101	Chassis & Cab	1030	3075	—
FC-101	Pickup	1085	3310	—
FC-101	Panel	1410	4010	—
FC-101	Canopy Exp.	1460	3990	—
FC-101	Suburban	1445	—	—
Series FC-102 — 1/2-Ton — 125.25 in. w.b.				
FC-102	Chassis	865	2560	—
FC-102	Chassis & Cab	1050	3055	—
FC-102	Pickup	1120	3325	—
FC-102	Platform	1175	3605	—
Series FC-152 — 3/4-Ton — 125.25 in. w.b.				
FC-152	Chassis	940	2820	—
FC-152	Chassis & Cab	1125	3315	—
FC-152	Pickup	1195	3585	—
FC-152	Platform	1250	3865	—
Series FC-251 — 1-Ton — 116 in. w.b.				
FC-251	Chassis	985	3165	—
Series FC-252 — 1-Ton — 125.25 in. w.b.				
FC-252	Chassis	1005	3195	—
FC-252	Chassis & Cab	1190	3690	—
Series FCL-253 — 1-Ton — 137 in. w.b.				
FCL-253	Chassis	1020	3240	—
FCL-253	Chassis & Cab	1205	3735	—
FCL-253	Pickup	1305	4050	—
FCL-253	Panel	1645	4835	—
FCL-253	Platform Stake	1385	4563	—
FCL-253	Platform	1320	4313	—
FCL-253	Canopy	1720	4775	—
Series FCL-281 — 1-Ton — 137 in. w.b.				
FC-281	Chassis	1115	3710	—
FC-281	Chassis & Cab	1300	4205	—
FC-281	Platform Stake	1480	5033	—
FC-281	Platform	1415	4783	—
Series FCL-283 — 1-Ton — 161 in. w.b.				
FC-283	Chassis	1145	3885	—
FC-283	Chassis & Cab	1330	4380	—
FC-283	Platform Stake	1545	5424	—
FC-283	Platform	1465	5129	—
FC-283	Platform Express	1550	5510	—

ENGINE: Inline. OHV. Six-cylinder. Cast iron block. Bore & stroke: 3.5625 in. x 3.8125 in. Displacement: 228 cid. Brake hp: 93 at 3200 rpm. Four main bearings. Hydraulic valve lifters. Carburetor: one-barrel.
CHASSIS [Series FC-101]: Wheelbase: 116 in. Overall length: 196.575 in. Tires: 6.00 x 16 six-ply.
CHASSIS [Series FC-102]: Wheelbase: 125.25 in. Overall length: 206 in. Tires: 6.00 x 16 six-ply.
CHASSIS [Series FC-152]: Wheelbase: 125.25 in. Overall length: 206 in. Tires: 15 in. six-ply.
CHASSIS [Series FC-251]: Wheelbase: 116 in. Overall length: 196.575 in. Tires: 7.00 x 17 six-ply.
CHASSIS [Series FC-152]: Wheelbase: 125.25 in. Overall length: 206 in. Tires: 15 in. six-ply.
CHASSIS [Series FC-251]: Wheelbase: 116 in. Overall length: 196.575 in. Tires: 7.00 x 17 six-ply.
CHASSIS [Series FC-252]: Wheelbase: 125.25 in. Overall length: 206 in. Tires: 7.00 x 17 six-ply.
CHASSIS [Series FC-253]: Wheelbase: 137 in. Overall length: 223.875 in. Tires: 7.00 x 17 six-ply.
CHASSIS [Series FC-281]: Wheelbase: 137 in. Overall length: 223.875 in. Tires: 6.50 x 20.
CHASSIS [Series FC-283]: Wheelbase: 161 in. Overall length: 265 in. Tires: 6.50 x 20.
TECHNICAL: Manual transmission. Speeds: 3F/1R. Floor mounted gear shift lever. Single dry-disc clutch. Hypoid, semi-floating rear axle. Overall ratio: [EC-100]: 4.11:1, [EC-150]: 4.55:1. Hydraulic, four-wheel brakes. Pressed steel wheels. Four-speed transmission.

OPTIONS: Double-acting shock absorbers. Economy rear axle. Rearview mirrors and brackets. Oil-bath air cleaner. Heavy-duty clutch. Governor. Bumper guards. Tail and stop lamp equipment. Heavy-duty cooling system and radiator. Right-hand front seat in panel, canopy. Double-acting rear springs. Radiator with overflow return tank. Heavy-duty three-speed transmission. Heavy-duty four-speed transmission. Tru-Stop brake equipment. Inside cab fuel tank. Wide runningboards. Fresh air ventilator heater and defroster. Chrome radiator grille. Rear cab corner windows. Deluxe cab and equipment.
HISTORICAL: Calendar year registrations: [All series] 49,187.

1948 GMC

1948 GMC Cantrell Station Wagon (OCW)

GMC — LIGHT-DUTY — SIX-CYLINDER: The new postwar trucks introduced midway through 1947 continued to be marketed. The appearance was unchanged. Large GMC letters were above the simple horizontal bar grille. The headlights were in the front fenders. Small, circular parking lights were positioned directly below the headlights. The trucks had two-piece windshields, alligator hoods, one-piece door windows. There was also GMC lettering on the rear corners of the hoodsides. The gas tank on pickups was mounted under the frame, though an inside-the-cab tank was optional. The Model EF delivery vans had new 102 in. and 132 in. wheelbases.
I.D. DATA: Serial number located stamped on plate positioned on left door hinge pillar. Starting: [EF-241] EF-241-1559 to 3982; [EFP-241] EFP-241-1559 to 3982; [EF-242] EF-242-1559 to 3982; [EFP-242] EFP242-1559 to 3982; [FC-101] FC-101-2430 to 25886; [FC-102] FC-102-2430 to 25886; [FC-152] FC-152-601 to 6884; [FC-251] FC-251-517 to 8075; [FC-252] FC-252-517 to 8075; [FC-253] FC-253-517 to 8075. Engine numbers located on left-hand side of cylinder block behind oil filter. Starting: A24869253, C24875484, B270745183.

1948 GMC 1/2-Ton Model 101 Suburban Carryall (OCW)

Model	Body Type	Price	Weight	Prod. Total
Series FC-101 — 1/2-Ton — 116 in. w.b.				
FC-101	Chassis	915	2580	—
FC-101	Chassis & Cab	1135	3065	—
FC-101	Pickup	1200	3330	—
FC-101	Panel	1385	3500	—
FC-101	Canopy Express	1435	3500	—
FC-101	Suburban	1015	—	—
Series FC-102 — 1/2-Ton — 125.25 in. w.b.				
FC-102	Chassis	935	2560	—
FC-102	Chassis & Cab	1155	3045	—
FC-102	Pickup	1240	3335	—
FC-102	Stake	1300	3660	—
Series FC-152 — 3/4-Ton — 125.25 in. w.b.				
FC-152	Chassis	1025	2820	—
FC-152	Chassis & Cab	1245	3305	—
FC-152	Pickup	1330	3595	—
FC-152	Stake	1390	3910	—
Series EF-241 — 1-Ton — 102 in. w.b.				
EF-241	Package Delivery	2595	3120	—

Series EFP — 1-Ton — 102 in. w.b.

EFP-241	Package Delivery	2760	3310	—

Series FC-251 — 1-Ton — 116 in. w.b.

FC-251	Chassis	1095	3165	—

Series FC-252 — 1-Ton — 125.25 in. w.b.

FC-252	Chassis	1115	3195	—
FC-252	Chassis & Cab	1335	3680	—

Series FC-253 — 1-Ton — 137 in. w.b.

FC-253	Chassis	1130	3240	—
FC-253	Chassis & Cab	1350	3725	—
FC-253	Pickup	1460	4055	—
FC-253	Platform	1475	4260	—
FC-253	Stake	1550	4510	—
FC-253	Panel	1620	4335	—
FC-253	Canopy Express	1695	4340	—

ENGINE: Inline. OHV. 6-cylinder. Cast iron block. Bore & stroke: 3.5625 x 3.8125 in. Displacement: 228 cid. Brake horsepower: 93. NACC HP: 30.4. Mechanical valve lifters. Carburetor: Carter one-barrel.

CHASSIS [Series FC-101]: Wheelbase: 116 in. Overall length: 196.575 in. Tires: 6.00 x 16, six-ply.

CHASSIS [Series FC-102]: Wheelbase: 125.25 in. Overall length: 206 in. Tires: 6.00 x 16, six-ply.

CHASSIS [Series FC-152]: Wheelbase: 125.25 in. Overall length: 206 in. Tires: 15, six-ply.

CHASSIS [Series EF-241]: Wheelbase: 102 in. Tires: 7.00 x 16, six-ply.

CHASSIS [Series EF-242]: Wheelbase: 132 in. Tires: 8.25 x 16, 10-ply.

CHASSIS [Series EFP-241]: Wheelbase: 102 in. Tires: 7.00 x 16, six-ply.

CHASSIS [Series FC-251]: Wheelbase: 116 in. Overall length: 196.575 in. Tires: 7.00 x 17, six-ply.

CHASSIS [Series FC-252]: Wheelbase: 125.25 in. Overall length: 206 in. Tires: 7.00 x 17, six-ply.

CHASSIS [Series FC-253]: Wheelbase: 137 in. Overall length: 224.125 in. Tires: 7.00 x 17, six-ply.

1948 GMC 1/2-Ton Model FC-101 Pickup (LS)

TECHNICAL: Manual, synchromesh. Speeds: 3F/1R. Floor-mounted gearshift. Clutch: Single disc, diaphragm spring. Semi-floating [1/2-ton], full-floating [all others] rear axle. Overall ratio: 4.11.1 [FC-101]. Hydraulic, four-wheel brakes. Pressed steel wheels.

DRIVETRAIN OPTIONS: Four-speed manual transmission ($50). Oil bath air filter ($3.50). AC oil filter ($10). Vacuum pump on fuel pump ($8). Double action front shock absorbers ($10). Double action rear shock absorbers ($10).

OPTIONS: Double-acting shock absorbers. Economy rear axle. Rearview mirrors and brackets. Oil-bath air cleaner. Heavy-duty clutch. Governor. Oil filter. Bumper guard. Tail and stop lamp equipment. Heavy-duty cooling system and radiator. Right-hand front seat in panel, canopy. Double-acting rear springs. Radiator with overflow return tank. Heavy-duty three-speed transmission. Heavy-duty four-speed transmission. Tru-Stop brake equipment. Inside cab fuel tank. Wide runningboards. Fresh air ventilator heater and defroster. Chrome radiator grille. Rear cab corner windows. Deluxe cab and equipment.

HISTORICAL: Introduced: Summer, 1947. Calendar year registrations: [All series] 74,857.

1948 GMC 1/2-Ton Model FC-101 Panel Delivery (DSO)

1949 GMC

1949 GMC 1/2-Ton Model FC-100 Pickup (GMC)

GMC — LIGHT-DUTY — SIX-CYLINDER: GMC trucks were basically unchanged from 1948. There were some technical improvements. An inside-the-cab gas tank was now standard, so all 1948 pickups had the gas filler at the right rear of the cab instead of on the side of the cargo box.

I.D. DATA: Serial number located unchanged from 1948. Starting: FC-152-181 up; Oakland 601 up. EF-241 and EFP-241-3983 and up. FC-101-25887-64000. FC-102-25887-64000. FC-152-6885-20200. FC-251-8076-19101. FC-252-8076-19101. FC-253-8076-19101. Engine number location unchanged from 1948.

1949 GMC 1/2-Ton Model 101 Panel Delivery (OCW)

Model	Body Type	Price	Weight	Prod. Total
Series FC-101 — 1/2-Ton — 116 in. w.b.				
FC-101	Chassis	985	2580	—
FC-101	Chassis & Cab	1210	3065	—
FC-101	Pickup	1275	3330	—
FC-101	Panel	1455	3985	—
FC-101	Canopy Express	1505	3985	—
FC-101	Suburban	1685	—	—
Series FC-102 — 1/2-Ton — 125.25 in. w.b.				
FC-102	Chassis	1005	2560	—
FC-102	Chassis & Cab	1230	3045	—
FC-102	Pickup	1315	3335	—
FC-102	Stake	1375	3660	—
Series FC-152 — 3/4-Ton — 125.25 in. w.b.				
FC-152	Chassis	1080	2820	—
FC-152	Chassis & Cab	1305	3305	—
FC-152	Pickup	1390	3595	—
FC-152	Stake	1450	3910	—
Series FP-152 — 3/4-Ton — 125.25 in. w.b.				
FP-152	Chassis Delivery	1095	2575	—
Series EF-241 — 1-Ton — 102 in. w.b.				
EF-241	Delivery	2840	3120	—
Series EFP-241 — 1-Ton — 102 in. w.b.				
EFP-241	Delivery	—	3310	—
Series EFP-242 — 1-Ton — 132 in. w.b.				
EFP-242	Delivery	—	3450	—
Series FC-251 — 1-Ton — 116 in. w.b.				
FC-251	Chassis	1150	3165	—
Series FC-252 — 1-Ton — 125.25 in. w.b.				
FC-252	Chassis	1150	3195	—
FC-252	Chassis & Cab	1375	3680	—

Series FC-253 — 1-Ton — 137 in. w.b.

FC-253	Chassis	1150	3240	—
FC-253	Chassis & Cab	1375	3725	—
FC-253	Pickup	1485	4055	—
FC-253	Panel	1665	4820	—
FC-253	Stake	1575	4510	—
FC-253	Platform	1500	4260	—
FC-253	Canopy Express	1740	4825	—

ENGINE: Inline. OHV. 6-cylinder. Cast iron block. Bore & stroke: 3.5625 x 3.8125 in. Displacement: 228 cid. Brake horsepower: 93. NACC HP: 30.4. Mechanical valve lifters. Carburetor: Carter one-barrel.
CHASSIS [Series FC-101]: Wheelbase: 116 in. Overall length: 196.575 in. Tires: 6.00 x 16, six-ply.
CHASSIS [Series FC-102]: Wheelbase: 125.25 in. Overall length: 206 in. Tires: 6.00 x 16, six-ply.
CHASSIS [Series FC-152]: Wheelbase: 125.25 in. Overall length: 206 in. Tires: 15, six-ply.
CHASSIS [Series EF-241]: Wheelbase: 102 in. Tires: 7.00 x 16, six-ply.
CHASSIS [Series EF-242]: Wheelbase: 132 in. Tires: 8.25 x 16, 10-ply.
CHASSIS [Series EFP-241]: Wheelbase: 102 in. Tires: 7.00 x 16, six-ply.
CHASSIS [Series FC-251]: Wheelbase: 116 in. Overall length: 196.575 in. Tires: 7.00 x 17, six-ply.
CHASSIS [Series FC-252]: Wheelbase: 125.25 in. Overall length: 206 in. Tires: 7.00 x 17, six-ply.
CHASSIS [Series FC-253]: Wheelbase: 137 in. Overall length: 224.125 in. Tires: 7.00 x 17, six-ply.
TECHNICAL: Manual, synchromesh. Speeds: 3F/1R. Floor-mounted gearshift. Clutch: Single disc, diaphragm spring. Semi-floating [1/2-ton], full-floating [all others] rear axle. Overall ratio: 4.11.1 [FC-101]. Hydraulic, four-wheel brakes. Pressed steel wheels.
DRIVETRAIN OPTIONS: Four-speed manual transmission ($50). Oil bath air filter ($3.50). AC oil filter ($10). Vacuum pump on fuel pump ($8). Double action front shock absorbers ($10). Double action rear shock absorbers ($10).
OPTIONS: Double-acting shock absorbers. Economy rear axle. Rearview mirrors and brackets. Oil-bath air cleaner. Governor. Oil filter. Dual tail and stop lamp equipment. Heavy-duty clutch. Heavy-duty radiator. Right-hand front seat in panel, canopy. Heavy-duty three-speed transmission. Heavy-duty four-speed transmission. Tru-Stop brake equipment. Wide runningboards. Fresh air ventilator heater and defroster. Chrome radiator grille. Deluxe cab and equipment.
HISTORICAL: Calendar year registrations: [All series] 80,407.

1950 GMC

1950 GMC 1/2-Ton Model FC-101 Pickup (DFW)

GMC — LIGHT-DUTY — SIX-CYLINDER: No big design changes were made in the GMC light-duty truck line for 1950. However, the 228 cid six-cylinder engine was increased in horsepower to 96, new airplane type shock absorbers were introduced, improvements were made to electrical systems and the availability of some options and accessories changed.
I.D. DATA: Serial number stamped on plate located on left door hinge pillar. Engine number located on left side of cylinder block behind oil filler. GM trucks were not produced on a yearly model change basis. Serial numbers were not made available to industry recording sources.

1950 GMC 3/4-Ton FC-152 Pickup 6.5-ft. (GMC)

Standard Catalog of Light-Duty Trucks

Model	Body Type	Price	Weight	Prod. Total
Series FC-101 — 1/2-Ton — 116 in. w.b.				
FC-101	Chassis	975	2550	—
FC-101	Chassis & Cab	1200	2980	—
FC-101	Pickup	1265	—	—
FC-101	Panel	1445	—	—
FC-101	Canopy Express	1495	—	—
FC-101	Suburban	1675	—	—
Series FC-102 — 1/2-Ton — 125.25 in. w.b.				
FC-102	Chassis	995	2540	—
FC-102	Chassis & Cab	1220	2970	—
FC-102	Pickup	1305	—	—
FC-102	Stake	1365	—	—
Series FC-152 — 3/4-Ton — 125.25 in. w.b.				
FC-152	Chassis	1070	2775	—
FC-152	Chassis & Cab	1295	3225	—
FC-152	Pickup	1380	—	—
FC-152	Stake	1440	—	—
Series FP-152 — 3/4-Ton — 125.25 in. w.b.				
FP-152	Chassis Delivery	—	2515	—
Series FC-251 — 1-Ton — 116 in. w.b.				
FC-251	Chassis	—	3000	—
Series FC-252 — 1-Ton — 125.25 in. w.b.				
FC-252	Chassis	—	3040	—
FC-252	Chassis & Cab	—	3490	—
Series FC-253 — 1-Ton — 137 in. w.b.				
FC-253	Chassis	—	3084	—
FC-253	Chassis & Cab	—	3535	—
Series FC-281 — 1-Ton — 137 in. w.b.				
FC-281	Chassis	1210	3460	—
FC-281	Chassis & Cab	1435	3905	—
FC-281	Platform	1560	—	—
FC-281	Stake	1635	—	—

ENGINE: Inline. OHV. Six-cylinder. Cast iron block. Bore & stroke: 3.5625 x 3.8125 in. Displacement: 228 cid. Brake hp: 96 at 3200 rpm. Mechanical valve lifters. Carburetor: Carter one-barrel.

1950 GMC 3/4-Ton Model FP152 Forward Control Panel (RPZ)

CHASSIS [Series FC-101]: Wheelbase: 116 in. Overall length: 196.575 in. Tires: 6.00 x 16, six-ply.
CHASSIS [Series FC-102]: Wheelbase: 125.25 in. Overall length: 206 in. Tires: 6.00 x 16, six-ply.
CHASSIS [Series FC-151]: Wheelbase: 125.25 in. Tires: 15 in., six-ply.
CHASSIS [Series FC-152]: Wheelbase: 125.25 in. Overall length: 206 in. Tires: 15 in., six-ply.
CHASSIS [Series FC-251]: Wheelbase: 116 in. Overall length: 196.58 in. Tires: 7.00 x 17, six-ply.
CHASSIS [Series FC-252]: Wheelbase: 125.25 in. Overall length: 206 in. Tires: 7.00 x 17, six-ply.
CHASSIS [Series FC-253]: Wheelbase: 125.25 in. Overall length: 223.88 in. Tires: 7.00 x 17, six-ply.
CHASSIS [Series FC-281]: Wheelbase: 137 in. Overall length: 223.875 in. Tires: 7.00 x 20, eight-ply.

1950 GMC 1/2-Ton Model FC-101 Panel (DFW/ATA)

425

TECHNICAL: Manual, synchromesh. Speeds: 3F/1R. Floor-mounted gearshift. Single disc, diaphragm spring clutch. Rear axle: [1/2-ton] semi-floating; [Others] full-floating. Hydraulic, four-wheel brakes. Pressed steel wheels.

DRIVETRAIN OPTIONS: Four-speed manual transmission. Oil bath. Oil filter. AC oil filter. Vacuum pump on fuel pump. Double action front and rear shock absorbers.

OPTIONS: Double-acting shock absorbers. Long runningboards and rear fenders. Non-standard rear axle ratios. Rearview mirrors and brackets. Rear shock absorber shield. Hydrovac power brake. Oil bath air cleaner. Heavy-duty clutch. Oil filter. Governor. Dual tail and stop lamp. Heavy-duty rear springs. Heavy-duty radiator. Right-hand front seat (panel, canopy). Auxiliary rear springs. Heavy-duty three- and four-speed transmissions. Combination fuel/vacuum pump. Genuine leather trim. Chrome radiator grille. Deluxe cab equipment. Deluxe panel equipment.

HISTORICAL: Calendar year registrations: [All] 97,200. The year's big innovation was the more powerful six-cylinder engine.

1950 GMC 1-Ton FC-252 Delivery With Stand-up Controls (DFW/GHB)

1951 GMC

1951 GMC 1/2-Ton Series 101-22 Panel (OCW)

GMC — LIGHT-DUTY — SIX-CYLINDER: General styling was unchanged from 1950. Ventipanes were added and the door glass was smaller as a consequence. Seats had a new adjusting mechanism. Front suspension stabilizer bars on 1/2-ton models were redesigned. Braking improvements were also made.

1951 GMC 3/4-Ton Series 152-22 Pickup (OCW)

I.D. DATA: Serial number stamped on plate located on left door hinge pillar. Engine number located on left side of cylinder block behind oil filler. GM trucks were not produced on a yearly model change basis. Serial numbers were not made available to industry recording sources.

Model	Body Type	Price	Weight	Prod. Total
Series 101-22 — 1/2-Ton — 116 in. w.b.				
101-22	Chassis	1025	2615	—
101-22	Chassis & Cab	1265	3045	—
101-22	Pickup	1330	3275	—
101-22	Panel	1510	3575	—
101-22	Canopy Express	1560	3540	—
101-22	Suburban	1702	3860	—
Series 102-22 — 1/2-Ton — 125.25 in. w.b.				
102-22	Chassis	1045	2610	—
102-22	Chassis & Cab	1285	3040	—
102-22	Pickup	1370	3365	—
102-22	Stake Rack	1435	3655	—
Series 152-22 — 3/4-Ton — 125.25 in. w.b.				
152-22	Chassis	1150	2870	—
152-22	Chassis & Cab	1390	3320	—
152-22	Pickup	1475	3640	—
152-22	Stake Rack	1540	3925	—
Series P152-22 — 3/4-Ton — 125.25 in. w.b.				
P152-22	Chassis Delivery	1170	2550	—
Series 252-22 — 1-Ton — 125.25 in. w.b.				
252-22	Chassis	1222	3130	—
252-22	Chassis & Cab	1462	3580	—
Series 253-22 — 1-Ton — 137 in. w.b.				
253-22	Chassis	1222	3170	—
253-22	Chassis & Cab	1462	3620	—
253-22	Panel	1762	4385	—
253-22	Pickup	1572	4105	—
253-22	Platform	1587	4165	—
253-22	Stake Rack	1652	4395	—
253-22	Canopy Express	1837	4410	—

ENGINE: Inline. OHV. Six-cylinder. Cast iron block. Bore & stroke: 3.5625 x 3.8125 in. Displacement: 228 cid. Brake hp: 100 at 3400 rpm.

1951 GMC 1-Ton Series P252-22 Forward-Control Panel (RPZ)

CHASSIS [Series 101-22]: Wheelbase: 116 in. Overall length: 196.575 in. Tires: 6.00 x 16, six-ply.

CHASSIS [Series 102-22]: Wheelbase: 125.25 in. Overall length: 206 in. Tires: 6.00 x 16, six-ply.

CHASSIS [Series 151-22]: Wheelbase: 125.25 in. Tires: 15 in., six-ply.

CHASSIS [Series 152-22]: Wheelbase: 125.25 in. Overall length: 206 in. Tires: 15 in., six-ply.

CHASSIS [Series 252-22]: Wheelbase: 125.25 in. Overall length: 206 in. Tires: 7.00 x 17, six-ply.

CHASSIS [Series 253-22]: Wheelbase: 137 in. Overall length: 223.88 in. Tires: 7.00 x 17, six-ply.

TECHNICAL: Manual synchromesh transmission. Speeds: 3F/1R. Floor mount gearshift. Single disc, diaphragm spring clutch. Rear axle: [1/2-ton] semi-floating. [All others] full-floating. Hydraulic, four-wheel brakes. Pressed steel wheels.

DRIVETRAIN OPTIONS: Four-speed manual transmission. Oil bath. Oil filter. AC oil filter. Vacuum pump on fuel pump. Double action front and rear shock absorbers.

OPTIONS: Double-acting shock absorbers. Long runningboards and rear fenders. Non-standard rear axle ratios. Rearview mirrors and brackets. Rear shock absorber shield. Hydrovac power brake. Oil bath air cleaner. Rear bumper. Heavy-duty clutch. Oil filter. Governor. Dual tail and stop lamp. Heavy-duty rear springs. Heavy-duty radiator. Right-hand front seat (panel, canopy). Auxiliary rear springs. Vacuum reserve tank. Heavy-duty three- and four-speed transmissions. Heavy-duty generator. Stand-up driving controls (delivery models). Combination fuel/vacuum pump. Chrome front bumper. Spare wheel and carrier. Chrome radiator grille. Deluxe cab equipment. Deluxe panel equipment. Nu-Vue cab windows.

HISTORICAL: Calendar year registrations. [All] 100,285. The horsepower of the GMC 228 cid engine increased to 100.

1952 GMC

1952 GMC 1/2-Ton Series 101-22 Canopy Express (OCW)

GMC — LIGHT-DUTY — SIX-CYLINDER: The appearance of GMC trucks was unchanged from 1951. There were some technical refinements, including cooling system improvements. The chrome front bumper option was temporarily dropped due to Korean War material restrictions.

1952 GMC 3/4-Ton Series P152-22 Express/Pickup (DFW)

I.D. DATA: Serial number stamped on plate located on left door hinge pillar. Engine number located on left side of cylinder block behind oil filler. GM trucks were not produced on a yearly model change basis. Serial numbers were not made available to industry recording sources.

1952 GMC 1/2-Ton Series 101-22 Pickup (RPZ)

Model	Body Type	Price	Weight	Prod. Total
Series FC-100-22 — 1/2-Ton — 116 in. w.b.				
101-22	Chassis	1073	2640	—
101-22	Chassis & Cab	1317	3105	—
101-22	Pickup	1385	3365	—
101-22	Panel	1566	3575	—
101-22	Canopy Express	1617	3555	—
101-22	Suburban	1826	3890	—

Standard Catalog of Light-Duty Trucks

Series 102-22 — 1/2-Ton — 125.25 in. w.b.				
102-22	Chassis	1094	2635	—
102-22	Chassis & Cab	1338	3100	—
102-22	Pickup	1427	3465	—
102-22	Stake Rack	1496	3705	—
Series P52-22 — 3/4-Ton — 125.25 in. w.b.				
P152-22	Chassis	1204	2845	—
P152-22	Chassis & Cab	1448	3330	—
P152-22	Pickup	1537	3095	—
P152-22	Stake Rack	1606	3915	—
P152-22	Chassis Delivery	1225	—	—
Series PM-152-22 — 3/4-Ton — 125.25 in. w.b.				
PM152-22	Chassis Delivery	1380	2695	—
Series 250-22 — 1-Ton — 125.25 in. w.b.				
252-22	Chassis	1282	3110	—
252-22	Chassis & Cab	1526	3595	—
Series 253-22 — 1-Ton — 137 in. w.b.				
253-22	Chassis	1282	3135	—
253-22	Chassis & Cab	1526	3620	—
253-22	Panel	1641	4355	—
253-22	Pickup	1657	4130	—
253-22	Platform	1725	4170	—
253-22	Stake Rack	1831	4405	—
253-22	Canopy Express	1907	4300	—

ENGINE: Inline. OHV. Six-cylinder. Cast iron block. Bore & stroke: 3.5625 x 3.8125 in. Displacement: 228 cid. Brake hp: 100 at 3400 rpm.

CHASSIS [Series 101-22]: Wheelbase: 116 in. Overall length: 196.575 in. Tires: 6.00 x 16, six-ply.

CHASSIS [Series 102-22]: Wheelbase: 125.25 in. Overall length: 206 in. Tires: 6.00 x 16, six-ply.

CHASSIS [Series 151-22]: Wheelbase: 125.25 in. Tires: 15 in., six-ply.

CHASSIS [Series 152-22]: Wheelbase: 125.25 in. Overall length: 206 in. Tires: 15 in., six-ply.

CHASSIS [Series 252-22]: Wheelbase: 125.25 in. Overall length: 206 in. Tires: 7.00 x 17, six-ply.

CHASSIS [Series 253-22]: Wheelbase: 137 in. Overall length: 223.88 in. Tires: 7.00 x 17, six-ply.

TECHNICAL: Manual synchromesh transmission. Speeds: 3F/1R. Floor mount gearshift. Single disc, diaphragm spring clutch. Rear axle: [1/2-ton] semi-floating. [All others] full-floating. Hydraulic, four-wheel brakes. Pressed steel wheels.

DRIVETRAIN OPTIONS: Four-speed manual transmission. Oil bath. Oil filter. AC oil filter. Vacuum pump on fuel pump. Double action front and rear shock absorbers.

OPTIONS: Double-acting shock absorbers. Long runningboards and rear fenders. Non-standard rear axle ratios. Rearview mirrors and brackets. Rear shock absorber shield. Hydrovac power brake. Oil bath air cleaner. Rear bumper. Heavy-duty clutch. Oil filter. Governor. Dual tail and stop lamp. Heavy-duty rear springs. Heavy-duty radiator. Right-hand front seat (panel, canopy). Auxiliary rear springs. Vacuum reserve tank. Heavy-duty three- and four-speed transmissions. Heavy-duty generator. Stand-up driving controls (delivery models). Combination fuel/vacuum pump. Chrome front bumper. Spare wheel and carrier. Chrome radiator grille. Deluxe cab equipment. Deluxe panel equipment. Nu-Vue cab windows.

HISTORICAL: Calendar year registrations. [All] 79,612.

1952 GMC 1/2-Ton Series 101-22 Pickup (RLH)

1953 GMC

GMC — LIGHT-DUTY — SIX-CYLINDER: The GMC light-duty trucks would be extensively restyled in 1954, but there were no important alterations in appearance this year. The big news for 1953 was the availability of GM's famous four-speed Hydra-Matic transmission as a new option. This transmission, which was available on all 1/2-ton to 1-1/2-ton models was standard on the GMC Package Delivery model. Other new options were tinted glass and side-mounted spare tire carriers. Models with automatic transmission carried Hydra-Matic identification plates on their side hood panels.

1953 GMC 1/2-Ton Series 101-22 Pickup (CW)

I.D. DATA: Serial number stamped on plate located on left door hinge pillar. Engine number located on left side of cylinder block behind oil filler. GM trucks were not produced on a yearly model change basis. Serial numbers were not made available to industry recording sources.

1953 GMC 1/2-Ton Series 101-22 U.S. Navy Survey Panel (D. Russel/CPC)

Model	Body Type	Price	Weight	Prod. Total
Series 101-22 — 1/2-Ton — 116 in. w.b.				
101-22	Chassis & Cowl	1073	2615	—
101-22	Chassis & Cab	1317	3080	—
101-22	Pickup	1385	3340	—
101-22	Panel	1566	3550	—
101-22	Canopy Express	1617	3530	—
101-22	Suburban	1834	3865	—
Series 102-22 — 1/2-Ton — 125.25 in. w.b.				
102-22	Chassis & Cowl	1094	2610	—
102-22	Chassis & Cab	1338	3075	—
102-22	Pickup	1427	3440	—
102-22	Stake Rack	1496	3680	—
Series 150-22 — 3/4-Ton — 125.25 in. w.b.				
152-22	Chassis & Cowl	1204	2825	—
152-22	Chassis & Cab	1448	3310	—
152-22	Pickup	1537	3675	—
152-22	Stake Rack	1606	3895	—
Series PM-150-22 — 3/4-Ton — 125.25 in. w.b.				
152-22	Chassis Package Delivery	1380	2080	—
Series 252-22 — 1-Ton — 125.25 in. w.b.				
252-22	Chassis & Cowl	1282	3090	—
252-22	Chassis & Cab	1526	3575	—
Series 253-22 — 1-Ton — 137 in. w.b.				
253-22	Chassis & Cowl	1282	3115	—
253-22	Chassis & Cab	1526	3600	—
253-22	Pickup	1641	4110	—
253-22	Platform	1657	4150	—
253-22	Stake Rack	1725	4385	—
253-22	Panel	1831	4335	—
253-22	Canopy Express	1907	4260	—

ENGINE: Inline. OHV. Six-cylinder. Cast iron block. Bore & stroke: 3.5625 x 3.8125 in. Displacement: 228 cid. Brake hp: 100 at 3400 rpm.

CHASSIS [Series 101-22]: Wheelbase: 116 in. Overall length: 196.575 in. Tires: 6.00 x 16, six-ply.

CHASSIS [Series 102-22]: Wheelbase: 125.25 in. Overall length: 206 in. Tires: 6.00 x 16, six-ply.

CHASSIS [Series 151-22]: Wheelbase: 125.25 in. Tires: 15 in., six-ply.

CHASSIS [Series 152-22]: Wheelbase: 125.25 in. Overall length: 206 in. Tires: 15 in., six-ply.

CHASSIS [Series 252-22]: Wheelbase: 125.25 in. Overall length: 206 in. Tires: 7.00 x 17, six-ply.

CHASSIS [Series 253-22]: Wheelbase: 137 in. Overall length: 223.88 in. Tires: 7.00 x 17, six-ply.

TECHNICAL: Manual synchromesh transmission. Speeds: 3F/1R. Floor mount gearshift. Single disc, diaphragm spring clutch. Rear axle: [1/2-ton] semi-floating. [All others] full-floating. Hydraulic, four-wheel brakes. Pressed steel wheels.

DRIVETRAIN OPTIONS: Dual Range Hydra-Matic (standard Model PM-152-22) transmission. Four-speed manual transmission. Oil bath. Oil filter. AC oil filter. Vacuum pump on fuel pump. Double action front and rear shock absorbers.

OPTIONS: Double-acting shock absorbers. Long runningboards and rear fenders. Non-standard rear axle ratios. Rearview mirrors and brackets. Rear shock absorber shield. Hydrovac power brake. Oil bath air cleaner. Rear bumper. Heavy-duty clutch. Oil filter. Governor. Dual tail and stop lamp. Heavy-duty rear springs. Heavy-duty radiator. Right-hand front seat (panel, canopy). Auxiliary rear springs. Vacuum reserve tank. Heavy-duty three- and four-speed transmissions. Heavy-duty generator. Stand-up driving controls (delivery models). Combination fuel/vacuum pump. Chrome front bumper. Spare wheel and carrier. Chrome radiator grille. Deluxe cab equipment. Deluxe panel equipment. Nu-Vue cab windows.

HISTORICAL: Calendar year registrations. [All] 82,296.

1953 GMC 1/2-Ton Series 101-22 Pickup [modern wheels/tires] (DFW)

1954 GMC

1954 GMC 1/2-Ton Series 101-24 Pickup (Rick Schnitzler)

GMC — LIGHT-DUTY — SIX-CYLINDER: GMC trucks were given their most extensive styling revisions since 1948. The familiar GMC grille format was continued, but the side bars were wider and flared at the bottom (where they extended out to serve as large, chrome parking light housings.) Even the front fenders were changed to incorporate rectangular depressions to accommodate the parking lights. Chrome grilles and bumpers were back, as Korean War material restrictions were eased. The chrome trim was optional, though, and cost extra. Therefore, most trucks had these parts painted. A unique rear bumper (unlike the 1947-1953 type) was new. It had a center dip to accommodate the license plate. Also found on the 1954 models was a one-piece windshield. The pickups' cargo box was redesigned, too. Its side and front panels, as well as the tailgate, were 18-1/2 in. high. The top rail was changed to a flat (not sloping) style. Taillights were square, instead of round. Chrome hubcaps returned, but the GMC letters stamped into them were painted white. This was the first year GMC trucks featured color-coordinated interiors. The power rating of the 248.5 cid six was increased to 125 hp and was the new standard engine for the light-duty GMC models.

I.D. DATA: Serial number stamped on plate located on left door hinge pillar. Engine number located on left side of cylinder block behind oil filler. GM trucks were not produced on a yearly model change basis. Serial numbers were not made available to industry recording sources.

Model	Body Type	Price	Weight	Prod. Total
Series 101-24 — 1/2-Ton — 116 in. w.b.				
101-24	Chassis & Cowl	—	—	—
101-24	Chassis & Cab	1317	3085	—
101-24	Pickup	1385	3355	—
101-24	Panel	1566	3535	—
101-24	Deluxe Panel	1615	—	—
101-24	Canopy	1617	3485	—
101-24	Suburban	1890	3820	—
Series 102-24 — 1/2-Ton — 125.25 in. w.b.				
102-24	Chassis & Cowl	—	—	—
102-24	Chassis & Cab	1338	3080	—
102-24	Pickup	1427	3370	—
102-24	Stake Rack	—	—	—
Series 150-24 — 3/4-Ton — 125.25 in. wb.				
152-24	Chassis & Cowl	—	—	—
152-24	Chassis & Cab	1448	3370	—
152-24	Pickup	1537	3720	—
152-24	Stake Rack	1606	4010	—
Series PM-152-24 — 3/4-Ton — 125.25 in. w.b.				
PM-152-24	Chassis Package Delivery	1380	2665	—
Series 250-24 — 1-Ton — 125.25 in. w.b.				
252-24	Chassis & Cowl	—	—	—
252-24	Chassis & Cab	1526	3660	—
Series 253-24 — 1-Ton — 137 in. w.b.				
253-24	Chassis & Cowl	—	—	—
253-24	Platform	1657	4260	—
253-24	Stake Rack	1725	4530	—
253-24	Panel	1831	4325	—
253-24	Deluxe Panel	1831	—	—
253-24	Canopy Express	1907	4270	—

ENGINE: Inline. OHV. Six-cylinder. Cast iron block. Bore & stroke: 3.718 x 3.08 in. Displacement: 248.5 cid. Brake hp: 125. Hydraulic valve lifters. Carburetor: one-barrel.)

CHASSIS [Series 101-24]: Wheelbase: 116 in. Overall length: 196.575 in. Tires: 6.00 x 16, six-ply.

CHASSIS [Series 102-24]: Wheelbase: 125.25 in. Overall length: 206 in. Tires: 6.00 x 16, six-ply.

CHASSIS [Series 151-24]: Wheelbase: 125.25 in. Tires: 15 in., six-ply.

CHASSIS [Series 152-24]: Wheelbase: 125.25 in. Overall length: 206 in. Tires: 15 in., six-ply.

CHASSIS [Series 252-24]: Wheelbase: 125.25 in. Overall length: 206 in. Tires: 7.00 x 17, six-ply.

CHASSIS [Series 253-24]: Wheelbase: 137 in. Overall length: 223.88 in. Tires: 7.00 x 17, six-ply.

TECHNICAL: Manual synchromesh transmission. Speeds: 3F/1R. Floor mount gearshift. Single disc, diaphragm spring clutch. Rear axle: [1/2-ton] semi-floating. [All others] full-floating. Hydraulic, four-wheel brakes. Pressed steel wheels.

DRIVETRAIN OPTIONS: Dual Range Hydra-Matic (standard Model PM-152-24) transmission. Four-speed manual transmission. Oil bath. Oil filter. AC oil filter. Vacuum pump on fuel pump. Double action front and rear shock absorbers.

OPTIONS: Directional signal. Double-acting shock absorbers. Long runningboards and rear fenders. Non-standard rear axle ratios. Rearview mirrors and brackets. Rear shock absorber shield. Hydrovac power brake. Propeller shaft brake. Oil bath air cleaner. Positive crankcase ventilation system. Painted rear bumper. Chrome rear bumper. Heavy-duty clutch. High-sill body. Oil filter. Governor. Dual tail and stop lamp. Heavy-duty rear springs. Heavy-duty radiator. Right-hand front seat (panel, canopy). Auxiliary rear springs. Vacuum reserve tank. Hydra-Matic transmission. Overdrive transmission. Electric windshield wipers. Power steering. Heavy-duty three- and four-speed transmissions. Heavy-duty generator. Solenoid starter. Combination fuel/vacuum pump. Chrome front bumper. Spare wheel and carrier. Deluxe equipment Chrome equipment. Deluxe cab. Deluxe panel. Nu-Vue cab windows. Lock package, includes key locks for left door and side-mounted spare wheel rim. Power brakes. Two-won paint (cab and panel models). E-Z-Eye tinted glass.

HISTORICAL: Calendar year registrations. [All] 66,644.

1955 GMC
(1st Series)

1955 GMC First Series 1/2-Ton Model 101-24 Pickup (GMC)

Standard Catalog of Light-Duty Trucks

GMC — LIGHT-DUTY — SIX-CYLINDER: The extensive styling revisions introduced on 1954 GMC trucks were continued on the 1955 First Series models. The wider, flared at the bottom grille with rectangular parking light housings, unique center dip rear bumper, one-piece windshield, higher cargo box with flat top rail and square taillights were carried over until the all-new series was ready for introduction at midyear. Some small revisions took place. The circular fender impressions in the new-for-1954 pickup bed were changed to make flat inner walls. The battery was moved from under the passenger side floorboard to below the hood.

I.D. DATA: Serial number stamped on plate located on left door hinge pillar. Engine number located on left side of cylinder block behind oil filler. GM trucks were not produced on a yearly model change basis. Serial numbers were not made available to industry recording sources.

1955 GMC First Series 1/2-Ton Model 101-24 Pickup (GMC)

Model	Body Type	Price	Weight	Prod. Total
Series 101-24 — 1/2-Ton — 116 in. w.b.				
101-24	Chassis & Cowl	—	—	—
101-24	Chassis & Cab	1317	3085	—
101-24	Pickup	1385	3355	—
101-24	Panel	1566	3535	—
101-24	Deluxe Panel	1615	—	—
101-24	Canopy	1617	3485	—
101-24	Suburban	1890	3820	—
Series 102-24 — 1/2-Ton — 125.25 in. w.b.				
102-24	Chassis & Cowl	—	—	—
102-24	Chassis & Cab	1338	3080	—
102-24	Pickup	1427	3370	—
102-24	Stake Rack	—	—	—
Series 150-24 — 3/4-Ton — 125.25 in. wb.				
152-24	Chassis & Cowl	—	—	—
152-24	Chassis & Cab	1448	3370	—
152-24	Pickup	1537	3720	—
152-24	Stake Rack	1606	4010	—
Series PM-152-24 — 3/4-Ton — 125.25 in. w.b.				
PM-152-24	Chassis Package Delivery	1380	2665	—
Series 250-24 — 1-Ton — 125.25 in. w.b.				
252-24	Chassis & Cowl	—	—	—
252-24	Chassis & Cab	1526	3660	—
Series 253-24 — 1-Ton — 137 in. w.b.				
253-24	Chassis & Cowl	—	—	—
253-24	Platform	1657	4260	—
253-24	Stake Rack	1725	4530	—
253-24	Panel	1831	4325	—
253-24	Deluxe Panel	1831	—	—
253-24	Canopy Express	1907	4270	—

ENGINE: Inline. OHV. Six-cylinder. Cast iron block. Bore & stroke: 3.718 x 3.08 in. Displacement: 248.5 cid. Brake hp: 125. Hydraulic valve lifters. Carburetor: one-barrel.

CHASSIS [Series 101-24]: Wheelbase: 116 in. Overall length: 196.575 in. Tires: 6.00 x 16, six-ply.

CHASSIS [Series 102-24]: Wheelbase: 125.25 in. Overall length: 206 in. Tires: 6.00 x 16, six-ply.

CHASSIS [Series 151-24]: Wheelbase: 125.25 in. Tires: 15 in., six-ply.

CHASSIS [Series 152-24]: Wheelbase: 125.25 in. Overall length: 206 in. Tires: 15 in., six-ply.

CHASSIS [Series 252-24]: Wheelbase: 125.25 in. Overall length: 206 in. Tires: 7.00 x 17, six-ply.

CHASSIS [Series 253-24]: Wheelbase: 137 in. Overall length: 223.88 in. Tires: 7.00 x 17, six-ply.

TECHNICAL: Manual synchromesh transmission. Speeds: 3F/1R. Floor mount gearshift. Single disc, diaphragm spring clutch. Rear axle: [1/2-ton] semi-floating. [All others] full-floating. Hydraulic, four-wheel brakes. Pressed steel wheels.

DRIVETRAIN OPTIONS: Dual Range Hydra-Matic (standard Model PM-152-24) transmission. Four-speed manual transmission. Oil bath. Oil filter. AC oil filter. Vacuum pump on fuel pump. Double-action front and rear shock absorbers.

OPTIONS: Directional signal. Double-acting shock absorbers. Long runningboards and rear fenders. Non-standard rear axle ratios. Rearview mirrors and brackets. Rear shock absorber shield. Hydrovac power brake. Propeller shaft brake. Oil bath air cleaner. Positive crankcase ventilation system. Painted rear bumper. Chrome rear bumper. Heavy-duty clutch. High-sill body. Oil filter. Governor. Dual tail and stop lamp. Heavy-duty rear springs. Heavy-duty radiator. Right-hand front seat (panel, canopy). Auxiliary rear springs. Vacuum reserve tank. Hydra-Matic transmission. Overdrive transmission. Electric windshield wipers. Power steering. Heavy-duty three- and four-speed transmissions. Heavy-duty generator. Solenoid starter. Combination fuel/vacuum pump. Chrome front bumper. Spare wheel and carrier. Deluxe equipment Chrome equipment. Deluxe cab. Deluxe panel. Nu-Vue cab windows. Lock package, includes key locks for left door and side-mounted spare wheel rim. Power brakes. Two-tone paint (cab and panel models). E-Z-Eye tinted glass.

HISTORICAL: All of General Motors cars and trucks were due for changeover in model year 1955. GM had trouble getting so many product revisions completed by new model introduction time in the fall of 1954. Therefore, it was decided to postpone the release of all-new 1955 Chevrolet and GMC trucks until the spring of 1955. With minor (but important to collectors) revisions to styling, finish and engineering, the Advance-Design series was continued as a "First Series" 1955 line.

1955 GMC
(2nd Series)

1955 GMC 1/2-Ton Model 101 Pickup Six-cylinder (GMC)

GMC — LIGHT-DUTY — SIX/V-8: GMC introduced both new styling and a new V-8 engine (actually a Pontiac V-8) in 1955. The first significant change since 1947 was dramatic. The front end featured a two-bar grille format suggesting that of the 1954 Oldsmobile. The grille carried 100 (1/2-ton), 150 (3/4-ton) or 250 (1-ton) numbers to indicate the series. Hooded headlights and a bumper with protruding circular guards reflected styling themes that had earlier been associated with Cadillac. No hood ornament was fitted. Traditon GMC lettering, more stylized than ever, was mounted on the lower hood surface in an oblong cove with a gridwork background. The use of a panoramic windshield and backlight substantially increased the glass area of the GMC pickups. The higher front fender line extended back through the full length of the cab. Joining the GMC truck line was the Suburban Pickup, GMC's version of the Chevrolet Cameo Carrier pickup.

1955 GMC 1/2-Ton Model 101-8 Pickup V-8 (OCW)

I.D. DATA: Serial number located inside cab or on truck firewall. Stamped on this "GMC Service Parts Identification" plate was the model of the engine, transmission, service brake and axle. Engine numbers located: [six] on left side of cylinder block behind oil filler; [V-8] On pad on front right-hand cylinder bank. GM trucks were not produced on a yearly model change basis. Serial numbers were not made available to industry recording sources.

Model	Body Type	Price	Weight	Prod. Total
Series 100 — 1/2-Ton — 114 in. w.b. — 6-cyl.				
101	Chassis & Cab	1398	3025	—
101	Pickup	1488	3375	—
101	Panel	1753	3605	—
101	Delivery Panel	1823	3605	—
101	Suburban Pickup	1923	3535	±
101	Suburban	2076	3830	—
Series 102 — 1/2-Ton — 123.25 in. w.b. — 6-cyl.				
102	Chassis & Cab	1419	3070	—
102	Pickup	1519	3450	—
102	Stake Rack	1604	3665	—
Series 100-8 — 1/2-Ton — 114 in. w.b. — V-8				
101-8	Chassis & Cab	1498	3135	—
101-8	Chassis & Cab	1498	3135	—
101-8	Pickup	1588	3485	—
101-8	Panel	1853	3715	—
101-8	Delivery Panel	1923	3715	—
101-8	Suburban	2176	3940	—
101-8	Suburban Pickup	2023	3645	—

Series 102-8 — 1/2-Ton — 123.25 in. w.b. — V-8				
102-8	Chassis & Cab	1519	3180	—
102-8	Pickup	1619	3560	—
102-8	Stake Rack	1704	3775	—
Series 150 — 3/4-Ton — 123.25 in. w.b. — 6-cyl.				
152	Chassis & Cab	1549	3370	—
152	Pickup	1649	3750	—
152	Stake Rack	1734	3965	—
Series 150-8 — 3/4-Ton — 123.25 in. w.b. — V-8				
152-8	Chassis & Cab	1649	3480	—
152-8	Pickup	1749	3860	—
152-8	Stake Rack	1834	4075	—
Series PM-151 — 3/4-Ton — 104 in. w.b. — 6-cyl.				
PM-151	For. Con. Chassis	1499	2865	—
Series PM-152 — 3/4-Ton — 125 in. w.b. — 6-cyl.				
PM-152	For. Con. Chassis	1499	2925	—
Series PM-153 — 1-Ton — 137 in. w.b.				
PM-153	For. Con. Chassis	1499	2945	—
Series 251 — 1-Ton — 114 in. w.b. — 6-cyl.				
251	Chassis & Cab	1653	3605	—
Series 252 — 1-Ton — 123.25 in. w.b. — 6-cyl.				
252	Chassis & Cab	1653	3630	—
Series 253 — 1-Ton — 135 in. w.b. — 6-cyl.				
253	Chassis & Cab	1653	3670	—
253	Pickup	1778	4120	—
253	Platform	1793	4235	—
253	Stake Rack	1873	4510	—
253	Panel	2053	4355	—
253	Delivery Panel	2123	4355	—
Series 251- 1-Ton — 114 in. w.b. — V-8				
251	Chassis & Cab	1753	3715	—
Series 252 — 1-Ton — 123.25 in. w.b. — V-8				
252	Chassis & Cab	1753	3740	—
Series 253 — 1-Ton — 135 in. w.b. — V-8				
253	Chassis & Cab	1753	3780	—
253	Pickup	1878	4230	—
253	Platform	1893	4345	—
253	Stake Rack	1973	4620	—
253	Panel	2153	4465	—
253	Delivery Panel	2223	4465	—
Series PM-251 — 1-Ton — 114 in. w.b. — 6-cyl.				
PM-251	For. Cont. Chassis	1601	2935	—
Series PM-252 — 1-Ton — 123.25 in. w.b. — 6-cyl.				
PM-252	For. Cont. Chassis	1601	3000	—
Series PM-253 — 1-Ton — 135 in. w.b. — 6-cyl.				
PM-253	For. Cont. Chassis	1601	3015	—

1955 GMC 1/2-Ton Model 101-8 Pickup V-8 (OCW)

ENGINE [Standard Six]: Inline. OHV. Six-cylinder. Cast iron block. Bore & stroke: 3.71875 x 3.8125 in. Displacement: 248 cid.. Compression: 7.5:1. Brake hp: 125 at 3600 rpm. **Max** torque: 214 lbs.-ft. at 1550 rpm. Carburetor: Holley one-barrel model 1904.

ENGINE [Standard V-8]: V-type. OHV. Eight-cylinder. Cast iron block. Bore & stroke: 3.75 x 3.25 in. Displacement: 287.2 cid.. Compression ratio: 7.4:1. Brake hp: 155 at 3600 rpm. Max torque: 246 lbs.-ft. at 2200-2600 rpm. Five main bearings. Hydraulic valve lifters. Carburetor: Carter or Rochester two-barrel.

1955 GMC 1/2-Ton Suburban Pickup V-8 [modern wheels/tires] (Ted Stevens/CPC)

CHASSIS [101]: Wheelbase: 114 in. Overall length: 193.56 [Pickup Suburban], 185.687 [all others]. Overall height: 74 in. Front/Rear tread: 61/61 in. Tires: 6.70 x 15, four-ply. GVW: 5,000 lbs.
CHASSIS [102]: Wheelbase: 123.25 in. Overall length: 205.5625 in. Front/Rear tread: 61/61 in. Tires: 6.70 x 15, four-ply. GVW: 5,000 lbs.
CHASSIS [152]: Wheelbase: 123.25 in. Overall length: 205.5625 in. Front/Rear tread: 61/61 in. Tires: 7.00 x 17.5, six-ply. GVW: 6,500 lbs.
CHASSIS [252]: Wheelbase: 135 in. Overall length: 215.8125 in. Front/Rear tread: 61/61 in. Tires: 8.00 x 17.5, six-ply. GVW: 8,800 lbs.
CHASSIS [253]: Wheelbase: 135 in. Overall length: 215.8125 in. Front/Rear tread: 61 in./61 in. GVW: 8,800 lbs.
CHASSIS [PM-151]: Wheelbase: 104 in. Tires: 8.00 x 19.5, six-ply. GVW: 7,000 lbs.
CHASSIS [PM-152]: Wheelbase: 125 in. GVW: 7,000 lbs.
CHASSIS [PM-153]: Wheelbase: 137 in. GVW: 7,000 lbs.
CHASSIS [PM-251]: Wheelbase: 104 in. Tires: 8.00 x 19.5, six-ply. GVW: 10,000 lbs.
CHASSIS [PM-252]: Wheelbase: 125 in. GVW: 10,000 lbs.
CHASSIS [PM-253]: Wheelbase: 137 in. GVW: 10,000 lbs.
TECHNICAL: Manual, synchromesh. Speeds: 3F/1R (4F/1R 1-ton models). Column-mounted three-speed gearshift. Floor-mounted four-speed gearshift. Diaphragm spring clutch, 10 in. diameter, (10.5 in. diameter on 3/4-ton and 1-ton models). Rear axle: [1/2-ton] semi-floating; [others] full-floating. Hydraulic four-wheel brakes: [1/2-ton] 11 x 2 in. front, 11 x 1.75 in. rear; [1-ton] 12 x 2 in. front, 14 x 2.5 in. rear. Pressed steel wheels.
DRIVETRAIN OPTIONS: Four-speed Hydra-Matic. (1/2-ton models only). Four-speed manual transmission. Power steering. Oil bath. Air cleaner. 55-amp generator. Heavy-duty suspension.
OPTIONS: Heater/defroster. Directional signal. Double-acting shock absorbers. Shock absorbers. Rearview mirrors and brackets. Rear shock absorber shield. Hydrovac power brake. Oil bath air cleaner. Positive crankcase ventilation system. Painted rear bumper. Chrome rear bumper. Heavy-duty clutch. Platform body. Oil filter. Governor. Dual tail and stop lamp. Heavy-duty rear springs. Heavy-duty radiator. Foam rubber seat cushion. Right-hand front seat (panel, canopy). Heavy-duty rear springs. Speedometer fittings. Hydra-Matic transmission. Overdrive transmission. Heavy-duty three- and four-speed transmissions. Electric windshield wipers. Power steering. Heavy-duty generator. Side-mounted spare wheel carrier. Heavy-duty battery. Heavy-duty seat trim. Front bumper. Spare wheel and carrier. Chrome trim. Panoramic rear window. Lock package, includes key locks for left door and side-mounted spare wheel rim. E-Z-Eye tinted glass. Auxiliary runningboard. Custom cab package. Custom panel package.
HISTORICAL: Calendar year registrations. [All] 84,877 . New innovations included introduction of V-8 engines for light-duty trucks. First year for 12-volt electrical system. Suburban Pickup also referred to as "Town and Country" model.

1956 GMC

1956 GMC Cantrell Wood-bodied Carryall (OCW)

GMC — LIGHT-DUTY — SIX/V-8: After the dramatic changes of 1955 the latest GMC trucks were virtually unchanged in appearance. As in 1955, the grille carried 100 (1/2-ton), 150 (3/4-ton) or 250 (1-ton) numbers to indicate the series. The 100/101 Series model lineup included the Suburban Pickup with deluxe trim and special "flush-side" fiberglass

outer fender panels. All the other 1955 trucks returned, too. Mechanical revisions were highlighted by larger six-cylinder and V-8 engines now displacing 269.5 and 316.6 cid. respectively. Trucks with the V-8 were no longer listed as a separate series; the V-8 engine was an option.
I.D. DATA: The GMC Service Parts Identification Plate is located inside the cab or on the truck firewall. Stamped on the plate is the model of engine, transmission, service brakes and front and rear axles. Engine numbers located: [six] on left side of cylinder block behind oil filler; [V-8] On pad on front right-hand cylinder bank. GM trucks were not produced on a yearly model change basis. Serial numbers were not made available to industry recording sources.

Model	Body Type	Price	Weight	Prod. Total
Series 101 — 1/2-Ton -114 in. w.b.				
101	Chassis & Cab	1629	3060	—
101	Panel	2028	3640	—
101	Panel Deluxe	2120	3640	—
101	Pickup	1732	3410	—
101	Canopy Express	—	3570	—
101	Suburban	2422	3865	—
Series 102 — 1/2-Ton — 123.25 in. w.b.				
102	Chassis & Cab	1651	3130	—
102	Pickup	1765	3510	—
102	Stake Rack	—	3725	—
Series 150 — 3/4-Ton — 123.25 in. w.b.				
152	Chassis & Cab	1808	3425	—
152	Pickup 7.5 ft.	1922	3805	—
152	Stake Rack 7.5 ft.	2013	4020	—
Series PM151 Forward-Control — 3/4-Ton — 104 in. w.b.				
151	Chassis	1756	2900	—
NOTE 1: PM152 (125 in. w.b.) and PM-153 (137 in. w.b.) also available.				
Series 251 — 1-Ton — 114 in. w.b.				
251	Chassis & Cab	1920	3615	—
Series 252 — 1-Ton — 123.25 in. w.b.				
252	Chassis & Cab	1920	3635	—
Series 253 — 1-Ton — 135 in. w.b.				
253	Chassis & Cab	1920	3660	—
253	Panel 9 ft.	2373	4345	—
253	Panel Deluxe 9 ft.	2465	4345	—
253	Pickup 9 ft.	2055	4110	—
253	Platform	—	4225	—
253	Stake Rack	2168	4500	—
Series PM251 Forward-Control — 1-Ton — 104 in. w.b.				
251	Chassis	1866	3030	—

NOTE 2: PM252 (125 in. w.b.) and PM253 (137 in. w.b.) also available.
NOTE 3: Add $129 and 160 lbs. for V-8 engine.

1956 GMC 3/4-Ton Model 152 Pickup 4x4 (RCA)

ENGINE [Base six]: Inline. OHV. Six-cylinder. Cast iron block. Bore & stroke: 3.78 x 4.0 in. Displacement: 269.5 cid.. Compression ratio: 7.5:1. Brake hp: 130 at 3600 rpm. Max. Torque: 238 lbs.-ft. at 1400 rpm. Carburetor: Holley one-barrel Model 1904.
ENGINE [Base V-8]: V-Type. OHV. Eight-cylinder. Cast iron block. Bore & stroke: 3.937 x 3.25 in. Displacement: 316.6 cid. Compression ratio: 7.8:1. Brake hp: 180 at 4400 rpm. Max. Torque: 276 lbs.-ft. at 2200 rpm. Five main bearings. Hydraulic valve lifters. Carburetor: Rochester two-barrel.
CHASSIS [Series 100]: Wheelbase: 114/123.25 in. Overall length: [pickup, suburban] 186 in.; [others] 194 in. Front/Rear tread: 61 in./61 in.. Tires: 6.70 x 15, four-ply.
CHASSIS [Series 150]: Wheelbase: 123.25 in. Overall length: 206 in. Front/Rear tread: 61 in./61 in.. Tires: 7 x 17.5, four-ply.
CHASSIS [Series PM150]: Wheelbase: 104/125/137 in. Tires: 8 x 19.5, six-ply.
CHASIS [Series 250]: Wheelbase: 114/123.25/135 in. Overall length: 186/206/216 in. Tires: 8 x 17.5, six-ply.
TECHNICAL: Manual, synchromesh. Speeds: 3F/1R (4F/1R 1-ton models). Column-mounted three-speed gearshift. Floor-mounted four-speed gearshift. Diaphragm spring clutch, 10 in. diameter, (10.5 in. diameter on 3/4-ton and 1-ton models). Rear axle: [1/2-ton] semi-floating; [others] full-floating. Hydraulic four-wheel brakes: [1/2-ton] 11 x 2 in. front, 11 x 1.75 in. rear; [1-ton] 12 x 2 in. front, 14 x 2.5 in. rear. Pressed steel wheels.
DRIVETRAIN OPTIONS: Four-speed Hydra-Matic. (1/2-ton models only). Four-speed manual transmission. Power steering. Oil bath. Air cleaner. 55-amp. generator. Heavy-duty suspension.

OPTIONS: Heater/defroster. Directional signals. Shock absorbers. Shock absorbers. Rear-view mirrors and brackets. Rear shock absorber shield. Hydrovac power brake. Oil bath air cleaner. Positive crankcase ventilation system. Painted rear bumper. Chrome rear bumper. Heavy-duty clutch. Platform body. Oil filter. Governor. Dual tail and stop lamp. Heavy-duty rear springs. Heavy-duty radiator. Foam rubber seat cushion. Right-hand front seat (panel, canopy). Heavy-duty rear springs. Speedometer fittings. Hydra-Matic transmission. Overdrive transmission. Heavy-duty three- and four-speed transmissions. Electric windshield wipers. Power steering. Heavy-duty generator. Side-mounted spare wheel carrier. Heavy-duty battery. Heavy-duty seat trim. Front bumper. Spare wheel and carrier. Chrome trim. Panoramic rear window. Lock package, includes key locks for left door and side-mounted spare wheel rim. E-Z-Eye tinted glass. Auxiliary runningboard. Custom panel package.

HISTORICAL: Calendar year registrations. [All] 82,266.

1957 GMC

1957 GMC 1/2-Ton Model 101 Suburban 4x4 (DFW)

GMC — LIGHT-DUTY — SIX/V-8: GMC trucks for 1957 featured a new grille design. Replacing the twin-bar arrangement was an insert with a center divider and horizontal bars. A model designation plaque was placed in the left section. The plaque carried 100 (1/2-ton), 150 (3/4-ton) or 250 (1-ton) numbers to indicate the series. The secondary grille mesh, which served as a backdrop for the GMC logo on the 1955 and 1956 models, was eliminated. The model line up was unchanged. It again included the stylish Suburban Pickup. Directional signals were now standard equipment.

I.D. DATA: The GMC Service Parts Identification Plate is located inside the cab or on the truck firewall. Stamped on the plate is the model of engine, transmission, service brakes and front and rear axles. Engine numbers located: [six] on left side of cylinder block behind oil filler; [V-8] On pad on front right-hand cylinder bank. GM trucks were not produced on a yearly model change basis. Serial numbers were not made available to industry recording sources.

Model	Body Type	Price	Weight	Prod. Total
Series 101 — 1/2-Ton — 114 in. w.b.				
101	Chassis & Cab	1743	3040	—
101	Panel	2147	3620	—
101	Deluxe Panel	2239	3620	—
101	Pickup	1846	3390	—
101	Canopy Express	—	3550	—
101	Suburban	2498	3845	—
Series 102 — 1/2-Ton — 123.25 in. w.b.				
102	Chassis & Cab	1782	3110	—
102	Pickup	1896	3490	—
Series 150 — 3/4-Ton — 123.25 in. w.b.				
152	Chassis & Cab	1928	3435	—
152	Pickup 7.5 ft.	2042	3815	—
152	Stake Rack 7.5 ft.	2133	—	—
Series PM151 Forward-Control — 3/4-Ton — 104 in. w.b.				
151	Chassis	1839	2915	—
Series PM152 Forward-Control — 3/4-Ton — 123.23 in. w.b.				
152	Chassis	1877	2970	—
Series PM153 Forward-Control — 3/4-Ton — 137 in. w.b.				
153	Chassis	1909	2995	—
Series 251 — 1-Ton — 114 in. w.b.				
251	Chassis & Cab	2056	3635	—
Series 252 — 1-Ton — 123.25 in. w.b.				
252	Chassis & Cab	2056	3655	—
Series 253 — 1-Ton — 135 in. w.b.				
253	Chassis & Cab	2056	3680	—
253	Panel 9 ft.	2519	4365	—
253	Panel Deluxe 9 ft.	2572	4365	—
253	Pickup 9 ft.	2191	4130	—
253	Stake Rack	2304	4520	—

NOTE 1: Four-wheel drive (4x4) available on Series 100/150/250 conventionals.
NOTE 2: Add $136 and 110 lbs. for V-8 engine.

ENGINE [Base six]: Inline. OHV. Six-cylinder. Cast iron block. Bore & stroke: 3.78 x 4.0 in. Displacement: 269.5 cid.. Compression ratio: 7.5:1. Brake hp: 130 at 3600 rpm. Carburetor: Holley one-barrel model 1904.

ENGINE [Base V-8]: V-type. OHV. Eight-cylinder. Cast iron block. Bore & stroke: 3.94 x 3.56 in. Displacement: 347 cid. Brake hp: 206 at 4400 rpm. Max torque: 317 lbs.-ft. at 2000-2200 rpm. Five main bearings. Hydraulic valve lifters. Carburetor: two-barrel.

CHASSIS [Series 101]: Wheelbase: 114 in. Overall length: [Pickup/Suburban] 194 in.; [Others] 186 in. Front/Rear tread: 61 in./61 in. Tires: 6.70 x 15, four-ply.

CHASSIS [Series 102]: Wheelbase: 123.25 in. Overall length: 206 in. Front/Rear tread: 61 in./61 in. Tires: 6.70 x 15, four-ply.

CHASSIS [Series 150]: Wheelbase: 123.25 in. Overall length: 206 in. Front/Rear tread: 61 in./61 in. Tires: 7.00 x 17.5, six-ply.

CHASSIS [Series PM151]: Wheelbase: 104 in. Tires: 8.00 x 19.5, six-ply.

CHASSIS [Series PM150]: Wheelbase: 125 in. Tires: 8.00 x 19.5, six-ply.

CHASSIS [Series PM150]: Wheelbase: 137 in. Tires: 8.00 x 19.5, six-ply.

CHASSIS [Series 251]: Wheelbase: 114 in. Overall length: 186 in. Tires: 8.00 x 17.5, six-ply.

CHASSIS [Series 252]: Wheelbase: 123.25. Overall length: 206 in. Tires: 8.00 x 17.5, six-ply.

CHASSIS [Series 253]: Wheelbase: 135 in. Overall length: 216 in. Tires: 8.00 x 17.5, six-ply.

CHASSIS [Series PM251]: Wheelbase: 104 in. Tires: 8.00 x 19.5, six-ply.

CHASSIS [Series PM252]: Wheelbase: 125 in. Tires: 8.00 x 19.5, six-ply.

CHASSIS [Series PM253]: Wheelbase: 137 in. Tires: 8.00 x 19.5, six-ply.

TECHNICAL: Manual, synchromesh. Speeds: 3F/1R (4F/1R 1-ton models). Column-mounted three-speed gearshift. Floor-mounted four-speed gearshift. Diaphragm spring clutch, 10 in. diameter, (10.5 in. diameter on 3/4-ton and 1-ton models). Rear axle: [1/2-ton] semi-floating; [others] full-floating. Hydraulic four-wheel brakes: [1/2-ton] 11 x 2 in. front, 11 x 1.75 in. rear; [1-ton] 12 x 2 in. front, 14 x 2.5 in. rear. Pressed steel wheels.

DRIVETRAIN OPTIONS: Four-speed Hydra-Matic. (1/2-ton models only). Four-speed manual transmission. Power steering. Oil bath. Air cleaner. 55-amp. generator. Heavy-duty suspension.

OPTIONS: Heater/defroster. Directional signals. Shock absorbers. Shock absorbers. Rear-view mirrors and brackets. Rear shock absorber shield. Hydrovac power brake. Oil bath air cleaner. Positive crankcase ventilation system. Painted rear bumper. Chrome rear bumper. Heavy-duty clutch. Platform body. Oil filter. Governor. Heavy-duty front springs. Heavy-duty rear springs. Heavy-duty radiator. Foam rubber seat cushion. Right-hand front seat (panel, canopy). Heavy-duty rear springs. Speedometer fittings. Hydra-Matic transmission. Overdrive transmission. Heavy-duty three- and four-speed transmissions. Electric windshield wipers. Power steering. Heavy-duty generator. Side-mounted spare wheel carrier. Heavy-duty battery. Side-mounted spare wheel carrier. Chrome trim. Panoramic rear window. Lock package, includes key locks for left door and side-mounted spare wheel rim. E-Z-Eye tinted glass. Four-barrel carburetor. Auxiliary runningboard. Custom Cab package. Custom Panel package. Full-width third seat (Suburban). Positraction. Four-wheel drive.

HISTORICAL: Calendar year registrations. [All] 62,165.

1958 GMC

1958 GMC 1/2-Ton Series 100 [Model 101] Suburban (DFW/GHB)

GMC — LIGHT-DUTY — SIX/V-8: A new Wide-Side pickup body looked like the Suburban Pickup, but featured all-steel construction. Dual headlights and a restyled grille also highlighted the exterior appearance of the 1958 GMC trucks. The grille again carried 100 (1/2-ton), 150 (3/4-ton) or 250 (1-ton) numbers to indicate the series. A broad, creased body feature line on the "Wide-Side" models was suggestive of a similar styling treatment used by Cadillac in 1956. The front hood GMC logo was slimmed down and series numeral identification was placed in the center of the grille. Also found on the 1958 models were new hubcaps that looked less ornate than those used from 1955 through 1957.

I.D. DATA: Serial number located: A GMC Service Parts Identification Plate was installed inside the cab or on the firewall. Engine numbers located: [six] on left side of cylinder block behind oil filler; [V-8] On pad on front right-hand cylinder bank. GM trucks were not produced on a yearly model change basis. Serial numbers were not made available to industry recording sources.

432

1958 GMC 1/2-Ton Series 100 [Model 101] Pickup 4x4 (RCA)

Model	Body Type	Price	Weight	Prod. Total
Series 101 — 1/2-Ton — 114 in. w.b.				
101	Chassis & Cab	1815	3050	—
101	Panel 7 ft.	2230	3650	—
101	Panel Deluxe 7 ft.	2322	3655	—
101	Pickup 6.5 ft.	1929	3400	—
101	Wide-Side Pickup (6.5 ft.)	1950	3450	—
101	Suburban	2581	3990	—
Series 102 — 1/2-Ton — 123.25 in. w.b.				
102	Chassis & Cab	1864	3120	—
102	Pickup	1978	3540	—
102	Wide-Side Pickup	1999	3590	—
Series 152 — 3/4-Ton — 123.25 in. w.b.				
152	Chassis & Cab	2000	3400	—
152	Pickup	2114	3820	—
152	Wide-Side Pickup	2135	3870	—
152	Stake Rack	2205	4020	—
Series PM151 Forward-Control — 3/4-Ton — 104 in. w.b.				
151	Chassis	1855	2760	—
151	Panel 8 ft.	3322	—	—
Series PM152 Forward-Control — 3/4-Ton — 125 in. w.b.				
152	Chassis	1893	2815	—
152	Panel 10 ft.	3409	—	—
Series PM151 Forward-Control — 3/4-Ton — 137 in. w.b.				
153	Chassis	1925	2860	—
153	Panel 12 ft.	3524	—	—
Series 251 — 1-Ton — 114 in. w.b.				
251	Chassis & Cab	2128	3635	—
Series 252 — 1-Ton — 123.25 in. w.b.				
252	Chassis & Cab	2128	3655	—
Series 253 — 1-Ton — 135 in. w.b.				
253	Chassis & Cab	2128	3680	—
253	Panel 9 ft.	2591	4450	—
253	Panel Deluxe 9 ft.	2683	4455	—
253	Pickup	2263	4130	—
253	Stake Rack	2376	4520	—
Series PM251 Forward-Control — 1-Ton — 104 in. w.b.				
251	Chassis	2021	3005	—
251	Panel 8 ft.	3488	—	—
Series PM252 Forward-Control — 1-Ton — 125 in. w.b.				
252	Chassis	2058	3080	—
252	Panel 10 ft.	3574	—	—
Series PM253 Forward-Control — 1-Ton — 137 in. w.b.				
253	Chassis	2091	3125	—
253	Panel 9 ft.	3090	—	—

1958 GMC 1/2-Ton Series 100 [Model 101] Panel 4x4 (RCA)

Standard Catalog of Light-Duty Trucks

NOTE 1: Four-wheel drive (4x4) option available for Series 100/150/250 conventional trucks.
NOTE 2: Add $49 and 70 lbs. for base V-8.
ENGINE [Base six]: Inline. OHV. Six-cylinder. Cast iron block. Bore & stroke: 3.78 x 4.0 in. Displacement: 269.5 cid.. Compression ratio: 7.5:1. Brake hp: 130 at 3600 rpm. Carburetor: Holly one-barrel model 1904.
ENGINE [Base V-8]: V-type. OHV. Eight-cylinder. Cast iron block. Bore & stroke: 3.875 x 3.5625 in. Displacement: 336.1 cid. Brake hp: 200 at 4400 rpm. Max torque: 307 lbs.-ft. at 2000-2400 rpm.
CHASSIS [Series 101]: Wheelbase: 114 in. Overall length: [Pickup/Suburban] 194 in.; [Others] 186 in. Front/Rear tread: 61 in./61 in. Tires: 6.70 x 15, four-ply.
CHASSIS [Series 102]: Wheelbase: 123.25 in. Overall length: 206 in. Front/Rear tread: 61 in./61 in. Tires: 6.70 x 15, four-ply.
CHASSIS [Series 150]: Wheelbase: 123.25 in. Overall length: 206 in. Front/Rear tread: 61 in./61 in. Tires: 7.00 x 17.5, six-ply.
CHASSIS [Series PM151]: Wheelbase: 104 in. Tires: 8.00 x 19.5, six-ply.
CHASSIS [Series PM150]: Wheelbase: 125 in. Tires: 8.00 x 19.5, six-ply.
CHASSIS [Series PM150]: Wheelbase: 137 in. Tires: 8.00 x 19.5, six-ply.
CHASSIS [Series 251]: Wheelbase: 114 in. Overall length: 186 in. Tires: 8.00 x 17.5, six-ply.
CHASSIS [Series 252]: Wheelbase: 123.25. Overall length: 206 in. Tires: 8.00 x 17.5, six-ply.
CHASSIS [Series 253]: Wheelbase: 135 in. Overall length: 216 in. Tires: 8.00 x 17.5, six-ply.
CHASSIS [Series PM251]: Wheelbase: 104 in. Tires: 8.00 x 19.5, six-ply.
CHASSIS [Series PM252]: Wheelbase: 125 in. Tires: 8.00 x 19.5, six-ply.
CHASSIS [Series PM253]: Wheelbase: 137 in. Tires: 8.00 x 19.5, six-ply.
TECHNICAL: Manual, synchromesh. Speeds: 3F/1R (4F/1R 1-ton models). Column-mounted three-speed gearshift. Floor-mounted four-speed gearshift. Diaphragm spring clutch, 10 in. diameter, (10.5 in. diameter on 3/4-ton and 1-ton models). Rear axle: [1/2-ton] semi-floating; [others] full-floating. Hydraulic four-wheel brakes: [1/2-ton] 11 x 2 in. front, 11 x 1.75 in. rear; [1-ton] 12 x 2 in. front, 14 x 2.5 in. rear. Pressed steel wheels.
DRIVETRAIN OPTIONS: Four-speed Hydra-Matic. (1/2-ton models only). Four-speed manual transmission. Power steering. Oil bath. Air cleaner. 55-amp. generator. Heavy-duty suspension.
OPTIONS: Heater/defroster. Shock absorbers. Shock absorbers. Rearview mirrors and brackets. Rear shock absorber shield. Hydrovac power brake. Oil bath air cleaner. Positive crankcase ventilation system. Painted rear bumper. Chrome rear bumper. Heavy-duty clutch. Platform body. Oil filter. Governor. Heavy-duty front springs. Heavy-duty rear springs. Heavy-duty radiator. Foam rubber seat cushion. Right-hand front seat (Panel, Canopy). Heavy-duty rear springs. Speedometer fittings. Hydra-Matic transmission. Over-drive transmission. Heavy-duty three- and four-speed transmissions. Electric windshield wipers. Power steering. Heavy-duty generator. Side-mounted spare wheel carrier. Heavy-duty battery. Side-mounted spare wheel carrier. Chrome trim. Panoramic rear window. Lock package, includes key locks for left door and side-mounted spare wheel rim. E-Z-Eye tinted glass. Four-barrel carburetor. Auxiliary runningboard. Custom Cab package. Custom Panel package. Full-width third seat (Suburban). Positraction. Four-wheel drive.
HISTORICAL: Calendar year registrations. [All] 55,950. Model year production: 64,216 . New innovations included a larger displacement V-8.

1959 GMC

1959 GMC 1/2-Ton Series 100 [Model 101] Pickup (GMC)

GMC — LIGHT-DUTY — SIX/V-8: Not found on the 1959 GMC models was the pseudo-automotive front bumper with its twin pod-like bumper guards. Instead a more functional straight-line bumper was used.
I.D. DATA: Serial number located: A GMC Service Parts Identification Plate was installed inside the cab or on the firewall. Engine numbers located: [six] on left side of cylinder block behind oil filler; [V-8] On pad on front right-hand cylinder bank. GM trucks were not produced on a yearly model change basis. Serial numbers were not made available to industry recording sources.

Model	Body Type	Price	Weight	Prod. Total
Series 101 — 1/2-Ton — 114 in. w.b.				
101	Chassis & Cab	1880	3050	—
101	Panel	2295	3650	—
101	Panel Deluxe	2387	3655	—
101	Pickup 6.5 ft.	1994	3400	—
101	Wide-Side Pickup	2015	3450	—
101	Suburban	2678	3990	—
Series 102 — 1/2-Ton — 123.25 in. w.b.				
102	Chassis & Cab	1929	3120	—
102	Pickup 8 ft.	2043	3540	—
102	Wide-Side Pickup 8 ft.	2064	3590	—
Series 150 — 3/4-Ton — 123.25 in. w.b.				
152	Chassis & Cab	2064	3400	—
152	Pickup	2178	3820	—
152	Wide-Side Pickup	2199	3870	—
152	Stake Rack	2209	4020	—
Series PM-151 Forward-Control — 3/4-Ton — 104 in. w.b.				
151	Chassis	1919	2760	—
151	Panel 8 ft.	3386	—	—
Series PM-151 Forward-Control — 3/4-Ton — 125 in. w.b.				
152	Chassis	1957	2815	—
152	Panel 10 ft.	3473	—	—
Series PM-151 Forward-Control — 3/4-Ton — 137 in. w.b.				
153	Chassis	1989	2860	—
Series 251 — 1-Ton — 123.25 in. w.b.				
251	Chassis & Cab	2192	3635	—
Series 252 — 1-Ton — 114 in. w.b.				
252	Chassis & Cab	2192	3655	—
Series 253 — 1-Ton — 135 in. w.b.				
253	Chassis & Cab	2192	3680	—
253	Panel 10 ft.	2655	—	—
253	Panel Deluxe 10 ft.	2747	—	—
253	Pickup	2327	4130	—
253	Stake Rack	2440	4520	—
Series PM-251 Forward-Control — 1-Ton — 104 in. w.b.				
251	Chassis	2085	3005	—
251	Panel	3553	—	—
Series PM-152 Forward-Control — 1-Ton — 125 in. w.b.				
252	Chassis	2123	3080	—
252	Panel	3639	—	—
Series PM-153 Forward-Control — 1-Ton — 137 in. w.b.				
253	Chassis	2155	3125	—
253	Panel	3754	—	—

ENGINE [Base six]: Inline. OHV. Six-cylinder. Cast iron block. Bore & stroke: 3.78 x 4.0 in. Displacement: 269.5 cid.. Compression ratio: 7.5:1. Brake hp: 130 at 3600 rpm. Carburetor: Holly one-barrel model 1904.

ENGINE [Base V-8]: V-type. OHV. Eight-cylinder. Cast iron block. Bore & stroke: 3.875 x 3.5625 in. Displacement: 336.1 cid. Brake hp: 200 at 4400 rpm. Max torque: 307 lbs.-ft. at 2000-2400 rpm.

CHASSIS [Series 101]: Wheelbase: 114 in. Overall length: [Pickup/Suburban] 194 in.; [Others] 186 in. Front/Rear tread: 61 in./61 in. Tires: 6.70 x 15, four-ply.

CHASSIS [Series 102]: Wheelbase: 123.25 in. Overall length: 206 in. Front/Rear tread: 61 in./61 in. Tires: 6.70 x 15, four-ply.

CHASSIS [Series 150]: Wheelbase: 123.25 in. Overall length: 206 in. Front/Rear tread: 61 in./61 in. Tires: 7.00 x 17.5, six-ply.

CHASSIS [Series PM151]: Wheelbase: 104 in. Tires: 8.00 x 19.5, six-ply.

CHASSIS [Series PM150]: Wheelbase: 125 in. Tires: 8.00 x 19.5, six-ply.

CHASSIS [Series PM150]: Wheelbase: 137 in. Tires: 8.00 x 19.5, six-ply.

CHASSIS [Series 251]: Wheelbase: 114 in. Overall length: 186 in. Tires: 8.00 x 17.5, six-ply.

CHASSIS [Series 252]: Wheelbase: 123.25. Overall length: 206 in. Tires: 8.00 x 17.5, six-ply.

CHASSIS [Series 253]: Wheelbase: 135 in. Overall length: 216 in. Tires: 8.00 x 17.5, six-ply.

CHASSIS [Series PM251]: Wheelbase: 104 in. Tires: 8.00 x 19.5, six-ply.

CHASSIS [Series PM252]: Wheelbase: 125 in. Tires: 8.00 x 19.5, six-ply.

CHASSIS [Series PM253]: Wheelbase: 137 in. Tires: 8.00 x 19.5, six-ply.

TECHNICAL: Manual, synchromesh. Speeds: 3F/1R (4F/1R 1-ton models). Column-mounted three-speed gearshift. Floor-mounted four-speed gearshift. Diaphragm spring clutch, 10 in. diameter, (10.5 in. diameter, 3/4-ton and 1-ton models). Rear axle: [1/2-ton] semi-floating; [others] full-floating. Hydraulic four-wheel brakes: [1/2-ton] 11 x 2 in. front, 11 x 1.75 in. rear; [1-ton] 12 x 2 in. front, 14 x 2.5 in. rear. Pressed steel wheels.

DRIVETRAIN OPTIONS: Four-speed Hydra-Matic. (1/2-ton models only). Four-speed manual transmission. Power steering. Oil bath. Air cleaner. 55-amp generator. Heavy-duty suspension.

OPTIONS: Air cleaner. Positraction. Optional axle ratios. Heavy-duty battery. Rear bumper. Custom Cab. Heavy-duty clutch. Directional signal switch. Heater and defroster. Recirculating heater and defroster. Free-wheeling hubs. Right-hand door lock. Spare tire carrier lock. Right-hand door lock and spare tire carrier lock package. Maximum economy option. Exterior mirror. Oil filter. (one-quart). Oil filter (two-quart). Custom Panel body. Heavy-duty radiator. Short runningboard. Auxiliary seat (Canopy Express and Panel). Bostrom type seat. Foam rubber seat cushion. Shock absorber shields. Heavy-duty rear springs. Hydra-Matic transmission. Heavy-duty three- and four-speed transmissions. Electric windshield wipers. Power steering. Heavy-duty generator. Side-mounted spare wheel carrier. Side-mounted spare wheel carrier. Panoramic rear window. E-Z-Eye tinted glass. Radio. Four-barrel carburetor. Auxiliary runningboard. Custom Cab package. Full-width third seat Suburban. Four-wheel drive.

HISTORICAL: Calendar year registrations. [All] 69,509. Model year production: 77,473 (all series).

434

1960 GMC

GMC — LIGHT-DUTY — I-6/V-6: GMC trucks had a completely new appearance combining a modern cab with lower overall height. A "pinched-waist" feature line ran along the hood and doors (and rear quarters of panels, Suburbans and Wide-Side pickups). The massive, full-width hood had jet-pod styling. A screenlike grillework filled the upper front end with rectangular parking lamps inside the pods at each end. The lower grille had a "barbell" look with GMC letters in the center and dual headlamps at each end. Trim consisted of a circular medallion on the fendersides, behind the headlamps with a V through the circle to indicate use of the V-6. The roof of the cab had an overhang at the rear. Up front, there was a wraparound windshield. Deluxe and Custom Cabs were available. A side trim molding option was available. The molding ran across the cowlside and doors of all models and the rear quarters of the flush-fendered Wide-Side pickups. Along with a new suspension system, the GMC light-duty trucks had stronger, yet lighter, frames. As a replacement for the inline six-cylinder engine, GMC offered a new V-6 engine displacing 305 cid. It was standard in all light-duty models, except a small new van. Listed in the 1/2-ton class, this was called the Junior Delivery Van. It was on a short 98 in. wheelbase with forward-control design. The larger 3/4-ton and 1-ton walk-in delivery vans disappeared from conventional light-duty truck listings, though such models were still available.

I.D. DATA: The serial number is stamped on the identification plate mounted on the cowl left side panel inside the cab or on the left door hinge pillar. Data on the plate includes truck model number, chassis serial number, certified gross and maximum gross vehicle weight and net horsepower. Engine numbers located: [six] on left side of cylinder block behind oil filler. [V-8] stamped on top of cylinder block ahead of right-hand bank of cylinder head.

1960 GMC 1/2-Ton Wide-Side Pickup (GMC)

Model	Body Type	Price	Weight	Prod. Total
Series PV1000 — 1/2-Ton — 98 in. w.b.				
PV1001	Junior Delivery Van	2658	3900	
Series P1000 — 1/2-Ton — 115 in. w.b.				
P1001	Chassis & Cab	1958	3415	—
P1001	Panel 7.5-ft.	2389	3970	—
P1001	Custom Panel 7.5-ft.	2486	3985	—
P1001	Wide-Side Pickup 6.5-ft.	2093	3835	—
P1001	Fender-Side Pickup 6.5-ft.	2072	3785	—
P1001	Suburban	2821	4300	—
Series P1000 — 1/2-Ton — 127 in. w.b.				
P1002	Chassis & Cab	2008	3485	—
P1002	Wide-Side Pickup 8-ft.	2143	3955	—
P1002	Fender-Side Pickup 8-ft.	2122	3905	—
Series P1500 — 3/4-Ton — 127 in. w.b.				
P1502	Chassis & Cab	2142	3720	—
P1502	Wide-Side Pickup 8-ft.	2277	4190	—
P1502	Fender-Side Pickup 8-ft.	2256	4140	—
P1502	Stake 8-ft.	2347	4380	—
Series P2502 — 1-Ton — 127 in. w.b.				
P2502	Chassis & Cab	2281	3955	—
Series P2503 — 1-Ton — 133 in. w.b.				
P2503	Chassis & Cab	2281	3970	—
P2503	Panel 10.5-ft.	2841	4687	—
P2503	Custom Panel 10.5-ft.	2938	4700	—
P2503	Pickup	2416	4415	—
P2503	Stake	2529	4810	—

NOTE 1: Series 1000 add $650 for 4x4 option.
NOTE 2: Series 1500 add $700 for 4x4 option.
NOTE 3: "K" series/model prefix for 4x4 trucks.

1960 GMC 1-Ton Series 2500 Platform Stake (GMC)

ENGINE [Standard All Conventionals]: V-type. OHV. "305 A". Six-cylinder. Cast iron block. Bore & stroke: 4.25 x 3.58. Displacement: 304.7 cid.. Compression ratio: 7.75:1. Brake hp: 150 at 3600 rpm. Max torque: 260 lbs.-ft. at 1600 rpm. Four main bearings. Carburetor: Holley one-barrel, model 1904.

ENGINE [Standard PV1001]: Inline. OHV. Six-cylinder. Cast iron block. Bore & stroke: 3.78 x 4.0 in. Displacement: 269.5 cid.. Compression ratio: 7.5:1. Brake hp: 133 at 3600 rpm. Max torque: 244 lbs.-ft. at 1300-2000 rpm. Carburetor: one-barrel.

1960 GMC Crew Cab Pickup/Track Cleaner (GMC)

CHASSIS [Series 1000]: Wheelbase: 98/115/127 in. Overall length: 186.75 to 206.25 in. Tires: 7.10 x 15, four-ply.

CHASSIS [Series 1500]: Wheelbase: 127 in. Overall length: 206.25 in. Tires: 7.00 x 17.5, six-ply.

CHASSIS [Series 2500]: Wheelbase: 127/133 in. Overall length: 206.25 to 216.25 in. Tires: 8.00 x 17.5, six-ply.

TECHNICAL: Manual, synchromesh transmission. Speeds: 3F/1R (4R/1R-Series 2500). Column (floor-Series 2500) mounted gearshift. Rear axle: [1/2-ton] semi-floating Full-floating [all others] rear axle. Hydraulic, four-wheel brakes. Pressed steel wheels.

DRIVETRAIN OPTIONS: Hydra-Matic. Auxiliary rear springs (1/2-ton, 3/4-ton models). Limited-slip differential. Full-lock differential.

OPTIONS: Air cleaner. Air conditioning. Positraction rear axle. Vacuum power brakes. Economy carburetor. Heavy-duty clutch. E-Z-Eye glass. Heavy-duty generator. Heater and defroster. Inside mirror. Oil filter. Padded instrument panel. Radio. Foam rubber seat cushion. Heavy-duty rear springs. Power steering. Steering wheel. Hydra-Matic automatic transmission ($253). Overdrive transmission. Wheel discs. Windshield washers. Electric windshield wipers. Dual exhausts. "K" four-wheel drive option. Four-speed synchromesh transmission ($92).

HISTORICAL: Calendar year registrations. [All] 82,546. Model year production. [All] 104,310. New innovations included Introduction of V-6 engine.

GMC — SERIES 1000/K1000 [1/2-TON]/ 1500/K1500 [3/4-TON]/ 25000 [1-TON]/V3000-V3500 FORWARD CONTROL — I-6/V-6: GMC trucks were not produced on a model year change basis. Production of the 1960 designs continued into model year 1961. You would have to see the title to tell the trucks apart.

I.D. DATA: Serial number located stamped on identification plate mounted on cowl left side panel inside the cab or on left door hinge pillar. Serial number includes truck model number, chassis serial number, certified gross and maximum gross vehicle weight and net horsepower. Engine numbers located: [I-6] stamped on a boss on crankcase adjacent to the distributor; [V-6] stamped on top of cylinder block ahead of right-hand bank cylinder head. The 305 engines for Series 1000/1500 trucks have a C prefix for identification purposes.

Model	Body Type	Price	Weight	Prod. Total
Series 1000 — 1/2-Ton — 98 in. w.b. — (I-6)				
1001	Delivery Van Jr.	2701	3900	—
Series 1000 — 1/2-Ton — 115 in. w.b. — (V-6)				
1001	Chassis & Cab	1958	3400	—
1001	Wide-Side Pickup	2093	3795	—
1001	Fender-Side Pickup	2072	3760	—
1001	Custom Panel 7.5 ft.	2389	4050	—
1001	Custom Panel 7.5 ft.	2486	4060	—
1001	Suburban	2821	4385	—

NOTE 1: 127 in. wheelbase Series 1002 chassis & cab and pickups available.
NOTE 2: Add $693 for K1000 4x4 models.

Model	Body Type	Price	Weight	Prod. Total
Series 1500 — 3/4-Ton — 127 in. w.b. — (V-6)				
1502	Chassis & Cab	2142	3740	—
1502	Wide-Side Pickup 8-ft.	2277	4210	—
1502	Fender-Side Pickup 8-ft.	2256	4160	—
1502	Stake 8-ft.	2347	4400	—

NOTE 3: Add $710 for K1500 4x4 models.

Model	Body Type	Price	Weight	Prod. Total
Series 2502 — 1-Ton — 121 in. w.b. — (V-6)				
2502	Chassis & Cab	2281	4045	—
Series 2503 — 1-Ton — 133 in. w.b. — (V-6)				
2503	Chassis & Cab	2336	—	—
2503	Pickup	2416	4620	—
2503	Panel 12.5-ft.	2841	4845	—
2503	Panel 10.5-ft.	2938	4860	—
2503	Stake	2529	4885	—

ENGINE [V-6]: V-type. Ohv. Six-cylinder. Cast iron block. Bore & stroke: 4.25 in. x 3.58 in. Displacement: 304.7 cid.. Compression ratio: 7.75:1. Brake hp: 150 at 3600 rpm. Max. Torque: 260 lbs.-ft. at 1600-2000 rpm. Four main bearings. Hydraulic valve lifters. Carburetor: Holley one-barrel (downdraft model 1904).

ENGINE [V1001]: Inline. Ohv. Six-cylinder. Cast iron block. Bore & stroke: 3.78 in. x 4 in. Displacement: 269.5 cid.. Compression ratio: 7.75:1. Brake hp: 133 at 3600 rpm. Max. Torque: 244 lbs.-ft. at 1300-2000 rpm. Hydraulic valve lifters. Carburetor Holley model 1904 FS.

CHASSIS [V1000]: Wheelbase: 98 in. Tires: 7.10-15 in.

CHASSIS [Series 1000]: Wheelbase: 115-127 in. Length: [1001] 206 in. Front tread: 63.1 in. Rear tread: 61 in. Tires: 7.10-15 in.

CHASSIS [Series 1500]: Wheelbase: 127 in. Front tread: 63.1 in. Rear tread: 61.1 in. Tires: 7-17.5 in.

CHASSIS [Series 2500]: Wheelbase: 121-133 in. Tires: 8-17.5 in.

TECHNICAL: Manual transmission. Speeds: 3 F/1R. Column-mounted gearshift. Clutch: [1000] Borg & Beck 10-1/2 in. single-plate dry-disc clutch: [1500] Borg & Beck 11 in. single plate dry disc (optional in K1000). Rear axle: [1000] hypoid, semi-floating rear axle. Overall axle ratio: [1000] 3.38 or 3.07; [K-1000/K-1500] 3.54; [1500] 4.56. Optional axle ratios: [1500] 4.10; [2500] 4.57, 5.14. Hydraulic, four-wheel brakes. Steel, disc wheels.

DRIVETRAIN OPTIONS: Automatic tranmission: [1000/1500/2500] four-speed Hydra-Matic ($253). Transmission: [Standard on 2500; optional on 1000/K1000/1500/K1500] four-speed manual.

OPTIONS: Air cleaner. Air conditioning. Positraction rear axle. Heavy-duty battery. Spare wheel carrier. Painted bumper. Heavy-duty clutch. Directional signal switch. Extra-cooling fan. Amp. and oil pressure gauges. E-Z-Eye glass. Heavy-duty generator. Heater and defroster. Towing hooks. Exterior sideview mirror. Oil filter. Heavy-duty radiator. Radio. Bostrom seat. Heavy-duty shock absorbers. Heavy-duty rear springs. Tachometer. Special crankcase ventilation system. Panoramic rear window. Electric windshield wipers. Alternator. Ammeter. Maximum economy carburetor.

HISTORICAL: Calendar year production: 74,996.

1961 GMC

1961 GMC 1/2-Ton Fender-Side Pickup (GMC)

1962 GMC

1962 GMC 1/2-Ton Wide-Side Pickup (GMC)

GMC — SERIES 1000/K1000 [1/2-TON]/ 1500/K1500 [3/4-TON]/ 25000 [1-Ton]/V3000-V3500 FORWARD CONTROL — I-6/V-6: The hood was lowered and rounded off in front so that it now carried the upper bodyside feature line horizontally around the front of the trucks. This eliminated the upper grille. Twin air slots were seen between the parking lamps on the front face of the hood. The lower grille was similar to before. Emblems on the hood-sides had a 6 inside an oval inside a V. This gave them a piece-of-pie shape when viewed from afar. The emblems were raised to the forward hoodside, just behind the parking lamps. New hubcaps were seen. They had a dark-colored, round center medallion with a white circle and GMC lettering on them. Standard equipment on 1000 Series trucks included a fuel filter, oil bath air filter, painted front bumper, electric windshield wipers, fuel filter, left-hand outside rearview mirror, left-hand inside sun visor and five 7.10 x 15 four-ply black sidewall tubelss tires. Series 1500 trucks included fuel filter, painted front bumper, electric wipers, left-hand outside rearview mirror, left-hand interior sun visor and four 7-17.5 six-ply black sidewall tubeless tires.

I.D. DATA: Serial number located stamped on identification plate mounted on cowl left side panel inside the cab or on left door hinge pillar. Number includes truck model number, Chassis serial number, certified gross and maximum gross vehicle weight and net horse power. Engine numbers located: [I-6] stamped on a boss or crank case adjacent to the distributor; [V-6] stamped on top of cylinder block ahead of right-bank cylinder head. 305 engines for 1000/1500 have a C for identification purpose (i.e. 305C 137 786). A suffix D was used to indicate heavy-duty.

Model	Body Type	Price	Weight	Prod. Total
Series 1000 — 1/2-Ton — 98 in. w.b. — (I-6)				
1001	Junior Delivery	2752	3900	—
Series 1001 — 1/2-Ton — 115 in. w.b. — (V-6)				
1001	Chassis & Cab,	2009	3400	—
1001	Wide-Side Pickup	2144	3795	—
1001	Fender-Side Pickup	2123	3760	—
1001	Panel 7.5-ft.	2440	4050	—
1001	Custom Panel 7.5-ft.	2537	4060	—
1001	Suburban	2882	4385	—

NOTE 1: 127 in. wheelbase Series 1002 chassis & cab and pickups available.
NOTE 2: Add $665 for K1000 4x4 trucks.

Model	Body Type	Price	Weight	Prod. Total
Series 1500 — 3/4-Ton — 127 in. w.b. — (V-6)				
1502	Chassis & Cab	2194	3740	—
1502	Wide-Side Pickup 8-ft.	2329	4210	—
1502	Fender-Side Pickup 8-ft.	2308	4160	—
1502	Stake 8-ft.	2399	4400	—

NOTE 3: Add $693 to for K1500 4x4 trucks.

Model	Body Type	Price	Weight	Prod. Total
2502	Chassis & Cab	2336	4045	—
Series 2503 — 1-Ton — 133 in. w.b. — (V-6)				
2503	Chassis & Cab	2336	4045	—
2503	Pickup	2471	4620	—
2503	Panel 10.5-ft.	2896	4845	—
2503	Custom Panel 10.5-ft.	2993	4860	—
2503	Stake	2584	4885	—

1962 GMC 1/2-Ton Suburban Carryall (GMC)

ENGINE [V-6]: V-type. Ohv. Six-cylinder. Cast iron block. Bore & stroke: 4.25 in. x 3.58 in. Displacement: 304.7 cid.. Compression ratio: 7.75:1. Brake hp: 165 at 3800 rpm. Max. Torque: 280 lbs.-ft. at 1600 rpm. Four main bearings. Hydraulic valve lifters. Carburetor: Bendix-Stromberg model WW 381031.
ENGINE [Junior Delivery]: Inline. Ohv. Six-cylinder. Cast iron block. Bore & stroke: 3.78 in. x 4 in. Displacement: 269.5 cid.. Compression ratio: 7.75:1. Brake hp: 133 at 3600 rpm. Max. Torque: 244 lbs.-ft. at 1300-2000 rpm. Hydraulic valve lifters. Carburetor: Holley model 1904 FS.
CHASSIS [Junior Delivery]: Wheelbase: 98 in. Tires: 7.10-15 in.
CHASSIS [1000]: Wheelbase: 115-127 in. Overall length: 206 in. Front tread: 63.1 in. Rear tread: 61.0 in. Tires: 7.10-15 in.
CHASSIS [1500]: Wheelbase: 127 in. Front tread: 63.1 in. Rear tread: 61.0 in. Tires: 7-17.5 in.
CHASSIS [2500]: Wheelbase: 121-133 in. Tires: 8-17.5 in.
TECHNICAL: Manual transmission. Speeds: 3F/1R. Column-mounted gearshift. Clutch: [100/1500] Borg & Beck 10-1/2 in. single-plate dry-disc; [K1000/K1500] 11 in. (optional 1000/1500). Rear axle: [1000] hypoid, semi-floating. Overall gear ratio: [1000] 3.38.1 or 3.07; [K1000/K1500] 3.54:1; [1500] 4.56:1; [2500] 4.10: [optional all] 4.57:1 or 5.10:1. Steel disc wheels.
DRIVETRAIN OPTIONS: Automatic transmission: [1000/1500/2500] four-speed Hydra-Matic ($196.50). Power-Lok differential. Four-speed manual, 1000 Series ($62.80); 1500 Series ($71.10); 2500 Series (standard equipment). Auxiliary rear spring. Choice of rear axle ratio.
OPTIONS: Rear bumper. Code 0440 Power-lok rear axle, 1000 Series ($50.30); 1500 Series ($68.57). Code 1206 70-amp. heavy-duty battery, all ($5.87). Code 0113 Custom cab package including chrome equipment, all except panel ($75.25). Code 1304 front end chrome equipment, all including Custom Cab ($41.80). Code 0612 heavy-duty 11 in. clutch, all ($4.30). Code 0649 crankcase ventilation system, all ($5.87). Code 0618 heavy-duty fuel pump, all ($6.30). Code 0609 35-amp. generator, all ($29.30). Code 0611, 50-amp.

generator, all ($75.25). Code 0602 velocity type generator, all without Hydra-Matic or heavy-duty V-6 ($13.44). Code 1406 airflow heater, all ($57.69). Code 1405, recirculating heater, all ($41.80). Code 0148, chrome front fender and cab moldings, all with Custom Cab option required ($10). Code 0149, Wide-Side Pickup fender and side moldings. Code 0601 one-quart oil bath air cleaner, all ($3.40). Code 0605 full-flow oil filter, all ($9.21). Code 0721 oil cooler for Hydra-Matic, all ($33.45). Code 0144 left door lock, all ($1.29). Code 0143 full-width rear window, all ($33.45). Code 0135 folding rear auxiliary seat, panels ($31.78). Code 0437 Soft-Ride rear coil springs, all ($4.20). Code 1220 right-hand tail-lamp, stake ($7.54). Code 0706 four-speed transmission, 1000 Series ($62.80); 1500 Series ($71.10). Code 0701 Hydra-Matic transmission, all except 1-ton ($196.50). Code 1045, sidemount tire carrier, Fender-Side Pickup ($12.17); Wide-Side pickup ($10.88). Optional tires: [1000 Series] five 7.10 x 15 four-ply whitewalls ($28); five 7.10 x 15 six-ply blackwalls ($34.05); five 7-17.5 six-ply blackwalls ($101.50); five 6.50 x 16 six-ply ($47.86); five 6.50 x 16 six-ply whitewalls ($79.46). Note: Dealer cost prices for options are given in brackets above.

HISTORICAL: Calendar year production: 89,789.

1962 GMC 3/4-Ton Wide-Side "Camper Special" Pickup (DFW)

1963 GMC

1963 GMC 1/2-Ton Handi-Van (GMC)

GMC — SERIES 1000/K1000 [1/2-TON]/ 1500/K1500 [3/4-TON]/ 25000 [1-Ton]/V3000-V3500 FORWARD CONTROL — I-6/V-6: The 1963 trucks were in the same group as the 1962 models, as GMC continued its policy of ignoring annual model year changes. The low, beveled, rounded-in-front hood again carried the upper bodyside feature line horizontally around the front of the trucks. Two air slots were seen between the parking lamps on the front face of the hood. The lower grille had a barbell shape. Emblems on the hoodsides had a 6 inside an oval inside a V. This gave them a piece-of-pie shape when viewed from afar. They were on the forward side of the hood, just behind the parking lamps. Hubcaps had a dark-colored, round center medallion with a white circle and GMC lettering on them. Standard equipment on 1000 Series trucks included a fuel filter, oil bath air filter, painted front bumper, electric windshield wipers, fuel filter, left-hand outside rearview mirror, left-hand inside sun visor and five 7.10 x 15 four-ply black sidewall tubelss tires. Series 1500 trucks included fuel filter, painted front bumper, electric wipers, left-hand outside rearview mirror, left-hand interior sun visor and four 7-17.5 six-ply black sidewall tubeless tires. The Junior Delivery Van was dropped, while a 102 in. wheelbase forward-control utility truck was new.

I.D. DATA: Serial number located on plate mounted on left cab door hinge pillar. Consists of a four digit vehicle code prefix followed by a five digit serial number. Starting: 10001 and up. GMC did not produce vehicles on the basis of annual model change. No yearly serial number ranges are available. Engine numbers located: [V-6] stamped on top of the cylinder head ahead of the right-cylinder head. It consists of an engine number prefix, (i.e. TDGOC) followed by a five digit serial number identified to the vehicle serial number. If under-sized

main and connecting rod bearings are used, an "A" suffix added. A "B" suffix is used for over-sized pistons. "AB" means a combination of "A" and "B". A plate indicating the vehicle's trim and paint numbers is located on engine side of firewall in back of hood hinge on the right side of the body. Production of 1964 model Handi-Vans began late in calendar year 1963.

1963 GMC 1/2-Ton Fender-Side Pickup (OCW)

Model	Body Type	Price	Weight	Prod. Total
Series 1000 — 1/2-Ton — 115 in. w.b. — (V-6)				
1001	Chassis & Cab	2007	3340	—
1001	Wide-Side Pickup	2142	3735	—
1001	Fender-Side Pickup	2121	3700	—
1001	Panel 7.5-ft.	2438	3980	—
1001	Panel Custom 7.5-ft.	2535	3990	—
1001	Suburban	2824	4230	—

NOTE 1: 127 in. wheelbase Series 1002 chassis & cab and pickups available.
NOTE 2: Add $665 for K1000 4x4 models.

Series PB1000 Forward-Control — 1/2-Ton — 102 in. w.b. — (I-6)				
PB1001	Package Van	2535	3540	
Series 1500 — 3/4-Ton — 127 in. w.b. — (V-6)				
1502	Chassis & Cab	2193	3760	—
1502	Wide-Side Pickup 8-ft.	2328	4230	—
1502	Fender-Side Pickup 8-ft.	2307	4200	—
1502	Stake 8-ft.	2398	4395	—

NOTE 3: Add $693 for K1500 4x4

Series PB1500 Forward-Control — 3/4-Ton — 104-137 in. w.b. — (I-6)				
PB1501	Package Van	3153	4545	
Series PB2500 Forward-Control — 1-Ton — 104-137 in. w.b. — (I-6)				
PB2501	Package Van	3345	4855	
Series 2502 — 1-Ton — 121 in. w.b. — (V-6)				
2502	Chassis & Cab	2352	3900	
Series 2503 — 1-Ton — 133 in. w.b. — (V-6)				
2503	Panel 10.5-ft.	2912	4785	—
2503	Custom Panel 10.5-ft.	3009	4800	—
2503	Pickup 9-ft.	2487	4385	—
2503	Stake	2600	4755	—

ENGINE [Standard: Series 1000/1500/2500]: V-type. Ohv. Six-cylinder. Cast iron block. Bore & stroke: 4.25 in. x 3.58 in. Displacement: 304.7 cid.. Compression ratio: 7.75:1. Brake hp: 165 at 3800 rpm. Max. Torque: 280 lb.-ft. at 1600 rpm. Four main bearings. Hydraulic valve lifters. Carburetor: Stromberg model WW 23-151.
ENGINE [Standard: Series P1000/PB1000]: Inline. Ohv. Four-cylinder. Cast iron block. Bore & stroke: 3.875 in. x 3.25 in. Displacement: 153 cid.. Compression ratio: 8.5. Brake hp: 90 at 4000 rpm. Max. Torque: 152 lbs.-ft. at 2400 rpm. Five main bearings. Hydraulic valve lifters. Carburetor: Rochester one-barrel model 7020103.
ENGINE [Standard: Series PB-1500 and PB-2500]: Inline. OHV. Six-cylinder. Cast iron block. Bore & stroke: 3.875 in. x 3.25 in. Displacement: 230 cid.. Compression ratio: 8.5:1. Brake hp: 140 at 4400 rpm. Max. Torque: 220 lbs.-ft. at 1600 rpm. Five main bearings. Hydraulic valve lifters. Carburetor: Rochester one-barrel model 7023003.

1963 GMC 1/2-Ton Suburban Carryall w/custom wheels (R. Schultz)

CHASSIS [1000]: Wheelbase: 115-127 in. Overall length: 206 in. Front tread: 63.1 in. Rear tread: 61.0 in. Tires: 7.10 x 15 in.
CHASSIS [PB1000]: Wheelbase: 102 in. Tires: 6.70 x 15 in.
CHASSIS [1500]: Wheelbase: 127 in. Tires: 7 x 17.5 in.
CHASSIS [PB1500]: Wheelbase: 104-137 in. Tires: 7 x 17.5 in.
CHASSIS [2500]: Wheelbase: 121-133 in. Tires: 8 x 17.5 in.
CHASSIS [PB2500]: Wheelbase: 104-137 in. Tires: 7 x 17.5 in.

Standard Catalog of Light-Duty Trucks

TECHNICAL: Manual transmission, General Motors SM318. Speeds: 3F/1R. Column-mounted gearshift. Clutch: Borg & Beck, 10.5 in. disc, single-plate, dry-disc. Rear axles: [1000] semi-floating, hypoid gear rear axle. Overall axle ratios: [1000]: 3.07:1 (opt. 3.54:1); [1500]: 4.10:1 (opt. 4.56:1); [K1500]: 4.56:1. Hydraulic, four-wheel brakes. Steel disc wheels. Power-Lok differential. Transmissions: New process Model 745-G, heavy-duty three-speed manual. GM model SM424 four-speed manual. [Package Vans] Model AT-218, Pow-R-Flo automatic. [100/1500/2500] Hydra-Matic automatic trans. Power steering: $135.
OPTIONS: Rear bumper. Code 0440 Power-Lok rear axle, 1000 Series ($50.30); 1500 Series ($68.57). Code 1206 70-amp. heavy-duty battery, all ($5.87). Code 0113 Custom cab package including chrome equipment, all except Panel ($75.25). Code 1304 front end chrome equipment, all including Custom Cab ($41.80). Code 0612 heavy-duty 11 in. clutch, all ($43.91). Code 0649 crankcase ventilation system, all ($5.87). Code 0618 heavy-duty fuel pump, all ($6.30). Code 0609 35-amp. generator, all ($29.30). Code 0611, 50-amp. generator, all ($75.25). Code 0602 velocity type generator, all without Hydra-Matic or heavy-duty V-6 ($13.44). Code 1406 airflow heater, all ($57.69). Code 1405, recirculating heater, all ($41.80). Code 0148, chrome front fender and cab moldings, all with Custom Cab option required ($10). Code 0149, Wide-Side Pickup fender and side moldings. Code 0601 one-quart oil bath air cleaner, all ($3.40). Code 0605 full-flow oil filter, all ($9.21). Code 0721 oil cooler for Hydra-Matic, all ($33.45). Code 0144 left door lock, all ($1.29). Code 0143 full-width rear window, all ($33.45). Code 0135 folding rear auxiliary seat, panels ($31.78). Code 0437 Soft-Ride rear coil springs, all ($4.20). Code 1220 right-hand taillamp, stake ($7.54). Code 0706 four-speed transmission, 1000 Series ($62.80); 1500 Series ($71.10). Code 0701 Hydra-Matic transmission, all except 1-ton ($196.50). Code 1045, sidemount tire carrier, Fender-Side Pickup ($12.17); Wide-Side Pickup ($10.88). Optional tires: [1000 Series] five 7.10 x 15 four-ply whitewalls ($28); five 7.10 x 15 six-ply blackwalls ($34.05); five 7-17.5 six-ply blackwalls ($101.50); five 6.50 x 16 six-ply ($47.86); five 6.50 x 16 six-ply whitewalls ($79.46). Note: Dealer cost prices for options are given in brackets above).
HISTORICAL: Calendar year production: 101,234

1964 GMC 1/2-Ton Suburban Carryall (GMC)

GMC — SERIES 1000/K1000 [1/2-TON]/ 1500/K1500 [3/4-TON]/ 25000 [1-TON]/V3000-V3500 FORWARD CONTROL — I-6/V-6: An important new truck-line was the G Series of small, forward-control Handi-Vans marking GMC's entry into the light van market. The Handi-Van had a base four-cylinder engine and an inline six-cylinder motor was an option. For conventional 1964 models, GMC made some extensive changes to the "greenhouse" section of the truck cab. The wraparound windshield of 1960-1963 was replaced with a non-wraparound one-piece curved glass. This changed the slant of the windshield/front door pillar from forward-slanting to rearward-slanting. Ventipanes (vent windows) also had an entirely new triangular shape. A low, beveled, rounded-in-front hood still carried the upper bodyside feature line horizontally around the front of the trucks. A larger air slot sat between the parking lamps on the front face of the hood. The lower grille had the same barbel shape and same horizontal dual headlamp arrangement. Emblems on the hoodsides still had the piece-of-pie shape. New hubcaps with rotor-shaped center embossments flanking a dark, round GMC center medallion were seen. Standard equipment on 1000 Series trucks included a fuel filter, oil bath air filter, painted front bumper, electric windshield wipers, fuel filter, left-hand outside rearview mirror, left-hand inside sun visor and five 7.10 x 15 four-ply black sidewall tubelss tires. The V-6 was still standard, but a new option for 1000 Series models was an inline six-cylinder engine. This was most likely a reaction to the GMC V-6's bad reputation for long-lasting service, although the I-1000 models with this motor were $16 less expensive. Series 1500 trucks included fuel filter, painted front bumper, electric wipers, left-hand outside rearview mirror, left-hand interior sun visor and four 7-17.5 six-ply black sidewall tubeless tires. While V-6 power was standard, the 3/4-ton trucks could also be had as I-1500s with the inline six. One-tons were also offered as I-2500s. The four-wheel drive option was not offered for inline six-cylinder powered trucks.
I.D. DATA: Serial number located on plate mounted on left cab door hinge pillar. Engine numbers located: [V-6] stamped on top of the cylinder block ahead of the right cylinder head. Serial numbers are not used on I-6 inline engines. Numbers appearing on crankcase boss at rear of distributor are building date code.

Model	Body Type	Price	Weight	Prod. Total
G1000 — 1/2-Ton — 90 in. w.b. — (I-4)				
G1001	Handi-Van	2042	2820	
I1000 — 1/2-Ton — 115 in. w.b. — (I-6)				
I1001	Chassis & Cab	1890	2910	
I1001	Wide-Side Pickup	2025	3305	—
I1001	Fender-Side Pickup	2004	3255	—
I1001	Deluxe Panel 7.5-ft.	2321	3490	—
I1001	Custom Panel 7.5-ft.	2418	3490	—
I1001	Suburban	2719	3745	—

NOTE 1: 127 in. wheelbase Series I-1002 chassis & cab and pickups available.

1000 — 1/2-Ton — 115 in. w.b. — (V-6)

Model	Body Type	Price	Weight	Prod. Total
1001	Chassis & Cab	2006	3340	—
1001	Wide-Side Pickup	2141	3735	—
1001	Fender-Side Pickup	2130	3685	—
1001	Custom Panel 7.5-ft.	2437	3920	—
1001	Suburban	2834	4175	—

NOTE 2: 127 in. wheelbase Series 1002 chassis & cab and pickups available.
NOTE 3: Add $676 for K1000 4x4.

PB1000 Forward-Control — 1/2-Ton — 102 in. w.b. — (I-6)

PB1001	Package Van 7 ft.	2537	3520	—

I1500 — 3/4-Ton — 127 in. w.b. — (I-6)

I1500	Chassis & Cab	2075	3330	—
I1500	Wide-Side Pickup 8-ft.	2210	3810	—
I1500	Fender-Side Pickup 8-ft.	2189	3770	—
I1500	Stake 8-ft.	2397	4395	—

1500 — 3/4-Ton — 127 in. w.b. — (V-6)

1502	Chassis & Cab	2192	3760	—
1502	Wide-Side Pickup 8-ft.	2327	4240	—
1502	Fender-Side Pickup 8-ft.	2306	4200	—
1503	Stake 8-ft.	2397	4395	—

NOTE 4: Add $676 for K1500 4x4.

PB1500 Forward Control — 3/4-Ton — 125 in. w.b. — (I-6)

PB1502	Package Van	3244	5050	—

PB1503 Forward Control — 3/4-Ton — 137 in. w.b. — (I-6)

PB1503	Package Van	—	—	—

PB2502 Forward Control — 1-Ton — 125 in. w.b. — (I-6)

PB2502	Package Van	3436	5270	—

PB2503 Forward Control — 1-Ton — 137 in. w.b. — (I-6)

PB2503	Package Van			

I2502 — 1-Ton — 121 in. w.b. — (I-6)

I2502	Chassis & Cab	2231	3495	—

I2502 — 1-Ton — 133 in. w.b. — (I-6)

I2503	Deluxe Panel 10.5-ft.	2791	4330	—
I2503	Custom Panel 10.5-ft.	2888	4330	—
I2503	Fender-Side Pickup 9-ft.	2366	3990	—
I2503	Stake 9-ft.	2479	4350	—

Series 2500

2502 — 1-Ton — 121 in. w.b. — (I-6)

2502	Chassis & Cab	2351	3925	—

2502 — 1-Ton — 133 in. w.b. — (I-6)

2503	Deluxe Panel 10.5-ft.	2911	4760	—
2503	Custom Panel 10.5-ft.	3008	4760	—
2503	Fender-Side Pickup 9-ft.	2486	4420	—
2503	Stake 9-ft.	2599	4780	—

ENGINE [Standard: I1000/I1500]: Inline. OHV. Six-cylinder. Cast iron block. Bore & stroke: 3.875 in. x 3.25 in. Displacement: 230 cid.. Compression ratio: 8.5:1. Net horsepower: 120 at 3600 rpm. Max. Torque: 220 lbs.-ft. at 1600 rpm. Four main bearings. Hydraulic valve lifters. Carburetor: Rochester downdraft model B10Z3011 or 7024009.
ENGINE [Standard: 1000/1500/K1000/K1500]: V-type. OHV. Six-cylinder. Cast iron block. Bore & stroke: 4.25 in. x 3.58 in. Displacement: 304.7 cid.. Compression ratio: 7.75:1. Brake hp: 165 at 3800 rpm. Max. Torque: 280 lbs.-ft. at 1600 rpm. Four main bearings. Hydraulic valve lifters. Carburetor: Bendix-Stromberg downdraft two-barrel, [early] model WW381094; [late] WW 381123.
ENGINE [Standard: Series P1000/PB1000]: Inline. OHV. Four-cylinder. Cast iron block. Bore & stroke: 3.875 in. x 3.25 in. Displacement: 153 cid. Brake hp: 90 at 4000 rpm. Max. Torque: 152 lbs.-ft. at 2400 rpm. Five main bearings. Hydraulic valve lifters. Carburetor: Rochester one-barrel model 7020103.
CHASSIS [G1000]: Wheelbase: 90 in. Tires: 6.50 x 13 in.
CHASSIS [Series I1000]: Wheelbase: 115-127 in. Overall length: 206 in. Height: 71 in. Front tread: 63.1 in. Rear tread: 61.1 in. Tires: 6.70 x 15 in.
CHASSIS [1000]: Wheelbase: 115-127 in. Overall length: 206 in. Height: 71 in. Front tread: 63.1 in. Rear tread: 61.1 in. Tires: 7.10 x 15 in.
CHASSIS [I1500]: Wheelbase: 127 in. Front tread: 63.1 in. Rear tread: 61.1 in. Tires: 7 x 17.5 in.
CHASSIS [1500]: Wheelbase: 127 in. Height: 71 in. Front tread: 63.1 in. Rear tread: 61.1 in. Tires: 7 x 17.5 in.
CHASSIS [PB1500]: Wheelbase: 125-137 in. Tires: 7 x 17.5 in.
CHASSIS [PB2500]: Wheelbase: 125-137 in. Tires: 8 x 19.5 in.
CHASSIS [I2500]: Wheelbase: 121-133 in. Tires: 8 x 17.5 in.
CHASSIS [2500]: Wheelbase: 121-133 in. Tires: 8 x 17.5 in.
TECHNICAL: Transmission: [1/2- to 3/4-ton]. GM no. SM318 three-speed manual. Column-mounted gear shift lever. Single-plate dry-disc clutch. Clutch: [I1000/I1500] GM 10 in. dry disc standard (11 in. optional.); [1000] Borg & Beck 10-1/2 in.; [all 4x4] Borg & Beck 11 in. (optional 1000/1500). Hypoid, semi-floating rear axle. Overall ratio: [1000]: 3.07:1 (opt. 3.54:1); [I-1000]: 3.54:1 (opt. 3.09, 3.92:1); [I1500/1500/K1500] 4.56:1. (optional 4.10). Hydraulic four-wheel brakes. Steel disc wheels.
OPTIONS: Rear bumper. Code 0440 Power-Lok rear axle, 1000 Series ($50.30); 1500 Series ($68.57). Code 1206 70-amp. heavy-duty battery, all ($5.87). Code 0113 Custom cab package including chrome equipment, all except Panel ($75.25). Code 1304 front end chrome equipment, all including Custom Cab ($41.80). Code 0612 heavy-duty 11 in. clutch, all ($4.30). Code 0649 crankcase ventilation system, all ($5.87). Code 0618 heavy-duty fuel pump, all ($6.30). Code 0609 35-amp. generator, all ($29.30). Code 0611, 50-amp. generator, all ($75.25). Code 0602 velocity type generator, all without Hydra-Matic or heavy-duty V-6 ($13.44). Code 1406 airflow heater, all ($57.69). Code 1405, recirculating heater, all ($41.80). Code 0148, chrome front fender and cab moldings, all with Custom Cab option required ($10). Code 0149, Wide-Side Pickup fender and side moldings, all ($71.10). Code 0601 one-quart oil bath air cleaner, all ($3.40). Code 0605 full-flow oil filter, all ($9.21). Code 0721 oil cooler for Hydra-Matic, all ($33.45). Code 0144 left door lock, all ($1.29). Code 0143 full-width rear window, all ($33.45). Code 0135 folding rear auxiliary seat, panels ($31.78). Code 0437 Soft-Ride rear coil springs, all ($4.20). Code 1220 right-hand taillamp, stake ($7.54). Code 0706 four-speed transmission, 1000 Series ($62.80); 1500 Series ($71.10). Code 0701 Hydra-Matic transmission, all except 1-ton ($196.50). Code 1045, sidemount tire carrier, Fender-Side Pickup ($12.17); Wide-Side Pickup ($10.88).

438

Optional tires: [1000 Series] five 7.10 x 15 four-ply whitewalls ($28); five 7.10 x 15 six-ply blackwalls ($34.05); five 7-17.5 six-ply blackwalls ($101.50); five 6.50 x 16 six-ply ($47.86); five 6.50 x 16 six-ply whitewalls ($79.46). Note: Dealer cost prices for options are given in brackets above).
HISTORICAL: Calendar year production: 110,521.

1965 GMC

1965 GMC 1/2-Ton Wide-Side Pickup, Deluxe Cab (GMC)

GMC — LIGHT-DUTY — ALL ENGINES: Still avoiding model year changes for the sake of change, GMC continued the 1964 series for another industry model year. Sometime in 1965 or 1966, the grille emblem "GMC" was modestly changed with squarer-shaped letters. In the 90 in. wheelbase forward-control van series, there was a new windowed model called a Handi-Bus.
I.D. DATA: Serial number located on plate mounted on left cab door hinge pillar. Engine numbers located: [V-6]: stamped on top of the cylinder block ahead of the right-cylinder head. Serial numbers not used on inline engines. Numbers appearing on crankcase boss at rear of distributor are building date codes.

1965 GMC 1/2-Ton Handi-Van (JAG)

Model	Body Type	Price	Weight	Prod. Total
G1000 — 1/2-Ton — 90 in. w.b.				
G1001	Handi-Van	2080	2825	—
G1101	Handi-Bus	2330	3040	—
I1000 — 1/2-Ton — 115 in. w.b.				
I1001	Chassis & Cab	1890	2910	—
I1001	Wide-Side Pickup	2025	3305	—
I1001	Fender-Side Pickup	2004	3255	—
I1001	Deluxe Panel 7.5-ft.	2321	3490	—
I1001	CustomPanel 7.5-ft.	2418	3490	—
I1001	Suburban	2718	3745	—

NOTE 1: 127 in. wheelbase Series I-1002 chassis & cab and pickups available.

1000 — 1/2-Ton — 115 in. w.b.

1001	Chassis & Cab	2006	3340	—
1001	Wide-Side Pickup	2141	3735	—
1001	Fender-Side Pickup	2120	3685	—
1001	Deluxe Panel 7.5-ft.	2437	3920	—
1001	Custom Panel 7.5-ft.	2534	3920	—
1001	Suburban	2834	4175	—

NOTE 2: 127 in. wheelbase Series I-1002 chassis & cab and pickups available.
NOTE 3: Add $665 Series K-1000.

PB1000 — 1/2-Ton — 102 in. w.b.

PB1001	Package Van	2534	3520	—

I1500 — 3/4-Ton — 127 in. w.b.

I1502	Chassis & Cab	2075	3330	—
I1502	Wide-Side Pickup 8-ft.	2210	3810	—
I1502	Fender-Side Pickup 8-ft.	2189	3770	—
I1502	Stake Rack 8-ft.	2280	3965	—

1500 — 3/4-Ton — 127 in. w.b.

1502	Chassis & Cab	2193	3760	—
1502	Wide-Side Pickup 8-ft.	2328	4240	—
1502	Fender-Side Pickup 8-ft.	2307	4200	—
1502	Stake Rack 8-ft.	2398	4395	—

NOTE 4: $692 for K1500.

PB1500 — 3/4-Ton — 104-137 in. w.b.

PB1502	Package Van	3238	5050	—

PB2500 — 1-Ton — 104-137 in. w.b.

PB2502	Package Van	3434	5270	—

I2502 — 1-Ton — 121 in. w.b. — (I-6)

I2502	Chassis & Cab	2232	3495	—

I2502 — 1-Ton — 133 in. w.b. — (I-6)

I2503	Deluxe Panel 10.5-ft.	2792	4330	—
I2503	Custom Panel 10.5-ft.	2889	4330	—
I2503	Fender-Side Pickup 9-ft.	2367	3990	—
I2503	Stake 9-ft.	2480	4350	—

2502 — 1-Ton — 121 in. w.b. — (I-6)

2502	Chassis & Cab	2351	3925	—

2502 — 1-Ton — 133 in. w.b. — (I-6)

2503	Deluxe Panel 10.5-ft.	2911	4760	—
2503	Custom Panel 10.5-ft.	3008	4760	—
2503	Fender-Side Pickup 9-ft.	2486	4420	—
2503	Stake 9-ft.	2599	4780	—

ENGINE [Standard: I1000/I1500]: Inline. OHV. Six-cylinder. Cast iron block. Bore & stroke: 3.875 in. x 3.25 in. Displacement: 230 cid.. Compression ratio: 8.5:1. Net horsepower: 120 at 3600 rpm. Max. Torque: 220 lbs.-ft. at 1600 rpm. Four main bearings. Hydraulic valve lifters. Carburetor: Rochester downdraft model B10Z3011 or 7024009.
ENGINE [Standard: 1000/1500/K1000/K1500]: V-type. OHV. Six-cylinder. Cast iron block. Bore & stroke: 4.25 in. x 3.58 in. Displacement: 304.7 cid.. Compression ratio: 7.75:1. Brake hp: 165 at 3800 rpm. Max. Torque: 280 lbs.-ft. at 1600 rpm. Four main bearings. Hydraulic valve lifters. Carburetor: Bendix-Stromberg downdraft two-barrel WW 381123.
ENGINE [Standard: Series P1000/PB1000]: Inline. OHV. Four-cylinder. Cast iron block. Bore & stroke: 3.875 in. x. 3.25 in. Displacement: 153 cid. Brake hp: 90 at 4000 rpm. Max. Torque: 152 lbs.-ft. at 2400 rpm. Five main bearings. Hydraulic valve lifters. Carburetor: Rochester one-barrel model 7020103.

1965 GMC 1/2-Ton Wide-Side Pickup (GMC)

CHASSIS [Handi-Van]: Wheelbase: 90 in. Tires: 6.50 x 13 in.
CHASSIS [I1000]: Wheelbase: 115-127 in. Overall length: 206 in. Height: 71 in. Front tread: 63.1 in. Rear tread: 61.1 in. Tires: 6.70 x 15 in.
CHASSIS [1000]: Wheelbase: 115-127 in. Overall length: 206 in. Height: 71 in. Front tread: 63.1 in. Rear tread: 61.1 in. Tires: 7.10 x 15 in.
CHASSIS [I1500]: Wheelbase: 127 in. Front tread: 63.1 in. Rear tread: 61.1 in. Tires: 7 x 17.5 in.
CHASSIS [1500]: Wheelbase: 127 in. Height: 71 in. Front tread: 63.1 in. Rear tread: 61.1 in. Tires: 7 x 17.5 in.
CHASSIS [PB-1500]: Wheelbase: 125-137 in. Tires: 7 x 17.5 in.
CHASSIS [PB-2500]: Wheelbase: 125-137 in. Tires: 8 x 19.5 in.
CHASSIS [I2500]: Wheelbase: 121-133 in. Tires: 8 x 17.5 in.
CHASSIS [2500]: Wheelbase: 121-133 in. Tires: 8 x 17.5 in.
TECHNICAL: Transmission: [1/2- to 3/4-ton]. CM no. SM318 three-speed manual. Column-mounted gear shift lever. Single-plate dry-disc clutch. Clutch: [I1000/I1500] GM 10 in. dry disc standard (11 in. optional.); [1000] Borg & Beck 10-1/2 in.; [all 4x4] Borg & Beck 11 in. (optional 1000/1500). Hypoid, semi-floating rear axle. Overall ratio: [1000]: 3.07:1 (opt. 3.54:1); [I-1000]: 3.54:1 (opt. 3.09, 3.92:1); [I1500/1500/K1500] 4.56:1. (optional 4.10). Hydraulic four-wheel brakes. Steel disc wheels.
OPTIONS: Rear bumper. Code 0440 Power-Lok rear axle, 1000 Series ($50.30); 1500 Series ($68.57). Code 1206 70-amp. heavy-duty battery, all ($5.87). Code 0113 Custom cab package including chrome equipment, all except Panel ($75.25). Code 1304 front end chrome equipment, all including Custom Cab ($41.80). Code 0612 heavy-duty 11 in. clutch, all ($4.30). Code 0649 crankcase ventilation system, all ($5.87). Code 0618 heavy-duty fuel pump, all ($6.30). Code 0609 35-amp. generator, all ($29.30). Code 0611, 50-amp. generator, all ($75.25). Code 0602 velocity type generator, all without Hydra-Matic or heavy-duty V-6 ($13.44). Code 1406 airflow heater, all ($57.69). Code 1405, recirculating heater, all ($41.80). Code 0148, chrome front fender and cab moldings, all with Custom Cab option required ($10). Code 0149, Wide-Side Pickup fender and side moldings. Code 0601 one-quart oil bath air cleaner, all ($3.40). Code 0605 full-flow oil filter, all ($9.21). Code 0721 oil cooler for Hydra-Matic, all ($33.45). Code 0144 left door lock, all ($1.29).

Code 0143 full-width rear window, all ($33.45). Code 0135 folding rear auxiliary seat, panels ($31.78). Code 0437 Soft-Ride rear coil springs, all ($4.20). Code 1220 right-hand taillamp, stake ($7.54). Code 0706 four-speed transmission, 1000 Series ($62.80); 1500 Series ($71.10). Code 0701 Hydra-Matic transmission, all except 1-ton ($196.50). Code 1045, sidemount tire carrier, Fender-Side Pickup ($12.17); Wide-Side Pickup ($10.88). Optional tires: [1000 Series] five 7.10 x 15 four-ply whitewalls ($28); five 7.10 x 15 six-ply blackwalls ($34.05); five 7-17.5 six-ply blackwalls ($101.50); five 6.50 x 16 six-ply ($47.86); five 6.50 x 16 six-ply whitewalls ($79.46). Note: Dealer cost prices for options are given in brackets above).

HISTORICAL: Calendar year production: 136,705.

1966 GMC

GMC — LIGHT-DUTY — ALL ENGINES: This was the last year of the styling cycle that started back in 1964. No design changes were made in the GMC truck design. The windowed Handi-Bus was made available with 3/4-ton and 1-ton payload ratings. Some engine changes were made. The base engine for 1/2-ton and 3/4-ton Handi-Vans and 1/2-ton Package Delivery models was switched from the 153 cid four-cylinder to the 194 cid inline six. A new 250 cid inline six was standard in larger Package Delivery trucks and also optional in 1/2-ton through 1-ton conventionals. The V-6 that was standard in conventional trucks up to 1-ton now had 170 hp. The 230 cid inline six was an economy option for the conventionals and an extra-cost option for Handi-Vans. Standard equipment on 1000 Series trucks included a fuel filter, oil bath air filter, painted front bumper, electric windshield wipers, fuel filter, left-hand outside rearview mirror, left-hand inside sun visor and five 7.10 x 15 four-ply black sidewall tubelss tires. Series 1500 trucks included fuel filter, painted front bumper, electric wipers, left-hand outside rearview mirror, left-hand interior sun visor and four 7-17.5 six-ply black sidewall tubeless tires.

I.D. DATA: Serial number located on plate mounted on left cab door hinge pillar. Starting: GMC trucks were not formally produced on a year-to-year model change. Engine numbers located: [V-6] Stamped on top of the cylinder block ahead of the right cylinder head. Serial numbers not used on inline engines. Numbers appearing on crankcase boss at rear of distributor are building date codes.

1966 GMC 1/2-Ton Model 1001 Wide-Side Pickup (G. Clarey)

Model	Body Type	Price	Weight	Prod. Total
G1001— 1/2-Ton — 90 in. w.b.				
G1001	Handi-Van	2116	2690	—
G1011	Handi-Bus	2363	3040	—
G1021— 3/4-Ton — 90 in. w.b.				
G1021	Handi-Bus	2496	3135	—
G1031— 1-Ton — 90 in. w.b.				
G1021	Handi-Bus	2722	3195	—
I1000 — 1/2-Ton — 115 in. w.b.				
I1001	Chassis & Cab	1927	2910	—
I1001	Wide-Side Pickup	2071	3305	—
I1001	Fender-Side Pickup	2050	3255	—
I1001	Deluxe Panel 7.5-ft.	2361	3490	—
I1001	Custom Panel 7.5-ft.	2458	3490	—
I1001	Suburban	2706	3745	—

NOTE 1: 127 in. wheelbase Series I-1002 chassis & cab and pickups available.

1000 — 1/2-Ton — 115 in. w.b.				
1001	Chassis & Cab	2054	3340	—
1001	Wide-Side Pickup	2199	3735	—
1001	Fender-Side Pickup	2177	3685	—
1001	Deluxe Panel 7.5-ft.	2488	3920	—
1001	Custom Panel 7.5-ft.	2585	3920	—
1001	Suburban	2830	4175	—

NOTE 2: 127 in. wheelbase Series I-1002 chassis & cab and pickups available.
NOTE 3: Add $665 Series K-1000.

PB1000 — 1/2-Ton — 102 in. w.b.				
PB1001	Package Van	2618	3520	

I1500 — 3/4-Ton — 127 in. w.b.			
I1502	Chassis & Cab	2111	3330	—
I1502	Wide-Side Pickup 8-ft.	2255	3810	—
I1502	Fender-Side Pickup 8-ft.	2234	3770	—
I1502	Stake Rack 8-ft.	2327	3965	—
1500 — 3/4-Ton — 127 in. w.b.			
1502	Chassis & Cab	2240	3760	—
1502	Wide-Side Pickup 8-ft.	2385	4240	—
1502	Fender-Side Pickup 8-ft.	2363	4200	—
1502	Stake Rack 8-ft.	2456	4395	—

NOTE 4: $693 for K1500.

PB1500 — 3/4-Ton — 104-137 in. w.b.			
PB1502	Package Van	3284	5070	—
PB2500 — 1-Ton — 104-137 in. w.b.			
PB2502	Package Van	3480	5295	—
I2502 — 1-Ton — 121 in. w.b. — (I-6)			
I2502	Chassis & Cab	2258	3495	—
I2502 — 1-Ton — 133 in. w.b. — (I-6)			
I2503	Deluxe Panel 10.5-ft.	2831	4330	—
I2503	Custom Panel 10.5-ft.	2928	4330	—
I2503	Fender-Side Pickup 9-ft.	2413	3990	—
I2503	Stake 9-ft.	2527	4350	—
2502 — 1-Ton — 121 in. w.b. — (I-6)			
2502	Chassis & Cab	2399	3925	—
2502 — 1-Ton — 133 in. w.b. — (I-6)			
2503	Deluxe Panel 10.5-ft.	2926	4760	—
2503	Custom Panel 10.5-ft.	3059	4760	—
2503	Fender-Side Pickup 9-ft.	2544	4420	—
2503	Stake 9-ft.	2658	4780	—

1966 GMC 1/2-Ton Fender-Side Pickup (RPZ)

ENGINE [Standard: Series G-1000, except Model G-1031]: Inline. OHV. Six-cylinder. Cast iron block. Bore & stroke: 3.56 in. x 3.25 in. Displacement: 194 cid. Brake hp: 120 at 4400 rpm. Max. Torque: 177 lbs.-ft. at 2400 rpm. Seven main bearings. Hydraulic valve lifters. Carburetor: Rochester one-barrel model.

ENGINE [Standard: G1031/PB1000]: Inline. OHV. Six-cylinder. Cast iron block. Bore & stroke: 3.875 in. x 3.25 in. Displacement: 230 cid.. Compression ratio: 8.5:1. Net horsepower: 120 at 3600 rpm. Max. Torque: 220 lbs.-ft. at 1600 rpm. Four main bearings. Hydraulic valve lifters. Carburetor: Rochester downdraft model B10Z3011 or 7024009.

1966 GMC 1/2-Ton Carryall Suburban (RPZ)

ENGINE [Standard: I1000/I1500/I2500]: Inline. OHV. Model 250-6. Six-cylinder. Cast iron block. Bore & stroke: 3.87 in. x 3.53 in. Displacement: 250 cid.. Compression ratio: 8.5:1. Brake hp: 150 at 4200 rpm. Max. Torque: 235 lbs.-ft. at 1600 rpm. Seven main bearings. Hydraulic valve lifters. Carburetor: Rochester one-barrel model B.

ENGINE [Optional: PB1500/PB2500]: Inline. OHV. Model 292-6. Six-cylinder. Cast iron block. Bore & stroke: 3.87 in. x 4.12 in. Displacement: 292 cid.. Compression ratio: 8.5:1. Brake hp: 170 at 4000 rpm. Max. Torque: 275 lbs.-ft. at 1600 rpm. Seven main bearings. Hydraulic valve lifters. Carburetor: Rochester.

ENGINE [Standard: 1000/1500/K1000/K1500]: V-type. OHV. Six-cylinder. Cast iron block. Bore & stroke: 4.25 in. x 3.58 in. Displacement: 304.7 cid.. Compression ratio: 7.75:1. Brake hp: 170 at 4000 rpm. Max. Torque: 277 lbs.-ft. at 1600 rpm. Four main bearings. Hydraulic valve lifters. Carburetor: Bendix-Stromberg downdraft two-barrel WW 381123.

VALUE VAN

1966 GMC 1/2-Ton Model PB-1000 Value Van Package Delivery (RPZ)

1966 GMC 1/2-Ton Panel Delivery (RPZ)

CHASSIS [Handi-Van]: Wheelbase: 90 in. Tires: 6.50 x 13 in.

1966 GMC 1/2-Ton Handi-Bus (RPZ)

CHASSIS [I1000]: Wheelbase: 115-127 in. Overall length: 206 in. Height: 71 in. Front tread: 63.1 in. Rear tread: 61.1 in. Tires: 6.70 x 15 in.

CHASSIS [1000]: Wheelbase: 115-127 in. Overall length: 206 in. Height: 71 in. Front tread: 63.1 in. Rear tread: 61.1 in. Tires: 7.10 x 15 in.

CHASSIS [PB1000]: Wheelbase: 102 in. Tires: 7.75 x 15 in.

1966 GMC 3/4-Ton PB1500 Value Van Package Delivery (RPZ)

CHASSIS [I1500]: Wheelbase: 127 in. Front tread: 63.1 in. Rear tread: 61.1 in. Tires: 7 x 17.5 in.

CHASSIS [1500]: Wheelbase: 127 in. Height: 71 in. Front tread: 63.1 in. Rear tread: 61.1 in. Tires: 7 x 17.5 in.

CHASSIS [PB1500]: Wheelbase: 125-137 in. Tires: 7 x 17.5 in.

CHASSIS [PB-2500]: Wheelbase: 125-137 in. Tires: 8 x 19.5 in.

CHASSIS [I2500]: Wheelbase: 121-133 in. Tires: 8 x 17.5 in.

CHASSIS [2500]: Wheelbase: 121-133 in. Tires: 8 x 17.5 in.

1966 GMC 1/2-Ton Handi-Van (RPZ)

TECHNICAL: Transmission: [1/2- to 3/4-ton]. CM no. SM318 three-speed manual. Column-mounted gear shift lever. Single-plate dry-disc clutch. Clutch: [I1000/I1500] GM 10 in. dry disc standard (11 in. optional.); [1000] Borg & Beck 10-1/2 in.; [all 4x4] Borg & Beck 11 in. (optional 1000/1500). Hypoid, semi-floating rear axle. Overall ratio: [1000]: 3.07:1 (opt. 3.54:1); [I-1000]: 3.54:1 (opt. 3.09, 3.92:1); [I1500/1500/K1500] 4.56:1. (optional 4.10). Hydraulic four-wheel brakes. Steel disc wheels.

OPTIONS: Rear bumper. Code 0440 Power-Lok rear axle, 1000 Series ($50.30); 1500 Series ($68.57). Code 1206 70-amp. heavy-duty battery, all ($5.87). Code 0113 Custom cab package including chrome equipment, all except Panel ($75.25). Code 1304 front end chrome equipment, all including Custom Cab ($41.80). Code 0612 heavy-duty 11 in. clutch, all ($4.30). Code 0649 crankcase ventilation system, all ($5.87). Code 0618 heavy-duty fuel pump, all ($6.30). Code 0609 35-amp. generator, all ($29.30). Code 0611, 50-amp. generator, all ($75.25). Code 0602 velocity type generator, all without Hydra-Matic or heavy-duty V-6 ($13.44). Code 1406 airflow heater, all ($57.69). Code 1405, recirculating heater, all ($41.80). Code 0148, chrome front fender and cab moldings, all with Custom Cab option required ($10). Code 0149, Wide-Side Pickup fender and side moldings. Code 0601 one-quart oil bath air cleaner, all ($3.40). Code 0605 full-flow oil filter, all ($9.21). Code 0721 oil cooler for Hydra-Matic, all ($33.45). Code 0144 left door lock, all ($1.29). Code 0143 full-width rear window, all ($33.45). Code 0135 folding rear auxiliary seat, panels ($31.78). Code 0437 Soft-Ride rear coil springs, all ($4.20). Code 1220 right-hand taillamp, stake ($62.80); 1500 Series ($71.10). Code 0701 Hydra-Matic transmission, all except 1-ton ($196.50). Code 1045, sidemount tire carrier, Fender-Side Pickup ($12.17); Wide-Side Pickup ($10.88). Optional tires: [1000 Series] five 7.10 x 15 four-ply whitewalls ($28); five 7.10 x 15 six-ply blackwalls ($34.05); five 7-17.5 six-ply blackwalls ($101.50); five 6.50 x 16 six-ply ($47.86); five 6.50 x 16 six-ply whitewalls ($79.46). Note: Dealer cost prices for options are given in brackets above).

HISTORICAL: Calendar year production: 127,294.

Standard Catalog of Light-Duty Trucks

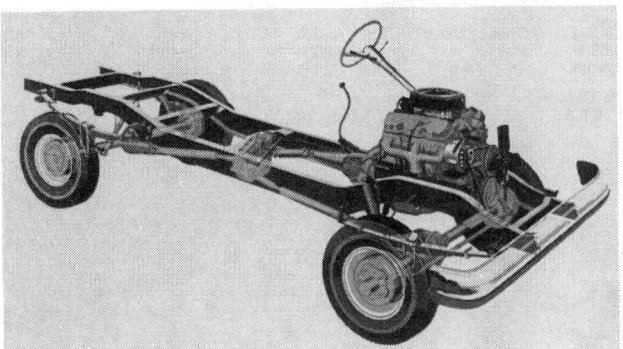

1966 GMC 1/2-Ton K1001 4x4 Truck Chassis (RCA)

1967 GMC

New styling and numerous technical refinements made 1967 a banner year for GMC. Replacing the angular-shaped bodies used since 1960 were units with rounded edges, smooth surfaces and lower body areas/chrome accents. The GMC's grillework was very neat, consisting of a wide center bar bearing GMC lettering, a center divider and encompassing the dual headlight system.

Numerous standard safety features were standard on the 1967 models. Among these was an energy-absorbing instrument panel and steering column, dual braking system, seat belts and four-way hazard flashing lights.

I.D. DATA: Serial number located on plate mounted on left cab door hinge pillar. Starting: GMC trucks were not formally produced on a year-to-year model change. Engine numbers located: [V-6]: stamped on top of the cylinder block ahead of the right-cylinder head. Serial numbers not used on inline engines. Numbers appearing on crankcase boss at rear of distributor are building date codes.

Model	Body Type	Price	Weight	Prod. Total
Series G1500 — 1/2-Ton — 90-108 in. w.b.				
GS1600G	Handi-Van	2252	2900	—
GS1600K	Handi-Bus	2430	3095	—
GS1600W	Deluxe Handi-Bus	2565	3190	—
GS1600X	Custom Handi-Bus	2754	3225	—
Series G-2500 — 3/4-Ton — 90-108 in. w.b.				
GS2630G	Handi-Van	2585	3140	—
GS2630K	Handi-Bus	2708	3285	—
GS2630W	Custom Handi-Bus	2843	3385	—
GS2630X	Deluxe Handi-Bus	3032	3435	—
Series P1500 — 1/2-Ton — 102 in. w.b.				
PS1500H	Van	2746	3650	—
Series P2500 — 3/4-Ton — 104-137 in. w.b.				
PS2590J	Van Round	3292	4715	—
PS2630H	Van Square	3380	5025	—
P3500 — 1-Ton — 104-137 in. w.b.				
PS3590J	Van Round	3489	4940	—
PS3630H	Van Square	3576	5250	—
PT2500 (Diesel) — 3/4-Ton — 104-137 in. w.b.				
PT2590J	Van Round	5234	5435	—
PT2630H	Van Square	5321	5745	—
PT3500 (Diesel) — 1-Ton — 104-137 in. w.b.				
PT3590J	Van Round	5339	5590	—
PT3630H	Van Square	5426	5905	—
C1500 — 1/2-Ton — 115 in. w.b.				
CS1570V	Chassis & Cab	2057	2975	—
CS1570C	Fender-Side Pickup 6.5 ft.	2182	3320	—
CS1570D	Wide-Side Pickup 6.5 ft.	2225	3385	—
C1500 — 1/2-Ton — 127 in. w.b. — (I-6)				
CS1590C	Fender-Side Pickup 8-ft.	2232	3400	—
CS1590D	Wide-Side Pickup 8-ft.	2275	3490	—
CS1590G	Panel	2948	3760	—
CS1590K	Suburban	2979	3980	—

NOTE 1: Add $680 for K1500 4x4 models.
NOTE 2: Same models $120 more in Series CM1500 with 305 cid V-6.
NOTE 3: Same models $95 more in Series CE1500 with 283 cid V-8.

Model	Body Type	Price	Weight	Prod. Total
Series C2500 — 3/4-Ton — 127 in. w.b.				
CS2590V	Chassis & Cab	2233	3415	—
CS2590C	Fender-Side Pickup	2359	3815	—
CS2590D	Wide-Side Pickup	2402	3905	—
CS2590F	Stake	2448	4040	—
CS2590G	Panel	2739	4165	—
CS2590K	Suburban	2969	4385	—

NOTE 4: Add $680 for K2500 4x4 models.
NOTE 5: Same models $120 more in Series CM2500 with 305 cid V-6.
NOTE 6: Same models $95 more in Series CE2500 with 283 cid V-8.

441

Series C3500 — 1-Ton — 133 in. w.b.

CS3600V	Chassis & Cab	2389	3600	—
CS3600C	Pickup	2536	4030	—
CS3600F	Stake Rack	2647	4430	—

NOTE 7: Same models $120 more in Series CM3500 with 305 cid V-6.
NOTE 8: Same models $95 more in Series CE2500 with 283 cid V-8.

1967 GMC 1/2-Ton Wide-Side Pickup w/modern camper shell (JLC)

ENGINE [Standard: G1500/G2500/P1500]: Inline. OHV. Six-cylinder. Cast iron block. Bore & stroke: 3.875 in. x 3.25 in. Displacement: 230 cid.. Compression ratio: 8.5:1. Brake hp: 140 at 4400 rpm. Max. Torque: 220 lbs.-ft. at 1600 rpm. Net horsepower: 120 at 3600 rpm. Seven main bearings. Hydraulic valve lifters. Carburetor: Rochester one-barrel model M 7028006/7028010.
ENGINE [Standard: P2500/P3500/C1500/C2500/C3500]: Inline. OHV. Six-cylinder. Cast iron block. Bore & stroke: 3.875 in. x 3.53 in. Displacement: 250 cid.. Compression ratio: 8.5:1. Brake hp: 155 at 4200 rpm. Seven main bearings. Hydraulic valve lifters. Carburetor: Carter downdraft one-barrel model 3891593.

1967 GMC 1/2-Ton Suburban Carryall (OCW)

ENGINE [Standard: Series CM1500/CM2500/CM3500]: V-type. OHV. Six-cylinder. Cast iron block. Bore & stroke: 4.25 in. x 3.58 in. Displacement: 304.7 cid.. Compression ratio: 7.75:1. Brake hp: 170 at 4000 rpm. Max. Torque: 277 lbs.-ft. at 1600 rpm. Four main bearings. Hydraulic valve lifters. Carburetor: Stromberg 2-bbl. model WW 23-161.
ENGINE [Standard: Diesel P2500/P3500]: Inline. OHV. diesel. Three-cylinder. Cast iron block. Bore & stroke: 3.875 in. x 4.5 in. Displacement: 159 cid. Brake hp: 82 at 2500 rpm.
ENGINE [Optional Handi-Van/Conventionals]: V-type. OHV. Eight-cylinder. Cast iron block. Bore & stroke: 3.875 in. x 3.0 in. Displacement: 283 cid. Brake hp: 175 at 4400 rpm. Max. Torque: 275 lbs.-ft. at 2400 rpm. Five main bearings. Hydraulic valve lifters.
ENGINE [Optional: Series P1500/P2500/P3500/C1500/C2500/C3500]: Inline. OHV. Six-cylinder. Cast iron block. Bore & stroke: 3.875 in. x 4.5 in. Displacement: 292 cid. Compression ratio: 8.1:1. Brake hp: 170 at 4000 rpm. Max. Torque: 275 lbs.-ft. at 1600 rpm. Seven main bearings. Hydraulic valve lifters. Carburetor: Rochester one-barrel modell 7028012/7028013.
CHASSIS [G1500]: Wheelbase: 90-108 in. Tires: 6.95 x 14 in.
CHASSIS [P1500]: Wheelbase: 102 in. Tires: 8.15 x 15 in.
CHASSIS [P3500]: Wheelbase: 104-137 in. Tires: 8 x 19.5 in.
CHASSIS [C2500/CM2500]: Wheelbase: 127 in. Length: 200.5 in. Height: 74.5 in. Tires: 7 x 17.5 in.
CHASSIS [G2500]: Wheelbase: 108 in. Tires: 7.75 x 15 in.
CHASSIS [P2500]: Wheelbase: 104-137 in. Tires: 7 x 17.5 in.
CHASSIS [C1500/CM1500]: Wheelbase: 115-127 in. Length: 200.5 in. Height: 74.5 in. Tires: 7.75 x 15 in.
CHASSIS [C3500]: Wheelbase: 133-157 in. Tires: 8 x 17.5 in.
TECHNICAL: Three-speed, synchromesh transmission. Speeds: 3F/1R. Column-mounted gearshift. Clutch: Single-plate-dry disc. (230/250 cid engines), coil spring single dry plate (292/283 cid engines). Rear axle: [1/2-ton] semi-floating; [3/4-ton and 1-ton] full-floating. Hydraulic four-wheel brakes. Kelsey-Hayes pressed steel wheels. Turbo-Hydramatic automatic transmission. Four-speed manual transmission. Auxiliary rear springs. No-Spin Differential. Heavy-duty suspension. Camper-Cruiser Package.
OPTIONS: Air cleaner. Heavy-duty air cleaner. Air conditioning. Positraction rear axle. Optional ratio rear axle. Heavy-duty battery. Mounting brackets. Vacuum power brakes. Bumper. Hubcaps. Spare wheel carrier. Heavy-duty clutch. Heavy-duty cooling. Custom side molding. Pickup box floor. Fuel filter. Gauge package. Generator. Soft-Ray glass. GM air injector reactor. Governor. Shoulder harness. Heater and defroster. Towing hooks. Side marker lamps. Lock. Exterior mirror. Custom Camper package and trim. Fuel and vacuum booster pump. Radiator. Radio. Bucket seats. Heavy-duty shocks. Speed warning indica-

tor. Auxiliary rear springs. Heavy-duty front springs. Heavy-duty rear springs. Front stabilizer bar. Heavy-duty starter. Power steering. Tachometer. Throttle control. Closed crankcase ventilation. Full wheelcovers. Full-view rear window.
HISTORICAL: Calendar year production: 130,659.

1968 GMC

1968 GMC 3/4-Ton Wide-Side Pickup w/modern camper shell (DFW)

Minor changes were made to the GMC trucks introduced in 1967. GMC letters decorating the front end of trucks were relocated from the center of the grille crossbars to the front center of the hood, just above the grille. Nameplates attached to the sides of the cowl were of a more horizontal design. A new 307 cid V-8 replaced the previous 283 cid V-8. New 327 cid and 396 cid V-8 engines were optional.
I.D. DATA: Serial number located on plate mounted on left cab door hinge pillar. Starting: GMC trucks were not formally produced on a year-to-year model change. Engine numbers located [V-6]: stamped on top of the cylinder block ahead of the right cylinder head. Serial numbers not used on in-line engines. Numbers appearing on crank case boss at rear of distributor are building date codes.

1968 GMC 3/4-Ton Model KS2500 Wide-Side Pickup 4x4 (RCA)

Model	Body Type	Price	Weight	Prod. Total
Series G1500 — 1/2-Ton — 90-108 in. w.b.				
GS1600G	Handi-Van	2306	2900	—
GS1600K	Handi-Bus	2546	3095	—
GS1600W	Deluxe Handi-Bus	2674	3190	—
GS1600X	Custom Handi-Bus	2865	3225	—
Series G-2500 — 3/4-Ton — 90-108 in. w.b. — (V-8)				
GE2630G	Handi-Van	2712	3290	—
GE2630K	Handi-Bus	2942	3435	—
GE2630W	Custom Handi-Bus	3069	3535	—
GE2630X	Deluxe Handi-Bus	3260	3585	—
NOTE 1: Above prices/weights for 3/4-ton "GE" van with V-8				
Series P1500 — 1/2-Ton — 102 in. w.b.				
PS1500H	Van	2824	3710	—
Series P2500 — 3/4-Ton — 104-137 in. w.b.				
PS2580H	Steel Van	3586	5180	—
P3500 — 1-Ton — 104-137 in. w.b.				
PS3580H	Steel Van	3766	5395	—
PT2500 (Diesel) — 3/4-Ton — 104-137 in. w.b.				
PT2580H	Steel Van	5528	6070	—
PT2630H	Van Square	5321	5745	—
PT3500 (Diesel) — 1-Ton — 104-137 in. w.b.				
PT3580H	Steel Van	5608	6170	—

C1500 — 1/2-Ton — 115 in. w.b.

CS1570V	Chassis & Cab	2210	2975	—
CS1570C	Fender-Side Pickup 6.5 ft.	2319	3320	—
CS1570D	Wide-Side Pickup 6.5 ft.	2362	3385	—

C1500 — 1/2-Ton — 127 in. w.b. — (I-6)

CS1590C	Fender-Side Pickup 8-ft.	2369	3400	—
CS1590D	Wide-Side Pickup 8-ft.	2412	3490	—
CS1590G	Panel	2689	3760	—
CS1590K	Suburban	2934	3980	—

NOTE 2: Add $665 for K1500 4x4 models.
NOTE 3: Same models $120 more in Series CM1500 with 305 cid V-6.
NOTE 4: Same models $95 more in Series CE1500 with 307 cid V-8.

Series C2500 — 3/4-Ton — 127 in. w.b.

CS2590V	Chassis & Cab	2389	3415	—
CS2590C	Fender-Side Pickup	2498	3815	—
CS2590D	Wide-Side Pickup	2541	3905	—
CS2590F	Stake	2591	4040	—
CS2590G	Panel	2831	4165	—
CS2590K	Suburban	3188	4385	—

NOTE 4: Add $680 for K2500 4x4 models.
NOTE 5: Same models $120 more in Series CM2500 with 305 cid V-6.
NOTE 6: Same models $95 more in Series CE2500 with 307 cid V-8.

Series C3500 — 1-Ton — 133 in. w.b.

CS3600V	Chassis & Cab	2545	3600	—
CS3600C	Pickup	2680	4030	—
CS3600F	Stake Rack	2860	4430	—

NOTE 7: Same models $120 more in Series CM3500 with 305 cid V-6.
NOTE 8: Same models $95 more in Series CE2500 with 307 cid V-8.

ENGINE [Standard: G1500/G2500/P1500]: Inline. Six-cylinder. Cast iron block. Bore & stroke: 3.875 in. x 3.25 in. Displacement: 230 cid. Compression ratio: 8.5:1. Brake hp: 140 at 4400 rpm. Seven main bearings. Hydraulic valve lifters. Carburetor: Rochester one-barrel model 7028017.
ENGINE [Standard: C1500/C2500/C3500/P2500/P3500]: Inline. OHV. Six-cylinder. Cast iron block. Bore & stroke: 3.875 in. x 3.53 in. Displacement: 250 cid. Compression ratio: 8.5:1. Brake hp: 155 at 4200 rpm. Seven main bearings. Hydraulic valve lifters. Carburetor: Carter downdraft one-barrel model 3891593.
ENGINE [Standard: CM1500/CM2500/CM3500]: V-type. OHV. Six-cylinder. Cast iron block. Bore & stroke: 4.25 in. x 3. 58 in. Displacement: 304.7 cid. Compression ratio: 7.75:1. Brake hp: 170 at 4000 rpm. Max. Torque: 277 lbs.-ft. at 1600 rpm. Four main bearings. Hydraulic valve lifters. Carburetor: Stromberg two-barrel model WW23-161.
ENGINE [Standard: Diesel P2500/P3500]: Inline. OHV. Diesel. Three-cylinder. Cast iron block. Bore & stroke: 3.875 in. x 4.5 in. Displacement: 159 cid. Brake hp: 82 at 2500 rpm.
ENGINE [Optional: G1500/G2500]: V-type. OHV. Eight-cylinder. Bore & stroke: 3.875 in. x 3.25 in. displacement: 307 cid. Compression ratio: 9.0:1. Brake hp: 200 at 4600 rpm. Five main bearings. Hydraulic valve lifters. Carburetor: Rochester two-barrel.
ENGINE [Optional: C1500/C2500/C3500]: V-type. OHV. Eight-cylinder. Cast iron block. Bore & stroke: 4.09 in. x 3.76 in. Displacement: 396 cid. Compression ratio: 9.0:1. Brake hp: 310 at 4800 rpm. Max. Torque: 400 lbs.-ft. at 3200 rpm. Five main bearings. Hydraulic valve lifters. Carburetor: Rochester 4MV7028211.
ENGINE [Optional: P1500/P2500/P3500/C1500/C2500/C3500; 4x4 models]: Inline. OHV. Six-cylinder. Cast iron block. Bore & stroke: 3.875 in. x 4.12 in. Displacement: 292 cid. Compression ratio: 8.1:1. Brake hp: 170 at 4000 rpm. Max. Torque: 275 lbs.-ft. at 1600 rpm. Seven main bearings. Hydraulic valve lifters. Carburetor: Rochester one-barrel model M7028021/7028013.

CHASSIS [G1500]: Wheelbase: 90-108 in. Tires: 6.95 x 14 in.
CHASSIS [G2500]: Wheelbase: 108 in. Tires: 7.75 x 15 in.
CHASSIS [P1500]: Wheelbase: 102 in. Tires: 8.15 x 15 in.
CHASSIS [C2500]: Wheelbase: 127 in. Tires: 7 x 17.5 in.
CHASSIS [P2500]: Wheelbase: 125-133 in. Tires: 8 x 17.5 in.
CHASSIS [P3500]: Wheelbase: 125-157 in. Tires: 8 x 17.5 in.
CHASSIS [C1500]: Wheelbase: 115-127 in. Tires: 8.15 x 15 in.
CHASSIS [C3500]: Wheelbase: 133-157 in. Tires: 8 x 17.5 in.
TECHNICAL: Manual, synchromesh transmission. Speeds: 3F/1R. Column-mounted gear shift lever. Clutch: [230/250 cid] single-plate, dry-disc clutch; [292/307/396 cid] coil spring single plate. Rear axle: [1/2-ton] semi-floating [3/4-ton/1-ton] full-floating. Hydraulic four-wheel brakes. Kelsey-Hayes, pressed steel wheels. Overdrive (C-1500 only). Power steering. Turbo Hydra-Matic. Four-speed manual transmission. Camper package ($71): C-2500, C-3500. Auxlilary rear spring. No-spin differential. Heavy-duty suspension. Power brakes. Heavy-duty clutch.
OPTIONS: Air cleaner. Heavy-duty air cleaner. Air conditioning. Positraction rear axle. Optional ratio rear axle. Heavy-duty battery. Mounting brackets. Vacuum power brakes. Bumper. Hubcaps. Spare wheel carrier. Heavy-duty clutch. Heavy-duty cooling. Custom side molding. Pickup box floor. Fuel filter. Gauge package. Generator. Soft-Ray glass. GM air injector reactor. Governor. Shoulder harness. Heater and defroster. Towing hooks. Side marker lamps. Lock. Exterior mirror. Custom Camper package and trim. Fuel and vacuum booster pump. Radiator. Radio. Bucket seats. Heavy-duty shocks. Speed warning indicator. Auxiliary rear springs. Heavy-duty front springs. Heavy-duty rear springs. Front stabilizer bar. Heavy-duty starter. Power steering. Tachometer. Throttle control. Closed crankcase ventilation. Full wheelcovers. Full-view rear window.
HISTORICAL: Calendar year production: 148,479.

1969 GMC

There were no significant styling changes for 1968 GMC products. However, there were many new options, as the list of factory extras grew very large. They included the Interior Convenience group with special seat trim; roof trim; sunshades; door trim and color-coordinated floor mat. The Custom Trim package included custom seat trim, sunshades and headliner; cigar lighter; chrome hubcaps; horn blow ring; coat hooks and full-width rear window. The Custom Appearance group included chrome grille; extra chrome moldings; a cab trim panel; custom steering wheel (with bright horn ring); and bright windshield moldings. The Custom Comfort & Convenience group included a foam seat cushion; nylon

upholstery; cigar lighter; door armrests; door locks; sunshades; and extra cab insulation. One of the technical revisions this year was a reduction of engine choices. Inline sixes came in 230 and 250 cid options. The V-6 continued. V-8s included the 307 cid and a new 350 cid engines. Lower horsepower ratings indicated work going on in the fuel economy and air pollution areas.

1969 GMC 1/2-Ton Wide-Side Pickup (RPZ)

I.D. DATA: Serial number located on plate mounted on left cab door hinge pillar. Starting: GMC trucks were not formally produced on a year-to-year model change. Engine numbers located: [V-6] stamped on top of the cylinder block ahead of the right cylinder head. Serial numbers not used on in-line engines. Numbers appearing on crank case boss at rear of distributor are building date codes.

1969 GMC 3/4-Ton Model KS2500 Wide-Side Pickup 4x4 (RCA)

Model	Body Type	Price	Weight	Prod. Total
Series G1500 — 1/2-Ton — 90-108 in. w.b.				
GS1600G	Handi-Van	2387	2900	—
GS1600K	Handi-Bus	2654	3095	—
GS1600W	Custom Handi-Bus	2781	3190	—
GS1600X	Custom Deluxe Handi-Bus	2972	3225	—
Series G2500 — 3/4-Ton — 108 in. w.b. (V-8)				
GE2630G	Handi-Van	2764	3290	—
GE2630K	Handi-Bus	3021	3435	—
GE2630W	Custom Handi-Bus	3149	3535	—
GE2630X	Custom Deluxe Handi-Bus	3340	3585	—

NOTE 1: Above prices/weights for 3/4-ton "GE" van with V-8

Series P1500 — 1/2-Ton — 115-127 in. w.b.				
PS1550H	Van	2904	3710	—
Series P2500 — 3/4-Ton — 125-133 in. w.b.				
PS2580H	Steel Van	3682	5180	—
PS2580S	Aluminum Van	4470	—	—
Series P3500 — 1-Ton — 125-157 in. w.b.				
PS3580H	Steel Van	3858	5395	—
PS3580S	Aluminum Van	4646	—	—
Series C1500 — 1/2-Ton — 115 in. w.b.				
CS1570V	Chassis & Cab	2260	2990	—
CS1570C	Fender-Side Pickup 6.5-ft.	2370	3335	—
CS1570D	Wide-Side Pickup 6.5-ft.	2413	3400	—
Series C1500 — 1/2-Ton — 127 in. w.b.				
CS1590C	Fender-Side Pickup 8-ft.	2420	3415	—
CS1590D	Wide-Side Pickup 8-ft.	2463	3505	—
CS1590G	Panel	2823	3775	—
CS1590K	Surburban	3059	3750	—

NOTE 2: Add $700 average for K1500 4x4 models.
NOTE 3: Same models $150 more in Series CM1500 with 305 cid V-6.
NOTE 4: Same models $100 more in Series CE1500 with 307 cid V-8.

Series C2500 — 3/4-Ton — 127 in. w.b.				
CS2590V	Chassis & Cab	2491	3430	—
CS2590C	Fender-Side Pickup 8-ft.	2601	3830	—
CS2590D	Wide-Side Pickup 8-ft.	2644	3920	—
CS2600D	Wide-Side Pickup 8.5-ft.	2707	3980	—
CS2590G	Panel	3035	3660	—
CS2590K	Surburban	3312	4140	—

NOTE 5: Add $700 average for K1500 4x4 models.
NOTE 6: Same models $150 more in Series CM2500 with 305 cid V-6.
NOTE 7: Same models $100 more in Series CE2500 with 307 cid V-8.

Series C-3500 — 1-Ton — 133 in. w.b.

CS3600V	Chassis & Cab	2626	3615	—
CS3600C	Fender-Side Pickup 9-ft.	2759	4045	—
CS3600D	Wide-Side Pickup 8.5 ft.	2821	4105	—

NOTE 8: Same models $150 more in CM3500 with 305 cid V-6.
NOTE 9: Same models $100 more in Series CE3500 with 307 cid V-8.

1969 GMC 3/4-Ton Model C2500 Panel Delivery (RPZ)

ENGINE [G1500/G2500/P1500]: Inline. OHV. Six-cylinder. Cast iron block. Bore & stroke: 3.875 in. x 3.25 in. Displacement: 230 cid. Compression ratio: 8.5:1. Brake hp: 140 at 4400 rpm. Seven main bearings. Hydraulic valve lifters. Carburetor: Rochester one-barrel model 7028017.
ENGINE [Standard: P2500/P3500/C1500/C2500/C3500]: Inline. OHV. Six-cylinder. Cast iron block. Bore & stroke: 3.875 in. x 3.53 in. Displacement: 250 cid. Compression ratio: 8.5:1. Brake hp: 155 at 4200 rpm. Seven main bearings. Hydraulic valve lifters. Carburetor: Carter downdraft one-barrel model 3891593.

1969 GMC 1/2-Ton Model C1500 Suburban Carryall (RPZ)

ENGINE [Standard CM1500/CM2500/CM3500]: V-type. OHV. Six-cylinder. Cast iron block. Bore & stroke: 4.25 in. x 3.58 in. Displacement: 304.7 cid. Compression ratio: 7.75:1. Brake hp: 170 at 4600 rpm. Max. Torque: 277 lbs.-ft. at 1600 rpm. Four main bearings. Hydraulic valve lifters. Carburetor: Stromberg two-barrel model WW23-161.
ENGINE [Optional: G1500/G2500]: V-type. OHV. Eight-cylinder. Cast iron block. Bore & stroke: 3.875 in. x 3.25 in. Displacement: 307 cid. Compression ratio: 9.0:1. Brake hp: 200 at 4600 rpm. Five main bearings. Hydraulic valve lifters. Carburetor: Rochester four-barrell.
ENGINE [Optional: C1500/C2500/C3500]: V-type. OHV. Eight-cylinder. Cast iron block. Bore & stroke: 4.0 in. x 3.5 in. Displacement: 350 cid. Compression ratio: 9.0:1. Brake hp: 255 at 4800 rpm. Five main bearings. Hydraulic valve lifters. Carburetor: Rochester model 4MV7028211.
CHASSIS [G1500]: Wheelbase: 90-108 in. Tires: 6.95 x 14 in.

1969 GMC 3/4-Ton Model KS2500 Wide-Side Pickup 4x4 (RPZ)

CHASSIS [G2500]: Wheelbase: 108 in. Tires: 7.15 x 15 in.
CHASSIS [P1500]: Wheelbase: 102 in. Tires: 8.25 x 15 in.
CHASSIS [P2500]: Wheelbase: 125-133 in. Tires: 8 x 16.5 in.
CHASSIS [P3500]: Wheelbase: 125-157 in. Tires: 8 x 16.5 in.
CHASSIS [C1500]: Wheelbase: 115-127 in. Length: 200.5 in. Height: 74.5 in. Tires: 8.25 x 15 in.

CHASSIS [C2500]: Wheelbase: 127-133 in. Length: 200.5 in. Height: 74.5 in. Tires: 8 x 16.5 in.
CHASSIS [C3500]: Wheelbase: 133-157 in. Height: 74.5 in. Tires: 8 x 16.5 in.

1969 GMC 3/4-Ton Model G2500 Handi-Van (RPZ)

TECHNICAL: Manual, synchromesh transmission. Speeds: 3F/1R. Column-mounted gear shift lever. Clutch: [230/250 cid engines] single plate, dry-disc clutch; [292/307/396 cid engines] coil spring single-plate dry-disc. Rear axle: [1/2-ton] semi-floating; [3/4-ton and 1-ton] full-floating. Hydraulic four-wheel brakes. Kelsey-Hayes pressed steel wheels. Overdrive for C1500 only. Turbo Hydramatic. Four-speed manual transmission. Auxiliary rear spring. Camper package. No-spin differential. Power steering. Heavy-duty suspension. Heavy-duty three-speed manual.
OPTIONS: All-weather air conditioning. Roof air conditioner. Front door armrest. Right sunshade. Left sunshade. Junior West Coast mirror (bright or painted). Senior West Coast mirror (bright or painted). Rearview mirror. Remote-control outside rearview mirror. Visor vanity mirror. Non-glare inside mirror. Front cross-view mirror. Body paint stripe. Fixed or swing-arm outside mirrors; right- and left-hand swinging. Heavy-duty cab lifting torsion bar. Assist handles. Forward-Control P10 body; P20/P30 aluminum body; P20-P30 square body. Platform and stake rack. Platform only. Pickup box mounting. Floorboard. Bodyside door. Heavy-duty frame, frame reinforcements and special frame equipment. Heavy-duty front axles. Front stabilizer bar. Heavy-duty front/rear springs. Auxiliary rear springs. Rear shock absorbers. Helper springs. Optional rear axle ratios. Positraction rear axle. Vacuum power brake. Front disc brakes. Heavy-duty brake system. Air brakes. Special parking brakes. Brake system moisture ejection system. Special brake equipment. Fan drive. Two-quart oil filter. Engine block heater. Heavy-duty oil filter. Air injection reactor. Controlled combustion system. Positive crankcase ventilation. Cruise control. Fuel filter. Fuel and vacuum booster pump. Manual throttle control. Heavy-duty and oil bath air cleaners. Heavy-duty generators. Oversize gas tanks. Dual exhausts. Tilt steering. Woodgrain steering wheel. Power steering. 22 in. steering wheel. 21 in. steering wheel. Heavy-duty manual steering. Full wheelcovers. Deluxe wheel trim cover. Chrome hubcaps. Wheel trim ring. Spare wheel carrier. Side-mounted spare wheel carrier. Heavy-duty batteries. Parking lamps. Camper electrical system. Roof marker and identification lamps. Air horn. Dual horns. Voltmeter. Speed warning buzzer. Tachometer. Oil pressure gauge. Ammeter. Class A directionals. Double-faced front directional lamps. Manual, push-button and AM/FM push-button radios. Trailer towing equipment. Heavy-duty radiator. Front bumper. Chrome bumper. Rear painted bumper. Rear step bumper. Front chrome bumper. Heavy-duty cooling system. Deluxe roof rack. PTO equipment. Hazzard flasher system. Side marker lamps. Front tow hook. Engine alarm system. Interior convenience group. Custom interior (includes convenience equipment features). Cab insulation. Custom Cab package. Custom Appearance package. Custom comfort and convenience package. Rally wheel rims. Stake body. Auxiliary seats (Panel/Suburban, one or two). Cab corner windows. Foam seat cushions. Tinted glass. Two-speed wipers. Interior convenience group. More.

1969 GMC 3/4-Ton Model KS2500 Wide-Side Pickup 4x4 (RCA)

HISTORICAL: Calendar year production: 150,180.

1970 GMC

GMC — LIGHT-DUTY — SIX/V-8: Joining the GMC line in 1970 was the Jimmy model. Available in either two- or four-wheel drive and with a removable hardtop the Jimmy was GMC's entry into the expanding off-road recreational vehicle market. With a standard six-cylinder engine and two-wheel drive, its starting price was $2,377. There was also a new Heavy 3/4-ton ("heavy" meaning heavy-duty) on the longer 1-ton wheelbase with an 8.5-ft. long cargo box.

1970 GMC Model C15904 1/2-Ton Wide-Side Pickup (RPZ)

I.D. DATA: Serial number located on plate mounted on left cab door hinge pillar. Starting: GMC trucks were not formally produced on a year-to-year model change. Engine numbers located: [V-6]: stamped on top of the cylinder block ahead of the right-cylinder head. Serial numbers not used on inline engines. Numbers appearing on crankcase boss at rear of distributor are building date codes. Model/engine prefixes: GS/CS/KS/PS (S= six-cylinder [V-6]); CSI/KSI (SI=six-cylinder inline); GE/CE/KE/PE (E=eight-cylinder).

Model	Body Type	Price	Weight	Prod. Total
C1550 (4x2) Jimmy — 1/2-Ton — 104 in. w.b. — 6-cyl.				
CS15514	Open Utility	2375	3310	—
K1550 (4x4) Jimmy — 1/2-Ton — 104 in. w.b.				
KS15514	Open Utility	2947	3595	—

NOTE 1: Add $95 for base V-8 (CE/KE prefix).

Model	Body Type	Price	Weight	Prod. Total
G1500 Handi-Van — 1/2-Ton — 90 in./108 in. w.b. — 6-cyl.				
GS1600G	Handi-Van	2464	2975	—
GS1600K	Handi-Bus	2758	3165	—
GS1600W	Custom Handi-Bus	2886	3275	—
GS1600X	Custom Deluxe Handi-Bus	3077	3310	—

NOTE 2: Add average $280 for G1630 (108 in. w.b.) Handi-Van.
NOTE 3: Add $95 for base V-8 (GE prefix)

Model	Body Type	Price	Weight	Prod. Total
G2500 Handi-Van — 3/4-Ton — 108 in. w.b. — V-8				
GE2630G	Handi-Van 2840	3370	—	—
GE2630K	Handi-Bus 3126	3510	—	—
GE2630W	Custom Handi-Bus 3253	3640	—	—
GE2630X	Custom Deluxe Handi-Bus 3444	3690	—	—
P1500 Package Van — 1/2-Ton — 102 in. w.b. — 6-cyl.				
PS15535	Van	3099	3715	—
P2500 Package Van — 3/4-Ton — 125 in./133 in. w.b. — 6-cyl.				
PS25835	Steel Van	3864	5085	—
PS25885	Aluminum Van	4652	—	—
P3500 Package Van — 1-Ton — 125in./133 in. w.b. — 6-cyl.				
PS35835	Steel Van	4038	5255	—
PS35855	Aluminum Van	4826	—	—
C1500 Conventional — 1/2-Ton — 115 in. w.b. — 6-cyl.				
CS15703	Chassis & Cab	2381	3025	—
CS15734	Wide-Side Pickup 6.5-ft.	2534	3440	—
CS15704	Fender-Side Pickup 6.5-ft.	2496	3365	—
C1500 Conventional — 1/2-Ton — 127 in. w.b. — 6-cyl.				
CS15934	Wide-Side Pickup 8-ft.	2571	3540	—
CS15904	Fender-Side Pickup 8-ft.	2534	3445	—
CS15905	Panel	3047	3650	—
CS15916	Suburban	3287	3790	—

NOTE 4: Add $575 for KS1500/KE1500 4x4
NOTE 5: Add $95 for base V-8 (CE/KE Prefix)

Model	Body Type	Price	Weight	Prod. Total
C2500 Conventional — 3/4-Ton — 127 in. w.b. — 6-cyl.				
CS25903	Chassis & Cab	2628	3430	—
CS25904	Fender-Side Pickup 8-ft.	2728	3830	—
CS25934	Wide-Side Pickup 8-ft.	2766	3925	—
CS25905	Panel	3245	4040	—
CS25906	Suburban	3417	4165	—

(4x4 models: KS prefix)

Model	Body Type	Price	Weight	Prod. Total
C2600 Conventional — 3/4-Ton H-D — 133 in. w.b. -6-cyl.				
CS26904	Wide-Side Pickup 8.5-ft.	2830	3965	—

NOTE 6: Add $575 for KS2500/KE2500 4x4
NOTE 7: Add $95 for base V-8 (CE/KE Prefix)

Model	Body Type	Price	Weight	Prod. Total
C3500 Conventional — 1-Ton — 133 in. w.b. — 6-cyl.				
CS36003	Chassis & Cab	2712	3575	—
CS36004	Fender-Side Pickup 9-ft.	2850	4005	—
CS36034	Wide-Side Pickup 8.5-ft.	2911	4090	—

NOTE 8: Add $575 for KS3500/KE3500 4x4
NOTE 9: Add $95 for base V-8 (CE/KE Prefix)

1970 GMC 1/2-Ton Jimmy Open Utility With Hardtop 4x4 (RCA)

ENGINE [Standard: all Models]: Inline. OHV. Six-cylinder. Cast iron block. Bore & stroke: 3.875 in. x 3.53 in. Displacement: 250 cid.. Compression ratio: 8.5:1. Brake hp: 155 at 4200 rpm. Seven main bearings. Hydraulic valve lifters. Carburetor: Carter downdraft one-barrel model 3891593.

ENGINE [Base V-8]: V-type. OHV. Eight-cylinder. Cast iron block. Bore & stroke: 3.875 in. x 3.25 in. Displacement: 307 cid.. Compression ratio: 9.0:1. Brake hp: 200 at 4600 rpm. Five main bearings. Hydraulic valve lifters. Carburetor: Rochester 2-bbl.

ENGINE [Optional: P1500/P2500/P3500/C1500/C2500/C3500]: Inline. OHV. Six-cylinder. Cast iron block. Bore & stroke: 3.875 in. x 4.12 in. Displacement: 292 cid.. Compression ratio: 8.1:1. Brake hp: 170 at 4000 rpm. Max. Torque: 275 lbs.-ft. at 1600 rpm. Seven main bearings. Hydraulic valve lifters. Carburetor: Rochester one-barrel model M7028012/7028013.

ENGINE [Standard CM1500/CM2500/CM3500]: V-type. OHV. Six-cylinder. Cast iron block. Bore & stroke: 4.25 in. x 3.58 in. Displacement: 304.7 cid.. Compression ratio: 7.75:1. Brake hp: 170 at 4600 rpm. Max. Torque: 277 lbs.-ft. at 1600 rpm. Four main bearings. Hydraulic valve lifters. Carburetor: Stromberg two-barrel model WW23-161.

ENGINE [Optional: C1500/C2500/C3500]: V-type. OHV. Eight-cylinder. Cast iron block. Bore & stroke: 4.0 in. x 3.48 in. Displacement: 350 cid.. Compression ratio: 9.0:1. Brake hp: 225 at 4800 rpm. Max. Torque: 365 lbs.-ft. at 3200 rpm. Five main bearings. Hydraulic valve lifters. Carburetor: Rochester 2-bbl.

CHASSIS (Series Jimmy K-1550): Wheelbase: 104 in. Length: 177.5 in. Height: 68.7 in. Front tread: 60.4 in. Rear tread: 60.4 in. Tires: E78 x 15 in.

CHASSIS [Series G1500]: Wheelbase: 90-108 in. Tires: 6.95 x 14 in.

CHASSIS [Series G2500]: Wheelbase: 108 in. Tires: 7.75 x 15 in.

CHASSIS [Series C1500]: Wheelbase: 115-127 in. Tires: G78 x 15 in.

CHASSIS [Series P1500]: Wheelbase: 102 in. Tires: G78 x 15 in.

CHASSIS [Series P2500]: Wheelbase: 125-133 in. Tires: 8.75 x 16.5 in.

CHASSIS [Series P3500]: Wheelbase: 125-151 in. Tires: 8.75 x 16.5 in.

CHASSIS [Series C2500]: Wheelbase: 127-133 in. Tires: 8.75 x 16.5 in.

CHASSIS [Series C3500]: Wheelbase: 133-157 in. Tires: 8.75 x 16.5 in.

TECHNICAL: Manual, synchromesh transmission. Speeds: 3F/1R. Column mounted gearshift. Clutch: [250 cid] single-plate, dry-disc; [others] coil spring dry plate. Rear axle: [1/2-ton] semi-floating; [3/4-ton/1-ton] full-floating rear axle. Hydraulic, four-wheel brakes. Kelsey-Hayes pressed steel wheels. Turbo-Hydramatic automatic transmission. Camper Package for C2500/C3500. Wide ratio Muncie three-speed manual. Free-wheeling hubs (4x4). No spin differential. Power steering. Front stabilizer bar. Rear leaf springs. 42 amp. generator. Heavy-duty battery. Heavy-duty rear spring. Heavy-duty front shocks. Auxiliary full tank.

OPTIONS: All-weather air conditioning. Roof air conditioner. Front door armrest. Right sunshade. Left sunshade. Junior West Coast mirror (bright or painted). Senior West Coast mirror (bright or painted). Rearview mirror. Remote-control outside rearview mirror. Visor vanity mirror. Non-glare inside mirror. Front cross-view mirror. Body paint stripe. Fixed or swing-arm outside mirrors; right- and left-hand swinging. Heavy-duty cab lifting torsion bar. Assist handles. Forward-Control P10 body; P20/P30 aluminum body; P20-P30 square body. Platform and stake rack. Platform only. Pickup box mounting. Floorboard. Body side door. Heavy-duty frame, frame reinforcements and special frame equipment. Heavy-duty front axles. Front stabilizer bar. Heavy-duty front/rear springs. Auxiliary rear springs. Rear shock absorbers. Helper springs. Optional rear axle. Positraction rear axle. Vacuum power brake. Front disc brakes. Heavy-duty brake system. Air brakes. Special parking brakes. Brake system moisture ejection system. Special brake equipment. Fan drive. Two-quart oil filter. Engine block heater. Heavy-duty oil filter. Air injection reactor. Controlled combustion system. Positive crankcase ventilation. Cruise control. Fuel filter. Fuel and vacuum booster pump. Manual throttle control. Heavy-duty and oil bath air cleaners. Heavy-duty generators. Oversize gas tanks. Dual exhausts. Tilting steering. Woodgrain steering wheel. Power steering. 22 in. steering wheel. 21 in. steering wheel. Heavy-duty manual steering. Full wheelcovers. Deluxe wheel trim cover. Chrome hubcaps. Chrome wheel trim ring. Spare wheel carrier. Side-mounted spare wheel carrier. Heavy-duty batteries. Parking lamps. Camper electrical system. Roof marker and identification lamps. Air horn. Dual horns. Voltmeter. Speed warning buzzer. Tachometer. Oil pressure gauge. Ammeter. Class A directionals. Double-faced front directional lamps. Manual, push-button and AM/FM push-button radios. Trailer towing equipment. Heavy-duty radiator. Front bumper. Chrome bumper. Rear painted bumper. Rear step bumper. Front chrome bumper. Heavy-duty cooling system. Deluxe roof rack. PTO equipment. Hazzard flasher system. Side marker lamps. Front tow hook. Engine alarm system. Interior convenience group. Custom interior (includes convenience equipment features). Cab insulation. Custom Cab package. Custom Appearance package. Custom comfort and convenience package. Rally wheel rims. Stake body. Auxiliary seats (Panel/Suburban, one or two). Cab corner windows. Foam seat cushions. Tinted glass. Two-speed wipers. Interior convenience group. More.

HISTORICAL: Calendar year production: 121,833. First year for Jimmy model.

1971 GMC

1971 GMC 1/2-Ton Jimmy Open Utility With Hardtop 4x4 (RCA)

GMC — LIGHT-DUTY — SIX/V-8: The big news for 1971 at GMC was the introduction of the Sprint. Based on the Chevrolet El Camino, this was a sedan-pickup that combined passenger car sheet metal with a pickup box. The first Sprint had a two-tier grille and double horizontal-slot front parking lamps as visual characteristics. The idea behind this example of GM badge engineering was to achieve more sales of the El Camino-type model by making it available at GM dealerships. No major appearance changes were introduced on the 1971 GMC conventional trucks. They were highlighted by the use of new blacked-out grille sections and a new two-tone color scheme for Wide-Side Pickups. Added to the GMC lineup were new vans with extended hoods for easier services and sliding side doors. They were equipped with single headlamps and grilles with narrow horizontal bars. The '71s can be spotted by their single rectangular front side marker lamps.

I.D. DATA: Serial number combination GVW and serial number plate located on left door hinge pillar. Example: [pickup] CE-140()100001 and up. Model/engine prefixes: GS/CS/KS/PS (S=six-cylinder); GE/CE/KE/PE (E=eight-cylinder). Engine number indicates manufacturing plant, month, and day of manufacture and transmission type. [Six]: located on pad at right-hand side of cylinder block at rear of distributor. [V-8]: located on pad at front, right-hand side of cylinder block.

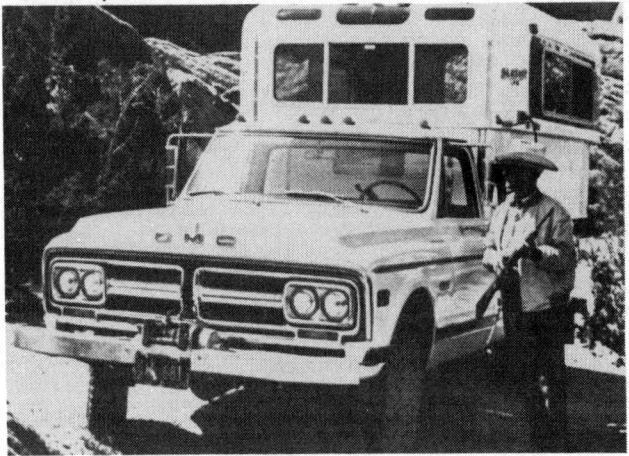

1971 GMC 1-Ton K3500 Wide-Side Pickup 4x4 (RCA)

Model	Body Type	Price	Weight	Prod. Total
Sprint 1/2-Ton — 116 in. w.b. — V-8				
53480	Sedan-Pickup	2988	3418	—
53680	Custom Sedan-Pickup	3074	3442	—
Jimmy 4x2 C1550 — 1/2-Ton — 104 in. w.b. — V-8				
CE15514	Open Utility	2795	3440	—
Jimmy 4x4 K1550 — 1/2-Ton — 104 in. w.b. — V-8				
KE15514	Open Utility	3374	3730	—
G1500 Van — 1/2-Ton — 110 in. w.b. — V-8				
GE16005	Vandura	3053	3445	—
GE16006	Rally	3503	3750	—
G1503 Van — 1/2-Ton — 125 in. w.b. — V-8				
GE16036	Rally STX	3790	3420	—
G2500 Van — 3/4-Ton — 110 in. w.b. — V-8				
GE26005	Vandura	3196	3625	—
GE26006	Rally	3581	3900	—
G2503 Van — 3/4-Ton — 125 in. w.b. — V-8				
GE26036	Rally STX	3808	4010	—
G3500 Van — 1-Ton — 110 in. w.b. — V-8				
GE36005	Vandura	3307	3695	—
G3503 Van — 1-Ton — 125 in. w.b. — V-8				
GE36306	Rally	3824	4280	—
GE36336	Rally STX	4111	4505	—
C1500 Conventional — 1/2-Ton — 115 in. w.b. — V-8				
CE15703	Chassis & Cab	2786	3160	—
CE15704	Fender-Side Pickup 6.5-ft	2946	3500	—
CE15734	Fender-Side Pickup 6.5-ft	2946	3575	—
C1500 Conventional — 1/2-Ton — 127 in. w.b. — V-8				
CE15904	Fender-Side Pickup 8-ft.	2983	3575	—
CE15934	Wide-Side Pickup 8-ft.	2983	3665	—
CE15916	Suburban	3757	3910	—
C2500 Conventional — 3/4-Ton — 127 in. w.b.				
CE25903	Chassis & Cab	3027	3570	—
CE25904	Fender-Side Pickup 8-ft.	3188	3970	—
CE25934	Wide-Side Pickup 8-ft.	3188	4055	—
CE25906	Suburban	3886	4295	—
C2600 Conventional — H-D 3/4-Ton — 133 in. w.b. — V-8				
CE26034	Wide-Side Pickup 8.5-ft.	3252	4100	—
C3500 Conventional — 1-Ton — 133 in. w.b. — V-8				
CE36003	Chassis & Cab	3118	3695	—
CE36004	Fender-Side Pickup 9-ft.	3171	4125	—
C3500 Conventional — H-D 1-Ton — 157 in. w.b. — V-8				
CE36034	Wide-Side Pickup 8.5-ft.	3332	4215	—
P1500 Package Van — 1/2-Ton — 102 in. w.b. — 6-cyl.				
PS15535	Van	2415	3740	—
P2500 Package Van — 3/4-Ton — 127 in./133 in. w.b. — V-8.				
PE25835	Van	4312	5200	—
P3500 Package Van — 1-Ton — 127 in./133 in. w.b. — V-8.				
PE35835	Van	4486	5375	—

NOTE 1: Add average $720 for 4x4 (KS1500/KE1500/KS2500/KE2500 prefix)
NOTE 2: An E in model codes above means prices/specifications given are for trucks with base V-8. Deduct $150 average for six-cylinder models (E in model code becomes S for six). Six-cylinder data for models that came with six only.

1971 GMC 1/2-Ton K1500 Suburban 4x4 (RCA)

ENGINE [Standard: Sprint 380/most others]: Inline. OHV. Six-cylinder. Cast iron block. Bore & stroke: 3.875 in. x 3.53 in. Displacement: 250 cid.. Compression ratio: 8.5:1. Brake hp: 145 at 4200 rpm. Seven main bearings. Hydraulic valve lifters. Carburetor: Rochester one-barrel
ENGINE [Suburban base six]: Inline. OHV. Six-cylinder. Cast iron block. Bore & stroke: 3.875 in. x 4.12 in. Displacement: 292 cid. Compression ratio: 8.1:1. Brake hp: 170 at 4000 rpm. Max. Torque: 275 lbs.-ft. at 1600 rpm. Seven main bearings. Hydraulic valve lifters. Carburetor: Rochester one-barrel model M7028012/7028013.
ENGINE [Base V-8: Sprint 480/CE1500/PE2500/PE3500]: V-type. OHV. Eight-cylinder. Cast iron block. Bore & stroke: 3.875 in. x 3.25 in. Displacement: 307 cid. Compression ratio: 8.5:1. Brake hp: 200 at 4600 rpm. Five main bearings. Hydraulic valve lifters. Carburetor: Rochester two-barrel.
ENGINE [Base V-8 GE2500/GE3500/all Suburbans; optional in others]: V-type. OHV. Eight-cylinder. Cast iron block. Bore & stroke: 4.0 in. x 3.5 in. Displacement: 350 cid.. Compression ratio: 8.5:1. Brake hp: 250 at 4600 rpm. Max Torque: 350 lb. ft at 3000 rpm. Net horsepower: 170 at 3600 rpm. Five main bearings. Hydraulic valve lifters. Carburetor: Rochester two-barrel.
ENGINE [Special order option]: V-type. OHV. Eight-cylinder. Cast iron block. Bore & stroke: 4.125 in. x 3.75 in. Displacement: 402 cid.. Compression ratio: 8.5:1. Brake hp: 300 at 4800 rpm. Net horsepower: 240 at 4400 rpm. Five main bearings. Hydraulic valve lifters. Carburetor: Rochester four-barrel.
CHASSIS [Sprint]: Wheelbase: 116 in. Overall length: 206.8 in. Height: 54.4 in. Front tread: 60.2 in. Rear tread: 59.2 in. Tires: E78-14B.
CHASSIS [Jimmy]: Wheelbase: 104 in. Overall length: 177.5 in. Height: 68.7 in. Front tread: 60.4 in. Rear tread 60.4 in. Tires: E78-15B.
CHASSIS [Series G1500]: Wheelbase: 110 in. Overall length: 178 in. Height: 80 in. Tires: F78 x 14B in.
CHASSIS [G1503]: Wheelbase: 125 in. Overall length: 202.2 in. Height: 80 in. Tires: F78 x 14B in.
CHASSIS [G2500]: Wheelbase: 110 in. Overall length: 178 in. Height: 80 in. Tires: G78 x 15B in.
CHASSIS [G2503]: Wheelbase: 125 in. Overall length: 202.2 in. Height: 80 in. Tires: G78 x 15B in.
CHASSIS [G3500]: Wheelbase: 110 in. Overall length: 178 in. Height: 80 in. Tires: 8 x 16.5C in.
CHASSIS [G3503]: Wheelbase: 125 in. Overall length: 202.2 in. Height: 80 in. Tires: 8 x 16.5C in.

CHASSIS [P1500]: Wheelbase: 102 in. Height: 75 in. Tires: G78 x 15B in.

CHASSIS [P2500/P3500]: Wheelbase: 125 in. Overall length: 220.75 in. Tires: 8.75 x 16.5C in.

CHASSIS [P2503/P3503]: Wheelbase: 133 in. Overall length: 244.75 in. Tires: 8.75 x 16.5C in.

CHASSIS [C1500]: Wheelbase: 115-127 in. Tires: G78 x 15B in.

CHASSIS [C1503]: Wheelbase: 127 in. Tires: G78 x 15B in.

CHASSIS [C2500]: Wheelbase: 127 in. Tires: 8.75 x 16.5C in.

CHASSIS [C2503]: Wheelbase: 133 in. Tires: 8.75 x 16.5C in.

CHASSIS [C3500]: Wheelbase: 133 in. Overall length: 244.75. Tires: 8.75 x 16C in.

CHASSIS [C3503]: Wheelbase: 157 in. Overall length: 265.75 in. Tires: 8.75 x 16C in.

TECHNICAL: Steering: Saginaw manual. Transmission: 3F/1R fully-synchronized transmission. Column-mounted gear shift lever. Clutch: [250 cid] single-plate, dry-disc clutch; [all others] coil spring single dry plate. Rear axle: [1/2-Ton] semi-floating; [3/4-Ton/1-Ton] full floating. Hydraulic, four-wheel brakes. Kelsey-Hayes pressed steel wheels. Turbo Hydramatic automatic transmission 350 and 400 ($258.25). Wide-ratio Muncie three-speed manual. Four-speed manual has floor-mounted shifter.

OPTIONS: All-weather air conditioning. Roof air conditioner. Front door armrest. Right sunshade. Left sunshade. Junior West Coast mirror (bright or painted). Senior West Coast mirror (bright or painted). Rearview mirror. Remote-control outside rearview mirror. Visor vanity mirror. Non-glare inside mirror. Front cross-view mirror. Body-paint stripe. Fixed or swing-arm outside mirrors; right- and left-hand swinging. Heavy-duty cab lifting torsion bar. Assist handles. Forward-Control P10 body; P20/P30 aluminum body; P20-P30 square body. Platform and stake rack. Platform only. Pickup box mounting. Floorboard. Panel/Van side door. Heavy-duty frame, frame reinforcements and special frame equipment. Heavy-duty front axles. Front stabilizer bar. Heavy-duty front/rear springs. Auxiliary rear springs. Rear shock absorbers. Helper springs. Optional rear axle ratios. Positraction rear axle. Vacuum power brake. Front disc brakes. Heavy-duty brake system. Air brakes. Special parking brakes. Brake system moisture ejection system. Special brake equipment. Fan drive. Two-quart oil filter. Engine block heater. Heavy-duty oil filter. Air injection reactor. Controlled combustion system. Positive crankcase ventilation. Cruise control. Fuel filter. Fuel and vacuum booster pump. Manual throttle control. Heavy-duty and oil bath air cleaners. Heavy-duty generators. Oversize gas tanks. Dual exhausts. Tilt steering. Woodgrain steering wheel. Power steering. 22 in. steering wheel. 21 in. steering wheel. Heavy-duty manual steering. Full wheelcovers. Deluxe wheel trim cover. Chrome hubcaps. Wheel trim ring. Spare wheel carrier. Side-mounted spare wheel carrier. Heavy-duty batteries. Parking lamps. Camper electrical system. Roof marker and identification lamps. Air horn. Dual horns. Voltmeter. Speed warning buzzer. Tachometer. Oil pressure gauge. Ammeter. Class A directionals. Double-faced front directional lamps. Manual, push-button and AM/FM push-button radios. Trailer towing equipment. Heavy-duty radiator. Front bumper. Chrome bumper. Rear painted bumper. Rear step bumper. Front chrome bumper. Heavy-duty cooling system. Deluxe roof rack. PTO equipment. Hazzard flasher system. Side marker lamps. Front tow hook. Engine alarm system. Interior convenience group. Custom interior (includes convenience equipment features). Cab insulation. Custom Cab package. Custom Appearance package. Custom comfort and convenience package. Rally wheel rims. Stake body. Auxiliary seats (panel/suburban, one or two). Cab corner windows. Foam seat cushions. Tinted glass. Two-speed wipers. Interior convenience group. Clock. Radio antenna. Seat covers. SP Package (Spring) $365. Sierra package (C1500/C2500/C3500). [Jimmy] Super Custom package. Dome light switch.

HISTORICAL: First year for Sprint model.

1972 GMC 1/2-Ton Sprint Sport Coupe-Pickup (GMC)

GMC — LIGHT-DUTY — SIX/V-8: Conventional GMC trucks were unchanged in any significant way from 1971. The grille had a body-color vertical center strip separating two large rectangular openings. Inside the outer end of each opening were twin headlamps mounted horizontally in massive rectangular housings. A thick horizontal bar ran across the center of each grille opening, from the center strip to the headlamps. There were large GMC letters on the nose. Sprints had a new three-tier grille, with two thin chrome horizontal moldings running full-width across the center of each tier. The tiers were separated by thicker, full-width chrome horizontal moldings. There was GMC lettering in the middle of the center tier of the grille. The front parking lamps were larger, one-piece lenses, more or less square, but angled to wrap around the front body corners to do double-duty as side marker lamps. Vans looked much like 1971 except for a change to double-slot style side marker lights.

I.D. DATA: Serial number vehicle identification located on top of instrument panel, left front. Body numbers, trim and paint plate-left upper portion of horizontal surface of shroud under hood (see bottom for sample).* Starting: 50001. Model/engine prefixes: GS/CS/KS/PS (S=six-cylinder); GE/CE/KE/PE (E=eight-cylinder). Engine numbers located [Six]: on pad at right-hand side of cylinder block at rear of distributor. [V-8]: on pad at front, right-hand side of cylinder block, on boss above filler plug. Early in 1972, GMC vehicles had five symbol model codes shown in first column of chart below. During the year, the company switched to an alpha-numerical model code on VIN plates. Examples: Model 53380 VIN would read 5C80D2B500001; Model 53480 VIN would read 5C80F2B500001; Model 53680 VIN would read 5C80H2B500001. Explanation: first symbol 5=GMC; second symbol indicates truck-

line (C=Sprint; D=Custom Sprint); third and fourth symbols indicate body style (80=sedan-pickup); fourth symbol indicates engine (D=250 cid six; F=327 cid four-barrel V-8; H=350 cid two-barrel V-8; J=350 cid four-barrel V-8; U=402 cid four-barrel V-8; W=454 cid four-barrel V-8); fifth symbol indicates model year, 2=1972. Sixth symbol indicates assembly plant: B=Baltimore, Md.; K=Leeds, Mo.; L=Van Nuys, Calif.; last six symbols are sequential production number staring with 500001 for each model at each plant.

4-Wheel-Drive K-Model Picku

1972 GMC 3/4-Ton K2534 Wide-Side Pickup 4x4 (RCA)

Model	Body Type	Price	Weight	Prod. Total
Sprint — 1/2-Ton — 116 in. w.b. — 6-cyl.				
53380	Sedan-Pickup	2790	3302	—
Sprint — 1/2-Ton — 116 in. w.b. — V-8				
53480	Sedan-Pickup	2880	3418	—
Sprint — 1/2-Ton — 116 in. w.b. — V-8				
53680	Custom Sedan-Pickup	2960	3442	—
Sprint — 1/2-Ton — 116 in. w.b.				
Jimmy 4x2 C1550 — 1/2-Ton — 104 in. w.b. — V-8				
CE15514	Open Utility	2720	3440	—
Jimmy 4x4 K1550 — 1/2-Ton — 104 in. w.b. — V-8				
KE15514	Open Utility	3275	3730	—
G1500 Van — 1/2-Ton — 110 in. w.b. — V-8				
GE16005	Vandura	2895	3445	—
GE16006	Rally	3405	3750	—
GE16036	Rally STX	3685	3420	—
G1503 Van — 1/2-Ton — 125 in. w.b. — V-8				
GE16005	Vandura	3039	3610	—
GE16006	Rally	3530	3860	—
GE16036	Rally STX	3805	3925	—
Series G2500 — 3/4-Ton — 110 in. w.b. — V-8				
GE26005	Vandura	3035	3625	—
GE26006	Rally	3335	3675	—
GE26036	STX	3760	4010	—
Series G2530 — 3/4-Ton — 125 in. w.b. — V-8				
GE26305	Vandura	3165	3790	—
GE26306	Rally	3605	4070	—
GE26336	STX	3880	4210	—
Series G3500 — 1-Ton — 110 in. w.b. — V-8				
GE36305	Vandura	3140	3920	—
Series G3530 — 1-Ton — 125 in. w.b. — V-8				
GE36305	Vandura	3275	4090	—
GE36306	Rally	3720	4280	—
GE36336	Rally STX	4000	4505	—
P1500 Value Van — 1/2-Ton — 102 in. w.b. — 6-cyl.				
PS15535	Package Van	3259	3810	—
P2500 Value Van — 3/4-Ton — 125 in./133 in. w.b. — 6-cyl.				
PE25835	Package Van	4113	5280	—
P3500 Value Van — 3/4-Ton — 125 in./133 in. w.b. — 6-cyl.				
PE35835	Package Van	4279	5445	—
C1570 Conventional — 1/2-Ton — 115 in. w.b. — V-8				
CE15703	Chassis & Cab	2660	3280	—
CE15704	Fender-Side Pickup 6.5-ft	2804	3620	—
CE15734	Wide-Side Pickup 6.5-ft	2804	3690	—
C1590 Conventional — 1/2-Ton — 127 in. w.b. — V-8				
CE15904	Fender-Side Pickup 8-ft.	2840	3695	—
CE15934	Wide-Side Pickup 8-ft.	2840	3775	—
CE15916	Suburban	3655	4090	—
C2590 Conventional — 3/4-Ton — 127 in. w.b. — V-8				
CE25903	Chassis & Cab (127 in. w.b.)	2890	3585	—
CE25904	Fender-Side Pickup 8-ft.	3035	3990	—
CE25934	Wide-Side Pickup 8-ft.	3035	4070	—
CE25906	Suburban	3782	4510	—
C2690 Conventional — H-D 3/4-Ton — 133 in. w.b. — V-8				
CE26034	Wide-Side Pickup 8.5-ft.	3096	4125	—
C3500 Conventional — 1-Ton — 133 in. w.b. — V-8				
CE36003	Chassis & Cab	2977	3705	—
CE36004	Fender-Side Pickup 9-ft.	3113	4135	—
C3600 Conventional — H-D 1-Ton — 157 in. w.b. — V-8				
CE36034	Wide-Side Pickup 9.5-ft.	3172	4215	—

NOTE 1: Add average $720 for 4x4 (KS1500/KE1500/KS2500/KE2500 prefix)
NOTE 2: An E in model codes above means prices/specifications given are for trucks with base V-8. Deduct $150 average for six-cylinder models (E in model code becomes S for six). Six-cylinder data for models that came with six only.

1972 GMC 3/4-Ton K2534 Wide-Side Pickup 4x4 (RCA)

ENGINE [Base six: most]: Inline. OHV. Six-cylinder. Cast iron block. Bore & stroke: 3.9 in. x 4.5 in. Displacement: 250 cid. Compression ratio: 8.5:1. Brake hp: 155 at 4200 rpm. Max. Torque: 230 lbs.-ft. at 1600 rpm. Net horsepower: 110 at 4000 rpm. Seven main bearings. Hydraulic valve lifters. Carburetor: Rochester one-barrel.
ENGINE [Suburban base six]: Inline. OHV. Six-cylinder. Cast iron block. Bore & stroke: 3.875 in. x 4.12 in. Displacement: 292 cid. Compression ratio: 8.1:1. Brake hp: 170 at 4000 rpm. Max. Torque: 275 lbs.-ft. at 1600 rpm. Seven main bearings. Hydraulic valve lifters. Carburetor: Rochester one-barrel model M7028012/7028013.
ENGINE [Base V-8: Sprint/CE1500/CE2500/CE3500/PE2500/PE3500]: V-type. OHV. Eight-cylinder. Cast iron block. Bore & stroke: 3.875 in. x 3.25 in. Displacement: 307 cid. Compression ratio: 8.5:1. Brake hp: 200 at 4600 rpm. Max. Torque: 300 lbs.-ft. at 2400 rpm. Net horsepower: 135 at 4000 rpm. Five main bearings. Hydraulic valve lifters. Carburetor: Rochester two-barrel.
ENGINE [Base V-8 GE2500/GE3500/Suburbans/optional others]: V-type. OHV. Eight-cylinder. Cast iron block. Bore & stroke: 4.0 in. x 3.5 in. Displacement: 350 cid. Compression ratio: 8.5:1. Brake hp: 250 at 4600 rpm. Max Torque: 350 lbs.-ft. at 3000 rpm. Net horsepower: 170 at 3600 rpm. Five main bearings. Hydraulic valve lifters. Carburetor: Rochester two-barrel.
ENGINE [Option]: V-type. OHV. Eight-cylinder. Cast iron block. Bore & stroke: 4.125 in. x 3.75 in. Displacement: 402 cid. Compression ratio: 8.5:1. Brake hp: 300 at 4800 rpm. Net horsepower: 240 at 4400 rpm. Five main bearings. Hydraulic valve lifters. Carburetor: Rochester four-barrell.
ENGINE [Sprint option]: V-type. OHV. Eight-cylinder. Cast iron block. Bore & stroke: 4.251 in. x 4.0 in. Displacement: 454 cid. Compression ratio: 8.5:1. Net horsepower: 270 at 4000 rpm. Max. Torque: 390 lbs.-ft. at 3200 rpm. Five main bearings. Hydraulic valve lifters. Carburetor: Rochester four-barrell.
CHASSIS [Sprint]: Wheelbase: 116 in. Overall length: 206.8 in. Height: 54.4 in. Front tread: 60.2 in. Rear tread: 59.2 in. Tires: E78-14B.
CHASSIS [Jimmy]: Wheelbase: 104 in. Overall length: 177.5 in. Height: 68.7 in. Front tread: 60.4 in. Rear tread 60.4 in. Tires: E78-15B.
CHASSIS [Series G1500]: Wheelbase: 110 in. Overall length: 178 in. Height: 80 in. Tires: F78 x 14B in.
CHASSIS [G1503]: Wheelbase: 125 in. Overall length: 202.2 in. Height: 80 in. Tires: F78 x 14B in.
CHASSIS [G2500]: Wheelbase: 110 in. Overall length: 178 in. Height: 80 in. Tires: G78 x 15B in.
CHASSIS [G2503]: Wheelbase: 125 in. Overall length: 202.2 in. Height: 80 in. Tires: G78 x 15B in.
CHASSIS [G3500]: Wheelbase: 110 in. Overall length: 178 in. Height: 80 in. Tires: 8 x 16.5C in.
CHASSIS [G3503]: Wheelbase: 125 in. Overall length: 202.2 in. Height: 80 in. Tires: 8 x 16.5C in.
CHASSIS [P1500]: Wheelbase: 102 in. Height: 75 in. Tires: G78 x 15B in.
CHASSIS [P2500/P3500]: Wheelbase: 125 in. Overall length: 220.75 in. Tires: 8.75 x 16.5C in.
CHASSIS [P2503/P3503]: Wheelbase: 133 in. Overall length: 244.75 in. Tires: 8.75 x 16.5C in.
CHASSIS [C1500]: Wheelbase: 115-127 in. Tires: G78 x 15B in.
CHASSIS [C1503]: Wheelbase: 127 in. Tires: G78 x 15B in.
CHASSIS [C2500]: Wheelbase: 127 in. Tires: 8.75 x 16.5C in.
CHASSIS [C2503]: Wheelbase: 133 in. Tires: 8.75 x 16.5C in.
CHASSIS [C3500]: Wheelbase: 133 in. Overall length: 244.75. Tires: 8.75 x 16C in.
CHASSIS [C3503]: Wheelbase: 157 in. Overall length: 265.75 in. Tires: 8.75 x 16C in.
TECHNICAL: Steering: Saginaw manual. Transmission: 3F/1R fully-synchronized transmission. Column-mounted gear shift lever. Clutch: [250 cid] single plate, dry-disc clutch; [all others] coil spring single dry plate. Rear axle: [1/2-Ton] semi-floating; [3/4-Ton/1-Ton] full floating. Hydraulic, four-wheel brakes. Kelsey-Hayes pressed steel wheels. Turbo Hydra-matic automatic transmission 350 and 400 ($258.25). Wide-ratio Muncie three-speed manual. Four-speed manual has floor-mounted shifter.
OPTIONS: All-weather air conditioner. Roof air conditioner. Front door armrest. Right sunshade. Left sunshade. Junior West Coast mirror (bright or painted). Senior West Coast mirror (bright or painted). Rearview mirror. Remote-control outside rearview mirror. Visor vanity mirror. Non-glare inside mirror. Front cross-view mirror. Body paint stripe. Fixed or swing-arm outside mirrors; right- and left-hand swinging. Heavy-duty cab lifting torsion bar. Assist handles. Forward-Control P10 body; P20/P30 aluminum body; P20-P30 square body. Platform and stake rack. Platform only. Pickup box mounting. Floorboard. Panel/Van side door. Heavy-duty frame, frame reinforcements and special frame equipment. Heavy-duty front axles. Front stabilizer bar. Heavy-duty front/rear springs. Auxiliary rear springs. Rear shock absorbers. Helper springs. Optional rear axle ratios. Positraction rear axle. Vacuum power brake. Front disc brakes. Heavy-duty brake system. Air brakes. Special parking brakes. Brake system moisture ejection system. Special brake equipment. Fan drive. Two-quart oil filter. Engine block heater. Heavy-duty oil filter. Air injection reactor. Controlled combustion system. Positive crankcase ventilation. Cruise control. Fuel filter. Fuel and vacuum booster pump. Manual throttle control. Heavy-duty and oil bath air cleaners. Heavy-duty generators. Oversize gas tanks. Dual exhausts. Tilt steering. Woodgrain steering wheel. Power steering. 22 in. steering wheel. 21 in. steering wheel. Heavy-duty manual steering. Full wheelcovers. Deluxe wheel trim ring. Chrome hubcaps. Wheel trim ring. Spare wheel carrier. Side-mounted spare wheel carrier. Heavy-duty batteries. Parking lamps. Camper electrical system. Roof marker and identification lamps. Air horn. Dual horns. Voltmeter. Speed warning buzzer. Tachometer. Oil pressure gauge. Ammeter. Class A directionals. Double-faced front directional lamps. Manual, push-button and AM/FM

push-button radios. Trailer towing equipment. Heavy-duty radiator. Front bumper. Chrome bumper. Rear painted bumper. Rear step bumper. Front chrome bumper. Heavy-duty cooling system. Deluxe roof rack. PTO equipment. Hazzard flasher system. Side marker lamps. Front tow hook. Engine alarm system. Interior convenience group. Custom interior (includes convenience equipment features). Cab insulation. Custom Cab package. Custom Appearance package. Custom comfort and convenience package. Rally wheel rims. Stake body. Auxiliary seats (Panel/Suburban, one or two). Cab corner windows. Foam seat cushions. Tinted glass. Two-speed wipers. Interior convenience group. Clock. Radio antenna. Seat covers. SP Package (Spring) $365. Sierra package (C1500/C2500/C3500). [Jimmy] Super Custom package. Dome light switch.
HISTORICAL: Calendar year production: 132,243.

1973 GMC

1973 GMC 1/2-Ton Sprint "High Sierra" Pickup (RCA)

GMC — LIGHT-DUTY — SIX/V-8: The Sprint had totally new styling. The full-width grille was topped off with a heavier molding that dropped down the sides of the grille insert and extended horizontally under the headlamps. The insert had a fine mesh of thin vertical and horizontal moldings. There was a small GMC badge in the center and Sprint lettering at the lower left-hand side. Square headlamps were sunk into rectangular housings ahead of squarish "bulges" that flared into the hood/fender lines for a classic look. There were rectangular parking lights in the full-width bumper. There was a High Sierra trim option with woodgrain bodyside and tailgate paneling for the Sprint Custom. The Jimmy had new front end styling in 1973. It was similar to that of conventional cab trucks described below. The 1973 vans seemed externally unchanged from 1973 in any appreciable way. On the dash, the heater control panel retained its rectangular shape, but switched from a vertical to horizontal mounting in the dash. New styling appeared on conventional cab trucks. Single headlamps in square housings were seen. The front had three large square openings with a dark cross-hatched grillework in the background. There was GMC lettering in the center. Large rectangular parking lamps were positioned below the headlamps. Engine call-out plaques were installed in the right-hand grille section. Options included two-tone color schemes or a woodgrained bodyside trim. Value Vans were unchanged. They had single round headlamps, rectangular parking lamps, a grille with two narrow, full-width rectangular openings and GMC letters between the two grille sections. Steel and aluminum bodies came on a variety of wheelbases.
I.D. DATA: Serial number located: [Sprint] left-hand top of dash; [Package Vans] Dash and toe panel; [others] left door hinge pillar. First symbol: T=GMC truck. Second symbol indicated chassis type: C (passenger)=base Sprint; D (passenger)=Sprint Custom; C=Conventional; G=Rally Van; K=4x4 Conventional; P=Forward-Control. Third symbol indicated engine type: [Sprint] H=350 cid/145 hp V-8 two-barrel; L=350 cid/160 hp V-8 four-barrel; R=400 cid V-8/150 hp two-barrel; U=400 cid/180 hp V-8 four-barrel; Y=454 cid/235 hp V-8 four-barrel. [Others] L=454/245 hp V-8 four-barrel; N= 110 cid four-cylinder/75 hp two-barrel; Q=250 cid/100 hp six-cylinder one-barrel; S=292 cid six-cylinder (LPG); T=292 cid/120 hp six-cylinder one-barrel; V=350 cid/145 hp V-8 two-barrel; W=350 cid V-8 (LPG); Y=350 cid/160 hp V-8 four-barrel; Z=454 cid/230 hp V-8 four-barrel. Fourth symbol indicates series/tonnage: 1=1/2-Ton; 2=3/4-Ton; 3=1-Ton. Fifth symbol indicates body type: 2=Chassis & Cowl; 3=Chassis & Cab; 4=Cab & pickup box; 5=Package Van/Panel; 6=Rally Van/Suburban and 8=Jimmy Open Utility. Sixth symbol indicates model year 3=1973. Seventh symbol indicates assembly plant: B=Baltimore, Md.; K=Leeds, Mo.; V=Pontiac, Mich.; Z=Freemont, Calif. Next six symbols are sequential production number starting at 100001 for each model at factory.

Model	Body Type	Price	Weight	Prod. Total
Sprint — 1/2-Ton — 116 in. w.b. — V-8				
5AC80	Sedan-Pickup	2976	3625	—
5AD80	Custom Sedan-Pickup	3038	3635	—
Jimmy 4x2 — 1/2-Ton — 106.5 in. w.b. — V-8				
TC10514	Open Utility	—	—	—
Jimmy 4x4 — 1/2-Ton — 106.5 in. w.b. — V-8				
TK10514	Open Utility	3319	3757	—
G1500 — 1/2-Ton — 110 in. w.b. — V-8				
TG11005	Vandura	2942	3518	—
TG11006	Rally	3455	3822	—
TG11006	Rally STX	3785	3985	—

NOTE 1: Same vans available on 125 in. wheelbase.

G2500 — 3/4-Ton — 110 in. w.b. — V-8

TG21005	Vandura	3079	3658	—
TG21006	Rally	3531	3901	—
TG21006	Rally STX	3831	4064	—

NOTE 2: Same vans available on 125 in. wheelbase.

G3500 — 1-Ton — 110 in. w.b. — V-8

TG31005	Vandura	3188	3962	—
TG31306	Rally	3772	4358	—
TG31306	Rally STX	4102	4478	—

NOTE 3: Same vans available on 125 in. wheelbase.

P1500 Value Van — 1/2-Ton — 102 in. w.b.

TP10542	Van 7-ft.	3453	4040	—

P2500 Value Van — 3/4-Ton — 125-135 in. w.b.

TP20842	Van 10-ft.	4234	5278	—

P3500 Value Van — 1-Ton — 125-157 in. w.b.

TP30842	Van 10-ft.	4402	5548	—

C1500 Conventional — 1/2-Ton — 117-1/2 in. w.b. — V-8

TC10703	Chassis & Cab	2695	3296	—
TC10703	Fender-Side Pickup 6.5-ft	2882	3622	—
TX10703	Wide-Side Pickup 6.5-ft	2882	3741	—

C1503 Conventional — 1/2-Ton — 131-1/2 in. w.b. — V-8

TC10903	Fender-Side Pickup 8 ft.	2918	3718	—
TC10903	Wide-Side Pickup 8-ft.	2918	3843	—

C1506 Conventional — 1/2-Ton — 129-1/2 in. w.b. — V-8

TC10906	Suburban	3710	4136	—

C2503 Conventional — 3/4-Ton — 131-1/2 in. w.b. — V-8

TC20903	Chassis & Cab	2934	3650	—
TC20903	Fender-Side Pickup 8-ft.	3119	4045	—
TC20903	Wide-Side Pickup 8-ft.	3119	4170	—

C2506 Conventional — 3/4-Ton — 129-1/2 in. w.b. — V-8

TC20906	Suburban	4040	4624	—

C2603 Conventional — 3/4-Ton — 164-1/2 in. w.b. — V-8

TC20963	Pickup Crew Cab 8-ft.	4152	4423	—

C3503 Conventional — 1-Ton — 135.1 in. w.b. — V-8

TC30903	Chassis & Cab	3023	3810	—
TC30903	Fender-Side Pickup 8-ft.	3207	4236	—
TC30903	Wide-Side Pickup 8-ft. .	3207	4326	—

C2603 Conventional — 1-Ton — 164-1/2 in. w.b. — V-8

TC30963	Pickup crew cab 8 ft.	4226	4424	—

ENGINE [Standard: All models except Sprint]: Inline. OHV. Six-cylinder. Cast iron block. Bore & stroke: 3-7/8 in. x 3-1/2 in. Displacement: 250 cid. Compression ratio: 8.25:1. Net horsepower: 100 at 3600 rpm. Net Torque: 175 lbs.-ft. at 2000 rpm. Seven main bearings. Hydraulic valve lifters. Carburetor: Rochester one-barrel.

ENGINE [Standard: Sprint, optional: C1500/C2500/C3500]: V-type. OHV. Eight-cylinder. Cast iron block. Bore & stroke: 3-7/8 in. x 3-1/4 in. Displacement: 307 cid. Compression ratio: 8.5:1. Net horsepower: 115 at 3600 rpm. Net Torque: 205 lbs.-ft. at 2000 rpm. Five main bearings. Hydraulic valve lifters. Carburetor: two-barrel.

ENGINE [Optional: C1500/C2500/C3500/P1500/P2500/P3500]: Inline. OHV. Six-cylinder. Cast iron block. Bore & stroke: 3-7/8 in. x 4-1/8 in. Displacement: 292 cid. Compression ratio: 8.0:1. Net horsepower: 120 at 3600 rpm. Net Torque: 225 lbs.-ft. at 2000 rpm. Seven main bearings. Hydraulic valve lifters. Carburetor: one-barrel.

ENGINE [Optional: Sprint/Jimmy/G Series/P Series]: V-type. OHV. Eight-cylinder. Cast iron block. Bore & stroke: 4 in. x 3.48 in. Displacement: 350 cid. Compression ratio: 8.5:1. Net horsepower: 155 at 4000 rpm. Net Torque: 255 lbs.-ft. at 2400 rpm. Five main bearings. Hydraulic valve lifters. Carburetor: two-barrel.

CHASSIS [Sprint]: Wheelbase: 116 in. Overall length: 201.6 in. Height: 53.8 in. Front tread: 58.5 in. Rear tread: 57.8 in. Tires: G78 x 14B in.

CHASSIS [Jimmy]: Wheelbase: 106.5 in. Overall length: 184.5 in. Height: [4x2] 67.5 without top; 69.5 with top; [4x4] 69.5 without top; 71.5 with top. Tires: E78 x 15B in.

CHASSIS [G1500]: Wheelbase: 110-125 in. Overall length: 178 x 202.2 in. Tires: G78 x 14B in.

CHASSIS [G2500]: Wheelbase: 110-125 in. Overall length: 178 x 202.2 in. Tires: G78 x 15B in.

CHASSIS [G3500]: Wheelbase: 110-125 in. Overall length: 178 x 202.2 in. Tires: 8.00 x 16.5C in.

CHASSIS [P1500]: Wheelbase: 102 in. Height: 75 in. Tires: G78 x 15B in.

CHASSIS [P2500]: Wheelbase: 125-135 in. Tires: 8.75 x 16.5C in.

CHASSIS [P3500]: Wheelbase: 125-157 in. Overall length: 220.75 x 265.75 in. Tires: 9.50 x 16.5D in.

CHASSIS [C1500]: Wheelbase: 117.5-131.5 in. Overall length: 191-212 in. Height: 69.8 in. Front tread: 65.8 in. Rear tread: 62.7 in. Tires: G78 x 15B in.

CHASSIS [C2500]: Wheelbase: 131.5-164.5 in. Overall length: 212-244.43 in. Height: 71.8 in. Front tread: 65.8 in. Rear tread: 62.7 in. Tires: 8.75 x 16.5C in.

CHASSIS [C3500]: Wheelbase: 131.5-164.5 in. Overall length: 212-244.43 in. Height: 71.8 in. Front tread: 65.8 in. Rear tread: 62.7 in. Tires: 8.75 x 16.5C in.

TECHNICAL: Manual synchromesh transmission. Speeds: 3F/1R. Column mounted gearshift. Camper package. Dual rear wheels (C-3500). Turbo Hydramatic 350/ 400/475 transmissions optional. Various clutches and rear axle ratios. Four-speed manual transmission. Front stablizier bar (4x2).

OPTIONS: Sprint SP package. Sprint Custom High Sierra package. Sierra package for Jimmy/conventional. Sierra Grande package (conventionals). Below-eye-line mirrors. Drip moldings. Sliding rear window. Cargo lamp. Comfortilt steering wheel. Exterior tool and storage compartment. Whitewall tires. Woodgrain exterior trim. Glide-out spare tire carrier. All-weather air conditioning. Roof air conditioner. Front door armrest. Right sunshade. Left sunshade. Junior West Coast mirror (bright or painted). Senior West Coast mirror (bright or painted). Rearview mirror. Remote-control outside rearview mirror. Visor vanity mirror. Non-glare inside mirror. Front cross-view mirror. Body paint stripe. Fixed or swing-arm outside mirrors; right- and left-hand swinging. Heavy-duty cab lifting torsion bar. Assist handles. Forward-Control P10 body; P20/P30 aluminum body; P20-P30 square body. Platform and stake rack. Platform only. Pickup box mounting. Floorboard. Panel/Van side door. Heavy-duty frame. Frame reinforcements and special frame equipment. Heavy-duty front axles. Front stabilizer bar. Heavy-duty front/rear springs. Auxiliary rear springs. Rear shock

absorbers. Helper springs. Optional rear axle ratios. Positraction rear axle. Vacuum power brake. Front disc brakes. Heavy-duty brake system. Air brakes. Special parking brakes. Brake system moisture ejection system. Special brake equipment. Fan drive. Two-quart oil filter. Engine block heater. Heavy-duty oil filter. Air injection reactor. Controlled -combustion system. Positive crankcase ventilation. Cruise control. Fuel filter. Fuel and vacuum booster pump. Manual throttle control. Heavy-duty and oil bath air cleaners. Heavy-duty generators. Oversize gas tanks. Dual exhausts. Tilt steering. Woodgrain steering wheel. Power steering. 22 in. steering wheel. 21 in. steering wheel. Heavy-duty manual steering. Full wheelcovers. Deluxe wheel trim cover. Chrome hubcaps. Wheel trim ring. Spare wheel carrier. Side-mounted spare wheel carrier. Heavy-duty batteries. Parking lamps. Camper electrical system. Roof marker and identification lamps. Air horn. Dual horns. Voltmeter. Speed warning buzzer. Tachometer. Oil pressure gauge. Ammeter. Class A directionals. Double-faced front directional lamps. Manual, push-button and AM/FM push-button radios. Trailer towing equipment. Heavy-duty radiator. Front bumper. Chrome bumper. Rear painted bumper. Rear step bumper. Front chrome bumper. Heavy-duty cooling system. Deluxe roof rack. PTO equipment. Hazzard flasher system. Side marker lamps. Front tow hook. Engine alarm system. Interior convenience group. Rally wheel rims. Stake body. Auxiliary seat (Suburban). Foam seat cushions. Tinted glass. Two-speed wipers. Interior convenience group. Clock. Radio antenna. Seat covers.

HISTORICAL: Calendar year production: 166,733.

1974 GMC

1974 GMC High Sierra Wide-Side Camper Special Pickup (JAG)

GMC — LIGHT-DUTY — SIX/V-8: The Sprint now had GMC lettering in its center grille section. The wide "Mercedes" style grille with three separate horizontal tiers and a thin, vertical center molding continued. The square headlamps were sunk into rectangular housings ahead of squarish "bulges" that flared into the hood/fender lines for a classic look. There were rectangular parking lights below the main bar. A body-colored panel showed through below the middle of the front bumper. There was still a High Sierra trim option with woodgrain bodyside and tailgate paneling. The Jimmy kept the same new styling as 1973. The 1974 vans were unchanged from 1973 in any appreciable way. Last year's new styling continued. Single headlamps in square housings were seen. The front had three large square openings with a dark cross-hatched grillework in the background. There was GMC lettering in the center. Large rectangular parking lamps were positioned below the headlamps. Engine call-out plaques were installed in the right-hand grille section. Options included two-tone color schemes or a woodgrained bodyside trim. The package delivery vans were unchanged. They had single round headlamps, rectangular parking lamps, grille with two narrow, full-width rectangular openings and GMC letters between the two grille sections. Steel and aluminum bodies came on a variety of wheelbases.

1974 GMC K1500 Jimmy Open Utility With Hardtop 4x4 (RCA)

I.D. DATA: Serial number located: [Sprint] left-hand top of dash; [Package Vans] Dash and toe panel; [others] left door hinge pillar. First symbol T=GMC truck. Second symbol indicated chassis type: C=Conventional; G=Rally Van; K=4x4 Conventional; P=Forward-Control. Third symbol indicated engine type: [Sprint] H=350 cid/145 hp V-8 two-barrel; L=350 cid/160 hp V-8 four-barrel; R=400 cid V-8/150 hp two-barrel;; U=400 cid/180 hp V-8 four-barrel; Y=454 cid/235 hp V-8 four-barrel. [Others] L=454/245 hp V-8 four-barrel; N= 110 cid four-cylinder/75 hp two-barrel; Q=250 cid/100 hp six-cylinder one-barrel; S=292 cid six-cylinder (LPG); T=292 cid/120 hp six-cylinder one-barrel; V=350 cid/145 hp V-8 two-barrel; W=350 cid V-8 (LPG); Y=350 cid/160 hp V-8 four-barrel; Z=454 cid/230 hp V-8 four-barrel. Fourth symbol indicates series/tonnage: 1=1/2-Ton; 2=3/4-Ton; 3=1-Ton. Fifth symbol indicates body type: 2=Chassis & Cowl; 3=Chassis & Cab; 4=Cab & pickup box; 5=Package Van/Panel; 6=Rally Van/Suburban and 8=Jimmy Open Utility. Sixth symbol indicates model year 3=1973. Seventh symbol indicates assembly plant: B=Baltimore, Md.; K=Leeds, Mo.; V=Pontiac, Mich.; Z=Freemont, Calif. Next six symbols are sequential production number starting at 100001 for each model at factory.

Model	Body Type	Price	Weight	Prod. Total
Sprint — 1/2-Ton — 116 in. w.b. — V-8				
5AC80	Sedan-Pickup	3119	3817	—
5AD80	Classic Sedan-Pickup	3277	3832	—
Jimmy 4x2 — 1/2-Ton — 106.5 in. w.b. — V-8				
TC10514	Open Utility	—	—	—
Jimmy 4x4 — 1/2-Ton — 106.5 in. w.b. — V-8				
TK10514	Open Utility	3798	3796	—
G1500 — 1/2-Ton — 110 in. w.b. — V-8				
TG11005	Vandura	3238	3520	—
TG11006	Rally	3455	3867	—
TG11006	Rally STX	4232	4000	—

NOTE 1: Same vans available on 125 in. wheelbase.

Model	Body Type	Price	Weight	Prod. Total
G2500 — 3/4-Ton — 110 in. w.b. — V-8				
TG21005	Vandura	3377	3615	—
TG21006	Rally	3531	3965	—
TG21006	Rally STX	4330	4054	—

NOTE 2: Same vans available on 125 in. wheelbase.

Model	Body Type	Price	Weight	Prod. Total
G3500 — 1-Ton — 110 in. w.b. — V-8				
TG31005	Vandura	3495	3904	—
TG31306	Rally	4200	4364	—
TG31306	Rally STX	4565	4577	—

NOTE 3: Same vans available on 125 in. wheelbase.

Model	Body Type	Price	Weight	Prod. Total
G3503 — 1/Ton — 125 in. w.b. (only) — V-8				
TG31303	Rally Camper Special	4161	3662	—
TG31303	Magna Van 10-ft.	4643	4833	—
P1500 Value Van — 1/2-Ton — 102 in. w.b.				
TP10542	Van 7-ft.	3763	4064	—
P2500 Value Van — 3/4-Ton — 125-135 in. w.b.				
TP20842	Van 10-ft.	4634	5306	—
P3500 Value Van — 1-Ton — 125-157 in. w.b.				
TP30842	Van 10-ft.	4842	5485	—
C1500 Conventional — 1/2-Ton — 117-1/2 in. w.b. — V-8				
TC10703	Chassis & Cab	—	—	—
TC10703	Fender-Side Pickup 6.5-ft	3117	3653	—
TX10703	Wide-Side Pickup 6.5-ft	3117	3757	—
C1503 Conventional — 1/2-Ton — 131-1/2 in. w.b. — V-8				
TC10903	Fender-Side Pickup 8 ft.	3153	3761	—
TC10903	Wide-Side Pickup 8-ft.	3153	3871	—
C1506 Conventional — 1/2-Ton — 129-1/2 in. w.b. — V-8				
TC10906	Suburban	4026	4211	—
C2503 Conventional — 3/4-Ton — 131-1/2 in. w.b. — V-8				
TC20903	Chassis & Cab	3267	3714	—
TC20903	Fender-Side Pickup 8-ft.	3434	4109	—
TC20903	Wide-Side Pickup 8-ft.	3434	4219	—
C2506 Conventional — 3/4-Ton — 129-1/2 in. w.b. — V-8				
TC20906	Suburban	4933	4964	—
C2603 Conventional — 3/4-Ton — 164-1/2 in. w.b. — V-8				
TC20963	Pickup Crew Cab 8-ft.	4544	4458	—
C3503 Conventional — 1-Ton — 135.1 in. w.b. — V-8				
TC30903	Chassis & Cab	3364	3878	—
TC30903	Fender-Side Pickup 8-ft.	3531	4304	—
TC30903	Wide-Side Pickup 8-ft.	3531	4379	—
C2603 Conventional — 1-Ton — 164-1/2 in. w.b. — V-8				
TC30963	Pickup crew cab 8-ft.	4626	5002	—
TC30963	Stake 8-ft.	3677	4506	—
TC30963	Stake 9-ft.	3792	4728	—

NOTE: Add for K Series 4x4.

1974 GMC K1500 1/2-Ton Wide-Side Pickup 4x4 (RCA)

ENGINE [Standard: all Models except Sprint]: Inline. OHV. Six-cylinder. Cast iron block. Bore & stroke: 37/8 in. x 31/2 in. Displacement: 250 cid. Compression ratio: 8.25:1. Net horsepower: 100 at 3600 rpm. Torque: 175 lbs.-ft. at 1800 rpm. Seven main bearings. Hydraulic valve lifters. Carburetor: one-barrel.
ENGINE [Optional: C2500/C3500; Standard: G2500/G3500]: Inline. OHV. Six-cylinder. Cast iron block. Bore & stroke: 37/8 in. x 4.12 in. Displacement: 292 cid. Compression ratio: 8.0. Net horsepower: 120 at 3000 rpm. Torque: 215 lbs. ft. at 2000 rpm. Seven main bearings. Hydraulic valve lifters. Carburetor: one-barrel.
ENGINE [Optional: C1500/G1500; Standard: Sprint]: Inline. OHV. Eight-cylinder. Cast iron block. Bore & stroke: 4 in. x 3.48 in. Displacement: 350 cid. Compression ratio: 8.5. Brake hp: 5. Net horsepower: 145 at 3600 rpm. Torque: T-250 at 2200 rpm. Five main bearings. Hydraulic valve lifters. Carburetor: two-barrel.
ENGINE [Optional: C Series/G Series/Sprint]: Inline. OHV. Eight-cylinder. Cast iron block. Bore & stroke: 4 in. x 3.48 in. Displacement: 350 cid. Compression ratio: 8.5. Brake hp: 5. Net horsepower: 160 at 3800 rpm. Torque: 255 at 2400 rpm. Five main bearings. Hydraulic valve lifters. Carburetor: Rochester four-barrel.
ENGINE [Optional: C Series, Sprint]: Inline. OHV. Eight-cylinder. Cast iron block. Bore & stroke: 41/4 in. x 4 in. Displacement: 454 cid. Compression ratio: 8.5. Brake hp: 5. Net horsepower: 245 at 4000 rpm. Torque: 365 at 2800 rpm. Five main bearings. Hydraulic valve lifters. Carburetor: Rochester Quadra Jet four-barrel.

1974 GMC 1/2-Ton Sprint High Sierra Pickup (DFW/DPLW)

CHASSIS [Sprint]: Wheelbase: 116 in. Overall length: 201.6 in. Height: 53.8 in. Front tread: 58.5 in. Rear tread: 57.8 in. Tires: G78 x 14B in.
CHASSIS [Jimmy]: Wheelbase: 106.5 in. Overall length: 184.5 in. Height: [4x2] 67.5 without top; 69.5 with top; [4x4] 69.5 without top; 71.5 with top. Tires: E78 x 15B in.
CHASSIS [G1500]: Wheelbase: 110-125 in. Overall length: 178-202.2 in. Tires: G78 x 14B in.
CHASSIS [G2500]: Wheelbase: 110-125 in. Overall length: 178-202.2 in. Tires: G78 x 15B in.
CHASSIS [G3500]: Wheelbase: 110-125 in. Overall length: 178-202.2 in. Tires: 8.00 x 16.5C in.
CHASSIS [P1500]: Wheelbase: 102 in. Height: 75 in. Tires: G78 x 15B in.
CHASSIS [P2500]: Wheelbase: 125-135 in. Tires: 8.75 x 16.5C in.
CHASSIS [P3500]: Wheelbase: 125-157 in. Overall length: 220.75 x 265.75 in. Tires: 9.50 x 16.5D in.
CHASSIS [C1500]: Wheelbase: 117.5-131.5 in. Overall length: 191-212 in. Height: 69.8 in. Front tread: 65.8 in. Rear tread: 62.7 in. Tires: G78 x 15B in.
CHASSIS [C2500]: Wheelbase: 131.5-164.5 in. Overall length: 212-244.43 in. Height: 71.8 in. Front tread: 65.8 in. Rear tread: 62.7 in. Tires: 8.75 x 16.5C in.
CHASSIS [C3500]: Wheelbase: 131.5-164.5 in. Overall length: 212-244.43 in. Height: 71.8 in. Front tread: 65.8 in. Rear tread: 62.7 in. Tires: 8.75 x 16.5C in.

1974 GMC 1/2-Ton Sprint Sport Pickup (OCW)

TECHNICAL: Manual synchromesh transmission. Speeds: 3F/1R. Column mounted gearshift. Camper package. Dual rear wheels (C-3500). Turbo Hydramatic 350/ 400/475 transmissions optional. Various clutches and rear axle ratios. Four-speed manual transmission. Front stablizier bar (4x2).

OPTIONS: Sprint SP package. Sprint Custom High Sierra package. Sierra package for Jimmy/conventional. Sierra Grande package (conventionals). Below-eye-line mirrors. Drip moldings. Sliding rear window. Cargo lamp. Comfortilt steering wheel. Exterior tool and storage compartment. Whitewall tires. Woodgrain exterior trim. Glide-out spare tire carrier. All-weather air conditioning. Roof air conditioner. Front door armrest. Right sunshade. Left sunshade. Junior West Coast mirror (bright or painted). Senior West Coast mirror (bright or painted). Rearview mirror. Remote-control outside rearview mirror. Visor vanity mirror. Non-glare inside mirror. Front cross-view mirror. Body paint stripe. Fixed or swing-arm outside mirrors; right- and left-hand swinging. Heavy-duty cab lifting torsion bar. Assist handles. Forward-Control P10 body; P20-P30 aluminum body; P20-P30 square body. Platform and stake rack. Platform only. Pickup box mounting. Floorboard. Panel/Van side door. Heavy-duty frame, frame reinforcements and special frame equipment. Heavy-duty front axles. Front stabilizer bar. Heavy-duty front/rear springs. Auxiliary rear springs. Rear shock absorbers. Helper springs. Optional rear axle ratios. Positraction rear axle. Vacuum power brake. Front disc brakes. Heavy-duty brake system. Air brakes. Special parking brakes. Brake system moisture ejection system. Special brake equipment. Fan drive. Two-quart oil filter. Engine block heater. Heavy-duty oil filter. Air injection reactor. Controlled-combustion system. Positive crankcase ventilation. Cruise control. Fuel filter. Fuel and vacuum booster pump. Manual throttle control. Heavy-duty and oil bath air cleaners. Heavy-duty generators. Oversize gas tanks. Dual exhausts. Tilt steering. Woodgrain steering wheel. Power steering. 22 in. steering wheel. 21 in. steering wheel. Heavy-duty manual steering. Full wheelcovers. Deluxe wheel trim cover. Chrome hubcaps. Wheel trim ring. Spare wheel carrier. Side-mounted spare wheel carrier. Heavy-duty batteries. Parking lamps. Camper electrical system. Roof marker and identification lamps. Air horn. Dual horns. Voltmeter. Speed warning buzzer. Tachometer. Oil pressure gauge. Ammeter. Class A directionals. Double-faced front directional lamps. Manual, push-button and AM/FM push-button radios. Trailer towing equipment. Heavy-duty radiator. Front bumper. Chrome bumper. Rear painted bumper. Rear step bumper. Front chrome bumper. Heavy-duty cooling system. Deluxe roof rack. PTO equipment. Hazzard flasher system. Interior convenience group. Clock. Radio antenna. Seat covers.

HISTORICAL: Calendar year sales: 142,055.

1975 GMC

1975 GMC Sierra Classic Crew Cab Pickup (RPZ)

GMC — LIGHT-DUTY — SIX/V-8: The Sprint had a new grille pattern with bright vertical division bars creating 10 segments with a cross-hatch insert. A small, squarish badge was in the next to last left-hand segment. The square headlamps were still sunk into rectangular housings ahead of squarish "bulges" that flared into the hood and fender lines for the classic look. There were rectangular parking lights below the main bar. A body-colored panel showed through below the middle of the front bumper. The High Sierra trim option added woodgrain bodyside and tailgate paneling. On Jimmys, a revamped grille had two full-width, narrow horizontal slots. Each was divided into three sections. GMC letters were on the horizontal division bar between the two grille slots. The GMC Vandura, Rally and Rally STX vans continued to be popular. There was a new 1-ton Vandura Special model on the stretched 146 in. wheelbase. Conventional trucks continued to share front sheet metal with the Jimmy. This included the new grille with horizontal slots divided into three sections and GMC letters on the horizontal division bar. Single headlamps in square housings were seen. Options included two-tone color schemes or a woodgrained bodyside trim. High Sierra, Sierra Grande and Sierra Classic trim packages. The package delivery vans (Value-Vans) were unchanged. They had single round headlamps, rectangular parking lamps, grille with two narrow, full-width rectangular openings and GMC letters between the two grille sections. Steel and aluminum bodies came on a variety of wheelbases.

I.D. DATA: Serial number located: [Sprint] left-hand top of dash; [Package Vans] dash and toe panel; [others] left door hinge pillar. First symbol T=GMC truck. Second symbol indicated cab chassis type: C (passsenger series)=base Sprint; D=Sprint Classic; C=Conventional; G=Rally Van; K=4x4 Conventional; P=Forward-Control; C. Third symbol indicated engine type: [Sprint] H=350 cid/145 hp V-8 two-barrel; L=350 cid/165 hp V-8 four-barrel; R=400 cid V-8/165 hp two-barrel; U=400 cid/205 hp V-8 four-barrel; W=455 cid/205 hp V-8 four-barrel; [Others] L=454/245 hp V-8 four-barrel; N= 110 cid four-cylinder/75 hp two-barrel; Q=250 cid/100 hp six-cylinder one-barrel; S=292 cid six-cylinder (LPG); T=292 cid/120 hp six-cylinder one-barrel; V=350 cid/145 hp V-8 two-barrel; W=350 cid V-8 (LPG); Y=350 cid/160 hp V-8 four-barrel; Z=454 cid/230 hp V-8 four-barrel. Fourth symbol indicates series/tonnage: 1=1/2-Ton; 2=3/4-Ton; 3=1-Ton. Fifth symbol indicates body type: 2=Chassis & Cowl; 3=Chassis & Cab; 4=Cab & pickup box; 5=Package Van/Panel; 6=Rally Van/Suburban and 8=Jimmy Open Utility. Sixth symbol indicates model year 3=1973. Seventh symbol is plant code: A=Lakewood, Ga.; B=Baltimore, Md.; D=Doraville, Ga.; J=Janesville, Wis.; K=Leeds, Mo.; R=Arlington, Texas; U=Lordstown, Ohio; V=Pontiac, Mich.; Z=Fremont, Calif.; 1=Oshawa, Canada. Next six symbols are sequential production number starting at 100001 for each model at factory.

1975 GMC 1/2-Ton High Sierra Custom Pickup (JAG)

Model	Body Type	Price	Weight	Prod. Total
Sprint — 1/2-Ton — 116 in. w.b. — V-8				
5AC80	Sedan-Pickup	3828	3706	—
5AD80	Classic Sedan-Pickup	3966	3748	—
Jimmy 4x2 — 1/2-Ton — 106.5 in. w.b. — V-8				
TC10514	Open Utility	—	—	—
TC10514	Utility w/Top	—	—	—
Jimmy 4x4 — 1/2-Ton — 106.5 in. w.b. — V-8				
TK10514	Open Utility	4569	4026	—
TC10514	Utility w/Top	4998	4272	—
G1500 — 1/2-Ton — 110 in. w.b. — V-8				
TG11005	Vandura	3443	3584	—
TG11006	Rally	4103	3935	—
TG11006	Rally STX	4506	4098	—
NOTE 1: Same vans available on 125 in. wheelbase.				
G2500 — 3/4-Ton — 110 in. w.b. — V-8				
TG21005	Vandura	3653	3625	—
TG21006	Rally	4275	3910	—
TG21006	Rally STX	4678	4073	—
NOTE 2: Same vans available on 125 in. wheelbase.				
G3500 — 1-Ton — 110 in. w.b. — V-8				
TG31005	Vandura	3743	3917	—
TG31306	Rally	4477	4369	—
TG31306	Rally STX	4880	4583	—
NOTE 3: Same vans available on 125 in. wheelbase.				
G3503 — 1/Ton — 125 in. w.b. (only) — V-8				
TG31303	Vandura Special	4167	—	—
TG31303	Rally Camper Special	4377	—	—
TG31303	Steel Magna Van 10-ft.	4970	4998	—
P1500 Value Van — 1/2-Ton — 102 in. w.b.				
TP10542	Van 7-ft.	4532	4144	—
P2500 Value Van — 3/4-Ton — 125-135 in. w.b.				
TP20842	Van 10-ft.	5242	5382	—
P3500 Value Van — 1-Ton — 125-157 in. w.b.				
TP30842	Van 10-ft.	5499	5588	—
C1500 Conventional — 1/2-Ton — 117-1/2 in. w.b. — V-8				
TC10703	Chassis & Cab	3676	—	—
TC10703	Fender-Side Pickup 6.5-ft	3609	3783	—
TX10703	Wide-Side Pickup 6.5-ft	3609	3796	—
C1503 Conventional — 1/2-Ton — 131-1/2 in. w.b. — V-8				
TC10903	Fender-Side Pickup 8-ft.	3652	3774	—
TC10903	Wide-Side Pickup 8-ft.	3652	3844	—
C1506 Conventional — 1/2-Ton — 129-1/2 in. w.b. — V-8				
TC10906	Suburban	4707	4336	—
C2503 Conventional — 3/4-Ton — 131-1/2 in. w.b. — V-8				
TC20903	Chassis & Cab	3863	3737	—
TC20903	Fender-Side Pickup 8-ft.	4030	4137	—
TC20903	Wide-Side Pickup 8-ft.	4030	4207	—
TC2543 Bonus Cab — 3/4-Ton — 131-1/2 in. w.b.				
TC20943	Bonus Cab Pickup 8-ft.	4613	—	—
TC2563 Conventional — 3/4-Ton — 164.5 in. w.b.				
TC20963	Crew Cab Pickup 8-ft.	5002	4935	—
TC20963	Stake 8-ft.	4246	4365	—
C2506 Conventional — 3/4-Ton — 129-1/2 in. w.b. — V-8				
TC20906	Suburban	5045	4664	—
C2603 Conventional — 3/4-Ton — 164-1/2 in. w.b. — V-8				
TC20963	Pickup Crew Cab 8-ft.	4544	4458	—

C3503 Conventional — 1-Ton — 135.1 in. w.b. — V-8

TC30903	Chassis & Cab	3996	3913	—
TC30903	Fender-Side Pickup 8-ft.	4163	4344	—
TC30903	Wide-Side Pickup 8-ft.	4163	4379	—

C2603 Conventional — 1-Ton — 164-1/2 in. w.b. — V-8

TC30963	Pickup crew cab 8 ft.	5155	4987	—
TC30963	Stake 9-ft.	4498	4761	—

NOTE: Add $1007 for K Series 4x4 models (C prefix changes to K).

1975 GMC Jimmy Open Utility With Hardtop 4x4 (RCA)

1975 GMC Sierra Classic Suburban Carryall (OCW)

ENGINE [Standard: Series C1500/Jimmy/Sprint/G1500]: Inline. gasoline. Six-cylinder. Cast iron block. Bore & stroke: 3-7/8 in. x 3-1/2 in. Displacement: 250 cid. Compression ratio: 8.25:1. Net horsepower: 105 at 3800 rpm. Net Torque: 185 lbs.-ft. at 1200 rpm. Seven main bearings. Hydraulic valve lifters. Carburetor: one-barrel.
ENGINE [Optional: Series C1500/Sprint]: V-type. gasoline. Eight-cylinder. Cast iron block. Bore & stroke: 4 in. x 3-1/2 in. Displacement: 350 cid. Compression ratio: 8.5:1. Net horsepower: 145 at 3800 rpm. Net Torque: 250 lbs.-ft. at 2200 rpm. Five main bearings. Hydraulic valve lifters. Carburetor: two-barrel.
ENGINE [Optional: all models]: V-type. gasoline. Eight-cylinder. Cast iron block. Bore & stroke: 4 in. x 3-1/2 in. Displacement: 350 cid. Net horsepower: 160 at 3800 rpm. Net Torque: 250 lbs.-ft. at 2400 rpm. Five main bearings. Hydraulic valve lifters. Carburetor: four-barrel.

ENGINE [Standard: Series C2500/C3500/P1500/P2500/P3500/G2500/G3500]: Inline. OHV. Six-cylinder. Cast iron block. Bore & stroke: 3-7/8 in. x 4-1/8 in. Displacement: 292 cid. Compression ratio: 8.0:1. Net horsepower: 120 at 3600 rpm. Net Torque: 215 lbs.-ft. at 2000 rpm. Seven main bearings. Hydraulic valve lifters. Carburetor: one-barrel.
ENGINE [Optional: Sprint 4x4/C1500/C2500 Pickup]: V-type. OHV. Eight-cylinder. Cast iron block. Bore & stroke: 4-1/8 in. x 4 in. Displacement: 400 cid. Compression ratio: 8.5:1. Net horsepower: 175 at 3600 rpm. Five main bearings. Hydraulic valve lifters. Carburetor: four-barrel.
ENGINE [Optional: Series C1500/C2500/C3500/Sprint ($340)]: V-type. OHV. Eight-cylinder. Cast iron block. Bore & stroke: 4-1/8 in. x 4 in. Displacement: 454 cid. Compression ratio: 8.25:1. Brake hp: 5. Net horsepower: 245 at 4000 rpm. Net. Torque: 355 lbs.-ft. at 3000 rpm. Five main bearings. Hydraulic valve lifters. Carburetor: Rochester Quadra-Jet four-barrel.

CHASSIS [Sprint]: Wheelbase: 116 in. Length: 201.6 in. Height: 53.8 in. Front tread: 58.5 in. Rear tread: 57.8 in. Tires: GR78 x 15B in.
CHASSIS [Jimmy]: Wheelbase: 106.5 in. Length: 184.5 in. Height: [4x2] 66.75 in. without top, 68.75 in. with top; [4x4] 69 in. without top, 71 in. with top. Front tread: [4x2] 64.5 in.; [4x4] 65.75 in. Rear tread: [4x2] 63 in.; [4x4] 62.75 in. Tires: H78 x 15B in.

CHASSIS [G1500]: Wheelbase: 110in./125 in. Length: 178 in./202.2 in. Height: 78.8 x 81.2 in. Tires: E78 x 15B in.
CHASSIS [P2500]: Wheelbase: 125 in./133 in. Length: 220.75 in./244.75 in. Tires: 8.75 x 16.5C in.
CHASSIS [G2500]: Wheelbase: 110 in./125 in. Length: 178 in./202.2 in. Height: 78.8 x 81. 2 in. Tires: J78 x 15B in.
CHASSIS [G3500]: Wheelbase: 110 in./125 in. Tires: 8.00 x 16.5C in.
CHASSIS [P1500]: Wheelbase: 102 in. Height: 75 in. Tires: L78 x 15B. in.
CHASSIS [P3500]: Wheelbase: 125-151 in. Length: 220.75 x 268.75 in. Tires: 8.75 x 16.5C in.
CHASSIS [C1500]: Wheelbase: 117.5 in./131.5 in. Length: [Wide-Side] 191-1/4 in. x 211-1/4 in. [Fender-Side] 1901/4 in. x 2101/4 in. Tires: G78 x 15B in.
CHASSIS [C2500]: Wheelbase: 131.5 in./164.5 in. Length: [Wide-Side] 191-1/4 in./211-1/4 in./244-1/4 in. [Fender-Side] 210-1/4 in./244-1/4 in. Tires: 8.75 x 16.5C in.
CHASSIS [C3500]: Wheelbase: 131.5 in./164.5 in. Length: [Wide-Side] 211-1/4 in./244-1/4 in. [Fender-Side] 210-1/4 in./244-1/4 in. Tires: 8.75 x 16.5C in.

1975 GMC Sprint Pickup With Sport Trim (DFW)

TECHNICAL: Manual, all-synchromesh transmission. Speeds: 3F/1R. Column-mounted gearshift lever. Clutch: [C1500] 11 in. dia. (six/V-8); [C2500/C3500]: 11 in. diameter (six); 12 in. dia. (V-8). Sixes use single disc with either diaphragm or coil springs; V-8s have single disc with coil spring pressure plate. Rear axle: [1/2-ton] semi-floating; [3/4-ton/1-ton] full-floating. Overall ratio: [C1500]: 3.73 (six), 3.40 (V-8). [C2500]: 4.56 (six); 3.73 (V-8); 4.10 (Crew Cab). [C3500] 4.10:1. Pressed steel brakes: [1500] 7/16 in., 1/2 in. bolts; [2500/3500] 9/16 in. bolts.

TECHNICAL OPTIONS: Turbo-Hydramatic automatic transmission. Camper Package. Dual rear wheels (C3500). Four-speed manual transmission. Heavy-duty radiator. Heavy-duty generator. Heavy-duty battery.

OPTIONS: Chromed front bumper. Chromed rear bumper. Radio AM, AM/FM, windshield embedded antenna. Clock. Cigar Lighter. SP Package (Sprint) ($215). High Sierra Package (Sprint Classic) ($113). High Sierra Package (Jimmy/Series C). Sierra Classic Package (truck series C). Sierra Grande Package (truck series C). Gauge Package. Tachometer. Drip moldings. Exterior tool and storage compartment. Air conditioning. White sidewall tires (C1500 only). Below-Eyeline mirrors. Comfortilt steering wheel. Rear step bumper. Chrome front bumper with rubber impact strips. Woodgrain exterior trim (Wide-Side only). Sliding rear window. Cargo area lamp. Box-mounted spare tire. Glide-out spare tire carrier. Much more.

HISTORICAL: Calendar year sales: 140,423.

1975 GMC K2500 3/4-Ton Wide-Side High Sierra Pickup (RCA)

1976 GMC

1976 GMC K1500 Wide-Side High Sierra Pickup 4x4 (RCA)

GMC — LIGHT-DUTY — SIX/V-8: The Sprint had a new full-width grille with a fine mesh-patterned insert and a small nameplate at the center. The headlamps were changed to two squares stacked on top of each segment. The square headlamps were still sunk into rect-angular housings ahead. It came in base and Classic lines, with SP (Sport) and Sierra Madre Del Sur trim options. The "bulges" sculpted into the hood/fender lines looked great with the new grille. There were rectangular parking lights in the bumper. On Jimmys, there were no major styling changes. The grille again had two horizontal slots. Each was divided into three sections. GMC letters were on the horizontal division bar between the two grille slots. Reference sources began listing the 4x4 as an open utility with top, rather than just an open utility. A High-Sierra option was offered. The GMC Vandura, Rally and Rally STX van line remained the same. No new models were listed. Conventional trucks continued to share front sheet metal with the Jimmy. This included the '75 carryover style grille with hor-izontal slots divided into three sections and GMC letters on the horizontal division bar. Sin-gle headlamps in square housings were seen again. There were rectangular parking lamps, horizontally mounted, directly below them. High Sierra, Sierra Grande and Sierra Classic trim packages were available. New Bonus Cab 1-Ton models were added to the line. Value-Vans were unchanged. These package deliveries had single round headlamps, rectangular parking lamps, a grille with two narrow, full-width rectangular openings and GMC letters between the two grille sections. Steel and aluminum bodies by various inde-pendent contractors came on a variety of wheelbases.

1976 GMC Sprint Pickup (DFW)

I.D. DATA: Serial number a combination VIN and rating plate is located on the left door lock pillar. First symbol T=GMC. Second symbol indicates cab chassis type: C (passen-ger)=base Sprint; D (passenger)=Sprint Classic; C (light truck)=conventional cab; G=Vandura and Rally vans; K=conventional 4x4; P=Value-Van. The third symbol indicates engine: [Sprint] D=250 cid/105 hp L-6; Q=305 cid/170 hp four-barrel V-8; H=350 cid/145 hp two-barrel V-8; J=350 cid/165 hp four-barrel V-8; M=350 cid/155 hp two-barrel V-8; N=400 cid/170 hp two-barrel V-8; U=400 cid/175 hp four-barrel V-8. [Vans/Conventionals] D=250 cid/105 hp L6; T=292 cid/120 hp one-barrel L6; Q=305 cid/130 hp two-barrel V-8; V=350 cid/145 hp two-barrel V-8; L=350 cid/160 hp four-barrel V-8; U=400 cid/175 hp four-barrel V-8; S=454 cid/240 hp four-barrel V-8 (conventionals only); Y2=454 cid/245 hp four-barrel V-8 (Value-Vans). Fourth symbol indicates series: 1=1/2-ton; 2=3/4-ton; 3=1-ton. Fifth sym-bol indicates body type: 2=chassis & cowl; 3=chassis & cab; 4=cab & pickup box; 5=Vandura; 6=Rally Van/Rally Wagon/Suburban; 8=Jimmy. Sixth symbol 6=1976. Seventh symbol is plant code: A=Lakewood, Ga.; B=Baltimore, Md.; D=Doraville, Ga.; J=Janesville, Wis.; K=Leeds, Mo.; R=Arlington, Texas; U=Lordstown, Ohio; V=Pontiac, Mich.; Z=Fre-mont, Calif.; 1=Oshawa, Canada. The last six numbers are the sequential production code starting at 100001 for each factory.

1976 GMC Sierra Classic 25 Indy 500 Pickup (IMSC/JLM)

Model	Body Type	Price	Weight	Prod. Total
Sprint — 1/2-Ton — 116 in. w.b. — V-8				
5AC80	Sedan-Pickup	4333	3916	—
5AD80	Classic Sedan-Pickup	4468	3821	—
Jimmy 4x2 — 1/2-Ton — 106.5 in. w.b. — V-8				
TC10514	Utility w/Top	—	—	—
Jimmy 4x4 — 1/2-Ton — 106.5 in. w.b. — V-8				
TC10514	Utility w/Top	5364	4496	—
G1500 — 1/2-Ton — 110 in. w.b. — V-8				
TG11005	Vandura	3811	3703	—
TG11006	Rally	4509	4027	—
TG11006	Rally STX	5102	4403	—
NOTE 1: Same vans available on 125 in. wheelbase.				
G2500 — 3/4-Ton — 110 in. w.b. — V-8				
TG21005	Vandura	4022	3730	—
TG21006	Rally	4682	4013	—
TG21006	Rally STX	5220	4369	—
NOTE 2: Same vans available on 125 in. wheelbase.				
G3500 — 1-Ton — 110 in. w.b. — V-8				
TG31005	Vandura	4143	3971	—
TG31306	Rally	4915	4431	—
TG31306	Rally STX	5318	4618	—
NOTE 3: Same vans available on 125 in. wheelbase.				
G3503 — 1/Ton — 125 in. w.b. (only) — V-8				
TG31303	Vandura Special	4533	3698	—
TG31303	Rally Camper Special	4731	3767	—
TG31303	Steel Magna Van 10-ft.	5405	5100	—
P1500 Value Van — 1/2-Ton — 102 in. w.b.				
TP10542	Van 7-ft.	4855	4311	—
P2500 Value Van — 3/4-Ton — 125-135 in. w.b.				
TP20842	Van 10-ft.	5563	5465	—
P3500 Value Van — 1-Ton — 125-157 in. w.b.				
TP30842	Van 10-ft.	5864	5671	—
C1500 Conventional — 1/2-Ton — 117-1/2 in. w.b. — V-8				
TC10703	Chassis & Cab	3957	3532	—
TC10703	Fender-Side Pickup 6.5-ft	3863	3863	—
TX10703	Wide-Side Pickup 6.5-ft	3863	3931	—
C1503 Conventional — 1/2-Ton — 131-1/2 in. w.b. — V-8				
TC10903	Fender-Side Pickup 8 ft.	3908	3987	—
TC10903	Wide-Side Pickup 8-ft.	3908	4063	—
C1506 Conventional — 1/2-Ton — 129-1/2 in. w.b. — V-8				
TC10906	Suburban	5087	4469	—
C2503 Conventional — 3/4-Ton — 131-1/2 in. w.b. — V-8				
TC20903	Chassis & Cab	4139	3840	—
TC20903	Fender-Side Pickup 8-ft.	4306	4238	—
TC20903	Wide-Side Pickup 8-ft.	4306	4314	—
TC2543 Bonus Cab — 3/4-Ton — 131-1/2 in. w.b.				
TC20943	Bonus Cab Pickup 8-ft.	4953	4786	—
TC2563 Conventional — 3/4-Ton — 164.5 in. w.b.				
TC20963	Crew Cab Pickup 8-ft.	5327	5029	—
TC20963	Stake 8-ft.	4734	4468	—
C2506 Conventional — 3/4-Ton — 129-1/2 in. w.b. — V-8				
TC20906	Suburban	5375	4851	—
C2663 Conventional — 3/4-Ton — 164-1/2 in. w.b. — V-8				
TC20963	Pickup Crew Cab 8-ft.	5327	5029	—
C3503 Conventional — 1-Ton — 135.1 in. w.b. — V-8				
TC30903	Chassis & Cab	4279	3997	—
TC30903	Fender-Side Pickup 8-ft.	4446	4426	—
TC30903	Wide-Side Pickup 8-ft.	4446	4467	—
C2603 Conventional — 1-Ton — 164-1/2 in. w.b. — V-8				
TC30963	Pickup crew cab 8-ft.	5487	5081	—
TC30963	Stake 9-ft.	4939	4845	—

1976 GMC Wide-Side Pickup (JAG)

ENGINE [Standard: C1500/Sprint/Blazer/Vans]: Inline. OHV. Six-cylinder. Cast iron block. Bore & stroke: 3-7/8 in. x 3-1/2 in. Displacement: 250 cid. Compression ratio: 8.25:1. Net horsepower: 100 at 3600 rpm. Net Torque: 175 lbs.-ft. at 1800 rpm. Seven main bearings. Hydraulic valve lifters. Carburetor: one-barrel.

ENGINE [Standard: C2500/C3500/Value-Van]: Inline. OHV. Six-cylinder. Cast iron block. Bore & stroke: 3-7/8 in. x 4-1/8 in. Displacement: 292 cid. Compression ratio: 8.0:1. Net horsepower: 120 at 3600 rpm. Net Torque: 275 lbs.-ft. at 2000 rpm. Seven main bearings. Hydraulic valve lifters. Carburetor: one-barrel.

ENGINE [Optional: all]: V-type. OHV. Eight-cylinder. Cast iron block. Bore & stroke: 4 in. x 2/2 in. Displacement: 350 cid. Compression ratio: 8.5:1. Net horsepower: 165 at 3800 rpm. Net Torque: 255 lbs.-ft. at 2800 rpm. Five main bearings. Hydraulic valve lifters. Carburetor: four-barrel Mod-Quad.

ENGINE [Optional: C1500]: V-type. OHV. Eight-cylinder. Cast iron block. Bore & stroke: 4 in. x 2/2 in. Displacement: 350 cid. Compression ratio: 8.5:1. Net horsepower: 145 at 3800 rpm. Net Torque: 250 lbs.-ft. at 2200 rpm. Five main bearings. Hydraulic valve lifters. Carburetor: two-barrel.

ENGINE [Optional: K1500/K2500/Vans/Sprint]: V-type. OHV. Eight-cylinder. Cast iron block. Bore & stroke: 4-1/8 in. x 4 in. Displacement: 400 cid. Compression ratio: 8.5:1. Net horsepower: 175 at 3600 rpm. Net Torque: 290 lbs.-ft. at 2800 rpm. Five main bearings. Hydraulic valve lifters. Carburetor: four-barrel, Mod-Quad. ($148)

ENGINE [Optional: C1500/C2500/C3500]: V-type. OHV. Eight-cylinder. Cast iron block. Bore & stroke: 41/4 in. x 4 in. Displacement: 454 cid. Compression ratio: 8.25:1. Net horsepower: 240 at 3800 rpm. Max. Torque: 370 lbs.-ft. at 2800 rpm. Five main bearings. Hydraulic valve lifters. Carburetor: Rochester Mod Quad four-barrel.

CHASSIS [Sprint]: Wheelbase: 116 in. Length: 201.6 in. Height: 53.8 in. Front tread: 58.5 in. Rear tread: 57.8 in. Tires: GR78 x 15B in.

CHASSIS [Jimmy]: Wheelbase: 106.5 in. Length: 184.5 in. Height: [4x2] 66.75 in. without top; 68.75 in. with top. [4x4] 69 in. without top; 71 in. with top. Front tread: [4x2] 64.5 in.; [4x4] 65.75 in. Rear tread: [4x2] 63 in.; [4x4] 62.75. Tires: H78 x 15B in.

CHASSIS [G1500]: Wheelbase: 110 in./125 in. Length: 178 in./202.2 in. Height: 78.8 in./81. 2 in. Tires: E78 x 15B in.

CHASSIS [G2500]: Wheelbase: 110 in./125 in. Length: 178 in./202.2 in. Height: 78.8 in./81. 2 in. Tires: J78 x 15B in.

CHASSIS [G3500]: Wheelbase: 110 in./146 in. Tires: 8.00 x 16.5C in.

CHASSIS [P1500]: Wheelbase: 102 in. Height: 75 in. Tires: L78 x 15B. in.

CHASSIS [P2500]: Wheelbase: 125 in./133 in. Length: 220.75 in./244.75 in. Tires: 8.75 x 16.5C in.

CHASSIS [P3500]: Wheelbase: 125 in./157 in. Length: 220.75 in./268.75 in. Tires: 8.75 x 16.5C in.

CHASSIS [C1500]: Wheelbase: 117.5 in./131.5 in. Length: [Wide-Side] 191-1/4 in./211-1/4 in. [Fender-Side] 190-1/4 in./210-1/4 in. Height: 69.8 in. Front tread: 65.8 in. Rear tread: 62.7 in. Tires: G78 x 15B in.

CHASSIS [C2500]: Wheelbase: 131.5-164.5 in. Length: [Wide-Side] 211-1/4 in./244-1/4 in. [Fender-Side] 210-1/4 in./244-1/4 in. Height: 69.8 in. Front tread: 65.8 in. Rear tread: 62.7 in. Tires: 8.75 x 16.5C in.

CHASSIS [C3500]: Wheelbase: 131.5 in./164.5 in. Length: [Wide-Side] 211-1/4 in./244-1/4 in. [Fender-Side] 210-1/4 in./244-1/4 in. Height: 71.8 in. Front tread: 65.8 in. Rear tread: 62.7 in. Tires: 8.75 x 16.5C in.

1976 GMC K1500 High Sierra Suburban 4x4 (RCA)

TECHNICAL: Manual, synchromesh transmission. Speeds: [1500/2500 (except 2500 Crew Cab)] 3F/1R; [all 3500/2500 Crew Cab] Four-speed manual with floor-mounted shifter. Column mounted gearshift lever. Clutch: [262 cid six/two-barrel V-8s] 11 in. diameter; [four-bar-

rel V-8s] 12 in. diameter. Rear axle: [1500] Salisbury semi-floating; [2500/3500] full-floating. Hydraulic four-wheel brakes: [front] disc; [rear] air-cooled finned cast iron drums. Steel disc wheels.

TECHNICAL OPTIONS: Turbo-Hydramatic transmission. Heavy-duty suspension. Heavy-duty three-speed manual transmission. Four-speed manual transmission. Dual rear wheels (C3500 Wide-Side, Bonus and Crew Cab models). Camper Package. Heavy-duty chassis (C1500). Front stabilizer bar. Delco freedom battery. Locking differential.

OPTIONS: Radio AM. AM/FM radio. AM/FM/8-track tape radio. Clock. Bucket seats [two-door models only]. Sierra Classic Package (YE9/two-door models only). Sierra Grande Package, two-door only ($262). [RPO Z84] High Sierra package, (not available for Crew Cab/Bonus Cab). Gauge package. Tachometer. Headlamp warning system. Air conditioning. Full wheelcovers (15, 16 and 16.5 in. wheels). Comfortilt steering wheel. Full-width rear step bumper. Swing-out camper mirrors (painted or stainless steel). Rally wheel. Sliding rear window. Swing-out spare tire carrier. [Sprint] SP Package ($226). Sierra Madre Del Sur package ($128). Two-tone paint. Special two-tone with secondary. Neutral or contrasting color. Deluxe two-tone contrasting or complementary secondary color on roof and sides. Special and deluxe two-tones have upper and lowerside moldings.

HISTORICAL: Calendar year production: 223,805.

1977 GMC

1977 GMC Sierra Classic Wide-Side Pickup (OCW)

GMC — LIGHT-DUTY — SIX: Since it was the last year of this style Sprint, it made sense that the sedan-pickup had no changes to speak of. Base and Classic trim lines were seen again. Truck spotters identified the newest GMC light-duty models by the shape of their new ice-cube tray grille. It could make 10 giant ice-cubes in the segments formed by four vertical dividers and a broad horizontal bar with GMC lettering in the center. High Sierra, Sierra Grande and Sierra Classic options were marketed. Jimmys had the same new grille. They came with High Sierra trim as an options. The Vandura/Rally vans adopted the ice-cube tray grille look. New Gypsy Van and Gaucho Van packages appeared. Value-Van package delivery trucks saw little change again.

1977 GMC Jimmy With Casa Grande Camper Option (RCA)

I.D. DATA: Serial number a combination VIN and rating plate is located on the left door lock pillar. First symbol T=GMC. Second symbol indicates cab chassis type: C (passenger)=base Sprint; D (passenger)=Sprint Classic; C (light truck)=conventional cab; G=Vandura and Rally vans; K=conventional 4x4; P=Value-Van. The third symbol indicates engine: [Sprint] D=250 cid/100 hp L-6; H=350 cid/145 hp two-barrel V-8; J=350 cid/165 hp four-barrel V-8; M=350 cid/155 hp two-barrel V-8; N=400 cid/170 hp two-barrel V-8; U=400 cid/175 hp four-barrel V-8. [Vans/Conventionals] P/Q=250 cid/100 hp L6; R/T=292 cid/130 hp one-barrel L6; V=350 cid/145 hp two-barrel V-8; Y=350 cid/160 hp four-barrel V-8 L=350 cid/160 hp four-barrel V-8; U=350 cid/170 hp four-barrel V-8; Z=454 cid/230 hp four-barrel V-8

(conventionals only); L=454 cid/245 hp four-barrel V-8 (Value-Vans). Fourth symbol indicates series: 1=1/2-ton; 2=3/4-ton; 3=1-ton. Fifth symbol indicates body type: 2=chassis & cowl; 3=chassis & cab; 4=cab & pickup box; 5=Vandura; 6=Rally Van/Rally Wagon/Suburban; 8=Jimmy. Sixth symbol 7=1977. Seventh symbol is plant code: A=Lakewood, Ga.; B=Baltimore, Md.; D=Doraville, Ga.; J=Janesville, Wis.; K=Leeds, Mo.; R=Arlington, Texas; U=Lordstown, Ohio; V=Pontiac, Mich.; Z=Fremont, Calif.; 1=Oshawa, Canada. Symbols 8-13 are sequential production number.

Model	Body Type	Price	Weight	Prod. Total
Sprint — 1/2-Ton — 116 in. w.b. — V-8				
5AC80	Sedan-Pickup	4268	3791	—
5AD80	Classic Sedan-Pickup	4403	3821	—
Jimmy 4x2 — 1/2-Ton — 106.5 in. w.b. — V-8				
TC10514	Utility with Top	—	—	—
Jimmy 4x4 — 1/2-Ton — 106.5 in. w.b. — V-8				
TK10514	Utility with Top	5603	3914	—
TK10514	Open Utility	5503	3864	—
G1500 — 1/2-Ton — 110 in. w.b. — V-8				
TG11005	Vandura	4112	3586	—
TG11006	Rally	4885	3913	—
TG11006	Rally STX	5634	4314	—
NOTE 1: Same vans available on 125 in. wheelbase.				
G2500 — 3/4-Ton — 110 in. w.b. — V-8				
TG21005	Vandura	4375	3607	3730
TG21006	Rally	5110	3890	—
TG21006	Rally STX	5773	4267	—
NOTE 2: Same vans available on 125 in. wheelbase.				
G3500 — 1-Ton — 110 in. w.b. — V-8				
TG31005	Vandura	4496	3840	—
TG31306	Rally	5368	4300	—
TG31306	Rally STX	5871	4508	—
NOTE 3: Same vans available on 125 in. wheelbase.				
G3503 — 1/Ton — 125 in. w.b. (only) — V-8				
TG31303	Vandura Special	4950	3557	—
TG31303	Rally Camper Special	4499	3629	—
TG31303	Steel Magna Van 10-ft.	6275	4961	—
P1500 Value Van — 1/2-Ton — 102 in. w.b.				
TP10542	Van 7-ft.	5391	4176	—
P2500 Value Van — 3/4-Ton — 125 in./133 in. w.b.				
TP20842	Van 10-ft.	6287	5273	—
P3500 Value Van — 1-Ton — 125 in./157 in. w.b.				
TP30842	Van 10-ft.	6603	5493	—
C1500 Conventional — 1/2-Ton — 117-1/2 in. w.b. — V-8				
TC10703	Chassis & Cab	4206	3383	—
TC10703	Fender-Side Pickup 6.5-ft	4122	3585	—
TX10703	Wide-Side Pickup 6.5-ft	4122	3645	—
C1503 Conventional — 1/2-Ton — 131-1/2 in. w.b. — V-8				
TC10903	Fender-Side Pickup 8-ft.	4172	3700	—
TC10903	Wide-Side Pickup 8-ft.	4172	3791	—
C1506 Conventional — 1/2-Ton — 129-1/2 in. w.b. — V-8				
TC10906	Suburban	5279	4315	—

1977 GMC Sierra Classic Wide-Side Pickup (JAG)

C2503 Conventional — 3/4-Ton — 131-1/2 in. w.b. — V-8				
TC20903	Chassis & Cab	4399	3662	—
TC20903	Fender-Side Pickup 8-ft.	4624	4015	—
TC20903	Wide-Side Pickup 8-ft.	4624	4015	—
TC20943	Bonus Cab Pickup 8-ft.	5271	4644	—
TC2563 Conventional — 3/4-Ton — 164.5 in. w.b.				
TC20943	Bonus Cab Pickup 8-ft.	5271	4644	—
TC20943	Crew Cab Pickup 8-ft.	5645	5029	—
TC20943	Platform Stake 8-ft.	5039	4296	—
C2506 Conventional — 3/4-Ton — 129-1/2 in. w.b. — V-8				
TC20906	Suburban	5725	4649	—
C2663 Conventional — 3/4-Ton — 164-1/2 in. w.b. — V-8				
TC20963	Crew Cab Pickup 8-ft.	5327	5029	—

C3503 Conventional — 1-Ton — 135.1 in. w.b. — V-8				
TC30903	Chassis & Cab	4539	3803	—
TC30903	Fender-Side Pickup 8-ft.	4764	4238	—
TC30903	Wide-Side Pickup 8-ft.	4764	4283	—
C2643 Conventional — 1-Ton — 135.1 in. w.b. — V-8				
TC30943	Pickup Bonus Cab 8-ft.	5695	5081	—
TC30943	Crew Cab Pickup 8-ft.	5580	5029	—
TC30943	Platform Stake 9-ft.	5223	4650	—

NOTE 4: 4x4 models have TK prefix. Add $1,248 to factory price.

1977 GMC Jimmy 1/2-Ton Open Utility With Hardtop (RCA)

ENGINE [Standard C2500/C3500]: Inline. OHV. Six-cylinder. Cast iron block. Bore & stroke: 3.87 x 4.12 in. Displacement: 292 cid. Compression ratio: 8.0:1. Net horsepower: 120 at 3600 rpm. Net torque: 215 lbs.-ft. at 2000 rpm. Seven main bearings. Hydraulic valve lifters. Carburetor: one-barrel.

ENGINE [Standard C1500/C1500/F44]: Inline. OHV. Six-cylinder. Cast iron block. Bore & stroke: 3.87 x 3.53 in. Displacement: 250 cid. Compression ratio: 8.23:1. Net horsepower: 110 at 3800 rpm. Net torque: 195 lbs.-ft. at 1600 rpm. Seven main bearings. Hydraulic valve lifters. Carburetor: one-barrel.

ENGINE [Optional: C1500/C1500/C2500/C3500]: V-type. OHV. Eight-cylinder. Cast iron block. Bore & stroke: 4.00 x 3.48 in. Displacement: 350 cid. Compression ratio: 8.5:1. Net horsepower: 165 at 3800 rpm. Net torque: 260 lbs.-ft. at 2400 rpm. (255 at 2800 rpm. for 6001 GVW lbs. and above). Five main bearings. Hydraulic valve lifters. Carburetor: four-barrel.

1977 GMC 1/2-Ton Sprint Pickup (DFW)

1977 GMC Sierra Classic 25 Indy Hauler (IMSC/JLM)

ENGINE [Optional: C1500/C1500/F44/C2500/C3500]: V-type. OHV. Eight-cylinder. Cast iron block. Bore & stroke: 4.25 x 4.00. Displacement: 454 cid. Compression ratio: 8.25:1. Net horsepower: 245 at 3800 rpm. Net torque: 365 lbs.-ft. at 2800 rpm. Five main bearings. Hydraulic valve lifters. Carburetor: four-barrel. 6,001 lbs. and above GVW ratings: Brake hp: 240 at 2800 rpm. California ratings: Brake hp: 250 at 3800 rpm. Net torque: 385 lbs.-ft. at 2800 rpm.

ENGINE [4x4 (TK) trucks with 6,001 lbs. and above GVW only]: V-type. OHV. Eight-cylinder. Cast iron block. Bore & stroke: 4.13 x 3.75 in. Displacement: 400 cid. Compression ratio: 8.5:1. Net horsepower: 175 at 3600 rpm. Net torque: 290 lbs.-ft. at 2800 rpm. Five main bearings. Hydraulic valve lifters. Carburetor: four-barrel.

455

1977 GMC K3500 Crew Cab Wide-Side Pickup 4x4 (RCA)

CHASSIS [Sprint]: Wheelbase: 116 in. Overall length: 213.3 in. Overall height: 53.8 in. Front/Rear tread: 58.5/57.8 in. Tires: GR78 x 15B.

CHASSIS [Jimmy]: Wheelbase: 106.5 in. Overall length: 184.4 in. Overall height: 69.8 in. Front/Rear tread: 66.7/63.7 in. Tires H78 x 15B.

CHASSIS [G1500]: Wheelbase: 110/125 in. Overall length: 178 in./202.2 in. Overall height: 78.8 in./81.2 in. Tires: E or F78 x 15B.

CHASSIS [G2500]: Wheelbase: 110 in./125 in. Overall length: 178 in./202.2 in. Overall height: 78.8 x 81.2 in. Tires: J78 x 15B.

CHASSIS [G3500]: Wheelbase: 110 in./146 in. Tires: [Vandura/Rally] 8.00 x 16.5C; [Camper Special/Magna] 8.75 x 16.5D.

CHASSIS [P1500]: Wheelbase: 102 in. Overall length: 175 in. Tires: L78 x 15B.

CHASSIS [P2500]: Wheelbase: 125 in./133 in. Overall length: 220.75 in./244.75 in. Tires: 8.75 x 16.5C.

CHASSIS [P3500]: Wheelbase: 125 in./157 in. Overall length: 220.75/268.75 in. Tires: 8.75 x 16.5C.

CHASSIS [C1500]: Wheelbase: 117.5/12.5 in. Overall length: 191.3 in./212 in. Overall height: 69.8 in. Front/Rear tread: 65.8 in./62.7 in. Tires: G78 x 15B.

CHASSIS [C2500]: Wheelbase: 117.5 in./131.5 in./164.5 in. Overall length: 191.3 in./212 in./244.43 in. Overall height: 69.8 in. Front/Rear tread: 65.8 in./62.7 in. Tires: [Standard] 8.75 x 16.5C; [Bonus Cab] 8.75 x 16.5C (front); 8.75 x 16.5D (rear)/[Crew Cab] 9.50 x 16.5C (front); 9.50 x 16.5D (rear).

CHASSIS [C3500]: Wheelbase: 131.5 in./164.5 in. Overall length: 212 in./244.43 in. Overall height: 71.8 in. Front/Rear tread: 65.8 in./62.7 in. Tires: [Standard] 8.75 x 16.5C; [Bonus/Crew Cab] 9.50 x 16.5E.

1977 GMC K1500 Sierra Classic Fender-Side Pickup 4x4 (RCA)

TECHNICAL: Manual, synchromesh transmission. Speeds: [1500/2500 (except 2500 Crew Cab)] 3F/1R; [all 3500/2500 Crew Cab] Four-speed manual with floor-mounted shifter. Column mounted gearshift lever. Clutch: [262 cid six/two-barrel V-8s] 11 in. diameter; [four-barrel V-8s] 12 in. diameter. Rear axle: [1500] Salisbury semi-floating; [2500/3500] full-floating. Hydraulic four-wheel brakes: [front] disc; [rear] air-cooled finned cast iron drums. Steel disc wheels.

TECHNICAL OPTIONS: Turbo-Hydramatic transmission. Heavy-duty suspension. Heavy-duty three-speed manual transmission. Four-speed manual transmission. Dual rear wheels (C3500 Wide-Side, Bonus and Crew Cab models). Camper Package. Heavy-duty chassis (C1500). Front stablizier bar. Delco freedom battery. Locking differential. Larger size tires (tube and tubeless). Power steering. Power brakes (C1500). Engine oil cooler. 61 amp. generator. Heavy-duty shocks. Heavy-duty springs. Heavy-duty battery. Trailering package. Camper package. Dual rear wheels (C3500).

OPTIONS: Chrome front bumper. Chrome rear bumper. AM, AM/FM, AM/FM 8-track CB radio. Electric clock. Floor mats. Two-tone exterior paint. Intermittent windshield wipers. Interior hood release. Power windows. Power door locks. White sidewall tires. Pickup box side rails. Rear step bumper. Below eyeline mirrors. Rear step bumper. Cargo area lamp. Sliding rear window. Gauge package. Tachometer. Speed and cruise control. Air conditioning. Tilt steering wheel. 15, 16, 16.5 in. styled wheel. White letter tires. PA6 spoke wheel (C, K1500). Swing-out spare tire carrier.

HISTORICAL: Calendar year sales: [All series] 234,992.

1977 GMC K2500 Chassis & Cab With Utility Body 4x4 (RCA)

1978 GMC

1978 GMC Jimmy With Desert Fox

GMC — LIGHT-DUTY — SIX: The most important news from GMC was the new Caballero. It replaced the Sprint as GMC's entry in the sports-pickup field. The Caballero was nearly a foot shorter in overall length and nearly 600 lbs. lighter than the former model, but it possessed equal cargo carrying capacity. The Caballero also had a new V-6 engine as its base powerplant. Its new styling included a completely new roofline, small side quarter windows and a wraparound rear window. The front featured single rectangular headlights. The spare tire was carried under the pickup box floor and was accessible from the vehicle's interior. Although the Caballero was shorter on the outside it had greater interior roominess in all length and height dimensions. The pickup box length at the floor was virtually the same as before and longer at the top of the box. The truck still came in two series, which were renamed Pickup and Diablo Pickup. There was a Laredo option group. Jimmys, conventional cab trucks and Suburbans stuck with the ice-cube-tray grille introduced in 1977. It had 10 square openings and GMC letters at the center of the horizontal division bar. A new Street Coupe equipment package was released as an option for the C1500. GMC "Indy Hauler" trucks were also built to commemorate the company's involvement with the Indy 500. GMCs were "Official Speedway Trucks" during the race. Vans continued with the handsome ice-cube tray grille. The Gypsy and Gaucho packages returned. The Value-Vans were still around, too.

1978 GMC K-2500 Suburban

I.D. DATA: Serial number a combination VIN and rating plate is located on the left door lock pillar. First symbol T=GMC. Second symbol indicates cab chassis type: W=Caballero; C=conventional cab (incl. 106 in.); G=Vandura and Rally vans; K=conventional 4x4 (including 106 in.); P=Forward-Control (Value-Van). The third symbol indicates engine: [Caballero] A=231 cid two-barrel V-6; U=305 cid two-barrel V-8; L=350 cid four-barrel V-8; M=3.3L/200 cid two-barrel V-6 (Canada only). [Vans/Conventionals] D=250 cid one-barrel L6/115 hp

(under 6,000 lbs. GVW); 100 hp (over 6,000 lbs. GVW); T=292 cid/120 hp one-barrel L6; U=305 cid two-barrel V-8/145 hp (below 6,000 lbs. GVW); 140 hp (over 6,000 lbs. GVW); Z=350 cid (5.7 liter)/120 hp diesel V-8; L=350 cid/165 hp four-barrel V-8; S=454 cid four-barrel V-8/205 hp (under 6,000 lbs. GVW); 240 hp over 6,000 lbs. Fourth symbol indicates series: 1=1/2-ton; 2=3/4-ton; 3=1-ton; 4=1/2-ton. Fifth symbol indicates body type: 2=chassis & cowl; 3=chassis & cab; 4=cab & pickup box/van with Hi-Cube box; 5=Panel Van; 6=Passenger van/Suburban; 8=Jimmy. Sixth symbol 8=1978. Seventh symbol is plant code: A=Lakewood, Ga.; B=Baltimore, Md.; D=Doraville, Ga.; J=Janesville, Wis.; K=Leeds, Mo.; R=Arlington, Texas; U=Lordstown, Ohio; V=Pontiac, Mich.; Z=Fremont, Calif.; 1=Oshawa, Canada. Symbols 8-13 are sequential production number.

Model	Body Type	Price	Weight	Prod. Total
Caballero — 1/2-Ton — 117.1 in. w.b. — V-8				
5AW80	Sedan-Pickup	4774	3184	—
5AW80/YE7	Diablo Sedan-Pickup	4953	3184	—
Jimmy 4x2 — 1/2-Ton — 106.5 in. w.b. — V-8				
TC10514	Utility with Top	—	—	—
Jimmy 4x4 — 1/2-Ton — 106.5 in. w.b. — V-8				
TK10514	Utility with Top	6378	4280	—
TK10514	Open Utility	6278	4132	—
G1500 — 1/2-Ton — 110 in. w.b. — V-8				
TG11005	Vandura	4609	3652	—
TG11006	Rally	5468	3956	—
TG11006	Rally STX	6181	4132	—
NOTE 1: Same vans available on 125 in. wheelbase.				
G2500 — 3/4-Ton — 110 in. w.b. — V-8				
TG21005	Vandura	4905	3661	—
TG21006	Rally	5726	3944	—
TG21006	Rally STX	6439	4282	—
NOTE 2: Same vans available on 125 in. wheelbase.				
G3500 — 1-Ton — 110 in. w.b. — V-8				
TG31005	Vandura	5055	3896	—
TG31306	Rally	6037	4357	—
TG31306	Rally STX	6590	4530	—
NOTE 3: Same vans available on 125 in. wheelbase.				
G3503 — 1/Ton — 125 in. w.b. (only) — V-8				
TG31303	Vandura Special	5579	3944	—
TG31303	Rally Camper Special	5482	3639	—
TG31303	Steel Magna Van 10-ft.	6857	5047	—
P1500 Value Van — 1/2-Ton — 102 in. w.b.				
TP10542	Van 7-ft.	5771	4172	—
P2500 Value Van — 3/4-Ton — 125 in./133 in. w.b.				
TP20842	Van 10-ft.	6753	5283	—
P3500 Value Van — 1-Ton — 125 in./157 in. w.b.				
TP30842	Van 10-ft.	6978	5503	—

1978 GMC Fender-Side With High Sierra trim

Model	Body Type	Price	Weight	Prod. Total
C1500 Conventional — 1/2-Ton — 117-1/2 in. w.b. — V-8				
TC10703	Chassis & Cab	4543	3570	—
TC10703	Fender-Side Pickup 6.5-ft	4418	3579	—
TX10703	Wide-Side Pickup 6.5-ft	4418	3639	—
C1503 Conventional — 1/2-Ton — 131-1/2 in. w.b. — V-8				
TC10903	Fender-Side Pickup 8 ft.	4493	3694	—
TC10903	Wide-Side Pickup 8-ft.	4493	3775	—
C1506 Conventional — 1/2-Ton — 129-1/2 in. w.b. — V-8				
TC10906	Suburban	5800	4257	—
C2503 Conventional — 3/4-Ton — 131-1/2 in. w.b. — V-8				
TC20903	Chassis & Cab	4813	3665	—
TC20903	Fender-Side Pickup 8-ft.	5038	4054	—
TC20903	Wide-Side Pickup 8-ft.	5038	4135	—
TC20943	Bonus Cab Pickup 8-ft.	5512	4176	—
TC2563 Conventional — 3/4-Ton — 164.5 in. w.b.				
TC20943	Bonus Cab Pickup 8-ft.	5737	—	—
TC20943	Crew Cab Pickup 8-ft.	5886	—	—
TC20943	Platform Stake 8-ft.	5541	4299	—
C2506 Conventional — 3/4-Ton — 129-1/2 in. w.b. — V-8				
TC20906	Suburban	6381	4620	—
C2663 Conventional — 3/4-Ton — 164-1/2 in. w.b. — V-8				
TC20963	Crew Cab Pickup 8-ft.	6111	—	—

Model	Body Type	Price	Weight	Prod. Total
C3503 Conventional — 1-Ton — 135.1 in. w.b. — V-8				
TC30903	Chassis & Cab	5055	3792	—
TC30903	Fender-Side Pickup 8-ft.	5280	4181	—
TC30903	Wide-Side Pickup 8-ft.	5280	4262	—
C2643 Conventional — 1-Ton — 135.1 in. w.b. — V-8				
TC30943	Bonus Cab Pickup 8-ft.	6162	4909	—
TC20943	Crew Cab Pickup 8-ft.	6272	—	—
TC30943	Platform Stake 9-ft.	5886	4655	—

NOTE 4: 4x4 models have TK prefix. Adds to factory price.

1978 GMC Crew Cab With Sierra Classic trim

ENGINE [Standard C1500]: Inline. OHV. Six-cylinder. Cast iron block. Bore & stroke: 3.876 x 3.530 in. Displacement: 250 cid. Compression ratio: 8.25:1. Net horsepower: 115 at 3800 rpm. Net torque: 195 lbs.-ft. at 1800 rpm. (above 6,001 lb. GVW]. Net horsepower 100 at 3600 rpm., Net torque: 175 lbs.-ft. at 1800 rpm. Seven main bearings. Hydraulic valve lifters. Carburetor: Mono-Jet model 1ME.

ENGINE [Standard C2500/C3500]: Inline. OHV. Six-cylinder. Cast iron block. Bore & stroke: 3.8764 x 4.120 in. Displacement: 292 cid. Compression ratio: 8.0:1. Net horsepower: 120 at 3600 rpm. Net torque: 215 lbs.-ft. at 2000 rpm. Seven main bearings. Hydraulic valve lifters. Carburetor: one-barrel.

ENGINE [Optional C1500/Caballero]: V-type. OHV. Eight-cylinder. Cast iron block. Bore & stroke: 3.736 x 3.480 in. Displacement: 305 cid. Compression ratio: 8.5:1. Net horsepower: 145 at 3800 rpm. Net torque: 245 lbs.-ft. at 2400 rpm. Five main bearings. Hydraulic valve lifters. Carburetor: two-barrel. model 2GC.

ENGINE [Optional: all models]: V-type. OHV. Eight-cylinder. Cast iron block. Bore & stroke: 4.0 x 3.480 in. Displacement: 350 cid. Compression ratio: 8.5:1. Net horsepower: 165 at 3800 rpm. Net torque: 260 lbs.-ft. at 2400 rpm. Five main bearings. Hydraulic valve lifters. Carburetor: four-barrel model M4MC/MV.

ENGINE [Optional K1500/K2500/K3500]: V-type. OHV. Eight-cylinder. Cast iron block. Bore & stroke: 4.125 x 3.750 in. Displacement: 400 cid. Compression ratio: 8.5:1. Net horsepower: 175 at 3600 rpm. Net torque: 290 lbs.-ft. at 2800 rpm. Five main bearings. Hydraulic valve lifters. Carburetor: four-barrel model M4MC/MV.

ENGINE [Optional: C1500/C2500/C3500/K1500/K2500/K3500]: V-type. OHV. Eight-cylinder. Cast iron block. Bore & stroke: 4.250 x 4.0 in. Displacement: 454 cid. Compression ratio: 8.5:1. Net horsepower: 205 at 3600 rpm. Net torque: 355 lbs.-ft. at 2800 rpm. Five main bearings. Hydraulic valve lifters. Carburetor: four-barrel model M4MC/MV.

ENGINE [Optional C1500]: V-type. Diesel. Eight-cylinder. Cast iron block. Bore & stroke: 4.057 x 3.385 in. Displacement: 350 cid. Compression ratio: 20.5:1. Net horsepower: 120 at 3600 rpm. Net torque: 222 lbs.-ft. at 1900 rpm. Five main bearings. Hydraulic valve lifters.

ENGINE [Standard Caballero]: V-type. OHV. Six-cylinder. Cast iron block. Bore & stroke: 3.50 x 3.48 in. Displacement: 200 cid. Compression ratio: 8.2:1. Net horsepower: 95 at 3800 rpm. Net torque: 160 lbs.-ft. at 2000 rpm. Carburetor: Rochester two-barrel.

ENGINE [Optional Caballero]: (available with automatic transmission only). Standard engine for California delivery. V-6. OHV. Six-cylinder. Cast iron block. Bore & stroke: 3.80 x 3.40 in. Displacement: 235 cid. Compression ratio: 8.0:1. Net horsepower: 105 at 3400 rpm. Net torque: 185 lbs.-ft. at 2000 rpm. Hydraulic valve lifters. Carburetor: Rochester two-barrel.

1978 GMC Fender-Side With Desert Fox trim

CHASSIS [Caballero]: Wheelbase: 117.1 in. Overall length: 201.6 in. Overall height: 53.8 in. Front/Rear tread: 58.5 in./57.8 in. Tires: P205 x 75R14.

CHASSIS [Jimmy]: Wheelbase: 106.5 in. Overall length: 184.4 in. Overall height: 69.8 in. Front/Rear tread: 66.7/63.7 in. Tires H78 x 15B.

CHASSIS [G1500]: Wheelbase: 110/125 in. Overall length: 178 in./202.2 in. Overall height: 78.8 in./81.2 in. Tires: E or F78 15B.

CHASSIS [G2500]: Wheelbase: 110 in./125 in. Overall length: 178 in./202.2 in. Overall height: 78.8 in x 81.2 in. Tires: J78 15B.

CHASSIS [G3500]: Wheelbase: 110 in./146 in. Tires: [Vandura/Rally] 8.00 x 16.5C; [Camper Special/Magna] 8.75 x 16.5D.

CHASSIS [P1500]: Wheelbase: 102 in. Overall length: 175 in. Tires: L78 x 15B.

CHASSIS [P2500]: Wheelbase: 125 in./133 in. Overall length: 220.75 in./244.75 in. Tires: 8.75 x 16.5C.

CHASSIS [P3500]: Wheelbase: 125 in./157 in. Overall length: 220.75/268.75 in. Tires: 8.75 x 16.5C.

CHASSIS [C1500]: Wheelbase: 117.5/12.5 in. Overall length: 191.3 in./212 in. Overall height: 69.8 in. Front/Rear tread: 65.8 in./62.7 in. Tires: G78 x 15B.

CHASSIS [C2500]: Wheelbase: 117.5 in./131.5 in./164.5 in. Overall length: 191.3 in./212 in./244.43 in. Overall height: 69.8 in. Front/Rear tread: 65.8 in./62.7 in. Tires: [Standard] 8.75 x 16.5C; [Bonus Cab] 8.75 x 16.5C (front); 8.75 x 16.5D (rear)/[Crew Cab] 9.50 x 16.5C (front); 9.50 x 16.5D (rear).

CHASSIS [C3500]: Wheelbase: 131.5 in./164.5 in. Overall length: 212 in./244.43 in. Overall height: 71.8 in. Front/Rear tread: 65.8 in./62.7 in. Tires: [Standard] 8.75 x 16.5C; [Bonus/Crew Cab] 9.50 x 16.5E.

TECHNICAL: Manual, synchromesh transmission. Speeds: [1500/2500 (except 2500 Crew Cab)] 3F/1R; [all 3500/2500 Crew Cab] Four-speed manual with floor-mounted shifter. Column mounted gearshift lever. Clutch: [262 cid six/two-barrel V-8s] 11 in. diameter; [four-barrel V-8s] 12 in. diameter. Rear axle: [1500] Salisbury semi-floating; [2500/3500] full-floating. Hydraulic four-wheel brakes: [front] disc; [rear] air-cooled finned cast iron drums. Steel disc wheels.

TECHNICAL OPTIONS: Automatic transmission. CBC-350 three-speed automatic torque converter. Four-speed manual, model CH-465. Power steering. Power brakes (C1500). Trailering package. Camper special package. Heavy-duty generator. Engine oil cooler. Heavy-duty shock absorber. Heavy-duty front and rear springs. Heavy-duty Freedom battery. Dual rear wheels (C3500/K3500 Wide-Side 8-ft. box only). Front stabilizer bar.

1978 GMC JImmy High Sierra With PA6 wheels

OPTIONS: [All] Chrome front bumper. Chrome rear bumper. AM;AM/FM;AM/FM 8-track stereos. CB radio. Front bumper guards. Rear step bumper. Tilt steering wheel. Swing-out camper mirrors. Sliding rear window. White stripe tires. White letter tires. Spoke wheels. Wheelcovers. Swing-out spare tire carrier. [Sprint] Laredo package. [Vandura/Rally] Gypsy package ($1,050). Eight-passenger package ($180). Twelve-passenger package ($380). [C1500/Jimmy] Street Coupe equipment. [Conventional Cabs] Camper Special. High Sierra package ($781). Sierra Grande package. Sierra Classic package. Bucket seats. Cargo area lamp. Power windows. Power door locks. Pickup box side rails. Speed and cruise controls. Garage package. Air conditioning. Tachometer. Below eye-line mirrors. Auxiliary fuel tank. Color-keyed floor mats. Intermittent windshield wipers. Soft-ray tinted glass. Two-tone exterior paint combinations. [Value-Vans] Aluminum body.

1978 GMC Caballero "Diablo" Pickup (OCW)

HISTORICAL: Model year sales: 283,540. New innovations included new Caballero introduction.

1978 GMC Sierra Classic Wide-Side Diesel Pickup (OCW)

1979 GMC K-1500 Wide-Side Sierra Grande Pickup

GMC — LIGHT-DUTY — SIX/V-8: Styling refinements for 1979 included bright trim added to the lower grille portion and a black-colored mesh back-drop for the main grille section. The Caballero also received a new grille with a prominent horizontal emphasis. Pickup interiors had a new standard vinyl seat trim. All models except Caballero and P-series had a wider vent window post for added theft protection.

1979 GMC Jimmy

I.D. DATA: Serial number a combination VIN and rating plate is located on the left door lock pillar. First symbol T=GMC. Second symbol indicates cab chassis type: W=Caballero; C=conventional cab (incl. 106 in.); G=Vandura and Rally vans; K=conventional 4x4 (incl. 106 in.); P=Forward-Control (Value-Van). The third symbol indicates engine: [Caballero] A=231 cid two-barrel V-6; U=305 cid two-barrel V-8; L=350 cid four-barrel V-8; M=3.3L/200 cid two-barrel V-6 (Canada only). [Vans/Conventionals] D=250 cid one-barrel L6/115 hp (under 6,000 lbs. GVW); 100 hp (over 6,000 lbs. GVW); T=292 cid/120 hp one-barrel L6; U=305 cid two-barrel V-8/145 hp (below 6,000 lbs. GVW); 140 hp (over 6,000 lbs. GVW); Z=350 cid (5.7 liter)/120 hp diesel V-8; L=350 cid/165 hp four-barrel V-8; S=454 cid four-barrel V-8/205 hp (under 6,000 lbs. GVW); 240 hp over 6,000 lbs. Fourth symbol indicates series: 1=1/2-ton; 2=3/4-ton; 3=1-ton; 4=1/2-ton. Fifth symbol indicates body type: 2=chassis & cowl; 3=chassis & cab; 4=cab & pickup box/van with Hi-Cube box; 5=Panel Van; 6=Passenger van/Suburban; 8=Jimmy. Sixth symbol 8=1978. Seventh symbol is plant code: A=Lakewood, Ga.; B=Baltimore, Md.; D=Doraville, Ga.; J=Janesville, Wis.; K=Leeds, Mo.; R=Arlington, Texas; U=Lordstown, Ohio; V=Pontiac, Mich.; Z=Fremont, Calif.; 1=Oshawa, Canada. Symbols 8-13 are sequential production number.

Model	Body Type	Price	Weight	Prod. Total
Caballero — 1/2-Ton — 117.1 in. w.b. — V-8				
5AW80	Sedan-Pickup	5378	3188	—
5AW80/YE7	Diablo Sedan-Pickup	5580	3328	—
Jimmy 4x2 — 1/2-Ton — 106.5 in. w.b. — V-8				
TC10514	Utility with Top	—	—	—
Jimmy 4x4 — 1/2-Ton — 106.5 in. w.b. — V-8				
TK10514	Utility with Top	7373	4371	—
TK10514	Open Utility	7273	4457	—
G1500 — 1/2-Ton — 110 in. w.b. — V-8				
TG11005	Vandura	5312	3693	—
TG11006	Rally	6229	3998	—
TG11006	Rally STX	7030	4349	—

NOTE 1: Same vans available on 125 in. wheelbase.

Standard Catalog of Light-Duty Trucks

G2500 — 3/4-Ton — 110 in. w.b. — V-8

TG21005	Vandura	5606	3689	—
TG21006	Rally	6397	3970	—
TG21006	Rally STX	7186	4318	—

NOTE 2: Same vans available on 125 in. wheelbase.

G3500 — 1-Ton — 110 in. w.b. — V-8

TG31005	Vandura	5822	3914	—
TG31306	Rally	6774	4378	—
TG31306	Rally STX	7410	4556	—

NOTE 3: Same vans available on 125 in. wheelbase.

G3503 — 1/Ton — 125 in. w.b. (only) — V-8

TG31303	Vandura Special	5383	3547	—
TG31303	Rally Camper Special	6293	3688	—
TG31303	Steel Magna Van 10-ft.	7032	—	—

P1500 Value Van — 1/2-Ton — 102 in. w.b.

TP10542	Van 7-ft.	6339	4226	—

P2500 Value Van — 3/4-Ton — 125 in./133 in. w.b.

TP20842	Van 10-ft.	7642	5311	—

P3500 Value Van — 1-Ton — 125 in./157 in. w.b.

TP30842	Van 10-ft.	7867	5485	—

C1500 Conventional — 1/2-Ton — 117-1/2 in. w.b. — V-8

TC10703	Chassis & Cab	4943	3406	—
TC10703	Fender-Side Pickup 6.5-ft	5091	3570	—
TX10703	Wide-Side Pickup 6.5-ft	5091	3628	—

C1503 Conventional — 1/2-Ton — 131-1/2 in. w.b. — V-8

TC10903	Fender-Side Pickup 8 ft	5171	3693	—
TC10903	Wide-Side Pickup 8-ft.	5171	3767	—

C1506 Conventional — 1/2-Ton — 129-1/2 in. w.b. — V-8

TC10906	Suburban	6614	4285	—

C2503 Conventional — 3/4-Ton — 131-1/2 in. w.b. — V-8

TC20903	Chassis & Cab	5481	3676	—
TC20903	Fender-Side Pickup 8-ft.	5742	4061	—
TC20903	Wide-Side Pickup 8-ft.	5742	4135	—

TC2563 Conventional — 3/4-Ton — 164.5 in. w.b.

TC20943	Bonus Cab Pickup 8-ft.	6516	—	—
TC20943	Crew Cab Pickup 8-ft.	6918	—	—
TC20943	Platform Stake 8-ft.	6239	—	—

C2506 Conventional — 3/4-Ton — 129-1/2 in. w.b. — V-8

TC20906	Suburban	7075	4556	—

C2663 Conventional — 3/4-Ton — 164-1/2 in. w.b. — V-8

TC20963	Crew Cab Pickup 8-ft.	6918	—	—

C3503 Conventional — 1-Ton — 135.1 in. w.b. — V-8

TC30903	Chassis & Cab	5941	3899	—
TC30903	Fender-Side Pickup 8-ft.	6237	4284	—
TC30903	Wide-Side Pickup 8-ft.	6237	4358	—

C2643 Conventional — 1-Ton — 135.1 in. w.b. — V-8

TC30943	Bonus Cab Pickup 8-ft.	7023	—	—
TC20943	Crew Cab Pickup 8-ft.	7183	—	—
TC30943	Platform Stake 9-ft.	6856	4671	—

NOTE 4: 4x4 models have TK prefix. Adds to factory price.

1979 GMC Sierra Classic Wide-Side Pickup (JAG)

ENGINE [Standard C1500]: Inline. OHV. Six-cylinder. Cast iron block. Bore & stroke: 3.876 x 3.530 in. Displacement: 250 cid. Compression ratio: 8.25:1. Net horsepower: 115 at 3800 rpm. Net torque: 195 lbs.-ft. at 1800 rpm. (above 6,001 lb. GVW). Net horsepower 100 at 3600 rpm., Net torque: 175 lbs.-ft. at 1800 rpm. Seven main bearings. Hydraulic valve lifters. Carburetor: Mono-Jet model 1ME.

ENGINE [Standard C2500/C3500]: Inline. OHV. Six-cylinder. Cast iron block. Bore & stroke: 3.8764 x 4.120 in. Displacement: 292 cid. Compression ratio: 8.0:1. Net horsepower: 120 at 3600 rpm. Net torque: 215 lbs.-ft. at 2000 rpm. Seven main bearings. Hydraulic valve lifters. Carburetor: one-barrel.

ENGINE [Optional C1500/Caballero]: V-type. OHV. Eight-cylinder. Cast iron block. Bore & stroke: 3.736 x 3.480 in. Displacement: 305 cid. Compression ratio: 8.5:1. Net horsepower: 145 at 3800 rpm. Net torque: 245 lbs.-ft. at 2400 rpm. Five main bearings. Hydraulic valve lifters. Carburetor: two-barrel. model 2GC.

ENGINE [Optional: all models]: V-type. OHV. Eight-cylinder. Cast iron block. Bore & stroke: 4.0 x 3.480 in. Displacement: 350 cid. Compression ratio: 8.5:1. Net horsepower: 165 at 3800 rpm. Net torque: 260 lbs.-ft. at 2400 rpm. Five main bearings. Hydraulic valve lifters. Carburetor: four-barrel model M4MC/MV.

ENGINE [Optional K1500/K2500/K3500]: V-type. OHV. Eight-cylinder. Cast iron block. Bore & stroke: 4.125 x 3.750 in. Displacement: 400 cid. Compression ratio: 8.5:1. Net horsepower: 175 at 3600 rpm. Net torque: 290 lbs.-ft. at 2800 rpm. Five main bearings. Hydraulic valve lifters. Carburetor: four-barrel model M4MC/MV.

ENGINE [Optional: C1500/C2500/C3500/K1500/K2500/K3500]: V-type. OHV. Eight-cylinder. Cast iron block. Bore & stroke: 4.250 x 4.0 in. Displacement: 454 cid. Compression ratio: 8.5:1. Net horsepower: 205 at 3600 rpm. Net torque: 355 lbs.-ft. at 2800 rpm. Five main bearings. Hydraulic valve lifters. Carburetor: four-barrel model M4MC/MV.

ENGINE [Optional C1500]: V-type. Diesel. Eight-cylinder. Cast iron block. Bore & stroke: 4.057 x 3.385 in. Displacement: 350 cid. Compression ratio: 20.5:1. Net horsepower: 120 at 3600 rpm. Net torque: 222 lbs.-ft. at 1900 rpm. Five main bearings. Hydraulic valve lifters.

ENGINE [Standard Caballero]: V-type. OHV. Six-cylinder. Cast iron block. Bore & stroke: 3.50 x 3.48 in. Displacement: 200 cid. Compression ratio: 8.2:1. Net horsepower: 95 at 3800 rpm. Net torque: 160 lbs.-ft. at 2000 rpm. Carburetor: Rochester two-barrel.

ENGINE [Optional Caballero]: (available with automatic transmission only). Standard engine for California delivery. V-6. OHV. Six-cylinder. Cast iron block. Bore & stroke: 3.80 x 3.40 in. Displacement: 235 cid. Compression ratio: 8.0:1. Net horsepower: 105 at 3400 rpm. Net torque: 185 lbs.-ft. at 2000 rpm. Hydraulic valve lifters. Carburetor: Rochester two-barrel.

CHASSIS [Caballero]: Wheelbase: 117.1 in. Overall length: 201.6 in. Overall height: 53.8 in. Front/Rear tread: 58.5 in./57.8 in. Tires: P205 x 75R14.

CHASSIS [Jimmy]: Wheelbase: 106.5 in. Overall length: 184.4 in. Overall height: 69.8 in. Front/Rear tread: 66.7/63.7 in. Tires H78 x 15B.

CHASSIS [G1500]: Wheelbase: 110/125 in. Overall length: 178 in./202.2 in. Overall height: 78.8 in./81.2 in. Tires: E or F78 x 15B.

CHASSIS [G2500]: Wheelbase: 110 in./125 in. Overall length: 178 in./202.2 in. Overall height: 78.8/81.2 in. Tires: J78 x 15B.

CHASSIS [G3500]: Wheelbase: 110 in./146 in. Tires: [Vandura/Rally] 8.00 x 16.5C; [Camper Special/Magna] 8.75 x 16.5D.

CHASSIS [P1500]: Wheelbase: 102 in. Overall length: 175 in. Tires: L78 x 15B.

CHASSIS [P2500]: Wheelbase: 125 in./133 in. Overall length: 220.75 in./244.75 in. Tires: 8.75 x 16.5C.

CHASSIS [P3500]: Wheelbase: 125 in./157 in. Overall length: 220.75/268.75 in. Tires: 8.75 x 16.5C.

CHASSIS [C1500]: Wheelbase: 117.5/12.5 in. Overall length: 191.3 in./212 in. Overall height: 69.8 in. Front/Rear tread: 65.8 in./62.7 in. Tires: G78 x 15B.

CHASSIS [C2500]: Wheelbase: 117.5 in./131.5 in./164.5 in. Overall length: 191.3 in./212 in./244.43 in. Overall height: 69.8 in. Front/Rear tread: 65.8 in./62.7 in. Tires: [Standard] 8.75 x 16.5C; [Bonus Cab] 8.75 x 16.5C (front); 8.75 x 16.5D (rear)/[Crew Cab] 9.50 x 16.5C (front); 9.50 x 16.5D (rear).

CHASSIS [C3500]: Wheelbase: 131.5 in./164.5 in. Overall length: 212 in./244.43 in. Overall height: 71.8 in. Front/Rear tread: 65.8 in./62.7 in. Tires: [Standard] 8.75 x 16.5C; [Bonus/Crew Cab] 9.50 x 16.5E.

TECHNICAL: Manual, synchromesh transmission. Speeds: [1500/2500 (except 2500 Crew Cab)] 3F/1R; [all 3500/2500 Crew Cab] Four-speed manual with floor-mounted shifter. Column mounted gearshift lever. Clutch: [262 cid six/two-barrel V-8s] 11 in. diameter; [four-barrel V-8s] 12 in. diameter. Rear axle: [1500] Salisbury semi-floating; [2500/3500] full-floating. Hydraulic four-wheel brakes: [front] disc; [rear] air-cooled finned cast iron drums. Steel disc wheels.

TECHNICAL OPTIONS: Automatic transmission. CBC-350 three-speed automatic torque converter. Four-speed manual, model CH-465. Power steering. Power brakes (C1500). Trailering package. Camper special package. Heavy-duty generator. Engine oil cooler. Heavy-duty shock absorber. Heavy-duty front and rear springs. Heavy-duty Freedom battery. Dual rear wheels (C3500/K3500 Wide-Side 8-ft. box only). Front stabilizer bar.

OPTIONS: [All] Chrome front bumper. Chrome rear bumper. AM;AM/FM;AM/FM 8-track stereos. CB radio. Front bumper guards. Rear step bumper. Tilt steering wheel. Swing-out camper mirrors. Sliding rear window. White stripe tires. White letter tires. Spoke wheels. Wheelcovers. Swing-out spare tire carrier. N67 Rally wheels. PA6 styled wheels. [Sprint] Laredo package. Bucket seats. [Vandura/Rally] Gypsy package ($1,050). Eight-passenger package ($180). Twelve-passenger package ($380). [C1500/Jimmy] Street Coupe equipment. PH7 styled aluminum wheels (Street Coupe models only). [Conventional Cabs] Camper Special. High Sierra package ($781). Sierra Grande package. Sierra Classic package. Bucket seats. Cargo area lamp. Power windows. Power door locks. Pickup box side rails. Speed and cruise controls. Garage package. Air conditioning. Tachometer. Below eye-line mirrors. Auxiliary fuel tank. Color-keyed floor mats. Intermittent windshield wipers. Soft-ray tinted glass. Two-tone exterior paint combinations. [Value-Vans] Aluminum body.

HISTORICAL: Calendar year sales: [Vandura/Rally] 41,587; [Suburban] 6,984; [Jimmy] 11,804; [P] Series 5,045; [Caballero] 6,412; [C/K Series] 106,504.

1979 GMC Suburban

1980 GMC

1980 GMC Caballero Pickup (DFW)

GMC — LIGHT-DUTY — SIX/V-8: Changes for 1980 were essentially cosmetic in nature. The Caballero's grille had short, thin vertical blades arranged in three full-width horizontal rows. Slightly heavier horizontal moldings separated the rows and there was also a vertical denter molding. A stand-up hood ornament was used. Trim variations included the base and Diablo series and a Laredo option package. Jimmys, trucks and vans continued with the "ice-cube tray" type grille. The horizontal center strip with GMC letters was now done in body color. There was a custom grille treatment for some Sierras, some of which were used as Indianapolis Motor Speedway Official Trucks during the Indy 500. They were called "Indy Haulers." Also optional was a Deluxe frontal treatment with two vertically stacked headlamps replacing larger single headlamps and parking lamps. Trucks with the deluxe grille had parking lights in the bumper. Value-Vans could be had with a variety of bodies built by independent contractors (factory approved or local) in steel or aluminum. An inline six remained standard on the 1/2-ton; others had base V-8s.

I.D. DATA: [Caballero] Located on top of instrument panel. Serial number has 13 symbols. Serial number has 13 symbols. First symbol T=GMC. Second symbol indicates line/series: W=Caballero. Third and fourth symbols indicate body type: 80=two-door sedan-pickup; Fifth symbol indicates engine code: A=3.8 L (231 cid)/105 hp two-barrel V-6 built by Buick; H=5.0 L (305 cid)/140 hp four-barrel V-8; J=4.4 L (267 cid)/115 hp two-barrel V-8; K=3.8 L/ (231 cid) two-barrel V-6 built by Chevrolet. Sixth symbol indicates model year: A=1980; Seventh symbol indicates factory code: R=Arlington, Texas; B=Baltimore, Md.; D=Doraville, Ga.; K=Leeds, Mo. Last six symbols are production sequence number starting at 100001. Engine numbers located: [six] on pad on right-hand side of block at rear of distributor; [V-8] on pad on right-hand side of block.

I.D. DATA: [Conventionals/Vans] Located on plate attached to left top of instrument panel on C,K,G models; on front of dash and toe panel left of steering colum in Value-Van. First symbol T=GMC. Conventional Cab/Jimmy; G=Vandura/Rally Wagon; K=Conventional Cab 4x4/Jimmy 4x4; P=Forward-Control (Value-Van).; Third Symbol is engine code: D=4.1L (250 cid)/110 hp two-barrel six; T=4.8L (292 cid)/120 hp one-barrel six; G=5.0L (305 cid)/140 hp two-barrel V-8; L=5.7L (350 cid)/165 hp four-barrel V-8; M=5.7L (350 cid)/170 hp four-barrel V-8; P=5.7L (350 cid)/155 hp two-barrel V-8; R=6.6L (400 cid)/175 hp four-barrel V-8; S=7.4L (454 cid)/240 hp four-barrel V-8; X=6.6L (400 cid)/180 hp four-barrel V-8. Z=5.7L (350 cid)/120 hp diesel V-8. The fourth symbol indicates model: 1=1/2 ton; 2=3/4-ton; 3=1-ton; 4=1/2-ton (with heavy-duty suspension). Fifth symbol indicates body type: 2=Chassis & Cowl; 3=Chassis & Cab; 4=Cab w/pickup box or van with Hi-Cube box; 5=Panel Van (Vandura); 6=Rally Wagon or Suburban; 8=Jimmy Utility. The sixth symbol indicates model year A=1980. The seventh symbol indicates assembly plant; 1981 GMC models were sourced from: B=Baltimore, Md.; Z=Fremont, Calif.; J=Janesville, Wis.; S=St. Louis; 3=Detroit (Chevrolet), Mich. (Value-Vans built in Chevrolet plant); F=Flint, Mich.; V=Pontiac, Mich. (GMC headquarters). The last six symbols were the production sequence number starting at 100001. Engine numbers located: [six] on pad on right-hand side of block at rear of distributor; [V-8] on pad on right-hand side of block.

Model	Body Type	Price	Weight	Prod. Total
Caballero — 1/2-Ton — 117.1 in. w.b. — V-8				
AW80	Pickup	5911	3098	—
AW80YE7	Diablo Pickup	6129	—	—
Jimmy — 1/2-Ton — 106-1/2 in. w.b. — V-8				
TK10516	Open Utility with Hardtop	8078	4418	—
TK10516	Open Utility with Soft Top	7975		—

NOTE 1: 4x2 Jimmys have TC prefix.

1980 GMC Sierra Classic "Indy Hauler" Pickup (OCW)

1980 GMC Rally Wagon STX Passenger Van (OCW)

Model	Body Type	Price	Weight	
G1505 Vandura — 1/2-Ton — 110 in. w.b. — V-8				
TG11005	Vandura	5748	3652	—
G1506 Rally Wagon — 1/2-Ton — 110 in. w.b. — V-8				
TG11006	Rally	6747	3971	—
TG11306	Rally	7699	4153	—
G2505 (005) Vandura — 3/4-Ton — 110 in. w.b. — V-8				
TG21005	Vandura	6183	3756	—
G2500 (006/306) Rally Wagon — 3/4-Ton — 110 in. w.b. — V-8				
TG21006	Rally	7023	4012	—
TG11306	Rally STX	7975	4202	—
EG3500 (305) Vandura — 1-Ton — 110 in. w.b. — V-8				
TG2305	Vandura	7060	4154	—
G3500 (306) Rally Wagon — 1-Ton — 110 in. w.b. — V-8				
TG2306	Rally	7901	4450	—
TG2306	Rally STX	8680		—
NOTE 2: All vans available with 125 in. wheelbase option				
G3500 (332) Rally Camper — 1-Ton — 125 in. w.b. — V-8				
TG2332	Rally Camper Special	6808	3736	—
G3500 (303) Special Van — 1-Ton — 125 in. w.b. — V-8				
TG2303	Vandura Special	5860	3524	—
TG2303	Magna Van	7785	—	—
P1500 — 1/2-Ton — 102 in. w.b. — L6				
TP10542	Van 7-ft.	6785	4332	—
P2500 — 3/4-Ton — 125 in./133 in. w.b. — V-8				
TP20842	Van, 10-ft.	8139	5425	—
P3500 — 1-Ton — 125 in./157 in. w.b. — V-8				
TP30842	Van 10-ft.	8409	5599	—
C1500 (703) — 1/2-Ton — 117.5 in. w.b. — V-8				
TC10703	Chassis & Cab	5785	3243	—
TC10703	Fender-Side Pickup 6.5-ft.	5505	3612	—
TC10703	Wide-Side Pickup 6.5-ft.	5505	3609	—
C1500 (903) — 1/2-Ton — 131.5 in. w.b. — V-8				
TC10903	Chassis & Cab	5870	3627	—
TC10903	Fender-Side Pickup 8-ft.	5590	3692	—
TC10903	Wide-Side Pickup 8-ft.	5590	3767	—
C1500 (906) — 1/2-Ton — 131.5 in. w.b. — V-8				
TC10906	Suburban	7456	4208	—
C2500 (903) — 3/4-Ton — 129.5 in. w.b. — V-8				
TC20903	Chassis & Cab	6216	3625	—
TC20903	Fender-Side Pickup, 8-ft.	6326	4009	—
TC20903	Wide-Side Pickup, 8-ft.	6326	4084	—
C2500 (943) — 3/4-Ton — 164.5 in. w.b. — V-8				
TC20943	Chassis & Bonus Cab	6904	4330	—
TC20943	Wide-Side Bonus Cab Pickup	7241		—
TC20943	Chassis & Crew Cab	7218	—	—
TC20943	Wide-Side Crew Cab Pickup	7495	—	—
C2500 (906) — 3/4-Ton — 129.5 in. w.b. — V-8				
TC20906	Suburban	7923	4504	—
C3500 (903) — 1-Ton — 131.5 in. w.b.				
TC30903	Chassis & Cab	5941	3899	—
TC30903	Fender-Side Pickup 8-ft.	6687	4232	—
TC30903	Wide-Side Pickup 8-ft.	6687	4307	—
C3500 (943/003) — 3/4-Ton — 164.5 in. w.b. — V-8				
TC30943	Chassis & Bonus Cab	7120	4364	—
TC30943	Wide-Side Bonus Cab Pickup	7397	4823	—
TC30943	Chassis & Crew Cab	7374	—	—
TC30943	Wide-Side Crew Cab Pickup	7651	—	—
TC20003	Platform & Stake	7481	4708	—

TECHNICAL: Manual, synchromesh. Speeds: 3F/1R (Four-speed C3500). Column (floor-Four-speed) mounted gearshift. 11 in. diameter, 12 in. diameter with 350, 400, 454 cid. engines with four-barrel. carburetor clutch. Semi-floating (1/2-Ton models), Full-floating (all others) rear axle. Overall ratio: C1500 3.07:1, C1500 diesel 2.76:1, C2500, C3500 4.11:1. Front disc, rear drum, hydraulic, power assisted except brakes for C1500. Pressed steel

wheels. Automatic transmission CBC-350, three-speed automatic. Four-speed manual model CH-465. Power steering. Power brakes (C1500). Trailering package. Camper package. Heavy-duty generator. Engine oil cooler. Heavy-duty shock absorbers. Heavy-duty springs. Heavy-duty Freedom battery. Dual rear wheels. Front stabilizer bar. F-44 package.

1980 GMC High Sierra 4x4 Suburban (RCA)

ENGINE [Standard C1500]: Inline. OHV. Six-cylinder. Cast iron block. Bore & stroke: 3.876 x 3.530 in. Displacement: 250 cid. Compression ratio: 8.25:1. Net horsepower: 115 at 3800 rpm. Net torque: 195 lbs.-ft. at 1800 rpm. (above 6,001 lb. GVW). Net horsepower 100 at 3600 rpm., Net torque: 175 lbs.-ft. at 1800 rpm. Seven main bearings. Hydraulic valve lifters. Carburetor: Mono-Jet model 1ME.
ENGINE [Standard C2500/C3500]: Inline. OHV. Six-cylinder. Cast iron block. Bore & stroke. 3.8764 x 4.120 in. Displacement: 292 cid. Compression ratio: 8.0:1. Net horsepower: 120 at 3600 rpm. Net torque: 215 lbs.-ft. at 2000 rpm. Seven main bearings. Hydraulic valve lifters. Carburetor: one-barrel.
ENGINE [Optional C1500/Caballero]: V-type. OHV. Eight-cylinder. Cast iron block. Bore & stroke: 3.736 x 3.480 in. Displacement: 305 cid. Compression ratio: 8.5:1. Net horsepower: 145 at 3800 rpm. Net torque: 245 lbs.-ft. at 2400 rpm. Five main bearings. Hydraulic valve lifters. Carburetor: two-barrel. model 2GC.
ENGINE [Optional: all models]: V-type. OHV. Eight-cylinder. Cast iron block. Bore & stroke: 4.0 x 3.480 in. Displacement: 350 cid. Compression ratio: 8.5:1. Net horsepower: 165 at 3800 rpm. Net torque: 260 lbs.-ft. at 2400 rpm. Five main bearings. Hydraulic valve lifters. Carburetor: four-barrel model M4MC/MV.
ENGINE [Optional K1500/K2500/K3500]: V-type. OHV. Eight-cylinder. Cast iron block. Bore & stroke: 4.125 x 3.750 in. Displacement: 400 cid. Compression ratio: 8.5:1. Net horsepower: 175 at 3600 rpm. Net torque: 290 lbs.-ft. at 2800 rpm. Five main bearings. Hydraulic valve lifters. Carburetor: four-barrel model M4MC/MV.
ENGINE [Optional C1500/C2500/C3500/K1500/K2500/K3500]: V-type. OHV. Eight-cylinder. Cast iron block. Bore & stroke: 4.250 x 4.0 in. Displacement: 454 cid. Compression ratio: 8.5:1. Net horsepower: 205 at 3600 rpm. Net torque: 355 lbs.-ft. at 2800 rpm. Five main bearings. Hydraulic valve lifters. Carburetor: four-barrel model M4MC/MV.
ENGINE [Optional C1500]: V-type. Diesel. Eight-cylinder. Cast iron block. Bore & stroke: 4.057 x 3.385 in. Displacement: 350 cid. Compression ratio: 20.5:1. Net horsepower: 120 at 3600 rpm. Net torque: 222 lbs.-ft. at 1900 rpm. Five main bearings. Hydraulic valve lifters.
ENGINE [Standard Caballero]: V-type. OHV. Six-cylinder. Cast iron block. Bore & stroke: 3.50 x 3.48 in. Displacement: 200 cid. Compression ratio: 8.2:1. Net horsepower: 95 at 3800 rpm. Net torque: 160 lbs.-ft. at 2000 rpm. Carburetor: Rochester two-barrel.
ENGINE [Optional Caballero]: (available with automatic transmission only). Standard engine for California delivery. V-6. OHV. Six-cylinder. Cast iron block. Bore & stroke: 3.80 x 3.40 in. Displacement: 235 cid. Compression ratio: 8.0:1. Net horsepower: 105 at 3400 rpm. Net torque: 185 lbs.-ft. at 2000 rpm. Hydraulic valve lifters. Carburetor: Rochester two-barrel.

1980 GMC High Sierra Wide-Side Pickup (RCA)

CHASSIS [Caballero]: Wheelbase: 117.1 in. Overall length: 201.6 in. Overall height: 53.8 in. Front/Rear tread: 58.5 in./57.8 in. Tires: P205 x 75R14.
CHASSIS [Jimmy]: Wheelbase: 106.5 in. Overall length: 184.4 in. Overall height: 69.8 in. Front/Rear tread: 66.7/63.7 in. Tires H78 x 15B.
CHASSIS [G1500]: Wheelbase: 110/125 in. Overall length: 178 in./202.2 in. Overall height: 78.8 in./81.2 in. Tires: E or F78 x 15B.
CHASSIS [G2500]: Wheelbase: 110 in./125 in. Overall length: 178 in./202.2 in. Overall height: 78.8 in./81.2 in. Tires: J78 x 15B.
CHASSIS [G3500]: Wheelbase: 110 in./146 in. Tires: [Vandura/Rally] 8.00 x 16.5C; [Camper Special/Magna] 8.75 x 16.5D.
CHASSIS [P1500]: Wheelbase: 102 in. Overall length: 175 in. Tires: L78 x 15B.
CHASSIS [P2500]: Wheelbase: 125 in./133 in. Overall length: 220.75 in./244.75 in. Tires: 8.75 x 16.5C.
CHASSIS [P3500]: Wheelbase: 125 in./157 in. Overall length: 220.75/268.75 in. Tires: 8.75 x 16.5C.
CHASSIS [C1500]: Wheelbase: 117.5/12.5 in. Overall length: 191.3 in./212 in. Overall height: 69.8 in. Front/Rear tread: 65.8 in./62.7 in. Tires: G78 x 15B.
CHASSIS [C2500]: Wheelbase: 117.5 in./131.5 in./164.5 in. Overall length: 191.3 in./212 in./244.43 in. Overall height: 69.8 in. Front/Rear tread: 65.8 in./62.7 in. Tires: [Standard]

8.75 x 16.5C; [Bonus Cab] 8.75 x 16.5C (front); 8.75 x 16.5D (rear)/[Crew Cab] 9.50 x 16.5C (front); 9.50 x 16.5D (rear).
CHASSIS [C3500]: Wheelbase: 131.5 in./164.5 in. Overall length: 212 in./244.43 in. Overall height: 71.8 in. Front/Rear tread: 65.8 in./62.7 in. Tires: [Standard] 8.75 x 16.5C; [Bonus/Crew Cab] 9.50 x 16.5E.

1980 GMC G3500 Magna Van Cutaway Chassis (OCW)

TECHNICAL: Manual, synchromesh transmission, column mounted gearshift lever. Speeds: [1500/2500 (except 2500 Crew Cab)] 3F/1R; [all 3500/2500 Crew Cab] Four-speed manual with floor-mounted shifter. Clutch: 11 in. diameter; [with 350-4V/400-4V/454-4V V-8s] 12 in. diameter. Rear axle: [1500] Salisbury semi-floating; [2500/3500] full-floating. Overall ratio: [C1500] 3.07:1; [C1500] diesel 2.76:1; [C2500/C3500] 4.11:1. Hydraulic four-wheel brakes, power-assisted: [front] disc; [rear] air-cooled finned cast iron drums. Pressed steel disc wheels.
TECHNICAL OPTIONS: Automatic transmission CBC-350, three-speed automatic. Four-speed manual model CH-465. Power steering. Trailering package. Camper package. Heavy-duty generator. Engine oil cooler. Heavy-duty shock absorbers. Heavy-duty springs. Heavy-duty Freedom battery. Dual rear wheels. Front stabilizer bar. F-44 "Big Dooley" package.
OPTIONS: [All] Chrome front bumper. Rear bumper. AM and AM/FM radio. Electric clock. Air conditioning. Color-keyed floor mats. Tinted glass. Chrome grille. Tilt steering wheel. Intermittent wipers. Sliding rear windows. [Caballero] Loredo package ($165). [Vandura/Rally Wagon] Gypsy package. Eight-passenger package ($225). Twelve-passenger package ($480). [Jimmy/Conventional] High Sierra package. Sierra classic package ($895). Sierra Grande package. Street Coupe equipment. And more.
HISTORICAL: Calendar year sales: 141,030. Sales broke out as follows: [Pickups] 102,130; [Vandura/Rally] 21,007; [Suburban] 4,210; [Jimmy] 5,608; [P-models] 3,612; [Caballero] 4,463.

1980 GMC K1500 Jimmy Sierra Classic Sport Wagon 4x4 (RCA)

1981 GMC

1981 GMC Sierra Classic "Indy Hauler" Pickup (DFW)

GMC — LIGHT TRUCK — (ALL SERIES) — SIX-CYLINDER/V-8: A new grille in the Caballero had eight thin, full-width horizontal bars and bright upper and lower moldings. The Caballero name was on the lower left corner. New wheelcovers were seen. Inside was a restyled instrument panel with new pad and glossy applique, new seat trim and international symbols for controls. New options included a 55/45 split bench seat, trip odometer and resume-speed cruise control feature. The Diablo models came with contrasting lower body perimeter and the Diablo name on the door liners. There was a Caballero Amarillo package with roof and lower perimeter in a matching contrasting color. Also new were standard high-pressure tires that decreased rolling resistance and upped fuel economy. Powertrains were carried over from 1980, but with Computer Command Control on all engines. The Jimmy was still available with 4x2 or 4x4 chassis. New aerodynamic sheet metal was used from the cowl forward. The front fenders and hood were restyled with a new front bumper mounted air dam to improve fuel economy. The front fender skirts had attached shields to reduce engine compartment splash. A new grille and bumper were made of high-strength steel to reduce weight. A 4.1 liter/250 cid inline six was standard. There was also a new version of the 305 cid V-8. It had electronic spark control (ESC) and could be ordered outside California. The K Series (4x4) models had a new aluminum transfer case and automatic locking hubs allowing drivers to shift into 4x4 mode at speeds up to 20 mph. A new option was a quad shocks package for off-roaders. "Ice-cube tray" grilles were on the conventional trucks, Suburbans and vans again. The center divider was bright finished. A deluxe grille with vertically stacked headlamps and in-the-bumper parking lights was optional again. There were many important changes made in the latest GMC trucks that made them far more fuel efficient than in years past. Attractive new, aerodynamically designed front sheet metal had less wind drag. Overall, the GMC pickups weighed 87 to 300 lbs. less than in 1980, but there was no reduction in their payload capacities. Cabs and beds were about the same size, too. The front disc brakes on the C1500, C2500 and their 4x4 counterparts were of a low-drag design. Also introduced were rear springs on the 4x2 and 4x4 1/2-ton and 3/4-ton models. These springs were shot-peened for added strength. Most GMC trucks with the optional automatic transmission had re-engineered clutch plates for quieter operation. Interior changes included a higher grade standard interior with full foam seat cushions and a more attractive vinyl upholstery. The instrument panel now had a foam-padded pad with a GMC nameplate. Again this year, GMC was the official truck of the Indianapolis 500. The company provided 50 pickups, Suburbans and vans with "Indy Hauler" graphics for use as general transportation, safety and emergency vehicles during the race. New options included halogen high-beam headlamps and quartz clocks. The standard 4.1 liter six, three 5.0 liter V-8s and a 5.7 liter V-8 were available in trucks with GVWs below 8,500 lbs. that were governed by one set of emission standards. Above that, a 4.8 liter six and 7.4 liter V-8 were offered. There was also a new high-compression (9.2:1) 5.0 liter V-8 with ESC said to give the performance of a 5.7 liter V-8 combined with better fuel economy. There was a new water-in-fuel warning lamp for diesels, quad shocks for K1500/K2500s and a travel bed package consisting of a three-passenger bench seat with folding backrest and hinged backrest extension. GMC vans were essentially unchanged from 1980, but featured engineering refinements like the ESC V-8 and improved corrosion-proofing. On Rally STX vans, the beltline molding was positioned lower on the bodysides. This changed the two-tone paint scheme color breaks which were now right at the beltline and just above the wheel openings. A 5.0 liter V-8 or the ESC V-8 were standard in most models. The new travel bed option came in vans, too. Value-Vans were available again in steel and aluminum. However, the 1/2-ton Forward-Control chassis was dropped.

1981 GMC 1/2-Ton Caballero Diablo Sport Pickup (DFW/GMC)

I.D. DATA: In 1981, GM changed its VIN system to include country of origin, manufacturer's code, and GVWR/brake system information. This was the first year that Caballeros had the same coding system as trucks, except the engines in Caballeros used car coding. [Light-Duty Truck and Multi-purpose Passenger Vehicles (MPV)] Located on plate attached to left top of instrument panel; or on left-hand top of instrument panel; or on front of dash and toe panel left of steering colum in Value-Van. First symbol indicates country of origin: 1=USA; 2=Canada; 3=Japan. Second symbol indicates manufacturer: G=GM; 8=Isuzu (not applicable to GMC 1981). Third symbol indicates make: T=GMC truck; 5=GMC MPV (such as Suburban or Rally Wagon); O=GMC van with fourth seat. Fourth symbol indicates GVWR/brake system: B=3,001-4,000 lbs./hydraulic; C=4,001-5,000lbs./hydraulic; etc. through K=14,000-16,000 lbs./hydraulic. Fifth symbol indicates line and chassis: C=Conventional Cab/Jimmy; G=Vandura/Rally Wagon; K=Conventional Cab 4x4/Jimmy 4x4; P=Forward-Control (Value-Van); W=Caballero; Z=4x2 special body. The sixth symbol indicates model: 1=1/2 ton; 2=3/4-ton; 3=1-ton; 8=1/2-ton Caballero; 9=Chassis & Cowl. The seventh symbol indicates body type: 0=two-door sedan-pickup; 1=Hi-Cube or Cutaway Van; 2=Forward-Control; 3=four-door cab; 4=two-door cab; 5=van; 6=Suburban; 8=Jimmy (utility); 9=stake. The eighth symbol indicated engine: [Caballero] A=3.8L (231 cid)/110 hp V-6 two-barrel; H=5.0L (305 cid)/135 hp V-8 four-barrel; J=4.3L (267 cid)/120 hp V-8. [Light-Duty and MPV] D=4.1L (250 cid)/115 hp two-barrel L-6; F=5.0L (305 cid)/155 hp four-barrel V-8. H=5.0L (305 cid)/160 hp four-barrel V-8; G=5.0L (305 cid)/135 hp two-barrel V-8; L=5.7L (350 cid)/165 hp V-8; M=5.7L (350 cid)/185 hp four-barrel V-8; N=1.8L (111 cid)/75 hp Isuzu L-4 two-barrel; P=5.7L (350 cid)/161 hp four-barrel V-8; T=4.8L (292 cid)/115 hp one-barrel L-6); Z=7.4L (454 cid)/240 hp four-barrel V-8; Z=5.7L (350 cid)/105 hp diesel V-8. The ninth symbol is a check digit. The 10th symbol indicates model year B=1981. The eleventh symbol indicates assembly plant; GMC models were sourced from: B=Baltimore, Md.; Z=Fremont, Calif.; J=Janesville, Wis.; S=St. Louis; D=Detroit (Chevrolet), Mich. (Value-Vans built in Chevrolet plant); F=Flint, Mich.; V=Pontiac, Mich. (GMC headquarters) and possibly other factories. The last six symbols were the production sequence number starting at 100001.

Model	Body Type	Price	Weight	Prod. Total
Caballero — 1/2-Ton — 117.1 in. w.b. — V-8				
AW80	Pickup	6988	3181	—
AW80YE7	Diablo Pickup	7217	—	—

Jimmy — 1/2-Ton — 106-1/2 in. w.b. — V-8

TK10516	Open Utility with Hardtop	8856	4087	—
TK10516	Open Utility with Soft Top	8750	—	—

NOTE 1: 4x2 Jimmys have TC prefix.

G1505 Vandura — 1/2-Ton — 110 in. w.b. — V-8

TG11005	Vandura 6434	3577		—

G1506 Rally Wagon — 1/2-Ton — 110 in. w.b. — V-8

TG11006	Custom Rally	7465	3907	—
TG11306	Rally STX	7699	4153	—

G2500 (005) Vandura — 3/4-Ton — 110 in. w.b. — V-8

TG21005	Vandura	6756	3631	—

G2500 (006/306) Rally Wagon — 3/4-Ton — 110 in. w.b. — V-8

TG21006	Rally	7617	3928	—
TG11306	Rally STX	8456	4096	—

G3500 (305) Vandura — 1-Ton — 110 in. w.b. — V-8

TG31305	Vandura	8056	4285	—

G3506 (306) Rally Wagon — 1-Ton — 110 in. w.b. — V-8

TG31306	Rally	8997	4602	—
TG31306	Custom Rally	9653	4602	—
TG31306	Rally STX	9863	4602	—

NOTE 2: All vans available with 125 in. wheelbase option

G3500 (332) Rally Camper — 3/4-Ton — 125 in. w.b. — V-8

TG31332	Rally Camper Special	7765	3746	—

G3500 (303) Special Van — 3/4-Ton — 125 in. w.b. — V-8

TG31303	Vandura Special	6764	3578	—
TG31303	Magna Van	9053	—	—

P2500 — 3/4-Ton — 125 in./133 in. w.b. — V-8

TP20842	Van, 10-ft.	9711	5479	—

P3500 — 1-Ton — 125 in./157 in. w.b. — V-8

TP30842	Van 10-ft.	9959	5671	—

C1500 (703) — 1/2-Ton — 117.5 in. w.b. — V-8

TC10703	Chassis & Cab	6012	3348	—
TC10703	Fender-Side Pickup 6.5-ft.	6012	3391	—
TC10703	Wide-Side Pickup 6.5-ft.	5505	3609	—

C1500 (903) — 1/2-Ton — 131.5 in. w.b. — V-8

TC10903	Chassis & Cab	5870	3627	—
TC10903	Fender-Side Pickup 8-ft.	5590	3692	—
TC10903	Wide-Side Pickup 8-ft.	5590	3767	—

C1500 (906) — 1/2-Ton — 131.5 in. w.b. — V-8

TC10906	Suburban	7456	4208	—

C2500 (903) — 3/4-Ton — 129.5 in. w.b. — V-8

TC20903	Chassis & Cab	6216	3625	—
TC20903	Fender-Side Pickup, 8-ft.	6326	4009	—
TC20903	Wide-Side Pickup, 8-ft.	6326	4084	—

C2500 (943) — 3/4-Ton — 164.5 in. w.b. — V-8

TC20943	Chassis & Bonus Cab	6904	4330	—
TC20943	Wide-Side Bonus Cab Pickup	7241	—	—
TC20943	Chassis & Crew Cab	7218	—	—
TC20943	Wide-Side Crew Cab Pickup	7495	—	—

C2500 (906) — 3/4-Ton — 129.5 in. w.b. — V-8

TC20906	Suburban	7923	4504	—

C3500 (903) — 1-Ton — 131.5 in. w.b.

TC30903	Chassis & Cab	5941	3899	—
TC30903	Fender-Side Pickup 8-ft.	6687	4232	—
TC30903	Wide-Side Pickup 8-ft.	6687	4307	—

C3500 (943/003) — 1-Ton — 164.5 in. w.b. — V-8

TC30943	Chassis & Bonus Cab	7120	4364	—
TC30943	Wide-Side Bonus Cab Pickup	7397	4823	—
TC30943	Chassis & Crew Cab	7374	—	—
TC30943	Wide-Side Crew Cab Pickup	7651	—	—
TC20003	Platform & Stake	7481	4708	—

1981 GMC 1-Ton Indy 500 Wrecker (IMSC/JLM)

ENGINE [Caballero base V-6]: V-type. OHV. Six-cylinder. Cast iron block. Bore & stroke: 3.8 x 3.4 in. Displacement: 231 cid. Net horsepower: 110 at 3800 rpm. Net torque: 190 lbs.-ft. at 1600 rpm. Carburetor: Rochester two-barrel. Passenger engine code A. Source: Buick.
ENGINE [Optional Caballero]: (available with automatic transmission only). Standard engine for California delivery. V-6. OHV. Six-cylinder. Cast iron block. Bore & stroke: 4.80 x

462

3.48 in. Displacement: 262 cid. Compression ratio: 8.0:1. Net horsepower: 155 at 4000 rpm. Net torque: 230 lbs.-ft. at 2400 rpm. Hydraulic valve lifters. Carburetor: Rochester two-barrel. Passenger engine code S. Source: Chevrolet.

ENGINE [Optional Caballero]: V-8. OHV. Six-cylinder. Cast iron block. Bore & stroke: 3.74 x 3.48 in. Displacement: 305 cid. Net horsepower: 135 at 4200 rpm. Net torque: 235 lbs.-ft. at 2400 rpm. Hydraulic valve lifters. Carburetor: Rochester four-barrel. Passenger engine code A. Source: Chevrolet.

ENGINE [Optional Caballero]: V-8. OHV. Six-cylinder. Cast iron block. Bore & stroke: 3.5 x 3.48 in. Displacement: 267 cid. Net horsepower: 120 at 3600 rpm. Net torque: 215 lbs.-ft. at 2000 rpm. Hydraulic valve lifters. Carburetor: Rochester four-barrel. Passenger engine code J. Source: Chevrolet.

ENGINE [Optional Caballero]: V-type. OHV. Eight-cylinder. Cast iron block. Bore & stroke: 4.0 x 3.480 in. Displacement: 350 cid. Net horsepower: 105 at 3200 rpm. Net torque: 200 lbs.-ft. at 1600 rpm. Five main bearings. Hydraulic valve lifters. Diesel. Passenger engine code N. Source: Oldsmobile.

ENGINE [C1500 base six]: Inline. OHV. Six-cylinder. Cast iron block. Bore & stroke: 3.876 x 3.530 in. Displacement: 250 cid. Compression ratio: 8.25:1. Net horsepower: 115 at 3600 rpm. Net torque: 200 lbs.-ft. at 2000 rpm. [above 6,001 lb. GVW]. Net horsepower 100 at 3600 rpm. Net torque: 175 lbs.-ft. at 1800 rpm. Seven main bearings. Hydraulic valve lifters. Carburetor: Mono-Jet model 1ME. Engine code D. Source: Chevrolet.

ENGINE [C2500/C3500/P base six]: Inline. OHV. Six-cylinder. Cast iron block. Bore & stroke: 3.8764 x 4.120 in. Displacement: 292 cid. Compression ratio: 8.0:1. Net horsepower: 115 at 4000 rpm. Net torque: 210 lbs.-ft. at 1800 rpm. Seven main bearings. Hydraulic valve lifters. Carburetor: one-barrel. Engine code T. Source: Chevrolet.

ENGINE [Optional C1500]: V-type. OHV. Eight-cylinder. Cast iron block. Bore & stroke: 3.736 x 3.480 in. Displacement: 305 cid. Compression ratio: 8.5:1. Net horsepower: 155 at 4000 rpm. Net torque: 245 lbs.-ft. at 1600 rpm. Five main bearings. Hydraulic valve lifters. Carburetor: four-barrel model. Engine code F. Source: Chevrolet.

ENGINE [Optional C1500]: V-type. OHV. Eight-cylinder. Cast iron block. Bore & stroke: 3.736 x 3.480 in. Displacement: 305 cid. Compression ratio: 8.5:1. Net horsepower: 135 at 4200 rpm. Net torque: 235 lbs.-ft. at 2400 rpm. Five main bearings. Hydraulic valve lifters. Carburetor: two-barrel model 2GC. Engine code G. Source: Chevrolet.

ENGINE [Optional C1500]: V-type. OHV. Eight-cylinder. Cast iron block. Bore & stroke: 3.736 x 3.480 in. Displacement: 305 cid. Compression ratio: 8.5:1. Net horsepower: 160 at 4400 rpm. Net torque: 235 lbs.-ft. at 2000 rpm. Five main bearings. Hydraulic valve lifters. Carburetor: four-barrel. Code H. Source: Chevrolet.

ENGINE [Optional: all models]: V-type. OHV. Eight-cylinder. Cast iron block. Bore & stroke: 4.0 x 3.480 in. Displacement: 350 cid. Compression ratio: 8.5:1. Net horsepower: 165 at 3800 rpm. Net torque: 275 lbs.-ft. at 1600 rpm. Five main bearings. Hydraulic valve lifters. Carburetor: four-barrel model M4MC/MV. Engine code L. Source: Chevrolet.

ENGINE [Optional: all models]: V-type. OHV. Eight-cylinder. Cast iron block. Bore & stroke: 4.0 x 3.480 in. Displacement: 350 cid. Compression ratio: 8.5:1. Net horsepower: 185 at 4000 rpm. Net torque: 285 lbs.-ft. at 2400 rpm. Five main bearings. Hydraulic valve lifters. Carburetor: four-barrel model M4MC/MV. Engine code M. Source: Chevrolet.

ENGINE [Optional: all models]: V-type. OHV. Eight-cylinder. Cast iron block. Bore & stroke: 4.0 x 3.480 in. Displacement: 350 cid. Compression ratio: 8.5:1. Net horsepower: 161 at 3800 rpm. Net torque: 275 lbs.-ft. at 2400 rpm. Five main bearings. Hydraulic valve lifters. Carburetor: four-barrel model M4MC/MV. Engine code P. Source: Chevrolet.

ENGINE [Optional: all models]: V-type. OHV. Eight-cylinder. Cast iron block. Bore & stroke: 4.0 x 3.480 in. Displacement: 350 cid. Net horsepower: 105 at 3200 rpm. Net torque: 200 lbs.-ft. at 1600 rpm. Five main bearings. Hydraulic valve lifters. Oldsmobile diesel. Engine code Z. Source: Chevrolet.

ENGINE [Optional: C1500/C2500/C3500/K1500/K2500/K3500]: V-type. OHV. Eight-cylinder. Cast iron block. Bore & stroke: 4.250 x 4.0 in. Displacement: 454 cid. Compression ratio: 8.5:1. Net horsepower: 240 at 3800 rpm. Net torque: 375 lbs.-ft. at 3200 rpm. Five main bearings. Hydraulic valve lifters. Carburetor: four-barrel model M4MC/MV. Engine code W. Source: Chevrolet.

1981 GMC K1500 High Sierra Fender-Side Pickup (RCA)

CHASSIS [Caballero]: Wheelbase: 117.1 in. Overall length: 201.6 in. Overall height: 53.8 in. Front/Rear tread: 58.5 in./57.8 in. Tires: P205 x 75R14.

CHASSIS [Jimmy]: Wheelbase: 106.5 in. Overall length: 184.4 in. Overall height: 69.8 in. Front/Rear tread: 66.7 in./63.7 in. Tires H78 x 15B.

CHASSIS [G1500]: Wheelbase: 110 in./125 in. Overall length: 178 in./202.2 in. Overall height: 78.8 in./81.2 in. Tires: E78 x 15B or F78 x 15B.

CHASSIS [G2500]: Wheelbase: 110 in./125 in. Overall length: 178 in./202.2 in. Overall height: 78.8 x 81.2 in. Tires: J78 x 15B.

CHASSIS [G3500]: Wheelbase: 110 in./146 in. Tires: [Vandura/Rally] 8.00 x 16.5C; [Camper Special/Magna] 8.75 x 16.5D.

CHASSIS [P2500]: Wheelbase: 125 in./133 in. Overall length: 220.75 in./244.75 in. Tires: 8.75 x 16.5C.

CHASSIS [P3500]: Wheelbase: 125 in./157 in. Overall length: 220.75/268.75 in. Tires: 8.75 x 16.5C.

CHASSIS [C1500]: Wheelbase: 117.5/12.5 in. Overall length: 191.3 in./212 in. Overall height: 69.8 in. Front/Rear tread: 65.8 in./62.7 in. Tires: G78 x 15B.

CHASSIS [C2500]: Wheelbase: 117.5 in./131.5 in./164.5 in. Overall length: 191.3 in./212 in./244.43 in. Overall height: 69.8 in. Front/Rear tread: 65.8 in./62.7 in. Tires: [Standard] 8.75 x 16.5C; [Bonus Cab] 8.75 x 16.5C (front); 8.75 x 16.5D (rear)/[Crew Cab] 9.50 x 16.5C (front); 9.50 x 16.5D (rear).

CHASSIS [C3500]: Wheelbase: 131.5 in./164.5 in. Overall length: 212 in./244.43 in. Overall height: 71.8 in. Front/Rear tread: 65.8 in./62.7 in. Tires: [Standard] 8.75 x 16.5C; [Bonus/Crew Cab] 9.50 x 16.5E.

1981 GMC K1500 Sierra Wide-Side Pickup (RCA)

TECHNICAL: Manual, synchromesh transmission, column mounted gearshift lever. Speeds: [1500/2500 (except 2500 Crew Cab)] 3F/1R; [all 3500/2500 Crew Cab] Four-speed manual with floor-mounted shifter. Clutch: 11 in. diameter; [with 350-4V/400-4V/454-4V V-8s] 12 in. diameter. Rear axle: [1500] Salisbury semi-floating; [2500/3500] full-floating. Overall ratio: [C1500] 3.07:1; [C1500] diesel 2.76:1; [C2500/C3500] 4.11:1. Hydraulic four-wheel brakes, power-assisted: [front] disc; [rear] air-cooled finned cast iron drums. Kelsey-Hayes pressed steel disc wheels.

OPTIONS: [Caballero] Cloth bench seat (NC). Cloth bucket seats ($91) Cloth 55/45 seat ($181). Vinyl bench seat ($28). Vinyl bucket seats ($91). Vinyl 55/45 seat ($209). 4.4 liter two-barrel V-8 ($50) 5.0-liter four-barrel V-8 ($50). Air conditioning ($585). Performance rear axle ($19). Limited slip axle ($67). Heavy-duty battery ($20). Bumper rub strips ($43). Bumper guards ($48). Electric clock ($23). Conquista ($161). Console ($86). Heavy-duty cooling ($34 with A/C to $61 without). Tonneau cargo box cover ($113). Power locks ($93). California emissions ($46). Color-keyed mats ($13). Gauges and trip odometer ($92). 63-amp generator ($6 with A/C, $34 without). All tinted glass ($75). Halogen headlamps ($36). Special instrumentation ($159). Auxiliary lighting ($26). OSRV mirrors, left sport/left remote or right manual ($47). Twin remote sport mirrors ($73). Deluxe bodyside moldings ($53). Door edge guard moldings ($13). Front fender/bodyside/tailgate moldings ($49). Cargo box side rails ($77). Royal Knight package ($71). Power seat ($173). Cruise ($132). Tilt ($81). Sport suspension ($13). 22-gallon fuel tank ($22). Cargo box tie-downs ($20). Transmission: four-speed manual ($141); automatic ($349). Sport silver/or gold wheelcovers ($55). Wire wheelcovers ($135). Rally wheels ($49). Wheelcover locks ($34). Power windows ($140). Intermittent wipers ($41). [Jimmy/All Wide-Sides] Sierra Grande package, trucks with bucket seats ($290); others ($310). Plain High Sierra package, trucks with bucket seats ($394); others ($452); same on trucks with exterior decor package [and buckets] ($338); [and no buckets] ($395). Plain Sierra Classic package, trucks with bucket seats ($668); others ($718); same on trucks with exterior decor package [and buckets] ($642); [and no buckets] ($693). Vinyl bench seat (NC). Special custom cloth bench seat (NC). Street Coupe equipment ($231-$273). Two-tone paint (61); t/w High Sierra/Sierra Classic. Special two-tone paint ($256); t/w High Sierra ($222); t/w Sierra Grande ($185); t/w Sierra Classic ($138). Exterior Decor package: ($440); t/w High Sierra ($429); t/w Sierra Grande ($337); t/w Sierra Classic ($314). Special Sport two-tone with Street Coupe equipment (NC). Engines: 4.1L six (NC); 4.8L six (NC). 5.0L-2V V-8 ($295). 5.0L ESC V-8 ($345). 5.0L-4V V-8 ($345). 5.7L V-8 ($315). 7.4L V-8 ($425). Transmissions: automatic ($384); four-speed manual ($170). Optional axle ($26) 3.73 high-altitude axle ($26). Air conditioning ($591). Deluxe front appearance, included with Sierra Classic ($88). Locking rear axle ($88). Heavy-duty battery ($40). Auxiliary battery, 3500-watt ($101). Power brakes ($76). Bumpers: painted rear ($53); painted rear step, ($90) or t/w Street Coupe ($37); chrome front and rear, ($111) or t/w High Sierra, Sierra Classic or Sierra Grande ($82); chrome rear step ($151) or t/w Street Coupe ($98). Chrome front bumper guards ($34). Glide-out spare ($33). Side-mount spare ($24). Street Coupe equipment ($767); t/w bucket seats ($722). Electric clock with gauges ($60); or t/w Sierra Classic ($31). Engine oil cooler ($95). Heavy-duty transmission oil cooler ($47). Heavy-duty radiator cooler ($42). Power locks ($98). Dual exhausts ($41). Tachometer and gages ($90); or t/w Sierra Classic ($61). Heavy-duty generators ($47-51). Tinted glass ($35). Halogen headlamps ($26). Cargo lamps ($49); or t/w Street Coupe/Siera packages ($28). Roof marker lamps ($39). Cgar lighter ($24). Below-eye mirrors, painted ($39); stainless ($63). Camper mirror ($74). Sr. West Coast mirror ($50). Black bodyside moldings ($92). Bright bodyside moldings ($115) or t/w Sierra Grande ($12). Custom molding package ($126); or t/w High Sierra ($92); or t/w Sierra Grande ($23). Deluxe molding package ($138); or t/w High Sierra ($104); or t/w Sierra Grande ($35); or t/w special two-tone/deluxe two-tone/exterior decor package ($12). Door edge guards ($13). Wheel opening moldings ($23). Operating convenience package with door locks and power windows ($243). Fuel tank shield ($40); or with auxiliary fuel tank ($101). Heavy-duty shocks ($27). Pickup box side rails ($77). Cruise ($132) Front stabilizer ($27). Heavy-duty front stabilizer ($43). Power steering ($205); or included with Trailering Special. Tilt steering ($81). Custom steering wheel ($16). Auxiliary fuel tank ($177). Front towing device ($30). Weight distributing platform type trailer hitch ($127). Trailering Special package ($772); or t/w air conditioning ($725). Trim rings ($45) or standard with Rally wheels. C1500 or K1500 wheelcovers ($24). Forged aluminum wheels ($360). Rally wheels w/trim rings ($88). Styled wheels ($176). Power windows ($145). Sliding rear window ($88). Intermittant wipers ($34). Cold climate package ($98-$155, depending on trim level and trailering equipment). [Van] Custom high-back bucket seats $34). Swivel bucket seats ($420). Special two-tone paint ($185) Deluxe two-tone paint ($195). Exterior Decor package ($394). 5.0L-4V V-8 ($345); 5.7L V-8 ($345). Automatic transmission ($384). Locking rear axle ($191). Optional ratio axles ($26). Front air conditioning ($696). Front/rear air conditioning ($1,138). Heavy-duty battery ($40). Chrome front/rear bumpers ($58). Chrome bumper guards ($58). Chrome front bumper guards ($34). Electric clock ($27). Engine oil color ($95). Transmission oil cooler ($47). Heavy-duty cooling ($42). Power door locks ($147). California emissions ($80). Rear side door extender link ($29). Floor and wheelhouse carpeting ($145). Gauges ($29). Generators ($4-$75). Tinted glass all ($75). Tinted windshield ($25). One-way glass ($296). Swing-out rear door ($44). Halogen headlamps ($36). Rear heater ($156-189). Cigar lighter ($19). Auxiliary lighting ($77). Painted left/right below-eye-level mirrors ($39); stainless ($63). Black bodyside moldings ($102). Door edge guards ($13). Wheel opening moldings ($57). Operating convenience package ($292). Eight-passenger seating ($219). 12-passenger seating ($467). Swivel bucket seats ($426). Travel bed seating ($561-770). Heavy-duty shocks ($27). Cruise ($132). Heavy-duty rear springs ($26). Power steering ($217). Tilt wheel ($81). Custom wheel ($21). Rear door positive stop ($29). Front seat stowage compartment ($29). Body striping ($56) 33-gallon fuel tank ($68). Theft deterrent system ($146). Trailer hitch, deadweight type ($52); distribution platform type ($145). Trailering Special package ($456). Roof ventilator ($62). Special wheelcovers ($51). Forged aluminum wheels ($360). Rally wheels w/trim rings ($88). Styled wheels ($176). Power windows front side only ($145). Intemittent wipers ($34). STX trim ($516).

HISTORICAL: Calendar year sales: 141,335 distributed as follows: [Pickups] 97,599. [Vandura/Rally] 22,982; [Suburban] 4,349; [Jimmy] 4,689; [P-Series] 3,454. [Caballero] 3,994.

1981 GMC K1500 Jimmy Sport Utility Wagon 4x4 (RCA)

1982 GMC

1982 K1500 Jimmy Diesel Sport Utility Wagon 4x4 (OCW)

GMC — LIGHT TRUCK — (ALL SERIES) — SIX-CYLINDER/V-8: The latest Caballero had new front end styling with a cross-hatched grille design and dual rectangular headlights. A total of five new exterior colors were offered along with new two-tone combinations. Technical refinements included dual cowl-mounted fluidic windshield washers and a fender-mounted fixed mast radio antenna. A three-speed automatic transmission was standard on all 1982 Caballeros. Also included as regular equipment were a 3.8L V-6, power brakes, carpeting and a cloth bench seat. The Diablo added dual sport mirrors, front air dam, accent paint color on lower body and Rally wheels. Leading the 1982 GMC truck lineup were the new S15 models. Work on these trucks began in October, 1978 and they were regarded as GM's response to the increasing popularity of imported light trucks. Compared to the Chevy LUV, the new GMC S15 (and the Chevrolet S10) was 2 inches lower and had a wheelbase just 0.4 in. longer. Styling included single rectangular headlamps and a grille with three big square openings. Horizontal parking lamps were set in the bumper. The standard S15 came with a 1.9L four-cylinder engine, four-speed manual transmission, bench seat and dual OSRV mirrors. The Sierra version had a black bumper, less side trim and no GMC lettering in the center grille segment. There was a High Sierra and a Sierra Classic with chrome bumpers, GMC grille lettering, spoke wheelcovers and a lower body perimeter molding. Only Wide-Side boxes were offered, but they came in 6-ft. and 7.5-ft. lengths. Most mechanical components for the S15 were from General Motors' G-cars, which included the Chevrolet Monte Carlo and Pontiac Grand Prix. Its base four-cylinder engine and transmission were supplied by Isuzu. There was a sporty S15 Gypsy package, too. Regular trucks again had "ice-cube" tray grilles. Under the headlamps was a new grille extension with three vertical-slot type segments. Parking lamps were in the bumper. Other changes for 1982 included the 4.1 liter diesel engine which had as its standard transmission the same New Process four-speed transmission that was introduced during 1981 for the GMC Special Economy truck. Also available on some GMC models was a new four-speed automatic transmission, the THG-700R4, which had a lock-up torque converter that engaged in second, third and overdrive. Standard equipment included a 4.1 liter inline six (4.8 liter in C3500/K2500/K3500), three-speed manual transmission with column shift (four-speed floor shift on C3500/K3500), power brakes (C3500 and all 4x4s), and bench seat. A four-speed manual gearbox and power steering were standard on K1500s and all 4x4s included a two-speed transfer case. Jimmys included the 4.1 liter six, three-speed (four-speed on K1500), power brakes, vinyl bucket seats, chrome bumpers and, on 4x4s, automatic locking hubs and power steering.

I.D. DATA: In 1982, GM changed its VIN system only to add the S15 and revise engines offerings. Caballeros had the same coding system as trucks, except the engines in Caballeros used car coding. [Light-Duty Truck and Multi-purpose Passenger Vehicles (MPV)] Located on plate attached to left top of instrument panel; or on left-hand top of instrument panel; or on front of dash and toe panel left of steering colum in Value-Van. First symbol indicates country of origin: 1=USA; 2=Canada; 3=Japan. Second symbol indicates manufacturer: G=GM; 8=Isuzu (not applicable to GMC 1982). Third symbol indicates make: T=GMC truck; 5=GMC MPV (such as Suburban or Rally Wagon); 0=GMC van with fourth seat. Fourth symbol indicates GVWR/brake system: B=3001-4000 lbs./hydraulic; C=4001-5000/hydraulic; etc. through K=14,000-16,000 lbs./hydraulic. Fifth symbol indicates line and chassis: C=Conventional Cab/Jimmy; G=Vandura/Rally Wagon; K=Conventional Cab 4x4/Jimmy 4x4; P=Forward-Control (Value-Van).; S=S15 mini pickup; W=Caballero; Z=4x2 special body. The sixth symbol indicates model: 1=1/2 ton; 2=3/4-ton; 3=1-ton; 8=1/2-ton Caballero; 9=Chasis & Cowl. The seventh symbol indicates body type: 0=two-door sedan-pickup; 1=Hi-Cube or Cutaway Van; 2=Forward-Control; 3=four-door cab; 4=two-door cab; 5=van; 6=Suburban; 8=Jimmy (utility); 9=Stake. The eighth symbol indicated engine: [Caballero] K=3.8L (229 cid)/110 hp V-6 two-barrel; H=5.0L (305 cid)/135 hp V-8 four-barrel; J=4.4L (267 cid)/120 hp V-8. [Light-Duty and MPV] A=1.9L-2.0L Isuzu (119 cid)/82 hp two-barrel L4; B=2.8L (173 cid)/125 hp two-barrel V-6; C=6.2L (379 cid)/130 hp diesel V-8; J=6.2L (379 cid)/148 hp V-8; D=4.1L (250 cid)/115 hp two-barrel L-6; F=5.0L (305 cid)/155 hp four-barrel V-8; H=5.0L (305 cid)/160 hp four-barrel V-8; L=5.7L (350 cid)/165 hp V-8; M=5.7L (350 cid)/185 hp four-barrel V-8; N=1.8L (111 cid)/75 hp Isuzu L-4 two-barrel; P=5.7L (350 cid)/161 hp two-barrel V-8; S=2.2L (137 cid)/62 hp Isuzu L-4 diesel; T=4.8L (292 cid)/115 hp one-barrel L-6; W=7.4L (454 cid)/240 hp four-barrel V-8). The ninth symbol is a check digit. The 10th symbol indicates model year C=1982. The 11th symbol indicates assembly plant; GMC models were sourced from: B=Baltimore, Md.; Z=Fremont, Calif.; J=Janesville, Wis.; S=St. Louis; 3=Detroit (Chevrolet), Mich. (Value-Vans built in Chevrolet plant); F=Flint, Mich.; V=Pontiac, Mich. (GMC headquarters) and possibly other factories. The last six symbols were the production sequence number starting at 100001.

Model	Body Type	Price	Weight	Prod. Total
S15 — 1/2-Ton — 108 in./118 in. w.b. — V-6				
S14	Wide-Side Pickup 6-ft.	6270	2509	—
S14	Wide-Side Pickup 7.5-ft	6420	2584	—
Caballero — 1/2-Ton — 117.1 in. w.b. — V-6				
AW80	Pickup	7995	3294	—
AW80YE7	Diablo Pickup	8244	3300	—
K1500 Jimmy — 1/2-Ton — 106-1/2 in. w.b. — V-8				
K18	Utility Wagon	9874	4294	—
NOTE 1: 4x2 Jimmys have C18 prefix.				
G15 Vandura — 1/2-Ton — 110 in. w.b. — V-8				
TG11005	Vandura	6908	3708	—
TG11005	Rally	8122	4015	—
G1500 (006/306) Rally Wagon — 1/2-Ton — 125 in. w.b. — V-8				
TG11006	Custom Rally	9040	4273	—
TG11306	Rally STX	9268	4313	—
G2500 (005) Vandura — 3/4-Ton — 110 in. w.b. — V-8				
TG21005	Vandura	7256	3782	—
G2500 (006/306) Rally Wagon — 3/4-Ton — 125 in. w.b. — V-8				
TG21006	Rally	8486	4207	—
TG11306	Rally Custom	9204	4294	—
TG11306	Rally STX	9432	4334	—
G3500 (305) Vandura — 1-Ton — 125 in. w.b. — V-8				
TG31305	Vandura	8494	4251	—
G3500 (306) Rally — 1-Ton — 125 in. w.b. — V-8				
G3500 (331) Special Van — 1-Ton — 125 in. w.b. — V-8				
TG31303	Vandura Special	7261	3739	—
TG31306	Rally	10,228	4595	—
TG31306	Custom Rally	10,946	4682	—
TG31306	Rally STX	11,174	4854	—
NOTE 2: All vans available with 125 in. wheelbase option				
G3500 (331) Rally Camper — 1-Ton — 125 in. w.b. — V-8				
TG31331	Rally Camper Special	8452	3951	—
G3500 (331) Magna Van — 1-Ton — 125 in. w.b. — V-8				
TG31331	Magna Van 10-ft.	10,141	5515	—
G3500 (331) Magna Van — 1-Ton — 146 in. w.b. — V-8				
TG31331	Magna Van 12-ft.	11,607	5998	—
P2500 — 3/4-Ton — 125 in./133 in. w.b. — V-8				
TP20842	Van, 10-ft.	11,744	5777	—
P3500 — 1-Ton — 125 in./157 in. w.b. — V-8				
TP30842	Van 10-ft.	11,820	5998	—
C1500 (703) — 1/2-Ton — 117.5 in. w.b. — V-8				
TC10703	Chassis & Cab	—	—	—
TC10703	Fender-Side Pickup 6.5-ft.	6689	3418	—
TC10703	Wide-Side Pickup 6.5-ft.	6564	2584	—
C1500 (903) — 1/2-Ton — 131.5 in. w.b. — V-8				
TC10903	Wide-Side Pickup 8-ft.	6714	3613	—
C1500 (906) — 1/2-Ton — 131.5 in. w.b. — V-8				
TC10906	Suburban	9744	4295	—
C2500 (903) — 3/4-Ton — 129.5 in. w.b. — V-8				
TC20903	Chassis & Cab	7865	3661	—
TC20903	Fender-Side Pickup 8-ft.	7857	3956	—
TC20903	Wide-Side Pickup, 8-ft.	7732	3999	—
C2500 (943) — 3/4-Ton — 164.5 in. w.b. — V-8				
TC20943	Wide-Side Bonus Cab Pickup	9123	4748	—
TC20943	Wide-Side Crew Cab Pickup	9439	4809	—

	C2500 (906) — 3/4-Ton — 129.5 in. w.b. — V-8			
TC20906	Suburban	9978	4677	—

	C3500 (903) — 1-Ton — 131.5 in. w.b.			
TC30903	Chassis & Cab	7990	3973	—
TC30903	Fender-Side Pickup 8-ft.	8474	4323	—
TC30903	Wide-Side Pickup 8-ft.	8349	4394	—

	C3500 (943/003) — 1-Ton — 164.5 in. w.b. — V-8			
TC30943	Chassis & Bonus Cab	8943	4400	—
TC30943	Wide-Side Bonus Cab Pickup	9286	4817	—
TC30943	Chassis & Crew Cab	9259	4626	—
TC30943	Wide-Side Crew Cab Pickup	9602	4878	—

1982 GMC Sierra Classic Wide-Side Pickup (OCW)

ENGINE [Caballero base V-6]: V-type. OHV. Six-cylinder. Cast iron block. Bore & stroke: 3.8 x 3.4 in. Displacement: 231 cid/3.8 liter. Net horsepower: 110 at 3800 rpm. Net torque: 190 lbs.-ft. at 1600 rpm. Carburetor: Rochester two-barrel. Passenger car engine code A. Source: Buick.

ENGINE [Optional Caballero]: V-8. OHV. V-8. Cast iron block. Bore & stroke: 3.74 x 3.48 in. Displacement: 305 cid/5.0 liter. Net horsepower: 135 at 4200 rpm. Net torque: 235 lbs.-ft. at 2400 rpm. Hydraulic valve lifters. Carburetor: Rochester four-barrel. Passenger/truck engine code H. Source: Chevrolet.

ENGINE [Optional Caballero]: V-8. OHV. Six-cylinder. Cast iron block. Bore & stroke: 3.5 x 3.48 in. Displacement: 267 cid/4.4 liter. Net horsepower: 120 at 3600 rpm. Net torque: 215 lbs.-ft. at 2000 rpm. Hydraulic valve lifters. Carburetor: Rochester four-barrel. Passenger/truck engine code J. Source: Chevrolet.

ENGINE [S15 base]: Inline. OHC. Four-cylinder. Bore & stroke: 3.42 x 3.23 in. Displacement: 119 cid/sometimes called 1.9 liter or 2.0 liter. Net horsepower: 82 at 4600 rpm. Net torque: 101 lbs.-ft. at 3000 rpm. Hydraulic valve lifters. Carburetor: two-barrel. Light-duty truck engine code A. Source: Isuzu.

1982 GMC Caballero 1/2-Ton Sport Pickup (OCW)

1982 GMC Vandura Passenger Van (OCW)

ENGINE [Optional S15]: Inline. OHV. Six-cylinder. Bore & stroke: 3.5 x 2.99 in. Displacement: 173 cid/2.8 liter. Net horsepower: 125 at 4800 rpm. Net torque: 150 lbs.-ft. at 2200 rpm. Hydraulic valve lifters. Carburetor: two-barrel. Engine code B. Source: Chevrolet.

ENGINE [Optional diesel]: V-type. OHV. Eight-cylinder. Cast iron block. Bore & stroke: 3.98 x 3.82 in. Displacement: 379 cid/6.2 liter. Net horsepower: 130 at 3600 rpm. Net torque: 240 at 2000 rpm. Injected diesel. Engine code C. Source: Chevrolet.

ENGINE [C1500 base six]: Inline. OHV. Six-cylinder. Cast iron block. Bore & stroke: 3.876 x 3.530 in. Displacement: 250 cid/4.1 liter. Compression ratio: 8.25:1. Net horsepower: 115 at 3600 rpm. Net torque: 200 lbs.-ft. at 2000 rpm. [above 6,001 lb. GVW]. Net horsepower 100 at 3600 rpm. Net torque: 175 lbs.-ft. at 1800 rpm. Seven main bearings. Hydraulic valve lifters. Carburetor: Mono-Jet model 1ME. Engine code D. Source: Chevrolet.

ENGINE [Optional C1500]: V-type. OHV. Eight-cylinder. Cast iron block. Bore & stroke: 3.736 x 3.480 in. Displacement: 305 cid/5.0 liter. Compression ratio: 8.5:1. Net horsepower: 155 at 4000 rpm. Net torque: 245 lbs.-ft. at 1600 rpm. Five main bearings. Hydraulic valve lifters. Carburetor: four-barrel model. Engine code F. Source: Chevrolet.

ENGINE [Optional C1500/C2500/K1500/Vans/Suburbans]: (Not available in California). V-type. OHV. Eight-cylinder. Cast iron block. Bore & stroke: 3.736 x 3.480 in. Displacement: 305 cid/5.0 liter. Compression ratio: 9.2:1. Net horsepower: 160 at 4400 rpm. Max torque: 235 lbs.-ft. at 2000 rpm. C1500 Brake hp: 165 at 4400 rpm. Max torque: 240 lbs.-ft. at 2000 rpm. Five main bearings. Hydraulic valve lifters. Carburetor: Rochester Staged model four-barrel, Electronic Spark Control (ESC). Code H. Source: Chevrolet.

ENGINE [Optional diesel]: V-type. OHV. Eight-cylinder. Cast iron block. Bore & stroke: 3.98 x 3.82 in. Displacement: 379 cid/6.2 liter. Net horsepower: 148 at 3600 rpm. Net torque: 246 at 2000 rpm. Injected diesel. Engine code J. Source: Chevrolet.

ENGINE [Optional: all models]: V-type. OHV. Eight-cylinder. Cast iron block. Bore & stroke: 4.0 x 3.480 in. Displacement: 350 cid/5.7 liter. Compression ratio: 8.5:1. Net horsepower: 165 at 3800 rpm. Net torque: 275 lbs.-ft. at 1600 rpm. Five main bearings. Hydraulic valve lifters. Carburetor: four-barrel model M4MC/MV. Engine code L. Source: Chevrolet.

ENGINE [Optional: all models]: V-type. OHV. Eight-cylinder. Cast iron block. Bore & stroke: 4.0 x 3.480 in. Displacement: 350 cid/5.7 liter. Compression ratio: 8.5:1. Net horsepower: 185 at 4000 rpm. Net torque: 285 lbs.-ft. at 2400 rpm. Five main bearings. Hydraulic valve lifters. Carburetor: four-barrel model M4MC/MV. Engine code M. Source: Chevrolet.

ENGINE [S15]: Inline. OHC. OHV. Four-cylinder. Bore & stroke: 3.31 x 3.23 in. Displacement: 111 cid/1.8 liter. Net horsepower: 75 at 5000 rpm. Net torque: 88 at 3000 rpm. Hydraulic valve lifters. Carburetor: two-barrel. Engine code N. Source: Isuzu.

ENGINE [Optional: all models]: V-type. OHV. Eight-cylinder. Cast iron block. Bore & stroke: 4.0 x 3.480 in. Displacement: 350 cid/5.7 liter. Compression ratio: 8.5:1. Net horsepower: 161 at 3800 rpm. Net torque: 275 lbs.-ft. at 2400 rpm. Five main bearings. Hydraulic valve lifters. Carburetor: four-barrel model M4MC/MV. Engine code P. Source: Chevrolet.

ENGINE [S15]: Inline. OHC. OHV. Four-cylinder. Bore & stroke: 3.46 x 3.62 in. Displacement: 137 cid/2.2 liter. Net horsepower: 62 at 4300 rpm. Net torque: 96 at 2200 rpm. Hydraulic valve lifters. Injected diesel. Engine code S. Source: Isuzu.

ENGINE [C2500/C3500/P base six]: Inline. OHV. Six-cylinder. Cast iron block. Bore & stroke: 3.8764 x 4.120 in. Displacement: 292 cid/4.8 liter. Compression ratio: 8.0:1. Net horsepower: 115 at 4000 rpm. Net torque: 210 lbs.-ft. at 1800 rpm. Seven main bearings. Hydraulic valve lifters. Carburetor: one-barrel. Engine code T. Source: Chevrolet.

ENGINE [Optional: C1500/C2500/C3500/K1500/K2500/K3500]: V-type. OHV. Eight-cylinder. Cast iron block. Bore & stroke: 4.250 x 4.0 in. Displacement: 454 cid/7.4 liter. Compression ratio: 8.5:1. Net horsepower: 240 at 3800 rpm. Net torque: 375 lbs.-ft. at 3200 rpm. Five main bearings. Hydraulic valve lifters. Carburetor: four-barrel model M4MC/MV. Engine code W. Source: Chevrolet.

1982 GMC Vandura Panel Delivery Van (OCW)

CHASSIS [S15]: Wheelbase: 108.3/117.9 in. Overall length: 178.2/194.1 in. Overall heigth: 59 in. Front/Rear tread: 64.7 x 64.7 in. Tires: P195 x 75R14, fiberglass-belted. Optional: P195 x 75R14, steel-belted P205 x 75R14, P205 x 70R14.

CHASSIS [Caballero]: Wheelbase: 117.1 in. Overall length: 201.6 in. Overall height: 53.8 in. Front/Rear tread: 58.5 in./57.8 in. Tires: P205 x 75R14.

CHASSIS [Jimmy]: Wheelbase: 106.5 in. Overall length: 184.4 in. Overall height: 69.8 in. Front/Rear tread: 66.7 in./63.7 in. Tires H78 x 15B.

CHASSIS [G1500]: Wheelbase: 110 in./125 in. Overall length: 178 in./202.2 in. Overall height: 78.8 in./81.2 in. Tires: E78 x 15B or F78 x 15B.

CHASSIS [G2500]: Wheelbase: 110 in./125 in. Overall length: 178 in./202.2 in. Overall height: 78.8 x 81.2 in. Tires: J78 x 15B.

CHASSIS [G3500]: Wheelbase: 110 in./146 in. Tires: [Vandura/Rally] 8.00 x 16.5C; [Camper Special/Magna] 8.75 x 16.5D.

CHASSIS [P2500]: Wheelbase: 125 in./133 in. Overall length: 220.75 in./244.75 in. Tires: 8.75 x 16.5C.

CHASSIS [P3500]: Wheelbase: 125 in./157 in. Overall length: 220.75/268.75 in. Tires: 8.75 x 16.5C.

CHASSIS [C1500]: Wheelbase: 117.5/12.5 in. Overall length: 191.3 x/212 in. Overall height: 69.8 in. Front/Rear tread: 65.8 x/62.7 in. Tires: G78 x 15B.

CHASSIS [C2500]: Wheelbase: 117.5 in./131.5 in./164.5 in. Overall length: 191.3 x/212 in./244.43 in. Overall height: 69.8 in. Front/Rear tread: 65.8 x/62.7 in. Tires: [Standard] 8.75 x 16.5C; [Bonus Cab] 8.75 x 16.5C (front); 8.75 x 16.5D (rear) /[Crew Cab] 9.50 x 16.5C (front); 9.50 x 16.5D (rear).

465

CHASSIS [C3500]: Wheelbase: 131.5 in./164.5 in. Overall length: 212 in./244.43 in. Overall height: 71.8 in. Front/Rear tread: 65.8 in./62.7 in. Tires: [Standard] 8.75 x 16.5C; [Bonus/Crew Cab] 9.50 x 16.5E.

TECHNICAL: Manual, synchromesh. Speeds: 3F/1R; [S15] 4F/1R; [C3500/K2500/K3500] 4F/1R. Column-mounted three-speed gearshift; floor-mounted four-speed gearshift. [Clutch] 11 in. diameter in all full-sized models; 12 in. diameter clutch optional. Rear axle: [G1500/C1500/K1500/C2500/K2500] semi-floating; [all others] full-floating. Overall ratio: [C1500] 2.73:1; [C2500/K2500] 3.42:1; [K3500 Bonus/Crew] 4.56:1; all other full-sized models 4.10:1; [S15] 2.56/2.73/3.08/3.42/3.73, depending on rpm, engine, and transmission. [Brakes] Four-wheel hydraulic system, front disc, rear drum brakes. Kelsey-Hayes pressed steel wheels.

1982 GMC K2500 High Sierra Suburban (RCA)

OPTIONS: [Caballero/S15/C and K Jimmy and pickup]: [S15] 2.8L V-6 ($215) [Caballero] 4.4L V-8 ($61); 5.0L V-8 ($61). [C/K/G] 5.0L ESC V-8 ($147) [C/K/G] 5.7L V-8 ($281-296). [C/K] 6.2L diesel V-8 in Jimmy, C/K1500 and C2500 ($1,146); in K2500 ($999). Transmissions: four-speed, in C1500 ($170); four-speed manual overdrive, C1500 w/o Super Saver ($170); C2500/K1500/K2500 ($65); three-speed automatic, in S15/C1500 ($376); in C2500/K2500/C3500/K3500 ($391). Four-speed automatic, in C1500 Jimmy ($171); in K1500 Jimmy/C1500/K1500/C2500/K2500 ($547). Air conditioning ($532-581). Caballero Amirillo package ($183). Deluxe Jimmy/C/K front end appearance ($86). Cabarello limited-slip axle ($66). Optional axle ratios ($19-31). Auxiliary battery ($345). Heavy-duty battery ($22-39). S-15 power brakes ($75). Heavy-duty power brakes C/K ($62-137). C/K pickup chrome rear bumper ($83). C/K pickup rear step bumper, painted ($91); chrome ($152). S15 color-keyed front bumper ($49). S15 color-keyed rear bumper ($110). Jimmy front and rear deluxe chrome bumpers ($38). C/K glide-out spare ($24). Sidemount spare ($34). Electric quartz clock, Caballero ($28); Jimmy and pickup ($61); Jimmy and pickup t/w Sierra Classic ($32). S15 digital clock ($52). Cold Climate package ($98-186). S15 console ($83) Engine oil cooler, except Caballero ($96). Transmission oil cooler ($48-89). Heavy-duty cooling system ($35-61). Caballero cargo box tonneau cover ($112). Diesel equipment package: Jimmy ($996); C1500 ($1,105); C2500 ($1,093); C3500 ($1,093); K1500/K2500 ($894); K3500 ($673). Power door locks ($91-99). C/K dual exhaust system ($42). Exterior decor package, Jimmy/C/K ($240-433). Fuel tanks, S15 [20-gallon]/Caballero [22-gallon]/Jimmy [31-gallon] ($34/$22/$34). Cargo box tie-downs ($20). Sport Caballero and Diablo wheelcovers ($54). Wire wheelcovers ($132). Rally wheels ($49-89). Wheelcover locks ($34). Power windows ($143). Intermittent wipers ($41). S15 High Sierra ($279) S15 Sierra Classic ($473). Jimmy/C/K High Sierra package ($179-273). Jimmy/C/K Sierra Classic package ($513-799). Vinyl bench seat (NC). Special custom cloth bench seat (NC). Two-tone paint ($61); t/w High Sierra/Sierra Classic. Special two-tone paint ($256); t/w High Sierra ($222); t/w Sierra Grande ($185); t/w Sierra Classic ($138). Exterior Decor package ($440); t/w High Sierra ($429); t/w Sierra Grande ($337); t/w Sierra Classic ($314). Tachometer and gauges ($90); or t/w Sierra Classic ($61). Heavy-duty generators ($47-51). Tinted glass ($35). Halogen headlamps ($26). Cargo lamps ($49). Roof marker lamps ($39). Cigarette lighter ($24). Below-eye mirrors, painted ($39); stainless ($63). Camper mirror ($74). Sr. West Coast mirror ($50). Black bodyside moldings ($92). Bright bodyside moldings ($115) or t/w Sierra Grande ($12). Custom molding package ($126); or t/w High Sierra ($92); or t/w Sierra Grande ($23). Deluxe molding package ($138); or t/w High Sierra ($104); or t/w Sierra Grande ($35); or t/w special two-tone/deluxe two-tone/exterior decor package ($12). Door edge guards ($13). Wheel opening moldings ($23). Operating convenience package w/door locks and power windows ($243). Fuel tank shield ($40); or with auxiliary fuel tank ($101). Heavy-duty shocks ($27). Pickup box side rails ($77). Cruise ($132) Front stabilizer ($27). Heavy-duty front stabilizer ($43). Power steering ($205); or included with Trailering Special. Tilt steering ($81). Custom steering wheel ($16). Auxiliary fuel tank ($177). Front towing device ($30). Weight distributing platform type trailer hitch ($127). Trailering Special package ($772); or t/w air conditioning ($725). Trim rings ($45) or standard with Rally wheels. C1500 or K1500 wheelcovers ($24). Forged aluminum wheels ($360). Rally wheels w/trim rings ($88). Styled wheels ($176). Power windows ($145). Sliding rear window ($89). Intermittent wipers ($34). Cold climate package ($98-$155, depending on trim level and trailering equipment). [Van] Custom high-back bucket seats $34. Swivel bucket seats ($420). Special two-tone paint ($185) Deluxe two-tone paint ($195). Exterior Decor package ($394). 5.0L-4V V-8 ($345); 5.7L V-8 ($345). Automatic transmission ($384). Locking rear axle ($191). Optional ratio axles ($26). Front air conditioning ($696). Front/rear air conditioning ($1,138). Heavy-duty battery ($40). Chrome front/rear bumpers ($58). Chrome bumper guards ($34). Chrome front bumper guards ($34). Electric clock ($27). Engine oil color ($95). Transmission oil cooler ($47). Heavy-duty cooling ($42). Power door locks ($147). California emissions ($80). Rear side door extender link ($29). Floor and wheelhouse carpeting ($145). Gauges ($29). Generators ($4-$75). Tinted glass all ($75). Tinted windshield ($25). One-way glass ($296). Swing-out rear door ($44). Halogen headlamps ($36). Rear heater ($156-189). Cigarette lighter ($19). Auxiliary lighting ($77). Painted left/right below-eye-level mirrors ($39); stainless ($63). Black bodyside moldings ($102). Door edge guards ($13). Wheel opening moldings ($57). Operating convenience package ($292). Eight-passenger seating ($219). 12-passenger seating ($467). Swivel bucket seats ($426). Travel bed seating ($561-770). Heavy-duty shocks ($27). Cruise ($132). Heavy-duty rear springs ($26). Power steering ($217). Tilt wheel ($81). Custom wheel ($21). Rear door positive stop ($29). Front seat stowage compartment ($29). Body striping ($56) 33-gallon fuel tank ($68). Theft deterrent system ($146). Trailer hitch, deadweight type ($52); distribution platform type ($145). Trailering Special package ($456). Roof ventilator ($62). Special wheelcovers ($51). Forged aluminum wheels ($360). Rally wheels w/ trim rings ($88). Styled wheels ($176). Power windows front side only ($145). Intermittent wipers ($34). STX trim ($516).

(Notes on 1982 option listing: w/means with; w/o means without; t/w means teamed with; L, as in 5.0L, means engine displacement in liters; V, as in 5.0L-2V, means number of venturis (barrels) in carburetor. Above lists are for S15, Caballero, C/K pickup [typical of all pickups/Jimmy] and G2500 Rally Van [typical of G-Series vans]. Actual equipment availability and prices will vary for each line or even for body styles within a line.)

1982 GMC K1500 Jimmy Diesel Sport Utility Wagon 4x4 (RCA)

1983 GMC

1983 GMC High Sierra Wide-Side Pickup (OCW)

GMC — LIGHT-TRUCK — (ALL SERIES) — FOUR-CYLINDER/SIX-CYLINDER/V-8: Caballeros looked virtually the same as last year with a very tight-patterned "ice-cube tray" grille. The Amarillo trim package was back. The general appearance of S15s remained the same. Added to the S15 line were 4x4 and extended cab models. Vying for the attention of downsized truck buyers was the S15 Jimmy, which was 15.3 in. shorter and 14.8 in narrower than the full-sized Jimmy. It had an all-new 100.5 in. wheelbase and two-door wagon (with tailgate) type body. Sierra Classic and Gypsy options were offered for the S15 Jimmy, which was a 4x4 only model. In the unchanged full-size truck/Suburban/Jimmy bodies there were two new grilles. One had a horizontal center bar and two vertical dividers framing six rectangles with parking lamps in the lower, outer rectangles. Twin rectangular headlamps were stacked vertically. A fancier deluxe grille (standard in Sierra Classics) divided each of the rectangles into three smaller squares. Both grilles had GMC letters at the middle of the horizontal center divider. Moving the parking lamps to the grille eliminated the need for a different front bumper on trucks with the deluxe grille. Improving the trucks' resistance to corrosion was added use of galvanized steel in the pickup box front panel, plus a Zincrometal inner hood liner. High Sierra and Sierra Classic upgrades were optional. The G2500 and G3500 Vans and Sport Vans were now offered with the 6.2 liter diesel engine as well as the four-speed overdrive automatic transmission. Numerous refinements were also part of the 1983 GMC van scene. These included a revised steering wheel angle that was close to that used on pickup models and a floor-mounted manual transmission lever. Also installed on the vans were wet-arms windshield washers with wiper arm located nozzles, a new rear door hinge pivot, new rear latch and floating roller mechanism for the sliding door and an interior hood release. All vans with manual transmission could be ordered with a tilt steering wheel. Anti-chip coating was installed along the lower body from the front wheel wheels to the rear doors of all vans. Value-Vans were about the same.

I.D. DATA: The VIN is found on a plate attached to the top left of the instrument panel or sticker inside glove box. The VIN has 17 symbols. The first three symbols indicate country of origin, manufacturer and type of vehicle. The fourth symbol indicates GVW range. The fifth, sixth and seventh symbols indicate series, nominal (tonnage) rating and body style. The eighth symbol indicates engine: [All] A=1.9L-2.0L Isuzu (119 cid)/82 hp two-barrel L-4; B=2.8L (173 cid)/125 hp two-barrel V-6; C=6.2L (379 cid)/130 hp diesel V-8; D=4.1L (250 cid)/115 hp two-barrel L-6; F=5.0L (305 cid)/155 hp four-barrel V-8; H=5.0L (305 cid)/160 hp four-barrel V-8; J=6.2L (379 cid)/148 hp diesel V-8; L=5.7L (350 cid)/165 hp V-8; M=5.7L (350 cid)/185 hp four-barrel V-8; N=1.8L (111 cid)/75 hp Isuzu L-4 two-barrel; T=4.8L (292 cid)/115 hp one-barrel L-6; W=7.4L (454 cid)/240 hp four-barrel V-8. Y=2.0L (121 cid)/110 hp L4. Z (diesel) =5.7L (350 cid)/105 hp Olds diesel V-8. The ninth symbol is a check digit. The 10th symbol indicates model year D=1983. The eleventh symbol indicates assembly plant; GMC models were sourced from: B=Baltimore, Md.; Z=Fremont, Calif.; J=Janesville, Wis.; S=St. Louis; 3=Detroit (Chevrolet), Mich. (Value-Vans built in Chevrolet plant); F=Flint, Mich.; V=Pontiac, Mich. (GMC headquarters) and possibly other factories. The last six symbols were the production sequence number starting at 100001.

1983 GMC S15 Mini Sport Pickup (OCW)

1983 GMC Sierra Classic "Indy Hauler" Wide-Side Pickup (IMSC/JLM)

Model	Body Type	Price	Weight	Prod. Total
Caballero — 1/2-Ton Sedan-Pickup				
GW80	Base	8191	3372	—
GW80YE7	Diablo	8445	3337	—
K1500 Jimmy — 1/2-Ton — Sport Utility 4x4				
TK10516	Hardtop Utility	10,287	4426	—

1983 GMC S15 Jimmy Sport Utility Wagon (OCW)

S15 Jimmy — 1/2-Ton — Mini Sport Utility Wagon 4x4

TT10516	Hardtop Utility	9433	3206	—

NOTE 1: All 4x2 Jimmy/S15 Jimmy models have TC prefix.

G1500 — 1/2-Ton — Vandura/Rally Wagon

TG11005	Vandura	7101	3711	—
TG11006	Rally	8597	4039	—
TG11306	Rally Custom	9533	—	—
TG11306	Rally STX	9789	—	—

G2500 — 3/4-Ton — Vandura/Rally Wagon

TG21005	Vandura	7714	3812	—
TG21306	Rally	8968	4278	—
TG21306	Rally Custom	9701	—	—
TG21306	Rally STX	9957	—	—

Standard Catalog of Light-Duty Trucks

1983 GMC K1500 Jimmy Sport Utility Wagon (OCW)

G3500 — 1-Ton — Vandura/Rally Wagon

TG2305	Vandura	8718	4399	—
TG2306	Rally	11,371	4719	—
TG2306	Rally Custom	12,104	—	—
TG2306	Rally STX	12,306	—	—

P2500 — 3/4-Ton Forward-Control

P2500	Value Van	12,588	5860	—

P3500 — 1-Ton Forward- Control

TP30842	Value Van	12,107	5946	—

S15 — 1/2-Ton Mini-Pickup

TS10603	Wide-Side Pickup 6-ft.	6343	2537	—
TS10803	Wide-Side Pickup 7.5-ft.	6496	2618	—
TS10653	Extended Cab Pickup	6725	2647	—

C1500 — 1/2-Ton Conventional

TC10703	Fender-Side Pickup 6.5-ft.	6835	3408	—
TC10703	Wide-Side Pickup 6.5-ft.	6707	3471	—
TC10903	Wide-Side Pickup 8-ft.	6860	3633	—
TC10906	Suburban	9951	4293	—

C2500 — 3/4-Ton Conventional

TC20903	Chassis & Cab	8032	3614	—
TC20903	Fender-Side Pickup 8-ft.	8525	3964	—
TC20903	Wide-Side Pickup 8-ft.	8397	4025	—
TC20943	Crew Cab Pickup	9637	4806	—
TC20906	Suburban	10,187	4697	—

C3500 — 1-Ton Conventional

TC30903	Chassis & Cab	8160	3965	—
TC30903	Fender-Side Pickup 8-ft.	8654	429	—
TC30903	Wide-Side Pickup 8-ft.	8526	4380	—
TC30943	Chassis & Bonus Cab	912	4406	—
TC30943	Bonus Cab Pickup	9481	4815	—
TC30943	Chassis & Crew Cab	9453	4467	—
TC30943	Crew Cab Pickup	9803	4878	—

NOTE 2: All 4x4 conventional light-duty trucks have TK prefix.

ENGINE [Caballero base V-6]: V-type. OHV. Six-cylinder. Cast iron block. Bore & stroke: 3.8 x 3.4 in. Displacement: 231 cid/3.8 liter. Net horsepower: 110 at 3800 rpm. Net torque: 190 lbs.-ft. at 1600 rpm. Carburetor: Rochester two-barrel. Passenger car engine code A. Source: Buick.

1983 GMC Caballero 1/2-Ton Sport Diesel Pickup (OCW)

1983 GMC Rally Wagon Passenger Van (OCW)

ENGINE [Optional Caballero]: V-8. OHV. V-8. Cast iron block. Bore & stroke: 3.74 x 3.48 in. Displacement: 305 cid/5.0 liter. Net horsepower: 135 at 4200 rpm. Net torque: 235 lbs.-ft. at 2400 rpm. Hydraulic valve lifters. Carburetor: Rochester four-barrel. Passenger/truck engine code H. Source: Chevrolet.

1983 GMC Suburban Carryall (OCW)

ENGINE [Optional Caballero]: V-8. OHV. Six-cylinder. Cast iron block. Bore & stroke: 3.5 x 3.48 in. Displacement: 267 cid/4.4 liter. Net horsepower: 120 at 3600 rpm. Net torque: 215 lbs.-ft. at 2000 rpm. Hydraulic valve lifters. Carburetor: Rochester four-barrel. Passenger/truck engine code J. Source: Chevrolet.
ENGINE [S15 base]: Inline. OHC. Four-cylinder. Bore & stroke: 3.42 x 3.23 in. Displacement: 119 cid/sometimes called 1.9 liter or 2.0 liter. Net horsepower: 82 at 4600 rpm. Net torque: 101 lbs.-ft. at 3000 rpm. Hydraulic valve lifters. Carburetor: two-barrel. Light-duty truck engine code A. Source: Isuzu.
ENGINE [Optional S15]: Inline. OHV. Six-cylinder. Bore & stroke: 3.5 x 2.99 in. Displacement: 173 cid/2.8 liter. Net horsepower: 125 at 4800 rpm. Net torque: 150 lbs.-ft. at 2200 rpm. Hydraulic valve lifters. Carburetor: two-barrel. Engine code B. Source: Chevrolet.
ENGINE [Optional diesel]: V-type. OHV. Eight-cylinder. Cast iron block. Bore & stroke: 3.98 x 3.82 in. Displacement: 379 cid/6.2 liter. Net horsepower: 130 at 3600 rpm. Net torque: 240 at 2000 rpm. Injected diesel. Engine code C. Source: Chevrolet.
ENGINE [C1500 base six]: Inline. OHV. Six-cylinder. Cast iron block. Bore & stroke: 3.876 x 3.530 in. Displacement: 250 cid/4.1 liter. Compression ratio: 8.25:1. Net horsepower: 115 at 3600 rpm. Net torque: 200 lbs.-ft. at 2000 rpm. [above 6,001 lb. GVW]. Net horsepower 100 at 3600 rpm. Net torque: 175 lbs.-ft. at 1800 rpm. Seven main bearings. Hydraulic valve lifters. Carburetor: Mono-Jet model 1ME. Engine code D. Source: Chevrolet.
ENGINE [Optional C1500]: V-type. OHV. Eight-cylinder. Cast iron block. Bore & stroke: 3.736 x 3.480 in. Displacement: 305 cid/5.0 liter. Compression ratio: 8.5:1. Net horsepower: 155 at 4000 rpm. Net torque: 245 lbs.-ft. at 1600 rpm. Five main bearings. Hydraulic valve lifters. Carburetor: four-barrel model. Engine code F. Source: Chevrolet.

1983 GMC K2500 High Sierra Suburban 4x4 (RCA)

ENGINE [Optional: C1500/C2500/K1500/Vans/Suburbans]: (Not available in California.) V-type. OHV. Eight-cylinder. Cast iron block. Bore & stroke: 3.736 x 3.480 in. Displacement: 305 cid/5.0 liter. Compression ratio: 9.2:1. Net horsepower: 160 at 4400 rpm. Max torque: 235 lbs.-ft. at 2000 rpm. C1500 Brake hp: 165 at 4400 rpm. Max torque: 240 lbs.-ft. at 2000 rpm. Five main bearings. Hydraulic valve lifters. Carburetor: Rochester Staged model four-barrel, Electronic Spark Control (ESC). Code H. Source: Chevrolet.

ENGINE [Optional diesel]: V-type. OHV. Eight-cylinder. Cast iron block. Bore & stroke: 3.98 x 3.82 in. Displacement: 379 cid/6.2 liter. Net horsepower: 148 at 3600 rpm. Net torque: 246 at 2000 rpm. Injected diesel. Engine code J. Source: Chevrolet.
ENGINE [Optional: all models]: V-type. OHV. Eight-cylinder. Cast iron block. Bore & stroke: 4.0 x 3.480 in. Displacement: 350 cid/5.7 liter. Compression ratio: 8.5:1. Net horsepower: 165 at 3800 rpm. Net torque: 275 lbs.-ft. at 1600 rpm. Five main bearings. Hydraulic valve lifters. Carburetor: four-barrel model M4MC/MV. Engine code L. Source: Chevrolet.
ENGINE [Optional: all models]: V-type. OHV. Eight-cylinder. Cast iron block. Bore & stroke: 4.0 x 3.480 in. Displacement: 350 cid/5.7 liter. Compression ratio: 8.5:1. Net horsepower: 185 at 4000 rpm. Net torque: 285 lbs.-ft. at 2400 rpm. Five main bearings. Hydraulic valve lifters. Carburetor: four-barrel model M4MC/MV. Engine code M. Source: Chevrolet.
ENGINE [S15]: Inline. OHC. OHV. Four-cylinder. Bore & stroke: 3.31 x 3.23 in. Displacement: 111 cid/1.8 liter. Net horsepower: 75 at 5000 rpm. Net torque: 88 at 3000 rpm. Hydraulic valve lifters. Carburetor: two-barrel. Engine code N. Source: Isuzu.
ENGINE [Optional: all models]: V-type. OHV. Eight-cylinder. Cast iron block. Bore & stroke: 4.0 x 3.480 in. Displacement: 350 cid/5.7 liter. Compression ratio: 8.5:1. Net horsepower: 161 at 3800 rpm. Net torque: 275 lbs.-ft. at 2400 rpm. Five main bearings. Hydraulic valve lifters. Carburetor: four-barrel model M4MC/MV. Engine code P. Source: Chevrolet.
ENGINE [S15]: Inline. OHC. OHV. Four-cylinder. Bore & stroke: 3.46 x 3.62 in. Displacement: 137 cid/2.2 liter. Net horsepower: 62 at 4300 rpm. Net torque: 96 at 2200 rpm. Hydraulic valve lifters. Injected diesel. Engine code S. Source: Isuzu.
ENGINE [C2500/C3500/P base six]: Inline. OHV. Six-cylinder. Cast iron block. Bore & stroke: 3.8764 x 4.120 in. Displacement: 292 cid/4.8 liter. Compression ratio: 8.0:1. Net horsepower: 115 at 4000 rpm. Net torque: 210 lbs.-ft. at 1800 rpm. Seven main bearings. Hydraulic valve lifters. Carburetor: one-barrel. Engine code T. Source: Chevrolet.
ENGINE [Optional: C1500/C2500/C3500/K1500/K2500/K3500]: V-type. OHV. Eight-cylinder. Cast iron block. Bore & stroke: 4.250 x 4.0 in. Displacement: 454 cid/7.4 liter. Compression ratio: 8.5:1. Net horsepower: 240 at 3800 rpm. Net torque: 375 lbs.-ft. at 3200 rpm. Five main bearings. Hydraulic valve lifters. Carburetor: four-barrel model M4MC/MV. Engine code W. Source: Chevrolet.

1983 GMC S-15 Jimmy Sport Utility Wagon (RCA)

CHASSIS [S15]: Wheelbase: 108.3/117.9 in. Overall length: 178.2/194.1 in. Overall height: 59 in. Front/Rear tread: 64.7 x 64.7 in. Tires: P195 x 75R14, fiberglass-belted. Optional: P195 x 75R14, steel-belted P205 x 75R14, P205 x 70R14.
CHASSIS [Caballero]: Wheelbase: 117.1 in. Overall length: 201.6 in. Overall height: 53.8 in. Front/Rear tread: 58.5 in./57.8 in. Tires: P205 x 75R14.
CHASSIS [Jimmy]: Wheelbase: 106.5 in. Overall length: 184.4 in. Overall height: 69.8 in. Front/Rear tread: 66.7 in./63.7 in. Tires H78 x 15B.
CHASSIS [K15 Jimmy]: Wheelbase: 100.5 in. Overall length: 170.3 in. Overall height: 65 in. Front/Rear tread: 55.6/55.1 in. Tires: P195 x 75R15.
CHASSIS [S15 Extended Cab]: Wheelbase: 122.9 in. Overall height: 59.4 in. Front/Rear tread: 64.7/64.7 in. Tires: P195 x 75R14.

1983 GMC S15 Sierra Classic Club Cab Wide-Side Pickup (RCA)

CHASSIS [G1500]: Wheelbase: 110 in./125 in. Overall length: 178 in./202.2 in. Overall height: 78.8 in./81.2 in. Tires: E78 x 15B or F78 x 15B.
CHASSIS [G2500]: Wheelbase: 110 in./125 in. Overall length: 178 in./202.2 in. Overall height: 78.8 x 81.2 in. Tires: J78 x 15B.
CHASSIS [G3500]: Wheelbase: 110 in./146 in. Tires: [Vandura/Rally] 8.00 x 16.5C; [Camper Special/Magna] 8.75 x 16.5D.
CHASSIS [P2500]: Wheelbase: 125 in./133 in. Overall length: 220.75 in./244.75 in. Tires: 8.75 x 16.5C.
CHASSIS [P3500]: Wheelbase: 125 in./157 in. Overall length: 220.75/268.75 in. Tires: 8.75 x 16.5C.
CHASSIS [C1500]: Wheelbase: 117.5/12.5 in. Overall length: 191.3 in./212 in. Overall height: 69.8 in. Front/Rear tread: 65.8 in./62.7 in. Tires: G78 x 15B.

CHASSIS [C2500]: Wheelbase: 117.5 in./131.5 in./164.5 in. Overall length: 191.3 in./212 in./244.43 in. Overall height: 69.8 in. Front/Rear tread: 65.8 in./62.7 in. Tires: [Standard] 8.75 x 16.5C; [Bonus Cab] 8.75 x 16.5C (front); 8.75 x 16.5D (rear)/[Crew Cab] 9.50 x 16.5C (front); 9.50 x 16.5D (rear).

CHASSIS [C3500]: Wheelbase: 131.5 in./164.5 in. Overall length: 212 in./244.43 in. Overall height: 71.8 in. Front/Rear tread: 65.8 in./62.7 in. Tires: [Standard] 8.75 x 16.5C; [Bonus/Crew Cab] 9.50 x 16.5E.

TECHNICAL: Manual, synchromesh. Speeds: 3F/1R. [S15] 4F/1R. [C3500/K2500/K3500] 4F/1R. Column-mounted three-speed gearshift; floor-mounted four-speed gearshift. [Clutch] 11 in. diameter in all full-sized models; 12 in. diameter clutch optional. Rear axle: [G1500/C1500/K1500/C2500/K2500] semi-floating; [all others] full-floating. Overall ratio: [C1500] 2.73:1; [C2500/K2500] 3.42:1; [K3500 Bonus/Crew] 4.56:1; all other full-sized models 4.10:1; [S15] 2.56/2.73/3.08/3.42/3.73, depending rpm, engine, and transmission. [Brakes] Four-wheel hydraulic system, front disc, rear drum brakes. Kelsey-Hayes pressed steel wheels.

OPTIONS: Amarillo package (Caballero) ($189). Sierra Classic package (K1500 Jimmy) ($983). Sierra Classic package (S15 Jimmy) ($576). Gypsy package (S15 Jimmy). 8-passenger package (G-series) ($264). 12-passenger package (G-series) ($552). High Sierra equipment (S15, C-series). Sierra classic equipment (S15, C-series). Gypsy equipment (S15). For additional options refer to 1982 GMC section.

HISTORICAL: Calendar year sales: 238,411 divided as follows: [Full-sized pickups] 105,741. [S15] 40,491. [Vandura/Rally] 45,535. [Suburban] 11,292. [Jimmy] 7361, [S15-Jimmy] 21,760. [P-Series] 4071. [Caballero] 2160.

1983 K1500 Jimmy Sport Utility Wagon 4x4 (RCA)

1984 GMC

1984 GMC Sierra Classic Wide-Side Pickup

GMC — LIGHT-TRUCK — (ALL SERIES) — FOUR-CYLINDER/SIX-CYLINDER/V-8: S-15 Regular Cab models with 4x2 were now offered with a new Sport Suspension package that included quick-ratio power steering gear, special front stabilizer bar and larger-than-standard shock absorbers. Introduced on the full-size models were two-sided galvanized steel interior door panels. Also installed were semi-metallic front brake linings on C1500, K1500 and C2500 and K2500 models. Most of these GMC trucks also had new Non-asbestos rear brake linings. All C/K pickups and Chassis-Cabs had new plastic fuel tank stone shields.

I.D. DATA: The VIN is found on a plate attached to the top left of the instrument panel or sticker inside glove box. The VIN has 17 symbols. The first three symbols indicate country of origin, manufacturer and type of vehicle. The fourth symbol indicates GVW range. The fifth, sixth and seventh symbols indicate series, nominal (tonnage) rating and body style. The eighth symbol indicates engine: [All] A=1.9L-2.0L Isuzu (119 cid)/82 hp two-barrel L4; B=2.8L (173 cid)/125 hp two-barrel V-6; C=6.2L (379 cid)/130 hp diesel V-8; D=4.1L (250 cid)/115 hp two-barrel L-6; F=5.0L (305 cid)/155 hp four-barrel V-8; H=5.0L (305 cid)/160 hp four-barrel V-8; J=6.2L (379 cid)/148 hp diesel V-8; K=3.8L (229 cid)/110 hp V-6 two-barrel; L=5.7L (350 cid)/165 hp V-8; M=5.7L (350 cid)/185 hp four-barrel V-8; N=1.8L (111 cid)/75 hp Isuzu L-4 two-barrel; T=4.8L (292 cid)/115 hp one-barrel L-6; W=7.4L (454 cid)/240 hp four-barrel V-8. Y=2.0L (121 cid)/110 hp L4; Z (diesel) =5.7L (350 cid)/105 hp Olds diesel V-8. The ninth symbol is a check digit. The 10th symbol indicates model year E=1984. The 11th symbol indicates assembly plant; GMC models were sourced from:

B=Baltimore, Md.; Z=Fremont, Calif.; J=Janesville, Wis.; S=St. Louis; 3=Detroit (Chevrolet), Mich. (Value-Vans built in Chevrolet plant); F=Flint, Mich.; V=Pontiac, Mich. (GMC headquarters) and possibly other factories. The last six symbols were the production sequence number starting at 100001.

1984 GMC "Jimmy" Club Coupe (extended cab) Pickup (OCW)

Model	Body Type	Price	Weight	Prod. Total
Caballero — 1/2-Ton — Sedan Pickup				
1GW80	Base Pickup	8522	3298	—
1GW80	SS Diablo Pickup	8781	3305	—
Jimmy — 1/2-Ton — Sport Utility Wagon 4x4				
TK10516	Utility	10,819	4409	—
S15 Jimmy — 1/2-Ton — Mini Sport Utility Wagon 4x4				
TT10516	Utility	9685	3246	—
Series G1500 — 1/2-Ton — Vandura/Rally Wagon				
G11005	Vandura	7541	3732	—
G11006	Rally	9089	4085	—
G11306	Rally Custom	10,062	—	—
G11306	Rally STX	10,327	—	—
G2500 — 3/4-Ton — Vandura/Rally Wagon				
G21005	Vandura	8176	3813	—
G21306	Rally	9477	4276	—
G21306	Rally Custom	10,238	—	—
G21306	Rally STX	10,503	—	—
G3500 — 1-Ton — Vandura/Rally Wagon				
G2305	Vandura	9212	4305	—
G2306	Rally	11,964	4984	—
G2306	Rally Custom	12,724	—	—
G2306	Rally STX	12,990	—	—
G3500 — 1-Ton — Hi-Cube Van				
G2303	Hi-Cube 10-ft.	11,624	5423	—
G2603	Hi-Cube 12-ft.	12,894	5891	—
P2500 — (Step Van)				
P2500	Value Van 10.5-ft.	12,588	5860	—
P3500 — 1-Ton — Forward-Control				
P3500	Value Van 10.5-ft.	12,666	5998	—
S15 — 1/2-Ton — Mini Pickup				
S10603	Wide-Side Pickup 6-ft.	6398	2574	—
S10803	Wide-Side Pickup 7.5-ft.	6551	2649	—
S10653	Extended Cab Wide-Side Pickup	6924	2705	—
C1500 — 1/2-Ton — Conventional				
C10703	Fender-Side Pickup 6.5-ft.	7101	3434	—
C10703	Wide-Side Pickup 6.5-ft.	6970	3481	—
C10903	Wide-Side Pickup 8-ft.	7127	3644	—
C10906	Suburban	10,368	3420	—
C2500 — 3/4-Ton — Conventional				
C20903	Chassis & Cab	8342	3617	—
C20903	Fender-Side Pickup 8-ft.	829	3977	—
C20903	Wide-Side Pickup 8-ft.	8188	4039	—
C20943	Bonus Cab Pickup	9645	4742	—
C20943	Crew Cab Pickup	9975	4803	—
C20906	Suburban	10,599	4098	—
C3500 — 1-Ton — Conventional				
C30903	Chassis & Cab	8474	3990	—
C30903	Fender-Side Pickup 8-ft.	8966	4342	—
C30903	Wide-Side Pickup	8834	4404	—
C30943	Chassis & Bonus Cab	9471	4412	—
C30943	Bonus Cab Pickup	9815	4822	—
C30943	Chassis & Crew Cab	10,146	4883	—

NOTE 1: 4x4 GMC trucks have "K" prefix in model number.
NOTE 2: S15 Series: 6-ft. box=108.3 in. w.b.; 7.5-ft. box=122.9 in. w.b.
NOTE 3: Conventionals: 6.5-ft. box=117.5 in. w.b.; 8-ft. box=12.5 in. w.b.

Standard Catalog of Light-Duty Trucks

1984 GMC S-15 Mini-Pickup (OCW)

ENGINE [Caballero base V-6]: V-type. OHV. Six-cylinder. Cast iron block. Bore & stroke: 3.8 x 3.4 in. Displacement: 231 cid/3.8 liter. Net horsepower: 110 at 3800 rpm. Net torque: 190 lbs.-ft. at 1600 rpm. Carburetor: Rochester two-barrel. Passenger car engine code A. Source: Buick.

ENGINE [Optional Caballero]: V-8. OHV. V-8. Cast iron block. Bore & stroke: 3.74 x 3.48 in. Displacement: 305 cid/5.0 liter. Net horsepower: 135 at 4200 rpm. Net torque: 235 lbs.-ft. at 2400 rpm. Hydraulic valve lifters. Carburetor: Rochester four-barrel. Passenger/truck engine code H. Source: Chevrolet.

ENGINE [Optional Caballero]: V-8. OHV. Six-cylinder. Cast iron block. Bore & stroke: 3.5 x 3.48 in. Displacement: 267 cid/4.4 liter. Net horsepower: 120 at 3600 rpm. Net torque: 215 lbs.-ft. at 2000 rpm. Hydraulic valve lifters. Carburetor: Rochester four-barrel. Passenger/truck engine code J. Source: Chevrolet.

ENGINE [S15 base]: Inline. OHC. Four-cylinder. Bore & stroke: 3.42 x 3.23 in. Displacement: 119 cid/sometimes called 1.9 liter or 2.0 liter. Net horsepower: 82 at 4600 rpm. Net torque: 101 lbs.-ft. at 3000 rpm. Hydraulic valve lifters. Carburetor: two-barrel. Light-duty truck engine code A. Source: Isuzu.

ENGINE [Optional S15]: Inline. OHV. Six-cylinder. Bore & stroke: 3.5 x 2.99 in. Displacement: 173 cid/2.8 liter. Net horsepower: 125 at 4800 rpm. Net torque: 150 lbs.-ft. at 2200 rpm. Hydraulic valve lifters. Carburetor: two-barrel. Engine code B. Source: Chevrolet.

ENGINE [Optional diesel]: V-type. OHV. Eight-cylinder. Cast iron block. Bore & stroke: 3.98 x 3.82 in. Displacement: 379 cid/6.2 liter. Net horsepower: 130 at 3600 rpm. Net torque: 240 at 2000 rpm. Injected diesel. Engine code C. Source: Chevrolet.

ENGINE [C1500 base six]: Inline. OHV. Six-cylinder. Cast iron block. Bore & stroke: 3.876 x 3.530 in. Displacement: 250 cid/4.1 liter. Compression ratio: 8.25:1. Net horsepower: 115 at 3600 rpm. Net torque: 200 lbs.-ft. at 2000 rpm. [above 6,001 lb. GVW]. Net horsepower 100 at 3600 rpm. Net torque: 175 lbs.-ft. at 1800 rpm. Seven main bearings. Hydraulic valve lifters. Carburetor: Mono-Jet model 1ME. Engine code D. Source: Chevrolet.

ENGINE [Optional C1500]: V-type. OHV. Eight-cylinder. Cast iron block. Bore & stroke: 3.736 x 3.480 in. Displacement: 305 cid/5.0 liter. Compression ratio: 8.5:1. Net horsepower: 155 at 4000 rpm. Net torque: 245 lbs.-ft. at 1600 rpm. Five main bearings. Hydraulic valve lifters. Carburetor: four-barrel model. Source: Chevrolet.

ENGINE [Optional: C1500/C2500/K1500/Vans/Suburbans]: (Not available in California). V-type. OHV. Eight-cylinder. Cast iron block. Bore & stroke: 3.736 x 3.480 in. Displacement: 305 cid/5.0 liter. Compression ratio: 9.2:1. Net horsepower: 160 at 4400 rpm. Max horsepower: 235 lbs.-ft. at 2000 rpm. C1500 Brake hp: 165 at 4400 rpm. Max torque: 240 lbs.-ft. at 2000 rpm. Five main bearings. Hydraulic valve lifters. Carburetor: Rochester Staged model four-barrel, Electronic Spark Control (ESC). Code H. Source: Chevrolet.

1984 GMC S-15 "Indy Hauler" Pickup (IMSC/JLM)

ENGINE [Optional diesel]: V-type. OHV. Eight-cylinder. Cast iron block. Bore & stroke: 3.98 x 3.82 in. Displacement: 379 cid/6.2 liter. Net horsepower: 148 at 3600 rpm. Net torque: 246 at 2000 rpm. Injected diesel. Engine code J. Source: Chevrolet.

ENGINE [Optional: all models]: V-type. OHV. Eight-cylinder. Cast iron block. Bore & stroke: 4.0 x 3.480 in. Displacement: 350 cid/5.7 liter. Compression ratio: 8.5:1. Net horsepower: 165 at 3800 rpm. Net torque: 275 lbs.-ft. at 1600 rpm. Five main bearings. Hydraulic valve lifters. Carburetor: four-barrel model M4MC/MV. Engine code L. Source: Chevrolet.

ENGINE [Optional: all models]: V-type. OHV. Eight-cylinder. Cast iron block. Bore & stroke: 4.0 x 3.480 in. Displacement: 350 cid/5.7 liter. Compression ratio: 8.5:1. Net horsepower: 185 at 4000 rpm. Net torque: 285 lbs.-ft. at 2400 rpm. Five main bearings. Hydraulic valve lifters. Carburetor: four-barrel model M4MC/MV. Engine code M. Source: Chevrolet.

ENGINE [S15]: Inline. OHC. OHV. Four-cylinder. Bore & stroke: 3.31 x 3.23 in. Displacement: 111 cid/1.8 liter. Net horsepower: 75 at 5000 rpm. Net torque: 88 at 3000 rpm. Hydraulic valve lifters. Carburetor: two-barrel. Engine code N. Source: Isuzu.

ENGINE [Optional: all models]: V-type. OHV. Eight-cylinder. Cast iron block. Bore & stroke: 4.0 x 3.480 in. Displacement: 350 cid/5.7 liter. Compression ratio: 8.5:1. Net horsepower: 161 at 3800 rpm. Net torque: 275 lbs.-ft. at 2400 rpm. Five main bearings. Hydraulic valve lifters. Carburetor: four-barrel model M4MC/MV. Engine code P. Source: Chevrolet.

ENGINE [S15]: Inline. OHC. OHV. Four-cylinder. Bore & stroke: 3.46 x 3.62 in. Displacement: 137 cid/2.2 liter. Net horsepower: 62 at 4300 rpm. Net torque: 96 at 2200 rpm. Hydraulic valve lifters. Injected diesel. Engine code S. Source: Isuzu.

ENGINE [C2500/C3500/P base six]: Inline. OHV. Six-cylinder. Cast iron block. Bore & stroke: 3.8764 x 4.120 in. Displacement: 292 cid/4.8 liter. Compression ratio: 8.0:1. Net horsepower: 115 at 4000 rpm. Net torque: 210 lbs.-ft. at 1800 rpm. Seven main bearings. Hydraulic valve lifters. Carburetor: one-barrel. Engine code T. Source: Chevrolet.

ENGINE [Optional: C1500/C2500/C3500/K1500/K2500/K3500]: V-type. OHV. Eight-cylinder. Cast iron block. Bore & stroke: 4.250 x 4.0 in. Displacement: 454 cid/7.4 liter. Compression ratio: 8.5:1. Net horsepower: 240 at 3800 rpm. Net torque: 375 lbs.-ft. at 3200 rpm. Five main bearings. Hydraulic valve lifters. Carburetor: four-barrel model M4MC/MV. Engine code W. Source: Chevrolet.

1984 GMC S-15 High Sierra Mini-Pickup (JAG)

CHASSIS [S15]: Wheelbase: 108.3/117.9 in. Overall length: 178.2/194.1 in. Overall heigth: 59 in. Front/Rear tread: 64.7 x 64.7 in. Tires: P195 x 75R14, fiberglass-belted. Optional: P195 x 75R14, steel-belted P205 x 75R14, P205 x 70R14.

CHASSIS [Caballero] Wheelbase: 117.1 in. Overall length: 201.6 in. Overall height: 53.8 in. Front/Rear tread: 58.5 in./57.8 in. Tires: P205 x 75R14.

CHASSIS [Jimmy]: Wheelbase: 106.5 in. Overall length: 184.4 in. Overall height: 69.8 in. Front/Rear tread: 66.7 in./63.7 in. Tires H78 x 15B.

CHASSIS [K15 Jimmy]: Wheelbase: 100.5 in. Overall length: 170.3 in. Overall height: 65 in. Front/Rear tread: 55.6/55.1 in. Tires: P195 x 75R15.

CHASSIS [S15 Extended Cab]: Wheelbase: 122.9 in. Overall height: 59.4 in. Front/Rear tread: 64.7/64.7 in. Tires: P195 x 75R14.

CHASSIS [G1500]: Wheelbase: 110 in./125 in. Overall length: 178 in./202.2 in. Overall height: 78.8 in./81.2 in. Tires: E78 x 15B or F78 x 15B.

CHASSIS [G2500]: Wheelbase: 110 in./125 in. Overall length: 178 in./202.2 in. Overall height: 78.8 x 81.2 in. Tires: J78 x 15B.

CHASSIS [G3500]: Wheelbase: 110 in./146 in. Tires: [Vandura/Rally] 8.00 x 16.5C; [Camper Special/Magna] 8.75 x 16.5D.

CHASSIS [P2500]: Wheelbase: 125 in./133 in. Overall length: 220.75 in./244.75 in. Tires: 8.75 x 16.5C.

CHASSIS [P3500]: Wheelbase: 125 in./157 in. Overall length: 220.75/268.75 in. Tires: 8.75 x 16.5C.

CHASSIS [C1500]: Wheelbase: 117.5/12.5 in. Overall length: 191.3 in./212 in. Overall height: 69.8 in. Front/Rear tread: 65.8 in./62.7 in. Tires: G78 x 15B.

CHASSIS [C2500]: Wheelbase: 117.5 in./131.5 in.164.5 in. Overall length: 191.3 in./212 in./244.43 in. Overall height: 69.8 in. Front/Rear tread: 65.8 in./62.7 in. Tires: [Standard] 8.75 x 16.5C; [Bonus Cab] 8.75 x 16.5C (front); 8.75 x 16.5D (rear)/[Crew Cab] 9.50 x 16.5C (front); 9.50 x 16.5D (rear).

CHASSIS [C3500]: Wheelbase: 131.5 in./164.5 in. Overall length: 212 in./244.43 in. Overall height: 71.8 in. Front/Rear tread: 65.8 in./62.7 in. Tires: [Standard] 8.75 x 16.5C; [Bonus/Crew Cab] 9.50 x 16.5E.

1984 GMC "S-15 JImmy" Mini-Sport Utility (OCW)

TECHNICAL: Manual, synchromesh. Speeds: 3F/1R; [S15] 4F/1R; [C3500/K2500/K3500] 4F/1R. Column-mounted three-speed gearshift; floor-mounted four-speed gearshift. [Clutch] 11 in. diameter in all full-sized models; 12 in. diameter clutch optional. Rear axle: [G1500/C1500/K1500/C2500/K2500] semi-floating; [all others] full-floating. Overall ratio: [C1500] 2.73:1; [C2500/K2500] 3.42:1; [K3500 Bonus/Crew] 4.56:1; all other full-sized models 4.10:1; [S15] 2.56/2.73/3.08/3.42/3.73, depending rpm, engine, and transmission. [Brakes] Four-wheel hydraulic system, front disc, rear drum brakes. Kelsey-Hayes pressed steel wheels.

OPTIONS: [Caballero] Amarillo package ($189). [K1500/Jimmy] Sierra Classic package ($983). [S15 Jimmy] Sierra Classic package ($576). [S15 Jimmy] Gypsy package. [Vans] 8-passenger package ($264); 12-passenger package ($552). [S15/C/K] High Sierra equipment; Sierra classic equipment ($983). [S15] Gypsy equipment. Cargo area lamp. Color-keyed floor mats. Comfortilt steering wheel. Deluxe front appearance package. Dome light. Gauge package. Halogen headlights. Intermittent windshield wipers. Painted and stainless

steel below eyeline mirrors. Stainless steel camper mirrors. Black and brightmolding. Door edge guards. Special two-tone paint. Sliding rear window. Tinted glass. Rally wheels. Styled wheels. Electronic cruise control. Reclining bucket seats [Suburban]: Rear heater. Electric window tailgate. Chromed front bumper guards. Chromed or painted rear step bumper. Radio AM, AM/FM stereo with cassette player, Seek and Scan stereo. Quartz electric clock. Cigar lighter. For additional options refer to 1982 for typical examples.

1984 GMC Sierra Classic Suburban Carryall (OCW)

HISTORICAL: Calendar year sales: 280,52 divided as follows: [Safari] (introduced as 1985 model) 217. [Full-sized pickups] 121,704. [S-15] 43,742. [Vandura/Rally] 45,991. [Suburban] 16,132. [Jimmy] 8,488. [S15-Jimmy] 34,519. [P-Series] 7,036. [Caballero] 2,702.

1984 GMC Rally STX Passenger Van (OCW)

1985 GMC

1985 GMC Sierra Classic 10 Wide-Side Pickup (F.T. Taber)

GMC — LIGHT-TRUCK — (ALL SERIES) — FOUR/SIX/V-8: GMC's entry into the so-called mini-van market, the Safari, featured an integral body/frame design on a 111 in. wheelbase. Its standard powerplant was the 151 cid inline four with a new Vortex V-6 optional. A wide variety of exterior color and trim levels were offered. The Safari had a maximum capacity of 151.8 cu. ft. with the second and available rear seats removed. With room for five passengers load capacity was 86.2 ft. The Caballero had the new 4.3L Vortex V-6 as its standard engine. The optional 305 cid V-8 now had a 9.5:1 compression ratio and an electronic spark control (ESC). A 65-amp. generator was standard on Caballeros with air conditioning. New standard stainless steel full wheelcovers with a brushed-finish center

with GMC lettering were standard. A total of nine new exterior colors were offered. The Caballero's standard velour cloth interior was also new for 1985. Numerous changes were made in the S15 line for 1985. Like its larger counterparts, the S15 had a black chrome insert for its partitioned front grille. The Custom two-tone paint option included "Sunshine" striping. All models had restyled fender nameplates and a new paint scheme for the optional styled wheels. New optional custom vinyl and custom cloth seats trim was offered in any of four colors. Standard on all models, except the 4x2 short wheelbase conventional cab pickup, was the new 2.5 liter Tech IV engine with electronic fuel injection (EFI). Additional refinements included use of a partitioned fuse panel, two-side-galvanized steel for the hood inner panel and fender skirts, welded-on bumper brackets, adjust-on-release rear brake adjusters, new valving for the shock absorbers, new controls for the optional intermittent wipers and a new variable-ratio manual steering gear. The 1985 full-sized GMC models were identified by their new front end appearance featuring stacked rectangular headlights, a bold three-section grille format with blacked-out gridwork and red-letter GMC identification. Wide-Side models with single rear wheels were offered with a new optional custom two-tone color scheme. All models had wet-arm-type windshield washers. Both 4x2 and 4x4 models could be fitted with front tow hooks. Interior changes included a new seat cushion contour and seatback angle for the standard bench seat. Both the optional custom vinyl and custom cloth fabrics were new for 1985. A major technical development was the use of the 4.3 liter/262 cid Vortex V-6 as the base engine for the C1500/K1500 and light-duty-emission C2500 pickups.

I.D. DATA: The VIN is found on a plate attached to the top left of the instrument panel or sticker inside glove box. The VIN has 17 symbols. The first three symbols indicate country of origin, manufacturer and type of vehicle. The fourth symbol indicates GVW range. The fifth, sixth and seventh symbols indicate series, nominal (tonnage) rating and body style. The eighth symbol indicates engine: [All] A=1.9L-2.0L Isuzu (119 cid)/82 hp two-barrel L4; B=2.8L (173 cid)/125 hp two-barrel V-6; C=6.2L (379 cid)/130 hp diesel V-8; D=4.1L (250 cid)/115 hp two-barrel L-6; F=5.0L (305 cid)/155 hp four-barrel V-8; H=5.0L (305 cid)/160 hp four-barrel V-8; J=6.2L (379 cid)/148 hp diesel V-8; L=5.7L (350 cid)/165 hp V-8; M=5.7L (350 cid)/185 hp four-barrel V-8; N=1.8L (111 cid)/75 hp Isuzu L-4 two-barrel; T=4.8L (292 cid)/115 hp one-barrel L-6; W=7.4L (454 cid)/240 hp four-barrel V-8; Z=4.3L (262 cid)/140 hp two-barrel Vortex V-6. The ninth symbol is a check digit. The 10th symbol indicates model year F=1985. The 11th symbol indicates assembly plant; GMC models were sourced from: B=Baltimore, Md.; Z=Fremont, Calif.; J=Janesville, Wis.; S=St. Louis; 3=Detroit (Chevrolet), Mich. (Value-Vans built in Chevrolet plant); F=Flint, Mich.; V=Pontiac, Mich. (GMC headquarters) and possibly other factories. The last six symbols were the production sequence number starting at 100001.

Model	Body Type	Price	Weight	Prod. Total
Caballero — 1/2-Ton — Sedan-Pickup				
W80	Sedan Pickup	8933	3252	—
W80	Sedan SS Diablo	9198	3263	—
K1500 Jimmy — 1/2-Ton — Sport Utility 4x4				
K10	Utility Wagon	11,223	4462	—
S15 Jimmy — 1/2-Ton — Mini Sport Utility Wagon				
T10	Utility Wagon	9994	3256	—
Safari — 1/2-Ton — Mini-Van				
M10	Cargo Van	7821	3048	—
M10	Safari Wagon SL	8195	3277	—
M10	Safari Wagon SLX	8623	—	—
M10	Safari Wagon SLE	9359	—	—
G1500 — 1/2-Ton				
G11	Vandura	7987	3668	—
G11	Rally	9517	4037	—
G11	Rally Custom	10,514	—	—
G11	Rally STX	10,827	—	—
G2500 — 3/4-Ton — Vandura/Rally Wagon				
G21	Vandura	8581	3811	—
G21	Rally	9915	4277	—
G21	Rally Custom	10,695	—	—
G21	Rally STX	11,007	—	—
G3500 — 1-Ton — Vandura/Rally Wagon				
G2	Vandura	10,342	4402	—
G2	Rally	12,291	4988	—
G2	Rally Custom	13,071	—	—
G2	Rally STX	13,383	—	—
G2	Cutaway	8950	4372	—
G3500 — 1-Ton — Magnavan				
G2	10-ft. Cutaway	12,097	5054	—
G2	12-ft. Cutaway	13,351	5891	—
P2500 — 3/4-Ton — Forward-Control				
P20	Value Van	13,038	5860	—
P3500 — 1-Ton — Forward-Control				
P30	Value Van	13,119	5998	—
S15 — 1/2-Ton — Mini Pickup				
S10	Wide-Side Pickup 6-ft.	5990	2567	—
S10	Wide-Side Pickup 7.5-ft.	6702	2656	—
S10	Wide-Side Extended Cab Pickup	7167	2711	—
C1500 — 1/2-Ton — Conventional				
C10	Fender-Side Pickup 6.5-ft.	7428	3439	—
C10	Wide-Side Pickup 6.5-ft.	7295	3486	—
C10	Wide-Side Pickup 8-ft.	7461	3048	—
C10	Suburban	10,700	4219	—
C2500 — 3/4-Ton — Conventional				
C20	Chassis & Cab	8516	3626	—
C20	Fender-Side Pickup 8-ft.	8677	3986	—
C20	Wide-Side Pickup 8-ft.	8543	4048	—
C20	Wide-Side Bonus Cab Pickup	9902	4747	—
C20	Wide-Side Crew Cab Pickup	10,238	4808	—
C20	Suburban	10,953	4705	—

C3500 — 1-Ton — Conventional

C30	Chassis & Cab	8650	3994	—
C30	Fender-Side Pickup 8-ft.	9167	4347	—
C30	Wide-Side Pickup 8-ft.	9033	4409	—
C30	Chassis & Bonus Cab	9667	4418	—
C30	Wide-Side Bonus Cab Pickup	10,033	4829	—
C30	Chassis & Crew Cab	10,005	4479	—
C30	Wide-Side Crew Cab Pickup	10,371	4890	—

NOTE 1: 4x4 GMC trucks have "K" prefix in model number.
NOTE 2: S15 Series: 6-ft. box=108.3 in. w.b.; 7.5-ft. box=122.9 in. w.b.
NOTE 3: Conventionals: 6.5-ft. box=117.5 in. w.b.; 8-ft. box=12.5 in. w.b.

1985 GMC K-Jimmy Sierra Classic

ENGINE [Caballero base V-6]: V-type. OHV. Six-cylinder. Cast iron block. Bore & stroke: 3.8 x 3.4 in. Displacement: 231 cid/3.8 liter. Net horsepower: 110 at 3800 rpm. Net torque: 190 lbs.-ft. at 1600 rpm. Carburetor: Rochester two-barrel. Passenger car engine code A. Source: Buick.

ENGINE [Optional Caballero]: V-8. OHV. V-8. Cast iron block. Bore & stroke: 3.74 x 3.48 in. Displacement: 305 cid/5.0 liter. Net horsepower: 135 at 4200 rpm. Net torque: 235 lbs.-ft. at 2400 rpm. Hydraulic valve lifters. Carburetor: Rochester four-barrel. Passenger/truck engine code H. Source: Chevrolet.

ENGINE [Optional Caballero]: V-8. OHV. Six-cylinder. Cast iron block. Bore & stroke: 3.5 x 3.48 in. Displacement: 267 cid/4.4 liter. Net horsepower: 120 at 3600 rpm. Net torque: 215 lbs.-ft. at 2000 rpm. Hydraulic valve lifters. Carburetor: Rochester four-barrel. Passenger/truck engine code J. Source: Chevrolet.

ENGINE [S15 base]: Inline. OHC. Four-cylinder. Bore & stroke: 3.42 x 3.23 in. Displacement: 119 cid/sometimes called 1.9 liter or 2.0 liter. Net horsepower: 82 at 4600 rpm. Net torque: 101 lbs.-ft. at 3000 rpm. Hydraulic valve lifters. Carburetor: two-barrel. Light-duty truck engine code A. Source: Izusu.

ENGINE [Optional S15]: Inline. OHV. Six-cylinder. Bore & stroke: 3.5 x 2.99 in. Displacement: 173 cid/2.8 liter. Net horsepower: 125 at 4800 rpm. Net torque: 150 lbs.-ft. at 2200 rpm. Hydraulic valve lifters. Carburetor: two-barrel. Engine code B. Source: Chevrolet.

ENGINE [Optional diesel]: V-type. OHV. Eight-cylinder. Cast iron block. Bore & stroke: 3.98 x 3.82 in. Displacement: 379 cid/6.2 liter. Net horsepower: 130 at 3600 rpm. Net torque: 240 at 2000 rpm. Injected diesel. Engine code C. Source: Chevrolet.

ENGINE [C1500 base six]: Inline. OHV. Six-cylinder. Cast iron block. Bore & stroke: 3.876 x 3.530 in. Displacement: 250 cid/4.1 liter. Compression ratio: 8.25:1. Net horsepower: 115 at 3600 rpm. Net torque: 200 lbs.-ft. at 2000 rpm. [above 6,001 lb. GVW]. Net horsepower 100 at 3600 rpm. Net torque: 175 lbs.-ft. at 1800 rpm. Seven main bearings. Hydraulic valve lifters. Carburetor: Mono-Jet model 1ME. Engine code D. Source: Chevrolet.

ENGINE [Optional C1500]: V-type. OHV. Eight-cylinder. Cast iron block. Bore & stroke: 3.736 x 3.480 in. Displacement: 305 cid/5.0 liter. Compression ratio: 8.5:1. Net horsepower: 155 at 4000 rpm. Net torque: 245 lbs.-ft. at 1600 rpm. Five main bearings. Hydraulic valve lifters. Carburetor: four-barrel model. Engine code F. Source: Chevrolet.

ENGINE [Optional: C1500/C2500/K1500/Vans/Suburbans]: (Not available in California). V-type. OHV. Eight-cylinder. Cast iron block. Bore & stroke: 3.736 x 3.480 in. Displacement: 305 cid/5.0 liter. Compression ratio: 9.2:1. Net horsepower: 160 at 4400 rpm. Max torque: 235 lbs.-ft. at 2000 rpm. C1500 Brake hp: 165 at 4400 rpm. Max torque: 240 lbs.-ft. at 2000 rpm. Five main bearings. Hydraulic valve lifters. Carburetor: Rochester Staged model four-barrel, Electronic Spark Control (ESC). Code H. Source: Chevrolet.

ENGINE [Optional diesel]: V-type. OHV. Eight-cylinder. Cast iron block. Bore & stroke: 3.98 x 3.82 in. Displacement: 379 cid/6.2 liter. Net horsepower: 148 at 3600 rpm. Net torque: 246 at 2000 rpm. Injected diesel. Engine code J. Source: Chevrolet.

ENGINE [Optional: all models]: V-type. OHV. Eight-cylinder. Cast iron block. Bore & stroke: 4.0 x 3.480 in. Displacement: 350 cid/5.7 liter. Compression ratio: 8.5:1. Net horsepower: 165 at 3800 rpm. Net torque: 275 lbs.-ft. at 1600 rpm. Five main bearings. Hydraulic valve lifters. Carburetor: four-barrel model M4MC/MV. Engine code L. Source: Chevrolet.

ENGINE [Optional: all models]: V-type. OHV. Eight-cylinder. Cast iron block. Bore & stroke: 4.0 x 3.480 in. Displacement: 350 cid/5.7 liter. Compression ratio: 8.5:1. Net horsepower: 185 at 4000 rpm. Net torque: 285 lbs.-ft. at 2400 rpm. Five main bearings. Hydraulic valve lifters. Carburetor: four-barrel model M4MC/MV. Engine code M. Source: Chevrolet.

ENGINE [S15]: Inline. OHC. OHV. Four-cylinder. Bore & stroke: 3.31 x 3.23 in. Displacement: 111 cid/1.8 liter. Net horsepower: 75 at 5000 rpm. Net torque: 88 at 3000 rpm. Hydraulic valve lifters. Carburetor: two-barrel. Engine code N. Source: Isuzu.

ENGINE [Optional: all models]: V-type. OHV. Eight-cylinder. Cast iron block. Bore & stroke: 4.0 x 3.480 in. Displacement: 350 cid/5.7 liter. Compression ratio: 8.5:1. Net horsepower: 161 at 3800 rpm. Net torque: 258 lbs.-ft. at 2400 rpm. Five main bearings. Hydraulic valve lifters. Carburetor: four-barrel model M4MC/MV. Engine code P. Source: Chevrolet.

ENGINE [S15]: Inline. OHC. OHV. Four-cylinder. Bore & stroke: 3.46 x 3.62 in. Displacement: 137 cid/2.2 liter. Net horsepower: 62 at 4300 rpm. Net torque: 96 at 2200 rpm. Hydraulic valve lifters. Injected diesel. Engine code S. Source: Isuzu.

ENGINE [C2500/C3500/P base six]: Inline. OHV. Six-cylinder. Cast iron block. Bore & stroke: 3.8764 x 4.120 in. Displacement: 292 cid/4.8 liter. Compression ratio: 8.0:1. Net horsepower: 115 at 4000 rpm. Net torque: 210 lbs.-ft. at 1800 rpm. Seven main bearings. Hydraulic valve lifters. Carburetor: one-barrel. Engine code T. Source: Chevrolet.

ENGINE [Optional: C1500/C2500/C3500/K1500/K2500/K3500]: V-type. OHV. Eight-cylinder. Cast iron block. Bore & stroke: 4.250 x 4.0 in. Displacement: 454 cid/7.4 liter. Compression ratio: 8.5:1. Net horsepower: 240 at 3800 rpm. Net torque: 375 lbs.-ft. at 3200 rpm. Five main bearings. Hydraulic valve lifters. Carburetor: four-barrel model M4MC/MV. Engine code W. Source: Chevrolet.

ENGINE [Standard: C/K1500 and C2500 Pickups]: V-type. OHV. Six-cylinder. Cast iron block. Bore & stroke: 4.00 x 3.48 in. Displacement: 262 cid. Compression ratio: 9.3:1. Net horsepower: 155 at 4000 rpm. Net torque: 230 lbs.-ft. at 2400 rpm. Carburetor: Rochester Quadrajet, Electronic Spark Control. Engine code Z. Source: Chevrolet.

CHASSIS [Safari]: Wheelbase: 111 in. Overall length: 176.8 in. Overall height: 71.7 in. Tires: P195 x 75R15.

CHASSIS [S15]: Wheelbase: 108.3/117.9 in. Overall length: 178.2/194.1 in. Overall heigth: 59 in. Front/Rear tread: 64.7 x 64.7 in. Tires: P195 x 75R14, fiberglass-belted. Optional: P195 x 75R14, steel-belted P205 x 75R14, P205 x 70R14.

CHASSIS [Caballero]: Wheelbase: 117.1 in. Overall length: 201.6 in. Overall height: 53.8 in. Front/Rear tread: 58.5 in./57.8 in. Tires: P205 x 75R14.

CHASSIS [Jimmy]: Wheelbase: 106.5 in. Overall length: 184.4 in. Overall height: 69.8 in. Front/Rear tread: 66.7 in./63.7 in. Tires H78 x 15B.

CHASSIS [K15 Jimmy]: Wheelbase: 100.5 in. Overall length: 170.3 in. Overall height: 65 in. Front/Rear tread: 55.6/55.1 in. Tires: P195 x 75R15.

CHASSIS [S15 Extended Cab]: Wheelbase: 122.9 in. Overall height: 59.4 in. Front/Rear tread: 64.7/64.7 in. Tires: P195 x 75R14.

CHASSIS [G1500]: Wheelbase: 110 in./125 in. Overall length: 178 in./202.2 in. Overall height: 78.8 in./81.2 in. Tires: E78 x 15B or F78 x 15B.

CHASSIS [G2500]: Wheelbase: 110 in./125 in. Overall length: 178 in./202.2 in. Overall height: 78.8 x 81.2 in. Tires: J78 x 15B.

CHASSIS [G3500]: Wheelbase: 110 in./146 in. Tires: [Vandura/Rally] 8.00 x 16.5C; [Camper Special/Magna] 8.75 x 16.5D.

CHASSIS [P2500]: Wheelbase: 125 in./133 in. Overall length: 220.75 in./244.75 in. Tires: 8.75 x 16.5C.

CHASSIS [P3500]: Wheelbase: 125 in./157 in. Overall length: 220.75/268.75 in. Tires: 8.75 x 16.5C.

CHASSIS [C1500]: Wheelbase: 117.5/12.5 in. Overall length: 191.3 in./212 in. Overall height: 69.8 in. Front/Rear tread: 62.7 in. Tires: G78 x 15B.

CHASSIS [C2500]: Wheelbase: 117.5 in./131.5 in./164.5 in. Overall length: 191.3 in./212 in./244.43 in. Overall height: 69.8 in. Front/Rear tread: 65.8 in./62.7 in. Tires: [Standard] 8.75 x 16.5C; [Bonus Cab] 8.75 x 16.5C (front); 8.75 x 16.5D (rear)/[Crew Cab] 9.50 x 16.5C (front); 9.50 x 16.5D (rear).

CHASSIS [C3500]: Wheelbase: 131.5 in./164.5 in. Overall length: 212 in./244.43 in. Overall height: 71.8 in. Front/Rear tread: 65.8 in./62.7 in. Tires: [Standard] 8.75 x 16.5C; [Bonus/Crew Cab] 9.50 x 16.5E.

1985 GMC K-1500 High Sierra Fenderside Pickup

TECHNICAL: Manual, synchromesh. Speeds: 3F/1R; [S15] 4F/1R; [C3500/K2500/K3500] 4F/1R. Column-mounted three-speed gearshift; floor-mounted four-speed gearshift. [C1500/diesel] standard on selected models with V-6 and diesel: four-speed manual overdrive (synchromesh) transmission. Three-speed and four-speed automatic transmissions optional on different models. Floor-mounted gearshift. [Clutch] 11 in. diameter in all full-sized models; 12 in. diameter clutch optional. Rear axle: [G1500/C1500/K1500/C2500/K2500] semi-floating; [all others] full-floating. Overall ratio: [C1500] 2.73:1; [C2500/K2500] 3.42:1; [K3500 Bonus/Crew] 4.56:1; all other full-sized models 4.10:1; [S15] 2.56/2.73/3.08/3.42/3.73, depending rpm, engine, and transmission. [Brakes] Four-wheel hydraulic system, front disc, rear drum brakes. Kelsey-Hayes pressed steel wheels.

OPTIONS: [Caballero] Amarillo package ($189). [K1500/Jimmy] Sierra Classic package ($983). [S15 Jimmy] Sierra Classic package ($576). [S15 Jimmy] Gypsy package. [Vans] 8-passenger package ($264); 12-passenger package ($552). [S15/C/K] High Sierra equipment; Sierra classic equipment ($983). [S15] Gypsy equipment. Cargo area lamp. Color-keyed floor mats. Comfortilt steering wheel. Dome light. Gauge package. Halogen headlights. Intermittent windshield wipers. Painted and stainless steel below eyeline mirrors. Stainless steel camper mirrors. Black and bright molding. Door edge guards. Special two-tone paint. Sliding rear window. Tinted glass. Rally wheels. Styled wheels. Electronic cruise control. Reclining bucket seats [Suburban]: Rear heater. Electric window tailgate. Chromed front bumper guards. Chromed or painted rear step bumper. Radio AM, AM/FM stereo with cassette player, Seek and Scan stereo. Cigar electric clock. Rear bumper chromed. Radio: AM, AM/FM, AM/FM stereo, AM/FM stereo with cassette. Electric clock. Cigarette lighter. Air conditioning. Cast aluminum wheels (C/K1500). Bright wheelcovers. Styled wheels (C/K1500). Deluxe front end appearance package (includes dual headlights). Custom and deluxe molding packages. Power door locks. Power windows. Dome light. Camper mirrors. West Coast mirrors. Halogen hi-beam headlamps. Roof marker lamps. Cargo area lamp. Comfortilt steering wheel. Sliding rear window. Various exterior two-tone paint schemes. For additional options refer to 1982 for typical examples.

HISTORICAL: Calendar year production: 26,533 divided as follows: [Vandura/Rally Wagon] 22,805; [S15] 57,740; [S15] Jimmy 51,582; [Jimmy] 11,525; [Safari] 34,181; [Caballero] 3,057; [Suburban] 23,850; [C/K pickups] 105,651; [P-Series] 5,842.

1986 GMC

1986 GMC Vandura With Rank & Son Conversion (RSB)

GMC — LIGHT-TRUCK — (1986 SERIES) — ALL-ENGINES: The GMC Caballero offered a four-speed overdrive automatic transmission with the standard V-6 engine in 1986. Other changes were minor. New for the "S" series Jimmy was a revamped instrument cluster with warning lights on either side of the combination fuel/speedometer gauge. Added to the 1986 option list was a 2.8-liter V-6 with TBI. Technical changes were the same as for comparable Chevrolets, including a new Delcotron generator, lighter pistons, 30-degree exhaust valve seats, low-pressure gas shocks, new paint and trim options and a hinged rear-mounted spare tire carrier. S15 pickups had the same new instrument panel treatment as the S Series Blazer. It also included a new package tray and trim plates. The Insta-Trac 4x4 option provided off-road capability with a shift that could be switched from 4x2 to 4x4 at any speed. Engine improvements were also new.

Full-size K1500 Jimmys had new molded front-bucket seats with folding seatbacks. The cloth seat-trim option included a reclining seatback feature and the passenger seat included the slide-forward, easy-entry feature which had been standard on the smaller S15 series. Black and white tops were available with solid colors, while a new steel-gray top was available to match a similar exterior color. Full-size GMC pickups featured GM's 4.3-liter Vortex V-6 as standard equipment. A 50,000 mile warranty was offered for Diesel-engined trucks. The GMC Suburban had new bucket seats with outboard armrests as a 1986 extra. Of interest to collectors was the method used to promote GMC's 1986 models as the ultimate upscale trucks. The company contacted the Classic Car Club of America to arrange an advertising photograph that featured an S15 pickup truck towing an L-29 Cord to a stately looking mansion. Parked in the mansion's four-car garage were a 1937 Bugatti, 1930s Buick and a 1957 Cushman Eagle and Indian motorcycle. The Cord in the photo was borrowed from the well-known collection of the late Barney Pollard. The Bugatti was once one of Ettore Bugatti's personal cars, which was scheduled to be shown at Pebble Beach. The Buick was a "resto-rod," refurbished with modern appointments. Credit for this "The Classic No Enthusiast Should Be Without" ad theme belongs to McCann-Erickson, GMC's Detroit advertising agency. The Safari mini-van, introduced six months earlier, was unchanged, except for use of the new Delcotron. Without optional passenger seats, the Safari had 189.9 cu. ft. of payload space. Even with the seat, storage room was a respectable 83.7 cu. ft. A second optional passenger bench seat could also be ordered. Three trim levels: SL, SLX and SLE were available for passenger models. GMC vans and other big trucks used a new five-ribbed poly-vee generator accessory belt. Both the Rally Wagon and Vandura had modest refinements. The conventional sliding side door could be replaced, at no extra cost, with 60/40 swing-out doors incorporating a new sliding 90-degree door check system. This prevented fouling between the right front side door and forward side swing-out door.

Additional models covered in this section include the GMC Magnavan (King-size van) and the GMC Value Van (Step-Van type truck), which were both little changed from 1985.

1986 GMC S-15 Jimmy Sierra Classic

Standard Catalog of Light-Duty Trucks

I.D. DATA: The VIN is found on a plate attached to the top left of the instrument panel or sticker inside glove box. The VIN has 17 symbols. The first three symbols indicate country of origin, manufacturer and type of vehicle. The fourth symbol indicates GVW range. The fifth, sixth and seventh symbols indicate series, nominal (tonnage) rating and body style. The eighth symbol indicates engine: [All] B=2.8L (173 cid)/125 hp two-barrel V-6; C=6.2L (379 cid)/130 hp diesel V-8; D=4.1L (250 cid)/115 hp two-barrel L-6; E=2.5L (151 cid)/92 hp L-4 two-barrel; F=5.0L (305 cid)/155 hp four-barrel V-8; H=5.0L (305 cid)/160 hp four-barrel V-8; J=6.2L (379 cid)/148 hp diesel V-8; L=5.7L (350 cid)/165 hp V-8; M=5.7L (350 cid)/185 hp four-barrel V-8; N=1.8L (111 cid)/75 hp Isuzu L-4 two-barrel; T=4.8L (292 cid)/115 hp one-barrel L-6; W=7.4L (454 cid)/240 hp four-barrel V-8); Z=4.3L (262 cid)/140 hp two-barrel Vortex V-6. The ninth symbol is a check digit. The 10th symbol indicates model year G=1986. The 11th symbol indicates assembly plant; GMC models were sourced from: B=Baltimore, Md.; Z=Fremont, Calif.; J=Janesville, Wis.; S=St. Louis; 3=Detroit (Chevrolet), Mich. (Value-Vans built in Chevrolet plant); F=Flint, Mich.; V=Pontiac, Mich. (GMC headquarters) and possibly other factories. The last six symbols were the production sequence number starting at 100001.

Model	Body Type	Price	Weight	Prod. Total
Caballero — 1/2-Ton — 117.1 in. w.b. — V-6				
W80	Sport Pickup	9623	3234	—
W80	Diablo Pickup	9936	3239	—
K1500 Jimmy — 1/2-Ton — 4x4 — 106.5 in. w.b. — V-8				
K18	Sport Utility	12085	4444	—
S15 Jimmy — 1/2-Ton — 4x4 — 100 in. w.b.				
T18	Mini Sport Utility	10,745	3125	—
Safari — 1/2-Ton — 111 in. w.b. — V-6				
M10	Cargo Van	8945	3258	—
M10	SL Wagon	9086	3434	—
M10	SLX Wagon	9541	3509	—
M10	SLE Wagon	10,265	3569	—
G1500 Van — 1/2-Ton — 110 in./125 in. w.b. — V-6				
G15	Vandura	8677	3700	—
G15	Rally	10,283	4052	—
G15	Custom Rally	11,341	4153	—
G15	Rally STX	11,673	4196	—
G2500 Van — 3/4-Ton — 110 in./125 in. w.b. — V-6				
G25	Vandura	9308	3786	—
G25	Rally	10,706	4244	—
G25	Custom Rally	11,533	4345	—
G25	Rally STX	11,864	4388	—
G3500 Van — 1-Ton — 110 in./125 in. — V-8				
G35	Vandura	11,129	4526	—
G35	Rally	13,173	4526	—
G35	Custom Rally	14,001	5117	—
G35	Rally STX	14,32	5261	—
Magnavan — 1-Ton — 125 in./146 in. w.b. — V-8				
G2	10-ft. Van	13,492	5209	—
G2	12-ft. Van	14,803	5886	—
Value Van — 3/4-Ton — 125 in./133 in./178 in. w.b. — I-6				
P22	Panel 10.5-ft.	14,338	5869	—
Value Van — 1-Ton — 125 in./133 in./178 in. w.b. — I-6				
P32	Panel 10.5-ft.	14,422	6022	—
S10 Pickup — 1/2-Ton — 108.3 in./122.9 in. w.b. — V-6				
S14	Wide-Side Spec. 6-ft.	5990	2574	—
S14	Wide-Side 6-ft.	7046	2574	—
S14	Wide-Side 7.5-ft.	7281	2645	—
S14	Bonus Cab 6-ft.	7733	2713	—
C1500 Pickup — 1/2-Ton — 117.5 in./12.5 in. w.b. — V-6				
C14	Fenderside 6.5-ft.	7955	3385	—
C14	Wide-Side 6.5-ft.	7815	3432	—
C14	Wide-Side 8-ft.	7989	3595	—
C14	Suburban V-8	11,528	4279	—
C2500 Pickup — 3/4-Ton — 131.5 in. w.b. — V-6				
C24	Chassis & Cab	9667	3607	—
C24	Fenderside 8-ft.	9304	3930	—
C24	Wide-Side 8-ft.	9164	3992	—
C23	Bonus Cab Wide-Side 8-ft.	11,154	4773	—
C23	Crew Cab Wide-Side 8-ft.	11,502	4834	—
C26	Suburban V-8	12,349	4771	—
C3500 Pickup — 1-Ton — 134.5 in./164.5 in. — V-6				
C34	Chassis & Cab	9843	4011	—
C34	Fenderside	10,381	4426	—
C34	Wide-Side	10,242	4426	—
C33	Bonus Cab Chassis	10,901	4451	—
C33	Bonus Cab Wide-Side	11,282	4862	—
C33	Crew Cab Chassis	11,253	4512	—
C33	Crew Cab Wide-Side	11,633	4923	—

NOTE 1: S-10 Jimmy also available with 4x2.
NOTE 2: 4x4 GMC trucks have "K" prefix in model number.
NOTE 3: S15 Series: 6-ft. box=108.3 in. w.b.; 7.5-ft. box=122.9 in. w.b.
NOTE 4: Conventionals: 6.5-ft. box=117.5 in.; 8-ft. box=12.5 in. w.b.
NOTE 5: All 1-ton pickups listed above are models with 8-ft. long pickup boxes.
ENGINE [Optional S15]: Inline. OHV. Six-cylinder. Bore & stroke: 3.5 x 2.99 in. Displacement: 173 cid/2.8 liter. Net horsepower: 125 at 4800 rpm. Net torque: 150 lbs.-ft. at 2200 rpm. Hydraulic valve lifters. Carburetor: two-barrel. Engine code B. Source: Chevrolet.
ENGINE [Optional diesel]: V-type. OHV. Eight-cylinder. Cast iron block. Bore & stroke: 3.98 x 3.82 in. Displacement: 379 cid/6.2 liter. Net horsepower: 130 at 3600 rpm. Net torque: 240 at 2000 rpm. Injected diesel. Engine code C. Source: Chevrolet.
ENGINE [C1500 base six]: Inline. OHV. Six-cylinder. Cast iron block. Bore & stroke: 3.876 x 3.530 in. Displacement: 250 cid/4.1 liter. Compression ratio: 8.25:1. Net horsepower: 115 at 3600 rpm. Net torque: 200 lbs.-ft. at 2000 rpm. [above 6,001 lb. GVW]. Net horsepower 100 at 3600 rpm. Net torque: 175 lbs.-ft. at 1800 rpm. Seven main bearings. Hydraulic valve lifters. Carburetor: Mono-Jet model 1ME. Engine code D. Source: Chevrolet.

ENGINE [Safari]: V-type. OHV. Six-cylinder. Cast iron block. Bore & stroke: 4 x 3 in. Displacement: 151 cid/2.5 liter. Net horsepower: 92 at 4000 rpm. Net torque: 134 lbs.-ft. at 2800 rpm. Five main bearings. Hydraulic valve lifters. Carburetor: two-barrel model. Engine code E. Source: Pontiac.

ENGINE [Optional C1500]: V-type. OHV. Eight-cylinder. Cast iron block. Bore & stroke: 3.736 x 3.480 in. Displacement: 305 cid/5.0 liter. Compression ratio: 8.5:1. Net horsepower: 155 at 4000 rpm. Net torque: 245 lbs.-ft. at 1600 rpm. Five main bearings. Hydraulic valve lifters. Carburetor: four-barrel model. Engine code F. Source: Chevrolet.

ENGINE [Optional: C1500/C2500/K1500/Vans/Suburbans]: (Not available in California). V-type. OHV. Eight-cylinder. Cast iron block. Bore & stroke: 3.736 x 3.480 in. Displacement: 305 cid/5.0 liter. Compression ratio: 9.2:1. Net horsepower: 160 at 4400 rpm. Net torque: 235 lbs.-ft. at 2000 rpm. C1500 Brake hp: 165 at 4400 rpm. Max torque: 240 lbs.-ft. at 2000 rpm. Five main bearings. Hydraulic valve lifters. Carburetor: Rochester Staged model four-barrel, Electronic Spark Control (ESC). Code H. Source: Chevrolet.

ENGINE [Optional diesel]: V-type. OHV. Eight-cylinder. Cast iron block. Bore & stroke: 3.98 x 3.82 in. Displacement: 379 cid/6.2 liter. Net horsepower: 148 at 3600 rpm. Net torque: 246 at 2000 rpm. Injected diesel. Engine code J. Source: Chevrolet.

ENGINE [Optional: all models]: V-type. OHV. Eight-cylinder. Cast iron block. Bore & stroke: 4.0 x 3.480 in. Displacement: 350 cid/5.7 liter. Compression ratio: 8.5:1. Net horsepower: 165 at 3800 rpm. Net torque: 275 lbs.-ft. at 1600 rpm. Five main bearings. Hydraulic valve lifters. Carburetor: four-barrel model M4MC/MV. Engine code L. Source: Chevrolet.

ENGINE [Optional: all models]: V-type. OHV. Eight-cylinder. Cast iron block. Bore & stroke: 4.0 x 3.480 in. Displacement: 350 cid/5.7 liter. Compression ratio: 8.5:1. Net horsepower: 185 at 4000 rpm. Net torque: 285 lbs.-ft. at 2400 rpm. Five main bearings. Hydraulic valve lifters. Carburetor: four-barrel model M4MC/MV. Engine code M. Source: Chevrolet.

ENGINE [S15]: Inline. OHC. OHV. Four-cylinder. Bore & stroke: 3.31 x 3.23 in. Displacement: 111 cid/1.8 liter. Net horsepower: 75 at 5000 rpm. Net torque: 88 at 3000 rpm. Hydraulic valve lifters. Carburetor: two-barrel model. Engine code N. Source: Isuzu.

ENGINE [C2500/C3500/P base six]: Inline. OHV. Six-cylinder. Cast iron block. Bore & stroke: 3.8764 x 4.120 in. Displacement: 292 cid/4.8 liter. Compression ratio: 8.0:1. Net horsepower: 115 at 4000 rpm. Net torque: 210 lbs.-ft. at 1800 rpm. Seven main bearings. Hydraulic valve lifters. Carburetor: one-barrel model. Engine code T. Source: Chevrolet.

ENGINE [Optional: C1500/C2500/C3500/K1500/K2500/K3500]: V-type. OHV. Eight-cylinder. Cast iron block. Bore & stroke: 4.250 x 4.0 in. Displacement: 454 cid/7.4 liter. Compression ratio: 8.5:1. Net horsepower: 240 at 3800 rpm. Net torque: 375 lbs.-ft. at 3200 rpm. Five main bearings. Hydraulic valve lifters. Carburetor: four-barrel model M4MC/MV. Engine code W. Source: Chevrolet.

ENGINE [Standard: C/K1500 and C2500 Pickups]: V-type. OHV. Six-cylinder. Cast iron block. Bore & stroke: 4.00 x 3.48 in. Displacement: 262 cid. Compression ratio: 9.3:1. Net horsepower: 155 at 4000 rpm. Net torque: 230 lbs.-ft. at 2400 rpm. Carburetor: Rochester Quadrajet, Electronic Spark Control. Engine code Z. Source: Chevrolet.

1986 GMC Sierra Classic Wide-Side

CHASSIS [Caballero]: Wheelbase: 117.1 in. Overall length: 201.6 in. Height: 53.8 in. Tires: P205/75R14 in.
CHASSIS [S-15 Pickup]: Wheelbase: 108.3/122.9 in. Overall length: 178.2/194.2 in. Height: 61.3 in. Tires: P195/75R14 in.
CHASSIS [S-15 Jimmy]: Wheelbase: 100.5 in. Overall length: 170.3 in. Height: 64.7 in.

Tires: P195/75R15 in.
CHASSIS [C1500 Pickup]: Wheelbase: 117.5/12.5 in. Overall length: 193.5/213.4 in. Height: 69.2 in. Tires: P195/75R15 in.
CHASSIS [C2500 Pickup]: Wheelbase: 12.5 in. Overall length: 213.4 in. Height: 72.2 in. Tires: LT215/85R16 in.
CHASSIS [C3500 Pickup]: Wheelbase: 12.5 in. Overall length: 213.4 in. Height: 73.6 in. Tires: LT235/85R16D-E in.
CHASSIS [T18 Jimmy 4x4]: Wheelbase: 106.5 in. Overall length: 184.8 in. Height: 73.8 in. Tires: P215/75R15 in.
CHASSIS [C1500 Suburban]: Wheelbase: 129.5 in. Overall length: 219.1 in. Height: 72.0 in. Tires: P235/75R15 in.
CHASSIS [G1500 Van]: Wheelbase: 110/125 in. Overall length: 178.2/202.2 in. Height: 79.4 in. Tires: P205/75R15 in.
CHASSIS [Safari]: Wheelbase: 111 in. Overall length: 176.8 in. Height: 71.7 in. Tires: P195/75R15 in.

TECHNICAL: Manual, synchromesh. Speeds: 3F/1R; [S15] 4F/1R; [C3500/K2500/K3500] 4F/1R. Column-mounted three-speed gearshift; floor-mounted four-speed gearshift. [C1500/diesel] standard on selected models with V-6 and diesel: four-speed manual overdrive (synchromesh) transmission. Three-speed and four-speed automatic overdrive transmissions optional on different models. Floor-mounted gearshift. [Clutch] 11 in. diameter in all full-sized models; 12 in. diameter clutch optional. Rear axle: [G1500/C1500/K1500/C2500/K2500] semi-floating; [all others] full-floating. Overall ratio: [C1500] 2.73:1; [C2500/K2500] 3.42:1; [K3500 Bonus/Crew] 4.56:1; all other full-sized models 4.10:1; [S15] 2.56/2.73/3.08/3.42/3.73, depending on rpm, engine, and transmission. [Brakes] Four-wheel hydraulic system, front disc, rear drum brakes. Kelsey-Hayes pressed steel wheels.

OPTIONS: [Caballero] Amarillo package ($225). V-8 engine. [K18 Jimmy] Silverado package ($1015). 6.2L diesel engine. [S15 Jimmy] Sierra Classic package ($595). Gypsy package. [Safari] Tilt steering ($115). Cruise control ($195). [Vans] V-8 engine. Diesel engine. 12-passenger package. [Value Vans] 11,000-pound rear axle. 5.7L V-8 engine. Diesel engine. [S10 Pickup] High Sierra package. Sierra Classic package. Gypsy package. [Pickup/Suburban] High Sierra package. Sierra Classic package. V-8 engine (except Suburbans). Diesel engine.

HISTORICAL: Introduced: Oct., 1985. Model year sales: [Vans] 39,099; [Safari] 29,743; [S15 Pickup] 49,139; [S15 Jimmy] 43,710; [Jimmy] 9686; [Caballero] 2795; [Suburban] 19,287; [Pickups] 114,115; [Value Vans] 4158. [Total, through Sept., 1986] 21,732. Innovations: Redesigned "S" Series instrument panel. Lighter weight alloy pistons in 2.8-liter V-6. Throttle Body Injection (TBI) used on 2.8 liter V-6. Full-size light-duty trucks have new type generator belt. Vortec six standard for full-size pickups. GMC's model year sales (through Sept., 1986) were almost 7,000 units higher than the all-time record set in 1985. During 1986, GMC announced that a new line of smaller conventional pickups would be introduced in May, 1987.

1986 GMC K-Jimmy Sierra Classic

IHC
1907-1980

1961 IHC Scout 1/4-Ton Sport Utility

By John Gunnell

The history of International Harvester Co. traces back to the invention of the McCormick reaper, in 1831. This researcher's grandfather sold such farm machines, for Cyrus McCormick, in the 1880s. It was in 1902, that the IHC merger took place.

By 1907, series production of the IHC high-wheel Auto-Buggy began. Almost immediately, grain box models were offered. These were called Auto-Wagons and were actually light-duty trucks. Vans, buses and more substantial express wagons were on the road by 1912. A year later, the company decided that its motor vehicle operations should be concentrated on the manufacture of trucks.

In 1915, a new line of four-cylinder trucks with a "shovel-nose" hood — like Renaults of the day — was brought out. These had payloads ranging upwards from 3/4-ton. A unique feature was placement of the radiator behind the engine.

A line of famous IHC models, new for 1921, was designated the "S" series. These trucks became popularly known as "Red Babies," due to their small size and bright red finish. They were marketed through IHC farm equipment dealers and caught on with American farmers. The "S" stood for speed-truck and they could zip along at up to 30 mph. A popular configuration was the 1/2-ton pickup.

Production of 50,000 units, in 1929, put IHC in the big leagues. With 170 sales branches, the company blanketed the country and ranked high against major competitors. In fact, for a while, only Chevy and Ford outdid IHC in truck business. It would be years before Dodge and GMC overtook International.

Through the 1930s, IHC adopted alphabetical designations, producing the A- (1930-1932), B- (1933-1934) and C- (1934-1936) series. By this time, there were 217 agencies nationwide.

The "C" series trucks are famous for being the first IHCs to sport car-like styling. They had a v-type aluminum grille and slanted windshield.

A significant light-duty model evolved for 1937. It brought a more modern, streamlined appearance to the line, with its fat-fendered look and turret top styling. Handsome pickups and panel trucks were joined by a wood-bodied station wagon that received lots of promotional attention.

Introduced in 1940, the graceful-looking "K" series carried IHC through the World War II era in grand style. It survived, with just modest changes, through 1949. Also notable was a 1938 innovation, the Metro-bodied multi-stop delivery van. This small businessman's dream truck would soon be available in bakery truck, milk truck and mini-bus styles.

Postwar buyers were treated to a new "KB" model in 1949. It had a steering column mounted gearshift and 82 hp "Green Diamond" six. It was also about this time that the Travelall, a station wagon-like panel truck, debuted.

During the early 1950s, handsomely styled "R" and "S" series trucks were produced. They pioneered such features as one-piece wraparound windshields, two-tone paint jobs and 12-volt electrical systems. Continuing to do yeoman's duties were a wide variety of Metros, with styling much like that of prewar times.

IHC went back to the "A" designation in 1957-1958. This time the letter stood for "anniversary," as this was considered the company's 50th anniversary of truck-making. New for 1959, were "C" models with quad headlights, V-8 engines and optional "Bonus Load" styling. These trucks had slab-sided rear quarters, instead of pontoon fenders. IHC advertised "the box is as wide as the cab" and "25 percent more cargo room."

For 1960, the "B" series moved the quad headlamps sideways, for a lower appearance. Independent front suspension and an hydraulic clutch were technical advances. V-8s became standard for awhile. Before long, the Metro took on a boxier look and a smaller Metro-Mite series bowed.

Making its debut, in 1961, was the Scout. Powered by a slant-mounted half-a-V-8, this Jeep-like utility vehicle started the modern, sporty, four-wheel-drive craze. The base model was a convertible with removable doors. There were soft-top, hardtop and Traveltop versions, too. Sales leaped off to a strong start.

Booming truck sales, in the '60s, left little time for product development. IHC boasted of not believing in model-year changes for the sake of change. But, by 1970, this philosophy started to wither. The light-duty trucks became more modern and boxier-looking. In addition, a larger, longer, lower and more luxurious Scout II entered the picture in late 1971. It quickly found 30,000 buyers.

The energy crunches and economic recessions of the 1970s hurt IHC. By 1975, the company's famous Metro and Travelall models were disappearing — or gone. The Scout seemed to be IHC's best hope. It was treated to countless different decal and trim options. In 1979, IHC introduced the first turbo diesel engine in a 4x4 sports/utility vehicle. It wasn't enough to turn the tide.

In the early 1980s, the company incurred a financial crisis which took it to the brink of bankruptcy in the truck, agricultural and construction equipment markets. To survive the crisis, the Scout was dropped and IHC abandoned the light-duty truck market completely.

In 1986, the company changed its name to Navistar.

1905 IHC Auto Wagon (Mike Carbonella Photo)

1951 IHC Pickup (J.R. Faureau)

1922 IHC Model S "Red Baby" (Hope Emerich)

1954 International Pickup (OCW)

1961 IHC C-120 4x4 Pickup (RCA)

1963 IHC Series 1200 Travelall (RCA)

1964 International Metro Delivery Van (RPZ)

1965 International Travelall (RPZ)

Standard Catalog of Light-Duty Trucks

1968 IHC Model 1200B 4x4 (RCA)

1976 IHC Travelall

1977 IHC Scout II Sport Utility

1978 IHC Scout Terra Sport Pickup (RCA)

1907-1909 IHC

1907 IHC Auto Wagon Panel Delivery (J. Small)

AUTO WAGON — MODEL A — TWO-CYLINDER: International Harvester Co. was formed in 1907. The company's first light-duty truck was the Auto Wagon, a commercial version of the Auto Buggy passenger car. Both vehicles were high-wheeler types using a 20 hp air-cooled two-cylinder engine. The Auto Wagons had a wagon-like express body mounted on the steel frame behind a high platform on which the two-passenger seat was placed. Most of the bodywork was of wood. While early Auto Buggies employed a tiller steering system, a steering wheel seems to have been standardized with the appearance of the 1908 sales catalog. Thus, all of these trucks probably had steering wheels. Speeds up to 20 mph were possible, although 10-12 mph was the regular cruising speed range. Accessory rear seats were available to change the Auto Wagon into a part-time passenger car.

I.D. DATA: Serial number located on manufacturer's plate. Auto Buggy and Auto Wagon serial numbers were in the same sequence. Serial numbers appear to be consecutive and carried over from year-to-year through 1912. An Auto Wagon belonging to the Indianapolis Motor Speedway Hall of Fame museum bears serial number 2551. This corresponds with information that 2,700 IHCs were built between October 1907 and March 1910. Specific starting and ending numbers, by year, are not available.

1907 IHC Auto Wagon Panel Delivery (OCW)

Model	Body Type	Price	Weight	Prod. Total
A	Auto Wagon 2P	600	1600	Note 1

NOTE 1: See serial number data.
ENGINE: Horizontal-opposed. Four-cycle. Air-cooled. Two-cylinder. Cast iron block. Displacement: 196.25 cid.. Bore & stroke: 5 in. x 5 in. ALAM horsepower: 14-20 hp. Cooling: Double fan system. Ignition: Via six battery cells. Carburetor: Described as "reliable and simple." Induction system ued a "reliable" carburetor.

CHASSIS: Wheelbase: 84 in. Front tread: 56 in. Rear tread: 56 in. Tires: Various sizes up to 44 in. diameter.
TECHNICAL: Planetary transmission. Speeds: 2F/1R. Outboard-mounted gearshift lever. Positive type clutch. Chain-drive. Rear wheel brakes. Wood spoke wheels.
OPTIONS: Single front-mounted acetylene gas headlamp. Front-mounted gas tank. Rear passenger seat. Front seat cushions.
HISTORICAL: Introduced during 1909. First IHC commercial vehicle. The Auto Wagon is said to be the first IHC automobile to carry a model designation. It was not considered a motor truck until 1912. IHC specifications and serial numbers were not listed with the Association of Licensed Automobile Manufacturers indicating that the firm was not a member of ALAM. This truck was designed by Mr. E.A. Johnson.

1909 IHC Auto Wagon Express (OCW)

1910 IHC

1910 IHC Auto Wagon Express (OCW)

AUTO WAGON — MODEL A — TWO-CYLINDER: The Model A IHC Auto Wagon was carried into 1910 without major changes. In 1910, model numbers were begun as a means of parts identification, but not to designate particular models. There was a special "wide track" model-option featuring 60 in. wide front and rear treads which were better-suited for use on roads in Southern states.
I.D. DATA: Serial number located on manufacturer's plate. Serial numbers above 2700 appeared after March, 1910. Starting and ending numbers, by year, are not available.

Model	Body Type	Price	Weight	Prod. Total
A	Auto Wagon 2P	800	1600	Note 1

NOTE 1: Total production of IHC high-wheelers between 1907 and 1912 was approximately 4,500. This includes both Auto Buggies and Auto Wagons. Production included 2,700 built through March, 1910 and about 1,800 built thereafter.
ENGINE: Horizontally-opposed. Four-cycle. Air-cooled. Two-cylinder. Cast iron block. Displacement: 196.5 cid.. Bore & stroke: 5 in. x 5 in. ALAM horsepower: 14-20 hp. Cooling: Double fan system. Ignition: Via six battery cells. Carburetor: Described as "reliable and simple."
CHASSIS: Wheelbase: 84 in. Front tread: 56 in. Rear tread: 56 in. Tires: Various sizes up to 44 in. diameter.
TECHNICAL: Planetary transmission. Speeds: 1F/2R. Outboard-mounted gearshift lever. Positive type clutch. Chain-drive. Rear wheel brakes. Wood spoke wheels.
OPTIONS: Single center front acetylene gas headlamp. Front-mounted gas tank. Rear passenger seat. Front seat cushion.
HISTORICAL: The initials IHC came into widespread use for these vehicles during 1910. The company built some four-cylinder passenger cars this year. After 1911, the IHC automobile department was shut down.

Standard Catalog of Light-Duty Trucks

1911 IHC

AUTO WAGON — MODEL A — TWO-CYLINDER: The Model A IHC Auto Wagon entered its final year of production in 1911. By this time, dual brass headlamps and even cowl lamps were showing up on these primitive trucks. Although the name Auto Wagon would be replaced by the designation Motor Truck, and some refinements would occur, the IHC high-wheel commercial vehicles did not disappear.

1911 IHC Auto Wagon Utility Express (MVMA/DFW)

I.D. DATA: Serial number located on manufacturer's plate. All 1911 serial numbers were above 2700. Number 4500 was the approximate ending number for the series, as far as can be determined.

Model	Body Type	Price	Weight	Prod. Total
A	Auto Wagon 2P	800	1600	Note 1

NOTE 1: It appears that approximately 1,800 vehicles were built in the 1911 series.

ENGINE: Horizontal-opposed. Four-cycle. Air-cooled. Two-cylinder. Cast iron block. Displacement: 196.5 cid.. Bore & stroke: 5 in. x 5 in. ALAM horsepower: 14-20 hp. Cooling: Double fan system. Ignition: Six battery cells.

CHASSIS: Wheelbase: 84 in. Front tread: 56 in. Rear tread: 56 in. Tires: Various sizes up to 44 in. diameter.

TECHNICAL: Planetary transmission. Speeds: 2F/1R. Outboard-mounted gearshift lever. Positive type clutch. Chain-drive. Rear wheel brakes. Wood spoke wheels.

OPTIONS: Single center-mounted front acetylene headlamp. Dual side-mounted acetylene headlamps. Sunday-go-to-meeting type rear passenger seat. Front seat cushions.

HISTORICAL: Final year for IHC automobile production.

1912 IHC

MOTOR TRUCK — AW/MW — TWO-CYLINDER: In its 1912 Directory of Automobiles the motoring publication *AUTOMOBILE TRADE JOURNAL* referenced some new models bearing the familiar IHC logo. "The International Harvester Co., Harvester Building, Chicago, Ill. is exhibiting at the Chicago Show its 1,000 lb. delivery wagon, with open panel express," the report began, going on to describe a larger, more powerful high-wheel commercial vehicle that replaced the original Auto Wagon. The 1912 line actually consisted of AW and MW series and several new body types. An IHC-built air-cooled engine was used in the AW series. The MW models at first utilized a British-American-built water-cooled powerplant. This year, in addition to the open delivery, there were panel trucks, hucksters, canopy wagons, mail trucks and auto-buses. The high-wheelers were now called Motor Trucks and featured a short hood in the front, dual acetylene headlamps, cowl lamps and a horn. Many models were also fitted with full or partial side curtains, upholstered seats, fenders, folding windshields, tool boxes and auxiliary seats.

I.D. DATA: Serial number located on manufacturer's plate.

Model	Body Type	Price	Weight	Prod. Total
1,000 lb. Motor Truck — 1/2-Ton				
AA	Delivery Wagon - 2P	800	2500	—
AW	Panel Express - 2P	900	2540	—
MW	Panel Express - 2P	950	2695	—
MW	Canopy Express - 9P	1050	2600	—
MA	Delivery Wagon - 2P	850	2610	—

1912 IHC Motor Truck 1/2-Ton Panel Express (HAC/DFW)

ENGINE [AW]: Horizontal-opposed. Four-cycle. Air-cooled. Two-cylinder. Cast iron block. Displacement: 196.5 cid.. Bore & stroke: 5 in. x 5 in. ALAM horsepower: 18-20 hp. Ignition: Bosch magneto. Lubrication: Mechanical oiler system.
ENGINE [MW]: Horizontal-opposed. Water-cooled. Two-cylinder. Cast iron alloy. Displacement: 196.5 cid.. Bore & Stroke: 5 in. x 5 in. ALAM Horsepower: 15 hp.

1912 IHC 1/2-Ton Motor Truck Delivery Wagon (OCW)

CHASSIS: Wheelbase: 90 in. Overall Length: 96 in. Height: 48 in. Front tread: 56 in. Rear tread: 56 in. Tires: Various sizes up to 44 in. diameter.
TECHNICAL: Individual clutch type transmission. Speeds: 2F/1R. Outboard-mounted gearshift lever. Positive type clutch. Chain-drive rear axle. Expanding/contracting rear wheel brakes. Wood spoke wheels.
OPTIONS: Dual acetylene headlamps. Cowl lamps. Side curtains. Upholstered seat. Auxiliary seats. 60 inch southern tread. Leather fenders. Acetylene tank. Tool box. Folding windshield. Tool boxes. Express box tarpaulin. Canopy style top.
HISTORICAL: First true IHC trucks this year. New water-cooled engine available. Last year for right-hand drive only. Some Auto Wagons still made through 1916.

1913-1914 IHC

MOTOR TRUCK — AW/MW — TWO-CYLINDER: There were four Motor Trucks offered by International Harvester Co. for the 1913 and 1914 model years. All were listed in used car reference books as panel express vehicles. At least some left-hand drive units appeared in 1913. Photos from the period suggest that many purpose-built bodies appeared and that open delivery wagons were still available.

1913 IHC Model MW 1/2-Ton Flareboard Express (R. Theimer)

I.D. DATA: Serial number located on manufacturer's plate.

479

1914 IHC Motor Truck 1/2-Ton Curtained Flareboard Express (OCW)

Model	Body Type	Price	Weight	Prod. Total
1,000 lb. Motor Truck — 1/2-Ton				
AA	Panel Express - 2P	800	2500	—
AW	Panel Express - 2P	900	2695	—
MA	Panel Express - 3P	850	2610	—
MW	Panel Express - 2P	950	2695	—

NOTE 1: Models AA and AW were rated for 800 lb. capacity
NOTE 2: Models MA and MW were rated for 1,000 lb. capacity.
NOTE 3: Gross vehicle weights were as follows: [Model AA] 3,300 lbs.; [Model AW] 3,340 lbs.; [Model MA] 3,610 lbs. and [Model MW] 3,695 lbs.

1913 IHC Motor Wagon 1/2-Ton Flareboard Express (OCW)

ENGINE: Horizontally-opposed. Four-cycle. Air-cooled. Two-cylinder. Cast iron block. Displacement: 196.5 cid.. Bore & stroke: 5 in. x 5 in. ALAM horsepower: 18-20 hp. Ignition: Bosch magneto. Lubrication: Mechanical oiler system. (Note. A first in model designation indicates use of air-cooled engine.)
ENGINE: Horizontally-opposed. Four-cycle. Water-cooled. Two-cylinder. Cast iron block. Displacement: 196.5 cid.. Bore & stroke: 5 in. x 5 in. ALAM horsepower: 18-20 hp. Ignition: Bosch magneto. Lubrication: Mechanical oiler system. (Note: M first in model designation indicates use of water-cooled engine.)

1914 IHC Model MW 1/2-Ton Flareboard Express (OCW)

CHASSIS: Wheelbase: 90 in. Overall Length: 96 in. Height: 48 in. Front tread: 56 in. Rear tread: 56 in. Tires: Sizes up to 44 in. diameter.
TECHNICAL: Individual clutch type transmission. Speeds: 2F/1R. Outboard-mounted gearshift lever. Positive type clutch. Chain-drive to rear axle. Expanding/contracting rear wheel brakes. Wood spoke wheels.

OPTIONS: Acetylene tank. Acetylene headlamps. Cowl lamps. Kerosene taillamp. Upholstered seat. Auxiliary seats. 60 in. Southern tread. Leather fenders. Tool box. Two-piece folding windshield. Side curtains. Tool box. Express box tarpaulin. Canopy style top.

1914 IHC Model MA 1/2-Ton Flareboard Express (OCW)

HISTORICAL: First appearance of left-hand steering. Final full production year for air-cooled models as a contemporary product. Some Model As were built through 1916. In 1914, the name International began to appear on the company's trucks, replacing the initials IHC.

1915 IHC

1915 IHC Model AW 1/2-Ton Flareboard Express (D. Christie)

MOTOR TRUCK — MODEL E/F — TWO-CYLINDER: Different reference sources list different trucks in the IHC product line for 1915. There is a Model M 1/2-ton listed in one used car price book, along with the 3/4-ton Model E. A vehicle weight guide from the State of Wisconsin shows only the 3/4-ton Model E and one-ton Model F. And a *BRANHAM AUTOMOBILE REFERENCE BOOK* shows only the 1-ton Model F. The Model M was a carryover of the 1913-1914 Model MW. The Model E was probably a transitional model. However, the Model F was more revolutionary. It was an all-new, larger vehicle that was only nominally a light-duty truck. In most configurations, it was clearly intended for heavy-duty usage. Among its innovations were a unique sloping hood, rear-mounted (behind engine) radiator, artillery wheels with hard rubber tires and built-in fenders. Also, below the hood was a new four-cylinder powerplant.
I.D. DATA: Serial number located on manufacturer's plate on dashboard. Model F (only): Starting number 501. Ending number: 600.

Model	Body Type	Price	Weight	Prod. Total
M	1/2-Ton Chassis - 2P	750	2700	—
E	3/4-Ton Chassis - 2P	1000	3300	—
F	1-Ton Chassis - 2P	1500	3950	99

NOTE 1: *BRANHAM AUTOMOBILE REFERENCE BOOK* lists serial numbers 501 to 600 for the 1915 Model F, suggesting production of 99 units for the year.
NOTE 2: Capacity Ratings: [Model E] 1,500 lbs.; [Model F] 2,000 lbs.
NOTE 3: Gross Pounds: [Model E] 4,800 lbs.; [Model F] 5,950 lbs.
ENGINE [Model M]: Horizontally-opposed. Four-cycle. Water-cooled. Two-cylinder. Cast iron block. Displacement: 196.5 cid.. Bore & stroke: 5 in. x 5 in. ALAM horsepower: 18-20 hp. Ignition: Bosch magneto. Lubrication: Mechanical oiler system.
ENGINE [Models E/F]: Inline. Cast en bloc. Four-cylinder. Cast iron block. Bore & stroke: 3-1/2 in. x 5 in. ALAM horsepower: 19.60 hp. Bosch or Dixie magneto ignition.
CHASSIS [Model M]: Wheelbase: 90 in. Overall Length: 96 in. Height: 48 in. Front tread: 56 in. Rear tread: 56 in. Tires: Sizes up to 44 in. diameter.
CHASSIS [Model E/F]: Wheelbase: 128 in. Front tread: 56 in. Rear tread: 56 in. Tires: 36 in. diameter.

TECHNICAL: Selective sliding transmission. Speeds: 3F/1R. Floor-mounted gearshift lever. Internal gear rear axle. Overall ratios: [Model F] 7.91:1. Expanding and contracting rear wheel brakes. Artillery spoke wheels.

OPTIONS: Headlamps. Cowl lamps. Taillights. Pneumatic tires ($55). Windshield. Side curtains. Electric lighting ($75).

HISTORICAL: The new-for-1915 four-cylinder engine had the same bore and stroke measurements as the Model 8-16 International farm tractor engine. The Model F found favor with many fire apparatus builders as the basis of a light-duty fire truck combining faster road speeds with rugged and durable construction. IHC held approximately four percent of the total domestic truck market.

1916-1920 IHC

1916-1920 IHC 3/4-ton Model H Screenside (Goodyear)

MOTOR TRUCK — MODEL H/F — FOUR-CYLINDER: International Harvester Co. was primarily involved in the heavy-duty truck building market through 1920. Models between 1-ton and 3-1/2-tons represented the mainstay products during this period. The lightest models were the 3/4-ton Model H and 1-ton Model F. The Model F specifications remained unchanged from 1915. The Model H was a similar looking vehicle, but on a slightly smaller scale. It featured the characteristic sloping, Renault-style hood, a behind-the-engine radiator and the IHC 20 hp four-cylinder engine. After its introduction in 1916, this 3/4-tonner was carried over, through 1920, with the main change each season being the manufacturer's suggested retail price.

I.D. DATA: Serial number located on manufacturer's plate on the dashboard. Annual starting and ending numbers were as follows, [Model F]: (1916) 601-1417; (1917) 1418-3956; (1918) 3957-7385; (1919) 5305-5999; (1920) 8977-& up [Model H]: (1916) 501-1096; (1917) 1097-3300; (1918) 3301-5304; (1919) 7386-8976; (1920) 6000-& up.

Model	Body Type	Price	Weight	Prod. Total
1916				
F	Express	1550	3950	816
H	Express	1250	3650	595
1917				
F	Chassis	1500	3950	2538
H	Chassis	1225	3650	2203
1918				
F	Chassis	1750	3950	3428
H	Chassis	1450	3650	2200
1919				
F	Chassis	1750	3950	1590
H	Chassis	1450	3650	694
1920				
F	Chassis	—	3950	—
H	Chassis	—	3650	—

NOTE 1: Model H=3/4-ton; Model F=1-ton.
NOTE 2: GVW Ratings: [Model F] 5,950 lbs.; [Model H] 5,150 lbs.
NOTE 3: Production estimates above based on serial numbers.
ENGINE: Inline. Cast en bloc. Four-cylinder. Cast iron block. Bore & stroke: 3-1/2 in. x 5-1/4 in. ALAM horsepower: 19.60 hp. Holley carburetor. Magneto ignition by Bosch or Dixie.
CHASSIS [Model F]: Wheelbase: 128 in. Front tread: 56 in. Rear tread: 56 in. Tires: 36 in. diameter.
CHASSIS [Model H]: Wheelbase: 115 in. Front tread: 56 in. Rear tread: 56 in.
TECHNICAL: Selective sliding transmission. Speeds: 3F/1R. Floor-mounted gearshift lever. Internal gear rear axle. Overall ratio: [Model F] 7.91:1; [Model H] 6.8:1. Expanding and contracting rear wheel brakes. Artillery spoke wheels.
OPTIONS: Headlamps. Cowl lamps. Taillights. Pneumatic tires ($55). Windshield. Side curtains. Electric lighting ($75).
HISTORICAL: Like other U.S. truck manufacturers, IHC made a formidable effort to support the Allied Operations in Europe during World War I. On June 14, 1916 an IHC Model F became the first truck to climb Pike's Peak in Colorado. The last of the original Auto Wagons left the IHC Akron works in Akron, Ohio in 1916. In 1919, IHC purchased the Parlin & Orendorff Co. of Canton, Ill., a major farm equipment manufacturer. This strengthened the entire company.

1921 IHC

1921 IHC Model S "Red Baby" Express (OCW)

MOTOR TRUCK — MODELS S AND 21 — FOUR-CYLINDER: Like other truck manufacturers, International Harvester Co. introduced a line of smaller, faster "speed" trucks in 1921. The new Model S was one of these. It was rated for 3/4-ton and featured a conventional style hood, flat radiator and pneumatic tires. The engine used was a Lycoming KB four-cylinder with the radiator in front. Standard features included electric starting and lighting, a storage battery, power tire pump and electric horn. These trucks were painted bright red at the factory and they became known as "Red Babies." Their scaled-down size and lighter weight made road speeds of 25 to 30 mph possible. A 1-ton Model 21 truck was also offered to replace the earlier and similar Model H. This truck retained the sloping hood and rear-of-engine radiator mounting. It was not a true light-duty truck in today's meaning of the term, but some light commercial vehicle buffs do collect such rigs that fall into the borderline 1-ton class.

I.D. DATA: Serial number located on manufacturer's plate on dash. [Model S] Serial numbers 101 through 2600 were used in 1921. [Model 21] Serial numbers through 567 were used in 1921, but the beginning number is unavailable. Engine numbers located on left-hand side at base of engine block.

Model	Body Type	Price	Weight	Prod. Total
Model S — 3/4-Ton — 115 in. w.b.				
S	Chassis	—	2600	2499
Model 21 — 1-Ton — 128 in. w.b.				
21	Chassis	—	3030	566

NOTE 1: Production totals are estimates based on serial number references.
NOTE 2: Prices "available upon application" as dealer discounts were common.
NOTE 3: [S] Net Wt.=3,511 lbs.; Load Capacity=1,500 lbs.; GVW=5,011 lbs.
NOTE 4: [21] Net Wt.=3,980 lbs.; Load Capacity=2,000 lbs.; GVW=5,980 lbs.

ENGINE: Inline. L-head. Four-cylinder. Cast iron block. Bore & stroke: 3-1/2 in. x 5-1/4 in. Displacement: 192.4 cid.. Brake horsepower: 35 at 2100 rpm. Net horsepower: 19.60 (ALAM). Main bearings: Two. Valve lifters: Solid. Carburetor: Ensign model.
CHASSIS [Model S]: Wheelbase: 115 in. Front tread: 56 in. Rear tread: 56 in. Tires: 30 x 5.25 pneumatic.
CHASSIS [Model 21]: Wheelbase: 115 in. Front tread: 56 in. Rear tread: 56 in. Tires: 30 x 5.25 pneumatic.
TECHNICAL [Model S]: Selective sliding transmission. Speeds: 3F/1R. Floor-mounted gearshift. Clutch: Multiple disc type. Semi-floating rear axle. Overall ratio: 6.3:1. Rear wheel brakes. Artillery spoke wheels.
NOTE 5: Technical data for the Model 21 is similar to the 1916-1920 Model H. Exception: 6.8:1 final gear ratio.
OPTIONS: Full-length runningboards. Speedometer. Variety of cabs and bodies. Wire spoke wheels. Taillight.
HISTORICAL: Production: Over 33,000 IHC Model S trucks were built between 1921 and 1926. Innovations: During this period, IHC had a large force of field representatives to maintain contact with its farm implement dealers and agents nationwide. They were called blockmen and drove red Model S pickups as service trucks. Before long, these "Red Babies" seemed as common in rural areas as Model T Fords. A cast iron promotional model toy version was made. In addition, the Buddy L toy company also sold a toy version of the Model S. Both of these toys are collectible items now. During 1921, IHC Model S truck manufacturing moved to the Springfield Works, Springfield, Ohio.

1922 IHC

MOTOR TRUCK — MODELS S AND 21 — FOUR-CYLINDER: Both the Model S and Model 21 were carried over, basically unchanged, for 1922. The weights of both saw a slight increase, suggesting the inclusion of more standard equipment. An Inspection Service Policy was offered to buyers this season.

I.D. DATA: Serial number located on manufacturer's plate on dash. Serial numbers 2601 to 9900 were used on 1922 Model S trucks. Serial numbers 568 to 787 were used on 1922 Model 21 trucks. Engine numbers located on left side of motor at base.

Model	Body Type	Price	Weight	Prod. Total
Model S Series — 3/4-Ton — 115 in. w.b.				
S	Chassis	—	2761	7299
Model 21 Series — 1-Ton — 128 in. w.b.				
21	Chassis	—	3030	219
21	Chassis	—	3160	219

NOTE 1: Production totals are estimates based on serial number references.
NOTE 2: Prices "available upon application" due to dealer discount programs.
NOTE 3: [S] Net. Wt.=3,661 lbs.; Load Capacity=1,500 lbs.; GVW=5,661 lbs.
NOTE 4: [21] Net Wt.=4,030 lbs.; Load Capacity=2,000 lbs.; GVW=6,030 lbs.

1922 IHC Model S "Red Baby" Express (John Scott)

ENGINE: Inline. L-head. Four-cylinder. Cast iron block. Bore & stroke: 3-1/2 in. x 5-1/4 in. Displacement: 192.4 cid.. Brake horsepower: 35 at 2100 rpm. ALAM horsepower: 19.60 hp. Two main bearings. Solid valve lifters. Ensign carburetor.
CHASSIS [Model S]: Wheelbase: 115 in./124-1/8 in. Front tread: 56 in. Rear tread: 56 in. Tires: 30 x 5.25 pnuematic.
CHASSIS [Model 21]: Wheelbase: 115 in. Front tread: 56 in. Rear tread: 56 in. Tires: 30 x 5.25 pneumatic.
TECHNICAL [Model S]: Selective sliding transmission. Speeds: 3F/1R. Floor-mounted gearshift lever. Multiple disc type clutch. Semi-floating rear axle. Overall ratio: 6.3:1. Rear wheel brakes. Artillery spoke wheels.
NOTE: Technical data for Model 21 similar to 1916-1920 Model H. Final gear ratio changed to 7.0:1 this year.
OPTIONS: Full-length runningboards. Speedometer. Variety of cabs and bodies. Wire spoke wheels. Front bumper. Taillight.
HISTORICAL: Approximately 7,500 of the 3/4-ton and 1-ton trucks were made this year. Free inspection service policy was offered this year.

1923 IHC

MOTOR TRUCK — MODEL S AND MODEL 21 — FOUR-CYLINDER: The Model S had a slightly lower shipping weight, but higher hood and load capacity this season. It was up-rated to a 1-ton. There was no basic change in design, however. The Model 21 was carried over from 1922 with unchanged specifications. Serial and motor number locations changed this year.

1923 IHC Model S 1-Ton Panel (Giant Mfg. Co./DFW)

I.D. DATA: Serial number located on floorboard in right side of driving compartment. Serial numbers 9901 to 20644 were used on 1923 Model S trucks. Serial numbers for the Model 21 started at 787, with ending number not available. Engine numbers located on left-hand side of crankcase.

Model	Body Type	Price	Weight	Prod. Total
Model S Series — 1-Ton — 115 in./124-1/8 in. w.b.				
S	Chassis	—	2700	10,743
Model 21 Series — 1-Ton — 128 in. w.b.				
21	Chassis	—	3030	—

NOTE 1: Model S production total estimated based on serial numbers.
NOTE 2: Prices "available upon application" due to dealer discount program.
NOTE 3: [S] Net Wt.=3,650 lbs.; Load Capacity=2,000 lbs.; GVW=5,650 lbs.
NOTE 4: [21] Net Wt.=3,980 lbs.; Load Capacity=2,000 lbs.; GVW=5,980 lbs.
ENGINE: Inline. L-head. Four-cylinder. Cast iron block. Bore & stroke: 3-1/2 in. x 5-1/4 in. Displacement: 192.4 cid.. Brake horsepower: 35 at 2100 rpm. Net horsepower: 19.60 (ALAM). Main bearings: Two. Valve lifters: Solid. Carburetor: Ensign.
CHASSIS [Model S]: Wheelbase: 115 in./128 in. Front tread: 56 in. Rear tread: 56 in. Tires: 30 x 5.25 pneumatic.
CHASSIS [Model 21]: Wheelbase: 115 in./128 in. Front tread: 56 in. Rear tread: 56 in. Tires: 30 x 5.25 pneumatic.
TECHNICAL [Model S]: Selective sliding transmission. Speeds: 3F/1R. Floor-mounted gearshift. Clutch: Multiple disc type. Semi-floating rear axle. Overall ratio: 6.3:1. Rear wheel brakes. Artillery spoke wheels.
NOTE: Technical data for Model 21 similar to 1916-1920 Model H.
OPTIONS: Full-length runningboards. Speedometer. Variety of cabs and bodies. Wire spoke wheels. Front bumper. Taillight.
HISTORICAL: During 1923, a brand new IHC factory was built in Fort Wayne, Ind. This was the final season for production of the Model 21.

1924 IHC

1924 IHC Model S 1-Ton Panel (OCW)

1925 IHC

MOTOR TRUCK — MODEL S SPEED TRUCK — FOUR-CYLINDER: IHC identification was no longer used on International trucks, although it was still the corporate abbreviation. The Model S speed truck was carried over from 1923 without change. Please refer to the 1923 section for information about this model. The Model 21 was no longer available. Gone from all International trucks this season were sloped, French-style hoods and behind-the-engine radiators. The company now had a total of 102 factory branches and 1,500 dealers. An industrial tractor was introduced by IHC this year under its McCormick-Deering farm equipment nameplate. Serial numbers 15800 to 20645 were found on 1924 Model S trucks, suggesting production of some 4,845 units. This brought total production of this truck, over four years, to more than 25,000 units.
MOTOR TRUCK — SPECIAL DELIVERY — FOUR-CYLINDER: A new 3/4-ton Special Delivery model was introduced under the International truck nameplate this year. It had a 116 in. wheelbase and was powered by a four-cylinder Waukesha engine. This model carried the International name on the sides of its butterfly hood, above eight vertical louvers. The Model S had the name on the body sill behind the cab doors. Standard Special Delivery features included pneumatic tires, air cleaner, electric lights, electric starter and speedometer. Among a long list of extra-cost options were full-length runningboards, water pump and deluxe nickle-plated radiator shell. This model should not be confused with the SD, an updated version of the Model S 1-ton.
MOTOR TRUCK — MODELS S/SD/SL — FOUR-CYLINDER: The Model S continued to be available for 1-ton truck buyers in 1925. It was joined by two new variations, the SD and SL, which were produced in relatively small numbers. All of these continued to use the 20 hp (ALAM) Lycoming Model K engine. This was the only year that the SD and SL were rated at 1-ton. Both were uprated to 1-1/2-tons for 1926, when they became the basis for IHC's first tractor-trailer truck with a 110 in. wheelbase. IHC also started manufacturing buses this season and made at least several Lang-bodied buses on the Model S running gear, probably with an extended wheelbase.

1925 IHC Model S 1-Ton Flareboard Express (Mike Carbonella)

I.D. DATA: Serial number located on floorboard in right side of driving compartment. Serial numbers 501 and up were used on Special Delivery trucks. Serial numbers 20645 and up were used on Model S trucks. Serial numbers 501 and up were used on both Model SD and SL trucks. Engine numbers located on left side of crankcase.

Model	Body Type	Price	Weight	Prod. Total
Special Delivery Series — 3/4-Ton				
—	Special Delivery	—	1850	—
Model S Series — 1-Ton				
S	Chassis	—	2700	—
SD	Chassis	—	2855	—
SL	Chassis	—	3156	—

NOTE 1: Prices upon application due to dealer discount program.
NOTE 2: [S] Net. Wt.=3,650 lbs. (pneumatic tires); Load Capacity=2,000 lbs.; GVW=5,650 lbs.
NOTE 3: [SD] Net Wt.=3,720 lbs.; Load Capacity=2,000 lbs.; GVW=5,720 lbs.

ENGINE [Special Delivery]: Inline. L-head. Waukesha four-cylinder. Cast iron block. Bore & stroke: 3-1/4 in. x 4-1/2 in. Displacement: 149.3 cid.. Net horsepower: 16.90. Solid valve lifters. Carburetor: Own.

ENGINE [Model S/SD/SL]: Inline. L-head. Lycoming four-cylinder. Cast iron block. Bore & stroke: 3-1/2 in. x 5-1/4 in.. Displacement: 192.4 cid.. Brake horsepower: 35 at 2100 rpm. Net horsepower: 19.60 (ALAM) Two main bearings. Solid valve lifters. Ensign carburetor.

CHASSIS [Special Delivery]: Wheelbase: 116 in. Front tread: 56 in. Rear tread: 56 in. Tires: 30 x 5.25 pneumatic.

CHASSIS [Model S]: Wheelbase: 115 in./124 in. Front tread: 56 in. Rear tread: 56 in. Tires: 30 x 5.25 pneumatic.

TECHNICAL [Model S]: Selective sliding transmission. Speeds: 3F/1R. Floor-mounted gearshift lever. Multiple disc type clutch. Semi-floating rear axle. Rear wheel brakes. Artillery spoke wheels.

OPTIONS: Front bumper. Pneumatic tires. Full-length runningboards. Nickel plated radiator. Variety of bodies and cabs. Speedometer (standard on Special Delivery). Wire spoke wheels. Dual taillights. Water pump .

HISTORICAL: IHC began manufacturing buses in 1925.

1926 IHC

MOTOR TRUCK — MODEL S — FOUR-CYLINDER: The nearest thing to a light-duty International truck in 1926 was the 1-ton Model S speed chassis. A new shipping weight of 2,670 lbs. was given for this model, which continued to use the four-cylinder Lycoming engine, still found in the same locations, began with 27238-C. Little else about the truck seems to have changed. Consult the 1925 section of this catalog for additional information. The models SD and SL were up-rated to 1-1/2-tons and available as tractor-trailer trucks. The 1925 type Special Delivery model was no longer available, although a different truck using the same designation would be introduced in the spring of 1927 as the Series S Special Delivery. In general terms, this was the season that enclosed cabs began to appear in greater evidence on all IHC trucks.

1926 IHC Model S 1-Ton Express (NI/DFW)

1927-1928 IHC

1927 IHC 1-Ton Platform Stake (OCW)

SPECIAL DELIVERY — SERIES S — FOUR-CYLINDER: Featuring up-to-date, passenger car-like styling that set it apart from earlier IHC products, the second type of Special Delivery from International bowed in the spring of 1927. This 3/4-ton C-cab panel delivery was characterized by a longer, lower hood; wider and flatter cowl; crisper body sills with full-length runningboards; full crown fenders; drum headlights; a nickle-plated radiator shell; multiple vertical hood louvers; and a lower overall body height. The engine was a 20 hp Waukesha four-cylinder. A 116 in. wheelbase was featured in 1927, growing to 124 in. for 1928. Factory-crafted bodies were fitted.

I.D. DATA: Serial number located on plate on dash; also on right side of floorboard. Production started each year with number 501. A suffix was used to indicate series production. Motor numbers on left side of crankcase.

Model	Body Type	Price	Weight	Prod. Total
Special Delivery (SD) — Series S — 3/4-Ton				
SD	Panel	720	2188	—
SD	Pickup	—	—	—
SD	Canopy	—	—	—
SD	Screen	—	—	—
SD	Sedan Delivery	—	—	—

1927 IHC 1/2-Ton Special Delivery Pickup (Ferris State College)

ENGINE: Inline. L-head. Four-cylinder. Cast iron block. Bore & stroke: 3-1/2 in. x 4-1/2 in. Displacement: 173 cid.. Brake horsepower: 30 at 2700 rpm. Net horsepower: 19.60 (NACC). Valve lifters: Solid. Carburetor: Zenith.
CHASSIS: Wheelbase: [1927] 116 in.; [1928] 124 in. Front tread: 56 in. Rear tread: 56 in. Tires: 30 x 5 in.
TECHNICAL: Selective sliding transmission. Speeds: 3F/1R. Floor-mounted gearshift. Clutch: Multiple disc. Semi-floating rear axle. Rear wheel brakes. Artillery spoke wheels.
OPTIONS: Front bumper. Special paint. Sidemount spare tire. Dual taillamps. Auxiliary passenger seat.

1928 IHC 3/4- to 1-Ton Canopy Express (OCW)

HISTORICAL: Introduced: Spring 1927. Calendar year sales: [1927] 16,356 for all trucks. Calendar year production: A total of 25,000 IHC trucks were built in 1927, including all models from 3/4- to 5-tons. Innovations: "Six-Speed Special" introduced in heavy truck lineup and new generation of light-duty Special Delivery models appeared at midyear 1927. In December, 1927 a Special Delivery made a 6,618 mile trip from Nairobi to Algiers, in Africa, via the Sahara Desert. The truck averaged 15 mpg of gasoline for the 16 day journey.

1929 IHC

1929 IHC 3/4- to 1-Ton Platform Stake (Mike Carbonella photo)

SPECIAL DELIVERY — SERIES S — FOUR-CYLINDER: The Series S Special Delivery continued to be offered on the 3/4-ton chassis. There were no changes to speak of. This was a record season for International truck sales in all weight classes and categories. There were still several 1-ton series available.
I.D. DATA: Serial number located on plate on dash; also on right side of floorboard. Production started each year with number 501, with a suffix used to indicate series production. Motor numbers on left side of block.

Model	Body Type	Price	Weight	Prod. Total
Series S				
Special Delivery — Series S — 3/4-Ton				
SD	Panel	720	2188	—
SD	Pickup	—	—	—
SD	Canopy	—	—	—
SD	Screen	—	—	—
SD	Sedan Delivery	—	—	—

ENGINE: Inline. L-head. Four-cylinder. Cast iron block. Bore & stroke: 3-1/2 in. x 4-1/2 in. Displacement: 173 cid.. Brake horsepower: 30 at 2700 rpm. Net horsepower: 19.60 (NACC). Valve lifters: Solid. Carburetor: Zenith.
CHASSIS: Wheelbase: 124 in. Front tread: 56 in. Rear tread: 56 in. Tires: 30 x 5 in.
TECHNICAL: Selective sliding transmission. Speeds: 3F/1R. Floor-mounted gearshift. Clutch: Multiple disc. Semi-floating rear axle. Rear wheel brakes. Artillery spoke wheels.
OPTIONS: Front bumper. Special paint. Sidemount spare tire. Dual taillamps. Auxiliary passenger seat.

HISTORICAL: Introduced: December 1928. Calendar year sales: [All IHC trucks] 31,434. Calendar year production: [All IHC trucks] over 50,000 units. By 1929, International Harvester had expanded to 170 branches nationwide. Total production of all IHC trucks surpassed 50,000 units.

1930 IHC

1930 IHC 1/2-Ton Model AW-1 Panel (OCW)

LIGHT TRUCK — SERIES AW-1 — FOUR-CYLINDER: International trucks, large and small, came in a brand new "A" series this year. They were handsome vehicles with plated radiator shells of a square design, torpedo headlights, more rounded full-crown fenders, squarer hoods, wider diamond pattern runningboards, cowl vents and cowl lamps, and distinctive wraparound belt moldings. These were again 3/4-ton models using the same Waukesha engine. A choice of 124 in. or 136 in. wheelbases was available.
I.D. DATA: Serial number located on plate on dash; also on right side of floorboard. Production started with number 501. Motor numbers on left side of block.

Model	Body Type	Price	Weight	Prod. Total
Series AW-1 — 3/4-Ton				
AW-1	Chassis	720	2622	—
AW-1	Panel	720	2188	—
AW-1	Pickup	—	—	—
AW-1	Canopy	—	—	—
AW-1	Screen	—	—	—
AW-1	Sedan Delivery	—	—	—

ENGINE: Inline. L-head. Four-cylinder. Cast iron block. Bore & stroke: 3-1/2 in. x 4-1/2 in. Displacement: 173 cid.. Brake horsepower: 30 at 2700 rpm. Net horsepower: 19.60 (NACC). Solid valve lifters. Carburetor: Zenith.
CHASSIS: Wheelbase: 124 in./136 in. Front tread: 56 in. Rear tread: 56 in. Tires: 30 x 5 in.
TECHNICAL [Model S]: Selective sliding transmission. Speeds: 3F/1R. Floor-mounted gearshift lever. Multiple disc type clutch. Semi-floating rear axle. Rear wheel brakes. Artillery spoke wheels.
OPTIONS: Sidemounted spare. Special paint. Front bumper. Dual taillights. Cowl lamps. Deluxe trim package. Bed rails.
HISTORICAL: Introduced mid-1930. Calendar year sales: [All trucks] 23,703 units. After 1929, the economic depression sent IHC sales tumbling down to below the levels of the late 1920s. During this period, IHC was third in total U.S. truck sales. Its ranking in the light truck field was much lower and management became interested in marketing a 1/2-ton model.

1931 IHC

LIGHT TRUCK — SERIES AW-1/SERIES A-1 — FOUR-CYLINDER: For 1931, IHC offered 3/4-ton trucks in two series. Both looked the same, being similar in appearance and style to last season's AW-1. They both used a Waukesha four-cylinder engine and 136 in. wheelbase. However, the new A-1 Series 3/4-ton was slighty larger overall and a bit pricier. The engine used in the smaller line was Waukesha's XA model, while the larger truck had an XAH engine with a larger bore, but the same stroke. It had nine additional brake horsepower. Styling features included chrome radiator shells, torpedo headlights, vertical louver hoods, cadet sun visors, spider style spoke steel wheels and full runningboards. Tools, jack, tool box, ammeter, electric head and taillamps, radiator guard, front fenders and horn. The A-1 model still used a vacuum tank fuel system. It had its light switch on the steering column. A mechanical split-type universal joint was used The transmission was a four-speed manual unit. Line-bored main bearings and poured rods were used.
I.D. DATA: Serial number located on plate on dash and on floorboard at right side. Numbers 501 and up (both series). Motor number on left side of crankcase.

Model	Body Type	Price	Weight	Prod. Total
Series AW-1 — Special Delivery — 3/4-Ton				
AW-1	Chassis	650	2620	—
AW-1	Pickup	882	3542	—
AW-1	Canopy	900	3827	—
AW-1	Screen	900	3827	—
AW-1	Panel	1006	3910	—
AW-1	Sedan Delivery	1070	3781	—

Series A-1 — 3/4-Ton

Model	Body Type	Price	Weight	Prod. Total
A-1	Chassis	675	2740	—

NOTE 1: Prices for truck bodies were available upon application at IHC dealers.

ENGINE [Series AW-1]: Inline. L-head. Four-cylinder. Cast iron block. Bore & stroke: 3-1/2 in. x 4-1/2 in. Displacement: 173 cid.. Brake horsepower: 30 at 2700 rpm. Net horsepower: 19.6 (NACC). Line bored main bearings and rods. Solid valve lifters. Carburetor: Zenith.

ENGINE [Series A-1]: Inline. L-head. Four-cylinder. Cast iron block. Bore & stroke: 3-3/8 in. x 4-1/2 in. Displacement: 185.8 cid.. Brake horsepower: 39 at 2400 rpm. Net horsepower: 21.03 (NACC). Line bored main bearings. Poured rods. Solid valve lifters. Carburetor: Zenith.

CHASSIS [Series AW-1]: Wheelbase: 136 in. Front tread: 56 in. Rear tread: 56 in. Tires: 30 x 5 in.

CHASSIS [Series A-1]: Wheelbase: 136 in. Front tread: 56 in. Rear tread: 56 in. Tires: 30 x 5 in.

TECHNICAL: Selective sliding transmission. Speeds: 3F/1R. Floor-mounted gearshift lever. Multiple disc type clutch. Semi-floating rear axle. Bendix rear wheel brakes. Steel spoke wheels.

NOTE: The A-1 models had a four-speed manual transmission.

OPTIONS: Rearview mirror. Cowl lamps. Sidemounted spare. Front bumper. Rear bumper. Various cabs and bodies. Windshield wiper. Special paint. Dual taillights.

HISTORICAL: Introduced December, 1930. Calendar year registrations: [All IHC trucks] 21,073. The new Model A-1 Series was introduced in 1931. A total of 109,220 trucks of 3/4-ton or less capacity were produced by all companies in the United States and Canada this year. IHC trucks held 24 percent of the domestic truck market. Production was low due to the depression. IHC was the third-ranked truck-maker in the country, but no production breakouts are available. However, experts believe that the majority of sales went to smaller 3/4-tonners.

1932 IHC

1932 IHC 1/2-Ton Model AW-1 Panel (OCW)

LIGHT TRUCK — SERIES AW-1/A-1/M-2 — FOUR-CYLINDER: The AW-1 and A-1 lines continued to be offered as 3/4-ton trucks for 1932. There was little or no change in both products. A new model was the one ton M-2. It used the XAH Waukesha four-cylinder engine. Smaller International trucks used a windshield with an arched lower edge, while larger capacity models had rectangular windshields.

I.D. DATA: Serial number located on plate on dash and on floorboard at right side. [Both Series] Numbers 501 and up. Motor numbers on left side of crankcase.

Model	Body Type	Price	Weight	Prod. Total
Series AW-1 Special Delivery — 3/4-Ton				
AW-1	Chassis	600	2620	—
AW-1	Pickup	852	3542	—
AW-1	Canopy	870	3827	—
AW-1	Screen	870	3827	—
AW-1	Panel	956	3910	—
AW-1	Sedan Delivery	1020	3781	—
Series A-1 — 3/4-Ton				
A-1	Chassis	615	2740	—
A-1	Pickup	867	3562	—
A-1	Canopy	885	3947	—
A-1	Screen	885	3947	—
A-1	Panel	971	4030	—
A-1	Sedan Delivery	1035	3901	—
Series M-2 — 1-Ton				
M-2	Chassis	850	3081	—

NOTE 1: Truck body prices available upon application.

ENGINE [Series AW-1]: Inline. L-head. Four-cylinder. Cast iron block. Bore & stroke: 3-1/2 in. x 4-1/2 in. Displacement: 173 cid.. Brake horsepower: 30 at 2700 rpm. Net horsepower: 19.6 (NACC). Line bored main bearings and rods. Solid valve lifters. Carburetor: Zenith.

ENGINE [Series A-1/M-2]: Inline. L-head. Four-cylinder. Cast iron block. Bore & stroke: 3-3/8 in. x 4-1/2 in. Displacement: 185.8 cid.. Brake horsepower: 39 at 2400 rpm. Net horsepower: 21.03 (NACC). Line bored main bearings and poured rods. Solid valve lifters. Carburetor: Zenith.

CHASSIS [Series AW-1]: Wheelbase: 136 in. Front tread: 56 in. Rear tread: 56 in. Tires: 30 x 5 in.

CHASSIS [Series A-1]: Wheelbase: 136 in. Front tread: 56 in. Rear tread: 56 in. Tires: 30 x 5 in.

CHASSIS [Series M-2]: Wheelbase: 118 in. Front tread: 60 in. Rear tread: 60 in.

TECHNICAL [Series AW-1]: Selective sliding transmission. Speeds: 3F/1R. Floor-mounted gearshift lever. Multiple disc type clutch. Semi-floating rear axle. Bendix rear wheel brakes. Steel spoke wheels.

TECHNICAL [Series A-1/M-2]: Selective sliding transmission. Speeds: 3F/1R. Floor-mounted gearshift lever. Multiple disc type clutch. Semi-floating rear axle. Bendix rear wheel brakes. Steel spoke wheels.

OPTIONS: Rearview mirror. Cowl lamps. Side mount spare tire. Front bumper. Rear bumper. Various cabs and bodies. Windshield wiper. Special paint. Dual taillights.

HISTORICAL: Introduced December 1931. Calendar year registrations: [All IHC trucks] 15,752. New M-2 Series introduced. Truck-makers in the U.S. and Canada produced only 79,127 units of 3/4-ton and under capacity and only 1,618 units of 1-ton to 1-1/2-ton capacity. Obviously, the continuing depression is having a negative effect on the industry. IHC was still the nation's third largest seller of all kinds of trucks, but the lack of a 1/2-ton model was costing the loss of sales to firms like Ford and Chevrolet.

1933 IHC

1933 IHC 1/2-Ton Model D-1 Pickup (OCW)

LIGHT TRUCK — SERIES D-1/A-1/M-2 — ALL ENGINES: International needed a low-priced 1/2-ton truck to compete with Ford and Chevrolet during the Great Depression. The company did not have such a model or a factory set up to produce one. In 1931, Willys-Overland had introduced the Model C-113 in this market, just before entering receivership. So IHC made a deal to market a modified version of this 1/2-ton through International dealers for 1933. It was called the D-1 series and used the same 113 in. wheelbase as the Willys model with a slightly larger version of the same six-cylinder engine. Manufacturing was sourced from the Willys-Overland factory in Toledo, Ohio, but the trucks carried International nameplates. Styling was characterized by single-bar bumpers, more rounded rooflines and a visor-less windshield. Although the prices were very low for these models, they included wire wheels and a sidemounted spare tire as standard equipment. The 3/4-ton A-1 series continued to be available. Also carried over was the M-2 1-ton series. Both of the larger lines had little change from last season.

I.D. DATA: Serial number located on plate on dash and also on the right side of the floorboard. Serial numbers began at number 501 for all series. Ending numbers are not available. Engine numbers located on the left side of crankcase.

Model	Body Type	Price	Weight	Prod. Total
Series D-1 — 1/2-Ton				
D-1	Chassis	360	2100	—
D-1	Pickup	475	2698	—
D-1	Canopy	550	2775	—
D-1	Screen	550	2775	—
D-1	Panel	565	2882	—
D-1	Sedan Delivery	630	2725	—
Series A-1 — 3/4-Ton				
A-1	Chassis	615	2812	—
A-1	Pickup	867	3562	—
A-1	Screen	885	3947	—
A-1	Canopy	885	3947	—
A-1	Panel	971	4030	—
A-1	Sedan Delivery	1035	3901	—
Series M-2 — 1-Ton				
M-2	1-Ton Chassis	850	3081	—

NOTE 1: By early 1934, Willys-Overland reported that 17,000 series D-1 trucks had been built for International Harvester Corp.

1933 IHC 1/2-Ton Model D-1 Pickup (OCW)

ENGINE [Series D-1]: Inline. L-head. Six-cylinder. Cast iron block. Bore & stroke: 3-5/16 in. x 4-3/4 in. Displacement: 213 cid.. Brake horsepower: 70 at 3400 rpm. Net horsepower: 26.33 (NACC). Slip-in main bearings and rod bearings. Solid valve lifters.
ENGINE [Series A-1/M-2]: Inline. L-head. Four-cylinder. Cast iron block. Bore & stroke: 3-3/8 in. x 41/2 in. Displacement: 185.8 cid.. Brake horsepower: 39 at 2400 rpm. Net horsepower: 21.03 (NACC). Line bored main bearings and poured rods. Solid valve lifters. Carburetor: Zenith.
CHASSIS [Series D-1]: Wheelbase: 113 in. Front tread: 56 in. Rear tread: 56 in. Tires: 5.25 x 18 in.
CHASSIS [Series A-1]: Wheelbase: 136 in. Front tread: 56 in. Rear tread: 56 in. Tires: 30 x 5.00 in.
CHASSIS [Series M-2]: Wheelbase: 118 in. Front tread: 60 in. Rear tread: 60 in.
TECHNICAL [Series D-1]: Synchromesh transmission. Speeds: 3F/1R. Floor-mounted gearshift lever. Multiple disc type clutch. Semi-floating rear axle. Overall ratio: 4.18:1. Two-shoe Bendix brakes. Wire spoke wheels.

1933 IHC Canopy Delivery Truck (OCW)

TECHNICAL [Series A-1/M-2]: Selective sliding transmission. Speeds: 4F/1R. Floor-mounted gearshift lever. Multiple disc type clutch. Semi-floating rear axle. Overall ratio: 4.18:1. Bendix rear wheel brakes. Steel spoke wheels.
OPTIONS: Front bumper (standard on D-1). Rear bumper (standard on D-1). Single sidemount. Rearview mirror. Various cabs and bodies. Windshield wiper. Bumper guards. Shock absorbers (standard on D-1). Special paint. Dual taillights. Wire wheels. Various axle ratios. Seat covers. Pedestal mirror (for sidemounted spare). Spotlight. Cowl lamps.

1933 IHC Model A-1 3/4-Ton Panel (OCW)

HISTORICAL: Introduced January, 1933. Calendar year registrations: [All IHC trucks] 26,658. Calendar year production: Approximately 17,000 D-1 models. No breakouts for other models. New 1/2-ton series. Synchromesh manual tranmission. Production of 100 Series D-1 trucks per day was originally scheduled, but Willys-Overland's financial instability created problems. Ultimately, the 1/2-ton trucks were built in batches of 2,500 or 5,000 units at a time. Due to the extremely low prices, profits from this model were very low or non-existent.

1933 IHC 3/4-Ton Model A-1 Pickup (OCW)

1934 IHC

1934 IHC 1/2-Ton Model D-1 Pickup (OCW)

LIGHT TRUCK — SERIES C-1/D-1/A-1/M-2 — ALL ENGINES: Willys-Overland continued to produce the 1/2-ton D-1 series for International Harvester in early 1934. It was joined by an all-new 1/2-ton C-1 Series, built in IHC's factory. This model featured a raked V-type radiator, deluxe style sidemount spare, skirted fenders, and more streamlined cowl, cab and hood. Like the D-1, the new model had IHC's heavy-duty six of 213 cid displacement. However, it was tuned to give more horsepower and a higher rpm peak. The standard wheelbase was 113 in., but a 125 in. stance was optional. Other features included slip-in mains and rods, spark plug cables in conduits, two-shoe Bendix brakes, and three-speed conventional transmission. Also carried over, with only minor alterations, were the 3/4-ton A-1 and the 1-ton M-2 lines.

I.D. DATA: Serial number located on a plate on dash and also on right side of the floorboard. Serial numbers began at number 501 for all series. Ending numbers are not available. Engine numbers located on left side of crankcase.

1934 IHC 1/2-Ton Model D-1 Pickup (OCW)

Model	Body Type	Price	Weight	Prod. Total
Series D-1 — 1/2-Ton — 113 in. w.b.				
D-1	Chassis	360	2100	—
D-1	Pickup	475	2698	—
D-1	Canopy	550	2775	—
D-1	Screen	550	2775	—
D-1	Panel	565	2882	—
D-1	Sedan Delivery	630	2725	—
Series C-1 — 1/2-Ton — 113 in. w.b.				
C-1	Chassis SWB	445	2320	—
C-1	Pickup SWB	545	3005	—
Series C-1 — 1/2-Ton — 136 in. w.b.				
C-1	Chassis LWB	470	2330	—
Series A-1 — 3/4-Ton — 136 in. w.b.				
A-1	Chassis	615	2812	—
A-1	Pickup	867	3562	—
A-1	Screen	885	3947	—
A-1	Canopy	885	3947	—
A-1	Panel	971	4030	—
A-1	Sedan Delivery	1035	3081	—
Series M-2 — 1-Ton — 118 in. w.b.				
M-2	Chassis	850	3081	—

NOTE 1: SWB = short wheelbase; LWB = long wheelbase

1934 IHC Series 1-Ton M-2 Armored Car (OCW)

ENGINE [Series D-1/C-1]: Inline. L-head. Six-cylinder. Cast iron block. Bore & stroke: 3-5/16 in. x 43/4 in. Displacement: 213 cid. Brake horsepower: [D-1] 70 at 3400 rpm.; [C-1] 78 at 3600 rpm. Net horsepower: [D-1] 16.33; [C-1] 26.3 (NACC). Slip-in main bearings and rod bearings. Solid valve lifters.
ENGINE [Series A-1/M-2]: Inline. L-head. Four-cylinder. Cast iron block. Bore & stroke: 3-3/8 in. x 4-1/2 in. Displacement: 185.8 cid. Brake horsepower: 39 at 2400 rpm. Net horsepower: 21.03 (NACC). Line bored main bearings and poured rod bearings. Solid valve lifters. Carburetor: Zenith.
CHASSIS [Series D-1]: Wheelbase: 113 in. or 125 in. Front tread: 56 in. Rear tread: 56 in. Tires: 5.25 x 18 in.
CHASSIS [Series C-1]: Wheelbase: 113 in. Front tread: 56 in. Rear tread: 56 in. Tires: 5.25 x 18 in.
CHASSIS [Series A-1]: Wheelbase: 136 in. Front tread: 56 in. Rear tread: 56 in. Tires: 30 x 5.00 in.
CHASSIS [Series M-2]: Wheelbase: 118 in. Front tread: 61 in. Rear tread: 61 in.
TECHNICAL [Series C-1/D-1]: Synchromesh transmission. Speeds: 3F/1R. Floor-mounted gearshift lever. Multiple disc type clutch. Semi-floating rear axle. Overall ratio: 4.18:1. Two-shoe Bendix brakes. Wire spoke wheels.
TECHNICAL [Series A-1/M-2]: Selective sliding transmission. Speeds: 4F/1R. Floor-mounted gearshift lever. Multiple disc type clutch. Semi-floating rear axle. Overall ratio: 4.18:1. Two-shoe Bendix brakes. Steel spoke wheels.

1934 IHC 1/2-Ton Model D-1 Panel (NI/DFW)

OPTIONS: Front bumper (standard on D-1). Rear bumper (standard on D-1). Single sidemount. Rearview mirror. Various cabs and bodies. Windshield wiper. Bumper guards. Shock absorbers (standard on D-1). Special paint. Dual taillights. Wire wheels (standard on D-1). Various axle ratios. Seat covers. Pedestal mirror (for sidemount). Spotlight. Cowl lamps.
NOTE: Bumpers and shock absorbers were $25 extra on the new C-1.
HISTORICAL: Introduced: [C-1] April, 1934; [others] December, 1933. Calendar year registrations: [All IHC trucks] 31,555.

Standard Catalog of Light-Duty Trucks

NOTE: The C-1 line had a total production run of 75,000 units from 1934 to 1937. Breakouts for other models not available.
New C-1 1/2-ton series built by IHC. Improved six-cylinder engine. Improved ignition wiring system. New streamlined styling on C-1 models. The D-1/C-1 six-cylinder engine was a product of the Wilson Foundry & Machine Co. of Pontiac, Mich. The popular C-1 was well accepted by IHC buyers and led to a large increase in sales and production. International was again the nation's third-ranked truck builder.

1934 IHC 3/4-Ton Model A-1 Mail Delivery Truck (OCW)

1935 IHC

1935 IHC 1/2-Ton Model C-1 Pickup (NI/DFW)

LIGHT TRUCK — SERIES C-1/C-10/C-20/M-3 — ALL ENGINES: This was a year for expansion of the famous C Series trucks from IHC. The C-1 models were carried over as a 1/2-ton line. These had two chassis with 113- and 125-in. wheelbases. They were six-cylinder models. Also available were 3/4-ton C-10 models with a four-cylinder powerplant. These trucks had a 133 in. wheelbase. The C-20 models were actually large trucks with a 157 in. wheelbase and four-cylinder engines. They had a maximum 1-1/2-ton capacity, although they were nominally rated for 1-ton payloads. The M-2 became the M-3, with a 133 in. wheelbase and the four-cylinder engine. The larger trucks had a V dip in the front bumper, while the smaller ones again had straight bumpers.
I.D. DATA: Serial number located on a plate on dash and also on right side of the floorboard. Serial numbers began at number 501 for all series. Ending numbers are not available. Engine numbers located on left side of crankcase.

1935 IHC 1-Ton Model C-20 Platform Stake (OCW)

Model	Body Type	Price	Weight	Prod. Total
Series C-1 — 1/2-Ton — 113 in. w.b.				
C-1	Chassis	400	2050	—
Series C-1 — 1/2-Ton — 125 in. w.b.				
C-1	Chassis	425	2095	—
Series C-10 — 3/4-Ton — 133 in. w.b.				
C-10	Chassis	575	2870	—
C-10	Chassis	590	2867	—
Series C-20 — 1- to 1-1/2-Ton — 133 in. w.b.				
C-20	Chassis	575	2919	—
Series C-20 — 1- to 1-1/2-Ton — 157 in. w.b.				
C-20	Chassis	590	2867	—
Series M-3 — 1-Ton — 133 in. w.b.				
M-3	Chassis	850	3081	—

1935 IHC 1/2-Ton Model C-1 Pickup (OCW)

ENGINE [Series C-1]: Inline. L-head. Six-cylinder. Cast iron block. Bore & stroke: 3-5/16 in. x 43/4 in. Displacement: 213 cid.. Brake horsepower: 78 at 3600 rpm. Net horsepower: 26.3 (NACC). Slip-in main bearings and rod bearings. Solid valve lifters.
ENGINE [Series C-10/C-20/M-3]: Inline. L-head. Four-cylinder. Cast iron block. Bore & stroke: 3-3/8 in. x 4-1/2 in. Displacement: 185.8 cid. Brake horsepower: 39 at 2400 rpm. Net horsepower: 21.03 (NACC). Line bored main bearings and poured rod bearings. Solid valve lifters. Carburetor: Zenith.
CHASSIS [Series C-1]: Wheelbase: 113 in. or 125 in. Front tread: 56 in. Rear tread: 56 in. Tires: 5.25 x 18 in.
CHASSIS [Series C-10]: Wheelbase: 133 in.
CHASSIS [Series C-20]: Wheelbase: 133 in. or 157 in.
CHASSIS [Series M-3]: Wheelbase: 133 in.
TECHNICAL: Conventional transmission. Speeds: 3-4F/1R (*). Floor-mounted gearshift lever. Multiple disc type clutch. Semi-floating rear axle. Overall ratio: 4.18:1. Two-shoe Bendix brakes. Wire spoke wheels or steel spoke wheels. (*) Four-speed transmission in C-10 and C-20 model.

1935 IHC 1/2-Ton Model C-1 Canopy (D.H. Landis)

OPTIONS: Front bumper. Rear bumper. Single sidemount. Rearview mirror. Various cabs and bodies. Windshield wiper. Bumper guards. Shock absorbers. Special paint. Dual taillights. Wire wheels. Various axle ratios. Seat covers. Pedestal mirrors. Spotlight. Cowl lamps.
HISTORICAL: Introduced: January 1934. Calendar year registrations: (All IHC trucks] 53,471. During 1936, a total of 316,208 (38.6 percent) of the trucks made by U.S. and Canadian Manufacturers were 3/4-ton or less in payload capacity. Another 9,686 trucks were made in the 1-ton to under 1-1/2-ton class. This amounted to 1.1 percent of the North American total.

1935 IHC 1/2-Ton Model C-1 Pickup (OCW)

1936 IHC

1936 IHC 1-Ton Model CS-20 Dump Truck (OCW)

LIGHT TRUCK — SERIES C-5/C-1/C-10/CS-20/M-3/C-12 — ALL ENGINES: International Harvester again expanded its line of 1/2-ton to 1-ton trucks. There were seven different series within the range. Styling was carried over from 1935. The smaller trucks had skirted fenders and straight front bumpers while larger models had unskirted clamshell fenders and veed front bumpers. Four-cylinder Waukesha powerplants were used in the C-5/C-10/CS-20/M-3 series. Other models employed IHC-built six-cylinder engines. The C-1 had its own heavy-duty 213 cid six rated at 79 hp. The C-5 used a new FK engine with removable valve lifter clusters and a fuel pump in the valve door. It had Bendix hydraulic brakes and a three-speed synchromesh transmission. The C-10 and CS-20 models employed the XAH engine. Both had hydraulic brakes and four-speed transmissions. The C-15 used IHC's Heavy-Duty 2 engine and had hydraulic brakes and a three-speed transmission. The M-3 shared many features of the CS-20 line. A six-cylinder Heavy-Duty 3 powerplant was used in the 3/4-ton C-12, which also had hydraulic braking and a four-speed transmission.
I.D. DATA: Serial number located on plate on dash. Also, on right side of the floorboard. Engine numbers located on left side of crankcase. Serial and engine numbers unavailable.

1936 IHC 1-Ton Model C30 Platform Stake (OCW)

Standard Catalog of Light-Duty Trucks

Model	Body Type	Price	Weight	Prod. Total
Series C-5 — 1/2-Ton — 113 in. w.b.				
C-5	Chassis	415	1981	—
Series C-5 — 1/2-Ton — 125 in. w.b.				
C-5	Chassis	440	2026	—
Series C-1 — 1/2-Ton — 113 in. w.b.				
C-1	Chassis	415	2078	—
Series C-1 — 1/2-Ton — 125 in. w.b.				
C-1	Chassis	440	2123	—
Series C-10 — 3/4-Ton — 133 in. w.b.				
C-10	Chassis	590	3089	—
Series C-15 — 3/4-/1-Ton — 136 in. w.b.				
C-15	Chassis	545	2619	—
Series M-3 — 1-Ton — 118 in. w.b.				
M-3	Chassis	850	3163	—
Series CS-20 — 1-/1-1/2-Ton — 118 in. w.b.				
CS-20	Chassis	685	3000	—
Series C-12 — 3/4-Ton — 133 in. w.b.				
C-12	Chassis	616	3003	—

ENGINE [Series C-5]: Inline. L-head. Four-cylinder. Cast iron block. Bore & stroke: 31/4 in. x 4 in. Displacement: 132.7 cid.. Brake horsepower: 33 at 2800 rpm. Net horsepower: 16.9 (NACC). Slip-in main bearings and rod bearings. Solid valve lifters in crankcase.
ENGINE [Series C-1/C-15/C-12]: Inline. L-head. Six-cylinder. Cast iron block. Bore & stroke: 3-5/16 in. x 43/4 in. Displacement: 213 cid.. Compression ratio: 6.3:1. Brake horsepower: 78 at 3400 rpm. Net horsepower: 26.3 (NACC). Four main bearings (insert type). Solid valve lifters. Carburetor: Single downdraft.
ENGINE [Series C-10/CS-20/M-3]: Inline. L-head. Four-cylinder. Cast iron block. Bore & stroke: 3-3/8 in. x 4-1/2 in. Displacement: 185.8 cid.. Net horsepower: 21.03 (NACC). Solid valve lifters.
CHASSIS [Series C-5/C-1]: Wheelbase: 113 in./125 in. Tires: 5.25 x 18 in.
CHASSIS [Series C-10/C-12]: Wheelbase: 133 in.
CHASSIS [Series M-3/CS-20]: Wheelbase: 118 in.
CHASSIS [Series C-15]: Wheelbase: 136 in.
TECHNICAL [Series C-1/C-5/C-15]: Manual transmission. Speeds: 3F/1R. Floor-mounted gearshift lever. Multiple disc type clutch. Semi-floating rear axle. Overall ratio: 4.18 to 8.5. Bendix hydraulic brakes. Wire or steel spoke wheels.
NOTE: Synchromesh three-speed transmission in C-5 models.
TECHNICAL [Series C-10/C-20/C-12/M-3]: Manual transmission. Speeds: 4F/1R. Floor-mounted gearshift lever. Multiple disc type clutch. Semi-floating rear axle. Overall ratio: 4.18 to 8.5. Bendix hydraulic brakes. Steel spoke wheels.
OPTIONS: Front bumper. Rear bumper. Single sidemount. Rearview mirror. Pedestal mirror for sidemount. Wire spoke wheels. Bumper guards. Windshield wipers (dual). Special paint. Various bodies. Wheel trim rings. Dual taillights. Seat covers. Oversized (20 in.) tires. Spotlight. License plate frames.
HISTORICAL: Introduced: January 1936. Calendar year registrations: [All IHC trucks] 71,958. Calendar year production: [All IHC trucks] 86,563. Hydraulic brakes standardized for light-duty International trucks. IHC was once again America's third-ranked truck manufacturer and held 11.03 percent of the total market. The sales slump caused by the Great Depression was coming to an end.

1937-1938 IHC

LIGHT TRUCK — SERIES C-5/C-1/C-15//M-3 — ALL ENGINES: In early 1937, four series of IHC trucks rated for 1-ton or lower capacities were carried over virtually without change. The C-5 was now available only with the shorter 113 in. wheelbase. The same was true of the C-1. Both of these 1/2-tons used the same engines as last year. As in 1936, the C-15 was classified as a 3/4-ton to 1-ton model. It, too, was unaltered in any important sense. The M-3 was, likewise, unchanged as far as the basics went. All of these models were cataloged at the same prices in effect during 1936. However, all scaled-in at heavier shipping weights, suggesting some changes in standard equipment. The weight increases ranged from a modest two pound jump on the C-5 to a 127 lb. increase for the C-1 and C-15 models. The M-3 gained 117 lbs. Refer to the 1936 section of this catalog for additional specifications for these trucks.

1937 IHC 3/4-Ton Model D-15 Platform Stake (OCW)

LIGHT TRUCK — SERIES D-5/D-2/D-15/ — ALL ENGINES: A new Series D line of trucks was introduced in the spring of 1937. They featured all-steel cabs with turret top styling, the "fat fender" look and split windshields. The grille consisted of five groups of curved horizontal bars separated by bright metal moldings. Each group was wider than the one below it. The trim moldings above and below the top group extended back along the hoodsides. Long horizontal hood louvers were between them, with an International nameplate in the center. The nose above the grille was flat, rounded and finished in body color. An I-H emblem decorated the nose. Larger, torpedo-shaped headlamp buckets were attached to the catwalk area on the pedestals. There were short runningboards extending only to the rear of the cab. Single-bar front bumpers were used on all models and spare tires were hung on the passenger side of the body or box, behind the doors. The larger D-15 pickups had horizontal ribs on the boxsides. Steel spoke wheels were used on all models. A new commercial station wagon with wood body construction appeared. The D-2 used a Heavy-Duty 213 engine; the D-5 had an FC engine and the D-15 employed the Heavy-Duty 213A engine. All had slip-in mains and rods, Bendix hydraulic brakes and three-speed synchromesh transmission. The D-2 and D-15 had a hand-brake operating on the rear wheels.

I.D. DATA: Serial number located on plate on dash. Also on right floorboard. Engine numbers located on left side of crankcase. Serial and engine numbers unavailable.

1937 IHC 1/2-Ton Model D-5 Panel (NI/DFW}

Model	Body Type	Price	Weight	Prod. Total
Series D-5 — 1/2-Ton — 113 in./125 in. w.b.				
D-5	Chassis	470	2170	—
Series D-2 — 1/2-Ton — 113 in. w.b.				
D-2	Chassis	455	2290	—
Series D-15 — 3/4-Ton — 130 in. w.b.				
D-15	Chassis	570	2770	—

NOTE 1: Refer to 1936 for C and M Series data.
NOTE 2: 1938 chassis prices were: [D-5] $490; [D-2] $475 and [D-15] $605.
NOTE 3: Shipping weights for 1938 were unchanged.

ENGINE [Series D-5]: Inline. L-head. Four-cylinder. Cast iron block. Bore & stroke: 3-1/4 in. x 4 in. Displacement: 132.7 cid.. Brake horsepower: 33 at 2800 rpm. Net horsepower: 16.9 (NACC). Slip-in main bearings and rod bearings. Solid valve lifters.

ENGINE [Series D-2/D-15]: Inline. L-head. Six-cylinder. Cast iron block. Bore & stroke: 3-5/16 in. x 43/4 in. Displacement: 213 cid.. Compression ratio: 6.3:1. Brake horsepower: 78 at 3400 rpm. Net horsepower: 26.3 (NACC). Four main bearings (insert type). Solid valve lifters. Carburetor: Single downdraft.

1937 IHC 1-Ton Model D-5 Beverage Truck (OCW)

CHASSIS [Series D-5]: Wheelbase: 113/125 in.
CHASSIS [Series D-2]: Wheelbase: 113 in.
CHASSIS [Series D-15]: Wheelbase: 130 in.

TECHNICAL: Manual transmission. Speeds: 3F/1R. Floor-mounted gearshift lever. Multiple dry disc type clutch. Semi-floating rear axle. Bendix hydraulic brakes. Steel spoke wheels.

OPTIONS: Front bumper. Rear bumper. Single sidemount tire. Rearview mirror. Dual windshield wipers. Special paint. Bumper guards. Wheel trim rings. Dual taillights. Various bodies. Oversized tires. Spotlight. Windshield visor. License frames.

489

1937 IHC 1/2-Ton Model D-5 Deluxe Panel (J.H. Archives)

1938 IHC 1/2-Ton Model D-5 Panel (OCW)

HISTORICAL [Series D]: Introduced: March 1937. Calendar year registrations: [All IHC trucks] 76,174. Calendar year production: [All IHC trucks] 100,700. All-new D series introduced. Turret top cab styling with all-steel construction. Modernized design for the D series. During 1937, IHC increased its lead on Dodge in the U.S. truck market. The company now held 30.22 percent of total American truck output and broke the 100,000 units per year level for the first time. It was again the third largest maker of all types of trucks. For 1938, calendar year registrations for all IHC trucks dropped to 55,836 and calendar year production fell to 51,593 units. That gave IHC a 10.24 percent market share and, once again, third rank in the industry.

1938 IHC 1/2-Ton Model D-2 Commercial Station Wagon (OCW)

1939 IHC

HALF-TON TRUCK — SERIES D-2 — SIX-CYLINDER: More emphasis was placed on marketing IHC trucks with factory-built bodies starting in 1939. The products in the light-duty truck lines were still the D series models and there were no significant changes in styling or engineering. These trucks were promoted with the sales slogan Beauty Plus Dependability. The 1/2-ton D-2 models were still available with a choice of two wheelbases. The design features were the same as described in the 1937-1938 section of this catalog.

1939 IHC 1/2-Ton Model D-2 Commercial Station Wagon (OCW)

1/2-TON TRUCK — SERIES D-5 — FOUR-CYLINDER: International's D-5 series line was carried over without any important changes for model year 1939. This was the four-cylinder version of IHC's smallest truck. Several models such as the station wagon and Metro (bus) were not available with the smaller engine.

3/4 to 1-ton — SERIES D-15 — SIX-CYLINDER: IHC's larger D-15 light-duty truck was also carried over. There were no more than minor detail changes from previous D-15 models. Two wheelbases were also offered in this range: 113 in. and 130 in.

1939 IHC 1-Ton Model D-15 Stake (OCW)

I.D. DATA [Series D-2/D-5/D-15]: Serial number located on plate on dash. Also on floorboard on right side. Numbers for each series prefix began at 501. Engine numbers located on left side of crankcase. Starting numbers unavailable.

Model	Body Type	Price	Weight	Prod. Total
Series D-2 — 1/2-Ton — 113 in. w.b.				
D-2	Chassis	475	2290	—
D-2	Chassis & Cab	583	2725	—
D-2	Express	620	3565	—
D-2	Canopy	775	3565	—
D-2	Panel	713	3210	—
D-2	DM Body	860	3295	—
D-2	DB Body	860	3295	—
D-2	Station Wagon	930	3590	—
D-2	Metro Body	1200	—	—
Series D-2 — 1/2-Ton — 125 in. w.b.				
D-2	Chassis	500	2315	—
D-2	Chassis & Cab	608	2750	—
D-2	Express	640	3590	—
D-2	Stake	668	3625	—
D-2	Canopy	810	3590	—
D-2	Panel	750	3315	—

NOTE 1: DM Body=is a milk delivery truck.
NOTE 2: DB Body=is a bakery delivery truck.

Model	Body Type	Price	Weight	Prod. Total
Series D-5 — 1/2-Ton — 113 in. w.b.				
D-5	Chassis	450	2170	—
D-5	Chassis & Cab	557	2605	—
D-5	Express	595	3445	—
D-5	Canopy	750	3445	—
D-5	Panel	688	3090	—
D-5	DM Body	835	3175	—
D-5	DB Body	835	3175	—
Series D-5 — 1/2-Ton — 125 in. w.b.				
D-5	Chassis	475	2195	—
D-5	Chassis & Cab	583	2630	—
D-5	Express	635	3470	—
D-5	Stake	643	3505	—
D-5	Canopy	785	3470	—
D-5	Panel	725	3195	—

Series D-15 — 3/4-Ton to 1-Ton — 113 in. w.b.

Model	Body Type	Price	Weight	Prod. Total
D-15	Chassis	605	2770	—
D-15	Chassis & Cab	713	3205	—
D-15	Express	750	4140	—
D-15	DM Body	1000	3775	—
D-15	DB Body	1000	3775	—
D-15	Stordor	1330	—	—

Series D-15 — 3/4-Ton to 1-Ton 1 (130 in. w.b.)

Model	Body Type	Price	Weight	Prod. Total
D-15	Chassis	605	2800	—
D-15	Chassis & Cab	713	3235	—
D-15	Express	785	4170	—
D-15	Stake	788	4110	—
D-15	Canopy	930	4170	—
D-15	Panel	873	4000	—

1939 IHC 1-Ton Model D-15 Armored Car (OCW)

ENGINE [Series D-2]: Inline. L-head. Six-cylinder. Cast iron block. Bore & stroke: 3-5/16 in. x 4-3/4 in. Displacement: 213 cid.. Compression ratio: 6.3:1. Brake horsepower: 78 at 3400 rpm. Net horsepower: 26.3 (NACC). Four main bearings [insert type]. Solid valve lifters. Carburetor: Single downdraft.

ENGINE [Series D-5]: Inline. L-head. Four-cylinder. Cast iron block. Bore & stroke: 3-1/4 in. x 4 in. Displacement: 132.7 cid.. Brake horsepower: 33 at 2800 rpm. Net horsepower: 16.9 (NACC). Slip-in main bearings. Solid valve lifters.

ENGINE [Series D-15]: Inline. L-head. Six-cylinder. Cast iron block. Bore & stroke: 3-5/16 in. x 4-3/4 in. Displacement: 213 cid.. Compression ratio: 6.3:1. Brake horsepower: 78 at 3400 rpm. Net horsepower: 26.3 (NACC). Four main bearings [insert type]. Solid valve lifters. Carburetor: Single downdraft.

CHASSIS [Series D-2]: Wheelbase: 113/125 in.

CHASSIS [Series D-5]: Wheelbase: 113/125 in.

CHASSIS [Series D-15]: Wheelbase: 113/130 in.

TECHNICAL: Synchromesh transmission. Speeds: 3F/1R. Floor-mounted gearshift lever. Multiple dry disc type clutch. Hypoid rear axle. Bendix hydraulic brakes. Steel spoke wheels.

OPTIONS: Front bumper. Rear bumper. Single sidemount tire. Rearview mirror. Dual windshield wipers. Special paint. Bumper guards. Wheel trim rings. Dual taillights. Oversized tires. Spotlight. Windshield visor. License frames.

HISTORICAL [Series D]: Introduced: January 1939. Calendar year registrations: [All IHC trucks] 66,048. Calendar year production: [All IHC trucks] 81,960. IHC continued as America's number three truck maker. It had 11.38 percent of the total U.S. market. Commander Attilio Gatti used a fleet of IHC trucks on his 10th African expedition in 1938-1939. Five of these covered a combined total of 66,000 miles with repair costs totaling just $38. The explorer used several IHC commercial station wagons.

1940 IHC

1940 IHC Model 1/2-Ton D-2 Panel (OCW)

1/2-TON — SERIES D2/D2H — SIX-CYLINDER: The 1940 model year started October, 1939. The product line was a carryover of the D series. It featured a flat, rounded nose and a tall split grille with five horizontal segments having horizontal blades. The radiator badge on front said International through three diamonds. This was a six-cylinder line with seven models, including DM (milk) or DB (bakery) panels and a commercial station wagon on a 113 in. wheelbase and seven models including DM panel and stake (no station wagon) on a 125 in. wheelbase. A D2H designation was used for long (125 in.) wheelbase models. The express was now called the pickup. The D2 pickup had smooth box sides. A heavy-duty D2H 3/4-ton chassis option was available.

1/2-TON — SERIES D2M — SIX-CYLINDER: The Metro delivery van was listed as a separate D2M Series. It came with either a 102 in. or 113 in. wheelbase. General styling was continued from the 1937-1938 models. The same six used in the D2/D2H line was employed.

1/2-TON — SERIES D5 — FOUR-CYLINDER: Except for slightly increased prices, the D5 series was carried over, without change, as an early 1940 offering. It came in both 113 in. and 125 in. wheelbase lines. The bakery truck, on the shorter wheelbase, was no longer cataloged. A stake was included. The four-cylinder Waukesha powerplant was again found under the hoods of these trucks.

3/4-TON — SERIES D15/D15L/D15LL/D15H — SIX-CYLINDER: These series offered chassis, chassis & cab, express models on either 113 in. or 130 in. wheelbases. The milk and bread delivery trucks were also available on the small wheelbase only. Stake, panel and canopy models were offered on the long wheelbase only. The L, LL and H options were chassis GVW options of 3/4- or 1-ton. D15 pickups had horizontal ribs on the sides of their larger cargo box.

3/4-TON — SERIES D15M/D15ML — SIX-CYLINDER: These were 102 in. or 113 in. Metros of 3/4-ton or 1-ton payload ratings. They were similar to D2Ms, but with heftier chassis components.

3/4- to 1-TON — D29 — SIX-CYLINDER: A larger six-cylinder engine and longer wheelbase characterized this series of trucks rated between 3/4-ton and 1-ton (depending upon tires and chassis equipment.)

I.D. DATA [Series D2/D2H/D2M]: Serial number located on plate on dash. Also on floorboard on right side of driving compartment. Also on left front end of frame, left front spring hanger or front end of right runningboard shield. Starting: [Series D2]: 72819; [Series D2H] 72819; [Series D2M) 570; [D-5] 3504; [D15/D15L/D15LL/D15H] 23554; [D29] 661. Ending numbers not available. Engine numbers located on left side of crankcase.

Model	Body Type	Price	Weight	Prod. Total
Series D2 — 1/2-Ton — 113 in. w.b.				
D2	Chassis & Cowl	475	2187	—
D2	Chassis & Cab	583	2622	—
D2	Pickup	620	2900	—
D2	Canopy	775	3462	—
D2	Panel	713	3107	—
DM-2	Milk	860	3192	—
D2	Station Wagon	955	3487	—

NOTE 1: Also available as D2H (3/4-Ton heavy-duty).

Model	Body Type	Price	Weight	Prod. Total
Series D2 — 1/2-Ton — 125 in. w.b.				
D2	Chassis & Cowl	500	2212	—
D2	Chassis & Cab	608	2647	—
D2	Pickup	660	2925	—
D2	Canopy	810	3487	—
D2	Panel	750	3132	—
D2	Stake	668	3178	—

NOTE 2: Also available as D2H (3/4-Ton heavy-duty).

Model	Body Type	Price	Weight	Prod. Total
Series D2M — Metro Delivery -1/2-Ton — 102 in. w.b.				
D2M/B	Walk-in	1100	1942	—
Series D2M — Metro Delivery -1/2-Ton — 113 in. w.b.				
D2M/B	Walk-in	1170	1952	—
Series D5 — 1/2-Ton -113 in. w.b.				
D5	Chassis & Cowl	490	2067	—
D5	Chassis & Cab	598	2502	—
D5	Pickup	635	2780	—
D5	Canopy	790	3342	—
D5	Panel	728	2987	—
DM5	Milk Truck	875	3072	—
Series D5 — 1/2-Ton — 125 in. w.b.				
D5	Chassis & Cowl	515	2092	—
D5	Chassis & Cab	623	2527	—
D5	Pickup	675	2805	—
D5	Canopy	825	3367	—
D5	Panel	765	3012	—
DM/DB5	Walk-in	835	3072	—
Series D15L — 3/4- to 1-Ton — 113 in. w.b.				
D15L	Chassis & Cowl	605	2667	—
D15L	Chassis & Cab	712	3102	—
D15L	Pickup	750	3380	—
DM15L	Milk Truck	1000	3672	—
Series D15LL — 1/2- to 1-ton — 130 in. w.b.				
D15LL	Chassis & Cowl	605	2697	—
D15LL	Chassis & Cab	713	3132	—
D15LL	Pickup	785	3410	—
D15LL	Canopy	930	3972	—
D15LL	Panel	873	3617	—
D15LL	Stake	788	3663	—
Series D15M — Metro Delivery — 102 in. w.b.				
D15M	Walk-in	1240	2222	—
Series D15M — Metro Delivery — 113 in. w.b.				
D15M	Walk-in	1310	2321	—
Series D29 — 3/4-Ton to 1-Ton — 128 in. w.b.				
D29	Chassis & Cowl	650	3553	—
D29	Chassis & Cab	758	3788	—
Series D29 — 3/4-Ton — 155 in. w.b.				
D29	Chassis & Cowl	685	3398	—
D29	Chassis & Cab	793	—	—

Series D29 — 3/4-Ton — 173 in. w.b.

D29	Chassis & Cowl	710	3528	—
D29	Chassis & Cab	818	—	—

Series D15 — 1-Ton — 113 in. w.b.

D15	Chassis & Cowl	605	2667	—
D15	Chassis & Cowl	712	3102	—
D15	Pickup	750	3380	—
DM15	Milk Truck	1000	3672	—

Series D15H — 1-Ton — 130 in. w.b.

D15H	Chassis & Cowl	605	2697	—
D15H	Chassis & Cab	713	3132	—
D15H	Pickup	785	3410	—
D15H	Canopy	930	3972	—
D15H	Panel	873	3617	—
D15H	Stake	788	3663	—

Series D15M — Metro Delivery — 1-Ton — 102 in. w.b.

D15M	Panel	1240	2222	—

Series D15M — Metro Delivery — 1-Ton — 113 in. w.b.

D15M	Panel	1310	2321	—

ENGINE [Series D2/D2H/D2M]: Inline. L-head. Six-cylinder. Cast iron block. Bore & stroke: 3-5/16 in. x 4-1/8 in. Displacement: 213 cid.. Compression ratio: 6.3:1. Brake horsepower: 78 at 3400 rpm. Net horsepower: 26.3 (NACC). Four main bearings. Solid valve lifters. Carburetor: Single downdraft.

ENGINE [Series D5]: Inline. L-head. Four-cylinder. Cast iron block. Bore & stroke: 3-1/4 in. x 4 in. Displacement: 132.7 cid.. Brake horsepower: 33 at 2800 rpm. Net horsepower: 16.9 (NACC). Slip-in main bearings. Solid valve lifters.

ENGINE [Series D29]: Inline. L-head. Six-cylinder. Cast iron block. Bore & stroke: 3-5/16 in. x 4-1/2 in. Displacement: 232 cid.. Brake horsepower: 81 at 3200 rpm. Net horsepower: 26.3 (NACC). Solid valve lifters.

NOTE: The 81 hp. engine was used only in the D29 Series. The D15L/D15LL/D15M trucks used the same 78 hp six-cylinder engine as the D2/D2H/D2M 1/2-ton models. See specification above for this engine.

CHASSIS [Series D2]: Wheelbase: 113 in. Tires: 6.00 x 16 (four-ply).
CHASSIS [Series D2H]: Wheelbase: 125 in. Tires: 6.00 x 16 (four-ply).
CHASSIS [Series D5 SWB]: Wheelbase: 113 in. Tires: 6.00 x 16 (six-ply).
CHASSIS [Series D5 LWB]: Wheelbase: 125 in. Tires: 6.00 x 16 (six-ply).
CHASSIS [Series D2M]: Wheelbase: 102 in. Tires: 6.00 x 16 (four-ply).
CHASSIS [Series D2M]: Wheelbase: 113 in. Tires: 6.00 x 16 (four-ply).
CHASSIS [Series D15/D15L]: Wheelbase: 113 in. Tires: 7.00 x 16 (six-ply).
CHASSIS [Series D15LL/D15H]: Wheelbase: 130 in. Tires: 7.00 x 16 (six-ply).
CHASSIS [Series D15M]: Wheelbase: 102 in. Tires: 7.00 x 16 (six-ply).
CHASSIS [Series D15M]: Wheelbase: 113 in. Tires: 7.00 x 16 (six-ply).
CHASSIS [Series D29]: Wheelbase: 128 in. Tires: [Front] 30 x 5 in.; [Rear] 32 x 6 in.
CHASSIS [Series D29]: Wheelbase: 155 in. Tires: [Front] 30 x 5 in.; [Rear] 32 x 6 in.
CHASSIS [Series D29]: Wheelbase: 173 in. Tires: [Front] 30 x 5 in.; [Rear] 32 x 6 in.

TECHNICAL: Synchromesh transmission. Speeds: 3F/1R. Floor-mounted gearshift lever. Multiple dry disc type clutch. Hypoid rear axle. Bendix hydraulic brakes. Steel spoke wheels.

OPTIONS: Front bumper. Rear bumper. Single sidemount tire. Rearview mirror. Dual windshield wipers. Special paint. Bumper guards. Radio. Heater. Wheel trim rings. Dual taillights. Radio antenna. Seat covers. Oversized tires. Spotlight. Windshield visor. License frames. Cab clearance lights. Turn signals.

HISTORICAL: Introduced: October, 1939. Calendar year registrations: [All IHC trucks] 76,833. Calendar year production: [All IHC trucks] 81,753. Model year production: [All IHC trucks] 78,810. Industrywide truck production, by capacities, for 1940 was as follows: [3/4-Ton or less] 37.2 percent; [1-ton] 4.9 percent. International Harvester Co. slipped behind Dodge in truck production this year. Dodge had 12.39 percent of the total truck market to gain third rank. IHC had 10.41 percent and was the fourth largest producer. The company was now being threatened by GMC as well.
1940-1/2 IHC

1940-1/2 IHC

MODEL K TRUCK — SERIES K-1 — SIX-CYLINDER: An all-new Model K truck was introduced by IHC during model year 1940. The K1 was the 1/2-ton model having a gross vehicle weight (GVW) rating of 4,400 lbs. There was also a K-1H variation or option listed as a 3/4-ton. (The H suffix apparently meant heavy-duty.) All model Ks had modernized styling with wider front fenders and flush headlamps. A tall, straight, vertical grille featured bright, horizontal curved bars on either side of a vertical center divider. Rectangular parking lamps were incorporated into the upper corner of the grille. The single-bar bumper ran straight across the front and wider, half-length runningboards were seen. The front of the hood arched over to the grille to form a flat, rounded nose which was decorated with an International emblem. The badge had the company name running across three diamonds. Sculpturing appeared on the sides of the hood with an International name at the rear corner. The 213 cid six was promoted as a Green Diamond engine.

MODEL K TRUCK — SERIES K-2 — SIX-CYLINDER: The K-2 Series was the 3/4-ton version of the newly restyled International truck. Models in this line had a 5,200 pound GVW rating. The NADA actually listed the K-2 as a 1/2-ton in 1940, but it was uprated to 3/4-ton from 1941 on. Styling characteristics for all model Ks were similar. There were two variations or options for K-2 trucks. The K-2L was a 1/2-ton and the K-2H was a 1-ton. (The suffix L indicated light-duty and the suffix H indicated heavy-duty.)

MODEL K TRUCK — SERIES K-3 — SIX-CYLINDER: The new Model K styling was also seen on the 1-ton K-3 series. These trucks came with a standard 113 in. wheelbase or special 130 in. wheelbase. They had a 6,650 pound GVW rating. Two variations or options (K-3L at 1/2-ton or K-3H at 1-1/4-tons) were available. Two of the heavier-duty Model Ks offered 3/4-ton options with an L suffix. These were the K-4L (a variation of the 1-1/4-ton K-4) and the K-5L (a variation of the 11/2-ton K-5). These trucks had respective GVW ratings of 10,000 lbs. and 13,500 lbs. and could hardly be considered Light-duty models regardless of factory nomenclature.

I.D. DATA [Series K-1]: Serial number stamped on a plate on dash. Also on floorboard on right side of driving compartment. Also on left front end of frame, left front spring hanger or front end of right runningboard shield. Starting: 501. Ending: 5468. Engine numbers located on left side of crankcase. Starting and ending numbers not available.
I.D. DATA [Series K-2]: Serial number in same locations. Starting: 501. Ending: 3091. Engine numbers in same locations.
I.D. DATA [Series K-3]: Serial number in same locations. Starting: 501. Ending: 2308. Engine numbers in same locations.

Model	Body Type	Price	Weight	Prod. Total
Model K-1 (1/2-Ton)/K-1H (3/4-Ton) — 113 in. w.b.				
K-1	Chassis & Cowl	490	2250	—
K-1	Chassis & Cab	598	2645	—
K-1	Pickup	640	2923	—
K-1	Panel	733	3170	—
K-1	Station Wagon	1000	3350	—
Model K-1 (1/2-Ton)/K-1H (3/4-Ton) — 125 in. w.b.				
K-1	Chassis & Cowl	510	2275	—
K-1	Chassis & Cab	618	2670	—
K-1	Pickup	675	2978	—
K-1	Panel	765	3275	—
K-1	Station Wagon	678	3201	—

NOTE 1: Serial numbers indicate 4,967 trucks made in this series.

Model	Body Type	Price	Weight	Prod. Total
Model K-2/K-2L (1/2-Ton)/K-2H (1-Ton) — 125 in. w.b.				
K-2	Chassis & Cowl	520	2285	—
K-2	Chassis & Cab	628	2680	—
K-2	Pickup	685	2988	—
K-2	Panel	775	3285	—
K-2	Stake	688	3211	—

NOTE 2: Serial numbers indicate 2,590 trucks made in this series.

Model	Body Type	Price	Weight	Prod. Total
Model K-3/K-3L (1/2-Ton) — 113 in. w.b.				
K-3	Chassis & Cowl	620	3000	—
K-3	Chassis & Cab	728	3395	—
K-3	Pickup	770	3673	—
Model K-3/K-3L (1/2-Ton) — 130 in. w.b.				
K-3	Chassis & Cowl	620	3030	—
K-3	Chassis & Cab	728	3425	—
K-3	Pickup	805	3796	—
K-3	Panel	893	4230	—
K-3	Stake	803	4039	—

NOTE 1: Serial numbers indicate 1,807 truck made in this series.

ENGINE [Series K-1]: Inline. L-head. Six-cylinder. Cast iron block. Bore & stroke: 3-5/16 in. x 4-1/8 in. Displacement: 213 cid.. Compression ratio: 6.3:1. Brake horsepower: 78 at 3400 rpm. Net horsepower: 26.3 (NACC). Four main bearings. Solid valve lifters. Carburetor: Single downdraft.
ENGINE [Series K-2]: See Series K-1 engine data above.
ENGINE [Series K-3]: See Series K-1 engine date above.
CHASSIS [Series K-1]: Wheelbase: 113/125 in. Tires: 6.00 x 16 in.
CHASSIS [Series K-2]: Wheelbase: 125 in. Tires: 6.00 x 16 in.
CHASSIS [Series K-3]: Wheelbase: 113/130 in. Tires: 6.00 x 16 in.
TECHNICAL: Synchromesh transmission. Speeds: 3F/1R. Floor-mounted gearshift lever. Multiple dry disc type clutch. Hypoid rear axle. Overall ratio: [1/2-ton] 4.18:1; [3/4-1-ton] 4.875:1 to 6.5:1. Bendix hydraulic brakes. Steel disc wheels.
OPTIONS: Front bumper. Rear bumper. Bumper guards. Radio. Heater. Clock. Cigar lighter. Radio antenna. Seat covers. External sun shade. Spotlight.
HISTORICAL: See 1940 historical notes.

1941-1942 IHC

1941 IHC 1/2-Ton Model K-5 Commercial Station Wagob (OCW)

MODEL K — SERIES K-1 — SIX-CYLINDER: Running production changes of a minor nature were the only updates for IHC's 1941 Model K trucks. The 1/2-ton line was again designated the K-1 Series. A K-1H option, rated at 3/4-ton, could be had. This series continued to offer 113 and 125 in. wheelbases. The Green Diamond six-cylinder engine was used. One thing that changed from the 1940-1/2 introductory lineup was pricing, which increased $40 to $60 per model. Also new were several additional model offerings: the

canopy delivery and KM milk truck on the 113 in. wheelbase and the canopy delivery and KB bakery truck on the 125 in. wheelbase. The entire series was carried over into 1942, basically without change. However, some late-1942 models were built with a minimum of chrome plated parts due to wartime material restrictions.

MODEL K — SERIES K-2 — SIX-CYLINDER: The trucks in the K-2 Series were also little changed. This was again a 3/4-ton range having 1/2-ton [K-2L] and 1-ton [K-2H] variations. A canopy delivery truck and KB bakery truck were new models. All of the K-2s used the 125 in. w.b. and the 82 hp. Green Diamond six-cylinder engine. The same models were carried over for 1942 at the same prices and with slightly lower shipping weights. Some late '42s had wartime blackout trim.

MODEL K — SERIES K-3 — SIX-CYLINDER: The K-3 trucks were in the 1-ton series. There was a 1/2-ton K-3L option. Few changes from the 1940-1/2 versions were seen. Two wheelbases, 113 in. and 130 in., were available again. A Model KM milk truck was a new model on the smaller wheelbase. It was offered for 1941 and 1942. New 1941 models for the 130 in. wheelbase included a canopy delivery and station wagon. Both were carried over for 1942. The '42s again had the same prices and slightly lower shipping weights.

METRO DELIVERY — SERIES D2M/K-1M/D15M/K-3M — SIX-CYLINDER: Introduced in 1938, the Metro Delivery was a multi-stop truck featuring a body by Metro Body Co. (This firm later became an IHC subsidiary). These van-like vehicles came in four series. The D2M had a 1/2-ton rating and 4,600 pound GVW. The K-1M had a 1/2-ton rating and 4,600 pound GVW. The D15M had a 3/4-one ton rating and 7,000 pound GVW. The K-3M was a 1-ton with 7,000 pound GVW. All series offered 102 in. and 113 in. wheelbases and had Green Diamond powerplants. In Atlantic City, N.J., a fleet of Metro Delivery vans served many years as jitney buses. For 1942, only the K-1M (1/2-ton) and K-3M (1-ton) series were available.

I.D. DATA: [K-1] Serial number located on plate on dash. Also on floorboard on right side of driving compartment. Also on left front end of frame, left front spring hanger or right runningboard shield at front end. Starting: [1941] 5469. [1942] 26491. Ending: [1941] 26490. [1942] 28601. Engine numbers located on left side of crankcase. Engine numbers not available. [K-2] Serial numbers in the same locations. Starting: [1941] 3092. [1942] 13907. Ending: [1941] 13906. [1942] 14455. Engine numbers in the same locations. Starting and ending numbers not available. [K-3] Serial numbers in same locations. Starting: [1941] 2309. [1942] 12618. Ending: [1941] 12617. [1942] 13605. Engine numbers in same locations. Starting and ending numbers not available. [Metro] Serial numbers in the same locations. Starting: 1941: [D2M] 1592 and up. [K-1M] 501 to 1959. [D15M] 2076 and up. [K-3M] 501 to 2520. 1942: [K-1M] 1960 to 2008. [K-3M] 2521 to 2650. Engine numbers in same locations. Starting and ending numbers not available.

Model	Body Type	Price	Weight	Prod. Total
Model K-1 (1/2-Ton)/K-1H (3/4-Ton) — 113 in. w.b.				
K-1	Chassis & Cowl	550	2250	—
K-1	Chassis & Cab	663	2630	—
K-1	Pickup	710	2908	—
K-1	Canopy	900	3525	—
K-1	Panel	815	3170	—
KM-1	Milk Truck	970	3255	—
K-1	Station Wagon	1140	3250	—
Model K-1 (1/2-Ton)/K-1H — (3/4-Ton) — 125 in. w.b.				
K-1	Chassis & Cowl	570	2275	—
K-1	Chassis & Cab	683	2655	—
K-1	Pickup	745	2963	—
K-1	Canopy	930	3550	—
K-1	Panel	850	3275	—
K-1	Stake	753	3186	—
KB-1	Bakery Truck	1015	3271	—

NOTE 1: Serial numbering indicates 21,021 trucks built in the 1941 series and 2,110 trucks built in the 1942 series.

NOTE 2: In 1942, the same models were marketed at the same prices. However, the weights were reduced by some 45-60 lbs. per model.

Model	Body Type	Price	Weight	Prod. Total
Model K-2 (3/4-Ton)/K-2L (1/2-Ton)/K-2H (1-Ton) — 125 in. w.b.				
K-2	Chassis & Cowl	580	2285	—
K-2	Chassis & Cab	693	2665	—
K-2	Pickup	755	2973	—
K-2	Canopy	940	3560	—
K-2	Panel	860	3285	—
K-2	Stake	763	3196	—
KB-2	Bakery Truck	1025	3370	—

NOTE 3: Serial numbers indicate 10,814 trucks built in the 1941 Series and 548 trucks built in the 1942 series.

NOTE 4: The base shipping weights for 1942 were 2,235 lbs. for the chassis and cowl and 2,630 lbs. for the chassis and Cab Weights for other 1942 models not available.

Model	Body Type	Price	Weight	Prod. Total
Model K-3 (1-Ton)/K-3L (1/2-Ton) — 113 in. w.b.				
K-3	Chassis & Cowl	680	3000	—
K-3	Chassis & Cab	793	3380	—
K-3	Pickup	840	3658	—
KM-3	Milk Truck	1110	4005	—
Model K-3 (1-Ton)/K-3L (1/2-Ton) — 130 in. w.b.				
K-3	Chassis & Cowl	680	3030	—
K-3	Chassis & Cab	793	3410	—
K-3	Pickup	875	3781	—
K-3	Canopy	1060	4750	—
K-3	Panel	980	4230	—
K-3	Stake	873	4034	—
K-3	Station Wagon	1520	4330	—

NOTE 5: Serial numbers indicate 10,308 trucks built in the 1941 series and 987 trucks built in the 1942 series.

NOTE 6: Some 1942 weights were: Chassis & Cowl with 113 in. w.b. (2,667 lbs.); Chassis & Cab with 113 in. w.b. (3,062 lbs.); Chassis & Cowl with 130 in. w.b. (2,697 lbs.); Chassis & Cab with 130 in. w.b. (3,092 lbs.).

Model	Body Type	Price	Weight	Prod. Total
1941 Metro Delivery Series — 1/2-Ton — 102 in. w.b.				
D-2M	Walk-in	1100	1942	—
K-1M	Walk-in Chassis	560	—	—
K-1M	Walk-in	1170	—	—
1941 Metro Delivery Series — 1/2-Ton — 113 in. w.b.				
D-2M	Walk-in	1170	1952	—
K-1M	Walk-in Chassis	560	—	—
K-1M	Walk-in	1215	—	—
1941 Metro Delivery Series — 3/4-Ton — 102 in. w.b.				
D15M	Walk-in	1240	—	—
1941 Metro Delivery Series — 3/4-Ton — 113 in. w.b.				
D15M	Walk-in	1310	—	—
1941 Metro Delivery Series — 1-Ton — 102 in. w.b.				
K-3M	Walk-in Chassis	670	—	—
K-3M	Walk-in	1280	—	—
1941 Metro Delivery Series — 1-Ton — 113 in. w.b.				
K-3M	Walk-in Chassis	670	—	—
K-3M	Walk-in	1325	—	—
1942 Metro Delivery Series — 1/2-Ton — 102 in. w.b.				
K-1M	Walk-in Chassis	560	—	—
K-1M	Walk-in	1170	—	—
1942 Metro Delivery Series — 1/2-Ton — 113 in. w.b.				
K-1M	Walk-in Chassis	560	—	—
K-1M	Walk-in	1215	—	—
1942 Metro Delivery Series — 1-Ton — 102 in. w.b.				
K-3M	Walk-in Chassis	670	—	—
K-3M	Walk-in	1280	—	—
1942 Metro Delivery Series — 1-Ton — 113 in. w.b.				
K-3M	Walk-in Chassis	670	—	—
K-3M	Walk-in	1325	—	—

1942 IHC 1/2-Ton Model K-1 Pickup (OCW)

ENGINE [Series K-1/K-2/K-3/Metro]: Inline. L-head. Six-cylinder. Cast iron block. Bore & stroke: 3-5/16 in. x 4-1/8 in. Displacement: 213 cid.. Compression ratio: 6.3:1. Brake horsepower: 82 at 3400 rpm. Net horsepower: 26.3 (NACC). Four main bearings of insert type. Solid valve lifters. Carburetor: Single downdraft. Crankcase capacity: 6-1/2 quarts. (Full-pressure type.) Cooling system capacity: 14-3/4 quarts. Electrical system: six volts. Oil bath air cleaner.

CHASSIS [Series K-1]: Wheelbase: 113/125 in. Front tread: 58-9/32 in. Rear tread: 58-13/16 in. Tires: 6.00 x 16 in.

CHASSIS [Series K-2]: Wheelbase: 125 in. Front tread: 58-9/32 in. Rear tread: 58-13/16 in. Tires: 6.00 x 16 in.

CHASSIS [Series K-3]: Wheelbase: 113/130 in. Front tread: 58-9/32 in. Rear tread: 58-13/16 in. Tires: 6.00 x 16 in.

CHASSIS [1/2-Ton Metro Delivery]: Wheelbase: 102/113 in. Front tread: 58-9/32 in. Rear tread: 58-13/16 in. Tires: 6.00 x 16 (four-ply).

CHASSIS [3/4-Ton to 1-Ton Metro Delivery]: Wheelbase: 102/113 in. Front tread: 58-9/32 in. Rear tread: 58-13/16 in. Tires: 7.00 x 16 (six-ply).

TECHNICAL: Synchromesh transmission. Speeds: 3F/1R. Floor-mounted gearshift lever. 10 inch diameter single dry-plate clutch. Semi-floating rear axle. Overall ratio: 4.18:1. Four-wheel hydraulic internal expanding brakes. Steel disc wheels. Optional: Four-speed selective, with straight cut gears.

OPTIONS: Front bumper. Rear bumper. Rearview mirror. Wheel trim rings. Spotlight. Dual taillights. Bumper guards. Radio. Heater. Special paint. Oversize tires. Radio antenna. Seat covers. External sun shade. Spotlight. License plate bracket. Side mounted spare tire on station wagon. Dual windshield wiper. Fog lamps.

HISTORICAL: Introduced: [1941] November, 1940..[1942] October, 1941. Calendar year registrations all IHC trucks: [1941] 92,482; [1942] unavailable. Calendar year production all IHC trucks: [1941] 120,843. [1942] 42,126. Model year production all IHC trucks: [1941] 115,283. With 11.05 percent of the overall truck market, IHC was the fourth-largest truckmaker in calendar 1941. In calendar year 1942, the company's market penetration fell to 4.80 percent and its sales ranking dropped to seventh.

1946 IHC

MODEL K — SERIES K-1/K-1M/K-2/K-3/K-3M — SIX-CYLINDER: IHC made a major contribution to the Allied efforts, during World War II, through the manufacture of a wide range of military vehicles and armaments. For example, over 13,000 M-5 half-tracks were built at the company's Springfield Works between 1942 and 1944. In the light-duty truck

field, the 1943 models were a continuation of the 1942s. No light trucks were cataloged for 1944, but starting in November of 1945, the K-2 (3/4-ton) and the K-3 and K-3M models (both 1-ton) were produced in chassis and chassis and cab form. Also, the K-3 pickup was made. These trucks were basically the same as 1942 models, although some had blackout trim features. Many were fitted with special military bodies and equipment for armed forces use here and abroad. Others were released for sale to civilians with essential occupations such as doctors, farmers and armaments workers. The serial numbers and prices/weights of these trucks are given in this section. For other information, refer to the 1941-1942 section of this catalog.

I.D. DATA: Serial number located in the same places as on 1942 models. Starting: [K-2] 14456. [K-3] 13606. [K-3M] 2651. Ending: [K-2] 17100. [K-3] 19566. [K-3M] 2930. Engine numbers located in the same place. No numbers available.

Model	Body Type	Price	Weight	Prod. Total
Model K-2 — 3/4-Ton — 125 in. w.b.				
K-2	Chassis	768	2285	Note 1
K-2	Chassis & Cab	888	2680	Note 1
Model K-3 — 1-Ton — 113 in. w.b.				
K-3	Chassis	821	3000	Note 2
K-3	Chassis & Cab	941	3395	Note 2
Model K-3 — 1-ton — 130 in. w.b.				
K-3	Chassis	946	3425	Note 2
K-3	Chassis & Cab	1031	3815	Note 2
Model K-3M — 1-ton — 102 in. w.b.				
K-3M	Chassis	—	2585	Note 3

NOTE 1: Serial numbers indicate 2,644 trucks built in Series K-2.
NOTE 2: Serial numbers indicate 5,960 trucks built in Series K-3.
NOTE 3: Serial numbers indicate 279 trucks built in Series K-3M.
ADDITIONAL NOTE: See 1941-1942 section for technical specifications and pricing data.

MODEL K — K-1 SERIES — SIX-CYLINDER: The Model K line of IHC light-duty trucks was carried over for its final year in 1946. Styling was again unchanged. Characteristic appearance features included a domed cab roofline, long, pointed hood, flush headlights and a tall, barrel-shaped grille with curved horizontal bars and a vertical center divider. The International nameplate appeared at the lower rear edge of the hood. Decorating the nose was a badge having the company name across three diamonds. I-H Red was the company's traditional color for these trucks, but dark green, maroon and black finish was also available. The Green Diamond six-cylinder engine was used again. A heavy-duty suspension option coded as K-1H was available and uprated the trucks to 3/4-ton, although K-1s are generally considered 1/2-tonners. They were again available on two different wheelbases. A new 1/2-ton K-1M was also available on a 102 in. wheelbase. Due to the unstable postwar market, IHCs were sold as chassis or chassis-and-cabs with bodywork optional. GVW ratings were 4,400 lbs. for the K-1 and 4,600 lbs. for the K-1M.

1946 IHC 3/4-Ton Model K-2 Express (OCW)

MODEL K — K-1 SERIES — SIX-CYLINDER: The Model K line of IHC light-duty trucks was carried over for its final year in 1946. Styling was again unchanged. Characteristic appearance features included a domed cab roofline, long, pointed hood, flush headlights and a tall, barrel-shaped grille with curved horizontal bars and a vertical center divider. The International nameplate appeared at the lower rear edge of the hood. Decorating the nose was a badge having the company name across three diamonds. I-H Red was the company's traditional color for these trucks, but dark green, maroon and black finish was also available. The Green Diamond six-cylinder engine was used again. A heavy-duty suspension option coded as K-1H was available and uprated the trucks to 3/4-ton, although K-1s are generally considered 1/2-tons. They were again available on two different wheelbases. A new 1/2-ton K-1M was also available on a 102 in. wheelbase. Due to the unstable postwar market, IHCs were sold as chassis or chassis-and-cabs with bodywork optional. GVW ratings were 4,400 lbs. for the K-1 and 4,600 lbs. for the K-1M.

MODEL K — K-2 SERIES — SIX-CYLINDER: The K-2 Series continued to be available for 3/4-ton truck buyers in 1946. It could be had with light-duty K-2L (1/2-ton) and heavy-duty K-2H (1-ton) suspension options. The 125 in. wheelbase chassis was used for all models. Under the hood was the Green Diamond six-cylinder flathead engine. A heavy-duty Knox pickup box was used. Styling was similar to that of the K-1 trucks. The GVW rating was 5,200 lbs..

MODEL K — SERIES K-3 — SIX-CYLINDER: IHC 1-ton trucks were again designated K-3s. A light-duty K-3L suspension option (1/2-ton rated) was cataloged. These trucks came with 113 or 130 in. wheelbases and Green Diamond engines. Styling was similar to other models in larger proportion. A 6,650 pound GVW rating applied. There was also a new, 102 in. wheelbase K-3M model, with a 7,000 pound GVW rating.

I.D. DATA: Serial number located: See 1945 IHC. Starting: [K-1] 28611. [K-1M] 2009. Ending: [K-1] 49308. [K-1M] 4251. [K-2] Starting: 17101. Ending: 28480. Engine numbers located: See 1945 IHC. [K-3] Starting: 19567. Ending 31108. Engine numbers located: See 1945 IHC.

Model	Body Type	Price	Weight	Prod. Total
Series K-1 — 1/2-Ton — 113 in. w.b.				
K-1	Chassis & Cab	883	2645	—
K-1	Chassis	763	2250	—

Model	Body Type	Price	Weight	Prod. Total
Series K-1 — 1/2-Ton — 125 in. w.b.				
K-1	Chassis & Cab	—	2760	—
K-1	Chassis	883	2375	—
Series K-1M — 1/2-Ton — 102 in. w.b.				
K-1M	Chassis	773	2150	—

NOTE 1: Serial numbers indicate 20,697 trucks built in the K-1 series and 2,242 trucks built in the K-1M series.

Model	Body Type	Price	Weight	Prod. Total
Series K-2 — 3/4-Ton — 125 in. w.b.				
K-2	Chassis	768	2285	—
K-2	Chassis & Cab	888	2680	—
K-2	Express	958	3020	—

NOTE 2: Serial numbers indicate 11,379 trucks built in the K-2 Series.

Model	Body Type	Price	Weight	Prod. Total
Series K-3 — 1-ton — 113 in. w.b.				
K-3	Chassis	891	3000	—
K-3	Chassis & Cab	1011	3395	—
Series K-3 — 1-ton — 130 in. w.b.				
K-3	Express	1102	3739	—
K-3	Stake	1099	4049	—
Series K-3M — 1-ton — 102 in. w.b.				
K-3M	Chassis	—	2585	—

NOTE 3: Serial numbers indicate 11,541 trucks built in this series.

ENGINE [All]: Inline. L-head. Six-cylinder. Cast iron block. Bore & stroke: 3-5/16 in. x 4-1/8-in. Displacement: 213 cid.. Compression ratio: 6.3:1. Brake horsepower: 82 at 3400 rpm. Net horsepower: 26.3 (NACC). Maximum Torque: 160 lbs.-ft. at 1200 rpm. Four main bearings. Solid valve lifters. Carburetor: Zenith.
CHASSIS [Series K-1/K-1M*]: Wheelbase: 113/125/102(*) in.. Height: 49 in. Front tread: 58-9/32 in. Rear tread: 58-13/16 in. Tires: 6.00 x 16 in.
CHASSIS [Series K-2]: Wheelbase: 125 in. Front tread: 58-9/32 in. Rear tread: 58-13/16 in. Tires: 6.00 x 16 in.
CHASSIS [Series K-3/K-3M*]: Wheelbase: 113/130/102(*) in.. Tires: 7.00 x 16 in.
TECHNICAL: Synchromesh transmission. Speeds: 3F/1R. Floor-mounted gearshift lever. Single-plate dry disc clutch; 10 inch diameter, semi-floating rear axle. Overall ratio: 4.88:1. Four-wheel hydraulic internal expanding brakes. Steel disc wheels. Four-speed manual transmission, with straight cut gears. Rear axle ratios: 3.72:1 through 5.11:1.
OPTIONS: Dual wipers. Rear bumper (station wagon). Single sidemount (station wagon). Dual cab sunvisors. Electric wipers. Knox heavy-duty grain box. Bumper guards. Radio. Heater. Clock. Cigar lighters. Radio antenna. Seat covers. External sun shade. Spotlight. Wheel trim rings. License plate bracket. Turn signals. Dual taillights. Special paint. Oversized tires.
HISTORICAL: Introduced: January 1946. Calendar year registrations: [All IHC trucks] 78,392. Calendar year production: [All IHC trucks] 113,546. IHC became America's fourth largest truck-maker again in 1946, with a 12.05 percent share of the total market. Chevrolet, Ford and Dodge, in order, were the only companies to sell more commercial vehicles.

1947-1949 IHC

1947 IHC 1/2-Ton Model KB-1 Pickup (DSO)

MODEL KB — SERIES KB-1/KB-1M — SIX-CYLINDER: International introduced a new KB Series in January 1947. It remained in production, with no more than minor changes, through the close of the 1949 model year. Prices increased a bit each year and a few models had shipping weight changes. The KB was mainly an evolutionary series and brought no major alterations to the basically prewar design. The flush headlamps, domed cab roofs and long, pointed hoods continued to characterize the IHC look. There was even a crank hole at the bottom of the grille, through which a manual engine crank could be inserted. The grille was still tall and barrel-shaped, but wing-like side grille extensions were added. They brought the bottom seven grille members out towards the headlights, right over the fender sheet metal. The badge on the nose of the trucks was made larger and now attached to the upper grille bars. In its center was a depression containing a smaller emblem with the International name across three diamonds. A chrome molding was added

on the top of the nose of the hood and model call-outs were plated below the International name on the rear lower edge of the hood. Standard equipment included an adjustable bench seat, 80 mph speedometer, ammeter, water temperature gauge, glove box, Lovejoy refillable shock absorbers, solid front axle, solid rear axle, semi-elliptic rear leaf springs, single interior sun visor and single vacuum-operated windshield wiper. The Green Diamond six-cylinder engine was used again. The KB-1 was the 1/2-ton model on 113 in. or 125 in. wheelbases. There was also a KB-1M 1/2-ton on a 102 in. wheelbase. GVW ratings for the two series were 4,200 and 4,600 lbs., respectively.

1947 IHC 1/2-Ton Model KB-1 Pickup (OCW)

MODEL KB — SERIES KB-2 — SIX-CYLINDER: The KB-2 was the 3/4-ton version of the updated IHC truck. It was styled and equipped similar to the KB-1. Only the 125 in. wheelbase was available for this series. A popular option for the 3/4-ton series was a heavy-duty grain box with checkerplate bed surface promoted as the "Knox Box" after its manufacturer's name (which appeared on the tailgate). Like the KB-1, the KB-2 came in I-H red, dark green, maroon or black finish. These 3/4-tons had a 5,200 lb. GVW rating.

1947 IHC 3/4-Ton Model KB-2 Platform (OCW)

MODEL KB — SERIES KB-3/KB-3M — SIX-CYLINDER: The KB-3 was the 1-ton version of the updated IHC truck. It was styled and equipped similar to other light-duty 1947-1949 models, except for larger tires and a heavier-duty running gear. The KB-3M was a shorter wheelbase version. GVW ratings for these two lines were 5,200 and 6,650 lbs., respectively. Power came from the same Green Diamond engine used in other small IHC trucks. The KB-3M, like the KB-1M, came only in chassis form in 1947 and gained a Metro walk-in van body for 1948 and 1949.

I.D. DATA: Serial number located: See 1945 IHC. 1947 starting/ending numbers: [KB-1] 49309/70792. [KB-1M] 4252/6706. [KB-2] 28481/49056. [KB-3] 31109/41078. [KB-3M] 6235/10749. 1948 starting/ending numbers: [KB-1] 70793/93351. [KB-1M] 6707/10633. [KB-2] 49057/74329. [KB-3] 41079/51781. [KB-3M] 10750/16634. 1949 starting numbers: [KB-1] 93352-up. [KB-1M] 10634-up. [KB-2] 74330-up. [KB-3] 51782-up. [KB-3M] 16635-up. Ending numbers for 1949 not available. Engine numbers located: See 1945 IHC. Engine numbers not available.

1948 IHC 3/4-Ton Model KB-2 Express (OCW)

Standard Catalog of Light-Duty Trucks

Model	Body Type	Price	Weight	Prod. Total
1947				
Series KB-1 — 1/2-Ton — 113 in. w.b.				
KB-1	Chassis	874	2350	—
KB-1	Chassis & Cowl	1030	2645	—
KB-1	Express (Pickup)	1098	2959	—
KB-1	Panel	1238	3150	—
KB-1	KBM (Bakery/Milk)	1477	3650	—
Series KB-1 — 1/2-Ton — 125 in. w.b.				
KB-1	Chassis	900	2375	—
KB-1	Chassis & Cowl	1056	2670	—
KB-1	Express (Pickup)	1139	2984	—
KB-1	Panel	1290	3175	—
KB-1	Stake	1145	3201	—
Series KB-1M — 1/2-Ton — 102 in. w.b.				
KB-1M	Chassis	827	2150	—

NOTE 1: Serial numbers indicate 21,483 trucks built in 1947 Series KB-1 and 2,484 trucks built in 1947 Series KB-1M.

Model	Body Type	Price	Weight	Prod. Total
1948				
Series KB-1 — 1/2-Ton — 113 in. w.b.				
KB-1	Chassis	890	2250	—
KB-1	Chassis & Cowl	1098	2645	—
KB-1	Express (Pickup)	1186	2959	—
KB-1	Panel	1347	3545	—
KB-1	KBM (Bakery/Milk)	1560	3650	—
Series KB-1 — 1/2-Ton — 125 in. w.b.				
KB-1	Chassis	1066	2375	—
KB-1	Chassis & Cowl	1263	2670	—
KB-1	Express (Pickup)	1368	2984	—
KB-1	Panel	1581	3175	—
KB-1	Stake	1378	3201	—
Series KB-1M — 1/2-Ton — 102 in. w.b.				
KB-1M	Chassis	843	2150	—
KB-1M	Metro	1810	3955	—

NOTE 2: Serial numbers indicate 22,558 trucks built in 1948 Series KB-1 and 3,926 trucks built in 1948 Series KB-M1.

Model	Body Type	Price	Weight	Prod. Total
1949				
Series KB-1 — 1/2-Ton — 113 in. w.b.				
KB-1	Chassis	1045	2250	—
KB-1	Chassis & Cowl	1235	2645	—
KB-1	Express (Pickup)	1331	2959	—
KB-1	Panel	1534	3545	—
Series KB-1 — 1/2-Ton — 125 in. w.b.				
KB-1	Chassis	1071	2375	—
KB-1	Chassis & Cowl	1269	2670	—
KB-1	Express (Pickup)	1373	2984	—
KB-1	Panel	1586	3175	—
KB-1	Stake	1383	3201	—
Series KB-1M — 1/2-Ton — 102 in. w.b.				
KB-1M	Chassis	957	2150	—
KB-1M	Metro	2082	3955	—

NOTE 3: Production of 1949 models cannot be determined since ending serial numbers are not available.

1948 IHC 1-Ton Model KB-3 Stake (OCW)

Model	Body Type	Price	Weight	Prod. Total
1947				
Series KB-2 — 3/4-Ton — 125 in. w.b.				
KB-2	Chassis	916	2285	—
KB-2	Chassis & Cab	1066	2680	—
KB-2	Express (Pickup)	1155	3020	—
KB-2	Panel	1306	3245	—
KB-2	Stake	1160	3211	—

NOTE 4: Serial numbers indicate 20,575 trucks built in 1947 Series KB-2.

1948 IHC 1/2-Ton Model KB-1 Commercial Station Wagon (OCW)

1948

Series KB-2 — 3/4-Ton — 125 in. w.b.

KB-2	Chassis	931	2285	—
KB-2	Chassis & Cab	1139	2680	—
KB-2	Express (Pickup)	1243	3020	—
KB-2	Panel	1415	3640	—
KB-2	Stake	1254	3211	—

NOTE 5: Serial numbers indicate 25,272 trucks built in 1947 Series KB-2.

1948 IHC 1/2-Ton Metro Delivery Van (OCW)

1949

Series KB-2 — 3/4-Ton — 125 in. w.b.

KB-2	Chassis	1097	2285	—
KB-2	Chassis & Cab	1295	2680	—
KB-2	Express (Pickup)	1399	3020	—
KB-2	Panel	1612	3640	—
KB-2	Stake	1409	3211	—

NOTE 5: Production of 1949 models cannot be determined since ending serial numbers are not available.

1949 IHC 1/2-Ton Model KB-1 Panel (B. Heller)

1947

Series KB-3 — 1-Ton — 113 in. w.b.

KB-3	Chassis	1067	3000	—
KB-3	Chassis & Cowl	1217	3395	—
KB-3	Express (Pickup)	1291	3709	—
KB-3	KM (Milk)	1671	4005	—

Series KB-3 — 1-Ton — 130 in. w.b.

KB-3	Chassis	1067	3130	—
KB-3	Chassis & Cowl	1223	3425	—
KB-3	Express (Pickup)	1334	3739	—
KB-3	Panel	1483	4090	—
KB-3	Stake	1322	4049	—

Series KB-3M — 1-Ton — 102 in. w.b.

KB-3M	Chassis	990	2585	—

NOTE 6: Serial numbers indicate 9,969 trucks built in 1947 Series KB-3 and 4,514 trucks built in 1947 Series KB-3M.

1948

Series KB-3 — 1-Ton — 113 in. w.b.

KB-3	Chassis	1093	3000	—
KB-3	Chassis & Cowl	1301	3395	—
KB-3	Express (Pickup)	1390	3709	—
KB-3	KM (Milk)	1764	4005	—

Series KB-3 — 1-Ton — 130 in. w.b.

KB-3	Chassis	1244	3130	—
KB-3	Chassis & Cowl	1442	3425	—
KB-3	Express (Pickup)	1572	3739	—
KB-3	Panel	1785	4090	—
KB-3	Stake	1572	4049	—

Series KB-3M — 1-Ton — 102 in. w.b.

KB-3M	Chassis	1016	2585	—
KB-3M	Metro	1982	4390	—

NOTE 7: Serial numbers indicate 11,702 trucks built in 1948 Series KB-3 and 5,884 trucks built in 1948 Series KB-3M.

1949

Series KB-3 — 1-Ton — 113 in. w.b.

KB-3	Chassis	1249	3000	—
KB-3	Chassis & Cowl	1447	3395	—
KB-3	Express (Pickup)	1525	3709	—
KB-3	KBM (Bake/Milk)	2017	4400	—

Series KB-3 — 1-Ton — 130 in. w.b.

KB-3	Chassis	1249	3130	—
KB-3	Chassis & Cowl	1446	3425	—
KB-3	Express (Pickup)	1576	3815	—
KB-3	Panel	1790	4090	—
KB-3	Stake	1576	4049	—

Series KB-3M — 1-Ton — 102 in. w.b.

KB-3M	Chassis	1145	2585	—
KB-3M	Metro	2270	4390	—

NOTE 8: Production of 1949 models cannot be determined since ending serial numbers are not available.

1949 IHC 1/2-Ton Model KB-1 Pickup (OCW)

ENGINE [All 1947-1949 Series]: Inline. L-head. Six-cylinder. Cast iron block. Bore & stroke: 3-5/16 in. x 4-1/8 in. Displacement: 213 cid.. Compression ratio: 6.3:1. Brake horsepower: 82 at 3400 rpm. Net horsepower: 26.3 (NACC). Maximum Torque: 160 lbs.-ft. at 1200 rpm. Four main bearings. Solid valve lifters. Carburetor: Single downdraft, (model) Zenith.

CHASSIS [Series KB-1/KB-1M*]: Wheelbase: 113/125/102(*) in. Height: 49 in. Front tread: 58-9/32 in. Rear tread: 58-13/16 in. Tires: 6.00 x 16 in.

CHASSIS [Series KB-2]: Wheelbase: 125 in. Front tread: 58-9/32 in. Rear tread: 58-13/16 in. Tires: 6.00 x 16 in.

CHASSIS [Series KB-3/KB-3M*]: Wheelbase: 113/130/102(*) in. Tires: 7.00 x 16 in.

TECHNICAL: Synchromesh transmission. Speeds: 3F/1R. Floor-mounted gearshift lever. Single-plate dry disc clutch; 10 inch diameter, semi-floating rear axle. Overall ratio: 3.72:1 to 5.11:1. Four-wheel hydraulic internal expanding brakes. Steel spoke wheels. Four-speed manual transmission, with straight cut gears.

OPTIONS: Front bumper. Rear bumper. Single sidemount (station wagons). Dual cab interior sun visors. Dual electric wipers. Knox box. Bumper guards. Radio. Heater. Clock. Cigar lighters. Radio antenna. Seat covers. External sun shade. Spotlight. Wheel trim rings. License plate frame. Turn signals. Dual taillights. Special paint. Oversized tires. Deluxe panel station wagon Metro bus interior. Deluxe trim package.

HISTORICAL: Introduced: [1947] Jan. 1947; [1948] Jan. 1, 1948; [1949] Jan.1949. Calendar year production: All IHC products: [1947] 153,009; [1948] 166,784; [1949] 110,558. Model year production: Same as above calendar year totals. New KB series introduced in 1947. IHC industry ranking (and market share) for the three years was as follows: [1947] ranked fourth (12.37 percent); [1948] ranked fourth (12.18 percent); [1949] ranked fourth (9.77 percent). Mr. J.L. McCaffrey was president of IHC. W.V. Reese was engineering man-

ager. W.K. Perkins was manager of sales. All-time record truck sales were recorded in 1948. IHC had about 15,000 truck division employees. The company was headquartered in Chicago, Ill. IHC trucks were nicknamed "Corn-Binders."

1950-1952 IHC

MODEL L — ALL SERIES — SIX-CYLINDER: An all-new L Series line of trucks was introduced by IHC in January 1950. They were totally restyled and re-engineered. Styling characteristics included a one-piece windshield, two-section rear cab window, broad flat fenders and a wide and flat front end cap. Single headlamps were flush-mounted into keyhole-shaped recesses with rectangular parking lamps below. The new grille consisted of horizontal bars with 19 vertical slots above. The three outermost vertical blades on each side were shorter. A bright metal strip ran across the lower edge of the nose. The nose had an an IHC shield on it, plus a chrome molding running up the center of the hood. A painted, wraparound bumper protected the front. Under the hood was a new overhead valve inline six-cylinder engine. These models were first merchandised mainly as chassis and cab trucks. More information about body styles was released in 1952. A station wagon with wood body construction could be ordered. Metro vans, milk trucks, bakery trucks and small school buses were available, too. (Note: To estimate prices for 1950-1951 models, see cab and truck body prices listed below.)

1950 IHC 1/2-Ton Model L-110 Panel (DSO)

1950 IHC 1/2-Ton Model L-110 Pickup (HAS)

I.D. DATA: Serial number located same as 1945. These trucks were not produced on a yearly model basis. Year model determined by date of original sale to operator. Starting serial numbers were 501 up. Engine numbers located same as 1945. Engine numbers not available.

Model	Body Type	Price	Weight	Prod. Total
1950				
Series L-110/L-111/L-112 — 1/2 Ton				
L-11	Chassis & Cab	1304	2965	—
Series L-120/L-121/L-122 — 3/4-Ton				
L-12	Chassis & Cab	1439	3230	—
Series LM-120/LM-121/LM-122 — 3/4-Ton				
LM-12	Metro Chassis	1183	2370	—
Series L-150 - 1-Ton				
L-15	Chassis & Cab	1600	3880	—
Series L-153 — 1-Ton				
L-153	School Bus	1468	3540	—
Series LM-150 — 1-Ton				
LM-15	Heavy-Duty Metro Chassis	1354	2970	

Standard Catalog of Light-Duty Trucks

Model	Body Type	Price	Weight	Prod. Total
1951				
Series L-110/L-111/L-112 — 1/2-Ton				
L-11	Chassis & Cab	1350	2965	—
Series L-120/L-121/L-122 — 3/4-Ton				
L-12	Chassis & Cab	1490	3230	—
Series LM-120/LM-121/LM-122 — 3/4-Ton				
LM-12	Metro Chassis	1175	2370	—
Series LB-140 Metro — 1/2-Ton				
LB-14	Milk Truck	1980	3015	—
Series L-150/L-151 — 1-Ton				
L-15	Chassis & Cab	1657	3880	—
Series L-153 — 1-Ton				
L-153	1-Ton School Bus	1535	3540	—
Series LM-150 — 1-Ton				
LM-15	Heavy-Duty Metro Chassis	1350	2970	—
1952				
Series L-110/L-111/L-112 - 1/2-Ton				
L-11	Chassis & Cab	1375	2965	—
L-11	Pickup	1468	—	—
L-11	Panel	1658	—	—
Series L-120/L-121/L-122 - 3/4-Ton				
L-12	Chassis & Cab	1505	3230	—
L-12	Pickup	1598	—	—
L-12	Panel	1788	—	—
Series LM-120 — 102 in. w.b. — 1/2-Ton				
LM-12	Metro	2289	—	
Series LM-121 — 115 in. w.b. — 3/4-Ton				
LM-12	Metro	2344	—	
Series LM-122 — 122 in. w.b. — 1-Ton				
LM-12	Metro	2506	—	
Series LB-140 — 1/2-Ton				
LB-14	Milk Truck	2750	3015	—
Series L-150/L-151 — 1-Ton				
L-15	Chassis & Cab	1699	3880	—
Series L-153 — 130 in. w.b. — 1-Ton				
L-15	School Bus	1510	3540	—
Series LM-150 — 115 in. w.b. — 3/4-Ton				
LM-15	Heavy-Duty Metro	2519	—	
Series LM-151 — 122 in. w.b. — 1-Ton				
LM-15	Heavy-Duty Metro	2681	—	

1951 IHC 3/4-Ton Model L-120 Pickup (J.R. Faureau)

1951 IHC 1/2-Ton Model L-110 Panel (OCW)

Cab and Truck Body Prices

(Cab Price)

Series L-110	$230
Series L-120	$230
Series L-130	$230
Series L-150	$239

(Pickup Body)

Series L-110/115 in. w.b./6-1/2 ft. box.	$93
Series L-120/115 in. w.b./6-1/2 ft. box.	$93
Series L-110/127 in. w.b./8-ft. box.	$108
Series L-120/127 in. w.b./8-ft. box.	$108
Series L-130/134 in. w.b./9-ft. box.	$127

(Panel Body)

Series L-110/115 in. w.b./7-1/2 ft. cargo floor	$513
Series L-120/115 in. w.b./7-1/2 ft. cargo floor	$513

(Metro Van Body)

Series LM-120/102 in. w.b. with standard body	$2289
Series LM-120/115 in. w.b. with standard body	$2344
Series LM-120/122 in. w.b. with standard body	$2506
Series LM-150/115 in. w.b. with standard body	$2519
Series LM-150/122 in. w.b. with standard body	$2681
Series LM-150/134 in. w.b. with standard body	$2788

1952 IHC 3/4-Ton Model L-120 Pickup (OCW)

1952 IHC 1/2-Ton Model L-110 Pickup (OCW)

ENGINE [All Series]: Inline. Overhead valve. Six-cylinder. Cast iron block. Bore & stroke: 3-9/16 in. x 3-11/16 in. Displacement: 220 cid.. Brake horsepower: 101. Net horsepower: 30.4 (NACC).
CHASSIS [Series L-110/L-111]: Wheelbase: 115 in./127 in.
CHASSIS [Series L-112/L-120 Heavy-Duty]: Wheelbase: 127 in.
CHASSIS [Series L-130]: Wheelbase: 134 in.
CHASSIS [Metro Van]: Wheelbase: 102 in./115 in.
TECHNICAL: Synchromesh transmission. Speeds: 3F/1R. Column or floor-mounted gearshift lever. Single-plate dry-disc clutch; 10 in. diam. Semi-floating rear axle. Four-wheel hydraulic brakes. Steel disc wheels. Four-speed transmission.
OPTIONS: Front bumper. Rear bumper. Dual interior sun visors. Dual electric wipers. Turn signals. Fender skirts. Bumper guards. Radio. Heater. Clock. Cigar lighter. Radio antenna. Seat covers. External sun shade. Spotlight. Wheel trim rings. License plate frame. Special paint. Oversized tires. Deluxe trim packages. Station wagon.
HISTORICAL: Introduced: Jan. 1950. Calendar year registrations, all IHC models: [1950] 97,818; [1951] 95,184. Calendar year production: IHC models 5,000 lbs. and less: [1949] 18,368; [1950] 26,350; [1951] 31,588. IHC models 5,001 to 10,000 lbs.: [1949] 38,306; [1950] 27,330; [1951] 28,996. Model year production of all IHC: [1950] 106,418; [1951] 151,439. Innnovations: New L Series styling with modernized features. All-new overhead valve six-cylinder. First column shift availability. IHC held its fourth rank in the truck industry. The company's second best year in history was recorded in 1951. The company produced 5-ton trucks for the military this season. A new motor truck engineering lab was opened at Ft. Wayne, Ind. in 1951. In 1951, the company announced that one million trucks it had produced were still in service.

498

1952 IHC 1/2-Ton Model L110 Station Wagon (OCW)

1953-1955 IHC

1953 IHC 1/2-Ton Model R-11 Panel (L.T. Seeley)

MODEL R — 1/2-TON — SIX-CYLINDER: IHC R Series trucks were introduced in 1953. Light-duty models were marketed through 1955. Stylingwise, they looked like a modernized L Series. Front end panels were now slightly concave with an oval grille opening. A hefty single grille bar, with I-H in its center, spanned the opening horizontally. Single, round headlamp housings protruded slightly and had rectangular parking lamps underneath. An air slot was cut into the lower front edge of the hood. Trim items consisted of a hood ornament, hoodside handles and International nameplates (at the rear of the hood). Two-tone finish was optional. Half-ton lines were the light-duty R-100 (115 in. wheelbase) and heavy-duty R-110 (115 or 127 in. wheelbase). The R-100 had a 4,200 lbs. GVW rating, but could be ordered with an R-102 option that increased the GVW to 4,600 lbs. The R-110 also had a 4,200 lbs. GVW and two options; the R-111 (4,800 lbs. GVW) and R-112 (5,400 lbs. GVW). Standard equipment included gauges, a single interior sun visor, bench seat, small hubcaps, black sidewall tires and tire changing tools. The overhead valve Silver Diamond six-cylinder engine was carried over from 1952 for the new trucks. For 1953 and 1954 these trucks were identical in features, models, prices and weights. In 1955, a chassis without cab was added and prices increased slightly, although weights were unchanged.

1953 IHC Cantrell Woodie Station Wagon (OCW)

MODEL R — 3/4-TON — SIX-CYLINDER: The R-120 was the basic 3/4-ton series offered by IHC from 1953-1955. It had a 5,400 lbs. GVW rating. Also available were the R-121 (5,900 lbs. GVW) and R-122 (6,500 lbs. GVW) chassis options. The R-120/R-122 trucks could be had on either the 115 in. or 127 in. wheelbase. Styling and equipment features were similar to those of the 1/2-tons. Hydra-Matic automatic transmission was a new-for-1955 option for all light-duty IHC trucks. An identifying series designation appeared on the side of the hoods at the cowl. For 1953 and 1954, these trucks were identical in features, models, prices and weights. In 1955, a chassis & cowl only configuration was added and prices went up slightly, although weights were unchanged. Also available on the 3/4-ton chassis was the Metro Delivery van, with a choice of 102 in., 115 in. or 122 in. wheelbase. The Silver Diamond six was used in all of these trucks.

MODEL R — 1-TON — SIX-CYLINDER: The R-130 was the basic 1-ton series offered by IHC from 1953-1955. It had a 6,800 lbs. GVW rating. Also available were the R-131 (7,700 lbs. GVW) and R-132 (8,600 lbs. GVW) chassis options. The R-130/R-131/R-132 trucks could be had on either a 115 in., 122 in. or 134 in. wheelbase. Styling and equipment features were similar to those of other models. A four-speed transmission was, however, standard with the 1-tons. These trucks had series identification on the hoodsides near the cowl, below the International name.

1953 IHC 1/2-Ton Model R-100 Pickup(PM)

1953 IHC 1/2-Ton Model R-110 Travelall (DFW)

I.D. DATA: Serial number located on the left side frame rail behind front spring hanger. Also stamped on capacity plate attached to the left door pillar. Starting: Numbers began at 501 up for each series. Ending: Not available. Engine numbers located: Stamped on boss on left-hand upper-front side of crankcase. Engine numbers not available. International trucks were not produced on a yearly model basis change. Model year was determined by the date of original sale to operator, as shown by bill of sale or title. Serial numbers were continued from 1953.

1953 IHC 1/2-Ton Model R-110 Pickup (OCW)

Standard Catalog of Light-Duty Trucks

Model	Body Type	Price	Weight	Prod. Total
1953-1954				
Series R-100/R-102 — 1/2-Ton — 115 in. w.b.				
R-100	Chassis & Cab	1230	2980	—
R-100	Pickup	1324	3310	
Series R-110/R-111/R-112 — 1/2-Ton — 115 in. w.b.				
R-110	Chassis & Cab	1290	3115	—
R-110	Pickup	1384	3445	—
R-110	Panel	1576	3720	—
Series R-110/R-111/R-112 — 1/2-Ton — 127 in. w.b.				
R-110	Chassis & Cab	1315	3200	—
R-110	Pickup	1424	3585	—
R-110	Stake	1502	—	—

1954 IHC Milk Delivery Truck (OCW)

Model	Body Type	Price	Weight	Prod. Total
1955				
Series R-100/R-102 — 1/2-Ton — 115 in. w.b.				
R-100	Chassis & Cowl	1063	2490	—
R-100	Chassis & Cab	1305	2980	—
R-100	Pickup	1399	3310	—
Series R-110/R-111/R-112 — 1/2-Ton — 115 in. w.b.				
R-110	Chassis & Cowl	1123	2625	—
R-110	Chassis & Cab	1365	3115	—
R-110	Pickup	1459	3445	—
R-110	Stake	1552	—	—
R-110	Panel	1656	3720	—
Series R-110/R-111/R-112 — 1/2-Ton — 127 in. w.b.				
R-110	Chassis & Cowl	1148	2710	—
R-110	Chassis & Cab	1390	3200	—
R-110	Pickup	1484	3585	—
R-110	Stake	1577	—	—

Model	Body Type	Price	Weight	Prod. Total
1953-1954				
Series R-120/R-121/R-122 — 3/4-Ton — 115 in. w.b.				
R-120	Chassis & Cab	1372	3380	—
R-120	Pickup	1466	3710	—
R-120	Panel	1658	3985	—
Series R-120/R-121/R-122 — 3/4-Ton — 127 in. w.b.				
R-120	Chassis & Cab	1397	3410	—
R-120	Pickup	1506	3795	—
R-120	Stake	1584	—	—
Series RA-120/RA-121/RA-122 — 3/4-Ton — 115 in. w.b.				
RA-120	Metroette Chassis	2175	3158	—
Series RM-120/RM-121/RM-122 — 3/4-Ton — 102 in. w.b.				
RM-120	Standard Metro	2314	—	—
RM-120	Metro Flat Back	2374	—	—
Series RM-120/RM-121/RM-122 — 3/4-Ton — 115 in. w.b.				
RM-120	Standard Metro	2369	—	—
RM-120	Metro Flat Back	2429	—	—
RM-120	School Bus	3319	—	—
Series RM-120/RM-121/RM-122 — 3/4-Ton — 122 in. w.b.				
RM-120	Standard Metro	2531	—	—
RM-120	Metro Flat Back	2591	—	—
1955				
Series R-120/R-121/R-122 — 3/4-Ton — 115 in. w.b.				
R-120	Chassis & Cowl	1205	2890	—
R-120	Chassis & Cab	1447	3380	—
R-120	Pickup	1556	3710	—
R-120	Panel	1738	3985	—
Series R-120/R-121/R-122 — 3/4-Ton — 127 in w.b.				
R-120	Chassis & Cowl	1230	2920	—
R-120	Chassis & Cab	1472	3410	—
R-120	Pickup	1581	3740	—
R-120	Stake	1659	—	—
Series RA-120/RA-121/RA-122 — 3/4-Ton — 115 in. w.b.				
RA-120	Metroette Chassis	2225	3158	—

Series RM-120/RM-121/RM-122 — 3/4-Ton — 102 in. w.b.

| RM-120 | Metro Chassis | 1230 | 2520 | — |
| RM-120 | Metro Body | 2364 | — | — |

Series RM-120/RM-121/RM-122 — 3/4-Ton — 115 in. w.b.

RM-120	Metro Chassis	1230	2650	—
RM-120	Metro Body	2419	—	—
RM-120	Metro Flat Back	2479	—	—
RM-120	Metro-Lite Body	2990	—	—
RM-120	School Bus (forward seat)	3369	—	—
RM-120	School Bus (full seat)	3369	—	—

Series RM-120/RM-121/RM-122 — 3/4-Ton — 122 in. w.b.

RM-120	Metro Chassis	1255	2740	—
RM-120	Metro Flat Back	2641	—	—
RM-120	Metro-Lite Body	3040	—	—

NOTE 1: GVW rating for the Metroette was 9,000 lbs. GVW ratings for Metros were as follows: [RM-120] 5,400 lbs., [RM-121] 6,000 lbs., [RM-122] 6,600 lbs.

1953-1954

Series R-130/R-131/R-132 — 1-Ton — 115 in. w.b.

R-130	Chassis & Cab	1474	3610	—
R-130	Pickup	1700	—	—
R-130	Stake	1700	—	—

Series R-130/R-131/R-132 — 1-Ton — 134 in. w.b.

R-130	Chassis & Cab	1489	3650	—
R-130	Pickup	1617	4060	—
R-130	Stake	1715	—	—

1954 IHC 1/2-Ton Model R-110 Pickup (IOA)

1955

Series R-130/R-131/R-132 — 1-Ton — 122 in. w.b.

R-130	Chassis & Cowl	1322	3130	—
R-130	Chassis & Cab	1564	3620	—
R-130	Stake	1790	—	—

Series R-130/R-131/R-132 — 1-Ton — 134 in. w.b.

R-130	Chassis & Cowl	1322	3160	—
R-130	Chassis & Cab	1564	3650	—
R-130	Pickup	1692	4060	—
R-130	Stake	1790	—	—

1954 IHC 1/2-Ton Model R-110 Pickup 4x4 (OCW)

ENGINE: Inline. Overhead valve. Six-cylinder. Cast iron block. Bore & stroke: 3-9/16 in. x 3-11/16 in. Displacement: 220.5 cid.. Compression ratio: 6.5:1 (7.01 after 1954). Brake horsepower: 100 at 3600 rpm. (104 at 3600 after 1954). Net horsepower: 30.4 (NACC). Maximum Torque: 173.5 lbs.-ft. at 1200 rpm. Four main bearings. Solid valve lifters. The Silver Diamond six-cylinder engine featured rifle-drilled connecting rods, full-pressure lubrication and heat-treated aluminum alloy pistons with four piston rings.

1954 IHC 1/2-Ton Model R-110 Pickup (S. Soloy)

CHASSIS [1/2-Ton Series]: Wheelbase: 115 in./127 in. Height: 51-5/16 in. Front tread: 58-9/32 in. Rear tread: 58-13/16 in. Tires: 6.00 x 16 in.
CHASSIS [3/4-Ton Series]: Wheelbase: 102 in./115 in./122 in./127 in. Tires: 6.50 x 16 six-ply.
CHASSIS [1-Ton Series]: Wheelbase: 115 in./122 in./134 in. Tires: 7.50 x 16 in.

1955 IHC 1/2-Ton Model R-110 Pickup (OCW)

TECHNICAL [1/2-Ton and 3/4-Ton Series]: Synchromesh transmission. Speeds: 3F/1R. Floor mounted gearshift lever. Single-plate dry-disc clutch; 11 in. diam. Hotchkiss type full-floating hypoid rear axle. Overall ratio: 4.1:1. Pres-stop twin-shoe drum brakes. Steel disc wheels. Heavy-duty three-speed manual transmission optional all models. Hydra-Matic transmission optional 1955 models only.
TECHNICAL [1-Ton Series]: Sliding gear transmission with carburized gears. Speeds: 4F/1R. Floor mounted gearshift lever. Single-plate dry-disc clutch; 11 in. diam. Hotchkiss type full-floating hypoid rear axle. Overall ratio: 6.616:1. Pres-stop twin-shoe drum brakes. Steel disc wheels. Hydra-Matic transmission optional 1955 models only.

1955 IHC 1/2-Ton Model R-110 Pickup (S. Soloy)

OPTIONS: Chrome front bumper. Rear bumper. Dual sidemounted spares (bodyside). Full foam rubber seat padding. Dome light. Bumper guards. Radio (AM). Heater (fresh air or recirculating models). Clock. Cigar lighter. Radio antenna. Seat covers. External sun shade. Spotlight. Right-hand sunvisor. Door armrests. Electric windshield wipers. Lockable glove compartment. Special paint. Wheel trim rings. Turn signals. White sidewall tires. Pickup box side panels. Outside rearview mirror. Deluxe equipment package. Deluxe cab interior.

HISTORICAL: Introduced Jan. 1953. Calendar year registrations: [All 1953 models] 95,404; [all 1954 models] 84,222; [all 1955 models] 100,441. Calendar year registrations by weight class: [1953] 39,507 in 5,000 lbs. or less category and 21,083 in 5,001 lbs. to 10,000 lbs. class. (Total for all 1953 models 121,522). [1954] 29,322 in 5,000 lbs. or less category and 12,945 in 5,001 lbs. to 10,000 lbs. class. [1955] 35,330 in 5,000 lbs. or less category and 20,843 in 5,001 to 10,000 lbs. class. Innovations: Updated styling. Hydra-Matic transmission available in 1955 models. New Metroette and Metro-Lite models. J.L. McCaffrey was IHC president in 1953 when the R-100 series debuted. IHC was third-ranked in U.S. truck production for 1953, despite a Borg-Warner transmission plant strike that cost the company about 15,000 assemblies. During 1953, IHC introduced two four-wheel drive (4x4) Model R trucks. Other new products included LP gas attachments for certain R trucks and the Travelall station wagon. McCaffrey continued to head the company in

1954, when sales of all models slipped 20.9 percent. Three-speed fully automatic transmissions were made a late 1954 option for light-duty models and tubeless tires become standard equipment. IHC's output rose 37 percent in 1955, despite a 26 day factory strike. The company retained number three position in truck production.

1956 and Early 1957 IHC

1956 IHC 1/2-Ton Model S-110 Travelall (DFW/MVMA)

MODEL S — 1/2-TON — SIX-CYLINDER: A new S Series was brought out by IHC late in 1955 and continued through mid-1957. Since IHC trucks were not sold on a model year basis, some of these may have been registered as 1955 models, although they are usually thought of as 1956-1957 vehicles. They had a somewhat squarer, more sculptured look with their headlights mounted high on the fenders inside chrome rings. An opening at the front center edge of the wider, flatter hood formed a wide air scoop. The grille insert was somewhat trapezoid shaped and painted, rather than plated. It had a similarly shaped, but narrower, opening flanked by two rather large, round parking lights. A winged IH badge was on the nose and the hoodsides, near the cowl, carried the International name and a series designation. A new windshield permitted more visibility. It was comparable to the popular mid-'50s wraparound windshields. Regular and Deluxe cab interiors were available. The standard trim was in gray vinyl, coordinated with a gray interior color combination. These trucks still had separate pontoon rear fenders and full runningboards. Half-tons came in the light-duty (4,200 lbs. GVW) S-100 Series and the heavy-duty (also 4,200 lbs. GVW) S-110 series. The S-100 line had an S-102 option (5,000 lbs. GVW) and the S-110 had an S-112 option (5,400 lbs. GVW). There were two wheelbases for the S-110s and a new Travelall model that resembled a station wagon. The 1957 model had slightly increased prices and the same weights.

1956 IHC 1/2-Ton Model R-110 Pickup (RCA)

1956 IHC 1/2-Ton Model S-110 Panel (OCW)

MODEL S — 3/4-TON — SIX-CYLINDER: The S-120 was the basic 3/4-ton series offered by IHC in 1956-1957. It had a 5,400 lbs. GVW rating. Also available was an S-122 (6900 lbs. GVW) chassis option. These trucks came on either the 115 in. or 127 in. wheelbase,

when equipped with conventional rear wheel drive. In addition, there was a four-wheel drive (4x4) chassis option for 3/4-ton trucks on four different wheelbases: 115, 122, 127 or 134 inches. Also available on a 3/4-ton chassis, were Metro van-type trucks. Here, the base series was coded SM-120 and the heavier-duty chassis option was the SM-122. The Metros came on 102, 115 and 122 in. wheelbase with standard, flatback or Metro-Lite bodies. Gross vehicle weight ratings were 5,400 lbs. for the SM-120 and 6,600 lbs. for the SM-122. IHC also continued to market 3/4-ton milk/bakery delivery vans on the 115 in. wheelbase. These were in the SA-120 Series and had a 6,500 lbs. GVW rating. All of these trucks used the 240 Black Diamond engine. They were sold from late 1955 to mid-1957.

1956 IHC 1/2-Ton Model S-110 Travelall (OCW)

MODEL S — 1-TON — SIX-CYLINDER: S-130 was IHC's designation for the 7,000 lbs. GVW, 1-ton models that it produced from late 1955 to mid-1957. There was an S-132 chassis option to raise GVW ratings to a hefty 8,800 lbs. A 122 in. wheelbase chassis was marketed, plus a chassis and three factory bodies on a longer 134 in. wheelbase. One-ton versions of the Metro Delivery models were also offered. There was the basic 7,000 lbs. GVW lighter-duty version, plus an SM-132 option with a 9,000 lbs. GVW rating.

1956 IHC 3/4-Ton Model S-120 Pickup (OCW)

I.D. DATA: Serial number located on left side of frame rail behind front spring hanger. Also stamped on capacity plate attached to left door pillar. Serial numbers were continued from 1953. Numbers are not available. Engine numbers located stamped on boss on left-hand upper front side of crankcase. Engine numbers not available. IHC trucks were not produced on a yearly model basis change. Year model was determined by date of original sale to operator, as shown by bill of sale or title. Because of different state laws, 1955, 1956 and 1957 Model S titles can be found, although this series was built less than two years.

1956 IHC 1/2-Ton Model S-110 Pickup (DFW)

Model	Body Type	Price	Weight	Prod. Total
Series S-100/S-102 — 1/2-Ton — 115 in. w.b.				
S-100	Chassis & Cab	1370	2980	—
S-100	Pickup	1471	3310	—

Series S-110/S-112 — 1/2-Ton — 115 in. w.b.

S-110	Chassis & Cab	1465	3115	—
S-110	Pickup	1566	3445	—
S-110	Panel	1793	3720	—
S-110	Travelall	2066	4000	—

Series S-110/S-112 — 1/2-Ton — 127 in. w.b.

S-110	Chassis & Cab	1490	3200	—
S-110	Pickup	1607	3530	—
S-110	Stake	1681	3585	—
S-110	Platform	1628	—	—

NOTE 1: In 1957, the 1/2-ton trucks were $60 more expensive and had identical shipping weights as compared to the 1956 introductory prices above.

1956 IHC 3/4-Ton Model S-120 Travelall (RPZ)

Series S-120/S-122 — 3/4-Ton — 115 in. w.b.

S-120	Chassis & Cab	1547	3380	—
S-120	Pickup	1647	3710	—
S-120	Panel	1857	3985	—
S-120	Travelall	2148	4265	—

Series S-120/S-122 — 3/4-Ton — 127 in. w.b.

S-120	Chassis & Cab	1572	3410	—
S-120	Pickup	1689	3795	—
S-120	Stake	1763	3869	—
S-120	Platform	1710	—	—

Series S-120 — 3/4-Ton — 4x4 — 115 in. w.b.

S-120	Chassis & Cab	2027	3880	—
S-120	Pickup	2128	4210	—
S-120	Panel	2355	4485	—
S-120	Travelall	2628	4765	—

Series S-120 — 3/4-Ton — 4x4 — 122 in. w.b.

S-120	Chassis & Cab	2037	3908	—

Series S-120 — 3/4-Ton — 4x4 — 127 in. w.b.

S-120	Chassis & Cab	2047	3922	—
S-120	Platform	2185	—	—
S-120	Stake	2238	4527	—
S-120	Pickup	2164	4307	—

Series S-120 — 3/4-Ton — 4x4 — 134 in. w.b.

S-120	Chassis & Cab	2057	3938	—
S-120	Platform	2216	—	—
S-120	Stake	2294	4628	—
S-120	Pickup	2194	4348	—

Series SA-120/SA-122 — 3/4-Ton — 115 in. w.b.

SA-120	Milk Delivery	2490	2675	—
SA-120	Delivery Body	2490	2675	—

Series SM-120/SM-122 — 3/4-Ton — 102 in. w.b.

SM-120	Chassis	1298	2650	—
SM-120	Standard Metro Body	2523	3705	—

Series SM-120/SM-122 — 3/4-Ton — 115 in. w.b.

SM-120	Chassis	1298	2650	—
SM-120	Standard Metro Body	2582	4570	—
SM-120	Flat Back Metro	2647	4650	—
SM-120	Metro-Lite	3199	—	—

Series SM-120/SM-122 — 3/4-Ton — 122 in. w.b.

SM-120	Chassis	1323	2740	—
SM-120	Flat Back Metro	2820	4900	—
SM-120	Metro-Lite	3251	—	—

NOTE 2: Prices increased for 1957 3/4-ton models as follows: Conventional S-120/S-122 ($70); 4x4 S-120/S-122 ($150); SA-120 ($115); SM-120/SM-122 w/102 in. w.b. ($118); SM-120/SM-122 w/115 in. w.b. ($121) and SM-120/SM-122 w/122 in. w.b. ($133). Shipping weights were unchanged from 1956.

Series S-130/S-132 — 1-Ton — 122 in. w.b.

S-130	Chassis & Cab	1664	3620	—

Series S-130/S-132 — 1-Ton — 134 in. w.b.

S-130	Chassis & Cab	1664	3650	—
S-130	Pickup	1801	4060	—
S-130	Platform	1823	—	—
S-130	Stake	1901	—	—

Series SM-130/SM-132 — 1-Ton — 122 in. w.b.

S-130	Chassis	1495	2940	—
SM-130	Flat Back Steel Body	2992	5100	—
SM-130	Metro-Lite Body	3423	4210	—

Series SM-130/SM-132 — 1-Ton — 134 in. w.b.

SM-130	Chassis	1495	2980	—
SM-130	Flat Back Steel Body	3107	5390	—
SM-130	Metro-Lite Body	3623	4480	—

1956 IHC 1/2-Ton Model S-110 Pickup With High Sides (OCW)

ENGINE [Series S-100/S-102/S-120/SM-122/SM-130/SM-132]: Inline. Overhead valve. Six-cylinder. Cast iron block. Bore & stroke: 3-9/16 in. x 3-11/16 in. Displacement: 220.5 cid.. Compression ratio: 6.5:1. Brake horsepower: 100 at 3600 rpm. Net horsepower: 30.4 (NACC). Maximum Torque: 173.5 lbs.-ft. at 1200 rpm. Four main bearings. Solid valve lifters. (Silver Diamond engine).

ENGINE [Series S-110/S-112/S-120/S-122/S-130/S-132]: Inline. Overhead valve. Six-cylinder. Cast iron block. Bore & stroke: 3.56 in. x 4.018 in. Displacement: 240 cid.. Brake horsepower: 140.8 at 3800 rpm. Net horsepower: 30.4 (NACC). Maximum Torque: 223.5 lbs.-ft. at 2000 rpm. Four main bearings. Solid valve lifters. (240 Black Diamond engine).

CHASSIS [1/2-Ton Series]: Wheelbase: 115 in./127 in. Front tread: 58-9/32 in. Rear tread: 58-13/16 in. Tires: 6.00 x 16 in.

CHASSIS [3/4-Ton Series]: Wheelbase: 102 in./115 in./122 in./127 in. Tires: 6.50 x 16 six-ply.

CHASSIS [1-Ton Series]: Wheelbase: 122 in./134 in. Tires: 7.50 x 16 in.

TECHNICAL: Same as comparable 1955 models.

OPTIONS: Chrome front bumper. Rear bumper. Single sidemount (bodyside mounting). Deluxe cab interior. Foam rubber seats. Dome light. Bumper guards. Radio (AM). Heater. Clock. Cigar lighter. Radio antenna. Seat covers. External sun shade. Spotlight. Right-hand sun visor. Door armrests. Electric wipers. Lockable glove compartment. Special paint. Two-tone paint. Wheel trim rings. Turn signals. White sidewall tires. Pickup box side panels. Outside rearview mirror. Deluxe equipment package.

1957 IHC Atlantic City Jitney Bus (OCW)

HISTORICAL: Introduced mid to late 1955 through mid-1957. Calendar year registrations, all models: [1956] 108,014; [1957] 96,956. Calendar year production, all models: [1956] 137,839; [1957] 121,775. Calendar year registrations by weight class: [1956] 20,696 trucks in 5,000 lbs. or less category and 23,830 trucks in 5,001 lbs. to 10,000 lbs. class. [1957] 33,572 in 6,000 lbs. or less category and 18,296 in 6,001 lbs. to 10,000 lbs. class. Four-wheel drive introduced in 3/4-ton series. The Travelall became a standard factory model. IHC production for 1956 was up 5.7 percent over 1955. In 1956, V-8 engines were introduced for heavy-duty models. The company began celebrating its 50th year of truck production in 1957. From 1907-1956, IHC built more than 2.6 million trucks. They claimed that 1.1 million were still in use in 1957. An "A" for Anniversary series was introduced, in mid-1957, to commemorate the occasion. J.L. McCaffrey became chairman of the board and P.V. Moulder was president. The company retained number three position in the truck industry.

1957-1958 IHC

1957 IHC 1/2-Ton Model A-100 Golden Anniversary Pickup (OCW)

MODEL A — 1/2-TON — SIX-CYLINDER: IHC marked its 50th year of truck manufacturing with a modernized A Series. These Golden Anniversary models debuted in the early spring of 1957. They were dramatically changed and had a more contemporary look with integral front fenders. Styling revisions included a wider cab, a new sweep-around windshield and flatter roofs and hoods. The slab-sided bodies had sculptured front and rear fenders. The squarer front fenders had parking lamps tucked above the single round headlamps, inside the fender nacelles. The hood had a wider air scoop up front, with a larger winged IH emblem below it. The grille was shaped somewhat like the previous one, but without parking lights. A Custom pickup body with flush outer rear quarters appeared. This model actually used the rear fenders from the two-door Travelall and had a unique tailgate featuring spring-loaded cables to support it when in the lowered position. This was probably the first one-hand-operated tailgate. Customs were available only on the 114 in. wheelbase chassis. The inside dimensions of the box were the same as those of "Bonus Load" models with external fenders and a seven-foot box length. Customs had lightning bolt style side moldings and, often, two-tone finish. An International name appeared on the trailing edge of upper front fenders on all models. Series designations were moved to the front fendersides, behind the headlights. A 220 Black Diamond engine was used in A-100 models (also with A-102 chassis option) and the 240 Black Diamond powerplant was used in other half-tons. A new model was a Utility pickup with crew type cab.

1958 IHC 1/2-Ton Model A-100 Custom Pickup (S. Soloy)

MODEL A — 3/4-TON — SIX-CYLINDER: The A-120/A-122 Series offered one dozen conventional trucks on four different wheelbases. Styling changes were in the same mold as those on the 1/2-tons, except that proportions were somewhat larger. New models were crew-cab-like utility pickups. A new technical feature for all light-duty IHC trucks was a 12-volt electrical system. Also available on the 3/4-ton chassis were AB bakery trucks and AM Metro vans and coaches. A similarly styled new model was the AM-80 four-cylinder Metro-Mite mini-van. Although it was not a 3/4-ton truck, we're listing the Mite with other Metro-type models. It was a small truck with a 96 in. wheelbase and 3,800 lbs. GVW rating. The Metro-Lite, an aluminum body version of the full-size Metro, now came in 9 ft. 8 in. and 10 ft. 8 in. wheelbase 3/4-ton models.

MODEL A — 1-TON — SIX-CYLINDER: Two lines of 1-ton models were included in the A Series. The first included the big pickups and utility pickups with crew cabs. These were designated A-130s and an A-132 option was available. Their GVW ratings ranged from 7,000 to 8,000 lbs. and three wheelbases were available. The second line was comprised of various Metro vans which came with three different wheelbases. Designated AM-130s (or AM-132s with heavy-duty chassis options), the Metros had GVW ratings between 7,000 and 9,000 lbs.

Standard Catalog of Light-Duty Trucks

I.D. DATA: Serial number located on left side of frame rail behind front spring hanger. Also stamped on capacity plate attached to left door pillar. Serial numbers were continued from 1956-1957. Numbers are not available. Engine numbers located stamped on boss on left-hand upper front side of crankcase. Engine numbers not available. IHC trucks were not produced on a yearly model basis change. Year model was determined by date of original sale to operator, as shown by bill of sale or title.

Model	Body Type	Price	Weight	Prod. Total
Series A-100/A-102 — 1/2-Ton — 110 in. w.b.				
A-100	Chassis & Cab	1785	3120	—
Series A-100/A-102 — 1/2-Ton — 114 in. w.b.				
A-100	Chassis & Cab	1785	3130	—
A-100	Pickup 7-ft.	1905	3460	—
A-100	Custom Pickup 7-ft.	2212	3460	—
A-100	Panel 7-ft.	2198	3735	—
A-100	Travelall 7-ft.	2517	4015	—
Series A-110/A-112 — 1/2-Ton — 110 in. w.b.				
A-110	Chassis & Cab	1887	3140	—
Series A-110/A-112 — 1/2-Ton — 114 in. w.b.				
A-110	Chassis & Cab	1887	3150	—
A-110	Pickup 7-ft.	2008	3480	—
A-110	Custom Pickup 7-ft.	2314	3480	—
A-110	Panel 7-ft.	2300	3735	—
A-110	Travelall	2619	4035	—
Series A-110/A-112 — 1/2-Ton — 126 in. w.b.				
A-110	Chassis & Cab	1914	3170	—
A-110	Pickup 8-1/2 ft.	2052	3555	—
Series A-110/A-112 — 1/2-Ton — 129 in. w.b.				
A-110	Utility Chassis & Cab	3006	3634	—
A-110	Utility Chassis & Custom Cab	3114	—	—
A-110	Utility Pickup 6-ft.	3135	—	—
A-110	Custom Utility Pickup 6-ft.	3297	—	—
Series A-120/A-122 — 3/4-Ton — 110 in. w.b.				
A-120	Chassis & Cab	2002	3555	—
Series A-120/A-122 — 3/4-Ton — 114 in. w.b.				
A-120	Chassis & Cab	2002	3565	—
A-120	Pickup 7-ft.	2123	3895	—
A-120	Custom Pickup 7-ft.	2424	3895	—
A-120	Panel 7-ft.	2396	4170	—
A-120	Travelall 7-ft.	2691	4450	—
Series A-120/A-122 — 3/4-Ton — 126 in. w.b.				
A-120	Chassis & Cab	2029	3585	—
A-120	Pickup 8-1/2 ft.	2167	3970	—
Series A-120/A-122 — 3/4-Ton — 129 in. w.b.				
A-120	Chassis & Utility Cab	3125	—	—
A-120	Chassis & Utility Cab	3232	—	—
A-120	Utility Pickup 6-ft.	3254	—	—
A-120	Custom Utility Pickup 6-ft.	3415	—	—

NOTE 1: These trucks could also be ordered with IHC's four-wheel drive option. The 4x4 package added $642 to the factory prices and 270 lbs. to the shipping weight.

Model	Body Type	Price	Weight	Prod. Total
Series AM-80 Metro-Mite — 1/2-Ton — 96 in. w.b.				
AM-80	Walk-In Panel	2251	2800	—
Series AB-120 Metroette — 3/4-Ton — 115 in. w.b.				
AB-120	Panel	2891	4755	—
Series AM-120 Metro — 3/4-Ton — 102 in. w.b.				
AM-120	Chassis & Front Section	2075	2520	—
AM-120	Standard Metro 7-3/4 ft.	2930	4335	—
Series AM-120 Metro — 3/4-Ton — 115 in. w.b.				
AM-120	Chassis & Front Section	2075	2650	—
AM-120	Standard Metro 9-1/2 ft.	2996	4570	—
AM-120	Flat Back Metro 9-1/2 ft.	3070	4650	—
AM-120	Metro-Lite 9-3/4 ft.	3694	—	—
AM-120	Metro Coach (8-P)	4156	—	—
AM-120	Metro School Bus (12-P)	4308	—	—
AM-120	Metro School Bus 16-Pass.	4156	—	—
Series AM-120 Metro — 3/4-Ton — 122 in. w.b.				
AM-120	Metro-Lite 103/4 ft.	3747	—	—
AM-120	Flat Back Metro 10-1/2 ft.	3265	—	—
AM-120	Chassis & Front Section	2103	2740	—
Series A-130/A-132 — 1-Ton — 117 in. w.b.				
A-130	Chassis & Cab	2129	3765	—
Series A-130/A-132 — 1-Ton — 126 in. w.b.				
A-130	Chassis & Cab	2140	3785	—
A-130	Chassis & Cab	2277	4195	—
Series A-130/A-132 — 1-Ton — 129 in. w.b.				
A-130	Pickup 8-1/2 ft.	2150	3805	—
A-130	Utility Chassis & Cab	3226	—	—
A-130	Custom Utility Chassis & Cab	3334	—	—
Series AM-130/AM-132 — 1-Ton — 115 in. w.b.				
AM-130	Standard Metro 9-1/2 ft.	3202	—	—
AM-130	Flat Back Metro 9-1/2 ft.	3275	—	—

Series AM-130/AM-132 — 1-Ton — 122 in. w.b.

AM-130	Chassis & Front Section	2309	2940	—
AM-130	Metro Lite 10 ft. 8 in.	3957	4250	—
AM-130	Flat Back Metro 10-1/2 ft.	3471	5100	—

Series AM-130/AM-132 — 1-Ton — 134 in. w.b.

AM-130	Chassis & Front Section	2309	2980	—
AM-130	Flat Back Metro 12 ft. 7 in.	3601	5390	—
AM-130	Metro-Lite 12 ft. 8 in.	4183	4480	—

1958 IHC 1/2-Ton Model A-112 Travelette Utility Pickup (S. Soloy)

ENGINE [Series A-100/A-102/AB-120/AM-120/AM-130]: 220 Black Diamond. Inline. Overhead valve. Six-cylinder. Cast iron block. Bore & stroke: 3-9/16 in. x 3-11/16 in. Displacement: 220.5 cid.. Brake horsepower: 112.5 at 3800 rpm. Net horsepower: 30.4 (NACC). Maximum Torque: 194.4 lbs.-ft. at 1600-2000 rpm. Four main bearings. Solid valve lifters. (Models not shown in brackets here, except AM-80s, used the 240 Black Diamond as base engine. The A-100 could be optioned with a 240 Black Diamond or 264 Black Diamond engines. A 264 Black Diamond engine was optional in A-120s. The 240 Black Diamond engine was optional in AM-130s.)

ENGINE [Series A-110/A-112/A-120/A-130]: 240 Black Diamond. Inline. Overhead valve. Six-cylinder. Cast iron block. Bore & stroke: 3.56 in. x 4.018 in. Displacement: 240.3 cid.. Brake horsepower: 140.8 at 3800 rpm. Net horsepower: 30.4 (NACC). Maximum Torque: 223.5 lbs.-ft. at 2000 rpm. Four main bearings. Solid valve lifters. (Optional in AM-120/AM-130/A-100 models.)

ENGINE [Series AM-80 Metro-Mite]: Inline. Overhead valve. Four-cylinder. Cast iron block. Bore & stroke: 2-7/8 in. x 3-1/2 in. Displacement: 90.884 cid.. Brake horsepower: 59.6 at 4600-4800 rpm. Net horsepower: 13.2 (NACC). Maximum Torque: 87.4 lbs.-ft. at 1600-2400 rpm. (This engine was available in the Metro-Mite only).

ENGINE [Optional in A-100/A-110/A-120/A-130]: 264 Black Diamond: Inline. Overhead valve. Six-cylinder. Cast iron block. Bore & stroke: 3-11/16 in. x 4-1/8 in. Displacement: 264.3 cid.. Brake horsepower: 153.5 at 3800 rpm. Net horsepower: 32.6 (NACC). Maximum Torque: 248 lbs.-ft. at 2400 rpm. Four main bearings. Solid valve lifters.

CHASSIS [1/2-Ton Series]: Wheelbase: 110 in./114 in./126 in./129 in. Tires: [A-100] 6.70 x 15 in.; [A-110] 6.00 x 16 six-ply.

CHASSIS [3/4-Ton Series]: Wheelbase: 102 in./114 in./115 in./122 in./126 in./129 in. Tires: [A-120/AM-120] 7.00 x 17.5 six-ply; [AB-120] 7.00 x 17.5 six-ply.

CHASSIS [1-Ton Series]: Wheelbase: 115 in./117 in./122 in./126 in./129 in./134 in. Tires: [All] 8.00 x 17.5 six-ply.

CHASSIS [Metro-Mite Series]: Wheelbase: 96 in. Tires: 6.40 x 15 four-ply.

TECHNICAL: Same as comparable 1955 models.

OPTIONS: Chrome front bumper. Rear bumper. Deluxe cab interior. Foam rubber seats. Dome light. Door armrest. Bumper guards. Radio (AM). Heater (fresh air type or recirculating type). Clock. Cigar lighter. Radio antenna. Seat covers. Custom exterior trim. Spotlight. Right-hand sun visor. Electric wipers. Lockable glove box. Special paint. Two-tone paint. Wheel trim rings. Directional signals. White sidewall tires. Pickup box side panels. Outside rearview mirror. Right-hand outside rearview mirror.

HISTORICAL: Introduced mid-1957. See 1957 section for calendar year registrations and production of 1957 models. Calendar year 1958 registrations by weight class: 27,721 in 6,000 lbs. and less category; 14,270 in 6,001 to 10,000 lbs. class. Calendar year 1958 production: [All IHC] 81,213. Calendar year 1958 registrations [All IHC]: 89,721 units. Innovations: The new, lightweight Metro-Mite was introduced as the smallest multi-step vehicle in the U.S. Travel Crew six-man pickup truck cabs were introduced. A new truck sales processing center was opened in Ft. Wayne, Ind. The 1958 IHC products were promoted as Golden Anniversary models. The A Series prefix indicated anniversary models. F.W. Jenks became president of IHC during 1958. Calendar year production was the lowest total in the postwar era. In April 1958, IHC's Metro Body Co. produced its 150th unit since the firm became an IHC subsidiary in 1948. The company said 10.8 percent of all trucks, on the road were IH models.

504

1959 IHC

1959 IHC 1/2-Ton Model B-100 Travelall (OCW)

MODEL B — 1/2-TON — SIX-CYLINDER: IHC did a nice job of modernizing its products in 1959. Changes included a new '55 Chevy-like grille and quadruple headlights. These were stacked vertically inside a chrome-rimmed housing. Bright metal windshield moldings appeared. There were bright-rimmed, round parking lights below the headlights, too. The entire image was brighter and more up-to-date. Crew cab utility pickups were now called Travelettes. Chrome bumpers and whitewalls, once uncommon on IH pickups, were now nearly standard fare. There was even a V-8 engine option released during 1959. Standard 1/2-ton models were in the B-100 Series, which included the traditional heavy chassis option coded B-102. GVWs ranged from 4,200 to 5,000 lbs. as in 1958. There was again a heavy-duty 1/2-ton series, coded B-110 and having a B-112 option. These trucks had GVWs between 4,200 and 5,800 lbs. The Metro-Mite was also still available in the 1/2-ton range. It was unchanged in any regard and the 1958 section can be referred to for data on this model.

1959 IHC 3/4-Ton Model B-120 4x4 With Service Body (RCA)

MODEL B — 3/4-TON — SIX-CYLINDER: The 1959 IH 3/4-ton series was updated similar to the 1/2-ton models. Series designations corresponded to 1958 with "B" instead of "A" prefixes. The Custom versions of pickups were now an option instead of a separate model. A four-wheel drive (4x4) option was again available for 3/4-tons at a slightly higher price. Metroette panel trucks and Metro vans and coaches were unchanged in 3/4-ton AB and AM series, rather than the new B series. This is because they were unchanged from 1958, except for a price increase averaging about $130 per model. Readers interested in these trucks should refer to the 1958 section for weights, specifications and current values.

1959 IHC 3/4-Ton Model B-122 Travelette Utility Pickup (OCW)

MODEL B — 1-TON — SIX-CYLINDER: Changes in the Model B 1-tons were patterned after those for conventional light-duties in the 1/2- and 3/4-ton series. Models, wheelbases and GVW ratings corresponded to those of 1958's A-130 models. The AM-130 Metro vans were carried over without any changes except for higher prices. Readers interested in these trucks should refer to the 1958 section for weights, specifications and current values.

1959 1-Ton Model B-132 Travelette Utility Pickup (S. Soloy)

I.D. DATA: Serial number located on left side of frame rail behind front spring hanger. Also stamped on capacity plate attached to left door pillar. Serial numbers were continued from 1957-1958. Numbers are not available. Engine numbers located stamped on boss on left-hand upper front side of crankcase. Engine numbers not available. IHC trucks were not produced on a yearly model basis change. Year model was determined by date of original sale to operator, as shown by bill of sale or title.

1959 IHC 1/2-Ton Model B-100 Bonus Load Pickup (S. Soloy)

Model	Body Type	Price	Weight	Prod. Total
Series B-100/B-102 — 1/2-Ton — 110 in. w.b.				
B-100	Chassis & Cab	1927	3120	—
Series B-100/B-102 — 1/2-Ton — 114 in. w.b.				
B-100	Chassis & Cab	1927	3130	—
B-100	Pickup 7-ft.	2045	3460	—
B-100	Panel 7-ft.	2340	3735	—
B-100	Travelall	2659	4015	—
Series B-110/B-112 — 1/2-Ton — 110 in. w.b.				
B-110	Chassis & Cab	1998	3140	—
Series B-110/B-112 — 1/2-Ton — 114 in. w.b.				
B-110	Chassis & Cab	1998	3150	—
B-110	Pickup 7-ft.	2116	3480	—
B-110	Panel	2411	3755	—
B-110	Travelall	2730	4035	—
Series B-110/B-112 — 1/2-Ton — 126 in. w.b.				
B-110	Chassis & Cab	2025	3170	—
B-110	Pickup 8-1/2 ft.	2154	3555	—
Series B-110/B-112 — 1/2-Ton — 129 in. w.b.				
B-110	Travelette Chassis & Cab	3117	3634	—
B-110	Travelette 6-ft.	3244	—	—
Series B-120/B-122 — 3/4-Ton — 110 in. w.b.				
B-120	Chassis & Cab	2152	3555	—
Series B-120/B-122 — 3/4-Ton — 114 in. w.b.				
B-120	Chassis & Cab	2152	3565	—
B-120	Pickup 7-ft.	2270	3895	—
B-120	Panel 7-ft.	2548	4170	—
B-120	Travelall	2840	4450	—
Series B-120/B-122 — 3/4-Ton — 126 in. w.b.				
B-120	Chassis & Cab	2179	3585	—
B-120	Pickup 8-1/2 ft.	2308	3970	—
Series B-120/B-122 — 3/4-Ton — 129 in. w.b.				
B-120	Travelette Chassis & Cab	3274	—	—
B-120	Travelette 6-ft.	3401	—	—

NOTE 1: Add $765 and 270 lbs. for 4x4 trucks.
NOTE 2: Refer to 1958 for Metroette and Metro Delivery Van models. The 1959 Metroette was $3,051 and 1959 Metro vans ranged from $2,203 to $4,367 in price.

Model	Body Type	Price	Weight	Prod. Total
Series B-130/B-132 — 1-Ton — 117 in. w.b.				
B-130	Chassis & Cab	2217	3765	—
Series B-130/B-132 — 1-Ton — 126 in. w.b.				
B-130	Chassis & Cab	2228	3785	—
B-130	Pickup 8-1/2 ft.	2357	4195	—
Series B-130/B-132 — 1-Ton — 129 in. w.b.				
B-130	Chassis & Cab	2239	3805	—
B-130	Travelette Chassis & Cab	3315	—	—

NOTE 3: Refer to 1958 for Metro Delivery van models. Prices for 1959 Metro Vans (1-ton) ranged from $2,426 to $4,378.
ENGINE [B-100/AM-120/AM-130]: 220 Black Diamond. Inline. Overhead valve. Six-cylinder. Cast iron block. Bore & stroke: 3-9/16 in. x 3-11/16 in. Displacement: 220.5 cid.. Brake horsepower: 112.5 at 3800 rpm. Net horsepower: 30.4 (NACC). Maximum Torque: 194.4 lbs.-ft. at 1600-2200 rpm.
ENGINE [B-110/B-120/B-130]: 240 Black Diamond. Inline. Overhead valve. Six-cylinder. Cast iron block. Bore & stroke: 3.56 in. x 4.018 in. Displacement: 240.3 cid.. Brake horsepower: 140.8 at 3800 rpm. Net horsepower: 30.4 (NACC). Maximum Torque: 223.5 lbs.-ft. at 2000 rpm. (Optional in Metro Delivery vans in the AM-120/AM-130 series.)
ENGINE: 264 Black Diamond. Inline. Overhead valve. Six-cylinder. Cast iron block. Bore & stroke: 3-11/16 in. x 4-1/8 in. Displacement: 264.3 cid.. Brake horsepower: 153.5 at 3800 rpm. Net horsepower: 32.6 (NACC). Maximum Torque: 248 lbs.-ft. at 2400 rpm. (Optional in B-110/B-120/B-130).
ENGINE: V-266. Vee-block. Overhead valve. Eight-cylinder. Cast iron block. Bore & stroke: 3-7/8 in. x 3-7/32 in. Displacement: 265.761 cid.. Brake horsepower: 154.8 at 4400 rpm. Net horsepower: 42.1 (NACC). Maximum Torque: 227.1 lbs.-ft. at 2800 rpm. (Optional in B-100/B-110/B-120/B-130).
ENGINE [Metro-Mite]: The Metro-Mite for 1959 used the same engine as the 1958 Metro-Mite.
CHASSIS: Same as comparable 1958 models.
TECHNICAL: Same as comparable 1955 models.
OPTIONS: See 1958 options.
HISTORICAL: Calendar year registrations by weight: [1959] 42,963 in the 6,000 lbs. and less category; 17,183 in the 6,001 to 10,000 lbs. class. Calendar year registrations [All IHC models]: 108,828. Calendar year production: 143,199 (12.56 percent). The new B series introduced new styling, a Bonus Load pickup body, and heavier frame construction. In March, a 266 cid.. V-8 was introduced for the light-duty models. By November, the V-8 was made standard in all B lines. IH's share of the total U.S. truck market climbed to 12.74 percent in 1959. F.W. Jenks continued as president. Construction started, early in 1960, on a new 625,000 sq. ft. master motor truck parts depot at Ft. Wayne, Ind.

1959 3/4-Ton Model B-120 Panel 4x4 (OCW)

1960 IHC

1960 IHC 1/2-Ton Travelall (DFW)

MODEL B — 1/2-TON — EIGHT-CYLINDER: The B Series was carried over for 1960 with one major technical change, the V-266 engine was made standard equipment. Six-cylinder engines became a delete-option. Appearance changes were virtually non-existent, but the front emblem was given a new silver background to help distinguish the 1960 model. The International name appeared below the contour line at the rear front fenders and "V" emblems (with V-8 engines) were on the front sides of the fenders behind the headlights. The Metro-Mite was also still available in the 1/2-ton range and again unchanged even in price and weight. Refer to the 1958 section for data on this model.
MODEL B — 3/4-TON — EIGHT-CYLINDER: IHC's 3/4-ton trucks had the same basic changes as the 1/2-ton models. The price of the four-wheel-drive option increased slightly. Metroette panel trucks and Metro vans and coaches were again available as a continuation

of the old AB-120 and AM-120 series. These trucks continued to use the 220 cid six as base powerplant. Refer to the 1958 section for data on these models. Prices were the same as in 1959 for the 3/4-ton Metros.

MODEL B — 1-TON — EIGHT-CYLINDER: Changes for the 1960 Model B 1-tons followed those for conventional 1/2-tons and 3/4-tons. The new V-8 made these trucks modestly pricier than last year. AM-130 Metro Delivery vans were continued from 1958 models and specifications with only the factory prices being changed. These prices were still above 1958 levels but lower than the 1959 prices. This is probably a reflection of production economies realized by manufacturing the same model for several years. IHC was able to pass on its savings to buyers using lower prices to promote extra sales of its basically old-fashioned product. And, of course, the operators of these strictly commercial vehicles were more interested in low prices and reliability, than style. Please refer to the 1958 section for weights, specifications and current values of Metro vans.

I.D. DATA: Refer to the 1956-1957 section.

Model	Body Type	Price	Weight	Prod. Total
B-100/B-102 — 1/2-Ton — 110 in. w.b.				
B-100	Chassis & Cab	2032	3264	—
B-100 — B-102 — 1/2-Ton — 114 in. w.b.				
B-100	Chassis & Cab	2032	3274	—
B-100	Pickup 7-ft.	2151	3604	—
B-100	Panel 7-ft.	2425	3879	—
B-100	Travelall	2845	4159	—
B-110/B-112 — 1/2-Ton — 110 in. w.b.				
B-110	Chassis & Cab	2089	3262	—
B-110/B-112 — 1/2-Ton — 114 in. w.b.				
B-110	Chassis & Cab	2089	3272	—
B-110	Pickup 7-ft.	2208	3602	—
B-110	Panel	2480	3877	—
B-110	Travelall	2890	4155	—
B-110/B-112 — 1/2-Ton — 126 in. w.b.				
B-110	Chassis & Cab	2116	3292	—
B-110	Pickup 8-1/2 ft.	2245	3677	—
B-110-B-112 — 1/2-Ton — 129 in. w.b.				
B-110	Travelette Chassis & Cab	3208	—	—
B-110	Travelette 6 ft.	3335	—	—
B-120/B-122 — 3/4-Ton — 110 in. w.b.				
B-120	Chassis & Cab	2241	3677	—
B-120-B-122 — 3/4-Ton — 114 in. w.b.				
B-120	Chassis & Cab	2241	3687	—
B-120	Pickup 7-ft.	2359	4017	—
B-120	Panel 7-ft.	2637	4292	—
B-120	Travelall	3001	4572	—
B-120/B-122 — 3/4-Ton — 126 in. w.b.				
B-120	Chassis & Cab	2268	3707	—
B-120	Pickup 8-1/2-ft.	2397	4092	—
B-120-B-122 — 3/4-Ton — 129 in. w.b.				
B-120	Travelette Chassis & Cab	3359	—	—
B-120	Travelette 6-ft.	3490	—	—

NOTE 1: Add $783 and 270 lbs. for 4x4 trucks.
NOTE 2: Refer to 1958 for Metroette and Metro Delivery Van models. The 1960 Metroette was $3051 and 1960 Metro Vans were priced from $2,203 to $4,367.

B-130/B-132 — 1-Ton — 117 in. w.b.				
B-130	Chassis & Cab	2284	3887	—
B-130-B-132 — 1-Ton — 126 in. w.b.				
B-130	Chassis & Cab	2295	3907	—
B-130	Pickup 8-1/2 ft.	2424	4317	—
B-130/B-132 — 1-Ton — 129 in. w.b.				
B-130	Chassis & Cab	2305	3927	—
B-130	Travelette Chassis & Cab	3381	—	—

NOTE 3: Refer to 1958 for Metro Delivery van models. Prices for 1960 1-ton Metro vans ranged from $2,421 to $4,371.

ENGINES [All] : The V-266 engine standard in B-100/B-110/B-120/B-130 models. The "220 Black Diamond" engine was standard in AB-120/AM-120/AM-130 models. The "240 Black Diamond" engine was optional in the B-110/B-120/B-130 models. The "A55" four-cylinder engine was again used in International Metro-Mites. Refer to 1959 section for engine specifications.

CHASSIS: Same as comparable 1958 models.

TECHNICAL: Same as comparable 1955 models.

OPTIONS: See 1958 options.

HISTORICAL: Introduced Jan. 1960. Calendar year registrations by weight: [6,000 lbs. and under] 30,666; [6,001-10,000 lbs.] 16,223. Calendar year registration [All IHC models]: 110,349. Calendar year production 119,696. Market share: 9.99 percent. Innovations: V-8 engine now standard in conventional light-duty trucks up to 1-ton. Six-cylinder engines continued to be available as optional equipment. E.W. Jenks continued as company president, S.G. Johnson headed engineering and L.W. Pierson was sales manager.

1961 IHC

1961 IHC Scout With Steel Cab Top (S. Soloy)

MODEL 80 — 1/4-TON SCOUT — FOUR-CYLINDER: In 1961, International Harvester's truck division pioneered the development of the recreational vehicle market with the introduction of the International Scout, a totally new sport utility truck. It had rounded, boxy lines, a three-passenger cab and compact five-foot pickup bed. The grille was a rectangle with a mesh screen insert with IH in the center. It was flanked by round headlamps. A bright metal Scout script was on the front fendersides. The Cab Top was removable, as were the doors. The windshield could be lowered flat against the hood. Standard equipment included a front bumper, sealed beam headlights, combination tail and stoplamp, parking lights, electric horn, spare wheel and tire, four-wheel hydraulic brakes, 52 in. adjustable bench seat, side-mounted mirror, 12-volt electrical system and Comanche four-cylinder engine. The Scout came in colors of white, tan, metallic blue, red, metallic green or yellow with a black frame. The Cab Top or optional Travel-top could be painted white for two-toning at no charge. The Scout was marketed in 4x2 and 4x4 models. Pickup beds were integral with the cab and had full-length, square inner housings, covering the wheels and fuel tank(s), on which four passengers could sit. There was a drop tailgate and simple round taillamps at the rear. The GVW was 3,200 lbs. (4x2) and 3,900 lbs. (4x4).

1961 IHC Scout With Vinyl Cab Top (S. Soloy)

MODEL C — 1/2-TON — EIGHT-CYLINDER: The 1961 Model C International trucks had a lower, wider appearance. The front fender line was lowered and extended straight across in the front. The hood was widened and lowered accordingly. Its lower lip still formed an air-scoop-like opening and there were scallop-like contours molded into the top surface. A winged IH emblem decorated the front of the hood. Dual headlamps now sat side-by-side with each pair housed in bright metal trimmed ovals. Oval-shaped parking lights were directly below them. The grille was a wide, concave affair stamped out of anodized aluminum with six stacks of six oval-shaped openings. There was a new wraparound bumper. A V-8 series designation badge and International chrome script appeared on the rear sides of the hood (except when the optional six-cylinder engine was ordered). Doors and cabs were redesigned too. There was a standard C-100 line and C-102 option with GVW ratings of 4,200 lbs. to 5,000 lbs. The heavier 1/2-ton series was the C-110. And it came with a C-112 chassis option. These trucks had GVW ratings between 4,200 lbs. and 5,800 lbs. Wheelbases of 115, 119, 122, 131 and 140 inches were offered in the two lines, making them longer than previous models. The AM-80 Metro-Mite walk-in panel truck was also available. It was again a direct carryover of the 1958 model. (Refer to 1958 section)

1961 IHC Scout With Steel Travel-Top (S. Soloy)

MODEL C — 3/4-TON — EIGHT-CYLINDER: Styling changes for the 3/4-ton C line were similar to those appearing on the 1/2-ton C line. There was a base C-120 series and a C-122 chassis option. Models on 115, 119, 122, 131 and 140 in. wheelbases were offered. GVWs were 5,400 lbs. to 7,000 lbs. for conventional drive trucks and 7,000 lbs. for trucks with the 4x4 option. Again carried over from 1958 were the AB-120 (Metroette) and AM-120 (Metro Delivery) models. These were sold at the same prices as in effect during 1960 and shipping weights were unchanged. Refer to 1958 section for information about models, specifications and current values.

MODEL C — 1-TON — EIGHT-CYLINDER: As usual, the 1-ton C series followed the styling pattern of the light-duty conventional trucks. They were built on wheelbases of 122, 131, 134 and 140 in. There was a C-132 option with heavy-duty suspension system. GVW ratings ranged from 7,000 lbs. to 8,800 lbs. There was also a series of 1-ton Metro delivery vans which were an exact continuation of the 1958 line with 1960 prices. For model listings, specifications and current values on these AM-130 trucks consult the 1958 section of this catalog.

1961 IHC 1/2-Ton Model C-120 Travelall (RCA)

I.D. DATA: Serial number stamped on a plate on dash and on left front siderail. Numbers were a continuation of previous numbers. Starting and ending numbers are not available. The 1961 models had the suffix -1 following the serial number for 1961. Engine numbers were stamped on the right side of crankcase at the upper front. International trucks were not produced on a yearly model basis. Model year was determined by date of original sale as shown on Bill of Sale or title.

Model	Body Type	Price	Weight	Prod. Total
Scout — 1/4-Ton — 100 in. w.b.				
80	Utility Pickup 5-ft.	1771	2800	Note 1
Scout 4x4 — 1/4-Ton — 100 in. w.b.				
80	Utility Pickup 5-ft.	2139	3000	Note 1

NOTE 1: More than 28,000 Scouts were sold in 1961.
NOTE 2: For 1961, the AM-80 Metro-Mite was $2,251 and 2,800 lbs. See 1958 section for other data on this model.

Model	Body Type	Price	Weight	
C-100/C-102 Trucks — 1/2-Ton — 119 in. w.b.				
C-100	Chassis & Cab	2069	3265	—
C-100	Pickup 7-ft.	2187	3640	—
C-100	Panel 7-ft.	2502	4095	—
C-100	Travelall	2853	4240	—
C-100	Custom Travelall	3139	—	—
C-110/C-112 Trucks — 3/4-Ton — 115 in. w.b.				
C-110	Chassis & Cab	2092	3290	—
C-110/C-112 Trucks — 3/4-Ton — 119 in. w.b.				
C-110	Chassis & Cab	2092	3295	—
C-110	Pickup 7-ft.	2210	3670	—
C-110	Panel 7-ft.	2524	3850	—
C-110	Travelall	2876	3995	—
C-110	Custom Travelall	3162	—	—
C-110/C-112 Trucks — 3/4-Ton — 122 in. w.b.				
C-110	Chassis & Cab	2108	3301	—
C-110/C-112 Trucks — 3/4-Ton — 131 in. w.b.				
C-110	Chassis & Cab	2118	3325	—
C-110	Pickup 8-1/2 ft.	2248	3750	—
C-110/C-112 Trucks — 3/4-Ton — 140 in. w.b.				
C-110	Travelette Chassis & Cab	2699	3829	—
C-110	Travelette Pickup 6-ft.	2843	—	—
C-120/C-122 Trucks — 1-Ton — 115 in. w.b.				
C-120	Chassis & Cab	2247	3476	—
C-120/C-122 Trucks — 1-Ton — 119 in. w.b.				
C-120	Chassis & Cab	2247	3480	—
C-120	Pickup 7-ft.	2365	3855	—
C-120	Panel 7-ft.	2679	4035	—
C-120	Travelall	2970	4180	—
C-120	Custom Travelall	3249	—	—
C-120/C-122 Trucks — 1-Ton — 122 in. w.b.				
C-120	Chassis & Cab	2263	3486	—
C-120/C-122 Trucks — 1-Ton — 131 in. w.b.				
C-120	Chassis & Cab	2273	3604	—
C-120	Pickup 8-1/2 ft.	2403	4029	—
C-120/C-122 Trucks — 1-Ton — 140 in. w.b.				
C-120	Travelette Chassis & Cab	2854	4052	—
C-120	Travelette Pickup 6-ft.	2998	—	—

NOTE 3: Add $614 and 270 lbs.s for C-110/C-120 models with the 4x4 option.
NOTE 4: AB-120 Metroette is $3,056 and 4,755 lbs.; AM-120 Metro delivery same as 1958, except no standard Metro body on 102 in. wheelbase. Metro prices: $2,208-$4,372. Weights and specifications for these models same as 1958.

Model	Body Type	Price	Weight	
C-130/C-132 — 1-Ton — 122 in. w.b.				
C-130	Chassis & Cab	2346	3630	—
C-130/C-132 — 1-Ton — 131 in. w.b.				
C-130	Chassis & Cab	2357	3655	—
C-130	Pickup 8-1/2 ft.	3486	4080	—
C-130/C-132 — 1-Ton — 134 in. w.b.				
C-130	Chassis & Cab	2368	3666	—
C-130/C-132 — 1-Ton — 140 in. w.b.				
C-130	Travelette Chassis & Cab	2938	4114	—

NOTE 6: AM-130 Metro delivery same as 1958. Prices for 1-ton Metros: $2,421-$4,209. Weights and specifications for these models same as 1958.

1961 IHC 1/2-Ton Model C-120 Custom Travelall (OCW)

ENGINE [Scout]: Comanche Four. Inline. OHV. (Single bank of V-8). Four-cylinder. Cast iron block with aluminum intake manifold. Bore & stroke: 3-7/8 in. x 3-7/32 in. Displacement: 151.84 cid.. Compression ratio: 8.19:1. Brake horsepower: 93.4 at 4400 rpm. Net horsepower: 24.1 (NACC). Maximum Torque: 135 lbs.-ft. at 2400 rpm. Solid valve lifters. Carburetor: Downdraft. Features: Fuel pump. Fuel filter. 11-gallon fuel tank (left side ofbody). Oil bath air cleaner. Full-pressure lubrication. External gear oil pump. Wire mesh floating oil strainer. Deep sump oil pan. Engine derived from IH V-304 V-8. Used only in Scout.

ENGINE [AM-80]: A-55 Engine. Inline. Overhead valve. Four-cylinder. Cast iron block. Bore & stroke: 2-7/8 in. x 3-1/2 in. Displacement: 90.884 cid.. Brake horsepower: 59.6 at 4600-4800 rpm. Net horsepower: 13.2 (NACC). Maximum Torque: 87.4 lbs.-ft. at 1600-2400 rpm. Used in AM-80 Metro-Mite only; based on English Austin engine.

ENGINE [C-100/C-110/C-120/C-130]: V-266 Engine. Overhead valve. Vee-block. Eight-cylinder. Cast iron block. Bore & stroke: 3-3/8 in. x 3-7/32 in. Displacement: 154.8 cid.. Brake horsepower: 154.8 at 4400 rpm. Net horsepower: 42.1 (NACC). Maximum Torque: 227.1 lbs.-ft. at 2800 rpm. Solid valve lifters. Carburetor: Downdraft.

ENGINE [AB-120/AM-120/AM-130]: 220 Black Diamond. Inline. OHV. Six-cylinder. Cast iron block. Bore & stroke: 3-9/16 in. x 3-11/16 in. Displacement: 220.5 cid.. Brake horsepower: 112.5 at 3800 rpm. Net horsepower: 30.4. Maximum Torque: 194.4 lbs.-ft. at 1600-2000 rpm. Four main bearings. Solid valve lifters. Carburetor: Downdraft.

ENGINE [Optional AB-120/AM-120/AM-130/ all C series]: 240 Black Diamond. Inline. Overhead valve. Six-cylinder. Cast iron block. Bore & stroke: 3.56 in. x 4.018 in. Displacement: 240.3 cid.. Brake horsepower: 140.8 at 3800 rpm. Net horsepower: 30.4 (NACC). Maximum Torque: 223.5 lbs.-ft. at 2000 rpm. Four main bearings. Solid valve lifters. Carburetor: Downdraft.

CHASSIS [Scout 80]: Wheelbase: 100 in. Overall length: 154 in. Width: 68.6 in. Height: [4x2] 67 in.; [4x4] 68 in. Ground clearance: [Front] 4x2=9 in./4x4=9.3 in.; [Rear] All=9.3 in.; Four-ply tires: [4x2] 6.50 x 15 PC; [4x4] 6.00 x 16 PC, tube-type, non-directional.

CHASSIS [AM-80 Metro-Mite]: Wheelbase: 96 in. Tires: 6.50 x 14 four-ply.

CHASSIS [C-100/C-102]: Wheelbase: 119 in. Tires: 6.70 x 15 four-ply.

CHASSIS [C-110/C-112]: Wheelbase: 115/119/122/131/140 in. Tires: 7.10 x 15 four-ply.

CHASSIS [C-120/C-122]: Wheelbase: 115/119/122/131/140 in. Tires: 7.00 x 15.5 six-ply.

CHASSIS [C-130/C-132]: Wheelbase: 122/131/134/140 in. Tires: 8.00 x 17.5 six-ply.

CHASSIS [AB-120 Metroette]: Wheelbase: 115 in. Tires: 7.00 x 17.5 six-ply.

CHASSIS [AM-120/AM-122 Metro]: Wheelbase: 102/115/122 in. Tires: 7.00 x 17 six-ply.

CHASSIS [AM-130/AM-132 Metro]: Wheelbase: 115/122/134 in. Tires: 8.00 x 17.5 six-ply.

TECHNICAL [Scout]: Synchromesh transmission. Speeds: 3F/1R. Floor-mounted gearshift lever. Clutch: 10 in. diameter, single-plate, 6-spring, coil spring vibration damper. Single reduction hypoid type rear axle (2,300 lbs. capacity). Overall ratio: 4.27:1. Four-wheel hydraulic brakes. Wheels: [4x2] 15 in. disc. 4.50K rim with hubcaps; [4x4] 16 in. disc, 4.50E rim. Drivetrain options: Optional transfer case on 4x4 models controls engagement of front-wheel-drive and provides extra-low gear that multiplies torque power to the wheels. This unit mounted to the transmission and had a multi-ratio power divider. Three position shifting: (low) 3.333; (second) 1.851 to 1; (high) direct drive. Front axle on 4x4 models was a single-reduction type with 4.27:1 ratio. The 4x2 models used a 2,000 lbs. capacity I-beam type axle instead. Power take-off was available at extra cost for 4x4 models. Full torque type with front and rear output shafts mounted on transfer case, left side. Winch drive and mounting parts.

TECHNICAL [Trucks]: Same as previous model years since 1955.

1961 IHC Scout With Vinyl Travel-Top (S. Soloy)

OPTIONS [Scout]: Front axle locking hubs for 4x4 model, manual or automatic. Skid plate. Rear axle, 4.27:1 with Power-Lok differential. Full-length steel Travel-Top enclosure with lift-gate and windows. Vinyl-coated Sport-Top with snap-on curtains. Cushioned seats and backrests over wheelhousings. Sun visors. Armrests. Safety belts. Fresh air heater/defroster. Radio and aerial. Cigar lighter. Inside mirror. Seat covers. Bucket seats. Floor mat for 4x4 (standard 4x2). 60-amp. battery. Directional turn signals. 40-amp. alternator. Hand throttle control. Increased capacity cooling. Dual 11-gallon fuel tanks. Front tow hook. Grille guard. Rear bumper. Rear tow hook. Trailer hitch. Undercoating. Right-hand drive. Power take-off. Snowplow. Special tires. Ramsey model 200 winch, front-mounted with 150 ft. cable and hook.

OPTIONS [Trucks]: Chrome front bumper. Rear bumper. Outside rearview mirror(s). Undercoating. Trailer hitch. Grille guard. Bumper guards. Radio (AM). Heater (fresh air type or recirculating). Clock. Cigar lighter. Radio antenna. Seat covers. Dual sun visors. Spotlight. Electric wipers. Special paint. Two-tone finish. Custom trim package. Deluxe cab package. Front-mounted winch. Directional turn signals. Safety belts. High-side pickup box panels. Clearance marker lights. Armrests. Increased capacity cooling. Heavy-duty battery. Power-Lok differential. Foam seat cushions. Floor mat. 40-amp. alternator. Snow plow. Power steering. Power brakes. Automatic transmission.

1961 IHC Scout Convertible With Doors (S. Soloy)

HISTORICAL: Introduced Nov. 1, 1960. Calendar year registrations: [All IHC trucks] 116,538. Calendar year registrations by weight class: [6,000 lbs. and under] 48,997; [6,001-10,000 lbs.] 13,085. Calendar year production: [All models] 142,816. New styling. Independent front suspension. International Scout introduced. F.W. Jenks continued as IHC president. R.M. Buzard was vice-president of the Motor Truck Div. The company was headquartered in Chicago, Ill. and had plants in Emeryville, Calif., Ft. Wayne, Ind., Indianapolis, Ind., Springfield, Ohio, and Bridgeport, Conn. IHC increased its market share, although overall truck sales were down.

1961 IHC 3/4-Ton Model C-120 Travelette Pickup 4x4 (S. Soloy)

1962 IHC

MODEL 80 — 1/4-TON SCOUT — FOUR-CYLINDER: The Scout was carried over for 1962 with no major alterations. Roll-up windows became a new option. As in 1961, the standard model came with a Sport-Top made of vinyl-coated material, which was removable. The doors could also be removed for Jeep-like off-roading with the windshield up or folded flat. The Sport-Top full body enclosure gave the buyer a full-length vinyl-coated roof covering with snap-on curtains to cover the five-foot pickup box. A full-length steel

Travel-Top was the ultimate option. It, too, was removable. Like the original version, the '62 carried its spare tire and wheel mounted vertically at the center of the box wall, behind the driver's seat.

MODEL C — 1/2-TON — EIGHT-CYLINDER: There were no obvious changes in the C series 1/2-tons. Styling and engineering was carried over from 1961. Featured in both lines was the Bonus Load pickup truck with 7-ft. box. This style pickup also came in the C-110 with an 8-1/2 ft. box. The Metro-Mite was dropped in 1962.

MODEL C — 3/4-TON — EIGHT-CYLINDER: The C series 3/4-tons were also carried over from 1961. Bonus Load pickups were available with both the 7-foot and 8-1/2 ft. boxes. The AB-120 Metroette and AM-120 Metros were again offered as a continuation of the series introduced in 1958.

MODEL C — 1-TON — EIGHT-CYLINDER: The 1-ton C series was another carryover from 1961. It had the 8-1/2 ft. box. Bonus Load pickup included. The 1-ton Metros were also offered as a continuation of the 1958 series. Four-wheel drive (4x4) was made available for the C-130 models this season.

I.D. DATA: Serial numbers located in the same locations. The numbering system was basically the same. The 1962 models had the suffix -2 following the serial number for 1962.

1962 IHC Scout 1/4-Ton Sport Utility (DFW/MVMA)

Model	Body Type	Price	Weight	Prod. Total
Scout — 1/4-Ton — 100 in. w.b.				
80	Utility Pickup 5-ft.	1754	2800	—
Scout 4x4 — 1/4-Ton — 100 in. w.b.				
80	Utility Pickup 5-ft.	2132	3000	—
C-100/C-102 — 1/2-Ton — 119 in. w.b.				
C-100	Chassis & Cab	2072	3265	—
C-100	Pickup 7-ft.	2191	3640	—
C-100	Bonus Load Pickup 7-ft.	2207	3630	—
C-100	Panel 7-ft.	2505	4095	—
C-100	Travelall	2795	4240	—
C-100	Custom Travelall	3075	—	—
C-110/C-112 — 1/2-Ton — 115 in. w.b.				
C-110	Chassis & Cab	2096	3290	—
C-110/C-112 — 1/2-Ton — 119 in. w.b.				
C-110	Chassis & Cab	2096	3295	—
C-110	Pickup 7-ft.	2214	3670	—
C-110	Bonus Load Pickup 7-ft.	2230	3660	—
C-110	Panel 7-ft.	2528	3850	—
C-110	Travelall	2819	3995	—
C-110	Custom Travelall	3099	—	—
C-110/C-112 — 1/2-Ton — 122 in. w.b.				
C-110	Chassis & Cab	2112	3301	—
C-110/C-112 — 1/2-Ton — 131 in. w.b.				
C-110	Chassis & Cab	2123	3325	—
C-110	Pickup 8-1/2 ft.	2252	3750	—
C-110	Bonus Load Pickup 8-1/2 ft.	2268	3740	—
C-110/C-112 — 1/2-Ton — 140 in. w.b.				
C-110	Travelette Chassis & Cab	2704	3829	—
C-110	Travelette Pickup 6 ft.	2847	—	—
C-110	Travelette Pickup 6 ft.	2847	—	—
C-120/C-122 — 3/4-Ton — 115 in. w.b.				
C-120	Chassis & Cab	2251	3476	—
C-120/C-122 — 3/4-Ton — 119 in. w.b.				
C-120	Chassis & Cab	2251	3480	—
C-120	Pickup 7-ft.	2369	3855	—
C-120	Bonus Load Pickup 7-ft.	2385	3845	—
C-120	Panel 7-ft.	2683	4035	—
C-120	Travelall	2974	4180	—
C-120	Custom Travelall	3254	—	—
C-120/C-122 — 3/4-Ton — 122 in. w.b.				
C-120	Chassis & Cab	2267	3486	—
C-120/C-122 — 3/4-ton — 131 in. w.b.				
C-120	Chassis & Cab	2278	3604	—
C-120	Pickup 8-1/2 ft.	2407	4029	—
C-120	Bonus Load Pickup 8-1/2 ft.	2423	4019	—
C-120/C-122 — 3/4-Ton — 140 in. w.b.				
C-120	Travelette Chassis & Cab	2859	4052	—
C-120	Travelette Pickup 6 ft.	3002	—	—

NOTE 1: Add $614 and 270 lbs. for 4x4.
NOTE 2: AB-120 Metroette/AM-120 Metro had same prices and weights as 1961.

C-130/C-132 — 1-Ton — 122 in. w.b.				
C-130	Chassis & Cab	2350	3630	—
C-130/C-132 — 1-Ton — 131 in. w.b.				
C-130	Chassis & Cab	2361	3655	—
C-130	Pickup 8-1/2 ft.	2490	4080	—
C-130	Bonus Load Pickup 8-1/2 ft.	2507	4070	—
C-130/C-132 — 1-Ton — 134 in. w.b.				
C-130	Chassis & Cab	2372	3666	—
C-130/C-132 — 1-Ton — 140 in. w.b.				
C-130	Travelette Chassis & Cab	2942	4114	—

NOTE 3: Add $1,109 and 285 lbs. for C-130 4x4 models.
NOTE 4: AM-130 Metro delivery models were priced from $2,431 to $4,220.

1962 IHC Scout Sport Utility With Steel Travel-Top (S. Soloy)

ENGINE [Scout]: Comanche Four. Inline. OHV. (Single bank of V-8). Four-cylinder. Cast iron block with aluminum intake manifold. Bore & stroke: 3-7/8 in. x 3-7/32 in. Displacement: 151.84 cid.. Compression ratio: 8.19:1. Brake horsepower: 93.4 at 4400 rpm. Net horsepower: 24.1 (NACC). Maximum Torque: 135 lbs.-ft. at 2400 rpm. Solid valve lifters. Carburetor: Downdraft. Features: Fuel pump. Fuel filter. 11-gallon fuel tank (left side of body). Oil bath air cleaner. Full-pressure lubrication. External gear oil pump. Wire mesh floating oil strainer. Deep sump oil pan. Engine derived from IH V-304 V-8. Used only in Scout.
ENGINE [AM-80]: A-55 Engine. Inline. Overhead valve. Four-cylinder. Cast iron block. Bore & stroke: 2-7/8 in. x 3-1/2 in. Displacement: 90.88 cid.. Brake horsepower: 59.6 at 4600-4800 rpm. Net horsepower: 13.2 (NACC). Maximum Torque: 87.4 lbs.-ft. at 1600-2400 rpm. Used in AM-80 Metro-Mite only; based on English Austin engine.
ENGINE [C-100/C-110/C-120/C-130]: V-266 Engine. Overhead valve. Vee-block. Eight-cylinder. Cast iron block. Bore & stroke: 3-3/8 in. x 3-7/32 in. Displacement: 154.8 cid.. Brake horsepower: 154.8 at 4400 rpm. Net horsepower: 42.1 (NACC). Maximum Torque: 227.1 lbs.-ft. at 2800 rpm. Solid valve lifters. Carburetor: Downdraft.
ENGINE [AB-120/AM-120/AM-130]: 220 Black Diamond. Inline. OHV. Six-cylinder. Cast iron block. Bore & stroke: 3-9/16 in. x 3-11/16 in. Displacement: 220.5 cid.. Brake horsepower: 112.5 at 3800 rpm. Net horsepower: 30.4. Maximum Torque: 194.4 lbs.-ft. at 1600-2000 rpm. Four main bearings. Solid valve lifters. Carburetor: Downdraft.
ENGINE [Optional AB-120/AM-120/AM-130/ all C series]: 240 Black Diamond. Inline. Overhead valve. Six-cylinder. Cast iron block. Bore & stroke: 3.56 in. x 4.018 in. Displacement: 240.3 cid.. Brake horsepower: 140.8 at 3800 rpm. Net horsepower: 30.4 (NACC). Maximum Torque: 223.5 lbs.-ft. at 2000 rpm. Four main bearings. Solid valve lifters. Carburetor: Downdraft.
CHASSIS [Scout 80]: Wheelbase: 100 in. Overall length: 154 in. Width: 68.6 in. Height: [4x2] 67 in.; [4x4] 68 in. Ground clearance: [Front] 4x2=9 in./4x4=9.3 in.; [Rear] all=9.3 in.; Four-wheel tires: [4x2] 6.50 x 15 PC; [4x4] 6.00 x 16 PC, tube-type, non-directional.
CHASSIS [C-100/C-102]: Wheelbase: 119 in. Tires: 6.70 x 15 four-ply.
CHASSIS [C-110/C-112]: Wheelbase: 115/119/122/131/140 in. Tires: 7.10 x 15 four-ply.
CHASSIS [C-120/C-122]: Wheelbase: 115/119/122/131/140 in. Tires: 7.00 x 15.5 six-ply.
CHASSIS [C-130/C-132]: Wheelbase: 122/131/134/140 in. Tires: 8.00 x 17.5 six-ply.
CHASSIS [AB-120 Metroette]: Wheelbase: 115 in. Tires: 7.00 x 17.5 six-ply.
CHASSIS [AM-120/AM-122 Metro]: Wheelbase: 102/115/122 in. Tires: 7.00 x 17 six-ply.
CHASSIS [AM-130/AM-132 Metro]: Wheelbase: 115/122/134 in. Tires: 8.00 x 17.5 six-ply.
TECHNICAL [Scout]: Synchromesh transmission. Speeds: 3F/1R. Floor-mounted gearshift lever. Clutch: 10 in. diameter, single-plate, 6-spring, coil spring vibration damper. Single hypoid type rear axle (2,300 lbs. capacity). Overall ratio: 4.27:1. Four-wheel hydraulic brakes. Wheels: [4x2] 15 in. disc. 4.50K rim with hubcaps; [4x4] 16 in. disc, 4.50E rim. Drivetrain options: Optional transfer case on 4x4 models controls engagement of front-wheel-drive and provides extra-low gear that multiplies torque power to the wheels. This unit mounted to the transmission and had a multi-ratio power divider. Three position shifting: (low) 3.333; (second) 1.851 to 1; (high) direct drive. Front axle on 4x4 models was a single-reduction type with 4.27:1 ratio. The 4x2 models used a 2,000 lbs. capacity I-beam type axle instead. Power take-off was available at extra cost for 4x4 models. Full torque type with front and rear output shafts mounted on transfer case, left side. Winch drive and mounting parts.
TECHNICAL [Trucks]: Same as previous model years since 1955.
OPTIONS [Scout]: Front axle locking hubs for 4x4 model, manual or automatic. Skid plate. Rear axle, 4.27:1 with Power-Lok differential. Full-length steel Travel-Top enclosure with lift-gate and windows. Vinyl-coated Sport-Top with snap-on curtains. Cushioned seats and backrests over wheelhousings. Sun visors. Armrests. Safety belts. Fresh air heater/defroster. Radio and aerial. Cigar lighter. Inside mirror. Seat covers. Bucket seats. Floor mat for 4x4 (standard 4x2). 60-amp. battery. Directional turn signals. 40-amp. alternator. Hand throttle control. Increased capacity cooling. Dual 11-gallon fuel tanks. Front tow hook. Grille guard. Rear bumper. Rear tow hook. Trailer hitch. Undercoating. Right-hand drive. Power take-off. Snowplow. Special tires. Ramsey model 200 winch, front mounted with 150 ft. cable and hook. New roll-up windows.
OPTIONS [Trucks]: Chrome front bumper. Rear bumper. Outside rearview mirror(s). Under coating. Trailer hitch. Grille guard. Bumper guards. Radio (AM). Heater (fresh air type or recirculating). Clock. Cigar lighter. Radio antenna. Seat covers. Dual sun visors.

Spotlight. Electric wipers. Special paint. Two-tone finish. Custom trim package. Deluxe cab package. Front-mounted winch. Directional turn signals. Safety belts. High side pickup box panels. Clearance marker lights. Armrests. Increased capacity cooling. Heavy-Duty battery. Power-Lok differential. Foam seat cushions. Floor mat. 40-amp. alternator. Snowplow. Power steering. Power brakes. Automatic transmission.
HISTORICAL: Introduced Nov. 1, 1961. Calendar year registrations: [All IHC models] 130,959. Calendar year production: [All IHC models] 147,285. Market share: [All IHC models] 11.47 percent. Innovations: Scout gets roll-up windows. Metro-Mite dropped temporarily for new design changeover. Historically, the company introduced its heavy-duty Load Star line in March of 1962. Also received was a government order for 3,224 five-ton 6x6 tactical motor trucks to be produced in Ft. Wayne through September 1962. An additional 300 workers were hired. On Nov. 8, 1961, the order had 4,000 more trucks added to it.

1963 IHC

1963 IHC 3/4-Ton Model C-1200 Travelette Pickup (RCA)

MODEL 80 — 1/4-TON SCOUT — FOUR-CYLINDER: The Scout for 1963 looked like the Scout for 1962 and had the same engine specifications. The 4x2 version was lower in price, while the 4x4 edition was more expensive.
MODEL CM — METRO-MITE/METRO — FOUR-CYLINDER: The Metro-Mite was offered in a new CM Series, the base model being the CM-75. A walk-in version was called the CM-80. The main change from the earlier Metro-Mite was a horizontal bar grille without vertical center divider and a new powerplant. The Scout's 4-152 engine was used. These trucks had a 4,000 lbs. GVW. Also new was a 1/2-ton Metro delivery van, the CM-110 (with a CM-112 chassis option). It had the same type of new grille as the Mite and shared the 4-152 engine. The wheelbase was 6 inches longer, however, and GVW was 4,500 to 5,500 lbs. The larger Metros were still AM models based on 1958 designs.
MODEL C — 1/2-TON — SIX-CYLINDER: A new C-1000 style light-duty truck line was introduced in November 1962. The IH hood badge lost its wings and single headlamps returned. The grille was now a gridwork of two horizontal bars intersected by nine vertical members with the International name spelled out between the bars at the center. There were twin air slots between the grille and somewhat less chrome trimmings. Six-cylinder engines became standard equipment and a V-8 was optional. Wheelbases and GVWs were the same as comparable 1962 models. The Travelette Crew cabs got the Bonus Load treatment, too.
MODEL C — 3/4-TON — SIX-CYLINDER: The C-1200 was the 3/4-ton version of the 1963 IHC light-truck. Here, too, the six-cylinder replaced the V-8 as the standard engine. A Bonus Load version of the Travelette model was new. All else was comparable to 1962 offerings. The AM-120 Metros and AB-120 Metroette continued to be based on the 1958 series. Refer back to the 1958 section for this data. Model offerings were trimmed to the standard 9 ft. 6 in. Metro, Flat Back Metro, Metro Van and Metro Lite on 115 or 122 in. wheelbases with 5,400 lbs. to 6,000 lbs. GVWs.
MODEL C — 1-TON — SIX-CYLINDER: The 1-ton had the same basic changes as lighter IHC trucks. The 8-1/2 pickup was issued in Bonus Load configuration and the six-cylinder became standard. The AM-130 Metro line was a continuation of the 1958 series including the standard Metro on a 115 in. wheelbase and the Flat Back, Van and Metro-Lite on 115/122 in. w.heelbase. Refer to the 1958 section for basic Metro data.
I.D. DATA: Serial numbers were in the same locations. The 1963 models had the suffix -3 following the serial number to indicate 1963.

1963 IHC 1/2-Ton Model C-1000 Fenderside Pickup (S. Soloy)

Model	Body Type	Price	Weight	Prod. Total
Scout 80 — 1/4-Ton — 100 in. w.b. — 4x4				
80	Pickup 5-ft.	1701	2800	—
80	Pickup 5-ft.	2188	3000	—
Metro-Mite CM-75/CM-80 — 1/2-Ton — 96 in. w.b.				
CM-75	Metro-Mite Panel 7-ft.	2345	—	—
CM-80	Metro-Mite Walk-in 7-ft.	2372	—	—
Metro-Mite CM-110 — 1/2-Ton — 102 in. w.b.				
CM-110	Metro-Mite Walk-in 8-ft.	2675	—	—
Trucks C-1000 — 1/2-Ton — 119 in. w.b.				
C-1000	Chassis & Cab	1941	3265	—
C-1000	Pickup 7-ft.	2061	3640	—
C-1000	Bonus Load Pickup 7-ft.	2077	3630	—
C-1000	Travelall/Panel 7-ft.	2373	3820	—
C-1100 — Heavy-Duty 1/2-Ton — 115 in. w.b.				
C-1100	Chassis & Cab	1965	3290	—
C-1100 — Heavy-Duty 1/2-Ton — 119 in. w.b.				
C-1100	Pickup 7-ft.	2086	3675	—
C-1100	Bonus Load Pickup 7-ft.	2102	3665	—
C-1100	Travelall/Panel 7-ft.	2398	3855	—
C-1100 — Heavy-Duty 1/2-Ton — 131 in. w.b.				
C-1100	Chassis & Cab	1965	3290	—
C-1100	Pickup 8-1/2 ft.	2086	3675	—
C-1100	Bonus Load Pickup 8-1/2 ft.	2102	3665	—
C-1100 — Heavy-Duty 1/2-Ton — 140 in. w.b.				
C-1100	Travelette Chassis & Cab	2571	3830	—
C-1100	Travelette Bonus Load Pickup	2714	—	—
Trucks C-1200 — 3/4-Ton — 115 in. w.b.-131 in. w.b.				
C-1200	Chassis & Cab	2089	3475	—
Series C-1200 — 3/4-Ton — 119-131 in. w.b.				
C-1200	Pickup 7-ft.	2086	3675	—
C-1200	Bonus Load Pickup 7-ft.	2102	3665	—
C-1200	Panel 7-ft./119 in.	2398	3855	—
Series C-1200 — 3/4-Ton — 140 in. w.b.				
C-1200	Travelette Chassis & Cab	2571	3830	—
C-1200	Bonus Load Travelette Pickup	2714	—	—

NOTE 1: Add $638 for 4x4 models.
NOTE 2: Metroette AB-120 was $3,105 and 4,755 lbs.
NOTE 3: Metro AM-120S were $3,072-$3,789 and 4,570-4,650 lbs.

Model	Body Type	Price	Weight	Prod. Total
Series C-1300 — 1-Ton — 122-134 in. w.b.				
C-1300	Chassis & Cab	2190	3630	—
Series C-1300 — 1-Ton — 131 in. w.b.				
C-1300	Pickup 8-1/2 ft.	2327	4080	—
C-1300	Bonus Load Pickup 8-1/2 ft.	2838	—	—

NOTE 4: Add $1,147 for 4x4 models.
NOTE 5: Metro AM-130s were $3,270-$4,048 and 4,320 lbs. for Metro-Lite.

ENGINE [Scout/Metro-Mite/CM-110/CM-112]: Comanche Four. Inline. OHV. (Single bank of V-8.) Four-cylinder. Cast iron block with aluminum intake manifold. Bore & stroke: 3-7/8 in. x 3-7/32 in. Displacement: 151.84 cid.. Compression ratio: 8.19:1. Brake horsepower: 93.4 at 4400 rpm. Net horsepower: 24.1 (NACC). Maximum torque: 135 lbs.-ft. at 2400 rpm. Solid valve lifters. Carburetor: Downdraft.
ENGINE [C-1000/C-1110/C-1200]: BG-241 (formerly 240 Black Diamond). Inline. Overhead valve. Six-cylinder. Cast iron block. Bore & stroke: 3.56 in. x 4.018 in. Displacement: 240.3 cid.. Brake horsepower: 140.8 at 3800 rpm. Net horsepower: 30.4 (NACC). Maximum Torque: 223.5 lbs.-ft. at 2000 rpm. Four main bearings. Solid valve lifters. Carburetor: Downdraft. (Optional in AB-120/AM-120/AM-130 models.)
ENGINE [AB-120/AM-120/AM-130]: BG-220 (formerly 220 Black Diamond). Inline. Six-cylinder. Cast iron block. Bore & stroke: 3-9/16 in. x 3-11/16 in. Displacement: 220.5 cid.. Brake horsepower: 112.5 at 3800 rpm. Net horsepower: 30.4. Maximum Torque: 194.4 lbs.-ft. at 1600-2000 rpm. Four main bearings. Solid valve lifters. Carburetor: Downdraft. (Optional in CM-75/CM-80/CM-110 models.)
ENGINE [Optional V-8]: V-266 Engine. Overhead valve. Vee-block. Eight-cylinder. Cast iron block. Bore & stroke: 3-3/8 in. x 3-7/32 in. Displacement: 154.8 cid.. Brake horsepower: 154.8 at 4400 rpm. Net horsepower: 42.1 (NACC). Maximum Torque: 227.1 lbs.-ft. at 2800 rpm. Solid valve lifters. Carburetor: Downdraft. (Optional in C-1000/C-1100/C-1200/C-1300 models.)

1963 IHC 1/2-Ton Model C-1100 Custom Travelall (S. Soloy)

CHASSIS [Scout Series]: Wheelbase: 100 in. Tires: [4x2] 6.50 x 15; [4x4] 6.00 x 16.
CHASSIS [Metro-Mite Series]: Wheelbase: 96 in. Tires: 6.50 x 15 in.

CHASSIS [CM-110 Metro]: Wheelbase: 102 in. Tires: 6.70 x 15 in.
CHASSIS [AM-120 Metro]: Wheelbase: 115 in./122 in. Tires: 7.00 x 17.5 in.
CHASSIS [AM-130 Metro]: Wheelbase: 115 in./122 in./134 in. Tires: 8.00 x 17.5 in.
CHASSIS [AB-120 Metroette]: Wheelbase: 115 in. Tires: 7.00 x 15 in.
CHASSIS [C-1000]: Wheelbase: 119 in. Tires: 6.70 x 15 in.
CHASSIS [C-1100]: Wheelbase: 115 in./119 in./131 in./140 in. Tires: 7.10 x 15 in.
CHASSIS [C-1200]: Wheelbase: 115 in./119 in./131 in./140 in. Tires: 7.00 x 17.5 in.
CHASSIS [C-1300]: Wheelbase: 122 in./131 in./134 in. Tires: 8.00 x 17.5 in.

TECHNICAL [Scout]: Synchromesh transmission. Speeds: 3F/1R. Floor-mounted gearshift lever. Clutch: 10 in. diameter, single-plate, 6-spring, coil spring vibration damper. Single reduction hypoid type rear axle (2,300 lbs. capacity). Overall ratio: 4.27:1. Four-wheel hydraulic brakes. Wheels: [4x2] 15 in. disc. 4.50K rim with hubcaps; [4x4] 16 in. disc. 4.50E rim. Drivetrain options: Optional transfer case on 4x4 models controls engagement of front-wheel drive and provides extra-low gear that multiplies torque power to the wheels. This unit mounted to the transmission and had a multi-ratio power divider. Three position shifting: (low) 3.333; (second) 1.851 to 1; (high) direct drive. Front axle on 4x4 models was a single-reduction type with 4.27:1 ratio. The 4x2 models used a 2,000 lbs. capacity I-beam type axle instead. Power take-off was available at extra cost for 4x4 models. Full torque type with front and rear output shafts mounted on transfer case, left side. Winch drive and mounting parts.
TECHNICAL [1/2-Ton and 3/4-Ton]: Synchromesh transmission. Speeds: 3F/1R. Floor-mounted gearshift lever. Single-plate dry-disc clutch. Full-floating rear axle. Overall ratio: 4.1:1. Four-wheel drum brakes. Heavy-duty three-speed transmission and Hydra-Matic transmission optional on all models.
TECHNICAL [1-Ton]: Synchromesh transmission. Speeds: 4F/1R. Floor-mounted gearshift lever. Single-plate dry-disc clutch. Full-floating rear axle. Overall ratio: 6.616:1. Four-wheel drum brakes. Hydra-Matic transmission optional on all models.

1963 IHC 1/2-Ton Model C-1100 Bonus Load Pickup (D. Sagvold)

OPTIONS [Scout]: Front axle locking hubs for 4x4 model, manual or automatic. Skid plate. Rear axle, 4.27:1 with Power-Lok differential. Full-length steel Travel-Top enclosure with lift-gate and windows. Vinyl-coated Sport-Top with snap-on curtains. Cushioned seats and backrests over wheelhousings. Sun visors. Armrests. Safety belts. Fresh air heater/defroster. Radio and aerial. Cigar lighter. Inside mirror. Bucket seats. Floor mat for 4x4 (standard 4x2). 60-amp. battery. Directional turn signals. 40-amp. alternator. Hand throttle control. Increased capacity cooling. Dual 11-gallon fuel tanks. Front tow hook. Grille guard. Rear bumper. Rear tow hook. Trailer hitch. Undercoating. Right-hand drive. Power take-off. Snowplow. Special tires. Ramsey model 200 winch, front-mounted with 150 ft. cable and hook. New roll-up windows.
OPTIONS [Trucks]: Chrome front bumper. Rear bumper. Outside rearview mirror(s). Undercoating. Trailer hitch. Grille guard. Bumper guards. Radio (AM). Heater (fresh air type or recirculating). Clock. Cigar lighter. Radio antenna. Seat covers. Dual sun visors. Spotlight. Electric wipers. Special paint. Two-tone finish. Custom trim package. Deluxe cab package. Front-mounted winch. Directional turn signals. Safety belts. High side pickup box panels. Clearance marker lights. Armrests. Increased capacity cooling. Heavy-duty battery. Power-Lok differential. Foam seat cushions. Floor mat. 40-amp. alternator. Snowplow. Power steering. Power brakes. Automatic transmission. Power steering ($174.)

HISTORICAL: Introduced Nov. 1, 1962. Calendar year registrations: [All IHC trucks] 145,105. Calendar year registrations by weight class: [up to 6,000 lbs.] 57,497; [6,001 to 10,000 lbs.] 14,294. Calendar year production: [All IHC models] 168,296. Market share: [All IHC] 11.50 percent. Innovations: New Metro-Mite series uses four-cylinder Scout engine. Six-cylinder engines become standard equipment in C series trucks again. C series has modernized styling. H.O. Bercher was now president of IHC, while R.M. Buzard remained executive vice-president of the Truck Div. During the summer of 1963, a three-year program for expansion and improvement of the Ft. Wayne, Ind. works began. This was an all-time record year for the company.

1963 IHC 1/4-Ton Scout Sport Utility (RCA)

1964 IHC

I.D. DATA: Serial Number located on plate on dash; on right-hand floorboard inside cab; on left front frame side rail; and on front right-hand runningboard shield. Numbers for 1964 had a 4 suffix to indicate model year. Numbers are not available. Engine numbers located on right upper front side of six-cylinder engine crankcase. On left upper front of V-8 engine crankcase. (Diesel engine: plate on left side.) The original Bill of Sale determined model year, since IHC trucks were not manufactured on a yearly model basis.

1964 IHC 3/4-Ton Model AM-120 Metro Coach School Bus (RPZ)

1964 IHC 3/4-Ton Model C-1200 Custom Travelall (S. Soloy)

SCOUT — SERIES 80 — FOUR-CYLINDER: The 1964 International Scout looked the same as the 1963 model. There were no major technical changes. Under the hood once again was the Comanche four-cylinder engine. Prices for both the 4x2 and 4x4 models underwent a modest increase.

METRO-MITE — SERIES CM — FOUR-CYLINDER: The small Metro-Mite delivery vans in the CM series were of modern, boxy design with full-across horizontal grille bars. The CM-75/CM-80 lines featured a 4,000 lbs. GVW rating and had a 96 in. wheelbase. With a 102 in. wheelbase and 4,500 lbs. GVW, plus larger tires, the CM-110 Metro-Mite was a bit larger. It shared the modern, boxy styling. All of these models had single front and rear wheels as base equipment.

METRO/METROETTE — SERIES A — SIX-CYLINDER: The Metro delivery van series was an important part of IHC truck offerings in payload capacities up to 1-ton. Series A trucks were, technically, a direct continuation of the 1958 line. There were some updated features, but they were of a relatively minor nature. The AB-120 Metroette was an old-fashioned looking milk/bakery delivery truck with styling that dated back to 1956. The lighter version was considered a medium-duty (3/4-ton) truck. It was coded the AB-120, used a 115 in. wheelbase and had a 5,400 lbs. GVW. The regular Metros were AM models. The AM-120 was the 3/4-ton line and the AM-130 was the 1-ton. These trucks were available on a variety of wheelbases: 102 in., 115 in., 122 in. and 134 in. GVWs ranged between 5,400 lbs. and 6,500 lbs. for AM-120s and 7,000 lbs. to 9,000 lbs. for AM-130s. Base engine was the 220.5 cid six. The BG-241 engine was optionally available.

LIGHT-TRUCK — C-900 — FOUR-CYLINDER: An all-new IHC product for 1964 was the C-900 compact truck. This unique and somewhat advanced vehicle was basically a smaller-than-standard pickup with the Scout's four-cylinder engine, a 107 in. wheelbase and a 6-ft. long pickup box. It had the same general styling as the standard-size C Series models, except it was not a slab-side pickup. Instead, it had rear fenders that protruded from the pickup box. It was one of the first downsized pickup trucks. However, buyers could also order a C-900 chassis-and-cab and have aftermarket stake and platform bodies added.

1/2-TON TRUCKS — SERIES C-1000/C-1100 — SIX/V-8: The C series IHC pickups for 1964 looked similar to the redesigned 1963 models. These "corn binders" came in two 1/2-ton lines (C-1000 and C-1100) both using the BG-241 six-cylinder engine as standard equipment. All of the C-1000s had a 119 in. wheelbase and GVWs between 3,265 and 3,965 lbs. The C-1100s came with 115 in., 119 in., 131 in. and 140 in. wheelbases. These 1/2-tons had GVW ratings from 3,290 to 3,845 lbs. The BG-241 engine was standard. Both 1/2-ton series came with standard 4x2 drivetrains. The 1/2-ton C-1100 series was also offered with a 4x4 option costing $572.

3/4-TON TRUCKS — SERIES C-1200 — SIX/V-8: The C-1200 was the 3/4-ton. It came with the same wheelbases as before. A 4x4 drivetrain option was $610 extra.

1-TON TRUCKS — SERIES C-1300 — SIX/V-8: For 1-ton buyers, the C-1300 line was available, too. It offered 122 in., 131 in. and 134 in. wheelbases, plus wheelbases of 120 in. and 129 in. with 4x4. The 4x4 option was $1,122 extra for C-1300s. They had GVWs ranging as high as 10,000 lbs.

1964 IHC 1/2-Ton Model C-1000 Custom Travelall (S. Soloy)

Model	Body Type	Price	Weight	Prod. Total
Scout 80 — 4x2 — 1/4-Ton — 100 in. w.b.				
80	Pickup 5-ft.	1722	2800	—
Scout 80 — 4x4 — 1/4-Ton — 100 in w.b.				
80	Pickup 5-ft.	2210	3000	—
CM-75 Metro-Mite — 1/2-Ton — 96 in w.b.				
CM-75	Metro-Mite Body	2345	2955	—
CM-80 Metro-Mite — 1/2-Ton — 96 in. w.b.				
CM-80	Metro-Mite Body	2372	2955	—
CM-110 Metro — 1/2-Ton — 102 in. w.b.				
CM-110	Metro-Mite Body	2675	3345	—
AB-120 Metro — 3/4-Ton — 115 in. w.b.				
AB-120	Milk Delivery Body	3105	4755	—
AM-120 Metro — 3/4-Ton — 102 in./115 in./134 in./122 in.				
AM-120	Metro 102/115 in. w.b.	3072	4570	—
AM-120	Flat Back 115/134 in. w.b.	3150	4650	—
AM-120	Metro-Van 115/122 in. w.b.	3276	5080	—
AM-120	Metro-Lite 115/122 in. w.b.	3789	—	—
AM-120	Metro-Coach 115 in. w.b.	4440	—	—
AM-130 Metro — 1-Ton — 115 in./134 in./122 in.				
AM-130	Metro 115 in. w.b.	3270	—	—
AM-130	Flat Back 115/134 in. w.b.	3483	—	—
AM-130	Metro-Van 115/122 in. w.b.	3475	—	—
AM-130	Metro-Lite 122/134 in. w.b.	4048	4160	—
C-900 — 1/2-Ton — 107 in. w.b.				
C-900	Chassis & Cab	1837	2875	—
C-900	Pickup 6-ft.	1952	3210	—
C-1000 — 1/2-Ton — 119 in.				
C-1000	Chassis & Cab	2003	3265	—
C-1000	Pickup	2124	3640	—
C-1000	Bonus Load Pickup	2135	3650	—
C-1000	Panel	2427	3820	—
C-1000	Travelall	2631	3965	—
C-1100 — 1/2-Ton — 115 in. to 140 in.				
C-1100	Chassis & Cab 115/131 in. w.b.	2003	3290	—
C-1100	Pickup 115/131 in. w.b.	2124	3665	—
C-1100	Bonus Load Pickup 119/131 in. w.b.	2135	3655	—
C-1100	Travelette Cab 140 in. w.b.	2631	3830	—
C-1100	Panel 119 in. w.b.	2427	3845	—
C-1100	Travelette Pickup 140 in. w.b.	2770	—	—
C-1100	Custom Travelall 119 in. w.b.	2731	3990	—

NOTE 1: Add $572 for 4x4 option C-1100.

Model	Body Type	Price	Weight	Prod. Total
C-1200 — 3/4-Ton — 115-140 in. w.b.				
C-1200	Chassis & Cab 115-131 in. w.b.	2126	3475	—
C-1200	Pickup 115-131 in. w.b.	2246	3850	—
C-1200	Bonus Load Pickup 119-131 in. w.b.	2258	3840	—
C-1200	Panel 119 in. w.b.	2550	4035	—
C-1200	Travelette Cab 140 in. w.b.	2754	4050	—
C-1200	Travelette Pickup 140 in. w.b.	2893	4797	—
C-1200	Custom Travelall 119 in. w.b.	2854	4255	—

NOTE 2: Add $638 for 4x4 option C-1200.

C-1300 — 1-Ton — 122-134 in. w.b.

C-1300	Chassis & Cab 122-134 in. w.b.	2226	3630	—
C-1300	Pickup 131 in. w.b.	2362	4080	—
C-1300	Bonus Load Pickup 131 in. w.b.	2374	4070	—

NOTE 3: Add $1,147 for 4x4 option. (C-1300)

NOTE 4: All factory prices include truck cab price and Federal Excise Tax. Prices listed are for minimum wheelbase. Prices for major items of optional equipment should be added to the base chassis-and-cab price to arrive at built-up prices. Specifications apply to basic standard chassis.

ENGINE [Scout/Metro-Mite/CM-110/C-900]: Comanche Four. Inline. OHV. (Single bank of V-8). Four-cylinder. Cast iron block with aluminum intake manifold. Bore & stroke 3-7/8 in. x 3-7/32 in. Displacement: 151.84 cid.. Compression ratio: 8.19:1. Brake horsepower: 93.4 at 4400 rpm. Net horsepower: 24.1 (NACC). Maximum Torque: 135 lbs.-ft. at 2400 rpm. Solid valve lifters. Carburetor: Downdraft.

ENGINE [C-1000/C-1110/C-1200/C-1300]: BG-241. Inline. Overhead valve. Six-cylinder. Cast iron block. Bore & stroke: 3.56 in. x 4.018 in. Displacement: 240.3 cid.. Brake horsepower: 140.8 at 3800 rpm. Net horsepower: 30.4 (NACC). Maximum Torque: 223.5 lbs.-ft. at 2000 rpm. Four main bearings. Solid valve lifters. Carburetor: Downdraft. (Optional in AB-120/AM-120/AM-130 models.)

ENGINE [AB-120/AM-120/AM-130]: BG-220. Inline. OHV. Six-cylinder. Cast iron block. Bore & stroke: 3-9/16 in. x 3-11/16 in. Displacement: 220.5 cid.. Brake horsepower: 112.5 at 3800 rpm. Net horsepower: 30.4. Maximum Torque: 194.4 lbs.-ft. at 1600-2000 rpm. Four main bearings. Solid valve lifters. Carburetor: Downdraft. (Optional in CM-75/CM-80/CM-110 models.)

ENGINE [Optional V-8]: V-266 Engine. Overhead valve. Vee-block. Eight-cylinder. Cast iron block. Bore & stroke: 3-3/8 in. x 3-7/32 in. Displacement: 154.8 cid.. Brake horsepower: 154.8 at 4400 rpm. Net horsepower: 42.1 (NACC). Maximum Torque: 227.1 lbs.-ft. at 2800 rpm. Solid valve lifters. Carburetor: Downdraft. (Optional in C-1000/C-1100/C-1200/C-1300 models.)

ENGINE [Optional V-8]: V-304 engine. Vee-block. Overhead valves. Bore & stroke: 3-7/8 in. x 3-7/32 in.. Displacement: 303.682 cid.. Brake horsepower: 193.1 at 4400 rpm. SAE horsepower: 48.1. Maximum Torque: 272.4 lbs.-ft. at 2800 rpm. Solid valve lifters. Downdraft carburetor. (First made available for C-1100/C-1200 models.)

CHASSIS [Scout Series]: Wheelbase. 100 in. Tires: [4x2] 6.50 x 15 in.; [4x4] 6.00 x 16 in.

CHASSIS [Metro-Mite Series]: Wheelbase. 96 in./102 in. Tires: [CM-75/CM-80] 6.50 x 15 in.; [CM-112] 6.70 x 15 in.

CHASSIS [AM-120 Metro]: Wheelbase. 115 in./122 in. Tires. 7.00 x 17.5 in.

CHASSIS [AM-130 Metro]: Wheelbase. 115 in./122 in./134 in. Tires. 8.00 x 17.5 in.

CHASSIS [AB-120 Metroette]: Wheelbase. 115 in. Tires. 7.00 x 17.5 in.

CHASSIS [C-900 Compact Truck]: Wheelbase. 107 in. Tires. 6.50 x 15 in.

CHASSIS [C-1000]: Wheelbase. 119 in. Tires. 6.70 x 15 in.

CHASSIS [C-1100]: Wheelbase. 115 in./119 in./131 in./140 in. Tires. 7.10 x 15 in.

CHASSIS [C-1200]: Wheelbase. 115 in./119 in./131 in./140 in. Tires. 7.00 x 17.5 in.

CHASSIS [C-1300]: Wheelbase. 122 in./131 in./134 in. Tires. 8.00 x 17.5 in.

TECHNICAL [C-900]: Manual. Synchromesh. Speeds: 3F/1R. Floor-mounted gearshift lever. Single dry disc clutch. Hypoid rear axle. Four-wheel hydraulic brakes. Steel disc wheels.

TECHNICAL [Scout]: Synchromesh transmission. Speeds: 3F/1R. Floor-mounted gearshift lever. Clutch: 10 in. diameter, single-plate, 6-spring, coil spring vibration damper. Single reduction hypoid type rear axle (2,300 lbs. capacity). Overall ratio: 4.27:1. Four-wheel hydraulic brakes. Wheels: [4x2] 15 in. disc, 4.50K rim with hubcaps; [4x4] 16 in. disc, 4.50E rim. Drivetrain options: Optional transfer case on 4x4 models controls engagement of front-whee drive and provides extra-low gear that multiplies torque power to the wheels. This unit mounted to the transmission and had a multi-ratio power divider. Three position shifting: (low) 3.333; (second) 1.851 to 1; (high) direct drive. Front axle on 4x4 models was a single-reduction type with 4.27:1 ratio. The 4x2 models used a 2,000 lbs. capacity I-beam type axle instead. Power take-off was available at extra cost for 4x4 models. Full torque type with front and rear output shafts mounted on transfer case, left side. Winch drive and mounting parts.

TECHNICAL [1/2-Ton and 3/4-Ton]: Synchromesh transmission. Speeds: 3F/1R. Floor-mounted gearshift lever. Single-plate dry disc clutch. Full-floating rear axle. Overall ratio: 4.1:1. Four-wheel drum brakes. Heavy-duty three-speed transmission and Hydra-Matic transmission optional on all models.

TECHNICAL [1-Ton]: Synchromesh transmission. Speeds: 4F/1R. Floor-mounted gearshift lever. Single dry-disc clutch. Full-floating rear axle. Overall ratio: 6.616:1. Four-wheel drum brakes. Hydra-Matic transmission optional on all models.

OPTIONS [Scout]: Panel top in lieu of standard cab ($139). R-14 Power-Lok rear axle ($38). R-23 Power-Lok rear axle ($92).

OPTIONS [Metro]: Six-cylinder engine. T-28 Metro-Matic transmission ($250). Outside rearview mirror. Grille guard. Special paint. Radio. Rear bumper. Heater.

OPTIONS: Power steering ($175). Power brakes ($61). BG-241 engine ($37). T-28 Metro-Matic transmission ($220). Outside rearview mirrors. Grille guard. Special paint. Rear bumper. Radio. Heater. Oversize tires.

OPTIONS [C-1000/C-1100/C-1200]: Power steering ($174). Power brakes ($51). 8-ft. platform except C-1000 ($186). 8-ft. stake except C-1000 ($257). V-266 engine ($118). V-304 engine for C-1100 and C-1200 ($179). V-304 LPG engine for C-1100 and C-1200 ($374). T-28 automatic transmission, except 4x4 ($244). T-15 four-speed transmission, except 4x4 ($65). T-16 transmission, C-1200 4x4 ($179). Power-Lok transmission ($60, average). Overdrive ($143). [C-1300] Power brakes ($61). 9-ft. stake ($319). 9-ft. platform ($215). V-266 engine ($118). V-304 engine ($179). V-304 LPG engine, with 4x2 only, ($370) and T-28 automatic transmission, C-1300 with 4x2 only, ($220).

HISTORICAL: Introduced November, 1963. Calendar year registrations: [All IHC truck models] 148,008. Calendar year registrations by GVW: [6,000 lbs. and under] 58,534 units; [6,001-10,000 lbs.] 15,366 units. Calendar year production: [All IHC truck models] 166,892. Market share: 10.69 percent. Innovations: New C-900 compact pickup introduced. Champagne Edition Scout released. The 304 cid. V-8 was first made available as an option for trucks under 1-ton this year. This was the fourth year in a row that IHC truck sales increased. A new 1,400,000 sq.-ft. truck plant was under construction in Springfield, Ohio. H.O. Bercher was company president. R.M. Buzard continued to head the Motor Truck Div.

1965 IHC

1965 IHC 1/2-Ton Model D-1100 Bonus Load Pickup 4x4 (RCA)

SCOUT — SERIES 800 — FOUR-CYLINDER: The 1965 Scout 800 had a new, car-like anodized aluminum grille with the word International spelled out horizontally along its center. An IH emblem was on the front of the hood. A new, permanently-fixed, leak-proof windshield made for a tighter interior. Dual variable-speed wipers were now bottom-mounted. Standard equipment included a safety-styled steering wheel, roll-down windows, tension-adjustable vent wings, rotary door locks that could be actuated from inside or outside, push-button door handles with separate key locks, suspended pedals, new Vibradamp acoustical headliner (with steel Traveltop) and sound-deadening outer door panel liners. Drip moldings were redesigned to carry water below the windows and there was a new, one-hand tailgate latch release lever. Two-stage support straps were featured on models with tailgate mounted spare tires to prevent full drop from the weight of the tire. Utility models came with hard and soft Cab Tops, Panel Tops or hard and soft Traveltops. They featured full-width rubber padded seat, all-vinyl, champagne-colored upholstery, an ashtray and a silver front bumper. Custom models came with hard and soft Cab Tops or hard and soft Traveltops. Deep contoured bucket seats were standard in Traveltop models. Other custom features included all-vinyl, champagne-colored upholstery, harmonizing vinyl-covered door panels, dual sun visors and armrests, front floor mat, cigar lighter, chrome outside rearview mirror, chrome wheel discs and chrome front bumper. There was also a new Easy View instrument panel.

METRO-MITE — CM SERIES — FOUR-CYLINDER: The Metro-Mite models were carried over from 1964 more or less intact. Changes, if any, were of a very minor nature.

METRO/METROETTE — SERIES A — SIX-CYLINDER: The full-size Metros and the Metroette milk and bakery trucks were carried over from 1964 practically without change.

LIGHT-TRUCK — D-900 — FOUR-CYLINDER: The compact size International 900 Series pickup was carried over for 1965. This truck, now called a D-900, featured the company's Bonus Load (slab-sided) look only. There was little change from last season. Even prices and weights remained the same. These trucks had a tall, flat rear end with single round taillights mounted high on the fenders. The International name was lettered across the top of the tailgate.

TRUCKS — SERIES D — SIX/V-8: International's standard 1/2-, 3/4- and 1-ton trucks were restyled up front for 1965. They had a new "electric shaver" grille with 31 vertical bars. Running horizontally across the 13 center bars was an International nameplate. These trucks came with a choice of conventional styling with flared rear fenders or Bonus Load styling and boxsides flush with the cab. Except for the new grille, they were virtually unchanged from 1964 appearances.

1965 IHC 1-Ton D-1300 Fenderside Pickup 4x4 (G. Gudeman)

I.D. DATA: Serial and engine numbers are in the same location as 1964. Numbers for 1965 had a -5 suffix to indicate model year. Numbers are not available.

Model	Body Type	Price	Weight	Prod. Total
Scout 800 — 1/4-Ton — 100 in. w.b. — 4x2				
800	Pickup 5-ft.	1720	2800	—
Scout 800 — 1/4-Ton — 100 in. w.b. — 4x4				
800	Pickup 5-ft.	2210	3000	—
Metro CM-75 — 1/2-Ton — 96 in w.b.				
CM	Metro-Mite Body	2345	2955	—

Metro CM-80 — 1/2-Ton — 96 in. w.b.				
CM	Metro-Mite Body	2370	2995	—

Metro CM-110 — 1/-Ton — 102 in. w.b.				
CM	Metro-Mite Body	2675	3345	—

Metroette AB-120 — 3/4-Ton — 115 in. w.b.				
AB-120	Milk Delivery Body	3105	4755	—

Metro AM-120 — 3/4-Ton — 115 in./122 in. w.b.				
AM-120	Metro	3070	4570	—
AM-120	Flatbad	3150	4650	—
AM-120	Metro-Van	3275	5080	—
AM-120	Metro-Lite	3790	—	—
AM-120	Metro Coach 115 in. w.b.	4440	—	—

Metro AM-130 — 1-Ton — 115 in./122 in./134 in. w.b.				
AM-130	Metro 115 in. w.b.	3270	—	—
AM-130	Flat Back 115-134 in. w.b.	3345	5050	—
AM-130	Metro-Van 115-122 in. w.b.	3475	5320	—
AM-130	Metro-Lite 122-134 in. w.b.	4050	4210	—

D-900 Trucks — 1/2-Ton — 107 in w.b.				
D-900	Chassis & Cab	1835	2875	—
D-900	Pickup 6-ft.	1950	3270	—

D-1000 Trucks — 1/2-Ton — 119 in w.b.				
D-1000	Chassis & cab	1975	3265	—
D-1000	Pickup	2100	3640	—
D-1000	Bonus Load Pickup	2110	3630	—
D-1000	Panel	2400	5150	—
D-1000	Travelall	2705	5440	—

D-1100 Trucks — 1/2-Ton — 115-131 in. w.b.				
D-1100	Chassis & Cab	2005	3290	—
D-1100	Bonus Load Pickup 119 in. w.b.	2135	3655	—
D-1100	Travelall	2730	5475	—
D-1100	Panel	2425	5185	—

D-1100 Trucks — 1/2-Ton — 119-131 in. w.b.				
D-1100	Pickup	2125	3665	—

D-1100 Trucks — 1/2-Ton — 140 in. w.b.				
D-1100	Travelette Pickup	2770	—	—
D-1100	Travelette Pickup	2630	3830	—

NOTE 1: Add $569 and 305 lbs. for 4x4 option on D-1100.

D-1200 Trucks — 3/4-Ton — 115-131 in. w.b.				
D-1200	Chassis & Cab	2125	3475	—

D-1200 Trucks — 3/4-Ton — 119 in. w.b.				
D-1200	Travelall	2855	5655	—
D-1200	Panel	2550	5365	—

D-1200 Trucks — 3/4-Ton — 119-131 in. w.b.				
D-1200	Pickup	2245	3855	—
D-1200	Bonus Load Pickup	2260	3845	—

D-1200 Trucks — 3/4-Ton — 140 in. w.b.				
D-1200	Travelette Cab	2755	4050	—
D-1200	Travelette Pickup	2895	—	—

NOTE 2: Add $609 and 410 lbs. for 4x4 D-1200.

D-1300 Trucks — 1-Ton — 122-134 in. w.b.				
D-1300	Chassis & Cab	2225	3660	—

D-1300 Trucks — 1-Ton — 131 in. w.b.				
D-1300	Pickup	2360	4090	—
D-1300	Bonus Load Pickup	2375	4080	—

NOTE 3: Add $1,123 and 745 lbs. for 4x4 D-1300.

ENGINE [Scout/Metro-Mite/CM-110/C-900]: Comanche 93. Inline. OHV. (Single bank of V-8). Four-cylinder. Cast iron block with aluminum intake manifold. Bore & stroke: 3-7/8 in. x 3-7/32 in. Displacement: 151.84 cid.. Compression ratio: 8.19:1. Brake horsepower: 93.4 at 4400 rpm. Net horsepower: 24.1 (NACC). Maximum Torque: 135 lbs.-ft. at 2400 rpm. Solid valve lifters. Carburetor: Downdraft.

ENGINE [Scout Turbo III Option]: Inline. OHV. Turbocharged. Four-cylinder. Cast iron block. Bore & stroke: 3-7/8x3-7/32 in. Displacement: 151.84 cid.. Brake horsepower: 111.3 at 4000 rpm. Maximum Torque: 166.5 lbs.-ft. at 3200 rpm.

ENGINE [C-1000/C-1100/C-1200/C-1300]: BG-241. Inline. Overhead valve. Six-cylinder. Cast iron block. Bore & stroke: 3.56 in. x 4.018 in. Displacement: 240.3 cid.. Brake horsepower: 140.8 at 3800 rpm. Net horsepower: 30.4 (NACC). Maximum Torque: 223.5 lbs.-ft. at 2000 rpm. Four main bearings. Solid valve lifters. Carburetor: Downdraft. (Optional in AB-120/AM-120/AM-130 models.)

ENGINE [AM-120/AM-130]: BG-220. Inline. OHV. Six-cylinder. Cast iron block. Bore & stroke: 3-9/16 in. x 3-11/16 in. Displacement: 220.5 cid.. Brake horsepower: 112.5 at 3800 rpm. Net horsepower: 30.4. Maximum Torque: 194.4 lbs.-ft. at 1600-2000 rpm. Four main bearings. Solid valve lifters. Carburetor: Downdraft. (Optional in CM-75/CM-80/CM-110 models.)

ENGINE [Optional V-8]: V-266 Engine. Overhead valve. Vee-block. Eight-cylinder. Cast iron block. Bore & stroke: 3-3/8 in. x 3-7/32 in. Displacement: 266.8 cid.. Brake horsepower: 154.8 at 4400 rpm. Net horsepower: 42.1 (NACC). Maximum Torque: 227.1 lbs.-ft. at 2800 rpm. Solid valve lifters. Carburetor: Downdraft. (Optional in C-1000/C-1100/C-1200/C-1300 models.)

ENGINE [Optional V-8]: V-304 engine. Vee-block. Overhead valves. Bore & stroke: 3-7/8 in. x 3-7/32 in. Displacement: 303.682 cid.. Brake horsepower: 193.1 at 4400 rpm. SAE horsepower: 48.1. Maximum Torque: 272.4 lbs.-ft. at 2800 rpm. Solid valve lifters. Downdraft carburetor. (Optional in C-1100/C-1300 models.)

CHASSIS [Scout Series]: Wheelbase: 100 in. Tires: [4x2] 6.50 x 15 in.; [4x4] 6.00 x 16 in.

CHASSIS [Metro-Mite Series]: Wheelbase: 96 in./102 in. Tires: [CM-75/CM-80] 6.50 x 15 in.; [CM-112] 6.70 x 15 in.

CHASSIS [AM-120 Metro]: Wheelbase: 115 in./122 in. Tires: 7.00 x 17.5 in.

CHASSIS [AM-130 Metro]: Wheelbase: 115 in./122 in./134 in. Tires: 8.00 x 17.5 in.

CHASSIS [AB-120 Metroette]: Wheelbase: 115 in. Tires: 7.00 x 17.5 in.

CHASSIS [C-900 Compact Truck]: Wheelbase: 107 in. Tires: 6.50 x 15 in.

CHASSIS [C-1000]: Wheelbase: 119 in. Tires: 6.70 x 15 in.

CHASSIS [C-1100]: Wheelbase: 115 in./119 in./131 in./140 in. Tires: 7.10 x 15 in.

CHASSIS [C-1200]: Wheelbase: 115 in./119 in./131 in./140 in. Tires: 7.00 x 17.5 in.

CHASSIS [C-1300]: Wheelbase: 122 in./131 in./134 in. Tires: 8.00 x 17.5 in.

TECHNICAL [C-900]: Manual. Synchromesh. Speeds: 3F/1R. Floor-mounted gearshift lever. Single dry disc clutch. Hypoid rear axle. Four-wheel hydraulic brakes. Steel disc wheels.

TECHNICAL [Scout]: Synchromesh transmission. Speeds: 3F/1R. Floor-mounted gearshift lever. Clutch: 10 in. diameter, single-plate, 6-spring, coil spring vibration damper. Single reduction hypoid type rear axle (2,300 lbs. capacity). Overall ratio: 4.27:1. Four-wheel hydraulic brakes. Wheels: [4x2] 15 in. disc. 4.50K rim with hubcaps; [4x4] 16 in. disc. 4.50E rim. Drivetrain options: Optional transfer case on 4x4 models controls engagement of front-wheel-drive and provides extra-low gear that multiplies torque power to the wheels. This unit mounted to the transmission and had a multi-ratio power divider. Three position shifting: (low) 3.333; (second) 1.851 to 1; (high) direct drive. Front axle on 4x4 models was a single-reduction type with 4.27:1 ratio. The 4x2 models used a 2,000 lbs. capacity I-beam type axle instead. Power take-off was available at extra cost for 4x4 models. Full torque type with front and rear output shafts mounted on transfer case, left side. Winch drive and mounting parts.

TECHNICAL [1/2-Ton and 3/4-Ton]: Synchromesh transmission. Speeds: 3F/1R. Floor-mounted gearshift lever. Single-plate dry-disc clutch. Full-floating rear axle. Overall ratio: 4.1:1. Four-wheel drum brakes. Heavy-duty three-speed transmission and Hydra-Matic transmission optional on all models.

TECHNICAL [1-Ton]: Synchromesh transmission. Speeds: 4F/1R. Floor-mounted gearshift lever. Single-plate dry-disc clutch. Full-floating rear axle. Overall ratio: 6.616:1. Four-wheel drum brakes. Hydra-Matic transmission optional on all models.

OPTIONS [Scout]: Steel Cab Top. Soft Cab Top. Steel Traveltop. Soft Traveltop. Steel Panel Top. (All tops were removable). Heavy-duty rear axle. Oversized tires. Undercoating. Flashing parking and taillights. Ten-gallon auxiliary gas tank. Windshield washers. Full-width upholstered rear seat. Full transistor push-button radio. Fresh air heater and defroster. Four-speed synchromesh transmission. Power take-off. Panel Top in lieu of standard Cab Top ($140). R-14 Power-Lok rear axle, all models ($40). R-23 Power-Lok rear axle, 4x4 models only ($90). Rear compartment seating for custom Traveltop models incuded custom-trim full-width seat with armrests and rear floor mat. Cushions for benches over wheelhousings, all models. Driver's or dual armrests for utility models. Silver rear bumper for custom models. Chrome rear bumper for custom models. Exterior paint options for 1965 included: (1) Champagne Metallic; (2) Aspen green; (3) Apache gold; (4) white; (5) red; (6) light yellow and (7) Moonstone blue.

OPTIONS [Metro-Mite]: Power brakes ($60). T-28 Metro-Matic transmission ($250). RA-23 rear axle on CM-75/CM-80 ($80). RA-23 rear axle on CM-110 ($50). Outside rearview mirror. Grille guard. Special paint. Radio. Rear bumper. Heater.

OPTIONS [Metro]: Power steering ($174). Overdrive ($143). Power brakes ($60). BG-241 engine ($40). BG-265 engine ($60). T-28 Metro-Matic transmission ($220). RA-11 rear axle on AM-120 ($65). Outside rearview mirror. Grille guard. Special paint. Rear bumper. Radio. Heater. Oversize tires.

OPTIONS [D-1000/D-1100/D-1200]: Power brakes ($50). V-266 engine ($120). V-304 engine ($180). V-304 LPG engine, in D-1100/1200 except Travelall ($375). BG-241 LPG engine in D-1100 4x2 models ($150). T-28 automatic transmission, except 4x4 models ($245). T-15 four-speed transmission, except 4x4 models ($65). T-16 four-speed transmission, 4x4 models only ($75). T-8 overdrive transmission, D-1000/1100 4x2 models ($145). 8-ft. platform except D-1000 ($185). 8-ft. stake except D-1000 ($205). [D-1300]: Power brakes ($60). V-266 engine ($120). V-304 engine ($180). V-304 LPG engine in D-1300 4x2 models ($370). BG-241 LPG engine, D-1300 4x2 models ($150). T-28 automatic transmission in D-1300 4x2 models. ($220). T-16 four-speed transmission in D-1300 4x4 models ($50). 9-ft. platform ($215). 9-ft. stake ($320).

HISTORICAL: Introduced October 1964. Calendar year registrations by GVW class: [6,000 lbs. or less] 58,833; [6,001 to 10,000 lbs.] 16,381. Calendar year production: [All IHC trucks] 171,638. Market share: 9.62 percent. Factory shipments: IHC shipped 64,500 trucks in the under-6,000 lbs. GVW category and 19,700 trucks in the 6,001 to 10,000 lbs. GVW category. Innovations: Improved Scout 800 models. Scout has new options including four-speed transmission with 4.07:1 rear axle, bucket seats and contoured floor covering. New turbocharged Comanche four-cylinder engine. Scout available in new Utility and Custom truck lines. Surveys taken in 1965 showed that nearly 75 percent of all Scouts were purchased primarily for non-business use and that 82 percent of these trucks were ordered with four-wheel drive. Station wagons and sports cars made up better than one-third of all trade-ins on new Scouts and nearly one-half of Scout buyers had never purchased an International product before. Production for the calendar year was an all-time high record for the Chicago-based truck-maker. Output in calendar 1965 included 26,962 gas powered four-cylinder engines. H.O. Bercher was IHC president and R.M. Buzard continued to head the company's Motor Truck Div. as executive vice-president. S.G. Johnson was engineering manager.

1966 IHC 1/4-Ton Scout 800 Sportop Utility (RCA)

SCOUT — SERIES 800 — FOUR-CYLINDER: The Scout "Sportop" models, introduced in 1966, reflected the trend toward more consumer luxury items. Interior features included bucket seats, matching rear seats, trim panels over the rear wheelhousings, a trimmed transmission console and a champagne colored interior. Later that year, a larger four-cylinder engine and a 155 hp V-8 were made available. The turbocharged Comanche III engine was also used in some 1966 models.

METRO — SERIES M — ALL ENGINES: The Metro-Mites and Metros were redesignated M models for 1966. The smaller trucks were four-cylinder models and came on two different wheelbases. Those on a 102 in. wheelbase were called M-700s and M-800s. There was also an M-1100 model with a 108 in. wheelbase. Larger Metros used the BG-220 six-cylinder powerplant. They were called M-1200s and had wheelbases between 119 and 127 in. Gross vehicle weights ranged from 4,500 to 5,500 lbs. for M-700/M-800 models and 4,500 to 6,000 lbs. for M-1100s. Also available was the larger M-1200 Metro with wheelbases of 119 to 127 in. These had GVW ratings in the 8,000 to 9,000 lbs. class.

LIGHT-TRUCK — 900A SERIES — FOUR-CYLINDER: The 900A compact pickup was again available in 1966. This was the final season for the small, four-cylinder pickup, which sold for under $2,000. Consequently, there was little change in the product. It's too bad that International didn't keep it going until the early 1970s, when the nationwide fuel shortages occurred. However, the market for such a truck simply wasn't very large in the mid-1960s. The 900A continued to use a 107 in. wheelbase and had a 4,000 lbs. GVW.

TRUCKS — SERIES A — SIX-CYLINDER: The standard size pickups for 1966 were characterized by a minor alteration to the grille. A center strip was now used to carry the International company name. It ran full-width across the trucks, from headlight to headlight. The upper sides of the box, on pickups, now carried a trim molding on fancier models. Available truck lines included the 1000A and 1100A 1/2-tons, the 1200A 3/4-ton and the 1300A 1-ton.

I.D. DATA: Serial numbers and engine numbers for all IHC vehicles were in the same locations. Numbers for 1966 had a -6 suffix to indicate model year. Numbers are not available.

1966 IHC 3/4-Ton Model 1200 A Fenderside Pickup 4x4 (OCW)

Model	Body Type	Price	Weight	Prod. Total
Scout 800 — 1/4-Ton — 100 in. w.b. — 4x2				
800	Utility Roadster	1731	2800	—
800	Utility Traveltop	1904	2900	—
800	Custom Roadster	1858	2800	—
800	Custom Traveltop	2124	2900	—
800	Sportop Soft Top	2442	2800	—
800	Sportop Hardtop	2408	2900	—
800	Utility Pickup	1802	2800	—
800	Custom Pickup	1939	2900	—
NOTE 1: Add $752 and 200 lbs. for 4x4 models.				
Metro-Mite M-700/M-800 — 1/2-Ton — 102 in w.b.				
M-700	Walk-in Panel	2549	3655	—
M-800	Walk-in Panel	2549	3705	—
Metro M-1100 — 1/2-Ton — 108 in. w.b.				
M-1100	Walk-in Panel	2883	4095	—
Metro M-1200 — 3/4-Ton — 119-127 in w.b.				
M-1200	Walk-in Panel	3249	4940	—
900A Pickup — 1/2-Ton — 4x2 — 107 in. w.b.				
900A	Chassis & Cab	1865	2875	—
900A	Pickup	1980	3210	—
1000A Trucks — 1/2-Ton — 119 in. w.b.				
1000A	Chassis & Cab	2005	3130	—
1000A	Pickup 7-ft.	2126	3500	—
1000A	Bonus Load Pickup 7-ft.	2138	—	—
1000A	Panel 7-ft.	2429	3800	—
1100A Trucks — 1/2-Ton — 115-140 in. w.b.				
1100A	Chassis & Cab	2035	3180	—
1100A Trucks — 1/2-Ton — 119-131 in. w.b.				
1100A	Pickup	2156	3550	—
1100A	Bonus Load Pickup	2168	—	—
1100A Trucks — 1/2-Ton — 119 in. w.b.				
1100A	Panel 7-ft.	2460	3850	—
1100A Trucks — 1/2-Ton — 140 in. w.b.				
1100A	Travelette Cab	2672	3625	—
1100A	Bonus Load Travelette	2811	3900	—
NOTE 2: Add $569 for 1100A 4x4.				
1000A Travelall Custom — 1/2-Ton — 119 in. w.b.				
1000A	Travelall 4x2	2766	3980	—
1100A Travelall Custom — 1/2-Ton — 119 in. w.b.				
1100A	Travelall 4x2	2796	4030	—
1100A	Travelall 4x4	3365	—	—
1200A Travelall Custom — 3/4-Ton — 119 in. w.b.				
1200A	Travelall 4x2	2913	4260	—
1200A	Travelall 4x4	3518	—	—
1200A Trucks — 3/4-Ton — 115-140 in. w.b.				
1200A	Chassis & Cab	2155	3410	—
1200A Trucks — 3/4-Ton — 119-131 in. w.b.				
1200A	Pickup	275	3780	—
1200A	Bonus Load Pickup	2287	—	—
1200A Trucks — 3/4-Ton — 119 in. w.b.				
1200A	Panel 7-ft.	2579	4080	—
1200A Truck — 3/4-Ton — 140 in. w.b.				
1200A	Travelette Cab	2791	3850	—
1200A	Bonus Load Travelette	930	4185	—
NOTE 3: Add $609 for 1200A 4x4.				
1300A Trucks — 1-Ton — 122-140 in w.b.				
1300A	Chassis & Cab	2254	3610	—
1300A Trucks — 1-Ton — 131 in. w.b.				
1300A	Pickup 8-1/2-ft.	2390	4020	—
1300A	Bonus Load Pickup 8-1/2-ft.	2402	4035	—
1300A Trucks — 1-Ton — 140 in w.b.				
1300A	Travelette Cab	2874	4055	—
1300A	Bonus Load Travelette	3016	4390	—

NOTE 4: Add $1,124 for 1300A 4x4.

ENGINE [Scout/Metro-Mite/M-1100/900A]: Comanche Four. Inline. OHV. (Single bank of V-8). Four-cylinder. Cast iron block with aluminum intake manifold. Bore & stroke: 3-7/8 in. x 3-7/32 in. Displacement: 151.84 cid.. Compression ratio: 8.19:1. Brake horsepower: 93.4 at 4400 rpm. Net horsepower: 24.1 (NACC). Maximum Torque: 135 lbs.-ft. at 2400 rpm. Solid valve lifters. Carburetor: Downdraft.

ENGINE [Scout Turbo III Option]: Inline. OHV. Turbocharged. Four-cylinder. Cast iron block. Bore & stroke: 3-7/8x3-7/32 in. Displacement: 151.84 cid.. Brake horsepower: 111.3 at 4000 rpm. Maximum Torque: 166.5 lbs.-ft. at 3200 rpm. (Also optional in M-700/M-800/M-1100/900A models in 1966.)

ENGINE [Optional Scout]: 4-196. Inline. Overhead valve. Four-cylinder. Cast iron block. Bore & stroke: 4-1/8 in. x 3-21/32 in. Displacement: 195.44 cid.. Brake horsepower: 110.8 at 4000 rpm. Net horsepower: 27.2. Maximum Torque: 180.2 lbs.-ft. at 2000 rpm. Carburetor: Single downdraft. (The 4-196 engine option was introduced in mid-1966.)

ENGINE [C-1000/C-1110/C-1200/C-1300]: BG-241. Inline. Overhead valve. Six-cylinder. Cast iron block. Bore & stroke: 3.56 in. x 4.018 in. Displacement: 240.3 cid.. Brake horsepower: 140.8 at 3800 rpm. Net horsepower: 30.4 (NACC). Maximum Torque: 223.5 lbs.-ft. at 2000 rpm. Four main bearings. Solid valve lifters. Carburetor: Downdraft. (Optional in M-1200 Metros.)

ENGINE [M-1200]: BG-220. Inline. OHV. Six-cylinder. Cast iron block. Bore & stroke: 3-9/16 in. x 3-11/16 in. Displacement: 220.5 cid.. Brake horsepower: 112.5 at 3800 rpm. Net horsepower: 30.4. Maximum Torque: 194.4 lbs.-ft. at 1600-2000 rpm. Four main bearings. Solid valve lifters. Carburetor: Downdraft. (Optional in M-700/M-800 models.)

ENGINE [Optional V-8]: V-266 Engine. Overhead valve. Vee-block. Eight-cylinder. Cast iron block. Bore & stroke: 3-3/8 in. x 3-7/32 in. Displacement: 266.76 cid.. Brake horsepower: 154.8 at 4400 rpm. Net horsepower: 42.1 (NACC). Maximum Torque: 227.1 lbs.-ft. at 2800 rpm. Solid valve lifters. Carburetor: Downdraft. (Optional in M-1200 models and in Scout at midyear.)

ENGINE [Optional V-8]: V-304 engine. Vee-block. Overhead valves. Bore & stroke: 3-7/8 in. x 3-7/32 in. Displacement: 303.682 cid.. Brake horsepower: 193.1 at 4400 rpm. SAE horsepower: 48.1. Maximum Torque: 272.4 lbs.-ft. at 2800 rpm. Solid valve lifters. Downdraft carburetor. (Optional C-1100/C-1200 models.)

CHASSIS [Series Scout 800]: Wheelbase: 100 in. Tires: [4x2] 7.35 x 15 in; [4x4] 6.00 x 16 in.

CHASSIS [Series M-700/M-800]: Wheelbase: 102 in. Tires: 7.35 x 15 in.

CHASSIS [Series M-1100]: Wheelbase: 108 in. Tires: 7.75 x 15 in.

CHASSIS [Series M-1200]: Wheelbase: 119-127 in. Tires 7.00 x 17.5 in.

CHASSIS [Series 900A]: Wheelbase: 107 in. Tires: 7.35 x 15 in.

CHASSIS [Series 1000A]: Wheelbase: 119 in. Tires: 7.75 x 15 in.

CHASSIS [Series 1100A]: Wheelbase: 115 to 140 in. Tires: 8.15 x 15 in.

CHASSIS [Series 1200A]: Wheelbase: 115-140 in. Tires: 7.00 x 17.5 in.

CHASSIS [Series 1300A]: Wheelbase: 122-140 in. Tires: 8.00 x 17.5 in.

TECHNICAL [C-900]: Manual. Synchromesh. Speeds: 3F/1R. Floor-mounted gearshift lever. Single-plate, dry-disc clutch. Hypoid rear axle. Four-wheel hydraulic brakes. Steel disc wheels.

TECHNICAL [Scout]: Synchromesh transmission. Speeds: 3F/1R. Floor-mounted gearshift lever. Clutch: 10 in. diameter, single-plate, 6-spring, coil spring vibration damper. Single reduction hypoid type rear axle (2,300 lbs. capacity). Overall ratio: 4.27:1. Four-wheel hydraulic brakes. Wheels: [4x2] 15 in. disc. 4.50K rim with hubcaps; [4x4] 16 in. disc. 4.50E rim. Drivetrain options: Optional transfer case on 4x4 models controls engagement of front-wheel-drive and provides extra-low gear that multiplies torque power to the wheels. This unit mounted to the transmission and had a multi-ratio power divider. Three position shifting: (low) 3.333; (second) 1.851 to 1; (high) direct drive. Front axle on 4x4 models was a single-reduction type with 4.27:1 ratio. The 4x2 models used a 2,000 lbs. capacity I-beam type axle instead. Power take-off was available at extra cost for 4x4 models. Full torque type with front and rear output shafts mounted on transfer case, left side. Winch drive and mounting parts.

TECHNICAL [1/2-Ton and 3/4-Ton]: Synchromesh transmission. Speeds: 3F/1R. Floor-mounted gearshift lever. Single-plate dry-disc clutch. Full-floating rear axle. Overall ratio: 4.1:1. Four-wheel drum brakes. Heavy-duty three-speed transmission and Hydra-Matic transmission optional on all models.

TECHNICAL [1-Ton]: Synchromesh transmission. Speeds: 4F/1R. Floor-mounted gearshift lever. Single-plate dry-disc clutch. Full-floating rear axle. Overall ratio: 6.616:1. Four-wheel drum brakes. Hydra-Matic transmission optional on all models.

OPTIONS [Scout]: Steel Cab Top. Soft Cab Top. Steel Traveltop. Soft Traveltop. Steel Panel Top. (All tops were removable). Heavy-duty rear axle. Oversized tires. Undercoating. Flashing parking and taillights. Ten-gallon auxiliary gas tank. Windshield washers. Full-width upholstered rear seat. Full transistor push-button radio. Fresh air heater and defroster. Four-speed synchromesh transmission. Power take-off. Panel Top in lieu of standard Cab Top ($140). R-14 Power-Lok rear axle, all models ($40). R-23 Power-Lok rear axle, 4x4 models only ($90). Rear compartment seating for custom Traveltop models incuded custom-trim full-width seat with armrests and rear floor mat. Cushions for benches over wheelhousings, all models. Driver's or dual armrests for utility models. Silver rear bumper for utility models. Chrome rear bumper for custom models.

OPTIONS [Metro-Mite]: Power brakes ($60). T-28 Metro-Matic transmission ($250). RA-23 rear axle on CM-75/CM-80 ($80). RA-23 rear axle on CM-110 ($50). Outside rearview mirror. Grille guard. Special paint. Radio. Rear bumper. Heater.

OPTIONS [Metro]: Power steering ($174). Overdrive ($143). Power brakes ($60). BG-241 engine ($40). BG-265 engine ($60). T-28 Metro-Matic transmission ($220). RA-11 rear axle on AM-120 ($65). Outside rearview mirror. Grille guard. Special paint. Rear bumper. Radio. Heater. Oversize tires.

OPTIONS [D-1000/D-1100/D-1200]: Power brakes ($50). V-266 engine ($120). V-304 engine ($180). V-304 LPG engine, in D-1100/1200 except Travelall ($375). BG-241 LPG engine in D-1100 4x2 models ($150). T-28 automatic transmission, except 4x4 models ($245). T-15 four-speed transmission, except 4x4 models ($65). T-16 four-speed transmission, 4x4 models only ($75). T-8 overdrive transmission, D-1000/1100 4x2 models ($145). 8-ft. platform except D-1000 ($185). 8-ft. stake except D-1000 ($255). [D-1300]: Power brakes ($60). V-266 engine ($120). V-304 engine ($180). V-304 LPG engine in D-1300 4x2 models ($370). BG-241 LPG engine, D-1300 4x2 models ($150). T-28 automatic transmission in D-1300 4x2 models. T-16 four-speed transmission in D-1300 4x4 models ($50). 9-ft. platform($215). 9-ft. stake($320).

HISTORICAL: Introduced: Nov.r 1, 1965. Calendar year registrations by GVW class: [6,000 lbs. or less] 62,254; [6,001 to 10,000 lbs.] 15,004. Calendar year production: [All IHC Trucks] 170,385. Market share: 9.66 percent share of market. Innovations: Scout made available in two new luxury convertible and hardtop models with bucket seats and other passenger car appointments. New, 20 percent more powerful, big six released for Scout 800 models. A new line of pickups with camper conversions introduced. New Metro series truck with aluminum bodies introduced. Scout V-8 option released at midyear. Worldwide sales of IHC trucks, service parts and service set a new record in 1966, climbing to $1.2 billion. There was a problem with parts shortages this year, resulting from lack of supplier capacity.

1966 IHC 1/4-Ton Scout 80 Traveltop Utility (RCA)

1967 IHC

1967 IHC 1/2-Ton Model 1100B Bonus Load Pickup 4x4 (RCA)

SCOUT — 800 SERIES — FOUR-CYLINDER: The 1967 Scout was similar to last year's model. It continued to be marketed in three different trim levels: Utility, Custom and Sportop. Utility models had bench seats and silver-gray front bumpers. Custom models had vinyl-covered door panels, dual sunvisors, armrests, front floor mats, a cigar lighter, chrome outside rearview mirror, chrome wheel discs and a chrome front bumper. Deep contoured bucket seats were standard in Customs with soft or all-steel full-length Travetops. The top series included the slanted-back Sportop (hard or soft), roll-down front windows with chrome moldings, wing-out rear quarter windows with chrome moldings, dual variable-speed wipers, front bucket seats, deluxe front and rear floor mats; chrome outside and inside mirrors, chrome front bumper, chrome rear bumperettes, chrome wheel discs and other luxury appointments. Promotional emphasis was placed on the V-8 model brought out late in calendar year 1966. About 50 lbs. of safety equipment was added this season to meet new government regulations. Colors available for 1967 were: Apache gold, red, Bahama blue, Alpine white, Malibu beige, Tahitian yellow and Aspen green.

METRO — SERIES M — ALL ENGINES: The light-duty IHC Metro vans came in the same series available in 1966. The M-700 and M-800 models were on the 102 in. wheelbase with standard four-cylinder power. M-1100s were on a 108 in. wheelbase with four-cylinder engines as base equipment. The larger M-1200 and MA-1200 models had a choice of

wheelbases between 119 and 134 in. The BG-220 six-cylinder engine was standard in the 1200 series models.

LIGHT-DUTY — SERIES 900A/908B — ALL-ENGINES: A new, V-8 powered compact pickup series called the 908B joined the IHC truck lineup in 1967. This truck had a slightly larger 115 in. wheelbase and came in two models. The first was a conventional pickup with flared-type rear fenders and a 6-ft. 8-in. long pickup box. The second was a slab-sided Bonus Load model with the same box. There seems to be some confusion over the continuation of the 900A series. The NADA used car guide of January 1968 showed this model being available as a 1967 truck. However, other reference books indicate the 900A went out of production after the 1966 model year. Possibly, some 1966 versions were carried over and sold as 1967s until the supply was gone.

CONVENTIONAL TRUCKS — SERIES B — SIX-CYLINDER: A new grille characterized the conventional (standard size) light-duty trucks from IHC for 1967. It featured a segmented bright metal surround over a darker appearing insert. The International name was stamped on a horizontal bar that spanned the center of the grille opening. All else was about the same as in 1966. The 1000B series included four models with 4,200 lbs. to 5,000 lbs. GVW ratings. There were eight models with GVWs of 4,700-5,800 lbs. in the 1100B lineup. Also having eight models was the 1200B series, with GVWs ranging from 5,500 to 7,300 lbs. There were four-more light-duty trucks, with 7,000 lbs. to 8,800 lbs. GVWs, in the 1300B series. The 1000B and 1100B were lighter, and heavier, 1/2-tons. The 1200B was the 3/4 ton and the 1300B was a 1-ton. IHC referred to the various models as light-, medium- and heavy- light-duty trucks which sounds a little confusing.

I.D. DATA: Serial number located on the left door pillar. The serial number consisted of 13 symbols. The first six identify the serial number. The seventh digit indicates the manufacturing plant. The last six digits are sequential production numbers. Numbers are not available. Engine numbers took the form of a prefix to the engine serial numbers. For example, a V-266 engine serial number would read V-266-000000. Engine numbers are located on machined boss on cylinder block.

1967 IHC 1/4-Ton Scout 800 Traveltop Utility 4x4 (JAG)

Model	Body Type	Price	Weight	Prod. Total
Scout 800 — 1/4 — Ton — 4x2 — 100 in w.b.				
800	Utility Roadster	1830	2850	—
800	Utility Traveltop	2043	2950	—
800	Custom Roadster	1998	2850	—
800	Custom Traveltop	2263	2950	—
800	Soft Top Sportop	2592	2850	—
800	Hardtop Sportop	2558	2950	—
800	Utility Pickup	1945	2850	—
800	Custom Pickup	2082	2950	—
Scout 800 — 1/4-Ton — 4x4 — 100 in w.b.				
800	Utility Roadster	2622	—	—
800	Utility Traveltop	2796	3615	—
800	Custom Roadster	2745	—	—
800	Custom Traveltop	3010	—	—
800	Soft Top Sportop	3344	—	—
800	Hardtop Sportop	3310	—	—
800	Utility Pickup	2715	3515	—
800	Custom Pickup	2846	—	—
Metro M-700/M-800 — 1/2-Ton — 102 in. w.b.				
M-700	Walk-in Panel	2549	3655	—
M-800	Walk-in Panel	2549	3705	—
Metro M-1100 — 1/2-Ton — 108 in. w.b.				
M-1100	Walk-in Panel	2883	4095	—
Metro M-1200 — 3/4-Ton — 119-127 in. w.b.				
M-1200	Walk-in Panel	3249	4940	—
Metro MA-1200 — 3/4-Ton — 119-134 in. w.b.				
MA-1200	Walk-in Panel	3907	—	—
900A Pickup — 1/2-Ton — 107 in. w.b. — six				
900A	Chassis & Cab	1865	2875	—
900A	Pickup 6-ft.	1980	3210	—
908B Pickup — 1/2-Ton — 115 in. w.b. — V-8				
908B	Pickup 6-ft. 8 in.	2126	3815	—
908B	Bonus Load Pickup 6-ft. 8-in.	2138	3815	—
1000B Trucks — 1/2-Ton — 119 in. w.b.				
1000B	Chassis & Cab	2182	3245	—
1000B	Pickup 7-ft.	2303	3615	—
1000B	Bonus Load Pickup 7-ft.	2315	3615	—
1000B	Panel 7-ft.	2623	3915	—
1000B Travelall Custom — 1/2-Ton — 119 in. w.b.				
1000B	Travelall 4x2	2985	5440	—
1100B Travelall Custom — 1/2-Ton — 119 in. w.b.				
1100B	Travelall 4x2	2980	5475	—
1100B	Travelall 4x4	3600	—	—

1200B Travelall Custom — 3/4-Ton — 119 in. w.b.

1200B	Travelall 4x2	3110	5655	—
1200B	Travelall 4x4	3600	5990	—

1100B Trucks — 1/2-Ton — 115-140 in w.b.

1100B	Chassis & Cab	2139	3225	—
1100B	Pickup 6.75-ft.	2260	3595	—
1100B	Bonus Load Pickup 6.75-ft.	2272	3595	—
1100B	Pickup 8.5-ft.	2292	3675	—
1100B	Bonus Load Pickup 8-ft.	2304	3660	—
1100B	Panel 7-ft.	2612	3895	—
1100B	Travelette Cab	2846	3670	—
1100B	Bonus Load Travelette 6-ft.	2985	4005	—

NOTE 1: Add $569 for Series 1100B 4x4s.

1200B Trucks — 3/4-Ton — 119-166 in. w.b.

1200B	Chassis & Cab	2309	3460	—
1200B	Pickup 7-ft.	2430	3830	—
1200B	Bonus Load Pickup 7-ft.	2442	3830	—
1200B	Pickup 8.5-ft.	2462	3900	—
1200B	Bonus Load Pickup 8-ft.	2474	3885	—
1200B	Panel 7-ft.	2750	4130	—
1200B	Travelette Cab	2984	3895	—
1200B	Bonus Load Travelette 6-ft.	3123	4230	—

NOTE 2: Add $606 for Series 1200B 4x4s.

1300B Trucks — 1-Ton — 131-156 in. w.b.

1300B	Chassis & Cab	2419	3671	—
1300B	Pickup 8.5-ft.	2545	4196	—
1300B	Travelette Cab	3066	4196	—
1300B	Bonus Load Travelette 6-ft.	3208	4435	—

NOTE 3: Add $1,123 for Series 1300 B 4x4s.
NOTE 4: Factory prices for V-8 if offered; deduct $62 for six-cylinder.

ENGINE [Base: Scout 800/M-700/M-800/M-1100/900A]: 4-152. Inline. OHV. Four-cylinder. Cast iron block. Bore & stroke: 3-7/8 in. x 3-7/32 in. Displacement: 151.84 cid.. Compression ratio: 8.19:1. Brake horsepower: 93 at 4400 rpm. Net horsepower: 24.1. Maximum Torque: 143 lbs.-ft. at 2400 rpm. Hydraulic valve lifters. Carburetor: Holley 1904 model 3479 single-barrel.

ENGINE [Optional: Scout 800]: Turbo III. Inline. OHV. Turbocharged. Four-cylinder. Cast iron block. Bore & stroke: 3-7/8 in. x 3-7/32 in. Displacement: 151.84 cid.. Compression ratio: 8.19:1. Brake horsepower: 111 at 4000 rpm. Maximum Torque: 166 lbs.-ft. at 3200 rpm. Hydraulic valve lifters. Carburetor: Holley 1904 model 3862 single-barrel.

ENGINE [Optional Scout]: 4-196. Inline. OHV. Four-cylinder. Cast iron block. Bore & stroke: 4-1/8 in. x 3-21/32 in. Displacement: 195.44 cid.. Compression ratio: 8.1:1. Brake horsepower: 111 at 4000 rpm. Net horsepower: 27.2. Maximum Torque: 180 lbs.-ft. at 2000 rpm. Hydraulic valve lifters. Carburetor: Holley 1904 model 3716 single-barrel.

ENGINE [Base: M-1200/MA-1200]: BG-220. Inline. Overhead Valve. Six-cylinder. Cast iron block. Bore & stroke: 3-9/16 in. x 3-11/16 in. Displacement: 220.5 cid.. Compression ratio: 7.5:1. Brake horsepower: 112.5 at 3800 rpm. Net horsepower: 30.4. Maximum Torque: 194.4 lbs.-ft. at 2000 rpm. Solid valve lifters (barrel-type). Carburetor: Holley model 1904 single-barrel. (Optional: M-700/M-800/M-1100).

ENGINE [Base: 1000B/1100B/1200B/1300B]: BG-241. Inline. Overhead valve. Six-cylinder. Cast iron block. Bore & stroke: 3.56 in. x 4.018 in. Displacement: 240.3 cid.. Compression ratio: 7.5:1. Brake horsepower: 140.8 at 3800 rpm. Net horsepower: 30.4. Maximum Torque: 223.5 lbs.-ft. at 2000 rpm. Solid valve lifters (barrel-type). Carburetor: Holley single barrel model 1904. (Optional: M-1200/MA-1200 Metro models.)

ENGINE [Optional/V-266]: Vee block. OHV. Eight-cylinder. Cast iron block. Bore & stroke: 3-3/8 in. x 3-7/32 in. Displacement: 266.76 cid.. Compression ratio: 8.4:1. Brake horsepower: 155 at 4400 rpm. Net horsepower: 42.1. Maximum Torque: 227.1 lbs.-ft. at 2800 rpm. Hydraulic valve lifters. Carburetor: Holley 2300 model 1710 two-barrel. (Optional in Scout 800/M-1200/MA-1200/908B/1000B/1100B/1200B/1300B).

CHASSIS [Scout 800 Series]: Wheelbase: 100 in. Tires 7.35 x 15 in.

CHASSIS [Series M-700/M-800]: Wheelbase: 102 in. Tires: 7.35 x 15 in.

CHASSIS [Series M-1100]: Wheelbase: 108 in. Tires: 7.75 x 15 in.

CHASSIS [Series M-1200/MA-1200]: Wheelbase: 119-134 in. Tires: 7.00 x 17.5 in.

CHASSIS [Series 900A]: Wheelbase: 107 in. Tires: 7.35 x 15 in.

CHASSIS [Series 908B]: Wheelbase: 115 in. Tires: 7.75 x 15 in.

CHASSIS [Series 1000B]: Wheelbase: 119 in. Tires: 8.15 x 15 in.

CHASSIS [Series 1100B]: Wheelbase: 115/118/131/140 in. Tires: 8.15 x 15 in.

CHASSIS [Series 1200B]: Wheelbase: 115/119/131/140 in. Tires: 7.00 x 17.5 in.

CHASSIS [Series 1300B]: Wheelbase: 122/131/140 in. [4x4] wheelbase: 120, 129 and 132 in. Tires: 8.00 x 17.5 in.

1967 IHC 1/4-Ton Scout 800 Traveltop Utility 4x4 (JAG)

TECHNICAL: Manual synchromesh transmission. Speeds: 3F/1R or 4F/1R. Floor-mounted gearshift lever. Hydraulic clutch. Single-reduction rear axle. Overall ratio: Various. Hydraulic four-wheel brakes. Disc wheels. Drivetrain options: Automatic transmission. Overdrive. Transmissions used in IHC trucks were identified by an AT or T code listed on the vehicle inspection card attached to left sun visor. The T-1 and T-2 transmissions were produced by IHC. Models T-4 through T-16 were made by Borg-Warner. The T-17 and T-18 models were by New Process. Models T-30 through T-39 were made by Fuller.

OPTIONS [Scout 800 Series]: White sidewall tires. Solid state radio. Fresh air heater-defroster. Parking and taillight flasher switch. Ten gallon auxiliary gas tank. Windshield washer. Heavy-duty axles, springs, tires and other special equipment. Rear compartment seating for Traveltop models. Cushions for wheelhouse benches. Driver's or dual armrests for Utility models. Silver gray rear bumper for Utility models. Chrome rear bumper for Custom models. Undercoating.

OPTIONS [Metro Series]: Grille guard. Rear bumper. Outside rearview mirror or mirrors. Radio. Special paint. Oversize tires. Overdrive ($200). Power steering. Automatic transmission. Metro-Matic transmissions ($211). Four-speed transmission.

OPTIONS [Series 908B]: Rear bumper. Radio. Fresh-air heater-defroster. White sidewall tires. Outside rearview mirror(s). Special paint.

OPTIONS: Whitewall tires. Rear Bumper. Power steering. Roof rack [Travelall]. Deluxe interior appointments. Custom interior package. Bumper guards. Transistor radio. Fresh-air heater and defroster. Clock. Cigar lighter. Radio antenna. Seat covers. Outside rearview mirror(s). Custom exterior trim. Wheel trim rings. Two-tone paint. California towing mirrors. Oversize tires. Vinyl top (Travelall). Foam rubber seat cushions. Pickup box rails. Automatic transmission. Four-speed transmission.

HISTORICAL: Introduced: Nov. 1, 1966. Calendar year registrations by GVW class: [6,000 lbs. or less] 62,148; [6,001 to 10,000 lbs.] 13,579. Calendar year production: [All IHC trucks] 167,940. Market share: 10.59 percent. Innovations: New compact V-8 powered pickup truck line introduced. Revised styling on B series conventional trucks. Safety features added to some models to satisfy new government standards. Worldwide sales by IHC in fiscal-year 1967 topped the $2.5 billion mark for the second year in a row. Truck sales were down five percent from 1966's all-time record. H.O. Bercher continued as company president, while R.O. Musgjerd took over as general manager of the Motor Truck Div.

1967 IHC 1/4-Ton Scout 800 Traveltop Utility 4x4 (S. Soloy)

1968 IHC

1968 IHC 1/2-Ton Model 1100C Travelall 4x4 (RCA)

SCOUT — 800 SERIES — FOUR-CYLINDER: Any changes in the 1968 Scout were of a minor nature. The Custom roadster, Sportop hardtop and Custom pickup disappeared as separate models. Engine offerings included the 152 cid four-cylinder as base equipment and the 196 cid four-cylinder and 266 cid V-8 as options. The turbocharged four-cylinder option was discontinued. Standard equipment followed the 1967 pattern.

METRO — SERIES M — ALL ENGINES: Models in the lighter-capacity Metro Series were basically unchanged, but the M-700 model was discontinued. The M-800, M-1100, M-1200 and MA-1200 models continued to be available. The trucks in the M-1200 series had a base six-cylinder engine, while the others came standard with the Scout's Comanche slant four.

CONVENTIONAL LIGHT TRUCKS — SERIES C — ALL ENGINES: The biggest change in IHC's 1968 conventional light trucks seems to be that the IH badge was removed from the hood above the grille center. Travelall models could also be had with a contrast panel on the rear-quarter panels, between the chrome belt moldings and with chrome moldings extending across the doors and front fendersides.

I.D. DATA: Serial number located on the left door pillar. The serial number consisted of 13 symbols. The first six identify the serial number. The seventh digit indicates the manufacturing plant. The last six digits are sequential production numbers. Numbers are not available. Engine numbers took the form of a prefix to the engine serial numbers. For example, a V-266 engine serial number would read V-266-000000. Engine numbers are located on machined boss on cylinder block.

1968 IHC 1/4-Ton Scout 800 Sport Utility 4x4 (DFW)

Model	Body Type	Price	Weight	Prod. Total
Scout 800 — 1/4-Ton 4x4 — 100 in w.b.				
800	Utility Roadster	2875	3465	—
800	Traveltop Utility	3048	3615	—
800	Traveltop Custom	3263	3615	—
800	Softop Spor ttop	3492	3515	—
800	Utility Pickup	2973	—	—

NOTE 1: Scout price and weights for 4x4s with V-8.

Model	Body Type	Price	Weight	Prod. Total
Metro M-800 — 1/2-Ton — 102 in. w.b.				
M-800	Walk-in Panel 7-ft.	2876	3660	—
Metro M-1100 — 1/2-Ton — 108 in. w.b.				
M-1100	Walk-in Panel 8-ft.	3271	3830	—
Metro M-1200 — 3/4-Ton — 119/134 in. w.b.				
M-1200	Walk-in Panel 9.75-ft.	3739	5005	—
MA-1200	Walk-in Panel 9-ft.	4170	4475	—

NOTE 2: M-1200/MA-1200 prices include base V-8.

Model	Body Type	Price	Weight	Prod. Total
908C Pickup — 1/2-Ton — 115 in. w.b.				
908C	Pickup 6-ft. 8 in.	2451	3815	—
908C	Bonus Load Pickup 6-ft. 8 in.	2463	3815	—
1000C Trucks — 1/2-Ton — 119 in. w.b.				
1000C	Chassis & Cab	2444	3245	—
1000C	Pickup 7-ft.	2564	3625	—
1000C	Bonus Load Pickup 7-ft.	2576	3625	—
1000C	Panel 7-ft.	2968	3915	—
1000C Travelall — 1/2-Ton — 119 in. w.b.				
1000C	Travelall 4x2	3170	5440	—
1100C Travelall Custom — 1/2-Ton — 119 in. w.b.				
1100C	Travelall 4x2	3160	5475	—
1100C	Travelall 4x4	3785	—	—
1200C Travelall Custom — 3/4-Ton — 119 in. w.b.				
1200C	Travelall 4x2	3240	5655	—
1200C	Travelall 4x4	3880	5990	—
1100C Trucks — 1/2-Ton — 115-140 in. w.b.				
1100C	Chassis & Cab	2398	3225	—
1100C	Pickup 6.75-ft.	2519	3585	—
1100C	Bonus Load Pickup 6-ft. 8 in.	2531	3585	—
1100C	Pickup 8.75-ft	2651	3675	—
1100C	Bonus Load Pickup 8-ft. 6 in.	2563	3660	—
1100C	Panel 7-ft.	2900	3895	—
1100C	Travelette Cab	3105	3670	—
1100C	Bonus Load Travelette 6-ft.	3244	4005	—

NOTE 3: Add $569 for 4x4s.

Model	Body Type	Price	Weight	Prod. Total
1200C Trucks — 3/4-Ton — 119-166 in. w.b.				
1200C	Chassis & Cab	2531	3460	—
1200C	Pickup 7-ft.	2651	3830	—
1200C	Bonus Load Pickup 7-ft.	2663	3830	—
1200C	Pickup 8.5-ft.	2684	3900	—
1200C	Bonus Load Pickup 8-ft.	2696	3885	—
1200C	Panel 7-ft.	3000	4130	—
1200C	Travelette Cab	3205	3895	—
1200C	Bonus Load Travelette 6-ft.	3344	4230	—

NOTE 4: Add $609 for 4x4s.

Model	Body Type	Price	Weight	Prod. Total
1300C Trucks — 1-Ton — 131-156 in. w.b.				
1300C	Chassis & Cab	2613	3675	—
1300C	Pickup 8-ft. 6 in.	2739	4100	—
1300C	Travelette Cab	3261	4100	—
1300C	Bonus Load Travelette 6-ft.	3403	4435	—

NOTE 5: Add $1,123 for 4x4s.
NOTE 6: All truck prices/weights are for V-8 models.

1968 IHC 3/4-Ton Model 1200C Travelette Pickup 4x4 (RCA)

ENGINE [Base: Scout 800/M-700/M-800/M-1100/900A]: 4-152. Inline. OHV. Four-cylinder. Cast iron block. Bore & stroke: 3-7/8 in. x 3-7/32 in. Displacement: 151.84 cid.. Compression ratio: 8.19:1. Brake horsepower: 93 at 4400 rpm. Net horsepower: 24.1. Maximum Torque: 143 lbs.-ft. at 2400 rpm. Hydraulic valve lifters. Carburetor: Holley 1904 model 3479 single-barrel.
ENGINE [Optional Scout]: 4-196. Inline. OHV. Four-cylinder. Cast iron block. Bore & stroke: 4-1/8 in. x 3-21/32 in. Displacement: 195.44 cid. Compression ratio: 8.1:1. Brake horsepower: 111 at 4000 rpm. Net horsepower: 27.2. Maximum Torque: 180 lbs.-ft. at 2000 rpm. Hydraulic valve lifters. Carburetor: Holley 1904 model 3716 single-barrel.
ENGINE [Base: M-1200/MA-1200]: BG-220. Inline. Overhead Valve. Six-cylinder. Cast iron block. Bore & stroke: 3-9/16 in. x 3-11/16 in. Displacement: 220.5 cid.. Compression ratio: 7.5:1. Brake horsepower: 112.5 at 3800 rpm. Net horsepower: 30.4. Maximum Torque: 194.4 lbs.-ft. at 2000 rpm. Solid valve lifters (barrel-type). Carburetor: Holley model 1904 single-barrel. (Optional: M-700/M-800/M-1100.)
ENGINE [Base: 1000B/1100B/1200B/1300B]: BG-241. Inline. Overhead valve. Six-cylinder. Cast iron block. Bore & stroke: 3.56 in. x 4.018 in. Displacement: 240.3 cid.. Compression ratio: 7.5:1. Brake horsepower: 140.8 at 3800 rpm. Net horsepower: 30.4. Maximum Torque: 223.5 lbs.-ft. at 2000 rpm. Solid valve lifters (barrel-type). Carburetor: Holley single-barrel model 1904. (Optional: M-1200/MA-1200 Metro models.)
ENGINE [Optional/V-266]: Vee block. OHV. Eight-cylinder. Cast iron block. Bore & stroke: 3-3/8 in. x 3-7/32 in. Displacement: 266.76 cid.. Compression ratio: 8.4:1. Brake horsepower: 155 at 4400 rpm. Net horsepower: 42.1. Maximum Torque: 227.1 lbs.-ft. at 2800 rpm. Hydraulic valve lifters. Carburetor: Holley 2300 model 1710 two-barrel. (Optional in Scout 800/M-1200/MA-1200/908B/1000B/1100B/1200B/1300B).
CHASSIS [Scout 800]: Wheelbase: 100 in. Tires 7.35 x 15 in.
CHASSIS [M-700/M-800]: Wheelbase: 102 in. Tires: 7.35 x 15 in.
CHASSIS [M-1100]: Wheelbase: 108 in. Tires: 7.00 x 15 in.
CHASSIS [M-1200/MA-1200]: Wheelbase: 119-134 in. Tires: 7.00 x 17.5 in.
CHASSIS [900A]: Wheelbase: 107 in. Tires: 7.35 x 15 in.
CHASSIS [908B]: Wheelbase: 115 in. Tires: 7.75 x 15 in.
CHASSIS [1000B]: Wheelbase: 119 in. Tires: 8.15 x 15 in.
CHASSIS [1100B]: Wheelbase: 115/118/131/140 in. Tires: 8.15 x 15 in.
CHASSIS [1200B]: Wheelbase: 115/119/131/140 in. Tires: 7.00 x 17.5 in.
CHASSIS [1300B]: (4x2) wheelbase: 122/131/140 in.; (4x4) wheelbase: 120/129/132 in. Tires: 8.00 x 17.5 in.
TECHNICAL: Manual synchromesh transmission. Speeds: 3F/1R or 4F/1R. Floor-mounted gearshift lever. Hydraulic clutch. Single-reduction rear axle. Overall ratio: Various. Hydraulic four-wheel brakes. Disc wheels. Drivetrain options: Automatic transmission. Overdrive. Transmissions used in IHC trucks were identified by an AT or T code listed on the vehicle inspection card attached to the left sun visor. The T-1 and T-2 transmissions were produced by IHC. Models T-4 through T-16 were made by Borg-Warner. The T-17 and T-18 models were by New Process. Models T-30 through T-39 were made by Fuller.

1968 IHC 1/2-Ton Model 1100C Custom Travelall (S. Soloy)

OPTIONS [Scout 800 Series]: White sidewall tires. Solid state radio. Fresh air heater-defroster. Parking and taillight flasher switch. Ten gallon auxiliary gas tank. Windshield washer. Heavy-duty axles, springs, tires and other special equipment. Rear compartment seating for Traveltop models. Cushions for wheelhouse benches. Driver's or dual armrests for Utility models. Silver gray rear bumper for Utility models. Chrome rear bumper for Custom models. Undercoating.
OPTIONS [Metro Series]: Grille guard. Rear bumper. Outside rearview mirror or mirrors. Radio. Special paint. Oversize tires. Overdrive ($200). Power steering. Automatic transmission. Metro-Matic transmissions ($211). Four-speed transmission.
OPTIONS [Series 908B]: Rear bumper. Radio. Fresh-air heater-defroster. White sidewall tires. Outside rearview mirror(s). Special paint.
OPTIONS: Whitewall tires. Rear Bumper. Power steering. Roof rack [Travelall]. Deluxe interior appointments. Custom interior package. Bumper guards. Transistor radio. Fresh-air heater and defroster. Clock. Cigar lighter. Radio antenna. Seat covers. Outside rearview mirror(s). Custom exterior trim. Wheel trim rings. Two-tone paint. California towing mirrors. Oversize tires. Vinyl top (Travelall). Foam rubber seat cushions. Pickup box rails. Automatic transmission. Four-speed transmission.

HISTORICAL: Introduced Nov. 1, 1967. Calendar year registrations by GVW: [6,000 lbs. or less] 48,200; [6,001-10,000 lbs.] 20,461. Calendar year production: [All IHC trucks] 145,549. By 1968, the 200,000th IHC Scout had been built at the Fort Wayne, Ind. factory. Worldwide sales of trucks in fiscal 1968 were up 2.5 percent from the previous year.

1968 IHC 3/4-Ton Model 1200C Bonus Load Pickup 4x4 (RCA)

1969-1970 IHC

1969 IHC 1/4-Ton Scout 800A Sport Utility 4x4 (JAG)

1969 IHC 1/2-Ton Model 1100D Bonus Load Pickup 4x4 (RCA)

SCOUT — SERIES 800A — FOUR-CYLINDER: 1969 was a year for special limited-edition versions of the Scout. The new Scout Aristocrat featured two-tone metallic paint, wide tires, chrome wheels, a padded and carpeted interior and special coachman roof rack. IHC promoted this model as a classic in its own time. External changes for 1969 models included squarish, chrome trimmed headlight housings. The International nameplate on the mesh grille was smaller in size and moved to the lower left-hand corner. Round side-marker reflectors appeared on the front and rear fendersides. Some other changes included an enlarged window area in steel Traveltops; energy-absorbing steering column; refined

steering mechanism; broader power range; new 304 cid V-8 option; aluminized muffler; softer, lower-rate rear springs; and factory installed rear step bumper. Standard equipment consisted of padded dash and sun visors; seat belts on all seats; safety door latches; four-way emergency flashers; windshield washer; variable-speed wipers with non-glare arms; fresh air heater and defroster; inside and outside mirrors, back-up lights; front and rear side relfectors; dual brake system; self-adjusting brakes with heavy-duty linings; and 3,500 lbs. capacity rear axle. Interior appointments included black vinyl bench seat; insulated rubber floor mat; ashtray; and driver's armrest. A silver-gray front bumper was standard. Colors available included Alpine white, Plum metallic, red, medium blue metallic, Lime green metallic, Copper metallic and gold metallic. These models were carried over, basically without change, for 1970.

METRO — SERIES M — FOUR-CYLINDER: In 1969, the 196 cid four-cylinder engine (4-196) was made standard equipment for all light-duty Metro Vans. Only three models under 1-ton were available. Their GVW ratings were as follows: M-1100 (5,500-6,000 lbs.); M-1200 (8,000 lbs.) and MA-1200 (9,000 lbs.). Additional government mandated safety features were made standard equipment. These models were carried over, basically without change, for 1970.

CONVENTIONAL LIGHT TRUCKS — SERIES D — ALL ENGINES: All-new styling was seen for conventional light-duty IHC trucks in 1969. The new look was patterned after the design of the Scout with slab-sided fenders, a flat wide hood, Scout-like grille and squarer "greenhouse" area. Other changes included the addition of side safety lights and, usually, the use of contrasting lower bodyside panels. There were four model lines. The 1000D models had 115 to 131 in. wheelbases and 4,800-5,400 lbs. GVW ratings. Then came the 1100Ds, with the same wheelbase and GVWs. The 1200D trucks had 115 to 164 in. wheelbases and a 6,100-7,500 lbs. GVW range. Rated for 7,000 lbs.-10,000 lbs. GVWs were the 1300Ds on wheelbases of 131-156 in.

1969 IHC 1/2-Ton Model 1100D Travelall 4x4 (RCA)

I.D. DATA: Serial number located on the left door pillar. The serial number consisted of 13 symbols. The first six identify the serial number. The seventh digit indicates the manufacturing plant. The last six digits are sequential production numbers. Numbers are not available. Engine numbers took the form of a prefix to the engine serial numbers. For example, a V-266 engine serial number would read V-266-000000. Engine numbers are located on machined boss on cylinder block.

1969 IHC 1/2-Ton Model 1100D Custom Travelall (JAG)

Model	Body Type	Price	Weight	Prod. Total
Scout 800A — 4x4 — 100 in. w.b.				
800A	Roadster	3040	3465	—
800A	Pickup	3139	3515	—
800A	Traveltop	3213	3615	—

NOTE 1: Prices and weights for 1969 4x4 with V-8.
NOTE 2: Prices for comparable 1970 models average $193 higher.
NOTE 3: Weights for comparable 1970 models average 310 lbs. lighter.

Model	Body Type	Price	Weight	Prod. Total
Metro M-1100 — 4x2 — 108 in. w.b.				
M-1100	Walk-in Panel 8-ft.	3446	3830	
Metro M-1200 — 4x2 — 119-134 in. w.b.				
M-1200	Walk-in Panel 9.75-ft.	3893	5157	
MA-1200	Walk-in Panel 9-ft.	4372	4627	

NOTE 4: M/MA-1200 prices/weights include optional V-304 V-8 engine.
NOTE 5: 1970 prices about $107 higher.
NOTE 6: Weights for 1970 models were the same as 1969.

1000D Trucks — 4x2 — 115-131 in. w.b.

Model	Body Type			
1000D	Chassis & Cab	2524	3417	—
1000D	Pickup 6-1/2-ft.	2645	3777	—
1000D	Bonus Load Pickup 6-1/2-ft.	2683	3777	—
1000D	Panel 7-ft.	3158	4087	—
1000D	Pickup 8-ft.	2682	3827	—
1000D	Bonus Load Pickup 8-ft.	2721	3852	—

1100D Trucks — 4x2 — 115-131 in. w.b.

Model	Body Type			
1100D	Chassis & Cab	2479	3397	—
1100D	Pickup 6.5-ft.	2599	3757	—
1100D	Bonus Load Pickup 6.5-ft.	2638	3757	—
1100D	Panel 7-ft.	3113	4067	—
1100D	Pickup 8-ft.	2637	3807	—
1100D	Bonus Load Pickup 8-ft.	2675	3832	—

NOTE 7: Add for 1100D 4x4 models.

1000D Travelall — 1/2-Ton — 119 in. w.b.

Model	Body Type			
1000D	Travelall 4x2	3315	5440	—

1100D Travelall Custom — 1/2-Ton — 119 in. w.b.

Model	Body Type			
1100D	Travelall 4x2	3270	5475	—
1100D	Travelall 4x4	3940	—	—

1200D Travelall Custom — 3/4-Ton — 119 in. w.b.

Model	Body Type			
1200D	Travelall 4x2	3410	5655	—
1200D	Travelall 4x4	3940	5990	—

1200D Trucks — 4x2 — 115-164 in. w.b.

Model	Body Type			
1200D	Chassis & Cab	2564	3410	—
1200D	Pickup 6.5-ft.	2685	3720	—
1200D	Bonus Load Pickup 6.5-ft.	2724	3720	—
1200D	Panel 7-ft.	3198	4080	—
1200D	Pickup 8-ft.	2722	3820	—
1200D	Bonus Load Pickup 8-ft.	2761	3836	—
1200D	Travelette Cab	3226	3815	—
1200D	Travelette Pickup 6.5-ft.	3394	4025	—
1200D	Bonus Load Travelette 8-ft.	3544	4225	—

NOTE 8: Add for 1200D 4x4 models.

1300D — 4x2 — 134-156 in. w.b.

Model	Body Type			
1300D	Chassis & Cab	2749	3635	—
1300D	Pickup 9-ft.	2880	4306	—
1300D	Travelette Cab	3384	4261	—
1300D	Bonus Load Travelette 6.5-ft.	3544	4621	—

NOTE 9: Add for 1300D 4x4 models.
NOTE 10: Prices above for 4x2 trucks with conventional drive and 304 cid V-8.
NOTE 11: [1000D] 1970 prices average $142 higher ($209 panel); weights same.
NOTE 12: [1100D] 1970 prices average $146 higher ($212 panel); weights same.
NOTE 13: [1200D] 1970 prices average $160 higher ($228 panel); weights same.
NOTE 14: [Series 1300D] 1970 prices average $184 more; weights vary slightly.

1969 IHC 1/4-Ton Scout 800A Sport Utility (RCA)

1969 IHC 1/2-Ton Model 1100D Custom Bonus Load Pickup (JAG)

Standard Catalog of Light-Duty Trucks

ENGINE [Optional]: Vee-block, OHV. Eight-cylinder. Cast iron block. Bore & stroke: 3-7/8 in. x 3-7/32 in. Displacement: 304 cid.. Compression ratio: 8.19:1 in. Brake horsepower: 180 at 4400 rpm. Net horsepower: 48.1. Maximum Torque: 262 lbs.-ft. at 2400 rpm. Hydraulic valve lifters. Carburetor: Holley model 2300G. (This was the only optional engine for 1969 Scouts.)

ENGINE [1000D]: Model PT-6-232. Inline, OHV. Six-cylinder. Cast iron block. Bore & stroke: 33/4 in. x 3-1/2 in. Displacement: 232 cid.. Compression ratio: 8.5:1. Brake horsepower: 145 at 4300 rpm. Maximum Torque: 215 lbs.-ft. at 1600 rpm. Hydraulic valve lifters. Carburetor: Single Barrel. (This new six-cylinder engine was used in 1000D models and 1100D 4x4s.)

ENGINE [1100D]: The BG-241 six-cylinder engine was standard in 4x2 models in the 1100D Series. (Standard 1200/1300D Series.)

ENGINE: The V-266 V-8, was standard in the 1200D and 1300D models with conventional 4x2 or optional 4x4 drivetrains. See 1967 engine specifications.

ENGINE [Optional]: Available options for 1969 IHC trucks included the BG-265 six-cylinder and V-304 V-8. See 1968 engines for more data.

1970 IHC 3/4-Ton AM-1200 Metro Van (DFW)

CHASSIS [Scout Series 800A]: Wheelbase: 100 in. Tires: [1969] 7.35 x 15 in.; [1970] E78 x 15 in.

CHASSIS [Series M-1100]: Wheelbase: 108 in. Tires: 7.00 x 15 in.

CHASSIS [Series M-1200/MA-1200]: Wheelbase: 119 to 134 in. Tires: 7.00 x 17.5 in.

CHASSIS [Series 1000D]: Wheelbase: 115-131 in. Tires: [1969] 8.25 x 15 in.; [1970] G78 x 15 in.

CHASSIS [Series 1100D]: Wheelbase: 115-131 in. Tires: [1969] 8.25 x 15 in.; [1970] G78 x 15 in.

CHASSIS [Series 1200D]: Wheelbase: 115-164 in. Tires: 8.00 x 16.5 in.

CHASSIS [Series 1300D]: Wheelbase: 134-156 in. Tires: 8.00 x 16.5 in.

1970 IHC 1/2-Ton Model 1100D Bonus Load Pickup 4x4 (RCA)

TECHNICAL: Manual synchromesh transmission. Speeds: 3F/1R or 4F/1R. Floor-mounted gearshift lever. Hydraulic clutch. Single-reduction rear axle. Overall ratio: Various. Hydraulic four-wheel brakes. Disc wheels. Drivetrain options: Automatic transmission. Overdrive. Transmissions used in IHC trucks were identified by an AT or T code listed on the vehicle inspection card attached to left sun visor. The T-1 and T-2 transmissions were produced by IHC. Models T-4 through T-16 were made by Borg-Warner. The T-17 and T-18 models were by New Process. Models T-30 through T-39 were made by Fuller.

1970 IHC Metro Forward-Control Interior (DFW)

OPTIONS [Scout Series]: Chrome front bumper. Solid-state push-button radio. Eight-track stereo tape player. Radio antenna package. Dash courtesy lamps. Rear seat for custom Traveltop and Roadster models. Inside or outside spare tire mounting. Wheelwell covers/seats (models without rear seat). Four-speed transmission. Limited-slip differential. Factory installed integral utility step-bumper and trailer hitch. Dual 10-gallon auxiliary fuel tanks. Increased capacity electrical system. Dual electric horns. Skid plate. Front wheel locking hubs for all-wheel drive. Increased capacity cooling for four-cylinder engine. Engine governor and hand throttle. Transfer case mounted power-take-off. Chrome full wheel discs. Silver-gray rear bumper. Front tow hook. Rear tow loop. Various sizes of tires and rims. Custom interior package including: color interior; bucket seats in black vinyl; matching padded door panels; dual armrests; textured vinyl front floor mat; cigar lighter and headliner in Traveltop models. Aristocrat trim package.

OPTIONS [Metro Series]: Grille guard. Rear bumper. Outside rearview mirror or mirrors. Radio. Special paint. Oversize tires. Overdrive ($200). Power steering. Automatic transmission. Metro-Matic transmissions ($211). Four-speed transmission.

OPTIONS [Series 908B]: Rear bumper. Radio. Fresh-air heater-defroster. White sidewall tires. Outside rearview mirror(s). Special paint.

OPTIONS [Conventional Light Trucks]: Outside rearview mirror(s). Dual California trailer mirrors. Custom exterior trim package. Full wheel discs. Camper package ($69). Wheel trim rings. Foam rubber seat cushions. Tinted-glass. Air conditioning. Solid-state push-button radio. Eight-track tape player. Antenna package. Roof rack. High-side pickup box package. Pickup box rails. Rear bumper. Whitewall tires. Power steering. Power brakes. Back-up lights. Auxiliary gas tank. Spare tire. Automatic transmission. Four-speed manual transmission.

HISTORICAL: Introduced November, 1968. Calendar year registrations by GVW Class: (1969) [6,000 lbs. or less] 41,174; [6,001-10,000 lbs.] 18,634. (1970) [6,000 lbs. or less] 44,713; [6,001-10,000 lbs.] 19,764. Calendar year production all IHC trucks: (1969) 160,255; (1970) 155,353. Innovations: Scout Aristocrat model introduced in the summer of 1969. Scout gets new 304 cid V-8. New three pass muffler gives 10 percent power increase. New Silent-Bloc front spring bushings for Scout models. Conventional trucks completely redesigned. New PT-6-232 engine introduced; six-cylinder with hydraulic valve lifters. By 1969, a number of competitive makes had entered in the sport/utility vehicle class. As a result, Scout sales leveled off at 15,000 to 18,000 units annually. In the IHC Motor Truck Div., J.P. Kaine was assistant to the vice-president for 1969-1970, with R.L. McCaffre as division sales manager.

1970 IHC 1/2-Ton Model 1100D Travelall 4x4 (RCA)

1971 IHC 1/2-Ton Model 1110 Travelall 4x4 (RCA)

SCOUT — SERIES 800B — FOUR-CYLINDER: The IH badge from the nose of the regular Scout was now moved onto the left-hand side of the grille. New special paint and striping packages were introduced. This was to be the Scout 800's last season.
SCOUT — SERIES II: A new Scout II was introduced in the spring of 1971. The vehicle was completely redesigned and now offered power brakes, power steering, air conditioning, automatic transmission, larger V-8s, a bigger clutch, a wider choice of rear axle ratios, more axle capacity, bigger brakes, automatic or manual locking front hubs for 4x4 models and increased cooling. The body was lower and longer than the Scout 800 with a five cu. ft. increase in load space. The rear seat was lowered and increased in width to accomodate three passengers. Sales of the new model exceeded 30,000 units in its first year.
METRO — SERIES M — FOUR-CYLINDER: There were no styling changes to speak of in the 1971 Metro models. Everything was about the same as in 1969-1970 except for revised prices and weights and a new base six-cylinder engine in M-1200 and MA-1200 models. These trucks had used the 196 cid four-cyliner powerplant as base equipment in 1969-1970, but the PT-6-232 six-cylinder engine, which first appeared in 1969, was now standardized.

1971 IHC 1/2-Ton Model 1010 Travelall (NI)

CONVENTIONAL LIGHT TRUCK — SERIES D — SIX-CYLINDER: "We haven't had a model year since 1907," International Harvester explained in a 1971 advertisement. The ad went on to explain that the company didn't believe in planned obsolesence. However, it also mentioned that the 1971 pickups had a new grille, different tailgate treatment, new rocker panel trim and several new colors. The grille revision followed the conservative Scout pattern in simply moving the company's name badge to the left-hand side of the mesh grille insert. At the rear of light-duty models there were new, vertically-mounted rectangular taillights. Hubcaps were now lacking the small fins found on the 1969-1970 type. Model designation badges were also added on the front fendersides, above the side-marker reflectors. Two sets of air vents at the cowl was another minor change. All series used the PT-6-232 engine as standard equipment.
I.D. DATA: Serial number located on left door pillar post. The serial number consists of 13 symbols. The first six symbols identify the serial number. The seventh symbol designates the manufacturing plant. The last six symbols are the sequential production number.

Model	Body Type	Price	Weight	Prod. Total
Scout 800B — 1/4 Ton — 4x4 — 100 in. w.b.				
800B	Roadster	3376	—	—
800B	Traveltop	3564	3480	—
800B	Pickup	3483	3380	—
NOTE 1: Prices/weights for 4x4s with V-8.				
Scout II — 1/4-Ton — 4x4 — 100 in. w.b.				
S-II	Traveltop	3608	3794	—
S-II	Pickup	3528	3694	—
NOTE 2: Prices/weights for 4x4 with V-8.				
Metro M-1100 — 1/2-Ton — 4x2 — 108 in. w.b.				
M-1100	Walk-in Panel 8-ft.	3794	3830	—

Metro M-1200 — 3/4-Ton — 4x2 — 119 in. w.b.

M-1200	Walk-in Panel 9-ft. 8 in.	4744	4410	—

Metro MA-1200 — 3/4-Ton — 4x2 — 134 in. w.b.

MA-1200	Walk-in Panel 9-ft.	4820	4485	—

1000D Trucks — 1/2-Ton — 4x2 — 115-131 in. w.b.

1010	Chassis & Cab	2815	3417	—
1010	Pickup 6.5-ft.	2962	3777	—
1010	Bonus Load Pickup 6.5-ft.	2974	3777	—
1010	Panel 7-ft.	3627	4087	—
1010	Travelall	3853	5440	—
1010	Pickup 8-ft.	3000	3827	—
1010	Bonus Load Pickup 8-ft.	3012	3827	—

NOTE 3: Prices for trucks with V-304 V-8.

1100D — 1/2-Ton — 4x2 — 115-131 in. w.b.

1110	Chassis & Cab	2795	3397	—
1110	Pickup 6.5-ft.	2941	3757	—
1110	Bonus Load Pickup 6.5-ft.	2953	3757	—
1110	Panel 7-ft.	3605	4067	—
1110	Travelall	3831	5475	—
1110	Pickup 8-ft.	2978	3807	—
1110	Bonus Load Pickup 8-ft.	2990	3807	—

NOTE 4: Prices for trucks with V-304 V-8.
NOTE 5: Add $613-705 for 4x4.

1200D Trucks — 3/4-Ton — 4x2 — 115-164 in. w.b.

1210	Chassis & Cab	2930	3627	—
1210	Pickup 6.5-ft.	3078	3987	—
1210	Bonus Load Pickup 6.5-ft.	3089	3987	—
1210	Panel 7-ft.	3742	4297	—
1210	Pickup 8-ft.	3115	4037	—
1210	Bonus Load Pickup 8-ft.	3127	4037	—
1210	Travelette Cab 6.5-ft.	3592	4067	—
1210	Travelette Pickup 6.5-ft.	3748	4427	—
1210	Bonus Load Travelette Pickup 8-ft.	3919	4477	—
1210	Travelall	3961	5655	—

NOTE 6: Prices for trucks with V-304 V-8.
NOTE 7: Add $785-973 for 4x4.

1300D Trucks — 1-Ton — 4x2 — 134-156 in. w.b.

1310	Chassis & Cab	3108	3852	—
1310	Pickup 9-ft.	3267	4312	—
1310	Travelette Cab	3743	4272	—
1310	Bonus Load Travelette Pickup 6.5-ft.	3903	4632	—

NOTE 8: Prices for trucks with V-304 V-8.
NOTE 9: 4x4 option not available for 1300D trucks.

1971 IHC 1/2-Ton Model 1110 Custom Travelall (NI)

ENGINE [Base: Scout 800/M-700/M-800/M-1100/900A]: 4-152. Inline. OHV. Four-cylinder. Cast iron block. Bore & stroke: 3-7/8 in. x 3-7/32 in. Displacement: 151.84 cid.. Compression ratio: 8.19:1. Brake horsepower: 93 at 4400 rpm. Net horsepower: 24.1. Maximum Torque: 143 lbs.-ft. at 2400 rpm. Hydraulic valve lifters. Carburetor: Holley 1904 model 3479 single-barrel.
ENGINE [Base: Scout II/M-1100]: 4-196. Inline. OHV. Four-cylinder. Cast iron block. Bore & stroke: 4-1/8 in. x 3-21/32 in. Displacement: 195.44 cid.. Compression ratio: 8.1:1. Brake horsepower: 111 at 4000 rpm. Net horsepower: 27.2. Maximum Torque: 180 lbs.-ft. at 2000 rpm. Hydraulic valve lifters. Carburetor: Holley 1904 model 3716 single-barrel.
ENGINE [Standard: 1000/1100/1200/1300/M-1200/MA-1200; Optional: Scout II]: PT-6-232. Inline. Six-cylinder. Overhead valve. Cast iron block. Bore and stroke: 3-3/4 x 3-1/2 in. Displacement: 232 cid.. Gross horsepower: 145 at 4300 rpm. Gross Torque: 215 lbs.-ft. at 1600 rpm. Taxable horsepower: 33.75.
ENGINE [Optional V-8]: V-304. Vee block. Overhead valve. Cast iron block. Bore and stroke: 3-7/8 x 3-7/32 in. Displacement: 303.68 cid.. Net horsepower: 140 at 3800 rpm. Net torque: 243 lbs.-ft. at 2400 rpm. Taxable horsepower: 48.1. (Optional in Scout II and Metros.)
ENGINE [Optional LNG V-8]: V-304-LPG. Vee block. Overhead valve. Cast iron block. Bore and stroke: 3-7/8 x 3-7/32 in. Displacement: 303.68 cid.. Net horsepower: 140 at 3800 rpm. Net torque: 243 lbs.-ft. at 2400 rpm. Taxable horsepower: 48.1. (Liquid natural gas fueled engine optional in 1300 series 1-ton 4x2 trucks.)
ENGINE [Optional V-8]: Model V-345. Vee-block, OHV. Eight-cylinder. Cast iron block. Bore & stroke: 3-7/8 in. x 3-21/32 in. Displacement: 344.96 cid.. Compression ratio: 8.05:1. Brake horsepower: 196.7 at 4000 rpm. Net horsepower: 48.1. Maximum Torque: 309 lbs.-ft. at 2200 rpm. Hydraulic valve lifters. Carburetor: Holley model 2300G two-barrel. (This was a new option for the Scout II, but was not a new engine. It had been used previously in some other models.)
CHASSIS [Scout 800]: Wheelbase: 100 in. Tires: E78-15. GVW: 3,200 lbs.
CHASSIS [Scout II]: Wheelbase: 100 in. Tires: E78-15. GVW: 3,200 lbs.
CHASSIS [M-1100]: Wheelbase: 108 in. Tires: 7.00 x 15. GVW: 5,500-6,000 lbs.

CHASSIS [MA-1200]: Wheelbase: 119 in. Tires: 7.00 x 17.5. GVW: 8,000-9,000 lbs.
CHASSIS [MA-1500]: Wheelbase: 119 in./127 in./134 in. Tires: 8.00 x 19.5. GVW: 10,000-14,000 lbs.
CHASSIS [1000D]: Wheelbase: 115 in./(Travelall & Panel) 119 in. Tires: G78-15. GVWs: [Travelall] 4,200-5,000 lbs.; [Others]: 4,800-5,400 lbs.
CHASSIS [1100D 4x2]: Wheelbase: 115 in./(Travelall & Panel) 119 in./131 in. Tires: G78-15. GVWs: [Travelall] 4,700-5,800 lbs.; [Others]: 4,800-5,400 lbs.
CHASSIS [1100D 4x4]: Wheelbase: 115 in./(Travelall & Panel) 119 in./131 in. Tires: G78-15. GVWs: [Travelall] 5,600 lbs.; [Others]: 4,800-5,600 lbs.
CHASSIS [1200D 4x2]: Wheelbase: 115 in./(Travelall & Panel) 119 in./131 in./(Travelette) 140 in. Tires: 8.00 x 16.5. GVWs: [Travelall] 5,500-7,300 lbs.; [Others]: 6,100-7,500 lbs.
CHASSIS [1200D 4x4]: Wheelbase: 115 in./(Travelall & Panel) 119 in./131 in./(Travelette) 140 in. Tires: 8.00 x 16.5. GVWs: [Travelall] 7,000 lbs.; [Others]: 6,100-7,700 lbs.
CHASSIS [1300D]: Wheelbase: 134 in./(Travelette) 140 in. Tires: 8.00 x 16.5. GVWs: [All]: 7,000-8,800 lbs.
OPTIONS [Scout]: Six-cylinder engine ($87). 304 cu. in V-8 engine ($164). RA-28 rear axle ($61). Custom package, Traveltop ($249).
OPTIONS [Scout II]: Six-cylinder engine ($87). 304 cu. in. V-8 ($164). RA-28 rear axle ($61). Custom Travelette package ($249).
OPTIONS: [Metros] Power steering, all models ($258). V-304 eight-cylinder engine ($83). Automatic transmission ($265 average). RA-15 rear axle ($155). RA-126 rear axle ($280). Aluminum body.
OPTIONS: [1010/1110/1200/1300] V-304 engine ($60). V-304 LPG engine, 1110/1210 4x2 models ($195). Five-speed transmission, all 4x2 models ($300). RA-1700 rear axle, all 1210 models ($140). (Series 1310) V-304 engine ($60). V-304 LPG engine, 4x2 models only ($230). T-34 transmission, 4x2 models only ($245).
HISTORICAL: Introduced: Fall of 1970. Calendar year registrations by GVW: [6,000 lbs. or less] 53,077; [6,001-10,000 lbs.] 23,834. Calendar year production: [All IHC trucks] 185,859. Market share: 8.97 percent. Innovations: All-new Scout II model introduced. Larger V-8 available in Scout II. PT-6-232 engine standard in large Metros and other light-duty trucks. New five-speed transmission in some 4x2 models. Air conditioning, power steering and deluxe interior trim for the Scout II. Brooks McCormick became president and chief executive officer of IHC this year. K.P. Mazurek was vice president in charge of the Motor Truck Div. Truck sales accounted for $1,522.8 million. V-8 models accounted for 135,269 assemblies out of the calendar year total.

1972 IHC

1972 IHC 1/4-Ton Scout II Compact Sport Utility Wagon 4x4 (RCA)

SCOUT — SERIES II — ALL ENGINES: The Scout II was the only Scout available in 1972. Styling characteristics of this model included the longer, lower utility body introduced in mid-1971 and a grille treatment with three horizontal slots stacked on top of each other within a full-width rectangular panel. Round headlights were inside this panel, at the edge of the slots. An International nameplate was placed between the two lower slots at the lower left-hand side. A lower perimeter molding trimmed both sides of the body. There were Traveltop and pickup models, plus a Custom trim package and several decaling options. Base engine was the 196 cid four-cylinder. Options included a 232 cid six and two V-8s. The four-cylinder engine was not available in California.
METRO — SERIES M — ALL ENGINES: A new 258 cid six-cylinder base engine was the big change for 1972 Metro models. It replaced both the M-1100's four-cylinder powerplant and the PT-6-232 engine that came with last season's 1200 series models. The MA-1200 model was no longer being marketed. American Motors was the manufacturer of the new engine.
CONVENTIONAL TRUCKS — SERIES 1010/1110/1210/1310 — ALL ENGINES: Styling changes for 1972 included a new dashboard and grille. The grille consisted of five horizontal bars on either side of a vertical center divider. It ran fully across the front of the truck, with a single round headlight on either end. There were four series; the 1010 (1/2-ton), the 1110 (1/2-ton), 1210 (3/4-ton) and 1310 (1-ton). Various wheelbases were available in each line. All Travelalls and Panels had a 119 in. wheelbase. In Sept. 1971, *MOTOR TREND* road tested a Travelall and called it "far and away the best of the real station wagons in design, comfort and quality." Standard Travelall equipment included bench seats, seat belts, full instrumentation, safety side markers, front and rear bumpers and a 77 cu. ft. cargo area (124 cu. ft. with seat folded flush to the floor). A 4x4 driveline was available. Other Travelall chassis features included recirculating ball steering with 17.5: ratio; front torsion bars with shocks and stabilizer bar; rear longitudinal leaf springs with shocks; and a 19-gallon fuel tank. (Parallel leaf spring front suspension could be substituted for struts and torsion bars.) Cab models had various wheelbases: 115 in for 6-ft. regular or Bonus Load pickup bodies; 131 in. for 8-ft.; 134 in. for 9-ft. regular pickup, dump, stake or platform bodies; 140 in. for Travelettes; and 156 in. for 12-foot stake, dump, platform or van bodies. Standard equipment included bench seats, seat belts, full instrumentation, safety side markers, and front bumper. The 1110s and 1210s could be had with 4x4 equipment.

1972 IHC 3/4-Ton Model 1210 Travelette Pickup (Erwin Knapp)

I.D. DATA: Serial number located on the left front door pillar post. The serial number consists of 13 symbols. The first six identify the serial number. The seventh (digit) designates the manufacturing plant. The last six (digits) are sequential production numbers. Engine model identification takes the form of a prefix to the engine serial number. For example, a V-266 engine serial number would read V-266-000000. Engine numbers are located on a machined boss on the cylinder block. Serial numbers and engine numbers are not available.

Model	Body Type	Price	Weight	Prod. Total
Scout II — 1/4-Ton — 4x2 — 100 in. w.b.				
SII	Traveltop	2560	2950	—
SII	Pickup	2415	2850	—
Scout II — 1/4-Ton — 4x4 — 100 in. w.b.				
SII	Traveltop	3340	3050	—
SII	Pickup	3185	3150	—
Metro M-1100 — 1/2-Ton — 4x2 — 108 in. w.b.				
M-1100	Walk-in Panel 8-ft.	3865	3830	—
Metro M-1200 — 3/4-Ton — 4x2 — 119-127 in. w.b.				
M-1200	Walk-in Panel 9-ft.	4168	4410	—
M-1200	Walk-in Panel 10-ft.	4300	4485	—
Travelall/Panel 1010 — 1/2-Ton — 4x2 — 119 in. w.b.				
1010	Station Wagon	3650	5440	—
Travelall/Panel 1010 — 1/2-Ton — 119 in. w.b.				
1110	Station Wagon 4x2	3580	5475	—
1110	Station Wagon 4x4	4295	5475	—
1110	Panel 4x2	3522	2475	—
1110	Panel 4x4	4135	2900	—
Travelall/Panel 1010 — 3/4-Ton — 119 in. w.b.				
1210	Station Wagon 4x2	3705	5655	—
1210	Station Wagon 4x4	4515	5990	—
1110	Panel 4x2	3659	2550	—
1110	Panel 4x4	4450	3125	—
1010 Trucks — 1/2-Ton — 4x2 — 115 in. w.b.				
1010	Chassis & Cab	2731	1900	—
1010	Pickup	2879	2025	—
1110 Trucks — 1/2-Ton — 4x2 — 115-131 in. w.b.				
1110	Chassis & Cab	2575	3180	—
1110	Pickup	2715	3555	—
1110 Trucks — 1/2-Ton — 4x2 — 115-131 in. w.b.				
1110	Chassis & Cab	3120	3485	—
1110	Pickup	3265	3860	—
1210 Trucks — 3/4-Ton 4x2 — 115-131 in. w.b.				
1210	Chassis & Cab	3355	3850	—
1210	Pickup	3510	4215	—
1210	Travelette Cab	3120	3485	—
1210	Travelette Pickup	3265	3860	—
Series 1210 — 3/4-Ton — 4x4 — 115-131 in. w.b.				
1210	Chassis & Cab	3440	3820	—
1210	Pickup	3580	4195	—
1210	Travelette Cab	4245	4245	—
1210	Travelette Pickup	4410	4635	—
Series 1310 — 1-Ton — 4x2 — 131-150 in. w.b.				
1310	Chassis & Cab	3090	3610	—
1310	Pickup	3100	3630	—
1310	Travelette Cab	3560	3695	—
1310	Travelette Pickup	3715	4045	—

NOTE 1: Price of a Bonus Load pickup over the standard pickups listed above was $15.
ENGINE [Base: Scout II]: 4-196. Inline. OHV. Four-cylinder. Cast iron block. Bore & stroke: 4-1/8 in. x 3-21/32 in. Displacement: 195.44 cid.. Compression ratio: 8.1:1. Brake horsepower: 111 at 4000 rpm. Net horsepower: 27.2. Maximum Torque: 180 lbs.-ft. at 2000 rpm. Hydraulic valve lifters. Carburetor: Holley 1904 model 3716 single-barrel.
ENGINE [Base: Metro/Travelall/Conventionals]: Model 6-258. Inline, OHV, Six-cylinder. Cast iron block. Bore & stroke: 3.75 in. x 3.9 in. Displacement: 258.1 cid.. Brake horsepower: 135 at 3800 rpm. Net horsepower: 33.75. Maximum Torque: 235 lbs.-ft. at 2000 rpm. Hydraulic valve lifters. Carburetor: Holley Model 1940C. (AMC engine.)
ENGINE [Optional V-8]: V-304. Vee block. Overhead valve. Cast iron block. Bore and stroke: 3-7/8 x 3-7/32 in. Displacement: 303.68 cid.. Net horsepower: 140 at 3800 rpm. Net torque: 243 lbs.-ft. at 2400 rpm. Taxable horsepower: 48.1. (Optional in Scout II/Metro/ Travelall/Conventionals.)
ENGINE [Optional LNG V-8]: V-304-LPG. Vee block. Overhead valve. Cast iron block. Bore and stroke: 3-7/8 x 3-7/32 in. Displacement: 303.68 cid.. Net horsepower: 140 at 3800

rpm. Net torque: 243 lbs.-ft. at 2400 rpm. Taxable horsepower: 48.1. (Liquid natural gas fueled engine optional in 1300 series 1-ton 4x2 trucks.)

ENGINE [Optional V-8]: Model V-345. Vee-block, OHV. Eight-cylinder. Cast iron block. Bore & stroke: 3-7/8 in. x 3-21/32 in. Displacement: 344.96 cid Compression ratio: 8.05:1. Brake horsepower: 196.7 at 4000 rpm. Net horsepower: 48.1. Maximum Torque: 309 lbs.-ft. at 2200 rpm. Hydraulic valve lifters. Carburetor: Holley model 2300G two-barrel. (This was a new option for the Scout II and conventional trucks, but was not a new engine. It had been used previously in some other models.)

ENGINE [Optional]: V-392. V-8. Overhead valve. Cast iron block. Bore and stroke: 4.12 x 3.66 in. Displacement: 390,89 cid.. Brake horsepower: 253.4 at 4200 rpm. Net horsepower: 54.5. Maximum Torque: 381.3 lbs.-ft. at 2800 rpm. Hydraulic valve lifters. Carburetor: Two-barrel model Holley 4150. (Optional in Travelall.)

CHASSIS [Scout 800]: Wheelbase: 100 in. Tires: E78-15. GVW: 3,200 lbs.

CHASSIS [Scout II]: Wheelbase: 100 in. Tires: E78-15. GVW: 3,200 lbs.

CHASSIS [M-1100]: Wheelbase: 108 in. Tires: 7.00 x 15. GVW: 5,500-6,000 lbs.

CHASSIS [MA-1200]: Wheelbase: 119 in. Tires: 7.00 x 17.5. GVW: 8,000-9,000 lbs.

CHASSIS [MA-1500]: Wheelbase: 119 in./127 in./134 in. Tires: 8.00 x 19.5. GVW: 10,000-14,000 lbs.

CHASSIS [1000D]: Wheelbase: 115 in./(Travelall & Panel) 119 in. Tires: G78-15. GVWs: [Travelall] 4,200-5,000 lbs.; [Others]: 4,800-5,400 lbs.

CHASSIS [1100D 4x2]: Wheelbase: 115 in./(Travelall & Panel) 119 in./131 in.

TECHNICAL [All]: Manual, synchromesh transmission. Speeds: 3F/1R. Column mounted gearshift lever. Single-plate dry-disc clutch. Single reduction rear axle. Overall ratio: various. Front and rear drum brakes. Steel disc wheels. Automatic transmission.

OPTIONS [Scout II]: Power brakes. Power steering. Air conditioning. Custom Traveltop package ($245). RA-28 rear axle ($60). Solid-state push-button radio. Heater and defroster. Single or dual Outside rearview mirror(s). Roof luggage rack. Tinted windshield. Bucket seats. Radio antenna package. Eight-track tape player. Automatic transmission. Spare tire and carrier. Special paint. Sport decal packages. Full wheel discs. White sidewall tires. Oversize tires. Three-speed manual transmission. Four-speed manual transmission.

OPTIONS [Metro]: Power steering ($258). Automatic transmission ($225 average). RA-15 rear axle, in 1200 series ($75). Radio. Special paint. Outside rearview mirrors. Oversize tires.

OPTIONS [Conventional Trucks]: Chrome front bumper. Rear bumper. Custom trim package. Outside rearview mirror(s). Two-tone paint. Special paint. Bumper guards. Radio. Heater. Clock. Cigar lighter. Radio antenna. Seat covers. Clearance lights. Dual California mirrors. Deluxe hub caps. White sidewall tires. Power steering. Power brakes. License plate frames. V-304 engine, all except 1310 ($75). V-304 engine, all 4x2 except 1310 ($240). Five-speed transmission, all 4x2 ($310). RA-17 rear axle, 1200 Series ($140). V-304 engine, 1310 only ($80). V-304 LPG engine, 1300 Series 4x2 ($260). T-34 transmission, 1300 Series 4x2 ($220).

HISTORICAL: Introduced Fall 1971. Calendar year registrations: [6,000 lbs. or less] 65,815; [6,001-10,000 lbs.] 27,110. Calendar year production: [All IHC trucks] 212,654 (8.60 percent). Innovations: New grille styling with horizontal-bar theme for most models. Worldwide sales in fiscal 1972 totaled $3,493,000,000. This was the fifth consecutive year that sales eclipsed a previous record sales year. Plans for increased participation in world markets were announced by IH, which acquired a one-third interest in DAF of Eindhoven, The Netherlands.

1972 IHC 3/4-Ton Model 1210 Bonus Load Pickup (DFW)

1973 IHC

SCOUT — SERIES II — ALL ENGINES: The 1973 Scout II had a new front end treatment. There was still a rectangular front panel with single, round headlamps at each end. Between the headlamps there were now two grilles, one on each side of a narrow, body-colored vertical divider. Each grille had a rectangular opening with a chrome surround and six, vertical bars finished in body color. An International nameplate ran horizontally across the lower section of the outer four bars on the left-hand grille. All else was about the same as in 1972.

1973 IHC 3/4-Ton Bonus Load Pickup 4x4 (Erwin Knapp)

METRO — SERIES MS — SIX-CYLINDER: The Metro line was designated the MS series this season. There was only one 1-ton-or-under model left. This was the MS-1210 chassis. Longer wheelbases ranging from a low of 125 in. to a high of 159 in. were available. Upon ordering a chassis, the buyer could add one of several different sized Walk-in panel bodies.

1973 IHC 1/2-Ton Model 1110 Custom Bonus Load Pickup (JAG)

CONVENTIONAL TRUCKS — SERIES 1010/1110/1210 — SIX-CYLINDER: The big styling change for 1973 was really pretty small potatoes. It consisted of narrowing the front fender tip badges to put slightly more room between them and the side-markers. There was also a new hubcap design with more pointed center. Standard trim featured a minimum of tinsel with no side moldings. Deluxe trim trucks had a molding along the lower bodyside feature line from behind the front wheel cutout to the rear. Custom trim had a molding around the front wheel cutouts, up the fender and back down the body along the upper beltline. The area inside the moldings was often finished in a contrasting color or with a woodgrain insert on Travelalls. The taillights were tall, narrow trapezoids positioned base-to-base with the top lens pointing up and the bottom one pointing downwards. A similarly shaped white backup light was incorporated into the bottom lens. Travelalls also featured a drop-down tailgate with lowerable rear window glass. Many units wore vinyl tops and the roof rack was a popular option, too. The Travelall was actually merchandised as a passenger car. The 119 in. wheelbase panel truck was disconinued. One-tons were now available with four-wheel drive.

1973 IHC 1/2-Ton Model 1110 Custom Bonus Load Pickup (JAG)

Standard Catalog of Light-Duty Trucks

I.D. DATA: Serial number located on the left front door pillar post. The serial number consists of 13 symbols. The first six identify the serial number. The seventh (digit) designates the manufacturing plant. The last six (digits) are sequential production numbers. Engine model identification takes the form of a prefix to the engine serial number. For example, a V-266 engine serial number would read V-266-000000. Engine numbers are located on a machined boss on the cylinder block. Serial numbers and engine numbers are not available.

1973 IHC 1/4-Ton Scout II Compact Sport Utility Wagon (RCA)

Model	Body Type	Price	Weight	Prod. Total
Scout II — 1/4-Ton — 4x2 — 100 in. w.b.				
SII	Traveltop	2752	3370	—
SII	Cab Top	2605	3290	—
Scout II — 1/4-Ton — 4x4 — 100 in. w.b.				
SII	Traveltop	3549	3600	—
SII	Cab Top	3394	3500	—
Metro MS-1200 — 3/4-Ton — 4x2 — 125-159 in. w.b.				
MS-1210	Chassis	2545	2280	—
Travelall 1010 — 1/2-Ton -119 in. w.b.				
1010	Station Wagon 4x2	3775	5440	—
Travelall 1110 — 3/4-Ton — 119 in. w.b.				
1110	Station Wagon 4x2	3700	5475	—
1110	Station Wagon 4x4	4375	5655	—
Travelall 1210 — 3/4-Ton — 119 in. w.b.				
1210	Station Wagon 4x2	3820	5475	—
1210	Station Wagon 4x4	4600	5990	—
1010 Trucks — 1/2-Ton — 4x2 — 131 in. w.b.				
1010	Pickup	2925	3735	—
1110 Trucks — 1/2-Ton — 4x2 — 115-131 in. w.b.				
1110	Chassis & Cab	2710	3180	—
1110	Pickup	2856	3555	—
1110 Trucks — 1/2-Ton — 4x4 — 115-131 in. w.b.				
1110	Chassis & Cab	3269	3485	—
1110	Pickup	3411	3860	—
1210 Trucks — 3/4-Ton — 4x2 — 115-149 in. w.b.				
1210	Chassis & Cab	2831	3410	—
1210	Pickup	2973	3785	—
1210	Travelette Cab	3470	3850	—
1210	Travelette Pickup	3621	4215	—
1210 Trucks — 3/4-Ton — 4x4 — 115-149 in. w.b.				
1210	Chassis & Cab	3544	3820	—
1210	Pickup	3687	4195	—
1210	Travelette Cab	4352	4270	—
1210	Travelette Pickup	4814	4635	—
1310 Trucks — 1-Ton — 4x2 — 131-150 in. w.b.				
1310	Chassis & Cab	3155	3610	—
1310	Pickup	3166	3630	—
1310	Travelette Cab	3626	3695	—
1310	Travelette Pickup	3780	4045	—
1310 — 1-Ton — 4x4 — 132 in. w.b.				
1310	Chassis & Cab	4369	4375	—
1310	Pickup 9 ft.	4522	4375	—

NOTE 1: Bonus Load pickups were $11 over the cost of standard pickups.
ENGINE [Base: Scout II]: 4-196. Inline. OHV. Four-cylinder. Cast iron block. Bore & stroke: 4-1/8 in. x 3-21/32 in. Displacement: 195.44 cid.. Net horsepower: 86 at 3800 rpm. Taxable horsepower: 27.2. Maximum Torque: 157 lbs.-ft. at 2200 rpm. Hydraulic valve lifters. Carburetor: Holley 1904 model 3716 single-barrel.
ENGINE [Base: Metro/Travelall/Conventionals]: Model 6-258. Inline, OHV. Six-cylinder. Cast iron block. Bore & stroke: 3.75 in. x 3.9 in. Displacement: 258.1 cid.. Brake horsepower: 115 at 3800 rpm. Net horsepower: 33.75. Maximum Torque: 199 lbs.-ft. at 2000 rpm. Hydraulic valve lifters. Carburetor: Holley Model 1940C. (AMC engine.)
ENGINE [Optional V-8]: V-304. Vee block. Overhead valve. Cast iron block. Bore & stroke: 3-7/8 x 3-7/32 in. Displacement: 303.68 cid.. Net horsepower: 140 at 3800 rpm. Net torque: 243 lbs.-ft. at 2400 rpm. Taxable horsepower: 48.1. (Optional in Scout II/Metro/Travelall/Conventionals.)
ENGINE [Optional LNG V-8]: V-304-LPG. Vee block. Overhead valve. Cast iron block. Bore and stroke: 3-7/8 x 3-7/32 in. Displacement: 303.68 cid.. Net horsepower: 140 at 3800 rpm. Net torque: 243 lbs.-ft. at 2400 rpm. Taxable horsepower: 48.1. (Liquid natural gas fueled engine optional in 1300 series 1-ton 4x2 trucks.)

ENGINE [Optional V-8]: Model V-345. Vee-block, OHV. Eight-cylinder. Cast iron block. Bore & stroke: 3-7/8 in. x 3-21/32 in. Displacement: 344.96 cid.. Net horsepower: 154.8 at 4400 rpm. Net horsepower: 48.1. Net Torque: 227.1 lbs.-ft. at 2200 rpm. Hydraulic valve lifters. Carburetor: Holley model 2300G two-barrel.

ENGINE [Optional V-392]: V-8. Overhead valve. Cast iron block. Bore and stroke: 4.12 x 3.66 in. Displacement: 390.89 cid.. Horsepower: 191 at 3600 rpm. Net horsepower: 54.5. Net Torque: 2433 lbs.-ft. at 2800 rpm. Hydraulic valve lifters. Carburetor: Two-barrel model Holley 4150. (Optional in Travelall.)

CHASSIS [Scout II]: Wheelbase: 100 in. Tires: E78 x 15 in.

CHASSIS [MS-1210]: Wheelbase: 125-159 in. Tires: 8.75 x 16 in.

CHASSIS [1010]: Wheelbase: 131 in. Tires: G78 x 15 in.

CHASSIS [1110]: Wheelbase: 115-131 in. Tires: G78 x 15 in.

CHASSIS [1210]: Wheelbase: 115/119/131/149/156 in. Tires: 8.00 x 16.5 in.

CHASSIS [1310]: Wheelbase: 131/132/134/149/150 in. Tires: 8.00 x 16.5 in.

1973 IHC 1-Ton Model 1310 Cab & Utility Body (JAG)

TECHNICAL [All, 4x2, typical]: Manual (synchromesh) transmission. Speeds: 3F/1R. Column mounted gearshift lever. Single-plate dry-disc clutch. Single reduction rear axle. Overall ratio: 3.31:1; 3.73:1 or 4.27:1. Four-wheel hydraulic brakes. Steel disc wheels. Technical options: Four-speed transmission. Five-speed transmission. Automatic transmission. Overdrive. Four-wheel drive running gear. On 4x4 models the front-drive axle was full-floating.

OPTIONS [Scout II]: V-304 engine ($85). V-345 engine ($120). RA-28 Trac-Lok rear axle ($60). Custom Traveltop package ($245). Power steering. Power brakes. Air conditioning. Dual outside rearview mirrors. Radio. Radio antenna. Roof rack. Deluxe wheels. Sliding side windows. Whitewall tires. Spare tire and carrier. Special paint. Oversize tires. Bucket seats. Console.

OPTIONS [Metro]: Power steering, all ($135). V-304 engine, all ($85). V-392 engine ($235). T-34 or T-36 five-speed transmission in all 4x2 models ($310). Automatic transmission, all 4x2 models, average ($240). RA-17 rear axle, all 1200 models ($140). Power brakes. Air conditioning. Roof rack. Vinyl top. Deluxe wheelcovers. Custom wheelcovers. Wood grain side trim. White sidewall tires. Custom interior package. Dual outside rearview mirrors. Towing package. Bumper hitch. California trucker mirrors. Oversize tires.

OPTIONS [Conventionals]: V-304 engine, all ($80). V-304 LPG engine, Series 1300, 4x2 only ($260). T-34 transmission, Series 1300 4x2 only ($220). Power steering ($135). Automatic transmission (average $240). Power brakes. Air conditioning. Tinted glass. Deluxe trim package. Custom trim package. White sidewall tires. Dual outside rearview mirrors. Dual California trucker mirrors. Custom interior package. Cab clearance lights. Tow package. Camper package. V-345 engine. V-392 engine. Oversize tires. Two-tone paint. Special paint. Floor mats. Spare tire and carrier.

1973 IHC 1/2-Ton Custom Travelall Station Wagon (RCA)

HISTORICAL: Introduced Fall 1972. Calendar year registrations: [All IHC trucks] 199,875. Calendar year production: [Light-duty trucks]: 105,569. Calendar year production: [All IHC trucks]: 207,547. Market share: 6.91 percent. Innovations: New front styling for all models. Engines de-tuned to operate on low-lead fuel. IHC was America's fifth largest truck-maker behind Chevrolet, Ford, Dodge and GMC in order. B. McCormick was the company's president and chief executive officer. K.P. Mazurek was president and Corporate VP of the Motor Truck Div.

1973 IHC 1/2-Ton Model 1110 Custom Bonus Load Pickup (JAG)

1974 IHC

1974 IHC 1/2-Ton Model 100 Bonus Load Pickup 4x4 (RCA)

SCOUT — SERIES II — ALL ENGINES: There were no changes in the 1974 Scout, but a few more decal options and equipment packages came out. The grille was also slightly revised. It now had an "electric shaver" look with vertical blades all across it.

METRO — SERIES MS — SIX-CYLINDER: The Metro van line was again carried over as the MS-1210. These trucks were sold as a stripped chassis with hydraulic brakes. Three wheelbases were available. A variety of optional Step-Van bodies could be added, including steel and aluminum versions. The 1200 designation indicated 3/4-ton capacity.

CONVENTIONAL TRUCKS — SERIES 100/200 — V-8 ENGINE: Travelalls and conventional light-duty trucks had revised series designations for 1974. They were available as 100 (1/2-ton) or 200 (3/4-ton) models. A 345 cid V-8 was now standard equipment in the 4x2 Series 100 Travelall. Other Travelalls used the 392 cid V-8 as base engine. The 258 cid six-cylinder was standard in all other models, except 4x4s used the 304 cid V-8 as base engine. There was a new grille with five full-width horizontal bars. Also, the rectangular badges ahead of the front wheel openings were moved down closer to the side-markers. The regular pickups had the narrower box and flared rear fenders. Bonus Load Pickups had a wider box that was flush with the sides of the cab. Travelette (crew cab) models came both ways. Deluxe and Custom exterior trim packages were offered again. Custom trim had a molding around the front wheel cutouts, up the fender and back down the body along the upper beltline. The area inside the moldings was often finished in a contrasting color or with a woodgrain insert on Travelalls.

I.D. DATA [All]: Located on left door hinge pillar. Serial numbers for 1974 conventional trucks began with 4 (H) 1 (A) ODHB and up.

1974 IHC 1/4-Ton Scout II Compact Sport Utility Wagon (IHC)

Model	Body Type	Price	Weight	Prod. Total
Scout II — 1/2-Ton — 100 in. w.b.				
SII	Traveltop 4x2	2979	3462	—
SII	Traveltop 4x4	3943	3717	—
SII	Cab Top 4x2	2832	3316	—
SII	Cab Top 4x4	3788	3571	—

NOTE 1: Above prices include Hydra-Matic and power brakes.

Model	Body Type	Price	Weight	Prod. Total
Metro				
MS-1210	Step-Van Chassis 125 in.	2695	3328	—
MS-1210	Step-Van Chassis 137 in.	2705	3340	—
MS-1210	Step-Van Chassis 159 in.	2736	3362	—
Travelall 100 — 1/2-Ton — 119 in. w.b.				
100	Station Wagon 4x2	4338	4450	—
100	Station Wagon 4x4	5320	4795	—
Travelall 200 — 3/4-Ton — 119 in. w.b.				
200	Station Wagon 4x2	4798	4696	—
200	Station Wagon 4x4	5498	4899	—
100 Trucks — 1/2-Ton — 4x2 — 115 in. w.b.				
100	Chassis & Cab	3106	3381	—
100	Fender Pickup	3258	3753	—
100	Bonus Load Pickup	3258	3806	—
100 Trucks — 1/2-Ton — 4x2 — 132 in. w.b.				
100	Chassis & Cab	3258	3422	—
100	Fender Pickup	3294	3842	—
100	Bonus Load Pickup	3294	3902	—
100 Trucks — 1/2-Ton — 4x4 — 115 in. w.b.				
100	Chassis & Cab	3877	3571	—
100	Fender Pickup	4031	4143	—
100	Bonus Load Pickup	4031	4196	—
100 Trucks — 1/2-Ton — 4x4 — 132 in. w.b.				
100	Chassis & Cab	3903	3794	—
100	Fender Pickup	4067	4214	—
100	Bonus Load Pickup	4067	4274	—
200 Trucks — 3/4-Ton — 4x2 — 132 in. w.b.				
200	Chassis & Cab	3362	3745	—
200	Bonus Load Pickup	3526	4225	—
200	Fender Pickup	3526	4165	—
200	Chassis & Cab	3372	3708	—
200 Trucks — 3/4-Ton — 4x2 — 149 in. w.b.				
200	Travelette Chassis & Cab	4093	4302	—
200	Travelette Fender Pickup	4255	4674	—
200	Travelette Bonus Load Pickup	4255	4727	—
200 Trucks — 3/4-Ton — 4x2 — 158 in. w.b.				
200	Chassis & Cab	3422	3780	—
200 Trucks — 3/4-Ton — 4x2 — 166 in. w.b.				
200	Travelette Chassis & Cab	4244	4369	—
200	Travelette Fender Pickup	4408	4789	—
200	Travelette Bonus Load Pickup	4408	4849	—
200 Trucks — 3/4-Ton — 4x4 — 132				
200	Chassis & Cab	4016	3993	—
200	Fender Pickup	4181	4413	—
200	Bonus Load Pickup	4181	4473	—

ENGINE [Base: Scout II]: 4-196. Inline. OHV. Four-cylinder. Cast iron block. Bore & stroke: 4-1/8 in. x 3-21/32 in. Displacement: 195.44 cid.. Net horsepower: 86 at 3800 rpm. Taxable horsepower: 27.2. Maximum Torque: 157 lbs.-ft. at 2200 rpm. Hydraulic valve lifters. Carburetor: Holley 1904 model 3716 single-barrel.

ENGINE [Base: Metro/Travelall/Conventionals]: Model 6-258. Inline, OHV, Six-cylinder. Cast iron block. Bore & stroke: 3.75 in. x 3.9 in. Displacement: 258.1 cid.. Brake horsepower: 115 at 3800 rpm. Net horsepower: 33.75. Maximum Torque: 199 lbs.-ft. at 2000 rpm. Hydraulic valve lifters. Carburetor: Holley Model 1940C. (AMC engine).

ENGINE [Base: Series 10 4x4s V-8]: V-304. V-8. Overhead valve. Cast iron block. Bore and stroke: 3-7/8 x 3-7/32 in. Displacement: 303.68 cid.. Net horsepower: 140 at 3800 rpm. Net torque: 243 lbs.-ft. at 2400 rpm. Taxable horsepower: 48.1. (Optional in Scout II/Metro/Travelall/other conventionals.)

ENGINE [Optional LNG V-8]: V-304-LPG. Vee block. Overhead valve. Cast iron block. Bore and stroke: 3-7/8 x 3-7/32 in. Displacement: 303.68 cid.. Net horsepower: 140 at 3800 rpm. Net torque: 243 lbs.-ft. at 2400 rpm. Taxable horsepower: 48.1. (Liquid natural gas fueled engine optional in 1300 series 1-ton 4x2 trucks.)

ENGINE [Base: Travelall 100 4x2]: Model V-345. Vee-block, OHV. Eight-cylinder. Cast iron block. Bore & stroke: 3-7/8 in. x 3-21/32 in. Displacement: 344.96 cid.. Net horsepower: 154.8 at 4400 rpm. Net horsepower: 48.1. Net Torque: 227.1 lbs.-ft. at 2200 rpm. Hydraulic valve lifters. Carburetor: Holley model 2300G two-barrel.

ENGINE [Optional] V-392]: V-8. Overhead valve. Cast iron block. Bore and stroke: 4.12 x 3.66 in. Displacement: 390.89 cid.. Net horsepower: 191 at 3600 rpm. Net horsepower: 54.5. Net Torque: 2433 lbs.-ft. at 2800 rpm. Hydraulic valve lifters. Carburetor: Two-barrel model Holley 4150. (Optional in Travelall.)

CHASSIS [Scout II]: Wheelbase: 100 in. Tires: F78 x 15 in.
CHASSIS [Metro]: Wheelbase: 125-159 in. Tires: 8.75 x 16.5 in.
CHASSIS [Series 100]: Wheelbase: 115-132 in. Tires: G78 x 15 in.
CHASSIS [Series 200]: Wheelbase: 132-158 in. Tires: 8.00 x 16.5 in.
TECHNICAL [All 4x2 (typical)]: Manual synchromesh transmission. Speeds: 3F/1R. Column mounted gearshift lever. Single-plate dry-disc clutch. Single reduction rear axle. Overall axle ratio: 3.31:1, 3.73:1 or 4.27:1. Four-wheel hydraulic brakes. Steel disc wheels. Technical options: Four-speed transmission. Five-speed transmission. Automatic transmission. Overdrive. Four-wheel drive running gear. On 4x4 models the front drive axle was full-floating.

OPTIONS [Scout II]: Automatic transmission ($238 average). Air conditioning ($500 average). AM radio ($70). Deluxe exterior trim package 500 ($69.) Deluxe exterior trim package, other models ($120 average). V-304 engine ($100). V-345 engine ($135). Other options similar to 1973.

OPTIONS [Metro]: T-407 three-speed automatic transmission ($238 average). Power steering. Power brakes. AM radio ($70). V-304 engine ($100 average). V-345-2 heavy-duty engine ($131). Dual outside rearview mirrors. Four-speed transmission. Special paint.

TRAVELALL 200: Automatic transmission (39.9 percent); power disc brakes (100.0 percent); power steering (51.1 percent); radio AM only (22.4 percent); radio AM/FM stereo (6.1 percent); air conditioning (82.3 percent); limited-slip differential (36.1 percent); tinted glass (24.9 percent); wheelcovers (22.6 percent); interior trim package (59.7 percent); exterior trim package (53.5 percent); four-wheel drive (86.1 percent) rates based on total output of 29,238 Series 200 Travelalls.

OPTIONS [Conventionals]: V-392 engine in 200 Travelall ($185). V-392 engine in 100 Travelall ($255). V-400 engine in 200 Travelall (deduct $55). V-400 engine in 100 Travelall ($131). Power brakes. Roof rack. Vinyl top. Deluxe wheelcovers. Custom wheelcovers. Woodgrain side trim. Custom interior package. Dual outside rearview mirrors. Two-tone paint. Custom interior. 304 cid.. V-8 in 100/4x2 ($100). 304 cid.. V-8 in 200 ($100). 345 cu. in V-8 in Series 100 and all-series with 4x4 ($245). 392 cid.. V-8 in Series 100 ($255). 400 cid.. V-8, in Series 100 ($255); in Series 100 Travelette ($131). Power steering. Automatic tansmission ($238). Power brakes. Air conditioning ($500). Deluxe wheelcovers. Custom wheels. Whitewall tires. Dual outside rearview mirrors. Towing package ($410). Bumper hitch. California trucker mirrors. Clearance marker lights (except 1/2-ton). Oversize tires. Tinted glass ($70). Deluxe exterior trim package ($120). Custom exterior trim package ($275). Camper special package with 200 series ($275).

HISTORICAL: Introduced Fall 1973. Calendar year registrations by GVW Class: [6,000 lbs. or less] 50,089; [6,001 to 10,000 lbs.] 23,567. Calendar year production: [All IHC trucks] 177,915. Market share: 6.29 percent. Model year production: [All IHC trucks] 161,375. Model year production: [Scout II] 29,657. Model year production: [Pickups] 36,584. Innovations: "Electric Shaver" grilles for Scout II. New series designations for light-duty trucks. V-8 engines become standard equipment in some series. Although production of light-duty pickups was continued in 1975, this was the last year for IHC as a major light-duty pickup manufacturer. Only 6,329 pickups would be made in 1975, the final year for that series.

OPTION INSTALLATION RATES: The following data indicates percentage of total IHC production having the specified factory options installed.

SERIES 100: Automatic transmission (62.7 percent); power disc brakes (100.0 percent); power steering (70.7 percent); radio AM only (62.7 percent); radio AM/FM stereo (2.4 percent); V-8 engines 350 cid or less (51.7 percent); V-8 engines over 350 cid (51.7 percent); air conditioning (21.9 percent); limited-slip differential (19.5 percent); tinted glass (21.9 percent); wheelcovers (57.6 percent); interior trim package (43.6 percent); exterior trim package (55.4 percent); four-wheel drive (25.8 percent) rates based on total output of 20,062 Series 100 1/2-ton cab models.

SERIES 200: Automatic transmission (44.2 percent); power disc brakes (100.0 percent); power steering (70.9 percent); radio AM only (48.3 percent); radio AM/FM stereo (2.1 percent); V-8 engines 350 cid or less (74.0 percent); V-8 engines over 350 cid (20.1 percent); air conditioning (13.6 percent); limited-slip differential (17.8 percent); dual rear wheels (18.6 percent); tinted glass (13.6 percent); wheelcovers (30.9 percent); interior trim package (29.3 percent); exterior trim package (32.1 percent); four-wheel drive (39.6 percent) rates based on total output of 21,996 Series 200 3/4-ton cab models.

SCOUT II: Automatic transmission (53.6 percent); power disc brakes (100.0 percent); power steering (61.4 percent); radio AM only (70.8 percent); radio AM/FM stereo (6.7 percent); V-8 engines 350 cid or less (62.7 percent); air conditioning (26.3 percent); limited-slip differential (37.2 percent); tinted glass (26.3 percent); wheelcovers (64.0 percent); interior trim package (83.5 percent); exterior trim package (82.6 percent); four-wheel drive (17.1 percent) rates based on total output of 6,714 Scout IIs.

TRAVELALL 100: Automatic transmission (95.5 percent); power disc brakes (100.0 percent); power steering (95.4 percent); radio AM only (47.3 percent); radio AM/FM stereo (39.9 percent); V-8 engines 350 cid or less (15.1 percent); V-8 engines over 350 cid (84.9 percent); air conditioning (82.8 percent); limited-slip differential (20.3 percent); tinted glass (82.8 percent); wheelcovers (82.5 percent); interior trim package (72.8 percent); exterior trim package (71.8 percent); four-wheel drive (40.2 percent) rates based on total output of 1,138 Series 100 Travelalls.

1975 IHC

SCOUT XLC — SERIES II — ALL ENGINES: The 1975 Scout XLC was basically unchanged from the 1974 model. However, there were a couple of powertrain changes. The slant-four engine was further detuned and the G-258 engine was dropped. Available options included two V-8s with slightly less horsepower.

1975 IHC 1/2-Ton Scout II Compact Sport Utility Wagon (RCA)

METRO — SERIES MS — V-8: This was the last year of production for the IH Metro Vans. As a result, there was no change for the new year, except in base engine. Since the six-cylinder engine was dropped, the 345 cid.. V-8 became standard equipment.

1975 IHC 1/4-Ton Scout II Compact Sport Utility Wagon (IHC)

TRAVELALL — SERIES 150/200 — V-8: This was also the final season for the famous Travelall. Any changes were of a minor nature. As in 1974, the wheelbase was 120 in. However, the 100 Series was redesignated the 150. Two V-8s, the V-345A and V-392 were optional. Standard, Deluxe and Custom trim levels were available again.

1975 IHC 1/4-Ton Scout II Compact Sport Utility Wagon (IHC)

PICKUP TRUCKS — SERIES 150/200 — V-8: IHC's 1975 Light-duty pickups were similar to 1974 models, except that the 1/2-ton models were now designated the 150 series. The 200 designation still applied to 3/4-ton models. A small V-8 was standard equipment in both lines. These trucks could be optionally equipped with deluxe or custom trim packages. All of the conventional pickups and all of the crew-cab Travelette pickups were now of the fenderless Bonus Load style.

I.D. DATA: Serial number located on the left front door pillar post. The serial number consists of 13 symbols. The first six identify the serial number. The seventh (digit) designates the manufacturing plant. The last six (digits) are sequential production numbers. Engine model identification takes the form of a prefix to the engine serial number. For example, a V-266 engine serial number would read V-266-000000. Engine numbers are located on a machined boss on the cylinder block. Serial numbers and engine numbers are not available.

Model	Body Type	Price	Weight	Prod. Total
Scout II XLC — 1/4-Ton — 100 in. w.b.				
SII	Traveltop 4x2	3760	3471	—
SII	Traveltop 4x4	4712	3551	—
SII	Cab Top 4x2	3285	3376	—
SII	Cab Top 4x4	4489	3549	—
Metro M-1210 — 3/4-Ton — 125 in./137 in./159 in. w.b.				
MS-1210	Chassis	3452	3328	—
MS-1210	Chassis	3462	3340	—
MS-1210	Chassis	3493	3362	—
Travelall 150 — 1/2-Ton — 120 in. w.b.				
150	Station Wagon 4x2	4973	4597	—
150	Station Wagon 4x4	5836	4803	—
Travelall 200 — 3/4-Ton — 120 in. w.b.				
200	Station Wagon 4x2	5172	4831	—
200	Station Wagon 4x4	6024	5051	—
150 — 4x2 — 1/2-Ton — 115 in. w.b.				
150	Chassis & Cab	3800	3624	—
150	Bonus Load Pickup	3952	4029	—
150 — 4x2 1/2-Ton — 132 in. w.b.				
150	Chassis & Cab	3824	3687	—
150	Bonus Load Pickup	3988	4143	—
Series 150 — 4x4 — 1/2-Ton — 115 in. w.b.				
150	Chassis & Cab	4575	3872	—
150	Bonus Load Pickup 115 in. w.b.	4729	4283	—
Series 150 — 4x4 — 1/2-Ton — 132 in. w.b.				
150	Chassis & Cab	4601	3938	—
150	Bonus Load Pickup	4765	4394	—

Series 200 — 4x2 — 3/4-Ton — 132 in. w.b.				
200	Chassis & Cab	4166	3922	—
200	Bonus Load Pickup	4330	4378	—
Series 200 — 4x2 — 3/4-Ton — 149 in. w.b.				
200	Chassis & Cab	4176	3984	—
200	Travelette Chassis & Cab	4897	4377	—
200	Bonus Load Travelette Pickup	5059	4788	—
Series 200 — 4x2 — 3/4-Ton — 158 in. w.b.				
200	Chassis & Cab	4226	4024	—
Series 200 — 4x4 — 3/4-Ton — 166 in. w.b.				
200	Travelette Chassis & Cab 5048	4435	—	
200	Bonus Load Travelette Pickup	5212	4891	—
Series 200 — 4x4 — 3/4-Ton — 132 in. w.b.				
200	Chassis & Cab	5008	4136	—
200	Bonus Load Pickup	5173	4592	—

ENGINE [Scout II XLC, Base]: Inline, OHV. Four-cylinder. Cast iron block. Bore & stroke: 4-1/8 in. x 3-21/32 in. Displacement: 196 cid.. Compression ratio: 8.02:1. Brake horsepower: 86 at 3800 rpm. Net horsepower: 27.2. Maximum Torque: 157 lbs.-ft. at 2200 rpm. Hydraulic valve lifters. Carburetor: Holley model 1920.

ENGINE [Scout II XLC, Optional]: Vee-block, OHV. Eight-cylinder. Cast iron block. Bore & stroke: 3-7/8 in. x 3-7/32 in. Displacement: 304 cid.. Compression ratio: 8.2:1. Brake horsepower: 140 at 3800 rpm. Net horsepower: 48.1. Maximum Torque: 243 lbs.-ft. at 2400 rpm. Hydraulic valve lifters. Carburetor: Holley model 2210C.

ENGINE [Scout II XLC, Optional]: Vee-block, OHV. Eight-cylinder. Cast iron block. Bore & stroke: 3-7/8 in. x 3-21/32 in. Displacement: 345 cid.. Compression ratio: 8.05:1. Brake horsepower: 158 at 3600 rpm. Net horsepower: 48.1. Maximum Torque: 288 lbs.-ft. at 2000 rpm. Hydraulic valve lifters. Carburetor: Holley two-barrel model 2210. (Also available with Holley 2300 four-barrel carb. The four-barrel engine also had 8.05:1 compression. It was rated 168 hp at 3800 rpm and developed 288 lbs.-ft of torque at 2000 rpm.)

ENGINE [Travelall, Optional]: Vee-block, OHV. Eight-cylinder. Cast iron block. Bore & stroke: 4-1/8 in. x 3-21/32 in. Displacement: 392 cid.. Compression ratio: 8.02:1. Brake horsepower: 187 at 3600 rpm. Maximum Torque: 307 lbs.-ft. at 2400 rpm. Hydraulic valve lifters. Carburetor: Holley four-barrel model 4150. (Also available with 8.0:1 compression ratio; 191 hp at 3600 rpm and 307 lbs.-ft. of torque at 2400 rpm.)

CHASSIS [Scout II XLC]: Wheelbase: 100 in. Tires: H78 x 15 in.

CHASSIS [Metro]: Wheelbase: 125-159 in. Tires: 8.75 x 16 in.

CHASSIS [Series 150]: Wheelbase: 115-132 in. Tires: H78 x 15 in.

CHASSIS [Series 200]: Wheelbase: 132-166 in. Tires: 8.00 x 16.5 in.

TECHNICAL [4x2 Models, Typical]: Manual (synchromesh) transmission. Speeds: 3F/ 1R. Column mounted gearshift lever. Single-plate dry-disc clutch. Single reduction rear axle. Four-wheel hydraulic brakes. Steel disc wheels. Four-speed transmission. Automatic transmission. Overdrive.

OPTIONS: Chrome front bumper, Series 200. Rear bumper. Air conditioning ($540). Automatic transmission ($287). Power steering ($154). Power brakes. Bumper guards. AM radio ($77). Heater. Clock. Cigar lighter. Radio antenna. Seat covers. Trailer towing package ($451). Deluxe exterior trim package ($144). Custom exterior trim package ($299). Camper Special Package, Series 200 with 4x4 ($302). Tinted glass. V-345 V-8 engine ($40). V-392 V-8 engine ($167). Wheel trim rings. Clearance lamps, Series 200 cab. Dual outside rearview mirrors. California trucker mirrors. Rear step bumper. Spare tire and carrier. AM/FM radio.

OPTION INSTALLATION RATES: The following data indicates the percentage of total IHC truck production having the specified options installed. Data is arranged according to series. Percentage figures, in brackets, indicate installation rate. Total series output is given at end of each data block.

SERIES 150: Automatic transmission (64.4 percent); power disc brakes (100.0 percent); power steering (83.9 percent); V-8 engines 350 cid or less (90.3 percent); V-8 engines over 350 cid (9.7 percent); limited-slip rear axle (68.3 percent); four-wheel drive (43.7 percent); interior trim package (12.1 percent); exterior trim package (30.0 percent); AM radio (71.5 percent); AM/FM stereo radio (0.7 percent); tinted glass (22.1 percent); air conditioning (58.6 percent). Total output 6,618 trucks.

SERIES 200: Automatic transmission (39.1 percent); power disc brakes (100.0 percent); power steering (83.7 percent); V-8 engines 350 cid or less (76.3 percent); V-8 engines over 350 cid (23.7 percent); limited-slip rear axle (19.5 percent); dual rear wheels (0.3 percent); four-wheel drive (46.2 percent); interior trim package (6.6 percent); exterior trim package (12.5 percent); AM radio (57.0 percent); AM/FM stereo radio (0.5 percent); tinted glass (13.3 percent); air conditioning (33.5 percent); total output 10,418.

TRAVELALL 150: Automatic transmission (95.3 percent); power disc brakes (100.0 percent); power steering (93.8 percent); V-8 engines 350 cid or less (36.1 percent); V-8 engines over 350 cid (63.9 percent); limited-slip rear axle (11.7 percent); four-wheel drive (18.3 percent); interior trim package (71.4 percent); exterior trim package (37.4 percent); AM radio (55.6 percent); AM/FM stereo radio (4.6 percent); tinted glass (78.6 percent); air conditioning (86.1 percent). Total output 4,224 trucks.

TRAVELALL 200: Automatic transmission (22.2 percent); power disc brakes (100.0 percent); power steering (31.0 percent); V-8 engines 350 cid or less (43.3 percent); V-8 engines over 350 cid (56.7 percent); limited-slip rear axle (44.8 percent); four-wheel drive (52.0 percent) interior trim package (11.5 percent); exterior trim package (5.7 percent); AM radio (13.8 percent); AM/FM stereo radio (2.7 percent); tinted glass (26.8 percent); air conditioning (16.9 percent). Total output 563 trucks.

SCOUT II: Automatic transmission (58.2 percent); power disc brakes (100.0 percent); power steering (79.3 percent); V-8 engines 350 cid or less (82.1 percent); limited-slip rear axle (39.2 percent); four-wheel drive (88.9 percent); steel-belted radial tires (11.2 percent); wheelcovers (64.5 percent); interior trim package (61.8 percent); exterior trim package (63.5 percent); AM radio (73.5 percent); AM/FM stereo radio (10.2 percent); tinted glass (38.5 percent); air conditioning (32.3 percent). Total output 21,366 trucks.

HISTORICAL: Introduced Fall 1974. Calendar year production: [All IHC trucks]: 111,352. Model year production [Scout]: 25,904. Model year production: [Pickups]: 6,329. Innovations: New 150 Series replaces 100 Series in 1/2-ton lineup. This was the final year of production of IHC Metro vans and conventional light-duty pickups, Travelall and Travelette models.

1975 IHC 1/2-Ton Model 150 Custom Travelall Station Wagon (RCA)

1976 IHC

1976 IHC 1/4-Ton Scout II Terra Compact Sport Pickup (JAG)

SCOUT — SERIES XLC — FOUR-CYLINDER: International Harvester Co. decided to concentrate on its heavy-duty truck line in 1976. As a result, all Metro vans, Travelall station wagons and regular pickups were dropped from production. The only light-duty models available were in the Scout line. Two new Scouts were introduced. They had a longer 118 in. wheelbase. The hatchback station wagon was called a Traveler. A pickup truck with a 6-ft. box and 11 cu. ft. of behind-the-seat storage was called the Terra. Also available was the 100 in. wheelbase Scout II with its familiar Traveltop station wagon configuration. All three Scout models had a restyled grille design. It was divided into three vertical segments, each of which was filled with five horizontal bars. They offered special side appliques. These included white panels, woodgrain with cork finish, a stylized red feather design and Rallye racing stripes extending along the sides and up onto the hood. Nine exterior colors now included Winter white, Terra Cotta, Fire orange, Dark brown metallic, Solar yellow, Pewter metallic, Grenoble green, Buckskin, and Glacier blue. Interiors included carpeting, bucket seats and vinyl panels in Ivy green, Wedgewood blue, Parchment, Tanbark and Custom Saddle. Among standard equipment features were power disc brakes, chrome dual mirrors, chrome front and rear bumpers and wheelcovers, day/night mirror, increased capacity cooling and undercoating. Four-wheel drive was available in two versions: a dash-operated single-speed transfer case and a floor-mounted two-speed transfer case. A diesel engine was a new option.

I.D. DATA: Serial number located on the left door pillar. The serial number consists of 13 symbols. The first six symbols identify the serial number. The seventh (digit) designates the manufacturing plant. The last six digits are sequential production numbers. Numbers are not available.

1976 IHC 1/4-Ton Scout II Terra Compact Sport Pickup (JAG)

Model	Body Type	Price	Weight	Prod. Total
Scout II — Four-cylinder (Gas) — 1/4-Ton — 100 in. w.b.				
XLC	Traveltop 4x2	4793	3746	Note 1
XLC	Traveltop 4x4	5751	3846	Note 1
Scout II — Six-cylinder (Diesel) — 1/4-Ton — 100 in. w.b.				
XLC	Traveltop 4x2	7381	3983	Note 1
XLC	Traveltop 4x4	8394	4083	Note 1

Terra — Four-cylinder (Gas) — 1/4-Ton — 118 in. w.b.				
XLC	Terra Pickup 4x2	4612	3761	Note 2
XLC	Terra Pickup 4x4	5637	3861	Note 2
Terra — Six-Cylinder (Diesel) — 1/4-Ton — 118 in. w.b.				
XLC	Terra Pickup 4x2	7200	4026	Note 2
XLC	Terra Pickup 4x4	8285	4126	Note 2
Traveler — Four-cylinder (Gas) — 1/4-Ton — 118 in. w.b.				
XLC	Station Wagon 4x2	5172	4101	Note 3
XLC	Station Wagon 4x4	6122	4201	Note 3
Traveler — Six-cylinder (Diesel) — 1/4-Ton — 118 in. w.b.				
XLC	Station Wagon 4x2	7760	4101	Note 3
XLC	Station Wagon 4x4	8770	4202	Note 3

NOTE 1: Model year production of Scout II models totaled 17,506 units.
NOTE 2: Model year production of Scout/Terra models totaled 6,496 units.
NOTE 3: Model year production of Scout/Traveler models totaled 7,635 units.

1976 IHC 1/4-Ton Scout II Compact Sport Utility Wagon (RCA)

ENGINE [Base]: Inline. OHV. Slanted mounting. Four-cylinder. Cast iron block. Bore & stroke: 4-1/8 in. x 3-21/32 in. Displacement: 196 cid.. Compression ratio: 8.02:1. Brake horsepower: 86 at 3800 rpm. Net horsepower: 27.2. Maximum Torque: 157 lbs.-ft at 2200 rpm. Hydraulic valve lifters. Carburetor: Holley one-barrel model 1904.

ENGINE [Diesel]: Inline. OHV. Slant-mounted diesel. Six-cylinder. Cast iron block. Bore & stroke: 3.27 in. x 3.94 in. Displacement: 198 cid.. Brake horsepower: 92. (This 6-33 engine was built by Nissan of Japan.)

ENGINE [Optional]: Vee-block. OHV. Eight-cylinder. Cast iron block. Bore & stroke: 3-7/8 in. x 3-7/32 in. Displacement: 304 cid.. Compression ratio: 8.2:1. Brake horsepower: 140 at 3800 rpm. Net horsepower: 48.1. Maximum Torque: 243 lbs.-ft at 2400 rpm. Hydraulic valve lifters. Carburetor: Holley two-barrel 2210.

ENGINE [Optional]: Vee-block. OHV. Eight-cylinder. Cast iron block. Bore & stroke: 3-7/8 in. x 3-21/32 in. Displacement: 345 cid.. Compression ratio: 8.05:1. Brake horsepower 168 at 3800 rpm. Maximum Torque: 288 lbs.-ft at 2000 rpm. Hydraulic valve lifters. Carburetor: Holley four-barrel model 2300.

1976 IHC 1/4-Ton Scout II Compact Sport Utility Wagon (JAG)

CHASSIS [Scout II]: Wheelbase: 100 in. Overall length: 166.2 in. Height: 65.7 in. Front tread: 58.5 in. Rear tread: 57.62 in. Tires: H78 x 15 LRB.

CHASSIS [Scout Terra]: Wheelbase: 118 in. Overall length: 184.2 in. Height: 66 in. Front tread: 58.5 in. Rear tread: 57.62 in. Tires: H78 x 15 LRB.

CHASSIS [Scout Traveler]: Wheelbase: 118 in. Overall length: 184.2 in. Height: 66 in. Front tread: 58.5 in. Rear tread: 57.62 in. Tires: H78 x 15 LRB.

Other dimensions [all models]. Overall width, 70 in. Tailgate opening width, 54.8 in. Tailgate opening height, 40 in. width between wheel well housings, 42 in. Minimum ground clearance, 7.6 in. The turning diameter was 33 ft. 10 in for the Scout II and 38 ft. 10 in for other models.

527

1976 IHC 1/4-Ton Scout II Compact Sport Utility Wagon (JAG)

TECHNICAL [4x2]: Manual (synchromesh) transmission. Speeds: 3F/1R. Floor-mounted gearshift lever. 11-inch angle link, 2,000 lbs. plate pressure clutch. Dana-44 rear axle. Overall ratio: 3.54:1 or 3.73:1. Power front disc/rear drum brakes. Steel disc wheels. Drivetrain options: Trac-Lok limited-slip differential. Heavy-duty clutch. Four-speed transmission. Automatic transmission.

TECHNICAL [4x4]: Manual synchromesh transmission. Speeds: 3F/1R. Floor-mounted gearshift lever. 11-inch angle link, 2,000 lbs. plate pressure clutch. Dana-44, 3,500 lbs. driving rear axle. Overall ratio: 3.54:1 or 3.73 to 1. Front power disc/rear drum brakes. Five-stud steel disc wheels with 6.00 JK rims.

1976 IHC 1/4-Ton Scout II Compact Sport Utility Wagon — Diesel (RCA)

OPTIONS: Four-speed transmission ($165). Automatic transmission, except diesel ($306); with diesel ($141). Two-speed transfer case, 4x4, standard with diesel ($67). Right-hand drive ($144). Power steering, with 4x2 ($172); with 4x4 ($189). Air conditioning/heater package ($497). Trailering package ($183). Rally package, with 4x2 ($631); with 4x4 ($648). Custom interior trim, with Traveltop ($221); with Terra ($198); with Traveler ($261). Radial tire chrome wheel package ($366). Deluxe exterior trim package ($60). Deluxe interior trim package ($134). California emissions, without air pump ($39); with air pump ($80). AM radio ($83). AM/FM radio ($184). Cruise control ($80). Console, requires bucket seats ($48). Electric clock ($24). Tilt steering wheel, standard with diesel ($73). Door edge guards ($8). Bumper step with hitch ball ($37). Bodyside moldings ($31). Skid plate protector ($39). Automatic front locking hubs with 4x4 ($72). Dual mirrors ($48). Luggage rack, except Terra ($92). Chrome tie-down rails on Terra ($70). 61-amp. alternator ($42). Trac-Lok axle ($82). Optional axle ratios ($17). 72-amp. battery ($19). Heavy-duty shocks ($13). Heavy-duty front springs and shocks, with 4x4 ($17); Terra with 4x4 ($19); Terra & Traveler with 4x2 ($45). Heavy-duty rear springs & shocks, Traveltop with 4x4 ($29). Heavy-duty front & rear springs & shocks, Traveler ($38). Modulated fan ($41). Tu Tone paint ($115). Tan vinyl bucket seats ($79); other colors ($101). Rear folding seat, except Terra ($160). Cargo area mat, except Terra ($32). Sliding rear quarter window, Traveltop ($51); Traveler ($66).

OPTION INSTALLATION RATES: The following data indicates the percentage of total IHC truck production having the specified options installed. Data is arranged according to series. Percentage figures, in brackets, indicate installation rate.

TERRA PICKUP: 350 cid and less V-8 (60.1 percent); six-cylinder (5.6 percent); automatic transmission. (41.0 percent); four-speed (36.3 percent); power disc brakes (100.0 percent); power steering (75.9 percent); limited-slip rear differential (34.8 percent); four-wheel drive (54.7 percent); radial tires (4.5 percent); trailer tow equipment (2.5 percent); rear bumper (100.0 percent); wheelcovers (95.7 percent); styled wheels (4.3 percent); trim groups interior (47.0 percent); exterior (47.7 percent); bucket seats (9.9 percent); tinted glass (100.0 percent); air conditioning (15.9 percent); adjustable steering column (7.2 percent); radios AM (78.9 percent); AM/FM (7.3 percent).

SCOUT II: 350 cid and less V-8 (80.6 percent); six-cylinder engines (1.5 percent); automatic transmission (61.7 percent); four-speed (22.6 percent); power disc brakes (100.0 percent); power steering (86.6 percent); limited-slip rear differential (31.8 percent); four-wheel drive (93.3 percent); radial tires (11.5 percent); trailer tow equipment (3.4 percent); rear bumper (100.0 percent); wheelcovers (92.3 percent); styled wheels (7.7 percent); interior trim groups (74.5 percent); exterior trim groups (66.6 percent); bucket seats (44.1 percent); tinted glass (100.0 percent); air conditioning (37.3 percent); adjustable steering column (20.1 percent); radios AM (59.5 percent); AM/FM (23.0 percent).

TRAVELER: 350 cid and less V-8 (88.3 percent); six-cylinder engines (6.1 percent); automatic transmission. (83.7 percent); four-speed (12.0 percent); power disc brakes (100.0 percent); power steering (96.0 percent); limited-slip rear differential (32.5 percent); four-wheel drive (77.2 percent); radial tires (35.9 percent); trailer tow equipment (25.8 percent);

rear bumper (100.0 percent); wheelcovers (84.1 percent); styled wheels (15.9 percent); interior trim groups (90.0 percent); exterior trim groups (86.9 percent); bucket seats (48.2 percent); tinted glass (100.0 percent); air conditioning (65.9 percent); adjustable steering column (50.7 percent); radios AM (54.2 percent); AM/FM (38.8 percent).

1976 IHC 1/4-Ton Scout II Terra Compact Sport Pickup (JAG)

HISTORICAL: Introduced Fall 1975. Calendar year registrations [All IHC trucks]: 100,657. Market share: 3.29 percent. Calendar year registrations by weight class: [Under 6,000 lbs.] none; [6,001 to 10,000 lbs.] 34,100. Calendar year production [All IHC trucks]: 114,855. Calendar year retail sales [Scout]: 30,555. Calendar year production [Scout II]: 25,840. Calendar year production [Terra Pickups]: 15,732. Innovations: New series of light trucks (Terra) and station wagons (Traveler) introduced. IH became the first American manufacturer to offer diesel power as an option on the Scout II, Traveler and Terra. B. McCormick continued as IH President and Chief executive officer. J.P. Kaine became, president of the Truck Group. The company operated four U.S. plants in Springfield, Ohio; Fort Wayne, Ind., Indianapolis, Ind. and Shadyside, Ohio during 1976. It had 14,358 employees in these plants. Another 1,482 workers were employed at a fifth plant in Chatham, Ont., Canada. During calendar year 1976, IH built 42,683 trucks in Springfield, 72,172 trucks in Ft. Wayne and 13,500 trucks in Canada.

1976 IHC 1/4-Ton Scout II Traveler Sport Utility (JAG)

1977 IHC

SCOUT — SERIES XLC — FOUR (GAS)/SIX (DIESEL): For 1977, the Scout's headlamp buckets were made a bit squarer. A new grille design featured two, thin rectangular loops stacked on top of each other with thin vertical blades behind them. The International nameplate appeared on the left-hand side between the loops. A new SSII package was introduced and priced at $5,251. Standard equipment included all standard safety, anti-theft, convenience and emission control equipment; 196 cid.. four-cylinder engine (except diesel models); three-speed manual synchronized floor shift; power front disc and rear drum brakes; H78 x 15 LRB blackwall tires; stainless steel wheels; undercoating; dual chrome door-mounted mirrors; tinted glass; dual electric horns; vinyl interior; cigar lighter; manual locking hubs (4x4 models); steel cab with fiberglass top (Terra); and full-length white top with integral headliner (Traveler). New options for 1977 models included cruise control and tilt steering.

1977 IHC 1/4-Ton Scout XLC Traveler Sport Utility (JAG)

1977 IHC 1/4-Ton Scout XLC Traveler Sport Utility (RCA)

1977 IHC 1/4-Ton Scout XLC Safari Sport Utility (Dick Bova)

ENGINE [Base]: Inline. OHV. Slanted mounting. Four-cylinder. Cast iron block. Bore & stroke: 4-1/8 in. x 3-21/32 in. Displacement: 196 cid.. Compression ratio: 8.02:1. Brake horsepower: 86 at 3800 rpm. Net horsepower: 27.2. Maximum Torque: 157 lbs.-ft at 2200 rpm. Hydraulic valve lifters. Carburetor: Holley one-barrel model 1904.

ENGINE [Diesel]: Inline, OHV. Slant-mounted diesel. Six-cylinder. Cast iron block. Bore & stroke: 3.27 in. x 3.94 in. Displacement: 198 cid.. Brake horsepower: 92. (This 6-33 engine was built by Nissan of Japan.)

ENGINE [Optional]: Vee-block. OHV. Eight-cylinder. Cast iron block. Bore & stroke: 3-7/8 in. x 3-7/32 in. Displacement: 304 cid.. Compression ratio: 8.2:1. Brake horsepower: 140 at 3800 rpm. Net horsepower: 48.1. Maximum Torque: 243 lbs.-ft at 2400 rpm. Hydraulic valve lifters. Carburetor: Holley two-barrel model 2210.

ENGINE [Optional]: Vee-block. OHV. Eight-cylinder. Cast iron block. Bore & stroke: 3-7/8 in. x 3-21/32 in. Displacement: 345 cid.. Compression ratio: 8.05:1. Brake horsepower 168 at 3800 rpm. Maximum Torque: 288 lbs.-ft at 2000 rpm. Hydraulic valve lifters. Carburetor: Holley four-barrel model 2300.

CHASSIS [Scout II]: Wheelbase: 100 in. Length: 166.2 in. Height: 65.7 in. Front tread: 58.5 in. Rear tread: 57.62 in. Tires: H78 x 15 LRB.

CHASSIS [Scout Terra]: Wheelbase: 118 in. Length: 184.2 in. Height: 66 in. Front tread: 58.5 in. Rear tread: 57.62 in. Tires: H78 x 15 LRB.

CHASSIS [Scout Traveler]: Wheelbase: 118 in. Length: 184.2 in. Height: 66 in. Front tread: 58.2 in. Rear tread: 57.62 in. Tires: H78 x 15 LRB.

TECHNICAL [4x2]: Manual (synchromesh) transmission. Speeds: 3F/1R. Floor-mounted gearshift lever. 11-inch angle link, 2,000 lbs. plate pressure clutch. Dana-44 rear axle. Overall ratio: 3.54:1 or 3.73:1. Power front disc/rear drum brakes. Steel disc wheels. Drivetrain options: Trac-Lok limited-slip differential. Heavy-duty clutch. Four-speed transmission. Automatic transmission.

TECHNICAL [4x4]: Manual synchromesh transmission. Speeds: 3F/1R. Floor-mounted gearshift lever. 11-inch angle link, 2,000 lbs. plate pressure clutch. Dana-44, 3,500 lbs. driving rear axle. Overall ratio: 3.54:1 or 3.73 to 1. Front power disc/rear drum brakes. Five-stud steel disc wheels with 6.00 JK rims.

OPTIONS: Four-speed transmission ($165). Automatic transmission, except diesel ($306); with diesel ($141). Two-speed transfer case, 4x4 standard with diesel ($67). Right-hand drive ($144). Power steering, with 4x2 ($172); with 4x4 ($189). Air conditioning/heater package ($497). Trailering package ($183). Rally package, with 4x2 ($631); with 4x4 ($648). Custom interior trim, with Traveltop ($221); with Terra ($198); with Traveler ($261). Radial tire chrome wheel package ($366). Deluxe exterior trim package ($50). Deluxe interior trim package ($134). California emissions, without air pump ($39); with air pump ($80). AM radio ($83). AM/FM radio ($184). Cruise control ($80). Console, requires bucket seats ($48). Electric clock ($24). Tilt steering wheel, standard with diesel ($73). Door edge guards ($8). Bumper step with hitch ball ($37). Bodyside moldings ($31). Skid plate protector ($39). Automatic front locking hubs with 4x4 ($72). Dual mirrors ($48). Luggage rack, except Terra ($92). Chrome tie-down rails on Terra ($70). 61-amp. alternator ($42). Trac-Lok axle ($82). Optional axle ratios ($17). 72-amp. battery ($19). Heavy-duty shocks ($13). Heavy-duty front springs & shocks, Traveltop with 4x4 ($17); Terra & Traveler with 4x2 ($45). Heavy-duty rear springs & shocks, Traveltop with 4x4 ($29). Heavy-duty front & rear springs & shocks, Traveler ($38). Modulated fan ($41). Tu-tone paint ($115). Tan vinyl bucket seats ($79); other colors ($101). Rear folding seat, except Terra ($160). Cargo area mat, except Terra ($32). Sliding rear quarter window, Traveltop ($51); Traveler ($66).

OPTION INSTALLATION RATES: The following data indicates the percentage of factory options installed on 1977 IHC trucks according to series. Percentage figures in brackets indicate installation rate. Series production for model year is given at the end of each data block.

TERRA: V-8 engine (64.2 percent); diesel (14.1 percent); automatic transmission (45.6 percent); four-speed transmission. (37.6 percent); front disc brakes (100 percent); power steering (82.3 percent); limited-slip (42 percent); four-wheel drive (77.8 percent); styled wheels (10.1 percent); standard wheelcovers (89.9 percent); towing package (0.2 percent); rear bumper, standard (32.9 percent); rear bumper, step type (67.1 percent); custom interior trim (47.6 percent); custom exterior trim (46.6 percent); bucket seats (15.1 percent); air conditioning (17.7 percent); tilt steering (11.6 percent); speed control (5.8 percent); AM radio (56.2 percent); AM/FM radio (24.6 percent); radial tires (4.6 percent). Total output: 2,688 trucks.

SCOUT II: V-8 engine (87.5 percent); diesel engine (1.7 percent); automatic transmission. (68.7 percent); four-speed transmission. (23.7 percent); front disc brakes (100 percent); power steering (94.3 percent); limited-slip (38.5 percent); four-wheel drive (96.2 percent); styled wheels (37.8 percent); standard wheelcovers (56.8 percent); towing package (1.9 percent); rear bumper, standard (48.1 percent); rear bumper, step type (51.4 percent); custom interior trim (61.1 percent); custom exterior trim (58.9 percent); bucket seats (41.4 percent); air conditioning (31.1 percent); tilt steering (20.6 percent); speed control (19.3 percent); AM radio (50.3 percent); AM/FM radio (24.6 percent); radial tires (9.5 percent). Total output: 27,074 trucks.

TRAVELER: V-8 engine (93.3 percent); diesel engine (5.2 percent); automatic transmission (89.3 percent); four-speed transmission (9.2 percent); front disc brakes (100 percent); power steering (98.1 percent); limited-slip (30.2 percent); four-wheel drive (89.7 percent); styled wheels (30.4 percent); standard wheel cover (69.6 percent); towing package (23.5 percent); rear bumper, standard (71.9 percent); rear bumper, step type (28.1 percent); custom interior trim (94 percent); custom exterior trim (81.8 percent); bucket seats (65.5 percent); air conditioning (68 percent); tilt steering (56.9 percent); speed control (57.5 percent); AM radio (41.1 percent); AM/FM radio (46.6 percent); radial tires (38.1 percent). Total output: 9,620 trucks.

I.D. DATA: Serial number located on the left door pillar. The serial number consists of 13 symbols. The first six symbols identify the serial number. The seventh (digit) designates the manufacturing plant. The last six digits are sequential production numbers. Numbers are not available.

Model	Body Type	Price	Weight	Prod. Total
Scout II — 1/4-Ton — Four-cylinder (Gas) — 100 in. w.b.				
XLC	Traveltop 4x2	4793	3746	Note 1
XLC	Traveltop 4x4	5751	3846	Note 1
Scout II — 1/4-Ton — Six-Cylinder (Diesel) — 100 in. w.b.				
XLC	Traveltop 4x2	7381	3983	Note 1
XLC	Traveltop 4x4	8394	4083	Note 1
Terra — 1/4-Ton — Four-cylinder (Gas) — 118 in. w.b.				
XLC	Pickup 4x2	4612	3761	Note 2
XLC	Pickup 4x4	5637	3861	Note 2
Terra — 1/4-Ton — Six-cylinder (Diesel) — 118 in. w.b.				
XLC	Pickup 4x2	7200	4026	Note 2
XLC	Pickup 4x4	8285	4126	Note 2
Traveler — 1/4-Ton — Four-cylinder (Gas) — 118 in. w.b.				
XLC	Station Wagon 4x2	5172	4101	Note 3
XLC	Station Wagon 4x4	6122	4201	Note 3
Traveler — 1/4-Ton — Six-cylinder (Diesel) — 118 in. w.b.				
XLC	Station Wagon 4x2	7760	4101	Note 3
XLC	Station Wagon 4x4	8770	4201	Note 3

NOTE 1: Model year production of Scout II models totaled 27,074 units.
NOTE 2: Model year production of Scout/Terra models totaled 2,688 units.
NOTE 3: Model year production of Scout/Traveler models totaled 9,620 units.

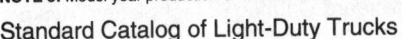

Standard Catalog of Light-Duty Trucks

1977 IHC 1/4-Ton Scout SS II Sport Utility (OCW)

HISTORICAL: Introduced Fall 1976. Calendar year registrations: [All IHC trucks]: 107,564. Calendar year retail sales: [Scout II]: 32,004. Calendar year production: [All IHC trucks]: 110,894. Market share: 3.18 percent. Calendar year registrations by weight class: [6,000 to 10,000 lbs.]: 32,046. Model year production by model: [Terra] 2,688; [Scout II] 27,074; [Traveler] 9,620; [Total]: 39,382. Innovations: New grille. New Scout SSII model.

1978 IHC

1978 IHC 1/4-Ton Scout XLC Rallye Sport Utility Wagon (JAG)

SCOUT — SERIES XLC — ALL ENGINES: The Scouts from IHC had a slightly revised grille design for 1978. Basically, the vertical blades were removed from the grille ensemble and the rectangular-shaped bright metal surround was made thicker. Inside the surround were two thin, horizontal loops of chrome stacked one on top of the other. The single, round headlamps were housed in large squares on either side of the grille and these were also trimmed with bright metal moldings. The SSII model had its own distinct grille with seven vertical members. Standard equipment included all safety, anti-theft and emissions items required to meet government standards; 196 cid.. four-cylinder engine; three-speed manual synchronized floor shift; manual steering; power-front disc and rear drum brakes; H78 x 15 LRB blackwall tires; stainless steel wheels; undercoating; dual chrome door-mounted mirrors; tinted glass; dual electric horns; vinyl interior; cigar lighter; manual locking hubs (4x4 models); steel cab with fiberglass top (Terra models); and full-length white top with integral headliner (Traveler models). The diesel engine was strictly an extra-cost option this year. It had a $2,581 pricetag.

1978 IHC 1/4-Ton Scout XLC Compact Sport Utility Wagon (RCA)

I.D. DATA: Serial number located on left door pillar post. The serial number consisted of 13 symbols. The first six symbols identified the serial number. The seventh digit designated the manufacturing plant. The last six digits were sequential production numbers. Numbers are not available.

Model	Body Type	Price	Weight	Prod. Total
Scout — V-8 — 4x4				
XLC	Scout II Traveltop	6329	3846	—
XLC	Scout Terra Pickup	6284	3861	—
XLC	Scout SSII	5563	3455	—
XLC	Traveler Station Wagon	6975	4200	—

NOTE 1: Prices/weights for 4x4 models with the 304 cid V-8 ($170 option).
NOTE 2: 4x4 running gear was around $1,000 extra.

1978 IHC 1/4-Ton Scout XLC SSII Sport Utility (RCA)

ENGINE [Base]: Inline. OHV. Slanted mounting. Four-cylinder. Cast iron block. Bore & stroke: 4-1/8 in. x 3-21/32 in. Displacement: 196 cid.. Compression ratio: 8.02:1. Brake horsepower: 86 at 3800 rpm. Net horsepower: 27.2. Maximum Torque: 157 lbs.-ft. at 2200 rpm. Hydraulic valve lifters. Carburetor: Holley one-barrel model 1904.
ENGINE [Diesel]: Inline. OHV. Slant-mounted diesel. Six-cylinder. Cast iron block. Bore & stroke: 3.27 in. x 3.94 in. Displacement: 198 cid.. Brake horsepower: 92. (This 6-33 engine was built by Nissan of Japan.)
ENGINE [Optional]: Vee-block. OHV. Eight-cylinder. Cast iron block. Bore & stroke: 3-7/8 in. x 3-7/32 in. Displacement: 304 cid.. Compression ratio: 8.2:1. Brake horsepower: 140 at 3800 rpm. Net horsepower: 48.1. Maximum Torque: 243 lbs.-ft. at 2400 rpm. Hydraulic valve lifters. Carburetor: Holley two-barrel model 2210.
ENGINE [Optional]: Vee-block. OHV. Eight-cylinder. Cast iron block. Bore & stroke: 3-7/8 in. x 3-21/32 in. Displacement: 345 cid.. Compression ratio: 8.05:1. Brake horsepower 168 at 3800 rpm. Maximum Torque: 288 lbs.-ft. at 2000 rpm. Hydraulic valve lifters. Carburetor: Holley four-barrel model 2300.
CHASSIS [Scout II]: Wheelbase: 100 in. Length: 166.2 in. Height: 65.7 in. Front tread: 58.5 in. Rear tread: 57.62 in. Tires: H78 x 15 LRB.
CHASSIS [Scout SSII]: Wheelbase: 100 in. Length: 166.2 in. Front tread: 58.5 in. Rear tread: 57.62 in. Tires: H78 x 15 LRB.
CHASSIS [Terra/Traveler]: Wheelbase: 118 in. Length: 184.2 in. Height: 66.0 in. Front tread: 58.5 in. Rear tread: 57.62 in. Tires: H78 x 15 LRB.
TECHNICAL: Manual (synchromesh) transmission. Speeds: 3F/1R. Floor-mounted gearshift lever. Clutch: 11 in. angle link, 2,000 lbs. plate pressure. Dana-44 3500 lbs. capacity rear driving axle. Overall ratio: 3.73:1. Front power disc/rear drum brakes. Five-stud disc wheels. Four-speed manual transmission (wide-ratio). Four-speed manual transmission (close-ratio). Three-speed automatic tranmission. Transmission oil cooler. Four-wheel drive (4x4).
OPTIONS: Optional equipment was similar to 1977 models at similar prices. The 6-33 (Nissan-built) diesel engine was $2,581 extra. A new Rallye trim package was $687 extra. The 345 cid V-8 cost $123 over the price of a 304 cid V-8.
OPTION INSTALLATION RATES: The following data indicates the percentage of factory options installed on 1977 IHC trucks according to series. Percentage figures in brackets indicate installation rate. Series production for model year is given at the end of each data block.
[TERRA]: Engines: V-8 under 350 cid (72.6 percent); diesel (7.4 percent); L-4 (20.0 percent); automatic transmission (40.9 percent); four-speed (46.1 percent); power front disc brakes (100.0 percent); power steering (78.5 percent); radial tires (3.3 percent); four-wheel drive (88.7 percent); limited-slip rear differential (38.7 percent); styled wheels (15.8 percent); wheelcovers, standard (84.2 percent); regular bumpers (34.0 percent) step bumper (66.0 percent); trailer towing equipment (2.2 percent); trim groups interior (54.5 percent), exterior (61.8 percent); two-tone paint (NA); exterior stripes (NA); bucket seats (21.5 percent); tinted glass (100.0 percent); air conditioning (18.1 percent); speed regulator (7.5 percent); adjustable steering column (13.3 percent); AM audio equipment (50.9 percent), AM/FM (11.8 percent); sun roof (1.4 percent). Total output: 2,966 trucks.
SCOUT II: Engines: V-8 under 350 cid (87.7 percent); diesel (2.0 percent); L-4 (10.3 percent); automatic transmission (73.0 percent); four-speed transmission (20.2 percent); power front disc brakes (100.0 percent); power steering (94.3 percent); radial tires (7.6 percent); four-wheel drive (97.4 percent); limited-slip rear differential (34.8 percent); styled wheels (21.6 percent); wheelcovers, standard (78.4 percent); regular bumpers (47.3 percent); step bumper (52.7 percent); trailer towing equipment (2.7 percent); trim groups, interior (76.8 percent), exterior (80.3 percent); two-tone paint (NA); exterior stripes (NA); bucket seats (63.4 percent); tinted glass (100.0 percent); air conditioning (40.3 percent); speed regulator (26.5 percent); adjustable steering column (31.3 percent); audio equipment AM (44.4 percent), AM/FM (24.9 percent); sun roof (0.6 percent). Total output: 26,369 trucks.
TRAVELER: Engines: V-8 under 350 cid (90.8 percent); diesel (7.6 percent); L-4 (1.6 percent); transmission, automatic (88.3 percent); four-speed (10.6 percent); power front disc brakes (100.0 percent); power steering (93.9 percent); radial tires (52.9 percent); four-wheel drive (96.4 percent); limited-slip rear differential (28.6 percent); styled wheels (22.8 percent); wheelcovers, standard (77.2 percent); regular bumpers (75.5 percent), step bumper (24.5 percent); trailer towing equipment (30.3 percent); trim groups, interior (91.3 percent), exterior (91.7 percent); two-tone paint (NA); exterior stripes (NA); bucket seats (70.9 percent); tinted glass (100.0 percent); air conditioning (66.4 percent); speed regulator (55.0 percent); adjustable steering column (54.2 percent); audio equipment AM (33.7 percent), AM/FM (41.8 percent); sun roof (3.6 percent). Total output: 9,856 trucks.

HISTORICAL: Introduced Fall 1977. Calendar year registrations by GVW: [6,000 to 10,000 lbs.] 36,065. Calendar year sales: [Scout II] 35,794. Calendar year production: [All IHC]: 123,123. Market share: 3.31 percent. Model year production: [Scout II] 26,369; [Terra pickup] 2,966; [Traveler] 9,856; [Total] 39,191. Innovations: New grille design. Diesel engine now merchandised as a separate option instead of a model option. Brook McCormick was company president. J. Patrick Kaine was president of the truck group. IHC's truck production in calendar 1978 rose to 122,282 units from 1977's 110,894 but was still one of the company's weaker years. Output of the light-duty Scouts saw an increase, however.

1979 IHC

1979 IHC 1/4-Ton Scout XLC Terra Suntanner Pickup (OCW)

SCOUT — SERIES XLC — ALL ENGINES: The 1979 Scouts had no significant changes from the 1978 models, although various new decal and striping packages were available. Standard equipment was the same as last season.

1979 IHC 1/4-Ton Scout XLC SSII Sport Utility Wagon (RCA)

I.D. DATA: Serial number located on the left door pillar. The serial number consists of 13 symbols. The first six symbols identify the serial number. The seventh (digit) designates the manufacturing plant. The last six digits are sequential production numbers. Numbers are not available.

1979 IHC 1/4-Ton Scout XLC Rallye Sport Utility Wagon (OCW)

Model	Body Type	Price	Weight	Prod. Total
Scout — 1/4-Ton — 100 in. w.b. — V-8 — 4x4				
XLC	Scout II Traveltop	7212	3846	—
XLC	Scout Terra Pickup	7263	3861	—
XLC	Scout SSII	6406	3455	—
XLC	Traveler Station Wagon	7657	4200	—

NOTE 1: Prices/weights for 4x4 models with 304 cid V-8 ($170 option).
NOTE 2: 4x4 running gear was around $1,000 extra.

ENGINE [Base]: Inline. OHV. Slanted mounting. Four-cylinder. Cast iron block. Bore & stroke: 4-1/8 in. x 3-21/32 in. Displacement: 196 cid.. Compression ratio: 8.02:1. Brake horsepower: 86 at 3800 rpm. Net horsepower: 27.2. Maximum Torque: 157 lbs.-ft. at 2200 rpm. Hydraulic valve lifters. Carburetor: Holley one-barrel model 1904.

ENGINE [Diesel]: Inline, OHV. Slant-mounted diesel. Six-cylinder. Cast iron block. Bore & stroke: 3.27 in. x 3.94 in. Displacement: 198 cid.. Brake horsepower: 92. (This 6-33 engine was built by Nissan of Japan.)

ENGINE [Optional]: Vee-block. OHV. Eight-cylinder. Cast iron block. Bore & stroke: 3-7/8 in. x 3-7/32 in. Displacement: 304 cid.. Compression ratio: 8.2:1. Brake horsepower: 140 at 3800 rpm. Net horsepower: 48.1. Maximum Torque: 243 lbs.-ft. at 2400 rpm. Hydraulic valve lifters. Carburetor: Holley two-barrel model 2210.

ENGINE [Optional]: Vee-block. OHV. Eight-cylinder. Cast iron block. Bore & stroke: 3-7/8 in. x 3-21/32 in. Displacement: 345 cid.. Compression ratio: 8.05:1. Brake horsepower 168 at 3800 rpm. Maximum Torque: 288 lbs.-ft. at 2000 rpm. Hydraulic valve lifters. Carburetor: Holley four-barrel model 2300.

1979 IHC 1/4-Ton Scout XLC Rallye Sport Utility Wagon (RCA)

CHASSIS [Scout II]: Wheelbase: 100 in. Length: 166.2 in. Height: 65.7 in. Front tread: 58.5 in. Rear tread: 57.62 in. Tires: H78 x 15 LRB.

CHASSIS [Scout SSII]: Wheelbase: 100 in. Length: 166.2 in. Front tread: 58.5 in. Rear tread: 57.62 in. Tires: H78 x 15 LRB.

CHASSIS [Terra/Traveler]: Wheelbase: 118 in. Length: 184.2 in. Height: 66.0 in. Front tread: 58.5 in. Rear tread: 57.62 in. Tires: H78 x 15 LRB.

1979 IHC 1/4-Ton Scout XLC Terra Pickup (OCW)

TECHNICAL: Manual (synchromesh) transmission. Speeds: 3F/1R. Floor-mounted gearshift lever. Clutch: 11 in. angle link, 2,000 lbs. plate pressure. Dana-44 3,500 lbs. capacity rear driving axle. Overall ratio: 3.73:1. Front power disc/rear drum brakes. Five-stud disc wheels. Four-speed manual transmission (wide-ratio). Four-speed manual transmission (close-ratio). Three-speed automatic tranmission. Transmission oil cooler. Four-wheel drive (4x4).

1979 IHC 1/4-Ton Scout XLC Rallye Sport Utility Wagon (JAG)

OPTIONS: Optional equipment was similar to 1977 models at similar prices. The 6-33 (Nissan-built) diesel engine was $2,581 extra. A new Rallye trim package was $687 extra. The 345 cid V-8 cost $123 over the price of a 304 cid V-8.

1979 IHC 1/4-Ton Scout XLC Rallye Sport Utility Wagon (JAG)

OPTION INSTALLATION RATES: The following data indicates the percentage of factory options installed on 1977 IHC trucks according to series. Percentage figures in brackets indicate installation rate. Series production for model year is given at the end of each data block.

1979 IHC 1/4-Ton Scout XLC SSII Sport Utility (OCW)

OPTION INSTALLATION RATES: The following data indicates the percentage of factory options installed on 1979 IHC trucks according to series. Percentage figures in brackets indicate installation rate. Model year totals for series production are given at the end of each data block.

TERRA: Engine: V-8 301-349 cid (81.3 percent); four-cylinder engines (13.5 percent); diesel engines (5.2 percent); transmissions, automatic (54.9 percent), four-speed (40.8 percent); 4x4 drive (100.0 percent); power front disc brakes (100.0 percent); power steering (84.4 percent); steel styled wheels (37.1 percent); wheelcovers (62.9 percent); steel radial tires (7.1 percent); trailer tow equipment (3.3 percent); trim groups interior (62.3 percent), exterior (64.5 percent); bucket seats (30.8 percent); tinted glass (100.0 percent); air conditioning (31.3 percent); speed regulator (12.2 percent); adjustable steering column (20.1 percent); audio equipment AM (41.3 percent), AM/FM (6.8 percent), stereo (8.1 percent), radio with tape deck (5.4 percent); sun roof (2.6 percent); rear bumper conversion (40.9 percent), step (59.1 percent). Total output: 2,437 trucks.

1979 IHC 1/4-Ton Scout XLC Rallye Sport Utility Wagon (JAG)

1979 IHC 1/4-Ton Scout XLC Traveler Utility Wagon (OCW)

SCOUT II: Engine: V-8 301-349 (92.1 percent); four-cylinder engines (6.7 percent); diesel engines (1.2 percent); transmissions, automatic (75.3 percent), four-speed (19.3 percent); 4x4 drive (99.0 percent); power front disc brakes (100.0 percent); power steering (95.3 percent); steel styled wheels (29.9 percent); wheelcovers (70.1 percent); steel radial tires (15.3 percent); trailer tow equipment (2.7 percent); trim groups interior (79.8 percent), exterior (84.1 percent); bucket seats (65.3 percent); tinted glass (100.0 percent); air conditioning (43.6 percent); speed regulator (29.8 percent); adjustable steering column (35.1 percent); audio equipment AM (34.7 percent), AM/FM (13.0 percent), stereo (13.0 percent), radio with tape deck (9.2 percent); sun roof (0.6 percent); rear bumper conversion (52.3 percent), step (47.7 percent). Total output: 35,286 trucks.

1979 IHC 1/4-Ton Scout XLC Terra Sport Pickup (OCW)

TRAVELER: Engine: four-cylinder engines (0.2 percent); diesel engines (3.1 percent); transmissions, automatic (89.7 percent), four-speed (9.7 percent); 4x4 drive (99.0 percent); power front disc brakes (100.0 percent); power steering (87.3 percent); steel styled wheels (34.3 percent); wheelcovers (65.7 percent); steel radial tires (32.9 percent); trailer tow equipment (27.0 percent); trim groups interior (90.3 percent), exterior (95.7 percent); bucket seats (72.2 percent); tinted glass (100.0 percent); speed regulator (57.6 percent); adjustable steering column (61.4 percent); audio equipment AM (25.8 percent), AM/FM (14.8 percent), stereo (14.9 percent), radio with tape deck (19.6 percent); sun roof (3.8 percent); rear bumper conversion (73.5 percent), step (26.5 percent). Total output: 6,620 trucks.

HISTORICAL: Introduced: Fall 1978. Calendar year registrations by GVW Class: [6,000 to 10,000 lbs.] 23,464. Calendar year sales [Scouts]: 24,567. Calendar year production [All IHC trucks]: 115,453. Market share: 3.78 percent. Model year production: [Scout II] 35,286; [Terra pickup] 2,437; [Traveler] 6,620; [Total] 44,343. Innovations: Over 99 percent of all 1979 Scouts had four-wheel drive (4x4) running gear. This was the last year for Scout 4x2 models. Company retained its leadership in heavy truck market and took number one spot

in medium-duty field away from Ford. A lengthy strike began on Nov. 1, 1979 and continued into calendar 1980. It kept production five percent lower than last season. Scout sales also dropped by nearly one-third for the calendar year. This was attributed to a downturn in the once booming 4x4 truck market.

1980 IHC

1980 IHC 1/4-Ton Scout XLC Compact Sport Utility Wagon (JAG)

SCOUT XLC SERIES — ALL ENGINES: A new optional turbocharged diesel engine, extensive new corrosion protection, and a redesigned grille headlined the features of the 1980 Scout line of four-wheel drive sports/utility vehicles. Models included the Scout II, a 100 in. wheelbase vehicle with a full steel top; the Traveler, a 118 in. wheelbase hatchback wagon; and the Terra, a 6-ft. bed pickup on a 118 in. wheelbase. Part-time four-wheel drive was standard on all 1980 Scouts. Gasoline engine choices included a 196 cid four-cylinder and 304 and 345 cid V-8s. Corrosion protection was significantly increased on all Scouts through the use of zinc-rich primers, zincrometal, galvanized steel and hot wax applications. The front end had a new look with a black bumper and a restyled black grille with bright trim which incorporated rectangular headlights. A bright grille and chrome bumper was optional. Distinctive new side appliques were available including Spear, See-Thru Flare and Rallye stripe patterns. Traveler models could have woodgrain trim. Six new exterior colors were also offered: Black Canyon black; Copper; Dark brown; Saffron yellow; green metallic; and Concord blue. Improvements for 1980 included a redesigned air conditioning unit with improved cooling and quieter operation, power steering as standard on all models, a new 15 inch styled steering wheel, a satin finish dashboard with new graphic identification for gauges, and new optional wheels with turbine-spoke styling.

1980 IHC 1/4-Ton Scout XLC Compact Sport Utility Wagon (JAG)

SCOUT II/TRAVELER/TERRA — STANDARD EQUIPMENT — [Front axle]: Dana-44, 3,200 lbs. capacity driving axle. Warn manual locking hubs. [Rear axle]: Dana-44, 3,500 lbs. capacity, driving axle. [Brakes]: Dual operation hydraulic power brakes, with warning light. Front disc: 11.75 in. rotor with 3.1 in. piston, self-adjusting. Total swept area was 226 sq. in. Rear drum 11-1/32 x 2-1/4 in. DSSA self-adjusting. Total lining area was 101.8 sq. in. [Bodies]: All steel welded construction. Scout II includes steel top with integral headliner and side trim panels. Traveler includes full-length white fiberglass top with integral headliner. Terra includes white fiberglass top with integral headliner. All bodies have: Corrosion protection. Left and right air intake vents. Fresh air heater and defroster. Inside mounted spare tire carrier (bed-mounted on Terra). Windshield-mounted rearview mirror. Two-speed electric windshield wipers and washer. Suspended brake, clutch and accelerator pedals. Padded instrument panel. Padded sun visors. Front floor mat. Black vinyl front seat with seat belts. Seat belt retractors. Direct-reading gauges for ammeter, oil, water and fuel.

Push-button door locks. Inside hood release. Black steel-framed roll-down windows and vent wings. Push-button locking vent wings. Push-button tailgate with locking latch on liftgate. Push-button tailgate (Terra). Locking, energy-absorbing steering column. Ashtray in instrument panel. Chrome door-mounted mirror (dual chrome mirrors on Traveler models). Two coat hooks (one on Terra). Armrests for driver and passenger doors. [Clutch]: 11 in. angle link, 2,000 lbs. plate pressure. [Cooling System]: Radiator frontal area: 477 sq. in. Permanent type (- 20 f.) antifreeze. [Electrical System]: 12-volt, 37-amp. 10 si alternator. 12-volt, 40 amp. alternator (diesel engines). 300 CCA Battery. 625 CCA battery (diesel engines). Dual stop and taillights. Glow plug indicator (diesel engines). Electric horn. Courtesy lights-dash mounted. Front axle engaged indicator light. Parking brake warning light. Dome light with driver and passenger door switches (two dome lights on Traveler). Cargo light (Terra only). Directional signals. Back-up lights. Traffic hazard flashers. Front and rear side marker lights. [Engine]: (Scout II/Terra) 4-196 four-cylinder gasoline engine; (Traveler) V-304 gasoline V-8 engine. Diesels: Nissan 6-33T six-cylinder turbocharged diesel. [Transmissions]: Three-speed synchromesh for gasoline models; not available in Traveler. Four-speed synchromesh in diesel models. Three-speed automatic standard in Traveler.

1980 IHC 1/4-Ton Scout XLC Compact Sport Utility Wagon (JAG)

Model	Body Type	Price	Weight	Prod. Total
Scout — V-8 — 4x4				
XLC	Scout II Traveltop	8116	3840	—
XLC	Scout Terra Pickup	8017	3864	—
XLC	Traveler Station Wagon	8630	4201	—

NOTE 1: All 1980 Scouts were 4x4 models.
NOTE 2: Prices/weights include 304 cid V-8 (standard in Traveler).

1980 IHC 1/4-Ton Scout XLC Terra Compact Sport Pickup (OCW)

ENGINE [4-196]: Displacement: 196 cid.. Bore & stroke: 4-1/8 in. x 3-21/32 in. Compression ratio: 8.02 to 1. Net horsepower: 76.5 at 3600 rpm. Maximum Torque: 153.3 lbs.-ft. at 2000 rpm. Unleaded fuel.
ENGINE [V-304A]: Displacement: 304 cid.. Bore & stroke: 3-7/8 in. x 3-7/32 in. Compression ratio: 8.19 to 1. Net horsepower: 122.3 at 3400 rpm. Maximum Torque: 226.3 lbs.-ft. at 2000 rpm. Unleaded fuel.
ENGINE [V-345A]: Displacement: 345 cid.. Bore & stroke: 3-7/8 in. x 3-21/32 in. Compression ratio: 8.05 to 1. Net horsepower: 148 at 3600 rpm. Maximum Torque: 265 lbs.-ft. at 2000 rpm. Unleaded fuel.
ENGINE [6-33T Diesel]: Displacement: 198 cid.. Bore & stroke: 3.27 in. x 3.94 in. Compression ratio: 22 to 1. Net horsepower: 101 at 3800 rpm. Maximum Torque: 175 lbs.-ft. at 2200 rpm. Diesel fuel.
CHASSIS [Scout II]: Wheelbase: 100 in. Length: 166.2 in. Width: 70 in. Height: 65.7 in. Tailgate opening width: 54.8 in. Tailgate opening height: 40 in. Width between rear wheel housings: 42 in. Front tread: 58.5 in. Rear tread: 57.62 in. Minimum ground clearance: 7.6 in. Turning diameter: 33 ft. 10 in. (to clear bumper) 36 ft. 4 in. Cargo capacity: 82 cu. ft. Weight (with standard equipment): [Gasoline] front 2,074 lbs.; rear 1,766 lbs; total 3,840 lbs.; [Diesel] front 2,286 lbs.; rear 1,797 lbs.; total 4,083 lbs.
CHASSIS [Terra]: Wheelbase: 118 in. Length: 184.2 in. Width: 70 in. Height: 66 in. Tailgate opening width: 54.8 in. Width between wheelwells 42 in. Bed length: 72 in. Front tread: 58.5 in. Rear tread: 57.62 in. Minimum ground clearance: 7.6 in. Turning diameter: (to clear tire) 38 ft. 10 in.; (to clear bumper) 40 ft. 5 in. Weight (with standard equipment): [Gasoline] front 2,241 lbs.; rear 1,623 lbs.; total 3,864 lbs. [Diesel] front 2,470 lbs.; rear 1,647 lbs.; total 4,117 lbs.
CHASSIS [Scout Traveler]: Wheelbase: 118 in. Length: 184.2 in. Width: 70 in. Height: 66 in. Tailgate opening width: 54.8 in. Tailgate opening height: 40 in. Width between wheel wells 42 in. Front tread: 58.5 in. Rear tread: 57.62 in. Minimum ground clearance: 7.6 in. Turning diameter: (to clear tire) 38 ft. 10 in.; (to clear bumper) 40 ft. 5 in. Weight (with standard equipment): [Gasoline] front 2,437 lbs.; rear 1,764 lbs.; total 4,201 lbs. [Diesel] front 2,437 lbs.; rear 1,765 lbs.; total 4,202 lbs.

1980 IHC 1/4-Ton Scout XLC Terra Compact Sport Pickup (RCA)

OPTIONAL EQUIPMENT: [Axle, Front]: Twist-Lok manual locking hubs. Automatic locking hubs. [Axle, Rear]: Trac-Lok limited-slip differential. [Body]: Air conditioning (includes 63 amp. alternator and 390 CCA battery on gasoline engines; not available on 4-196 engine). Bright finish exterior (see package contents). Cargo area mat (included with rear seat and Deluxe and Custom interiors; not available on Terra). Chrome tie-down rails (Terra only). Console (bucket seats only). Custom Interior trim (see package contents). Day/night mirror (included with Custom interior). Deluxe Exterior trim (see package contents). Deluxe Interior trim (see Package Contents). Door edge guards. Dual 7 in. x 10 in. low-profile, mirrors with four-inch extensions. Folding rear seat (includes cargo area mat; not available on Terra). Front bucket seats. Luggage rack (not available on Terra). Sliding rear quarter windows (not available on Terra). Spare tire lock. Dual chrome door-mounted mirrors. Tinted glass in all windows. Full bright-finish wheelcovers. [Clutch]: Heavy-duty 11 in. angle link, 2,200 lbs. plate pressure (required with V-345). [Electrical]: 63 amp. (10 si) alternator (included with air conditioning and Trailer Towing package). 12 volt 390 CCA battery (included with air conditioning and Trailer Towing package; not available on diesels). 12 volt 500 CCA maintenance-free battery (not available on diesels). AM Radio with single speaker. AM-FM radio with single speaker. AM-FM Stereo radio with three speakers. AM-FM Stereo with 8-track tape player, with three speakers. Electric clock. Six-way trailer wiring (included in Trailer Towing package). Cigar lighter. Dual electric horns. [Engines]: V-304 gasoline engine, two-barrel carburetor, electronic ignition (standard on Traveler). V-345 gasoline engine, four-barrel carburetor, electronic ignition. Automatic cruise control (V-8 engines, automatic transmissions only). California exhaust emission and evaporative system certification (required for California 4-196, V-304 and V-345 gasoline engines and 6-33T diesel engine). Modulated fan (not available on diesels). [Finish]: Midnight brown top (Traveler and Terra). Spear applique: green/blue or orange/orange. Rallye applique (not available Scout II): white/yellow/orange or black/yellow/orange. See-Thru Flare applique (not available Traveler): orange/white or orange/black. Woodgrain applique (Traveler only). Gold Rallye applique (Scout II only). Silver Rallye applique (Scout II only). [Frame]: Heavy-duty rear step bumper. [Fuel Tank]: Skid plate protector (not available Traveler). [Steering]: Sport steering wheel. Tilt steering wheel (standard on diesels). Right-hand drive. [Suspension]: Heavy-duty front and rear springs with heavy-duty (1-3/16 in. bore) front and rear

shock absorbers (not available Terra). Heavy-duty (1-2/16 in. bore) front and rear shock absorbers, not available Terra. Heavy-duty front springs with heavy-duty (1-3/16 in. bore) front and rear shock absorbers, Terra only. [Trailer Towing]: Trailer towing package: includes 63-amp. alternator, 390 CCA battery, Class III equalizer hitch, six-way trailer wiring (less connector). Requires V-8 engines. [Transmissions]: Three-speed automatic (V-8 engines only). Ratios: (first) 2.45; (second) 1.45; (third) 1.00; (reverse) 2.20. Wide-ratio four-speed manual. Ratios: (first) 6.32; (second) 3.09; (third) 1.68; (fourth) 1.00; (reverse) 6.96. Close-ratio four-speed manual. Ratios: (first) 4.02; (second) 2.41; (third) 1.41; (fourth) 1.00; (reverse) 4.42. Transmission auxiliary oil cooler (automatic transmission only). [Wheels and Tires]: H78-15-LRB white sidewall, 6.00 in. rim, regular tread. H78-15-LRB, 6.00 in. rim, mud and snow tread. H78-15-LRB, white sidewall, 6.00 in. rim, mud and snow tread. P225/75R-15 Goodyear Tiempo radial, white sidewall, 6.00 in. rim, all-season tread. P225/75R-15 Goodyear Tiempo radial, white sidewall, 7.00 in. styled wheel rims, all-season tread.

OPTION PACKAGES: [Bright Finish Exterior]: Silver color grille with bright trim. Chrome front and rear bumpers. Bright vent and side glass frames. Bright windshield molding. Tinted glass in all windows. [Deluxe Exterior]: Silver color grille with bright trim. Chrome front and rear bumpers. Bright vent and side glass frames. Bright windshield molding. Bright/black side trim molding. Tinted glass in all windows. [Deluxe Interior]: Color-keyed inner door trim panels. Vinyl cargo mat (not available on Terra). Vinyl floor mats. Vinyl spare tire cover (not available on Terra or with 10-15 tires). Armrests. Kick panels. Choice of: Tartan blue nylon seats with vinyl trim. Russet nylon seats with vinyl trim. Sierra Tan all-vinyl seats with pillow effect. Black all-vinyl seats with pillow effect. Bright satin finish trim on the instrument panel and transmission shift tower. Cigar lighter. Dual electric horns. [Custom Interior]: Color-Keyed: Day/night mirror. Inner door trim panels with carpet and map pocket. Vinyl cargo mat (not available on Terra). Vinyl spare tire cover (not available on Terra or with 10-15 tires). Armrests. Carpeting on floor in passenger areas. Carpeting on rear inner quarter panels (not available on Terra). Kick panels. Choice of: Tartan blue nylon seats with vinyl trim. Russet nylon seats with vinyl trim. Sierra tan all-vinyl seats with pillow effect. Black all-vinyl seats with pillow effect. Bright satin finish trim on the instrument panel and transmission shift tower. Cigar lighter. Dual electric horns. [Styled Wheel Radial Tire Package]: Five 15 in. 7.00 JJ turbine-spoke styled wheels. Five P225/75R-15 Goodyear Tiempo radial tires. Chrome lug nuts. Black rear axle end plates. [Off-Road Tire Package]: Five 15 in 8.00 JJ white spoke wheels. Five 10-15 LRB outlined white letter tires, on-off highway tread. Chrome lug nuts. [Trailer Towing]: not available 4-196, diesel, three-speed manual transmission, 2.72 axle ratio. 63-amp. alternator. 390 CCA Battery. Equalizer hitch (Class III). Six-way trailer wiring (less connector).

HISTORICAL: Introduced Fall 1979. Calendar year registrations by GVW Class: [6,000-10,000 lbs.] 17,724. Calendar year sales [Scouts]: 18,805. Calendar year production: [All IHC trucks]: 67,857. Market share: 4.15 percent. Calendar year production: [Scout only]: 30,059. Innovations: New turbocharged diesel engine. All Scouts were 4x4 models in 1980. Power steering is standard equipment on regular Scouts. Improved rust protection on all models. Technical refinements to rear axle, transfer case, electrical system and air conditioner. Final year for light-duty IHC trucks. After 1980, the company concentrated on heavy-duty truck market. There had been plans to bring out a new line of light-duty Scout models for 1982 after IHC's exemption from certain federal standards expired at the end of the 1981 model year. Following failure of negotiations to sell both the Scout business and the Ft. Wayne, Ind. factory (where Scouts were built), IHC ended production of the line on Oct. 31, 1980. In mid-1986, International Harvester company's Truck Group adopted the new name Navistar International.

JEEP
1945-1986

1960 Jeep 1-Ton Forward Control (FC-170) Heavy-Duty Pickup 4x4 (RCA)

By Robert C. Ackerson
Additional research by John A. Gunnell

When the dust settled after World War II, Willys-Overland was in an admirable position. Identified in the public's view as the creator of the well-known military Jeep, it quickly moved to begin peacetime production of a civilian version of that remarkable vehicle. Beginning in 1947, Willys-Overland began offering a new series of Brooks Stevens designed, Jeep-like trucks that moved the company into the 1/2-ton and 1-ton classes with vehicles that captured the charisma, charm and stamina of the famous fighting 4x4.

While these trucks enjoyed the benefits of a consistent policy of product improvement, the Jeep models were, by no means, ignored by Willys-Overland or the public. Eager to assure the dominant position in the still embryonic 4x4 truck market, Willys-Overland went to great lengths to tailor Jeep accessories and options to the needs of its customers.

The CJ-2A Universal Jeep was replaced by the CJ-3A model in 1950. The following year a new Farm Jeep model was offered. Two years later, the first of the F-head models, the CJ-3B, was introduced.

Ironically, in 1953, which was Willys-Overland's 50th anniversary, the company was purchased by industrialist Henry J. Kaiser for $62 million. Edgar F. Kaiser then became president of Willys Motors, which operated as part of Kaiser Mfg. Co. He held that position until 1959.

Kaiser Industries was the sponsor of James Garner's popular television Western "Maverick." Those who remember the series can also recall a time when there wasn't a mass market for 4x4 vehicles. Going off-road in those days, meant taking a trip to your Kaiser showroom to purchase a Jeep, Jeep wagon, Jeep pickup or Forward Control Jeep truck.

The purchase of Willys had its good and bad sides for Kaiser. It gained some innovative product developments, a foothold in a growing world vehicle market and was able to keep America's 1/4-ton "war hero" alive when it was ailing. On the minus side, there was the sobering fact that the forthcoming boom in off-road and recreational vehicle interest was a few years too far down the road to benefit Kaiser and make its new venture a total success.

Nevertheless, there was solid reasoning behind Henry J. Kaiser's deal. His former partner, Joe Frazer, had once served (1939-1943) as president of Willys-Overland and used the association to induce the Toledo-based firm to become a supplier of engines for Kaiser cars. Then, too, Kaiser's other businesses, including aluminum and ship-building, were worldwide in scope. This fit right in with the Jeep's international popularity. In addition, military orders, during the Korean War era, provided extra incentive for Kaiser to purchase the ailing Jeep-maker.

At first, Willys was operated as a subsidiary of Kaiser. After the purchase, all production was transferred from Willow Run, Mich. to Toledo. For a while, Kaiser and Henry J autos were built on the same assembly lines as Jeeps. By

1955, however, several elements faded from the picture. Kaiser stopped building cars, the Korean War ended and civilian demand for 4x4 vehicles was being somewhat substantially filled by cheap, war surplus units. Calendar year registrations of Jeeps were averaging only 24,000 annually throughout the '50s.

The market eventually warranted a change in direction, with sales promotions and product advances geared to the light-duty truck and family-car markets. Although Jeep's CJ models were little altered (they still said "Willys" on front), new emphasis began to be placed on expanding the appeal of the overall line to more typical car and truck users.

The station wagon models that Willys developed after World War II were dressed-up with Nike missile-shaped side moldings, chrome bumpers, bright hubcaps...even basketweave body textures. Deluxe versions of the conventional pickups were released, in addition to all-new, cab-forward FC models. Names such as Harlequin, Surrey, Gala and Maverick were applied to fancier models for upscale imaging. Before long, even the CJ was gussied-up with chrome, bright colored paint and a fringed surrey top. A 4x2 version was produced as a mail delivery special and a new line of parcel vans was introduced.

Cruse W. Moss, president of Kaiser-Frazer's automotive division, would later tell historians that the Brooks Stevens' designed Jeepster nearly made it back to life in the mid-'50s too. He said the company, aware of the model's popularity, was all set to "green light" its return, but a search failed to turn up the jigs and dies needed to build the Jeepster.

Even without another model, the lineup was full. As the '60s dawned, there were no less than six Universals, 19 Jeep pickups and wagons and three "FC" trucks available. By 1961, this climbed to 31 models and, by 1963, there were 49 different varieties of Jeeps, including the all-new Gladiator/Wagoneer series.

The change to a more up-to-date appearance in 1963 was accompanied by a corporate realignment. The company was renamed Kaiser-Jeep Corp. S.A. Girard, who had been president of Willys since 1959, assumed that title at Kaiser-Jeep. Towards the end of the model year, the Kaiser name also began showing up on some of the vehicles.

Kaiser's growing product line did not reflect any major popularity gains for Jeep vehicles. Calendar year registrations averaged 31,500 units per year from 1960-1962 and increased by only an average 12,000 in the 1963-1966 period. Even that gain came mostly on the strength of the Gladiator/Wagoneer. By the time 1967 rolled around, the tooling for the Jeepster had been found. A modernized version, labeled the Jeepster Commando, was released with heavy promotional backing. It was aimed at the same type of weekend off-roaders that made the International Scout a success. The Commando, however, did not find quite as many buyers waiting as the Scout had.

Even with the Commando, Kaiser-Jeep experienced a business downturn. Yearly registrations averaged about 38,100 units between 1967-1969. As a result, Kaiser-Jeep Corp. was merged into American Motors during 1970 and put under new AMC management. Formerly a supplier of Kaiser V-8 powerplants, AMC took over as parent company of the Jeep vehicle line.

American Motors purchased Jeep from Kaiser Industries in February, 1970. At first, AMC retained such established model designations as CJ (Civilian Jeep), Wagoneer, Gladiator and Jeepster Commando. Almost immediately, the new owner began a program of dressing-up its products and streamlining marketing techniques to widen the Jeep models' appeal.

By 1971, offerings had been pared-down from 38 to 22 models. The following season, the venerable four-cylinder Jeep engine disappeared. In its place came AMC-built inline sixes and overhead valve V-8s, the top option being a 360 cid (5.9-liter) V-8 offering up to 195 hp.

The die for the future was cast in 1973. That's when the AMC-Jeep line was neatly divided into truck and non-truck models, all with names as well as numerical designations. The trucks came in single-wall Thriftside and double-wall Townside configurations. They were simply called Jeep Trucks and were no longer referred to as Gladiators. Jeep, Commando and Wagoneer labels were applied to other models. Wagoneers and four of the lighter-duty pickups had AMC's new Quadra-Trac full-time four-wheel drive setup. With this system, four-wheel drive was always in use, but each wheel could spin at its own speed making two-wheel drive unnecessary.

Optional exterior woodgrain trims, bright bodyside moldings and new two-tone paint treatments were made available to spruce-up appearances. Color-coded instruments were marked with international symbols and included two new types of gauges: an ammeter and a clock. A full-width "electric shaver" type grille was seen again, too.

AMC's first all-new offering, a two-door sports utility vehicle, bowed in the 1974 Cherokee. It replaced the Commando and was much better suited to slugging it out with Broncos and Blazers in the sales wars. By this time, the line was down to a pair each of Wagoneers, Cherokees and Jeeps, plus three Townside pickups. It totaled nine models, each with a distinct identity. There was just enough variety for practically everyone and a lot less confusion and crossover.

Calendar year registrations reflected the success that AMC's easier-to-understand marketing program was achieving. They stood at 36,354 vehicles in 1970, but leaped to 50,926 in 1972; 68,227 in 1973; and 96,835 for 1974. Model year production surpassed the magic 100,000 unit level during 1975, when some 62,000 CJs, 14,000 pickups, 17,000 Wagoneers and 16,000 Cherokees were built.

Corporately, Jeep continued to operate as a wholly-owned subsidiary of AMC, with operations still based in Toledo. W.H. Jean was plant manager; J.E. MacAfee was in charge of engineering; Charles Mashigan was styling chief and E.V. Amoroso headed-up sales. John A. Conde, today a well-known automotive historian, was director of public relations.

In the later '70s, there were a number of technical changes such as adopting power disc brakes (made standard equipment in 1977) and larger six- and eight-cylinder engines. A luxurious Wagoneer Limited model-option debuted in 1979 and all other vehicles were provided with a wide choice of trim options. There was the Renegade package for CJ models and Honcho or Golden Eagle options for pickups. Cherokee S and Chief options could also be had. Such extras cost up to $1,300 in 1979. The steep prices made some extras rare, one reason they have strong appeal to collectors today.

Despite the bold prices, many high-optioned Jeeps performed well in the marketplace during this booming period for Jeep sales. Calendar year registrations went to 107,487 in 1976; 124,843 in 1977; and 168,548 in 1978. Even in off-year 1979, a season of industry-wide slack, Jeep saw 145,583 of its vehicles titled in the U.S. Then came the early '80s.

The years 1980-1982 were disastrous, not only for Jeep, but for AMC and the entire American car and truck industry. By the fall of 1983, American Motors had registered its 14th

consecutive business quarter with figures written in red ink. Despite crisp new styling touches and the release of a new Scrambler model (in 1981), registrations averaged no better than 67,400 units over this three-year period.

A high note was sounded at the beginning of 1984 when the down-sized Cherokee and Wagoneer Sport Wagons were added to the AMC lineup. By this time, the company had also inked an historic agreement to produce Jeeps in China on a joint-venture basis.

A two-wheel drive version of the Cherokee was offered for the first time in 1985 and, for 1986, down-sized and modernized Commanche pickups took their place in a revitalized and expanded Jeep product stable. Entering the stage, in mid-1986 (as a 1987 model), was a totally revised type of Universal Jeep known as the Wrangler. AMC claimed that this CJ-like new model "carries the illustrious badge of Jeep's off-road durability and ruggedness, but also holds out the promise of the smoothest on-road ride yet offered in a small sport utility."

1953 Willys-Overland Military M38 Universal Jeep 4x4

1960 Jeep 1/4-Ton CJ-5 Universal 4x4 (OCW)

1957 Willys-Jeep 3/4-Ton FC-150 Pickup 4x4 (SM)

1960 Jeep 1-Ton FA-134 Pickup (OCW)

1960 Jeep 1-Ton FA-134 Pickup 4x4

Standard Catalog of Light-Duty Trucks

1960 Jeep 3/4-Ton FC-150 Pickup (RCA)

1960 Jeep 1/4-Ton CJ-3B Universal 4x4 (RCA)

1962 Jeep 1/4-Ton CJ-3B Universal 4x4 (RCA)

1962 Jeep 1/2-Ton L6-226 Utility Wagon 4x4 (RCA)

1962 Jeep 1/2-Ton CJ-6 Universal 4x4 (RCA)

538

1966 Jeep Super Wagoneer (RCA)

1982 Jeep 1/2-Ton CJ-7 "Jamboree" 4x4 (RCA)

1986 Jeep Comanche Pioneer Shortbed 4WD

1945 JEEP

WILLYS — SERIES CJ-2A — FOUR-CYLINDER: The GI's workhorse, the 1/4-ton Jeep utility vehicle (reconaissance truck in U.S. Army lingo), donned civilian garb for the first time in 1945. The civilian Jeep (CJ) had the same engine as its military counterpart, but the gear ratios in the transmission and axle were changed. A significant change in the civilian Jeep was an available power-take-off attachment. Geared to the Jeep's transmission, it could drive farm equipment, shred corn, fill a silo, operate a winch, etc. There were also better shock absorbers and springs. Other refinements were made in combustion chamber and radiator shrouding designs. Standard equipment included a remote gas filler (military models filled by lifting the driver's seat), seven-inch headlights, an automatic windshield wiper and rear tailgate.

I.D. DATA: Serial number located on plate at left side of driver's seat on floor riser in Jeep. Starting: 10001. Ending: 11824. Military Jeeps were produced 1941-1944. No numbers were released for the civilian market in these years. Engine numbers located on right side of cylinder block; stamped on water pump boss on front of cylinder block. On most Jeep models the engine and serial numbers were the same.

Model	Body Type	Price	Weight	Prod. Total
Willys Jeep — 2/5-Ton — 4-cyl.- 4x4				
CJ-2A	Universal	1090	2037	—

ENGINE [All]: Inline. L-head. Four-cylinder. Cast iron block. Bore & stroke: 3-1/8/in. x 4-3/8 in. Displacement: 134.2 cid. Compression ratio: 6.5:1. Brake hp: 60 at 4000 rpm. Net hp: 15.63 (NACC) Max. Torque: 105 lbs.-ft. at 2000 rpm. Three main bearings. Solid valve lifters. Carburetor: Carter model WA-1 (613S).

CHASSIS [Jeep CJ-2A]: Wheelbase: 80-1/6 in. Length: 129-7/8 in. Height: 67-1/4 in. Front and rear tread: 48-7/16 in. Tires: 6.00 x 16 four-ply.

TECHNICAL: Synchromesh transmission. Speeds: 3F/1R. Transfer case: two-speeds. Floor-mounted gearshift lever. Single-plate, dry-disc with torsional dampening clutch. Hypoid axles: full-floating front, semi-floating rear. Bendix hydraulic brakes. Five disc type 5-stud wheels, size 4.50 x 16 in.

OPTIONS: Power-take-off ($96.25). Pulley drive ($57.40). Motor governor ($28.65). Special wheels and 7-in. tires ($40). Front canvas top ($57.80). Hydraulic lift ($225).

HISTORICAL: Introduced: July 1945. Calendar year production: 1,823. Production of civilian Jeeps started in 1945. Unsold 1941-1942 trucks were made available to "approved" buyers (such as doctors, munitions workers, etc.) during World War II. By Nov. 1945, the Steyr Autoplant, in Austria, was building about 25 winterized Jeeps per day in Europe. Willys-Overland was always a leader in export marketing and the Jeep was truly a "World Class" vehicle.

1946 JEEP

1946 Willys-Overland CJ-2A Universal Jeep 4x4 (OCW)

WILLYS — SERIES CJ-2A — FOUR-CYLINDER: The 1946 Jeep was part of the same series that first hit the market in 1945. There were no changes. By the end of 1946, over 71,000 examples were built for the civilian market.

I.D. DATA: Serial number located on plate at left side of driver's seat on floor riser in 1946-1948 model CJ-2A. Starting: 11,825. Ending: 83,379. Engine numbers located on right side of cylinder block; stamped on water pump boss on front of cylinder block. On most Jeep models the engine and serial numbers were the same.

Model	Body Type	Price	Weight	Prod. Total
Willys Jeep — 2/5-Ton — 4-cyl. — 4x4				
CJ-2A	Jeep Universal	1146	2074	

Standard Catalog of Light-Duty Trucks

ENGINE: Inline. L-head. Four-cylinder. Cast iron block. Bore & stroke: 3-1/8 in. x 4-3/8 in. Displacement: 134.2 cid. Compression ratio: 6.5:1. Brake hp: 60 at 4000 rpm. Net hp: 15.63 (NACC) Max. Torque: 105 lbs.-ft. at 2000 rpm. Three main bearings. Solid valve lifters. Carburetor: Carter model WA-1 (613S).

CHASSIS: Wheelbase: 80 in. Length: 129-7/8 in. Height: 67-1/4 in. Front tread: 55-1/4 in. Rear tread: 57 in. Tires: 6.00 x 15 four-ply.

TECHNICAL: Synchromesh transmission. Speeds: 3F/1R. Two-speed transfer case. Floor-mounted gearshift lever. Single-plate, dry-disc clutch. Hypoid rear axle. Bendix hydraulic brakes. Disc wheels.

OPTIONS: [*] Power-take-off ($96.25). [*] Pulley drive ($57.40). [*] Motor governor ($28.65). Special wheels and 7-in. tires ($40). Front canvas top ($57.80). Hydraulic lift ($225). Metal top (Varies).

NOTE: [*] Also applicable to Model 473 four-wheel drive trucks.

HISTORICAL: Introduced: Jan. 1946. Calendar year production: [Station Wagon] 6,533. [Jeeps] 71,455; [Trucks] 1. The Willys Station Wagons and Panel Delivery trucks bowed late this year. Most historians consider the station wagon a car instead of a truck. The 1946-1954 Willys-Overland Jeep 4x2 station wagons were considered cars. Information about them is available in Krause Publication's *STANDARD CATALOG of AMERICAN CARS* 1946-1975. In 1955, following Kaiser's purchase of Willys, this model was renamed the Utility Wagon and certified as a truck. Therefore, 1955 and up station wagons are included in this catalog.

1947 JEEP

1947 Willys-Overland Jeep 4x4 Pickup (RCA)

WILLYS — JEEP SERIES — FOUR-CYLINDER: New this year was a line of Jeep trucks with a new 63 hp engine. There was a pickup and a panel delivery. They had an all-steel cab, split window and full doors with indentation panels. There was a molding down the hood center, chrome bumpers were available front and rear. There were even optional chrome hubcaps with Willy's "W" symbol in the center. Three decorative, painted moldings trimmed the lower edges of the door, mid-quarter panel and rear quarter panel. Frontal styling followed the theme of the Universal Jeep, but the grille was taller and had 10 vertical slots compared to seven for the CJ-2A Universal model. The CJ-2A was, once again, basically identical to the previous model.

I.D. DATA: Serial number located on plate at left side of driver's seat on floor riser in 1946-1948 model CJ-2A; on left side of dash under hood in 4x2 and 4x4 models; on left floor riser in back of seat in 1947-1949 models 4-63. Serial numbers: [Jeep] 83381 to 148459; [Panel] 16535 to H4044; [Trucks] 10001 to 12346. Engine numbers located on right side of cylinder block; stamped on water pump boss on front of cylinder block. On most Jeep models the engine and serial numbers were the same.

Model	Body Type	Price	Weight	Prod. Total
Willys Jeep — 2/5-Ton — 4-cyl. — 4x4				
CJ-2A	Jeep Universal	1241	2074	—
Willys Truck — 1/2-Ton — 4-cyl. — 4x4				
463	Panel	1358	2587	—
Willys Truck — 1-Ton — 4-cyl. — 4x4				
4x4	Chassis	1175	1974	—
4x4	Chassis & Cab	1529	2809	—
4x4	Pickup	1620	3129	—
4x4	Platform Stake	1685	3431	—

1947 Willys-Overland Universal Jeep 4x4 (OCW)

539

ENGINE [CJ-2A]: Inline. L-head. Four-cylinder. Cast iron block. Bore & stroke: 3-1/8 in. x 4-3/8 in. Displacement: 134.2 cid. Compression ratio: 6.5:1. Brake hp: 60 at 4000 rpm. Net hp: 15.63 (NACC) Max. Torque: 105 lbs.-ft. at 2000 rpm. Three main bearings. Solid valve lifters. Carburetor: Carter type WA-1 model 613S.

ENGINE [Model 463]: Inline. L-head. Four-cylinder. Cast iron block. Bore & stroke: 3-1/8 in. x 4-3/8 in. Displacement: 134.2 cid. Compression ratio: 6.48:1. Brake hp: 63 at 4000 rpm. Net hp: 15.63 (NACC) Max. Torque: 105 lbs.-ft. at 2000 rpm. Three main bearings. Solid valve lifters. Carburetor: Carter type WA-1 model 613S.

CHASSIS [Jeep CJ-2A]: Wheelbase: 80 in. Tires: 6.00 x 15 in.

CHASSIS [Model 463]: Wheelbase: 104 in. Front tread: 55-1/4 in. Rear tread: 57 in. Tires: 6.50 x 15 in.

TECHNICAL: Synchromesh transmission. Speeds: 3F/1R. Floor-mounted gearshift lever. Single-plate, dry-disc clutch. Hypoid rear axle. Bendix hydraulic brakes. Disc wheels.

OPTIONS: [*] Power-take-off ($96.25). [*] Pulley drive ($57.40). [*] Motor governor ($28.65). Special wheels and 7-in. tires ($40). Front canvas top ($57.80). Hydraulic lift ($225). Metal top (Varies).

NOTE: [*] Also applicable to Model 473 four-wheel drive trucks.

HISTORICAL: Introduced: Jan. 1947. Calendar year production: [Station Wagon] 33,214. [Jeeps] 77,958; [Trucks] 8,747. Two- and four-wheel drive trucks were introduced by Willys in 1947. Sales were brisk and the company reopened its West Coast factory.

1947 Willys-Overland Jeep 1/2-Ton 4x4 Pickup (RCA)

1948 JEEP

WILLYS — JEEP SERIES — FOUR-CYLINDER: The CJ-2A Universal Jeep was again carried over as a 1/4-ton utility truck available only with 4x4 running gear. There were no big changes. The two-wheel drive 1/2-ton panel was also available once more. The 1-ton 4x4 Jeep truck line included a pickup and platform stake truck.

I.D. DATA: Serial number located on plate at left side of driver's seat on floor riser in 1946-1948 model CJ-2A; on left side of dash under hood in 1948-1951 models 4x2 and 4x4; on left floor riser in back of seat in 1947-1949 models 463. Serial numbers: [CJ-2A] 148,459 to 219,588; [463] 44,045-79,715; [4x2] 12,643-21,010 and [4x4] 12,347-30,575. Engine numbers located on right side of cylinder block; stamped on water pump boss on front of cylinder block. On most Jeep models the engine and serial numbers were the same.

Model	Body Type	Price	Weight	Prod. Total
Willys Jeep — 2/5-Ton — 4-cyl. — 4x4				
CJ-2A	Jeep Universal	1262	2037	—
Willys Truck — 1/2-Ton — 4-cyl. — 4x2				
463	Panel	1477	2587	—
Willys Truck — 1-Ton — 4-cyl. — 4x2				
4x2	Chassis & Cab	1334	2677	—
4x2	Pickup	1427	2995	—
4x2	Platform	1493	3299	—
Willys Truck — 1-Ton — 4-cyl. — 4x4				
4x4	Chassis & Cab	1652	2809	—
4x4	Pickup	1743	3129	—
4x4	Platform	1807	3431	—

540

1948 Willys-Overland CJ-2A Universal Jeep 4x4 (OCW)

ENGINE [CJ-2A]: Inline. L-head. Four-cylinder. Cast iron block. Bore & stroke: 3-1/8 in. x 4-3/8 in. Displacement: 134.2 cid. Compression ratio: 6.5:1. Brake hp: 60 at 4000 rpm. Net hp: 15.63 (NACC) Max. Torque: 105 lbs.-ft. at 2000 rpm. Three main bearings. Solid valve lifters. Carburetor: Carter model WA-1 (613S).

ENGINE [Model 463]: Inline. L-head. Four-cylinder. Cast iron block. Bore & stroke: 3-1/8 in. x 4-3/8 in. Displacement: 134.2 cid. Compression ratio: 6.48:1. Brake hp: 63 at 4000 rpm. Net hp: 15.63 (NACC) Max. Torque: 105 lbs.-ft. at 2000 rpm. Three main bearings. Solid valve lifters. Carburetor: Carter WA-1 model 613S.

CHASSIS [Jeep CJ-2A]: Wheelbase: 80 in. Front tread: 55-1/4 in. Rear tread: 57 in. Tires: 6.00 x 15 in.

CHASSIS [Model 463]: Wheelbase: 104 in. Front tread: 55-1/4 in. Rear tread: 57 in. Tires: 6.00 x 15 in.

CHASSIS [Other]: Wheelbase: 118 in. Front tread: 55-1/4 in. Rear tread: 57 in. Tires: [4x2] 6.50 x 16 in.; [4x4] 7.00 x 16 in.

TECHNICAL: Synchromesh transmission. Speeds: 3F/1R (4x4 Transfer case: two-speed). Floor-mounted gearshift lever. Single-plate, dry-disc clutch. Hypoid rear axle. Hydraulic brakes. Disc wheels.

OPTIONS: [*] Power-take-off ($96.25). [*] Pulley drive ($57.40). [*] Motor governor ($28.65). Special wheels and 7-in. tires ($40). Front canvas top ($57.80). Hydraulic lift ($225). Metal top (Varies).

NOTE: [*] Also applicable to Model 473 four-wheel-drive trucks.

HISTORICAL: Introduced: Nov. 1947. Calendar year production: [Station Wagon] 22,309; [Jeeps] 63,170; [Trucks] 41,462. The Willys Jeepster was introduced (See Krause Publication's *STANDARD CATALOG of AMERICAN CARS 1946-1975* for information about Jeepsters.)

1949 JEEP

1949 Willys-Overland Jeep 4x4 Panel Delivery Truck (OCW)

WILLYS — JEEP SERIES — FOUR-CYLINDER: There were no major changes in the 1949 Jeep line. Some trucks formerly available only as 4x4s could now be had as 4x2s.

I.D. DATA: Serial number located on right side of dash under hood in 1949-1954 models CJ-2A and CJ-3A/CJ-3B; on left side of dash under hood in 1948-1951 models 4x2 and 4x4; on left floor riser in back of seat in 4-63. Serial numbers: [CJ-2A] 219,589-224,764; [CJ-3A] 10,001 to 35,688; [463] 79,716-106,503; [4x2] 21,011-26,562 and [4x4] 30,576-43,586. Engine numbers located on right side of cylinder block; stamped on water pump boss on front of cylinder block.

Model	Body Type	Price	Weight	Prod. Total
Willys Jeep — 2/5-Ton — 4-cyl. — 4x4				
CJ-2A	Jeep Universal	1270	2037	—
CJ-3A	Jeep Universal	1270	2110	—
Willys Truck — 1/2-Ton — 4-cyl. — 4x4				
463	Panel	1375	2587	—

Willys Truck — 1-Ton — 4-cyl. — 4x2

4x2	Chassis & Cab	1282	2677	—
4x2	Pickup	1375	2995	—
4x2	Platform	1442	3299	—

Willys Truck — 1-Ton — 4-cyl. — 4x4

4x4	Chassis & Cab	1700	2809	—
4x4	Pickup	1792	3129	—
4x4	Platform Stake	1856	3431	—

ENGINE [CJ-2A/CJ-3A]: Inline. L-head. Four-cylinder. Cast iron block. Bore & stroke: 3-1/8 in. x 4-3/8 in. Displacement: 134.2 cid. Compression ratio: 6.5:1. Brake hp: 60 at 4000 rpm. Net hp: 15.63 (NACC) Max. Torque: 105 lbs.-ft. at 2000 rpm. Three main bearings. Solid valve lifters. Carburetor: [CJ models] Carter type WA-1 model 613S.

ENGINE [Model 463]: Inline. L-head. Four-cylinder. Cast iron block. Bore & stroke: 3-1/8 in. x 4-3/8 in. Displacement: 134.2 cid. Compression ratio: 6.48:1. Brake hp: 63 at 4000 rpm. Net hp: 15.63 (NACC) Max. Torque: 105 lbs.-ft. at 2000 rpm. Three main bearings. Solid valve lifters. Carburetor: [2x2] Carter type WA-1 model 613S; [4x4] Carter type WO models 596S or 636S.

CHASSIS [Jeep]: Wheelbase: 80 in. Front tread: 55-1/4 in. Rear tread: 57 in. Tires: 6.00 x 15 in.

CHASSIS [Model 463]: Wheelbase: 104 in. Front tread: 55-1/4 in. Rear tread: 57 in. Tires: 6.50 x 16 in.

CHASSIS [Other models]: Wheelbase: 118 in. Front tread: 55-1/4 in. Rear tread: 57 in. Tires: [4x2] 6.50 x 16 in.; [4x4] 7.00 x 16 in.

TECHNICAL: Synchromesh transmission. Speeds: 3F/1R (4x4s have two-speed transfer case). Floor-mounted gearshift lever. Single-plate, dry-disc clutch. Hypoid rear axle. Four-wheel hydraulic brakes. Disc wheels.

OPTIONS: [*] Power-take-off ($96.25). [*] Pulley drive ($57.40). [*] Motor governor ($28.65). Special wheels and 7-in. tires ($40). Front canvas top ($57.80). Hydraulic lift ($225). Metal top (price varies).

NOTE: [*] Also applicable to Model 473 four-wheel drive trucks.

HISTORICAL: Introduced: Nov. 1949. Calendar year production: [Station Wagon] 29,290; [Jeeps] 18,342; [Trucks] 18,342.

1950 JEEP

1950 Willys-Overland Jeep 4x2 Pickup (OCW)

WILLYS — JEEP SERIES — FOUR-CYLINDER: For Jeep, there was a lot new this year. The CJ-3A replaced the CJ-2A as the basic Universal Jeep. In the truck and station wagon line, there was new front end styling. The fenders had a "peaked," rather than flat flare to them. The grille consisted of five horizontal bright metal moldings running across nine vertical moldings. There was a chrome ornament on the tip of the hood. Two new engines, the "Hurricane" four and the "Lightning" six were offered in wagons, but not (yet) trucks. There was, however a new 1/2-ton 4x2 truck with the grille revisions.

I.D. DATA: Serial number located on right side of dash under hood in 1949-1954 models CJ-2A and CJ-3A/CJ-3B; on left side of dash under hood in 1948-1951 models 4x2 and 4x4. Serial numbers: [CJ-3A] 35,689-63,784; [463] 106,504-112,402; [1/2-ton] 26,563-27,787 and [1-ton] 43,587-47,709. Engine numbers located on right side of cylinder block; stamped on water pump boss on front of cylinder block. On most Jeep models the engine and serial numbers were the same.

Model	Body Type	Price	Weight	Prod. Total
Willys Jeep — 1/4-Ton — 4-cyl. — 4x4				
CJ-3A	Jeep Universal	1270	2110	—
Willys Truck — 1/2-Ton — 4-cyl. — 4x2				
463	1/2-Ton Panel	1374	2587	—
Willys Truck — 1/2-Ton — 4-cyl. — 4x4				
4x4	Chassis & Cab	1282	2677	—
4x4	Pickup	1375	2995	—
4x4	Platform Stake	1441	3299	—
Willys Truck — 1-Ton — 4-cyl. — 4x4				
4x4	Chassis & Cab	1700	2809	—
4x4	Pickup	1792	3129	—
4x4	Platform Stake	1856	3431	—

1950 Willys-Overland VJ-3 Military Jeep 4x4 (OCW)

ENGINE [CJ-3A]: Inline. L-head. Four-cylinder. Cast iron block. Bore & stroke: 3-1/8 in. x 4-3/8 in. Displacement: 134.2 cid. Compression ratio: 6.5:1. Brake hp: 60 at 4000 rpm. Net hp: 15.63 (NACC) Max. Torque: 105 lbs.-ft. at 2000 rpm. Three main bearings. Solid valve lifters. Carburetor: [4x2] Carter type WA-1 model 613S; [4x4] Carter type WO models 596S or 636S.

ENGINE [Model 463]: Inline. L-head. Four-cylinder. Cast iron block. Bore & stroke: 3-1/8 in. x 4-3/8 in. Displacement: 134.2 cid. Compression ratio: 6.48:1. Brake hp: 63 at 4000 rpm. Net hp: 15.63 (NACC) Max. Torque: 105 lbs.-ft. at 2000 rpm. Three main bearings. Solid valve lifters. Carburetor: Carter type WA-1 model 613S.

CHASSIS [Jeep]: Wheelbase: 80 in. Front tread: 55-1/4 in. Rear tread: 57 in. Tires: 6.00 x 15 in.

CHASSIS [Model 463]: Wheelbase: 104 in. Front tread: 55-1/4 in. Rear tread: 57 in. Tires: 6.50 x 16 in.

CHASSIS [Model 473]: Wheelbase: 118 in. Front tread: 55-1/4 in. Rear tread: 57 in. Tires: [4x2] 6.50 x 16 in.; [4x4] 7.00 x 16 in.

TECHNICAL: Synchromesh transmission. Speeds: 3F/1R (4x4s have two-speed transfer case). Floor-mounted gearshift lever. Single-plate, dry-disc clutch. Hypoid front axle with 4x4. Hypoid rear axle. Four-wheel hydraulic brakes. Disc wheels.

OPTIONS: [*] Power-take-off ($96.25). [*] Pulley drive ($57.40). [*] Motor governor ($28.65). Special wheels and 7-in. tires ($40). Front canvas top ($57.80). Hydraulic lift ($225). Metal top (Varies).

NOTE: [*] Also applicable also to Model 473 four-wheel drive trucks.

HISTORICAL: Introduced: Nov. 1949 and continued. Calendar year production: [Station Wagon] 32,218; [Jeeps] 26,624; Trucks] 22,282. Production of military Jeeps for the Korean War resumed.

1951 JEEP

1951 Willys-Overland Jeep 1-Ton 4x4 Pickup (RCA)

WILLYS — JEEP SERIES — FOUR-CYLINDER: For 1951, Willys continued the 80 in. wheelbase Universal Jeep, Model CJ-3A, which retained the war-proven 134 cid L-head four-cylinder engine. Identifying features included its one-piece windshield design with stamped panels on the lower section of the windshield frame. A military version, the updated M-38, would serve admirably with U.S. Armed Forces in the Korean War. In civilian form, it was made available as a stripped chassis or with the open utility body or as a new model called the "Farm Jeep" with a power-take-off (PTO) attachment. Only three stripped chassis and 62 Farm Jeeps were built. This year's Jeep trucks retained the slightly "veed" eggcrate grille design introduced in 1950. They were all on a 118 in. wheelbase, except the sedan delivery, which had a 104 in. wheelbase. The Sedan Delivery came only as a 4x2 truck. Available on the longer wheelbase, with either 4x2 or 4x4 running gear, were a stripped chassis, Chassis & Cab, Pickup and Platform Stake truck. The Sedan Delivery had a 4,000 lb. GVW rating. All other 4x2 trucks had a 4,250 lb. GVW and the 4x4s were rated for 5,300 lbs. (The CJ-3A had a 3,500 lb. GVW rating). Power for the trucks was provided by the hotter F-head four-cylinder engine. The 4x4 equipped trucks had "4-Wheel-Drive" call-outs on the side of the hood.

I.D. DATA: Serial number located on plate on right side of dash under hood in 1949-1954 models CJ-2A and CJ-3A/CJ-3B; on left side of dash under hood in 1948-1951 models 4x2 and 4x4. Serial numbers: [FJ] 451-GC1 — 10,001 to 10,062; [CJ-3(S)] 451-GA1 — 10,001

to 10,003; [CJ-3(O)] 451-GB1 — 10,001 to 54,158; [473 chassis] CA-1 10,001 to 15,440; [473 Chassis & Cab] DB1 — 10,001 to 10,530; [473 pickup] DC1 — 10,001 to 13,016; [473 stake] DD1 — 10,001 to ending; [473E Chassis & Cab] — EB1 — 10,001 to 11,894; [473E pickup] — EC1 — 10,001 to 26,029; [473E Stake] — ED1 — 10,001 to 10,420. Engine numbers located on right side of cylinder block; stamped on water pump boss on front of cylinder block. Beginning around 1951 and continuing through at least 1953, each model had a specific serial number prefix such as 451-4GC. The first number indicated the number of cylinders. The second and third numbers indicated model year. The first letter indicated the basic chassis and body type. The second letter indicated model. The fourth number indicated series in any one model year. On most Jeep models the engine and serial numbers were the same.

1951 Willys-Overland Jeep 1-Ton Rail Utility Truck 4x4

Model	Body Type	Price	Weight	Prod. Total
Willys Jeep — 1/4-Ton — 4-cyl. — 4x4				
FJ	Farm Jeep	1550	2280	—
CJ-3	Chassis	1055	1692	—
CJ-3	Jeep Universal	1290	2110	—
Jeep Trucks — 1/2-Ton — 4-cyl. — 4x2				
473-SD	Sedan Delivery	1469	2406	—
Jeep Trucks — 1-Ton — 4-cyl. — 4x2				
473-D	Chassis	865	1716	—
473-D	Chassis & Cab	1220	2406	—
473-D	Pickup	1295	2722	—
473-D	Platform Stake	1365	2963	—
Jeep Trucks — 1-Ton — 4-cyl. — 4x4				
473-E	Chassis	1205	2109	—
473-E	Chassis & Cab	1595	2799	—
473-E	Pickup	1678	3115	—
473-E	Platform Stake	1736	3356	—

ENGINE [CJ-2A]: Inline. L-head. Four-cylinder. Cast iron block. Bore & stroke: 3-1/8 in. x 4-3/8 in. Displacement: 134.2 cid. Compression ratio: 6.5:1. Brake hp: 60 at 4000 rpm. Net hp: 15.63 (NACC) Max. Torque: 105 lbs.-ft. at 2000 rpm. Three main bearings. Solid valve lifters. Carburetor: Carter type YF models 832S or 832SA.

ENGINE [473]: Inline. L-head. Four-cylinder. Cast iron block. Bore & stroke: 3-1/8 in. x 4-3/8 in. Displacement: 134.2 cid. Compression ratio: 7.4:1. Brake hp: 72 at 4000 rpm. Net hp: 15.63 (NACC) Max. Torque: 114 lbs.-ft. at 2000 rpm. Three main bearings. Solid valve lifters. Carburetor: Carter type YF model 832S/832SA one-barrel.

CHASSIS [FJ/CJ-3A]: Wheelbase: 80-1/16 in. Length: 129-7/8 in. Height: 67-1/4 in. (top up). Front and rear tread: 48-7/16 in. Tires: 6.00 x 16 in.

CHASSIS [473 sedan delivery]: Wheelbase: 104.5 in. Length: 176.25 in. Height: 73.62 in. Front and rear tread: 57 in. Tires: 6.70 x 15 in.

CHASSIS [473 trucks]: Wheelbase: 118 in. Length: 183.7 in. Height: 74.3 in. Front and rear tread: 57 in. Tires: [4x2] 6.70 x 15 in.; [4x4] 7.00 x 15 in.

TECHNICAL: Synchromesh transmission. Speeds: 3F/1R (4x4 models have two-speed transfer case). Floor-mounted gearshift lever. Single-plate, dry-disc clutch. Hypoid rear axle. Overall ratio: 5.38:1. Four-wheel hydraulic brakes. Disc wheels. The 4x4 models had two hypoid axles with a full-floating type in front; semi-floating rear. Axle capacity [CJ-3A] 2,000 lbs. front; 2,500 lbs. rear.

OPTIONS: [*] Power-take-off ($96.25). [*] Pulley drive ($57.40). [*] Motor governor ($28.65). Special wheels and 7-in. tires ($40). Front canvas top ($57.80). Hydraulic lift ($225). Metal top (Varies). Other options available for Jeep trucks included: Chrome front bumper. Chrome rear bumper. Rearview mirrors. Chrome wheel discs. Bumper guards. Clearance lights.

HISTORICAL: Introduced: [Farm Jeep] July 1951; [451] Nov. 1950. Calendar year registrations: 24,292 [All Trucks]. Calendar year production: [Jeeps] 76,571; [Station Wagons] 25,316; [Trucks] 20,244. Military and civilian orders for Willys-Overland vehicles exceeded a quarter-billion dollars in 1951. There was a backlog for Jeep orders that Willys had trouble keeping up with. First half sales figures, of which 90 percent were for the civilian market, set an all-time record and were up 168 percent over the comparable 1950 period.

1952 JEEP

WILLYS — JEEP SERIES — FOUR-CYLINDER: Willys was producing like crazy to fill military orders for Korean War Jeeps. Civilian models also sold well this year. There wasn't time to worry about changing the products' basic designs. However, all trucks listed in used car guides were 4x4 models. It seems that among Jeep-Trucks, only the sedan delivery was

offered with conventional 4x2 running gear. (By the way, a 2,000 lbs. capacity I-beam front axle was used on the 4x2 models). The 4x4 trucks had "4-Wheel-Drive" on the sides of their hoods near the cowl.

1952 Willys-Overland Jeep 1-Ton Pickup 4x4 (D. Sagvold)

I.D. DATA: Serial number located on right side of dash under hood in 1949-1954 models CJ-2A and CJ-3A/CJ-3B; on left side of dash under hood in models 473. Starting: [CJ-3A] 452-GA1-10,001 to 10,013; [CJ-3A open] 452-GB1-10,001 to 39,652; [473-SD] 452-GA1-10,001 to 12,091; [473 chassis] 452-FA1-10,001 & up; [473 chassis & cab] 452-EB1-10,001 to 11,085; [473 pickup] 452-EC1-10,001 to 23,183; [473 stake] 452-ED1-10,001 to 10,358. Engine numbers located on right side of cylinder block; stamped on water pump boss on front of cylinder block. Beginning around 1951 and continuing through at least 1953, each model had a specific serial number prefix such as 451-4GC. The first number indicated the number of cylinders. The second and third numbers indicated model year. The first letter indicated the basic chassis and body type. The second letter indicated model. The fourth number indicated series in any one model year. On most Jeep models the engine and serial numbers were the same.

Model	Body Type	Price	Weight	Prod. Total
Willys Jeep — 1/4-Ton — 4-cyl. — 4x4				
CJ-3A	Chassis	1224	1692	—
CJ-3A	Jeep Universal	1352	2108	—
Jeep Trucks — 1/2-Ton — 4-cyl. — 4x2				
473-SD	Sedan Delivery	1469	2406	—
Jeep Trucks — 1-Ton — 4-cyl. — 4x4				
473	Chassis Stripped	1296	2109	—
473	Chassis & Cab	1712	2799	—
473	Pickup	1805	3115	—
473	Platform Stake	1870	3356	—

ENGINE [CJ-2A]: Inline. L-head. Four-cylinder. Cast iron block. Bore & stroke: 3-1/8 in. x 4-3/8 in. Displacement: 134.2 cid. Compression ratio: 6.5:1. Brake hp: 60 at 4000 rpm. Net hp: 15.63 (NACC) Max. Torque: 105 lbs.-ft. at 2000 rpm. Three main bearings. Solid valve lifters. Carburetor: Carter type YF model 938S or 938SA.

ENGINE [473-SW]: Inline. F-head. Four-cylinder. Cast iron block. Bore & stroke: 3-1/8 in. x 4-3/8 in. Displacement: 134.2 cid. Compression ratio: 7.4:1. Brake hp: 72 at 4000 rpm. Net hp: 15.63 (NACC) Max. Torque: 114 lbs.-ft. at 2000 rpm. Three main bearings. Solid valve lifters. Carburetor: Carter type YF model 951S.

CHASSIS [CJ-3A]: Wheelbase: 80-1/16 in. Length: 129-7/8 in. Height: 67-1/4 in. (top up). Front and rear tread: 48-7/16 in. Tires: 6.00 x 16 in.

CHASSIS [Sedan Delivery]: Wheelbase: 104 in. Length: 176-1/4 in. Height: 73.62 in. Front and rear tread: 57 in. Tires: [4x2] 6.70 x 15 in.

CHASSIS [Trucks]: Wheelbase: 118 in. Length: 183.7 in. Height: 74.3 in. Front and rear tread: 57 in. Tires: [4x4] 7.00 x 15 in.

TECHNICAL: Synchromesh transmission. Speeds: 3F/1R (4x4 models have two-speed transfer case). Floor-mounted gearshift lever. Single-plate, dry-disc clutch. Hypoid rear axle. Overall ratio: 5.38:1. Four-wheel hydraulic brakes. Disc wheels. The 4x2 models had a 2,000 lbs. capacity front I-beam axle. The 4x4 models had a 2,000 lbs. capacity, full-floating type hypoid front axle. A 2,500 lbs. capacity, semi-floating hypoid rear axle was used on both 4x2 and 4x4 models.

OPTIONS: [CJ] Power-take-off ($96.25). Pulley drive ($57.40). Motor governor ($28.65). Special wheels and 7-in. tires ($40). Front canvas top ($57.80). Hydraulic lift ($225). Metal top (various prices). [4x4 Trucks]: Power-take-off ($96.25). Pulley drive ($57.40). Motor governor ($28.65). Rearview mirror. Sidemount spare on pickups/stakes. Chrome bumper. License frame. [Sedan Delivery]: Chrome front bumper. Chrome rear bumper. License frame. Chrome wheel disc. Bumperettes. Bumper guards. Wheel trim rings. Whitewall tires. Rearview mirror. Radio and antenna.

HISTORICAL: Introduced: Dec. 10, 1951. Calendar year registrations: 20,356 [Trucks]. Calendar year production: [Jeeps] 88,098; [Station Wagons] 12,890; [Trucks] 31,273. New "Hurricane" F-head engine in Jeeps (late 1952 for 1953 models). Grille styling revised. New M38A1 military jeep introduced. This became the civilian CJ-5. The one-millionth Jeep was built March 19, 1952. Defense contracts awarded in 1952 totaled $200,556,116 and included a front-line Jeep ambulance project.

1953 JEEP

WILLYS — JEEP SERIES — FOUR-CYLINDER: The CJ-3B bowed as an added civilian model for 1953. It was basically the same as the carryover CJ-3A, but had a higher hood and grille to fit the new 70 hp "Hurricane Four" F-head engine. Willys lettering appeared on the front and the raised hoodside panels. The famous Korean War military MD/M38A1 Jeep also entered production late in 1952 as a 1953 model. This would be the basis for the civilian CJ-5 of later years. The CJ-3B used a 70 hp version of the truck engine. It had slightly lower compression. Attempts to market a special "Farm Jeep" were revived this season. In the Jeep truck line, the primary change was the addition of a new, 4x4 sedan delivery, which joined the 4x2 model. The chassis-only configuration was dropped. Henry J. Kaiser purchased the company, in the spring, changing the name to Willys Motors, Inc.

1953 Willys-Jeep CJ-3B Universal 4x4 (RCA)

I.D. DATA: Serial number located on plate at left side of driver's seat on floor riser on right side of dash under hood in 1949-1954 models CJ-2A and CJ-3A/CJ-3B; on left side of dash under hood on Model 473 trucks. Serial numbers: [CJ-3B open] 453-GB2-10,001 to 37,550; [CJ-3B Farm] 453-GC2-10,001 & up; [CJ-3A] 453-GB1-10,001 & up; [4x2 Sedan Delivery] 453-CA2-10,001 to 12,347; [4x4 Sedan Delivery] 453-RA2-10,001 to 10,992; [4x4 Chassis] 453-EB2-10,001 to 11,516; [4x4 Pickup] 453-EC2-10,001 to 24,128 and [4x4 Stake] 453-ED2-10,001 to 10,694. Engine numbers located on right side of cylinder block; stamped on water pump boss on front of cylinder block. Beginning around 1951 and continuing through at least 1953, each model had a specific serial number prefix such as 451-4GC. The first number indicated the number of cylinders. The second and third numbers indicated model year. Letters indicated the model code. The fourth number indicated series in any one model year. On most Jeep models the engine and serial numbers were the same.

Model	Body Type	Price	Weight	Prod. Total
Willys Jeep — 1/4-Ton — 4-cyl. — 4x4				
CJ-3B	Jeep Universal	1377	2098	—
CJ-3B	Farm Jeep	1439	2098	—
CJ-3A	Jeep Universal	1352	2108	—
Jeep Sedan Delivery — 1/2-Ton — 4-cyl. — 4x2				
475	Sedan Delivery	1469	2620	—
Jeep Sedan Delivery — 1/2-Ton — 4-cyl. — 4x4				
475SD	Sedan Delivery	1920	2976	—
Jeep Trucks — 1-Ton — 4-cyl/ — 4x4				
475	Chassis & Cab	1712	2799	—
475	Pickup	1805	3115	—
475	Platform Stake	1870	3356	—

ENGINE [CJ-3A]: Inline. L-head. Four-cylinder. Cast iron block. Bore & stroke: 3-1/8 in. x 4-3/8 in. Displacement: 134.2 cid. Compression ratio: 6.48:1. Brake hp: 60 at 4000 rpm. Net hp: 15.63 (NACC) Max. Torque: 105 lbs.-ft. at 2000 rpm. Three main bearings. Solid valve lifters. Carburetor: Carter type model YF models 938S; 938SA.

ENGINE [CJ-3B]: Inline. F-head. Four-cylinder. Cast iron block. Bore & stroke: 3-1/8 in. x 4-3/8 in. Displacement: 134.2 cid. Compression ratio: 6.90:1. Brake hp: 70 at 4000 rpm. Net hp: 15.63 (NACC) Max. Torque: 114 lbs.-ft. at 2000 rpm. Three main bearings. Solid valve lifters. Carburetor: Carter type YF model 951S.

ENGINE [475]: Inline. F-head. Four-cylinder. Cast iron block. Bore & stroke: 3-1/8 in. x 4-3/8 in. Displacement: 134.2 cid. Compression ratio: 7.40:1. Brake hp: 72 at 4000 rpm. Net hp: 15.63. Max. Torque: 114 lbs.-ft. at 2000 rpm. Three main bearings. Solid valve lifters. Carburetor: Carter type YF model 951S.

CHASSIS [CJ-3A/CJ-3B]: Wheelbase: 80-1/16 in. Length: 129-7/8 in. Height: 67-1/4 in. Front and rear tread: 48-7/16 in. Tires: 6.00 x 16 in.

CHASSIS [Sedan Delivery 4x2]: Wheelbase: 104 in. Length: 176-1/4 in. Height: 73.62 in. Front and rear tread: 57 in. Tires: [4x2] 6.70 x 15 in.

CHASSIS [Sedan Delivery 4x4]: Wheelbase: 104-1/2 in. Length: 176-1/4 in. Height: 73.62 in. Front and rear tread: 57 in. Tires: [4x4] 7.00 x 15 in.

CHASSIS [Trucks 4x4]: Wheelbase: 118 in. Length: 183.7 in. Height: 74.3 in. Front and rear tread: 57 in. Tires: 7.00 x 15 in.

TECHNICAL: Synchromesh transmission. Speeds: 3F/1R (4x4 models with two-speed transfer case). Floor-mounted gearshift lever. Single-plate, dry-disc clutch. Hypoid rear axle. Overall ratio: 5.38:1. Four-wheel hydraulic brakes. Disc wheels. The 4x2 models have I-beam front axle. The 4x4 models have full-floating hypoid front axle. All models have semi-floating hypoid rear axle.

OPTIONS: [CJ]: Power-take-off ($96.25). Pulley drive ($57.40). Motor governor ($28.65). Special wheels and 7-in. tires ($40). Front canvas top ($57.80). Hydraulic lift ($225). Metal top (various prices). [4x4Trucks]: Power-take-off ($96.25). Pulley drive ($57.40). Motor governor ($28.65). Rearview mirror. Sidemount spare on pickups/stakes. Chrome bumper. License frame. [Sedan Delivery]: Chrome front bumper. Chrome rear bumper. License frame. Chrome wheel disc. Bumperettes. Bumper guards. Wheel trim rings. Whitewall tires. Rearview mirror. Radio and antenna.

HISTORICAL: Introduced: [CJ-3B] Jan. 28, 1953; [others] Oct. 20, 1952. Calendar year registrations: 17,712 [Trucks]. Calendar year production: [Jeeps/Trucks] 88,650; [Station Wagons] 5,417. New CJ-3B featured higher hood/grille design to accomodate 71 hp "Hurricane Four" F-head engine. On April 28, 1953, Kaiser Manufacturing Co. formally purchased Willys-Overland at a cost of $62,381,175. This was Willys-Overland's "Golden Jubilee" year, celebrating the company's 50th anniversary. Production averaged 8,800 trucks monthly. On Sept. 2, 1953 an assembly point in Japan was established. On the same day, Chase Aircraft Co., of Trenton, N.J., became a wholly owned subsidiary of Willys Motors. On Sept. 5, the U.S. Army cut its Jeep orders back by 50 percent. On Sept. 22, vehicle production at a Kaiser plant in the Netherlands was announced.

1953 Willys-Jeep Military Front Line Ambulance (OCW)

1954 JEEP

1954 Willys-Jeep 1/2-Ton Sedan Delivery 4x4 (RCA)

WILLYS — JEEP SERIES — ALL ENGINES: Willys-Overland was now Willys Motors, a division of Kaiser Industries which sold the Willys-Jeep and Jeep-Truck lines. The CJ-3A was dropped. All three Universal Jeeps offered this season were CJ-3B models. They still said "Willys" above the grille and on the hoodsides. The powerplant was the F-head four-cylinder. Jeep-Truck models had another new grille. It had only three bright metal moldings, running horizontally across the top, middle and bottom. Nine vertical bars, in body color, were behind the bright moldings. All four-cylinder trucks were 4x4s. They were designated 454 models and used the 72 hp F-head engine. Three body styles: chassis and cab, pickup and platform stake came in this 1-ton series. All-new were two six-cylinder lines of trucks powered by a 115 hp L-head six. This was called a "Super Hurricane" engine.

I.D. DATA: Serial number located on right side of dash under hood; on front frame crossmember; on left floor riser in back of driver's seat. Serial numbers: [CJ-5 chassis] 54-10,001 to 12,600 and 454-GA2-10,601 up; [CJ-3B-OB] 54-10,001 to 12,600 and 454-GB2-12,001 up; [454-GC2] 10,001 to 10,012; [454-FA2] 10,001 to 13,528; [454-EC2] 10,001 to 13,606; [454-ED2] 10,001 to 10,185; [454-EB2] 10,001 to 10,681; [654-CA2] 10,001 to 10,308; [654-EC2] 10,001 to 14,927; [654-EB2] 10,001 to 10,439; [654-RA2] 10,001 to 10,243 and [654-FA2] 10,001 to 13,528. Engine numbers located on right side of cylinder block and stamped on water pump boss on front of cylinder block. On most Jeep models the engine and serial numbers are the same.

Model	Body Type	Price	Weight	Prod. Total
Willys Jeep — 1/4-Ton — 4-cyl. — 4x4				
CJ-3B	Chassis	1145	1718	—
CJ-3B	Jeep Universal	1377	2306	—
CJ-3B	Farm Jeep	1439	2184	—
Jeep Sedan Delivery — 1/2-Ton — 4-cyl. — 4x4				
454-CA2	Sedan Delivery	1520	2711	—

| Jeep Trucks — 1-Ton — 4-cyl. — 4x2 | | | | |

454-EB2	Chassis & Cab	1712	2774	—
454-EC2	Pickup	1805	3135	—
454-ED2	Platform Stake	1870	3356	—

Jeep Sedan Delivery — 1/2-Ton — 6-cyl. — 4x4

654-RA2	Sedan Delivery	2009	3055	—

Jeep Trucks — 1-Ton — 6-cyl. — 4x4

654-EB2	Chassis & Cab	1802	2850	—
654-EC2	Pickup	1895	3141	—
654-ED2	Platform Stake	1960	3362	—

ENGINE [CJ-3B]: Inline. F-head. Four-cylinder. Cast iron block. Bore & stroke: 3-1/8 in. x 4-3/8 in. Displacement: 134.2 cid. Compression ratio: 6.90:1. Brake hp: 70 at 4000 rpm. Net hp: 15.63. Max. Torque: 114 lbs.-ft. at 2000 rpm. Three main bearings. Solid valve lifters. Carburetor: Carter YF model 938S or 938SA one-barrel.

ENGINE [Series 454]: Inline. F-head. Four-cylinder. Cast iron block. Bore & stroke: 3-1/8 in. x 4-3/8 in. Displacement: 134.2 cid. Compression ratio: 7.40:1. Brake hp: 72 at 4000 rpm. Net hp: 15.63. Max. Torque: 114 lbs.-ft. at 2000 rpm. Three main bearings. Solid valve lifters. Carburetor: Carter YF model 951S one-barrel.

ENGINE [Model CA]: Inline. F-head. Six-cylinder. Cast iron block. Bore & stroke: 3-1/8 in. x 3-1/2 in. Displacement: 161.5 cid. Compression ratio: 7.6:1. Brake hp: 90 at 4200 rpm. Net hp: 23.44. Max. Torque: 135 lbs.-ft. at 2000 rpm. Four main bearings. Solid valve lifters. Carburetor: Carter YF model 924S or 2071S one-barrel.

ENGINE [6-226]: Inline. L-head. Six-cylinder. Cast iron block. Bore & stroke: 3-5/16 in. x 4-3/8 in. Displacement: 226.2 cid. Compression ratio: 6.86:1. Brake hp: 115 at 3650 rpm. Net hp: 26.3. Max. Torque: 190 lbs.-ft. at 1800 rpm. Four main bearings. Solid valve lifters. Carburetor: Carter WDG model 2052S or 2052SA one-barrel.

CHASSIS [CJ-3B]: Wheelbase: 80-1/16 in. Length: 129-7/8 in. Height: 67-1/4 in. Front and rear tread: 48-7/8 in. Tires: 6.00 x 16 in.

CHASSIS [Sedan Delivery 4x2]: Wheelbase: 104 in. Length: 176-1/4 in. Height: 73.62 in. Front and rear tread: 57 in. Tires: 6.70 x 15 in.

CHASSIS [Sedan Delivery 4x4]: Wheelbase: 104-1/2 in. Length: 176-1/4 in. Height: 73.62 in. Front and rear tread: 57 in. Tires: 7.00 x 15 in.

CHASSIS [Trucks 4x4]: Wheelbase: 118 in. Length: 183.7 in. Height: 74.3 in. Front and rear tread: 57 in. Tires: 7.00 x 15 in.

TECHNICAL: Synchromesh transmission. Speeds: 3F/1R (4x4 models have two-speed transfer case). Floor-mounted gearshift lever. Single-plate, dry-disc clutch. Hypoid rear axle. Overall ratio: 5.38:1. Four-wheel hydraulic brakes. Disc wheels. The 4x2 models had I-beam front axle. The 4x4 models have full-floating hypoid front axle. All models have semi-floating hypoid rear axle.

OPTIONS: [Jeep]: Power-take-off ($96.25). Pulley drive ($57.40). Motor governor ($28.65). Special wheels and 7-in. tires ($40). Front canvas top ($57.80). Hydraulic lift ($225). Metal top (various prices). [4x4 trucks]: Power-take-off ($96.25). Pulley drive ($57.40). Motor governor ($28.65). Rearview mirror. Sidemount spare on pickups/stakes. Chrome bumper. License frame. [Sedan Delivery]: Chrome front bumper. Chrome rear bumper. License frame. Chrome wheel disc. Bumperettes. Bumper guards. Wheel trim rings. Whitewall tires. Rearview mirror. Radio and antenna.

HISTORICAL: Introduced: [Jeep] Dec. 1, 1953; [four-cylinder trucks] Feb. 3, 1954; [six-cylinder trucks] June 30 or May 10, 1954; [CJ-5] Nov. 12, 1954. Calendar year registrations: [Trucks] 9,925; [Jeeps] 7,598. Calendar year production: [Commercial Vehicles] 75,434. Innovations included a new six-cylinder engine. The EC/ED/EB models bowed May 10 and the RA/FA models bowed June 30. The six was called "Super-Hurricane" engine. Truck grilles was redesigned. The CJ-5 was a demilitarized version of the famous M-38 Jeep. On Feb. 23, 1954 the 500,000th postwar Jeep was built. E.F. Kaiser was president of Willys. C.A. Watson was general sales manager. On July 19, 1954 some 400 workers were recalled for increased truck programming and car-building assembly lines were temporarily closed for truck erecting. Four days later, Kaiser-Willys announced plans to liquidate surplus facilities and concentrate all car-truck operations in the Toledo, Ohio area. The Maywood, Calif. factory, opened in 1928, was closed on July 29. It was first converted to a warehouse and later sold. On Oct. 5, Kaiser-Willys signed a contract to produce Jeeps in Argentina. Jeep production begins in Brazil, too.

1954 Willys-Jeep 1-Ton Pickup 4x4 (RCA)

1955 JEEP

WILLYS — JEEP SERIES — ALL ENGINES: The military M38 became the civilian CJ-5 in model-year 1955. It had entirely new body work with lower, squarer-cornered door openings, sunk-in headlights, redesigned fenders and an 81 in. (versus CJ-3's 80 in.) wheelbase. The new front fenders were fuller and had front "flaps" for more protection. A variation from military specifications was a one-piece windshield. Trucks used the grille that came out in 1954. There were four new 4x2 models, two with four-cylinder engines and two with six-cylinder engines. One was a sedan delivery and the other was called a Utility Wagon. This was actually the same as the earlier station wagon, which was considered a

car. Willys Motors had stopped making the conventional passenger cars (Ace/Lark/Bermuda) made by Willys-Overland. The new owners of the company were intent on being "imaged" as truck-makers. So, the station wagon was renamed and certified as a truck.

1955 Willys-Jeep CJ-5 Universal 4x4 (OCW)

I.D. DATA: Serial number located on right side of dash under hood; on front frame cross-member; on left floor riser in back of driver's seat. Serial numbers began with "55" (1955) or "54" (1954 Carryover) followed by three digits designating a specific model. Next came a hyphen and four or five digits indicating production sequence. Starting: [All] 5001. Ending: numbers are not available. A typical serial number looked like this: 55268-5001. The 55268 designated the model number (see chart below) and the 5001 was the beginning sequential number. Engine numbers located on right side of cylinder block; stamped on water pump boss on front of cylinder block. On most Jeep models the engine and serial numbers are the same.

1955 Willys-Jeep 1-Ton Pickup 4x4 (RCA)

Model	Body Type	Price	Weight	Prod. Total
Model 57348 Willys Jeep — 1/4-Ton — 4-cyl. — 4x4				
CJ-3B	Jeep	1411	2134	—
Model 57548 Willys Jeep — 1/4-Ton — 4-cyl. — 4x4				
CJ-5	Jeep	1476	2164	—
Model 54247 Sedan Delivery — 1/2-Ton — 4-cyl. — 4x2				
475	Sedan Delivery	1494	2786	—
Model 54147 Utility Wagon — 1/2-Ton — 4-cyl. — 4x2				
475	Utility Wagon	1748	3009	—
Model 54268 Sedan Delivery — 1/2-Ton — 6-cyl. — 4x2				
685	Sedan Delivery	1545	2633	—
Model 54827 Sedan Delivery — 1/2-Ton — 6-cyl. — 4x4				
6-226	Sedan Delivery	2036	3055	—
Trucks (*) — 1-Ton — 6-cyl. — 4x2				
6-226	Chassis & Cab	1833	2782	—
6-226	Pickup	1927	3141	—
6-226	Platform Stake	1992	3355	—
Model 54267 Sedan Delivery — 6-cyl. — 4x2				
6-226	Sedan Delivery	1584	2890	—
Model 54167 Utility Wagon — 1/2-Ton — 6-cyl. — 4x2				
6-226	Utility Wagon	1837	3113	—

(*) Model numbers for 1955 1-ton trucks are: [Chassis] 54168; [pickup] 54268; [platform] 54368. The first number (5) indicated model year. The others were the model number.

ENGINE [CJ-3B/CJ-5]: Inline. F-head. Four-cylinder. Cast iron block. Bore & stroke: 3-1/8 in. x 4-3/8 in. Displacement: 134.2 cid. Compression ratio: 6.9:1. Brake hp: 70 at 4000 rpm. Net hp: 15.63. Max. Torque: 114 lbs.-ft. at 2000 rpm. Three main bearings. Solid valve lifters. Carburetor: Carter YF model 938S or 938SA one-barrel.

ENGINE [475]: Inline. F-head. Four-cylinder. Cast iron block. Bore & stroke: 3-1/8 in. x 4-3/8 in. Displacement: 134.2 cid. Compression ratio: 7.4:1. Brake hp: 72 at 4000 rpm. Net hp: 15.63. Max. Torque: 114 lbs.-ft. at 2000 rpm. Three main bearings. Solid valve lifters. Carburetor: Carter YF model 951S one-barrel.

ENGINE [685]: Inline. F-head. Six-cylinder. Cast iron block. Bore & stroke: 3-1/8 in. x 3-1/2 in. Displacement: 161.5 cid. Compression ratio: 7.6:1. Brake hp: 90 at 4200 rpm. Net hp: 23.4. Max. Torque: 114 lbs.-ft. at 2000 rpm. Four main bearings. Solid valve lifters. Carburetor: Carter YF model 924S or 2071S one-barrel.

ENGINE [6-226]: Inline. Six-cylinder. Cast iron block. Bore & stroke: 3-5/16 in. x 4-3/8 in. Displacement: 226.2 cid. Compression ratio: 6.86:1. Brake hp: 115 at 3650 rpm. Net hp: 26.3. Max. Torque: 190 lbs.-ft. at 1800 rpm. Four main bearings. Solid valve lifters. Carburetor: Carter WDG model 2052S or 2052SA one-barrel.

CHASSIS [CJ-5]: Wheelbase: 81 in. Length: 135-1/2 in. Height: 69-1/2 in. Front and rear tread: 48-7/16 in. Tires: 6.00 x 16 in.

CHASSIS [CJ-3B]: Wheelbase: 80-1/16 in. Length: 129-7/8 in. Height: 67-1/4 in. Front and rear tread: 48-7/16 in. Tires: 6.00 x 16 in.

CHASSIS [Sedan Delivery 4x2]: Wheelbase: 104 in. Length: 176-1/4 in. Height: 73.62 in. Front and rear tread: 57 in. Tires: 6.70 x 15 in.

CHASSIS [Sedan Delivery 4x4]: Wheelbase: 104-1/2 in. Length: 176-1/4 in. Height: 73.62 in. Front and rear tread: 57 in. Tires: 7.00 x 15 in.

CHASSIS [Trucks 4x4]: Wheelbase: 118 in. Length: 183.7 in. Height: 74.3 in. Front and rear tread: 57 in. Tires: 7.00 x 15 in.

TECHNICAL [CJ-5]: Synchromesh transmission. Speeds: 3F/1R (with two-speed transfer case). Floor-mounted gearshift lever. Single-plate, dry-disc clutch with torsional dampening, 72 sq. in. area. Full-floating hypoid front axle. Semi-floating hypoid rear axle. Overall ratio: 5.38:1. Bendix hydraulic 9 in. drum brakes. Five 4.50 x 16 five-stud disc wheels.

TECHNICAL [Other models]: Synchromesh transmission. Speeds: 3F/1R (4x4 models have two-speed transfer case). Floor-mounted gearshift lever. Single-plate, dry-disc clutch. Hypoid rear axle. Overall ratio: 5.38:1. Four-wheel hydraulic brakes. Disc wheels. The 4x2 models had I-beam front axle. The 4x4 models have full-floating hypoid front axle. All models have semi-floating hypoid rear axle.

OPTIONS [CJ-5]: Five metal and fabric-top options. Ventilating windshield. Power-take-off. Eight body color choices. Approved snow plow. Winch. 36 x 39-1/4 in. all-steel cargo box.

OPTIONS: [CJs]: Power-take-off ($96.25). Pulley drive ($57.40). Motor governor ($28.65). Special wheels and 7-in. tires ($40). Front canvas top ($57.80). Hydraulic lift ($225). Metal top (various prices). [4x4 trucks]: Power-take-off ($96.25). Pulley drive ($57.40). Motor governor ($28.65). Rearview mirror. Sidemount spare on pickups/stakes. Chrome bumper. License frame. [Sedan Delivery]: Chrome front bumper. Chrome rear bumper. License frame. Chrome wheel disc. Bumperettes. Bumper guards. Wheel trim rings. Whitewall tires. Rearview mirror. Radio and antenna.

1955 Willys-Jeep Utility Wagon 4x4 (RCA)

HISTORICAL: Introduced: [CJ-3B/685] Oct. 11, 1954; [CJ-5] Nov. 12, 1954; [475] May 26, 1955; [6-226 with 118 in. wheelbase] Oct. 11, 1954; [Other 6-226 models] May 26, 1955. Calendar year registrations: [Trucks] 16,811; [Jeeps] 10,441. Calendar year production: [commercial vehicles] 78,922. This included 47,432 Jeeps. Innovations included the restyled CJ-5, (short wheelbase) and CJ-6 (long wheelbase) Willys Jeeps. Also new was the 4x2 Dispatcher, a Jeep-like vehicle with the L-head four-cylinder engine that bowed Oct. 26, 1955 as a 1956 model. Willys withdrew as a U.S. automaker in 1955. The Jeep was now the company's mainstay product. In Dec. 1955 the one-millionth Willys commercial vehicle since World War II was produced. Approximately 46 percent of the company's 1955 commercial units had four-cylinder powerplants. Eighty-six percent of Jeep output in calendar 1955 was for the civilian market. Effective with Willy's withdrawal from the passenger car market, reference sources began listing Jeep Station Wagons with trucks, sometimes referring to them as Utility Wagons. We will follow this practice in this catalog.

1956 JEEP

WILLYS — JEEP SERIES — ALL ENGINES: The big news from Willys this season was a new 4x4 Jeep called the CJ-6 and a new line of Jeep-like 4x2 models named Dispatchers. The CJ-6 was a stretched version of last year's new CJ-5. Like that model, it had the more aesthetically pleasing curved hood and fenders along with a slightly curved windshield header. There was a 20 in. longer wheelbase. The pickup box was also lengthened enough to add twin benches along the inner sidewalls and provide room for up to eight people. The new Dispatcher was designated the DJ-3A model. It had the old-style straight front fenders and seven vertical slots in its grille. The front axle was a solid I-beam type. This was the predecessor of the DJ-5 Postal Jeep. It came in open, soft top and hardtop models. Also new for 1955 was the addition of Sedan Delivery, Utility Wagon and Pickup models with a four-cylinder engine and 4x4 running gear. By this time, some models were wearing the Jeep name instead of the Willys name. The CJ-3B said "Willys" on the grille and hoodsides. The CJ-5/CJ-6/DJ-3A said "Jeep" on the sides of the cowl. The trucks with 4x4 running gear said "4-Wheel-Drive" on the side of the hood near the cowl. Four different engines were standard in specific models.

1956 Jeep CJ-5 Universal 4x4 (RCA)

I.D. DATA: Serial number located on right side of dash under hood; on front frame crossmember; on left floor riser in back of driver's seat. Engine numbers located on right side of cylinder block; stamped on water pump boss on front of cylinder block. On most Jeep models the engine and serial numbers are the same.

Model	Body Type	Price	Weight	Prod. Total
Willys Jeep — 1/4-Ton — 4-cyl. — 4x4 — 80 in. w.b.				
CJ-3B	Jeep Universal	2134	—	
Willys Jeep — 1/4-Ton — 4-cyl. — 4x4 — 81 in. w.b.				
CJ-5	Jeep Universal	2164	—	
Willys Jeep — 1/2-Ton — 4-cyl. — 4x4 — 101 in. w.b.				
CJ-6	Jeep Universal	2305	—	
Dispatcher — 1/4-Ton — 4-cyl. — 4x2 — 80 in. w.b.				
DJ-3A	Basic	1205	1968	—
DJ-3A	Canvas Top	1261	2016	—
DJ-3A	Hardtop	1397	2205	—
Jeep Trucks — 1/2-Ton — 4-cyl. — 4x2 — 104.5 in. w.b.				
475	Utility Wagon	2012	2944	—
475	Sedan Delivery	1700	2746	—
Jeep Trucks — 1/2-Ton — 6-cyl. — 4x2 — 104.5 in. w.b.				
L6-226	Utility Wagon	2118	3057	—
L6-226	Sedan Delivery	2311	2859	—
Jeep Trucks — 1/2-Ton — 4-cyl. — 4x4 — 104.5 in. w.b.				
475	Sedan Delivery	2114	2951	—
475	Station Wagon	2287	3174	—
475	Pickup	1997	3065	—
Jeep Trucks — 1/2-Ton — 6-cyl. — 4x4 — 104.5 in. w.b.				
L6-226	Sedan Delivery	2176	3055	—
L6-226	Station Wagon	2250	3278	—
Jeep Trucks — 1-Ton — 6-cyl. — 4x4 — 118 in. w.b.				
L6-226	Pickup	2187	3176	—
L6-226	Stake	2118	3341	—

ENGINE [CJ-3B/CJ-5]: Inline. F-head. Four-cylinder. Cast iron block. Bore & stroke: 3-1/8 in. x 4-3/8 in. Displacement: 134.2 cid. Compression ratio: 6.9:1. Brake hp: 70 at 4000 rpm. Net hp: 15.63. Max. Torque: 114 lbs.-ft. at 2000 rpm. Three main bearings. Solid valve lifters. Carburetor: Carter YF models 938S or 938SA one-barrel.

ENGINE [CJ-6/475]: Inline. F-head. Four-cylinder. Cast iron block. Bore & stroke: 3-1/8 in. x 4-3/8 in. Displacement: 134.2 cid. Compression ratio: 7.4:1. Brake hp: 72 at 4000 rpm. Net hp: 15.63. Max. Torque: 114 lbs.-ft. at 2000 rpm. Three main bearings. Solid valve lifters. Carburetor: Carter YF models 938S or 938SA one-barrel.

ENGINE [DJ-3]: Inline. L-head. Four-cylinder. Cast iron block. Bore & stroke: 3-1/8 in. x 4-3/8 in. Displacement: 134 cid. Compression ratio: 7.4:1. Brake hp: 75 at 4000 rpm. Net hp: 15.63. Max. Torque: 114 lbs.-ft. at 2000 rpm. Three main bearings. Solid valve lifters. Carburetor: Carter YF model 2392S one-barrel.

ENGINE [6-226]: Inline. L-head. Six-cylinder. Cast iron block. Bore & stroke: 3-5/16 in. x 4-3/8 in. Displacement: 226.2 cid. Compression ratio: 6.86:1. Brake hp: 115 at 3650 rpm. Net hp: 26.3. Max. Torque: 190 lbs.-ft. at 1800 rpm. Four main bearings. Solid valve lifters. Carburetor: Carter WDG model 2052S or 2052SA one-barrel; Carter WCD model 2204S two-barrel.

CHASSIS [CJ-3B]: Wheelbase: 80-1/16 in. Length: 129-7/8 in. Height: 67-1/4 in. Front and rear tread: 48-7/16 in. Tires: 6.00 x 16 in.

CHASSIS [CJ-5]: Wheelbase: 81 in. Length: 135-1/2 in. Height: 69-1/2 in. Front and rear tread: 48-7/16 in. Tires: 6.00 x 16 in.

CHASSIS [CJ-6]: Wheelbase: 101 in. Length: 155-1/2 in. Height: 68-1/4 in. Front and rear tread: 48-7/16 in. Tires: 6.00 x 16 in. all-service type.

CHASSIS [DJ-3]: Wheelbase: 80.09 in. Length: 125.45 in. Height: 62.74 in. (windshield raised). Front and rear tread: 48.25 in. Tires: 6.50 x 15 four-ply tubeless.

CHASSIS [Sedan Delivery 4x2]: Wheelbase: 104 in. Length: 176-1/4 in. Height: 73.62 in. Front and rear tread: 57 in. Tires: 6.70 x 15 in.

CHASSIS [Sedan Delivery 4x4]: Wheelbase: 104-1/2 in. Length: 176-1/4 in. Height: 73.62 in. Front and rear tread: 57 in. Tires: 7.00 x 15 in.

CHASSIS [Trucks 4x4]: Wheelbase: 118 in. Length: 183.7 in. Height: 74.3 in. Front and rear tread: 57 in. Tires: 7.00 x 15 in.

TECHNICAL [Basic, all models]: Synchromesh transmission. Speeds: 3F/1R. Floor-mounted gearshift lever. Single-plate, dry-disc clutch. Hypoid semi-floating rear axle. Overall ratio: 3.54:1, 4.56:1 or 5.38:1. Four-wheel hydraulic brakes. Disc wheels. 4x4 models have two-speed transfer case. 4x2 models have I-beam type front axle. 4x4 models have full-floating hypoid front axle.

OPTIONS, JEEP: [CJs] Power-take-off ($96.25). Pulley drive ($57.40). Motor governor ($28.65). Special wheels and 7-in. tires ($40). Front canvas top ($57.80). Hydraulic lift ($225). Metal top (various prices). [CJ-5]: Five metal and fabric-top options. Ventilating

windshield. Power-take-off. Eight body color choices. Approved snow plow. Winch. All-steel cargo box (36 x 39-1/4 in.). [CJ-6]: All-weather canvas tops. New body colors. Oversize tires.

OPTIONS, DISPATCHER: [DJ-3A] Convertible top. 40 cu. ft. hardtop with rippled fiberglass roof and 36 in. wide gate opening. Whitewall tires. Chrome wheel discs. Chrome front bumper. Chrome rear bumper. Eight standard body colors. "Law Enforcement" package.

OPTIONS, JEEP-TRUCKS: [4x4 trucks] Power-take-off ($96.25). Pulley drive ($57.40). Motor governor ($28.65). Rearview mirror. Sidemount spare on pickups/stakes. Chrome bumper. License frame. [Sedan Delivery]: Chrome front bumper. Chrome rear bumper. License frame. Chrome wheel disc. Bumperettes. Bumper guards. Wheel trim rings. Whitewall tires. Rearview mirror. Radio and antenna.

HISTORICAL: Introduced: Aug. 17, 1955 except Dispatcher, which bowed Oct. 26, 1955. Calendar year registrations: 23,488 [All Trucks and Jeeps]. This year's main innovation was the new-for-1956 Dispatcher model. It was available with canvas top or fiberglass roof with sliding doors, as well as basic open model. The 60 hp L-head four-cylinder engine was called the "Go-Devil" powerplant.

1957 JEEP

1957 Jeep FC-150 3/4-Ton Pickup 4x4 (RCA)

WILLYS — JEEP SERIES — ALL ENGINES: The major innovation of 1957 was the introduction of the Forward Control (FC) Jeep. This was a model that resembled the cab of a modern van with a pickup or stake body behind it. It was a cab-over-engine truck. There were actually several passenger-van prototypes done by famed industrial designer Brooks Stevens. One of these is said to survive on the island estate of Henry Kaiser in upper Michigan. The production versions came as the FC-150, a 1/4-ton on an 81 in. wheelbase and the FC-170, a 1-ton with 103-1/2 in. wheelbase. Willys' L-head engines were used as powerplants with the 72 hp four in the FC-150 and the 115 hp six for the FC-170. Universal Jeeps available this year included the CJ-3B/CJ-5/CJ-6. None had significant changes. There were three Dispatchers. Trucks continued to offer the 1954 style grille. The only really new models were 4x4s in chassis-with-windshield and chassis-with-flat face-cowl configurations. However, the line was greatly expanded through engine, running gear and wheelbase selections, to 13 models with four-wheel drive (4x4) and four with conventional drive (4x2); a total of 15 models not counting Jeeps or Forward Control models.

I.D. DATA: Serial number located on right side of dash under hood; on front frame crossmember; on left floor riser in back of driver's seat. Engine numbers located on right side of cylinder block; stamped on water pump boss on front of cylinder block. On most Jeep models the engine and serial numbers are the same.

1957 Jeep FC-150 1-Ton Stake 4x4 (RCA)

Model	Body Type	Price	Weight	Prod. Total
Willys Jeep — 1/4-Ton — 4-cyl. — 4x4 — 80 in. w.b.				
CJ-3B	Jeep Universal	1799	2132	—
Willys Jeep — 1/4-Ton — 4-cyl. — 4x4 — 81 in. w.b.				
CJ-5	Jeep Universal	1886	2163	—
Willys Jeep — 1/2-Ton — 4-cyl. — 4x4 — 101 in. w.b.				
CJ-6	Jeep Universal	2068	2225	—

Model	Body Type		Price	Weight	Prod. Total
Dispatcher — 1/4-Ton — 4-cyl. — 4x2 — 80 in. w.b.					
DJ-3A	Basic		1303	1709	—
DJ-3A	Soft Top		1363	1769	—
DJ-3A	Hardtop		1511	2004	—
Jeep Trucks — 1/2-Ton — 4-cyl. — 4x2 — 104.5 in. w.b.					
F4-134	Delivery		1843	2746	—
F4-134	Utility Wagon		2152	2944	—
Jeep Trucks — 1-Ton — 4-cyl. — 4x4 — 104.5 in. w.b.					
F4-134	Delivery		2391	2895	—
F4-134	Pickup		2256	3065	—
FC-150 — 3/4-Ton — 4-cyl. — 4x4 — 81 in. w.b.					
FC-150	Chassis & Cab		2217	2764	—
FC-150	Pickup		2320	3020	—
FC-150	Stake		2410	3187	—
Jeep Trucks — 1/2-Ton — 6-cyl. — 4x4 — 104.5 in. w.b.					
L6-226	Chassis		1822	1963	—
L6-226	Chassis & F.F. Cowl		2122	2140	—
L6-226	Delivery		2505	3008	—
L6-226	Utility Wagon		2265	3057	—
Jeep Trucks — 1/2-Ton — 6-cyl. — 4x2 — 104.5 in. w.b.					
L6-226	Delivery		1958	2859	—
L6-226	Utility Wagon		2764	3206	—
Jeep Trucks — 1-Ton — 6-cyl. — 4x4 — 118 in w.b.					
L6-226	Chassis		1824	2127	—
L6-226	Chassis & F.F. Cowl		2124	2237	—
L6-226	Chassis with windshield		2150	2256	—
L6-226	Chassis & Cab		2251	2817	—
L6-226	Pickup		2370	3176	—
L6-226	Stake		2453	3341	—
FC-170 — 1-Ton — 6-cyl. — 4x4 — 103.5 in. w.b.					
FC-170	Chassis & Cab		2593	2901	—
FC-170	Pickup		2713	3331	—
FC-170	Stake		2896	3564	—

1957 Jeep 1-Ton Pickup Truck 4x4 (OCW)

ENGINE [CJ-3B/CJ-5]: Inline. F-head. Four-cylinder. Cast iron block. Bore & stroke: 3-1/8 in. x 4-3/8 in. Displacement: 134.2 cid. Compression ratio: 6.9:1. Brake hp: 70 at 4000 rpm. Net hp: 15.63. Max. Torque: 114 lbs.-ft. at 2000 rpm. Three main bearings. Solid valve lifters. Carburetor: Carter YF model 938S or 938SA.

ENGINE [CJ6/F4-134]: Inline. F-head. Four-cylinder. Cast iron block. Bore & stroke: 3-1/8 in. x 4-3/8 in. Displacement: 134.2 cid. Compression ratio: 7.4:1. Brake hp: 72 at 4000 rpm. Net hp: 15.63. Max. Torque: 114 lbs.-ft. at 2000 rpm. Three main bearings. Solid valve lifters. Carburetor: Carter YF models 938S or 938SA one-barrel.

ENGINE [FC-150]: Inline. L-head. Four-cylinder. Cast iron block. Bore & stroke: 3-1/8 in. x 4-3/8 in. Displacement: 134.2 cid. Compression ratio: 7.40:1. Brake hp: 72 at 4000 rpm. Net hp: 15.63. Max. Torque: 114 lbs.-ft. at 2000 rpm. Three main bearings. Solid valve lifters. Carburetor: Carter YF model 2392S one-barrel.

ENGINE [6-226/FC-170]: Inline. L-head. Six-cylinder. Cast iron block. Bore & stroke: 3-5/16 in. x 4-3/8 in. Displacement: 226.2 cid. Compression ratio: 6.86:1. Brake hp: 115 at 3650 rpm. Net hp: 26.3. Max. Torque: 190 lbs.-ft. at 1800 rpm. Four main bearings. Solid valve lifters. Carburetor: Carter WDG model 2052S or 2052SA one-barrel; Carter WC model 2204S two-barrel.

CHASSIS [CJ-3B]: Wheelbase: 80-1/16 in. Length: 129-7/8 in. Height: 67-1/4 in. Front and rear tread: 48-7/16 in. Tires: 6.00 x 16 in.

CHASSIS [CJ-5]: Wheelbase: 81 in. Length: 135-1/2 in. Height: 69-1/2 in. Front and rear tread: 48-7/16 in. Tires: 6.00 x 16 in.

CHASSIS [CJ-6]: Wheelbase: 101 in. Length: 155-1/2 in. Height: 68-1/4 in. Front and rear tread: 48-7/16 in. Tires: 6.00 x 16 in. all-service type.

CHASSIS [DJ-3]: Wheelbase: 80.09 in. Length: 125.45 in. Height: 62.74 in. (windshield raised). Front and rear tread: 48.25 in. Tires: 6.50 x 15 four-ply tubeless.

CHASSIS [Sedan Delivery 4x2]: Wheelbase: 104 in. Length: 176-1/4 in. Height: 73.62 in. Front and rear tread: 57 in. Tires: 6.70 x 15 in.

CHASSIS [Sedan Delivery 4x4]: Wheelbase: 104-1/2 in. Length: 176-1/4 in. Height: 73.62 in. Front and rear tread: 57 in. Tires: 7.00 x 15 in.

CHASSIS [Trucks 4x4]: Wheelbase: 118 in. Length: 183.7 in. Height: 74.3 in. Front and rear tread: 57 in. Tires: 7.00 x 15 in.

CHASSIS [FC-150]: Wheelbase: 81 in. Length: 147-1/2 in. Height: 77-3/8 in. Front tread: 48-1/4 in. Rear tread: 48-1/4 in. Tires: 7.00 x 16 in. four-ply All-Service.

CHASSIS [FC-170]: Wheelbase: 103-5/8 in. Length: 203 in. Height: 79-1/8 in. Front tread: 63-1/2 in. Rear tread: 63-1/2 in. Tires: 7.00 x 16 in. six-ply.

TECHNICAL [All except FC]: Synchromesh transmission. Speeds: 3F/1R. Floor-mounted gearshift lever. Single-plate, dry-disc clutch. Hypoid semi-floating rear axle. Overall ratio: 3.54:1, 4.56:1 or 5.38:1. Four-wheel hydraulic brakes. Disc wheels. 4x4 models have two-speed transfer case. 4x2 models have I-beam type front axle. 4x4 models have full-floating hypoid front axle.

TECHNICAL [FC]: Synchromesh transmission. Speeds: 3F/1R (four-speed optional). Floor-mounted gearshift lever. Single-plate, dry-disc clutch (heavy-duty on FC-170). Rear axle: [FC-150] Semi-floating hypoid; [FC-170] full-floating hypoid rear axle. Overall axle ratio: [FC-150] 5.38:1; [FC-170] 4.89:1. Four-wheel hydraulic brakes (heavy-duty on FC-170). Disc wheels (dual rear available on FC-170).

OPTIONS [CJ-5]: Five metal and fabric-top options. Ventilating windshield. Power-take-off. Eight body color choices. Approved snow plow. Winch. 36 x 39-1/4 in. all-steel cargo box.

OPTIONS, JEEP: [All CJs] Power-take-off ($96.25). Pulley drive ($57.40). Motor governor ($28.65). Special wheels and 7-in. tires ($40). Front canvas top ($57.80). Hydraulic lift ($225). Metal top (various prices). [4x4 Trucks]: Power-take-off ($96.25). Pulley drive ($57.40). Motor governor ($28.65). Rearview mirror. Sidemount spare on pickups/stakes. Chrome bumper. License frame. [Sedan Delivery]: Chrome front bumper. Chrome rear bumper. License frame. Chrome wheel disc. Bumperettes. Bumper guards. Wheel trim rings. Whitewall tires. Rearview mirror. Radio and antenna. [CJ-6]: All-weather canvas tops. New body colors. Oversize tires.

OPTIONS, DISPATCHER: [DJ-3A] Convertible top. 40 cu. ft. hardtop with rippled fiberglass roof and 36 in. wide gate opening. Whitewall tires. Chrome wheel discs. Chrome front bumper. Chrome rear bumper. Eight standard body colors. "Law Enforcement" package.

OPTIONS, FC: [FC-150/FC-170]: Fresh air heater. Radio. Tu-tone paint. Front bumper guards. Direction signals. E-Z-Eye glass. Windshield washer. Front air vent. Double passenger seat. Oil bath air cleaner. Oil filter. High altitude cylinder head (no charge). Four-speed transmission. Power-Lok differential. Heavy-duty rear axle. Heavy-duty springs and shocks. Transmission brake. Hot climate radiator. Power-take-off (center and rear). Governor. Various size/type tires. Draw-Bar. Stabilizer bar. Rear bumperettes. Selective drive hubs. Bed and/or front mount winch. Snow plow. Dozer blade. Wrecker equipment. Jeep-A-Trench. Service bodies.

HISTORICAL: Introduced: [FC-150] Nov. 27, 1956; [FC-170] May 20, 1957; [others] Aug. 16-17, 1956. Calendar year registrations: 22,005 [All Trucks and Jeeps]. Forward-control Jeeps (FC-150/FC-170) were introduced. The new Continental type L-head six was derived from Kaiser's passenger car motor. A special Civil Defense rescue truck and Cargo/Personnel Carrier, both with 4x4 running gear, were marketed this year. A version of the long wheelbase CJ6 was the M-170 a military 1/4-ton 4x4 front line ambulance.

1958 JEEP

1958 Jeep FC-170 1-Ton Pickup (DFW)

WILLYS — JEEP SERIES — ALL ENGINES: After several years of (for Jeep) major changes, 1958 was the time to settle back and make minor refinements in styling, marketing and pricing. All models, except wagons, deliveries and pickups, now had one-piece windshields. No longer cataloged, except in the big 1-ton truck series and the FC Series, were chassis type configurations. The four-cylinder Utility Wagon was made available with 4x4 running gear. In addition, most prices were around $100 to $110 higher.

I.D. DATA: Serial number located on right side of dash under hood; on front frame crossmember; on left floor riser in back of driver's seat. Engine numbers located on right side of cylinder block; stamped on water pump boss on front of cylinder block. On most Jeep models the engine and serial numbers are the same.

Model	Body Type	Price	Weight	Prod. Total
Willys Jeep — 1/4-Ton — 4-cyl. — 4x4 — 80 in. w.b.				
CJ-3B	Jeep Universal	1888	2132	—
Willys Jeep — 1/4-Ton — 4-cyl. — 4x4 — 81 in. w.b.				
CJ-5	Jeep Universal	1979	2163	—
Willys Jeep — 1/2-Ton — 4-cyl. — 4x4 — 101 in. w.b.				
CJ-6	Jeep Universal	2171	2225	—
Dispatcher — 1/4-Ton — 4-cyl. — 4x2 — 80 in. w.b.				
DJ-3A	Basic	1367	1709	—
DJ-3A	Soft Top	1430	1769	—
DJ-3A	Hardtop	1586	2004	—
Jeep Trucks — 1/2-Ton — 4-cyl. — 4x2 — 104.5 in. w.b.				
FA-134	Delivery	1934	2746	—
FA-134	Utility Wagon	2152	2944	—
Jeep Trucks — 1/2-Ton — 4-cyl. — 4x4 — 104.5 in. w.b.				
4F-134	Delivery	2510	2893	—
4F-134	Utility Wagon	2654	3093	—
Jeep Trucks — 1-Ton — 4-cyl. — 4x4 — 118 in. w.b.				
4F-134	Pickup	2367	3065	—
FC Forward Control — 3/4-Ton — 4-cyl — 4x4 — 81 in. w.b.				
FC-150	Chassis	2327	2764	—
FC-150	Pickup	2444	3020	—
FC-150	Stake	2545	3187	—
Jeep Trucks — 1/2-Ton — 6-cyl. — 4x2 — 104.5 in. w.b.				
L6-226	Delivery	2055	2859	—
L6-226	Utility Wagon	2265	3057	—
Jeep Trucks — 1/2-Ton — 6-cyl. — 4x4 — 104.5 in. w.b.				
L6-226	Delivery	2630	3008	—
L6-226	Utility Wagon	2764	3206	—
Jeep Trucks — 1-Ton — 6-cyl. — 4x2 — 118 in. w.b.				
L6-226	Chassis & Cab	2363	2817	—
L6-226	Pickup	2488	3176	—
L6-226	Stake	2575	3341	—
Forward Control — 1-Ton — 6-cyl. — 4x4 — 103.5 in. w.b.				
FC-170	Chassis & Cab	2722	2901	—
FC-170	Pickup	2858	3331	—
FC-170	Stake	3065	3000	—

ENGINE [CJ-3B/CJ-5]: Inline. F-head. Four-cylinder. Cast iron block. Bore & stroke: 3-1/8 in. x 4-3/8 in. Displacement: 134.2 cid. Compression ratio: 6.9:1. Brake hp: 70 at 4000 rpm. Net hp: 15.63. Max. Torque: 114 lbs.-ft. at 2000 rpm. Three main bearings. Solid valve lifters. Carburetor: Carter YF models 938S or 938SA.

ENGINE [CJ6/F4-134]: Inline. F-head. Four-cylinder. Cast iron block. Bore & stroke: 3-1/8 in. x 4-3/8 in. Displacement: 134.2 cid. Compression ratio: 7.4:1. Brake hp: 72 at 4000 rpm. Net hp: 15.63. Max. Torque: 114 lbs.-ft. at 2000 rpm. Three main bearings. Solid valve lifters. Carburetor: Carter YF models 938S or 938SA one-barrel.

ENGINE [FC-150]: Inline. L-head. Four-cylinder. Cast iron block. Bore & stroke: 3-1/8 in. x 4-3/8 in. Displacement: 134.2 cid. Compression ratio: 7.40:1. Brake hp: 72 at 4000 rpm. Net hp: 15.63. Max. Torque: 114 lbs.-ft. at 2000 rpm. Three main bearings. Solid valve lifters. Carburetor: Carter YF models 2392S one-barrel.

ENGINE [6-226/FC-170]: Inline. L-head. Six-cylinder. Cast iron block. Bore & stroke: 3-5/16 in. x 4-3/8 in. Displacement: 226.2 cid. Compression ratio: 6.86:1. Brake hp: 115 at 3650 rpm. Net hp: 26.3. Max. Torque: 190 lbs.-ft. at 1800 rpm. Four main bearings. Solid valve lifters. Carburetor: Carter WDG model 2052S or 2052SA one-barrel; Carter WC model 2204S two-barrel.

CHASSIS [CJs]: Wheelbase: [CJ3B] 80 in.; [CJ5] 81 in.; [CJ6] 101 in. Length: [CJ3B] 129-7/8 in.; [CJ5] 135-1/2 in.; [CJ6] 155-1/2 in. Height: [CJ3B] 67-1/4 in.; [CJ5] 69-1/2 in.; [CJ6] 68-1/4 in. Front tread: [All] 48-7/16 in. Rear tread: [All] 48-7/16 in. Tires: 6.00 x 16 four-ply.

CHASSIS [Dispatcher]: Wheelbase: 80.09 in. Length: 125.45 in. Height: 62.74 in. Front tread: 55-1/4 in. Tires: 6.40 x 15 in.

CHASSIS [Trucks]: Wheelbase: [SWB] 104-1/2 in.; [LWB] 118 in. Length: [SWB] 176.2 in.; [LWB] 183.7 in. Height: [SWB] 72.1 in.; [LWB] 74.3 in. Front tread: [SWB] 57 in.; [LWB] 57 in. (except 1-ton). Rear tread: [SWB] 57 in.; [LWB] 63.5 in. (except 1-ton). Tires: 6.70 x 15; 7.00 x 15; 7.00 x 16 (4x4). (SWB=short wheelbase; LWB=long wheelbase).

CHASSIS [FC-150]: Wheelbase: 81 in. Length: 147.3 in. Height: 78 in. Front tread: 57 in. Rear tread: 57 in. Tires: 7.00 x 15 four-ply.

CHASSIS [FC-170]: Wheelbase: 103-1/2 in. Length: 181.4 in. Height: 79.4 in. Front tread: 63.4 in. Rear tread: 63.8 in. Tires: 7.00 x 16.

TECHNICAL [All except FCs]: Synchromesh transmission. Speeds: 3F/1R. Floor-mounted gearshift lever. Single-plate, dry-disc clutch. Hypoid semi-floating rear axle. Overall ratio: 3.54:1, 4.56:1 or 5.38:1. Four-wheel hydraulic brakes. Disc wheels. 4x4 models have two-speed transfer case. 4x2 models have I-beam type front axle. 4x4 models have full-floating hypoid front axle.

TECHNICAL [FCs]: Synchromesh transmission. Speeds: 3F/1R (four-speed optional). Floor-mounted gearshift lever. Single-plate, dry-disc clutch (heavy-duty on FC-170). Rear axle: [FC-150] Semi-floating hypoid; [FC-170] full-floating hypoid rear axle. Overall axle ratio: [FC-150] 5.38:1; [FC-170] 4.89:1. Four-wheel hydraulic brakes (heavy-duty on FC-170). Disc wheels. Dual rear wheels available on FC-170.

OPTIONS, CJs: [CJ] Power-take-off ($96.25). Pulley drive ($57.40). Motor governor ($28.65). Special wheels and 7-in. tires ($40). Front canvas top ($57.80). Hydraulic lift ($225). Metal top (various prices). [CJ-5]: Five metal and fabric-top options. Ventilating windshield. Power-take-off. Eight body color choices. Approved snow plow. Winch. 36 x 39-1/4 in. all-steel cargo box. [CJ-6]: All-weather canvas tops. New body colors. Oversize tires.

OPTIONS, DJs: [DJ-3A] Convertible top. 40 cu. ft. hardtop with rippled fiberglass roof and 36 in. wide gate opening. Whitewall tires. Chrome wheel discs. Chrome front bumper. Chrome rear bumper. Eight standard body colors. "Law Enforcement" package.

OPTIONS, TRUCKS: [4x4]: Power-take-off ($96.25). Pulley drive ($57.40). Motor governor ($28.65). Rearview mirror. Sidemount spare on pickups/stakes. Chrome bumper. License frame. [Sedan Delivery]: Chrome front bumper. Chrome rear bumper. License frame. Chrome wheel disc. Bumperettes. Bumper guards. Wheel trim rings. Whitewall tires. Rearview mirror. Radio and antenna.

OPTIONS, FCs: [FC-150/FC-170] Fresh air heater. Radio. Tu-tone paint. Front bumper guards. Direction signals. E-Z-Eye glass. Windshield washer. Front air vent. Double passenger seat. Oil bath air cleaner. Oil filter. High altitude cylinder head (no charge). Four-speed transmission. Power-Lok differential. Heavy-duty rear axle. Heavy-duty springs and shocks. Transmission brake. Hot climate radiator. Power-take-off (center and rear). Governor. Various size/type tires. Draw-Bar. Stabilizer bar. Rear bumperettes. Selective drive hubs. Bed and/or front mount winch. Snow plow. Dozer blade. Wrecker equipment. Jeep-A-Trench. Service bodies.

HISTORICAL: Introduced: Aug. 15, 1957. Calendar year registrations: 22,523 [All Trucks and Jeeps]. One-piece windshield on all models. The JA-3CB was a unique Jeep variant available in Argentina this year. It had built-in step plates, chrome bumpers, chrome "bottle cap" wheelcovers, a convertible top and detachable doors. This 4x2 was not marketed in the U.S.

1959 JEEP

WILLYS — JEEP SERIES — ALL ENGINES: New this season was a fringe-top version of the Dispatcher named the Surrey. It was similar to the Jeep Gala, an export model available for rental at beach front resorts. Features included a fringed-and-striped surrey top, chrome bumpers, wheel discs and other bright trim. The striped top came in pink, green or blue contrasted with white. Some model lineups were also shuffled around or trimmed a bit. Along with names like Surrey and Gala, some traditional models got new two-tone trim packages with names. The two-wheel drive Utility Wagon was called the Maverick. This was probably related to Kaiser Industries being a sponsor of James Garner's television Western series called "Maverick." Jeep stylists also turned out the Harlequin, an all-steel wagon with special trim including Kaiser's three-diamond logo on the doors. On the Maverick wagon, the main body below the bright metal beltline molding was done in contrasting color. The contrasting section continued onto the front fendersides in the form of a matching inverted triangle, also trimmed with bright moldings. The "greenhouse" was then done in a color that matched the insert panel.

Model	Body Type	Price	Weight	Prod. Total
Jeep — 1/4-Ton — 4-cyl. — 4x4 — 80 in. w.b.				
CJ-3B	Jeep Universal	1888	2132	—
Jeep — 1/4-Ton — 4-cyl. — 4x4 — 81 in. w.b.				
CJ-5	Jeep Universal	1976	2163	—
Jeep — 1/2-Ton — 4-cyl. — 4x4 — 101 in. w.b.				
CJ-6	Jeep Universal	2171	2225	—
Dispatcher — 1/4-Ton — 4-cyl. — 4x2 — 80 in. w.b.				
DJ-3A	Soft Top	1430	1769	—
DJ-3A	Hardtop	1586	2004	—
Jeep Trucks — 1/2-Ton — 4-cyl. — 4x2 — 104.5 in. w.b.				
F4-134	Chassis	1582	1855	—
F4-134	Delivery	1934	2746	—
Jeep Trucks — 1-Ton — 4-cyl. — 4x4 — 118 in. w.b.				
F4-134	Chassis	2510	2893	—
F4-134	Pickup	2368	3065	—
Forward Control — 3/4-Ton — 4-cyl. — 4x4 — 81 in. w.b.				
FC-150	Chassis & Cab	2416	2764	—
FC-150	Pickup	2533	3024	—
FC-150	Stake	2634	3187	—
Jeep Trucks — 1/2-Ton — 6-cyl. — 4x2 — 104.5 in. wheelbase				
L6-226	Delivery	2055	2859	—
L6-226	Wagon	2378	3057	—
Jeep Trucks — 1/2-Ton — 6-cyl. — 4x4 — 104.5 in. wheelbase				
L6-226	Delivery	2630	3008	—
L6-226	Wagon	2901	3206	—
Jeep Trucks — 1-Ton — 6-cyl. — 4x4 — 118 in. wheelbase				
L6-226	Chassis & Cab	2363	2817	—
L6-226	Pickup	2488	3176	—
L6-226	Stake	2575	3341	—
Forward Control — 1-Ton — 6-cyl. — 4x4 — 103.5 in. w.b.				
FC-170	Chassis & Cab	2722	2901	—
FC-170	Pickup	2858	3331	—
FC-170	Stake	3065	3564	—

1959 Jeep FC-170 1-Ton Pickup 4x4 (DFW)

1959 Jeep 1/4-Ton CJ-3B Universal Jeep 4x4 (RCA)

I.D. DATA: Serial number located on right side of dash under hood; on front frame crossmember; on left floor riser in back of driver's seat. Engine numbers located on right side of cylinder block; stamped on water pump boss on front of cylinder block. On most Jeep models the engine and serial numbers are the same.

1959 Jeep 1/4-Ton CJ-5 Universal Jeep 4x4 (RCA)

1959 Jeep 1/2-Ton Utility Wagon 4x4 (RCA)

ENGINE [CJ-3B/CJ-5]: Inline. F-head. Four-cylinder. Cast iron block. Bore & stroke: 3-1/8 in. x 4-3/8 in. Displacement: 134.2 cid. Compression ratio: 6.9:1. Brake hp: 70 at 4000 rpm. Net hp: 15.63. Max. Torque: 114 lbs.-ft. at 2000 rpm. Three main bearings. Solid valve lifters. Carburetor: Carter YF model 938S or 938SA.

ENGINE [CJ6/F4-134]: Inline. F-head. Four-cylinder. Cast iron block. Bore & stroke: 3-1/8 in. x 4-3/8 in. Displacement: 134.2 cid. Compression ratio: 7.4:1. Brake hp: 72 at 4000 rpm. Net hp: 15.63. Max. Torque: 114 lbs.-ft. at 2000 rpm. Three main bearings. Solid valve lifters. Carburetor: Carter YF model 938S or 938SA one-barrel.

ENGINE [FC-150]: Inline. L-head. Four-cylinder. Cast iron block. Bore & stroke: 3-1/8 in. x 4-3/8 in. Displacement: 134.2 cid. Compression ratio: 7.40:1. Brake hp: 72 at 4000 rpm. Net hp: 15.63. Max. Torque: 114 lbs.-ft. at 2000 rpm. Three main bearings. Solid valve lifters. Carburetor: Carter YF model 2392S one-barrel.

ENGINE [6-226/FC-170]: Inline. L-head. Six-cylinder. Cast iron block. Bore & stroke: 3-5/16 in. x 4-3/8 in. Displacement: 226.2 cid. Compression ratio: 6.86:1. Brake hp: 115 at 3650 rpm. Net hp: 26.3. Max. Torque: 190 lbs.-ft. at 1800 rpm. Four main bearings. Solid valve lifters. Carburetor: Carter WDG model 2052S or 2052SA one-barrel; Carter WC model 2204S two-barrel.

CHASSIS [CJs]: Wheelbase: [CJ-3B] 80 in.; [CJ-5] 81 in.; [CJ-6] 101 in. Length: [CJ-3B] 129-7/8 in.; [CJ-5] 135-1/2 in.; [CJ-6] 155-1/2 in. Height: [CJ-3B] 67-1/4 in.; [CJ-5] 69-1/2 in.; [CJ-6] 68-1/4 in. Front tread: [All] 48-7/16 in. Rear tread: [All] 48-7/16 in. Tires: 6.00 x 16 in.

CHASSIS [DJ]: Wheelbase: 80.09 in. Length: 125.45 in. Height: 62.74 in. Front tread: 55-1/4 in. Rear tread: 57 in. Tires: 6.40 x 15 in.

CHASSIS [Jeep-Trucks]: Wheelbase: [SWB] 104.5 in.; [LWB] 118 in. Length: [SWB] 176.2 in.; [LWB] 183.7 in. Height: [SWB] 72.1 in.; [LWB] 74.3 in. Front tread: [SWB] 57 in.; [LWB] 57 in. Rear tread: [SWB] 57 in.; [LWB] 63.5 in. (except 1-tons). Tires: 7.00 x 15 in. or others. (SWB=short wheelbase; LWB=long wheelbase).

CHASSIS [Series FC-150]: Wheelbase: 81 in. Length: 147.3 in. Height: 78 in. Front tread: 57 in. Rear tread: 57 in. Tires: 7.00 x 15 in.

CHASSIS [Series FC-170]: Wheelbase: 103-1/2in. Length: 181.4 in. Height: 79.4 in. Front tread: 63.4 in. Rear tread: 63.8 in. Tires: 7.00 x 16 in. (Dual rear wheels available on heavy-duty models).

1959 Jeep 1/2-Ton "Maverick" Utility Wagon 4x2 (OCW)

TECHNICAL [All except FC]: Synchromesh transmission. Speeds: 3F/1R. Floor-mounted gearshift lever. Single-plate, dry-disc clutch. Hypoid semi-floating rear axle. Overall ratio: 3.54:1, 4.56:1 or 5.38:1. Four-wheel hydraulic brakes. Disc wheels. 4x4 models have two-speed transfer case. 4x2 models have I-beam type front axle. 4x4 models have full-floating hypoid front axle.

TECHNICAL [FC-150/FC-170]: Synchromesh transmission. Speeds: 3F/1R (four-speed optional). Floor-mounted gearshift lever. Single-plate, dry-disc clutch (heavy-duty on FC-170). Rear axle: [FC-150] Semi-floating hypoid; [FC-170] full-floating hypoid rear axle. Overall ratio: [FC-150] 5.38:1; [FC-170] 4.89:1. Four-wheel hydraulic brakes (heavy-duty on FC-170). Disc wheels (dual rear on heavy-duty FC-170).

OPTIONS [CJs]: Three different color striped tops for Surrey. [Gala] Chrome front bumper. Chrome rear bumper. Chrome bumperettes. Chrome wheel discs. Power-take-off ($96.25). Pulley drive ($57.40). Motor governor ($28.65). Special wheels and 7-in. tires ($40). Front canvas top ($57.80). Hydraulic lift ($225). Metal top (various prices). [CJ-5]: Five metal and fabric-top options. Ventilating windshield. Power-take-off. Eight body color choices. Approved snow plow. Winch. All-steel cargo box (36 x 39-1/4 in.). [CJ-6]: All-weather canvas tops. New body colors. Oversize tires.

OPTIONS [DJ]: Convertible top. 40 cu. ft. hardtop with rippled fiberglass roof and 36 in. wide gate opening. Whitewall tires. Chrome wheel discs. Chrome front bumper. Chrome rear bumper. Eight standard body colors. "Law Enforcement" package.

OPTIONS, TRUCKS: [4x4] Standard and deluxe cab trim. Power-take-off ($96.25). Pulley drive ($57.40). Motor governor ($28.65). Rearview mirror. Sidemount spare on pickups/ stakes. Chrome bumper. License frame. [Sedan Delivery] Chrome front bumper. Chrome rear bumper. License frame. Chrome wheel disc. Bumperettes. Bumper guards. Wheel trim rings. Whitewall tires. Rearview mirror. Radio and antenna. New two-tone paint combinations.

OPTIONS [FC-150/FC-170]: Fresh air heater. Radio. Tu-tone paint. Front bumper guards. Direction signals. E-Z-Eye glass. Windshield washer. Front air vent. Double passenger seat. Oil bath air cleaner. Oil filter. High altitude cylinder head (no charge). Four-speed transmission. Power-Lok differential. Heavy-duty rear axle. Heavy-duty springs and shocks. Transmission brake. Hot climate radiator. Power-take-off (center and rear). Governor. Various size/type tires. Draw-Bar. Stabilizer bar. Rear bumperettes. Selective drive hubs. Bed and/or front mount winch. Snow plow. Dozer blade. Wrecker equipment. Jeep-A-Trench. Service bodies.

1959 Jeep 1/2-Ton CJ-6 Universal Jeep 4x4 (OCW)

HISTORICAL: Introduced: Fall, 1958. Calendar year registrations: [Jeeps] 10,576; [trucks to 6,000 lbs.] 11,920; [trucks 6,001-10,000 lbs.] 8,130. Calendar year production: [All Models, domestic]: 114,881. Willys registered a 10.08 percent market share. Willys worldwide sales included: [Jeeps] 58,238; [Trucks] 56,643. Of this total, 50.7 percent were Jeeps. Innovations included the new Surrey model. The Maverick version of the 4x2 Station Wagon was introduced on May 7, 1959. It was a dressed-up version of the base model. A Jeep fleet sales ad of this year printed a list of over 150 companies that used Jeep vehicles and said, "Known by the companies they keep . . . Jeep vehicles." E.F. Kaiser was president of Willys Motors, Inc., a subsidiary of Kaiser Industries, Corp. Willys, on Feb. 26, signed an agreement with its Brazilian affilliate to produce French Renaults in a plant near Sao Paulo. On April 6, Mitsubishi, of Japan, paid $1,790,000 for the rights to build Jeeps there. On Aug. 21, Willys of Canada began production of the CJ-5 at Windsor, Ontario. Jeeps outsold trucks on a worldwide basis this year, but trucks did better in the United States.

1959 Jeep FC-170 1-Ton Pickup 4x4 (RCA)

1960 JEEP

WILLYS — JEEP SERIES — ALL ENGINES: New body trim treatments, similar to those introduced on the mid-1959 Maverick, were now available on all Jeep trucks, except Foward Control models. (The FC models had their own standard and deluxe treatments for the exteriors and interiors of their "Safety-View" cabs.) A new "economy" delivery truck made its appearance in the two-wheel drive 1/2-ton lineup. A new Fleetvan was also developed for the U.S. Post Office.

1960 Jeep 1/4-Ton CJ-5 Enclosure Top Universal 4x4 (RCA)

1960 Jeep 1/2-Ton CJ-6 Universal 4x4 (RCA)

1960 Jeep 1/2-Ton Utility Wagon 4x4 (RCA)

I.D. DATA: Serial number located on right side of dash under hood; on front frame cross-member; on left floor riser in back of driver's seat. Engine numbers located on right side of cylinder block; stamped on water pump boss on front of cylinder block. On most Jeep models the engine and serial numbers are the same.

Model	Body Type	Price	Weight	Prod. Total
Jeep — 1/4-Ton — 4-cyl. — 4x4 — 80 in. w.b.				
CJ-3B	Jeep Universal	1888	2132	—
Jeep — 1/4-Ton — 4-cyl. — 4x4 — 81 in. w.b.				
CJ-5	Jeep Universal	1979	2163	—
Jeep — 1/2-Ton — 4-cyl. — 4x4 — 101 in. w.b.				
CJ-6	Jeep Universal	2171	2225	—
Dispatcher — 1/4-Ton — 4-cyl. — 4x2 — 80 in. w.b.				
DJ-3A	Soft Top	1430	1769	—
DJ-3A	Hardtop	1586	2004	—
DJ-3A	Surrey	1650	1819	—
Jeep Trucks — 1/2-Ton — 4-cyl. — 4x2 — 104.5 in. w.b.				
FA-134	Economy Delivery	1582	1855	—
FA-134	Station Wagon	1995	2858	—
FA-134	Utility Wagon	2258	2944	—
FA-134	Utility Delivery	1934	2746	—
Jeep Trucks — 1/2-Ton — 4-cyl. — 4x4 — 104.5 in. w.b.				
FA-134	Utility Wagon	2782	3093	—
FA-134	Utility Delivery	2510	2895	—
Jeep Trucks — 1-Ton — 4-cyl. — 4x4 — 118 in. w.b.				
FA-134	Pickup	2368	3065	—
FA-134	Stake	2455	3230	—
Jeep FC-150 — 3/4-Ton — 4-cyl. — 4x4 — 81 in. w.b.				
FC-150	Chassis & Cab	2416	2896	—
FC-150	Pickup	2533	3152	—
FC-150	Stake	2634	3319	—
Jeep Trucks — 1/2-Ton — 6-cyl. — 4x2 — 104.5 in. w.b.				
L6-226	Station Wagon	2258	2971	—
L6-226	Utility Wagon	2378	3057	—
L6-226	Utility Delivery	2055	2859	—
Jeep Trucks — 1/2-Ton — 6-cyl. — 4x4 — 104.5 in. w.b.				
L6-226	Utility Wagon	2901	3206	—
L6-226	Utility Delivery	2630	3008	—
Jeep Trucks — 1-Ton — 6-cyl. — 4x4 — 118 in. w.b.				
L6-226	Chassis & Cab	2363	2817	—
L6-226	Pickup	2488	3176	—
L6-226	Stake	2575	3341	—
FC-170 — 1-Ton — 6-cyl. — 4x4 — 103.5 in. w.b.				
FC-170	Chassis & Cab	2722	2901	—
FC-170	Pickup	2858	3331	—
FC-170	Stake	3065	3564	—

1960 Jeep 1-Ton Pickup Truck 4x4 (OCW)

ENGINE [CJ-3B/CJ-5]: Inline. F-head. Four-cylinder. Cast iron block. Bore & stroke: 3-1/8 in. x 4-3/8 in. Displacement: 134.2 cid. Compression ratio: 6.9:1. Brake hp: 70 at 4000 rpm. Net hp: 15.63. Max. Torque: 114 lbs.-ft. at 2000 rpm. Three main bearings. Solid valve lifters. Carburetor: Carter YF model 938S or 938SA.

ENGINE [CJ6/F4-134]: Inline. F-head. Four-cylinder. Cast iron block. Bore & stroke: 3-1/8 in. x 4-3/8 in. Displacement: 134.2 cid. Compression ratio: 7.4:1. Brake hp: 72 at 4000 rpm. Net hp: 15.63. Max. Torque: 114 lbs.-ft. at 2000 rpm. Three main bearings. Solid valve lifters. Carburetor: Carter YF model 938S or 938SA one-barrel.

ENGINE [FC-150]: Inline. L-head. Four-cylinder. Cast iron block. Bore & stroke: 3-1/8 in. x 4-3/8 in. Displacement: 134.2 cid. Compression ratio: 7.40:1. Brake hp: 72 at 4000 rpm. Net hp: 15.63. Max. Torque: 114 lbs.-ft. at 2000 rpm. Three main bearings. Solid valve lifters. Carburetor: Carter YF model 2392S one-barrel.

ENGINE [6-226/FC-170]: Inline. L-head. Six-cylinder. Cast iron block. Bore & stroke: 3-5/16 in. x 4-3/8 in. Displacement: 226.2 cid. Compression ratio: 6.86:1. Brake hp: 115 at 3650 rpm. Net hp: 26.3. Max. Torque: 190 lbs.-ft. at 1800 rpm. Four main bearings. Solid valve lifters. Carburetor: Carter WDG model 2052S or 2052SA one-barrel; Carter WC model 2204S two-barrel.

1960 Jeep Panel Delivery 4x2 (OCW)

CHASSIS [CJ-3-B]: Wheelbase: 80 in. Length: 129-7/8 in. Height: 67-1/4 in. Front tread: 48-7/16 in. Rear tread: 48-7/16 in. Tires: 6.00 x 16 in.

CHASSIS [CJ-5]: Wheelbase: 81.09 in. Length: 135.50 in. Height: 69.50 in. Front tread: 48-7/16 in. Rear tread: 48-7/16 in. Tires: 6.00 x 16 in.

CHASSIS [CJ-6]: Wheelbase: 101 in. Length: 155-1/2 in. Height: 68-1/4 in. Front tread: 48-7/16 in. Rear tread: 48-7/16 in. Tires: 6.00 x 16 in.

CHASSIS [DJ-3]: Wheelbase: 80.1 in. Length: 125.4 in. Height: 59.8 in. Front tread: 48.2 in. Rear tread: 48.5 in. Tires: 6.50 x 15 in.

CHASSIS [SWB trucks]: Wheelbase: 104.5 in. Length: 176.2 in. Height: 72.1 in. Front tread: 57 in. Rear tread: 57 in. Tires: 7.00 x 15 in. (6.70 x 15 on Station Wagon)

CHASSIS [LWB trucks]: Wheelbase: 118 in. Length: 183.7 in. Height: 74.3 in. Front tread: 57 in. Rear tread: 63.5 in. Tires: 7.00 x 16 in.

NOTE: SWB=short wheelbase; LWB=long wheelbase.

CHASSIS [FC-150]: Wheelbase: 81 in. Tires: 7.00 x 15 in.

CHASSIS [FC-170]: Wheelbase: 103-1/2 in. Tires: 7.00 x 16 in.

TECHNICAL [All except FC]: Synchromesh transmission. Speeds: 3F/1R. Floor-mounted gearshift lever. Single-plate, dry-disc clutch. Hypoid semi-floating rear axle. Overall ratio: 3.54:1, 4.56:1 or 5.38:1. Four-wheel hydraulic brakes. Disc wheels. 4x4 models have two-speed transfer case. 4x2 models have I-beam type front axle. 4x4 models have full-floating hypoid front axle.

TECHNICAL [FC-150/FC-170]: Synchromesh transmission. Speeds: 3F/1R (four-speed optional). Floor-mounted gearshift lever. Single-plate, dry-disc clutch (heavy-duty on FC-170). Rear axle: [FC-150] Semi-floating hypoid; [FC-170] full-floating hypoid rear axle. Overall ratio: [FC-150] 5.38:1; [FC-170] 4.89:1. Four-wheel hydraulic (heavy-duty on FC-170) brakes. Disc wheels (dual rear on FC-170 heavy-duty model).

OPTIONS [CJ]: Three different color striped tops for Surrey. [Gala] Chrome front bumper. Chrome rear bumper. Chrome bumperettes. Chrome wheel discs. Power-take-off. Pulley drive. Motor governor. Special wheels and 7-in. tires. Front canvas top. Hydraulic lift. Metal top. [CJ-6]: All-weather canvas tops. New body colors. Oversize tires. [CJ-5]: Five metal and fabric-top options. Ventilating windshield. Power-take-off. Eight body color choices. Approved snow plow. Winch. All-steel cargo box (36 x 39-1/4 in.).

OPTIONS [DJ]: Convertible top. 40 cu. ft. hardtop with rippled fiberglass roof and 36 in. wide gate opening. Whitewall tires. Chrome wheel discs. Chrome front bumper. Chrome rear bumper. Eight standard body colors. "Law Enforcement" package.

OPTIONS, TRUCKS: [4x4] Standard and deluxe cab trim. Power-take-off. Pulley drive. Motor governor. Rearview mirror. Sidemount spare on pickups/stakes. Chrome bumper. License frame. [Sedan Delivery] Chrome front bumper. Chrome rear bumper. License frame. Chrome wheel disc. Bumperettes. Bumper guards. Wheel trim rings. Whitewall tires. Rearview mirror. Radio and antenna. New two-tone paint combinations.

OPTIONS [FC]: Fresh air heater. Radio. Tu-tone paint. Front bumper guards. Direction signals. E-Z-Eye glass. Windshield washer. Front air vent. Double passenger seat. Oil bath air cleaner. Oil filter. High altitude cylinder head (no charge). Four-speed transmission. Power-Lok differential. Heavy-duty rear axle. Heavy-duty springs and shocks. Transmission brake. Hot climate radiator. Power-take-off (center and rear). Governor. Various size/type tires. Draw-Bar. Stabilizer bar. Rear bumperettes. Selective drive hubs. Bed and/or front mount winch. Snow plow. Dozer blade. Wrecker equipment. Jeep-A-Trench. Service bodies.

1960 Jeep FC-170 1-Ton Pickup 4x4 (OCW)

HISTORICAL: Introduced: Fall, 1959. Calendar year registrations: [All Trucks and Jeeps] 31,385. Calendar year production: [All Models, domestic] 122,446. Of this total, 51.9 percent were Jeeps. Note: 71,159 Willys vehicles made in 1960 were four-cylinder models and 51,287 were six-cylinder vehicles. Station Wagons and Panel Trucks got new body trim treatments. Barney Roos, who is sometimes called "The Father of the Willys Jeep," died of a heart attack in New York City. Sales of Jeep 4x4s reached an all-time high in 1960. In July, 1960, Willys was awarded the first of a series of contracts to build Fleetvans for the U.S. Post Office. By Feb. 1961, the number of these units ordered rose to 6,025.

Standard Catalog of Light-Duty Trucks

1961 JEEP

1961 Jeep 1/2-Ton Utility Wagon 4x4 (OCW)

WILLYS — JEEP SERIES — ALL ENGINES: In 1961, Willys introduced the Fleetvan to the regular commercial vehicle market. It had an 80 in. wheelbase, 133 in. overall length and 4x2 running gear. It was well-suited for multi-stop delivery work and featured sit-or-stand driving accomodations. The four-cylinder F-head engine was used. Other changes included deletion of the 1-ton 4x4 stake truck with the four-cylinder engine. Also, the Jeep-Surrey 4x2 was temporarily discontinued .

I.D. DATA: Serial number located on right side of dash under hood; on front frame cross-member; on left floor riser in back of driver's seat. Engine numbers located on right side of cylinder block; stamped on water pump boss on front of cylinder block. On most Jeep models the engine and serial numbers are the same.

1961 Jeep 1/4-Ton CJ-5 Universal 4x4 (OCW)

Model	Body Type	Price	Weight	Prod. Total
Jeep — 1/4-Ton — 4-cyl. — 4x4 — 80 in. w.b.				
CJ-3B	Jeep Universal	1890	2220	—
Jeep — 1/4-Ton — 4-cyl. — 4x4 — 81 in. w.b.				
CJ-5	Jeep Universal	1980	2251	—
Jeep — 1/2-Ton — 4-cyl. — 4x4 — 101 in. w.b.				
CJ-6	Jeep Universal	2170	2313	—
Dispatcher — 1/4-Ton — 4-cyl. — 4x4 — 80 in. w.b.				
DJ-3A	Basic	1365	2797	—
DJ-3A	Soft Top	1430	1857	—
DJ-3A	Hardtop	1585	2092	—
Fleetvan — 1/2-Ton — 4-cyl. — 4x2 — 81 in. w.b.				
FJ-3A	Fleetvan	2380	3045	—
Jeep Trucks — 1/2-Ton — 4-cyl. — 4x2 — 104.5 in. w.b.				
F4-134	Economy Delivery	1580	1987	—
F4-134	Station Wagon	1995	2990	—
F4-134	Utility Wagon	2260	3076	—
F4-134	Utility Delivery	1935	2878	—
Jeep Trucks — 1/2-Ton — 4-cyl. — 4x4 — 104.5 in. w.b.				
F4-134	Utility Wagon	2780	3225	—
F4-134	Utility Delivery	2510	3025	—
Jeep Trucks — 1-Ton — 4-cyl. — 4x4 — 118 in. w.b.				
F4-134	Pickup	2365	3197	—
FC-150 — 3/4-Ton — 4-cyl. — 4x4 — 81 in. w.b.				
FC-150	Chassis & Cab	2415	2884	—
FC-150	Pickup	2535	3140	—
FC-150	Platform Stake	2635	3307	—
Jeep Truck — 1/2-Ton — 6-cyl. — 4x2 — 104.5 in. w.b.				
L6-226	Utility Wagon	2380	3172	—
L6-226	Utility Delivery	2055	2974	—
L6-226	Station Wagon	2260	3103	—
Jeep Truck — 1/2-Ton — 6-cyl. — 4x4 — 104.5 in. w.b.				
L6-226	Utility Wagon	2900	3321	—
L6-226	Utility Delivery	2630	3123	—
Jeep Truck — 1-Ton — 6-cyl. — 4x4 — 118 in. w.b.				
L6-226	Pickup	2490	3291	—
L6-226	Platform Stake	2575	3456	—
L6-226	Chassis & Cab	2365	2932	—
FC-170 — 1-Ton — 6-cyl. — 4x4 — 103.5 in. w.b.				
FC-170	Chassis & Cab	2720	3056	—
FC-170	Pickup	2855	3486	—
FC-170	Platform Stake	3065	3719	—
FC-170 (Dual Rear — 1-Ton — 6-cyl. — 4x4 — 103.5 in. w.b.				
FC-170	Chassis & Cab	3395	3726	—
FC-170	Pickup	3531	4156	—
FC-170	Platform Stake	3835	4505	—

1961 Jeep FJ-3A Fleetvan Walk-in Delivery Truck (OCW)

ENGINE [CJ-3B/CJ-5]: Inline. F-head. Four-cylinder. Cast iron block. Bore & stroke: 3-1/8 in. x 4-3/8 in. Displacement: 134.2 cid. Compression ratio: 6.9:1. Brake hp: 70 at 4000 rpm. Net hp: 15.63. Max. Torque: 114 lbs.-ft. at 2000 rpm. Three main bearings. Solid valve lifters. Carburetor: Carter YF model 938S or 938SA.

ENGINE [CJ6/F4-134]: Inline. F-head. Four-cylinder. Cast iron block. Bore & stroke: 3-1/8 in. x 4-3/8 in. Displacement: 134.2 cid. Compression ratio: 7.4:1. Brake hp: 72 at 4000 rpm. Net hp: 15.63. Max. Torque: 114 lbs.-ft. at 2000 rpm. Three main bearings. Solid valve lifters. Carburetor: Carter YF model 938S or 938SA one-barrel.

ENGINE [Fleetvan]: Inline. F-head. Four-cylinder. Cast iron block. Bore & stroke: 3-1/8 in. x 4-3/8 in. Displacement: 134.2 cid. Compression ratio: 7.4:1. Brake hp: 75 at 4000 rpm. Net hp: 15.63. Max. Torque: 115 lbs.-ft. at 2000 rpm. Three main bearings. Solid valve lifters. Carburetor: Carter model YF.

ENGINE [FC-150]: Inline. L-head. Four-cylinder. Cast iron block. Bore & stroke: 3-1/8 in. x 4-3/8 in. Displacement: 134.2 cid. Compression ratio: 7.40:1. Brake hp: 72 at 4000 rpm. Net hp: 15.63. Max. Torque: 114 lbs.-ft. at 2000 rpm. Three main bearings. Solid valve lifters. Carburetor: Carter YF model 2392S one-barrel.

ENGINE [6-226/FC-170]: Inline. L-head. Six-cylinder. Cast iron block. Bore & stroke: 3-5/16 in. x 4-3/8 in. Displacement: 226.2 cid. Compression ratio: 6.86:1. Brake hp: 115 at 3650 rpm. Net hp: 26.3. Max. Torque: 190 lbs.-ft. at 1800 rpm. Four main bearings. Solid valve lifters. Carburetor: Carter WDG model 2052S or 2052SA one-barrel; Carter WC model 2204S two-barrel.

CHASSIS [CJ-3-B]: Wheelbase: 80 in. Length: 129-7/8 in. Height: 67-1/4 in. Front tread: 48-7/16. Rear tread: 48-7/16 in. Tires: 6.00 x 16 in.

CHASSIS [CJ-5]: Wheelbase: 81.09 in. Length: 135.50 in. Height: 69.50 in. Front tread: 48-7/16 in. Rear tread: 48-7/16 in. Tires: 6.00 x 16 in.

CHASSIS [CJ-6]: Wheelbase: 101 in. Length: 155-1/2 in. Height: 68-1/4 in. Front tread: 48-7/16 in. Rear tread: 48-7/16 in. Tires: 6.00 x 16 in.

CHASSIS [DJ-3]: Wheelbase: 80.1 in. Length: 125.4 in. Height: 59.8 in. Front tread: 48.2 in. Rear tread: 48.5 in. Tires: 6.50 x 15 in.

CHASSIS [Fleetvan]: Wheelbase: 81 in. Length: 154 in. Height: 90.12 in. Front tread: 48-9/16 in. Rear tread: 48-9/16 in. Tires: 6.70 x 15 four-ply tubeless.

CHASSIS [SWB trucks]: Wheelbase: 104.5 in. Length: 176.2 in. Height: 72.1 in. Front tread: 57 in. Rear tread: 57 in. Tires: 7.00 x 15 in. (6.70 x 15 on Station Wagon).

CHASSIS [LWB trucks]: Wheelbase: 118 in. Length: 183.7 in. Height: 74.3 in. Front tread: 57 in. Rear tread: 63.5 in. Tires: 7.00 x 16 in. Note: SWB=short wheelbase; LWB=long wheelbase.

CHASSIS [FC-150]: Wheelbase: 81 in. Tires: 7.00 x 15 in.

CHASSIS [FC-170]: Wheelbase: 103-1/2 in. Tires: 7.00 x 16 in.

TECHNICAL [FC-150/FC-170]: Synchromesh transmission. Speeds: 3F/1R (four-speed optional). Floor-mounted gearshift lever. Single-plate, dry-disc clutch (heavy-duty on FC-170). Rear axle: [FC-150] Semi-floating hypoid; [FC-170] full-floating hypoid rear axle. Overall ratio: [FC-150] 5.38:1; [FC-170] 4.89:1. Four-wheel hydraulic brakes (heavy-duty on FC-170). Disc wheels (dual rear on FC-170 heavy-duty models).

TECHNICAL [Fleetvan]: Synchromesh transmission. Speeds: 3F/1R. Floor-mounted gearshift lever. Single-plate, dry-disc clutch, 72 sq. in. frictional area. Hypoid, semi-floating rear axle. Overall ratio: 4.56:1. Hydraulic 9 in. drum brakes. Four 15 x 5.00 five stud disc wheels.

TECHNICAL [All other models]: Synchromesh transmission. Speeds: 3F/1R. Floor-mounted gearshift lever. Single-plate, dry-disc clutch. Hypoid semi-floating rear axle. Overall ratio: 3.54:1, 4.56:1 or 5.38:1. Four-wheel hydraulic brakes. Disc wheels. 4x4 models have two-speed transfer case. 4x2 models have I-beam type front axle. 4x4 models have full-floating hypoid front axle.

OPTIONS [CJ]: Three different color striped tops for Surrey. [Gala] Chrome front bumper. Chrome rear bumper. Chrome bumperettes. Chrome wheel discs. Power-take-off. Pulley drive. Motor governor. Special wheels and 7-in. tires. Front canvas top. Hydraulic lift. Metal top. [CJ-5]: Five metal and fabric-top options. Ventilating windshield. Power-take-off. Eight body color choices. Approved snow plow. Winch. 36 x 39-1/4 in. all-steel cargo box. [CJ-6]: All-weather canvas tops. New body colors. Oversize tires.

OPTIONS [DJ]: Convertible top. 40 cu. ft. hardtop with rippled fiberglass roof and 36 in. wide gate opening. Whitewall tires. Chrome front bumper. Chrome rear bumper. Eight standard body colors. Law Enforcement package.

OPTIONS, FLEETVAN: Two-tone finish. Ladder racks. Heater. Stake model available. Dual rear wheel platform stake model available in 8,000 lb. GVW option.

OPTIONS, TRUCKS: [4x4s]: Standard and deluxe cab trim. Power-take-off. Pulley drive. Motor governor. Rearview mirror. Sidemount spare on pickups/stakes. Chrome bumper. License frame. [Sedan Delivery]: Chrome front bumper. Chrome rear bumper. License frame. Chrome wheel disc. Bumperettes. Bumper guards. Wheel trim rings. Whitewall tires. Rearview mirror. Radio and antenna. New two-tone paint combinations.

OPTIONS [FC]: Fresh air heater. Radio. Tu-tone paint. Front bumper guards. Direction signals. E-Z-Eye glass. Windshield washer. Front air vent. Double passenger seat. Oil bath air cleaner. Oil filter. High altitude cylinder head (no charge). Power-Lok differential. Heavy-duty rear axle. Heavy-duty springs and shocks. Transmission brake. Hot climate radiator. Power-take-off (center and rear). Governor. Various size/type tires. Draw-Bar. Stabilizer bar. Rear bumperettes. Selective drive hubs. Bed and/or front mount winch. Snow plow. Dozer blade. Wrecker equipment. Jeep-A-Trench. Service bodies.

HISTORICAL: Introduced: Fall, 1960. Calendar year registrations: 32,644 [All Trucks and Jeeps]. Calendar year production: [All Models, domestic]: 123,755 (10.98 percent). This included 68,116 Jeeps (55 percent) and 55,639 (45 percent) Jeep-trucks. The breakout for engine types was 72,913 four-cylinders and 50,842 six-cylinders. A four-cylinder Perkins diesel engine was made available in Universal Jeeps. The company set new sales records in 1961. In Canada, Willys underwent expansions including larger production facilities.

1962 JEEP

WILLYS — JEEP SERIES — ALL ENGINES: For 1962, the Surrey returned as part of the Dispatcher 4x2 series. The station wagons with either 4x2 or 4x4 running gear were now described as Traveller models. They could be had in solid colors or with two types of two-tone trim. One style was similar to that described for the 1959-1/2 Maverick, except that only the roof was in contrasting color; the windshield and door pillars were not. The second treatment is often described as "Rocket" style trim. With this, a contrast panel running the full-length of the bodyside was shaped somewhat like a Nike missile and the roof was finished to match it. Both 4x2 and 4x4 Travellers came with double doors in the rear, plus auxiliary passenger benches hinged to the inner sidewalls. However, the 4x2 had a carpeted cargo floor and spare tire behind the driver's seat. The 4x4 model carried its spare on the roof and had "Jeep 4-wheel Drive" lettering on the right rear door. In May 1962, a new overhead cam six-cylinder engine was introduced for Jeep vehicles. "Who put the Big 6 in '62?" asked a sales brochure. The new engine was available in the Jeep utility wagon, Station Wagon, Pickup and Panel Delivery trucks only.

1962 Jeep 1/2-Ton CJ-6 Universal 4x4 (OCW)

1962 Jeep FC-150 3/4-Ton Stake Bed 4x4 (OCW)

I.D. DATA: Serial number located on right side of dash under hood; on front frame cross-member; on left floor riser in back of driver's seat. Engine numbers located on right side of cylinder block; stamped on water pump boss on front of cylinder block. On most Jeep models the engine and serial numbers are the same.

1962 Jeep FC-170 Heavy-Duty 1-Ton Stake Bed 4x4 (OCW)

Model	Body Type	Price	Weight	Prod. Total
Jeep — 1/4-Ton — 4-cyl. — 4x4 — 80 in. w.b.				
CJ-3B	Jeep Universal	1960	2220	—
Jeep — 1/4-Ton — 4-cyl. — 4x4 — 81 in. w.b.				
CJ-5	Jeep Universal	2055	2251	—
Jeep — 1/2-Ton — 4-cyl. — 4x4 — 101 in. w.b.				
CJ-6	Jeep Universal	2150	2313	—
Dispatcher — 1/4-Ton — 4x2 — 4-cyl. — 80 in. w.b.				
DJ-3A	Basic	1435	1797	—
DJ-3A	Soft Top	1505	1857	—
DJ-3A	Hardtop	1665	2092	—
DJ-3A	Surrey	1775	2007	—
Fleetvan — 1/2 - Ton — 4-cyl. — 4x2 — 81 in. w.b.				
FJ-3A	Fleetvan	2380	3045	—
Jeep Trucks — 1/2-Ton — 4-cyl. — 4x2 — 104.5 in. w.b.				
F4-134	Economy Delivery	1695	1987	—
F4-134	Station Wagon	2095	2990	—
F4-134	Utility Wagon	N.A.	3076	—
F4-134	Utility Delivery	2005	2878	—
Jeep Trucks — 1/2-Ton — 4-cyl. — 4x4 — 104.5 in. w.b.				
F4-134	Utility Wagon	2885	3225	—
F4-134	Utility Delivery	2605	3025	—
Jeep Truck — 1-Ton — 4-cyl. — 4x4 — 118 in. w.b.				
F4-134	Pickup	2370	3197	—
FC-150 -3/4-Ton — 4-cyl. — 4x4 — 81 in. w.b.				
FC-150	Chassis & Cab	2505	2884	—
FC-150	Pickup	2625	3140	—
FC-150	Platform Stake	2725	3307	—
Jeep Trucks — 1/2-Ton — 6-cyl. — 4x2 — 104.5 in. w.b.				
L6-226	Utility Wagon	2345	3172	—
L6-226	Utility Delivery	2130	2974	—
L6-226	Station Wagon	2345	3103	—
Jeep Trucks — 1/2-Ton — 6-cyl. — 4x4 — 104.5 in. w.b.				
L6-226	Utility Wagon	3010	3321	—
L6-226	Utility Delivery	2730	3123	—
Jeep Trucks — 1-Ton — 6-cyl. — 4x4 — 118 in. w.b.				
L6-226	Pickup	2490	3291	—
L6-226	Platform Stake	2575	3456	—
L6-226	Chassis & Cab	2365	2932	—
FC-170 — 1-Ton — 6-cyl. — 4x4 — 103.5 in. w.b.				
(Single rear wheels)				
FC-170	Chassis & Cab	2825	3056	—
FC-170	Pickup	2960	3486	—
FC-170	Platform Stake	3165	3719	—
(Dual rear wheels/8,000 lbs. GVW)				
FC-170	Chassis & Cab	3315	3726	—
(Dual rear wheels/9,000 lbs. GVW)				
FC-170	Chassis & Cab	3525	3726	—

1962 Jeep DJ-3 1/4-Ton "Gala" Surrey-Top Universal 4x2

ENGINE [CJ-3B/CJ-5]: Inline. F-head. Four-cylinder. Cast iron block. Bore & stroke: 3-1/8 in. x 4-3/8 in. Displacement: 134.2 cid. Compression ratio: 6.9:1. Brake hp: 70 at 4000 rpm. Net hp: 15.63. Max. Torque: 114 lbs.-ft. at 2000 rpm. Three main bearings. Solid valve lifters. Carburetor: Carter YF model 938S or 938SA.

ENGINE [CJ6/F4-134]: Inline. F-head. Four-cylinder. Cast iron block. Bore & stroke: 3-1/8 in. x 4-3/8 in. Displacement: 134.2 cid. Compression ratio: 7.4:1. Brake hp: 72 at 4000 rpm. Net hp: 15.63. Max. Torque: 114 lbs.-ft. at 2000 rpm. Three main bearings. Solid valve lifters. Carburetor: Carter YF model 938S/938SA one-barrel.

ENGINE [Fleetvan]: Inline. F-head. Four-cylinder. Cast iron block. Bore & stroke: 3-1/8 in. x 4-3/8 in. Displacement: 134.2 cid. Compression ratio: 7.4:1. Brake hp: 75 at 4000 rpm. Net hp: 15.63. Max. Torque: 115 lbs.-ft. at 2000 rpm. Three main bearings. Solid valve lifters. Carburetor: Carter model YF.

ENGINE [FC-150]: Inline. L-head. Four-cylinder. Cast iron block. Bore & stroke: 3-1/8 in. x 4-3/8 in. Displacement: 134.2 cid. Compression ratio: 7.40:1. Brake hp: 72 at 4000 rpm. Net hp: 15.63. Max. Torque: 114 lbs.-ft. at 2000 rpm. Three main bearings. Solid valve lifters. Carburetor: Carter YF model 2392S one-barrel.

ENGINE [6-226/FC-170]: Inline. L-head. Six-cylinder. Cast iron block. Bore & stroke: 3-5/16 in. x 4-3/8 in. Displacement: 226.2 cid. Compression ratio: 6.86:1. Brake hp: 115 at 3650 rpm. Net hp: 26.3. Max. Torque: 190 lbs.-ft. at 1800 rpm. Four main bearings. Solid valve lifters. Carburetor: Carter WDG model 2052S or 2052SA one-barrel; Carter WC model 2204S two-barrel.

ENGINE [Tornado 230]: Inline. Overhead valve/overhead cam. Six-cylinder. Cast iron with extensive use of aluminum components. Bore & stroke: 3.34 x 4.38 in. Displacement: 230 cid. Compression ratio: 8.5:1. Brake hp: 140 at 4000 rpm. Max. Torque: 210 lbs.-ft. and 1750 rpm. Overhead valve lifters.

1962 Jeep "Traveller" 1/2-Ton Utility Wagon 4x4

CHASSIS [CJ-3B]: Wheelbase: 80 in. Length: 129-7/8 in. Height: 67-1/4 in. Front tread: 48-7/16 in. Rear tread: 48-7/16 in. Tires: 6.00 x 16 in.

CHASSIS [CJ-5]: Wheelbase: 81.09 in. Length: 135.50 in. Height: 69.50 in. Front tread: 48-7/16 in. Rear tread: 48-7/16 in. Tires: 6.00 x 16 in.

CHASSIS [CJ-6]: Wheelbase: 101 in. Length: 155-1/2 in. Height: 68-1/4 in. Front tread: 48-7/16 in. Rear tread: 48-7/16 in. Tires: 6.00 x 16 in.

CHASSIS [DJ-3]: Wheelbase: 80.1 in. Length: 125.4 in. Height: 59.8 in. Front tread: 48.2 in. Rear tread: 48.5 in. Tires: 6.50 x 15 in.

CHASSIS [Fleetvan]: Wheelbase: 81 in. Length: 154 in. Height: 90.12 in. Front tread: 48-9/16 in. Rear tread: 48-9/16 in. Tires: 6.70 x 15 four-ply tubeless.

CHASSIS [SWB trucks]: Wheelbase: 104.5 in. Length: 176.2 in. Height: 72.1 in. Front tread: 57 in. Rear tread: 57 in. Tires: 7.00 x 15 in. (6.70 x 15 on Station Wagon).

CHASSIS [LWB trucks]: Wheelbase: 118 in. Length: 183.7 in. Height: 74.3 in. Front tread: 57 in. Rear tread: 63.5 in. Tires: 7.00 x 16 in. (SWB=short wheelbase; LWB=long wheelbase).

CHASSIS [FC-150]: Wheelbase: 81 in. Tires: 7.00 x 15 in.

CHASSIS [FC-170]: Wheelbase: 103-1/2 in. Tires: 7.00 x 16 in.

1962 Jeep CJ-3B 1/4-Ton Universal 4x4

TECHNICAL [FC-150/FC-170]: Synchromesh transmission. Speeds: 3F/1R (four-speed optional). Floor-mounted gearshift lever. Single-plate, dry-disc clutch (heavy-duty on FC-170). Rear axle: [FC-150] Semi-floating hypoid; [FC-170] full-floating hypoid rear axle. Overall ratios: [FC-150] 5.38:1; [FC-170] 4.89:1. Four-wheel hydraulic brakes (heavy-duty on FC-170). Disc wheels (dual rear on FC-170 Heavy-Duty model).

TECHNICAL [Fleetvan]: Synchromesh transmission. Speeds: 3F/1R. Floor-mounted gearshift lever. Single-plate, dry-disc clutch, 72 sq. in. frictional area. I-beam front axle. Hypoid, semi-floating rear axle. Overall ratio: 4.56:1. Hydraulic 9 in. drum brakes. Four 15 x 5.00 five stud disc wheels.

TECHNICAL [Other models]: Synchromesh transmission. Speeds: 3F/1R. Floor-mounted gearshift lever. Single-plate, dry-disc clutch. Hypoid semi-floating rear axle. Overall ratio: 3.54:1, 4.56:1 or 5.38:1. Four-wheel hydraulic brakes. Disc wheels. 4x4 models have two-speed transfer case. 4x2 models have I-beam type front axle. 4x4 models have full-floating hypoid front axle.

1962 Jeep 1/2-Ton Panel Delivery 4x2

OPTIONS [CJ]: Three different color striped tops for Surrey. [Gala] Chrome front bumper. Chrome rear bumper. Chrome bumperettes. Chrome wheel discs. Power-take-off. Pulley drive. Motor governor. Special wheels and 7-in. tires. Front canvas top. Hydraulic lift. Metal top. [CJ-5]: Five metal and fabric-top options. Ventilating windshield. Power-take-off. Eight body color choices. Approved snow plow. Winch. 36 x 39-1/4 in. all-steel cargo box. [CJ-6]: All-weather canvas tops. New body colors. Oversize tires.

1962 Jeep 1-Ton Pickup 4x4 (OCW)

OPTIONS [DJ-3A]: Convertible top. 40 cu. ft. hardtop with rippled fiberglass roof and 36 in. wide gate opening. Whitewall tires. Chrome wheel discs. Chrome front bumper. Chrome rear bumper. Eight standard body colors. "Law Enforcement" package.

OPTIONS [FJ]: [Fleetvan]: Two-tone finish. Ladder racks. Heater. Stake model available. Dual rear wheel platform stake model available in 8,000 lb. GVW option.

1962 Jeep FJ-3A Fleetvan Walk-in Delivery (OCW)

OPTIONS [TRUCKS]: [4x4]: Standard and deluxe cab trim. Power-take-off. Pulley drive. Motor governor. Rearview mirror. Sidemount spare on pickups/stakes. Chrome bumper. License frame. [Sedan Delivery]: Chrome front bumper. Chrome rear bumper. License frame. Chrome wheel disc. Bumperettes. Bumper guards. Wheel trim rings. Whitewall tires. Rearview mirror. Radio and antenna. New Tu-tone paint combinations.

OPTIONS [FC]: Fresh air heater. Radio. Tu-tone paint. Front bumper guards. Direction signals. E-Z-Eye glass. Windshield washer. Front air vent. Double passenger seat. Oil bath air cleaner. Oil filter. High altitude cylinder head (no charge). Four-speed transmission. Power-Lok differential. Heavy-duty rear axle. Heavy-duty springs and shocks. Transmission brake. Hot climate radiator. Power-take-off (center and rear). Governor. Various size/type tires. Draw-Bar. Stabilizer bar. Rear bumperettes. Selective drive hubs. Bed and/or front mount winch. Snow plow. Dozer blade. Wrecker equipment. Jeep-A-Trench. Service bodies.

APPROVED SPECIAL EQUIPMENT: Jeep Approved Special Equipment and Accessory Options for 1962 included steel or canvas tops for Jeep Universals, Ramsey or Koenig winches for all Jeeps, wrecker equipment for Universals, Pickups and FC models, Meyer angle-dozer plows, "Jeep-A-Trench" trench-diggers, a tailgate loader for all Jeep-trucks and a convertible top for Universals.

1962 Jeep FC-150 3/4-Ton Stake Bed 4x4 (OCW)

HISTORICAL: Introduced: Fall, 1961. Calendar year registrations: 30,426 [All Trucks and Jeeps]. Calendar year production: [All Models] 85,623 Market share: 6.83 percent. The "Tornado OHC" six-cylinder engine was introduced on May 2, 1962. This was the last year for the Willys-Jeep. After Kaiser's purchase of Willys on April 28, 1953, the products were still called "Willys-Jeep" models. There was a totally restyled line of commercial vehicles known as the Gladiator series. The earliest 1963 Gladiators said only "Jeep" on the front fendersides, but before long they said "Kaiser-Jeep."

1962 Jeep FC-170 1-Ton Platform 4x4 (OCW)

UNIVERSAL/DISPATCHER — SERIES CJ/DJ — FOUR-CYLINDER: In 1963, Kaiser Industries changed the name of its Willys Motors, Inc. subsidiary. It was now called Kaiser-Jeep Corp. and the Willys name was removed from the vehicles. There were three Jeep Universal models, all rated for 1/4-ton and featuring four-wheel drive. The CJ-3B was available again. It was characterized by its seven slot grille, slightly raised hood, flat fenders and short hood length. Power came from a 72 hp version of the Hurricane four-cylinder engine. Larger headlamps, touching the outer grille slots near the top, were one sign of the CJ-5 model. It also had a longer hood, curved fenders and hood, door opening with straighter front edge and sculptured body sides. Base engine was a 75 hp Hurricane four-cylinder. The CJ-6 was a stretched version of the CJ-5, with the CJ-3B engine under its hood. Three 4x2 Dispatcher models were also available. They looked similar to CJ-3Bs, but had an I-beam front axle and the 60 hp "Lightning" L-head four. Models included the Jeep version with open-side convertible top, the hardtop with a full-enclosure fiberglass top and sliding doors or the soft top with a full-enclosure fabric top.

JEEP-TRUCK — SERIES F-134/L6-226/6-230 — ALL ENGINES: There were three series of the old-fashioned looking Jeep Wagons, Pickups and Panels available in 1963. Series designations revealed type of engine and displacement. Some consider the 4x2 Station Wagon and 4x4 Utility Wagon to be passenger cars, but Kaiser had them certified as trucks in 1955. The Pickups and Panel Deliveries were on a longer 118 in. wheelbase and rated for 1-ton payloads. Station Wagons were offered in standard or custom trim levels. All of these models were basically carryovers from the early 1950s, but now had a circular badge with Kaiser's corporate logo above the center of the grille. In the truck lineup, platform stake bed models were available, too. Another choice buyers had was between 4x2 and 4x4 chassis. The grille had nine vertical bars crossed at the top, center and bottom with horizontal chrome moldings and was slightly V-shaped. General body styling was straight from the Jeep "family" with spare tires carried on the sides of Pickups, inside 4x2 Wagons and on the roof of 4x4 Wagons and Vans.

FORWARD CONTROL — SERIES FC — ALL ENGINES: The Forward Control Jeep series were carried over for 1963. A four-cylinder engine was standard in the 3/4-ton FC-150 line. Other standard equipment included dual wipers, key locks on both doors, dispatch box, color-toned interiors, cool Plasti-Strand upholstery, ashtray, left-hand sun visor, dome light, rearview mirror and adjustable driver's seat. Deluxe equipment added dual sunvisors, armrests, rear quarter windows, acoustical trim, vinyl windshield trim, chrome safety handrail, foam rubber seats, cigarette lighter, and front panel kick pads. The 1-ton came standard with the 226 cid "Hurricane" L-head six. It was designated the FC-170 and came in three basic models. Also available were two FC-170 heavy-duty chassis configurations with dual rear wheels. Customers could have platform, stake or special bodies mounted on this rugged chassis. Both cab-overs were 4x4 trucks and four-speed transmission was optional. Standard equipment also included a Safety-View cab, acoustical trim panels on doors and headlining, heavy glass fiber engine cover insulation, console-type instrument panel, vinyl covered dash, flat-plane steering wheel, feather-light steering, safety door latches, foam rubber seats, suspended pedals and a single-control transfer case lever.

WAGONEER/GLADIATOR — SERIES J — SIX-CYLINDER: New for 1963 was a wide range of Jeep carryall-type station wagons and trucks with totally updated styling. The carryalls were called Wagoneers. The trucks were called Gladiators and came in chassis-and-cab, pickup and platform stake models. Pickups were further separated into Thriftside (flared fender) and Townside (slab fender) model-options. Automatic transmission was available for the first time with a four-wheel drive chassis. Two-wheel-drive Wagoneers and Gladiators were also offered. All of these vehicles had more conventional styling than other Jeep products, but the center-grille, with its 12 vertical slots, identified them as Jeep Family members. Overall styling was boxy, but very crisp and clean. There were nine basic series on three wheelbases: 110, 120 and 126 inches. 1/2-ton, 3/4-ton and 1-ton models were offered. Four 1/2-ton series had GVW ratings of 4,200-4,500, 4,000, 5,600 and 5,000 lbs. Three 3/4-ton series had GVWs of 6,000, 6,600 or 7,600 lbs. Both 1-ton series had GVWs of 8,600 lbs. The 230 cid overhead cam six-cylinder engine was standard in all lines.

I.D. DATA: [CJ] Serial number located on floor riser. Starting numbers were distinct for each model: [CJ-3B] 57348-59127 and up; [CJ-5] 57548-90027 and up; [CJ-6] 57748-18221 and up; [DJ-3A] 56337-15704 and up. Ending numbers not available. [F-134/L6-226/6-230] Serial number located on door hinge pillar post. Each model had a distinct starting number for 37 variations. The first five digits of the serial numbers, as listed in the chart below, identified the model. These were followed by a dash and the sequential number. [FC] Serial number located on door hinge pillar. Unlike other Jeeps, the FC-150 was numbered by series with 65548-20683 the starting number for all models. The FC-170 starting number was 61568-15897. However, the heavy-duty chassis each had distinct starting numbers, 61368-13-10001 for the chassis with windshield and 61568-13-10479 for the chassis and cab. [J Series] Serial number located on left-hand door hinge pillar. The first four digits indicated the truck-line. The fifth symbol was a letter, followed by the sequential number. Starting number for each series was 10001 up. [All Series] Engine numbers located on right-hand corner of block.

Model	Body Type	Price	Weight	Prod. Total
CJ-3B — 1/4-Ton — 4x4 — 80 in. w.b.				
CJ-3B	Jeep Universal	2015	2132	14,544
CJ-5 — 1/4-Ton — 4x4 — 81 in. w.b.				
CJ-5	Jeep Universal	2109	2163	11,304
CJ-6 — 1/2-Ton — 4x4 — 101 in. w.b.				
CJ-6	Jeep Universal	2204	2225	2108
DJ-34 — 1/4-Ton — 4x2 — 80 in. w.b.				
DJ-3A	Jeep	1492	1709	Note 2
DJ-3A	Hardtop	1723	2004	Note 2
DJ-3A	Soft Top	1559	1769	Note 2

NOTE 1: All Jeep production estimated by comparing 1963-1964 starting numbers.
NOTE 2: Total DJ-3A production was 1,552.

Series F-134 — 1/2-Ton — 104.5 in. w.b.

58147	Station Wagon (4x2)	2095	2858	566
54347	Traveler (4x2)	2561	3077	Note 3
54147	Utility Wagon (4x2)	2258	2944	Note 4
54148	Utility Wagon (4x4)	2887	3093	448
54247	Panel Delivery (4x2)	2007	2746	224
54248	Panel Delivery (4x4)	2605	2893	606

Series F-134 — 1-Ton — 118 in. w.b.

55248	Pickup (4x4)	2369	3065	937

Series L6-226 — 1/2-Ton — 104.5 in. w.b.

58167	Station Wagon (4x2)	2344	2971	1053
54167	Utility Wagon (4x2)	2738	3057	Note 4
54367	Traveler (4x2)	2378	2939	Note 4
54168	Utility Wagon (4x4)	3010	3206	7273
54467	Utility Chassis (4x2)	1814	1968	Note 4
54267	Panel Delivery (4x2)	2132	2859	Note 4
55468	Chassis (4x4)	2232	2281	Note 4
54268	Panel Delivery (4x4)	2728	3008	Note 4
54468	Utility Chassis (4x4)	2311	2228	Note 4

Series L6-226 — 1-Ton — 118 in. w.b.

55168	Chassis & Cab (4x4)	2365	2817	Note 4
55268	Pickup (4x4)	2490	3176	1335
55368	Platform Stake (4x4)	2577	3341	Note 4

Series 6-230 — 1/2-Ton — 104.5 in. w.b.

58177	Station Wagon (4x2)	2450	3047	11
54377	Traveler (4x2)	2792	3240	19
54178	Utility Wagon (4x4)	3117	3307	35
54378	Traveler (4x4)	3389	3410	73
54278	Panel Delivery (4x4)	2835	3561	Note 4
54277	Panel Delivery (4x2)	—	3147	50

Series 6-230 — 1-Ton — 118 in. w.b.

55178	Chassis & Cab (4x4)	2472	2872	1042
55278	Pickup (4x4)	2597	3238	31
55378	Stake (4x4)	2684	3373	45

NOTE 3: Model not offered 1964; production cannot be estimated.
NOTE 4: Starting number for 1964 is identical suggesting none made.

Series FC-150 — 3/4-Ton — 4x4 — 81 in. w.b.

65548	Chassis & Cab	2507	2764	1091
65548	Pickup	2624	3020	Note 5
65548	Plat. Stake	2725	3187	Note 5

Series FC-170 — 1-Ton — 4x4 — 103.5 in. w.b.

61568	Chassis & Cab	2824	2901	2031
61568	Pickup	2960	3331	Note 5
61568	Platform Stake	3167	3564	Note 5

Series FC-170HD — 1-Ton — 6x6 — 103.5 in. w.b.

61368	Chassis & Windshield	3144	3028	174
61568	Chassis & Cab	3315	3561	Note 5

NOTE 5: Combined series production shown as Chassis & Cab total.

Series J-100 — 1/2-Ton — 4x2 — 110 in. w.b.

1314	4d Wagoneer	2589	3480	—
1312	2d Wagoneer	2546	3453	—
1314C	4d Custom Wagoneer	2783	3515	—
1312C	2d Custom Wagoneer	2738	3488	—
1313	Panel Delivery	2438	3253	—

Series J-100 — 1/2-Ton — 4x4 — 110 in. w.b.

1414	4d Wagoneer	3332	3623	—
1412	2d Wagoneer	3278	3596	—
1414C	4d Custom Wagoneer	3526	3658	—
1412C	2d Custom Wagoneer	3472	3631	—
1413	Panel Delivery	2996	3396	—

Series J-200 — 1/2-Ton — 4x2 — 120 in. w.b.

2306F	Chassis & Cab	1913	2901	—
2306F	Thriftside Pickup	2014	3196	—
2306F	Townside Pickup	2041	3304	—

Series J-200 — 1/2-Ton — 4x4 — 120 in. w.b.

2406F	Chassis & Cab	2596	3061	—
2406F	Thriftside Pickup	2696	3361	—
2406F	Townside Pickup	2722	3461	—

Series J-210 — 1/2-Ton — 4x2 — 120 in. w.b.

2306A	Chassis & Cab	1977	2941	—
2306A	Thriftside Pickup	2078	3236	—
2306A	Townside Pickup	2105	3344	—

Series J-210 — 1/2-Ton — 4x4 — 120 in. w.b.

2406A	Chassis & Cab	2653	3096	—
2406A	Thriftside Pickup	2734	3396	—
2406A	Townside Pickup	2781	3496	—

Series J-300 — 1/2-Ton — 4x2 — 126 in. w.b.

3306E	Chassis & Cab	2017	2943	—
3306E	Thriftside Pickup	2133	3263	—
3306E	Townside Pickup	2160	3371	—

Series J-300 — 1/2-Ton — 4x4 — 126 in. w.b.

3406E	Chassis & Cab	2654	3091	—
3406E	Thriftside Pickup	2769	3441	—
3406E	Townside Pickup	2796	3541	—

Series J-220 — 3/4-Ton — 4x2 — 120 in. w.b.

2306B	Chassis & Cab	2062	3024	—
2306B	Thriftside Pickup	2163	3319	—
2306B	Townside Pickup	2189	3427	—
2306B	Platform Stake	2368	3680	—

Series J-220 — 3/4-Ton — 4x4 — 120 in. w.b.

2406B	Chassis & Cab	2753	3214	—
2406B	Thriftside Pickup	2854	3514	—
2406B	Townside Pickup	2881	3614	—
2406B	Platform Stake	3060	3894	—

Series J-310 — 3/4-Ton — 4x2 — 126 in. w.b.

3306B	Chassis & Cab	2128	3067	—
3306B	Thriftside Pickup	2243	3387	—
3306B	Townside Pickup	2270	3495	—
3306B	Platform Stake	2468	3771	—

Series J-310 — 3/4-Ton — 4x4 — 126 in. w.b.

3406B	Chassis & Cab	2771	3239	—
3406B	Thriftside Pickup	2886	3589	—
3406B	Townside Pickup	2913	3689	—
3406B	Platform Stake	3111	3979	—

Series J-320 — 3/4-Ton — 4x2 — 126 in. w.b.

3306C	Chassis & Cab	2283	3168	—
3306C	Thriftside Pickup	2398	3488	—
3306C	Townside Pickup	2425	3596	—
3306C	Platform Stake	2623	3872	—

Series J-320 — 3/4-Ton — 4x4 — 126 in. w.b.

3406C	Chassis & Cab	2931	3377	—
3406C	Thriftside Pickup	3046	3727	—
3406C	Townside Pickup	3073	3827	—
3406C	Platform Stake	3271	4117	—

Series J-230 — 1-Ton — 4x2 — 120 in. w.b.

2406D	Chassis & Cab	3578	3874	—
2406D	Platform Stake	3970	4714	—

Series J-330 — 1-Ton — 4x2 — 126 in. w.b.

3406D	Chassis & Cab	3597	3899	—
3406D	Platform Stake	4011	4799	—

NOTE 6: Explanation of J-Series model number suffixes: A=5,600 lb. GVW; B=6,600 lb. GVW; C=7,600 lb. GVW; D=8,600 lb. GVW; E=5,000 lb. GVW; F=4,000 lb. GVW.

1963 Jeep J-300 Gladiator 1-Ton Townside Pickup (RCA)

ENGINE [CJ-3B/CJ-6/F-134]: Inline. F-head. Four-cylinder. Cast iron block. Bore & stroke: 3-1/8 in. x 4-3/8 in. Displacement: 134.2 cid. Compression ratio: 6.9:1. Brake hp: 72 at 4000 rpm. Net hp: 15.63. Torque: 114 lbs.-ft. at 2000 rpm. Solid valve lifters. Carburetor: Carter.
ENGINE [CJ-5/FC-150]: Inline. F-head. Four-cylinder. Cast iron block. Bore & stroke: 3-1/8 in. x 4-3/8 in. Displacement: 134.2 cid. Compression ratio: 7.4:1. Brake hp: 75 at 4000 rpm. Net hp: 15.63. Torque: 114 lbs.-ft. at 2000 rpm. Solid valve lifters. Carburetor: Carter.
ENGINE [DJ-3A]: Inline. L-head. Four-cylinder. Cast iron block. Bore & stroke: 3-1/8 in. x 4-3/8 in. Displacement: 134.2 cid. Compression ratio: 7.00:1. Brake hp: 60 at 4000 rpm. Net hp: 15.63. Torque: 114 lbs.-ft. at 2000 rpm. Solid valve lifters. Carburetor: Carter.
ENGINE [L6-226/FC-170]: Inline. L-head. Six-cylinder. Cast iron block. Bore & stroke: 3-5/16 in. x 4-3/8 in. Displacement: 226.2 cid. Compression ratio: 6.86:1 (7.3:1 optional). Brake hp: 105 at 3600 rpm. Net hp: 26.3. Torque: 190 lbs.-ft. at 1400 rpm. Solid valve lifters. Carburetor: Carter.
ENGINE [6-230/J-Series]: Overhead Cam. Inline. Six-cylinder. Cast iron block. Bore & stroke: 3.34 in. x 4.38 in. Displacement: 230 cid. Compression ratio: 8.5:1. Brake hp: 140 at 4000 rpm. Net hp: 26.77. Torque: 210 lbs.-ft. at 1750 rpm. Solid valve lifters. Carburetor: Carter model two-barrel.

1963 Jeep J-310 Gladiator 3/4-Ton Townside Pickup (OCW)

CHASSIS: See model charts above for wheelbases. Overall length: [CJ-3B] 129.9 in.; [CJ-5] 135.5. in.; [CJ-6] 155.5 in.; [DJ-3A] 125.4 in.; [F-134/L6-226/6-230] 1/2-ton 176.2 in.; 1-ton 183.7 in.; [FC-150] 147.3 in.; [FC-170] 181.4 in.; [J-100] 183.66 in. Front tread: [CJ-3B]

48.4 in.; [CJ-5] 48.4 in.; [CJ-6] 48.4 in.; [DJ-3A] 48.2 in.; [F-134, L6-226, 6-230] 1/2-Ton: 57 in.; 1-Ton: 57 in.; [FC-150] 57 in.; [FC-170] 63.4 in.; [J-100] 57 in. Rear tread: [CJ-3B] 48.4 in.; [CJ-5] 48.4 in.; [CJ-6] 48.4 in.; [DJ-3A] 48.5 in.; [F-134/L6-226/6-230] 1/2-Ton: 57 in.; 1-Ton: 63.5 in.; [FC-150] 57 in.; [FC-170] 63.8 in.; [J-100] 57 in. Tires: [CJ-all models] 6.00 x 16 in.; [DJ-3A] 6.50 x 15 in.; [F-134/L6-226/6-230] 1/2-Ton 4x2: 6.70 x 15 in.; 1/2-Ton 4x4: 7.00 x 15 in.; 1-Ton 7.00 x 16 in.; [FC-150] 7.00 x 15 in.; [FC-170] 7.00 x 16 in.; [J-100, J-200] 6.70 x 15 in.; [J-210] 7.60 x 15 in.; [J-300] 7.10 x 15 in.; [J-320] 7.50 x 16 in.; [other models] 7.00 x 16 in.

1963 Jeep J-100 Two-Door Wagoneer 4x2 (KJC)

TECHNICAL: Synchromesh transmission. Speeds: 3F/1R. Floor-mounted gearshift lever. Single-plate, dry-disc clutch. Semi-floating rear axle. Four-wheel hydraulic brakes. Steel disc wheels. 4x2 models have I-beam front axle. 4x4 models have hypoid, semi-floating front axle and two-speed transfer case with ratios of 1.00:1 and 2.46:1.

OPTIONS: [CJ/DJ] Convertible top; all-weather canvas top; fiberglass cab top; metal cab top. Four-speed transmission ($194). [All models] Rearview mirror. Radio. Antenna package. Ramsey or Koenig winches for front, rear or bed mount. Warn or Cutlas selective drive hubs. Canfield wrecker for Universals, 4x4 pickup or Forward Control models. Meyer angle dozers. Jeep-A-Trench. Tailgate loader for 600 lb. or 1,000 lb. rated models. Deluxe cab on Forward Control models. Fresh air heater. Tu-tone paint. Front bumper guards. Directional signals. E-Z-Eye glass. Windshield washer. FC-150 front air vent. FC-150 double passenger seat. Oil bath air cleaner. Oil filter. High-altitude cylinder head (no charge). Powr-Lok rear differential. Heavy-duty rear axle. Heavy-duty springs and shock absorbers. Transmission brake. Hot-Climate radiator. Variable and constant-speed governors. Various size and type tires including whitewalls in available sizes. Draw-Bar. Stabilizer bar. Rear bumper-ettes. Automatic transmission in Travelalls and Gladiators. Full wheel discs.

1963 Jeep J-100 Four-Door Wagoneer 4x2 (KJC)

HISTORICAL: Introduced: Fall, 1963. Calendar year production: 110,457 (this included 55,215 four-cylinder and 55,242 six-cylinders). Also included in the total were 12,615 Jeep Universal models and 25,156 Jeep trucks. Innovations: Wagoneer station wagon introduced; Gladiator truck series debuted. First automatic transmission and independent front suspension on four-wheel drive (4x4 vehicles). First ohc engine mass-produced in U.S. Sales of Jeeps established all-time records in 1963. Corporate dollar sales achieved record $221,000 (up 42 percent from 1962).

1964 JEEP

Plain? You bet it is! But it's also the toughest little buggy on the automotive scene!

1964 Jeep CJ-5 1/4-Ton Universal (RCA)

UNIVERSAL/DISPATCHER — SERIES CJ/DJ — FOUR-CYLINDER: Introduced as "the new idea in sports cars," two new models were added to the Jeep Universal lineup in 1964. The CJ-5A and CJ-6A Tuxedo Park packages were upscale versions of the two base models with features like turbine-style full wheel discs, whitewall tires and spare tire covers. Trim items like windshield hinges, the rearview mirror and bumpers were made of bright metal. Also new for the year (but actually a reincarnation) was the DJ-3A Surrey with stripes and fringe on top and extra chrome goodies. Everything else was much the same as 1963. The 75 hp four-cylinder Hurricane engine was used in CJs, while Dispatchers had the 60 hp Lightning L-head four as base equipment.

JEEP — SERIES F-134/L6-226/6-230 — ALL ENGINES: Jeep Station Wagons, Pickups and Panel Trucks continued to be sold in 1964. Several models in the L6-226 series were cut, leaving only the standard wheelbase 4x2 Station Wagon, 4x4 Utility Wagon and long-wheelbase 1-ton Pickup Truck. The other model lines, as well as the styling of all models, were left unchanged. A lower (133 hp) version of the ohc six-cylinder engine was available in 6-230 models, as well as last season's 140 hp job.

FORWARD CONTROL/FLEETVAN — SERIES FC/FJ — ALL ENGINES: The Forward Control 3/4-ton and 1-ton series were carried over for 1963 with one minor "model" change. The FC-170 heavy-duty configuration, with dual rear wheels, was available in chassis-and-cab form only. Standard equipment was similar to that of 1963. Returning this season was the Jeep Fleetvan in FJ-3 and FJ-3A models. Specifically designed for light-duty, multi-stop operation, the Fleetvan was popular with the U.S. Post Office. Its backbone was the tough Jeep chassis in 4x2 configuration with four-cylinder Hurricane engine. With only 81 in. of wheelbase, the boxy little trucks could carry payloads up to 1,000 lbs. It was 64.7 in. wide and 154 in. long. The load space of 87.5 in. supported a cargo capacity of 170 cu. ft. The height of the sliding side doors (one on each side) was 70 in. for easy walk-through ability. Rear loading height was just 26-3/8 in. from the ground, with cargo area access via double rear doors. The engine was located up front and a single seat was provided for the driver. Kaiser advertised that "five Fleetvans take up less garage space than four nationally adver-tised competitive vehicles."

with a lively new ap

1964 Jeep CJ5A 1/4-Ton "Tuxedo Park" 4x4 (RCA)

WAGONEER/GLADIATOR — SERIES J — SIX-CYLINDER: Kaiser's Jeep Wagoneer for 1964 came in two- or four-door wagons and looked just like the original 1963 version. New options included the lower compression 133 hp edition of the ohc Hurricane six-cylinder engine and air conditioning. Standard drivetrain was the 140 hp six linked to a three-speed manual transmission with gearshift lever on the steering column. Optional overdrive and an automatic transmission could be ordered on 4x2 Wagoneers, while only the automatic was optional on 4x4s. A choice of suspension systems was offered on both 4x2 and 4x4 models. Independent front suspension with torsion bars and rear leaf springs was one option. The other was leaf springs all around. Other extras included deluxe trim, power-take-off, power steering, power brakes and a series of dash-mounted lights to indicate whether the Wagoneer was in 4x4 or 4x2 modes. A floor-mounted knob engaged the 4x4 system. Also carried over from 1963 were the Gladiator trucks, which shared basic styling with the Wagoneer. They came in 1/2-ton, 3/4-ton and 1-ton configurations. The 1-tons were 4x4s only, while the others were available with 4x2 or 4x4 running gear. Wheelbases of 120 or 126 in. were available in all lines. Body styles were the same as 1963.

I.D. DATA: [All] VINs located: right side of dash under hood; left side of dash under hood; left floor riser in back of driver's seat; or on left door post. Except for the J-series, early 1964 models used the 1963 numbering system, with the first five digits indicating series and model and the five digits after the dash representing the sequential number. On late-1964 and up J-Series models, the number of digits ahead of the dash was four. The four digit numbers are used in the charts below. For early 1964 models see 1963 codes. Engine numbers located on right-hand front of block.

Model	Body Type	Price	Weight	Prod. Total
CJ-3B — 1/4-Ton — 4x4 — 80 in. w.b.				
CJ-3B	Jeep Universal	2117	2132	—
CJ-5 — 1/4-Ton — 4x4 — 81 in. w.b.				
CJ-5	Jeep Universal	2211	2163	—
CJ-5A	Jeep Universal Tuxedo	2306	2163	—
CJ-6 — 1/2-Ton — 4x4 — 101 in. w.b.				
DJ-3A	Jeep Universal	1518	1709	—
DJ-3A	Jeep Hardtop	1747	2004	—
DJ-3A	Jeep Soft Top	1660	1769	—
DJ-3A	Jeep Surrey	—	1819	—
Series F-134 — 1/2-Ton — 104.5 in. w.b.				
4112	Station Wagon (4x2)	2357	2858	—
54147	Utility Wagon (4x2)	2258	2944	—
4212	Utility Wagon (4x4)	3030	3093	—
4215	Traveler (4x4)	3302	3077	—
4113	Panel Delivery (4x2)	2143	2746	—
4213	Panel Delivery (4x4)	2741	2893	—
Series F-134 — 1-Ton — 118 in. w.b.				
4307	Pickup (4x4)	2514	3065	—

556

Series L6-226 — 1/2-Ton — 104.5 in. w.b.

58167	Station Wagon (4x2)	2344	2971	—
54168	Utility Wagon (4x4)	3010	3206	—
4113	Panel Delivery (4x2)	2143	2746	—
4213	Panel Delivery (4x4)	2741	2893	—

Series L6-226 — 1-Ton — 118 in. w.b.

4307	Pickup (4x4)	2514	3065	—

Series 6-230 — 1/2-Ton — 104.5 in. w.b.

6412	Station Wagon (4x2)	2596	2858	—
6415	Utility Traveler (4x2)	2938	3240	—
6512	Utility Wagon (4x4)	3263	3307	—
6515	Utility Traveler (4x4)	3534	3410	—
6513	Panel Delivery (4x4)	2973	3028	—
6413	Panel Delivery (4x2)	2377	3147	—

Series 6-230 — 1-Ton — 4x4 — 118 in. w.b.

6606	Chassis & Cab	2619	2872	—
6607	Pickup	2744	3238	—
6608	Stake	2831	3873	—

Series FC-150 — 3/4-Ton — 4x4 — 81 in. w.b.

9209	Chassis & Cab	2735	2764	—
9209	Pickup	2853	3020	—
9209	Platform Stake	2954	3187	—

Series FC-170 — 1-Ton — 4x4 — 103.5 in. w.b.

9309	Chassis & Cab	3056	2901	—
9309	Pickup	3192	3331	—
9309	Platform Stake	3399	3564	—

Series FC-170HD — 1-Ton — 6x6 — 103.5 in. w.b.

9325	Chassis & Cab	3547	3561	—

Series FJ-3 Fleetvan — 1/2-Ton — 80 in. w.b.

62847	Step-in Delivery	2360	2900	—

Series FJ-3A Fleetvan — 1/2-Ton — 81 in. w.b.

62147	Step-in Delivery	2380	2910	—

Series J-100 — 1/2-Ton — 4x2 — 110 in. w.b.

1314	4d Wagoneer	2673	3480	—
1312	2d Wagoneer	2629	3453	—
1314C	4d Custom Wagoneer	2871	3515	—
1312C	2d Custom Wagoneer	2827	3488	—
1313	Panel Delivery	2511	3253	—

Series J-100 — 1/2-Ton — 4x4 — 110 in. w.b.

1414	4d Wagoneer	3434	3623	—
1412	2d Wagoneer	3379	3596	—
1414C	4d Custom Wagoneer	3633	3658	—
1412C	2d Custom Wagoneer	3578	3631	—
1413	Panel Delivery	3082	3396	—

Series J-200 — 1/2-Ton — 4x2 — 120 in. w.b.

2306F	Chassis & Cab	1980	2901	—
2306F	Thriftside Pickup	2081	3196	—
2306F	Townside Pickup	2108	3304	—

Series J-200 — 1/2-Ton — 4x4 — 120 in. w.b.

2406F	Chassis & Cab	2679	3061	—
2406F	Thriftside Pickup	2779	3361	—
2406F	Townside Pickup	2806	3461	—

Series J-210 — 1/2-Ton — 4x2 — 120 in. w.b.

2306A	Chassis & Cab	2046	2941	—
2306A	Thriftside Pickup	2147	3236	—
2306A	Townside Pickup	2173	3344	—

Series J-210 — 1/2-Ton — 4x4 — 120 in. w.b.

2406A	Chassis & Cab	2738	3096	—
2406A	Thriftside Pickup	2839	3396	—
2406A	Townside Pickup	2866	3496	—

Series J-300 — 1/2-Ton — 4x2 — 126 in. w.b.

3306E	Chassis & Cab	2087	2943	—
3306E	Thriftside Pickup	2202	3263	—
3306E	Townside Pickup	2229	3371	—

Series J-300 — 1/2-Ton — 4x4 — 126 in. w.b.

3406E	Chassis & Cab	2739	3091	—
3406E	Thriftside Pickup	2854	3441	—
3406E	Townside Pickup	2881	3541	—

Series J-220 — 3/4-Ton — 4x2 — 120 in. w.b.

2306B	Chassis & Cab	2132	3024	—
2306B	Thriftside Pickup	2233	3319	—
2306B	Townside Pickup	2260	3427	—
2306B	Platform Stake	2439	3680	—

Series J-220 — 3/4-Ton — 4x4 — 120 in. w.b.

2406B	Chassis & Cab	2841	3214	—
2406B	Thriftside Pickup	2942	3514	—
2406B	Townside Pickup	2969	3614	—
2406B	Platform Stake	3148	3894	—

Series J-310 — 3/4-Ton — 4x2 — 126 in. w.b.

3306B	Chassis & Cab	2201	3067	—
3306B	Thriftside Pickup	2316	3387	—
3306B	Townside Pickup	2343	3495	—
3306B	Platform Stake	2541	3771	—

Series J-310 — 3/4-Ton — 4x4 — 126 in. w.b.

3406B	Chassis & Cab	2860	3239	—
3406B	Thriftside Pickup	2975	3589	—
3406B	Townside Pickup	3002	3689	—
3406B	Platform Stake	3200	3979	—

Series J-320 — 3/4-Ton — 4x2 — 126 in. w.b.

3306C	Chassis & Cab	2359	3168	—
3306C	Thriftside Pickup	2474	3488	—
3306C	Townside Pickup	2501	3596	—
3306C	Platform Stake	2699	3872	—

Series J-320 — 3/4-Ton — 4x4 — 126 in. w.b.

3406C	Chassis & Cab	3024	3377	—
3406C	Thriftside Pickup	3139	3727	—
3406C	Townside Pickup	3166	3827	—
3406C	Platform Stake	3364	4117	—

Series J-230 — 1-Ton — 4x4 — 120 in. w.b.

2406D	Chassis & Cab	3687	3874	—
2406D	Platform Stake	4079	4714	—

Series J-330 — 1-Ton — 4x4 — 126 in. w.b.

3406D	Chassis & Cab	3706	3899	—
3406D	Platform Stake	4120	4790	—

NOTE 1: Explanation of "J" series model number suffixes: A=5,600 lb. GVW; B=6,600 lb. GVW; C=7,600 lb. GVW; D=8,600 lb. GVW, E=5,000 lb. GVW; F=4,000 lb. GVW.

1964 Jeep J-100 Two-Door Wagoneer 4x4 (KJC)

ENGINE [CJ-3B/CJ-6/F-134]: Inline. F-head. Four-cylinder. Cast iron block. Bore & stroke: 3-1/8 in. x 4-3/8 in. Displacement: 134.2 cid. Compression ratio: 6.9:1. Brake hp: 72 at 4000 rpm. Net hp: 15.63. Torque: 114 lbs.-ft. at 2000 rpm. Solid valve lifters. Carburetor: Carter.

ENGINE [CJ-5/FC-150/FJ-3(A)]: Inline. F-head. Four-cylinder. Cast iron block. Bore & stroke: 3-1/8 in. x 4-3/8 in. Displacement: 134.2 cid. Compression ratio: 7.4:1. Brake hp: 75 at 4000 rpm. Net hp: 15.63. Torque: 114 lbs.-ft. at 2000 rpm. Solid valve lifters. Carburetor: Carter.

ENGINE [DJ-3A]: Inline. L-head. Four-cylinder. Cast iron block. Bore & stroke: 3-1/8 in. x 4-3/8 in. Displacement: 134.2 cid. Compression ratio: 7.00:1. Brake hp: 60 at 4000 rpm. Net hp: 15.63. Torque: 114 lbs.-ft. at 2000 rpm. Solid valve lifters. Carburetor: Carter.

ENGINE [L6-226/FC-170]: Inline. L-head. Six-cylinder. Cast iron block. Bore & stroke: 3-5/16 in. x 4-3/8 in. Displacement: 226.2 cid. Compression ratio: 6.86:1 (7.3:1 optional). Brake hp: 105 at 3600 rpm. Net hp: 26.3. Torque: 190 lbs.-ft. at 1400 rpm. Solid valve lifters. Carburetor: Carter.

ENGINE [6-230/J-Series]: Overhead Cam. Inline. Six-cylinder. Cast iron block. Bore & stroke: 3.34 in. x 4.38 in. Displacement: 230 cid. Compression ratio: 8.5:1. Brake hp: 140 at 4000 rpm. Net hp: 26.77. Torque: 210 lbs.-ft. at 1750 rpm. Solid valve lifters. Carburetor: Carter model two-barrel.

ENGINE [6-230/J-Series Economy Option]: Inline. Overhead camshaft. Six-cylinder. Cast iron block. Bore & stroke: 3.344 in. x 4.375 in. Displacement: 230.5 cid. Compression ratio: 7.5:1. Brake hp: 133 at 4000 rpm. Net hp: 26.77. Torque: 199 lbs.-ft. at 2400 rpm. Solid valve lifters. Carburetor: Carter model two-barrel.

1964 Jeep J-100 Two-Door Wagoneer 4x4 (KJC)

CHASSIS: For wheelbase see chart above. Overall length: [CJ-3B] 129.9 in.; [CJ-5] 135.5. in.; [CJ-6] 155.5 in.; [DJ-3A] 125.4 in.; [F-134/L6-226/6-230] 1/2-ton 176.2 in.; 1-ton 183.7 in.; [FC-150] 147.3 in.; [FC-170] 181.4 in.; [J-100] 183.66 in.; [Fleetvan] 154 in. Front tread: [CJ-3B] 48.4 in.; [CJ-5] 48.4 in.; [CJ-6] 48.4 in.; [DJ-3A] 48.2 in.; [F-134, L6-226, 6-230] 1/2-Ton: 57 in.; 1-Ton: 57 in.; [FC-150] 57 in.; [FC-170] 63.4 in.; [J-100] 57 in.; [Fleetvan] 48-9/15 in. Rear tread: [CJ-3B] 48.4 in.; [CJ-5] 48.4 in.; [CJ-6] 48.4 in.; [DJ-3A] 48.5 in.; [F-134/L6-226/6-230] 1/2-Ton: 57 in.; 1-Ton: 63.5 in.; [FC-150] 57 in.; [FC-170] 63.8 in.; [J-100] 57 in.; [Fleetvan] 48-9/16 in. Tires: [CJ-all models] 6.00 x 16 in.; [DJ-3A] 6.50 x 15 in.; [Fleetvan] 6.70 x 15; [F-134/L6-226/6-230] 1/2-Ton 4x2: 6.70 x 15 in.; 1/2-Ton 4x4: 7.00 x 15 in;

1-Ton 7.00 x 16 in.; [FC-150] 7.00 x 15 in.; [FC-170] 7.00 x 16 in.; [J-100, J-200] 6.70 x 15 in.; [J-210] 7.60 x 15 in.; [J-300] 7.10 x 15 in.; [J-320] 7.50 x 16 in.; [Other J-Series models] 7.00 x 16 in.

TECHNICAL: Synchromesh transmission. Speeds: 3F/1R. Floor-mounted gearshift lever. Single-plate dry-disc clutch. Semi-floating rear axle. Four-wheel hydraulic brakes. Steel disc wheels. 4x2 models have I-beam front axle. 4x4 models have hypoid, semi-floating front axle and two-speed transfer case with ratios of 1.00:1 and 2.46:1.

OPTIONS: [CJ/DJ] Convertible top; all-weather canvas top; fiberglass cab top; metal cab top. Four-speed transmission ($194). [All models] Air conditioning. Power steering ($81). Overdrive ($126). Four-speed transmission ($109). Rearview mirror. Radio. Antenna package. Ramsey or Koenig winches for front, rear or bed mount. Warn or Cutlas selective drive hubs. Canfield wrecker for Universals, 4x4 pickup or Forward Control models. Meyer angle dozers. Jeep-A-Trench. Tailgate loader for 600 lb. or 1,000 lb. rated models. Deluxe cab on Forward Control models. Fresh air heater. Tu-tone paint. Front bumper guards. Directional signals. E-Z-Eye glass. Windshield washer. FC-150 front air vent. FC-150 double passenger seat. Oil bath air cleaner. Oil filter. High-altitude cylinder head (no charge). Powr-Lok rear differential. Heavy-duty rear axle. Heavy-duty springs and shock absorbers. Transmission brake. Hot-Climate radiator. Variable and constant-speed governors. Various size and type tires including whitewalls in available sizes. Draw-Bar. Stabilizer bar. Rear bumperettes. Automatic transmission in Travelalls and Gladiators. Full wheel discs.

HISTORICAL: Introduced: Fall 1963. Calendar year registrations: [Universals] 11,915; [Trucks] 59,180. Calendar year production: 120,830 (including 58,755 four-cylinders and 62,075 six-cylinders). Innovations: Tuxedo Park IV introduced as a sporty version of the Jeep Universal. Kaiser-Jeep Corp. received an $81 million Army contract for production of trucks and purchased Studebaker's Chippewa plant in South Bend, Ind. Sales again set new records, with $255,582,000 registered for model year 1964. Sales of Jeep approved accessories also increased. The number of U.S. dealers leaped by 15 percent.

1964 Jeep J-100 Four-Door Wagoneer 4x2 (KJC)

1965 JEEP

UNIVERSAL/DISPATCHER — SERIES CJ/DJ — FOUR-CYLINDER: The name "Kaiser Jeep" was added to the front sides of the hood or fenders of all models this year. On CJ/DJ models, it was accompanied by Jeep lettering on the side of the cowl. A new model for 1965 was the DJ-5, which had a lower grille and hood line. Its distinctive, five-slot grille corresponded with the "DJ-5" designation for easy identification. It was a Dispatcher 4x2 type vehicle used primarily for light-duty courier service, mostly by the U.S. Post Office. A unique accessory was a strangely twisted convex rearview mirror mounted to the left-hand front fender near the front corner of the hood. It had a modified suspension system and, often, came with right-hand drive. There was also a full-cab enclosure with sliding side doors and a rear door. A single bucket seat was provided for the operator. Accompanying the new 81 in. wheelbase DJ-5 was a 101 inch wheelbase DJ-6. All other 1964 models in this dual series were carried over, with the exceptions of the DJ-3 soft top and surrey. The Tuxedo Park models featured exclusive all-white finish, special rolled-and-pleated upholstery and chrome ornamentation.

1965 Jeep CJ-5 1/4-Ton Universal 4x4 (OCW)

JEEP — SERIES F-134/6-230 — ALL ENGINES: The utility type Jeep Station Wagons, Panels and Pickups also carried "Kaiser Jeep" badges this season. The L6-226 models disappeared and the L-head six-cylinder engine was now used only for the FC-170 trucks. This was the final appearance of the F-134 line.

FORWARD CONTROL — SERIES FC — ALL ENGINES: There was no Fleetvan series for 1965, but the Forward Control models remained available in 3/4-ton (FC-150) and 1-ton (FC-170) configurations. They were very little changed, except for the addition of Kaiser-Jeep identification nameplates.

WAGONEER/GLADIATOR — SERIES J — SIX-CYLINDER: Kaiser-Jeep nameplates replaced the Jeep name on the front fendersides of the 1965 Wagoneers and Gladiators. There were actually two separate series of Gladiators this year. The first was comprised of the J-200, J-210, J-300, J-220, J-310, J-320, J-230 and J-330 lines, all of which were car-

ried over from 1964 with no changes in prices, weights or other specifications. For data on these trucks, please refer to the 1964 listings for the same models. The second series of Gladiators was comprised of the J-2500, J-2600, J-3500, J-3600, J-2700, J-3700, J-2800 and J-3800 lines. These trucks had the same general styling as the early Gladiators and used the same 230 cid ohc six-cylinder engine as standard equipment. A new option was a 327 cid V-8. The GVW ratings for the later series were also slightly higher, in most cases, than the comparable models in the original Gladiator series.

I.D. DATA: Serial number located in the same locations. The new Gladiators used model numbers identical to those for the "old" Gladiators, except for the alphabetical suffix. Codes for other models were the same as 1964. Engine numbers located in the same places.

1965 Jeep J-3000 Gladiator Townside Pickup (RCA)

Model	Body Type	Price	Weight	Prod. Total
CJ-3B — 1/4-Ton -4x4 — 80 in. w.b.				
8105	Jeep Universal	2117	2132	—
CJ-5 — 1/4-Ton — 4x4 — 81 in. w.b.				
8305	Jeep Universal	2211	2163	—
8322	Tuxedo Park	2306	2163	—
CJ-6 — 1/2-Ton — 4x4 — 101 in. w.b.				
8405	Jeep Universal	2306	2225	—
8422	Tuxedo Park	2401	2225	—
DJ-3(A) — 1/2-Ton — 4x2 — 101 in. w.b.				
8201	Soft Top	1518	1709	—
8203	HardTop	1747	2004	—
8505	Special	1744	1823	—
DJ-6 — 1/4-Ton — 4x2 — 81 in. w.b.				
8505	Soft Top	1818	1823	—
Series F-134 — 1/2-Ton — 104.5 in. w.b.				
4112	Station Wagon (4x2)	2357	2858	—
4212	Utility Wagon (4x4)	3030	3093	—
4215	Traveler (4x4)	3302	3077	—
4113	Panel Delivery (4x2)	2143	2746	—
4213	Panel Delivery (4x4)	2741	2893	—
Series F-134 — 1-Ton — 118 in. w.b.				
4307	Pickup (4x4)	2514	3065	—
Series 6-230 — 1/2-Ton — 104.5 in. w.b.				
6412	Station Wagon (4x2)	2596	3047	—
6512	Utility Wagon (4x4)	3263	3307	—
6513	Panel Delivery (4x4)	2973	3028	—
6413	Panel Delivery (4x2)	2377	3147	—
Series 6-230 — 1-Ton — 4x4 — 118 in. w.b.				
6606	Chassis & Cab	2619	2872	—
6607	Pickup	2744	3238	—
6608	Stake	2831	3373	—
Series FC-150 — 3/4-Ton — 4x4 — 81 in. w.b.				
9209	Chassis & Cab	2735	2764	—
9209	Pickup	2853	3020	—
9209	Platform Stake	2954	3187	—
Series FC-170 — 1-Ton — 4x4 — 103.5 in. w.b.				
9309	Chassis & Cab	3056	2901	—
9309	Pickup	3192	3331	—
9309	Platform Stake	3399	3564	—
Series FC-170HD — 1-Ton — 6x6 — 103.5 in. w.b.				
9325	Chassis & Cab	3547	3561	
Series J-100 — 1/2-Ton — 4x2 — 110 in. w.b.				
1314	4d Wagoneer	2701	3480	—
1312	2d Wagoneer	2658	3453	—
1314C	4d Custom Wagoneer	2896	3515	—
1312C	2d Custom Wagoneer	2853	3488	—
1313	Panel Delivery	2511	3253	—
Series J-100 — 1/2-Ton — 4x4 — 110 in. w.b.				
1414	4d Wagoneer	3449	3623	—
1412	2d Wagoneer	3395	3596	—
1414C	4d Custom Wagoneer	3644	3658	—
1412C	2d Custom Wagoneer	3590	3631	—
1413	Panel Delivery	3082	3396	—
Series J-2500 — 1/2-Ton — 4x2 — 120 in. w.b.				
2306W	Chassis & Cab	2149	2919	—
2306W	Thriftside Pickup	2250	3214	—
2306W	Townside Pickup	2277	3322	—

558

Series J-2500 — 1/2-Ton — 4x4 — 120 in. w.b.

2406W	Chassis & Cab	2802	3128	—
2406W	Thriftside Pickup	2903	3423	—
2406W	Townside Pickup	2930	3531	—

Series J-2600 — 1/2-Ton — 4x2 — 120 in. w.b.

2306X	Chassis & Cab	2263	3060	—
2306X	Thriftside Pickup	2364	3355	—
2306X	Townside Pickup	2390	3463	—

Series J-2600 — 1/2-Ton — 4x4 — 120 in. w.b.

2406X	Chassis & Cab	2923	3269	—
2406X	Thriftside Pickup	3024	3564	—
2406X	Townside Pickup	3050	3672	—

Series J-3500 — 1/2-Ton — 4x2 — 126 in. w.b.

3306W	Chassis & Cab	2168	2943	—
3306W	Thriftside Pickup	2282	3263	—
3306W	Townside Pickup	2309	3371	—

Series J-3500 — 1/2-Ton — 4x4 — 126 in. w.b.

3406W	Chassis & Cab	2821	3152	—
3406W	Thriftside Pickup	2935	3472	—
3406W	Townside Pickup	2962	3580	—

Series J-3600 — 1/2-Ton — 4x2 — 126 in. w.b.

3306X	Chassis & Cab	2282	3081	—
3306X	Thriftside Pickup	2396	3401	—
3306X	Townside Pickup	2423	3509	—
3306X	Platform Stake	2620	3785	—

Series J-3600 — 1/2-Ton — 4x4 — 126 in. w.b.

3406X	Chassis & Cab	2942	3081	—
3406X	Thriftside Pickup	3056	3401	—
3406X	Townside Pickup	3083	3509	—
3406X	Platform Stake	3280	3785	—

Series J-2700 — 3/4-Ton — 4x2 — 120 in. w.b.

2306Y	Chassis & Cab	2422	3147	—
2306Y	Thriftside Pickup	2523	3442	—
2306Y	Townside Pickup	2549	3550	—
2306Y	Platform Stake	2748	3803	—

Series J-2700 — 3/4-Ton — 4x4 — 120 in. w.b.

2406Y	Chassis & Cab	3087	3356	—
2406Y	Thriftside Pickup	3188	3651	—
2406Y	Townside Pickup	3215	3759	—
2406Y	Platform Stake	3393	4012	—

Series J-3700 — 3/4-Ton — 4x2 — 126 in. w.b.

3306Y	Chassis & Cab	2441	3168	—
3306Y	Thriftside Pickup	2555	3488	—
3306Y	Townside Pickup	2582	3596	—
3306Y	Platform Stake	2779	3872	—

Series J-3700 — 3/4-Ton — 4x4 — 126 in. w.b.

3406Y	Chassis & Cab	3106	3377	—
3406Y	Thriftside Pickup	3220	3697	—
3406Y	Townside Pickup	3247	3805	—
3406Y	Platform Stake	3444	4081	—

Series J-2800 — 1-Ton — 4x4 — 120 in. w.b.

2406Z	Chassis & Cab	3770	3789	—
2406Z	Platform Stake	4163	4534	—

Series J-3800 — 1-Ton — 4x4 — 126 in. w.b.

3406Z	Chassis & Cab	3788	3822	—
3406Z	Platform Stake	4203	4620	—

NOTE 1: Explanation of "J" series model number suffix: W=5,000 lb. GVW; X=6,000 lb. GVW; Y=7000 lb. GVW; Z=8,600 lb. GVW.

ENGINE [CJs/FC-150/FJ-3(A)]: Inline. F-head. Four-cylinder. Cast iron block. Bore & stroke: 3-1/8 in. x 4-3/8 in. Displacement: 134.2 cid. Compression ratio: 7.4:1. Brake hp 75 at 4000 rpm. Net hp: 15.63. Torque: 114 lbs.-ft. at 2000 rpm. Solid valve lifters. Carburetor: Carter.

ENGINE [DJ-3A]: Inline. L-head. Four-cylinder. Cast iron block. Bore & stroke: 3-1/8 in. x 4-3/8 in. Displacement: 134.2 cid. Compression ratio: 7.00:1. Brake hp 60 at 4000 rpm. Net hp: 15.63. Torque: 114 lbs.-ft. at 2000 rpm. Solid valve lifters. Carburetor: Carter.

ENGINE [FC-170]: Inline. L-head. Six-cylinder. Cast iron block. Bore & stroke: 3-5/16 in. x 4-3/8 in. Displacement: 226.2 cid. Compression ratio: 6.86:1 (7.3:1 optional). Brake hp: 105 at 3600 rpm. Net hp: 26.3. Torque: 190 lbs.-ft. at 1,400 rpm. Solid valve lifters. Carburetor: Carter.

ENGINE [6-230/J-Series]: Overhead Cam. Inline. Six-cylinder. Cast iron block. Bore & stroke: 3.34 in. x 4.38 in. Displacement: 230 cid. Compression ratio: 8.5:1. Brake hp: 140 at 4000 rpm. Net hp: 26.77. Torque: 210 lbs.-ft. at 1,750 rpm. Carburetor: Carter model two-barrel.

ENGINE [6-230/J-Series Economy Option]: Inline. Overhead camshaft. Six-cylinder. Cast iron block. Bore & stroke: 3.344 in. x 4.375 in. Displacement: 230.5 cid. Compression ratio: 7.5:1. Brake hp: 133 at 4000 rpm. Net hp: 26.77. Torque: 199 lbs.-ft. at 2400 rpm. Solid valve lifters. Carburetor: Carter model two-barrel.

ENGINE [Optional]: Ohv. Vee-block. Eight-cylinder. Cast iron block. Bore & stroke: 4.00 in. x 3.25 in. Displacement: 327 cid. Brake hp: 250 at 4700 rpm. Net hp: 51.2. Torque: 340 lbs.-ft. at 2600 rpm. Hydraulic valve lifters. Carburetor: Carter.

1965 Jeep J-100 Four-Door Wagoneer (KJC)

1965 Jeep J-100 Four-Door Super Wagoneer (KJC)

CHASSIS: For wheelbase see chart above. Overall length: [CJ-3B] 129.9 in.; [CJ-5] 135.5 in.; [CJ-6] 155.5 in.; [DJ-3A] 125.4 in.; [F-134/L6-226/6-230] 1/2-ton 176.2 in.; 1-ton 183.7 in.; [FC-150] 147.3 in.; [FC-170] 181.4 in.; [J-100] 183.66 in.; [Fleetvan] 154 in. Front tread: [CJ-3B] 48.4 in.; [CJ-5] 48.4 in.; [CJ-6] 48.4 in.; [DJ-3A] 48.2 in.; [F-134, L6-226, 6-230] 1/2-Ton: 57 in.; 1-Ton: 57 in.; [FC-150] 57 in.; [FC-170] 63.4 in.; [J-100] 57 in.; [Fleetvan] 48-9/15 in. Rear tread: [CJ-3B] 48.4 in.; [CJ-5] 48.4 in.; [CJ-6] 48.4 in.; [DJ-3A] 48.5 in.; [F-134/L6-226/6-230] 1/2-Ton: 57 in.; 1-Ton: 63.5 in.; [FC-150] 57 in.; [FC-170] 63.8 in.; [J-100] 57 in.; [Fleetvan] 48-9/16 in. Tires: [CJ-all models] 6.00 x 16 in.; [DJ-3A] 6.50 x 15 in.; [Fleetvan] 6.70 x 15; [F-134/L6-226/6-230] 1/2-Ton 4x2: 6.70 x 15 in.; 1/2-Ton 4x4: 7.00 x 15 in; 1-Ton 7.00 x 16 in.; [FC-150] 7.00 x 15 in.; [FC-170] 7.00 x 16 in.; [J-100, J-200] 6.70 x 15 in.; [J-210] 7.60 x 15 in.; [J-300] 7.10 x 15 in.; [J-320] 7.50 x 16 in.; [Other J-Series models] 7.00 x 16 in.

TECHNICAL: Synchromesh transmission. Speeds: 3F/1R. Floor-mounted gearshift lever. Single-plate dry-disc clutch. Semi-floating rear axle. Four-wheel hydraulic brakes. Steel disc wheels. 4x2 models have I-beam front axle. 4x4 models have hypoid, semi-floating front axle and two-speed transfer case with ratios of 1.00:1 and 2.46:1.

OPTIONS: [CJ/DJ] Convertible top; all-weather canvas top; fiberglass cab top; metal cab top. Four-speed transmission ($194). [All models] Air conditioning. Power steering ($81). Overdrive ($126). Four-speed transmission ($109). Rearview mirror. Radio. Antenna package. Ramsey or Koenig winches for front, rear or bed mount. Warn or Cutlas selective drive hubs. Canfield wrecker for Universals, 4x4 pickup or Forward Control models. Meyer angle dozers. Jeep-A-Trench. Tailgate loader for 600 lb. or 1,000 lb. rated models. Deluxe cab on Forward Control models. Fresh air heater. Tu-tone paint. Front bumper guards. Directional signals. E-Z-Eye glass. Windshield washer. FC-150 front air vent. FC-150 double passenger seat. Oil bath air cleaner. Oil filter. High-altitude cylinder head (no charge). Powr-Lok rear differential. Heavy-duty rear axle. Heavy-duty springs and shock absorbers. Transmission brake. Hot-Climate radiator. Variable and constant-speed governors. Various size and type tires including whitewalls in available sizes. Draw-bar. Stabilizer bar. Rear bumperettes. Automatic transmission in Travelalls and Gladiators. Full wheel discs.

HISTORICAL: Introduced: Fall, 1964. Calendar year production: 108,601 (This included 40,846 fours, 50,578 sixes and 17,167 V-8s. Factory shipments totaled 87,900 vehicles 6,000 lbs. and under and 5,800 vehicles 6,001 to 10,000 lbs. Innovations: Fleetvan introduced. A new M606 Jeep would be produced for foreign markets under foreign aid programs. Eight-cylinder (V-8) engine introduced. Jeep sales to the U.S. Government hit record levels, thanks to the Fleetvan postal trucks.

1966 JEEP

UNIVERSAL/DISPATCHER — SERIES CJ/DJ — FOUR-CYLINDER: As usual, the 1966 Jeeps looked like last year's models. There were no changes in the lineup of CJ 4x4s and DJ 4x2s and the basic specifications were familiar. In the options department, a V-6 was made available for the CJ-5/CJ-6/CJ-5A/CJ-6A/DJ-5/DJ-6. The four-cylinder base engines were carried over as standard equipment with the 75 hp version used in all models except the DJ-3A, which used the 60 hp edition. Dropped from production this season were the

Jeep wagons and trucks of the early postwar style in the F-134 and 6-230 series. This completed the phaseout of these old-fashioned looking models which always seemed to be part truck/part passenger car.

1966 Jeep CJ-5 1/4-Ton Universal 4x4 (OCW)

FORWARD CONTROL — SERIES FC — ALL ENGINES: Now in their last season, the cute-looking Jeep Forward Control models were unchanged in appearance, features or models. The 3/4-ton FC-150 continued to be powered by the F-head four-cylinder Hurricane engine, while the 1-ton FC-170 relied on the L-head six-cylinder Lightning engine.
WAGONEER/GLADIATOR — SERIES J — SIX-CYLINDER: Two faces were again seen on Jeep Wagons. Two-door models shared the Gladiator look with tall vertical bars in the center only. Four-door Wagoneers had a full-across grille more car-like than truck-like. It had an "electric shaver" appearance with veed vertical bars. The bodysides were slightly more sculptured. The center bulge hood ended with a dummy air scoop. A new model called the Super Wagoneer came standard with four-wheel drive, larger tires and V-8 engine. New contrasting side spears, vinyl roofs, mag wheels and roof carriers were optional. Gladiator trucks did not adopt the new frontal treatment and looked much the same as they did when introduced in 1963.

1966 Jeep CJ-5 1/4-Ton Universal 4x4 (OCW)

I.D. DATA: Serial number located on left front door hinge pillar post and left firewall. The VIN consists of from nine to 11 symbols. The first five symbols indicate series and body style. The last five or six are sequential production numbers. Engine numbers located on right-hand front of block.

1966 Jeep CJ-5 1/4-Ton Universal Hardtop 4x4 (OCW)

Model	Body Type	Price	Weight	Prod. Total
CJ-3B — 1/4-Ton — 4x4 — 80 in. w.b.				
8105	Jeep Universal	2190	2132	—
CJ-5 — 1/4-Ton — 4x4 — 81 in. w.b.				
8305	Jeep Universal	2284	2163	—
CJ-5A — 1/4-Ton — 4x4 — 81 in. w.b.				
8322	Tuxedo Park	2379	2163	—
CJ-6 — 4x4 — 101 in. w.b.				
8405	Jeep Universal	2379	2225	—
CJ-6A — 1/2-Ton — 4x4 — 101 in. w.b.				
8422	Tuxedo Park	2475	2225	—
DJ-5 — 1/4-Ton — 4x2 — 81 in. w.b.				
8505	Dispatcher	1744	1823	—
DJ-6 — 1/2-Ton — 4x2 — 101 in. w.b.				
8201	Soft Top	1519	1709	—
8203	Hardtop	1748	2004	—
Series FC-150 — 3/4-Ton — 4x4 — 81 in. w.b.				
9209	Chassis & Cab	2735	2896	—
9209	Pickup	2853	3152	—
9209	Platform Stake	2954	3319	—
Series FC-170 — 1-Ton — 4x4 — 103.5 in. w.b.				
9309	Chassis & Cab	3056	2901	—
9309	Pickup	3192	3331	—
9309	Platform Stake	3399	3564	—
Series FC-170HD — 1-Ton — 6x6 — 103.5 in. w.b.				
9325	Chassis & Cab	3547	3561	—
Series J-100 — 1/2-Ton — 4x2 — 110 in. w.b.				
1314	4d Wagoneer	2838	3480	—
1312	2d Wagoneer	2794	3453	—
1314C	4d Custom Wagoneer	3033	3515	—
1312C	2d Custom Wagoneer	2989	3488	—
1313	Panel Delivery	2650	3253	—
Series J-100 — 1/2-Ton — 4x4 — 110 in. w.b.				
1414	4d Wagoneer	3585	3623	—
1412	2d Wagoneer	3531	3596	—
1414C	4d Custom Wagoneer	3780	3658	—
1412C	2d Custom Wagoneer	3726	3631	—
1413	Panel Delivery	3223	3396	—
1414D	4d Super Wagoneer	5943	4241	—
Series J-2500 — 1/2-Ton — 4x2 — 120 in. w.b.				
2306W	Chassis & Cab	2207	2919	—
2306W	Thriftside Pickup	2308	3214	—
2306W	Townside Pickup	2335	3322	—
Series J-2500 — 1/2-Ton — 4x4 — 120 in. w.b.				
2406W	Chassis & Cab	2861	3128	—
2406W	Thriftside Pickup	2961	3423	—
2406W	Townside Pickup	2988	3531	—
Series J-2600 — 1/2-Ton — 4x2 — 120 in. w.b.				
2306X	Chassis & Cab	2321	3060	—
2306X	Thriftside Pickup	2421	3355	—
2306X	Townside Pickup	2448	3463	—
2306X	Platform Stake	2626	3716	—
Series J-2600 — 1/2-Ton — 4x4 — 120 in. w.b.				
2406X	Chassis & Cab	2981	3269	—
2406X	Thriftside Pickup	3082	3564	—
2406X	Townside Pickup	3109	3672	—
2406X	Platform Stake	3287	3925	—
Series J-3500 — 1/2-Ton — 4x2 — 126 in. w.b.				
3306W	Chassis & Cab	2226	2943	—
3306W	Thriftside Pickup	2340	3263	—
3306W	Townside Pickup	2367	3371	—
Series J-3500 — 1/2-Ton — 4x4 — 126 in. w.b.				
3406W	Chassis & Cab	2879	3152	—
3406W	Thriftside Pickup	2994	3472	—
3406W	Townside Pickup	3021	3580	—
Series J-3600 — 1/2-Ton — 4x2 — 126 in. w.b.				
3306X	Chassis & Cab	2340	3081	—
3306X	Thriftside Pickup	2454	3401	—
3306X	Townside Pickup	2481	3509	—
3306X	Platform Stake	2678	3785	—
Series J-3600 — 1/2-Ton — 4x4 — 126 in. w.b.				
3406X	Chassis & Cab	3000	3290	—
3406X	Thriftside Pickup	3114	3610	—
3406X	Townside Pickup	3141	3718	—
3406X	Platform Stake	3338	3994	—
Series J-2700 — 3/4-Ton — 4x2 — 120 in. w.b.				
2306Y	Chassis & Cab	2480	3147	—
2306Y	Thriftside Pickup	2580	3442	—
2306Y	Townside Pickup	2607	3550	—
2306Y	Platform Stake	2785	3803	—
Series J-2700 — 3/4-Ton — 4x4 — 120 in. w.b.				
2406Y	Chassis & Cab	3146	3356	—
2406Y	Thriftside Pickup	3246	3651	—
2406Y	Townside Pickup	3273	3759	—
2406Y	Platform Stake	3451	4012	—

Series J-3700 — 3/4-Ton — 4x2 — 126 in. w.b.

3306Y	Chassis & Cab	2498	3168	—
3306Y	Thriftside Pickup	2613	3488	—
3306Y	Townside Pickup	2640	3596	—
3306Y	Platform Stake	2837	3872	—

Series J-3700 — 3/4-Ton — 4x4 — 126 in. w.b.

3406Y	Chassis & Cab	3164	3377	—
3406Y	Thriftside Pickup	3279	3697	—
3406Y	Townside Pickup	3305	3805	—
3406Y	Platform Stake	3502	4081	—

Series J-2800 — 1-Ton — 4x4 — 120 in. w.b.

2406Z	Chassis & Cab	3831	3789	—
2406Z	Platform Stake	4223	4534	—

Series J-3800 — 1-Ton — 4x4 — 126 in. w.b.

3406Z	Chassis & Cab	3849	3822	—
3406Z	Platform Stake	4264	4620	—

1966 Jeep J-100 Four-Door Super Wagoneer (KJC)

ENGINE [CJs/DJ-6/FC-150/FJ-3(A)]: Inline. F-head. Four-cylinder. Cast iron block. Bore & stroke: 3-1/8 in. x 4-3/8 in. Displacement: 134.2 cid. Compression ratio: 7.4:1. Brake hp: 75 at 4000 rpm. Net hp: 15.63. Torque: 114 lbs.-ft. at 2000 rpm. Solid valve lifters. Carburetor: Carter.

ENGINE [DJ-3A]: Inline. L-head. Four-cylinder. Cast iron block. Bore & stroke: 3-1/8 in. x 4-3/8 in. Displacement: 134.2 cid. Compression ratio: 7.00:1. Brake hp: 60 at 4000 rpm. Net hp: 15.63. Torque: 114 lbs.-ft. at 2000 rpm. Solid valve lifters. Carburetor: Carter.

ENGINE [Optional CJ/DJ/Commando]: Vee-block. Overhead valve. Six-cylinder. Bore & stroke: 3.75 in. x 3.40 in. Displacement: 225 cid. Compression ratio: 9.0:1. Brake hp: 155 at 4400 rpm. Net hp: 33.75. Torque: 225 lbs.-ft. at 2400 rpm. Four main bearings. Hydraulic valve lifters. Carburetor: Carter model two-barrel.

ENGINE [FC-170]: Inline. L-head. Six-cylinder. Cast iron block. Bore & stroke: 3-5/16 in. x 4-3/8 in. Displacement: 226.2 cid. Compression ratio: 6.86:1 (7.3:1 optional). Brake hp: 105 at 3600 rpm. Net hp: 26.3. Torque: 190 lbs.-ft. at 1400 rpm. Solid valve lifters. Carburetor: Carter.

ENGINE [J-Series]: Overhead Cam. Inline. Six-cylinder. Cast iron block. Bore & stroke: 3.34 in. x 4.38 in. Displacement: 230 cid. Compression ratio: 8.5:1. Brake hp: 140 at 4000 rpm. Net hp: 26.77. Torque: 210 lbs.-ft. at 1750 rpm. Solid valve lifters. Carburetor: Carter model two-barrel.

ENGINE [J-Series Economy Option]: Inline. Overhead camshaft. Six-cylinder. Cast iron block. Bore & stroke: 3.344 in. x 4.375 in. Displacement: 230.5 cid. Compression ratio: 7.5:1. Brake hp: 133 at 4000 rpm. Net hp: 26.77. Torque: 199 lbs.-ft. at 2400 rpm. Solid valve lifters. Carburetor: Carter model two-barrel.

ENGINE [Super Wagoneer]: OHV. Vee-block. Eight-cylinder. Cast iron block. Bore & stroke: 4.00 in. x 3.25 in. Displacement: 327 cid. Brake hp: 250 at 4700 rpm. Net hp: 51.2. Torque: 340 lbs.-ft. at 2600 rpm. Hydraulic valve lifters. Carburetor: Carter. (Optional in other J-Series trucks.)

1966 Jeep J-100 Four-Door Super Wagoneer (JAG)

Standard Catalog of Light-Duty Trucks

CHASSIS: For wheelbase see chart above. Overall length: [CJ-3B] 129.9 in.; [CJ-5] 135.5. in.; [CJ-6] 155.5 in.; [DJ-3A] 125.4 in.; [FC-150] 147.3 in.; [FC-170] 181.4 in.; [J-100] 183.66 in.; [Fleetvan] 154 in. Front tread: [CJ-3B] 48.4 in.; [CJ-5] 48.4 in.; [CJ-6] 48.4 in.; [DJ-3A] 48.2 in.; [F-134, L6-226, 6-230] 1/2-Ton: 57 in.; 1-Ton: 57 in.; [FC-150] 57 in.; [FC-170] 63.4 in.; [J-100] 57 in.; [Fleetvan] 48-9/16 in. Rear tread: [CJ-3B] 48.4 in.; [CJ-5] 48.4 in.; [CJ-6] 48.4 in.; [DJ-3A] 48.5 in.; [FC-150] 57 in.; [FC-170] 63.8 in.; [J-100] 57 in.; [Fleetvan] 48-9/16 in. Tires: [CJ-all models] 6.00 x 16 in.; [DJ-3A] 6.50 x 15 in.; [Fleetvan] 6.70 x 15; [FC-150] 7.00 x 15 in.; [FC-170] 7.00 x 16 in.; [J-100, J-200] 6.70 x 15 in.; [J-210] 7.60 x 15 in.; [J-300] 7.10 x 15 in.; [J-320] 7.50 x 16 in.; [Other J-Series models] 7.00 x 16 in.

1966 Kaiser-Jeep GladiatorTownside Pickup

TECHNICAL: Synchromesh transmission. Speeds: 3F/1R. Floor-mounted gearshift lever. Single-plate dry-disc clutch. Semi-floating rear axle. Four-wheel hydraulic brakes. Steel disc wheels. 4x2 models have I-beam front axle. 4x4 models have hypoid, semi-floating front axle and two-speed transfer case with ratios of 1.00:1 and 2.46:1.

1966 Jeep J-100 Four-Door Wagoneer Ambulance 4x4

OPTIONS: [CJ/DJ] Convertible top; all-weather canvas top; fiberglass cab top; metal cab top. Four-speed transmission ($194). [All models] Air conditioning. Power steering ($81). Overdrive ($126). Four-speed transmission ($109). Rearview mirror. Radio. Antenna package. Ramsey or Koenig winches for front, rear or bed mount. Warn or Cutlas selective drive hubs. Canfield wrecker for Universals, 4x4 pickup or Forward Control models. Meyer angle dozers. Jeep-A-Trench. Tailgate loader for 600 lb. or 1,000 lb. rated models. Deluxe cab on Forward Control models. Fresh air heater. Tu-tone paint. Front bumper guards. Directional signals. E-Z-Eye glass. Windshield washer. FC-150 front air vent. FC-150 double passenger seat. Oil bath air cleaner. Oil filter. High-altitude cylinder head (no charge). Powr-Lok rear differential. Heavy-duty rear axle. Heavy-duty springs and shock absorbers. Transmission brake. Hot-Climate radiator. Variable and constant-speed governors. Various size and type tires including whitewalls in available sizes. Draw-Bar. Stabilizer bar. Rear bumperettes. Automatic transmission in Travelalls and Gladiators. Full wheel discs. V-6 ($191).

HISTORICAL: Introduced: Fall, 1965. Calendar year production: 99,624 (This included 25,400 fours, 50,578 sixes and 16,800 V-8s). Innovations: New V-6 engine introduced. This was known as the "Dauntless" V-6. The automotive division posted a profit of $7,180,000 before interest expense. This was up, although model year sales declined 8.3 percent.

1966 Jeep J-100 Two-Door Wagoneer Panel Delivery (OCW)

1967 JEEP

1967 Jeep Universal M-715 Military (ATC)

UNIVERSAL/DISPATCHER — SERIES CJ/DJ — FOUR-CYLINDER: The CJ-3B and both DJ-3A models were discontinued in 1967. The venerable CJ-5, offshoot of the M-38A1 Korean War Army Jeep, was now the mainstay of the 1/4-ton utility vehicle lineup. The CJ-5A was again the sportier, more luxurious edition. Basically the same, except for their 20 in. longer wheelbase and stretched bodies, were the CJ-6 and CJ-6A. Also remaining available were the 4x2 Jeeps coded the DJ-5 and DJ-6, which had their characteristic five-slot grilles. Base powerplant in all models was the 134.2 cid 75 hp F-head four-cylinder engine. Optional in all Jeep Universals was the 225 cid 90-degree V-6, which now cranked-out 160 hp.

1967 Jeep Commando Convertible (OCW)

JEEPSTER COMMANDO — SERIES 8700 — FOUR-CYLINDER: An all-new line of Jeepster Commando models was introduced in January 1967. This was a modernized version of the early postwar Jeepster based on the original Brooks Stevens' design concept with some updating. The hood was widened to overlap the front fenders, which protruded only slightly on the sides and curved downwards, CJ-5-style, at the front. There was a simple, Jeep-like flat front with seven slots, which curved out, over the fenders, at the top. Circular parking lights were mounted outboard of the headlights, over the fenders. There were no actual rear fenders, only a flared contour that ran along the lower edge of the and over the wheel wells. The horizontally pleated vinyl upholstery covered two bucket seats in front and a small bench seat at the rear. At the angular back of the phaeton-like body was a rear-mounted spare tire and wheel. The Jeepster Commando came in four models: Roadster Coupe; Convertible Phaeton; Station Wagon and Pickup Truck. They were rated at 1/4-ton and had a 3,550 lb. GVW rating (pickup). All were 4x4 models with the 134.2 cid/75 hp four-cylinder as base engine. The 225 cid/160 hp V-6 was optional. Jeepster Commando paint options: were: Sprucetip green; President red; Empire blue; Gold beige; Glacier white and prairie gold.

1967 Jeep Commando Convertible (OCW)

WAGONEER/GLADIATOR — SERIES J — SIX-CYLINDER: For model-year 1967, there was some paring down of the numerous series and models in the Wagoneer/Gladiator range. This was accomplished by eliminating nearly all 4x2 models, except in the J-100 series. Base engine for all series was the 232 cid ohc six-cylinder with 145 hp. The 327 cid V-8 with 250 hp was optional once again.

1967 Jeep Commando Hardtop (OCW)

I.D. DATA: Serial number located on left front door hinge pillar post and left firewall. The VIN consists of from nine to 11 symbols. The first four-or five symbols indicate series and style. The last five or six are sequential production numbers.

1967 Jeep Commando Convertible (OCW)

Model	Body Type	Price	Weight	Prod. Total
CJ-5 — 1/4-Ton — 4x4 — 81 in. w.b.				
8305	Jeep	2361	2163	—
CJ-5A — 1/4-Ton — 4x4 — 81 in. w.b.				
8322	Jeep	2458	2163	—
CJ-6 — 1/2-Ton — 4x4 — 101 in. w.b.				
8405	Jeep	2457	2217	—
CJ-6A — 1/2-Ton — 4x4 — 101 in. w.b.				
8422	Jeep	2553	2217	—
DJ-5 — 1/4-Ton — 4x2 — 81 in. w.b.				
8505	Dispatcher	1821	1823	
DJ-6 — 1/4-Ton — 4x2 — 101 in. w.b.				
8605	Dispatcher	1917	1956	

	Jeepster Commando — 1/4-Ton — 4x4 — 101 in. w.b.			
8701	Convertible	3186	2724	—
8705F	Station Wagon	2749	2673	—
8705	Roadster	2466	2461	—
8705H	Pickup	2548	2610	—

	Series J-100 — 1/2-Ton — 4x2 — 110 in. w.b.			
1314	4d Wagoneer	2953	3497	—
1312	2d Wagoneer	2909	3470	—
1314C	4d Custom Wagoneer	3150	3532	—
1312C	2d Custom Wagoneer	3106	3505	—
1313	Panel Delivery	2783	3270	—

	Series J-100 — 1/2-Ton — 4x4 — 110 in. w.b.			
1414	4d Wagoneer	3702	3654	—
1412	2d Wagoneer	3648	3627	—
1414C	4d Custom Wagoneer	3898	3689	—
1412C	2d Custom Wagoneer	3844	3662	—
1413	Panel Delivery	3357	3427	—
1414D	Super Wagoneer	6048	4241	—

	Series J-2500 — 1/2-Ton — 4x4 — 120 in. w.b.			
2406W	Chassis & Cab	2957	3096	—
2406W	Thriftside Pickup	3058	3391	—
2406W	Townside Pickup	3085	3499	—

	Series J-2600 — 1/2-Ton — 4x4 — 120 in. w.b.			
2406X	Chassis & Cab	3078	3237	—
2406X	Thriftside Pickup	3178	3532	—
2406X	Townside Pickup	3205	3640	—
2406X	Platform Stake	3383	3893	—

	Series J-2700 — 3/4-Ton — 4x4 — 120 in. w.b.			
2406Y	Chassis & Cab	3242	3324	—
2406Y	Thriftside Pickup	3343	3619	—
2406Y	Townside Pickup	3369	3727	—
2406Y	Platform Stake	3548	3980	—

	Series J-2800 — 1-Ton — 4x4 — 120 in. w.b.			
2406Z	Chassis & Cab	3920	3757	—
2406Z	Platform Stake	4312	4502	—

	Series J-3500 — 1/2-Ton — 4x2 — 126 in. w.b.			
3406W	Chassis & Cab	2976	3120	—
3406W	Thriftside Pickup	3091	3440	—
3406W	Townside Pickup	3117	3548	—

	Series J-3600 — 1/2-Ton — 4x4 — 126 in. w.b.			
3406X	Chassis & Cab	3096	3258	—
3406X	Thriftside Pickup	3211	3578	—
3406X	Townside Pickup	3238	3686	—
3406X	Platform Stake	3435	3962	—

	Series J-2700 — 3/4-Ton — 4x4 — 126 in. w.b.			
3406Y	Chassis & Cab	3261	3345	—
3406Y	Thriftside Pickup	3375	3665	—
3406Y	Townside Pickup	3402	3773	—
3406Y	Platform Stake	3599	4049	—

	Series J-3800 — 1-Ton — 4x4 — 126 in. w.b.			
3406Z	Chassis & Cab	3938	3790	—
3406Z	Platform Stake	4353	4588	—

1967 Jeep J-100 Four-Door Super Wagoneer (OCW)

ENGINE [CJ/DJ-3A/DJ-6/Commando]: Inline. F-head. Four-cylinder. Cast iron block. Bore & stroke: 3-1/8 in. x 4-3/8 in. Displacement: 134.2 cid. Compression ratio: 7.4:1. Brake hp: 75 at 4000 rpm. Net hp: 15.63. Torque: 114 lbs.-ft. at 2000 rpm. Solid valve lifters. Carburetor: Carter.

ENGINE [DJ-3A]: Inline. L-head. Four-cylinder. Cast iron block. Bore & stroke: 3-1/8 in. x 4-3/8 in. Displacement: 134.2 cid. Compression ratio: 7.00:1. Brake hp: 60 at 4000 rpm. Net hp: 15.63. Torque: 114 lbs.-ft. at 2000 rpm. Solid valve lifters. Carburetor: Carter.

ENGINE [Optional CJ/DJ/Commando]: Vee-block. Overhead valve. Six-cylinder. Bore & stroke: 3.75 in. x 3.40 in. Displacement: 225 cid. Compression ratio: 9.0:1. Brake hp: 155 at 4400 rpm. Net hp: 33.75. Torque: 225 lbs.-ft. at 2400 rpm. Four main bearings. Hydraulic valve lifters. Carburetor: Carter model two-barrel.

ENGINE [J-Series]: Overhead Cam. Inline. Six-cylinder. Cast iron block. Bore & stroke: 3.34 in. x 4.38 in. Displacement: 230 cid. Compression ratio: 8.5:1. Brake hp: 140 at 4000 rpm. Net hp: 26.77. Torque: 210 lbs.-ft. at 1750 rpm. Solid valve lifters. Carburetor: Carter model two-barrel.

ENGINE [J-Series Economy Option]: Inline. Overhead camshaft. Six-cylinder. Cast iron block. Bore & stroke: 3.344 in. x 4.375 in. Displacement: 230.5 cid. Compression ratio: 7.5:1. Brake hp: 133 at 4000 rpm. Net hp: 26.77. Torque: 199 lbs.-ft. at 2400 rpm. Solid valve lifters. Carburetor: Carter model two-barrel.

ENGINE [Custom/Super Wagoneer]: OHV. Vee-block. Eight-cylinder. Cast iron block. Bore & stroke: 4.00 in. x 3.25 in. Displacement: 327 cid. Brake hp: 250 at 4700 rpm. Net hp: 51.2. Torque: 340 lbs.-ft. at 2600 rpm. Hydraulic valve lifters. Carburetor: Carter. (Optional in other J-Series trucks).

CHASSIS: For wheelbase see chart above. Overall length: [CJ-3B] 129.9 in.; [CJ-5] 135.5. in.; [CJ-6] 155.5 in.; [DJ-3A] 183.66 in. Front tread: [CJ-3B] 48.4 in.; [CJ-5] 48.4 in.; [CJ-6] 48.4 in.; [DJ-3A] 48.2 in.; [J-100] 57 in.; [Fleetvan] 48-9/15 in. Rear tread: [CJ-3B] 48.4 in.; [CJ-5] 48.4 in.; [CJ-6] 48.4 in.; [DJ-3A] 48.5 in.; [J-100] 57 in.; [Fleetvan] 48-9/16 in. Tires: [CJ-all models] 6.00 x 16 in.; [DJ-3A] 6.50 x 15 in.; [J-100, J-200] 6.70 x 15 in.; [J-210] 7.60 x 15 in.; [J-300] 7.10 x 15 in.; [J-320] 7.50 x 16 in.; [Other J-Series models] 7.00 x 16 in. [Jeepster Commando]: Wheelbase: 101. Cargo area: 63.8 in. Tires: 7.35 x 15 in.

TECHNICAL: Synchromesh transmission. Speeds: 3F/1R. Floor-mounted gearshift lever. Single-plate dry-disc clutch. Semi-floating rear axle. Four-wheel hydraulic brakes. Steel disc wheels. 4x2 models have I-beam front axle. 4x4 models have hypoid, semi-floating front axle and two-speed transfer case with ratios of 1.00:1 and 2.46:1.

TECHNICAL [Jeepster Commando]: Synchromesh transmission. Speeds: 3F/1R. Floor-mounted gearshift lever. Single-plate dry-disc clutch with torsional dampening. Axles: Hypoid gears, full-floating front, semi-floating rear. Overall ratio: 3.54:1. Four-wheel hydraulic brakes. Disc wheels.

1967 Jeep J-100 Four-Door Wagoneer (OCW)

OPTIONS: [CJ/DJ] Convertible top; all-weather canvas top; fiberglass cab top; metal cab top. Four-speed transmission ($194). [All models] Air conditioning. Power steering ($81). Overdrive ($126). Four-speed transmission ($109). Rearview mirror. Radio. Antenna package. Ramsey or Koenig winches for front, rear or bed mount. Warn or Cutlas selective drive hubs. Canfield wrecker for Universals, 4x4 pickup. Meyer angle dozers. Jeep-A-Trench. Tailgate loader for 600 lb. or 1,000 lb. rated models. Fresh air heater. Tu-tone paint. Front bumper guards. Directional signals. E-Z-Eye glass. Windshield washer. Oil bath air cleaner. Oil filter. High-altitude cylinder head (no charge). Powr-Lok rear differential. Heavy-duty rear axle. Heavy-duty springs and shock absorbers. Transmission brake. Hot-Climate radiator. Variable and constant-speed governors. Various size and type tires including whitewalls in available sizes. Draw-Bar. Stabilizer bar. Rear bumperettes. Automatic transmission in Travelalls and Gladiators. Full wheel discs. V-6 ($191).

1967 Jeep Commando Hardtop (JAG)

HISTORICAL: Introduced: Fall 1966. Calendar year production: 116,744 (This included 29,858 Jeep vehicles and 86,886 military trucks.) Engine installations broke-out as 28,994 fours, 75,715 sixes and 12,035 V-8s. Innovations: New V-6 engine introduced. This was known as the Dauntless V-6. Jeepster reintroduced in Jan. 1967. Turbo-Hydra-Matic transmission available in conjunction with V-6. Kaiser-Jeep's operating profit was $14,530,000; over double that of the previous year. E.F. Kaiser replaced H.J. Kaiser as Chairman of the Board. B.J. Heard was Executive Vice-President and general manager of the Commercial Products Div.

1968 JEEP

UNIVERSAL/DISPATCHER — SERIES CJ/DJ — FOUR-CYLINDER: The Universal Jeep continued to resist fadish model year changes for the sake of change. For 1968, the lineup was unaltered and both styling and mechanical features were generally the same as in 1967. However, a new option was a diesel engine. Gas engine selections were unchanged. All models gained a few pounds when government-mandated safety equipment was added to the vehicles, along with emissions control hardware.

1968 Jeep CJ-5 Universal 4x4 (JAG)

1968 Jeep CJ-5 Universal 4x4 Family Camper (JAG)

JEEPSTER COMMANDO — SERIES 8700 — FOUR-CYLINDER: Changes for the Jeepster Commandos for 1968 included a new top for the convertible, hinged tailgates for better rear seat access, full metal doors with roll-up windows for the convertible and ventipanes on appropriate models. There was also a slight redesign of the name badges on the sides of the hood and newly styled wheelcovers. The Jeepster engine options were the same as in 1967. Turbo-Hydra-Matic transmission was available with the optional V-6.

1968 Jeep CJ-5 Universal 4x4 (KJC)

WAGONEER/GLADIATOR — SERIES J — SIX-CYLINDER/V-8: The Wagoneers and Gladiators were carried over with some additional cutting of models. Gone from the long-wheelbase series was the flared-rear-fender Thriftside pickup trucks. This reduced the model count to a total of eight Wagoneers and 24 Gladiators. Wagoneers came only in 4x4 form. There was one new Wagoneer, called the Custom V-8, which joined the V8-only Super Wagoneer in a separate sub-series. They represented the marque's luxury models. Both were priced at above $6,000 in standard form, which included many features that normally sold for extra-cost. A camper package for J-3600 Gladiators was a $267 option.

1968 Jeep Commando Convertible 4x4 (OCW)

I.D. DATA: Serial number located on left front door hinge pillar post and left firewall. The VIN consists of from nine to 11 symbols. The first four or five symbols indicate series and body style. The last five or six are sequential production numbers. Starting serial numbers: [CJ-5] 8305S or 8305015 or 8305C15-228800 and up. [CJ-5A] 8322S-17423 and up. [CJ-6] 8405015 or 8405S-33935 and up. [CJ-6A] 8422S-10462 and up. [DJ-5] 8505015 or 8505S-12261 and up. [DJ-6] 8605015 or 8605S-11461 and up. [Series 8700] [Model] 15-19027 and up. [Convertible] 8701-12215 and up. [Pickup] 8705H15-19027 and up. [Wagoneers] 1414017 or 1414S-205868 and up; 1412017 or 1412S-200358 and up; 1414017 or 1414CS-200621 and up; 1412C17 or 1412CS-200015 and up; 1414D19 or 1414DS-101078 and up; 1414X19-30001 and up; 1413S-200583 and up (V-8 100060 and up). [Gladiator] 2406W17 or 2406WS-202456 and up (V-8 101447 and up); 2406X1or 2406XS-20257 and up (V-8 101447 and up); 2406Y17 or 2460Y or 2406YS-201297 and up (V8 100235 and up); 2406Z17 or 2406Z or 2406ZS-200020 and up (V-8 100010 and up); 3406W17 or 3406WS-21022 and up (V-8 101794 and up); 3406X17 or 3406XS-200669 and up (V-8 102974 and up); 3406Y17 or 3406Y or 3406YS-200725 up (V-8 100514 and up); 3406Z17 or 3406ZN or 3406ZS-200150 and up (V-8 100139 and up).

1968 Jeep Commando Station Wagon 4x4 (JAG)

Model	Body Type	Price	Weight	Prod. Total
CJ-5 — 1/4-Ton — 4x4 — 81 in. w.b.				
8305	Jeep Universal	2683	2212	—
CJ-5A — 1/4-Ton — 4x4 — 81 in. w.b.				
8322	Jeep Universal	2778	2212	—
CJ-6 — 1/2-Ton — 4x4 — 101 in. w.b.				
8405	Jeep Universal	2778	2274	—
CJ-6A — 1/2-Ton — 4x4 — 101 in. w.b.				
8422	Jeep Universal	2875	2274	—
DJ-5 — 1/4-Ton — 4x2 — 81 in. w.b.				
8505	Jeep Dispatcher	2153	1872	—
DJ-6 — 1/4-Ton — 4x2 — 101 in. w.b.				
8605	Jeep Dispatcher	2249	2005	—
Jeepster Commando — 1/4-Ton — 4x4 — 101 in. w.b.				
8702	2d Convertible	3442	2853	—
8705F	Station Wagon	3005	2722	—
8705	Roadster Coupe	2730	2510	—
8705H	Pickup Truck	2817	2659	—
Series J-100 — 1/2-Ton — 4x4 — 110 in. w.b.				
1414S	4d Wagoneer	3869	3710	—
1412S	2d Wagoneer	3815	3683	—
1414CS	4d Custom Wagoneer	4065	3745	—
1412CS	2d Custom Wagoneer	4011	3718	—
1413S	Panel Delivery	3457	3483	—
Series J-100 V-8 — 1/2-Ton — 4x4 — 110 in. w.b.				
1414D	Super Wagoneer	6163	4263	—
1414X	4d Custom Wagoneer	5671	3907	—
Series J-2500 — 1/2-Ton — 4x4 — 120 in. w.b.				
2406W	Chassis & Cab	3119	3152	—
2406W	Thriftside Pickup	3225	3447	—
2406W	Townside Pickup	3253	3555	—

Series J-2600 — 1/2-Ton — 4x4 — 120 in. w.b.

2406X	Chassis & Cab	3240	3293	—
2406X	Thriftside Pickup	3345	3588	—
2406X	Townside Pickup	3373	3696	—
2406X	Platform Stake	3560	3949	—

Series J-2700 — 3/4-Ton — 4x4 — 120 in. w.b.

2406Y	Chassis & Cab	3404	3380	—
2406Y	Thriftside Pickup	3510	3675	—
2406Y	Townside Pickup	3538	3785	—
2406Y	Platform Stake	3725	4036	—

Series J-2800 — 1-Ton — 4x4 — 120 in. w.b.

2406Z	Chassis & Cab	3996	3813	—
2406Z	Platform Stake	4411	4558	—

Series J-3500 — 1/2-Ton — 4x4 — 126 in. w.b.

3406W	Chassis & Cab	3138	3176	—
3406W	Townside Pickup	3286	3604	—

Series J-3600 — 1/2-Ton — 4x4 — 126 in. w.b.

3406X	Chassis & Cab	3258	3314	—
3406X	Townside Pickup	3407	3742	—
3406X	Platform Stake	3614	4018	—

Series J-3700 — 3/4-Ton — 4x4 — 126 in. w.b.

3406Y	Chassis & Cab	3423	3401	—
3406Y	Townside Pickup	3571	3829	—
3406Y	Platform Stake	3778	4105	—

Series J-3800 — 1-Ton — 4x4 — 126 in. w.b.

3406Z	Chassis & Cab	4015	3846	—
3406Z	Platform Stake	4429	4644	—

1968 Jeep Commando Hardtop (JAG)

ENGINES: The diesel was a four-cylinder with 3.5 x 5 in. bore and stroke. It was rated at 19.6 taxable hp.

ENGINE [CJ/DJ-3A/DJ-6/Commando]: Inline. F-head. Four-cylinder. Cast iron block. Bore & stroke: 3-1/8 in. x 4-3/8 in. Displacement: 134.2 cid. Compression ratio: 7.4:1. Brake hp: 75 at 4000 rpm. Net hp: 15.63. Torque: 114 lbs.-ft. at 2000 rpm. Solid valve lifters. Carburetor: Carter.

ENGINE [DJ-3A]: Inline. L-head. Four-cylinder. Cast iron block. Bore & stroke: 3-1/8 in. x 4-3/8 in. Displacement: 134.2 cid. Compression ratio: 7.00:1. Brake hp: 60 at 4000 rpm. Net hp: 15.63. Torque: 114 lbs.-ft. at 2000 rpm. Solid valve lifters. Carburetor: Carter.

ENGINE [Optional CJ/DJ/Commando]: Vee-block. Overhead valve. Six-cylinder. Bore & stroke: 3.75 in. x 3.40 in. Displacement: 225 cid. Compression ratio: 9.0:1. Brake hp: 155 at 4400 rpm. Net hp: 33.75. Torque: 225 lbs.-ft. at 2400 rpm. Four main bearings. Hydraulic valve lifters. Carburetor: Carter model two-barrel.

ENGINE [J-Series]: Overhead Cam. Inline. Six-cylinder. Cast iron block. Bore & stroke: 3.34 in. x 4.38 in. Displacement: 230 cid. Compression ratio: 8.5:1. Brake hp: 140 at 4000 rpm. Net hp: 26.77. Torque: 210 lbs.-ft. at 1750 rpm. Solid valve lifters. Carburetor: Carter model two-barrel.

Standard Catalog of Light-Duty Trucks

ENGINE [J-Series Economy Option]: Inline. Overhead camshaft. Six-cylinder. Cast iron block. Bore & stroke: 3.344 in. x 4.375 in. Displacement: 230.5 cid. Compression ratio: 7.5:1. Brake hp: 133 at 4000 rpm. Net hp: 26.77. Torque: 199 lbs.-ft. at 2400 rpm. Solid valve lifters. Carburetor: Carter model two-barrel.

ENGINE [Custom/Super Wagoneer]: OHV. Vee-block. Eight-cylinder. Cast iron block. Bore & stroke: 4.00 in. x 3.25 in. Displacement: 327 cid. Brake hp: 250 at 4700 rpm. Net hp: 51.2. Torque: 340 lbs.-ft. at 2600 rpm. Hydraulic valve lifters. Carburetor: Carter. (Optional in other J-Series trucks.)

1968 Jeep J-100 Four-Door Wagoneer (KJC)

CHASSIS: For wheelbase see chart above. Overall length: [CJ-3B] 129.9 in.; [CJ-5] 135.5. in.; [CJ-6] 155.5 in.; [DJ-3A] 125.4 in.; [J-100] 183.66 in. Front tread: [CJ-3B] 48.4 in.; [CJ-5] 48.4 in.; [CJ-6] 48.4 in.; [DJ-3A] 48.2 in.; [J-100] 57 in.; [Fleetvan] 48-9/15 in. Rear tread: [CJ-3B] 48.4 in.; [CJ-5] 48.4 in.; [CJ-6] 48.4 in.; [DJ-3A] 48.5 in.; [J-100] 57 in.; [Fleetvan] 48-9/16 in. Tires: [CJ-all models] 6.00 x 16 in.; [DJ-3A] 6.50 x 15 in.; [J-100, J-200] 6.70 x 15 in.; [J-210] 7.60 x 15 in.; [J-300] 7.10 x 15 in.; [J-320] 7.50 x 16 in.; [Other J-Series models] 7.00 x 16 in. [Jeepster Commando]: Wheelbase: 101 in. Cargo area: 63.8 in. Tires: 7.35 x 15 in.

TECHNICAL: Synchromesh transmission. Speeds: 3F/1R. Floor-mounted gearshift lever. Single-plate dry-disc clutch. Semi-floating rear axle. Four-wheel hydraulic brakes. Steel disc wheels. 4x2 models have I-beam front axle. 4x4 models have hypoid, semi-floating front axle and two-speed transfer case with ratios of 1.00:1 and 2.46:1.

TECHNICAL [Jeepster Commando]: Synchromesh transmission. Speeds: 3F/1R. Floor-mounted gearshift lever. Single-plate dry-disc clutch with torsional dampening. Axles: Hypoid gears, full-floating front, semi-floating rear. Overall ratio: 3.54:1. Four-wheel hydraulic brakes. Disc wheels.

OPTIONS: [CJ/DJ] Convertible top; all-weather canvas top; fiberglass cab top; metal cab top. Four-speed transmission ($194). [All models] Air conditioning. Power steering ($81). Overdrive ($126). Four-speed transmission ($109). Rearview mirror. Radio. Antenna package. Ramsey or Koenig winches for front, rear or bed mount. Warn or Cutlas selective drive hubs. Canfield wrecker for Universals, 4x4 pickup. Meyer angle dozers. Jeep-A-Trench. Tailgate loader for 600 lb. or 1,000 lb. rated models. Fresh air heater. Tu-tone paint. Front bumper guards. Directional signals. E-Z-Eye glass. Windshield washer. Oil bath air cleaner. Oil filter. High-altitude cylinder head. Powr-Lok rear differential. Heavy-duty rear axle. Heavy-duty springs and shock absorbers. Transmission brake. Hot-Climate radiator. Variable and constant-speed governors. Various size and type tires including white-walls in available sizes. Draw-Bar. Stabilizer bar. Rear bumperettes. Automatic transmission in Travelalls and Gladiators. Full wheel discs. V-6 ($191).

HISTORICAL: Introduced: Fall, 1967. Calendar year production: 117,573 (This included a much higher 86,886 Jeep vehicles and only 29,858 military trucks). Engine breakouts were: [4-cyl.] 24,458; [6-cyl.] 76,220 and [V-8] 16,895. Innovations: Diesel engine available in some models during 1968 only. Historical notes: New V-6 manufacturing plant opens. A marine version of this engine was also supplied to a major boat engine manufacturer. (Jeeps were built at Toledo, Ohio and Army trucks at South Bend, Ind. The new V-6 manufacturing facility was also in Toledo). J.R. Cody became V.P. and General Manager of the Commercial Division.

1969 JEEP

UNIVERSAL/DISPATCHER — SERIES CJ/DJ — FOUR-CYLINDER: To conform with federal safety regulations, Jeep products had new side-marker lamps this year. They were mounted on the sides of the hood and rear quarter of the body. The CJ-5A and CJ-6A Tuxedo Park models were deleted as was the CJ-6. There was a new, limited-edition "462" model-option including a roll bar, swing-out spare tire carrier, polyglass tubeless tires, skid plate, electric ammeter and oil gauges. It was designed for some serious off-roading. This was the final season for the Jeep by Kaiser. The brand name left Kaiser Industries in 1970, becoming Jeep Corp., a division of American Motors.

1969 Jeep "462" Universal 4x4 (OCW)

JEEPSTER COMMANDO — SERIES 8700 — FOUR-CYLINDER: A more luxurious version of the Jeepser Commando was added to the line in 1969. It was simply called the Jeepster and came only in the convertible body style. New side-marker lights were the main styling change.

1969 Jeep Gladiator Townside "Family Camper" Pickup

WAGONEER/GLADIATOR — SERIES J — SIX-CYLINDER/V-8: The Wagoneer and Gladiator models were little-changed for 1969. The Wagoneers were all four-door models. New side-marker lamps were added to the sides of the front and rear fenders. The 1-ton trucks on both the 120 and 126 in. wheelbase were dropped. Actually, the J-3800 chassis was still available, but it was down-rated to 3/4-tons and an 8,000 lbs. GVW. It could be equipped with the camper package for $148 extra.
I.D. DATA: Serial number located on left front door hinge pillar post and left firewall. The VIN consists of from nine to 11 symbols. The first four to six indicated series and body style. The last five or six are sequential production numbers. Starting serial numbers: [CJ-5] 8305015 or 8305C15-244728 and up. [CJ-6] 8405015-35264 and up. [DJ-5] 8505015-12871 and up. [Jeepster Convertible] 8701015-12545 and up. [Commandos] [Model] 15-28002 and up; [Convertible] 15-10001 and up; [Pickup] 8705H15-28002 and up. [J-2500] 2406W17-202937 and up; [J-2600] 2406X17-202823 and up; [J-2700] 2406Y17-203184 and up; [J-3500] 3406W17-201152 and up; [J-3600] 3406X17-200866 and up; [J-3700] 3406Y17-200848 and up; [J-3800] 3407Z19-300001 and up.

Model	Body Type	Price	Weight	Prod. Total
CJ-5 — 1/4-Ton — 4x4 — 81 in. w.b.				
8305	Jeep Universal	2823	2212	—
CJ-6 — 1/2-Ton — 4x4 — 101 in. w.b.				
8405	Jeep Universal	2918	2274	—
DJ-5 — 1/4-Ton — 4x2 — 81 in. w.b.				
8505	Jeep Dispatcher	2292	1872	—
Jeepster Commando — 1/4-Ton — 4x4 — 101 in. w.b.				
8702	2d Convertible	3005	2707	—
8705F	Station Wagon	3113	2722	—
8705	Roadster Coupe	2824	2510	—
8705H	Pickup	2914	2659	—
Jeepster — 1/4-Ton — 4x4 — 101 in. w.b.				
8701	2d Convertible	3537	2773	—
Series J-100 — 1/2-Ton — 4x4 — 110 in. w.b.				
1414O	Wagoneer (6-cyl.)	4145	3710	—
1414C	Custom Wagoneer (6-cyl.)	4342	3745	—
1414X	Wagoneer (V-8)	5671	3907	—
1414D	Custom Wagoneer (V-8)	6163	4263	—

Series J-2500 — 1/2-Ton — 4x4 — 120 in. w.b.				
2406W	Chassis & Cab	3243	3152	—
2406W	Thriftside Pickup	3348	3447	—
2406W	Townside Pickup	3376	3555	—
Series J-2600 — 1/2-Ton — 4x4 — 120 in. w.b.				
2406X	Chassis & Cab	3363	3293	—
2406X	Thriftside Pickup	3469	3588	—
2406X	Townside Pickup	3497	3696	—
2406X	Stake	3684	3949	—
Series J-2700 — 3/4-Ton — 4x4 — 120 in. w.b.				
2406Y	Chassis & Cab	3528	3380	—
2406Y	Thriftside Pickup	3633	3675	—
2406Y	Townside Pickup	3661	3783	—
2406Y	Stake	3849	4036	—
Series J-3500 — 1/2-Ton — 4x4 — 126 in. w.b.				
3406W	Chassis & Cab	3261	3176	—
3406W	Townside Pickup	3410	3604	—
Series J-3600 — 1/2-Ton — 4x4 — 126 in. w.b.				
3406X	Chassis & Cab	3382	3314	—
3406X	Townside Pickup	3530	3742	—
3406X	Stake	3737	4018	—
Series J-3700 — 3/4-Ton — 4x4 — 126 in. w.b.				
3406Y	Chassis & Cab	3546	3401	—
3406Y	Townside Pickup	3695	3829	—
3406Y	Stake	3902	4105	—
Series J-3800 — 3/4-Ton — 4x4 — 126 in. w.b.				
3406Z	Chassis & Cab	4184	3792	—

ENGINE [CJ/DJ-3A/Commando]: Inline. F-head. Four-cylinder. Cast iron block. Bore & stroke: 3-1/8 in. x 4-3/8 in. Displacement: 134.2 cid. Compression ratio: 7.4:1. Brake hp: 75 at 4000 rpm. Net hp: 15.63. Torque: 114 lbs.-ft. at 2000 rpm. Solid valve lifters. Carburetor: Carter.

ENGINE [DJ-3A]: Inline. L-head. Four-cylinder. Cast iron block. Bore & stroke: 3-1/8 in. x 4-3/8 in. Displacement: 134.2 cid. Compression ratio: 7.00:1. Brake hp: 60 at 4000 rpm. Net hp: 15.63. Torque: 114 lbs.-ft. at 2000 rpm. Solid valve lifters. Carburetor: Carter.

ENGINE [Optional CJ/DJ/Commando]: Vee-block. Overhead valve. Six-cylinder. Bore & stroke: 3.75 in. x 3.40 in. Displacement: 225 cid. Compression ratio: 9.0:1. Brake hp: 155 at 4400 rpm. Net hp: 33.75. Torque: 225 lbs.-ft. at 2400 rpm. Four main bearings. Hydraulic valve lifters. Carburetor: Carter model two-barrel.

ENGINE [J-Series]: Overhead Cam. Inline. Six-cylinder. Cast iron block. Bore & stroke: 3.34 in. x 4.38 in. Displacement: 230 cid. Compression ratio: 8.5:1. Brake hp: 140 at 4000 rpm. Net hp: 26.77. Torque: 210 lbs.-ft. at 1,750 rpm. Solid valve lifters. Carburetor: Carter model two-barrel.

ENGINE [J-Series Economy Option]: Inline. Overhead camshaft. Six-cylinder. Cast iron block. Bore & stroke: 3.344 in. x 4.375 in. Displacement: 230.5 cid. Compression ratio: 7.5:1. Brake hp: 133 at 4000 rpm. Net hp: 26.77. Torque: 199 lbs.-ft. at 2400 rpm. Solid valve lifters. Carburetor: Carter model two-barrel.

ENGINE [Custom/Super Wagoneer]: OHV. Vee-block. Eight-cylinder. Cast iron block. Bore & stroke: 4.00 in. x 3.25 in. Displacement: 327 cid. Brake hp: 250 at 4700 rpm. Net hp: 51.2. Torque: 340 lbs.-ft. at 2600 rpm. Hydraulic valve lifters. Carburetor: Carter. (Optional in other J-Series trucks.)

CHASSIS: For wheelbase see chart above. Overall length: [CJ-3B] 129.9 in.; [CJ-5] 135.5. in.; [CJ-6] 155.5 in.; [DJ-3A] 125.4 in.; [J-100] 183.66 in. Front tread: [CJ-3B] 48.4 in.; [CJ-5] 48.4 in.; [CJ-6] 48.4 in.; [DJ-3A] 48.2 in.; [J-100] 57 in.; [Fleetvan] 48-9/15 in. Rear tread: [CJ-3B] 48.4 in.; [CJ-5] 48.4 in.; [CJ-6] 48.4 in.; [DJ-3A] 48.5 in.; [J-100] 57 in.; [Fleetvan] 48-9/16 in. Tires: [CJ-all models] 6.00 x 16 in.; [DJ-3A] 6.50 x 15 in.; [J-100, J-200] 6.70 x 15 in.; [J-210] 7.60 x 15 in.; [J-300] 7.10 x 15 in.; [J-320] 7.50 x 16 in.; [Other J-Series models] 7.00 x 16 in. [Jeepster Commando]: Wheelbase: 101 in. Cargo area: 63.8 in. Tires: 7.35 x 15 in.

TECHNICAL: Synchromesh transmission. Speeds: 3F/1R. Floor-mounted gearshift lever. Single-plate dry-disc clutch. Semi-floating rear axle. Four-wheel hydraulic brakes. Steel disc wheels. 4x2 models have I-beam front axle. 4x4 models have hypoid, semi-floating front axle and two-speed transfer case with ratios of 1.00:1 and 2.46:1.

TECHNICAL [Jeepster Commando]: Synchromesh transmission. Speeds: 3F/1R. Floor-mounted gearshift lever. Single-plate dry-disc clutch with torsional dampening. Axles: Hypoid gears, full-floating front, semi-floating rear. Overall ratio: 3.54:1. Four-wheel hydraulic brakes. Disc wheels.

OPTIONS: [CJ/DJ] Convertible top; all-weather canvas top; fiberglass cab top; metal cab top. Four-speed transmission ($194). [All models] Air conditioning. Power steering ($81). Overdrive ($126). Four-speed transmission ($109). Rearview mirror. Radio. Antenna package. Ramsey or Koenig winches for front, rear or bed mount. Warn or Cutlas selective drive hubs. Canfield wrecker for Universals, 4x4 pickup. Meyer angle dozers. Jeep-A-Trench. Tailgate loader for 600 lb. or 1,000 lb. rated models. Fresh air heater. Tu-tone paint. Front bumper guards. Directional signals. E-Z-Eye glass. Windshield washer. Oil bath air cleaner. Oil filter. High-altitude cylinder head (no charge). Powr-Lok rear differential. Heavy-duty rear axle. Heavy-duty springs and shock absorbers. Transmission brake. Hot-Climate radiator. Variable and constant-speed governors. Various size and type tires including whitewalls in available sizes. Draw-Bar. Stabilizer bar. Rear bumperettes. Automatic transmission in Travelalls and Gladiators. Full wheel discs. V-6 ($191).

HISTORICAL: Introduced: Fall, 1968. Calendar year production: 93,160 in the U.S. and 2,048 in Canada. (This included 61,652 civilian trucks made in Toledo and 29,929 military vehicles built in South Bend.) Innovations: New sporty '462' Jeep model was released. Historical notes: On Feb. 5, 1970 Kaiser-Jeep was purchased for approximately $70 million by AMC.

1969 Jeep CJ-5 Universal 4x4 (JAG)

1970 JEEP

1970 AMC Jeep, J-2500 Gladiator Pickup (OCW)

JEEP — 1970 SERIES — ALL ENGINES: After American Motors purchased Kaiser-Jeep from Kaiser Industries, in February, 1970, it renamed it the Jeep Corp. With the acquisition of Jeep, which had sales of over $400 million, American Motors gained entry into the four-wheel drive market, which had grown by almost 500 percent in the previous decade. Although Jeep's share of the market had fallen as other competitors had entered this field, its 20 percent share of the market was strong enough to serve as a base to re-establish Jeep as a sales leader. American Motors organized a new product development group which was assigned the long range task of developing completely new Jeep models, while making improvements in the current line. For 1970 the most significant changes to be found were a new grille, for the Gladiator truck, as well as optional Tu-tone color combinations.

1970 AMC Jeep, Custom Wagoneer Station Wagon (OCW)

I.D. DATA: The VIN is located on the left front door hinge pillar and left firewall. The VIN has 13 symbols. The first five digits indicate series and style. The sixth and seventh desig-

Standard Catalog of Light-Duty Trucks

nate engine type. The last six digits are sequential serial numbers. The starting number varies per model.

Model	Body Type	Price	Weight	Prod. Total
J-100 — 1/4-Ton — 4x4 — 110 in. w.b.				
1414	4d Station Wagon	4284	3710	—
1414C	4d Station Wagon	4526	3745	—
1414X	4d Custom Station Wagon	5876	3907	—
Jeepster Commando				
8705F	2d Station Wagon	3208	2722	—
8705C	2d Roadster	2917	2510	—
Jeepster				
8701	2d Convertible	3822	2853	—
8702	Convertible Commando	3328	2787	—
CJ-5 — 1/4-Ton — 4x4 — 81 in. w.b.				
8305C15	Jeep	2930	2212	—
CJ-6 — 101 in. w.b.				
8405C15	Jeep	3026	2274	—
DJ-5 — 1/4-Ton — 2x2 — 81 in. w.b.				
8505C15	Jeep	2396	1872	—
Jeepster — 1/4-Ton — 4x4 — 101 in. w.b.				
8705H15	Pickup	3014	2659	—
Series J-2500 — 1/2-Ton — 4x4				
2406W17	Chassis & Cab	3361	3152	—
2406W17	Thriftside Pickup	3488	3447	—
2406W17	Townside Pickup	3516	3555	—
Series J-2600 — 1/2-Ton — 4x4				
2406X17	Chassis & Cab	3483	3293	—
2406X17	Thriftside Pickup	3610	3588	—
2406X17	Townside Pickup	3638	3696	—
2406X17	Platform Stake	3804	3949	—
Series J-2700 — 1/2-Ton — 4x4				
2406Y17	Chassis & Cab	3649	3380	—
2406Y17	Thriftside Pickup	3776	3675	—
2406Y17	Townside Pickup	3804	3783	—
2406Y17	Platform Stake	3790	4036	—
Series J-3500 — 1/2-Ton — 4x4				
3406W17	Chassis & Cab	3381	3176	—
3406W17	Townside Pickup	3544	3604	—
Series J-3600 — 1/2-Ton — 4x4				
3406X17	Chassis & Cab	3505	3314	—
3406X17	Townside Pickup	3667	3742	—
3406X17	Platform Stake	3860	4018	—
Series J-3700 — 1/2-Ton — 4x4				
3406Y17	Chassis & Cab	3668	3401	—
3406Y17	Townside Pickup	3831	3829	—
3406Y17	Platform Stake	4024	4105	—
Series J-3800 — 1/2-Ton — 4x4				
3407Z19	Chassis & Cab	4320	3792	—
Series J-4500 — 1/2-Ton — 4x4				
3408W17	Chassis & Cab	3381	3130	—
3408W17	Townside Pickup	3544	3558	—
Series J-4600 — 3/4-Ton — 4x4				
3408X17	Chassis & Cab	3505	3268	—
3408X17	Townside Pickup	3668	3696	—
Series J-4700 — 3/4-Ton — 4x4				
3408Y17	Chassis & Cab	3668	3355	—
3408Y17	Townside Pickup	3831	3783	—

1970 AMC Jeep, XJ001 Concept Vehicle (OCW)

ENGINE [Standard CJ-5/CJ-6/DJ-5/Jeepster]: Inline. F-head. Four-cylinder. Cast iron block. Bore & stroke: 3.125 x 4.375 in. Displacement: 134.2 cid. Compression ratio: 6.9:1. Brake horsepower: 72 at 4000 rpm. Torque: 114 lb.-ft. at 2000 rpm. Three main bearings. Mechanical valve lifters. Carburetor: Single one-barrel.

1970 AMC Jeep, Commando Station Wagon (RPZ)

1970 AMC Jeep, Jeepster Interior (RPZ)

ENGINE [Optional all models except CJ-5, CJ-6, DJ-5, Jeepster]: V-type. OHV. Eight-cylinder. Cast iron block. Bore & stroke: 3.8 x 3.85 in. Displacement: 350 cid. Compression ratio: 9.0:1. Brake horsepower: 230 at 4400 rpm. Max. Torque: 314 lb.-ft. at 2600 rpm. Five main bearings. Hydraulic valve lifters. Carburetor: Two-barrel.

ENGINE [Standard except CJ/DJ/Jeepster]: Inline. OHV. Six-cylinder. Cast iron block. Bore & stroke: 3.75 x 3.51 in. Displacement: 232 cid. Compression ratio: 8.5:1. Brake horsepower: 145 at 4300 rpm. Torque: 215 lb.-ft. at 1600 rpm. Seven main bearings. Hydraulic valve lifters. Carburetor: Carter one-barrel model YF.

1970 AMC Jeep, CJ-5 Universal Jeep (RPZ)

ENGINE [Optional]: Vee-block. Overhead valve. Six-cylinder. Cast iron block. Bore & stroke: 3.75 x 3.40 in. Displacement: 225 cid. Compression ratio: 9.0:1. Brake horsepower: 160 at 4200 rpm. Max Torque: 235 lb.-ft. at 2400 rpm. Hydraulic valve lifters. Carburetor: Two-barrel.

1970 AMC Jeep, Jeepster Commando Pickups (RPZ)

CHASSIS [J-100]: Wheelbase: 110. Tires: 7.75 x 15
CHASSIS [Jeepster/Jeepster Commando]: Wheelbase: 101 in. Overall length: 168.5 in. Tires: 7.35 x 15.
CHASSIS [CJ-5]: Wheelbase: 81 in. Overall length: 133 in. Front tread: 48.25 in. Rear tread: 48.25 in. Tires: 6.00 x 16 in.
CHASSIS [CJ-6]: Wheelbase: 101 in. Tires: 6.00 x 16 in.
CHASSIS [DJ-5]: Wheelbase: 80 in. Overall length: 126 in. Front tread: 48.25 in. Rear tread: 48.25 in. Tires: 6.85 x 15 in.
CHASSIS [Jeepster]: Wheelbase: 101 in. Overall length: 168.40 in. Height: 64.2 in. Front tread: 50 in. Rear tread: 50 in. Tires: 7.35 x 15 in.
CHASSIS [J-2500/J-2600/J-2700]: Wheelbase: 120 in. Overall length: 193.6 in. Front tread: 63.5 in. Rear tread: 63.8 in. Tires: (J-2500) 8.25 x 15 in.; (J-2600) 7.00 x 16 in.; (J-2700) 7.50 x 16 in.
CHASSIS [J-3500/J-3600/J-3700]: Wheelbase: 126 in. Tires: (J-3500) 8.25 x 15 in.; (J-3600) 7.00 x 16 in.; (J-3700) 7.50 x 16 in.
CHASSIS [J-3800/J-4500/J-4600/J-4700]: Wheelbase: 132 in. Overall length: 205.6 in. Front tread: 63.9 in. Rear tread: 64.4 in. Tires: (J-3800) 7.50 x 16 in.; (J-4500) 8.25 x 15 in.; (J-4600) 7.00 x 16 in.; (J-4700) 7.50 x 15 in.

1970 AMC Jeep, CJ-5 Universal Jeep (RPZ)

TECHNICAL: Manual, synchromesh transmission. Speeds: 3F/1R. Column-mounted gearshift. Single-plate, dry-disc clutch. (1/2-Ton Jeep models) semi-floating rear axle; (all others) full-floating rear axle. Hydraulic, four-wheel, drum brakes. Pressed steel wheels. Automatic transmission. Technical Options: Power steering. Four-speed manual transmission. Camper Package ($163).
OPTIONS: Rear bumper. Rear step bumper. AM radio. Clock. Camper Package ($163). West Coast mirror.

1970 AMC Jeep, J-100 Wagoneer Station Wagon (RPZ)

HISTORICAL: Introduced: Fall 1969. Calendar year sales: 30,842 (All series and models). Calendar year production: 45,805 (All series and models).

1971 JEEP

JEEP — 1971 SERIES — ALL ENGINES: No appearance changes were made for either the Jeep CJ or J-series trucks for 1971. Early in 1971, the AMC 304 cid and 360 cid V-8 engines became optional for the J-series trucks, while the AMC 258 cid six-cylinder became their standard powerplant. Of interest to modern day collectors are several special, limited-edition versions of the Jeepster issued in 1971. The first was the Hurst/Jeepster Special, which had a special air scoop hood with a tachometer on top of it. Also featured on this low-production car were Rally stripes on the cowl and tailgate, fat tires and either a Hurst Dual-Gate automatic transmission selector or manual transmission with a Hurst T-handle shifter. Also available was the SC-1 Jeepster station wagon with Butterscotch gold finish, a white top, black Rally stripes and a V-6 engine.

I.D. DATA: The VIN is located on the left front door hinge pillar and left firewall. The VIN has 13 symbols. The first five digits indicate series and style. The sixth and seventh designate engine type. The last six digits are sequential serial numbers. The starting number varies per model.

1971 AMC Jeep Commando Station Wagon (OCW)

Model	Body Type	Price	Weight	Prod. Total
J-100 — 1/4-Ton — 4x4 — 110 in. w.b.				
1414	4d Station Wagon	4447	3661	—
1414C	4d Custom Station Wagon	4526	3696	—
1414X	4d Special Station Wagon	6114	3982	—
Jeepster Commando — 4x4				
8705F	2d Station Wagon	3446	2722	—
8705O	2dr Roadster	3197	2510	—
Jeepster Commando Six				
8705F	2dr Station Wagon	3546	2802	—
8705O	2dr Roadster	3297	2590	—
87020	2dr Convertible	3465	2787	—
na	2dr SC-1 Station Wagon	na	na	—
na	2dr Hurst Special Wagon	na	na	—
CJ-5 — 1/4-Ton — 4x4				
8305015	Jeep	2886	2112	—
CJ-6 — 1/2-Ton — 4x4				
8405015	Jeep	2979	2274	—
DJ-5 — 1/4-Ton — 2x2				
8505015	Open	2382	1872	—
Jeepster — 1/2-Ton				
8705H15	Pickup	3291	2659	—
J-2500 — 1/2-Ton — 4x4				
2406W17	Chassis & Cab	3251	3125	—
2406W17	Thriftside Pickup (7-ft.)	3406	3420	—
2406W17	Townside Pickup (7-ft.)	3406	3528	—
J-3800 — 1/2-Ton — 4x4				
3407Z19	Chassis & Cab	4113	3792	—
3407Z19	Townside Pickup	4264	4220	—
J-4500 — 1/2-Ton — 4x4				
3408W17	Chassis & Cab	3281	3151	—
3408W17	Townside Pickup (8-ft.)	3443	3579	—
J-4600 — 1/2-Ton — 4x4				
3408X17	Chassis & Cab	3405	3289	—
3408X17	Townside Pickup (8-ft.)	3567	3717	—
J-4700 — 3/4-Ton — 4x4				
3408Y17	Chassis & Cab	3567	3378	—
3408Y17	Townside Pickup (8-ft.)	3729	3806	—
J-4800 — 3/4-Ton — 4x4				
3407Z19	Chassis & Cab	4218	3806	—
3407Z19	Townside Pickup (8-ft.)	4370	4294	—

1971 AMC Jeep, J-100 Wagoneer Station Wagon (OCW)

ENGINE [Standard J-100 Wagoneer]: Inline. OHV. Six-cylinder. Cast iron block. Bore & stroke: 3.75 x 3.5 in. Displacement: 232 cid. Brake horsepower: 145 at 4300 rpm.
ENGINE [Optional Wagoneer V-8]: Vee-block. OHV. Cast iron block. Bore & stroke: 3.8 x 3.85 in. Displacement: 350 cid. Brake horsepower: 230 at 4400 rpm.
ENGINE [Standard CJ-5/CJ-6/DJ-5/Jeepster/Commando]: Inline. F-head. Four-cylinder. Cast iron block. Bore & stroke: 3.125 x 4.375 in. Displacement: 134.2 cid. Compression ratio: 6.9:1. Brake horsepower: 72 at 4000 rpm. Torque: 114 lb.-ft. at 2000 rpm. Three main bearings. Mechanical valve lifters. Carburetor: One-barrel.

1971 AMC Jeep, Commando SC-1 Station Wagon (OCW)

ENGINE [Optional Commando V-6]: Vee-block. OHV. Bore & stroke: 3.75 x 3.4 in. Displacement: 225 cid. Brake horsepower: 160 at 4200 rpm.
ENGINE [Standard: J-2500, J-4500, J-4600, J-4700]: Inline. OHV. Six-cylinder. Cast iron block. Bore & stroke: 3.75 x 3.9 in. Displacement: 258 cid. Compression ratio: 8.0:1. Brake horsepower: 110 at 3500 rpm. Seven main bearings. Hydraulic valve lifters. Carburetor: Carter one-barrel model YF.
ENGINE [Standard: J-3808, J-4800]: V-type. OHV. Eight-cylinder. Cast iron block. Bore & stroke: 4.08 x 3.44 in. Displacement: 360 cid. Brake horsepower: 175. Five main bearings. Hydraulic valve lifters. Carburetor: Two-barrel.

1971 AMC Jeep, Hurst Jeepster Special (C&C)

CHASSIS [J-100]: Wheelbase: 110 in. Overall length: 183.66 in. Width: 75.60 in. Tires: 7.75 x 15.
CHASSIS [3700]: Wheelbase: 101 in. Overall length: 168.5. Tires: 7.35 x 15.
CHASSIS [Jeepster]: Wheelbase: 101 in. Overall length: 168.40 in. Height: 64.2 in. Front tread: 50 in. Rear tread: 50 in. Tires: 7.35 x 15 in.
CHASSIS [J-2500]: Wheelbase: 120 in. Overall length: 193.6 in. Front tread: 63.5 in. Rear tread: 63.8 in. Tires: 8.25 x 15 in.
CHASSIS [J-3800/J-4500/J-4600/J-4700/J-4800]: Wheelbase: 132 in. Overall length: 205.6 in. Front tread: 63.9 in. Rear tread: 64.4 in. Tires: (J-4500) 8.25 x 15 in.; (J-4600) 7.00 x 16 in.; (J-4700) 7.50 x 16 in.; (J-4800) 7.50 x 16 in.
CHASSIS [CJ-5]: Wheelbase: 81 in. Overall length: 133 in. Front tread: 48.25 in. Rear

1971 AMC Jeep, J-100 Super Wagoneer Station Wagon (RPZ)

TECHNICAL: Manual, synchromesh transmission. Speeds: 3F/1R. Column-mounted gearshift. Single-plate, dry-disc clutch. (1/2-Ton Trucks, all CJ-5/CJ-6/DJ-5) semi-floating rear axle; (all others) full-floating rear axle. Four-wheel hydraulic, drum brakes. Pressed steel wheels. Technical Options: Four-speed manual transmission. Power steering. Camper Package ($163).

1971 AMC Jeep, CJ-5 Renegade II Universal Jeep (OCW)

OPTIONS: Rear bumper. Rear step bumper. AM radio. Clock. Cigar lighter. Camper Package ($163). 327 V-8 ($220). Power steering ($135). Four-speed transmission ($105). Turbo-Hydra-Matic transmission ($280). Thriftside pickup (add $105). 225 six-cylinder engine in CJ (average $215). Four-speed transmission in CJ (average $180). CJ camper kit ($2,200). 350 cid V-8 in J-100 ($220).

HISTORICAL: Introduced: Fall 1970. Calendar year sales: 38,979 (All series). Calendar year production: 54,480 (All series). At the same time the evidence was clear that American Motors' efforts to broaden the Jeep's appeal were paying off. For the first six months of 1971, Jeep wholesale sales were up 26 percent over the same 1970 period. Overall, sales for the same period totalled 17,878 compared to 14,186 in 1970.

1972 JEEP

1972 AMC Jeep, Commando Station Wagon (OCW)

JEEP — 1972 SERIES — ALL ENGINES: Numerous styling and option changes were included in the Jeep picture for 1972. The Commando got the most attention with a new front end design and interior changes. The wheelbase grew, and both the body and tread got wider.

Continuing the wave of change for 1972 at Jeep was a new line of engines for the CJ models. Although the vintage F-head four-cylinder was still offered for export, the "Dauntless" V-6 was no longer available. The standard CJ engine now was the AMC 232 cid six-cylinder with the larger 258 cid six-cylinder and 304 cid and 360 cid V-8 engines available as options. The CJ-5 and CJ-6 retained their familiar look, but now had longer wheelbases and increased length. In addition, their front and rear treads were increased by three and 1.5 inches respectively. Also adopted was a new Dana model 30 open-end front axle and a rear axle with a capacity of 3,000 pounds, which was 500 pounds greater than the unit used in 1971. Use of a Dana model 20 transfer case reduced overall noise and provided a smoother shifting precedure. Appreciated by long-time Jeep fans, was the latest model's larger diameter clutch, improved heater and suspended clutch and brake pedals. Numerous new options were listed for the CJ Jeeps including a fixed rear tailgate with a rear-mounted spare, a vinyl-coated full fabric top, 15 in. wheelcovers and oil and ammeter gauges.

The Commando also had a longer wheelbase and the same engine lineup as the CJ models. Its appearance was changed due to a new front end with a stamped steel grille that enclosed both the head and parking lights. The Commando, like the CJ Jeep, also was equipped with an open-ended front axle, larger brakes and increased capacity clutch. Changes to the Commando's interior included repositioned front seats and reshaped rear wheelhousings.

The J-series trucks now could be ordered with a new 6000 GVW capacity on the 120 in. wheelbase chassis. Common to all J-trucks were larger clutches and brakes. No styling changes were made in their appearance, but interiors featured new seat trim patterns.

I.D. DATA: The VIN is located on the left front door hinge pillar and left firewall as before, but the format was changed. The VIN still has 13 symbols. The first indicates Jeep Corp. The second indicates model year. The third indicates transmission, drivetrain, and assembly plant. The fourth and fifth indicate series or model. The sixth symbol identifies body style. The seventh symbol indicates model type and GVW. The eighth symbol indicates the engine. Engine codes were: E=232 cid six-cylinder; A=258 cid six-cylinder; H=304 cid V-8; N=360 cid V-8. The next five symbols are the sequential production number.

Model	Body Type	Price	Weight	Prod. Total
J-100 — 1/4-Ton — 4 x 4				
1414	4d Station Wagon	4398	3808	—
1414C	4d Custom Station Wagon	4640	3843	—
Jeepster Commando — 1/4-Ton — 4 x 4				
8705F	Station Wagon	3408	3002	—
87050	Roadster	3257	2790	—
CJ-5 — 1/4-Ton — 4x4				
83050	Jeep	2955	2437	—
CJ-6 — 1/4-Ton — 4x4				
84050	Jeep	3045	2499	—
DJ-5 — 1/4-Ton — 2x2				
85050	Open	2475	2255	—
Commando — 1/2-Ton — 4x4				
8705H	Pickup	3284	2939	—
J-2500 — 1/2-Ton — 4x4				
2406W	Chassis & Cab	3181	3272	—
2406W	Thriftside Pickup	3328	3567	—
2406W	Townside Pickup	3328	3675	—
Series J-2600 — 1/2-Ton — 4x4				
2406X	Thriftside Pickup	3449	3689	—
2406X	Townside Pickup	3449	3797	—
Series J-4500 — 1/2-Ton — 4x4				
3408W	Chassis & Cab	3210	3298	—
3408W	Townside Pickup	3365	3726	—
Series J-4600 — 1/2-Ton — 4x4				
3408X	Chassis & Cab	3331	3436	—
3408X	Townside Pickup	3486	3864	—
Series J-4700 — 1/2-Ton — 4x4				
3408Y	Chassis & Cab	3698	3732	—
3408Y	Townside Pickup	3853	4160	—
Series J-4800 — 1/2-Ton — 4x4				
3407Z	Chassis & Cab	4107	4013	—
3407Z	Townside Pickup	4262	4441	—

1972 AMC Jeep, CJ-5 Universal Jeep With Hardtop (OCW)

ENGINE [Standard J-100 Wagoneer]: Inline. OHV. Six-cylinder. Cast iron block. Bore & stroke: 3.75 x 3.5 in. Displacement: 232 cid. Brake horsepower: 145 at 4300 rpm. Torque: 185 lb.-ft. at 1800 rpm. Seven main bearings. Hydraulic valve lifters. Carburetor: One-barrel.

ENGINE [Standard Commando V-6]: Vee-block. OHV. Bore & stroke: 3.75 x 3.4 in. Displacement: 225 cid. Brake horsepower: 160 at 4200 rpm.

ENGINE [Standard CJ-5/CJ-6/DJ-5]: Inline. OHV. Six-cylinder. Cast iron block. Bore & stroke: 3.75 x 3.5 in. Displacement: 232 cid. Brake horsepower: 145 at 4300 rpm. Torque: 185 lb.-ft. at 1800 rpm. Seven main bearings. Hydraulic valve lifters. Carburetor: One-barrel.

ENGINE [Standard: J-2500, J-2600, J-4500, J-4600]: Inline. OHV. Six-cylinder. Cast iron block. Bore & stroke: 3.75 x 3.9 in. Displacement: 258 cid. Compression ratio: 8.0:1. Brake horsepower: 110 at 3500 rpm. Max torque: 195 lb.-ft. at 2000 rpm. Seven main bearings. Hydraulic valve lifters. Carburetor: Carter one-barrel model YF.

ENGINE [Optional J-2500, J-4500, J-4600, $165]: V-block. OHV. Eight-cylinder. Cast iron block. Bore & stroke: 3.75 x 3.44 in. Displacement: 304 cid. Compression ratio: 8.4:1. Net horsepower: 150 at 4400 rpm. Net torque: 245 lb.-ft. at 2500 rpm. Five main bearings. Hydraulic valve lifters. Carburetor: Autolite two-barrel model 2100.

ENGINE [Standard J-4700, J-4800; Optional $212]: J-2500, J-2600, J-4500, J-4600): V-type. OHV. Eight-cylinder. Cast iron block. Bore & stroke: 4.08 x 3.44 in. Displacement: 360 cid. Compression ratio: 8.5:1. Net horsepower: 175 at 4000 rpm. Net torque: 285 lb.-ft. at 2400 rpm. Five main bearings. Hydraulic valve lifters. Carburetor: Autolite two-barrel.

1972 AMC Jeep, J-100 Wagoneer Station Wagon (JAG)

CHASSIS [Wagoneer]: Wheelbase: 110 in. Overall length: 183.66 in. Width: 75.6 in.

CHASSIS [Commando]: Wheelbase: 104 in. Overall length: 174.5 in.

CHASSIS [CJ-5]: Wheelbase: 84 in. Overall length: 138.9 in. Front tread: 51.5 in. Rear tread: 50 in. Tires: (with 232 cid six) 8.45 x 15; (with 258 cid six) H78 x 15; (with V-8) 6.00 x 16.

CHASSIS [CJ-6]: Wheelbase: 104 in. Overall length: 158.9 in. Front tread: 51.5 in. Rear tread: 50 in. Tires: 7.35 x 15 in.

CHASSIS [DJ-5]: Wheelbase: 84 in. Overall length: 138.9 in. Tires: 7.35 x 15 in.

CHASSIS [J-4500/J-4600/J-4700/J-4800]: Wheelbase: 132 in. Overall length: 205.6 in. Front tread: 63.9 in. Rear tread: 64.4 in. Tires: [J-4500] 8.25 x 15 in.; [J-4600] 7.00 x 16 in.; [J-4700] 7.50 x 16 in.; [J-4800] 7.50 x 16 in.

CHASSIS [Commando]: Wheelbase: 104 in. Overall length: 174.5 in. Front tread: 51.5 in. Rear tread: 50 in. Tires: 7.35 x 15 in.

CHASSIS [J-2500/J-2600]: Wheelbase: 120 in. Overall length: 193.6 in. Front tread: 63.5 in. Rear tread: 63.8 in. Tires: [J-2500] 8.25 x 15 in.; [J-2600] 7.00 x 16 in.

TECHNICAL [J-Series]: Manual, synchromesh transmission. Speeds: 3F/1R (J-4800 4F/1R). Column (floor J-4800) mounted gearshift. Single-plate, dry-disc clutch. (1/2-Ton Trucks, DJ-5, CJ-5, CJ-6) semi-floating rear axle; (all others) full-floating rear axle. Hydraulic drum (four-wheel) brakes. Pressed steel wheels. Technical Options: Three-speed automatic transmission. Four-speed manual transmission. Power steering. Power brakes. Trac-Lok differential. Heavy-duty cooling system. Heavy-duty alternator. Heavy-duty battery. Semi-automatic front hubs. Reserve fuel tank. Fuel tank skid plate. Heavy-duty snow plow. Winches.

TECHNICAL [CJ-5, CJ-6]: Manual synchromesh transmission. Speeds: 3F/1R. Floor-mounted gearshift. Single-plate, dry-disc clutch. Technical Options: Four-speed manual transmission. Power brakes. Power steering. Heavy-duty springs. Heavy-duty shock absorbers. Trac-Lok differential. Semi-automatic front hubs. Heavy-duty cooling system.

TECHNICAL [Commando Series]: Manual synchromesh transmission. Speeds: 3F/1R. Floor-mounted gearshift. Single-plate, dry-disc clutch. Technical Options: Three-speed automatic transmission (column shift). Four-speed (floor shift) manual transmission. Power brakes. Power steering. Heavy-duty springs. Heavy-duty shock absorbers. Heavy-duty alternator. Heavy-duty battery. Trac-Lok differential. Semi-automatic. Heavy-duty cooling system. Heavy-duty snow plow. Winches. Power-take-off.

OPTIONS: Power steering ($151). Power brakes ($48). 327 cid V-8 engine ($220). Four-speed transmission ($112). Turbo-Hydra-Matic transmission ($280). Thriftside pickup on J2500 chassis (add $155). Townside pickup on 120 in. wheelbase chassis (add $135). Townside pickup on 132 in. wheelbase chassis (add $165). Gladiator camper on chassis and cab ($4218). Pickup body for Gladiator chassis and cab ($160).

HISTORICAL: Business was up over 30 percent in 1972, with retail sales of 51,621 Jeeps. Production was up to 71,255 units, a 34 percent boost. Deliveries for the season included 18,744 CJs, 9,115 Commandos, 14,524 Wagoneers and 9,238 trucks. For the first time, Jeep built more V-8s than other types of engines. The totals were: 134 cid four — 6,968; 232 cid L-6 9,021; 304 cid V-8 — 17,696; 360 cid V-8 -18,215.

1973 AMC Jeep, CJ-5 Universal Jeep (JAG)

JEEP — 1973 SERIES — ALL ENGINES: 1973 was the year that the full impact of American Motor's development plan was apparent in the design of Jeep vehicles. The J-series trucks had new double-wall side panels for the bed, a wider tailgate (operable with one hand) and a new mechanical clutch linkage that had a longer service life and required less maintenance. The interior was distinguished by a redesigned instrument panel with increased padding and easier-to-read gauges, including "direct-reading" oil and ammeter gauges. But, the big news for the J-trucks was the availability of the full-time Quadra-Trac four-wheel drive option. This system, offered on J-2500/2600/4500 and 4600 models, included the 360 cid V-8 and automatic transmission as standard equipment. An optional low range unit was available, either as a dealer-installed feature or as original equipment, direct from the factory. Quadra-Trac allowed all four wheels to operate at their own speeds, each receiving the proper portion of driving power. The key to this system was a limited-slip differential that transmitted power to the front and rear wheels.

The CJ Jeeps were given a new, more stylish instrument panel with a large center gauge encompassing the speedometer and the temperature and fuel gauges. Mounted to the left and right of this unit were the ammeter and oil pressure gauges. Beginning in January, 1973, the Jeep "Renegade" was available. It had a standard 304 cid V-8, H78 x 16 tires on styled wheels, blacked-out hood, racing stripes, fender lip extensions, dual mirrors and visors, a custom vinyl interior, rear-mounted spare tire, plus transmission and fuel tank skid plates.

In its last year of production, the Commando was given standard upgraded tires and new axle joints.

1973 AMC Jeep, J-2500 Gladiator Townside Pickup (CW)

I.D. DATA: VIN located on the left front door hinge pillar and left firewall. VIN still has 13 symbols. The first indicates Jeep Corp. The second indicates model year. The third indicates transmission, drivetrain and assembly plant. The fourth and fifth indicate series or model. The sixth symbol identifies body style. The seventh symbol indicates model type and GVW. The eighth symbol indicates the engine. Engine codes were: E=232 cid six-cylinder; A=258 cid six-cylinder; H=304 cid V-8; N=360 cid V-8; P=360 cid V-8. Z=401 cid V-8. The next five symbols are the sequential production number.

Model	Body Type	Price	Weight	Prod. Total
Jeep Wagoneer — 1/2-Ton — 4x4				
14	4dr Standard Station Wagon	4501	3810	—
15	4dr Custom Station Wagon	4739	3850	—
Jeep Commando — 1/2-Ton — 4x4				
89	2dr Station Wagon	3506	3010	—
87	2dr Roadster	3355	2800	—
CJ-5 — 1/4-Ton — 4x4				
83	Jeep	3086	2450	—

CJ-6 — 1/4-Ton — 4x4				
84	Jeep	3176	2510	—
DJ-5 — 1/4-Ton — 4x2				
85	Jeep	2606	2270	—
Commando — 1/2-Ton — 4x4				
88	Pickup	3382	2950	—
Series J-2500 — 1/2-Ton — 4x4				
25	Thriftside Pickup	3353	3570	—
25	Townside Pickup	3353	3715	—
Series J-2600 — 1/2-Ton — 4x4				
26	Chassis & Cab	3327	3395	—
26	Thriftside Pickup	3474	3690	—
26	Townside Pickup	3474	3835	—
Series J-4500 — 3/4-Ton — 4x4				
45	Chassis & Cab	3235	3300	—
45	Townside Pickup	3390	3760	—
Series J-4600 — 3/4-Ton — 4x4				
46	Chassis & Cab	3356	3435	—
46	Townside Pickup	3511	3895	—
Series J-4700 — 3/4-Ton — 4x4				
47	Chassis & Cab	3723	3730	—
Series J-4800 — 3/4-Ton — 4x4				
48	Chassis & Cab	4132	4015	—
48	Townside Pickup	4287	4475	—

ENGINE [Standard: Commando/CJ-5/CJ-6]: Inline. OHV. Six-cylinder. Cast iron block. Bore & stroke: 3.75 x 3.5 in. Displacement: 232 cid. Compression ratio: 8.0:1. Brake horsepower: 145 at 4300 rpm. Torque: 215 lb.-ft. at 1600 rpm. Net horsepower: 100 at 3600 rpm. Torque: 185 lb.-ft. at 1800 rpm. Seven main bearings. Hydraulic valve lifters. Carburetor: Single Carter one-barrel model YF.

ENGINE [Standard: Cherokee and J-2500/J-4500/J-4600. Optional: Commando/J-4800]: Inline. Six-cylinder. Cast iron block. Bore & stroke: 3.75 x 3.9 in. Displacement: 258 cid. Compression ratio: 8.0:1. Net horsepower: 110 at 3500 rpm. Net torque: 195 lb.-ft. at 2000 rpm. Seven main bearings. Hydraulic valve lifters. Carburetor: Single Carter one-barrel model YF.

1973 AMC Jeep, J-2600 Gladiator Townside Pickup (JAG)

ENGINE [Optional: Commando/CJ-5/CJ-6; Standard: CJ-5/Renegade]: V-type. OHV. Eight-cylinder. Cast iron block. Bore & stroke: 3.75 x 3.44 in. Displacement: 304 cid. Compression ratio: 8.4:1. Net horsepower: 150 at 4200 rpm. Net torque: 245 lb.-ft. at 2500 rpm. Five main bearings. Hydraulic valve lifters. Carburetor: Single two-barrel.

ENGINE [Standard: Wagoneer. Optional: J-2500/J-2600/J-4500/J-4700/J-4800]: V-type. OHV. Eight-cylinder. Cast iron block. Bore & stroke: 4.08 x 3.44 in. Displacement: 360 cid. Compression ratio: 8.5:1. Net horsepower: 175 at 4000 rpm. Net torque: 285 lb.-ft. at 2400 rpm. Five main bearings. Hydraulic valve lifters. Carburetor: Single two-barrel.

ENGINE [Optional: J-2500/J-2600/J-4500/J-4700/J-4800]: V-type. OHV. Eight-cylinder. Cast iron block. Bore & stroke: 4.08 x 3.44 in. Displacement: 360 cid. Compression ratio: 8.5:1. Net horsepower: 195 at 4400 rpm. Net torque: 295 lb.-ft. at 2900 rpm. Five main bearings. Hydraulic valve lifters. Carburetor: Single four-barrel.

1973 AMC Jeep, Super Wagoneer Station Wagon (JAG)

CHASSIS [Wagoneer]: Wheelbase: 110 in. Overall length: 183.66 in. Width: 75.6 in.

CHASSIS [Commando]: Wheelbase: 104 in. Overall length: 174.5 in. Front tread: 51.5 in. Rear tread: 50.0 in. Tires: F78-15B.

CHASSIS [J-2500]: Wheelbase: 120 in. Overall length: 193.6 in. Front tread: 63.5 in. Rear tread: 63.8 in. Tires: F78-15 in.

CHASSIS [J-2600]: Wheelbase: 120 in. Overall length: 193.6 in. Front tread: 63.5 in. Rear tread: 63.8 in. Tires: 7.00 x 16 in.

CHASSIS [J-4500]: Wheelbase: 132 in. Overall length: 205.6 in. Front tread: 63.9 in. Rear tread: 64.4 in. Tires: F78-15 in.

CHASSIS [J-4600]: Wheelbase: 132 in. Overall length: 205.6 in. Front tread: 63.9 in. Rear tread: 64.4 in. Tires: 7.00 x 16 in.

CHASSIS [J-4700]: Wheelbase: 132 in. Overall length: 205.6 in. Front tread: 63.9 in. Rear tread: 64.4 in. Tires: 7.50 x 16 in.

CHASSIS [J-4800]: Wheelbase: 132 in. Overall length: 205.6 in. Front tread: 63.9 in. Rear tread: 64.4 in. Tires: 7.50 x 16 in.

CHASSIS [CJ-5]: Wheelbase: 84 in. Overall length: 138.9 in. Front tread: 51.5 in. Rear tread: 50.0 in. Tires: F78-15B, four-ply.

CHASSIS [CJ-6]: Wheelbase: 104 in. Overall length: 158.9 in. Front tread: 51.5 in. Rear tread: 50.0 in. Tires: F78-15B, four-ply.

1973 AMC Jeep, Wagoneer Station Wagon (AMC)

TECHNICAL [CJ-5, CJ-6]: Manual synchromesh transmission. Speeds: 3F/1R. Floor-mounted gearshift. Semi-floating rear axle. Hydraulic drum brakes. Pressed steel wheels. Technical options: Four-speed manual transmission. Power brakes. Power steering. Heavy-duty springs. Heavy-duty shock. Variety of tire sizes. Trac-Lok differential. Semi-automatic front hubs. Heavy-duty cooling system.

TECHNICAL [Commando]: Synchronized, manual transmission. Speeds: 3F/1R. Floor-mounted gearshift. Semi-floating rear axle. Technical options: Automatic Transmission. Four-speed manual transmission. Power brakes. Power steering. Heavy-duty springs. Heavy-duty shock absorbers. Heavy-duty alternator. Heavy-duty battery. Trac-Lok differential. Semi-automatic front hubs. Heavy-duty cooling system. Power-take-off. Reserve fuel tank (J-Series).

TECHNICAL [J-2500/J-2600/J-4500/J-4600/J-4700/J-4800]: Synchronized, manual transmission. Speeds: 3F/1R (J-4800: 4F/1R). Column-mounted gearshift (J-4800: floor-mounted). Technical options: Automaitc Transmission. Power brakes. Power steering. Four-speed manual transmission. Trac-Lok differential. Heavy-duty cooling system. Heavy-duty alternator. Heavy-duty battery. Power-take-off. Semi-automatic hubs.

OPTIONS: Chrome front bumper (CJ). Chrome rear bumper (CJ). AM Radio. Electric clock. Cigar lighter. Wheel covers. Full-width split front seat (Commando). Tinted glass. Air conditioning. Special Decor Group (Commando). Bucket seats with center armrest (J-Series). West Coast Mirrors (J-Series). Courtesy lights. Custom Decor Group (J-Series). Outside passenger side mirror. Dual horns (J-Series). Tonneau cover (J-Series). Rear step bumper (J-Series). Two-tone paint (J-Series). Woodgrain trim (J-Series). Safari top (Commando Roadster/CJ). Meta top (CJ). Fabric top (CJ). Front bucket seats (CJ). Rear bench seat (Commando). Power brakes ($45). 304 cid V-8 ($126-165). 258 cid six ($45). Custom Decor package ($179). Four-speed manual transmission ($107).

HISTORICAL: Introduced: Fall, 1972. Calendar year sales: (Jeep sales) 68,430. Calendar year production: (all models) 94,035.

1974 JEEP

JEEP — 1974 SERIES — ALL ENGINES: For 1974, the Cherokee was introduced into the sports-utility field. It was a two-door station wagon with a Gladiator truck type grille. Wagoneers received a new front end treatment with the parking lamps in the grille. The Jeepster Commando line was discontinued. Renegades, which were previously available as a limited edition option, were made a regular production CJ model. In addition to the 304 cid V-8, they had special paint and graphics, a rear-mounted spare, roll bar, passenger assist rail, dual sun visors, oil and amp. gages and styled aluminum wheel rims. The Quadra-Trac four-wheel-drive system was offered on all J-series trucks with either six- or eight-cylinder engines. Other improvements included larger brakes and a shorter turning radius for the J-trucks.

1974 AMC Jeep, CJ-5 Renegade Universal Jeep (AMC)

JEEP — 1974 SERIES — ALL ENGINES: For 1974, the Cherokee was introduced into the sports-utility field. It was a two-door station wagon with a Gladiator truck type grille. Wagoneers received a new front end treatment with the parking lamps in the grille. The Jeepster Commando line was discontinued. Renegades, which were previously available as a limited edition option, were made a regular production CJ model. In addition to the 304 cid V-8, they had special paint and graphics, a rear-mounted spare, roll bar, passenger assist rail, dual sun visors, oil and amp. gages and styled aluminum wheel rims. The Quadra-Trac four-wheel-drive system was offered on all J-series trucks with either six- or eight-cylinder engines. Other improvements included larger brakes and a shorter turning radius for the J-trucks.

I.D. DATA: VIN located on the left front door hinge pillar and left firewall. VIN still has 13 symbols. The first indicates Jeep Corp. The second indicates model year. The third indicates transmission, drivetrain and assembly plant. The fourth and fifth indicate series or model. The sixth symbol identifies body style. The seventh symbol indicates model type and GVW. The eigth symbol indicates the engine. Engine codes were: E=232 cid six-cylinder; A=258 cid six-cylinder; H=304 cid V-8; N=360 cid V-8; P=360 cid V-8. Z=401 cid V-8. The next five symbols are the sequential production number.

1974 AMC Jeep, J-10 Townside Pickup (CW)

Model	Body Type	Price	Weight	Prod. Total
Wagoneer — 1/2-Ton — 4x4				
14	4dr Station Wagon	5406	4270	—
15	4dr Custom Station Wagon	5704	4290	—
Cherokee — 1/2-Ton — 4x4				
16	2dr Station Wagon	4161	3870	—
17	2dr "S" Station Wagon	4724	3870	—
CJ-5 — 1/4-Ton — 4x4				
83	Jeep	3574	2540	—
CJ-6 — 1/4-Ton — 4x4				
84	Jeep	3670	2600	—
J-10 — 1/2-Ton — 4x4				
25	Townside Pickup (SWB)	3776	3770	—
45	Townside Pickup (LWB)	3837	3820	—
J-20 — 3/4-Ton — 4x4				
46	Townside Pickup (LWB)	4375	4390	—

1974 AMC Jeep, Cherokee 'S' Two-Door Station Wagon (OCW)

ENGINE [Standard: Cherokee and J-10; Optional: CJ-5/CJ-6]: Inline. OHV. Six-cylinder. Cast iron block. Bore & stroke: 3.85 x 3.90 in. Displacement: 258 cid. Compression ratio: 8.0:1. Net horsepower: 110 at 3500 rpm. Torque: 195 lb.-ft. at 2000 rpm. Seven main bearings. Hydraulic valve lifters. Carburetor: Carter one-barrel model YF.

ENGINE [Standard: Wagoneer and J-20; Optional: J-10]: V-type. OHV. Eight-cylinder. Cast iron block. Bore & stroke: 4.08 x 3.44 in. Displacement: 360 cid. Compression ratio: 8.5:1. Net horsepower: 175 at 4000 rpm. Net torque: 285 lb.-ft. at 2400 rpm. Five main bearings. Hydraulic valve lifters. Carburetor: Single two-barrel.

ENGINE [Optional: J-10/J-20]: V-type. OHV. Eight-cylinder. Cast iron block. Bore & stroke: 4.17 x 3.68 in. Displacement: 401 cid. Net horsepower: 235 at 4600 rpm. Five main bearings. Hydraulic valve lifters. Carburetor: Four-barrel.

ENGINE [Standard: CJ-5/CJ-6]: Inline. OHV. Six-cylinder. Cast iron block. Bore & stroke: 3.75 x 3.50 in. Displacement: 232 cid. Compression ratio: 8.0:1. Net horsepower: 100 at 3600 rpm. Net torque: 185 lb.-ft. at 1800 rpm. Seven main bearings. Hydraulic valve lifters. Carburetor: Carter one-barrel model YF.

ENGINE [Optional: CJ-5/CJ-6; Standard: Renegade]: V-type. OHV. Eight-cylinder. Cast iron block. Bore & stroke: 3.75 x 3.44 in. Displacement: 304 cid. Compression ratio: 8.4:1. Net horsepower: 150 at 4200 rpm. Net torque: 245 lb.-ft. at 2500 rpm. Five main bearings. Hydraulic valve lifters. Carburetor: Autolite two-barrel model 2100.

1974 AMC Jeep, J-2600 Pioneer Townside Pickup (AMC)

CHASSIS [Cherokee]: Wheelbase: 109 in. Overall length: 183.7 in. Tires: F78-15.

CHASSIS [Wagoneer]: Wheelbase: 109 in. Overall length: 183.7 in. Tires: F78-15.

CHASSIS [CJ-5]: Wheelbase: 84 in. Overall length: 138.9 in. Front tread: 51.5 in. Rear tread: 50.0 in. Tires: F78-15, four-ply.

CHASSIS [CJ-6]: Wheelbase: 104 in. Overall length: 158.9 in. Front tread: 51.5 in. Rear tread: 50.0 in. Tires: F78-15, four-ply.

CHASSIS [J-10]: Wheelbase: 118.7/130.7 in. Overall length: 192.5/204.5 in. Height: 69.3/69.1 in. Front tread: 63.3 in. Rear tread: 63.8 in. Tires: G78-15 in.

CHASSIS [J-20]: Wheelbase: 130.7 in. Overall length: 204.5 in. Height: 70.7 in. Front tread: 63.3 in. Rear tread: 63.8 in. Tires: 8.00 x 16.5D in.

TECHNICAL [CJ-5, CJ-6, J-10, J-20]: Same as 1973, except new option: Quadra-Trac full-time four-wheel-drive for J-10 and J-20 models.

OPTIONS: 258 cid six-cylinder engine in CJ-5/CJ-6 ($54). 360 cid V-8 engine in J-10 ($201). 401 cid V-8 engine, in Wagoneer ($94); in J-10 ($295); in J-20 ($94). 304 cid V-8 engine in CJ-5/CJ-6, except Renegade ($126). Four-speed transmission in CJs ($107). Renegade option package ($701). Wagoneer woodgrain trim ($179). CJ metal cab ($425). Power disc brakes for Cherokee ($65). Power brakes for CJ ($45).

1974 AMC Jeep Custom Wagoneer Station Wagon (AMC)

HISTORICAL: Introduced: Fall, 1973. Calendar year sales: (all Jeep models) 67,110. Calendar year production: (all models) 92,283. Model year production: 96,763. Business was up 16.6 percent. Model year output included 15,350 Wagoneers; 43,137 CJ-5s; 2,826 CJ-6s; 18,277 Cherokees; and 13,874 Jeep trucks. Jeep Corp. operated as a subsidiary of American Motors Corp., with its headquarters in Detroit. The main Jeep factory was located in Toledo, Ohio. C. Mashigan was director of design. Now famous automotive historian John A. Conde was manager of public relations. The Jeep Cherokee won the Sports Car Club of America's Pro-Rally series in 1974. There was a slight rise in popularity of six-cylinder powered Jeep vehicles in 1974, up to 49 percent of production (versus 37.8 percent in 1973).

1975 JEEP

JEEP — 1975 SERIES — ALL ENGINES: Cherokees received sporty new trim options for 1975. At midyear, the Cherokee Chief was introduced at the Detroit Auto Show. It had a wider-than-normal track, fat tires and specific trim. The special graphics included model callouts on the rocker panels. New-for-1975 Cherokee options included Cruise Command speed control, AM/FM quadraphonic sound system and a rear window defogger. Wagoneers got electronic ignition, a new power steering system and suspension revisions. Leading the list of appearance changes for the 1975 CJ models was the availability of the Levi's vinyl front bucket and rear bench seat feature. This was standard for the Renegade model with optional for the CJ-5. The Renegade also had a new body stripe format. Added to the CJ option list was a factory-installed AM radio with a weatherproof case and a fixed length whip-type antenna. The full soft top was of a new design with improved visibility and larger door openings.

The J-Series pickup trucks were available with a new Pioneer trim package consisting of woodgrain exterior trim, deep pile carpeting, pleated fabric seats, chrome front bumpers, bright exterior window moldings, deluxe door trim pads, bright wheelcovers (J-10), bright hub caps (J-20), dual horns, locking glove box, cigar lighter, woodgrain instrument cluster trim and bright armrest overlays.

1975 AMC Jeep, CJ-5 Levis Renegade (AMC)

I.D. DATA: VIN located on the left front door hinge pillar and left firewall. VIN still has 13 symbols. The first indicates Jeep Corp. The second indicates model year. The third indicates transmission, drivetrain and assembly plant. The fourth and fifth indicate series or model. The sixth symbol identifies body style. The seventh symbol now indicates the engine. Engine codes were: E=232 cid six-cylinder; A=258 cid six-cylinder; H=304 cid V-8; N=360 cid V-8; P=360 cid V-8. Z=401 cid V-8. The next six symbols are the sequential production number beginning at 000001.

1975 AMC Jeep, J-20 Townside Pioneer Pickup (AMC)

Model	Body Type	Price	Weight	Prod. Total
Wagoneer — 1/2-Ton — 4x4				
14	4dr Standard Station Wagon	6013	4240	—
15	4dr Custom Station Wagon	6246	4256	—
Cherokee — 1/2-Ton — 4x4				
16	2dr Station Wagon	4851	3657	—
17	2dr "S" Station Wagon	5399	3677	—
CJ-5 — 1/4-Ton — 4x4 — 84 in. w.b.				
83	Jeep	4099	2648	32,486
CJ-6 — 1/4-Ton — 4x4 — 104 in. w.b.				
84	Jeep	4195	2714	2,935
J-10 — 1/2-Ton — 4x4 — 119/131 in. w.b.				
25	Townside Pickup (SWB)	4228	3712	2,258
45	Townside Pickup (LWB)	4289	3770	4,721
J-20 — 3/4-Ton — 4x4 — 131 in. w.b.				
46	Townside Pickup	4925	4333	2,977

NOTE: See "Historical" for additional production data.

ENGINE [Standard: Cherokee and J-10; Optional: CJ-5/CJ-6]: Inline. OHV. Six-cylinder. Cast iron block. Bore & stroke: 3.75 x 3.9 in. Displacement: 258 cid. Compression ratio: 8.0:1. Net horsepower: 110 at 3500 rpm. Torque: 195 lb.-ft. at 2000 rpm. Seven main bearings. Hydraulic valve lifters. Carburetor: Single Carter one-barrel. (Note: This engine was not available in California where a four-barrel version of the 360 cid V-8 was standard.)

1975 AMC Jeep, Cherokee 'S' Station Wagon (AMC)

ENGINE [Standard: Wagoneer and J-20; Optional: J-10]: V-type. OHV. Eight-cylinder. Cast iron block. Bore & stroke: 4.08 x 3.44 in. Displacement: 360 cid. Compression ratio: 8.5:1. Net horsepower: 175 at 4000 rpm. Net torque: 285 lb.-ft. at 2400 rpm. Five main bearings. Hydraulic valve lifters. Carburetor: Single two-barrel.

ENGINE [Optional: J-10/J-20]: V-type. OHV. Eight-cylinder. Cast iron block. Bore & stroke: 4.08 x 3.44 in. Displacement: 360 cid. Net horsepower: 195 at 4400 rpm. Five main bearings. Hydraulic valve lifters. Carburetor: Single four-barrel.

ENGINE [Optional: J-10/J-20]: V-type. OHV. Eight-cylinder. Cast iron block. Bore & stroke: 4.17 x 3.68 in. Displacement: 401 cid. Net horsepower: 235 at 4600 rpm. Five main bearings. Hydraulic valve lifters. Carburetor: Single four-barrel.

ENGINE [Standard: CJ-5/CJ-6]: Inline. OHV. Six-cylinder. Cast iron block. Bore & stroke: 3.75 x 3.50 in. Displacement: 232 cid. Compression ratio: 8.0:1. Net horsepower: 100 at 3600 rpm. Net torque: 185 lb.-ft. at 1800 rpm. Seven main bearings. Hydraulic valve lifters. Carburetor: Carter one-barrel model YF.

ENGINE [Standard: Renegade; Optional CJ-5/CJ-6]: V-type. OHV. Eight-cylinder. Cast iron block. Bore & stroke: 3.75 x 3.44 in. Displacement: 304 cid. Compression ratio: 8.4:1. Net horsepower: 150 at 4200 rpm. Net torque: 245 lb.-ft. at 2500 rpm. Seven main bearings. Hydraulic valve lifters. Carburetor: Autolite two-barrel model 2100.

CHASSIS [Wagoneer]: Wheelbase: 109 in. Overall length: 183.7 in. Tires: F78-15.

CHASSIS [Cherokee]: Wheelbase: 109 in. Overall length: 183.7 in. Tires: F78-15.

CHASSIS [CJ-5]: Wheelbase: 84 in. Overall length: 138.9 in. Height: 69.5 in. Front tread: 51.5 in. Rear tread: 50.0 in. Tires: F78-15B in.

CHASSIS [CJ-6]: Wheelbase: 104 in. Overall length: 158.9 in. Height: 68.3 in. Front tread: 51.5 in. Rear tread: 50.0 in. Tires: F78-15B in.

1975 AMC Jeep Cherokee Chief Station Wagon (AMC)

CHASSIS [J-10 SWB]: Wheelbase: 119.0 in. Overall length: 193.6 in. Height: 65.9 in. Front tread: 63.1 in. Rear tread: 64.9 in. Tires: H78-15B in.

CHASSIS [J-10/J-20 LWB]: Wheelbase: 131.0 in. Overall length: 205.6 in. Height: 71.3 in. Front tread: 64.8 in. Rear tread: 66.1 in. Tires: (J-10) H78-15B; (J-20/6,500-lb. GVW) 8.00 x 16.5; (J-20/7,200-lb. GVW) 8.75 x 16.5 in.

TECHNICAL [CJ-5/CJ-6]: Manual, synchromesh transmission. Speeds: 3F/1R. Floor-mounted gearshift. Single-plate, dry-disc clutch. Semi-floating rear axle. Overall ratio: 3.73:1, (optional) 4.27:1. Manual four-wheel hydraulic drum brakes. Pressed steel, five-bolt design wheels. Technical options: Warn locking hubs. Winches (mechanical or electric). Four-speed manual transmission (with 258 cid, one-barrel engine only). Heavy-duty cooling system. Heavy-duty springs and shock absorbers (front and rear). Rear Trac-Lok differential. 70-amp. battery. 62-amp. alternator. Cold climate group. Draw-Bar. Helper springs.

TECHNICAL [Cherokee/Wagoneeer/J-10/J-20]: Fully synchronized. Speeds: 3F/1R. Floor-mounted gearshift. Clutch: (J-10) 10.5 in., 106.75 sq. in. area, (J-20) 11.0 in., 110.96 sq. in. area. (J-10) Semi-floating rear axle; (J-20) full-floating rear axle. Overall ratio: (J-10) 3.54, 4.09:1, (J-20) 3.73:1, 4.09:1 optional. Brakes: (J-10) Hydraulic, 11 in. x 2 in.; (J-20) front power disc, 12.5 in. Wheels: (J-10) 6-bolt; (J-20) 8-bolt steel disc. Technical options: Automatic transmission Turbo Hydra-Matic. Front power disc 12.0 in. brakes (J-10). Auxiliary fuel tank. Power steering. Quadra-Trac. Rear Trak-Lok Differential (not available with Quadra-Trac). Camper Special Package. Heavy-duty battery and alternator. Four-speed transmission. Heavy-duty cooling system. Cold climate group. Heavy-duty springs and shock absorbers. Helper springs.

OPTIONS [Wagoneer/Cherokee/CJ-5]: Rear Bumperettes. Radio AM, Citizen's Band. Cigar lighter and ashtray. Swing-out tire carrier. Roll bar. Power steering, except standard in Wagoneer ($169). Four-speed transmission ($129). Power brakes. Rear seat. Renegade package ($725). Forged aluminum wheels (standard with Renegade Package). Padded instrument panel (standard with Renegade package). Passenger safety Rail. Air conditioning ($421). 304 cid V-8 in CJ ($126). 360 cid V-8 engine in Cherokee and J-10 ($201). 360 cid four-barrel V-8 engine in J-10 ($295); in J-20 ($94). Tachometer. Metal top (full or half). Push bumper. Outside passenger mirror. Woodgrain wagon ($108).

OPTIONS [J-10/J-20]: Rear bumper. Rear step bumper. Bumper guards with nerf strips. Radio AM, AM/FM stereo. Air conditioning. Sliding rear window. Cruise control. Power steering. Sport steering wheel. Leather-wrapped steering wheel. Tilt steering wheel. Steel-belted radial tires (not available for J-20). Tinted glass. Custom trim package. Light group. Convenience group. Wheel hub caps (J-20). Wheel covers (J-10). Outside passenger mirror. Two-tone paint. Aluminum cargo cap. CJ metal cab ($430).

1975 AMC-Jeep Wagoneer Station Wagon (AMC)

HISTORICAL: Introduced: Fall, 1974. Calendar year sales: (Jeep sales) 69,834. Calendar year production: (All Jeep vehicles) 105,833. (Worldwide wholesale sales) 104,936. Innovations: Introduction of Levi's seat trim. New calendar year production mark of 110,844. Model year production totaled 67,780 Jeep vehicles. This included 32,486 CJ-5s, 2,935 CJ-6s, 12,925 Cherokees, 9,296 Wagoneers, 2,258 J-2500s, 182 J-2600s, 4,721 J-4500s and 2,977 J-4600s. Use of electronic ignition system on J-Series models also started this year. In the CJ-5 series, 60.3 percent of the Jeeps had six-cylinder engines; 27 percent had AM radios and 39.7 percent had the 360 cid V-8. In the Cherokee series 71.6 percent had automatic transmission; 81 percent had power disc brakes; 73.9 percent had 360 cid or 401 cid V-8s and 14.7 percent had power steering. In the Wagoneer line, 66.8 percent had wheelcovers, 48.6 percent had an adjustable steering and 34 percent had an AM/FM stereo.

1976 JEEP

1976 AMC Jeep, CJ-5 Renegade Universal Jeep (JAG)

JEEP — 1976 SERIES — ALL ENGINES: The major story from Jeep for 1976 was the new CJ-7 model. It was described as "the most exciting vehicle to hit the four-wheel drive market in years." With a 93.5 in. wheelbase, the CJ-7 offered more front and rear legroom, more cargo space and larger, 33.8 in. wide door openings. It was available with a one-piece removable hardtop, steel side doors and a rear liftgate. A soft top was another option. The CJ-7 made Jeep history by being the first CJ model available with an automatic transmission and Quadra-Trac. The smaller Jeep CJ-5 was also available.

Wagoneers featured a new, more rugged frame that facilitated direct steering gear mounting. The woodgrained side trim package was of a new, narrower design. The Cherokee had a new design that made extensive use of box-section side rail construction. The Cherokee Chief, with standard power disc brakes, power steering and fuel tank skid plate was a regular production model this season.

The Renegade package, again available for both CJ models, was upgraded to include courtesy lights under the dash, an eight-in. day/night mirror, sports steering wheel, instrument panel overlay and bright rocker panel protection molding between the front and rear wheel wells. The CJ frame was also upgraded with splayed side rails (wider in front than back) to allow for wider spacing of the rear springs. In addition, the frame had stronger crossmembers and an integral skid plate. Other revisions included use of longer and wider multi-springs, new shock absorbers and newhold-down mounts.

The J-series trucks also had a new frame with splayed rear side rails, hold-down mounts, springs and shocks. Its crossmembers and box section side rails were also of stronger construction. All J-trucks were equipped with an improved windshield washer system having two spray nozzles.

In January, 1976 the "Honcho" package for J-10 short wheelbase models was introduced. Its primary features included five 10 x 15 in. Tracker A-T Goodyear tires with raised white lettering mounted on eight-inch slotted wheels; gold striping on the side, tailgate and fenders (with black and white accents); blue Levi's denim interior; rear step bumper; and special blue Sports steering wheel. The Honcho was offered in a choice of six exterior colors.

1976 AMC Jeep, CJ-5 Renegade Universal Jeep

575

1976 AMC Jeep, CJ-7 Universal Jeep (JAG)

I.D. DATA: VIN located on the left front door hinge pillar and left firewall. VIN still has 13 symbols. The first indicates Jeep Corp. The second indicates model year. The third indicates transmission, drivetrain and assembly plant. The fourth and fifth indicate series or model. The sixth symbol identifies body style. The seventh symbol indicates the engine. Engine codes were: E=232 cid six-cylinder; A=258 cid six-cylinder; H=304 cid V-8; N=360 cid V-8; P=360 cid V-8. Z=401 cid V-8. The next six symbols are the sequential production number beginning at 000001.

Model	Body Type	Price	Weight	Prod. Total
Wagoneer — 1/2-Ton — 4x4				
14	4dr Standard Station Wagon	6339	4329	—
15	4dr Custom Station Wagon	6572	4345	—
Cherokee — 1/2-Ton — 4x4				
16	2dr Station Wagon	5258	3918	—
17	2dr Station Wagon	5806	3938	—
CJ-5 — 1/4-Ton — 4x4 — 84 in. w.b.				
83	Jeep	4199	2641	31,116
CJ-7 — 1/4-Ton — 4x4 — 94 in. w.b.				
93	Jeep	4299	2683	21,016
J-10 — 1/2-Ton — 4x4 — 119/131 in. w.b.				
25	Townside Pickup (SWB)	4643	3773	—
45	Townside Pickup (LWB)	4704	3873	—
J-20 — 3/4-Ton — 4x4 — 131 in. w.b.				
46	Townside Pickup	5290	4285	3,210

NOTE: See "Historical" for additional production data.

1976 AMC Jeep, CJ-7 Universal Jeep With Hardtop (JAG)

ENGINE [Standard: Cherokee and J-10; Optional: CJ-5/CJ-6]: Inline. OHV. Six-cylinder. Cast iron block. Bore & stroke: 3.75 x 3.9 in. Displacement: 258 cid. Compression ratio: 8.0:1. Net horsepower: 110 at 3500 rpm. Torque: 195 lb.-ft. at 2000 rpm. Seven main bearings. Hydraulic valve lifters. Carburetor: Single Carter one-barrel. (Note: This engine was not available in California where a four-barrel version of the 360 cid V-8 was standard.)
ENGINE [Standard: Wagoneer and J-20; Optional: J-10]: V-type. OHV. Eight-cylinder. Cast iron block. Bore & stroke: 4.08 x 3.44 in. Displacement: 360 cid. Compression ratio: 8.5:1. Net horsepower: 175 at 4000 rpm. Net torque: 285 lb.-ft. at 2400 rpm. Five main bearings. Hydraulic valve lifters. Carburetor: Single two-barrel.

1976 AMC Jeep, J-10 Townside Pickup (AMC)

ENGINE [Optional: J-10/J-20]: V-type. OHV. Eight-cylinder. Cast iron block. Bore & stroke: 4.08 x 3.44 in. Displacement: 360 cid. Net horsepower: 195 at 4400 rpm. Five main bearings. Hydraulic valve lifters. Carburetor: Single four-barrel.
ENGINE [Optional: J-10/J-20]: V-type. OHV. Eight-cylinder. Cast iron block. Bore & stroke: 4.17 x 3.68 in. Displacement: 401 cid. Net horsepower: 235 at 4600 rpm. Five main bearings. Hydraulic valve lifters. Carburetor: Single four-barrel.
ENGINE [Standard: CJ-5/CJ-6]: Inline. OHV. Six-cylinder. Cast iron block. Bore & stroke: 3.75 x 3.50 in. Displacement: 232 cid. Compression ratio: 8.0:1. Net horsepower: 100 at 3600 rpm. Net torque: 185 lb.-ft. at 1800 rpm. Seven main bearings. Hydraulic valve lifters. Carburetor: Carter one-barrel model YF.
ENGINE [Standard: Renegade; Optional CJ-5/CJ-6]: V-type. OHV. Eight-cylinder. Cast iron block. Bore & stroke: 3.75 x 3.44 in. Displacement: 304 cid. Compression ratio: 8.4:1. Net horsepower: 150 at 4200 rpm. Net torque: 245 lb.-ft. at 2500 rpm. Seven main bearings. Hydraulic valve lifters. Carburetor: Autolite two-barrel model 2100.

1976 AMC Jeep, Honcho Pickup (OCW)

CHASSIS [Wagoneer]: Wheelbase: 109 in. Overall length: 183.7 in. Tires: F78-15.
CHASSIS [Cherokee]: Wheelbase: 109 in. Overall length: 183.7 in. Tires: F78-15.
CHASSIS [CJ-5]: Wheelbase: 83.5 in. Overall length: 138.5 in. Height: 67.6 in. Front tread: 51.5 in. Rear tread: 50.0 in. Tires: F78-15B in.
CHASSIS [CJ-7]: Wheelbase: 93.5 in. Overall length: 147.9 in. Height: 67.6 in. Front tread: 51.5 in. Rear tread: 50.0 in. Tires: F78-15B in.
CHASSIS [J-10]: Wheelbase: 118.7 in. Overall length: 192.5 in. Front tread: (J-10) 63.3 in., (Honcho) 65.4 in. Rear tread: (J-10) 63.8 in., (Honcho) 65.8 in. Tires: H78-15B in.
CHASSIS [J-10/J-20 LWB]: Wheelbase: 130.7 in. Overall length: 204.5 in. Front tread: 64.6 in. Rear tread: 65.9 in. Tires: (J-10) H78-15B; (J-20/6500-lb. GVW) 8.00 x 16.5; (J-20/7200-lb. GVW) 9.50 x 16.5.

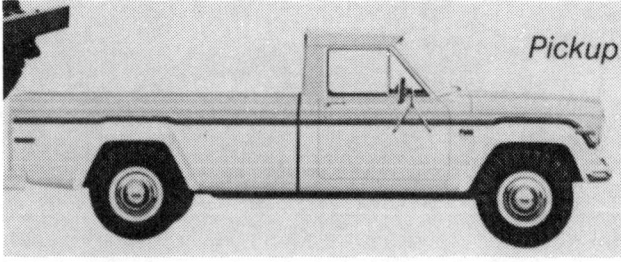

1976 AMC Jeep, J-10 Townside Pickup (JAG)

TECHNICAL [Wagoneer/Cherokee/J-10/J-20]: Manual, synchromesh transmission. Speeds: 3F/1R. Floor-mounted gearshift. Clutch: (J-10) 10.5 in. diameter, 106.75 sq. in., (J-20) 11.0 in. diameter, 110.96 sq. in. Rear axle: (J-10) Semi-floating; (J-20) full-floating. Overall ratio: (J-10) 3.54:1 or 4.09:1; (J-20) 3.73:1. (J-10) Four-wheel hydraulic drum brakes. (J-20) Front disc/rear drum brakes with power assist. Pressed steel wheels. Technical Options: Automatic transmission Turbo Hydra-Matic. Four-speed manual transmission. Quadra-Trac (available with automatic transmission only). 12-in. power front disc brakes (J-10). Snow Boss plow package. Winches (mechanical or 12-volt). Auxiliary fuel tank (20 gallon, for long wheelbase only, not available for California). Rear Trac-Lok differential. Camper special package. Fuel tank skid plate. Heavy-duty battery and alternator. Heavy-duty shock absorbers. Heavy-duty springs. Heavy-duty cooling system. Cold climate package. Locking hubs (not available with Quadra-Trac). Trailer Towing Package.

1976 AMC Jeep, Chrokee Station Wagon (JAG)

TECHNICAL [CJ-Series]: Manual, synchromesh transmission. Speeds: 3F/1R. Floor-mounted gearshift. Single-plate, dry-disc clutch. Semi-floating rear axle. Overall ratio: 3.54:1. Manual, hydraulic brakes. Pressed steel, five-bolt wheels. Technical Options: Automatic Transmission. Turbo Hydra-Matic transmission. Quadra-Trac (available with automatic transmission only). Four-speed manual transmission. Extra-duty suspension system. Front stabilizer bar. Power drum brakes (available with "304" V-8 only). Low range for Quadra-Trac (available for CJ-7 only). Heavy-duty cooling system. Rear Trac-Lok differential. 70-amp. battery. Heavy-duty alternator. Cold climate group. Steel belted radial ply tires. Winches. Snow plow. Free-running front hubs.

1976 AMC Jeep, Wagoneer Station Wagon (JAG)

OPTIONS [Wagoneer/Cherokee/Trucks]: 401 cid V-8 ($94). Power steering, except standard in Wagoneer ($179). Turbo-Hydra-Matic, except standard on Wagoneer ($325). Four-speed transmission in Cherokee ($136). Luggage rack, Wagoneer ($80). Factory air conditioning ($480). Front bumper guards with Nerf strips. Rear step bumper. Convenience group. Light group. Custom trim package. Radios: AM/FM stereo ($209); Citizens Band; AM. Forged aluminum styled wheels (J-10 only). Bucket seats (Custom, Pioneer and Honcho only). Cruise control. Power steering. Tilt steering wheel. Sports steering wheel. Leather wrapped steering wheel. Sliding rear window. Dual low profile mirror. Aluminum cargo cap. Wheelcovers. Honcho package. Pioneer package.

1976 AMC Jeep, Custom Wagoneer Station Wagon (JAG)

OPTIONS [CJ-Series]: Rear step bumper. Roll bar. Full soft top. Carpeting. Convenience group. Decor group. Radios: AM or Citizens Band. Sports steering wheel. Leather wrapped sports steering wheel. Rear seat. Swing-out tire carrier. Passenger grab rail. Tachometer and Rally clock. Padded instrument panel. Removable top, injection-molded (CJ-7 only). Outside passenger mirror. Renegade package.

1976 AMC Jeep, J-20 Townside Pickup (131 in. w.b.)

HISTORICAL: Introduced: Fall, 1975. Calendar year sales: (all models and series) 95,506. Calendar year production: 126,125. Worldwide wholesale sales: 125,879. Model year production totaled 102,450 Jeep vehicles. This included 16,520 Wagoneers; 18,859 Cherokees; 21,016 CJ-7s; 2,431 CJ-6s (export only); 31,116 CJ-5s; 9,298 J-10s and 3,210 J-20s.

1976 AMC Jeep, Cherokee Chief Two-Door Wagon (rear view)

1977 JEEP

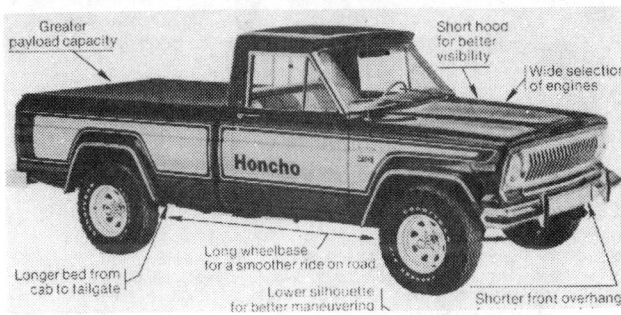

1977 AMC Jeep, Honcho Townside Pickup (JAG)

JEEP — 1977 SERIES — ALL ENGINES: This was a year of changes for Jeep CJs. Probably most exciting was the midyear introduction of the "Golden Eagle" trim package for the CJ-5 and CJ-7. It included a roll bar, white-letter off-road tires and a tachometer with either the inline six or V-8. Worthwhile and noteworthy technical improvements were made. For the first time the CJ models were available with factory air conditioning. Also debuting, as a CJ option, were power front disc brakes. To faciliate their use, the CJ Jeeps had stronger front axles and wheel spindles, as well as wider wheels and tires. Also revised was the frame. It now had fully boxed side rails. All rear panels were also strengthened. The optional four-speed manual transmission had a new 6.32:1 low gear ratio. The popular Renegade package for the CJ-5 and CJ-7 models was continued. It now included new 9.00 x 15 Goodyear "Tracker" tires. More all-new options were a center console and tilt steering. A four-door wagon was added to the Cherokee sports/utility series, which gained power front disc brakes and the 258 cid "Big Six" as standard equipment. The Cherokee two-door wagon continued and was now offered with a sporty Chief trim package and in standard and wide-stance versions. The latter featured fat raised-white-letter tires.

The most significant change made to the J-series trucks was their higher standard and optional GVW payload rating. The standard rating was increased to 6,800 pounds from 6500 and the optional ratings were increased by 400 pounds to 7,200 and 8,000 pounds. Available once more was the Honcho package for the 119 inch wheelbase J-10. It included Levi's blue denim upholstery and door inserts, a chrome front bumper, blue sports steering wheel and Honcho graphics and lettering.

1977 AMC Jeep, Cherokee Two-Door Station Wagon (OCW)

I.D. DATA: VIN located on the left front door hinge pillar and left firewall. VIN still has 13 symbols. The first indicates Jeep Corp. The second indicates model year. The third indicates transmission, drivetrain and assembly plant. The fourth and fifth indicate series or model. The sixth symbol identifies body style. The seventh symbol indicates the engine.

577

Engine codes were: E=232 cid six-cylinder; A=258 cid six-cylinder; H=304 cid V-8; N=360 cid V-8; P=360 cid V-8. Z=401 cid V-8. The next six symbols are the sequential production number beginning at 000001.

Model	Body Type	Price	Weight	Prod. Total
Wagoneer — 1/2-Ton — 4x4				
15	4dr Station Wagon	6966	4345	19,900
Cherokee — 1/2-Ton — 4x4				
16	2dr Station Wagon	5636	3971	—
17	2dr Wide Stance	6059	3991	—
18	4dr Station Wagon	5736	4106	—
CJ-5 — 1/4-Ton — 4x4 — 84 in. w.b.				
83	Jeep	4399	2659	32,996
CJ-7 — 1/4-Ton — 4x4 — 94 in. w.b.				
93	Jeep	4499	2701	25,414
J-10 — 1/2-Ton — 4x4 — 119/131 in. w.b.				
25	Townside Pickup (SWB)	4995	3826	—
45	Townside Pickup (LWB)	5059	3926	—
J-20 — 3/4-Ton — 4x4 — 131 in. w.b.				
46	Townside Pickup	5607	4285	3,343

NOTE: See "Historical" for additional production data.

1977 AMC Jeep, Cherokee Four-Door Station Wagon (OCW)

ENGINE [Standard: Cherokee and J-10; Optional: CJ-5/CJ-6]: Inline. OHV. Six-cylinder. Cast iron block. Bore & stroke: 3.75 x 3.9 in. Displacement: 258 cid. Compression ratio: 8.0:1. Net horsepower: 110 at 3500 rpm. Torque: 195 lb.-ft. at 2000 rpm. Seven main bearings. Hydraulic valve lifters. Carburetor: Single Carter one-barrel. (Note: This engine was not available in California where a four-barrel version of the 360 cid V-8 was standard.)

ENGINE [Standard: Wagoneer and J-20; Optional: J-10]: V-type. OHV. Eight-cylinder. Cast iron block. Bore & stroke: 4.08 x 3.44 in. Displacement: 360 cid. Compression ratio: 8.5:1. Net horsepower: 175 at 4000 rpm. Net torque: 285 lb.-ft. at 2400 rpm. Five main bearings. Hydraulic valve lifters. Carburetor: Single two-barrel.

1977 AMC Jeep, CJ-5 Universal Jeep (OCW)

ENGINE [Optional: J-10/J-20]: V-type. OHV. Eight-cylinder. Cast iron block. Bore & stroke: 4.08 x 3.44 in. Displacement: 360 cid. Net horsepower: 195 at 4400 rpm. Five main bearings. Hydraulic valve lifters. Carburetor: Single four-barrel.

ENGINE [Optional: J-10/J-20]: V-type. OHV. Eight-cylinder. Cast iron block. Bore & stroke: 4.17 x 3.68 in. Displacement: 401 cid. Net horsepower: 235 at 4600 rpm. Five main bearings. Hydraulic valve lifters. Carburetor: Single four-barrel.

ENGINE [Standard: CJ-5/CJ-6]: Inline. OHV. Six-cylinder. Cast iron block. Bore & stroke: 3.75 x 3.50 in. Displacement: 232 cid. Compression ratio: 8.0:1. Net horsepower: 100 at 3600 rpm. Net torque: 185 lb.-ft. at 1800 rpm. Seven main bearings. Hydraulic valve lifters. Carburetor: Carter one-barrel model YF.

ENGINE [Standard: Renegade; Optional CJ-5/CJ-6]: V-type. OHV. Eight-cylinder. Cast iron block. Bore & stroke: 3.75 x 3.44 in. Displacement: 304 cid. Compression ratio: 8.4:1. Net horsepower: 150 at 4200 rpm. Net torque: 245 lb.-ft. at 2500 rpm. Seven main bearings. Hydraulic valve lifters. Carburetor: Autolite two-barrel model 2100.

1977 AMC Jeep, CJ-7 Universal Jeep With Hardtop (OCW)

CHASSIS [Wagoneer]: Wheelbase: 109 in. Overall length: 183.7 in. Tires: F78-15.

CHASSIS [Cherokee]: Wheelbase: 109 in. Overall length: 183.7 in. Tires: F78-15.

CHASSIS [CJ-5]: Wheelbase: 83.5 in. Overall length: 138.5 in. Height: 67.6 in. Front tread: 51.5 in. Rear tread: 50.0 in. Tires: F78-15 in.

CHASSIS [CJ-7]: Wheelbase: 93.5 in. Overall length: 147.9 in. Height: 67.6 in. Front tread: 51.5 in. Rear tread: 50.0 in. Tires: F78-15 in.

CHASSIS [J-10]: Wheelbase: 118.7 in. Overall length: 192.5 in. Front tread: (J-10) 63.3 in.; (Honcho) 65.4 in. Rear tread: (J-10) 63.8 in.; (Honcho) 65.8 in. Tires: H78-15 in.

CHASSIS [J-10/J-20 LWB]: Wheelbase: 130.7 in. Overall length: 204.5 in. Front tread: 64.6 in. Rear tread: 65.9 in. Tires: (J-10) F78-15; (J-20/6,800 lb. GVW) 8.00 x 16.5; (J-20/7,600-8,200 lb. GVW) 9.50 x 16.5 in.

1977 AMC Jeep, J-20 Townside Pickup (OCW)

TECHNICAL [Wagoneer/Cherokee/J-10/J-20]: Manual, synchromesh transmission. Speeds: 3F/1R. Floor-mounted gearshift. Clutch (J-10) 10.5 in. diameter, 106.75 sq. in., (J-20) 11.0 in. diameter, 110.96 sq. in. Rear axle: (J-10) Semi-floating; (J-20) full-floating. Overall ratio: (J-10) 3.54:1 or 4.09:1; (J-20) 3.73:1. (J-10) Four-wheel hydraulic drum brakes. (J-20) Front disc/rear drum brakes with power assist. Pressed steel wheels. Technical Options: Automatic transmission Turbo Hydra-Matic. Four-speed manual transmission. Quadra-Trac (available with automatic transmission only). 12-in. power front disc brakes (J-10). Snow Boss plow package. Winches (mechanical or 12-volt). Auxiliary fuel tank (20 gallon, for long wheelbase only, not available for California). Rear Trac-Lok differential. Camper special package. Fuel tank skid plate. Heavy-duty battery and alternator. Heavy-duty shock absorbers. Heavy-duty springs. Heavy-duty cooling system. Cold climate package. Locking hubs (not available with Quadra-Trac). Trailer Towing Package.

TECHNICAL [CJ-Series]: Manual, synchromesh transmission. Speeds: 3F/1R. Floor-mounted gearshift. Single-plate, dry-disc clutch. Semi-floating rear axle. Overall ratio: 3.54:1; 4.09:1. Manual, hydraulic four-wheel-drum brakes. Pressed steel wheels. Technical options: Automatic transmission Turbo Hydra-Matic. Quadra-Trac (available with Turbo Hydra-Matic only). Free-running front hubs ($95). Power steering ($166). Power front disc brakes ($73). Front stabilizer bar ($27). Four-speed manual transmission (6.32:1 low gear). Extra-duty suspension system. Low-range for Quadra-Trac (CJ-7 only). Heavy-duty cooling system. Rear Trac-Lok differential. 70-amp. battery. Heavy-duty alternator. Cold climate group. Steel-belted radial ply tires. Winches. Snow plow.

OPTIONS [Wagoneer/Cherokee/Trucks]: 401 cid V-8 ($94). Power steering, except standard in Wagoneer ($190). Turbo-Hydra-Matic with Quadra-Trac, except standard on Wagoneer ($345). Four-speed transmission in Cherokee ($144). Cherokee Chief package for Model 17 ($469). Luggage rack, Wagoneer ($85). Factory air conditioning ($509). Front bumper guards with Nerf strips. Rear step bumper. Convenience group. Light group. Custom trim package. Radios: AM/FM stereo ($222); Citizens Band; AM. Forged aluminum styled wheels (J-10 only). Bucket seats (Custom, Pioneer and Honcho only). Cruise control ($80). Power steering. Tilt steering wheel. Sports steering wheel. Leather wrapped steering wheel. Sliding rear window. Dual low profile mirror. Aluminum cargo cap. Wheelcovers. Honcho package. Pioneer package.

OPTIONS [CJ-Series]: Rear step bumper. Roll bar. Full soft top ($275). Carpeting ($63). Convenience group. Decor group. AM radio ($73). Citizens Band Radio. Cigar lighter and ashtray. Renegade package, CJ-5 ($839). Outside passenger mirror. Center console ($62). Air conditioning ($499). Tachometer and Rally clock ($73). Sports steering wheel. Leather wrapped sports steering wheel. Rear seat. Swing-out tire carrier. Padded instrument panel. Injection-molded removable top (CJ-7).

HISTORICAL: Introduced: Fall, 1976. Calendar year sales: (all Jeep models and series) 115,079. Calendar year production: (Worldwide wholesales) 153,485. Model year output was 127,996 units. This included 19,900 Wagoneers; 31,308 Cherokees; 32,966 CJ-5s; 2,754 CJ-6s (export only); 25,414 CJ-7s; 12,191 J-10s and 3,343 J-20s. Innovations: Improved frame, brakes and suspension. New tires for Renegade series. Air conditioning made available for first time on CJs. "Golden Eagle" option introduced at mid-year. Historical notes: Jeep sales reached an all-time record high level in model year 1977.

1978 JEEP

1978 AMC Jeep, CJ-7 Renegade (JAG)

JEEP — 1978 SERIES — ALL ENGINES: For 1978, Jeep Corp. stayed away from new models and made minimal design changes to the existing line. More comfort and convenience options were offered for all Jeeps. The Wagoneer got a new, midyear special edition. This Wagoneer Limited featured a luxury interior, woodgrain exterior trim and added sound insulation.

Technical and appearance changes for 1978 were limited. Continued into 1978, was the "Golden Eagle" option, which had been introduced in mid-1977. This year it was offered in a wider choice of colors and featured a large golden eagle decal on the hood and special striping on the grille, plus fender flares and gold-colored wheels. All CJ models were fitted with an improved heating system that distributed heat more efficiently, provided better fresh air ventilation and gave higher defroster temperatures. Engine efficiency was improved, due to a new ambient air intake system.

The J-series trucks were also available with the Golden Eagle package. For the J-trucks it included a chrome front bumper; rear step bumper; gold eight inch spoked wheels (with black accents); 10 x 15 inch all-terrain tires; bright window frames; pickup box-mounted roll bar (with off-road driving lights); steel grille guard; Levi's bucket seats; custom interior and an engine-turned instrument cluster. Other interior appointments were tan carpeting, sports steering wheel and bright armrest overlays. A golden eagle decal was positioned on the hood and lower door panel. Gold, green and orange striping was found on the door, cab and upper box sides.

A new trim package, the "10-4" option, was available for J-10 models on the short wheelbase chassis. It could be ordered in any of 10 colors with two-tone orange and black accent striping. A two-tone orange "10-4" decal was located on the side, just ahead of the rear wheels. Other features included 10 x 15 inch Tracker tires, white 15 x 8 inch wheels (with red pinstriping), a bed-mounted roll bar and rear step bumper.

The J-series trucks had an additional 2.5 inch of legroom due to a modified toeboard and relocated accelerator. J-10 GVW rating for the J-10 was moved up to 6,200 pounds.

I.D. DATA: VIN located on the left front door hinge pillar and left firewall. VIN still has 13 symbols. The first indicates Jeep Corp. The second indicates model year. The third indicates transmission, drivetrain and assembly plant. The fourth and fifth indicate series or model. The sixth symbol identifies body style. The seventh symbol indicates the engine. Engine codes were: E=232 cid six-cylinder; A=258 cid six-cylinder; C=258 six-cylinder; E=232 six-cylinder; G=121 cid four-cylinder; H=304 cid V-8; N=360 cid V-8; P=360 cid V-8; Z=401 cid V-8. The next six symbols are the sequential production number beginning at 000001.

Model	Body Type	Price	Weight	Prod. Total
Wagoneer — 1/2-Ton — 4x4				
15	4dr Station Wagon	7695	4345	24,274
Cherokee — 1/2-Ton — 4x4				
16	2dr Station Wagon	6229	3971	—
17	2dr Wide Stance	6675	4084	—
18	4dr Station Wagon	6335	4106	—
CJ-5 — 1/4-Ton — 4x4 — 84 in. w.b.				
83	Jeep	5095	2738	37,611
CJ-7 — 1/4-Ton — 4x4 — 94 in. w.b.				
93	Jeep	5195	2782	38,274
J-10 — 1/4-Ton — 4x4 — 119/131 in. w.b.				
25	Townside Pickup (SWB)	5675	3831	—
45	Townside Pickup (LWB)	5743	3898	—
J-20 — 3/4-Ton — 4x4 — 131 in. w.b.				
46	Townside Pickup	6324	4269	8,085

NOTE: See "Historical" for additional production data.

ENGINE [Four]: Inline. OHV. Four-cylinder. Bore & stroke: 3.41 x 3.23 in. Displacement: 121 cid. Compression: 8.2:1. Brake horsepower: 80 at 5000 rpm.

ENGINE [Standard: CJ-5/CJ-6]: Inline. OHV. Six-cylinder. Cast iron block. Bore & stroke: 3.75 x 3.50 in. Displacement: 232 cid. Compression ratio: 8.0:1. Net horsepower: 100 at 3600 rpm. Net torque: 185 lb.-ft. at 1800 rpm. Seven main bearings. Hydraulic valve lifters. Carburetor: Carter one-barrel model YF.

ENGINE [Standard: Cherokee and J-10; Optional: CJ-5/CJ-6]: Inline. OHV. Six-cylinder. Cast iron block. Bore & stroke: 3.75 x 3.9 in. Displacement: 258 cid. Compression ratio: 8.0:1. Net horsepower: 110 at 3500 rpm. Torque: 195 lb.-ft. at 2000 rpm. Seven main bearings. Hydraulic valve lifters. Carburetor: Single Carter one-barrel. (Note: This engine was not available in California where a four-barrel version of the 360 cid V-8 was standard.)

ENGINE [Optional: Cherokee/J-10/CJ-5/CJ-6]: Inline. OHV. Six-cylinder. Cast iron block. Bore & stroke: 3.75 x 3.9 in. Displacement: 258 cid. Compression ratio: 8.0:1. Net horsepower: 120 at 3600 rpm. Torque: 195 lb.-ft. at 2000 rpm. Seven main bearings. Hydraulic valve lifters. Carburetor: Single Carter two-barrel.

ENGINE [Standard: Renegade; Optional CJ-5/CJ-6]: V-type. OHV. Eight-cylinder. Cast iron block. Bore & stroke: 3.75 x 3.44 in. Displacement: 304 cid. Compression ratio: 8.4:1. Net horsepower: 150 at 4200 rpm. Net torque: 245 lb.-ft. at 2500 rpm. Seven main bearings. Hydraulic valve lifters. Carburetor: Autolite two-barrel model 2100.

ENGINE [Standard: Wagoneer and J-20; Optional: J-10]: V-type. OHV. Eight-cylinder. Cast iron block. Bore & stroke: 4.08 x 3.44 in. Displacement: 360 cid. Compression ratio: 8.5:1. Net horsepower: 175 at 4000 rpm. Net torque: 285 lb.-ft. at 2400 rpm. Five main bearings. Hydraulic valve lifters. Carburetor: Single two-barrel.

ENGINE [Optional: J-10/J-20]: V-type. OHV. Eight-cylinder. Cast iron block. Bore & stroke: 4.08 x 3.44 in. Displacement: 360 cid. Net horsepower: 195 at 4400 rpm. Five main bearings. Hydraulic valve lifters. Carburetor: Single four-barrel.

ENGINE [Optional: J-10/J-20]: V-type. OHV. Eight-cylinder. Cast iron block. Bore & stroke: 4.17 x 3.68 in. Displacement: 401 cid. Net horsepower: 235 at 4600 rpm. Five main bearings. Hydraulic valve lifters. Carburetor: Single four-barrel.

ENGINE [Standard: CJ-5/CJ-6]: Inline. OHV. Six-cylinder. Cast iron block. Bore & stroke: 3.75 x 3.50 in. Displacement: 232 cid. Compression ratio: 8.0:1. Net horsepower: 100 at 3600 rpm. Net torque: 185 lb.-ft. at 1800 rpm. Seven main bearings. Hydraulic valve lifters. Carburetor: Carter one-barrel model YF.

ENGINE [Standard: Renegade; Optional CJ-5/CJ-6]: V-type. OHV. Eight-cylinder. Cast iron block. Bore & stroke: 3.75 x 3.44 in. Displacement: 304 cid. Compression ratio: 8.4:1. Net horsepower: 150 at 4200 rpm. Net torque: 245 lb.-ft. at 2500 rpm. Seven main bearings. Hydraulic valve lifters. Carburetor: Autolite two-barrel model 2100.

CHASSIS [Wagoneer]: Wheelbase: 108.7 in. Overall length: 186 in. Width: 76 in. Tires: F78-15.

CHASSIS [Cherokee]: Wheelbase: 108.7 in. Overall length: 186 in. Tires: F78-15.

CHASSIS [CJ-5]: Wheelbase: 83.5 in. Overall length: 138.5 in. Height: 67.6 in. Front tread: 51.5 in. Rear tread: 50.0 in. Tires: H78-15 in.

CHASSIS [CJ-7]: Wheelbase: 93.5 in. Overall length: 147.9 in. Height: 67.6 in. Front tread: 51.5 in. Rear tread: 50.0 in. Tires: H78-15 in.

CHASSIS [J-10]: Wheelbase: 118.7 in. Overall length: 192.5 in. Front tread: (J-10) 63.3 in.; (Honcho) 65.4 in. Rear tread: (J-10) 63.8 in.; (Honcho) 65.8 in. Tires: H78-15 in.

CHASSIS [J-10/J-20 LWB]: Wheelbase: 130.7 in. Overall length: 204.5 in. Front tread: 64.6 in. Rear tread: 65.9 in. Tires: (J-10) F78-15; (J-20/6800 lb. GVW) 8.00 x 16.5; (J-20/7600-8200 lb. GVW) 9.50 x 16.5 in.

CHASSIS: All chassis measurements were the same as 1977. The CJ-5 and CJ-7 had new H78-15 size tires. The J-10 had the same new size tires.

TECHNICAL [Wagoneer/Cherokee/J-10/J-20]: Manual, synchromesh transmission. Speeds: 3F/1R. Floor-mounted gearshift. Clutch: (J-10) 10.5 in. diameter, 106.75 sq. in., (J-20) 11.0 in. diameter, 110.96 sq. in. Rear axle: (J-10) Semi-floating; (J-20) full-floating. Overall ratio: (J-10) 3.54:1 or 4.09:1; (J-20) 3.73:1. (J-10) Four-wheel hydraulic drum brakes. (J-20) Front disc/rear drum brakes with power assist. Pressed steel wheels. Technical Options: Automatic transmission Turbo Hydra-Matic. Four-speed manual transmission. Quadra-Trac (available with automatic transmission only). 12-in. power front disc brakes (J-10). Snow Boss plow package. Winches (mechanical or 12-volt). Auxiliary fuel tank (20 gallon, for long wheelbase only, not available for California). Rear Trac-Lok differential. Camper special package. Fuel tank skid plate. Heavy-duty battery and alternator. Heavy-duty shock absorbers. Heavy-duty springs. Heavy-duty cooling system. Cold climate group. Locking hubs (not available with Quadra-Trac). Trailer Towing Package.

TECHNICAL [CJ-Series]: Manual, synchromesh transmission. Speeds: 3F/1R. Floor-mounted gearshift. Single-plate, dry-disc dry disc clutch. Semi-floating rear axle. Overall ratio: 3.54:1; 4.09:1. Manual, hydraulic four-wheel-drum brakes. Pressed steel wheels. Technical options: Automatic transmission Turbo Hydra-Matic. Quadra-Trac (available with Turbo Hydra-Matic only). Free-running front hubs ($95). Power steering ($166). Power front disc brakes ($73). Steering damper ($10). Front stabilizer bar ($27). Four-speed manual transmission (6.32:1 low gear). Extra-duty suspension system. Low-range for Quadra-Trac (CJ-7 only). Heavy-duty cooling system. Rear Trac-Lok differential. 70-amp. battery. Heavy-duty alternator. Cold climate group. Steel-belted radial ply tires. Winches. Snow plow.

OPTIONS: Most convenience and appearance options were unchanged for 1978. However, many items previously optional on the CJ models were now standard equipment. These included an ashtray and cigar lighters, passenger assist bar and passenger side exterior mirror. Standard tires were now H78-15 Suburbanite fiberglass belted types. Included in the convenience group option was an underhood light. Added to the option list for the J-series pickups was the "10-4" appearance package. New options for the J-trucks included an AM/FM Multiplex 8-track tape, 7-inch chrome-plated spoked steel wheels for J-10 models. A grille guard and a pickup bed mounted roll bar.

OPTIONS [Wagoneer/Cherokee]: Automatic transmission with Quadra-Trac, except standard in Wagoneer ($345). Wagoneer Limited trim package ($3,120).

OPTIONS [J-Series]: Bumper guards AM/FM stereo/Citizen's Band ($349). AM Radio ($86). AM/Citizen's Band ($229). AM/FM stereo ($229). AM/FM stereo w/tape player ($329). Sliding rear window ($79). Tinted glass ($32). "10-4" package ($619). Levis Fabric Bucket Seats ($175). Bucket seats ($155). Roll bar ($105). Air conditioning ($557). Brush guard ($69). Pickup box cap ($324). Convenience group ($83). Cruise control ($100). Custom package ($95). Golden Eagle package, J-10 (SWB) only, with driving lights ($999); without ($974). Honcho package, J-10 (SWB) only. Light group ($46).

OPTIONS [CJ-Series]: AM radio ($86). Standard soft top ($253). Levis soft top ($292). Vinyl bucket Levis seats ($73). Vinyl bench seat ($35). Rear seat ($106). Moon roof for CJ-7 ($149). Roll bar ($70). Air conditioning ($529). Metal cab for CJ-5 ($471). Removable front carpet ($44). Removable front and rear carpet ($73). Convenience group ($27). Decor group ($105). Golden Eagle package ($1249). Hardtop with doors, CJ-7 ($610). Renegade package ($799).

HISTORICAL: Introduced: Fall, 1977. Calendar year sales: (all models and series) 161,912. Model year production included 36,945 Cherokees; 24,274 Wagoneers; 37,611 CJ-5s; 743 CJ-6s (export); 38,274 CJ-7s; 9,167 J-10s and 8,085 J-20s. Innovations: Many new options released. Legroom in the Jeep pickup trucks was increased. GVW ratings of Jeep trucks increased. Historical notes: To commemorate the 25th anniversary of the CJ-5 a limited-edition "Silver Anniversary" CJ-5 was offered. A total of 3,000 copies were produced with Quick silver metallic finish, silver-toned Renegade accent striping black soft top, black vinyl bucket seats, silver accents and a special dashboard plaque.

1979 JEEP

1979 AMC Jeep, CJ-5 Renegade Universal Jeep (RPZ)

JEEP — 1979 SERIES — ALL ENGINES: This was not a year of dramatic change for Jeep vehicles. Sales were up so much, that the outdated, ex-Willys factory in Toledo could hardly keep up. The CJ series was carried over virtually unchanged. The Renegade package featured new exterior graphics. Revisions made in the J-series trucks consisted of a new front end appearance with rectangular headlights set in a grille with a slightly protruding center section and vertical blades. The front bumper no longer had a recessed middle portion. Available for all pickups was a new "high style" box enclosure. The Honcho trim package was revised.

I.D. DATA: VIN located on the left front door hinge pillar and left firewall. VIN still has 13 symbols. The first indicates Jeep Corp. The second indicates model year. The third indicates transmission, drivetrain and assembly plant. The fourth and fifth indicate series or model. The sixth symbol identifies body style. The seventh symbol indicates the engine. Engine codes were: E=232 cid six-cylinder; A=258 cid six-cylinder; C=258 six-cylinder; E=232 six-cylinder; G=121 cid four-cylinder; H=304 cid V-8; N=360 cid V-8. The next six symbols are the sequential production number beginning at 000001.

1979 AMC Jeep, CJ-7 Renegade Universal Jeep (RPZ)

Model	Body Type	Price	Weight	Prod. Total
Wagoneer — 1/2-Ton — 4x4				
15	4dr Station Wagon	9065	4034	—
15	4dr Limited Station Wagon	12,485	4181	—
Cherokee — 1/2-Ton — 4x4				
16	2d Station Wagon	7328	3653	—
17	2dr Wide Stance	7671	3774	—
18	4dr Station Wagon	7441	3761	—
CJ-5 — 1/4-Ton — 4x4 — 84 in. w.b.				
83	Jeep	5588	2623	21,308
CJ-7 — 1/4-Ton — 4x4 — 94 in. w.b.				
93	Jeep	5732	2666	24,580
J-10 — 1/2-Ton — 4x4 — 119/131 in. w.b.				
25	Townside Pickup (SWB)	6172	3693	—
45	Townside Pickup (LWB)	6245	3760	—
J-20 — 3/4-Ton — 4x4 — 131 in. w.b.				
46	Townside Pickup	6872	4167	10,403

NOTE: See "Historical" for additional production data.
ENGINE [Four]: Inline. OHV. Four-cylinder. Bore & stroke: 3.41 x 3.23 in. Displacement: 121 cid. Compression: 8.2:1. Brake horsepower: 80 at 5000 rpm.
ENGINE [Standard: CJ-5/CJ-6]: Inline. OHV. Six-cylinder. Cast iron block. Bore & stroke: 3.75 x 3.50 in. Displacement: 232 cid. Compression ratio: 8.0:1. Net horsepower: 100 at 3600 rpm. Net torque: 185 lb.-ft. at 1800 rpm. Seven main bearings. Hydraulic valve lifters. Carburetor: Carter one-barrel model YF.

ENGINE [Standard: Cherokee and J-10; Optional: CJ-5/CJ-6]: Inline. OHV. Six-cylinder. Cast iron block. Bore & stroke: 3.75 x 3.9 in. Displacement: 258 cid. Compression ratio: 8.0:1. Net horsepower: 110 at 3500 rpm. Torque: 195 lb.-ft. at 2000 rpm. Seven main bearings. Hydraulic valve lifters. Carburetor: Single Carter one-barrel. (Note: This engine was not available in California where a four-barrel version of the 360 cid V-8 was standard.)
ENGINE [Optional: Cherokee/J-10/CJ-5/CJ-6]: Inline. OHV. Six-cylinder. Cast iron block. Bore & stroke: 3.75 x 3.9 in. Displacement: 258 cid. Compression ratio: 8.0:1. Net horsepower: 120 at 3600 rpm. Torque: 195 lb.-ft. at 2000 rpm. Seven main bearings. Hydraulic valve lifters. Carburetor: Single Carter two-barrel.
ENGINE [Standard: Renegade; Optional CJ-5/CJ-6]: V-type. OHV. Eight-cylinder. Cast iron block. Bore & stroke: 3.75 x 3.44 in. Displacement: 304 cid. Compression ratio: 8.4:1. Net horsepower: 150 at 4200 rpm. Net torque: 245 lb.-ft. at 2500 rpm. Seven main bearings. Hydraulic valve lifters. Carburetor: Autolite two-barrel model 2100.
ENGINE [Standard: Wagoneer and J-20; Optional: J-10]: V-type. OHV. Eight-cylinder. Cast iron block. Bore & stroke: 4.08 x 3.44 in. Displacement: 360 cid. Compression ratio: 8.5:1. Net horsepower: 175 at 4000 rpm. Net torque: 285 lb.-ft. at 2400 rpm. Five main bearings. Hydraulic valve lifters. Carburetor: Single two-barrel.
ENGINE [Optional: J-10/J-20]: V-type. OHV. Eight-cylinder. Cast iron block. Bore & stroke: 4.08 x 3.44 in. Displacement: 360 cid. Net horsepower: 195 at 4400 rpm. Five main bearings. Hydraulic valve lifters. Carburetor: Single four-barrel.
ENGINE [Optional: J-10/J-20]: V-type. OHV. Eight-cylinder. Cast iron block. Bore & stroke: 4.17 x 3.68 in. Displacement: 401 cid. Net horsepower: 235 at 4600 rpm. Five main bearings. Hydraulic valve lifters. Carburetor: Single four-barrel.
ENGINE [Standard: CJ-5/CJ-6]: Inline. OHV. Six-cylinder. Cast iron block. Bore & stroke: 3.75 x 3.50 in. Displacement: 232 cid. Compression ratio: 8.0:1. Net horsepower: 100 at 3600 rpm. Net torque: 185 lb.-ft. at 1800 rpm. Seven main bearings. Hydraulic valve lifters. Carburetor: Carter one-barrel model YF.
ENGINE [Standard: Renegade; Optional CJ-5/CJ-6]: V-type. OHV. Eight-cylinder. Cast iron block. Bore & stroke: 3.75 x 3.44 in. Displacement: 304 cid. Compression ratio: 8.4:1. Net horsepower: 150 at 4200 rpm. Net torque: 245 lb.-ft. at 2500 rpm. Seven main bearings. Hydraulic valve lifters. Carburetor: Autolite two-barrel model 2100.

1979 AMC Jeep, Golden Eagle With Hardtop (RPZ)

CHASSIS [Wagoneer]: Wheelbase: 108.7 in. Overall length: 186 in. Width: 76 in. Tires: F78-15.
CHASSIS [Cherokee]: Wheelbase: 108.7 in. Overall length: 186 in. Tires: F78-15.
CHASSIS [J-10 SWB]: Wheelbase: 118.7 in. Overall length: 192.5 in. Height: 69.3 in. Front tread: 63.3 in. Rear tread: 63.8 in. Tires: H78-15 in.
CHASSIS [J-10/J-20 LWB]: Wheelbase: 130.7 in. Overall length: 204.5 in. Height: 69.1/70.7 in. Front tread: (J-10) 63.3 in., (J-20) 64.6 in. Rear tread: (J-10) 63.8 in., (J-20) 65.9 in. Tires: (J-10) H78-15, (J-20) 8.75 x 16.5 in.
CHASSIS [CJ-5]: Wheelbase: 83.5 in. Overall length: 134.8 in. Height: 67.6 in. Front tread: 51.5 in. Rear tread: 50.0 in. Tires: H78-15 in.
CHASSIS [CJ-7]: Wheelbase: 93.5 in. Overall length: 144.3 in. Height: 67.6 in. Front tread: 57.5 in. Rear tread: 50.0 in. Tires: H78-15 in.

1979 AMC Jeep, Honcho Townside Pickup (RPZ)

TECHNICAL [CJ-Series]: Manual, synchronized transmission. Speeds: 3F/1R. Floor-mounted gearshift. Single-plate, dry-disc clutch. Semi-floating rear axle. Four-wheel drum brakes. Pressed steel wheels. Options: Turbo-Hydra-Matic with Quadra-Trac (CJ-7 only). Four-speed manual transmission. Quadra-Trac low range. Rear Trac-Lok differential. Free-wheeling hubs. Heavy-duty cooling system. Extra-duty suspension package. Steering damper. Front stabilizer bar. Heavy-duty 70-amp. battery. Heavy-duty 63-amp. alternator. Cold Climate group.

1979 AMC Jeep, Honcho Townside Pickup (CW)

TECHNICAL [Wagoneer/Cherokee/J-10/J-20]: Fully synchronized manual transmission. Speeds: 3F/1R. Floor-mounted gearshift. Single-plate, dry-disc clutch. (J-10) Semi-floating rear axle; (J-20) full-floating rear axle. Power front disc/rear drum brakes. Steel disc wheels. Options: Turbo-Hydra-Matic with Quadra-Trac. Four-speed manual transmission ($161). Quadra-Trac low range. Rear Trac-Lok differential. Free-wheeling hubs. Heavy-duty cooling system. Extra-duty suspension system. Heavy-duty shock absorbers. Front stabilizer bar. Heavy-duty 70-amp. battery. Heavy-duty 63-amp. alternator. Cold Climate group. "Snow Boss" package. 304 cid V-8 ($342).

OPTIONS [Wagoneer/Cherokee]: Power steering, standard in Wagoneer ($226). 360 cid V-8, standard in Wagoneer ($378). Turbo-Hydra-Matic with Quadra-Trac, standard in Wagoneer ($396). AM/FM stereo ($241). AM/FM stereo with tape ($346). Cherokee "S" package ($699). Cherokee Chief package ($600). Golden Eagle package ($970).

OPTIONS [Trucks]: Radios: AM, AM/FM, AM/CB, AM/FM/CB and AM/FM/Tape. Electric clock. Custom package ($126). Honcho package, SWB/J-10 ($824). Golden Eagle package, SWB/J-10 ($1224). "10-4" Package, SWB/J-10. 10-4 Package (J-10, 118.7 in. wheelbase only). Soft-Feel sports steering wheel. Leather-wrapped sports steering wheel. Aluminum wheels (not available J-20). 15 inch wheelcovers (not available J-20). Hubcaps (J-20). Convenience group. Air conditioning. Tinted glass. Tilt steering wheel. Cruise control. Light group. Low profile mirrors. Bucket seats. Rear step bumper. Sliding rear window. Cargo cap. Roll bar. Fuel tank skid plate. Front bumper guards. Brush guards. Floor mats. Spare tire lock. Rear bumperettes.

1979 AMC Jeep, Wagoneer Limited Four-Door Wagon (RPZ)

OPTIONS [CJ Series]: Renegade package ($825). Golden Eagle Package. Hardtop ($656). CJ-5 side-mounted spare and tailgate. (CJ-7) Swing-away spare tire carrier. Injection molded hardtop (CJ-7). Full metal cab (CJ-5). Removable carpet. AM radio. Moon roof (with hardtop only). Body side step. Power front disc brakes. Power steering. Tachometer and Rally clock. Tilt steering wheel. Air conditioning. Convenience group. Decor group. 15 inch wheelcovers. Soft-Feel steering wheel (black). Soft top. Padded instrument panel. Four-speed transmission ($161). 304 cid V-8 ($342).

1979 AMC Jeep, Cherokee 'S' Four-Door Station Wagon (RPZ)

HISTORICAL: Introduced: Fall, 1978. Calendar year registrations: 145,583. Calendar year sales: (all models and series) 140,431. Calendar year production reached an all-time record of 177,575 units at the Jeep Corp. Toledo, Ohio plant. Model year output totaled 152,992 units. This included 36,195 Wagoneers; 48,813 Cherokees; 21,308 CJ-5s; 24,580 CJ-7s; 11,693 J-10s and 10,403 J-20s. Innovations: New Renegade graphics. Jeep pickups get new front end treatment. Optional "high-style" box enclosure released.

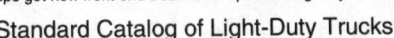

1979 AMC Jeep, Cherokee Chief Two-Door Station Wagon (RPZ)

1980 JEEP

1980 AMC Jeep, Cherokee Special Police Wagon (JAG)

JEEP — 1980 SERIES — ALL ENGINES: American Motors' response to the dramatic upswing in gasoline prices and its inverse relationship to sales of off-road vehicle and four-wheel-drive light-duty trucks was pronounced. Throughout the Jeep line, transmissions were made more efficient and lighter in weight. Many models had freewheeling front hubs and fuel conserving driveline designs. Quadra-Trac was improved by replacement of cone clutches with viscous drives.

For the CJ models, the most dramatic news was use of the General Motors 151 cid, four-cylinder engine as standard powerplant. Also new, was a standard, lightweight four-speed, close-ratio manual transmission. A new chassis design was adopted. It was both stronger and lighter than the unit it replaced. Free-wheeling front hubs were standard. Also installed on all CJ Jeeps was a roll bar. If the 258 cid six-cylinder or 304 cid V-8 were ordered for the CJ-7, they were available with a lightweight automatic transmission, part-time four-wheel drive system and freewheeling hubs.

Appearance changes were lead by a new soft top with steel doors and roll-up windows. Either CJ model was available with a new "Laredo" package. It included specially trimmed high-back bucket seats, chrome grille and accents, special striping and Wrangler radial tires.

For 1980, the J-trucks had a new lightweight, more efficient drivetrain, free-wheeling front hubs, front stabilizer bar and a high-density blow-molded fuel tank. Numerous new options were offered, including power windows and an electronic digital clock. Like the CJ models, the Jeep trucks were available with the improved Quadra-Trac, Laredo package and part-time four-wheel-drive (with either a standard four-speed manual or automatic transmission). The short-wheelbase Sportside model was available in an optional "highline" version with Honcho graphics, wooden cargo box rails and a styled roll bar.

I.D. DATA: VIN located on the left front door hinge pillar and left firewall. VIN has 13 symbols. The first indicates Jeep Corp. The second indicates model year. The third indicates transmission, drivetrain and assembly plant. The fourth and fifth indicate series or model. The sixth symbol identifies body style. The seventh symbol indicates the engine. Engine codes were: B=151 cid four-cylinder engine; C=258 cid six-cylinder engine; H=304 cid V-8; N=360 cid V-8. The next six symbols are the sequential production number beginning at 000001.

Model	Body Type	Price	Weight	Prod. Total
Wagoneer — 1/2-Ton — 4x4				
15	4dr Station Wagon	9732	3964	—
15	4dr Limited Station Wagon	13,653	3990	—
Cherokee — 1/2-Ton — 4x4				
16	2dr Station Wagon	8180	3780	—
17	2dr Wide Stance	8823	3868	—
18	4dr Station Wagon	8380	3849	—
CJ-5 — 1/4-Ton — 4x4 — 84 in. w.b.				
83	Jeep	6195	2439	14,156

581

CJ-7 — 1/4-Ton — 4x4 — 94 in. w.b.				
93	Jeep	6445	2464	20,191
J-10 — 1/2-Ton — 4x4 — 119/131 in. w.b.				
25	Townside Pickup (SWB)	6874	3714	—
45	Townside Pickup (LWB)	6972	3776	—
J-20 — 3/4-Ton — 4x4 — 131 in. w.b.				
46	Townside Pickup	7837	4246	2,004

NOTE: See "Historical" for additional production data.

ENGINE [Standard: CJ]: Inline. OHV. Four-cylinder. Cast iron block. Bore & stroke: 4.00 x 3.00 in. Displacement: 151 cid. Compression ratio: 8.2:1. Taxable horsepower: 21.70. Hydraulic valve lifters. Carburetor: Two-barrel.
ENGINE [Standard: J-10/CJ]: Inline. OHV. Six-cylinder. Cast iron block. Bore & stroke: 3.75 x 3.90 in. Displacement: 258 cid. Compression ratio: 8.0:1. Net horsepower: 110. Taxable horsepower: 33.75. Seven main bearings. Hydraulic valve lifters. Carburetor: Single two-barrel.
ENGINE [Standard: Renegade; Optional CJ-5/CJ-6]: V-type. OHV. Eight-cylinder. Cast iron block. Bore & stroke: 3.75 x 3.44 in. Displacement: 304 cid. Compression ratio: 8.4:1. Net horsepower: 150 at 4200 rpm. Net torque: 245 lb.-ft. at 2500 rpm. Seven main bearings. Hydraulic valve lifters. Carburetor: Autolite two-barrel model 2100.
ENGINE [Standard: CJ-20; Optional: J-10]: Vee-block. OHV. Eight-cylinder. Cast iron block. Bore & stroke: 4.08 x 3.44 in. Displacement: 360 cid. Compression ratio: 8.25:1. Net horsepower: 175. Taxable horsepower: 53.27. Five main bearings. Hydraulic valve lifters. Carburetor: Single two-barrel.

CHASSIS [Wagoneer]: Wheelbase: 108.7 in. Overall length: 186 in. Width: 76 in. Tires: F78-15.
CHASSIS [Cherokee]: Wheelbase: 108.7 in. Overall length: 186 in. Tires: F78-15.
CHASSIS [CJ-5]: Wheelbase: 83.5 in. Overall length: 144.3 in. Height: 67.6 in. Front tread: 51.5 in. Rear tread: 50.0 in. Tires: H78-15 in.
CHASSIS [CJ-7]: Wheelbase: 93.5 in. Overall length: 153.2 in. Height: 67.6 in. Front tread: 51.5 in. Rear tread: 50.0 in. Tires: H78-15 in.
CHASSIS [J-10 SWB]: Wheelbase: 118.7 in. Overall length: 192.7 in. Height: 69.3 in. Front tread: 63.3 in. Rear tread: 63.8 in. Tires: H78-15 in.
CHASSIS [J-10/J-20 LWB]: Wheelbase: 130.7 in. Overall length: 204.5 in. Height: 69.1/70.7 in. Front tread: (J-10) 63.3 in.; (J-20) 63.3 in. Rear tread: (J-10) 63.8 in.; (J-20) 64.9 in. Tires: (J-10) H78-15; (J-20) 8.75 x 16.5 in.
CHASSIS [J-10 Sportside]: Wheelbase: 118.7 in. Overall length: 196.9 in. Height: 69.1 in. Front tread: 63.3 in. Rear tread: 63.8 in. Tires: H78-15 in.

TECHNICAL [CJ-Series]: Manual, synchronized transmission. Speeds: 4F/1R. Floor-mounted gearshift. Single-plate, dry-disc clutch. Semi-floating rear axle. Overall ratio: (four-cylinder) 3.73:1, (six-cylinder) 3.07:1, (V-8) 3.07:1. Manual front disc/rear drum brakes. Steel wheels. Technical Options: Automatic transmission (CJ-7). Quadra-Trac with automatic transmission. Heavy-duty shock absorbers. Steering stabilizer. Automatic hubs. Air overload kit. Heavy-duty cooling system. Snow plows.
TECHNICAL [Wagoneer/Cherokee/J-Series]: Fully synchronized, manual transmission. Speeds: 4F/1R. Floor-mounted gearshift. Single-plate, dry-disc clutch. (J-10) Semi-floating rear axle; (J-20) full-floating rear axle. Front disc/rear drum brakes. Pressed steel wheels. Technical Options: Automatic transmission, column mounted. Quadra-Trac (with automatic transmission). Heavy-duty cooling system. Heavy-duty shock absorbers. Helper springs. Cruise control. Automatic hubs (not available with Quadra-Trac). Engine block heater. Extra-duty suspension package. Heavy-duty battery. Heavy-duty alternator. Cold climate group. Snow Boss package.

OPTIONS [CJ-5/CJ-7]: Safari soft top. Skyviewer soft top. Top boot. Sun bonnet. M3 metal cab (CJ-5 only). Cab with vertical rear door (CJ-5 only). Deluxe M3 cab (CJ-5 only). Renegade package ($899). Golden Hawk package. Laredo package. Hardtop ($676). Hand held searchlight (all models). Passenger assist handle. Ski rack. Bug screen. Automatic transmission ($333). 304 cid V-8 engine ($383). 258 cid six-cylinder engine ($129).
OPTIONS [Wagoneer/Cherokee]: Power steering, included with models 15 and 17; other models ($233). Automatic transmission, standard in Wagoneer. AM/FM stereo ($245). AM/FM stereo with tape ($355). AM/FM stereo with CB radio ($495). Cruise control. Rear window defroster. Tilt steering wheel. Luggage rack. Aluminum wheels (standard on Wagoneer Limited). Wagoneer woodgrain exterior trim package ($139). Removable moon roof ($300). Power door locks. Power windows. Cherokee S package, model 16 and 18 ($784). Cherokee Chief package for model 17 ($799). Golden Eagle or Golden Hawk package for Cherokee. Cherokee Laredo package ($1,600). Custom or Tu-Tone paint. 360 cid V-8 engine ($420). Air conditioning.
OPTIONS [J-Series Trucks]: Custom package ($149). Honcho package, model 25 ($849). Laredo package, model 25 ($1,600). Sportside package, model 25 ($899). Honcho Sportside package, model 25 ($1,325). Automatic transmission ($333). 360 V-8 engine ($420).

HISTORICAL: Introduced: Fall, 1979. Calendar year registrations: 81,923. Calendar year sales: (all models and series) 77,852 including: (CJ models) 47,304, (J Series pickup) 8,656. Model year production totaled 66,520 units. This included 10,234 Wagoneers; 11,541 Cherokees; 14,156 CJ-5s; 20,191 CJ-7s; 8,394 J-10s and 2,004 J-20s. Innovations: Four-cylinder engine returns to CJ Series. New top-of-the-line Laredo package available for pickup and CJ models. Jeep dealers recorded an average of 45 sales per outlet in 1980, down from an average of 77 sales per outlet in 1979 and 93 per outlet in 1978. Jeep vehicles continued to be produced exclusively in the company's Toledo, Ohio factory. The 151 cid four, a Pontiac-built powerplant, was made standard equipment in the CJs and 9,347 got it. Jeep Corp. also constructed 1,028 CJs with a four-cylinder diesel engine, but these were made strictly for export. Also, the 258 cid six was re-introduced as an economy option for the Wagoneer.

1981 JEEP

JEEP — 1981 SERIES — ALL ENGINES: The Wagoneer continued as Jeep's six-passenger, four-wheel drive, four-door station wagon. A 258 cid (4.2-liter) six was standard (360 cid V-8 in California), as was automatic transmission with Quadra-Trac.
Cherokees continued to come in three basic models. Model 16 was a five-passenger two-door station wagon with part-time four-wheel drive and a standard 258 cid six-cylinder engine. Model 17 was the same basic vehicle in "Wide-Stance" format with fatter wheels and tires. Model 18 was the four-door Cherokee wagon.
CJ-5s represented a two/four-passenger four-wheel drive sports utility vehicle in open body or optional hardtop versions. Standard engine was the 151 cid (2.5-liter) four-cylinder linked to a four-speed manual transmission.
CJ-7s represented a longer wheelbase two/four-passenger four-wheel drive sports utility vehicle in open body or optional hardtop versions with rear-mounted or swing-away spare tire. Standard engine was again the 151 cid (2.5-liter) four-cylinder linked to a four-speed manual transmission.

The CJ-8 was a new-for-1981 sporty model, aimed at the younger or young-at-heart buyer.

CJ Jeeps for 1981 were fitted with a longer side step. CJ-7 models with the optional soft/metal top feature had a new vent window. The Renegade package, again available for either CJ-5 or CJ-7 Jeeps, had a new graphics package in gradations of yellow, blue or red. All CJ models had a steering damper and a front anti-roll bar, plus a new front axle assembly with gas-filled upper and lower ball joint sockets.

1981 AMC Jeep, CJ-5 Renegade Universal Jeep (OCW)

The major physical change made to the J-trucks was a new lightweight, all-plastic slotted grille. Less noticeable, but important to the J-trucks' fuel economy, was a standard front air dam and the elimination of the pickups roof lip. The J-10 model was lowered by 1.25 inches, due to redesigned front and rear springs. Power steering was now standard on the J-10 models. All J-series models had low-drag brakes.

The Jeep's optional automatic transmission, which since 1980 had been the Chrysler TorqueFlite unit, now had a locking torque converter. The American Motors 258 cid six-cylinder engine was redesigned to reduce its overall weight from 535 to 445 pounds.

An important addition to the Jeep line was the Scrambler pickup, which was depicted as an import fighter.

1981 AMC Jeep, CJ-7 Laredo Univeral Jeep (OCW)

I.D. DATA: VIN located on the top left surface of the instrument panel. There are 17 symbols. The first three symbols indicate the manufacturer, make and vehicle type. The engine type is indicated by the fourth symbol: B=151 cid four-cylinder; C=258 cid six-cylinder; N=360 cid V-8. The next letter identifies the transmission type. The series and type of vehicle are identified by the sixth and seventh symbols, which are the same as the model number. The eighth character identifies the GVW rating with the next serving as the check digit. Then follows the model year and assembly point codes. The last six digits are sequential production numbers.

1981 AMC Jeep, Cherokee Chief Four-Door Station Wagon (OCW)

Model	Body Type	Price	Weight	Prod. Total
Wagoneer — 1/2-Ton — 4x4				
15	4dr Station Wagon	10,464	3779	—
15	4dr Limited Station Wagon	15,164	3800	—
Cherokee — 1/2-Ton — 4x4				
16	2dr Station Wagon	9574	3699	—
17	2dr Wide Stance	9837	3748	—
18	4dr Station Wagon	10,722	3822	—
CJ-5 — 1/4-Ton — 4x4 — 84 in. w.b.				
85	Jeep	7240	2495	13,477
CJ-7 — 1/4-Ton — 4x4 — 94 in. w.b.				
87	Jeep	7490	2520	27,767
CJ-8 Scrambler — 1/4-Ton — 4x4 — 104 in. w.b.				
88	Jeep	7288	2650	8,355
J-10 — 1/2-Ton — 4x4 — 119/131 in. w.b.				
25	Townside Pickup (SWB)	7960	3702	—
26	Townside Pickup (LWB)	8056	3764	—
J-20 — 3/4-Ton — 4x4 — 131 in. w.b.				
27	Townside Pickup	8766	4308	1,534

NOTE: See "Historical" for additional production data.

1981 AMC Jeep, J-10 Laredo Townside Pickup

ENGINE [Standard: CJ]: Inline. OHV. Four-cylinder. Cast iron block. Bore & stroke: 4.00 x 3.00 in. Displacement: 151 cid. Compression ratio: 8.2:1. Taxable horsepower: 21.70. Hydraulic valve lifters. Carburetor: Two-barrel.

ENGINE [Standard: J-10/CJ]: Inline. OHV. Six-cylinder. Cast iron block. Bore & stroke: 3.75 x 3.90 in. Displacement: 258 cid. Compression ratio: 8.0:1. Net horsepower: 110. Taxable horsepower: 33.75. Seven main bearings. Hydraulic valve lifters. Carburetor: Single two-barrel.

ENGINE [Standard: CJ-20; Optional: J-10]: Vee-block. OHV. Eight-cylinder. Cast iron block. Bore & stroke: 4.08 x 3.44 in. Displacement: 360 cid. Compression ratio: 8.25:1. Net horsepower: 175. Taxable horsepower: 53.27. Five main bearings. Hydraulic valve lifters. Carburetor: Single two-barrel.

1981 AMC Jeep, J-10 Honcho Sportside Pickup (JAG)

TECHNICAL [CJ/Scrambler]: Manual, synchronized transmission. Speeds: 4F/1R. Floor-mounted gearshift. Single-plate, dry-disc clutch. Semi-floating rear axle. Overall ratio: (four-cylinder) 3.73:1, (six-cylinder) 3.07:1, (V-8) 3.07:1. Manual front disc/rear drum brakes. Steel wheels. Technical Options: Automatic transmission (CJ-7). Quadra-Trac with automatic transmission (CJ-7). Heavy-duty shock absorbers. Steering stabilizer. Automatic hubs. Air overload kit. Heavy-duty cooling system. Snow plows.

TECHNICAL [Wagoneer/Cherokee/J-Series]: Fully synchronized, manual transmission. Speeds: 4F/1R. Floor-mounted gearshift. Single-plate, dry-disc clutch. (J-10) Semi-floating rear axle; (J-20) full-floating rear axle. Front disc/rear drum brakes. Pressed steel wheels. Technical Options: Automatic transmission, column mounted. Quadra-Trac (with automatic transmission). Heavy-duty cooling system. Heavy-duty shock absorbers. Helper springs. Cruise control. Automatic hubs (not available with Quadra-Trac). Engine block heater. Extra-duty suspension package. Heavy-duty battery. Heavy-duty alternator. Cold climate group. Snow Boss package.

1981 AMC Jeep, Wagoneer Limited Four-Door Station Wagon (JAG)

CHASSIS [Wagoneer]: Wheelbase: 108.7 in. Overall length: 183.5 in. Width: 75.6 in. Height: 65.9 in. GVW maximum: 6,100 lbs. Cargo capacity: 95.1 cu. ft. Front overhang: 29.9 in. Rear overhang: 44.9 in. Front suspension: Leaf springs on live axle with stabilizer bar. Rear suspension: Leaf springs on live axle with tube shocks. Front brakes: power disc. Rear brakes: drum. Steering: Power-assisted; 17.1 ratio. Turning circle: 37.7 ft. Fuel: 20.3 gallons.

CHASSIS [Cherokee]: Wheelbase: 108.7 in. Overall length: 183.5 in. Width: 75.6 in. Height: 66.8 in. GVW: 6,100 lbs. maximum. Cargo capacity: 95.1 cu. ft. without rear seat. Front overhang: 29.9 in. Rear overhang: 44.9 in. Front suspension: Leaf springs on live axle with stabilizer bar. Rear suspension: Leaf springs on live axle with tube shocks. Front brakes: power disc. Rear brakes: drum. Steering: Power-assisted; 17.1 ratio. Turning circle: 37.7 ft. Fuel: 20.3 gallons.

CHASSIS [CJ-5]: Wheelbase: 83.5 in. Overall length: 144.3 in. standard or 134.8 in. with rear-mounted spare; Width: 68.6 in. Height with open body, 67.6 in. GVW maximum: 3,700 lbs. Cargo capacity: 10.2 cu. ft. without rear seat. Front overhang: 23.5 in. Rear overhang: 37.3 in. standard or 27.8 in. with rear-mounted spare. Front suspension: leaf spring on live axle with tube shocks. Rear suspension: leaf springs on live axle with tube shocks. Front brakes: manual discs. Rear brakes: drum. Steering: manual re-circulating ball, 24:1 ratio, 34.1 ft. turning circle. Fuel: 15.5 gallons.

CHASSIS [CJ-7]: Wheelbase: 93.5 in. Overall length: 153.2 in. standard or 144.3 in. with rear-mounted spare; Width: 68.6 in. Height with open body, 67.6 in. GVW maximum: 4,100 lbs. Cargo capacity: 13.6 cu. ft. without rear seat. Front overhang: 23.5 in. Rear overhang: 36.2 in. standard or 27.3 in. with rear-mounted spare. Front suspension: leaf spring on live axle with tube shocks. Rear suspension: leaf springs on live axle with tube shocks. Front brakes: manual discs. Rear brakes: drum. Steering: manual re-circulating ball, 24:1 ratio, 38 ft. turning circle. Fuel: 15.5 gallons.

CHASSIS [CJ-8 Scrambler]: Wheelbase: 103.5 in. Overall length: 177.3 in. Height: 67.6 in. (70.5 w/hardtop). Front tread: 51.5 in. Rear tread: 50.0 in. Tires: H78-15 in.

CHASSIS [J-10 SWB]: Wheelbase: 118.8 in. Overall length: 194.0 in. Height: 68.5 in. Front tread: 63.3 in. Rear tread: 63.8 in. Tires: H78-15.

CHASSIS [J-10 LWB]: Wheelbase: 130.8 in. Overall length: 206 in. Height: 68.3 in. Front tread: 63.3 in. Rear tread: 63.8 in. Tires: H78-15.

CHASSIS [J-10 Sportside]: Wheelbase: 118.8 in. Overall length: 194 in. Height: 69.1 in. Front tread: 63.3 in. Rear tread: 63.8 in. Tires: H78-15.

CHASSIS [J-20]: Wheelbase: 130.8 in. Overall length: 206 in. Height: 70.7 in. Front tread: 64.9 in. Rear tread: 65.9 in. Tires: 8.75 x 16.5.

1981 AMC Jeep, Scrambler Pickup (OCW)

OPTIONS [CJ-5]: Special color combo paint ($29). Vinyl bucket seats with denim trim ($104). Optional axle ratios ($29). Center console without Laredo package ($60). Rear seat without Renegade or Laredo packages ($170). 258 cid six-cylinder engine ($136). 304 cid V-8 engine ($345). California emissions ($80). Rear Trac-Loc ($179). Laredo package soft top ($2,049). Renegade package, soft top ($945). Power front disc brakes ($79). Power steering, required with air conditioning ($206). AM radio and antenna ($90). AM/FM stereo with antenna and two speakers ($224). 63-ampere alternator, except included with Climate Group ($53). High-output battery, except included with Climate group ($42). Cold climate group without air conditioning ($104); with air conditioning ($52). Heavy-duty cooling system, included free with air conditioning ($104). Extra-heavy-duty suspension, with Laredo ($69); without Laredo ($98). Front and rear heavy-duty shocks ($30). Body side step ($24). Draw-Bar ($41). Roll bar accessory package ($104). Side-mount spare and removable tailgate ($25). Black or white vinyl soft top ($288). Denim vinyl soft top, blue or nutmeg color, with denim interior only ($333). Bumperettes, included in Laredo package ($28). Bumper accessory package, not available with Laredo package ($104). Front and rear floor carpet ($100). Padded dashboard, included with Renegade or Laredo packages ($52). Air conditioning, plus power steering, carpeting and six or V-8 engine required ($591). Convenience group, included with Renegade and Laredo packages ($32). Halogen fog lamps ($83). Halogen headlamps ($48). Stowage box, not available with sun roof ($94). Tachometer and Rally clock, included in Laredo package for no extra cost ($89). Tilt steering wheel ($81). Soft-Feel steering wheel, except included in Renegade package ($47). Decor group, except included in Laredo ($132). Four 15-inch wheelcovers ($46). Five chrome-plated 15x18 inch styled steel wheels ($147).

1981 AMC Jeep, Wagoneer Brougham Four-Door Station Wagon (JAG)

OPTIONS [CJ-7]: Special color combo paint ($29). Vinyl bucket seats with denim trim ($104). Optional axle ratios ($29). Center console without Laredo package ($60). Rear seat without Renegade or Laredo packages ($170). 258 cid six-cylinder engine ($136). 304 cid V-8 engine ($345). California emissions ($80). Rear Trac-Loc ($179). Laredo package soft top ($2,049). Renegade package, soft top ($945). Power front disc brakes ($79). Power steering, required with air conditioning ($206). AM radio and antenna ($90). AM/FM stereo with antenna and two speakers ($224). 63-ampere alternator, except included with Climate Group ($53). High-output battery, except included with Climate group ($42). Cold climate group without air conditioning ($104); with air conditioning ($52). Heavy-duty cooling system, included free with air conditioning ($104). Extra-heavy-duty suspension, with Laredo ($69); without Laredo ($98). Front and rear heavy-duty shocks ($30). Body side step ($24). Draw-Bar ($41). Roll bar accessory package ($104). Side-mount spare and removable tailgate ($25). Black or white vinyl soft top ($288). Denim vinyl soft top, blue or nutmeg color, with denim interior only ($333). Bumperettes, included in Laredo package ($28). Bumper accessory package, not available with Laredo package ($104). Front and rear floor carpet ($100). Padded dashboard, included with Renegade or Laredo packages ($52). Air conditioning, plus power steering, carpeting and six or V-8 engine required ($591). Convenience group, included with Renegade and Laredo packages ($32). Halogen fog lamps ($83). Halogen headlamps ($48). Stowage box, not available with sun roof ($94). Tachometer and Rally clock, included in Laredo package for no extra cost ($89). Tilt steering wheel ($81). Soft-Feel steering wheel, except included in Renegade package ($47). Decor group, except included in Laredo ($132). Four 15-inch wheelcovers ($46). Five chrome-plated 15x18 inch styled steel wheels ($147). Automatic transmission with part-time four-wheel drive ($350). Laredo package with hardtop ($2,520). Sun roof, rear seat mandatory ($249). Metal doors for optional soft top ($190). Black or white hardtop with doors ($710). Nutmeg hardtop with doors and bronze-toned glass ($837).

OPTIONS [Wagoneer]: Two-tone paint ($184). Special non-recommended color combinations ($29). Vinyl or fabric bucket seat with center armrest ($158). Optional axle ratio ($29). 360 V-8 ($345). California emissions ($80). Automatic transmission and part-time four-wheel drive ($350). Automatic Quadra-Trac transmission ($350). Trac-Loc, except not available with Quadra-Trac ($179). Wagoneer Brougham package ($935). Snow Boss package ($1,323). Trailer towing package A ($86). Trailer towing package B ($168). Power door locks ($147). Power side windows and door locks ($372). Power tailgate window, included in Brougham package; without Brougham option ($67). Power six-way driver's bucket seat ($158). Power six-way bucket seats ($263). AM push-button radio with antenna ($90). AM/FM stereo radio with antenna and four speakers ($224). AM/FM CB stereo with antenna and four speakers ($420). AM/FM casette stereo with antenna and four speakers ($325). AM/FM 8-Track with antenna and four speakers ($320). Premium audio system, FM only ($100). 70-Amp. Heavy-duty alternator; standard with air conditioning, rear window defroster and Cold Climate group; otherwise ($53). Heavy-duty battery, except standard with Cold Climate group ($42). Cold Climate group with air conditioning or rear window defroster ($52). Auxiliary automatic transmission oil cooler ($48). Heavy-duty cooling system ($46). Extra-duty suspension ($132). Extra-heavy-duty front springs ($13). Soft Ride suspension ($44). Heavy-duty shocks ($30). Inside spare tire mount and cover ($69). Roof rack with adjustable top bars, included with Brougham; otherwise ($109). Removable sun roof ($349). Bumper guards ($72). Bumper guards and nerfing strips ($113). Retractable cargo area cover ($62). Carpeted cargo floor and insulation ($81). Extra quiet insulation, standard with Brougham; otherwise ($136). Front and rear protective floor mats, standard with Brougham package; otherwise ($21). Scuff moldings, standard with Brougham package; otherwise ($92). Air conditioning, including heavy-duty cooling and alternator ($591). All tinted glass ($75). Convenience group, standard with Brougham option; otherwise ($71). Cruise control ($132). Halogen fog lamps ($83). Light group ($73). Left- and right-hand remote-control mirrors ($132). Dual mirrors ($69). Rear window defroster ($108). Tilt steering ($81). Visibility group ($143). Leather sport steering wheel ($69). Four chrome styled wheels ($226). Four forged aluminum wheels ($339); same with Brougham option ($124). Woodgrain side panels ($146); same with Brougham option ($75).

OPTIONS [Cherokee two-door]: Special non-recommended color combinations ($29). 360 V-8 ($345). California emissions ($80). Automatic transmission and part-time four-wheel drive ($350). Automatic Quadra-Trac transmission ($350). Trac-Loc, except not available with Quadra-Trac ($179). Snow Boss package ($1,323). Trailer towing package A ($86). Trailer towing package B ($168). Power tailgate window ($67). Power six-way driver's bucket seat ($158). Power six-way bucket seats ($263). AM push-button radio with antenna ($90). AM/FM stereo radio with antenna and four speakers ($224). AM/FM CB stereo with antenna and four speakers ($420). AM/FM casette stereo with antenna and four speakers ($325). AM/FM 8-Track with antenna and four speakers ($320). Premium audio system, FM only ($100). 70-Amp. Heavy-duty alternator; standard with air conditioning, rear window defroster and Cold Climate group; otherwise ($53). Heavy-duty battery, except standard with Cold Climate group ($42). Cold Climate group with air conditioning or rear window defroster ($52). Auxiliary automatic transmission oil cooler ($48). Heavy-duty cooling system ($46). Extra-duty suspension ($132). Extra-heavy-duty front springs ($13). Soft Ride suspension ($44). Heavy-duty shocks ($30). Inside spare tire mount and cover ($69). Roof rack with adjustable top bars ($109). Removable sun roof ($349). Bumper guards ($72). Bumper guards and nerfing strips ($113). Retractable cargo area cover ($62). Carpeted cargo floor and insulation ($81). Extra quiet insulation ($136). Front and rear protective floor mats otherwise ($21). Air conditioning, including heavy-duty cooling and alternator ($591). All tinted glass ($75). Convenience group ($71). Cruise control ($132). Halogen fog lamps ($83). Light group ($73). Left- and right-hand remote-control mirrors ($132). Dual mirrors ($69). Rear window defroster ($108). Tilt steering ($81). Visibility group ($143). Four styled chrome wheels included in Laredo; on Cherokee Chief ($156). Fabric bucket seats ($53). Cherokee Chief package ($839). Laredo package ($1,680). Chrome grille, standard with Laredo; other models ($53). Power door locks ($98). Power side windows and door locks ($243). Cold climate package ($104). Fixed center armrest ($67). Dual heavy-duty front shocks with heavy-duty rears ($90). Rear quarter vent window, included in Cherokee Chief/Laredo; otherwise ($79). Power sun roof, reg. Laredo ($1,460). Soft-Feel steering wheel ($47). Vinyl bodyside moldings ($75).

OPTIONS [Cherokee four-door]: Special non-recommended color combinations ($29). 360 V-8 ($345). California emissions ($80). Automatic transmission and part-time four-wheel drive ($350). Automatic Quadra-Trac transmission ($350). Trac-Loc, except not available with Quadra-Trac ($179). Snow Boss package ($1,323). Trailer towing package A ($86). Trailer towing package B ($168). Power tailgate window ($67). Power six-way driver's bucket seat ($158). Power six-way bucket seats ($263). AM push-button radio with antenna ($90). AM/FM stereo radio with antenna and four speakers ($224). AM/FM CB stereo with antenna and four speakers ($420). AM/FM casette stereo with antenna and four speakers ($325). AM/FM 8-Track with antenna and four speakers ($320). Premium audio system, FM only ($100). 70-Amp. Heavy-duty alternator; standard with air conditioning, rear window defroster and Cold Climate group; otherwise ($53). Heavy-duty battery, except standard with Cold Climate group ($42). Cold Climate group with air conditioning or rear window defroster ($52). Auxiliary automatic transmission oil cooler ($48). Heavy-duty cooling system ($46). Extra-duty suspension ($132). Extra-heavy-duty front springs ($13). Soft Ride suspension ($44). Heavy-duty shocks ($30). Inside spare tire mount and cover ($69). Roof rack with adjustable top bars ($109). Removable sun roof ($349). Bumper guards ($72). Bumper guards and nerfing strips ($113). Retractable cargo area cover ($62). Carpeted cargo floor and insulation ($81). Extra Quiet insulation ($136). Front and rear protective floor mats ($21). Air conditioning, including heavy-duty cooling and alternator ($591). All tinted glass ($75). Convenience group ($71). Cruise control ($132). Halogen fog lamps ($83). Light group ($73). Left- and right-hand remote-control mirrors ($132). Dual mirrors ($69). Rear window defroster ($108). Tilt steering ($81). Visibility group ($143). Four styled chrome wheels included in Laredo; on Cherokee Chief ($156). Fabric bucket seats ($53). Cherokee Chief package ($839). Laredo package ($1,680). Chrome grille, standard with Laredo; other models ($53). Power door locks ($138). Power side windows and door locks ($358). Cold climate package ($104). Fixed center armrest ($67). Dual heavy-duty front shocks with heavy-duty rears ($90). Rear quarter vent window, included in Cherokee Chief/ Laredo; otherwise ($79). Power sun roof, reg. Laredo ($1,460). Soft-Feel steering wheel ($47). Vinyl bodyside moldings ($75). Forged aluminum wheels ($239).

OPTIONS [J-Series Trucks]: Tu-Tone paint, not available with Honcho or Laredo; other models ($183). Special paint ($29). Fabric bench seat cushions included in Laredo; in other models ($24). Vinyl bucket seats, included with Laredo; in other models ($177). Fabric bucket seats, included with Honcho Sportside; with regular Honcho ($177); with other models ($200). Axle ratios ($29). 360 cid V-8 ($345). California emissions system ($80). Automatic transmission with part-time four-wheel drive ($350). Quadra-Trac ($350). Trac-Loc ($179). Sportside truck package ($944). Honcho Sportside truck package ($1,392). Custom package ($157). Honcho package ($892). Laredo ($1,680). Cap for Townside box ($638). Painted rear step bumper, included in Honcho and Sportside packages ($90). Chrome rear step bumper ($151). Townside box delete ($140 credit). Brush guard instead of bumper guard, with Laredo ($38); other models ($80). 15 x 8 chrome styled wheels ($118). Chrome grille ($53).

HISTORICAL: Introduced: Fall, 1979. Calendar year registrations: 81,923. Calendar year sales: (all models and series) 77,852 including: (CJ models) 47,304, (J Series pickup) 8,656. Model year production totaled 66,520 units. This included 10,234 Wagoneers; 11,541 Cherokees; 14,156 CJ-5s; 20,191 CJ-7s; 8,394 J-10s and 2,004 J-20s. Innovations: Four-cylinder engine returns to CJ Series. New top-of-the-line Laredo package available for pickup and CJ models. Jeep dealers recorded an average of 45 sales per outlet in 1980, down from an average of 77 sales per outlet in 1979 and 93 per outlet in 1978. Jeep vehicles continued to be produced exclusively in the company's Toledo, Ohio factory. The 151

cid four, a Pontiac-built powerplant, was made standard equipment in the CJs and 9,347 got it. Jeep Corp. also constructed 1,028 CJs with a four-cylinder diesel engine, but these were made strictly for export. Also, the 258 cid six was re-introduced as an economy option for the Wagoneer.

HISTORICAL: Introduced: March 25, 1981 (Scrambler). Calendar year registrations: 58,257. Calendar year sales: (all models and series) 63,275 divided as follows: (CJ models) 30,564; (Scrambler) 7,840; (J-Series Pickups) 6,516. Model year production totaled 77,560 vehicles, including: 13,594 Wagoneers; 6,557 Cherokees; 13,447 CJ-5s; 380 CJ-6 exports; 27,767 CJ-7s; 8,335 CJ-8/Scramblers; 5,916 J-10s and 1,534 J-20s. Innovations: Renegade package revised. Improvements to CJ front suspension. Power steering becomes standard and on J-10. All-new "Scrambler" model introduced. Historical notes: AMC had a total of 1,589 dealers in 1981. The company posted a loss of $160.9 million for the year. Worldwide unit sales of Jeeps totaled $104,628 million. Jeep sales per outlet continued to fall, sliding to an average of 34 units.

1982 JEEP

JEEP — 1982 SERIES — ALL ENGINES: Like other manufacturers, Jeep Corp. was becoming more and more involved with the marketing of specialty models created by adding options to the Wagoneer, Cherokee, Jeep and Jeep truck.
In the Wagoneer line, the Custom Wagoneer came with power steering; full wheelcovers; carpets; vinyl bench seats; bodyside moldings; a cargo mat; chrome grille and electronic ignition. The Wagoneer Brougham added cloth or deluxe vinyl upholstery; custom door trim; woodgrained dash trim; power tailgate window; styled wheels; lower tailgate molding; light group; halogen headlamps; woodgrain bodyside rub strips; convenience options group and visibility group. The Wagoneer Limited also included: full bodyside and tailgate woodgrain trim; special woodgrained luggage rack; 15-inch forged aluminum wheels; Goodyear Arriva white sidewall tires; bucket seats; woodgrained door trim; air conditioning; cruise control; tilt steering; premium AM/FM sound system; power windows and power door locks.
The Cherokee continued to be available in regular and "Wide-Wheel" two-door wagons and a four-door wagon. The base Cherokee included power steering, power brakes, four-speed manual transmission and a part-time four-wheel dive system. The Cherokee Chief added upper and lower black-out treatments; bodyside and tailgate striping; a blacked-out grille; Sun Valley front bucket seats and a Soft-Feel sports steering wheel. Additional equipment in the Cherokee Laredo package (available for the four-door or "Wide-Wheel" two-door) included special exterior striping; 15 x 8 chrome styled wheels with black hubs; Goodyear Wrangler radial tires (Wide-Wheel) or Goodyear Arriva white sidewall tires (four-door); bright moldings; roof rack; special folding bucket seats; Cara vinyl or Western Weave upholstery fabrics; extra carpeting; and a leather-wrapped steering wheel.

1982 AMC Jeep, CJ-7 Laredo Universal Jeep (RPZ)

Both the CJ-7 and J-series trucks were offered in new trim packages for 1982. The most refined CJ, the CJ-7 Limited, was depicted as the Jeep intended for "that special breed of drivers who want to blend an upgraded level of comfort and decor with their sports action on road and off." The Limited package included all base CJ-7 equipment, plus power steering and brakes; AM/FM radio with two speakers; a monochromatic paint scheme with color-keyed hardtop and wheel lip extensions; special dual-color bodyside striping; a blacked-out grille panel; exterior Limited nameplates; and a host of other features. Of these, the most controversial was the special improved ride package, which gave the Limited a far softer ride than any other CJ in history.
Both the CJ-7 and Scrambler now had a wider front and rear tread. Respective increases were 3.4 inches and 4.6 in. All models, except the CJ-5 with the 258 cid six-cylinder engine, were available with a five-speed manual T5 transmission supplied by Warner Gear. All six-cylinder CJ Jeeps were also available with the wide-ratio, three-speed automatic transmission with a lock-up converter. CJs with manual transmissions were also available with cruise control.
The new Pioneer Townside package, available for both the J-10 and J-20, included all features found in the Custom package, plus upper side scuff molding; tailgate stripes; "Pioneer" decals; dark argent-painted grille; carpeted cab floor; front bumper guards; and full wheelcovers (J-10 only), plus several other interior and exterior features. Otherwise, changes to the J-series trucks were extremely limited. The most important drivetrain development was the availability of the five-speed gearbox.
The Scrambler was now delivered with a new Space-Saver spare tire mounted on the roll bar, instead of on the tailgate (as in 1981). The older arrangement, with a standard full-sized spare, was available as an option.

I.D. DATA: VIN located on the top left surface of the instrument panel. There are 17 symbols. The first three symbols indicate the manufacturer, make and vehicle type. The engine type is indicated by the fourth symbol: B=151 cid four-cylinder; C=258 cid six-cylinder; N=360 cid V-8. The next letter identifies the transmission type. The series and type of vehicle are identified by the sixth and seventh symbols, which are the same as the model number. The eighth character identifies the GVW rating with the next serving as the check digit. Then follows the model year (tenth symbol C) and assembly point codes. The last six digits are sequential production numbers.

Model	Body Type	Price	Weight	Prod. Total
Wagoneer — 1/2-Ton — 4x4				
15	4dr Station Wagon	11,114	3797	—
15	4dr Station Wagon Brougham	12,084	—	—
15	4dr Station Wagon Limited	15,964	—	—
Cherokee — 1/2-Ton — 4x4				
16	2dr Station Wagon	9849	3692	—
17	2dr Wide Stance Wagon	10,812	3741	—
18	4dr Station Wagon	11,647	3296	—
CJ-5 — 1/4-Ton — 4x4 — 84 in. w.b.				
85	Jeep	7515	2489	6,080
CJ-7 — 1/4-Ton — 4x4 — 93.4 in. w.b.				
87	Jeep	7765	2555	23,820
Scrambler — 1/2-Ton — 4x4 — 103.4 in. w.b.				
88	Pickup	7588	2093	7,759
J-10 — 1/2-Ton — 4x4 — 119/131 in. w.b.				
25	Townside Pickup (SWB)	8610	3656	—
26	Townside Pickup (LWB)	8756	3708	—
J-20 — 3/4-Ton — 4x4 — 131 in. w.b.				
27	Townside Pickup	9766	4270	1,418

NOTE 1: See "Historical" for additional production totals.
NOTE 2: J-10 Sportside option has 118.8 in. w.b.
ENGINE [Standard: Wagoneer/Cherokee/J-10/Optional Scrambler/CJ-5/CJ-7]: Inline. OHV. Six-cylinder. Cast iron block. Bore & stroke: 3.75 x 3.90 in. Displacement: 258 cid Compression ratio: 8.3:1. Net horsepower: 110 at 3000 rpm. Net torque: 205 lbs.-ft. at 1800 rpm. Seven main bearings. Hydraulic valve lifters. Carburetor: Single two-barrel.
ENGINE [Standard: Scrambler/CJ-5/CJ-7]: Inline. OHV. Four-cylinder. Cast iron block. Bore & stroke: 4.00 x 3.00 in. Displacement: 151 cid. Compression ratio: 8.2:1. Net horsepower: 82 at 4000 rpm. Torque: 125 lbs.-ft. at 2600 rpm. Hydraulic valve lifters. Carburetor: Single Two-barrel.

1982 AMC Jeep J-10 Honcho Pickup (RPZ)

ENGINE [Standard: J-20; Optional: Wagoneer/Cherokee/J-10]: Vee-block. OHV. Eight-cylinder. Cast iron block. Bore & stroke: 4.08 x 3.44 in. Displacement: 360 cid. Compression ratio: 8.25:1. Net horsepower: 150 at 3400 rpm. Net torque: 205 lbs.-ft. at 1500 rpm. Five main bearings. Hydraulic valve lifters. Carburetor: Single two-barrel.
CHASSIS [Wagoneer]: Wheelbase: 108.7 in. Overall length: 183.5 in. Width: 75.6 in. Height: 65.9 in. GVW maximum: 6,100 lbs. Cargo capacity: 95.1 cu. ft. Front overhang: 29.9 in. Rear overhang: 44.9 in. Front suspension: Leaf springs on live axle with stabilizer bar. Rear suspension: Leaf springs on live axle with tube shocks. Front brakes: power disc. Rear brakes: drum. Steering: Power-assisted; 17.1 ratio. Turning circle: 37.7 ft. Fuel: 20.3 gallons.
CHASSIS [Cherokee]: Wheelbase: 108.7 in. Overall length: 183.5 in. Width: 75.6 in. Height: 66.8 in. GVW: 6,100 lbs. maximum. Cargo capacity: 95.1 cu. ft. without rear seat. Front overhang: 29.9 in. Rear overhang: 44.9 in. Front suspension: Leaf springs on live axle with stabilizer bar. Rear suspension: Leaf springs on live axle with tube shocks. Front brakes: power disc. Rear brakes: drum. Steering: Power-assisted; 17.1 ratio. Turning circle: 37.7 ft. Fuel: 20.3 gallons.
CHASSIS [CJ-5]: Wheelbase: 83.5 in. Overall length: 144.3 in. standard or 134.8 in. with rear-mounted spare; Width: 68.6 in. Height with open body, 67.6 in. GVW maximum: 3,700 lbs. Cargo capacity: 10.2 cu. ft. without rear seat. Front overhang: 23.5 in. Rear overhang: 37.3 in. standard or 27.8 in. with rear-mounted spare. Front suspension: leaf spring on live axle with tube shocks. Rear suspension: leaf springs on live axle with tube shocks. Front brakes: manual discs. Rear brakes: drum. Steering: manual re-circulating ball, 24:1 ratio, 34.1 ft. turning circle. Fuel: 15.5 gallons.
CHASSIS [CJ-7]: Wheelbase: 93.5 in. Overall length: 153.2 in. standard or 144.3 in. with rear-mounted spare; Width: 68.6 in. Height with open body, 67.6 in. GVW maximum: 4,100 lbs. Cargo capacity: 13.6 cu. ft. without rear seat. Front overhang: 23.5 in. Rear overhang: 36.2 in. standard or 27.3 in. with rear-mounted spare. Front suspension: leaf spring on live axle with tube shocks. Rear suspension: leaf springs on live axle with tube shocks. Front brakes: manual discs. Rear brakes: drum. Steering: manual re-circulating ball, 24:1 ratio, 38 ft. turning circle. Fuel: 15.5 gallons.
CHASSIS [CJ-8 Scrambler]: Wheelbase: 103.5 in. Overall length: 177.3 in. Height: 67.6 in. (70.5 w/hardtop). Front tread: 51.5 in. Rear tread: 50.0 in. Tires: H78-15 in.
CHASSIS [J-10 SWB]: Wheelbase: 118.8 in. Overall length: 194.0 in. Height: 68.5 in. Front tread: 63.3 in. Rear tread: 63.8 in. Tires: H78-15.
CHASSIS [J-10 LWB]: Wheelbase: 130.8 in. Overall length: 206 in. Height: 68.3 in. Front tread: 63.3 in. Rear tread: 63.8 in. Tires: H78-15.
CHASSIS [J-10 Sportside]: Wheelbase: 118.8 in. Overall length: 194 in. Height: 69.1 in. Front tread: 63.3 in. Rear tread: 63.8 in. Tires: H78-15.
CHASSIS [J-20]: Wheelbase: 130.8 in. Overall length: 206 in. Height: 70.7 in. Front tread: 64.9 in. Rear tread: 65.9 in. Tires: 8.75 x 16.5.

1982 AMC Jeep, Cherokee Two-Door Station Wagon (RPZ)

TECHNICAL: Selective synchromesh transmission. Speeds: 4F/1R. Floor-mounted gearshift. Single-plate, dry-disc clutch. Shaft drive. Rear axle: (J-20) full-floating; (others) semifloating. Overall drive ratio: 3.54:1. Four-wheel hydraulic front disc/rear drum power brakes. (* Power brakes optional on models 85/87/88). Steel disc wheels.

1982 AMC Jeep, Scrambler Pickup (RPZ)

1982 AMC Jeep, Wagoneer Limited (RPZ)

OPTIONS: 258 cid six-cylinder engine, models 85/87/88 ($150). 360 cid V-8 engine, standard w/J-20 ($351). Five-speed transmission, except J-20 ($199). Automatic transmission ($409). Automatic Quadra-Trac ($455). Air conditioning ($681). Heavy-duty alternator ($59). Optional axle ratio, without wide wheels ($33). Heavy-duty battery ($47). Power brakes, models 85/87/88 ($99). Bumper accessory package, models 85/87/88 ($113). Retractable cargo area cover ($75). Townside box cap for pickups ($684). Cold Climate group ($115). Heavy-duty cooling system ($49). Cruise control ($159). Custom package, Townside pickups ($169). Decor Group, models 85/87/88 ($86). Trac-Loc differential ($219). Doors for Scrambler/CJ-7 with soft top ($229). California emissions system ($80). Tinted glass, pickups ($48). Chrome grille, pickups ($57). Halogen headlights on CJs ($56). Honcho Package, model 25 ($949). Honcho Sportside Package, J-10 Sportside ($470). Scrambler padded instrument panel ($56). Laredo Package, model 25 ($1,749). Laredo Package for CJ, with soft top ($2,149); with hardtop ($2,599). Light group, J-10/J-20 with roll bar ($49); without roll bar ($71). CJ-7 Limited package ($2895). Pioneer package, on J-10 Townside ($599); on J-20 ($577); on Scrambler/CJ ($950). AM radio ($99). AM/FM stereo ($229). AM/FM stereo w/CB ($456). AM/FM w/cassette, pickups ($339). AM/FM ETR stereo w/cassette, pickups ($479). Premium audio system, Limited ($115). CJ Renegade package ($979). Roll bar on pickups ($135). Roll bar access package, CJs ($979). Scrambler "SL" package, with soft top ($1,999); with hardtop ($2,399). Scrambler "SR" Sport package ($799). Pickup cloth bench seat trim ($25). Cloth bucket seats, J-10 w/ Pioneer package ($181); other pickups ($205). Vinyl bucket seats, Townside pickups ($181); Scrambler including Denim trim ($106). Dual low-profile mirrors (except Scrambler), with visibility group ($26); without visibily group ($85). Dual electric remote mirrors (except Scrambler), with visibility group ($83); without visibility group ($142). Heavy-duty shocks, regular ($35); with dual fronts ($119). Air adjustable rear shocks, except Scrambler and J-20 ($66). Snow Boss package, except Scrambler ($1,399). Scrambler spare tire lock ($9). Heavy-duty rear springs, pickups ($48). Heavy-duty front springs, J-10 ($59). Extra heavy-duty front springs, pickups ($79). Power steering on Scrambler and CJs ($229). Tachometer and Rally clock, Scrambler and CJs ($96). Hardtop with doors, Scrambler ($695); CJ ($775). Scrambler soft denim top ($300). Scrambler soft vinyl top ($280).

CJ soft vinyl top ($330). Scrambler tonneau cover ($122). Visibility group, except Scrambler ($152). Wheelcovers, all models ($55). Forged aluminum wheels, J-10 Townside ($399). Forged aluminum wheels, J-10 Honcho or Sportside ($200). Power side windows and door locks, J-10/J-20 ($288). Sliding rear window, J-10/J-20 ($97). Wood side rails, Scrambler ($92). Chrome styled steel wheels, models 85/87/88 ($349); J-10 ($150).
HISTORICAL: Introduced: Fall, 1981. Innovations: Wider tread for CJ and Scrambler models. New option packages released. Five-speed manual transmission available. Total calendar year production: 75,269 (includes Wagoneer and Cherokee). Calendar year registrations: 62,097 (includes Wagoneer and Cherokee). Calendar year production by model: (CJ) 37,221; (Pickups) 6,113; (Scrambler) 6,315. Calendar year sales: 67,646 (U.S. and Canada). Model year production totaled 64,965 units. This included 14,489 Wagoneers; 6,013 Cherokees; 6,080 CJ-5s; 23,820 CJ-7s; 7,759 CJ-8/Scramblers; 5,026 J-10s; and 1,418 J-20s. W. Paul Tippett, Jr. became chairman of American Motors in 1982, replacing Gerald C. Meyers. Tippett was born Dec. 27, 1932 and graduated from Wabash College, in Cincinnati, Ohio. The company posted Jeep dollar sales of $90.7 million for Jeep vehicles in calendar 1982. AMC reported a net loss of $153.5 million on its cars and trucks during this period. Texans were the leading buyers of Jeep vehicles, based on the state's registration of 6,492 vehicles. California was second with 4,132 registrations and Pennsylvania was third with 3,568 registration. Unit sales of Jeep vehicles, for the calendar year, were 67,646 for the U.S./Canadian market and an additional 23,083 for the international market.

1983 JEEP

JEEP — 1983 SERIES — ALL ENGINES: The most important Jeep developments for 1983 were technical in nature. A new full-time four-wheel/two-wheel drive system, called Selec-Trac, replaced Quadra-Trac, which had been introduced in 1973. Selec-Trac was optional on J-10 pickups with either six-cylinder or V-8 engines. Selec-Trac featured a two-speed capability in the transfer case for added torque. To engage either two- or four-wheel drive, the driver of a Selec-Trac J-10 stopped the vehicle and activated a switch on the instrument panel. A safety catch was provided to avoid accidental movement of the Selec-Trac switch. Technical refinements to the 258 cid six-cylinder engine included an increase in compression ratio to 9.2:1 from 8.6:1 and the addition of a fuel feedback system and knock sensor to improve performance and efficiency.
Appearance changes were held to a minimum. Both the Renegade package, for the CJ-5 and CJ-7, as well as the Scrambler's SR trim package, had new striping arrangements.
A new XJ model was in the works for introduction during 1983, but delays in the production startup led to the XJ line being introduced in the fall of 1983 as a new-for-1984 series.
I.D. DATA: VIN located on the top left surface of the instrument panel. There are 17 symbols. The first three symbols indicate the manufacturer, make and vehicle type. The engine type is indicated by the fourth symbol: B=151 cid (2.5 liter) four-cylinder; C=258 cid (4.2 liter) six-cylinder; N=360 cid (6.0 liter) V-8; U=150 cid (2.5 liter) four-cylinder. The next letter identifies the transmission type. The series and type of vehicle are identified by the sixth and seventh symbols, which are the same as the model number. The eighth character identifies the GVW rating with the next serving as the check digit. Then follows the model year (tenth symbol D) and assembly point codes. The last six digits are sequential production numbers.

1983 AMC Jeep, CJ-5 Renegade Universal (RPZ)

Model	Body Type	Price	Weight	Prod. Total
Wagoneer — 1/2-Ton — 4x4				
15	4dr Brougham Station Wagon	13,173	3869	—
15	4dr Limited Station Wagon	16,889	—	—
Cherokee — 1/2-Ton — 4x4				
16	2dr Station Wagon	10,315	3764	6,186
CJ-5 — 1/4-Ton — 4x4 — 83.4 in. w.b.				
85	Jeep	7515	2099	3,085
CJ-7 — 1/4-Ton — 4x4 — 93.4 in. w.b.				
87	Jeep	6995	2595	37,673
Scrambler — 1/2-Ton — 4x4 — 103.4 in. w.b.				
88	Pickup	6765	2733	5,407
J-10 — 1/2-Ton — 4x4 — 119/131 in. w.b.				
25	Townside Pickup (SWB)	9082	3728	—
26	Townside Pickup (LWB)	9227	3790	—
J-20 — 3/4-Ton — 4x4 — 131 in. w.b.				
27	Townside Pickup	10,117	4336	2,740

NOTE: See "Historical" for additional production totals.

1983 AMC Jeep, J-10 Laredo Townside Pickup (RPZ)

ENGINE [Standard: 88; Optional: 85/87]: Inline. OHV. Four-cylinder. Cast iron block. Bore & stroke: 4.0 x 3.0 in. Displacement: 151 cid. Compression ratio: 9.6:1. Net horsepower: 92. Five main bearings. Hydraulic valve lifters. Carburetor: Single two-barrel.
ENGINE [Standard: 85/25/26; Optional: 88/87]: Inline. OHV. Six-cylinder. Cast iron block. Bore & stroke: 3.75 x 3.90 in. Displacement: 258 cid. Compression ratio: 9.2:1. Net horsepower: 102 at 3000 rpm. Net Torque: 204 lbs.-ft. at 1650 rpm. Seven main bearings. Hydraulic valve lifters. Carburetor: Single Two-barrel.
ENGINE [Standard: 27; Optional: 25/26]: Vee-block. OHV. Eight-cylinder. Cast iron block. Bore & stroke: 4.08 x 3.44 in. Displacement: 360 cid. Brake horsepower: 170 at 4000 rpm. Taxable: 280 lbs.-ft. at 2400 rpm. Five main bearings. Hydraulic valve lifters. Carburetor: Two-barrel.
CHASSIS [Wagoneer]: Wheelbase: 108.7 in. Overall length: 183.5 in. Width: 75.6 in. Height: 65.9 in. GVW maximum: 6100 lbs. Cargo capacity: 95.1 cu. ft. Front overhang: 29.9 in. Rear overhang: 44.9 in. Front suspension: Leaf springs on live axle with stabilizer bar. Rear suspension: Leaf springs on live axle with tube shocks. Front brakes: power disc. Rear brakes: drum. Steering: Power-assisted; 17.1 ratio. Turning circle 37.7 ft. Fuel: 20.3 gallons.
CHASSIS [Cherokee]: Wheelbase: 108.7 in. Overall length: 183.5 in. Width: 75.6 in. Height: 66.8 in. GVW: 6100 lbs. maximum. Cargo capacity: 95.1 cu. ft. without rear seat. Front overhang: 29.9 in. Rear overhang: 44.9 in. Front suspension: Leaf springs on live axle with stabilizer bar. Rear suspension: Leaf springs on live axle with tube shocks. Front brakes: power disc. Rear brakes: drum. Steering: Power-assisted; 17.1 ratio. Turning circle: 37.7 ft. Fuel: 20.3 gallons.
CHASSIS [CJ-5]: Wheelbase: 83.4 in. Overall length: 142.9 in. standard. Width: 68.6 in. Height with open body, 69.3 in. Front tread: 52.4 in. (53.9 in. with styled wheels). Rear tread: 50.5 in. GVW maximum: 3700 lbs. Cargo capacity: 10.2 cu. ft. without rear seat. Front overhang: 23.5 in. Rear overhang: 37.3 in. standard or 27.8 in. with rear-mounted spare. Front suspension: leaf spring on live axle with tube shocks. Rear suspension: leaf springs on live axle with tube shocks. Front brakes: manual discs. Rear brakes: drum. Steering: manual re-circulating ball, 24:1 ratio, 34.1 ft. turning circle. Fuel: 15.5 gallons. Tires: G78-15.
CHASSIS [CJ-7]: Wheelbase: 93.4 in. Overall length: 153.5 in. standard and 144.3 in. with rear-mounted spare; Width: 68.6 in. Front tread: 55.1 in. Rear tread: 55.1 in. Height with open body, 69.3 in. GVW maximum: 4,100 lbs. Cargo capacity: 13.6 cu. ft. without rear seat. Front overhang: 23.5 in. Rear overhang: 36.2 in. standard or 27.3 in. with rear-mounted spare. Front suspension: leaf spring on live axle with tube shocks. Rear suspension: leaf springs on live axle with tube shocks. Front brakes: manual discs. Rear brakes: drum. Steering: manual re-circulating ball, 24:1 ratio, 38 ft. turning circle. Fuel: 15.5 gallons. Tires: G78-15.
CHASSIS [CJ-8 Scrambler]: Wheelbase: 103.4 in. Overall length: 168.9 in. Height: 69.5 in. (70.5 w/hardtop). Front tread: 55.8 in. Rear tread: 55.1 in. Tires: G78-15 in.
CHASSIS [Model 25]: Wheelbase: 118.7 in. Overall length: 192.5 in. Height: 67.4 in. Front tread: 64 in. Rear tread: 63.8 in. Tires: P225-75R15.
CHASSIS [Model 26]: Wheelbase: 130.7 in. Overall length: 204.5 in. Height: 67.5 in. Front tread: 66.0 in. Rear tread: 65.8 in. Tires: P225-75R15.
CHASSIS [Model 27]: Wheelbase: 130.7 in. Overall length: 204.5 in. Height: 67.6 in. Front tread: 64.6 in. Rear tread: 65.9 in. Tires: 8.75 x 16.5.

1983 AMC Jeep, Scrambler SL Sport Pickup (RPZ)

TECHNICAL: Selective synchromesh transmission. Speeds: 4F/1R. Floor-mounted gearshift. Single-plate, dry-disc clutch. Shaft drive. Rear axle: (J-20) full-floating; (others) semi-floating. Ratio: 3.54:1. Four-wheel hydraulic front disc/rear drum power brakes. (* Power brakes optional on models 85/87/88.) Steel disc wheels.
OPTIONS [Wagoneer/Cherokee]: Automatic transmission (standard in Wagoneer); Five-speed transmission ($225). AM/FM stereo, standard in Wagoneer Limited; in other models ($199). AM/FM stereo with tape ($329). Cruise control, standard in Wagoneer Limited; in other models ($184). Rear window defroster, standard in Wagoneer Limited; in other models ($134). Tilt steering wheel, standard in Wagoneer Limited; in other models ($106). Roof rack, standard on Wagoneer Limited; on other models ($122). Aluminum wheels (standard for Wagoneer Limited). Sun roof ($389). Power sun roof ($1,637). Power door locks. Power windows. Power seats, standard in Wagoneer Limited; in other models ($290). Laredo package ($1,128). Pioneer package ($1,131). Custom or two-tone paint. 360 cid V-8 engine ($393). Air conditioning.

OPTIONS [CJ/Scrambler]: Renegade package ($1,011). Laredo package ($2220). Limited package ($3,595). Scrambler "SR" Sport package ($825). Scrambler "SL" Sport package ($2,065). Soft top. Hardtop. Automatic transmission. Five-speed manual transmission. 258 cid six-cylinder engine.
OPTIONS [J10/J20]: Custom package ($175). Pioneer package ($619). Laredo package ($1,807). Automatic transmission. Five-speed manual transmission. 360 cid V-8 engine.

HISTORICAL: Introduced: Fall, 1982. Innovations: New Select-Trac full-time four-wheel-drive system introduced. Higher compression, fuel feedback system and knock sensor added to 258 cid six-cylinder engine. Calendar year U.S. registrations: 76,453. Calendar year sales, U.S. and Canada: 93,169. U.S. Calendar year production: (total) 75,534; (CJ) 40,758; (Pickups) 4705; (Scrambler) 5407. Worldwide Calendar year production (Toledo plant): 113,263.

Model year output totaled 64,965. This total included: 14,849 Wagoneer; 6,013 Cherokee; 6,080 CJ-5s; 23,820 CJ-7s; 7,759 CJ-8/Scramblers; 5,026 J-10s and 1,418 J-20s. Company president was Paul W. Tippett, Jr. Historical notes: Sales of four-wheel-drive Jeep vehicles in 1983 were the best since 1979 and up 29 percent from the previous year. Chairman Tippett and president Jose J. Dedeurwaerder reported, in late 1983, that a particularly encouraging sign was the fact that "Jeep production at our Toledo plant is now higher than at any time since the plant was acquired from Kaiser in 1970." Worldwide wholesale unit sales of Jeeps totaled $113,443 million, up 25 percent from 1982. Worldwide unit sales of Jeeps, in the calendar year, peaked at 93,169 vehicles in the U.S. and Canada and 20,274 more for the international market. In state-by-state registrations, California leaped to second place with 6,004 Jeeps registered for calendar 1982. Texas was still first with 6,970 registrations.

On the international scene, the May, 1983 signing of an agreement with Beijing Jeep Corp. opened the door for a joint-venture in which AMC would help build Jeeps in the People's Republic of China. Efforts to strengthen the Latin American export market were also made by AMC-Jeep.

1984 JEEP

1984 AMC Jeep, Wagoneer Limited Four-Door Station Wagon (AMC)

JEEP — 1984 SERIES — ALL ENGINES: The all-new, down-sized Cherokee and Wagoneer Sportwagons in the XJ series bowed as a 1984 models and nearly doubled the retail sales of Jeep vehicles by the end of the year.

The Cherokee came in two-door and four-door versions, while the Wagoneer Sportwagon was a four-door only. The new bodies had a short, squarish, but neatly tailored look. Large, square headlamps sat atop the horizontally-mounted rectangular parking lamps up front. The grille featured tall, vertical bars. There was a "glassy" greenhouse and flared wheel openings. Bright bumpers with black rubber end caps were seen in front. The XJs were 21 inches shorter, six inches narrower, four inches lower and 1,000 pounds lighter than the "senior" Grand Wagoneer.

At the time, the smaller new models were the only compact sports utility vehicles offering the four-door body style and two types of four-wheel drive systems. The systems were the SelectTrac and shift-o-the-fly CommandTrac.

Now representing somewhat of a luxury station wagon, the Grand Wagoneer was again based on the old, first-seen-in-1963, body. Many equipment items that cost extra on other Jeeps were standard in the Grand Wagoneer. The Grand Wagoneer's standard equipment included automatic transmission; cruise control; rear window defroster; tilt steering wheel; luggage rack; aluminum wheels; power door locks; power windows and power seats.

The elimination of the CJ-5 from the Jeep lineup was of considerable historic importance. This was a reflection of the ever-rising popularity of the roomier CJ-7. It also reduced production complexity at Toledo. Significant to the future of Jeep vehicles was the introduction of the first four-cylinder engine ever produced by AMC. This 2.5-liter engine was the base powerplant for both the CJ-7 and the Scrambler. Unlike many other contemporary truck engines the new four-cylinder was intended specifically for use in Jeep vehicles.

Jeep's 4.2-liter (258 cid) inline six continued as base engine for the J-10 pickup. The J-20 three-quarter ton pickup continued to use the 5.9-liter (360 cid) V-8 as its sole engine choice.

GVWs for the various models were 4150-pounds for CJ-7s and Scramblers; 6,200-pounds for the J-10 pickups and 7,600-8,400-pounds for the J-20s. The payload range for these models, in the same order, was: (CJ-7) 1,227-pounds; (Scrambler) 1,146-pounds; (J-10) 2,156-pounds and (J-20) 3,745-pounds.

587

1984 AMC Jeep, CJ-7 Laredo (AMC)

I.D. DATA: VIN located on the top left surface of the instrument panel. There are 17 symbols. The first three symbols indicate the manufacturer, make and vehicle type. The engine type is indicated by the fourth symbol: U=150 cid (2.5-liter) four-cylinder; W=173 cid (2.8 liter) V-6; C=258 cid (4.2 liter) six-cylinder; N=360 cid (5.9 liter) V-8. The next letter identifies the transmission type. The series and type of vehicle are identified by the sixth and seventh symbols, which are the same as the model number. The eighth character identifies the GVW rating with the next serving as the check digit. Then follows the model year (tenth symbol E) and assembly point codes. The last six digits are sequential production numbers.

Model	Body Type	Price	Weight	Prod. Total
Wagoneer Sport Wagon L-4 — 1/2-Ton — 4x4				
75	4dr Station Wagon	12,444	3047	—
75	4dr Limited Station Wagon	17,076	3222	—
Wagoneer Sport Wagon V-6 — 1/2-Ton — 4x4				
75	4dr Station Wagon	12,749	3065	—
75	4dr Limited Station Wagon	17,381	3240	—
Grand Wagoneer V-8 — 1/2-Ton — 4x4				
15	4dr Station Wagon	19,306	4221	—
Cherokee L-4 — 1/2-Ton — 4x4				
77	2dr Station Wagon	9995	2817	—
78	4dr Station Wagon	10,295	2979	—
Cherokee V-6 — 1/2-Ton — 4x4				
77	2dr Station Wagon	10,300	2963	—
78	4dr Station Wagon	10,600	3023	—
CJ-7 — L-4 — 1/4-Ton — 4x4 — 93.4 in. w.b.				
87	Jeep	7563	2598	42,644
Scrambler — L-4 — 1/2-Ton — 4x4 — 103.4 in. w.b.				
88	Pickup	7563	2679	4,130
J-10 Pickup — L-6 — 1/2-Ton — 4x4 — 118.8/130.7 in. w.b.				
25	Townside (SWB)	9967	3724	—
26	Townside (LWB)	10,117	3811	—
J-20 Pickup — V-8 — 3/4-Ton — 4x4 — 130.7 in. w.b.				
27	Townside Pickup	11,043	4323	—

NOTE: See "Historical" for additional production data.

1984 AMC Jeep Scrambler Pickup (OCW)

ENGINE [standard in Cherokee XJ/Wagoneer XJ/CJ-7/Scrambler]: Inline. OHV. Four-cylinder. Cast iron block. Bore & stroke: 3.875 x 3.188 in. Displacement: 150.4 cid. Compression ratio: 9.2:1. Taxable horsepower: 24.04. Net horsepower: 86 at 3650 rpm. Net torque: 132 lbs.-ft. at 3200 rpm. Five main bearings. Hydraulic valve lifters. Carburetor: One-barrel with electronic FFB.
ENGINE [optional]: Vee-block. OHV. Six-cylinder. Bore & stroke: 3.50 x 2.99 in. Displacement: 173 cid. Compression ratio: 8.5:1. Horsepower rating: not advertised. Carburetor: two-barrel.
ENGINE [standard in Grand Wagoneer/J-10; optional in CJ-7/Scrambler]: Inline. OHV. Six-cylinder. Cast iron block. Bore & stroke: 3.75 x 3.90 in. Displacement: 258 cid. Compression ratio: 9.2:1. Taxable horsepower: 33.75. Net horsepower: 102 at 3000 rpm. Net Torque: 204 lbs.-ft. at 1650 rpm. Seven main bearings. Hydraulic valve lifters. Carburetor: Two-barrel.

ENGINE [standard in J-20; optional in Grand Wagoneer/J-10]: Vee-block. OHV. Eight-cylinder. Cast iron block. Bore & stroke: 4.08 x 3.44 in. Displacement: 360 cid. Taxable horsepower: 53.27. Brake horsepower: 175. Five main bearings. Hydraulic valve lifters. Carburetor: Two-barrel.

1984 AMC Jeep, Laredo Scrambler pickup (AMC)

CHASSIS [Wagoneer XJ]: Wheelbase: 101.4 in. Width: 70.5 in. Overall length: 165.3 in. Height: 64.1 in.

CHASSIS [Cherokee XJ]: Wheelbase: 101.4 in. Width: 69.3 in. Overall length: 165.3 in. Height: 64.1 in.

CHASSIS [Grand Wagoneer]: Wheelbase: 108.7 in. Width: 74.8 in. Overall length: 186.4 in. Height: 66.4 in. Tires: P225/75R-15.

CHASSIS [CJ-7]: Wheelbase: 93.4 in. Width: 65.3 in. Overall length: 153.2 in. Height: 70.9 in. Front tread: 55.8 in. Rear tread: 55.1 in. Tires: P205/75R15 in.

CHASSIS [Scrambler]: Wheelbase: 103.4 in. Width: 65.3 in. Overall length: 166.2 in. Height: 70.8 in. Front tread: 55.8 in. Rear tread: 55.1 in. Tires: P205/75R15 in.

CHASSIS [J-10/Model 25]: Wheelbase: 118.7 in. Width: 78.9 in. Overall length: 194 in. Height: 69 in. Front tread: 64.0 in. Rear tread: 63.8 in. Tires: P225/75R15 in.

CHASSIS [J-10/Model 26]: Wheelbase: 130.7 in. Width: 78.9 in. Overall length: 206 in. Height: 69 in. Front tread: 64.0 in. Rear tread: 63.8 in. Tires: P225/75R15 in.

CHASSIS [J-20]: Wheelbase: 130.7 in. Width: 78.9 in. Overall length: 206 in. Height: 70 in. Front tread: 64.6 in. Rear tread: 65.9 in. Tires: 8.25 x 16.5 in.

1984 AMC Jeep, Laredo Townside Pickup (AMC)

TECHNICAL: Selective synchromesh transmission. Speeds: 4F/1R. Floor-mounted gearshift. Single-plate, dry-disc clutch. Rear axle: (J-20) full-floating; (others) semi-floating. Overall ratio: 3.54:1. Power assisted hydraulic front disc/rear drum brakes. (* Power assist optional on CJ-7 and Scrambler). Steel disc wheels.

TECHNICAL [Cherokee]: Selective synchromesh transmission. Speeds: 4F/1R. Floor-mounted gearshift. Single-plate, dry-disc clutch. Shaft drive. Rear axle: semi-floating. Quadra-Link front suspension. Two "shift-on-the-fly" 2WD/4WD systems. UniFrame construction. Power front disc brakes/rear drum. Stabilizer bars front and rear.

TECHNICAL [Wagoneer]: Three-speed automatic transmission. Speeds: 3F/1R. Column-mounted gearshift. Shaft drive. Rear axle: full-floating. Power front disc/rear drum brakes. Four-wheel drive "shift-on-the-fly" system. Selec-Trac all-road surface 2WD/4WD system optional.

OPTIONS [Wagoneer XJ/Cherokee XJ/Grand Wagoneer]: Limited package ($3,595). Automatic transmission, standard in Grand Wagoneer and Limited; optional in other models. Five-speed transmission (standard in base Wagoneer XJ). AM/FM stereo, standard in Wagoneer XJ Limited; optional in other XJs. AM/FM stereo with tape, standard in Grand Wagoneer; optional in other models. Cruise control, standard in Grand Wagoneer; optional in other models ($191). Rear window defroster, standard in Grand Wagoneer and Limited; optional in other models ($140). Tilt steering wheel, standard in Grand Wagoneer and Limited; optional in other models ($110). Luggage rack, standard on Grand Wagoneer and Limited; optional on other models ($119). Power sun roof ($1,694). Power door locks, standard in Grand Wagoneer and Limited; optional in other models. Power windows, standard in Grand Wagoneer and Limited; optional in other models ($300). Power seats, standard on Grand Wagoneer and Limited; optional in other models. Cherokee Chief package ($1,310). Pioneer package ($1,000). 360 cid V-8.

OPTIONS [CJ-7]: Renegade package ($1,124). (Scrambler): "SR" Sport package ($932). Hardtop ($829). (Pickups): Pioneer package ($456). Laredo package ($2,129).

HISTORICAL: Introduced: Fall, 1983. Calendar year sales: 153,801 (all Series), includes: (CJ-7) 39,547; (Scrambler) 2846; (J-Series Pickup) 3404. Model year production was 152,931 units. This included: 58,596 Cherokee XJs; 20,940 Wagoneer XJs; 42,644 CJ-7s; 4,130 Scramblers; 4,085 Jeep trucks; and 22,536 Grand Wagoneers. Innovations: First four-cylinder AMC engine introduced. The new Jeep Cherokee and Wagoneer Sport wagons were the first all-new Jeep line in 20 years. The 1984 Cherokee was honored with "4x4 of the year" awards by all three leading off-road magazines. As a result of increased Jeep production, all laid-off employees were recalled at Toledo and the Jeep work force was increased by new hires.

1985 JEEP

1985 AMC Jeep, Scrambler Pickup (JAG)

JEEP — 1985 SERIES — ALL ENGINES: The latest CJ-7, available in base, Renegade and Laredo levels, had new, optional fold and tumble rear seats in place of the older fixed-back type. Both the Laredo and Renegade CJ-7 Jeeps featured new exterior tape stripe patterns, three new exterior colors and one new interior color. High-back bucket seats were now standard.

Highlights of the 1985 Scrambler included replacement of the SR Sport version by the Renegade and the introduction of the Scrambler Laredo, which filled the position previously occupied by the soft and hardtop SL Sport. Both the Renegade and Laredo had new exterior and interior decor, a new interior color and new soft and hardtop colors. All Scramblers, including the base model, had high-back bucket seats.

Again available was the downsized Cherokee XJ two-door sport utility wagons, with an inline four-cylinder engine standard and an overhead cam four-cylinder diesel engine optional. The four-door Wagoneer XJ was back again, too, offering the 2.5 liter inline four or 2.8 liter V-6 below its hood.

Customers who wanted a larger vehicle were not left out. They could order the Grand Wagoneer station wagon, which had the 4.2 liter "Big Six" standard and offered the 5.9 liter V-8 at extra-cost.

J-series trucks were unchanged for 1985 as the company geared up to produce a compact Commanche pickup for 1986. However, there was a new two-wheel drive Cherokee released at midyear as a 1985-1/2 model. It was aimed at giving buyers in the Sun Belt states a Jeep pickup that cost $1,200 less than the four-wheel drive model.

1985 AMC Jeep, CJ-7 Universal Jeep (JAG)

I.D. DATA: VIN located on the top left surface of the instrument panel. There are 17 symbols. The first three symbols indicate the manufacturer, make and vehicle type. The engine type is indicated by the fourth symbol: B=126 cid (2.1 liter) OHC-4 turbo diesel; U=150 cid (2.5-liter) four-cylinder; W=173 cid (2.8 liter) V-6; C=258 cid (4.2 liter) six-cylinder; N=360 cid (5.9 liter) V-8. The next letter identifies the transmission type. The series and type of vehicle are identified by the sixth and seventh symbols, which are the same as the model number. The eighth character identifies the GVW rating with the next serving as the check digit. Then follows the model year (tenth symbol F) and assembly point codes. The last six digits are sequential production numbers.

1985 AMC Jeep, CJ-7 Renegade (AMC)

Model	Body Type	Price	Weight	Prod. Total
Wagoneer Sport Wagon — L-4 — 1/2-Ton — 4x4				
75	4d Station Wagon	13,255	3,063	—
75	4d Limited Station Wagon	17,953	3,222	—
Wagoneer Sport Wagon — V-6 — 1/2-Ton — 4x4				
75	4dr Station Wagon	13,604	3,106	—
75	4dr Limited Station Wagon	18,302	3,265	—
Grand Wagoneer — L-6 — 1/2-Ton — 4x4				
15	4dr Station Wagon	20,462	4,228	9,010
Cherokee Sport Wagon — L-4 — 1/2-Ton — 4x2				
73	2dr Station Wagon	9195	2777	—
74	4dr Station Wagon	9766	2828	—
Cherokee Sport Wagon — L-4 — 1/2-Ton — 4x4				
77	2dr Station Wagon	10,405	2923	—
78	4dr Station Wagon	10,976	2984	—
Cherokee Sport Wagon — V-6 — 1/2-Ton — 4x2				
73	2dr Station Wagon	9544	2852	—
74	4dr Station Wagon	10,115	2903	—
Cherokee Sport Wagon — V-6 — 1/2-Ton — 4x4				
77	2dr Station Wagon	10,754	2998	—
78	4dr Station Wagon	11,325	3059	—
CJ-7 — 1/4-Ton — 4x4 — 93.5 in. w.b.				
87	Jeep	7282	2601	21,770
Scrambler — 1/2-Ton — 4x4 — 103.5 in. w.b.				
88	Jeep	7282	2701	1,050
J-10 Pickup — 1/2-Ton — 4x4 — 131 in. w.b.				
26	Pickup	10,311	3799	—
J-20 Pickup — 3/4-Ton — 4x4 — 131 in. w.b.				
27	Pickup	11,275	4353	—

NOTE: See historical for additional production data.

ENGINE [Optional Cherokee XJ/Wagoneer XJ]: Inline. Overhead cam. OHV. Turbocharged. Diesel. Four-cylinder. Bore & stroke: 2.99 x 3.56 in. Displacement: 126 cid. Compression: 21.5:1. Fuel system: Indirect injection. Brake hp: not advertised. Taxable hp: 18.34.

ENGINE [Standard: CJ-7/Scrambler/Cherokee XJ/Wagoneer XJ]: Inline. OHV. Four-cylinder. Cast iron block. Bore & stroke: 3.88 x 3.19 in. Displacement: 150 cid. Compression ratio: 9.2:1. Taxable horsepower: 24.04. Net horsepower: 86 at 3650 rpm. Net torque: 132 lbs.-ft. at 3200 rpm. Five main bearings. Hydraulic valve lifters. Carburetor: One-barrel.

ENGINE [Optional Wagoneer/Cherokee]: Vee-block. OHV. Six-cylinder. Bore & stroke: 3.50 x 2.99 in. Displacement: 173 cid. Compression ratio: 8.5:1. Horsepower rating: not advertised. Carburetor: two-barrel.

ENGINE [Standard: Grand Wagoneer/J-10; Optional: CJ-7/Scrambler]: Inline. OHV. Six-cylinder. Cast iron block. Bore & stroke: 3.75 x 3.90 in. Displacement: 258 cid. Compression ratio: 9.2:1. Taxable horsepower: 33.75. Net horsepower: 102 at 3000 rpm. Net torque: 204 lbs.-ft. at 1650 rpm. Seven main bearings. Hydraulic valve lifters. Carburetor: Two-barrel.

ENGINE [Standard: J-20/Optional: J-10/Grand Wagoneer]: Vee-block. OHV. Eight-cylinder. Cast iron block. Bore & stroke: 4.08 x 3.44 in. Displacement: 360 cid. Compression ratio: 8.25:1. Taxable horsepower: 53.27. Five main bearings. Hydraulic valve lifters. Carburetor: Two-barrel.

Jeep Cherokee Pioneer 4-door...the only 4-door in its class!

1985 AMC Jeep, Cherokee Pioneer Four-Door Station Wagon (JAG)

CHASSIS [CJ-7]: Wheelbase: 93.4 in. Overall length: 153.2 in. Height: (hardtop) 71.0 in.; (open) 69.1 in. Front tread: 55.8 in. Rear tread: 55.1 in. Tires: P205/75R15 in. "Arriva", steel-belted.
CHASSIS [Wagoneer XJ]: Wheelbase: 101.4 in. Width: 70.5 in. Overall length: 165.3 in. Height: 64.1 in.
CHASSIS [Cherokee XJ]: Wheelbase: 101.4 in. Width: 69.3 in. Overall length: 165.3 in. Height: 64.1 in.
CHASSIS [Grand Wagoneer]: Wheelbase: 108.7 in. Width: 74.8 in. Overall length: 186.4 in. Height: 66.4 in. Tires: P225/75R-15
CHASSIS [CJ-7]: Wheelbase: 93.4 in. Width: 65.3 in. Overall length: 153.2 in. Height: 70.9 in. Front tread: 55.8 in. Rear tread: 55.1 in. Tires: P205/75R15 in.
CHASSIS [Scrambler]: Wheelbase: 103.4 in. Width: 65.3 in. Overall length: 166.2 in. Height: 70.8 in. Front tread: 55.8 in. Rear tread: 55.1 in. Tires: P205/75R15 in.
CHASSIS [J-10/Model 25]: Wheelbase: 118.7 in. Width: 78.9 in. Overall length: 194 in. Height: 69 in. Front tread: 64.0 in. Rear tread: 63.8 in. Tires: P225/75R15 in.
CHASSIS [J-10/Model 26]: Wheelbase: 130.7 in. Width: 78.9 in. Overall length: 206 in. Height: 69 in. Front tread: 64.0 in. Rear tread: 63.8 in. Tires: P225/75R15 in.
CHASSIS [J-20]: Wheelbase: 130.7 in. Width: 78.9 in. Overall length: 206 in. Height: 70 in. Front tread: 64.6 in. Rear tread: 65.9 in. Tires: 8.25 x 16.5 in.

TECHNICAL [CJ-7/Scrambler]: Selective synchromesh transmission. Speeds: 4F/1R. Floor-shift. Single-plate, dry-disc clutch. Shaft drive. Semi-floating rear axle. Overall ratio: 3.54:1. Manual front disc/rear drum brakes. 15 x 6 in., five-bolt pressed steel wheels.
TECHNICAL [J-10]: Selective synchromesh transmission. Speeds: 4F/1R. Floor-mounted gearshift. Single-plate, dry-disc clutch. Shaft drive. Rear axle: semi-floating. Overall ratio: 2.73:1. Power front disc/rear drum brakes. 15 x 6 in. pressed steel wheels.
TECHNICAL [J-20]: Automatic transmission. Speeds: 3F/1R. Column-mounted gearshift. Shaft drive. Rear axle: full-floating. Overall ratio: 3.73:1. Power front disc/rear drum brakes. 16.5 x 6 in. pressed steel wheels.
TECHNICAL [Cherokee]: Selective synchromesh transmission. Speeds: 4F/1R. Floor-mounted gearshift. Single-plate, dry-disc clutch. Shaft drive. Rear axle: semi-floating. Quadra-Link front suspension. Two "shift-on-the-fly" 2WD/4WD systems. UniFrame construction. Power front disc brakes/rear drum. Stabilizer bars front and rear.
TECHNICAL [Wagoneer]: Three-speed automatic transmission. Speeds: 3F/1R. Column-mounted gearshift. Shaft drive. Rear axle: full-floating. Power front disc/rear drum brakes. Four-wheel drive "shift-on-the-fly" system. Selec-Trac all-road surface 2WD/4WD system optional.

OPTIONS [CJ-7/Scrambler]: Renegade package. Laredo package. Variable-ratio power steering (required with air conditioning. Five-speed manual transmission with overdrive. Power front disc brakes. Cold Climate Group. Heavy-duty alternator. Heavy-duty battery. Heavy-duty cooling system. Coolant recovery system. Automatic/part-time four-wheel-drive (not available with four-cylinder) Rear Trac-Lok differential. Heavy-duty shock absorbers. Extra-duty suspension package. Soft ride suspension (not available for base models). Front chrome bumper (Scrambler only, standard Laredo). Chrome rear step bumper (Scrambler only, standard Laredo). Painted rear step bumper (Scrambler only, not available Laredo). Bumper accessory package (not available for Laredo). Rear bumperettes (standard Laredo). Doors for soft and fiberglass tops. Outside passenger side mirror. Bodyside step. Full soft top. Vinyl soft tops. Radios: AM/AM-FM Stereo/AM-FM Stereo/Cassette player (require factory hard or soft top). Hardtop. Air conditioning (not available with four-cylinder) Cruise Control. Fog lamps (clear lens). Halogen headlamps. Extra Quiet Insulation (hardtop only). Styled steel chrome wheels. Styled steel painted wheels. Bumper accessory package (not available Laredo). Carpeting (front and rear) (standard Laredo). Center Console (standard Laredo). Convenience Group (base model only, standard all others). Decor Group (standard Renegade, not available for Laredo). Roll Bar Accessory package. Fold and tumble rear seat (standard on Renegade and Laredo) CJ-7 only. Soft-Feel sport steering wheel (standard on Renegade, not available Laredo). Leather-wrapped steering wheel (standard on Laredo). Rear storage box. Tachometer and Rally clock (standard on Laredo). Tilt steering wheel. Various wheel and tire combinations.
OPTIONS [Pickups]: Heavy-duty alternator. Heavy-duty battery. Cold Climate Group. Heavy-duty cooling system. Heavy-duty GVW options: 8400 GVW (J-20); 6200 GVW (J-10). Rear Trac-Lok differential. Heavy-duty shock absorber. Extra heavy-duty springs. Radios: AM/AM-FM Stereo/Electronically-tuned AM/FM with cassette. Automatic transmission. 5.9-liter V-8 engine. Pioneer package ($475). White styled wheels. Visibility Group. Tilt steering wheel (not available with manual transmission). Light Group. Insulation package. Protective floor mats. Grain vinyl bench seat (included in Pioneer package). Soft-Feel sport steering wheel. Leather-wrapped steering wheel. Chrome front grille. Dual low-profile exterior mirrors. Sliding rear window. Air conditioning. Convenience Group.
OPTIONS [Wagoneer/Cherokee]: Stereo tape. Cruise control (*). Tilt steering wheel (*). Custom wheelcovers (*). Power sun roof. Sun roof. Power door locks (*). Power windows (*). Power seat (*). Chief package (Cherokee). Laredo package (Cherokee). Pioneer package (Cherokee). Turbo diesel engine. Six-cylinder engine (Standard in Grand Wagoneer). Power steering. Air conditioning.

HISTORICAL: Introduced: Fall, 1984. Calendar year production: (all Jeep vehicles including AM General) 236,277. Includes: (CJ-Series) 46,553. (J-Series Pickup) 1,953. Model year production of AMC Jeep light-duty trucks (excluding AM General) was 92,310 units. This includes 48,540 Chrokee XJs; 10,620 Wagoneer XJs; 21,720 CJ-7s; 1,050 Scramblers; 9,010 Grand Wagoneers; 1,320 J-10/J-20 pickups. Innovations: New Scrambler "Renegade" model introduced. CJ-7 gets new fold-and-tumble rear seat option. New trim packages. Historical notes: Paul W. Tippett continued as chairman of Renault/AMC/Jeep.

1986-1/2 AMC Jeep, Wrangler Laredo (OCW)

JEEP — 1986 SERIES — ALL ENGINES: An historic milestone in light-duty truck history was the end of production of the CJ Universal Jeep during model year 1986. At the start of the season, the 1986 sales brochure gave little hint that the CJ series would be phased-out. "CJ has always been special," said the promotional copy. "And for 1986 it makes more sense when you consider its long list of standard features, its exceptional fuel economy and its affordable price." The end came in Jan. 1986, closing 40 years of civilian production during which some 1.6 million units were built. Naturally, there were no significant changes in the 1986 CJ-7 model.

Its replacement, seen as early as February at the Chicago Auto Show, carried a May 13, 1986 showroom release date. It was known as the Wrangler (or Jeep YJ in Canada). Although the basic Jeep CJ silhouette was apparent in the Wrangler, the forward half of the vehicle, including hood, fender lines and grille, were more contemporary in appearance. Characteristics included a seven-slot, horizontally "veed" grille, square headlamps and parking lamps, a raised hood center panel, modern instrumentation and doors. It had a 93.4 in. wheelbase, 152-153 in. overall length, 66 in. width and 58 in. front/rear tread. The Wrangler was merchandised as a 1987 model and came in base, Sport Decor and Laredo trim levels. Standard equipment included a fuel-injected version of AMC's 2.5-liter four-cylinder engine, five-speed manual transmission; power brakes; P215/75R-15 tires; high-back front bucket seats; fold-and-tumble rear seat; mini front carpet mat, column-mounted wiper/washer controls; padded roll bar with side bars extending to windshield frame; swing-away rear tailgate; soft top with metal half-doors and tinted windshield.

New, and promoted as a 1986 model, was a compact Comanche pickup truck. This slab-sided, sporty pickup was designed to meet the Japanese imports head-on. It had a grille with 10 vertical segments between its rectangular headlamps and a sleek cab with trim panels on the rear corners. A Jeep UniFrame with 120 in. wheelbase used a Quadra-link front suspension and Hotchkiss rear layout with semi-elliptical multi-leaf springs. Standard equipment included a throttle-body-injected 2.5-liter four, five-speed manual transmission, power assisted front disc/rear drum brakes and P195/75R15 steel radial tires. With the 4 x 4 models, Jeep's "Command-Trac" shift-on-the-fly system was used.

The Cherokee XJ continued as AMC's compact sports utility wagon with two-door and four-door versions available. The 1985-1/2 two-wheel drive version of the two-door, which had earned seven percent of total 1985 Cherokee sales, was back again. It and the four-wheel drive four-door model used the 2.5 liter L-4 with throttle-body-injection as standard engine. The 2.1 liter turbo diesel and 2.8 liter V-6 were optional.

The Wagoneer XJ four-door, four-wheel drive sport utility wagon offered the same power-train choices as the Cherokee.

For 1986, the Grand Wagoneer had a distinctive new front end with twin horizontal openings and vertically arranged dual headlamps. Power steering; power brakes; a mini console; carpets; gages; body and hood stripes; wheel trim rings; and P205/75R15 radial whitewalls were standard. A Wagoneer Limited package added air conditioning; heavy-duty electrical system; bumper guards; cruise control; power windows; power door locks; AM/FM radio; roof rack; woodgrain bodysides; Michelin tires and more.

"An enormous capacity for work" was promised for 1986 buyers of the J-10/J-20 series of standard pickups. These 4x4 only models had few appearance changes, other than new graphics treatments. They again had the Townside look set off by rectangular headlamps and a 13 slot "electric shaver" grille. Base engines were the 4.2-liter six in the half-ton J-10 and the 5.9-liter V-8 in the 3/4-ton J-20.

I.D. DATA: VIN located on the top left surface of the instrument panel. There are 17 symbols. The first three symbols indicate the manufacturer, make and vehicle type. The engine type is indicated by the fourth symbol: B=126 cid (2.1 liter) OHC-4 turbo diesel; H=150 cid (2.5-liter) four-cylinder TBI engine; W=173 cid (2.8 liter) V-6; C=258 cid (4.2 liter) six-cylinder; N=360 cid (5.9 liter) V-8. The next letter identifies the transmission type. The series and type of vehicle are identified by the sixth and seventh symbols, which are the same as the model number. The eighth character identifies the GVW rating with the next serving as the check digit. Then follows the model year (tenth symbol G) and assembly point codes. The last six digits are sequential production numbers.

Standard Catalog of Light-Duty Trucks

1986 Jeep Wrangler Laredo (OCW)

Model	Body Type	Price	Weight	Prod. Total
Wagoneer Sport Wagon — L4/TBI — 1/2-Ton — 4x4				
75	4d Station Wagon	13,360	3,039	—
75	4d Limited Station Wagon	18,600	3,234	—
Wagoneer Sport Wagon — V-6 — 1/2-Ton — 4x4				
75	4dr Station Wagon	14,607	3,104	—
75	4dr Limited Station Wagon	19,037	3,299	—
Grand Wagoneer — L-6 — 1/2-Ton — 4x4				
15	4dr Station Wagon	21,350	4,252	16,252
Cherokee Sport Wagon — L4/TBI — 1/2-Ton — 4x2				
73	2dr Station Wagon	9335	2751	—
74	4dr Station Wagon	9950	2802	—
Cherokee Sport Wagon — L4/TBI — 1/2-Ton — 4x4				
77	2dr Station Wagon	10,695	2917	
78	4dr Station Wagon	11,320	2968	
Cherokee Sport Wagon — V-6 — 1/2-Ton — 4x2				
73	2dr Station Wagon	9772	2847	—
74	4dr Station Wagon	10,387	2898	—
Cherokee Sport Wagon — V-6 — 1/2-Ton — 4x4				
77	2dr Station Wagon	11,132	3013	—
78	4dr Station Wagon	11,757	3064	—
CJ-7 — 1/4-Ton — 4x4 — 93.5 in. w.b.				
87	Jeep	7500	2596	25,929
Wrangler — 1/4-Ton — 4-cyl — 93.4 in. w.b.				
81	Jeep	8396	—	—
Wrangler — 1/4-Ton — V-6 — 93.4 in. w.b.				
81	Jeep	9899	—	—
Comanche — 1/2-Ton — 4x2 — 120 in. w.b.				
66	Pickup	7049	2931	—
Comanche — 1/2-Ton — 4x4 — 120 in. w.b.				
65	Pickup	8699	3098	—
J-10 — 1/2-Ton — 4x4 — 131 in. w.b.				
26	Pickup	10,870	3808	—
J-20 — 1/2-Ton — 4x4 — 131 in. w.b.				
27	Pickup	12,160	4388	—

NOTE: See historical for additional production data.

1986 AMC Jeep, Commanche Pickup (JAG)

ENGINE [Turbo Diesel; Optional: 65/66]: Inline. OHV. Four-cylinder. Cast iron block. Bore & stroke: 2.99 x 3.5 in. Displacement: 126 cid/2.1L. Taxable horsepower: 18.34. Hydraulic valve lifters. Turbo charged.
ENGINE [Standard: Wrangler/66; 65; 87]: Inline. OHV. Four-cylinder. Cast iron block. Bore & stroke: 3.88 x 3.19 in. Displacement: 150 cid/2.5L. Compression ratio: 9.2:1. Brake horsepower: 117 at 5000 rpm. Taxable horsepower: 24.04. Hydraulic valve lifters. Throttle Body Injection (EFI). Torque (Compression): 135 lbs.-ft. at 3500 rpm.

Standard Catalog of Light-Duty Trucks

ENGINE [Optional: 65/66]: Vee-block. Six-cylinder. Cast iron block. Bore & stroke: 3.5 x 2.99 in. Displacement: 173 cid/2.8L. Brake horsepower: 115 at 4800 rpm. Taxable horsepower: 29.45. Hydraulic valve lifters. Two-barrel carburetor. Torque (Compression) 150 lbs.-ft. at 2100 rpm.
ENGINE [Standard: J-10; Optional: 66/65/Wrangler]: Inline. OHV. Six-cylinder. Cast iron block. Bore & stroke: 3.75 x 3.9 in. Displacement: 258 cid/4.2L. Compression ratio: 9.2:1. Brake horsepower: 112 at 3000 rpm. Taxable horsepower: 33.75. Hydraulic valve lifters. Two-barrel carburetor. Torque (Compression) 210 lbs.-ft. at 3000 rpm.
ENGINE [Standard: 27; Optional: 26]: Vee-block. Eight-cylinder. Cast iron block. Bore & stroke: 4.08 x 3.44 in. Displacement: 360 cid/5.9L. Taxable horsepower: 53.27. Hydraulic valve lifters. Four-barrel carburetor.

1986 AMC Jeep, Grand Wagoneer Limousine (OCW)

CHASSIS [CJ-7]: Wheelbase: 93.5 in. Overall length: 153.2 in. Height: (hardtop) 71.0 in. Front tread: 55.8 in. Rear tread: 55.1 in. Tires: P205/75R-15 in.
CHASSIS [Scrambler]: Wheelbase: 103.4 in. Width: 65.3 in. Overall length: 166.2 in. Height: 70.8 in. Front tread: 55.8 in. Rear tread: 55.1 in. Tires: P205/75R15 in.
CHASSIS [Wrangler]: Wheelbase: 93.4 in. Overall length: 152 in. Height: (hardtop) 69.3 in. Front tread: 58 in. Rear tread: 58 in. Tires: P215/75R-15 in.
NOTE: Comanche and Wrangler 4x4s use P225/75R-15 in. tires.
CHASSIS [Wagoneer XJ]: Wheelbase: 101.4 in. Width: 70.5 in. Overall length: 165.3 in. Height: 64.1 in.
CHASSIS [Cherokee XJ]: Wheelbase: 101.4 in. Width: 69.3 in. Overall length: 165.3 in. Height: 64.1 in.
CHASSIS [Grand Wagoneer]: Wheelbase: 108.7 in. Width: 74.8 in. Overall length: 186.4 in. Height: 66.4 in. Tires: P225/75R-15
CHASSIS [J-10]: Wheelbase: 131 in. Overall length: 206 in. Height: 70.7 in. Front tread: 63.3 in. Rear tread: 63.8 in. Tires: P225/75R-15 in.
CHASSIS [J-20]: Wheelbase: 131 in. Overall length: 206 in. Height: 70.7 in. Front tread: 63.3 in. Rear tread: 63.8 in. Tires: P225/75R-15 in.
TECHNICAL [Wrangler]: Selective synchromesh transmission. Speeds: (Standard) 5F/1R. Floor controls. Single-plate, dry-disc clutch. Shaft drive. Semi-floating rear axle. Overall drive ratio: (Standard) 4.11.1. Brakes: Disc front/drum rear with power assist. Wheels: 15 x 7.0 disc wheels.
NOTE: For Standard 4x2 model w/2.5L four.
TECHNICAL [CJ-7/Scrambler]: Selective synchromesh transmission. Speeds: 4F/1R. Floor-shift. Single-plate, dry-disc clutch. Shaft drive. Semi-floating rear axle. Overall ratio: 3.54:1. Manual front disc/rear drum brakes. 15 x 6 in., five-bolt pressed steel wheels.
TECHNICAL [J-10]: Selective synchromesh transmission. Speeds: 4F/1R. Floor-mounted gearshift. Single-plate, dry-disc clutch. Shaft drive. Rear axle: semi-floating. Overall ratio: 2.73:1. Power front disc/rear drum brakes. 15 x 6 in. pressed steel wheels.
TECHNICAL [J-20]: Automatic transmission. Speeds: 3F/1R. Column-mounted gearshift. Shaft drive. Rear axle: full-floating. Overall ratio: 3.73:1. Power front disc/rear drum brakes. 16.5 x 6 in. pressed steel wheels.
TECHNICAL [Cherokee]: Selective synchromesh transmission. Speeds: 4F/1R. Floor-mounted gearshift. Single-plate, dry-disc clutch. Shaft drive. Rear axle: semi-floating. Quadra-Link front suspension. Two "shift-on-the-fly" 2WD/4WD systems. UniFrame construction. Power front disc brakes/rear drum. Stabilizer bars front and rear.
TECHNICAL [Wagoneer]: Three-speed automatic transmission. Speeds: 3F/1R. Column-mounted gearshift. Shaft drive. Rear axle: full-floating. Power front disc/rear drum brakes. Four-wheel drive "shift-on-the-fly" system. Selec-Trac all-road surface 2WD/4WD system optional.
OPTIONAL: Chrysler A-3 automatic transmission available only with six-cylinder engine.
TECHNICAL [Comanche Pickup]: Selective synchromesh transmission. Speeds: 5F/1R. Floor controls. Single dry disc clutch. Shaft drive. Hotchkiss solid rear axle. Overall drive ratio: 3.73:1. Brakes: Power assisted front disc/rear drum. Wheels: 15 x 6 in. five-bolt pressed steel wheels.
NOTE: For Standard 4x2 model w/base engine.
OPTIONS [Wrangler]: Carbureted 4.2L six-cylinder engine. Three-speed automatic transmission. Hardtop (standard with Laredo). Tilt steering. (Sport Decor Group): includes, most standard features, plus AM/FM monaural radio; black side cowl carpet; special Wrangler hood decals; special Wrangler lower bodyside stripes; P215/75R15 Goodyear all-terrain Wrangler tires; conventional size spare with lock and convenience group. (Laredo Hardtop Group): includes richer interior trim; AM/FM monaural radio; Buffalo-grain vinyl upholstery; front and rear carpeting; center console; extra-quiet insulation; leather-wrapped Sport steering wheel; special door trim panels and map pockets; chrome front bumper; rear bumperettes; grille panel; headlamp bezels; tow hooks; color-keyed wheel flares; full-length mud guards; integrated steps; deep tinted glass; OSRV door mirrors; bumper accessory package; special hood and body side stripes; convenience group; 15 x 7 in. aluminum wheels; P215/75R-15 Goodyear Wrangler RWL radial tires, spare tire and matching aluminum spare wheel. Rear trac-lok differential. Air conditioning. Extra-quiet insulation. Full-carpets. Halogen fog lamps. Power steering. Cruise Control (6-cyl. only). Leather-wrapped Sport steering wheel. Electric rear window defogger (hardtop). Heavy-duty suspension. Heavy-duty cooling. Aluminum wheels. Off-Road equipment package. Conventional spare tire. Metallic exterior paints.
OPTIONS [CJ-7/Scrambler]: Renegade package. Laredo package. Variable-ratio power steering (required with air conditioning. Five-speed manual transmission with overdrive. Power front disc brakes. Cold Climate Group. Heavy-duty alternator. Heavy-duty battery. Heavy-duty cooling system. Coolant recovery system. Automatic/part-time four-wheel-drive (not available with four-cylinder) Rear Trac-Lok differential. Heavy-duty shock absorbers. Extra-duty suspension package. Soft ride suspension (not available for base models). Front chrome bumper (Scrambler only, standard Laredo). Chrome rear step bumper (Scrambler only, standard Laredo). Painted rear step bumper (Scrambler only, not available Laredo). Bumperettes (not available for Laredo). Rear bumperettes (standard Laredo). Doors for soft and fiberglass tops. Outside passenger side mirror. Bodyside step. Full soft top. Vinyl soft tops. Radios: AM/AM-FM Stereo/AM-FM Stereo/Cassette player (require factory hard or soft top). Hardtop. Air conditioning (not available with four-cylinder) Cruise Control. Fog lamps (clear lens). Halogen headlamps. Extra Quiet Insulation (hardtop only). Styled steel chrome wheels. Styled steel painted wheels. Bumper accessory package (not available Laredo). Carpeting (front and rear) (standard Laredo).

Center Console (standard Laredo). Convenience Group (base model only, standard all others). Decor Group (standard Renegade, not available for Laredo). Roll Bar Accessory package. Fold and tumble rear seat (standard on Renegade and Laredo) CJ-7 only. Soft-Feel sport steering wheel (standard on Renegade, not available for Laredo). Leather-wrapped steering wheel (standard on Laredo). Rear storage box. Tachometer and Rally clock (standard on Laredo). Tilt steering wheel. Various wheel and tire combinations.

OPTIONS [Wagoneer/Cherokee]: Stereo tape. Cruise control (*). Tilt steering wheel (*). Custom wheelcovers (*). Power sun roof. Sun roof. Power door locks (*). Power windows (*). Power seat (*). Chief package (Cherokee). Laredo package (Cherokee). Pioneer package (Cherokee). Turbo diesel engine. Six-cylinder engine (Standard in Grand Wagoneer). Power steering. Air conditioning.

OPTIONS [Comanche]: "X" package. "XLS" package. 2.8L six-cylinder engine. 2.1L turbo diesel engine. 2205-pound payload package. Power steering w/17.5:1 ratio. P225/75R15 radial tires. 24-gallon fuel tank. Automatic transmission. Command-Trac 4x4 system (Standard on 4x4 models). Selec-Trac 4x4 system (optional on 4x4 models). 4:11.1 rear axle ratio.

HISTORICAL: Introduced: Fall, 1985; (Wrangler) May, 1986. Innovations: New Comanche mini-pickup series. New Wrangler replaces CJ-Series in Jan., 1986 (considered a 1987 model). Model year production (excluding AM General products) totaled 243,406. This included: 25,929 CJ-7s; 122,968 Cherokee XJs; 13,716 Wagoneer XJs; 45,219 Comanche pickups; 1,657 J-10/J-20 pickups; 17,665 Grand Wagoneers and 16,252 of the 1987 Wranglers. A California Jeep dealer launched an unsuccessful nationwide publicity campaign to "Save the Jeep CJ." Joseph E. Cappy became president of AMC during 1986. Cappy referred to the new Comanche as "AMC's first state-of-the-art-product in the two-wheel-drive market, which accounts for 75 percent of the light truck market." Other names considered for the new compact pickup were Renegade, Commando, Wrangler and Honcho. AMC also announced that a total of five years had been spent in development of the 1987 Wrangler as an up-to-date replacement for the famous Jeep CJ.

PLYMOUTH
1930-1986

1941 Plymouth Pickup

By Jim Benjaminson (Prewar)
By Charles Webb (Postwar)

From 1935 to 1942, commercial versions of Chrysler's low-priced Plymouth were offered, alongside Dodge trucks, to give dealers with joint Chrysler-Plymouth franchises extra sales.

A "pilot" version Plymouth truck appeared as early as 1930. It failed to see production. This was most likely due to the fact that Chrysler's non-Dodge outlets had the Fargo truck to sell in the U.S. at the time. However, after 1935, the Fargo became a badge-engineered Dodge marketed in Canada and as an export to other nations. This again created the need for a non-Dodge commercial vehicle line.

Plymouth tested the waters. Then, in 1935, it began offering a Commercial Car series. This consisted of a modified two-door sedan passenger car, which was converted into a Sedan Delivery truck. It had essentially the same status as a Business Coupe. Other "business" models included taxicabs, aftermarket station wagons and ambulances. A Commercial Sedan, with blanked-out rear quarters and a side-hinged cargo door, earned less than 150 sales. Nevertheless, a Panel Delivery (with a split seatback and inner panels) was added to the Commercial Car series in 1936.

Sales were encouraging enough to continue the truck-line in 1938 and expand it the following season. For 1939, an added series used the smallest Dodge truck chassis.

This Road King line included a four-door sedan-ambulance conversion, a coupe with a cargo box, a two-door Commercial Sedan and a Sedan Delivery. All had a 114 in. wheelbase. A two-inch longer stance characterized the new P81 Series, which had Chassis & Cab, and Pickup models. For 1940, the Plymouth Commercial Car line again offered models on two wheelbases.

Interestingly, the largest Plymouth truck had the car chassis and sheet metal. The smaller model was a true truck. It carried over the 1939 sheet metal, but had its headlights mounted on the fender crease in "bug-eye" fashion.

The fact that the real trucks were more compact than the Commercial Cars seemed illogical. Perhaps even more surprising was the continuation of this system in 1941. This was the final prewar year for dual wheelbases. Again, the light-duty trucks had year-old styling and a 116 in. wheelbase, while the passenger-based Commercial Cars adopted new-for-1941 sheet metal and rode a longer 117 in. wheelbase.

War-shortened model-year 1942 saw both the Commercial Car and light-duty truck series discontinued. However, sales of left-over units went on. The small number of units finding buyers were registered (at least in some states) as 1942 models. Some new Commercial Sedans may also have been assembled, probably on a built-to-order basis.

Plymouth trucks did not return immediately following the end of hostilities. In fact, it wasn't until 1974 that the company's name would appear on a truck. The new model's

impact on the overall truck market would turn out to be minor.

At first, the entire Plymouth light-duty truck line consisted of the Trail Duster 4x4 Sport Utility vehicle and the Voyager. The latter was a driver-forward passenger van marketed as a "Wagon." The Trail Duster was intended to cash-in on the the booming market for off-road machines and recreational vehicles in the 1970s. Like typical Sport Utility trucks, it was pretty Spartan in basic form. However, it could be optioned-out to almost the luxury car level. The Voyager Wagon was an attractive people-hauler that could carry as many as 15 passengers.

Both Trail Duster and Voyager were made on the same assembly lines as the nearly identical Dodge versions of the same vehicles. Although as good or better-looking than most competitors, there was nothing particularly special about them. Since Plymouth did not have as many dealers as Chevrolet, Ford, Dodge and others, sales remained modest.

In 1979, Plymouth expanded its truck offerings by including the Arrow Mini-Pickup. Arrow, like its twin the Dodge

500, was made by Mitsubishi Motors Corp. in Japan. These trucks soon gained a reputation for being among the best (if not the best) compact trucks on the market.

When Chevrolet and Ford phased-out their imported small trucks and replaced them with domestically-produced versions, Plymouth did not follow the trend. However, Plymouth did drop the Arrow after the 1982 model year. It was replaced by the new Scamp. The Scamp was less of a standard Pickup and more like a miniature version of the Ranchero/El Camino Coupe-Pickup genre. Despite its sporty good looks, the Scamp lasted just one year.

In 1984, Plymouth found a winner in the light-duty truck field. It was the new Voyager. Part car/part station wagon/part truck, this new front-wheel drive vehicle was unlike anything that Ford or Chevrolet offered. It was also an instant success. For once, Plymouth was out front. Other truck-makers had to play "catch-up ball."

By 1986, the only light-duty truck offered by Plymouth was the Voyager. Although MoPar truck lovers could still turn to Dodge for a variety of commercial vehicles, Plymouth no longer offered something to fit every light-duty need.

1932 Plymouth Model PA Ambulance (CHC)

1933 Plymouth Model PC Business Coupe (CHC)

1934 Plymouth Model PE Westchester Suburban (CHC)

1940 Plymouth Roadking Utility Sedan (JAW)

1940 Plymouth PT105 Pickup (Ron Barker)

1940 Plymouth PT105 Pickup (Ron Barker)

594

1941 Plymouth Pickup Truck (Sonny Glasbrenner)

1974 Plymouth Trail Duster 4x4 Utility Wagon (CW)

1974 Plymouth Voyager Custom Wagon (CW)

1975 Plymouth Trailduster Open Utility (CW)

Standard Catalog of Light-Duty Trucks

1980 Plymouth Trailduster Utility Wagon (CW)

1980 Plymouth Voyager Wagon (OCW)

1983 Plymouth Scamp Sport Mini-Pickup (CW)

1982 Plymouth Arrow Mini-Pickup (OCW)

1930-1931 PLYMOUTH

1930 Plymouth Pilot Model Delivery Car (CHC)

COMMERCIAL SEDAN — SERIES 30U — FOUR-CYLINDER: Plymouth's first entry into the commercial field was a rather half-hearted entry using a passenger car chassis. The Commercial Sedan was a modification of a two-door sedan, with the addition of a door at the rear of the body and the deletion the rear seat. The rear quarter windows were blanked out through the use of removable panels. The idea behind the vehicle was to provide a commercial/passenger vehicle to the small businessman who needed both types of vehicles, but could afford to purchase only one. With the rear seat available as an option, it was possible to convert the vehicle into a family car when needed. With the window blanks in place and the rear seat removed, it became the perfect delivery vehicle and its passenger car styling allowed it to go where commercial vehicles were prohibited. At a time when Chrysler Corp. was still building a Fargo commercial car in the same line, as well as a similar vehicle from sister division DeSoto, the Plymouth 30U Commercial Sedan met with little success and the idea was dropped at the end of the year. By then, only 80 vehicles had been sold.

I.D. DATA: Serial number located on right front door post. Starting: Detroit, Mich. — 1,500,001. Ending: Detroit, Mich. — 1,570,188. Engine number located on left front corner of cylinder block, directly above generator mounting. Starting: U200,001. Ending: U277,000. (The engine number is found on a boss on the left front corner of the cylinder block, usually directly above the generator. The numbers indicate the engine sequential serial number and may also include a series of code letters to advise mechanics that the engine was factory installed with under- or over-sized components. In addition, the model code was stamped into the serial number, indicating the model year of the engine. A typical engine code example is: T50-123456-AB. The letters T50 indicate the model code (1937 Model PT50). The next group (i.e., 123456) is the sequential number. The suffix AB indicates over- and under-size engine components per the following code: A=.020 over-size cylinder bore; B=.010 under-size main and connecting rod bearings; C=.005 over-size rod bearings; AB=.020 over-size cylinders and .010 under-size mains and rods; E=Economy engine with smaller carburetor and intake manifold; X=small bore export engine.

1931 Plymouth Red Top Taxicab (CHC)

Model	Body Type	Price	Weight	Prod. Total
Series 30U				
30U	Commercial Sedan	750	—	80

ENGINE: Inline. L-head. Four-cylinder. Cast iron block. Bore & stroke: 3-5/8-in. x 4-3/4 in. Displacement: 196.1 cid. Compression ratio: 4.6. Brake horsepower: 48 at 2800 rpm. SAE Horsepower: 21.03. Three main bearings. Solid valve lifters. Carburetor: Carter model 130S, Carter model 130SA, Carter model 156-S or Carter model 158-S (export). Torque: 120 lbs.-ft. at 1200 rpm.

CHASSIS [Series 30U]: Wheelbase: 109-3/4 in. Overall length: 169 in. Front tread: 56-1/4 in. Rear tread: 56-1/8 in. Tires: 4.75 x 19 in.

TECHNICAL: [Early models] sliding spur gears; [later models] helical cut gears. Speeds: 3F/1R. Floor shift gearshift lever. Single dry-disc clutch. Shaft drive. Semi-floating, spiral bevel. Overall ratio: 4.3 to 1. Four-wheel hydraulic brakes. Wood spoke, (wire optional) wheels. Rim Size: 4.75 x 19 in.

OPTIONS: Front bumper. Rear bumper. Single sidemount. Windshield defroster. Spring covers. Five- or six-bolt lug pattern wire wheels.

HISTORICAL: Production began April 8, 1930; ended June 8, 1931. Model year production: 80 commercial sedans were built. F.L. Rockelman was president of Plymouth in 1930 and 1931.

1935 PLYMOUTH

1935 Plymouth Commercial Sedan (C.Schreckenberg)

COMMERCIAL SEDAN — SERIES PJ — SIX-CYLINDER: After an absence from the commercial field since 1931, Plymouth re-entered the market with another Sedan Delivery conversion from a standard passenger car body. Based on the two-door flatback sedan, a single rear door was fitted at the rear. Like its 30U counterpart, the PJ's interior was gutted and the rear quarter windows were filled with blanks, which were removable. A complete interior was offered, as an option, to convert the vehicle into a standard passenger model. While the 30U version had been the highest priced body style in the vehicle lineup, the PJ version had an asking price of only $100 more than the passenger sedan on which it was based. It was cheaper than sedans in the Deluxe series. This version met with considerably more success than the 30U and 1,142 found buyers.

1935 Plymouth Commercial Station Wagon (CHC)

I.D. DATA: Serial number located on right front door post. Starting: Detroit, Mich.: 1,039,101; Windsor, Ontario: 9,396,076; Los Angeles, Calif.: 3,151,501. Ending: Detroit, Mich.: 1,111,645; Windsor, Ontario: 9,397,345; Los Angeles, Calif.: 3,157,116. Engine number located on left front corner of cylinder block, directly above generator mounting. Starting: PJ-1001. Ending: PJ-359025.

1935 Plymouth High-Speed Safety Armored Car (SSP)

Model	Body Type	Price	Weight	Prod. Total
Series PJ				
651-B	Sedan Delivery	635	2735	1142

ENGINE: Inline. L-head. Six-cylinder. Cast iron block. Bore & stroke: 3-1/8 in. x 4-3/8 in. Displacement: 201.3 cid. Compression ratio: 6.7. Brake horsepower: 82 at 3600 rpm. SAE Horsepower: 23.44. Four main bearings. Solid valve lifters. Carburetor: Carter model BB439S. Torque: 145 lbs.-ft. at 1200 rpm.

CHASSIS: [Series PJ Business Six]: Wheelbase: 113 in. Overall length: 187-7/8 in. Front tread: 56-1/4 in. Rear tread: 58 in. Tires: 6.00 x 16 in.

1935 Plymouth Commercial Sedan Delivery (CHC)

TECHNICAL: Sliding gear transmission with helical cut gears. Speeds: 3F/1R. Floor shift gearshift lever. 9-1/2 in. single-plate dry-disc clutch. Shaft drive. Semi-floating, spiral bevel. Overall ratio: 4.125 to 1. Four-wheel hydraulic brakes. Steel spoke artillery wheels. Rim Size: 6.00 x 16 in.

OPTIONS: Front and rear bumper as a package, including spare tire, ($33). Single sidemount (standard). Dual sidemount. Sidemount cover(s). Fender skirts ($9 pair). Bumper guards. Philco Transitone radio ($39.95). Heaters. Glove box door clock ($11.75). Cigar lighter ($1.). Seat covers. Spotlight ($15.95). Clock mirror ($3.95). Locking gas cap ($2.25). Dual air tone external horns ($12.). Kool Kushion ($2.95). License plate frames ($2.45). Radiator grille cover ($1.25). Right-hand sun visor ($1.75). Metal spring covers ($6.). Wheel trim rings ($1.35). Right-hand windshield wiper ($4.95). Oil bath air cleaner ($2.50). Sailing ship radiator ornament ($3.50). Duo-Airstream heater ($19.95). Deluxe hot water heater ($15.95). Standard hot water heater ($12.95). 20 in. high-clearance wheels.

HISTORICAL: Production starting date unknown. Production ended Aug. 15, 1935. Model year production: 1,142 Commercial Sedans. Dan S. Eddins was president of Plymouth in 1935.

1936 PLYMOUTH

1936 Plymouth Sedan Delivery (DFW)

COMMERCIAL SEDAN — SERIES P1 — SIX-CYLINDER: Again basing its commercial model on the passenger car chassis, Plymouth saw fit to treat the 1936 Commercial Sedan to its own body. No longer was the practice of converting a two-door sedan body followed. Based on the cheaper "Business Car" chassis, the model's price was reduced $20 from the 1935 version. An improved business climate saw a doubling in sales of this particular body style. For those buyers not wishing to purchase this special style, Plymouth offered several unique options for its regular passenger models. They included special ambulance and hearse conversions for the four-door sedan and a removable pickup box for use on the business coupe.

I.D. DATA: Serial number located on right front door post. Starting: Detroit, Mich.: 1,111,701; Evansville, Ind.: 9,000,101; Los Angeles, Calif.: 3,157,151; Windsor, Ontario: 9,397,351. Ending: Detroit, Mich.: 1,183,569; Evansville, Ind.: 9,012,724; Los Angeles, Calif.: 3,162,365; Windsor, Ontario: 9,400,000. Engine number located on left front corner of cylinder block, above generator mount. Starting: P2-1001. Ending: P-2532087.

Model	Body Type	Price	Weight	Prod. Total
Series P1				
P1	Commercial Sedan	605	2880	3527

1936 Plymouth Westchester Suburban (CHC)

ENGINE: [Standard] Inline. Six-cylinder. Cast iron block. Bore & stroke: 3-1/8 in. in. x 4-3/8 in. Displacement: 201.3 cid. Compression ratio: 6.7. Brake horsepower: 82 at 3600 rpm. SAE Horsepower: 23.44. Four main bearings. Solid valve lifters. Carburetor: Carter BB439S; Carter B6F1; Carter C6E1-2. Torque: 145 lbs.-ft. at 1200 rpm.

ENGINE: [Optional] Economy version with one-inch carburetor and smaller intake manifold developed 65 hp at 3000 rpm. Identified by engine code P2E. Export versions had a 2-7/8 in. x 4-3/8 in. bore and stroke and displacement of 170.4 cid. They were identified by engine code P2X.

CHASSIS: [Series P1 Business Six]: Wheelbase: 113 in. Overall length: 190 in. Front tread: 55-7/8 in. Rear tread: 58 in. Tires: 5.25 x 17 in.

TECHNICAL: Sliding gear transmission with helical cut gears. Speeds: 3F/1R. Floor shift gearshift lever. 9-1/4 in. single-plate dry-disc clutch. Shaft drive. Semi-floating, spiral bevel. Overall ratio: 4.125 to 1. Steel artillery spoke wheels. Rim Size: 6.25 x 17 in.

OPTIONS: Front and rear bumper sold as a package. Single sidemount (standard). Dual sidemount. Fender skirts ($9 pair). Heater (several hot water types available). Spotlight ($15.95). Heavy-duty air cleaner ($2.50). Radiator ornament ($3.50). Metal rear spring covers ($16). Wheels ($15). Deluxe steering wheel ($5). 20 in. high-clearance wheels ($15). Glove box lock ($1). Locking gas cap ($1.50). Deluxe external Airtone horns ($12). Right-hand taillamp. ($2.85). Right-hand inside sun visor ($1.50). Radiator grill cover ($1.25). Hand brake extension lever ($1.50). Exhaust extension ($1). Chrome wheel discs ($2.30 each). License plate frames ($2.45 pair). Defroster ($1.50). Electric defrost fan ($6.50).

HISTORICAL: Production began Sept. 19, 1935; ending Aug. 21, 1936. Model year production: 3,527. Dan S. Eddins was president of Plymouth.

1937 PLYMOUTH

1937 Plymouth PT50 Pickup (OCW/IOCS)

COMMERCIAL CAR — SERIES PT-50 — SIX-CYLINDER: Plymouth entered the commercial field in 1937 with its own truck chassis. It was built on a 116 in. ladder type frame. There was little doubt in anyone's mind that the Plymouth Commercial car, as it was called, was a clone of its sister Dodge truck. The reasons for building such a vehicle lay within the corporate structure of Chrysler. Plymouth dealerships were always "dualed" with another corporate offerings (either Chrysler, DeSoto or Dodge) to give dealers more than one line to sell. For those dualed with Dodge, there was no need for another commercial vehicle. However, those dealers dualed with DeSoto or Chrysler had no commercial vehicle to sell. In cities where a Plymouth dealership was found on nearly every street corner, the loss of sales did not sit well. In addition, rural areas not served by a Dodge-Plymouth dealership also lost sales to the competition. Offered on the Commercial car chassis was a Sedan Delivery, the Express (Pickup) and a Chassis & Cab complete with runningboards and rear fenders. For this one year only, the wood-bodied station wagon would ride on the commercial car chassis. (From its inception in 1935, the woodie wagon was considered by the factory to be a commercial vehicle, rather than a passenger car, but this was the first, last and only station wagon on a commercial chassis. The new Pickups were met with a fair amount of enthusiasm. Yet, 1937 would prove to be their best sales year. For the first two

years of its existence, the Commercial Car would be built in three factories (in Detroit, Evansville and Los Angeles). In its final years, the Evansville plant would discontinue manufacture. Remaining on the passenger car chassis was the ambulance conversion (the hearse version was discontinued) and a removable pickup box for the Business Coupe.

1937 Plymouth Sedan Delivery (D. Hermany/DB)

I.D. DATA: Serial number located on right front door post. Serial numbers: Detroit, Mich.: 8,850,101 to 8,861,664; Los Angeles, Calif.: 9,206,601 to 9,208,113; Evansville, Ill.: 9,182,701 to 9,185,187. Engine number located on left front corner of block, directly above generator. Starting: T50-1001 on up.

1937 Plymouth Sedan Delivery (D.W. Hermany)

Model	Body Type	Price	Weight	Prod. Total
Series PT50				
N/A	Chassis & cab	495	2400	158
K-82-LR	Pickup	525	3100	10,709
N/A	Station Wagon	740	2920	602
K-1-3	Sedan Delivery	655	3100	3256

1937 Plymouth PT50 Commercial Station Wagon (JB)

ENGINE: Inline. L-head. Six-cylinder. Cast iron block. Bore & stroke: 3-1/8 in. x 4-3/8 in. Displacement: 201.3 cid. Compression ratio: 6.7. Brake horsepower: 70 at 3000 rpm. SAE Horsepower: 23.44. Four main bearings. Solid valve lifters. Carburetor: Chandler Groves model A2.

1937 Plymouth Pickup (S.W. Tiernan/DB)

CHASSIS [PT-50]: Wheelbase: 116 in. Tires: 6.00 x 16 in.

1937 Plymouth Model PT57 Pickup (JB/POC)

TECHNICAL: Sliding gear transmission. Speeds: 3F/1R. Floor shift gearshift lever. Single-plate dry-disc 10 in. clutch. Shaft drive. Hypoid, semi-floating rear axle. Overall ratio: 4.1. Four-wheel hydraulic brakes. Steel disc wheels. Rim Size: 6.00 x 16 in.

1937 Plymouth Model PT50 Chassis & Cab (JB)

OPTIONS: Chrome plated rear bumper ($8.50). Single sidemount (standard right side). Dual sidemount: left sidemount optional including tire, tube & tire lock ($10). Bumper guards ($1.50 pair). Chassis accessory group including chrome radiator shell, chrome headlamps and double-acting shock absorbers, front and rear ($17). Dual horns ($7.50). Coach lamps for Commercial Sedan ($8.50). Long-arm stationary rearview mirror ($1.50). Long-arm adjustable rearview mirror ($2.50). Sun visors ($2 each). Metal spare tire cover ($6.50). Chrome windshield frame ($3). Right-hand taillamp. ($4). Economy engine package Group 1 ($2.50); same Group 2 ($3). Four-speed transmission ($25). Painted sheet metal including fenders, splash aprons, runningboards ($5). Oil bath air cleaner ($3.75). Vortex air cleaner with standard cap ($17.50); with Vortex cap ($19.50). Governor ($5). Chrome headlamps ($2.75). Oil filter ($3.25). Chrome radiator shell ($6.). Auxiliary seat, Commercial Sedan ($10). Double-acting shocks, front ($4.75); rear ($4.75). Right-hand windshield wiper ($4).

1937 Plymouth Seven-Passenger Yellow Taxicab (CHC)

HISTORICAL: Production began Sept. 16, 1937; ended Aug. 17, 1938. Model year production: 14,725 Commercial Sedans. Dan S. Eddins was again president of Plymouth.

1938 PLYMOUTH

1938 Plymouth P57 Commercial Sedan Delivery (OCW)

COMMERCIAL car — SERIES PT-57 — SIX-CYLINDER: The Plymouth Commercial car for 1938 was a slightly restyled version of the 1937 offering. The grille was now squatter to approximate the styling of the 1938 Plymouth passenger cars, but, that was the only change. Both the 1937 and 1938 Commercial Cars closely resembled the passenger car line, yet there was no interchangability of sheetmetal or trim between the two series. Prices were considerably higher for the 1938 models, but the recession of 1938, coupled with the fact that dealers lots were full of trade-ins from the previous record year, spelled disaster as far as production went. Sales dropped to nearly half their 1937 levels. Models offered in the PT57 series included a Sedan Delivery, the Express and the Chassis & Cab. The wood-bodied Station Wagon once more rode the passenger car chassis. Plymouth continued to offer its ambulance conversion in the regular sedan line, while the removable pickup box was still available for the Business Coupe.

1938 Plymouth P57 Commercial Sedan Delivery (JB/POC)

I.D. DATA: Serial number located on right front door post. Serial numbers: Detroit, Mich.: 8,618,701 to 8,624,135; Los Angeles, Calif.: 9,208,201 to 9,208,797; Evansville, Ind.: 9,185,301 to 9,186,416. Starting: T57-1001 and up.

Model	Body Type	Price	Weight	Prod. Total
Series PT57				
N/A	Chassis & Cab	560	1850	95
K8-2-LR	Express	585	1850	4620
K-1-3	Sedan Delivery	695	1850	1601

1938 Plymouth Model P5 Business Coupe-Pickup (JB)

ENGINE: Inline. L-head. Six-cylinder. Cast iron block. Bore & stroke: 3-1/8 in. x 4-3/8 in. Displacement: 201.3 cid. Compression ratio: 6.7. Brake horsepower: 70 at 3000 rpm. SAE Horsepower: 23.44. Four main bearings. Solid valve lifters. Carburetor: Chandler Groves model A2. Torque: 145 lbs.-ft. at 1200 rpm.

1938 Plymouth PT57 Pickup Truck (D.J. Phillips)

CHASSIS [PT57]: Wheelbase: 116 in. Tires: 6.00 x 16 in.

1938 Plymouth Commercial Station Wagon (CHC)

TECHNICAL: Sliding gear transmission. Speeds: [Standard] 3F/1R, [Optional] 4F/1R with power-take-off opening. Floor shift gearshift lever. Single-plate dry-disc 10 in. clutch. Shaft drive. Hypoid, semi-floating rear axle. Overall ratio: 4.1. Four-wheel hydraulic brakes. Steel disc wheels. Rim Size: 6.00 x 16 in.

1938 Plymouth PT57 Pickup (JB/POC)

OPTIONS: Chrome plated rear bumper ($8.50). Single sidemount (standard right side only). Dual sidemount: left hand optional, including tire, tube and tire lock ($10). Bumper guards ($1.50 pair). Chassis accessory group including chrome radiator shell, chrome headlamps and double-acting shock absorbers, front and rear ($17). Dual horns ($7.50). Coach lamps for Commercial Sedan ($8.50). Long-arm stationary rearview mirror ($1.50). Long-arm adjustable rearview mirror ($2.50). Sun visors ($2 each). Metal spare tire cover ($6.50). Chrome windshield frame ($3). Right-hand taillamp. ($4). Economy engine package Group 1 ($2.50); same, Group 2 ($3). Four-speed transmission ($25). Painted sheet metal, including fenders, splash aprons, runningboards ($5). Oil bath air cleaner ($3.75). Vortex air cleaner with standard cap ($17.50); with Vortex cap ($19.50). Governor ($5). Chrome headlamps ($2.75). Oil filter ($3.25). Chrome radiator shell ($6.). Auxiliary seat, Commercial Sedan ($10). Double-acting shocks, front ($4.75); rear ($4.75). Right-hand windshield wiper ($4).

HISTORICAL: Production began Sept. 16, 1937; ended Aug. 17, 1938. Model year production: 6,316. Dan S. Eddins was again president of Plymouth.

599

1939 PLYMOUTH

1939 Plymouth PT81 Chassis & Cab With Cargo Body (CHC)

ROADKING — SERIES P7 — SIX-CYLINDER: For reasons unexplained, Plymouth decided to offer two different lines of commercial vehicles this year. They came on both the passenger car and commercial car chassis. Reverting back to the passenger car line was the Panel Delivery. Made up of its own special body on the P7 Roadking chassis, the Panel offered two doors at the rear, while carrying the spare tire in a single sidemounted fender. The interior consisted of a single seat, although a second seat was optional. The rear cargo area was paneled. The windows in both rear doors could also be rolled down if desired. Also offered this year was the familiar Commercial Sedan, now called a Utility Sedan. Still based on the two-door passenger car this version varied in that it didn't have a regular door at the rear like the previous model. Instead, the opening was through the trunk lid and there was no dividing partition between the trunk area and the rear compartment. The interior was lined and a lockable screen partition could be installed behind the driver's seat. If needed, a full set of seats could be installed to turn the Utility Sedan into a five-passenger vehicle for normal use. Sales of the Panel Delivery were up from 1938, but sales of the Utility Sedan were a disappointing 341 units. The company also continued to offer the ambulance conversion on sedans, as well as the pickup box for the Business Coupe.

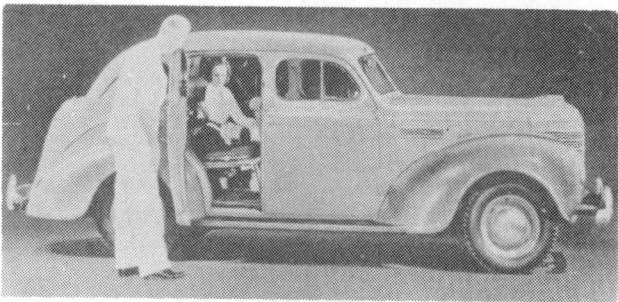

1939 Plymouth Sedan-Ambulance (OCW)

I.D. DATA: Serial number located on right front door post. Serial numbers: Detroit, Mich.: 1,298,001 to 1,377,475; Los Angeles, Calif.: 3,110,001 to 3,114,680; Evansville, Ind.: 9,150,401 to 9,164,593; Windsor, Ontario: 9,603,586 to 9,607,605. Engine number located on left front corner of block, directly above generator. Starting engine number: P8-1001. Ending engine number: P8-411923.

Model	Body Type	Price	Weight	Prod. Total
Series P7 (Roadking)				
723	Panel Delivery	715	1985	2270
N/A	Utility Sedan	685	2844	341

ENGINE: Inline. L-head. Six-cylinder. Cast iron block. Bore & stroke: 3-1/8 in. x 4-3/8 in. Displacement: 201.3 cid. Compression ratio: 6.7:1. Brake horsepower: 82 at 3600 rpm. SAE Horsepower: 23.44. Four main bearings. Solid valve lifters. Carburetor: Carter models B6K1, B6M1, DGA1-2 or D6C1-1. Torque: 145 lbs.-ft. at 1200 rpm.

1939 Plymouth Sedan Delivery (DFW/MVMA)

600

OPTIONAL ENGINE: Aluminum high-compression head gives 7.0 compression ratio and 86 horsepower at 3600 rpm. Export engine: Bore & stroke: 2-7/8 in. x 4-3/8 in. (Engines coded P8X).

1939 Plymouth Roadking Utility Sedan (DFW)

COMMERCIAL CAR — SERIES PT81 — SIX-CYLINDER: A completely restyled vehicle was the order of the day for the 1939 Plymouth Commercial Car. Styled to closely match its sister Dodge, the new Plymouth no longer looked like a truck version of a passenger car. It now looked like a big and brawny truck. To some it was not as attractive a vehicle as it had been before. Outside of emblems and hubcaps, as well as a three-piece front end ensemble, the Plymouth Commercial Car could easily be mistaken for a Dodge (the Dodge had a two-piece front end) or its Canadian sister, the Fargo (which also had three-piece front end). With the removal of the Sedan Delivery to the passenger car chassis, the PT81 Commercial Car consisted of only the Express-Pickup and the Cab & Chassis. Prices were lowered slightly and sales increased slightly for the year. The cab of this new vehicle sat several inches further forward on the chassis. It was advertised as a real three-man cab. The pickup box increased in size slightly, as well. Throughout their lifetime, the Plymouth Commercial Cars would all ride a 116 in. wheelbase. Unique to the design of the new cab was a latch located at the top of the door frame. It was claimed this helped to keep the doors from popping open during operation over rough terrain. Fender-mounted spare tires were no longer offered on the commercial vehicles. The spare now rode in a hanger, beneath the pickup box at the rear of the frame rails. However, a few vehicles are known to have had the spare tire mounted forward of the right rear fender, on the runningboard.

I.D. DATA: Serial number located on right front door post. Serial numbers: Detroit, Mich.: 8,624,201 to 8,630,418; Los Angeles, Calif.: 9,208,851 to 9,209,340. Engine number located on left front corner of block, directly above generator. Starting engine number: T81-1001 and up.

Model	Body Type	Price	Weight	Prod. Total
Series PT81				
N/A	Chassis & Cab	545	2075	140
N/A	Sedan Delivery	654	2800	13
M-1-2	Pickup	575	2800	6181

ENGINE: Inline. L-head. Six-cylinder. Cast iron block. Bore & stroke: 3-1/8 in. x 4-3/8 in. Displacement: 201.3 cid. Compression ratio: 6.7:1. Brake horsepower: 70 at 3000 rpm. SAE Horsepower: 23.44. Four main bearings. Solid valve lifters. Torque: 145 lbs.-ft. at 1200 rpm.
CHASSIS [P7]: Wheelbase: 114 in. Overall length: 182-3/16 in. (without bumpers). Front tread: 56-1/4 in. Rear tread: 60 in. Tires: 5.50 x 16 in.
CHASSIS [PT81]: Wheelbase: 116 in. Overall length: 182 in. Tires: 6.00 x 16 in.
TECHNICAL [P7]: Sliding gear transmission. Speeds: 3F/1R. Floor-mounted gearshift lever. Single-plate dry-disc 9-1/4 in. clutch. Shaft drive. Hypoid, semi-floating rear axle. Overall ratio: 3.9:1. Four-wheel hydraulic brakes. Steel disc wheels. Rim Size: 5.50 x 16 in.
TECHNICAL [PT81]: Sliding gear transmission. [Standard] 3F/1R; [Optional] 4F/1R with power-take-off opening. Floor-mounted gearshift lever. Single-plate dry-disc clutch. Shaft drive. Hypoid, semi-floating rear axle. Overall ratio: 4.1:1. Four-wheel hydraulic brakes. Four steel disc wheels. Rim Size: 6:00 x 16 in.

1939 Plymouth PT81 Pickup (OCW)

OPTIONS [P7]: Single sidemount (standard on Sedan Delivery and Utility Sedan). Dual sidemount (optional on Sedan Delivery and Utility Sedan). Fender skirts ($8.25). Bumper guards ($4.50 pair). Electric clock in glove box door ($10). Cigar lighter ($2). Spotlight ($14.50). Chrome wheel discs ($8). Economy engine, group 1 ($2.50). Economy engine, group 2 ($3). Stone deflector, Utility Sedan only ($1). Whitewall tires 6.00 x 16 in. ($15.75). 5.50 x 16 in. ($13.75). Heavy-duty air cleaner ($2). 20 in. high-clearance wheels ($18). Glove box lock ($11.75). Oil filter ($2.75). Deluxe steering wheel ($5). Rear spring covers ($3). Clock mirror ($3.95). Dual trumpet horns, under hood mount ($8.25). Right-hand inside sun visor ($1.75). License plate frames ($1.75). Fog lamps ($12). Outside rearview mirror ($1.95). Runningboard side mouldings ($1.50). Exhaust extension ($1). Locking gas cap ($1.50). Heaters: Super Airstream ($24.45); Tri Airstream ($21.45); Deluxe ($18.45); Dual Airstream ($15.45). Defroster ($4.50). Manual radio with Skyway antenna ($41.50); with Roadway antenna, under runningboard mounting ($43.95).

1939 Plymouth Sedan Delivery (DFW/MVMA)

OPTIONS [PT81]: Oil bath air cleaner ($3.25). Right-hand taillamp. ($4). Chrome head-lamps ($2.75). Dual horns ($7.50). Colored sheet metal ($5). Chrome radiator shell ($6). Long-arm stationary mirror ($1.50). Long-arm adjustable mirror ($2.50). Sun visor ($2). Four-speed transmission ($17.50). Chrome windshield frame ($3). Right-hand windshield wiper ($4). Express type rear bumper ($6). Spare wheel lock ($1.50).

1939 Plymouth Utility Coupe With Extendable Box (CHC)

HISTORICAL [PT81]: Production began Nov. 1, 1938; ended Aug. 31, 1939. Model year production: 6,321 units. [P7]: Production began Aug. 18, 1938; ending Aug. 18, 1939. Model year production: 2,270 Sedan Deliveries and 341 Utility Sedans were built. Of the 341 Utility Sedans, production was broken down as follows: [Detroit] Left-hand drive, for domestic market=308; [Detroit] Left-hand drive, for export market=1; [Evansville] Left-hand drive, for domestic market=18; [Los Angeles] Left-hand drive, for domestic market=14. Of the 2,270 Panel Delivery trucks, production was broken down as follows: [Detroit] Left-hand drive, for domestic market=1,779; [Detroit] left-hand drive, for export market=52; [Detroit] right-hand drive, for export market=50; [Evansville] Left-hand drive, for domestic market=180; [Los Angeles] Left-hand drive, for domestic market=137; [Completely Knocked-Down] For export, left-hand drive=54; [Completely Knocked-Down] For export, right-hand drive=18. In 1939, Dan S. Eddins continued as president of Plymouth.

1940 PLYMOUTH

1940 Plymouth Roadking Utility Sedan (CHC)

ROADKING — SERIES P9 — SIX-CYLINDER: The Plymouth passenger car commercial line once again consisted of the Panel Delivery and the Utility Sedan. Both vehicles were restyled to match the normal passenger car line. The only other difference between the 1939 and 1940 models was that the spare tire of the Panel Delivery could no longer be mounted in the fenders. The spare was now carried forward of the right rear fender, in a special indentation in the body. Both body styles offered the same options as the previous

Standard Catalog of Light-Duty Trucks

year, including the screen partition for the Utility Sedan. The ambulance conversion was offered on either the Deluxe or Roadking chassis. Sales of the Utility Sedan nearly doubled, while sales of the Panel Delivery remained nearly static. While the ambulance conversion of the regular Passenger Sedan was still offered, it would appear that the removable pickup box for the Business Coupe was no longer available.

1940 Plymouth Road King Sedan-Ambulance (CHC)

I.D. DATA: Serial number located on right front door post. Serial numbers: Detroit, Mich.: 1,378,001 to 1,454,303; Los Angeles, Calif.: 3,114,801 to 3,121,385; Evansville, Ind.: 9,062,201 to 9,081,375; Windsor, Ontario: 9,368,516 to 9,373,193. Engine number located on left front corner of block, directly above generator. Starting engine number: P9-1001. Ending engine number: P9-415462.

1940 Plymouth Panel Delivery (CHC)

Model	Body Type	Price	Weight	Prod. Total
Series P9 (Roadking)				
N/A	Utility Sedan	699	2769	589
755	Panel Delivery	720	1941	2889

ENGINE: Inline. L-head. Six-cylinder. Cast iron block. Bore & stroke: 3-1/8 in. x 4-3/8 in. Displacement: 201.3 cid. Compression ratio: 6.7:1. Brake horsepower: 84 at 3600 rpm. Horsepower: 23.44. Four main bearings. Solid valve lifters. Carburetor: Carter model D6A1, model D6C1, or model D6P1. Torque: 154 lbs.-ft. at 1200 rpm.

OPTIONAL ENGINE: High-compression aluminum head. Compression ratio 7.0 to 1. 87 horsepower at 3600 rpm. 158 lbs.-ft. torque at 1200 rpm. Export engines: Bore & stroke: 2-7/8 in. x 4-3/8 in., 170.4 cid., 70 horsepower. (Export engines were code numbered P9X.)

1940 Plymouth PT105 Pickup (JB/POC)

COMMERCIAL CAR — SERIES PT105 — SIX-CYLINDER: Plymouth's truck chassis offering this year was a very slightly updated version of the 1939 model. Visually, the only external changes were the addition of sealed beam headlamps, which resulted in the parking lamps being mounted in small pods atop the headlamp shell. Three horizontal strips of bright trim also adorned the radiator shell, to approximate the grille design of the passenger car line. The line still consisted of only the Express-Pickup and the Chassis & Cab. Both were sold with full runningboards and rear fenders. Prices were up $10 over 1939, yet sales were also up slightly.

I.D. DATA: Serial number located on right front door post. Serial numbers: Detroit, Mich.: 8,631,001 to 8,637,730; Los Angeles, Calif.: 9,209,351 to 9,210,053. Engine number located on left front corner of block, directly above generator. Starting engine number: PT105-1001. Ending engine number: PT105-34654.

1940 Plymouth PT105 Yacht Basin Delivery Truck (CHC)

Model	Body Type	Price	Weight	Prod. Total
Series PT105				
N/A	Chassis & Cab	555	2600	174
4012	Express-Pickup	585	2800	6879

ENGINE: Inline. L-head. Six-cylinder. Cast iron block. Bore & stroke: 3-1/8 in. x 4-3/8 in. Displacement: 201.3 cid. Compression ratio: 6.7:1. Brake horsepower: 79 at 3000 rpm. Horsepower: 23.44. Four main bearings. Solid valve lifters. Torque: 154 lbs.-ft. at 1200 rpm.

CHASSIS [P9]: Wheelbase: 117 in. Front tread: 57 in. Rear tread: 60 in. Tires: 5.50 x 16 in.

CHASSIS [PT105]: Wheelbase: 116 in. Overall length: 182 in. Tires: 6.00 x 16 in.

TECHNICAL [P9]: Sliding gear transmission. Speeds: 3F/1R. Column-mounted gearshift lever. Dry, single 9-1/4 in. disc clutch. Shaft drive. Hypoid, semi-floating rear axle. Overall ratio: 3.9:1. Four-wheel hydraulic brakes. Steel disc wheels. Rim Size: 5.50 x 16 in.

TECHNICAL [PT105]: Sliding gear transmission. Speeds: [std.] 3F/1R; [opt.] 4F/1R with power-take-off opening. Floor-mounted gearshift lever. Single, dry 10 in. disc clutch. Shaft drive. Hypoid, semi-floating rear axle. Overall ratio: 4.1:1. Four-wheel hydraulic brakes. Steel disc wheels. Rim Size: 6.00 x 16 in.

OPTIONS [P9]: Push-button radio ($47.50). All Weather heater system ($45.50). Electric clock in glove box door ($12). Spotlight, right- or left-hand ($14.50 each). Backup lamp. ($2.95). Exhaust extension ($1). Fender grille guard ($11.20). Fender protectors ($6.25). Fog lamps ($12). Locking gas cap ($1.50). Grille guard ($6.95). Dual trumpet horns (under-hood-mounted) ($8.50). License plate frames ($1.50). Outside rearview mirror ($1.95). Deluxe steering wheel ($8.50). Front center bumper Superguard ($1.75). Wheel discs ($1.50) each. Wheel trim rings ($1.50 each). 20 in. high-clearance wheels.

OPTIONS [PT105]: Oil bath air cleaner ($2.50). Vortex air cleaner ($17.50 with standard cap or $19.50 with Vortex cap). Airfoam seat cushions ($10). Right-hand taillamp. ($2.50). Domelamp. ($3.50). Glove box lock ($1.50). 32 amp. generator for slow speed operation ($4). Governor ($5). Chrome headlamps ($3.50). Grille guard ($7.50). Dual horns ($7.50). Heater & defroster ($25). Deluxe Purolator oil filter ($5). Colored sheet metal ($5). Long-arm stationary mirror ($1.50); same for right-hand side ($3). Sun visor ($2). Inside rearview mirror ($1). Four-speed transmission ($17.50). Chrome windshield frame ($3). Right-hand vacuum windshield wiper ($4). Left-hand electric windshield wiper ($6). Dual electric wipers ($13). Express type rear bumper ($6). Spare wheel lock ($1.50). Economy engine package, group 1 ($2.50), group 2 ($3). Tires: Five 5.25 x 20 four-ply ($18). Five 5.25 x 20 six-ply ($35). Five 6.00 x 16 six-ply ($14.50). Five 6.00 x 18 six-ply (price not listed). Five 6.25 x 16 six-ply ($23.50). Five 6.50 x 16 four-ply ($13.50). Five 6.50 x 16 six-ply ($28.25).

1940 Plymouth PT105 Pickup (D. Kostansek/DFW)

HISTORICAL [P9]: Production began Aug. 15, 1939; ended July 12, 1940. Model year production: 106,738. Of these, 2,889 were Sedan Delivery trucks, 589 Utility Sedans. Of the 589 Utility Sedans, production was broken down as follows: [Detroit] left-hand drive domestic market=502; [Detroit] left-hand drive export=6; [Detroit] right-hand drive export=2; [Evansville] left-hand drive domestic=63; [Los Angeles] left-hand drive domestic=16. Of the 2,889 Panel Deliverys built, production was broken down as follows: [Detroit] left-hand drive domestic market=2,278; [Detroit] left-hand drive export=39; [Detroit] right-hand drive export=5; [Evansville] left-hand drive domestic=312; [Los Angeles] left-hand drive domestic=255. [PT105]: Production began Sept. 26, 1939; ended Aug. 20. 1940. Model year production: 7,053. Dan S. Eddins continued as president of Plymouth.

COMMERCIAL CAR — SERIES PT125 — SIX-CYLINDER: 1941 would prove to be the final year for Plymouth's truck chassis Commercial Car. While the reasons for this have never been fully explained by Chrysler Corp., it would appear that low sales, plus the demand on the Dodge factories for increased production of military vehicles, worked together to sound the death knoll for the Plymouth truck. The 1941s were slightly restyled to give them a more expensive look. Pricewise, they were more expensive by $35. Production of the Express dipped by 800 units, while the Chassis & Cab found 22 more purchasers than it had in 1940. At the front, the PT125 series featured an overlay of chrome trim on the same nose piece used since 1939. This resulted in appearance not unlike the 1941 passenger car. The front bumper had a V-shape to it and the headlamps were moved out to the crown of the fenders. This resulted in a more "bug-eyed" appearance. The parking lamps were moved back to the cowl and the familiar Plymouth script moved from the radiator shell, to the center of the hood panels. As the last Plymouth truck rolled off the assembly line, late in 1941, the end of an era in Plymouth truck production had come to a close. It wouldn't be until 1974 that Plymouth would again offer such a vehicle. When it did, it, too, would be based on its sister division, Dodge.

1941 Plymouth Fire & Rescue Squad Pickup (OCW)

I.D. DATA: Serial number located on right front door post. Serial numbers: Detroit, Mich.: 81,000,101 to 81,006,107; Los Angeles, Calif.: 9,210,101 to 9,210,700. Engine number located on left front corner of block, directly above generator. Starting engine number: PT125-1001 and up.

1941 Plymouth P11 Sedan Delivery (JB/POC)

Model	Body Type	Price	Weight	Prod. Total
Series PT125				
N/A	Chassis & Cab	590	2600	196
4112	Pickup	625	2800	6073
N/A	Panel Delivery	720	2800	

1941 Plymouth Pickup (Clyde "Buck" Jones)

NOTE: The PT125 Panel Delivery is listed in contemporary used car price books, although it appears that none may have actually been built.
ENGINE: Inline. L-head. Six-cylinder. Cast iron block. Bore & stroke: 3-1/8 in. x 4-3/8 in. Displacement: 201.3 cid. Brake horsepower: 87 at 3800 rpm. SAE Net horsepower: 23.44. Four main bearings. Solid valve lifters. Carburetor: Ball & Ball.

1941 Plymouth Pickup Truck (JB)

DELUXE — SERIES P11/P11D — SIX-CYLINDER: Plymouth's passenger car-based commercial vehicles once again included the Panel Delivery and the Utility Sedan. For the most part, both were based on the P11 Plymouth chassis. In a rare move, Plymouth offered three passenger car series in 1941, including the P11 Plymouth, the P11D Deluxe and the P12 Special Deluxe. For reasons unknown, while 99.9 percent of the Utility Sedan and Panel Delivery production took place on the P11 chassis, someone with pull at the factory had a single model of each built on the P11D chassis. In addition, two Utility Sedans were built on the P12 Special Deluxe chassis. Outside of restyling to match the regular passenger car line, these commercial vehicles did not differ from the previous year's offerings.
I.D. DATA: Serial number located on right front door post. Serial numbers: Detroit, Mich.: 15,000,101 to 15,135,030; Los Angeles, Calif.: 3,121,501 to 3,133,962; Evansville, Ind.: 22,001,001 to 22,036,667; Windsor, Ontario: 9,821,241 to 9,829,853. Engine number located on left front corner of block, directly above generator. Engine numbers: P11-1001 to P11-535085.

1941 Plymouth Sedan Delivery (D.S. Olsen photo)

Model	Body Type	Price	Weight	Prod. Total
Series P11				
N/A	Utility Sedan	739	2600	174
820	Sedan Delivery	760	2794	468
Series P11D				
N/A	Deluxe Utility Sedan	—	—	1
820	Deluxe Sedan Delivery	—	—	1
Series P12				
820	Utility Sedan	—	—	2

ENGINE: Inline. L-head. Six-cylinder. Cast iron block. Bore & stroke: 3-1/8 in. x 4-3/8 in. Displacement: 201.3 cid. Brake horsepower: 87 at 3800 rpm. SAE Net horsepower: 23.44. Four main bearings. Solid valve lifters. Carburetor: Ball & Ball.
CHASSIS [P11/P11D]: Wheelbase: 117 in. Overall length: 195 in. Front tread: 57 in. Rear tread: 60 in. Tires: 6:00 x 16 in.
CHASSIS [PT125]: Wheelbase: 116 in. Overall length: 182 in. Tires: 6:00 x 16 in.
TECHNICAL [PT125]: Sliding gear transmission. Speeds: [Standard] 3F/1R; [Optional] 4F/1R with power-take-off opening. Floor-mounted gearshift lever. Single-plate dry-disc single 10 in. clutch. Shaft drive. Hypoid, semi-floating rear axle. Overall ratio: 4.1:1. Four-wheel hydraulic brakes. Steel disc wheels. Rim Size: 6:00 x 16 in.
TECHNICAL [P11/P12]: Sliding gear transmission. Speeds: 3F/1R. Column-mounted gearshift lever. Single-plate dry-disc 9-1/4 in. clutch. Shaft drive. Hypoid, semi-floating rear axle. Overall ratio: 4.1:1. Four-wheel hydraulic brakes. Steel disc wheels. Rim Size: 6:00 x 16 in.
OPTIONS [PT125]: Oil bath air cleaner ($2.50). Vortex air cleaner with standard cap ($17.50); with Vortex cap ($19.50). Airfoam seat cushions ($10). Right-hand taillamp. ($2.50). Dome lamp. ($3.50). Glove box lock ($1.50). 32 amp. generator for slow speed operation ($4). Governor ($5). Chrome headlamps, including cowl lamps ($3.50). Grille guard ($7.50). Dual horns ($7.50). Heater and defroster ($25). Deluxe Purolator oil filter ($5). Colored sheet metal, (no charge). Long-arm stationary mirror ($1.50); same for right-hand side ($3). Sunvisor ($2). Inside rearview mirror ($1). Four-speed transmission ($17.50). Chrome windshield frame ($3). Right-hand vacuum windshield wiper ($4). Left-hand electric windshield wiper ($6). Dual electric windshield wipers ($13). Express type rear bumper ($6). Spare wheel lock ($1.50). Economy engine package, group 1 ($4.25); same, group 2 ($3). All tire sets sold in groups of 5: Five 5.25 x 20 four-ply ($18). Five 5.25 x 20 six-ply ($35). Five 6.00 x 16 six-ply ($14.50). Five 6.00 x 16 eight-ply (Price not listed). Five 6.25 x 16 six-ply ($23.50). Five 6.50 x 16 four-ply ($13.50). Five 6.50 x 16 six-ply ($28.25).
OPTIONS [P11/P11D]: Accessory group B including cigar lighter, glove box lock with steel glove box and stainless steel wheel trim rings ($10). Accessory group C including right-hand windshield wiper and right-hand sun visor ($5). Bumper fender guards ($8). Bumper center guards ($3). Chrome wheel discs, set of four ($6). Chrome wheel trim rings, set of five ($7.50). Front door armrest ($1.75). Front door vent wings ($12). Glove box lock with steel glove box ($1). Dual horns ($5). Powermatic shifting ($6.50). Eight tube push-button radio ($46.75). Six tube radio ($35.15). Cowl-mounted antenna ($6.20). Economy engine, group 1 ($2.50) including smallbore carburetor and intake manifold ($3.73). Rear axle ratio ($2.50). Economy engine group 2, same as group 1 except includes throttle stop and heat shields ($3.50). Back-up signal, emergency brake alarm, cigarette lighter, Kool Kushion, exhaust extension, fog lights, six different hot water heaters, cowl-mounted outside rearview mirrors, grille guard, insect screen, seat covers, left-hand or right-hand spotlight.
HISTORICAL [PT125]: Production began Sept. 18, 1940. End of production not recorded. Model year production: 6,269. [Series P11/Deluxe P11D]: Production began Aug. 8, 1940; ended July 16, 1941. Model year production: [P11 Sedan Delivery] 3,200; [P11 Utility Sedans] 468; [P11D Utility Sedan] 1; [P11D Sedan Delivery] 1. Dan S. Eddins was still the president of Plymouth. Of the 468 P11 Utility Sedans, production was broken down as follows: [Detroit] left-hand drive export Market=1; [Detroit] right-hand drive export=10; [Detroit] left-hand drive domestic=383; [Evansville] left-hand drive domestic=45; [Los Angeles] left-hand drive domestic=29; [Detroit] P11D Utility Sedan=1. Of the 3,200 P11 Panel Delivery's production was broken down as follows: [Detroit] left-hand drive domestic Market=2,537; [Detroit] left-hand drive export=54; [Detroit] right-hand drive export=1; [Evansville] left-hand drive domestic=344; [Los Angeles] left-hand drive domestic=258; Knock Down export left-hand drive=6; [Detroit] P11D Panel Delivery=1. Two P12 Utility Sedans were also Detroit built.

1942 PLYMOUTH

DELUXE — SERIES P14S — SIX-CYLINDER: Plymouth's first entry into the commercial field began in 1930, with the conversion of 80 passenger cars to Commercial Sedans. Ironically, Plymouth's last prewar entry into the commercial field would also be based on a converted passenger car body style. This time the vehicle was called a Utility Sedan. The idea behind the two vehicles was the same. Even more ironic, was the final production total: the same 80 unit figure. Plymouth's passenger car lineup for 1942 consisted of the P14S Deluxe and the P14C Special Deluxe. All of the Utility Sedans were based on the Deluxe series. Production of all 1942 models would be short-lived since the U.S. became involved in World War II and production of the commercial offerings from Plymouth would be completely curtailed. When production resumed, late in 1945, no commercial vehicles would be offered.
I.D. DATA: Serial number located on right front door post. Serial numbers: Detroit, Mich.: 15,135,501 to 15,153,935; Los Angeles, Calif.: 3,134,501 to 3,136,266; Evansville, Ind.: 22,037,001 to 22,041,356; Windsor, Ontario: 9,829,856 to 9,836,986. Engine numbers located on left front corner of block, directly above generator. Starting engine number: P14-1001. Ending engine number: P14-149161.

Model	Body Type	Price	Weight	Prod. Total
Deluxe Series P14S				
N/A	Utility Sedan	842	2985	80

ENGINE [P14S]: Inline. L-head. Six-cylinder. Cast iron block. Bore & stroke: 3-1/4 in. x 4-3/8 in. Displacement: 217.8 cid. Compression ratio: 6.8:1. Brake horsepower: 95 at 3400 rpm. SAE horsepower: 25.35. Four main bearings. Solid valve lifters. Carburetor: Carter model B6P1 or B6G1. Torque: 172 lbs.-ft. at 1600 rpm.
CHASSIS [P14S]: Wheelbase: 117 in. Tires: 16 x 6.00 in.
TECHNICAL [P14S]: Sliding gear transmission. Speeds: 3F/1R. Column-mounted gearshift lever. Single-plate dry-disc 9-1/4 in. clutch. Driveshaft. Hypoid, semi-floating rear axle. Overall ratio: 3.9:1 (3.73 with economy engine). Four-wheel hydraulic brakes. Steel disc wheels. Rim Size: 6:00 x 16 in. Power-Matic shifting — vacuum/operated self-shifting ($7.85 option).
OPTIONS: Fender skirts ($12.50). Eight tube push-button radio ($54.85). All Weather heating system ($49.20). Electric clock ($9.75). Cigar lighter ($2). Right-hand or left-hand spotlight ($15.80). License plate frames ($2.20). Windshield washer ($3.95). Hand brake alarm ($2.50). Locking gas cap ($1.80). Outside rearview mirror ($2.35). Powermatic shifting ($7.85). Direction signals ($10). Exhaust extension. Wheel trim discs. Wheel trim rings. Buzzer type hand brake alarm. Flashing light type hand brake alarm. Six tube push-button radio. Universal mount radio. Skyway external radio antenna. Internal cowl-mounted antenna. Crank-operated cowl-concealed antenna. Power operated cowl-concealed antenna.

HISTORICAL [P14S]: Production began July 25, 1941; ending Jan. 31, 1942. Model year production: 27,645. Of these, 80 were Utility Sedans. Production broke down as follows: Detroit left-hand drive domestic Market=63; Detroit left-hand drive export=2; Evansville left-hand drive domestic=9; Los Angeles left-hand drive domestic=6. Dan S. Eddins continued as president of Plymouth.

1974 PLYMOUTH

1974 Plymouth Trail Duster Sport Utility 4x4 (CHC)

TRAIL DUSTER — SERIES PW-100 — ALL ENGINES: The new Trail Duster was a handsome sports/utility vehicle. Its two round headlights were slightly recessed into the simple, but appealing, grille (which was outlined in bright trim). The Plymouth name, printed in bright letters, appeared to float in the blacked-out center of the grille. The large, vertical wraparound taillights had backup lights incorporated into their upper section. Standard Trail Duster features included: Full-time four-wheel drive; a single all-vinyl bucket seat with seat belt and retractor; armrest pads; color-keyed padded instrument panel; electronic ignition; power front disc brakes; heavy-duty 9-1/4 in. rear axle; under-the-hood tool storage; five shift positions transfer case: 1) Low-lock, for use only on low-traction surfaces such as deep snow, mud or soft sand. 2) Low, for normal operation when additional power is needed on high-traction surfaces. 3) Neutral, with vehicle stopped, both axles are disengaged for power-take-off operation. 4) High, for all normal operation in direct drive on paved or unpaved surfaces. 5) High-lock, for use only on low-traction surfaces such as snow, mud or soft sand; and three-speed manual transmission.

1974 Plymouth Trail Duster Open Body 4x4 Utility (CHC)

Model	Body Type	Price	Weight	Prod. Total
Trail Duster — 4x4 — 1/2-Ton				
PW100	Topless Utility	3964	3910	5015

CHASSIS: Wheelbase: 106 in. Overall length: 184.62 in. Overall width: 79.5 in. Overall height with roof: 72 in. Tires: E78-15B in. GVW rating: 4,900-6,000 lbs.

TECHNICAL: Four-speed manual transmission. TorqueFlite automatic transmission. 360 cid V-8 with four-barrel carburetor. 400 cid V-8 with two-barrel carburetor (not available in California). 440 cid V-8 with four-barrel carburetor.

1974 Plymouth Trail Duster With Full Vinyl Enclosure Top

OPTIONS: Sport package: includes deluxe front bucket seats with special trim and a lockable center console with a removable beverage chest; bright front and rear bumper and windshield molding; unique bodyside and tailgate trim; color-keyed door trim panels with map pockets. Inner and outer double-walled steel roof. AM radio. AM/FM radio. Air-conditioning. Power steering. Convenience package: Glove box lock; glove box light; ash receiver light; inside hood lock release; and a 12 in. day/night rearview mirror. Tachometer. Bright wheelcovers. Trailer towing package: Includes light or heavy equipment. Oil pressure gauge. Non-adjustable and forward tilting passenger seat (includes sun visor and seatbelt). Deluxe seats (includes console, sun visors and seat belts). Rear bench seat. Outside-mounted tire carrier. Vented rear side window. Skid plates (fuel tank shield and transfer case shield). Tinted glass, windshield or all glass. High output heater. Increased cooling. Engine block heater. Hand throttle (not available with TorqueFlite automatic transmission). Step-type rear bumper. Front bumper guards. Steel roof (available in color, vinyl-textured white or black). Two-tone (includes moldings and bright tail lamp bezels). Dual horn. Bright hubcaps. Dealer installed soft top. Roll bar.

HISTORICAL: Trail Dusters were built by Dodge. They were offered in the following exterior colors: Light gold. Medium gold. Dark Green metallic. Light blue. Bright red. Light green. Yellow. Avocado metallic. Medium blue metallic. Sunstone. Bronze metallic. Medium gold metallic. White.

1974 Plymouth Voyager Sport Maxi-Wagon (CHC)

VOYAGER — SERIES PB100 — ALL ENGINES: The attractive new Voyager was a van made on the same assembly line as the Dodge Sportsman. It had two round headlights each encased in a large square shaped piece of bright trim. The blacked-out grille was outlined by bright molding. Four horizontal bright trim pieces ran from headlight to headlight. Sandwiched between them, in the center, was the word Plymouth. On either side were the rectangular signal lights. The rectangular taillights had backup lights incorporated into them. Standard features included: Forty-one amp. alternator; driver and front passenger armrests; driver's compartment ashtray; forty-eight amp.-hr. battery; passenger side double doors with vented glass; electronic ignition; twenty-three gallon fuel tank; glove box door with push-button operated latch; fresh air heater with defrosters; dual electric horns; bumper jack; oil pressure indicator light; driver and front passenger bucket seats (in blue, green, parchment, or black); three-passenger bench seat; two padded sun visors; spare tire carrier; traffic hazard warning switch; two-speed windshield wipers and dual jet washers; power front disc brakes; Argent silver and black grille; front and rear painted bumpers (white); dual 5 x 7 in. painted exterior mirrors; black driver compartment floor mat; driver compartment headliner; Voyager nameplates; and three-speed manual transmission. Standard sized Voyagers on both short and long wheelbases were promoted as Wagons. Stretched versions, on the long wheelbase only, were Maxi-Wagons.

I.D. DATA: A combination of 13 symbols are used. The first seven identify the model, series, GVW Class (A=6,000 lbs. or less. B=over 6,000 lbs.) engine, model year and assembly plant. The last six are sequential serial numbers. (They begin each year at 000,001.) The symbols for the engines are A=440 V-8; B=225 six; C=225 six; D=440 V-8; E=318 V-8; F=360 V-8 with two-barrel carb; G=318 V-8; H=243 Diesel; J=400 V-8; K=360 V-8; T=360 V-8 with four-barrel carb; X=Special L-6; and Y=Special V-8. The VIN symbols were BA=PB100.

1974 Plymouth Model PB100 Voyager Wagon (CHC)

Model	Body Type	Price	Weight	Prod. Total
Voyager Van — 1/2-Ton — 109 in. w.b.				
PB100	Wagon	3855	3685	Note 1
Voyager Van — 1/2-Ton — 127 in. w.b.				
PB100	Wagon	4003	3820	Note 1

NOTE 1: Van production was 11,701 units for all series.

ENGINE: Six-cylinder. Displacement: 225 cid. Brake horsepower: 95 at 3600 rpm. Bore & stroke: 3.40 in. x 4.12 in. Compression ratio: 8.4:1. Carburetor: One-barrel. Displacement: 318 cid. V-8. Brake horsepower: 150 at 4000 rpm. Bore & stroke: 3.91 in. x 3.31 in. Compression ratio: 8.6:1. Carburetor: two-barrel.

VOYAGER — SERIES PB200 — ALL ENGINES: The PB200 came in three sizes and could haul heavier payloads than the PB100. It came equipped with the same standard features.

I.D. DATA: A combination of 13 symbols are used. The first seven identify the model, series, GVW Class (A=6,000 lbs. or less. B=over 6,000 lbs.) engine, model year and assembly plant. The last six are sequential serial numbers. (They begin each year at 000,001.) The symbols for the engines are A=440 V-8; B=225 six; C=225 six; D=440 V-8; E=318 V-8; F=360 V-8 with two-barrel carb; G=318 V-8; H=243 Diesel; J=400 V-8; K=360 V-8; T=360 V-8 with four-barrel carb; X=Special L-6; and Y=Special V-8. The VIN symbols were BB=PB200.

Model	Body Type	Price	Weight	Prod. Total
Voyager Van — 3/4-Ton — 109 in. w.b.				
PB200	Wagon	3955	3805	Note 1
Voyager Van — 3/4-Ton — 127 in. w.b.				
PB200	Wagon	4294	4025	Note 1
PB200	Maxi-Wagon	4494	4280	Note 1

NOTE 1: Van production was 11,701 units for all series.

ENGINE: Six-cylinder. Displacement: 225 cid. Brake horsepower: 95 at 3600 rpm. Bore & stroke: 3.40 in. x 4.12 in. Compression ratio: 8.4:1. Carburetor: One-barrel. Displacement: 318 cid. V-8. Brake horsepower: 150 at 4000 rpm. Bore & stroke: 3.91 in. x 3.31 in. Compression ratio: 8.6:1. Carburetor: two-barrel.

VOYAGER — SERIES PB300 — ALL ENGINES: The PB300 came in two sizes, both had a 127 in. wheelbase. The ultimate was the extended body version. It could carry more people and heavier loads than any other Voyager. In addition to the standard features found on the PB100 and PB200, the PB300 came with larger brakes and TorqueFlite automatic transmission.

I.D. DATA: A combination of 13 symbols were used. The first seven identify the model, series, GVW Class (A=6,000 lbs. or less. B=over 6,000 lbs.) engine, model year and assembly plant. The last six are sequential serial numbers. (They begin each year at 000,001.) The symbols for the engines are A=440 V-8; B=225 six; C=225 six; D=440 V-8; E=318 V-8; F=360 V-8 with two-barrel carburetor; G=318 V-8; H=243 Diesel; J=400 V-8; K=360 V-8; T=360 V-8 with four-barrel carburetor; X=Special L-6; and Y=Special V-8. The VIN symbols were BC=PB300.

Model	Body Type	Price	Weight	Prod. Total
Voyager Van — 1-Ton — 127 in. w.b.				
PB300	Wagon	4934	4315	Note 1
PB300	Maxi-Wagon	5130	4435	Note 1

NOTE 1: Van production was 11,701 units for all series.

ENGINE: [Trail Duster PW100]: Displacement: 318 cid. V-8. Brake horsepower: 155 at 4000 rpm. Bore & stroke: 3.91 in. x 3.31 in. Compression ratio: 8.6:1. Carburetor: two-barrel.

CHASSIS: Wheelbase [PB100/PB200]: 109 in.; [PB100/PB200/PB300]: 127 in. Overall width: 79.8 in. Overall length: [109 in. wheelbase] 176 in.; [127 in. wheelbase] 194 in.; [127 in. wheelbase extended] 212 in. Overall height: [PB100 109 in. wheelbase] 77.2 in.; [PB100 127 in. wheelbase] 77.3 in.; [PB200 109 in. wheelbase] 78.4; [PB200 127 in. wheelbase and 127 in. wheelbase extended] 78.6 in.; [PB300] 79.1 in. Tires [PB100]: E78-15B; [PB200] G78-15B, [PB300] 8.00-16.5D.

OPTIONS [PACKAGES]: Convenience package. Insulation package. Trailer towing package. Sport package: Includes argent and black grille with bright molding around grille; dual bright finish 5 x 7 in. exterior mirrors; bright finish hubcaps; Voyager Sport nameplates; bright taillamp bezels; exterior upper front, side and rear moldings; Sport seat trim (in blue, green, parchment, or black); vinyl side-trim panels; armrests at both sides of the rear bench seat; color-keyed carpeting; cigarette lighter; added insulation; full headliner; padded instrument panel; front and rear bright finish bumpers; fiberglass window trim; bright finish windshield moldings; horn bar; spare tire cover. Optional Sport interior package: Includes cloth-and-vinyl front bucket seats with matching rear bench seat and interior trim. Custom package: Includes Argent and black grille; front and rear painted bumpers; exterior dual 5 x 7 in. painted mirrors; bright finish hubcaps; Custom nameplates; bright taillamp. bezel; upper front and side exterior moldings; color-keyed interior trim; color-keyed floor mats throughout; full headliner; padded instrument panel; instrument cluster trim dress-up; horn bar; cigarette lighter; fiberglass window trim; and spare tire cover.

OPTIONS: Air-conditioning (V-8 models only). Automatic speed control (available with V-8 engines and automatic transmission only). Fifty-nine or 70 amp.-hr. battery. Front and rear bright finish bumpers. Cigarette lighter. Heavy-duty clutch (six-cylinder only). Vented glass rear doors. Tinted glass, windshield or all windows. Passenger compartment headliner. Deluxe heater. Auxiliary heater. Horn bar. Bright finish hubcaps. Padded instrument panel. Interior day/night prismatic mirror. Increased cooling. Oil pressure gauge. Power steering. AM radio. AM/FM radio. Eight-passenger seating (PB200/PB300). Twelve-passenger seating (PB300 with 127 in. wheelbase); 15-passenger seating (PB300 extended). Heavy-duty front and rear shock absorbers. Bright finish wheelcovers (except on PB300). Low-mount exterior mirrors. Inside hood release. Heavy-duty alternator. Sliding side door.

HISTORICAL: Voyager buyers had their choice of 13 exterior colors: Medium blue metallic; Medium gold metallic; Avocado metallic; turquoise; Medium gold; Bright red; Light green; Light blue; yellow; Dark green metallic; Light gold; Bronze metallic; and white. A pair of two-tone paint options were offered: 1) Main color on top, secondary color on bottom. 2) Main color on top and bottom, secondary color in between.

1975 Plymouth Trail Duster With Fiberglass Top

TRAIL DUSTER — PD-100 UTILITY VEHICLE: Big news for the Trail Duster in 1975 was the addition of a two-wheel drive model It looked virtually the same as last year's four-wheel drive version. But it was 2-1/2 in. lower. It also featured independent front suspension.

I.D. DATA: A combination of 13 symbols were used. The first seven identify the model, series, GVW Class (A=6,000 lbs. or less. B=over 6,000 lbs.) engine, model year and assembly plant. The last six are sequential serial numbers. (They begin each year at 000,001.) The symbols for the engines are A=440 V-8; B=225 six; C=225 six; D=440 V-8; E=318 V-8; F=360 V-8 with two-barrel carburetor; G=318 V-8; H=243 Diesel; J=400 V-8; K=360 V-8; T=360 V-8 with four-barrel carburetor; X=Special L-6; and Y=Special V-8.

Model	Body Type	Price	Weight	Prod. Total
Trail Duster — 4x2 — 1/2-Ton				
PD100	Utility	3640	3570	666

ENGINE [Base]: Six-cylinder. Displacement: 225 cid. Brake horsepower: 105 at 3600 rpm. Bore & stroke: 3.40 in. x 4.12 in. Compression ratio: 8.4:1. Carburetor: one-barrel.
ENGINE [Optional]: Displacement: 318 cid. V-8. Brake horsepower: 150 at 4000 rpm. (155 horsepower in California). Bore & stroke: 3.91 in. x 3.31 in. Compression ratio: 8.6:1. Carburetor: two-barrel.

1975 Plymouth Trail Duster With Full Vinyl Enclosure

TRAIL DUSTER PW100 UTILITY VEHICLE: To say the four-wheel drive Trail Duster was little changed for 1975 would be an understatement. The sales catalog used the same cover photo as it had for 1974. Even the new dash looked similar to the old one.

Model	Body Type	Price	Weight	Prod. Total
Trail Duster — 4x4 — 1/2-Ton				
PW100	Utility	4546	4085	3877

CHASSIS: Wheelbase: 106 in. Overall length: 184.6 in. Overall width: 79.5 in. Overall height with roof: [PD100]: 70 in.; [PW100] 72 in. Tires: [Six] E78-15B in.; [V-8] E78-15B. GVW rating: 4,900-6,000 lbs.
TECHNICAL: Four-speed manual transmission (PW100). Three-speed TorqueFlite automatic. Two V-8 engines: 360 cid with two-barrel carburetor and a 440 cid with four-barrel carburetor.
OPTIONS: Sport package: Includes unique bodyside and tailgate trim; bright front and rear bumpers, accents and windshield molding; full foam all-vinyl driver and passenger bucket seats; color-keyed door trim panels with map pockets; console and sun visors. Air-conditioning. Power steering. Automatic speed control. Tachometer. Bright wheelcovers. Trailer towing package. Oil pressure gauge. Passenger seat. Deluxe seats including console, sun visors and seat belts. Rear bench seat. Skid plates. Tinted glass (windshield or all glass). High output heater. Increased cooling. Engine block heater. Hand throttle (not available with TorqueFlite automatic). Step-type rear bumper. Front bumper guards. Steel roof (in body color or vinyl textured white or black). Two-tone (includes moldings and bright taillamp bezels). Dual horn. Bright hubcaps. AM or AM/FM radio. Dealer installed soft top. Thirty-five gallon fuel tank. Front stabilizer bar (PD-100). Heavy-duty shock absorbers. Heavy-duty battery. Heavy-duty alternator. Roll bar. Front passengers seat.

1975 Plymouth Trail Duster With Fiberglass Top

VOYAGER — PB100 WAGON: Styling was identical to 1974, but that wasn't bad. Standard features included: Electronic ignition, driver and front passenger armrests, power front brakes, argent and black grille, front and rear painted bumpers, white hubcaps, dual electric horns, 23-gal. fuel tank, fresh air heater with defrosters, three-passenger bench seat, padded sun visors, spare tire carrier, ashtray, driver compartment headliner, black driver compartment floor mat, Voyager nameplates, and dual painted exterior mirrors.

I.D. DATA: A combination of 13 symbols were used. The first seven identify the model, series, GVW Class (A=6,000 lbs. or less. B=over 6,000 lbs.) engine, model year and assembly plant. The last six are sequential serial numbers. (They begin each year at 000,001.) The symbols for the engines are A=440 V-8; B=225 six; C=225 six; D=440 V-8; E=318 V-8; F=360 V-8 with two-barrel carburetor; G=318 V-8; H=243 Diesel; J=400 V-8; K=360 V-8; T=360 V-8 with four-barrel carburetor; X=Special L-6; and Y=Special V-8. The VIN symbols were BA=PB100.

Model	Body Type	Price	Weight	Prod. Total
Voyager Van — 1/2-Ton — 109 in. w.b.				
PB100	Wagon	4568	3715	3261
Voyager Van — 1/2-Ton — 127 in. w.b.				
PB100	Wagon	4680	3820	1103

ENGINE [Base]: Six-cylinder. Displacement: 225 cid. Brake horsepower: 95 at 3600 rpm. Bore & stroke: 3.40 in. x 4.12 in. Compression ratio: 8.4:1. Carburetor: one-barrel.
ENGINE [Optional]: Displacement: 318 cid. V-8. Brake horsepower: 150 at 4000 rpm.. Bore & stroke: 3.91 in. x 3.31 in. Compression ratio: 8.6:1. Carburetor: two-barrel.

1975 Plymouth PB300 Voyager Sport Wagon (CPD)

VOYAGER — PB200 WAGON: The PB200 came with the same standard features as the PB100. But buyers had their choice of three sizes. In addition, the payload allowances were much higher.
I.D. DATA: A combination of 13 symbols were used. The first seven identify the model, series, GVW Class (A=6,000 lbs. or less. B=over 6,000 lbs.) engine, model year and assembly plant. The last six are sequential serial numbers. (They begin each year at 000,001.) The symbols for the engines are A=440 V-8; B=225 six; C=225 six; D=440 V-8; E=318 V-8; F=360 V-8 with two-barrel carburetor; G=318 V-8; H=243 Diesel; J=400 V-8; K=360 V-8; T=360 V-8 with four-barrel carburetor; X=Special L-6; and Y=Special V-8. The VIN symbols were BB=PB200.

Model	Body Type	Price	Weight	Prod. Total
Voyager Van — 3/4-Ton — 109 in. w.b.				
PB200	Wagon	4668	3805	399
Voyager Van — 3/4-Ton — 127 in. w.b.				
PB200	Wagon	5102	4025	4237
PB200	Maxi-Wagon	5300	4280	1441

ENGINE: Same as PB100.
VOYAGER — PB300 WAGON: For maximum load capacities, buyers ordered the PB300 Voyager. In addition to the standard features found on the PB100, it came with the axle jack and TorqueFlite automatic transmission.
I.D. DATA: A combination of 13 symbols are used. The first seven identify the model, series, GVW Class (A=6,000 lbs. or less. B=over 6,000 lbs.) engine, model year and assembly plant. The last six are sequential serial numbers. (They begin each year at 000,001.) The symbols for the engines are A=440 V-8; B=225 six; C=225 six; D=440 V-8; E=318 V-8; F=360 V-8 with two-barrel carb; G=318 V-8; H=243 Diesel; J=400 V-8; K=360 V-8; T=360 V-8 with four-barrel carb; X=Special L-6; and Y=Special V-8. The VIN symbols were BC=PB300.

Model	Body Type	Price	Weight	Prod. Total
Voyager Van — 1-Ton — 127 in. w.b.				
PB300	Wagon	5634	4140	802
PB300	Maxi-Wagon	5811	4435	3305

ENGINE: See PB100 (318 cid V-8 specifications).
CHASSIS: Wheelbase [PB100/PB200]: 109 in.; [PB100/PB200/PB300]: 127 in. Overall width: 79.8 in. Overall length: [109 in. wheelbase 176 in.; [127 in. wheelbase] 194 in.; [127 in. wheelbase extended] 212 in. Overall height: [PB100/109 in. wheelbase]: 77.2 in.; [PB100/127 in. wheelbase] 77.3 in.; [PB200/109 in. wheelbase] 78.4 in.; [PB200/127 in. wheelbase] 78.6 in.; [PB300] 79.1 in. Tires: [PB100/109 in. wheelbase]: E78-15B; [PB100/127 in. wheelbase] F78-15B; [PB200] G78-15B; [PB300] 8.00-16.5D.
TECHNICAL: [PB100/PB200] TorqueFlite automatic transmission.
OPTION PACKAGES: Convenience package. Trailer-towing package (two). Custom Package: includes Argent silver and black grille; front and rear painted bumpers; white-painted dual 5 x 7 in. exterior mirrors; bright finish hubcaps; Voyager Custom nameplates; bright taillamp bezels; upper front and side exterior moldings; color-keyed interior, side trim panels, and floor mats; full headliner; padded instrument panel; instrument cluster trim dress-up; horn bar; cigarette lighter; fiberglass window trim; and spare tire cover. Sport Package: includes Argent silver and black grille with bright molding around grille; dual bright finish 5 x 7 in. mirrors; bright finish hubcaps; Voyager and Sport nameplates; bright taillamp bezels; exterior upper front, side and rear moldings; Sport seat trim; color-keyed carpeting; full headliner; padded instrument panel; bright finish instrument cluster trim; padded vinyl trim bodyside panel with woodgrain; front and rear bright finish bumpers; fiberglass window trim; added insulation; bright finish windshield molding; bright finish side and rear window moldings; horn bar; cigarette lighter; Spare tire cover; all-vinyl front bucket seats in blue, green, parchment, or black; optional cloth-and-vinyl seats in the same colors. Premium Trim Package: includes (for Sport) cloth and vinyl seats; parchment or gold vinyl trim on doors; carpeted floors, engine housing, seat risers, legs; and more.
CONVENIENCE OPTIONS: Single rear door. Left- and right-side low-mount mirrors. Steel-belted, radial-ply white sidewall tires. Push-button AM/FM radio. Air-conditioning (V-8 models only.) Automatic speed control. (Available with V-8 engines and automatic transmission only.) Front and rear bright finish bumpers (standard or Voyager Sport). Heavy-duty clutch (six-cylinder only.) Vented glass rear doors. Tinted glass (windshield only or all windows). Passenger compartment headliner. Deluxe heater. Auxiliary heater. Horn bar. Bright finish hubcaps. Padded instrument panel. Interior day/night prismatic mirror. Increased cooling. Oil pressure gauge. Power steering. AM radio. Eight-passenger seating (PB200/PB300). Twelve-passenger seating (PB300 127 in. wheelbase and extended body models). Fifteen-passenger seating (PB300 extended. Front and rear heavy-duty shock absorbers. Bright finish wheelcovers (PB100/PB200). Inside hood release. Heavy-duty alternator (55 amp. and 72 amp.). Sliding side door. Heavy-duty rear leaf springs (PB100/PB300). Five-stud disc wheels, [PB100/PB200] 15 in. x 6.50 in.; [PB300] 16.5 in. x 6.75 in. Two-tone paint (main color on top, secondary color on bottom or main color on top and bottom, secondary color in between).

1976 PLYMOUTH

TRAIL DUSTER — SERIES PD-100 — ALL ENGINES: The attractive styling of last year's model was unchanged. In fact, some of the same photos used in the 1975 Trail Duster literature showed up in the 1976 sales catalog. Standard features included: Full-foam all-vinyl bucket seats; armrest pads; color-keyed padded instrument panel; bright front and rear bumpers; fuse box located on top of glove box; three-speed manual transmission; and 24-gal. fuel tank.
I.D. DATA: A combination of 13 symbols were used. The first seven identify the model, series, GVW Class (A=6,000 lbs. or less. B=over 6,000 lbs.) engine, model year and assembly plant. The last six are sequential serial numbers. (They begin each year at 000,001.) The symbols for the engines are A=440 V-8; B=225 six; C=225 six; D=440 V-8; E=318 V-8; F=360 V-8 with two-barrel carburetor; G=318 V-8; H=243 Diesel; J=400 V-8; K=360 V-8; T=360 V-8 with four-barrel carburetor; X=Special L-6; and Y=Special V-8.

Model	Body Type	Price	Weight	Prod. Total
Trail Duster — 4x2 — 1/2-Ton				
PD100	Utility	3702	3570	4255

NOTE 1: Production total is for both 4x2 and 4x4 Trail Dusters.
ENGINE [Base]: Six-cylinder. Displacement: 225 cid. Brake horsepower: 100 at 3600 rpm. Bore & stroke: 3.40 in. x 4.12 in. Compression ratio: 8.4:1. Carburetor: one-barrel.
ENGINE [Optional]: Displacement: 318 cid. V-8. Brake horsepower: 150 at 4000 rpm. (155 horsepower in California). Bore & stroke: 3.91 in. x 3.31 in. Compression ratio: 8.6:1. Carburetor: two-barrel.

1976 Plymouth Trail Duster SE 4x4 Utility

TRAIL DUSTER — SERIES PW100 — ALL ENGINES: Sales literature called the four-wheel drive Trail Duster "a pure adventure machine that could take you to all those places in this world you haven't been yet." The PW100 came with the same standard features as

the two-wheel drive PD100, plus it had a front stabilizer bar and higher capacity front axle. This full-time four-wheel drive vehicle had five shift positions for on-road cruising and off road use: 1) Low-lock for deep snow, mud, sand. 2) Low for mountainous and hilly terrain. 3) Neutral. 4) High for paved surfaces. 5) High-lock for snow, mud sand.

I.D. DATA: A combination of 13 symbols were used. The first seven identify the model, series, GVW Class (A=6,000 lbs. or less. B=over 6,000 lbs.) engine, model year and assembly plant. The last six are sequential serial numbers. (They begin each year at 000,001.) The symbols for the engines are A=440 V-8; B=225 six; C=225 six; D=440 V-8; E=318 V-8; F=360 V-8 with two-barrel carb; G=318 V-8; H=243 Diesel; J=400 V-8; K=360 V-8; T=360 V-8 with four-barrel carb; X=Special L-6; and Y=Special V-8.

Model	Body Type	Price	Weight	Prod. Total
Trail Duster — 4x4 — 1/2-Ton				
PW100	Utility	4834	3980	Note 1

NOTE 1: See Trail Duster production total above.

CHASSIS: Wheelbase: 106 in. Overall length: 184.6 in. Overall width: 79.5 in. Overall height with roof: 72 in. Tires: E78-15B. GVW Rating: 4,900-6,100 lbs.

TECHNICAL: Four-speed manual transmission (PW100). Three-speed TorqueFlite automatic transmission. Three V-8 engines: 360 cid with two-barrel carburetor (available in California only); 400 cid with two-barrel carburetor; 440 cid with four-barrel carburetor.

CONVENIENCE OPTIONS: Sport package: Deluxe full-foam all-vinyl front bucket seats; color-keyed door trim panels with map pockets; center console with removable styrofoam beverage chest; windshield moldings; and unique bodyside, tailgate and inteior trim. Air-conditioning. Power steering. Automatic speed control. Tachometer. Bright finish or premium wheelcovers. Trailer towing package, includes 52 amp. alternator; 70 amp.-hr. battery; wiring harness; heavy-duty variable load flasher; and increased engine cooling system. Sno-Fiter package (PW100). Convenience package (standard on Sport). Oil pressure gauge. Electric clock. Rear bench seat. Skid plates. Tinted glass (windshield or all glass). High output heater. Increased cooling. Engine block heater. Hand throttle (not available with TorqueFlite automatic). Step type rear bumper. Protection package (includes front bumper guards and door edge protectors). Steel roof (available in body color or vinyl textured white or black). Two-tone paint (includes moldings and bright taillamp bezels). Dual horn. Bright hubcaps. AM or AM/FM radio. Dealer installed soft top. Thirty-five gallon fuel tank. Heavy-duty shocks. Roll bar. Heavy-duty front stabilizer bar. Low mount mirrors. Cigar lighter. Boca Raton cloth-and-vinyl seats in parchment (hardtops with Sport option only).

1976 Plymouth Voyager Sport Wagon (JAG)

VOYAGER — SERIES PB100 — ALL ENGINES: Voyager styling was carried over from the previous model year. Standard equipment included: Forty-eight amp. alternator; driver and front passenger armrest; driver's compartment ashtray; passenger-side double doors with vented glass; door locks, all doors; electronic ignition system; a 22.1 gal. fuel tank; glove box door with push-button operated latch; fresh air heater with defrosters; dual electric horns; bumper jack; interior mirror; oil pressure indicator light; driver and front passenger bucket seats; three-passenger rear bench seat; padded sun visors; spare tire carrier; two-speed windshield wipers with arm-mounted washers; power front disc brakes; Argent and black grille; front and rear white painted bumpers; white painted hubcaps; dual 5 in. x 7 in. painted exterior mirrors; black driver's compartment floor mat; driver compartment headliner; Voyager nameplates; and three-speed manual transmission.

I.D. DATA: A combination of 13 symbols were used. The first seven identify the model, series, GVW Class (A=6,000 lbs. or less. B=over 6,000 lbs.) engine, model year and assembly plant. The last six are sequential serial numbers. (They begin each year at 000,001.) The symbols for the engines are A=440 V-8; B=225 six; C=225 six; D=440 V-8; E=318 V-8; F=360 V-8 with two-barrel carburetor; G=318 V-8; H=243 Diesel; J=400 V-8; K=360 V-8; T=360 V-8 with four-barrel carburetor; X=Special L-6; and Y=Special V-8.

Model	Body Type	Price	Weight	Prod. Total
Voyager Van — 1/2-Ton — 109 in. w.b.				
PB100	Wagon	4768	3715	Note 1
Voyager Van — 1/2-Ton — 127 in. w.b.				
PB100	Wagon	4877	3820	Note 1

NOTE 1: Production was 10,819 units for all three Voyager series.

ENGINE [Base]: Six-cylinder. Displacement: 225 cid. Brake horsepower: 95 at 3600 rpm. Bore & stroke: 3.40 in. x 4.12 in. Compression ratio: 8.4:1. Carburetor: one-barrel.

ENGINE [Optional]: Displacement: 318 cid. V-8. Brake horsepower: 150 at 4000 rpm.. Bore & stroke: 3.91 in. x 3.31 in. Compression ratio: 8.6:1. Carburetor: two-barrel.

VOYAGER — SERIES PB200 — ALL ENGINES: The allowable driver, passenger, luggage and load weight for the lowest price 109 in. wheelbase PB200 wagon was nearly 70 percent greater than that for the equivalent PB100 Voyager. Buyers had their pick of three sizes of PB200s. Standard features were the same as those for the PB100.

I.D. DATA: A combination of 13 symbols were used. The first seven identify the model, series, GVW Class (A=6,000 lbs. or less. B=over 6,000 lbs.) engine, model year and assembly plant. The last six are sequential serial numbers. (They begin each year at 000,001.) The symbols for the engines are A=440 V-8; B=225 six; C=225 six; D=440 V-8; E=318 V-8; F=360 V-8 with two-barrel carb; G=318 V-8; H=243 Diesel; J=400 V-8; K=360 V-8; T=360 V-8 with four-barrel carb; X=Special L-6; and Y=Special V-8.

Model	Body Type	Price	Weight	Prod. Total
Voyager Van — 3/4-Ton — 109 in. w.b.				
PB200	Wagon	4863	3805	Note 1
Voyager Van — 3/4-Ton — 127 in. w.b.				
PB200	Wagon	4956	4025	Note 1
PB200	Maxi-Wagon	5177	4280	Note 1

NOTE 1: Production was 10,819 units for all three Voyager series.

ENGINE [Base]: Six-cylinder. Displacement: 225 cid. Brake horsepower: 95 at 3600 rpm. Bore & stroke: 3.40 in. x 4.12 in. Compression ratio: 8.4:1. Carburetor: one-barrel.

ENGINE [Optional]: Displacement: 318 cid. V-8. Brake horsepower: 150 at 4000 rpm. Bore & stroke: 3.91 in. x 3.31 in. Compression ratio: 8.6:1. Carburetor: two-barrel.

VOYAGER — SERIES PB300 — ALL ENGINES: The PB300 may have looked like the other series, but it was capable of hauling much heavier loads. TorqueFlite automatic transmission, an axle jack and larger brakes were standard. In addition to the equipment listed for the PB100.

I.D. DATA: A combination of 13 symbols were used. The first seven identify the model, series, GVW Class (A=6,000 lbs. or less. B=over 6,000 lbs.) engine, model year and assembly plant. The last six are sequential serial numbers. (They begin each year at 000,001.) The symbols for the engines are A=440 V-8; B=225 six; C=225 six; D=440 V-8; E=318 V-8; F=360 V-8 with two-barrel carburetor; G=318 V-8; H=243 Diesel; J=400 V-8; K=360 V-8; T=360 V-8 with four-barrel carburetor; X=Special L-6; and Y=Special V-8.

Model	Body Type	Price	Weight	Prod. Total
Voyager Van — 1-Ton — 127 in. w.b.				
PB300	Wagon	5644	4140	Note 1
PB300	Maxi-Wagon	5841	4280	Note 1

NOTE 1: Production was 10,819 units for all three Voyager series.

ENGINE [Optional]: Displacement: 318 cid. V-8. Brake horsepower: 150 at 4000 rpm. Bore & stroke: 3.91 in. x 3.31 in. Compression ratio: 8.6:1. Carburetor: two-barrel.

CHASSIS: Wheelbase [PB100/PB200] 109 in.; [PB100/PB200/PB300] 127 in. Overall width: 79.8 in. Overall length: [109 in. wheelbase] 176 in.; [127 in. wheelbase] 194 in.; [127 in. wheelbase Maxi-Wagon] 212 in. Overall height: 80.8 in. Tires: [PB100/109 in. wheelbase]: E78-15B; [PB100/127 in. wheelbase] F78-15B; [PB200/109 in. wheelbase and 127 in. wheelbase] G78-15B; [B200/127 in. wheelbase] H78-15B; [PB300] 8.00-16.5D.

1976 Plymouth Voyager Sport Maxi-Wagon (OCW)

OPTIONAL PACKAGES: Convenience. Insulation. Trailer Towing: Light and heavy-duty. Includes 52 amp. alternator, 70 amp.-hr. battery, increased cooling, heavy-duty variable load flasher and wiring harness. Heavy-duty shock absorbers and 15 in. heavy-duty rims. Eight-passenger seating: (PB200;PB300). Twelve-passenger seating (PB300). Fifteen-passenger seating (PB300). Custom: Argent and black grille. Front and rear white painted bumpers. Dual white painted exterior mirrors (5 in. x 7 in.). Bright finish hubcaps. Custom nameplates. Bright taillamp bezels. Upper front and side exterior moldings. Color-keyed interior trim. Color-keyed floor mats throughout. Full headliner. Padded instrument panel. Instrument cluster trim dress-up. Horn bar. Cigarette lighter. Fiberglass window trim. Spare tire cover. Low-back front bucket seats in blue, green, parchment or black. Sport Option: Argent silver and black grille with bright molding around grille. Dual bright finish 5 in. x 7 in. exterior mirrors. Bright finish hubcaps. Voyager Sport nameplates. Bright taillamp. Bezels. Exterior upper front, side, and rear moldings. Deluxe vinyl seat trim. Color-keyed carpeting. Full headliner. Padded instrument panel with simulated wood-grain insert. Bright finish instrument cluster trim. Padded vinyl trim side panel with wood grain. Front and rear bright finish bumpers. Fiberglass window trim. Added insulation. Bright finish windshield molding. Bright finish side and rear window moldings. Horn bar. Cigarette lighter. Spare tire cover. Sport optional interior: Cloth-and-vinyl high-back front bucket seats with inboard fold-down front armrests in a woven texture available in blue, green or parchment. Matching three-passenger rear bench seat. Color-keyed carpeting, padded side panel and door trim. Premium trim: Bright front and rear bumpers. Dual bright 5 in. x 7 in. exterior mirrors. Bright finish hubcaps. Bright taillamp bezels. Voyager and Sport nameplates. Bright molding around grille, windshield, side and rear windows (except front doors). High-back deluxe cloth-and-vinyl bucket seats with fold down armrests and deluxe cloth-and-vinyl bench seats. Bright instrument cluster trim. Driver and passenger compartment special door and side panels carpeting. Carpeting on lower engine compartment. Full headliner. Spare tire cover. Additional insulation. Cigarette lighter. Fiberglass window trim.

CONVENIENCE OPTIONS: Air-conditioning (front or front and rear, V-8 models only). A 59 amp. or 70 amp.-hr. battery. Bright finish front and rear bumpers. Cigarette lighter. Heavy-duty clutch (225 six-cylinder only). Vented glass rear doors. Tinted glass, windshield only or all windows. Passenger compartment headliner. Deluxe heater. Auxiliary rear heater. Horn bar. Bright finish hubcaps. Padded instrument panel. Interior day/night prismatic mirror. Increased cooling. Oil pressure gauge. Power steering. AM or AM/FM radio. Thirty-six gallon gas tank. Front and rear heavy-duty shock absorbers. Two bright finish wheelcovers (except on PB300). Left and right low-mount exterior mirrors. Inside hood release. Heavy-duty alternator (52 and 63 amp.). Sliding side door. One piece rear door with fixed glass. Chrome style road wheels (except PB300). Automatic speed control, available with V-8 automatic transmission models only.

POWERTRAIN OPTIONS: TorqueFlite automatic transmission (PB100/PB200). 360 cid V-8. 440 cid V-8 (PB200/PB300).

NOTE: The 1976 Plymouth Voyager was available in 14 exterior colors: Bright red; yellow; russet; Light blue; Light gold; Bright blue metallic; Medium gold metallic; Light green metallic; Sunstone; Bright green metallic; Bright tan metallic; Dark green metallic; Silver Cloud metallic; and white. Buyers had their choice of a pair of two-tone paint procedures; 1) Main color on top, secondary color on bottom. 2) Main color on top and bottom, secondary color in between.

1977 PLYMOUTH

TRAIL DUSTER — SERIES PD100 — ALL ENGINES: The Trail Duster received a facelift for 1977. Vertical signal lights were integrated into the new, horizontal bar grille. The Plymouth nameplate was moved to the face of the hood. A different style of two toning was used. It sandwiched the contrasting color in a wide band, on the sides and lower grille. Standard features included: Low-back front bucket seats; power disc brakes; electronic ignition system; dual outside mirrors; painted hubcaps; and three-speed manual transmission.

I.D. DATA: A combination of 13 symbols were used. The first seven identify the model, series, GVW Class (A=6,000 lbs. or less. B=over 6,000 lbs.) engine, model year and assembly plant. The last six are sequential serial numbers. (They begin each year at 000,001.) The symbols for the engines are A=440 V-8; B=225 six; C=225 six; D=440 V-8; E=318 V-8; F=360 V-8 with two-barrel carburetor; G=318 V-8; H=243 Diesel; J=400 V-8; K=360 V-8; T=360 V-8 with four-barrel carburetor; X=Special L-6; and Y=Special V-8.

Model	Body Type	Price	Weight	Prod. Total
Trail Duster — 4x2 — 1/2-Ton				
PD100	Utility	4030	3570	—

ENGINE: Six-cylinder. Displacement: 225 cid. Brake horsepower: 95 at 3600 rpm. Bore & stroke: 3.40 in. x 4.12 in. Compression ratio: 8.4:1. Carburetor: one-barrel.

TRAIL DUSTER — SERIES PW100 — ALL ENGINES: The four-wheel drive Trail Duster had the same basic features as the standard version, plus a front stabilizer bar. It was also a couple inches taller.

I.D. DATA: A combination of 13 symbols were used. The first seven identify the model, series, GVW Class (A=6,000 lbs. or less. B=over 6,000 lbs.) engine, model year and assembly plant. The last six are sequential serial numbers. (They begin each year at 000,001.) The symbols for the engines are A=440 V-8; B=225 six; C=225 six; D=440 V-8; E=318 V-8; F=360 V-8 with two-barrel carburetor; G=318 V-8; H=243 Diesel; J=400 V-8; K=360 V-8; T=360 V-8 with four-barrel carburetor; X=Special L-6; and Y=Special V-8.

Model	Body Type	Price	Weight	Prod. Total
Trail Duster — 4x4 — 1/2-Ton				
PW100	Utility	5045	3940	—

ENGINE: Same as PD100 (except in California where standard engine was: 318 cid V-8. Brake horsepower: 150 at 4000 rpm. Bore & stroke: 3.91 in. x 3.31 in. Compression ratio: 8.6:1. Carburetor: two-barrel.

CHASSIS: Wheelbase: 106 in. Overall length: 184.6 in. Overall width: 79.5 in. Overall height [PD100] 70 in.; [PW100] 72 in. Tires: E78-15B. GVW Rating: 4,900-6,100 lbs.

1977 Plymouth Trail Duster 4x4 Open Utility (OCW)

TECHNICAL: Four-speed manual transmission with either wide- or close-ratio (PW100). Three-speed TorqueFlite automatic transmission. 318 cid V-8 with two-barrel carburetor. 360 cid V-8 with two-barrel carburetor. 400 cid V-8 with two-barrel carburetor. 440 cid V-8 with four-barrel carburetor.

1977 Plymouth Trail Duster Sport Utility (CHC)

CONVENIENCE OPTIONS: Sport interior package: Includes deluxe vinyl bucket seats with matching padded door trim and a console beverage chest with removable insulated liner; high-back Command seats in striped cloth-and-vinyl with matching padded door trim with pull handles and carpeted lower panels; lockable console; inboard fold-down armrests; color-keyed carpeting; Removable steel roof. Soft vinyl roof with roll-up windows. Three-passenger rear bench seat. Sport padded instrument panel with rosewood-grain applique and panel trim molding. Air-conditioning. Power steering. Speed control. Sno-plow package (PW100). Roll bar. Outside spare tire carrier. Eight-spoke white-painted road wheels with raised white lettering on wide tires. Chrome-styled slotted road wheels with raised white lettering on wide all-terrain 10.00-15 LT tires. Trailer-assist package: Includes 63 amp. alternator; 7 amp.-hr. battery; wiring harness; heavy-duty variable load flasher; and increased engine cooling system. Low-mount mirrors. Convenience package. Oil pressure gauge. Electric clock (not available with tachometer). High output heater. Engine block heater. Hand throttle. Step type rear bumper. Protection package (front bumper guards and door edge protectors). Two-tone body with moldings. Dual electric horn. Bright hubcaps. AM radio. AM/FM radio. Thirty-five gallon fuel tank. Heavy-duty shock absorbers. Cigar lighter. Heavy-duty front stabilizer bar.

NOTE: 1977 Trail Dusters were available in 14 colors: Harvest gold; yellow; russet; Light green metallic; Bright red; Medium green sunfire metallic; Russet sunfire metallic; Bright tan metallic; Light tan; Silver cloud metallic; white; Light blue; Black sunfire metallic; Medium blue metallic.

1977 Plymouth PB100 Voyager Custom Wagon (CPD)

VOYAGER — SERIES PB100 — ALL ENGINES: The 1977 Voyager looked the same as last year's model. Standard features included: Vinyl interior; driver and front passenger armrests; passenger-side double doors with vented glass; electronic ignition system; 22-gal. fuel tank; dual electric horns; padded sun visors; spare tire carrier; two-speed windshield wipers with washers; power front disc brakes; Argent silver and black grille; painted front and rear bumpers; dual painted mirrors; painted hubcaps; black driver and passenger compartment floor mat; driver compartment headliner; and three-speed manual transmission.

I.D. DATA: A combination of 13 symbols are used. The first seven identify the model, series, GVW Class (A=6,000 lbs. or less. B=over 6,000 lbs.) engine, model year and assembly plant. The last six are sequential serial numbers. (They begin each year at 000,001.) The symbols for the engines are A=440 V-8; B=225 six; C=225 six; D=440 V-8; E=318 V-8; F=360 V-8 with two-barrel carb; G=318 V-8; H=243 Diesel; J=400 V-8; K=360 V-8; T=360 V-8 with four-barrel carb; X=Special L-6; and Y=Special V-8.

Model	Body Type	Price	Weight	Prod. Total
Voyager Van — 1/2-Ton — 109 in. w.b.				
PB100	Wagon	5198	3715	—
Voyager Van — 1/2-Ton — 127 in. w.b.				
PB100	Wagon	5307	3820	—

ENGINE [Base]: Six-cylinder. Displacement: 225 cid. Brake horsepower: 95 at 3600 rpm. Bore & stroke: 3.40 in. x 4.12 in. Compression ratio: 8.4:1. Carburetor: one-barrel.
ENGINE [Optional]: Displacement: 318 cid. V-8. Brake horsepower: 150 at 4000 rpm.. Bore & stroke: 3.91 in. x 3.31 in. Compression ratio: 8.6:1. Carburetor: two-barrel.

1977 Plymouth Voyager Sport Wagon (OCW)

VOYAGER — SERIES PB200 — ALL ENGINES: The PB200 came with many of the same features as the PB100 Voyager. The maximum weight loads in PB200 wagons were more than double those in the standard line.

I.D. DATA: A combination of 13 symbols were used. The first seven identify the model, series, GVW Class (A=6,000 lbs. or less. B=over 6,000 lbs.) engine, model year and assembly plant. The last six are sequential serial numbers. (They begin each year at 000,001.) The symbols for the engines are A=440 V-8; B=225 six; C=225 six; D=440 V-8; E=318 V-8; F=360 V-8 with two-barrel carb; G=318 V-8; H=243 Diesel; J=400 V-8; K=360 V-8; T=360 V-8 with four-barrel carburetor; X=Special L-6; and Y=Special V-8.

Model	Body Type	Price	Weight	Prod. Total
Voyager Van — 3/4-Ton — 109 in. w.b.				
PB200	Wagon	5266	3805	

Voyager Van — 3/4-Ton — 127 in. w.b.

PB200	Wagon	5384	4025	—
PB200	Maxi-Wagon	5539	4280	—

ENGINE: Same as PB100.

VOYAGER — SERIES PB300 — ALL ENGINES: Buyers who wanted maximum load carrying capacity order this series. LoadFlite automatic transmission with fluid level warning light was standard.

I.D. DATA: A combination of 13 symbols were used. The first seven identify the model, series, GVW Class (A=6,000 lbs. or less. B=over 6,000 lbs.) engine, model year and assembly plant. The last six are sequential serial numbers. (They begin each year at 000,001.) The symbols for the engines are A=440 V-8; B=225 six; C=225 six; D=440 V-8; E=318 V-8; F=360 V-8 with two-barrel carburetor; G=318 V-8; H=243 Diesel; J=400 V-8; K=360 V-8; T=360 V-8 with four-barrel carburetor; X=Special L-6; and Y=Special V-8.

Model	Body Type	Price	Weight	Prod. Total
Voyager Van — 1-Ton — 127 in. w.b.				
PB300	Wagon	6085	4140	—
PB300	Maxi-Wagon	6240	4280	—

ENGINE: Displacement: 318 cid. V-8. (See PB100).

CHASSIS: Wheelbase [PB100/PB200] 109 in.; [PB100/PB200/PB300]: 127 in. Overall width: 79.8 in. Overall length: [109 in. wheelbase] 176 in.; [127 in. wheelbase] 194 in.; [127 in. wheelbase extended] 212 in. Overall height: 80.8 in. Tires: [109 in. wheelbase]: E78-15B; [PB100/127 in. wheelbase] F78-15B; [PB200] H78-15B; [PB300] 8.00 x 16.5D.

TECHNICAL: Four-speed manual, overdrive (PB100). LoadFlite automatic transmission. 360 cid V-8. 400 cid V-8 (PB200/PB300) and 440 cid V-8 (PB200/PB300).

OPTIONAL PACKAGES: Convenience. Ignition time delay light. Cigar lighter and light. Courtesy light front door. Glove box light. 10 in. day/night rearview mirror. In-cab actuated hood lock release. Premium Trim: (127 in. wheelbase V-8 models only). Bright front and rear bumpers. Dual 5 x 7 in. bright mirrors. Bright finish hubcaps and taillamp bezels. Bright molding around grille, windshield, side and rear windows. High-back deluxe cloth and vinyl bucket seats with fold down armrests and matching bench seat. Bright instrument cluster trim. Carpeting. Vinyl covered full headliner. Spare tire cover. Additional insulation. Cigarette lighter. Fiberglass window trim. Exterior upper front, side and rear bright moldings. Padded instrument panel with woodgrain inserts. Horn bar. Voyager Sport optional interior: Woven texture cloth and vinyl high back Command seats with inboard fold-down armrests. Three-passenger rear bench seat. Swivel front seats optional. Dual armrest on passenger seat. Color-keyed carpeting, padded side panel trim and door trim. (Available on 127 in. wheelbase V-8 models only.) Easy Order Package: Automatic transmission. Convenience package. Dual 5 x 7 in. bright mirrors. Two-tone paint. Power steering. AM radio. Scuff pads. Dome lamps witches, side and rear door operated. Wheelcovers. Luxury Package: Automatic transmission. Convenience package. AM/FM radio. Scuff pads. Power steering. Dome lamp switches. Premium wheelcovers. Air-conditioning. Tinted glass. Speed control. Door edge protection. High back cloth and vinyl Command front bucket seats. Two-tone paint. Sport Interior: (127 in. wheelbase V-8 models only) Deluxe pleated all vinyl front bucket seats. A matching three-passenger rear seat. Color-keyed vinyl door trim with padded side panels. carpeting. Dual bright finish 5 x 7 in. mirrors. Voyager Sport nameplates. Full vinyl covered headliner. Padded instrument panel with simulated woodgrain insert. Bright finish front and rear bumpers. Added insulation. Bright finish windshield, side, and rear window moldings. Cigarette lighter. Spare tire cover. Custom Package: Low-back all vinyl front bucket seat (in blue, green, parchment and black). Padded dash. Horn bar. Cigarette lighter. Bright finish hubcaps. Custom nameplates. Bright taillamp bezel. Upper front and side exterior moldings. Color-keyed floor mats. Full length headliner. Instrument cluster trim dress up. Fiberglass window trim. Spare tire cover.

CONVENIENCE OPTIONS: Trailer towing (light- or heavy-duty) setup, includes 63 amp. alternator, 70 amp.-hr. battery, increased cooling, heavy-duty variable load flasher and wiring harness. Heavy-duty shock absorbers. Air-conditioning (front or front and rear). Automatic speed control (available with V-8 automatic transmission models only). Front and rear bright finish bumpers. Cigarette lighter. Heavy-duty 11 in. clutch (225 six-cylinder only). Vented glass in optional dual rear doors. Tinted glass, windshield only or all windows. Sunscreen glass in rear compartment windows and side door glass (five- and eight-passenger wagons only). Passenger compartment headliner. Deluxe heater. Auxiliary rear heater. Horn bar. Bright finish hubcaps. Padded instrument panel. Interior day/night prismatic 10 in. mirror. Increased cooling. Oil pressure gauge. Tape stripes. Power steering. AM or AM/FM radio. Thirty-six gallon fuel tank. Eight-passenger seating (PB200/PB300). Twelve-passenger seating (PB300). Fifteen-passenger seating (PB300 Maxi-Wagon). Driver and passenger swivel seats with dual armrests on passenger seat and inboard armrest on driver's seat (Sport and Premium Package only). Bright finish wheelcovers. Exterior mirrors, white painted or bright finish. Inside hood release. Heavy-duty alternator. Sliding side door (127 in. wheelbase only). Dual rear door with fixed or vented glass. Chrome-style road wheels (PB100, PB200). Wide sport road wheels, chrome disc or white painted spoke (PB100, PB200). Fuel pacer system. Front door edge protectors.

1978 PLYMOUTH

TRAIL DUSTER — SERIES PD100 — ALL ENGINES: After major restyling in 1977, the Trail Duster exterior design was left alone for 1978. New optional items included: different seats; sunscreen glass; Hurst transfer case gear selector; three-spoke Tuff steering wheel and tilt steering column; CB radio integrated with an AM/FM stereo; and a skylight sun roof. Among the standard equipment was: full-foam deluxe-vinyl bucket seats; armrest pads; padded instrument panel; 10 in. day/night inside rearview mirror; dual 5 x 7 in. bright exterior mirrors; and bright front and rear bumpers.

I.D. DATA: A combination of 13 symbols were used. The first seven identify the model, series, GVW Class (A=6,000 lbs. or less. B=over 6,000 lbs.) engine, model year and assembly plant. The last six are sequential serial numbers. (They begin each year at 000,001.) The symbols for the engines are A=440 V-8; B=225 six; C=225 six; D=440 V-8; E=318 V-8; F=360 V-8 with two-barrel carburetor; G=318 V-8; H=243 Diesel; J=400 V-8; K=360 V-8; T=360 V-8 with four-barrel carburetor; X=Special L-6; and Y=Special V-8.

Model	Body Type	Price	Weight	Prod. Total
Trail Duster — 4x2 — 1/2-Ton				
PD100	Utility	4647	3570	—

ENGINE: Six-cylinder. Displacement: 225 cid. Brake horsepower: 100 at 3600 rpm. Bore & stroke: 3.4 in. x 4.12 in. Compression ratio: 8.4:1. Carburetor: two-barrel.

TRAIL DUSTER — SERIES PW100 — ALL ENGINES: The PW100 featured full-time four-wheel drive. It had an inter-axle differential that proportioned power to both the front and rear axles. That allowed the wheels on one axle to travel at a different rate of speed from those on the other axle. This supposedly cut down on tire wear and improved the vehicle's handling. A new color offered this year on the PW100 and PD100, was sunrise orange.

I.D. DATA: A combination of 13 symbols were used. The first seven identify the model, series, GVW Class (A=6,000 lbs. or less. B=over 6,000 lbs.) engine, model year and assembly plant. The last six are sequential serial numbers. (They begin each year at 000,001.) The symbols for the engines are A=440 V-8; B=225 six; C=225 six; D=440 V-8; E=318 V-8; F=360 V-8 with two-barrel carburetor; G=318 V-8; H=243 Diesel; J=400 V-8; K=360 V-8; T=360 V-8 with four-barrel carburetor; X=Special L-6; and Y=Special V-8.

Model	Body Type	Price	Weight	Prod. Total
Trail Duster — 4x4 — 1/2-Ton				
PW100	Utility	5684	4085	—

ENGINE: Same as PD100.

1978 Plymouth Trail Duster 4x4 Utility (OCW)

CHASSIS: Wheelbase: 106 in. Overall length: 184.6 in. Overall width: 79.5 in. Overall height (PW100): 74.2 in. Tires: H78-15B (bias polyester). BSW GVW Rating: 6,100 lbs.

TECHNICAL: Four-speed manual transmission with either wide or close space ratio. Three-speed LoadFlite automatic transmission. Four V-8 engines: 318 cid. with two-barrel carburetor; 360 cid. with two-barrel carburetor; 400 cid. with two-barrel carburetor and 440 cid. V-8 with four-barrel carburetor.

CONVENIENCE OPTIONS: Air-conditioning. Tinted glass. Sunscreen glass for quarter and rear windows. Step type rear bumper. Cigar lighter. Electric clock. Thirty-five gallon fuel tank. Oil pressure gauge. Deluxe heater. Dual electric horn. Increased cooling. Low mount mirrors (with or without extended arm). Power steering. Radios: AM, AM/FM, AM/FM stereo, AM/FM stereo with 8-track, AM with CB transceiver, AM/FM with CB transceiver. Roll bar. Removable steel hardtop roof. Soft top roof (dealer installed). Skylite sun roof. Three-passenger rear bench seat. Heavy-duty shock absorbers. Skid plate. Automatic speed control. Heavy-duty front stabilizer bar. Tuff steering wheel. Tilt steering column. Tachometer. Hand throttle. Two-tone Bright hubcaps. Bright finish or premium wheelcovers. Chrome slotted or eight-spoke white painted wide sport road wheels. Sport package: Deluxe all-vinyl front bucket seats or cloth and vinyl bucket seats with optional hardtop roof. Color-keyed door trim panels. Lockable console with removable styrofoam beverage chest. Convenience package. Oil pressure gauge. Cigar lighter. Dual horns. Simulated woodgrain instrument panel faceplate. Bright exterior moldings on the windshield, drip rail, wideside with black paint fill, and partial front and rear wheel lip. Protection package. Bright hubcaps. Sport medallion on front fender. Other packages available on 1978 Trail Dusters were: convenience, easy order, luxury, protection, Sno-Plow, sound control and light or heavy-duty trailer towing.

1978 Plymouth Voyager Wagon (OCW)

VOYAGER — SERIES PB100 — ALL ENGINES: The new Voyager looked about the same as last year's model from the front. However, changes were made in side and rear-styling. The sidemarker lights were raised from the lower rear quarter panels to the middle and larger, vertical taillights were used. Five-passenger seating, a 22-gal. fuel tank, and a three-speed manual transmission were among the standard features.

I.D. DATA: A combination of 13 symbols were used. The first seven identify the model, series, GVW Class (A=6,000 lbs. or less. B=over 6,000 lbs.) engine, model year and assembly plant. The last six are sequential serial numbers. (They begin each year at 000,001.) The symbols for the engines are A=440 V-8; B=225 six; C=225 six; D=440 V-8; E=318 V-8; F=360 V-8 with two-barrel carburetor; G=318 V-8; H=243 Diesel; J=400 V-8; K=360 V-8; T=360 V-8 with four-barrel carburetor; X=Special L-6; and Y=Special V-8.

Model	Body Type	Price	Weight	Prod. Total
Voyager Van — 1/2-Ton — 109 in. w.b.				
PB100	Wagon	5302	3715	—

Voyager Van — 1/2-Ton — 127 in. w.b.

Model	Body Type	Price	Weight	Prod. Total
PB100	Wagon	5413	3880	—

ENGINE [Base]: Six-cylinder. Displacement: 225 cid. Brake horsepower: 90 at 3600 rpm. Bore & stroke: 3.40 in. x 4.12 in. Compression ratio: 8.4:1. Carburetor: one-barrel.

ENGINE [Optional]: Displacement: 318 cid. V-8. Brake horsepower: 140 at 4000 rpm.. Bore & stroke: 3.91 in. x 3.31 in. Compression ratio: 8.5:1. Carburetor: two-barrel.

VOYAGER — SERIES PB200 — ALL ENGINES: Although the wheelbase remained at 127 in., the largest of the three sizes of PB200 vans, the Maxi-Wagon, was several inches longer than the 1977 version. It also came with snazzy new wraparound rear quarter windows.

I.D. DATA: A combination of 13 symbols were used. The first seven identify the model, series, GVW Class (A=6,000 lbs. or less. B=over 6,000 lbs.) engine, model year and assembly plant. The last six are sequential serial numbers. (They begin each year at 000,001.) The symbols for the engines are A=440 V-8; B=225 six; C=225 six; D=440 V-8; E=318 V-8; F=360 V-8 with two-barrel carburetor; G=318 V-8; H=243 Diesel; J=400 V-8; K=360 V-8; T=360 V-8 with four-barrel carburetor; X=Special L-6; and Y=Special V-8.

Voyager Van — 3/4-Ton — 109 in. w.b.

Model	Body Type	Price	Weight	Prod. Total
PB200	Wagon	5371	3805	—

Voyager Van — 3/4-Ton — 127 in. w.b.

Model	Body Type	Price	Weight	Prod. Total
PB200	Wagon	5491	3930	—
PB200	Maxi-Wagon	5649	4280	—

ENGINE: Same as PB100.

VOYAGER — SERIES PB300 — ALL ENGINES: The PB300 series was the most practical choice among buyers who hauled heavy loads. As before, it was available in two sizes, big and huge. Fortunately for drivers, power steering was standard, as was a three-speed automatic transmission.

I.D. DATA: A combination of 13 symbols were used. The first seven identify the model, series, GVW Class (A=6,000 lbs. or less. B=over 6,000 lbs.) engine, model year and assembly plant. The last six are sequential serial numbers. (They begin each year at 000,001.) The symbols for the engines are A=440 V-8; B=225 six; C=225 six; D=440 V-8; E=318 V-8; F=360 V-8 with two-barrel carburetor; G=318 V-8; H=243 Diesel; J=400 V-8; K=360 V-8; T=360 V-8 with four-barrel carburetor; X=Special L-6; and Y=Special V-8.

Voyager Van — 1-Ton — 127 in. w.b.

Model	Body Type	Price	Weight	Prod. Total
PB300	Wagon	6569	4140	—
PB300	Maxi-Wagon	6893	4280	—

ENGINE: Displacement: 318 cid. V-8. (See PB100).

CHASSIS: Wheelbase [PB100/PB200] 109 in.; [PB100/PB200/PB300] 127 in. Overall width: 79.8 in. Overall length: [109 in. wheelbase] 179.1 in.; [127 in. wheelbase] 197 in.; [Maxi-Wagon] 223.1 in. Overall height: [109 in. wheelbase] 79.6 in.; [127 in. wheelbase] 80.9 in.; [Maxi-Wagon] 80.6 in. Tires: [PB100] FR78 x 15B; [PB200/109 in. wheelbase] J78 x 15B; [PB200/127 in. wheelbase] H78 x 15B and [PB300] 8.00 x 16.5D in.

TECHNICAL: Four-speed manual, overdrive (PB100). LoadFlite automatic transmission (PB100, PB200). 360 cid V-8. 400 cid V-8 (PB200/PB300) and 440 cid V-8 (PB200/PB300).

OPTIONAL PACKAGES: Convenience Package: Includes cigar lighter; glove box light; in-cab-actuated hood lock release; and 10 in. day/night rearview mirror. Custom Package: Includes Custom nameplates; bright molding around windshield, side and rear windows (except driver and passenger door windws); color-keyed floor mat; instrument panel lower skirts; low-back vinyl bucket seats. Sport Package: Includes, deluxe all-vinyl front bucket seats; matching three-passenger rear seat; color-keyed vinyl door trim with padded side panels; carpeting; dual bright finish 5 x 7 in. mirrors; Sport nameplates; vinyl-covered headliner; spare tire cover; padded instrument panel with simulated woodgrain insert; added insulation; cigar lighter; and bright hubcaps. Easy order package: Includes, automatic transmission; Convenience package; dual 5 x 7 in. bright mirrors; two-tone paint; power steering; AM radio; scuff pads; dome lamp; switches, side and rear door-operated; and wheelcovers. Luxury package: Includes automatic transmission; Convenience package; two-tone paint; AM/FM radio; power steering; scuff pads; bright finish wheelcovers; air-conditioning; tinted glass; speed control; and high-back Command bucket seats. Trailer towing package: Includes either light- or heavy-duty. Premium trim package (127 in. wheelbase V-8 models only): Includes bright front and rear bumpers; high-back deluxe cloth-and-vinyl bucket seats with matching bench seat; bright molding around grille; color-keyed carpeting with floor insulation; dash liner insulation; and dual electric horns.

CONVENIENCE OPTIONS: Sky Lite sun roof. Air-conditioning. Heavy-duty shocks. Automatic speed control. Front and rear bright finish bumpers. Cigarette lighter. Heavy-duty clutch. Tinted glass, windshield only or all windows. Sunscreen glass in rear compartment windows and side door glass. Passenger compartment headliner. Deluxe heater. Horn bar. Bright finish hubcaps. Interior day/night prismatic mirror. Increased cooling. Oil pressure gauge. Power steering. AM or AM/FM radio. Thirty-six gallon fuel tank. Eight-passenger seating (PB200/PB300). Twelve-passenger seating (PB300). Fifteen-passenger seating (PB300 extended body Maxi-Wagon). Driver and passenger swivel seats. Bright finish wheelcovers. Inside hood release. Heavy-duty alternator. Sliding side door (127 in. wheelbase only). Chrome-style road wheels. Wide sport road wheels, chrome disc or white-painted spoke.

1979 Plymouth Arrow Mini-Pickup (OCW)

ARROW PICKUP: This was the first year for the sporty Arrow Pickup. It was made, for Plymouth, by Mitsubishi Motors Corp. in Japan. Styling for this compact truck was clean, yet pretty. The two rectangular headlights were slightly recessed in a honeycomb rectangular grille. The signal lights were integrated into the front bumper. The large, vertical wraparound taillamps seemed almost out of proportion to the size of the truck. There was no rear bumper. Standard features included: Tubular cargo tie-down bars on the inside of the 81.5 in. long box; four-speed manual transmission; power front disc brakes; adjustable steering column with lock; vinyl folding bench seat; color-keyed door trim panels; dual sun visors; cashmere headliner; padded instrument panel; black racing type exterior rearview mirror; Argent silver painted front bumper with black rubber ends; upper level vent outlets; two-speed windshield wipers with washers; bright hubcaps; dome light; electronic ignition system; two-spoke steering wheel; tinted glass; passenger assist grip; AM radio; cigarette lighter; cargo lamp; armrests; bright windshield molding; bright drip rail molding; extra sound insulation.

I.D. DATA: A combination of 17 symbols were used by Mitsubishi. The first three identify the country of origin, manufacturer and type of vehicle. The fourth symbol indicates the restraint system. The fifth, sixth and seventh symbols indicate the model. The eighth digit indicates the engine. The ninth symbol is a check digit. The 10th symbol indicates model year. The 11th symbol indicates the assembly plant. The last five symbols are the sequential production numbers. The symbols for the engines are: K or 3=97.5 cid (1.6 liter) four; U=135 cid (2.0 liter) four.

Model	Body Type	Price	Weight	Prod. Total
OJL4	Pickup Sweptline	4819	2410	—

ENGINE: Four-cylinder. Displacement: 122 cid. Brake horsepower: 90 at 5000 rpm. Bore & stroke: 3.30 in. x 3.54 in. Compression ratio: 8.5:1. Carburetor: two-barrel.

ARROW SPORT PICKUP: As good looking as the basic Arrow was, it didn't really seem necessary to offer an even flashier version, but one was available. The Arrow Sport featured: Bodyside tape stripes; five-speed manual transmission; vinyl high-back bucket seats; console; loop-pile carpet; tachometer; oil pressure gauge and ammeter; three-spoke sport-styled steering wheel; white-spoke sport wheels; and AM/FM stereo radio.

I.D. DATA: A combination of 17 symbols were used by Mitsubishi. The first three identify the country of origin, manufacturer and type of vehicle. The fourth symbol indicates the restraint system. The fifth, sixth and seventh symbols indicate the model. The eighth digit indicates the engine. The ninth symbol is a check digit. The 10th symbol indicates model year. The 11th symbol indicates the assembly plant. The last five symbols are the sequential production numbers. The symbols for the engines are: K or 3=97.5 cid (1.6 liter) four; U=135 cid (2.0 liter) four.

Model	Body Type	Price	Weight	Prod. Total
OJP4	Sport Pickup Sweptline	5608	2410	—

ENGINE: Four-cylinder. Displacement: 156 cid. Brake horsepower: 105 at 5000 rpm. Bore & stroke: 3.59 in. x 3.86 in. Compression ratio: 8.2:1. Carburetor: two-barrel.

CHASSIS: Wheelbase: 109.4 in. Overall length: 184.6 in. Overall width: 65 in. Overall height: 60.8 in. Box length: 81.5 in. Box width: 64.2 in. GVW Rating: 3,880 lbs. Payload: 1,400 lbs. Tires: [Arrow] 6.00 x 14-C in. white sidewall bias-ply; [Arrow Sport] 185SR-14 raised white-letter radial.

TECHNICAL: Three-speed automatic transmission.

CONVENIENCE OPTIONS: Step type rear bumper. Grille guard. Roll bar. Sky Lite sun roof, Dual low-mount mirrors. Black racing-type mirror for passenger side.

NOTE: The Arrow Pickup was offered in a choice of three exterior colors: Light tan, Canyon red metallic or Warm white. The Arrow Sport could be had in black, Spitfire orange or a two-tone combination of yellow and low-luster black.

1979 Plymouth Trail Duster 4x4 Utility (OCW)

1979 Plymouth Voyager Maxi-Wagon (OCW)

TRAIL DUSTER — SERIES PD100 — (UTILITY VEHICLE): The rugged Trail Duster received a new one-piece honeycomb theme aluminum grille. It was divided horizontally in the center. Smaller signal lights were now located below the grille, under the headlights. Among standard features were: A three-speed manual transmission; deluxe vinyl low-back front bucket seats; color-keyed instrument panel and door trim panels; and black soft-touch vinyl steering wheel and horn pad.

I.D. DATA: A combination of 13 symbols were used. The first seven identify the model, series, GVW Class (A=6,000 lbs. or less; B=over 6,000 lbs.) engine, model year and assembly plant. The last six are sequential serial numbers. (They begin each year at 000,001.) The symbols for the engines are A=440 V-8; B=225 six; C=225 six; D=440 V-8; E=318 V-8; F=360 V-8 with two-barrel carburetor; G=318 V-8; H=243 Diesel; J=400 V-8; K=360 V-8; T=360 V-8 with four-barrel carburetor; X=Special L-6; and Y=Special V-8.

Model	Body Type	Price	Weight	Prod. Total
PD100	Utility Vehicle	5645	3570	—

ENGINE: Six-cylinder. Displacement: 225 cid. Brake horsepower: 90 at 3600 rpm. Bore & stroke: 3.40 in. x 4.12 in. Compression ratio: 8.4:1. Carburetor: one-barrel. (Engine not available in California.)

TRAIL DUSTER — SERIES PW100 — (UTILITY VEHICLE): The PW100 had full-time four-wheel drive. That eliminated the need to shift in or out of four-wheel drive or to lock or unlock the front free-wheeling hubs. It also came with a 3,280 lbs. capacity front leaf spring suspension, high capacity 3,600 lbs. rear axle and front stabilizer bar.

I.D. DATA: A combination of 13 symbols were used. The first seven identify the model, series, GVW Class (A=6,000 lbs. or less; B=over 6,000 lbs.) engine, model year and assembly plant. The last six are sequential serial numbers. (They begin each year at 000,001.) The symbols for the engines are A=440 V-8; B=225 six; C=225 six; D=440 V-8; E=318 V-8; F=360 V-8 with two-barrel carburetor; G=318 V-8; H=243 diesel; J=400 V-8; K=360 V-8; T=360 V-8 with four-barrel carburetor; X=Special L-6; and Y=Special V-8.

Model	Body Type	Price	Weight	Prod. Total
PW100	Utility Vehicle	7286	4150	—

ENGINE: Displacement: 318 cid V-8. Brake horsepower: 120 at 3600 rpm. Bore & stroke: 3.91 in. x 3.31 in. Compression ratio: 8.5:1. Carburetor: two-barrel.

CHASSIS: Wheelbase: 106 in. Overall length: 184.6 in. Overall width: 79.5 in. GVW Rating: [PD100] 4,800-6,050 lbs.; [PW100] 6,050 lbs. Tires: [PD100] FR78-15B; [PW100] L78-15B.

OPTIONAL PACKAGES: Sno-Commander package (PW100 only): Includes power angling blade; power lift; and seven-way control valve. Trail Duster Sport package: Includes dual vertically stacked quad rectangular headlights; bright windshield molding and taillight bezels; Sport nameplates on front fender; bucket seats; color-keyed vinyl door trim panels with assist strap; locking console with removable beverage chest; and woodgrain instrument panel face plate with bright trim.

CONVENIENCE OPTIONS: Tilt steering column. Sky Lite sun roof. Radios: AM with 40 channel CB; AM/FM/MX stereo with 40-channel CB; AM/FM/MX stereo with eight-track tape. Electric door locks. Five-slot chrome disc wide sport road wheels. White-painted steel spoke wide sport road wheels. Chrome-styled road wheels. Vinyl soft top. Air-conditioning. Outside spare tire carrier. Automatic speed control. Power steering. Inside hood lock release. Three-passenger deluxe vinyl split back front bench seat. Low-back cloth-and-vinyl front bucket seats. Three-passenger bench rear seat in matching front seat trim. High-back cloth-and-vinyl Command front bucket seats (Trail Duster Sport only). Front stabilizer bar (PD100). Heavy-duty front stabilizer bar (PW100).

TECHNICAL: [PW100] 318 cid V-8; [PW100] 360 cid V-8. Three-speed automatic transmission. [PW100] NP435 four-speed manual transmission; [PW100] NP445 four-speed manual transmission.

NOTE: Trail Duster buyers had their choice of 15 exterior colors in 1979: Formal black; white; cashmere; Medium canyon red; Sunburst orange; Yellow flame; Light silver metallic; Cadet blue metallic; Ensign blue metallic; Teal frost metallic; Citron green metallic; Medium tan metallic; Teal green sunfire metallic; Canyon red sunfire metallic; and Sable brown sunfire metallic.

VOYAGER — SERIES PB100 — WAGON: Styling refinements were made to the Voyager front end in 1979. The new criss-cross theme grille had full length, wraparound signal lights. The Plymouth name was now centered above the grille, rather than to one side (as on last year's model). The front bumper was also new. The overall effect of these changes was to jazz up the Voyager's somewhat plain appearance. And it succeeded. Other less noticeable new features included a coolant reserve system and larger front suspension control arm rubber bushings. Among the standard equipment were: Air vent doors; driver and front-passenger armrests; ashtray; painted front and rear bumpers; automatic choke; power front disc brakes; door locks; 22 gal. fuel tank; Argent silver finished grille with seven-inch round headlamps; hardboard headliner in driver's compartment; fresh air heater with defrosters; color-keyed horn pad; painted hubcaps; dual painted 5 x 7 in. exterior rearview mirrors; low-back vinyl front bucket seats and three-passenger bench seat; two-spoke color-keyed steering wheel; padded sun visors; single rear door with fixed glass; double hinged-passenger side doors with vented glass; spare tire carrier; Voyager nameplates on both front fenders; electric wiper arm mounted windshield washers; and two-speed windshield wipers.

I.D. DATA: A combination of 13 symbols were used. The first seven identify the model, series, GVW Class (A=6,000 lbs. or less; B=over 6,000 lbs.) engine, model year and assembly plant. The last six are sequential serial numbers. (They begin each year at 000,001.) The symbols for the engines are A=440 V-8; B=225 six; C=225 six; D=440 V-8; E=318 V-8; F=360 V-8 with two-barrel carburetor; G=318 V-8; H=243 Diesel; J=400 V-8; K=360 V-8; T=360 V-8 with four-barrel carburetor; X=Special L-6; and Y=Special V-8.

Model	Body Type	Price	Weight	Prod. Total
Voyager Van — 1/2-Ton — 109.6 in. w.b.				
PB100	Van	5978	3715	—
Voyager Van — 1/2-Ton — 127 in. w.b.				
PB100	Van	6138	3880	—

ENGINE: Six-cylinder. Displacement: 225 cid. Brake horsepower: 90 at 3600 rpm. Bore & stroke: 3.40 in. x 4.12 in. Compression ratio: 8.4:1. Carburetor: one-barrel.

VOYAGER — SERIES PB200 — WAGON: The PB200 came with most of the same features as the PB100. However, this more heavy-duty series also offered the spacious, extended body Maxi-Wagon.

I.D. DATA: A combination of 13 symbols are used. The first seven identify the model, series, GVW Class (A=6,000 lbs. or less; B=over 6,000 lbs.) engine, model year and assembly plant. The last six are sequential serial numbers. (They begin each year at 000,001.) The symbols for the engines are A=440 V-8; B=225 six; C=225 six; D=440 V-8; E=318 V-8; F=360 V-8 with two-barrel carburetor; G=318 V-8; H=243 Diesel; J=400 V-8; K=360 V-8; T=360 V-8 with four-barrel carburetor; X=Special L-6; and Y=Special V-8.

Model	Body Type	Price	Weight	Prod. Total
Voyager Van — 3/4-Ton — 109 in. w.b.				
PB200	Van	6310	3805	—
Voyager Van — 3/4-Ton — 127 in. w.b.				
PB200	Van	6472	3930	—
PB200	Maxi-Wagon	6870	4280	—

ENGINE: Displacement: 318 cid. Brake horsepower: 140 at 4000 rpm. Bore & stroke: 3.91 in. x 3.31 in. Compression ratio: 8.6:1. Carburetor: two-barrel.

VOYAGER — SERIES PB300 — WAGON: The top-of-the-line PB300 could be ordered in either the standard or extended-length (Maxi-Wagon) versions. Both were on a 127 in. wheelbase. Both were made for heavy-duty use. Power steering and automatic transmission were standard.

I.D. DATA: A combination of 13 symbols are used. The first seven identify the model, series, GVW Class (A=6,000 lbs. or less; B=over 6,000 lbs.) engine, model year and assembly plant. The last six are sequential serial numbers. (They begin each year at 000,001.) The symbols for the engines are A=440 V-8; B=225 six; C=225 six; D=440 V-8; E=318 V-8; F=360 V-8 with two-barrel carburetor; G=318 V-8; H=243 Diesel; J=400 V-8; K=360 V-8; T=360 V-8 with four-barrel carburetor; X=Special L-6; and Y=Special V-8.

Model	Body Type	Price	Weight	Prod. Total
Voyager Van — 1-Ton — 127.6 in. w.b.				
PB300	Van	7641	4140	—
PB300	Maxi-Wagon	7950	4280	—

ENGINE: Displacement: 318 cid. Brake horsepower: 140 at 4000 rpm. Bore & stroke: 3.91 in. x 3.31 in. Compression ratio: 8.5:1. Carburetor: two-barrel.

CHASSIS: Wheelbase [PB100/PB200]: 109.6 in.; [PB100/PB200/PB300] 127.6 in. Overall width: 79.8 in. Overall length: [109.6 in. wheelbase] 179.1 in.; [127.6 in. wheelbase] 197.1 in.; [Maxi-Wagon] 223.1 in. Overall height: [109.6 in. wheelbase] 79.6 in.; [127.6 in. wheelbase] 80.9 in.; [Maxi-Wagon] 80.6 in. Tires: [PB100] ER78 x 15B; [PB200/109 in. wheelbase] J78 x 15B; [PB200/127.6 in. wheelbase] H78 x 15B; [PB300] 8.00 x 16.5D in. GVW Ratings (lbs.): 4,900-6,000 (PB100); 6,050-6,400 (PB200); 6,700-7,800 (PB300).

TECHNICAL: [PB100] 318 cid V-8. [PB200/PB300] 360 cid V-8. [PB100/PB200] Four-speed manual transmission. [PB100/PB200] Three-speed automatic transmission.

OPTIONAL PACKAGES: Custom package: Includes Voyager Custom nameplates on front doors; bright molding around windshield, side and rear windows (except driver and-passenger door windows); bright taillamp bezels; bright hubcaps; right- and left-hand instrument panel lower skirts; cigar lighter; white non-vinyl-covered headliner in driver and-

passenger compartment; vinyl door and side trim panels with plaid insert; color-keyed floor mat with floor insulation; dash liner insulation; and garnish trim over front door headers and around rear compartment windows. Sport package: Includes Voyager Sport nameplates on front doors; bright lower side and rear moldings; bright moldings around windshield, side and rear windows (except driver and-passenger door windows); bright finish grille with seven-inch round headlamps and grille medallion; bright taillamp bezels; bright hubcaps; bright front and rear bumpers; dual 5 x 7 in. bright exterior mirrors; woodgrain appliques on lower face of instrument panel; left- and right-side instrument panel lower skirts; cigar lighter; horn pad with woodgrain insert; vinyl-covered, color-keyed, insulated headliner in driver and-passenger compartments; color-keyed spare tire cover; deluxe vinyl seat trim; vinyl door and side trim panels with woodgrain trim; color-keyed carpeting with floor insulation; dash liner insulation; dome light switches, door operated on all doors; garnish rims over front door headers, around rear compartment windows, and on A-pillar and windshield; and dual electric horns. Sport Premium Trim package: Includes Voyager Sport nameplates on front doors; bright lower side and rear moldings; bright molding around windshield, side and rear windows (except driver and passenger door windows); dual vertically stacked quad rectangular headlamps with bright grille and grille medallion; bright taillamp bezels; bright hubcaps; bright front and rear bumpers; dual 5 x 7 in. bright exterior mirrors; woodgrain appliques on lower face of instrument panel; instrument panel lower skirts, left and right; cigar lighter; horn pad with woodgrain insert; vinyl-covered, color-keyed, insulated headliner in driver and-passenger compartments; color-keyed spare tire cover; high-back deluxe cloth-and-vinyl reclining Command bucket seats and deluxe cloth-and-vinyl bench seat; vinyl door and side trim panels with woodgrain trim and front door appliques and pull strap; color-keyed carpeting with floor insulation; color-keyed carpeted engine housing cover; dash liner insulation; dome light switches, door-operated on all doors; garnish trim over front door headers, around rear compartment windows and on A-pillar and windshield; and dual electric horns. Convenience package: Includes cigar lighter; glove box lock; 10 in. day/night rearview mirror; and in-cab-actuated hood lock release. Light package: Includes, ignition switch light with time delay; glove box light; cigar lighter light; automatic door switches for interior dome lights; and courtesy lamps on front and side doors. Luxury package: Includes automatic transmission; Convenience package; two-tone paint; AM/FM radio including front and rear speakers; power steering; bright finish wheelcovers with PB300 or premium Class II bright finish wheelcovers with PB100 or PB200; integral front-mounted air-conditioning; automatic speed control; tinted glass, all windows; front door edge protectors; high-back cloth-and-vinyl Command bucket seats and cloth-and vinyl bench seat; light package; bumper guards front and rear; and 15 in. diameter vinyl steering wheel. Easy Order package: Includes automatic transmission; Convenience package; two-tone paint; AM radio; bright front and rear bumpers; bright dual 5 x 7 in. exterior rearview mirrors; power steering; scuff pads front- and side-passenger doors; wheelcovers; bumper guards front and rear; 15 in. diameter vinyl steering wheel; and automatic door switches for interior dome lights. Exterior Molding package: Includes upper side and rear molding; lower side and rear molding; upper side and rear and lower side and rear moldings.

CONVENIENCE OPTIONS: Bright front and rear bumpers. Bumper guards front and rear. Heavy-duty alternator. Heavy-duty battery. Cigar lighter. Digital clock. Increased cooling. Automatic transmission oil-to-air auxiliary cooler. Rear window electric defroster (for single rear door). Dual rear doors, hinged type. Sliding-passenger door. Door metal check arms. Front doors door edge protectors. Rear doors inside handle and lock button. Thirty-six gallon fuel tank. Instrumentation: oil pressure gauge and trip odometer, dual calibrated speedometer and odometer. Tinted glass, windshield or all windows. Sun screen privacy glass. Banded glass, front door glass and vent wings. Bright finish grille with seven-inch round headlamps and grille medallion. Dual quad rectangular vertically stacked headlamps. Passenger compartment headliner. Deluxe high-output heater. Auxiliary heater in passenger compartment. Dual electric horns. In-cab-actuated hood lock release. Ten-inch day/night prismatic type rearview mirror. Dual short-arm 5 x 7 in. bright finish exterior mirrors. Dual low-mount 6 x 9 in. paint finish exterior mirrors. Dual low-mount 6 x 9 in. bright finish exterior mirrors. Wheel lip molding. Choice of three two-tone paint procedures: 1) Upper and lower (50/50 two-tone); 2) Mid-section in secondary color, rest of the body in main color.; 3) Roof and mid-section in secondary color, rest of body in main color. Power steering. Rear radio speaker. Side step sill scuff pads. Heavy-duty shock absorbers, front and rear. Spare tire cover. Dome lamp switches, all doors. Unibelt restraint system. Deluxe windshield wipers, two-speed with intermittent wipe. Wheels: chrome-styled road type; 15 x 6.00 in. wide sport road-type; white-painted steel-spoke 15 x 7.00 in.; or five-slot chrome-styled disc, 15 x 7.00 in. Bright hubcaps. Tilt steering column. Radios: AM, AM/FM, AM/FM/MX stereo, AM/FM MX stereo/eight-track tape, AM/40-channel CB transceiver, AM/FM/MX stereo/40-channel CB transceiver. Automatic speed control. Sky Lite sun roofs (available over driver's compartment of five- and eight-passenger models, and over passenger compartment of 127.6 in. wheelbase five- and eight-passenger models). Eight-passenger seating (PB100 with 225 cid six-cylinder, 6,000 lbs. GVW and LR78 x 15-B tires; PB200 and PB300 models). Twelve-passenger seating (127.6 in. wheelbase PB300, requires optional 7,200 lbs. GVW package). Fifteen-passenger seating (PB300 Maxi-Wagon with 7,800 lbs. GVW package). Air-conditioning. Electric door locks. Light- or heavy-duty trailer towing packages.

1980 PLYMOUTH

ARROW PICKUP: The attractive styling was unchanged for 1980. It still offered the largest payload in the Mini-Pickup class. That, along with ample legroom, improved steering and good gas mileage, helped make the Arrow an excellent value. Standard features included: Power front disc brakes; adjustable steering column; vinyl folding bench seat; dual sun visors; padded dash; dual racing-type side mirrors; two-speed wipers and washers; tubular cargo tie-down bars in pickup box; electronic ignition; tinted glass; two-spoke steering wheel; passenger assist grip; AM radio; cigarette lighter cargo lamp; armrests; bright windshield and drip rail moldings; and a four-speed manual transmission.

I.D. DATA: A combination of 17 symbols were used by Mitsubishi. The first three identify the country of origin, manufacturer and type of vehicle. The fourth symbol indicates the restraint system. The fifth, sixth and seventh symbols indicate the model. The eighth digit indicates the engine. The ninth symbol is a check digit. The 10th symbol indicates model year. The 11th symbol indicates the assembly plant. The last five symbols are the sequential production numbers. The symbols for the engines are: K or 3=97.5 cid (1.6 liter) four; U=135 cid (2.0 liter) four.

1980 Plymouth Arrow Mini-Pickup (CPD)

Model	Body Type	Price	Weight	Prod. Total
OJL4	Pickup Sweptline	4821	2573	—

ENGINE: Four-cylinder. Displacement: 122 cid. Brake horsepower: 90 at 5000 rpm. Bore & stroke: 3.30 in. x 3.54 in. Compression ratio: 8.5:1. Carburetor: two-barrel.

ARROW SPORT PICKUP: A step up from the standard Arrow was the Sport. It came with many of the same features plus: flashy tape striping; low-luster black painted front bumper; raised white-lettered steel-belted radial tires; wide spoke wheels; two-tone high back vinyl bucket seats in cashmere and dark cashmere or black and gray; three-spoke steering wheel; floor console; loop pile carpeting; AM/FM stereo radio; tachometer; oil pressure gauge and ammeter; and a five-speed manual transmission with overdrive.

I.D. DATA: A combination of 17 symbols were used by Mitsubishi. The first three identify the country of origin, manufacturer and type of vehicle. The fourth symbol indicates the restraint system. The fifth, sixth and seventh symbols indicate the model. The eighth digit indicates the engine. The ninth symbol is a check digit. The 10th symbol indicates model year. The 11th symbol indicates the assembly plant. The last five symbols are the sequential production numbers. The symbols for the engines are: K or 3=97.5 cid (1.6 liter) four; U=135 cid (2.0 liter) four.

1980 Plymouth Arrow Sport Mini-Pickup (CPD)

Model	Body Type	Price	Weight	Prod. Total
OJP4	Sport Pickup Sweptline	5627	2648	—

ENGINE: Four-cylinder. Displacement: 156 cid. Brake horsepower: 105 at 5000 rpm. Bore & stroke: 3.59 in. x 3.86 in. Compression ratio: 8.2:1. Carburetor: two-barrel.

CHASSIS: Wheelbase: 109.4 in. Overall length: 184.6 in. Overall width: 65 in. Overall height: [Arrow] 60.6 in.; [Arrow Sport] 59.8 in.. Tires: [Arrow] 6.00 x 14-C in.; [Arrow Sport] 185S x 14. Box length: 81.5 in. Box width: 64.2 in. Maximum payload: [Arrow] 1,527 lbs.; [Arrow Sport] 1,557 lbs.. GVW Rating: [Arrow] 4,045 lbs.; [Arrow Sport] 4,120 lbs.

TECHNICAL: Automatic transmission.

CONVENIENCE OPTIONS: Sky Lite sun roof. Cargo box roll bar. Air-conditioning. Bodyside and tailgate tape stripes (Arrow only). Front grille guard. Mud guards. Low-mount black left and right mirrors. Power steering. Sliding rear window. Low-luster black step-type rear bumper. Vinyl bodyside moldings. Wheel trim rings (Arrow only).

1980 Plymouth Trail Duster SE 4x4 Utility Wagon (CPD)

TRAIL DUSTER — SERIES PD100: Styling was the same as last year and that wasn't bad. Among the standard features were: An insulated dash liner; dual exterior mirrors; power front disc brakes; deluxe vinyl low-back bucket seats; two seven-inch round headlights; rear compartment floor mat and rear courtesy lamps; independent front coil spring

suspension; electronic ignition; 24-gal. fuel tank; dual jet windshield washers and two-speed windshield wipers; and three-speed automatic transmission.

I.D. DATA: A combination of 13 symbols were used. The first seven identify the model, series, GVW Class (A=6,000 lbs. or less; B=over 6,000 lbs.) engine, model year and assembly plant. The last six are sequential serial numbers. (They begin each year at 000,001.) The symbols for the engines are A=440 V-8; B=225 six; C=225 six; D=440 V-8; E=318 V-8; F=360 V-8 with two-barrel carburetor; G=318 V-8; H=243 diesel; J=400 V-8; K=360 V-8; T=360 V-8 with four-barrel carburetor; X=Special L-6; and Y=Special V-8.

Model	Body Type	Price	Weight	Prod. Total
PD100	Utility Vehicle	6793	3570	—

ENGINE: Six-cylinder. Displacement: 225 cid. Brake horsepower: 90 at 3600 rpm. Bore & stroke: 3.40 in. x 4.12 in. Compression ratio: 8.4:1. Carburetor: one-barrel.

TRAIL DUSTER — SERIES PW100: A new part-time four-wheel drive system replaced the full-time unit on the 4x4 Trail Duster. It used a new transfer case design that resulted in less driveline noise, reduced weight and improved fuel economy. Standard features included: leaf spring front suspension; four-speed manual transmission; manual locking hubs; power steering; and front stabilizer bar.

I.D. DATA: A combination of 13 symbols were used. The first seven identify the model, series, GVW Class (A=6,000 lbs. or less; B=over 6,000 lbs.) engine, model year and assembly plant. The last six are sequential serial numbers. (They begin each year at 000,001.) The symbols for the engines are A=440 V-8; B=225 six; C=225 six; D=440 V-8; E=318 V-8; F=360 V-8 with two-barrel Carburetor; G=318 V-8; H=243 Diesel; J=400 V-8; K=360 V-8; T=360 V-8 with four-barrel. Carburetor; X=Special L-6; and Y=Special V-8.

Model	Body Type	Price	Weight	Prod. Total
PW100	Utility Vehicle	8298	4150	—

ENGINE: Displacement: 318 cid V-8. Brake horsepower: 120 at 3600 rpm. Bore & stroke: 3.91 in. x 3.31 in. Compression ratio: 8.5:1. Carburetor: two-barrel.

CHASSIS: Wheelbase: 106 in. Overall length: [Without bumper guards] 184.62 in. [With bumper guards]; 186.16 in. Overall width: 79.5 in. GVW Rating: [PD100] 5,300 lbs.; [PW100] 5,850 lbs.; [PW100 with Sno-Commander] 6,050 lbs. Tires: [PD100] P225/75-R15B glass-belted radials; [PW100] P235/75-15B polyester bias-belted.

TECHNICAL: [PD100] 318 cid V-8 with two-barrel Carburetor (PD100). [PW100] 360 cid V-8 with four-barrel Carburetor. Three-speed automatic transmission.

OPTION PACKAGES: Sno-Commander package [PW100 only]: Includes power angling blade; power lift; seven-way control valve; plow lights; 35-gal. fuel tank; and heavy-duty front leaf springs. Trail Duster Sport package: Includes dual vertically-stacked quad rectangular headlamps with halogen high-beam lamp; bright windshield, drip rail, quarter side window and liftgate window moldings; bright taillamp bezels; Sport medallion on front fenders; tailgate surround molding with vinyl tape insert appliques; woodtone appliques on door trim panels with assist strap and carpeting on lower door panel; cloth-and-vinyl bucket seats; lockable console with removable styrofoam beverage chest; perforated white hardboard headliner; carpeting; woodtone appliques on instrument panel faceplate; Trail Duster Sport nameplate on instrument panel; black horn pad with woodtone appliques insert and black two-spoke steering wheel; color-keyed spare tire cover; dual electric horns; and bright door sill tread plate. Trail Duster Macho 4x4 package [PW100 only]: Includes 15 x 7 in. white-painted steel spoke road wheels; Sport four-spoke steering wheel; low-luster black painted front and rear bumpers; special low-luster black paint treatment and black/orange tape stripes on lower portion of vehicle; tailgate decals "4WD" and "Plymouth" in black with color accent; limited monotone exterior paint color selection; and five 10-15LT outline white-letter tires.

CONVENIENCE OPTIONS: Aluminum radial ribbed road wheels. AM/FM stereo with cassette tape player. AM/FM stereo with search-tune. Bright hitch-type rear bumper. Tilt steering column. Skid plate. Fold-up rear bench seat. Power windows. Deluxe vinyl split-back front bench seat. Air-conditioning. Front stabilizer bar (PD100). Heavy-duty front stabilizer bar (PW100). Aluminum radial ribbed wheels. White-painted steel spoke wheels. Five-slot chrome disc wheels. Step type rear bumper. Hitch type rear bumper. Electric clock. Cigar lighter. Lockable console. Auxiliary transmission oil to air cooler. 35-gal. fuel tank. Oil pressure gauge. Tinted glass. Quad rectangular dual vertically-stacked headlights. Engine block heater. Deluxe heater. In-cab-actuated hood lock release. Dual electric horns. Rubber mats. Dual low-mount mirrors. Exterior moldings. Power door locks. Power steering. AM/FM stereo with 40-channel CB transceiver. Roll bar. Heavy-duty front and rear shock absorbers. Fuel tank shield. Transfer case shield. Sun roof. Speed control. Outside-mounted swing-out tire carrier. Bright wheelcovers. Premium wheelcovers. Light- and heavy-duty trailer towing packages.

1980 Plymouth Voyager PB200 Wagon (CPD)

VOYAGER — SERIES PB100 — WAGON: Exterior styling was the same as last year's model However, some changes were made to upholstery designs. Among standard Voyager features were: Electronic ignition, seven-inch round headlights, color-keyed horn pad, bright hubcaps, padded sun visors, full width black floor mat, windshield washers, two-speed windshield wipers, low-back vinyl bucket seats up front and a three-passenger bench seat in the back, 22 gal. fuel tank, four-speed manual transmission with overdrive, power front disc brakes, argent finish grille and painted front and rear bumpers.

I.D. DATA: A combination of 13 symbols were used. The first seven identify the model, series, GVW Class (A=6,000 lbs. or less; B=over 6,000 lbs.) engine, model year and assembly plant. The last six are sequential serial numbers. (They begin each year at 000,001.) The symbols for the engines are A=440 V-8; B=225 six; C=225 six; D=440 V-8; E=318 V-8; F=360 V-8 with two-barrel carburetor; G=318 V-8; H=243 Diesel; J=400 V-8; K=360 V-8; T=360 V-8 with four-barrel carburetor; X=Special L-6; and Y=Special V-8.

Model	Body Type	Price	Weight	Prod. Total
Voyager Van — 1/2-Ton — 109 in. w.b.				
PB100	Van	6564	3715	—
Voyager Van — 1/2-Ton — 127.6 in. w.b.				
PB100	Van	6736	3880	—

ENGINE: Six-cylinder. Displacement: 225 cid. Brake horsepower: 90 at 3600 rpm. Bore & stroke: 3.40 in. x 4.12 in. Compression ratio: 8.4:1. Carburetor: one-barrel.

VOYAGER — SERIES PB200 — WAGON: Buyers had their choice of three sizes in this slightly more heavy-duty Voyager series. Top of the line was the spacious Maxi-Wagon. It had over three feet more interior room than the 109.6 in. wheelbase model. Automatic transmission was standard in the Maxi-Wagon.

I.D. DATA: A combination of 13 symbols were used. The first seven identify the model, series, GVW Class (A=6,000 lbs. or less; B=over 6,000 lbs.) engine, model year and assembly plant. The last six are sequential serial numbers. (They begin each year at 000,001.) The symbols for the engines are A=440 V-8; B=225 six; C=225 six; D=440 V-8; E=318 V-8; F=360 V-8 with two-barrel carburetor; G=318 V-8; H=243 Diesel; J=400 V-8; K=360 V-8; T=360 V-8 with four-barrel carburetor; X=Special L-6; and Y=Special V-8.

Model	Body Type	Price	Weight	Prod. Total
Voyager Van — 3/4-Ton — 109.6 in. w.b.				
PB200	Van	6876	3805	—
Voyager Van — 3/4-Ton — 127.6 in. w.b.				
PB200	Van	7051	3930	—
PB200	Maxi-Wagon	8152	4280	—

ENGINE: [Wagon] Six-cylinder. Displacement: 225 cid. Brake horsepower: 90 at 3600 rpm. Bore & stroke: 3.40 in. x 4.12 in. Compression ratio: 8.4:1. Carburetor: one-barrel. (Not available in California).

ENGINE: [Maxi-Wagon] V-8. 318 cid. Brake horsepower: 120 at 3600 rpm. Bore & stroke: 3.91 in. x 3.31 in. Compression ratio: 8.5:1. Carburetor: two-barrel.

VOYAGER — SERIES PB300 — WAGON: Both PB300 Voyagers had a 127.6 in. wheelbase. They were made for hauling heavy loads. Power steering and a three-speed automatic transmission were standard. The brakes were also bigger on this Voyager series than the other two.

I.D. DATA: A combination of 13 symbols were used. The first seven identify the model, series, GVW Class (A=6,000 lbs. or less; B=over 6,000 lbs.) engine, model year and assembly plant. The last six are sequential serial numbers. (They begin each year at 000,001.) The symbols for the engines are A=440 V-8; B=225 six; C=225 six; D=440 V-8; E=318 V-8; F=360 V-8 with two-barrel carburetor; G=318 V-8; H=243 Diesel; J=400 V-8; K=360 V-8; T=360 V-8 with four-barrel carburetor; X=Special L-6; and Y=Special V-8.

Model	Body Type	Price	Weight	Prod. Total
Voyager Van — 1-Ton — 127.6 in. w.b.				
PB300	Wagon	8364	4140	—
PB300	Maxi-Wagon	8664	4280	—

ENGINE: Displacement: 318 cid V-8. Brake horsepower: 120 at 3600 rpm. Bore & stroke: 3.91 in. x 3.31 in. Compression ratio: 8.5:1. Carburetor: two-barrel.

CHASSIS: Wheelbase [Wagon] 109.6 in.; [Wagon and Maxi-Wagon] 127.6 in. Overall length: [Wagon] 178.9 in.; [Wagon] 196.9 in.; [Maxi-Wagon] 222.9 in. Overall width: 79.8 in. Overall height: [109.6 in. wheelbase] 79.6 in.; [127.6 in. wheelbase Wagon] 80.9 in.; [Maxi-Wagon] 80.6 in. Tires: [PB100] P195/75R-15B glass-belted radial; [PB200/109.6 in. wheelbase Wagon]: P225/75R-15B glass-belted radial; [PB200/127.6 in. wheelbase Wagon]: P235/75R-15C glass-belted radial; [PB300 Wagon]: 8.00 x 16.5E polyester bias-belted; [PB300 Maxi-Wagon] 8.75 x 16.5E polyester bias-belted. GVW Rating (lbs.): [PB100] 5,100; [PB200 Wagons] 6,050 lbs.; [PB200 Maxi-Wagon] 6,400 lbs.; [PB300] 7,200 lbs.

TECHNICAL: [PB100/PB200 Wagons] 318 cid V-8; [PB200/PB300 Wagons] 360 cid V-8. [PB100/PB200 Wagons] Three-speed automatic transmission.

OPTION PACKAGES: Voyager Custom package: Includes nameplates; bright molding around windshield, side and rear windows; bright taillamp bezels; cigar lighter; instrument panel lower skirts; perforated color-keyed hardboard headliner with overprint pattern; vinyl door and side trim panels with plaid insert; color-keyed floor mat and floor insulation; trim over front door headers and around rear compartment window; and plaid vinyl low-back front bucket seats with matching three-passenger rear seat. Voyager Sport package for 127.6 in. wheelbase models only: Includes, nameplates; bright lower side and rear molding; dual vertically stacked quad rectangular headlamps with halogen high-beam and bright grille and grille medallion; bright front and rear bumpers; dual bright exterior mirrors; woodtone appliques on lower face of instrument panel; horn pad with woodtone insert; spare tire cover; vinyl door and side trim panels with woodtone trim; color-keyed carpeting with floor insulation; dome light switches, door-operated, on all doors; trim over front door headers, around rear compartment windows and low back front bucket seats (high-back plaid cloth-and-vinyl front buckets optional); A-pillar and windshield moldings; and dual electric horns. Voyager Sport package with Premium Trim package: Includes, soft cloth-covered headliner over the driver and-passenger compartment; vinyl door and side trim panels with woodtone trim and front door appliques; pull strap; color-keyed carpeted engine housing cover; high-back front bucket seats; and heavy-duty insulation (with PB100, this package requires optional 5,400 lbs. GVW option). Voyager Sport and Voyager Sport with Premium Trim package: Includes interior lower fiberglass insulation panels and additional insulation under floor covering. Voyager Custom with Premium Trim package: Same as previous, plus full-length headlining with insulation. Voyager with Premium Trim package: Same as previous, plus interior lower trim panels in passenger compartment; color-keyed garnish trim over front door headers, sliding door track, around headliner and around rear compartment window; jute insulation under floor mat; and dash liner insulation. Eight-passenger Seating package [PB200/PB300 Wagons and Maxi-Wagons]: Includes one additional quick-release three-passenger bench seat and eight-passenger Travel Seat. Twelve-passenger Seating package [PB300 Wagon and Maxi-Wagon]: Includes two additional bench seats (one three-passenger and one four-passenger and tire carrier relocated under third bench seat (requires rear door/doors with optional vented glass at extra cost). Fifteen-passenger Seating [PB300 Maxi-Wagon]: Includes three additional seats (two three-passenger and one four-passenger) and tire carrier relocated under fourth seat (Requires optional 8,550 lbs. GVW package and rear door/doors with optional vented glass at extra cost). Light-Duty Trailer Towing package: Includes Maximum Cooling equipment; heavy-duty variable load flasher; seven-wire harness; bright hitch type rear bumper; and Class 1 ball hitch. Heavy-duty Trailer Towing package for PB200 and PB300: Includes, Maximum Cooling equipment; 63-amp. alternator; 70 amp.-hr./430 amp. cold-crank battery; seven-wire harness; Class IV tow bar hitch; heavy-duty variable load flasher; and heavy-duty front and rear shock absorbers.

CONVENIENCE OPTIONS: Air-conditioning (integral front and auxiliary rear). Bright front and rear bumpers. Hitch type rear bumper. Front and rear bumper guards on nerf strips. Cigar lighter. Digital clock. Auxiliary transmission oil-to-air cooling. Electric rear window defroster. Dual rear doors with fixed or vented glass. Single rear door with vented glass. Sliding door on passenger side. 36-gal. fuel tank. Oil pressure and trip odometer gauges. Tinted glass. Dual quad rectangular headlamps, vertically-stacked, with halogen high beams. Bright grille (includes quad headlamps). Passenger compartment headliner. Auxiliary rear heater. Deluxe front heater. Dual electric horns. Interior reading lamp in driver's compartment. In-cab-actuated hood release lock. Color-keyed rubber floor mats in driver's compartment. Illuminated vanity mirror. Exterior dual low-mount mirrors. Exterior dual short

arm mirrors. Wheel lip, lower, and/or upper moldings. Power windows, steering and/or door locks. AM, AM/FM, AM/FM stereo, AM/FM stereo with Search-Tune, AM/FM stereo with eight-track tape player, AM/FM stereo with cassette tape player and Dolby noise reduction system, AM/FM stereo with 40-channel CB transceiver, rear speaker. Heavy-duty shock absorbers. Sky Lite sun roof. Color-keyed spare tire cover. Speed control. Front stabilizer bar. Tilt steering column. Door-operated dome light switch. Radial-ribbed aluminum, five-slot chrome disc, or white-painted spoke wheels. Bright and premium wheelcovers. Deluxe windshield wipers.

1981 PLYMOUTH

ARROW PICKUP: The Arrow's good looks weren't tampered with in 1981. Among the standard features were: Argent painted front bumper with black rubber ends; cargo lamp; cigarette lighter; dome light with driver and passenger side door switches; emergency flashers; 15.1-gal. fuel tank; bright Argent silver grille; color-keyed headliner; inside hood release; bright hubcaps; interior rearview mirror; dual black racing-type exterior mirrors; bright drip rail molding; bright windshield molding; AM radio; adjustable steering column with lock; dual sun visors; tubular cargo tie-down bars on both sides of the interior of the pickup box; tinted glass; trip odometer; two-speed windshield wipers with washers; four-speed manual transmission; cashmere interior; and choice of three exterior colors: White, tan or black.
I.D. DATA: There are 17 symbols. The first three indicate the manufacturer, make and type of vehicle. The fourth the GVW range. The next three tell the series and body style. The eighth tells the engine. After that is the check digit and a letter representing the model year. The 11th symbol identifies the assembly plant. The remaining six digits are the sequential production numbers.

Model	Body Type	Price	Weight	Prod. Total
OJL4	Pickup Sweptline	6202	2520	—

ENGINE: Four-cylinder. Displacement: 122 cid. Brake horsepower: 90 at 5000 rpm. Bore & stroke: 3.30 in. x 3.54 in. Compression ratio: 8.5:1. Carburetor: two-barrel. (This engine was rated at 88 hp in California.)
ARROW CUSTOM PICKUP: This was a new model for 1981. It came with many of the same standard features as the basic Arrow plus, chrome front bumper with black rubber ends; five-speed manual transmission; carpeting; 18-gal. fuel tank; and vinyl bodyside moldings. The Custom was offered in three exterior colors: Medium blue metallic, Warm white and black. All had blue interiors.
I.D. DATA: There are 17 symbols. The first three indicate the manufacturer, make and type of vehicle. The fourth the GVW range. The next three tell the series and body style. The eighth tells the engine. After that is the check digit and a letter representing the model year. The 11th symbol identifies the assembly plant. The remaining six digits are the sequential production numbers.

Model	Body Type	Price	Weight	Prod. Total
OJH4	Pickup Sweptline	6681	2565	—

ENGINE: Four-cylinder. Displacement: 156 cid. Brake horsepower: 105 at 5000 rpm. Bore & stroke: 3.59 in. x 3.86 in. Compression ratio: 8.2:1. Carburetor: two-barrel. (This engine was rated at 103 hp in California.)
ARROW SPORTS PICKUP: Top of the Arrow line was the Sport. Exclusive to this model were: a center console with oil pressure gauge, ammeter, and transmission shift lever; gold grille; AM/FM stereo radio; gold-painted wide spoke road wheels; bodyside tape stripes; and a five-speed manual transmission. The Sport was available in two exterior colors, red and Ballast sand metallic. The interior and high-back bucket seats were only available in two-tone cashmere and black.
I.D. DATA: There are 17 symbols. The first three indicate the manufacturer, make and type of vehicle. The fourth the GVW range. The next three tell the series and body style. The eighth tells the engine. After that is the check digit and a letter representing the model year. The 11th symbol identifies the assembly plant. The remaining six digits are the sequential production numbers.

Model	Body Type	Price	Weight	Prod. Total
OJP4	Pickup Sweptline	7240	2565	—

ENGINE: Four-cylinder. Displacement: 156 cid. Brake horsepower: 105 at 5000 rpm. Bore & stroke: 3.59 in. x 3.86 in. Compression ratio: 8.2:1. Carburetor: two-barrel. (This engine was rated at 103 hp in California.)
CHASSIS: Wheelbase: 109.4 in. Overall length: 184.6 in. Overall width: 65 in. Overall height: [Arrow] 60.6 in. [Arrow Custom/Arrow Sport] 59.8 in. Box length: 81.5 in. Box width: 64.2 in. GVW Rating: [Arrow] 4,045 lbs.; [Arrow Custom/Arrow Sport] 4,120 lbs. Payload (including driver and passengers): [Arrow] 1,525 lbs.; [Arrow Custom/Arrow Sport] 1,555 lbs. Tires: [Arrow] 6.00 x 14C white sidewall; [Arrow Custom] 185SR14 steel-belted radial white sidewall; [Arrow Sport] 185SR14 steel-belted radial raised white letter.
TECHNICAL: Three-speed automatic transmission.

1981 Plymouth Arrow Mini-Pickup (OCW)

CONVENIENCE OPTIONS: Air-conditioning. Chrome rear step bumper. Low-luster black rear step bumper. Front bumper guards (not available with grille guard). Electronic digital clock. Front floor mats (Arrow Custom and Arrow Sport). 18-gal. fuel tank (Arrow). Front grille guard (not available with Air-conditioning). Low-mount chrome exterior mirrors. Vinyl bodyside molding (Arrow). Vinyl pickup box top edge molding. Front and rear wheel openings moldings. Mud guards. Power steering. Sliding rear window. Sport bar in cargo box. Sky Lite sun roof. Bodyside tape stripe (Arrow and Arrow Custom). Wheel trim rings (Arrow and Arrow Custom).
NOTE: Chrysler Corp. was so sure buyers would like the 1981 Arrow pickup truck, it offered a money-back guarantee. If you weren't completely satisfied, you could bring it back in good condition, with no metal damage, within 30 days or 1,000 miles for a refund.
TRAIL DUSTER — SERIES PD150: The 4x2 Trail Duster received a new look for 1981 at its front, rear and side. It featured a flashier rectangular-section style grille with larger rectangular signal lights directly below the headlights. The backup lights were now on the lower level of the taillights. The two-piece tailgate of previous years was replaced with a one-piece fiberglass liftgate. The new, larger wraparound quarter windows were a real stand out feature. Even the instrument panel was changed. Standard equipment included: bright finish front and rear bumpers; automatic choke; Cleaner Air system; coolant reserve system; insulated dash liner; color-keyed inner door trim panels and armrests; electronic ignition system; black front floor mat with padding; 35-gal. fuel tank; tinted glass, all windows; aluminum grille with painted plastic insert and headlamp doors; single rectangular headlamps; fresh air heater with defrosters; single electric horn; bright hubcaps; padded instrument panel; combination map/courtesy light on instrument panel; rear compartment courtesy lights; dual bright finish short arm 5 x 7 in. exterior mirrors; power front disc brakes; AM radio; rear roof vent; deluxe vinyl low-back bucket seats; driver and-passenger color-keyed sun visors; bright quarter side window moldings; dual jet windshield washers; two-speed windshield wipers; and rear liftgate-open warning light.
I.D. DATA: There are 17 symbols. The first three indicate the manufacturer, make and type of vehicle. The fourth the GVW range. The next three tell the series and body style. The eighth tells the engine. After that is the check digit and a letter representing the model year. The 11th symbol identifies the assembly plant. The remaining six digits are the sequential production numbers.

Model	Body Type	Price	Weight	Prod. Total
PD150	Utility Vehicle	8257	3570	—

ENGINE: Displacement: 318 cid V-8. Brake horsepower: 120 at 3600 rpm. Bore & stroke: 3.91 in. x 3.31 in. Compression ratio: 8.5:1. Carburetor: two-barrel.
TRAIL DUSTER — SERIES PW150 — UTILITY VEHICLE: The part-time four-wheel drive PW150 shared most of the same features as the two-wheel drive PD150. In addition, it had: Power steering; front stabilizer bar; two-speed NP208 transfer case; locking front wheel hubs; and an NP435 four-speed manual transmission.
I.D. DATA: There are 17 symbols. The first three indicate the manufacturer, make and type of vehicle. The fourth the GVW range. The next three tell the series and body style. The eighth tells the engine. After that is the check digit and a letter representing the model year. The 11th symbol identifies the assembly plant. The remaining six digits are the sequential production numbers.

Model	Body Type	Price	Weight	Prod. Total
PW150	Utility Vehicle	9508	4126	—

ENGINE: Same as Trail Duster PD150.
CHASSIS: Wheelbase: 106 in. Overall length: 184.62 in. Overall width: 79.5 in. GVW Rating: [PD150] 5,300 lbs.; [PW150] 5,850 lbs. Tires: [PD150] P235/75R15 BSW GBR; [PW150] P235/75R15B BSW GBR.
TECHNICAL: [PW150] Three-speed automatic transmission. [PW150] 318 cid V-8 with four-barrel Carburetor. [PW150] 360 cid V-8 with four-barrel Carburetor.
OPTIONAL PACKAGES: Sno-Commander package: Includes snow removal equipment custom fitted to the vehicle. PW150 Convenience package: Includes two-speed intermittent windshield wipers; day/night interior 10 in. rearview mirror; glove box lock and light; ash receiver light; and in-cab-actuated hood lock release. Protection package: Includes door edge protectors; bright front bumper and guards with nerf strips; and bright rear bumper with nerf strips. Sport package: Includes bright windshield and drip rail molding and taillamp bezels; bright aluminum grille with chrome plastic insert and headlamp doors; upper and lower liftgate moldings with bright applique panel; power steering on PD150 models; woodtone trim applique on interior doors; assist straps; carpeting on lower door panels; color-keyed driver and front-passenger high-back Command bucket seats with cloth-and-vinyl trim; inboard fold-down armrests on seats; lockable console with removable styrofoam beverage chest; color-keyed folding rear bench seat with cloth-and-vinyl trim; color-keyed soft headliner, carpeting and rear side and liftgate inner trim panels; woodtone instrument cluster faceplate; black leather-wrapped steering wheel with black horn pad and woodtone insert; color-keyed spare tire cover (not available with 10R15 tires); cigar lighter; dual horns; bright front door sill scuff plate; underhood insulation panel; oil pressure, engine temperature gauges; color-keyed cowl side trim panels; and trip odometer. Macho package: Sport interior; special tu-tone exterior paint; Macho tape stripe; high-gloss black front and rear bumpers; five outline white-lettered steel-belted radial tires; four radial-ribbed aluminum wheels on PD150; steel spoke orange wheels and black accent on PW150; and heavy-duty stabilizer bar (PW150). Trailer Towing package: Light-duty for PD150/PW150 or heavy-duty for PW150.
CONVENIENCE OPTION: Air-conditioning. Heavy-duty alternator. Heavy-duty battery. Step type painted rear bumper. Electric digital clock. Lockable console. Auxiliary transmission oil-to-air cooler. Maximum engine cooling. Oil pressure, engine temperature and trip odometer gauges. Sunscreen privacy glass. Bright insert grille and headlamp doors. Halogen headlamps. Deluxe bi-level heater. Engine block heater. In-cab-actuated hood lock release. Two accessory type rubber mats. Dual bright 6 x 9 in. low mount mirrors. Bright 7-1/2 x 10-1/2 in. low mount extended mirrors. Lower exterior moldings. Upper exterior moldings. Power door locks. Power steering. Power windows. Radios: AM/FM, AM/FM stereo, AM/FM stereo/cassette tape player. Dolby noise reduction system. AM/FM stereo/eight-track tape player. AM/FM stereo/electronic search tune. AM/FM stereo with 40-channel CB transceiver. Heavy-duty front and rear shocks. Fuel tank shield. Transfer case shield (not available in PD150). Automatic speed control. Sport bar. Front stabilizer bar (PW150). Tilt type steering column. Four-spoke Sport steering wheel. Sky Lite sun roof. Bright wheelcovers. Premium wheelcovers (PD150). Wheels: 15 x 7 in. aluminum radial ribbed; five-slot chrome disc; white-painted steel spoke; road-type spare wheel. Two-speed/intermittent wipe windshield wiper.
NOTE: Trail Duster exterior colors for 1981 were: Bright silver metallic; Coffee brown metallic; Daystar blue metallic; Graphic yellow; Nightwatch blue; Impact orange; Impact blue; Impact red; Light seaspray green metallic; Medium crimson red; Medium seaspray green metallic; Black; cashmere; Pearl white; and Ginger.
VOYAGER — SERIES PB150 — WAGON: The newest thing about the 1981 Voyager was a couple of extra-cost seating options called Quad Command (bucket seats) and Converta-Bed (bench seat). Design-wise, it was the same as last year's model Standard features included: air vent doors; driver and front-passenger armrests; driver's compartment ashtray; front disc brakes; painted front and rear bumpers; Cleaner Air system; right-side double doors with vented glass; single rear door with fixed glass and inside door handle and lock button; electronic ignition system; black full-width floor mat; 22-gal. fuel tank; Argent silver finished grille; seven-inch round headlamps; perforated hardboard headliner with overprint pattern in the driver's compartment; fresh air heater with defroster; single electric horn; color-keyed horn pad; bright hubcaps; padded instrument panel and sun visors; electric windshield washers and wipers; brake system warning light; dual 5 x 7 in. painted exterior mirrors; nameplate on front doors; AM radio; driver and front-passenger low-back vinyl

bucket seats; three-passenger quick-release vinyl rear bench seat including three seat belts; spare tire carrier; color-keyed 16-1/2 in. diameter steering wheel; and four-speed manual transmission.

I.D. DATA: There are 17 symbols. The first three indicate the manufacturer, make and type of vehicle. The fourth the GVW range. The next three tell the series and body style. The eighth tells the engine. After that is the check digit and a letter representing the model year. The 11th symbol identifies the assembly plant. The remaining six digits are the sequential production numbers.

Model	Body Type	Price	Weight	Prod. Total
Voyager Van — 1/2-Ton — 109.6 in. w.b.				
PB150	Van	7701	3493	—
Voyager Van — 1/2-Ton — 127.6 in. w.b.				
PB150	Van	7890	3764	—

ENGINE: Six-cylinder. Displacement: 225 cid. Brake horsepower: 90 at 3600 rpm. Bore & stroke: 3.40 in. x 4.12 in. Compression ratio: 8.4:1. Carburetor: one-barrel.

VOYAGER — SERIES PB250 — WAGON: The mid-level Voyager had the same good looks as the basic model, but greater load capacity. This was especially true in the 127.6 in. wheelbase, extended body Maxi-Wagon, which sales literature claimed was America's roomiest wagon. A three-speed automatic transmission was standard in the Maxi-wagon.

I.D. DATA: There are 17 symbols. The first three indicate the manufacturer, make and type of vehicle. The fourth the GVW range. The next three tell the series and body style. The eighth tells the engine. After that is the check digit and a letter representing the model year. The 11th symbol identifies the assembly plant. The remaining six digits are the sequential production numbers.

Model	Body Type	Price	Weight	Prod. Total
Voyager Van — 3/4-Ton — 109.6 in. w.b.				
PB250	Van	6579	3805	—
Voyager Van — 3/4-Ton — 127.6 in. w.b.				
PB250	Van	6735	3930	—
PB250	Maxi-Wagon	7696	4280	—

ENGINE: [Wagon; 109.6 in. wheelbase] Six-cylinder. Displacement: 225 cid. Brake horsepower: 90 at 3600 rpm. Bore & stroke: 3.40 in. x 4.12 in. Compression ratio: 8.4:1. Carburetor: one-barrel.

ENGINE: [Maxi-Wagon; 127.6 in. wheelbase] 318 cid V-8. Brake horsepower: 120 at 3600 rpm. Bore & stroke: 3.91 in. x 3.31 Compression ratio: 8.5:1. Carburetor: two-barrel. (The 318 cid V-8 was not available in California. In that state, a 360 cid V-8 with four-barrel Carburetor was standard on the Maxi-Wagon.)

VOYAGER — SERIES PB350 — WAGON: Power steering and a three-speed automatic transmission were standard on the PB350. So were a color-keyed 15 in. diameter steering wheel and larger brakes. As before, the PB350 was for people who had to haul heavy loads on a regular basis.

I.D. DATA: There are 17 symbols. The first three indicate the manufacturer, make and type of vehicle. The fourth the GVW range. The next three tell the series and body style. The eighth tells the engine. After that is the check digit and a letter representing the model year. The 11th symbol identifies the assembly plant. The remaining six digits are the sequential production numbers.

Model	Body Type	Price	Weight	Prod. Total
Voyager Van — 1-Ton — 127.6 in. w.b.				
PB350	Wagon	8018	4140	—
PB350	Maxi-Wagon	8333	4280	—

ENGINE: [Wagon/Maxi-Wagon; 127.6 in. wheelbase] 318 cid V-8. Brake horsepower: 120 at 3600 rpm. Bore & stroke: 3.91 in. x 3.31 Compression ratio: 8.5:1. Carburetor: two-barrel. (The 318 cid V-8 was not available in California. In that state, a 360 cid V-8 with four-barrel Carburetor was standard on the Maxi-Wagon.)

CHASSIS: Wheelbase: [Wagon] 109.6 in.; [Wagon and Maxi-Wagon] 127.6 in. Overall height: [109.6 in. wheelbase] 79.6 in.; [127.6 in. wheelbase] 80.9 in.; [Maxi-Wagon] 80.6 in. Overall width: 79.8 in. Overall length: [109.6 in. wheelbase] 178.9 in.; [127.6 in. wheelbase] 196.9 in.; [Maxi-Wagon] 222.9 in. Tires: [PB150]: P205/75R15 glass-belted radial; [PB250 109.6 in. wheelbase] P225/75R15 glass-belted radial; [PB250 127.6 in. wheelbase Wagon] P235/75R15 glass-belted radial; [PB250 Maxi-Wagon] P235/75R15XL steel-belted radial; [PB350 Wagon] 8.00 x 16.5E (10PR) polyester bias-belted. GVW Rating: [PB150] 5,300 lbs.; [PB250] 5,800-6,400 lbs.; [PB350] 7,200-8,510 lbs.

TECHNICAL: [PB150/PB250] 318 cid V-8 with two-barrel Carburetor. [PB150/PB250/PB350] 318 cid V-8 with four-barrel Carburetor; [PB250/PB350] 360 cid V-8 with four-barrel Carburetor.

OPTION PACKAGES: Custom package: Includes, Voyager nameplates; bright molding around windshield, side and rear windows (except driver and passenger door windows); bright taillamp bezels; quad rectangular headlamps with halogen high beams; instrument panel lower skirts; cigar lighter; color-keyed headliner in driver and-passenger compartment; vinyl door and side trim panels with plaid insert; color-keyed carpeting; dash liner insulation; garnish trim over front door and compartment windows; and frames around rear compartment windows. Sport package: Includes, bright lower side and rear moldings; quad rectangular headlamps with halogen high-beams and bright grille; bright front and rear bumpers; dual 5 x 7 in; bright exterior mirrors; woodtone applique on lower face of instrument panel; horn pad with woodtone insert; spare tire cover; vinyl door and side trim panels with woodtone trim; dome light switches, door-operated on all doors; garnish trim over front doors and compartment windows, headers around rear compartment windows and pillars and windshield; dual electric horns; color-keyed unibelt restraint system; driver and front-passenger bucket seats and three-passenger rear bench seat in deluxe vinyl trim; soft cloth-covered driver and-passenger compartment headliner; accessory floor mats in driver's compartment; and electronic digital clock. Premier package: Includes bright upper side and rear and lower side and rear moldings; bright bumpers and bumper guards with nerf strips front and rear; bodyside and rear woodtone tape applique with dual gold accent strips; vinyl door and side trim panels with woodtone trim and front door applique pull-strap; carpeted engine housing cover; oil pressure gauge and trip odometer; power steering; leather-wrapped steering wheel; day/night interior mirror; glove box lock and light; deluxe windshield wipers (two-speed with intermittent wipe); inside actuated hood release lock; ignition and headlight switch with time delay; cigar lighter light; courtesy step well lamp (front and side doors); driver and front-passenger high-back reclining Command bucket seats; and a three-passenger rear bench seat (all in cloth-and-vinyl trim). Heavy-duty Insulation package: [For Sport and Premier Wagons] Includes interior lower fiberglass insulation panels (not offered on standard single rear door or optional sliding side door) and insulation under floor covering; [For Custom wagons] Includes all previous items, plus full-length headlining with insulation; [For Wagons] includes all the previous items, plus interior lower trim panels in-passenger compartment (blue or cashmere), garnish trim over front door headers and around headliner and rear compartment window, dash liner insulation and sliding door track cover. Eight-passenger seating package: [All PB250/PB350 models] Includes one additional quick-release three-passenger bench seat with three seat belts (not available teamed with 6,100 lbs. GVW package on 109.6 in. wheelbase PB250 model with six or on PB350 Maxi-Wagon with 8,510 lbs. GVW package). Quad Command Seating package: Includes four Command high-back bucket seats in blue, cashmere, or red cloth-and-vinyl trim. Eight-passenger Travel Seating package: Includes five-, seven-, or eight-passenger Converta-bed seating. Twelve-passenger Seating package: Includes two additional bench seats (second is three-passenger quick-release, third is four-passenger) and tire carrier located under third bench seat [not available on PB350 Maxi-Wagon with 8,510 lbs. GVW package and requires window retention and rear door(s) with optional vented glass in PB350]. Fifteen-passenger seating for PB350 Maxi-Wagon: Includes three additional bench seats (second and third are three-passenger, fourth four-passenger) and tire carrier relocated under fourth and fifth bench seat. [Requires window retention and rear door/doors with vented glass.] Convenience package: Includes, cigar lighter; glove box lock; 10 in. day/night rearview mirror; in-cab-actuated hood lock release; and two-speed windshield wipers with intermittent wiper. Light package: Includes ignition and headlight switch with time delay (Requires cigar lighter at extra cost.)

CONVENIENCE OPTIONS: Air-conditioning. Heavy-duty alternator (63 amp. or 117 amp.). 59 amp.-hr./375 amp. Cold Crank heavy-duty battery. 70 amp.-hr./430 amp. Cold Crank maintenance-free battery. 85 amp.-hr./500 amp. Cold Crank long-life battery. Hitch type bright rear bumper. Bright front and rear bumper. Bright front and rear bumper with guards and nerf strips. Cigar lighter. Electronic digital clock. Auxiliary transmission oil to air cooling. Maximum engine cooling. Rear window electric defroster for single rear door. Dual rear doors with fixed or vented glass. Single rear door with vented glass. Sliding-passenger side door. 36-gal. fuel tank. Oil pressure and trip odometer gauges. Sun screen privacy glass. All windows tinted. Bright grille (includes quad rectangular headlamps with halogen high beams.) Passenger compartment headliner. Auxiliary rear heater. Deluxe front heater. Dual electric horns. Interior reading lamp in driver's compartment. In-cab-actuated hood release. Two color-keyed accessory type rubber mats in driver's compartment. Dual exterior low-mount 6 x 9 in. painted or bright mirrors. Dual exterior short arm 5 x by 7 in. bright mirrors. Illuminated vanity. Interior day/night mirror. Lower moldings (includes side and rear). Upper moldings (includes side, rear and bright taillamp bezels). Upper and lower moldings. Electric door locks. Power steering. Electric front doors windows. Radios: AM/FM. AM/FM stereo. AM/FM stereo with cassette tape player and Dolby noise reduction system. AM/FM stereo with eight-track tape player. AM/FM stereo with electronic search-tune. AM/FM stereo with 40-channel CB transceiver. Rear speaker for AM or AM/FM radio only. Heavy-duty front and rear shock absorbers. Color-keyed spare tire cover. Automatic speed control. Front stabilizer bar. Tilt-type steering column. Leather-wrapped steering wheel. Sky Lite driver's compartment sun roof. Door operated dome light switch. Color-keyed unibelt restraint system. Wheels: Road-type 15 x 7 in. Radial ribbed aluminum. Five-slot chrome disc. White painted spoke. Road type spare wheel. Bright wheelcovers. Premium wheelcovers. Deluxe windshield wipers with intermittent wipe.

NOTE: 1981 Voyagers were offered in the following colors: Cashmere; Graphic yellow (not offered on Sport or Premier); Impact red; Medium crimson red; Ginger (not offered on Sport or Premier); Coffee brown metallic; Impact blue (not offered on Sport or Premier); Nightwatch blue; Medium seaspray green metallic (not offered on Sport or Premier); Daystar blue metallic; Bright silver metallic; Pearl white; and black. There were two styles of two-toning.

1982 PLYMOUTH

1982 Plymouth Arrow Mini-Pickup (OCW)

ARROW CUSTOM PICKUP: The Arrow Custom dropped a notch to become the basic pickup in the Arrow line. A blacked-out grille and headlamp trim were the only major styling changes for 1982. Standard features included: Argent painted front bumper with black rubber ends; cargo lamp; cigarette lighter; dome light with driver and-passenger side door switches; emergency flashers; 18-gal. fuel tank; tinted glass; flat-black grille; color-keyed headliner; inside hood release; bright hubcaps; left and right side black sport type exterior mirrors; interior rearview mirror; bright drip rail molding; bright windshield molding; AM radio; adjustable angle steering column; dual sun visors; tubular low-mount tie-down bars on both sides of the interior of the pickup box; trip odometer; two-speed windshield wipers with washers; and four-speed manual transmission. Three exterior colors were offered: white, light tan or red.

I.D. DATA: There are 17 symbols. The first three indicate the manufacturer, make and type of vehicle. The fourth the GVW range. The next three tell the series and body style. The eighth tells the engine. After that is the check digit and a letter representing the model year. The 11th symbol identifies the assembly plant. The remaining six digits are the sequential production numbers.

Model	Body Type	Price	Weight	Prod. Total
OJL4	Pickup Sweptline	6408	2540	—

ENGINE: Four-cylinder. Displacement: 122 cid. Brake horsepower: 90 at 5000 rpm. Bore & stroke: 3.30 in. x 3.54 in. Compression ratio: 8.5:1. Carburetor: two-barrel. (This engine was rated at 88 hp in California.)

ARROW ROYAL PICKUP: The new Arrow Royal had a slightly higher payload rating than the Custom. It also came with steel-belted radial white sidewall tires; chrome front bumper; vinyl bodyside moldings; carpeting; a blue tweed cloth-and-vinyl bench seat; and a five-speed manual transmission. Royal buyers had their choice of three exterior colors: Dark blue metallic, white or Medium blue metallic.

I.D. DATA: There are 17 symbols. The first three indicate the manufacturer, make and type of vehicle. The fourth the GVW range. The next three tell the series and body style. The eighth tells the engine. After that is the check digit and a letter representing the model year. The 11th symbol identifies the assembly plant. The remaining six digits are the sequential production numbers.

Model	Body Type	Price	Weight	Prod. Total
OJH4	Pickup Sweptline	6892	2565	—

ENGINE: Four-cylinder. Displacement: 156 cid. Brake horsepower: 105 at 5000 rpm. Bore & stroke: 3.59 in. x 3.86 in. Compression ratio: 8.2:1. Carburetor: two-barrel. (This engine was rated at 103 hp in California.)

ARROW SPORT PICKUP: This was the flashiest and plushest Arrow. In addition to many of the standard features offered on the other two models, it also came with: center console with oil pressure gauge, ammeter and transmission shift lever; AM/FM stereo radio; wide spoke color-keyed road wheels; tape stripes on the bodyside, tailgate, wheel lips and air dam; red/tan two-tone velour cloth bucket seats; and five-speed manual transmission. Two exterior colors were available: Dark red or Corsica brown.

I.D. DATA: There are 17 symbols. The first three indicate the manufacturer, make and type of vehicle. The fourth the GVW range. The next three tell the series and body style. The eighth tells the engine. After that is the check digit and a letter representing the model year. The 11th symbol identifies the assembly plant. The remaining six digits are the sequential production numbers.

Model	Body Type	Price	Weight	Prod. Total
OJP4	Pickup Sweptline	7474	2585	—

ENGINE: Four-cylinder. Displacement: 156 cid. Brake horsepower: 105 at 5000 rpm. Bore & stroke: 3.59 in. x 3.86 in. Compression ratio: 8.2:1. Carburetor: two-barrel. (This engine was rated at 103 hp in California.)

CHASSIS: Wheelbase: 109.4 in. Overall length: 194.6 in. Overall width: 65 in. Overall height: [Arrow Custom] 60.6 in.; [Arrow Royal/Arrow Sport] 59.8 in. Box length: 81.5 in. Box width: 64.2 in. GVW Rating: [Arrow Custom] 4,025 lbs.; [Arrow Custom with five-speed manual] 3,595 lbs.; [Arrow Royal/Arrow Sport] 4,120 lbs. Payload: [Arrow Custom with four-speed manual] 1,505 lbs.; [Arrow Custom with five-speed manual] 1,055 lbs.; [Arrow Royal] 1,555 lbs.; [Arrow Sport] 1,535 lbs. Tires: [Arrow Custom with four-speed manual] 6.00 x 14C white sidewall; [Arrow Custom/Arrow Royal with five-speed manual] 185SR14 steel-belted radial white sidewall; [Arrow Sport] 185SR14 steel-belted radial raised white-letter.

TECHNICAL: [Arrow Custom] Five-speed manual transmission. [Arrow Royal/Arrow Sport] Three-speed automatic transmission.

CONVENIENCE OPTIONS: Air-conditioning (not available with grille guard). Rear step chrome bumper. Rear step low-luster black bumper. Front bumper guards (not available with grille guard). Electronic digital clock. High-altitude emissions package: Arrow Royal/ Arrow Sport. Front floor mats: Arrow Royal/Arrow Sport. Grille guard. Exterior low-mount chrome mirrors. Vinyl bodyside molding on Custom. Vinyl pickup box top edge molding. Front and rear wheel openings moldings: Arrow Custom/Arrow Royal. Mud guards. Power steering. Sliding rear window. Automatic speed control: Arrow Royal/Arrow Sport). Sport bar. Skylite sun roof. Bodyside tape stripe on Custom and Royal. Sport tape stripe package on Sport. Wheel trim rings for Custom and Royal. Tonneau cover. Pickup bed liner. Side-wall liners. Runningboards.

1982 Plymouth Voyager Family Van (OCW)

VOYAGER — SERIES PB150 — WAGON: Voyager styling was carried over from the previous year. Standard features included: Driver and front-passenger armrests; driver's compartment ashtray; front disc brakes; painted front and rear bumper; cigar lighter; Cleaner Air system; right side double doors with vented glass; single rear door with fixed glass and inside door handle and lock button; electronic ignition system; black full-width floor mat; 22-gal.; glove box with door; Argent silver finish grille; seven-inch; round headlamps; color-keyed driver's compartment headliner; fresh air heater with defroster; in-cab-activated hood release; dual electric horns; bright hubcaps; driver and passenger compartment lights with door-operated switches; locks, all doors; day/night rearview mirror; dual bright 5 x 7 in; exterior mirrors; nameplate on front doors; power steering; AM radio; driver and front-passenger low-back vinyl bucket seats; three-passenger quick-release vinyl rear bench seat; color-keyed five-inch diameter steering wheel; padded color-keyed sun visors; inside-mounted spare tire carrier; two-speed (non-intermittent) windshield wipers with washer; padded dash; brake system warning light; dual braking system with separate brake fluid reservoirs in the master cylinder; energy-absorbing steering column; and four-speed manual transmission with overdrive.

I.D. DATA: There are 17 symbols. The first three indicate the manufacturer, make and type of vehicle. The fourth the GVW range. The next three tell the series and body style. The eighth tells the engine. After that is the check digit and a letter representing the model year. The 11th symbol identifies the assembly plant. The remaining six digits are the sequential production numbers.

Model	Body Type	Price	Weight	Prod. Total
Voyager Van — 1/2-Ton — 109.6 in. w.b.				
PB150	Van	8482	3604	—
Voyager Van — 1/2-Ton — 127.6 in. w.b.				
PB150	Van	8682	3604	—

ENGINE: Six-cylinder. Displacement: 225 cid. Brake horsepower: 90 at 3600 rpm. Bore & stroke: 3.40 in. x 4.12 in. Compression ratio: 8.4:1. Carburetor: one-barrel.

VOYAGER — SERIES PB250 — WAGON: This was the perfect Voyager for large families or people who did a lot of hauling, yet were concerned with fuel economy. It was the heaviest Voyager available with six-cylinder powerplant. As before, three sizes were offered. The largest was the Maxi-Wagon.

I.D. DATA: There are 17 symbols. The first three indicate the manufacturer, make and type of vehicle. The fourth the GVW range. The next three tell the series and body style. The eighth tells the engine. After that is the check digit and a letter representing the model year. The 11th symbol identifies the assembly plant. The remaining six digits are the sequential production numbers.

Model	Body Type	Price	Weight	Prod. Total
Voyager Van — 3/4-Ton — 109.6 in. w.b.				
PB250	Van	8767	3805	—
Voyager Van — 3/4-Ton — 127.6 in. w.b.				
PB250	Van	8895	3930	—
PB250	Maxi-Wagon	9980	4280	—

ENGINE: [109.6 in./standard 127.6 in. wheelbase Wagons] Six-cylinder. Displacement: 225 cid. Brake horsepower: 90 at 3600 rpm. Bore & stroke: 3.40 in. x 4.12 in. Compression ratio: 8.4:1. Carburetor: one-barrel.

ENGINE: [Maxi-Wagon] 318 cid V-8. Brake horsepower: 120 at 3600 rpm. Bore & stroke: 3.91 in. x 3.31 Compression ratio: 8.5:1. Carburetor: two-barrel. (The 318 cid V-8 with two-barrel Carburetor was not available in California.)

VOYAGER — SERIES PB350 — WAGON: The ultimate Voyager for big payloads was the PB350. Larger brakes and a three-speed automatic transmission were standard. The Maxi-Wagon came with heavy-duty shocks.

I.D. DATA: There are 17 symbols. The first three indicate the manufacturer, make and type of vehicle. The fourth the GVW range. The next three tell the series and body style. The eighth tells the engine. After that is the check digit and a letter representing the model year. The 11th symbol identifies the assembly plant. The remaining six digits are the sequential production numbers.

Model	Body Type	Price	Weight	Prod. Total
Voyager Van — 1-Ton — 127.6 in. w.b.				
PB350	Van	10,159	4140	—
PB350	Maxi-Wagon	10,687	4280	—

ENGINE: [Maxi-Wagon] 318 cid V-8. Brake horsepower: 120 at 3600 rpm. Bore & stroke: 3.91 in. x 3.31 Compression ratio: 8.5:1. Carburetor: two-barrel. (The 318 cid V-8 with two-barrel Carburetor was not available in California.)

CHASSIS: Wheelbase: [Wagon] 109.6 in.; [Wagon/Maxi-Wagon] 127.6 in. Overall height: [109.6 in. wheelbase] 79.6 in.; [127.6 in. wheelbase Wagon] 80.9 in.; [Maxi-Wagon] 80.6 in. Overall width: 79.8 in. Overall length: [109.6 in. wheelbase] 178.9 in.; [127.6 in. wheelbase Wagon] 196.9 in.; [Maxi-Wagon] 222.9 in. Tires: [PB150] P205/75R15 glass-belted radial; [PB250 127.6 in. wheelbase 6,010 lbs. GVW] P225/75R15 glass-belted radial; [PB250 109.6 in. wheelbase 6,010 lbs. GVW and 127.6 in. wheelbase with 6,400 lbs. GVW] P235/ 75R15 glass-belted radial; [PB250 Maxi-Wagon] P235/75R15XL; [PB350 Wagon 127.6 in. wheelbase] 8.00 x 16.5E (10PR) polyester bias-belted; [PB350 Maxi-Wagon] 8.75 x 16.5E (10PR) polyester bias-belted. GVW Rating: [PB150] 5,300 lbs.; [PB250/109.6 in. wheel-base and 127.6 in. wheelbase Wagon] 6,010 lbs.; [PB250/127.6 in. wheelbase Wagon/ Maxi-Wagon] 6,400 lbs.; [PB350 127.6 in. wheelbase Wagon/Maxi-Wagon] 7,500 lbs. and [PB350 Maxi-Wagon] 8,510 lbs.

TECHNICAL: [PB150/PB250] 318 cid V-8 with two-barrel Carburetor. [PB150/PB250/ PB350] 318 cid V-8 with four-barrel Carburetor. [PB350] 360 cid V-8 with four-barrel Carburetor. [PB150/PB250] Three-speed automatic transmission.

OPTIONAL PACKAGES: Sport package: Includes bright exterior nameplates, lower side and rear moldings; dual vertically-stacked quad rectangular headlamps with halogen high beams and bright grille; bright front and rear bumpers; bright molding around windshield, side and rear windows (except driver and-passenger door windows); bright taillamp bezels; woodtone applique on lower face of instrument panel; spare tire cover; vinyl door and side trim panels with woodtone trim; garnish moldings over front doors and passenger compartment windows; headers around rear compartment windows and front pillar and windshield; driver and front passenger color-keyed low-back bucket seats and bench seat in deluxe vinyl trim; soft cloth-covered headliner with insulation in driver and passenger compartment; accessory floor mats in driver's compartment; electronic digitial clock; instrument panel lower skirts; color-keyed carpeting; dash liner insulation; and luxury steering wheel with woodtone rim insert. Premier package: Includes, bright exterior nameplate, upper side and rear moldings; bright bumper guards with rub strips, front and rear; body-side and rear woodtone tape applique with dual gold accent strips; vinyl door and side trim panels with woodtone trim and front door pull straps; color-keyed carpeted engine housing cover; oil pressure gauge and trip odometer; glove box lock and light; deluxe two-speed windshield wipers with intermittent wipe; ignition and headlight switch with time delay; cigar lighter light; courtesy step well lamp, front and side doors; driver and front-passenger color-keyed high-back reclining Command bucket seats; and a three-passenger bench seat with matching cloth-and-vinyl trim. Exterior appearance package: Includes, bright grille; bright front and rear bumpers; bright taillamp bezels; bright windshield molding; dual vertically-stacked quad rectangular headlamps with halogen high beams; and bright side and rear window moldings (except driver and front-passenger door windows). Insulation package: [For Sport and Premier Wagons] Includes interior lower fiberglass insulation panels, except on standard single rear door or optional sliding side door, and insulation under floor covering; [For Voyager wagons] includes the items listed for Sport/Premier wagons, plus interior lower trim panels in-passenger compartment in blue or cashmere color; color-keyed garnish moldings over front door headers and around headliner and rear compartment window; dash liner insulation; sliding side door track cover; and white hardboard headliner in-passenger compartment. Quad Command seating package: Includes four high-back Command bucket seats and five- or eight-passenger Converta-bed seating. Eight-passenger travel seating package for PB250/PB350: Includes, eight-passenger seating with one additional quick-release three-passenger bench seat with three seat belts (Not available on PB350 Maxi-Wagon with 8,510 lbs. GVW package). Twelve-passenger seating for all PB350s: Includes two additional bench seats (the second a three-passenger quick-release bench seat; the third a four-passenger seat) and spare tire carrier relocated under third bench seat. Requires window retention and rear door(s) with optional vented glass (not available on PB350 Maxi-Wagon with 8,510 lbs. GVW package). Fifteen-passenger seating for PB350 Maxi-Wagon only: Includes three additional bench seats (second and third three-passenger seats with quick-release; the fourth, of four-passenger design), plus tire carrier relocated under fourth bench seat. Requires 8,510 lbs. GVW package and window retention and rear door/doors with optional vented glass at extra cost. Heavy-duty trailer towing package for PB250/PB350: Includes Maximum Cooling equipment; 60 amp. alternator; 430 amp. maintenance-free battery; seven-wire harness; Class IV tow bar hitch; heavy-duty variable load flasher; and heavy-duty shocks (requires the following at extra cost: automatic transmission, 318 cid four-barrel V-8 or 360 cid four-barrel V-8; transmission auxiliary oil cooler; and 36-gal. fuel tank. Convenience package: Includes cigar lighter; glove box lock and light; ignition and headlight switch with time delay (not available with tilt steering); two-speed windshield wipers with intermittent wipe; and courtesy step well lamps for front and side doors (available teamed with Sport package only).

CONVENIENCE OPTIONS: Air-conditioning (integral front, auxiliary rear with or without auxiliary heater). Heavy-duty alternators. Heavy-duty batteries. Bright front and rear bumpers, guards and rub strips. Bright front and rear bumpers. Electronic digital clock. Auxiliary transmission oil to air cooling. Maximum engine cooling. Electric rear window defroster for single rear door. Dual rear doors with vented glass. Single rear door with vented glass. Sliding-passenger side door. 36-gal. fuel tank. Oil pressure and trip odometer gauges. Sun screen privacy glass. Tinted glass, all windows. Bright grille with dual quad rectangular headlamps, vertically-stacked with halogen high beams. Auxiliary rear heater. Deluxe front heater. Engine block heater. Two color-keyed (accessory type) rubber mats in driver's compartment. Dual low-mount 6 x 9 in. bright exterior mirrors. Lower moldings (includes side, rear and bright taillamp bezel moldings). Upper moldings (includes side, rear and bright taillamp bezels). Upper and lower moldings with bright taillamp bezels. Electronic display warning indicator for engine oil level, transmission oil level, radiator coolant level and transmission oil temperature. Electric door locks. Power front door windows. Radios: AM/FM stereo. AM/FM stereo with cassette tape player, electronic tuning and Dolby noise reduction system. AM/FM stereo with Search-Tune and electronic tuning. AM/FM stereo with eight-track tape player. AM/FM stereo with 40-channel CB transceiver. Heavy-duty shock absorbers. Automatic speed control. Front stabilizer bar. Tilt type steering column. Luxury type steering wheel. Bright deluxe wheelcovers. Wheels: (Road type 15 x 7 in.) Aluminum radial ribbed. Five-slot chrome disc. Deluxe two-speed windshield wipers with intermittent wipe.

1983 PLYMOUTH

SCAMP PICKUP: "The dashing good looks of a sporty car...the carry-all utility of a small truck." That's how sales literature described Plymouth's new Scamp. This front-wheel drive vehicle was more like a mini El Camino than a traditional pickup. From the front it looked just like the Plymouth Turismo. The two rectangular headlights were recessed into the front fenders. The aggressive looking "missing teeth" grille and thin front bumper seemed molded into the aerodynamic body. The large, vertical taillights had backup lights in their lower section. Standard equipment included: cigarette lighter; Cleaner Air system; clock and trip odometer; coat hooks; directional signals with lane-change feature; black exterior door handle inserts; hazard warning flashers; electronic fuel control system; 13-gal. fuel tank; tinted glass, all windows; halogen headlights; cloth-covered headliner; heater and defroster; inside hood release; hood silencer pad; dual horns; electronic ignition and voltage regulator; instrument panel padding; glove box lock; driver's side remote exterior mirror; interior day/night rearview mirror; passenger side visor vanity mirror; cargo box flange trim molding; bright wheel lip and sill moldings; black windshield and rear window moldings; package tray; rack-and-pinion steering; color-keyed four-spoke sport steering wheel; bodyside and rear stripes; leaf spring rear suspension; four-speed manual transmission; electric windshield washers; and deluxe windshield wipers with intermittent wipe.

I.D. DATA: There are 17 symbols. The first three indicate the manufacturer, make and type of vehicle. The fourth the GVW range. The next three tell the series and body style. The eighth tells the engine. After that is the check digit and a letter representing the model year. The 11th symbol identifies the assembly plant. The remaining six digits are the sequential production numbers.

Model	Body Type	Price	Weight	Prod. Total
MH28	Pickup	6683	2305	—

ENGINE: Four-cylinder. Displacement: 135 cid. Brake horsepower: 84 at 4800 rpm. Bore & stroke: 3.44 in. x 3.62 in. Compression ratio: 8.5:1. Carburetor: two-barrel.

SCAMP GT PICKUP: Scamp buyers who wanted something with a bit more flash could step up to the GT. It came with most of the same standard features as the basic model plus: simulated hood scoop; Rallye instrument cluster that included a tachometer, clock and trip odometer; AM radio; GT tape graphics stripes; Rallye wheels (14 in. Argent silver steel with trim rings); and five-speed manual transmission. Buyers had a choice of two interiors. The first had cloth-and-vinyl high-back bucket seats with integral head restraints and reclining seatbacks in black with a wide vertical red stripe. The second had solid black versions of the same seats.

I.D. DATA: There are 17 symbols. The first three indicate the manufacturer, make and type of vehicle. The fourth the GVW range. The next three tell the series and body style. The eighth tells the engine. After that is the check digit and a letter representing the model year. The 11th symbol identifies the assembly plant. The remaining six digits are the sequential production numbers.

Model	Body Type	Price	Weight	Prod. Total
MS28	Pickup	7204	2340	—

ENGINE: Four-cylinder. Displacement: 135 cid. Brake horsepower: 84 at 4800 rpm. Bore & stroke: 3.44 in. x 3.62 in. Compression ratio: 8.5:1. Carburetor: two-barrel.

CHASSIS: Wheelbase: 104.2 in. Overall length: 183.6 in. Overall width: 66.8 in. Overall height: 51.8 in. Box length: 63.7 in. Payload: [Scamp] 1,145 lbs.; [Scamp GT] 2,110 lbs. Tires: [Scamp] P175/75R13 BSW glass-belted radials; [Scamp GT] P195/60R14 BSW steel-belted radial with raised black letters.

TECHNICAL: Five-speed manual transmission (Scamp.). Three-speed automatic transmission.

CONVENIENCE OPTIONS: Light package: Includes, ash receiver light; glove box light; headlamps-on warning buzzer; ignition switch light with time delay; and map/courtesy light. Protection package: Includes vinyl lower bodyside corrosion protection; undercoating; and front floor mats. Cold weather package: Includes 430 amp. maintenance-free battery; engine block heater; air-conditioning; front license plate bracket; Rallye cluster, includes tachometer, clock and trip odometer. Painted remote-control mirror. Power steering. Radios: AM. AM/FM stereo, manually-tuned. AM/FM stereo, electronically tuned. AM/FM stereo with cassette tape player and Dolby system, electronically tuned. Cargo box side rails. Automatic speed control. Tonneau cover. Cast aluminum wheels, 14 in.; Rallye wheels, 13 in.; or Rallye wheels, 14 in.

Standard Catalog of Light-Duty Trucks

1983 Plymouth Voyager Wagon (OCW)

VOYAGER — SERIES PB150 — WAGON: Voyager styling was basically unchanged for 1983. However, there was now only one two-tone paint procedure. Standard features included: Brake warning light; dual braking system with separate brake fluid reservoirs in the master cylinder; electric windshield washers and wipers; fade-resistant front disc brakes; inside hood release; padded instrument panel and sun visors; traffic hazard warning flasher system; air vent doors; driver and front passenger armrests; driver's compartment ashtray; a 370 amp. maintenance-free battery; painted front and rear bumper; cigar lighter; Cleaner Air system; right side double doors with vented and banded glass; single rear door with fixed glass and side door handle and lock button; electronic ignition system; full-width black floor mat; 22-gal. fuel tank; tinted glass, all windows; Argent silver finished grille; round headlamps; color-keyed driver's compartment headliner; deluxe fresh air heater with defroster; in-cab activated hood release; dual electric horns; bright hubcaps; bumper type jack; interior rearview day/night mirror; dual bright 5 x 7 in. exterior mirrors; nameplates on front doors; power steering; AM radio; deluxe driver and front-passenger high-back vinyl Command bucket seats; three-passenger quick-release deluxe vinyl rear bench seat with three seat belts; color-keyed 15 in. diameter steering wheel; inside-mounted spare tire carrier; and four-speed manual transmission with overdrive.

I.D. DATA: There are 17 symbols. The first three indicate the manufacturer, make and type of vehicle. The fourth the GVW range. The next three tell the series and body style. The eighth tells the engine. After that is the check digit and a letter representing the model year. The 11th symbol identifies the assembly plant. The remaining six digits are the sequential production numbers.

Model	Body Type	Price	Weight	Prod. Total
Voyager Van — 1/2-Ton — 109.6 in. w.b.				
PB150	Wagon	8885	3604	—
Voyager Van — 1/2-Ton — 127.6 in. w.b.				
PB150	Wagon	9085	3764	—

ENGINE: Six-cylinder. Displacement: 225 cid. Brake horsepower: 90 at 3600 rpm. Bore & stroke: 3.40 in. x 4.12 in. Compression ratio: 8.4:1. Carburetor: one-barrel.

VOYAGER — SERIES PB250 — WAGON: The mid-line PB250 came with the same standard features as the PB150, but it could haul heavier loads. It also offered an additional body size. This was the Maxi-Wagon, with a 127 in. wheelbase and extended body. Maxi-wagons came equipped with automatic transmission.

I.D. DATA: There are 17 symbols. The first three indicate the manufacturer, make and type of vehicle. The fourth the GVW range. The next three tell the series and body style. The eighth tells the engine. After that is the check digit and a letter representing the model year. The 11th symbol identifies the assembly plant. The remaining six digits are the sequential production numbers.

Model	Body Type	Price	Weight	Prod. Total
Voyager Van — 3/4-Ton — 127.6 in. w.b.				
PB250	Wagon	9486	3930	—
PB250	Maxi-Wagon	10,030	4280	—

ENGINE: [Wagon] Six-cylinder. Displacement: 225 cid. Brake horsepower: 90 at 3600 rpm. Bore & stroke: 3.40 in. x 4.12 in. Compression ratio: 8.4:1. Carburetor: one-barrel.

ENGINE: [Maxi-Wagon] 318 cid V-8. Brake horsepower: 120 at 3600 rpm. Bore & stroke: 3.91 in. x 3.31 Compression ratio: 8.5:1. Carburetor: two-barrel. (The 318 cid V-8 with two-barrel Carburetor was not available in California.)

VOYAGER — SERIES PB350 — WAGON: The PB350 was the Voyager for buyers who wanted maximum load capacity. It could be had in a standard 127.6 in. wheelbase Wagon version or the extra-roomy extended Maxi-Wagon. Both came equipped with automatic transmission, larger brakes and axle type jacks.

I.D. DATA: There are 17 symbols. The first three indicate the manufacturer, make and type of vehicle. The fourth the GVW range. The next three tell the series and body style. The eighth tells the engine. After that is the check digit and a letter representing the model year. The 11th symbol identifies the assembly plant. The remaining six digits are the sequential production numbers.

Model	Body Type	Price	Weight	Prod. Total
Voyager Van — 1-Ton — 127.6 in. w.b.				
PB350	Wagon	10,708	4140	—
Voyager Van — 1-Ton — 127.6 in. w.b.				
PB350	Maxi-Wagon	11,260	4280	—

ENGINE: [Maxi-Wagon] 318 cid V-8. Brake horsepower: 120 at 3600 rpm. Bore & stroke: 3.91 in. x 3.31 Compression ratio: 8.5:1. Carburetor: two-barrel. (The 318 cid V-8 with two-barrel Carburetor was not available in California.)

CHASSIS: Wheelbase [Wagon] 109.6 in.; [Wagon and Maxi-Wagon] 127.6 in. Overall height: [109.6 in. wheelbase] 79.6 in.; [127.6 in. wheelbase Wagon] 80.9 in.; [Maxi-Wagon] 80.6 in. Overall width: 79.8 in. Overall length: [109.6 in. wheelbase] 178.9 in.; [127.6 in. wheelbase Wagon] 196.9 in.; [Maxi-Wagon] 222.9 in. Tires: [PB150] P205/75R15 glass-belted radial; [PB250/127.6 in. wheelbase Wagon] P225/75R15 glass-belted radial; [PB250 Maxi-Wagon] P235/75R15XL steel-belted radial; [PB350 Wagon] 8.00 x 16.5E polyester bias-belted; [PB350 Maxi-Wagon] 8.75 x 16.5E polyester bias-belted. GVW Ratings: [PB150] 5,300-6,010 lbs.; [PB250] 6,010-6,400 lbs.; [PB350] 7,500-8,510 lbs.

TECHNICAL: [PB150/PB250] 318 cid V-8 with two-barrel Carburetor. [PB150/PB250/PB350] 318 cid V-8 with four-barrel Carburetor. [PB350] 360 cid V-8 with four-barrel Carburetor. [PB150/PB250] Three-speed automatic transmission.

OPTIONAL PACKAGES: Sport package: Includes bright exterior nameplates, lower side and rear moldings; dual vertically-stacked quad rectangular headlamps with halogen high beams and bright grille; bright front and rear bumpers; bright molding around windshield, side and rear windows (except driver and-passenger door windows); bright taillamp; bezels; woodtone applique on lower face of instrument panel; spare tire cover; vinyl door and side trim panels with woodtone trim; garnish moldings over front doors and passenger compartment windows; headers around rear compartment windows and front pillar and windshield; driver and front passenger color-keyed low-back bucket seats and bench seat in deluxe vinyl trim; soft cloth-covered headliner with insulation in driver and passenger compartment; accessory floor mats in driver's compartment; electronic digitial clock; instrument panel lower skirts; color-keyed carpeting; dash liner insulation; and luxury steering wheel with woodtone rim insert. Premier package: Includes, bright exterior nameplate, upper side and rear moldings; bright bumper guards with rub strips, front and rear; body-side and rear woodtone tape applique with dual gold accent strips; vinyl door and side trim panels with woodtone trim and front door pull straps; color-keyed carpeted engine housing cover; oil pressure gauge and trip odometer; glove box lock and light; deluxe two-speed windshield wipers with intermittent wipe; ignition and headlight switch with time delay; cigar lighter light; courtesy step well lamp, front and side doors; driver and front-passenger color-keyed high-back reclining Command bucket seats; and a three-passenger bench seat with matching cloth-and-vinyl trim. Exterior appearance package: Includes, bright grille; bright front and rear bumpers; bright taillamp bezels; bright windshield molding; dual vertically-stacked quad rectangular headlamps with halogen high beams; and bright side and rear window moldings (except driver and front-passenger door windows). Insulation package: [For Sport and Premier Wagons] Includes interior nylon fiberglass insulation panels, except on standard single rear door or optional sliding side door, and insulation under floor covering; [For Voyager wagons] includes the items listed for Sport/Premier wagons, plus interior lower trim panels in-passenger compartment in blue or cashmere color; color-keyed garnish moldings over front door headers and around headliner and rear compartment window; dash liner insulation; sliding side door track cover; and white hardboard headliner in-passenger compartment. Quad Command seating package: Includes four high-back Command bucket seats and five- or eight-passenger Converta-bed seating. Eight-passenger travel seating package for PB250/PB350: Includes, eight-passenger seating with one additional quick-release three-passenger bench seat with three seat belts (Not available on PB350 Maxi-Wagon with 8,510 lbs. GVW package). Twelve-passenger seating for all PB350s: Includes two additional bench seats (the second a three-passenger quick-release bench seat; the third a four-passenger seat) and spare tire carrier relocated under third bench seat. Requires window retention and rear door(s) with optional vented glass (not available on PB350 Maxi-Wagon with 8,510 lbs. GVW package). Fifteen-passenger seating for PB350 Maxi-Wagon only: Includes three additional bench seats (second and third three-passenger seats with quick-release; the fourth, of four-passenger design), plus tire carrier relocated under fourth bench seat. Requires 8,510 lbs. GVW package and window retention and rear door/doors with optional vented glass at extra cost. Heavy-duty trailer towing package for PB250/PB350: Includes Maximum Cooling equipment; 60 amp. alternator; 430 amp. maintenance-free battery; seven-wire harness; Class IV tow bar hitch; heavy-duty variable load flasher; and heavy-duty shocks (requires the following at extra cost: automatic transmission, 318 cid four-barrel V-8 or 360 cid four-barrel V-8; transmission auxiliary oil cooler; and 36-gal. fuel tank. Convenience package: Includes cigar lighter; glove box lock and light; ignition and headlight switch with time delay (not available with tilt steering); two-speed windshield wipers with intermittent wipe; and courtesy step well lamps for front and side doors (available teamed with Sport package only).

CONVENIENCE OPTIONS: Air-conditioning (integral front, auxiliary rear with or without auxiliary heater). Heavy-duty alternators. Heavy-duty batteries. Bright front and rear bumpers, guards and rub strips. Bright front and rear bumpers. Electronic digital clock. Auxiliary transmission oil to air cooling. Maximum engine cooling. Electric rear window defroster for single rear door. Dual rear doors with vented glass. Single rear door with vented glass. Sliding-passenger side door. 36-gal. fuel tank. Oil pressure and trip odometer gauges. Sun screen privacy glass. Tinted glass, all windows. Bright grille with dual quad rectangular headlamps, vertically-stacked with halogen high beams. Auxiliary rear heater. Deluxe front heater. Engine block heater. Two color-keyed (accessory type) rubber mats in driver's compartment. Dual low-mount 6 x 9 in. bright exterior mirrors. Lower moldings (includes side, rear and bright taillamp bezel moldings). Upper moldings (includes side, rear and bright taillamp bezels). Upper and lower moldings with bright taillamp bezels. Electronic display warning indicator for engine oil level, transmission oil level, radiator coolant level and transmission oil temperature. Electric door locks. Power front door windows. Radios: AM/FM stereo. AM/FM stereo with cassette tape player. AM/FM stereo with cassette tape player and Dolby noise reduction system. AM/FM stereo with Search-Tune and electronic tuning. AM/FM stereo with eight-track tape player. AM/FM stereo with 40-channel CB transceiver. Heavy-duty shock absorbers. Automatic speed control. Front stabilizer bar. Tilt-type steering column. Luxury type steering wheel. Bright deluxe wheelcovers. Wheels: (Road type 15 x 7 in.) Aluminum radial ribbed. Five-slot chrome disc. Deluxe two-speed windshield wipers with intermittent wipe.

NOTE: The 1983 Voyager was available in a choice of 13 exterior colors: Graphic red; Beige sand; Crimson red; Spice metallic; Nightwatch blue; Sable brown; Light blue metallic; Charcoal gray metallic; Burnished silver metallic; Pearl white; and black.

1984 Plymouth Voyager Passenger Wagon (CPD)

VOYAGER WAGON: The Voyager was dramatically changed for 1984. It became less like a traditional van and more like a station wagon. Yet, its exterior resembled the previous year's model from the front. This shrunken Voyager had front-wheel-drive. The thin horizontal bars grille had dual, vertically- stacked, quad rectangular headlights. Large wrap-around signal lights were integrated into it. A Chrysler star emblem rose above the grille on the sloping hood. The tall vertical taillights had backup lights built into their lower section. Standard features included: Halogen headlamps; inside hood release; five-speed manual transmission with overdrive; side window de-misters; tinted glass; cigarette lighter; power brakes; power steering; electronic digital clock; AM electronic tune radio; front and rear bumper rub strips; day/night rearview mirrors; tethered fuel cap; headlamps-on chime; left-side remote control exterior mirror; single note horn; 15-gal. fuel tank; bright grille; two-speed windshield wipers with wet arm washers; and color-keyed seat belts with automatic release on front bucket seats.

I.D. DATA: There are 17 symbols. The first three indicate the manufacturer, make and type of vehicle. The fourth the GVW range. The next three tell the series and body style. The eighth tells the engine. After that is the check digit and a letter representing the model year. The 11th symbol identifies the assembly plant. The remaining six digits are the sequential production numbers.

Model	Body Type	Price	Weight	Prod. Total
L36	Mini-Van	8280	2937	—

ENGINE: Four-cylinder. Displacement: 122 cid. Brake horsepower: 90 at 5000 rpm. Bore & stroke: 3.30 in. x 3.54 in. Compression ratio: 8.5:1. Carburetor: two-barrel.

1984 Plymouth Voyager Passenger Wagon (CPD)

VOYAGER SE WAGON: The Voyager SE (Special Edition) came with the same standard features as the basic model, plus: Road wheels; a dual note horn; front folding armrests; and soft cloth trim panels with carpeted lower inserts.

I.D. DATA: There are 17 symbols. The first three indicate the manufacturer, make and type of vehicle. The fourth the GVW range. The next three tell the series and body style. The eighth tells the engine. After that is the check digit and a letter representing the model year. The 11th symbol identifies the assembly plant. The remaining six digits are the sequential production numbers.

Model	Body Type	Price	Weight	Prod. Total
H36	Mini-Van	8517	2984	—

ENGINE: Four-cylinder. Displacement: 122 cid. Brake horsepower: 90 at 5000 rpm. Bore & stroke: 3.30 in. x 3.54 in. Compression ratio: 8.5:1. Carburetor: two-barrel.

1984 Plymouth Voyager Passenger Wagon (CPD)

VOYAGER LE WAGON: This was the top-of-the-line model most often seen in Voyager "Magic Wagon" advertisements. In addition to the standard features found in the other two versions the LE (Limited Edition) had: Deluxe sound insulation; high-back front reclining bucket seats; dual black remote-control exterior mirrors; luxury steering wheel; center woodgrain applique; and upper and lower bodyside moldings.

I.D. DATA: There are 17 symbols. The first three indicate the manufacturer, make and type of vehicle. The fourth the GVW range. The next three tell the series and body style. The eighth tells the engine. After that is the check digit and a letter representing the model year. The 11th symbol identifies the assembly plant. The remaining six digits are the sequential production numbers.

Model	Body Type	Price	Weight	Prod. Total
P36	Mini-Van	9105	3026	—

ENGINE: Four-cylinder. Displacement: 122 cid. Brake horsepower: 90 at 5000 rpm. Bore & stroke: 3.30 in. x 3.54 in. Compression ratio: 8.5:1. Carburetor: two-barrel.

CHASSIS: Wheelbase: 112 in. Overall length: 175.9 in. Overall width: 69.6 in. Overall height: 64.6 in. Tires: P185/75R14 steel-belted radial black sidewall.

TECHNICAL: TorqueFlite three-speed automatic transmission. Four-cylinder 2.6 liter Mitsubishi built engine.

1984 Plymouth Voyager Passenger Wagon (CPD)

OPTIONAL PACKAGES: Gauge package with gauge alert: Includes engine coolant temperate gauge with high temperature warning light; oil pressure gauge with low pressure warning light; low-voltage warning light; and trip odometer with push-button reset. Light package: Includes ash receiver light; front map/reading lights; headlamp switch call-out light; ignition switch light with time delay; instrument panel door-ajar light; low fuel warning light; low washer fluid light; underhood compartment light; liftgate-mounted dual floodlights. Basic group package: Includes light package; deluxe intermittent windshield wipers; dual note horns; power liftgate release; a 500-amp. battery; dual remote-control exterior mirrors; deluxe sound insulation; cruise control; 20-gal. fuel tank; sliding door outside lock; liftgate wiper/washer; luxury steering wheel; and gauge package with gauge alert. Luxury equipment discount package: Includes, tilt steering column; power windows; and power front door locks and drivers' seat; and Basic group options. Travel equipment discount package for Voyager SE/Voyager LE: Includes, Mitsubishi 2.6 liter engine; seven-passenger seating package; sunscreen glass; remote-control rear vent windows; 20-gal. fuel tank; and 500 amp. battery. Seven-passenger seating package for Voyager SE/Voyager LE: Includes second seat (two-passenger bench with fixed back, side armrests and quick-release attachments); third seat (three-passenger bench with folding back, side armrests, adjustable feature and quick-release attachments); three storage bins (in third seat armrests and right rear trim panel); ash receiver in C-pillar below belt; heavy-duty suspension and rear brakes; and P195/75R14 steel-belted radial black sidewall tires.

CONVENIENCE OPTIONS: Air-conditioning. Heavy-duty suspension. 500 amp. battery. Tonneau cover. 20-gal. fuel tank. Sunscreen privacy glass. Electric rear window defroster. Power door locks. Luggage rack. Vinyl bodyside moldings. Two-tone paint (Voyager SE). Radios: AM/FM stereo with electronic tuning. AM/FM stereo with electronic tuning and cassette tape player. Cruise control. Dual black remote control exterior mirror. Tilt-steering column. Wire wheelcovers (Voyager SE, Voyager LE). Power windows (Voyager SE, Voyager LE). Sport road wheels. Rear quarter vent with remote-control. Deluxe windshield wipers. Rear window wiper. High-back bucket seats with vinyl trim (Voyager SE). Power driver's seat.

HISTORICAL: According to a *POPULAR MECHANIC's* magazine survey of Plymouth Voyager/Dodge caravan owners, the SE was the most popular series (60.4 percent). Most buyers (90.3 percent) ordered automatic transmission. The majority of owners (66.3 percent) were age 30 to 49. The three things owners liked best about their vehicle were; handling (52.2 percent), comfort (39.9 percent) and roominess (33.4 percent).

1985 Plymouth Voyager With Magic Camper Option (CPD)

VOYAGER WAGON: After the dramatic changes made in 1984, Voyager styling was basically untouched for the new model year. Standard features included: Front air dam; 60 amp. alternator and 335 amp. maintenance-free battery; power front disc brakes; color-keyed front and rear bumper end caps; bright front and rear bumpers with protective rub strips; carpeting; warning chimes for key in "fasten seat belts" and "headlamps on;" cigar lighter; coolant overflow reservoir; corrosion protection; front door windows de-misters; sliding right side cargo compartment door with vented glass; electronic ignition and voltage regulator; remote cable release fuel filler door; 15-gal. fuel tank; tinted glass all windows; vented bodyside glass; bright grille; halogen low and high beam headlamps; cloth-covered driver and passenger compartment headliner; bi-level ventilation heater; inside hood release; single note horn; liftgate with fixed glass; driver and passenger compartments dome lights; day/night rearview mirror; black left-side remote control exterior mirror; black rear window and windshield molding; AM radio with electronic tuning, digital display and integral digital clock; color-keyed seat belts with automatic release on front bucket seats; rack-and-pinion power steering; vinyl two-spoke steering wheel; compact spare tire; cable winch system underslung tire carrier; five-speed manual transmission with overdrive; deluxe wheelcovers; two-speed windshield wipers with wet arm washers; liftgate wiper/washer; brake fluid pressure loss warning light; turn signals with lane-change feature; and dual braking system.

Model	Body Type	Price	Weight	Prod. Total
L36	Mini-Van	9147	2911	—

ENGINE: Four-cylinder. Displacement: 122 cid. Brake horsepower: 90 at 5000 rpm. Bore & stroke: 3.30 in. x 3.54 in. Compression ratio: 8.5:1. Carburetor: two-barrel.

VOYAGER SE WAGON: The SE was a step up from the standard Voyager. It came with most of the same basic features plus: deluxe cloth low-back front bucket seats; bright upper bodyside and lift gate moldings; and luxury wheelcovers.

I.D. DATA: There are 17 symbols. The first three indicate the manufacturer, make and type of vehicle. The fourth the GVW range. The next three tell the series and body style. The eighth tells the engine. After that is the check digit and a letter representing the model year. The 11th symbol identifies the assembly plant. The remaining six digits are the sequential production numbers.

Model	Body Type	Price	Weight	Prod. Total
H36	Mini-Van	9393	2984	—

ENGINE: Four-cylinder. Displacement: 122 cid. Brake horsepower: 90 at 5000 rpm. Bore & stroke: 3.30 in. x 3.54 in. Compression ratio: 8.5:1. Carburetor: two-barrel.

VOYAGER LE WAGON: It was easy to tell which was the top of the line Voyager. The LE came with distinctive woodgrain exterior appliques and body surround moldings. The interior featured luxury cloth high-back front bucket seats with integral headrests, armrests, seatback storage pockets and driver and passenger recliners. It also had a luxury steering wheel.

I.D. DATA: There are 17 symbols. The first three indicate the manufacturer, make and type of vehicle. The fourth the GVW range. The next three tell the series and body style. The eighth tells the engine. After that is the check digit and a letter representing the model year. The 11th symbol identifies the assembly plant. The remaining six digits are the sequential production numbers.

Model	Body Type	Price	Weight	Prod. Total
P-36	Mini-Van	10,005	9105	—

ENGINE: Four-cylinder. Displacement: 122 cid. Brake horsepower: 90 at 5000 rpm. Bore & stroke: 3.30 in. x 3.54 in. Compression ratio: 8.5:1. Carburetor: two-barrel.

CHASSIS: Wheelbase: 112 in. Overall length: 175.9 in. Overall width: 69.6 in. Overall height: 64.6 in, Tires: P185/75Rl4 steel-belted radial black sidewall.

OPTIONAL PACKAGES: [Voyager] Light package: Includes, deluxe intermittent windshield wipers; dual-note horns; power liftgate release; a 500 amp. battery; dual remote-control mirrors; deluxe sound insulation package. Popular Equipment discount package: [Voyager SE and Voyager LE] Includes, light package; gauge with gauge alert package; deluxe intermittent windshield wipers; AM/FM stereo radio with clock; dual note horns; automatic speed control; power liftgate release; dual remote mirrors; deluxe sound insulation; luxury steering wheel; illuminated visor vanity mirror; and overhead console (for Voyager LE models only). Luxury equipment Discount package: [Voyager LE] Includes, Popular Equipment package; tilt-steering column; power mirrors; power front door windows; door locks; and driver's seat. Travel equipment discount package: [Voyager SE/Voyager LE] Includes, Mitsubishi 2.6-liter engine (requires automatic transaxle at extra cost). Seven-passenger seating package; sunscreen glass; remote-control rear vent windows; 20-gal. fuel tank; and 500 amp. battery. Sport wheel package: Includes, P205/70Rl4 steel-belted radial raised black-letter tires and cast aluminum wheels. Gauge with gauge alert package: Includes, engine coolant temperature gauge with high temperature warning light;

oil pressure gauge with low pressure warning light; low-voltage warning light; and trip odometer with push-button reset. Light package: Includes, ash receiver light; front map/reading lights; headlamp switch call-out light; ignition switch light with time delay; instrument panel door-ajar light; low-fuel warning light; low washer fluid light; underhood compartment light; and liftgate-mounted dual floodlights. Deluxe sound insulation package: Includes, door-to-sill seals and liftgate, passenger floor, underhood, under instrument panel, and wheelhousing silencers. Seven-passenger seating package: [Voyager SE/Voyager LE] Includes second seat (two-passenger bench with fixed back, side armrests and quick-release attachments); third seat (three-passenger bench with folding back, side armrests, adjustable feature [slides front to rear on tracks]) and quick-release attachments; three storage bins (in third seat armrests and right rear trim panel); ash receiver in C-pillar below belt; heavy-duty suspension and rear brakes; and P195/75RI4 steel-belted radial black sidewall tires.

CONVENIENCE OPTIONS: Air-conditioning with bi-level ventilation. A 500 amp. maintenance-free heavy-duty battery. Black and front and rear bumper guards. Forward storage console. Converta-Bed rear seating option (Voyager/Voyager SE). Electrically-heated liftgate window defroster. Accessory type front and rear floor mats. 20-gal. fuel tank. Sun screen glass, all windows except windshield and front doors. Roof-mounted luggage rack. Dual black remote-control exterior mirrors. Dual back power remote-control exterior mirrors. Color-keyed bodyside vinyl molding. Power door locks. Power liftgate release. Power driver's seat. Power windows (Voyager SE/Voyager LE). AM/FM stereo with electronic tuning, digital display, four speakers and integral digital clock. Premium AM/FM stereo radio with electronic tuning, digital display, seek-and- scan, cassette tape player with automatic reverse, Dynamic Noise Reduction, four speakers and integral digital clock. AM stereo/FM stereo radio with electronic tuning, digital display, 36-watt Ultimate Sound System, memory scan, up-and-down scan, cassette player with automatic reverse and metal tape capability, Dynamic Noise Reduction, five-channel graphic equalizer, joy stick balance/fader control, ambience sound control, four speakers and integral digital clock. Automatic speed control. Tilt-steering column. Heavy-duty suspension (includes P195/75RI4 tires). Conventional spare tire. Tires: P195/75R14 steel-belted radial black sidewall; P205/70RI4 steel-belted radial raised black letter; P205/70RI4 steel-belted radial white sidewall. Rear cargo compartment tonneau cover. Remote-control rear quarter windows vent. Wire wheelcovers (Voyager SE/Voyager LE).

TECHNICAL: TorqueFlite three-speed automatic transmission. Four-cylinder 2.6 liter Mitsubishi-built engine.

1986 Plymouth Voyager Mini-Wagon (CPD)

VOYAGER: Voyager styling was carried over from 1985. Among changes made for 1986 were: new brake proportioning valve; integrated wraparound front air dam; outside lock on sliding side door; and improved manual transmission. Standard features included: Front-wheel drive; maintenance-free battery; power front disc brakes; carpeting; "Fasten seat belts," "headlights on," and "key in ignition" warning chimes; electronic digital clock; cigar lighter; coolant overflow reservoir; corrosion protection (extensive use of galvanized steel; urethane protective coating on lower body panels); front door window de-misters; sliding right-side door with vented glass; electronic ignition and voltage regulation; stainless steel

exhaust system; remote release fuel filler door; 15-gal. fuel tank; tinted glass; bright grille; quad halogen headlights; headliner; bi-level ventilation heater; inside hood release; single note horn; liftgate with fixed glass; left remote-control exterior mirror; black rear window and windshield moldings; AM radio with electronic tuning; rack-and-pinion power steering; compact spare tire; five-speed manual transmission with overdrive; wheelcovers; two-speed windshield wipers with wet arm washers; and lift-gate wiper/washer with intermittent wipe.

VOYAGER SE: The SE (Special Edition) came with most of the same items as the base Voyager, plus, or in place of base: soft cloth trim panels with carpeted lower insert; assist strap on front passenger seatback; bright upper bodyside and liftgate moldings; Deluxe cloth-and-vinyl seats with front folding armrests; styled road wheels with bright trim ring; hub cover and nut covers.

VOYAGER LE: The Voyager LE (Luxury Edition) lived up to its name. It came with most of the same features found on the SE, plus, or in place of SE: Deluxe sound insulation; dual power-remote-control exterior rearview mirrors; dual note horn; woodtone bodyside and liftgate moldings; and woodtone bodyside applique (omitted with monotone paint).

I.D. DATA: There are 17 symbols. The first three indicate the manufacturer, make and type of vehicle. The fourth the GVW range. The next three tell the series and body style. The eighth tells the engine. After that is the check digit and a letter representing the model year. The 11th symbol identifies the assembly plant. The remaining six digits are the sequential production numbers.

Model	Body Type	Price	Weight	Prod. Total
H21	Mini-Van	9506	3005	—
H41	SE Mini-Van	9785	3046	—
H51	LE Mini-Van	10,528	3071	—

ENGINE: Displacement: 2.2 liters (135 cid). OHC. Four-cylinder. Brake horsepower: 101 at 5600 rpm. Compression ratio: 9.0:1. Carburetor: two-barrel.

CHASSIS: Wheelbase: 112 in. Overall length: 175.9 in. Overall width: 69.6 in. Overall height: 64.2 in. GVW Rating: 4,450-4,600 lbs. Tires: P185/75RI4.

TECHNICAL: 2.6 liter (156 cid) OHC. Four-cylinder. Three-speed automatic transmission.

OPTIONAL PACKAGES: Basic group: [Voyager] Includes, 20-gal. fuel tank; illuminated vanity mirror; 500 amp. maintenance-free battery; deluxe intermittent windshield wipers; deluxe sound insulation; dual remote-control outside rearview mirrors; and sliding side door with outside key lock. Light package; Includes power liftgate release and dual note horns. Gauge Package: Includes cruise control. Popular equipment discount package: [SE/LE] Includes, AM stereo/FM stereo radio with integral clock; 500 amp. battery; deluxe sound insulation; deluxe intermittent windshield wipers; dual non-power remote-control mirrors (SE); dual note horns; and electronic speed control. Gauge and gauge alert package, includes illuminated visor vanity mirror; light package; luxury steering wheel; overhead console (LE); power liftgate release; remote control rear quarter vent windows; and sliding side door outside key lock. Luxury equipment discount package: [LE] Includes popular equipment package; power door locks; power driver's bucket seat; power front door windows; and tilt steering column. Travel equipment discount package: [SE/LE] Includes 500 amp. battery; dual note horns; 20-gal. fuel tank; 2.6 liter engine; automatic transmission; and remote-control rear quarter vent windows. Seven-passenger seating package: Includes, sliding side door with outside key lock; sunscreen glass. Gauge alert package: Includes engine coolant temperature gauge and high temperature warning light; low voltage warning light; oil pressure gauge and low pressure warning light; trip odometer with push-button reset. Light package: Includes, ash receiver light; front map/reading lights (two); headlight switch call-out light with time delay; ignition switch light with time delay; instrument panel "door ajar," "low-fuel," and "low washer fluid" lights; liftgate-mounted dual floodlights; and underhood light. Seven-passenger seating package: [SE/LE] Includes second seat (two-passenger bench); third rear seat (three-passenger bench); ash receiver in right C-pillar below belt; heavy-duty rear brakes; heavy-duty suspension; P195/75RI4 SBR BSW tires; and dual rear storage bins with armrest covers incorporated into wheel wells. Eight-passenger seating package: [SE] Includes, three-passenger front bench seat; second seat (two-passenger bench); third seat (three-passenger bench); ash receiver in C-pillar; heavy-duty rear brakes; heavy-duty suspension; P195/75RI4 SBR BSW tires; and dual rear storage bins with armrest covers incorporated into wheel wells. Sport wheel package: Includes 14 in. cast aluminum wheels; and P195/75RI4 SBR/BSW tires with 2.2-liter engine or P205/70RI4 SBR/BLT tires with 2.6-liter engine.

CONVENIENCE OPTIONS: Air-conditioning. Coverta-Bed rear seating. Electric liftgate window defroster. 20-gal. fuel tank. Sunscreen glass. Roof-mounted luggage rack. Dual remote-control exterior mirrors. Vinyl bodyside molding. Power door locks. Power liftgate release. AM/FM stereo radio. Premium AM/FM stereo radio with cassette tape player. AM/FM stereo with Ultimate Sound System. Electronic speed control. Tilt steering column. Conventional spare tire. Rear cargo compartment tonneau cover. Wire wheelcovers (SE/LE). Sport wheelcovers (SE/LE). Deluxe windshield wipers with intermittent wipe and wet arm washers.

NOTE: Voyager exterior colors for 1986 included: Light cream; black; Golden bronze pearl coat; Dark cordovan pearl coat; Gunmetal blue pearl coat (extra cost); Gold dust; Garnet red pearl coat (extra cost); Radiant silver; white; and Ice blue. Two-tone color combinations were: Gold dust/Golden bronze pearl coat; Garant red pearl coat/black; Radiant silver/black; Light cream/Golden bronze pearl coat; Gunmetal blue pearl coat/black; and Ice blue/Gunmetal blue pearl coat.

PONTIAC
1926-1953

1953 Pontiac Sedan Delivery (Dick Choler)

By John Gunnell

Although it is not widely known, Pontiac made trucks at several stages in its history prior to introduction of the current Trans Sport multi purpose vehicle as a production model in 1990.

The first Pontiac was a "companion" car to the Oakland, made by Oakland Motor Car Co. (The Oakland factory was in the City of Pontiac, which lies in Oakland County, Mich.) No commercial vehicles were offered under the Oakland name, but nearly as soon as the Pontiac appeared, a commercial version was added to the line.

This 1926 model was actually a commercial car (truck based on the car chassis and running gear). It shared the twin-head "Chief-of-the-Sixes" Pontiac engine, three-speed gearbox, and 110 in. wheelbase with passenger models. Assembly line photos show long rows of these trucks being manufactured alongside the cars.

Called the Deluxe Delivery, the truck was nicely appointed and trimmed for its modest price of $770. It was offered for two or two-and-one-half years, during which time 3,500 were built. Only two are known to survive today.

Sometime during 1928, the Pontiac Deluxe Delivery became the GMC T-11. Both were virtually identical, except for their radiator badges. The GMC home factory was also in Pontiac, Mich. Some GMC truck engines of the 1930s were sourced from Pontiac Motor Car Co. From about 1931

on, the Pontiac chassis became popular with builders of "professional" vehicles (ambulances and funeral cars). These lie out of the scope of our study.

During the 1930s and 1940s, General Motors of Canada offered a Pontiac commercial car with passenger car front sheet metal and a Sedan Delivery body. Following normal Canadian practice, the running gear used in these models was sourced from Chevrolet.

There are photos of 1935 and 1939 U.S. models with commercial bodies in the Pontiac Historic Collection. They indicate that a series of prototypes were constructed, although Pontiac commercial cars were not mass-produced in the U.S. prior to World War II.

Apparently, Sedan Delivery versions of the Chevy-based Canadian Pontiacs reappeared after World War II. Then, in 1949, a Sedan Delivery was introduced in the U.S. It had the front sheet metal, chassis and running gear of the domestic model and could be had with a flathead six or eight, both of inline design.

Designed as a one-step-up business vehicle for the butcher, the baker and candlestick maker, the Pontiac Sedan Delivery soon became fancier, adopting the trim of Deluxe cars from 1950 on. Sales were not substantial and the model lasted only through 1953. Under 9,000 were made in all.

Canada continued to be a better market for Pontiac commercial vehicles. The Pontiac trimmed Chevrolet-based Sedan Delivery lasted there until at least 1958 when 449

were produced. Later, in the 1970s, a badge-engineered Chevy Vega was sold north of the border as the Pontiac Astre panel. It was little more than an Astre Safari station wagon with panel sides. When the Astre came to the U.S., the panel version did not.

By the late 1950s, there were hints that Pontiac wanted to test the waters of the U.S. commercial vehicle market for a third time. Several prototypes of a car-based pickup were put together in 1959-1960. This "El Catalina" looked very attractive, but was not approved for production. PMD employees recall that a prototype was later employed as a push-car to move vehicles around the factory grounds. Other prototype Pontiac trucks, such as a mid-1980s Grand Am pickup, surfaced as well.

1927 Pontiac Deluxe Delivery assembly line (PMD)

1935 Pontiac Sedan Delivery Prototype (JMS)

1938 Pontiac (Canadian) Sedan Delivery (RJ)

1939 Pontiac Sedan Delivery Prototype (PMD)

1939 Pontiac Sedan Delivery Prototype, rear (PMD)

1949 Pontiac Streamliner Eight Sedan Delivery (JMS/PMD)

1949 Pontiac Streamliner Eight Sedan Delivery (PMD)

1950 Pontiac Streamliner Eight Sedan Delivery (PMD)

Standard Catalog of Light-Duty Trucks

1926 PONTIAC

1926 Pontiac 1/2-Ton Deluxe Delivery (PMD)

DELUXE SIX — SERIES 6-27 — SIX-CYLINDER: The 1/2-ton Pontiac Six Deluxe Delivery car was introduced, in October, 1926, as the lowest priced six-cylinder commercial car on the U.S. market. The chassis was the regular passenger car unit with thicker rear springs and heavy-duty commercial balloon tires. Rated payload was 1,000 lbs. Up front, the driver's compartment was nearly identical to that of the Pontiac two-door sedan. Standard Fisher Body parts included seats, a Vision-and-Ventilating (VV) windshield, instrument board, cowl, door parts and other fittings. Seats were upholstered in leather-like fabrikoid. Panel body construction was of the composite type, employing one-piece side panels. "Due to the use of steel braces, mortised joints and the special side panels, the body is unusually sound-proof and vibration-free," reported the Oct. 14, 1926 issue of *AUTOMOTIVE INDUSTRIES*. The body had Duco finish in Balsam blue with a contrasting wide belt of orange extending entirely around the panel body. Standard equipment included a rearview mirror, cowl lights, radiator emblem, gasoline gauge, 12-gallon fuel tank, sun visors, plate glass windows with high-speed regulators and nickeled door handles. The roof was covered with a rubberized material supplied by DuPont. A drip molding extended around the entire roof, while lengthwise steel strips protected the hardwood flooring. The body was designed to be exceptionally low at the rear for easy access. Twin, tight-closing doors with rectangular windows were provided at the rear.

I.D. DATA: Serial number located on right side of rear frame crossmember or on frame under left front fender. Starting: 00001-26. Ending: 84261-26. Engine numbers located on left side of crankcase or near left front corner of cylinder block.

Model	Body Type	Price	Weight		Prod. Total
6-27	Panel Delivery	770	2470		Note 1

NOTE 1: According to contemporary registration data, a total of 3,611 Pontiac Deluxe Delivery were registered in the U.S. between 1926 and 1928. This is probably close to total production of this model.
ENGINE: Inline. L-head. Six-cylinder. (Twin head). Cast iron & block. Bore & stroke: 3-1/4 in. x 3-3/4 in. Displacement: 186.5 cid. Compression ratio: 4.8:1. Brake horsepower: 36 at 2400 rpm. Net horsepower: 25.35. Three main bearings. Solid valve lifters. Carburetor: Carter one-barrel.
CHASSIS [6-26]: Wheelbase: 110 in. Overall length: 151.25 in. Height: 43 in. Front tread: 56 in. Rear tread: 56 in. Tires: 29 x 4.75 in.
TECHNICAL: Selective sliding transmission. Speeds: 3F/1R. Floor-mounted gearshift lever. Ventilated single disc dry clutch. Shaft drive. Semi-floating rear axle. Overall ratio: 4.18:1. Two-wheel mechanical brakes. Wood-spoke wheels.
OPTIONS: Front bumper. Rear bumper. Single sidemount. Bumper guards. Heater.
HISTORICAL: Introduced October, 1926. Calendar year registrations: [Series three-year total] 3,611. Innovations: First Pontiac model year and first Pontiac truck. Lowest cost six-cylinder truck in America. Historical notes: Built as part of Oakland's new "companion car series." The truck's GVW rating was 3,470 lbs. The Deluxe Delivery car was promoted as a truck with the comfort of a passenger car.

1927 PONTIAC

DELUXE DELIVERY — SERIES 6-27 — SIX-CYLINDER: As the 1926 Pontiac car-line was carried over into 1927 practically unchanged, the company's handsome-looking truck followed suit. The name of the model was again the Deluxe Delivery and a brand new screenside body type was introduced at the New York Auto Show in January, 1927. Instead of a panel body, it had heavy metal screening material on the sides and rear, a drop-down tailgate and rolled leather curtains to cover the screening. The panel truck continued to come with standard Balsam blue Duco body, black running gear and a wide contrast belt finished in Burning Bush orange. An ad in *SATURDAY EVENING POST*, in the spring of 1927 said, "Only 5 months old and now you see it everywhere" about the Pontiac truck. Indeed, factory photos indicate that a goodly number of the these trucks were built, although they are rarities today. Standard equipment for 1927 models was as follows: Fisher VV one-piece windshield with automatic cleaner, sun visor, cowl parking lights, individual sedan seats providing passenger car comfort, plate glass windows with high-speed regulators, nickeled door handles, 12-gallon gas tank located in the rear for convenience in refueling, special heavy-duty springs and heavy-duty balloon tires. The trucks also had Delco-Remy

ignition and rear wheel mechanical brakes. The trucks featured semi-elliptic leaf springs measuring 29 x 1.75 in. in front and 54 x 1.75 in. at the rear. Tires were of extra-ply, non-skid design.

1927 Pontiac Series 6-27 Screenside Delivery (Jerry Bougher)

I.D. DATA: Serial number located on right side of rear frame crossmember or on frame under left front fender. Starting: 145000-27. Ending: 204000-27. Engine numbers located on left side of crankcase or near left front corner of block. Starting: P156250. Ending: P220000 (approximate).

Model	Body Type	Price	Weight	Prod. Total
6-27	Panel Delivery	770	2470	Note 1
6-27	Screen Delivery	760	2440	Note 1

NOTE 1: A total of 3,611 trucks were registered between 1926 and 1928.
ENGINE: Inline. L-head. Six-cylinder. (Twin head). Cast-iron block. Bore & stroke: 3-1/4 in. x 3-3/4 in. Displacement: 186.5 cid. Compression ratio: 4.8:1. Brake horsepower: 36 at 2400 rpm. Net horsepower: 25.35. Three main bearings. Solid valve lifters. Carburetor: Carter one-barrel.
CHASSIS [6-27]: Wheelbase: 110 in. Overall length: 151.25 in. Height: 43 in. Front tread: 56 in. Rear tread: 56 in. Tires: 29 x 4.75 extra-ply.
TECHNICAL: Selective sliding transmission. Speeds: 3F/1R. Floor-mounted gearshift lever. Ventilated single disc dry clutch. Semi-floating rear axle. Overall ratio: 4.18:1. Two-wheel mechanical brakes. Wood-spoke wheels.
OPTIONS: Front bumper. Rear bumper. Single sidemount. Bumper guards. Heater.
HISTORICAL: Introduced Jan. 1927. Calendar year registrations: [three year total] 3,611. Innovations: New screenside delivery introduced. A.R. Glancey was president of Oakland Motor Car Co., which produced Pontiac cars and trucks.

1928 PONTIAC

1928 Pontiac Deluxe Delivery/GMC T-11 (PMD)

DELUXE DELIVERY — SERIES 6-27/6-28 — SIX-CYLINDER: Judging by serial numbers, the Series 6-27 Pontiac truck (like the company's cars) continued into the early part of the 1928 model year. Here, the facts get a little confusing. Some 6-28 Series Pontiac trucks may have been built, but 1928 was the last year for the Pontiac Deluxe Delivery. In 1929, this vehicle became a GMC model through the simple changing of the radiator shell and name badges. GMC continued to use the Pontiac six-cylinder engine.
I.D. DATA: Serial number located on right side of rear frame crossmember or on frame under left front fender. Starting: 145000-27. Ending: 2040000-28. Engine numbers located on left side of crankcase.

Model	Body Type	Price	Weight	Prod. Total
Deluxe Delivery - 1/2-Ton - 110 in. w.b.				
6-28	Chassis	585	1820	Note 1
6-28	Panel Delivery	770	2455	Note 1
6-28	Canopy Delivery	760	2465	Note 1
6-28	Screen Delivery	760	2465	Note 1
6-28	Pickup	—	—	Note 1
6-28	Sedan Delivery	—	—	Note 1

NOTE 1: A total of 3,611 trucks were registered between 1926 and 1928.

ENGINE: Inline. L-head. Six-cylinder. (Twin head). Cast-iron block. Bore & stroke: 3-1/4 in. x 3-3/4 in. Displacement: 186.5 cid. Compression ratio: 4.8:1. Brake horsepower: 36 at 2400 rpm. Net horsepower: 25.35. Three main bearings. Solid valve lifters. Carburetor: Carter one-barrel.

CHASSIS [6-27]: Wheelbase: 110 in. Overall length: 151.25 in. Height: 43 in. Front tread: 56 in. Rear tread: 56 in. Tires: 29 x 4.75 extra-ply.

TECHNICAL: Selective sliding transmission. Speeds: 3F/1R. Floor-mounted gearshift lever. Ventilated single disc dry clutch. Semi-floating rear axle. Overall ratio: 4.18:1. Two-wheel mechanical brakes. Wood-spoke wheels.

OPTIONS: Front bumper. Rear bumper. Single sidemount. Bumper guards. Heater.

HISTORICAL: Introduced Jan. 1928. A.R. Glancey was president of Oakland Motor Car Co., which produced Pontiac cars and trucks. This would be the last year for production type Pontiac trucks until 1949.

1949 PONTIAC

1949 Pontiac Streamliner Eight Sedan Delivery (OCW)

STREAMLINER — SERIES 25/27 — SIX-CYLINDER/EIGHT-CYLINDER: Pontiac re-entered the light-truck field with a handsome Sedan Delivery. It was the first true Pontiac truck produced in the U.S. since the late 1920s. Although much similar to a station wagon in size and shape, it was a two-door vehicle with a curb-side opening third door (with fixed window) at the rear. Pontiac trimmed it as a standard model having black rubber gravel shields and painted headlamp surrounds. It was cataloged in the standard series. Publicity photos of a deluxe version with bright metal trim and side spears exist, but this was probably a prototype. Features of 1949 Pontiacs included wider seats, a horizontal curved windshield, new sealed airplane-type shock absorbers and low-pressure tires. The trucks came with a choice of two flathead engines, a 90 hp inline six and 104 hp inline eight. The Sedan Delivery had a 9-1/2 in. step-up in the floor level, behind the twin bucket seats. The cargo area was 85-3/4 in. long and the roof was 64-1/4 in. high. Color choices included all offered for other 1949 Pontiacs, except Blue Lake blue or Coventry gray. The 1949 grille consisted of a full-width center horizontal wing with an ornament in a housing at the center. There were short horizonal teeth below the bar, but none above it. Rectangular parking lights were mounted at either end, below the single headlamps. Silver Streak moldings and an Indian head mascot finished the motif. Upholstery was brown imitation leather.

I.D. DATA: Serial number located on left-hand door pillar. Starting: [Six] P-6R-1001 and up; [Eight] P-8R-1001 and up. Engine numbers located on left side of cylinder block. The engine number is the VIN and should match the number on the door pillar. Starting: [Six] P-6R-1001 and up; [Eight] P-8R-1001 and up.

Model	Body Type	Price	Weight	Prod. Total
Streamliner Six - 1/2-Ton - 120 in. w.b.				
6R	Sedan Delivery	1749	3230	Note 1
Streamliner Eight - 1/2-Ton - 120 in. w.b.				
8R	Sedan Delivery	1817	3295	Note 1

NOTE 1: Calendar year production totaled 2,488 units.

ENGINE: Inline. L-head. Six-cylinder. Cast iron block. Bore & stroke: 3-9/16 in. x 4 in. Displacement: 239.2 cid. Compression ratio: [standard] 6.5:1. Brake horsepower: 90 at 3400 rpm. Net horsepower: 30.4. Four main bearings. Solid valve lifters. Carburetor: Carter one-barrel model WAL-537S.

NOTE: Optional 7.5:1 high-compression head used with Hydra-Matic transmission. Hydra-Matic equipped trucks had 93 horsepower at 3400 rpm.

ENGINE: Inline. L-head. Eight-cylinder. Cast iron block. Bore & stroke: 4-1/4 in. x 4-3/4 in. Displacement: 248.9 cid. Compression ratio: [standard] 6.5:1. Brake horsepower: 103 at 3800 rpm. Net horsepower: 33.8. Five main bearings. Solid valve lifters. Carburetor: Carter two-barrel model WCD.

NOTE: Optional 7.5:1 head used with Hydra-Matic transmission. Hydra-Matic equipped trucks had 106 horsepower at 3800 rpm.

CHASSIS [Streamliner Series]: Wheelbase: 120 in. Overall length: 203.8 in. Height: 64-1/4 in. Front tread: 58 in. Rear tread: 59 in. Tires: 7.60 x 15 in.

TECHNICAL: Synchromesh transmission. Speeds: 3F/1R. Column-mounted gearshift lever. Single-plate dry disc clutch. Semi-floating rear axle. Overall ratio: 4.1:1. Four-wheel hydraulic brakes. Steel disc wheels. Automatic transmission (optional Hydra-Matic Drive).

OPTIONS: Mast antenna. Seven-tube Chieftain radio. No-Blow wind deflectors. Venti-Seat underseat heater. Windshield sun visor. Traffic light viewer. License frames. Light-up hood ornament. Full wheel discs. Wheel trim rings. White sidewall discs. Deluxe steering wheel. Visor vanity mirror. Directional signals. Compass. Windshield washers. Deluxe electric clock. Glove compartment light. Seat covers. Safti-Jack. Outside rearview mirror. Back-up lights. Spotlight. Foglights. Bumper guards. Master grille guard. Exhaust deflector. No-Mar gas filler door trim. Underhood trouble lamp. Jack bag. Tool kit.

HISTORICAL: Introduced Jan. 1949. Calendar year production: 2,488. Innovations: First U.S. built Pontiac truck since 1928. New dial cluster dash. New broad rims. New airplane-type shock absorbers. Historical notes: Pontiac sold 21.2 percent of all cars in its price range, but held only .20 percent of the light-duty truck market.

624

1950 PONTIAC

1950 Pontiac Streamliner Six Sedan Delivery (JAG)

STREAMLINER — SERIES 25/27 — SIX-CYLINDER/EIGHT-CYLINDER: A Sedan Delivery truck was again part of Pontiac's Streamliner Six (Series 25) and Streamliner Eight (Series 27) product offerings. The 1950 models were upgraded with additional bright metal trim parts including three-quarter length body side moldings, rocker panel moldings, rear gravel shields and headlight rims. New for the year was a radiator grille with five teeth spaced across a massive horizontal bar. In the center of this arrangement was a circular red plastic disc bearing an Indian brave's image. Corner bar extensions and parking lamps now curved around the front fenders. The hood ornament was an outward thrusting brave's head in chrome. An illuminated mascot was an accessory for the second year in a row. A nameplate below the hood Silver Streaks bore the Pontiac name. A Silver Streak script decorated the front fendersides, above the midside molding. On eight-cylinder trucks, a number "8" separated the two words. Sedan deliveries were offered in 11 solid colors and five two-tone combinations. Interior trim was now in tan, instead of brown, imitation leather. The 1950 models were slightly heavier and modestly shorter than '49s. Inside panels were brown masonite, painted light gray. A tan imitation leather headliner was fitted. Rubber mats were used on the driving compartment floor and the rear cargo area was covered with linoleum. Standard equipment included a finger-tip starter, low pressure-tires, Tru-Arc steering system, Duflex rear springs, triple-sealed brakes and built-in lifetime oil filter.

1950 Pontiac Streamliner Eight Sedan Delivery (Jack Hughes)

I.D. DATA: Serial number located on left-hand front door pillar; also on lip on front of cylinder block at left side. Starting: [Six] P-6T-1001 and up; [Eight] P-8T-1001 and up. Engine numbers located on lip on front of cylinder block at left side. Engine stamping and door pillar stamping should match.

Model	Body Type	Price	Weight	Prod. Total
Streamliner Series 6				
2571	Sedan Delivery	1733	3309	Note 1
Streamliner Series 8				
2571	Sedan Delivery	1801	3379	Note 1

NOTE 1: A total of 2,158 sedan deliveries were built in calendar year 1950.

1950 Pontiac Streamliner Eight Sedan Delivery (Jack Hughes)

ENGINE: Inline. L-head. Six-cylinder. Cast iron block. Bore & stroke: 3-9/16 in. x 4 in. Displacement: 239.2 cid. Compression ratio: [standard] 6.5:1. Brake horsepower: 90 at 3400 rpm. Net horsepower: 30.4. Torque: 178 lbs.-ft. at 1200 rpm. Four main bearings. Solid valve lifters. Carburetor: Carter one-barrel model WA1-717-S.
NOTE: Optional 7.5:1 cylinder head with Hydra-Matic gives 93 hp at 3400 rpm and 183 lbs.-ft. torque at 1200 rpm.

1950 Pontiac Streamliner Eight Sedan Delivery (POCI)

ENGINE: Inline. L-head. Eight-cylinder. Cast iron block. Bore & stroke: 3-3/8 in. x 3-3/4 in. Displacement: 268.2 cid. Compression ratio: [standard] 6.5:1. Brake horsepower: 108 at 3600 rpm. Net horsepower: 36.4. Torque: 208 lbs.-ft. at 1800 rpm. Five main bearings. Solid valve lifters. Carburetor: Carter two-barrel model WCD-719-S.
NOTE: Optional 7.5:1 cylinder head with Hydra-Matic gives 113 hp at 3600 rpm and 214 lbs.-ft. torque at 2000 rpm.
CHASSIS [Streamliner Series]: Wheelbase: 120 in. Overall length: 202-7/8 in. Height: 62.5 in. Front tread: 58 in. Rear tread: 59 in. Tires: 7.10 x 15 six-ply; [No cost option] 7.60 x 15 four-ply.
TECHNICAL: Synchromesh transmission. Speeds: 3F/1R. Column-mounted gearshift lever. Single-plate dry disc clutch. Semi-floating rear axle. Overall ratio: 4.1:1. Four-wheel hydraulic brakes. Steel disc wheels. Hydra-Matic Drive optional.
OPTIONS: Mast antenna. Seven-tube Chieftain radio. No-Blow wind deflectors. Venti-Seat underseat heater. Windshield sun visor. Traffic light viewer. License frames. Light-up hood ornament. Full wheel discs. Wheel trim rings. White sidewall discs. Deluxe steering wheel. Visor vanity mirror. Directional signals. Compass. Windshield washers. Deluxe electric clock. Glove compartment light. Seat covers. Safti-Jack. Outside rearview mirror. Back-up lights. Spotlight. Foglights. Bumper guards. Master grille guard. Exhaust deflector. No-Mar gas filler door trim. Underhood trouble lamp. Jack bag. Tool kit.
HISTORICAL: Introduced Nov. 10, 1949. Calendar year production: 2,158. Innovations: Larger displacement, more powerful straight eight. New model Carter carburetor on eight-cylinder engine. Combination fuel pump/vacuum pump added to sixes. New dashboard type heater and carbon core ignition cables. Deluxe trim used on Sedan Delivery, although it was not part of Pontiac's Deluxe series. Most 1950 Pontiacs were eights and more than half had Hydra-Matic Drive. Rio red was a color choice limited to Sedan Deliveries, station wagons and convertibles.

1951 PONTIAC

STREAMLINER — SERIES 25/27 — SIX-CYLINDER/EIGHT-CYLINDER: New Silver Anniversary trim commemorated the Pontiac nameplate's 25th year in 1951. In honor of the occasion the red plastic circular disc in the center of the grille had a gold Indian head and gold band (the same part with silver trim was used other years.) Also changed was the grille ensemble. It now consisted of two wing-shaped stampings stretching out from a short centerpiece that housed the Indian medallion. There was also a full-width horizontal lower bar with two shorter vertical bars between it and the wings on each side. A sure way to identify 1951 models is by the feather-shaped tips added to the front of the bodyside moldings. At the rear, the Sedan Delivery had a curb-side opening door decorated with a Pontiac script above a short Silver Streak molding. Three stars were embossed on these tips.

Standard Catalog of Light-Duty Trucks

Circular taillights were mounted in slightly protruding housings at each rear body corner, inboard of the fenders. There were also Silver Streaks on the hood. The trucks came in any of 12 solid colors or four two-tone combinations. Two-tone choices were Berkshire green over Palmetto green; Saturn gold over Lido beige; Imperial maroon over Sand gray or Palmetto green over Berkshire green. Upholstery was again tan imitation leather. The trucks came with an adjustable driver's seat and folding passenger seat. Bright metal trim was again used on the bodysides, rocker panels, headlights and gravel shields, although the trucks were not listed with other Deluxe models. A solid chrome Indian hood mascot was standard, with the light-up version optional.

1951 Pontiac Streamliner Eight Sedan Delivery (Jack Samples)

I.D. DATA: Serial number located on left-hand front door pillar. Starting: P-6T-1001 and up. Engine numbers located on lip on front of cylinder block at left side. Engine stamping and door pillar stamping should match.

Model	Body Type	Price	Weight	Prod. Total
Streamliner Six - 1/2-Ton - 120 in. w.b.				
2571	Sedan Delivery	1811	3403	Note 1
Streamliner Eight - 1/2-Ton - 120 in. w.b.				
2571	Sedan Delivery	1879	3508	Note 1

NOTE 1: Calendar year production was 1,822 units.

1951 Pontiac Streamliner Eight Sedan Delivery (Jack Samples)

ENGINE: Inline. L-head. Six-cylinder. Cast iron block. Bore & stroke: 3-9/16 in. x 4 in. Displacement: 239.2 cid. Compression ratio: [standard] 6.5:1. Brake horsepower: 96 at 3400 rpm. Net horsepower: 30.4. Torque: 191 lbs.-ft. at 1200 rpm. Four main bearings. Solid valve lifters. Carburetor: Rochester one-barrel model BC.
NOTE: Optional 7.5:1 cylinder head with Hydra-Matic gave 100 hp at 3400 rpm and 195 lbs.-ft. torque at 1200 rpm.

1951 Pontiac Streamliner Six Sedan Delivery (Bill Morton)

ENGINE: Inline. L-head. Eight-cylinder. Cast iron block. Bore & stroke: 3-3/8 in. x 3-3/4 in. Displacement: 268.4 cid. Compression ratio: [standard] 6.5:1. Brake horsepower: 116 at 3600 rpm. Net horsepower: 36.4. Torque: 220 lbs.-ft. at 2000 rpm. Five main bearings. Solid valve lifters. Carburetor: Carter two-barrel model WCD-720S or WCD-720SA.

NOTE: Optional 7.5:1 compression cylinder head with Hydra-Matic gives 120 hp at 3600 rpm and 225 lbs.-ft. torque at 2000 rpm.

CHASSIS [Streamliner Series]: Wheelbase: 120 in. Overall length: 202.2 in. Height: 63.4 in. Front tread: 58 in. Rear tread: 59 in. Tires: 7.10 x 15 six-ply.; [No cost option] 7.60 x 15 four-ply.

TECHNICAL: Synchromesh transmission. Speeds: 3F/1R. Column-mounted gearshift lever. Single-plate dry disc clutch. Semi-floating rear axle. Overall ratio: 3.6:1; 3.9:1; 4.1:1. Four-wheel hydraulic brakes. Steel disc wheels. Hydra-Matic Drive optional at $165.

OPTIONS: Mast antenna. Seven-tube Chieftain radio. No-Blow wind deflectors. Venti-Seat underseat heater. Windshield sun visor. Traffic light viewer. License frames. Light-up hood ornament. Full wheel discs. Wheel trim rings. White sidewall discs. Deluxe steering wheel. Visor vanity mirror. Directional signals. Compass. Windshield washers. Deluxe electric clock. Glove compartment light. Seat covers. Safti-Jack. Outside rearview mirror. Back-up lights. Spotlight. Foglights. Bumper guards. Master grille guard. Exhaust deflector. No-Mar gas filler door trim. Underhood trouble lamp. Jack bag. Tool kit.

1951 Pontiac Streamliner Eight Sedan Delivery (PMD)

HISTORICAL: Introduced Dec. 11, 1950. Calendar year production: 1,822. Innovations: Stainless steel trim introduced. Increased engine horsepower. New carburetors. Improved Hydra-Matic with quick reverse feature. New 7-lbs. psi radiator cap. Six-inch longer rear springs. Low-gravity type 6-volt battery. Historical notes: Due to Korean War start-up, the National Production Agency put a .20 percent (market share) cap on Pontiac's truck production. Arnold Lenz replaced Harry J. Klinger as Pontiac general manager this year. Pontiac Motor Div. began production of the Otter, a continuous-track military amphibious vehicle, after opening a new plant on April 30, 1951.

1951 Pontiac Streamliner Six Sedan Delivery (Bill Morton)

1952 PONTIAC

1952 Pontiac Chieftain Six Sedan Delivery (PMD)

CHIEFTAIN — SERIES 25/27 — SIX-CYLINDER/EIGHT-CYLINDER: Characteristics of 1952 Pontiacs included a new front end ensemble. Between the nameplate and the grille molding was a four-vertical section grille. Model designations were eliminated from the bodysides, as were the trim plates extending outboard of the parking lamps. The side moldings had a small, parallel strip on top extending into the front door. Since the Pontiac Streamliner model name was eliminated this year, the Sedan Delivery truck became a

Chieftain. It came in both the Chieftain Six (Series 25) and Chieftain Eight (Series 27) product lines. The truck again had Deluxe type trim, but a standard model number and small bottle cap hubcaps. Upholstery was now dark gray imitation leather. As in the past, certain colors (Cherokee red and four two-tone choices) were pretty much exclusive to trucks and station wagons, although the convertible could also be had in the red.

1952 Pontiac (Canadian) Sedan Delivery (OCW)

I.D. DATA: Serial number data same as 1949 to 1951. Truck starting numbers were: [six-cylinder] P-6W-1001 and up and [eight-cylinder] P-8W-1001 up. "W" code indicated Wilmington, Del. factory, suggesting all trucks were sourced from that plant.

Model	Body Type	Price	Weight	Prod. Total
Chieftain Six - 1/2-Ton - 120 in. w.b.				
2571	Sedan Delivery	1850	3308	Note 1
Chieftain Eight - 1/2-Ton - 120 in. w.b.				
2571	Sedan Delivery	1920	3413	Note 1

NOTE 1: Calendar year production was 984 units.

1952 Pontiac (Canadian) Sedan Delivery (OCW)

ENGINE: Inline. L-head. Six-cylinder. Cast iron block. Bore & stroke: 3-9/16 in. x 4 in. Displacement: 239.2 cid. Compression ratio: [standard] 6.8:1. Brake horsepower: 100 at 3400 rpm. Net horsepower: 30.4. Torque: 189 lbs.-ft. at 1400 rpm. Four main bearings. Solid valve lifters. Carburetor: Rochester one-barrel model BC.

NOTE: Optional 7.7:1 cylinder head with Hydra-Matic gave 102 hp at 3400 rpm and 194 lbs.-ft. torque at 1400 rpm.

ENGINE: Inline. L-head. Eight-cylinder. Cast iron block. Bore & stroke: 3-3/8 in. x 3-3/4 in. Displacement: 268.4 cid. Compression ratio: [standard] 6.8:1. Brake horsepower: 118 at 3600 rpm. Net horsepower: 36.4. Torque: 222 lbs.-ft. at 2200 rpm. Five main bearings. Solid valve lifters. Carburetor: Carter two-barrel model WCD-720S or WCD-720SA.

NOTE: Optional 7.7:1 cylinder head with Hydra-Matic gave 122 hp at 3600 rpm and 227 lbs.-ft. torque at 2200 rpm.

CHASSIS [Chieftain Series]: Wheelbase: 120 in. Overall length: 202.5 in. Height: 63.1 in. Front tread: 58 in. Rear tread: 59 in. Tires: 7.10 x 15 six-ply.; [No cost option] 7.60 x 15 four-ply.

TECHNICAL: Synchromesh transmission. Speeds: 3F/1R. Column-mounted gearshift lever. Single-plate dry disc clutch. Semi-floating rear axle. Overall ratio: [with Hydra-Matic] 3.63; [with Synchromesh] 4.1:1. Four-wheel hydraulic brakes. Steel disc wheels. Automatic transmission Dual-range Hydra-Matic ($178).

OPTIONS: Mast antenna. Seven-tube Chieftain radio. No-Blow wind deflectors. Venti-Seat underseat heater. Windshield sun visor. Traffic light viewer. License frames. Light-up hood ornament. Full wheel discs. Wheel trim rings. White sidewall discs. Deluxe steering wheel. Visor vanity mirror. Directional signals. Compass. Windshield washers. Deluxe electric clock. Glove compartment light. Seat covers. Safti-Jack. Outside rearview mirror. Back-up lights. Spotlight. Foglights. Bumper guards. Master grille guard. Exhaust deflector. No-Mar gas filler door trim. Underhood trouble lamp. Jack bag. Tool kit.

HISTORICAL: Introduced: Nov. 2, 1951. Calendar year production: 984. Innovations: Dual-Range Hydra-Matic Drive. Higher compression cylinder heads. New standard rear axle ratios. Lock ring type pistons. Nylon plastic speedometer gears. Redesigned U-joints. New type brake linings. Fuse and wiring revisions. Extruded generator housing. New Delco 44-5 spark plugs. Recalibrated distributor curve. The Office of Price Stability (OPS) was a government agency charged with protecting the economy during the Korean Conflict. The OPS placed a cap of .18 percent on light-truck production by Pontiac. As a result, the company was limited to that share of the overall market in light-duty models. This made the 1952 Pontiac Sedan Delivery rarer than others. General manager Arnold Lenz was killed in a car-train crash. Robert M. Critchfield was appointed to fill the position.

1953 PONTIAC

CHIEFTAIN — SERIES 25/26 — SIX-CYLINDER/EIGHT-CYLINDER: New dual streak trimmings, all-new body styling, a one-piece curved windshield, twin-feather Indian hood ornament, more massive chrome headlight doors and new front grille (which encircled the parking lights) were characteristics of 1953 Pontiacs. Dual-streak styling referred to arranging the hood Silver Streaks in two thinner bands separated by a wide, color panel. While cars had step-up design rear fenders, the Sedan Delivery (and station wagon) had fenders extending to the rear in an uninterrupted sweep. Special taillamp assemblies with oval bezels and round lenses were housed in the fenders. The trucks did not have round Indian head medallions on the rear fenders. Also, the bumper guard arrangement on trucks and wagons was unique and similar to that used in 1952. There was no built-in crossbar guard; the license lamp was attached to the rear bumper apron. The license plate was held by a bracket at the center of the panel below the rear door. As previous, the Sedan Delivery was marketed as a base Special model although it had Deluxe moldings and chrome gravel guards (without rear panel extensions). The interior (Trim Code 83) was beige and black imitation leather. A new two-tone Special model steering wheel with finger indentations on the spokes was used in trucks. Inside was an adjustable driver's seat and separate hinged passenger seat, tough ribbed synthetic rubber floor mat, dual sun visors and coated fabric material headliner in lighter beige. The rear compartment had black linoleum floor coverings. Walls were covered with painted Masonite panel board, while wheelhousings, rear corner panels and the inside of the rear door were painted to match the interior. The truck's GVW rating, including driver, was 2,320 lbs. It had a 16-gallon gas tank.

1953 Pontiac Chieftain Sedan Delivery (Dick Choler)

I.D. DATA: Serial number located on left-hand door pillar. Starting: [six-cylinder] P-6X-1001; [eight-cylinder] P-8X-1001. Engine numbers located on lip on left side of cylinder block. Block stamping and door pillar stamping should match.

Model	Body Type	Price	Weight	Prod. Total
Chieftain Six - 1/2-Ton - 122 in. w.b.				
2517	Sedan Delivery	1850	3406	Note 1
Chieftain Eight - 1/2-Ton - 122 in. wb.				
2517	Sedan Delivery	1920	3481	Note 1

NOTE 1: Calendar year production was 1,324 units.

ENGINE: Inline. L-head. Six-cylinder. Cast iron block. Bore & stroke: 3-9/16 in. x 4 in. Displacement: 239.2 cid. Compression ratio: [standard] 7.0:1. Brake horsepower: 115 at 3800 rpm. Net horsepower: 30.4. Torque: 193 lbs.-ft. at 2000 rpm. Four main bearings. Solid valve lifters. Carburetor: Carter two-barrel model WCD-2010-S.

NOTE: Optional 7.7:1 high-compression cylinder head with Hydra-Matic Drive gave 118 hp at 3800 rpm and 197 lbs.-ft. of torque at 2000 rpm.

ENGINE: Inline. L-head. Eight-cylinder. Cast iron block. Bore & stroke: 3-3/8 in. x 3-3/4 in. Displacement: 268.4 cid. Compression ratio: [standard] 6.8:1. Brake horsepower: 118 at 3600 rpm. Net horsepower: 36.4. Torque: 222 lbs.-ft. at 2200 rpm. Five main bearings. Solid valve lifters. Carburetor: Carter WCD two-barrel model 719-SA.

NOTE: Optional 7.7:1 compression cylinder head with Hydra-Matic Drive gave 122 hp at 3600 rpm and 227 lbs.-ft. torque at 2200 rpm.

CHASSIS [Chieftain Special Series]: Wheelbase: 122 in. Overall length: 202.6 in. Height: 65.2 in. Front tread: 58 in. Rear tread: 59.05 in. Tires: 7.10 x 15 six-ply. [front] 28 psi; [rear] 30 psi; [special equipment] 7.60 x 15. Other measurements: Overall length with rear door open (229.9 in.); Step-up in floor level back of driver's seat (7.3 in.); Driver's seat to rear door (76 in.); Dash to rear door (135.6 in.); Average height floor to ceiling (41.8 in.); Inside width above wheelhousings (46.5 in.); Top of wheelhousings above floor (12 in.).

TECHNICAL: Synchromesh transmission. Speeds: 3F/1R. Column-mounted gearshift lever. Single-plate dry disc clutch. Semi-floating rear axle. Overall ratio: [six-cylinder/synchromesh] 4.1:1; [eight-cylinder/synchromesh] 3.9:1; [all Hydra-Matic] 3.08:1. Four-wheel mechanical brakes. Steel disc wheels. Automatic transmission Dual-Range Hydra-Matic Drive ($178).

1953 Pontiac Chieftain Sedan Delivery (OCW)

OPTIONS: Power steering ($134). Venti-seat underseat heater/defroster. Chieftain 7-tube radio. Directional signals. Autronic-Eye. Back-up lamps. Non-glare rearview mirror. Rear fender panels (skirts). Exhaust deflector. No-Mar fuel guard door. Deluxe steering wheel. Illuminated hood ornament. Windshield sun visor. Traffic light viewer. Latex foam seat cushions. Windshield washers. Outside rearview mirror(s). Visor vanity mirror. Glovebox lamp. Underhood lamp. Lighted ashtray. Hand-brake-on signal lamp. Master grille guard. Wing guards. E-Z-Eye glass. Dual fog lamps. Rear speaker. Electric antenna. Safety spot lamp. Chrome trim rings. Safti-jack. Oil bath air cleaner.

DEALER-INSTALLED OPTIONS: Seat covers. Hand spot lamp. Venti-shades. Draft deflectors. Tissue dispenser. Magna tray. Fuel door lock. Simulated wire wheel discs. Illuminated car compass.

HISTORICAL: Introduced Dec. 6, 1952. Calendar year production: 1,324. Innovations: New styling. Longer wheelbase. One-piece windshield. New Uni-steel Higher horsepower ratings. Two-barrel carburetor with six. Revised intake manifold. Dip stick relocated. Some Pontiacs made with Chevrolet Powerglide transmissions following Hydra-Matic factory fire. This was the last year for the Sedan Delivery. Some collectors believe a 1954 model was planned and, perhaps, built in very small numbers. Pontiac sedan deliveries were produced in Canada at least through 1958. Production of Canadian light-duty trucks totaled 1,407 in 1954; 1,022 in 1955; 1,385 in 1956; 682 in 1957 and 449 in 1958.

STUDEBAKER

1908-1963

1957 Studebaker Transtar Pickup

By Fred K. Fox

Long before the advent of motorized light-duty trucks, Studebaker was manufacturing horse-drawn commercial vehicles in South Bend, Ind. The H&C Studebaker blacksmith shop was opened in February, 1852. During their first year of business, Henry and Clem Studebaker constructed two wagons which they sold to local farmers. The carrying capacity of these wagons, by today's standards, would classify them as light-duty vehicles, but the term "light-duty truck" was unknown in 1852.

The small blacksmith shop grew quickly from its humble beginnings. By the time of our country's centennial in 1876, Studebaker was the largest producer of horse-drawn vehicles in the world. Studebaker experimented with some automobile designs in the late 1890s. In 1902 they introduced their first car, an electric. In 1904 they brought out a gasoline-powered automobile that featured a chassis built by Garford.

A very limited number of Studebaker Electrics and Garford powered Studebaker gasoline vehicles were sold as commercial units. One of the more interesting models from this period was the Suburban, which was introduced in 1908. The Studebaker Suburban was an open passenger car that could be easily converted to a baggage car by simply removing the rear seat. Studebaker called it "The Adaptable Car."

In late 1908, Studebaker became the sales agent for the new EMF 30 automobile. In 1911, the Studebaker Brothers Manufacturing Co. and the EMF Co. merged and formed the Studebaker Corp.

From late 1911 to early 1913, the new corporation produced a limited number of Flanders 20 half-ton panel deliveries. Selling for $800, the fragile 102 in. wheelbase Flanders deliveries were powered by a 154.8 cid (3-5/8 in. bore x 3-3/4 in. stroke) L-head four-cylinder engine that produced 20 hp.

Studebaker factories in Detroit used custom built EMF 30 and Flanders 20 pickups to transport small parts around the plant. These roadster pickups were actually called pickups (with no hyphen) in 1913 company literature. This was probably one of the earliest uses of the non-hyphenated pickup name in reference to a motorized light-duty vehicle with a box on the back.

Studebaker formally entered the light-duty vehicle field in 1914 when they introduced their 3/4-ton Model Three Delivery Car. The Delivery Car was available as a closed Panel Side Delivery or open Express Body Delivery. Each was priced at $1,150. Studebaker Delivery Cars were powered by a 192.4 cid (3-1/2 in. bore x 5 in. stroke) L-head four-cylinder engine that produced 30 hp. They had a wheelbase of 108-1/2 in. and were fitted with 34 x 4-1/2 tires.

Studebaker Delivery Cars were available from 1914 to 1917. Prices were lowered to $1,085 in 1915 and in 1916 the Panel Delivery was $875 and the Express Delivery

$825. Because of World War I, prices were raised $50 in 1917. The 1915 was a Model Five and the 1916-1917 was a Model SF. In 1916, the wheelbase was increased to 112 in. and the load rating was reduced to 1/2-ton. The same basic engine was used all four years, but for 1916-1917 the cylinder bore was increased to 3-7/8 in. The larger bore increased the displacement to 235.8 cid and the horsepower to 40. Production figures for the 1914-1917 Studebaker Delivery Cars do not exist, but they certainly were not very high. It is unlikely that many have survived.

In 1918, Studebaker discontinued all motorized commercial vehicle production. Larger models were introduced in 1925, but it was not until 1927 that light-duty commercial vehicles returned to Studebaker's lineup.

Between 1927 and 1931, a wide range of Studebaker and Erskine open and closed delivery cars were offered by Studebaker. Most Studebaker versions used Dictator chassis. No pickup-bodied trucks were among the styles offered in 1927-1931. As in 1914-1917, sales of the 1927-1931 light-duty Studebaker commercial cars were not great. In 1932 they again abandoned (except for funeral cars and ambulance chassis) light-duty commercial vehicle production. Experimental vehicles, including even a Rockne

pickup, were built in the early 1930s. But, it was not until 1937, that Studebaker again entered the light-duty commercial vehicle field.

This time, Studebaker wisely decided to produce a pickup style truck. In contrast to earlier ventures, the 1937 undertaking attracted many buyers and established Studebaker as a viable producer of light-duty trucks. Except for 1940 and the World War II period, Studebaker built a continuous line of light-duty trucks right up to the time of the South Bend plant's closing in December, 1963.

Among Studebaker's famous models were the 1937-1939 Coupe-Express, the 1941-1948 M series models, the 1949-1954 R series trucks and the 1955-1964 E series models. The last years of the E series, 1960 to 1964, included the popular Lark-bodied Champ models.

As we have shown, Studebaker built some light-duty commercial vehicles prior to 1937, but it was not until the introduction of the Coupe-Express pickup in 1937 that the company gained recognition for being a producer of light-duty trucks. Because of this, my cataloging of Studebaker light-duty trucks will start with the 1937 model year, although you will see earlier models illustrated in this introduction.

1914 Studebaker Panel Body Delivery (OCW)

1915 Studebaker Delivery Car — Express Body (ASC)

1915 Studebaker Model "S" Light Delivery (OCW)

1916 Studebaker 1000 lb. Commercial Car — Model SF

1915 Studebaker Delivery Car — Panel Side Body (ASC)

Standard Catalog of Light-Duty Trucks

1929 Studebaker "Arlington" Funeral Coach (DFW/ASC)

1930 Studebaker Open Express (A&A)

1933 Rockne Panel Delivery (A&A)

1930 Studebaker Fifth-wheel Trailer Combo (DFW/KCMS)

1933 & 1934 Studebaker Panel Delivery Trucks (A&A)

1931 Studebaker 1-Ton Beverage Truck (A&A)

1934 Studebaker 1-Ton Panel Delivery (A&A)

1932 Rockne Panel Delivery (A&A)

1934 Studebaker 1-Ton Panel Delivery (A&A)

1937 STUDEBAKER

1937 Studebaker Coupe-Express (A&A)

MODEL J5 — SIX-CYLINDER: In 1937, Studebaker introduced its first light-duty pickup, the Coupe-Express. Front end sheet metal, most of the cab, the instrument panel, engine and basic chassis components, came directly from the 1937 Studebaker 5A Dictator passenger car. Since the Coupe-Express was based on a car styling, it had vent windows in the doors, something not offered on most other pickups of the era. It also had dual windshield wipers, dual sun visors, a rearview mirror, dome light and an adjustable seat. The 1937 Coupe-Express was fitted with a double-walled, six-foot long, 16-gauge all-steel pickup box. It featured a contoured outer shell that flowed into the rear fenders. The tailgate was smooth and had no name on it. The bed floor was all-steel. The Coupe-Express came with a spare tire mounted in the right front fenderwell. Front and rear chrome bumpers were also standard. Like the 5A Dictator, the Coupe-Express had an I-beam front axle. The Coupe-Express could be ordered without a pickup box. Another variant was the Suburban Car, a woody station wagon which was based on a J5 windshield cowl chassis. Larger Standard series Studebaker trucks used the same cab as the Coupe-Express. Included in the Standard series was a 1-1/2-ton J15 Express Pickup and Panel Van.

I.D. DATA: The serial number was located on the left side of the frame under the front fender. The engine number was located on the top left side of the cylinder block above the distributor. The beginning serial numbers for the J5 Coupe-Express were J5-001 in South Bend and J5-5,001 in Los Angeles. The beginning engine number was T-701.

Model	Body Type	Price	Weight	Prod. Total
J5 Series — 1/2-Ton				
J5	Pickup	647	3168	3125

ENGINE: Six-cylinder. L-head. Cast iron block. Displacement: 217.8 cid. Bore & Stroke: 3-1/4 in. x 4-3/8 in. Compression ratio: 6.01. Brake horsepower: 86 at 3600 rpm. Taxable horsepower: 25.38. Maximum Torque: 160 lbs.-ft. at 1200 rpm. Main bearings: Four. Valve lifters: Solid. Carburetor: Stromberg Model EX-23 one-barrel, Carter Model W1-371S one-barrel or Carter Model WA1-414S one-barrel.

CHASSIS & BODY: Wheelbase: 116 in. Overall length: 193 in. Height: 67 in. Width: 71.75 in. Interior pickup box dimensions: 71.75 in. long x 48.6 in. wide x 14.6 in. high. Front tread: 57.4 in. Rear tread: 60.4 in. Tires: 6.00 x 16. GVW: [J5] 4,500 lbs.

TECHNICAL: Sliding gear transmission. Speeds: 3F/1R. Synchromesh in second and third. Floor shift control. Single-plate dry-disc clutch. I-beam front axle. Hypoid semi-floating rear axle. Overall ratio: 4.55:1. Hydraulic brakes. Automatic Hill Holder standard. Steel disc wheels. Two-stage rear springs. Front and rear tubular shocks. Variable ratio steering gear.

OPTIONS: Overdrive transmission. Radio. Heater. Electric clock. Leather upholstery. Cigarette lighter. Rear axle: 4.82:1. Tires: 6.50 x 16. Steel spoke wheels. Cab-high tarpaulin pickup box cover. Locking gas cap. License plate frames. Spotlight. Clear road or amber fog lights. Wig-wag stoplight.

HISTORICAL: With sales of over 3,000, the 1937 Coupe-Express was, up to that time, the best selling truck model ever produced by Studebaker. Quite a few 1937 Coupe-Expresses have survived, but there are evidently no surviving J5 Suburban Cars.

1938 STUDEBAKER

MODEL K5 — SIX-CYLINDER: As in 1937, the 1938 K5 Coupe-Express pickup was based on current year Studebaker car styling. In 1938, Studebaker dropped the Dictator name and returned the Commander model name. The 1938 Coupe-Express front end and cab styling was based on the 1938 Commander Model 7A (identified during the early part of the year as the Studebaker Six). The Commander 7A, in contrast to the State Commander 8A and President 4C, had free-standing headlights instead of the faired-in headlights used on the more expensive models. Raymond Loewy's rakish 1938 car windshield was incorporated into the 1938 Coupe-Express. Restyled front fenders and a shorter front end resulted in the spare wheel and tire sitting much higher than it did in 1937. The rear fenders were unchanged from 1937, but the pickup box was lengthened 5-1/2 in. to make up for the shortened front end. As on the 7A Commander, the K5's front suspension featured Studebaker's independent Planar transverse spring suspension system. This system was first introduced on top line Studebaker cars in 1935. Tubular shocks were replaced by Houdaille lever arm shocks. The six-cylinder engine was bored out an extra 1/16 in. in 1938. The K5's

Standard Catalog of Light-Duty Trucks

---

instrument panel was like that used in the 7A Commander. The Suburban Car woody wagon was continued in 1938. A K10 one-ton Fast-Transport with pickup box or panel body was offered in 1938. K10 and larger standard series trucks continued with the 1937 cab styling.

1938 Studebaker Walk-in Delivery Van (A&A)

1938 Studebaker K-10 Stake Bed (A&A)

I.D. DATA: Serial number location: same as 1937. Engine numbers were located on the top left side rear corner of the cylinder block on early models and on the top left side front corner of the cylinder block on later models. The beginning serial numbers for the K5 Coupe-Express were K5-001 in South Bend and K5-7,501 in Los Angeles. The beginning engine numbers were T-4301 and H-7801 (both H and T engines were built in South Bend). Some production figure records indicate that no 1938 K5s were actually produced in Los Angeles.

Model	Body Type	Price	Weight	Prod. Total
K5 Series — 1/2-Ton				
K5	Pickup	850	3250	1000

ENGINE: Six-cylinder. L-head. Cast iron block. Displacement: 226.2 cid. Bore & stroke: 3-5/16 in. x 4-3/8 in. Compression ratio: 6.0:1. Brake horsepower: 90 at 3400 rpm. Taxable horsepower: 26.35. Main bearings: Four. Valve lifters: Solid. Carburetor: Stromberg Model BXO-26 one-barrel.

1938 Studebaker K-10 Pickup (A&A)

CHASSIS & BODY: Wheelbase: 116.5 in. Overall length: 193.75 in. Height: 67.75 in. Width: 73 in. Interior pickup box dimensions: 77.25 in. long x 48.6 in. wide x 14.6 in. high. Front tread: 59.4 in. Rear tread: 59.6 in. Tires: 6.00 x 16. GVW; [K5] 4,500 lbs.

1938 Studebaker Furniture Van (A&A)

TECHNICAL: Sliding gear transmission. Speeds: 3F/1R. Synchromesh in second and third. Floor shift control. Single-plate dry-disc clutch. Planar independent front suspension. Hypoid semi-floating rear axle. Overall ratio: 4.55:1. Hydraulic brakes. Steel disc wheels. Two-stage rear springs. Front and rear Houdaille lever arm shocks. Variable-ratio steering gear.

1938 Studebaker Specialty Van (A&A)

OPTIONS: Overdrive transmission. Automatic Hill Holder. Radio. Heater. Electric clock. Leather upholstery. Cigarette lighter. Rear axle: 4.82:1. Tires: 6.50 x 16. Cab-high tarpaulin pickup box cover. Locking gas cap. License plate frames. Spotlight. Clear road or amber fog lights. Wig-wag oscillating stoplight. Windshield washer. Bumper and grille guards. Fender guide. Fabric radiator cover.

1938 Studebaker K-10 Fire & Rescue Truck (A&A)

HISTORICAL: In 1938 the K5 used both "T" (truck) prefix engine numbers and regular Commander "H" prefix engine numbers. The recession of 1938 helped cut Coupe-Express sales to one-third of what they were in 1937. No K5 Suburban Car woody wagons are known to have survived.

1938 Studebaker Coupe-Express (A&A)

1939 STUDEBAKER

MODEL L5 — SIX-CYLINDER: For the second year in a row, the Coupe-Express front sheet metal was restyled to match the current year Studebaker car. As on Commanders and Presidents, and later Champions, the headlights of the 1939 Coupe-Express were built into the front fenders. The front fenders were an all new design, although the high-mounted spare was retained in the right wheel well. The Commander/President split grille was also adopted on the Coupe-Express. The cab styling, pickup box and instrument panel remained unchanged from 1938 and the original 1937 rear fenders were retained. No significant mechanical changes were made from 1938. The L5 Suburban Car woody wagon and 1-ton K10 Fast-Transport were continued. The K10 and larger Standard series trucks continued with the cab style introduced on the 1937 Coupe-Express. Edwards Iron Works, of South Bend, Ind., offered a small pickup box that could fit into the back of a Champion coupe with its trunk lid removed. Unlike the Coupe-Express box, the Edwards box had "STUDEBAKER" on the tailgate. Edwards called it both the pickup Coupe and the Coupe-Delivery. Rated at only 1/4-ton, the Coupe-Delivery did not really fall into the light-duty truck classification.

I.D. DATA: Serial number location: same as 1937-38. Engine number location: same as late 1938. The beginning serial numbers for the L5 Coupe-Express were L5-001 in South Bend and no 1939 Coupe-Express models were assembled in Los Angeles. The beginning engine number was H-42,501.

Model	Body Type	Price	Weight	Prod. Total
L5 Series				
L5	Pickup	850	3250	1200

1939 Studebaker Coupe-Express (A&A)

ENGINE: Six-cylinder. L-head. Cast iron block. Displacement: 226.2 cid. Bore & stroke: 3-5/16 in. x 4-3/8 in. Compression ratio: 6.0:1. Brake horsepower: 90 at 3400 rpm. Taxable horsepower: 26.35. Main bearings: Four. Valve lifters: Solid. Carburetor: Stromberg Model BXO-26 one-barrel.

CHASSIS & BODY: Wheelbase: 116.5 in. Overall length: 195.4 in. Height: 67.75 in. Width: 73 in. Interior pickup box dimensions: 77.25 in. long x 48.6 in. wide x 14.6 in. high. Front tread: 59.4 in. Rear tread: 59.6 in. Tires: 6.00 x 16. GVW: 4,500 lbs.

TECHNICAL: Sliding gear transmission. Speeds: 3F/1R. Synchromesh in second and third. Floor or column shift controls. Single-plate dry-disc clutch. Planar independent front suspension. Hypoid semi-floating rear axle. Overall ratio: 4.55:1. Hydraulic brakes. Steel disc wheels. Two-stage rear springs. Front and rear Houdaille lever arm shocks. Variable-ratio steering gear.

OPTIONS: Overdrive transmission. Automatic Hill Holder. Radio. Heater. Electric clock. Leather upholstery. Cigarette lighter. Rear axle: 4.82:1. Tires: 6.50 x 16. Cab-high tarpaulin pickup box cover. Locking gas cap. License plate frames. Spotlight. Clear road or amber fog lights. Wig-wag oscillating stoplight. Windshield washer. Bumper and grille guards. Fender guide. Fabric radiator cover.

HISTORICAL: As in 1937 and 1938, no 1939 L5 Suburban Car woody wagons are known to have survived. The Suburban Car production is included in the Coupe-Express production figures and no breakdowns have been discovered. The economy took a definite upturn in 1939, but Coupe-Express sales only increased 20 percent over 1938 and were still way below the 1937 figure.

1940 STUDEBAKER

1940 Studebaker Champion Sedan Delivery (A&A)

For the 1940 model year, Studebaker produced no light-duty trucks. The inability of the 1939 Coupe-Express to show a significant sales increase over the 1938 model, convinced Studebaker executives that they were on the wrong track. A pickup with car styling, independent front suspension and a "pretty" pickup box had limited sales appeal in the late '30s. Studebaker was working on a more truck-like light-duty pickup, but it was not ready for the 1940 model year. In the interim, all they could offer was the 1/4-ton Champion Coupe-Delivery with the small (68 in. long x 30 in. wide x 18.6 in. high) Edwards Iron Works pickup box in the back and the large (6,750 GVW) 1-ton K10 Fast-Transport. The Fast-Transport was available with a panel body or two different 8-foot pickup boxes. The Fast-Transport Custom Express came with a smooth sided box and steel floor, while the cheaper Fast-Transport Standard Express came with a conventional cargo box and a wooden floor. Both of these styles of trucks had "STUDEBAKER" on the tailgate. A few Fast-Transports have survived and at least one restored 1940 Champion Coupe-Delivery exists.

1941 STUDEBAKER

1941 Studebaker Deluxe Pickup Truck (FKF)

MODEL M5 — SIX-CYLINDER: For the 1941 model year, Studebaker introduced a whole new line of commercial vehicles. Called the M series, they all featured the same cab and front end styling. Some of the cab components, including the instrument panel, were borrowed from the 1941 Champion car, but the front end styling was unique to the new truck line. The light-duty pickup version of the M series was the 1/2-ton M5 Coupe-Express (same spelling as the 1937-1939 models, but generally without the hyphen). To save tooling money, the M5 had runningboards that were interchangeable from side to side and fenders that were interchangeable, on a given side, from front to rear. The all-steel pickup box was of contemporary design. The Coupe-Express was available with or without the box. The name "STUDEBAKER" was pressed into the tailgate and on a nameplate on the front of the hood. All M series trucks featured an interior hood release. M5 hubcaps were the same as those used on 1940-1941 Commander cars. The M5 was powered by the same small six-cylinder engine that was used in the Champion car, but it had an I-beam front axle instead of the Champion's Planar independent front suspension. The Standard trim M5 was not nearly as plush as the 1937-1939 Coupe-Express models. It had only one interior sun visor, one windshield wiper, no dome light and no rear bumper. It was also about 10 in. higher than the earlier style. With a base price of $664, it was $186 less than the 1939 Coupe-Express. A Deluxe M5 Coupe-Express was offered. A Deluxe version was created by adding a $24.47 Deluxe Equipment Group option to a Standard trim model. The Deluxe Equipment Group included stainless steel grille bar overlays, a hood ornament, bright metal side moldings, chrome

exterior rearview mirror, dome light, and body color fenders (Standard trim models had black fenders). A 1-ton M15 Standard Express with an 8-ft. pickup box was also produced.

I.D. DATA: Serial numbers were located on a plate on the left front door hinge pillar or on the left side of the seat riser. Engine numbers were located on the top, left side, front corner of the cylinder block. The beginning serial number for the 1941 M5 Coupe-Express was M5-001. The ending serial number was M5-4685. The starting engine number was 1M-001. All domestic M5s were assembled in South Bend, Indiana.

Model	Body Type	Price	Weight	Prod. Total
M5 Series				
M5	Pickup	644	2660	4685*

(**) Estimate based on serial number span.

ENGINE: Six-cylinder. L-head. Cast iron block. Displacement: 169.6 cid.. Bore & stroke: 3 in. x 4 in. Compression ratio: 6.5:1. Brake horsepower: 80 at 4000 rpm. Taxable horsepower: 21.6. Maximum torque: 134 lbs.-ft. Main bearings: Four. Valve lifters: Solid. Carburetor: Carter Model WA1-496S one-barrel.

1941 Studebaker Pickup Truck (A&A)

CHASSIS & BODY: Wheelbase: 113 in. Overall length: 181.25 in. Height: 77 in. Width: 75.3 in. Interior pickup box dimensions: 78.2 in. long x 48.5 in. wide x 13.4 in. high. Front tread: 59.9 in. Rear tread: 59.6 in. Tires: 6.00 x 16 four-ply. GVW: 4,500 lbs.

TECHNICAL: Sliding gear transmission. Speeds: 3F/1R. Synchromesh in second and third. Floor shift control. Single-plate dry-disc clutch. I-beam front axle. Hypoid semi-floating rear axle. Overall ratio: 4.82:1. Hydraulic brakes. Steel disc wheels. Lever arm shock absorbers. Variable-ratio steering gear.

OPTIONS: Four-speed transmission with floor shift control. Overdrive with three-speed transmission and steering column shift control. Hill Holder. Radio. Heater. Electric clock. Leather upholstery. Door armrests. Right-hand sun visor. Right-hand windshield wiper. Dome light. Interior rearview mirror. Cigarette lighter. Deluxe steering wheel. Dual horns. Deluxe Equipment Group. Caravan Top. Body color fenders. Chrome rear bumper. Bumper guards. Extra taillight. License plate frames. Locking gas cap. Spotlight. Fog lights. Service light. Windshield washer. Wheel trim rings. Whitewall tires. Six-ply tires. 6.25 x 16, 6.50 x 16 or 7.00 x 16 tires. Two-stage rear springs. 4.55:1 rear axle. Fram oil filter. Oil bath air cleaner.

HISTORICAL: The 1941 M series, with total sales of 8,439 for all models from 1/2-ton to 1-1/2-tons, set a new high water mark for Studebaker truck production. The M5, with its lower price, I-beam front axle, conventional pickup box and non-car front end, proved to be much more popular than the earlier Coupe-Express. A few M5s were fitted with Montpelier panel bodies or factory stake bodies, but most were sold with pickup boxes. Very few 1941 Deluxe Coupe-Express models were sold and they are extremely rare today.

1941-1943 STUDEBAKER (MILITARY)

During World War II, Studebaker assembled 197,678 model US6 2-1/2 -ton Hercules-powered 6x6 and 6x4 military trucks. Over 100,000 of these trucks were sent to Russia via Lend-lease. The Studebaker military trucks used a slightly modified M series truck cab. After World War II, the GAZ factory in Gorky, Russia, started production of a series of trucks that were close copies of the Studebaker US6 models. The GAZ cabs were almost identical to the cabs used on the M5 Coupe-Express. Many GAZ trucks with M series style cabs are still in use around the world. Studebaker also produced 67,789 Wright Cyclone R-1820 aircraft engines for the Boeing B-17 Flying Fortress and 15,890 tracked Weasel light personnel carriers. 10,647 of the Weasels were the amphibious M-29C version. The Weasel was designed by Studebaker engineers and all were built in Studebaker plants. The Weasel was powered by the same Champion engine that was used in the M5 Coupe-Express.

1942 STUDEBAKER

1942 Studebaker Standard Model M5 Pickup (FKF)

MODEL M5 — SIX-CYLINDER: The basic Coupe-Express was continued unchanged in 1942. However, the war in Europe and America's entrance into the war in December, 1941, had effects on M5 trim and production. The 1942 production started in September 1941 and near that time the Deluxe Equipment Group with its stainless steel grille overlays was discontinued. This was because of the government's need for critical metals for domestic and export military material production. Not long after America's entrance into the war, all chrome-plated trim was replaced by painted trim. Cars and trucks with painted trim were called "blackout" models. All light-duty Studebaker commercial vehicle production was indefinitely suspended on Jan. 31, 1942.

I.D. DATA: Serial number and engine number locations: same as 1941. The starting serial number for the 1942 M5 Coupe-Express was M5-4686. The ending serial number was on or before M5-5000. Engine numbers were continuous from 1941 to 1948 and year breaks are not available.

Model	Body Type	Price	Weight	Prod. Total
M5 Series				
M5	Pickup	687	2660	315*

(*) This is the maximum figure possible based on the serial number span.

ENGINE: Six-cylinder. L-head. Cast iron block. Displacement: 169.6 cid. Bore & stroke: 3 in. x 4 in. Compression ratio: 6.5:1. Brake horsepower: 80 at 4000 rpm. Taxable horsepower: 21.6. Maximum torque: 134 lbs.-ft. Main bearings: Four. Valve lifters: Solid. Carburetor: Carter Model WA1-496S one-barrel.

CHASSIS & BODY: Wheelbase: 113 in. Overall length: 181.25 in. Height: 77 in. Width: 75.3 in. Interior pickup box dimensions: 78.2 in. long x 48.5 in. wide x 13.4 in. high. Front tread: 59.9 in. Rear tread: 59.6 in. Tires: 6.00 x 16 four-ply. GVW: 4,200 lbs.

TECHNICAL: Sliding gear transmission. Speeds: 3F/1R. Synchromesh in second and third. Floor shift control. Single-plate dry-disc clutch. I-beam front axle. Hypoid semi-floating rear axle. Overall ratio: 4.82:1. Hydraulic brakes. Steel disc wheels. Lever arm shock absorbers. Variable-ratio steering gear.

OPTIONS: Four-speed transmission with floor shift control. Overdrive with three-speed transmission and steering column shift control. Hill Holder. Radio. Heater. Electric clock. Leather upholstery. Door armrests. Right-hand sun visor. Right-hand windshield wiper. Dome light. Interior rearview mirror. Cigarette lighter. Deluxe steering wheel. Dual horns. Caravan Top. Body color fenders. Chrome rear bumper. Bumper guards. Extra taillight. License plate frames. Locking gas cap. Spotlight. Fog lights. Service light. Windshield washer. Wheel trim rings. Six-ply tires. 6.25 x 16, 6.50 x 16 or 7.00 x 16 tires. Two-stage rear springs. 4.55:1 rear axle. Fram oil filter. Oil bath air cleaner.

HISTORICAL: Because of World War II, very few 1942 M5 Coupe-Express pickups were built. Today they are extremely rare, especially the blackout models. Larger model trucks were considered more important to domestic commerce, so Studebaker was allowed to build many more 1942 1-1/2-ton trucks than Coupe-Express models.

1944-1945 STUDEBAKER

By late 1944, the need for civilian trucks on the home front was very critical. Because of this, the War Production Board authorized some companies to make a limited number of medium-duty trucks. No light-duty models were allowed, but Studebaker, starting in the spring of 1945, produced a few blackout 1-ton Model M15-20 Express trucks with eight-foot pickup boxes. They were like the prewar M15s, except they used the modified military US6 cab (C9 type) that featured a swing windshield and metal door and kick panels. Built in much larger numbers was the 1-ton Model M15-28 truck with dual rear wheels. The 1945 M15s were fitted standard with heavy-duty wheels and springs. They had two windshield wipers, two sun visors, an oil bath air cleaner and an oil filter. The later items were standard on all subsequent M series trucks. Altogether, Studebaker produced 4,000 of the 1945 M15s, but, as mentioned, only a small percentage of those were the Express model with a pickup box. At least two 1945 M15-20 Expresses are known to have survived.

1946 STUDEBAKER

1946 Studebaker Truck

MODEL M5 — SIX-CYLINDER: After the conclusion of World War II, Studebaker brought back its full line of M series trucks, including the popular 1/2-ton M5 Coupe-Express. Except for a few minor items, the 1946 M5 was identical to the 1941 M5. The Deluxe Equipment Group did not return, but two windshield wipers, two sun visors, an oil filter and an oil bath air cleaner were made standard on the M5. Also added to the M5 standard list were body color fenders, 6.50 x 16 six-ply tires, two-stage rear springs, a dome light and armrests. Because of tire shortages, early 1946 models came with a spare wheel, but no spare tire. Early 1946s also had painted hubcaps that were similar in design to those used on 1942 Commander and President cars. The prewar style chrome hubcaps returned early in the model year. The 1-ton pickup, now also called a Coupe-Express, was continued from 1945. It, like all 1946 M series models, came with the fixed windshield C2 cab that had cardboard door and kick panels. The year's 1-ton trucks were called M15As. They lacked some of the heavy-duty equipment that was standard in 1945.

I.D. DATA: Serial number and engine number locations: Same as 1941-1942. The starting serial number for the 1946 M5 Coupe-Express was M5-5001. The ending serial number was on or before M5-19052. Engine numbers were continuous from 1941 to 1948 and year-breakouts are not available.

Model	Body Type	Price	Weight	Prod. Total
M5 Series				
M5	Pickup	929	2710	14,052

NOTE 1: Because of changing regulations from the Office of Price Administration, M5 prices were raised several times during 1946. They started at $832 in January and were up to $968 by the end of the model year. Production is based on the serial number span.

ENGINE: Six-cylinder. L-head. Cast iron block. Displacement: 169.6 cid. Bore & stroke: 3 in. x 4 in. Compression ratio: 6.5:1. Brake horsepower: 80 at 4000 rpm. Taxable horsepower: 21.6. Maximum torque: 134 lbs.-ft. Main bearings: Four. Valve lifters: Solid. Carburetor: Carter Model WE-532S one-barrel.

CHASSIS & BODY: Wheelbase: 113 in. Overall length: 181.25 in. Height: 77 in. Width: 75.3 in. Interior pickup box dimensions: 78.2 in. long x 48.5 in. wide x 13.4 in. high. Front tread: 59.9 in. Rear tread: 59.6 in. Tires: 6.50 x 16 six-ply. GVW: [M5] 4,500 lbs.

TECHNICAL: Sliding gear transmission. Speeds: 3F/1R. Synchromesh in second and third. Floor shift control. Single-plate dry-disc clutch. I-beam front axle. Hypoid semi-floating rear axle. Overall ratio: 4.82:1. Hydraulic brakes. Steel disc wheels. Lever arm shock absorbers. Variable-ratio steering gear.

OPTIONS: Four-speed transmission with floor shift control. Overdrive with three-speed transmission and steering column shift control. Hill Holder. Radio. Heater. Electric clock. Interior rearview mirror. Cigarette lighter. Dual horns. Mattex seat covers. Caravan Top. Chrome rear bumper. Heavy-duty bumper. Heavy-duty grille and light guard. Bumper guards. Extra taillight. License plate frames. Locking gas cap. Spotlight. Fog lights. Service light. Hood light. Glove compartment light. Turn signals. Windshield washer. Wheel trim rings. Six blade fan. Extension rearview mirror. Heavy-duty springs. No optional tire sizes were available in 1946.

HISTORICAL: The strong postwar seller's market meant that Studebaker could sell as many M5 pickups as they could build. The larger 6.50 x 16 six-ply tires allowed the GVW to be raised 300 lbs. over 1941-42.

1947 STUDEBAKER

MODEL M5 — SIX-CYLINDER: For the 1947 model year, the M5 Coupe-Express was little changed from 1946. A few more options were added and a hood ornament, like the prewar deluxe ornament, was added to all models during midyear. As with every year, new exterior colors were made available in 1947. Grease fittings were changed from Zerk brand to Alemite brand. M5 windshield cowl chassis with Cantrell woody station wagon bodies were produced for export sales.

1947 Studebaker Mail Delivery Truck (A&A)

I.D. DATA: Serial number and engine number locations: Same as 1941-1946. The starting serial number for the 1947 M5 Coupe-Express was M5-19053. The ending serial number was on or before M5-42429. Engine numbers were continuous from 1941 to 1948 and year breaks are not available.

Model	Body Type	Price	Weight	Prod. Total
M5 Series				
M5	Pickup	1082	2635	23,377*

(*) Production estimate is based on serial number span.

1947 Studebaker Cantrell Station Wagon (A&A)

ENGINE: Six-cylinder. L-head. Cast iron block. Displacement: 169.6 cid. Bore & stroke: 3 in. x 4 in. Compression ratio: 6.5:1. Brake horsepower: 80 at 4000 rpm. Taxable horsepower: 21.6. Maximum torque: 134 lbs.-ft. Main bearings: Four. Valve lifters: Solid. Carburetor: Carter Model WE-532S one-barrel or Zenith Model 28BV10 one-barrel.
CHASSIS & BODY: Wheelbase: 113 in. Overall length: 181.25 in. Height: 77 in. Width: 75.3 in. Interior pickup box dimensions: 78.2 in. long x 48.5 in. wide x 13.4 in. high. Front tread: 59.9 in. Rear tread: 59.6 in. Tires: 6.50 x 16 six-ply. GVW: [M5] 4,500 lbs.
TECHNICAL: Sliding gear transmission. Speeds: 3F/1R. Synchromesh in second and third. Floor shift control. Single-plate dry-disc clutch. I-beam front axle. Hypoid semi-floating rear axle. Overall ratio: 4.82:1. Hydraulic brakes. Steel disc wheels. Lever arm shock absorbers. Variable-ratio steering gear.

1947 Studebaker Pickup (A&A)

OPTIONS: Four-speed transmission with floor shift control. Overdrive with three-speed transmission and steering column shift controls. Hill Holder. Radio. Heater. Electric clock. Interior rearview mirror. Cigarette lighter. Dual horns. Mattex seat covers. Caravan Top.

Chrome rear bumper. Heavy-duty bumper. Heavy-duty grille and light guard. Bumper guards. Extra taillight. License plate frames. Locking gas cap. Spotlight. Fog lights. Service light. Hood light. Glove compartment light. Turn signals. Windshield washer. Wheel trim rings. Six blade fan. Extension rearview mirror. Heavy-duty springs. Early cut-in generator. Vacuum booster for windshield wiper. Hood ornament (early). Glare proof interior rearview mirror. Visor vanity mirror. Fire extinguisher. No optional tire sizes were available in 1947.

HISTORICAL: By building large quantities of trucks during World War II, Studebaker gained valuable mass truck production experience. This proved beneficial in the early post-war years. During the 1946 calendar year, Studebaker produced 43,196 commercial vehicles. In 1947 the figure climbed to 67,811. The 1947 figure was greater than the total of all motorized commercial vehicles produced by Studebaker before World War II.

1948 STUDEBAKER

1948 Studebaker Pickup (FKF)

MODEL M5 — SIX-CYLINDER: M series Studebaker truck production continued into 1948 with few changes from 1947. The standard exterior left-hand mirror was switched from one with a fixed-length arm to one with an extension arm. Model year production started in the fall of 1947 and ended in March, 1948. The early ending date was necessary because of the introduction of the new 1949 series 2R trucks. Besides having new styling, the new models were to be produced in a different plant. This required moving much of the M series production equipment to the new plant. The former M series assembly building was converted into a press shop.

I.D. DATA: Serial number and engine number locations: Same as 1941-1947. The starting serial number for the 1948 M5 Coupe-Express was M5-42,430. The ending serial number was on or before M5-52,682. Engine numbers were continuous from 1941 to 1948 and year breaks are not available.

Model	Body Type	Price	Weight	Prod. Total
M5 Series				
M5	Pickup	1107	2635	10,253*

(*) Production estimate is based on serial number span.

1948 Studebaker Pickup (OCW)

ENGINE: Six-cylinder. L-head. Cast iron block. Displacement: 169.6 cid. Bore & stroke: 3 in. x 4 in. Compression ratio: 6.5:1. Brake horsepower: 80 at 4000 rpm. Taxable horsepower: 21.6. Maximum torque: 134 lbs.-ft. Main bearings: Four. Valve lifters: Solid. Carburetor: Zenith Model 2BV10 one-barrel or Carter Model WE-661S one-barrel.

1948 Studebaker Pickup, modified (L. Rowell)

CHASSIS & BODY: Wheelbase: 113 in. Overall length: 181.25 in. Height: 77 in. Width: 75.3 in. Interior pickup box dimensions: 78.2 in. long x 48.5 in. wide x 13.4 in. high. Front tread: 59.9 in. Rear tread: 59.6 in. Tires: 6.50 x 16 six-ply. GVW: [M5] 4,500 lbs.
TECHNICAL: Sliding gear transmission. Speeds: 3F/1R. Synchromesh in second and third. Floor shift control. Single-plate dry-disc clutch. I-beam front axle. Hypoid semi-floating rear axle. Overall ratio: 4.82:1. Hydraulic brakes. Steel disc wheels. Lever arm shock absorbers. Variable-ratio steering gear.
OPTIONS: Four-speed transmission with floor shift control. Overdrive with three-speed transmission and steering column shift control. Hill Holder. Radio. Heater. Electric clock. Interior rearview mirror. Cigarette lighter. Dual horns. Mattex seat covers. Caravan Top. Chrome rear bumper. Heavy-duty bumper. Heavy-duty grille and light guard. Bumper guards. Extra taillight. License plate frames. Locking gas cap. Spotlight. Fog lights. Service light. Hood light. Glove compartment light. Turn signals. Windshield washer. Wheel trim rings. Six blade fan. Right-hand extension rearview mirror. Heavy-duty springs. Early cut-in generator. Vacuum booster for windshield wiper. Glare proof interior rearview mirror. Visor vanity mirror. Fire extinguisher. No optional tire sizes were available in 1948.
HISTORICAL: Serial numbers indicate a maximum total of 52,682 M5s being built from 1941 to 1948, but a separate factory figure indicates a total of 52,541. This means a few serial numbers in the range were not assigned to any trucks. Most of the missing numbers were probably at the end of the 1942 production run. Prior to the introduction of the 1949 2R series trucks, Studebaker put a lot of effort into a proposed line of R series trucks. The R5 version was to include torsion bar suspension and fenders that blended into the doors like on the new postwar Dodge trucks. The R series trucks were never put into production.

1949 STUDEBAKER

1949 Studebaker Pickup (FKF)

MODELS 2R5 AND 2R10 — SIX-CYLINDER: For the 1949 model year, Studebaker introduced an all new line of trucks in the 2R series. An R series had been planned, but it never got beyond the prototype stage. The new 2R models were designed by Raymond Loewy's styling chief Robert Bourke. He worked at the Studebaker factory in South Bend, Ind. Bourke is the same stylist who later created the famous 1953 Studebaker Starliner and Starlight. The new truck styling, like Studebaker's postwar car styling, was ahead of the competition. It was low and featured no exterior runningboards and a smooth double wall pickup box. Unlike earlier Studebaker pickups, it borrowed no sheet metal from any Studebaker cars. The only contemporary car parts it used were Commander hubcaps and inverted Champion headlight rims. Shortly after production started, the Champion hood ornament was adopted. The M series steering wheel, which dated back to the 1941 Champion, was retained. The instruments were similar to the ones used in the M series and all 1941 cars, plus 1942 and 1946 Champions. Unlike the M series, the back sides of the instruments were accessible from under the hood, instead of from under the instrument panel. Interior door panels were made of steel instead of cardboard. A new addition to the lineup was a 3/4-ton 2R10 model. The 2R10 was available with an eight-foot, all-steel pickup box and a full-floating rear axle. The larger 1-ton model, called the 2R15, was retained. It was also available with an eight-foot pickup box. The 1/2-ton 2R5 continued with a 6-1/2-foot all-steel pickup box. The "STUDEBAKER" name on the pickup boxes was painted a Tusk ivory accent color. The same accent color was used to highlight the grille and painted bumper. Of course, all could be ordered without the pickup box or with a stake

bed. Chassis, Chassis & Cowl or Chassis, Cowl & Windshield configurations were also available for special body applications. The Coupe-Express name was discontinued in 1949. Mechanically, the 2R series was little changed from the M series. The standard three-speed transmission on light-duty models now had a steering column shift instead of a floor shift.

1949 Studebaker Stake Bed (A&A)

I.D. DATA: The serial number was located on a plate on the left side of the seat riser. The engine number was located on the top, left side, front corner of the cylinder block. The starting serial number for the 2R5 was R5-001 (HR5-001 in Canada). The starting serial number for the 2R10 was R10-001. The starting engine number for the 2R5 and 2R10 was 1R-001 (H1R-001 for the Canadian 2R5).

Model	Body Type	Price	Weight	Prod. Total
2R Series — 1/2-Ton				
2R5	Pickup	1262	2675	Note 1
2R10 Series — 3/4-Ton				
2R10	Pickup	1367	3040	Note 1

NOTE 1: Exact model year breakdowns of 1949-53 2R series truck production is impossible to give because the model year designation depended on a serial number/date of sale formula. Total domestic production for the five years was very close to the following: 2R5=110,500; 2R10=37,300.

1949 Studebaker 1/2-Ton Pickup (IMSC)

ENGINE: Six-cylinder. L-head. Cast iron block. Displacement: 169.6 cid. Bore & stroke: 3 in. x 4 in. Compression ratio: 6.5:1. Brake horsepower: 80 at 4000 rpm. Taxable horsepower: 21.6. Maximum torque: 134 lbs.-ft. Main bearings: Four. Valve lifters: Solid. Carburetor: Carter Model BBR1-633S one-barrel.
CHASSIS & BODY [2R5]: Wheelbase: 112 in. Overall length: 185.6 in. Height: 69.75 in. Width: 75.6 in. Interior pickup box dimensions: 77.8 in. long x 48.5 in. wide x 17.1 in. high. Front tread: 60.8 in. Rear tread: 59.6 in. Tires: 6.00 x 16 four-ply. GVW: [2R] 4,600 lbs.; [2R10] 6,100 lbs.

1949 Studebaker Pickup (A&A)

CHASSIS & BODY [2R10]: Wheelbase: 122 in. Overall length: 203.6 in. Height: 69.9 in. Width: 75.6 in. Interior pickup box dimensions: 95.8 in. long x 48.5 in. wide x 17.1 in. high. Front tread: 60.8 in. Rear tread: 60.4 in. Tires: 6.50 x 16 six-ply.

TECHNICAL: Sliding gear transmission. Speeds: 3F/1R. Synchromesh in second and third. Steering column shift control. Single-plate dry-disc clutch. I-beam front axle. 2R5 rear axle: Hypoid semi-floating with 4.82:1 overall ratio. 2R10 rear axle: Spiral bevel full-floating with 5.57:1 overall ratio. Hydraulic brakes. Steel disc wheels; slotted on 2R10. Lever arm shock absorbers. Variable-ratio steering.

1949 Studebaker 3/4-Ton Pickup (H. Bower)

OPTIONS: Four-speed transmission with floor shift control. Overdrive [first only on 2R5, but later on both 2R5 and 2R10]. Hill Holder. Radio. Climatizer heater/defroster. Interior rearview mirror. Glare-proof interior rearview mirror. Visor vanity mirror. Cigarette lighter. Dual horns. Caravan Top. Steel stake rack. Chrome front bumper. Chrome or painted rear bumper. Bumper guards. Heavy-duty grille and lamp guard. Extra taillight. License plate frames. Locking gas cap. Right-hand exterior rearview mirror. Spotlight. Fog lights. Turn signals. Exhaust deflector. Windshield washer. Mattex seat covers. Armrest covers. Hand throttle. Windshield wiper vacuum booster. Fram oil filter. Heavy-duty oil bath air cleaner. Six blade fan. Early cut-in generator. 19 plate battery. Heavy-duty radiator. Two-stage rear springs. Heavy-duty rear springs. Spare tire chain and lock. Optional items specific to the 2R5: Wheel trim rings. 6.00 x 16 six-ply tires. 6.50 x 16 six-ply tires. Optional items specific to the 2R10: 7.00 x 16 six-ply tires. 7.50 x 16 eight-ply tires. Final drive ratio of 4.86:1.

1949 Studebaker Cantrell Station Wagon (A&A)

HISTORICAL: All domestic 2R series trucks were assembled in a giant plant [called the "Chippewa Avenue Plant"] outside of South Bend, Inc. Built by the government at the outset of World War II, Studebaker used the plant during the war for assembling 63,789 Wright Cyclone R-1820 aircraft engines. Studebaker purchased the plant after the war and set it up for truck production during early 1948. Model 2R truck production started there in mid-1948. Starting in February, 1949 production of 2R5 models was also carried on in Studebaker's Canadian plant in Hamilton, Ontario. A total of 1,498 series 2R5 trucks were built in Canada during the 1949 calendar year. As the seller's market started to fade away, in 1949 and the early 1950s, some Studebaker dealers ended up with more trucks than they could quickly sell. Since the basic styling was unchanged from 1949 to 1953, Studebaker established a year model registration procedure that allowed late 1949 models to be sold as 1950s, late '50 models to be sold as '51s and so on. This is why no definite serial number breaks can be given for 2R series model year. To accurately date a 1949-53 Studebaker truck, the serial number and date it was sold to a retail customer needs to be known. Sales in 1949 were very good. Total 2R series (1/2-ton to 2-ton) sales for the 1949 calendar year were 63,473.

1950 STUDEBAKER

MODELS 2R5/2R6/2R10/2R11 — SIX-CYLINDER: The 2R series proved to be a big sales hit in 1949, so no big changes were made in 1950. Early in the model year, a sliding seat mechanism was adopted on all models. A kit allowed this seat to be installed on earlier models. Also, early in the year the horn button medallion was changed from script to block letters. Another early change was the switching of the standard shock absorbers from the lever arm type to the direct action tubular type. The compression ratio was raised from 6.5:1 to 7:1 on the 170 cid. engine. This raised the horsepower from 80 to 85. On April 11, 1950, it was announced that the larger 245 cid Commander six-cylinder engine could be ordered in the 1/2-, 3/4- and 1-ton models. It was already standard in the larger models. The 1/2-ton

with the "245" was called a 2R6 and the 3/4-ton with the "245" was called a 2R11. The 2R6 and 2R11 came standard with heavy-duty front springs. Very few 2R6s or 2R11s were sold during the 1950 model year. As in the past, some new exterior colors were announced each year during 2R series production.

1950 Studebaker Pickup (FKF)

I.D. DATA: The serial number was located on a plate on the left side of the seat riser. The engine number was located on the top, left side, front corner of the cylinder block. Exact serial number breaks between 1949 and 1950 2R5 and 2R10 models were not established. The starting serial number for the 2R6 was R6-101. The starting serial number for the 2R11 was R11-101. The starting engine number for the 2 R6 and 2R11 was 6R-101. The year of a 2R series truck depended on its serial number and when it was first sold to a retail customer.

Model	Body Type	Price	Weight	Prod. Total
1/2-Ton — 2R5				
2R5	Pickup	1262	2675	Note 1
1/2-Ton — 2R6				
2R6	Pickup	1312	2900	Note 1
3/4-Ton — 2R10				
2R10	Pickup	1367	3040	Note 1
2R11	Pickup	1417	3265	Note 1

NOTE 1: Exact model year breakdowns of 1949-53 2R series truck production is impossible to give because the model year designation depended on a serial number/date of sale formula. Total domestic production for the five years was very close to the following: 2R5=110,500; 2R6=12,150; 2R10=37,300; 2R11=10,350.

1950 Studebaker Pickup Truck (D.A. Derr)

ENGINE: [2R5 and 2R10] Six-cylinder. L-head. Cast iron block. Displacement: 169.6 cid. Bore & stroke: 3 in. x 4 in. Compression ratio: 7.0:1. Brake horsepower: 85 at 4000 rpm. Taxable horsepower: 21.6. Maximum torque: 138 lbs.-ft. Main bearings: Four. Valve lifters: Solid. Carburetor: Carter Model BBR1-633S one-barrel.
ENGINE [Big Six]: [2R6 and 2R11] Six-cylinder. L-head. Cast iron block. Displacement: 245.6 cid. Bore & stroke: 3-5/16 in. x 4-3/4 in. Compression ratio: 7.0:1. Brake horsepower: 102 at 3200 rpm. Taxable horsepower: 26.3. Maximum torque: 205 lbs.-ft. Main bearings: Four. Valve lifters. Solid. Carburetor: Carter Model BBR1-777SA one-barrel.
CHASSIS & BODY [2R5/2R6]: Wheelbase: 112 in. Overall length: 185.6 in. Height: 69.75 in. Width: 75.6 in. Interior pickup box dimensions: 77.8 in. long x 48.5 in. wide x 17.1 in. high. Front tread: 60.8 in. Rear tread: 59.6 in. Tires: 6.00 x 16 four-ply. GVW: [1/2-ton] 4,600 lbs.; [3/4-ton] 6,100 lbs.
CHASSIS & BODY [2R10/2R11]: Wheelbase: 122 in. Overall length: 203.6 in. Height: 69.9 in. Width: 75.6 in. Interior pickup box dimensions: 95.8 in. long x 48.5 in. wide x 17.1 in. high. Front tread: 60.8 in. Rear tread: 60.4 in. Tires: 6.50 x 16 six-ply.
TECHNICAL: Sliding gear transmission. Speeds: 3F/1R. Synchromesh in second and third. Steering column shift control. Single-plate dry-disc clutch. I-beam front axle. 2R5 and 2R6 rear axle: Hypoid semi-floating with 4.82:1 [2R5] and 4.09:1 [2R6] overall ratios. 2R10 and 2R11 rear axle: Spiral bevel full-floating with 5.57:1 (2R10) and 4.86:1 (2R11) overall ratios. Hydraulic brakes. Steel disc wheels (slotted on 2R10/2R11). Lever arm or direct acting tubular shock absorbers. Variable-ratio steering.
OPTIONS: Four-speed transmission with floor shift control (available on special order only). Overdrive. Hill Holder. Radio. Climatizer heater/defroster. Interior rearview mirror. Glare-proof interior rearview mirror. Visor vanity mirror. Cigarette lighter. Dual horns. Caravan Top. Steel stake rack. Chrome front bumper. Chrome or painted rear bumper. Bumper guards. Heavy-duty grille and lamp guard. Extra taillight. License plate frames. Locking gas cap. Right-hand exterior rearview mirror. Left and right exterior extension rearview mirrors. Spotlight. Fog lights. Turn signals. Underhood light. Service light. Tailgate step. Step for one or both sides of the pickup box. Rear fender gravel shields. Front splash guards.

Standard Catalog of Light-Duty Trucks

637

Exhaust deflector. Windshield washer. Mattex seat covers. Armrest covers. Hand throttle. Windshield wiper vacuum booster. Fram oil filter. Heavy-duty oil bath air cleaner. Six-blade fan. Early cut-in generator. 19-plate battery. Heavy-duty radiator. Two-stage rear springs. Heavy-duty rear springs. Spare tire chain and lock. [Options specific to 2R5/2R6] Wheel trim rings. 6.00 x 16 six-ply tires. 6.50 x 16 six-ply tires. 7.10 x 15 four-ply tires. Optional items specific to the 2R10 and 2R11: 7.00 x 16 six-ply tires. 7.50 x 16 eight-ply tires. Final drive ratio of 4.86:1 (2R10).

1950 Studebaker 3/4-Ton Utility Truck (A&A)

HISTORICAL: Total 2R series [1/2- to 2-ton] production for the 1950 calendar year was 50,323. This was down a little from 1949, which indicated that the strong postwar American demand for commercial vehicles was finally being fulfilled. Studebaker would never again reach the truck production levels it achieved in 1947-49. The Canadian plant produced 1,823 Model 2R5s during the 1950 calendar year.

1951 STUDEBAKER

1951 Studebaker Pickup (DSSC)

MODELS 2R5/2R6/2R10/2R11 — SIX-CYLINDER: Basic 1/2- and 3/4-ton models were continued unchanged from late 1950. A new 2R6 1/2-ton off-road Trailblazer was introduced in 1951. The Trailblazer used four- or six-ply low pressure 9.00 x 13 tires. The Trailblazer was recommended for use in sand or snow. Various companies, including Montpelier, built panel bodies for light-duty Studebaker trucks. Export woody station wagons were built by Cantrell Body Co. of Huntington, N.Y. They used 1/2- or 3/4-ton windshield cowl chassis. Because of inflation caused by the Korean War, prices were raised about seven percent. Studebaker introduced a V-8 engine for its Commander car models in 1951, but they did not use it in any domestic commercial vehicles.
I.D. DATA: The serial number was located on a plate on the left side of the seat riser. The engine number was located on the top, left side, front corner of the cylinder block. Exact serial number breaks between 1950 and 1951 models were not established. The year of a 2R series truck depended on its serial number and when it was first sold to a retail customer.

Model	Body Type	Price	Weight	Prod. Total
2R Series — 1/2-Ton				
2R5	Pickup	1352	2675	Note 1
2R6	Pickup	1402	2900	Note 1
2R Series — 3/4-Ton				
2R10	Pickup	1467	3040	Note 1
2R11	Pickup	1517	3265	Note 1

NOTE 1: Exact model year breakdowns of 1949-53 2R series truck production is impossible to give because the model year designation depended on a serial number/date of sale formula. Total domestic production for the five years was very close to the following: 2R5=110,500; 2R6=12,150; 2R10=37,300; 2R11=10,350.
ENGINE [2R5/2R10]: Six-cylinder. L-head. Cast iron block. Displacement: 169.6 cid. Bore & stroke: 3 in. x 4 in. Compression ratio: 7.0:1. Brake horsepower: 85 at 4000 rpm. Taxable horsepower: 21.6. Maximum torque: 138 lbs.-ft. Main bearings: Four. Valve lifters: Solid. Carburetor: Carter Model BBR1-633S one-barrel.

ENGINE [2R6/2R11]: Six-cylinder. L-head. Cast iron block. Displacement: 245.6 cid. Bore & stroke: 3-5/16 in. x 4-3/4 in. Compression ratio: 7.0:1. Brake horsepower: 102 at 3200 rpm. Taxable horsepower: 26.3. Maximum torque: 205 lbs.-ft. Main bearings: Four. Valve lifters: Solid. Carburetor: Carter Model BBR1-777SA one-barrel.
CHASSIS & BODY [2R5/2R6]: Wheelbase: 112 in. Overall length: 185.6 in. Height: 69.75 in. Width: 75.6 in. Interior pickup box dimensions: 77.8 in. long x 48.5 in. wide x 17.1 in. high. Front tread: 60.8 in. Rear tread: 59.6 in. Tires: 6.00 x 16 four-ply. GVW: 4,600 lbs.
CHASSIS & BODY [2R10/2R11]: Wheelbase: 122 in. Overall length: 203.6 in. Height: 69.9 in. Width: 75.6 in. Interior pickup box dimensions: 95.8 in. long x 48.5 in. wide x 17.1 in. high. Front tread: 60.8 in. Rear tread: 60.4 in. Tires: 6.50 x 16 six-ply. GVW: 6,100.

1951 Studebaker Trailblazer Pickup (FKF)

TECHNICAL: Sliding gear transmission. Speeds: 3F/1R. Synchromesh in second and third. Steering column shift control. Single-plate dry-disc clutch. I-beam front axle. Rear axle: [2R5] 4.89:1 (late) overall ratio; [2R6] Hypoid semi-floating with 4.82:1 (early) or 4.09:1 (late) overall ratio; [2R10] 5.57:1 overall ratio. [2R11] Spiral bevel type, full-floating with 4.86:1 overall ratio. Hydraulic brakes. Steel disc wheels (slotted on 2R10/2R11). Direct acting tubular shock absorbers. Variable-ratio steering.

OPTIONS: Four-speed transmission with floor shift control available on special order only. Overdrive. Hill Holder. Radio. Climatizer heater/defroster. Interior rearview mirror. Glare-proof interior rearview mirror. Visor vanity mirror. Cigarette lighter. Dual horns. Caravan Top. Steel stake rack. Chrome front bumper. Chrome or painted rear bumper. Bumper guards. Heavy-duty grille and lamp guard. Extra taillight. License plate frames. Locking gas cap. Right-hand exterior rearview mirror. Left and right exterior extension rearview mirrors. Spotlight. Fog lights. Turn signals. Underhood light. Service light. Tailgate step. Step for one or both sides of the pickup box. Rear fender gravel shields. Front splash guards. Exhaust deflector. Windshield washer. Mattex seat covers. Armrest covers. Hand throttle. Windshield wiper vacuum booster. Fram oil filter. Heavy-duty oil bath air cleaner. Six blade fan. Early cut-in generator. 19-plate battery. Heavy-duty radiator. Two-stage rear springs. Heavy-duty rear springs. Spare tire chain and lock. [2R5/2R6 only] Wheel trim rings. 6.00 x 16 six-ply tires. 6.50 x 16 six-ply tires. 7.10 x 15 four-ply tires. Final drive ratio: [2R5] 4.55:1 or 4.09:1 ; [2R6] 4.55:1 or 4.89:1. Trailblazer package for 2R6 only. [2R10/2R11 only] 7.00 x 16 six-ply tires. 7.50 x 16 eight-ply tires. [2R10] Final drive ratio of 4.86:1.

HISTORICAL: Total 2R series [1/2- to 2-ton] production for the 1951 calendar year was 51,814. The Canadian plant produced 1,546 Model 2R5s during the 1951 calendar year.

1952 STUDEBAKER

1952 Studebaker 3/4-Ton Pickup (FKF)

MODELS 2R5/2R6/2R10/2R11 — SIX-CYLINDER: The 2R series was continued another year with only minor changes. In January 1952, the interior accent color was changed from Tuscan tan to Pilot gray. At the same time, the seat frame was changed from Tuscan tan to maroon and the interior vinyl covered weather stripping was changed from brown to maroon.

I.D. DATA: The serial number was located on a plate on the left side of the seat riser. The engine number was located on the top, left side, front corner of the cylinder block. Exact serial number breaks between 1951 and 1952 models were not established. The year of a 2R series truck depended on its serial number and when it was first sold to a retail customer.

Model	Body Type	Price	Weight	Prod. Total
2R Series — 1/2-Ton				
2R5	Pickup	1404	2675	Note 1
2R6	Pickup	1454	2900	Note 1
2R Series — 3/4-Ton				
2R10	Pickup	1527	3040	Note 1
2R11	Pickup	1574	3265	Note 1

NOTE 1: Exact model year breakdowns of 1949-53 2R series truck production is impossible to give because the model year designation depended on a serial number/date of sale formula. Total domestic production for the five years was very close to the following: 2R5=110,500; 2R6=12,150; 2R10=37,300; 2R11=10,350.

ENGINE [2R5/2R10]: Six-cylinder. L-head. Cast iron block. Displacement: 169.6 cid. Bore & stroke: 3 in. x 4 in. Compression ratio: 7.0:1. Brake horsepower: 85 at 4000 rpm. Taxable horsepower: 21.6. Maximum torque: 138 lbs.-ft. Main bearings: Four. Valve lifters: Solid. Carburetor: Carter Model BBR1-633S one-barrel.

ENGINE [2R6/2R11]: Six-cylinder. L-head. Cast iron block. Displacement: 245.6 cid. Bore & stroke: 3-5/16 in. x 4-3/4 in. Compression ratio: 7.0:1. Brake horsepower: 102 at 3200 rpm. Taxable horsepower: 26.3. Maximum torque: 205 lbs.-ft. Main bearings: Four. Valve lifters: Solid. Carburetor: Carter Model BBR1-777SA one-barrel.

CHASSIS & BODY [2R5/2R6]: Wheelbase: 112 in. Overall length: 185.6 in. Height: 69.75 in. Width: 75.6 in. Interior pickup box dimensions: 77.8 in. long x 48.5 in. wide x 17.1 in. high. Front tread: 60.8 in. Rear tread: 59.6 in. Tires: 6.00 x 16 four-ply. GVW: 4,600 lbs.

CHASSIS & BODY [2R10/2R11]: Wheelbase: 122 in. Overall length: 203.6 in. Height: 69.9 in. Width: 75.6 in. Interior pickup box dimensions: 95.8 in. long x 48.5 in. wide x 17.1 in. high. Front tread: 60.8 in. Rear tread: 60.4 in. Tires: 6.50 x 16 six-ply. GVW: 6,100 lbs.

TECHNICAL: Sliding gear transmission. Speeds: 3F/1R. Synchromesh in second and third. Steering column shift control. Single-plate dry-disc clutch. I-beam front axle. Rear axle: [2R5/2R6] Hypoid semi-floating with 4.89:1 (2R5) and 4.09:1 (2R6) overall ratios; [2R10/2R11] Spiral bevel full-floating with 5.57:1 (2R10) and 4.86:1 (2R11) overall ratios. Hydraulic brakes. Steel disc wheels (slotted on 2R10/2R11.) Direct acting tubular shock absorbers. Variable-ratio steering.

OPTIONS: Four-speed transmission with floor shift control available on special order only. Overdrive. Hill Holder. Radio. Climatizer heater/defroster. Interior rearview mirror. Glare-proof interior rearview mirror. Visor vanity mirror. Cigarette lighter. Dual horns. Caravan Top. Steel stake rack. Chrome front bumper. Chrome or painted rear bumper. Bumper guards. Heavy-duty grille and lamp guard. Extra taillight. License plate frames. Locking gas cap. Right-hand exterior rearview mirror. Left and right exterior extension rearview mirrors. Spotlight. Fog lights. Turn signals. Underhood light. Service light. Tailgate step. Step for one or both sides of the pickup box. Rear fender gravel shields. Front splash guards. Exhaust deflector. Windshield washer. Mattex seat covers. Armrest covers. Hand throttle. Windshield wiper vacuum booster. Fram oil filter. Heavy-duty oil bath air cleaner. Six blade fan. Early cut-in generator. 19-plate battery. Heavy-duty radiator. Two-stage rear springs. Heavy-duty rear springs. Spare tire chain and lock. [2R5/2R6 only] Wheel trim rings. 6.00 x 16 six-ply tires. 6.50 x 16 six-ply tires. 7.10 x 15 four-ply tires. Final drive ratios of 4.55:1 or 4.09:1 (2R5); 4.55:1 or 4.89:1 (2R6). Trailblazer package (2R6 only). [Options 2R10/2R11 only] 7.00 x 16 six-ply tires. 7.50 x 16 eight-ply tires. Final drive ratio of 4.86:1 (2R10).

HISTORICAL: Total 2R series (1/2- to 2-ton) production for the 1952 calendar year was 58,873. The Canadian plant produced 963 Model 2R5s during the 1952 calendar year.

1953 Studebaker Pickup With Caravan Top (FKF)

MODELS 2R5/2R6/2R10/2R11 — SIX-CYLINDER: The final year of 2R production again saw few changes from the previous year. Some new exterior colors were introduced and tinted glass was introduced as a new extra cost option.

I.D. DATA: The serial number was located on a plate on the left side of the seat riser. The engine number was located on the top, left side, front corner of the cylinder block. Exact serial number breaks between 1952 and 1953 models were not established. The year of a 2R series truck depended on its serial number and when it was first sold to a retail customer.

Model	Body Type	Price	Weight	Prod. Total
2R Series 1/2-Ton				
2R5	Pickup	1404	2675	Note 1
2R6	Pickup	1454	2900	Note 1
2R Series 3/4-Ton				
2R10	Pickup	1527	3040	Note 1
2R11	Pickup	1574	3265	Note 1

NOTE 1: Exact model year breakdowns of 1949-53 2R series truck production is impossible to give because the model year designation depended on a serial number/date of sale formula. Total domestic production for the five years was very close to the following: 2R5=110,500; 2R6=12,150; 2R10=37,300; 2R11=10,350.

ENGINE [2R5/2R10]: Six-cylinder. L-head. Cast iron block. Displacement: 169.6 cid. Bore & stroke: 3 in. x 4 in. Compression ratio: 7.0:1. Brake horsepower: 85 at 4000 rpm. Taxable horsepower: 21.6. Maximum torque: 138 lbs.-ft. Main bearings: Four. Valve lifters: Solid. Carburetor: Carter Model BBR1-633S one-barrel.

ENGINE [2R6/2R11]: Six-cylinder. L-head. Cast iron block. Displacement: 245.6 cid. Bore & stroke: 3-5/16 in. x 4-3/4 in. Compression ratio: 7.0:1. Brake horsepower: 102 at 3200 rpm. Taxable horsepower: 26.3. Maximum torque: 205 lbs.-ft. Main bearings: Four. Valve lifters: Solid. Carburetor: Carter Model BBR1-777SA one-barrel.

CHASSIS & BODY [2R5/2R6]: Wheelbase: 112 in. Overall length: 185.6 in. Height: 69.75 in. Width: 75.6 in. Interior pickup box dimensions: 77.8 in. long x 48.5 in. wide x 17.1 in. high. Front tread: 60.8 in. Rear tread: 59.6 in. Tires: 6.00 x 16 four-ply. GVW: 4,600 lbs.

CHASSIS & BODY [2R10/2R11]: Wheelbase: 122 in. Overall length: 203.6 in. Height: 69.9 in. Width: 75.6 in. Interior pickup box dimensions: 95.8 in. long x 48.5 in. wide x 17.1 in. high. Front tread: 60.8 in. Rear tread: 60.4 in. Tires: 6.50 x 16 six-ply. GVW: 6,100 lbs.

TECHNICAL: Sliding gear transmission. Speeds: 3F/1R. Synchromesh in second and third. Steering column shift control. Single-plate dry-disc clutch. I-beam front axle. 2R5 and 2R6 rear axle: Hypoid semi-floating with 4.89:1 (2R5) and 4.09:1 (2R6) overall ratios. 2R10 and 2R11 rear axle: Spiral bevel full-floating with 5.57:1 (2R10) and 4.86:1 (2R11) overall ratios. Hydraulic brakes. Steel disc wheels (slotted on 2R10 and 2R11). Direct acting tubular shock absorbers. Variable-ratio steering.

OPTIONS: Four-speed transmission with floor shift control available on special order only. Overdrive. Hill Holder. Radio. Climatizer heater/defroster. Interior rearview mirror. Glare-proof interior rearview mirror. Visor vanity mirror. Cigarette lighter. Dual horns. Caravan Top. Steel stake rack. Chrome front bumper. Chrome or painted rear bumper. Bumper guards. Heavy-duty grille and lamp guard. Extra taillight. License plate frames. Locking gas cap. Right-hand exterior rearview mirror. Left and right exterior extension rearview mirrors. Tinted glass. Spotlight. Fog lights. Turn signals. Underhood light. Service light. Tailgate step. Step for one or both sides of the pickup box. Rear fender gravel shields. Front splash guards. Exhaust deflector. Windshield washer. Mattex seat covers. Armrest covers. Hand throttle. Windshield wiper vacuum booster. Fram oil filter. Heavy-duty oil bath air cleaner. Six blade fan. Early cut-in generator. 19-plate battery. Two-stage rear springs. Heavy-duty rear springs. Spare tire chain and lock. [2R5/2R6 options only] Wheel trim rings. 6.00 x 16 six-ply tires. 6.50 x 16 six-ply tires. 7.10 x 15 four-ply tires. Final drive ratios of 4.55:1 or 4.09:1 (2R5); 4.55:1 or 4.89:1 (2R6). Trailblazer package for 2R6 only. [2R10/2R11 options only] 7.00 x 16 six-ply tires. 7.50 x 16 eight-ply tires. Final drive ratio of 4.86:1 (2R10).

HISTORICAL: Total 2R series (1/2- to 2-ton) production for the 1953 calendar year was 32,012. This was way down from 1952. Many factors caused the decline, including less demand, old-fashioned styling, reduced car sales (thus less floor room traffic) and non-competitive pricing because of higher per unit expenses. These problems plagued Studebaker from 1953 on. The Canadian plant produced 772 Model 2R5s in 1953.

1954 STUDEBAKER

1954 Studebaker Pickup (FKF)

MODELS 3R5/3R6/3R10/3R11 — SIX-CYLINDER: After five years (1949-1953) of the same styling and trim, Studebaker finally gave their trucks a minor facelift in 1954. The restyled models were called the 3R series and were introduced in March 1954. Except for a new grille with fewer horizontal openings, all the sheet metal was the same as 1949-53. The major changes were in trim and a switch to a curved, one-piece windshield. The headlight rims, side nameplates and hubcaps (3R5 and 3R6) were restyled for 1954. The hood ornament was made an extra-cost option and the outside mirror was switched from round to square. The bumper was made solid body color and the grille was painted completely in the accent color. On the inside, the glove box door was restyled and the instruments were rearranged and changed from rectangular to round dials. A V-8 engine was introduced in larger models, but the light-duty trucks continued with the same engines that were offered in 1953. The compression ratio of the 170 cid engine was raised from 7:1 to 7.5:1, but no change in horsepower was reported. An electric windshield wiper kit was added to the options list. An adaptor plate allowed this wiper kit to be fitted to 1949-53 models. Vacuum type wipers continued as standard equipment.

I.D. DATA: The serial number was located on a plate on the left side of the seat riser. The engine number was located on the top, left side, front corner of the cylinder block. The starting serial number for the 3R5 and R5 was 111,401 (HR5-6,601 in Canada). The starting serial number for the 3R6 was R6-12,651. The starting serial number for the 3R10 was R10-37,501. The starting serial number for the 3R11 was R11-10,651. The starting engine number for the 3R5 and 3R10 was 1R-149,001. The starting engine number for the 3R6 and 3R11 was 6R-24,701.

639

Model	Body Type	Price	Weight	Prod. Total
3R Series — 1/2-Ton				
3R5	Pickup	1469	2665	Note 1
3R6	Pickup	1522	2890	Note 1
3R Series — 3/4-Ton				
3R10	Pickup	1622	3040	Note 1
3R11	Pickup	1675	3265	Note 1

NOTE 1: Production breakdowns are not available. Total production of all 3R models (1/2- to 2-ton) was 12,003.

1954 Studebaker Pickup (DFW/SI)

ENGINE [3R5/ 3R10]: Six-cylinder. L-head. Cast iron block. Displacement: 169.6 cid. Bore & stroke: 3 in. x 4 in. Compression ratio: 7.5:1. Brake horsepower: 85 at 4000 rpm. Taxable horsepower: 21.6. Maximum torque: 138 lbs.-ft. Main bearings: Four. Valve lifters: Solid. Carburetor: Carter Model BBR1-633S one-barrel.
ENGINE [3R6/3R11]: Six-cylinder. L-head. Cast iron block. Displacement: 245.6 cid. Bore & stroke: 3-5/16 in. x 4-3/4 in. Compression ratio: 7.0:1. Brake horsepower: 102 at 3200 rpm. Taxable horsepower: 26.3. Maximum torque: 205 lbs.-ft. Main bearings: Four. Valve lifters. Solid. Carburetor: Carter Model BBR1-777SA one-barrel.
CHASSIS & BODY [3R5/3R6]: Wheelbase: 112 in. Overall length: 185.6 in. Height: 69.75 in. Width: 75.6 in. Interior pickup box dimensions: 77.8 in. long x 48.5 in. wide x 17.1 in. high. Front tread: 60.8 in. Rear tread: 59.6 in. Tires: 6.00 x 16 four-ply. GVW: [3R5] 4,600 lbs.; [3R6] 4,800 lbs.
CHASSIS & BODY [3R10/3R11]: Wheelbase: 122 in. Overall length: 203.6 in. Height: 69.9 in. Width: 75.6 in. Interior pickup box dimensions: 95.8 in. long x 48.5 in. wide x 17.1 in. high. Front tread: 60.8 in. Rear tread: 60.4 in. Tires: 6.50 x 16 six-ply. GVW: [3R10] 6,100 lbs.; [3R11] 6,300 lbs.
TECHNICAL: Sliding gear transmission. Speeds: 3F/1R. Synchromesh in second and third. Steering column shift control. Single-plate dry-disc clutch. I-beam front axle. 3R5 and 3R6 rear axle: Hypoid semi-floating with 4.89:1 (3R5) and 4.09:1 (3R6) overall ratios. 3R10 and 3R11 rear axle: Spiral bevel full-floating with 5.57:1 (3R10) and 4.86:1 (3R11) overall ratios. Hydraulic brakes. Steel disc wheels; slotted on 3R10 and 3R11. Direct acting tubular shock absorbers. Variable-ratio steering.
OPTIONS: Four-speed synchromesh transmission with floor shift control. Overdrive. Hill Holder. Radio. Climatizer heater/defroster. Interior rearview mirror. Glare-proof interior rear-view mirror. Visor vanity mirror. Cigarette lighter. Dual horns. Caravan Top. Chrome front bumper. Chrome or painted rear bumper. Extra taillight. Hood ornament. License plate frames. Locking gas cap. Right-hand exterior rearview mirror. Left and right exterior exten-sion rearview mirrors. Tinted glass. Spotlight. Turn signals. Underhood light. Service light. Tailgate step. Step for one or both sides of the pickup box. Rear fender gravel shields. Front splash guards. Exhaust deflector. Windshield washer. Mattex seat covers. Armrest covers. Hand throttle. Windshield wiper vacuum booster. Electric windshield wiper kit. Fram oil filter. Heavy-duty oil bath air cleaner. Five- or six-blade fan. Early cut-in generator. 19-plate battery. Heavy-duty radiator. Two-stage rear springs. Heavy-duty rear springs. 7.5:1 compression ratio ("245" engine). Spare tire chain and lock. [Optional items specific to the 3R5/3R6] 6.00 x 16 six-ply tires. 6.50 x 16 six-ply tires. 7.10 x 15 four-ply tires. Final drive ratios of 4.55:1 or 4.09:1 (3R5); 4.55:1 or 4.89:1 (3R6). [Optional items specific to the 3R10/3R11] 7.00 x 16 six-ply tires. 7.50 x 16 eight-ply tires. Final drive ratios of 4.86:1 (3R10) and 4.11:1 (3R11).
HISTORICAL: Studebaker truck sales, like their car sales, continued to decline in 1954. Total 1954 truck (1/2-ton to 2-ton) calendar year production was only 15,608, about one-half of 1953 and one-quarter of 1949. Studebaker joined forces with Packard in October, 1954 to form the Studebaker-Packard Corp., but neither company gained from the consoli-dation. The Canadian plant produced 263 model 3R5s in 1954.

1955 STUDEBAKER

MODELS E5/E7/E10/E12 — ALL ENGINES: Styling changes were limited in 1955, but mechanical changes were the most numerous since 1941. Because of all the mechanical changes, the old R designation was dropped and a new E series introduced. Styling changes included a larger rear window, a larger front name plate and V-8 hoodside emblems on models powered by the V-8 engine. A new hood ornament had an "8" on V-8 engine models and an "S" on six-cylinder engine models. Exterior door visors and a padded dash pad were fitted as standard equipment on all but a few early models. Vinyl and rayon upholstery materials replaced the earlier all-vinyl upholstery. The sliding tracks for the seat cushion were discontinued and the 1949 style, with three positioning studs, returned. The sliding seat was available as an extra-cost option. Grille and wheel accent colors were color-keyed to the body colors. In midyear, a red and white two-tone paint combination was offered on 1/2-ton models. Exterior door handles were made larger. Mechanical changes included making the V-8 engine available in light-duty models, increasing the stroke of the small six and dropping the "245" six from the domestic lineup. The lower end of the small six

was also beefed up. The new 1/2-ton V-8 was called the E7 and the new 3/4-ton V-8 was named the E12. Studebaker's Automatic Drive transmission was made an extra-cost option on the E7 and E12. Automatic Drive models were started with a button on the instrument panel, but all others continued with the starter button under the clutch pedal, a method Studebaker had used for many years. Tubeless tires on 1/2-ton models were introduced during the year. Dry element air cleaners were made standard on all models.

1955 Studebaker Pickup (DS)

I.D. DATA: The serial number was located on a plate on the left side of the seat riser. The engine number was located on the top, left side, front corner of the cylinder block. The V-8 engine number was located on the top, front end of the cylinder block, next to the oil filler tube. The starting serial number for the E5 was E5-114,001 (HE5-101 in Canada). The starting serial number for the E7 was E7-101. The starting serial number for the E10 was E10-38,001. The starting serial number for the E12 was E12-101. The starting engine num-ber for the E5 and E10 was 1E-101. The starting engine number for the E7 and E12 was 2E-101.

Model	Body Type	Price	Weight	Prod. Total
E Series — 1/2-Ton				
E5	Pickup	1510	2695	Note 1
E7	Pickup	1595	2970	Note 1
E Series — 3/4-Ton				
E10	Pickup	1690	3070	Note 1
E12	Pickup	1775	3345	Note 1

NOTE 1: Production breakdowns are not available. Total production of all E models (1/2- to 2-ton) was 27,119. Serial number spans for a particular model give a rough estimate of how many of that model were built in a year.

1955 Studebaker 3/4-Ton Pickup (A&A)

ENGINE [E5/E10]: Six-cylinder. L-head. Cast iron block. Displacement: 185.6 cid. Bore & stroke: 3 in. x 4-3/8 in. Compression ratio: 7.5:1. Brake horsepower: 92 at 3800 rpm. Tax-able horsepower: 21.6. Maximum torque: 152 lbs.-ft. Main bearings: Four. Valve lifters: Solid. Carburetor: Carter Model BBR1-2125S one-barrel.
ENGINE [E7/E12]: Eight-cylinder. OHV V-8. Cast iron block. Displacement: 224.3 cid. Bore & stroke: 3-9/16 in. x 2-13/16 in. Compression ratio: 7.5:1. Brake horsepower: 140 at 4500 rpm. Taxable horsepower: 40.6. Maximum torque: 202 lbs.-ft. Main bearings: Five. Valve lifters: Solid. Carburetor: Stromberg Model WW two-barrel.
CHASSIS & BODY [E5/E7]: Wheelbase: 112 in. Overall length: 185.6 in. Height: 69.75 in. Width: 75.6 in. Interior pickup box dimensions: 77.8 in. long x 48.5 in. wide x 17.1 in. high. Front tread: 60.8 in. Rear tread: 59.6 in. Tires: 6.00 x 16 four-ply. GVW: [3R5] 4,600 lbs.; [3R6] 4,800 lbs.
CHASSIS & BODY [E10/E12]: Wheelbase: 122 in. Overall length: 203.6 in. Height: 69.9 in. Width: 75.6 in. Interior pickup box dimensions: 95.8 in. long x 48.5 in. wide x 17.1 in. high. Front tread: 60.8 in. Rear tread: 60.4 in. Tires: 6.50 x 16 six-ply. GVW: [3R10] 6,100 lbs.; [3R11] 6,300 lbs.
TECHNICAL: Sliding gear transmission. Speeds: 3F/1R. Synchromesh in second and third. Steering column shift control. Single-plate dry-disc clutch. I-beam front axle. E5 and E7 rear axle: Hypoid semi-floating with 4.09, 4.27 or 4.55:1 (E5) and 3.73, 4.09, 4.27 or 4.55:1 (E7) overall ratios. E10 or E12 rear axle: Spiral bevel full-floating with 4.86 or 5.57:1 (E10) and 4.11 or 4.86:1 (E12) overall ratios. Hydraulic brakes. Steel disc wheels; slotted on E10 and E12. Direct acting tubular shock absorbers. Variable-ratio steering.

1955 Studebaker 3/4-Ton Pickup (FKF)

OPTIONS: Automatic Drive (E7 and E12 only). Four-speed synchromesh transmission with floor shift control. Overdrive. Hill Holder. Radio. Climatizer heater/defroster. Sliding seat mechanism. Interior rearview mirror. Map light. Accelerator pedal cover. Kleenex dispenser. Cigarette lighter. 3-D Booster horn. Red and white two-tone paint job (midyear, 1/2-ton only). Caravan Top. Chrome front bumper. Chrome or painted rear bumper. Extra taillight. License plate frames. Locking gas cap. Right-hand exterior rearview mirror. Left and right exterior extension rearview mirrors. Tinted glass. Spotlight. Directional signals. Underhood light. Tailgate step. Step for one or both sides of the pickup box. Rear fender gravel shields. Front splash guards. Exhaust deflector. Windshield washer. Mattex seat covers. Hand throttle. Electric windshield wiper kit. Fram oil filter. Oil bath air cleaner. Five- or six-blade fan. Headbolt engine heater. Early cut-in generator. 19 -plate battery. Heavy-duty radiator. Two-stage rear springs. Heavy-duty springs. [Optional tires specific to the E5/E7] 6.00 x 16 six-ply, 6.50 x 16 six ply and 7.10 x 15 four-ply. [Optional tires specific to the E10/E12] 7.00 x 16 six-ply and 7.50 x 16 eight-ply.

1955-1/2 Studebaker Pickups (FKF)

HISTORICAL: Total 1955 truck (1/2- to 2-ton) calendar year sales climbed to 19,793. The slight improvement can be credited to a good year for the whole industry and the V-8 option in light-duty models. The Canadian plant discontinued all truck production after producing 256 of the 1955 Model E5 trucks.

1956 STUDEBAKER

1956 Studebaker Transtar Pickup (FKF)

MODELS 2E5/2E7/2E12 — ALL ENGINES: Ever since it was formed in October 1954, the Studebaker-Packard Corp. had been losing money. Because of this, the Studebaker Truck

Div. was forced to continue with the same basic design. In an effort to attract some new interest, the 1956 2E series trucks were given a slight face lift and all were labeled "Transtars." Transtar nameplates were put on the doors. This was the first time Studebaker attached a model nameplate to the outside of one of its light-duty trucks. Working within their limited budget, they actively promoted the Transtar name. It proved to be a popular name. In fact, International picked it up after Studebaker quit the truck business. Design changes included a new, more rounded hood with a large "STUDEBAKER" nameplate set in an opening in the front. Large, separate parking lights were added in the front and the pickup box was made three-inches wider. The wider box made it necessary to increase the rear tread by three-inches. A longer 122 in. wheelbase option was added to the 1/2-tons so they could be fitted with an eight-foot pickup box. Full wheelcovers were added to the 1/2-ton option list and whitewall tires were promoted on 2E5s and 2E7s. Two-tones in several different color combinations were offered. The break line between the two colors was relocated from where it was on the 1955-1/2 trucks with two-tone finish. An optional C4 Deluxe Cab was introduced, but its introduction was actually a sales ploy. It had about the same features as the old 2R series cab. The 1956 standard cab was stripped of armrests, the right sun visor and the ashtray. In 1955, the map light and sliding seat tracks had been dropped from the standard equipment list. The 1956 Deluxe Cab returned all these items, except the right armrest. It also featured a perforated headliner with fiberglass insulation. Both standard and Deluxe cabs continued with the dash pad and door visors. Mechanical options introduced included a four-barrel carburetor for the V-8 engine (possibly available on late 1955 models) and a Twin-Traction, limited-slip differential for 1/2-ton models. Studebaker was the first make to offer a limited-slip differential on a light-duty truck. The 3/4-ton model was switched to a hypoid-type final drive. A one-pint oil bath air cleaner was returned as standard equipment. Early in the model year, the Automatic Drive transmission option was replaced by Flightomatic. Two stage rear springs were made standard equipment. The electrical system was switched from 6-volt to 12-volt and key starting was introduced. The 3/4-ton six-cylinder E10 model was dropped from domestic sales. The old 245 cid six-cylinder engine was available on special order. The 224 cid V-8 was continued on the 2E7 and 2E12, but at least one person special-ordered a 2E7 with a 259 cid V-8 and a five-speed transmission. Both of these items were available in larger models. The larger 1-ton Pickup was continued on a 131 in. wheelbase chassis with a nine-foot pickup box.

1956 Studebaker Pickup (DSSC)

I.D. DATA: The serial number was located on a plate on the left side of the seat riser. The engine number was located on the top, left side, front corner of the cylinder block. The starting serial number for the 2E5 was E5-119,501. The starting serial number for the 2E7 was E7-4,601. The starting serial number for the 2E12 was E12-2,101. The starting engine number for the 2E5 was 1E-6,501. The starting engine number for the 2E7 and 2E12 was 2E-7,001.

Model	Body Type	Price	Weight	Prod. Total
2E Series — 1/2-Ton				
2E5-112	Pickup	1641	2740	Note 1
2E5-122	Pickup	1677	2880	Note 1
2E7-112	Pickup	1738	3025	Note 1
2E7-122	Pickup	1774	3165	Note 1
2E Series — 3/4-Ton				
2E12	Pickup	1915	3410	Note 1

NOTE 1: Production breakdowns are not available. Total production of all 2E models (1/2- to 2-ton) was 20,218. Serial number spans for a particular model give a rough estimate of how many of that model were built in a year.

ENGINE [2E5]: Six-cylinder. L-head. Cast iron block. Displacement: 185.6 cid. Bore & stroke: 3 in. x 4-3/8 in. Compression ratio: 7.5:1. Brake horsepower: 92 at 3800 rpm. Taxable horsepower: 21.6. Maximum torque: 152 lbs.-ft. Main bearings: Four. Valve lifters: Solid. Carburetor: Carter Model BBR1-2125S one-barrel.

ENGINE [2E7/2E12]: Eight-cylinder. OHV V-8. Cast iron block. Displacement: 224.3 cid. Bore & stroke: 3-9/16 in. x 2-13/16 in. Compression ratio: 7.5:1. Brake horsepower: 140 at 4500 rpm. (160 hp with optional four-barrel carburetor). Taxable horsepower: 40.6. Maximum torque: 202 lbs.-ft. Main bearings: Five. Valve lifters: Solid. Carburetor: Stromberg Model WW two-barrel (optional: Carter Model WCFB four-barrel).

CHASSIS & BODY [2E5-112/2E7-112]: Wheelbase: 112 in. Overall length: 185.6 in. Height: 69.75 in. Width: 77.5 in. Interior pickup box dimensions: 77.8 in. long x 51.5 in. wide x 17.1 in. high. Front tread: 60.8 in. Rear tread: 62.6 in. Tires: 6.00 x 16 four-ply. GVW: [2E5-112] 4,800 lbs.; [2E5-122] 4,800 lbs.; [2E7-112] 5,000 lbs. [2E7-122] 5,000 lbs.

1956 Studebaker 3/4-Ton Transtar Pickup (FKF)

CHASSIS & BODY [2E5-122/2E7-122/2E12]: Wheelbase: 122 in. Overall length: 203.6 in. Height: 69.75 in. (69.6 in. for 2E12). Width: 77.5 in. Interior pickup box dimensions: 95.8 in. long x 51.5 in. wide x 17.1 in. high. Front tread: 60.8 in. Rear tread: 62.6 in. (63 in. for 2E12). Tires: 6.00 x 16 four-ply (7.00 x 16 six-ply on 2E12). GVW: [2E12] 7,000 lbs.

TECHNICAL: Sliding gear transmission. Speeds: 3F/1R. Synchromesh in second and third. Steering column shift control. Single-plate dry-disc clutch. I-beam front axle. 2E5 and 2E7 rear axle: Hypoid semi-floating with 4.27 or 4.55:1 (2E5) and 3.73, 4.09 or 4.27:1 (2E7) overall ratios. 2E12 rear axle: Hypoid full-floating with 4.11 or 4.88:1 overall ratios. Hydraulic brakes. Steel disc wheels; slotted on 2E12. Direct acting tubular shock absorbers. Variable-ratio steering.

OPTIONS: Automatic transmission (2E7 and 2E12 only). Four-speed synchromesh transmission with floor shift control. Overdrive. Hill Holder. Twin-Traction (1/2-ton models only). Deluxe Cab. Radio. Climatizer heater/defroster. Sliding seat mechanism. Interior rearview mirror. Ashtray. Right-hand sun visor. Seat pad. Safety seat belts. Armrests. Compass. Traffic light viewer. Map light. Accelerator pedal cover. Kleenex dispenser. Cigarette lighter. Dual horns. Two-tone paint. Caravan Top. Painted rear bumper. Extra taillight. Full wheel covers (1/2-ton only). License plate frames. Locking gas cap. Right-hand exterior rearview mirror. Left and right exterior extension rearview mirrors. Tinted glass. Spotlight. Directional signals. Underhood light. Tailgate step. Step for one or both sides of the pickup box. Rear fender gravel shields. Front splash guards. Exhaust deflector. Windshield washer. Mattex seat covers. Hand throttle. Electric windshield wipers (standard on V-8 with automatic transmission). Fram oil filter. One-quart oil bath air cleaner. Governor (V-8 two-barrel models only). V-8 power package (four-barrel carburetor and large air cleaner). Five- or six-blade fan. Headbolt engine heater. Heavy-duty battery. Heavy-duty radiator. Heavy-duty springs. Heavy-duty shock absorbers. Brake fluid reservoir. [Optional tires specific to the 2E5 and 2E7] 6.00 x 16 six-ply, 6.50 x 16 six-ply and 7.10 x 15 four-ply (black or whitewall). [Optional tires specific to the 2E12] 7.50 x 16 eight-ply and 7.50 x 17 eight-ply.

HISTORICAL: Production was only a little off of 1955, but way below the record set in 1947-52. Fancy two-tones and numerous options did not help improve sales. The product was good, but prices were not competitive and people were afraid Studebaker-Packard was going out of business. During the year, the Chippewa Ave. plant was leased to Curtiss-Wright and Studebaker truck production was moved back to the main plant.

1957 STUDEBAKER

MODELS 3E5/3E6/3E7/3E11/3E12 — ALL ENGINES: During the mid-'50s, Studebaker felt it needed annual styling changes for its trucks, so the 1957 Series 3E Transtar models included several changes from 1956, although the basic 1949 body was still being used. A new fiberglass grille with three "buck teeth" and a much larger front bumper gave the light-duty models a new appearance. The parking lights were moved to the top of the front fenders and two-tone models were again given a different paint color separation line. Check mark trim strips were used on the cab to separate the two colors. A safety swing-away taillight was made standard equipment. The right-hand taillight was still an extra-cost option. On the inside, new instruments, with warning (idiot) lights for oil pressure and charge/discharge, were adopted. The optional Climatizer controls were moved to the center of the dash, thus forcing the optional radio to be hung under the instrument panel. A chrome Transtar dash nameplate, chrome door visors, chrome exterior mirrors and chrome parking lights were added to the C4 Deluxe Cab package. The hood nameplate was now painted on standard trim models and chrome on Deluxe models. The sliding seat tracks were returned as standard equipment. On V-8s, the 224 cid V-8 was replaced by the longer stroke 259 cid V-8. Also, the 245 cid six was returned as a standard option. Power brakes were added as an option on all models. A heavy-duty engine with chrome top rings, heavy-duty valves, valve rotary caps, etc., was optional on V-8 models.

I.D. DATA: The serial number was located on a plate on the left side of the seat riser. The engine number was located on the top, left side, front corner of the cylinder block. Starting serial numbers: [3E5] E5-123,001; [3E6] E6-15,501; [3E7] E7-7,601; [3E11] E11-12,401; [3E12] E12-3,001. Starting engine numbers: [3E5] 1E-10,101; [3E6/3E11] 4E-3,401; [3E7/3E12] 3E-2,701*

* Heavy-duty 259 engines had a "5E" engine number prefix.

Model	Body Type	Price	Weight	Prod. Total
3E Series — 1/2-Ton				
3E5-112	Pickup	1722	2745	Note 1
3E5-122	Pickup	1758	2875	Note 1
3E6-112	Pickup	1754	2950	Note 1
3E6-122	Pickup	1789	3075	Note 1
3E7-112	Pickup	1853	3020	Note 1
3E7-122	Pickup	1888	3160	Note 1
3E Series — 3/4-Ton				
3E11	Pickup	1911	3310	Note 1
3E12	Pickup	2010	3395	Note 1

NOTE 1: Production breakdowns are not available. Total production of all 1957 3E models (1/2- to 2-ton) was 11,185. Serial number spans for a particular model give a rough estimate of how many of that model were built in a year.

1957 Studebaker Transtar Pickup (A&A)

ENGINE [3E5]: Six-cylinder. L-head. Cast iron block. Displacement: 185.6 cid. Bore & stroke: 3 in. x 4-3/8 in. Compression ratio: 7.5:1. Brake horsepower: 92 at 3800 rpm. Taxable horsepower: 21.6. Maximum torque: 152 lbs.-ft. Main bearings: Four. Valve lifters: Solid. Carburetor: Carter Model BBR1-2125S one-barrel. GVW: [3E5-112] 4,800 lbs.; [3E5-122] 4,800 lbs.; [Others] 5,000 lbs.

ENGINE [3E6/3E11]: Six-cylinder. L-head. Cast iron block. Displacement: 245.6 cid. Bore & stroke: 3-5/16 in. x 4-3/4 in. Compression ratio: 7.5:1. Brake horsepower: 106 at 3400 rpm. Taxable horsepower: 26.3. Maximum torque: 204 lbs.-ft. Main bearings: Four. Valve lifters: Solid. Carburetor: Carter Model BBR1-777SA one-barrel.

ENGINE [3E7/3E12]: Eight-cylinder. OHV V-8. Cast iron block. Displacement: 259.2 cid. Bore & stroke: 3-9/16 in. x 3-1/4 in. Compression ratio: 7.5:1. Brake horsepower: 170 at 4200 rpm. (178 horsepower with optional four-barrel carburetor.) Taxable horsepower 40.6. Maximum torque: 250 lbs.-ft. Main bearings: Five. Valve lifters: Solid. Carburetor: Stromberg Model WW two-barrel (optional: Carter Model WCFB four-barrel).

CHASSIS & BODY [3E5-112/3E6-112/3E7-112]: Wheelbase: 112 in. Overall length: 185.6 in. Height: 69.75 in. Width: 77.5 in. Interior pickup box dimensions: 77.8 in. long x 51.5 in. wide x 17.1 in. high. Front tread: 60.8 in. Rear tread: 62.6 in. Tires: 6.00 x 16 four-ply. GVW: [3E5-112] 4,800 lbs.; [Others] 5,000 lbs.

CHASSIS & BODY [3E5-122/3E6-122/3E7-122/3E11/3E12]: Wheelbase: 122 in. Overall length: 203.6 in. Height: 69.75 in. (69.6 in. for 3E11/3E12). Width: 77.5 in. Interior pickup box dimensions: 95.8 in. long x 51.5 in. wide x 17.1 in. high. Front tread: 60.8 in. Rear tread: 62.6 in. (63 in. for 3E11/3E12). Tires: 6.00 x 16 four-ply (7.00 x 16 six-ply on 3E11/3E12). [3E5-122] 4,800 lbs.; [Other 3E5/3E6/3E7] 5,000 lbs.; [3E11/3E12] 7,000 lbs.

1957 Studebaker Walk-In Bakery Delivery (A&A)

TECHNICAL: Sliding gear transmission. Speeds: 3F/1R. Synchromesh in second and third. Steering column shift control. Single-plate dry-disc clutch. I-beam front axle. 3E5/3E6/3E7 rear axle: Hypoid semi-floating with 4.27 or 4.55:1 (3E5), 4.09 or 4.27:1 (3E6) and 3.73, 4.09 or 4.27:1 (3E7) overall ratios. 3E11/3E12 rear axle: Hypoid full-floating with 4.10 or 4.88:1 overall ratios. Hydraulic brakes. Steel disc wheels. Direct acting tubular shock absorbers. Variable-ratio steering.

OPTIONS: Flightomatic transmission (3E7 and 3E12 only). Four-speed synchromesh transmission with floor shift control. Overdrive. Hill Holder. Power brakes. Twin-Traction (1/2-ton models only). Deluxe Cab. Radio. Climatizer heater/defroster. Interior rearview mirror. Ashtray. Right-hand sun visor. Seat pad. Safety seat belts. Armrests. Compass. Traffic light viewer. Map light. Accelerator pedal cover. Kleenex dispenser. Cigarette lighter. Dual horns. Two-tone paint. Caravan Top. Painted rear bumper. Extra taillight. License plate frames. Locking gas cap. Right-hand exterior rearview mirror. Left and right exterior extension rearview mirrors. Tinted glass. Spotlight. Directional signals. Underhood light. Front splash guards. Exhaust deflector. Windshield washer. Mattex seat covers. Hand throttle. Electric windshield wipers (standard on V-8 with automatic transmission). Fram oil filter. One-quart oil bath air cleaner. Governor (V-8 two-barrel models only). Heavy-duty engine (V-8 models only). V-8 power package (four-barrel carburetor and large air cleaner). Five- or six-blade fan. Headbolt engine heater. Heavy-duty battery. Heavy-duty radiator.

Heavy-duty springs. Heavy-duty shock absorbers. Brake fluid reservoir. [Optional tires specific to the 3E5/3E6/3E7] 6.00 x 16 six-ply, 6.50 x 16 six-ply and 7.10 x 15 four-ply (black or whitewall). [Optional tires specific to the 3E11/3E12] 8.00 x 17 eight-ply and 8.00 x 19.5 eight-ply.

HISTORICAL: Sales continued to fall while production costs forced price increases for all models. Studebaker-Packard was close to going out of business in 1957.

1958 STUDEBAKER

MODELS 3E1/3E5/3E6/3E7/3E11/3E12 — ALL ENGINES: Studebaker-Packard's precarious position forced the Studebaker Truck Div. to continue the 3E series into 1958, but this did not stop them from making two major introductions for the 1958 model year. The first was a four-wheel drive option for 1/2-, 3/4- and 1-ton models powered by the 245 cid six and V-8 engines. The four-wheel-drive front axle was manufactured by Napco. Models fitted with four-wheel-drive had a "D" suffix added to their model number. A scalloped right rear fender allowed room for mounting the spare tire on the side of the pickup box on four-wheel-drive models. This type of spare tire mounting was made optional on other models. The four-wheel-drive option cost about $1,100, a sizable sum in 1958. The other introduction was a stripped down 1/2-ton called the Scotsman. The Scotsman name was first introduced by Studebaker in mid-1957 for their new bare-bones car model. The 1958 Scotsman pickup (3E1) was only available with the 185 cid six. The Scotsman used a modified 2R series grille, small front bumper and plaid name decals on the hood front, instrument panel and rear apron. The Scotsman came with an inside rearview mirror, but outside ones were extra-cost. The Scotsman cab was labeled the C1 cab. It had no glove box door, a non-sliding seat, painted hubcaps and headlight rims and many other cost-cutting features. All the trimming-down allowed Studebaker to sell the Scotsman pickup for only $1,595. It was the lowest price full-sized pickup sold in the U.S. The regular Transtar models remained unchanged from 1957. More effort was made in 1958 to promote sales of non-pickup bodies for their light-duty trucks. Special Powers bodies on 3E6 and 3E11 models were advertised for use by plumbers, contractors and public utility companies.

I.D. DATA: The serial number was located on a plate on the left side of the seat riser. The engine number was located on the top, left side, front corner of the cylinder block. Starting serial numbers: [3E5]: E5-125,401; [3E1]: E1-101; [3E6]: E6-16,901; [3E7]: E7-9,801; [3E11] E11-13,001; [3E12] E12-3,601. Starting engine numbers: [3E1/3E5] 1E-12,601; [3E6/3E11] 4E-5,701; [3E7/3E12] 3E-6,301*

* Heavy-duty 259 engines had a "5E" engine number prefix.

1958 Studebaker 3/4-Ton Transtar 4x4 Pickup (FKF)

Model	Body Type	Price	Weight	Prod. Total
3E Series — 1/2-Ton				
3E1-112	Pickup	1595	2600	Note 1
3E5-112	Pickup	1773	2745	Note 1
3E5-122	Pickup	1808	2875	Note 1
3E6-112	Pickup	1804	2950	Note 1
3E6-122	Pickup	1839	3075	Note 1
3E7-112	Pickup	1903	3020	Note 1
3E7-122	Pickup	1938	3160	Note 1
3E Series — 3/4-Ton				
3E11	Pickup	1961	3310	Note 1
3E12	Pickup	2060	3395	Note 1

NOTE 1: Production breakdowns are not available. Total production of all 1958 Series 3E models (1/2- to 2-ton) was 7,085. Serial number spans for a particular model give a rough estimate of how many of that model were built in a year.

ENGINE [3E1/3E5]: Six-cylinder. L-head. Cast iron block. Displacement: 185.6 cid. Bore & stroke: 3 in. x 4-3/8 in. Compression ratio: 7.5:1. Brake horsepower: 92 at 3800 rpm. Taxable horsepower: 21.6. Maximum torque: 152 lbs.-ft. Main bearings: Four. Valve lifters: Solid. Carburetor: Carter Model BBR1-2125S one-barrel.

ENGINE [3E6/3E11]: Six-cylinder. L-head. Cast iron block. Displacement: 245.6 cid. Bore & stroke: 3-5/16 in. x 4-3/4 in. Compression ratio: 7.5:1. Brake horsepower: 106 at 3400 rpm. Taxable horsepower: 26.3. Maximum torque: 204 lbs.-ft. Main bearings: Four. Valve lifters: Solid. Carburetor: Carter Model BBR1-777SA one-barrel.

ENGINE [3E7/3E12]: Eight-cylinder. OHV V-8. Cast iron block. Displacement: 259.2 cid. Bore & stroke: 3-9/16 in. x 3-1/4 in. Compression ratio: 7.5:1. Brake horsepower: 170 at 4200 rpm. [178 horsepower with optional four-barrel carburetor]. Taxable horsepower 40.6. Maximum torque: 250 lbs.-ft. Main bearings: Five. Valve lifters: Solid. Carburetor: Stromberg Model WW two-barrel (optional: Carter Model WCFB four-barrel).

CHASSIS & BODY [3E1-112/3E5-112/3E6-112/3E7-112]: Wheelbase: 112 in. Overall length: 185.6 in. Height: 69.75 in. Width: 77.5 in. Interior pickup box dimensions: 77.8 in. long x 51.5 in. wide x 17.1 in. high. Front tread: 60.8 in. Rear tread: 62.6 in. Tires: 6.00 x 16 four-ply. GVW: 4,800-5,000 lbs.

CHASSIS & BODY [3E5-122/3E6-122/3E7-122/3E11/3E12]: Wheelbase: 122 in. Overall length: 203.6 in. Height: 69.75 in. (69.6 in. for 3E11 and 3E12). Width: 77.5 in. Interior pickup box dimensions: 95.8 in. long x 51.5 in. wide x 17.1 in. high. Front tread: 60.8 in.

Rear tread: 62.6 in. (63 in. for 3E11 and 3E12). Tires: 6.00 x 16 four-ply (7.00 x 16 six-ply on 3E11 and 3E12). GVW: 4,800; 5,000; 7,000 lbs.

1958 Studebaker Scotsman Pickup (FKF)

TECHNICAL: Sliding gear transmission. Speeds: 3F/1R. Synchromesh in second and third. Steering column shift control. Single-plate dry-disc clutch. I-beam front axle. 3E1/3E5/3E6/3E7 rear axle: Hypoid semi-floating with 4.27 or 4.55:1 (3E1/3E5); 4.09 or 4.27:1 (3E6) and 3.73, 4.09 and 4.27:1 (3E7) overall ratios. 3E11/3E12 rear axle: Hypoid full-floating with 4.10 or 4.88:1 overall ratios. Hydraulic brakes. Steel disc wheels. Direct acting tubular shock absorbers. Variable-ratio steering.

OPTIONS: Flightomatic transmission (3E7/3E12 only). Four-speed synchromesh transmission with floor shift control. Overdrive. Four-wheel drive (3E6/3E7/3E11/3E12 models). Hill Holder. Power brakes. Twin-Traction (1/2-ton models only). Deluxe Cab. Radio. Climatizer heater/defroster. Interior rearview mirror. Ashtray. Right-hand sun visor. Seat pad. Safety seat belts. Armrests. Compass. Traffic light viewer. Map light. Accelerator pedal cover. Kleenex dispenser. Cigarette lighter. Dual horns. Two-tone paint. (Transtar models only). Caravan Top. Painted rear bumper. Extra taillight. License plate frames. Locking gas cap. Right-hand exterior rearview mirror. Left and right exterior extension rearview mirrors. Tinted glass. Spotlight. Directional signals. Underhood light. Right rear fender kit for spare tire. Front splash guards. Exhaust deflector. Windshield washer. Mattex seat covers. Hand throttle. Electric windshield wipers kit (standard on V-8 with automatic transmission). Fram oil filter. One-quart oil bath air cleaner. Governor (V-8 two-barrel models only). Heavy-duty engine (V-8 models only). V-8 power package (four-barrel carburetor and large air cleaner). Five- or six-blade fan. Headbolt engine heater. Heavy-duty battery. Heavy-duty radiator. Heavy-duty springs. Heavy-duty shock absorbers. Brake fluid reservoir. [Special options for the Scotsman 3E1] Oil bath air cleaner. Outside rearview mirror(s). Spare tire. Two-stage rear springs. [Optional tires specific to the 3E1/3E5/3E6/3E7] 6.00 x 16 six-ply, 6.50 x 16 six-ply and 7.10 x 15 four-ply (black or whitewall). [Optional tires specific to the 3E11/3E12] 8.00 x 17 eight-ply and 8.00 x 19.5 eight-ply.

HISTORICAL: The year 1958 could very well have been Studebaker-Packard's last year. Car and truck sales for the model year were the lowest since 1945. Then, in the fall of 1958, Studebaker introduced its 1959 Lark car and everything turned around. The Lark sold well and the profits began to roll in.

1958 Studebaker Transtar Pickup (DFW)

1959 STUDEBAKER

MODELS 4E1/4E2/4E3/4E7/4E11/4E12 — ALL ENGINES: For some odd reason, Studebaker decided not to use the Transtar name in 1959. The former Transtar models with the "buck tooth" fiberglass grille were now known as the Deluxe Series. All domestic Deluxe Series models were fitted with a C4 Deluxe Cab. Deluxe models now had key locks on both doors and Studebaker door nameplates in place of Transtar names. In contrast to 1957-58, single-tone Deluxe Series models had body color grilles, instead of the off-white grilles used the previous two years. Also, the parking lights were moved from the top of the fenders down into the grille. The Scotsman series was expanded to include a 245 cid six Model 4E3 and a 259 cid V-8 Model 4E2. The plaid name decals were dropped and a simple chrome "S"

was added to the front of the hood. The Scotsman was also upgraded somewhat. It got a glove compartment door, electric windshield wipers, a spare tire, optional 122 in. wheelbase and a few other extra amenities. Partially because of this, Studebaker raised the price of the Scotsman 185 model 1/2-ton from $1,595 to $1,791. Studebaker's success with the perky Lark car changed the company's philosophy about developing an austere reputation. Because of the 4E1 and the 4E3 Scotsmans, the six-cylinder engines were not offered as standard powerplants for any 1959 domestic 1/2-ton Deluxe Series models. The four-wheel drive option was continued in 1959. It was available on all 1/2- to 1-ton models powered by the 245 cid six or 259 cid V-8, including the 4E2 and 4E3 Scotsman models. The standard V-8 engine for the 4E7 (1/2-ton) and 4E12 (3/4-ton) V-8 Deluxe Series models was upgraded to the 289 cid V-8. The old Champion six used in the 4E1 Scotsman was reduced to 169.6 cid. All domestic models now came standard with electric windshield wipers.

1959 Studebaker Transtar 4x4 Pickup (OCW)

I.D. DATA: The serial number was located on a plate on the left side of the seat riser. The engine number was located on the top, left side, front corner of the cylinder block. Starting serial numbers: [4E1] E1-1,001; [4E2] E2-101; [4E3] E3-101; [4E7] E7-11,001; [4E11] E11-13,501; [4E12] E12-3,901. Starting engine numbers: [4E1] 1E-15,001 (170 six); [4E3/4E11] 4E-7,301 (245 six); [4E2] 3E-8,001 (259 V-8)*; [4E7/4E12] 7E-101 (289 V-8)**.
* Heavy-duty 259 engines had a "5E" engine number prefix.
** Heavy-duty 289 engines had a "6E" engine number prefix.

Model	Body Type	Price	Weight	Prod. Total
4E Series — 1/2-Ton				
4E1-112	Pickup	1791	2660	Note 1
4E1-122	Pickup	1826	2800	Note 1
4E2-112	Pickup	1939	2960	Note 1
4E2-122	Pickup	1974	3150	Note 1
4E3-112	Pickup	1868	2920	Note 1
4E3-122	Pickup	1902	3060	Note 1
4E7-112	Pickup	2071	3000	Note 1
4E7-122	Pickup	2105	3140	Note 1
4E Series — 3/4-Ton				
4E11	Pickup	2103	3245	Note 1
4E12	Pickup	2247	3360	Note 1

NOTE 1: Production breakdowns are not available. Total production of all 1959 4E models (1/2- to 2-ton) was 7,737. Serial number spans for a particular model give a rough estimate of how many of that model were built in a year.

ENGINE [4E1]: Six-cylinder. L-head. Cast iron block. Displacement: 169.6 cid. Bore & stroke: 3 in. x 4 in. Compression ratio: 8.0:1. Brake horsepower: 90 at 4000 rpm. Taxable horsepower: 21.6. Maximum torque: 145 lbs.-ft. Main bearings: Four. Valve lifters: Solid. Carburetor: Carter Model AS, one-barrel.

1959 Studebaker Deluxe Pickup (FKF)

ENGINE [4E3/4E11]: Six-cylinder. L-head. Cast iron block. Displacement: 245.6 cid. Bore & stroke: 3-5/16 in. x 4-3/4 in. Compression ratio: 7.5:1. Brake horsepower: 118 at 3400 rpm. Taxable horsepower: 26.3. Maximum torque: 204 lbs.-ft. Main bearings: Four. Valve lifters: Solid. Carburetor: Carter Model BBR1-777SA one-barrel.
ENGINE [4E2]: Eight-cylinder. OHV V-8. Cast iron block. Displacement: 259.2 cid. Bore & stroke: 3-9/16 in. x 3-1/4 in. Compression ratio: 7.5:1. Brake horsepower: 180 at 4500 rpm. (195 horsepower with optional four-barrel carburetor.) Taxable horsepower 40.6. Maximum torque: 260 lbs.-ft. Main bearings: Five. Valve lifters: Solid. Carburetor: Stromberg Model WW two-barrel (optional: Carter Model WCFB four-barrel).
ENGINE [4E7/4E12]: Eight-cylinder. OHV V-8. Cast iron block. Displacement: 289 cid. Bore & stroke: 3-9/16 in. x 3-5/8 in. Compression ratio: 7.5:1. Brake horsepower: 210 at 4500 rpm. (225 horsepower with optional four-barrel carburetor.) Taxable horsepower 40.6. Maximum torque: 300 lbs.-ft. Main bearings: Five. Valve lifters: Solid. Carburetor: Stromberg Model WW two-barrel (optional: Carter Model WCFB four-barrel).

1959 Studebaker Lark Panel Wagon (A&A)

CHASSIS & BODY [4E1-112/4E2-112/4E3-112/4E7-112]: Wheelbase: 112 in. Overall length: 185.6 in. Height: 69.75 in. Width: 77.5 in. Interior pickup box dimensions: 77.8 in. long x 51.5 in. wide x 17.1 in. high. Front tread: 60.8 in. Rear tread: 62.6 in. Tires: 6.00 x 16 four-ply (7.10 x 15 on 4E7). GVW: 5,000 lbs.-5,200 lbs.

CHASSIS & BODY [4E1-122/4E2-122/4E3-122/4E7-122/4E11/4E12]: Wheelbase: 122 in. Overall length: 203.6 in. Height: 69.75 in. (69.6 in. for 4E11/4E12). Width: 77.5 in. Interior pickup box dimensions: 95.8 in. long x 51.5 in. wide x 17.1 in. high. Front tread: 60.8 in. Rear tread: 62.6 in. (63 in. for 4E11 and 4E12). Tires: 6.00 x 16 four-ply (7.10 x 15 on 4E7; 7.00 x 16 six-ply on 4E11 and 4E12). GVW: 5,000 lbs.; 5,200 lbs.; 7,000 lbs.

TECHNICAL: Sliding gear transmission. Speeds: 3F/1R. Synchromesh in second and third. Steering column shift control. Single-plate dry-disc clutch. I-beam front axle. 4E1/4E2/4E3/4E7 rear axle: Hypoid semi-floating with 4.27 at 4.55:1 (4E1); 4.09, 4.27 or 4.55:1 (4E2/4E3) and 4.09 or 4.27:1 (4E7). 4E11/4E12 rear axle: Hypoid full-floating with 4.10 at 4.88:1 overall ratios. Hydraulic brakes. Steel disc wheels. Direct acting tubular shock absorbers. Variable-ratio steering.

1959 Studebaker Scotsman Pickup (FKF)

OPTIONS: Flightomatic transmission (4E2/4E7/4E12 only). Four-speed synchromesh transmission with floor shift control. Overdrive. Four-wheel-drive (4E2/4E3/4E7/4E11/4E12 models). Hill Holder. Power brakes. Twin-Traction. Radio. Climatizer heater/defroster. Seat pad. Safety seat belts. Compass. Traffic light viewer. Accelerator pedal cover. Kleenex dispenser. Cigarette lighter. Dual horns. Two-tone paint (Deluxe Series only). Caravan Top. Painted rear bumper. Extra taillight. License plate frames. Locking gas cap. Right-hand exterior rearview mirror. Left and right exterior extension rearview mirrors. Tinted glass. Spotlight. Directional signals. Underhood light. Right rear fender kit for spare tire. Front splash guards. Five- or six-blade fan. Headbolt engine heater. Heavy-duty battery. Heavy-duty radiator. Heavy-duty springs. Heavy-duty shock absorbers. Brake fluid reservoir. Special options for the Scotsman (4E1/4E2/4E3): outside rearview mirror(s), right-hand sun visor, map light, sliding seat, two-stage rear springs. [Optional tires specific to the 4E1/4E2/4E3/4E7] 6.50 x 16 six-ply (also 7.10 x 15 four-ply on Scotsman), whitewalls. [Optional tires specific to the 4E11/4E12] 7.00 x 17 eight-ply, 7.50 x 17 eight-ply and 8.00 x 17.5 eight-ply.

HISTORICAL: Although Lark sales were good in 1959, Studebaker truck sales made no big improvement over 1958. Many Larks were sold by "Big Three" dealers who had their own trucks to sell. Also, after 11 model years, Studebaker was still marketing the same basic truck

1960 STUDEBAKER

1960 Studebaker Champ Pickup (FKF)

MODELS 5E5/5E6/5E7/5E11/5E12 — ALL ENGINES: Profits from the Lark car finally gave Studebaker's Truck Div. a little money to work with. One-ton and larger models continued with the old design (again called the Transtar), but light-duty 1/2- and 3/4-ton models finally got a new styling. Borrowing from the concept of the original 1937-39 Coupe-Express, Studebaker took the Lark body and converted it to a truck front end and cab. Except for being chopped off behind the front door and featuring a brawnier grille and bumper, the styling, including the instrument panel, was identical to a 1959-1960 Lark four-door sedan. The new cab was called the "T" cab. The old pickup box was continued. Unlike the original Coupe-Express, the new model, called the Champ, used a truck chassis instead of a car chassis. The same wheelbases as offered in 1959 were continued. For 1960, the four-wheel drive was only offered on the 1-ton Transtar C cab models. One-ton pickups with a nine-foot box were still offered in 1960, but very few were sold. The new Champ was available with a standard T4 cab or a Deluxe T6 cab. The standard cab had painted hubcaps, gas cap, grille, side air intakes and headlight rims. These items were chrome or stainless steel on the Deluxe models. Deluxe models also had side fender moldings, dash pad, sliding rear window, two armrests, dome light, dual sun visors and bright metal window trim. Studebaker was one of the first companies to offer a pickup with a sliding rear cab window. All 1/2-ton models had new hubcaps with an "S" in the middle. Hubcaps were optional on 3/4-ton models. The Scotsman series was discontinued and the standard engine for the 1/2- and 3/4-ton V-8 models was again the 259 cid version. The 259 cid heavy-duty engine and the 289 cid engine, standard or heavy-duty, were extra-cost options. Dry type air cleaners were standard on all models. The new styling was much lower than older design. Because of this, the Champ had less drag and greater fuel economy. Custom flat-front Studebaker delivery vans were given some promotion during the year. They had bodies built by an outside firm, but a Lark grille and a 1955 truck nameplate. Very few were sold.

I.D. DATA: The 1960 5E T-cab serial number was on a plate mounted on the left door lock pillar post. Engine number locations were the same as 1955-1959. Starting serial numbers: [5E5] E5-127,301; [5E6] E6-18,201; [5E7] E7-12,301; [5E11] E11-13,901; [5E12] E12-4,301. Starting engine numbers: [5E5] 1E-18,301 (170 six); [5E6/5E11] 4E-9,401 (245 six); [5E7/5E12] 3E-9,201 (259 V-8)*
* Heavy-duty 259 cid engines had a "5E" engine number prefix; 289 engines had a "7E" engine number prefix; and heavy-duty 289 cid engines had a "6E" engine number prefix.

1960 Studebaker (modified) Champ 4x4 Pickup (DFW)

Model	Body Type	Price	Weight	Prod. Total
5E Series — 1/2-ton				
5E5-112	Pickup	1875	2775	Note 1
5E5-122	Pickup	1912	2915	Note 1
5E6-112	Pickup	1960	2980	Note 1
5E6-122	Pickup	1996	3120	Note 1
5E7-112	Pickup	2046	3060	Note 1
5E7-122	Pickup	2081	3200	Note 1
5E Series — 3/4-Ton				
5E11	Pickup	2108	3340	Note 1
5E12	Pickup	2220	3425	Note 1

NOTE 1: Production breakdowns are not available. Total production of all 1960 5E models (1/2- to 2-ton) was 8,294. Serial number spans for a particular model give a rough estimate of how many of that model were built in a year.

1960 Studebaker Transtar 4x4 Pickup (A&A)

ENGINE [5E5]: Six-cylinder. L-head. Cast iron block. Displacement: 169.6 cid. Bore & stroke: 3 in. x 4 in. Compression ratio: 8.0:1. Brake horsepower: 90 at 4000 rpm. Taxable horsepower: 21.6. Maximum torque: 145 lbs.-ft. Main bearings: Four. Valve lifters: Solid. Carburetor: Carter Model AS one-barrel.
ENGINE [5E6/5E11]: Six-cylinder. L-head. Cast iron block. Displacement: 245.6 cid. Bore & stroke: 3-5/16 in. x 4-3/4 in. Compression ratio: 7.5:1. Brake horsepower: 118 at 3400 rpm. Taxable horsepower: 26.3. Maximum torque: 204 lbs.-ft. Main bearings: Four. Valve lifters: Solid. Carburetor: Carter Model AS one-barrel.
ENGINE [5E7/5E12]: Eight-cylinder. OHV V-8. Cast iron block. Displacement: 259.2 cid. Bore & stroke: 3-9/16 in. x 3-1/4 in. Compression ratio: 7.5:1. Brake horsepower: 180 at 4500 rpm. (195 horsepower with optional four-barrel carburetor). Taxable horsepower 40.6. Maximum torque: 260 lbs.-ft. Main bearings: Five. Valve lifters: Solid. Carburetor: Stromberg Model WW two-barrel (optional: Carter Model WCFB four-barrel).
ENGINE [5E7/5E12; optional engine]: Eight-cylinder. OHV V-8. Cast iron block. Displacement: 289 cid. Bore & stroke: 3-9/16 in. x 3-5/8 in. Compression ratio: 7.5:1. Brake horsepower: 210 at 4500 rpm. (225 horsepower with optional four-barrel carburetor). Taxable horsepower 40.6. Maximum torque: 300 lbs.-ft. Main bearings: Five. Valve lifters: Solid. Carburetor: Stromberg Model WW two-barrel (optional: Carter Model WCFB four-barrel).
CHASSIS & BODY [5E5-112/5E6-112/5E7-112]: Wheelbase: 112 in. Overall length: 179.8 in. Height: 68 in. Width: 77.5 in. Interior pickup box dimensions: 77.8 in. long x 51.5 in. wide x 17.1 in. high. Front tread: 58 in. Rear tread: 62.6 in. Tires: 6.00 x 16 four-ply. GVW: [5E5-112] 5,000 lbs.; [5E6-112] 5,200 lbs.; [5E7-112] 5,200 lbs.

1960 Studebaker Champ Pickup (A&A)

CHASSIS & BODY [5E5-122/5E6-122/5E7-122/5E11/5E12]: Wheelbase: 122 in. Overall length: 197.8 in. Height: 68 in. (69 in. for 5E11/5E12). Width: 77.5 in. Interior pickup box dimensions: 95.8 in. long x 51.5 in. wide x 17.1 in. high. Front tread: 58 in. Rear tread: 62.6 in. (63 in. for 5E11/5E12). Tires: 6.00 x 16 four-ply (7.00 x 16 six-ply on 5E11/5E12). GVW: [5E5-122] 5,000 lbs.; [5E6-122] 5,200 lbs.; [5E7-122] 5,200 lbs. GVW: [5E5-11] 7,000 lbs.; [5E6-12] 7,000 lbs.
TECHNICAL: Sliding gear transmission. Speeds: 3F/1R. Synchromesh in second and third. Steering column shift control. Single-plate dry-disc clutch. I-beam front axle. Rear axle: [5E5/5E6/5E7] Hypoid semi-floating with 4.27 or 4.55:1 (5E5); 3.73, 4.09, 4.27 or 4.55:1 (5E6/5E7) overall ratios; [5E11/5E12] Hypoid full-floating with 4.10 or 4.88:1 overall ratios. Hydraulic brakes. Steel disc wheels. Direct acting tubular shock absorbers. Variable-ratio steering.
OPTIONS: Flightomatic transmission (5E7/5E12 only). Four-speed synchromesh transmission with floor shift control. Overdrive. Twin-Traction. Hill Holder. Power brakes. Deluxe T6 Cab. Radio. Clock. Climatizer heater/defroster. Safety seat belts. Kleenex dispenser. Cigarette lighter. Dual door locks. Dual horns. Caravan Top. Painted rear bumper. Right-hand taillight. License plate frames. Locking gas cap. Left- and right-hand exterior rearview mirrors. Left and right exterior extension rearview mirrors. Tinted glass. Spotlight. Directional signals. Right rear fender kit for spare tire. Inside pickup box tire carrier. Hubcaps (3/4-ton models). Front splash guards. Windshield washer. Cushion toppers. Oil filter. One-quart oil bath air cleaner. Engine governor. Inline gas filter. 289 or heavy-duty engines (V-8 models only). 7.0:1 compression ratio. Four-barrel carburetor (V-8s only). Heavy-duty 11 in. clutch (V-8 only). Heavy-duty generator. Leece-Neville alternator. Heavy-duty battery. Heavy-duty fan. Heavy-duty radiator. Heavy-duty front springs (5E5). Heavy-duty rear springs. Heavy-duty shock absorbers. Brake fluid reservoir. Items for non-Deluxe Cab: seat pads, padded dash, sliding rear window, right-hand sun visor, armrests, dome light. [Optional tires specific to the 5E5/5E6/5E7] 7.10 x 15 four-ply (black or whitewall), 6.00 x 16 six-ply and 6.50 x 16 six-ply. Optional tires specific to the 5E11/5E12: 7.50 x 16 six-ply and 8.00 x 17.5 eight-ply.

1960 Studebaker Champ Pickup (OCW)

HISTORICAL: Production delays and steel strikes held up the introduction of the 5E Champ until the spring of 1960. A short model year kept 5E production from showing any significant increases. No matter what Studebaker did, they had no luck in increasing truck sales. The Champ cab turned out to be poorly designed in regard to rust prevention.

1960 Studebaker Champ Pickup (A & A)

1961 STUDEBAKER

1961 Studebaker Champ Deluxe Pickup (FKF)

MODELS 6E5/6E7/6E10/6E12 — ALL ENGINES: The big news for 1961 was the introduction of the overhead valve version of the old 170 cid engine. In truck form, the new engine produced 110 hp; 20 more than its L-head predecessor. With the introduction of the OHV six, the 245 cid L-head six was discontinued for the last time. The 3/4-ton "10" model returned as the 6E10. As on 1961 Lark cars, the side trim was raised above the contour line on Deluxe Cab (T6) models. The 1961 Champ side grille styling was the same as used on 1959 Lark cars, while the 1960 Champ side grilles were the same design as used on 1960 Lark cars. In January 1961, a new wide Spaceside pickup box was made available. The basic box styling had previously been used by Dodge. Dodge called it the Sweptline box. The dies to manufacture the box were purchased from Dodge and the box was modified to fit the Champ. The front panel next to the cab was redesigned and a tailgate with "STUDEBAKER" on it was added. The older, narrow box with external fenders was retained. The new single wall Spaceside box was identified as the P2 box and the older box, now called the "Double Wall" box, was listed as the P1 box. Fifteen-inch wheels were made standard on 1/2-ton Champs. A few Champ pickups with Studebaker Cruiser chassis were built for export sales only.

I.D. DATA: The 1961 6E T-cab serial number and engine number locations were the same as 1960. Starting serial numbers: [6E5] E5-129,601; [6E7] E7-13,801; [6E10] E10-39,001; [6E12] E12-4,701. Starting engine numbers: [6E5/6E10] 1E-20,601 (170 six); [6E7/6E12] 3E-11,601 (259 V-8)*

* Heavy-duty 259 engines had a "5E" engine number prefix; 289 engines had a "7E" engine number prefix; and heavy-duty 289 engines had a "6E" engine number prefix.

Model	Body Type	Price	Weight	Prod. Total
6E Series — 1/2-ton				
6E5-112	Pickup	1875	2816	Note 1
6E5-122	Pickup	1913	2956	Note 1
6E7-112	Pickup	2050	3080	Note 1
6E7-122	Pickup	2082	3220	Note 1
6E Series — 3/4-Ton				
6E10	Pickup	2035	3155	Note 1
6E12	Pickup	2205	3450	Note 1

NOTE 1: Production breakdowns are not available. Total production of all 1961 6E models (1/2- to 2-ton) was 7,641. Serial number spans for a particular model give a rough estimate of how many of that model were built in a year.

ENGINE [6E5 and 6E10]: Six-cylinder. OHV in-line six. Cast iron block. Displacement: 169.6 cid. Bore & stroke: 3 in. x 4 in. Compression ratio: 8.0:1. Brake horsepower: 110 at 4500 rpm. Taxable horsepower: 21.6. Maximum torque: 156 lbs.-ft. Main bearings: Four. Valve lifters: Solid. Carburetor: Carter Model AS, one-barrel.

ENGINE [6E7/6E12]: Eight-cylinder. OHV V-8. Cast iron block. Displacement: 259.2 cid. Bore & stroke: 3-9/16 in. x 3-1/4 in. Compression ratio: 7.5:1. Brake horsepower: 180 at 4500 rpm. (195 horsepower with optional four-barrel carburetor). Taxable horsepower: 40.6. Maximum torque: 260 lbs.-ft. Main bearings: Five. Valve lifters: Solid. Carburetor: Stromberg Model WW two barrel (optional: Carter Model WCFB four-barrel).

ENGINE [6E7/6E12; optional engine]: Eight-cylinder. OHV V-8. Cast iron block. Displacement: 289 cid. Bore & stroke: 3-9/16 in. x 3-5/8 in. Compression ratio: 7.5:1. Brake horsepower: 210 at 4500 rpm. (225 horsepower with optional four-barrel carburetor). Taxable horsepower: 40.6. Maximum torque: 300 lbs.-ft. Main bearings: Five. Valve lifters: Solid. Carburetor: Stromberg Model WW two-barrel (optional: Carter Model WCFB four-barrel).

CHASSIS & BODY [6E5-112/6E7-112]: Wheelbase: 112 in. Overall length: 179.8 in. Height: 65 in. Width: 77.5 in. P1 pickup box interior dimensions: 77.8 in. long x 51.5 in. wide x 17.1 in. high. P2 Spaceside pickup box interior dimensions: 78.75 in. long x 70.75 in. wide x 20 in. high. Front tread: 58 in. Rear tread: 62.6 in. Tires: 6.70 x 15 four-ply. GVW: [6E5-112] 5,000 lbs.; [6E7-112] 5,200 lbs.

CHASSIS & BODY [6E5-122/6E7-122/6E10/6E12]: Wheelbase: 122 in. Overall length: 197.8 in. Height: 65 in. (66 in. for 6E11/6E12). Width: 77.5 in. P1 pickup box interior dimensions: 95.8 in. long x 51.5 in. wide x 17.1 in. high. P2 Spaceside pickup box interior dimensions: 99 in. long x 70.75 in. wide x 20 in. high. Front tread: 58 in. Rear tread: 62.6 in. (63 in. for 6E11/6E12). Tires: 6.70 x 15 four-ply (7.00 x 16 six-ply on 6E11/6E12). GVW: [6E10] 7,000 lbs.; [6E11] 7,000 lbs.

TECHNICAL: Sliding gear transmission. Speeds: 3F/1R. Synchromesh in second and third. Steering column shift control. Single-plate dry-disc clutch. I-beam front axle. 6E5 and 6E7 rear axle: Hypoid semi-floating with 4.09, 4.27 or 4.55:1 (6E5); 3.73, 4.09, 4.27 or 4.55:1 (6E7) overall ratios. 6E10 and 6E12 rear axle: Hypoid full-floating with 4.56 or 4.88:1 (6E10); 4.10, 4.56 or 4.88:1 (6E12) overall ratios. Hydraulic brakes. Steel disc wheels. Direct acting tubular shock absorbers. Variable-ratio steering.

OPTIONS: Flightomatic transmission (6E7/6E12 only). Four-speed synchromesh transmission with floor shift control. Overdrive. Twin-Traction. Hill Holder. Power brakes. P2 Spaceside pickup box. Deluxe T6 Cab. Radio. Clock. Climatizer heater/defroster. Safety seat belts. Kleenex dispenser. Cigarette lighter. Dual door locks. Dual Horns. Caravan top. Painted rear bumper. Right-hand taillight. License plate frames. Locking gas cap. Left- and right-hand exterior rearview mirrors. Left and right exterior extension rearview mirrors. Tinted glass. Spot light. Directional signals. Right rear fender kit for spare tire (P1 box only). Inside pickup box tire carrier. Hubcaps (3/4-ton models). Front splash guards. Windshield washer. Cushion toppers. Oil filter. One-quart oil bath air cleaner. Engine governor. Inline gas filter. 289 or heavy-duty engines (V-8 models only). 7.0:1 compression ratio (V-8s only). Positive crankcase ventilation. Four-barrel carburetor (V-8s only). Heavy-duty 11 in. (V-8 only). Heavy-duty generator. Leece-Neville alternator. Heavy-duty battery. Heavy-duty fan. Heavy-duty radiator. Heavy-duty front springs (6E5/6E10). Heavy-duty rear springs. Heavy-duty shock absorbers. Brake fluid reservoir. [Items for non-Deluxe Cab] seat pads, padded dash, sliding rear window, right-hand sun visor, armrests, dome light. [Optional tires specific to the 6E5/6E7] 7.10 x 15 four-ply, 6.00 x 16 four-ply, 6.00 x 16 six-ply, 6.50 x 16 six-ply and whitewalls. [Optional tires specific to the 6E10/6E12] 7.50 x 16 six-ply.

HISTORICAL: The new OHV six and wide Spaceside box did not help sales. Problems with cracked valve seats on the six-cylinder engine hurt the reputation of the new engine.

1962 STUDEBAKER

MODELS 7E5/7E7/7E10/7E12 — ALL ENGINES: Although the Lark car front end was restyled in 1961 and again in 1962, the Champ light-duty trucks continued with the 1959-60 Lark front end styling. Changes for the 1962 model year were minimal. On Deluxe Cab models the side fender trim was again lowered back to the contour line as in 1960. For the first time, the Flightomatic automatic transmission was made an extra-cost option on six-cylinder models. The older P1 narrow pickup with the exterior fenders was continued, but the newer Spaceside box was made standard equipment.

1962 Studebaker Champ Deluxe Pickup (A&A)

I.D. DATA: The 1962 7E T-cab serial number and engine number locations were the same as 1960-61. Starting serial numbers: [7E5] E5-132,601; [7E7] E7-16,201; [7E10] E10-39,301; [7E12] E12-5,201. Starting engine numbers: [7E5/7E10] 1E-23,901 (170 six); [7E7/7E12] 3E-14,801 (259 V-8)*

* Heavy-duty 259 cid engines had a "5E" engine number prefix; 289 cid engines had a "7E" engine number prefix; and heavy-duty 289 cid engines had a "6E" engine number prefix.

Model	Body Type	Price	Weight	Prod. Total
7E Series — 1/2-ton				
7E5-112	Pickup	1870	2790	Note 1
7E5-122	Pickup	1915	2930	Note 1
7E7-112	Pickup	2050	3075	Note 1
7E7-122	Pickup	2084	3215	Note 1
7E Series — 3/4-Ton				
7E10	Pickup	2035	3355	Note 1
7E12	Pickup	2205	3440	Note 1

NOTE 1: Production breakdowns are not available. Total production of all 1962 Series 7E models (1/2- to 2-ton) was 8,742. Serial number spans for a particular model give a rough estimate of how many of that model were built in a year.

1962 Studebaker Champ Deluxe Pickup (FKF)

ENGINE [7E5/7E10]: Six-cylinder. OHV in-line six. Cast iron block. Displacement: 169.6 cid. Bore & stroke: 3 in. x 4 in. Compression ratio: 8.0:1. Brake horsepower: 110 at 4500 rpm. Taxable horsepower: 21.6. Maximum torque: 156 lbs.-ft. Main bearings: Four. Valve lifters: Solid. Carburetor: Carter Model AS, one-barrel.
ENGINE [7E7/7E12]: Eight-cylinder. OHV V-8. Cast iron block. Displacement: 259.2 cid. Bore & stroke: 3-9/16 in. x 3-1/4 in. Compression ratio: 7.5:1. Brake horsepower: 180 at 4500 rpm. (195 horsepower with optional four-barrel carburetor). Taxable horsepower: 40.6. Maximum torque: 260 lbs.-ft. Main bearings: Five. Valve lifters: Solid. Carburetor: Stromberg Model WW two-barrel (optional: Carter Model WCFB four-barrel).
ENGINE [7E7/7E12; optional engine]: Eight-cylinder. OHV V-8. Cast iron block. Displacement: 289 cid. Bore & stroke: 3-9/16 in. x 3-5/8 in. Compression ratio: 7.5:1. Brake horsepower: 210 at 4500 rpm. (225 horsepower with optional four-barrel carburetor). Taxable horsepower 40.6. Maximum torque: 300 lbs.-ft. Main bearings: Five. Valve lifters: Solid. Carburetor: Stromberg Model WW two-barrel (optional: Carter Model WCFB four-barrel).
CHASSIS & BODY [7E5-112/7E7-112]: Wheelbase: 112 in. Overall length: 180.7 in. Height: 65 in. Width: 77.5 in. P1 pickup box interior dimensions: 77.8 in. long x 51.5 in. wide x 17.1 in. high. P2 Spaceside pickup box interior dimensions: 78.75 in. long x 70.75 in. wide x 20 in. high. Front tread: 58 in. Rear tread: 62.6 in. Tires: 6.70 x 15 four-ply. GVW: [7E5-112] 5,000 lbs.; [7E7-112] 5,200 lbs.
CHASSIS & BODY [7E5-122/7E7-122/7E10/7E12]: Wheelbase: 122 in. Overall length: 201 in. Height: 65 in. (66 in. for 7E11/7E12). Width: 77.5 in. P1 pickup box interior dimensions: 95.8 in. long x 51.5 in. wide x 17.1 in. high. P2 Spaceside pickup box interior dimensions: 99 in. long x 70.75 in. wide x 20 in. high. Front tread: 58 in. Rear tread: 62.6 in. (63 in. for 7E11/7E12). Tires: 6.70 x 15 four-ply (7.00 x 16 six-ply on 7E11/7E12). GVW: [7E10] 7,000 lbs.; [7E11] 7,000 lbs.
TECHNICAL: Sliding gear transmission. Speeds: 3F/1R. Synchromesh in second and third. Steering column shift control. Single-plate dry-disc clutch. I-beam front axle. 7E5, and 7E7 rear axle: Hypoid semi-floating with 4.09, 4.27 or 4.55:1 (7E5); 3.73, 4.09, 4.27 or 4.55:1 (7E7) overall ratios. 7E10/7E12 rear axle: Hypoid full-floating with 4.56 or 4.88:1 (7E10); 4.10, 4.56, or 4.88:1 (7E12) overall ratios. Hydraulic brakes. Steel disc wheels. Direct acting tubular shock absorbers. Variable-ratio steering.
OPTIONS: Flightomatic transmission. Four-speed synchromesh transmission with floor shift control. Overdrive. Twin-Traction. Hill Holder. Power brakes. P1 Double Wall pickup box. Deluxe T6 Cab. Radio. Clock. Climatizer heater/defroster. Safety seat belts. Kleenex

---

dispenser. Cigarette lighter. Dual door locks. Dual horns. Caravan Top. Painted rear bumper. Right-hand taillight. License plate frames. Locking gas cap. Left- and right-hand exterior rearview mirrors. Left and right exterior extension rearview mirrors. Tinted glass. Spotlight. Directional signals. Right rear fender kit for spare tire (P1 box only). Inside pickup box tire carrier. Hubcaps (3/4-ton models). Front splash guards. Windshield washer. Cushion toppers. Oil filter. One-quart oil bath air cleaner. Engine governor. In-line gas filter. 289 or heavy-duty engines (V-8 models only). 7.0:1 compression ratio (V-8s only). Positive crankcase ventilation. Four-barrel carburetor (V-8s only). Heavy-duty 11 in. clutch (V-8 only). Heavy-duty generator. Leece-Neville alternator. Heavy-duty battery. Heavy-duty fan. Heavy-duty radiator. Heavy-duty front springs (7E5 & 7E10). Heavy-duty rear springs. Heavy-duty shock absorbers. Brake fluid reservoir. Items for non-Deluxe Cab: seat pads, padded dash, sliding rear window, right-hand sun visor, armrests, dome light. Optional tires specific to the 7E5, and 7E7: 7.10 x 15 four-ply, 6.00 x 16 four-ply, 6.00 x 16 six-ply, 6.50 x 16 six-ply and whitewalls. Optional tires specific to the 7E10 and 7E12: 7.50 x 16 six-ply.

HISTORICAL: Sales increased slightly in 1962. Studebaker dealers who were proficient at selling trucks found the Champ an easy pickup to market. With a base price of $1,870 for the six-cylinder with the 6-1/2-foot box, the Champ was the lowest-priced domestic 5,000 lb. GVW pickup sold in the U.S. in 1962. The problem was that most Studebaker dealers in the early 1960s made little effort to sell trucks.

1963-1964 STUDEBAKER

MODELS 8E5/8E7/8E10/8E12 — ALL ENGINES: Studebaker's last trucks were the 8E series models that were produced during the 1963 and shortened 1964 model years. The last Studebaker civilian truck was assembled on Dec. 27, 1963. Although the 8E Champ was the end of the line, it had several improvements over the 1962 Series 7E trucks. Steering geometry was all-new and a new type of constant-ratio steering gear was adopted. Brake and clutch pedals were switched to the swing type. Front shock absorbers were mounted in a new "sea leg" fashion. Wider and longer front springs were adopted. Full-flow oil filters were made standard equipment on all models and the six-cylinder engine was fitted with a new style carburetor. The optional V-8 four-barrel carburetor was also changed. The brake master cylinder was moved from the frame to the firewall. Positive crankcase ventilation was made standard equipment. The old narrow P1 "Double Wall" pickup box was discontinued. Air conditioning and a Conestoga camper were added to the option list. During the model year, a five-speed transmission was made an extra-cost option. One option never offered on 1/2-or 3/4-ton Studebaker trucks was power steering. During 1963-64, Studebaker assembled an 8E5 forward-control van called the Zip-Van. Produced in fairly large quantities, the Zip-Van was built specifically for the U.S. Post Office Dept. The Zip-Van had right-hand controls and used Transtar truck instruments. For the 1964 model year, Studebaker introduced the Service Champ. The Service Champ featured fiberglass utility bodies for plumbers, electricians, tire servicemen, etc. Service Champs were available only on 122 in. wheelbase models.

I.D. DATA: The 1963-64 8E T-cab serial number and engine number locations were the same as 1960-62. Starting serial numbers: [8E5] E5-136,001; [8E7] E7-18,901; [8E10] E10-39,901; [8E12] E12-5,901. Starting engine numbers: [8E5/8E10] 1E-27,801 (170 six); [8E7/8E12] 3E-18,901 (259 V-8)*

* Heavy-duty 259 cid engines had a "5E" engine number prefix; 289 cid engines had a "7E" engine number prefix; and heavy-duty 289 cid engines had a "6E" engine number prefix.

1963 Studebaker Champ Deluxe Pickup (FKF)

Model	Body Type	Price	Weight	Prod. Total
8E Series — 1/2-ton				
8E5-112	Pickup	1915	2790	Note 1
8E5-122	Pickup	1957	2930	Note 1
8E7-112	Pickup	2083	3075	Note 1
8E7-122	Pickup	2120	3215	Note 1
8E Series — 3/4-Ton				
8E10	Pickup	2075	3355	Note 1
8E12	Pickup	2244	3440	Note 1

NOTE 1: Production breakdowns are not available. Total 1963 calendar year production of all models (1/2- to 2-ton) was 13,117.
ENGINE [8E5/8E10]: Six-cylinder. OHV in-line six. Cast iron block. Displacement: 169.6 cid. Bore & stroke: 3 in. x 4 in. Compression ratio: 8.0:1. Brake horsepower: 110 at 4500 rpm. Taxable horsepower: 21.6. Maximum torque: 156 lbs.-ft. Main bearings: Four. Valve lifters: Solid. Carburetor: Carter Model RBS one-barrel.
ENGINE [8E7/8E12]: Eight-cylinder. OHV V-8. Cast iron block. Displacement: 259.2 cid. Bore & stroke: 3-9/16 in. x 3-1/4 in. Compression ratio: 7.5:1. Brake horsepower: 180 at 4500 rpm. (195 horsepower with optional four-barrel carburetor). Taxable horsepower: 40.6. Maximum torque: 260 lbs.-ft. Main bearings: Five. Valve lifters: Solid. Carburetor: Stromberg Model WW two-barrel (optional: Carter Model AFB four-barrel).

ENGINE [8E7/8E12; optional engine]: Eight-cylinder. OHV V-8. Cast iron block. Displacement: 289 cid. Bore & stroke: 3-9/16 in. x 3-5/8 in. Compression ratio: 7.5:1. Brake horsepower: 210 at 4500 rpm. (225 horsepower with optional four-barrel carburetor). Taxable horsepower 40.6. Maximum torque: 300 lbs.-ft. Main bearings: Five. Valve lifters: Solid. Carburetor: Stromberg Model WW two-barrel (optional: Carter Model AFB four-barrel).

1964 Studebaker Postal Zip Van (A&A)

CHASSIS & BODY [8E5-112/8E7-112]: Wheelbase: 112 in. Overall length: 180.7 in. Height: 65 in. Width: 77.5 in. P2 Spaceside pickup box interior dimensions: 78.75 in. long x 70.75 in. wide x 20 in. high. Front tread: 58 in. Rear tread: 62.6 in. Tires: 6.70 x 15 four-ply. GVW: [8E5-112] 5,000 lbs.; [8E7-112] 5,200 lbs.

CHASSIS & BODY [8E5-122/8E7-122/8E10/8E12]: Wheelbase: 122 in. Overall length: 201 in. Height: 65 in. (66 in. for 8E11 and 8E12). Width: 77.5 in. P2 Spaceside pickup box interior dimensions: 99 in. long x 70.75 in. wide x 20 in. high. Front tread: 58 in. Rear tread: 62.6 in. (63 in. for 8E11 and 8E12). Tires: 6.70 x 15 four-ply (7.00 x 16 six-ply on 8E11 and 8E12). GVW: [8E10] 7,000 lbs.; [8E11] 7,000 lbs.

TECHNICAL: Sliding gear transmission. Speeds: 3F/1R. Synchromesh in second and third. Steering column shift control. Single-plate dry-disc clutch. I-beam front axle. 8E5, and 8E7 rear axle: Hypoid semi-floating with 4.09, 4.27 or 4.55:1 (8E5); 3.73, 4.09, 4.27 or 4.55:1 (8E7) overall ratios. 8E10 and 8E12 rear axle: Hypoid full-floating with 4.56 or 4.88:1 (8E10); 4.10, 4.56, or 4.88:1 (8E12) overall ratios. Hydraulic brakes. Steel disc wheels. Direct acting tubular shock absorbers. Constant ratio steering.

OPTIONS: Flightomatic transmission. Four-speed synchromesh transmission with floor shift control. Five-speed synchromesh transmission with floor shift control. Overdrive. Twin-Traction. Hill Holder. Power brakes. Air conditioning. Deluxe T6 Cab. Radio. Clock. Climatizer heater/defroster. Safety seat belts. Kleenex dispenser. Cigarette lighter. Dual door locks. Dual horns. Standard or Deluxe Conestoga camper. Caravan Top. U2 or U3 Service Champ fiberglass bodies (in 1964, 122 in. wheelbase only). Painted rear bumper. Heavy-duty wraparound cadmium-toned diamond embossed rear step bumper. Right-hand taillight. License plate frames. Locking gas cap. Left and right-hand exterior rearview mirrors. Left and right exterior extension rearview mirrors. Tinted glass. Spotlight. Directional signals. Inside pickup box tire carrier. Hubcaps (3/4-ton models). Front splash guards. Windshield washer. Cushion toppers. One-quart oil bath air cleaner. Engine governor. In-line gas filter. 289 or heavy-duty engines (V-8 models only). 7.0:1 compression ratio (V-8s only). Four-barrel carburetor (V-8s only). Heavy-duty 11 in. clutch (V-8 only). Heavy-duty generator. Alternator. Heavy-duty battery. Heavy-duty fan. Heavy-duty radiator. Heavy-duty front springs (8E5/8E10). Heavy-duty rear springs. Heavy-duty shock absorbers. Items for non-Deluxe Cab: seat pads, padded dash, sliding rear window, right-hand sun visor, armrests, dome light. Optional tires specific to the 8E5/8E7: 7.10 x 15 four-ply, 6.00 x 16 four-ply, 6.00 x 16 six-ply, 6.50 x 16 six-ply and whitewalls. Optional tires specific to the 8E10/8E12: 7.50 x 16 six-ply.

HISTORICAL: When the Avanti production facilities were sold to Nathan Altman in 1964-65, he also obtained the Champ and Transtar truck rights, but no trucks were ever produced by the Avanti Motor Corp. Except for the M and 2R series models, Studebaker light-duty trucks were never produced in large quantities, but hundreds of post-1936 models of all types have been saved by dedicated Studebaker enthusiasts.

WILLYS-OVERLAND
1911-1942

1938 Willys-Overland Model 77 Pickup (OCW)

By Robert C. Ackerson

A fleet of postal delivery wagons, for service in Indianapolis, was built by Overland in 1909. The following March, the Ohio automaker expanded operations into the light-duty commercial vehicle field with its Model 37 Covered Delivery Wagon. Some 391 of these passenger car-based trucks were assembled through 1911, the same year a 1-ton truck appeared.

John North Willys guided the firm's rising fortunes and, in March 1912, Willys-Overland purchased controlling interest in Gramm Motor Truck Co. of Lima, Ohio. In August, Garford Automobile Co., of Elyria, Ohio, was acquired. (Garford also built 1-ton trucks, as well as larger models.)

In August, 1912, Willys initiated a court battle against Gramm. Willys had charged company founder B.A. Gramm with stock manipulation schemes. When the lawsuit was settled, Gramm left to form several other truck firms, such as Gramm-Bernstein. Willys consummated the purchase of Gramm Motor Truck.

A 3/4-ton truck called the Model 65 Willys Utility was introduced by Gramm Motor Truck in January, 1913. Some literature refers to this model as a Willys-Overland product, but the vehicle nameplates were stamped with the Gramm name. Among heavier models, Gramm also offered a 1-ton, while Willys-Overland concurrently marketed an 800 lbs. delivery vehicle with open or closed body types.

At the start of calendar 1915, Willys-Overland sold its interest in both Garford and Gramm. However, Overland dealers continued to handle sales of both brands. In 1916, the Willys Utility was marketed as the Garford Model 64, but it did not return the following season. No longer involved in heavy truck-making, Willys-Overland remained active in the light-duty field. Its products included the 800 lbs. payload Model 83 of 1916; the 750 lbs. payload Model 75 of 1916-1917 and a 1200 lbs. payload truck. The latter, built in 1916, was fittingly called the Model 1200. A light panel and express truck were available, on the Model 90 chassis, for 1918.

Willys commercial vehicle production ceased during the 1921 recession year. It resumed in 1922. Starting that year, the Overland Four chassis was used as the basis for a Light Delivery. These trucks appeared on a list published by *MOTOR WORLD* on Oct. 25, 1923. They were designated the Overland Model 91C and 91E and had a 1/2-ton payload rating. A 1-ton Garford, the Model 15, was also offered that year.

Willys-Overland continued this line through the 1920s. Later, between 1927 and 1931, the company resumed active marketing of Gramm-built trucks featuring Knight sleeve-valve engines. When the Whippet was introduced for model year 1927, a light-duty truck version soon followed. These vehicles were stylish performers that came in both four- and six-cylinder versions.

The depression years were rough ones for Willys-Overland. In spite of the best efforts of its management, the firm

entered into receivership in early 1933. This took place about the same time that Willys-Overland introduced an important new model. This Willys 77 truck, a derivative of a revised passenger car line, was extremely handsome with its sloping front end, flowing fender lines and faired-in headlights.

The original 77 remained in production until 1938. During its tenure, it received numerous styling touches, apparently inspired by both Buicks and LaSalles. When a replacement (also identified as a 77) appeared, it was apparent that the Willys-Overland designers had not lost their ability to create fresh new lines that borrowed from no one. The new Willys

looked like no other truck on the road and featured such items as an alligator type hood, forward-sloping front fenders and a ship's prow front end.

This body style was continued until the end of production in 1942. As the years passed, its appearance became somewhat more conventional. In 1942, Willys-Overland (the Overland part of the name was revived in 1939) stopped making trucks. It was too busy producing military Jeeps for the U.S. Army. In the postwar era, civilian versions of the Jeep (see Jeep section) made up Willys' commercial model line.

1909 Overland Screenside Delivery (DFW/DPL)

1914 Overland Model 79-DE Open Flareboard (OCW)

1911-1912 WILLYS-OVERLAND

1911-1912 Overland Mail Delivery Truck (DFW/SI)

OVERLAND/GRAMM — MODEL 37/1-TON — FOUR-CYLINDER: The Overland Model 37 was first listed in 1910 as an 800 lbs. commercial car. The 37 was a commercial version of the Overland passenger car. Most of these trucks featured panel bodies. A year later, the Willys-Overland Co. came out with a 1-ton truck. Willys historian Duane Perrin believes neither was sold as an Overland until 1912. A 1-ton model was carried over into 1912. It had solid tires and a driver's seat perched in front over the engine.

I.D. DATA: Serial number located on plate on heel board under left front cushion; on right frame member; on spring hanger, right rear; on right rear frame member and/or under left front fender. Engine numbers located on right front corner of cylinder block and/or left side of engine. The 1911 to 1912 serial numbers are not available.

Model	Body Type	Price	Weight	Prod. Total
Overland Model 37 — 800 lbs. — 102 in. w.b.				
37	Special Delivery	1000	—	—
37	Delivery	800	—	—
Overland 2000 lb. — 1-Ton				
1T	Truck	1500	—	—
Gramm — 2000 lb. — 1-Ton				
1T	Truck (1911)	1800	—	—
1T	Truck (1912)	2000	—	—

ENGINE: L-head. Inline. Four-cylinder. Cast iron block. Bore & stroke: 3-3/4 in. x 4-1/2 in. Displacement: 198.8 cid. NACC horsepower: 25. Solid valve lifters. Carburetor: one-barrel.
CHASSIS: (Model 37) Wheelbase: 102 in. Tires: 32 x 3-1/2 in. (1-ton) Wheelbase: 120 in.
TECHNICAL: Selective sliding transmission. Speeds: 3F/1R. Outboard-mounted gearshift lever. Chain-drive system. Rear wheel brakes. Wood spoke wheels.
OPTIONS: Bulb horn. Brass sidelights. Headlamps. Taillamps. Special paint. Aftermarket bodies.
HISTORICAL: Driver-over-engine 1-ton truck with solid tires introduced. Overland moved production from Indianapolis, Ind. to Toledo, Ohio this year. Willys historian Duane Perrin reports that Express Delivery and Panel Delivery versions of the 1912 Overland Model 59 were available. Our research turned up no data on these models.

1913 WILLYS-OVERLAND

1913 Willys Utility (by Gramm) 3/4-Ton Covered Express (OCW)

Standard Catalog of Light-Duty Trucks

WILLYS-OVERLAND — MODEL 69/1-TON — FOUR-CYLINDER: The first appearance of the Willys Utility name on a truck came in 1913. This truck was made by Gramm at Lima, Ohio. Gramm was not officially part of the Willys-Overland Co., although John North Willys controlled both firms, as well as numerous others. A 1-1/2-ton model is beyond the scope of this catalog, but two other 1913 models were 1-ton or less. Gramm produced a 1-ton truck which is included in this section. Available data is sketchy. Marketed as an Overland gasoline truck was a commercial vehicle of the year's Model 69 four-cylinder passenger car. It came with an open express (large pickup) body or as a full panel van-type truck. The Gramm-built Willys Utility was advertised in the July 1913 *LITERARY DIGEST*. It was said to be priced 30-50 percent lower than similar vehicles and described as "practical and up-to-date." It used a 30 hp motor governed for a top speed of 18 mph. Pneumatic tires were mounted in front, with two-inch larger diameter solid tires at the rear. This truck was advertised under the Willys-Overland Co. name and address and used many Model 69 components.

I.D. DATA: Serial number located on plate on heel board under left front cushion; on right frame member; on spring hanger, right rear; on right rear frame member and/or under left front fender. Engine numbers located on right front corner of cylinder block and/or left side of engine. Serial numbers for the Overland 69 began at number 1 and ended at 30,026. This series included both passenger cars and trucks.

Model	Body Type	Price	Weight	Prod. Total
Overland Model 69 — 800 lbs. — 110 in. w.b.				
69	Open Express	950	—	—
69	Full Panel	1000	—	—
Gramm 1-Ton — 2000 lbs.				
1T	Chassis	1750	—	—
Willys Utility — 1500 lbs. (3/4-Ton)				
WU	Chassis	1250	—	—

ENGINE [Overland]: L-head. Inline. Four-cylinder. Cast iron block. Bore & stroke: 4 in. x 4-1/2 in. Displacement: 226.2 cid. NACC horsepower: 30.
ENGINE [Willys Utility]: Literature mentions a "powerful 30 horsepower motor — controlled by our patented governor. It cannot operate over 18 miles per hour."
CHASSIS [Overland Model 69]: Wheelbase: 110 in. Tires: 32 x 3-1/2 in.
CHASSIS [Gramm/Willys Utility]: Tires: [front] 34 x 4-1/2 in.; [rear] 36 x 3-1/2 in.
TECHNICAL: An advertisement read: "The pressed steel frame is built to stand the most severe strains of heavy loads and the worst possible road conditions. It is thoroughly reinforced. Both the front and rear axles are unusually rugged, and are made in our drop forge plant. It has a three-speed transmission — three forward and one reverse. We found that 34 in. x 4-1/2 in. pneumatic tires on the front wheels and 36 in. x 3-1/2 in. solid tires on the rear give the most practical service, so we equipped the truck accordingly. It is a big practical commercial truck — built purely and simply for commercial purposes."
OPTIONS: 60 in. Southern gauge. Special paint. Brass side lamps. Bulb horn. Headlamps. Taillamps.
HISTORICAL: Innovations: New open express available from factory. Three-speed selective transmission replaces two-speed; pedal controlled planetary type. Historical notes: First use of Willys name on a truck occurred this year. Built by Gramm, it followed Overland practice but had side-chain final drive.

1914 WILLYS-OVERLAND

1914 Overland Model 79-DS Panel (OCW)

OVERLAND — MODEL 79/MODEL 65 — FOUR-CYLINDER: The Model 79 Overland was a commercial car variation of the Model 79 passenger car. It was cataloged as an 800 lbs. commercial chassis. Most likely, buyers would have purpose-built bodies custom made for a chassis. Most were turned out as light vans. Produced only as a commercial vehicle, the Model 65 was a 1500 lbs. gasoline truck offered in both 1914 and 1915. It came in chassis-only form or with a factory express This was the same truck listed by the Association of Licensed Automobile Manufacturers (ALAM) as the Willys Utility in the ALAM's 1915 handbook. It was actually made at the Gramm plant in Lima, Ohio.

I.D. DATA: Serial number located on plate on heel board under left front cushion; on right frame member; on spring hanger, right rear; on right rear frame member and/or under left front fender. Engine numbers located on right front corner of cylinder block and/or left side of engine. Serial numbers for the Overland 65 are not available. Serial numbers for the Overland 79 began at number 1 and ended at 45,005. This series included both cars and trucks.

Model	Body Type	Price	Weight	Prod. Total
Overland Model 79 — 800 lbs. — 114 in. w.b.				
79	Chassis	900	2765	—

Willys-Utility — Model 65 — 3/4-Ton — 120 in. w.b.

| 65 | Chassis | 1350 | 2882 | — |

ENGINE: Vertical. Four-cylinder. Cast iron block. Bore & stroke: 4-1/8 in. x 4-1/2 in. Displacement: 240.5 cid. Net horsepower: 27.2 (NACC). Solid valve lifters. Carburetor: one-barrel.
CHASSIS [Overland Model 79]: Wheelbase: 114 in. Tires: 33 x 4 in.
CHASSIS [Overland Model 65]: Wheelbase: 120 in. Front tread: 56 in. Rear tread: 58 in. Tires: [front] 34 x 4-1/2 in.; [rear] 36 x 3-1/2 in.
TECHNICAL: Selective sliding transmission. Speeds: 3F/1R. Outboard-mounted gearshift lever. Cone clutch. Double side chain-drive. Contracting and expanding brakes. Wood spoke wheels.
OPTIONS: Bulb horn. Brass sidelights. Headlamps. Taillamps. Special paint. Aftermarket bodies.
HISTORICAL: New Model 79 introduced. Willys-Knight was introduced as a new car-line this year. Some Willys-Knight taxicabs and trucks were built later. A Willys-Overland facility became the first auto agency established in Iceland.

1915 WILLYS-OVERLAND

WILLYS-OVERLAND — MODEL 65 — FOUR-CYLINDER: Willys historian Duane Perrin believes that the Willys Utility Model 65 commercial chassis was carried over only in Canada for 1915. There was also a Gramm 65 the same year. The Gramm offered the same two body styles as the Overland (identical prices), plus a more expensive 65A chassis. This was an example of badge-engineering (selling the same product under two nameplates). The Gramm-made Willys Utility had a four-cylinder engine with separately-cast blocks arranged vertically under its rounded hood. It was water-cooled, via a cellular radiator. It also had jump spark ignition with a magneto and dry batteries as the electric source. The driver sat on the right side and controls were center-mounted. The covered express featured a paneled box. A long, flat top was supported on beams at each corner of the box. The top extended over the driver's compartment.
I.D. DATA: Serial number located on plate on heel board under left front cushion; on right frame member; on spring hanger, right rear; on right rear frame member and/or under left front fender. Engine numbers located on right front corner of cylinder block and/or left side of engine. The Gramm Motor Truck Co., of Lima, Ohio was controlled by John N. Willys at this time and produced a model described as the Willys Utility 1500 lbs. truck. Serial or model numbers for this product are unavailable.

Model	Body Type	Price	Weight	Prod. Total
Overland Model 65 — 3/4-Ton — 120 in. w.b.				
65	Chassis	1350	2882	—
65	Express	1500	2985	—
Willys-Utility — Model 65 — 3/4-Ton — 120 in. w.b.				
65	Chassis	1350	2882	—
65	Express	1500	2985	—
65A	Chassis	1800	3000	—

NOTE 1: Willys Utility made by Gramm.
ENGINE: Vertical. Four-cylinder. Cast iron block. Bore & stroke: 4-1/8 in. x 4-1/2 in. Displacement: 240.5 cid. Horsepower: 27.2 (NACC). Solid valve lifters. Carburetor: one-barrel.
CHASSIS: Wheelbase: 120 in. Tread: [front] 56 in.; [rear] 58 in. Tires: [front] 34 x 4-1/2 in. pneumatic; [rear] 36 x 3-1/2 in. solid.
TECHNICAL: Selective sliding transmission. Speeds: 3F/1R. Outboard-mounted gearshift lever. Cone clutch. Drive system: Double side chain-drive. Contracting and expanding rear wheel brakes. Wood spoke wheels.
OPTIONS: 60 in. Southern gauge. Bulb horn. Brass sidelights. Brass headlamps. Carbide taillamps. Side curtains. Special paint. Aftermarket bodies.
HISTORICAL: New 65A model introduced. Full electrics also available. There was a 1-ton heavy-duty model, too. Overland introduced left-hand drive this year.
The firm had profits of $10 million this year.

1916 WILLYS-OVERLAND

1916 Overland Open Flareboard Express (DFW/IPC)

WILLYS-OVERLAND — MODEL 83 — FOUR-CYLINDER: Overland's Model 83 passenger car was the basis for a new commercial vehicle line of 1916. This model had an angular, cathedral-shaped radiator, rounded cowl and large sweeping fenders. The body sills were rather high on this model. Also based on a current passenger car, was the Model 75 commercial chassis. The Overland 75 looked like a slightly scaled-down version of the 83. However, it had much lower body sills and a much shorter hood line. Standard equipment for both models included windshield, speedometer, ammeter and demountable rims. The 83 came in two 800 lbs. models: Express Delivery and Special Delivery, plus a 1200 lbs. Open Express truck. The 75 came with a 750 lbs. payload rating as a Panel Delivery or Screenside Delivery. Standard colors for passenger cars were Brewster green body with fenders and radiator black.
I.D. DATA: Serial number located on plate on heel board under left front cushion; on right frame member; on spring hanger, right rear; on right rear frame member and/or under left front fender. Engine numbers located on right front corner of cylinder block and/or left side of engine. [Overland 83] 1-102,840; [Overland 75] 1-25,000. There was also a 75B with approximate numbers 25,001 to 65,694. The 75B had 30 hp, five more than the 75. Both series included both passenger cars and trucks.

Model	Body Type	Price	Weight	Prod. Total
Overland Model 83 — 800 lbs. — 106 in. w.b.				
83	Express	725	2780	—
83	Special	750	2790	—
Overland Model 83B — 1200 lbs. — 106 in. w.b.				
83B	Open Express	850	3329	—
Overland Model 75 — 750 lbs. (1/4-Ton) — 104 in. w.b.				
75LD	Screen	595	3268	—
75PLD	Panel	625	3268	—

ENGINE [Model 83]: Cast en bloc. Inline. Side-valve (L-head). Four-cylinder. Cast iron block. Bore & stroke: 4-1/8 in. x 4-1/2 in. Displacement: 240.5 cid. Horsepower: 27.25 (NACC). Five main bearings. Solid valve lifters. Carburetor: Tillotson. Gravity feed. Splitdorf ignition (single system with two units.) Six-volt. Auto-Lite six-volt starter and generator. Willard 80 battery. Helical camshaft drive. Pump cooling. Splash cooling.
ENGINE [Model 75]: Cylinders cast in blocks of two. Inline. Side-valve. Four-cylinder. Cast iron block. Bore & stroke: 3-1/8 in. x 5 in. Displacement: 153.4 cid. Horsepower: 15.63 (NACC). Two main bearings. Solid valve lifters. Carburetor: Tillotson. Gravity feed. Splitdorf ignition (single system with two units.) Six-volt. Auto-Lite six-volt starter and generator. Gould 80 battery. Chain camshaft drive. Pump cooling. Splash oiling.
CHASSIS [Overland Model 83]: Wheelbase: 106 in. Front and rear tread: 50 or 60 in. Tires: 33 x 4 in.
CHASSIS [Overland Model 75]: Wheelbase: 104 in. Front and rear tread: 50 or 60 in. Tires: 31 x 4 in.
TECHNICAL: Selective transmission on axle. Speeds: 3F/1R. Floor-mounted gearshift lever. Cone clutch. [Model 83] 3/4-floating; [Model 75] full-floating rear axle. High gear ratio: [Model 83] 3.75:1; [Model 75] 4.00:1. Contracting on jackshaft/expanding rear wheel brakes. Wood spoke wheels. The 83 had semi-elliptic front springs and 3/4-elliptic rears. The 75 had semi-elliptic front springs and cantilever rear springs.
OPTIONS: 60 in. Southern gauge. Bulb horn. Brass sidelights. Brass headlamps. Carbide taillamps. Side curtains. Special paint. Aftermarket bodies.
HISTORICAL: Innovations: New L-head monobloc engine. Overland 83 commercial vehicles introduced. New Special Delivery and screenside delivery bow. Willys-Overland produced 140,111 passenger vehicles in calendar 1916.

1917 WILLYS-OVERLAND

WILLYS-OVERLAND — MODEL 75 — FOUR-CYLINDER: Again based on a current passenger car was the Model 75 commercial chassis. The Overland 75 looked like a slightly scaled-down version of the 83. However, it had much lower body sills and a much shorter hood line. Standard equipment for both models included windshield, speedometer, ammeter and demountable rims. The 75 came with a 750 lbs. payload rating as a Panel Delivery or Screenside Delivery. Standard colors for passenger cars were Brewster green body with fenders and radiator black.
WILLYS-OVERLAND — MODEL 83 — FOUR-CYLINDER: This model was carried over from 1916. It again sported an angular, cathedral-shaped radiator, rounded cowl and large sweeping fenders. The body sills were rather high on this model. The 83 came in two 800 lbs. models: Express Delivery and Special Delivery, plus as a 1200 lbs. Open Express truck.
WILLYS-OVERLAND — SERIES 90 — FOUR-CYLINDER: The 90 was produced mainly in Panel Delivery form and remained a staple Willys-Overland product into the early-1920s, when the Light Four replaced it. As compared to the previous models, the 90 had a higher, straighter hood and cowl line-both being at the same level on the top surface. However, it resembled the 83 as far as size, sharing the same 106 in. wheelbase. According to Willys historian Duane A. Perrin, a 104 in. wheelbase was available, too. Standard equipment included a Stewart speedometer, Kellogg power tire pump, Willard storage battery, Auto-Lite horn, Stan weld wheel rims, Champion spark plugs and Goodyear or Fisk tires. Perrin adds that the Overland 75 series was carried over for 1917, as well as the Model 83B, a 1,200 lbs. Express.
I.D. DATA: Serial number located on plate on heel board under left front cushion; on right frame member; on spring hanger, right rear; on right rear frame member and/or under left front fender. Engine numbers located on right front corner of cylinder block and/or left side of engine. Serial numbers for the 1917 Overland Model 90 began at number 1 and ended at 87,008. This series included both trucks and passenger cars.

Model	Body Type	Price	Weight	Prod. Total
Overland Model 75 — 750 lbs. (1/4-Ton) — 104 in. w.b.				
75LD	Screen	595	3268	—
75PLD	Panel	625	3268	—
Overland Model 83 — 800 lbs. — 106 in. w.b.				
83	Express	725	2780	—
83	Special	750	2790	—
Overland Model 83B — 1200 lbs. — 106 in. w.b.				
83B	Open Express	850	3329	—

Overland Model 90 — 750 lbs. — 104 in./106 in. w.b.

90PLD	Panel	700	2895	—

ENGINE [Model 75]: Cylinders cast in blocks of two. Inline. Side-valve. Four-cylinder. Cast iron block. Bore & stroke: 3-1/8 in. x 5 in. Displacement: 153.4 cid. Horsepower: 15.63 (NACC). Two main bearings. Solid valve lifters. Carburetor: Tillotson. Gravity feed. Splitdorf ignition (single system with two units.) Six-volt. Auto-Lite six-volt starter and generator. Gould 80 battery. Chain camshaft drive. Pump cooling. Splash oiling.

ENGINE [Model 83]: Cast en bloc. Inline. Side-valve (L-head). Four-cylinder. Cast iron block. Bore & stroke: 4-1/8 in. x 4-1/2 in. Displacement: 240.5 cid. Horsepower: 27.25 (NACC). Five main bearings. Solid valve lifters. Carburetor: Tillotson. Gravity feed. Splitdorf ignition (single system with two units.) Six-volt. Auto-Lite six-volt starter and generator. Willard 80 battery. Helical camshaft drive. Pump cooling. Splash oiling.

ENGINE [Series 90]: Vertical. Separate cast cylinders. Valves on right side. Four-cylinder. Cast iron block. Bore & stroke: 3-1/8 in. x 5 in. Displacement: 178.8 cid. Horsepower: 32 (NACC). Two main bearings. Solid valve lifters. Carburetor: Tillotson model V. Other features: Helical drive camshaft. Inlet manifold outside and bolted-on. Iron pistons with three diagonal rings. Thermo-syphon cooling. Circulation splash oiling. Stewart fuel feed. Connecticut ignition. Auto-Lite six-volt starter.

CHASSIS [Overland Model 75]: Wheelbase: 104 in. Front and rear tread: 50 or 60 in. Tires: 31 x 4 in.

CHASSIS [Overland Model 83]: Wheelbase: 106 in. Front and rear tread: 50 or 60 in. Tires: 33 x 4 in.

CHASSIS [Overland Model 90]: Wheelbase: 104-106 in. Front and rear tread: [Standard] 50 in.; [Optional] 60 in. Tires: 31 x 4 in.

TECHNICAL [All]: Selective transmission on axle. Speeds: 3F/1R. Floor-mounted gearshift lever. Cone clutch. [Model 83] 3/4-floating; [Model 75] full-floating rear axle. High gear ratio: [Model 83] 3.75:1; [Model 75] 4.00:1. Contracting on jackshaft/expanding rear wheel brakes. Wood spoke wheels. The 83 had semi-elliptic front springs and 3/4-elliptic rears. The 75 had semi-elliptic front springs and cantilever rear springs. [Model 90] Selective sliding transmission. Speeds: 3F/1R. Floor-mounted gearshift lever. Cone type clutch. Three-quarter floating rear axle. High gear ratio: 3.75:1. Rear wheel brakes. Wood spoke wheels. Rear springs of cantilever design.

OPTIONS: 60 in. Southern gauge. Special paint. Aftermarket bodies.

HISTORICAL: Innovations: Series 90 comes out. New, modernized styling. Priced competitively with Model T. Historical notes: The Series 90 engine was the basis for some famous later Willy's powerplants. Curtiss Aviation Co. became part of Willys Corp., but was completely separate from Willys-Overland, Co.

1918 WILLYS-OVERLAND

WILLYS-OVERLAND — SERIES 90 — FOUR-CYLINDER: The Overland 90 was carried over into 1918 basically unchanged, except that a group of heavy-duty models rated for 1200 lbs. payloads was added. A new body style, in both weight classes, was an open express.

WILLYS-OVERLAND — MODEL 83 — FOUR-CYLINDER: This model was carried over from 1917. It again sported an angular, cathedral-shaped radiator, rounded cowl and large sweeping fenders. The body sills were rather high on this model. The 83 came in two 800 lbs. models: Express Delivery and Special Delivery, plus as a 1200 lbs. Open Express truck.

I.D. DATA: Serial number located on plate on heel board under left front cushion; on right frame member; on spring hanger, right rear; on right rear frame member and/or under left front fender. Engine numbers located on right front corner of cylinder block and/or left side of engine. Serial numbers for the 1918 Overland 90/90B were 87,009-140,643 passenger cars and trucks inclusive.

Model	Body Type	Price	Weight	Prod. Total
Overland 90				

Overland Model 83 — 800 lbs. — 106 in. w.b.

Model	Body Type	Price	Weight	Prod. Total
83	Express	725	2780	—
83	Special	750	2790	—

Overland Model 83B — 1200 lbs. — 106 in. w.b.

83B	Open Express	850	3329	—

Overland Model 90 — 800 lbs. — 106 in. w.b.

90	Chassis	800	2876	—
90	Express	840	2923	—
90	Panel	865	3110	—

Overland Model 90B — 1200 lbs. — 106 in. w.b.

90B	Chassis	915	3249	—
90B	Express	975	3400	—

ENGINE [Model 83]: Cast en bloc. Inline. Side-valve (L-head). Four-cylinder. Cast iron block. Bore & stroke: 4-1/8 in. x 4-1/2 in. Displacement: 240.5 cid. Horsepower: 27.25 (NACC). Five main bearings. Solid valve lifters. Carburetor: Tillotson. Gravity feed. Splitdorf ignition (single system with two units.) Six-volt. Auto-Lite six-volt starter and generator. Willard 80 battery. Helical camshaft drive. Pump cooling. Splash oiling.

ENGINE [Model 90/90B]: Vertical. Cylinder cast en bloc. Four-cylinder. Cast iron block. Bore & stroke: 3-3/8 in. x 5 in. Displacement: 178.8 cid. Horsepower: 32 (NACC). Two main bearings. Solid valve lifters. Carburetor: Tillotson model V.

CHASSIS [Overland Model 83]: Wheelbase: 106 in. Front and rear tread: 50 or 60 in. Tires: 33 x 4 in.

CHASSIS [Overland 90]: Wheelbase: 106 in. Front and rear tread: [Standard] 50 in. [Optional] 60 in. Tires: 31 x 4 in.

TECHNICAL: Selective sliding transmission. Speeds: 3F/1R. Floor-mounted gearshift lever. Cone type clutch. Three-quarter floating rear axle. High gear ratio: 3.75:1. Rear wheel brakes. Wood spoke wheels.

OPTIONS: 60 in. Southern gauge. Special paint. Aftermarket bodies.

HISTORICAL: John North Willys had over extended himself in building up his company. This set the stage for a financial reorganization in 1919.

1919 WILLYS-OVERLAND

WILLYS-OVERLAND — MODEL 83B — FOUR-CYLINDER: This model was carried over from 1917. It again sported an angular, cathedral-shaped radiator, rounded cowl and large sweeping fenders. The body sills were rather high on this model.

WILLYS-OVERLAND — SERIES 90/90CE — FOUR-CYLINDER: The Overland 90 continued to be a staple product for Willys-Overland in 1919. Models were the same offered in 1918. The Model 83B (see 1916-1918) was also continued until 1920.

I.D. DATA: Serial number located on plate on heel board under left front cushion; on right frame member; on spring hanger, right rear; on right rear frame member and/or under left front fender. Engine numbers located on right front corner of cylinder block and/or left side of engine. Serial numbers are not available.

Model	Body Type	Price	Weight	Prod. Total
Overland Model 83B — Payload 1200 lbs. — 106 in. w.b.				
83B	Open Express	850	3329	—
Overland 90 — 800 lbs. — 106 in. w.b.				
90	Chassis	800	2876	—
90	Express	840	2923	—
90	Panel	865	3110	—
90CE	Chassis	915	3249	—
90CE	Express	975	3400	—

ENGINE [Model 83]: Cast en bloc. Inline. Side-valve (L-head). Four-cylinder. Cast iron block. Bore & stroke: 4-1/8 in. x 4-1/2 in. Displacement: 240.5 cid. Horsepower: 27.25 (NACC). Five main bearings. Solid valve lifters. Carburetor: Tillotson. Gravity feed. Splitdorf ignition (single system with two units.) Six-volt. Auto-Lite six-volt starter and generator. Willard 80 battery. Helical camshaft drive. Pump cooling. Splash oiling.

ENGINE [Model 90/90B]: Vertical. Cylinder cast en bloc. Four-cylinder. Cast iron block. Bore & stroke: 3-3/8 in. x 5 in. Displacement: 178.8 cid. Horsepower: 32 (NACC). Two main bearings. Solid valve lifters. Carburetor: Tillotson Model V.

CHASSIS [Overland Model 83]: Wheelbase: 106 in. Front and rear tread: 50 or 60 in. Tires: 33 x 4 in.

CHASSIS [Overland 90]: Wheelbase: 106 in. Front and rear tread: [standard] 50 in. [optional] 60 in. Tires: 31 x 4 in.

TECHNICAL [All]: Selective sliding transmission. Speeds: 3F/1R. Floor-mounted gearshift lever. Cone type clutch. Three-quarter floating rear axle. High gear ratio: 3.75:1. Rear wheel brakes. Wood spoke wheels.

OPTIONS: 60 in. Southern gauge. Special paint. Aftermarket bodies.

HISTORICAL: The Willys Corp. was organized in 1919. It was a holding company for takeovers of firms such as Moline Plow, Tillotson Carburetor, Stephens, Curtiss Aeroplane Co. and many others. The Willys Corp. did not include Willys-Overland Co. The company itself, although controlled by John North Willys, was run by a management team picked by Chase National Bank (the note holder). The bank eventually put Walter P. Chrysler in charge of day-to-day operations.

1920 WILLYS-OVERLAND

OVERLAND — LIGHT-FOUR — FOUR-CYLINDER: The Overland Light-Four was a Classic motor truck. This model introduced a dimunitive four-cylinder engine that survived, in some Willys models, until 1963. It was seen mostly in delivery van form. Standard equipment included a Stewart speedometer, Stanweld wheel rims, hand tire pump, Auto-Lite horn, Auto-Lite lamps, Duratex upholstery and four Fisk or Federal Grand tires.

I.D. DATA: Serial number located on plate on heel board under left front cushion; on right frame member; on spring hanger, right rear; on right rear frame member and/or under left front fender. Engine numbers located on right front corner of cylinder block and/or left side of engine. Serial numbers are not available.

Model	Body Type	Price	Weight	Prod. Total
Overland Light-Four — 800 lbs. — 100 in. w.b.				
4	Chassis	450	—	—
4	Express	—	—	—
4	Panel	—	—	—
4	Chassis	—	—	—
4	Express	—	—	—

ENGINE: Inline. L-head. Four-cylinder. Cast iron block. Bore & stroke: 3-3/8 in. x 4 in. Displacement: 143.1 cid. Horsepower: 27 (NACC). Two main bearings. Solid valve lifters. Carburetor: Tillotson one-barrel. Features of this engine included: detachable head; cylinders cast en bloc design; cast iron valves; helical camshaft drive; aluminum pistons; diagonally-split piston rings, three per cylinder; splash oiling; gravity fuel feed; Connecticut ignition; six-volt Auto-Lite ignition.

CHASSIS: Wheelbase: 100 in. Tires: 30 x 3-1/2 in.

TECHNICAL: Selective sliding gear transmission, unit type. Speeds: 3F/1R. Floor-mounted gearshift lever. Plate type clutch. Three-quarter floating rear axle. Overall ratio: 4.50:1. Two wheel rear brakes. Wood spoke wheels.

OPTIONS: Front bumper. Rear bumper. Single sidemount. Special paint. Rearview mirror. Cowl lamps. Side curtains.

HISTORICAL: New Light-Four series was introduced.

1921 WILLYS-OVERLAND

OVERLAND — LIGHT-FOUR — FOUR-CYLINDER: The Light-Four continued unchanged from 1920. The commercial car line included the same models; three in the 800 lbs. payload class and two 1/2-tons. The one seen most was the panel truck.

I.D. DATA: Serial number located on plate on heel board under left front cushion; on right frame member; on spring hanger, right rear; on right rear frame member and/or under left front fender. Engine numbers located on right front corner of cylinder block and/or left side of engine. Serial numbers are not available.

Model	Body Type	Price	Weight	Prod. Total
Overland Model Four — 800 lbs. — 100 in. w.b.				
4	Chassis	450	—	—
4	Express	—	—	—
4	Panel	—	—	—
Overland Model Four — 1000 lbs. — 100 in. w.b.				
4	Chassis	—	—	—
4	Express	—	—	—

ENGINE: Inline. L-head. Four-cylinder. Cast iron block. Bore & stroke: 3-3/8 in. x 4 in. Displacement: 143.1 cid. Horsepower: 27 (NACC). Two main bearings. Solid valve lifters. Carburetor: Tillotson.

CHASSIS: Wheelbase: 100 in. Tires: 30 x 3-1/2 in.

TECHNICAL: Selective sliding gear transmission, unit type. Speeds: 3F/1R. Floor-mounted gearshift lever. Plate type clutch. Three-quarter floating rear axle. Overall ratio: 4.50:1. Rear wheel brakes. Wood spoke wheels.

OPTIONS: Special paint. Rearview mirror. Cowl lamps. Side curtains.

HISTORICAL: Willys-Overland sold less than 50,000 passenger cars and even fewer trucks in 1921. It had an indebtedness of $20 million. The future was bright, however. The period from 1921-1925 would be turnaround years.

1922 WILLYS-OVERLAND

1922 Overland Vestibule Panel Delivery (Broadway Cleaners)

OVERLAND — LIGHT-FOUR — FOUR-CYLINDER: The Light-Four was virtually the same as the 1921 version. This model helped pull Willys-Overland out of receivership.

I.D. DATA: Serial number located on plate on heel board under left front cushion; on right frame member; on spring hanger, right rear; on right rear frame member and/or under left front fender. Engine numbers located on right front corner of cylinder block and/or left side of engine. Serial numbers are not available.

Model	Body Type	Price	Weight	Prod. Total
Overland Model Four — 800 lbs. — 100 in. w.b.				
4	Chassis	450	—	—
4	Express	—	—	—
4	Panel	—	—	—
Overland Model Four — 1000 lbs. — 100 in. w.b.				
4	Chassis	—	—	—
4	Express	—	—	—

ENGINE: Inline. L-head. Four-cylinder. Cast iron block. Bore & stroke: 3-3/8 in. x 4 in. Displacement: 143.1 cid. Horsepower: 27 (NACC). Two main bearings. Solid valve lifters. Carburetor: Tillotson.

CHASSIS: Wheelbase: 100 in. Tires: 30 x 3-1/2 in.

TECHNICAL: Selective sliding gear transmission. Speeds: 3F/1R. Floor-mounted gearshift lever. Plate type clutch. Three-quarter floating rear axle. Overall ratio: 4.50:1. Rear wheel brakes. Wood spoke wheels.

OPTIONS: Special paint. Spare tire. Rearview mirror. Windshield wiper. Cowl lamps. Side curtains.

1923 WILLYS-OVERLAND

OVERLAND — SERIES 91CE — FOUR-CYLINDER: The 1923 Overland 91CE model was much similar to the previous Light-Four. The year's main changes included a revamped body style range with four 1/2-ton models: a traditional open express, a panel, a canopy and a screenside. The designation Overland 91CE was used for the commercial vehicles; cars were 91s. Standard equipment included a Stewart speedometer, Duratex upholstery and Trico automatic windshield cleaner. Other features were an Auto-Lite starting and lighting system, Indiana headlamps, Corcolite taillamps, Nagel ammeter and Schwarze horn. A six-volt U.S.L. 80-amp. storage battery was used. Average gasoline economy for the Series 91 passenger car was 20 mpg. It can be assumed the truck version was economical, too.

I.D. DATA: Serial number located on plate on heel board under left front cushion; on right frame member; on spring hanger, right rear; on right rear frame member and/or under left front fender. Engine numbers located on right front corner of cylinder block and/or left side of engine.

Serial numbers for the 1923 Overland 91 began at number 1 and ended at 133,200, passenger cars inclusive.

Model	Body Type	Price	Weight	Prod. Total
Overland Model 91CE — 1/2-Ton — 100 in. w.b.				
91CE	Chassis	425	2020	—

ENGINE: Vertical. Inline. L-head. Four-cylinder. Cast iron block. Bore & stroke: 3-3/8 in. x 4 in. Displacement: 143.1 cid. Compression ratio: 4.00:1. Brake horsepower: 27 at 2200 rpm. Three main bearings. Solid valve lifters. Carburetor: Tillotson one-barrel.

CHASSIS [Overland Series 91]: Wheelbase: 100 in. Tires: 30 x 3-1/2 in.

TECHNICAL: Selective sliding gear transmission. Speeds: 3F/1R. Floor-mounted gearshift lever. Borg & Beck 8-in. disc clutch. Semi-floating SB rear axle. Overall ratio: 4.50:1. Rear wheel brakes. Hayes wood spoke wheels.

OPTIONS: 60 in. Southern gauge. Special paint. Aftermarket bodies. Rearview mirror(s). Front bumper. Rear fender guards. Side curtains.

HISTORICAL: A 1-ton truck based on the Overland four-cylinder car chassis was produced at Willys' Stockport branch in England. It was not offered here.

1924 WILLYS-OVERLAND

1924 Overland Screenside Delivery (Linda Clark)

OVERLAND — SERIES 91CE — FOUR-CYLINDER: The commercial car (light-truck) version of the Overland 91 was again the 91CE. There were only minor changes. A new eight-plate clutch replaced the disc type of 1923. A slight increase in cylinder bore size increased engine displacement to 153.9 cid. Horsepower was up to 30. A new Outlook brand windshield cleaner (wiper) was used.

I.D. DATA: Serial number located on plate on heel board under left front cushion; on right frame member; on spring hanger, right rear; on right rear frame member and/or under left front fender. Engine numbers located on right front corner of cylinder block and/or left side of engine. Serial numbers for the 1924 Overland 91 were 133,201-240,271 (passenger cars included).

Model	Body Type	Price	Weight	Prod. Total
Overland Model 91CE — 1/2-Ton — 100 in. w.b.				
91CE	Chassis	395	2040	—

ENGINE: Vertical. Inline. L-head. Four-cylinder. Cast iron block. Bore & stroke: 31/2 in. x 4 in. Displacement: 153.9 cid. Compression ratio: 4.00:1. Brake horsepower: 30 at 2400 rpm. NACC horsepower: 19.6 (taxable). Three main bearings. Solid valve lifters. Carburetor: Tillotson one-barrel.

CHASSIS [Overland Series 91CE]: Wheelbase: 100 in. Tires: 30 x 3-1/2 in.

TECHNICAL: Selective sliding gear transmission. Speeds: 3F/1R. Floor-mounted gearshift lever. Eight-plate clutch. Semi-floating rear axle. Overall ratio: 4.50:1. Rear wheel brakes. Wood spoke wheels.

OPTIONS: 60 in. Southern gauge. Special paint. Aftermarket bodies. Rearview mirror(s). Front bumper. Rear fender guards. Side curtains. Pines tire lock. Spotlight. Crolan gas gauge. Radiator shield. Wind wings. Shock absorbers.
HISTORICAL: Both four-and six-cylinder taxicabs were made available on the Willys-Knight chassis.

1925
WILLYS-OVERLAND

OVERLAND — SERIES 91CE — FOUR-CYLINDER: The 91CE line of trucks was again carried over. There were no major specifications changes.
I.D. DATA: Serial number located on plate on heel board under left front cushion; on right frame member; on spring hanger, right rear; on right rear frame member and/or under left front fender. Engine numbers located on right front corner of cylinder block and/or left side of engine. Serial numbers for the 1925 Overland 91/91A were 240,272 to 339,655, passenger cars inclusive.

Model	Body Type	Price	Weight	Prod. Total
Overland Model 91CE — 1/2-Ton — 100 in. w.b.				
91CE	Chassis	395	2040	—

ENGINE: Inline. L-head. Four-cylinder. Cast iron block. Bore & stroke: 3-1/2 in. x 4 in. Displacement: 153.9 cid. Compression ratio: 4.00:1. Brake horsepower: 30 at 2400 rpm. NACC horsepower: 19.6. Three main bearings. Solid valve lifters. Carburetor: Tillotson one-barrel.
CHASSIS [Overland Series 91CE]: Wheelbase: 100 in. Tires: 30 x 3-1/2 in.
TECHNICAL: Selective sliding gear transmission. Speeds: 3F/1R. Floor-mounted gearshift lever. Eight-plate type clutch. Semi-floating rear axle. Overall ratio: 4.50:1. Rear wheel brakes. Wood spoke wheels.
OPTIONS: 60 in. Southern gauge. Special paint. Aftermarket bodies. Rearview mirror(s). Front bumper. Rear fender guards. Side curtains. Pines tire lock. Spotlight. Gas gauge. Radiator shield. Wind wings. Shock absorbers.
HISTORICAL: In contrast to the bleak year of 1921, Willys sold plenty of cars (200,000) and trucks in 1925. Annual profits were nearly as high as the debt of $20 million reported only four years earlier.

1926
WILLYS-OVERLAND

OVERLAND — SERIES 91CE — FOUR-CYLINDER: The Light-Four, Model 91CE was carried over for its final season in 1926. It was still marketed as a 1/2-ton chassis to which customers could add bodies made by aftermarket firms. Shown are estimated prices for typical body styles of this era in this catalog.
I.D. DATA: Serial number located on plate on heel board under left front cushion; on right frame member; on spring hanger, right rear; on right rear frame member and/or under left front fender. Engine numbers located on right front corner of cylinder block and/or left side of engine. Serial numbers for the 1926 Overland 91/91A were 339,656-364,569 (passenger cars included.)

Model	Body Type	Price	Weight	Prod. Total
Overland Model 91 — 1/2-Ton — 100 in.				
91CE	Chassis	395	2040	—

ENGINE: Inline. L-head. Four-cylinder. Cast iron block. Bore & stroke: 3-1/2 in. x 4 in. Displacement: 153.9 cid. Compression ratio: 4.00:1. Brake horsepower: 30 at 2400 rpm. NACC horsepower: 19.6. Three main bearings. Solid valve lifters. Carburetor: Tillotson one-barrel.
CHASSIS [Overland Series 91]: Wheelbase: 100 in. Tires: 30 x 3-1/2 in.
TECHNICAL: Selective sliding gear transmission. Speeds: 3F/1R. Floor-mounted gearshift lever. Eight-plate type clutch. Semi-floating rear axle. Overall ratio: 4.50:1. Rear wheel brakes. Wood spoke wheels.
OPTIONS: 60 in. Southern gauge. Special paint. Aftermarket bodies. Rearview mirror(s). Front bumper. Rear fender guards. Side curtains.
HISTORICAL: Innovations: Whippet replaces the Light-Four effective with 1927 model year (introduced in calendar 1926). Six-cylinder engine optional in Whippet. Last year for Light-Four model.

1927
WILLYS-OVERLAND

WHIPPET — SERIES 96 — FOUR-CYLINDER: The Whippet was America's smallest car when introduced in the fall of 1926 as a 1927 model. But, it was a fast and strong runner. These were qualities that made Whippet-based commercial vehicles a natural development. The Whippet replaced the Overland in Willys-Overland Co.'s marketing program and is often referred to as the Willys' Whippet, after 1929. One advanced feature was four-wheel mechanical brakes. The base engine was a 2.2-litre side-valve four. Later, a 2.4-liter six was made an option. A full range of models was available. Styling features included a bright metal rounded radiator shell, vertical hood louvers inside a slightly raised panel and drum type headlights on 1927 models. There was a vacuum feed fuel system and Auto-Lite ignition. The 1927 version had raised panel fenders. The Whippet hood mascot was a racing dog. Whippet trucks with the optional six-cylinder engine used the same motor as the Model 93A passenger car.

I.D. DATA: Serial number located on plate on dash; also on left side of frame member ahead of front spring rear hanger; also on right side of frame at rear end; also under driver's seat cushion. Engine numbers located on either front or rear on upper corner of cylinder block on right side. Serial numbers for 1927 Whippets were numbers 1-110,344 with passenger cars and trucks included.

Model	Body Type	Price	Weight	Prod. Total
Whippet Model 96 — 1/2-Ton — 100.25 in. w.b.				
96	Chassis	370	1469	—
96	Pickup	—	—	—
96	Canopy	—	—	—
96	Screen	—	—	—
96	Panel	—	—	—
96	Sedan	—	—	—

ENGINE [Base]: Inline. L-head. Four-cylinder. Cast iron block. Bore & stroke: 3-1/8 in. x 4-3/8 in. Displacement: 134.2 cid. Brake horsepower: 30 at 2800 rpm. Net horsepower: 15.6 (NACC). Three main bearings. Solid valve lifters. Carburetor: Tillotson model one-barrel.
ENGINE [Optional]: Inline. L-head. Six-cylinder. Cast iron block. Bore & stroke: 3 in. x 4 in. Displacement: 169.6 cid. Brake horsepower: 40 at 2800 rpm. Net horsepower: 21.6 (NACC). Seven main bearings. Solid valve lifters. Carburetor: Tillotson model one-barrel.
CHASSIS [Whippet 96]: Wheelbase: 100.25 in. Tires: 28 x 4.75 in.
CHASSIS [Whippet 93A]: Wheelbase: 100.25 in. Tires: 29 x 4.75 in.
TECHNICAL: Selective sliding transmission. Speeds: 3F/1R. Floor-mounted gearshift lever. Overall ratio: 4.5:1. Four-wheel mechanical brakes. Wood spoke wheels.
OPTIONS: Front bumper. Rear bumper. Single sidemount. Special paint. Rearview mirror.
HISTORICAL: Whippet replaces the Overland. Whippet features included four-wheel mechanical brakes, European-like styling and full-pressure lubrication. The six-cylinder engine had seven main bearings and invar strut pistons. A Whippet passenger car averaged 52.52 mph for 24 hours during an endurance run at Indianapolis Motor Speedway.

1928
WILLYS-OVERLAND

WHIPPET — SERIES 96 — FOUR-CYLINDER: The 1928 Whippets looked nearly identical to the original, but a plain radiator cap was used. The entire radiator was somewhat higher and narrower, although of similar design. New features included a bango type rear axle, new-sized tires and smoother front fenders without a raised panel. Trucks with the base four-cylinder engine were Model 96s. The optional six-cylinder engine was taken from the Model 6-98 passenger car.
I.D. DATA: Serial number located on plate on dash; also on left side of frame member ahead of front spring rear hanger; also on right side of frame at rear end; also under driver's seat cushion. Engine numbers located on either front or rear on upper corner of cylinder block on right side. Serial numbers for 1928 Whippets were 110,345-227,902 passenger cars and trucks inclusive.

Model	Body Type	Price	Weight	Prod. Total
Whippet Model 96 — 1/2-Ton — 100.25 in. w.b.				
96	Chassis	370	1469	—
96	Pickup	—	—	—
96	Canopy	—	—	—
96	Screen	—	—	—
96	Panel	—	—	—
96	Sedan	—	—	—

ENGINE [Base]: Inline. L-head. Four-cylinder. Cast iron block. Bore & stroke: 3-1/8 in. x 4-3/8 in. Displacement: 134.2 cid. Brake horsepower: 32 at 2800 rpm. NACC horsepower: 15.6. Three main bearings. Solid valve lifters. Carburetor: Tillotson model one-barrel.
ENGINE [Optional]: Inline. L-head. Six-cylinder. Cast iron block. Bore & stroke: 3-1/8 in. x 3-7/8 in. Displacement: 178.3 cid. Brake horsepower: 43 at 2800 rpm. NACC horsepower: 23.4. Seven main bearings. Solid valve lifters. Carburetor: Tillotson model one-barrel.
CHASSIS [Whippet Series 96]: Wheelbase: 100-1/4 in. Tires: 28 x 4.75 in.
TECHNICAL: Selective sliding gear transmission. Speeds: 3F/1R. Floor-mounted gearshift lever. Borg & Beck clutch. Bango type rear axle. Overall ratio: 4.5:1. Four-wheel mechanical brakes. Wood spoke wheels.
OPTIONS: Front bumper. Rear bumper. Single sidemount. Special paint. Rearview mirror.
HISTORICAL: Introduced: [four-cylinder] Aug. 1927; [six-cylinder] April 1928. A new plant in Maywood, Calif. was built this year.

1929
WILLYS-OVERLAND

WHIPPET — SERIES 96/96A — FOUR-CYLINDER: The new Superior Whippet 96A line was promoted for 1929. This series featured a new radiator that was peaked, instead of rounded, at the top. There was full-crown front fenders and torpedo headlights, too. A heavier molding ran down the edge of the hood and cowl sides, curving up across the cowl right at the base of the windshield. There was a longer wheelbase, enlarged standard four-cylinder engine and also a larger optional six. Truck models offered on the Whippet 1/2-ton commercial chassis were the same available in the past. Fingertip controls mounted in a new unit-grouped instrument cluster were another highly-touted 96A feature. The early 1929 models were a carryover of the 1928 series.
I.D. DATA: Serial number located on plate on dash; also on left side of frame member ahead of front spring rear hanger; also on right side of frame at rear end; also under driver's seat cushion. Engine numbers located on either front or rear on upper corner of cylinder block on right side. The 1929 Whippet 96 had serial numbers 227,903-321,000. The 1929 Whippet 96A had serial numbers 321,001-435,092. Both series included both passenger cars and motor trucks.

Model	Body Type	Price	Weight	Prod. Total
Whippet Model 96 — 1/2-Ton — 100.25 in. w.b.				
96	Chassis	370	1469	—
96	Pickup	—	—	—
96	Screen	—	—	—
96	Canopy	—	—	—
96	Panel	—	—	—
96	Sedan	—	—	—
Whippet Model 96A — 1/2-Ton — 100.25 in. w.b.				
96A	Chassis	405	1691	—
96A	Pickup	—	—	—
96A	Canopy	—	—	—
96A	Screen	—	—	—
96A	Panel	—	—	—
96A	Sedan	—	—	—

ENGINE [Base Model 96A]: Inline. L-head. Four-cylinder. Cast iron block. Bore & stroke: 3-1/8 in. x 4-3/4- in. Displacement: 145.7 cid. Compression ratio: 5.4:1. Brake horsepower: 40 at 3200 rpm. Horsepower: 15.6 (NACC). Three main bearings. Solid valve lifters. Carburetor: Tillotson model one-barrel.
ENGINE [Optional Model 98A]: Inline. L-head. Six-cylinder. Cast iron block. Bore & stroke: 3-1/8 in. x 3-7/8 in. Displacement: 178.3 cid. Compression ratio: 5.12:1. Brake horsepower: 50 at 3000 rpm. Horsepower: 23.4 (NACC). Seven main bearings. Solid valve lifters. Carburetor: Tillotson model one-barrel. This was the engine from the 112.50 in. wheelbase Whippet 98A passenger car. The engine was optional in trucks.
CHASSIS [Whippet 96]: Wheelbase: 100.25 in. Tires: 28 x 4.75 in.
CHASSIS [Whippet 96A]: Wheelbase: 103.25 in. Tires: 28 x 4.75 in. or 4.75 x 19 in.
TECHNICAL: Selective sliding gear transmission. Speeds: 3F/1R. Floor-mounted gearshift lever. Borg & Beck clutch. Semi-floating rear axle. Overall ratio: 4.5:1. Four-wheel mechanical brakes. Wood spoke wheels.
OPTIONS: Front bumper. Sidemounted spare tire. Special paint. Deluxe equipment. Rearview mirror. Side curtains. Auxiliary passenger seat. Aftermarket bodies. Fog lamps.
HISTORICAL: Introduced [Models 96/98] Aug. 1928; [Model 96A] Nov. 1928; [Model 98A] Dec. 1928.

1930 WILLYS-OVERLAND

WILLYS-WHIPPET — SERIES 96A/SERIES 98B — ALL ENGINES: The Whippet 96A was carried over for 1930 in the same line of six truck models. These were all of the New Superior style. A newly-listed feature was a single-lever controlled windshield. A change of this year was a new line of 110 in. wheelbase trucks, merchandised as the Willys' Six Model 98B. This was technically the Whippet 98 passenger car converted to commercial vehicle form and equipped with a bored-out six-cylinder engine that now displaced 193 cid. Stylingwise, the Willys six looked distinct from the Whippet. It had a taller, more rounded radiator shell, bright metal torpedo headlights, front parking lamps (unusually mounted below the headlights on the tie-bar) and a hood with vertical louvers arranged in three separate groups.
I.D. DATA: Serial number located on plate on dash; also on left side of frame member ahead of front spring rear hanger; also on right side of frame at rear end; also under driver's seat cushion. Engine numbers located on either front or rear on upper corner of cylinder block on right side. The 1930 Whippet had serial numbers 435,093-465,000. The 1930 Willys 98B had serial numbers 131,001-154,843. Both series included both passenger cars and motor trucks.

Model	Body Type	Price	Weight	Prod. Total
Whippet Model 96A — 1/2-Ton — 103.25 in. w.b. — Four				
96A	Chassis	405	1691	—
96A	Pickup	—	—	—
96A	Canopy	—	—	—
96A	Screen	—	—	—
96A	Panel	—	—	—
96A	Sedan	—	—	—
Willys Model 98B — 1/2-Ton — 110 in. w.b. — Six				
98B	Chassis	525	1903	—
98B	Pickup	—	—	—
98B	Canopy	—	—	—
98B	Screen	—	—	—
98B	Panel	—	—	—
98B	Sedan	—	—	—

ENGINE [Base Model 96A]: Inline. L-head. Four-cylinder. Cast iron block. Bore & stroke: 3-1/8 in. x 4-3/4 in. Displacement: 145.7 cid. Compression ratio: 5.4:1. Brake horsepower: 40 at 3200 rpm. Horsepower: 15.6 (NACC). Three main bearings. Solid valve lifters. Carburetor: Tillotson model one-barrel.
ENGINE [Optional, Model 96A]: Inline. L-head. Six-cylinder. Cast iron block. Bore & stroke: 3.125 in. x 3.875 in. Displacement: 178.3 cid. Compression ratio: 5.12:1. Brake horsepower: 50 at 3000 rpm. Horsepower: 23.4 (NACC). Seven main bearings. Solid valve lifters. Carburetor: Tillotson model one-barrel. This was designated the 98A engine and was still an option for the Whippet 96A, even though the new Willys 98B had a larger six-cylinder engine.
ENGINE [Model 98B]: Inline. L-head. Six-cylinder. Cast iron block. Bore & stroke: 3-1/4 in. x 3-7/8 in. Displacement: 192.9 cid. Brake horsepower: 65 at 3400 rpm. Horsepower: 25.35 (NACC). Seven main bearings. Solid valve lifters. Carburetor: Tillotson model J1A.
CHASSIS [Whippet 96A]: Wheelbase: 103.25 in. Tires: 4.75 x 19 in.
CHASSIS [Willys 98B]: Wheelbase: 110 in. Tires: 5.00 x 19 in.
TECHNICAL: Selective sliding gear transmission. Speeds: 3F/1R. Floor-mounted gearshift lever. Borg & Beck clutch. Semi-floating rear axle. Four-wheel mechanical brakes. Wood spoke or wire spoke wheels.
OPTIONS: Front bumper. Sidemounted spare tire. Special paint. Deluxe equipment. Rearview mirror. Side curtains. Passenger auxiliary seat. Fog lamps. Aftermarket bodies.
HISTORICAL: Introduced: [Whippet] Oct. 1929; [Willys Six] Dec. 1929. Calendar year registrations: [all trucks] 4,264. John North Willys stepped down from the presidency this year. Linwood A. Miller, formerly a high-ranking vice president, took over the top spot. In March, Mr. Willys became the first U.S. Ambassador to Poland.

1931 WILLYS-OVERLAND

WILLYS-WHIPPET — SERIES C-113 — ALL ENGINES: The 96A and 98B were carried over as early 1931 models. In January 1931, a new C-113 model superseded or joined the other series. This new line offered the same truck body styles equipped with the 193 cid six-cylinder engine on a new 113 in. wheelbase chassis. Four-wheel mechanical brakes and an Autolite ignition system remained standard equipment. Styling characteristics included a high, narrow radiator with rounded top, torpedo headlights, vertically louvered hood and split windshield.
I.D. DATA: Serial number located on plate on dash; also on left side of frame member ahead of front spring rear hanger; also on right side of frame at rear end; also under driver's seat cushion. Engine numbers located on either front or rear on upper corner of cylinder block on right side.
Serial numbers, passenger cars and trucks: [96A] 465,001-470,247; [98B] 154,844-ending number; [C-113] 1001-2399. (C-113 is truck only.)

Model	Body Type	Price	Weight	Prod. Total
Whippet Model 96A — 1/2-Ton — 103.25 in. w.b. — Four				
96A	Chassis	360	1665	—
96A	Pickup	—	—	—
96A	Screen	—	—	—
96A	Canopy	—	—	—
96A	Panel	—	—	—
96A	Sedan	—	—	—
Willys Model 98B — 1/2-Ton — 110 in. w.b. — Six				
98B	Chassis	525	1905	—
98B	Pickup	—	—	—
98B	Canopy	—	—	—
98B	Screen	—	—	—
98B	Panel	—	—	—
98B	Sedan	—	—	—
Willys Model C-113 — 1/2-Ton — 113 in. w.b. — Six				
C-113	Chassis	395	1923	—
C-113	Pickup	—	—	—
C-113	Canopy	—	—	—
C-113	Screen	—	—	—
C-113	Panel	—	—	—
C-113	Sedan	—	—	—

ENGINE [Model 96A]: Inline. L-head. Four-cylinder. Cast iron block. Bore & stroke: 3-1/8 in. x 4-3/4 in. Displacement: 145.7 cid. Compression ratio: 5.4:1. Brake horsepower: 40 at 3200 rpm. Horsepower: 15.6 (NACC). Three main bearings. Solid valve lifters. Carburetor: Tillotson model one-barrel. The 50 hp six-cylinder engine was optional; see 1930 specifications.
ENGINE [Model 98B]: Inline. L-head. Six-cylinder. Cast iron block. Bore & stroke: 3-1/4 in. x 3-7/8 in. Displacement: 192.9 cid. Compression ratio: 5.6:1. Brake horsepower: 65 at 3400 rpm. Horsepower: 25.35 (NACC). Four main bearings. Solid valve lifters. Carburetor: Tillotson model J1A.
ENGINE [Model C-113]: Inline. L-head. Six-cylinder. Cast iron block. Bore & stroke: 3-1/4 in. x 3-7/8 in. Displacement: 192.9 cid. Compression ratio: 5.6:1. Brake horsepower: 65 at 3400 rpm. Horsepower: 25.35 (NACC). Four main bearings. Solid valve lifters. Carburetor: Tillotson model J1A.
CHASSIS [Whippet 96A]: Wheelbase: 103-1/4 in. Tires: 28 x 4.75 in.
CHASSIS [Willys 98B]: Wheelbase: 110 in. Tires: 29 x 5.00 in.
CHASSIS [Willys C-113]: Wheelbase: 113 in. Tires: 29 x 5.00 in.
TECHNICAL [All]: Selective sliding gear transmission. Speeds: 3F/1R. Floor-mounted gearshift lever. Borg & Beck clutch. Semi-floating rear axle. Four-wheel mechanical brakes. Wood spoke or wire wheels.
OPTIONS: Front bumper. Sidemounted spare tire. Special paint. Deluxe equipment. Rearview mirror. Side curtains. Passenger auxiliary seat. Fog lamps. Aftermarket bodies.
HISTORICAL: Introduced: [Whippet] Sept. 1930; [Willys Six] Sept. 1930; [C-113] Jan. 1931. Calendar year registrations: 3,131 [all trucks].
The C-113 superseded the Whippet 96A and Willys six 98B in Jan. 1931.

1932 WILLYS-OVERLAND

WILLYS — SERIES C-113 — SIX-CYLINDER: Carried over for 1932 for Willys truck customers wanting light-duty models was the C-113. This 1/2-ton again came as a chassis only, or with any of five factory-approved truck bodies. There were the three other models in the C series, but the 113 was the only light-duty. The C-101, C-131 and C-157 were rated for 1-1/2-tons.
I.D. DATA: Serial number located on plate on dash; also on left side of frame member ahead of front spring rear hanger; also on right side of frame at rear end; also under driver's seat cushion. Engine numbers located on either front or rear on upper corner of cylinder block on right side. Serial numbers 2400-3893 were used for 1932-1933 models.

Model	Body Type	Price	Weight	Prod. Total
Willys Model C-113 — 1/2-Ton — 113 in. w.b. — Six				
C-113	Chassis	415	1923	—
C-113	Pickup	—	—	—
C-113	Canopy	—	—	—
C-113	Screen	—	—	—
C-113	Panel	—	—	—
C-113	Sedan	—	—	—

ENGINE [Model C-113]: Inline. L-head. Six-cylinder. Cast iron block. Bore & stroke: 3-1/4 in. x 3-7/8 in. Displacement: 192.9 cid. Compression ratio: 5.26:1. Brake horsepower: 65 at 3400 rpm. Horsepower: 25.35 (NACC). Four main bearings. Solid valve lifters. Carburetor: Tillotson model J1A.

CHASSIS [Willys C-113]: Wheelbase: 113 in. Tires: 29 x 5.00 in.

TECHNICAL: Selective sliding gear transmission. Speeds: 3F/1R. Floor-mounted gearshift lever. Borg & Beck clutch. Semi-floating rear axle. Four-wheel mechanical brakes. Steel spoke wheels.

OPTIONS: Front bumper. Sidemounted spare tire. Special paint. Deluxe equipment. Rear-view mirror. Side curtains. Passenger auxiliary seat. Fog lamps. Aftermarket bodies.

HISTORICAL: Introduced: Jan. 1932. Calendar year registrations: [All trucks] 1,132. The C-113 was listed as the Willys Six. At the request of President Hoover, John North Willys returned to Toledo to manage Willys-Overland, since the depression had badly hurt the firm.

1933 WILLYS-OVERLAND

WILLYS — SERIES 77 — FOUR-CYLINDER: New from Willys for 1933 was a stylish new 77 light-duty series rated for 1/2-ton. These trucks had a highly streamlined appearance with a hood that sloped down in the front to meet a new teardrop-shaped, veed radiator grille. Four slanted vent doors decorated the rear of the hoodsides, near the cowl. Front fenders had skirted valances and fared-in headlights. There was a veed, single-bar front two-piece bumper. Rear fenders were also streamlined and flared outward at the rear. There was a fin-like hood ornament, one-piece windshield and new steel artillery wheels. These were rather small trucks, perched on a short 100 in. wheelbase. The sole factory model was a panel delivery. The side-opening rear door (it opened towards the street) had a small window and rear-mounted spare tire carrier.

I.D. DATA: Serial number located on plate on dash; also on left side of frame member ahead of front spring rear hanger; also on right side of frame at rear end; also under driver's seat cushion. Engine numbers located on either front or rear on upper corner of cylinder block on right side. Same serial numbers as 1932.

Model	Body Type	Price	Weight	Prod. Total
Willys Model 77 — 1/2-Ton — 100 in. w.b.				
77	Panel	415	—	—

ENGINE: Inline. L-head. Four-cylinder. Cast iron block. Bore & stroke: 3-1/8 in. x 4-3/8 in. Displacement: 134.2 cid. Compression ratio: 5.13:1. Brake horsepower: 48 at 3200 rpm. Horsepower: 15.63 (NACC). Three main bearings. Solid valve lifters. Carburetor: Tillotson model one-barrel.

CHASSIS [Willys 77]: Wheelbase: 100 in. Tires: 17 x 5.00 in.

TECHNICAL: Selective sliding gear transmission. Speeds: 3F/1R. Floor-mounted gearshift lever. Four-wheel mechanical brakes. Steel artillery wheels.

OPTIONS: Front bumper. Sidemounted spare tire. Special paint. Deluxe equipment. Rear-view mirror. Side curtains. Passenger auxiliary seat. Fog lamps. Aftermarket bodies.

HISTORICAL: Introduced: Jan. 1933. Calendar year registrations: [All trucks] 233. Willys 77 introduced and available in panel delivery form. Most C-113 models titled in 1933 were built in the 1932 calendar year. Willys trucks built in 1933 are very rare. In 1932, the company was on the verge of receivership and dropped all of its current model lines in place of a new 1933 product called the Willys 77. In February 1933, the firm officially entered bank receivership.

1934 WILLYS-OVERLAND

WILLYS — SERIES 77 — FOUR-CYLINDER: The Willys 77 was again marketed in 1934. Yearly changes included new wire spoke wheels and redesigned hood louvers. There were four slightly curved, horizontal louvers on the rear sides of the hood. Each was shorter than the one above it. A panel delivery represented the factory's model lineup.

I.D. DATA: Serial number located on left frame ahead of front spring rear hanger; also on tag attached to left front door sill; also on plate on front right-hand side of front frame cross-member at center. Starting: 13,821. Ending: 27,005. Engine numbers located on right side, front upper corner of cylinder block.

Model	Body Type	Price	Weight	Prod. Total
Willys Model 77 — 1/2-Ton — 100 in. w.b. — Four				
77	Panel	415	2130	—

ENGINE [Model 77]: Inline. L-head. Four-cylinder. Cast iron block. Bore & stroke: 3-1/8 in. x 4-3/8 in. Displacement: 134.2 cid. Compression ratio: 5.13:1. Brake horsepower: 48 at 3200 rpm. Horsepower: 15.63 (NACC). Three main bearings. Solid valve lifters. Carburetor: Tillotson model one-barrel.

CHASSIS [Willys 77]: Wheelbase: 100 in. Tires: 17 x 5.00 in.

TECHNICAL: Selective sliding gear transmission. Speeds: 3F/1R. Floor-mounted gearshift lever. Four-wheel mechanical brakes. Wire spoke wheels.

HISTORICAL: Calendar year registrations: [all trucks] 25. Most trucks of the 1934 design were built late in calendar year 1933. These are still quite rare. Total registrations of trucks in the two calendar years came to just 258 vehicles.

1935 WILLYS-OVERLAND

WILLYS — SERIES 77 — FOUR-CYLINDER: For 1935, the Willys 77 truck had a higher, more-conventional veed grille and straighter (non-sloping) hoodline. The grille looked somewhat Buick-like. Decorating the sides of the hood were five slanted, oblong bubbles for air venting. They looked LaSalle-like. Someone at Willys seemed to appreciate GM design. Parking lights were placed alongside the radiator, under the fared-in headlights. The bumper was again a two-piece affair. It was veed towards the center. Wire wheels continued. The fenders were done in black; the rest of the truck in body color. A new cab pickup model came out this season. Both it and the panel were priced below $500.

I.D. DATA: Serial number located on left frame ahead of front spring rear hanger; also on tag attached to left front door sill; also on plate on front right-hand side of front frame cross member at center. Starting: [pickup]: 27,001 up. Starting: [panel]: 27,001 up. Engine numbers located on right side, front upper corner of cylinder block.

Model	Body Type	Price	Weight	Prod. Total
Willys Model 77 — 1/2-Ton — 100 in. w.b. — Four				
77	Pickup	475	2040	—
77	Panel	495	2195	—

ENGINE [Model 77]: Inline. L-head. Four-cylinder. Cast iron block. Bore & stroke: 3-1/8 in. x 4-3/8 in. Displacement: 134.2 cid. Compression ratio: 5.23:1. Brake horsepower: 48 at 3400 rpm. Horsepower: 15.63 (NACC). Three main bearings. Solid valve lifters. Carburetor: Tillotson model one-barrel.

CHASSIS [Willys 77]: Wheelbase: 100 in. Tires: 17 x 5.00 in.

TECHNICAL: Selective sliding gear transmission. Speeds: 3F/1R. Floor-mounted gearshift lever. Overall ratio: 4.3:1. Four-wheel mechanical brakes. Wire spoke wheels.

HISTORICAL: Introduced: Jan. 1, 1935. Calendar year registrations: [All trucks] 2,280. In January 1935, John North Willys was again elected as company president, but five months later he suffered a heart attack. He died in August. By December, reorganization of his firm was completed by others.

1936 WILLYS-OVERLAND

1936 Willys Series 77 1/2-Ton Panel (DFW/MVMA)

WILLYS — SERIES 77 — FOUR-CYLINDER: Changes to the 1936 Willys 77 trucks were minor. There was a curvier bumper and artillery style steel spoke wheels made their reappearance. Handles were seen on the sides of the hood, underneath the rearmost pair of bubble vents. Weights and prices of both models fell a little. The depression was probably responsible for some reduction in standard equipment that allowed lower prices and resulted in less bulk.

I.D. DATA: Serial number located on left frame ahead of front spring rear hanger; also on tag attached to left front door sill; also on plate on front right-hand side of front frame cross-member at center. Starting: [pickup]: 37,426 up. Starting: [delivery]: 35,939 up. Engine numbers located on right side, front upper corner of cylinder block.

Model	Body Type	Price	Weight	Prod. Total
Willys Model 77 — 1/2-Ton — 100 in. w.b. — Four				
77	Pickup	395	2000	—
77	Panel	415	2130	—

ENGINE [Model 77]: Inline. L-head. Four-cylinder. Cast iron block. Bore & stroke: 3-1/8 in. x 4-3/8 in. Displacement: 134.2 cid. Compression ratio: 5.7:1. Brake horsepower: 48 at 3200 rpm. Horsepower: 15.63 (NACC). Three main bearings. Solid valve lifters. Carburetor: Tillotson model one-barrel.

CHASSIS [Willys 77]: Wheelbase: 100 in. Tires: 17 x 5.00 in.

TECHNICAL: Selective sliding gear transmission. Speeds: 3F/1R. Floor-mounted gearshift lever. Overall ratio: 4.3:1. Four-wheel mechanical brakes. Steel artillery spoke wheels.

HISTORICAL: Introduced: Sept. 10, 1935. Calendar year registrations: [All trucks] 2,441. Calendar year production: Willys produced 23,831 vehicles of all types (cars and trucks) in calendar 1936. Willys-Overland's receivership status ended in February 1936.

1937 WILLYS-OVERLAND

1937 Willys 1/2-Ton Pickup (DFW/WRHS)

WILLYS — SERIES 77 — FOUR-CYLINDER: The Willys 77 was completely restyled in 1937. Features included an all-steel body and top, rounded ship's prow front having a grille that was integral with the hood, and a hood that was hinged at the cowl to open in alligator fashion. There were actually two grilles, one on each side of the prow. They consisted of vertical louvers following the rounded hood contour with three louvers near (but below) the top louver extending back to the cowl. The rounded fenders extended outwards at the top contour to form bee hive-shaped headlight housings which were faired into the fenders and decorated with horizontal ribs on either side. The bumper was a one-piece, single-bar design with guards at each frame horn. These were unusual, but cute-looking trucks. Pickup and panel bodies were again made available.

I.D. DATA: Serial number located on left frame ahead of front spring rear hanger; also on tag attached to left front door sill; also on plate on front right-hand side of front frame cross member at center. Starting: 61,000. Ending: 64,467. Engine numbers located on right side, front upper corner of cylinder block.

Model	Body Type	Price	Weight	Prod. Total
Willys Model 77 — 1/2-Ton — 100 in. w.b. — Four				
77	Pickup	395	2000	—
77	Panel	415	2130	—

ENGINE [Model 77]: Inline. L-head. Four-cylinder. Cast iron block. Bore & stroke: 3-1/8 in. x 4-3/8 in. Displacement: 134.2 cid. Compression ratio: 5.7:1. Brake horsepower: 48 at 3200 rpm. Horsepower: 15.63 (NACC). Three main bearings. Solid valve lifters. Carburetor: Tillotson model one-barrel.
CHASSIS [Willys 77]: Wheelbase: 100 in. Tires: 16 x 5.50 in.
TECHNICAL: Manual transmission. Speeds: 3F/1R. Floor-mounted gearshift lever. Overall ratio: 4.3:1. Four-wheel mechanical brakes. Steel disc wheels.
HISTORICAL: Introduced: Nov. 1936. Calendar year registrations: 1,122 [All trucks]. Calendar year production: Willys produced 63,465 vehicles of all types (cars and trucks) in calendar 1937. The redesigned Model 77 debuted as a 1937 truck.

1938 WILLYS-OVERLAND

1938 Willys Model 77 Pickup

WILLYS — MODEL 38 — FOUR-CYLINDER: Characteristics of the new 1938 Willys 38 trucks included a newly designed radiator, rain troughs over the doors and a water temperature indicator installed separately from other instruments. The rounded grille and general styling of body and fenders was practically the same as the 1937 model. A new stake truck was cataloged, plus three chassis models. These were: chassis-only; chassis and cowl and chassis cowl and cab. The pickup and panel continued.

I.D. DATA: Serial number located on left frame ahead of front spring rear hanger; also on tag attached to left front door sill; also on plate on front right-hand side of front frame cross member at center. Starting: 65,001. Ending: 89,000. Engine numbers located on right side, front upper corner of cylinder block.

Model	Body Type	Price	Weight	Prod. Total
Willys Model 38 — 1/2-Ton — 100 in. w.b. — Four				
38	Chassis	330	1285	—
38	Chassis & Cowl	400	1677	—
38	Chassis & Cab	490	1908	—
38	Pickup	530	2226	—
38	Stake	545	2220	—
38	Panel	824	2568	—

1938 Willys-Overland Model 77 Pickup (OCW)

ENGINE [Model 38]: Inline. L-head. Four-cylinder. Cast iron block. Bore & stroke: 3-1/8 in. x 4-3/8 in. Displacement: 134.2 cid. Brake horsepower: 48 at 3200 rpm. Horsepower: 15.63 (NACC). Three main bearings. Solid valve lifters. Carburetor: Tillotson model one-barrel.
CHASSIS [Willys Model 38]: Wheelbase: 100 in. Tires: 16 x 5.50 in.
TECHNICAL: Manual transmission. Speeds: 3F/1R. Floor-mounted gearshift lever. Overall ratio: 4.3:1. Four-wheel mechanical brakes. Steel disc wheels.
OPTIONS: Rear bumper. Grille guard. Dual taillamps. Dual windshield wipers. Dual sun visors. Rearview mirror(s). Ashtray (front). Rear fender protection guards. Locking gas cap. Tailpipe extension. Wheel trim rings. Dual horns. License plate frames. Radio antenna. Radio. Radiator cap with blow-off valve. Mirror clock. Glove compartment with door. Grille cover. Seat covers. Aluminum cylinder head. Heater. Heater/defroster. Custom radio with aerial. Windshield wiper vacuum booster pump.
HISTORICAL: Introduced: Sept. 20, 1937. Calendar year registrations: [All trucks] 1,889. Calendar year production: Willys produced 26,286 vehicles of all types [cars and trucks] in calendar 1938. Barney Roos, a former president of the Society of Automotive engineers, came to Willys-Overland this year after a stint with the Rootes automotive companies in England. He assumed the title of chief engineer.

1939 WILLYS-OVERLAND

1939 Willys Walk-In Panel Delivery Van (DFW/MVMA)

WILLYS-OVERLAND — SERIES 38/SERIES 48 — FOUR-CYLINDER: The Overland name was revived for a time in 1939. Later in the year, it was changed to Willys-Overland again. The front end was revamped into a more conventional ship's prow design with horizontal louvers from only the middle down. Other louvers were punched into the front fender apron on either side of center. A chrome molding, at beltline height, extended across the sides of the hood and dipped down at the front. The hood ornament looked like a backwards fin. The headlamp housings were thinner and less rounded; the lenses

themselves were shield-shaped and rather unusual. The front bumper was a single-bar type without guards. However, guards, dual windshield wipers, dual sun visors and dual taillights were made part of a Deluxe equipment package. Deluxe models were known as 48s. A 440 cab-over-engine delivery van is also mentioned in some sources as a 1939 product.

I.D. DATA: Serial number located on left frame ahead of front spring rear hanger; also on tag attached to left front door sill; also on plate on front right-hand side of front frame cross member at center. Starting: [model 38] 89,001; [model 48] 91,751. Ending: [model 38] 91,750; [model 48] 94,375. Engine numbers located on right side, front upper corner of cylinder block.

1939 Willys Model 38 1/2-Ton Pickup (DFW/MVMA)

Model	Body Type	Price	Weight	Prod. Total
Willys Model 38 — 1/2-Ton — 100 in. w.b. — Four				
38	Chassis	330	1285	—
38	Chassis & Cowl	400	1677	—
38	Chassis & Cab	490	1908	—
38	Pickup	530	2226	—
38	Stake	545	2220	—
38	Panel	824	2568	—
Willys Model 48 — 1/2-Ton — 100 in. w.b. — Four				
48	Pickup	530	2226	—
48	Stake	545	2220	—
48	Panel	824	2568	—

ENGINE [Both Series]: Inline. L-head. Four-cylinder. Cast iron block. Bore & stroke: 3-1/8 in. x 4-3/8 in. Displacement: 134.2 cid. Brake horsepower: 48 at 3200 rpm. Horsepower: 15.6 (NACC). Three main bearings. Solid valve lifters. Carburetor: Tillotson model one-barrel.
ENGINE [Optional]: Inline. L-head. Four-cylinder. Cast iron block. Bore & stroke: 3-1/8 in. x 4-3/8 in. Displacement: 134.2 cid. Brake horsepower: 61 at 3600 rpm. Horsepower: 15.6 (NACC). Three main bearings. Solid valve lifters. Carburetor: Carter model WO-4505.
CHASSIS [Willys Model 38]: Wheelbase: 100 in. Tires: 16 x 5.50 in.
CHASSIS [Willys Model 48]: Wheelbase: 100 in. Tires: 16 x 5.00 in.
TECHNICAL: Manual transmission. Speeds: 3F/1R. Floor mounted gearshift lever. Overall ratio: [standard] 4.3:1; [optional] 4.55:1. Four-wheel brakes. Steel disc wheels.
OPTIONS: Rear bumper. Grille guard. Dual taillamps. Dual windshield wipers. Dual sun visors. Rearview mirror(s). Ashtray (front). Rear fender protection guards. Locking gas cap. Tailpipe extension. Wheel trim rings. Dual horns. License plate frames. Radio antenna. Radio. Radiator cap with blow-off valve. Mirror clock. Glove compartment with door. Grille cover. Seat covers. Aluminum cylinder head. Heater. Heater/defroster. Custom radio with aerial. Windshield wiper vacuum booster pump.
HISTORICAL: Introduced: Oct. 1938. Calendar year registrations: [All trucks] 1,634. Calendar year production: Willys produced 18,150 cars and trucks in calendar 1939. Innovations: The Model 77 was given hydraulic brakes. The Overland name was temporarily revived, then dropped.

1940 WILLYS-OVERLAND

WILLYS — SERIES 440 — FOUR-CYLINDER: The 1940 Willys 440 trucks still had a 100 in. wheelbase, although cars in this series were up to a stance of 102 in. Styling changes included a more vertical nose; the name Willys in capital letters on the upper rear corner of the hood and new teardrop-shaped headlights. Each side of the prow was trimmed with four chrome speed lines, largest on top, extending to the cowl and descending in size downward. There were two lower grilles, with horizontal bars and rounded outer edges, on the front below the nose. The hood ornament was round with speed lines emanating back from it. The bumper had two oblong openings punched in it, near the center. Deluxe models had dual

windshield wipers, taillights, sun visors and bumper guards. Two four-cylinder engines, 48 hp and 58 hp, were offered as SC-440 and SCOF-440 economy options. Willys trucks finally got hydraulic brakes.

1940 Willys "Quad" Jeep Prototype (OCW)

I.D. DATA: Serial number located on left frame ahead of front spring rear hanger; also on tag attached to left front door sill; also on plate on front right-hand side of front frame crossmember at center. Starting: 17,001. Ending: 49,341. Engine numbers located on right side, front upper corner of cylinder block.

Model	Body Type	Price	Weight	Prod. Total
Willys Model 440 — 1/2-Ton — 102 in. w.b. — Four				
440	Pickup	535	2207	—
440P	Panel	799	2624	—

ENGINE [Model 440]: Inline. L-head. Four-cylinder. Cast iron block. Bore & stroke: 3-1/8 in. x 4-3/8 in. Displacement: 134.2 cid. Brake horsepower: 61 at 3600 rpm. Horsepower: 15.6 (NACC). Three main bearings. Solid valve lifters. Carburetor: Carter model WO-450S.
CHASSIS [Willys Model 440]: Wheelbase: 102 in. Length: 181 in. Front tread: 55 in. Rear tread: 56 in. Tires: 5.50 x 16 in.
TECHNICAL: Manual transmission. Speeds: 3F/1R. Floor-mounted gearshift lever. Single dry disc clutch. Bango rear axle. Overall ratio: [standard] 4.3:1; [optional] 4.55:1; 4.7:1; 5.11:1. Four-wheel hydraulic brakes. Steel disc wheels.
OPTIONS: Rear bumper. Grille guard. Dual taillamps. Dual windshield wipers. Dual sun visors. Rearview mirror(s). Ashtray (front). Rear fender protection guards. Locking gas cap. Tailpipe extension. Wheel trim rings. Dual horns. License plate frames. Radio antenna. Radio. Radiator cap with blow-off valve. Mirror clock. Glove compartment with door. Grille cover. Seat covers. Aluminum cylinder head. Heater. Heater/defroster. Custom radio with aerial. Windshield wiper vacuum booster pump.
HISTORICAL: Introduced: Oct. 1939. Calendar year registrations: [all trucks] 2,291. Calendar year production: Willys produced 32,930 cars, trucks and Jeeps in calendar 1940. The American predecessor of the Jeep was assembled in 1940.

1941 WILLYS-OVERLAND

1941 Willys MA Jeep Universal (OCW)

659

WILLYS — SERIES 441 — FOUR-CYLINDER: A new Willys 441 Americar series of trucks was introduced Feb. 1, 1941. The Willys-Americar trade name went along with numerous technical and styling changes. There was a longer 104 in. wheelbase, more powerful engine and new one-piece "electric shaver" lower grille. There were no longer speed lines on the hoodsides; just a beltline extension molding. The cab-over-engine walk-in delivery truck was continued, too. It had art deco rounded front fenders, a split windshield, bug-eye headlamps and a grille with a window sash appearance and the Willys name on top. These vans are supposed to be quite scarce.

I.D. DATA: Serial number located on left frame ahead of front spring rear hanger; also on tag attached to left front door sill; also on plate on front right-hand side of front frame cross-member at center. Starting: 50,001. Ending: 80,100. Engine numbers located on right side, front upper corner of cylinder block.

Model	Body Type	Price	Weight	Prod. Total
Willys Model 441 — 1/2-Ton — 104 in. w.b. — Four				
441	Chassis	360	1285	—
441	Chassis & Cowl	442	1677	—
441	Chassis & Cab	542	1908	—
441	Pickup	587	2207	—
441	COE Panel	869	2624	—

ENGINE [Series 441]: Inline. L-head. Four-cylinder. Cast iron block. Bore & stroke: 3-1/8 in. x 4-3/8 in. Displacement: 134.2 cid. Compression ratio: 6.48:1. Brake horsepower: 63 at 3800 rpm. Horsepower: 15.6 (NACC). Three main bearings. Solid valve lifters. Carburetor: Carter model WO-507S.

CHASSIS [Willys Model 441]: Wheelbase: 104 in. Length: 181 in. Front tread: 55 in. Rear tread: 56 in. Tires: 5.50 x 16 in.

TECHNICAL: Manual synchromesh transmission. Speeds: 3F/1R. Floor-mounted gearshift lever. Single dry disc clutch. Hypoid rear axle. Overall ratio: 4.3:1 and others. Four-wheel hydraulic brakes. Steel disc wheels.

OPTIONS: Rear bumper. Grille guard. Dual taillamps. Dual windshield wipers. Dual sun visors. Rearview mirror(s). Front ashtray. Rear fender protection guards. Locking gas cap. Tailpipe extension. Wheel trim rings. Dual horns. License plate frames. Radio antenna. Radio. Radiator cap with blow-off valve. Mirror clock. Glove compartment with door. Grille cover. Seat covers. Aluminum cylinder head. Heater. Heater/defroster. Custom radio with aerial. Windshield wiper vacuum booster pump.

HISTORICAL: Introduced: Aug. 28, 1940. Calendar year registrations: [all trucks] 2,031. Calendar year production: Willys produced 28,014 vehicles of all types in calendar 1941. Hypoid rear axle adopted. Willys-Overland finished its 1941 model run on July 30, 1941. Production of 1942 models commenced on Aug. 2, 1941. Willys-Overland spent $2,170,000 expanding its Toledo factory in 1941. In its 1941 financial statement assets of $7,358,162 were listed against liabilities of $5,551,075. Working capital was $1,807,087. Earnings per common share were .86 and book value of a share of common stock was $3.54. Company officers included chairman of the board W.M. Canaday, president J.W. Frazer, sales manager G.H. Bell and chief engineer D.G. Roos.

1942 WILLYS-OVERLAND

WILLYS — SERIES 442 — FOUR-CYLINDER: Among characteristics of its 1942 trucks, Willys noted that the four-cylinder "Go-Devil" motor was the same one used in U.S. Army Jeeps. Overdrive was standard on some models this year, but probably just an option for trucks. Styling was identical to 1941, unless some blackout models were built late-in-the-year. These would have had painted trim, of course.

I.D. DATA: Serial number located on left frame ahead of front spring rear hanger; also on tag attached to left front door sill; also on plate on front right-hand side of front frame cross-member at center. Starting: 80,101. Ending: 92,020. Engine numbers located on right side, front upper corner of cylinder block.

Model	Body Type	Price	Weight	Prod. Total
Willys Model 442 — 1/2-Ton — 104 in. w.b. — Four				
442	Chassis	410	1272	—
442	Chassis & Cowl	525	1670	—
442	Chassis & Cab	642	1900	—
442	Pickup	732	2238	—
442	Panel	950	2708	—

1942 Willys MB Jeep Universal (Stan Brown)

WILLYS — SERIES 442 — FOUR-CYLINDER: Among characteristics of its 1942 trucks, Willys noted that the four-cylinder "Go-Devil" motor was the same one used in U.S. Army Jeeps. Overdrive was standard on some models this year, but probably just an option for trucks. Styling was identical to 1941, unless some blackout models were built late-in-the-year. These would have had painted trim, of course.

I.D. DATA: Serial number located on left frame ahead of front spring rear hanger; also on tag attached to left front door sill; also on plate on front right-hand side of front frame cross-member at center. Starting: 80,101. Ending: 92,020. Engine numbers located on right side, front upper corner of cylinder block.

Model	Body Type	Price	Weight	Prod. Total
Willys Model 442 — 1/2-Ton — 104 in. w.b. — Four				
442	Chassis	410	1272	—
442	Chassis & Cowl	525	1670	—
442	Chassis & Cab	642	1900	—
442	Pickup	732	2238	—
442	Panel	950	2708	—

ENGINE [Series 442]: Inline. L-head. Four-cylinder. Cast iron block. Bore & stroke: 3-1/8 in. x 4-3/8 in. Displacement: 134.2 cid. Compression ratio: 6.48:1. Brake horsepower: 63 at 3800 rpm. Horsepower: 15.6 (NACC). Three main bearings. Solid valve lifters. Carburetor: Carter model WO-507S.

CHASSIS [Willys Model 442]: Wheelbase: 104 in. Length: 181 in. Front tread: 55 in. Rear tread: 58 in. Tires: 5.50 x 16 in.

TECHNICAL: Manual synchromesh transmission. Speeds: 3F/1R. Floor-mounted gearshift lever. Single dry disc clutch. Hypoid rear axle. Overall ratio: [standard] 4.3:1. Four-wheel hydraulic brakes. Steel disc wheels. Overdrive.

OPTIONS: Rear bumper. Grille guard. Dual taillamps. Dual windshield wipers. Dual sun visors. Rearview mirror(s). Front ashtray. Rear fender protection guards. Locking gas cap. Tailpipe extension. Wheel trim rings. Dual horns. License plate frames. Radio antenna. Radio. Radiator cap with blow-off valve. Mirror clock. Glove compartment with door. Grille cover. Seat covers. Aluminum cylinder head. Heater. Heater/defroster. Custom radio w/ aerial. Windshield wiper vacuum booster pump.

HISTORICAL: Introduced: Sept. 1941. Willys-Overland ended production of 1942 civilian models on Jan. 24, 1942. A truck manufacturing stop order was issued by the War Production Board on March 4. During WWII, together with Ford, the company manufactured the Jeep vehicle originated by American Bantam.

THE DIRECTORY

1916 Rush 1,000 lb. (1/2-Ton) Gasoline Delivery Car (*OLD CARS WEEKLY* Photo)

This section of *THE STANDARD CATALOG of AMERICAN LIGHT-DUTY TRUCKS* is called "The Directory." It presents an alphabetical listing of additional North American companies that manufactured trucks with payload capacities up to and including 1-ton.

Some of these firms are small manufacturers that produced vehicles only for a single year. Others survived in the business for decades. Some are still manufacturing trucks. While the roles they played in the light-duty truck market were not major ones in all cases, they have jointly contributed to its history.

Trucks made by these companies range from commercial versions of golf carts to some rather large 1-ton models. We decided to use the 1-ton cut-off largely because the Antique Automobile Club of America's *OFFICIAL JUDGING MANUAL* specifies a class division at that point. We have not attempted to draw a fine line to define what constitutes a light-duty or heavy-duty 1-ton. Truck collectors will likely consider any "extraneous" facts and photos a bonus, rather than a liability.

The Directory represents an extensive effort to provide light-duty truck enthusiasts with basic information about non-mainstream truck manufacturers. Also included are models from companies, better known for making cars or larger trucks, that produced some light-duty models. Over 100 new listings have been added for this edition. More than 50 of the previous entries have been improved or expanded. There are 25 or more new illustrations.

No claims are made as to this being a complete roster of light-duty truck manufacturers. All of our "standard catalogs" are intended to serve as collectors' guides, rather than history textbooks or encyclopedias. Their purpose is to make a great deal of information available now, not to delay publication until every "missing link" in the chain of history is clasped. As all motor vehicle collectors know, tracing missing links can become a never-ending project.

The Directory is arranged with the brand names of the trucks in alphabetical order. Where several brands used the same trade name, they are sorted both alphabetically and

Standard Catalog of Light-Duty Trucks

661

chronologically. This makes the material self-indexing, so that users can readily find information on a certain marque they wish to read about. In most cases, illustrations of a truck appear below its listing, unless the page layout dictated an above-text position. The pictures are captioned according to either contemporary sources or facts supplied by contributors. Credits for photos are in coded form, which is explained elsewhere. Photos of an actual collector's vehicle indicate the owner's first initial and surname, if known.

In certain cases, the payload capacities of trucks in the illustrations cannot be verified as 1-ton or less. However, in most cases trucks with different GVW ratings made by the same manufacturer will tend to look similar, so the photos will still be a useful identification aid.

Most listings for The Directory in the first edition were compiled by Professor Donald F. Wood, of the Center For World Business, School of Business, San Francisco State University. *THE ENCYCLOPEDIA OF COMMERCIAL VEHICLES*, compiled by G.N. Georgano for Krause Publications in 1978, was a primary reference for the original listings. Additional facts and photos came from automotive and truck historians, including William L. Bailey, Ralph Dunwoodie, John A. Gunnell, Elliott Kahn, Walter O. MacIlvain, John Perala, William Pollock, Willard J. Prentice, James J. Schild, Dennis Schrimpf, Donald J. Summar, J.H. Valentine, Raymond A. Wawryzyniak and James A. Wren.

Krause Publications would welcome any additional photos and information from readers, pertaining to either the models listed in The Directory, or others that should be.

1900 Riker Delivery Van (OCW)

1901 Clark Delivery Van (JAW)

1897 American Electric Vehicle Van (JAW)

1898 Browning Touring Cart (DPL/NAHC)

1902 New Era Commercial Runabout (DPL)

662

1908 Duplex Power-Wagon Stake Bed (JAW)

1911 Rovan Light Delivery Wagon (JAW)

1911 Torbenson Auto Delivery Wagon (JAW)

1912 Brockway Light Delivery Wagon (JAW)

Standard Catalog of Light-Duty Trucks

1936 Stewart 1-Ton Panel Delivery (S. Glasbrenner)

1937 Mack Jr. Cab Express (DFW)

1938 Mack Jr. Pickup (Sonny Glasbrenner)

1939 Fargo Panel Delivery (RPZ)

A

A.B.C. — St. Louis, Mo. — (1908-1911) — This auto manufacturer also turned out 1/2-ton delivery vans. They were powered by two-cylinder engines.

ACASON — Detroit, Mich. — (1915-1922) — This company made assembled trucks. Several 1/2- to 1-ton models were produced by Acason Motor Truck Co. Only the earliest products were in the 1/2-ton class. Later, the firm concentrated on heavier vehicles. These included the Model R 1-ton of 1918-1919; the Model RR 1-ton of 1920-1921; and the "Fast Four," which was a 1922 model with a 3/4-ton rating. Though previously thought to have survived through 1925, a weight book published by the State of Wisconsin in that year states "went out of business in 1922."

ACME — Reading, Pa. — (1905-1906) — The Acme Motor Car Co. also built a small delivery truck.

1906 Acme Delivery Wagon (JAW)

ACME — Cadillac, Mich. — (1915-1931) — This moderately well-known truck was available in sizes ranging from 3/4-ton up to six tons. The manufacturer was named the Cadillac Auto Truck Co.; then the Acme Motor Truck Co. The 1-ton Model B was offered from 1916-1921. It had a four-cylinder engine with a 3-3/4 x 5 in. bore and stroke and 22.5 ALAM horsepower. In 1921, the firm's 3/4-ton Model G was introduced. It was powered by the same motor and stayed in the line for 1922 as the Model 20. There was also a 1922 1-ton called the Model 30. For 1923, the "20" was uprated to 1-ton; the "30" to 1-1/2-tons. For 1925, there was a new 1-ton called the Model 21. It had a new four-cylinder engine with 4-1/4 x 4-1/2 in. dimensions and 28.90 hp.

1925 Acme Laundry Delivery Truck (HACJ/LIAM)

1925 Acme 1-Ton Canopy Top Express (DFW/MG)

1926 Acme Model 21 1-Ton Flyer Express (OCW)

ACME WAGON CO. — Emigsville, Pa. — (1916-1917) — A typical assembled 1-ton truck, this one had a four-cylinder, 17 hp engine, a dry plate clutch, three-speed transmission and bevel gear drive. It was produced as a sideline to the firm's farm wagon business.

ACORN — Cincinnati, Ohio — (1910-1912) — This was a delivery wagon, with 1,000 lb. capacity, manufactured by the Acorn Motor Car Co.

1910 Acorn Commercial Car (OCW)

ACORN — Chicago, Ill. — (1925-1931) — This company made a line of assembled trucks ranging up to 5-tons. The lightest was a 1-ton with a four-cylinder engine.

ADAMS — Findlay, Ohio — (1910-1916) — The Adams Brothers Co.'s first product was a 3/4-ton delivery van; later models were larger, up to 2-1/2-tons.

Standard Catalog of Light-Duty Trucks

1912 Adams 1-Ton Truck (RAW)

1914 Adams Model A Covered Flareboard Express (OCW)

AKRON — Akron, Ohio — (1912-1914) — The Akron Motor Car & Truck Co. offered the 3/4-ton Model 20. It had a four-cylinder Hinkley engine, three-speed transmission, pneumatic tires, bevel gear drive and a 133 in. wheelbase.

ALL-AMERICAN — Chicago, Ill. (1918-1922)/Fremont, Ohio (1922-1925) — The All-American offerings included conventional 1-ton trucks with four-cylinder Herschell-Spillman engines. They had three-speed transmissions, internal gear drives and 130 in. wheelbasea. There was the Model A of 1918-1919; the Model 1 of 1920-1921; and the Model 10 of 1923-1925. All-American Truck Co. manufactured trucks in the former Ogren car factory, in Chicago. In August, 1922, the Fremont Motors Corp. of Ohio took over its production. Though previously thought to have disappeared in 1923, new information indicates the company survived through 1925. The trucks were better-known in some foreign countries as AAs.

1918 All-American Model A 1-Ton Stake (OCW)

ALTER — Cincinnati, Ohio — (1914-1916) — Cincinnati Motors Mfg. Co. built a line including 1,000 lb. (1/2-ton) and 1,800 lb. models. They had four-cylinder engines. The firm later moved to Grand Haven, Mich., and was built by Hamilton Motors Co. It then became part of Panhard and Apex.

AMERICAN — LaFayette, Ind. — (1918) — Little is known about the American Motor Vehicle Co. except that, for a short time, it marketed a 1/2-ton truck. It also built light vehicles for juveniles.

AMERICAN — Detroit, Mich. — American Motor Truck Co. built this 1-ton with a four-cylinder Continental engine and a 108 in. wheelbase. It had a three-speed Brown-Lipe gearbox and double-reduction drive axle.

AMERICAN-ARGO — Saginaw, Mich. — (1912-1918) — Also known as Argo Electric and the American Electric. The Argo Electric Vehicle Co. produced electric trucks in 1/2-ton and 1-ton series. They were conventional machines with 40-cell batteries, shaft drive and a top speed of 16 mph. They had an 86 in. wheelbase, 34 x 3 in. tires and $1,200 chassis price.

Standard Catalog of Light-Duty Trucks

1915 American Argo Model K-10 Express (OCW)

AMERICAN AUSTIN — Butler, Pa. — (1930-1934) — Based on the English Austin Seven, this company's truck line included coupe and panel deliveries through 1933, in which year a Bantam van was added. The panel delivery, a pickup and the Pony Express were in the 1933 line and 1934's series featured a pickup and panel delivery. All had a 14 hp four-cylinder engine and 75 in. wheelbase. Prices were in the $330 to $450 range and weights between 1,035 and 1,300 lbs. were listed. About 8,558 units were built before a bankruptcy that led to reorganization under the name Austin Bantam.

1931 American Austin Panel Delivery (DFW/CC)

1931 American Austin Pickup (DFW/MVMA)

1931 American Austin Model 375 Pickup (F. Alduk)

665

1933 American Austin Service Car (OCW)

AMERICAN BANTAM — Butler, Pa. — (1937-1941) — Restyled by Count Alexis de Sakhnoffsky, the Bantam reappeared in 1937. These mini-trucks retained the Austin wheelbase and engine and came as pickups and panels. Introductory prices of below $400 began to increase to as high as $497 for the fancy Boulevard Delivery of 1938-1939. A business coupe was also available in 1938, at $439, as was a chassis-only. The chassis, pickup and panel survived through 1941, with slightly increased horsepower the final two years. In 1940, Bantam also developed a 1/4-ton light 4x4 for the U.S. Army, which became the prototype for the World War II Jeep. Bantam built 2,500 military Jeeps in 1941, before the demand out-paced its production capability. During the war, the company built two-wheel trailers, but motor vehicle manufacturing ceased.

1938 American Bantam Pickup (OCW)

1938 American Bantam Boulevard Delivery (JAW)

1938 American Bantam Panel Express (WLB)

1938 American Bantam Model 60 Boulevard Delivery

1939 American Bantam Pickup (OCW)

1940 American Bantam Boulevard Delivery (DFW)

666

Standard Catalog of Light-Duty Trucks

1940 American Bantam Boulevard Delivery (OCW)

1940 American Bantam Pickup (F. Alduk)

AMERICAN ELECTRIC — Saginaw, Mich. — (1912-1918) — For information about the American Electric Car Co. see American-Argo.

ANDERSON — Anderson, Ind. — (1909-1910) — This was a high-wheeler, with chain-drive and a two-cylinder engine, built by the Anderson Carriage Manufacturing Co.

1909 Anderson Model B High-Wheel Commercial (WLB)

ANN ARBOR — Ann Arbor, Mich. — (1911-1912) — The Huron River Manufacturing Co. built this open delivery van, powered by a two-cylinder engine, and rated at 3/4-ton.

APEX — Grand Haven, Mich. — (1918-1921) — Hamilton Motors Co.'s models included a 1-ton with a 130 in. wheelbase. It was related to the Alter and the Panhard.

ARGO — Saginaw, Mich. — (1911-1915) — The Argo Electric Vehicle Co. built autos and electric trucks in the 1/2- and 1-ton sizes. For more information see the American Argo listing above.

1914 Argo Model K-10 Platform/Stake (OCW)

1914 Argo Model K-20 Express (OCW)

ARKLA — Little Rock, Ark. — (1965) — The Arkansas-Louisiana Gas Co. built 100 light (840 lb. capacity) trucks for their own use. They had a two-cylinder, 45.5 hp air-cooled pancake engine. Cabs and hoods were made of fiberglass.

ARMLEDER — Cincinnati, Ohio — (1910-1938) — A former wagon maker, this firm built 3/4-ton to 3-1/2-ton trucks through the 1920s and 1-ton to 3-1/2-tons later. Early models were chain-drive fours. Worm drive appeared in 1917 and sixes in 1927. Production was 50-100 units per year. In 1928, Armleder became a division of LeBlond-Schacht.

1914 Armleder Model B Screenside Express (OCW)

ATCO — Kankakee, Ill. — (1919-1923) — In 1920, The American Truck & Trailer Corp. made a four-cylinder, Buda-engined 1-ton truck. It was uprated to 1-1/2-tons for 1921.

ATLANTIC — Newark, N.J. — (1912-1921) — After starting with production of larger trucks, this firm produced 1/2-ton and 1-ton electrics in 1914. There was no basic change until 1920, when the 1/2-ton was dropped. A 1-ton electric with chain-drive was available in 1921.

1914 Atlantic Model C-10 Covered Flareboard (OCW)

1914 Atlantic Model 1-C Covered Flareboard (OCW)

ATLAS — Springfield, Mass. — (1907-1908 to 1912) — Atlas Motor Car Co. first produced large trucks and a 15-passenger sightseeing bus. A new product for 1909 was a 1,250 lb. delivery van with a 20 hp two-cylinder, two-stroke engine listed for $1,900 along with a taxi. Only the taxi was sold in 1910. In 1911, a 3/4-ton Model L delivery van with three-speed gearbox, shaft drive and pneumatic tires was offered for $2,000. It was carried over for 1912, but with a lower price of $1,750.

ATLAS — York, Pa. — (1916-1923) — The Martin Carriage Works manufactured the Atlas. It was a successor to the Martin truck. By 1925, the company name was Atlas Truck Corp. In 1916, the four-cylinder Model 16 was marketed as a 1/2-ton. The Atlas models of 1917 were the Model 17A 1/2-ton and Model 17 3/4-ton delivery trucks powered by Lycoming engines. These were followed by the Model 18 (1/2-ton) and Model 18B (3/4-ton) in 1918. The next year, only the 3/4-ton returned as the Model 19. There were two 3/4-tons...Models 20 and 20C...in 1920. The Model 21 1-ton was offered in 1921-1922 and evolved into the Model 22 for the 1922-1923 selling season. Later trucks were larger. By 1925, the firm was in liquidation. It eventually became part of Selden.

1918 Atlas No. 938 Furniture Body (DFW/SI)

1918 Atlas 1500 Lb. Bakery Delivery (OCW)

1918 Atlas 1500 Lb. Panel Delivery (OCW)

ATTERBURY — Buffalo, N.Y. — (1910-1935) — Started as the Buffalo truck. By 1911, a 1-ton was marketed. There was a 3/4-ton Model A in 1912; a 1-ton Model B in 1913-1914; a 1-ton Model BW in 1915; and the 1-ton GB in 1916. Sales were concentrated near Buffalo. Production was low and the 1-tons disappeared. After 1916, only 2-ton and up models were manufactured.

1914 Atterbury Model B Covered Flareboard (OCW)

AUBURN — Auburn, Ind. — (1936) — Near the end of its life, the Auburn Automobile Co., a well-known auto manufacturer built commercial chassis for ambulance and hearse bodies. Few were sold. The firm was also connected with the Stutz Pak-Age Car.

AUGLAIZE — New Bremen, Ohio — (1911-1916) — This company's light-duty trucks included the Model B 1/2-ton express van with water-cooled two-cylinder engine. It looked like a high-wheeler with small wheels and featured double chain-drive and a planetary transmission. Other 1912 Agalize products were the Model C, a 1,500 lb. Express that sold for $1,650 and the Model D, a 1-ton Express with a $2,200 pricetag. In 1913, the Model B (which was actually rated for 1,200 lbs., rather than an even 1/2-ton) was continued. The price was raised $50 to $1,050. However, the "D" designation was then applied to a 3,000 lb. truck, rather than a 2,000 pounder. In 1914, the company went to the chassis-only configuration with the Model H and Model G. The first was a 1,500 pounder with two-cylinder gas engine priced at $1,000. The other was a $1,400 1-ton In 1915, the price of the Model H was dropped to $950 for the chassis-only, while an Express Wagon could be had for $990. The Model D was also continued at $1,700 for the chassis and $1,750 for the Express Wagon. In Auglaize Motor Car Co.'s final year of truck-making, the 1916 models were marketed without alphabetical designations. They appear to have been basically the same trucks with new prices; $975 for the 3/4-ton and $1,200 for the 1-ton. Period photos show that some of the models looked very automobile-like.

Standard Catalog of Light-Duty Trucks

1914 Auglaize Model G Flareboard (OCW)

1914 Auglaize Model H Flareboard (OCW)

AURORA — Aurora, Ill. — (1908) — The Aurora Motor Works built this 3/4-ton (1,500 lb.) open delivery van with a two-stroke air-cooled twin-cylinder engine, planetary transmission and shaft drive. The wheelbase was 80 in.

AUTOCAR — Ardmore, Pa. — (1908-1954) — Best known for larger trucks, Autocar made a 1-ton Model XVIII electrics 1-ton chassis in 1909 and the 1-ton XX-IRO the next year. The Model E-1F, a 1-ton electric truck, was also offered between 1923-1925. Other Autocars were of heavier capacity. The company did produce a handsome panel delivery which had much more of a "light-duty" look than other Autocars, but it was rated for a 1-1/2-ton payload. Autocar later became part of the White Motor Co.

1927 Autocar Model A 1-1/2-Ton Panel Delivery (OCW)

AUTOMATIC — Buffalo, N.Y. — (1922) — Automatic Transportation Co. built this diminutive electric van with a 65 in. wheelbase and 102 in. overall length. A 24-volt motor drove the truck via chain-drive. Tiller steering was featured.

AUTO-TRUCK — Bangor, Pa. — (1916) — This 1-ton stake truck with a 20 hp Buda four-cylinder engine was $1,250.

AVAILABLE — Chicago, Ill. — (1910-1957) — Though mainly a large truck maker, Available Truck Co. offered a 2,000 lb. (1-ton) model from 1916-1918 designated the Model 1. Later, in 1923-1925, the company introduced a 1-ton "speed" truck called the Hustler.

AVERY — Peoria, Ill. — (1910-1923) — This tractor and farm equipment company built a 1-ton with open cab, four-cylinders and chain-drive in 1910-1911. For 1914-1916, there was a gas-powered 3/4-ton that listed for $2,000 with enclosed panel or express bodies. In the same years, there was a 1-ton Model 41, priced at $1,690 for the chassis. Heavier trucks were built thereafter.

Standard Catalog of Light-Duty Trucks

1914 Avery Model C Covered Flareboard (OCW)

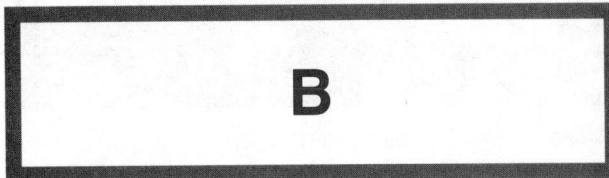

B

BABCOCK — Watertown, N.Y. — (1911-1913) — H.H. Babcock Co. made a 3/4-ton (1,500 lb.) Model G delivery van with a two-cylinder engine under the driver's seat. It used a three-speed transmission and double chain-drive. Wheelbase for this $1,650 truck was 102 in.

BAILEY — Boston, Mass. — (1912-1914) — Bailey & Co. built a 300 lb. rated, battery-powered electric van based on its cyclecar. It had a 106 in. wheelbase, pneumatic tires and a top speed of 20 mph. A light-duty service car was also offered.

1914 Bailey Model E Cyclecar Delivery (OCW)

BAKER — Cleveland, Ohio — (1908-1916) — This company started as Baker Motor Vehicle Co. and built a Model W 1-ton electric truck chassis in 1908. It sold for $2,300. There was no 1909 series. In 1910, a new 1/2-ton electric came in chassis ($1,900) and express ($2,200) configurations. A 1-ton electric was also available in chassis ($2,300); truck ($2,650); and delivery ($2,800) formats. In 1911, the 1/2-ton (now dubbed the Model X) sold only as a $1,200 delivery. The 1-ton was called the 1911-1912 Model O and came as a chassis ($2,300) or delivery ($2,650). It 1912, just the 1/2-ton chassis for $1,900 was listed. During 1913-1914 the Model X and Model O chassis were carried over at the same prices, while a new 500 lb. (1/4-ton) Model W was introduced. It came in panel or open express styles for $1,800. In 1915, the 1/2-ton and the Model O were carried over unchanged. The next year brought a new 1,000 lb. (1/2-ton) delivery priced at $2,175. That season, the company changed its name to R. & L. Baker Co. The last year was 1916. However, Baker Motors, Inc., which built steam-powered buses from 1926-1928 is sometimes linked to the earlier firm's dates.

BAKER-BELL — Philadelphia, Pa. — (1913-1914) — The Baker-Bell Motor Co. also built small, closed, delivery vans with capacities between 500 lbs. and 1,500 lbs.

BARKER — Norwalk, Conn. — (1912-1917) — This firm, the C.L. Barker Co., built large trucks. However, for a short time, it also marketed a model of 1/2-ton capacity.

1914 Barker Model U Flareboard (OCW)

669

BATTRONIC — Boyertown, Pa. — (1964-1978) — Battronic Truck Corp. made step-in type vans and larger buses. They were battery-powered. The first models represented a joint venture between Exxide Battery, Boyertown Auto Body Works and the English truck-maker Smith Delivery Vehicles. After 1969, Battronic was a subsidiary of Boyertown Auto Body Works. The other firms had withdrawn their support. The van has a 2,500 lb. payload and 25 mph top speed.

1975 Battronic Walk-in Delivery Van (OCW)

BAUER — Kansas City, Mo. — (1914-1917) — The Bauer Machine Works Co. built trucks in the 1/2- to 3/4-ton range. The Bauer Model A, a 1,000 lb. gas-powered truck, was offered in 1915-1916 as a chassis only. It was priced at $900. In 1916, it also came as a flareboard express at $1,050. Added to the product line, in 1916, was the Model B. It was another 1/2-ton. It was also $1,050 in chassis form and $1,175 in the flareboard model.

BEARDSLEY — Los Angeles, Calif. — (1914-1915) — These battery-powered trucks were sold in the 1/2-ton to 1-ton ranges. They were built by the Beardsley Electric Co.

1914 Beardsley Electric Express (JHV)

1914 Beardsley 750 Lb. Panel Delivery (JHV)

BELL — York, Pa. — (1915-1918) — The Bell Motor Car Co. built both autos and trucks. In 1917, their 1/2-ton Model 17 sold for $825 as an open delivery and $875 as a closed delivery. It used a gasoline engine.

BELMONT — Lewistown, Pa. — (1919-1926) — Belmont Motors Corp. made a 3/4-ton (1,500 lb.) truck in 1920. It sold for $1,150 and used a four-cylinder 26 hp Continental motor. Belmont later became part of Kearns.

BERGDOLL — Philadelphia, Pa. — (1910-1913) — The Louis J. Bergdoll Motor Car Co. offered delivery vans on their passenger car chassis. A contemporary insurance guide described the company's 1912 model as a 1,000 to 1,500 lb. delivery for $1,500. A truck of similar capacity, with an enclosed body, was offered in 1913. It was then called the Model C and had a $1,600 pricetag.

BESSEMER — Grove City, Pa. — (1911-1923)/Plainfield, N.J. — (1923-1926) — This was primarily a heavy truck, but in some years a 3/4-ton model was offered. For example, in 1918 the 3/4-ton Bessemer chassis sold for $975. The Bessemer Motor Truck Co. was the initial manufacturer. In its later years, the firm went through several mergers.

1914 Bessemer 1-Ton Chassis (GEM/DJS)

1914 Bessemer Model C Slatside Delivery (OCW)

1914 Bessemer Model B Covered Flareboard (OCW)

BEST — Flint, Mich. — (1912-1915) — The Durant-Dort Carriage Co. built these small, 76 in. wheelbase, open and closed delivery vans.

1912 Best Panel Delivery Van (HACJ/LIAM)

1914 Best Model A Panel Body Delivery (OCW)

BEST — San Leandro, Calif. — (1913-1914) — The Best Manufacturing Co.'s smallest truck was a 1-ton with a two-cylinder engine mounted under the body. It had a friction transmission and double chain-drive. Best of California seems to have built only electric trucks. On Jan. 18, 1913, *THE SAN LEANDRO REPORTER* commented that Best had recently made its first carload shipment of "electric motor trucks."

BETHLEHEM — Allentown, Pa. — (1917-1927) — Bethlehem Motor Corp. introduced a 1-ton in 1920, but most of its trucks were larger types.

1920 Bethelehem 3/4-Ton Express (OCW)

BETZ — Hammond, Ind. — (1919-1929) — A 1-ton was added to Betz Motor Truck's line in 1924. It had a 136 in. wheelbase and a Buda engine.

BELLSTROM — Battle Creek, Mich. — (1915-1916)/Detroit, Mich. (1916-1921) — This company's earliest truck was a 3/4-ton. Later, larger models were seen.

BEYSTER-DETROIT — Detroit, Mich. — (1910-1913) — These were light delivery trucks, mounted on a 105 in. wheelbase. They were built by the Beyster-Detroit Motor Car Co.

1911 Beyster-Detroit Panel Body Delivery Van (OCW)

BIMEL — Sidney, Ohio — (1916) — A 1,000 lb. (1/2-ton) chassis was cataloged by Bimel Buggy Co. in 1916. It was gasoline-powered and sold for $485. This firm also promoted a six-cylinder automobile which, it appears, was never actually produced. However, the Elco automobile was made by the same company between 1915 and 1917.

BINGHAM — Cleveland, Ohio — (1914-1915) — The Bingham Mfg. Co. offered a light-duty truck with 1,250 lb. capacity. Stake, panel or open express bodies were available.

Standard Catalog of Light-Duty Trucks

BIRCH — Chicago, Ill. — (1916-1923) — Birch Motor College, Inc., had its Model 24 truck on the market for just one year, in 1918. It was a 1/2-ton powered by a four-cylinder gas engine. The chassis was $735 and a box body model was $795. This company was connected to a technical school and its cars and trucks were assembled by students. Trucks were not listed until 1918 and may have been offered for one season only.

BLACK CROW — Chicago, Ill. — (1909-1912)/Elkhart, Ind. — (1912) — The Black Manufacturing Co., which moved to Elkhart, Ind. in 1912, built high-wheeler 1/2-ton delivery trucks. After the move, the firm's name was Crow Motor Car Co.

BLACKER — Chillicothe, Ohio — (1910-1912) — Blackers came in sizes ranging from 1/2-ton to 3-tons. They were built by John H. Blacker & Co.

BOARD — Alexandria, Va. — (1911-1913) — These were open panel vehicles in capacities ranging from 1,000 lbs. to 6,000 lbs., built by the B.F. Board Motor Truck Co.

BORLAND — Chicago, Ill. — (1912-1914) — The Borland-Grannis Co. built electric trucks with 3/4-ton capacity.

BOSS — Reading, Pa. — (1905-1906) — Powered by steam, these 1,000 lb. capacity delivery trucks had wheelbases of 72 in. They were built by the Boss Knitting Machine Works, which apparently was diversifying.

BOSWORTH — Saugus, Mass. — (1903-1904) — Frank C. Bosworth built this 7-1/2 hp, steam-powered vehicle. It had what appears to have been a large cargo box mounted at the rear. No series production seems to have ensued.

1903 Bosworth Delivery Box Model (WLB)

BRAMWELL — Springfield, Ohio — (1904-1905) — These were small delivery vans with a 76 in. wheelbase built by the Springfield Auto Co.

1904 Bramwell Commercial Car Chassis (GR)

BRASIE — Minneapolis, Minn. — (1913-1917) — Frank E. Brasie made large trucks first. By 1914, the Packet light delivery was offered. It had a 12 hp four-cylinder engine, friction transmission and belt drive. In 1916, Brasie Motor Truck Co. became Packet Motor Car Mfg. Co.

1916 Brasie Packet Flareboard Express (OCW)

BRECHT — St. Louis, Mo. — (1904) — The Brecht Automobile Co. made steam-powered automobiles and included a light delivery body truck in its list of model offerings.

BRINTON — Coatesville, Pa. — (1913-1926) — While operating as Chester County Motor Co. (1913-1916) this firm made a 1,500 lb. (3/4-ton) prototype truck with a Renault style hood and chain-drive. Production models were bigger. Later, as Brinton Motor Truck Co., of Philadelphia, a 1-ton truck was produced.

BRISCOE — Jackson, Mich. — (1915-1919) — The Briscoe Motor Corp., an auto manufacturer, offered a 1/2-ton truck on its passenger car chassis.

BROC — Cleveland, Ohio — (1909-1914) — These battery-powered light trucks came with either open or closed bodies. Initially, they were built by the Broc Carriage & Wagon Co. which, after some reorganizations, became the Broc Electric Car Co.

BROCKWAY — Cortland, N.Y. — (1912-1977) — The Brockway Motor Truck Co. was primarily a manufacturer of medium- and heavy-duty trucks. But, at various times, the smallest trucks in their model offerings qualified for inclusion in this book. For example, in 1916, their 3/4-ton chassis, with chain-drive and a 124 in. wheelbase, sold for $1,200. This price included "Front seat and fenders, two oil dash lamps and oil taillamp, horn, and set of tools." In the 1930s, Brockway also built a line of electric delivery trucks, ranging in capacity from 1- to 7-tons. There was also a Brockway-Indiana model.

1912 Brockway Commercial Express (OCW)

1914 Brockway Model B Flareboard (OCW)

1914 Brockway Model A Panel Delivery (OCW)

1929 Brockway Type JF Express (DFW/FLP)

1930 Brockway-Indiana Compressor Truck (OCW)

1936 Brockway Electric Walk-in Milk Truck (DFW/HAC)

Standard Catalog of Light-Duty Trucks

BRODESSER — Milwaukee, Wis. — (1910-1911) — This truck was built by a firm named P.H. & Co. in Milwaukee, Wis. Peter H. Brodesser, a German immigrant who made elevators, began building trucks as a sideline. His firm produced models in capacities ranging from 1- to 3-tons. The 1910 lineup included the Model A 1-ton delivery for $1,400. It had a horizontally opposed two-cylinder engine with force-feed lubrication. This truck, with a $100 price increase, was also offered in 1911. The Model C1 joined it. This was another 1-ton with a $1,700/pricetag. In 1912, the name "Juno" was adopted. The Juno Motor Truck Co., of Juneau, Wis., later evolved.

BRONX — Bronx, N.Y. — (1912-1913) — One photo shows this 800 lb. truck parked outside the Bronx Motor Vehicle plant. The light truck was on a 76 in. wheelbase and could make 14 mph or 50 miles-per-charge. A 2-ton was also made.

BRONX ELECTRIC — Bronx, N.Y. — (1912-1913) — The Bronx Electric Vehicle Co. made these electrics, with the smallest having a 76 in. wheelbase and a capacity of 800 lbs.

1912 Bronx Electric Express (OCW)

1914 Bronx Light-Duty Express Wagon (JAW)

BROOKS — Saginaw, Mich. — (1911-1913) — These high-wheelers were available with either open or closed bodies. They were powered by an air-cooled engine. During its short production span, the firm had two names. First it was the Brooks Manufacturing Co., then the Brooks Motor Wagon Co. The latter name was in use by 1912, when an 800 lb. rated two-cylinder model was available. It came as a screenside express, for $500, or a full panel body truck, for $550. By 1912, only the screenside model, called the "B" and priced at $650, was marketed.

1912 Brooks Express Wagon (OCW)

BROWN — Peru, Ind. — (1912-1914) — A number of firms built autos and trucks named "Brown." The Brown Commercial Car Co. built delivery vans in the 3/4-ton to 1-ton size range.

1913 Brown Standard Express with Screens (RAW)

1914 Brown Flareboard with Screens (DFW/MVMA)

1914 Brown Model F Covered Flareboard (OCW)

BROWN — Cincinnati, Ohio — (1916) — Based on their passenger car chassis, the Brown Carriage Co. assembled this light delivery truck.

BROYHILL — Wayne, Neb. — (1986 — ?) — Historian Elliott Kahn reports that this articulated (it bends in the middle) cab-over utility was built by Broyhill Mfg. Co. and featured a 4x4 drivetrain. The Park Maintenance Dept. of Clearwater, Fla. utilizes one of the trucks.

1986 Broyhill Utility Park Service Truck (EK)

BRUNNER — Buffalo, N.Y. — (1910) — This truck was built by the Brunner Motor Car Co. in a number of sizes, with 1/2-ton being the smallest.

1910 Brunner Light Delivery Van (WOM)

BRUSH — Detroit, Mich. — (1908-1913) — A branch of the N.Y. City based United States Motor Co., Brush produced a number of light delivery vans. Offered in 1908 and 1909, at $600, was a 500 lb. payload, 1cylinder model. In 1910, there was a Model BC, which was a 600 lb. truck at the same price. In 1911-1912, this model continued to sell, but at a higher $650. The earliest vans were based on the Brush automobile, which had a six horsepower engine, wooden frame and axles, chain-drive, full coil spring suspension and solid tires. In 1912, pneumatic tires were adopted. There was also a light taxi, known as the Titan, which used the same chassis.

1911 Brush Light Delivery Van (OCW)

BUCKLEN — Elkhart, Ind. — (1912-1916) — This firm's Model A was a 3/4-ton truck with an open express body, stake body or delivery van body. Larger Models B and C were also produced.

BUCKMOBILE — Utica, N.Y. — (1905) — This company's 1-ton Business Wagon was $1,100. It had an open delivery body, 83 in. wheelbase and two-cylinder engine with 15 hp. Extremely long chains were used to carry drive to the rear wheels.

BUFFALO — Buffalo, N.Y. — (1908-1910) — Along with larger trucks that were related to Autocar models, the Atterbury Mfg. Co. made a 1/2-ton with solid rubber tires and chain-drive. Also available was the Model C 1-ton delivery van.

1910 Buffalo Canopy Top Delivery Wagon (JAW)

1910 Buffalo Canopy Top Delivery Wagon (WOM)

BUFFALO — Buffalo, N.Y. — (1914-1915) — These were battery-powered electrics, rated at 3/4-ton and 1-ton, and built by the Buffalo Electric Vehicle Co. In 1914, the 1,500 lb. chassis was priced at $2,200, while the 1-ton chassis sold for $2,400. In 1915, the Model CCA 1-ton was also sold for $2,400 in chassis-only form. There was also a 1/2-ton with its engine under the hood. These trucks had solid rubber tires and double chain-drive.

1914 Buffalo Closed Body Delivery Van (OCW)

BUICK — Flint, Mich. — (1910-1918/1922-1923) — This well-known automobile manufacturer built trucks early in its history. The Buick passenger car chassis was utilized for the commercial cars. The most common models were delivery vans. Military ambulances on Buick chassis were common sights during World War I. In 1918, the firm's smallest truck sold for $790, which included the body. Buick also offered trucks during the 1922-1923 model years. Its commercial chassis continued to be used for many years, carrying ambulances, hearses, paddy wagons and, even fire apparatus.

1911 Buick Express Body Delivery (E. Chattfield/DFW)

1913 Buick Telephone Company Express (DFW/IBT)

1914 Buick Model 4 Stake Body Express (OCW)

1914 Buick Model 4 Covered Flareboard (OCW)

1915 Buick Two-Cylinder Light Delivery (DFW/MVMA)

1914 Buick Model 4 Flareboard Express (OCW)

1915 Buick Light Delivery Van (DFW/IBC)

1914 Buick Model 3 Panel Body Delivery (OCW)

Standard Catalog of Light-Duty Trucks

1916 Buick Flareboard Express (VHTM)

1917 Buick Roadster Express Conversion (DFW/HEPO)

1928 Buick Panel Delivery (DFW)

BUTLER — Butler, Pa. — (1913-1914) — Built by the Huselton Automobile Co., the Butler light-duty truck could carry a 3/4-ton load.

BYRON — Denver, Colo. — (1912) — This company's products included a gasoline powered 1-ton model.

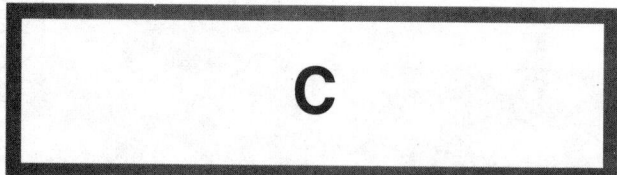

C

CADILLAC — Detroit, Mich. — (1904 to date) — This famous GM division marketed light trucks from 1904 through 1909. During its entire history, Cadillac also supplied commercial chassis for ambulances, hearses, flower cars, airport buses, etc. Because of their sturdy construction, many Cadillac passenger cars, late in their lives, were converted into commercial vehicles, with the most typical example being a tow-truck.

1903 Cadillac Commercial Car (DFW/SBT)

1906 Cadillac 9 HP Delivery Van (OCW)

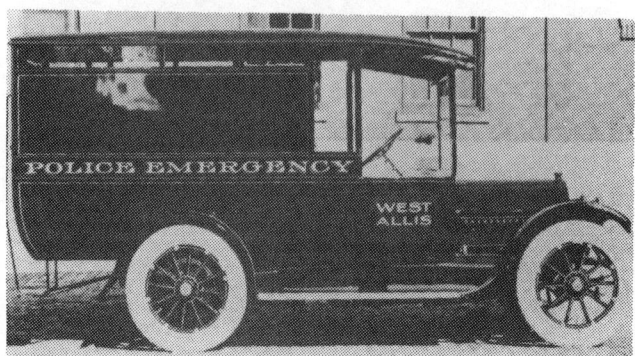

1913 Cadillac Screenside Ambulance (OCW)

1913 Cadillac Screenside Patrol Wagon (OCW)

1920 Cadillac Military Express Model (DFW/ACE)

CADILLAC — Cadillac, Mich. — (pre-World War I) — This brand was listed in *AUTOMOBILE TRADE JOURNAL* as a product of the Cadillac Auto Truck Co. One offering was a 3/4-ton model with a 128 in. wheelbase and $1,290 price.

CAPITOL — Washington, D.C. — (1910-1912) — These were chain-driven, battery-powered electric delivery trucks, built by the Washington Motor Vehicle Co.

1910 Capitol 1/2-Ton Electric Delivery Van (WJP)

CAPITOL — Denver, Colo. — (1914) — These electric delivery vans, built by the Capitol Truck Mfg. Co., were powered by General Electric motors.

1914 Capitol Electric Express Wagon (JAW)

CARLSON — Philadelphia, Pa. — (1904-1910) — This company's first trucks were 1-tons that also weighed 1-ton. They had four-cylinder, four-cycle, double-opposed horizontal engines that produced 20 hp. Larger models were built later on.

CARTERCAR — Pontiac, Mich. — (1906-1912) — These were light-duty trucks marketed on Cartercar's passenger car chassis. Like the automobiles, these trucks used friction-drive transmissions. This system would ultimately prove unreliable in the commercial vehicle field. The Model C delivery of 1908 was a handsome-looking C-cab van with a $1,400 pricetag. The company also produced taxis on the same 96-110 in. wheelbase chassis.

1908 Cartercar Model C Delivery Van (JAW)

Standard Catalog of Light-Duty Trucks

1911 Cartercar Bus-Back Roadster (OCW)

CASE — New Bremen, Ohio — (1910-1913) — These were 1,200 lb. capacity delivery vans built by the Case Motor Car Co.

CASS — Port Huron, Mich. — (1910-1915) — The Cass Motor Truck Co. built small trucks, ranging in size from 3/4-ton to 1-1/2-ton.

1910 Cass Panel Delivery Van (DPL/NAHC)

CAVAC — Plymouth, Mich. — (1910-1911) — These were three-wheel delivery cars built by the Small Motor Co.

CECO — Chicago, Ill. — (1914) — These "trucks" put a van body on a cyclecar. They were built by the Continental Engineering Co.

CHADWICK — Pottstown, Pa. — (1915-1916) — The Chadwick Engineering Works, of Pottstown, Pa., made this light-duty truck in the mid-teens. It was rated for a 1,000 lb. payload capacity. Price for the chassis-only configuration, in 1916, was $620. A delivery body was also offered on this running gear, which was essentially a beefed-up version of the firm's automobile chassis. The engine used was a 16 hp LeRoi four-cylinder. This was the company's last shot at manufacturing before its factory was taken over for war work. It had just 13 assemblers.

CHAMPION — Oswego, N.Y. — (1904-1905) — The Champion Wagon Works was among several firms using the Champion name on its products. One truck was a battery-powered electric with forward control configuration and double chain-drive. It came only as an open-sided van with a top and a 1-ton payload rating.

CHAMPION — Cleveland, Ohio — (1907) — The McCrea Motor Truck Co. built 1/2-ton and two-ton trucks under the Champion name. Apparently, they were built for just one year. The Model L (which probably stood for "light truck") had a delivery type body and sold for $1,850. It was an electric-powered vehicle. The manufacturer may have moved to Chicago later.

CHAMPION — Milwaukee, Wis. — (1912-1913) — Milwaukee Auto Truck Manufacturing Co. was another firm that used the Champion name to designate three models built in 1912. The firm's Model A was a gasoline-engined 1-ton that cost $2,000, while its "B" and "C" models were rated for 2- and 3-ton payloads, respectively.

1913 Champion 1-Ton Panel Delivery (JAW)

CHAMPION — Fulton, Ill. — (1917) — Champion Motor Co. produced four versions of its gas-powered 1,000 lb. Model A truck. The chassis was $725, an Open Express was $750, an Open Express with top was $765 and a Panel was $785. The power team was an L-head four with three-speed transmission attachment.

CHASE — Syracuse, N.Y. — (1907-c.1917) — The Chase Motor Truck Co. built trucks in the 3/4-ton and up range. In the firm's early years, a business runabout — which could be converted from a four-seat auto to a light-duty truck — was also marketed. In 1916, the firm's 3/4-ton model sold for $1,500.

1911 Chase Open Express

1912 Chase Panel Delivery Van (DFW/SI)

1913 Chase Panel Delivery Van (DFW/PTC)

1913 Chase Stakeside Express Wagon (DFW/PTC)

1914 Chase Model D Flareboard Express (OCW)

1914 Chase Model H Panel Delivery (OCW)

CHAUTAUQUA — Jamestown, N.Y. — (1914) — The Chautauqua Cyclecar Co. placed a van body on some of their cyclecars.

CHECKER — Joliet, Ill. — (1920-1923)/Kalamazoo, Mich. — (1923-1984) — The Checker Cab Mfg. Co. built taxicabs, but sometimes their chassis are used for other commercial purposes. In the early 1930s, the company made a model that was very much like the mod-

ern Chevrolet/GMC Suburban, though General Motors often gets credit for innovating this type of truck.

CHELSEA — Newark, N.J. — (1915) — The Chelsea Mfg. Co.'s sole model was a Panel Van that carried 800 lb. loads. It had a 102 in. wheelbase and four-cylinder, 15 hp engine. The standard color scheme was a dark blue body with black fenders and running gear.

CHICAGO — Chicago, Ill. — (1910-1911) — The Chicago Commercial Car Co. built 3/4- and 1-ton vans.

CHICAGO — Chicago, Ill. — (1919-1932) — This firm operated as Chicago Motor Truck Co. and Robert M. Cutting Co. A Hercules four-cylinder engine powered the 1-ton truck it produced in the 1920s.

CHICAGO BUSINESS — Chicago, Ill. — (1912) — A single model was made by the Chicago Business Car Co. It was a truck with a two-cylinder 14 hp engine and an 87 in. wheelbase that was rated for 800 lb. loads.

CHICAGO MOTOR WAGON — Chicago, Ill. — (1910-1912) — This two-cylinder, 20 hp truck was rated 3/4-ton to 1-ton. It had a 90 in. wheelbase, friction transmission and double chain-drive. Its chassis weight was 2,300 lbs. Price for an open express bodied model was $1,000.

CINO — Cincinnati, Ohio — (1910-1913) — This was a 1/2-ton on a 113 in. wheelbase featuring a 40 hp engine. A $1,300 truck rated for 1/4-ton was offered in 1913.

CLARK — Lansing, Mich. — (1910-1912) — These were open express vans built by the Clark Power Wagon Co. This firm made delivery vans and express vans of 1,500 lbs. and 2,000 lbs. They had planetary transmissions and shaft drive. In 1911, Clark & Co. combined with Ferguson Motor Co. to form the Clark Power Wagon Co.

CLARK POWER WAGON — Lansing, Mich. — (1910-1912) — These were open express vans built by the Clark Power Wagon Co.

1911 Clark Power Wagon (WOM)

CLARK — Chicago, Ill. — (1910-1914) — The Clark Delivery Wagon Co. built small vans.

1910 Clark 1-Ton Stake Body Express (DFW/SI)

Standard Catalog of Light-Duty Trucks

1914 Clark Stake Platform (OCW)

1914 Clark Flareboard With Stakes (OCW)

CLEVELAND — Jackson, Mich. — (1913-1914) — This truck was also known as the "New Cleveland." It was a 3/4-ton of mostly conventional design, but powered by an unusual four-cylinder engine having an overhead camshaft and overhead valves. The valves were installed at a 45-degree angle. The Cleveland was of delivery wagon style, with a single driver's seat. Other features included pneumatic tires and shaft drive. The company was known as the E.C. Clark Motor Co. and its tradename was derived by C.D. Paxton, a Cleveland-based marketing firm.

1913 Cleveland Open Express (RAW)

CLIMAX — Sandusky, Ohio — (1907) — The Dunbar Mfg. Co. built a light chassis on which either a passenger car or delivery body could be built. The Climax Commercial Car was advertised in *THE AUTOMOBILE* as a "convertible light delivery." It had a capacity of 1,000 lbs. and three-inch solid tires. It sold for $860 without top and $900 with top. It was promoted as "simple, light and durable" and a Sandusky, Ohio dealer, Hinde & Dauch, said that the Climax Commercial Car "fills a long-felt want."

CLYDESDALE — Clyde, Ohio — (1916-1938) — The original Clydesdale line of 1916-1917 had only heavy trucks. The Model 125, a 3/4-ton assembled truck, was marketed in 1917-1918. The lightest 1919 model was the "32," which had a 1-ton payload rating. It was continued as the 32-C for 1920-1921. In 1921, a 3/4-ton Model 20 was also released. For 1922, the 3/4-ton was called the Model 10 and the "20" was uprated to 1-1/2-tons. Later, Clydesdale made mostly larger trucks, but a 1-ton model was kept in the line for years.

COLEMAN — Olean, N.Y. — (1910-1915) — Light trucks were made by F. Coleman Carriage & Harness Co. They included 1,200 lb. vans designated Models A-1 and A-2, which had 20 hp, air-cooled two-cylinder engines under the body. There was also a Model B 1-ton with 107 in. wheelbase and water-cooled four. In 1914 and 1915, the 1-ton Model D was offered. It came with stake or express bodies, at $1,950 and $2,100, respectively. The small vans had planetary transmissions and double chain-drive.

1914 Coleman Model B Covered Express (OCW)

COLLIER — Cleveland, Ohio — (1917) — The Collier Co. built a light delivery van in 1917. It was designated the Model M and resembled a passenger car in overall design, although the company did not build autos. This 1,500 lb. (3/4-ton) truck used a four-cylinder gasoline engine and sold for $885 in chassis form. Panel delivery and open express bodies were available. The following season, the firm relocated to Bellevue, Ohio.

COLLIER — Bellevue, Ohio — (1918-1922) — After the Collier Co. moved to Bellevue, Ohio, the price of its 3/4-ton chassis rose by $100 to $985. It was still powered by a four-cylinder gasoline engine. Models once again available included a panel delivery or an open express. In 1919, a 1-ton truck was added to the line. It featured a Continental powerplant and a worm drive system. Even larger trucks were brought to market in 1921 and 1922.

1919 Collier Model 18 1-Ton Chassis (OCW)

COLLINS — Scranton, Pa. — (1900) — Patrick J. Collins probably made a single 1-ton truck to demonstrate his unique chassis design. It used electric motors for both driving and steering functions. A delivery type body was fitted.

COLUMBIA — Hartford, Conn. — (1899-1907) — This was a very popular make of electric truck, built by the Electric Vehicle Co., which was the successor to the Columbia Automobile Co. Many of their chassis were used for buses. In 1907, the firm concentrated on building gasoline-powered automobiles.

1904 Columbia Electric Panel Delivery (DFW/SI)

COLUMBIA — Pontiac, Mich. — (1916-1926) — Columbia Motor Truck & Trailer Co. sold a 1-ton Model F truck in 1920 and 1923 only. It was a four-cylinder powered truck with a curb weight around 6,000 lbs.

COLUMBIA CARRIAGE — Portland, Ore. — (1915) — Columbia Carriage & Auto Works "GMC Utility" car could carry up to 11 passengers or a ton of cargo. It came with four seats, the three rear-most being removable. The canopy style top was also detachable. Without the canopy top, the truck became a freight wagon. It had pneumatic tires and could be ordered in any color. The price was $1,400 f.o.b. Portland.

1915 Columbia Carriage GMC 1-Ton Freight Wagon

COMET — Indianapolis, Ind. — (1914) — The Comet Cyclecar Co. attached a delivery box to one of its models.

1914 Comet Cyclecar Model A Delivery Wagon (OCW)

1914 Comet Cyclecar Model B Box Body (OCW)

COMMERCE — Detroit, Mich. — (1911-1926)/Lima, Ohio — (1927-1932) — The Commerce Motor Car Co., of Detroit, built light delivery trucks and canopy express models. A 1,000 lb. truck came out in 1912 with prices of $850 for the closed panel and $800 for an open delivery. In 1913-1914, there were four 1/2-ton trucks with three-cylinder gas engines. The Model K chassis listed for $875, the KA flareboard express was $950, the KC panel was $975 and the KH covered flareboard express was $975. In 1915, the trucks were up-rated to 1,500 lbs. (3/4-ton) and marketed as the SA express, SC panel and SH stake, all priced at $975. The Model S brought the end of production for the earlier 1/2-ton friction drive trucks. It also introduced the use of a Continental four-cylinder L-head engine with 3-1/2 x 5 in. bore and stroke that could produce speeds in excess of 15 mph. It had a 107 in. wheelbase and 56 in. track. An article in *MOTOR FIELD'S* November 1914 issue said, "The new wagon has been very well received and many dealers throughout the West have already taken on this new line." For 1916, there was a Model N 1,500 lb. chassis costing $875. The addition of the A/C/H suffix was again used to identify the express/panel/stake bodies, which were again $975. A variety of 1-ton models started with the "E" ($1,340) of 1917. The Model E lineup included the EA open express ($1,375), the EH canopy top ($1,456) and ES stake ($1,490). The E series continued through 1920. Then came the "T" of 1921 and the "11-A" of 1924-1925. All were four-cylinder powered. They also built bus chassis. In 1927, the firm was acquired by Relay Motors Corp., of Lima, Ohio and thus became linked with other moderately well-known makes: Garford, Relay and Service. However, by this time they were no longer marketing "light-duty" trucks.

1911 Commerce Light Delivery Van (OCW)

1914 Commerce Model KH Covered Flareboard Express

1914 Commerce Model KC Panel Delivery (OCW)

1914 Commerce Model KA Flareboard Express (OCW)

Standard Catalog of Light-Duty Trucks

1926 Commerce Model 7 Distributor 1-Ton Chassis

COMMERCIAL — New York, N.Y. — (1906-1912) — Commercial Motor Car Co.'s line included a 1-ton truck with a four-cylinder engine, chain-drive and solid rubber tires.

COMPOUND — Middletown, Conn. — (1906) — Eisenhuth Horseless Vehicle Co. made a $1,400 Model Nine delivery van on a 98-1/2 in. wheelbase It had a unique three-cylinder engine with a larger center cylinder that received exhaust gases from the outer, conventional ones. Features included a three-speed transmission and double chain-drive.

CONCORD — Concord, N.H. — (1916-1933) — Built by Abbott & Downing Co., and Abbott-Downing Truck & Body Co., this marque had in its line a 1-ton model powered by a Buda engine.

CONESTOGA — Connorsville, Ind. — (1914-1916) — Connorsville Buggy Co. built a 1,250 lb. payload, battery-powered electric truck.

CONTINENTAL — Superior, Wis. — (1912-1918) — The 1918 model line included a 1-ton with worm drive and a four-cylinder motor. It was called Continental Truck Mfg., Co.

CONTINENTAL — Chicago, Ill. — (1915-1917) — Continental Motor Truck Co. included a 1-ton in its line. Features included a four-cylinder engine, three-speed transmission and worm-gear final drive.

COOK — Kankakee, Ill. — (1920-1923) Cook Motors Corp. built only a 1-ton in 1920 and 1921. It was replaced by a 2-ton in 1922.

COPPOCK — Marion, Ind. (1907)/Decatur, Ind. (1908-1909) — This "Sterling quality" 1-ton stake had an 87 in. wheelbase, solid tires and a two-cycle, two-cylinder engine with copper water jackets. A three-speed progressive transmission was used. It was referred to as a commercial car.

CORBIN — New Britain, Conn. — (1902-1905) — This automaker built a 1,500 lb. (3/4-ton) light truck with an eight-horsepower single-cylinder engine.

CORBITT — Henderson, N.C. — (1913-1958) — Corbitt made well-known regional trucks until well after the end of World War II. While they were mostly large models, a 1-ton Model F ($2,000) appeared as early as 1916. Another "light" four-cylinder job, the Model E, bowed at $1,300 in 1917. It then went to $1,800 the next season. The Model E survived until 1925, being joined by the 3/4-ton Model H in 1922. The following year, a slightly less powerful 3/4-ton Model S was marketed. Also, in 1926, there was the Model 20, with an 18.23 hp four-cylinder. One-ton Corbitts were also manufactured in the 1930s.

1914 Corbitt Model F Flareboard (OCW)

CORTLAND — Cortland, N.Y. (1911)/Pittsfield, Mass. (1912) — A driver-over-engine 3/4-ton delivery wagon was offered by Cortland Motor Wagon Co. It had a 15 hp two-cylinder engine, planetary transmission and double chain-drive. Open side ($1,100) and closed side ($1,750) vans were available.

1911 Cortland 1,500 lb. Delivery Wagon (GMN)

COUPLE GEAR — Grand Rapids, Mich. — (1904-1922) — This company specialized in heavy, slow-moving trucks powered by motors in the wheels. In 1908, a 1-ton gas/electric model was made. It had drive on the front wheels only and could make nine mph. In 1914, another small-sized product was a three-wheel electric contractor's wagon.

1914 Couple Gear 3-Wheel Contractor's Wagon (OCW)

COVERT — Lockport, N.Y. — (1906-1907) — The Covert Motor Vehicle Co. built small delivery trucks with wire-side bodies. Its 1907 two-cylinder, forward-control model was a 1,000 lb. delivery truck which was priced at $1,000. The body was of the van type with screened side panels. Other features included an 84 in. wheelbase, two-speed gearbox and shaft drive.

C.P.T. — Chicago, Ill. — (1912) — The Chicago Pneumatic Tool Company produced a gasoline powered 1,500-to 2,000 lb. truck chassis under its corporate initials. It lasted for one year. The truck was marketed at $950. This company also made the Duntley and Giant/Little Giant trucks.

CRANE & BREED — Cincinnati, Ohio — (1909-1924) — Founded in 1850, this former carriage-maker was one of the pioneering firms in the field of purpose-built hearses and ambulances. These were rather heavy vehicles with 1-ton or higher payload ratings. In 1915, the least expensive 1-ton sold for $2,000 in chassis form, $3,650 as an ambulance and $3,750 as a hearse. During that same year, there was also the 1-ton Model 48. It was $2,850 for the chassis, $4,500 for the ambulance and $5,085 for the top-level of hearse. Pre-1912 models were four-cylinder vehicles with magneto ignition, three-speed gearboxes and chain-drive. After 1912, the company concentrated on making only the bodies, which were mounted on a six-cylinder Winton chassis. Such models were produced until 1924.

CRAWFORD — Hagerstown, Md. — (1911-1917) — The Crawford Automobile Co. offered a 1,200 lb. capacity van on their automobile chassis.

1909 Crawford Commercial Roadster (EK)

CRESCENT — Middletown, Ohio (1912-1913)/Hamilton, Ohio (1913) — Crescent Motor Truck Co. made 1-tons along with its 2-ton and 3-ton models.

CRETORS — Chicago, Ill. — (1915) — C. Cretors & Co. built nine special popcorn wagons powered by 22.5 hp four-cylinder Buda engines. One of the originals is in the National Automobile Museum (formerly Harrah's Automobile Collection) in Reno, Nev.

CRICKETT — Detroit, Mich. — (1915) — The Cyclecar Co. of Detroit produced a gasoline-engined Package Delivery model with a low $345 pricetag.

CROCE — Asbury Park, N.J. — (circa 1914-1918) — The Croce Automobile Co. also marketed a line of delivery trucks. Among its models was the "A," which sold for $1,700 in 1914. It was a 3/4-ton gasoline-engined truck. For 1915, the Model A came as a $1,650 chassis or $1,800 open or closed cab van. There was also a Model C 1-ton chassis ($1,850) in 1914 and an A-1 1-ton chassis ($1,800) in 1915. After skipping one season, Croce returned to the market, in 1917, with three light-duty models. The "18" (open) and "19" (closed) body models were both 3/4-tons costing $950, while the "20" was a 1-ton selling for $1,250 with either an open or closed type

1914 Croce Panel Body Delivery Car (OCW)

1915 Croce Panel Body Delivery Car (DFW/SI)

Standard Catalog of Light-Duty Trucks

1916 Croce Panel Body Delivery Car (DFW/MVMA)

CROFTON — San Diego, Calif. — (1959-1961) — This was a jeep-type vehicle built by the Crofton Marine Engine Co. It was derived from the Crosley, after that marque disappeared.

1960 Crofton-Bug Utility (Reggie Rapp)

CROW — Elkhart, Ind. — (1912-1913) — This was a delivery van offered on an automaker's chassis. The manufacturer was the Crow Motor Co.

CROWN — Milwaukee, Wis. — (1910-1915) — The Crown Commercial Car Co. started out building 1/2-ton model trucks. It then began building larger capacity models.

CROWTHER-DURYEA — Rochester, N.Y. — (1916) — This light truck was developed by Charles Duryea and built by the Crowther Motor Co.

CROXTON — Washington, Pa. — (1911-1913) -This company's light-duty commercial vehicles are claimed to all have been taxicabs, but at least one panel body truck was constructed. A characteristic of the make was a sloping hood and behind-the-engine radiator.

1913 Croxton Model A Panel Body Delivery (OCW)

Standard Catalog of Light-Duty Trucks

C.T. — Philadelphia, Pa. — (1908-1928) — This company was known as Commercial Truck Co. of America through 1916 and the name C.T. was used for model listings thereafter. Its well-known electric trucks can often be spotted in old photos showing traffic scenes in large Eastern cities. The 1909 line included a 1/2-ton delivery van priced at $2,200. This model was carried over, for 1910, with two more light-duty trucks and various heavier-duty models. The smallest was a 1/2-ton delivery that sold for $2,000. A 1-ton truck was also marketed for $2,800. By 1911, the 500 pounder was lowered in price to $1,900, while the 1/2-ton increased to $2,250. Price for the 1-ton model remained unchanged. In 1912, the three models were $2,000, $2,200 and $2,800 in order. Alphabetical designations were adopted in 1913, the Model A being a 750 lb. panel priced at $2,000 and the Model B being a 1,500 lb. panel for $2,200. The following season the "A" was down-rated to 500 lbs. again. It sold for $1,440 in chassis form or $2,000 with the panel body. For 1916, the lightest version was the 1-ton Model C, at $1,800 for the chassis. The 1/2-ton returned, in 1918, with prices varying from $2,005 to $2,540, depending on the type of battery. This truck could travel 13 mph. In 1925, the C.T. 1/2-ton chassis was $1,900.

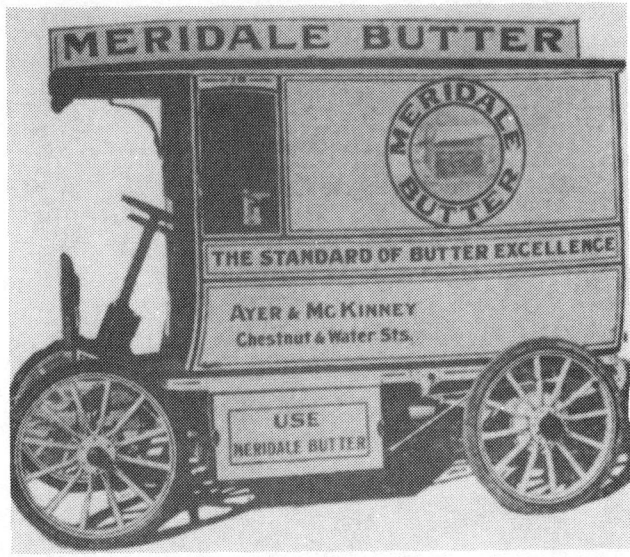

1914 C.T. 1,000 lb. Panel Body Delivery (OCW)

1922 C.T. Electric Flat-Front Panel Delivery (DFW/MVMA)

1922 C.T. Electric Panel Delivery (DFW/MVMA)

1925 C.T. Electric Walk-in Delivery (DFW/NA)

CUSHMAN — Lincoln, Neb. — (1936 to date) — Cushman Motors, manufacturer of the well-known scooters, outfitted some of their scooters with commercial and freight-carrying bodies.

1965 Cushman 3-Wheel Police/Utility Scooter (WJP)

1984 Cushman 3-Wheel Police Special Scooter (EK)

684

DAIN — Ottumwa, Iowa — (1912-1917) — Joseph Dain's Dain Mfg. Co. built a line of 1-ton trucks with the driver's seat set to the left of the hood. All had vertical four-cylinder engines with 4-3/4 x 5 in. bore and strokes and 22.5 ALAM hp, K-W ignition, force-feed lubrication, dual friction transmission and 36 x 3-1/2 in. tires. The wheelbase was 100 in.; the frame length 162 in. The loading space was 114 in. long and 54 in. wide. The 1-ton was offered all years.

DANIELSON — Chicago, Ill. — (1912-1914) — Danielson Engine Works made the Model A 1-ton with a 113 in. wheelbase. It had a four-cylinder engine, three-speed transmission and chain-drive.

DARBY — St. Louis, Mo. — (1910) — This was a small delivery van produced by the Darby Motor Car Co.

DART — Waterloo, Ia. — (1903 to date) — This is an old name in the truck business and the manufacturer's name has changed eight times. The firm was in Anderson, Ind. from 1903- 1907 and then in Waterloo from 1907-1925. It then moved to Kansas City, Mo., where it exists today. Presently, it builds mainly large off-highway construction vehicles. At one time, it did build light-duty trucks. In 1916, it sold a Model D with an express rated at 1/2-ton capacity, for $675. The Model A was rated at 1/2-ton capacity and the Model BB at 3/4-ton capacity.

1914 Dart Model B Flareboard Express (OCW)

1914 Dart Model B Flareboard Express (DFW/HCC)

DAY-ELDER — Irvington, N.J. — (1919-1937) — This was a moderately well-known make of truck and bus made by the Day-Elder Motor Truck Co. in sizes up to 5- or 6-tons. From 1916 to 1918, they offered a 3/4-ton Day-Elder "Junior," which sold for $950. A 1-ton "Senior" model was available at the same time.

1916 Day-Elder 1-Ton Stake Body (OCW)

1916 Day-Elder Junior 1,250 Lb. Chassis (RAW)

1916 Day-Elder Senior 1-Ton Chassis (RAW)

DAYTON — Joliet, Ill. — (1914) — Like many cyclecar makers, this firm turned out commercial versions of its product for light delivery work. An 18 hp four-cylinder engine powered this 105 in. wheelbase machine which, with a delivery box mounted aft, became a light-duty truck. Chicagoan William O. Dayton gave his name to the short-lived venture.

1914 Dayton Flareboard Express (OCW)

DAYTON — Dayton, Ohio — (1915) — The Model 51 was an electric-powered truck with a 750 lb. payload capacity. It came as a chassis for $1,200 or a closed panel at $1,600. Dayton Electric Car Co. built it.

DAY UTILITY — Detroit, Mich./Milwaukee, Wis. — (1912-1914) — The Day Automobile Co. introduced its 1/2-ton Special Delivery at a price of $1,150. In 1913, the 1/2-ton Model C ($1,500) was produced in Mich., while the 3/4-ton Model D was made in both states, but at different prices. The Detroit built version, with a delivery body, was $1,500. The Milwaukee made Model D (a chassis only) was $1,850. In 1914, the Model D — now called a "convertible," — was built in Michigan only. It sold for the $1,500 price.

DEARBORN — Chicago, Ill. — (1919-1924) — In 1923 and 1924, this firm made a 1-ton with a 133 in. wheelbase and pneumatic tires.

DECATUR — Decatur, Ind. — (1909-1912)/Grand Rapids, Mich. — (1912-1915) — The Decatur Motor Car Co., and several succeeding firms, built various models of trucks. They included a delivery van designed so that the driver rode in the rear, over the load-carrying body.

1914 Decatur Cyclecar Parcel Post Delivery Wagon

DEFIANCE — Defiance, Ohio — (1917-1931) — In 1921-1922 the four-cylinder Model G2/GL2 made by Defiance-Century Motor Truck Co. from 1921 to at least 1925 had a 1-ton payload capacity. This truck weighed about 2,700 lbs.

DELCAR — Troy, N.Y. — (1947-1949) — This was a short (60 in. wheelbase) delivery van built by a firm named American Motors, Inc.

1947 Delcar Mini Walk-in Van (OCW)

DE MARTINI — San Francisco, Calif. — (1915-c. 1934) — F.J. DeMartini & Co. were wagon-makers and the DeMartini Motor Truck Co. was formed in 1916. The *MOTOR TRUCK* magazine of July, 1917, stated that DeMartini built trucks of 1-, 2-, 3- and 4-ton capacity. Trucks were seen at West Coast auto shows as late as 1934. George DeMartini continued to operate a truck repair shop in his factory on Pacific Ave. until 1978.

DE MOTTE — Valley Forge, Pa. — (1904) — This automaker built a two-cylinder (10 hp) delivery wagon and a four-cylinder (20 hp) truck. The latter was constructed on a DeMotte touring car chassis with the driver's seat perched precariously above the engine.

DENBY — Detroit, Mich. — (1914-1930) — Usually associated with larger sizes of trucks, the Denby Motor Truck Co. did, in some years of the early 1920s, produce models as small as 3/4-ton capacity.

1915 Denby Flareboard Express Wagon (NACH/DPL)

1915 Denby 3/4-Ton Express (OCW)

1916 Denby 1-Ton Open Flareboard Express (WOM)

1916 Denby Type U 3/4-Ton Stake (D. Sagvold)

1917 Denby 1-Ton Express Box Body (Myron Stone)

1925 Denby Model 41 1-Ton Chassis (OCW)

DENMO — Cleveland, Ohio — (1916-1918) — The Denneen Motor Co., of Cleveland, announced its first line of trucks late in 1916. A four-cylinder Wisconsin engine powered these conventional models. It was attached to a three-speed tranmission and Torbensen internal gear drive axle. Pneumatic tires were used in front with solid tires at the rear. In 1917 only, the company produced its Model 12, a flareboard express with a 1,250 lb. payload. It sold for $995. By 1918, the firm became Grant Motor Car Corp. and the Grant name was then used on the trucks.

DENNISTON — Buffalo, N.Y. — (1911-1912) — The E.E. Denniston Co. built small delivery vans with a two-cylinder engine.

DE SCHAUM — Buffalo, N.Y. — (1908-1909) — This was a small delivery van, with an 84 in. wheelbase, that was sold by the DeSchaum Motor Syndicate Co. for a brief period.

DEPENDABLE — Galesburg, Ill. — (1914-1925) — Dependable Truck & Tractor Co. made a 1-ton with a Buda engine, three-speed transmission and worm-drive rear axle through 1921.

DESOTO — Detroit, Mich. — (1930-present) — The first commercial vehicle made by DeSoto was the rare Model K Commercial Sedan. This 1/2-ton rated "sedan delivery" had blanked-out rear side windows and a rear access door. Only one was known to exist in 1956! DeSoto components were also used in Chrysler's Fargo truck line. Depot hacks and taxicabs also rode DeSoto chassis. Starting in 1938, the DeSoto name was used by Chrysler to identify a line of Dodge-like trucks. These were intended to be sold by foreign based dealers of Chrysler products who lacked a Dodge franchise. They were first seen in European countries and spread into the Australian market after World War II. They were virtually identical to the Dodges offered in the same areas, except for nameplates. While use of the name was discontinued in most countries after the demise of DeSoto cars in 1961, certain models assembled in Turkey continued to use this identification.

1958 DeSoto 4x4 Pickup Truck (DFW/DPL)

Standard Catalog of Light-Duty Trucks

1958 DeSoto 1-Ton Stake (DFW/DPL)

DETROIT — Detroit, Mich. — (1914-1915) — Anderson Electric Car Co. produced a 1-ton electric truck under this name in 1914. It was designated the Model 2 and sold for $1,500 in chassis form. This firm also built the Detroit Electric trucks (see next listing) and automobiles.

1914 Detroit Model 2 Truck Chassis (OCW)

1914 Detroit Model 1 Panel Body Delivery (OCW)

DETROIT ELECTRIC — Detroit, Mich. — (1909-1927) — This was a long-lived electric. It was manufactured at first by the Anderson Carriage Co.; then the Anderson Electric Car Co. and, finally, by the Detroit Electric Car Co. In some years the smallest models were rated at 1/2-ton capacity.

1910 Detroit Electric 10CWT Delivery Van (OCW)

DETROIT MOTOR WAGON — Detroit, Mich. — (1912-1913) — The Motor Wagon Co., of Detroit, Mich., produced several light-duty vans of 800 lb. and 1,000 lb. capacity in 1912. The four-cylinder engine sat in a 102 in. wheelbase and was attached to a planetary transmission. Final drive was by chain. The smaller wagon was $610; the larger one $900. Four different 1,000 lb. (1/2-ton) models were marketed in 1913. The line included an Express Wagon and Stake-bodied truck, which both sold for $950, plus two panel deliveries. The first panel was $975 and the second, probably a closed cab version, was $985.

DE WITT — North Manchester, Ind. — (1984-1986) — This is a replica of the DeWitt auto-buggy, produced in the same town as the original, but many years later. The company tried to generate interest in this beautiful copy of a high-wheeler among car collectors. Though promoted primarily as a passenger vehicle, a cargo box was available for the rear deck.

1984 DeWitt Flareboard Express (EK)

DIAMOND T — Chicago, Ill. — (1911-1966) — Diamond T's origins go back to 1905 when C.A. Tilt built his first car. He continued that line until 1911, when one of his buyers wanted a truck. The first was a 1-1/2-ton conventional four-cylinder truck. Diamond T built some trucks rated as small as 1,500 lbs. capacity. In 1916, the model JA, rated at 3/4-ton, sold for $1,175. This evolved into the 1-ton J-5 of 1919, with a 3-1/3 x 4 in. 20 hp four-cylinder engine. There was no 1-ton for 1920, but 1921-1922 brought the Model 03, a 1-ton with a 3-3/4 x 5-1/4 in. four and 3,800 lb. shipping weight. In 1923, the 03 was up-rated to 1-1/2-tons, but a new 3/4-ton to 1-ton Model 75 appeared. It had a 4 x 5 in. four and weighed 1,000 lbs. less. The Model 75 continued in 1924 and was then up-rated to 1-ton only for 1925. The trucks grew larger until 1936, when C.A. Tilt restyled the line with new streamlined looks for many models. The 3/4-ton Model 80 was introduced with a list price of $560. It had a 3-1/4 x 4-1/8 in. Hercules six generating 25.35 net horsepower and offered pickup and panel models with flashy styling and chrome wheels. The model 301 and 304 one-ton trucks were also available. In 1938, the Model 80 trucks were continued as 80S (standard) or 80D (deluxe) versions at $560 and $620 respectively. There was also a new Model 201 1-ton, plus "S" and "D" versions of the Model 301, and 1-ton Models 305, 304S, 304D and 212 ADL (the latter a light version of the 1-1/2-ton. The Model 231, a 1-ton Dor-to-Dor delivery was listed, too. For 1939-1940, the line was cut-back to a single 1-ton conventional (201) and a pair of Stutz-designed 1-ton Pak-Age-Car deliveries. Starting in 1941, a pair of 1/2-ton Diamond Ts were marketed: Model 91 and Model 117. Both utilized a 3-5/16 x 3-7/8 in 17.55 hp six. Apparently, the model numbers designated wheelbase length, the smaller trucks weighing 3,150 lbs. and the larger tipping the scales at 3,400 lbs. There were also a 1/2-ton 201L/201CL versions of the Model 201 1-ton conventional, plus 1-ton versions of Diamond T's 300 and 400 series 1-1/2-tons. The range of civilian models was continued after WWII, when production hit an all-time peak. Then, in 1951, the

company began to focus exclusively on heavy-duty trucks, dropping its smaller models. In 1958, the company was acquired by White Motor Co., which had purchased Reo the previous year. This led to some wonderful large Diamond-Reo models, but the days of the handsome Diamond T pickups were gone forever.

1935 Diamond T 1-Ton Wrecker (Joe Egle)

1937 Diamond T Model 80D 3/4-Ton Pickup (PM)

1940 Diamond T 1-Ton Pickup (JAG)

1948 Diamond T 1-Ton Pickup (M. Stowell)

1949 Diamond T 1-Ton Pickup (H.F. Fugitt)

DISPATCH — Minneapolis, Minn. — (1910-1919) — The Dispatch Motor Car Co. built both autos and small trucks, styled with Renault-type hoods. In 1918, their 3/4-ton truck sold for $1,100.

DIEHL — Philadelphia, Pa. — (1918-1927) — Diehl Motor Truck Works made a 1-ton from 1918-1920. It had a Continental engine.

DIVCO — Detroit, Mich./Delaware, Ohio — (1926 to date) — The originator of the Divco milk truck was George Bacon, chief engineer of Detroit Electric Car Co. These stand-up, forward-control vans came in many configurations and sizes. The firm also went through numerous mergers.

1927 Divco Walk-in Milk Delivery Truck (OCW)

1947 Divco Van with Charles Wacker body (DFW/CWC)

Standard Catalog of Light-Duty Trucks

1948 Divco Helm's Bakery Van (OCW)

1948 Divco Walk-in Milk Truck (RAW)

DORRIS — St. Louis, Mo. — (1912-1925) — At the 1912 Chicago Auto Show, Dorris Motor Car Co. exhibited a 1,500 lb. Model G delivery car available in chassis ($2,000) and closed panel body ($2,400) models. It had a four-cylinder, 30 hp motor and selective sliding transmission. The loading space inside the panel was 46 in. wide, 70 in. long and 60 in. high. It had contracting/expanding rear wheel brakes and 35 x 4-1/2 in. tires. In 1913, the 3/4-ton was marketed as a chassis for $2,100. It reappeared in 1915 ($1,950) and 1916 ($1,900). The latter year, it was identified as the Model IA-4. Heavier Dorris trucks were made later. The lightest was the 1-ton Model K-2 of 1922 to 1924.

1912 Dorris Model G 1,500 lb. Delivery Car (OCW)

1912 Dorris Commercial Car

Standard Catalog of Light-Duty Trucks

1914 Dorris Screenside Delivery (DFW/MPC)

1914 Dorris Panelside Delivery Van (OCW)

1914 Dorris Platform Stake (OCW)

DORT — Flint, Mich. — (1921-c.1924) — The Dort Motor Car Co. built autos and, in some years, also marketed a panel truck.

1921 Dort 1-Ton Panel Van (OMM)

DOWAGIAC — Dowagiac, Mich. — (1909-1912) — This was a light van built by the Dowagiac Motor Car Co.

DOWNING — Detroit, Mich. — (1914) — The Downing Cyclecar Co. built a light van on their cyclecar chassis.

DUDLY — Menominee, Mich. — (1914-1915) — This was a cyclecar with a light van body and known as the "Dudly Bug." It was built by the Dudly Tool Co.

DUER — Chicago, Ill. — (1910) — This was a high-wheeler, steered by a tiller, and made by the Chicago Coach & Carriage Co.

1908 Duer High-Wheel Light Delivery Wagon (JAW)

DUNLAP — Columbus, Ohio — (1914-1915) — The Dunlap Electric Co. built a 1/2-ton capacity, battery-powered truck.

DUNTLEY — (See Little Giant)

DUPLEX — Lansing, Mich. — (1908 to date) — This make of truck has survived for many years, being built by a succession of firms in Charlotte and Lansing, Mich. and then in Winona, Minn. Most of its trucks were very heavy and had all-wheel drive. In their early days a 3/4-ton four-wheel drive delivery wagon was built. This two-cylinder vehicle was called the Model A and was a 1,500 lb. delivery model. It was offered in 1910-1911 for $1,250 as a product of Power Car Co. of Charlotte, Mich. By 1915, the company had become the Duplex Truck Co., of Lansing, Mich.

1914 Duplex Light Express Wagon (DFW/WRHS)

DURANT — Flint, Mich. — (1928-1929) — In January 1928, Durant Motors announced a restyled line of its passenger cars. The name Star was used on four-cylinder models and the Durant name, which had been dropped from use in mid-1926, appeared again on the three six-cylinder models. At the company's Toronto, Canada factory, the Star commercial line was revived using the Durant name and featuring a variety of body styles similar to those available on the Star chassis in 1926-1927. Production at the Elizabeth, N.J. factory listed only the bare chassis and the convertible roadster under the Durant name on the price list, but it is believed the complete line was also available from the Elizabeth factory. The small, 1/2-ton, commercial line was powered by the same Continental four-cylinder engine used in the Star. The trucks featured only updated styling and paint schemes as the change for 1928. A second line of trucks, this a 3/4-ton series built on the model 65 Durant chassis, would be produced only in the Lansing, Mich. plant. These would bear the Rugby name, not Durant. This series had only six-cylinder models. Having started in late March 1928, production of trucks under the Durant name continued for only a few months and by summer, all commercial production would change to the Rugby name. (Prior to this, the Rugby name had been used on Star cars that were made for export sale.) However, these Series M-2 Durant trucks continued to be sold as new models in 1929. This was probably because sales of trucks remaining in inventory carried over into calendar 1929.

1928 Durant Closed Cowl Cab w/Express Body (JG/DFR)

DURO/DUROCAR — Los Angeles (Alhambra), Calif. — (1910-1916) — Apparently, the first truck offered by this company was a 3/4-ton covered delivery that sold for $1,600. It had a 110 in. wheelbase and 56 in. track. The 26 hp engine was a 5-1/2 x 5 in. bore and stroke side-valve two-cylinder linked to a selective, sliding three-speed transmission, leather-faced cone clutch and shaft drive system. It had thermo-syphon cooling, dual jump spark ignition and a Remy magneto and dry cell electrical system. Semi-elliptic springs were used in front, with full-elliptics at the rear. Tires were 34 x 3-1/2 in. all around. This truck was listed in *MOTOR* magazine as late as Feb. 1910. In its July 23, 1910 issue, *PACIFIC MOTORING* featured an ad featuring the new four-cylinder products of Durocar Mfg. Co., 935 So. Los Angeles St. Trucks and cars were featured. The Durocar Light Truck apparently used the Duro "Little Four," a four-cylinder engine with 35 hp. It was among several different body styles (probably including passenger cars) that were offered for $1,750. However, the ad boldly indicated that they were "worth $500 more" because they had power to spare. The second new series was the Duro "Big Four," which produced 50 hp. It was promoted as "an ideal seven-passenger family car." A price of $3,500 was listed for the Big Four, but there's no indication as to whether a commercial version was available. Apparently, the company was reorganized sometime after 1910. By 1914, the model name was shortened to Duro and the manufacturer was listed as Amalgamated Motors Corp. of Alhambra. The only model was a 1-1/2-ton truck chassis with a $2,000 pricetag.

DURYEA — Reading, Pa. — (1896-1917) — There were several firms associated with this famous name. They built some trucks, although not on a regular basis. A pair of two-cylinder models were made under the Chas. E. Duryea Co. name in 1910 and 1911. The 1910 model was a 500 lb. delivery selling for $800. A 700 lb. delivery, priced at $725, was marketed the next season. Also available, in 1911, was a one-cylinder model called the Tri-Van. It was rated for 400 lbs. and sold for $400. After a brief absence from the truck market, a 1/2-ton chassis priced at $600 was offered by Duryea Laboratories in 1916. During 1918, the Duryea Motor Co., of Saginaw, Mich., cataloged four light-duty commercial vehicles, all with 800 lb. payload ratings. They included a chassis for $600, the Model A open express for $625, the Model B convertible truck for $650 and the Model C panel body delivery for $675. All Duryea trucks were gasoline powered models.

1896 Duryea Military Field Car (DFW/HCHS)

DUTCHER PTV — San Diego, Calif. — (1984) — The Dutcher PTV was a commercial mini-van made by Dutcher Industries, Inc. It had a rear-mounted gasoline engine, automatic transmission and low maintenance, corrosion-resistant chassis structure with replaceable fiberglass body panels and independent suspension system. The truck could accomodate a driver, seven passengers and 20 cu. ft. of luggage. It could also be converted to transport two wheelchairs and four passengers.

1984 Dutcher PTV Mini-Van (OCW)

E

EAGLE — St. Louis, Mo. — (1920-1928) — The Eagle Motor Truck Corp. built trucks in a range of sizes, some as small as 1/2-ton capacity.

ECLIPSE — Franklin, Pa. — (1911-1913) — Eclipse Motor Truck Co. sold a four-cylinder 1-ton truck. It had a compressed air starter.

ECLIPSE — Cleveland, Ohio — The Eclipse Motor Co. was listed in *AUTOMOBILE TRADE JOURNAL* as a maker of 1-ton trucks, but little else is recorded concerning the firm.

ECONOMY — Joliet, Ill. — (1909-1912) — The Economy Motor Car Co. built high-wheel vans with two-cylinder engines. The company's 1910 truck-line was comprised of the Model 1 and the Model 2, both of which used two-cylinder gasoline engines. In chassis only form, the first sold for $850, while the second was $1,200. The designations Model 2 and Model 3 were used in 1911. This Model 2 was a 1-ton delivery vehicle with a $1,400 price-tag, while the Model 3 was a 1/2-ton delivery selling at $1,150. After reorganizing as the Economy Motor Co. and moving to Tiffin, Ohio, the firm came up with a two truck line for 1918. This included the Model 36-T, a 1,200 lb. express for $1,095, and the 1-36-T, a 1-ton chassis-only priced at $1,295.

1911 Economy 1,000 lb. Motor Truck (OCW)

ELECTRIC VEHICLE ASSOCIATION — New York, N.Y. — (c. 1918) — This appears to be a trade organization, rather than a truck manufacturer. The EVA ran advertisements promoting the use of electric delivery trucks. A 1918 advertisement told how Mandel Bros., of Chicago, Ill., adapted electric delivery wagons, which cost only $5.80 per day in total operating costs. The association also had offices in Boston and Chicago.

Standard Catalog of Light-Duty Trucks

1918 Electric Vehicle Association Panel Delivery (OCW)

ELLSWORTH — Keokuk, Ia. — (1916-1920) — The Mills-Ellsworth Co. built light delivery vans.

ELMIRA — Elmira, N.Y. — (1916-1921) — The Elmira Commercial Motor Car Co. built a 1/2-ton truck.

ELYSEE — Hagerstown, Md. — (1926-1932) — This product of the M.P. Moller auto empire was a Panel Delivery truck. It came in Band Box, Fifth Avenue, Courier and Mercury models designed for delivering high-class goods to wealthy homes. It was based on Moller's Standish brand passenger cars and used the same radiator grille and Continental Red Seal six-cylinder engine.

ERSKINE — South Bend, Ind. — (1928-1930) — Erskines were a smaller auto built by Studebaker. They offered 1/2-ton capacity chassis, panels, and screen bodies. In 1929, the six-cylinder chassis sold for $675; the screenside for $860 and the panel for $875. (For additional information, see the Studebaker section in this catalog.)

1927 Erskine Model 50 Closed Panel Delivery (OCW)

1928 Erskine Model 51 Sedan Delivery (OCW)

ESSEX — Detroit, Mich. — (1919-1933) — Hudson Motor Car Co. offered the Essex as a lower price auto. In some years light trucks were built on their chassis. In 1933, 1/2-ton Essex trucks, on 106 in. wheelbases, were in the $440-$545 price range. By this time, the trucks were also called Essex-Terraplane. (For additional information, see the Hudson section in this catalog.)

EUGOL — Kenosha, Wis. — (1921-1923) — Eugol Motor Truck Co.'s Model 752 was a four-cylinder, 1-ton with pneumatic tires and three-speed transmission.

EVANS LIMITED — Detroit, Mich. — (1912-1913) — Automobile Manufacturing & Engineering Co. produced the 1,000 lb. (1/2-ton) Model 1 with four-cylinder engine. It had a three-speed transmission and shaft drive. This $1,200 model had a 112 in. wheelbase.

F

FALCON — Detroit, Mich. — (1915-1916) — This was a 1/2-ton truck built by the Falcon Motor Truck Co.

FAMOUS — St. Joseph, Mich. — (1917-1923) — Famous Trucks, Inc.'s Model B10 was a 1-ton with a 10 ft. wheelbase and Continental four-cylinder engine. It sold for $1,690.

FARGO — Chicago, Ill. — (1913-1921) — The Fargo Motor Car Co. built a line of trucks in the 3/4-ton to 1-ton capacity range.

FARGO — Detroit, Mich. — (1930-1972) — The Fargo line of commercial vehicles from Chrysler has had a long and varied history. Its origins began in the early days of the company, yet the Fargo name is barely known in the country of its origin. It is nearly a household word elsewhere in the world. In his early plans for the corporation, Walter P. Chrysler knew he had to fill all segments of the marketplace. Using the popular, mid-priced Chrysler car as his base, he branched out in all directions. For the commercial buyer, he decided to organize a new and separate company. It was known as Fargo Motor Corp. Fargo was not an automatic offering to Chrysler franchise holders. In a bulletin issued July 9, 1928, J.E. Fields (Chrysler vice-president in charge of sales) stated "only where local conditions warrant, where finances are adequate and where a commercial car activity will not detract from passenger car operations, will the Fargo franchise be offered to Chrysler distributors and dealers." The Fargo franchise was next offered to DeSoto dealers and, then, to dealers outside the Chrysler organization. The Fargo line initially consisted of 1/2-ton and 3/4-ton chassis, with a choice of bodies including a Panel and Sedan Delivery (sedan body with windows). Further expansion of the initial line included plans for trucks up to 2-tons, but only a 1-ton would eventually see the light of day. Chrysler Corp. was, by the end of July 1928, able to purchase the huge Dodge Brothers' holdings. These included not only Dodge trucks, but Graham Brothers trucks as well (Graham was the line's medium-and heavy-duty offering). This resulted in a new "ballgame." Chrysler found itself literally swimming in truck lines. The depression of late 1929 brought a need to rationalize the lineup. It was easy to drop the Graham Brothers name (the Grahams had already resigned to begin production of an automobile under their own name). By 1930, the original Fargo would be gone as well. Yet, the name was destined to live for another 42 years. Following the shutting down of Fargo production lines, the Fargo Motor Corp. became Chrysler's national fleet sales organization. In 1931, it absorbed the national fleet sales division of Dodge Brothers and Chrysler Corp. Fargo's new function was to further sales of Chrysler-built cars and trucks to national fleet users, federal and state governments and certain larger counties and cities by making vehicles meeting specified customer requirements. Although the Fargo Corp. was to handle fleet sales of all Chrysler-built products, it wasn't long before a need began to appear for the re-emergence of the Fargo truck line. From 1933-1935, over 3,500 Fargo 1-1/2-ton trucks were built in Detroit and exported around the world. Then came 1936 and Canada, where the Fargo name got a new, long-term lease on life. Because of its size, Chrysler-Canada's method of providing its dealers with dual brands to sell was unique. Chrysler and Plymouth were paired in one division, with DeSoto-Dodge paired in the other. (In the U.S., each division was individually structured.) Because of the pairings in Canada, Chrysler-Plymouth was "out in the cold" as far as truck sales were concerned. So, for 1936, the Fargo truck line made its debut in Canada. It was added to the Chrysler Div. The first Fargo pickups, of 1936, were little more than Plymouth passenger cars with Dodge pickup cabs. The hood, fenders, headlamps, running boards were pure Plymouth, yet the vehicle was fitted with a unique grille insert and radiator ornament. Fargo even shared Dodge's new truck assembly plant on Tecumseh Road in Detroit. For 1937, the Fargo was based solely on Dodge sheet metal (as was the Plymouth Commercial Car line here). But, there was a difference. While the Plymouth Commercial Car was offered only in 1/2-ton configurations, the Fargo lineup included models of 1/2- to 3-tons. The Plymouth Commercial Car lasted only through 1941, but Fargo remained a Canadian offering through 1972. While those in the know tend to think of the Fargo as a purely Canadian truck from this point on, production actually took place (with the exception of World War II) in Detroit as well as Canada. However, the trucks were sold only in Canada and other export markets. As the years passed, Fargos differed less and less from Dodges on which they were based. By the end, the nameplates read Fargo, while the hubcaps read Dodge. By 1972, the need to rationalize the line once again came to Chrysler Corp. As the model year ended, so, too, came the end of the line for the once proud Fargo name. (To muddy the waters a little further, it should be mentioned in passing that some export commercial vehicles were sold under the DeSoto nameplate long after the passenger car by the same name had passed from the scene. The DeSoto truck, like the Fargo, was merely a Dodge under its skin.)

1937 Fargo 1/2-Ton Pickup (C.D. Clayton)

1939 Fargo 1-Ton Pickup (RPZ)

1939 Fargo 1/2-Ton Panel (RPZ)

1929 Fargo Clipper "Suburban" (CHC)

1941 Fargo 1/2-Ton Pickup (B. Roycroft/JB)

1947 Fargo 1-Ton Military Type 4x4 Power Wagon (RPZ)

1957 Fargo Deluxe 1/2-Ton Utiline Pickup (CHC/JB)

1962 Fargo F100 Sweptline Pickup (RPZ)

1968 Fargo F100 Utiline Pickup (RPZ)

1969 Fargo FW100 Power Wagon 4x4 Utiline Pickup (RPZ)

Standard Catalog of Light-Duty Trucks

FAWICK — Sioux Falls, S.D. — (1913-1916) — Not exactly a household word, this was a make of light truck built by the Fawick Motor Car Co.

FEDERAL — Detroit, Mich. — (1910-1959) — The Federal Motor Truck Co., manufacturer of well-known make of trucks attempted to offer 3/4-ton models in the 1930s. An article in *SPECIAL INTEREST AUTOS* (1980) questioned whether actual production ever commenced. Only drawings (no photos) of these models have been seen. Federal did offer a 3/4-ton in 1949. One-tons were unquestionably produced for many years.

1930 Federal Walk-in Panel (DFW/NAHC)

1939 Federal 3/4-Ton Panel (DFW/MVMA)

1939 Federal 3/4-Ton Pickup (DFW/MVMA)

1940 Federal Walk-in Delivery Van (DFW/SI)

1949 Federal Model 15M Utility Express (DFW/MVMA)

FEDERAL-KNIGHT — Detroit, Mich. — (1924-1928) — In June, 1924, Federal (see above listing) introduced the Willys-Knight sleeve-valve engine to the motor truck industry. A light-duty chassis was engineered to accept this powerplant and sell for just $1,095. The Federal-Knight was continued until 1928, at which time Willys-Knight started putting the engine in its own trucks. The model designation "FK" was used to identify those trucks which utilized the Knight "sleeve-valve" engine under license. The powerplant was a four-cylinder version with a bore and stroke of 3-5/8 x 4 in. and an NACC (National Automobile Chamber of Commerce) rating of 21.03 hp. The Model FK trucks had a 2,300 lb. curb weight and 1-ton payload rating. The 40 bhp produced by the novel sleeve-valve engine looked impressive on paper, although its reliability for long-term usage was a point of debate among truck fleet operators.

1924 Federal-Knight Fully-Closed Panel Delivery (OCW)

1925 Federal-Knight 1-Ton Chassis (OCW)

1925 Federal-Knight Semi-Enclosed Panel Delivery (OCW)

1925 Federal-Knight Open Cab Panel Delivery (OCW)

FINDLEY — Geneva, Ohio — (1909-1912) — The Findley Motor Co. was the same as the Ewing Auto Co. and built a number of light-duty trucks and taxis. The Ewing Model C of 1909-1910 was a $3,000 five-passenger taxi. In 1911, Models A and B were made. The "A" was a 1/2-ton delivery priced at $2,000. The "B" was a two-cylinder delivery rated for 500 lbs. and selling for $950. For 1912, the products included express models of "A" and "B" with payload ratings of 750 and 2,000 lbs., respectively. The first was still $2,000, but the cheaper truck now had a $1,125 pricetag.

FIRESTONE-COLUMBUS — Columbus, Ohio — (1912) — The Columbus Buggy Co. built a vehicle which could be converted from a light van to a passenger car.

FISHER-STANDARD — Detroit, Mich. — (1912-1933) — Built by the Standard Motor Truck Co., whose larger models were called Standards, the Fisher-Standard Junior was a small 3/4-ton to 1-1/2-ton model offered in the early 1930s.

FLANDERS — Detroit, Mich. — (1912-1913) — Flanders Motor Co., which was to become a part of Studebaker, built autos. However, some of their automobile chassis were outfitted with truck bodies.

1912 Flanders Panel Delivery (OCW)

1912 Flanders Panel Delivery (OCW)

FLINT — Flint, Mich. — (1912-1915) — The Flint was a companion car to the Best. It was built by Durant-Dort Carriage Co. A four-cylinder engine was used and the light-duty chassis sold in the $1,285 to $1,375 range.

1914 Flint Model C Panel (OCW)

FORT WAYNE — Fort Wayne, Ind. — (1911-1913) — Fort Wayne Auto Mfg. Co.'s Model A was a 1-ton with a four-cylinder engine, three-speed gearbox and double chain-drive.

FOSTORIA — Fostoria, Ohio — (1916) — The Fostoria Light Car Co. made a gasoline-powered 1,500 lb. (3/4-ton) truck chassis that sold for $485.

1916 Fostoria Canopy Delivery Truck (DFW)

FRANKLIN — Syracuse, N.Y. — (1902-1935) — The Franklin Automobile Co. is known best for its air-cooled autos. Up until 1912, it also marketed a line of light trucks. In addition, some of their later auto chassis were outfitted with truck and other commercial bodies.

1911 Franklin Commercial Car with pneumatics (OCW)

1911 Franklin B.F. Goodrich Express (DFW/SI)

Standard Catalog of Light-Duty Trucks

1910 Franklin 1-Ton Delivery (OCW)

FRAYER-MILLER — Columbus, Ohio — (1906-1910) — This nameplate was a product of Oscar Lear Auto Co. from 1906-1910 and made by Kelly Motor Truck Co. in 1910. A 1-ton gasoline truck was a product of 1910. It sold for $2,600 as a chassis.

1907 Frayer-Miller Canopy Stake Bed Express (JAW)

FRITCHLE — Denver, Colo. — (1911-1916) — This was an delivery van version of a battery-powered electric automobile. It was built by the Fritchle Auto & Battery Co.

1914 Fritchle Panel Body Delivery (OCW)

FRONTMOBILE — Camden, N.J. — (1918-1919) — The Camden Motors Corp. built both autos and light trucks.

F-S — Milwaukee, Wis. — (1912) — The F-S Motors Co. built a short-lived line of trucks, the smallest being a model rated at 3/4-tons.

FULTON — New York, N.Y. — (1916-1925) Fulton Motor Truck Co. had offices in New York City and a factory in Farmingdale, Long Island. Though mainly a large truck builder (up to 4-1/2 tons), from 1921 to 1925 it built a 1-ton with an interesting play off the company's name. It was called the "Full-Ton Express." Features included a four-cylinder engine, 130 in. wheelbase and characteristically round Fulton radiator. Called the Model A, it had 35 x 5 pneumatic tires.

G

GABRIEL AUTO CO. — Cleveland, Ohio — (1910-1915) — This firm produced many light-duty models in chassis-only form. Its K of 1914-1915 was a 1/2-ton priced at $1,000 and $1,200. The 3/4-ton Model H sold for $1,500 in 1914 and $1,600 in 1915-1916. The 1-ton model J was $2,000 in both 1914 and 1915. A lower-priced ($1,800) Model O 1-ton bowed in 1916. The firm evolved from the W.H. Gabriel Carriage & Wagon Co. and built cars under that name until 1912. With introduction of a 1-ton truck in 1913, the Gabriel Motor Truck Co. was formed. However, it appears that Gabriel Auto Co. continued producing commercial cars and trucks up to 2-tons, under the original name, until 1916.

1914 Gabriel Model K Flareboard (OCW)

1914 Gabriel Model H Covered Flareboard (OCW)

1914 Gabriel Model J Covered Flareboard (OCW)

GABRIEL — Cleveland, Ohio — (1913-1920) — Although this company can be dated to 1913 for trucks built under another variation of its name (see previous entry), the name Gabriel Motor Truck Co. was separately attached to several 1-ton and under commercial vehicles. The first of these appeared in model year 1917. Available for that season only was the Model B, a gas-powered 1,500 lb. model priced at a modest $800. It was accompanied by the 2,000 lb. Model C, another gasoline-engined truck with a price that was twice as high. In 1918, the 1-ton (Model C) was the lightest model, but the price of its chassis-only configuration was raised to $1,750.

GAETH — Cleveland, Ohio — (1906-1910) — The Gaeth Automobile Works also produced some light trucks.

1908 Gaeth 1-Ton Delivery Van (OCW)

GALE — Galesburg, Ill. — (1905-1906) — This was a small van, with a 73 in. wheelbase, built by the Western Tool Works.

GALLOWAY — Waterloo, Iowa — (1908-1911) — Agricultural equipment was the first product of this firm. The company was organized in 1906. An 18.22 hp two-cylinder, solid tire, chain-drive farm wagon type vehicle was sold. It could be fitted with "Sunday-go-to-meeting" seats for passenger transport. This truck was introduced in 1908. During the week, its express body could handle heavy cargo-carrying chores. It had a load space 78 in. long and 42 in. wide that could carry between 1,000 lbs. and 1,500 lbs. Other features included a two-speed planetary transmission and 85 in. wheelbase. The price was $570 or $12 more with the extra seat. One of these rare trucks survives in Bill Pollock's "Automobile Showcase" in Pottstown, Pa.

1909 Galloway Flareboard Express (Pollock Auto Showcase)

GARFORD — Lima, Ohio — (1909-1933) — The Garford Motor Truck Co. built a moderately well-known large truck. Late in its corporate life, it became part of a combine which also made Relay, Service and Commerce trucks. In some years a 3/4-ton capacity Garford was offered. In 1916, the Garford Model 64, rated at 3/4-ton capacity, had chain-drive, a four-cylinder engine, and came with a choice of solid or pneumatic tires. As a chassis, it sold for $1,350.

1921 Garford 1- to 1-1/2-Ton Livestock Delivery (JAW)

Standard Catalog of Light-Duty Trucks

1923 Garford Model 15 Chassis & Cowl (JAW)

1924 Garford Covered Flareboard Express (OCW)

GARY — Gary, Ind. — (1916-1927) — The Gary Motor Truck Co. built trucks ranging in capacity from 3/4-ton to 5-tons. The first 1-ton was the Model F four-cylinder of 1916-1920. There was no 1-ton model in the 1921 line, but the "F" returned in 1922. For 1923, the Model W 1-ton was brought out. This became the WLD in 1925.

1917 Gary Model E 3/4-Ton Panel Delivery (DFW/SI)

GAY — Ottawa, Ill. — (1913-1915) — S.G. Gay Co. made 3/4-ton and 1-ton models. Both had four-cylinder engines, three-speed transmissions, solid rubber tires, semi-elliptic springs all around and double chain-drive.

GAYLORD — Gaylord, Mich. — (1910-1913) — This was a utility model based on the firm's regular passenger cars selling for $1,000 to $1,500. A variety of 20-40 hp four-cylinder engines were employed.

GEM — Grand Rapids, Mich. — (1917-1919) — This was a light delivery van, made by the Gem Motor Car Corp.

1917 GEM 1/2-Ton Panel Delivery (HAC)

GENERAL — Cleveland, Ohio — (1903) — This was a van version of a runabout, built by the General Automobile & Manufacturing Co.

GENERAL VEHICLE CO. — Long Island City, N.Y. — (1906-1920) — Battery-powered electrics were built by this company under the trade-name "G.V." See listings under that name below.

GENEVA — Geneva, N.Y. — (1912-1919) — The Geneva Wagon Co. produced a line of small trucks. In 1918, their 3/4-ton capacity chassis sold for $700. This appeared to be the lowest price of any 3/4-ton chassis on a list of about 25 makes of that era.

GIANT — Chicago Heights, Ill. — (1911-1923) — Early reference sources, such as the *MANUAL OF AUTOMOBILE LIABILITY INSURANCE*, listed this truck as the "Little Giant." Later sources, such as the *BRANHAM AUTOMOBILE REFERENCE BOOK*, call it the "Giant." The first year for model listings was 1911, although the Imperial Palace Hotel and Casino has a 1909 Giant on display in its Las Vegas auto collection. Chicago Pneumatic Tool Co. was actually the manufacturer and BRANHAM clearly indicates that Giant Truck Corp. went "out of business" after 1923. Chicago Pneumatic, of course, is still with us, today, as a maker of air compressors. The Giant Truck Co.'s first product line consisted of a 3/4-ton delivery wagon with a two-cylinder engine and $1,000 pricetag. By 1912, a pair of two-cylinder gas-powered models were available. The 3/4-ton was the Model C, selling at $1,100 for the chassis. Also offered was a 1-ton Model D that came as an open flareboard ($1,100), canvas top ($1,150), standard body ($1,150) or full-panel ($1,200). In 1913, there were two 3/4-tons, the Models A and B, both at $950, and two 1-tons, the Model C ($1,050) and Model D ($1,150). Models available for 1914 were all 1-tons priced at $1,050. They were labeled the D, F and H. The H was carried over for 1915 and 1916 (as the H-3) with a $1,350 pricetag. From this point on, mostly 1-1/2 to 5-ton models were marketed, but a 3/4-ton called the Model 15 was available until 1918. It used a four-cylinder engine with 3-1/2 x 5 in. bore and stroke that produced 19.60 hp. A 3,425 lb. curb weight was registered. According to serial numbers, about 800 to 1,300 units were produced.

1909 Giant Express Wagon (Imperial Palace)

GILLIG — Hayward, Calif. — (1912-1913) — Before Gillig Bros. began building buses, Leo Gillig built an experimental truck at his shop in San Francisco in 1912. The Nov. 10, 1912 issue of the *OAKLAND TRIBUNE* reported he had made a 3/4-ton truck and "arrangements to place at least 50 of the light trucks on the market for the 1913 season." The truck used chain-drive and patented differentials of the simplest design, the paper noted. Gillig was prepared to build bodies to order for his trucks, but any production beyond the experimental stage is uncertain. The firm later made buses for many years. In 1976, Gillig Bros. became the Gillig Corp.

G.J.G. — White Plains, N.Y. — (1912-1913) — The G.J.G. Motor Car Co. also built a small van.

GLIDE — Peoria, Ill. — (1911-1912) — The Bartholomew Co. built both autos and small trucks for a short period of time.

GLOBE — Northville, Mich. — (1916-1919) — The Globe Furniture Co. organized Globe Motor Truck Co. One model was a 1,500 lb. (3/4-ton) truck. Six-cylinder engines were used at first, but after 1918, a four-cylinder Continental motor was adopted.

Standard Catalog of Light-Duty Trucks

GOLDEN STATE — San Francisco, Calif. — (1918-1937) — William Goldman began selling truck attachments for Ford cars in 1918 and organized Golden State Truck Co. around 1922. Ten years later, the firm relocated operations to the Doane Motor Truck Co. plant on the city's Third St. Both companies made low-bed trucks and, apparently, consolidated their operations during the depression. The last directory listings for Golden State appeared in 1937.

GRABOWSKY — Detroit, Mich. — (1908-1913) — Max Grabowsky, founder of the Grabowsky Power Wagon Co., was the designer of the Rapid truck. The smallest of his models were 1-tons made in 1910-1911 ($2,300) and 1912-1913 ($2,200). A 22 hp two-cylinder engine was used through 1912.

1909 Grabowsky Power Wagon (Pollock Auto Showcase)

GRAHAM BROS. — Evansville, Ind. — (1919-1928) — This firm became associated with Dodge Bros. in the 1920s and built light trucks (called commercial cars) and medium trucks based on the Dodge automobile. Eventually the Graham Brothers truck became the Dodge truck. In 1928, the Model SD (108 in. wheelbase) 1/2-ton was marketed for $645 along with a series of 3/4-ton DD/DDX models offering pickup, canopy, panel, screenside and sedan delivery bodies. These used a 212 cid Dodge four-cylinder engine and had a 116 in. wheelbase. These models returned in 1929 as SE/SEW (1/2-ton) and DE/DEW (3/4-ton) trucklines. After Jan. 1929, these Graham Bros. "commercial cars" changed to Dodge Bros. models. (See Dodge.)

1925 Graham Bros. 1-Ton Panel Delivery

1925 Graham Bros. United Parcel Truck (DFW/UPS)

1927 Graham Bros. 1-Ton Express (OCW)

1929 Graham Brothers Model DEW 3/4-Ton Panel

GRAMM — Delphos, Ohio — (1926-1942) — The name "Gramm" was associated with several Ohio-built trucks and, in 1915, the Gramm Motor Truck Co. built the first "Willys Utility" model. This company was not a part of Willys-Overland, although John North Willys was, for a time, a majority stockholder in Gramm. The Model 65 Willys Utility was rated at 3/4-ton. In the late 1930s, Gramm Motor Truck Co. had a close relationship with Bickle, of Canada.

1915 Gramm Model 65 1,500 lb. Canopy Express (OCW)

GRAMM-BERNSTEIN — Lima, Ohio — (1912-1930) — Truck pioneer B.A. Gramm joined with Max Bernstein to start this firm which built mostly large trucks. A 1-ton ($1,750); 3/4- to 1-ton ($1,350) and 1-ton ($1,500) were made in 1914-1915-1916, respectively. The Model 10 was offered, in 1921-1922, as a 1-ton. then, it was down-rated to 3/4-ton capacity for 1923-1924.

1914 Gramm-Bernstein Model 1 One-Ton Chassis (OCW)

GRAMM-KINCAID — Lima, Ohio (1925)/Delphos, Ohio (1925-1928) — A separate firm formed by B.A. Gramm in partnership with R.M. Kincaid. It produced 1-ton and larger trucks, as well as buses.

GRANT — Cleveland, Ohio — (1918-1923) — The Grant Motor Car Corp. built both light-duty and medium-duty trucks. All used four-cylinder Continental engines. The light-duty 3/4-ton was dropped in 1920.

GRANT-FERRIS — Troy, N.Y. — (1901) — This early truck company produced a 1/4-ton light van with horizontally-opposed two-cylinder engine and a fast-and-loose pulley transmission. It had a top speed of 12 mph.

GRASS-PREMIER — Sauk City, Wis. — (1923-1937) — This was an assembled truck, made by the Grass-Premier Truck Co. They sometimes offered a 3/4-ton capacity model.

GRAY — Detroit, Mich. — (1923-1925) — The Gray Motor Corp. built autos, and also offered a light van.

1925 Gray 1-Ton Chassis (OCW)

GREAT EAGLE — Columbus, Ohio — (1911-1914) — The United States Carriage Co. built autos and supplied commercial chassis.

1910 Great Eagle Commercial Limousine (NAHC)

GREYHOUND — Toledo, Ohio — (1914-1915) — The Greyhound Cyclecar Co. fitted a van body to its regular chassis to make a truck with a 104 in. wheelbase. The 650 lb. vehicle had a four-cylinder, 10 hp water-cooled engine and sold for $385.

GRUMMAN-OLSON — Garden City, N.Y. — (1963 to date) — Grumman Aerospace company bought the J.B. Olson Corp., which built aluminum-alloy truck bodies under the "Kurb-master" tradename. These trucks used the chassis of other manufacturers with distinctive walk-in van and cube-van type bodies. Smaller models had 102 in. wheelbases.

1983 Grumman-Olson Kurbvan Aluminum Minivan (G-O)

G.V. — Long Island City, N.Y. — (1906-1920) — The General Vehicle Co. built a wide range of battery-powered trucks, usually equipped with General Electric motors. As early as 1907, nine different types were offered. They ranged from flatbed trucks to buses and included light-duty models with a payload capacity of 750 lbs. In 1914, the 750 lb. chassis sold for $1,370, while a 1/2-ton chassis was $1,700 and a 1-ton went for $2,100. The following season, the smallest truck was dropped and the two other 1-ton-or-under models were joined by a new 1/2-ton featuring worm drive. Listings for 1915 and 1917 specified "with G.V. batteries," indicating that the firm manufactured its own wet-cell batteries. In other years, however, the brand of batteries was not specified. For 1916, there were two

1/2-ton models, plus a 1-ton. The smaller truck could go 12 m.p.h. and had a range of 45 miles. G.V.s came with a "mechanical hand horn, taillamp, hub odometer, kit of tools, charging receptacle and plug with 12 feet of cable." Features of one 1/2-ton included an 88 in. wheelbase and chain-drive at a price of $1,700 in 1916. Another one, with a 20 in. longer wheelbase, had worm drive and a $1,950 pricetag. The 1-ton continued to sell for $2,100. Also marketed in that year were two electric freight trucks, of 1-ton capacity, with G.V.X. batteries. The smaller, on a six-foot long chassis, sold for $1,350. The larger, on a 10-foot chassis, was $1,400. Light trucks in the 1918 line included a $1,360 1/2-ton and the $2,100 1-ton. The company, which started under the name Vehicle Equipment Co., survived only until 1920.

1914 G.V. 750-lb. Electric Panel Delivery (OCW)

1914 G.V. 1,000-lb. Electric Panel Delivery (RAW)

1914 G.V. 1-Ton Flareboard Express (OCW)

Standard Catalog of Light-Duty Trucks

1915 G.V. Panel Body Electric Delivery (RAW)

1915 G.V. Naval Gun Factory Truck Crane (RAW)

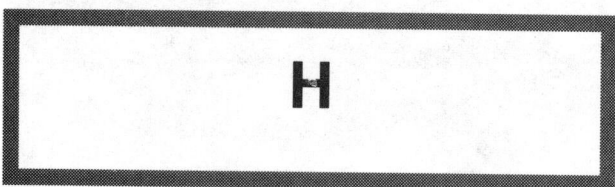

HAHN — Hamburg, Pa. — (1907-date) — Now known as a builder of fire apparatus, Hahn Motors, Inc. at one time built a full range of trucks. From time to time, their smallest model would be less than 1-ton. In 1916, their 3/4-ton chassis was powered by a Continental motor, had a 102 in. wheelbase, worm gear drive, and sold for $1,000. (It also had a Klaxon horn.)

1917 Hahn 1-Ton Model C Canopy Van (JAW)

HANDY WAGON — Auburn, Ind. — (1911-1916) — This was the name of a truck built in Auburn, Ind., a city best known for its Auburn, Cord and Duesenberg cars. Both high-wheeler type delivery wagons and conventional 1/2-tons were produced by the Auburn Motor Chassis Co. The high-wheelers used an air-cooled twin-cylinder engine and chain-drive, while the 1/2-ton was four-cylinder powered.

HANNIBAL — Hannibal, Mo. — (1916) — This truck from Mark Twain's hometown was a 1-ton built by Hannibal Motor Car Co.

HARLEY-DAVIDSON — Milwaukee, Wis. — (1914-to date) — This well-known motorcycle company has made many commercial versions of its products. Most commonly seen are three-wheel delivery vehicles, some with full cab enclosures. These are particularly useful to and popular with traffic law enforcement agencies. In the late 1920s, and possibly at other times, Harley-Davidson also produced a motorcycle ambulance.

1914 Harley-Davidson Box Body Tricar (OCW)

1927 Harley-Davidson Ambulance (HD)

1972 Harley-Davidson Golf Cart Utility Scooter (EK)

HART-KRAFT — York, Pa. — (1907-1913) — Early models built by the Hart-Kraft Motor Co. were high-wheelers. Only 1/2-ton delivery wagons were produced through 1910, with trucks and truck chassis leaving the factory thereafter. For 1909, the line consisted of three two-cylinder deliveries, the A1 ($1,100); A2 ($1,175) and A3 ($1,200). In the following year, the B3 ($1,000), B5 ($1,175) and B6 ($1,100) were offered. Only one light truck, the 1/2-ton BX4 ($1,425) was listed for 1911. Then, for the next two years, models included the 1/2-ton B, 3/4-ton BX, 3/4-ton G and 1-ton E. While prices of $1,800 for the G and $2,000 for the E applied both seasons, the others changed considerably in price. The Model B was $1,175 in 1912 and $825 in 1913, while the BX went from $1,250 to $900. The G and E were part of a new four-cylinder line, introduced in 1911, which took the firm into receivership. Thereafter, Continental engines were used.

1910 Hart-Kraft 1,000 lb. Canopy Express

1911 Hart-Kraft Light-Duty Bus (JBY/DJS)

HATFIELD — Miamisburg, Ohio — (1907-1908) — Hatfield Motor Vehicle Co. built high-wheeler type light open delivery vans. They featured a two-cylinder engine, friction transmission and double chain-drive. This truck tipped the scales at 1,100 lbs. and could handle an 800 lb. payload.

HATFIELD — Cortland, N.Y. (1910)/Cornwall-On-Hudson, N.Y. (1911)/Elmira, N.Y. (1911-1914) — These light trucks were made by Hatfield Automobile Truck Co. after 1911. They were small 1/2-ton and 1-ton vehicles with three-cylinder engines.

1917 Hatfield Model I 1,000 lb. Suburban (HAC) .

HAWKEYE — Sioux City, Iowa — (1916-1933) — This company's line consisted mainly of 1-1/4 to 3-1/2-ton trucks. However, from 1922 to 1925, the 1-ton Model O "speed truck" was marketed. It had a four-cylinder Buda engine.

HENDERSON — North Cambridge, Mass. — (1916-c. 1926) — Henderson Brothers produced two light-duty models as early as 1916. Both were gas-engined and marketed in chassis-only form. The 1,200 lb. model was $1,100 and the 1-tonn sold for $1,500. One industry trade index indicates that other Henderson chassis in the 3/4- to 1-1/2-ton range were available through the middle of the "Roaring '20s."

HENNEGIN — Chicago, Ill. — (1908) — This was a high-wheeler van built by the Commercial Automobile Co. It was listed in the *MANUAL OF AUTOMOBILE LIABILITY INSURANCE* for only one model year. Designated the Model A (a designation applied to the initial efforts of many manufacturers), this one was a two-cylinder, gas-fueled delivery rated for a 600 lb. payload and selling for $650. The engine was mounted beneath the body and linked to a friction type transmission. Double chain-drive carried power to the rear wheels. An 87 in. wheelbase chassis was used.

Standard Catalog of Light-Duty Trucks

1908 Hennegin Model F Physician's Car (NAHC)

HERCULES — South Boston, Mass. — (1913-1915) — Hercules Motor Truck Co. made a 1-ton model priced at $1,175 that came with express or stake bodies.

HERRESHOFF — Detroit, Mich. — (1911-1912) These were small vans (98 in. wheelbase) made by the Herreshoff Motor Co.

HEWITT — New York, N.Y. — (1905-1906) — Edward Ringwood Hewitt's first commercial vehicles were light vans on a single-cylinder passenger car chassis. Some sources show this trade name used through 1909, although the *MANUAL OF AUTOMOBILE LIABILITY INSURANCE* suggests that the identity Hewitt International (see listing below) had actually been adopted by 1907, which is five years earlier than some secondary references indicate.

HEWITT-INTERNATIONAL — N.Y. City — (1907-1912) — This firm evolved from E.R. Hewitt's original effort (listed above). Its products were primarily heavy trucks, although a 1-ton Model 20D was built in 1911 and 1912. It sold for $1,500 in chassis-only form.

HEWITT-LINDSTROM — Chicago, Ill. — (1900-1901) — Financier John Hewitt and engineer Charles A. Lindstrom formed this company to make electric runabouts, town cars, trucks and buses.

1900 Hewitt-Lindstrom Electric Stage Coach (GR)

HEWITT-LUDLOW — San Francisco, Calif. — (c. 1912- c. 1926) — The Hewitt-Ludlow Auto Co. built trucks in the 3/4-ton to 3-1/2-ton capacity range. Their 1916 3/4-ton chassis had Buda power, worm drive, a 120 in. wheelbase and a $1,650 price.

1917 Hewitt-Ludlow 1- to 1-1/2-Ton Gasoline Tanker (JAW)

701

HEWITT-METZGER — N.Y. City — (1913-1914) — When E.R. Hewitt's International Motor Co. (see listing above) merged with Metzger Motor Car Co., a gasoline-engined 1-ton was part of the model lineup. It sold for $1,800. Other models ranged up to 10 tons.

HIGRADE — Grand Rapids, Mich. — (1917-1921) — Highgrade Motors Co. made trucks in the 3/4-ton to 1-1/2-ton capacity range.

HIND & DAUCH — Sandusky, Ohio — (1907-1908) — Hind & Dauch built a 1/2-ton capacity delivery van.

HOLSMAN — Chicago, Ill. — (1908-1910) — These were commercial versions of the high-wheeler car built by Holsman Automobile Co. The 1909 Model 14K was a 1/2-ton gas-engined delivery for $650 and the H14 was a similar model for $850. In 1910, the price of the 14K dropped to $700, while the new 1/2-ton Model H-14-O delivery truck was $1,050.

1900 Holsman Telephone Utility Wagon (DFW/WEPS)

HOOVER — York, Pa. — (1911; 1917-1920) — Hoover Wagon Co. filled one order for 1,500 lb. (3/4-ton) trucks as early as 1911. The company's mainstay business, though, was building York-Hoover car and truck bodies. In 1917, a 1-ton truck with a Continental four-cylinder engine was assembled by the firm. The 1919 version of the 1-ton sold for $1,435. Many Hoovers had postal delivery type bodies, which were a company specialty.

HORNER — Wyandotte, Mich. — (1913-1918) — Detroit-Wyandotte Motor Co. made a 1-ton, but it had a long 145 in. wheelbase for a light-duty model. A screenside express van was offered. The cost was a hefty $2,000-$2,200.

HOUGHTON — Marion, Ohio — (1915-1917) — This firm's assembled type 1-ton truck had a 22 hp four-cylinder engine and pneumatic tires. Many were built as hearses.

1916 Houghton 1-Ton Panel Delivery (DFW/HAC)

HOWARD — Yonkers, N.Y. — (1903) -The Howard Automobile Co. also made a line of trucks, including a 1/2-ton unit with a three-cylinder engine. These trucks were designed by W.S. Howard, who had previously worked for Grant-Ferris Co. Two models were offered; one for carrying passengers and the other for hauling cargo loads up to 1,000 lbs. The company also produced a 4-ton gas/electric truck, which lies beyond the scope of this catalog.

1895 Howard Canopy Top Suburban (NAHC/OPC)

HOWARD — Boston, Mass. — (c. 1916) — This company listed a 1,500 lb. (3/4-ton) truck chassis in 1916. It was priced $940.

HUEBNER — Brooklyn, N.Y. — (c. 1914) — O.E. Huebner Co.'s Model 6 was an electric-powered truck with a closed parcel van body. It had a 500 lb. load capacity and cost $500.

HUPMOBILE — Detroit, Mich. — (1912-1925) — Sources differ as to the range of years the Hupp Motor Co. also manufactured light-duty trucks and commercial chassis.

1914 Hupmobile Model 32 Panel Body (OCW)

1925 Hupmobile Model R Panel Delivery (DFW/OHS)

Standard Catalog of Light-Duty Trucks

1927 Hupmobile Commercial Station Wagon (DFW/CTA)

HUPP-YEATS — Detroit, Mich. — (1911-1912) — The R.C.H. Corp. produced this 1/2-ton electric with open or closed bodies. A screenside express was $1,600.

HURLBURT — New York, N.Y. (1914-1915)/Bronx, N.Y. (1915-1919)/Harrisburg, Pa. (1919-1927) — Hurlburt Motor Truck Co.'s lightest truck was a 1-ton. But, most models were larger. The 1-ton cost $1,750 in 1915 and 1916. The company later became Harrisburg Mfg. & Boiler Co.

IDEAL — Fort Wayne, Ind. — (c. 1911-1916) — Ideal Auto Co. of Fort Wayne introduced a pair of two-cylinder trucks in 1911. The Model C delivery body had a 1,200 lb. load capacity and $1,050 price. The Model D delivery had a 1-ton load capacity and $1,350 price. The 1-ton remained available as the Model I stake or express (1912); Model H chassis (1913); Model I chassis (1914); and Model M chassis (1915-1916). There was also a 1912 Model H 3/4-ton open express ($1,500) and 1913 Model I 3/4-ton chassis (also $1,500).

1914 Ideal Model I 1-Ton Covered Flareboard (OCW)

IMP — Auburn, Ind. — (1913-1915) — This rig was on a cyclecar chassis and built by W.H. McIntyre Co. The Closed Delivery model of 1914 sold for just $395.

1914 Imp Light Closed Delivery Car (OCW)

INDEPENDENT — Plano, Ill. — (1911) — The manufacturer of this $750 gasoline-powered Business Model No. 22 was listed as the Harvester Co.

INDEPENDENT — Port Huron, Mich. — (1915-1918) — Independent Motors Co. marketed the 1,500- to 2,000 lb. Model F chassis for four years at a price of $1,285 to $1,385. It was gas-engined.

INDEPENDENT — Davenport, Ia. — (1917-1921) — This firm built 1-ton assembled trucks with Continental engines, Fuller three-speed gearboxes and Russel bevel gear rear axles. One was the Model B of 1921-1922. It had a 135 in. wheelbase. There was also a Model J 1-ton in 1923-1924.

INDEPENDENT — Youngstown, Ohio — (1918-1923) — A 1-ton was always a part of this company's line. It was another assembled job with a Continental four, three-speed Fuller transmission and worm drive axle.

INDIANA — Marion, Ind. — (1911-1932)/Cleveland, Ohio (1932-1939) — The Indiana was made by Harwood-Barley Mfg. Co. which was later absorbed by White Motor Co. It was a well-known assembler of trucks. A 3/4-ton model was sold in 1915, at a price of $1,200 for the chassis. The firm also made several 1-tons. They included the Model B (1915-1916); Model S (1916); and Model T (1918). The S was particularly interesting, as it came with both 19.6 and 22.5 (ALAM) hp four-cylinder engines, as well as a 21.6 hp six. A Highway Express "speed truck" came out in the year 1922. It was a 1-ton with a 3-3/4 x 5-1/4 in. bore and stroke four that developed 22.5 hp. In 1923, it was marketed as the Model 10. In 1924-1925, a Model 11 with a 4 x 5 in. four and 25.6 hp, was marketed in the 1-ton category.

1914 Indiana Model B-30 Flareboard Express (OCW)

1932 Indiana 1-Ton to 1-1/2-Ton Dump Truck (NSPC/JE)

1932 Indiana Model 70 1-Ton Milk Van (DFW/VWC)

1937 Indiana Walk-in Milk Delivery (DFW/Volvo-White)

1937 Indiana Model 80 Bakery Van (DFW/Volvo-White)

INLAND — Evansville, Ind. — (1919-1921) — One model made by Inland Motor Co. was a 1-ton truck.

INTER-STATE — Muncie, Ind. — (1916-1917) — In 1917, this company introduced a light commercial vehicle rated 850 lbs. with a four-cylinder engine, pneumatic tires and an $850 price.

INTERBORO — Philadelphia, Pa. (1914) — The Interboro Motor Truck Co.'s Model A was a 2,000 lb. (1-ton) payload-rated chassis that sold for $1,850. It had a four-cylinder, 23 hp engine.

IROQUOIS — Buffalo, N.Y. — (1906) — The Iroquois Iron Works built two sizes of trucks: a 4-ton and a 1/2-ton.

J

JACKSON — Jackson, Mich. — (c. 1907-1923) — The Jackson Motor Car Co. had built passenger cars since 1903. It then started building light-duty trucks. Later, it built heavy trucks.

1908 Jackson Panel Delivery Van (NAHC/DPL)

JAMIESON — Warren, Penna. — (1901-1902) — This was a small delivery truck that was made by the Jamieson Automobile Works.

JEFFERY — Kenosha, Wis. — (1914-1917) — The Thomas B. Jeffery Co. is best-known as the builder of the Jeffery Quad, a heavy four-wheel drive and steer truck that became famous in World War I. It also built a lighter 3/4-ton truck, which sold for $1,325 in chassis form in 1914. This model rode on 35 x 4-1/2 in. pneumatic tires and had an electric starter. Also marketed in 1914 was a 1-ton stake bed priced $1,575. No trucks of these capacities were listed for 1915. Then, in 1916, Jeffery added two gas-engined trucks of lighter construction. The Model 1016 was a stake rated for 1,000 lbs. to 1,500 lbs. and selling for $875. The Model 2016 had a 1-ton to 1-1/2-ton rating and a $1,650 pricetag. In 1917, Jeffery was acquired by Nash.

1914 Jeffery 1,500 lb. Flareboard Express (OCW)

1914 Jeffery 1-Ton Flareboard With Stakes (OCW)

1915 Jeffery Police Paddy Wagon (DFW/NAHC)

1916 Jeffery Model 1016 1,500 lb. Panel (DFW/MVMA)

1916 Jeffery 1,500 lb. Flareboard Express (DFW/MVMA)

JOHNSON KANSAS CITY — Kansas City, Mo. — (1905-1917) — These were light vans, sometimes known as the "Kansas City Car," built by the Kansas City Motor Car Company.

JOHNSON — Milwaukee, Wis. -(1901-1912). A fleet of at least four of Professor Johnson's steam-powered 1-ton vans were used for mail delivery service. Later, under Renault licensure, he built gasoline models, too. A 1/2-ton gas-engined delivery truck was offered in 1911 for $1,500. One year later, the model name was changed to "1,000 lb. truck" and it came in delivery ($1,500) and full wood body ($1,600) models. There was also a 1912 one-ton model priced at $2,000.

JOLIET — Joliet, Ill. — (1912) — These lightweight electric delivery vans were made by Joliet Auto Truck Co. The Model E with a 500 lb. load capacity panel body was $900. The Model D with a 1,250 lb. full panel body cost $1,500.

JOLY & LAMBERT — Anderson, Mass. — (c. 1916) — The Joly & Lambert Electric Auto Co. made a 1,000 lb. chassis model priced at $925 and a 1-ton chassis for $1,590.

JONZ — New Albany, Ind. — (1911-1912) — The American Automobile Mfg. Co. also built a line of light trucks with three-cylinder powerplants. The 1-ton gas-engined platform body was $1,500. Also offered for $1,250 were flat or express bodies rated for a 1/2-ton load capacity.

K

KANSAS CITY — Kansas City, Mo. — (1905-1917) — These were light vans sometimes known as the "Kansas City Car." They were built by the Kansas City Motor Car Co.

KARIVAN — Wheatland, Pa. — (1955) — This was a three-wheeled van, outfitted by Tri-Car, Inc.

KEARNS — Beavertown, Pa. — (1909-1928) — The Kearns Motor Car Co. started out building larger trucks. Just after World War I, it introduced some smaller models including one rated at 1/2-ton capacity. Prior to this, there was a 1-ton Model 35 that sold for $2,950 in 1911, plus a $2,100 1-ton of 1912 and the Model 30, another 1-ton of 1914-1915 that retailed for $2,000 to $2,100. Also in 1914, the company sold its Model A. This was a 3/4-ton truck. It was priced at $950 for the chassis, $1,000 for a flareboard, $1,050 for a stake bed and $1,100 for a panel. In 1916, the name Kearns Motor Truck Co. was used for a small chassis with a 1,000 lb. payload rating which sold for $600. The postwar 1/2-ton used a Lycoming engine, dry-plate clutch and internal gear drive. It was $850.

1914 Kearns Model A Panel Delivery Van (OCW)

1918 Kearns Model DU Covered Flareboard Express (DFW)

1920 Kearns Flareboard Express (B. Crowley)

KELLAND — Newark, N.J. — (1922-c. 1926) — The Kelland Motor Car Co. built small, battery-powered vans. Their 1/2-ton chassis sold for $1,750 and their 3/4-ton chassis sold for $1,850.

1920 Kelland Electric Walk-in Delivery Van (DFW/HAC)

KELLY-SPRINGFIELD — Springfield, Ohio — (1910-1929) — This make suceeded the Frayer-Miller and continued to use air-cooled engines through 1912; water-cooled fours thereafter. Characteristics included sloped hoods, behind-the-engine radiators and a three-speed transmission. One-tons were offered through 1916 as the $2,000 Model K-30.

1914 Kelly-Springfield K-30 1-Ton Chassis (OCW)

KENAN — Long Beach, Calif. — (1915) — One of three models produced by Kenan Manufacturing Co. was a 1,500 lb. (3/4-ton) chassis with a gasoline engine and $1,600 price-tag.

KENWORTH — Seattle, Wash. — (1925 to date) — This firm evolved from Gerlinger Motor Car Co. and took its name from H.W. Kent and E.K. Worthington, who were executives for the predecessor firm which built the Gersix truck. Most Kenworths were in the 1-1/2- to 18-ton range, but 1-tons were produced in the middle 1920s. From the 1940s on, the firm has been best known mainly for its tractor trailer trucks.

1926 Kenworth 1-Ton Model OS Van (OCW)

KEYSTONE — Philadelphia, Pa. — (1919-1923) — This company started as the Commercial Car Unit Co. in Philadelphia and later became Keystone Motor Truck Co. of Oaks, Pa. (Montgomery County). At first, the sole product was a 2-ton. A 1-ton model was available in 1920 only. This truck was named the Model 20, which indicated its 2,000 lb. capacity, rather than model year. It had a four-cylinder Buda engine with 3-5/8 x 4 in. bore and stroke, 18.23 hp and a curb weight of 2,040 lbs.

KING — Chicago, Ill. — (c. 1899-1900) — Built by machinist A.W. King, this high-wheel runabout resembled a wagon with flatbed rear deck. It was suitable for light-duty cargo hauling and truck use, as well as passenger carrying.

1896 King High-Wheeler With Platform Deck (NAHC)

KING ZEITLER — Chicago, Ill. — (1919-c. 1929) — The King-Zeitler Co. made trucks of between 3/4-ton to 5-ton capacity.

1924 King Zeitler Chassis & Cab (Reynolds Museum)

KISSEL — Hartford, Wis. — (1908-1931) — The Kissel Motor Car Co. was known for both its autos and trucks, and they are sometimes called "Kissel-Kars." Some of their chassis were used for buses, fire apparatus and professional cars. In 1916, their 1/2-ton delivery chassis with a 115 in. wheelbase sold for $950; their next larger chassis was rated at 3/4 to 1-ton. It had a 125 in. wheelbase and sold for $1,250. Trade directories from the late 1920s show that the smallest Kissel truck, then, was rated at 1-ton.

1912 Kissel 1,500 lb. Platform (KM/HW)

1912 Kissel 1,500 lb. Rack Body (KM/HW)

1913 Kissel 1,500 lb. Delivery Van (DFW/SI)

1914 Kissel 1-Ton Platform Stake (OCW)

1914 Kissel 1,500 lb. Panel Body Delivery (OCW)

1915 Kissel 1,500 lb. Panel Delivery (OCW)

1916 Kissel 3/4-Ton to 1-Ton Express With Stakes (KM/HW)

KLEIBER — San Francisco, Calif. — (1914-1937) — The Kleiber Motor Truck Co. built a full-sized range of trucks, although in its later years it was also an important West Coast distributor for Studebaker. For at least two years, 1929 and 1930, their smallest chassis was rated at 3/4-ton capacity and sold for $1,170.

1930 Kleiber 1-Ton Ice Truck (DFW/SI)

KNOX — Springfield, Mass. — (1901-1924) — Best-known for its three- and four-wheel tractors, the Knox Automobile Co. also made light-duty delivery trucks and ambulances.

1902 Knox Waterless Light Delivery (JAW)

1904 Knox Canopied Express Delivery (JAW)

KOEHLER — Newark, N.J. — (1913-1916) — The H.J. Koehler Sporting Goods Co. produced a line of 1-tons under this company name for four years. The 1913-1915 Model A came as a stake-side open flareboard truck (&750); an express ($790); a canvas-side ($800) or a panel delivery ($900). The Model K of 1915-1916 was produced in chassis-only form ($895); as well as open-flare ($935) or express ($980). All were powered by four-cylinder, overhead valve gasoline engines. By 1917, the name was changed to H.J. Koehler Motor Corp. and trucks over 1-ton were the only products made. Relatives of H.J. Koehler are still active in the truck collecting hobby.

1914 Koehler 1-Ton Express Wagon (OCW)

1915 Krebs Model F 3/4-Ton Light Express (JAW)

KOPP — Buffalo, N.Y. — (1911-1916) — Kopp Motor Truck Co.'s lightest model was a 1-ton truck.

KOSMATH — Detroit, Mich. — (1914-1916) — The Kosmath was a continuation of the Miller Car Co.'s 1914 Model A 1/2-ton panel truck. The first Kosmath was a 1,250 lb. gasoline powered truck that sold for $900 with a panel In 1915, a 1/2-ton Model 14 was offered in chassis form for $850. This became the Model 15 the following season, which sold for $675 in chassis form and $750 as a panel or express.

K.R.I.T. — Detroit, Mich. — (1911-1914) — The Krit Motor Car Co. built autos, and also a light delivery body on one of the auto chassis.

1914 KRIT Model KD 1/2-Ton Panel Body Delivery (OCW)

1914 Kosmath 1,250 lb. Panel Body Van (OCW)

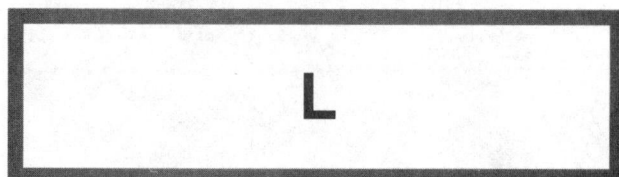

L

LAMBERT — Anderson, Ind. — (1912-1917) — The Buckeye Manufacturing Co. built mainly autos, but also produced some commercial chassis and trucks. The first year for truck production seems to be 1912, when a 1-ton express was offered at $1,600. The Model V-3, of 1913-1914, was a 1-ton chassis with an $1,800 pricetag. For 1915, the line was expanded to include the V-1 with an 800 lb. payload rating. It came as a chassis for $900 or a panel at $950. The same year, the V-2 was offered in the 1,500 lb. class. It sold for $1,125 in chassis form and $1,200 as an express. The V-3 was also carried over at $1,700.

KREBS — Bellevue, Ohio — (1922-1925) — The Krebs Motor Truck Co. built trucks in sizes ranging from 3/4 to six-tons. A 1916 trade directory also mentions a Krebs Commercial Car Co., of Clyde, Ohio, which built trucks with Renault-style hoods. Their 1916 3/4-ton chassis on a 120 in. wheelbase with worm drive, pneumatic tires and a 22.5 hp. engine, sold for $1,600.

1914 Krebs Model BB 1,500 lb. Panel Body (OCW)

1912 Lambert Panel Delivery (DFW/MVMA)

Standard Catalog of Light-Duty Trucks

1914 Lambert Model V-3 Flareboard Express (OCW)

LANDSHAFT — Chicago, Ill. — (1911-1920) — In its early years, the William Landshaft & Son firm built a 1/2-ton truck. The company's 1912 line included the Model A, a gas-engined 1,000 lb. open delivery selling for $950, the Model B, a 1,000 lb. panel top with a $1,000 pricetag, the Model C 1-ton open delivery at $1,250 and the Model D panel top for $1,300. All used two-cylinder engines. There were 1/2-, 3/4- and 1-tons in 1913, all being of open express style with prices between $950 and $1,700. For 1914 and 1915, the 3/4-ton and 1-ton models were continued. By 1916, the smallest Landshaft truck was the 1-ton.

1914 Landshaft Model C Flareboard Express (OCW)

LANE — Kalamazoo, Mich. — (1916-1920) — The Lane Motor Truck Co.'s first product was a 3/4-ton truck with a four-cylinder engine. Other models the firm built were heavier trucks.

LANGE — Pittsburgh, Pa. — (1911-1931) — In 1913, the Lange Motor Truck Co. produced a 1-ton chassis identified as the Model C. It was a gas-engined truck with a $2,250 price. The Model C was made through at least 1918. Thereafter, all of the company's products appear to be 1-1/2-tons or heavier.

1914 Lange Model C Flareboard Express (OCW)

LANPHER — Carthage, Mo. — (1910) — Lanpher Motor Buggy Co. produced the Model L light-delivery for just one season. It was a high-wheel van with a 14 hp two-cylinder engine and a $550 price. The truck featured a 76 in. wheelbase, planetary transmission and chain-drive.

LANSDEN — Danbury, Conn. — (1905-1928) — This is a moderately-well-known battery-powered electric truck, manufactured by the Lansden Co. at four successive sites: Newark, N.J.; Allentown, Pa.; Brooklyn, N.Y. and Danbury. Their trucks ranged in capacity from 1/2-ton to 6-tons. A 1907 listing identifies a 1,000 lb. payload electric delivery truck selling for $2,350. Other 1/2-tons were made as late as 1915 and sold for $2,535 in express form. In 1918, their 1/3-ton chassis was priced at $1,400 with battery and $1,150 without. The batteries weighed 1,050 lbs. (more than the truck's payload!). The truck's range (loaded) was 50 miles; unloaded, 60 miles. It could travel at 15 mph.

LARRABEE — Binghamton, N.Y. — (1916-1932) -The Larrabee Co. was named for H. Chester Larrabee and R.H. Deyo, president. It was one of many companies producing standard asssembled trucks with the general range of 1- to 5-tons. Its Model M, of 1917-1918, was a 1-ton chassis powered by a four-cylinder gasoline engine. It sold for $1,600 the first year, but was up to $1,950 by 1918. In 1922, the company offered a 1-ton "Speed Truck" with a six-cylinder Continental engine and pneumatic tires. The 1-ton of 1919 was $1,950. Four-cylinder taxicabs were also manufactured in the late 1920s.

LA SALLE-NIAGARA — Niagara Falls, N.Y. — (1906) — This company's truck was a 1-ton flatbed delivery van with a 90 in. wheelbase, two-cylinder engine and $1,500 price-tag.

LAUTH — Chicago, Ill. — (1907-1910) — This company had Magnus Hendrickson trucks built expressly for use at its tanning factory. They were light conventionals with gas engines, chain-drive, cab roofs and closed delivery bodies. From 1908, cars and trucks were made in limited numbers. Hendrickson designed the first hollow-spoke wheel, several transmissions and the first worm drive axle.

LAUTH-JUERGENS — Fremont, Ohio — (1910-1915) — Theodore Juergens joined J. Lauth & Co. (see prior listing) in 1908. By 1910, the firm moved to Ohio as the Lauth-Juergens Motor Car Co., which was exclusively a truck-maker. Magnus Hendrickson was chief engineer. The Model K, of 1913-1914, sold for $2,100 in 1-ton chassis form. It had a guaranteed-for-life motor. Larger models were built until 1914, when H.G. Burford Co. purchased the firm.

1914 Lauth-Juergens Model K Canopy Express (OCW)

LAVIGNE — Detroit, Mich. — (1914-1915) -The Lavigne Cyclecar Co. offered a delivery model with an eight-foot wheelbase. It was powered by an air-cooled four and had a planetary transmission and shaft drive. The $600 vehicle had a 650 lb. GVW.

L.A.W. — Findlay, Ohio — (1912-1913) — The smallest of this company's models was a 1-ton with French type sloping hood. A four-cylinder engine, shaft drive and double-reduction axle were featured in the $2,200 truck.

LAWSON — Pittsburgh, Pa. — (1917-1918) — The Lawson Manufacturing Co. built a 1/2-ton truck. It also made a 3/4-ton model with a 120 in. wheelbase and 34 x 4 in. tires.

LEACH — Everitt, Mass. — (1899-1900) — This was a steam-powered delivery van on an auto chassis produced by the Leach Motor Vehicle Co.

LE MOON — Chicago, Ill. — (1910-1939) — Nelson & LeMoon, of Chicago, claimed to have built its first truck in 1906. By 1910, the firm had a 1-ton on the market. Its D1, of 1913, was a 1-ton express with a $2,000 asking price. Most of its products were, however, heavier-duties.

LESCINA — Newark, N.J. — (pre-World War I) — This firm made a 1/2-ton truck with a 112 in. wheelbase, three-speed transmission and 32 x 3-1/2 in. tires.

LIBERTY — Detroit, Mich. — (1916-1923) — The Liberty Motor Car Co. built a six-cylinder automobile and some pictures have been found of a light truck, probably built on a commercial chassis.

1918 Liberty Pickup Truck (DFW/OHS)

LIGHT — New York City — (1914) — This was a three-wheel parcel delivery van built by Light Commercial Car Co. Some sources trace this firm to Marietta, Pa. in 1913. However the *MANUAL OF AUTOMOBILE LIABILITY INSURANCE* indicates that 1914 was the only year of production under this corporate name. There were a pair of two-cylinder models having 750 lb. payloads. The first was a chassis at $460. A box model was $15 more.

1914 Light Tri-Car Box Body Delivery (OCW)

LIMA — Lima, Ohio — (1915-1916) — This was a 1/2-ton truck built by the Lima Light Car Manufacturing Co.

LINCOLN — Chicago, Ill. — (1912-1913) — These were light vans, built by the Lincoln Motor Car Works, a successor to the Sears. For 1912, there were two models, both with 800 lb. payloads. The "27" was a closed panel. It sold for $750. The "29" was a $650 express. The two were carried over, for 1913, at prices of $685 and $585, respectively. These trucks used a 14 hp two-cylinder engine which was air-cooled. They featured a friction type transmission and single chain-drive. Solid or pneumatic tires were optional.

LINCOLN — Detroit, Mich./Pontiac, Mich. — (1916) — The only size truck offered by the Lincoln Motor Truck Co. was a 3/4-ton capacity model. It was probably a 3/4- to 1-ton type in reality, as some sources simply list it as a 1-ton. It sold for $925 in chassis form and $985 as an open express. Its features included a four-cylinder ohv engine, three-speed gearbox and 122 in. wheelbase. Lincoln absorbed the O.K. Motor Truck Co. in 1916.

LINDSLEY — Indianapolis, Ind. — (1908) — This was a high-wheeled, 3/4-ton delivery van offered by J. V. Lindsley & Co. It used a two-cylinder gas engine and sold for $500.

LION — New York City — (1920-1921) — The Lion Motor Truck Corp., of New York, N.Y., produced just one model. It was a 3/4-ton truck.

LIPPARD-STEWART — Buffalo, N.Y. — (1911-1919) — The Lippard-Stewart Motor Car Co. built light trucks, with Renault-style sloped hoods. In 1916, their 1/2-ton model was on a 106 in. wheelbase and sold for $1,000. Their 3/4-ton model sold for $1,600 and was available with three wheelbases: 115 in., 125 in. and 135 in.. Some individuals associated with this firm left, and formed a new firm which built Stewart trucks, a make which lasted until World War II.

1911 Lippard-Stewart Light Express (OCW)

1914 Lippard-Stewart Model B Panel Delivery (OCW)

LITTLE GIANT — Chicago, Ill. — (1912-1918) — The Chicago Pneumatic Tool Co. manufactured trucks ranging from 3/4-ton to 31/2-tons. These were first called "Little Giants," although reference sources contemporary to the 1920s use the name "Giant." The 1916

3/4-ton model sold for $1,500. It was on a 120 in. wheelbase. It came with "electric side and taillights, demountable rim, horn, tools, jack and mud guards." (See Giant listing)

1911 Little Giant Light Express Wagon (OCW)

1911 Little Giant Canopied Delivery (OCW)

1914 Little Giant Model F Platform (OCW)

1914 Little Giant Model H Flareboard (OCW)

1915 Little Giant 3/4-Ton Chassis & Cowl (OCW)

1916 Little Giant 1-Ton Worm Drive Delivery (OCW)

LITTLEMAC — Muscatine, Iowa — (1929-1935) — According to historian Jeff Gillis, Muscatine Mayor Herbert Thompson and his brother Ralph promoted Clayton Frederick's pint-sized auto in an effort to bring industry to their town. In Nov., 1929, Thompson Motors was incorporated at $1,000,000. The Littlemac rode an 80 in. wheelbase (later increased to 82 in.) and had a Continental four-cylinder engine. Six "truckette" versions of the vehicle were manufactured, including a very boxy panel delivery. They cost about $500. The first was delivered to a local baker in August, 1931.

1932 Littlemac Panel Truckette (Jeff Gillis)

1932 Littlemac Panel Truckette (Jeff Gillis)

Standard Catalog of Light-Duty Trucks

1932 Littlemac Panel Truckette (Jeff Gillis)

LOCOMOBILE — Bridgeport, Conn. — (1901-1929) — Just after the turn of the century, the Locomobile Co. of America built a 1/2-ton capacity "Locodelivery" powered by steam, with a 12-1/2-gallon fuel tank, a 50-gallon water tank and 16 in. boiler. It sold for $2,000. They also built heavy trucks just before World War I. In addition, their auto chassis were sometimes outfitted with commercial bodies.

1918 Locomobile Sightseeing Bus (DFW/OHS)

LOGAN — Chillicothe, Ohio — (1907-1908) — This firm was undoubtedly connected to the company in the following listing, although, in this case, the name Logan Construction Co. was used. The 1907 line included the Model N, a 1,200 pounder and the 2-1/2-ton Model M. In 1908, there was a 1-ton Model T. They used two-cylinder gasoline engines. The "N" sold for $1,000, while the "T" was $2,250.

LOGAN EXPRESS — Chillicothe, Ohio — (1904-1908) — Benjamin A. Gramm started this firm as a part of his Motor Storage & Mfg. Co. It produced two- and four-cylinder cars with both air- and water-cooled engines. The 1905 Logan Express was a commercial version of the two-cylinder Model D touring car. By 1907, trucks became the company's mainstay product. After a 1908 bankruptcy, B.A. Gramm moved to Bowling Green, Ohio, to establish Gramm-Logan Motor Car Co., which built only trucks. The firm then became Gramm-Bernstein and Gramm, both headquartered in Lima, Ohio.

1905 Logan Model E Express Wagon (JAW)

LOOMIS — Westfield, Massachusetts — (1901) — The Loomis Automobile Co. produced light vans powered by a single-cylinder engine.

LORD BALTIMORE — Baltimore, Md. — (1911-1914) — This company's first light-duty truck was the 1/2-ton Model D truck chassis of 1913, which sold for $1,300. A 1-ton priced at $2,250 and called the Model C was also a part of the line. For 1914 a 1-ton Model B had a $2,000 pricetag. While some sources indicate the firm survived until 1916, still building 1-tons, contemporary insurance manuals have no listings later than 1914.

1914 Lord Baltimore Model B Covered Express (OCW)

LOYAL — Lancaster, Ohio — (1918-1920) — The Loyal Motor Truck Co. built light trucks during its short life. Its 1918 1/2-ton model sold for $800 and was on a 110 in. wheelbase. The 3/4-ton model was on a 120 in. wheelbase and sold for $850.

LUCK UTILITY — Cleburne, Texas — (1913-1914) — The Cleburne Motor Car Manufacturing Co. built a 1/2-ton truck. It sold for $750. The four-cylinder engine was under a hood between the individual seats. Other features included a three-speed transmission and shaft drive.

1912 Luck Utility Commercial Roadster (D.J. Kava)

LUVERNE — Luverne, Minn. — (c. 1912-1925) — This firm began in 1906, evolving out of a carriage-building operation of two brothers, Al and Ed Leicher. The new firm built both autos and trucks. In 1913, they built a motorized fire pumper for the City of Luverne. They stopped building autos in 1917 and trucks in 1923. However, they continued to outfit fire-fighting apparatus, a function the firm still performs.

1917 Luverne 1-Ton Farm Wagon (DFW)

M

MACCAR — Allentown, Pa. — (1912-1935) — The Maccar Truck Co. can be traced to one of the original Mack Brothers. It is best known for its medium and large trucks, although, for a few years, its smallest model was rated at 3/4-ton. In 1914, the 1,500 lb. Model A was $1,650. The same year the Model B 1-ton, at $1,900 for a chassis, was marketed. Strangely, the "B" designation was also used on 1-1/2 and 2-ton models. The 3/4-ton Model A was also carried over for 1915-1916. By 1916, the 1-ton Model E was replaced by the Model K. Priced

at $2,100, it lasted one year. It wasn't until 1920 that 1-tons (Models S, S-1 and S-2) returned to the line. They survived until 1922, when the 1-1/2-ton Model S-A joined them. After 1922, the smallest Maccars were 1-1/2-tons.

1914 Maccar Model A Semi Panel Delivery (OCW)

1914 Maccar Model A Flareboard Express (OCW)

1914 Maccar Model A Covered Flareboard (OCW)

1914 Maccar Model B Chassis (OCW)

MACK — Allentown, Pa. — (1902 to date) — This is one of the best-known of all U.S. trucks, buses and fire apparatus. Sometimes its smallest chassis would be rated at under 1-ton. In the period 1936-1938, Mack Jrs. were marketed in sizes as small as 1/2-ton; (they were actually manufactured by Reo, but had minor trim changes). One Mack Jr. was sold as an attractive 1/2-ton pickup. This model is highly sought by old truck fans who want to own a Mack but don't have a large garage.

1914 Mack Covered Flareboard Express (OCW)

1936 Mack Junior Milk Delivery Van (DFW/DPL)

1937 Mack Junior Cab Express (EK)

MACKBILT — New York, N.Y. — (1917) — Founded by William C. Mack of Mack Bros., this company's 3/4-ton had a 115 in. wheelbase, pneumatic tires and a four-cylinder Buda engine.

MAHONING — Youngstown, Ohio — (c. 1904-1905) — Mahoning Motor Car Co. produced a $950 delivery car as part of its four model line. It was powered by a nine horsepower, one-cylinder engine and had an 82 in. wheelbase.

1901 Mahoning Closed Top Delivery Van (JAW)

MAIS — Peru/Indianapolis, Ind. — (1911-1916) -This company produced mainly large trucks, but is believed to have offered a 3/4-ton and 1-ton in its early years. For 1914, a 1/2-ton flareboard express was marketed for $825. Premier Motor Mfg., of Indianapolis, acquired Mais in 1916.

1914 Mais Covered Flareboard Express (OCW)

MARATHON — Nashville, Tenn. — (1912-1913) — Marathon Motor Works built trucks in a variety of sizes, the smallest of which was rated at 1/4-ton. This was listed as the "Runner" model. It was a light delivery with a gasoline fueled engine and an $850 price.

MARMON — Indianapolis, Ind. — (1912-1935) — Nordyke & Marmon, the prestige auto-maker, produced several light-duty trucks. One model was a 1/4-ton light delivery van with a T-head four-cylinder engine, three-speed gearbox and shaft drive, which had a top speed of 20 mph. The Model 3, of 1913-1914, was a gas-powered 3/4-ton selling for $2,500 in chassis-only form. This van had a long 10-ft. wheelbase, but a small cargo area.

1914 Marmon Covered Flareboard Express (OCW)

1914 Marmon Panel Body Delivery (OCW)

MARMON-HERRINGTON — Indianapolis, Ind. — (1913-1963) — Marmon-Herrington, Inc. is best known for its large, all-wheel drive off-road trucks and for its all-wheel drive axle conversion kits for Ford trucks. However, after World War II, they also built a small step-van called the "Delivr-All." Production of Delivr-Alls continued until 1952.

1936 Marmon-Herrington "Delivr-All" Panel (DFW/BAC)

MARTIN — York, Pa. — (1909-1915) — The Martin Carriage Works built high-wheelers with 1/2-ton capacity and two-cylinder engines. Models offered in 1910-1912 included the 3/4-ton "E" panel ($1,500); the 1/2-ton "J" panel ($1,400); the 3/4-ton "G" full-panel ($1,650); the 3/4-ton "F2" shift-top ($1,450); the 3/4-ton "G2" full-panel ($1,600); the 3/4-ton "G3" full-panel ($1,840); the 3/4-ton "G4" full-panel ($1,600) and the "H," a 1-ton panel priced at $1,750. However, after 1912, the smallest truck was a 1-ton. The Martin name was discontinued in 1915 and replaced by Atlas.

MARYLAND — Luke, Md. — (1900-1901) — The Maryland Automobile Mfg. Co. sold delivery vans with a 1,000 lb. payload. They used a two-cylinder, double slide-valve steam engine. The top speed was 30 mph.

MASON — Waterloo, Iowa — (1912-1914) — This company evolved out of Maytag (see separate listing below) and the two are sometimes referred to as Mason-Maytag. The Model 12 was a closed delivery offered at $800 in 1912. It was carried over for 1913-1914 as an open flareboard express with similar price. Also offered then was the Model 13, a $1,000 open flareboard express. All had two-cylinder, gasoline engines.

MAYTAG — Waterloo, Iowa — (1908-1911) — The name survives as a maker of washing machines. The Maytag-Mason Motor Co. built a light auto with a body which could be converted into a light truck.

1910 Maytag Model 10 Light Delivery Van (OCW)

1910 Maytag Light Express Wagon (DFW/ACTHR)

1911 Maytag Light Delivery Wagon (DFW/ACTHR)

1911 Maytag Light Delivery Car (DFW/ACTHR)

MAXFER — Chicago, Ill. — (1917-1919) — Maxfer Truck & Tractor Co. made rear ends to convert Model T Fords into trucks. It also manufactured its own 1-ton truck with a 31 hp four-cylinder engine.

MAXIM — Port Jefferson, N.Y. — (1913-1914) — The Maxim Tri-Car Co., headquartered in New York City, built a Model F three-wheel light truck ($425) and a Model E delivery model ($395). Payload ratings were 750 lbs. and 500 lbs., respectively. Both the Tri-Car and the Delivery had two-cylinder powerplants.

Standard Catalog of Light-Duty Trucks

1911 Maxim Box Body Tri-Car (OCW/DPL)

1914 Maxim Tri-Car Delivery Van (OCW)

MAXWELL — Detroit, Mich. — (1905-1925) — Starting out as Maxwell-Briscoe and eventually becoming part of Chrysler, the Maxwell Motor Co. produced autos, taxicabs, fire apparatus, delivery vans and some other light trucks. There was a two-cylinder (gas) delivery truck offered in 1907 for $1,450. In 1909, the similar Model OD sold for $1,400. Apparently, truck manufacturing was discontinued for a while (or "commercial car" bodies were made an option for Maxwell cars). After 1917, Maxwell listed trucks again. One was a 1-ton called the Model 4. The year 1918 brought a 750 lb. version of this truck, joining the 1-ton. In 1919, there was only the 1-ton; in 1920, only a 1-1/2-ton. No trucks were produced again in 1921-1922. For 1923, the 1/2-ton Model 25 was introduced. This was a true light-duty truck with a curb weight of 3,210 lbs. In terms of total trucks registered in the U.S. in late 1921, Maxwells were 10th from the top. By 1925, the company was out of business. It was then absorbed into Chrysler.

1909 Maxwell Model A Canopy Express (W. Pollock)

Standard Catalog of Light-Duty Trucks

1917 Maxwell 1-Ton Express (VHTM)

1925 Maxwell Merchant's Car-Panel Body (OCW)

McINTYRE — Auburn, Ind. — (1909-1915) — The W. H. McIntyre Co. dated from 1880, building both autos and trucks. Its early trucks were high-wheelers. The company made many, many light-duty commercial styles including an 1,800 lb. delivery ($800), 1-ton delivery ($1,200), 1,200 lb. delivery ($1,000), 600 lb. delivery ($550) and 800 lb. chassis ($600).

1912 McIntyre Express (Skip Marketti/ACD Museum)

MEISELBACH — North Milwaukee, Wis. — (1904-1909) — This company began with a 1-ton powered by a water-cooled, horizontally-opposed two-cylinder engine. It had a friction transmission and chain-drive. The price of the 1-ton in 1908-1909, was $2,000.

MENOMINEE — Menominee, Mich. — (1913-1918) — D. F. Poyer & Co. built a number of 1-ton and under trucks with this nameplate. The Model A, of 1913, was a 1,500 lb. (3/4-ton) that came in chassis ($1,125) or express ($1,200) forms. Rated for 2,000 lbs. (1-ton) was the Model B of the same year. It retailed at $1,400 for the chassis and $1,500 for an express body. Both were carried over, for 1914, as the A-3 and B-3 with similar prices. For 1915, the line was substantially expanded in terms of body styles. The 3/4-ton MA-3 came as a chassis ($1,125), or exprees/stake/panel (all $1,200), while the 1-ton MB-3 was $1,400 for the chassis and $1,500 for any of the other three styles. The 1916 line included the 3/4-ton Model E and 1-ton Model FW, which were $1,125 and $1,575, respectively, for chassis-only models. In 1917, the firm was reorganized as Menominee Motor Truck Co. The M-EW, a 3/4-ton for $1,425 and the M-FW, a 1-ton for $1,790, were offered in chassis-only format that year. In 1918, there were two models, the EW (now up-rated to 1-ton and priced $1,650) and a second 1-ton ($1,775) called the "Hurry Ton," which was of the popular (at the time) "speed wagon" type.

715

1914 Menominee Model A-3 Flareboard Express (OCW)

1914 Menominee Model B-3 Flareboard Express (OCW)

MENOMINEE — Clintonville, Wis. — (1911-1937) — This was a well-known "regional" truck, offered in a small and medium capacities. The 1918 3/4-ton capacity 124 in. wheelbase chassis sold for $1,525. The firm was acquired by FWD, which still exists in Clintonville. (Reference was also found to an apparently unrelated 1916 Menominee 3/4-ton truck, built by the D. F. Poyer Co. of Menominee, Mich.)

MERCURY — Chicago, Ill. — (1911-1916) — These were 1/2-ton high-wheelers built by the Mercury Manufacturing Co. The first models were a delivery ($750) and closed express ($850), all powered by a two-cylinder gas engine. In 1912, five 1,000 lb. models were offered at prices from $750 to $900. In 1914-1915, four versions of the 1,000 lb. Model P were marketed in the same price range. Strangely, the 1916 line included a small 1/2-ton Model P delivery ($750), plus a larger electric tractor and a very huge 10-ton chassis.

1911 Mercury Flareboard Express (DFW/ATA)

1914 Mercury Flareboard Express (OCW)

MERCURY — Detroit, Mich. — (1915) — This was a van body on a cyclecar chassis, offered by the Mercury Cyclecar Co. It had a gasoline engine and a $400 pricetag. The engine, which was air-cooled, produced 10 hp. Drive was taken, from a friction transmission, via long double belts, to the rear wheels. It had a 100 in. wheelbase.

MERCURY (FORD OF CANADA) — (1946-1967) -From 1946-1957, Canadian Ford dealers sold Ford-type trucks under the Mercury name. They had trim variations from the domestic products, but were basically badge-engineered Fords. The names Monarch and Frontenac were also used, in Canada, for other badge-engineered Ford trucks.

1949 Mercury (Canadian) M47 Pickup (OCW)

1950 Mercury (Canadian) 1-Ton Stake (OCW)

MERIT — Waterville, Ohio — (1911) — The Waterville Tractor Co. built a 1/2-ton capacity delivery truck. It was designated the Model B and used a two-cylinder, air-cooled gasoline engine. An 84 in. wheelbase was featured, along with friction transmission and double chain-drive. The price was $1,000.

MERZ — Indianapolis, Ind. — (1913-1915) — This was a light van body on a cyclecar chassis. It was built by the Merz Cyclecar Co. The vehicle had a seven-foot wheelbase with a 3-1/4-foot tread. The air-cooled, two-cylinder engine generated 10 hp. Like others of its type, Merz used a friction transmission and belt drive.

MESSERER — Newark, N.J. — (1898) — This early delivery truck was built by S. Messerer. It had a 1,000 lb. payload capacity. The 4 x 6 in. bore and stroke four-cylinder gas engine developed six hp at 350 rpm. Drive was by six inch pulley.

METROPOLITAN — New York, N.Y. — (1917) — Metropolitan Motors produced three 3/4-tons in 1917. The chassis was priced at $895. The Model AA canopy top was $995. Last, but not least, they had the Model AB, a $1,035 full-panel.

METZ — Waltham, Mass. — (1916-1917) — Metz Motor Car Co. had a small 800 lb. chassis on the market in 1916. It cost only $535. By 1917, the product line had not grown, but the product had. The sole model, then, was a 1-ton priced at $695. This truck was connected to the Hewitt (see separate listing).

1916 Metz Commercial Delivery Car (DFW/HAC)

MICHAELSON — Minneapolis, Minn. — (1914) — This cyclecar company evolved from a motorcycle firm. The base model, using a 15 hp air-cooled engine, sold for $400. A box-bodied Tri-Car, tagged at $375, was depicted in the company's catalog. However, actual production has not been verified. A pilot model appeared at the Minneapolis Auto Show in Jan. 1914. By the following April, Joseph M. Michaelson left the firm.

1914 Michaelson Box Body Tri-Car (OCW)

MILBURN — Toledo, Ohio — (1915) — The Milburn Wagon Co. produced a $985 electric-powered 750 lb. truck. It had an underslung chassis and 90 in. wheelbase. Solid rubber tires were mounted.

MILLER — Bridgeport, Conn. — (1907-1908) — This firm produced Model A, B and D sightseeing buses with two-cylinder engines. The smallest sat 12 passengers.

MILLER — Detroit, Mich. — (1913-1914) — This was a 1/2-ton delivery van made by the Miller Car Co. of Detroit, a branch of the Milwaukee Auto Truck Mfg. Co. This firm also made one of the Champion trucks listed separately in this catalog. A 1914 offering was the Model A, a 1/2-ton panel with $850 price.

1914 Miller Model A Panel Body (OCW)

MILWAUKEE — Milwaukee, Wis. — (1901-1902) — The Milwaukee Automobile Co. built steam passenger cars and two different trucks. Only one fell into the "light-duty" category. It was a light delivery based on the firm's current automobile, which had a two-cylinder, five hp engine. It was rated for a payload of 800 lbs.

1902 Milwaukee Steam Delivery Wagon (GNG)

Standard Catalog of Light-Duty Trucks

MINNEAPOLIS — Minneapolis, Minn. — (1912-1913) — This line of three-wheel delivery vans was built by the Minneapolis Motor Cycle Co. It included a $350 chassis, $395 wood box body model and $425 metal box body truck. The designation "14C" was used on all and all shared a payload range rating of 350-400 lbs. Power came from a two-cylinder gas engine.

1914 Minneapolis Box Body Tri-Car (OCW)

MINO — New Orleans, La. — (1914) — A modified cyclecar with a four-cylinder air-cooled engine on a 100 in. wheelbase, the Mino came with a small, closed delivery body.

MITCHELL — Racine, Wis. — (1903-1923) — This was a passenger car, built by the Mitchell Motor Co. Sometimes, commercial bodies were placed on their chassis. Also, in 1907, the company cataloged a 1-ton truck. It sold for $2,000.

1919 Mitchell Panel Delivery (T. Donahue)

MOBILETTE — Chicago, Ill. — (1913-1914) — This very light delivery van was built on the cyclecar made by Woods Mobilette Co. It had a four-cylinder engine.

MODERN — Bowling Green, Ohio — (1911-1919) — This make was manufactured by the Bowling Green Motor Car Co. Capacities ranged from 1/2-ton to 3-1/2-ton. In 1913, the 1,000 lb. BV model sold for $1,325, while the Model AX, a 3/4-ton, was highest at $1,625.

1914 Modern Model F Flareboard Express (OXW)

1914 Modern Model G Panel Body Delivery (OCW)

MONITOR — Chicago, Ill. — (1910) — The Monitor Automobile Works made a 1/2-ton wicker delivery van. It was identified as the Model L and sold for $1,050. The engine was a two-cylinder job. Also available was the 1-ton Model G Delivery, selling for $1,450.

MONITOR — Janesville, Wis. — (1910-1916) — Monitor Automobile Works produced two 1-tons in 1911. Both had two-cylinder engines. The B-109 was $1,500 and the D-110 was $1,600. A 1,500 lb. truck, the A-109 express, was marketed, in 1912, at a price of $1,000. Thereafter, the company produced light-duties in both of these sizes (at around the same prices), plus some heavier models.

1914 Monitor Model E Chassis (OCW)

1914 Monitor Model A Panel Body Delivery (OCW)

MOON — St. Louis, Mo. — (1914-1918) — This was a 1/2-ton truck built by the J.W. Moon Buggy Co. It was called the Model A and came as a $1,600 panel for 1914. In 1915, the same model was marketed as a chassis ($1,300), convertible truck ($1,450) and express ($1,550). It was up-rated to 1,500 lbs. in 1917 and called the "23-1/2 Express," with a pricetag of $1,150. In 1918, only 2-tons were offered.

1928 Moon Model 672 Chassis-Only (OCW)

MOORE — Philadelphia, Pa. — (1912-1914) — The Moore Motor Truck Co.'s first offering was the Model C, a 3/4-ton. By 1914, the line began at the 1-1/2 ton limit.

MOORE — Syracuse, N.Y. — (1913-1914) — Just to confuse people, this company, with the same trade-name as the previous firm, also built a 3/4-ton Model C. However, it had an unusual three-cylinder engine, which was air-cooled. Its hood was French styled. Other features included a planetary transmission and double chain-drive. It cost $1,300. Palmer-Moore was the corporate name. (See separate Palmer-Moore listing.)

MORA — Cleveland, Ohio — (1912-1914) — A 3/4-ton open express was built by the Mora Power Wagon Co. Called the Model 20, it was a two-cylinder model with a $1,000 price. There was also Models 24 and 25, which were 1-tons in the $1,400-$1,500 price range.

1914 Mora Model 24 Standard Open Express Body (OCW)

MORELAND — Los Angeles, Calif. — (1912-1941) — This company produced the Model D, a 1,500- to 2,000 lb. chassis in 1914. It was $1,700. In 1915-1916, a 1-ton chassis model was also offered. It was priced $1,850 the earlier year, but then dropped to $1,550.

MORSE — Pittsburgh, Penna. — (1914-1916) — This company made the Morse Cyclecar, which was available with commercial body options. The truck version had a 400 lb. load capacity and 105 in. wheelbase. Other features included a two-cylinder motor and 28 x 3 in. tires.

MOTOKART — New York City — (1914) — This box-bodied cyclecar was made by the Tarrytown Motor Car Co. and sold for $400. It was powered by a two-cylinder gas engine and had a load capacity of 500 lbs. Contemporary sources listed it under the Tarrytown Motor Car Co. name.

1914 Motokart Box Body Delivery (OCW)

MOTORETTE — Hartford, Conn. — (1913) — These were three-wheeled delivery wagons made by the C.W. Kelsey Manufacturing Co. Both the Model L1 ($450) and Model N1 ($500) were powered by a two-cylinder engine. The first could carry 250 lb. loads and the other hauled twice that weight.

1913 Mottorette Model R-1 Rickshaw (HAC)

MOTOR WAGON — Detroit, Mich. — (1912-1913) — These were light vans, built by the Motor Wagon Co. of Detroit. Both the Express ($610) and Full Panel ($700) were two-cylinder powered and rated for 800 lb. loads.

1911 Motor Wagon Light Express Wagon (OCW)

M&P — Detroit, Mich. — (1911-1913) — These were battery-powered trucks which used Westinghouse motors. They were built by the M & P Electric Vehicle Co. Rated at 1,500 lbs., the chassis model sold for $1,450.

1914 M & P Flareboard Express (OCW)

1914 M & P Panel Body Delivery (OCW)

MUSKEGON — Muskegon, Mich. — (1917-1920) -The Muskegon Engine Co. is believed to have made one model called the "20." A modern reference says it was a 1-ton, but a contemporary (to the era) insurance guide identifies it as a 2-ton for $2,145. If this is correct, it would not qualify as a "light-duty."

MYERS — Sheboygan, Wis. (pre-World War I) — This firm made a 3/4-ton truck. However, this fact does not seem to have attracted widespread attention and little else is known.

MYERS — Pittsburgh, Pa. — (1918-1919) -The E.A. Meyer's Co.'s smallest model was a 1-ton. Not much about this model is known. It is not listed in contemporary insurance guides covering the 1912-1918 period.

N

NAPOLEON — Napoleon, Ohio/Traverse City, Mich. — (1917-1922) — This firm offered the Model 1727 in 1917. It was a four-cylinder powered 1,000 lb. (1/2-ton) truck selling at $735. The gas engine was made by Gray and had overhead valves. Other features included a

three-speed gearbox and bevel-gear axle. Some sources give a later starting date for the firm, which operated under the names Napoleon Auto Mfg. Co. (1917-1918); Napoleon Motors Co. (1919-1920) and Napoleon Motor Cars & Trucks (post-1921).

NASH — Kenosha, Wis. — (1917-1954) — Nash produced a 1-ton Model 2017 in 1918. It listed for $1,595 in chassis form. The company concentrated on heavier trucks later, but some 1-tons were built in the 1920s. After World War II, a 2/3-ton model was built, mainly for export, although it saw limited stateside distribution. It had a six-cylinder ohv engine. The Nash name was also linked to Jeffery, Rambler and AMC/Jeep, which are listed separately in this catalog.

1917 Nash Model 2017 Canopy Express (OCW)

1920 Nash 1-Ton Express (John Scott)

1921 Nash 1-Ton Express (WOM)

1946 Nash (customized) 1-Ton Pickup (P.B. Grenier)

NATCO — Bay City, Mich. — (1912-1916) — A 1-ton gas engine truck was sold 1913-1916. Known as Model 15, it sold for $1,925 in chassis form.

1914 NATCO Type 15 Covered Flareboard Express (OCW)

NELSON & LeMOON CO. — Chicago, Ill. — (1910-1939) — This firm operated under the above name through 1927 and as the Nelson & LeMoon Truck Co. thereafter. It claimed to have made a 1906 model, but records start at 1910, in which year a four-cylinder 1-ton with double-chain-drive was offered. Two trucks of similar capacity, Models D-1 and E-1, were sold at $1,800 in 1914 and 1915, the E-1 continuing, through 1917, at a lower $1,700 price. It used a four-cylinder (33/4x5-1/4) Continental engine rated for 22.40 hp and weighed around 3,200 lbs. In 1919-1920, this became the F-1, which was much the same, but about 200 lbs heavier. The G-1, another model with a larger (4.0x5-1/4 in.) four — rated at 27.23 hp — returned a 1-ton to the line in 1923 and remained through at least 1925. In 1928, six-cylinder Continental engines were adopted for a new, eight-model lineup of smaller trucks. They included a $1,500 1-ton. Later series were made up entirely of larger models.

1914 Nelson & Lemoon Model D-1 Panel (OCW)

NEUSTADT — St. Louis, Mo. — (1911-1914) — This company made motorized fire apparatus as early as 1905. The Model A, a 1-ton, was introduced in 1911. It had a four-cylinder engine and came with either solid or pneumatic tires.

NEWARK — Newark, N.J. — (1911-1912) — These were small, open vans. They were built by the Newark Automobile Manufacturing Co. Payloads included 1/2-ton and 3/4-ton. They had water-cooled fours, three speed gearboxes and shaft drive. Wheelbases of 96 and 106 inches were available. The 1000 lb. Commercial Car had a 1,700 lb. curb weight and $1,250 pricetag.

NEW ERA — Dayton, Ohio — (1911-1912) — This was a three-wheeler, built by the New Era Auto Cycle Co. A one-cylinder, air-cooled engine drove the single rear wheel. The cargo box could handle a 400 lb. payload. It had handle-bar steering.

NEW ERA — Joliet, Ill. — (1917) — The New Era Engineering Co. built a gasoline-engine 1/2-ton Light Delivery that sold for $685. There appears to be no connection between this manufacturer and the earlier company producing tricars under the same name.

NEW YORK — Nutley, N.J. — (1912) — The New York Motor Works built trucks ranging in size from 3/4-ton to 5-tons. The smaller models were four-cylinder powered. The company's motto was "Made in the East for the East."

NILES — Niles, Ohio — (1916-1920) — This company built a 1-ton through 1918. It was called the Model B and was a four-cylinder truck. The chassis was $1,175 the initial season, $1,500 in 1917 and $1,600 the final year. A 1-1/2 ton continued to leave the factory thereafter.

NOBLE — Kendallville, Ind. — (1917-1931) — This company produced some 1-ton models. Most of its trucks, however, were in the 2-1/2-ton to 5-ton range.

NOLAND — Edgewater, Fla. — (c. 1985) — Commercial vehicle historian Elliott Kahn says this gas engined utility cart is a three-wheeler which includes four-passenger accomodations (on two bench seats) and a molded cargo bin at the rear of its fiberglass or plastic body. Rack style side-rails appear to be one option intended to increase the cargo capacity.

1985 Noland Covered Utility Cart (EK)

NORTHERN — Detroit, Mich. — (1906-1908) — This was a light delivery van built by the Northern Motor Car Co. Designated the Model C, it used a 20 hp two-cylinder engine, planetary transmission and shaft drive. The $1,600 truck rode on a 106 in. wheelbase.

NORWALK — Martinsburg, W.V. — 1918-1919 — This company's 1-ton truck chassis sold for $1,295 in 1918. It had a four-cylinder Lycoming Model K gasoline engine, three-speed gearbox and worm drive. These trucks had a 130 in. wheelbase and did not come with electric lights in a period when most makers offered them.

NYBERG — Chicago, Ill. — (1912-1913) — Nyberg Automobile Works produced a couple of 1-ton-or-under commercial vehicles. The 1912 Model 35 was a 1,500 lb. closed delivery selling for $1,300. Its price rose to $1,500 the next season. In 1912, the Model 38 1-ton was also marketed. This delivery truck also had a $1,500 pricetag.

OHIO — Cincinnati, Ohio — (1912) — The Ohio Motor Car Co. built autos and used the same chassis for a light truck.

O.K. — Detroit, Mich. — (1913-1916) — These were small, open vans built by the O.K. Motor Truck Co.

1914 O.K. 1,200 lb. Delivery (OCW)

OLD HICKORY — Louisville, Ken. — (1915-1923) — This was a Southern-built light truck, made by the Kentucky Wagon Manufacturing Co. In 1918, its 3/4-ton chassis on a 124 in. wheelbase with a four-cylinder 17 hp engine, sold for $875.

Standard Catalog of Light-Duty Trucks

1918 Old Hickory Covered Flareboard Express (DFW)

OLDSMOBILE — Lansing, Mich. — (1904 — c.1975) — The first of many light-duty commercial vehicles produced by Oldsmobile was a delivery van version of the company's famous Curved Dash model. It appeared as early as 1904. Between 1905 and 1907, the company produced heavier trucks. The firm became a branch of General Motors and, for a while, stuck chiefly to making passenger cars. However, in 1918, a 1-ton truck using an overhead valve four-cylinder Northway engine, came on the market for a short stay. It survived until about 1924, after which time the Oldsmobile truck was seen only in export markets. In the 1930s, Oldsmobile engines were used in some GMC truck models. The company's chassis was also used by some "professional car" builders as a platform for ambulance and hearse conversions. Though never the most popular choice of professional car makers, these conversions were available at least through the mid-1970s from firms like Superior and, especially, Cotner-Bevington. Also of interest, was the development of a prototype Oldsmobile sedan delivery in 1950. Only one of these was ever built. From 1968-1970, the American Quality Coach Co. also produced an airport limousine based on the front-wheel-drive Oldsmobile Toronado. It had twin rear axles, eight doors and seating accomodations for 15 people.

1904 Oldsmobile Box Body Runabout (OCW)

1919 Oldsmobile 1-Ton Rack Body Express (DFW)

Standard Catalog of Light-Duty Trucks

1919 Oldsmobile "Economy" Canopy Express (OCW)

1919 Oldsmobile Stake (C.D. Peck/CPC)

1920 Oldsmobile 1-Ton Canopy Express (J. Vann/CPC)

1920 Oldsmobile 1-Ton Canopy Express (OCW)

OLIVER — Detroit, Mich. — (1910-1913) — The Oliver Motor Car Co. built high-wheeled delivery vans.

OLSON — Garden City, N.Y. — (1963-date) — J.B. Olson was a truck-making concern that produced lightweight aluminum bodies for platforms built by other manufacturers, such as Chevrolet's Step-Van chassis. In 1963, the company was purchased by Grumman Aerospace. A new line of aluminum bodied Grumman Kurbmaster vans was launched. While Olson Kurbmaster trucks used running gear supplied by makers like Ford, Chevrolet and GMC, they were of distinctive design and sold exclusively through Grumman dealers.

1983 Olson Kurbmaster 1-Ton Panel De;livery (EK)

ONEIDA — Green Bay, Wis. — (1917-1923) — The first series of Oneidas included a 1-ton model. It was called the Model A and returned again in 1918. In 1919, the Model B Oneida was down-rated to add a second 1-ton to the line. Later models were larger. Continental four-cylinder engines were used first, then Hercules. Though some sources list the company through 1931, a Wisconsin vehicle weight guide of 1926 notes "not in production since 1923."

OVERLAND — Toledo, Ohio — (1909-1939) — See the Willys-Overland section in the forward section of the catalog. Trucks bearing only the Overland name were made at various times, but were a Willys-Overland related product.

OWOSSO — Owosso, Mich. — (1910-1914) — This company's first offering was a 1-ton panel delivery. It had a two-cylinder engine that produced 20 hp. Other features included a planet gear transmission, double chain-drive setup and 106 in. wheelbase. The truck had the engine mounted below its floor. Solid rubber tires were used. Springs were semi-elliptics at all four corners.

1910 Owosso 1-Ton Panel Delivery (Steve Schmidt)

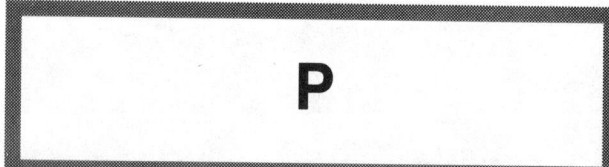

P

PACKARD — Detroit, Mich. — (1905-1923) — The Packard Motor Car Co. built medium and large trucks in the years indicated; in addition, their large auto chassis were sometimes used for commercial bodies. The Packard Model 1D (1915) was the company's first 1-ton. It evolved into the Model E Packard 1-ton sold from 1916 thru 1919. The smallest model available in 1920 was a 1-1/2-ton. From 1922 on, truck offerings started at 2-tons.

1910 Packard Police Patrol Wagon (DFW/MVMA)

1910 Packard Light Panel Bodied Delivery (DFW/MVMA)

1912 Packard Goodyear Tire Mail Delivery Van (GYTR)

1916 Packard 2,000 lb. "ID" Truck Chassis (OCW)

1920 Packard Twin Six Ambulance (DFW/HEPO)

1922 Packard Motion Picture Film Truck (IMSC/DFW)

1933 Packard Armored Car (JE/NSPC)

PACKET — See Brasie Packet.

PACO — Chicago, Ill. — (1908) — This was a small delivery van made by the Pietsch Auto & Marine Co.

PAIGE — Detroit, Mich. — (1930-1941) — Graham-Paige Motors Corp. marketed a sedan delivery on their passenger car chassis. Prices in 1930 for the 3/4-ton units were: chassis $860; panel delivery, $1,095; and screen delivery, $1,095.

PAK-AGE-CAR — Chicago, Ill. — (1926-1941) — This was a small stand-up van. Its manufacturing was associated with a number of prominent companies including Stutz, Auburn and Diamond-T. The vehicles were box-like in appearance and used for home deliveries in cities. Drivers often stood while driving. In the late 1920s, models sold for just under $1,000.

Standard Catalog of Light-Duty Trucks

1927 Pak-Age-Car Panel Delivery (DFW/SI)

1927 Pak-Age-Car Panel Delivery Van (OCW)

1935 Pak-Age-Car Panel Delivery Van (DFW/MVMA)

1940 Pak-Age-Car Walk-in Delivery Van (DFW/SI)

PALMER — St. Louis, Mo. — (1912-1915) — This truck, manufactured by the Palmer-Meyer Motor Truck Co., ranged in capacity from 3/4-ton to 1-1/2-tons. Early in its history, the firm offered a 1-ton gas-engined chassis for $1,600. The 1914 edition could also be had as a covered flareboard express that came with a large cape-type top resting on four posts; one at each corner of the express box. Roll-down curtains were provided for weather protection. The engine was a side-valve (L-head) design attached to a three-speed gearbox. Double chains carried drive to the rear wheels. Other features included headlamps and cowl lamps. This same type of truck was carried over in 1915, at the same price. However, shaft drive was adopted in 1915. By 1916, the brand name became Palmer-Meyer.

1914 Palmer-Moore Model C Flareboard Express (OCW)

1914 Palmer Covered Flareboard Express (OCW)

PALMER-MEYER — St. Louis, Mo. — (1916-1918) — The Palmer-Meyer Motor Truck Co. manufactured both light and heavy trucks. Some of these were marketed under the Palmer name alone (see listing above). However, an insurance guide dated Jan. 1, 1916, listed the brand name as Palmer-Meyer. In 1916, the price of a 1-ton truck chassis was $1,500 and a 1,500 lb. (3/4-ton) chassis was $950. For 1917-1918, the line included a 1-ton internal gear chassis-only model with a four-cylinder engine. It sold for $1,350 the first year and $1,685 the second, which was the nameplate's last. The lightest truck made by Palmer-Meyer was the 3/4-ton Model B. A frontal type hood was used and platform/stake bodies were available.

PALMER-MOORE — Syracuse, N.Y. — (1913-c. 1916) — The Palmer-Moore Co. built 3/4-ton and 1-ton trucks. In 1916, their 3/4-ton model K sold for $1,150 with a front. It had a Renault-style sloped hood, a 106 in. wheelbase and was powered by a four-cylinder Buda engine.

1914 Palmer-Moore Model C Panel Delivery (OCW)

PANHARD — Grand Haven, Mich. — 1918-1919. Panhard Motors built assembled trucks, including a 1-ton model with a Gray four-cylinder engine, Fuller gearbox and Torbenson rear axle. There was no connection with the French Panhard.

PARKER — Milwaukee, Wis. — (1918-1933) — Parker Motor Truck Co. offered some 1-tons. They included the C-22 of 1922 and the B-23 of 1923-1924. Both trucks used four-cylinder engines. The company was originally called Stegman.

PATHFINDER — Indianapolis, Ind. — (1912-1914) — The Motor Car Manufacturing Co. built mainly autos, but also sold a light van on their auto chassis. This 3/4-ton model had a 120 in. wheelbase, a four-cylinder engine, three-speed transmission and shaft drive. Later, a 1-ton truck was offered on the same chassis. With a closed van body, the price was $2,000.

PATRIOT — Lincoln, Neb. — (1918-1926) — These were 3/4-ton to 4-ton trucks built by the Patriot Motors Co. Their models had patriotic names, such as "Revere," "Lincoln," and "Washington." The Revere was the 3/4-ton unit. It had a 129 in. wheelbase, a Continental four-cylinder motor and a dashboard of selected oak, iron bound, with "special provisions for attaching windshield and cab roof irons." The company first operated under the name Hebb Motors Co., introducing its first truck (a 1918 model) on Oct. 1, 1917. In 1920, the name Patriot Motors Co. was adopted and used on trucks produced in Lincoln through 1922. In the latter year, the firm relocated to Havelock, Neb. and took the name Patriot Manufacturing Co. These trucks were marketed with heavy emphasis on agricultural use and were said to be popular with farmers because of the many purpose built bodies available.

1914 Palmer-Moore Open Flareboard Express (OCW)

1914 Palmer-Moore Model C Platform Stake (OCW)

1918 Patriot 1- to 1-1/2-Ton Lincoln Truck (SCC/TL)

Standard Catalog of Light-Duty Trucks

PAULDING — St. Louis, Mo. — (1913-1916) — The St. Louis Motor Truck Co. built trucks ranging in capacity from less than 1/2-ton to three-tons. An 800 lb. model with double chain-drive was sold through 1916. Shaft drive was then adopted.

PENN — Pittsburgh, Pa. — (1911-1913) — This was a light truck version of the auto manufactured by the Penn Motor Car Co. The 1,500 lb. (3/4-ton) delivery had a four-cylinder, 22 (ALAM) hp motor, shaft drive and a $1,200 pricetag in 1912.

PENTON — Cleveland, Ohio — (1921-1928) — The Penton Motor Co.'s Cantilever Truck was an early type of walk-in delivery van. A four-cylinder engine and front-wheel drive were featured in this model.

PERFEX — Los Angeles, Calif. — (1913-1914) — The Perfex Co. built both autos and a 1/2-ton truck. The truck was called the Model 19. It had a 116 in. wheelbase, T-head four-cylinder engine, three-speed transmission, shaft drive and pneumatic tires. Its price was $875.

1913 Perfex Express Wagon (JDV)

PHILADELPHIA — Philadelphia, Pa. — (1911-1912) — This was a 3/4-ton delivery van made by the Philadelphia Truck Co. The four-cylinder, forward-control truck was rated for 1,500 lb. payloads. It had a 102 in. wheelbase and weighed 2,065 lbs. The price was $2,200.

PHIPPS-GRINELL — Detroit, Mich. — (1910-1911) — The Phipps-Grinell Auto Co. built a small, battery-powered electric van that had a hood like a gas-powered truck. It was rated for just 800 lbs. and was the company's only commercial vehicle. Double chain-drive and solid tires were other features.

PHOENIX — Phoenixville, Pa. — (1908-1910) — These were high-wheeler delivery trucks produced by the Phoenix Auto Works. They had 12 hp, two-cylinder DeTamble air-cooled engines. A friction-type transmission was used and chains carried drive to the rear axles. The truck cost $800 in 1908 and $900 later.

P.H.P. — Westfield, Mass. — (1911-1912) — During its short life, the P.H.P. Motor Truck Co. built light trucks. Its Model 25 was a 3/4-ton on a 102 in. wheelbase. There was also a 1-ton, called the Model 28, that rode a 115 in. wheelbase. Both featured 30 hp four-cylinder engines, three-speed transmission, and shaft drive. They cost $1,050 and $1,500, respectively.

PIERCE-ARROW — Buffalo, N.Y. — (1910-1938) — The Pierce-Arrow Motor Car Co. built a high-quality line of medium and large trucks and bus chassis until the early 1930s. In addition, their passenger car chassis was often used for mounting ambulance, hearse, small bus and fire apparatus bodies. For example, both the Milwaukee and Minneapolis fire departments used substantial numbers of fire apparatus built on Pierce-Arrow chassis.

1933 Pierce-Arrow 1-Ton Hose Truck (DFW/WS)

PITTSBURG — Pittsburg, Pa. — (1908-1911) — These were light electric trucks, built by the Pittsburg Motor Vehicle Co., (the "h" apparently was not used in spelling the city's name at that time).

PLYMOUTH — Toledo, Ohio/Plymouth, Ohio — (1906-1914) — This company built friction-drive trucks. A 1/2-ton model was sold in 1906-1907. It had a Continental four-cylinder engine and double chain-drive. By 1908, sightseeing buses with 50 hp were available. Most companies did not make such large engines with friction-drive. Only two models, including a 26.5 hp 1-ton with "cyclops" headlight, were 1912 offerings. The 1-ton chassis sold for $1,850 in 1914, when 2- and 3-tons were also marketed.

Standard Catalog of Light-Duty Trucks

1914 Plymouth Model D-3 Covered Flareboard (OCW)

PONY — Minneapolis, Minn. — (1919-1923) — This was a 1/4-ton delivery van. Later, the manufacturer attempted to market a cyclecar-based truck. It had a small, four-cylinder, water-cooled engine, friction transmission, chain-drive and a 90 in. wheelbase. The price was just $350.

POPE-HARTFORD — Hartford, Conn. — (1906-1914) — The Pope Manufacturing Co. built large trucks and its auto chassis were sometimes fitted with commercial bodies.

1917 Pope-Hartford Motor Ambulance (DFW/HAC)

POPE-WAVERLY — Indianapolis, Ind. — (1904-1908) — Electric light delivery vans were included in the line, plus a 96 in. wheelbase 1-ton with an unusually wide 82 in. track. In 1906, there were six models, including one open delivery, two closed vans and a 1-ton truck.

POSS — Detroit, Mich. — (1912-1914) — Poss Motor Co. made only a 1/2-ton truck with an open delivery body. It had a 98 in. wheelbase and weighed 1,350 lbs. Features included a water-cooled four-cylinder engine and choice of solid or pneumatic tires. The price was $850.

1911 Poss Model A 1/2-Ton Express Truck (NAHC)

POWELL — Compton, Calif. — (1954-1956) — The Powell Mfg. Co. built a small pickup based on old Plymouth components. The pickup's top rail was a long cylinder, rumored to be built for carrying disassembled fly fishing rods.

1955 Powell Sport Wagon (JAG)

1956 Powell Sport Wagon (DFW/HTM)

POWER — Detroit, Mich. — (1917-1923) — Power Truck & Tractor Co. began with a 2-ton truck. By 1918, a smaller 1-ton was available. It had a four-cylinder engine and lasted until 1921.

POYER — Menominee, Mich. — (pre World War I) — The D.F. Poyer Co. made a 3/4-ton truck and a 1-ton model, too.

PRACTICAL PIGGINS — Racine, Wis. — (1913) — The Piggins Motor Truck Co.'s line included a 1-ton, gas-engined chassis that sold for $1,750. It used a 4-cylinder engine, three-speed gearbox and shaft drive system.

PRECEDENT — Calif. — (1984) — The Precedent was a luxury mini-van/limousine unveiled at the National Automobile Dealers Association (NADA) convention in Feb. 1984. It was created by Alain Clenet, who is best known for his Ford-based neo-Classic car. Artist Mark P. Stehrenberger collaborated with Fred L. Lands, of Lands Design in Elkhart, Ind., to style the vehicle. Dick Gulstrand, of racing fame, was chassis consultant. The platform of Chevrolet's S10 pickup was used in combination with Camaro and Lincoln Continental drivetrain components. The frame and doors were taken from the French-built Citroen, while the chassis and body panels were totally unique.

1984 Precedent Luxury Mini-Van (JAG)

PROGRESS — Milwaukee, Wis. — (1911-1914) — This company's smallest model was a 3/4-ton with a four-cylinder engine, forward-control chassis layout, three-speed transmission andf double chain-drive.

PULLMAN — York, Pa. — (1917) — This automaker (Pullman Motor Car Corp.) produced the Model 424-32 1/2-ton truck in 1917. It came in open express ($750) or panel delivery ($775) form.

PURITY — St. Paul, Minn. — (1914-1915) — The Purity Bread Co. apparently built some small electrics for its own use and then offered some for sale. These were battery-powered units on a 102 in. wheelbase. Payload capacities were 1,200 or 2,000 lbs. Pneumatic tires were featured.

QUAKERTOWN — Quakertown, Pa. — (1916) — Quakertown Auto Manufacturing Co. sold its only commercial vehicle for $500. This was a 1/2-ton model with a 35 hp four-cylinder engine.

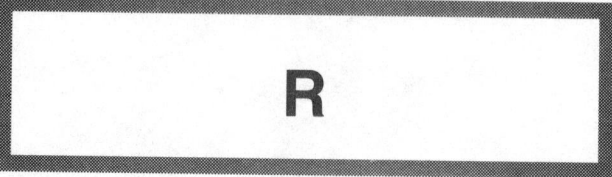

RAINIER — New York, N.Y. — (1916-1924)/Flushing, N.Y. (1924-1927) — The first model made by this company was a 1/2-ton with either closed or open express bodies available. It had a Rainier built four-cylinder engine and worm drive. Along with larger models, a 3/4-ton was added in 1918. By 1925, there were seven models from 3/4-ton up.

RALSTON — Omaha, Neb. — (1913) — During its short existence, the Ralston Motor Co. built a 1/2-ton open van. It had a four-cylinder air-cooled engine, friction transmission, wood frame, 36 x 2 in. solid tires and double chain-drive. Price was $750 for the 108 in. wheelbased truck.

RAMBLER — Kenosha, Wis. — (1897-1913) — Named for an early bicycle made by Thomas B. Jeffery, the Rambler was Jeffery's first car and became a best-seller. In 1904, a Rambler Delivery Wagon was cataloged. An advertisement said it was fitted with "81 in. wheelbase and four full elliptic springs, insuring safe conveyence for delicate packages." The ad also added that it could "carry one-quarter cubic yards of merchandise, accessible front and rear of wagon." A detachable delivery top was provided with brass sidelamps and a horn. It sold for $850 at the factory. Some Ramblers were also converted into dealer service cars. In 1914, the firm was renamed Jeffery and introduced a 3/4-ton express.

1904 Rambler Type 1 Delivery Van (OCW)

1905 Rambler Panel Delivery Van (OCW)

Standard Catalog of Light-Duty Trucks

1911 Rambler Model 63 Pickup (AMC)

RANDOLPH — Flint, Mich./Chicago, Ill. — (1908-1912/1913) — This truck (a.k.a. the "Strenuous Randolph") was the 1-ton Model 14. It had its forward-control driver's bench seat behind a high, flat radiator. A huge headlamp sat, cyclops-style, atop the radiator. Also available were two-cylinder light delivery models. Other features included double chain-drive, solid tires and three-speed gearboxes.

1910 Randolph Model 14 1-Ton Truck (NAHC)

RANIER — Flushing, N.Y. — (1916-1927) — This was a moderately well-known Eastern truck, manufactured by the Ranier Motor Corp. The first model was rated at 1/2-ton; eventually the firm made trucks up to 6-tons in capacity. In 1918, they produced both a 1/2-ton chassis on a 115 in. wheelbase, selling for $995 and a 3/4-ton chassis on a 125 in. wheelbase, selling for $1,150. In 1927, their last year, they produced a 3/4-ton chassis, selling for $1,970.

1918 Rainier Screenside Express (DFW/SI)

RAPID — Detroit, Mich. — (1904-1912) — The Rapid Motor Vehicle Co. started out building light vans. It then concentrated on medium-sized trucks. One-tons were produced as early as 1906. The 1907 line included a 1-ton delivery van. By 1909, some 17 different trucks were available, including ambulances and funeral cars. A police patrol wagon was another product that met with some success. By 1909, the line was down to a pair of 1-tons and a large 1-1/2-ton. One-, 2- and 3-ton trucks were available for 1910. General Motors Truck (GMC) absorbed Rapid in 1912.

Standard Catalog of Light-Duty Trucks

1910 Rapid Police Patrol Wagon (DFW/MVMA)

RASSEL — Toledo, Ohio — (1911-1912) — E.C. Rassel Mfg. Co. produced these models. The 1911 Model A truck was a $1,600 1-ton. It was carried over for 1912 at a $100 higher price. Also available the second year, in chassis form, was the 3/4-ton Model O. It had a $1,500 pricetag. Both were gasoline-engined trucks.

READING STEAMER — Reading, Pa. — (1901-1902) — The Steam Vehicle Co. of America offered two light enclosed deliveries. The smaller truck's carrying space was only 48 x 29 x 36 in. and it sold for $1,200. The larger one's space was 36 x 36 x 51 in. and it could carry 750 lbs.

REAL — Anderson, Ind. — (1914) — This was a small cyclecar van built by the H. Paul Prigg Co. It sold for $395. It had a two-cylinder engine, friction transmission and belt-drive. The wheelbase was 78 in. The tread was 36 in. The frame was made of wood.

RED SHIELD HUSTLER — Detroit, Mich. — (1912) — The Red Shield Hustler Power Co. built small high-wheelers in the 500 to 1,200 lb. capacity range. They had two-cylinder engines mounted below the body. A planetary transmission passed drive back to double chains at the rear. Wheelbases of 75 in. and 86 in. were offered in two models.

REGAL — Detroit, Mich. — (1911-1912) Regal Motor Car Co. made some 1/2-ton trucks. They were not based directly on the Regal automobiles. A wheelbase of 107 in. was used. The powerplant was a 30 hp four-cylinder engine. This model was only built for about one year.

RELAY — Lima, Ohio — (1927-1933) — Relay Motors Corp. is noted mainly for large trucks. However, in the early 1930s, its smallest model was rated at 3/4-ton capacity. This 1931 model used a Continental engine. In earlier years, the firm had offered a six-cylinder engined 1-ton truck using a Buda engine and four-speed transmission.

RELIABLE-DAYTON — Chicago, Ill. — (1906-1909) — This firm made a high-wheeler truck. It carried an engine under the seat and featured tiller steering, a transmission with two forward speeds and reverse and a $1,000 list price. The company's main product was passenger cars of similar style.

RENVILLE — Minneapolis, Minn. — (1912) -These trucks were products of the Renville Buggy Manufacturing Co. A two-cylinder engine was the powerplant. The 1,500 lb. platform model went for $800. The 1-ton platform was $1,150.

REO — Lansing, Mich. — (1908-1967) — This firm operated under four names during its long history. It was known as Reo Motor Car Co. from 1908-1939. It then became Reo Motors, Inc., a name that persisted between 1940 and 1957. In the latter year, it became part of White Motor Co. known as Reo Div. By 1961, this was modified to Reo Motor Div. of White Motor Co. It was a well-known make of truck. In fact, its most reknowned model was the Reo Speedwagon, a name which was adopted, later, by a rock musical group that is popular today. (However, the name has been changed in pronunciation to "R-E-O Speedwagon.") In the late 1920s, Reo registrations were fifth highest in the country. The smallest Reo Speedwagon was generally rated at 1-ton; sometimes 3/4-ton. In 1918, Reo's 3/4-ton Speedwagon chassis on a 128 in. wheelbase sold for $1,100. In the late 1920s, the firm made a "junior" Speedwagon rated at 1/2-ton and up. The Reo Motor Car Co. also produced autos up until the mid-1930s and, in many years, the lightest Reo truck offered was based on the passenger car chassis. For example, in the mid-'30s, the firm built light trucks which were marketed by Mack. The Reo firm built a full range of both truck and bus chassis and is probably better known for its medium-sized units.

1909 Reo Light Flareboard Express (BWA)

1916 Reo Model F 3/4-Ton Flareboard Express (OCW)

1918 Reo Speedwagon Ambulance (DFW/HCC)

1922 Reo Speedwagon Open Cab Express (W. Peguin)

1923 Reo Speedwagon Closed Cab Express (F. Morby)

1923 Reo Speedwagon Enclosed Cab High Side Express

1924 Reo Open Cab Panelside Delivery (DFW/HAC)

1925 Reo Speedwagon Canopy Top Express (OCW)

Standard Catalog of Light-Duty Trucks

1930 Reo Fremont Town Car Delivery (DFW/MVMA)

1931 Reo Speedwagon Cab Express (R. Kingston/DFW)

1934 Reo Speedwagon Cab Express (DFW/DPL)

1934 Reo Speedwagon Panel Body Delivery (DFW/DPL)

Standard Catalog of Light-Duty Trucks

1938 Reo Speedwagon Pickup (OCW/VAN)

1938 Reo Speedwagon Pickup (OCW/VAN)

1940 Reo Model 19AS Express Body (A & A)

1949 Reo Model 19AS Express Body (OCW)

REPUBLIC — Alma, Mich. — (1914-1929) — These were fairly well-known "assembled" trucks, produced by the Republic Motor Truck Co. According to registrations of trucks in use on Dec. 31, 1921, Republics were the second most widely used trucks in the U.S., trailing only Ford. The company's first product, the 1914 Model C, was rated for 2,000 lbs. (1-ton). With standard express or special express bodies, it sold for $1,425. In 1915, there was a 3/4-ton Model F express for $995 and a 1-ton Model L chassis for $1,350. In 1916, only a 2-ton truck was listed. The express truck sold for $995. It was on a 124 in. wheelbase . The F was back, joined by the 3/4-ton Model 9 and 1-ton Models E and 10. The 1917-1919 offerings included a 3/4-ton Model 9; a 1-ton Model 9-S and the 1-ton Model 10. Two 1-tons, the "10" and "10E" appeared in 1920 and 1921, joined by the 3/4-ton Model 75

the latter year. For 1922, there were 3/4-ton 75/75R models and 1-ton 10/10A/10D and 10ER models. For 1923, the smalled Republic product was the Model 75, but it was uprated to 1-1/4-tons. In its last year, Republic was associated with two other well-known makes: Linn (a builder of half-tracks) and American-LaFrance.

1914 Republic Model B Flareboard Express (OCW)

1914 Republic Model B Stake Platform Truck (OCW)

1915 Republic 1-Ton Canopy Express (V. Kovlak)

1919 Republic Model 10 1-Ton Platform (Dennis Hurry)

1920 Republic Canopied Express (DFW/WRHS)

1925 Republic Model 10F 3/4-Ton Open Cab Express (OCW)

REX — Chicago, Ill. — (1921-1923) — One of six trucks made by this firm was a 1-ton. It had a 4cylinder Buda engine. The company was called Royal Rex Motors Co. The firm's logo badge showed a swastika. Many of its worm-drive trucks went into the export market.

REYA — Napolean, Ohio — (1917-1919) — This rarely heard of company produced a 1-ton truck.

RIKER — Brooklyn, N.Y. — (1898-1903) — These were electric vans built by the Riker Electric Vehicle Co. It was in 1898, that Andrew L. Riker proudly exhibited the first electric truck that he built for B. Altman & Co., of New York City. Much larger trucks were also built, as well as cabs and buses.

1900 Riker Delivery Wagon (HACJ/LIAM)

ROBINSON — Minneapolis, Minn. — (1909-1920) — Thomas F. Robinson, Robinson-Loomer Truck Co. and Robinson Motor Truck Co. were among names used by this Midwestern firm. The "Gopher," an $1,800 1-ton, was the initial product. All of 57 units were made before a switch to larger models only was made.

ROCKFORD — Rockford, Ill. — (1914) — The Rockford Motor Truck Co. made 3/4-ton and 1-ton chassis-only trucks with custom bodies. The firm may have survived through 1916.

ROCKNE — (See the Studebaker section in the forward part of this catalog).

RODEFELD — Richmond, Ind. — (1915-1917) — This firm produced a 1-ton, apparently for three years. It was available in "chassis" and "optional" versions. In 1915, the respective prices for the two models were $1,100 and $1,300. In 1916, the chassis dropped $100, the option $150. The line was carried over into 1917 without change.

ROGERS — Omaha, Neb. — (1912-1914) — The Rogers Motor Car Co. built a 1/4-ton truck. This vehicle was actually rated at 600 lbs. A two-cylinder, 18 hp gas-engine was used. The light-delivery model sold for $850. It had a 100 in. wheelbase.

ROVAN — Columbus, Ohio — (1911-1914) — This was a light truck with front-wheel-drive produced by the Kinnear Mfg. Co. of Columbus, Ohio and, later, by James Boyd & Brothers, of Philadelphia, Pa. (a firm best known for its fire apparatus). Models with 104 and 124 in. wheelbases were available. They featured a flat, two-cylinder engine, three-speed gearbox bolted to the front axle and final worm gear drive. They were rated for 3/4-ton and had solid tires. A top speed of 22 mph was possible. The standard model sold for $1,600.

1911 Rovan Flareboard Express (JAW)

ROWE — Coatsville, Pa. — (1911-1914) — The Rowe Motor Co. built autos, then introduced trucks. The 1911 line included two 1,500 lb. deliveries. The first sold for $2,500. A Model A, for $1,800, was the cheaper version. There was also a 1-ton Model B delivery for $2,250. Heavier trucks were made in 1912. In 1913, two light express trucks appeared. One was the new 1,500 lb., $1,800 Model A. Also, the Model B was available at the same price as the 1911 delivery version. In 1914, the name Rowe Motor Mfg. Co. was adopted and production moved to Downington, Pa.

1911 Rowe Model A 3/4-Ton Covered Express (DJS)

ROWE — Downington, Pa. — (1914-1925) — Rowe Motor Mfg. Co. evolved from Rowe Motor Co. (see listing above). For 1914, the Model A (at $1,690) and Model B (at $2,175) were continued as truck chassis. Heavier models were cataloged in 1915 and one of these — the "CW" — was down-rated to 1-ton for 1916. In chassis form, it was $2,450. This was carried over for 1917, but the 1918 line started with a 2-ton truck.

1914 Rowe Flareboard Express (OCW)

Standard Catalog of Light-Duty Trucks

1914 Rowe Covered Flareboard Express (OCW)

1921 Rowe Vestibuled Canopy Delivery (DJS)

R.S. — Reading, Pa. — (1915-1916) — This firm made a three-wheel delivery car in Reading. It used a standard motorcycle engine. The transmission was a three-speed. A chain carried drive power to the single rear wheel.

RUGBY — (Related to Durant and Star; see Durant).

RUGGLES — Saginaw, Mich. — (1921-1928) — The Ruggles Motor Truck Co. built trucks in sizes ranging from 3/4-ton to 3-tons and also built bus chassis. The 3/4-ton Model 15 was produced in 1920 and 1921 only. A 1-ton Model 20 was offered in 1921-1922. The bus chassis was used to make models capable of hauling from 16-29 people from point A to point B. The company made its own engines until 1924.

1922 Ruggles "Go-Getter" Canopied Top Express (OCW)

RUSH — Philadelphia, Pa. — (1915-1918) — These were delivery trucks assembled by the Rush Delivery Car Co. The company's 1,000 lb. chassis sold for $625 in 1916. For 1917, the product line consisted of three versions of the 1/2-ton Model F. The chassis was $895, the Express $965 and the Panel $985.

$625

1916 Rush Light 1/2-Ton Delivery Car (WOM)

1917 Rush Light 1/2-Ton Delivery Car (OCW)

S

SAMPSON — Pittsfield, Mass. — (1905-1910) — This company operated in its first location through 1910, then moved West. Most trucks made by Alden Sampson were real "goliaths," but 1/2-ton and 1-ton versions were seen, the smaller truck having an 18 hp flat-twin engine and shaft drive. Alden Sampson Mfg. Co. relocated to Detroit, Mich. in 1910.

SAMPSON — Detroit, Mich. — (1910-1913) — Alden Sampson Manufacturing Co. offered a 1-ton truck for $2,100 in 1911. This model had a $2,100 pricetag. Also available, during the same year, was a 3/4-ton delivery model selling for $1,175. This was a rather handsome, open crescent-cab van known as the "Hercules." It used a four-cylinder Continental engine that developed 30 hp. The 3/4-ton was carried over as a 1913 model, but with a decrease in price to $1,450. By this time, the firm had become part of United Motor Co. and the Sampson nameplate disappeared.

1912 Sampson 1-Ton Delivery Van (OCW)

SAMSON — Janesville, Wis. — (1920-1923) — The Samson Tractor Co. made a 3/4-ton cab-over-engine light-duty truck. This Model A was offered in both 1920 and 1921. There was a new Model 15 3/4-ton truck for 1922. Samson was part of General Motors, so these trucks utilized the Chevrolet 490's engine. They were promoted primarily for on-the-farm use. The company went out of business in 1922. Upon its liquidation in 1923, the factory became a Chevrolet assembly plant.

1920 Samson Model 15 3/4-Ton Chassis (EEH)

SANBERT — Syracuse, N.Y. — (1911-1912) — The Sanbert-Herbert Co.'s three-cylinder engined truck was a 1-ton available with three body types. The standard delivery was $1,500. The open box model was identically priced. A panel could also be had for $1,625. (Note: Also see Sanford)

SANDOW — Chicago, Ill. — (1914-1928) — This firm sporadically made 1-ton trucks, at least through 1921. The Model I, of 1914, sold for $1,800 as a bare chassis. 1-tons returned, in 1917, with the $1,485 Model A. In 1918, the 4-cylinder Model G was priced at $2,050. The range continued until 1928 with 4-cylinder Buda or Continental engines, apparently including additional 1-ton models.

1914 Sandow Model I Panel Delivery (OCW)

SANDUSKY — Sandusky, Ohio — (1911-1914) — For its initial year, the Sandusky Auto Parts & Motor Truck Co. sold only a 1-ton closed express which was up-rated to 1-1/2 tons in 1912. The Model B, of 1914, was another light-duty available as a 3/4-ton chassis truck priced at $1 per pound. Common body styles seen on the 1914 chassis included the flare-board express and panel delivery van. These trucks used the shovel-nose type styling, which was popular in the light-duty truck industry at this time and used by other makers such as IHC. Other features included brass headlights and cowl lamps, wood-spoke wheels and left-hand drive. Double chains were used to carry power to the rear axle. One of the firm's customers was the Catawba Candy Co. of Sandusky.

1914 Sandusky Model B Panel Delivery (OCW)

SANFORD — Syracuse, N.Y. — (1914-1918) — Sanford Motor Truck Co. offered 3/4- and 1-ton trucks. In 1914, the 1-ton Model K came as a chassis, for $1,660, or as a stake body or flareboard, for $1,750. The Model O, of 1915, had a 3/4-ton payload rating and a $1,290 chassis price. For $60 extra, an express box could be added. The "O" and "K" were carried over for 1916 at the same prices and the "O" (now considered a 3/4- to 1-ton) was marketed again, in 1917, with no change in price. The company lasted until 1924, but made no light trucks after 1917.

1914 Sanford Model K Flareboard Express (OCW)

SAUER — New York, N.Y. — (1911-1918) — This truck was actually a machine imported from Germany, with final assembly taking place here. In its first year of business, a 1-ton called the Model A was sold. It was gasoline-engined. The chassis model carried a steep $5,000 pricetag. Later models were heavy-duty trucks up to 7-tons.

SAVIANO SCAT — Warren, Mich. — (c. 1955-1960) — Arnold P. Saviano, owner of a tool and die company, created this Jeep-like utility vehicle.

SAXON — Detroit, Mich. — (1914-1916) — Automobiles were the Saxon Motor Co.'s main product, although it also offered light-duty trucks built off the automobile chassis. The company's 400 lb. Light Delivery model, of 1915, carried a $395 retail price. It used a gasoline engine. Two 500 lb. models...Panel and Curtain Delivery... were marketed in the Model 6 line during 1917-1918. They sold for $800.

SCHACHT — Cincinnati, Ohio — (1911-1938) — The G.A. Schacht Motor Truck Co. built a moderately well-known truck, although only in the early years were light-duty models offered. In 1911, the firm's first line included the 1-ton Model D4 Delivery for $1,385. It had a two-cylinder engine. By 1912, the truck was down-rated to 3/4-tons. With a closed delivery body it cost $1,585. Also available were two 1/2-tons, the "D" closed delivery ($975) and the "E" open delivery ($850). For 1913, the D4 was up-rated to 1,800 lbs. payload and cost $1,600 in delivery van form. A chassis model, the "16," was a $2,000 1-ton. After 1914, only larger trucks were built.

SCHMIDT — Crossing, Ill. — (1911-1913) — Schmidt Brothers Co. made 1/2-, 3/4- and 1-ton trucks. The 1911s included the 1/2-ton Model F delivery ($975) and a 1-ton delivery ($1,325). Both had two-cylinder gas engines. Up-rated to 3/4-tons, the Model F was priced $1,100 in 1912. Also marketed, in "optional" form, was the 2,000 lb. Model C, priced at $1,375. These were carried over, in 1913, at $1,025 for the Model F and $1,375 for the Model C.

SCHNEER — San Francisco, Calif. — (c. 1916) — The J. J. Schneer Co. was a short-lived auto manufacturer. Some of its chassis were used for fire apparatus. One restored firefighting rig still survives. We don't know whether light-duty Schneer chassis were used for other commercial purposes.

SCHURMEIER — St. Paul, Minn. — (1911) — The Schurmeier Wagon Co.'s two-cylinder Model C was a 1,500 lb. payload truck for $1,800. Contemporary reference sources listed this commercial vehicle for only one year.

SCRIPPS-BOOTH — Detroit, Mich. — (1914-1915) -This automaker also produced a Box Body cyclecar having a 750 lb. payload rating. It used a 10 hp air-cooled two-cylinder engine that drove through a planetary transmission. The unit had a $395 retail price and featured a 100 in. wheelbase.

SEARS — Chicago, Ill. — (1909-1911) — These were high-wheelers distributed by Sears, Roebuck & Co. The commercial model was called a Light Farm Wagon. Its features included tiller steering, chain-drive, full-elliptic springs and front and rear fenders. The two-cylinder, horizontally-opposed engine was located under the seat. Like the Sears car, these trucks were marketed through the company's retail merchandise catalogs and were designed to be assembled by the owner. The high-wheel type of vehicle was very popular in rural areas, where roads had not yet been "improved" (paved). The tall, narrow, spoke wheels could wind their way through the deepest mud, muck and mire without getting stuck. In most cases, the wheels were fitted with hard rubber tires, although pneumatic tires were optionally available.

1911 Sears High-Wheeler Farm Wagon (OCW)

Standard Catalog of Light-Duty Trucks

SEITZ — Detroit, Mich. — (1911-1913) — Seitz Automobile Transmission Co. was another of the lesser known light-duty truck-makers. The 1,500 lb. delivery, of 1911, sold for $1,200. Products in 1912 included a 1,500 lb. closed delivery ($1,500) and 1-ton truck ($2,000). The latter, coded as the Model C, was carried over in 1913.

SELDEN — Rochester, N.Y. — (1913-1932) — George Selden's claim to fame was his automobile patent, which Henry Ford successfully contested. During the controversy, Selden constructed a vehicle from the patent drawings which would have to be considered a light truck. Interestingly, the truck is now in the Henry Ford Museum at Dearborn, Mich. Later in his life, Selden actively produced larger trucks. His firm was called the Selden Truck Corp. In 1918, he produced a 3/4-ton chassis. It had a 110 in. wheelbase and sold for $1,075.

1877 Selden Motor Wagon Replica (DFW/HFM)

1914 Selden Model J Covered Flareboard (OCW)

1914 Selden Model J-L Platform Stake (OCW)

1925 Selden Model 20-6 1- to 1-1/4 Ton Stake (OCW)

SENECA — Fostoria, Ohio — (1917-1918) — A four-post-top commercial vehicle was produced by the Seneca Motor Car Co. in 1917. It had a 1,275 lb. load capacity and $695 list price. Also available was a vestibuled (closed) cab version for $725. The firm's 1918 lineup included the $825 Model F 1/2-ton open delivery and $850 Model G 1/2-ton panel delivery, both with a new four-cylinder engine.

SERVICE — Detroit, Mich./Wabash, Ind. — (1911-1913/1914-1932) — Service Motor Truck Co. started in Detroit. Models for 1911 included the "D" 1/2-ton delivery ($750); "E" 1-ton delivery ($950); "H" 9-passenger bus ($850); and "C" 1/2-ton business car ($850). All used two-cylinder gas engines. In 1912-1913, offerings were the "J" 3/4-ton chassis ($1,400) and "K-L" 1-ton chassis ($1,550). The firm relocated, to Wabash, Ind., during 1914. That year the "J" (at $1,350) and "K" (at $1,475) were made again. A 1-ton Model W chassis with worm drive was $2,000 in 1915. For 1916, two 1-ton chassis, the "20" ($1,400) and "W" ($1,300) were available. For 1918, the four-cylinder "220" 1-ton chassis (at $1,900) was sold. One-tons were built in all years 1916-1921. They survived until 1921. There was also a 3/4-ton, called the Model 15 in 1921 and another called the Model 12 in 1922. Then, only heavier models were made until 1925, when the "25F" and "25H" 1-tons bowed.

1914 Service Model J Flareboard Express (OCW)

1914 Service Model K Covered Flareboard (OCW)

1915 Service Model J Flareboard Express (DFW)

1915 Service C-Cab Panel Delivery (JAW)

SHAW — Chicago, Ill. — (1918-1920) — The Walden W. Shaw Livery Co. built taxicabs and automobiles. In 1918, they introduced a line of trucks in both 3/4- and 2-ton sizes. The light-duty 3/4-ton model had a Continental engine, a 116.5 in. wheelbase and $1,650 price-tag.

1916 Shaw Model M2 3/4-Ton Stake Body (RAW)

SHELBY — Shelby, Ohio — (1917-1918) — These Shelbys came out a long time before the famous high-performance Mustangs and Dodges. Shelby Tractor and Truck Co. produced them. Both had four-cylinder engines. A 3/4-ton chassis was $900. The same price was charged for a 9 horsepower tractor.

SHERIDAN — Chicago, Ill. — (1916-1917) — The Sheridan Commercial Car Co. made the Model A in 1916. It was a gasoline-powered open delivery rated for 650 lb. payloads and selling for $465. In 1917, the company produced 1/2-ton stake bed and canopy models for $540. It would also sell you a chassis for just $490.

SIEBERT — Toledo, Ohio — (1911-1916) — Two light-duty models, a 1,200 pounder and a 1-ton, were the first trucks from The Shop of Siebert. A two-cylinder engine powered the smaller model, while the 1-ton (on a 10-ft. wheelbase), used a four-cylinder powerplant. The 1914 Model H 1-ton flareboard truck went for $1,350. In 1915, it was down-rated to become a 3/4-ton delivery priced at $1,250. In 1916, the final offering was a $1,350 chassis truck, the Model I. This firm later became a body builder for commercial vehicles, ambulances and funeral cars.

1914 Siebert Model H Covered Flareboard (OCW)

SIGNAL — Detroit, Mich. — (1913-1923) — Starting with a 1-1/2-ton truck, this firm made its 3/4-ton light-duty available in 1914 at $1,350 for the chassis. Four 1-ton models (D/DL/F/FL) were marketed in 1915 at $1,400-$1,700. An FS-F model of 1917 was a $1,700 1-ton with a choice of 10- or 12-ft. chassis. Also available, concurrently, was the FL 1-ton. It had a 14-ft. chassis and $1,775 pricetag. A 1-ton "F" returned to the line in 1920. It had a 4-1/8 x 5-1/4 in. bore and stroke Continental four-cylinder engine that produced 27.23 (ALAM) hp. The truck scaled-in at 4,500 lbs. Also available was the lighter (3,575 pound) Model NF, which used the same engine. Both were carried over into 1921. The following season, the NF got a new 22.50 hp engine of 3-3/4 x 5 in. bore and stroke, which remained available in 1923. By 1924, the company had stopped listing its model in references like *BRANHAM*.

1914 Signal Screenside Flareboard (OCW)

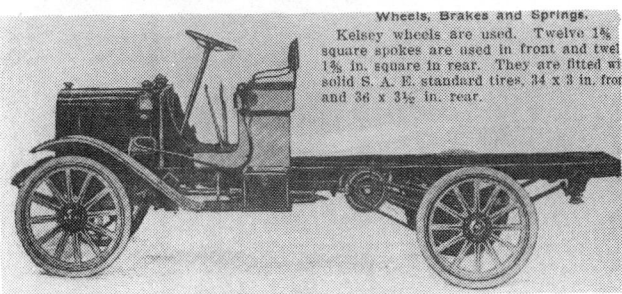

1914 Signal 1,500 lb. Motor Truck Chassis (OCW)

SIMPLO — St. Louis, Mo. — (1908-1909) — The Cook Motor Vehicle Co. built a small delivery van. It had an 86 in. wheelbase and sold for $700. The payload of this vehicle was 1,000 lbs. Power came from a 16 hp two-cylinder engine. Other features included a friction-drive transmission system and double chains.

SMITH FORM-A-TRUCK — Chicago, Ill. — (1917) — This firm built a unit for attachment to Ford Model Ts. It converted the Model T into a 1-ton truck. Ford's entry into the light truck field brought an end to the need for such a unit.

SNYDER — Cleveland, Ohio — (1914) — This was a cyclecar delivery van, produced by the Snyder Motor & Mfg. Co. It was designed with a 100 in. wheelbase. A water-cooled four-cylinder engine drove through a three-speed transmission, with power carried to the rear via shaft drive. It was priced to sell for $425.

SOULES — Grand Rapids, Mich. — (1905-1915) — Soules Motor Car Co. made a 1-ton truck with a horizontally-opposed 22 hp two-cylinder engine. It featured shaft drive. After moving to Detroit, the firm apparently continued production, a line of larger 3-, 4- and 6-tons was reported for 1915.

1907 Soules Light Delivery Wagon (JAW)

SOUTH BEND — South Bend, Ind. — (1914-1915) — South Bend Motor Works offered a 3/4-ton Model 28 gas-engined truck in its first season. In chassis form, it sold for $1,375. The following year, a 1-1/2 ton truck was the smallest one from this company.

SOUTHERN — Greensboro, N.C. — (1919-1921) -This company is known to have produced a 1-ton truck, but further details about the firm or its product are not known at this time.

SPAULDING — Grinnell, Iowa — (1913) — Grinnell, Iowa's contribution to light-duty trucking was a 3/4-ton chassis made by Spaulding Mfg. Co. It sold for $1,100 and had a gasoline engine.

SPEEDWELL — Dayton, Ohio — (1908-1915) — In its early years, the Speedwell Motor Car Co. produced light trucks. Later, it switched to building heavier ones.

SPHINX — York, Pa. — (1914-1916) — This short-lived make of light truck was produced by the Sphinx Motor Car Co., of York (a community which contributed more than its share of early auto and truck manufacturers). The three-year-only model was a 1/2-ton chassis priced at $600. It had a 17 hp, four-cylinder Lycoming engine. Other features included a cone type clutch and bevel gear drive.

Standard Catalog of Light-Duty Trucks

SPOERER — Baltimore, Md. — (1914) — This was a light, closed delivery van. It was built by Carl Spoerer's Sons Co. Price for the 3/4-ton truck, in its chassis-only form, was $2,250. This was not cheap. It had a four-cylinder 8.5-liter engine, 10 ft. wheelbase and shaft hp.

1912 Spoerer Model 40 C Delivery Wagon (WJP)

SPRINGFIELD — Springfield, Mass. — (1901) — This company produced a steam-powered delivery van in 1/2-ton configuration. For a relatively light-duty machine, it was very complex. It had two compound engines, one on each side of the vehicle. A travel range of 50 miles was claimed.

ST. LOUIS — St. Louis, Mo. — (1900-1901) — These were light vans made by the St. Louis Motor Carriage Co. They had a six horsepower, two-cylinder "pancake" engines, two forward speeds and bevel-gear drive.

STANDARD [FISHER STANDARD] — Detroit, Mich. — (1912-1934) — Standard Motor Truck Co. manufactured the Model 56 1-ton truck in 1919-1920. Its other models ranged from 2-tons to 6-tons.

STANDARD — Warren, Ohio — (1914) — During its short life, the Standard Motor Truck Co. built trucks between 1-ton and 1-1/2-ton capacity. Two models called the "A" (2,000 lbs.) and the "B" (3,000 lbs.) were marketed. The 1-ton Model A, in chassis configuration, carried an $1,800 pricetag.

STANLEY — Newton, Mass. — (1909-1916) — The Stanley Motor Carriage Co. was well-known for its steamers. They also offered bus and light truck chassis.

1914 Stanley Model 713 Panel Body Delivery (OCW)

1914 Stanley Express Wagon (WOM)

STAR — Elizabeth, N.J. — (See Durant).

STAR — Ann Arbor, Mich. — (1914) — No relation to the later Durant products, this firm's Model B could be ordered in two weight classes. Both versions were marketed as chassis-only models. The 3/4-ton version was $1,500 and the 1-ton version was $1,600. Both used gas engines.

STAR-TRIBUNE — Detroit, Mich. — (1914) — This company's name sounds like that of a newspaper. Its big news in light-duty trucks was the "O.K." model, a truck chassis with a 1,250-lb. payload rating and $850 list price. Also offered was the Model B 1-ton chassis. It cost $1,500. Star Tribune Motor Sales Co. was the official corporate title. (Also see O.K.)

STEARNS — Cleveland, Ohio — (1901-1916) — The 1901 Stearns Utility Wagon was advertised as a truck that made "no sound but the slight 'tif-tif' of the engine." Features of the curved-cab delivery included tiller steering; automatic spark control and an 11 hp one-

cylinder engine. Its five gallon gas tank was located under the floor. Standard equipment included a top, side curtains, full set of tools, twin oil lamps and a "well-modulated gong." The four-inch diameter pneumatic tires were mounted on 32 in. wheels. A unique idea was that it had no carburetor or mixing chamber. Gas moved directly to the engine through a needle valve with the throttle providing constant fuel mixture. Fuel economy of 20 mpg was claimed. This truck was easy on brake lining wear, too. The engine was used for this function, in addition to the pedal-operated differential brake. In later years, the firm made larger trucks under two other names: Stearns in 1914-1915 and Stearns-Knight in 1916.

1901 Stearns Utility Wagon (JAW)

STEEL SWALLOW — Jackson, Mich. — (1908) — These were small, enclosed vans built by the Steel Swallow Auto Co. They had a seven-foot long wheelbase. The engine was a two-cylinder job that generated all of eight horsepower. A friction type transmission was used.

1908 Steel Swallow RFD Postal Delivery Car (WLB)

STEGEMAN — Milwaukee, Wis. — (1911-1918) — This make of truck, produced by the Stegeman Motor Car Co., ranged in size from 3/4-ton to 5-tons. The firm's first 1-ton was the $2,250 chassis sold in 1912. It was carried over, in 1913, and joined by a 3/4-ton truck priced at $1,600. Both were seen again in 1914. By then, the larger truck could be had in open cab form for a reduced price of $2,100. The closed cab remained $2,250. The 3/4-ton lasted until 1915. For 1916, there was a new 1-ton at $1,680 for the chassis. Trucks of 2-tons and up were available in 1917-1918, but there were no light-duties.

1914 Stegeman Panel Body Delivery (OCW)

1914 Stegeman Covered Flareboard (OCW)

STEINMETZ — Baltimore, Md. — (1922-1926) — These were electric trucks built by the Steinmetz Electric Motor Car Corp. In the mid-1920s, their 1/2-ton chassis sold for $1,700; their 3/4-ton chassis for $1,850.

1920 Steinmetz Light-Duty Chassis & Cowl (OCW)

STEPHENSON — Milwaukee, Wis. — (1912) — One of three models listed for this Milwaukee, Wis. company was the $2,000 Model B 1-ton which came with express or stake bodies.

STERLING — Milwaukee, Wis. — (1916-1953) — The Sterling, built by the Sterling Motors Corp., was a very high-quality medium- to large-sized truck. (It originally had been named "Sternberg" but the name was changed because of anti-German sentiment during World War I.) For a few years, the lightest models were rated at under 1-ton. For example, in 1916, they sold a 3/4-ton chassis with a 127 in. wheelbase for $895 (an electric starter was an additional $75). However, the bulk of the firm's products were large models. In 1928, Sterling changed to a high-speed six-cylinder engine and brought out a "speed wagon" type 1-ton. This truck made a handsome enclosed panel delivery van. Its styling features included a side hood design with three stacks of short horizontal louvers, a one-piece windshield, sun visor, drum style headlights, six-spoke steel spyder wheels and bright metal radiator shell. During 1934, the firm became Sterling Motos Corp. of Milwaukee. The company's later trucks were virtually all larger models, some resembling Brockway and Indiana trucks. In 1951, Sterling was sold to White Motor Co. of Cleveland, Ohio. The following season, operations in Wisconsin were shut down and moved to Cleveland. About 12,000 Sterlings were built. The firm's boom period was in the 1920s.

1916 Sterling 1,500 lb. Enclosed Panel (OCW)

Standard Catalog of Light-Duty Trucks

1929 Sterling Model DB-7 Panel Delivery (DFW/DPL)

STERNBERG — Milwaukee, Wis. — (1908-1915) — This company later became Sterling (see separate listing above). Light-duty trucks were made some years. One year was 1909, when two-cylinder powered 1/2-ton ($985) and 1-ton ($1,650) trucks were offered. Another 1-ton was offered in 1912 at $2,300. Also, in 1915, there was a 1/2-ton express or flareboard model for $875.

STEWART — Buffalo, N.Y. — (1912-1941) — The Stewart Motor Corp. built a well-known line of trucks. They were available in a wide range of sizes. A note in one old catalog indicated that Stewart "will have ready for shipment in March 1916, a 1,000 lb. truck for $750." In the same year, Stewart's 3/4-ton chassis on a 118 in. wheelbase sold for $1,290. A 1918 publication indicated the firm offered a 3/4-ton chassis, with a 110 in. wheelbase, for $845. In the early 1920s, the lightest Stewart models were referred to as "speed trucks." In the later 1920s, they were designated Buddy Stewarts. From 1926-1929, the Buddy Stewart 3/4-ton chassis, powered by a six-cylinder engine, sold for $895. During much of the 1930s, the lightest Stewarts were rated at 1/2-ton. By 1936, the Buddy Stewart chassis price had dropped to $495.

1912 Stewart "Chronicle" Panel Delivery (JAW)

1914 Stewart 1,500 lb. Panel Delivery (OCW)

Standard Catalog of Light-Duty Trucks

1914 Stewart Model B Covered Flareboard (OCW)

1914 Stewart Model F Screenside Express (OCW)

1914 Stewart Model A Panel Delivery (OCW)

1926 Stewart Model 16 1-Ton Speed Truck (OCW)

1927 Buddy Stewart Canopy Express (J.Everitt/DFW)

1927 Buddy Stewart 1-Ton Panel Delivery (OCW)

1935 Stewart Light-Duty Panel Delivery (OCW)

1936 Stewart 1-Ton Panel (Sonny Glesbrenner)

1936 Buddy Stewart Panel Delivery (MVMA/DFW)

1936 Buddy Stewart Standard Pickup (MVMA/DFW)

STEWART — Covington, Ken. — (1912-1916) — Stewart Iron Works made cast iron fences, plus a 1-ton truck called the Model 1. It had a four-stroke, two-cylinder engine and 96 in. wheelbase. The frame had steel side rails and hickory crossmembers. It was of forward-control design with double chain-drive.

STEWART — Cincinnati, Ohio — (1914) — Two 1-ton models came from Stewart Iron Works Co., in 1914. Both used two-cylinder gas engines and had $1,150 list prices. The Model C was an express and the Model D a stake.

STODDARD-DAYTON — Dayton, Ohio — (1911-1912) — This high-quality automaker built trucks during its last two years of operation. The 1911 line included a 1-ton. The 1912 line had a light delivery van and a truck on the company's 28 hp automobile chassis.

STORMS — Detroit, Mich. — (1915) — Storms Electric Car Co. made the only battery-powered U.S. cyclecar. A 1/4-ton delivery van was also offered on the same chassis.

STOUGHTON — Stoughton, Wis. — (1920-1928) — The Stoughton Wagon Co. built both conventional trucks (in the 1- to 2-ton range) and fire apparatus. In 1921, the firm offered its 1-ton Model A, with a 3-3/4 x 5-1/4 in. bore and stroke Midwest four-cylinder engine developing 22.5 hp. This rig weighed-in at 3,300 lbs. For 1922, the smaller Model C, weighing 2,480 lbs. was added. It had a 3-1/2 x 5 in. engine, also produced by Midwest Motor Co. and capable of 19.60 hp. The "C" actually had a 3/4- to 1-1/4-ton rating, probably based on wheelbase options. It was carried over for 1923 in this manner, but with a smaller 18.23 hp engine of 3-3/8 x 4-1/2 in. For 1924, the truck was available only in 3/4-ton format, in which it scaled-in at 2,480 lbs. From this point on, all models seem to be heavy-duty trucks only.

SULLIVAN — Rochester, N.Y. — (1910-1923) — This firm was first called Sullivan Motor Car Co. and later Sullivan Motor Truck Co. The name change did not occur until after 1918. An 800 lb. delivery with a 16 hp horizontally-opposed twin-cylinder engine was the first Sullivan truck. Its features included a planetary transmission and double chain-drive. By 1912, a pair of 1,000-1,500 lb. capacity trucks with different one-cylinder engines was offered. In 1914, the line consisted of four two-cylinder models: the 1/2-ton Model 20 (chassis $925; panel $1,050); the 1-ton Model 51 (chassis $1,050; express ($1,100); the 1-ton Model 51-D (chassis $1,050; express ($1,140) and the 1-ton Model 51-J (chassis $1,050; express $1,200). In 1915, the 1-ton offering was the Model G, a $1,600 chassis truck. Thereafter, 1-1/2 tons were the firm's smallest products.

1914 Sullivan Model 51 Platform Stake (OCW)

SULTAN — Springfield, Mass. — (1911) — Fidelity and Casualty Co. of New York listed this company's taxicab in the truck section of its *MANUAL OF AUTOMOBILE LIABILITY INSURANCE* (1916 edition). It was made by Sultan Motor Car Co. The taxi used a gasoline engine and sold for $2,400.

SUPERIOR — Detroit, Mich. — (1911-1913) — In 1911, Superior Motor Car Co. produced a gas engined 1,200 lb. delivery truck which it sold for $1,500. In 1913, the company's product was a 1-ton called the Model A. It came with "optional" body work for $1,700.

SUPERIOR — Lansing, Mich. — (1912-1914) — F.G. Clark built this marque. The Superior Model A was a 1-ton with an express truck body. It had a 110 in. wheelbase and weighed just 2,500 lbs. The price of $1,700 included a three-speed transmission, double chain-drive and solid rubber tires.

SWEEPLITE — Clearwater, Fla. — (c. 1986) — This compact utility vehicle is marketed by American Sweeping Service Co. It uses a John Deere, four-cylinder diesel as its powerplant. The circular street sweeping brushes are mounted below the center of the vehicle. On the back is a hydraulically-operated dumpster type box. The cab, which is offset to the left, accomodates only the driver. The engine is mounted directly to the right of the cab. The Coke can on the hood is not a factory option.

1986 Sweeplite Utility Dumpster (EK)

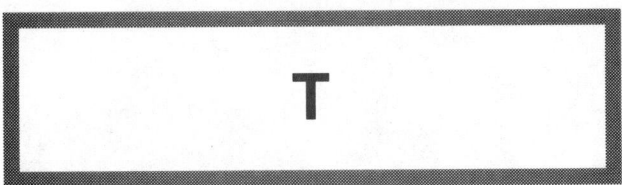

T

TARRYTOWN — New York, N.Y. — (1914) — The Tarrytown Motor Co. produced a box body delivery truck based on its cyclecar. The $400 machine used a two-cylinder gasoline engine. It had a 500 lb. load capacity. This model was listed in 1914 only.

TAYLOR — Fremont, Ohio — (1917-1918) — After purchasing the H.G. Burford Co. of Fremont, this firm made trucks up to 5-tons. Its smallest model was a 1-ton. Like the rest, it used a four-cylinder Continental engine, Covert gearbox and Timken worm drive rear axle. It had a 130 in. wheelbase.

THOMPSON — Providence, R.I. — (1905-1906) — Thompson Auto Co.'s Model A was a steam-powered truck. It used a burner made by Stanley Brothers, the well-known steam car maker. The engine was a 10 hp job by Fitzhenry. It had a 96 in. wheelbase, solid tires and an $1,800 price. The only body style was a delivery van.

THORNE — Chicago, Ill. — (1929-c. 1938) — These were stand-up vans, built by the Thorne Motor Corp. They were powered by an 18 hp, four-cylinder Continental engine which was front-mounted. It drove via a 90-volt electric motor, just ahead of the rear axle. Lockheed four-wheel brakes were a feature.

1930 Thorne Walk-in Panel Delivery (ATHS/DFW)

TIFFIN — Tiffin, Ohio — (1914-1918) — These were light to medium trucks built by the Tiffin Wagon Co. The company's 1914 line included a 1,250 lb. Model A chassis that sold for $1,600 and a 1-ton Model G priced at $2,000 for the chassis. A 1915-1916 pickup sold for $1,600. A 1-ton for $2,000 was continued for these years, too. The 1916 3/4-ton chassis, with a 110 in. wheelbase, sold for $1,250. The same size truck was also listed in 1918; it rode on 34 x 4-1/2 in. pneumatic tires.

1914 Tiffin Model A Platform Stake (OCW)

1914 Tiffin Model G Covered Flareboard (OCW)

TIGER — Detroit, Mich. — (1914-1915) — These were delivery bodies on cyclecar chassis, built by the Automobile Cyclecar Co. They were constructed on an 86 in. wheelbase. The four-cylinder, 12 hp engine featured water cooling. Factory list price was $300.

TITAN — Milwaukee, Wis. — (1918-1932) — As its name indicates, this firm built huge trucks. A 1-ton model was offered in 1925, however. It was the smallest Titan product. It had a four-cylinder, Buda-built engine.

TOLEDO — Toledo, Ohio — (1913) — The Toledo Motor Truck Co. marketed the Model A, a 1-ton truck, in 1913. It was gasoline-engine powered. As a chassis-only, it sold for $1,700. Stake or open express models were both $1,850. For an extra $100 you could get a full-panel body. A 2-ton was also sold.

TORBENSEN — Bloomfield, N.J. — (1906-1910) — These were high-wheel 3/4-ton vans built by the Torbensen Motor Car Co. The first models used a two-stroke, three-cylinder engine, which was air-cooled. Later, a two-cylinder engine was substituted. Other features were a planetary transmission, double chain-drive and a 92 in. wheelbase. By 1907, the firm's two-cylinder Model T was on the market. It was a 1-ton having a list price of $1,400. Three years later, another 1-ton, the Torbenson Delivery Truck, became available at no change in price.

1907 Torbenson 3/4-Ton Light Delivery Wagon (OCW)

TOURAINE — Philadelphia, Pa. — (1914) — A one-year-only model, Touraine Co.'s 550 lb. panel delivery truck carried a $550 pricetag.

TOURIST — Los Angeles, Calif. — (1902-1910) — The Auto Vehicle Co. produced mainly passenger cars, although its chassis were also used for fire apparatus and commercial trucks.

1906 Tourist Light Delivery Car (JDV)

TOWER — Greenville, Mich. — (1917-1923) — In its first year of operations, Tower Motor Truck Co. built a four-cylinder light-duty truck. Dubbed the Model A, the gas-engined chassis model had a $1,150 list price. Other trucks made by the firm were heavy-duty models.

TRABOLD — Johnstown, Pa. — (1911-1932) -The first Trabold Truck Mfg. Co. product was a four-cylinder cab-over-engine truck with chain-drive. A Buda-built four-cylinder engine was used in 1913. The company listed several chassis-only models of 1-ton and under capacity. They included a $975 three-quarter ton in 1914, a $1,475 1-ton the same year, a $1,250 1-ton in 1916 and a 3/4- to 1-ton priced at $1,150 in 1917. Truck bodies were actually made by the company until 1960.

1914 Trabold Panel Delivery Truck (OCW)

TRACTOR — Atlanta, Ga. — (1912) — Denlock Mfg. Co. produced the Tractor Truck. But, it was not a "tractor-truck" (as in tractor trailer). It was a 1-ton model with a $1,200 pricetag. A gas-fired powerplant was utilized.

TRANSIT — Keene, N.H. — (1902) — This truck was built by an automaker called Steamobile Co. Chances are good that it was a commercial version of the firm's Steamobile passenger vehicle. The two-cylinder engine cranked out six horsepower, which was transmitted to the rear wheels via a single chain. This was a truck with a rear driving position, the cargo hold being ahead of the operator.

TRANSIT — Louisville, Ken. — (1912-1916) — Beginnning in the 3-ton class, this firm introduced a 1-ton in 1913 and the 1-ton Model E ($1,200) in 1914 and 1915. This truck had an under-the-floor engine and double chains for drive.

1914 Transit Model E Covered Flareboard (OCW)

TRANSPORT — Mt. Pleasant, Mich. — (1919-1923) — This firm produced a 1-ton called the Model 20 between 1919 and 1921. It had a four-cylinder engine with 22.5 hp. The curb weight was 3,070 lbs. The Continental powerplant had a 3-3/4 x 5 in. bore and stroke. This

truck was replaced by the Model 15 series, which used the same motor and had a lighter 2,775 lbs. curb weight. A "15A" was added in 1923. The "A" indicated a longer wheelbase. It was about 100 lbs. heavier. These two models were built through 1925.

TRAYLOR — Allentown, Pa. — (1920-1928) — Traylor Engineering and Mfg. Co. was primarily in the heavy truck business, but made a 1-ton Model A in 1920. It was an assembled unit using a four-cylinder 3-3/4 x 5-1/8 in. bore and stroke Buda engine that developed 22.5 hp. Other components included a Brown-Lipe gearbox and Seldon worm drive rear axle. In 1925, a second 1-ton, the Model A, was introduced. It had the same engine and a 300 lbs. heavier (3,800 lbs.) curb weight.

TRIANGLE — St. John's, Mich. — (1917-1925) — Triangle Motor Truck Co.'s smallest model, introduced as a 3/4-ton in 1919, was an assembled unit with a Waukesha AC engine. This Model AA was produced as a 1-ton from 1920 until 1925, then up-rated to 1-1/2-tons afterwards. The motor had a 3-1/4 x 5 in. bore and stroke and produced 16.9 hp. Shipping weight for the 3/4-ton was 2,400 lbs. and, for the 1-ton, 2,400-2,600 lbs.

TRIUMPH — Chicago, Ill. — (1909-1912) — This was no sports car! Triumph Motor Car Co.'s first commercial vehicle was a light-delivery van with a two-cylinder, horizontally-opposed Monarch engine below the seat. Other features included a planetary transmission and double chain-drive. Air or water cooling systems were optional. They sold for $650 to $850. The company also offered the Model D to 1-ton truck buyers. It was also powered by a two-cylinder gas engine and sold for $1,200 in delivery van form.

TRIVAN — Frackville, Pa. — (1962-1964) — These were three-wheelers (one in the rear), which could carry 1/2-ton. Built by Roustabout Co., one of their uses was for in-plant hauling of industrial materials. They used a three-speed gearbox to transmit power to a single rear wheel. The steel tube frame had an air bag suspension. Production totaled all of 150 units.

1962 Trivan 1/2-Ton 3-Wheel Utility Pickup (JAG)

1963 Trivan 1/2-Ton 3-Wheel Utility Pickup (DJS)

1963 Trivan 1/2-Ton 3-Wheel Utility Pickup (DJS)

TROJAN — Toledo, Ohio — (1914-1920) — Toledo Carriage Woodwork Co. made this 3/4-ton. The chassis price was $1,500. A 1-ton model was added in 1916, when the firm became Commercial Truck Co. of Cleveland. The larger truck cost $1,600. Both had four-cylinder engines. (Wonder if they developed "Trojan-Horse" power?)

TRUMBULL — Bridgeport, Conn. — (1914-1916) — The Trumball Motor Car Co. also offered a light truck on one of its auto chassis. The 1/4-ton was powered via a 20 hp, four-cylinder engine and had a three-speed transmission and shaft drive. The $395 list price was the same one used for Trumbull's Model B and Model 168 roadster passenger cars.

TULSA — Tulsa, Okla. — (1913-1916) — The Tulsa Automobile & Mfg. Co. is believed to have built trucks in the 3/4-ton to 1-1/2 ton capacity range. The company's 1913 Model 10 was definitely a 3/4-ton. Its list price was $1,500. The company evolved out of two other firms — Harmon Motor Truck Co. (of Chicago) and Pioneer Automobile Co. (of Oklahoma City). A 1-ton truck was also produced, according to some sources.

TWIN COACH — Kent, Ohio — (1927-1933) — The Twin Coach Co. was formed by William B. and Frank R. Fageol to produce and market a large, urban transit type bus. Smaller vehicles, which were somewhat of a cross between a bus and a truck, were produced between 1929 and 1936. Included were a number of 1-ton delivery vans that were used by many milk and bakery companies, as well as by United Parcel Service. They were walk-in type trucks with sit-or-stand driving positions and were available in both electric and gas-powered versions. Also optional, was the buyer's choice of front- or rear-wheel-drive. Such units were manufactured for about seven years, until this operation was sold to Continental-Divco in 1936. Thereafter, Twin Coach concentrated almost exclusively on the building of larger buses again.

1935 Twin Coach Milk Delivery Van (J. Mattis)

U

UNION — St. Louis, Mo. — (1905) — This was a small, closed van built by the Union Automobile Mfg. Co. It used a two-cylinder engine that developed 16 hp. Other features included a friction type transmission, shaft drive and a 92 in. wheelbase. Solid or pneumatic tires were optional. The list price of the vehicle was $1,275.

1905 Union Light Delivery Car (JAW)

UNITED — Detroit, Mich. — (1914-1915) — This was a delivery van on a cyclecar, built by the National United Service Co. It had a friction type transmission and double chain-drive system. The $425 truck rode an eight-foot wheelbase and had a 40 in. tread. The engine was a four-cylinder powerplant and used water as its coolant.

UNITED — Grand Rapids, Mich. — (1916-1926) — This firm had four name changes. It began under the name United Motor Truck Co. In 1918, as United Motors Co., it built the four-cylinder Model AX, which was an $1,850-priced 1-ton. It became United Motor Products Co. in 1922 and merged with Acme Motor Truck Co. (of Cadillac, Mich.) in 1927. Other 1-ton models were built in the 1920s.

1926 United 1-Ton Panel Delivery (OCW)

URBAN — Louisville, Ken. — (1911-1918) — These were 1/2-ton battery electrics, built by the Kentucky Wagon Mfg. Co., which also built "Old Hickory" trucks. The company's 1913 line was made up of express ($1,800) and panel ($1,900) versions of the Model 10 1/2-ton electric. For 1914, a 1-ton called the Model 20 was retailed at $2,300 for an express body. A 3/4-ton, the Model 15A, came along in 1915. The chassis model was $1,562.50. Express or panel bodies were $600 more. As its final shot, the company offered three versions of a gas-engined Model M for 1917. The chassis was $825. With a "body only" this jumped to $865. For $60 more, buyers could get a "body fully-equipped." In 1918, the name Old Hickory (see separate listing) was adopted.

1914 Urban Model 10 Panel Delivery Body (OCW)

1914 Urban Model 20 Covered Flareboard (OCW)

U.S. — Cincinnati, Ohio — (1909-1930) — In its early years, the United States Motor Truck Co. built light models of trucks. Then, it switched to building heavier ones. One-tons were in the 1911-1912 line. The former was designated the Model A (how original!) and was a $2,000 delivery. Then, along came the Model B (how totally innovative!) for the second year. It was an express model with the same price. Both had two-cylinder gasoline engines. A 20 hp two-cylinder "pancake" engine was located under the seat and double chains carried drive to the rear wheels.

UTILITY — Milwaukee, Wis. — (1910-1911) — The Stephenson Motor Car Co. built trucks with this brand name. A Model B designation was used for a 1-ton Delivery that sold for $1,700 in 1910 and $2,000 in 1911. It featured a four-cylinder gasoline engine, forward-control driving position, friction transmission and double chain-drive system.

UTILITY — Gaylord, Mich. — (1912) — Don't confuse this 1/2-ton chassis model with the Milwaukee-built truck using a similar name one year earlier. This one was produced by Gaylord Motor Car Co. It sold for $1,500.

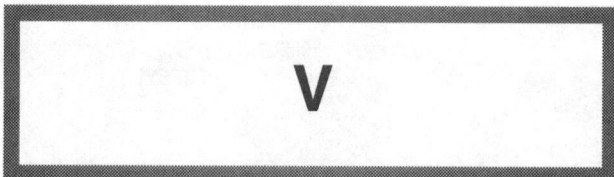

V

VAN AUKEN — Connersville, Ind. — (1914) — These were small electrics, manufactured by the Van Auken Electric Car Co. Having the oft-used designation "Model A," they were electric-powered chassis-trucks with a 750 lb. load capacity and an 80 in. wheelbase. The price was $1,000. General Electric supplied the motor, which provided four forward speeds. A tubular front axle was used. The rear axle was a worm drive unit. The chassis tipped the scales at 1,240 pounds.

1913 Van Auken 1-Ton Electric Delivery Van (HHB)

1914 Van Aukem Model A Stake Body (OCW)

VAN DYKE — Detroit, Mich. — (1910-1912) — The Van Dyke Motor Car Co. built delivery vans. All of them had two-cylinder gas-fueled engines. The 1/2-ton was $750 in 1910 and $850 in 1911. Closed delivery models were offered in five configurations during 1912, all with 1/2-ton payload ratings. They were: Model E-A ($1,000); Model E-C ($975); Model E-D ($1,050); Model E-F ($1,100) and Model E-G ($1,150).

1910 Van Dyke Open Cab Panel Delivery (MVMA/DFW)

VAN-L — Grand Rapids, Mich. — (1911-1912) — This company's name was Van-L Commercial Car Co. As a model name, it sounds like some kind of trim package for a late-model travel van. However, the light-duty product was a rather large 1-ton truck with four-cylinder engine, three-speed gearbox and double chain-drive. In fact, the only thing it had in common with today's vans was a forward-control driving configuration.

VAN WANBEKE — Elgin, Ill. — (1909) — This company produced two delivery models of which one, called the Model A, had a less-than-1-ton rating. Its load capacity was 1,800 lbs. and its price a modest $850. H.F. Wambeke & Sons used a two-cylinder gasoline engine in its trucks.

VEERAC — Minneapolis, Minn. — (1911-1914) — The Veerac Motor Co. built 3/4-ton and 1-ton trucks, plus an early 1/2-ton model. The latter, seen only in 1911, was a delivery for $850. It was called the Model A and, like all of Veerac Motor Co.'s products, utilized a two-cylinder gasoline engine. For 1912, the 1,500 lb. truck came in express ($850); stake ($875) and enclosed ($950) models. In 1913, the 1-ton Model B was available in express ($1,125) and stake ($1,250) styles. The 3/4-ton edition of the Model A had a $925 chassis price in 1914, when a platform version of the 1-ton Model B sold for $1,125. "Veerac" was an acronym for "valveless explosion every other revolution, air-cooled."

1912 Verrac 1,500 lb. Open Flareboard Express (OCW)

1912 Veerac 1,500 lb. Platform Stake Body (OCW)

1914 Veerac Model B Platform Stake Body (OCW)

Standard Catalog of Light-Duty Trucks

VELIE — Moline, Ill. — (1911-1929) — This well-respected automaker produced a 1-ton truck in 1914-1915. It was called the Model X and had a chassis price of $2,000. The powerplant was a 4-5/8 x 5-1/2 in. bore and stroke four-cylinder producing 34.23 hp. Also produced, in 1916-1917, was a 3/4-ton flareboard express at $890. It had a smaller four-cylinder engine with 3-1/8 x 4-1/2 in. cylinder dimensions and 15.63 hp. Shipping weights of the two trucks were far different; 4,200 lbs. for the larger and 2,320 lbs. for the smaller. In 1928 and 1929, Velie offered a 3/4-ton chassis, which sold for $1,595. Velie automobile commercial chassis were frequently used to carry ambulance and hearse bodies. In addition, some larger trucks (up to 5-tons) were built by the firm.

1914 Velie Model X Open Cab Flareboard Express (OCW)

1914 Velie 1-Ton Gravity Dump Truck (OCW)

VIALL — Chicago, Ill. — (1914-1917) — The lightest trucks made by Viall Motor Car Co. fit our criteria for "The Directory." They were gas-engined 1-tons called Model B1s. As a chassis-model, the B1 sold for $1,400.

VICTOR — Buffalo, N.Y. — (1911-1912) — It was $1,650 for Victor Motor Truck Co.'s 1,500 lb. Model A Delivery in 1911. Buyers who waited until 1912 had to spend $50 (express/stake) or $100 (panel) more for carryover versions of the same model. Also seen that season was the 1-ton Model B, available in express or stake bed models for $2,100. Bigger (up to 10-ton) trucks were also built.

VICTOR — St. Louis, Mo. — (1913-1914) — These 1/2-ton capacity electric trucks were made by Victor Automobile Mfg. Co. They utilized an electric motor manufactured by Westinghouse. Features included a 92 in. wheelbase and $1,500 list price.

VIM — Philadelphia, Pa. — (1913-1926) — The Touraine Co. of Philadelphia (see separate listing.) made Vims. Most were of 1-1/2-ton capacity. However, the only 1914 product was a light-delivery truck that sold for $585. It had a gasoline engine and a 1/2-ton payload rating. The engine, made by Northway, had four-cylinders and put out 14 hp. From 1915-1922, there were 1/2-ton models with higher numerical designations each year: Model 16 (1915); Model 18 (1916); Models 20/21 (1917); Models 21/26/28 (1918); Models 29-C/30-SC (1919); Model 29-C (1921); and Models 29-C/30-SC (1922). In 1918, a typical 1/2-ton chassis, on a 108 in. wheelbase, sold for $765. This was the lowest price for any similar-sized trucks in a trade directory of the era. Trucks in Vim's Model 50 series, with 1,500 lb. payloads, were offered from 1922-1924. The Model 50C was marketed all three years, while the 50F and 50D appeared only in 1923. In the mid-1920s, prices for Vim's 3/4-ton models were: (chassis) $995; (open express) $1,220 and (closed panel) $1,260. There were also 1-tons available, including the Model 25 of 1920-1922 and the Model 31 of 1920 only.

1916 Vim Open Cab 1/2-Ton Express (OCW)

Standard Catalog of Light-Duty Trucks

1916 Vim Canopy Top Stage Coach (HACJ/LIAM)

1920 Vim 3/4-Ton Panel Delivery Van (OMM)

VIXEN — Milwaukee, Wis. — (1915) — Davis Mfg. Co. built trucks under this trade name. The light delivery of 1915 held a 400 lb. load and cost $395. It used a gas-fueled powerplant.

VOLTCAR — New York, N.Y. — (1914-1916) — Cyclo-Lectric Car Co. produced this electric-powered parcel delivery van. Its payload capacity was 800 lbs. The price was $585. Features included a 68 in. wheelbase and worm gear drive.

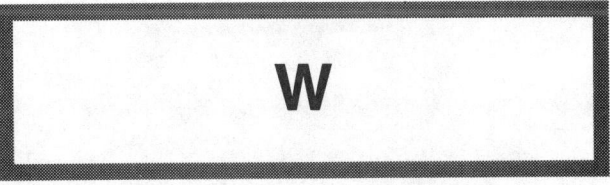

W

WACHUSETT — Fitchburg, Mass. — (1922-1930) — This company was started by one of the partners that founded New England Truck Co. (NETCO). It was built in a building that Fred Suthergreen built across the street from the NETCO plant. A 1-ton model was a conventional type truck manufactured as an "assembled" product (one made of parts sourced from other firms). Some features included a Continental powerplant, Brown-Lipe transmission and Timken rear axle.

WADE — Holly, Mich. — (1913-1914) — The Wade Commercial Car Co. made crude-looking high-wheelers with open express bodies. They had an air-cooled, one-cylinder engine mounted under the body. They were linked to a friction drive system and double drivechains. Perched on a six-foot wheelbase, the $400 model of 1913 carried 800 lb. loads. For 1914, the price dropped to $300, the capacity to 500 lbs.

1914 Wade Flareboard Express (OCW)

WAGENHALS — St. Louis, Mo. — (1910-1914) — This firm began as Wagenhals Mfg. Co. of St. Louis (1910-1911) and, then, moved north to operate as Wagenhals Motor Car Co. in Detroit. The design was a three-wheel delivery with driver behind the delivery box. The 1914-1915 Model 20 was available in open or closed body form at $690. It had a gas engine and 800 lb. payload. Also offered, the second year, was the Model 30. It was an electric priced at $575 and suitable for 800 lb. cargos. Other features included a planetary transmission and chain-drive to the single rear wheel. The U.S. Post Office used these as mail trucks.

1914 Wagenhals Box Body Tricar (OCW)

WALKER — Chicago, Ill. — (1906-1942) — This was a very well-known make of electric truck built by the Walker Vehicle Co. They built trucks in the size range from about 1/2-ton to 7-tons. In addition to the box-shape one associates with most electrics, they also built light delivery trucks with an engine-forward design which looked like "regular" trucks. In 1916, their 1/2-ton model M had a 82 in. wheelbase and was available with longer wheelbases as well. It had five forward and five reverse speeds and a range of up to 75 miles. In 1918, their 1/2-ton-capacity chassis was on a 93 in. wheelbase and sold for $1,600 with tires, but without a battery. Beginning in the mid-1920s, the smallest chassis was rated at 3/4-ton capacity and sold for about $1,750.

1914 Walker Model F Panel Body (OCW)

1914 Walker Model G Service Wagon (OCW)

1915 Walker Model G Service Wagon (DPL)

1918 Walker Walk-in Delivery Van (DPL/DFW)

1940 Walker UPS Walk-in Delivery Van (OCW)

WALTHAM — Waltham, Mass. — (1906-1908/1922) — Waltham Mfg. Co. made cyclecars sometimes known as Waltham-Orients. Commercial versions with 600-800 lb. payloads were available. They used one- or two-cylinder (6-8 hp) engines and friction drive transmission. Eight light delivery vans were offered on 98 or 99 in. wheelbases. In 1922, the com-

pany was reorganized and building the Master Six passenger car. A few of these were converted into "speed wagons" having commercial type bodies such as a 15-passenger tour bus.

1919 Waltham Speed Wagon Tourist Bus (NDC)

WARD — Mt. Vernon, N.Y. — (1910-1934) — Built by the Ward Motor Vehicle Co., this electric was well-known in the East. In 1918, their lightest chassis was rated at 3/8-ton capacity and was on an 88 in. wheelbase. They also offered a 1/2-ton model on a 90 in. chassis (as well as other trucks up to 5-tons in capacity). During the mid-1920s, Ward sold a 1/2-ton chassis for $1,460 and a 3/4-ton chassis for $1,770.

1913 Ward Electric Delivery Van (OHS/DFW)

1914 Ward Model EA Electric Delivery Van (OCW)

Standard Catalog of Light-Duty Trucks

1914 Ward Model EO Electric Platform Truck (OCW)

1914 Ward Model G2A Covered Flareboard (OCW)

1914 Ward Model EB Flareboard Express (OCW)

1916 Ward Electric Bakery Delivery Van (OCW)

1929 Ward Electric Walk-in Milk Delivery Van (OCW)

WARE — St. Paul, Minn. — (1912-1915) — This early type of 4x4 truck was designed by J.J. Ware, founder of Ware Motor Vehicle Co. A prop shaft was used to transmit power from the four-cylinder engine to the rear axle. From there, power dividers on both sides of the differential were connected to long shafts that drove the front axle. The firm later became Twin City Four Wheel Drive Co. It made models down to 3/4-ton in size.

WARNER — Beloit, Wis. — (1917) — This firm made truck trailers of 1,250 lbs. to 1,500 lbs. capacity for hauling such things as packages, steers, poles and lumber. Prices ranged from $100 to $325 for these models.

WARREN — Warren, Ohio — (1912-1913) — The Warren Motor Truck Co. built a 1/2-ton open express truck. It was called the Model 30. The wheelbase was 110 in. A 30 hp four-cylinder engine supplied the go-power. The firm offered other models through 1916, when a pair of 1-tons were marketed, as well as larger trucks. In chassis form, these 1916 "1-tons" were $1,700 and $1,900, respectively.

WARREN — Detroit, Mich. — (1911-1913) — The Warren light delivery vans were 1/2-tons and based on the firm's passenger car chassis. They came with open- or closed body styles. Their "Winged Express" models went for $1,300.

WASHINGTON — Washington, D.C. — (1909-1912) — These were electrics, ranging from less than 1/2-ton to 2-tons in capacity. They were built by the Washington Motor Vehicle Co. Four models were available in all. The smallest was rated for 750 lb. payloads. They used Edison alkaline batteries that could provide a driving range as high as 50 miles before requiring recharging.

1910 Washington Open Express (WJP)

WATSON — Canastota, N.Y. — (1917-1925) — The Watson Wagon Co. built or assembled large trucks. However, for a few years, their lightest model was rated at 3/4-ton in capacity. Starting in 1920, the company also built a 1-ton C-cab truck. It had a four-cylinder Buda engine, electric lights, left-hand drive and spring-loaded front bumper.

1920 Watson Model B 3/4- to 1-Ton Stake (ATV)

WAVERLEY ELECTRIC — Indianapolis, Ind. — (1899-1916) — Built first by the Indiana Bicycle Co. (which eventually became the Waverley Co.) these were moderately well-known electrics. In 1916, their 1/2-ton chassis on a 90 in. wheelbase sold for $1,800, a price which included: "Top for driver's seat, two head lamps, charging plug, Hubodometer, Sangamo ampere hour meter or regular volt ammeter, bell or horn and regular tool equipment." The price apparently also included a 42-cell, 11-plate battery.

1914 Waverley Electric Panel Body Delivery (OCW)

1914 Waverley Electric Covered Flareboard Express (OCW)

Standard Catalog of Light-Duty Trucks

1915 Waverley Electric Screenside Delivery (ELC/DFW)

WAYNE — New York, N.Y. — (1914) — The Wayne Light Commercial Car Co. built a truck on a light tricycle chassis. This model had an 800 lb. payload rating. An air-cooled two-cylinder engine was the powerplant. Belts carried drive to the single rear wheel. Other features included a two-speed gearbox and handle-bar steering system. It sold for $495.

WEEKS — Chicago, Ill. — (1907-1908) — These were 1/2-ton delivery trucks built by the Weeks Commercial Vehicle Co. The body style was that of a closed delivery van. The two-cylinder engine, made by Advance Engine & Mfg. Co., was positioned below the floorboards. It was vapor-cooled and capable of producing 20 hp. A friction disc drive system and double chains completed the powertrain. A curb weight of 1,500 lbs. was registered.

1907 Weeks Light-Delivery Van (JAW)

WESTCOASTER — Stockton, Calif. — (1927-1975) — Built by the West Coast Machinery Co., these light trucks were mounted on three- and four-wheel chassis. They were used for mail deliveries and by messengers within factories.

WEYHER — Whitewater, Wis. — (1910) — This obscure make of small truck was built by the Weyher Mfg. Co. Only a single model, rated for 1/2-ton, was offered. It had a 16 hp twin-cylinder engine, friction transmission and double chain-drive. Poised on a 94 in. wheelbase, the water-cooled truck rode on solid rubber tires.

WHITE — Cleveland, Ohio — (1901 to date) — This well-known make of trucks and buses is now associated with Volvo and most of its operations are in South Carolina. In its early days, it built light delivery trucks and autos (until 1918). They included several 3/4-ton models: the GTB delivery ($2,254) of 1911; the GBE of 1912-1913 (chassis $2,100/express and platform $2,250); and the GBBE of 1914-1918 (same prices as GBE). White stuck to bigger models in 1919, but returned to 3/4-tons by introducing the Model 15 In late 1921. This model stayed on the market through at least 1926. In terms of trucks registered in the U.S., Whites were the fifth most popular. Though not often thought of as a light truck maker, up until about 1925, White was a big factor in that market.

1900 White Steamer Light Delivery Car (JAW)

1909 White 3/4-Ton Dealer Service Car (DFW/VWC)

1910 White 3/4-Ton Domestic Express (DFW/VWC)

1911 White 3/4-Ton 9-Passenger Tour Bus (DFW/VWC)

1914 White Model GBBE Covered Flareboard (OCW)

1918 White 3/4-Ton Tourist Bus (Strozier Archives)

1915 White 3/4-Ton Hotel Bus (DFW/VWC)

1919 White 3/4-Ton Deluxe Panel Delivery (OCW)

1915 White Model GBBE 3/4-Ton Covered Flare (OCW)

1920 White 3/4-Ton Tourist Bus (Strozier Archives)

1916 White 3/4-Ton Panel Delivery (D. Sagvold)

1925 White Model 15 3/4-Ton Covered Flareboard (OCW)

Standard Catalog of Light-Duty Trucks

1926 White Model 15 3/4-Ton Panel Delivery (OCW)

1927 White Model 15A Open Express (J. Markey)

WHITE HICKORY — Atlanta, Ga. — (1918) — A 1-ton chassis-truck was produced by White Hickory Wagon Mfg. Co. in 1918. This four-cylinder, called the Model F, sold for $1,800.

WHITESIDES — Franklin, Ind. — (1911-1912) — This commercial vehicle was a four-cylinder powered 1-ton. It used a water-cooled 30 hp engine. Body styles available from the Whitesides Commercial Car Co. included a flat-bed "dray" model, vestibuled delivery van and stake bed truck. Prices ranged from $1,265 to $1,285.

WHITE STAR — Brooklyn, N.Y. — (1912-1914) — The White Star Motor & Engineering Co. made its 1-ton model in 1914. It was gas-engined and weighed in at 1,900 lbs. in chassis-only form. Other White Stars were heavier-duty trucks with three- and four-speed gearboxes.

1914 White Star Model 1 Covered Flareboard (OCW)

WICHITA — Wichita Falls, Texas — (1911-1932) — A 1-ton was about the smallest product of this regional manufacturer from the Southwest. The Model A of 1913-1914 was $1,650, the same price as the chain-drive model of 1915-1916. Also available, in 1915 and 1916, was the four-wheel drive Model K. Both had the same prices. In 1917, both models were continued with a higher $1,800 retail price.

Standard Catalog of Light-Duty Trucks

1914 Wichita Model A Bottle Body Truck (OCW)

1914 Wichita Model A Platform Stake Truck (OCW)

WILCOX — Minneapolis, Minn. — (1910-1927) — The H.E. Wilcox Motor Co. built trucks and buses, with the smallest truck rated at 3/4-ton capacity. The 1916-1918 Wilcox 3/4-ton Model U chassis, on a 120 in. wheelbase, sold for $1,200. There was also a 1-ton Model S in the same years. The 1-ton Model A was introduced in 1919 and carried into 1920. The Model AA replaced it for 1921-1922. A new 1-ton Model Y appeared in 1923. From then on, only bigger vehicles were built. In the late 1920s, the firm was reorganized and switched to building buses, mainly for Greyhound.

1914 Wilcox Model L Covered Flareboard (OCW)

1917 Wilcox Petroleum Tank Body Truck (JAW)

WILLET — Buffalo, N.Y. — (1911-1915) — Prior to 1913, the Willet Engine & Carburetor Co. offered just low-capacity delivery vans with two- or three-cylinder engines. The Model M, a 3/4-ton chassis, sold for $1,650 in 1914. For 1915, only the 3/4-ton was made. It featured a 133 in. wheelbase, shaft drive, pneumatic tires and $2,100 pricetag.

1914 Willet Model M Screenside Express (OCW)

WILSON — Detroit, Mich. — (1914-1925) — J.C. Wilson Co. made horsedrawn wagons. A Model F 1-ton, with four-cylinder powerplant, was marketed in 1916 through 1918. It sold for $1,375 the first two years and $1,450 the last year. It came in chassis form and a worm-drive system was used.

1925 Wilson Model C 1-Ton Stake Body (OCW)

WINKLER — South Bend, Ind. — (1911-1912) — Winkler Brothers Mfg. Co.'s truck-line included a 1-ton model. It had a 25 hp engine, but did not use the three-speed progressive gearbox of the firm's larger trucks. Features included a forward-control configuration and open cab styling.

WINTHER — Kenosha, Wis. — (1917-1927) — The Winther Motor Truck Co. built trucks as large as 7-tons capacity, as well as automobiles. Most of its smaller trucks were in the range of 1-1/2 to 2-tons. However, in 1923, the firm brought a 3/4-ton model to market. Designated the Model 751, it had a four-cylinder engine.

WINTON — Cleveland, Ohio — (1896-1924) — By the end of 1898, Alexander Winton had sold 22 cars. Sales of his product climbed to 850 vehicles by 1903. Though passenger cars were the mainstay, Winton at various times built military trucks. The earliest of these was the Wagonette, a 1904 model designed for the U.S. Army Signal Corps. The firm is also said to have moved heavily into military vehicle production during World War I.

1904 Winton Signal Corps Wagonette (SI/OCW)

WISCONSIN — Loganville, Wis. — (1912-1926) — This truck was built by three different firms located in three different Wisconsin communities. In 1916, while being built by the Myers Machine Co., of Sheboygan, a 3/4-ton capacity chassis was offered for $1,500.

1918 Wisconsin Petroleum Tanker Body Truck (JAW)

WITT-WILL — Washington, D.C. — (1911-1931) — Most of the Witt-Will Co.'s products were heavy trucks and beyond the scope of this light-duty truck catalog. However, in 1914 and 1915, there was the E series of trucks. The 1-ton used a gasoline-powered engine and was priced at $1,850 for a chassis-only.

1914 Witt-Will Model E-13 Flareboard (OCW)

1914 Witt-Will Model E-13 Open Panel Body (OCW)

WOLVERINE — Detroit, Mich. — (1918-1922) — The American Commercial Car Co. built trucks in the 3/4-ton to 1-1/2-ton size range. The 3/4-ton was a delivery van with pneumatic tires. It was offered only until 1918.

WOLVERINE-DETROIT — Detroit, Mich. — (1912-1913) — The Pratt, Carter, Sigsbee Co. produced this brand of truck. The 1912 offering was an open express model with a water-cooled single-cylinder engine, friction transmission and double chain-drive setup. Buyers had the option of ordering solid or pneumatic tires. The express had an 89 in. wheelbase. It sold for $775 in chassis-only configurtaion. For 1913, a 1/2-ton truck called the Model C was produced. It was a one-cylinder job with a 96 in. wheelbase and worm drive system. It came as a flareboard express and had the engine mounted underneath the body.

Standard Catalog of Light-Duty Trucks

1913 Wolverine Model C Flareboard (OCW)

WONDER — Chicago, Ill. — (c. 1917) — This company was listed in a 1918 auto insurance manual as the maker of two 1-ton trucks. The Model 1 open truck sold for $800. The Model 2 was a truck "with top" for $850. Both used gasoline engines.

WOODS — Havelock and Lincoln, Neb. — (1927-1931) — Although not thought of primarily as a light-duty truck-maker, this firm produced a 1-ton model. The company originally operated as Patriot Manufacturing, in Havelock. It then (1929) became a division of Arrow Aircraft & Motors Corp.

WOOLSTON — Riverton, N.J. — (1913) — Another firm whose 1-ton and under models was limited to a 1-ton truck was C.T. Woolston's company. It came as an express (or pickup) called the Model A. Features included a four-cylinder powerplant, three-speed gearbox and solid tires. A governor was used to limit the maximum road speed to 15 mph.

WORTH — Chicago, Ill. — (c. 1900) — Both W.O. Worth and W.R. Donaldson were old traction engine manufacturers so it was not unusual that an item in the April, 1900 issue of THE AUTOMOBILE REVIEW compared the construction of their two new vehicles, a surrey and a light delivery wagon, to the sturdiness of the agricultural equipment they built. The two joined with J.E. Keith and their old friend H.W. Kellogg to get a new company off the ground. Features of the Worth light delivery wagon included a panel body with open driver's compartment, tiller steering and wood spoke artillery wheels (smaller wheels in front).

X

XENIA — Xenia, Ohio — (1914) — This cyclecar came with a delivery box type It was powered by a two-cylinder air-cooled engine rated for 10 hp. A planet-type transmission passed the motive power to a pair of belts linked to the rearmost wheels. Equipment on the $395 mini-truck included a single headlight.

Y

YELLOW CAB — Chicago, Ill. (1915-1928)/Pontiac, Mich. (1928-1929) — The Yellow Cab business was started by John Hertz in Chicago in 1910. Five years later, the taxicab company began building its own taxis. In 1923, production of coaches and buses began. The company was taken over by General Motors in 1925. In 1924-1925, a 1-ton truck was marketed. It was called the Yellow Cab Truck. Together with a Yellow-Knight truck, the products ranged from 1,500 lb. (3/4-Ton) delivery vans to huge 4-ton trucks. The Model T2 Yellow-Knight truck of 1926 was a 1-ton with a 124 in. wheelbase. It used a four-cylinder Knight Sleeve-Valve four-cylinder engine with 18.9 ALAM hp. Features included a three-speed selective sliding transmission, semi-floating rear axle and 32 x 4-1/2 in. tires. The smaller models used Continental engine and came with some attractive panel bodies.

1923 Yellow Cab Panel Delivery Van (DFW/MCC)

Standard Catalog of Light-Duty Trucks

1924 Yellow Cab Panel Delivery Van (Upjohn/DFW)

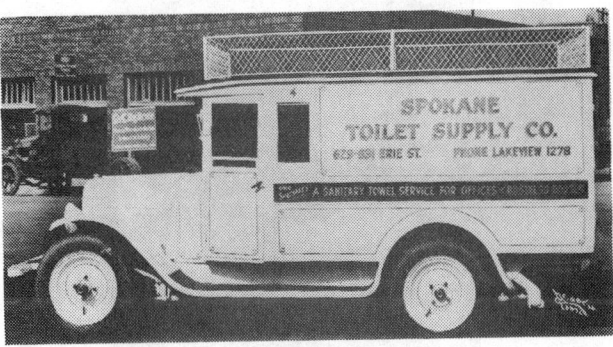

1926 Yellow-Knight T-2 1-Ton Delivery Van (GMC)

1926 Yellow-Knight T-2 1-Ton Chassis (OCW)

Z

ZEITLER & LAMSON — Chicago, Ill. — (1914-1916) — Zeitler & Lamson Motor Truck Co. produced a line of five different size and weight class trucks. One of them was a 1-ton model priced at $1,550. It used a Continental engine. Production stopped in 1917, but the design was reintroduced under the name King-Zeitler, in 1919.

ZIMMERMAN — Auburn, Ind. — (1912-1916) — This was a 1/2-ton high-wheeler, built by the Zimmerman Mfg. Co. It was, of course, based on the firm's passenger car and shared the same two-cylinder engine, planetary transmission and double chain-drive system. Three-quarter elliptic springs were used at the front of the truck, with full-elliptic types at the rear. By 1915, this vehicle was up-rated to 1-1/2 tons, quite a large jump from its introductory form.

VEHICLE CONDITION SCALE

EXCELLENT CONDITION

FINE CONDITION

VERY GOOD CONDITION

GOOD CONDITION

RESTORABLE CONDITION

PARTS TRUCK

1) EXCELLENT: Restored to current maxiumum professional standards of quality in every area, or perfect original with components operating and appearing as new. A 95-plus point show vehicle that is not driven.

2) FINE: Well-restored, or a combination of superior restoration and excellent original. Also, an *extremely* well-maintained original showing very minimal wear.

3) VERY GOOD: Completely operable original or "older restoration" showing wear. Also, a good amateur restoration, all presentable and serviceable inside and out. Plus, combinations of well-done restoration and good operable components or a partially restored vehicle with all parts necessary to complete and/or valuable NOS parts.

4) GOOD: A driveable vehicle needing no or only minor work to be functional. Also, a deteriorated restoration or a very poor amateur restoration. All components may need restoration to be "excellent," but the vehicle is mostly useable "as is."

5) RESTORABLE: Needs *complete* restoration of body, chassis and interior. May or may not be running, but isn't weathered, wrecked or stripped to the point of being useful only for parts.

6) PARTS VEHICLE: May or may not be running, but is weathered, wrecked and/or stripped to the point of being useful primarily for parts.

HOW TO USE THE LIGHT-DUTY TRUCK PRICING GUIDE

On the following pages is a **LIGHT-DUTY TRUCK PRICING GUIDE.** The value of a truck is a "ballpark" estimate at best. The estimates contained here are based upon national and regional data compiled by the editors of *Old Cars Weekly* and *Old Cars Price Guide*. These data include actual bids and prices at collector car auctions and sales, classified and display advertising of such vehicles, verified reports of private sales and input from experts.

Value estimates are listed for trucks in six different states of condition. These conditions (1-6) are illustrated and explained in the **VEHICLE CONDITION SCALE** on the page next following. Modified-truck values are not included, but can be estimated by figuring the cost of restoring to original condition and adjusting the figures shown here.

Appearing below is a section of chart taken from the **LIGHT-DUTY TRUCK PRICING GUIDE** to illustrate the following elements:

A. **MAKE** The make of truck, or marque name, appears in large, boldface type at the beginning of each value section.

B. **DESCRIPTION** The extreme left-hand column indicates truck year, model name, body type, engine configuration and, in some cases, wheelbase.

C. **CONDITION CODE** The six columns to the right are headed by the numbers one through six (1-6) which correspond to the conditions described in the **VEHICLE CONDITION SCALE** on the following page.

D. **VALUE** The value estimates, in dollars, appear below their respective condition code headings and across from the truck descriptions.

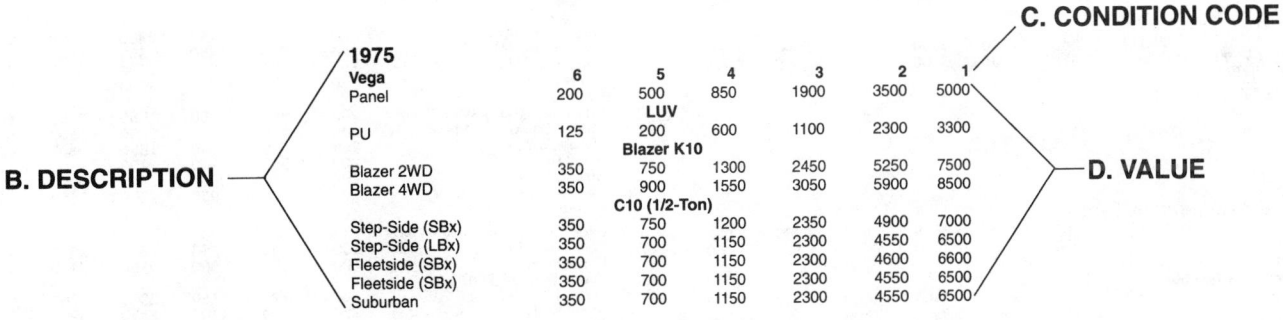

A. MAKE ——————— **CHEVROLET**

C. CONDITION CODE

1975	6	5	4	3	2	1
Vega						
Panel	200	500	850	1900	3500	5000
LUV						
PU	125	200	600	1100	2300	3300
Blazer K10						
Blazer 2WD	350	750	1300	2450	5250	7500
Blazer 4WD	350	900	1550	3050	5900	8500
C10 (1/2-Ton)						
Step-Side (SBx)	350	750	1200	2350	4900	7000
Step-Side (LBx)	350	700	1150	2300	4550	6500
Fleetside (SBx)	350	700	1150	2300	4600	6600
Fleetside (SBx)	350	700	1150	2300	4550	6500
Suburban	350	700	1150	2300	4550	6500

B. DESCRIPTION ——————— **D. VALUE**

AUSTIN

	6	5	4	3	2	1
1931						
Austin Series A						
Cpe Dly	750	2400	4000	8000	14,000	20,000
Panel Dly	850	2650	4400	8800	15,400	22,000
1932						
Austin Series A						
Cpe Dly	750	2400	4000	8000	14,000	20,000
Panel Dly	850	2650	4400	8800	15,400	22,000
1933						
Austin 275						
Cpe Dly	700	2300	3800	7600	13,300	19,000
Panel Dly	800	2500	4200	8400	14,700	21,000
Bantam Van	750	2400	4000	8000	14,000	20,000
Austin 375						
Panel Dly	750	2400	4000	8000	14,000	20,000
PU	700	2300	3800	7600	13,300	19,000
Pony Exp	700	2150	3600	7200	12,600	18,000
Cpe Dly	800	2500	4200	8400	14,700	21,000
1934						
Austin 375						
PU	600	1900	3200	6400	11,200	16,000
Panel Dly	700	2150	3600	7200	12,600	18,000
1935						
Austin 475						
PU	550	1800	3000	6000	10,500	15,000
Panel Dly	650	2050	3400	6800	11,900	17,000
1936						
No vehicles manufactured.						

BANTAM

	6	5	4	3	2	1
1937						
American Bantam 575						
PU	700	2300	3800	7600	13,300	19,000
Panel Dly	850	2750	4600	9200	16,100	23,000
1938						
American Bantam 60						
Bus Cpe	650	2050	3400	6800	11,900	17,000
PU Exp	700	2300	3800	7600	13,300	19,000
Panel Exp	850	2750	4600	9200	16,100	23,000
Boulevard Dly	1700	5400	9000	18,000	31,500	45,000
1939						
American Bantam 60						
PU Exp	700	2300	3800	7600	13,300	19,000
Panel Exp	850	2750	4600	9200	16,100	23,000
Boulevard Dly	1700	5400	9000	18,000	31,500	45,000
1940						
American Bantam 65						
PU	700	2300	3800	7600	13,300	19,000
Panel	850	2750	4600	9200	16,100	23,000
Boulevard Dly	1700	5400	9000	18,000	31,500	45,000
1941						
American Bantam 65						
PU	700	2300	3800	7600	13,300	19,000
Panel	850	2750	4600	9200	16,100	23,000

CHEVROLET

	6	5	4	3	2	1
1918						
Series "490"						
1/2-Ton Light Dly	450	1100	1700	3650	6650	9500
Series "T"						
1-Ton Flare Exp	350	725	1200	2350	4800	6800
1-Ton Covered Flare	350	725	1200	2350	4850	6900
1919						
Series "490"						
1/2-Ton Light Dly	450	1100	1700	3650	6650	9500
Series "T"						
1-Ton Flare Exp	350	725	1200	2350	4800	6800
1-Ton Covered Flare	350	725	1200	2350	4850	6900
1920						
Series "490"						
Light Dly Wag 1-Seat	450	1100	1700	3650	6650	9500
Light Dly Wag 2-Seat	450	1100	1700	3650	6650	9500
Model T						
Flareboard Exp	350	725	1200	2350	4800	6800
Covered Flare	350	725	1200	2350	4850	6900
1921						
Series "490"						
Open Exp	450	1100	1700	3650	6650	9500
Canopy Exp 3 Seat	450	1150	1800	3800	6800	9700
Series G						
Open Exp	350	800	1450	2750	5600	8000
Canopy Exp	350	850	1500	2900	5700	8200
Series T						
Open Exp	350	725	1200	2350	4800	6800
Canopy Exp	350	725	1200	2350	4850	6900

	6	5	4	3	2	1
1922						
Series "490"						
Dly Wag	450	1100	1700	3650	6650	9500
Panel Dly	400	1200	2000	3950	7000	10,000
Sta Wag	450	1450	2400	4800	8400	12,000
Series G						
Exp	350	800	1450	2750	5600	8000
Canopy Exp	350	850	1500	2900	5700	8200
Series T						
Open Exp	350	725	1200	2350	4800	6800
Canopy Exp	350	725	1200	2350	4850	6900
Canopy Exp w/curtains	350	750	1200	2350	4900	7000
1923						
Series B Superior						
Canopy Exp	400	1200	2000	3950	7000	10,000
Panel Dly	400	1200	2000	3950	7000	10,000
Sta Wag	450	1450	2400	4800	8400	12,000
Series D Superior						
Utl Dly (Exp)	350	725	1200	2350	4800	6800
Cattle Body (Stake)	350	750	1250	2400	5100	7300
Dly Wag	350	750	1200	2350	4900	7000
Panel Body	350	750	1300	2450	5250	7500
Gravity Dump	350	750	1350	2600	5400	7700
Petroleum Tanker	350	750	1350	2650	5450	7800
1924						
Series F						
Open Exp	350	725	1150	2300	4700	6700
Canopy Exp	350	750	1200	2350	4900	7000
Panel Dly	350	750	1200	2350	4900	7000
Sta Wag	350	900	1550	3000	5850	8400
Series H						
Open Cab Grain/Stock Body	200	500	850	1950	3600	5100
Closed Cab Grain/Stock Body	200	550	900	2000	3600	5200
Flareboard Exp	200	500	850	1850	3350	4900
Panel Body	200	550	900	2100	3700	5300
Dump/Coal Body	200	550	900	2150	3800	5400
Tanker (3 compartment)	200	600	950	2150	3850	5500
1925						
Series M - (1924-25) - (1-Ton)						
Flareboard Exp	200	500	850	1850	3350	4900
Panel Body	200	550	900	2100	3700	5300
Series K - (1/2-Ton)						
Flareboard Exp	350	725	1150	2300	4700	6700
Panel Body	350	750	1200	2350	4900	7000
Sta Wag	350	900	1550	3000	5850	8400
Series R - (1-Ton)						
Flareboard Exp	200	500	850	1850	3350	4900
Panel Body	200	550	900	2100	3700	5300
Grain Body	200	550	900	2000	3600	5200
Stake-Platform	200	500	850	1950	3600	5100
Tanker (3 compartment)	200	600	950	2150	3850	5500
Dump Body	200	550	900	2150	3800	5400
Wrecker	350	725	1150	2300	4700	6700
1926						
Series V						
Rds PU (Factory)	350	725	1150	2300	4700	6700
Commercial Rds (Factory)	350	700	1150	2300	4550	6500
Hercules Panel Dly	350	750	1200	2350	4900	7000
Springfield Ctry Clb Suburban	450	1450	2400	4800	8400	12,000
Springfield Panel Dly	400	1200	2000	3950	7000	10,000
Series X - (1926-27)						
Flareboard Exp (Factory)	350	750	1200	2350	4900	7000
Canopy Exp (Factory)	350	750	1300	2450	5250	7500
Screenside Exp (Factory)	350	750	1300	2450	5250	7500
Peddler's Wag (Factory)	350	750	1350	2650	5450	7800
Mifflinburg Depot Hack	400	1200	2000	3950	7000	10,000
Springfield 12P Suburban	400	1200	2000	3950	7000	10,000
Proctor-Keefe Dump	350	750	1350	2600	5400	7700
Mifflinburg Jitney/Exp	350	750	1300	2450	5250	7500
Platform Stake	350	750	1250	2400	5100	7300
Rack Body w/Coach Front	350	750	1250	2400	5100	7300
1927						
Capitol AA Series						
Rds PU	450	1150	1900	3850	6850	9800
Commercial Rds	450	1150	1900	3850	6850	9800
Open Exp	450	1100	1700	3650	6650	9500
Sta Wag	500	1550	2600	5200	9100	13,000
Panel Dly	400	1250	2100	4200	7400	10,500
Series LM						
Open Exp	350	750	1300	2450	5250	7500
Panel Dly	350	800	1450	2750	5600	8000
Dump	350	800	1450	2750	5600	8000
Suburban (Sta Wag)	450	1450	2400	4800	8400	12,000
School Bus	350	800	1450	2750	5600	8000
Peddler's Wagon	350	900	1550	3050	5900	8500
Cattle Body/Stake	350	750	1300	2450	5250	7500
Canopy Exp	350	850	1500	2900	5700	8200
Screenside Exp	350	850	1500	2900	5700	8200
1928						
Series National AB						
Rds w/Slip-in PU Box	400	1200	2000	3950	7000	10,000
Rds w/Panel Carrier	450	1450	2400	4800	8400	12,000
PU Exp	450	1150	1800	3800	6800	9700
Canopy Dly	400	1300	2200	4400	7700	11,000
Screenside Dly	400	1300	2200	4400	7700	11,000

754

	6	5	4	3	2	1
Panel Dly	400	1250	2100	4200	7400	10,500
Sed Dly	400	1300	2200	4400	7700	11,000
Henney Hearse	350	800	1450	2750	5600	8000
Henney Ambulance	350	900	1550	3050	5900	8500
Series LO/LP						
Open Exp Dly	400	1250	2100	4200	7400	10,500
Canopy Exp	400	1300	2200	4400	7700	11,000
Screenside Exp	400	1300	2200	4400	7700	11,000
Panel Dly	400	1200	2000	3950	7000	10,000
Platform Stake	350	750	1350	2600	5400	7700
Dump Body	350	800	1450	2750	5600	8000
Peddler's Wag	450	1100	1700	3650	6650	9500
Tow Truck	400	1200	2000	3950	7000	10,000
Tank Truck	400	1200	2000	3950	7000	10,000
1929						
International Series AC						
Rds w/Slip-in Cargo Box	450	1450	2400	4800	8400	12,000
Rds w/Panel Carrier	450	1450	2400	4800	8400	12,000
Open Exp	400	1200	2000	3950	7000	10,000
Canopy Exp	400	1300	2200	4400	7700	11,000
Sed Dly	450	1400	2300	4600	8100	11,500
Screenside Exp	400	1300	2200	4400	7700	11,000
Panel Dly	400	1300	2200	4400	7700	11,000
Ambassador Panel Dly	500	1550	2600	5200	9100	13,000
1930						
Rds PU	450	1500	2500	5000	8800	12,500
PU Exp	400	1300	2200	4400	7700	11,000
Panel Dly	400	1300	2200	4400	7700	11,000
DeL Panel Dly	500	1550	2600	5200	9100	13,000
Sed Dly	500	1600	2700	5400	9500	13,500
DeL Sed Dly	550	1700	2800	5600	9800	14,000
Canopy Exp	450	1450	2400	4800	8400	12,000
Screenside Exp	450	1450	2400	4800	8400	12,000
1931						
Open Cab PU	450	1450	2400	4800	8400	12,000
Closed Cab PU	400	1200	2000	3950	7000	10,000
Panel Dly	400	1300	2200	4400	7700	11,000
Canopy Dly (curtains)	450	1450	2400	4800	8400	12,000
Canopy Dly (screens)	450	1450	2400	4800	8400	12,000
Sed Dly	500	1600	2700	5400	9500	13,500
DeL Sta Wag	500	1550	2600	5200	9100	13,000

NOTE: Add 5 percent for Deluxe 1/2-Ton models.

	6	5	4	3	2	1
1932						
Open Cab PU	500	1550	2600	5200	9100	13,000
Closed Cab PU	400	1300	2200	4400	7700	11,000
Canopy Exp	450	1500	2500	5000	8800	12,500
Screenside Exp	450	1500	2500	5000	8800	12,500
Panel Dly	450	1400	2300	4600	8100	11,500
Spl Panel Dly	450	1500	2500	5000	8800	12,500
Sed Dly	550	1700	2800	5600	9800	14,000
Spl Sed Dly	550	1800	3000	6000	10,500	15,000

NOTE: Add 5 percent for Special Equipment on models other than those noted as "Specials" above. Add 2 percent for Canopy Tops on both pickups.

	6	5	4	3	2	1
1933						
Sed Dly	450	1450	2400	4800	8400	12,000
Spl Sed Dly	500	1600	2700	5400	9500	13,500
Closed Cab PU	400	1200	2000	3950	7000	10,000
Panel Dly	400	1200	2000	3950	7000	10,000
Spl Panel Dly	400	1300	2200	4400	7700	11,000
Canopy Exp	450	1100	1700	3650	6650	9500
Spl Canopy Exp	400	1300	2200	4400	7700	11,000
Screenside Exp	400	1300	2200	4400	7700	11,000

NOTE: Add 2 percent for canopied pickups.

	6	5	4	3	2	1
1934						
Closed Cab PU	400	1200	2000	3950	7000	10,000
Canopy PU	450	1100	1700	3650	6650	9500
Canopy Exp (curtains)	400	1200	2000	3950	7000	10,000
Canopy Exp (screens)	400	1200	2000	3950	7000	10,000
Panel Dly	450	1000	1650	3350	6300	9000
Sed Dly	400	1300	2200	4400	7700	11,000

NOTE: Add 5 percent for "Special" models.

	6	5	4	3	2	1
1935						
Series EB						
Closed Cab PU	400	1200	2000	3950	7000	10,000
Spl PU	400	1200	2000	3950	7000	10,000
Canopy Top PU	450	1100	1700	3650	6650	9500
Panel Dly	450	1000	1650	3350	6300	9000
Spl Panel Dly	450	1100	1700	3650	6650	9500
Canopy (curtains)	400	1200	2000	3950	7000	10,000
Canopy (screens)	400	1200	2000	3950	7000	10,000
Series EC						
Sed Dly	400	1300	2200	4400	7700	11,000
Suburban	400	1200	2000	3950	7000	10,000
1936						
Series FC						
Sed Dly	400	1250	2100	4200	7400	10,500
Series FB (1/2-Ton)						
PU	400	1200	2000	3950	7000	10,000
Panel Dly	450	1000	1650	3350	6300	9000
Suburban	450	1100	1700	3650	6650	9500
1937						
Series GB						
Sed Dly	400	1300	2200	4400	7700	11,000
Series GC						
PU	400	1200	2000	3950	7000	10,000
Panel	350	800	1450	2750	5600	8000
Canopy Exp	450	1100	1700	3650	6650	9500
Carryall Suburban	450	1100	1700	3650	6650	9500
Series GD						
PU	450	1000	1650	3350	6300	9000
Stake	350	725	1150	2300	4700	6700
Series GE						
PU	350	800	1450	2750	5600	8000
Stake	200	675	1050	2250	4300	6100
1938						
Series HB						
Cpe PU	450	1000	1650	3350	6300	9000
Sed Dly	450	1400	2300	4600	8100	11,500
Series HC						
PU	400	1200	2000	3950	7000	10,000
Panel	450	1000	1650	3350	6300	9000
Canopy Exp	400	1200	2000	3950	7000	10,000
Suburban	400	1250	2100	4200	7400	10,500

	6	5	4	3	2	1
Series HD						
PU	350	800	1450	2750	5600	8000
Panel	350	750	1350	2600	5400	7700
Stake	350	725	1200	2350	4800	6800
Series HE						
PU	350	750	1200	2350	4900	7000
Panel	350	700	1150	2300	4600	6600
Stake	350	700	1150	2300	4550	6500
1939						
Series JB						
Cpe PU	450	1000	1650	3350	6300	9000
Sed Dly	450	1450	2400	4800	8400	12,000
Series JC						
PU	400	1200	2000	3950	7000	10,000
Panel	350	900	1550	3050	5900	8500
Canopy Exp	450	1000	1650	3350	6300	9000
Suburban	450	1100	1700	3650	6650	9500
Series JD						
PU	350	900	1550	3050	5900	8500
Panel	350	800	1350	2700	5500	7900
Stake	350	725	1200	2350	4800	6800
Series VA						
Panel	350	700	1150	2300	4600	6600
1940						
Series KB						
Cpe PU	450	1100	1700	3650	6650	9500
Sed Dly	450	1500	2500	5000	8800	12,500
Series KH						
Sed Dly	450	1450	2400	4800	8400	12,000
Cpe PU	400	1200	2000	3950	7000	10,000
Series KC						
PU	400	1200	2000	3950	7000	10,000
Panel	350	900	1550	3050	5900	8500
Canopy Exp	450	1100	1700	3650	6650	9500
Suburban	400	1200	2000	3950	7000	10,000
Series KP						
Panel	200	675	1100	2250	4400	6300
Series KD						
PU	350	750	1350	2650	5450	7800
Panel	350	800	1350	2700	5500	7900
Platform	350	725	1200	2350	4800	6800
Stake	350	725	1200	2350	4850	6900
Series KF						
Panel	350	750	1250	2400	5100	7300
Platform	200	675	1100	2250	4400	6300
Stake	350	700	1100	2300	4500	6400
Series WA						
Open Exp	350	800	1450	2750	5600	8000
Panel	350	700	1150	2300	4600	6600
Canopy	350	750	1300	2450	5250	7500
1941						
Series AG						
Cpe PU	450	1000	1650	3350	6300	9000
Sed Dly	450	1500	2500	5000	8800	12,500
Series AJ						
Panel Dly	350	750	1300	2450	5250	7500
Series AK						
PU	400	1250	2100	4200	7400	10,500
Panel Dly	450	1000	1650	3350	6300	9000
Canopy	450	1000	1650	3350	6300	9000
Suburban	450	1100	1700	3650	6650	9500
Series AL						
PU	350	900	1550	3050	5900	8500
Panel Dly	350	800	1450	2750	5600	8000
Platform	350	725	1200	2350	4850	6900
Stake	350	750	1200	2350	4900	7000
Series AN						
Exp	350	750	1300	2400	5200	7400
Panel Dly	350	750	1300	2450	5250	7500
Platform	350	700	1100	2300	4500	6400
Stake	350	700	1150	2300	4550	6500
Series YR						
Canopy	350	750	1300	2450	5250	7500
1942						
Series BG						
Cpe PU	450	1050	1650	3500	6400	9200
Sed Dly	400	1300	2200	4400	7700	11,000
Series BJ						
Double-Duty Pkg Dly	350	750	1300	2450	5250	7500
Series BK						
PU	450	1000	1650	3350	6300	9000
Canopy	350	900	1550	3000	5850	8400
Suburban	350	900	1550	3050	5900	8500
Series BL						
PU	350	800	1450	2750	5600	8000
Panel Dly	350	800	1450	2750	5600	8000
Platform	350	725	1200	2350	4850	6900
Stake	350	750	1200	2350	4900	7000
Series BN						
Panel Dly	350	750	1300	2400	5200	7400
1944-1946						
Series DJ						
Sed Dly	400	1300	2200	4400	7700	11,000
Series BK/CK						
PU	400	1200	2000	3950	7000	10,000
Panel	450	950	1600	3250	6150	8800
Suburban	450	1000	1650	3350	6300	9000
Canopy	450	1000	1650	3350	6300	9000

NOTE: The Coupe Express was listed in the DJ Series, but none are believed to have been built. Therefore, no prices are given for this model.

	6	5	4	3	2	1
1946						
Series DJ						
Sed Dly	450	1400	2300	4600	8100	11,500
Series DP						
PU	400	1200	2000	3950	7000	10,000
Panel	350	900	1550	3100	6000	8600
Canopy	450	1000	1650	3350	6300	9000
Suburban	450	1000	1650	3350	6300	9000
Series DR						
PU	350	900	1550	3050	5900	8500
Panel	350	800	1350	2700	5500	7900
Platform	350	725	1200	2350	4800	6800
Stake	350	725	1200	2350	4850	6900

	6	5	4	3	2	1
Series DS						
Exp	350	750	1250	2400	5100	7300
Panel	350	750	1200	2350	4900	7000
Canopy Exp	350	750	1250	2400	5050	7200
1947						
Series 1500						
Sed Dly	450	1450	2400	4800	8400	12,000
Series 3100						
PU	400	1250	2100	4200	7400	10,500
Panel	350	750	1300	2450	5250	7500
Canopy Exp	350	800	1450	2750	5600	8000
Suburban	350	800	1450	2750	5600	8000
Series 3600						
PU	350	750	1300	2450	5250	7500
Platform	350	700	1150	2300	4600	6600
Stake	350	700	1150	2300	4600	6600
Series 3800						
PU	350	750	1200	2350	4900	7000
Panel	350	725	1150	2300	4700	6700
Canopy Exp	350	750	1200	2350	4900	7000
Platform	350	700	1100	2300	4500	6400
Stake	350	700	1150	2300	4550	6500
1948						
Series 1500						
Sed Dly	450	1450	2400	4800	8400	12,000
Series 3100						
PU	450	1500	2500	5000	8800	12,500
Panel	450	1000	1650	3350	6300	9000
Canopy Exp	450	1100	1700	3650	6650	9500
Suburban	450	1100	1700	3650	6650	9500
Series 3600						
PU	450	1100	1700	3650	6650	9500
Platform	350	800	1450	2750	5600	8000
Stake	350	850	1500	2800	5650	8100
Series 3800						
PU	350	900	1550	3050	5900	8500
Panel	350	850	1500	2800	5650	8100
Canopy Exp	350	900	1550	3050	5900	8500
Platform	350	750	1350	2650	5450	7800
Stake	350	800	1350	2700	5500	7900
1949						
Series 1500						
Sed Dly	450	1450	2400	4800	8400	12,000
Series 3100						
PU	450	1500	2500	5000	8800	12,500
Panel Dly	350	900	1550	3100	6000	8600
Canopy Exp	450	1100	1700	3650	6650	9500
Suburban Carryall	450	1100	1700	3650	6650	9500
Cantrell Sta Wag	550	1800	3000	6000	10,500	15,000
Olsen Kurbside Van	200	650	1050	2250	4200	6000
Series 3600/3700						
PU	450	1100	1700	3650	6650	9500
Platform	350	800	1450	2750	5600	8000
Stake Bed	350	850	1500	2800	5650	8100
Series 3800/3900						
PU	350	900	1550	3050	5900	8500
Panel Dly	350	850	1500	2800	5650	8100
Canopy Exp	350	900	1550	3050	5900	8500
Platform	350	750	1350	2650	5450	7800
Stake Bed	350	800	1350	2700	5500	7900
1950						
Series 1500						
Sed Dly	450	1500	2500	5000	8800	12,500
Series 3100						
PU	450	1500	2500	5000	8800	12,500
Panel Dly	350	900	1550	3100	6000	8600
Suburban Carryall	450	1100	1700	3650	6650	9500
Canopy Exp	450	1100	1700	3650	6650	9500
Series 3600/3700						
PU	450	1100	1700	3650	6650	9500
Platform	350	800	1450	2750	5600	8000
Stake Bed	350	850	1500	2800	5650	8100
Series 3800/3900						
PU	350	900	1550	3050	5900	8500
Panel Dly	350	850	1500	2800	5650	8100
Platform	350	750	1350	2650	5450	7800
Stake Bed	350	800	1350	2700	5500	7900
1951						
Series 1500						
Sed Dly	450	1500	2500	5000	8800	12,500
Series 3100						
PU	450	1500	2500	5000	8800	12,500
Panel Dly	350	900	1550	3100	6000	8600
Suburban Carryall	450	1100	1700	3650	6650	9500
Canopy Exp	450	1100	1700	3650	6650	9500
Series 3600/3700						
PU	450	1100	1700	3650	6650	9500
Platform	350	800	1450	2750	5600	8000
Stake Bed	350	850	1500	2800	5650	8100
Series 3800/3900						
PU	350	900	1550	3050	5900	8500
Panel Dly	350	850	1500	2800	5650	8100
Platform	350	750	1350	2650	5450	7800
Stake Bed	350	800	1350	2700	5500	7900
1952						
Series 1500						
Sed Dly	450	1500	2500	5000	8800	12,500
Series 3100						
PU	450	1500	2500	5000	8800	12,500
Panel Dly	350	900	1550	3100	6000	8600
Suburban Carryall	450	1100	1700	3650	6650	9500
Canopy Exp	450	1100	1700	3650	6650	9500
Series 3600/3700						
PU	450	1100	1700	3650	6650	9500
Platform	350	800	1450	2750	5600	8000
Stake Bed	350	850	1500	2800	5650	8100
Series 3800/3900						
PU	350	900	1550	3050	5900	8500
Panel Dly	350	850	1500	2800	5650	8100
Platform	350	750	1350	2650	5450	7800
Stake Bed	350	800	1350	2700	5500	7900
1953						
Series 1500						
Sed Dly	500	1550	2600	5200	9100	13,000

	6	5	4	3	2	1
Series 3100						
PU	450	1500	2500	5000	8800	12,500
Panel Dly	350	900	1550	3100	6000	8600
Suburban Carryall	450	1100	1700	3650	6650	9500
Canopy Exp	450	1100	1700	3650	6650	9500
Series 3600/3700						
PU	450	1100	1700	3650	6650	9500
Platform	350	800	1450	2750	5600	8000
Stake Bed	350	850	1500	2800	5650	8100
Series 3800/3900						
PU	350	900	1550	3050	5900	8500
Panel Dly	350	850	1500	2800	5650	8100
Platform	350	750	1350	2650	5450	7800
Stake Bed	350	800	1350	2700	5500	7900
1954						
Series 1500						
Sed Dly	500	1550	2600	5200	9100	13,000
Series 3100						
PU	450	1500	2500	5000	8800	12,500
Panel	350	950	1600	3200	6050	8700
Suburban	450	1000	1600	3300	6250	8900
Canopy	450	1100	1700	3650	6650	9500
Series 3600						
PU	450	1100	1700	3650	6650	9500
Platform	350	850	1500	2800	5650	8100
Stake	350	850	1500	2900	5700	8200
Series 3800						
PU	350	900	1550	3050	5900	8500
Panel	350	850	1500	2800	5650	8100
Canopy	450	1000	1650	3350	6300	9000
Platform	350	800	1450	2750	5600	8000
Stake	350	850	1500	2800	5650	8100
1955						
First Series						
Series 3100						
PU	500	1500	2550	5100	8900	12,700
Panel	350	950	1600	3200	6050	8700
Suburban	450	1100	1700	3650	6650	9500
Canopy	450	1100	1700	3650	6650	9500
Series 3600						
PU	450	1150	1800	3800	6800	9700
Platform	350	850	1500	2800	5650	8100
Stake	350	850	1500	2900	5700	8200
Series 3800						
PU	350	900	1550	3050	5900	8500
Panel	350	850	1500	2800	5650	8100
Canopy	450	1000	1650	3350	6300	9000
Platform	350	800	1450	2750	5600	8000
Stake	350	850	1500	2800	5650	8100
Second Series						
Series 1500						
Sed Dly	550	1700	2800	5600	9800	14,000
Series 3100						
PU	500	1550	2600	5200	9100	13,000
Cus Cab PU	500	1600	2700	5400	9500	13,500
Panel Dly	450	1150	1900	3900	6900	9900
Suburban	450	1100	1700	3650	6650	9500
Cameo Carrier	650	2050	3400	6800	11,900	17,000
Cantrell Sta Wag	500	1550	2600	5200	9100	13,000
Series 3400/3500/3700						
Walk-In Dly Van	350	750	1200	2350	4900	7000
School Bus	200	650	1050	2250	4200	6000
Series 3200						
PU (LBx)	350	900	1550	3000	5850	8400
Series 3600						
PU	350	800	1450	2750	5600	8000
Cus Cab PU	350	900	1550	3050	5900	8500
Platform	350	750	1200	2350	4900	7000
Platform & Stake	350	750	1300	2450	5250	7500
Cantrell Sta Wag	450	1500	2500	5000	8800	12,500
Series 3800						
PU	350	750	1350	2600	5400	7700
Panel Dly	350	900	1550	3050	5900	8500
Platform	350	700	1100	2300	4500	6400
Platform & Stake	350	725	1150	2300	4700	6700

NOTE: 1955-up prices based on top of the line models. Deduct 10 percent for 6-cyl.

	6	5	4	3	2	1
1956						
Series 1500						
Sed Dly	500	1550	2600	5200	9100	13,000
Series 3100						
PU	450	1450	2400	4800	8400	12,000
Cus Cab PU	450	1500	2500	5000	8800	12,500
Panel Dly	450	1000	1650	3350	6300	9000
Suburban	400	1200	2000	3950	7000	10,000
Cameo Carrier	650	2050	3400	6800	11,900	17,000
Cantrell Sta Wag	550	1700	2800	5600	9800	14,000
Series 3400/3500/3700						
Walk-In Dly Van	350	750	1200	2350	4900	7000
School Bus	200	650	1050	2250	4200	6000
Series 3200						
PU (LBx)	350	900	1550	3000	5850	8400
Series 3600						
PU	350	800	1450	2750	5600	8000
Cus Cab PU	350	900	1550	3050	5900	8500
Platform	350	750	1200	2350	4900	7000
Platform & Stake	350	750	1300	2400	5200	7400
Cantrell Sta Wag	500	1550	2600	5200	9100	13,000
Series 3800						
PU	350	750	1350	2600	5400	7700
Panel Dly	350	900	1550	3050	5900	8500
Platform	350	700	1100	2300	4500	6400
Platform & Stake	350	725	1150	2300	4700	6700

NOTE: 1955-up prices based on top of the line models. Deduct 10 percent for 6-cyl.

	6	5	4	3	2	1
1957						
Series 1500						
Sed Dly	550	1750	2900	5800	10,200	14,500
Series 3100						
PU	500	1550	2600	5200	9100	13,000
Cus Cab PU	500	1600	2700	5400	9500	13,500
Panel Dly	450	1000	1650	3350	6300	9000
Suburban	400	1300	2200	4400	7700	11,000
Cameo Carrier	650	2050	3400	6800	11,900	17,000
Cantrell Sta Wag	550	1750	2900	5800	10,200	14,500

	6	5	4	3	2	1
Series 3400/3500/3700						
Walk-In Dly Van	350	750	1200	2350	4900	7000
School Bus	200	650	1050	2250	4200	6000
Series 3200						
PU (LBx)	350	900	1550	3000	5850	8400
Series 3600						
PU	350	800	1450	2750	5600	8000
Cus Cab PU	350	900	1550	3050	5900	8500
Platform	350	750	1200	2350	4900	7000
Platform & Stake	350	750	1300	2400	5200	7400
Cantrell Sta Wag	500	1550	2600	5200	9100	13,000
Series 3800						
PU	350	800	1450	2750	5600	8000
Panel Dly	350	900	1550	3050	5900	8500
Platform	350	700	1100	2300	4500	6400
Platform & Stake	350	725	1150	2300	4700	6700

NOTE: 1955-up prices based on top of the line models.
Deduct 10 percent for 6-cyl.

1958

	6	5	4	3	2	1
Series 1100						
Sed Dly	450	1400	2300	4600	8100	11,500
Series 3100						
Stepside PU	450	1000	1650	3350	6300	9000
Fleetside PU	450	1100	1700	3650	6650	9500
Cameo PU	550	1800	3000	6000	10,500	15,000
Panel	350	900	1550	3000	5850	8400
Suburban	350	950	1600	3200	6050	8700
Series 3200						
Stepside (LBx)	350	900	1550	3000	5850	8400
Fleetside (LBx)	350	900	1550	3100	6000	8600
Series 3400/3500						
Step Van (104" wb)	350	800	1450	2750	5600	8000
Step Van (125" wb)	350	850	1500	2900	5700	8200
Series 3600						
Stepside PU	350	800	1450	2750	5600	8000
Fleetside PU	350	850	1500	2950	5800	8300
Stake	350	750	1200	2350	4900	7000
Series 3700						
Step Van (137" wb)	350	750	1300	2500	5300	7600
Series 3800						
PU	350	750	1300	2400	5200	7400
Panel	350	750	1250	2400	5050	7200
Stake	350	750	1200	2350	4900	7000

NOTE: 1955-up prices based on top of the line models.
Deduct 10 percent for 6-cyl.

1959

	6	5	4	3	2	1
Series 1100						
Sed Dly	400	1250	2100	4200	7400	10,500
El Camino	450	1400	2300	4600	8100	11,500
Series 3100						
Stepside PU	450	1000	1650	3350	6300	9000
Fleetside PU	450	1100	1700	3650	6650	9500
Cameo PU	550	1700	2800	5600	9800	14,000
Panel	350	900	1550	3000	5850	8400
Suburban	350	900	1550	3100	6000	8600
Series 3200						
Stepside PU	350	900	1550	3000	5850	8400
Fleetside PU	350	900	1550	3100	6000	8600
Series 3400/3500						
Panel (104" wb)	350	800	1350	2700	5500	7900
Panel (125" wb)	350	800	1450	2750	5600	8000
Series 3600						
Stepside PU	350	800	1350	2700	5500	7900
Fleetside PU	350	850	1500	2800	5650	8100
Series 3700						
Panel (137" wb)	350	750	1300	2500	5300	7600
Series 3800						
PU	350	750	1300	2400	5200	7400
Panel	350	750	1200	2350	4900	7000
Stake	350	725	1200	2350	4850	6900

NOTE: 1955-up prices based on top of the line models.
Deduct 10 percent for 6-cyl.

1960

	6	5	4	3	2	1
Series 1100						
Sed Dly	400	1300	2200	4400	7700	11,000
El Camino	450	1400	2300	4600	8100	11,500
Series C14 - (1/2-Ton)						
Stepside PU	450	1000	1650	3350	6300	9000
Fleetside PU	450	1100	1700	3650	6650	9500
Panel	350	900	1550	3000	5850	8400
Suburban	350	950	1600	3200	6050	8700
Series C15 "Long Box" - (1/2-Ton)						
Stepside PU	350	900	1550	3000	5850	8400
Fleetside PU	350	900	1550	3100	6000	8600
Series C25 - (3/4-Ton)						
Stepside PU	350	900	1550	3000	5850	8400
Fleetside PU	350	900	1550	3100	6000	8600
8-ft. Stake	350	725	1200	2350	4850	6900
Series C36 - (1-Ton)						
Stepside	350	750	1300	2400	5200	7400
Panel	350	750	1200	2350	4900	7000
9-ft. Stake	350	725	1200	2350	4850	6900
Step Vans						
Walk-In Dly (104" wb)	350	800	1350	2700	5500	7900
Walk-In Dly (125" wb)	350	800	1450	2750	5600	8000
Walk-In Dly (137" wb)	350	750	1300	2500	5300	7600

NOTE: 1955-up prices based on top of the line models.
Deduct 10 percent for 6-cyl.

1961

	6	5	4	3	2	1
Corvair Series 95						
Loadside	200	650	1000	2200	4100	5800
Rampside	200	675	1050	2250	4300	6100
Corvan Series						
Corvan Panel	200	650	1050	2250	4200	6000
Greenbriar Spt Van	350	700	1150	2300	4550	6500
Fleetside Pickups						
C10 PU (SBx)	400	1200	2000	3950	7000	10,000
C10 PU (LBx)	450	1150	1800	3800	6800	9700
K10 PU (SBx)	450	1100	1800	3700	6700	9600
K10 PU (LBx)	450	1100	1700	3650	6650	9500
C20 PU (LBx)	350	900	1550	3000	5850	8400
K20 PU (LBx)	350	850	1500	2800	5650	8100
Stepside Pickups						
C10 PU (SBx)	450	1150	1800	3800	6800	9700
C10 PU (LBx)	450	1100	1800	3700	6700	9600
K10 PU (SBx)	450	1100	1700	3650	6650	9500
K10 PU (LBx)	450	1050	1700	3600	6600	9400
C20 PU (LBx)	350	850	1500	2950	5800	8300
K20 PU (LBx)	350	800	1450	2750	5600	8000
C30 PU (8-1/2 ft. bed)	350	800	1350	2700	5500	7900
Step Vans						
P10 Walk-In	200	650	1000	2200	4100	5800
P20 Walk-In	200	650	1000	2200	4150	5900
P30 Walk-In	200	650	1050	2250	4200	6000
Panel/Suburban/Stake-Bed						
C10 Panel	200	600	1000	2200	4000	5700
C10 Suburban	350	725	1200	2350	4850	6900
C20 Panel	200	550	900	2150	3800	5400
C20 Suburban	350	725	1150	2300	4700	6700
C20 Stake	200	550	900	2150	3800	5400
C30 Panel (10-1/2 ft. bed)	200	600	950	2150	3850	5500
C30 Stake	200	600	950	2150	3850	5500

NOTE: 1955-up prices based on top of the line models. C is conventional drive model. K is 4-wheel drive (4WD) model. 10 is the 1/2-Ton series. 30 is the 1-Ton series. Short box has 6-1/2 ft. bed. Long box has 8-ft. bed.

1962

	6	5	4	3	2	1
Corvair Series 95						
Loadside	200	650	1000	2200	4100	5800
Rampside	200	675	1050	2250	4300	6100
Corvan Series						
Corvan Panel Van	200	600	1000	2200	4000	5700
Greenbriar Spt Van	350	700	1150	2300	4550	6500
Fleetside Pickups						
C10 PU (SBx)	450	1150	1900	3850	6850	9800
C10 PU (LBx)	450	1150	1800	3800	6800	9700
K10 PU (SBx)	450	1100	1800	3700	6700	9600
K10 PU (LBx)	450	1100	1700	3650	6650	9500
C20 PU (LBx)	350	900	1550	3000	5850	8400
K20 PU (LBx)	350	850	1500	2800	5650	8100
Stepside Pickups						
C10 PU (SBx)	450	1150	1800	3800	6800	9700
C10 PU (LBx)	450	1100	1800	3700	6700	9600
K10 PU (SBx)	450	1100	1700	3650	6650	9500
K10 PU (LBx)	450	1050	1700	3600	6600	9400
C20 PU (LBx)	350	850	1500	2950	5800	8300
K20 PU (LBx)	350	800	1450	2750	5600	8000
C30 PU (8-1/2 ft. bed)	350	800	1350	2700	5500	7900
Step Vans						
P10 Walk-In	200	650	1000	2200	4100	5800
P20 Walk-In	200	650	1000	2200	4150	5900
P30 Walk-In	200	650	1050	2250	4200	6000
Panel/Suburban/Stake-Bed						
C10 Panel	200	600	1000	2200	4000	5700
C10 Suburban	350	725	1200	2350	4850	6900
K10 Panel	200	550	900	2150	3800	5400
K10 Suburban	350	725	1150	2300	4700	6700
C20 Stake	200	550	900	2150	3800	5400
C30 Panel (10-1/2 ft. bed)	200	600	950	2150	3850	5500
C30 Stake	200	600	950	2150	3850	5500

NOTE: 1955-up prices based on top of the line models. C is conventional drive model. K is 4-wheel drive (4WD) model. 10 is 1/2-Ton series. 20 is 3/4-Ton series. 30 is 1-Ton series. Short box has 6-1/2 ft. bed. Long box has 8-ft. bed.

1963

	6	5	4	3	2	1
Corvair Series 95						
Loadside	200	650	1000	2200	4100	5800
Rampside	200	675	1050	2250	4300	6100
Corvan Series						
Corvan Panel Van	200	600	1000	2200	4000	5700
Greenbriar Spt Van	350	700	1150	2300	4600	6600
Fleetside Pickups						
C10 PU (SBx)	450	1150	1900	3850	6850	9800
C10 PU (LBx)	450	1150	1800	3800	6800	9700
K10 PU (SBx)	450	1100	1800	3700	6700	9600
K10 PU (LBx)	450	1100	1700	3650	6650	9500
C20 PU (LBx)	350	900	1550	3000	5850	8400
K20 PU (LBx)	350	850	1500	2800	5650	8100
Stepside Pickups						
C10 PU (SBx)	450	1150	1800	3800	6800	9700
C10 PU (LBx)	450	1100	1800	3700	6700	9600
K10 PU (SBx)	450	1100	1700	3650	6650	9500
K10 PU (LBx)	450	1050	1700	3600	6600	9400
C20 PU (LBx)	350	850	1500	2950	5800	8300
K20 PU (LBx)	350	800	1450	2750	5600	8000
C30 PU (8-1/2 ft. bed)	350	800	1350	2700	5500	7900
Step Vans						
P10 Walk-In	200	650	1000	2200	4100	5800
P20 Walk-In	200	650	1000	2200	4150	5900
P30 Walk-In	200	650	1050	2250	4200	6000
Panel/Suburban/Stake-Bed						
C10 Panel	200	600	1000	2200	4000	5700
C10 Suburban	350	725	1200	2350	4850	6900
K10 Panel	200	550	900	2150	3800	5400
K10 Suburban	350	725	1150	2300	4700	6700
C20 Stake	200	550	900	2150	3800	5400
C30 Panel (10-1/2 ft. bed)	200	600	950	2150	3850	5500
C30 Stake	200	600	950	2150	3850	5500

NOTE: 1955-up prices based on top of the line models. C is conventional drive model. K is 4-wheel drive (4WD) model. 10 is 1/2-Ton series. 20 is 3/4-Ton series. 30 is the 1-Ton series. Short box has 6-1/2 ft. bed. Long box has 8-ft. bed.

1964

	6	5	4	3	2	1
El Camino						
Spt PU	400	1200	2000	3950	7000	10,000
Cus Spt PU	400	1250	2100	4200	7400	10,500
Corvair Series 95						
Loadside	200	650	1000	2200	4100	5800
Rampside	200	675	1050	2250	4300	6100
Corvan Series						
Panel Van	200	600	1000	2200	4000	5700
Greenbriar Spt Van	350	725	1150	2300	4700	6700
Fleetside Pickups						
C10 PU (SBx)	450	1150	1900	3850	6850	9800
C10 PU (LBx)	450	1150	1800	3800	6800	9700
K10 PU (SBx)	450	1100	1800	3700	6700	9600
K10 PU (LBx)	450	1100	1700	3650	6650	9500
C20 PU (LBx)	350	900	1550	3000	5850	8400
K20 PU (LBx)	350	850	1500	2800	5650	8100

	6	5	4	3	2	1
Stepside Pickups						
C10 PU (SBx)	450	1150	1800	3800	6800	9700
C10 PU (LBx)	450	1100	1800	3700	6700	9600
K10 PU (SBx)	450	1100	1700	3650	6650	9500
K10 PU (LBx)	450	1050	1700	3600	6600	9400
C20 PU (LBx)	350	850	1500	2950	5800	8300
C30 PU (8-1/2 ft. bed)	350	800	1350	2700	5500	7900
G10 Chevy Van Series						
Panel Van	200	675	1050	2250	4300	6100
Step Van Series						
P10 Walk-In	200	650	1000	2200	4100	5800
P20 Walk-In	200	650	1000	2200	4150	5900
P30 Walk-In	200	650	1050	2250	4200	6000
Panel/Suburban/Stake-Bed						
C10 Panel	200	600	1000	2200	4000	5700
C10 Suburban	350	725	1200	2350	4850	6900
K10 Panel	200	550	900	2150	3800	5400
K10 Suburban	350	725	1150	2300	4700	6700
C20 Stake	200	550	900	2150	3800	5400
C30 Panel (10-1/2 ft. bed)	200	600	950	2150	3850	5500
C30 Stake	200	600	950	2150	3850	5500

NOTE: 1955-up prices based on top of the line models. C is conventional drive model. K is 4-wheel drive (4WD) model. 10 is 1/2-Ton series. 20 is 3/4-Ton series. 30 is 1-Ton series. Short box has 6-1/2 ft. bed. Long box has 8-ft. bed.

1965

	6	5	4	3	2	1
El Camino						
Spt PU	400	1200	2000	3950	7000	10,000
Cus Spt PU	400	1250	2100	4200	7400	10,500
Corvair Series 95						
Greenbriar Spt Van	350	725	1200	2350	4800	6800
Fleetside Pickups						
C10 PU (SBx)	450	1150	1900	3850	6850	9800
C10 PU (LBx)	450	1150	1800	3800	6800	9700
K10 PU (SBx)	450	1100	1800	3700	6700	9600
K10 PU (LBx)	450	1100	1700	3650	6650	9500
C20 PU (LBx)	350	900	1550	3000	5850	8400
K20 PU (LBx)	350	850	1500	2800	5650	8100
Stepside Pickups						
C10 PU (SBx)	450	1150	1800	3800	6800	9700
C10 PU (LBx)	450	1100	1800	3700	6700	9600
K10 PU (SBx)	450	1100	1700	3650	6650	9500
K10 PU (LBx)	450	1050	1700	3600	6600	9400
C20 PU (LBx)	350	850	1500	2950	5800	8300
C30 PU (8-1/2 ft. bed)	350	800	1350	2700	5500	7900
G12 Chevy Van Series						
Panel Van	200	650	1000	2200	4150	5900
Spt Van	200	650	1050	2250	4200	6000
Cus Spt Van	200	675	1050	2250	4300	6100
DeL Spt Van	200	675	1050	2250	4350	6200
Step Van Series						
P10 Panel	200	650	1000	2200	4100	5800
P20 Panel	200	650	1000	2200	4150	5900
P30 Panel	200	650	1050	2250	4200	6000
Panel/Suburban/Stake-Bed						
C10 Panel	200	600	1000	2200	4000	5700
C10 Suburban	350	725	1200	2350	4850	6900
K10 Panel	200	550	900	2150	3800	5400
K10 Suburban	350	725	1150	2300	4700	6700
C20 Stake	200	550	900	2150	3800	5400
C30 Panel	200	600	950	2150	3850	5500
C30 Stake	200	600	950	2150	3850	5500

NOTE: Greenbriar remained available in 1965. 1955-up prices based on top of the line models. C is conventional drive model. K is 4-wheel drive (4WD) model. 10 is 1/2-Ton series. 20 is 3/4-Ton series. 30 is 1-Ton series. Short box has 6-1/2 ft. bed. Long box has 8-ft. bed.

1966

	6	5	4	3	2	1
El Camino						
Spt PU	400	1200	2000	3950	7000	10,000
Cus Spt PU	400	1250	2100	4200	7400	10,500
Fleetside Pickup Series C10/C20						
C14 PU (SBx)	450	1150	1900	3850	6850	9800
C15 PU (LBx)	450	1150	1800	3800	6800	9700
K14 PU (SBx)	450	1100	1800	3700	6700	9600
K15 PU (LBx)	450	1100	1700	3650	6650	9500
C25 PU (LBx)	350	900	1550	3000	5850	8400
K25 PU (LBx)	350	850	1500	2800	5650	8100
Stepside Pickup Series C10/C20/C30						
C14 PU (SBx)	450	1150	1800	3800	6800	9700
C15 PU (LBx)	450	1100	1800	3700	6700	9600
K14 PU (SBx)	450	1100	1700	3650	6650	9500
K15 PU (LBx)	450	1050	1700	3600	6600	9400
C25 PU (LBx)	350	850	1500	2950	5800	8300
K25 PU (LBx)	350	800	1450	2750	5600	8000
1-Ton PU (8-1/2 ft. bed)	350	800	1350	2700	5500	7900
Chevy Van Series						
G12 Panel Van	200	650	1000	2200	4150	5900
G12 Spt Van	200	650	1050	2250	4200	6000
G12 Cus Spt Van	200	675	1050	2250	4300	6100
G12 DeL Spt Van	200	675	1050	2250	4350	6200
Step Van Series						
P10 Panel	150	300	750	1350	2700	3900
P20 Panel	150	350	750	1350	2800	4000
P30 Panel	150	350	750	1450	2900	4100
Panel/Suburban/Stake-Bed						
C14 Panel	150	300	700	1250	2650	3800
C14 Suburban	200	500	850	1900	3500	5000
K14 Panel	125	250	700	1150	2450	3500
K14 Suburban	150	450	800	1800	3300	4800
C25 Stake	125	250	700	1150	2450	3500
C36 Panel	125	250	700	1150	2500	3600
C36 Stake	125	250	700	1150	2500	3600

NOTE: C is conventional drive model. K is 4-wheel drive (4WD) model. 14 is 1/2-Ton Short box (6-1/2 ft. bed). 15 is 1/2-Ton Long box (8-ft. bed). 25 is 3/4-Ton. 36 is 1-Ton.

1967

	6	5	4	3	2	1
El Camino Series						
Spt PU	400	1200	2000	3950	7000	10,000
Cus Spt PU	400	1250	2100	4200	7400	10,500
Fleetside Pickups						
C10 PU (SBx)	400	1300	2200	4400	7700	11,000
C10 PU (LBx)	400	1200	2000	3950	7000	10,000
K10 PU (SBx)	450	1150	1800	3800	6800	9700
K10 PU (LBx)	450	1100	1700	3650	6650	9500
C20 PU (LBx)	450	950	1600	3250	6150	8800
C20 PU (8-1/2 ft. bed)	350	950	1600	3200	6050	8700
K20 PU (LBx)	350	950	1600	3200	6050	8700
K20 PU (8-1/2 ft. bed)	350	900	1550	3100	6000	8600
C30 PU (8-1/2 ft. bed)	350	750	1350	2650	5450	7800
Stepside Pickups						
C10 PU (SBx)	400	1200	2000	3950	7000	10,000
C10 PU (LBx)	450	1100	1800	3700	6700	9600
C20 PU (LBx)	350	950	1600	3200	6050	8700
K20 PU (LBx)	350	900	1550	3100	6000	8600
C30 PU (8-1/2 ft. bed)	350	750	1350	2650	5450	7800
Chevy Van Series						
G10 Panel Van	200	650	1000	2200	4100	5800
G10 Spt Van	200	650	1050	2250	4200	6000
G10 Cus Spt Van	200	675	1100	2250	4400	6300
G10 DeL Spt Van	350	700	1150	2300	4600	6600
G20 Panel Van	200	600	950	2200	3900	5600
G20 Spt Van	200	650	1000	2200	4100	5800
G20 Cus Spt Van	200	650	1050	2250	4200	6000
G20 DeL Spt Van	200	675	1100	2250	4400	6300
Step Van Series (Code "P")						
P10 Steel Panel	200	650	1000	2200	4100	5800
P20 Steel Panel	200	600	1000	2200	4000	5700
P30 Steel Panel	200	600	950	2200	3900	5600
Panel/Suburbans/Stakes						
C10 Panel	200	650	1050	2250	4200	6000
C10 Suburban	350	750	1250	2400	5100	7300
C20 Stake	200	675	1050	2250	4350	6200
C20 Panel	200	650	1000	2200	4100	5800
C20 Suburban	200	675	1100	2250	4400	6300
C30 Stake	200	675	1100	2250	4400	6300

NOTE: 1955-up prices based on top of the line models. Add 5 percent for 4WD. C is conventional drive model. K is 4-wheel drive (4WD) model. 10 is 1/2-Ton series. 20 is 3/4-Ton series. 30 is 1-Ton series. Short box has 6-1/2 ft. bed. Long box has 8-ft. bed.

1968

	6	5	4	3	2	1
El Camino Series						
Spt PU	400	1200	2000	3950	7000	10,000
Cus Spt PU	400	1250	2100	4200	7400	10,500

NOTE: Add 15 percent for SS-396 option.

	6	5	4	3	2	1
Fleetside PU						
C10 PU (SBx)	400	1300	2200	4400	7700	11,000
C10 PU (LBx)	400	1200	2000	3950	7000	10,000
K10 PU (SBx)	450	1150	1800	3800	6800	9700
K10 PU (LBx)	450	1100	1700	3650	6650	9500
C20 PU (LBx)	450	950	1600	3250	6150	8800
C20 PU (8-1/2 ft. bed)	350	950	1600	3200	6050	8700
K20 PU (LBx)	350	950	1600	3200	6050	8700
K20 PU (8-1/2 ft. bed)	350	900	1550	3100	6000	8600
Stepside Pickups						
C10 PU (SBx)	400	1200	2000	3950	7000	10,000
C10 PU (LBx)	450	1100	1800	3700	6700	9600
K10 PU (SBx)	450	1100	1700	3650	6650	9500
K10 PU (LBx)	450	1050	1700	3600	6600	9400
C20 PU (LBx)	350	950	1600	3200	6050	8700
K20 PU (LBx)	350	900	1550	3100	6000	8600
C30 PU (8-1/2 ft. bed)	350	750	1350	2650	5450	7800
Chevy Van Series						
G10 Panel Van	200	650	1000	2200	4100	5800
G10 Spt Van	200	650	1050	2250	4200	6000
G10 Cus Spt Van	200	675	1100	2250	4400	6300
G10 DeL Spt Van	350	700	1150	2300	4600	6600
G20 Panel Van	200	600	950	2200	3900	5600
G20 Spt Van	200	650	1000	2200	4100	5800
G20 Cus Spt Van	200	650	1050	2250	4200	6000
G20 DeL Spt Van	200	675	1100	2250	4400	6300
Step Van Series						
P10 Panel	200	650	1000	2200	4100	5800
P20 Panel	200	600	1000	2200	4000	5700
P30 Panel	200	600	950	2200	3900	5600
Panel/Suburban/Stake-Bed						
C10 Panel	200	650	1050	2250	4200	6000
C10 Suburban	350	750	1250	2400	5100	7300
C20 Stake	200	650	1000	2200	4100	5800

NOTE: 1955-up prices based on top of the line models. C is conventional drive model. K is 4-wheel drive (4WD) model. 10 is 1/2-Ton series. 20 is 3/4-Ton series. 30 is 1-Ton series. Short box has 6-1/2 ft. bed. Long box has 8-ft. bed.

1969

	6	5	4	3	2	1
El Camino Series						
Spt PU	400	1200	2000	3950	7000	10,000
Cus Spt PU	400	1250	2100	4200	7400	10,500

NOTE: Add 15 percent for SS-396 option.

	6	5	4	3	2	1
Blazer Series - (4WD)						
Blazer	400	1300	2200	4400	7700	11,000
Fleetside Series						
C10 PU (SBx)	450	1450	2400	4800	8400	12,000
C10 PU (LBx)	450	1400	2300	4600	8100	11,500
K10 PU (SBx)	400	1200	2000	3950	7000	10,000
K10 PU (LBx)	450	1150	1900	3850	6850	9800
C20 PU (LBx)	450	950	1600	3250	6150	8800
C20 PU (long horn)	350	900	1550	3100	6000	8600
K20 PU (LBx)	450	1100	1800	3700	6700	9600
K20 PU (long horn)	450	1150	1800	3800	6800	9700
C30 PU (long horn)	350	750	1350	2650	5450	7800
Stepside Series						
C10 PU (SBx)	400	1200	2000	3950	7000	10,000
C10 PU (LBx)	450	1100	1700	3650	6650	9500
K10 PU (SBx)	450	1150	1900	3900	6900	9900
K10 PU (LBx)	450	1150	1800	3800	6800	9700
C20 PU (LBx)	450	1150	1900	3850	6850	9800
C20 PU (long horn)	450	1150	1800	3800	6800	9700
K20 PU (LBx)	450	1150	1800	3800	6800	9700
K20 PU (long horn)	450	1100	1800	3700	6700	9600
C30 PU (long horn)	350	750	1350	2650	5450	7800
Chevy Van Series G10 - (1/2-Ton) - (90" wb)						
Panel Van	200	650	1050	2250	4200	6000
Spt Van	350	700	1150	2300	4600	6600
Cus Spt Van	350	700	1150	2300	4550	6500
DeL Spt Van	350	725	1150	2300	4700	6700
Chevy Van Series G20 - (3/4-Ton) - (108" wb)						
Panel Van	200	650	1000	2200	4100	5800
Spt Van	350	700	1100	2300	4500	6400
Cus Spt Van	200	675	1100	2250	4400	6300
DeL Spt Van	350	700	1150	2300	4550	6500
Step Vans						
P10 - (1/2-Ton) - (102"wb)	200	650	1000	2200	4100	5800
P20 - (3/4-Ton) - (125"wb)	150	350	750	1450	2900	4100
P30 - (1-Ton) - (125"wb)	150	350	750	1450	3000	4200

	6	5	4	3	2	1
Panel/Suburban Series C10/K10 - (115" wb)						
C10 Panel	350	750	1350	2650	5450	7800
C10 Suburban	450	1050	1700	3550	6500	9300
K10 Panel	350	750	1300	2500	5300	7600
K10 Suburban	450	1000	1650	3400	6350	9100
Panel/Suburban Series C20/K20 - (127" wb)						
C20 Panel	350	750	1300	2500	5300	7600
C20 Suburban	350	850	1500	2950	5800	8300
K20 Panel	350	750	1300	2400	5200	7400
K20 Suburban	350	850	1500	2800	5650	8100

NOTE: 1955-up prices based on top of the line models. C is conventional drive model. K is 4-wheel drive (4WD) model. 10 is 1/2-Ton series. 20 is 3/4-Ton series. 30 is 1-Ton series. Short box pickup has 6-1/2 ft. bed and 115" wb. Long box pickup has 8-ft. bed and 127" wb. Long horn pickup has 8-1/2 to 9-ft. bed and 133" wb.

1970

	6	5	4	3	2	1
El Camino Series						
Spt PU	400	1200	2000	3950	7000	10,000
Cus Spt PU	400	1250	2100	4200	7400	10,500

NOTE: Add 15 percent for SS-396 option.

	6	5	4	3	2	1
Blazer Series K10 - (4WD)						
Blazer	400	1200	2000	3950	7000	10,000
Pickup						
Fleetside Pickups						
C10 PU (SBx)	450	1450	2400	4800	8400	12,000
C10 PU (LBx)	450	1400	2300	4600	8100	11,500
K10 PU (SBx)	400	1200	2000	3950	7000	10,000
K10 PU (LBx)	450	1150	1900	3850	6850	9800
C20 PU (LBx)	450	950	1600	3250	6150	8800
C20 PU (long horn)	350	900	1550	3100	6000	8600
K20 PU (LBx)	450	1100	1800	3700	6700	9600
K20 PU (long horn)	450	1150	1800	3800	6800	9700
C30 PU (long horn)	350	750	1350	2650	5450	7800
Stepside Pickups						
C10 PU (SBx)	400	1250	2100	4200	7400	10,500
C10 PU (LBx)	400	1200	2000	3950	7000	10,000
K10 PU (SBx)	450	1150	1900	3900	6900	9900
K10 PU (LBx)	450	1150	1800	3800	6800	9700
C20 PU (LBx)	450	1150	1900	3850	6850	9800
K20 PU (LBx)	450	1150	1800	3800	6800	9700
C30 PU (long horn)	350	750	1350	2650	5450	7800
Chevy Van Series G10 - (1/2-Ton) - (90" wb)						
Panel Van	200	650	1050	2250	4200	6000
Spt Van	350	700	1150	2300	4600	6600
Cus Spt Van	350	700	1150	2300	4550	6500
DeL Spt Van	350	725	1150	2300	4700	6700
Chevy Van Series G20 - (3/4-Ton) - (108" wb)						
Panel Van	200	650	1000	2200	4100	5800
Spt Van	350	700	1100	2300	4500	6400
Cus Spt Van	200	675	1100	2250	4400	6300
DeL Spt Van	200	675	1100	2250	4400	6300
Step Vans						
P10 - (102" wb)	200	650	1000	2200	4100	5800
P20 - (125" wb)	150	350	750	1450	2900	4100
P30 - (125" wb)	150	350	750	1450	3000	4200
Panel/Suburban Series C10/K10 - (115" wb)						
C10 Panel	200	650	1050	2250	4200	6000
C10 Suburban	350	750	1300	2450	5250	7500
K10 Panel	200	650	1000	2200	4100	5800
K10 Suburban	350	750	1250	2400	5100	7300
Panel/Suburban Series C20/K20 - (127" wb)						
C20 Panel	200	650	1000	2200	4100	5800
C20 Suburban	350	700	1150	2300	4550	6500
K20 Panel	200	600	950	2200	3900	5600
K20 Suburban	200	675	1100	2250	4400	6300
Series C30 - (133" wb)						
1-Ton Stake (9-ft. bed)	200	500	850	1900	3500	5000

NOTE: C is conventional drive model. K is 4-wheel drive (4WD) model. 10 is 1/2-Ton series. 20 is 3/4-Ton series. 30 is 1-Ton series. Short box pickup has 6-1/2 ft. bed and 115" wb. Long box pickup has 8-ft. bed and 127" wb. Long horn pickup has 8-1/2 to 9-ft. bed and 133" wb.

1971

	6	5	4	3	2	1
Vega Panel Series						
Panel Exp	200	500	850	1900	3500	5000
El Camino (V-8)						
Spt PU	400	1200	2000	3950	7000	10,000
Cus Spt PU	400	1250	2100	4200	7400	10,500
Blazer Series K10 - (4WD)						
Blazer	400	1250	2100	4200	7400	10,500
Fleetside Pickups						
C10 PU (SBx)	450	1500	2500	5000	8800	12,500
C10 PU (LBx)	450	1450	2400	4800	8400	12,000
K10 PU (SBx)	400	1250	2100	4200	7400	10,500
K10 PU (LBx)	400	1250	2050	4100	7200	10,300
C20 PU (LBx)	450	1150	1900	3850	6850	9800
C20 PU (long horn)	450	1100	1700	3650	6650	9500
K20 PU (LBx)	450	1100	1800	3700	6700	9600
K20 PU (long horn)	450	1150	1800	3800	6800	9700
C30 PU (long horn)	350	750	1350	2650	5450	7800
Stepside Pickups						
C10 PU (SBx)	400	1250	2100	4200	7400	10,500
C10 PU (LBx)	400	1200	2000	3950	7000	10,000
K10 PU (SBx)	450	1100	1800	3700	6700	9600
K10 PU (LBx)	450	1050	1700	3550	6500	9300
C20 PU (LBx)	450	1050	1700	3550	6500	9300
K20 PU (LBx)	450	1050	1650	3500	6400	9200
C30 PU (long horn)	450	1000	1650	3400	6350	9100
Chevy Van Series G10 - (1/2-Ton) - (110" wb)						
Panel Van	350	750	1200	2350	4900	7000
Spt Van	350	750	1250	2400	5100	7300
Beauville	350	750	1350	2650	5450	7800
Chevy Van Series G20 - (3/4-Ton) - (110" wb)						
Panel Van	350	700	1150	2300	4550	6500
Spt Van	350	750	1250	2350	5000	7100
Beauville	350	750	1250	2400	5100	7300
Chevy Van Series G30 - (1-Ton) - (110" wb)						
Panel Van	200	675	1100	2250	4400	6300
Spt Van	350	700	1150	2300	4550	6500
Beauville	350	725	1200	2350	4800	6800
Step Vans						
P10 Step Van	200	650	1050	2250	4200	6000
P20 Step Van	200	675	1050	2250	4300	6100
P30 Step Van	200	675	1050	2250	4350	6200
Panels/Suburbans/Stakes						
C10 Suburban	400	1200	2000	3950	7000	10,000
K10 Suburban	350	900	1550	3050	5900	8500
C20 Suburban	350	900	1550	3050	5900	8500
K20 Suburban	350	750	1350	2650	5450	7800
C20 Stake	350	725	1200	2350	4800	6800
C30 Stake	350	725	1200	2350	4800	6800

NOTE: 1955-up prices based on top of the line models.
See previous notes for 1969-1970 explaining "model" information.

1972

	6	5	4	3	2	1
Vega (1/2-Ton)						
Panel Exp	200	500	850	1900	3500	5000
LUV Pickup (1/2-Ton)						
PU	150	450	800	1750	3250	4700
El Camino (V-8)						
Spt PU	400	1250	2100	4200	7400	10,500
Cus Spt PU	400	1300	2200	4400	7700	11,000
Blazer (4WD)						
C10 Blazer	450	1000	1650	3350	6300	9000
K10 Blazer	400	1300	2200	4400	7700	11,000
Fleetside Pickups						
C10 PU (SBx)	450	1500	2500	5000	8800	12,500
C10 PU (LBx)	450	1450	2400	4800	8400	12,000
K10 PU (SBx)	400	1300	2150	4300	7600	10,800
K10 PU (LBx)	400	1250	2100	4200	7400	10,500
C20 PU (SBx)	450	1150	1900	3850	6850	9800
C20 PU (LBx)	400	1200	2000	3950	7000	10,000
K20 PU (SBx)	450	1100	1800	3700	6700	9600
K20 PU (LBx)	450	1150	1800	3800	6800	9700
C30 PU (long horn)	350	750	1350	2650	5450	7800
Stepside Pickups						
C10 PU (SBx)	400	1300	2200	4400	7700	11,000
C10 PU (LBx)	400	1250	2100	4200	7400	10,500
K10 PU (SBx)	450	1150	1900	3850	6850	9800
K10 PU (LBx)	450	1100	1700	3650	6650	9500
K10 PU (LBx)	450	1150	1900	3850	6850	9800
K20 PU (LBx)	450	1050	1700	3550	6500	9300
C30 PU (long horn)	450	1000	1650	3400	6350	9100
Chevy Van						
G10 Panel Van	350	750	1200	2350	4900	7000
G10 Spt Van	350	750	1250	2400	5100	7300
G10 Beauville	350	750	1350	2650	5450	7800
G20 Panel Van	350	725	1200	2350	4800	6800
G20 Spt Van	350	750	1200	2350	4900	7000
G20 Beauville	350	750	1250	2400	5100	7300
Step Vans						
P10	200	650	1000	2200	4100	5800
P20	200	600	950	2200	3900	5600
P30	200	550	900	2150	3800	5400
Suburban						
C10 Suburban	400	1200	2000	3950	7000	10,000
K10 Suburban	350	900	1550	3050	5900	8500
C20 Suburban	350	900	1550	3050	5900	8500
K20 Suburban	350	750	1350	2650	5450	7800
Stake Bed						
C20 Stake	350	725	1200	2350	4800	6800
C30 Stake	350	725	1200	2350	4800	6800

NOTE: 1955-up prices based on top of the line models.

1973

	6	5	4	3	2	1
Vega						
Panel	200	500	850	1900	3500	5000
LUV						
PU	125	200	600	1100	2300	3300
El Camino						
PU	200	600	950	2150	3850	5500
Cus PU	200	650	1050	2250	4200	6000
Blazer K10						
Blazer 2WD	350	750	1300	2450	5250	7500
Blazer 4WD	350	900	1550	3050	5900	8500
C10 (1/2-Ton)						
Stepside (SBx)	350	900	1550	3050	5900	8500
Stepside (LBx)	350	800	1450	2750	5600	8000
Fleetside (SBx)	450	1000	1650	3350	6300	9000
Fleetside (LBx)	350	900	1550	3050	5900	8500
Suburban	350	750	1200	2350	4900	7000
K10 - 4WD - (1/2-Ton)						
Stepside (SBx)	200	600	1000	2200	4000	5700
Stepside (LBx)	200	650	1000	2200	4100	5800
Fleetside (SBx)	200	650	1000	2200	4150	5900
Fleetside (LBx)	200	650	1050	2250	4200	6000
Suburban	200	650	1050	2250	4200	6000
C20 - (3/4-Ton)						
Stepside (LBx)	200	600	950	2150	3850	5500
Fleetside (LBx)	200	600	1000	2200	4000	5700
6P (LBx)	200	550	900	2100	3700	5300
Suburban	200	650	1050	2250	4200	6000
K20 - 4WD - (3/4-Ton)						
Stepside (LBx)	200	650	1000	2200	4100	5800
Fleetside (LBx)	200	650	1000	2200	4150	5900
6P (LBx)	200	600	950	2150	3850	5500
Suburban	200	675	1050	2250	4350	6200
C30 - (1-Ton)						
Stepside (LBx)	200	550	900	2100	3700	5300
Fleetside (LBx)	200	600	950	2150	3850	5500
6P (LBx)	200	550	900	2000	3600	5200
Series CG Panels/Vans (1/2-Ton)						
Panel	150	400	750	1650	3150	4500
Spt Van	200	600	950	2150	3850	5500
Beauville	200	600	1000	2200	4000	5700
Series CG Panels/Vans (3/4-Ton)						
Panel	150	400	750	1550	3050	4300
Spt Van	200	550	900	2100	3700	5300
Beauville	200	600	950	2150	3850	5500
Series CG Panels Vans (1-Ton)						
Panel	150	350	750	1450	2900	4100
Spt Van	200	500	850	1950	3600	5100
Beauville	200	550	900	2100	3700	5300
Step Vans						
P10 Panel	150	350	750	1350	2800	4000
P20 Panel	150	300	750	1350	2700	3900
P30 Panel	150	300	700	1250	2650	3800

NOTE: 1955-up prices based on top of the line models.

1974

	6	5	4	3	2	1
Vega						
Panel	200	500	850	1900	3500	5000

	6	5	4	3	2	1
LUV						
PU	125	200	600	1100	2300	3300
El Camino						
PU	200	600	950	2150	3850	5500
Cus PU	200	650	1050	2250	4200	6000
Blazer K10						
Blazer 2WD	350	750	1300	2450	5250	7500
Blazer 4WD	350	900	1550	3050	5900	8500
C10 - (1/2-Ton)						
Stepside (SBx)	350	750	1200	2350	4900	7000
Stepside (LBx)	350	700	1150	2300	4550	6500
Fleetside (SBx)	350	750	1300	2450	5250	7500
Fleetside (LBx)	350	750	1250	2400	5050	7200
Suburban	350	725	1200	2350	4800	6800
K10 - 4WD - (1/2-Ton)						
Stepside (SBx)	200	600	1000	2200	4000	5700
Stepside (LBx)	200	650	1000	2200	4100	5800
Fleetside (SBx)	200	650	1000	2200	4150	5900
Fleetside (SBx)	200	650	1050	2250	4200	6000
Suburban	200	650	1050	2250	4200	6000
C20 - (3/4-Ton)						
Stepside (LBx)	200	600	950	2150	3850	5500
Fleetside (LBx)	200	600	1000	2200	4000	5700
6P (LBx)	200	550	900	2100	3700	5300
Suburban	200	650	1050	2250	4200	6000
K20 - 4WD - (3/4-Ton)						
Stepside (LBx)	200	650	1000	2200	4100	5800
Fleetside (LBx)	200	650	1000	2200	4150	5900
6P (LBx)	200	600	950	2150	3850	5500
Suburban	200	675	1050	2250	4350	6200
C30 - (1-Ton)						
Stepside (LBx)	200	550	900	2100	3700	5300
Fleetside (LBx)	200	600	950	2150	3850	5500
6P (LBx)	200	550	900	2000	3600	5200
Series CG Panels/Vans (1/2-Ton)						
Panel	150	400	750	1650	3150	4500
Spt Van	200	600	950	2150	3850	5500
Beauville	200	600	1000	2200	4000	5700
Series CG Panels/Vans (3/4-Ton)						
Panel	150	400	750	1550	3050	4300
Spt Van	200	550	900	2100	3700	5300
Beauville	200	600	950	2150	3850	5500
Series CG Panels/Vans (1-Ton)						
Panel	150	350	750	1450	2900	4100
Spt Van	200	500	850	1950	3600	5100
Beauville	200	550	900	2100	3700	5300
Step Vans						
P10 Panel	150	350	750	1350	2800	4000
P20 Panel	150	300	750	1350	2700	3900
P30 Panel	150	300	700	1250	2650	3800

NOTE: 1955-up prices based on top of the line models.

1975
	6	5	4	3	2	1
Vega						
Panel	200	500	850	1900	3500	5000
LUV						
PU	125	200	600	1100	2300	3300
El Camino						
PU	200	600	950	2150	3850	5500
Cus PU	200	650	1050	2250	4200	6000
Blazer K10						
Blazer 2WD	350	750	1300	2450	5250	7500
Blazer 4WD	350	900	1550	3050	5900	8500
C10 (1/2-Ton)						
Stepside (SBx)	350	750	1200	2350	4900	7000
Stepside (LBx)	350	700	1150	2300	4550	6500
Fleetside (SBx)	350	700	1150	2300	4600	6600
Fleetside (LBx)	350	700	1150	2300	4550	6500
Suburban	350	700	1150	2300	4550	6500
K10 - 4WD - (1/2-Ton)						
Stepside (SBx)	200	600	1000	2200	4000	5700
Stepside (LBx)	200	650	1000	2200	4100	5800
Fleetside (SBx)	200	650	1000	2200	4150	5900
Fleetside (LBx)	200	650	1050	2250	4200	6000
Suburban	200	650	1050	2250	4200	6000
C20 - (3/4-Ton)						
Stepside (LBx)	200	600	950	2150	3850	5500
Fleetside (LBx)	200	600	1000	2200	4000	5700
6P (LBx)	200	550	900	2100	3700	5300
Suburban	200	650	1050	2250	4200	6000
K20 - 4WD - (3/4-Ton)						
Stepside (LBx)	200	650	1000	2200	4100	5800
Fleetside (LBx)	200	650	1000	2200	4150	5900
6P (LBx)	200	600	950	2150	3850	5500
Suburban	200	675	1050	2250	4350	6200
C30 (1-Ton)						
Stepside (LBx)	200	550	900	2100	3700	5300
Fleetside (LBx)	200	600	950	2150	3850	5500
6P (LBx)	200	550	900	2000	3600	5200
Panels/Vans (1/2-Ton)						
Panel	150	400	750	1650	3150	4500
Spt Van	200	600	950	2150	3850	5500
Beauville	200	600	1000	2200	4000	5700
Panels/Vans (3/4-Ton)						
Panel	150	400	750	1550	3050	4300
Spt Van	200	550	900	2100	3700	5300
Beauville	200	600	950	2150	3850	5500
Panels/Vans (1-Ton)						
Panel	150	350	750	1450	2900	4100
Spt Van	200	500	850	1950	3600	5100
Beauville	200	550	900	2100	3700	5300
Step Vans						
P10 Panel	150	350	750	1350	2800	4000
P20 Panel	150	300	750	1350	2700	3900
P30 Panel	150	300	700	1250	2650	3800

NOTE: 1955-up prices based on top of the line models.

1976
	6	5	4	3	2	1
LUV						
PU	125	200	600	1100	2300	3300
El Camino						
PU	200	600	950	2150	3850	5500
Cus PU	200	650	1050	2250	4200	6000
Blazer K10						
Blazer 2WD	200	650	1050	2250	4200	6000
Blazer 4WD	350	750	1200	2350	4900	7000

	6	5	4	3	2	1
C10 (1/2-Ton)						
Stepside (SBx)	200	650	1000	2200	4150	5900
Stepside (LBx)	200	650	1050	2250	4200	6000
Fleetside (SBx)	200	675	1050	2250	4300	6100
Fleetside (LBx)	200	675	1050	2250	4350	6200
Suburban	200	650	1050	2250	4200	6000
K10 - 4WD - (1/2-Ton)						
Stepside (SBx)	200	600	1000	2200	4000	5700
Stepside (LBx)	200	650	1000	2200	4100	5800
Fleetside (SBx)	200	650	1000	2200	4150	5900
Fleetside (LBx)	200	650	1050	2250	4200	6000
Suburban	200	650	1000	2200	4100	5800
C20 (3/4-Ton)						
Stepside (LBx)	200	600	950	2150	3850	5500
Fleetside (LBx)	200	600	1000	2200	4000	5700
6P (LBx)	200	550	900	2100	3700	5300
Suburban	200	600	950	2200	3900	5600
K20 - 4WD - (3/4-Ton)						
Stepside (LBx)	200	650	1000	2200	4100	5800
Fleetside (LBx)	200	650	1000	2200	4150	5900
6P (LBx)	200	600	950	2150	3850	5500
Suburban	200	650	1000	2200	4100	5800
C30 (1-Ton)						
Stepside (LBx)	200	550	900	2100	3700	5300
Fleetside (LBx)	200	600	950	2150	3850	5500
6P (LBx)	200	550	900	2000	3600	5200
Panels/Vans (1/2-Ton)						
Panel	150	400	750	1650	3150	4500
Spt Van	200	600	950	2150	3850	5500
Beauville	200	600	1000	2200	4000	5700
Panels/Vans (3/4-Ton)						
Panel	150	400	750	1550	3050	4300
Spt Van	200	550	900	2100	3700	5300
Beauville	200	600	950	2150	3850	5500
Panels/Vans (1-Ton)						
Panel	150	350	750	1450	2900	4100
Spt Van	200	500	850	1950	3600	5100
Beauville	200	550	900	2100	3700	5300
Step Vans						
P10 Steel Panel	150	350	750	1350	2800	4000
P20 Steel Panel	150	300	750	1350	2700	3900
P30 Steel Panel	150	300	700	1250	2650	3800

NOTE: 1955-up prices based on top of the line models.

1977
	6	5	4	3	2	1
LUV						
PU	100	150	450	1000	1900	2700
El Camino						
PU	200	550	900	2000	3600	5200
Cus PU	200	600	1000	2200	4000	5700
SS PU	350	725	1200	2350	4850	6900
Blazer K10						
Blazer 4WD	350	725	1150	2300	4700	6700
Chevy Van 10						
Panel	150	350	750	1450	3000	4200
Spt Van	200	550	900	2000	3600	5200
Beauville Spt Van	200	600	950	2150	3850	5500
Chevy Van 20						
Panel	150	350	750	1350	2800	4000
Spt Van	200	500	850	1900	3500	5000
Beauville Spt Van	200	550	900	2000	3600	5200
Chevy Van 30						
Panel	150	300	750	1350	2700	3900
Spt Van	200	500	850	1850	3350	4900
Beauville Spt Van	200	500	850	1950	3600	5100
Cube Van	150	300	700	1250	2650	3800
Step Vans						
P10	125	250	700	1150	2500	3600
P20	125	250	700	1150	2450	3500
P30	125	200	600	1100	2250	3200
C10 (1 2-Ton)						
Stepside (SBx)	200	600	950	2150	3850	5500
Stepside (LBx)	200	600	950	2200	3900	5600
Fleetside (SBx)	200	600	950	2200	3900	5600
Fleetside (LBx)	200	600	1000	2200	4000	5700
Suburban	200	650	1000	2200	4100	5800
C20 (3 4-Ton)						
Stepside PU	200	550	900	2000	3600	5200
Fleetside PU	200	550	900	2150	3800	5400
Bonus Cab PU	200	550	900	2100	3700	5300
Crew Cab PU	200	550	900	2000	3600	5200
Suburban	200	550	900	2150	3800	5400
C30 (1-Ton)						
Stepside PU	200	500	850	1900	3500	5000
Fleetside PU	200	550	900	2000	3600	5200
Bonus Cab PU	200	500	850	1950	3600	5100
Crew Cab PU	200	500	850	1900	3500	5000

NOTE: 1955-up prices based on top of the line models.
Add 5 percent for 4WD Pickups & Suburbans.

1978
	6	5	4	3	2	1
LUV						
PU	100	150	450	1000	1900	2700
LBx	100	175	525	1050	1950	2800
El Camino - (V-8)						
PU	200	550	900	2000	3600	5200
SS PU	200	600	1000	2200	4000	5700
Blazer - K10 - (V-8)						
Blazer 4WD	350	725	1150	2300	4700	6700
Chevy Van 10						
Panel	150	350	750	1450	3000	4200
Spt Van	200	550	900	2000	3600	5200
Beauville Spt Van	200	600	950	2150	3850	5500
Chevy Van 20						
Panel	150	350	750	1350	2800	4000
Spt Van	200	500	850	1900	3500	5000
Beauville Spt Van	200	550	900	2000	3600	5200
Chevy Van 30						
Panel	150	300	750	1350	2700	3900
Spt Van	200	500	850	1850	3350	4900
Beauville Spt Van	200	500	850	1950	3600	5100
Hi-Cube	150	300	700	1250	2650	3800
Step Vans						
P10	125	250	700	1150	2500	3600
P20	125	250	700	1150	2450	3500

	6	5	4	3	2	1
P30	125	200	600	1100	2250	3200
C10 (1/2-Ton)						
Stepside (SBx)	200	600	950	2150	3850	5500
Stepside (LBx)	200	600	950	2200	3900	5600
Fleetside (SBx)	200	600	950	2200	3900	5600
Fleetside (LBx)	200	600	1000	2200	4000	5700
Suburban	200	650	1000	2200	4100	5800
C20 (3/4-Ton)						
Stepside PU	200	550	900	2000	3600	5200
Fleetside PU	200	550	900	2150	3800	5400
Bonus Cab PU	200	550	900	2100	3700	5300
Crew Cab PU	200	550	900	2000	3600	5200
Suburban	200	550	900	2150	3800	5400
C30 (1-Ton)						
Stepside PU	200	500	850	1900	3500	5000
Fleetside PU	200	550	900	2000	3600	5200
Bonus Cab PU	200	500	850	1950	3600	5100
Crew Cab PU	200	500	850	1900	3500	5000
"Big Dooley"	200	600	1000	2200	4000	5700

NOTE: 1955-up prices based on top of the line models.
Add 5 percent for 4WD models.

1979

	6	5	4	3	2	1
LUV						
PU	100	150	450	1000	1900	2700
LBx	100	175	525	1050	1950	2800
El Camino - (V-8)						
PU	200	550	900	2000	3600	5200
Cus PU	200	600	1000	2200	4000	5700
SS PU	200	650	1000	2200	4100	5800
Blazer - K10 - (V-8)						
Blazer 4WD	350	725	1150	2300	4700	6700
Chevy Van 10						
Panel	150	350	750	1450	3000	4200
Spt Van	200	550	900	2000	3600	5200
Beauville Spt Van	200	600	950	2150	3850	5500
Chevy Van 20						
Panel	150	350	750	1350	2800	4000
Spt Van	200	500	850	1900	3500	5000
Beauville Spt Van	200	550	900	2000	3600	5200
Caravan	200	600	1000	2200	4000	5700
Chevy Van 30						
Panel	150	300	750	1350	2700	3900
Spt Van	200	500	850	1850	3350	4900
Beauville Spt Van	200	500	850	1950	3600	5100
Hi-Cube Van	150	300	700	1250	2650	3800
Step Vans						
P10	125	250	700	1150	2500	3600
P20	125	250	700	1150	2450	3500
P30	125	200	600	1100	2250	3200
C10 - (V-8)						
Stepside (SBx)	200	600	950	2150	3850	5500
Stepside (LBx)	200	600	950	2200	3900	5600
Fleetside (SBx)	200	600	950	2200	3900	5600
Fleetside (LBx)	200	600	1000	2200	4000	5700
Suburban	200	650	1000	2200	4100	5800
C20 - (V-8)						
Stepside PU	200	550	900	2000	3600	5200
Fleetside PU	200	550	900	2150	3800	5400
Bonus Cab PU	200	550	900	2100	3700	5300
Crew Cab PU	200	550	900	2000	3600	5200
Suburban	200	550	900	2150	3800	5400
C30 - (V-8)						
Stepside PU	200	500	850	1900	3500	5000
Fleetside PU	200	550	900	2000	3600	5200
Bonus Cab PU	200	500	850	1950	3600	5100
Crew Cab PU	200	500	850	1900	3500	5000
"Big Dooley"	200	650	1000	2200	4100	5800

NOTE: 1955-up prices based on top of the line models.
Add 5 percent for 4WD models.

1980

	6	5	4	3	2	1
LUV						
PU	100	175	525	1050	1950	2800
LBx PU	100	175	525	1050	2050	2900
El Camino - (1/2-Ton) - (117" wb)						
PU	200	550	900	2100	3700	5300
Cus PU	200	650	1000	2200	4100	5800
SS PU	200	650	1000	2200	4150	5900
Blazer - K10						
Blazer 4WD	350	725	1200	2350	4800	6800
G10 Chevy Van - (1/2-Ton) - (110" or 125" wb)						
Panel	150	350	750	1450	3000	4200
Spt Van	200	550	900	2000	3600	5200
Beauville Spt Van	200	600	950	2150	3850	5500
G20 Chevy Van - (3/4-Ton) - (110" or 125" wb)						
Panel	150	350	750	1350	2800	4000
Spt Van	200	500	850	1900	3500	5000
Beauville Spt Van	200	550	900	2000	3600	5200
Nomad	200	600	950	2150	3850	5500
G30 Chevy Van - (1/2-Ton) - (125" or 146" wb)						
Panel	150	300	750	1350	2700	3900
Spt Van	200	500	850	1850	3350	4900
Beauville Spt Van	200	500	850	1950	3600	5100
Hi-Cube Van	150	300	700	1250	2650	3800
C10 - (1/2-Ton) - (117" or 131" wb)						
Stepside SBx PU	200	600	950	2200	3900	5600
Stepside LBx PU	200	600	1000	2200	4000	5700
Fleetside SBx PU	200	600	1000	2200	4000	5700
Fleetside LBx PU	200	650	1000	2200	4100	5800
Suburban	200	650	1000	2200	4150	5900
C20 - (3/4-Ton) - (131" or 164" wb)						
Stepside PU	200	550	900	2100	3700	5300
Fleetside PU	200	600	950	2150	3850	5500
Bonus Cab PU	200	550	900	2150	3800	5400
Crew Cab PU	200	550	900	2100	3700	5300
Suburban	200	600	950	2150	3850	5500
C30 - (1-Ton) - (131" or 164" wb)						
Stepside PU	200	500	850	1900	3500	5000
Fleetside PU	200	550	900	2000	3600	5200
Bonus Cab PU	200	500	850	1950	3600	5100
Crew Cab PU	200	500	850	1900	3500	5000
"Big Dooley	200	600	950	2150	3850	5500
Step- Vans (V-8)						
Step-Van (1/2-Ton)	125	250	700	1150	2500	3600
Step-Van (3/4-Ton)	125	250	700	1150	2450	3500
Step-Van (1-Ton)	125	200	600	1100	2250	3200

1981

	6	5	4	3	2	1
Luv - (1/2-Ton) - (104.3" or 117.9" wb)						
PU SBx	100	175	525	1050	2050	2900
PU LBx	100	175	525	1050	2100	3000
El Camino - (1/2-Ton) - (117" wb)						
PU	200	650	1000	2200	4100	5800
SS PU	200	650	1000	2200	4150	5900
Blazer K10 - (1/2-Ton) - (106.5" wb)						
Blazer 4WD	350	750	1200	2350	4900	7000
G10 Chevy Van - (1/2-Ton) - (110" or 125" wb)						
Chevy Van	150	400	750	1550	3050	4300
Spt Van	200	550	900	2000	3600	5200
Bonaventure	200	550	900	2150	3800	5400
Beauville	200	600	950	2200	3900	5600
G20 Chevy Van - (1/2-Ton) - (110" or 125" wb)						
Chevy Van	150	350	750	1450	3000	4200
Spt Van	200	500	850	1950	3600	5100
Bonaventure	200	550	900	2100	3700	5300
Beauville	200	600	950	2150	3850	5500
Nomad	200	600	950	2150	3850	5500
Step Van	150	300	750	1350	2700	3900
G30 Chevy Van - (1-Ton) - (125" or 146" wb)						
Chevy Van	150	350	750	1450	2900	4100
Spt Van	200	500	850	1900	3500	5000
Bonaventure	200	550	900	2000	3600	5200
Beauville	200	550	900	2150	3800	5400
Hi Cube 10	200	500	850	1850	3350	4900
Hi Cube 12	200	500	850	1850	3350	4900
Step Van	150	350	750	1350	2800	4000
C10 - (1/2-Ton) - (117" or 131" wb)						
Stepside PU SBx	200	650	1000	2200	4100	5800
Stepside PU LBx	200	600	1000	2200	4000	5700
Fleetside PU SBx	200	650	1000	2200	4150	5900
Fleetside PU LBx	200	650	1050	2250	4200	6000
Suburban	200	675	1050	2250	4350	6200
C20 - (3/4-Ton) - (131" or 164" wb)						
Stepside PU LBx	200	600	1000	2200	4000	5700
Fleetside PU LBx	200	650	1000	2200	4100	5800
Fleetside PU Bonus Cab LBx	200	650	1050	2250	4200	6000
Fleetside PU Crew Cab LBx	200	650	1000	2200	4150	5900
Suburban	200	675	1050	2250	4350	6200
C30 - (1-Ton) - (131" or 164" wb)						
Stepside PU LBx	200	600	950	2200	3900	5600
Fleetside PU LBx	200	600	1000	2200	4000	5700
Fleetside PU Bonus Cab LBx	200	650	1000	2200	4100	5800
Fleetside PU Crew Cab LBx	200	600	1000	2200	4000	5700

NOTE: Add 15 percent for 4WD.

1982

	6	5	4	3	2	1
Luv - (1/2-Ton) - (104.3" or 117.9" wb)						
PU SBx	75	100	400	750	1350	1900
PU LBx	75	100	425	800	1400	2000
El Camino - (1/2-Ton) - (117" wb)						
PU	150	450	800	1800	3300	4800
SS PU	200	500	850	1850	3350	4900
Blazer K10 - (1/2-Ton) - (106.5" wb)						
HdTp 4WD	200	650	1050	2250	4200	6000
G10 Chevy Van - (1/2-Ton) - (110" or 125" wb)						
Chevy Van	125	200	600	1100	2300	3300
Spt Van	150	350	750	1450	3000	4200
Bonaventure	150	400	750	1600	3100	4400
Beauville	150	450	750	1700	3200	4600
G20 Chevy Van - (3/4-Ton) - (110" or 125" wb)						
Chevy Van	125	200	600	1100	2250	3200
Spt Van	125	250	700	1150	2450	3500
Bonaventure	150	400	750	1550	3050	4300
Beauville	150	400	750	1650	3150	4500
Step-Van	100	175	525	1050	2050	2900
G30 Step Van - (1-Ton) - (125" or 146" wb)						
Chevy Van	125	200	600	1100	2200	3100
Spt Van	150	350	750	1350	2800	4000
Bonaventure	150	350	750	1450	3000	4200
Beauville	150	400	750	1600	3100	4400
Hi Cube 10	125	250	700	1150	2400	3400
Hi Cube 12	125	250	700	1150	2400	3400
Step-Van	100	175	525	1050	2100	3000
S10 - (1/2-Ton) - (108" or 118" wb)						
Fleetside PU SBx	100	125	475	900	1600	2300
Fleetside PU LBx	100	125	500	950	1700	2400
C10 - (1/2-Ton) - (117" or 131" wb)						
Stepside PU SBx	150	450	800	1800	3300	4800
Fleetside PU SBx	200	500	850	1850	3350	4900
Fleetside PU LBx	150	450	750	1700	3200	4600
Suburban	200	550	900	2100	3700	5300
C20 - (3/4-Ton) - (131" or 164" wb)						
Stepside PU LBx	150	450	800	1750	3250	4700
Fleetside PU LBx	150	450	800	1800	3300	4800
Fleetside PU Bonus Cab LBx	200	500	850	1950	3600	5100
Fleetside PU Crew Cab LBx	150	450	800	1750	3250	4700
Suburban	200	550	900	2100	3700	5300
C30 - (1-Ton) - (131" or 164" wb)						
Stepside PU LBx	150	400	750	1650	3150	4500
Fleetside PU LBx	150	450	750	1700	3200	4600
Fleetside PU Bonus Cab LBx	200	500	850	1850	3350	4900
Fleetside PU Crew Cab LBx	150	450	800	1750	3250	4700

NOTE: Add 15 percent for 4WD.

1983

	6	5	4	3	2	1
El Camino - (1/2-Ton) - (117" wb)						
PU	150	450	800	1800	3300	4800
SS PU	200	500	850	1850	3350	4900
S10 - (1/2-Ton) - (100.5" wb)						
Blazer 2WD	100	175	525	1050	2100	3000
Blazer 4WD	150	300	750	1350	2700	3900
Blazer K10 - (1/2-Ton) - (106.5" wb)						
Blazer 4WD	200	650	1050	2250	4200	6000
G10 Chevy Van - (1/2-Ton) - (110" or 125" wb)						
Chevy Van	125	200	600	1100	2300	3300
Spt Van	150	350	750	1450	3000	4200
Bonaventure	150	400	750	1600	3100	4400
Beauville	150	450	750	1700	3200	4600
G20 Chevy Van - (3/4-Ton) - (110" or 125" wb)						
Chevy Van	125	200	600	1100	2250	3200
Spt Van	150	350	750	1450	2900	4100
Bonaventure	150	400	750	1550	3050	4300
Beauville	150	400	750	1650	3150	4500
Step Van	100	150	450	1000	1900	2700

	6	5	4	3	2	1
G30 Chevy Van - (1-Ton) - (125" or 146" wb)						
Chevy Van	125	200	600	1100	2200	3100
Spt Van	150	350	750	1350	2800	4000
Bonaventure	150	350	750	1450	3000	4200
Beauville	150	400	750	1600	3100	4400
Hi Cube 10	125	200	600	1100	2250	3200
Hi Cube 12	125	200	600	1100	2250	3200
Step Van	100	150	450	1000	1900	2700
			Pickup			
S10 - (1/2-Ton) - (108" or 122" wb)						
Fleetside PU SBx	100	125	450	900	1550	2200
Fleetside PU LBx	100	125	475	900	1600	2300
Fleetside PU Ext Cab	100	150	450	1000	1750	2500
C10 - (1/2-Ton) - (117" or 131" wb)						
Stepside PU SBx	150	450	800	1800	3300	4800
Fleetside PU SBx	200	500	850	1850	3350	4900
Fleetside PU LBx	150	450	750	1700	3200	4600
Suburban	200	550	900	2100	3700	5300
C20 - (3/4-Ton) - (131" or 164" wb)						
Stepside PU LBx	150	450	800	1750	3250	4700
Fleetside PU LBx	150	450	800	1800	3300	4800
Fleetside PU Bonus Cab LBx	200	500	850	1950	3600	5100
Fleetside PU Crew Cab LBx	150	450	750	1700	3200	4600
Suburban	200	550	900	2100	3700	5300
C30 - (1-Ton) - (131" or 164" wb)						
Stepside PU LBx	150	400	750	1650	3150	4500
Fleetside PU LBx	150	450	750	1700	3200	4600
Fleetside PU Bonus Cab LBx	150	450	800	1800	3300	4800
Fleetside PU Crew Cab LBx	150	450	800	1750	3250	4700

NOTE: Add 15 percent for 4WD.

1984

	6	5	4	3	2	1
El Camino - (1/2-Ton) - (117" wb)						
PU	200	550	900	2150	3800	5400
SS PU	200	600	950	2200	3900	5600
S10 - (1/2-Ton) - (100.5" wb)						
Blazer 2WD	150	300	750	1350	2700	3900
Blazer 4WD	200	500	850	1850	3350	4900
K10 Blazer - (1/2-Ton) - (106.5" wb)						
Blazer 4WD	350	700	1150	2300	4600	6600
G10 Chevy Van - (1/2-Ton) - (110" or 125" wb)						
Chevy Van	150	300	750	1350	2700	3900
Spt Van	150	450	800	1750	3250	4700
Bonaventure	200	500	850	1850	3350	4900
Beauville	200	500	850	1950	3600	5100
G20 Chevy Van - (3/4-Ton) - (110" or 125" wb)						
Chevy Van	150	300	700	1250	2650	3800
Spt Van	150	450	750	1700	3200	4600
Bonaventure	150	450	800	1800	3300	4800
Beauville	200	500	850	1900	3500	5000
Step-Van	125	200	600	1100	2250	3200
G30 Chevy Van - (1/2-Ton) - (125" or 146" wb)						
Chevy Van	150	300	700	1250	2600	3700
Spt Van	150	400	750	1650	3150	4500
Bonaventure	150	450	800	1750	3250	4700
Beauville	200	500	850	1850	3350	4900
Hi Cube 10	150	300	700	1250	2600	3700
Hi Cube 12	150	300	700	1250	2600	3700
Step-Van	125	200	600	1100	2250	3200
S10 - (1/2-Ton) - (108" or 118" wb)						
Fleetside PU SBx	100	175	525	1050	1950	2800
Fleetside PU LBx	100	175	525	1050	2050	2900
Fleetside PU Ext Cab	125	200	600	1100	2200	3100
C10 - (1/2-Ton) - (117" or 131" wb)						
Stepside PU SBx	200	550	900	2150	3800	5400
Stepside PU LBx	200	600	950	2150	3850	5500
Fleetside PU LBx	200	550	900	2100	3700	5300
Suburban	200	650	1000	2200	4150	5900
C20 - (3/4-Ton) - (131" or 164" wb)						
Stepside PU LBx	200	550	900	2100	3700	5300
Fleetside PU LBx	200	550	900	2150	3800	5400
Fleetside PU Bonus Cab LBx	200	600	1000	2200	4000	5700
Fleetside PU Crew Cab LBx	200	600	950	2200	3900	5600
Suburban	200	650	1000	2200	4150	5900
C30 - (1-Ton) - (131" or 164" wb)						
Stepside PU LBx	200	500	850	1950	3600	5100
FLeetside PU LBx	200	550	900	2000	3600	5200
FLeetside PU Bonus Cab LBx	200	550	900	2100	3700	5300
Fleetside PU Crew Cab LBx	200	550	900	2000	3600	5200

NOTE: Add 15 percent for 4WD.

1985

	6	5	4	3	2	1
El Camino - (1/2-Ton) - (117" wb)						
PU	200	600	950	2200	3900	5600
SS PU	200	650	1000	2200	4100	5800
S10 Blazer - (1/2-Ton) - (100.5" wb)						
Blazer 2WD	200	500	850	1850	3350	4900
Blazer 4WD	200	650	1000	2200	4150	5900
K10 Blazer - (1/2-Ton) - (106.5" wb)						
Blazer 4WD	350	750	1200	2350	4900	7000
Astro - (1/2-Ton) - (111" wb)						
Cargo Van	150	350	750	1350	2800	4000
Van	150	450	750	1700	3200	4600
CS Van	150	450	800	1800	3300	4800
CL Van	200	500	850	1900	3500	5000
G10 Chevy Van - (1/2-Ton) - (110" or 125" wb)						
Chevy Van	150	400	750	1650	3150	4500
Spt Van	200	500	850	1850	3350	4900
Bonaventure	200	500	850	1950	3600	5100
Beauville	200	550	900	2100	3700	5300
G20 Chevy Van - (3/4-Ton) - (110" or 125" wb)						
Chevy Van	150	350	750	1450	2900	4100
Spt Van	150	450	800	1800	3300	4800
Bonaventure	200	500	850	1900	3500	5000
Beauville	200	550	900	2000	3600	5200
Nomad	200	500	850	1900	3500	5000
Step-Van	150	250	700	1150	2400	3400
G30 Chevy Van - (1-Ton) - (125" or 146" wb)						
Chevy Van	150	300	700	1250	2650	3800
Spt Van	150	350	750	1450	3000	4200
Bonaventure	150	400	750	1600	3100	4400
Beauville	200	500	850	1950	3600	5100
Hi Cube 10	150	300	700	1250	2650	3800
Hi Cube 12	150	300	700	1250	2650	3800
Step-Van	125	200	600	1100	2250	3200

	6	5	4	3	2	1
S10 - (1/2-Ton) - (108.3" or 123" wb)						
Fleetside PU SBx	125	250	700	1150	2450	3500
Fleetside PU LBx	125	250	700	1150	2400	3400
Fleetside PU Ext Cab	150	300	700	1250	2650	3800
C10 - (1/2-Ton) - (117" or 131" wb)						
Stepside PU SBx	200	500	850	1950	3600	5100
Fleetside PU SBx	200	550	900	2000	3600	5200
Fleetside PU LBx	200	500	850	1900	3500	5000
Suburban	200	675	1100	2250	4400	6300
C20 - (3/4-Ton) - (131" or 164" wb)						
Stepside PU LBx	200	500	850	1950	3600	5100
Fleetside PU LBx	200	550	900	2000	3600	5200
Fleetside PU Bonus Cab LBx	200	600	1000	2200	4000	5700
Fleetside PU Crew Cab LBx	200	650	1000	2200	4150	5900
Suburban	350	700	1100	2300	4500	6400
C30 - (1-Ton) - (131" or 164" wb)						
Stepside PU LBx	200	500	850	1900	3500	5000
Fleetside PU LBx	200	500	850	1950	3600	5100
Fleetside PU Bonus Cab LBx	200	500	850	1950	3600	5100
Fleetside PU Crew Cab LBx	200	650	1000	2200	4100	5800

NOTE: Add 15 percent for 4WD.

1986

	6	5	4	3	2	1
El Camino - (1/2-Ton) - (117" wb)						
PU	200	550	900	2150	3800	5400
SS PU	200	650	1000	2200	4100	5800
S10 Blazer - (1/2-Ton) - (100.5" wb)						
Blazer 2WD	200	600	950	2150	3850	5500
Blazer 4WD	350	700	1150	2300	4550	6500
K10 Blazer - (1/2-Ton) - (106.5" wb)						
Blazer 4WD	350	800	1450	2750	5600	8000
Astro - (1/2-Ton) - (111" wb)						
Cargo Van	150	400	750	1550	3050	4300
Van	200	600	950	2200	3900	5600
CS Van	200	650	1000	2200	4100	5800
CL Van	200	650	1050	2250	4200	6000
G10 Van - (1/2-Ton) - (110" or 125" wb)						
Chevy Van	200	500	850	1850	3350	4900
Short Van	200	650	1000	2200	4150	5900
Bonaventure	200	675	1050	2250	4300	6100
Beauville	200	675	1100	2250	4400	6300
G20 Van - (3/4-Ton) - (110" or 125" wb)						
Chevy Van	150	450	800	1800	3300	4800
Spt Van	200	650	1000	2200	4100	5800
Bonaventure	200	650	1050	2250	4200	6000
Beauville	200	675	1050	2250	4350	6200
Step-Van	150	350	750	1450	2900	4100
G30 Van - (1-Ton) - (125" wb)						
Chevy Van	150	450	800	1750	3250	4700
Spt Van	200	600	1000	2200	4000	5700
Bonaventure	200	650	1000	2200	4150	5900
Beauville	350	750	1200	2350	4900	7000
Hi Cube 10	200	600	950	2150	3850	5500
Hi Cube 12	200	600	950	2150	3850	5500
Step-Van	200	500	850	1900	3500	5000
S10 - (1/2-Ton) - (108" or 123" wb)						
Fleetside PU SBx	150	400	750	1650	3150	4500
Fleetside PU LBx	150	450	750	1700	3200	4600
Fleetside PU Ext Cab	200	500	850	1850	3350	4900
C10 - (1/2-Ton) - (117.5" or 131.5" wb)						
Stepside PU SBx	200	600	1000	2200	4000	5700
Fleetside PU SBx	200	650	1000	2200	4100	5800
Fleetside PU LBx	200	600	950	2200	3900	5600
Suburban	350	750	1200	2350	4900	7000
C20 - (3/4-Ton) - (131.5" or 164.5" wb)						
Stepside PU LBx	200	650	1000	2200	4100	5800
Fleetside PU LBx	200	650	1000	2200	4150	5900
Fleetside PU Bonus Cab LBx	200	675	1050	2250	4350	6200
Fleetside PU Crew Cab LBx	350	700	1100	2300	4500	6400
Suburban	350	700	1100	2300	4500	6400
C30 - (1-Ton) - (131.5" or 164.5" wb)						
Stepside PU LBx	200	600	1000	2200	4000	5700
Fleetside PU LBx	200	650	1000	2200	4100	5800
Fleetside PU Bonus Cab LBx	200	675	1050	2250	4300	6100
Fleetside PU Crew Cab LBx	200	675	1100	2250	4400	6300

NOTE: Add 15 percent for 4WD.

CROSLEY

	6	5	4	3	2	1
1940						
Crosley Commercial						
Panel Dly	125	250	700	1150	2450	3500
1941						
Crosley Commercial						
PU Dly	125	250	700	1150	2400	3400
Parkway Dly	125	250	700	1150	2500	3600
Panel Dly	125	250	700	1150	2450	3500
1942						
Crosley Commercial						
PU Dly	125	250	700	1150	2400	3400
Parkway Dly	125	250	700	1150	2500	3600
Panel Dly	125	250	700	1150	2450	3500
1947						
Crosley Commercial						
PU	125	250	700	1150	2400	3400
1948						
Crosley Commercial						
PU	125	250	700	1150	2400	3400
Panel	100	175	525	1050	2100	3000
1949						
Series CD						
PU	125	250	700	1150	2450	3500
Panel	125	250	700	1150	2500	3600
1950						
Crosley Commercial Series CD						
PU	125	250	700	1150	2450	3500
Panel	125	250	700	1150	2500	3600
Farm-O-Road	150	300	700	1250	2600	3700

1951

Crosley Commercial Series CD

	6	5	4	3	2	1
PU	125	250	700	1150	2450	3500
Panel	125	250	700	1150	2500	3600
Farm-O-Road	150	300	700	1250	2600	3700

1952

Crosley Commercial Series CD

	6	5	4	3	2	1
PU	125	250	700	1150	2450	3500
Panel	125	250	700	1150	2500	3600
Farm-O-Road	150	300	700	1250	2600	3700

1959-1962

Crofton Bug Series

	6	5	4	3	2	1
Bug Utl	125	250	700	1150	2500	3600
Brawny Bug Utl	150	300	750	1350	2700	3900

DODGE

1917

Commercial Car - (1/2-Ton)

	6	5	4	3	2	1
Screenside	200	650	1000	2200	4150	5900

1918

Commercial/Business Car - (1/2-Ton)

	6	5	4	3	2	1
Screenside	200	650	1000	2200	4150	5900
Panel	200	650	1000	2200	4100	5800

1919

Commercial/Business Car - (1/2-Ton)

	6	5	4	3	2	1
Screenside	200	650	1000	2200	4100	5800
Panel	200	600	1000	2200	4000	5700

1920

Commercial/Business Car - (1/2-Ton)

	6	5	4	3	2	1
Screenside	200	600	950	2200	3900	5600
Panel	200	600	950	2150	3850	5500

1921

Commercial/Business Car - (1/2-Ton)

	6	5	4	3	2	1
Screenside	200	600	1000	2200	4000	5700
Panel	200	600	950	2200	3900	5600

1922

Commercial/Business Car - (1/2-Ton)

	6	5	4	3	2	1
Screenside	200	600	1000	2200	4000	5700
Panel	200	600	950	2200	3900	5600

1923

Commercial/Business Car - (3/4-Ton)

	6	5	4	3	2	1
Screenside	200	650	1000	2200	4100	5800
Panel	200	600	1000	2200	4000	5700

1924

Commercial/Business Car - (3/4-Ton)

	6	5	4	3	2	1
Screenside	200	650	1000	2200	4100	5800
Panel	200	600	1000	2200	4000	5700

1925

Commercial/Business Car - (3/4-Ton)

	6	5	4	3	2	1
Screenside	200	650	1000	2200	4100	5800
Panel	200	600	1000	2200	4000	5700

1926

Commercial/Business Car - (3/4-Ton) - (116" wb)

	6	5	4	3	2	1
Screenside	200	600	1000	2200	4000	5700
Panel (72" wb)	200	600	950	2150	3850	5500

Business Car - (3/4-Ton) - (140" wb)

	6	5	4	3	2	1
Panel (96" wb)	200	550	900	2150	3800	5400

1927

Series DC - (3/4-Ton) - (116" wb)

	6	5	4	3	2	1
Exp	200	600	1000	2200	4000	5700
Canopy	200	600	950	2200	3900	5600
Screen	200	600	1000	2200	4000	5700
Panel	200	550	900	2100	3700	5300

Series BD - (1-Ton) - (126" wb)

	6	5	4	3	2	1
Exp	200	500	850	1900	3500	5000
Farm Box	150	450	750	1700	3200	4600
Canopy	200	500	850	1850	3350	4900
Panel	150	450	800	1800	3300	4800
Stake	150	450	750	1700	3200	4600

Series ID - (1-Ton) - (137" wb)

	6	5	4	3	2	1
Exp	200	500	850	1850	3350	4900
Canopy	150	450	800	1800	3300	4800
Panel	150	450	800	1750	3250	4700

1928-1929

Series SE - (1/2-Ton)

	6	5	4	3	2	1
Panel	200	550	900	2150	3800	5400

Series DA-120 - (3/4-Ton)

	6	5	4	3	2	1
PU Exp	200	600	950	2150	3850	5500
Canopy Dly	200	550	900	2100	3700	5300
Screen Dly	200	550	900	2150	3800	5400
Panel Dly	200	550	900	2000	3600	5200
Platform	200	500	850	1900	3500	5000
Stake	200	500	850	1850	3350	4900

Series DA-130 - (1-Ton)

	6	5	4	3	2	1
PU Exp	200	500	850	1900	3500	5000
Farm	150	400	750	1650	3150	4500
Canopy Dly	150	450	800	1800	3300	4800
Screen Dly	200	500	850	1850	3350	4900
Panel Dly	150	450	800	1750	3250	4700
Platform	150	400	750	1650	3150	4500
Stake	150	400	750	1600	3100	4400

Series DA-140 - (1-Ton)

	6	5	4	3	2	1
PU Exp	200	500	850	1900	3500	5000
Canopy Dly	150	450	800	1750	3250	4700
Screen Dly	150	450	800	1800	3300	4800
Panel Dly	150	450	750	1700	3200	4600
Side Door Panel	150	400	750	1650	3150	4500
Carryall	150	450	750	1700	3200	4600
Platform	150	400	750	1600	3100	4400
Stake	150	400	750	1600	3100	4400

1929

Merchant's Exp - (1/2-Ton) - (109" wb)

	6	5	4	3	2	1
Panel	200	600	950	2150	3850	5500

1930

Series UI-A-109 - (1/2-Ton)

	6	5	4	3	2	1
PU	200	650	1000	2200	4100	5800
Canopy	200	550	900	2100	3700	5300
Screen	200	550	900	2150	3800	5400
Panel	200	550	900	2000	3600	5200

Series UI-B-124 - (4-cyl) - (3/4-Ton)

	6	5	4	3	2	1
PU	200	500	850	1900	3500	5000
Canopy	150	450	800	1800	3300	4800
Screen	200	500	850	1850	3350	4900
Panel	150	450	800	1750	3250	4700
Platform	150	350	750	1350	2800	4000
Stake	150	350	750	1450	3000	4200

Series DA1-B-124 - (6-cyl) - (3/4-Ton) - Note 1

Series UI-C-133 - (4-cyl) - (1-Ton)

	6	5	4	3	2	1
Farm	150	350	750	1450	2900	4100
Exp	200	500	850	1850	3350	4900
Canopy	150	450	800	1750	3250	4700
Screen	150	450	800	1800	3300	4800
Panel	150	450	750	1700	3200	4600
Platform	150	300	750	1350	2700	3900
Stake	150	350	750	1450	2900	4100

Series DA1-C-133 - (6-cyl) - (1-Ton) - Note 2

Series DA1-C-140 - (1-Ton) - (140" wb)

	6	5	4	3	2	1
Exp	150	350	750	1450	2900	4100
Canopy	150	450	800	1750	3250	4700
Screen	150	450	800	1800	3300	4800
Panel	150	450	750	1700	3200	4600
Side Door Panel	150	400	750	1650	3150	4500
Carryall	150	450	800	1800	3300	4800
Platform	150	300	750	1350	2700	3900
Stake	150	350	750	1450	2900	4100

NOTE 1: For 6-cyl. models, add 5 percent from figure given for equivalent 4-cyl. (UI-B-124).
NOTE 2: For 6-cyl. models, add 5 percent from figure given for equivalent 4-cyl. (UI-C-133).

1931

Series UF-10 - (4-cyl) - (1/2-Ton)

	6	5	4	3	2	1
PU	200	675	1050	2250	4300	6100
Canopy	200	600	950	2200	3900	5600
Screen	200	600	1000	2200	4000	5700
Panel	200	600	950	2150	3850	5500

Series F-10 - (6-cyl) - (1/2-Ton) - Note 1

Series UI-B-124 - (4-cyl) - (3/4-Ton)

	6	5	4	3	2	1
PU	200	500	850	1900	3500	5000
Canopy	150	450	800	1800	3300	4800
Screen	200	500	850	1850	3350	4900
Panel	150	450	800	1750	3250	4700
Platform	150	350	750	1350	2800	4000
Stake	150	350	750	1450	3000	4200

Series DA1-B-124 - (6-cyl) - (3/4-Ton) - Note 2

Series UI-C-133 - (4-cyl) - (1-Ton)

	6	5	4	3	2	1
Exp	200	500	850	1850	3350	4900
Farm	150	350	750	1450	2900	4100
Canopy	150	450	800	1750	3250	4700
Screen	150	450	800	1800	3300	4800
Panel	150	450	750	1700	3200	4600
Platform	150	300	750	1350	2700	3900
Stake	150	350	750	1450	2900	4100

Series DA1-C-133 - (6 cyl) - (1 Ton) - Note 3

NOTE 1: For 6-cyl. model F-10, add 5 percent from figure given for equivalent 4-cyl. (UF-10).
NOTE 2: For 6-cyl. model DA1-B-124, add 5 percent from figure given for equivalent 4-cyl. (UI-B-124).
NOTE 3: For 6-cyl. model DA1-C-133, add 5 percent from figure given for equivalent 4-cyl. (UI-C-133).

1932

Series UF-10 - (4-cyl) - (1/2-Ton)

	6	5	4	3	2	1
PU	200	650	1050	2250	4200	6000
Canopy	200	600	950	2200	3900	5600
Screen	200	600	1000	2200	4000	5700
Panel	200	600	950	2150	3850	5500

Series F-10 - (6-cyl) - (1/2-Ton) - Note 1

Series UI-B-124 - (4-cyl) - (3/4-Ton)

	6	5	4	3	2	1
PU	200	500	850	1900	3500	5000
Canopy	150	450	800	1800	3300	4800
Screen	200	500	850	1850	3350	4900
Panel	150	450	800	1750	3250	4700
Platform	150	350	750	1350	2800	4000
Stake	150	350	750	1450	3000	4200

Series DA1-B-124 - (6-cyl) - (3/4-Ton) - Note 2

Series UI-C-133 - (4-cyl) - (1-Ton)

	6	5	4	3	2	1
Exp	200	500	850	1850	3350	4900
Farm	150	350	750	1450	2900	4100
Canopy	150	450	800	1750	3250	4700
Screen	150	450	800	1800	3300	4800
Panel	150	450	750	1700	3200	4600
Platform	150	300	750	1350	2700	3900
Stake	150	350	750	1450	2900	4100

Series DA1-C-133 - (6-cyl) - (1-Ton) - Note 3

NOTE 1: For 6-cyl. model F-10, add 5 percent from figure given for equivalent 4-cyl. (UF-10).
NOTE 2: For 6-cyl. model DA1-B-124, add 5 percent from figure given for equivalent 4-cyl. (UI-B-124).
NOTE 3: For 6-cyl. model DA1-C-133, add 5 percent from figure given for equivalent 4-cyl. (UI-C-133).

1933

Series HC - (1/2-Ton) - (111-1/4" wb)

	6	5	4	3	2	1
PU	200	650	1050	2250	4200	6000
Canopy	200	600	950	2200	3900	5600
Comm Sed	200	600	1000	2200	4000	5700
Panel	200	600	950	2150	3850	5500

Series HCL - (1/2-Ton) - (119" wb)

	6	5	4	3	2	1
Panel	200	550	900	2150	3800	5400

Series UF-10 - (1/2-Ton) - (109" wb)

	6	5	4	3	2	1
PU	200	650	1000	2200	4150	5900
Canopy	200	600	1000	2200	4000	5700
Screen	200	650	1000	2200	4100	5800
Panel	200	600	950	2200	3900	5600

Series F-10 - (1/2-Ton) - (109" wb) - Note 1

Series H-20 - (3/4 - 1 Ton) - (131" wb)

	6	5	4	3	2	1
Panel	200	550	900	2100	3700	5300

Series UG-20 - (3/4 - 1 Ton) - (131" wb)

	6	5	4	3	2	1
PU	200	600	950	2150	3850	5500
Canopy	200	550	900	2150	3800	5400
Sed Dly	200	600	1000	2200	4000	5700
Panel	200	550	900	2000	3600	5200

Series G-20 - (3/4 or 1 Ton) - (131" wb) - Note 2

NOTE 1: For 6-cyl. model F-10, add 5 percent to figure given for equivalent 4-cyl. (UF-10).
NOTE 2: For 6-cyl. model G-20, add 5 percent to figure given for equivalent 4-cyl. (UG-20).

1934

Series KC - (1/2-Ton) - (111-1/4" wb)

	6	5	4	3	2	1
PU	200	650	1050	2250	4200	6000
Canopy	200	600	950	2200	3900	5600
Comm Sed	200	600	1000	2200	4000	5700
Panel	200	600	950	2150	3850	5500

	6	5	4	3	2	1
Series KCL - (1/2-Ton) - (119" wb)						
Panel	200	550	900	2150	3800	5400
Series K-20 - (3/4-Ton) - (131" wb)						
PU	200	650	1000	2200	4150	5900
Canopy	200	600	1000	2200	4000	5700
Screen	200	650	1000	2200	4100	5800
Panel	200	600	950	2200	3900	5600
Series K-20X - (1-Ton) - (131" wb)						
PU	200	600	950	2150	3850	5500
Canopy	200	550	900	2150	3800	5400
Screen	200	600	950	2150	3850	5500
Panel	200	550	900	2100	3700	5300
Series K-30 - (1-Ton) - (131" wb)						
PU	200	600	950	2150	3850	5500
Canopy	200	550	900	2150	3800	5400
Screen	200	600	950	2150	3850	5500
Panel	200	550	900	2100	3700	5300

1935

	6	5	4	3	2	1
Series KC - (1/2-Ton) - (111-1/4" wb)						
PU	200	650	1050	2250	4200	6000
Canopy	200	600	950	2200	3900	5600
Screen	200	600	1000	2200	4000	5700
Comm Sed	200	600	950	2150	3850	5500
Suburban Sed	200	650	1000	2200	4150	5900
Series KCL - (1/2-Ton) - (119" wb)						
Panel	200	650	1050	2250	4200	6000
Series KH-15 - (3/4-Ton) - (131" wb)						
PU	200	650	1000	2200	4150	5900
Canopy	200	600	1000	2200	4000	5700
Screen	200	650	1000	2200	4100	5800
Panel	200	600	950	2200	3900	5600
Series KH-20 - (1-Ton) - (131" wb)						
PU	200	600	950	2150	3850	5500
Canopy	200	550	900	2150	3800	5400
Screen	200	600	950	2150	3850	5500
Panel	200	550	900	2100	3700	5300

1936

	6	5	4	3	2	1
Series LC/D2 - (1/2-Ton)						
PU	200	675	1050	2250	4300	6100
Canopy	200	600	1000	2200	4000	5700
Screen	200	650	1000	2200	4100	5800
Comm Sed	200	650	1000	2200	4150	5900
Panel	200	600	950	2200	3900	5600
Westchester Suburban	200	675	1050	2250	4350	6200
Series LE-16 - (3/4-Ton) - (136" wb)						
PU	200	650	1000	2200	4150	5900
Canopy	200	600	950	2200	3900	5600
Screen	200	600	1000	2200	4000	5700
Panel	200	650	1000	2200	4100	5800
Platform	150	450	800	1800	3300	4800
Stake	200	500	850	1900	3500	5000
Series LE-17 - (3/4-Ton) - (162" wb)						
Platform	150	400	750	1650	3150	4500
Stake	150	450	800	1800	3300	4800
Series LE-21 - (1-Ton) - (136" wb)						
PU	200	600	1000	2200	4000	5700
Canopy	200	600	950	2150	3850	5500
Screen	200	600	950	2200	3900	5600
Panel	200	550	900	2150	3800	5400
Platform	150	350	750	1450	3000	4200
Stake	150	400	750	1650	3150	4500
Series LE-22 - (1-Ton) - (162" wb)						
Platform	150	350	750	1350	2800	4000
Stake	150	400	750	1550	3050	4300

1937

	6	5	4	3	2	1
Series MC - (1/2-Ton) - (116" wb)						
PU	350	750	1350	2650	5450	7800
Canopy	350	750	1250	2400	5050	7200
Screen	350	750	1250	2400	5100	7300
Comm Sed	200	675	1050	2250	4350	6200
Panel	350	750	1300	2400	5200	7400
Westchester Suburban	350	725	1150	2300	4700	6700
Series MD - (3/4-Ton) - (120" wb)						
PU	350	750	1250	2400	5050	7200
Platform	350	700	1150	2300	4550	6500
Stake	200	650	1050	2250	4200	6000
Series MD - (3/4-Ton) - (136" wb)						
PU	350	750	1200	2350	4900	7000
Canopy	350	700	1100	2300	4500	6400
Screen	350	700	1150	2300	4550	6500
Panel	350	700	1150	2300	4600	6600
Platform	200	500	850	1900	3500	5000
Stake	200	550	900	2100	3700	5300
Series MD - (1-Ton) - (120" wb)						
PU	350	700	1150	2300	4550	6500
Platform	200	650	1000	2200	4100	5800
Stake	200	650	1050	2250	4200	6000
Series MD - (1-Ton) - (136" wb)						
PU	200	600	1000	2200	4000	5700
Canopy	200	600	950	2150	3850	5500
Screen	200	600	950	2200	3900	5600
Panel	200	550	900	2150	3800	5400
Platform	150	350	750	1450	3000	4200
Stake	150	400	750	1650	3150	4500

1938

	6	5	4	3	2	1
Series RC - (1/2-Ton) - (116" wb)						
PU	350	750	1350	2650	5450	7800
Canopy	350	750	1250	2400	5050	7200
Screen	350	750	1250	2400	5100	7300
Comm Sed	200	675	1050	2250	4350	6200
Panel	350	750	1300	2400	5200	7400
Westchester Suburban	350	725	1150	2300	4700	6700
Series RD-15 - (3/4-Ton) - (120" wb)						
PU	350	750	1250	2400	5050	7200
Platform	350	700	1150	2300	4550	6500
Stake	200	650	1050	2250	4200	6000
Series RD-16 - (3/4-Ton) - (136" wb)						
PU	350	750	1200	2350	4900	7000
Canopy	350	700	1100	2300	4500	6400
Screen	350	700	1150	2300	4550	6500
Panel	350	700	1150	2300	4600	6600
Platform	200	500	850	1900	3500	5000
Stake	200	550	900	2100	3700	5300
Series RD-20 - (1-Ton) - (120" wb)						
PU	350	700	1150	2300	4550	6500
Platform	200	650	1000	2200	4100	5800
Stake	200	650	1050	2250	4200	6000
Series RD-21 - (1-Ton) - (136" wb)						
PU	200	600	1000	2200	4000	5700
Canopy	200	600	950	2150	3850	5500
Screen	200	600	950	2200	3900	5600
Panel	200	550	900	2150	3800	5400
Platform	150	350	750	1450	3000	4200
Stake	150	400	750	1650	3150	4500

1939

	6	5	4	3	2	1
Series TC - (1/2-Ton) - (116" wb)						
PU	350	900	1550	3050	5900	8500
Canopy	350	900	1550	3100	6000	8600
Screen	350	900	1550	3100	6000	8600
Panel	450	950	1600	3250	6150	8800
Series TD - (3/4-Ton) - (120" wb)						
PU	350	750	1350	2600	5400	7700
Platform	350	750	1300	2400	5200	7400
Stake	350	750	1300	2400	5200	7400
Series TD-20 - (1-Ton) - (120" wb)						
PU	350	750	1300	2450	5250	7500
Platform	350	750	1250	2350	5000	7100
Stake	350	750	1250	2350	5000	7100
Series TD-21 - (1-Ton) - (133" wb)						
PU	350	750	1300	2450	5250	7500
Canopy	350	750	1300	2450	5250	7500
Screen	350	750	1300	2500	5300	7600
Panel	350	750	1350	2650	5450	7800
Platform	350	750	1250	2350	5000	7100
Stake	350	750	1250	2350	5000	7100

1940

	6	5	4	3	2	1
Series VC - (1/2-Ton) - (116" wb)						
PU	350	900	1550	3050	5900	8500
Canopy	350	900	1550	3100	6000	8600
Screen	350	900	1550	3100	6000	8600
Panel	450	950	1600	3250	6150	8800
Series VD-15 - (3/4-Ton) - (120" wb)						
PU	350	750	1350	2600	5400	7700
Platform	350	750	1300	2400	5200	7400
Stake	350	750	1300	2400	5200	7400
Series VD-20 - (1-Ton) - (120" wb)						
PU	350	750	1300	2450	5250	7500
Platform	350	750	1250	2350	5000	7100
Stake	350	750	1250	2350	5000	7100
Series VD-21 - (1-Ton) - (133" wb)						
PU	350	750	1300	2450	5250	7500
Canopy	350	750	1300	2450	5250	7500
Screen	350	750	1300	2500	5300	7600
Panel	350	750	1350	2650	5450	7800
Platform	350	750	1250	2350	5000	7100
Stake	350	750	1250	2350	5000	7100

1941

	6	5	4	3	2	1
Series WC - (1/2-Ton)						
PU	350	700	1150	2300	4600	6600
Canopy	350	725	1150	2300	4700	6700
Screen	350	725	1200	2350	4800	6800
Panel	200	675	1050	2250	4350	6200
Series WD - (3/4-Ton)						
PU	200	675	1050	2250	4300	6100
Platform	200	650	1000	2200	4100	5800
Stake	200	650	1000	2200	4150	5900
Series WD-20 - (1-Ton)						
PU	200	650	1050	2250	4200	6000
Platform	200	600	950	2200	3900	5600
Stake	200	600	1000	2200	4000	5700
Series WD-21 - (1-Ton)						
PU	200	600	1000	2200	4000	5700
Canopy	200	650	1050	2250	4200	6000
Screen	200	675	1050	2250	4350	6200
Panel	200	600	1000	2200	4000	5700
Platform	150	450	800	1800	3300	4800
Stake	200	600	950	2150	3850	5500

1942

	6	5	4	3	2	1
Series WC - (1/2-Ton)						
PU	350	700	1150	2300	4600	6600
Canopy	350	725	1150	2300	4700	6700
Screen	350	725	1200	2350	4800	6800
Panel	200	675	1050	2250	4350	6200
Series WD - (3/4-Ton)						
PU	200	675	1050	2250	4300	6100
Platform	200	650	1000	2200	4100	5800
Stake	200	650	1000	2200	4150	5900
Series WD-20 - (1-Ton)						
PU	200	650	1050	2250	4200	6000
Platform	200	600	950	2200	3900	5600
Stake	200	600	1000	2200	4000	5700
Series WD-21 - (1-Ton)						
PU	200	600	1000	2200	4000	5700
Canopy	200	650	1050	2250	4200	6000
Screen	200	675	1050	2250	4350	6200
Panel	200	600	1000	2200	4000	5700
Platform	150	450	800	1800	3300	4800
Stake	200	600	950	2150	3850	5500

1946

	6	5	4	3	2	1
Series WC - (1/2-Ton) - (116" wb)						
PU (6-1/2 ft.)	350	700	1150	2300	4600	6600
Canopy	350	725	1150	2300	4700	6700
Panel	200	675	1050	2250	4350	6200
Series WD-15 - (3/4-Ton) - (120" wb)						
PU (7-1/2 ft.)	200	675	1050	2250	4300	6100
Platform	200	650	1000	2200	4100	5800
Stake	200	650	1000	2200	4150	5900
Series WD-20 - (1-Ton) - (120" wb)						
PU	200	650	1000	2200	4100	5800
PU (7-1/2 ft.)	200	650	1050	2250	4200	6000
Platform	200	600	950	2200	3900	5600
Stake	200	600	1000	2200	4000	5700
Series WD-21 - (1-Ton) - (133" wb)						
PU (9-1/2 ft.)	200	600	1000	2200	4000	5700
Canopy	200	650	1050	2250	4200	6000
Panel	200	600	1000	2200	4000	5700

	6	5	4	3	2	1
Platform	150	450	800	1800	3300	4800
Stake	200	600	950	2150	3850	5500
Power Wag WDX - (1-Ton) - (126" wb)						
Chassis & Cab	200	650	1050	2250	4200	6000
PU	450	1000	1650	3350	6300	9000

1947
Series WC - (1/2-Ton) - (116" wb)

	6	5	4	3	2	1
PU	350	700	1150	2300	4600	6600
Canopy	350	725	1150	2300	4700	6700
Panel	200	675	1050	2250	4350	6200
Series WD-15 - (3/4-Ton) - (120" wb)						
PU	200	675	1050	2250	4300	6100
Platform	200	550	900	2100	3700	5300
Stake	200	650	1000	2200	4150	5900
Series WD-20 - (1-Ton) - (120" wb)						
PU	200	650	1000	2200	4100	5800
Platform	200	600	950	2200	3900	5600
Stake	200	600	1000	2200	4000	5700
Series WD-21 - (1-Ton) - (133" wb)						
PU	200	600	1000	2200	4000	5700
Canopy	200	650	1050	2250	4200	6000
Platform	150	450	800	1800	3300	4800
Stake	200	600	950	2150	3850	5500
Power-Wagon WDX - (1-Ton)						
PU	450	1000	1650	3350	6300	9000

1948-1949
Series B-1-B - (1/2-Ton) - (108" wb)

	6	5	4	3	2	1
PU	200	650	1050	2250	4200	6000
Panel	200	600	950	2150	3850	5500
Series B-1-C - (3/4-Ton) - (116" wb)						
PU	200	600	1000	2200	4000	5700
Platform	200	500	850	1900	3500	5000
Stake	200	500	850	1950	3600	5100
Series B-1-D - (1-Ton) - (116" wb)						
PU	200	550	900	2150	3800	5400
Platform	150	450	800	1750	3250	4700
Stake	150	450	800	1800	3300	4800
Series B-1-D - (1-Ton) - (126" wb)						
PU	200	550	900	2100	3700	5300
Platform	150	450	750	1700	3200	4600
Stake	150	450	800	1750	3250	4700
Series B-1-Power Wag - (1-Ton) - (126" wb)						
PU	450	1000	1650	3350	6300	9000
Series B-1-DU - (1 Ton)						
7-ft. body (102" wb)	150	300	700	1250	2650	3800
9-1/2 ft. body (117" wb)	150	300	700	1250	2600	3700
Series B-1-EU - (1-Ton)						
7-ft. body (102" wb)	150	300	700	1250	2650	3800
9-1/2 ft. body (117" wb)	150	300	700	1250	2600	3700
12-1/2 ft. body (142" wb)	125	250	700	1150	2500	3600

1950
Series B-2-B - (1/2-Ton) - (108" wb)

	6	5	4	3	2	1
PU	200	650	1050	2250	4200	6000
Panel	200	600	950	2150	3850	5500
Series B-2-C - (3/4-Ton) - (116" wb)						
PU	200	600	1000	2200	4000	5700
Platform	200	500	850	1900	3500	5000
Stake	200	500	850	1950	3600	5100
Series B-2-D - (1-Ton) - (116" wb)						
PU	200	550	900	2150	3800	5400
Platform	150	450	800	1750	3250	4700
Stake	150	450	800	1800	3300	4800
Series B-2-D - (1-Ton) - (126" wb)						
PU	200	550	900	2100	3700	5300
Platform	150	450	750	1700	3200	4600
Stake	150	450	800	1750	3250	4700
Series B-2-PW Power-Wagon - (1-Ton) - (126" wb)						
PU	450	1000	1650	3350	6300	9000
Series B-2-DU/EU Route-Van - (1-Ton)						
7-ft. body (102" wb)	150	300	700	1250	2650	3800
9-1/2 ft. body (117" wb)	150	300	700	1250	2600	3700
12-1/2 ft. body (142" wb)	125	250	700	1150	2500	3600

NOTE: Add 3 percent for Fluid Drive.

1951
Series B-3-B - (1/2-Ton) - (108" wb)

	6	5	4	3	2	1
PU	200	650	1050	2250	4200	6000
Panel	200	600	950	2150	3850	5500
Series B-3-C - (3/4-Ton) - (116" wb)						
PU	200	600	950	2200	3900	5600
Platform	200	500	850	1850	3350	4900
Stake	200	500	850	1900	3500	5000
Series B-3-D - (1-Ton) - (116" wb)						
PU	200	550	900	2100	3700	5300
Platform	150	450	750	1700	3200	4600
Stake	150	450	800	1750	3250	4700
Series B-3-D - (1-Ton) - (126" wb)						
PU	200	550	900	2000	3600	5200
Platform	150	400	750	1650	3150	4500
Stake	150	450	750	1700	3200	4600
Series B-3-PW Power-Wagon - (1-Ton) - (126" wb)						
PU	450	1000	1650	3350	6300	9000
Series B-3-DU/EU						
7-ft. body (102" wb)	150	300	700	1250	2650	3800
9-1/2 ft. body (117" wb)	150	300	700	1250	2600	3700
12-1/2 ft. body (142" wb)	125	250	700	1150	2500	3600

NOTE: Add 3 percent for Fluid Drive.

1952
Series B-3-B - (1/2-Ton) - (108" wb)

	6	5	4	3	2	1
PU	200	650	1050	2250	4200	6000
Panel	200	600	950	2150	3850	5500
Series B-3-C - (3/4-Ton) - (116" wb)						
PU	200	600	950	2200	3900	5600
Platform	200	500	850	1850	3350	4900
Stake	200	500	850	1900	3500	5000
Series B-3-D - (1-Ton) - (116" wb)						
PU	200	550	900	2100	3700	5300
Platform	150	450	750	1700	3200	4600
Stake	150	450	800	1750	3250	4700
Series B-3-D - (1-Ton) - (126" wb)						
PU	200	550	900	2000	3600	5200
Platform	150	400	750	1650	3150	4500
Stake	150	450	800	1750	3200	4600

Series B-3-PW Power-Wagon - (1-Ton) - (126" wb)

	6	5	4	3	2	1
PU	450	1000	1650	3350	6300	9000
Series B-3-DU/EU Route-Van						
7-ft. body (102" wb)	150	300	700	1250	2650	3800
9-1/2 ft. body (117" wb)	150	300	700	1250	2600	3700
Series B-3-EU Route-Van - (142" w.b.)						
12-1/2 ft. body	125	250	700	1150	2500	3600

NOTE: Add 3 percent for Fluid Drive.

1953
Series B-4-B - (1/2-Ton) - (108" wb)

	6	5	4	3	2	1
PU	200	650	1050	2250	4200	6000
Panel	200	600	950	2150	3850	5500
Series B-4-B - (1/2-Ton) - (116" wb)						
PU	200	650	1000	2200	4100	5800
Series B-4-C - (3/4-Ton) - (116" wb)						
PU	200	600	950	2200	3900	5600
Platform	200	500	850	1850	3350	4900
Stake	200	500	850	1900	3500	5000
Series B-4-D - (1-Ton) - (116" wb)						
PU	200	550	900	2100	3700	5300
Platform	150	450	750	1700	3200	4600
Stake	150	450	800	1750	3250	4700
Series B-4-D - (1-Ton) - (126" wb)						
PU	200	550	900	2000	3600	5200
Platform	150	400	750	1650	3150	4500
Stake	150	450	750	1700	3200	4600
Series B-4-PW Power-Wagon - (1-Ton) - (126" wb)						
PU	450	1000	1650	3350	6300	9000
Series B-4-DU/EU Route-Van						
7-ft. body (102" wb)	150	300	700	1250	2650	3800
9-1/2 ft. body (117" wb)	150	300	700	1250	2600	3700
12-1/2 ft. body (142" wb)	125	250	700	1150	2500	3600

NOTE: Add 3 percent for Fluid Drive.

1954
Series C-1-B - (1/2-Ton) - (108" wb)

	6	5	4	3	2	1
PU	350	700	1150	2300	4600	6600
Twn Panel	200	675	1050	2250	4300	6100
Series C-1-B - (1/2-Ton) - (116" wb)						
PU	200	675	1050	2250	4350	6200
Series C-1-C - (3/4-Ton) - (116" wb)						
PU	200	600	950	2200	3900	5600
Platform	200	500	850	1850	3350	4900
Stake	200	500	850	1900	3500	5000
Series C-1-D - (1-Ton) - (116" wb)						
PU	200	550	900	2100	3700	5300
Platform	150	450	750	1700	3200	4600
Stake	150	450	800	1750	3250	4700
Series C-1-D - (1-Ton) - (126" wb)						
PU	200	550	900	2000	3600	5200
Platform	150	400	750	1650	3150	4500
Stake	150	450	750	1700	3200	4600
Series C-1-PW Power-Wagon - (1-Ton) - (126" wb)						
PU	350	800	1450	2750	5600	8000
Series C-1-DU/EU Route-Van						
7-ft. body (102" wb)	150	300	700	1250	2650	3800
9-1/2 ft. body (117" wb)	150	300	700	1250	2600	3700
12-1/2 ft. body (142" wb)	125	250	700	1150	2500	3600

NOTES: Add 15 percent for V-8 engine.
Add 5 percent for automatic transmission.
Add 5 percent for Fluid Drive.

1955
Series C-3-BL - (1/2-Ton) - (108" wb)

	6	5	4	3	2	1
Lowside PU	350	750	1200	2350	4900	7000
Series C-3-B - (1/2-Ton) - (108" wb)						
Lowside PU	350	725	1200	2350	4800	6800
Highside PU	350	725	1200	2350	4850	6900
Panel	200	675	1050	2250	4350	6200
Series C-3-B - (1/2-Ton) - (116" wb)						
Lowside PU	350	700	1150	2300	4550	6500
Highside PU	350	700	1150	2300	4600	6600
Platform	200	600	950	2150	3850	5500
Stake	200	600	950	2200	3900	5600
Series C-3-C - (3/4-Ton) - (116" wb)						
PU	200	650	1000	2200	4150	5900
Platform	200	500	850	1850	3350	4900
Stake	200	500	850	1900	3500	5000
Series C-3-D - (1-Ton) - (116" wb)						
PU	200	600	950	2150	3850	5500
Platform	150	450	800	1800	3300	4800
Stake	200	500	850	1850	3350	4900
Series C-3-D - (1-Ton) - (126" wb)						
PU	200	500	850	1900	3500	5000
Platform	150	400	750	1650	3150	4500
Stake	150	450	750	1700	3200	4600
Series C-3-PW Power-Wag - (1-Ton) - (126" wb)						
PU	350	800	1450	2750	5600	8000

NOTES: Add 15 percent for V-8 engine.
Add 5 percent for automatic transmission.

1956
Series C-4-BL - (1/2-Ton) - (108" wb)

	6	5	4	3	2	1
Lowside PU	350	750	1200	2350	4900	7000
Series C-4-B - (1/2-Ton) - (108" wb)						
Lowside PU	350	725	1200	2350	4800	6800
Highside PU	350	725	1200	2350	4850	6900
Panel	200	675	1050	2250	4350	6200
Series C-4-B - (1/2-Ton) - (116" wb)						
Lowside PU	350	725	1150	2300	4700	6700
Highside PU	350	725	1200	2350	4800	6800
Platform	200	600	950	2150	3850	5500
Stake	200	600	950	2200	3900	5600
Series C-4-C - (3/4-Ton) - (116" wb)						
PU	200	650	1000	2200	4150	5900
Platform	200	500	850	1850	3350	4900
Stake	200	500	850	1900	3500	5000
Series C-4-D - (1-Ton) - (116" wb)						
PU	200	600	950	2150	3850	5500
Platform	150	450	800	1800	3300	4800
Stake	200	500	850	1850	3350	4900
Series C-4-D - (1-Ton) - (126" wb)						
PU	200	500	850	1900	3500	5000
Platform	150	400	750	1650	3150	4500
Stake	150	450	750	1700	3200	4600

	6	5	4	3	2	1
Series C-4-PW Power-Wagon - (1-Ton) - (126" wb)						
PU	350	800	1450	2750	5600	8000

NOTES: Add 15 percent for V-8 engine.
Add 5 percent for automatic transmission.

1957

	6	5	4	3	2	1
Series K6-D100 - (1/2-Ton) - (108" wb)						
PU	350	750	1200	2350	4900	7000
Panel	200	675	1100	2250	4400	6300
6P Wag	350	700	1100	2300	4500	6400
8P Wag	350	700	1100	2300	4500	6400
Series K6-D100 - (1/2-Ton) - (116" wb)						
PU	350	725	1200	2350	4850	6900
Platform	200	600	1000	2200	4000	5700
Stake	200	650	1000	2200	4100	5800
Series K6-D100 - (3/4-Ton) - (116" wb)						
PU	200	650	1050	2250	4200	6000
Platform	200	500	850	1950	3600	5100
Stake	200	550	900	2000	3600	5200
Series K6-D100 - (1-Ton) - (126" wb)						
PU	200	600	950	2200	3900	5600
Platform	150	450	750	1700	3200	4600
Stake	150	450	800	1750	3250	4700
Series K6-D100 4WD - (1/2-Ton) - (108" wb)						
PU	350	700	1150	2300	4550	6500
Panel	200	650	1050	2250	4200	6000
6P Wag	200	675	1050	2250	4300	6100
8P Wag	200	675	1050	2250	4300	6100
Series K6-W100 4WD - (1/2-Ton) - (116" wb)						
PU	350	700	1100	2300	4500	6400
Platform	200	550	900	2150	3800	5400
Stake	200	600	950	2150	3850	5500
Series K6-W200 4WD - (3/4-Ton) - (116" wb)						
PU	200	675	1050	2250	4350	6200
Platform	200	550	900	2100	3700	5300
Stake	200	550	900	2150	3800	5400
Series K6-W300 - (1-Ton) - (126" wb)						
PU	350	750	1300	2450	5250	7500

NOTES: Add 10 percent for V-8 engine.
Add 5 percent for automatic transmission.

1958

	6	5	4	3	2	1
Series L6-D100 - (1/2-Ton) - (108" wb)						
PU	350	750	1250	2350	5000	7100
Twn Panel	350	700	1100	2300	4500	6400
6P Wag	350	700	1150	2300	4550	6500
8P Wag	350	700	1150	2300	4550	6500
Series L6-D100 - (1/2-Ton) - (116" wb)						
PU	350	750	1200	2350	4900	7000
Sweptside PU	350	800	1450	2750	5600	8000
Platform	200	600	1000	2200	4000	5700
Stake	200	650	1000	2200	4100	5800
Series L6-D200 - (3/4-Ton) - (116" wb)						
PU	200	650	1050	2250	4200	6000
Platform	200	500	850	1950	3600	5100
Stake	200	550	900	2000	3600	5200
Series L6-D300 - (1-Ton) - (126" wb)						
PU	200	600	950	2200	3900	5600
Platform	150	450	750	1700	3200	4600
Stake	150	450	800	1750	3250	4700
Series L6-W100 4WD - (1/2-Ton) - (108" wb)						
PU	350	700	1150	2300	4550	6500
Twn Panel	200	650	1050	2250	4200	6000
6P Wag	200	675	1050	2250	4300	6100
8P Wag	200	675	1050	2250	4300	6100
Series L6-W100 4WD - (1/2-Ton) - (116" wb)						
PU	350	700	1100	2300	4500	6400
Platform	200	550	900	2150	3800	5400
Stake	200	600	950	2150	3850	5500
Series L6-W200 4WD - (3/4-Ton) - (116" wb)						
PU	200	675	1050	2250	4350	6200
Platform	200	550	900	2100	3700	5300
Stake	200	550	900	2150	3800	5400
Series L6-W300 4WD - (1-Ton) - (129" wb)						
PU	200	650	1050	2250	4200	6000
Platform	200	500	850	1950	3600	5100
Stake	200	550	900	2000	3600	5200
L6-W300M Power-Wagon - (1-Ton) - (126" wb)						
PU	350	750	1300	2450	5250	7500

NOTES: Add 10 percent for V-8 engine.
Add 5 percent for automatic transmission.

1959

	6	5	4	3	2	1
Series M6-D100 - (1/2-Ton) - (108" wb)						
Utiline PU	350	725	1200	2350	4850	6900
Sweptline PU	350	750	1250	2400	5050	7200
Twn Panel	350	700	1100	2300	4500	6400
6P Wag	350	700	1150	2300	4550	6500
8P Wag	350	700	1150	2300	4550	6500
Series M6-D100 - (1/2-Ton) - (116" wb)						
Utiline PU	350	725	1200	2350	4800	6800
Sweptline PU	350	750	1250	2400	5100	7300
Sweptside PU	350	800	1450	2750	5600	8000
Platform	200	600	1000	2200	4000	5700
Stake	200	650	1000	2200	4100	5800
Series M6-D200 - (3/4-Ton) - (116" wb)						
Utiline PU	200	650	1050	2250	4200	6000
Sweptline PU	200	675	1050	2250	4350	6200
Platform	200	500	850	1950	3600	5100
Stake	200	550	900	2000	3600	5200
Series M6-D300 - (1-Ton) - (126" wb)						
Utiline PU	200	600	950	2200	3900	5600
Sweptline PU	200	650	1000	2200	4100	5800
Platform	150	450	750	1700	3200	4600
Stake	150	450	800	1750	3250	4700
Series M6-W100 4WD - (1/2-Ton) - (108" wb)						
Utiline PU	350	700	1150	2300	4550	6500
Twn Panel	200	650	1050	2250	4200	6000
6P Wag	200	675	1050	2250	4300	6100
8P Wag	200	675	1050	2250	4300	6100
Series M6-W100 4WD - (1/2-Ton) - (116" wb)						
Utiline PU	350	700	1100	2300	4500	6400
Platform	200	550	900	2150	3800	5400
Stake	200	600	950	2150	3850	5500
Series M6-W200 4WD - (3/4-Ton) - (116" wb)						
Utiline PU	200	675	1050	2250	4350	6200
Platform	200	550	900	2100	3700	5300
Stake	200	550	900	2150	3800	5400
Series M6-W300 4WD - (1-Ton) - (129" wb)						
Utiline PU	200	650	1050	2250	4200	6000
Platform	200	500	850	1950	3600	5100
Stake	200	550	900	2000	3600	5200
Series M6-W300M Power-Wagon - (1-Ton) - (126" wb)						
PU	350	750	1300	2450	5250	7500

NOTES: Add 10 percent for V-8 engine.
Add 5 percent for automatic transmission.

1960

	6	5	4	3	2	1
Series P6-D100 - (1/2-Ton) - (108" wb)						
Utiline PU	350	725	1200	2350	4850	6900
Sweptline PU	350	750	1250	2400	5050	7200
Twn Panel	350	700	1100	2300	4500	6400
6P Wag	350	700	1150	2300	4550	6500
8P Wag	350	700	1150	2300	4550	6500
Series P6-D100 - (1/2-Ton) - (116" wb)						
Utiline PU	350	725	1200	2350	4800	6800
Sweptline PU	350	750	1250	2400	5100	7300
Platform	200	600	1000	2200	4000	5700
Stake	200	650	1000	2200	4100	5800
Series P6-D200 - (3/4- Ton) - (116" wb)						
Utiline PU	200	650	1050	2250	4200	6000
Sweptline PU	200	675	1050	2250	4350	6200
Platform	200	500	850	1950	3600	5100
Stake	200	550	900	2000	3600	5200
Series P6-D300 - (1- Ton) - (126" wb)						
Utiline PU	200	600	950	2200	3900	5600
Sweptline PU	200	650	1000	2200	4100	5800
Platform	150	450	750	1700	3200	4600
Stake	150	450	800	1750	3250	4700
Series P6-W100 4WD - (1/2-Ton) - (108" wb)						
Utiline PU	350	700	1150	2300	4550	6500
Sweptline PU	350	725	1150	2300	4700	6700
Twn Panel	200	650	1050	2250	4200	6000
6P Wag	200	675	1050	2250	4300	6100
8P Wag	200	675	1050	2250	4300	6100
Series P6-W100 4WD - (1/2-Ton) - (116" wb)						
Utiline PU	350	700	1100	2300	4500	6400
Sweptline PU	350	700	1150	2300	4600	6600
Platform	200	550	900	2150	3800	5400
Stake	200	600	950	2150	3850	5500
Series P6-W200 4WD - (3/4-Ton) - (116" wb)						
Utiline PU	200	675	1050	2250	4350	6200
Sweptline PU	350	700	1100	2300	4500	6400
Platform	200	550	900	2100	3700	5300
Stake	200	550	900	2150	3800	5400
Series P6-W300 - (1-Ton) - (129" wb)						
Utiline PU	200	650	1050	2250	4200	6000
Sweptline PU	200	675	1050	2250	4350	6200
Platform	200	500	850	1950	3600	5100
Stake	200	550	900	2000	3600	5200
Series P6-WM300 Power-Wagon - (1-Ton) - (126" wb)						
Utiline PU	350	750	1300	2450	5250	7500

NOTES: Add 5 percent for automatic transmission.
Add 10 percent for V-8 engine.

1961

	6	5	4	3	2	1
Series R6-D100 - (1/2-Ton) - (114" wb)						
Utiline PU	200	600	1000	2200	4000	5700
Sweptline PU	200	600	950	2200	3900	5600
Twn Panel	200	650	1000	2200	4100	5800
6P Wag	200	650	1000	2200	4150	5900
8P Wag	200	650	1000	2200	4150	5900
Series R6-D100 - (1/2-Ton) - (122" wb)						
Utiline PU	200	600	950	2200	3900	5600
Sweptline PU	200	650	1000	2200	4100	5800
Platform	200	500	850	1900	3500	5000
Stake	200	500	850	1950	3600	5100
Series R6-D200 - (3/4-Ton) - (122" wb)						
Utiline PU	200	550	900	2100	3700	5300
Sweptline PU	200	600	950	2150	3850	5500
Platform	200	500	850	1850	3350	4900
Stake	200	500	850	1900	3500	5000
Series R6-D300 - (1-Ton) - (133" wb)						
Utiline PU	200	500	850	1900	3500	5000
Platform	150	450	800	1800	3300	4800
Stake	200	500	850	1850	3350	4900
Series R6-W100 4WD - (1/2-Ton) - (114" wb)						
Utiline PU	200	650	1000	2200	4100	5800
Sweptline PU	200	600	1000	2200	4000	5700
Twn Panel	200	650	1000	2200	4150	5900
6P Wag	200	675	1050	2250	4350	6200
8P Wag	200	675	1050	2250	4350	6200
Series R6-W200 4WD - (3/4-Ton) - (122" wb)						
Utiline PU	200	600	950	2150	3850	5500
Sweptline PU	200	600	1000	2200	4000	5700
Platform	200	500	850	1950	3600	5100
Stake	200	550	900	2000	3600	5200
Series R6-W200 4WD - (1-Ton) - (133" wb)						
Utiline PU	200	550	900	2000	3600	5200
Platform	200	500	850	1850	3350	4900
Stake	200	500	850	1950	3600	5100
Series R6-WM300 - (1-Ton) - (126" wb)						
PU	350	900	1550	3050	5900	8500

NOTES: Add 10 percent for V-8 engine.
Add 5 percent for automatic transmission.

1962

	6	5	4	3	2	1
Series S6-D100 - (1/2- Ton) - (114" wb)						
Utiline PU	200	600	1000	2200	4000	5700
Sweptline PU	200	600	950	2200	3900	5600
Twn Panel	200	650	1000	2200	4100	5800
6P Wag	200	650	1000	2200	4150	5900
8P Wag	200	650	1000	2200	4150	5900
Series S6-D100 - (1/2-Ton) - (122" wb)						
Utiline PU	200	600	950	2200	3900	5600
Sweptline PU	200	650	1000	2200	4100	5800
Platform	200	500	850	1900	3500	5000
Stake	200	500	850	1950	3600	5100
Series S6-D200 - (3/4-Ton) - (122" wb)						
Utiline PU	200	550	900	2100	3700	5300
Sweptline PU	200	600	950	2150	3850	5500
Platform	200	500	850	1850	3350	4900
Stake	200	500	850	1900	3500	5000
Series S6-D300 - (1-Ton) - (133" wb)						
Utiline PU	200	500	850	1900	3500	5000
Platform	150	450	800	1800	3300	4800
Stake	200	500	850	1850	3350	4900

Series S6-W100 4WD - (1/2-Ton) - (114" wb)

	6	5	4	3	2	1
Utiline PU	200	650	1000	2200	4100	5800
Sweptline PU	200	600	1000	2200	4000	5700
Twn Panel	200	650	1000	2200	4150	5900
6P Wag	200	675	1050	2250	4350	6200
8P Wag	200	675	1050	2250	4350	6200

Series S6-W200 4WD - (3/4-Ton) - (122" wb)

	6	5	4	3	2	1
Utiline PU	200	600	950	2150	3850	5500
Sweptline PU	200	600	1000	2200	4000	5700
Platform	200	500	850	1950	3600	5100
Stake	200	550	900	2000	3600	5200

Series S6-W300 4WD - (1-Ton) - (133" wb)

	6	5	4	3	2	1
Utiline PU	200	550	900	2000	3600	5200
Platform	200	500	850	1850	3350	4900
Stake	200	500	850	1950	3600	5100

S6-WM300 Power-Wagon - (1-Ton) - (126" wb)

	6	5	4	3	2	1
PU	350	900	1550	3050	5900	8500

NOTES: Add 10 percent for V-8 engine.
Add 5 percent for automatic transmission.

1963

Series T6-D100 - (1/2-Ton) - (114" wb)

	6	5	4	3	2	1
Utiline PU	200	600	1000	2200	4000	5700
Sweptline PU	200	600	950	2200	3900	5600
Twn Panel	200	650	1000	2200	4100	5800
6P Wag	200	650	1000	2200	4150	5900
8P Wag	200	650	1000	2200	4150	5900

Series T6-D100 - (1/2-Ton) - (122" wb)

	6	5	4	3	2	1
Utiline PU	200	600	950	2200	3900	5600
Sweptline PU	200	650	1000	2200	4100	5800
Platform	200	500	850	1900	3500	5000
Stake	200	500	850	1950	3600	5100

Series T6-D200 - (3/4-Ton) - (122" wb)

	6	5	4	3	2	1
Utiline PU	200	550	900	2100	3700	5300
Sweptline PU	200	600	950	2150	3850	5500
Platform	200	500	850	1850	3350	4900
Stake	200	500	850	1900	3500	5000

T6-D200 Crew Cab - (3/4-Ton) - (146" wb)

	6	5	4	3	2	1
Utiline PU	200	500	850	1950	3600	5100
Sweptline PU	200	550	900	2000	3600	5200

Series T6-D300 - (1-Ton) - (133" wb)

	6	5	4	3	2	1
Utiline PU	200	500	850	1900	3500	5000
Platform	150	450	800	1800	3300	4800
Stake	200	500	850	1850	3350	4900

Series T6-W100 4WD - (1/2-Ton) - (114" wb)

	6	5	4	3	2	1
Utiline PU	200	650	1000	2200	4100	5800
Sweptline PU	200	600	1000	2200	4000	5700
Twn Panel	200	650	1000	2200	4150	5900
6P Wag	200	675	1050	2250	4350	6200
8P Wag	200	675	1050	2250	4350	6200

Series T6-W200 4WD - (3/4-Ton) - (122" wb)

	6	5	4	3	2	1
Utiline PU	200	600	950	2150	3850	5500
Sweptline PU	200	600	1000	2200	4000	5700
Platform	200	500	850	1950	3600	5100
Stake	200	550	900	2000	3600	5200

T6-W200 Crew Cab - (3/4-Ton) - (146" wb)

	6	5	4	3	2	1
Utiline PU	200	500	850	1900	3500	5000
Sweptline PU	200	500	850	1950	3600	5100

Series T6-W300 - (1-Ton) - (133" wb)

	6	5	4	3	2	1
Utiline PU	200	500	900	2000	3600	5200
Platform	200	500	850	1850	3350	4900
Stake	200	500	850	1950	3600	5100

T6-WM300 Power-Wagon - (1-Ton) - (126" wb)

	6	5	4	3	2	1
Utiline PU	350	900	1550	3050	5900	8500

NOTES: Add 10 percent for V-8 engine.
Add 5 percent for automatic transmission.

1964

Series V6-A100 - (1/2- Ton) - (90" wb)

	6	5	4	3	2	1
PU	200	600	950	2200	3900	5600
Van	200	550	900	2000	3600	5200
Wag	200	600	1000	2200	4000	5700

Series V6-D100 - (1/2-Ton) - (114" wb)

	6	5	4	3	2	1
Utiline PU	200	600	1000	2200	4000	5700
Sweptline PU	200	600	950	2200	3900	5600
Twn Panel	200	650	1000	2200	4100	5800
6P Wag	200	650	1000	2200	4150	5900
8P Wag	200	650	1000	2200	4150	5900

Series V6-D100 - (1/2-Ton) - (122" wb)

	6	5	4	3	2	1
Utiline PU	200	600	950	2200	3900	5600
Sweptline PU	200	650	1000	2200	4100	5800
Platform	200	500	850	1900	3500	5000
Stake	200	500	850	1950	3600	5100

Series V6-D200 - (3/4-Ton) - (122" wb)

	6	5	4	3	2	1
Utiline PU	200	550	900	2100	3700	5300
Sweptline PU	200	600	950	2150	3850	5500
Platform	200	500	850	1850	3350	4900
Stake	200	500	850	1900	3500	5000

V6-D200 Crew Cab - (3/4-Ton) - (146" wb)

	6	5	4	3	2	1
Utiline PU	200	500	850	1950	3600	5100
Sweptline PU	200	550	900	2000	3600	5200

Series V6-D300 - (1-Ton) - (133" wb)

	6	5	4	3	2	1
Utiline PU	200	500	850	1900	3500	5000
Platform	150	450	800	1800	3300	4800
Stake	200	500	850	1850	3350	4900

Series V6-W100 4WD - (1/2-Ton) - (114" wb)

	6	5	4	3	2	1
Utiline PU	200	650	1000	2200	4100	5800
Sweptline PU	200	600	1000	2200	4000	5700
Twn Panel	200	650	1000	2200	4150	5900
6P Wag	200	675	1050	2250	4350	6200
8P Wag	200	675	1050	2250	4350	6200

Series V6-W200 4WD - (3/4-Ton) - (122" wb)

	6	5	4	3	2	1
Utiline PU	200	600	950	2150	3850	5500
Sweptline PU	200	600	1000	2200	4000	5700
Platform	200	500	850	1950	3600	5100
Stake	200	550	900	2000	3600	5200

V6-W200 Crew Cab 4WD - (3/4-Ton) - (146" wb)

	6	5	4	3	2	1
Utiline PU	200	500	850	1900	3500	5000
Sweptline PU	200	500	850	1950	3600	5100

Series V6-W300 4WD - (1-Ton) - (133" wb)

	6	5	4	3	2	1
Utiline PU	200	550	900	2000	3600	5200
Platform	200	500	850	1850	3350	4900
Stake	200	500	850	1950	3600	5100

V6-WM300 Power-Wagon - (1-Ton) - (126" wb)

	6	5	4	3	2	1
Utiline PU	350	900	1550	3050	5900	8500

NOTES: Add 10 percent for V-8 engine.
Add 5 percent for automatic transmission.
Add 4 percent for power winch.

1965

A6-A100 Compact - (1/2-Ton) - (90" wb)

	6	5	4	3	2	1
PU	200	600	950	2200	3900	5600
Van	200	550	900	2000	3600	5200
Panel Van	200	550	900	2100	3700	5300
Sportsman	200	600	1000	2200	4000	5700
Cus Sportsman	200	650	1000	2200	4100	5800

Series A6-D100 - (1/2-Ton) - (114" wb)

	6	5	4	3	2	1
Utiline PU	200	600	1000	2200	4000	5700
Sweptline PU	200	600	950	2200	3900	5600
Twn Panel	200	650	1000	2200	4100	5800
6P Wag	200	650	1000	2200	4150	5900
8P Wag	200	650	1000	2200	4150	5900

Series A6-D100 - (1/2-Ton) - (122" or 128" wb)

	6	5	4	3	2	1
Utiline PU	200	600	950	2200	3900	5600
Sweptline PU	200	650	1000	2200	4100	5800
Platform	200	500	850	1900	3500	5000
Stake	200	500	850	1950	3600	5100

Series A6-D200 - (3/4-Ton) - (122" or 128" wb)

	6	5	4	3	2	1
Utiline PU	200	550	900	2100	3700	5300
Sweptline PU	200	600	950	2150	3850	5500
Platform	200	500	850	1850	3350	4900
Stake	200	500	850	1900	3500	5000

A6-D200 Crew Cab - (3/4-Ton) - (146" wb)

	6	5	4	3	2	1
Utiline PU	200	500	850	1950	3600	5100
Sweptline PU	200	550	900	2000	3600	5200

Series A6-D300 - (1-Ton) - (133" wb)

	6	5	4	3	2	1
Utiline PU	200	500	850	1900	3500	5000
Platform	150	450	800	1800	3300	4800
Stake	200	500	850	1850	3350	4900

Series A6-W100 4WD - (1/2-Ton) - (114" wb)

	6	5	4	3	2	1
Utiline PU	200	650	1000	2200	4100	5800
Sweptline PU	200	600	1000	2200	4000	5700
Twn Panel	200	650	1000	2200	4150	5900
6P Wag	200	675	1050	2250	4350	6200
8P Wag	200	675	1050	2250	4350	6200

Series A6-W200 4WD - (3/4-Ton) - (122" or 128" wb)

	6	5	4	3	2	1
Utiline PU	200	600	950	2150	3850	5500
Sweptline PU	200	600	1000	2200	4000	5700
Platform	200	500	850	1950	3600	5100
Stake	200	550	900	2000	3600	5200

A6-W200 Crew Cab 4WD - (3/4-Ton) - (146" wb)

	6	5	4	3	2	1
Utiline PU	200	500	850	1900	3500	5000
Sweptline PU	200	500	850	1950	3600	5100

Series A6-W300 4WD - (1-Ton) - (133" wb)

	6	5	4	3	2	1
Utiline PU	200	550	900	2000	3600	5200
Platform	200	500	850	1850	3350	4900
Stake	200	500	850	1950	3600	5100

A6-WM300 Power-Wagon - (1-Ton) - (126" wb)

	6	5	4	3	2	1
Utiline PU	350	900	1550	3050	5900	8500

NOTES: Add 10 percent for V-8 engine.
Add 5 percent for automatic transmission.
Add 4 percent for power winch.

1966

B6-A100 Compact - (1/2-Ton) - (90" wb)

	6	5	4	3	2	1
PU	200	600	950	2200	3900	5600
Panel Van	200	550	900	2100	3700	5300
Van	200	550	900	2000	3600	5200
Sportsman	200	600	1000	2200	4000	5700
Cus Sportsman	200	650	1000	2200	4100	5800

Series B6-D100 - (1/2-Ton) - (114" wb)

	6	5	4	3	2	1
Utiline PU	200	600	1000	2200	4000	5700
Sweptline PU	200	600	950	2200	3900	5600
Twn Panel	200	650	1000	2200	4100	5800
6P Wag	200	650	1000	2200	4150	5900
8P Wag	200	650	1000	2200	4150	5900

Series B6-D100 - (1/2-Ton) - (122" or 128" wb)

	6	5	4	3	2	1
Utiline PU	200	600	950	2200	3900	5600
Sweptline PU	200	650	1000	2200	4100	5800
Platform	200	500	850	1900	3500	5000
Stake	200	500	850	1950	3600	5100

Series B6-D200 - (3/4-Ton) - (122" or 128" wb)

	6	5	4	3	2	1
Utiline PU	200	550	900	2100	3700	5300
Sweptline PU	200	600	950	2150	3850	5500
Platform	200	500	850	1850	3350	4900
Stake	200	500	850	1900	3500	5000

B6-D200 Crew Cab - (3/4-Ton) - (146" wb)

	6	5	4	3	2	1
Utiline PU	200	500	850	1950	3600	5100
Sweptline PU	200	550	900	2000	3600	5200

Series B6-D300 - (1-Ton) - (133" wb)

	6	5	4	3	2	1
Utiline PU	200	500	850	1900	3500	5000
Platform	150	450	800	1800	3300	4800
Stake	200	500	850	1850	3350	4900

Series B6-W100 4WD - (1/2-Ton) - (114" wb)

	6	5	4	3	2	1
Utiline PU	200	650	1000	2200	4100	5800
Sweptline PU	200	600	1000	2200	4000	5700
Twn Panel	200	650	1000	2200	4150	5900
6P Wag	200	675	1050	2250	4350	6200
8P Wag	200	675	1050	2250	4350	6200

Series B6-W200 4WD - (3/4-Ton) - (122" or 128" wb)

	6	5	4	3	2	1
Utiline PU	200	600	950	2150	3850	5500
Sweptline PU	200	600	1000	2200	4000	5700
Platform	200	500	850	1950	3600	5100
Stake	200	550	900	2000	3600	5200

B6-W200 Crew Cab 4WD - (3/4-Ton) - (146" wb)

	6	5	4	3	2	1
Utiline PU	200	500	850	1900	3500	5000
Sweptline PU	200	500	850	1950	3600	5100

Series B6-W300 4WD - (1-Ton) - (133" wb)

	6	5	4	3	2	1
Utiline PU	200	550	900	2000	3600	5200
Platform	200	500	850	1850	3350	4900
Stake	200	500	850	1950	3600	5100

B6-WM300 Power-Wagon - (1-Ton) - (126" wb)

	6	5	4	3	2	1
Utiline PU	350	900	1550	3050	5900	8500

NOTES: Add 10 percent for V-8 engine.
Add 5 percent for automatic transmission.
Add 4 percent for power winch.

1967

A100 Compact - (1/2-Ton) - (90" wb)

	6	5	4	3	2	1
PU	200	600	950	2200	3900	5600
Panel Van	200	550	900	2000	3600	5200
Van	200	500	850	1950	3600	5100

A108 Compact - (1/2-Ton) - (108" wb)

	6	5	4	3	2	1
Panel Van	200	550	900	2100	3700	5300
Van	200	550	900	2000	3600	5200

	6	5	4	3	2	1
Series D100 - (1/2-Ton) - (114" wb)						
Utiline PU	200	650	1000	2200	4100	5800
Sweptline PU	200	650	1000	2200	4150	5900
Series D100 - (1/2-Ton) - (128" wb)						
Utiline PU	200	600	1000	2200	4000	5700
Sweptline PU	200	650	1000	2200	4100	5800
Platform	200	500	850	1900	3500	5000
Stake	200	500	850	1950	3600	5100
Series D200 - (3/4-Ton) - (128" wb)						
Utiline PU	200	600	950	2150	3850	5500
Sweptline PU	200	600	950	2200	3900	5600
Platform	200	500	850	1850	3350	4900
Stake	200	500	850	1900	3500	5000
D200 Crew Cab - (3/4-Ton) - (146" wb)						
Utiline PU	200	550	900	2150	3800	5400
Sweptline PU	200	600	950	2150	3850	5500
Series D300 - (1-Ton) - (133" wb)						
Utiline PU	200	500	850	1900	3500	5000
Platform	150	450	800	1800	3300	4800
Stake	200	500	850	1850	3350	4900
Series W100 4WD - (1/2-Ton) - (114" wb)						
Utiline PU	200	650	1000	2200	4150	5900
Sweptline PU	200	650	1050	2250	4200	6000
Series W200 4WD - (3/4-Ton) - (128" wb)						
Utiline PU	200	600	1000	2200	4000	5700
Sweptline PU	200	650	1000	2200	4100	5800
Platform	200	500	850	1900	3500	5000
Stake	200	500	850	1950	3600	5100
W200 Crew Cab 4WD - (3/4-Ton) - (146" wb)						
Utiline PU	200	500	850	1950	3600	5100
Sweptline PU	200	550	900	2000	3600	5200
Series W300 4WD - (1-Ton) - (133" wb)						
Utiline PU	200	500	850	1950	3600	5100
Platform	200	500	850	1850	3350	4900
Stake	200	500	850	1900	3500	5000
WM300 Power-Wagon - (1-Ton) - (126" wb)						
Utiline PU	350	900	1550	3050	5900	8500

NOTES: Add 10 percent for V-8 engine.
Add 5 percent for automatic transmission.
Add 4 percent for power winch.

1968

	6	5	4	3	2	1
A100 Compact - (1/2-Ton) - (90" wb)						
PU	200	600	950	2200	3900	5600
Panel Van	200	550	900	2000	3600	5200
Van	200	500	850	1950	3600	5100
A108 Compact - (1/2-Ton) - (108" wb)						
Panel Van	200	550	900	2100	3700	5300
Van	200	550	900	2000	3600	5200
Series D100 - (1/2-Ton) - (114" wb)						
Utiline PU	200	650	1000	2200	4100	5800
Sweptline PU	200	650	1000	2200	4150	5900
Series D100 - (1/2-Ton) - (128" wb)						
Utiline PU	200	600	1000	2200	4000	5700
Sweptline PU	200	650	1000	2200	4100	5800
Platform	200	500	850	1900	3500	5000
Stake	200	500	850	1950	3600	5100
Series D200 - (3/4-Ton) - (128" wb)						
Utiline PU	200	600	950	2150	3850	5500
Sweptline PU	200	600	950	2200	3900	5600
Platform	200	500	850	1850	3350	4900
Stake	200	500	850	1900	3500	5000
D200 Crew Cab - (3/4-Ton) - (146" wb)						
Utiline PU	200	550	900	2150	3800	5400
Sweptline PU	200	600	950	2150	3850	5500
Series D300 - (1-Ton) - (133" wb)						
Utiline PU	200	500	850	1900	3500	5000
Platform	150	450	800	1800	3300	4800
Stake	200	500	850	1850	3350	4900
Series W100 4WD - (1/2-Ton) - (114" wb)						
Utiline PU	200	650	1000	2200	4150	5900
Sweptline PU	200	650	1050	2250	4200	6000
Series W200 4WD - (3/4-Ton) - (128" wb)						
Utiline PU	200	600	1000	2200	4000	5700
Sweptline PU	200	650	1000	2200	4100	5800
Platform	200	500	850	1900	3500	5000
Stake	200	500	850	1950	3600	5100
W200 Crew Cab 4WD - (3/4-Ton) - (146" wb)						
Utiline PU	200	500	850	1950	3600	5100
Sweptline PU	200	550	900	2000	3600	5200
Series W300 4WD - (1-Ton) - (133" wb)						
Utiline PU	200	500	850	1950	3600	5100
Platform	200	500	850	1850	3350	4900
Stake	200	500	850	1900	3500	5000
WM300 Power-Wagon - (1-Ton) - (126" wb)						
Utiline PU	350	900	1550	3050	5900	8500

NOTES: Add 10 percent for V-8 engine.
Add 5 percent for automatic transmission.
Add 4 percent for power winch.

1969

	6	5	4	3	2	1
A100 Compact - (1/2-Ton) - (90" wb)						
PU	200	600	950	2200	3900	5600
Panel Van	200	550	900	2000	3600	5200
Van	200	500	850	1950	3600	5100
A108 Compact - (1/2-Ton) - (108" wb)						
Panel Van	200	550	900	2100	3700	5300
Van	200	550	900	2000	3600	5200
Series D100 - (1/2-Ton) - (114" wb)						
Utiline PU	200	650	1000	2200	4100	5800
Sweptline PU	200	650	1000	2200	4150	5900
Series D100 - (1/2-Ton) - (128" wb)						
Utiline PU	200	600	1000	2200	4000	5700
Sweptline PU	200	650	1000	2200	4100	5800
Platform	200	500	850	1900	3500	5000
Stake	200	500	850	1950	3600	5100
Series D200 - (3/4-Ton) - (128" wb)						
Utiline PU	200	600	950	2150	3850	5500
Sweptline PU	200	600	950	2200	3900	5600
Platform	200	500	850	1850	3350	4900
Stake	200	500	850	1900	3500	5000
D200 Crew Cab - (3/4-Ton) - (146" wb)						
Utiline PU	200	550	900	2150	3800	5400
Sweptline PU	200	600	950	2150	3850	5500
Series D300 - (1-Ton) - (133" wb)						
Utiline PU	200	500	850	1900	3500	5000
Platform	150	450	800	1800	3300	4800
Stake	200	500	850	1850	3350	4900
D300 Crew Cab - (1-Ton) - (159" wb)						
Utiline PU	200	500	850	1950	3600	5100
Sweptline PU	200	550	900	2000	3600	5200
Series W100 4WD - (1/2-Ton) - (114" wb)						
Utiline PU	200	650	1000	2200	4150	5900
Sweptline PU	200	650	1050	2250	4200	6000
Series W200 4WD - (3/4-Ton) - (128" wb)						
Utiline PU	200	500	850	1950	3600	5100
Sweptline PU	200	550	900	2000	3600	5200
Platform	200	500	850	1850	3350	4900
Stake	200	500	850	1900	3500	5000
W200 Crew Cab 4WD - (3/4-Ton) - (146" wb)						
Utiline PU	200	500	850	1900	3500	5000
Sweptline PU	200	500	850	1950	3600	5100
Series W300 4WD - (1-Ton) - (133" wb)						
Utiline PU	200	500	850	1950	3600	5100
Platform	150	450	800	1800	3300	4800
Stake	200	500	850	1850	3350	4900

1970

	6	5	4	3	2	1
A100 Compact - (1/2-Ton) - (90" wb)						
PU	200	600	950	2200	3900	5600
Panel Van	200	550	900	2000	3600	5200
Van	200	500	850	1950	3600	5100
A108 Compact - (1/2-Ton) - (108" wb)						
Panel Van	200	550	900	2100	3700	5300
Van	200	550	900	2000	3600	5200
Series D100 - (1/2-Ton) - (114" wb)						
Utiline PU	200	650	1000	2200	4100	5800
Sweptline PU	200	650	1000	2200	4150	5900
Series D100 - (1/2-Ton) - (128" wb)						
Utiline PU	200	600	1000	2200	4000	5700
Sweptline PU	200	650	1000	2200	4100	5800
Platform	200	500	850	1900	3500	5000
Stake	200	500	850	1950	3600	5100
Series D200 - (3/4-Ton) - (128" wb)						
Utiline PU	200	600	950	2150	3850	5500
Sweptline PU	200	600	950	2200	3900	5600
Platform	200	500	850	1850	3350	4900
Stake	200	500	850	1900	3500	5000
D200 Crew Cab - (3/4-Ton) - (146" wb)						
Utiline PU	200	550	900	2150	3800	5400
Sweptline PU	200	600	950	2150	3850	5500
Series D300 - (1-Ton) - (133" wb)						
Utiline PU	200	500	850	1900	3500	5000
Platform	150	450	800	1800	3300	4800
Stake	200	500	850	1850	3350	4900
D300 Crew Cab - (1-Ton) - (159" wb)						
Utiline PU	200	500	850	1950	3600	5100
Sweptline PU	200	550	900	2000	3600	5200
Series W100 4WD - (1/2-Ton) - (114" wb)						
Utiline PU	200	650	1000	2200	4150	5900
Sweptline PU	200	650	1050	2250	4200	6000
Series W100 4WD - (1/2-Ton) - (128" wb)						
Utiline PU	200	650	1050	2250	4200	6000
Sweptline PU	200	675	1050	2250	4300	6100
Series W200 4WD - (3/4-Ton) - (128" wb)						
Utiline PU	200	500	850	1950	3600	5100
Sweptline PU	200	550	900	2000	3600	5200
Platform	200	500	850	1850	3350	4900
Stake	200	500	850	1900	3500	5000
W200 Crew Cab 4WD - (3/4-Ton) - (146" wb)						
Utiline PU	200	500	850	1900	3500	5000
Sweptline PU	200	500	850	1950	3600	5100
Series W300 4WD - (1-Ton) - (133" wb)						
Utiline PU	200	500	850	1950	3600	5100
Platform	150	450	800	1800	3300	4800
Stake	200	500	850	1850	3350	4900

NOTE: Add 10 percent for V-8 engine.

1971

	6	5	4	3	2	1
Series B100 Van - (1/2-Ton)						
Van (109" wb)	150	300	750	1350	2700	3900
Van (127" wb)	150	350	750	1450	2900	4100
Series B200 Van - (3/4-Ton)						
Van (109" wb)	150	300	700	1250	2600	3700
Van (127" wb)	150	300	750	1350	2700	3900
Series B300 Van - (1-Ton)						
Van (109" wb)	125	250	700	1150	2500	3600
Van (127" wb)	150	300	700	1250	2650	3800
Series D100 - (1/2-Ton) - (114" wb)						
Utiline PU	200	650	1000	2200	4100	5800
Sweptline PU	200	650	1000	2200	4150	5900
Series D100 - (1/2-Ton) - (128" wb)						
Utiline PU	200	600	1000	2200	4000	5700
Sweptline PU	200	650	1000	2200	4100	5800
Series D200 - (3/4-Ton) - (128" wb)						
Utiline PU	200	600	950	2150	3850	5500
Sweptline PU	200	600	950	2200	3900	5600
D200 Crew Cab - (3/4-Ton)						
Utiline PU (146" wb)	200	500	850	1850	3350	4900
Sweptline PU (146" wb)	200	500	850	1900	3500	5000
Utiline PU (160" wb)	150	450	800	1750	3250	4700
Sweptline PU (160" wb)	150	450	800	1750	3250	4700
Series D300 - (1-Ton) - (133" or 159" wb)						
Utiline PU	200	500	850	1900	3500	5000
Crew Utiline	150	450	800	1800	3300	4800
Series W100 4WD - (1/2-Ton)						
Utiline PU (114" wb)	200	650	1000	2200	4150	5900
Sweptline PU (114" wb)	200	650	1050	2250	4200	6000
Utiline PU (128" wb)	200	650	1050	2250	4200	6000
Sweptline PU (128" wb)	200	675	1050	2250	4300	6100
Series W200 4WD - (3/4-Ton) - (128" wb)						
Utiline PU	200	500	850	1950	3600	5100
Sweptline PU	200	550	900	2000	3600	5200
W200 Crew Cab 4WD - (3/4-Ton) - (146" wb)						
Utiline PU	200	500	850	1900	3500	5000
Sweptline PU	200	500	850	1950	3600	5100
Series W300 4WD - (1-Ton) - (133" wb)						
Utiline PU	200	500	850	1950	3600	5100
Platform	150	450	800	1800	3300	4800
Stake	200	500	850	1850	3350	4900

NOTES: Add 10 percent for V-8 engine.
Add 10 percent for Maxivan package.

1972

	6	5	4	3	2	1
Series B100 Van - (1/2-Ton)						
Van (109" wb)	125	250	700	1150	2500	3600
Van (127" wb)	150	300	700	1250	2650	3800
Series B200 Van - (3/4-Ton)						
Van (109" wb)	125	250	700	1150	2400	3400
Van (127" wb)	125	250	700	1150	2500	3600
Maxivan	150	300	700	1250	2650	3800
Series B300 Van - (1-Ton)						
Van (109" wb)	125	200	600	1100	2250	3200
Van (127" wb)	125	250	700	1150	2400	3400
Maxivan	125	250	700	1150	2500	3600
Series D100 - (1/2-Ton)						
Utiline PU (115" wb)	200	500	850	1950	3600	5100
Sweptline PU (115" wb)	200	550	900	2000	3600	5200
Utiline PU (131" wb)	200	550	900	2000	3600	5200
Sweptline PU (131" wb)	200	550	900	2100	3700	5300
Series D200 - (3/4-Ton) - (131" wb)						
Utiline PU	200	500	850	1900	3500	5000
Sweptline PU	200	500	850	1950	3600	5100
D200 Crew Cab - (3/4-Ton)						
Utiline PU (149" wb)	150	450	800	1800	3300	4800
Sweptline PU (149" wb)	200	500	850	1850	3350	4900
Utiline PU (165" wb)	150	450	800	1750	3250	4700
Sweptline PU (165" wb)	150	450	800	1800	3300	4800
Series D300 - (1-Ton) - (135" wb)						
Utiline PU	150	400	750	1650	3150	4500
Series W100 4WD - (1/2-Ton)						
Utiline PU (115" wb)	200	550	900	2150	3800	5400
Sweptline PU (115" wb)	200	600	950	2150	3850	5500
Utiline PU (131" wb)	200	550	900	2100	3700	5300
Sweptline PU (131" wb)	200	550	900	2150	3800	5400
Series W200 4WD - (3/4-Ton) - (131" wb)						
Utiline PU	200	500	850	1950	3600	5100
Sweptline PU	200	550	900	2000	3600	5200
W200 Crew Cab 4WD - (3/4-Ton) - (149" wb)						
Utiline PU	200	500	850	1900	3500	5000
Sweptline PU	200	500	850	1950	3600	5100
Series W300 4WD - (1-Ton) - (135" wb)						
Utiline PU	200	500	850	1850	3350	4900
Platform	150	450	750	1700	3200	4600
Stake	150	450	800	1750	3250	4700

NOTE: Add 10 percent for V-8 engine.

1973

	6	5	4	3	2	1
Series B100 Van - (1/2-Ton)						
Van (109" wb)	125	250	700	1150	2500	3600
Van (127" wb)	150	300	700	1250	2650	3800
Series B200 Van - (3/4-Ton)						
Van (109" wb)	125	250	700	1150	2400	3400
Van (127" wb)	125	250	700	1150	2500	3600
Maxivan	150	300	700	1250	2650	3800
Series B300 Van - (1-Ton)						
Van (109" wb)	125	200	600	1100	2250	3200
Van (127" wb)	125	250	700	1150	2400	3400
Maxivan	125	250	700	1150	2500	3600
Kary Van	150	300	700	1250	2600	3700
Series D100 - (1/2-Ton)						
Utiline PU (115" wb)	200	500	850	1950	3600	5100
Sweptline PU (115" wb)	200	550	900	2000	3600	5200
Utiline PU (131" wb)	200	550	900	2000	3600	5200
Sweptline PU (131" wb)	200	550	900	2100	3700	5300
Series D200 - (3/4-Ton) - (131" wb)						
Utiline PU	200	500	850	1900	3500	5000
Sweptline PU	200	500	850	1950	3600	5100
D200 Crew Cab - (3/4-Ton)						
Utiline PU (149" wb)	150	450	800	1800	3300	4800
Sweptline PU (149" wb)	200	500	850	1850	3350	4900
Utiline PU (165" wb)	150	450	800	1750	3250	4700
Sweptline PU (165" wb)	150	450	800	1800	3300	4800
D100 Club Cab - (1/2-Ton)						
Sweptline PU (133" wb)	200	500	850	1900	3500	5000
Sweptline PU (149" wb)	200	500	850	1950	3600	5100
D200 Club Cab - (3/4-Ton) - (149" wb)						
Sweptline PU	200	500	850	1850	3350	4900
Series D300 - (1-Ton) - (135" wb)						
Utiline PU	150	400	750	1650	3150	4500
Series W100 4WD - (1/2-Ton)						
Utiline PU (115" wb)	200	550	900	2150	3800	5400
Sweptline PU (115" wb)	200	600	950	2150	3850	5500
Utiline PU (131" wb)	200	550	900	2100	3700	5300
Sweptline PU (131" wb)	200	550	900	2150	3800	5400
Series W200 4WD - (3/4-Ton) - (131" wb)						
Utiline PU	200	500	850	1950	3600	5100
Sweptline PU	200	550	900	2000	3600	5200
W200 Crew Cab 4WD - (3/4-Ton) - (149" wb)						
Utiline PU	200	500	850	1900	3500	5000
Sweptline PU	200	500	850	1950	3600	5100
Series W300 4WD - (1-Ton) - (135" wb)						
Utiline PU	200	500	850	1850	3350	4900
Platform	150	450	750	1700	3200	4600
Stake	150	450	800	1750	3250	4700

NOTE: Add 10 percent for V-8 engine.

1974

	6	5	4	3	2	1
AW100 Ramcharger 4WD - (1/2-Ton) - (106" wb)						
Spt	200	650	1000	2200	4100	5800
Series B100 Van - (1/2-Ton)						
Van (109" wb)	125	250	700	1150	2500	3600
Van (127" wb)	150	300	700	1250	2650	3800
Series B200 Van - (3/4-Ton)						
Van (109" wb)	125	250	700	1150	2400	3400
Van (127" wb)	125	250	700	1150	2500	3600
Maxivan	150	300	700	1250	2650	3800
Series B300 Van - (1-Ton)						
Van (109" wb)	125	200	600	1100	2250	3200
Van (127" wb)	125	250	700	1150	2400	3400
Maxivan	125	250	700	1150	2500	3600
Series CB Kary Van - (1-Ton) - (127" or 145" wb)						
10-ft. body	150	300	700	1250	2600	3700
12-ft. body	125	250	700	1150	2500	3600
Series D100 - (1/2-Ton)						
Utiline PU (115" wb)	200	500	850	1950	3600	5100
Sweptline PU (115" wb)	200	550	900	2000	3600	5200
Utiline PU (131" wb)	200	550	900	2000	3600	5200
Sweptline PU (131" wb)	200	550	900	2100	3700	5300

	6	5	4	3	2	1
Series D100 Club Cab - (1/2-Ton)						
Sweptline PU (133" wb)	200	500	850	1900	3500	5000
Sweptline PU (149" wb)	200	500	850	1950	3600	5100
Series D200 - (3/4-Ton) - (131" wb)						
Utiline PU	200	500	850	1900	3500	5000
Sweptline PU	200	500	850	1950	3600	5100
D200 Club Cab - (3/4-Ton) - (149" wb)						
Sweptline PU	200	500	850	1850	3350	4900
D200 Crew Cab - (3/4-Ton)						
Utiline PU (149" wb)	150	450	800	1800	3300	4800
Sweptline PU (149" wb)	200	500	850	1850	3350	4900
Utiline PU (165" wb)	150	450	800	1750	3250	4700
Sweptline PU (165" wb)	150	450	800	1800	3300	4800
Series D300 - (1-Ton) - (135" wb)						
Utiline PU	150	400	750	1650	3150	4500
Series W100 4WD - (1/2-Ton)						
Utiline PU (115" wb)	200	550	900	2150	3800	5400
Sweptline PU (115" wb)	200	600	950	2150	3850	5500
Utiline PU (131" wb)	200	550	900	2100	3700	5300
Sweptline PU (131" wb)	200	550	900	2150	3800	5400
Series W100 Club Cab 4WD - (1/2-Ton)						
Sweptline PU (133" wb)	200	550	900	2100	3700	5300
Sweptline PU (149" wb)	200	500	850	1950	3600	5100
Series W200 4WD - (3/4-Ton)						
Utiline PU (131" wb)	200	500	850	1950	3600	5100
Sweptline PU (131" wb)	200	550	900	2000	3600	5200
Sweptline Clb Cab (149" wb)	200	550	900	2100	3700	5300
Series W200 Crew Cab 4WD - (3/4-Ton) - (149" wb)						
Utiline PU	200	500	850	1900	3500	5000
Sweptline PU	200	500	850	1950	3600	5100
Series W300 4WD - (1-Ton) - (135" wb)						
Utiline PU	200	500	850	1850	3350	4900

NOTES: Add 10 percent for V-8 engine.
Add 12 percent for 440 CID V-8.

1975

	6	5	4	3	2	1
Ramcharger - (1/2-Ton) - (106" wb)						
AD100 2WD	200	550	900	2000	3600	5200
AW100 4WD	200	650	1000	2200	4100	5800
Series B100 Van - (1/2-Ton)						
Van (109" wb)	125	250	700	1150	2500	3600
Van (127" wb)	150	300	700	1250	2650	3800
Series B200 Van - (3/4-Ton)						
Van (109" wb)	125	250	700	1150	2400	3400
Van (127" wb)	125	250	700	1150	2500	3600
Maxivan	150	300	700	1250	2650	3800
Series B300 Van - (1-Ton)						
Van (109" wb)	125	200	600	1100	2250	3200
Van (127" wb)	125	250	700	1150	2400	3400
Maxivan	125	250	700	1150	2500	3600
Series CB Kary Van - (1-Ton) - (127" or 145" wb)						
10-ft. body	150	300	700	1250	2600	3700
12-ft. body	125	250	700	1150	2500	3600
Series D100 - (1/2-Ton)						
Utiline PU (115" wb)	200	500	850	1950	3600	5100
Sweptline PU (115" wb)	200	550	900	2000	3600	5200
Utiline PU (131" wb)	200	550	900	2000	3600	5200
Sweptline PU (131" wb)	200	550	900	2100	3700	5300
Series D100 Club Cab - (1/2-Ton)						
Sweptline PU (133" wb)	200	500	850	1900	3500	5000
Sweptline PU (149" wb)	200	500	850	1950	3600	5100
Series D200 - (3/4-Ton) - (131" wb)						
Utiline PU	200	500	850	1900	3500	5000
Sweptline PU	200	500	850	1950	3600	5100
Sweptline Clb Cab	200	500	850	1850	3350	4900
D200 Crew Cab - (3/4-Ton)						
Utiline PU (149" wb)	150	450	800	1800	3300	4800
Sweptline PU (149" wb)	200	500	850	1850	3350	4900
Utiline PU (165" wb)	150	450	800	1750	3250	4700
Sweptline PU (165" wb)	150	450	800	1800	3300	4800
Series D300 - (1-Ton) - (135" wb)						
Utiline PU	150	400	750	1650	3150	4500
Series W100 4WD - (1/2-Ton)						
Utiline PU (115" wb)	200	550	900	2150	3800	5400
Sweptline PU (115" wb)	200	600	950	2150	3850	5500
Utiline PU (131" wb)	200	550	900	2100	3700	5300
Sweptline PU (131" wb)	200	550	900	2150	3800	5400
Series W100 Club Cab 4WD - (1/2-Ton)						
Sweptline PU (133" wb)	200	550	900	2100	3700	5300
Sweptline PU (149" wb)	200	500	850	1950	3600	5100
Series W200 4WD- (3/4-Ton)						
Utiline PU (131" wb)	200	500	850	1950	3600	5100
Sweptline PU (131" wb)	200	550	900	2000	3600	5200
Sweptline Clb Cab (149" wb)	200	550	900	2100	3700	5300
Series W200 Crew Cab 4WD - (3/4-Ton) - (149" wb)						
Utiline PU	200	500	850	1900	3500	5000
Sweptline PU	200	500	850	1950	3600	5100
Series W300 4WD - (1-Ton) - (135" wb)						
Utiline PU	200	500	850	1850	3350	4900

NOTES: Add 10 percent for V-8 engine.
Add 12 percent for 440 CID V-8.

1976

	6	5	4	3	2	1
Ramcharger - (1/2-Ton) - (106" wb)						
AD100 2WD	200	500	850	1900	3500	5000
AW100 4WD	200	600	950	2200	3900	5600
Series B100 Van - (1/2-Ton)						
Van (109" wb)	125	250	700	1150	2450	3500
Van (127" wb)	150	300	700	1250	2600	3700
Series B200 Van - (3/4-Ton)						
Van (109" wb)	125	200	600	1100	2250	3200
Van (127" wb)	125	250	700	1150	2400	3400
Maxivan	125	250	700	1150	2500	3600
Series B300 Van - (1-Ton)						
Van (109" wb)	100	175	525	1050	2100	3000
Van (127" wb)	125	200	600	1100	2250	3200
Maxivan	125	250	700	1150	2400	3400
Series CB300 Kary Van - (1-Ton) - (127" or 145" wb)						
10-ft. body	125	200	600	1100	2300	3300
12-ft. x 80 in. body	125	250	700	1150	2400	3400
12-ft. x 94 in. body	125	250	700	1150	2500	3600
Series D100 - (1/2-Ton)						
Utiline PU (115" wb)	200	500	850	1850	3350	4900
Sweptline PU (115" wb)	200	500	850	1900	3500	5000
Utiline PU (131" wb)	200	500	850	1900	3500	5000
Sweptline PU (131" wb)	200	500	850	1950	3600	5100

	6	5	4	3	2	1
D100 Club Cab - (1/2-Ton)						
Sweptline PU (133" wb)	150	450	800	1800	3300	4800
Sweptline PU (149" wb)	200	500	850	1850	3350	4900
Series D200 - (3/4- Ton)						
Utiline PU (131" wb)	150	450	800	1750	3250	4700
Sweptline PU (131" wb)	150	450	800	1800	3300	4800
Sweptline Clb PU (149" wb)	200	500	850	1900	3500	5000
D200 Crew Cab - (3/4-Ton)						
Utiline PU (149" wb)	150	400	750	1650	3150	4500
Sweptline PU (149" wb)	150	450	750	1700	3200	4600
Utiline PU (165" wb)	150	400	750	1600	3100	4400
Sweptline PU (165" wb)	150	400	750	1650	3150	4500
Series D300 - (1-Ton)						
Sweptline P.U. (131" wb)	150	350	750	1450	3000	4200
Sweptline Clb (149" wb)	150	400	750	1600	3100	4400
Series W100 4WD - (1/2-Ton)						
Utiline PU (115" wb)	200	550	900	2100	3700	5300
Sweptline PU (115" wb)	200	600	950	2150	3850	5500
Utiline PU (131" wb)	200	550	900	2150	3800	5400
Sweptline PU (131" wb)	200	600	950	2200	3900	5600
W100 Club Cab 4WD - (1/2-Ton)						
Sweptline PU (133" wb)	200	500	850	1850	3350	4900
Sweptline PU (149" wb)	150	450	800	1800	3300	4800
Series W200 4WD - (3/4-Ton)						
Utiline PU (131" wb)	150	450	800	1750	3250	4700
Sweptline PU (131" wb)	150	450	800	1800	3300	4800
Sweptline Clb (149" wb)	200	500	850	1850	3350	4900
W200 Crew Cab 4WD - (3/4-Ton) - (149" wb)						
Utiline PU	150	450	800	1800	3300	4800
Sweptline PU	200	500	850	1850	3350	4900

NOTES: Add 10 percent for V-8 engine.
Add 12 percent for 440 CID V-8 engine.

1977

	6	5	4	3	2	1
Ramcharger - (1/2-Ton) - (106" wb)						
AD100 2WD	200	500	850	1900	3500	5000
AW100 4WD	200	600	950	2200	3900	5600
Series B100 Tradesman Van - (1/2-Ton)						
Van (109" wb)	125	250	700	1150	2450	3500
Van (127" wb)	150	300	700	1250	2600	3700
Series B200 Tradesman Van - (3/4-Ton)						
Van (109" wb)	125	200	600	1100	2250	3200
Van (127" wb)	125	250	700	1150	2400	3400
Maxivan	125	250	700	1150	2500	3600
Series B300 Tradesman Van - (1-Ton)						
Van (109" wb)	100	175	525	1050	2100	3000
Van (127" wb)	125	200	600	1100	2250	3200
Maxivan	125	250	700	1150	2400	3400
Series CB300 Kary Van - (1-Ton) - (127" or 145" wb)						
10-ft. body	125	200	600	1100	2300	3300
12-ft. body	125	250	700	1150	2400	3400
Series D100 - (1/2-Ton)						
Utiline PU (115" wb)	200	500	850	1850	3350	4900
Sweptline PU (115" wb)	200	500	850	1900	3500	5000
Utiline PU (131" wb)	200	500	850	1900	3500	5000
Sweptline PU (131" wb)	200	500	850	1950	3600	5100
D100 Club Car - (1/2-Ton)						
Sweptline PU (133" wb)	150	450	800	1800	3300	4800
Sweptline PU (149" wb)	200	500	850	1850	3350	4900
Series D150 - (HD 1/2-Ton)						
Utiline PU (115" wb)	150	400	750	1650	3150	4500
Sweptline PU (115" wb)	150	450	750	1700	3200	4600
Utiline PU (131" wb)	150	450	800	1750	3250	4700
Sweptline PU (131" wb)	150	450	800	1800	3300	4800
D150 Club Cab - (1/2-Ton)						
Sweptline PU (133" wb)	200	500	850	1900	3500	5000
Sweptline PU (149" wb)	150	450	800	1750	3250	4700
Series D200 - (3/4-Ton) - (131" wb)						
Utiline PU	200	500	850	1850	3350	4900
Sweptline PU	200	500	850	1900	3500	5000
D200 Club or Crew Cab - (3/4-Ton) - (149" or 165" wb)						
Utiline Clb	150	400	750	1650	3150	4500
Sweptline Crew	150	450	750	1700	3200	4600
Utiline Crew (165" wb)	150	350	750	1350	2800	4000
Sweptline Crew (165" wb)	150	350	750	1450	2900	4100
Series D300 - (1-Ton)						
Sweptline PU (131" wb)	150	300	700	1250	2650	3800
Sweptline Clb (149" wb)	150	300	750	1350	2700	3900
Series W100 4WD - (1/2-Ton)						
Utiline PU (115" wb)	200	550	900	2100	3700	5300
Sweptline PU (115" wb)	200	600	950	2150	3850	5500
Utiline PU (131" wb)	200	550	900	2150	3800	5400
Sweptline PU (131" wb)	200	600	950	2200	3900	5600
Series W100 Club Cab 4WD - (1/2-Ton)						
Sweptline PU (133" wb)	200	500	850	1850	3350	4900
Sweptline PU (149" wb)	150	450	800	1800	3300	4800
Series W150 4WD - (1/2-Ton)						
Utiline PU (115" wb)	150	450	800	1750	3250	4700
Sweptline PU (115" wb)	150	450	800	1800	3300	4800
Utiline PU (131" wb)	150	450	800	1800	3300	4800
Sweptline PU (131" wb)	200	500	850	1850	3350	4900
W150 Club Cab 4WD - (1/2-Ton)						
Sweptline PU (133" wb)	150	450	750	1700	3200	4600
Sweptline PU (149" wb)	150	400	750	1650	3150	4500
Series W200 4WD - (3/4-Ton) - (131" wb)						
Utiline PU	150	450	800	1800	3300	4800
Sweptline PU	200	500	850	1850	3350	4900
W200 Club or Crew Cab 4WD - (3/4-Ton) - (149" wb)						
Sweptline Clb	200	500	850	1900	3500	5000
Utiline Crew	150	450	800	1800	3300	4800
Sweptline Crew	200	500	850	1850	3350	4900

NOTE: Add 10 percent for V-8 engine.

1978

	6	5	4	3	2	1
Ramcharger - (1/2-Ton) - (106" wb)						
AD100 2WD	200	500	850	1900	3500	5000
AW100 4WD	200	600	950	2200	3900	5600
Series B100 Tradesman Van - (1/2-Ton)						
Van (109" wb)	125	250	700	1150	2450	3500
Van (127" wb)	150	300	700	1250	2600	3700
Series B200 Tradesman Van - (3/4-Ton)						
Van (109" wb)	125	200	600	1100	2250	3200
Van (127" wb)	125	250	700	1150	2400	3400
Maxivan	125	250	700	1150	2500	3600
Series B300 Tradesman Van - (1-Ton)						
Van (109" wb)	100	175	525	1050	2100	3000
Van (127" wb)	125	200	600	1100	2250	3200
Maxivan	125	250	700	1150	2400	3400
Series CB300 Kary Van - (1-Ton) - (127" or 145" wb)						
10-ft. body	125	200	600	1100	2300	3300
12-ft. body	125	250	700	1150	2400	3400
Series D100 - (1/2-Ton)						
Utiline PU (115" wb)	200	500	850	1850	3350	4900
Sweptline PU (115" wb)	200	500	850	1900	3500	5000
Utiline PU (131" wb)	200	600	950	2150	3850	5500
Sweptline PU (131" wb)	200	500	850	1950	3600	5100
D100 Club Cab - (1/2-Ton)						
Sweptline PU (133" wb)	150	450	800	1800	3300	4800
Sweptline PU (149" wb)	200	500	850	1850	3350	4900
Series D150 - (HD - 1/2-Ton)						
Utiline PU (115" wb)	150	400	750	1650	3150	4500
Sweptline PU (115" wb)	150	450	750	1700	3200	4600
Utiline PU (131" wb)	150	450	800	1750	3250	4700
Sweptline PU (131" wb)	150	450	800	1800	3300	4800

NOTE: Add 40 percent for Li'l Red Express.
Add 20 percent for Warlock option.
Add 20 percent for Macho Power-Wagon option.

	6	5	4	3	2	1
D150 Club Cab - (1/2-Ton)						
Sweptline PU (133" wb)	200	500	850	1900	3500	5000
Sweptline PU (149" wb)	150	450	800	1750	3250	4700
Series D200 - (3/4-Ton) - (131" wb)						
Utiline PU	200	500	850	1850	3350	4900
Sweptline PU	200	500	850	1900	3500	5000
D200 Club or Crew Cab - (3/4-Ton)						
Utiline Clb (149" wb)	150	400	750	1650	3150	4500
Utiline Crew (149" wb)	150	450	750	1700	3200	4600
Sweptline Crew (149" wb)	150	400	750	1600	3100	4400
Utiline Crew (165" wb)	150	350	750	1350	2800	4000
Sweptline Crew (165" wb)	150	350	750	1450	2900	4100
Series D300 - (1-Ton)						
Sweptline PU (131" wb)	150	300	700	1250	2650	3800
Sweptline PU (149" wb)	150	300	750	1350	2700	3900
Sweptline Crew	150	300	700	1250	2600	3700
Series W150 4WD - (1/2-Ton)						
Utiline PU (115" wb)	200	550	900	2100	3700	5300
Sweptline PU (115" wb)	200	600	950	2150	3850	5500
Utiline PU (131" wb)	200	550	900	2150	3800	5400
Sweptline PU (131" wb)	200	600	950	2200	3900	5600
W150 Club Cab 4WD						
Sweptline PU (133" wb)	200	550	900	2000	3600	5200
Sweptline PU (149" wb)	200	500	850	1900	3500	5000
Series W200 4WD - (3/4-Ton) - (131" wb)						
Utiline PU	150	450	800	1800	3300	4800
Sweptline PU	200	500	850	1850	3350	4900
W200 Club or Crew Cab 4WD - (3/4-Ton) - (149" wb)						
Clb Sweptline	200	500	850	1900	3500	5000
Crew Sweptline	150	450	800	1800	3300	4800

NOTE: Add 10 percent for V-8 engine.

1979

	6	5	4	3	2	1
Series D50 Mini Pickup - (1/4-Ton) - (109.4" wb)						
Sweptline	150	350	750	1450	3000	4200
Spt	150	400	750	1650	3150	4500
Ramcharger - (1/2-Ton) - (106" wb)						
AD100 2WD	200	500	850	1900	3500	5000
AW100 4WD	200	600	950	2200	3900	5600
Series B100 Tradesman Van - (1/2-Ton)						
Van (109" wb)	125	250	700	1150	2450	3500
Van (127" wb)	150	300	700	1250	2600	3700
Series B200 Tradesman Van - (3/4-Ton)						
Van (109" wb)	125	200	600	1100	2250	3200
Van (127" wb)	125	250	700	1150	2400	3400
Maxivan	125	250	700	1150	2500	3600
Series B300 Tradesman Van - (1-Ton)						
Van (109" wb)	100	175	525	1050	2100	3000
Van (127" wb)	125	200	600	1100	2250	3200
Maxivan	125	250	700	1150	2400	3400
Series CB300 Kary Van - (1-Ton) - (127" or 145" wb)						
10-ft. body	125	200	600	1100	2300	3300
12-ft. body	125	250	700	1150	2400	3400
Series D100 - (1/2-Ton)						
Utiline PU (115" wb)	200	550	900	2150	3800	5400
Sweptline PU (115" wb)	200	500	850	1900	3500	5000
Utiline PU (131" wb)	200	500	850	1900	3500	5000
Sweptline PU (131" wb)	200	500	850	1950	3600	5100
D100 Club Cab - (1/2-Ton)						
Sweptline PU (133" wb)	150	450	800	1800	3300	4800
Sweptline PU (149" wb)	200	500	850	1850	3350	4900
Series D150 - (HD - 1/2-Ton)						
Utiline PU (115" wb)	200	500	850	1900	3500	5000
Sweptline PU (115" wb)	150	450	750	1700	3200	4600
Utiline PU (131" wb)	150	450	800	1750	3250	4700
Sweptline PU (131" wb)	150	450	800	1800	3300	4800

NOTE: Add 40 percent for Li'l Red Express.
Add 20 percent for Warlock option.
Add 20 percent for Macho Power-Wagon option.

	6	5	4	3	2	1
D150 Club Cab - (1/2-Ton)						
Sweptline PU (133" wb)	200	500	850	1900	3500	5000
Sweptline PU (149" wb)	150	450	800	1750	3250	4700
Series D200 - (3/4-Ton) - (131" wb)						
Utiline PU	200	500	850	1850	3350	4900
Sweptline PU	200	500	850	1900	3500	5000
D200 Club or Crew Cab Pickup - (3/4-Ton)						
Sweptline Clb (149" wb)	150	400	750	1650	3150	4500
Utiline Crew (149" wb)	150	450	750	1700	3200	4600
Sweptline Crew (149" wb)	150	400	750	1600	3100	4400
Utiline Crew (165" wb)	150	350	750	1350	2800	4000
Sweptline Crew (165" wb)	150	350	750	1450	2900	4100
Series D300 - (1-Ton)						
Sweptline PU (131" wb)	150	300	700	1250	2650	3800
Sweptline Clb (149" wb)	150	300	750	1350	2700	3900
Sweptline Crew (165" wb)	150	300	700	1250	2600	3700
Series W150 4WD - (1/2-Ton)						
Utiline PU (115" wb)	200	550	900	2100	3700	5300
Sweptline PU (115" wb)	200	600	950	2150	3850	5500
Utiline PU (131" wb)	200	550	900	2150	3800	5400
Sweptline PU (131" wb)	200	600	950	2200	3900	5600
W150 Club Cab 4WD						
Sweptline PU (133" wb)	200	550	900	2000	3600	5200
Sweptline PU (149" wb)	200	500	850	1900	3500	5000
Series W200 4WD - (3/4-Ton) - (131" wb)						
Utiline PU	150	450	800	1800	3300	4800
Sweptline PU	200	500	850	1850	3350	4900

	6	5	4	3	2	1
W200 Club or Crew Cab 4WD - (3/4-Ton) - (149" wb)						
Sweptline Clb	200	500	850	1900	3500	5000
Sweptline Crew	150	450	800	1800	3300	4800

NOTE: Add 10 percent for V-8 engine.

1980

	6	5	4	3	2	1
Series D50 Mini Pickup - (1/4-Ton) - (109.4" wb)						
Sweptline	150	400	750	1550	3050	4300
Spt	150	450	750	1700	3200	4600
Ramcharger HdTp - (1-Ton) - (106" wb)						
AD100 2WD	200	550	900	2000	3600	5200
AW100 4WD	200	650	1000	2200	4100	5800
Series B100 Van/Sportsman - (1/2-Ton)						
Van (109" wb)	125	250	700	1150	2500	3600
Van (127" wb)	150	300	700	1250	2600	3700
Wag (109" wb)	150	300	750	1350	2700	3900
Wag (127" wb)	150	350	750	1450	2900	4100
Series B200 Van/Sportsman - (3/4-Ton)						
Van (109" wb)	125	250	700	1150	2400	3400
Van (127" wb)	125	250	700	1150	2450	3500
Wag (109" wb)	150	300	700	1250	2600	3700
Wag (127" wb)	150	300	750	1350	2700	3900
Maxivan	150	300	700	1250	2650	3800
Maxiwagon	150	350	750	1450	2900	4100
Series B300 Van/Sportsman - (1-Ton) - (127.6" wb)						
Van	125	200	600	1100	2300	3300
Maxivan	125	250	700	1150	2400	3400
Wag	125	250	700	1150	2450	3500
Maxiwagon	125	250	700	1150	2500	3600
Series D150 - (1/2-Ton)						
Utiline PU (115" wb)	150	450	750	1700	3200	4600
Sweptline PU (115" wb)	150	450	800	1750	3250	4700
Utiline PU (131" wb)	150	450	800	1750	3250	4700
Sweptline PU (131" wb)	150	450	800	1800	3300	4800
D150 Club Cab - (1/2-Ton)						
Sweptline PU (133" wb)	200	500	850	1900	3500	5000
Sweptline PU (149" wb)	200	500	850	1850	3350	4900
Series D200 - (3/4-Ton) - (131" wb)						
Utiline PU	200	500	850	1850	3350	4900
Sweptline PU	200	500	850	1900	3500	5000
D200 Club Cab - (3/4-Ton) - (149" wb)						
Sweptline PU	150	450	800	1750	3250	4700
D200 Crew Cab - (3/4-Ton)						
Sweptline PU (149" wb)	150	350	750	1450	3000	4200
Sweptline PU (165" wb)	150	350	750	1350	2800	4000
Series D300 - (1-Ton)						
Sweptline PU (131" wb)	150	350	750	1350	2800	4000
Sweptline Clb (149" wb)	150	350	750	1450	2900	4100
Sweptline Crew (165" wb)	150	450	750	1700	3200	4600
Series W150 4WD - (1/2-Ton)						
Utiline PU (115" wb)	200	550	900	2150	3800	5400
Sweptline PU (115" wb)	200	600	950	2200	3900	5600
Utiline PU (131" wb)	200	600	950	2150	3850	5500
Sweptline PU (131" wb)	200	650	1000	2200	4100	5800
Series W150 Club Cab 4WD - (1/2-Ton)						
Sweptline PU (133" wb)	200	600	1000	2200	4000	5700
Sweptline PU (149" wb)	200	600	950	2200	3900	5600
Series W200 4WD - (3/4-Ton) - (131" wb)						
Utiline PU	200	600	950	2150	3850	5500
Sweptline PU	200	600	1000	2200	4000	5700
W200 Club or Crew Cab 4WD - (3/4-Ton)						
Sweptline Clb (149" wb)	200	500	850	1900	3500	5000
Sweptline Crew (149" wb)	150	450	800	1800	3300	4800

1981

	6	5	4	3	2	1
Ram 50						
Cus PU	75	100	425	800	1400	2000
Royal PU	75	100	425	800	1400	2000
Spt PU	75	100	450	850	1500	2100
Ramcharger						
2WD	200	500	850	1900	3500	5000
4WD	200	650	1050	2250	4200	6000
B150						
Van	125	250	700	1150	2400	3400
Long Range Van	125	200	600	1100	2300	3300
Wag	150	400	750	1600	3100	4400
Mini-Ram Wag	150	400	750	1550	3050	4300
B250						
Van	125	250	700	1150	2400	3400
Wag	150	400	750	1650	3150	4500
Mini-Ram Wag	150	400	750	1550	3050	4300
B350						
Van	125	250	700	1150	2400	3400
Wag	150	400	750	1600	3100	4400
D150						
Utiline PU SBx	100	125	500	950	1700	2400
Sweptline PU SBx	100	150	450	1000	1750	2500
Club Cab PU SBx	100	175	525	1050	2050	2900
Utiline PU LBx	100	150	450	1000	1750	2500
Sweptline PU LBx	100	150	450	1000	1800	2600
Clb Cab PU LBx	100	175	525	1050	2100	3000
D250						
Utiline PU LBx	100	125	475	900	1600	2300
Sweptline PU LBx	100	125	500	950	1700	2400
Clb Cab PU LBx	100	175	525	1050	2050	2900
Crew Cab PU SBx	100	175	525	1050	1950	2800
Crew Cab PU LBx	100	175	525	1050	2050	2900
D350						
Sweptline PU LBx	100	125	475	900	1600	2300
Clb Cab PU LBx	100	175	525	1050	2050	2900
Crew Cab PU	100	175	525	1050	1950	2800

NOTE: Add 15 percent for 4WD.

1982

	6	5	4	3	2	1
Rampage FWD						
PU	75	100	400	750	1350	1900
Spt PU	75	100	400	750	1350	1900
Ram 50						
PU	75	100	400	750	1350	1900
Cus PU	75	100	400	750	1350	1900
Royal PU	75	100	450	850	1500	2100
Spt PU	100	125	450	900	1550	2200
Ramcharger						
2WD	200	500	850	1900	3500	5000
4WD	200	650	1050	2250	4200	6000
B150						
Wag	150	450	800	1750	3250	4700
Van	125	200	600	1100	2250	3200
Mini-Ram Wag	150	450	750	1700	3200	4600
Long Range Ram Van	125	250	700	1150	2400	3400
B250						
Wag	150	450	800	1800	3300	4800
Mini-Ram Wag	150	450	750	1700	3200	4600
Van	125	200	600	1100	2200	3100
B350						
Wag	150	450	800	1750	3250	4700
Van	100	175	525	1050	2100	3000
D150						
Utiline PU SBx	75	100	450	850	1500	2100
Sweptline PU SBx	100	125	450	900	1550	2200
Utiline PU LBx	75	100	450	850	1500	2100
Sweptline PU LBx	100	125	475	900	1600	2300
Sweptline Ram Miser SBx	100	125	475	900	1600	2300
Sweptline Ram Miser LBx	75	100	450	850	1500	2100
Sweptline Clb Cab LBx	100	125	500	950	1700	2400
D250						
Utiline PU LBx	100	125	450	900	1550	2200
Sweptline PU LBx	100	125	475	900	1600	2300
Sweptline Clb Cab LBx	100	125	500	950	1700	2400
D350						
Sweptline PU LBx	75	100	450	850	1500	2100
Sweptline Clb Cab PU LBx	100	125	475	900	1600	2300
Sweptline Crew Cab PU SBx	100	125	450	900	1550	2200
Sweptline Crew Cab PU LBx	100	125	475	900	1600	2300

NOTE: Add 15 percent for 4WD.

1983

	6	5	4	3	2	1
Rampage FWD						
PU	75	100	400	750	1350	1900
GT PU	75	100	425	800	1400	2000
Ram 50						
PU	75	100	450	850	1500	2100
Cus PU	100	125	450	900	1550	2200
Royal PU	100	125	475	900	1600	2300
Spt PU	100	125	500	950	1700	2400
Ramcharger						
2WD	200	600	950	2150	3850	5500
4WD	350	700	1150	2300	4550	6500
B150						
Wag	200	600	950	2150	3850	5500
Van	150	350	750	1350	2800	4000
Mini-Ram Wag	200	550	900	2150	3800	5400
Long Ram Van	150	350	750	1450	3000	4200
B250						
Wag	200	600	950	2150	3850	5500
Ram Van	150	400	750	1650	3150	4500
B350						
Wag	200	550	900	2150	3800	5400
Ram Van	150	400	750	1600	3100	4400
D150						
Utiline PU SBx	125	200	600	1100	2200	3100
Sweptline PU SBx	125	200	600	1100	2250	3200
Utiline PU LBx	125	200	600	1100	2200	3100
Sweptline PU LBx	125	200	600	1100	2300	3300
Sweptline Ram Miser PU SBx	100	175	525	1050	2100	3000
Sweptline Ram Miser PU LBx	125	200	600	1100	2200	3100
D250						
Utiline PU LBx	125	200	600	1100	2250	3200
Sweptline PU LBx	125	200	600	1100	2300	3300
D350						
Sweptline PU LBx	125	200	600	1100	2200	3100
Sweptline Crew Cab PU SBx	125	200	600	1100	2300	3300
Sweptline Crew Cab PU LBx	125	250	700	1150	2400	3400

NOTE: Add 15 percent for 4WD.

1984

	6	5	4	3	2	1
Rampage FWD						
PU	100	125	450	900	1550	2200
PU 2.2	100	125	475	900	1600	2300
Ram 50						
Cus PU	100	150	450	1000	1750	2500
Royal PU	100	150	450	1000	1800	2600
Spt PU	100	150	450	1000	1900	2700
Ramcharger						
2WD	200	650	1050	2250	4200	6000
4WD	350	750	1200	2350	4900	7000
Mini-Ram Van FWD						
Van	125	250	700	1150	2450	3500
Royal Van	150	300	700	1250	2600	3700
Caravan	200	600	950	2150	3850	5500
Caravan SE	200	650	1050	2250	4200	6000
Caravan LE	350	700	1150	2300	4550	6500
B150						
Wag	200	650	1050	2250	4200	6000
Value Wag	350	725	1150	2300	4700	6700
Ram Van	200	500	850	1900	3500	5000
Long Ram Van	200	550	900	2000	3600	5200
B250						
Wag	200	650	1050	2250	4200	6000
Ram Van	200	500	850	1950	3600	5100
B350						
Wag	200	650	1050	2250	4200	6000
Ram Van	200	500	850	1950	3600	5100
D100						
Sweptline PU SBx	150	350	750	1450	2900	4100
Sweptline PU LBx	150	350	750	1450	3000	4200
D150						
Utiline PU SBx	150	350	750	1450	2900	4100
Sweptline PU SBx	150	350	750	1450	3000	4200
Utiline PU LBx	150	350	750	1450	3000	4200
Sweptline PU LBx	150	400	750	1550	3050	4300
D250						
Utiline PU LBx	150	400	750	1550	3050	4300
Sweptline PU LBx	150	400	750	1600	3100	4400
D350						
Sweptline PU LBx	150	400	750	1600	3100	4400
Sweptline Crew Cab PU SBx	150	450	750	1700	3200	4600
Sweptline Crew Cab PU LBx	150	450	800	1750	3250	4700

NOTE: Add 15 percent for 4WD.

		6	5	4	3	2	1

1985

Ram 50

	6	5	4	3	2	1
Cus PU	125	250	700	1150	2450	3500
Royal PU	150	300	700	1250	2600	3700
Spt PU	150	300	700	1250	2650	3800
Ramcharger						
2WD	200	650	1050	2250	4200	6000
4WD	350	750	1200	2350	4900	7000
Mini-Ram Van FWD						
Van	150	400	750	1650	3150	4500
Royal Van	150	450	800	1750	3250	4700
Caravan	200	600	950	2150	3850	5500
Caravan SE	200	650	1050	2250	4200	6000
Caravan LE	350	700	1150	2300	4550	6500
B150						
Wag	350	700	1150	2300	4550	6500
Value Wag	350	725	1150	2300	4700	6700
Ram Van	200	500	850	1900	3500	5000
Long Ram Van	200	550	900	2000	3600	5200
B250						
Wag	350	700	1150	2300	4600	6600
Ram Van	200	500	850	1950	3600	5100
B350						
Wag	350	725	1150	2300	4700	6700
Ram Van	200	500	850	1900	3500	5000
D100						
Sweptline PU SBx	150	350	750	1450	2900	4100
Sweptline PU LBx	150	350	750	1450	3000	4200
D150						
Utiline PU SBx	150	350	750	1450	3000	4200
Sweptline PU SBx	150	400	750	1550	3050	4300
Utiline PU LBx	150	350	750	1450	2900	4100
Sweptline PU LBx	150	350	750	1450	3000	4200
D250						
Utiline PU LBx	150	400	750	1550	3050	4300
Sweptline PU LBx	150	400	750	1600	3100	4400
D350						
Sweptline PU LBx	150	400	750	1600	3100	4400
Sweptline Crew Cab PU SBx	150	450	750	1700	3200	4600
Sweptline Crew Cab PU LBx	150	450	800	1750	3250	4700

NOTE: Add 15 percent for 4WD.

1986

Ram 50

	6	5	4	3	2	1
PU	125	250	700	1150	2450	3500
Spt PU	150	300	700	1250	2600	3700
Ramcharger						
2WD	350	750	1200	2350	4900	7000
4WD	350	800	1450	2750	5600	8000
Mini-Ram Van FWD						
Van	200	600	950	2150	3850	5500
Royal Van	200	600	1000	2200	4000	5700
Caravan	350	700	1150	2300	4550	6500
Caravan SE	350	750	1200	2350	4900	7000
Caravan LE	350	750	1300	2450	5250	7500
B150						
Wag	350	750	1300	2450	5250	7500
Value Wag	350	750	1350	2600	5400	7700
Ram Van	200	650	1050	2250	4200	6000
Long Ram Van	200	675	1050	2250	4350	6200
B250						
Wag	350	750	1300	2500	5300	7600
Ram Van	200	675	1050	2250	4300	6100
B350						
Wag	350	750	1350	2600	5400	7700
Ram Van	200	675	1050	2250	4350	6200
D100						
Sweptline PU SBx	200	500	850	1950	3600	5100
Sweptline PU LBx	200	550	900	2000	3600	5200
D150						
Sweptline PU SBx	200	550	900	2000	3600	5200
Sweptline PU LBx	200	550	900	2100	3700	5300
D250						
Sweptline PU LBx	150	450	800	1800	3300	4800
D350						
Sweptline PU LBx	200	500	850	1850	3350	4900

NOTE: Add 15 percent for 4WD.

FORD

1905
Model E, 78" wb

	6	5	4	3	2	1
Dly Car	700	2300	3800	7600	13,300	19,000

1906
Model T, 84" wb

	6	5	4	3	2	1
PU	550	1700	2800	5600	9800	14,000
Dly Van	600	1900	3200	6400	11,200	16,000

1907
Model T, 84" wb

	6	5	4	3	2	1
PU	550	1700	2800	5600	9800	14,000
Dly Van	600	1900	3200	6400	11,200	16,000

1908
Model T, 84" wb

	6	5	4	3	2	1
PU	550	1700	2800	5600	9800	14,000
Dly Van	600	1900	3200	6400	11,200	16,000

1909
Model T, 100" wb

	6	5	4	3	2	1
PU	550	1700	2800	5600	9800	14,000
Dly Van	600	1900	3200	6400	11,200	16,000

1910
Model T, 100" wb

	6	5	4	3	2	1
PU	550	1700	2800	5600	9800	14,000
Dly Van	600	1900	3200	6400	11,200	16,000

1911
Model T, 100" wb

	6	5	4	3	2	1
PU	550	1700	2800	5600	9800	14,000
Dly Van	600	1900	3200	6400	11,200	16,000

NOTE: The 1906-1911 Ford trucks were commercial adaptations of passenger car chassis. As there were no factory truck bodies, the above prices should be used as a general guide only.

1912
Model T, 84" wb

	6	5	4	3	2	1
Commercial Rds	600	1900	3200	6400	11,200	16,000
Dly Van	550	1700	2800	5600	9800	14,000

NOTE: In 1912 the company marketed a true commercial roadster and also built Delivery Car (Van) prototypes that were tested by firms such as Bell Telephone, John Wanamaker and Milwaukee Novelty Dye Works.

1913
Model T, 84" wb

	6	5	4	3	2	1
Dly Van	400	1300	2200	4400	7700	11,000
Panel truck	550	1700	2800	5600	9800	14,000

NOTE: Ford again stopped making factory truck bodies. Trucks built on the 1913-1916 Model T Chassis have aftermarket bodies. Therefore, prices given here should be considered only a general guide to typical body styles that exist.

1914
Model T, 84" wb

	6	5	4	3	2	1
C-Cab Dly	550	1700	2800	5600	9800	14,000
Panel truck	400	1200	2000	3950	7000	10,000
Fire truck (TT)	450	1450	2400	4800	8400	12,000

1915
Model T, 84" wb

	6	5	4	3	2	1
C-Cab Dly	400	1300	2200	4400	7700	11,000
Panel truck	400	1200	2000	3950	7000	10,000
Express	450	1100	1700	3650	6650	9500

1916
Model T, 100" wb

	6	5	4	3	2	1
Panel truck	400	1200	2000	3950	7000	10,000
Swellside Panel	400	1200	2000	3950	7000	10,000
Fire truck	450	1450	2400	4800	8400	12,000

1917
Model T, 100" wb

	6	5	4	3	2	1
Box Body Dly	400	1200	2000	3950	7000	10,000
Open Front Panel	400	1200	2000	3950	7000	10,000
Enclosed Panel	450	1100	1700	3650	6650	9500
Huckster	400	1200	2000	3950	7000	10,000
Model TT, 124" wb						
Exp	350	900	1550	3050	5900	8500
Stake	350	800	1450	2750	5600	8000
Open Front Panel	400	1200	2000	3950	7000	10,000
Enclosed Panel	350	800	1450	2750	5600	8000

1918
Model T, 100" wb

	6	5	4	3	2	1
Rds PU	400	1300	2200	4400	7700	11,000
Box Body Dly	400	1200	2000	3950	7000	10,000
Open Front Panel	400	1250	2100	4200	7400	10,500
Enclosed Panel	450	1100	1700	3650	6650	9500
Huckster	400	1200	2000	3950	7000	10,000
Model TT, 124" wb						
Exp	350	800	1450	2750	5600	8000
Stake	350	750	1300	2450	5250	7500
Open Front Panel	450	1000	1650	3350	6300	9000
Enclosed Panel	350	800	1450	2750	5600	8000
Huckster	450	1000	1650	3350	6300	9000

1919
Model T, 100" wb

	6	5	4	3	2	1
Rds PU	400	1300	2200	4400	7700	11,000
Box Body Dly	400	1200	2000	3950	7000	10,000
Open Front Panel	400	1250	2100	4200	7400	10,500
Enclosed Panel	400	1200	2000	3950	7000	10,000
Huckster	400	1250	2100	4200	7400	10,500
Model TT, 124" wb						
Exp	350	900	1550	3050	5900	8500
Stake	350	800	1450	2750	5600	8000
Open Front Panel	400	1200	2000	3950	7000	10,000
Enclosed Panel	450	1000	1650	3350	6300	9000
Huckster	450	1100	1700	3650	6650	9500

1920
Model T, 100" wb

	6	5	4	3	2	1
Rds PU	400	1300	2200	4400	7700	11,000
Box Body Dly	400	1200	2000	3950	7000	10,000
Open Front Panel	400	1250	2100	4200	7400	10,500
Enclosed Panel	400	1200	2000	3950	7000	10,000
Huckster	400	1250	2100	4200	7400	10,500
Model TT, 124" wb						
Exp	350	900	1550	3050	5900	8500
Stake	350	800	1450	2750	5600	8000
Open Front Panel	400	1200	2000	3950	7000	10,000
Enclosed Panel	450	1000	1650	3350	6300	9000
Huckster	450	1100	1700	3650	6650	9500

1921
Model T, 100" wb

	6	5	4	3	2	1
Rds PU	400	1300	2200	4400	7700	11,000
Box Body Dly	400	1200	2000	3950	7000	10,000
Open Front Panel	400	1250	2100	4200	7400	10,500
Enclosed Panel	450	1100	1700	3650	6650	9500
Huckster	400	1200	2000	3950	7000	10,000
Model TT, 124" wb						
Exp	350	900	1550	3050	5900	8500
Stake	350	800	1450	2750	5600	8000
Open Front Panel	400	1200	2000	3950	7000	10,000
Enclosed Panel	450	1000	1650	3350	6300	9000
Huckster	450	1100	1700	3650	6650	

1922
Model T, 100" wb

	6	5	4	3	2	1
Rds PU	400	1300	2200	4400	7700	11,000
Box Body Dly	400	1200	2000	3950	7000	10,000
Open Front Panel	400	1250	2100	4200	7400	10,500
Enclosed Panel	450	1100	1700	3650	6650	9500
Huckster	400	1200	2000	3950	7000	10,000
Model TT, 124" wb						
Exp	350	900	1550	3050	5900	8500
Stake	350	800	1450	2750	5600	8000
Open Front Panel	400	1200	2000	3950	7000	10,000
Enclosed Panel	450	1100	1700	3650	6650	9500
Huckster	400	1200	2000	3950	7000	10,000

1923
Model T, 100" wb

	6	5	4	3	2	1
Rds PU	450	1450	2400	4800	8400	12,000
Box Body Dly	450	1100	1700	3650	6650	9500
Panel	400	1200	2000	3950	7000	10,000
Model TT, 124" wb						
C-Cab Exp	350	900	1550	3050	5900	8500
C-Cab Canopy Exp	350	800	1450	2750	5600	8000
C-Cab Screenside	350	900	1550	3050	5900	8500

	6	5	4	3	2	1
C-Cab Stake	350	900	1550	3050	5900	8500
Enclosed Front Panel	350	800	1450	2750	5600	8000
Open Front Panel	400	1200	2000	3950	7000	10,000

NOTE: Ford announced it would start building factory truck bodies Oct. 23, 1923. Ford designed C-Cab for Model TT, announced Jan. 9, 1924. Model T trucks (100" wb) still had aftermarket bodies. Use prices as general guide to values of models.

1924

	6	5	4	3	2	1
Model T, 100" wb						
Rds PU	450	1450	2400	4800	8400	12,000
Box Body Dly	450	1100	1700	3650	6650	9500
Panel	400	1200	2000	3950	7000	10,000
Model TT, 124" wb						
C-Cab Exp	350	900	1550	3050	5900	8500
C-Cab Canopy Exp	350	800	1450	2750	5600	8000
C-Cab Screenside	350	900	1550	3050	5900	8500
C-Cab Stake	350	750	1300	2450	5250	7500
Enclosed Front Panel	350	800	1450	2750	5600	8000
Open Front Panel	400	1200	2000	3950	7000	10,000

1925

	6	5	4	3	2	1
Model T, 100" wb						
Rds PU	450	1450	2400	4800	8400	12,000
Model TT, 124" wb						
C-Cab Exp	350	900	1550	3050	5900	8500
Enclosed Cab Exp	350	800	1450	2750	5600	8000
C-Cab Canopy Exp	350	800	1450	2750	5600	8000
Enclosed Cab Canopy Exp	350	750	1300	2450	5250	7500
C-Cab Screenside Exp	350	800	1450	2750	5600	8000
Enclosed Cab Screenside Exp	350	800	1450	2750	5600	8000
C-Cab Panel	400	1200	2000	3950	7000	10,000
Enclosed Cab Panel	450	1100	1700	3650	6650	9500
C-Cab Stake	350	750	1300	2450	5250	7500
Enclosed Cab Stake	350	750	1200	2350	4900	7000

NOTE: Model T pickup (factory) introduced April 15, 1925. Model TT Enclosed Cab introduced as an $85. option in spring of 1925. From 1925 listings on, all prices given are for factory-bodied trucks.

1926

	6	5	4	3	2	1
Model T, 100" wb						
Rds PU	450	1500	2500	5000	8800	12,500
Model TT, 124" wb						
C-Cab Exp	450	1000	1650	3350	6300	9000
Enclosed Cab Exp	350	900	1550	3050	5900	8500
C-Cab Canopy Exp	350	800	1450	2750	5600	8000
Enclosed Cab Canopy Exp	350	750	1350	2600	5400	7700
C-Cab Screenside Exp	450	1000	1650	3350	6300	9000
Enclosed Cab Screenside Exp	350	750	1300	2450	5250	7500
C-Cab Panel	400	1200	2000	3950	7000	10,000
Enclosed Cab Panel	350	800	1450	2750	5600	8000
C-Cab Stake	350	750	1300	2450	5250	7500
Enclosed Cab Stake	350	750	1200	2350	4900	7000

1927

	6	5	4	3	2	1
Model T, 100" wb						
Rds PU	450	1450	2400	4800	8400	12,000
Model TT, 124" wb						
C-Cab Exp	450	1000	1650	3350	6300	9000
Enclosed Cab Exp	350	900	1550	3050	5900	8500
C-Cab Canopy Exp	350	800	1450	2750	5600	8000
Enclosed Cab Canopy Exp	350	750	1350	2600	5400	7700
C-Cab Screenside Exp	450	1000	1650	3350	6300	9000
Enclosed Cab Screenside Exp	350	750	1300	2450	5250	7500
C-Cab Panel	400	1200	2000	3950	7000	10,000
Enclosed Cab Panel	350	800	1450	2750	5600	8000
C-Cab Stake	350	750	1300	2450	5250	7500
Enclosed Cab Stake	350	750	1200	2350	4900	7000

1928

	6	5	4	3	2	1
Model A, 103" wb						
Sed Dly	550	1700	2800	5600	9800	14,000
Open Cab PU	500	1550	2600	5200	9100	13,000
Closed Cab PU	350	900	1550	3050	5900	8500
Canopy Exp	450	1000	1650	3350	6300	9000
Screenside Exp	450	1000	1650	3350	6300	9000
Panel	400	1200	2000	3950	7000	10,000

1929

	6	5	4	3	2	1
Model A, 103" wb						
Sed Dly	550	1700	2800	5600	9800	14,000
Open Cab PU	500	1550	2600	5200	9100	13,000
Closed Cab PU	350	900	1550	3050	5900	8500
Panel	400	1200	2000	3950	7000	10,000

1930

	6	5	4	3	2	1
Model A, 103" wb						
Sed Dly	550	1700	2800	5600	9800	14,000
Twn Car Dly	950	3000	5000	10,000	17,500	25,000
Open Cab PU	450	1450	2400	4800	8400	12,000
Closed Cab PU	350	900	1550	3050	5900	8500
Panel	400	1200	2000	3950	7000	10,000

NOTE: Sedan Delivery officially called "Deluxe Delivery".

1931

	6	5	4	3	2	1
Model A, 103" wb						
Sed Dly	550	1700	2800	5600	9800	14,000
Twn Car Dly	950	3000	5000	10,000	17,500	25,000
Spl Panel	450	1450	2400	4800	8400	12,000
Std Panel	400	1200	2000	3950	7000	10,000
Drop Floor Panel	400	1200	2000	3950	7000	10,000
Open Cab PU	450	1450	2400	4800	8400	12,000
Closed Cab PU	350	900	1550	3050	5900	8500
DeL PU	450	950	1600	3250	6150	8800

NOTE: Town Car Delivery had coach lamps - only 196 built. Special Panel had natural wood body - only 900 built. Drop Floor Panel - only 1954 built. Deluxe Pickup had high bed sides with chrome rails - only 293 built.

1932

	6	5	4	3	2	1
Model B, 4-cyl, 106" wb						
Sed Dly	550	1750	2900	5800	10,200	14,500
Open Cab PU	450	1500	2500	5000	8800	12,500
Closed Cab PU	350	750	1350	2600	5400	7700
Std Panel	450	1100	1700	3650	6650	9500
DeL Panel	400	1200	2000	3950	7000	10,000
Model B-18, V-8, 106" wb						
Sed Dly	600	1900	3200	6400	11,200	16,000
Open Cab PU	500	1600	2700	5400	9500	13,500
Closed Cab PU	350	950	1600	3200	6050	8700
Std Panel	400	1250	2100	4200	7400	10,500
DeL Panel	400	1300	2200	4400	7700	11,000

1933

	6	5	4	3	2	1
Model 46, 4-cyl, 112" wb						
Sed Dly	500	1550	2600	5200	9100	13,000
Panel	350	900	1550	3050	5900	8500
DeL Panel	450	1000	1650	3350	6300	9000
PU	350	750	1300	2450	5250	7500
Model 46, V-8, 112" wb						
Sed Dly	550	1700	2800	5600	9800	14,000
Panel	450	1100	1700	3650	6650	9500
DeL Panel	400	1200	2000	3950	7000	10,000
PU	350	900	1550	3050	5900	8500

1934

	6	5	4	3	2	1
Model 46, 4-cyl, 112" wb						
Sed Dly	500	1550	2600	5200	9100	13,000
Panel	350	900	1550	3050	5900	8500
DeL Panel	450	1000	1650	3350	6300	9000
PU	350	750	1300	2450	5250	7500
Model 46, V-8, 112" wb						
Sed Dly	550	1700	2800	5600	9800	14,000
Panel	450	1100	1700	3650	6650	9500
DeL Panel	400	1200	2000	3950	7000	10,000
PU	350	900	1550	3050	5900	8500

1935

	6	5	4	3	2	1
Model 48, V-8, 112" wb						
Sed Dly	500	1550	2600	5200	9100	13,000
Model 50, V-8, 112" wb						
Panel	350	900	1550	3050	5900	8500
DeL Panel	450	1000	1650	3350	6300	9000
PU	350	750	1300	2450	5250	7500

1936

	6	5	4	3	2	1
Model 68, V-8, 112" wb						
Sed Dly	500	1550	2600	5200	9100	13,000
Model 67, V-8, 112" wb						
Panel	350	800	1450	2750	5600	8000
DeL Panel	350	900	1550	3050	5900	8500
PU	350	750	1200	2350	4900	7000

1937

	6	5	4	3	2	1
Model 74, V-8, 60 hp, 112" wb						
Cpe PU	450	1000	1650	3350	6300	9000
Sed Dly	450	1400	2300	4600	8100	11,500
Model 73, V-8, 60 hp, 112" wb						
PU	350	725	1200	2350	4800	6800
Platform	350	700	1150	2300	4550	6500
Stake	350	700	1150	2300	4550	6500
Panel	350	725	1200	2350	4800	6800
DeL Panel	350	750	1200	2350	4900	7000
Model 78, V-8, 85 hp, 112" wb						
Cpe PU	400	1250	2100	4200	7400	10,500
DeL Cpe PU	450	1400	2300	4600	8100	11,500
Sed Dly	450	1400	2350	4700	8300	11,800
Model 77, V-8, 85 hp, 112" wb						
PU	350	750	1200	2350	4900	7000
Platform	350	700	1150	2300	4600	6600
Stake	350	700	1150	2300	4600	6600
Panel	350	750	1200	2350	4900	7000
DeL Panel	350	750	1250	2400	5100	7300
Model 75, 1-Ton, V-8, 60 hp, 131.8" wb						
Platform	200	650	1050	2250	4200	6000
Stake	200	650	1050	2250	4200	6000
Panel	350	700	1150	2300	4550	6500

1938

	6	5	4	3	2	1
Model 82C, V-8, 60 hp, 112" wb						
PU	350	750	1200	2350	4900	7000
Platform	350	700	1150	2300	4550	6500
Stake	350	700	1150	2300	4550	6500
Panel Dly	350	750	1200	2350	4900	7000
Sed Dly	450	1400	2300	4600	8100	11,500
Model 82Y, 1-Ton, V-8, 60 hp, 122" wb						
Exp	350	700	1150	2300	4550	6500
Platform	200	650	1050	2250	4200	6000
Stake	200	650	1050	2250	4200	6000
Panel	350	700	1150	2300	4550	6500

NOTE: Add 10 percent for Model 81C 1/2-Ton or Model 81V 1-Ton with 85 hp V-8.

1939

	6	5	4	3	2	1
Model 922C, V-8, 60 hp, 112" wb						
PU	350	800	1450	2750	5600	8000
Platform	200	650	1050	2250	4200	6000
Stake	200	650	1050	2250	4200	6000
Panel	350	750	1200	2350	4900	7000
Sed Dly	450	1450	2400	4800	8400	12,000
Model 922D, 3/4-Ton, V-8, 60 hp, 122" wb						
Platform	200	650	1050	2250	4200	6000
Exp	200	650	1050	2250	4200	6000
Stake	200	650	1050	2250	4200	6000
Panel	350	750	1200	2350	4900	7000
Model 92Y, 1-Ton, V-8, 60 hp, 122" wb						
Platform	200	500	850	1900	3500	5000
Exp	200	500	850	1900	3500	5000
Stake	200	500	850	1900	3500	5000
Panel	200	650	1050	2250	4200	6000

NOTE: Add 10 percent for Model 91C 1/2-Ton; Model 910 3/4-Ton or Model 91Y 1-Ton with 85 hp, V-8.

1940

	6	5	4	3	2	1
Series OC1, 1/2-Ton, V-8, 60 hp, 112" wb						
PU	350	900	1550	3050	5900	8500
Platform	200	600	950	2150	3850	5500
Stake	200	650	1000	2200	4100	5800
Panel	350	750	1300	2450	5250	7500
Series O22A, 1/2-Ton, V-8, 60 hp, 112" wb						
Sed Dly	500	1600	2700	5400	9500	13,500
Series O2D, 3/4-Ton, V-8, 60 hp, 122" wb						
Platform	200	500	850	1900	3500	5000
Exp	350	700	1150	2300	4550	6500
Stake	200	600	950	2150	3850	5500
Panel	350	750	1300	2450	5250	7500
Series O2Y, 1-Ton, V-8, 60 hp, 122" wb						
Platform	150	450	800	1800	3300	4800
Exp	200	600	950	2150	3850	5500
Stake	200	500	850	1900	3500	5000
Panel	350	750	1300	2450	5250	7500

NOTE: Add 10 percent for Series 01C 1/2-Ton; Series 01A 1/2-Ton Sedan Delivery; Series 01D 3/4-Ton; and Series 01Y 1-Ton with 85 hp, V-8.

1941

	6	5	4	3	2	1
Model 1NC, 1/2-Ton, 4-cyl, 112" wb						
PU	350	800	1450	2750	5600	8000
Platform	200	550	900	2100	3700	5300
Stake	200	600	950	2200	3900	5600
Panel	350	750	1250	2400	5100	7300
Sed Dly	450	1500	2500	5000	8800	12,600

Standard Catalog Of Light-Duty Trucks 773

	6	5	4	3	2	1
Model 1ND, 3/4-Ton, 4-cyl, 122" wb						
Platform	150	450	800	1800	3300	4800
Exp	200	650	1050	2250	4200	6000
Stake	200	550	900	2100	3700	5300
Panel	350	750	1250	2400	5100	7300
Model 1NY, 1-Ton, 4-cyl, 122" wb						
Platform	150	400	750	1650	3150	4500
Exp	200	600	1000	2200	4000	5700
Stake	200	500	850	1900	3500	5000
Panel	350	750	1200	2350	4900	7000

NOTE: Add 10 percent for 85 hp, V-8 (Second symbol in V-8 Model number changes from N to G).

1942

	6	5	4	3	2	1
Model 2-GA, 1/2-Ton, 6-cyl, 114" wb						
Sed Dly	450	1500	2500	5000	8800	12,600
Model 2-NC, 1/2-Ton, 4-cyl, 114" wb						
PU	350	750	1350	2650	5450	7800
Platform	200	550	900	2100	3700	5300
Stake	200	600	950	2200	3900	5600
Panel	350	750	1250	2400	5100	7300
Model 2-ND, 3/4-Ton, 4-cyl, 122" wb						
Platform	150	450	800	1800	3300	4800
Exp	200	650	1050	2250	4200	6000
Stake	200	550	900	2100	3700	5300
Panel	350	750	1250	2400	5100	7300
Model 2-NY, 1-Ton, 4-cyl, 122" wb						
Platform	150	400	750	1650	3150	4500
Exp	200	600	1000	2200	4000	5700
Stake	200	500	850	1900	3500	5000
Panel	350	750	1200	2350	4900	7000

NOTE: Add 10 percent for 21-A Sedan Delivery with 90 hp, V-8. Add 10 percent for 29-A Sedan Delivery with 100 hp, V-8. Add 5 percent for other models with 6-cyl. (Second symbol in V-8 model number changes to G). Add 10 percent for other models with 90 hp, V-8. (Second symbol in V-8 model number changes to 1). Add 10 percent for other models with 100 hp, V-8 (second symbol in V-8 model number changes to 9).

1944

	6	5	4	3	2	1
1/2-Ton, 114" wb						
PU	350	700	1150	2300	4550	6500
Panel	200	675	1100	2250	4400	6300
Stake	200	650	1000	2200	4100	5800
3/4-Ton, 122" wb						
PU	200	650	1050	2250	4200	6000
Panel	200	650	1000	2200	4100	5800
Stake	200	600	950	2200	3900	5600

1945

	6	5	4	3	2	1
1/2-Ton, 114" wb						
PU	350	700	1150	2300	4550	6500
Panel	200	675	1100	2250	4400	6300
Stake	200	650	1000	2200	4100	5800
3/4-Ton, 122" wb						
PU	200	650	1050	2250	4200	6000
Panel	200	650	1000	2200	4100	5800
Stake	200	600	950	2200	3900	5600

1946

	6	5	4	3	2	1
Model 69GA, 1/2-Ton, 6-cyl, 114" wb						
Sed Dly	500	1600	2700	5400	9500	13,500
Model 6GC, 1/2-Ton, 6-cyl, 114" wb						
PU	350	900	1550	3050	5900	8500
Platform	200	650	1050	2250	4200	6000
Stake	200	675	1050	2250	4350	6200
Panel	400	1200	2000	3950	7000	10,000
Model 6GY, 1-Ton, 6-cyl, 122" wb						
PU	350	700	1150	2300	4550	6500
Platform	200	600	950	2150	3850	5500
Stake	200	600	1000	2200	4000	5700
Panel	350	900	1550	3050	5900	8500

NOTE: Add 5 percent for 69-A Sedan Delivery with 100 hp, V-8. Add 5 percent for other models with 100 hp, V-8 (second symbol in V-8 model number changes from G to 9).

1947

	6	5	4	3	2	1
Model 7GA, 1/2-Ton, 6-cyl, 114" wb						
Sed Dly	500	1600	2700	5400	9500	13,500
Model 7GC, 1/2-Ton, 5-cyl, 114" wb						
PU	350	900	1550	3050	5900	8500
Platform	200	650	1050	2250	4200	6000
Stake	200	675	1050	2250	4350	6200
Panel	400	1200	2000	3950	7000	10,000
Model 7GY, 1-Ton, 6-cyl, 122" wb						
PU	350	700	1150	2300	4550	6500
Stake	200	600	950	2150	3850	5500
Panel	350	900	1550	3050	5900	8500

Note: Add 5 percent for Model 79A Sedan Delivery with 100 hp, V-8. Add 5 percent for other models with 100 hp, V-8 (second symbol in V-8 model number changes from G to 9).

1948

	6	5	4	3	2	1
F-1 Model 8HC, 1/2-Ton, 6-cyl, 114" wb						
DeL Sed Dly	500	1600	2700	5400	9500	13,500
PU	350	900	1550	3050	5900	8500
Platform	200	650	1050	2250	4200	6000
Stake	200	675	1050	2250	4350	6200
Panel	400	1200	2000	3950	7000	10,000
F-2 Model 8HD, 3/4-Ton, 6-cyl, 122" wb						
PU	350	800	1450	2750	5600	8000
Platform	200	600	950	2150	3850	5500
Stake	200	600	1000	2200	4000	5700
F-3 Model 8HY, HD 3/4-Ton, 6-cyl, 122" wb						
PU	350	850	1500	2900	5700	8200
Platform	200	600	950	2200	3900	5600
Stake	200	650	1000	2200	4100	5800
F-4 Model 8HTL, 1-Ton, 6-cyl, 134" wb						
Platform	200	600	950	2150	3850	5500
Stake	200	600	1000	2200	4000	5700

NOTE: Add 5 percent for 100 hp, V-8, all models. (Second symbol in V-8 model number changes from H to R).

1949

	6	5	4	3	2	1
F-1 Model 9HC, 1/2-Ton, 6-cyl, 114" wb						
PU	350	900	1550	3050	5900	8500
Platform	200	650	1050	2250	4200	6000
Stake	200	675	1050	2250	4350	6200
Panel	400	1200	2000	3950	7000	10,000
F-2 Model 9HD, 3/4-Ton, 6-cyl, 122" wb						
PU	350	800	1450	2750	5600	8000
Platform	200	600	950	2150	3850	5500
Stake	200	600	1000	2200	4000	5700
F-3 Model 9HY, HD 3/4-Ton, 6-cyl, 122" wb						
PU	350	850	1500	2900	5700	8200
Platform	200	600	950	2200	3900	5600
Stake	200	650	1000	2200	4100	5800
F-3 Model 9HJ-104" wb; 9H2J-122" wb 3/4-Ton, 6-cyl						
Parcel Dly Van	150	350	750	1350	2800	4000
Model 9HTL, 1-Ton, 6-cyl, 134" wb						
Platform	200	600	950	2150	3850	5500
Stake	200	600	1000	2200	4000	5700

NOTE: Add 5 percent for all models with 100 hp, V-8. (Second symbol in V-8 model number changes from H to R).

1950

	6	5	4	3	2	1
F-1 Model 9HC, 1/2-Ton, 6-cyl, 114" wb						
PU	350	900	1550	3050	5900	8500
Platform	200	650	1050	2250	4200	6000
Stake	200	675	1050	2250	4350	6200
Panel	400	1200	2000	3950	7000	10,000
F-2 Model 9HD, 3/4-Ton, 6-cyl, 122" wb						
PU	350	800	1450	2750	5600	8000
Platform	200	600	950	2150	3850	5500
Stake	200	600	1000	2200	4000	5700
F-3 Model 9HY, HD 3/4-Ton, 6-cyl, 122" wb						
PU	350	850	1500	2900	5700	8200
Platform	200	600	950	2200	3900	5600
Stake	200	650	1000	2200	4100	5800
F-3 Model 9HJ-104" wb; Model 942J-122" wb 3/4-Ton, 6-cyl						
Parcel Dly	150	350	750	1350	2800	4000
F-4 Model 9HTL, 1-Ton, 6-cyl, 134" wb						
Platform	200	600	950	2150	3850	5500
Stake	200	600	1000	2200	4000	5700

NOTE: Add 5 percent to all models with 100 hp, V-8. (Second symbol in V-8 model number changes from H to R).

1951

	6	5	4	3	2	1
F-1 Model 1HC, 1/2-Ton, 6-cyl, 114" wb						
PU	350	900	1550	3050	5900	8500
Platform	200	650	1050	2250	4200	6000
Stake	200	675	1050	2250	4350	6200
Panel	400	1200	2000	3950	7000	10,000
F-2 Model 1HD, 3/4-Ton, 6-cyl, 122" wb						
PU	350	800	1450	2750	5600	8000
Platform	200	600	950	2150	3850	5500
Stake	200	600	1000	2200	4000	5700
F-3 Model 1HY, Heavy 3/4-Ton, 6-cyl, 122" wb						
PU	350	850	1500	2900	5700	8200
Platform	200	600	950	2200	3900	5600
Stake	200	650	1000	2200	4100	5800
F-3 Model 1HJ-104" wb; Model 1H2J-122" wb 3/4-Ton, 6-cyl						
Parcel Dly	150	350	750	1350	2800	4000
F-4 Model 1HTL, 1-Ton, 6-cyl, 134" wb						
Platform	200	600	950	2150	3850	5500
Stake	200	600	1000	2200	4000	5700

NOTE: Add 5 percent for all models with 100 hp, V-8. (Second symbol in V-8 model number changes from H to R.)

1952

	6	5	4	3	2	1
Courier Series, 1/2-Ton, 6-cyl, 115" wb						
Sed Dly	400	1200	2000	3950	7000	10,000
F-1 Series, 1/2-Ton, 6-cyl, 114" wb						
PU	350	900	1550	3050	5900	8500
Platform	200	650	1050	2250	4200	6000
Stake	200	675	1050	2250	4350	6200
Panel	400	1200	2000	3950	7000	10,000
F-2 Series, 3/4-Ton, 6-cyl, 122" wb						
PU	350	800	1450	2750	5600	8000
Platform	200	600	950	2150	3850	5500
Stake	200	600	1000	2200	4000	5700
F-3 Series, HD 3/4-Ton, 6-cyl, 122" wb						
PU	350	850	1500	2900	5700	8200
Platform	200	600	950	2200	3900	5600
Stake	200	650	1000	2200	4100	5800
F-3 Series, 3/4-Ton, 6-cyl, 104" or 122" wb						
Parcel Dly	150	350	750	1350	2800	4000
F-4 Series, 1-Ton, 6-cyl, 134" wb						
Platform	200	600	950	2150	3850	5500
Stake	200	600	1000	2200	4000	5700

NOTE: Add 5 percent for all models with 110 hp, V-8.

1953

	6	5	4	3	2	1
Courier Series, 1/2-Ton, 6-cyl, 115" wb						
Sed Dly	400	1200	2050	4100	7100	10,200
F-100 Series, 1/2-Ton, 6-cyl, 110" wb						
PU	350	950	1600	3200	6050	8700
Platform	350	700	1150	2300	4550	6500
Stake	350	725	1150	2300	4700	6700
Panel	450	1000	1650	3350	6300	9000
F-250 Series, 3/4-Ton, 6-cyl, 118" wb						
PU	350	900	1550	3050	5900	8500
Platform	200	600	950	2150	3850	5500
Stake	200	600	1000	2200	4000	5700
F-350 Series, 1-Ton, 6-cyl, 130" wb						
PU	350	750	1300	2450	5250	7500
Platform	150	400	750	1650	3150	4500
Stake	150	450	800	1750	3250	4700
P-350 Series, 1-Ton, 6-cyl, 104" or 122" wb						
Parcel Dly	150	350	750	1350	2800	4000

NOTE: Add 5 percent for V-8. All 1953 models have 50th Anniversary horn button.

1954

	6	5	4	3	2	1
Courier Series, 1/2-Ton, 6-cyl, 115" wb						
Sed Dly	400	1250	2100	4200	7400	10,500
F-100 Series, 1/2-Ton, 6-cyl, 110" wb						
PU	350	950	1600	3200	6050	8700
Platform	350	700	1150	2300	4550	6500
Stake	350	725	1150	2300	4700	6700
Panel	450	1000	1650	3350	6300	9000
F-100 DeL Series, 1/2-Ton, 6-cyl, 110" wb						
PU	350	900	1550	3050	5900	8500
Platform	200	600	950	2150	3850	5500
Stake	200	600	1000	2200	4000	5700
Panel	350	900	1550	3050	5900	8500
F-250 Series, 3/4-Ton, 6-cyl, 118" wb						
PU	350	800	1450	2750	5600	8000
Platform	200	600	950	2150	3850	5500
Stake	200	600	1000	2200	4000	5700
F-350 Series, 1-Ton, 6-cyl, 130" wb						
PU	350	750	1300	2450	5250	7500
Platform	150	400	750	1650	3150	4500
Stake	150	450	800	1750	3250	4700
P-350 Series, 1-Ton, 6-cyl, 104" or 122" wb						
Parcel Dly	150	300	750	1350	2700	3900

NOTE: Add 5 percent for V-8.

1955

	6	5	4	3	2	1
Courier, 1/2-Ton, 6-cyl, 115" wb						
Sed Dly	400	1300	2200	4400	7700	11,000
F-100 Series, 1/2-Ton, 6-cyl, 110" wb						
PU	350	900	1550	3050	5900	8500
Platform	200	600	950	2150	3850	5500
Stake	200	600	1000	2200	4000	5700
Panel	350	800	1450	2750	5600	8000
F-250 Series, 3/4-Ton, 6-cyl, 118" wb						
PU	350	800	1450	2750	5600	8000
Platform	200	500	850	1900	3500	5000
Stake	200	550	900	2000	3600	5200
F-350 Series, 1-Ton, 6-cyl, 130" wb						
PU	350	750	1200	2350	4900	7000
Platform	150	350	750	1450	3000	4200
Stake	150	400	750	1600	3100	4400
P-350 Series, 1-Ton, 6-cyl, 104" or 122" wb						
Parcel Dly	150	300	750	1350	2700	3900

NOTE: Add 5 percent for V-8. 1955 and up prices for Deluxe trim models.

1956

	6	5	4	3	2	1
Courier Series, 1/2-Ton, 6-cyl, 115.5" wb						
Sed Dly	450	1400	2300	4600	8100	11,500
F-100 Series, 1/2-Ton, 6-cyl, 110" wb						
PU	400	1200	2000	3950	7000	10,000
Platform	200	650	1050	2250	4200	6000
Stake	200	675	1050	2250	4350	6200
Panel	350	950	1600	3200	6050	8700
Cus Panel	450	1000	1650	3350	6300	9000
F-250 Series, 3/4-Ton, 6-cyl, 118" wb						
PU	350	900	1550	3050	5900	8500
Platform	200	550	900	2000	3600	5200
Stake	200	550	900	2150	3800	5400
F-350 Series, 1-Ton, 6-cyl, 130" wb						
PU	350	750	1300	2450	5250	7500
Platform	150	400	750	1600	3100	4400
Stake	150	450	750	1700	3200	4600

NOTE: Add 5 percent for V-8.

1957

	6	5	4	3	2	1
Courier Series, 1/2-Ton, 6-cyl, 116" wb						
Sed Dly	400	1200	2000	3950	7000	10,000
Ranchero Series, 1/2-Ton, 6-cyl, 116" wb						
PU	400	1250	2050	4100	7200	10,300
Cus PU	400	1300	2200	4400	7700	11,000
F-100 Series, 1/2-Ton, 6-cyl, 110" wb						
Flareside PU	350	900	1550	3050	5900	8500
Styleside PU--118" wb	450	1000	1650	3350	6300	9000
Styleside PU	450	1050	1650	3500	6400	9200
Platform	200	650	1050	2250	4200	6000
Stake	200	675	1050	2250	4350	6200
Panel	350	800	1450	2750	5600	8000
F-250 Series, 3/4-Ton, 6-cyl, 118" wb						
Flareside PU	350	750	1300	2450	5250	7500
Styleside PU	350	800	1450	2750	5600	8000
Platform	200	600	950	2150	3850	5500
Stake	200	600	1000	2200	4000	5700
F-350 Series, 1-Ton, 6-cyl, 130" wb						
Flareside PU	350	750	1200	2350	4900	7000
Styleside PU	350	750	1300	2450	5250	7500
Platform	200	500	850	1900	3500	5000
Stake	200	550	900	2000	3600	5200

NOTE: Add 5 percent for V-8.

1958

	6	5	4	3	2	1
Courier Series, 1/2-Ton, 6-cyl, 116" wb						
Sed Dly	450	1100	1700	3650	6650	9500
Ranchero Series, 1/2-Ton, 6-cyl, 116" wb						
PU	450	1100	1700	3650	6650	9500
Cus PU	400	1200	2000	3950	7000	10,000
F-100 Series, 1/2-Ton, 6-cyl, 110" wb						
Styleside PU, 6-1/2'	350	900	1550	3050	5900	8500
Flareside PU, 6-1/2'	450	1000	1650	3350	6300	9000
Platform	200	650	1050	2250	4200	6000
Stake	200	675	1050	2250	4350	6200
Panel	350	750	1350	2650	5450	7800
F-100 Series, 1/2-Ton, 6-cyl, 118" wb						
Styleside PU, 8'	350	900	1550	3000	5850	8400
Flareside PU, 8'	350	900	1550	3100	6000	8600
F-250 Series, 3/4-Ton, 6-cyl, 118" wb						
Styleside PU	350	800	1450	2750	5600	8000
Flareside PU	350	750	1350	2650	5450	7800
Platform	200	600	950	2150	3850	5500
Stake	200	600	1000	2200	4000	5700
F-350 Series, 1-Ton, 6-cyl, 130" wb						
Styleside PU	350	750	1300	2500	5300	7600
Flareside PU	350	750	1300	2450	5250	7500
Platform	200	500	850	1900	3500	5000
Stake	200	500	850	1900	3500	5000

NOTE: Add 5 percent for 292 cid/172 hp V-8, (all models). Add 10 percent for 352 cid/300 hp V-8, (Ranchero and Courier only).

1959

	6	5	4	3	2	1
Courier Series, 1/2-Ton, 6-cyl, 118" wb						
Sed Dly	450	1100	1700	3650	6650	9500
Ranchero Series, 1/2-Ton, 6-cyl, 118" wb						
Cus PU	400	1200	2000	3950	7000	10,000
F-100 Series, 1/2-Ton, 6-cyl, 110" wb						
Styleside PU, 6-1/2'	350	900	1550	3050	5900	8500
Flareside PU, 6-1/2'	450	1000	1650	3350	6300	9000
Platform	200	650	1050	2250	4200	6000
Stake	200	675	1050	2250	4350	6200
Panel	350	750	1350	2650	5450	7800
F-100 Series, 1/2-Ton, 6-cyl, 118" wb						
Styleside PU, 8'	350	900	1550	3000	5850	8400
Flareside PU, 8'	350	900	1550	3100	6000	8600
F-250 Series, 3/4-Ton, 6-cyl, 118" wb						
Styleside PU	350	800	1450	2750	5600	8000
Flareside PU	350	750	1350	2650	5450	7800
Platform	200	600	950	2150	3850	5500
Stake	200	600	1000	2200	4000	5700
F-350 Series, 1-Ton, 6-cyl, 130" wb						
Styleside PU	350	750	1300	2500	5300	7600
Flareside PU	350	750	1300	2450	5250	7500
Platform	200	500	850	1900	3500	5000
Stake	200	550	900	2000	3600	5200

NOTE: Add 5 percent for 292 cid/172 hp V-8, (all models). Add 10 percent for 352 cid/235 hp, V-8, (Courier only). Add 10 percent for 352 cid/300 hp, V-8, (Courier only). Add 5 percent for 4WD on F250 and F350 models only.

1960

	6	5	4	3	2	1
Courier Series, 1/2-Ton, 6-cyl, 116" wb						
Sed Dly	350	750	1300	2450	5250	7500
Falcon Ranchero Series 1/2-Ton, 6-cyl, 109.5" wb						
PU	200	650	1050	2250	4200	6000
Cus PU	200	675	1050	2250	4350	6200
F-100 Series, 1/2-Ton, 6-cyl, 110" wb						
Styleside PU, 6-1/2'	350	900	1550	3050	5900	8500
Flareside PU, 6-1/2'	450	1000	1650	3350	6300	9000
Platform	200	650	1050	2250	4200	6000
Stake	200	675	1050	2250	4350	6200
Panel	350	750	1350	2650	5450	7800
F-100 Series, 1/2-Ton, 6-cyl, 118" wb						
Styleside PU, 8'	350	900	1550	3000	5850	8400
Flareside PU, 8'	350	900	1550	3100	6000	8600
F-250 Series, 3/4-Ton, 6-cyl, 118" wb						
Styleside PU	350	800	1450	2750	5600	8000
Flareside PU	350	750	1350	2650	5450	7800
Platform	200	600	950	2150	3850	5500
Stake	200	600	1000	2200	4000	5700
F-350 Series, 1-Ton, 6-cyl, 130" wb						
Styleside PU	350	750	1300	2500	5300	7600
Flareside PU	350	750	1300	2450	5250	7500
Platform	200	500	850	1900	3500	5000
Stake	200	550	900	2000	3600	5200

NOTE: Add 5 percent for 292 cid/172 hp, V-8, (all models) except Ranchero. Add 5 percent for 352 cid/235 hp, V-8, (Courier only). Add 6 percent for 352 cid/300 hp, V-8, (Courier only). Add 5 percent for 4WD on F250 and F350 models only.

1961

	6	5	4	3	2	1
Econoline, Series E-100 1/2-Ton, 6-cyl, 90" wb						
PU	200	600	950	2150	3850	5500
Van	200	500	850	1900	3500	5000
Station Bus	200	600	950	2150	3850	5500
Falcon Series, 1/2-Ton, 6-cyl, 109.5" wb						
Ranchero PU	350	700	1100	2300	4500	6400
Sed Dly	200	650	1050	2250	4200	6000
F-100 Series, 1/2-Ton, 6-cyl, 110" wb						
Styleside PU, 6-1/2'	350	850	1500	2900	5700	8200
Flareside PU, 6-1/2'	350	800	1450	2750	5600	8000
Platform	200	650	1050	2250	4200	6000
Stake	200	675	1050	2250	4350	6200
Panel	350	750	1350	2650	5450	7800
F-100 Series, 1/2-Ton, 6-cyl, 118" wb						
Styleside PU, 8'	350	800	1450	2750	5600	8000
Flareside PU, 8'	350	750	1350	2650	5450	7800
F-250 Series, 3/4-Ton, 6-cyl, 118" wb						
Styleside PU	350	800	1450	2750	5600	8000
Flareside PU	350	750	1350	2650	5450	7800
Platform	200	600	950	2150	3850	5500
Stake	200	600	1000	2200	4000	5700
F-350 Series, 1-Ton, 6-cyl, 130" wb						
Styleside PU	350	750	1300	2500	5300	7600
Flareside PU	350	750	1300	2450	5250	7500
Platform	200	500	850	1900	3500	5000
Stake	200	550	900	2000	3600	5200

NOTE: Add 5 percent for Econoline/Falcon "Big Six". Add 10 percent for 292 cid/160 hp, V-8, all F-Series models. Add 5 percent for 4WD on F250 and F350 models only.

1962

	6	5	4	3	2	1
Econoline, E-100 Series 1/2-Ton, 6-cyl, 90" wb						
PU	200	600	950	2150	3850	5500
Van	200	500	850	1900	3500	5000
Falcon Series 1/2-Ton, 6-cyl, 109.5" wb						
Ranchero PU	200	675	1050	2250	4350	6200
Sed Dly	200	650	1000	2200	4100	5800
F-100 Series, 1/2-Ton, 6-cyl, 114" wb						
Styleside PU, 6-1/2' unit	350	800	1450	2750	5600	8000
Flareside PU, 6-1/2'	350	850	1500	2900	5700	8200
Styleside PU, 6-1/2', Sep.	350	900	1550	3050	5900	8500
Platform	200	600	950	2150	3850	5500
Stake	200	600	1000	2200	4000	5700
F-100 Series, 1/2-Ton, 6-cyl, 122" wb						
Styleside PU, 8', unit	350	750	1350	2650	5450	7800
Flareside PU, 8'	350	800	1450	2750	5600	8000
Styleside PU, 8', Sep.	350	850	1500	2950	5800	8300
F-250 Series, 3/4-Ton, 6-cyl, 122" wb						
Styleside PU, 8', unit	350	750	1300	2500	5300	7600
Flareside PU, 8'	350	750	1350	2650	5450	7800
Styleside PU, 8', Sep.	350	850	1500	2800	5650	8100
Platform	200	500	850	1900	3500	5000
Stake	200	550	900	2000	3600	5200
F-350 Series, 1-Ton, 6-cyl, 132" wb						
Flareside PU, 9'	350	750	1300	2450	5250	7500
Styleside PU, 9', Sep.	350	750	1350	2600	5400	7700
Platform	150	450	800	1800	3300	4800
Stake	200	500	850	1900	3500	5000

NOTE: Add 5 percent for Econoline/Falcon "Big Six". Add 5 percent for F-Series with V-8. Add 5 percent for 4WD on F250 and F350 models only.

1963

	6	5	4	3	2	1
Econoline, E-100 Series 1/2-Ton, 6-cyl, 90" wb						
PU	200	600	950	2150	3850	5500
Van	200	500	850	1900	3500	5000
Falcon Series 1/2-Ton, 6-cyl, 109.5" wb						
Ranchero PU	200	675	1050	2250	4350	6200
Sed Dly	200	650	1000	2200	4100	5800
F-100 Series, 1/2-Ton, 6-cyl, 114" wb						
Styleside PU, 6-1/2' unit	350	800	1450	2750	5600	8000
Flareside PU, 6-1/2'	350	850	1500	2900	5700	8200
Styleside PU, 6-1/2', Sep.	350	900	1550	3050	5900	8500
Platform	200	600	950	2150	3850	5500
Stake	200	600	1000	2200	4000	5700
F-100 Series, 1/2-Ton, 6-cyl, 122" wb						
Styleside PU, 8', unit	350	750	1350	2650	5450	7800
Flareside PU, 8'	350	800	1450	2750	5600	8000
Styleside PU, 8', Sep.	350	850	1500	2950	5800	8300
F-250 Series, 3/4-Ton, 6-cyl, 122" wb						
Styleside PU, 8', unit	350	750	1300	2500	5300	7600
Flareside PU, 8'	350	750	1350	2650	5450	7800
Styleside PU, 8', Sep.	350	850	1500	2800	5650	8100

	6	5	4	3	2	1
Platform	200	500	850	1900	3500	5000
Stake	200	550	900	2000	3600	5200
F-350 Series, 1-Ton, 6-cyl, 132" wb						
Flareside PU, 9'	350	750	1300	2450	5250	7500
Styleside PU, 9', Sep.	350	750	1250	2400	5050	7200
Platform	150	450	800	1800	3300	4800
Stake	200	500	850	1900	3500	5000

NOTE: Add 5 percent for Econoline/Falcon "Big Six". Add 5 percent for F-Series with V-8. Add 5 percent for 4WD on F250 and F350 models only.

1964

	6	5	4	3	2	1
Econoline E-100 1/2-Ton, 6-cyl, 90" wb						
PU	200	600	950	2150	3850	5500
Van	200	500	850	1900	3500	5000
Panel	150	400	750	1650	3150	4500
Falcon Series 1/2-Ton, 6-cyl, 109.5" wb						
Ranchero PU	200	600	1000	2200	4000	5700
Sed Dly	200	600	950	2150	3850	5500
F-100/Model F-101, 1/2-Ton, 6-cyl, 114" wb						
Flareside PU	350	800	1450	2750	5600	8000
Styleside PU	350	850	1500	2900	5700	8200
Platform	200	500	850	1900	3500	5000
Stake	200	550	900	2000	3600	5200
F-100/Model F-102, 1/2-Ton, 6-cyl, 128" wb						
Flareside PU LBx	350	750	1350	2650	5450	7800
Styleside PU LBx	350	800	1450	2750	5600	8000
F-250, 3/4-Ton, 6-cyl, 128" wb						
Flareside PU LBx	350	750	1250	2400	5050	7200
Styleside PU LBx	350	750	1300	2450	5250	7500
Platform	150	450	800	1800	3300	4800
Stake	200	500	850	1900	3500	5000
F-350, 1-Ton, 6-cyl, 132" wb						
Flareside PU 9'	350	750	1200	2350	4900	7000
Styleside PU 9'	350	750	1250	2400	5100	7300
Platform 9'	150	400	750	1650	3150	4500
Stake 9'	150	450	800	1750	3250	4700

NOTE: Add 5 percent for Econoline/Falcon "Big Six". Add 5 percent for Falcon 260 cid/164 hp, V-8. Add 5 percent for F-Series 292 cid/160 hp, V-8. Add 5 percent for 4WD on F250 and F350 models only.

1965

	6	5	4	3	2	1
Econoline E-100 1/2-Ton, 6-cyl, 90" wb						
PU	200	600	950	2150	3850	5500
Van	200	500	850	1900	3500	5000
Panel	150	400	750	1650	3150	4500
Falcon Series 1/2-Ton, 6-cyl, 109.5" wb						
Ranchero PU	200	600	1000	2200	4000	5700
Sed Dly	200	600	950	2150	3850	5500
F-100/Model F-101, 1/2-Ton, 6-cyl, 115" wb						
Flareside PU	350	800	1450	2750	5600	8000
Styleside PU	350	850	1500	2900	5700	8200
Platform	200	500	850	1900	3500	5000
Stake	200	550	900	2000	3600	5200
F-100/Model F-102, 1/2-Ton, 6-cyl, 129" wb						
Flareside PU LBx	350	750	1350	2650	5450	7800
Styleside PU LBx	350	800	1450	2750	5600	8000
F-250, 3/4-Ton, 6-cyl, 129" wb						
Flareside PU LBx	350	750	1250	2400	5050	7200
Styleside PU LBx	350	750	1300	2450	5250	7500
Platform	150	450	800	1800	3300	4800
Stake	200	500	850	1900	3500	5000
F-350, 1-Ton, 6-cyl, 132" wb						
Flareside PU 9'	350	750	1200	2350	4900	7000
Styleside PU 9'	350	750	1250	2400	5100	7300
Platform	150	400	750	1650	3150	4500
Stake	150	450	800	1750	3250	4700

NOTE: Add 5 percent for 240 cid/150 hp "Big Six", all models. Add 5 percent for base V-8, all models except Econoline. Add 10 percent for 289 cid/225 hp, 4 barrel V-8, Falcon. Add 5 percent for 4WD on F250 and F350 models only.

1966

	6	5	4	3	2	1
Bronco U-100, 1/2-Ton, 4WD, 6-cyl, 90" wb						
Rds	350	750	1250	2400	5050	7200
Spt Utl	350	750	1300	2450	5250	7500
Wag	350	750	1300	2450	5250	7500
Econoline E-100, 1/2-Ton, 90" wb						
PU	200	600	950	2150	3850	5500
Van	200	500	850	1900	3500	5000
Sup Van	150	450	750	1700	3200	4600
Panel Van	150	400	750	1650	3150	4500
Sup Panel Van	150	450	800	1750	3250	4700
Fairlane Ranchero, 1/2-Ton, 113" wb						
PU	350	750	1200	2350	4900	7000
Cus PU	350	750	1300	2450	5250	7500
F-100/Model F-101, 1/2-Ton, 115" wb						
Flareside PU	350	800	1450	2750	5600	8000
Styleside PU	350	850	1500	2900	5700	8200
Platform	200	500	850	1900	3500	5000
Stake	200	550	900	2000	3600	5200
F-100/Model F-102, 1/2-Ton, 129" wb						
Flareside PU	350	750	1350	2650	5450	7800
Styleside PU	350	800	1450	2750	5600	8000
F-250, 3/4-Ton, 129" wb						
Flareside PU	350	750	1250	2400	5050	7200
Styleside PU	350	750	1300	2450	5250	7500
Platform	150	450	800	1800	3300	4800
Stake	200	500	850	1900	3500	5000
F-350, 1-Ton, 132" wb						
Flareside PU	350	750	1200	2350	4900	7000
Styleside PU	350	750	1250	2400	5100	7300
Platform	150	400	750	1650	3150	4500
Stake	150	450	800	1750	3250	4700

NOTE: Add 5 percent for "Big Six" where available. Add 5 percent for base V-8 where available. Add 10 percent for optional V-8's where available. Add 5 percent for 4WD on F250 and F350 models only.

1967

	6	5	4	3	2	1
Bronco U-100, 1/2-Ton, 4WD, 6-cyl						
Rds	350	750	1250	2400	5050	7200
Spt Utl	350	750	1300	2450	5250	7500
Wag	350	750	1300	2450	5250	7500
Econoline E-100, 1/2-Ton, 6-cyl						
PU	200	600	950	2150	3850	5500
Van	200	500	850	1900	3500	5000
Sup Van	150	450	750	1700	3200	4600
Panel Van	150	400	750	1650	3150	4500
Sup Panel Van	150	450	800	1750	3250	4700
Fairlane Ranchero, 1/2-Ton, 6-cyl						
PU	350	750	1200	2350	4900	7000
500 PU	350	750	1300	2450	5250	7500
500 XL PU	350	800	1450	2750	5600	8000
F-100/Model F-101, 1/2-Ton, 6-cyl						
Flareside PU 6-1/2'	350	800	1450	2750	5600	8000
Styleside PU 6-1/2'	350	850	1500	2900	5700	8200
Platform	200	500	850	1900	3500	5000
Stake	200	550	900	2000	3600	5200
Flareside 8'	350	750	1350	2650	5450	7800
Styleside 8'	350	800	1450	2750	5600	8000
F-250, 3/4-Ton, 6-cyl						
Flareside PU 8'	350	750	1250	2400	5050	7200
Styleside PU 8'	350	750	1300	2450	5250	7500
Platform	150	450	800	1800	3300	4800
Stake	200	500	850	1900	3500	5000
F-350, 1-Ton, 6-cyl						
Flareside PU 9'	350	750	1200	2350	4900	7000
Styleside PU 9'	350	750	1250	2400	5100	7300
Platform 9'	150	400	750	1650	3150	4500
Stake 9'	150	450	800	1750	3250	4700

NOTE: Add 5 percent for "Big Six" where available. Add 5 percent for base V-8 where available. Add 10 percent for optional V-8's where available. Add 5 percent for 4WD on F250 and F350 models only.

1968

	6	5	4	3	2	1
Bronco U-100, 1/2-Ton, 6-cyl, 4WD						
Rds	350	750	1250	2400	5050	7200
Spt Utl	350	750	1300	2450	5250	7500
Wag	350	750	1300	2450	5250	7500
Fairlane/Torino 1/2-Ton, 6-cyl						
PU	350	750	1300	2450	5250	7500
500 PU	350	800	1450	2750	5600	8000
GT PU	350	900	1550	3050	5900	8500
F-100/Model F-101, 1/2-Ton, 6-cyl						
Flareside PU	350	800	1450	2750	5600	8000
Styleside PU	350	850	1500	2900	5700	8200
Platform	200	500	850	1900	3500	5000
Stake	200	550	900	2000	3600	5200
F-100/Model F-102, 1/2-Ton, 6-cyl						
Flareside PU LBx	350	750	1350	2650	5450	7800
Styleside PU LBx	350	800	1450	2750	5600	8000
F-250, 3/4-Ton, 6-cyl						
Flareside PU LBx	350	750	1250	2400	5050	7200
Styleside PU LBx	350	750	1300	2450	5250	7500
Platform	150	450	800	1800	3300	4800
Stake	200	500	850	1900	3500	5000
F-350, 1-Ton, 6-cyl						
Flareside PU 9'	350	750	1200	2350	4900	7000
Styleside PU 9'	350	750	1250	2400	5100	7300
Platform 9'	150	400	750	1650	3150	4500
Stake 9'	150	450	800	1750	3250	4700

NOTE: Add 5 percent for "Big Six" where available. Add 5 percent for base V-8 where available. Add 10 percent for optional V-8's where available. Add 5 percent for 4WD on F250 and F350 models only.

1969

	6	5	4	3	2	1
Fairlane/Torino, 1/2-Ton, 6-cyl						
PU	350	750	1300	2450	5250	7500
500 PU	350	800	1450	2750	5600	8000
GT PU	350	900	1550	3050	5900	8500
Club Wagon E-100, 1/2-Ton, 6-cyl						
Clb Wag	150	350	750	1350	2800	4000
Cus Clb Wag	150	400	750	1650	3150	4500
Chateau Wag	200	600	950	2150	3850	5500
Bronco U-100, 1/2-Ton, 6-cyl						
PU	350	750	1250	2400	5050	7200
Wag	350	750	1300	2450	5250	7500
Econoline E-100, 1/2-Ton, 6-cyl						
Cargo Van	125	250	700	1150	2450	3500
Window Van	150	350	750	1350	2800	4000
Display Van	150	350	750	1350	2800	4000
Econoline E-200, 3/4-Ton, 6-cyl						
Cargo Van	125	200	600	1100	2300	3300
Window Van	125	250	700	1150	2450	3500
Display Van	125	250	700	1150	2450	3500
Econoline E-300, HD 3/4-Ton, 6-cyl						
Cargo Van	100	175	525	1050	2100	3000
Window Van	125	250	700	1150	2450	3500
Display Van	125	250	700	1150	2450	3500
F-100, 1/2-Ton, 6-cyl						
Flareside PU 6-1/2'	350	750	1350	2650	5450	7800
Styleside PU 6-1/2'	350	750	1350	2600	5400	7700
Flareside PU 8'	350	750	1300	2500	5300	7600
Styleside PU 8'	350	750	1300	2450	5250	7500
F-250, 3/4-Ton, 6-cyl						
Flareside PU 8'	350	750	1300	2400	5200	7400
Styleside PU 8'	350	750	1250	2400	5100	7300
Platform 7-1/2'	200	500	850	1900	3500	5000
Stake 7-1/2'	200	550	900	2000	3600	5200
F-350, HD 3/4-Ton, 6-cyl						
Flareside PU	350	750	1250	2400	5050	7200
Styleside PU	350	750	1250	2350	5000	7100
Platform	150	450	800	1800	3300	4800
Stake	200	500	850	1900	3500	5000

NOTE: Add 5 percent for base V-8. Add 10 percent for optional V-8. Add 5 percent for 4WD on F250 and F350 models only.

1970

	6	5	4	3	2	1
Fairlane/Torino, 1/2-Ton, V-8						
PU	350	750	1200	2350	4900	7000
500 PU	350	750	1300	2450	5250	7500
Squire PU	350	800	1350	2700	5500	7900
GT PU	350	850	1500	2800	5650	8100
Club Wagon E-100, 1/2-Ton, 6-cyl						
Clb Wag	150	350	750	1350	2800	4000
Cus Clb Wag	150	400	750	1650	3150	4500
Chateau Wag	200	600	950	2150	3850	5500
Bronco U-100, 1/2-Ton, 6-cyl						
PU	350	750	1250	2400	5050	7200
Wag	350	750	1300	2450	5250	7500
Econoline E-100, 1/2-Ton, 6-cyl						
Cargo Van	125	250	700	1150	2450	3500
Window Van	150	350	750	1350	2800	4000
Display Van	150	300	700	1250	2650	3800
Econoline E-200, 3/4-Ton, 6-cyl						
Cargo Van	125	200	600	1100	2300	3300
Window Van	150	300	700	1250	2600	3700
Display Van	125	250	700	1150	2500	3600

	6	5	4	3	2	1
Econoline E-300, HD 3/4-Ton, 6-cyl						
Cargo Van	100	175	525	1050	2100	3000
Window Van	125	250	700	1150	2450	3500
Display Van	125	250	700	1150	2400	3400
F-100, 1/2-Ton, 6-cyl						
Flareside PU 6-1/2'	350	750	1350	2650	5450	7800
Styleside PU 6-1/2'	350	750	1350	2600	5400	7700
Flareside PU 8'	350	750	1300	2500	5300	7600
Styleside PU 8'	350	750	1300	2450	5250	7500
F-250, 3/4-Ton, 6-cyl						
Flareside PU	350	750	1300	2400	5200	7400
Styleside PU	350	750	1250	2400	5100	7300
Platform	200	500	850	1900	3500	5000
Stake	200	550	900	2000	3600	5200
F-350, HD 3/4-Ton, 6-cyl						
Flareside PU	350	750	1250	2400	5050	7200
Styleside PU	350	750	1250	2350	5000	7100
Platform	150	450	800	1800	3300	4800
Stake	200	500	850	1900	3500	5000

NOTE: Add 5 percent for base V-8. Add 10 percent for optional V-8. Add 5 percent for 4WD on F250 and F350 models only.

1971

	6	5	4	3	2	1
Fairlane/Torino, 1/2-Ton, V-8						
PU	350	750	1200	2350	4900	7000
500 PU	350	750	1300	2450	5250	7500
Squire PU	350	800	1350	2700	5500	7900
GT PU	350	850	1500	2800	5650	8100
Club Wagon E-100, 1/2-Ton, 6-cyl						
Clb Wag	150	350	750	1350	2800	4000
Cus Clb Wag	150	400	750	1650	3150	4500
Chateau Wag	200	600	950	2150	3850	5500
Bronco U-100, 1/2-Ton, 6-cyl						
PU	350	750	1250	2400	5050	7200
Wag	350	750	1300	2450	5250	7500
Econoline E-100, 1/2-Ton, 6-cyl						
Cargo Van	125	250	700	1150	2450	3500
Window Van	150	350	750	1350	2800	4000
Display Van	150	300	700	1250	2650	3800
Econoline E-200, 3/4-Ton, 6-cyl						
Cargo Van	125	200	600	1100	2300	3300
Window Van	150	300	700	1250	2650	3800
Display Van	125	250	700	1150	2500	3600
Econoline E-300, HD 3/4-Ton, 6-cyl						
Cargo Van	125	200	600	1100	2200	3100
Window Van	125	250	700	1150	2450	3500
Display Van	125	250	700	1150	2400	3400
F-100, 1/2-Ton, 6-cyl						
Flareside PU 6-1/2'	350	750	1350	2650	5450	7800
Styleside PU 6-1/2'	350	750	1350	2600	5400	7700
Flareside PU 8'	350	750	1300	2500	5300	7600
Styleside PU 8'	350	750	1300	2450	5250	7500
F-250, 3/4-Ton, 6-cyl						
Flareside PU	350	750	1300	2400	5200	7400
Styleside PU	350	750	1250	2400	5100	7300
Platform	200	500	850	1900	3500	5000
Stake	200	550	900	2000	3600	5200
F-350, HD 3/4-Ton, 6-cyl						
Flareside PU	350	750	1250	2400	5050	7200
Styleside PU	350	750	1250	2350	5000	7100
Platform	150	450	800	1800	3300	4800
Stake	200	500	850	1900	3500	5000

NOTE: Add 5 percent for base V-8. Add 10 percent for optional V-8. Add 5 percent for 4WD on F250 and F350 models only.

1972

	6	5	4	3	2	1
Courier, 1/2-Ton, 4-cyl						
PU	150	300	700	1250	2650	3800
Fairlane/Torino, 1/2-Ton, V-8						
PU	350	750	1200	2350	4900	7000
500 PU	350	750	1300	2450	5250	7500
Squire PU	350	800	1350	2700	5500	7900
GT PU	350	850	1500	2800	5650	8100
Club Wagon E-100, 1/2-Ton, 6-cyl						
Clb Wag	150	350	750	1350	2800	4000
Cus Clb Wag	150	400	750	1650	3150	4500
Chateau Wag	200	600	950	2150	3850	5500
Bronco U-100, 1/2-Ton, 6-cyl						
PU	350	750	1250	2400	5050	7200
Wag	350	750	1300	2450	5250	7500
Econoline E-100, 1/2-Ton, 6-cyl						
Cargo Van	125	250	700	1150	2450	3500
Window Van	150	350	750	1350	2800	4000
Display Van	125	250	700	1150	2500	3600
Econoline E-200, 3/4-Ton, 6-cyl						
Cargo Van	125	200	600	1100	2300	3300
Window Van	150	300	700	1250	2650	3800
Display Van	125	250	700	1150	2400	3400
Econoline E-300, HD 3/4-Ton, 6-cyl						
Cargo Van	125	200	600	1100	2200	3100
Window Van	150	300	700	1250	2600	3700
Display Van	125	200	600	1100	2300	3300
F-100, 1/2-Ton, 6-cyl						
Flareside PU 6-1/2'	350	850	1500	2800	5650	8100
Styleside PU 6-1/2'	350	800	1450	2750	5600	8000
Flareside PU 8'	350	750	1350	2650	5450	7800
Styleside PU 8'	350	750	1350	2600	5400	7700
F-250, 3/4-Ton, 6-cyl						
Flareside PU	350	750	1300	2400	5200	7400
Styleside PU	350	750	1250	2400	5100	7300
F-350, HD 3/4-Ton, 6-cyl						
Flareside PU	350	750	1250	2400	5050	7200
Styleside PU	350	750	1250	2350	5000	7100
Platform	150	450	800	1800	3300	4800
Stake	200	500	850	1900	3500	5000

NOTE: Add 5 percent for base V-8. Add 10 percent for optional V-8. Add 5 percent for 4WD on F250 and F350 models only.

1973

	6	5	4	3	2	1
Courier, 1/2-Ton, 4-cyl						
PU	150	350	750	1350	2800	4000
Fairlane/Torino, 1/2-Ton, V-8						
500 PU	350	750	1300	2450	5250	7500
Squire PU	350	800	1350	2700	5500	7900
GT PU	350	850	1500	2800	5650	8100
Club Wagon E-100, 1/2-Ton, 6-cyl						
Clb Wag	150	350	750	1450	3000	4200
Cus Clb Wag	150	400	750	1650	3150	4500
Chateau Wag	200	600	950	2150	3850	5500
Bronco U-100, 1/2-Ton, 6-cyl						
Wag	350	750	1300	2450	5250	7500
Econoline E-100, 1/2-Ton, 6-cyl						
Cargo Van	125	250	700	1150	2450	3500
Window Van	150	350	750	1350	2800	4000
Display Van	150	300	700	1250	2650	3800
Econoline E-200, 3/4-Ton, 6-cyl						
Cargo Van	125	250	700	1150	2400	3400
Window Van	150	300	750	1350	2700	3900
Display Van	150	300	700	1250	2600	3700
Econoline E-300, HD 3/4-Ton, 6-cyl						
Cargo Van	125	200	600	1100	2300	3300
Window Van	150	300	700	1250	2650	3800
Display Van	125	250	700	1150	2500	3600
F-100, 1/2-Ton, 6-cyl						
Flareside PU 6-1/2'	350	800	1450	2750	5600	8000
Styleside PU 6-1/2'	350	850	1500	2800	5650	8100
Flareside PU 8'	350	800	1350	2700	5500	7900
Styleside PU 8'	350	800	1450	2750	5600	8000
F-250, 3/4-Ton, 6-cyl						
Flareside PU	350	750	1300	2400	5200	7400
Styleside PU	350	750	1250	2400	5100	7300
Platform	200	500	850	1900	3500	5000
Stake	200	550	900	2000	3600	5200
F-350, HD 3/4-Ton, 6-cyl						
Flareside PU	350	750	1250	2400	5050	7200
Styleside PU	350	750	1250	2350	5000	7100
Platform	150	450	800	1800	3300	4800
Stake	200	500	850	1900	3500	5000

NOTE: Add 5 percent for base V-8. Add 10 percent for optional V-8. Add 5 percent for 4WD on F250 and F350 models only.

1974

	6	5	4	3	2	1
Courier						
PU	150	350	750	1350	2800	4000
Ranchero						
500 PU	200	675	1050	2250	4350	6200
GT PU	350	725	1150	2300	4700	6700
Sq PU	350	750	1250	2400	5050	7200
Bronco						
Wag	350	750	1200	2350	4900	7000
Econoline E-100						
Cargo Van	125	200	600	1100	2300	3300
Window Van	125	250	700	1150	2400	3400
Display Van	125	250	700	1150	2500	3600
Clb Wag	150	350	750	1450	2900	4100
Cus Clb Wag	150	400	750	1550	3050	4300
Chateau Clb Wag	150	400	750	1650	3150	4500
Econoline E-200						
Cargo Van	125	200	600	1100	2250	3200
Window Van	125	200	600	1100	2300	3300
Display Van	125	250	700	1150	2400	3400
Econoline E-300						
Cargo Van	100	175	525	1050	2050	2900
Window Van	125	200	600	1100	2200	3100
Display Van	125	200	600	1100	2300	3300
F-100 - (1/2-Ton)						
Flareside PU	200	675	1050	2250	4350	6200
Styleside PU	200	675	1100	2250	4400	6300
Sup Cab PU	200	650	1050	2250	4200	6000
F-250 - (3/4-Ton)						
Flareside PU	200	550	900	2100	3700	5300
Styleside PU	200	550	900	2150	3800	5400
Sup Cab	200	500	850	1950	3600	5100
F-350 - (1-Ton)						
PU	200	500	850	1950	3600	5100
Crew Cab PU	200	550	900	2100	3700	5300
Stake	200	500	850	1900	3500	5000

NOTE: Add 5 percent for 4WD on F250 and F350 models only.

1975

	6	5	4	3	2	1
Courier						
PU	150	350	750	1350	2800	4000
Ranchero						
500 PU	200	675	1050	2250	4350	6200
GT PU	350	725	1150	2300	4700	6700
Sq PU	350	750	1250	2400	5050	7200
Bronco						
Wag	350	750	1200	2350	4900	7000
Econoline E-100						
Cargo Van	125	200	600	1100	2250	3200
Window Van	125	250	700	1150	2400	3400
Display Van	125	250	700	1150	2500	3600
Clb Wag	150	350	750	1450	2900	4100
Cus Clb Wag	150	400	750	1550	3050	4300
Chateau Clb Wag	150	400	750	1650	3150	4500
Econoline E-200						
Cargo Van	125	200	600	1100	2200	3100
Window Van	125	200	600	1100	2300	3300
Display Van	125	250	700	1150	2450	3500
Econoline E-300						
Cargo Van	100	175	525	1050	2100	3000
Window Van	125	200	600	1100	2250	3200
Display Van	125	250	700	1150	2400	3400
F-100 - (1/2-Ton)						
Flareside PU	200	600	950	2150	3850	5500
Styleside PU	200	600	950	2200	3900	5600
Sup Cab PU	200	550	900	2000	3600	5200
F-250 - (3/4-Ton)						
Flareside PU	200	500	850	1900	3500	5000
Styleside PU	200	500	850	1950	3600	5100
Sup Cab	200	500	850	1900	3500	5000
F-350 - (1-Ton)						
PU	200	500	850	1850	3350	4900
Crew Cab PU	200	500	850	1900	3500	5000
Stake	200	500	850	1850	3350	4900

1976

	6	5	4	3	2	1
Courier						
PU	150	350	750	1350	2800	4000
Ranchero						
500 PU	200	675	1050	2250	4350	6200
GT PU	350	725	1150	2300	4700	6700
Sq PU	350	750	1250	2400	5050	7200
Bronco						
Wag	350	750	1200	2350	4900	7000
Econoline E-100						
Cargo Van	125	200	600	1100	2250	3200

(continued)

	6	5	4	3	2	1
Window Van	125	250	700	1150	2400	3400
Display Van	125	250	700	1150	2500	3600
Clb Wag	150	350	750	1450	2900	4100
Cus Clb Wag	150	400	750	1550	3050	4300
Chateau Clb Wag	150	400	750	1650	3150	4500
Econoline E-200						
Cargo Van	125	200	600	1100	2200	3100
Window Van	125	200	600	1100	2300	3300
Display Van	125	250	700	1150	2450	3500
Econoline E-300						
Cargo Van	100	175	525	1050	2100	3000
Window Van	125	200	600	1100	2250	3200
Display Van	125	250	700	1150	2400	3400
F-100 - (1/2-Ton)						
Flareside PU	200	500	850	1950	3600	5100
Styleside PU	200	550	900	2000	3600	5200
Sup Cab PU	200	500	850	1900	3500	5000
F-250 - (3/4-Ton)						
Flareside PU	200	500	850	1900	3500	5000
Styleside PU	200	500	850	1950	3600	5100
Sup Cab PU	200	500	850	1850	3350	4900
F-350 - (1-Ton)						
PU	200	500	850	1850	3350	4900
Crew Cab PU	200	500	850	1900	3500	5000
Stake	150	450	800	1800	3300	4800

1977
Courier
	6	5	4	3	2	1
PU	150	350	750	1350	2800	4000
Ranchero						
500 PU	200	650	1000	2200	4100	5800
GT PU	200	650	1050	2250	4200	6000
Sq PU	200	675	1050	2250	4350	6200
Bronco						
Wag	350	750	1200	2350	4900	7000
Econoline E-100						
Cargo Van	125	200	600	1100	2200	3100
Window Van	125	200	600	1100	2300	3300
Display Van	125	250	700	1150	2450	3500
Clb Wag	150	350	750	1350	2800	4000
Cus Clb Wag	150	350	750	1450	3000	4200
Chateau Clb Wag	150	400	750	1600	3100	4400
Econoline E-200						
Cargo Van	100	175	525	1050	2100	3000
Window Van	125	200	600	1100	2250	3200
Display Van	125	250	700	1150	2400	3400
Econoline E-300						
Cargo Van	100	175	525	1050	2050	2900
Window Van	125	200	600	1100	2200	3100
Display Van	125	200	600	1100	2300	3300
F-100 - (1/2-Ton)						
Flareside PU	200	500	850	1900	3500	5000
Styleside PU	200	500	850	1950	3600	5100
Sup Cab PU	200	500	850	1900	3500	5000
F-250 - (3/4-Ton)						
Flareside PU	200	500	850	1850	3350	4900
Styleside PU	200	500	850	1900	3500	5000
Sup Cab	200	500	850	1850	3350	4900
F-350 - (1-Ton)						
PU	150	450	800	1800	3300	4800
Crew Cab PU	200	500	850	1850	3350	4900
Stake	150	450	800	1800	3300	4800

1978
Courier
	6	5	4	3	2	1
PU	150	350	750	1350	2800	4000
Ranchero						
500 PU	200	650	1000	2200	4100	5800
GT PU	200	650	1050	2250	4200	6000
Sq PU	200	675	1050	2250	4350	6200
Bronco						
Wag	350	700	1150	2300	4550	6500
Econoline E-100						
Cargo Van	125	200	600	1100	2200	3100
Window Van	125	250	700	1150	2400	3400
Display Van	125	250	700	1150	2500	3600
Clb Wag	150	350	750	1450	2900	4100
Cus Clb Wag	150	400	750	1550	3050	4300
Chateau Clb Wag	150	400	750	1650	3150	4500
Econoline E-200						
Cargo Van	100	175	525	1050	2100	3000
Window Van	125	200	600	1100	2300	3300
Display Van	125	250	700	1150	2450	3500
Econoline E-300						
Cargo Van	100	175	525	1050	2050	2900
Window Van	125	200	600	1100	2250	3200
Display Van	125	250	700	1150	2400	3400
F-100 - (1/2-Ton)						
Flareside PU	200	500	850	1900	3500	5000
Styleside PU	200	500	850	1950	3600	5100
Sup Cab PU	200	500	850	1950	3600	5100
F-250 - (3/4-Ton)						
Flareside PU	200	500	850	1850	3350	4900
Styleside PU	200	500	850	1900	3500	5000
Sup Cab PU	200	500	850	1900	3500	5000
F-350 - (1-Ton)						
PU	150	450	800	1800	3300	4800
Crew Cab PU	200	500	850	1850	3350	4900
Stake	200	500	850	1850	3350	4900

1979
Courier
	6	5	4	3	2	1
PU	150	350	750	1350	2800	4000
Ranchero						
500 PU	200	650	1000	2200	4100	5800
GT PU	200	650	1050	2250	4200	6000
Sq PU	200	675	1050	2250	4350	6200
Bronco						
Wag	350	700	1150	2300	4550	6500
Econoline E-100						
Cargo Van	100	175	525	1050	2100	3000
Window Van	125	200	600	1100	2250	3200
Display Van	125	250	700	1150	2400	3400
Clb Wag	150	300	750	1350	2700	3900
Cus Clb Wag	150	350	750	1350	2800	4000
Chateau Clb Wag	150	350	750	1450	3000	4200

778

	6	5	4	3	2	1
Econoline E-200						
Cargo Van	100	175	525	1050	2050	2900
Window Van	125	200	600	1100	2200	3100
Display Van	125	200	600	1100	2250	3200
Econoline E-300						
Cargo Van	100	175	525	1050	1950	2800
Window Van	100	175	525	1050	2100	3000
Display Van	125	200	600	1100	2200	3100
F-100 - (1/2-Ton)						
Flareside PU	200	500	850	1900	3500	5000
Styleside PU	200	500	850	1950	3600	5100
Sup Cab	200	500	850	1950	3600	5100
F-250 - (3/4-Ton)						
Flareside PU	200	500	850	1850	3350	4900
Styleside PU	200	500	850	1900	3500	5000
Sup Cab	200	500	850	1900	3500	5000
F-350 - (1-Ton)						
PU	150	450	800	1800	3300	4800
Crew Cab PU	200	500	850	1850	3350	4900
Stake	200	500	850	1850	3350	4900

1980
Courier
	6	5	4	3	2	1
PU	150	350	750	1350	2800	4000
Ranchero						
500 PU	200	650	1000	2200	4100	5800
GT PU	200	650	1050	2250	4200	6000
Sq PU	200	675	1050	2250	4350	6200
Bronco						
Wag	350	700	1150	2300	4550	6500
Econoline E-100						
Cargo Van	100	175	525	1050	2100	3000
Window Van	125	200	600	1100	2250	3200
Display Van	125	250	700	1150	2400	3400
Clb Wag	150	300	750	1350	2700	3900
Cus Clb Wag	150	350	750	1450	2900	4100
Chateau Clb Wag	150	400	750	1550	3050	4300
Econoline E-200						
Cargo Van	100	175	525	1050	2050	2900
Window Van	125	200	600	1100	2200	3100
Display Van	125	200	600	1100	2250	3200
Econoline E-300						
Cargo Van	100	175	525	1050	1950	2800
Window Van	100	175	525	1050	2100	3000
Display Van	125	200	600	1100	2200	3100
F-100 - (1/2-Ton)						
Flareside PU	200	500	850	1900	3500	5000
Styleside PU	200	500	850	1950	3600	5100
Sup Cab	200	500	850	1950	3600	5100
F-250 - (3/4-Ton)						
Flareside PU	200	500	850	1850	3350	4900
Styleside PU	200	500	850	1900	3500	5000
Sup Cab	200	500	850	1900	3500	5000
F-350 - (1-Ton)						
PU	150	450	800	1800	3300	4800
Crew Cab PU	200	500	850	1850	3350	4900
Stake	150	400	750	1650	3150	4500

NOTE: Add 10 percent for 4WD.

1981
Bronco
	6	5	4	3	2	1
Bronco (4WD)	350	700	1150	2300	4550	6500
Econoline E-100						
Clb Wag	150	350	750	1450	2900	4100
Cargo Van	150	300	700	1250	2600	3700
Window Van	150	300	700	1250	2650	3800
Display Van	150	300	700	1250	2600	3700
Econoline E-150						
Clb Wag	150	350	750	1450	2900	4100
Sup Clb Wag	150	400	750	1550	3050	4300
Cargo Van	150	300	700	1250	2600	3700
Sup Cargo Van	150	300	750	1350	2700	3900
Window Van	150	300	700	1250	2650	3800
Sup Window Van	150	350	750	1350	2800	4000
Display Van	150	300	700	1250	2600	3700
Sup Display Van	150	300	750	1350	2700	3900
Econoline E-250						
Clb Wag	150	300	750	1350	2700	3900
Sup Clb Wag	150	350	750	1350	2800	4000
Cargo Van	125	250	700	1150	2450	3500
Sup Cargo Van	125	250	700	1150	2500	3600
Window Van	125	250	700	1150	2500	3600
Sup Window Van	150	300	700	1250	2600	3700
Display Van	125	250	700	1150	2450	3500
Sup Display Van	125	250	700	1150	2500	3600
Econoline E-350						
Sup Clb Wag	150	350	750	1450	2900	4100
Cargo Van	125	250	700	1150	2500	3600
Sup Cargo Van	150	300	700	1250	2600	3700
Window Van	150	300	700	1250	2600	3700
Sup Window Van	150	300	700	1250	2650	3800
Display Van	125	250	700	1150	2500	3600
Sup Display Van	150	300	750	1350	2700	3900
Courier						
Styleside PU SBx	100	150	450	1000	1900	2700
F-100						
Flareside PU SBx	200	550	900	2000	3600	5200
Styleside PU SBx	200	550	900	2100	3700	5300
Styleside PU LBx	200	500	850	1950	3600	5100
F-150						
Flareside PU SBx	200	550	900	2000	3600	5200
Styleside PU SBx	200	550	900	2100	3700	5300
Styleside PU LBx	200	500	850	1950	3600	5100
Styleside Sup Cab PU	200	550	900	2000	3600	5200
F-250						
Styleside PU LBx	150	450	800	1800	3300	4800
Styleside Sup Cab PU	200	500	850	1900	3500	5000
F-350						
Styleside PU LBx	200	500	850	1850	3350	4900
Styleside Crew Cab PU	150	450	800	1750	3250	4700

NOTE: Add 10 percent for 4WD.

1982
Bronco
	6	5	4	3	2	1
Bronco (4WD)	200	600	1000	2200	4000	5700
Econoline E-100						
Clb Wag	150	400	750	1650	3150	4500
Cargo Van	125	250	700	1150	2450	3500

	6	5	4	3	2	1
Window Van	125	250	700	1150	2500	3600
Display Van	125	250	700	1150	2450	3500
Econoline E-150						
Clb Wag	150	450	750	1700	3200	4600
Sup Clb Wag	150	450	800	1800	3300	4800
Cargo Van	125	250	700	1150	2500	3600
Sup Cargo Van	150	300	700	1250	2600	3700
Window Van	150	300	700	1250	2600	3800
Sup Window Van	150	300	700	1250	2650	3800
Display Van	125	250	700	1150	2500	3600
Sup Display Van	150	300	700	1250	2600	3700
Econoline E-250						
Clb Wag	150	400	750	1600	3100	4400
Sup Clb Wag	150	400	750	1650	3150	4500
Cargo Van	150	300	700	1250	2600	3700
Sup Cargo Van	150	300	700	1250	2650	3800
Window Van	150	300	700	1250	2650	3800
Sup Window Van	150	300	750	1350	2700	3900
Display Van	150	300	700	1250	2600	3700
Sup Display Van	150	300	700	1250	2650	3800
Econoline E-350						
Sup Clb Wag	150	450	750	1700	3200	4600
Cargo Van	150	300	700	1250	2650	3800
Sup Cargo Van	150	300	750	1350	2700	3900
Window Van	150	300	750	1350	2700	3900
Sup Window Van	150	350	750	1350	2800	4000
Display Van	150	300	700	1250	2650	3800
Sup Display Van	150	300	750	1350	2700	3900
Courier						
Styleside PU SBx	100	150	450	1000	1900	2700
Styleside PU LBx	100	175	525	1050	1950	2800
F-100						
Flareside PU SBx	200	550	900	2000	3600	5200
Styleside PU SBx	200	550	900	2100	3700	5300
Styleside PU LBx	200	550	900	2000	3600	5200
F-150						
Flareside PU SBx	200	500	850	1950	3600	5100
Styleside PU SBx	200	550	900	2000	3600	5200
Styleside PU LBx	200	500	850	1950	3600	5100
Styleside PU Sup Cab	200	550	900	2150	3800	5400
F-250						
Styleside PU LBx	200	500	850	1900	3500	5000
Styleside Sup Cab	200	550	900	2100	3700	5300
F-350						
Styleside PU LBx	200	500	850	1850	3350	4900

NOTE: Add 10 percent for 4WD.

1983

	6	5	4	3	2	1
Bronco						
Bronco (4WD)	350	700	1150	2300	4550	6500
Econoline E-100						
Cargo Van	125	250	700	1150	2450	3500
Window Van	150	300	700	1250	2600	3700
Display Van	125	250	700	1150	2450	3500
Econoline E-150						
Clb Wag	150	400	750	1650	3150	4500
Cargo Van	125	250	700	1150	2500	3600
Sup Cargo Van	150	300	700	1250	2600	3700
Window Van	150	300	700	1250	2650	3800
Sup Window Van	150	300	750	1350	2700	3900
Display Van	125	250	700	1150	2450	3500
Sup Display Van	125	250	700	1150	2500	3600
Econoline E-250						
Clb Wag	150	400	750	1550	3050	4300
Sup Clb Wag	150	400	750	1600	3100	4400
Cargo Van	150	300	700	1250	2600	3700
Sup Cargo Van	150	300	700	1250	2650	3800
Window Van	150	300	750	1350	2700	3900
Sup Window Van	150	350	750	1350	2800	4000
Display Van	125	250	700	1150	2500	3600
Sup Display Van	150	300	700	1250	2600	3700
Econoline E-350						
Sup Clb Wag	150	400	750	1650	3150	4500
Cargo Van	150	300	700	1250	2650	3800
Sup Cargo Van	150	300	750	1350	2700	3900
Window Van	150	350	750	1350	2800	4000
Sup Window Van	150	350	750	1450	2900	4100
Display Van	150	300	700	1250	2600	3700
Sup Display Van	150	300	700	1250	2650	3800
Ranger						
Styleside PU SBx	150	300	700	1250	2650	3800
Styleside PU LBx	150	300	750	1350	2700	3900
F-100						
Flareside PU SBx	200	550	900	2000	3600	5200
Styleside PU SBx	200	550	900	2100	3700	5300
Styleside PU LBx	200	550	900	2000	3600	5200
F-150						
Flareside PU SBx	200	500	850	1950	3600	5100
Styleside PU SBx	200	550	900	2000	3600	5200
Styleside PU LBx	200	550	900	1950	3600	5100
Styleside Sup Cab PU	200	550	900	2100	3700	5300
F-250						
Styleside PU LBx	200	500	850	1950	3600	5100
Styleside Sup Cab PU	200	550	900	2000	3600	5200
F-350						
Styleside PU LBx	200	500	850	1900	3500	5000
Styleside Crew Cab PU	200	500	850	1850	3350	4900

NOTE: Add 10 percent for 4WD.

1984

	6	5	4	3	2	1
Bronco II						
Bronco (4WD)	200	600	950	2200	3900	5600
Bronco						
Bronco (4WD)	350	750	1200	2350	4900	7000
Econoline E-150						
Clb Wag	150	400	750	1650	3150	4500
Cargo Van	150	350	750	1450	2900	4100
Window Van	150	350	750	1450	3000	4200
Sup Window Van	150	400	750	1600	3100	4400
Sup Cargo Van	150	400	750	1550	3050	4300
Display Van	150	350	750	1450	3000	4200
Econoline E-250						
Clb Wag	150	450	750	1700	3200	4600
Cargo Van	150	350	750	1450	3000	4200
Window Van	150	400	750	1550	3050	4300
Sup Window Van	150	400	750	1650	3150	4500

	6	5	4	3	2	1
Sup Cargo Van	150	400	750	1600	3100	4400
Display Van	150	400	750	1550	3050	4300
Sup Display Van	150	400	750	1600	3100	4400
Econoline E-350						
Clb Wag	150	450	800	1750	3250	4700
Cargo Van	150	400	750	1550	3050	4300
Window Van	150	400	750	1600	3100	4400
Sup Window Van	150	450	750	1700	3200	4600
Sup Cargo Van	150	400	750	1650	3150	4500
Display Van	150	400	750	1600	3100	4400
Sup Display Van	150	400	750	1650	3150	4500
Ranger						
Styleside PU SBx	100	175	525	1050	2100	3000
Styleside PU LBx	125	200	600	1100	2200	3100
Styleside Sup Cab PU	125	200	600	1100	2250	3200
F-150						
Flareside PU SBx	150	450	800	1800	3300	4800
Styleside PU SBx	200	500	850	1850	3350	4900
Styleside PU LBx	150	450	800	1800	3300	4800
Styleside Sup Cab SBx	200	500	850	1950	3600	5100
Styleside Sup Cab LBx	200	550	900	2000	3600	5200
F-250						
Styleside PU LBx	200	500	850	1900	3500	5000
Styleside Sup Cab PU LBx	200	550	900	2000	3600	5200
Styleside PU LBx	200	500	850	1850	3350	4900
Styleside Sup Cab PU LBx	200	500	850	1950	3600	5100

NOTE: Add 10 percent for 4WD.

1985

	6	5	4	3	2	1
Bronco II						
Bronco (4WD)	200	600	950	2200	3900	5600
Bronco						
Bronco (4WD)	350	750	1200	2350	4900	7000
Econoline E-150						
Clb Wag	200	650	1000	2200	4100	5800
Cargo Van	150	350	750	1450	2900	4100
Window Van	150	350	750	1450	3000	4200
Sup Window Van	150	400	750	1600	3100	4400
Sup Cargo Van	150	350	750	1450	3000	4200
Display Van	150	350	750	1450	2900	4100
Econoline E-250						
Clb Wag	200	600	950	2150	3850	5500
Cargo Van	150	350	750	1450	3000	4200
Window Van	150	400	750	1550	3050	4300
Sup Window Van	150	400	750	1650	3150	4500
Sup Cargo Van	150	400	750	1550	3050	4300
Display Van	150	350	750	1450	3000	4200
Econoline E-350						
Clb Wag	200	500	850	1900	3500	5000
Cargo Van	150	400	750	1550	3050	4300
Window Van	150	400	750	1600	3100	4400
Sup Window Van	150	450	750	1700	3200	4600
Sup Cargo Van	150	400	750	1600	3100	4400
Display Van	150	400	750	1550	3050	4300
Ranger						
Styleside PU SBx	150	300	700	1250	2600	3700
Styleside PU LBx	150	300	700	1250	2650	3800
Styleside Sup Cab PU	150	350	750	1350	2800	4000
F-150						
Flareside PU SBx	200	600	950	2150	3850	5500
Styleside PU SBx	200	600	950	2200	3900	5600
Styleside PU LBx	200	600	950	2150	3850	5500
Styleside Sup Cab PU SBx	200	600	1000	2200	4000	5700
Styleside Sup Cab PU LBx	200	650	1000	2200	4100	5800
F-250						
Styleside PU LBx	200	600	1000	2200	4000	5700
Styleside Sup Cab PU LBx	200	650	1000	2200	4100	5800
F-350						
Styleside PU LBx	200	600	950	2200	3900	5600
Styleside Sup Cab PU LBx	200	600	1000	2200	4000	5700

NOTE: Add 15 percent for 4WD.

1986

	6	5	4	3	2	1
Bronco II						
Bronco (2WD)	150	400	750	1650	3150	4500
Bronco (4WD)	200	600	1000	2200	4000	5700
Bronco						
Bronco (4WD)	350	750	1200	2350	4900	7000
Aerostar						
Panel Van	200	500	850	1900	3500	5000
Window Van	200	600	1000	2200	4000	5700
Wag	200	550	900	2000	3600	5200
Econoline E-150						
Clb Wag	200	650	1000	2200	4100	5800
Cargo Van	200	500	850	1950	3600	5100
Window Van	200	550	900	2100	3700	5300
Sup Cargo Van	200	550	900	2100	3700	5300
Sup Window Van	200	600	950	2150	3850	5500
Econoline E-250						
Clb Wag	200	600	1000	2200	4000	5700
Cargo Van	200	550	900	2000	3600	5200
Window Van	200	550	900	2150	3800	5400
Sup Cargo Van	200	550	900	2100	3700	5300
Econoline E-350						
Sup Clb Wag	200	600	950	2200	3900	5600
Cargo Van	200	550	900	2100	3700	5300
Window Van	200	550	900	2150	3800	5400
Sup Cargo Van	200	550	900	2150	3800	5400
Sup Window Van	200	600	950	2150	3850	5500
Ranger						
Styleside PU SBx	150	400	750	1550	3050	4300
Styleside PU LBx	150	400	750	1600	3100	4400
Styleside Sup Cab PU	150	400	750	1650	3150	4500
F-150						
Flareside PU SBx	200	600	950	2200	3900	5600
Styleside PU SBx	200	600	1000	2200	4000	5700
Styleside PU LBx	200	600	950	2200	3900	5600
Styleside Sup Cab PU SBx	200	650	1000	2200	4150	5900
Styleside Sup Cab PU LBx	200	650	1050	2250	4200	6000
F-250						
Styleside PU LBx	200	600	950	2150	3850	5500
Styleside Sup Cab PU LBx	200	650	1000	2200	4150	5900
F-350						
Styleside PU LBx	200	600	950	2150	3850	5500
Styleside Sup Cab PU LBx	200	600	1000	2200	4000	5700

NOTE: Add 15 percent for 4WD.

GMC

Model	6	5	4	3	2	1
1920-1926						
Canopy	350	700	1150	2300	4550	6500
1927						
Light Duty						
PU	350	700	1150	2300	4550	6500
Panel	200	675	1050	2250	4350	6200
1928						
Light Duty						
PU	350	700	1150	2300	4550	6500
Panel	200	675	1050	2250	4350	6200
1929						
Light Duty						
PU	350	700	1150	2300	4550	6500
Panel	200	675	1050	2250	4350	6200
1930						
Light Duty						
PU	350	700	1150	2300	4600	6600
Panel	350	700	1150	2300	4550	6500
Stake	200	650	1050	2250	4200	6000
1931						
Light Duty						
PU	350	750	1250	2400	5050	7200
Panel	350	750	1200	2350	4900	7000
Stake	200	650	1050	2250	4200	6000
1932						
Light Duty						
PU	350	750	1300	2450	5250	7500
Panel	350	750	1200	2350	4900	7000
Stake	200	650	1050	2250	4200	6000
1935						
Light Duty						
PU	450	1100	1700	3650	6650	9500
Panel	350	900	1550	3050	5900	8500
1936						
Light Duty						
PU	450	1100	1700	3650	6650	9500
Panel	350	900	1550	3050	5900	8500
1937						
Light Duty						
PU	450	1100	1700	3650	6650	9500
Panel	350	900	1550	3050	5900	8500
1938						
Light Duty - (1/2-Ton)						
PU	450	1100	1700	3650	6650	9500
Panel	350	900	1550	3050	5900	8500
Medium Duty						
3/4-Ton PU	350	750	1300	2450	5250	7500
3/4-Ton Panel	350	750	1250	2400	5050	7200
1-Ton PU	350	725	1200	2350	4850	6900
1-Ton Panel	350	700	1150	2300	4600	6600
Dly Van	200	675	1050	2250	4350	6200
1939						
Light Duty - (1/2-Ton)						
PU	450	1100	1700	3650	6650	9500
Panel	350	800	1450	2750	5600	8000
Medium Duty						
3/4-Ton PU	350	750	1300	2450	5250	7500
3/4-Ton Panel	350	750	1250	2400	5050	7200
1-Ton PU	350	725	1200	2350	4850	6900
1-Ton Panel	350	700	1150	2300	4600	6600
Dly Van	200	675	1050	2250	4350	6200
1940						
Light Duty - (1/2-Ton) - (113.5" wb)						
PU	450	1100	1700	3650	6650	9500
Panel	350	750	1300	2400	5200	7400
Canopy Dly	350	750	1300	2450	5250	7500
Screenside Dly	350	750	1300	2450	5250	7500
Suburban	350	750	1300	2500	5300	7600
Medium Duty - (123.75" wb)						
1/2-Ton PU	350	750	1300	2450	5250	7500
1/2-Ton Panel	350	750	1250	2400	5050	7200
1/2-Ton Stake	350	725	1200	2350	4800	6800
3/4-Ton PU	350	750	1200	2350	4900	7000
3/4-Ton Panel	350	725	1150	2300	4700	6700
3/4-Ton Stake	200	675	1100	2250	4400	6300
Medium Duty - (1-Ton) - (133" wb)						
PU	350	750	1200	2350	4900	7000
Panel	350	725	1200	2350	4800	6800
Canopy Dly	350	725	1200	2350	4850	6900
Screenside Dly	350	725	1200	2350	4850	6900
Stake	200	675	1050	2350	4300	6100
1941						
Light Duty - (1/2-Ton) - (115" wb)						
PU	400	1200	2000	3950	7000	10,000
Panel	350	900	1550	3050	5900	8500
Canopy Dly	350	900	1550	3100	6000	8600
Screenside Dly	350	950	1600	3200	6050	8700
Suburban	450	950	1600	3250	6150	8800
Stake	350	700	1150	2300	4550	6500
Light Duty - (1/2-Ton) - (125" wb)						
PU	350	750	1350	2600	5400	7700
Panel	350	750	1300	2450	5250	7500
Stake	350	725	1200	2350	4850	6900
Medium Duty - (3/4-Ton) - (125" wb)						
PU	350	750	1250	2400	5050	7200
Panel	350	750	1200	2350	4900	7000
Stake	350	700	1100	2300	4500	6400
Medium Duty - (1-Ton) - (134" wb)						
Stake	350	725	1150	2300	4700	6700
Panel	350	700	1150	2300	4550	6500
Canopy Dly	350	700	1150	2300	4600	6600
Screenside Dly	350	700	1150	2300	4600	6600
Stake	200	650	1050	2250	4200	6000
1942						
Light Duty - (1/2-Ton) - (115" wb)						
PU	350	900	1550	3050	5900	8500
Panel	350	800	1450	2750	5600	8000
Canopy Dly	350	750	1350	2600	5400	7700
Screenside Dly	350	750	1350	2600	5400	7700
Suburban	350	750	1350	2650	5450	7800
Stake	350	750	1200	2350	4900	7000
Light Duty - (1/2-Ton) - (125" wb)						
PU	350	750	1350	2600	5400	7700
Panel	350	750	1300	2450	5250	7500
Stake	350	725	1200	2350	4850	6900
Medium Duty - (3/4-Ton) - (125" wb)						
PU	350	750	1250	2400	5050	7200
Panel	350	750	1200	2350	4900	7000
Stake	350	700	1100	2300	4500	6400
Medium Duty - (1-Ton) - (134" wb)						
PU	350	725	1150	2300	4700	6700
Panel	350	700	1150	2300	4550	6500
Canopy Dly	350	700	1150	2300	4600	6600
Screenside Dly	350	700	1150	2300	4600	6600
Stake	200	650	1050	2250	4200	6000
1946						
Light Duty - (1/2-Ton) - (115" wb)						
PU	450	1100	1700	3650	6650	9500
Panel	350	900	1550	3100	6000	8600
Canopy Dly	350	950	1600	3200	6050	8700
Screenside Dly	350	950	1600	3200	6050	8700
Suburban	450	950	1600	3250	6150	8800
Stake	350	700	1150	2300	4550	6500
Light Duty - (1/2-Ton) - (125" wb)						
PU	350	750	1350	2600	5400	7700
Panel	350	750	1300	2450	5250	7500
Stake	350	725	1200	2350	4850	6900
Medium Duty - (3/4-Ton) - (125" wb)						
PU	350	750	1250	2400	5050	7200
Panel	350	750	1200	2350	4900	7000
Stake	350	700	1100	2300	4500	6400
Medium Duty - (1-Ton) - (134" wb)						
PU	350	725	1150	2300	4700	6700
Panel	350	700	1150	2300	4550	6500
Canopy Dly	350	700	1150	2300	4600	6600
Screenside Dly	350	700	1150	2300	4600	6600
Stake	200	650	1050	2250	4200	6000
1947						
Light Duty - (1/2-Ton) - (115" wb)						
PU	450	1100	1700	3650	6650	9500
Panel	350	750	1300	2500	5300	7600
Canopy Dly	350	750	1350	2600	5400	7700
Screenside Dly	350	750	1350	2600	5400	7700
Suburban	350	750	1350	2650	5450	7800
Stake	200	650	1050	2250	4200	6000
Light Duty - (1/2-Ton) - (125" wb)						
PU	350	750	1350	2600	5400	7700
Panel	350	750	1300	2450	5250	7500
Stake	350	725	1200	2350	4850	6900
Medium Duty - (3/4-Ton) - (125" wb)						
PU	350	750	1250	2400	5050	7200
Panel	350	750	1200	2350	4900	7000
Stake	350	700	1100	2300	4500	6400
Medium Duty - (1-Ton) - (134" wb)						
PU	350	725	1150	2300	4700	6700
Panel	350	700	1150	2300	4550	6500
Canopy Dly	350	700	1150	2300	4600	6600
Screenside Dly	350	700	1150	2300	4600	6600
Stake	200	650	1050	2250	4200	6000
1948						
Series FC-101						
PU	450	1400	2300	4600	8100	11,500
Panel	350	900	1550	3100	6000	8600
Canopy Exp	350	950	1600	3200	6050	8700
Suburban	450	950	1600	3250	6150	8800
Series FC-102						
PU	450	950	1600	3250	6150	8800
Stake	350	750	1200	2350	4900	7000
Series FC-152						
PU	350	900	1550	3050	5900	8500
Stake	350	850	1500	2800	5650	8100
Series EF-214						
Package Dly	350	800	1450	2750	5600	8000
Series EF-242						
Package Dly	350	750	1350	2650	5450	7800
Series EFP-241						
Package Dly	350	750	1350	2650	5450	7800
Series FC-253						
PU	200	675	1050	2250	4350	6200
Panel	200	650	1050	2250	4200	6000
Canopy Exp	200	675	1050	2250	4300	6100
Stake	200	650	1000	2200	4150	5900
Platform	200	650	1000	2200	4100	5800
1949						
Series FC-101						
PU	450	1400	2300	4600	8100	11,500
Panel	350	900	1550	3100	6000	8600
Canopy Exp	350	950	1600	3200	6050	8700
Suburban	450	950	1600	3250	6150	8800
Series FC-102						
PU	450	950	1600	3250	6150	8800
Stake	350	700	1150	2300	4550	6500
Series FC-152						
PU	350	900	1550	3050	5900	8500
Stake	350	850	1500	2800	5650	8100
Series EF-214						
Package Dly	350	800	1450	2750	5600	8000
Series EF-242						
Package Dly	350	750	1350	2650	5450	7800
Series EFP-241						
Package Dly	350	750	1300	2500	5300	7600
Series FC-253						
PU	350	850	1500	2900	5700	8200
Panel	350	800	1450	2750	5600	8000
Canopy Exp	350	850	1500	2800	5650	8100
Stake	350	800	1350	2700	5500	7900
Platform	350	750	1350	2650	5450	7800
1950						
Series FC-101						
PU	450	1400	2300	4600	8100	11,500
Panel	350	900	1550	3100	6000	8600
Canopy Exp	350	950	1600	3200	6050	8700
Suburban	450	950	1600	3250	6150	8800

	6	5	4	3	2	1
Series FC-102						
PU	450	950	1600	3250	6150	8800
Stake	350	700	1150	2300	4550	6500
Series FC-152						
PU	350	900	1550	3050	5900	8500
Stake	350	850	1500	2800	5650	8100
Series EF-214						
Package Dly	350	800	1450	2750	5600	8000
Series EF-242						
Package Dly	350	750	1350	2650	5450	7800
Series EFP-241						
Package Dly	350	750	1300	2500	5300	7600
Series FC-253						
PU	350	850	1500	2900	5700	8200
Panel	350	800	1450	2750	5600	8000
Canopy Exp	350	850	1500	2800	5650	8100
Stake	350	800	1350	2700	5500	7900
Platform	350	750	1350	2650	5450	7800

1951
Series 100-22 - (1/2-Ton) - (116" wb)

	6	5	4	3	2	1
PU	450	1400	2300	4600	8100	11,500
Panel	350	900	1550	3100	6000	8600
Canopy Exp	350	950	1600	3200	6050	8700
Suburban	450	950	1600	3250	6150	8800
Package Dly	350	800	1450	2750	5600	8000
Series 150-22 - (3/4-Ton) - (125.2" wb)						
PU	450	950	1600	3250	6150	8800
Stake	350	800	1450	2750	5600	8000
Package Dly	350	750	1350	2650	5450	7800
Series 250-22 - (1-Ton) - (137" wb)						
PU	350	850	1500	2900	5700	8200
Panel	350	800	1450	2750	5600	8000
Canopy Exp	350	850	1500	2800	5650	8100
Stake	350	800	1350	2700	5500	7900
Platform	350	750	1350	2650	5450	7800
Package Dly	350	750	1300	2500	5300	7600

1952
Series 100-22 - (1/2-Ton) - (116" wb)

	6	5	4	3	2	1
PU	450	1400	2300	4600	8100	11,500
Panel	350	900	1550	3100	6000	8600
Canopy Exp	350	950	1600	3200	6050	8700
Suburban	450	950	1600	3250	6150	8800
Series 150-22 - (3/4-Ton) - (125.2" wb)						
PU	350	725	1200	2350	4800	6800
Stake	200	675	1050	2250	4350	6200
Package Dly	200	675	1050	2250	4350	6200
Series 250-22 - (1-Ton) - (137" wb)						
PU	350	850	1500	2900	5700	8200
Panel	350	800	1450	2750	5600	8000
Canopy Exp	350	850	1500	2800	5650	8100
Stake	350	800	1350	2700	5500	7900
Platform	350	750	1350	2650	5450	7800
Package Dly	350	750	1300	2500	5300	7600

1953
Series 100-22 - (1/2-Ton) - (116" wb)

	6	5	4	3	2	1
PU	450	1400	2300	4600	8100	11,500
Panel	350	900	1550	3100	6000	8600
Canopy Exp	350	950	1600	3200	6050	8700
Suburban	450	950	1600	3250	6150	8800
Series 150-22 - (3/4-Ton) - (125.2" wb)						
PU	450	950	1600	3250	6150	8800
Stake	350	800	1450	2750	5600	8000
Package Dly	350	750	1350	2650	5450	7800
Series 250-22 - (1-Ton) - (137" wb)						
PU	350	850	1500	2900	5700	8200
Panel	350	800	1450	2750	5600	8000
Canopy Exp	350	850	1500	2800	5650	8100
Stake	350	800	1350	2700	5500	7900
Platform	350	750	1350	2650	5450	7800
Package Dly	350	750	1300	2500	5300	7600

1954
Series 100-22

	6	5	4	3	2	1
PU	350	850	1500	2900	5700	8200
Panel	350	725	1200	2350	4800	6800
Canopy Dly	350	725	1200	2350	4850	6900
Suburban	350	750	1200	2350	4900	7000
PU (LWB)	350	750	1300	2400	5200	7400
Stake Rack	350	700	1150	2300	4600	6600
Series 150-22						
PU	350	725	1200	2350	4800	6800
Stake Rack	200	675	1100	2250	4400	6300
Series 250-22						
PU	350	700	1150	2300	4550	6500
Panel	200	675	1100	2250	4400	6300
Canopy Exp	350	700	1100	2300	4500	6400
Stake Rack	200	650	1050	2250	4200	6000
Platform	350	800	1450	2750	5600	8000

1955
FIRST SERIES
Series 100-22

	6	5	4	3	2	1
PU	450	1400	2300	4600	8100	11,500
Panel	450	950	1600	3250	6150	8800
Canopy Exp	450	1000	1600	3300	6250	8900
Suburban	450	1000	1650	3350	6300	9000
PU (LWB)	450	1050	1700	3600	6600	9400
Stake Rack	350	900	1550	3100	6000	8600
Series 150-22						
PU	450	950	1600	3250	6150	8800
Stake Rack	350	850	1500	2950	5800	8300
Series 250-22						
PU	350	900	1550	3050	5900	8500
Panel	350	850	1500	2950	5800	8300
Canopy Exp	350	900	1550	3000	5850	8400
Stake Rack	350	850	1500	2800	5650	8100
Platform	350	800	1450	2750	5600	8000
SECOND SERIES						
Series 100						
PU	450	1450	2400	4800	8400	12,000
Panel	450	1000	1650	3350	6300	9000
Dly Panel	450	1100	1700	3650	6650	9500
Suburban PU	450	1500	2500	5000	8800	12,500
Suburban	350	900	1550	3050	5900	8500
Series 150						
PU	350	850	1500	2900	5700	8200
Stake Rack	350	750	1250	2400	5100	7300

	6	5	4	3	2	1
Series 250						
PU	350	750	1300	2500	5300	7600
Panel	350	850	1500	2950	5800	8300
Dly Panel	350	900	1550	3050	5900	8500
Stake Rack	350	700	1100	2300	4500	6400
Platform	200	675	1100	2250	4400	6300

1956
Series 100

	6	5	4	3	2	1
PU	400	1300	2200	4400	7700	11,000
Panel	350	900	1550	3050	5900	8500
Dly Panel	350	900	1550	3100	6000	8600
Suburban PU	450	1450	2400	4800	8400	12,000
Suburban	350	900	1550	3050	5900	8500
Series 150						
PU	350	850	1500	2900	5700	8200
Stake Rack	350	750	1250	2400	5100	7300
Series 250						
PU	350	750	1300	2500	5300	7600
Panel	350	850	1500	2950	5800	8300
Dly Panel	350	900	1550	3050	5900	8500
Stake Rack	350	700	1100	2300	4500	6400
Platform	200	675	1100	2250	4400	6300

1957
Series 100

	6	5	4	3	2	1
PU	450	1450	2400	4800	8400	12,000
Panel	350	900	1550	3050	5900	8500
Dly Panel	450	1000	1650	3350	6300	9000
Suburban PU	450	1500	2500	5000	8800	12,500
Suburban	400	1200	2000	3950	7000	10,000
Series 150						
PU	350	850	1500	2900	5700	8200
Stake Rack	350	750	1250	2400	5100	7300
Series 250						
PU	350	750	1300	2500	5300	7600
Panel	350	850	1500	2950	5800	8300
Dly Panel	350	900	1550	3050	5900	8500
Stake Rack	350	700	1100	2300	4500	6400
Platform	200	675	1100	2250	4400	6300

1958
Series 100

	6	5	4	3	2	1
PU	350	900	1550	3100	6000	8600
Wide-Side PU	350	950	1600	3200	6050	8700
PU (LWB)	350	850	1500	2950	5800	8300
Wide-Side PU (LWB)	350	900	1550	3000	5850	8400
Panel	350	900	1550	3050	5900	8500
Panel DeL	350	950	1600	3200	6050	8700
Suburban	450	950	1600	3250	6150	8800
Series 150						
PU	350	750	1200	2350	4900	7000
Wide-Side PU	350	750	1250	2400	5050	7200
Stake Rack	200	650	1050	2250	4200	6000
Series PM-150						
Panel (8-ft.)	350	750	1250	2400	5100	7300
Panel (10-ft.)	350	750	1250	2350	5000	7100
Panel (12-ft.)	350	725	1200	2350	4850	6900
Series 250						
PU	350	750	1250	2350	5000	7100
Panel	350	700	1150	2300	4550	6500
Panel DeL	350	700	1150	2300	4600	6600
Stake Rack	200	650	1000	2200	4100	5800
Series PM-250						
Panel (8-ft.)	350	750	1250	2350	5000	7100
Panel (10-ft.)	350	750	1200	2350	4900	7000

1959
Series 100

	6	5	4	3	2	1
PU	350	900	1550	3100	6000	8600
Wide-Side PU	350	950	1600	3200	6050	8700
PU (LWB)	350	850	1500	2950	5800	8300
Wide-Side PU (LWB)	350	900	1550	3000	5850	8400
Panel	350	900	1550	3050	5900	8500
Panel DeL	350	950	1600	3200	6050	8700
Suburban	450	950	1600	3250	6150	8800
Series 150						
PU	350	750	1200	2350	4900	7000
Wide-Side PU	350	750	1250	2400	5050	7200
Stake Rack	200	650	1050	2250	4200	6000
Series PM-150						
Panel (8-ft.)	350	750	1250	2400	5100	7300
Panel (10-ft.)	350	750	1250	2350	5000	7100
Panel (12-ft.)	350	725	1200	2350	4850	6900
Series 250						
PU	350	750	1250	2350	5000	7100
Panel	350	700	1150	2300	4550	6500
Panel DeL	350	700	1150	2300	4600	6600
Stake Rack	200	650	1000	2200	4100	5800
Series PM-250						
Panel (8-ft.)	350	750	1250	2350	5000	7100
Panel (10-ft.)	350	750	1200	2350	4900	7000

1960
(95" wb)

	6	5	4	3	2	1
Dly Van	150	400	750	1600	3100	4400
(1/2-Ton) - (115" wb)						
Fender-Side PU	350	800	1450	2750	5600	8000
Wide-Side PU	350	900	1550	3050	5900	8500
(1/2-Ton) - (127" wb)						
Fender-Side PU	350	750	1300	2450	5250	7500
Wide-Side PU	350	800	1450	2750	5600	8000
Panel	150	450	750	1700	3200	4600
Suburban	150	450	800	1800	3300	4800
(3/4-Ton) - (127" wb)						
Fender-Side PU	150	450	750	1700	3200	4600
Wide-Side PU	150	450	800	1750	3250	4700
Stake	150	400	750	1650	3150	4500
(1-Ton) - (121" or 133" wb)						
PU	150	400	750	1600	3100	4400
Panel	150	350	750	1450	3000	4200
Stake	150	350	750	1450	2900	4100

1961
(95" wb)

	6	5	4	3	2	1
Dly Van	150	400	750	1600	3100	4400
(1/2-Ton) - (115" wb)						
Fender-Side PU	350	900	1550	3050	5900	8500
Wide-Side PU	450	1000	1650	3350	6300	9000

(1/2-Ton) - (127" wb)

	6	5	4	3	2	1
Fender-Side PU	350	800	1450	2750	5600	8000
Wide-Side PU	350	900	1550	3050	5900	8500
Panel	150	450	750	1700	3200	4600
Suburban	150	450	800	1800	3300	4800

(3/4-Ton) - (127" wb)

	6	5	4	3	2	1
Fender-Side PU	150	450	750	1700	3200	4600
Wide-Side PU	150	450	800	1750	3250	4700
Stake	150	400	750	1650	3150	4500

(1-Ton) - (121" or 133" wb)

	6	5	4	3	2	1
PU	150	400	750	1600	3100	4400
Panel	150	350	750	1450	3000	4200
Stake	150	350	750	1450	2900	4100

1962

	6	5	4	3	2	1
(98" wb)						
Dly Van	150	400	750	1600	3100	4400
(1/2-Ton) - (115" wb)						
Fender-Side PU	350	800	1450	2750	5600	8000
Wide-Side PU	350	900	1550	3050	5900	8500
(1/2-Ton) - (127" wb)						
Fender-Side PU	350	750	1300	2450	5250	7500
Wide-Side PU	350	800	1450	2750	5600	8000
Panel	150	450	800	1750	3250	4700
Suburban	200	500	850	1850	3350	4900
(3/4-Ton) - (127" wb)						
Fender-Side PU	150	450	800	1750	3250	4700
Wide-Side PU	150	450	800	1800	3300	4800
Stake	150	400	750	1650	3150	4500
(1-Ton) - (121" or 133" wb)						
PU	150	400	750	1600	3100	4400
Panel	150	350	750	1450	3000	4200
Stake	150	350	750	1450	2900	4100

1963

	6	5	4	3	2	1
(98" wb)						
Dly Van	150	400	750	1600	3100	4400
(1/2-Ton) - (115" wb)						
Fender-Side PU	350	900	1550	3050	5900	8500
Wide-Side PU	450	1000	1650	3350	6300	9000
(1/2-Ton) - (127" wb)						
Fender-Side PU	350	800	1450	2750	5600	8000
Wide-Side PU	350	900	1550	3050	5900	8500
Panel	150	450	800	1750	3250	4700
Suburban	200	500	850	1850	3350	4900
(3/4-Ton) - (127" wb)						
Fender-Side PU	150	450	800	1750	3250	4700
Wide-Side PU	150	450	800	1800	3300	4800
Stake	150	400	750	1650	3150	4500
(1-Ton) - (121" or 133" wb)						
PU	150	400	750	1600	3100	4400
Panel	150	350	750	1450	3000	4200
Stake	150	350	750	1450	2900	4100
4WD						
Utl (1/2-Ton)	350	725	1200	2350	4800	6800
Utl (3/4-Ton)	150	450	750	1700	3200	4600
Utl (1-Ton)	150	400	750	1600	3100	4400

1964

	6	5	4	3	2	1
(98" wb)						
Dly Van	150	400	750	1600	3100	4400
(1/2-Ton) - (115" wb)						
Fender-Side PU	350	900	1550	3100	6000	8600
Wide-Side PU	350	950	1600	3200	6050	8700
(1/2-Ton) - (127" wb)						
Fender-Side PU	350	900	1550	3050	5900	8500
Wide-Side PU	350	900	1550	3100	6000	8600
Panel	150	450	800	1750	3250	4700
Suburban	200	500	850	1850	3350	4900
(3/4-Ton) - (127" wb)						
Fender-Side PU	150	450	800	1750	3250	4700
Wide-Side PU	150	450	800	1800	3300	4800
Stake	150	400	750	1650	3150	4500
(1-Ton) - (121" or 133" wb)						
PU	150	400	750	1600	3100	4400
Panel	150	350	750	1450	3000	4200
Stake	150	350	750	1450	2900	4100
4WD						
1/2-Ton	350	725	1200	2350	4800	6800
3/4-Ton	350	700	1100	2300	4500	6400
1-Ton	200	550	900	2150	3800	5400

1965

	6	5	4	3	2	1
(98" wb)						
Dly Van	150	400	750	1600	3100	4400
(1/2-Ton) - (115" wb)						
Fender-Side PU	350	900	1550	3050	5900	8500
Wide-Side PU	350	900	1550	3100	6000	8600
(1/2-Ton) - (127" wb)						
Fender-Side PU	350	900	1550	3000	5850	8400
Wide-Side PU	350	900	1550	3050	5900	8500
Panel	150	450	800	1750	3250	4700
Suburban	200	500	850	1850	3350	4900
(3/4-Ton) - (127" wb)						
Fender-Side PU	150	450	750	1700	3200	4600
Wide-Side PU	150	450	800	1750	3250	4700
Stake	150	400	750	1650	3150	4500
(1-Ton) - (121" or 133" wb)						
PU	150	400	750	1600	3100	4400
Panel	150	350	750	1450	3000	4200
Stake	150	350	750	1450	2900	4100
4WD						
1/2-Ton	350	725	1150	2300	4700	6700
3/4-Ton	200	675	1100	2250	4400	6300
1-Ton	200	550	900	2100	3700	5300

1966

	6	5	4	3	2	1
(90" wb)						
Window Van	150	450	800	1750	3250	4700
Dly Van	150	400	750	1600	3100	4400
(1/2-Ton) - (115" wb)						
Fender-Side PU	350	900	1550	3050	5900	8500
Wide-Side PU	350	900	1550	3100	6000	8600
(1/2-Ton) - (127" wb)						
Fender-Side PU	350	900	1550	3000	5850	8400
Wide-Side PU	350	900	1550	3050	5900	8500
Panel	150	450	800	1750	3250	4700
Suburban	200	500	850	1850	3350	4900
(3/4-Ton) - (127" wb)						
Fender-Side PU	150	450	800	1750	3250	4700
Wide-Side PU	150	450	800	1800	3300	4800
Stake	150	400	750	1650	3150	4500
(1-Ton) - (121" or 131" wb)						
PU	150	400	750	1600	3100	4400
Panel	150	350	750	1450	3000	4200
Stake	150	350	750	1450	2900	4100
4WD						
1/2-Ton	350	725	1150	2300	4700	6700
3/4-Ton	200	675	1100	2250	4400	6300
1-Ton	200	550	900	2100	3700	5300

1967

	6	5	4	3	2	1
(1/2-Ton) - (90" wb)						
Handi Van	150	450	800	1800	3300	4800
Handi Bus	200	500	850	1850	3350	4900
(1/2-Ton) - (102" wb)						
Van	150	450	750	1700	3200	4600
(1/2-Ton) - (115" wb)						
Fender-Side PU	450	1000	1650	3350	6300	9000
Wide-Side PU	400	1200	2000	3950	7000	10,000
(1/2-Ton) - (127" wb)						
Fender-Side PU	350	900	1550	3050	5900	8500
Wide-Side PU	450	1100	1700	3650	6650	9500
Panel	200	500	850	1900	3500	5000
Suburban	350	700	1150	2300	4550	6500
(3/4-Ton) - (127" wb)						
Fender-Side PU	350	800	1450	2750	5600	8000
Wide-Side PU	350	900	1550	3050	5900	8500
Panel	150	400	750	1650	3150	4500
Suburban	200	650	1050	2250	4200	6000
Stake	150	400	750	1600	3100	4400
(1-Ton) - (133" wb)						
PU	350	725	1200	2350	4800	6800
Stake Rack	350	700	1150	2300	4550	6500

1968

	6	5	4	3	2	1
(1/2-Ton) - (90" wb)						
Handi Van	150	450	800	1800	3300	4800
Handi Bus DeL	200	500	850	1850	3350	4900
(1/2-Ton) - (102" wb)						
Van	150	450	750	1700	3200	4600
(1/2-Ton) - (115" wb)						
Fender-Side PU	450	1000	1650	3350	6300	9000
Wide-Side PU	400	1200	2000	3950	7000	10,000
(1/2-Ton) - (127" wb)						
Fender-Side PU	350	900	1550	3050	5900	8500
Wide-Side PU	450	1100	1700	3650	6650	9500
Panel	200	500	850	1900	3500	5000
Suburban	350	700	1150	2300	4550	6500
(3/4-Ton) - (127" wb)						
Fender-Side PU	350	800	1450	2750	5600	8000
Wide-Side PU	350	900	1550	3050	5900	8500
Panel	150	400	750	1650	3150	4500
Suburban	200	650	1050	2250	4200	6000
Stake	150	400	750	1600	3100	4400
(1-Ton) - (133" wb)						
PU	350	725	1200	2350	4800	6800
Stake Rack	350	700	1150	2300	4550	6500

1969

	6	5	4	3	2	1
(1/2-Ton) - (90" wb)						
Handi Van	150	450	800	1800	3300	4800
Handi Bus DeL	200	500	850	1850	3350	4900
(1/2-Ton) - (102" wb)						
Van	150	450	750	1700	3200	4600
(1/2-Ton) - (115" wb)						
Fender-Side PU	400	1300	2200	4400	7700	11,000
Wide-Side PU	450	1400	2300	4600	8100	11,500
(1/2-Ton) - (127" wb)						
Fender-Side PU	400	1250	2100	4200	7400	10,500
Wide-Side PU	400	1300	2200	4400	7700	11,000
Panel	200	500	850	1900	3500	5000
Suburban	350	700	1150	2300	4550	6500
(3/4-Ton) - (127" wb)						
Fender-Side PU	350	900	1550	3050	5900	8500
Wide-Side PU	450	1000	1650	3350	6300	9000
Panel	150	400	750	1650	3150	4500
Suburban	200	650	1050	2250	4200	6000
Stake	150	400	750	1600	3100	4400
(1-Ton) - (133" wb)						
PU	350	725	1200	2350	4850	6900
Stake Rack	350	700	1150	2300	4600	6600

1970

	6	5	4	3	2	1
(1/2-Ton) - (90" wb)						
Handi Van	150	450	800	1800	3300	4800
Handi Bus DeL	200	500	850	1850	3350	4900
(1/2-Ton) - (102" wb)						
Van	150	450	750	1700	3200	4600
(1/2-Ton) - (115" wb)						
Fender-Side PU	400	1300	2200	4400	7700	11,000
Wide-Side PU	450	1400	2300	4600	8100	11,500
(1/2-Ton) - (127" wb)						
Fender-Side PU	400	1250	2100	4200	7400	10,500
Wide-Side PU	400	1300	2200	4400	7700	11,000
Panel	200	500	850	1900	3500	5000
Suburban	350	700	1150	2300	4550	6500
(3/4-Ton) - (127" wb)						
Fender-Side PU	350	900	1550	3050	5900	8500
Wide-Side PU	450	1000	1650	3350	6300	9000
Panel	150	400	750	1650	3150	4500
Suburban	200	650	1050	2250	4200	6000
Stake	150	400	750	1600	3100	4400
(1-Ton) - (133" wb)						
PU	350	725	1200	2350	4850	6900
Stake Rack	350	700	1150	2300	4550	6500
Jimmy (104" wb)						
Jimmy (2WD)	350	800	1450	2750	5600	8000
Jimmy (4WD)	450	1100	1700	3650	6650	9500

1971

	6	5	4	3	2	1
Sprint (1/2-Ton)						
PU	400	1250	2100	4200	7400	10,500
(1/2-Ton) - (90" wb)						
Handi Van	150	450	800	1800	3300	4800
Handi Bus DeL	200	500	850	1850	3350	4900

	6	5	4	3	2	1
(1/2-Ton) - (102" wb)						
Van	150	450	750	1700	3200	4600
(1/2-Ton) - (115" wb)						
Fender-Side PU	400	1250	2100	4200	7400	10,500
Wide-Side PU	450	1400	2300	4600	8100	11,500
(1/2-Ton) - (127" wb)						
Fender-Side PU	400	1200	2000	3950	7000	10,000
Wide-Side PU	400	1300	2200	4400	7700	11,000
Panel	200	550	900	2100	3700	5300
Suburban	350	900	1550	3050	5900	8500
(3/4-Ton) - (127" wb)						
Fender-Side PU	450	1000	1650	3350	6300	9000
Wide-Side PU	450	1100	1700	3650	6650	9500
Panel	200	550	900	2000	3600	5200
Suburban	350	800	1450	2750	5600	8000
Stake	150	450	750	1700	3200	4600
(1-Ton) - (133" wb)						
PU	350	725	1200	2350	4800	6800
Stake Rack	350	700	1150	2300	4550	6500
Jimmy (104" wb)						
Jimmy (2WD)	350	900	1550	3050	5900	8500
Jimmy (4WD)	400	1200	2000	3950	7000	10,000

1972

	6	5	4	3	2	1
Sprint (1/2-Ton)						
PU	400	1250	2100	4200	7400	10,500
(1/2-Ton) - (90" wb)						
Handi Van	150	450	800	1800	3300	4800
Handi Bus DeL	200	500	850	1850	3350	4900
(1/2-Ton) - (102" wb)						
Van	150	450	750	1700	3200	4600
(1/2-Ton) - (115" wb)						
Fender-Side PU	400	1250	2100	4200	7400	10,500
Wide-Side PU	450	1400	2300	4600	8100	11,500
(1/2-Ton) - (127" wb)						
Fender-Side PU	400	1200	2000	3950	7000	10,000
Wide-Side PU	400	1300	2200	4400	7700	11,000
Panel	200	550	900	2100	3700	5300
Suburban	350	900	1550	3050	5900	8500
(3/4-Ton) - (127" wb)						
Fender-Side PU	450	1000	1650	3350	6300	9000
Wide-Side PU	450	1100	1700	3650	6650	9500
Panel	200	550	900	2000	3600	5200
Suburban	350	800	1450	2750	5600	8000
Stake	150	450	750	1700	3200	4600
(1-Ton) - (133" wb)						
PU	350	725	1200	2350	4800	6800
Stake Rack	350	700	1150	2300	4550	6500
Jimmy (104" wb)						
Jimmy (2WD)	350	900	1550	3050	5900	8500
Jimmy (4WD)	400	1200	2000	3950	7000	10,000

1973

	6	5	4	3	2	1
(1/2-Ton) - (116" wb)						
Sprint Cus	200	600	950	2150	3850	5500
Jimmy - (1/2-Ton) - (106" wb)						
Jimmy (2WD)	350	700	1150	2300	4550	6500
Jimmy (4WD)	350	750	1300	2450	5250	7500
(1/2-Ton) - (110" wb)						
Rally Van	200	550	900	2000	3600	5200
(1/2-Ton) - (117" wb)						
Fender-Side PU	350	800	1450	2750	5600	8000
Wide-Side PU	350	900	1550	3050	5900	8500
(1/2-Ton) - (125" wb)						
Fender-Side PU	350	750	1300	2450	5250	7500
Wide-Side PU	350	800	1450	2750	5600	8000
Suburban	350	700	1150	2300	4550	6500
(3/4-Ton) - (125" wb)						
Fender-Side PU	200	650	1050	2250	4200	6000
Wide-Side PU	200	675	1050	2250	4350	6200
Suburban	200	675	1050	2250	4300	6100
Rally Van	200	650	1050	2250	4200	6000
(1-Ton) - (125" or 135" wb)						
PU	200	650	1050	2250	4200	6000
Crew Cab PU	200	600	1000	2200	4000	5700

1974

	6	5	4	3	2	1
(1/2-Ton) - (116" wb)						
Sprint Cus	200	600	950	2150	3850	5500
Jimmy - (1/2-Ton) - (106" wb)						
Jimmy (2WD)	350	700	1150	2300	4550	6500
Jimmy (4WD)	350	750	1300	2450	5250	7500
(1/2-Ton) - (110" wb)						
Rally Van	200	550	900	2000	3600	5200
(1/2-Ton) - (117" wb)						
Fender-Side PU	350	800	1450	2750	5600	8000
Wide-Side PU	350	900	1550	3050	5900	8500
(1/2-Ton) - (125" wb)						
Fender-Side PU	350	750	1300	2450	5250	7500
Wide-Side PU	350	800	1450	2750	5600	8000
Suburban	350	700	1150	2300	4550	6500
(3/4-Ton) - (125" wb)						
Fender-Side PU	200	650	1050	2250	4200	6000
Wide-Side PU	200	675	1050	2250	4350	6200
Suburban	200	675	1050	2250	4300	6100
Rally Van	200	650	1050	2250	4200	6000
(1-Ton) - (125" or 135" wb)						
PU	200	650	1050	2250	4200	6000
Crew Cab PU	200	600	1000	2200	4000	5700

1975

	6	5	4	3	2	1
(1/2-Ton) - (116" wb)						
Sprint Cus	200	600	950	2150	3850	5500
Jimmy - (1/2-Ton) - (106" wb)						
Jimmy (2WD)	350	700	1150	2300	4550	6500
Jimmy (4WD)	350	750	1300	2450	5250	7500
(1/2-Ton) - (110" wb)						
Rally Van	200	550	900	2000	3600	5200
(1/2-Ton) - (117" wb)						
Fender-Side PU	350	800	1450	2750	5600	8000
Wide-Side PU	350	900	1550	3050	5900	8500
(1/2-Ton) - (125" wb)						
Fender-Side PU	350	750	1300	2450	5250	7500
Wide-Side PU	350	800	1450	2750	5600	8000
Suburban	350	700	1150	2300	4550	6500
(3/4-Ton) - (125" wb)						
Fender-Side PU	200	650	1050	2250	4200	6000
Wide-Side PU	200	675	1050	2250	4350	6200
Suburban	200	675	1050	2250	4300	6100
Rally Van	200	650	1050	2250	4200	6000
(1-Ton) - (125" or 135" wb)						
PU	200	650	1050	2250	4200	6000
Crew Cab PU	200	600	1000	2200	4000	5700

1976

	6	5	4	3	2	1
(1/2-Ton) - (116" wb)						
Sprint Cus	200	600	950	2150	3850	5500
Jimmy - (1/2-Ton) - (106" wb)						
Jimmy (2WD)	350	700	1150	2300	4550	6500
Jimmy (4WD)	350	750	1300	2450	5250	7500
(1/2-Ton) - (110" wb)						
Rally Van	200	550	900	2000	3600	5200
(1/2-Ton) - (117" wb)						
Fender-Side PU	350	800	1450	2750	5600	8000
Wide-Side PU	350	900	1550	3050	5900	8500
(1/2-Ton) - (125" wb)						
Fender-Side PU	350	750	1300	2450	5250	7500
Wide-Side PU	350	800	1450	2750	5600	8000
Suburban	350	700	1150	2300	4550	6500
(3/4-Ton) - (125" wb)						
Fender-Side PU	200	650	1050	2250	4200	6000
Wide-Side PU	200	675	1050	2250	4350	6200
Suburban	200	675	1050	2250	4300	6100
Rally Van	200	650	1050	2250	4200	6000
(1-Ton) - (125" or 135" wb)						
PU	200	650	1050	2250	4200	6000
Crew Cab PU	200	600	1000	2200	4000	5700

1977

	6	5	4	3	2	1
Sprint - V-8 - (116" wb)						
Sprint PU	200	500	850	1900	3500	5000
Sprint Classic PU	200	600	950	2150	3850	5500
Jimmy - V-8 - (106" wb)						
Jimmy (4WD)	350	750	1300	2450	5250	7500
G1500 - Van - (1/2-Ton)						
Vandura	150	350	750	1350	2800	4000
Rally	200	500	850	1850	3350	4900
Rally STX	200	500	850	1950	3600	5100
P1500 Van	125	250	700	1150	2450	3500
G2500 - Van - (3/4-Ton)						
Vandura	150	300	750	1350	2700	3900
Rally	150	450	800	1800	3300	4800
Rally STX	200	500	850	1900	3500	5000
P2500 Van	125	250	700	1150	2400	3400
G3500 - Van - (1-Ton)						
Vandura	150	300	700	1250	2650	3800
Vandura Spl	150	300	750	1350	2700	3900
Rally Camper Spl	150	350	750	1450	2900	4100
Magna	125	250	700	1150	2500	3600
Rally	150	300	700	1250	2650	3800
Rally STX	150	300	750	1350	2700	3900
P3500 Van	125	200	600	1100	2300	3300
C1500 - (1/2-Ton)						
Fender-Side PU SBx	200	650	1000	2200	4150	5900
Wide-Side PU SBx	200	650	1050	2250	4200	6000
Fender-Side PU LBx	200	650	1000	2200	4100	5800
Wide-Side PU LBx	200	650	1050	2250	4150	5900
Suburban	200	650	1000	2200	4100	5800
C2500 - (3/4-Ton)						
Fender-Side PU	200	500	850	1950	3600	5100
Wide-Side PU	200	550	900	2100	3700	5300
Bonus Cab PU	200	550	900	2000	3600	5200
Crew Cab PU	200	500	850	1950	3600	5100
Stake	150	450	800	1800	3300	4800
Suburban	200	550	900	2100	3700	5300
C3500 - (1-Ton)						
Fender-Side PU	200	500	850	1850	3350	4900
Wide-Side PU	200	500	850	1950	3600	5100
Bonus Cab PU	200	500	850	1900	3500	5000
Crew Cab PU	200	500	850	1850	3350	4900
Stake	150	450	800	1750	3250	4700

1978

	6	5	4	3	2	1
Caballero - V-8 - (116" wb)						
Caballero PU	200	500	850	1900	3500	5000
Diablo PU	200	600	950	2150	3850	5500
Jimmy - V-8 - (106" wb)						
Jimmy (4WD)	350	700	1150	2300	4600	6600
G1500 - Van - (1/2-Ton)						
Vandura	150	350	750	1350	2800	4000
Rally	200	500	850	1850	3350	4900
Rally STX	200	500	850	1950	3600	5100
P1500 Van	125	250	700	1150	2450	3500
G2500 - Van - (3/4-Ton)						
Vandura	150	300	750	1350	2700	3900
Rally	150	450	800	1800	3300	4800
Rally STX	200	500	850	1900	3500	5000
P2500 Van	125	250	700	1150	2400	3400
G3500 - Van - (1-Ton)						
Vandura	150	300	700	1250	2650	3800
Vandura Spl	150	300	750	1350	2700	3900
Rally Camper Spl	150	350	750	1450	2900	4100
Magna	125	250	700	1150	2500	3600
Rally	150	300	700	1250	2650	3800
Rally STX	150	300	750	1350	2700	3900
P3500 Van	125	200	600	1100	2300	3300
C1500 - (1/2-Ton)						
Fender-Side PU SBx	200	550	900	2150	3800	5400
Wide-Side PU SBx	200	600	950	2150	3850	5500
Fender-Side PU LBx	200	600	950	2150	3850	5500
Wide-Side PU LBx	200	600	950	2200	3900	5600
Suburban	200	600	1000	2200	4000	5700
C2500 - (3/4-Ton)						
Fender-Side PU	200	500	850	1950	3600	5100
Wide-Side PU	200	550	900	2100	3700	5300
Bonus Cab PU	200	550	900	2000	3600	5200
Crew Cab PU	200	500	850	1950	3600	5100
Stake	150	450	800	1800	3300	4800
Suburban	200	550	900	2100	3700	5300
C3500 - (1-Ton)						
Fender-Side PU	200	500	850	1850	3350	4900
Wide-Side PU	200	500	850	1950	3600	5100
Bonus Cab PU	200	500	850	1900	3500	5000
Crew Cab PU	200	500	850	1850	3350	4900
Stake	150	450	800	1750	3250	4700

	6	5	4	3	2	1
1979						
Caballero - V-8 - (116" wb)						
Caballero PU	200	500	850	1900	3500	5000
Diablo PU	200	600	950	2150	3850	5500
Jimmy - V-8 - (106" wb)						
Jimmy (4WD)	350	700	1150	2300	4600	6600
G1500 - Van - (1/2-Ton)						
Vandura	150	350	750	1350	2800	4000
Rally	200	500	850	1850	3350	4900
Rally STX	200	500	850	1950	3600	5100
P1500 Van	125	250	700	1150	2450	3500
G2500 - Van - (3/4-Ton)						
Vandura	150	300	750	1350	2700	3900
Rally	150	450	800	1800	3300	4800
Rally STX	200	500	850	1900	3500	5000
P2500 Van	125	250	700	1150	2400	3400
G3500 - Van - (1-Ton)						
Vandura	150	300	700	1250	2650	3800
Vandura Spl	150	300	750	1350	2700	3900
Rally Camper Spl	150	350	750	1450	2900	4100
Magna	125	250	700	1150	2500	3600
Rally	150	300	700	1250	2650	3800
Rally STX	150	300	750	1350	2700	3900
P3500 Van	125	200	600	1100	2300	3300
C1500 - (1/2-Ton)						
Fender-Side PU SBx	200	550	900	2150	3800	5400
Wide-Side PU SBx	200	600	950	2150	3850	5500
Fender-Side PU LBx	200	600	950	2150	3850	5500
Wide-Side PU LBx	200	600	950	2200	3900	5600
Suburban	200	600	1000	2200	4000	5700
C2500 - (3/4-Ton)						
Fender-Side PU	200	500	850	1950	3600	5100
Wide-Side PU	200	550	900	2100	3700	5300
Bonus Cab PU	200	550	900	2000	3600	5200
Crew Cab PU	200	500	850	1950	3600	5100
Stake	150	450	800	1800	3300	4800
Suburban	200	550	900	2100	3700	5300
C3500 - (1-Ton)						
Fender-Side PU	200	500	850	1850	3350	4900
Wide-Side PU	200	500	850	1950	3600	5100
Bonus Cab PU	200	500	850	1900	3500	5000
Crew Cab PU	200	500	850	1850	3350	4900
Stake	150	450	800	1750	3250	4700
1980						
Caballero - V-8 - (116" wb)						
Caballero PU	200	500	850	1900	3500	5000
Diablo PU	200	600	950	2150	3850	5500
Jimmy - V-8 - (106" wb)						
Jimmy (4WD)	350	700	1150	2300	4600	6600
G1500 - Van - (1/2-Ton)						
Vandura	150	350	750	1350	2800	4000
Rally	200	500	850	1850	3350	4900
Rally STX	200	500	850	1950	3600	5100
P1500 Van	125	250	700	1150	2450	3500
G2500 - Van - (3/4-Ton)						
Vandura	150	300	750	1350	2700	3900
Rally	150	450	800	1800	3300	4800
Rally STX	200	500	850	1900	3500	5000
P2500 Van	125	250	700	1150	2400	3400
G3500 - Van - (1-Ton)						
Vandura	150	300	700	1250	2650	3800
Vandura Spl	150	300	750	1350	2700	3900
Rally Camper Spl	150	350	750	1450	2900	4100
Magna	125	250	700	1150	2500	3600
Rally	150	300	700	1250	2650	3800
Rally STX	150	300	750	1350	2700	3900
P3500 Van	125	200	600	1100	2300	3300
C1500 - (1/2-Ton)						
Fender-Side PU SBx	200	550	900	2150	3800	5400
Wide-Side PU SBx	200	600	950	2150	3850	5500
Fender-Side PU LBx	200	600	950	2150	3850	5500
Wide-Side PU LBx	200	600	950	2200	3900	5600
Suburban	200	600	1000	2200	4000	5700
C2500 - (3/4-Ton)						
Fender-Side PU	200	500	850	1950	3600	5100
Wide-Side PU	200	550	900	2100	3700	5300
Bonus Cab PU	200	550	900	2000	3600	5200
Crew Cab PU	200	500	850	1950	3600	5100
Stake	150	450	800	1800	3300	4800
Suburban	200	550	900	2100	3700	5300
C3500 - (1-Ton)						
Fender-Side PU	200	500	850	1850	3350	4900
Wide-Side PU	200	500	850	1950	3600	5100
Bonus Cab PU	200	500	850	1900	3500	5000
Crew Cab PU	200	500	850	1850	3350	4900
Stake	150	450	800	1750	3250	4700
1981						
Caballero - (1/2-Ton) - (117" wb)						
Caballero PU	100	175	525	1050	2050	2900
Diablo PU	100	175	525	1050	2100	3000
K1500 - (1/2-Ton) - (106.5" wb)						
Jimmy (4WD)	350	750	1200	2350	4900	7000
Jimmy Conv. Top (4WD)	350	750	1250	2400	5050	7200
G1500 Van - (1/2-Ton) - (110" or 125" wb)						
Vandura	150	400	750	1550	3050	4300
Rally	200	550	900	2000	3600	5200
Rally Cus	200	550	900	2150	3800	5400
Rally STX	200	600	950	2200	3900	5600
G2500 Van - (3/4-Ton) - (110" or 125" wb)						
Vandura	150	350	750	1450	3000	4200
Rally	200	500	850	1950	3600	5100
Rally Cus	200	550	900	2100	3700	5300
Rally STX	200	600	950	2150	3850	5500
Gaucho	200	600	950	2150	3850	5500
G3500 Van - (1-Ton) - (125" or 146" wb)						
Vandura	150	350	750	1450	2900	4100
Vandura Spl	200	500	850	1900	3500	5000
Rally Camper Spl	200	550	900	2000	3600	5200
Rally	200	550	900	2150	3800	5400
Rally Cus	200	600	950	2200	3900	5600
Rally STX	200	650	1000	2200	4100	5800
Magna Van 10	200	500	850	1850	3350	4900
Magna Van 12	200	500	850	1850	3350	4900
C1500 - (1/2-Ton) - (117.5" or 131.5" wb)						
Fender-Side PU SBx	200	650	1000	2200	4100	5800
Wide-Side PU SBx	200	650	1000	2200	4150	5900
Wide-Side PU LBx	200	600	1000	2200	4000	5700
Suburban 4d	200	675	1050	2250	4350	6200
C2500 - (3/4-Ton) - (131" wb)						
Fender-Side PU LBx	200	600	1000	2200	4000	5700
Wide-Side PU LBx	200	650	1000	2200	4100	5800
Bonus Cab 2d PU LBx	200	650	1050	2250	4200	6000
Crew Cab 4d PU LBx	200	650	1000	2200	4150	5900
Suburban 4d	200	675	1050	2250	4350	6200
C3500 - (1-Ton) - (131.5" or 164.5" wb)						
Fender-Side PU LBx	200	600	950	2200	3900	5600
Wide-Side PU LBx	200	600	1000	2200	4000	5700
Bonus Cab 2d PU LBx	200	650	1000	2200	4100	5800
Crew Cab 4d PU LBx	200	600	1000	2200	4000	5700

NOTE: Add 15 percent for 4WD.

	6	5	4	3	2	1
1982						
Caballero - (1/2-Ton) - (117.1" wb)						
Caballero PU	150	450	800	1800	3300	4800
Diablo PU	200	500	850	1850	3350	4900
K1500 - (1/2-Ton) - (106.5" wb)						
Jimmy (4WD)	200	650	1050	2250	4200	6000
G1500 Van - (1/2-Ton) - (110" or 125" wb)						
Vandura	125	200	600	1100	2300	3300
Rally	150	350	750	1450	3000	4200
Rally Cus	150	400	750	1600	3100	4400
Rally STX	150	450	750	1700	3200	4600
G2500 Van - (3/4-Ton) - (110" or 125" wb)						
Vandura	125	200	600	1100	2250	3200
Rally	125	250	700	1150	2450	3500
Rally Cus	150	400	750	1550	3050	4300
Rally STX	150	400	750	1650	3150	4500
G3500 Van - (1-Ton) - (125" or 146" wb)						
Vandura	125	200	600	1100	2200	3100
Vandura Spl	150	350	750	1350	2800	4000
Rally Camper Spl	150	350	750	1450	3000	4200
Rally	150	400	750	1600	3100	4400
Rally Cus	150	400	750	1600	3100	4400
Rally STX	150	400	750	1650	3150	4500
Magna Van 10	125	250	700	1150	2400	3400
Magna Van 12	125	250	700	1150	2400	3400
S15 - (1/2-Ton) - (108.3" or 122.9" wb)						
Wide-Side PU SBx	100	125	475	900	1600	2300
Wide-Side PU LBx	100	125	500	950	1700	2400
C1500 - (1/2-Ton) - (117.5" or 131.5" wb)						
Fender-Side PU SBx	150	450	800	1800	3300	4800
Wide-Side PU SBx	200	500	850	1850	3350	4900
Wide-Side PU LBx	150	450	750	1700	3200	4600
Suburban 4d	200	550	900	2100	3700	5300
C2500 - (3/4-Ton) - (131" wb)						
Fender-Side PU LBx	150	450	800	1750	3250	4700
Wide-Side PU LBx	150	450	800	1800	3300	4800
Bonus Cab 2d PU LBx	200	500	850	1950	3600	5100
Crew Cab 4d PU LBx	150	450	800	1750	3250	4700
Suburban 4d	200	550	900	2100	3700	5300
C3500 - (1-Ton) - (131.5" or 164.5" wb)						
Fender-Side PU LBx	150	400	750	1650	3150	4500
Wide-Side PU LBx	150	450	750	1700	3200	4600
Bonus Cab 2d PU LBx	200	500	850	1850	3350	4900
Crew Cab 4d PU LBx	150	450	800	1750	3250	4700

NOTE: Add 15 percent for 4WD.

	6	5	4	3	2	1
1983						
Caballero - (1/2-Ton) - (117.1" wb)						
Caballero PU	200	500	850	1850	3350	4900
Diablo PU	200	500	850	1900	3500	5000
S15 - (1/2-Ton) - (100.5" wb)						
Jimmy (2WD)	125	200	600	1100	2200	3100
Jimmy (4WD)	150	350	750	1350	2800	4000
K1500 - (1/2-Ton) - (106.5" wb)						
Jimmy (4WD)	200	675	1050	2250	4300	6100
G1500 Van - (1/2-Ton) - (110" or 125" wb)						
Vandura	125	250	700	1150	2400	3400
Rally	150	400	750	1550	3050	4300
Rally Cus	150	400	750	1650	3150	4500
Rally STX	150	450	800	1750	3250	4700
G2500 Van - (3/4-Ton) - (110" or 125" wb)						
Vandura	125	200	600	1100	2300	3300
Rally	150	350	750	1450	3000	4200
Rally Cus	150	400	750	1600	3100	4400
Rally STX	150	450	750	1700	3200	4600
G3500 Van - (1-Ton) - (125" or 146" wb)						
Vandura	125	200	600	1100	2250	3200
Rally	150	350	750	1450	2900	4100
Rally Cus	150	400	750	1550	3050	4300
Rally STX	150	400	750	1650	3150	4500
Magna Van 10	125	200	600	1100	2300	3300
Magna Van 12	125	200	600	1100	2300	3300
S15 - (1/2-Ton) - (108.3" or 122.9" wb)						
Wide-Side PU SBx	100	125	475	900	1600	2300
Wide-Side PU LBx	100	125	500	950	1700	2400
Wide-Side Ext Cab PU	100	150	450	1000	1800	2600
C1500 - (1/2-Ton) - (117.5" or 131.5" wb)						
Fender-Side PU SBx	200	500	850	1850	3350	4900
Wide-Side PU SBx	200	500	850	1900	3500	5000
Wide-Side PU LBx	150	450	800	1750	3250	4700
Suburban 4d	200	550	900	2150	3800	5400
C2500 - (3/4-Ton) - (131" wb)						
Fender-Side PU LBx	150	450	800	1800	3300	4800
Wide-Side PU LBx	200	500	850	1850	3350	4900
Bonus Cab 2d PU LBx	200	550	900	2000	3600	5200
Crew Cab 4d PU LBx	150	450	800	1750	3250	4700
Suburban 4d	200	550	900	2150	3800	5400
C3500 - (1-Ton) - (131.5" or 164.5" wb)						
Fender-Side PU LBx	150	450	750	1700	3200	4600
Wide-Side PU LBx	150	450	800	1750	3250	4700
Bonus Cab 2d PU LBx	200	500	850	1850	3350	4900
Crew Cab 4d PU LBx	150	450	800	1800	3300	4800

NOTE: Add 15 percent for 4WD.

	6	5	4	3	2	1
1984						
Caballero - (1/2-Ton) - (117.1" wb)						
Caballero PU	200	600	950	2150	3850	5500
SS Diablo PU	200	600	1000	2200	4000	5700
S15 - (1/2-Ton) - (100.5" wb)						
Jimmy (2WD)	150	450	800	1750	3250	4700
Jimmy (4WD)	150	450	800	1750	3250	4700

	6	5	4	3	2	1
K1500 - (1/2-Ton) - (106.5" wb)						
Jimmy (4WD)	350	725	1150	2300	4700	6700
G1500 Van - (1/2-Ton) - (110" or 125" wb)						
Vandura	150	350	750	1350	2800	4000
Rally	150	450	800	1800	3300	4800
Rally Cus	200	500	850	1900	3500	5000
Rally STX	200	550	900	2000	3600	5200
G2500 Van - (3/4-Ton) - (110" or 125" wb)						
Vandura	150	300	750	1350	2700	3900
Rally	150	450	800	1750	3250	4700
Rally Cus	200	500	850	1850	3350	4900
Rally STX	200	500	850	1950	3600	5100
G3500 Van - (1-Ton) - (125" or 146" wb)						
Vandura	150	300	700	1250	2650	3800
Rally	150	450	750	1700	3200	4600
Rally Cus	150	450	800	1800	3300	4800
Rally STX	200	500	850	1900	3500	5000
Magna Van 10	150	300	700	1250	2650	3800
Magna Van 12	150	300	700	1250	2650	3800
S15 - (1/2-Ton) - (108.3" or 122.9" wb)						
Wide-Side PU SBx	100	175	525	1050	2050	2900
Wide-Side PU LBx	100	175	525	1050	2100	3000
Wide-Side Ext Cab PU	125	200	600	1100	2250	3200
C1500 - (1/2-Ton) - (117.5" or 131.5" wb)						
Fender-Side PU SBx	200	550	900	2000	3600	5200
Wide-Side PU SBx	200	550	900	2100	3700	5300
Wide-Side PU LBx	200	500	850	1950	3600	5100
Suburban 4d	200	650	1050	2250	4200	6000
C2500 - (3/4-Ton) - (131" wb)						
Fender-Side PU LBx	200	500	850	1950	3600	5100
Wide-Side PU LBx	200	550	900	2000	3600	5200
Bonus Cab 2d PU LBx	200	600	950	2200	3900	5600
Crew Cab 4d PU LBx	200	600	950	2150	3850	5500
Suburban 4d	200	650	1000	2200	4100	5800
C3500 - (1-Ton) - (131.5" or 164.5" wb)						
Fender-Side PU LBx	200	500	850	1850	3350	4900
Wide-Side PU LBx	200	500	850	1900	3500	5000
Bonus Cab 2d PU LBx	200	500	850	1950	3600	5100
Crew Cab 4d PU LBx	200	500	850	1900	3500	5000

NOTE: Add 15 percent for 4WD.

1985

	6	5	4	3	2	1
Caballero - (1/2-Ton) - (117.1" wb)						
Caballero PU	200	650	1000	2200	4100	5800
SS Diablo PU	200	650	1050	2250	4200	6000
S15 - (1/2-Ton) - (100.5" wb)						
Jimmy (2WD)	200	600	950	2150	3850	5500
Jimmy (4WD)	350	700	1150	2300	4550	6500
K1500 - (1/2-Ton) - (106.5" wb)						
Jimmy (4WD)	350	750	1300	2450	5250	7500
Safari - (1/2-Ton) - (111" wb)						
Cargo Van	150	400	750	1600	3100	4400
SL Van	200	550	900	2150	3800	5400
SLT Van	200	600	950	2200	3900	5600
SLE Van	200	650	1000	2200	4100	5800
G1500 Van - (1/2-Ton) - (110" or 125" wb)						
Vandura	150	450	800	1800	3300	4800
Rally	200	550	900	2000	3600	5200
Rally Cus	200	550	900	2150	3800	5400
Rally STX	200	600	950	2200	3900	5600
G2500 Van - (3/4-Ton) - (110" or 125" wb)						
Vandura	150	450	800	1750	3250	4700
Rally	200	500	850	1950	3600	5100
Rally Cus	200	550	900	2100	3700	5300
Rally STX	200	600	950	2150	3850	5500
G3500 Van - (1-Ton) - (125" or 146" wb)						
Vandura	150	450	750	1700	3200	4600
Rally	200	500	850	1950	3600	5100
Rally Cus	200	550	900	2100	3700	5300
Rally STX	200	600	950	2150	3850	5500
Magna Van 10	150	400	750	1600	3100	4400
Magna Van 12	150	400	750	1600	3100	4400
S15 - (1/2-Ton) - (108.3" or 122.9" wb)						
Wide-Side PU SBx	125	250	700	1150	2500	3600
Wide-Side PU LBx	150	300	700	1250	2600	3700
Wide-Side Ext Cab PU	150	300	750	1350	2700	3900
C1500 - (1/2-Ton) - (117.5" or 131.5" wb)						
Fender-Side PU SBx	200	550	900	2000	3600	5200
Wide-Side PU SBx	200	550	900	2100	3700	5300
Wide-Side PU LBx	200	500	850	1950	3600	5100
Suburban 4d	200	675	1100	2250	4400	6300
C2500 - (3/4-Ton) - (131" wb)						
Fender-Side PU LBx	200	550	900	2000	3600	5200
Wide-Side PU LBx	200	550	900	2100	3700	5300
Bonus Cab 2d PU LBx	200	650	1000	2200	4100	5800
Crew Cab 4d PU LBx	200	650	1050	2250	4200	6000
Suburban 4d	350	700	1100	2300	4500	6400
C3500 - (1-Ton) - (131.5" or 164.5" wb)						
Fender-Side PU LBx	200	500	850	1950	3600	5100
Wide-Side PU LBx	200	550	900	2000	3600	5200
Bonus Cab 2d PU LBx	200	600	1000	2200	4000	5700
Crew Cab 4d PU LBx	200	650	1000	2200	4150	5900

NOTE: Add 15 percent for 4WD.

1986

	6	5	4	3	2	1
Caballero - (1/2-Ton) - (117.1" wb)						
Caballero PU	200	650	1050	2250	4200	6000
Diablo PU	350	700	1150	2300	4550	6500
S15 - (1/2-Ton) - (100.5" wb)						
Jimmy (2WD)	350	900	1550	3050	5900	8500
Jimmy (4WD)	450	1100	1700	3650	6650	9500
K1500 - (1/2-Ton) - (106.5" wb)						
Jimmy (4WD)	350	750	1250	2350	5000	7100
Safari - (1/2-Ton) - (111" wb)						
Cargo Van	200	650	1000	2200	4100	5800
SL Van	200	675	1050	2250	4350	6200
SLT Van	350	700	1100	2300	4500	6400
SLE Van	350	700	1150	2300	4600	6600
G1500 Van - (1/2-Ton) - (110" or 125" wb)						
Vandura	200	650	1000	2200	4150	5900
Rally	350	700	1150	2300	4550	6500
Rally Cus	350	725	1150	2300	4700	6700
Rally STX	350	725	1200	2350	4850	6900
G2500 Van - (3/4-Ton) - (110" or 125" wb)						
Vandura	200	600	1000	2200	4000	5700
Rally	350	700	1100	2300	4500	6400
Rally Cus	350	700	1150	2300	4600	6600
Rally STX	350	725	1200	2350	4800	6800
G3500 Van - (1-Ton) - (125" or 146" wb)						
Vandura	200	550	900	2100	3700	5300
Rally	200	675	1100	2250	4400	6300
Rally Cus	350	700	1150	2300	4550	6500
Rally STX	350	725	1150	2300	4700	6700
Magna Van 10	200	500	850	1900	3500	5000
Magna Van 12	200	500	850	1900	3500	5000
S15 - (1/2-Ton) - (108.3" or 122.9" wb)						
Wide-Side PU SBx	150	450	800	1800	3300	4800
Wide-Side PU LBx	200	500	850	1850	3350	4900
Wide-Side Ext Cab PU	200	500	850	1950	3600	5100
C1500 - (1/2-Ton) - (117.5" or 131.5" wb)						
Fender-Side PU SBx	200	675	1100	2250	4400	6300
Wide-Side PU SBx	350	700	1100	2300	4500	6400
Wide-Side PU LBx	200	675	1050	2250	4350	6200
Suburban 4d	350	900	1550	3050	5900	8500
C2500 - (3/4-Ton) - (131" wb)						
Fender-Side PU LBx	350	700	1100	2300	4500	6400
Wide-Side PU LBx	350	700	1150	2300	4550	6500
Bonus Cab 2d PU LBx	350	725	1200	2350	4800	6800
Crew Cab 4d PU LBx	350	750	1200	2350	4900	7000
Suburban 4d	450	1100	1700	3650	6650	9500
C3500 - (1-Ton) - (131.5" or 164.5" wb)						
Fender-Side PU LBx	200	675	1100	2250	4400	6300
Wide-Side PU LBx	350	700	1100	2300	4500	6400
Bonus Cab 2d PU LBx	350	725	1150	2300	4700	6700
Crew Cab 4d PU LBx	350	725	1150	2300	4700	6700

NOTE: Add 15 percent for 4WD.

HUDSON

1929

	6	5	4	3	2	1
Dover Series						
Canopy Exp	450	950	1600	3250	6150	8800
Screenside Dly	350	900	1550	3050	5900	8500
Panel Dly	450	1000	1650	3350	6300	9000
Flareboard PU	450	1100	1700	3650	6650	9500
Bed Rail PU	450	1450	2400	4800	8400	12,000
Sed Dly	400	1200	2000	3950	7000	10,000
Mail Truck w/sl. doors	750	2400	4000	8000	14,000	20,000

1930

	6	5	4	3	2	1
Essex Commercial Car Series						
PU	450	1100	1700	3650	6650	9500
Canopy Exp	350	850	1500	2900	5700	8200
Screenside Exp	350	900	1550	3050	5900	8500
Panel Exp	450	1000	1650	3350	6300	9000
Sed Dly	400	1200	2000	3950	7000	10,000

1931

	6	5	4	3	2	1
Essex Commercial Car Series						
PU	450	1100	1700	3650	6650	9500
Canopy Exp	350	850	1500	2900	5700	8200
Screenside Exp	350	900	1550	3050	5900	8500
Panel Dly	450	1000	1650	3350	6300	9000
Sed Dly	400	1200	2000	3950	7000	10,000

1933

	6	5	4	3	2	1
Essex-Terraplane Series						
PU Exp	350	850	1500	2900	5700	8200
Canopy Dly	350	750	1350	2600	5400	7700
Screenside Dly	350	800	1450	2750	5600	8000
Panel Dly	350	850	1500	2950	5800	8300
DeL Panel Dly	350	900	1550	3050	5900	8500
Sed Dly	450	1000	1650	3350	6300	9000
Mail Dly Van	550	1800	3000	6000	10,500	15,000

1934

	6	5	4	3	2	1
Terraplane Series						
Cab PU	350	900	1550	3050	5900	8500
Sed Dly	450	1000	1650	3350	6300	9000
Utl Coach	200	650	1050	2250	4200	6000
Com Sed Taxicab	350	750	1200	2350	4900	7000
Cantrell Sta Wag	500	1550	2600	5200	9100	13,000
Cotton Sta Wag	450	1450	2400	4800	8400	12,000

1935

	6	5	4	3	2	1
Terraplane Series GU						
Cab PU	350	900	1550	3050	5900	8500
Sed Dly	450	1000	1650	3350	6300	9000
Utl Coach	200	650	1050	2250	4200	6000
Com Sta Wag	500	1550	2600	5200	9100	13,000
Taxicab	350	750	1200	2350	4900	7000

1936

	6	5	4	3	2	1
Terraplane Series 61						
Cab PU	350	800	1450	2750	5600	8000
Cus Panel Dly	350	900	1550	3050	5900	8500
Utl Coach	200	600	950	2150	3850	5500
Cus Sta Wag	450	1450	2400	4800	8400	12,000
Taxicab	200	650	1050	2250	4200	6000

1937

	6	5	4	3	2	1
Terraplane Series 70 - (1/2 Ton)						
Utl Coach	200	550	900	2150	3800	5400
Utl Cpe PU	350	750	1350	2600	5400	7700
Terraplane Series 70 - (3/4 Ton)						
Cab PU	350	750	1300	2450	5250	7500
Panel Dly	350	750	1350	2650	5450	7800
Sta Wag	450	1400	2300	4600	8100	11,500
"Big Boy" Series 78 - (3/4 Ton)						
Cab PU	350	750	1200	2350	4900	7000
Cus Panel Dly	350	750	1300	2450	5250	7500
Big Boy Taxicab	200	650	1050	2250	4200	6000

1938

	6	5	4	3	2	1
Hudson-Terraplane Series 80						
Cab PU	350	750	1200	2350	4900	7000
Cus Panel Dly	350	800	1450	2750	5600	8000
Utl Cpe	200	650	1000	2200	4100	5800
Utl Coach	350	700	1100	2300	4500	6400
Utl Tr Coach	200	600	950	2150	3850	5500
Sta Wag	500	1550	2600	5200	9100	13,000
Hudson "Big Boy" Series 88						
Cab PU	350	800	1450	2750	5600	8000
Cus Panel Dly	350	900	1550	3050	5900	8500

	6	5	4	3	2	1
Hudson 112 Series 89						
Cab PU	350	750	1300	2450	5250	7500
Panel Dly	350	800	1450	2750	5600	8000
Utl Cpe	200	600	950	2150	3850	5500
Utl Coach	200	650	1050	2250	4200	6000
Utl Tr Coach	350	700	1100	2300	4500	6400
1939						
Hudson 112 Series						
PU	350	750	1300	2450	5250	7500
Cus Panel	350	800	1450	2750	5600	8000
(Business Cars)						
Utl Coach	200	650	1050	2250	4200	6000
Utl Cpe	350	700	1150	2300	4550	6500
Sta Wag	500	1550	2600	5200	9100	13,000
Hudson "Big Boy" Series						
PU	350	800	1450	2750	5600	8000
Cus Panel	350	900	1550	3050	5900	8500
Taxicab (86 HP)	450	1000	1650	3350	6300	9000
7P Partition Taxicab	350	700	1150	2300	4550	6500
Hudson Pacemaker Series						
Cus Panel	450	950	1600	3250	6150	8800
1940						
Hudson Six Series						
PU	350	700	1150	2300	4550	6500
Panel Dly	350	750	1300	2450	5250	7500
Traveler Line						
Utl Coach	200	600	950	2150	3850	5500
Utl Cpe	200	650	1050	2250	4200	6000
Sta Wag	500	1550	2600	5200	9100	13,000
Taxicab	200	600	950	2150	3850	5500
"Big Boy" Series						
PU	350	900	1550	3050	5900	8500
Panel Dly	350	800	1450	2750	5600	8000
9P Carryall Sed	200	650	1050	2250	4200	6000
7P Sed	200	600	950	2150	3850	5500
1941						
Hudson Six Series						
PU	350	900	1550	3050	5900	8500
All-Purpose Dly	350	900	1550	3050	5900	8500
Traveler Line						
Utl Cpe	200	650	1050	2250	4200	6000
Utl Coach	200	600	950	2150	3850	5500
"Big Boy" Series						
PU	350	900	1550	3050	5900	8500
9P Carryall Sed	200	650	1050	2250	4200	6000
Taxicab	200	600	950	2150	3850	5500
1942						
Traveler Series						
Utl Cpe	200	650	1050	2250	4200	6000
Utl Coach	200	600	950	2150	3850	5500
Hudson Six Series						
PU	350	900	1550	3050	5900	8500
Hudson "Big Boy" Series						
PU	350	750	1300	2450	5250	7500
1946						
Cab Pickup Series						
Cab PU	450	1000	1650	3350	6300	9000
1947						
Series 178						
PU	350	750	1200	2350	4900	7000

IHC

	6	5	4	3	2	1
1909						
Model A Series						
Auto Wag	650	2100	3500	7000	12,300	17,500
1910						
Model A Series						
Auto Wag	650	2100	3500	7000	12,300	17,500
1911						
Model A Series						
Auto Wag	650	2100	3500	7000	12,300	17,500
1912						
Series AA						
Dly Wag	700	2150	3600	7200	12,600	18,000
Series MW						
Dly Wag	700	2150	3600	7200	12,600	18,000
Panel Exp	700	2250	3750	7500	13,100	18,700
Series AW						
Panel Exp	700	2250	3750	7500	13,100	18,700
1913-1914						
Series AA						
Panel Exp	700	2150	3600	7200	12,600	18,000
Series AW						
Panel Exp	700	2150	3600	7200	12,600	18,000
Series MA						
Panel Exp	700	2250	3750	7500	13,100	18,700
Series MW						
Panel Exp	700	2250	3750	7500	13,100	18,700
1915						
Model M						
1/2-Ton Chassis	400	1200	2000	3950	7000	10,000
Model E						
3/4-Ton Chassis	450	1100	1700	3650	6650	9500
Model F						
1-Ton Chassis	450	1150	1900	3900	6900	9900
1916-1920						
Model F						
1-Ton Chassis	450	1150	1900	3900	6900	9900
Model H						
3/4-Ton Chassis	400	1200	2000	3950	7000	10,000
1921						
Model S Series - (3/4-Ton)						
Chassis	350	750	1200	2350	4900	7000
PU	450	1100	1700	3650	6650	9500
Exp	450	1000	1650	3350	6300	9000

	6	5	4	3	2	1
Stake	450	1000	1650	3350	6300	9000
Ambulance	450	1100	1700	3650	6650	9500
Panel	450	1100	1700	3650	6650	9500
Model 21 Series - (1-Ton)						
Chassis	350	700	1150	2300	4550	6500
Exp	350	800	1450	2750	5600	8000
Panel	350	900	1550	3050	5900	8500
Stake	350	800	1450	2750	5600	8000
Dump	350	900	1550	3050	5900	8500
Tank	450	1000	1650	3350	6300	9000
1922						
Model S Series - (3/4-Ton)						
Chassis	350	750	1200	2350	4900	7000
PU	450	1100	1700	3650	6650	9500
Exp	450	1000	1650	3350	6300	9000
Panel	450	1100	1700	3650	6650	9500
Stake	450	1000	1650	3350	6300	9000
Ambulance	450	1100	1700	3650	6650	9500
Model 21 Series - (1-Ton)						
Chassis	350	700	1150	2300	4550	6500
Exp	350	800	1450	2750	5600	8000
Panel	350	900	1550	3050	5900	8500
Stake	350	800	1450	2750	5600	8000
Dump	350	900	1550	3050	5900	8500
Tank	450	1000	1650	3350	6300	9000
1923						
Model S Series - (3/4-Ton)						
Chassis	350	750	1200	2350	4900	7000
PU	450	1100	1700	3650	6650	9500
Exp	450	1000	1650	3350	6300	9000
Panel	450	1100	1700	3650	6650	9500
Stake	450	1000	1650	3350	6300	9000
Ambulance	450	1100	1700	3650	6650	9500
Model 21 Series - (1-Ton)						
Chassis	350	700	1150	2300	4550	6500
Exp	350	800	1450	2750	5600	8000
Panel	350	900	1550	3050	5900	8500
Stake	350	800	1450	2750	5600	8000
Dump	350	900	1550	3050	5900	8500
Tank	450	1000	1650	3350	6300	9000
1925						
Special Delivery Series - (3/4-Ton)						
Chassis	350	800	1450	2750	5600	8000
Panel Dly	450	1000	1650	3350	6300	9000
Model S Series - (1-Ton)						
Chassis	350	750	1200	2350	4900	7000
PU	450	1000	1650	3350	6300	9000
Exp	350	900	1550	3050	5900	8500
Panel	450	1000	1650	3350	6300	9000
Stake	350	900	1550	3050	5900	8500
Ambulance	450	1000	1650	3350	6300	9000
Lang Bus	350	700	1150	2300	4550	6500
Model SD Series - (1-Ton)						
Chassis	350	700	1150	2300	4550	6500
Model SL Series - (1-Ton)						
Chassis	350	700	1150	2300	4550	6500
1927-1928						
Series S - (3/4-Ton)						
PU	450	1000	1650	3350	6300	9000
Canopy Dly	350	900	1550	3100	6000	8600
Screen Dly	350	850	1500	2900	5700	8200
Panel Dly	450	1050	1700	3600	6600	9400
Sed Dly	450	1150	1900	3900	6900	9900
1929						
Series S - (3/4-Ton)						
PU	450	1000	1650	3350	6300	9000
Canopy Dly	350	900	1550	3100	6000	8600
Screen Dly	350	850	1500	2900	5700	8200
Panel Dly	450	1050	1700	3600	6600	9400
Sed Dly	450	1150	1900	3900	6900	9900
1930						
Series AW-1 - (3/4-Ton) - (124" wb)						
Chassis	350	800	1450	2750	5600	8000
PU	450	950	1600	3250	6150	8800
Canopy Dly	450	950	1600	3250	6150	8800
Screen Dly	350	900	1550	3050	5900	8500
Panel Dly	450	1100	1700	3650	6650	9500
Sed Dly	400	1200	2000	3950	7000	10,000
Series AW-1 - (3/4-Ton) - (136" wb)						
Chassis	350	750	1200	2350	4900	7000
PU	350	900	1550	3100	6000	8600
Canopy Dly	350	850	1500	2900	5700	8200
Screen Dly	350	750	1350	2650	5450	7800
Panel Dly	450	1000	1650	3350	6300	9000
Sed Dly	450	1100	1700	3650	6650	9500
1931						
Series AW-1 - (3/4-Ton)						
Chassis	350	800	1450	2750	5600	8000
PU	450	1100	1700	3650	6650	9500
Canopy Dly	450	1050	1700	3600	6600	9400
Screen Dly	450	950	1600	3250	6150	8800
Panel	350	900	1550	3050	5900	8500
Sed Dly	400	1200	2000	3950	7000	10,000
Series A-1 - (3/4-Ton)						
Chassis	350	750	1300	2450	5250	7500
1932						
Series AW-1 - (3/4-Ton)						
Chassis	350	800	1450	2750	5600	8000
PU	450	1100	1700	3650	6650	9500
Canopy Dly	450	1050	1700	3600	6600	9400
Screen Dly	450	950	1600	3250	6150	8800
Panel	350	900	1550	3050	5900	8500
Sed Dly	400	1200	2000	3950	7000	10,000
Series A-1 - (3/4-Ton)						
Chassis	350	750	1300	2450	5250	7500
PU	350	800	1450	2750	5600	8000
Canopy Dly	350	800	1350	2700	5500	7900
Screen Dly	350	750	1250	2400	5100	7300
Panel	350	750	1200	2350	4900	7000
Sed Dly	350	900	1550	3050	5900	8500

	6	5	4	3	2	1
Series M-2 - (1-Ton)						
Chassis	350	725	1200	2350	4800	6800
1933						
Series D-1 - (1/2-Ton)						
Chassis	350	750	1300	2500	5300	7600
PU	350	850	1500	2800	5650	8100
Canopy Dly	350	800	1450	2750	5600	8000
Screen Dly	350	750	1300	2400	5200	7400
Panel	350	750	1250	2350	5000	7100
Sed Dly	350	900	1550	3100	6000	8600
Series A-1 - (3/4-Ton)						
Chassis	350	750	1300	2450	5250	7500
PU	350	800	1450	2750	5600	8000
Canopy Dly	350	800	1350	2700	5500	7900
Screen Dly	350	750	1250	2400	5100	7300
Panel	350	750	1200	2350	4900	7000
Sed Dly	350	900	1550	3050	5900	8500
Series M-2 - (1-Ton)						
Chassis	350	725	1200	2350	4800	6800
1934						
Series D-1 - (1/2-Ton)						
Chassis	350	750	1300	2500	5300	7600
PU	350	850	1500	2800	5650	8100
Canopy Dly	350	800	1450	2750	5600	8000
Screen Dly	350	750	1300	2400	5200	7400
Panel	350	750	1250	2350	5000	7100
Sed Dly	350	900	1550	3100	6000	8600
Series C-1 - (1/2-Ton)						
Chassis (113" wb)	350	750	1350	2650	5450	7800
Chassis (125" wb)	350	750	1350	2600	5400	7700
PU (113" wb)	350	900	1550	3050	5900	8500
Series A-1 - (3/4-Ton)						
Chassis	350	750	1300	2450	5250	7500
PU	350	800	1450	2750	5600	8000
Canopy Dly	350	800	1350	2700	5500	7900
Screen Dly	350	750	1250	2400	5100	7300
Panel	350	750	1200	2350	4900	7000
Sed Dly	350	900	1550	3050	5900	8500
Series M-2 (1-Ton)						
Chassis	350	725	1200	2350	4800	6800
1935						
Series C-1 - (1/2-Ton)						
Chassis (113" wb)	350	750	1350	2650	5450	7800
Chassis (125" wb)	350	750	1350	2600	5400	7700
Series C-10 - (3/4-Ton)						
Chassis	350	750	1300	2400	5200	7400
Chassis	350	750	1300	2450	5250	7500
Series C-20 - (1 or 1-1/2-Ton)						
Chassis (133" wb)	350	700	1150	2300	4550	6500
Chassis (157" wb)	200	650	1050	2250	4200	6000
Series M-3 - (1-Ton)						
Chassis	350	725	1200	2350	4800	6800
1936						
Series C-5 - (1/2-Ton)						
SWB Chassis	350	750	1300	2450	5250	7500
LWB Series	350	750	1300	2400	5200	7400
Series C-1 - (1/2-Ton)						
SWB Chassis	350	750	1350	2650	5450	7800
LWB Chassis	350	750	1350	2600	5400	7700
Series C-10 - (3/4-Ton)						
Chassis	350	750	1300	2400	5200	7400
Series C-15 - (3/4 or 1-Ton)						
Chassis	350	750	1250	2400	5100	7300
Series M-3 - (1-Ton)						
Chassis	200	650	1000	2200	4100	5800
Series CS-20 - (1 or 1-1/2-Ton)						
Chassis	200	600	950	2150	3850	5500
Series C-12 - (3/4-Ton)						
Chassis	350	750	1250	2400	5100	7300
1937-1938						
Series D-5 - (1/2-Ton)						
Chassis	350	750	1250	2400	5100	7300
Series D-2 - (1/2-Ton)						
Chassis	350	750	1300	2500	5300	7600
Series D-15 - (3/4 or 1-Ton)						
Chassis	350	750	1200	2350	4900	7000

NOTE: See 1936 for 1937 "C" and "M" Series values. The value estimates above are for Express (pickup) trucks. Check 1939 price guide for relative prices on other body styles.

	6	5	4	3	2	1
1939						
Series D-2 - (6-cyl) - (1/2-Ton) - (113" wb)						
Exp	350	850	1500	2950	5800	8300
Canopy Exp	350	900	1550	3000	5850	8400
Panel	350	900	1550	3050	5900	8500
DM Body	350	750	1350	2650	5450	7800
DB Body	350	750	1350	2650	5450	7800
Sta Wag	450	1000	1650	3350	6300	9000
Metro	200	500	850	1900	3500	5000
Series D-2 - (6-cyl) - (1/2-Ton) - (125" wb)						
Exp	350	850	1500	2800	5650	8100
Canopy Exp	350	850	1500	2900	5700	8200
Panel	350	850	1500	2950	5800	8300
Stake	350	750	1350	2600	5400	7700
1940						
Series D-2 - (6-cyl) - (1/2-Ton) - (113" wb)						
PU	350	850	1500	2950	5800	8300
Canopy	350	900	1550	3000	5850	8400
Panel	350	900	1550	3050	5900	8500
Milk Dly	350	750	1350	2650	5450	7800
Stake	350	750	1350	2600	5400	7700
Series D-2H - (6-cyl) - (1/2-Ton) - (125" wb)						
PU	350	850	1500	2800	5650	8100
Canopy	350	850	1500	2900	5700	8200
Panel	350	850	1500	2950	5800	8300
Stake	350	750	1350	2600	5400	7700
Series D-2M - (6-cyl) - (1/2-Ton) - (102" or 113" wb)						
Metro Panel (SWB)	350	725	1200	2350	4800	6800
Metro Panel (LWB)	350	725	1200	2350	4800	6800
Series D-5 - (4-cyl) - (1/2-Ton) - (113" wb)						
PU	350	750	1350	2650	5450	7800
Canopy	450	1150	1900	3900	6900	9900
Panel	350	800	1450	2750	5600	8000
Milk Dly	350	750	1250	2400	5100	7300

	6	5	4	3	2	1
Series D-5 - (4-cyl) - (1/2-Ton) - (125" wb)						
PU	350	750	1350	2600	5400	7700
Canopy	350	750	1350	2650	5450	7800
Panel	350	800	1350	2700	5500	7900
Stake	350	750	1250	2400	5100	7300
Series D-15L - (6-cyl) - (3/4-Ton) - (113" wb)						
PU	350	750	1300	2450	5250	7500
Milk Dly	350	750	1250	2350	5000	7100
Series D-15LL - (6-cyl) - (3/4-Ton) - (130" wb)						
PU	350	750	1300	2400	5200	7400
Canopy	350	750	1300	2450	5250	7500
Panel	350	750	1300	2500	5300	7600
Stake	350	750	1200	2350	4900	7000
Series D-15M - (6-cyl) - (3/4-Ton) - (102" or 113" wb)						
Panel (SWB)	350	700	1150	2300	4550	6500
Panel (LWB)	350	700	1150	2300	4550	6500
Series D-29 - (6-cyl) - (3/4-Ton)						
Chassis & Cowl (128" wb)	350	700	1150	2300	4550	6500
Chassis & Cab (128" wb)	350	700	1150	2300	4600	6600
Chassis & Cowl (155" wb)	200	675	1050	2250	4350	6200
Chassis & Cab (155" wb)	200	675	1100	2250	4400	6300
Chassis & Cowl (173" wb)	200	650	1000	2200	4150	5900
Chassis & Cab (173" wb)	200	650	1050	2250	4200	6000
Series D-15 - (6-cyl) - (1-Ton) - (113" wb)						
PU	350	700	1150	2300	4550	6500
Milk Dly	200	650	1000	2200	4150	5900
Series D-15H - (6-cyl) - (1-Ton) - (130" wb)						
PU	200	675	1100	2250	4400	6300
Canopy	200	675	1100	2250	4400	6300
Panel	350	700	1150	2300	4550	6500
Stake	200	650	1050	2250	4200	6000
Series 15M - (6-cyl) - (1-Ton) - (102" or 113" wb)						
Panel (SWB)	200	650	1050	2250	4200	6000
Panel (LWB)	200	650	1050	2250	4200	6000
Series K-1/K-1H - (1/2 or 3/4-Ton) - (113" wb)						
PU	350	900	1550	3050	5900	8500
Panel	350	900	1550	3100	6000	8600
Sta Wag	450	1500	2500	5000	8800	12,500
Series K-1/K-1H - (1/2 or 3/4-Ton) - (125" wb)						
PU	350	850	1500	2950	5800	8300
Panel	350	900	1550	3000	5850	8400
Stake	350	800	1350	2700	5500	7900
Series K-2L/K-2H - (1/2 or 1-Ton) - (125" wb)						
PU	350	850	1500	2900	5700	8200
Panel	350	850	1500	2950	5800	8300
Stake	350	800	1350	2700	5500	7900
Series K-3/K-3L - (1/2 or 1-Ton) - (113" wb)						
PU	350	900	1550	3100	6000	8600
Series K-3/K-3L - (1/2 or 1-Ton) - (130" wb)						
PU	350	900	1550	3050	5900	8500
Panel	350	900	1550	3100	6000	8600
Stake	350	750	1300	2500	5300	7600
1941-1942						
Series K-1 - (1/2-Ton) - (113" wb)						
PU	450	1000	1650	3350	6300	9000
Canopy	450	1050	1650	3500	6400	9200
Panel	450	1000	1650	3400	6350	9100
Milk Dly	350	750	1300	2450	5250	7500
Sta Wag	450	1500	2500	5000	8800	12,500
Series K-1 - (1/2-Ton) - (125" wb)						
PU	450	950	1600	3250	6150	8800
Canopy	450	1000	1650	3350	6300	9000
Panel	450	1000	1600	3300	6250	8900
Stake	350	800	1350	2700	5500	7900
Bakery Dly	350	750	1250	2400	5100	7300
Series K-2 - (3/4-Ton) - (125" wb)						
PU	350	900	1550	3050	5900	8500
Canopy	350	950	1600	3200	6050	8700
Panel	350	900	1550	3100	6000	8600
Stake	350	800	1350	2700	5500	7900
Bakery Dly	350	750	1250	2400	5050	7200
Series K-3 - (1-Ton) - (113" wb)						
PU	350	800	1450	2750	5600	8000
Milk Dly	350	750	1200	2350	4900	7000
Series K-3 - (1-Ton) - (130" wb)						
PU	350	750	1350	2650	5450	7800
Canopy	350	850	1500	2900	5700	8200
Panel	350	800	1450	2750	5600	8000
Stake	350	750	1300	2500	5300	7600
Sta Wag	450	1000	1650	3350	6300	9000
Metro Delivery - (102" wb)						
D-2M Panel	150	350	750	1350	2800	4000
K-1M Panel	150	300	750	1350	2700	3900
D-15M Panel	150	300	700	1250	2600	3700
K-3M Panel	125	250	700	1150	2450	3500
Metro Delivery - (113" wb)						
D-2M Panel	150	350	750	1450	2900	4100
K-1M Panel	150	350	750	1350	2800	4000
D-M15 Panel	150	300	700	1250	2650	3800
K-3M Panel	125	250	700	1150	2500	3600
Series K-1 - (1/2-Ton) - (113" wb)						
PU	350	725	1200	2350	4850	6900
Canopy	350	750	1200	2350	4900	7000
Panel	350	725	1150	2300	4700	6700
Milk Dly	150	300	700	1250	2600	3700
Sta Wag	450	1500	2500	5000	8800	12,500
Series K-1 - (1/2-Ton) - (125" wb)						
PU	350	725	1200	2350	4800	6800
Canopy	350	725	1200	2350	4850	6900
Panel	350	700	1150	2300	4600	6600
Stake	200	675	1050	2250	4350	6200
Bakery Dly	150	300	700	1250	2600	3700
Series K-2 - (3/4-Ton) - (125" wb)						
PU	350	725	1150	2300	4700	6700
Canopy	350	725	1200	2350	4800	6800
Panel	350	700	1150	2300	4550	6500
Stake	200	675	1050	2250	4300	6100
Bakery Dly	125	250	700	1150	2500	3600
Series K-3 - (1-Ton) - (113" wb)						
PU	350	700	1150	2300	4550	6500
Milk Dly	125	200	600	1100	2300	3300
Series K-3 - (1-Ton) - (130" wb)						
PU	200	600	950	2200	3900	5600
Canopy	200	650	1050	2250	4200	6000
Panel	200	600	950	2150	3850	5500
Stake	200	600	1000	2200	4000	5700
Sta Wag	450	1500	2500	5000	8800	12,500

Standard Catalog Of Light-Duty Trucks
787

1946

	6	5	4	3	2	1
Series K-1 - (1/2-Ton) - (113" wb)						
PU	350	700	1150	2300	4600	6600
Panel	200	500	850	1950	3600	5100
Series K-1 - (1/2-Ton) - (125" wb)						
PU	350	700	1150	2300	4550	6500
Panel	200	500	850	1900	3500	5000
Series K-1M - (1/2-Ton) - (102" wb)						
Metro Van	150	350	750	1450	3000	4200
Series K-2 - (3/4-Ton) - (125" wb)						
PU	200	650	1000	2200	4100	5800
Panel	150	350	750	1450	2900	4100
Series K-3 - (1-Ton) - (113" wb)						
PU	200	600	950	2150	3850	5500
Milk Dly	125	200	600	1100	2250	3200
Series K-3 - (1-Ton) - (130" wb)						
PU	200	550	900	2100	3700	5300
Stake	150	300	750	1350	2700	3900
Series K-3M - (1-Ton) - (102" wb)						
Metro Van	125	250	700	1150	2450	3500
Station Wagon						
Sta Wag	450	1500	2500	5000	8800	12,500

1947-1949

	6	5	4	3	2	1
Series KB-1 - (1/2-Ton) - (113" wb)						
Series KB-3M - (1Ton) - (102" wb)						
Panel	200	500	850	1950	3600	5100
KBM (Bake/Milk)	150	450	750	1700	3200	4600
Series KB-1 - (1/2-Ton) - (125" wb)						
Exp PU	350	700	1150	2300	4550	6500
Panel	200	500	850	1900	3500	5000
Stake	150	400	750	1650	3150	4500
Series KB-1M - (1/2-Ton) - (102" wb)						
Metro Van	125	250	700	1150	2400	3400
Series KB-2 - (3/4-Ton) - (125" wb)						
Exp PU	200	650	1000	2200	4100	5800
Panel	150	350	750	1450	2900	4100
Stake	150	350	750	1350	2800	4000
Series KB-3 - (1-Ton) - (113" wb)						
Exp PU	200	675	1050	2250	4350	6200
KM (Milk)	125	200	600	1100	2250	3200
Series KB-3 - (1-Ton) - (130" wb)						
Exp PU	200	600	950	2150	3850	5500
Panel	150	350	750	1350	2800	4000
Stake	150	300	750	1350	2700	3900
Series KB-3M - (1-Ton) - (102" wb)						
Metro Van	125	250	700	1150	2450	3500
Station Wagons (Cus Body)						
Sta Wag (all)	450	1500	2500	5000	8800	12,500

1950-1952

	6	5	4	3	2	1
Series L-110/L-111 - (1/2-Ton)						
PU (6-1/2 ft.)	200	675	1050	2250	4350	6200
PU (8-ft.)	200	675	1050	2250	4300	6100
Panel (7-1/2 ft.)	200	500	850	1850	3350	4900
Series L-112 - (3/4-Ton)						
PU (6-1/2 ft.)	200	650	1050	2250	4200	6000
PU (8-ft.)	200	650	1000	2200	4150	5900
PU (8-ft.)	150	450	750	1700	3200	4600
Series L-120 - (3/4-Ton)						
PU (6-1/2 ft.)	200	600	950	2150	3850	5500
PU (8-ft.)	200	500	850	1950	3600	5100
Panel (7-1/2 ft.)	150	350	750	1450	3000	4200
Series LM-120/LM-150/LM-151						
Metro (1/2-Ton)	125	250	700	1150	2450	3500
Metro (3/4-Ton)	125	250	700	1150	2400	3400
Metro (1-Ton)	100	150	450	1000	1900	2700
Series L-130 - (1-Ton)						
PU (9-ft.)	125	250	700	1150	2450	3500
Series L-153 - (1-Ton)						
School Bus	100	150	450	1000	1750	2500
Series LB-140						
Milk Truck	100	175	525	1050	1950	2800
Station Wagons						
Wood (1/2-Ton)	450	1500	2500	5000	8800	12,500
Wood (3/4-Ton)	450	1450	2400	4800	8400	12,000
Wood (1-Ton)	450	1400	2300	4600	8100	11,500

1953-1955

	6	5	4	3	2	1
Series R-100 Light Duty - (1/2-Ton) - (115" wb)						
PU (6-1/2 ft.)	200	675	1050	2250	4350	6200
Series R-110 Heavy Duty - (1/2-Ton) - (115" or 127" wb)						
PU (6-1/2 ft.)	200	675	1050	2250	4300	6100
Panel (7-1/2 ft.)	200	500	850	1850	3350	4900
PU (8-ft.)	200	650	1050	2250	4200	6000
Stake	200	550	900	2150	3800	5400
Series R-120 - (3/4-Ton) - (115" or 127" wb)						
PU (6-1/2 ft.)	200	650	1050	2250	4200	6000
Panel (7-1/2 ft.)	200	650	1000	2200	4150	5900
PU (8-ft.)	200	600	950	2150	3850	5500
Stake	200	550	900	2100	3700	5300
Series RA-120 - (3/4-Ton) - (115" wb)						
Metroette	125	200	600	1100	2200	3100
Series RM-120 - (3/4-Ton) - (102", 115" or 122" wb)						
Metro Dly (102" wb)	100	175	525	1050	2100	3000
Metro Flat Back (102" wb)	100	175	525	1050	2050	2900
Metro Dly (115" wb)	100	175	525	1050	2100	3000
Metro Flat Back (115" wb)	100	175	525	1050	2050	2900
Metro Bus (115" wb)	100	175	525	1050	2050	2900
Metro Dly (122" wb)	100	175	525	1050	2050	2900
Metro Flat Back (122" wb)	100	175	525	1050	1950	2800
Metro-Lite (115" wb)	100	150	450	1000	1900	2700
Metro-Lite (122" wb)	100	150	450	1000	1900	2700
Series R-130 - (1-Ton) - (115", 122" or 134" wb)						
PU (6-1/2 ft.)	125	200	600	1100	2250	3200
Stake (6-1/2 ft.)	100	175	525	1050	2100	3000
PU (9-ft.)	125	200	600	1100	2200	3100
Stake (8-ft.)	100	175	525	1050	2050	2900
Stake (9-ft.)	100	175	525	1050	1950	2800

1956-1957

	6	5	4	3	2	1
Series S-100 - (1/2-Ton) - (115" wb)						
PU (6-1/2 ft.)	350	700	1150	2300	4600	6600
Series S-110 - (Heavy Duty 1/2-Ton) - (115" or 127" wb)						
PU (6-1/2 ft.)	350	700	1150	2300	4550	6500
Panel	200	500	850	1900	3500	5000
Travelall	350	700	1150	2300	4600	6600
PU (8-ft.)	350	700	1100	2300	4500	6400
Stake	200	600	950	2150	3850	5500
Platform	200	550	900	2150	3800	5400
Series S-120 - (3/4-Ton) - (115" or 127" wb)						
PU (6-1/2 ft.)	200	675	1050	2250	4350	6200
Panel	150	350	750	1350	2800	4000
Travelall	200	600	950	2150	3850	5500
PU (8-ft.)	200	650	1050	2250	4200	6000
Stake	200	500	850	1900	3500	5000
Platform	200	500	850	1850	3350	4900
SA Milk Truck	100	175	525	1050	1950	2800
Metro Body (102" wb)	100	175	525	1050	2100	3000
Metro Dly (115" wb)	100	175	525	1050	2100	3000
Metro Flat Back (115" wb)	100	175	525	1050	2050	2900
Metro-Lite (115" wb)	100	175	525	1050	1950	2800
Metro Flat Back (122" wb)	100	150	450	1000	1900	2700
Metro-Lite (122" wb)	100	175	525	1050	1950	2800
Series S-130 - (1-Ton) - (122" wb)						
Chassis & Cab	100	175	525	1050	2100	3000
Series S-130 - (1-Ton) - (122" or 134" wb)						
PU (9-ft.)	125	200	600	1100	2300	3300
Platform (9-ft.)	125	200	600	1100	2200	3100
Stake (9-ft.)	125	200	600	1100	2250	3200
Metro Flat Back (122" wb)	100	150	450	1000	1900	2700
Metro-Lite (122" wb)	100	175	525	1050	1950	2800
Metro Flat Back (134" wb)	100	150	450	1000	1800	2600
Metro-Lite (134" wb)	100	150	450	1000	1900	2700

1957-1/2 - 1958

	6	5	4	3	2	1
Series A-100 - (1/2-Ton) - (7-ft.)						
PU	350	700	1150	2300	4550	6500
Cus PU	350	725	1150	2300	4700	6700
Panel	200	500	850	1950	3600	5100
Travelall	200	675	1050	2250	4300	6100
Series A-110 - (Heavy Duty) - (1/2-Ton)						
PU (7-ft.)	200	675	1050	2250	4350	6200
Cus PU (7-ft.)	350	700	1150	2300	4550	6500
Panel (7-ft.)	150	450	800	1750	3250	4700
Travelall	200	650	1050	2250	4200	6000
PU (8-1/2 ft.)	200	650	1050	2250	4200	6000
Utl PU (6-ft.)	200	600	950	2150	3850	5500
Cus Utl PU (6-ft.)	200	600	1000	2200	4000	5700
Series A-120 - (3/4-Ton)						
PU (7-ft.)	200	650	1050	2250	4200	6000
Cus PU (7-ft.)	200	675	1050	2250	4350	6200
Panel (7-ft.)	150	400	750	1550	3050	4300
Travelall (7-ft.)	200	650	1000	2200	4100	5800
PU (8-1/2 ft.)	200	650	1000	2200	4100	5800
Utl PU (6-ft.)	200	600	950	2200	3900	5600
Cus Utl PU (6-ft.)	200	600	1000	2200	4000	5700
Metro-Mite						
Walk-In Panel	125	200	600	1100	2200	3100
Metroette - (3/4-Ton)						
Milk/Bakery	100	175	525	1050	2100	3000
Metro Delivery Vans - (3/4-Ton)						
Metro (7-3/4 ft.)	125	200	600	1100	2250	3200
Metro (9-1/2 ft.)	125	200	600	1100	2200	3100
Flat Back (9-1/2 ft.)	100	175	525	1050	1950	2800
Metro-Lite (9-3/4 ft.)	100	150	450	1000	1900	2700
8P Coach	100	175	525	1050	2100	3000
12P Coach	100	175	525	1050	2100	3000
16P Coach	100	175	525	1050	2100	3000
Metro-Lite (10-3/4 ft.)	100	150	450	1000	1800	2600
Flat Back (10-1/2 ft.)	100	150	450	1000	1750	2500
Series A-130 - (1-Ton)						
PU (8-1/2 ft.)	150	400	750	1650	3150	4500
Utl PU	150	350	750	1350	2800	4000
Cus Utl PU	150	350	750	1450	3000	4200
Metro Delivery Vans - (1-Ton)						
Metro (9-1/2 ft.)	100	175	525	1050	2100	3000
Flat Back (9-1/2 ft.)	100	150	450	1000	1900	2700
Metro-Lite (10-ft. 8")	100	150	450	1000	1800	2600
Flat Back (10-1/2 ft.)	100	175	525	1050	1950	2800
Metro-Lite (12-ft. 8")	100	175	525	1050	2050	2900
Flat Back (12-ft. 7")	100	175	525	1050	1950	2800

1959

	6	5	4	3	2	1
Series B-100/B-102 - (3/4-Ton)						
PU (7-ft.)	200	650	1050	2250	4200	6000
Panel (7-ft.)	150	400	750	1650	3150	4500
Travelall	200	600	1000	2200	4000	5700
Series B-110/B-112 - (Heavy Duty) - (1/2-Ton)						
PU (7-ft.)	200	600	1000	2200	4000	5700
Panel	200	600	950	2150	3850	5500
Travelall	200	550	900	2000	3600	5200
PU (8-1/2 ft.)	200	500	850	1900	3500	5000
Travelette	200	500	850	1900	3500	5000

NOTE: Add 10 percent for Custom trim package.

	6	5	4	3	2	1
Series B-120/B-122 - (3/4-Ton)						
PU (7-ft.)	200	600	950	2150	3850	5500
Panel (7-ft.)	200	550	900	2150	3800	5400
Travelall	200	600	950	2150	3850	5500
PU (8-1/2 ft.)	200	500	850	1950	3600	5100
Travelette (6-ft.)	200	500	850	1850	3350	4900

NOTE: Add 5 percent for 4WD trucks.

	6	5	4	3	2	1
Series B-130/B-132 - (1-Ton)						
PU (8-1/2 ft.)	200	500	850	1900	3500	5000
Travelette	150	450	800	1800	3300	4800

NOTE: Add 5 percent for V-8 engines. Refer to 1958 section for Metro-Mite, Metroette and Metro Delivery Van prices.

1960

	6	5	4	3	2	1
Series B-100/B-102 - (1/2-Ton)						
PU (7-ft.)	350	700	1100	2300	4500	6400
Panel (7-ft.)	200	550	900	2000	3600	5200
Travelall	200	675	1050	2250	4350	6200
Series B-110/B-112 - (Heavy Duty) - (1/2-Ton)						
PU (7-ft.)	200	675	1050	2250	4350	6200
Panel	150	450	800	1750	3250	4700
Travelall	200	650	1000	2200	4150	5900
PU (8-1/2 ft.)	200	600	1000	2200	4000	5700
Travelette	200	550	900	2150	3800	5400

NOTE: Add 10 percent for Custom trim package.

	6	5	4	3	2	1
Series B-120/B-122 - (3/4-Ton)						
PU (7-ft.)	200	650	1050	2250	4200	6000
Panel (7-ft.)	150	350	750	1450	3000	4200
Travelall	200	600	950	2150	3850	5500
PU (8-1/2 ft.)	200	600	950	2150	3850	5500

	6	5	4	3	2	1
Travelette (6-ft.)	200	500	850	1950	3600	5100

NOTE: Add 5 percent for 4WD trucks.

	6	5	4	3	2	1
Series B-130/B-132 - (1-Ton)						
PU (8-1/2 ft.)	200	600	950	2150	3850	5500
Travelette	150	450	750	1700	3200	4600

NOTE: Deduct 5 percent for 6-cyl. engines. Refer to 1958 section for Metro-Mite, Metroette and Metro Delivery Van prices.

1961

	6	5	4	3	2	1
Series Scout 80 - (1/4-Ton) - (5-ft.)						
PU	200	600	950	2150	3850	5500
PU (4WD)	200	650	1000	2200	4100	5800

NOTE: Add 5 percent for vinyl Sport-Top (full enclosure).
Add 4 percent for steel Travel-Top.

	6	5	4	3	2	1
Series C-100 - (1/2-Ton)						
PU (7-ft.)	200	600	950	2150	3850	5500
Panel (7-ft.)	150	400	750	1650	3150	4500
Travelall	200	650	1050	2250	4200	6000
Cus Travelall	350	700	1150	2300	4550	6500
Series C-110 - (Heavy Duty) - (1/2-Ton)						
PU (7-ft.)	200	600	950	2200	3900	5600
Panel (7-ft.)	150	450	750	1700	3200	4600
Travelall	200	675	1050	2250	4300	6100
Cus Travelall	350	700	1150	2300	4600	6600
PU (8-1/2 ft.)	200	600	950	2150	3850	5500
Travelette PU	200	500	850	1900	3500	5000
Series C-120 - (3/4-Ton)						
PU (7-ft.)	200	500	850	1950	3600	5100
Panel (7-ft.)	150	350	750	1450	2900	4100
Travelall	200	600	950	2150	3850	5500
Cus Travelall	200	650	1000	2200	4150	5900
PU (8-1/2 ft.)	200	500	850	1900	3500	5000
Travelette PU	150	450	800	1800	3300	4800
Series C-130 - (1-Ton)						
PU (8-1/2 ft.)	150	450	800	1750	3250	4700
Travelette PU	150	400	750	1550	3050	4300

NOTE: Deduct 5 percent for 6-cyl. engine (all series "C"). Add 5 percent for 4WD option. See 1958 section for Metrolette, Metro Delivery and AM-130 Metro Delivery prices.

1962

	6	5	4	3	2	1
Scout 80 - (1/4-Ton) - (5-ft.)						
PU	200	650	1050	2250	4200	6000
PU (4WD)	200	675	1050	2250	4350	6200

NOTE: Add 5 percent for vinyl Sport-Top (full enclosure).
Add 4 percent for steel Travel-Top.

	6	5	4	3	2	1
Series C-100 - (1/2-Ton)						
PU (7-ft.)	200	650	1000	2200	4100	5800
Bonus PU (7-ft.)	200	650	1000	2200	4150	5900
Panel (7-ft.)	150	400	750	1650	3150	4500
Travelall	200	650	1050	2250	4200	6000
Cus Travelall	350	700	1150	2300	4550	6500
Series C-110 - (Heavy Duty) - (1/2-Ton)						
PU (7-ft.)	200	600	950	2200	3900	5600
Bonus PU (7-ft.)	200	600	1000	2200	4000	5700
Panel (7-ft.)	150	450	750	1700	3200	4600
Travelall	200	675	1050	2250	4300	6100
Cus Travelall	350	700	1150	2300	4600	6600
PU (8-1/2 ft.)	200	600	950	2150	3850	5500
Travelette PU	200	500	850	1900	3500	5000
Series C-120 - (3/4-Ton)						
PU (7-ft.)	200	500	850	1950	3600	5100
Bonus PU (7-ft.)	200	550	900	2000	3600	5200
Panel (7-ft.)	150	350	750	1450	2900	4100
Travelall	200	600	950	2150	3850	5500
Cus Travelall	200	650	1000	2200	4150	5900
PU (8-1/2 ft.)	200	500	850	1900	3500	5000
Bonus PU (8-1/2 ft.)	200	500	850	1900	3500	5000
Travelette PU	150	450	800	1800	3300	4800
Series C-130 - (1-Ton)						
PU (8-1/2 ft.)	150	450	800	1750	3250	4700
Bonus PU (8-1/2 ft.)	150	450	800	1800	3300	4800
Travelette PU	150	400	750	1550	3050	4300

NOTE: Deduct 5 percent for 6-cyl. engine (all series "C"). Add 5 percent for 4WD option (all series). See 1958 section for Metroette, Metro & AM-130 Metro prices.

1963

	6	5	4	3	2	1
Scout Series - (1/4-Ton)						
PU (2WD)	200	600	950	2150	3850	5500
PU (4WD)	200	650	1000	2200	4100	5800

NOTE: Add 5 percent for vinyl Sport-Top (full-length).
Add 10 percent for steel Travel-Top.

	6	5	4	3	2	1
Series CM-75/80 Metro-Mite - (1/4-Ton)						
Panel	150	300	700	1250	2600	3700
Walk-In Panel	125	250	700	1150	2500	3600
Series CM-110 Metro - (1/2-Ton)						
Walk-In Panel	150	300	700	1250	2650	3800
Series C-1000 - (1/2-Ton)						
PU (7-ft.)	200	550	900	2150	3800	5400
Bonus Load PU (7-ft.)	200	600	950	2150	3850	5500
Travelall	200	600	1000	2200	4000	5700
Panel	150	450	800	1750	3250	4700
Series C-1100 - (Heavy Duty) - (1/2-Ton)						
PU (7-ft.)	200	600	950	2150	3850	5500
Bonus Load PU (7-ft.)	200	600	950	2200	3900	5600
PU (8-ft.)	200	550	900	2150	3800	5400
Bonus Load PU (8-ft.)	200	600	950	2150	3850	5500
Panel	150	450	800	1800	3300	4800
Travelall	200	650	1000	2200	4100	5800
Travelette PU	200	500	850	1900	3500	5000
Bonus Load Travelette PU	200	500	850	1950	3600	5100

NOTE: Add 5 percent for V-8 (all "C" series).

1964

	6	5	4	3	2	1
Scout Series						
PU (2WD)	200	600	950	2150	3850	5500
PU (4WD)	200	650	1000	2200	4100	5800

NOTE: Add 5 percent for full-length vinyl Sport-Top. Add 10 percent for steel Travel-Top. Add 15 percent for "Champagne Edition" Scout.

	6	5	4	3	2	1
Metro-Mite						
CM-75 Panel	150	300	700	1250	2600	3700
CM-80 Walk-In	125	250	700	1150	2500	3600
CM-110 Panel	150	300	700	1250	2650	3800
Metro/Metroette - (3/4 or 1-Ton)						
Milk Dly	100	175	525	1050	1950	2800
Metro Body	100	175	525	1050	2100	3000
Flat Back	100	175	525	1050	2050	2900
Van	100	175	525	1050	1950	2800
Metro-Lite	100	175	525	1050	1950	2800
Metro Coach	125	200	600	1100	2200	3100
Series C-900 - (Compact)						
PU	150	450	800	1750	3250	4700
Series C-1000 - (1/2-Ton)						
PU	200	550	900	2150	3800	5400
Bonus Load PU	200	600	950	2150	3850	5500
Panel	150	450	800	1750	3250	4700
Travelall	200	600	1000	2200	4000	5700
Series C-1100 - (Heavy Duty) - (1/2-Ton)						
PU	200	550	900	2150	3800	5400
Bonus Load PU	200	600	950	2150	3850	5500
Travelette PU	150	450	800	1750	3250	4700
Panel	150	400	750	1650	3150	4500
Cus Travelall	200	600	1000	2200	4000	5700
Series C-1200 - (3/4-Ton)						
PU	200	550	900	2150	3800	5400
Bonus Load PU	200	600	950	2150	3850	5500
Travelette PU	150	450	800	1750	3250	4700
Travelette Camper	200	550	900	2150	3800	5400
Panel	150	400	750	1650	3150	4500
Cus Travelall	150	450	800	1800	3300	4800
Series C-1300 - (1-Ton)						
PU	200	500	850	1950	3600	5100
Bonus Load PU	200	550	900	2000	3600	5200

1965

	6	5	4	3	2	1
Scout 800 Series						
PU (2WD)	200	650	1000	2200	4100	5800
PU (4WD)	200	650	1050	2250	4200	6000

NOTE: Add 5 percent for full-length Sport-Top.
Add 7 percent for steel Travel-Top.

	6	5	4	3	2	1
Metro-Mite						
CM-75 Panel	150	300	700	1250	2600	3700
CM-80 Walk-In	125	250	700	1150	2500	3600
CM-110 Panel	150	300	700	1250	2650	3800
Metro/Metroette						
Milk Dly	125	250	700	1150	2500	3600
Metro Body	100	175	525	1050	2100	3000
Flat Back	100	175	525	1050	2050	2900
Van	100	175	525	1050	2100	3000
Metro-Lite	100	175	525	1050	1950	2800
8P Metro Coach	100	175	525	1050	2100	3000
Series D-900						
PU	200	500	850	1950	3600	5100
Series D-1000						
PU	200	600	950	2150	3850	5500
Bonus Load PU	200	600	950	2200	3900	5600
Panel	150	450	800	1800	3300	4800
Travelall	200	650	1000	2200	4100	5800
Series D-1100						
PU	200	600	950	2200	3900	5600
Bonus Load PU	200	600	1000	2200	4000	5700
Travelette PU	200	500	850	1950	3600	5100
Panel	200	500	850	1850	3350	4900
Cus Travelall	200	550	900	2000	3600	5200
Series D-1200						
PU	200	600	950	2150	3850	5500
Bonus Load PU	200	600	950	2200	3900	5600
Travelette PU	150	450	800	1800	3300	4800
Travelette Camper	200	650	1000	2200	4100	5800
Panel	150	450	800	1800	3300	4800
Cus Travelall	200	500	850	1900	3500	5000
Series C-1300						
PU	200	550	900	2000	3600	5200
Bonus Load PU	200	550	900	2100	3700	5300

NOTE: Add 5 percent for 4WD models (all series).

1966

	6	5	4	3	2	1
Scout 800 Series						
Utl PU	200	650	1000	2200	4150	5900
Cus PU	200	650	1050	2250	4200	6000
Utl Rds	200	650	1000	2200	4100	5800
Cus Rds	200	650	1000	2200	4150	5900
Utl Travel-Top	200	675	1100	2250	4400	6300
Cus Travel-Top	350	700	1100	2300	4500	6400
Soft Sport-Top	350	700	1150	2300	4550	6500
Hard Sport-Top	350	725	1150	2300	4700	6700

NOTE: Add 3 percent for Turbo-charged models.
Add 2 percent for V-8.

1967

	6	5	4	3	2	1
Scout 800 Series						
Utl PU	200	650	1000	2200	4150	5900
Cus PU	200	650	1050	2250	4200	6000
Utl Rds	200	650	1000	2200	4100	5800
Cus Rds	200	650	1000	2200	4150	5900
Utl Travel-Top	200	675	1100	2250	4400	6300
Cus Travel-Top	350	700	1100	2300	4500	6400
Spt Soft-Top	350	700	1150	2300	4550	6500
Spt HdTp	350	725	1150	2300	4700	6700

NOTE: Add 10 percent for 4WD model. Add 5 percent for soft Travel-Top. Add 4 percent for all steel Travel-Top. Add 2 percent for V-8 model. Add 3 percent for Turbo-charged 4-cyl.

	6	5	4	3	2	1
Metro Series						
M-700 Panel	150	300	700	1250	2600	3700
M-800 Panel	125	250	700	1150	2500	3600
M-1100 Panel	150	300	700	1250	2650	3800
M-1200 Panel	150	300	700	1250	2650	3800
MA-1200 Panel	150	350	750	1350	2800	4000
Series 900A						
PU	200	500	850	1950	3600	5100
Series 908B						
PU	200	550	900	2100	3700	5300
Bonus Load PU	200	550	900	2150	3800	5400
Series 1000B - (7-ft.)						
PU	200	600	950	2150	3850	5500
Bonus Load PU	200	600	950	2200	3900	5600
Panel	200	500	850	1850	3350	4900
Series 1100B						
PU (6-ft. 8")	200	600	1000	2200	4000	5700
Bonus Load PU (6-ft. 8")	200	650	1000	2200	4100	5800
PU (8-1/2 ft.)	200	600	950	2200	3900	5600
Bonus Load PU (8-ft.)	200	600	1000	2200	4000	5700
Panel (7-ft.)	200	500	850	1900	3500	5000
Travelette Cab	200	550	900	2000	3600	5200
B.L. Travelette PU (6-ft.)	200	550	900	2100	3700	5300

	6	5	4	3	2	1
Series 1200B						
PU (7-ft.)	200	600	950	2200	3900	5600
Bonus Load PU (7-ft.)	200	600	1000	2200	4000	5700
PU (8-1/2 ft.)	200	550	900	2150	3800	5400
Panel (7-ft.)	200	500	850	1850	3350	4900
Travelette PU	200	500	850	1850	3350	4900
B.L. Travelette PU (6-ft.)	200	500	850	1900	3500	5000
Series 1300B						
PU (8-1/2 ft.)	200	550	900	2100	3700	5300
Travelette	150	450	750	1700	3200	4600
B.L. Travelette PU (6-ft.)	150	450	800	1750	3250	4700

NOTE: Add 5 percent for 4WD (all Series 1100-1300).

1968

	6	5	4	3	2	1
Scout 800 Series						
Utl PU	200	650	1000	2200	4150	5900
Cus PU	200	650	1050	2250	4200	6000
Utl Rds	200	650	1000	2200	4100	5800
Cus Rds	200	650	1000	2200	4150	5900
Utl Travel-Top	200	675	1100	2250	4400	6300
Cus Travel-Top	350	700	1100	2300	4500	6400
Spt Soft-Top	350	700	1150	2300	4550	6500
Spt HdTp	350	725	1150	2300	4700	6700

NOTE: Add 10 percent for 4WD model. Add 5 percent for soft Travel-Top. Add 4 percent for all steel Travel-Top. Add 2 percent for V-8 model. Add 3 percent for Turbo-charged 4-cyl.

	6	5	4	3	2	1
Metro Series						
M-700 Panel	150	300	700	1250	2600	3700
M-800 Panel	125	250	700	1150	2500	3600
M-1100 Panel	150	300	700	1250	2650	3800
M-1200 Panel	150	300	700	1250	2650	3800
MA-1200 Panel	150	350	750	1350	2800	4000
Series 900A						
PU	200	500	850	1950	3600	5100
Series 908B						
PU	200	550	900	2100	3700	5300
Bonus Load PU	200	550	900	2150	3800	5400
Series 1000B - (7-ft.)						
PU	200	600	950	2150	3850	5500
Bonus Load PU	200	600	950	2200	3900	5600
Panel	200	500	850	1850	3350	4900
Series 1100B						
PU (6-ft. 8")	200	600	1000	2200	4000	5700
Bonus Load PU (6-ft. 8")	200	650	1000	2200	4100	5800
PU (8-1/2 ft.)	200	600	950	2200	3900	5600
Bonus Load PU (8-ft.)	200	600	1000	2200	4000	5700
Panel (7-ft.)	200	500	850	1900	3500	5000
Travelette Cab	200	550	900	2000	3600	5200
B.L. Travelette PU (6-ft.)	200	550	900	2100	3700	5300
Series 1200B						
PU (7-ft.)	200	600	950	2200	3900	5600
Bonus Load PU (7-ft.)	200	600	1000	2200	4000	5700
PU (8-1/2 ft.)	200	550	900	2150	3800	5400
Bonus Load PU (8-ft.)	200	600	950	2150	3850	5500
Panel (7-ft.)	200	500	850	1850	3350	4900
Travelette PU	200	500	850	1850	3350	4900
B.L. Travelette PU (6-ft.)	200	500	850	1900	3500	5000
Series 1300B						
PU (8-1/2 ft.)	200	550	900	2100	3700	5300
Travelette	150	450	750	1700	3200	4600
B.L. Travelette PU (6-ft.)	150	450	800	1750	3250	4700

NOTE: See 1967 for percent additions for special equipment, optional engines and 4WD models (all series).

1969-1970

	6	5	4	3	2	1
Scout 800A Series						
PU	350	700	1100	2300	4500	6400
Rds	200	650	1000	2200	4150	5900
Travel-Top	350	700	1150	2300	4550	6500
Aristocrat	350	750	1200	2350	4900	7000
Metro Series						
M-1100 Panel	150	300	700	1250	2650	3800
M-1200 Panel	150	300	700	1250	2650	3800
MA-1200 Panel	150	300	750	1350	2700	3900
Series 1000D						
PU (6-1/2 ft.)	200	600	950	2200	3900	5600
Bonus Load PU (6-1/2 ft.)	200	600	1000	2200	4000	5700
PU (8-ft.)	200	600	950	2150	3850	5500
Bonus Load PU (8-ft.)	200	600	950	2200	3900	5600
Panel	200	500	850	1900	3500	5000
Series 1100D						
PU (6-1/2 ft.)	200	650	1000	2200	4100	5800
Bonus Load PU (6-1/2 ft.)	200	650	1000	2200	4150	5900
PU (8-ft.)	200	550	900	2100	3700	5300
Bonus Load PU (8-ft.)	200	550	900	2150	3800	5400
Panel	200	500	850	1950	3600	5100
Series 1200D						
PU (6-1/2 ft.)	200	600	1000	2200	4000	5700
Bonus Load PU (6-1/2 ft.)	200	650	1000	2200	4100	5800
PU (8-ft.)	200	600	950	2150	3850	5500
Bonus Load PU (8-ft.)	200	600	950	2200	3900	5600
Panel	200	500	850	1900	3500	5000
Travelette (6-1/2 ft.)	200	500	850	1900	3500	5000
B.L. Travelette PU (8-ft.)	200	500	850	1950	3600	5100
Series 1300D						
PU (9-ft.)	200	550	900	2150	3800	5400
Travelette	150	450	800	1800	3300	4800
B.L. Travelette (6-1/2 ft.)	150	450	800	1750	3250	4700

NOTE: See 1967 for percent additions for special equipment, optional engines and 4WD models (all series).

1971

	6	5	4	3	2	1
Scout 800 Series						
PU	350	700	1100	2300	4500	6400
Rds	200	650	1000	2200	4150	5900
Travel-Top	350	700	1150	2300	4550	6500
Scout II Series						
PU	350	700	1150	2300	4550	6500
Travel-Top	350	725	1150	2300	4700	6700

NOTE: Add 5 percent for 4WD models. Add 5 percent for Custom trim package. Add 3 percent for V-8.

	6	5	4	3	2	1
Metro Series						
M-1100 Panel	150	300	700	1250	2650	3800
M-1200 Panel	150	300	700	1250	2650	3800
Series 1000D						
PU (6-1/2 ft.)	200	600	950	2200	3900	5600
Bonus Load PU (6-1/2 ft.)	200	600	1000	2200	4000	5700
PU (8-ft.)	200	600	950	2150	3850	5500
Bonus Load PU (8-ft.)	200	600	950	2200	3900	5600
Panel	200	500	850	1900	3500	5000
Travelall	200	600	950	2200	3900	5600

NOTE: Add 3 percent for V-8 engine. Add 5 percent for Custom trim package. Add 1 percent for 5-speed.

	6	5	4	3	2	1
Series 1100D						
PU (6-1/2 ft.)	200	650	1000	2200	4100	5800
Bonus Load PU (6-1/2 ft.)	200	650	1000	2200	4150	5900
PU (8-ft.)	200	550	900	2100	3700	5300
Bonus Load PU (8-ft.)	200	550	900	2150	3800	5400
Panel	200	500	850	1950	3600	5100
Travelall	200	650	1000	2200	4100	5800
Series 1200D						
PU (6-1/2 ft.)	200	600	1000	2200	4000	5700
Bonus Load PU (6-1/2 ft.)	200	650	1000	2200	4100	5800
PU (8-ft.)	200	600	950	2150	3850	5500
Bonus Load PU (8-ft.)	200	600	950	2200	3900	5600
Panel	200	500	850	1900	3500	5000
Travelette PU (6-1/2 ft).	200	500	850	1900	3500	5000
B.L. Travelette PU (8-ft).	200	500	850	1950	3600	5100

NOTE: Add 5 percent for 4WD (1100/1200 series only). Add 3 percent for V-8. Add 1 percent for 5-speed.

	6	5	4	3	2	1
Series 1300D						
PU (9-ft.)	200	550	900	2150	3800	5400
Travelette PU	150	450	800	1800	3300	4800
Bonus Load Travelette PU	150	450	800	1750	3250	4700

NOTE: Add 3 percent for V-8.
Add 1 percent for 5-speed.

1972

	6	5	4	3	2	1
Scout II (2WD)						
PU	350	700	1100	2300	4500	6400
Travel-Top	350	700	1150	2300	4550	6500
Scout II (4WD)						
PU	350	700	1150	2300	4600	6600
Travel-Top	350	725	1200	2350	4800	6800
Metro Series						
1110 Panel	150	300	700	1250	2650	3800
1200 Panel	150	300	700	1250	2650	3800
1200 Panel	150	300	750	1350	2700	3900
Travelall Series (2WD)						
1010 Sta Wag	200	600	950	2150	3850	5500
1110 Sta Wag	200	550	900	2150	3800	5400
1210 Sta Wag	200	550	900	2100	3700	5300
Travelall Series (4WD)						
1110 Sta Wag	200	650	1000	2200	4100	5800
1210 Sta Wag	200	600	1000	2200	4000	5700
Light Truck Series 1110 - (2WD)						
PU	200	600	950	2150	3850	5500
Bonus Load PU	200	600	950	2200	3900	5600
Light Truck Series 1110 - (4WD)						
PU	200	600	1000	2200	4000	5700
Bonus Load PU	200	650	1000	2200	4100	5800
Light Truck Series 1210 - (2WD)						
PU	150	450	800	1800	3300	4800
Bonus Load PU	200	500	850	1850	3350	4900
Travelette	150	450	800	1750	3250	4700
Light Truck Series 1210 - (4WD)						
PU	200	500	850	1850	3350	4900
Bonus Load PU	200	500	850	1900	3500	5000
Travelette	200	500	850	1900	3500	5000
Light Truck Series 1310 - (2WD)						
PU	200	550	900	2100	3700	5300
Bonus Load PU	150	450	800	1750	3250	4700
Travelette	150	450	750	1700	3200	4600

NOTE: Add 3 percent for V-8 engine (all series). Add 1 percent for 5-speed transmission. Add 5 percent for Custom trim packages.

1973

	6	5	4	3	2	1
Scout II (2WD)						
Travel-Top	350	700	1150	2300	4550	6500
Cab Top	350	700	1100	2300	4500	6400
Scout II (4WD)						
Travel-Top	350	725	1200	2350	4800	6800
Cab Top	350	700	1150	2300	4600	6600
Metro Series MS-1210 - (2WD)						
Walk-In Panel	150	300	750	1350	2700	3900
Travelall Series 1010 - (2WD)						
Sta Wag	200	600	950	2150	3850	5500
Travelall Series 1110						
Sta Wag (2WD)	200	550	900	2150	3800	5400
Sta Wag (4WD)	200	650	1000	2200	4100	5800
Travelall Series 1210						
Sta Wag (2WD)	200	550	900	2100	3700	5300
Sta Wag (4WD)	200	600	1000	2200	4000	5700
Light Truck Series 1010 - (2WD)						
PU (6-1/2 ft.)	200	600	950	2150	3850	5500
Bonus Load PU (6-1/2 ft.)	200	600	950	2200	3900	5600
PU (8-ft.)	200	550	900	2150	3800	5400
Bonus Load PU (8-ft.)	200	600	950	2150	3850	5500
Light Truck Series 1110 - (2WD)						
PU (6-1/2 ft.)	200	600	950	2150	3850	5500
Bonus Load PU (6-1/2 ft.)	200	600	950	2200	3900	5600
PU (8-ft.)	200	550	900	2150	3800	5400
Light Truck Series 1110 - (4WD)						
PU (6-1/2 ft.)	200	600	1000	2200	4000	5700
Bonus Load PU (6-1/2 ft.)	200	650	1000	2200	4100	5800
PU (8-ft.)	200	600	950	2150	3850	5500
Bonus Load PU (8-ft.)	200	550	900	2150	3800	5400
Light Truck Series 1210 - (2WD)						
PU (6-1/2 ft.)	150	450	800	1800	3300	4800
Bonus Load PU (6-1/2 ft.)	200	500	850	1850	3350	4900
PU (8-ft.)	150	400	750	1650	3150	4500
Bonus Load PU (8-ft.)	150	450	750	1700	3200	4600
Travelette PU (6-1/2 ft.)	150	450	750	1700	3200	4600
B.L. Travelette PU (6-1/2 ft.)	150	450	800	1750	3250	4700
Travelette PU (8-ft.)	200	500	850	1850	3350	4900
B.L. Travelette PU (8-ft.)	200	500	850	1900	3500	5000
Light Truck Series 1210 - (4WD)						
PU (6-1/2 ft.)	200	500	850	1850	3350	4900
Bonus Load PU (6-1/2 ft.)	200	500	850	1900	3500	5000
PU (8-ft.)	150	450	750	1700	3200	4600
Bonus Load PU (8-ft.)	150	450	800	1750	3250	4700
Travelette PU (6-1/2 ft.)	200	500	850	1900	3500	5000
B.L. Travelette PU (6-1/2 ft.)	200	500	850	1950	3600	5100
Travelette PU (8-ft.)	200	500	850	1900	3500	5000
B.L. Travelette PU (8-ft.)	200	500	850	1950	3600	5100
Light Truck Series 1310 - (2WD)						
PU (8-ft.)	200	550	900	2100	3700	5300
Bonus Load PU (8-ft.)	200	550	900	2150	3800	5400
PU (9-ft.)	200	500	850	1950	3600	5100
B.L. Travelette PU (6-1/2 ft.)	200	500	850	1850	3350	4900

	6	5	4	3	2	1
Light Truck Series 1310 - (4WD)						
PU (9-ft.)	150	450	800	1800	3300	4800

NOTE: Add 3 percent for 304 CID V-8. Add 4 percent for 345 CID V-8. Add 5 percent for 392 CID V-8. Add 5 percent for Custom trim package. Add 1 percent for 5-speed transmission.

1974
	6	5	4	3	2	1
Scout II - (2WD)						
Travel-Top	350	700	1150	2300	4550	6500
Cab Top	350	700	1100	2300	4500	6400
Scout II - (4WD)						
Travel-Top	350	725	1200	2350	4800	6800
Cab Top	350	700	1150	2300	4600	6600
Metro Series - (2WD)						
Step-Van	150	300	750	1350	2700	3900
Travelall Series 100						
Sta Wag (2WD)	200	600	950	2150	3850	5500
Sta Wag (4WD)	200	650	1000	2200	4100	5800
Travelall Series 200						
Sta Wag (2WD)	200	550	900	2100	3700	5300
Sta Wag (4WD)	200	600	1000	2200	4000	5700
Series 100 - (2WD)						
Fender PU (115" wb)	200	600	950	2150	3850	5500
Fender PU (132" wb)	200	550	900	2150	3800	5400
Bonus Load PU (115" wb)	200	600	950	2200	3900	5600
Bonus Load PU (132" wb)	200	600	950	2150	3850	5500
Series 100 - (4WD)						
Fender PU (115" wb)	200	600	1000	2200	4000	5700
Fender PU (132" wb)	200	600	950	2150	3850	5500
Bonus Load PU (115" wb)	200	650	1000	2200	4100	5800
Bonus Load PU (132" wb)	200	600	950	2200	3900	5600
Series 200 - (2WD)						
Fender PU (132" wb)	150	450	800	1800	3300	4800
Bonus Load PU (132" wb)	200	500	850	1850	3350	4900
Fender Travelette (149" wb)	150	450	750	1700	3200	4600
Fender Travelette (166" wb)	200	500	850	1850	3350	4900
B.L. Travelette (149" wb)	150	450	800	1750	3250	4700
B.L. Travelette (166" wb)	200	500	850	1900	3500	5000
Series 200 - (4WD)						
Fender PU (132" wb)	200	500	850	1850	3350	4900
Bonus Load PU (132" wb)	200	500	850	1900	3500	5000

NOTE: Add 2 percent for Deluxe exterior trim. Add 5 percent for Custom exterior trim. Add 4 percent for 345 or 392 CID V-8. Add 10 percent for Camper Special.

1975
	6	5	4	3	2	1
Scout Series XLC - (2WD)						
Travel-Top	350	700	1100	2300	4500	6400
Cab Top	200	675	1100	2250	4400	6300
Scout Series XLC - (4WD)						
Travel-Top	350	725	1200	2350	4800	6800
Cab Top	350	700	1150	2300	4600	6600
Metro Series						
Step-Van	150	300	750	1350	2700	3900
Travelall Series 150						
Sta Wag (2WD)	200	600	950	2150	3850	5500
Sta Wag (4WD)	200	650	1000	2200	4100	5800
Travelall Series 200						
Sta Wag (2WD)	200	550	900	2100	3700	5300
Sta Wag (4WD)	200	600	1000	2200	4000	5700
Series 150 - (2WD)						
Bonus Load PU (115" wb)	200	600	950	2200	3900	5600
Bonus Load PU (132" wb)	200	600	950	2150	3850	5500
Series 150 - (4WD)						
Bonus Load PU (115" wb)	200	650	1000	2200	4100	5800
Bonus Load PU (132" wb)	200	600	950	2200	3900	5600
Series 200 - (2WD)						
Bonus Load PU (132" wb)	200	500	850	1850	3350	4900
B.L. Travelette (149" wb)	150	450	800	1750	3250	4700
B.L. Travelette (166" wb)	200	500	850	1900	3500	5000
Series 200 - (4WD)						
Bonus Load PU	200	500	850	1900	3500	5000

NOTE: Add 2 percent for Deluxe exterior trim. Add 5 percent for Custom exterior trim. Add 4 percent for optional V-8. Add 10 percent for Camper Special.

1976
	6	5	4	3	2	1
Scout II						
Travel-Top (2WD)	200	650	1050	2250	4200	6000
Travel-Top (4WD)	200	675	1050	2250	4350	6200
Scout II Diesel						
Travel-Top (2WD)	200	600	1000	2200	4000	5700
Travel-Top (4WD)	200	650	1000	2200	4150	5900
Terra						
PU (2WD)	200	650	1050	2200	4100	5800
PU (4WD)	200	650	1050	2250	4200	6000
Terra Diesel						
PU (2WD)	200	600	950	2150	3850	5500
PU (4WD)	200	600	1000	2200	4000	5700
Traveler						
Sta Wag (2WD)	200	675	1050	2250	4350	6200
Sta Wag (4WD)	350	700	1100	2300	4500	6400
Traveler Diesel						
Sta Wag (2WD)	200	650	1000	2200	4150	5900
Sta Wag (4WD)	200	675	1050	2250	4300	6100

NOTE: Add 3 percent for V-8 engines. Add 3 percent for 4-speed transmission. Add 6 percent for Rally package. Add 4 percent for Custom trim. Add 2 percent for Deluxe trim.

1977
	6	5	4	3	2	1
Scout II						
Travel-Top (2WD)	200	650	1000	2200	4150	5900
Travel-Top (4WD)	200	675	1050	2250	4300	6100
Scout II Diesel						
Travel-Top (2WD)	200	600	950	2200	3900	5600
Travel-Top (4WD)	200	650	1000	2200	4100	5800
Terra						
PU (2WD)	200	600	1000	2200	4000	5700
PU (4WD)	200	650	1000	2200	4150	5900
Terra Diesel						
PU (2WD)	200	550	900	2150	3800	5400
PU (4WD)	200	600	950	2200	3900	5600
Traveler						
Sta Wag (2WD)	200	675	1050	2250	4300	6100
Sta Wag (4WD)	200	675	1100	2250	4400	6300
Traveler Diesel						
Sta Wag (2WD)	200	650	1000	2200	4100	5800
Sta Wag (4WD)	200	650	1050	2250	4200	6000

NOTE: Add 3 percent for V-8 engine. Add 3 percent for 4-speed transmission. Add 6 percent for Rally package. Add 8 percent for SSII. Add 2 percent for Deluxe trim. Add 4 percent for Custom trim.

1978
	6	5	4	3	2	1
Scout Series (2WD)						
Scout II	200	600	1000	2200	4000	5700
SS II	200	650	1000	2200	4150	5900
Terra PU	200	600	950	2200	3900	5600
Traveler Sta Wag	200	650	1050	2250	4200	6000

NOTE: Add 3 percent for V-8 engine. Deduct 4 percent for diesel engine. Add 6 percent for Rally package. Add 4 percent for Custom trim package. Add 2 percent for 4WD running gear.

1979
	6	5	4	3	2	1
Scout Series (2WD)						
Scout II	200	600	950	2200	3900	5600
SS II	200	650	1000	2200	4100	5800
Terra PU	200	600	950	2150	3850	5500
Traveler Sta Wag	200	650	1000	2200	4150	5900

NOTE: Add 3 percent for V-8 engine. Deduct 4 percent for 6-cyl. diesel. Add 6 percent for Rally package. Add 4 percent for Custom trim package. Add 2 percent for 4WD running gear.

1980
	6	5	4	3	2	1
Scout Series (4WD)						
Scout II	200	600	1000	2200	4000	5700
Terra PU	200	600	950	2200	3900	5600
Traveler Sta Wag	200	650	1050	2250	4200	6000

NOTE: Add 3 percent for V-8 engines. Add 5 percent for Turbo-charged diesel engine. Add 4 percent for Custom trim package. Add 6 percent for Rally trim.

JEEP

WILLYS-OVERLAND JEEP

1945
	6	5	4	3	2	1
Jeep Series (4WD)						
CJ-2 Jeep	400	1300	2150	4300	7500	10,700

NOTE: All Jeep prices in this catalog are for civilian models unless noted otherwise. Military Jeeps may sell for higher prices.

1946
	6	5	4	3	2	1
Jeep Series (4WD)						
CJ-2 Jeep	400	1300	2150	4300	7500	10,700

1947
	6	5	4	3	2	1
Willys Jeep (4WD)						
CJ-2 Jeep	400	1300	2150	4300	7500	10,700
Willys Jeep (2WD)						
Panel	200	650	1000	2200	4100	5800
Willys Truck (4WD)						
1-Ton PU	200	600	950	2150	3850	5500
1-Ton Platform	200	500	850	1900	3500	5000

1948
	6	5	4	3	2	1
Jeep Series (4WD)						
CJ-2 Jeep	400	1300	2150	4300	7500	10,700
Willys Jeep (2WD)						
PU	200	550	900	2100	3700	5300
Panel	200	650	1000	2200	4100	5800
Platform	200	500	850	1850	3350	4900
Willys Truck (4WD)						
PU	200	600	950	2150	3850	5500
Platform	200	500	850	1900	3500	5000

1949
	6	5	4	3	2	1
Jeep Series (4WD)						
CJ-2 Jeep	400	1300	2150	4300	7500	10,700
CJ-3 Jeep	400	1250	2100	4200	7400	10,500
Willys Truck (2WD)						
PU	200	550	900	2100	3700	5300
Panel	200	650	1000	2200	4100	5800
Platform	200	500	850	1850	3350	4900
Willys Truck (4WD)						
PU	200	600	950	2150	3850	5500
Platform	200	500	850	1900	3500	5000

1950
	6	5	4	3	2	1
Jeep Series (4WD)						
CJ-3 Jeep	400	1300	2150	4300	7500	10,700
Willys Truck (2WD)						
PU	200	600	950	2150	3850	5500
Panel	200	650	1000	2200	4100	5800
Stake	200	500	850	1850	3350	4900
Jeep Truck (4WD)						
PU	200	600	950	2150	3850	5500
Utl Wag	200	650	1000	2200	4100	5800
Stake	200	500	850	1900	3500	5000

1951
	6	5	4	3	2	1
Jeep Series (4WD)						
Farm Jeep	400	1250	2050	4100	7200	10,300
CJ-3 Jeep	400	1250	2100	4200	7400	10,500
Jeep Trucks (2WD)						
Chassis & Cab	200	500	850	1850	3350	4900
PU	200	550	900	2100	3700	5300
Sed Dly	200	650	1000	2200	4150	5900
Stake	200	500	850	1850	3350	4900
Jeep Trucks (4WD)						
PU	200	600	950	2150	3850	5500
Utl Wag	200	650	1000	2200	4100	5800
Stake	200	500	850	1900	3500	5000

1952
	6	5	4	3	2	1
Jeep Series (4WD)						
CJ-3 Open	400	1250	2100	4200	7400	10,500
Jeep Trucks (2WD)						
Sed Dly	200	650	1000	2200	4150	5900
Jeep Trucks (4WD)						
PU	200	600	950	2200	3900	5600
Utl Wag	200	650	1000	2200	4150	5900
Stake	200	500	850	1900	3500	5000

1953
	6	5	4	3	2	1
Jeep Series (4WD)						
CJ-3B Jeep	400	1300	2200	4400	7700	11,000
CJ-3B Farm Jeep	400	1300	2150	4300	7500	10,700
CJ-3A Jeep	400	1300	2150	4300	7500	10,700
Jeep Trucks (2WD)						
Sed Dly	200	650	1000	2200	4150	5900

	6	5	4	3	2	1
Jeep Trucks (4WD)						
Sed Dly	200	675	1100	2250	4400	6300
PU	200	600	1000	2200	4000	5700
Utl Wag	200	650	1050	2250	4200	6000
Stake	200	500	850	1900	3500	5000

1954

	6	5	4	3	2	1
Jeep Series (4WD)						
Open Jeep	400	1300	2200	4400	7700	11,000
Farm Jeep	400	1300	2150	4300	7500	10,700
Jeep Trucks (2WD)						
Sed Dly	200	650	1000	2200	4150	5900
Jeep Trucks (4WD)						
PU	350	700	1100	2300	4500	6400
Stake	200	500	850	1950	3600	5100
Sed Dly	350	700	1100	2300	4500	6400
Utl Wag	350	725	1150	2300	4700	6700
1-Ton PU	200	600	950	2150	3850	5500
1-Ton Stake	200	500	850	1900	3500	5000

NOTE: Add 3 percent for 6-cyl. trucks (not avail. in Universal Jeep).

1955

	6	5	4	3	2	1
Jeep Series (4WD)						
CJ-3B	400	1300	2200	4400	7700	11,000
CJ-5	400	1300	2200	4400	7700	11,000
Jeep Trucks (2WD)						
Sed Dly	200	675	1050	2250	4350	6200
Utl Wag	350	700	1150	2300	4550	6500
Jeep Trucks (4WD)						
Sed Dly	350	700	1150	2300	4550	6500
1-Ton PU	200	600	950	2200	3900	5600
Utl Wag	350	725	1200	2350	4800	6800
1-Ton Stake	200	500	850	1950	3600	5100

NOTE: Add 3 percent for 6-cyl. trucks (not avail. in CJ models).

1956

	6	5	4	3	2	1
Jeep Series (4WD)						
CJ-3B	400	1300	2200	4400	7700	11,000
CJ-5	400	1300	2200	4400	7700	11,000
CJ-6	400	1250	2100	4200	7400	10,500
Dispatcher Series (2WD)						
Open Jeep	200	675	1100	2250	4400	6300
Canvas Top	350	700	1150	2300	4550	6500
HdTp	350	725	1150	2300	4700	6700
Jeep Trucks (2WD)						
Utl Wag	350	700	1150	2300	4550	6500
Sed Dly	200	675	1050	2250	4350	6200
Jeep Trucks (4WD)						
Sed Dly	350	700	1150	2300	4600	6600
Sta Wag	350	725	1200	2350	4800	6800
PU	200	650	1050	2250	4200	6000
1-Ton PU	200	600	950	2200	3900	5600
1-Ton Stake	200	500	850	1950	3600	5100

NOTE: Add 3 percent for 6-cyl. trucks (not avail. in Jeeps).

1957

	6	5	4	3	2	1
Jeep Series (4WD)						
CJ-3B	400	1300	2200	4400	7700	11,000
CJ-5	400	1300	2200	4400	7700	11,000
CJ-6	400	1250	2100	4200	7400	10,500
Dispatcher Series (2WD)						
Open Jeep	200	675	1100	2250	4400	6300
Soft-Top	350	700	1150	2300	4550	6500
HdTp	350	725	1150	2300	4700	6700
Jeep Trucks (2WD)						
Dly	200	675	1050	2250	4350	6200
Utl Wag	350	700	1150	2300	4550	6500
Jeep Trucks (4WD)						
Dly	350	700	1150	2300	4600	6600
PU	200	650	1050	2250	4200	6000
Utl Wag	350	725	1200	2350	4800	6800
1-Ton PU	200	600	950	2200	3900	5600
1-Ton Stake	200	500	850	1950	3600	5100
Forward Control (4WD)						
3/4-Ton PU	200	650	1050	2250	4200	6000
3/4-Ton Stake	200	650	1000	2200	4100	5800
1-Ton PU	200	600	950	2200	3900	5600
1-Ton Stake	200	550	900	2150	3800	5400

NOTE: Add 3 percent for 6-cyl. trucks (not available in Jeep).

1958

	6	5	4	3	2	1
Jeep Series (4WD)						
CJ-3B	400	1250	2100	4200	7400	10,500
CJ-5	400	1300	2200	4400	7700	11,000
CJ-6	400	1250	2100	4200	7400	10,500
Dispatcher Series (2WD)						
Open Jeep	200	675	1100	2250	4400	6300
Soft-Top	350	700	1150	2300	4550	6500
HdTp	350	725	1150	2300	4700	6700
Jeep Trucks (2WD)						
Dly	200	550	900	2000	3600	5200
Utl Wag	200	550	900	2100	3700	5300
Jeep Trucks (4WD)						
Dly	200	600	950	2200	3900	5600
Utl Wag	200	600	1000	2200	4000	5700
1-Ton PU	150	450	750	1700	3200	4600
1-Ton Stake	150	350	750	1450	2900	4100
Forward Control (4WD)						
3/4-Ton PU	200	650	1050	2250	4200	6000
3/4-Ton Stake	200	650	1000	2200	4100	5800
1-Ton PU	200	600	950	2200	3900	5600
1-Ton Stake	200	550	900	2150	3800	5400

NOTE: Add 3 percent for 6-cyl. trucks (not available in Jeeps).

1959

	6	5	4	3	2	1
Jeep Series (4WD)						
CJ-3	400	1300	2150	4300	7500	10,700
CJ-5	400	1300	2200	4400	7700	11,000
CJ-6	400	1250	2100	4200	7400	10,600
Dispatcher Series (2WD)						
Soft-Top	350	700	1100	2300	4500	6400
HdTp	350	725	1200	2350	4800	6800
Jeep Trucks (2WD)						
Utl Wag	200	550	900	2150	3800	5400
Dly	200	550	900	2100	3700	5300
Jeep Trucks (4WD)						
Utl Dly	200	600	1000	2200	4000	5700
PU	200	500	850	1900	3500	5000

	6	5	4	3	2	1
Utl Wag	200	650	1000	2200	4150	5900
1-Ton PU	150	450	800	1750	3250	4700
1-Ton Stake	150	400	750	1650	3150	4500
Forward Control (4WD)						
3/4-Ton PU	200	675	1050	2250	4300	6100
3/4-Ton Stake	200	650	1000	2200	4150	5900
1-Ton PU	200	600	1000	2200	4000	5700
1-Ton Stake	200	600	950	2150	3850	5500

NOTE: Add 3 percent for 6-cyl. trucks (not available for Jeeps). Add 5 percent for "Maverick".

1960

	6	5	4	3	2	1
Jeep Series (4WD)						
CJ-3	400	1300	2150	4300	7500	10,700
CJ-5	400	1300	2200	4400	7700	11,000
CJ-6	400	1250	2100	4200	7400	10,600
Dispatcher Series (2WD)						
Soft-Top	350	700	1100	2300	4500	6400
HdTp	350	725	1200	2350	4800	6800
Surrey	350	750	1250	2400	5050	7200
Jeep Trucks (2WD)						
Economy Dly	150	450	800	1750	3250	4700
Sta Wag	200	600	1000	2200	4000	5700
Utl Wag	200	550	900	2150	3800	5400
Utl Dly	200	550	900	2000	3600	5200
Jeep Trucks (4WD)						
Utl Wag	200	600	1000	2200	4000	5700
Utl Dly	200	600	950	2150	3850	5500
1-Ton PU	200	550	900	2150	3800	5400
1-Ton Stake	200	500	850	1900	3500	5000
Forward Control (4WD)						
3/4-Ton PU	200	600	950	2200	3900	5600
3/4-Ton Stake	200	550	900	2150	3800	5400
1-Ton PU	200	550	900	2000	3600	5200
1-Ton Stake	200	500	850	1900	3500	5000

NOTE: Add 3 percent for 6-cyl. trucks. Add 5 percent for custom two-tone trim.

1961

	6	5	4	3	2	1
Jeep Series (4WD)						
CJ-3	400	1300	2150	4300	7600	10,800
CJ-5	400	1350	2250	4500	7800	11,200
CJ-6	400	1300	2150	4300	7500	10,700
Dispatcher Series (2WD)						
Jeep (Open)	350	700	1150	2300	4550	6500
Soft-Top	350	700	1150	2300	4600	6600
HdTp	350	725	1200	2350	4800	6800
Jeep Trucks (2WD)						
Fleetvan	150	450	800	1800	3300	4800
Economy Dly	150	450	800	1750	3250	4700
Sta Wag	200	600	950	2150	3850	5500
Utl Wag	200	550	900	2000	3600	5200
Utl Dly	200	500	850	1950	3600	5100
Jeep Trucks (4WD)						
Utl Wag	200	600	950	2150	3850	5500
Utl Dly	200	500	850	1900	3500	5000
1-Ton PU	150	450	800	1800	3300	4800
1-Ton Stake	150	400	750	1550	3050	4300
Forward Control (4WD)						
3/4-Ton PU	200	550	900	2000	3600	5200
3/4-Ton Stake	200	500	850	1900	3500	5000
1-Ton PU	150	450	800	1800	3300	4800
1-Ton Stake	150	450	750	1700	3200	4600

NOTE: Add 3 percent for 6-cyl. trucks.

1962

	6	5	4	3	2	1
Jeep Series (4WD)						
CJ-3	400	1300	2150	4300	7600	10,800
CJ-5	400	1350	2250	4500	7800	11,200
CJ-6	400	1300	2150	4300	7500	10,700
Dispatcher Series (2WD)						
Basic Jeep	350	700	1150	2300	4550	6500
Jeep w/Soft-Top	350	700	1150	2300	4600	6600
Jeep w/HdTp	350	725	1150	2300	4700	6700
Surrey	350	725	1200	2350	4800	6800
Jeep Trucks (2WD)						
Fleetvan	150	450	800	1800	3300	4800
Economy Dly	150	450	800	1750	3250	4700
Sta Wag	200	600	950	2150	3850	5500
Utl Wag	200	550	900	2000	3600	5200
Utl Dly	200	500	850	1950	3600	5100
Jeep Trucks (4WD)						
Utl Wag	200	600	950	2150	3850	5500
Utl Dly	200	500	850	1900	3500	5000
1-Ton PU	150	450	800	1800	3300	4800
1-Ton Stake	150	400	750	1550	3050	4300
Forward Control (4WD)						
3/4-Ton PU	200	550	900	2000	3600	5200
3/4-Ton Stake	200	500	850	1900	3500	5000
1-Ton PU	150	450	800	1800	3300	4800
1-Ton Stake	150	450	750	1700	3200	4600

NOTE: Add 3 percent for 6-cyl. trucks.

KAISER - JEEP

1963

	6	5	4	3	2	1
Jeep Universal - (4WD)						
CJ-3B Jeep	400	1300	2200	4400	7700	11,000
CJ-5 Jeep	450	1450	2400	4800	8400	12,000
CJ-6 Jeep	450	1400	2300	4600	8100	11,500
Dispatcher - (2WD)						
Jeep	350	700	1150	2300	4600	6600
HdTp	350	725	1150	2300	4700	6700
Soft Top	350	725	1200	2350	4800	6800
"Jeep" Wagons and Trucks - (1/2-Ton)						
Sta Wag	200	650	1050	2250	4200	6000
Traveller	200	675	1050	2250	4350	6200
Utl (2WD)	200	600	950	2150	3850	5500
Utl (4WD)	200	650	1050	2250	4200	6000
Panel (2WD)	200	550	900	2000	3600	5200
Panel (4WD)	200	650	1000	2200	4100	5800
"Jeep" Wagons and Truck - (1-Ton)						
PU (4WD)	150	450	800	1800	3300	4800
Stake (4WD)	200	500	850	1900	3500	5000

NOTE: Add 3 percent for L-Head 6-cyl.
Add 4 percent for OHC 6-cyl.

Forward-Control - (4WD) - (3/4-Ton)						
PU	200	550	900	2000	3600	5200
Stake	200	650	1000	2200	4150	5900

	6	5	4	3	2	1
Forward-Control - (1-Ton)						
PU	200	500	850	1950	3600	5100
Stake	200	650	1000	2200	4100	5800
HD PU	200	550	900	2000	3600	5200
HD Stake	200	500	850	1850	3350	4900
Fire Truck	350	700	1150	2300	4550	6500
Gladiator/Wagoneer - (1/2-Ton)						
2d Wag	200	650	1000	2200	4150	5900
4d Wag	200	650	1050	2250	4200	6000
2d Cus Wag	200	650	1050	2250	4200	6000
4d Cus Wag	200	675	1050	2250	4300	6100
Panel Dly	200	550	900	2100	3700	5300
Gladiator - (1/2-Ton) - (120" wb)						
Thriftside PU	200	600	950	2150	3850	5500
Townside PU	200	600	1000	2200	4000	5700
Gladiator - (1/2-Ton) - (126" wb)						
Thriftside PU	200	550	900	2100	3700	5300
Townside PU	200	600	950	2150	3850	5500
Gladiator - (3/4-Ton) - (120" wb)						
Thriftside PU	200	500	850	1950	3600	5100
Townside PU	200	550	900	2100	3700	5300
Stake	150	450	800	1750	3250	4700
Gladiator - (3/4-Ton) - (126" wb)						
Thriftside PU	200	500	850	1900	3500	5000
Townside PU	200	550	900	2000	3600	5200
Stake	150	450	750	1700	3200	4600
Gladiator - (1-Ton) - (120" wb)						
Stake	150	400	750	1650	3150	4500
Wrecker	200	550	900	2000	3600	5200
Fire Truck	200	675	1050	2250	4350	6200
Gladiator - (1-Ton) - (126" wb)						
Stake	150	400	750	1650	3150	4500
Wrecker	200	550	900	2100	3700	5300
Fire Truck	350	700	1150	2300	4550	6500

NOTE: Add 5 percent for 4WD.

1964

	6	5	4	3	2	1
Jeep Universal - (4WD)						
CJ-3B Jeep	400	1300	2200	4400	7700	11,000
CJ-5 Jeep	450	1450	2400	4800	8400	12,000
CJ-5A Tuxedo Park	450	1500	2500	5000	8800	12,500
CJ-6 Jeep	450	1450	2450	4900	8500	12,200
CJ-6A Jeep Park	450	1500	2500	5000	8700	12,400
Dispatcher - (2WD)						
Jeep	350	700	1150	2300	4600	6600
HdTp	350	725	1150	2300	4700	6700
Soft Top	350	725	1200	2350	4800	6800
Surrey	350	750	1200	2350	4900	7000
"Jeep" Wagons and Trucks - (1/2-Ton)						
Sta Wag	200	600	950	2150	3850	5500
Utl (2WD)	200	550	900	2100	3700	5300
Utl (4WD)	200	650	1000	2200	4100	5800
Traveler (2WD)	200	600	1000	2200	4000	5700
Traveler (4WD)	200	675	1050	2250	4350	6200
Panel (2WD)	200	500	850	1950	3600	5100
Panel (4WD)	200	600	950	2200	3900	5600
"Jeep" Wagons and Trucks - (1-Ton) - (4WD)						
PU	200	550	900	2100	3700	5300
Stake	200	500	850	1900	3500	5000

NOTE: Add 3 percent for L-Head 6-cyl.
Add 4 percent for OHC 6-cyl.

	6	5	4	3	2	1
Forward-Control - (3/4-Ton) - (4WD)						
PU	150	450	800	1750	3250	4700
Stake	150	400	750	1600	3100	4400
Forward-Control - (1-Ton)						
PU	150	450	750	1700	3200	4600
Stake	150	400	750	1550	3050	4300
HD PU	150	450	800	1750	3250	4700
HD Stake	150	400	750	1600	3100	4400
Fire Truck	200	675	1050	2250	4350	6200
Fleetvan - (4WD)						
FJ-3 Step-in Dly	150	400	750	1650	3150	4500
FJ-3A Step-in Dly	150	450	750	1700	3200	4600
Gladiator/Wagoneer - (1/2-Ton)						
2d Wag	200	650	1000	2200	4150	5900
4d Wag	200	650	1050	2250	4200	6000
2d Cus Wag	200	650	1050	2250	4200	6000
4d Cus Wag	200	675	1050	2250	4300	6100
Panel Dly	200	550	900	2100	3700	5300
Gladiator Pickup/Truck - (1/2-Ton) - (120" wb)						
Thriftside PU	200	500	850	1900	3500	5000
Townside PU	200	550	900	2000	3600	5200
Gladiator Pickup/Truck - (1/2-Ton) - (126" wb)						
Thriftside PU	150	450	800	1800	3300	4800
Townside PU	200	500	850	1900	3500	5000
Gladiator Pickup/Truck - (3/4-Ton) - (120" wb)						
Thriftside PU	150	450	750	1700	3200	4600
Townside PU	150	450	800	1800	3300	4800
Platform Stake	150	350	750	1450	3000	4200
Gladiator Pickup/Truck - (3/4-Ton) - (126" wb)						
Thriftside PU	150	400	750	1650	3150	4500
Townside PU	150	450	800	1750	3250	4700
Platform Stake	150	350	750	1450	2900	4100
Gladiator Pickup/Truck - (1-Ton) - (120" wb)						
Platform Stake	150	350	750	1350	2800	4000
Wrecker	150	450	800	1750	3250	4700
Fire Truck	200	650	1050	2250	4200	6000
Gladiator Pickup/Truck - (1-Ton) - (126" wb)						
Stake	150	350	750	1350	2800	4000
Wrecker	150	450	800	1800	3300	4800
Fire Truck	200	675	1050	2250	4350	6200

NOTE: Add 5 percent for 4WD.

1965

	6	5	4	3	2	1
Jeep Universal - (4WD)						
CJ-3B Jeep	400	1300	2200	4400	7700	11,000
CJ-5 Jeep	450	1400	2300	4600	8100	11,500
CJ-5A Tuxedo Park	450	1450	2400	4800	8400	12,000
CJ-6 Jeep	450	1400	2300	4600	8100	11,600
CJ-6A Tuxedo Park	450	1400	2350	4700	8300	11,800
Dispatcher - (2WD)						
DJ-5 Courier	200	600	950	2150	3850	5500
DJ-6 Courier	200	600	950	2200	3900	5600
DJ-3A Jeep	200	600	1000	2200	4000	5700
DJ-3A HdTp	200	650	1050	2250	4200	6000
"Jeep" Wagons and Trucks - (1/2-Ton)						
Sta Wag	200	600	950	2150	3850	5500
Utl Wag (4WD)	200	650	1000	2200	4100	5800
Traveler (4WD)	200	675	1050	2250	4350	6200
Panel (2WD)	200	500	850	1950	3600	5100
Panel (4WD)	200	600	950	2200	3900	5600
"Jeep" Wagons and Trucks - (1-Ton) - (4WD)						
PU	200	550	900	2100	3700	5300
Stake	200	500	850	1900	3500	5000

NOTE: Add 3 percent for L-Head 6-cyl. engine.

	6	5	4	3	2	1
Forward-Control - (4WD) - (3/4-Ton)						
PU	150	450	800	1750	3250	4700
Stake	150	400	750	1600	3100	4400
Forward-Control - (1-Ton)						
PU	150	450	750	1700	3200	4600
Stake	150	400	750	1550	3050	4300
HD PU	150	450	800	1750	3250	4700
HD Stake	150	400	750	1600	3100	4400
Fire Truck	200	675	1050	2250	4350	6200
Gladiator/Wagoneer - (1/2-Ton)						
2d Wag	200	650	1000	2200	4150	5900
4d Wag	200	650	1050	2250	4200	6000
2d Cus Wag	200	650	1050	2250	4200	6000
4d Cus Wag	200	675	1050	2250	4300	6100
Panel Dly	200	550	900	2100	3700	5300
Gladiator Pickup/Truck - (1/2-Ton) - (120" wb)						
Thriftside PU	200	500	850	1900	3500	5000
Townside PU	200	550	900	2000	3600	5200
Stake	150	400	750	1600	3100	4400
Gladiator Pickup/Truck - (1/2-Ton) - (126" wb)						
Thriftside PU	150	450	800	1800	3300	4800
Townside PU	200	500	850	1900	3500	5000
Stake	150	400	750	1550	3050	4300
Gladiator Pickup/Truck - (3/4-Ton) - (120" wb)						
Thriftside PU	150	450	750	1700	3200	4600
Townside PU	150	450	800	1800	3300	4800
Stake	150	350	750	1450	3000	4200
Gladiator Pickup/Truck - (3/4-Ton) - (126" wb)						
Thriftside PU	150	400	750	1650	3150	4500
Townside PU	150	450	800	1750	3250	4700
Stake	150	350	750	1450	2900	4100
Gladiator Pickup/Truck - (1-Ton) - (120" wb)						
Stake	150	350	750	1350	2800	4000
Wrecker	150	450	800	1750	3250	4700
Fire Truck	200	675	1050	2250	4350	6200
Gladiator Pickup/Truck - (1-Ton) - (126" wb)						
Stake	150	350	750	1350	2800	4000
Wrecker	150	450	800	1800	3300	4800
Fire Truck	200	675	1100	2250	4400	6300

NOTE: Add 5 percent for 4WD. Add 5 percent for V-8. For "first series" 1965 Gladiators refer to 1964 prices.

1966

	6	5	4	3	2	1
Jeep Universal - (4WD)						
CJ-3B Jeep	400	1300	2200	4400	7700	11,000
CJ-5 Jeep	450	1400	2300	4600	8100	11,500
CJ-5A Tuxedo Park	450	1450	2400	4800	8400	12,000
CJ-6 Jeep	450	1400	2300	4600	8100	11,600
CJ-6A Tuxedo Park	450	1400	2350	4700	8300	11,800
Dispatcher - (2WD)						
DJ-5 Courier	200	600	950	2150	3850	5500
DJ-6 Courier	200	600	950	2200	3900	5600
DJ-3A Jeep	200	600	1000	2200	4000	5700
DJ-3A HdTp	200	650	1050	2250	4200	6000

NOTE: Add 3 percent for V-6 engine.

	6	5	4	3	2	1
Forward-Control - (4WD) - (3/4-Ton)						
PU	150	450	800	1750	3250	4700
Stake	150	400	750	1600	3100	4400
Forward-Control - (1-Ton)						
PU	150	450	750	1700	3200	4600
Stake	150	400	750	1550	3050	4300
HD PU	150	450	800	1750	3250	4700
HD Stake	150	400	750	1600	3100	4400
Fire Truck	200	650	1050	2250	4200	6000
Wagoneer - (1/2-Ton)						
2d Wag	200	550	900	2150	3800	5400
4d Wag	200	600	950	2150	3850	5500
2d Cus Sta Wag	200	600	950	2150	3850	5500
4d Cus Sta Wag	200	600	950	2200	3900	5600
Panel Dly	150	450	800	1800	3300	4800
4d Super Wag	200	675	1100	2250	4400	6300
Gladiator - (1/2-Ton) - (120" wb)						
Thriftside PU	200	500	850	1900	3500	5000
Townside PU	200	550	900	2000	3600	5200
Stake	150	400	750	1600	3100	4400
Gladiator - (1/2-Ton) - (126" wb)						
Thriftside PU	150	450	800	1800	3300	4800
Townside PU	200	500	850	1900	3500	5000
Stake	150	400	750	1550	3050	4300
Gladiator - (3/4-Ton) - (120" wb)						
Thriftside PU	150	450	750	1700	3200	4600
Townside PU	150	450	800	1800	3300	4800
Stake	150	350	750	1450	3000	4200
Gladiator - (3/4-Ton) - (126" wb)						
Thriftside PU	150	400	750	1650	3150	4500
Townside PU	150	450	800	1750	3250	4700
Stake	150	350	750	1450	2900	4100
Gladiator - (1-Ton) - (120" wb)						
Stake	150	350	750	1350	2800	4000
Wrecker	150	450	800	1750	3250	4700
Fire Truck	200	650	1050	2250	4200	6000
Gladiator - (1-Ton) - (126" wb)						
Stake	150	350	750	1350	2800	4000
Wrecker	150	450	800	1750	3250	4700
Fire Truck	200	675	1050	2250	4300	6100
Gladiator - (1-Ton) - (126" wb)						
Stake	150	350	750	1350	2800	4000
Wrecker	150	450	800	1800	3300	4800
Fire Truck	200	675	1050	2250	4350	6200

NOTE: Add 5 percent for 4WD.
Add 5 percent for V-8.

1967

	6	5	4	3	2	1
Jeep Universal - (4WD)						
CJ-5 Jeep	400	1300	2200	4400	7700	11,000
CJ-5A Jeep	450	1400	2300	4600	8100	11,500
CJ-6 Jeep	450	1450	2400	4800	8400	12,000
CJ-6A Jeep	450	1500	2500	5000	8800	12,500
Dispatcher - (2WD)						
DJ-5 Courier	200	600	950	2150	3850	5500

	6	5	4	3	2	1
DJ-6 Courier	200	600	1000	2200	4000	5700
Jeepster Commando - (4WD)						
Conv	350	700	1150	2300	4600	6600
Sta Wag	200	650	1000	2200	4150	5900
Cpe-Rds	350	725	1200	2350	4800	6800
PU	200	600	950	2150	3850	5500
Wagoneer						
2d Wag	200	550	900	2150	3800	5400
4d Wag	200	600	950	2150	3850	5500
2d Cus Sta Wag	200	600	950	2150	3850	5500
4d Cus Sta Wag	200	600	950	2200	3900	5600
Panel Dly	150	450	800	1800	3300	4800
4d Sup Wag	200	650	1000	2200	4100	5800
Gladiator - (4WD) - (1/2-Ton) - (120" wb)						
Thriftside PU	200	500	850	1950	3600	5100
Townside PU	200	550	900	2000	3600	5200
Stake	150	400	750	1600	3100	4400
Gladiator - (3/4-Ton) - (120" wb)						
Thriftside PU	150	450	750	1700	3200	4600
Townside PU	150	450	800	1750	3250	4700
Stake	150	350	750	1450	3000	4200
Gladiator - (1-Ton) - (120" wb)						
Stake	150	350	750	1450	2900	4100
Gladiator - (1/2-Ton) - (126" wb)						
Thriftside PU	150	450	800	1800	3300	4800
Townside PU	200	500	850	1850	3350	4900
Stake	150	350	750	1350	2800	4000
Gladiator - (3/4-Ton) - (126" wb)						
Thriftside PU	150	450	750	1700	3200	4600
Townside PU	150	450	800	1750	3250	4700
Stake	150	350	750	1350	2800	4000
Gladiator - (1-Ton) - (126" wb)						
Stake	150	300	750	1350	2700	3900

NOTE: Add 5 percent for V-8 (except Super V-8). Add 5 percent for 2WD (Series 2500 only). Add 4 percent for V-6 engine. Add 5 percent for 4WD.

1968

	6	5	4	3	2	1
Jeep Universal - (4WD)						
CJ-5 Jeep	400	1300	2200	4400	7700	11,000
CJ-5A Jeep	450	1400	2300	4600	8100	11,500
CJ-6 Jeep	450	1450	2400	4800	8400	12,000
CJ-6A Jeep	450	1500	2500	5000	8800	12,500
Dispatcher - (2WD)						
DJ-5 Courier	200	550	900	2000	3600	5200
DJ-6 Courier	200	550	900	2100	3700	5300

NOTE: Add 4 percent for V-6 engine. Add 5 percent for diesel engine.

	6	5	4	3	2	1
Wagoneer - (V-8) - (4x4)						
4d Sta Wag	200	600	1000	2200	4000	5700
4d Sta Wag Cus	200	650	1000	2200	4100	5800
4d Sta Wag Sup	200	650	1000	2200	4150	5900
Jeepster Commando - (4WD)						
Conv	350	700	1150	2300	4600	6600
Sta Wag	200	650	1000	2200	4150	5900
Cpe-Rds	350	725	1200	2350	4800	6800
PU	200	600	950	2150	3850	5500

NOTE: Add 4 percent for V-6 engine.

1969

	6	5	4	3	2	1
Jeep						
CJ-5 Jeep	400	1300	2200	4400	7700	11,000
CJ-6 Jeep	450	1400	2300	4600	8100	11,500
DJ-5 Courier	200	600	950	2150	3850	5500
Wagon						
Jeepster Commando						
Conv	350	700	1150	2300	4600	6600
Sta Wag	200	650	1000	2200	4150	5900
Cpe-Rds	350	725	1200	2350	4800	6800
PU	200	600	950	2150	3850	5500
Conv	350	725	1200	2350	4850	6900
Wagoneer						
4d Wag	200	650	1000	2200	4100	5800
4d Cus Wag	200	650	1000	2200	4150	5900
Gladiator - (1/2-Ton) - (120" wb)						
Thriftside PU	200	600	950	2150	3850	5500
Townside PU	200	600	950	2200	3900	5600
Stake	150	400	750	1650	3150	4500
Gladiator - (3/4-Ton) - (120" wb)						
Thriftside PU	200	500	850	1850	3350	4900
Townside PU	200	500	850	1900	3500	5000
Stake	150	400	750	1600	3100	4400
Gladiator - (1/2-Ton) - (126" wb)						
Townside	200	500	850	1850	3350	4900
Stake	150	400	750	1550	3050	4300
Gladiator - (3/4-Ton) - (126" wb)						
Townside	150	450	800	1750	3250	4700
Stake	150	400	750	1550	3050	4300

NOTE: Add 4 percent for V-6 engine. Add 5 percent for V-8 engine. Add 10 percent for factory Camper Package.

AMC - JEEP

1970

	6	5	4	3	2	1
Model J-100, 110" wb						
4d Sta Wag	200	650	1000	2200	4100	5800
4d Cus Sta Wag	200	650	1000	2200	4150	5900
Model J-100, 101" wb						
4d Cus Sta Wag	200	600	950	2200	3900	5600
Jeepster Commando, 101" wb						
Sta Wag	200	650	1000	2200	4150	5900
Rds	350	725	1150	2300	4700	6700
Jeepster						
Conv	350	725	1200	2350	4800	6800
Conv Commando	350	725	1200	2350	4850	6900
CJ-5, 1/4-Ton, 81" wb						
Jeep	400	1200	2000	3950	7000	10,000
CJ-6, 101" wb						
Jeep	450	1100	1700	3650	6650	9500
DJ-5, 1/4-Ton, 81" wb						
Jeep	200	650	1050	2250	4200	6000
Jeepster, 1/4-Ton, 101" wb						
PU	200	650	1050	2250	4200	6000
Wagoneer V-8						
4d Cus Sta Wag	200	675	1050	2250	4350	6200

NOTE: Deduct 10 percent for 6-cyl.

	6	5	4	3	2	1
Series J-2500						
Thriftside PU	200	500	850	1850	3350	4900
Townside PU	200	500	850	1900	3500	5000
Series J-2600						
Thriftside PU	150	450	800	1750	3250	4700
Townside PU	150	450	800	1800	3300	4800
Platform Stake	150	400	750	1650	3150	4500
Series J-2700, 3/4-Ton						
Thriftside PU	150	350	750	1450	3000	4200
Townside PU	150	400	750	1550	3050	4300
Platform Stake	150	350	750	1450	2900	4100
Series J-3500, 1/2-Ton						
Townside PU	150	350	750	1450	3000	4200
Series J-3600, 1/2-Ton						
Townside PU	150	350	750	1450	3000	4200
Platform Stake	150	350	750	1350	2800	4000
Series J-3700, 3/4-Ton						
Townside PU	150	350	750	1450	2900	4100
Platform Stake	150	300	750	1350	2700	3900
Series J-4500						
Townside PU	150	350	750	1350	2800	4000
Series J-4600						
Townside PU	150	300	750	1350	2800	3900
Series J-4700						
Townside PU						

1971

	6	5	4	3	2	1
Model J-100, 110" wb						
4d Sta Wag	200	600	1000	2200	4000	5700
4d Cus Sta Wag	200	650	1000	2200	4150	5900
4d Spl Sta Wag	200	650	1000	2200	4100	5800
Jeepster Commando, 101" wb						
Sta Wag	200	650	1000	2200	4150	5900
Rds	350	725	1150	2300	4700	6700
Jeepster Commando Six						
Sta Wag	200	675	1050	2250	4300	6100
Rds	350	725	1200	2350	4800	6800
Conv	350	725	1200	2350	4850	6900
CJ-5, 1/4-Ton						
Jeep	400	1200	2000	3950	7000	10,000
CJ-6, 1/2-Ton						
Jeep	450	1100	1700	3650	6650	9500
DJ-5, 1/4-Ton						
Open	350	900	1550	3050	5900	8500
Jeepster, 1/2-Ton						
PU	200	650	1050	2250	4200	6000
Wagoneer V-8						
4d Sta Wag Cus	200	650	1000	2200	4150	5900

NOTE: Deduct 10 percent for 6-cyl.

	6	5	4	3	2	1
Series J-2500						
Thriftside PU	200	500	850	1850	3350	4900
Townside PU	150	450	800	1800	3300	4800
Series J-3800						
Townside PU	150	450	800	1750	3250	4700
Series J-4500						
Townside PU	150	450	750	1700	3200	4600
Series J-4600						
Townside PU	150	400	750	1650	3150	4500
Series J-4700						
Townside PU	150	400	750	1600	3100	4400
Series J-4800						
Townside PU	150	400	750	1550	3050	4300

1972

	6	5	4	3	2	1
Wagoneer, 6-cyl.						
4d Sta Wag	200	650	1000	2200	4100	5800
4d Cus Sta Wag	200	650	1050	2250	4200	6000
Commando, 1/2-Ton, 6-cyl, 101" wb						
4d Sta Wag	200	675	1050	2250	4300	6100
Rds	350	725	1200	2350	4800	6800
CJ-5, 1/4-Ton						
Jeep	400	1200	2000	3950	7000	10,000
CJ-6, 1/4-Ton						
Jeep	450	1100	1700	3650	6650	9500
DJ-5, 1/4-Ton, 2WD						
Open	200	650	1050	2250	4200	6000
Series J-2500, 1/2-Ton						
Thriftside PU	200	500	850	1850	3350	4900
Townside PU	150	450	800	1800	3300	4800
Series J-2600, 1/2-Ton						
Thriftside PU	150	450	800	1800	3300	4800
Townside PU	150	450	800	1750	3250	4700
Series J-4500, 3/4-Ton						
Townside PU	150	450	750	1700	3200	4600
Series J-4600, 3/4-Ton						
Townside PU	150	400	750	1650	3150	4500
Series J-4700, 3/4-Ton						
Townside PU	150	400	750	1600	3100	4400
Series J-4800, 3/4-Ton						
Townside PU	150	400	750	1550	3050	4300

1973

	6	5	4	3	2	1
Wagoneer, 6-cyl, 110" wb						
4d Sta Wag	200	650	1000	2200	4100	5800
4d Cus Sta Wag	200	650	1050	2250	4200	6000
Jeep Commando, 6-cyl						
2d Sta Wag	200	600	1000	2200	4000	5700
Rds	350	725	1150	2300	4700	6700
CJ-5, 1/4-Ton						
Jeep	400	1200	2000	3950	7000	10,000
CJ-6, 1/4-Ton						
Jeep	450	1100	1700	3650	6650	9500
Commando, 1/2-Ton, 104" wb						
PU	200	550	900	2100	3700	5300
Series J-2500, 1/2-Ton						
Thriftside PU	200	500	850	1900	3500	5000
Townside PU	200	500	850	1950	3600	5100
Series J-2600, 1/2-Ton						
Thriftside PU	200	500	850	1850	3350	4900
Townside PU	200	500	850	1900	3500	5000
Series J-4500, 3/4-Ton						
Townside PU	150	450	800	1800	3300	4800
Series J-4600, 3/4-Ton						
Townside PU	150	450	800	1750	3250	4700
Series J-4800, 3/4-Ton						
Townside PU	150	450	750	1700	3200	4600

	6	5	4	3	2	1
1974						
Wagoneer, V-8, 109" wb						
4d Sta Wag	200	650	1000	2200	4150	5900
4d Cus Sta Wag	200	675	1050	2250	4300	6100
Cherokee, 6-cyl, 109" wb						
2d Sta Wag	200	650	1000	2200	4100	5800
2d "S" Sta Wag	200	650	1000	2200	4150	5900
CJ-5, 1/4-Ton, 84" wb						
Jeep	400	1200	2000	3950	7000	10,000
CJ-6, 1/4-Ton, 104" wb						
Jeep	450	1100	1700	3650	6650	9500
Series J-10, 1/2-Ton, 110"-131" wb						
Townside PU, SWB	150	450	800	1800	3300	4800
Townside PU, LWB	150	450	800	1750	3250	4700
Series J-20, 3/4-Ton						
Townside PU, LWB	150	450	750	1700	3200	4600
1975						
Wagoneer, V-8						
4d Sta Wag	200	650	1000	2200	4150	5900
4d Cus Sta Wag	200	675	1050	2250	4300	6100
Cherokee, 6-cyl						
2d Sta Wag	200	650	1000	2200	4100	5800
2d "S" Sta Wag	200	650	1000	2200	4150	5900
CJ-5, 1/4-Ton, 84" wb						
Jeep	400	1200	2000	3950	7000	10,000
CJ-6, 1/4-Ton, 104" wb						
Jeep	450	1100	1700	3650	6650	9500
Series J-10, 1/2-Ton, 119" or 131" wb						
Townside PU, SWB	150	450	800	1800	3300	4800
Townside PU (LWB)	150	450	800	1750	3250	4700
Series J-20, 3/4-Ton, 131" wb						
Townside PU	150	450	750	1700	3200	4600
1976						
Wagoneer, V-8						
4d Sta Wag	200	650	1000	2200	4150	5900
4d Cus Sta Wag	200	675	1050	2250	4350	6200
Cherokee, 6-cyl.						
2d Sta Wag	200	650	1000	2200	4100	5800
2d "S" Sta Wag	200	650	1000	2200	4150	5900
CJ-5, 1/4-Ton, 84" wb						
Jeep	400	1200	2000	3950	7000	10,000
CJ-7, 1/4-Ton, 94" wb						
Jeep	450	1100	1700	3650	6650	9500
Series J-10, 1/2-Ton, 119" or 131" wb						
Townside PU, SWB	150	450	800	1750	3250	4700
Townside PU, LWB	150	450	750	1700	3200	4600
Series J-20, 3/4-Ton, 131" wb						
Townside PU, LWB	150	400	750	1650	3150	4500
1977						
Wagoneer, V-8						
4d Sta Wag	200	675	1050	2250	4300	6100
Cherokee, 6-cyl						
2d Sta Wag	200	650	1000	2200	4100	5800
2d "S" Sta Wag	200	650	1000	2200	4150	5900
4d Sta Wag	200	650	1000	2200	4100	5800
CJ-5, 1/4-Ton, 84" wb						
Jeep	450	1050	1650	3500	6400	9200
CJ-7, 1/4-Ton, 94" wb						
Jeep	450	1000	1650	3350	6300	9000
Series J-10, 1/2-Ton, 119" or 131" wb						
Townside PU, SWB	150	450	750	1700	3200	4600
Townside PU, LWB	150	400	750	1650	3150	4500
Series J-20, 3/4-Ton, 131" wb						
Townside PU	150	400	750	1600	3100	4400
1978						
Wagoneer, 108.7" wb						
4d Sta Wag	200	675	1050	2250	4300	6100
Cherokee, 6-cyl						
2d Sta Wag	200	650	1000	2200	4100	5800
2d "S" Sta Wag	200	650	1000	2200	4150	5900
4d Sta Wag	200	650	1000	2200	4100	5800
CJ-5, 1/4-Ton, 84" wb						
Jeep	450	1050	1650	3500	6400	9200
CJ-7, 1/4-Ton, 94" wb						
Jeep	450	1000	1650	3350	6300	9000
Series J-10, 1/2-Ton, 119" or 131" wb						
Townside PU, SWB	150	450	750	1700	3200	4600
Townside PU, LWB	150	400	750	1650	3150	4500
Series J-20, 3/4-Ton, 131" wb						
Townside PU	150	400	750	1600	3100	4400
1979						
Wagoneer, V-8, 108.7" wb						
4d Sta Wag	200	650	1050	2250	4200	6000
4d Ltd Sta Wag	200	675	1050	2250	4350	6200
Cherokee, 6-cyl						
2d Sta Wag	200	650	1000	2200	4100	5800
2d "S" Sta Wag	200	650	1000	2200	4150	5900
4d Sta Wag	200	650	1000	2200	4100	5800
CJ-5, 1/4-Ton, 84" wb						
Jeep	450	1000	1600	3300	6250	8900
CJ-7, 1/4-Ton, 94" wb						
Jeep	350	900	1550	3050	5900	8500
Series J-10, 1/2-Ton, 119" or 131" wb						
Townside PU, SWB	150	450	750	1700	3200	4600
Townside PU, LWB	150	400	750	1650	3150	4500
Series J-20, 3/4-Ton, 131" wb						
Townside PU	150	400	750	1600	3100	4400
1980						
Wagoneer, 6-cyl, 108.7" wb						
4d Sta Wag	200	650	1050	2250	4200	6000
4d Ltd Sta Wag	200	675	1050	2250	4350	6200
Cherokee, 6-cyl						
2d Sta Wag	200	600	950	2150	3850	5500
2d "S" Sta Wag	200	600	1000	2200	4000	5700
4d Sta Wag	200	650	1000	2200	4150	5900
CJ-5, 1/4-Ton, 84" wb						
Jeep	350	900	1550	3050	5900	8500
CJ-7, 1/4-Ton, 94" wb						
Jeep	350	800	1450	2750	5600	8000
Series J-10, 1/2-Ton, 119" or 131" wb						
Townside PU. SWB	150	450	750	1700	3200	4600
Townside PU, LWB	150	400	750	1650	3150	4500
Series J-20, 3/4-Ton, 131" wb	150	400	750	1650	3150	4500
Townside PU	150	400	750	1600	3100	4400
1981						
Wagoneer, 108.7" wb						
4d Sta Wag	200	650	1050	2250	4200	6000
4d Brgm Sta Wag	200	675	1050	2250	4350	6200
4d Ltd Sta Wag	350	700	1100	2300	4500	6400
Cherokee						
2d Sta Wag	200	500	850	1850	3350	4900
2d Sta Wag, Wide Wheels	200	500	850	1900	3500	5000
4d Sta Wag	200	500	850	1950	3600	5100
Scrambler, 1/2-Ton, 104" wb						
PU	125	250	700	1150	2450	3500
CJ-5, 1/4-Ton, 84" wb						
Jeep	150	350	750	1350	2800	4000
CJ-7, 1/4-Ton, 94" wb						
Jeep	150	350	750	1450	3000	4200
Series J-10, 1/2-Ton, 119" or 131" wb						
Townside PU, SWB	150	400	750	1650	3150	4500
Townside PU, LWB	150	400	750	1600	3100	4400
Series J-20, 3/4-Ton, 131" wb						
Townside PU	150	400	750	1550	3050	4300
1982						
Wagoneer, 6-cyl						
4d Sta Wag	200	650	1000	2200	4150	5900
4d Brgm Sta Wag	200	675	1100	2250	4400	6300
4d Ltd Sta Wag	350	725	1150	2300	4700	6700
Cherokee, 6-cyl						
2d Sta Wag	200	500	850	1850	3350	4900
4d Sta Wag	200	500	850	1950	3600	5100
Scrambler, 1/2-Ton, 103.4" wb						
PU	125	250	700	1150	2450	3500
CJ-5, 1/4-Ton, 84" wb						
Jeep	350	800	1450	2750	5600	8000
CJ-7, 1/4-Ton, 93.4" wb						
Jeep	350	750	1300	2450	5250	7500
Series J-10, 1/2-Ton, 119" or 131" wb						
Townside PU, SWB	150	400	750	1650	3150	4500
Townside PU, LWB	150	400	750	1600	3100	4400
Series J-20, 3/4-Ton, 131" wb						
Townside PU	150	400	750	1550	3050	4300
Series J-10, 1/2-Ton, 119" wb						
Sportside PU	150	450	750	1700	3200	4600
1983						
Wagoneer, 6-cyl						
4d Brgm Sta Wag	350	750	1200	2350	4900	7000
4d Ltd Sta Wag	350	750	1300	2450	5250	7500
Cherokee, 6-cyl						
2d Sta Wag	200	650	1050	2250	4200	6000
Scrambler, 1/2-Ton, 103.4" wb						
PU	125	250	700	1150	2500	3600
CJ-5, 1/4-Ton, 83.4" wb						
Jeep	350	800	1450	2750	5600	8000
CJ-7, 1/4-Ton, 93.4" wb						
Townside Pickup (4WD)						
Jeep	350	750	1300	2450	5250	7500
Series J-10, 1/2-Ton, 119" or 131" wb						
Townside PU, SWB	150	400	750	1600	3100	4400
Townside PU, LWB	150	400	750	1550	3050	4300
Series J-10, 1/2-Ton						
Sportside PU	150	400	750	1650	3150	4500
Series J-20, 3/4-Ton, 131" wb						
Townside PU	150	350	750	1450	3000	4200
1984						
Wagoneer, 4-cyl						
4d Sta Wag	350	750	1250	2400	5050	7200
4d Ltd Sta Wag	350	750	1200	2350	4900	7000
Wagoneer, 6-cyl						
4d Sta Wag	350	750	1300	2400	5200	7400
4d Ltd Sta Wag	350	750	1300	2450	5250	7500
Grand Wagoneer, V-8						
4d Sta Wag	350	750	1350	2650	5450	7800
Cherokee, 4-cyl						
2d Sta Wag	350	750	1250	2350	5000	7100
4d Sta Wag	350	750	1200	2350	4900	7000
Cherokee, 6-cyl						
2d Sta Wag	350	750	1250	2400	5100	7300
4d Sta Wag	350	750	1250	2400	5050	7200
Scrambler, 1/2-Ton, 103.4" wb						
PU	150	400	750	1600	3100	4400
CJ-7, 1/4-Ton, 93.4" wb						
Jeep	350	750	1350	2650	5450	7800
Series J-10, 1/2-Ton, 119" or 131" wb						
Townside PU	200	550	900	2000	3600	5200
Series J-20, 3/4-Ton, 131" wb						
Townside PU	200	550	900	2100	3700	5300
1985						
Wagoneer, 4-cyl, 101.4" wb						
4d Sta Wag	350	750	1200	2350	4900	7000
4d Ltd Sta Wag	350	750	1300	2450	5250	7500
Wagoneer, 8-cyl, 101.4" wb						
4d Sta Wag	350	750	1300	2450	5250	7500
4d Ltd Sta Wag	350	800	1450	2750	5600	8000
Grand Wagoneer, 108.7" wb						
4d Sta Wag	350	750	1200	2350	4900	7000
Cherokee, 4-cyl, 101.4" wb						
2d Sta Wag 2WD	200	650	1050	2250	4200	6000
4d Sta Wag 2WD	200	675	1050	2250	4350	6200
2d Sta Wag 4WD	350	700	1150	2300	4500	6500
4d Sta Wag 4WD	350	725	1150	2300	4700	6700
Cherokee, 6-cyl, 101.4" wb						
2d Sta Wag 2WD	200	675	1050	2250	4350	6200
4d Sta Wag 2WD	350	700	1100	2300	4500	6400
2d Sta Wag 4WD	350	725	1150	2300	4700	6700
4d Sta Wag 4WD	350	725	1200	2350	4850	6900
Scrambler, 1/2-Ton, 103.5" wb						
PU	200	675	1050	2250	4350	6200
CJ-7, 1/4-Ton, 93.5" wb						
Jeep	350	800	1450	2750	5600	8000
Series J-10, 1/2-Ton, 131" wb, 4WD						
Townside PU	200	650	1050	2250	4200	6000

	6	5	4	3	2	1
Series J-20, 3/4-Ton, 131" wb, 4WD						
Townside PU	350	700	1150	2300	4550	6500

1986
Wagoneer

	6	5	4	3	2	1
4d Sta Wag	350	900	1550	3050	5900	8500
4d Ltd Sta Wag	450	950	1600	3250	6150	8800
4d Grand Sta Wag	450	1000	1650	3350	6300	9000
Cherokee						
2d Sta Wag 2WD	350	750	1200	2350	4900	7000
4d Sta Wag 2WD	350	750	1300	2450	5250	7500
2d Sta Wag 4WD	350	750	1300	2450	5250	7500
4d Sta Wag 4WD	350	800	1450	2600	5600	8000
Wrangler, 1/4-Ton, 93.4" wb						
Jeep 2WD						
Comanche, 120" wb						
PU	350	700	1100	2300	4500	6400
CJ-7, 1/4-Ton, 93.5" wb						
Jeep	350	900	1550	3050	5900	8500
Series J-10, 131" wb, 4WD						
Townside PU	350	750	1200	2350	4900	7000
Series J-20, 131" wb, 4WD						
Townside PU	350	750	1300	2450	5250	7500

PLYMOUTH

1930-1931
Series 30U

	6	5	4	3	2	1
Commercial Sed	450	1000	1650	3350	6300	9000

1935
Series PJ

	6	5	4	3	2	1
Sed Dly	350	900	1550	3050	5900	8500

1936
Series P-1

	6	5	4	3	2	1
Commercial Sed	450	950	1600	3250	6150	8800

1937
Series PT-50

	6	5	4	3	2	1
PU	350	800	1450	2750	5600	8000
Sed Dly	450	1050	1700	3550	6500	9300
Sta Wag	600	1900	3200	6400	11,200	16,000

1938
Series PT-57

	6	5	4	3	2	1
PU	350	900	1550	3100	6000	8600
Sed Dly	450	1050	1700	3550	6500	9300

1939
Series P-7 Road King

	6	5	4	3	2	1
Utl Sed	350	750	1200	2350	4900	7000
Panel Dly	450	950	1600	3250	6150	8800
Series PT-81						
PU	350	950	1600	3200	6050	8700
Sed Dly	450	1050	1700	3550	6500	9300

1940
Series P-9 Road King

	6	5	4	3	2	1
Utl Sed	350	750	1200	2350	4900	7000
Panel Dly	450	950	1600	3250	6150	8800
Series PT-105						
PU	350	950	1600	3200	6050	8700

1941
Series PT-125

	6	5	4	3	2	1
PU	350	950	1600	3200	6050	8700
Panel Dly	450	1000	1600	3300	6250	8900
Series P-11						
Utl Sed	350	750	1300	2450	5250	7500
Sed Dly	450	1150	1800	3800	6800	9700

1942
Series P-14S

	6	5	4	3	2	1
Utl Sed	350	750	1350	2600	5400	7700

1974
Trail Duster - (4WD) - (1/2-Ton)

	6	5	4	3	2	1
Utl	150	350	750	1450	2900	4100
PB-100 Voyager Van - (1/2-Ton) - (109" wb)						
Wag	125	200	600	1100	2250	3200
(1/2-Ton) - (127" wb)						
Wag	125	200	600	1100	2300	3300
PB-200 Voyager Van - (3/4-Ton) - (109" wb)						
Wag	125	250	700	1150	2450	3500
(3/4-Ton) - (127" wb)						
Wag	125	250	700	1150	2500	3600
Maxi-Wagon	150	300	700	1250	2600	3700
PB-300 Voyager Van - (1-Ton) - (127" wb)						
Wag	150	300	700	1250	2600	3700
Maxi-Wagon	150	300	700	1250	2650	3800

1975
Trail Duster - (1/2-Ton)

	6	5	4	3	2	1
Utl (2WD)	150	350	750	1350	2800	4000
Utl (4WD)	150	400	750	1650	3150	4500
PB-100 Voyager Van - (1/2-Ton) - (109" wb)						
Wag	125	200	600	1100	2200	3100
(1/2-Ton) - (127" wb)						
Wag	125	200	600	1100	2250	3200
PB-200 Voyager Van - (3/4-Ton) - (109" wb)						
Wag	125	250	700	1150	2400	3400
(3/4-Ton) - (127" wb)						
Wag	125	250	700	1150	2450	3500
Maxi-Wagon	125	250	700	1150	2500	3600
PB-300 Voyager Van - (1-Ton) - (127" wb)						
Wag	125	250	700	1150	2500	3600
Maxi-Wagon	150	300	700	1250	2600	3700

1976
Trail Duster - (1/2-Ton)

	6	5	4	3	2	1
Utl (2WD)	150	350	750	1450	2900	4100
Utl (4WD)	150	450	750	1700	3200	4600
PB-100 Voyager Van - (1/2-Ton) - (109 wb)						
Wag	125	200	600	1100	2250	3200
(1/2-Ton) - (127" wb)						
Wag	125	200	600	1100	2300	3300
PB-200 Voyager Van - (3/4-Ton) - (109" wb)						
Wag	125	250	700	1150	2450	3500
(3/4-Ton) - (127" wb)						
Wag	125	250	700	1150	2500	3600
Maxi-Wagon	150	300	700	1250	2600	3700
PB-300 Voyager Van - (1-Ton) - (127" wb)						
Wag	150	300	700	1250	2600	3700
Maxi-Wagon	150	300	700	1250	2650	3800

1977
Trail Duster - (1/2-Ton)

	6	5	4	3	2	1
Utl (2WD)	150	350	750	1450	2900	4100
Utl (4WD)	150	450	750	1700	3200	4600
PB-100 Voyager Van - (1/2-Ton) - (109" wb)						
Wag	125	200	600	1100	2250	3200
(1/2-Ton) - (127" wb)						
Wag	125	200	600	1100	2300	3300
PB-200 Voyager Van - (3/4-Ton) - (109" wb)						
Wag	125	250	700	1150	2450	3500
(3/4-Ton) - (127" wb)						
Wag	125	250	700	1150	2500	3600
Maxi-Wagon	150	300	700	1250	2600	3700
PB-300 Voyager Van - (1-Ton) - (127" wb)						
Wag	150	300	700	1250	2600	3700
Maxi-Wagon	150	300	700	1250	2650	3800

1978
Trail Duster - (1/2-Ton)

	6	5	4	3	2	1
Utl (2WD)	150	400	750	1550	3050	4300
Utl (4WD)	150	450	800	1800	3300	4800
PB-100 Voyager Van - (1/2-Ton) - (109" wb)						
Wag	125	250	700	1150	2400	3400
(1/2-Ton) - (127" wb)						
Wag	125	200	600	1100	2300	3300
PB-200 Voyager Van - (3/4-Ton) - (109" wb)						
Wag	125	250	700	1150	2500	3600
(3/4-Ton) - (127" wb)						
Wag	150	300	700	1250	2600	3700
Maxi-Wagon	150	300	700	1250	2600	3700
PB-300 Voyager Van - (1-Ton) - (127" wb)						
Wag	150	300	750	1350	2700	3900
Maxi-Wagon	150	350	750	1350	2800	4000

1979
Arrow Series

	6	5	4	3	2	1
PU	100	175	525	1050	2100	3000
Spt PU	125	250	700	1150	2400	3400
Trail Duster Series PD-100						
Utl	150	400	750	1550	3050	4300
Trail Duster Series PW-100						
Utl	150	450	800	1800	3300	4800
Voyager Series						
PB-100 Van	125	250	700	1150	2400	3400
PB-200 Van	125	250	700	1150	2500	3600
PB-300 Van	150	300	750	1350	2700	3900

1980
Arrow Series

	6	5	4	3	2	1
PU	100	175	525	1050	2100	3000
Spt PU	125	250	700	1150	2400	3400
Trail Duster Series PD-100						
Utl	150	400	750	1550	3050	4300
Trail Duster Series PW-100						
Utl	150	450	800	1800	3300	4800
Voyager Series						
PB-100 Van	125	250	700	1150	2400	3400
PB-200 Van	125	250	700	1150	2500	3600
PB-300 Van	150	300	750	1350	2700	3900

1981
Arrow - (1/2-Ton) - (109.4" wb)

	6	5	4	3	2	1
Sweptline PU	75	100	425	800	1400	2000
Cus Sweptline PU	75	100	425	800	1400	2000
Spt Sweptline PU	75	100	425	800	1400	2000
Trail Duster - (1/2-Ton) - (106" wb)						
Utl (2WD)	200	500	850	1900	3500	5000
Utl (4WD)	200	650	1050	2250	4200	6000
PB-150 - (1/2-Ton) - (109.6" or 127.6" wb)						
Voyager	150	350	750	1350	2800	4000
PB-250 - (3/4-Ton) - (109.6" or 127.6" wb)						
Voyager	150	350	750	1450	2900	4100
PB-350 - (1-Ton) - (127.6" wb)						
Voyager	150	350	750	1350	2800	4000

1982
Arrow - (1/2-Ton) - (109.4" wb)

	6	5	4	3	2	1
Cus Sweptline PU	75	100	400	750	1350	1900
Royal Sweptline PU	75	100	400	750	1350	1900
Spt Sweptline PU	100	125	450	900	1550	2200
PB-150 - (1/2-Ton) - (109.6" or 127.6" wb)						
Voyager	150	350	750	1450	3000	4200
PB-250 - (3/4-Ton) - (109.6" or 127.6" wb)						
Voyager	150	400	750	1550	3050	4300
PB-350 - (1-Ton) - (127.6" wb)						
Voyager	150	350	750	1450	3000	4200

NOTE: Add 5 percent for premier option.

1983
Scamp FWD - (104.2" wb)

	6	5	4	3	2	1
PU	75	100	400	750	1350	1900
GT PU	75	100	425	800	1400	2000
PB-150 - (1/2-Ton) - (109.6" wb)						
Voyager	150	400	750	1650	3150	4500
PB-250 - (3/4-Ton) - (127.6" wb)						
Voyager	150	400	750	1650	3150	4500
PB-350 - (1-Ton) - (127.6" wb)						
Voyager	150	400	750	1600	3100	4400

1984
Voyager FWD - (112" wb)

	6	5	4	3	2	1
Voyager	150	300	700	1250	2650	3800
Voyager SE	150	350	750	1350	2800	4000
Voyager LE	150	400	750	1650	3150	4500

	6	5	4	3	2	1
1985						
Voyager FWD - (112" wb)						
Voyager	150	350	750	1350	2800	4000
Voyager SE	150	400	750	1650	3150	4500
Voyager LE	150	450	750	1700	3200	4600
1986						
Voyager FWD - (112.4" wb)						
Voyager	150	450	800	1750	3250	4700
Voyager SE	200	500	850	1900	3500	5000
Voyager LE	200	600	950	2150	3850	5500

PONTIAC

	6	5	4	3	2	1
1949						
Streamliner Series 6						
Sed Dly	400	1300	2200	4400	7700	11,000
Streamliner Series 8						
Sed Dly	450	1400	2300	4600	8100	11,500
1950						
Streamliner Series 6						
Sed Dly	400	1350	2250	4500	7800	11,200
Streamliner Series 8						
Sed Dly	450	1400	2350	4700	8200	11,700
1951						
Streamliner Series 6						
Sed Dly	450	1400	2300	4600	8100	11,500
Streamliner Series 8						
Sed Dly	450	1450	2400	4800	8400	12,000
1952						
Chieftain Series 6						
Sed Dly	400	1350	2250	4500	7800	11,200
Chieftain Series 8						
Sed Dly	450	1400	2350	4700	8200	11,700
1953						
Chieftain Series 6						
Sed Dly	500	1550	2550	5100	9000	12,800
Chieftain Series 8						
Sed Dly	500	1600	2650	5300	9300	13,300

STUDEBAKER

	6	5	4	3	2	1
1937						
Model 5A/6A, Dictator Six						
Cpe Exp	350	900	1550	3050	5900	8500
1938						
Model 7A, Commander Six						
Cpe Exp	350	900	1550	3050	5900	8500
1939						
Model 9A, Commander Six						
Cpe Exp	450	1100	1700	3650	6650	9500
1941						
Six-cyl. - (113" wb)						
1/2-Ton	350	750	1300	2450	5250	7500
1942						
Six-cyl. - (113" wb)						
1/2-Ton	350	750	1300	2450	5250	7500
1946						
Six-cyl.						
1/2-Ton	350	750	1300	2450	5250	7500
1947						
Six-cyl.						
1/2-Ton	350	750	1300	2450	5250	7500
1948						
Six-cyl.						
1/2-Ton	350	750	1300	2450	5250	7500
1949						
Six-cyl.						
1/2-Ton	150	450	800	1800	3300	4800
3/4-Ton	150	400	750	1550	3050	4300
1950						
Pickup - (1/2-Ton) - (6-cyl)						
2R5	150	450	800	1800	3300	4800
2R6	200	500	850	1850	3350	4900
Pickup - (3/4-Ton) - (6-cyl)						
2R10	150	400	750	1550	3050	4300
2R11	150	400	750	1600	3100	4400
1951						
Pickup - (1/2-Ton) - (6-cyl)						
2R5	150	450	800	1800	3300	4800
2R6	200	500	850	1850	3350	4900
Pickup - (3/4-Ton) - (6-cyl)						
2R10	150	400	750	1550	3050	4300
2R11	150	400	750	1600	3100	4400
1952						
Pickup - (1/2-Ton) - (6-cyl)						
2R5	150	450	800	1800	3300	4800
2R6	200	500	850	1850	3350	4900
Pickup - (3/4-Ton) - (6-cyl)						
2R10	150	400	750	1550	3050	4300
2R11	150	400	750	1600	3100	4400
1953						
Pickup - (1/2-Ton) - (6-cyl)						
2R5	150	450	800	1800	3300	4800
2R6	200	500	850	1850	3350	4900
Pickup - (3/4-Ton) - (6-cyl)						
2R10	150	400	750	1550	3050	4300
2R11	150	400	750	1600	3100	4400

	6	5	4	3	2	1
1954						
Pickup - (1/2-Ton) - (6-cyl)						
3R5	150	450	800	1800	3300	4800
3R6	200	500	850	1850	3350	4900
Pickup - (3/4-Ton) - (6-cyl)						
3R10	150	400	750	1550	3050	4300
3R11	150	400	750	1600	3100	4400
1955						
Pickup - (1/2-Ton) - (6-cyl)						
E5	200	500	850	1900	3500	5000
E7	200	500	850	1950	3600	5100
Pickup - (3/4-Ton) - (6-cyl)						
E10	150	450	750	1700	3200	4600
E12	150	450	800	1750	3250	4700
NOTE: Add 10 percent for V-8.						
1956						
Pickup - (1/2-Ton) - (6-cyl)						
2E5 (SWB)	200	550	900	2000	3600	5200
2E5 (LWB)	200	550	900	2000	3600	5200
2E7 (SWB)	200	600	950	2150	3850	5500
2E7 (LWB)	200	600	950	2150	3850	5500
Pickup - (3/4-Ton) - (6-cyl)						
2E12	200	500	850	1950	3600	5100
NOTE: Add 10 percent for V-8.						
1957						
Pickup - (1/2-Ton) - (6-cyl)						
3E5 (SWB)	200	500	850	1950	3600	5100
3E5 (LWB)	200	500	850	1950	3600	5100
3E6 (SWB)	200	550	900	2000	3600	5200
3E6 (LWB)	200	550	900	2000	3600	5200
3E7 (SWB)	200	650	1000	2200	4100	5800
3E7 (LWB)	200	650	1000	2200	4100	5800
Pickup - (3/4-Ton) - (6-cyl)						
3E11	150	450	750	1700	3200	4600
3E12	200	500	850	1950	3600	5100
NOTE: Add 10 percent for V-8.						
1958						
Pickup - (1/2-Ton) - (6-cyl)						
3E1 (SWB)	200	500	850	1900	3500	5000
3E5 (SWB)	200	550	900	2000	3600	5200
3E5 (LWB)	200	550	900	2000	3600	5200
3E6 (SWB)	200	550	900	2100	3700	5300
3E6 (LWB)	200	550	900	2100	3700	5300
3E7 (SWB)	200	650	1000	2200	4100	5800
3E7 (LWB)	200	650	1000	2200	4100	5800
Pickup - (3/4-Ton) - (6-cyl)						
3E11	150	450	750	1700	3200	4600
3E12	200	500	850	1950	3600	5100
NOTE: Add 10 percent for V-8.						
1959						
Pickup - (1/2-Ton) - (6-cyl)						
4E1 (SWB)	150	400	750	1650	3150	4500
4E1 (LWB)	150	400	750	1650	3150	4500
4E5 (SWB)	150	450	800	1750	3250	4700
4E5 (LWB)	150	450	800	1750	3250	4700
4E6 (SWB)	150	450	800	1800	3300	4800
4E6 (LWB)	150	450	800	1800	3300	4800
4E7 (SWB)	200	600	950	2150	3850	5500
4E7 (LWB)	200	600	950	2150	3850	5500
Pickup - (3/4-Ton) - (6-cyl)						
4E11	150	400	750	1550	3050	4300
4E12	150	450	800	1800	3300	4800
NOTE: Add 10 percent for V-8.						
1960						
Pickup - (1/2-Ton) - (6-cyl)						
5E5 (SWB)	200	550	900	2000	3600	5200
5E5 (LWB)	200	550	900	2000	3600	5200
5E6 (SWB)	200	550	900	2100	3700	5300
5E6 (LWB)	200	550	900	2100	3700	5300
5E7 (SWB)	200	600	950	2200	3900	5600
5E7 (LWB)	200	600	950	2200	3900	5600
Pickup - (3/4-Ton) - (6-cyl)						
5E11	150	400	750	1550	3050	4300
5E12	150	450	800	1800	3300	4800
NOTE: Add 10 percent for optional V-8 (210/225 HP).						
1961						
Pickup - (1/2-Ton) - (6-cyl)						
6E5 (SWB)	200	550	900	2000	3600	5200
6E5 (LWB)	200	550	900	2000	3600	5200
6E7 (SWB)	200	600	950	2200	3900	5600
6E7 (LWB)	200	600	950	2200	3900	5600
Pickup - (3/4-Ton) - (6-cyl)						
6E10	150	400	750	1550	3050	4300
6E12	150	450	800	1800	3300	4800
NOTE: Add 10 percent for optional V-8 (210/225 HP).						
1962						
Pickup - (1/2-Ton) - (6-cyl)						
7E5 (SWB)	200	550	900	2000	3600	5200
7E5 (LWB)	200	550	900	2000	3600	5200
7E7 (SWB)	200	600	950	2200	3900	5600
7E7 (LWB)	200	600	950	2200	3900	5600
Pickup - (3/4-Ton) - (6-cyl)						
7E10	150	400	750	1550	3050	4300
7E12	150	450	800	1800	3300	4800
NOTE: Add 10 percent for optional V-8 (210/225 HP).						
1963						
Pickup - (1/2-Ton) - (6-cyl)						
8E5 (SWB)	200	550	900	2000	3600	5200
8E5 (LWB)	200	550	900	2000	3600	5200
8E7 (SWB)	200	600	950	2200	3900	5600
8E7 (LWB)	200	600	950	2200	3900	5600
Pickup - (3/4-Ton) - (6-cyl)						
8E10	150	400	750	1550	3050	4300
8E12	150	450	800	1800	3300	4800
NOTE: Add 10 percent for optional V-8 (210/225 HP).						

Standard Catalog Of Light-Duty Trucks

1964
Pickup - (1/2-Ton) - (6-cyl)

	6	5	4	3	2	1
8E5 (SWB)	200	550	900	2000	3600	5200
8E5 (LWB)	200	500	850	1900	3500	5000
8E7 (SWB)	200	600	950	2200	3900	5600
8E7 (LWB)	200	600	950	2200	3900	5600

Pickup - (3/4-Ton) - (6-cyl)

	6	5	4	3	2	1
8E10	150	400	750	1550	3050	4300
8E12	150	450	800	1800	3300	4800

NOTE: Add 10 percent for optional V-8 (210/225 HP).

WILLYS-OVERLAND

1911-1912
Overland "37"

	6	5	4	3	2	1
Dly	350	900	1550	3050	5900	8500
Spl Dly	450	1100	1700	3650	6650	9500
Overland						
1-Ton Truck	200	675	1050	2250	4350	6200
Gramm						
1-Ton Truck	350	700	1150	2300	4550	6500

1913
Overland

	6	5	4	3	2	1
Open Exp	350	800	1450	2750	5600	8000
Full Panel	350	900	1550	3050	5900	8500
Gramm						
Chassis (1-Ton)	350	700	1150	2300	4550	6500
Willys						
Chassis (3/4-Ton)	350	750	1300	2450	5250	7500

1914
Overland "79"

	6	5	4	3	2	1
Exp	350	800	1450	2750	5600	8000
Panel	350	900	1550	3050	5900	8500
Willys Utility "65"						
Exp	350	750	1350	2650	5450	7800
Panel	350	850	1500	2950	5800	8300

1915
Willys Utility

	6	5	4	3	2	1
3/4-Ton Exp	350	750	1350	2650	5450	7800

1916
Overland "83"

	6	5	4	3	2	1
Exp Dly	350	900	1550	3050	5900	8500
Spl Dly	450	1100	1700	3650	6650	9500
Open Exp	350	800	1450	2750	5600	8000
Overland "75"						
Screen	450	1100	1800	3700	6700	9600
Panel	450	1150	1800	3800	6800	9700

1917
Overland "90"

	6	5	4	3	2	1
Panel	450	1000	1650	3350	6300	9000

1918
Overland "90"

	6	5	4	3	2	1
Exp (800 lbs.)	350	900	1550	3100	6000	8600
Panel (800 lbs.)	450	1000	1650	3350	6300	9000
Exp (1200 lbs.)	350	800	1450	2750	5600	8000

1919
Overland Light Four

	6	5	4	3	2	1
Exp (800 lbs.)	350	900	1550	3100	6000	8600
Panel (800 lbs.)	450	1000	1650	3350	6300	9000
Exp (1200 lbs.)	350	800	1450	2750	5600	8000

1920
Overland Model 5 - ("Light Four")

	6	5	4	3	2	1
Exp (800 lbs.)	350	950	1600	3200	6050	8700
Panel (800 lbs.)	450	1050	1650	3500	6400	9200
Exp (1000 lbs.)	350	850	1500	2800	5650	8100

1921
Overland Model Four

	6	5	4	3	2	1
Exp (800 lbs.)	350	950	1600	3200	6050	8700
Panel (800 lbs.)	450	1050	1650	3500	6400	9200
Exp (1000 lbs.)	350	850	1500	2800	5650	8100

1922
Overland Model Four

	6	5	4	3	2	1
Exp (800 lbs.)	350	950	1600	3200	6050	8700
Panel (800 lbs.)	450	1050	1650	3500	6400	9200
Exp (1000 lbs.)	350	850	1500	2800	5650	8100

1923
Overland "91CE"

	6	5	4	3	2	1
Exp	350	950	1600	3200	6050	8700
Canopy	450	1000	1650	3350	6300	9000
Screen	450	1000	1600	3300	6250	8900
Panel	450	1050	1650	3500	6400	9200

1924
Overland "91CE"

	6	5	4	3	2	1
Exp	350	950	1600	3200	6050	8700
Canopy	450	1000	1650	3350	6300	9000
Screen	450	1000	1600	3300	6250	8900
Panel	450	1050	1650	3500	6400	9200

1925
Overland "91CE"

	6	5	4	3	2	1
Open Exp	350	950	1600	3200	6050	8700
Canopy	450	1000	1650	3350	6300	9000
Screen	450	1000	1600	3300	6250	8900
Panel	450	1050	1650	3500	6400	9200

NOTE: (with aftermarket bodies).

1926
Overland Model 91

	6	5	4	3	2	1
Open Exp	350	950	1600	3200	6050	8700
Canopy	450	1000	1650	3350	6300	9000
Screen	450	1000	1600	3300	6250	8900
Panel	450	1050	1650	3500	6400	9200

NOTE: (with aftermarket bodies.)

1927
Whippet Model 96

	6	5	4	3	2	1
PU	200	675	1050	2250	4350	6200
Canopy	200	675	1100	2250	4400	6300
Screen	350	700	1100	2300	4500	6400
Panel	350	700	1150	2300	4600	6600
Sed Dly	350	725	1200	2350	4850	6900

NOTE: Add 12 percent for 6-cyl. engine.

1928
Whippet Series 96

	6	5	4	3	2	1
PU	200	675	1050	2250	4350	6200
Canopy	200	675	1100	2250	4400	6300
Screen	350	700	1100	2300	4500	6400
Panel	350	700	1150	2300	4600	6600
Sed Dly	350	725	1200	2350	4850	6900

NOTE: Add 12 percent for 6-cyl. engine.

1929
Whippet Series 96 - (100" wb)

	6	5	4	3	2	1
PU	200	675	1050	2250	4350	6200
Screen	200	675	1100	2250	4400	6300
Canopy	350	700	1100	2300	4500	6400
Panel	350	700	1150	2300	4600	6600
Sed Dly	350	725	1200	2350	4850	6900
Whippet Series 96A - (103" wb)						
PU	350	700	1100	2300	4500	6400
Canopy	350	700	1150	2300	4550	6500
Screen	350	700	1150	2300	4600	6600
Panel	350	725	1200	2350	4800	6800
Sed Dly	350	750	1250	2350	5000	7100

NOTE: Add 12 percent for Whippet Six.

Willys Series 98B

	6	5	4	3	2	1
PU	350	750	1300	2450	5250	7500
Canopy	350	750	1300	2500	5300	7600
Screenside	350	750	1350	2650	5450	7800
Panel	350	800	1450	2750	5600	8000
Sed Dly	350	900	1550	3100	6000	8600

1930
Whippet Series 96A

	6	5	4	3	2	1
PU	350	700	1100	2300	4500	6400
Canopy	350	700	1150	2300	4550	6500
Screenside	350	700	1150	2300	4600	6600
Panel	350	725	1200	2350	4800	6800
Screen Dly	350	750	1250	2350	5000	7100

1931
Whippet Series 96

	6	5	4	3	2	1
PU	350	700	1100	2300	4500	6400
Canopy	350	700	1150	2300	4550	6500
Screenside	350	700	1150	2300	4600	6600
Panel	350	725	1200	2350	4800	6800
Sed Dly	350	750	1250	2350	5000	7100

NOTE: Add 12 percent for Whippet Six.

Willys Series 98B

	6	5	4	3	2	1
PU	350	750	1300	2450	5250	7500
Canopy	350	750	1300	2500	5300	7600
Screenside	350	750	1350	2650	5450	7800
Panel	350	800	1450	2750	5600	8000
Sed Dly	350	900	1550	3100	6000	8600

Willys Series C-113

	6	5	4	3	2	1
PU	200	650	1050	2250	4200	6000
Canopy	200	675	1050	2250	4300	6100
Screenside	200	675	1050	2250	4350	6200
Panel	350	700	1100	2300	4500	6400
Sed Dly	350	725	1150	2300	4700	6700

1932
Willys Series C-113

	6	5	4	3	2	1
PU	200	650	1050	2250	4200	6000
Canopy	200	675	1050	2250	4300	6100
Screenside	200	675	1050	2250	4350	6200
Panel	350	700	1100	2300	4500	6400
Sed Dly	350	725	1150	2300	4700	6700

1933
Willys "77"

	6	5	4	3	2	1
Panel	350	725	1200	2350	4800	6800

1934
Willys Model 77

	6	5	4	3	2	1
Panel	350	725	1200	2350	4800	6800

1935
Willys Model 77

	6	5	4	3	2	1
PU	350	700	1150	2300	4550	6500
Panel	350	725	1200	2350	4850	6900

1936
Willys Model 77

	6	5	4	3	2	1
PU	350	700	1150	2300	4550	6500
Panel	350	725	1200	2350	4850	6900

1937
Willys Model 77

	6	5	4	3	2	1
PU	200	675	1050	2250	4300	6100
Panel	350	700	1150	2300	4600	6600

1938
Willys Model 38

	6	5	4	3	2	1
PU	200	675	1050	2250	4300	6100
Stake	200	600	950	2200	3900	5600
Panel	200	650	1050	2250	4200	6000

1939
Willys Model 38

	6	5	4	3	2	1
PU	200	650	1050	2250	4200	6000
Stake	200	600	950	2150	3850	5500
Panel	200	650	1000	2200	4150	5900

Willys Model 48

	6	5	4	3	2	1
PU	200	675	1050	2250	4300	6100
Stake	200	500	850	1900	3500	5000
Panel	200	650	1050	2250	4200	6000

1940
Willys Model 440

	6	5	4	3	2	1
PU	350	700	1150	2300	4550	6500
Panel Dly	200	675	1100	2250	4400	6300

1941
Willys Model 441

	6	5	4	3	2	1
PU	350	725	1150	2300	4700	6700
Panel Dly	350	700	1150	2300	4550	6500

1942
Willys Model 442

	6	5	4	3	2	1
PU	350	725	1150	2300	4700	6700
Panel Dly	350	700	1150	2300	4550	6500

For Collector Car Enthusiasts...

Catalogs For Car Collectors...

Standard Catalog of American Cars, 1805-1942
* 5,000 auto builders' makes and models from 1805-1942
* 4,500 photos present visual details to help restorers
ONLY $45.00

Standard Catalog of American Cars, 1946-1975
* Presenting more than 1,000 vehicle listings from 1946-1975
* Over 1,500 photographs aid in vehicle identification
ONLY $27.95

Standard Catalog of American Cars, 1976-1986
* Presents thousands of cars manufactured in America
* Helps pinpoint tomorrow's collector cars today
ONLY $19.95

Standard Catalog of American Light-Duty Trucks
* All new 2nd edition presents 500 truck listings, 1896-1986
* ID data, serial numbers, codes, specs, current pricing
ONLY $29.95

Standard Catalog of Ford
* Profiles every Ford make and model built from 1903-1990
* More than 500 photographs aid in identification
* ID data, serial numbers, codes, specs, current pricing
ONLY $19.95

Standard Catalog of Chevrolet
* Profiles every Chevy model manufactured from 1912-1990
* Over 500 photos bring restorers visual aid during projects
* ID data, serial numbers, codes, specs, current pricing
ONLY $19.95

Standard Catalog of Chrysler
* Profiles each Chrysler make and model in detail, from 1924-1990
* Presents I-to-6 conditional pricing through 1983 models
* ID data, serial numbers, codes, specs, production totals
ONLY $19.95

Standard Catalog of Buick
* Profiles every Buick model & make crafted from 1903-1990
* Chassis specs, body types, shipping weights, current pricing
* Fascinating stories, historical perspectives, photo profiles
ONLY $18.95

Standard Catalog of Cadillac
* All the makes that made Cadillac famous, from 1903-1990
* Photographic perspectives, codes, specs, ID and serial numbers
* Includes I-to-6 conditional pricing for current value comparisons
ONLY $18.95

Standard Catalog of American Motors
* Presents every model in the AMC family from 1903-1987
* Hudson, Nash, Metropolitan, Rambler, AMC/Jeep, AMX
* Factory prices, today's values, technical specifications
ONLY $19.95

Standard Guide to Automotive Restoration
* Matt Joseph's technical, hands-on guide for all restorers
* Complete system-by-system instructions for all makes & models
* More than 400 detailed photos aid in correct application
ONLY $24.95

MASTERCARD & VISA CUSTOMERS, CALL TOLL-FREE TO ORDER...
(800) 258-0929
Monday - Friday 6:30 am-8:00 pm, Saturday 8:00 am-2:00 pm Central Standard Time